DIRECTORY
OF
AMERICAN
SCHOLARS

DIRECTORY OF AMERICAN SCHOLARS

NINTH EDITION

VOLUME **I**

HISTORY

Rita C. Velázquez, Editor

The Gale Group

DETROIT • SAN FRANCISCO • LONDON • BOSTON • WOODBRIDGE, CT

Rita C. Velázquez, Editor

Project Associates and Contributing Editors: Michelle
Eads, Amanda Quick

Contributing Staff: Mary Alampi, Caryn Anders, Katy Balcer, Anja
Barnard, Donna Batten, Donna Craft, Andrea DeJong, Sarah DeMar, Sheila Dow, Kim
Forster, William Harmer, Kelly Hill, LySandra Hill, Sonya Hill, Crystal Holombo, Theresa
MacFarlane, Christine Maurer, Matthew Miskelly, Jacqueline Mueckenheim, Erin Nagel,
Lynn Pearce, Terry Peck, Maureen Puhl, Donna Wood.

Contributors: Chapter House, IMPS; The Electronic
Scriptorium, Ltd.

Managing Editor: Keith Jones

Manager, Technical Support Services: Theresa Rocklin
Programmer/Analyst: Jim Edwards

Manufacturing Manager: Dorothy Maki
Senior Buyer: Wendy Blurton

Product Design Manager: Cindy Baldwin
Art Director: Eric Johnson
Graphic Artist: Gary Leach

CONTENTS

PREFACE

First published in 1942 under the auspices of the American Council of Learned Societies, The Directory of American Scholars remains the foremost biographical reference to American humanities scholars. With the ninth edition, The Gale Group is continuing the tradition.

The directory is arranged for convenient use in four subject volumes: Volume I: History; Volume II: English, Speech, and Drama; Volume III: Foreign Languages, Linguistics, and Philology; Volume IV: Philosophy, Religion, and Law. Each volume of biographical listings contains a geographic index. Volume V contains an alphabetical index, a discipline index, an institutional index and a cumulative geographic index of scholars listed in the first four volumes.

The ninth edition of the Directory of American Scholars profiles more than 24,000 United States and Canadian scholars currently active in teaching, research, and publishing. The names of entrants were obtained from a variety of sources, including former entrants, academic deans, or citations in professional journals. In most cases, nominees received a questionnaire to complete, and selection for inclusion was made based on the following criteria:

1. Achievement, by reason of experience and training, of a stature in scholarly work equivalent to that associated with the doctoral degree, coupled with current activity in such work;

or

2. Achievement as evidenced by publication of scholarly works;

or

3. Attainment of a position of substantial responsibility by reason of achievement as outlined in (1) and (2).

Enhancements to the ninth edition include an index volume, simplifying the search for a particular scholar or a particular group of scholars. Indexing by discipline is sorted by primary and secondary majors, in some cases including majors that are not traditionally considered as humanities. Those individuals involved in several fields are cross-referenced into appropriate volumes.

The ninth edition of The Directory of American Scholars is produced by fully automated methods. Limitations in the printing method have made it necessary to omit most diacritics.

Individual entries can include place and year of birth, *primary discipline(s), vital statistics, education, honorary degrees, past and present professional experience, concurrent positions, *membership in international, national and regional societies, honors and awards, *research interest, *publications, and mailing address. Elements preceded by an asterisk are limited as to the number of items included. If an entrant exceeded these limitations, the editors selected the most recent information. Biographies received in the offices of The Gale Group after the editorial deadline were included in an abbreviated manner.

The editors have made every effort to include material as accurately and completely as possible within the confines of format and scope. However, the publishers do not assume and hereby disclaim any liability to any party for any loss or damage caused by errors or omissions in the Directory of American Scholars, whether such errors or omissions result from negligence, accident, or any other cause.

Thanks are expressed to those who contributed information and submitted nominations for the new edition. Many societies provided membership lists for the research process and published announcements in their journals or newsletters, and their help is appreciated.

Comments and suggestions regarding any aspect of the ninth edition are invited and should be addressed to The Editors, Directory of American Scholars, The Gale Group, 27500 Drake Road, Farmington Hills, MI 48333-3535.

ADVISORS

David M. Fahey
Professor of History
Miami University
Miami, Ohio

Patricia Hardesty
Humanities Reference/Liaison Libraran
George Mason University
Fairfax, Virginia

Stephen Karetzky
Library Director, Associate Professor
Felician College
Lodi, New Jersey

ABBREVIATIONS

AAAS American Association for the Advancement of Science
AAUP American Association of University Professors
abnorm abnormal
acad academia, academic, academica, academie, academique, academy
accad accademia
acct account, accountant, accounting
acoust acoustical, accounstic(s)
adj adjunct, adjutant
actg acting
activ activities, activity
addn addition(s), additional
AID Agency for International Development
adjust adjust
admin administration, administrative
adminr administrator(s)
admis admissions
adv advisor(s), advisory
advan advance(d), advancement
advert advertisement, advertising
aerodyn aerodynamic(s)
aeronaut aeronautic(s), aeronautical
aesthet aesthetics
affil affiliate(s), affiliation
agr agricultural, agriculture
agt agent
AFB Air Force Base
AHA American Historical Association
akad akademi, akademia
Ala Alabama
Algem algemeen, algemen
allergol allergological, allergology
allgem allgemein, allgemeine, allgemeinen
Alta Alberta
Am America, Americain, American, Americana, Americano, Amerika, Amerikaansch, Amerikaner, Amerikanisch, Amerikansk
anal analysis, analytic, analytical
analog analogue
anat anatomic, anatomical, anatomy
ann annal(s)
anthrop anthropological, anthropology
anthropom anthropometric, anthropometrical, anthropometry
antiq antiquaire(s), antiquarian, antiquary(ies), antiquities
app appoint, appointed, appointment
appl applied
appln application

approx approximate, approximately
Apr April
apt apartment(s)
arbit arbitration
arch archiv, archiva, archive(s), archivio, archivo
archaeol archaeological, archaeology
archaol archaologie, archaologisch
archeol archeological, archeologie, archeologique, archeology
archit architectural, architecture
Arg Argentina, Argentine
Ariz Arizona
Ark Arkansas
asn association
asoc asociacion
assoc(s) associate(s), associated
asst assistant
Assyriol Assyriology
astrodyn astrodynamics
astron astronomical, astronomy
astronaut astronautical, astronautics
astronr astronomer
attend attendant, attending
atty attorney
audiol audiology
Aug August
auth author(s)
AV audiovisual
ave avenue

b born
BC British Columbia
bd board
behav behavior, behavioral, behaviour, behavioural
Bibl Biblical, Biblique
bibliog bibliografia, bibliographic, bibligraphical, bibliography(ies)
bibliogr bibliographer
bibliot biblioteca, bibliotec, bibliotek, bibliotheca, bibliothek, bibliothequeca
biog biographical, biography
biol biological, biology
bk(s) books
bldg building
blvd boulevard
bol boletim, boletin
boll bollettino
bor borough

bot botanical, botany
br branch
Brit Britain, British
Bro(s) Brother(s)
bull bulletin
bur bureau
bus business
BWI British West Indies

c children
Calif California
Can Canada, Canadian, Canadien, Canadienne
cand candidate
cartog cartografic, cartographical, cartography
cartogra cartographer
Cath Catholic, Catholique
CBS Columbia Broadcasting System
cent central
Cent Am Central America
cert certificat, certificate, certified
chap chapter
chem chermical, chemistry
chg charge
chemn chairman
Cie Compagnie
cient cientifica, cientifico
class classical
clin(s) clinic(s)
Co Companies, Company, County
coauth coauth
co-dir co-director
co-ed co-editor
co-educ co-educational
col(s) colegio, college(s), collegiate
collab collaboration, collaborative, collaborating, collaborator
Colo Colorado
Comdr Commander
com commerce, commercial
commun communication(s)
comn(s) commission(s)
comnr commissioner
comp comparative, comparee
compos composition(s)
comput computer, computing
comt committee
conf conference
cong congress
Conn Connecticut

conserv conservacion,conservation, conservatoire, conservatory
consol consolidated, consolidation
const constitution, constitutional
construct construction
consult consultant, consulting
contemp contemporary
contrib contribute, contribution
contribur contributor
conv convention
coop cooperation, cooperative
coord coordinating, coordination
coordr coordinator
corresp corresponding
Corp Corporation
coun council, counsel, counseling
counr councillor, counselor
criminol criminology
Ct Court
ctr center
cult cultra, cultural, culturale, culture
cur curator
curric curriculum
cybernet cybernetics
CZ Canal Zone
Czeck Czechoslovakia

DC District of Columbia
Dec December
Del Delaware
deleg delegate, delegations
demog demographic, demography
demonstr demonstrator
dent dental, dentistry
dep deputy
dept department
Deut Deutsch, Deutschland
develop development
diag diagnosis, diagnostic
dialectol dialectology
dig digest
dipl diploma, diploma, diplomate, diplome
dir director(s), directory directory
Diss Abstr Dissertation Abstracts
dist district
distrib distributive
distribr distributors
div division, divorced
doc document, documentation
Dom Dominion
Dr Doctor, Drive
Drs Doctroandus

e east
ecol ecological, ecology
econ economic(s), economical, economy
ed edicion, edition, editor, editorial, edizione
educ education, educational
educr educator(s)
Egyptol Egyptology
elec electric, electrical, electricity electrical
elem elementary
emer emeriti, emeritus
encour encouragement
encycl encyclopedia
employ employment
Eng England
environ environment, environmental
EPDA Education Professions Development Act
equip equipment
ERIC Educational Resources Information Center
ESEA Elementary & Secondary Education Act
espec especially

estab established, establishment
estud estudante, estudas, estudianet, estudio(s), estudo(s)
ethnog ethnographical, ethnography
ethnol ethnological, ethnology
Europ European
eval evaluation
evangel evangelical
eve evening
exam examination
examr examiner
except exceptional
exec executive(s)
exeg exegesis(es), exegetic, exegetical, exegetics
exhib exhibition(s)
exp experiment, experimental, experimentation
exped expedition(s)
explor exploration(s)
expos exposition
exten extension

fac faculties, faculty
facil facilities, facility
Feb February
fed federal
fedn federation
fel(s) fellow(s), fellowship(s)
filol filologia, filologico
filos filosofia, filosofico
Fla Florida
FLES Foreign Languages in the Elementary Schools
for foreign
forsch forschung, forschungen
found foundation
Fr Francais(s), French
Ft Fort

Ga Georgia
gen general, generale
geneal genealogical, genealogy
genoot genootschap
geod geodesy, geodetic
geog geografia, geografico, geographer(s), geographic, geographie, geographical, geography
geogr geographer
geol geologic, geological, geology
geophys geophysical
Ger German, Germanic, Germanisch, Germany
Ges gesellschaft
gov governing, governors
govt government
grad graduate
Gr Brit Great Britain
guid guidance
gym gymnasium

handbk(s) handbooks
Hawaii
Hisp Hispanic, Hispanico, Hispano
hist historie, historia, historial, historic, historica, historical, historique, historische, history
histol histology, histological
Hoshsch Hoshschule
hon honorable, honorary
hosp(s) hospital(s)
hq headquarters
HumRRO Human Resources Research Office
hwy highway

Ill Illinois
illum illuminating, illumination

illus illustrate, illustration
illusr illustrator
imp imperial
improv improvement
Inc Incorporated
incl include, included, includes, including
Ind Indiana
indust(s) industrial, industry(ies)
infor information
inst institut, institrute(s), institution(s), instituto
instnl institutional, institutionalized
instr instruction, instructor(s)
instruct instructional
int internacional, international, internazionale
intel intelligence
introd introduction
invest investigacion, investiganda, investigation, investigative
investr investigator
ist istituto
Ital Italia, Italian, Italiana, Italiano, Italica, Italien, Italienisch, Italienne, Italy

J Journal
Jan January
jour journal, journalism
jr junior
jurisp jurisprudence
juv juvenile(s)

Kans Kansas
Koninki koninklijk
Ky Kentucky

La Louisiana
lab laboratorie, laboratorio, laboratorium, laboratory(ies)
lang language(s)
lect lecture(s)
lectr lecturer
legis legislacion, legislatief, legislation, legislative, legislativo, legislature, legislazione
lett letter(s), lettera, letteraria, letterature, lettere
lib liberal
libr libary(ies), librerio
librn librarian(s)
lic license, lecencia
ling linguistic(s), linguistica, linguistique
lit liteary, literatur, literatura, literature, littera, literature
Ltd Limited

m married
mach machine(s), machinery
mag magazine
Man Manitoba
Mar March
Mariol Mariological, Mariology
Mass Massachusetts
mat matematica, matematiche, matematico, matematik
math mathematics, mathematical, mathematics, mathematik, mathematique(s), mathematisch
Md Maryland
mech mechanical
med medical, medicine
Mediter Mediterranean
mem member, memoirs, memorial
ment mental, mentally
metrop metropolitan

Mex Mexican, Mexicano, Mexico
mfg manufacturing
mfr manufacture, manufacturer
mgr manager(s)
mgt management
Mich Michigan
mid middle
mil military
Minn Minnesota
Miss Mississippi
mitt mitteilung
mkt market, marketing
MLA Modern Language Association of America
Mo Missouri
mod modern,moderna, moderne, moderno
monatsh monatsheft(e)
monatsschr monatsschrift
monogr monograph
Mont Montana
morphol morphologica, morphologie, morphology
mt mount, mountain(s)
munic municipal
mus museum(s)
musicol musicological, musicology

n north
nac nacional
NASA National Aeronautics & Space Administration
nat nationaal, national, nationale, nationalis, naturalized
NATO North Atlantic Treaty Organization
naz nazionale
NB New Brunswick
NC North Carolina
MCTE National Council of Teachers of English
NDak North Dakota
NDEA National Defense Education Act
NEA National Education Association
Nebr Nebraska
Ned Nederland, Nederlandsch
Nev Nevada
Neth Netherlands
Nfld Newfoundland
NH New Hampshire
NJ New Jersey
NMex New Mexico
no number
nonres nonresident
norm normal, normale
Norweg Norwegian
Nov November
NS Nova Scotia
NSW New South Wales
NT Northwest Territories
numis numismatic, numismatico, numismatique
NY New York
NZ New Zealand

occas occasional
occup occupation, occupational
Oct October
Ohio
OEEC Organization for European Economic Cooperation
off office, officer(s), official(s)
Okla Oklahoma
Ont Ontario
oper operation(s), operational, operative
ord ordnance
Ore Oregon
orgn organization, organizational
orient oriental, orientale, orientalist,

orientalia
ornithol ornithological, ornithology

Pa Pennsylvania
Pac Pacific
paleontol paleontological, paleontology
PanAm Pan American
pedag pedagogia, pedagogic, pedagogical, pedagogico,
pedagogoie, pedagogik, pedagogique, pedagogy
Pei Prince Edward Island
penol penological, penology
phenomenol phenomenological, phenomenologie, phenomenology
philol philologica, philological, philologie, philologisch, philology
philos philosophia, philosophic, philosophical, philosophie,
philosophique, philosophisch, philosophical, philosohpy, philosozophia
photog photographic, photography
photogr photographer(s)
phys physical
pkwy parkway
pl place
polit politica, political, politicas, politico, politics,
politek, politike, politique, politsch, politisk
polytech polytechnic
pop population
Pontif Pontifical
Port Portugal, Portuguese
postgrad postgraduate
PR Puerto Rico
pract practice
prehist prehistoric
prep preparation, preparatory
pres president
Presby Presbyterian
preserv preservation
prev prevention, preventive
prin principal(s)
prob problem(s)
probtn probation
proc proceding
prod production
prof professional, professor, professorial
prog program(s), programmed, programming
proj project, projective
prom promotion
prov province, provincial
psychiat psychiatria, psychiatric, psychiatrica, psychiatrie, psychiatrique, psychiatrisch, psychiatry
psychol psychological
pt point
pub pub, publique
publ publication(s), published, publisher(s), publishing
pvt private

qm quartermaster
quad quaderni
qual qualitative, quality
quart quarterly
Que Quebec

rd road
RD Rural Delivery, Rural Free Delivery Rural Free Delivery
rec record(s), recording
rech recherche
redevelop redevelopment
ref reference
regist register, registered, registration

registr registrar
rehabil rehabilitation
rel(s) relacion, relation(s), relative, relazione
relig religion, religious
rep representative
repub republic
req requirement(s)
res research, reserve
rev review, revised, revista, revue
rhet rhetoric, rhetorical
RI Rhode Island
Rt Right
Rte Route
Russ Russian
rwy railway

s south
SAfrica South Africa
SAm South America, South American
Sask Saskatchewan
SC South Carolina
Scand Scandinavian
sch(s) school(s)
scholar scholarship
sci science(s), scientia, scientific, scientifico, scientifique, scienza
SDak South Dakota
SEATO Southeast Asia Treaty Organization
sec secondary
sect section
secy secretary
sem seminaire, seminar, seminario, seminary
sen senator, sneatorial
Sept September
ser serial, series
serv service(s)
soc social, sociedad, sociedade, societa, societas, societate,
societe, societet, society(ies)
soc sci social science(s)
sociol sociological, sociology
Span Spanish
spec special
sq square
sr senior
sr sister
St Saint, Street
sta station
statist statistical, statistics
Ste Sainte, Suite
struct structural, structure(s)
subcomt subcommittee
subj subject
substa substa
super superieur, superior, superiore
suppl supplement, supplementary
supt superintendent
supv supervising, supervision
supvr supervisor
supvry supervisory
surg surgical, surgery
surv survey
Swed Swedish
Switz Switzerland
symp symposium
syst system, systematic

tech technic(s), technica, technical, technicky, techniczny,
techniek, technik, technika, technikum, technique, technisch
technol technologic, technological, technologicke,
technologico, technologiczny, technologie, technologika,

technologique, technologisch, technology
tecnol   technologia, technologica, technologico
tel   telegraph(s), telephone
temp temporary
Tenn Tennessee
Terr Terrace
teol teologia, teologico
Tex Texas
textbk   textbook(s)
theol   theological, theologie, theologique, theologisch,
theology
theoret   theoretic(al)
ther therapy
trans   transactions
transp   transportation
transl   translation, translator(s)
treas   treasurer, treasury
trop tropical
TV   television
twp township

u   und
UAR   United Arab Republic
UK   United Kingdom
UN   United Nations

unemploy   unemployment
UNESCO   United Nations Educational, Scientific & Cultural Organization
UNICEF   United Nations Children's Fund
univ(s)   universidad, universite, university(ies)
UNRRA   United Nations Relief & Rehabilitation Administration
UNRWA   United Nations Relief & Works Agency
USA   United States of America
US   United States
USPHS   United States Public Health Service
USSR Union of Soviet Socialist Republics
Utah

Va   Virginia
var   various
veg   vegetable(s), vegetation
ver   vereeniging, verein, vereingt, vereinigung
vet   veteran, veterinarian, veterinary
VI   Virgin Islands

vis   visiting
voc   vocational
vocab   vocabulary
vol(s)   volume(s), voluntary, volunteer(s)
vchmn   vice chairman
vpres   vice president
Vt   Vermont

w   west
Wash Washington
wetensch   wetenschappelijk, wetenschappen
WHO   World Health Organization
WI   West Indies
wid   widow, widowed, widower
Wis Wisconsin
wiss   wissenschaft(en), wissenschaftliche(e)
WVa   West Virginia
Wyo   Wyoming

yearbk   yearbook(s)
YMCA Young Men's Christian Association
YMHA Young Men's Hebrew Association
YWCA Young Women's Christian Association
YWHA Young Women's Hebrew Association

z   zeitschrift

Biographies

A

AAGESON, JAMES W.
PERSONAL Born 11/24/1947, Havre, MT, m, 1970, 3 children **DISCIPLINE** NEW TESTAMENT STUDIES; HISTORY OF EARLY CHRISTIANITY **EDUCATION** MDiv, 76, MTh, 77, PhD, 84. **CAREER** Prof Relig, Concordia,Col. **MEMBERSHIPS** Soc Bibl Lit; Cath Bibl Asn **RESEARCH** Pauline Studies; New Testament Socio-linguistics; Jewish-Christian relations. **SELECTED PUBLICATIONS** Auth, Written Also for Our Sake: Paul and the Art of Biblical Interpretation, John Knox Press, 93; Paul's Gospel and the Language of Control: A Summary, Teaching at Concordia, 93; Judaizing and Lectionary, Early Jewish, Anchor Bible Dictionary; Typology, Correspondence, and the Application of Scripture in Romans 9-11, The Pauline Writings: A Sheffield Reader, Sheffield Acad Press, 95; Control in Pauline Language and Culture: A Study of Rom 6; New Testament Studies, 96; A Theoretical Context for Understanding I Cor 1:18-2:16, Teaching at Concordia, 96; 2 Timothy and Its Theology: In Search of a Theological Pattern, Soc of Bibl Lit Sem Papers, 97. **CONTACT ADDRESS** 901 S Eight St., Moorhead, MN, 56562. **EMAIL** aageson@cord.edu

AARON, DANIEL
PERSONAL Born 08/04/1912, Chicago, IL, m, 1937, 3 children **DISCIPLINE** AMERICAN STUDIES **EDUCATION** Univ Mich, AB, 33; Harvard Univ, PhD, 43. **CAREER** Instr English, Harvard Univ, 36-39, coun Am civilization, 37-39; from instr to prof English, Smith Col, 39-61, Jordan prof English lang & lit, 61-71; prof English, 71-75, chmn, Comt Higher Degrees in Hist Am Civilization, 71-79, V S THOMAS PROF ENGLISH & AM LIT & LANG, HARVARD UNIV, 75-, Guggenheim fel, 47; vis lectr, Bennington Col, 50-51; Smith-Mundt fel, 51-52; vis prof, Univ Helsinki, 51-52; Amherst Col, 54-55 & Univ Warsaw, 62-63; Fund for the Republic grant, 55; fel, Ctr Advan Study Behav Sci, 58-59; fel, Huntington Libr, 64; mem adv comt Am studies, Comt Int Exchange Persons, 66-; Fulbright prof, Univ Sussex, 68-69; Nat Humanities Inst fel, 75-76. **HONORS AND AWARDS** DrLet, Union Col, 68, Colby Col, 71, Univ Pa, 76. **MEMBERSHIPS** MLA; Am Acad Arts & Sci; Am Antiq Soc; Am Studies Asn (vpres, 67-68, pres, 71-73); fel Orgn Am Historians. **RESEARCH** American literature and history. **SELECTED PUBLICATIONS** Auth, Men of Good Hope, Oxford Univ; coauth, Ralph Waldo Emerson: A Modern Anthology, Houghton, 59; auth, Writers on the Left, Harcourt, 61, Oxford Univ, 77; ed, Paul Elmer More's Shelbourne Essays, Harcourt, 63; coauth, The United States: A History of the Republic, Prentice-Hall; co-ed, The Strenuous Decade: A Social and Intellectual Record of the 1930's, Doubleday, 70; auth, The Unwritten War: American Writers and the Civil War, Knopf, 73 & 76. **CONTACT ADDRESS** Harvard Univ, Warren House 23, Cambridge, MA, 02138.

ABADIE, HUBERT DALE
PERSONAL Born 05/18/1935, Edgard, LA, m, 1964, 3 children **DISCIPLINE** MODERN BRITISH HISTORY **EDUCATION** Loyola Univ La, BS, 57; La State Univ, MA, 61; Univ Calif, Los Angeles, PhD(Hist), 71. **CAREER** Actg asst prof, 62-64, asst prof, 67-72, assoc prof, 72-80, prof Hist, Univ Miss, 80-, assoc dean grad sch, 77-82; act dean, col Lib Arts, 82-84; assoc dean grad sch, 84; act assoc v chan Academic Affairs, 84-85; act dean, col Lib Arts, 85-86; dean, Col Lib Arts, 86-98; dean, Col of Lib Arts, prof History, 98; assoc dir, Croft Inst for Inter Studies, 98. **RESEARCH** Modern British political history; liberal imperialism in Britain; Victorian nonconformists. **SELECTED PUBLICATIONS** Co-ed, Sir Roger Casement, Theodore Roosevelt, and Congo reform: an unpublished letter, Mid Am, 1/65; A Song of Huey Lang, Louisiana History, XI, 70, 271-273. **CONTACT ADDRESS** Croft Inst for International Studies, Univ of Mississippi, General Delivery, University, MS, 38677-9999. **EMAIL** dabadi@olemiss.edu

ABBOT, WILLIAM WRIGHT
PERSONAL Born 05/20/1922, Louisville, GA, m, 1958, 2 children **DISCIPLINE** AMERICAN HISTORY **EDUCATION** Univ Ga, AB, 43; Duke Univ, MA, 49, PhD (hist), 53. **CAREER** From asst prof to assoc prof hist, Col William & Mary, 53-58; assoc prof, Northwestern Univ, 58-59 & Rice Univ, 61-63; prof, Col William & Mary, 63-66; PROF HIST, UNIV VA, 66-, Bk rev ed, William & Mary Quart, 55-61, ed, 63-66; assoc ed, J Southern Hist, 61-62, ed, 62-63; mem, Coun Inst Early Am Hist & Cult, 76-; ed, Papers of George Washington, 77- **MEMBERSHIPS** AHA; Orgn Am Historians; Southern Hist Asn. **RESEARCH** Eighteenth century America. **SELECTED PUBLICATIONS** Auth, The Royal Governors of Georgia, 1754-1775, Univ NC, 57; The Colonial Origins of the United States, 1607-1763, Wiley, 75. **CONTACT ADDRESS** Corcoran Dept of Hist, Univ of Va, Charlottesville, VA, 22903.

ABBOTT, ALBERT
PERSONAL Born 03/31/1922, Philadelphia, PA, m, 1950, 2 children **DISCIPLINE** AMERICAN HISTORY **EDUCATION** John Carroll Univ, BS, 52, MA, 58; Georgetown Univ, PhD(hist), 62. **CAREER** Teaching fel hist, Georgetown Univ, 58-61; ASST PROF HIST, FAIRFIELD UNIV, 61- **MEMBERSHIPS** Am Acad Polit & Soc Sci; Acad Polit Sci; AHA. **RESEARCH** American colonial and Negro history; American Civil War. **CONTACT ADDRESS** Dept of Hist, Fairfield Univ, Fairfield, CT, 06430.

ABBOTT, CARL
PERSONAL Born 12/03/1944, Knoxville, TN **DISCIPLINE** HISTORY **EDUCATION** Swarthmore Col, BA, 66; Univ Chicago, MA, 67; PhD, 71. **CAREER** Visg asst prof, hist, Univ Denver, 71-72; asst to assoc prof, hist and urban studies, Old Dominion Univ, 72-78; assoc dir, grad prog, pub hist, Portland State Univ, 78-79; assoc prof, urban studies and planning, Portland State Univ, 79-83; Aspinall prof, hist, polit sci, and pub affairs, Mesa Col, 85; Banneker prof, Washington area studies, vis prof, urban and reg planning, George Washington Univ, 87; prof, urban studies and planning, Portland State Univ, 83. **HONORS AND AWARDS** Pres, Urban Hist Asn, 98. **RESEARCH** History of U.S. cities and city planning; Regional growth and planning in American West. **SELECTED PUBLICATIONS** Coauth, Planning a New West: The Columbia River Gorge National Scenic Area, with Sy Adler and Margery P. Abbott, Corvallis, Ore State Univ Press, 97; auth, Planning the Oregon Way: A Twenty Year Evaluation, ed with Deborah Howe and Sy Adler, Corvallils, Ore State Univ Press, 94; The Metropolitan Frontier: Cities in the Modern American West, Tucson, Univ Ariz Press, 93; Articles, The International Cities Hypothesis: An Approach to American Urban History, Jour of Urban Hist, 24, Nov, 97; Thinking about Cities: The Central Tradition in U.S. Urban Histoty, Jour of Urban Hist, 22, Sep, 96; The Internationalization of Washington, D.C., Urban Affairs Rev, 31, May, 96; Beautiful Downtown Burbank: Changing Metropolitan Geography in the Modern West, Jour of the West, 34, Jul, 95; Reading Urban History: Influential Books and Historians, Jour of Urban Hist, 21, Nov, 94; Metropolitan Portland: Reputation and Reality, Built Environ, 20, 1, 94; The Politics of Land Use Law in Oregon: Senate Bill 100, Twenty Years After, Ore Hist Quart, 94, Spr, 93. **CONTACT ADDRESS** School of Urban Studies and Planning, Portland State Univ, Portland, OR, 97207. **EMAIL** abbottc@pdx.edu

ABBOTT, ELIZABETH
PERSONAL Ottawa, ON, Canada **DISCIPLINE** HISTORY **EDUCATION** Sir George Williams Univ, BA, 63; McGill Univ, MA, 66, PhD, 71. **CAREER** Res dir, Centre d'Etude Que, Concordia Univ, 66-84; prof hist, Dawson Col, 72-84; Reuters reporter, Haiti, 86-88; ed-in-chief, Chronicle Publ, 89-91; DEAN WOMEN, TRINITY COL, DEAN ST HILDA'S COL, UNIV TORONTO. **SELECTED PUBLICATIONS** Auth, Haiti: The Duvaliers and their Legacy, 88; ed, Racism or Responsible Government? The French Canadian Dilemma of the 1840's, 67; ed, Debates of the Legislative Assembly of United Canada 1841-1854, vols 1-19, 70-83; co-comp, Bibliographie pour Servir a l'Etude de l'Histoire du Canada Francais, 66; co-comp, L'inventaire de la Collection Louis-Hippolyte LaFontaine, 68. **CONTACT ADDRESS** 44 Devonshire Pl, Toronto, ON, M5S 2E2.

ABBOTT, RICHARD HENRY
PERSONAL Born 08/18/1936, Springfield, IL, m, 1976, 2 children **DISCIPLINE** UNITED STATES HISTORY **EDUCATION** Grinnell Col, BA, 58; Univ Mo, MA, 59; Univ Wis, PhD(US hist), 65. **CAREER** Asst prof US hist, Old Dominion Col, 63-66; from asst prof to assoc prof, prof Hist, Eastern Mich Univ, 73-. **HONORS AND AWARDS** Phi Beta Kappa. **RESEARCH** Civil War and Reconstruction; Negro history; history of the South. **SELECTED PUBLICATIONS** Auth, Ohio's Civil War Governors, Ohio Civil War Centennial Comn, 62; Yankee farmers in northern Virginia, 1840-1860, Va Mag Hist & Biog, 1/68; The agricultural press views the Yeoman, 1819-1859, Agr Hist, 1/68; Massachusetts and the Negro enlistment law of July, 1864, Civil War Hist, 9/68; Cobbler in Congress: Life of Henry Wilson, 1812-1875, Univ Ky, 72; chap on Republican party, In: Radical Republicans in the North, Johns Hopkins, 76; contribr, The Encycl of Southern History, La State Univ Press, 79; Coast Defense in the Spanish-American War, North Atlantic Squadron, United States Navy, and Afro-American Troops in the Philippine War in Bede, ed, The War of 1898 and US Interventions, 1898-1934, Garland publishers, 94; Henry Wilson, in The Vice Presidents: A Biographical Directory, Facts on File, 98. **CONTACT ADDRESS** Dept of History & Philosophy, Eastern Michigan Univ, 701 Pray Harrold, Ypsilanti, MI, 48197-2201. **EMAIL** his_abbott@online.emich.edu

ABEL, ELIE
PERSONAL Born 10/17/1920, Montreal, PQ, Canada **DISCIPLINE** HISTORY **EDUCATION** McGill Univ, BA, 41, LLD, 71; Columbia Univ, MS, 42; Univ Western Ont, LLD, 76. **CAREER** Journalist, vars publs, 41-70; dean, sch jour, Columbia Univ, 70-79; prof comm, Stanford Univ, 79-91; Mary Lou and George Boone Centennial prof & dir, Stanford in Washington, 93-94. **SELECTED PUBLICATIONS** Auth, The Missile Crisis, 66; coauth, Special Envoy to Churchill and Stalin 1941-46; coauth, Roots of Involvement: The U.S. in Asia 1784-1971; coauth, The Shattered Bloc: Behind the Upheaval in Eastern Europe, 90; ed, What's News: The Media in American Society, 81; ed, Leaking: Who Does It? Who Benefits? At What Cost?, 87. **CONTACT ADDRESS** 4101 Cathedral Ave NW, Apt 904, Washington, DC, 20016-3585.

ABEL, KERRY
DISCIPLINE SOCIAL AND CULTURAL HISTORY **EDUCATION** Queen's Univ, BA, PhD; Univ Manitoba, MA. **CAREER** Prof. **RESEARCH** Social and cultural history of the Canadian north. **SELECTED PUBLICATIONS** Co-ed, Aboriginal Resource Use in Canada: Historical and Legal Aspects, Univ Manitoba Press, 91; co-auth, Northern Athapaskan Oral Traditions and the White River Volcano, Catchpole, Ethnohist 39/2, 92; Colonies: A History of Canada before Confederation,

McGraw-Hill Ryerson, 92; auth, Drum Songs: Glimpses of Dene History, Montreal and Kingston: McGill-Queen's UP, 93; The Northwest and the North, Can Hist: A Reader's Guide, Vol 1, Univ Toronto Press, 94; Prophets, Priests and Preachers: Glimpses of Dene History, Out of the Background: Readings on Can Native Hist, Copp Clark, 96. **CONTACT ADDRESS** Dept of Hist, Carleton Univ, 1125 Colonel By Dr, Ottawa, ON, K1S 5B6. **EMAIL** kabel@ccs.carleton.ca

ABELS, RICHARD
PERSONAL Born 10/31/1951, Brooklyn, NY, m, 1975, 2 children **DISCIPLINE** HISTORY **EDUCATION** Columbia Univ, BA, 73; Columbia Univ, MA, 75; Columbia Univ, MPhil, 76; Columbia, PhD, 82. **CAREER** Asst prof, Cornell Col, 81-82; asst prof, USNA, 82-85; assoc prof, USNA 85-91; prof, USNA, 91-. **HONORS AND AWARDS** Teaching excellence award, USNA; Phi Beta Kappa; Magna Cum Laude, Columbia Univ. **MEMBERSHIPS** Charles Homer Haskins Soc for Anglo-Saxon, Norman, Angevin and Viking Hist; fel Royal Hist Soc; AHA; Medieval Academy. **RESEARCH** Anglo-Saxon hist; Anglo-Norman hist; medieval military hist; medieval heresy. **SELECTED PUBLICATIONS** Coauth, "The Participation of Women in Languedocian Catharism", in Mediaeval Studies 41, 97; auth, The Council of Whitby: A Study in Early Anglo Saxon Politics; auth, "the Devolution of Brookland in Ninth-Century Kent", in Archaeologia Cantiana 99, 83; auth, "Bookland and Fyrd Service in Late Saxon England", in Anglo-Norman Studies 7, 85; auth, Lordship and Military Obligation in Anglo-Saxon England, Univ Calif, 88; auth, Historical Introduction to Domesday Bedfordshire, Alecto Editions, 91; auth, "English Tactics and Strategy in the Late Tenth Century", in The Battle of Maldon A.D. 991, Oxford: Basil Blackwell, 91; auth, "King Alfred's Peace-Making Strategies with the Vikings", in The Haskins Society Journal: Studies in Medieval History 3, 92; auth, "English Logistics and Military Administration 871-1066: The Impact of the Viking Wars", in Military Aspects of Scandinavian Society in a European Perspective, AD 1-1300, 97; auth, "Sheriffs, Lord-Seeking and the Norman Settlement of the South-East Midlands", in Anglo-Norman Studies 19, 97; auth, Alfred the Great: War, Kingship and Culture in Ninth-Century England, Longman, 98. **CONTACT ADDRESS** History Department, U.S. Naval Academy, Annapolis, MD, 21402-5044. **EMAIL** abels@nadn.navy.mil

ABELSON, ELAINE S.
DISCIPLINE HISTORY **EDUCATION** NY Univ, PhD, 86. **CAREER** Fac, Eugene Lang Col. **RESEARCH** Dimensions of inequality; gender, urban women, and homelessness in the Great Depression. **SELECTED PUBLICATIONS** Auth, When Ladies Go A-Thieving: Middle-Class Shoplifters in the Victorian Department Store, 90. **CONTACT ADDRESS** Eugene Lang Col, New Sch for Social Research, 66 West 12th St, New York, NY, 10011.

ABOU-EL-HAJ, BARBARA
DISCIPLINE ART HISTORY **EDUCATION** UCLA, PhD, 75. **CAREER** Assoc prof/ch, SUNY Binghamton. **RESEARCH** Soc hist of medieval art and archit; monastic arts; political economy of building; cult of saints. **SELECTED PUBLICATIONS** Auth, The Medieval Cult of Saint in Formations and Transformations, Cambridge UP, 97; Artistic Integration Inside the Cathedrals, Social Consensus Outside? in Artistic Integration in Early Gothic Churches, Univ Toronto P, 95; Building and Decorating at Reims and Amiens in Europaische Skulptur im 12./13. Jahrhundert, Frankfurt am Main, 94. **CONTACT ADDRESS** SUNY Binghamton, PO Box 6000, Binghamton, NY, 13902-6000. **EMAIL** abouel@binghamton.edu

ABOU-EL-HAJ, RIFAAT ALI
PERSONAL Born 11/21/1933, Jerusalem, Palestine, m, 1967, 4 children **DISCIPLINE** EUROPEAN, NEAR EASTERN & COMPARATIVE HISTORY **EDUCATION** Washington & Lee Univ, AB, 56; Princeton Univ, MA, 59, PhD, 63. **CAREER** Asst instr, Princeton Univ, 60; from instr to asst prof, St Lawrence Univ, 62-64; from asst prof to assoc prof, 64-73, prof, Calif State Univ, Long Beach, 73-93; PROF, BINGHAMTON UNIV, BINGHAMTON, 93-; Consult, Choice, 64; assoc ed, The Hist Teach, 80-90. **MEMBERSHIPS** AHA; fel Royal Asiatic Soc; fel Mid East Studies Asn NAm. **RESEARCH** Ottoman Turkish history; Arab history; Modern European history; Comparative history. **SELECTED PUBLICATIONS** Auth, Closure of Ottoman Frontier in Europe: 1699-1703, 69 & Ottoman Vezir and Pasha households: 1683-1703, 74, J Am Oriental Soc; Ottoman attitudes toward negotiations, Der Islam, 74; The Narcissism of Mustafa II, 1695-1703, Studia Islamica, 74; The Rebellion of 1703 and the Structure of Ottoman Politics, Neth Inst Near East, 74; The Rebellion of 1703 and the Structure of Ottoman Politics, Istanbul, 84; The Formation of the Modern State: The Ottoman Empire from the 16th-18th Centuries, Albany, 92; auth & co-ed, The Ottoman City and Its Part: Urban Structure and Social Order, New Rochelle, 92; Theorizing beyond the nation-state: Ottoman society from 16th-19th Centuries, in Armagan: Festschrift fur Andreas Tietz, Prage, 95; Historiography in South West Asian and North African studies since Sa'id's Orientalism, in History after the Three Worlds: A Crisis in Historical Consciousness, forthcoming. **CONTACT ADDRESS** Hist Dept, SUNY, Binghamton, Binghamton, NY, 13902-6000. **EMAIL** 110430.1274@compuserve.com

ABRAHAM, DANIEL
PERSONAL Born 08/22/1968, Middletown, NY **DISCIPLINE** MUSICOLOGY **EDUCATION** Univ Mass, BM, 90;Univ Md, MM,95; PhD 99. **CAREER** Grad tchg asst, Univ Md, 94-98; vis prof mus, George Washington Univ, 98-99. **HONORS AND AWARDS** Conducting Fel, Ore Bach Festival,97; Irving Lowens Award for Student Musicol Res, 96. **MEMBERSHIPS** Am Musicol Soc; Soc 17th Century Mus; Am Bach Soc; Sonneck Soc Am Mus; Hist Brass Soc. **RESEARCH** 18th Century Music; Music in Society; Performance Practice; Music of Bach and Handel; Computer Application in Musicology; Choral Music. **SELECTED PUBLICATIONS** Auth, In Tuneful Muses: A Tribute to Henry Purcell,Univ Md, 95. **CONTACT ADDRESS** George Washington Univ, 1109 Devere Dr., Silver Spring, MD, 20903-1649. **EMAIL** dabraham@wam.umd.edu

ABRAMS, BRADLEY
DISCIPLINE RUSSIAN AND EAST CENTRAL EUROPEAN HISTORY **EDUCATION** Univ Tex, BA, 86; Stanford Univ, PhD, 97. **CAREER** Asst prof. **RESEARCH** Central and east central European history. **SELECTED PUBLICATIONS** Auth, Die Vertreibung der Sudetendeutschen und die tschechoslowakische Opposition in den 70er Jahren, Transit, 95; The Price of Retribution: The Trial of Jozef Tiso, E Europ Polit Soc, 96. **CONTACT ADDRESS** Dept of History, Columbia Col, New York, 2960 Broadway, New York, NY, 10027-6902.

ABRAMS, DOUGLAS CARL
PERSONAL Born 01/07/1950, Tarboro, NC, m, 1980 **DISCIPLINE** AMERICAN & EUROPEAN HISTORY **EDUCATION** Bob Jones Univ, BA, 72; NC State Univ, MA, 74; Sorbonne, Paris, dipl, 74; Univ Md, PhD, 81. **CAREER** Prof Am hist, Bob Jones Univ, 74-77; teaching asst, Univ Md, 77-81, instr, Univ Col, 81; PROF AM HIST, BOB JONES UNIV, 81- **MEMBERSHIPS** AHA; Orgn Am Historians. **RESEARCH** The New Deal era; twentieth century American political history; southern history. **SELECTED PUBLICATIONS** Auth, A progressive-conservative duel: The 1920 Democratic Gubernatorial primaries in NC, NC Hist Rev, autumn 78; THE UNBOUNDED COMMUNITY - NEIGHBORHOOD LIFE AND SOCIAL-STRUCTURE IN NEW-YORK-CITY, 1830-1875 - SCHERZER,KA/, HISTORIAN, Vol 0055, I DISSENT - THE LEGACY OF MCREYNOLDS,JAMES,CLARK - BOND,JE/, JOURNAL OF SOUTHERN HISTORY, Vol 0060, 1994 **CONTACT ADDRESS** 135A White Oak Dr, Greenville, SC, 29607.

ABRAMS, RICHARD M.
PERSONAL Born 07/12/1932, Brooklyn, NY, m, 1960, 3 children **DISCIPLINE** UNITED STATES HISTORY **EDUCATION** Columbia Univ, AB, 53, AM, 55 PhD, 62. **CAREER** Lectr hist, Columbia Univ, 57-60; from instr to assoc prof, 61-72, prof hist, Univ Calif, Berkeley, 72-, Soc Sci Res Coun fel, 64-65; Fulbright lectr, Inst of US Studies, Univ London, 68-69; Nat Endowment for Humanities fel, 72; dir, summer sem col teachers, Nat Endowment for Humanities, 77, 79, 81, & 84; vis prof hist, Normal Univ, Beijing, CHN, 95; dist vis prof hist, Innsbruck, AUT, 88; dist Fulbright prof US hist, Moscow State Univ, 89. **MEMBERSHIPS** AHA; Am Soc Legal Hist; Econ Hist Assn. **RESEARCH** History of business in American life; American business expansion abroad in the early 20th century; business and government relations in the United States since 1875. **SELECTED PUBLICATIONS** Auth, The failure of progressivism, In: The Shaping of 20th Century America, 2nd ed, Little, 71; co-ed, The Shaping of 20th Century America, 2nd ed, 71; Legal change and the legitimacy of the corporation in America, Stanford Law Rev, 4/72; coauth, The Unfinished Century, Little, 73; auth, The Burdens of Progress, Scott, 78; auth, The Reputation of Felix Frankfurter, The Am Bar Res Jour, Summer, 85; auth, The US Military & Higher Education, Annals, AAPSS, vol 502, 89; Business & Gout, Encycl of Am Pol Hist, ed by Jack Greene, Scribner's, 84; auth Not a Unity but a Miltiple: American Culture and the Modern Political (Dis)Order, Inst of Gov Stud, Berkeley, 94. **CONTACT ADDRESS** Dept of History, Univ of California, Berkeley, Berkeley, CA, 94720-2550. **EMAIL** abramsr@socrates.berkeley.edu

ABRAMSON, DANIEL
DISCIPLINE ART HISTORY **EDUCATION** Princeton Univ, BA 86; Harvard Univ, MA 90, PhD 93. **CAREER** Connecticut Col, asst prof 93-98; Tufts Col, asst prof 98-. **CONTACT ADDRESS** Dept of Art and Art History, Tufts Univ, 11 Talbot Ave, Medford, MA, 02155.

ABU-GHAZALEH, ADNAN M.
PERSONAL Born 07/22/1927, m, 1962, 3 children **DISCIPLINE** MIDDLE EAST HISTORY **EDUCATION** Univ London, BA, 58; NY Univ, MA, 61, PhD(mod hist), 67. **CAREER** Lectr Europ hist, Col Educ, Jordan, 58-60 & 61-63; dir, Am-Jordanian Cult Rels, Ministry Educ, Jordan, 63-64; from asst prof to assoc prof Mid E hist, 64-72, prof Mid E Hist, State Univ NY Col Plattsburgh, 72-. **MEMBERSHIPS** Fel, Mid E Studies Asn NAm. **RESEARCH** Palestine problem; Arab nationalism; Ottoman European diplomacy 1875-1914. **SELECTED PUBLICATIONS** Auth, Usua al-Mujtama al-Arabi (basic features of Arab society), al-Nahda Press, Jordan, 60; Nationalism and Literary Writing in Mandatory Palestine, Islamic Rev & Arab Affairs, London, England, 5/70; Al-Muarrikhun al-Falastiniuun al-Arab fi Zaman al-Intidab al-Baritani (Palestinian Arab historian during the British mandate), Shuun Falastiniyyah, Beirut, Lebanon, 5/71; Arab Cultural Nationalism in Palestine during the British mandate, J Palestine Studies, Beirut, Lebanon, 4/72; Arab Cultural Nationalism in Palestine, 1919-1948, Inst Palestine Studies, Beirut, 73; American Missions in Syria, 88; Palestinian-Arab Culture 1919-1960, 91; History and Culture of the Ancient Middle East and North Africa, 93. **CONTACT ADDRESS** Dept of Hist, SUNY Plattsburgh, Plattsburgh, NY, 12901.

ABZUG, ROBERT HENRY
PERSONAL Born 05/02/1945, New York, NY **DISCIPLINE** AMERICAN HISTORY **EDUCATION** Harvard Univ, BA, 67; Univ Calif, Berkeley, PhD, 77. **CAREER** Lectr hist, Univ Calif, Los Angeles, 77-78; ASST PROF HIST, UNIV TEX, AUSTIN, 78- . **MEMBERSHIPS** AHA; Orgn Am Historians; Soc Hist Early Am Repub. **RESEARCH** American social and intellectual history; history of religion. **SELECTED PUBLICATIONS** Auth, The influence of Garrisonian Abolitionists' fears of slave violence on the antislavery argument, 1829-1840, J Negro Hist, 1/70; The Copperheads: Historical approaches to Civil War dissent in the Midwest, Ind Mag Hist, 3/70; The Black family during Reconstruction, In: Key Issues in the Afro-American Experience II, Harcourt, 71; Passionate Liberator: Theodore Dwight Weld and the Dilemma of Reform, Oxford Univ, 80; Religious Tradition and American Culture, Wm & Mary Quart, Vol 0053, 96; American Reform and Reformers, A Biographical Dictionary, Jour S Hist, Vol 0063, 97; The Religious Critic in American Culture, Jour Amer Hist, Vol 0082, 95; Moralists and Modernizers, Amer Pre-Civil War Reformers, Church Hist, Vol 0065, 96; Freedoms Champion, Lovejoy, Elijah, Church Hist, Vol 0065, 96; The Abolitionist Sisterhood Womens Political Culture in Antebellum America, Am Hist Rev, Vol 0101, 96. **CONTACT ADDRESS** Dept of Hist, Univ Tex, Austin, TX, 78712-1026.

ACCAD, EVELYNE
PERSONAL Born 10/06/1943, Beirut, Lebanon **DISCIPLINE** FRANCOPHONE STUDIES, AFRICAN STUDIES **EDUCATION** Anderson Col, BA, 67; Ball State Univ, MA, 68; Ind Univ, Bloomington, PhD(comp lit), 73. **CAREER** From teaching asst to instr French, Anderson Col, 65-68; teacher English & girl's counr, Int Col, Beirut, 68-70; teaching asst comp lit, Ind Univ, 71-73; asst prof, 71-80, Assoc Prof French, Univ Ill, 80- **MEMBERSHIPS** African Lit Asn (pres, 78); African Studies Asn; MLA. **RESEARCH** Women in literature and society; African and Near Eastern literatures; 20th century French literature. **SELECTED PUBLICATIONS** Auth, Des Femmes, des Hommes et la Guerre: Fiction et realite au Proche-Orient, Paris: Study, 93; contribur, Bahithat: Women and Writing, v 2, 95-96; auth, Arab Women's Literary Inscriptions: A Note and Extended Bibliography, Col Lit, 95; auth, Truth Versus Loyalty, in Bell, ed, Radically Speaking: Feminism Reclaimed, Spinifex, 96; auth, Trois Chansons, in Ecritures de Femmes: Nouvelles Cartographies, Yale, 96; auth, Assia Djebar's Contribution to Arab Women's Literature: Rebellion, Maturity, Vision, World Lit Today, 96; auth, Wounding Words: A Woman's Journal in Tunisia, Heinemann, 96; auth, Saadawi's Woman at Point Zero, in, Oxford Companion to African Literature, Oxford, forthcoming; auth, Violence and Sexuality, in, Sexual Aggression: Key Research and Activism, Purdue, forthcoming; auth, Nawal El Saadawi, in, Fifty African and Caribbean Women Writers, Greenwood, forthcoming. **CONTACT ADDRESS** French Dept, Univ Ill, 707 S Mathews Ave, Urbana, IL, 61801-3625. **EMAIL** e_accad@uiuc.edu

ACCAMPO, ELINOR A.
DISCIPLINE HISTORY **EDUCATION** Univ Calif, Berkeley, PhD, 84. **CAREER** Assoc prof; Univ Southern Calif; prof, Colo Col, 79-81; prof, Denison Univ, 82-83; prof, USC, 83-; actg ch, Gender Stud Prog, USC, 88-89. **RESEARCH** Social and cultural history of modern France; history of gender; family, and sexuality. **SELECTED PUBLICATIONS** Auth, Industrialization, Family Life, and Class Relations: Saint Chamond, 1815-1914, Univ Calif Press, 89; The Rhetoric of Reproduction and the Reconfiguration of Womanhood in the French Birth Control Movement, 1890-1920, J Family Hist, Vol 21, 96; coauth, Gender and the Politics of Social Reform in France, 1870-1914, John Hopkins UP, 95. **CONTACT ADDRESS** Dept of History, Univ Southern Calif, University Park Campus, Los Angeles, CA, 90089. **EMAIL** accampo@usc.edu

ACHENBAUM, W. ANDREW
PERSONAL Born 03/02/1947, Philadelphia, PA, m, 1971, 2 children **DISCIPLINE** HISTORY; GERONTOLOGY **EDUCATION** Amherst Col, BA, 68; Univ Pa, MA, 70; Univ Mich, PhD, 76. **CAREER** Asst prof hist, Canisius Col, 76-80; asst res scientist, Inst Geront, Univ Mich, Ann Arbor, 78-80; ASST PROF HIST, CARNEGIE-MELLON UNIV, 80-, Consult hist & humanities, Inst Gerontology, 77-78. **MEMBERSHIPS** Orgn Am Historians; Geront Soc; Soc Sci Hist Asn. **RESEARCH** United States social and cultural history; history of aging; social welfare. **SELECTED PUBLICATIONS** Auth, Old Age in The New Land: The American Experience Since

1790, Johns Hopkins Univ, 78; coauth, Old age and modernization, Gerontologist, 6/78; auth, From womb through bloom to tomb, Rev Am Hist, 6/78; coauth, Images of Old Age in America, 1790-Present, Inst of Gerontology, 78; auth, Modern Values and Aging America, Little Brown, 82. **CONTACT ADDRESS** Dept of Hist, Carnegie Mellon Univ, Pittsburgh, PA, 15213.

ACHTENBERG, DEBORAH
DISCIPLINE HISTORY OF PHILOSOPHY, ANCIENT PHILOSOPHY **EDUCATION** New Schl for Soc Res, PhD, 82. **CAREER** Assoc prof, Univ Nev, Reno. **RESEARCH** Aristotle; ethics; political philosophy. **SELECTED PUBLICATIONS** Essays on Aristotle's ethics were recently published in Crossroads of Norm and Nature: Essays on Aristotle's 'Ethics' and 'Metaphysics' (Rowman & Littlefield Press), Essays in Ancient Greek Philosophy IV (SUNY) and Feminism and Ancient Philosophy (Routledge). **CONTACT ADDRESS** Univ Nev, Reno, Reno, NV, 89557. **EMAIL** achten@scs.unr.edu

ACKELSBERT, MARTHA A.
PERSONAL Born 06/05/1946, New York, NY **DISCIPLINE** POLITICAL SCIENCE **EDUCATION** Radcliffe Col, BA, 68; Princeton Univ, MA, 70, PhD, 76. **CAREER** From lectr to asst and assoc prof, and prof, Smith Col, 72- ; vis lectr, Sch of Soc Sci, Univ Sussex, UK, 77; vis prof, Soc Thought and Polit Econ, Univ Mass, Amherst, 89. **HONORS AND AWARDS** Phi Beta Kappa; NDEA Fel; AAUW post-doctoral res fel, Fel, Mary Ingraham Bunting Inst, Radcliffe Col, 83-84; vis fel, Ctr for Europ Stud, Harvard Univ, 83-84; vis fel, Walt Whitman Ctr for Culture and Polit of Democracy, Rutgers Univ, 92-93. **MEMBERSHIPS** Am Polit Sci Asn; Western Polit Sci Asn. **RESEARCH** Democratic theory; feminist political theory; women's activism; Spanish anarchism. **SELECTED PUBLICATIONS** Co-ed, Women, Welfare and Higher Education: Toward Comprehensive Policies, Smith, 88; auth, Free Women of Spain: Anarchism and the Struggle for the Emancipation of Women, Indiana, 91; auth, Models of Revolution: Rural Women and Anarchist Collectivisation in Civil War Spain, J of Peasant Stud, 93; auth, Dependency or Mutuality: A Feminist Perspective on Dilemmas of Welfare Policy, Rethinking Marxism, 94; coauth, Report of the Committee on the Status of Lesbians and Gays in the Political Science Profession, PS: Polit Sci and Polit, 95; auth, Identity Politics, Political Identities: Thoughts Toward a Multicultural Politics, Frontiers: J of Women's Stud, 96; auth, Toward a Multicultural Politics: A Jewish Feminist Perspective, in Brettschneider, ed, The Narrow Bridge: Jewish Views on Multiculturalism, Rutgers, 96; auth, Rethinking Anarchism/Rethinking Power: A Contemporary Feminist Perspective, in Shanley, ed, Reconstructing Political Theory: Feminist Perspectives, Polity, 97; auth, Privacy, Publicity and Power: A Feminist Rethinking of the Public-Private Distinction, in Hirschmann, ed, Revisioning the Political: Feminist Reconstructions of Traditional Concepts in Western Political Theory, Westview, 96. **CONTACT ADDRESS** Dept of Government, Smith Col, Northampton, MA, 01063. **EMAIL** mackelsb@sophia.smith.edu

ACKERMAN, JAMES SLOSS
PERSONAL Born 11/08/1919, San Francisco, CA, m, 1947, 4 children **DISCIPLINE** HISTORY/ARCHITECTURE **EDUCATION** Yale Univ, BA, 41; NY Univ, MA, 47, PhD, 52. **CAREER** Lectr hist art, 46 & 49, Yale Univ; from asst prof to prof hist art & archit, 52-60, Univ Calif, Berkeley; chmn dept, 63-68, prof, 60-, Harvard Univ;, chmn, 82-, ed-in-chief, Art Bull, 56-60; Coun Humanities fel, Princeton Univ, 60-61; mem, Coun Comt for Yale Art Gallery, 66-; Slade prof fine art, Cambridge Univ, 69-70; pres, Artists Found, 77-; mem, Coun Scholars, Libr Congr, 80-; Mellon Lectr, 85-, Natl Gallery of Art; Meyer Schapiro vis prof, Art Hist, 88. **HONORS AND AWARDS** Distinguished Teaching in Art Educ Medal, Nat Gallery Art, 66; Centennial Citation, Univ Calif, 67; Morey Award, Col Art Assn Am; Hitchcock Prize, Soc Archit Hist; Grand Off Italian Republic,72; DFA, Col of Art, 84; Gold Medal, Istituto di Storia dell'Arte Lombarda: Inst Honors, Amer Inst Archit,87; DArch, Univ Venice,88; Gold Medal,Istituto di Storia dell'Arte Lombarda, 87; Col Art Ass of Amer, Dist Tchng Award, 91; Premio Daria Borghese, 95; Paul Kristeller Career Achiev Award, Renaissance soc Amer., MA, Harvard Univ, 60; LHD, Kenyon Col, 61 & Univ Md Baltimore County, 76; DFA, Md Inst Col Art, 72. **MEMBERSHIPS** Col Art Assn Am; Soc Archit Hist; Renaissance Soc Am; fel Am Acad Rome; fel Am Acad Arts & Sci. **RESEARCH** Italian renaissance art and architecture; history of architectural theory. **SELECTED PUBLICATIONS** Auth, Architecture of Michelangelo, Viking, 61; coauth, Seventeenth Century Science and the Arts, Princeton, 61; auth, Art and Archaeology, Englewood Cliffs, 63; auth, Palladio, Harmondsworth, 66; Palladio's Villas, Augustin, 67; coauth, Views of Florence, Walker, 67; auth, The Villa: Form and Ideology of Country Houses, Princeton & London, 90; auth, Distance Points; Studies in Theory and Renaissance Art and Architecture, Cambridge, 91. **CONTACT ADDRESS** Harvard Univ, Sackler Museum, Cambridge, MA, 02138. **EMAIL** jsackerm@fas.harvard.edu

ACKERMAN, ROBERT M.
DISCIPLINE ALTERNATIVE DISPUTE RESOLUTION, LEGAL HISTORY, LEGAL PROFESSION **EDUCATION** Colgate Univ, BA, 73; Harvard Univ, JD, 76. **CAREER** Assoc, Holme, Roberts & Owen, Denver, Colo, 76-80; asst profr, Dickinson Univ, 80- 83; assoc prof, 83-85; prof, 85; vis lectr, Leicester Polytechnic Sch Law, Eng, 87; vis prof, Pa State Univ, 89; vis prof, Univ Vienna, 94; dean-. **MEMBERSHIPS** Mem, Phi Beta Kappa; Soc Prof(s) in Dispute Resolution. **SELECTED PUBLICATIONS** Auth, Instructor's Manual with Simulation and Problem Materials to Accompany Riskin Westbrook's Dispute Resolution and Lawyers. **CONTACT ADDRESS** Sch of Law, Willamette Univ, 900 State St, Salem, OR, 97301. **EMAIL** rackerma@willamette.edu

ADAMS, AFESA M.
PERSONAL Born 02/20/1936, Greenwood, Mississippi, m, 1975 **DISCIPLINE** PSYCHOLOGY **EDUCATION** Weber State College, BS, 1969; University of Utah, MS, 1973, PhD, 1975. **CAREER** University of Florida, asst professor, behavioral studies, 1974-79, acting chair, behavioral studies, 1976-78, assoc professor, psychology, 1976-80; University of Utah, dept of family & consumer studies, chair, 1980-83, assoc vice president, academic affairs, 1984-89, assoc professor, family & consumer studies, adjunct assoc professor, dept of psychology; University of North Florida, College of Arts & Sciences, dean, 1989-93; Professor of Psychology, 1993- currently. **HONORS AND AWARDS** Beehive Lodge, Elks, community service award, 1986; Phi Kappa Phi; United Way, Great Salt Lake Area, recognition for community service award, 1986; Hall of Fame, Granite High School, 1987-88; Civil Rights Worker of the Year, NAACP SL Branch, 1988; Featured in State Office of Educational Equity Unit film, Building on a Legacy: Contemporary Pioneering Women, 1988. **MEMBERSHIPS** American Psychological Assn; Utah Council on Family Relations; Natl Council of Negro Women Inc; Southeastern Psychological Assn; American Psychological Assn; Gainesville Women's Health Center, board of directors; State of Utah, Divison of Children, Youth & Families Day Care, advisory board, 1980-83; Governor's Committee for Exec Reorganization, 1983-85; Governor's Task Force, study financial barriers to health care, 1983-84, employer sponsored child care, 1984; several publications and papers; Daniel Memorial Institute, Inc, board of directors, 1989; Jacksonville Community Council, Inc; Hubbard House Programs for Spouse Abuse, board of directors, 1992-94; Advocates for a Better Jacksonville, 1989-, Jacksonville Art Museum, bd of dirs, 1990-93; Jacksonville Women's Network, 1989-; Raines High School, advisory council, 1989-; Andrew Jackson High School, accreditation team, 1989-; JCCI Study, Young Black Males, management team, 1989-; Chair, Implementation Community: JCCI Young Black Males Study, 1989-; National Council on Family Relations, 1989-; Popular Culture Association, 1989-; American Association for High Education, 1989-93; JCCI, bd of dirs, 1993-, sec, 1994-95, president elect 1996-97; Leadership Jacksonville Class, 1994; LJ, bd of dirs, 1994-95; Florida Theatre, board of directors, 1994-, vice pres, 1996-; UNF/NW Link: A Service Learning Monitoring Program, 1995-. **CONTACT ADDRESS** Psychology Department, Univ of North Florida, St Johns Bluff Rd, S, Jacksonville, FL, 32224-2645.

ADAMS, GRAHAM, JR.
PERSONAL Born 03/04/1928, New York, NY **DISCIPLINE** HISTORY **EDUCATION** Williams Col, BA, 48; Columbia Univ, MA, 54, PhD, 62. **CAREER** Lectr, Univ Aberdeen (Scotland), 62-63; asst prof, Barnard Col, Columbia Univ, 63-64; asst prof, Univ Mo, 64-66; assoc prof, Wayne State Univ, 66-67; assoc prof to prof, 67-93, head hist dept, 67-75, ch Am stud, 67-93, PROF EMER HISTORY, MT ALLISON UNIV. **HONORS AND AWARDS** Am Philos Soc res grant, 66; Can Coun res grant, 75-76; SSHRC grant, 82-83; US Embassy grant res Am stud, 89-90. **MEMBERSHIPS** Am Hist Asn; Orgn Am Hist; Can Hist Asn. **SELECTED PUBLICATIONS** Auth, Age of Industrial Violence 1910-1915, 66, 71; ed consult, Harvard Bus Hist Rev; ed consult, Can Rev Am Stud. **CONTACT ADDRESS** Dept of History, Mount Allison Univ, 63D York St, Sackville, NB, E4L 1G9.

ADAMS, HENRY
PERSONAL Born 05/12/1949, Boston, MA, m, 1989 **DISCIPLINE** AMERICAN ART OF THE 19TH CENTURY **EDUCATION** Harvard Univ, BA, 71; Yale Univ, PhD, 80. **CAREER** Prof, Case Western Reserve Univ; Curator, Am Painting, Cleveland Mus Art; Curator, Carnegie Mus of Art, Pittsburgh; Curator Am Art Nelson-Atkins Mus Art, Kansas City; Dir, Cummer Mus Art,Jacksonville; Fla; Interim dir,Kemper Mus Contemporary Art & Design,Kansas City. **HONORS AND AWARDS** Distinguished Service Medal, William Jewell Col, 89; Col Art Asn's Arthur Kingsley Porter Prize, 85; Frances Blanshard Prize. **SELECTED PUBLICATIONS** Auth, exhib cat, John La Farge, 87; Thomas Hart Benton: An American Original, 89; Thomas Hart Benton: Drawing from Life, 90; Albert Bloch: The American Blue Rider, 97; Dale Chihuly: Thirty Years in Glass, 97. **CONTACT ADDRESS** Case Western Reserve Univ, 10900 Euclid Ave, Cleveland, OH, 44106. **EMAIL** adams@cma-oh.org

ADAMS, LOUIS JEROLD
PERSONAL Born 06/01/1939, Logan, UT, m, 1963, 2 children **DISCIPLINE** POLITICAL SCIENCE, ASIAN POLITICS AND INTERNATIONAL LAW **EDUCATION** Univ Wa., Seattle, PhD, 72. **CAREER** Asst prof, Central Mo State Univ, 72-80; assoc prof, 80-90; prof, 90-. **MEMBERSHIPS** Amer Polit Sci Asn; Assoc for Asian Studies; Intl Studies Assoc. **RESEARCH** US-Japan trade relations. **SELECTED PUBLICATIONS** Auth, United States - Japan Trade Relations: The Function of Treaties, Chuo Law Rev, vol CIV, no 10-11, Aug, 98; The Law of United States - Japan Trade Relations, Jour of World Trade, Apr, 90. **CONTACT ADDRESS** Political Science Dept., Central Missouri State Univ, Warrensburg, MO, 64093. **EMAIL** jadams@cmsu1.cmsu.edu

ADAMS, MARILYN M.
DISCIPLINE HISTORICAL THEOLOGY **EDUCATION** Univ Ill, AB, 64; Cornell Univ, PhD, 67; Princeton Theol Sem, ThM, 84; ThM, 85. **HONORS AND AWARDS** NEH, Younger Humanist fel, 74-75; Am Coun Learned Soc fel, 88-89; UC Pres Coun Hum fel, 88-89; Guggenheim fel, 89-90. **SELECTED PUBLICATIONS** Auth, Ockham's Treatise on Predestination, God's Foreknowledge, and Future Contingents, Century-Crofts, 69; Paul of Venice: On the Truth and Falsity of Propositions and On the Significatum of a Proposition, Oxford Univ Press, 77; William Ockham, Notre Dame Univ Press, 87; Ed, The Philosophical Theology of John Duns Scotus: A Collection of Essays by Allan B. Wolter, Oxford Univ Press, 90; Couth, The Problem of Evil, Oxford Univ Press, 90. **CONTACT ADDRESS** Yale Univ, 409 Prospect St., New Haven, CT, 06511-2167.

ADAMS, MICHAEL CHARLES C
PERSONAL Born 07/26/1945, Chesterfield, England, m, 1969, 2 children **DISCIPLINE** AMERICAN STUDIES; HISTORY **EDUCATION** Univ Wales, BA, 66; Univ Sussex, Ph-D(Am studies), 73. **CAREER** Lectr English, North Nottinghamshire Col Further Educ, 70-71; asst prof hist, 72-77, asst to pres, 76-77, dir Grad Ctr, 77-78, assoc provost, 78-80, ASSOC PROF HIST & GEOG & CHAIRPERSON, NORTHERN KY UNIV, 81- . **MEMBERSHIPS** Southern Hist Asn; Am Studies Asn. **RESEARCH** United States and British cultural and military history; the Southern region of the United States; Victorian sexual attitudes. **SELECTED PUBLICATIONS** Auth, Our Masters the Rebels: A Speculation on Union Military Failure in the East 1861-1865, Harvard Univ, 78; Tennyson's Crimean War poetry: A crosscultural approach, J Hist Ideas, spring 79; The Transformation of War, Rev Am Hist, Vol 0021, 93; American Manhood Transformations in Masculinity from the Revolution to the Modern Era, Rev Am Hist, Vol 0022, 94; Voices from Captivity Interpreting the American POW Narrative, Jour Am Hist, Vol 0082, 95; In the Hands of Providence, Chamberlain, J L and the American Civil War, Jour Am Hist, Vol 0080, 93; The 1st Day at Gettysburg Essays on Confederate and Union Leadership, Jour S Hist, Vol 0059, 93; Burnside, Jour S Hist, Vol 0059, 93; Chancellorsville 1863, The Souls of the Brave, Am Hist Rev, Vol 0098, 93; Fatherhood in American, A History, Rev Am Hist, Vol 0022, 94; The 2nd Day at Gettysburg, Essays on Confederate The Union Leadership, Jour S Hist, Vol 0060, 94; The Boy-Man, The Life of Baden Powell, Jour Hist Sexuality, Vol 0003, 93; For Country , Cause and Leader, The Civil War Journal of Haydon, Charles B., Civil War Hist, Vol 0040, 94; Remembering War the American Way, Civil War Hist, Vol 0042, 96; The 3rd Day at Gettysburg and Beyond. Jour S Hist, Vol 0062, 96; The Civil Way Memoir of Stephenson, Philip, Civil Way Hist, Vol 0042, 96; Goodbye, Piccadilly, British War Brides in America, Rev Am Hist, Vol 0025, 97. **CONTACT ADDRESS** Dept of Hist & Geog, No Kentucky Univ, Highland Heights, KY, 41076.

ADAMS, NICHOLAS
PERSONAL New York, NY, s, 1977 **DISCIPLINE** HISTORY **EDUCATION** Cornell Univ, AB, 70; NY Univ, PhD, 77. **CAREER** Asst prof, 78-89, Lehigh Univ; Mary Conover Mellon Prof, 89-, Vassar Col. **RESEARCH** Architecture and Urbanism **CONTACT ADDRESS** Art Dept, Vassar Col, Poughkeepsie, NY, 12604. **EMAIL** niadams@vassar.edu

ADAMS, R.E.W.
PERSONAL Born 07/17/1931, Kansas City, MO, m, 1955, 4 children **DISCIPLINE** ANTHROPOLOGY AND ARCHAEOLOGY **EDUCATION** BA, anthrop, Univ NMex, 53; MA, anthrop, Harvard Univ, 60; PhD, anthrop, 63. **CAREER** Asst prof to prof, anthrop, Univ Minn, 63-72; dean, humanities and social sci, Univ Tex San Antonio, 72-79; prof, anthrop, Univ Tex San Antonio, 80-. **HONORS AND AWARDS** Fulbright scholar, resident fel, Rochefeller Ctr, Bellagio, Italy, overseas fel, Churchill Col, Cambridge Univ, England. **MEMBERSHIPS** Soc for Amer Archaeol; Registry of Prof Archaeol; Tex Archaeol Soc. **RESEARCH** New world archaeology; Primary ancient civilizations; Maya archaeology. **SELECTED PUBLICATIONS** Auth, Prehistoric Mesoamerica, 2nd ed; ed, The Origins of Maya Civilization; Ancient Civilizations of the New World, Rio Azul. **CONTACT ADDRESS** 14070 Mint Tr., San Antonio, TX, 78232-3509. **EMAIL** rewadams@jhno.com

ADAMS, RALPH JAMES QUINCY
PERSONAL Born 09/22/1943, Hammond, IN, m, 1979, 1 child **DISCIPLINE** MODERN BRITISH HISTORY **EDUCATION** Ind Univ, BS, 65; Valparaiso Univ, MA, 69; Univ Calif,

Santa Barbara, PhD, 72. **CAREER** Lectr hist, Univ Calif, Santa Barbara, 71-73; asst prof, Bethany Col, WVa, 73-74; asst prof, 74-79, ASSOC PROF HIST, TEX A&M UNIV, 79-, Assoc ed, ALBION, 82-; Am Philos Soc grant, 78. **MEMBERSHIPS** AHA; Conf Brit Studies; Rocky Mountain Conf Brit Studies (pres, 80). **RESEARCH** British political history; British military history. **SELECTED PUBLICATIONS** Auth, Delivering the Goods: Reappraising the Ministry of Munitions, 1915-1916, Albion, 1/76; New Men, New Ideas, Old Economics: Observations on the Labor Unrest in Great Britain, 1910-1914, Red River Valley Hist J, 1/77; Arms and the Wizard: Lloyd George and the Ministry of Munitions, 1915-1916, Cassell & Co, Ltd, London & Tex A&M Univ, 78; The War in Whitehall: The Prelude to the Ministry of Munitions, 1914-1915, Australian J Hist & Polit, 8/78; The Women's Part: Female Labor and the British Ministry of Munitions in the First World War, Red River Valley Hist J, 1/79; Defending the Empire, The Conservative Party and British Defense Policy, 1899-1915, Am Hist Rev, Vol 0097, 92; The Roots of Appeasement, The British Weekly Press and Nazi Germany During the 1930s, Vol 0024, 92; Dilemnas of Appeasement, British Detterrence and Defense, 1934-1937, Vol 0025, 93; Chamberlain and Appeasement, British Policy and the Coming of the 2nd World, Eng Hist Rev, Vol 0109, 94; Lords of Parliament, 1794-1914, Historian, Vol 0059, 96; A Liberal Chronicle - Journals and Papers of Pease, J A, First Lord-Gainford, 1908-1910, Albion, Vol 0028, 96. **CONTACT ADDRESS** Dept of Hist, Tex A&M Univ, 1 Texas A and M Univ, College Station, TX, 77843.

ADAMS, RUSSELL LEE
PERSONAL Born 08/13/1930, Baltimore, MD, m **DISCIPLINE** AFRICAN-AMERICAN STUDIES **EDUCATION** Morehouse College, BA, 1952; University of Chicago, MA, 1954, PhD, 1971. **CAREER** Fed City College, assoc professor, 1969-71; Howard University, assoc professor, 1971-, chairman, Dept of Afro-American Studies, currently. **MEMBERSHIPS** Private consultant, Afro-American Studies Career Program In-Serv & Dept, Montgomery County Board of Education; consultant for numerous facilities including: University of Pittsburgh, Center for Deseg, 1976-, Wilmington DE Public Schools, 1977, Newark-New Castle-Marshalton McKean School District, Jackson Public Schools, 1969-70; lecturer/consultant, US Info Agency, 1977; chairman, committee on status of blacks in profession Amer Pol Sci Assn, 1974-77; NAACP, Curr Eval Pool, Prince Georges County Bd of Ed 1976-. **SELECTED PUBLICATIONS** Auth, Great Negroes Past & Present, 1963-69, 1972; Leading American Negroes, 1965; Perceptual Difficulties Dev Pol Sci Varia, Spring 1976; publisher, Black Studies Movement, Assessment Journal of Negro Education, 1977. **CONTACT ADDRESS** Dept of Afro-American Studies, Howard Univ, 2400 Sixth St NW, Washington, DC, 20059-0002.

ADAMS, WINTHROP LINDSAY
PERSONAL Born 03/09/1947, Newport News, VA, 1 child **DISCIPLINE** ANCIENT GREEK & ROMAN HISTORY **EDUCATION** Univ Va, BA, 69, PhD, 75. **CAREER** Instr hist, Univ Va, 74; vis asst prof, 74-75, asst prof, 75-82, ASSOC PROF HIST, UNIV UTAH, 82-; vis assoc prof, Univ Mich, 84. **HONORS AND AWARDS** Univ Utah Pres Teaching Scholar; Ramona Cauron Award Teaching Excellence, Univ Utah. **MEMBERSHIPS** AHA; Am Philol Asn; Assoc Ancient Historians; Am Cath Hist Asn; Soc Ancient Military Hist **RESEARCH** Ancient Macedonia, Hellenistic Greek history, Roman Imperialism. **SELECTED PUBLICATIONS** Auth, The Dynamics of Internal Macedonian Politics in the Time of Cassander, Archaia Makedonia III, pages, 12-25; Cassander and the crossing of the Hellespont, Diordorus 17, 17, 4, Vol II, pages 111-115 & The royal Macedonian tomb at Vergina: An historical interpretation, Vol III, pages 67-72, Ancient World; co-ed, Philip II, Alexander the Great and the Macedonian Heritage, Univ Press Am, 4/82; Perseus and the Third Macedonian War, in Philip II, Alexander the Great and the Macedonian Heritage, Univ Press Am, 82; Macedonian Kingship and the Right of Petition, Archaia Makedonia, 86; Cassander, Alexander IV, and the Tombs at Vergina, Ancient World, 91; Philip V, Hannibal and the Origins of the First Macedonian War, Archaia Makedonia, 92; Cassander the the Greet City-States (319-317 B C), J Balkan Studies, 93; In the Wake of Alexander: Macedonia and the Agegean after the Death of Alexander the Great, Ancient World, 96; Historical Perspectives of Greco-Macedonian Ethnicity in the Hellenistic Age, Balkan Studies, 96; Philip II and the Thracian Frontier, in Proceedings of the II International Congress of Ancient Thrace, Komotini, Greece, 97; The Successors to Alexander, in The Greek World in the Fourth Century, Routlegde, 97; Philip II, the League of Corinth and the Governance of Greece, Archaia Makedonia, forthcoming. **CONTACT ADDRESS** Dept of Hist, Univ Utah, 217 Carlson Hall, Salt Lake City, UT, 84112-3124. **EMAIL** winthrop.adams@m.cc.utah.edu

ADAMSON, WALTER L.
PERSONAL Born 02/28/1946, Washington, DC, m, 1972, 2 children **DISCIPLINE** HISTORY **EDUCATION** Swarthmore Col, BA 68; Univ Calif Berk, MA 70; Brandeis Univ, PhD 76. **CAREER** Whitman Col, asst prof 75-77; Harvard Univ, Mellon Fel, 77-78; Emory Univ, asst, assoc, prof, Dobbs Prof, 78 to 87-. **HONORS AND AWARDS** Twice, Best Book in Italian Hist. **MEMBERSHIPS** AHA **RESEARCH** Modern Italy; Modern Europe; Intellectual History. **SELECTED PUBLICATIONS** Auth, Avant-Garde Florence: From Modernism to Fascism, Cambridge MA, Harv Univ Press, 93; auth, Futurism Mass Culture and Women: The Reshaping of the Artistic Vocation, 1909-1920, Modernism/Modernity, 97; auth, The Culture of Italian Fascism and the Fascist Crisis of Modernity: The Case of IL Selvaggio, Jour of Contemp Hist, 95; auth, The Impact of World War I on Italian Political Culture, Richard Stites, Aviel Roshwald, eds, European Culture in the Great War: The Arts Entertainment and Propaganda, NY, Cambridge Univ Press, forthcoming; auth, Modernism as Political Theory, In: Terrance Ball, Richard Bellamy, eds, The Cambridge History of Twentieth Century Political Thought, NY and Cambridge, Cambridge Univ Press, forthcoming; auth, The Liberal Democratic State: Critics, Thomas Baldwin, ed, The Cambridge History of Philosophy 1870-1945, NY and Cambridge, Cambridge Univ Press, forthcoming; auth, Luca Baccelli Praxis e poesis nella filosofia politica moderna, The European Legacy, forthcoming; Frank Manuel A. Requiem for Karl Marx, Jour of Modern History, 97. **CONTACT ADDRESS** Dept of History, Emory Univ, Bowden Hall, Atlanta, GA, 30322. **EMAIL** wadamso@emory.edu

ADAMSON, WALTER L.
DISCIPLINE HISTORY **EDUCATION** Swarthmore Col, BA, 68; Univ Calif Berkeley, MA, 69; Brandeis Univ, PhD, 76. **CAREER** Samuel Candler Dobbs Prof Intellectual His. **HONORS AND AWARDS** Marraro Prize (twice). **RESEARCH** Modern European intellectual and cultural history; modern Italian history. **SELECTED PUBLICATIONS** Auth, Avant-garde Florence: From Modernism to Fascism; Marx and the Disillusionment of Marxism; Hegemony and Revolution: Antonio Gramsci's Political and Cultural Theory. The first and third of these both received the as the best book in Italian history. **CONTACT ADDRESS** Dept History, Emory Univ, 221 Bowden Hall, 561 Kilgo Cir, Atlanta, GA, 30322-1950. **EMAIL** wadamso@emory.edu

ADAS, MICHAEL PETER
PERSONAL Born 02/04/1943, Detroit, MI, m, 1967, 2 children **DISCIPLINE** MODERN HISTORY **EDUCATION** Western MI Univ, BA, 65; Univ WI, MA, 66 & 67, PhD, 71. **CAREER** From asst prof to assoc prof, 70-78, chmn dept hist, 79-81, Abraham Voorhees prof hist, Rugers Univ, New Brunswick,78, Bd gov ch, 96-97; Carnegie Found res fel, 75. **HONORS AND AWARDS** Genevieve Gorst Herfurth Bk Award, Univ WI, 75; NJNEH Hum Bk Award, 90; Dexter Prize Hist Tech Soc, 91; Guggenheim Fel, 94-95. **MEMBERSHIPS** Asn Asian Studies; AAUP. **RESEARCH** Tech and western colonial domination; World War I as a global conflict **SELECTED PUBLICATIONS** Auth, The Burma Delta, Economic Development and Social Change on an Asian Rice Frontier, Univ Wis, 74; Prophets of Rebellion: Millenarian Protest against the European Colonial Order, Univ NC, 79, Cambridge, 86; Machines as the Measure of Men: Science, Technology and Western Dominance, Cornell Univ, 89, co-auth (with Peter Stearns and Stuart Schwartz), World Civilizations: The Global Experience, harperCollins, 92, and Turbulent Passage: A Global History of the Twentieth Century, HarperCollins, 93; ed, Islamic and European Expansion: The Forging of a Global Order, AHA/Temple, 93; ed, vol on Technology, In: An Expanding World, series, Variorum 96; State, Market and Peasant in South and Southeast Asian History, Variorum, 98. **CONTACT ADDRESS** Dept of Hist, Rutgers Col Rutgers Univ, PO Box 5059, New Brunswick, NJ, 08903-5059. **EMAIL** madas@rci.rutgers.edu

ADDINGTON, LARRY H.
PERSONAL Born 11/16/1932, Charlotte, NC, m, 1963, 1 child **DISCIPLINE** MILITARY & MODERN EUROPEAN HISTORY **EDUCATION** Univ NC, AB, 55, MA, 56; Duke Univ, PhD(hist), 62. **CAREER** Asst prof hist, San Jose State Col, 62-64; asst prof, 64-66, ASSOC PROF HIST, THE CITADEL, 66., Consult mil hist, US Army Combat Develop Command, 65-66 & 68-69; guest lectr, US Army War Col, 74; Citadel develop found fel, 82. **HONORS AND AWARDS** Moncado Award, Am Mil Inst, 68. **MEMBERSHIPS** AHA; AAUP; Southern Hist Asn. **RESEARCH** Nineteenth and twentieth century European political and Modern military history. **SELECTED PUBLICATIONS** Auth, From Moltke to Hitler: The Evolution of German Military Doctrine, 1865-1939, The Citadel, 66; The Welle annex and the German mobilization of 1939, Irish Defense J, 2/67; Operation sunflower, Rommell versus the general staff, Mil Affairs, fall 67; The Blitzkrieg Era and the German General Staff, 1865-1941, Rutgers Univ, 71; Antiaircraft artillery versus the fighter-bomber: the duel over North Vietnam, 1964-1968, Army Mag, 12/73; The Coast Artillary Corps and Artillery Organization, 1906-1950, Mil Affairs, 77; Field Marshal Lord Alexander, World Bk Encycl, 78; Field Marshal Lord Allenby, Biog Encycl of the World, 80; General Charles P Summerall, Dict Am Mil Biog, 81; The Roots of Blitzkrieg - Vonseeckt, Hans and German Military Reform, Jour Mil Hist, Vol 0057, 93; The Military in Politics and Society in France and Germany in the 20th Century, War in Hist, Vol 0003, 96. **CONTACT ADDRESS** Dept of Hist, The Citadel, Charleston, SC, 29409.

ADELSON, FRED B.
DISCIPLINE ART HISTORY **EDUCATION** Univ Mass, BA 70; Columbia Univ, MA, 71; PhD, 82. **CAREER** Adj lectr, Upsala Col, 72; adj instr, St Peter's Col, 72-73; adj instr, Rutgers Univ, New Brunswick, 72-73; adj instr, Kean Col NJ, 73-74; vis lectr, Rutgers Univ, Camden, 86-87; prof, Rowan Col, 74-. **HONORS AND AWARDS** Rockefeller Found fel, Columbia Univ, 78; res and develop grant, Glassboro State Col, 78; 83; 84; 87; 89; 91; fac fel prog, Princeton Univ, 89/90. **MEMBERSHIPS** Col Art Asn; Asn of Hist of Am Art ; Phi Kappa Phi. **SELECTED PUBLICATIONS** Auth, Architecture: Norman Jaffe, Archit Digest, 78; A New Look at Alvan Fisher, The Gilcrease Mag of Am Hist and Art, 84; An American Snowfall: Early Winter Scenes by Alvan Fisher, Arts in Va, 83-84; Art Under Cover: American Gift-Book Illustrations, The Mag ANTIQUES, 84; Con=struct=ures, Reading Pub Mus and Art Gallery, Reading, Pa, 85. Alvan Fisher in Maine: His Early Coastal Scenes, The Am Art J, 86; Home on La Grange: Alvan Fisher's Lithographs of Lafayette's Residence in France, The Mag ANTIQUES, 88; American Eclipse with Race Track, Masterworks of American Art from the Munson-Williams-Proctor Inst, Harry N. Abrams, 89; Dichotomy #18, The Painted Bride Art Ctr, Philadelphia, 89; Con=struct=ures, The Port of Hist Mus, Philadelphia, 93. Thomas Eakins and Walt Whitman, The Art of Thomas Eakins, Nat Portrait Gallery, London, Eng, 93. **CONTACT ADDRESS** Rowan Col of NJ, Glassboro, NJ, 08028-1701. **EMAIL** adelson@rowan.edu

ADELSON, ROGER
PERSONAL Born 07/11/1942, Abilene, KS, d **DISCIPLINE** HISTORY **EDUCATION** George Wash Univ, BA, 64; Washington Univ, MA, 68; Oxford Univ, B.Litt, 70; Washington Univ, PhD, 72 **CAREER** Senior Res Fel, St Anthony Col, Oxford Univ, 72-73; lctr, Harvard Univ, 74; asst prof, Ariz State Univ, 74-78; assoc prof, Ariz State Univ, 78-96; prof, Ariz State Univ, 96- **HONORS AND AWARDS** Alistair Horne Res Fel, 72-73; Outstanding Teacher Award, 79; Churchill Prize, 93; **MEMBERSHIPS** Amer Hist Assoc; North Amer Conf on Brit Studies; Council Foreign Relations; Middle East Studies Assoc; Conference Hist Jrn **RESEARCH** British and U.S. power in the Middle East in 20th Century; Comparative and Global History since 1500 **SELECTED PUBLICATIONS** Auth, Speaking of History: Conversations with Historians, East Lansing, 97; auth, London and the Invention of the Middle East: Money, Power and War, 1902-1922, New Haven, 95; auth, Mark Sykes: Portrait of an Amateur, London, 75 **CONTACT ADDRESS** Dept History, Arizona State Univ, Tempe, PO Box 872501, Tempe, AZ, 85287-2501. **EMAIL** adelsonr@asu.edu

ADKIN, NEIL
PERSONAL Born 07/04/1954, Hull, England **DISCIPLINE** CLASSICS **EDUCATION** Univ Col Oxford, BA, 76 (1st class), MA, 80; Univ Glasgow, PhD, 82. **CAREER** Thesarus Linguae fel, Bayerische Akademie Der Wissenschaften, 76-79; temporary lect in Medieval Latin, Univ Liverpool, 81-82; Univ Res fel, Univ Liverpool, 83-86; asst through assoc prof of Classics, Univ NE-Lincoln, 86-. **HONORS AND AWARDS** Hertford, De Paravicini, Ireland and Craven Scholarships, 73; Col of Arts and Sciences Award for Outstanding Teaching, 90. **MEMBERSHIPS** APA. **SELECTED PUBLICATIONS** Author of 127 articles on Patristic, Medieval, and Renaissance Latin, principally Jerome, Walter of Chatillon, and Erasmus. **CONTACT ADDRESS** Dept Classics, Univ of Nebraska, Lincoln, 237 Andrews Hall, PO Box 880337, Lincoln, NE, 68588-0337.

ADKINS, ARTHUR WILLIAM HOPE
PERSONAL Born 10/17/1929, Leicester, England, m, 1961, 2 children **DISCIPLINE** CLASSICS; PHILOSOPHY **EDUCATION** Oxford Univ, BA, 52, MA, 55, DPhil, 57. **CAREER** Asst lectr Latin humanities, Univ Glasgow, 54-56; lectr Greek, Bedford Col, Univ London, 56-61; fel class lang & lit, Exeter Col, Oxford, 61-65; prof classics, Univ Reading, 66-74; chmn, Dept Classics, 75-80, PROF GREEK, PHILOS & EARLY CHRISTIAN LIT, UNIV CHICAGO, 74- ; Vis sr fel classics Soc Humanities, Cornell Univ, 69-70. **MEMBERSHIPS** Soc Promotion Hellenic Studies; Class Asn Gt Brit; Am Philol Asn; Am Philos Asn; Asn Ancient Historians. **RESEARCH** Greek philosophy; Greek thought and religion; Greek literature. **SELECTED PUBLICATIONS** Auth, Merit and Responsibility: A Study in Greek Values, Clarendon, Oxford, 60; contribr, Greek religion, In: Historia Religionum Handbook for the History of Religions, Leiden, Brill, 69; auth, From the Many to the One: A Study of Personality and Views of Human Nature in the Context of Ancient Greek Society, Values and Beliefs, Constable, London & Cornell Univ, 70; Moral Values and Political Behavior in Ancient Greece, Chatto & Windus, London & Clark Irwin, Toronto, 72; Paralysis and Akrasia in Eth Nic 1102b16 ff, Am J Philos, Vol 97, 62-64; Polupragmosune and minding one's own business: A study in Greek social and political values, CP, 76; Callinus 1 and Tyrtaeus 10 as poetry, HSCP, 77; Lucretius I, 137 ff and the problems of writing Versus Latini, Phoenix, 77; Ethics with Aristotle, Classical Philol, Vol 0088, 93; Hybris- A Study in the Values of Honor and Shame in Ancient Greece, Class Jour, Vol 0090, 95; Aidos - The Psychology and Ethics of Honor and Shame in Ancient Greek Literature, Class Jour, Vol 0090, 95. **CONTACT ADDRESS** Dept of Classics, Univ of Chicago, 1050 E 59th St, Chicago, IL, 60637.

ADLER, PHILIP JOSEPH
PERSONAL Born 03/30/1930, Philadelphia, PA, m, 1971, 1 child **DISCIPLINE** MODERN HISTORY **EDUCATION** Loyola Univ, Los Angeles, BA, 54; Univ Vienna, PhD(hist), 61. **CAREER** Foreign serv officer, US Dept State, 62-66; assoc prof, 66-75, PROF HIST E CAROLINA UNIV, 75-, Lectr hist, Univ Md, 65-66; Fulbright-Hays fac res prog grant, 71-72; Nat Endowment for Humanities res fel, 76 & 79. **MEMBERSHIPS** AHA; Am Asn Advan Slavic Studies; Am Asn Southeastern Europ Studies. **RESEARCH** Ethnic culture in East Europe; Serbian history; Social Institutions. **SELECTED PUBLICATIONS** Auth, Notes on the beginning of modern Serbian literature, Southeastern Europe, Vol I, 74; Habsburg school reform among the Orthodox minorities, Slavic Rev, 74; German contractees in early 19th century Serbia, Sudost-Forsch Yearbk, 74; The introduction of public schooling for the Jews of Hungary (1849-1860), Jewish Social Studies, 74; Serbs, Magyars and Staatsinteresse in 18th century Austria, Austrian Hist Yearbk, 78; Nation and Nationalism Among the Serbs of Hungary, 1790-1870, E Europ Quart, 79; The South Slaves of the Habsburg Empire: An Annotated Bibliography, 1945-1980 (in prep); Broken Bonds- The Disintegration of Yugoslavia, Int Hist Rev, Vol 0016, 94; Bosnia-A Short History, Int Hist Rev, Vol 0018, 96. **CONTACT ADDRESS** Dept of Hist, East Carolina Univ, Greenville, NC, 27834.

ADOVASIO, J.M.
PERSONAL Born 02/17/1944, Youngstown, OH, w **DISCIPLINE** ANTHROPOLOGY **EDUCATION** Univ Arizona, BA, 65; Univ Utah, PhD, 70. **CAREER** Instr, asst prof anthrop, Youngstown State Univ,66-71; asst, 72-76, and assoc prof, 76-79, prof, 79-90, chemn 80-89, anthrop, assoc prof, 72-79, prof, 79-90, Latin Am Stud, dir Cultural Res Mgt Prog, 76-89, prof geol and planetary sci, 85-90, Univ Pittsburgh; res assoc Smithsonian Inst, 74- ; res assoc, Carnegie Museum, 78- ; exec dir Archaeol Res Prog, So Methodist Univ, 90-93; John E Boyle Prof Anthrop and Archaeol, Prof of Geol, dir Anthrop and Archaeol Dept, dir Archaeol Inst, dir Geol Dept, 91- Mercyhurst Col, 90- . **HONORS AND AWARDS** Honors Program, 63-65; Magna cum Laude, 65; Phi Eta Sigma; Phi Beta Kappa, 66; Rhodes Scholar finalist; NDEA Fel, 68-70; Smithsonian Inst Post-Doctoral Res Fel, 71-72; Sigma Xi; Outstanding Young Men of Am, 78; DSci (Honoris causa) Washington and Jefferson Univ, 83; Knight of the Sovereign Military Order of Malta, 95; J Alden Mason Award for Career Contrib to Penn Prehistory, 96. **MEMBERSHIPS** Am Anthrop Asn; Soc for Am Archaeol; Current Anthrop; Am Quaternary Asn; AAAS; Soc for Penn Archaeol; NY Acad of Sci; Am Sch for Oriental Res. **RESEARCH** Primitive technology especially lithics, basketry and textiles; early man in North America; the archaic stage in the Old and New World including subsistence, demography, technology, settlement patterns, etc; quaternary paleoecology; research methodology in the excavation of caves and rockshelters. **SELECTED PUBLICATIONS** Auth, The Ones That Will Not Go Away: A Biased View of Pre-Clovis Populations, in Soffer, ed, Kostenki to Clovis: Upper Paleolithic-Paleo-Indian Adaptations, Plenum, 93; coauth, On a Pleistocene Human Occupation at Pedra Furada, Brazil, Antiquity, 94; auth, Cordage and Cordage Impressions from Monte Verde, in Dillehay, ed, Monte Verde: A Late Pleistocene Site in Chile: The Archaeological Context, v.2, Smithsonian Inst, 96; auth, Upper Paleolithic Fibre Technology: Interlaced Woven Finds from Pavlov I, Czech Republic, c.26,000 Years Ago, Antiquity, 96; contribur to Fagan, ed, The Oxford Companion to Archaeology, Oxford, 96; coauth, The Origins of Perishables Production East of the Rockies, in Petersen, ed, Perishables Industries of the Eastern United States, Univ Tenn, 96; coauth, Textiles and Cordage: A Preliminary Assessment in Svoboda, Pavlov-Northwest: The Upper Paleolithic Burial and its Settlement Context, Academy of Sciences of the Czech Republic, 97; coauth, Environment and Excavations, Mercyhurst Archaeological Institute, 97; coauth, Perishable Industries from Nan Ranch, in Shafer, ed, The Archaeology of Nan Ranch, Univ New Mexico, 97; coauth, Archaeological Investigation of the Elk Creek Site, Girard Township, Erie County, Pennsylvania, Mercyhurst Archaeological Institute, 98; auth, The Miller Complex, in Gibbon, ed, Archaeology of Prehistoric North America: An Encyclopedia, Garland, in press. **CONTACT ADDRESS** Mercyhurst Archaeological Inst, 501 E 38 St, Erie, PA, 16546. **EMAIL** adovasio@mercyhurst.edu

AESCHBACHER, WILLIAM DRIVER
PERSONAL Born 01/12/1919, Tonganoxie, KS, m, 1944, 3 children **DISCIPLINE** AMERICAN HISTORY **EDUCATION** Univ Nebr, BS, 40, MA, 46, PhD(hist), 48. **CAREER** Assoc prof soc sci, Murray State Col, 48-56; dir, Nebr State Hist Soc & ed, Nebr Hist, 56-63; dir, Eisenhower Libr, 63-66; prof hist, Univ Utah, 66-68; PROF HIST, UNIV CINCINNATI, 68- **MEMBERSHIPS** Orgn Am Hist (secy-treas, 56-76); AHA; Southern Hist Asn; Western Hist Asn; Am Asn State & Local Hist. **RESEARCH** Western history; state and local history; agricultural history. **SELECTED PUBLICATIONS** Auth, Presidential libraries: New dimension in research facilities, Midwestern Quart, winter 65; The Mississippi Valley Historical Association 1870-1965, J Am Hist, 9/67; Allis-Chalmers - Farm Equipment 1914-1985, Jour of West, Vol 0035, 97. **CONTACT ADDRESS** Dept of Hist, Univ of Cincinnati, Cincinnati, OH, 45221.

AFRICA, THOMAS WILSON
PERSONAL Born 12/24/1927, Portland, OR, m, 1952, 2 children **DISCIPLINE** ANCIENT HISTORY **EDUCATION** Univ Calif, Los Angeles, AB, 56, MA, 57, PhD, 59. **CAREER** Instr hist, Univ Calif, Santa Barbara, 59-60; asst prof, La State Univ, 60-61; from asst prof to prof, Univ Southern Calif, 61-69; prof hist, State Univ NY, Binghamton, 69-80, chmn dept, 76; RES & WRITING, 80-, Res grant-in-aid, Am Coun Learned Soc, 60. **MEMBERSHIPS** AHA; Hist Sci Soc; Soc Promotion Hellenic Studies; Soc Prom Roman Studies. **RESEARCH** Historiography; Hellenistic age; effect of psychology in history. **SELECTED PUBLICATIONS** Auth, Phylarchus and the Spartan Revolution, Univ Calif, 61; Opium addiction of Marcus Aurelius, J Hist Ideas, 61; Rome of the Caesars, 65 & Science and the State in Greece and Rome, 67, Wiley; The Ancient World, Houghton, 69; The one-eyed man against Rome, Historia, 12/70; The Immense Majesty, Crowell, 74; Psychohistorical study of Brutus, J Interdisciplinary Hist, 78; The Owl at Dusk - 2 Centuries of Classical Scholarship, Jour of Hist of Ideas, Vol 0054, 93; The Wicked Knight and the Use of Anecdotes, Greece & Rome, Vol 0042, 95. **CONTACT ADDRESS** 421 African Rd, Vestal, NY, 13850.

AGEE, RICHARD J.
PERSONAL Born 05/02/1953, Oakland, CA **DISCIPLINE** MUSIC HISTORY **EDUCATION** Univ Calif Berkeley, BA, 76; Princeton, MFA, 78, PhD, 82. **CAREER** 1978-82, Asst instr, Princeton, 78-82; vis asst prof, Reed Col, 82-83; asst prof, 83-90, assoc prof, 90-97, prof,Colorado Col, 97-. **HONORS AND AWARDS** Fulbright fel, Italy, 78-79; Gladys Krieble Delmas Grant, Venice; Am Coun Learned Soc Grant-in-Aid, res at Civico Museo Bibliografico Musicale in Bologna and the Biblioteka Jagiellonska in Krakow, 87. Am Coun Learned Soc Grant-in-Aid (hon), Harvard, 86; NEH, Bologna and Modena, Italy, 85. **MEMBERSHIPS** Am Musicol Soc; Col Mus Asn. **RESEARCH** Italian Renaissance music printing; Italian madrigal. **SELECTED PUBLICATIONS** Auth, The Venetian Privilege and Music-Printing in the Sixteenth Century, in Early Music History: Studies in Medieval and Early Modern Music,83, p1-42; Ruberto Strozzi and the Early Madrigal, in Jour Am Musicol Soc, vol 36, 83, p1-17; Filippo Strozzi and the Early Madrigal, in Jour Am Musicol Soc, vol 38, 85, p227-37; A Venetian Music Printing Contract and Edition Size in the Sixteenth Century, in Studi Musicali, Rome, 86, p59-65; coauth, La Stampa della Musica Nova di Willaert, in the Rivista Italiana di Musicologia, Brandeis Univ, 89, p219-305; Studies in Medieval and Early Modern Music, 96, p1-58; A Costanzo Festa's Counterpoints on a Cantus Firmus,Madison, Wis, A-R Editions, Inc, 97; Costanzo Festa's Gradus ad Parnassum, in Early Music History: The Gardano Music Printing Firms, 1569-1611, Univ Rochester Press, 98. **CONTACT ADDRESS** Music Dept, The Colorado Col, Colorado Springs, CO, 80903. **EMAIL** ragee@ColoradoCollege.edu

AHERN, WILBERT H.
PERSONAL Born 07/12/1942, Greenville, IL, m, 1963, 2 children **DISCIPLINE** AMERICAN HISTORY **EDUCATION** Oberlin Col, BA, 63; Northwestern Univ, MA, 66, PhD, 68. **CAREER** Asst prof, 67-70, assoc prof, 70-79, actg acad dean, 78-79, prof Am Hist, Univ MN, Morris, 79-; chair div of Soc Sci, 87-95; co-dir, W Cent Minn Hist Res Ctr, 72-73, dir, 73-87, 96-; resident res fel, Newberry Libr, 74-75; coordr, Freshman Sem Prog, Univ Minn, Morris, 81-87; Danforth assoc, 81-96. **HONORS AND AWARDS** Horace T. Morse-Amoco Awd for Outstanding Contributions to Undergrad Educ, Univ Minn, 84; Solon J. Buck Awd for Best Article, Minnesota History 84. **MEMBERSHIPS** AAUP; Orgn Am Historians; AHA. **RESEARCH** United States, 1850-1917; race and nationality in America; social and intellectual history. **SELECTED PUBLICATIONS** Auth, "The Cox Plan of Reconstruction: A Case Study in Ideology and Race Relations," Civil War History, 70; "Assimilationist Racism: The Case of the Friends of the Indian," Journal of Ethnic Studies, summer 76; Laissiz Faire vs. Equal Rights: Liberal Republicans and Limits to Reconstruction," Phylon, 3/79; "The Returned Indians': Hampton Institute and Its Indian Alumni, 1878-1893," Journal of Ethnic Studies, 82; "Indian Education and Bureaucracy: The School at Morris," Minnesota History, 84; To Kill the Indian and Save the Man: The Boarding Scholar in American Indian Education, 86; "Enhancing the Faculty Development at Tribal College," Tribal College Journal, 96; "An Experiment Aborted: Returned Indian Students and the Indian School Service," Ethnohistory, 97. **CONTACT ADDRESS** Div of Soc Sci, Univ of Minnesota, 600 E 4th St, Morris, MN, 56267-2134. **EMAIL** ahernwh@cda.umn.mrs.edu

AHRENSDORF, PETER J.
DISCIPLINE CLASSICS **EDUCATION** Yale Univ, BA; Univ Chicago, PhD. **CAREER** Assoc prof pol sci and hum, Davidson Col, 89-. **RESEARCH** Plato and Thucydides; Thomas Pangle; theories of international rel(s) in the hist of polit philos. **SELECTED PUBLICATIONS** Auth, The Death of Socrates and the Life of Philosophy: An Interpretation of Plato's Phaedo, SUNY, 95. **CONTACT ADDRESS** Davidson Col, 102 N Main St, PO Box 1719, Davidson, NC, 28036. **EMAIL** peahrensdorf@davidson.edu

AIKIN, ROGER
DISCIPLINE ART HISTORY **EDUCATION** Univ Calif, Berkeley, PhD. **CAREER** Assoc prof & dept ch; Creighton Univ, 80-; stud photog in Oregon and Calif; work rep in Ansel Adams coll in the Ctr for Creative Photog in Tucson. **SELECTED PUBLICATIONS** Publ on, Calif art and photography of the 20th century; Renaissance and Baroque Art. **CONTACT ADDRESS** Dept of Fine and Performing Arts, Creighton Univ, 2500 California Plaza, Omaha, NE, 68178. **EMAIL** leca@creighton.edu

AINLEY, MARIANNE G.
PERSONAL Budapest, Hungary **DISCIPLINE** HISTORY OF SCIENCE/WOMEN'S STUDIES **EDUCATION** Sir George Williams Univ, BA, 64; Univ Montreal, MS, 80; McGill Univ, PhD, 85. **CAREER** Independent scholar, SSHRCC Can Strategic Grants Div, 86-87, 89-91; prin, Simone de Beauvoir Inst & Dir Women's Studs, Concordia Univ, 91-95; PROF & CHAIR, WOMEN'S STUDS, UNIV NORTHERN BC, 95-. **MEMBERSHIPS** McGill Ctr Tchr Women; Soc Can Ornithol; Can Hist Educ Soc; Can Women's Stud Asn; Can Sci Tech Hist Asn; Can Res Inst Advan Women; Hist Sci Soc Am. **SELECTED PUBLICATIONS** Auth, Uneasy Careers and Intimate Lives: Women in Science 1798-1979, 87; auth, Louise de Kiriline Lawrence & the World of Nature: A Tribute in the Can Field Naturalist, 94; auth, Canadian Women's Contributions to Chemistry, 1900-1970, in Can Chem News, 94; auth, Despite the Odds, Essays on Canadian Women and Science, The Emergence of Canadian Ornithology - An Historical Overview to 1950, in Contributions to the History of North American Ornithology, 95. **CONTACT ADDRESS** Women's Stud Prog, Univ of No British Columbia, 3333 University Way, Prince George, BC, V2N 4ZN. **EMAIL** ainley@ubc.edu.ca

AJOOTIAN, AILEEN
DISCIPLINE ANCIENT ART, CLASSICAL ARCHAEOLOGY **EDUCATION** SUNY, Oswego, BA; Univ OR, MA; Byrn Mawr Col, MA, PhD. **CAREER** Instr, Cleveland State Univ, Univ OR, McMaster Univ, Ontario; asst prof Classics and Art, Univ MS, 96-. **HONORS AND AWARDS** Anna C and Oliver C Colburn fel, Archaeological Institute of Am; fel, Whiting, Kress, Oscar Broneer, Bryne Rubel, Am Numis Soc. **RESEARCH** Sculptures and sculptors on the Pnyx. **SELECTED PUBLICATIONS** Among her many publ are those about Sparta and Praxiteles. **CONTACT ADDRESS** Univ MS, Oxford, MS, 38677.

AKE, DAVID
PERSONAL Born 05/11/1961, New Haven, CT **DISCIPLINE** MUSICOLOGY **EDUCATION** Calif Inst Arts, MFA, 87; UCLA, MA, 96. **CAREER** Asst prof mus, Univ Nevada-Reno, 99-. **HONORS AND AWARDS** Ki Mantle Hood Prize, Soc for Ethnomusico Southern Calif Chap, 97, 98. **MEMBERSHIPS** Am Musicol Soc; Soc for Ethnomusicol; Sonneck Soc; Broadcast Mus, Inc (BMI). **RESEARCH** Popular Music,twentieth-century music,jazz. **SELECTED PUBLICATIONS** Book Review of Music Grooves by Charles Keil and Steven Feld, Am Mus, vol 15, No 2, Summer 97, p252-4; Re-Masculating Jazz: Ornette Coleman, Lonely Woman, and the New York Jazz Scene in the Late 1950s, Am Mus, vol 16, No 1, Spring 98, p25-44; Louis Jordan, in Encyclopaedia Britannica (CD-ROM version), 98. **CONTACT ADDRESS** 932 N Croft Ave, Los Angeles, CA, 90069. **EMAIL** dake@ucla.edu

AKEHURST, F.R.P.
DISCIPLINE OLD FRENCH AND THE HISTORY OF FRENCH **EDUCATION** Univ Colo, PhD; Univ Minn, JD. **CAREER** Instr, Univ Minn, Twin Cities. **RESEARCH** Medieval French law. **SELECTED PUBLICATIONS** Ed, Handbook of the Troubadours, Univ Calif Press, 95; transl, "Coutumes de Beauvasis" of Philippe de Beaumanoir, Univ Pa Press, 92; published on the troubadours, the trouveres, and the fabliaux. **CONTACT ADDRESS** Univ Minn, Twin Cities, Minneapolis, MN, 55455.

AKIN, WILLIAM ERNEST
PERSONAL Born 12/15/1936, Chambers County, AL, m, 1971, 4 children **DISCIPLINE** HISTORY **EDUCATION** Univ of MD BA 61, Univ of MD MA 63, Univ of Rochester PhD 71. **CAREER** Instr SUNY Binghamton 66-69, Asst Prof Loyola College of Monteral 69-74, Assoc Prof and Dean of Hum Concordia Univ Montreal 74-79, Prof and Academic Vice Pres Ursinus College Collegeville PA 79-. **HONORS AND AWARDS** LLD Tohoko Gakuin Univ Sendai Japan. **MEMBERSHIPS** Soc for Baseball Res, Soc for Sports Hist, AHA. **RESEARCH** US Soc Hist, Sports Hist **SELECTED PUBLICATIONS** Technocracy and the American Dream 1900-1941, 77; Faculty Development in Liberal Arts Colleges, 85; History of the Town of Brighton NY:1814-1964, 64. **CONTACT ADDRESS** Ursinus Col, PO Box 1000, Collegeville, PA, 19426.

AKSAN, VIRGINIA
DISCIPLINE HISTORY **EDUCATION** Allegheny Col, BA; Berkley Col, MLS; Univ Toronto, MA, PhD. **HONORS AND AWARDS** SSHRC grant **MEMBERSHIPS** Turkish Studies Asn. **RESEARCH** 18th century Ottoman history. **SELECTED**

PUBLICATIONS Auth, An Ottoman Statesman in War and Peace: Ahmed Resmi Efendi 1700-1783; art, The One-Eyed Fighting the Blind: Mobilization, Supply and Command in the Russo-Turkish War of 1768-74, Int Hist Rev. **CONTACT ADDRESS** History Dept, McMaster Univ, 1280 Main St W, Hamilton, ON, L8S 4L9.

AL-MARAYATI, ABID AMIN
PERSONAL Born 10/14/1931, Baghdad, Iraq, 1 child **DISCIPLINE** POLITICAL SCIENCE, SOCIOLOGY, INTERNATIONAL RELATIONS, INTERNATIONAL LAW, I **EDUCATION** Bradley Univ, BA, 49-52, MA, 52-54; New York Univ, PhD, 54-59. **CAREER** Secy, Delegation Iraq, UN Gen Assembly, 55; secy, Delegation Yemen, UN Gen Assembly, 56-60; Instr, Govt, Univ Mass, 60; tech asst off, Int Atomic Energy Agency, Vienna, 60-62; assoc prof, SUNY, 62-64; res fel, Harvard Univ, 64-65; assoc prof, Ariz State Univ, 65-68; lectr & int educ consult, Am Inst For Trade, 65-68; PROF EMER, POLIT SCI, UNIV TOLEDO, 68-; vis prof, Univ Kuwait, 82-83; vis prof, Inst Public Admin, Riyadh, Saudi Arabia, 85-86; guest lectr, 90; vis prof, Beijing Stud Univ, 91. **MEMBERSHIPS** Assoc Student Educ; Middle East Studies Assoc N Amer; Phi Kappa Phi **RESEARCH** Psychological and Cultural Factors in the Iraq/Iran War; Shiism: A Study in Religion and Politics **CONTACT ADDRESS** Dept Polit Sci, Univ Toledo, 2109 Terr View West, Toledo, OH, 43607.

ALBERT, PETER J.
PERSONAL Born 07/24/1946, Racine, WI, m, 1991, 2 children **DISCIPLINE** AMERICAN HISTORY; LABOR HISTORY; THE AMERICAN REVOLUTION **EDUCATION** St. John's Univ, BA, 67; Univ of Wis at Madison, MA, 69; Univ of Md at Col Park, PhD, 76. **CAREER** Asst ed, 74-76, assic ed, 76-85, co-ed, Samuel Gompers Papers, Univ Md, Col Park, 85-. **SELECTED PUBLICATIONS** Co-ed, Samuel Gompers Papers-7 volumes-; co-ed, Perspectives on the American Revolution-14 volumes-. **CONTACT ADDRESS** History Dept, Univ of Maryland at Col Park, College Park, MD, 20742. **EMAIL** pa3@umail.umd.edu

ALBIN, THOMAS R.
PERSONAL Born 05/10/1951, Wakeeney, KS, m, 1971, 3 children **DISCIPLINE** CHURCH HISTORY **EDUCATION** Oral Roberts Univ, BA, 73, MA, 76; Fuller Theol Sem, MA, 77; Univ Cambridge, PhD 99. **CAREER** Vis lect, 87-88, Boston Univ School of Theol, adj fac, 89; asst prof, 88-92, Univ Dubuque Theol Sem, dir, contextual ed & instr in spiritual formation, 92-, Univ Dubuque Theol Sem. **HONORS AND AWARDS** BA, magna cum laude, 73; MA, 78; G. Lemuel Fenn Ministerial Scholar; John Wesley Fel, a Fund for Theol Ed, ATFE, 78-82; Bethune-Baker grant, fac of Div, Cambridge Univ; Pasadena Methodist Found Scholar; Charis Award for Excel in Tchng, UDTS, 90-91, 92-93. **MEMBERSHIPS** Am Academy of Relig; Charles Wesley Found; Oxford Inst for Methodist Theol Stud: Spiritual Dirs Int; Wesley Hist Soc, Eng. **SELECTED PUBLICATIONS** Auth, Spiritual Formation and Contextual Education, in the Report of the Proceedings of the Asn of Theol Field Ed, 93; auth, John and Charles Wesley, The Dict of Christian Ethics & Pastoral Theol, IVP, 95; auth, What We Believe and Why We Believe It: Understanding Our Doctrinal Standards and Our Theological Task, a 6 wk stud, pvtly printed, local United Methodist Churches, 96; rev, Of Laughter in the Amen Corner: The Life of Evangelist Sam Jones by Kathleen Minnix, 93, pub in Missiology: An Int Rev, vol XXV, no 2, 97; auth, One week of devotions in Disciplines 1999, Upper Room, 98; auth, The Charles Wesley Family in Bristol, Proceed of the Charles Wesley Soc, vol 4, 97, 98; auth, The Role of Small Groups in Early Methodist Spiritual Formation, in The Role of the Heart in N Amer Methodism, Scarecrow Press. **CONTACT ADDRESS** 1925 Carter Rd, Dubuque, IA, 52001. **EMAIL** talbin@univ.dbq.edu

ALBISETTI, JAMES C.
PERSONAL Born 03/03/1949, Wilmington, DE **DISCIPLINE** HISTORY **EDUCATION** Amherst Col, BA, 71; Yale Univ, PhD, 76. **CAREER** Lectr, Yale Univ, 77-78; vis asst prof, Hamilton Col, 78-79; from asst prof to assoc prof to prof, 79-, Univ Ky. **HONORS AND AWARDS** Phi Beta Kappa; NDEA Title IV Fel; German Stud Asn Book Prize, 85. **MEMBERSHIPS** Am Hist Asn; German Stud Asn; Hist of Educ Society; Conf Group Central European Hist; Int Standing Conf Hist Educ. **RESEARCH** German history; educational history; comparitive women's history. **SELECTED PUBLICATIONS** Auth, art, The Feminization of Teaching in the Nineteenth Century: A Comparative Perspective, 93; auth, art, The Decline of the German Mandarins After Twenty-Five Years, 94; auth, art, German Influence on the Higher Education of American Women, 95; auth, art, Professionalisierung Von Frauen im Lehrberuf, 96; auth, art, Female Education in German-Speaking Austria, Germany and Switzerland, 1866-1914, 96. **CONTACT ADDRESS** Univ of Kentucky, 1715 Patterson Tower, Lexington, KY, 40506-0027. **EMAIL** jcalbi01@pop.uky.edu

ALBRECHT, CATHERINE
DISCIPLINE HISTORY **EDUCATION** Indiana Univ, PhD. **CAREER** Asst prof, Univ Baltimore, 90-94; Assoc prof, Univ Baltimore, 94-. **MEMBERSHIPS** Am Hist Asn; Am Asn Advancement Slavic Studies. **SELECTED PUBLICATIONS** Auth, The Czech Economics Profession before 1914, Duncker und Humbolt, 65; auth, Two Czech Economists: Albin Braf and Josef Kaizl, E Central Europe, 92; auth, National Economy or Economic Nationalism in the Bohemian Crownlands, 1848-1914, Labyrinth of Nationalism/Complexities of Diplomacy: Essays in Honor of Barbara and Charles Jelavich, Slavica, 92; auth, Pride in Protection: The Jubilee Exhibition of 1891 and Economic Competition between Czechs and Germans in Bohemia, Austrian Hist Yearbook, 93; auth, Economic Nationalism Among German Bohemians, Nationalities Papers, 96. **CONTACT ADDRESS** Univ Baltimore, 1420 N. Charles Street, Baltimore, MD, 21201.

ALBRECHT, GARY LOUIS
PERSONAL Born 09/29/1937, Port Townsend, WA, m, 3 children **DISCIPLINE** SOCIOLOGY **EDUCATION** Gonzaga Univ, MA, 61; Fordham Univ, MA, 65; Emory Univ, PhD, 70. **CAREER** Vis scholar, Ctr for Health Svc & Policy, N Western Univ, assoc prof, Univ Illinois, Schl of Pub Health, 79-80; prof, schl of pub health, prof, disability & human devel, 81-, Univ ILL. **HONORS AND AWARDS** Mary E. Switzer Dist res fel, Natl Inst on Disability & Rehabilitation Res; Scholar Res, Maison des Sciences de L'Homme, Paris. **MEMBERSHIPS** Soc for Res in Rehab (UK); Amer Sociol Assn; Amer Anthrop Assn; Grant Review Panel; NIDDR; US Dept Ed. **RESEARCH** Sociology of disability & rehabilitation; social context of AIDS epidemic; social interaction between the ill, the public, & professional staff. **SELECTED PUBLICATIONS** Coauth, What Does AIDS Teach Us About Social Science?, Advances in Med Sociol 3, 93; auth, A Social Experience of Disability, Social Problems, McGraw Hill, 93; auth, A Sociological Evaluation of Our Experience With Aids: Research and Policy, ASA, Cong Briefing, 93; ed, Advances in Medical Sociology, Volume IV: A Reconsideration of Models of Health Behavior Change, JAI Press, 94; coauth, A Sociological Perspective of Health-Related Quality of Life Research, Advances in Med Sociol 5, 94; art, People at Risk: An Ethnography of Patients Presenting at Inner City Emergency Rooms, Ethnotes 4, 94; coauth, Organizational Theory in the Case and Care Management of Health Care, Advances in Med Sociol 6, 95; ed, Advances In Medical Sociology, Volume VI: Case and Case Management, JAI Press, 95; auth, Sociology, Encycl of Disability & Rehab, NY Macmillan, 96; art, Using Subjective Health Assessments in Practice and Policy-Making, Health Care Analysis 4, 96; art, The Health Politics of Disability, Health Pol & Policy, Delmar Pub, 97; coauth, Patient Satisfaction with an Emergency Department Chest Pain Observation Unit, Annals of Emerg Med 29, 97; coauth, Peer Intervention in Case Management Practice, J Case Manage 6:43, 97; art, Women and Disability, J Health Svc & Policy 2:1, 97; auth, The Marketing of Rehabilitation Goods and Services, Health Illness & Healing: Soc, Soc Context & Self, Roxbury Press, 99. **CONTACT ADDRESS** School of Public Health, Univ of Illinois at Chicago, 2035 W Taylor St, Chicago, IL, 60612. **EMAIL** Garya@uic.edu

ALBRIGHT, ANN COOPER
DISCIPLINE DANCE **EDUCATION** Bryn Mawr Col, BA, 81; Temple Univ, MFA, 83; NY Univ, PhD, 91. **CAREER** Assoc prof, Oberlin Coll, 90. **HONORS AND AWARDS** Individual Artist Awards, Ohio Arts Council in Dance Criticism **RESEARCH** Dancing and cultural theory. **SELECTED PUBLICATIONS** Au, Choreographing Difference: the Body and Identity in Comtemporary Dance, Weslyn Univ Press, 97. **CONTACT ADDRESS** Oberlin Col, Oberlin, OH, 44074.

ALDRETE, GREGORY S.
PERSONAL Born 09/08/1966, MN, s **DISCIPLINE** ANCIENT HISTORY **EDUCATION** Princeton, AB, 88; Univ Mich, PhD, 95. **CAREER** Asst Prof, Univ Wisc, 95-; Cic Minority fel, 88-90; Inst Hum Summer fel, 90; Mich Minority Merit fel, 90-91; Rackham Merit fel, 93-95; NEH fel, 96; Wisc Tchg fel, 97-98. **MEMBERSHIPS** Am Philol Asn; Am Hist Asn; Asn Ancient Hist **RESEARCH** Roman history; Rhetoric and oratory; Social and economic history. **SELECTED PUBLICATIONS** co-auth, Feeding the City: The Organization, Operation, and Scale of the Supply System for Rome, Life, Death, and Entertainment in the Roman Empire, Univ Mich Press, 98; auth, Making History Come Alive in the Classroom Through the Use of Role-Playing, Teaching Forum, 98; rev, Controlling Laughter: Political Humor in the Late Roman Republic, Hist Rev, 98. **CONTACT ADDRESS** Univ Wisc Green Bay, 2420 Nicolet Dr., Theatre Ha, Green Bay, WI, 54311. **EMAIL** aldreteg@gbms01.uwgb.edu

ALDRICH, MARK
PERSONAL Born 10/16/1941, Northhampton, MA, m, 1965 **DISCIPLINE** ECONOMIC HISTORY **EDUCATION** Middlebury Col, BA 63; Univ Calif Berk, MA 64; Univ Texas, PhD 69. **CAREER** Smith Col, asst prof, assoc prof, prof, 68 to 83-, Marilyn Carlson Nelson Prof of Econ, 95-. **MEMBERSHIPS** EHA; SHT. **RESEARCH** History of workplace safety. **SELECTED PUBLICATIONS** Auth, Safety First: Technology Business and Labor in the Transformation of Work Safety in America, Bal, John Hopkins Univ Press, 97; auth, The Peril of the Broken Rail: the Carriers the Steel Companies and Rail Technology, 1900-1945, Technology and Culture, forthcoming; Energy Conservation on Steam Railroads: Institutions Markets Technology, 1889-1943, Railroad History, 97; auth, The Perils of Mining Anthracite: Regulation Technology and Safety, 1870-1945, Penn History, 97; auth, The Cherry Mine Disaster of 1909: The Rest of the Story as told by George S. Rice, Mining History Jour, 97; auth, The Last Run of Engineer Peake: Work safety on the Rio Grande Southern Around the Time of World War I, Jour of the West, 97; Locomotive Inspection Materials at the National Archives, Railroad History, 96; auth, Preventing the Needless Peril of the Coal Miner: The Bureau of Mines and the Campaign to Prevent Coal Mine Explosions, Technology and Culture, 95; auth, Does Comparable Worth Correct for Discrimination?, David Saunders, ed, New Approaches to Employee Management, Greenwich CT, JAI, 94. **CONTACT ADDRESS** Smith Col, 10 Prospect St, Northampton, CT, 01063. **EMAIL** maldrich@smith.edu

ALDRICH, MICHELE
PERSONAL Born 10/06/1942, Seattle, WA, m, 1965 **DISCIPLINE** HISTORY AND GEOLOGY **EDUCATION** Univ Calif Berkeley, BA, geol, 64; Univ Tex Austin, PhD, hist, 74. **CAREER** Lectr, hist dept, Smith Col, 69-70; archiv, Valley Women's Ctr, 70-73; asst ed, Joseph Henry Papers, Smithsonian Inst, 74-75; consult, Aaron Burr Papers, NY Hist Soc, 75-76; fieldworker, Women's Hist Sources Survey, Univ Minn, 76-77; project dir, Women in Sci, AAAS, 77-83; dir, info svc, AAAS, 90-94; archiv, AAAS, 83-85, 95; visiting fel, dept of sci and tech, Cornell Univ, 96-; consult archiv, Winthrop Grp, 98-. **HONORS AND AWARDS** Geol Soc of Amer Hist of Geol award, 92. **MEMBERSHIPS** Orgn of Amer Hist; Hist of Sci Soc; New England Archiv. **RESEARCH** History of American Science. **SELECTED PUBLICATIONS** Co-ed, Theodore Hittell's California Academy of Sciences 1853-1906: A Narrative History, 97; auth, Scientific Association Records Programs: A Beginner's Guide AAAS: 95; co-ed, Directory of Historians of American Science, Forum for the History of America Sciene, 93; co-auth, Fishes of the Old Red Sandstone: Blossburg, Pennsylvania, 1830-1900, Earth Sci Hist, vol 11, 21-29, 92; auth, Women in Geology, Women of Science: Righting the Record, Ind Univ Press, 42-71, 90. **CONTACT ADDRESS** 24 Elm St., Hatfield, MA, 01038. **EMAIL** 73061.2420@compuserve.com

ALEXANDER, BOBBY C.
PERSONAL Born 12/03/1950, Shreveport, LA **DISCIPLINE** ANTHROPOLOGY **EDUCATION** Baylor Univ, BA, 73; Union Theol Sem, M.Div, 76; Columbia Univ, MPhil, 81, & Union Theol Sem, PhD, 85. **CAREER** Tchng asst, 79-81, Barnard Col; adj lectr, 81-85, adj asst prof, 85-86, Hunter Col, CUNY; asst prof, 86-93, Southern Methodist Univ; lectr, 93-97, sr lectr, 97-, Univ Texas, Dallas. **HONORS AND AWARDS** Student Choice Tchng Award, schl of soc sci, Univ Texas Dallas, 96; Jr Scholar Award SW Comm on Relig Stud, SW region of Amer Acad of Relig, 89-90; Res Asst Grant, AAR, 88-89. **MEMBERSHIPS** Amer Anthrop Assn; AAR, Soc for Sci Stud of Relig. **RESEARCH** Relig & polit culture; religion in contemp Amer soc; religious community & its contribution to cultural reproduction among Mexican migrant workers in the US global economy. **SELECTED PUBLICATIONS** Ed asst, The Encycl of Relig, 84-86; auth, "Ceremony", Encycl of Relig, Macmillan, 87; art, Pentecostal Ritual Reconsidered: 'Anti-structural' Dimension of Possession, J of Ritual Stud, 351:109, 89; art, Turner's Definition of Ritual Reconsidered: Grotowski's Experimental Theater as Secular Rituals of Spiritual Healing, Method & Theory in Stud of Relig, 3,1,31:62, 91; art, Correcting Misinterpretations of Turner's Theory: An African-American Pentecostal Illustration, J for Sci Stud of Relig, 30,1: 26, 91; art, An Afterward on Ritual in Biblical Studies, Semeia, 67:209, 95; ed, sect on ritual, Anthrop of Relig: A Handbk; auth, Ritual and Current Studies of Ritual: Overview, Anthrop of Relig: A Handbk, Greenwood Press, 97; auth, Televangelism Reconsidered: Ritual Within a Larger Social Drama, Rethinking Media, Relig, & Culture, Sage Pub, 97; auth, Victor Turner Revisited: Ritual As Social Change, Scholars Press, AAR, 91; auth, Televangelism Reconsidered: Ritual in the Search for Human Community, Scholars Press, AAR, 91. **CONTACT ADDRESS** School of Social Sciences, Univ of Texas, PO Box 830688, Richardson, TX, 75083. **EMAIL** bcalex@utdallas.edu

ALEXANDER, CHARLES C.
PERSONAL Born 10/24/1935, Cass Co, TX, m, 1960, 1 child **DISCIPLINE** UNITED STATES HISTORY **EDUCATION** Lamar State Col Tech, BA, 58; Univ Tex, MA, 59, PhD, 62. **CAREER** From instr to asst prof hist, Univ Houston, 62-66; assoc prof, Univ Ga, 66-70; Vis assoc prof, Univ Tex, 68-69; from prof to Distinguished Prof Hist, Ohio Univ, 70-. **HONORS AND AWARDS** LR Bryan Jr Award, Tex Gulf Coast Hist Asn, 62. **MEMBERSHIPS** Orgn Am Hist; Southern Hist Asn. **RESEARCH** American society thought and culture in the 20th century. **SELECTED PUBLICATIONS** Auth, Crusade for Conformity: The Ku Klux Klan in Texas, 1920-1930, Tex Gulf Coast Hist Asn, 62; The Ku Klux Klan in the Southwest, Univ Ky, 65; coauth, This New Ocean: A History of Project Mercury, US Govt Printing Off, 66; auth, Nationalism in American Thought, 1930-1945, Rand McNally, 69; Holding the Line: The Eisenhower Era, 1952-1961, Ind Univ, 75; Here the Country Lies: Nationalism and the Arts in Twentieth-Century America, Ind Univ Press, 80; Ty Cobb, Oxford Univ Press, 84; John McGraw, Viking, 88; Our Game: An American Baseball Histo-

ry, Holt, 91; Rogers Hornsby, Holt, 95. **CONTACT ADDRESS** Dept of Hist, Ohio Univ, Athens, OH, 45701-2979. **EMAIL** alexande@oak.cats.ohiou.edu

ALEXANDER, JOHN T.
PERSONAL Born 01/18/1940, Cooperstown, NY, m, 1964, 2 children **DISCIPLINE** MODERN RUSSIAN HISTORY **EDUCATION** Wesleyan Univ, AB, 61; Ind Univ, AM, 63, PhD(hist), 66. **CAREER** From asst prof to assoc prof, 66-74, PROF HIST, UNIV KANS, 74-. **HONORS AND AWARDS** Int Res & Exchange Bd exchange fel to USSR, 71 & 75; prin investr res grant, Nat Libr, Med, US Publ Health Serv, 72-73 & 75; vis fel, Kennan Inst Adv Russ Study, 81; Byron Caldwell Smith Award, for best work by Kans auth in all fields, 89; Balfour Jeffrey Higuchi Endowment Award for research achievement in the humanities, 92. **MEMBERSHIPS** AHA; Am Asn Advan Slavic Studies; Cent States Slavic Conf; Rocky Mountain Asn Slavic Studies; Brit Study Group 18 century Russia. **RESEARCH** Eighteenth century Russian society; early modern Russia; Russian medical history. **SELECTED PUBLICATIONS** Auth, Autocratic Politics in a National Crisis: The Imperial Russian Government and Pugachev's Revolt, 1773-1775, Ind Univ, 69; ed, S F Platonov, The Time of Troubles, Univ Kans, 70; auth, Western views of the Pugachev rebellion, Slavonic & E Europ Rev, 70; Emperor of the Cossacks: Pugachev and the Frontier Jacquerie of 1773-1775, Coronado, 73; S F Platonov: eminence and obscurity, introd to Rex Pyles transl, S F Platonov, Boris Godunov, Acad Int, 73; Cath II, Bubonic Plague and industry in Moscow, Am Hist Rev, 74; Bubonic Plague in Early Modern Russia, Johns Hopkins, 80; Catherine the Great and Public Health, J Hist Med, 81; Catherine the Great: Life and Legend, Oxford, 89; transl, E.V. Anisimov, The Reforms of Peter the Great, Sharpe, 93; auth, Anisimov, Empress Elizabeth, Acad Int, 95; Aeromania, Fire Balloons, and Catherine the Great's Ban of 1783, The Hist, 96; The Petrine Era and After, In: Freeze, Russia, A History, Oxford, 97; Ivan Shuvalov and Russian Court Politics, In: Literature, Lives, Astra, 94. **CONTACT ADDRESS** Dept of Hist, Univ of Kans, Lawrence, KS, 66045-0001. **EMAIL** jatalex@falcon.cc.ukans.edu

ALEXANDER, JON
PERSONAL Born 03/31/1943, Harrisburg, PA **DISCIPLINE** HISTORY **EDUCATION** Temple Univ, PhD, 71; Harvard Univ, MTS, 74. **CAREER** Assoc Prof, 98-, Providence College; Asst Prof, 75-78, Aquiwas Inst; Asst Prof, 70-71, Jackson State Univ. **MEMBERSHIPS** AAR; AHA. **RESEARCH** US Religious Autobiography and Biography. **SELECTED PUBLICATIONS** Auth, American Personal Religious Accounts 1600-1980: Toward an Inner History of America's Faiths, NY, Edward Mellen Press, 83; William Porcher DuBose: Selected Writings, Mahwah, Paulist Press, 88; Job Considered as a Conversion Account, Spirituality Today, 90. **CONTACT ADDRESS** History Dept, Providence Col, Providence, RI, 02918-0001.

ALEXANDER, MICHAEL C.
PERSONAL Born 01/28/1947, Geneva, NY, m, 1968, 2 children **DISCIPLINE** ANCIENT HISTORY **EDUCATION** Swarthmore Col, BA, 68; U of Toronto, MA, 70, PhD, 77. **CAREER** Univ of Alberta, sess lecrt, 74-75; Swarthmore Col, inst, 75-76; Univ of Ill, Chicago, asst prof, assoc prof, 76-. **HONORS AND AWARDS** NEH Fell, NHC Fell, U of Ill Fel. **MEMBERSHIPS** APA, AHA, ASLH **RESEARCH** Roman repub hist and law. **SELECTED PUBLICATIONS** Auth, Trials in the Late Roman Republic, 146 BC to 50 BC, U of T Press, 90; Hortensius' Speech in Defence of Verres, in: Phoenix, 76; The legatio Asiatica of Scaurus: Did It Take Place?, in: Trans of APA, 81; Repetition of Prosecution, and the Scope of Prosecution, in the Standing Criminal Courts of the Late Republic, in: Classical Antiquity, 82. **CONTACT ADDRESS** Dept of History, Univ of Illinois, Chicago, IL, 60607-7109. **EMAIL** micalexa@uic.edu

ALEXANDER, RALPH H.
PERSONAL Born 09/03/1936, Tyler, TX, m, 1964, 3 children **DISCIPLINE** SEMITICS AND OLD TESTAMENT; ARCHAEOLOGY **EDUCATION** Rice Univ, AB, 59; Dallas Theol Sem, ThM, 63, ThD, 68. **CAREER** Instr, S Bible Training School, 63-64, 65-66; asst prof of Bible and Archaeology, Wheaton Col, 66-72; prof Hebrew Scripture, dir summer quart Israel Prog, 74 & 78, W Baptist Sem, 73-87; assoc archaeologist, Albright Inst Archaeology, 77-78; dir, Advan Trng Studies Coordr Old Testament Concentration Bibl Educ Exten Int Austria, 87-95; dir, educ develop & advan trng studies, cis, bibl educ exten int, Moscow, 95-. **HONORS AND AWARDS** US Govt Fulbright grant, Israel, 64-65; Henry Thiessen Award New Testament; Outstanding Young Men Amer, 70; Outstanding Educ Amer; Who's Who Relig. **MEMBERSHIPS** Amer Schools Oriental Res; Archeol Inst Amer; Evangel Theol Soc; Fel Evangel Europ Tchrs; Inst Bibl Res; Israel Explor Soc; Nat Asn Hebrew Prof; Near East Archeol Soc; Soc Bibl Lit. **RESEARCH** Psalms; Old Testament Archaeology; Old Testament Law & Prophets. **SELECTED PUBLICATIONS** Contribur, New Commentary on the Whole Bible, Tyndale, 94; auth, Marriage and Divorce, Dictionary of Old Testament Ethics, Baker, 96; A New Covenant and An Eternal People, Israel: The Land and the People, Kregel, 98. **CONTACT ADDRESS** Box 3366, Gresham, OR, 97030. **EMAIL** ralphmyrna@earthlink.net

ALEXANDER, RONALD R.
PERSONAL Born 01/03/1942, London, WV, m, 1964, 3 children **DISCIPLINE** HISTORY **EDUCATION** WVa Inst Technol, BA, 64; Univ Ky, MA, 67, PhD, 76. **CAREER** Prof hist, WVA Inst Technology, 66-. **RESEARCH** American Civil War period; history of West Virginia Institute of Technology; First World War period. **SELECTED PUBLICATIONS** Auth, To hell with the Hapsburgs and Hohenzollerns, J WVa Hist Assn, spring 77; auth, West Virginia Tech, a History, Pictrial Histories Pub Co, Charleston, WV, 92. **CONTACT ADDRESS** Dept of History, West Virginia Univ Inst of Tech, 405 Fayette Pike, Montgomery, WV, 25136-2436. **EMAIL** dsoliv@wvit.wvnet.edu

ALEXANDER, THEODORE THOMAS, JR.
PERSONAL Born 11/24/1937, Los Angeles, California, d **DISCIPLINE** EDUCATION **EDUCATION** Los Angeles Community College, Los Angeles, CA, AA, electronics, 1958; California State University, Los Angeles, CA, BA, education, 1960, MA, education, 1964; University of Southern California, Los Angeles, CA, EdD, education, 1975. **CAREER** Los Angeles Board of Education, principal, 1971-75, administrative coord, 1975-76, administrative consultant, 1976-77, deputy area administrator, 1977-78, asst dir, 1978-82, asst superintendent, 1982-; University of Southern California, adjunct associate professor, 1971-. **HONORS AND AWARDS** USC Ebonics Support Group Outstanding Black Alumni Award, 1984; USC General Alumni Assn Tommy Statue Volunteer Service Award, 1984; National Achievement Award, Lamba Kappa Mu Sorority, 1985; Hilburn Award, Human Relations Award, City of Los Angeles Human Relations Committee, 1969; Award for Contribution to the field of education, The Assn of Black Law Enforcement Executives, 1991; Community Service Award, Kappa Alpha Psi National Award, 1988. **MEMBERSHIPS** President, Council of Black Administrators, 1983-85; president, Education Alumni Assn, USC, 1980-81; member, board of governors, General Alumni Assn, USC, 1986-89; president, polemarch, Los Angeles Alumni Chapter Kappa Alpha Psi Fraternity, 1986-89; president, Educare Support Group, USC, 1985-86. **CONTACT ADDRESS** Los Angeles Board of Education, 450 N Grand, Rm G-353, Los Angeles, CA, 90012.

ALEXANDER, THOMAS G.
PERSONAL Born 08/08/1935, Logan, UT, m, 1959, 5 children **DISCIPLINE** HISTORY **EDUCATION** Weber State Univ, AS 55; Utah State Univ, BS 60, MS 61; Univ Cal Berk, PhD 65. **CAREER** Brigham Young Univ, Lemuel Hardison Redd Jr Prof, prof, assoc prof, asst prof, 64 to 92-; SO IL Univ, adj assoc prof, 70-71; Univ Nebraska, vis lectr, 66. **HONORS AND AWARDS** AASLH Awd of Merit; NSDAR Amer Hist Medal Awd; Grace Arrington Awd; David W Beatrice C Evans Awd; NHPRC Fel; USHS Fel; USHS dist Awd. **MEMBERSHIPS** USHS; USDA; UASAL; NSDAR **RESEARCH** Auth, Western history; Amer environ history; Utah history; Latter-day Saint history **SELECTED PUBLICATIONS** Keeping Company with Wilford Woodruff, Jour of Morm Hist, 97; Reflections On Utah's Kingdom, Colony and Commonwealth, Rough Draft, 97; The Transformation of Utah from a Colony of Wall Street to Colony of Washington, The Thetean, 96; YX Company, and Woodruff, Wilford, and United States Versus Reynolds, and Salt Lake City Utah, and Kearns, Thomas, and Grant Heber Jour, Encycl of the American West, eds, Charles Phillip, Alan Axlerod, NY, Simon and Schuster Macmillan, 96; Utah's Constitution: A Reflection of the Territorial Experience, UT Hist Quart, 96. **CONTACT ADDRESS** Dept of History, Brigham Young Univ, Provo, UT, 84602-4446. **EMAIL** Thomas_Alexander@BYU.EDU

ALFORD, TERRY L.
PERSONAL Born 10/07/1945, Mobile, AL, m, 2 children **DISCIPLINE** AMERICAN HISTORY **EDUCATION** MS State Univ, BA, 66, MA 67, PhD, 70. **CAREER** Prof hist, Northern VA Community Col, 72-, Nat Endowment for Hum fel hist, 78-79. **MEMBERSHIPS** Surratt Soc; Lincoln grp of DC; Lincoln Inst of mid-Atlantic. **RESEARCH** Old South; Civil War; John Wilkes Booth; Lincoln Assassination. **SELECTED PUBLICATIONS** Auth, Prince Among Slaves, Harcourt Brace Jovanovich, 77; ed, John Wilkes Booth: A Sisters Memoir, univ Pres of MS, 96; ed board, Lincoln Herald; consul to Time Life Books, ABC News. **CONTACT ADDRESS** Dept of Hist, No Virginia Comm Col, 8333 Little River Tp, Annandale, VA, 22003-3743. **EMAIL** nvalfot@nv.cc.va.us

ALI, KAMAL HASSAN
PERSONAL Born 09/03/1944, Springfield, Massachusetts, m, 1966 **DISCIPLINE** EDUCATION **EDUCATION** Hunter College, 1963-64; New York Univ, 1964-65; Univ of Massachusetts, Amherst, MEd, 1977, EdD, 1981. **CAREER** Human Resources Admin, sr human resource specialist, 1967-71; Harlem East-Harlem Model Cities, project liason, 1971-74; Univ of Massachusetts, Amherst, graduate research and teaching asst, 1974-78; Vantage Consultants, Hartford, CT, training program developer, 1978-79; Westfield State College, dir, minority/bilingual vocational teacher educ programs, 1980-81, dir minority affairs, beginning 1981-, associate dean of academic affairs, currently. **HONORS AND AWARDS** Producer, host, cable television program "Coll Journal," Springfield, MA, 1983-; public speaking on educ, foreign policy, apartheid, 1984-86. **MEMBERSHIPS** Vice pres, Islamic Soc of Western Massachusetts, 1983-; Dunbar Community Center, chmn, bd of dir, 1984-86, chmn, New Bldg Comm, 1986-. **SELECTED PUBLICATIONS** Author, "Islamic Education in the United States: An Overview of Issues, Problems and Possible Approaches," 1984, "The Shariah and Its Implications to Muslim School Planning," 1986, Amer Journal of Islamic Social Studies. **CONTACT ADDRESS** Office of Multicultural Devt, Westfield State Col, Western Ave, Westfield, MA, 01086.

ALLEE, MARK
DISCIPLINE HISTORY **EDUCATION** Univ Pa, PhD, 87. **CAREER** Hist, Loyola Univ. **RESEARCH** Early modern 16th-19th centuries history; soc history; local history; law and society. **SELECTED PUBLICATIONS** Auth, Law and Society in Late Imperial China: Northern Taiwan in the Nineteenth Century, Stanford UP, 94; Code, Culture, Custom: Foundations of Civil Case Verdicts in a Nineteenth Century Court, In Civil Law in Chinese History, Stanford UP, 94. **CONTACT ADDRESS** Fine Arts Dept, Loyola Univ, Chicago, 6525 N. Sheridan Rd., Chicago, IL, 60626. **EMAIL** mallee@orion.it.luc.edu

ALLEN, BERNARD LEE
PERSONAL Born 07/19/1937, Weston, WV, m, 1964, 2 children **DISCIPLINE** HISTORY, PHILOSOPHY **EDUCATION** WVa Univ, BS, 59; Southern Ill Univ, MA, 64; WVa Univ, PhD(hist), 71. **CAREER** Instr hist & philos, WVa Univ, Parkersburg, 66-68 & WVa Univ, 70-71; asst prof hist & philos, 71-74, actg asst dean arts & sci, 75-76; assoc prof, 74-81, dean arts & sci & actg dean occup tech, 76, asst dean instr, 79-80, PROF HIST & PHILOS, PARKERSBURG COMMUNITY COL, 81-;adj instr, Wheeling Jesuit Univ, 93-98; adj instr, Washington St Comm Coll, 93-98. **HONORS AND AWARDS** Bd of Dir, WV Hum Fnd, Outstand Svc to Higher Edu, WV Prof of the Yr. **MEMBERSHIPS** Appalachian Stud Assn, WV Hist Assn of Col and Univ Tchrs of Hist; Oil, Gas, and Indus Hist Assn. **RESEARCH** John Dewey's philosophy of history; mid-Ohio valley; women of the Ohio valley; U.S. social and ideological history; the Virginias and the Carolinas. **SELECTED PUBLICATIONS** Auth, John Dewey's Views on History, 1859-1971, Univ Microfilms, 71; Oarkersburg: A Bicentennial History, Parkersburg Bicentennial Commission, 85; Lessons, Data Day, 90; Compassion: A History of the Harry Logan Children's Home, Harry Logan Children's Home Fnd, 92; co-auth, Where It All Began, 94. **CONTACT ADDRESS** Parkersburg Community Col, 300 Campus Dr, Box 167-A, Parkersburg, WV, 26101-8647. **EMAIL** ballen@alha.wuup.wvnet.edu

ALLEN, GARLAND E.
PERSONAL Born 02/13/1936, Louisville, KY, d, 2 children **DISCIPLINE** HISTORY OF SCIENCE **EDUCATION** Univ Louisville, BA, 57. **CAREER** Instr 65-76, Harvard Univ; Asst Prof, Assoc Prof, 67-, Washington Univ; vis Prof, 89-91, Harvard Univ. **HONORS AND AWARDS** Warren Cen Fel; Sigma Xi Ntl Lectr, Sigma Xi Bicentenn Lectr, Marine Biol Lab Trustee; George Sarton Awd. **MEMBERSHIPS** HSS; ISH; PSSB; BSHS. **RESEARCH** History of Genetics in 20th Century; Eugenics in the US. **SELECTED PUBLICATIONS** Auth, Nature versus Nurture, in: Encyc of Applied Ethics, NY, Academic Press, 97; Genetics and Behavior, in: Encyc of Applied Ethics, NY, Academic Press, 97; The social economic origins of genetic determination: a case history of the American Eugenics Movement, 1900-1940 and its lessons for today, Genetica, 97; The Double-Edged Sword of Genetic Determinism: Social and Political Agendas in Genetic Studies of Homosexuality, 1940-1994, in: Vernon A Rosario ed, Science and Homosexualities, NY, Routledge, 97; rev, Biologists Under Hitler, by Ute Deichmann, trans by T Dunlap, Endeavor, 98. **CONTACT ADDRESS** Biology Dept, Wash Univ, St. Louis, MO, 63130. **EMAIL** allen@brodec.wustl.edu

ALLEN, IRVING L.
DISCIPLINE SOCIOLOGY **EDUCATION** Univ Iowa, PhD 65. **CAREER** Univ Connecticut, prof emer, 63-. **RESEARCH** Social History of Culture and Language **SELECTED PUBLICATIONS** The City in Slang: New York Life and Popular Speech, NY, Oxford Univ Press, 93. **CONTACT ADDRESS** Box 138, Storrs, CT, 06268-0138.

ALLEN, JACK
PERSONAL Born 06/18/1914, Prestonsburg, KY, m, 1941, 3 children **DISCIPLINE** HISTORY **EDUCATION** Eastern Ky State Teachers Col, AB, 35; George Peabody Col, AM, 38, PhD, 41. **CAREER** Asst prof hist, Eastern Ky State Teachers Col, 40-46; assoc prof, 46-54, chmn dept hist & polit sci, 56-74, chmn div soc sci, 63-74, actg exec dean acad affairs, 74-75, dir prog educ policy specialists, 74-77, prof, 54-80, EMER PROF HIST, GEORGE PEABODY COL, 80-, Vis prof, Univ Colo, 59; consult, pub sch, Phoenix, Ariz, 60, Nova Sch, Ft Lauderdale, Fla, 63-67, pub sch, Oak Ridge, Tenn, 65-67 & Tri-Univ proj elem educ, 67-68; social studies specialist, Repub of Korea, 61 & 69; evaluator, title XI Insts Hist, 65; ad hoc comt soc sci/social studies, US Off Educ, 65-66; mem coun, Thirteen Original States Fund, 78-. **HONORS AND AWARDS** Am Asn State & Local Hist Award, 61. **MEMBERSHIPS** Nat Coun So-

cial Studies (pres, 58); Am Coun Educ; Orgn Am Historians; Am Studies Asn. **RESEARCH** Recent American history; social education. **SELECTED PUBLICATIONS** Coauth, Nations Around the Globe, 66 & The Earth and Our States, 66, Prentice-Hall; History: USA, 67 & 76, auth, Documents: USA, 67, coauth, USA: History With Documents, Vols I & II, 71, auth, American Society in Civic Issues, 73, American Society, 78 & Americans, 79, Am Bk Co; Education in the 80's: Social Studies, Nat Educ Asn, 81. **CONTACT ADDRESS** 3705 Hilldale Dr, Nashville, TN, 37215.

ALLEN, LEE NORCROSS
PERSONAL Born 04/16/1926, Valley, AL, m, 1963, 2 children **DISCIPLINE** HISTORY **EDUCATION** Auburn Univ, BS, 48, MS, 49; Univ Penn, PhD, 55. **CAREER** Instr to prof, 52-61, Eastern Col; prof, 61, dean, grad schl, 65-86, dean, arts & sci, 75-90, Samford Univ. **RESEARCH** Baptist hist, local hist, political hist of 1920's in USA. **CONTACT ADDRESS** Samford Univ, Mail Sub OX 2257, Birmingham, AL, 35229. **EMAIL** lnallen@samford.edu

ALLEN, MARK
DISCIPLINE FINE ARTS AND HUMANITIES **EDUCATION** St Norbert Col, BA; AR State Univ, MA; Univ IL at Champaign-Urbana, PhD. **CAREER** Assoc prof; taught at, Univ IL, AR State Univ & UTSA; taught in, UTSA London Semr Prog, 94; bibliogr, New Chaucer Soc; des & moderator, Online Chaucer Bibliog. **HONORS AND AWARDS** TX System's Chancellor's Coun Outstanding Tchg Awd, 90., Contrib, Annotated Bibliog for Eng Stud CD-ROM. **RESEARCH** Medieval lit and cult; Chaucer; Arthurian lit, the hist of the Eng lang; fantasy lit; technol applications in the hum. **SELECTED PUBLICATIONS** Coauth, The Essential Chaucer: An Annotated Bibliography of Major Modern Studies, G K Hall, 87; articles in, Stud in the Age of Chaucer, S Cent Rev, Arthurian Interpretations & Lit Onomastics Stud. **CONTACT ADDRESS** Col of Fine Arts and Hum, Univ Texas at San Antonio, 6900 N Loop 1604 W, San Antonio, TX, 78249. **EMAIL** mallen@lonestar.utsa.edu

ALLEN, MICHAEL I.
DISCIPLINE MEDIEVAL HISTORY **EDUCATION** Tufts Univ, BA, 85; Yale Univ, MA, 86; Univ Toronto, PhD, 94. **CAREER** Asst prof, Univ Chicago. **HONORS AND AWARDS** Phi Beta Kappa; Seymour Simches Sch; Yale Univ Fel; Borsa di studio; Doctoral Fel, Soc Scis & Hum Res Coun Canada. Queen Elizabeth II Ontario Fel; George C. Metcalf Fel; Postdoctoral Fel, Soc Scis & Hum Res Coun Canada. **RESEARCH** Early medieval cultures, literatrures and societies; medieval historical writing; books, script, and learning in medieval Europe; role of women in medievil education; Latin paleography. **SELECTED PUBLICATIONS** Auth, The Metrical Passio Crispini et Crispiniani of Henry of Avranches, Analecta Bollandiana, 90; Bede and Frechulf at Medieval St. Gallen, Beda Venerabilis: Historian, Monk and Northumbrian, 96. **CONTACT ADDRESS** Dept of Classics, Univ Chicago, 1010 E 50th St, Chicago, IL, 60637. **EMAIL** frechulf@uchicago.edu

ALLEN, ROBERT L.
PERSONAL Born 05/29/1942, Atlanta, GA, m, 1995 **DISCIPLINE** AFRICAN-AMERICAN STUDIES **EDUCATION** Attended Univ of Vienna, 1961-62; Morehouse College, BS, 1963; attended Columbia Univ, 1963-64; New School for Social Research, New York NY, MA, 1967; Univ of California, San Francisco, PhD, 1983. **CAREER** Guardian Newsweekly NYC, staff reporter 1967-69; San Jose State Coll, asst prof new coll & black studies dept 1969-72; The Black Scholar Mag, editor; Mills College, Oakland CA, began as lecturer, became asst prof of ethnic studies, 1973-84; Wild Trees Press, gen mgr, 1984-90; THE BLACK SCHOLAR, SENIOR ED, 1990-; AFRICAN-AMERICAN & ETHNIC STUDIES, UNIVERSITY OF CALIFORNIA-BERKELEY, VISITING PROF, 1994-. **HONORS AND AWARDS** Guggenheim fellowship, 1978; Winner American Book Award, 1995. **MEMBERSHIPS** Pres, Black World Foundation; mem, American Sociological Assn; mem, American Historical and Cultural Society; mem, Association of Black Sociologists; mem, Pacific Sociological Assn; mem, Council for Black Studies; Bay Area Black Journalists; bd mem, Oakland Men's Project; bd mem, San Francisco Book Council. **SELECTED PUBLICATIONS** Auth, "Black Awakening in Capitalist Amer" Doubleday, 1969, "Reluctant Reformers, The Impact of Racism on Amer Social Reform Movements" Howard Univ Press, 1974; contributor to periodicals; author, The Port Chicago Mutiny, Warner Books, 1989; coeditor Brotherman Ballantine, 1995. **CONTACT ADDRESS** The Black Scholar, PO Box 2869, Oakland, CA, 94618.

ALLEN, WILLIAM BARCLAY
PERSONAL Born 03/18/1944, Fernandina Beach, Florida, m **DISCIPLINE** POLITICAL SCIENCE **EDUCATION** Pepperdine Coll, BA 1967; Claremont Grad School, MA 1968, PhD 1972. **CAREER** Univ de Rouen, lecteur 1970-71; The Amer Univ, asst prof 1971-72; Harvey Mudd Coll, asst prof 1972-76, assoc prof 1976-83; St John's Coll Grad Inst, visiting tutor 1977-; Harvey Mudd Coll, prof of govt, 1983-94; Michigan State University, James Madison College, dean, 1993-. **HONORS AND AWARDS** Fulbright Fellowship 1970-71; Kellogg Natl Fellow WK Kellogg Found 1984-87; Prix Montesquieu Academic France 1986; Pi Sigma Alpha, Sigma Alpha; LID, Pepperdine University, 1988. **MEMBERSHIPS** Mem Claremont Rotary 1980-86; mem pres Claremont Unified School Dist Bd 1981-84; bd mem CA Assembly Fellowship Prog 1982-92; prog dir Liberty Fund Inc1982-89; chmn CA Scholars for Reagan 1984; bd mem LeRoy Boys Home; mem Natl Council for the Humanities, 1984-87; mem Am Pol Sci Assoc, Academie Montesquieu; mem, Chair US Commission on Civil Rights, 1987-92; US Civil Rights Commission, CA State Adv Committee, 1985-87. **CONTACT ADDRESS** Dean, James Madison Col, East Lansing, MI, 48825-1205.

ALLEN, WILLIAM SHERIDAN
PERSONAL Born 10/05/1932, Evanston, IL, m, 1982, 4 children **DISCIPLINE** MODERN GERMAN HISTORY **EDUCATION** Univ Mich, AB, 55; Univ Conn, MA, 56; Univ Minn, PhD(Ger hist), 62. **CAREER** Instr Hist, Bay City Jr Col, 58-59 & Mass Inst Technol, 60-61; from asst prof to assoc prof, Univ Mo, 61-67; assoc prof, Wayne State Univ, 67-70; PROF HIST, STATE UNIV NY BUFFALO, 74-, Univ Mo res coun grant, 63; Am Philos Soc grants, 63-64 & 65-66; Alexander von Humboldt Found fel, 65-66; res grants res coun, State Univ NY, 71-72 & 72-73; mem, Conf Group German Polit; mem, Nat Arch Liaison Comt, 69-78; Nat Endowment for the Humanities summer fel, 79. **HONORS AND AWARDS** Chancellors Award Excellence Teaching, State Univ NY, 76. **MEMBERSHIPS** Am Conf for Irish Stud; AHA; Conf Group Cent Europ Hist. **RESEARCH** Socialist underground in Nazi Germany; social history of Weimar and Nazi Germany; nineteenth century Irish nationalism. **SELECTED PUBLICATIONS** Auth, The Nazi Seizure of Power, Quadrangle, 65; contribr, Widerstand, Verfolgung, Emigration, Bod Godesberg, 67; The German Church Struggle and the Holocaust, Wayne Univ, 73; Reappraisals of Fascism, Franklin Watts, 75; auth, The Infancy of Nazism, Franklin Watts, 76; contribr, Totalitarianism Reconsidered, Nat Univ Publ, 81; Die Reihen fast Geschlossen, Hammer, 81. **CONTACT ADDRESS** Dept of History, State Univ NY, Buffalo, NY, 14260.

ALLIN, CRAIG WILLARD
PERSONAL Born 10/03/1946, Two Harbors, MN, m, 1977 **DISCIPLINE** POLITICAL SCIENCE **EDUCATION** Grinnell Coll, BA, 65; Princeton Univ, MA, 70, PhD, 76. **CAREER** Asst prof, Polit Sci, Cornell Coll, 72-79; assoc prof, Cornell Coll, 79-85; PROF, POLIT SCI, CORNELL COLL, 85-. **MEMBERSHIPS** Policy Stud Org **RESEARCH** Environmental politics; Management of wilderness areas & federal conservation lands. **SELECTED PUBLICATIONS** co-edr, Natural Resources, Salem Press, 98; "National Parks and Nature Reserves of the World," World Book Encyclopedia, Chic: World Bk Publ, 96; "Wilderness Policy," West Publ Lands & Envir Polit, Westview Press, 96; "Sex Discrimination, Encyc of Civil Rights Am, Salem Press, 97. **CONTACT ADDRESS** Dept Polit, Cornell Col, 600 First St W, Mount Vernon, IA, 52314-1098. **EMAIL** allin.craig@worldnet.ztt.net

ALLINGTON, RICHARD LLOYD
PERSONAL Born 05/13/1947, Grand Rapids, MI, m, 1980, 5 children **DISCIPLINE** EDUCATION **EDUCATION** Western Mich Univ, BA, 68; Mich St Univ, PhD, 73. **CAREER** Prof, 73-, SUNY Albany. **HONORS AND AWARDS** Harris Award, Intl Reading Asn; Johnston Award, Center for Literacy and Disability; Pres Award for re Excel, Who's Who in Amer Ed; Pres Natl Reading Conf; Bd of Dir, Intl Reading Asn; Res Grants from: Office of Ed Res and Improvement, Office of Special Ed and Rehabilitation, Natl Inst on Aging; Res Scientist at NRC, TLL & NRCELA. **RESEARCH** Literacy development; learning disabilities; education policy. **SELECTED PUBLICATIONS** Coauth, No Quick Fix: Rethinking Literacy Instruction In America's Elementary Schools, Tchrs Col Pres, 95; coauth, Schools That Work: All Children Readers And Writers, Longmans, 96; coauth, The Handbook of Special and Remedial Education, Elsevier Science, 96; coauth, Handbook of Research on Teaching Literacy through the Communicative and Visual Arts, Macmillan, 97; auth, Help for Struggling Readers, Intl Reading Asn, 98; coauth, The Politics of literacy teaching: How Research Shaped Educational Policy-Making, Ed Resr, 99. **CONTACT ADDRESS** SUNY, Albany, 400 Washington, ED 333, Albany, NY, 12222. **EMAIL** dickasunya@aol.com

ALLITT, PATRICK N.
DISCIPLINE HISTORY **EDUCATION** Oxford Univ, BA, 77; Univ Calif Berkeley, MA, 81, PhD, 86. **CAREER** Prof **RESEARCH** History of American religion; American political and intellectual history of the twentieth century. **SELECTED PUBLICATIONS** Auth, Catholic Intellectuals and Conservative Politics in America, 1950-1985; Catholic Converts: British and American Intellectuals Turn to Rome. **CONTACT ADDRESS** Dept History, Emory Univ, 221 Bowden Hall, 561 Kilgo Cir, Atlanta, GA, 30322-1950. **EMAIL** pallitt@emory.edu

ALLMAN, JEAN M.
DISCIPLINE HISTORY **EDUCATION** Northwestern Univ, PhD, 87. **CAREER** Assoc prof, 94-. **RESEARCH** West African history. **SELECTED PUBLICATIONS** Auth, The Quills of the Porcupine: Asante Nationalism in An Emergent Ghana, 93; Making Mothers: Missionaries, Medical Officers and Women's Work in Colonial Asante, Hist Workshop, 94; Hewers of Wood, Carriers of Water: Islam, Class and Politics on the Eve of Ghana's Independence, African Studies Rev, 91; Of Spinsters, Concubines and Wicked Women: Reflections on Gender and Social Change in Colonial Asante, Gender Hist, 91; The Youngmen and the Porcupine: Class, Nationalism and Asante's Struggle for Self-Determination, J African Hist, 90; co-ed, Social History of Africa, Heinemann. **CONTACT ADDRESS** History Dept, Univ of Minnesota, Twin Cities, 614 Social Sciences Tower, 267 19th Ave. S, Minneapolis, MN, 55455. **EMAIL** allma002@tc.umn.edu

ALOFSIN, ANTHONY
DISCIPLINE ART HISTORY, ARCHITECTURAL HISTORY/MODERN **EDUCATION** Philips Acad, dipl, 67; Harvard Coll, AB, 71; Harvard Grad School Design, M archit, 81; Columbia Univ, M philos, 83; Columbia Univ PhD, 87. **CAREER** Adj prof Art History, Coll Fine Arts, Martin Kermacy Centennial prof, School Archit, Univ Tex Austin, 87-. **HONORS AND AWARDS** Vasari Awardard, Univ Tex Austin, 90; Fac Research Awardard, Univ Research Inst, 93-4, Int Assoc Art Critics, Best Archit Show, 93-94; Book Awardard, Am Inst Archit, 94; Fac Research Awardard, Univ Research Inst, 95; Competitive Award, Univ Tex Austin, 97-98. **MEMBERSHIPS** Am Inst Archit; Coll Art Assoc; Hist Ger Cent Europ Art Archit; Soc Archit Hist; Soc Hist E Europ Russ Art Archit. **RESEARCH** Modernism; Historiography; modern European, Central European and American Architecture. **SELECTED PUBLICATIONS** Auth, Frank Lloyd Wright: The Lost Years, 1910-1922, 93; introd to Studies and Executed Buildings, 98; Frank Lloyd Wright: Europe and Beyond, 98; ed, Frank Lloyd Wright: An Index to the Taliesin Correspondence, 88; contrubur, American National Biography, 94; co-ed, center, A J for Archit , Am, 93. **CONTACT ADDRESS** School of Archit, Univ of Tex Austin, Goldsmith Hall, Austin, TX, 78712. **EMAIL** alofsin@uts.cc.utexas.edu

ALPERN ENGEL, BARBARA
DISCIPLINE HISTORY **EDUCATION** City Col NY, BA, 65; Harvard Univ, MA, 67; Columbia Univ, PhD, 74. **CAREER** Asst prof, 76-92, assoc prof, 82-92, prof, 92-, dir, Central and Eastern European Stu, 93-95, dept ch, 95-. **SELECTED PUBLICATIONS** Auth, Between the Fields and the City: Women, Work and Family in Russia, 1861-1914, Cambridge, 94; Women, Men and the Languages of Peasant Resistance, 1870-1917, Princeton, 94. **CONTACT ADDRESS** History Dept, Univ of Colorado, Boulder, Boulder, CO, 80309. **EMAIL** barbara.engel@colorado.edu

ALSOP, JAMES
DISCIPLINE HISTORY **EDUCATION** Winnipeg Univ, BA; Univ Western Ontario, MA; Cambridge Univ, PhD. **RESEARCH** English taxation **SELECTED PUBLICATIONS** Co-auth, English Seamen and Trader in Guinea 1553-1565, 92. **CONTACT ADDRESS** History Dept, McMaster Univ, 1280 Main St W, Hamilton, ON, L8S 4L9.

ALTER, GEORGE
PERSONAL Born 03/02/1949, Boston, MA, m, 1992, 1 child **DISCIPLINE** HISTORY **EDUCATION** Univ Penn, BA, 71; Univ Penn, PhD, hist, 78; Univ Mich, MA, applied econ, 78. **CAREER** Asst prof, dept of hist, Ind Univ, 79-87; assoc prof, dept of hist, Ind Univ, 87-; acting dir, Population Inst for Res and Training, Ind Univ, 87-88; dir, undergrad studies, dept of hist, Ind Univ, 96-98; dir, Population Inst for Res and Training, Ind Univ, 91-. **HONORS AND AWARDS** Internal Acad Residential fel, Ind Univ Inst for Adv Study, 95; Ind Univ summer facul fel, 95; Nat Res Svc award, Nat Inst on Aging, 89; Ind Heritage Res grant, 88; Ind Univ summer facul fel, 86; Nat Endow for the Humanities fel at Newberry Libr, 85; Lilly postdoctoral teaching fel, 82-83; Ind Univ summer facul fel, 80; post-doctoral fel, econ demography, Population Studies Ctr, Univ Mich, 77-78, 78-79; Penfield fel, 75-76; teaching asst, Univ Penn, 74-75; Univ Penn pre-doctoral fel, 71-75. **MEMBERSHIPS** Soc Sci Hist Asn; Population Asn of Amer; Econ Hist Asn; Cliometrics Soc; Soc de Demographi Hist. **RESEARCH** Historical demography; Family history; Economic history. **SELECTED PUBLICATIONS** Article, co-auth, Mortality and Economic Stress: Individual and Household Reponses in a Nineteenth-Century Belgian Village, Population and Economy: From Hunger to Modern Economic Growth, Oxford Univ Press, 98; article, co-auth, The sick and the well: adult health in Britain during the health transition, Health Trans Rev, suppl to vol 6, 19-44, 96; article, The European Marriage Pattern as Solution and Problem: Households of the Elderly in Verviers Belgium, 1831, Intl Jour of Family Hist, 1, 123-138, 96; article, Infant and Child Mortality in the United States and Canada, Infant and Child Mortality in the Past, Oxford, Clarendon Press, 91-108, 97; article, co-auth, Household Patterns of the Elderly and the Proximity of Children in a Nineteenth-Century City, Verviers, Belgium, 1831-1846, Aging and Generational Relations, Walter de Gruyter, 30-52, 96; article, Trends in United States Old Age Mortality, 1900-1935: Evidence from Railroad Pensions, Aging in the Past: Society, Demography, and Old Age, 328-59, Univ Calif Press, 95; article, co-auth, The Savings

of Ordinary Americans: The Philadelphia Saving Fund Society in the Mid-nineteenth Century, Jour of Econ Hist, 54, 735-67, 94. **CONTACT ADDRESS** Dept. of History, Indiana Univ, Bloomington, Bloomington, IN, 47405. **EMAIL** alter@indiana.edu

ALTHOLZ, JOSEF L.
PERSONAL Born 08/14/1933, New York, NY **DISCIPLINE** HISTORY **EDUCATION** Cornell Univ, BA, 54; Columbia Univ, MA, 55, PhD, 60. **CAREER** Instr to asst prof to assoc prof to prof, 59-, Univ Minn; vis prof, 70-71, Univ Wi. **HONORS AND AWARDS** Guggenheim Fel, 64-65; Fel Royal Hist Soc, 73. **MEMBERSHIPS** Amer Hist Assoc; Amer Catholic Hist Assoc; Res Soc for Victorian Periodicals; N Amer Conf on British Stud. **RESEARCH** Britain; 19th cent; religious hist. **SELECTED PUBLICATIONS** Auth, The Liberal Catholic Movement in England, Burns & Oates, 62; auth, The Religious Press in Britain, 1760-1900, Greenwood Press, 89; auth, Anatomy of a Controversy: The Debate over Essays and Reviews, 1860-1864, Scolar Press, 94; auth, The Tractarian Moment: The Incidental Origins of the Oxford Movement, Albion, 94; art, Lord Acton and the Plan of the Cambridge Modern History, Hist J, 96. **CONTACT ADDRESS** Dept of History, Univ Mn, Minneapolis, MN, 55455. **EMAIL** altho001@tc.umn.edu

ALTMAN, IDA
PERSONAL Born 04/30/1950, Washington, DC, s **DISCIPLINE** HISTORY **EDUCATION** Univ Mich, BA, 71; Univ Tex, MA, 72; Johns Hopkins Univ, PhD, 82. **CAREER** Instr, 82-, prof, Dept of History, 93-, Univ of New Orleans. **HONORS AND AWARDS** Herbert E Bolton Prize; Spain and America in the Quincentennial of the Discovery Prize, both for book Emigrants and Society. **MEMBERSHIPS** Amer Hist Asn; Conference on Latin Amer History; Soc for Spanish and Portuguese Historical Soc. **RESEARCH** Colonial Spanish Amer; Mexico; early modern Spain; emigration. **SELECTED PUBLICATIONS** Coauth, To Make America, European Emigration in the Early Modern Period, Univ of CA Press, 91; art, Spanish Society in Mexico City after Conquest, Hispanic Amer Hist Rev 71:3, 91; coauth, The Contact of Cultures Perspectives on the Quincentenary, Amer Hist Rev 99, 94. **CONTACT ADDRESS** Dept of History, Univ of New Orleans, New Orleans, LA, 70148.

ALTSCHUL, MICHAEL
PERSONAL Born 09/29/1936, Brooklyn, NY, 2 children **DISCIPLINE** MEDIEVAL & RENAISSANCE HISTORY **EDUCATION** NY Univ, AB, 57; Johns Hopkins Univ, PhD, 62. **CAREER** Instr & asst prof, Univ Mich, 62-67; assoc prof, 67-77, prof hist, Case Western Reserve Univ, 77-; Mem adv bd, Speculum: J Mediaeval Acad Am, 78-81. **MEMBERSHIPS** Renaissance Soc Am; Mediaeval Acad Am; fel Royal Hist Soc; Conf British Studies. **RESEARCH** Medieval political history; medieval England. **SELECTED PUBLICATIONS** Auth, A Baronial Family in Medieval England: The Clares, 1217-1314, Johns Hopkins, 65; auth, Anglo-Norman England, Cambridge, 68; ed, M & M, Medievalia et Humanistica, 70; contribr, Glamorgan County History, Ill: The Middle Ages, Univ Wales, 71. **CONTACT ADDRESS** Dept of History, Case Western Reserve Univ, 10900 Euclid Ave, Cleveland, OH, 44106-4901. **EMAIL** mxa6@po.cwru.edu

ALTSTADT, AUDREY L.
DISCIPLINE HISTORY **EDUCATION** Univ Chicago, PhD, 83. **CAREER** Assoc prof, Univ MA Amherst. **RESEARCH** Soviet hist. **SELECTED PUBLICATIONS** Auth, The Azerbaijani Turks, Stanford, 92; **CONTACT ADDRESS** Dept of Hist, Univ Massachusetts Amherst, Mass Ave, Amherst, MA, 01003.

ALVEY, RICHARD GERALD
PERSONAL Born 11/08/1935, Evansville, IN, m, 1967 **DISCIPLINE** FOLKLORISTICS, ENGLISH **EDUCATION** Univ Ky, BA, 69, MSLA, 70; Univ Pa, AM, 71, PhD(folkloristics), 74. **CAREER** Asst prof, 74-80, assoc prof folklore, Univ KY, 80-. **HONORS AND AWARDS** Mem, Coun on Exp Educ, 74-; Nat Endowment Humanities res grant, 76. **MEMBERSHIPS** Am Folklore Soc; Folklore Soc (British); Appalachian Studies Conf, 78; Asn Folklorists in South; Int Soc for Folk Narrative Res; bd mem, Appalachian Studies Conf, 78-. **RESEARCH** Folkloristics; Appalachian studies, regional studies; English. **SELECTED PUBLICATIONS** Auth, Phillips Barry and Anglo-American Folksong Scholarship, J Folklore Inst, 73; Folk beliefs about food & eating in Kentucky, Ky Hospitality, 76; A second look at the secondary ballad, Southern Folklore Quart, 78; Coyote tales, Enzyklopadie des Marchen **CONTACT ADDRESS** Dept of English, Univ of Kentucky, 500 S Limestone St, Lexington, KY, 40506-0003.

AMAN, MOHAMMED M.
PERSONAL Born 01/03/1940, Alexandria, Egypt, m, 1972 **DISCIPLINE** MIDDLE EASTERN STUDIES **EDUCATION** Cairo Univ Egypt, BA (with honors), 1961; Columbia Univ New York NY, MS, 1965; Univ of Pittsburgh, PhD, 1968; New York Univ, postdoctoral studies in Comp Sci, 1970-71. **CAREER** Univ of Pittsburgh, research asst, 1965-66; Duquesne Univ Pittsburgh, reference librarian, 1966-68; Pratt Inst NY, asst prof; St Johns Univ NY, asst and assoc prof 1969-73, dir and prof 1973-76; Long Island Univ, Greenvale Long Island NY, dean & prof 1976-79; Univ of Wisconsin-Milwaukee, dean and prof, 1979-. **HONORS AND AWARDS** Beta Phi Mu Intl Lib & Info Sci Honor Soc; award of appreciation from the Black Caucus of the Amer Library Assn, 1986; Award of Serv, Assn for Library and Information Science Educ, 1988; UNESCO consultant on the Revival of the Alexandrian Library Project, 1988-; John Ames Humphry/OCLC-Forest Press Award for Outstanding Contributions to Intl Librarianship, Amer Library Assn, 1989; Black Caucus of the Amer Library Assn (BCALA), Leadership Award, 1994; the WLA Special Service Award, 1992; Black Caucus of The ALA Award of Excellence, 1995; Prof Kaula Medal & Citation, 1996; WLA, Librarian of the Year, 1998. **MEMBERSHIPS** Info mgmt consultant UNIDO 1978-; UNESCO 1982-, US-AID 1984-96; chmn Intl Relations Comm Amer Lib Assn 1984-86, Assn Lib & Info Sci Ed 1985-86; Amer Soc for Info Science Intl Rel Comm; chair, Intl Issues in Information Special Interest Group; life mem, founding exec bd mem, NAACP 1984-; mem Amer Arab Affairs Council 1983-; mem Egyptian Amer Scholars Assn 1971-; bd member, A Wisconsin African Relief Effort (AWARE), 1986-89; bd member, Wisconsin African Historical Society/Museum, 1988-, member, Audience Development Committee, Milwaukee Art Museum; founder, Milwaukee Leader's Forum. **SELECTED PUBLICATIONS** Auth, contrib consult, Intl Library Review, 1969-91; ed-in-chief, Digest of Middle East Studies (DOMES), Arab Serials & Periodicals, 1979; Cataloging & Classification of Non-Western Library Material, 1980; Librarianship in the Third World, 1976, Developing Computer Based Library Sys 1984, Online Access to Database 1984, Information Services 1986; Urban Library Management, 1990. **CONTACT ADDRESS** Sch Libr & Info Sci, Univ of Wisconsin, PO Box 413, Enderis Hall, Milwaukee, WI, 53201.

AMAR, JOSEPH P.
PERSONAL Born 12/29/1946, Grand Rapids, MI, s **DISCIPLINE** SEMITIC LANGUAGES; HISTORY **EDUCATION** The Catholic Univ of America, PhD, 88. **CAREER** PROF, UNIV NOTRE DAME, 88-, CHAIR, CLASSICS DEPT, 97-. **MEMBERSHIPS** North Amer Patristics Soc (NAPS); Middle East Studies Assoc (MESA). **RESEARCH** Cultural/linguistic interplay; Syriac language & lit; medieval Christian Arabic; Islamic history. **CONTACT ADDRESS** Dept of Classics, Univ Notre Dame, 304 O'Shaughnessy Hall, Notre Dame, IN, 46556. **EMAIL** Joseph.P.Amar.1@nd.edu

AMBLER, EFFIE
DISCIPLINE EUROPEAN/RUSSIAN HISTORY **EDUCATION** Bryn Mawr Col, AB, 58; Ind Univ, Bloomington, PhD, 68. **CAREER** Asst prof hist, 65-66, Hollins Col; instr, 66-68, asst prof, 68-, assoc prof, 78-, Wayne St Univ. **MEMBERSHIPS** AAUP; Assn Advan Slavic Studies; AHA. **RESEARCH** Social and cultural history of the Russian Empire. **SELECTED PUBLICATIONS** Auth, Russian Journalism and Politics, 1861-81, The Career of Aleksei S Suvorin, Wayne State Univ, 72. **CONTACT ADDRESS** Dept of History, Wayne State Univ, 3094 FAB, Detroit, MI, 48202-3919.

AMBROSE, LINDA M.
DISCIPLINE HISTORY **EDUCATION** Univ Waterloo, BA, MA, PhD. **CAREER** Asst prof. **SELECTED PUBLICATIONS** Auth, For Home and Country, the Centennial His of the Women's Institutes in ontario, Boston Mills, 96. **CONTACT ADDRESS** Dept of History, Laurentian Univ, 935 Ramsey Lake Rd, Sudbury, ON, P3E 2C6.

AMBROSE, Z. PHILIP
PERSONAL Born 06/09/1936, Ponca City, OK, m, 2 children **DISCIPLINE** CLASSICAL LANGUAGES **EDUCATION** Princeton Univ, PhD, 63. **CAREER** Roberts Prof Of Classical Languages And Lit, 62-, Univ Vt **HONORS AND AWARDS** Phi Beta Kappa; CANA Barlow Beach Award for Dist Serv, 85. **MEMBERSHIPS** CANE; APA; Soc for Ancient Greek Philos. **RESEARCH** Greek drama; classical tradition, J. S. Bach. **SELECTED PUBLICATIONS** Auth, The Homeric Telos, Glotta, 48, 65; auth, The Lehythian and the Anagram of Frogs 1203, AJP 89, 68; auth, Two Textual Notes on the Miks Gloriosus, CJ, 72; auth, The Etymology and Geneology of Palinusus, AJP 101, 80; auth, Weinen, Klagen, Sorgen, Fayen und die antike Redekunst, Bach Sakrbuch, 80; auth, Socrates and Prodieus in the Clouds, Essays in Ancient Greek Philos, vol 2, 83; auth, Did Women Sing in the Thesmophoriazousae?, Didascalia Sup I; transl, The Texts to Johann Sebastian Bach's Church Cantatas, Stuttgart, 84; auth, Euripides Heraclisae, Bryn Mawr, 90; auth, Ganymede in Euripides' Cyclops, N Eng Class J, 96; auth, The Complete Texts to J. S. Bach's Vocal Works, transl and commentary, 98. **CONTACT ADDRESS** Dept of Classics, Univ of Vermont, 481 Main St, Burlington, VT, 05405. **EMAIL** zambrose@zoo.uvm.edu

AMBROSIUS, LLOYD
DISCIPLINE U.S. DIPLOMATIC HISTORY **EDUCATION** Univ Ill, Urbana-Champaign, PhD, 67. **CAREER** Prof, ch, dept Hist, Univ Nebr, Lincoln, 93-97. **HONORS AND AWARDS** Fulbright fel, Univ Heidelberg, Ger, 96. **RESEARCH** Diplomatic relations between the U S and the Weimar Republic. **SELECTED PUBLICATIONS** Auth, Woodrow Wilson and the American Diplomatic Tradition: The Treaty Fight in Perspective, Cambridge UP, 87; Wilsonian Statecraft: Theory and Practice of Liberal Internationalism during World War I, Scholarly Resrcs, 91. **CONTACT ADDRESS** Univ Nebr, Lincoln, 618 Oldfat, Lincoln, NE, 68588-0417. **EMAIL** lea@unlinfo.unl.edu

AMDUR, KATHRYN E.
DISCIPLINE HISTORY **EDUCATION** Cornell Univ, BA, 69; Stanford Univ, MA, 71, PhD, 78. **CAREER** Assoc prof **RESEARCH** Modern European social and political history, especially the history of labor movements in twentieth-century France; French trade unionism and industrial transformation in the 1930s through the 1950s. **SELECTED PUBLICATIONS** Auth, Syndicalist Legacy: Trade Unions and Politics in Two French Cities in the Era of World War I. **CONTACT ADDRESS** Dept History, Emory Univ, 221 Bowden Hall, 561 Kilgo Cir, Atlanta, GA, 30322-1950. **EMAIL** kamdur@emory.edu

AMIJI, HATIM M.
PERSONAL Born 06/11/1939, Zanzibar **DISCIPLINE** HISTORY **EDUCATION** London, BA (Hons) 1964; Princeton Univ, MA, PhD. **CAREER** Univ of MA Dept of History, assoc prof. **HONORS AND AWARDS** E African Railways & Harbours Rsch Awd 1963; Rockefeller Found Fellow 1965-67; Princeton Univ Fellow 1969-70; Zanzibar Govt Scholar 1961-64; Superior Merit Awd Univ of MA. **MEMBERSHIPS** Sec gen Zanzibar Youth League 1960; lecturer Trinity Coll Nabingo Uganda 1964; lecturer Princeton Univ 1969-70; rsch assoc Dept of History Univ of Nairobi Kenya 1967-68; lecturer Dept of History & Centre for African Studies Boston Univ 1972; dir African Studies Workshop World Affairs Council Boston 1972; mem Middle Eastern Studies Assoc; fellow E African Acad; mem African Studies Assoc of USA; ed bd Gemini Review; founder mem Pan-African Univ Org. **CONTACT ADDRESS** Dept History, Univ of Massachusetts, Harbor Campus Univ of MA, Boston, MA, 02125.

AMMON, THEODORE G.
DISCIPLINE HISTORY OF PHILOSOPHY, EPISTEMOLOGY, PHILOSOPHY AND LITERATURE **EDUCATION** Miss State Univ, BA; Wash Univ, MA, PhD. **CAREER** Dept Philos, Millsaps Col **SELECTED PUBLICATIONS** Publ on, ethical duties of teachers; philos underpinnings of lit of Jorge Luis Borges; teaching strategies for moral develop. **CONTACT ADDRESS** Dept of Philosophy, Millsaps Col, 1701 N State St, Jackson, MS, 39210. **EMAIL** ammontg@okra.millsaps.edu

AMOS, ORIS ELIZABETH CARTER
PERSONAL Martinsville, VA, m **DISCIPLINE** EDUCATION **EDUCATION** VA State Coll, BA 1951; OH State Univ, MA 1963, PhD 1971. **CAREER** VA Pub Schools, teacher 1951-55; Columbus OH Pub Sch, teacher 1963-66; OH State Univ, instr 1966-69; Otterbein Coll, asst prof 1971-75; Council for Exceptional Children, pres 1975; Coll of Educ, chmn Human Rel Comm 1975; Wright State Univ, prof of educ 1975-88; educ development consultant, 1988-. **HONORS AND AWARDS** Named Outstanding Educator of Yr 1972; Award for Distinguished Comm Serv Delta Sigma Theta Sorority 1972; Special Award Serv to Black Students at Otterbein Coll 1973; Teacher Excellence Award Wright State Univ 1979; Educator of Yr OH Fed Council of Exceptional Children 1982; Coord of Special Educ 1978-87; WSU Trustees Award, 1987; Greene County Hall of Fame for Women, Greene County OH, 1988. **MEMBERSHIPS** Teachers Adv Comm State of OH 1975; adv Black Students Otterbein Coll 1975; adv bd Miami Valley Reg Res Ctr; adv bd Dayton Area United Cerebral Palsy Professional Serv; adv bd Sinclair Comm Coll Special Educ; Panel of Experts to review proposals St Bd of Educ Columbus, OH 1975; mem Delta Sigma Theta Sorority; Pi Lambda Theta Women's Honorary in Educ; Central Chapel Church Yellow Springs. **CONTACT ADDRESS** Education, Wright State Univ, PO Box 416, Yellow Springs, OH, 45387.

AMUSSEN, SUSAN
DISCIPLINE HISTORY **EDUCATION** Princeton Univ, BA; Brown Univ, MA, PhD. **CAREER** Prof. **RESEARCH** Literature and history; women's studies; history of Christianity; feminist theology; feminist and critical pedagogy. **SELECTED PUBLICATIONS** Auth, Crime, loi, et justice rurale en Angleterre a l'epoque moderne, Etudes Rurales, 86; An Ordered Society: Gender and Class in Early Modern England, 88; Elizabeth I and Alice Balstone: Gender, Class, and the Exceptional Woman in Early Modern England, 94; Being Stirred To Much Unquietness: Violence and Domestic Violence in Early Modern England, J Women's Hist, 94; Discipline and Punish: The Uses and Meaning of Violence in Early Modern England, J British Studies, 95. **CONTACT ADDRESS** History Dept, Union Inst, 440 E McMillan St, Cincinnati, OH, 45206-1925.

ANCTIL, PIERRE
PERSONAL Born 07/28/1952, Quebec, PQ, Canada **DISCIPLINE** HISTORY **EDUCATION** Univ Laval, BA, 73, MA, 75; New Sch Soc Res (NY), PhD, 80. **CAREER** Res, Inst quebcois de recherche sur la culture, 80-88; dir, Fr Can stud & asst prof, Jewish stud, McGill Univ, 88-91; conseiller en services aux communautes culturelles, Min Educ, Govt Que, 91-93; CONSEILLER EN RELATIONS INTERCULTURELLES, MIN DES RELATIONS AVEC LES CITOYENS ET DE L'IMMIGRATION, GOVT QUE, 93-. **HONORS AND AWARDS** Can res fel, SSHRCC, 88-91. **MEMBERSHIPS** Asn Can Jewish Stud; Inst quebecois d'etudes sur la culture juive; Can Ethnic Studies Asn; vice pres, Can Multicultur Adv Comt, 90-91; mem bd govs, Montreal Holocaust Mem Ctr, 90-91. **RESEARCH** Canadian-Jewish studies; French Canadian studies. **SELECTED PUBLICATIONS** Auth, Le Rendez-vous manque les Juifs de Montreal face au Quebec de l'entre-deux-guerres, 88; auth, Le Devoir, les Juifs et l'immigration: De Bourassa a Laurendeau, 88; ed, Juifs et realites juives au Quebec, 84; ed, Un Homme Grand: Jack Kerouac at the Crossroads of Many Cultures, 90; ed, An Everyday Miracle, Yiddish Culture in Montreal, 90; ed, If One Were to Write a History... Selected Writings by Robert F. Harney, 91; transl, Poemes yiddish (J.I. Segal), 92; transl, Le Montreal juif d'autrefois (Israel Medresh), 97. **CONTACT ADDRESS** 360 McGill St, Montreal, PQ, H2Y 2E9.

ANDERSON, CHARLES SAMUEL
PERSONAL Born 03/04/1930, Madison, WI, m, 1951, 2 children **DISCIPLINE** HISTORICAL THEOLOGY **EDUCATION** St Olaf Col, BA, 51; Univ Wis, MA, 54; Luther Theol Sem, BD, 57; Union Theol Sem, NY, PhD (Hist Theol & Reformation Studies), 62. **CAREER** Teaching asst English, Univ Wis, 53-54; from asst prof to prof Hist Theol, Luther Theol Sem, 61-77, dir Grad Studies, 68-72, vpres Acad Affairs & dean, 77-80, pres, Augsburg Col, 80-97, clergyman, Am Lutheran Church, 57-; mem, Rockefeller Scholar Area Selection Comt, 63, 69; comn Inter Church Affairs, Am Lutheran Church, 64; vis lectr, Northwestern Lutheran Theol Sem, 64; Am Asn Theol Sch sabbatical studies grant, 67-68; vis lectr, Concordia Theol Sem, 68; Bush Found fel, 71-; chmn div Theol Studies, Lutheran Coun USA, 72-. **HONORS AND AWARDS** Phi Betta Kappa, Rockefeller & Martin Luther fell; Bush Leadership fell. **MEMBERSHIPS** Am Soc Church Hist; Renaissance Soc Am; Soc Reformation Res. **RESEARCH** Reformation theology; the military aspects of the Reformation; improvement of education for ministry. **SELECTED PUBLICATIONS** Auth, International Luther studies, Ecumenist, 66; Will the real Luther please stand up, Dialog, 67; The Reformation Then and Now, 67; The Augsburg Historical Atlas of Christianity in the Middle Ages and Reformation, 67, 72 & ed, Readings in Luther for Laymen, 67, Augsburg; auth, Robert Barnes, In: Interpretors of Luther, 68 & ed, Facet Books Reformation Series, 69-, Fortress; auth, Faith and Freedom: The Christian Faith According to the Lutheran Confessions, Augsburg, 78. **CONTACT ADDRESS** 1377 Grantham St, St. Paul, MN, 55108. **EMAIL** andersoc@visi.com

ANDERSON, CHARLES W.
PERSONAL Born 06/28/1934, Maniiowoc, WI, m, 1955 **DISCIPLINE** POLITICAL SCIENCE **EDUCATION** Grinnell Col, BA, 55; Johns Hopkins Univ, MA, 57; Univ Wisconsin, PhD, 60. **CAREER** Asst prof, prof, prof emer, polit sci, Univ Wisconsin, Madison, 60-96. **HONORS AND AWARDS** LLD, Grinnell Col, 88; Spitz Prize, 92. **RESEARCH** Political philosophy; political economy. **SELECTED PUBLICATIONS** Auth, The Political Economy of Mexico, 63; auth, Politics and Economic Change in Latin America, 67; auth, The Political Economy of Modern Spain, 70; auth, Issues of Political Development, 74; auth, Statecraft, 77; auth, Value Judgment and Income Distribution, 81; auth, Pragmatic Liberalism, 90; auth, Prescribing the Life of the Mind, 93. **CONTACT ADDRESS** Dept of Political Science, Univ of Wisconsin, Madison, 1304 Nishishin Trl, Monona, WI, 53716.

ANDERSON, DAVID ATLAS
PERSONAL Born 04/28/1930, Cincinnati, Ohio, m **DISCIPLINE** EDUCATION **EDUCATION** Rochester Inst of Tech, BFA 1960; Syracuse Univ, MA 1962; Union Grad School, PhD 1975. **CAREER** Urban League of Rochester, deputy exec dir 1967-70; State Univ of NY Brockport, lecturer Afro-Amer studies; Rochester Inst of Tech, visiting asst prof 1981-, dir parent educ, Rochester City School District. **HONORS AND AWARDS** Community Leadership Awd Urban League of Rochester 1982; Outstanding Community Serv, Health Assn of Rochester 1984; Distinguished Volunteer, Mental Health Assn Rochester 1986. **MEMBERSHIPS** Assoc Comm Health Univ of Rochester Medical Sch 1970-82; bd mem vice pres Mental Health Assoc 1980-86; lecturer Correctional Institutions at Sonyea and Oatka NY 1983-85; bd of dirs Rochester Museum & Sci Ctr 1986-90; Natl Assn of Black Storytellers, 1988-89. **CONTACT ADDRESS** Dir Parent Education, Rochester City School District, 131 W Broad St, Rochester, NY, 14614.

ANDERSON, DAVID L.
PERSONAL Born 08/10/1946, Pampa, TX, m, 1973, 1 child **DISCIPLINE** HISTORY **EDUCATION** Rice Univ, BA, 68; Univ Va, MA, 71, PhD, 74. **CAREER** Asst prof to assoc prof to prof, Univ Indianapolis, Ind, 81- . **HONORS AND AWARDS** Prof of the year, Coun for Advancement & support of Educ, 91; Robert H. Ferrell Book Award, Soc for Hist of Amer Foreign Relation, 92. **MEMBERSHIPS** Amer Hist Assoc; Org of Amer Hist; Soc for Hist of Amer Foreign Relations. **RESEARCH** US E Asian Relations; Vietnam War. **SELECTED PUBLICATIONS** Auth, The United States and Vietnam, in The Vietnam War, Macmillan, 98; Imperialism and Idealism: American Diplomats in China, 1861-1898, Ind Univ Press, 85; Trapped by Success: The Eisenhower Administration and Vietnam, 1953-1961, Columbia Univ Press, 91; Shadow on the White House: Presidents and the Vietnam War, 1945-1975, Univ Press Ks, 93; Facing My Lai: Moving Beyond the Massacre, Univ Press Ks, 98. **CONTACT ADDRESS** Dept of History, Univ Indianapolis, Indianapolis, IN, 46227. **EMAIL** anderson@uindy.edu

ANDERSON, EARL ROBERT
PERSONAL Born 09/16/1943, Virginia, MN, m, 1967, 2 children **DISCIPLINE** OLD & MIDDLE ENGLISH **EDUCATION** Univ Minn, BA, 65; Univ Ore, MA, 67, PhD, 70. **CAREER** Asst prof, 70-74, assoc prof Eng, Cleveland State Univ, 74-. **MEMBERSHIPS** Medieval Acad Am; MLA. **RESEARCH** Old English poetry; Middle English poetry. **SELECTED PUBLICATIONS** Auth, Cynewolf: Style, Structure and Theme on His Poetry, Fairleigh Dickinson University Press, 98. **CONTACT ADDRESS** Dept of English, Cleveland State Univ, 1983 E 24th St, Cleveland, OH, 44115-2440. **EMAIL** anderson_earl@hotmail.com

ANDERSON, FRED
DISCIPLINE HISTORY **EDUCATION** Colo State Univ, BA, 71; Harvard Univ, MA, 73; PhD, 81. **CAREER** Lec, Harvard, 81-83; asst prof, 83-89, assoc prof, Univ Colo, 89-. **SELECTED PUBLICATIONS** Auth, A People's Army: Massachusetts Soldiers and Society in the Seven Years' Warm Univ NC, 84; Why Did Colonial New Englanders Make Bad Soldiers? Contractual Principles and Military Conduct during the Seven Years' War, 81; A People's Army: Provincial Military Service in Massachusetts during the Seven Years' War, William Mary Quarterly, 83; Bringing the War Home: The Revolutionary Experience of Newport and New York, Rev Am Hist, 87; The Colonial Background to the American Victory, Greenwood, 88; co-auth, The Problem of Fragmentation and the Prospects for Synthesis in Early American Social History, William Mary Quarterly, 93. **CONTACT ADDRESS** History Dept, Univ of Colorado, Boulder, Boulder, CO, 80309. **EMAIL** andersof@spot.colorado.edu

ANDERSON, GREG
PERSONAL Born 10/24/1962, Weston Super Mare, England **DISCIPLINE** CLASSICS **EDUCATION** Univ of Newcastle UK, BA, 86; Univ of London UK, MA, 88; Yale Univ PhD, 97. **CAREER** Asst Prof, 97-98, Elmira College; Asst Prof, 98-, Univ of IL, Chicago. **MEMBERSHIPS** APA **RESEARCH** Ancient Grecian political & cultural history, sports history, nationalism. **SELECTED PUBLICATIONS** Auth, The Making of Democratic Athens, Politics and Culture in the Age of Cleisthenes, Ann Arbor, Univ of Mich Press, forthcoming; Alcmeonid Homelands Political Exile and the Unification of Attica, in: Historia, forthcoming; Games for Heros, Greek Athletics and the Invention of the Olympic Tradition, in: Report of the Yale-Smithsonian Annual Seminar on Material Culture, 97. **CONTACT ADDRESS** Dept of History, Univ of Ill Chicago, 601 S Morgan St, Chicago, IL, 60607-7109. **EMAIL** gregand@uic.edu

ANDERSON, JAMES C., JR.
PERSONAL Born 04/15/1951, Malden, MA, m, 1978, 2 children **DISCIPLINE** CLASSICS **EDUCATION** Colo Col, BA, 73; Univ NC, Chapel Hill, MA, 76, PhD, 80. **CAREER** From asst prof to assoc prof to prof, 80-, Univ Ga; Mellon prof in charge, Intercollegiate Ctr Classical Stud, Rome, 93-94; dir, Classical Summer Sch Am Acad, Rome, 92-94. **HONORS AND AWARDS** NEH Summer Stipend, 83; NEH Fel Col Tchrs, 94-95; Gen S. Beaver Tchg Prof, 96-99, Univ Ga., Fel, 78-79, Am Acad Rome; Thomas J. Watson Fel, 73-74, Greece, Britain; Phi Beta Kappa, 73. **MEMBERSHIPS** Archaeol Inst Am; Soc Fel Am Acad, Rome; Classical Assoc Middle West and South. **RESEARCH** Roman archaeology; Roman art and architecture; Latin Epigraphy. **SELECTED PUBLICATIONS** Auth, Historical Topography of the Imperial Fura, 84; auth, Roman Brick Stamps: The Thomas Ashby Collection, 91; auth, Roman Architecture and Society, 97. **CONTACT ADDRESS** Dept of Classics, Univ of Georgia, Park Hall, Athens, GA, 30602-6203. **EMAIL** janderso@arches.uga.edu

ANDERSON, JAMES D.
DISCIPLINE HISTORY **EDUCATION** Univ Ill, PhD, 73. **CAREER** Prof, Univ Ill Urbana Champaign **RESEARCH** History American education; history of African-American educatio; race in American life and culture. **SELECTED PUBLICATIONS** Auth, Race, Meritocracy, and the American Academy During the Immediate Post World War II Era, Hist Edu Quarterly, 93; How We Learn About Race Through History, Univ Minn, 94; Literacy and Education in the African American Experience, Hampton, 95. **CONTACT ADDRESS** History Dept, Univ Ill Urbana Champaign, 52 E Gregory Dr, Champaign, IL, 61820. **EMAIL** janders@uiuc.edu

ANDERSON, JANET A.
PERSONAL Born 03/29/1934, Washington, DC, s **DISCIPLINE** ART HISTORY **EDUCATION** Pa State Univ, BA, 57, MA, 59; Univ Mich, PhD, 70. **CAREER** Penn Hall Jr Col, 59-67; Univ of Wisc-Whitewater, 69-. **RESEARCH** Women artists; 17th century art. **SELECTED PUBLICATIONS** Women in the Fine Arts: A Bibliography and Illustration Guide, 90; auth, articles in Dictionary of Women Artists, 97; Pedro de Mena: 17th Century Spanish Sculptor, Edwin Meller Press, 98. **CONTACT ADDRESS** N7750 Engel Rd, Rte 3, Whitewater, WI, 53190.

ANDERSON, MARK
DISCIPLINE AMERICAN HISTORY **EDUCATION** Univ Calif, PhD, 95. **CAREER** Asst prof. **RESEARCH** Role of the mass media in the Mexican Revolution. **SELECTED PUBLICATIONS** Pub(s), nineteenth-century Amer lit. **CONTACT ADDRESS** Dept of Hist, Brock Univ, 500 Glenridge Ave, St Catharines, ON, L2S 3A1. **EMAIL** manderso@spartan.ac.BrockU.CA

ANDERSON, MARVIN W.
PERSONAL Born 01/12/1933, Montevideo, MN, m, 1961, 2 children **DISCIPLINE** THEOLOGY, HISTORY **EDUCATION** Univ Wash, BA, 55; Bethel Sem, BD, 59; Aberdeen Univ, PhD(Reformation hist), 64. **CAREER** Instr hist, Bethel Col, Minn, 60-61; instr hist & Greek, Northwestern Col, Minn, 61-62; from asst prof to assoc prof, 64-73, prof hist theol, Bethel Sem, 73-93, Am Coun Learned Socs grant-in-aid, 69-70; Am Asn Theol Schs fel, 70-71, res fel, 77-78; prof church hist, Southern Baptist Seminary, 94-. **MEMBERSHIPS** Am Soc Church Hist; Am Soc Reformation Res; Renaissance Soc Am; Ecclesiastical Hist Soc, England. **RESEARCH** Renaissance Europe from 1300 to 1500; Reformation studies from 1500 to 1563; Italian Reformation from 1519 to 1563. **SELECTED PUBLICATIONS** Auth, Luther's Sola Fide in Italy 1542-1551, Church Hist, 3/69; Gregorio Cortese and Roman Catholic Reform, 16th Century Essays & Studies, 70; Gospel and Authority, Augsburg, 71; Peter Martyr, Reformed Theologian (1542-1562): His Letters to Bullinger and Calvin, 16th Century J, 4/73; Peter Martyr: A Reformer in Exile (1542-1562), Degraaf, 75; The Battle for the Gospel: Bible and Reformation 1444-1589, Baker, 78; Royal Idolatry, Arch Reformations-Geschichte, 78; Evangelical Foundations: Religion in England, 1378-1683, Peter Lang, 87. **CONTACT ADDRESS** Southern Baptist Sem, 2825 Lexington Rd, Louisville, KY, 40280.

ANDERSON, MICHAEL JOHN
PERSONAL Born 05/30/1967, London, England, m, 1993 **DISCIPLINE** CLASSICAL LANGUAGES; LITERATURE **EDUCATION** Princeton Univ, AB, 89; Univ Oxford, DPhil, 94. **CAREER** Vis asst prof, Univ Oregon, 93/94; Mellon post-doctoral fel in humanities, Columbia Univ 94-96; asst prof, Yale Univ, 97- . **HONORS AND AWARDS** Fulbright Sch for study in Freiburg, GER, 89/90; Marshall Scholarship for study in Oxford, ENG, 90-93. **MEMBERSHIPS** APA **RESEARCH** Greek literature; Greek art. **SELECTED PUBLICATIONS** The Fall of Troy in Early Greek Poetry and Art, 97; The Sophrosyne of Persinna and the Romantic Strategy of Heliodorus' Aethiopica, Classical Philology, 97. **CONTACT ADDRESS** Dept of Classics, Yale Univ, New Haven, CT, 06520-8266. **EMAIL** michael.j.anderson@yale.edu

ANDERSON, NANCY FIX
PERSONAL Born 08/23/1941, Dallas, TX, m, 2 children **DISCIPLINE** HISTORY **EDUCATION** Stanford Univ, BA, 65; Univ Calif Irvine, MA, 67; Tulane Univ, 73. **CAREER** Loyola Univ, New Orleans, assoc prof history, 87-97, prof history, 97-. **HONORS AND AWARDS** Dux Academicas Award, Loyola Univ, 94. **MEMBERSHIPS** Amer Historical Assn; Southern Conf on British Studies; Southern Assn of Women Historians. **RESEARCH** Victorian English women and the family; Annie Besant. **SELECTED PUBLICATIONS** Auth, Woman against Women in Victorian England: A Life of Eliza Lynn Linton, 87; "Bridging Cross-Cultural Feminisms: Annie Besant and Women's Rights in England and India, 1874-1933," Women's History Review, no. 3, 94; "Not a Fit and Proper Person: Annie Besant's Struggle for Child Custody, 1878-9," in Maternal Instincts: Visions of Motherhood and Sexuality in Britain, 1875-1925, 97. **CONTACT ADDRESS** Dept of History, Loyola Univ, New Orleans, 6363 St Charles Ave, Box 65, New Orleans, LA, 70118. **EMAIL** anderson@loyno.edu

ANDERSON, ROBERT MAPES
PERSONAL Born 04/06/1929, New York, NY **DISCIPLINE** AMERICAN SOCIAL HISTORY & FOREIGN RELATIONS **EDUCATION** Wagner Col, BA, 59; Columbia Univ, MA, 62, PhD, 69. **CAREER** Hist ed, Monarch Press, New York, 62-64; lectr hist, 64-65, from instr to assoc prof, 65-77, chmn, Dept Hist & Polit Sci, 70-75, prof hist, Wagner Col, 77-. **MEMBERSHIPS** AHA; Orgn Am Historians; AAUP. **RESEARCH** American religious history. **SELECTED PUBLICATIONS**

Ed, United States Since 1865, Monarch, 63; Vision of the Disinherited: The Making of American Pentecostalism, Oxford Univ Press, 79, 2nd ed, Hendrickson Press, 92. **CONTACT ADDRESS** Wagner Col Grymes Hill, 631 Howard Ave, Staten Island, NY, 10301-4428. **EMAIL** rmander877@aol.com

ANDERSON, STANFORD OWEN
PERSONAL Born 11/13/1934, Redwood Falls, MN **DISCIPLINE** HISTORY OF ARCHITECTURE AND CITIES **EDUCATION** Univ Minn, Minneapolis, BA, 57; Univ Calif, Berkeley, MA (Archit), 58; Columbia Univ, PhD(hist art & archit), 68. **CAREER** Unit master archit design, Archit Asn, London, 62-63; asst prof, 63-68, assoc prof, 68-71, prof hist of archit & archit, Mass Inst Technol, 71-, asst prof, Exten & Summer Sch, Harvard Univ, 63-64; proj res dir, Inst Archit & Urban Studies, New York, 70-72; vis lectr, Archit Asn, London, 74-78; comnr, Boston Landmarks Comn, 80-87. **HONORS AND AWARDS** Fulbright (Germany), 61-62; Guggenheim, 69-70; ACLS, 77-78. **MEMBERSHIPS** Asn Col Schs Archit; Brit Soc Philos Sci; Col Art Asn Am; Soc Archit Historians; Bd Dir, Fulbright Assoc, 98-. **RESEARCH** History of modern architecture and urbanism; analysis and design of urban space; historiography. **SELECTED PUBLICATIONS** Auth, Architecture and tradition, L'Architettura, 4/65 & Archit Asn J, 5/65; Louis I Kahn in the 1960's, Boston Soc Architects J, 6/67; ed, Planning for Diversity and Choice, MIT Press, 69 & Verlag Rombach, 71; auth, Peter Behrens' changing concept of life as art, Archit Design, 2/69; Modern architecture and industry: Peter Behrens, Oppositions, winter 77, summer 80 & winter 81; ed, On Streets, MIT Press, 78 & G Gili, Barcelona, 81; auth, The plan of Savannah: city plan as resource, Harvard Archit Rev 2, 81; Types and conventions in time, Perspecta 18, 82; Architectural Design as a System of Research Programmes, Design Stud, vol V, 146-150; Peter Behren's Highest Kultursymbol, the Theater, Perspecta 26, 103-134; Memory in Architecture/Erinnerung in der Architektur, Daidalos, 58, 95; The New Empiricism-Bay Region-Axis': Kay Fisker and Postwar Debates on Functionalism, Regionalism, and Monumentality, J Archit Educ, L, 3, 203-213. **CONTACT ADDRESS** Dept of Archit, 77 Massachusetts Ave, Cambridge, MA, 02139-4307.

ANDERSON, TERRY HOWARD
PERSONAL Born 12/08/1946, Kankakee, IL **DISCIPLINE** AMERICAN HISTORY **EDUCATION** Univ MN, BA, 71; Univ MO, MA, 73; Ind Univ, PhD, 78. **CAREER** Assoc Instr Am hist and Asst Oral Historian, IN Univ, 74-76; asst prof, VA Polytech Inst & State Univ, 78-79; from Asst Prof to Prof Recent Am Hist, TX A&M Univ, 79, Oral Histarian, 79-88, Systems Asst Prof, TX A&M System, Prairie View A&M, 81, TX A&M-Koriyama, Japan, 91. **HONORS AND AWARDS** Fulbright Lectr, China, 94-95. **MEMBERSHIPS** Orgn Am Historians; Oral Hist Asn; Soc Historians Am For Rels; Am Hist Asn. **RESEARCH** Cold War; sixty's--soc movements of 1960's and early 1970's; oral hist. **SELECTED PUBLICATIONS** Auth, Becoming sane with psychohistory, Historian, 11/78; The United States, Great Britain, and the Cold War, 1944-1947, Univ Mo Press, 81; A guide to the oral history collection of Texas A&M, Sterling Evans Libr, 81; coauth, A Flying Tiger's Diary, Tex A&M Univ Press, 84; auth, The Movement and the Sixties, Oxford Univ Press, 95; The Sixties, Addison Wesley Longman, 98. **CONTACT ADDRESS** Dept Hist, Texas A&M Univ, 1 Texas A&M Univ, Col Station, TX, 77843. **EMAIL** tha@tamu.edu

ANDERSON, THOMAS JEFFERSON
PERSONAL Born 08/17/1928, Coutesville, PA, m **DISCIPLINE** MUSIC **EDUCATION** West Virginia State College, BM, 1950, D Music, 1984; Pennsylvania State University, MEd, 1951; University of Iowa, PhD, 1958; Holy Cross College, DMA, 1983. **CAREER** High Pt City Public School, teacher, 1951-54; West Virginia State College, instructor, 1955-56; Langston University, professor & chairman, 1958-63; Tennessee State University, professor of music, 1963-69; Atlanta Symphony Orchestra, composer-in-residence, 1969-71; Morehouse College, Danforth visiting professor of music, 1971-72; Tufts University, professor of music & chairman, 1972-80, Austin Fletcher professor of music, starting 1976; DeKalb University, Dept of Fine Arts, professor, currently. **HONORS AND AWARDS** Fellow, MacDowell Colony, 1960-83; fellow, Yhaddo 1970-77; Copley Foundation Award, 1964; Fromm Foundation Award, 1964-71; Phi Beta Kappa, honorary member, 1977; over 50 published compositions; artistic residency, University of Salvador, 1988; 60th Birthday Concert, Videmus, Harvard University, 1989; fellow, John Simon Guggenheim Foundation, 1989; bd mem, Harvard Musical Assn, 1989. **MEMBERSHIPS** Founder/president, Black Music Caucus MENC; board member, Elma Lewis School of Fine Arts, 1975-; advisory bd, Meet The Composer, 1980; chair, Comm of the Status of Minorities, College Music Society, 1976-80; Music Council the Arts & Humanities 1978-81; Harvard Musical Assn, 1976-; St Botolph Club, 1980. **CONTACT ADDRESS** Dept Fine Arts, Dekalb Col, 555 N Indian Creek Dr, Clarkston, GA, 30021-2361.

ANDERSON, WILLIAM L.
DISCIPLINE CHEROKEE HISTORY **EDUCATION** Univ AL, PhD. **CAREER** Hist Dept, Western Carolina Univ **SELECTED PUBLICATIONS** Auth, . Cherokee Removal: Before and After, 91. **CONTACT ADDRESS** Western Carolina Univ, Cullowhee, NC, 28723.

ANDERSON, WILLIAM SCOVIL
PERSONAL Born 09/16/1927, Brookline, MA, m, 1983, 5 children **DISCIPLINE** CLASSICS **EDUCATION** Yale Univ, BA, 50, PhD, 54; Cambridge Univ, BA, 52, MA, 56. **CAREER** Instr classics, Yale Univ, 55-60; from asst prof to assoc prof Latin, 60-65, chmn dept classics, 70-73, Prof Latin & Comp Lit Univ CA, Berkeley, 65-; prof in charge, Intercol Ctr Class Studies, Rome, 67-68; ed Vergilius, 65; res prof, Univ Melbourne, 84; Robson Lectr, Victoria Col, Toronto, 87; Blegen Res Prof, Vassar Col, 89-90; Vis Distinguished Prof, FL State Univ, 95. **HONORS AND AWARDS** Prix de Rome, 54; Morse fel, 59; Am Coun Learned Soc grant to deliver lect at Int Cong Satire, Rostock, Ger, 65; Nat Endowment Hum sr fel, 73-74; classicist-in-residence, Am Acad, Rome, 73-74. **MEMBERSHIPS** Am Philol Asn (pres, 77); Soc Relig Higher Educ; Philol Asn Pac Coast. **RESEARCH** Roman satire and comedy; Vergil; Ovid. **SELECTED PUBLICATIONS** Auth, The Art of the Aeneid, Prentice-Hall, 69; Ovid's Metamorphoses: Books 6-10, Univ OK, 72, Books 1-5, Univ OK, 96; Ovidius, Metamorphoses, Leipzig: Teubner, 77; Essays on Roman Satire, Princeton Univ, 82; Barbarian Play: Platus' Roman Comedy, Toronto, 93. **CONTACT ADDRESS** Dept of Class, Univ of California, 7212 Dwinelle Hall, Berkeley, CA, 94720-2521. **EMAIL** wsa@socrates.berkeley.edu

ANDERSON-TANNER, FREDERICK T., JR.
PERSONAL Born 02/17/1937, Winston-Salem, NC, d **DISCIPLINE** EDUCATION **EDUCATION** Morgan State Univ, BS 1959; Atlanta Univ, MA 1964; VA Poly Inst & State Univ, EdD 1975. **CAREER** Kathmandu Nepal, Fulbright scholar prof of English, 1962-63; Bd of Educ Sandersville GA, reading consult 1962; Clark Coll, instructor of English 1963-64; Morehouse Coll, reading specialist, 1965-66; Rosewood State Hosp, adult educ teacher 1966-67; Rosewood School for Retarded Children, vice principal, 1967-69; Coppin State Coll, Loyola Coll, visiting prof 1968; Bowie State Coll, prof 1968-69; Federal City Coll, dep dir skills center, 1969-70; State Dept of Health & Mental Hygiene, principal, 1970-72; Federal City Coll, assoc prof 1972-73; Gov Commn on Structure & Governance of Educ in MD, asst dir 1973-75; Gov of MD, educ aide 1975; Morgan State Univ, assoc prof of educ 1975-. **HONORS AND AWARDS** Fulbright Scholar to Nepal India, 1962-63; Natl Honor Soc; Exceptional Childrens Leadership Awd 1975; pres Black Caucus of Special Educators; Intl Council for Exceptional Children; 10 Yr Serv Award, State of MD; dissertation A Modified Delphi Study of Political Feasibility of Critical Issues Affecting Educ Reform in MD 1975. **MEMBERSHIPS** Life mem Alpha Phi Alpha; Masonic Order; Natl Educ Assn; Natl Cncl Tchrs of English; Cncl for Exceptional Children; Natl Rehab Counseling Assn; Phi Delta Kappa; natl Assn of State Dirs of Spec Educ; Assn for Supervision & Curriculum Devel; MD Consortium for Cooperative Planning in Spec Educ. **CONTACT ADDRESS** Morgan State Univ, Coldspring Lane, Baltimore, MD, 21207.

ANDO, CLIFFORD
DISCIPLINE CLASSICAL STUDIES **EDUCATION** Univ Mich, PhD, 96. **CAREER** Asst prof, York Univ, 96-98; asst prof, 98-. **MEMBERSHIPS** Am Philol Asn; North Am Patristics Soc. **RESEARCH** Roman history; Latin and Greek historiography. **SELECTED PUBLICATIONS** Auth, "Pagan Apologetics and Christian Intolerance in the Ages of Themistius and Augustine" in J of Early Christian Studies, 96; "Tacticus, Annales VI: Beginning and End" in Am J of Philol, 97. **CONTACT ADDRESS** Classics Dept, Univ of Southern California, Taper Hall 224, Los Angeles, CA, 90089-0352. **EMAIL** cando@usc.edu

ANDREA, ALFRED J.
PERSONAL Born 11/18/1941, Boston, MA, m, 1965, 2 children **DISCIPLINE** HISTORY **EDUCATION** Boston Col, AB (magna cum laude), 63; Cornell Univ, PhD, 69. **CAREER** INSTR, 67-69, ASST PROF, 69-75, ASSOC PROF, 75-82, DIR, MEDIEVAL-RENAISSANCE PROG, LIVING/LEARNING CENTER, 75-77, CO-DIR & ASSOC PROF IN ITALY, 78-79, DIR OF GRAD STUDIES, DEPT OF HIST, 92-94, PROF, 82-, DIR OF UNDERGRAD STUDIES, DEPT OF HIST, UNIV OF VT, 96-; Eli Lilly Exchange prof, univ of Pugent Sound, 78-79. **HONORS AND AWARDS** Fourth Annual Donald B. hoffman Fac Advisor Awd, Phi Alpha Theta Int Honor Soc in Hist, 91; Alexander von Humboldt Fel, 65-. **MEMBERSHIPS** World Hist Asn; Medieval Acad of Am; New England Medieval Confr; Am Soc of Church Hist; Phil Alpha Theta Honor Soc in Hist; New England Regional World Hist Asn; Soc for the Study of the Crusades and the Latin East. **RESEARCH** Medieval Europe, 300-1500; Global History to 1700; Medieval Ecclesiastical History; Papal-Byzantine Relations, 330-1453; The Crusades. **SELECTED PUBLICATIONS** Auth, The Medieval Record: Sources of Medieval European History, Houghton Mifflin Co., 98; The Anonymous Chronicler of Halberstadt's Account of the Fourth Crusade: Popular Religiosity in the Early Thirteenth Century, Historical Reflections/Reflexions Historiques, 96; The Sources for the Fourth Crusade, An Appendix to Donald E. Queller and Thomas Madden, the Fourth Crusade, Univ of Pa Press, 96; The Devastatio Constantinopolitana, A Special Perspective on the Fourth Crusade: An Analysis, new Edition, and Translation, Historical Reflections/Reflexions Historiques, 93; contribur, Using the Human Record: Suggestions from the Editors, a new manual on tchg global history to accompany The Human Record, 98. **CONTACT ADDRESS** Dept of Hist, Univ of Vermont, Burlington, VT, 05405. **EMAIL** aandrea@zoo.uvm.edu

ANDREW, JOHN ALFRED
PERSONAL Born 01/16/1943, Boston, MA, m, 1966, 2 children **DISCIPLINE** HISTORY **EDUCATION** Univ NH, BA, 65, MA, 67; Univ Tex, PhD, 73. **CAREER** PROF, FRANKLIN & MARSHALL COLL. **HONORS AND AWARDS** Ford Found Schol, 61-66; John Pine Grad Stud Schol Awd, 71-72; Phi Alpha Theta; Pi Sigma Alpha; Pi Gamma Mu; American Philosophical Soc Res Gra, 75; Moody Gra, LBJ Found, 93, 97. **MEMBERSHIPS** Org of Amer Historians, Penn Hist Assn, Amer Studies Assn, Soc for Historian of the Early Amer Republic. **RESEARCH** Social and political history **SELECTED PUBLICATIONS** Auth, Rebuilding the Christian Commonwealth: New England Congregationalists and Foreign Missions, 1800-1830, Univ Ky, 76; auth, From Revivals to Removal: Jeremiah Evarts, the Cherokee Nation and the Search for the Soul of America, Univ Ga, 92; auth, The Other Side of the Sixties: Young Americans for Freedom and the Rise of Conservative Politics, Rutgers Univ, 97; auth, Lyndon Johnson and the Great Society, Ivan R Dee, 98; auth, Betsey Stockton: Strangers in a Strange Land, J of Presbyterian Hist, 74; auth, AD Recalls: Betsey Stockton, in AD, 76; auth, Educating the Heathen: The Foreign Mission School Controversy and American Ideals, in J Amer Studies, 78; auth, Dear Prexy: Letters from the War Years, in F&M Today, 82; auth, Impending Crises of the 1960's: National Goals and National Purpose, in Viet Nam Generation, 94; auth, Struggle for the Republican Party in 1960, in Historian, 97; auth, Cracks in the Consensus: The Rockefeller Brothers Fund Special Studies Project and Eisenhower America, in Presidential Studies Quart, 98; auth, Pro-War and Anti-Draft: Young Americans for Freedom and the War in Viet Nam, in The Viet Nam War on Campus: Other Voices, More Distant Drums, forthcoming. **CONTACT ADDRESS** Dept of History, Franklin and Marshall Col, Lancaster, PA, 17604. **EMAIL** j_andrew@acad.fandm.edu

ANDREWS, ANTHONY P.
PERSONAL Born 08/23/1949, Washington, DC, m, 1989, 2 children **DISCIPLINE** ANTHROPOLOGY/ARCHAEOLOGY **EDUCATION** Harvard Univ, BA, 72; Univ Arizona, MA, 76; Univ Arizona, PhD, 80 **CAREER** Asst prof Anthro, Hamilton Col, 80-81; asst prof Anthro, New Col of USF, 81-85; assoc prof Anthro, New Col of USF, 85-89; prof Anthro, New Col of USF, 89-; Chair, Div of Soc Sci, New Col of USF, 89-95 **HONORS AND AWARDS** Magna Cum Laude, 72; multiple res grants; State of Florida Teaching Award **MEMBERSHIPS** Soc Amer Archeol; Amer Anthro Assoc; Sociedad Mexicana de Antropologia; Sociedad Espanola de Estudios Mayas **RESEARCH** Archaeology; Ethnohistory; Historical Archaelogy of Southern Mesoamerica **SELECTED PUBLICATIONS** First Cities, St Remy, 95; "A Brief History of Underwater Archaelogy in the Maya Area." Ancient Mesoamerica; "Late Postclassic Lowland Maya Archaeology." Jrnl World Prehistory **CONTACT ADDRESS** Division of Soc Sci, New Col of the Univ of So Florida, Sarasota, FL, 34243. **EMAIL** andrews@sar.usf.edu

ANDREWS, AVERY D.
PERSONAL Born 09/06/1927, New York, NY **DISCIPLINE** HISTORY **EDUCATION** Harvard Univ, AB, 50; Univ Pa, LLB, 53, MA, 58, PhD, 62. **CAREER** Instr, 61-62, Haverford Col, Bryn Mawr Col; instr, 62-63, Univ Del; instr, 63, Univ Pa; asst prof to assoc prof, 65-77, asst dean, grad sch of arts and sci, 75-92, George Washington Univ; acad admin, Columbian Sch of Arts & Sci, 92-95. **MEMBERSHIPS** Amer Hist Assoc; Medieval Acad of Amer, Renaissance Soc of Amer. **RESEARCH** Italian & other western involvement in eastern Mediterranean, 14th & 15th cent, & its effects on western culture, soc & politics **SELECTED PUBLICATIONS** Coauth, The Lost Fifth Book of the Life of Pope Paul II, Stud in the Renaissance, 70; art, Caffa, Pera, Dictionary of the Middle Ages, New York, 82-89. **CONTACT ADDRESS** Dept of History, George Washington Univ, Washington, DC, 20052. **EMAIL** aandrews@gwu.edu

ANDREWS, GEORGE REID
PERSONAL Born 04/10/1951, New Haven, CT, m, 1974, 3 children **DISCIPLINE** LATIN AMERICAN HISTORY **EDUCATION** Dartmouth Col, BA, 72; Univ WI-Madison, MA, 74, PhD(hist), 78. **CAREER** Librn, Shattuck Libr, 77-78; staff assoc, Social Sci Res Coun, 78-81; asst prof to prof hist, Univ Pittsburgh, 81-. **HONORS AND AWARDS** Herfurth Award, Univ WI-Madison, 81; Whitaker Prize, Middle Atlantic Coun on Latin Am Studies, 93; Guggenheim fel, 96. **MEMBERSHIPS** Latin Am Studies Asn; Conf Latin Am Hist; AHA. **RESEARCH** Race and class relations; Spanish American independence movements; urbanization. **SELECTED PUBLICATIONS** Auth, Toward a Re-evaluation of the Latin American Family Firm, Inter-Am Econ Affairs, 76; Race Ver-

sus Class Association: The Afro-Argentines of Buenos Aires, 1850-1900, J Latin Am Studies, 79; The Afro-Argentine Officers of Buenos Aires Province, 1800-1860, J of Negro Hist, 79; The Afro-Argentines of Buenos Aires, 1800-1900, Univ WI Press, 80; Spanish American Independence: A Structural Analysis, Latin Am Perspectives, 85; Latin American Workers, J of Soc Hist, 87; Comparing the Comparers: White Supremacy in the United States and South Africa, J of Soc Hist, 87; Black and White Workers: Sao Paulo, Brazil, 1888-1928, Hispanic Am Hist Rev, 88; coauth, The Abolition of Slavery and the Aftermath of Emancipation in Brazil, Duke Univ Press, 88, auth, Blacks and Whites in Sao Paulo, Brazil, 1888-1988, Univ WI Press, 91; Black Political Protest in Sao Paulo, Brazil, 1888-1988, J of Latin Am Studies, 92; Racial Inequality in Brazil and the United States: A Statistical Comparison, J of Soc Hist, 92; co-ed, The Social Construction of Democracy, 1870-1990, NY Univ Press, 95; auth, Brazilian Racial Democracy: An American Counterpoint, J of Contemp Hist, 96; Black Workers in the Export Years: Latin American, 1880-1930, Int Labor and Working- Class Hist, 97. **CONTACT ADDRESS** Dept Hist, Univ Pittsburgh, 3p38 Forbes Quad, Pittsburgh, PA, 15260-0001. **EMAIL** reid1@vms.cis.pitt.edu

ANDREWS, MAXINE RAMSEUR
PERSONAL Fayetteville, North Carolina **DISCIPLINE** EDUCATION **EDUCATION** Fayetteville State Univ, BS 1956; North Carolina Central Univ, MEd 1963; East Carolina Univ EdS 1975; Univ of NC at Greensboro, EdD 1985. **CAREER** Cumberland County Schools, teacher 1956-66, school social worker 1966-69; Elizabeth City State Univ, title III coord 1969-71; Fayetteville State Univ, adj prof 1985-; Sincerely Yours Writing & Specialty Svcs, proprietor 1986-; Cumberland County Schools, elem supervisor 1971-84, supervisor secondary educ 1984-90; Fayetteville State University, assistant professor/ coordinator of secondary education, coordinator of educational administration/curriculum/instruction, director, teaching fellows program; coordinator, master of school admin degree program, currently. **HONORS AND AWARDS** Distinguished Alumnae Fayetteville State Univ Natl Assoc for Equal Oppor in Higher Educ 1986. **MEMBERSHIPS** Member, Natl Educ Assoc; member, Assoc for Supervision and Curriculum Div; member, NC Assoc for Educators; member, Phi Delta Kappa; member, NC Assoc of Administrators; member, Delta Sigma Theta Sor; member, NC Historical Preservation Soc; member, Fayetteville State Alumni Assoc; president, 1987-90, secretary, 1988-91, North Carolina Association of Supervision and Curriculum Development; Master of School Administration, Fay State University, coordinator, 1997-. **CONTACT ADDRESS** Coordinator, Master of School Administration Degree Program, Fayetteville State Univ, Fayetteville, NC, 28301.

ANDRIEN, KENNETH JAMES
PERSONAL Born 03/15/1951, Upper Darby, PA, m, 2 children **DISCIPLINE** LATIN AMERICAN HISTORY, SPANISH HISTORY **EDUCATION** Trinity Col, BA, 73; Duke Univ, MA, 75, PhD(hist), 77. **CAREER** Asst prof Hist, 78-84, assoc prof , 85-94, prof hist, OH State Univ, 95-. **HONORS AND AWARDS** Phi Beta Kappa. **MEMBERSHIPS** AHA; Latin Am Studies Asn; Conf Latin Am Hist. **RESEARCH** Political, social and economic history of the Andrean Region, 16th-19th centuries. **SELECTED PUBLICATIONS** Auth, Crisis and Decline: The Viceroyalty of Peru in the Seventeenth Century, Univ NM Press, 85; The Kingdom of Quito, 1690-1830: The State and Regional Development, Cambridge Univ Press, 95; co-ed, with Rolena Adorno, Transatlantic Encounters: Europeans and Andreans in the Sixteenth century, Univ CA Press, 91; with Lyman L. Johnson, The Political Economy of Spanish America in the Age of Revolution, 1750-1850, Univ NM Press, 94; and articles in Past and Present, Hispanic Am Hist Rev, J Latin Am Studies, and The Americas. **CONTACT ADDRESS** Dept Hist, Ohio State Univ, 230 W 17th Ave, Columbus, OH, 43210-1367. **EMAIL** andrien.1@osu.edu

ANDRONICA, JOHN LOUIS
PERSONAL Born 10/06/1942, Boston, MA, m, 1966, 2 children **DISCIPLINE** CLASSICAL LANGUAGES **EDUCATION** Col of the Holy Cross, AB, 63; Boston Col, MA, 66; Johns Hopkins Univ, PhD, 69. **CAREER** Asst prof classic lang, 69-72, dir, Wake Forest-in-Venice Prog, 71-72 & 81, assoc prof class lang, Wake Forest Univ, 72-. **MEMBERSHIPS** Am Philol Assn; Class Assn Midwest & South; Vergiliam Soc; Petronian Soc. **RESEARCH** Latin love elegy; Latin epic. **CONTACT ADDRESS** Dept of Class Lang, Wake Forest Univ, PO Box 7343, Winston Salem, NC, 27109-7343. **EMAIL** andy@wfu.edu

ANGEL, MARC D.
PERSONAL Born 07/25/1945, Seattle, WA, m, 1967, 3 children **DISCIPLINE** HISTORY **EDUCATION** Yeshivs Col BA 67; Yeshiva Univ Grad Sch, MS 70, PhD 75; City Col NY, MA 70. **CAREER** Shearith Israel NYC, rabbi 69-. **HONORS AND AWARDS** Nat Jewish Book Awd **MEMBERSHIPS** RCA **RESEARCH** Hist and culture of Jews, Spanish and Portuguese backgrounds. **SELECTED PUBLICATIONS** Auth, Rhythms of Jewish Living, Northvale NJ, Jason Aronson Pub 97; The Orphaned Adult, NV NJ, Jason Aronson Pub 97; Seeking Good Speaking Peace: Collected Essays of Rabbi Marc D. Angel, ed, Hayyim J. Angel, Hoboken NJ, KTAV Pub 94; Voices in Exile: A Study in Sephardic Intellectual History, Hoboken NJ, KTAV pub 91; Exploring the Thought of Rabbi Joseph B. Soloveitchik, ed, Hoboken NJ, 97; The Essential Pele Yoetz, condensed/trans, NY, Sepher-Hermon Press 91. **CONTACT ADDRESS** Shearith Israel, 8 West 70th Street, New York, NY, 10023.

ANGELOU, MAYA
PERSONAL Born 04/04/1928, St. Louis, MO, d **DISCIPLINE** LITERATURE, HISTORY **CAREER** Author, poet, playwright, stage and screen producer, director, actress, 1954-; Southern Christian Leadership Conference, coordinator, 1959-60; Arab Observer Egypt, associate editor, 1961-62; University of Ghana, asst administrator, 1963-66; African Review, editor, 1964-66; California State University, Wichita State University, visiting professor; WAKE FOREST UNIVERSITY, DEPARTMENT OF HUMANITIES, REYNOLDS PROFESSOR OF AMERICAN STUDIES, 1974-. **HONORS AND AWARDS** 32 Honorary Degrees; Pulitzer Prize Nomination, "Just Give Me A Cool Drink of Water 'fore I Diiie," 1972; Tony Award Nomination, "Look Away," 1975; Ladies Home Journal, one of the Women of the Year in Communications, 1976; Emmy Award Nomination, Performance, "Roots," 1977; Distingushed Woman of North Carolina, 1992; Essence Magazine, Woman of the Year, 1992; Horatio Alger Award, 1992; Women In Film, Crystal Award, 1992; American Academy of Achievement, Golden Plate Award, 1990; Horatio Alger Awards Dinner Chairman, 1993; National Society for the Prevention of Cruelty to Children, London, England, NSPCC Maya Angelou CPT and Family Centre, London, England, center dedication, June 20, 1991; NAACP, Image Award, Literary Work, Nonfiction, 1998. **MEMBERSHIPS** American Federation of Television & Radio Artists; board of trustees, American Film Institute, 1975-; Directors Guild; Actors' Equity; Women's Prison Assn. **SELECTED PUBLICATIONS** Author, works include: I Know Why the Caged Bird Sings, 1970; Just Give Me A Cool Drink of Water 'Fore I Die, 1971; Gather Together in My Name, 1974; Oh Pray My Wings Are Gonna Fit Me Well, 1975; Singin & Swingin & Getting Merry Like Christmas, 1976; And Still I Rise, 1978; The Heart of a Woman, 1981; Shaker, Why Don't You Sing? 1983; All God's Children Need Traveling Shoes, 1986; Mrs Flowers: A Moment of Friendship, 1986; Wouldn't Take Nothing for My Journey Now, Random, 1993; poems: Maya Angelou, 1986; Now Sheba Sings the Song, 1987; I Shall Not Be Moved, Random House, 1990; plays include: Cabraret for Freedom, 1960; The Least of These, 1966; Ajax, 1974; And Still I Rise, 1976; screenplays include: Georgia Georgia, 1972; All Day Long, 1974; PBS-TV Documentaries: "Who Cares About Kids" "Kindred Spirits," KERA-TV, Dallas, TX; "Rainbow In The Clouds," series, host, writer, WTVS-TV, Detroit, MI; "To The Contrary," Maryland Public Television; lecturer: Nancy Hanks Lecture, American Council for the Arts, 1990; contributing writer: "Brewster Place," mini-series, HARPO Productions; panelist: Institute for the Study of Human Systems, Zermatt, Switzerland, 1990; lyricist: "King Now," theatrical project, London, England; has appeared in numerous plays and TV productions as both an actress and singer; wrote and presented a poem for President Clinton's Swearing-In Ceremonies, 1993; Down in the Delta, director; named UNICEF National Ambassador, 1996. **CONTACT ADDRESS** Dept of Humanities, Wake Forest Univ, PO Box 7314, Winston-Salem, NC, 27109.

ANGLIN, DOUGLAS G.
PERSONAL Born 12/16/1923, Toronto, ON, Canada **DISCIPLINE** POLITICAL SCIENCE/HISTORY **EDUCATION** Univ Toronto, BA, 48; Corpus Christi Col & Nuffield Col, Univ Oxford, BA, 50, MA, 54, DPhil, 56. **CAREER** Asst to assoc prof polit sci, Univ Man, 51-58; assoc prof to prof, 58-89, PROF EMER, CARLETON UNIV, 93-; assoc res fel, Nigerian Inst Soc Econ Res, Univ Ibadan, 62-63; vice chancellor, Univ Zambia, 65-69; res assoc, Ctr Int Stud, Princeton Univ, 69-70. **MEMBERSHIPS** African Stud Asn (US); Can Inst Int Affairs; Can Polit Sci Asn; Can Asn African Stud (pres 73-74). **SELECTED PUBLICATIONS** Auth, The St Pierre and Miquelon Affaire of 1941, 66; auth, Zambia Crisis Behaviour: Confronting Rhodesia's Unilateral Declaration of Independence 1965-1966, 94; coauth, Zambia's Foreign Policy: Studies in Diplomacy and Dependence, 79; co-ed, Africa: The Political Pattern, 61; co-ed, Canada, Scandinavia and Southern Africa, 79; co-ed, Conflict and Change in Southern Africa, 79. **CONTACT ADDRESS** Dept of Political Science, Carleton Univ, 1125 Colonel By Dr, Ottawa, ON, K1S 5B6.

ANGUS, MARGARET
PERSONAL Born 05/23/1908, Chinook, MT **DISCIPLINE** HISTORY **EDUCATION** Univ Mont, BA, 30; Queen's Univ, LLD, 73. **CAREER** Dir radio, Queen's Univ, 57-68; mus cur, 68-85; dir, Ont Hist Stud Ser, 72-88; pres, Frontenac Hist Found, 73-76, 79-81; gov, Heritage Can, 74-79; dir, Ont Heritage Found, 75-81. **MEMBERSHIPS** Ont Hist Soc (pres 69-71); Archit Conservancy Ont; Kingston Hist Soc (pres 72-74); Cataraqui Archaeol Res Found (dir 83-84). **SELECTED PUBLICATIONS** Auth, The Old Stones of Kingston, 66; auth, The Story of Bellevue House, 67; auth, History of Kingston General Hospital, vol I, 72, vol II, 94; contribur, Oliver Mowat's Ontario, 72; contribur, Kingston 300, 73; contribur, John A. Lived Here, 84; contribur, Queen's History in Names, 91; contribur, Summerhill, Queen's University at Kingston, 97; ser ed, Buildings of Architectural and Historic Significance in Kingston. **CONTACT ADDRESS** 1201-322 Brock St, Kingston, ON, K7L 1S9.

ANISE, LADUN OLADUNJOYE E.
PERSONAL Born 03/24/1940 **DISCIPLINE** POLITICAL SCIENCE **EDUCATION** Albion College, BA, 1967; Syracuse Univ, MA 1968, PhD Political Science 1970; Univ of Pittsburgh, MA 1975. **CAREER** Syracuse Univ, African Studies-Minority Studies, lecturer 1968-70; Educ Policy & Resource Devel Center, Syracuse Univ, rsch assoc 1969-70; Univ of Pittsburgh, asst prof 1970-75; Univ of Ife Nigeria, visiting sr lecturer 1979-83; Hill Dist Catholic School System & Educ Devel Center, Pittsburgh PA, consultant 1972-75; Univ of Pittsburgh, assoc prof 1975-, African Studies Group, coord 1982-88, Black Studies Dept, chmn (summers) 1987, 1989. **HONORS AND AWARDS** ASPAU Achievement & Scholastic Award 1967; Omicron Delta Kappa 1967; Maxwell Fellow 1967-70; Woodrow Wilson Doctoral Fellow 1970; Meritorious Achievement Award Univ of Pittsburgh 1974. **MEMBERSHIPS** Mem Current Issues Comm African Studies Assoc 1968-, Amer Political Science Assoc, Natl Org of Black Political Science, African Heritage Studies Assoc, Natl Acad of Social Science. **CONTACT ADDRESS** Dept of Political Science, Univ of Pittsburgh, 4T25 Forbes Quad, Pittsburgh, PA, 15260.

ANNA, TIMOTHY
PERSONAL Born 11/03/1944, Lexington, KY **DISCIPLINE** HISTORY **EDUCATION** Duke Univ, BA, 66, MA, 68, PhD, 69. **CAREER** Asst prof to prof, 69-97, DISTINGUISHED PROF HISTORY, UNIV MANITOBA, 97-. **HONORS AND AWARDS** Rh Inst res award hum, 84; Killam res fel, 94-96; fel, Royal Soc Can, 95. **RESEARCH** Latin American history, 19th and 20th centuries; Mexico, Peru, Spain. **SELECTED PUBLICATIONS** Auth, The Fall of the Royal Government in Mexico City, 78; auth, The Fall of the Royal Government in Peru, 79; auth, Spain and the Loss of America, 83; auth, The Mexican Empire of Iturbide, 90; auth, Forging Mexico 1821-1835, 98. **CONTACT ADDRESS** Dept of History, Univ of Manitoba, 28 Trueman Walk, Winnipeg, MB, R3T 5V5.

ANTHONY, DAVID HENRY, III
PERSONAL Born 04/28/1952, Brooklyn, New York, m **DISCIPLINE** HISTORY **EDUCATION** NY Univ, AB 1968-72; Univ of WI-Madison, MA History 1975, DPhil History 1983. **CAREER** Fulbright Fellow Dept of State, rsch assoc 1976-77; Univ of Dar es Salaam Tanzania, rsch assoc 1976-77; Clark Univ, visiting prof 1979; Coppin State Coll, instructor of history 1980-84; Univ of Oregon, Eugene, OR, assistant professor of history, 1984-88; Univ of California, Oakes College, Santa Cruz, assistant professor, currently. **HONORS AND AWARDS** Fulbright Hays Awd Fulbright Found Dept of State 1976-77; President's Humanities Fellowship, University of California, 1990-91. **MEMBERSHIPS** Curr spec Madison Metro Sch Dist 1977-78; consul Swahili Anteiro Pietila Helen Winternitz 1980; rsch affiliate Univ of FL Ctr for African studies 1982; visiting prof History Dept Towson State Univ 1982-83; judge Gr Baltimore History Fair 1982-84; mem Phi Alpha Theta 1983-; mem Fulbright Alumni Assn 1981-. **CONTACT ADDRESS** Univ of California, 1156 High St, Santa Cruz, CA, 95064.

ANTHONY, WILLIAM PHILIP
PERSONAL Born 01/30/1943, Chicago, IL, m, 1968, 2 children **DISCIPLINE** MANAGEMENT **EDUCATION** PhD 71, MBA, 67, BBA, 65, OH State Univ. **CAREER** Prof of Mgt, FL State Univ, 70-. **HONORS AND AWARDS** Beta Gamma Sigma **MEMBERSHIPS** Acad of Mgt; Southern Mgt Assoc. **RESEARCH** Top Mgt Teams, Hum Res. **SELECTED PUBLICATIONS** Books with Pam Perrewe and Micki Kacmar, Strategic Human Resource Management, 3rd ed Ft Worth, HBJ/ Dryden, 93, 96, 99(ant); B.J. Hodge and Larry Gales, Organization Theory, 5th ed, Boston MA, Allyn and Bacon Inc, 79, 84, 88, 91, 96; Articles with Erich Brockman, The Influence of Tacit Knowledge and Collective Mind on Strategic Planning, Journal of Managerial Issues, Vol X No2 pp204-222, 98; Marc street, A Conceptual Framework Establishing the Relationship Between Groupthink and Escalating Commitment Behavior, Small Group Research Vol23 No2, pp267-293, 97; Nick Maddox, Robert Bennett and Walt Wheatley, The Mind's Eye and the Practice of Management, Envisioning the Ambiguous, Management Decision Vol 32 No2, pp21-29,94. **CONTACT ADDRESS** Coll of Bus, Florida State Univ, Tallahassee, FL, 32306-1110. **EMAIL** banthon@cob.fsu.edu

ANTIA, KERSEY H.
PERSONAL Born 01/07/1936, Surat, India, m, 1966, 3 children **DISCIPLINE** PSYCHOLOGY **EDUCATION** Tata Inst of Social Svcs, MA; N.C. State Univ, MS, 69; Indiana Northern Univ, PhD, 74. **CAREER** Univ of N. C., res asst, 67-69; Behavior Systems Inc., Proj Dir, 69-70; State of IL, Clin Psychologist, 70-86; private practice as Psychologist, 86-. **MEMBERSHIPS** CPS, APS, SPM, AAP, AOS, AAR/WPR. **RESEARCH** Mind-body relations; interface between psychology and religion; interrelations and similarities between Zoroastrianism and Judeo-

Christian traditions. **SELECTED PUBLICATIONS** Auth, Contributions of the Interview to the Selection of Higher-Level Personnel, Experimental Publication System, Wash. D.C. Am Psych Assoc, 69; auth, Job Satisfaction: Facts versus Fiction, Experimental Pub Sys, Wash D.C. Am Psych Assoc, 69; auth, A Dimensional Analysis of Instructor Ratings and Peer Nominations, Experimental Pub Sys, Wash D.C. Amer Psych Assoc, 70; auth, Consequences of Early Rejection and Social Deprivation on Later Speech Development, IL Jour of Speech & Hearing, 75; auth, Cognitive Climate of an Organization & Cognitive Style of Its Leader, Behavior, 93. **CONTACT ADDRESS** 8318 W. 138th Pl, Orland Park, IL, 60462. **EMAIL** antia@juno.com

ANTLIFF, MARK
DISCIPLINE ART HISTORY **EDUCATION** Yale Univ, PhD. **CAREER** Assoc prof, Duke Univ. **RESEARCH** Art in Europe before 1945; interrelation of art and philos. **SELECTED PUBLICATIONS** Auth, Inventing Bergson: Cultural Politics and the Parisian Avant-Garde; co-auth, Fascist Visions: Art and Ideology in France and Italy. **CONTACT ADDRESS** Dept of Art and Art Hist, Duke Univ, East Duke Building, Durham, NC, 27706.

ANTOKOLETZ, ELLIOTT MAXIM
PERSONAL Born 08/13/1942, Jersey City, NJ, m, 1972, 1 child **DISCIPLINE** MUSICOLOGY **EDUCATION** Juilliard Sch Music, 60-65; Hunter Coll CUNY, AB, 68; MA, 70; CUNY, PhD, 75. **CAREER** Lectr, Chamber Music, Queens Coll CUNY, 73-76; PROF, MUSICOL, UNIV TX-AUSTIN, 76-. **MEMBERSHIPS** Queens Coll String Quartet; Am Musicol Soc; Sonneck Soc; Coll Music Soc; Int Music Soc **RESEARCH** Bela Bartock, 20th century music **SELECTED PUBLICATIONS** The Music of Be'la Barto'k, Univ Calif Press, 84; Be'la Barto'k: A Guide to Research, Garland Press, 88; Twentieth Century Music, Prentice Hall, 97. **CONTACT ADDRESS** Dept Music, Univ Texas-Austin, Austin, TX, 78712. **EMAIL** antokoletz@mail.utexas.edu

ANTONIO, ROBERT
PERSONAL Born 06/20/1945, New Haven, CT, s **DISCIPLINE** SOCIOLOGY **EDUCATION** Miami of Ohio, BA, 67; Notre Dame, MA, 70, PhD, 72. **CAREER** Asst prof, 71, assoc prof, 75, prof, 86-, Univ of KS. **HONORS AND AWARDS** Younger Humanist Fel-Natl Endowment of the Humanities, 74-75; Chancellors Club Award for Teaching Excellence, 79; Chancellors Club Career Teaching Award, 88; Chancellors Club Teaching Professorship, 89; Motor Board Honors Society-Outstanding Educator 75, 88, 91, 96. **MEMBERSHIPS** Amer Sociological Assn; Midwest Sociological Assn. **RESEARCH** Social Theory **SELECTED PUBLICATIONS** Auth, Max Weber, The Encyclopedia of Democracy, 95; Nietzsche's Antisociology: Subjectified Culture and the End of History, American Journal of Sociology, 95; Post-Fordism in the United States: The Poverty of Market Centered Democracy, Current Perspectives in Social Theory, 96; Mapping Postmodern Social Theory, in What is Social Theory? The Philosophical Debates, forthcoming; Karl Marx, Blackwell Companion to the Major Social Theorists, forthcoming. **CONTACT ADDRESS** Dept of Sociology, Univ Kansas, 732 Fraser, Lawrence, KS, 66045. **EMAIL** anto@falcon.cc.ukans.edu

APENA, IGHO ADELINE
DISCIPLINE AFRICAN HISTORY **EDUCATION** Ibadan. Nigeria, BA; Univ London, MA; Univ Lagos, Nigeria, PhD. **CAREER** Off, Dept of Hea and Soc Security, Brit Coun, Greater London Coun, Manager Crothal and Co; instr, Univ Guyana; libr off, Univ Aberdeen, Scotland; instr, res fel, Univ the West Indies, Jamaica; consult, Women Non-Governmental orgn, African Caribbean Inst of Jamaica; instr, Russell Sage Col. **HONORS AND AWARDS** Spec Female Award (Nigeria); British Coun Overseas Award. **MEMBERSHIPS** African Stud Asn of the US; Soc for the Comp Stud of Civilization. **RESEARCH** African history; women in Africa; the African Caribbean diaspora; historiography **SELECTED PUBLICATIONS** Auth, Guyanese Women's Reactions to Structural Adjustment Program, 95. **CONTACT ADDRESS** Russell Sage Col, Troy, NY, 12180. **EMAIL** apenaa@sage.edu

APONIUK, NATALIA
PERSONAL Gronlid, SK, Canada **DISCIPLINE** UKRAINIAN CANADIAN STUDIES **EDUCATION** Univ Sask, BA, 62; Univ Toronto. MA, 63, PhD, 74. **CAREER** Tchg asst, Slavic Langs, Univ Toronto, 63-65, 66-67, 73-74; asst prof, Reed Col, 67-72; lectr, Univ Alta, 74-75; instr, ESL, 75-77; asst prof, 77-86, DIR, CTR UKRAINIAN CAN STUDS 82-93, ASSOC PROF, GERMAN & SLAVIC STUDS, UNIV MANITOBA, 86-. **HONORS AND AWARDS** Hantelman Postgrad Fel, Univ Sask, 62-63; Prov Ont Govt Fel, 63-67; Taras Schevchenko Memorial Scholar, 64-65; Ukrainian Woman of Year, Winnipeg, 86; Univ Man Outreach Award, 92; Univ Man Award Serv, 93. **MEMBERSHIPS** Conf Ukrainian Studs; Can Asn Slavists; Can Women's Studs Asn. **SELECTED PUBLICATIONS** Auth, Perspectives on an Ethnic Bestseller: All of Baba's Children, in Can Ethnic Studs, 10, 78; auth, Some Images of Ukrainian Women in Canadian Literature, in J Ukrainian Studs, 8, 83; auth, Ukrainian Canadian Heritage Studies, in Horizons, 1, 92. **CONTACT ADDRESS** Dept of German & Slavic Stud, Univ Man, Winnipeg, MB, R3T 2N2. **EMAIL** aponiuk@cc.UManitoba.CA

APOSTOLOS-CAPPADONA, DIANE
PERSONAL Born 05/10/1948, Trenton, NJ **DISCIPLINE** AMERICAN CULTURAL HISTORY; RELIGION AND CULTURE **EDUCATION** Cath Univ of Amer, MA, 79; George Wash Univ, BA, 70, MA, 73, PhD, 88. **CAREER** Lectr, relig, Mt Vernon Col, 80-85; lectr, relig, George Wash Univ, 81-86; adj facul, christ and art, Pacific Sch of Relig, 85-86, 88-92; adj prof, art and culture, Liberal Studies prog, Georgetown Univ, 85-; res prof, Ctr for Muslim-Christian understanding, Georgetown Univ, 96-. **HONORS AND AWARDS** Sr fel, Ctr for the Study of World Relig, Harvard Univ, 96-97; res grant, Amer Acad of Relig; res grant, Amer Coun of Learned Soc; NEH grant. **MEMBERSHIPS** Amer Acad of Relig; Amer Asn of Mus; Amer Asn of Univ Women; Amer Studies Asn; Col Art Asn; Col Theol Soc; Congress on Res in Dance; Soc for Art, Relig, and Contemporary Culture. **RESEARCH** Images of women in religious art; Iconography of the Black Madonna; Relationship between art, gender, religion and culture; Iconography of Mary Magdalene. **SELECTED PUBLICATIONS** Auth, Dictionary of Women in Religious Art, Oxford Univ Press, 98; auth, Dictionary of Christian Art, Continuum Publ, 98; auth, Beyond Belief: The Artistic Journey and two entries in Beyond Belief: Modern Art and the Religious Imagination, The Nat Gallery of Victoria, Melbourne, 98; entries, Encycl of Comparative Iconography, 98; auth, Picturing Devotion: Rogier's Saint Luke Drawing the Virgin and Child, Saint Luke Drawing the Virgin and Child: Essays in Context, Brepols, 97; auth, Encyclopedia of Women in Religious Art, Continuum Publ, 96; auth, Picasso's Guernica as Mythic Iconoclasm: An Eliadean Reading of Modern Art, Myth and Method, Univ Va Press, 96; entries, The Dictionary of Art and The New Catholic Encyclopedia, vol 19: suppl, 96; auth, The Spirit and the Vision: The Influence of Christian Romanticism on the Development of 19th-century American Art, Scholar's Press, 95; co-ed, Women, Creativity and the Arts, Contiuum Publ, 95; ed, Art, Creativity, and the Sacred, Continuum Publ, 95; entries, Harper's Dictionary of Religion, 95; auth, Dictionary of Christian Art, Continuum Publ, 94; co-ed, Isamu Noguchi: Essays and Conversations, 94; auth, Noguchi at the Dance! Dance Collection, NY Publ Libr for the Performing Arts, 94. **CONTACT ADDRESS** Center for Muslim-Christian Understanding, Georgetown Univ, ICC #260, Washington, DC, 20057-1052. **EMAIL** apostold@gusun.georgetown.edu

APPEL, SUSAN K.
PERSONAL Born 07/07/1946, Toledo, OH **DISCIPLINE** ART HISTORY **EDUCATION** BFA, Bowling Green State Univ, 68; MA, art hist, Univ Iowa, Iowa City, 72; PhD, art history, Univ Ill at Urbana-Champaign, 90. **CAREER** Tchg asst, Univ Iowa, Iowa City, Iowa, 69-72; photographer and archit surv, Iowa State Hist Preserv Prog ,Iowa City, Iowa, 74; cons archit hist, City of Muscatine, Iowa, 74; cons archit hist, Environ Res Ctr, Iowa City, Iowa, 74-77; instr, art, Augustana Col, Rock Island, Ill, 74-76; asst prof, art, Phillips Univ, Enid, Okla, 76-79; visiting lectr, 82-83, course coord, 81-82, tchg asst, 79-81, Univ of Ill at Urbana-Champaign, 79-83; cons archit hist, The Urbana Grp, Urbana, Ill, 92; acting assoc chair, 98-99, assoc prof, art hist, 92-, asst prof, art hist, 89-92, lectr and instr, 83-89, Ill State Univ, Normal, Ill. **HONORS AND AWARDS** Univ Small Grant, Ill State Univ, 98; Reader, Advan Placement Test in Art Hist, Educ Testing Svc, Trenton, NJ State Col, 94-98; Preserv Svc Heritage Award, Preserv and Conserv Asn of Champaign, 97; Appointed Mem of the City of Champaign, Ill, Hist Preserv Comn, 97-; nominee outstanding tchr, Dept of Art as Col of Fine Arts, 96; Appointed mem of the Ill Hist Sites Adv Coun, 93-96; Univ Tchg Initiative Award, Ill State Univ, 95; Col Outstanding Res Award, Col of Fine Arts, Ill State Univ, 94; Soc for Indust Archaeol/Hist Amer Eng Record Fel, 92-93; Univ Res Grant and Small Grant, Ill State Univ, 92-93; Univ Res Grant, Ill State Univ, 90-91; Col of Fine Arts Facul Res Initiative, Ill State Univ, 88; Computerized Instr Rev Grant, Col of Fine Arts, Ill State Univ, summer, 86; Rosann S. Berry Fel, Soc of Archit Hist, 85; Res Travel Grants, Sch of Art and Design, Univ Ill, 84, 85; Dissertation Res Grant, Grad Col, Univ Ill, summer 83; Allerton Amer Traveling Scholar, Sch of Archit, Univ Ill, summer, 80; Victorian Soc in Amer Scholar to its summer sem in Victorian archit, Boston, 80; Honor Soc of Phi Kappa Phi, Univ Ill, Univ fel and res asst, Univ Ill, 81-82; participant, NEH Summer Sem for Col Tchrs, Urban Hist of the Mediterranean and Near East, Univ Calif Berkeley, summer, 78; Univ Iowa scholar, Delta Phi Delta, Nat Art Hon, Bowling Green State Univ; Two-Dimensional Design and Life Drawing awards, Bowling Green State Univ. **MEMBERSHIPS** Col Art Asn; Landmarks Preserv Coun of Ill; Midwest Art Hist Soc; Nat Trust for Hist Preserv; Soc for Indust Arheol; Soc of Archit Hist; Vernacular Archit Forum; Victorian Soc in Amer; Women's Caucus for Art. **RESEARCH** Architectural development of pre-Prohibition American breweries; American architectural history, including vernacular architecture; Historic preservation issues related to American architecture. **SELECTED PUBLICATIONS** Auth, Historic Breweries in the Contemporary Landscape, From Industry to Industrial Heritage, Proceedings of the Ninth International Conference on the Conservation of the Industrial Heritage in Montreal/Ottawa, Canada, May 29-June 2, 1994, 99-110, Ottawa, Can Soc for Indust Heritage, 98; Chicago and the Rise of Brewery Architecture, Chicago Hist, Mag of the Chicago Hist Soc, XXIV, 1, 4-19, spring, 95; Building Milwaukee's Breweries: an Overview of Pre-Prohibition Brewery Architecture in the Cream City, Wisc Mag of Hist, 78, 3, 163-199, spring, 95; book rev, Breweries of Wisconsin, by Jerry Apps, Madison, Univ Wisc Press, 1992, in Monatshefte fur deutschen Unterricht, deutsche Sprache und Litatur, LXXXVI, 2, 262-264, summer 94; contrib, Chicago: An Industrial Guide, Chicago, Pub Works Hist Soc, 91. **CONTACT ADDRESS** 307 N. Garfield Av., Champaign, IL, 61821-2615.

APPIAH, KWAME ANTHONY
DISCIPLINE AFRO-AMERICAN STUDIES AND PHILOSOPHY **EDUCATION** Cambridge Univ, England, BA, PhD. **CAREER** Prof. **MEMBERSHIPS** Past pres, Socr African Philos in NAm & is an ed of Transition. **RESEARCH** Epistemology and philosophy of language; African philosophy; philosophical problems of race and racism; Afro-American and African literature and literary theory. **SELECTED PUBLICATIONS** Auth, My Father's House: Africa in the Philosophy of Culture, 92 & Color Conscious: The Political Morality of Race, 96. **CONTACT ADDRESS** Dept of Philosophy, Harvard Univ, 8 Garden St, Cambridge, MA, 02138. **EMAIL** appiah@fas.harvard.edu

APPLEBAUM, DAVID
DISCIPLINE MODERN EUROPEAN HISTORY **EDUCATION** Brooklyn Col, BA; Univ Wis, PhD, 73. **CAREER** Instr, coordr, semester abroad prog, Rowan Col of NJ. **RESEARCH** French cultural, social, and legal history. **SELECTED PUBLICATIONS** Published a number of articles in French cultural, social, and legal history. **CONTACT ADDRESS** Rowan Col of NJ, Glassboro, NJ, 08028-1701.

APPLEBY, JOYCE
PERSONAL Born 04/09/1929, Omaha, NE, w, 3 children **DISCIPLINE** HISTORY **EDUCATION** Stanford Univ, BA, 50; Univ CA, MA, 59; PhD, 66, Claremont Graduate Sch. **CAREER** Asst prof, 67-70, assoc prof, 70-73, assoc dean, coll of arts and letters, 74-75, prof, 73-81 San Diego State Univ; chair of the dept of hist, 87-88, UCLA; harmsworth prof, 90-91, prof, 81-, Oxford. **MEMBERSHIPS** Elected member, Amer Philosophical Soc, 93; UCLA Coll of Letters and Sci distinguished Prof Award, 93; Council of the Smithsonian Institution, 94-98; delegate, Amer Council of Learned Societies, 94-98; John Simon Guggenheim Memorial Found Fel, 94-95; council, Amer Historical Assn, 96-99; Pres, Amer Historical Assn, 97. **RESEARCH** Early modern England, France, US. **SELECTED PUBLICATIONS** Ed, The Popular Sources of American Capitalism, Studiesin American Political Development, 96;Recollections of the Early Republic: Selected Autobiographies, 97; auth, The Personal Roots of the First American Temperance Movement, American Philosophical Society Proceedings for 1997; The Power of History, American Historical Review, 98; Ed with Terence Ball, The Political Writings of Thomas Jefferson, forthcoming. **CONTACT ADDRESS** 615 Westholme Ave., Los Angeles, CA, 90024.

ARAV, RAMI
PERSONAL Born 10/21/1947, Israel, m, 1980, 3 children **DISCIPLINE** ARCHAEOLOGY **EDUCATION** Tel Aviv Univ, MA 80; New York Univ, PhD 86. **CAREER** Univ Nebraska Omaha, vis prof, 94-98; and Dir of excavations at Bethsaida. **MEMBERSHIPS** SBL; ASOR. **RESEARCH** Archaeology of the Land of Israel. **SELECTED PUBLICATIONS** Auth, Jesus and His World, coauth, 95; Bethsaida, A City By the Northern Shore of the Sea of Galilee, co-ed, vol 1 95, vol 2 98. **CONTACT ADDRESS** Dept of Philosophy and Religion, Univ of Nebraska, Omaha, 4814 Capitol Ave, Omaha, NE, 68132. **EMAIL** rarav@cwis.unomaha.edu

ARBAGI, MARTIN GEORGE
PERSONAL Born 02/16/1940, Brooklyn, NY, m, 1971, 3 children **DISCIPLINE** BYZANTINE HISTORY, EARLY MEDIEVAL HISTORY **EDUCATION** Georgetown Univ, AB, 61; Rutgers Univ, New Brunswick, MA, 63, PhD(hist), 69. **CAREER** Asst prof hist, Univ Maine, Orono, 67-69; asst prof, 69-85, assoc prof, Wright State Univ, 85-, Mem exec comt, Conf Greek, Roman & Byzantine Studies, 75-77, 80- **MEMBERSHIPS** Mediaeval Acad Am, Nat Assoc of Schol, Ohio Class Conf. **RESEARCH** Byzantine East and Latin West to 1100. **SELECTED PUBLICATIONS** Auth, A Tenth-Century Emperor Michael of Constantinople, Speculum, 7/73; The Celibacy of Basil II, Byzantine Studies, 7/75; Byzantium, Germany, the Regnum Italicum and the Magyars in the Tenth-Century, Byzantine Studies, 1/79; Urbs Regia, Continuity, #10, 85. **CONTACT ADDRESS** Dept of Hist, Wright State Univ, 3640 Colonel Glenn, Dayton, OH, 45435-0002. **EMAIL** marbagi@gemair.com

ARBINO, GARY P.
PERSONAL m **DISCIPLINE** ARCHAEOLOGY, OLD TESTAMENT INTERPRETATION **EDUCATION** Humboldt State Univ, BA; Golden Gate Baptist Theol Sem, MDiv, PhD.

CAREER Asst curator, design dir, Marian Eakins Archaeol Coll, 91; adj prof, 92-96; guest asst prof, 96-98; curator, Marian Eakins Archaeol Coll, 98; asst prof, Golden Gate Baptist Theol Sem-. **HONORS AND AWARDS** Will Edd Langford Memorial scholar, 92; Who's Who Among Students In Amer Univ(s) and Col(s), 89, 92; Broadman Seminarian Award, 89; National Dean's List, 87, 92., Supvr, Sem library's audio-visual dept and video production studio, 90-96; Lib Circulation Svc, 94-96. **MEMBERSHIPS** Mem, Amer Sch(s) of Oriental Res; Soc Biblical Lit; member adv bd, Nat Assn prof(s)of Hebrew. **SELECTED PUBLICATIONS** Pub(s), Biblical Illustrator. **CONTACT ADDRESS** Golden Gate Baptist Theol Sem, 201 Sem Dr, Mill Valley, CA, 94941-3197. **EMAIL** GaryArbino@ggbts.edu

ARBURY, STEVE
DISCIPLINE ART HISTORY **EDUCATION** Albion Col, BA magna cum laude, 75; Rutgers Univ, MA, 78, PhD, 92. **CAREER** Librn asst, Albion Col Libr, 74-75; intern/asst to the cur, The Jewish Mus, NY, 76; librn asst, Art Libr, 75-76, instr, 78-80, asst tchr, 79, cofounder/ed, Rutgers Art Rev, 79-81, curatorial asst, Fine Arts Coll, Rutgers Univ, 80-81; instr, Univ Urbino, Italy, 81; adj prof, 84-88, hd, Fine Arts Libr, 84-88, instr, Roanoke Mus Fine Arts, 85; gallery dir, Roanoke Col, 86-88; assoc prof, 88-, cur, Art Hist Vis Rsrc Ctr, 88-, cur, Dorothy Gillespie Coll, Radford Univ, 97-. **HONORS AND AWARDS** Phi Beta Kappa, Albion Col, 75; Mary Bartlett Cowdrey fel, Rutgers Univ, 79-80; NJ State Grant, Rutgers Univ, 79-80, 80-81; Louis Bevier grad fel, Rutgers Univ, 80-81; Fulbright scholar/Span Govt grant, 81-82, 82-83; Outstanding Young Men of Am Award, 85; Distinguished Leadership Award, 86; Men of Achievement Award, 87; grant, Radford Univ, 93; fac prof develop leave, Radford Univ, 97; Award of Excellence, The Kemper A. Dobbins Annual Art Exhib, Va Mus of Transp, 97. **MEMBERSHIPS** Col Art Asn of Am; Midwest Art Hist Soc; Southeastern Col Art Conf; Am Soc for Hisp Art Hist Stud; Am Acad of Res Hist of Medieval Spain; Vis Rsrcs Asn; 16th Century Stud Conf; Am Asn of Mus; AAUP. **SELECTED PUBLICATIONS** Auth, Gifford Beal, Arthur B. Frost, Jr, Samuel Halpert, Marsden Hartley, Kinetic Art, Jonas Lie, Joseph Pickett, Joshua Shaw, Maurice Sterne, in ed Matthew Baigell, Dictionary of American Art, Harper & Row, 79; Slide Computerization with FileMaker II Software and the Apple Macintosh SE, Vis Rsrc Assn Bull 17, no 1, 90; Slide Computerization with FileMaker Plus and the Apple Macintosh SE, Southeastern Col Art Conf Rev XI, no 5, 90; Spanish Catafalques of the Golden Age, Rutgers Art Rev 12/13, 91-92; ASA Slide Classification System and Computerized Cataloging: Reference Manual, Newly rev ed, 95; Catafalque, Alonso de Mena, in The Dictionary of Art, 34 vols, MacMillan, 96. **CONTACT ADDRESS** Art Dept, Radford Univ, PO Box 6965, Radford, VA, 24142. **EMAIL** sarbury@runet.edu

ARCHDEACON, THOMAS JOHN
PERSONAL Born 07/05/1942, New York, NY, m, 1968, 3 children **DISCIPLINE** HISTORY **EDUCATION** Fordham Univ, BA, 64; Columbia Univ, MA, 65, PhD, 71. **CAREER** Capt, asst prof, 69-72, US Military Acad; asst prof, 72-76, assoc prof, 76-82, prof, 82-, Univ Wisc-Madison. **MEMBERSHIPS** Amer Hist Assn; Org of Amer Hist; Irish Amer Cult Inst; Amer Conf for Irish Stud; Ctr for Migration Stud. **RESEARCH** Immigration. **SELECTED PUBLICATIONS** Auth, Correlation and Regression Analysis: A Historian's Guide, Univ Wisc Press, 94; auth, Becoming American: An Ethnic History, Free Press, 83; auth, New York City, 1664-1710: Conquest and Change, Cornell Univ Press, 76. **CONTACT ADDRESS** Dept of History, Univ of Wisconsin, 455 N Park St, Madison, WI, 53706. **EMAIL** tjarchde@fcestaff.wisc.edu

ARCHER, CHALMERS, JR.
PERSONAL Born 04/21/1938, Tchula, Mississippi **DISCIPLINE** EDUCATION **EDUCATION** Saints Junior College, Associate, art; Tuskegee Inst, Alabama, BS 1972, MEd 1973; Auburn University, Alabama, PhD 1979; Univ of Alabama, Post Doctorate Certificate, 1979; MIT, Cambridge MA, Certificate 1982. **CAREER** Saints Jr College, asst to the pres, 1968-70; Tuskegee Inst, asst vice pres & asst prof 1970-83; Northern Virginia Community College, admin/prof, 1983-; Jackson Advocate, contributing editor. **HONORS AND AWARDS** Honorary Doctorate of Letters, Saints Jr Coll, Lexington MS, 1970; Phi Delta Kappa Award for Leadership; Exemplary Research & Program Development, 1981; cited for community contribution; lectured at Cambridge Univ, England, and five major universities on teaching and learning interdisciplinary studies, 1988-89; architect of Comp Counseling Ctr & Weekend College at Tuskegee Inst; Architect of Reading & Language Arts Special Emphasis Curriculum for public schs; developed successful multi-level Educ Alliance to Adv Equal Access with public schs; author of 22 educational & other publications; Robert F Kennedy Book Awards; The Francis B Simkins Award; Martha Albrand Award; The Sidney Hillman Foundation Award; participated in President-elect Clinton's "A Call for Reunion" Opening Ceremony; President Clinton's Task Force, Americans for Change, charter member; Democratic National Committee; Clinton/Gore Rapid Response Team. **MEMBERSHIPS** Natl Assn of Coll Deans, Registrars, and Admissions Officers; Phi Delta Kappa; Kappa Delta Pi; APGA; NAACP; charter mem Kiwanis Intl of Macon Coll; AAUP; AACRAO; Southeastern Assoc of Community Coll; Cooperative Educ; vice pres, Saints Jr Coll Alumni; past bd mem, Natl Consortium for the Recruitment of Black Students from Northern Cities; past chmn, State of Alabama's Steering Comm for Advanced Placement of High School Students; consultant, Department of Education on Retention, 1990-92. **SELECTED PUBLICATIONS** Author: Growing Up Black in Rural Mississippi, 1992; On the Shoulders of Giants, 1994; Growing Up With the Green Berets, 1998. **CONTACT ADDRESS** Dept of Music, Virginia State Univ, No Va Comm Coll, Manassas Campus, 6901 Sudley Rd, Manassas, VA, 22110.

ARCISZEWSKA, BARBARA
DISCIPLINE ART HISTORY **EDUCATION** Courtauld Inst, London, MA, 86; Univ Toronto, PhD, 94. **CAREER** Post-doctoral fel, Univ Toronto, 94-96; Yale Ctr for British Art, 96; Canadian Ctr for Archit, 97-. **HONORS AND AWARDS** SSHRC post-doctoral fel, 94-96; res fel, Yale Univ Mellon Ctr for British Art, 96. **MEMBERSHIPS** Col Art Assoc; Soc of Archit Hist; Soc for Eighteenth Century Stud. **RESEARCH** Art and architectural history from the Renaissance to the eighteenth century. **SELECTED PUBLICATIONS** Auth, A Villa Fit for A King: The Role of Palladian Architecture in the Ascending of the House of Hanover under George I, in Mandel, ed, Artas Propagande, RACAR, 92; auth, the Church of Sint Jan in Hertogenbosch: Defining the Boundaries of Patronage in Late Medieval Methelandith Architecture, in Wilkins, ed, The Search for a Patron in the Middle Ages and Renaissance, Mellen, 96. **CONTACT ADDRESS** 162-4020 Dundas St West, Toronto, ON, M6S 4W6. **EMAIL** arciszew@chass.utoronto.ca

ARDREY, SAUNDRA CURRY
PERSONAL Born 08/26/1953, Louisville, GA, m **DISCIPLINE** POLITICAL SCIENCE **EDUCATION** Winston-Salem State University, BA, 1975; Ohio State University, MA, 1976, PhD, 1983. **CAREER** University of North Carolina Chapel Hill, visting lecturer 1979-80; Jefferson Community College, University of Kentucky, instructor, 1980-81; Furman University, asst prof 1983-88; WESTERN KENTUCKY UNIVERSITY, DEPT OF GOVERNMENT, PROFESSOR, 1988-. **HONORS AND AWARDS** Western Kentucky University, Outstanding Achievement in Service Award, 1990; Outstanding Paper Awd, National Conference of Black Political Scientists, Annual Conference, 1994; Elections Analyst for Kentucky Public TV, 1995-; campaign consultant, 1995-. **MEMBERSHIPS** American Political Science Assn, 1975-87; Natl Conference of Black Political Science, 1978-; Southern Political Science Assn, 1983-87; American Assn of University Professor, 1983-85; bd mem, Greenville City Urban League, 1983-87; Greenville City United Way, 1983-84; exec comm, Greenville City Democratic Party, 1984-85; pres, Greenville City Young Democrats, 1984-85; pres, Bowling Green NOW; NAACP, Bowling Green Branch, 1990-; Alpha Kappa Alpha Sorority, 1989-. **CONTACT ADDRESS** Dept of Govt, Western Kentucky Univ, Grise Hall, Bowling Green, KY, 42101.

ARIETI, JAMES ALEXANDER
PERSONAL Born 05/12/1948, New York, NY, m, 1976, 1 child **DISCIPLINE** CLASSICS, HISTORY **EDUCATION** Grinnell Col, BA, 69; Stanford Univ, MA, 72, PhD(classics), 72. **CAREER** Asst prof classics, Stanford Univ, 73-74; asst prof, Pa State Univ, 74-75; asst prof classics & hist, Cornell Col, 75-77; asst prof, 78-81, assoc prof, 81-88, prof classics, Hampden-Sydney Col, 88-95, Thompson Prof Classics, 95-; asst bibliographer ling, MLA, 74-75; NEH fel, classics, 77-78; chemn bd & sr fel, Hesperis Inst for Humanistic Studies, 77-. **HONORS AND AWARDS** Phi Beta Kappa, 69; Woodrow Wilson fel, 69; McHaver Res Award, 86, 97; John Templeton Prize for Science & Religion, 96. **MEMBERSHIPS** Am Philol Asn; Class Asn of Middle West & South; VA Classical Asn. **RESEARCH** Ancient historiography and philosophy; ancient literary criticism; Septuagint. **SELECTED PUBLICATIONS** Auth, The Vocabulary of Septuagint Amos, J Biblical Lit, 74; Nudity in Greek Athletics, Class World, 75; coauth, The Dating of Longinus, Studia Classica, 75; co-ed, MLA Int Bibliography, In; 1974 Vol III, MLA, 76; contrib, Two Studies in Latin Phonology, Studia Ling et Philol, 76; coauth, Love Can Be Found, Harcourt Brace Jovanovich, 77; auth, Epedocles in Rome: Rape and the Roman Ethos, Clio, 81; A Heorodtean Source for Rasselas, Note & Queries, 81; coauth, Longinus on the Sublime, Edwin Meller pub, 85; co-ed, Hamartia: The Concept of Error in the Western Tradition, Edwin Mellen Pub, 83; auth, Interpreting Plato: The Dialogues as Drama, Rowman & Littlefield, 91; Discourses on the First Book of Herodotus, Littlefield Adams Books, 95; numerous articles and reviews. **CONTACT ADDRESS** Dept of Classics, Hampden-Sydney Col, Hampden Sydney, VA, 23943. **EMAIL** jina@tiger.hsc.edu

ARIS, RUTHERFORD
PERSONAL Born 09/15/1929, Bournemouth, England, m, 1958 **DISCIPLINE** MATHEMATICS **EDUCATION** Univer of London, BS, 48, PhD 60, DSC, 64. **CAREER** Tech Officer, ICI Birm, 50-55; Lectr, Univ of Edinburg, 56-58; Lectr, Univ MN, 58, Regents' Prof Emeritus, Univ MN, 96-. **HONORS AND AWARDS** Guggenheim Fel, 71-72; Sherman Fairchild Distinguished Scholar, 80-81; Fel Amer Acad Arts Sci, 88. **RESEARCH** Paleography of the 12th century book **SELECTED PUBLICATIONS** Auth, Medieval Scholarship: Biographical Studies on the Formation of a Discipline, Volume 1: History, Jean Mabillon, Garland Pub, NY, 95; New Literary Hist, Complementary viewpoints: Some thoughts on binocular vision in mathematical modelling and Latin paleography, 95; Chem. Engng. Sci., Reflections on Keats' equation, 97; Mathl. and Comp. Modelling, Dissections, transgressions and perilous paths, 98. **CONTACT ADDRESS** Dept of Chem Engineering, Univ of MN - Twin Cities, Minneapolis, MN, 55455. **EMAIL** raris@tc.umn.edu

ARLIN, MARY I.
DISCIPLINE MUSIC THEORY **EDUCATION** Ithaca Col, BS; Univ Ind, PhD. **CAREER** Prof. **MEMBERSHIPS** Soc Music Theory; Am Viola Soc. **SELECTED PUBLICATIONS** Auth, Interval Tutor: A Computer Program for Ear Training, Pendragon; Frustrating Fundamentals: A Computer Program for Theory, Pendragon; Esquisse de l'histoire de l'harmonie: An English-Language Translation of the Francois-Joseph Fitis History of Harmony, Pendragon; co-auth, Music Sources, Prentice Hall, 89; Supplement, Sightsinging I and II, Lyceum. **CONTACT ADDRESS** Dept of Music History, Theory and Composition, Ithaca Col, 100 Job Hall, Ithaca, NY, 14850. **EMAIL** arlin@ithaca.edu

ARMITAGE, DAVID
DISCIPLINE HISTORY **EDUCATION** Cambridge, PhD, 92. **CAREER** Res fel, Emmanuel Col, Cambridge, 90-93; asst prof Hist, 93-97, assoc prof Hist, Columbia Univ, 97-. **HONORS AND AWARDS** Irene Samuel Memorial Award of the Milton Soc of Am, 95; Phillip and Ruth Hettleman Award for Jr Fac, Columbia Univ, 96, 98; fel, Nat Humanities Center, 96-97; Georges Lurcy Jr Fac fel, 96-97; fel, Royal Hist Soc, 97-. **MEMBERSHIPS** Hakluyt Soc; Am Hist Asn; North Am Conference on British Studies; Assocs of the John Carter Brown Library; Assocs of the Omohundro Inst of Early Am Hist and Culture; Eighteenth-Century Scottish Studies Soc; Forum for European Expansion and Global Interaction. **RESEARCH** Early modern British hist; hist of the first British Empire; history of political thought. **SELECTED PUBLICATIONS** Co-ed, Milton and Republicanism, Cambridge, 95, paperback, 98; ed, Bolingbroke: Political Writings, Cambridge, 97; ed, Theories of Empire, 1450-1800, Aldershot, 98; recent essays in: Karen Ordahl Kupperman, ed, American in European Consciousness, 1493-1750, 95; John Robertson, ed, A Union for Empire, 95; Past and Present, 97; Journal of British Studies, 97; and Nicholas Canny, ed, The Oxford History of the British Empire, vol 1, 98. **CONTACT ADDRESS** Dept of History, Columbia Univ, Fayerweather Hall, New York, NY, 10027. **EMAIL** da56@columbia.edu

ARMITAGE, SUSAN
DISCIPLINE US WOMEN'S HISTORY **EDUCATION** Univ London, PhD, 68. **CAREER** Prof, Washington State Univ. **SELECTED PUBLICATIONS** Coaut, Out of Many, Prentice Hall, 94; co-ed, The Women's West, 87; So Much To Be Done: Women Settlers on the Mining and Ranching Frontier, 90 & Writing the Range:Race, Classs, and Culture in the Women's West, 98. **CONTACT ADDRESS** Dept of History, Washington State Univ, 301 Wilson Hall, PO Box 644030, Pullman, WA, 99164-4030. **EMAIL** armitage@wsu.edu

ARMSTRONG, BRIAN G
PERSONAL Born 08/01/1936, Titusville, PA, m, 1959, 2 children **DISCIPLINE** HISTORY **EDUCATION** Houghton Col, AB, 58; Gordon Div Sch, BD, 61; Princeton Theol Sem, ThM, 62, OhD, 67. **CAREER** Tch fel, Princeton Theol Sem, 65-67; asst prof, 67-70, assoc prof, Ga State Univ, 70-89; vis ACLS schol Univ Geneva, 72-73; actg ch, hist, 73-74, asst dean, 74-75, actg ch, For Lang, 79-80, ch, hon prg cmt, 80-84, ch bach of interdisc stu cmt, 84-86, grad dir, coll of arts & scis, 84-85, prof, Ga State Univ, 91-. **MEMBERSHIPS** AHA, ASCH, ASRR, Calvin Stu Soc, ICCR, NAS, RSA, SCSC, SHA **RESEARCH** History of reference; early modern France; Calvin and Calvinism, 17th century France. **SELECTED PUBLICATIONS** Auth, Calvinism and the Amyraut Heresu, Univ Wisc, 69; auth, Bibliographia Molinaei: An Alphabetical and Descriptive Bibliography: The Works of Pierre du Moulin, 94. **CONTACT ADDRESS** Dept Hist., Georgia State Univ, Univ Plaza, Athens, GA, 30303-4117. **EMAIL** shisbga@panther.gsu.edu

ARMSTRONG, CHARLES
DISCIPLINE MODERN KOREAN AND EAST ASIAN HISTORY **EDUCATION** Yale Univ, BA, 84, Univ Chicago, PhD, 94. **CAREER** Asst prof. **SELECTED PUBLICATIONS** Auth, Surveillance and Punishment in Post-Liberation North Korea, Positions, East Asia Cult Critique 3:3, 96; A Socialism of Our Style: North Korean Idology in a Post-Communist Era, North Korean Foreign Policy in the Post-Cold War Era, 97. **CONTACT ADDRESS** Dept of Hist, Columbia Col, New York, 2960 Broadway, New York, NY, 10027-6902.

ARMSTRONG, FREDERICK H.
PERSONAL Born 03/27/1926, Toronto, ON, Canada **DISCIPLINE** HISTORY **EDUCATION** Univ Toronto, BA, 49, MA, 51, PhD, 65. **CAREER** Instr, Univ Toronto, 62-63; fac mem,

63-75, prof, 75-89, res prof, 89-91, PROF EMER HISTORY, UNIV WESTERN ONTARIO, 91-. **HONORS AND AWARDS** Univ Western Ont Pres Medal, 79; Am Soc State Local Hist Award Merit, 84. **MEMBERSHIPS** Champlain Soc (coun 74-, vice pres 80-88, pres 88-91); Ont Hist Soc (dir 63-65, 72-80, pres 77-79); Royal Hist Soc. **SELECTED PUBLICATIONS** Auth, Handbook of Upper Canadian Chronology, 67, 2nd ed, 85; auth, Organizing for Preservation, 78; auth, Toronto: The Place of Meeting, 83; auth, The Forest City: An Illustrated History of London, Canada, 86; auth, A City in the Making, 89; coauth, Reflections on London's Past, 75. **CONTACT ADDRESS** Dept of History, Univ of Western Ontario, London, ON, N6A 5C2.

ARMSTRONG, JOE C.W.
PERSONAL Born 01/30/1934, Toronto, ON, Canada **DISCIPLINE** HISTORY/CARTOGRAPHY **EDUCATION** Bishop's Univ, BA, 58. **CAREER** Sr Indust Develop Off, Govt Can, 72-96; Prop, Canadiana Collection, Art & Discovery Maps of Canada, 78-93. **HONORS AND AWARDS** Fel, Royal Geog Soc (UK), 80; fel, Royal Geog Soc (Can), 81; Hon dir, Can Inst Surveyors, 83. **MEMBERSHIPS** Champlain Soc. **SELECTED PUBLICATIONS** Auth, From Sea Unto Sea/Art & Discovery Maps of Canada, 82; auth, Champlain, Eng ed 87, Fr ed 88; auth, Farewell the Peaceful Kingdom: The Seduction and Rape of Canada 1963-1994, 95. **CONTACT ADDRESS** 347 Keewatin Ave, Toronto, ON, M4P 2A4.

ARMSTRONG, PAT
DISCIPLINE CANADIAN STUDIES **EDUCATION** Carleton Univ, PhD. **CAREER** Prof, dir Can Stud, Carleton Univ. **RESEARCH** Transformations in the Canadian social security system; changes in the organization and structure of work. **SELECTED PUBLICATIONS** Co-auth, Wasting Away: Warning Signals for Canadian Health Care, Garamond, 97; Take Care: Warning Signals for the Canadian Health System, Garamond, 94; The Double Ghetto: Canadian Women and Their Segregated Work, McClelland and Stewart, 94; auth, Restructuring Pay Equity for a Restructured Workforce: Canadian Perspectives, Gender Work and Organisations 4, 96; From Caring and Sharing to Greedy and Mean, Language, Culture and Value at the Dawn of the 21st Century, Carleton UP, 96; Unravelling the Safety Net: Transformations in Health Care and Their Impact on Women, Women and Canadian Public Policy, Harcourt Brace, 96; Women and Health: Challenges and Changes, Feminist Issues: Race, Class and Sexuality, Prentice-Hall, 95; Caring and Women's Women's Work, Health and Can Soc, 94; Caring and Women's Work, Health and Can Soc, 94; Gender Relations, The Social World, McGraw-Hill Ryerson, 94. **CONTACT ADDRESS** Carleton Univ, 1125 Colonel By Dr, Ottawa, ON, K1S 5B6.

ARNOLD, BILL T.
PERSONAL Born 09/01/1955, Lancaster, KY, m, 1977, 3 children **DISCIPLINE** OLD TESTAMENT AND ANCIENT NEAR EASTERN STUDIES **EDUCATION** Asbury Col, BA, 77; Asbury Theol Sem, M Div, 80; Hebrew Union Col, PhD, 85. **CAREER** Assoc prof, old testament and bibl lang, Wesley Bibl Sem, 85-89; prof, old testament and bibl lang, Wesley Bible Sem, 89-91; assoc prof, old testament and semitic lang, Ashland Theol Sem, 91-93; prof, old testament and semitic lang, Ashland Theol Sem, 93-95; prof, old testament and semitic lang, Asbury Theol Sem, 95-. **HONORS AND AWARDS** Lykins Found Scholar, 77-78; Magee Christ Educ Found Scholar, 73-79; Intl Hon Soc of Theta Phi, 79; Joseph and Helen Regenstein Found fel, 80-81; S. H. and Helen R. Scheuer grad fel, 82-84; Nat Endow for the Humanities, summer stipend, 88; Eta Beta Rho, Nat Hon Soc of Students of Hebrew Lang and Culture, 92. **MEMBERSHIPS** Amer Oriental Soc; Amer Sch of Orient Res; Inst for Bibl Res; Nat Asn of the Prof of Hebrew; Soc of Bibl Lit; Wesleyan Theol Soc. **RESEARCH** Genesis; History of Israelite religion; Israelite historiography. **SELECTED PUBLICATIONS** Auth, What Has Nebuchadnezzar to do with David? On the Neo-Babylonian Period and Early Israel, Syria-Mesopotamia and the Bible, Sheffield Acad Press, 98; articles, The New Intl Dict of Old Testament Theol and Exegesis, Zondervan Publ House, 97; auth, The Use of Aramaic in the Hebrew Bible: Another Look at Bilingualism in Ezra and Daniel, Jour of Northwest Semitic Lang, 22, 2, 1-16, 96; auth, Luke's Characterizing Use of the Old Testament in the Book of Acts, 300-323, Hist, Lit, and Soc in the Book of Acts, Cambridge Univ Press, 96; auth, Age, Old (the Aged), Daniel, Theology of Manna Vision, Evang Dict of Bibl Theol, Baker Book House, 96; auth, Forms of Prophetic Speech in the Old Testament: A Summary of Claus Westermann's Contributions, Ashland Theol Jour, 27, 30-40, 95; auth, Babylonians, 43-75, Peoples of the Old Testament World, Baker Book House, 94; auth, The Weidner Chronicle and the Idea of History is Israel and Mespotamia, 129-148, Faith, Tradition, and History: Old Testament Historiography in Its Near Eastern Context, Eisenbrauns, 94. **CONTACT ADDRESS** Asbury Theol Sem, 204 N Lexington Ave, Wilmore, KY, 40390-1199. **EMAIL** Bill_Arnold@ats.wilmore.ky.us

ARNOLD, ERIC ANDERSON
PERSONAL Born 12/04/1939, Cleveland, OH, 3 children **DISCIPLINE** MODERN EUROPEAN & FRENCH HISTORY **EDUCATION** Oberlin Col, AB, 61; Columbia Univ, MA, 63, PhD(hist), 69. **CAREER** Lectr Europ hist, Newark England Col, 64-65; instr hist, Ohio State Univ, 65-69; asst prof, 69-80, assoc prof French & Europ Hist, Univ Denver, 80-. **MEMBERSHIPS** AHA; Western Soc Fr Hist; Soc Fr Hist Studies. **RESEARCH** Revolutionary and Napoleonic France. **SELECTED PUBLICATIONS** Auth, Some Observations on the French Opposition to Napoleonic Conscription, 1804-1806, Fr Hist Studies; Administrative Leadership in a Dictatorship: The Position of Joseph Fouche in the Napoleonic Police, 1800-1810, Rocky Mountain Soc Sci J, spring 74; Rouget de Lisle and the Maiseillaise, In: Western Society for French History, Vol 5, spring 78; Fouche, Napoleon and the General Police, Univ Press Am, 79; Some observations on the interdisciplinary teaching of eighteenth century French civilization, Teaching Hist: J Methods, fall 79; articles, in An Historical Dictionary of the French Revolution (in prep), An Historical Dictionary of Napoleonic France (in prep) & An Historical Dictionary of the French Second Empire (in prep), Greenwood Press; ed and trans, A Documentary Sruvey of Napoleonic France, Lanham, Md, 94 and A Documentary Survey of Napoleonic France: Supplement, Lanham, MD, 96. **CONTACT ADDRESS** Dept of History, Univ of Denver, 2199 S University, Denver, CO, 80210-4711. **EMAIL** earnold@du.edu

ARNOLD, JOSEPH L.
DISCIPLINE HISTORY **EDUCATION** OH State Univ, PhD. **CAREER** Prof, Univ MD Balitmore County. **RESEARCH** Am urban hist. **SELECTED PUBLICATIONS** Auth, The New Deal in the Suburbs: A History of the Greenbelt Town Program; Maryland: Old Line to New Prosperity; pubs on flood control and the Army Corps of Engineers. **CONTACT ADDRESS** Dept of Hist, Univ MD Baltimore County, Hilltop Circle, PO Box 1000, Baltimore, MD, 21250. **EMAIL** arnold@umbc7.umbc.edu

ARNOLD, STEVEN H.
DISCIPLINE INTERNATIONAL DEVELOPMENT THEORY **EDUCATION** Occidental Col, BA; John Hopkins Sch Adv Int Studies, MA, PhD. **CAREER** Prof, Am Univ. **HONORS AND AWARDS** Dir, Int Develop Div, dir, Hubert H. Humphrey North-South Fel Prog. **RESEARCH** International Development Theory & Institutions, Development Management, and Development Education. **SELECTED PUBLICATIONS** Auth, Responsibility Without Resources: The Dilemmas of Grassroots Managers, Grassroots Develop, 96; Our Global Vision: Development as Transformation, Educ Global Change, 91. **CONTACT ADDRESS** American Univ, 4400 Massachusetts Ave, Washington, DC, 20016.

ARNOULT, SHARON
PERSONAL Born 05/26/1954, San Antonio, TX, m, 1978 **DISCIPLINE** HISTORY **EDUCATION** Univ Tx Austin, BS, 76, BA, 84, MA, 91, PhD, 97 **CAREER** Instr, 83-90, Austin Comm Col; teaching asst, 87-93, Univ Tx Austin; instr to asst prof, 91-, SW Tx St Univ. **HONORS AND AWARDS** Meadows Fel in Fine Arts, S Methodist Univ, 79-80, 80-81; Dora Bonham Grad Scholar, 85; Sheffield Fund Award for Europ Hist, 91; Jr Fel, Univ Tx Austin, 97. **MEMBERSHIPS** Amer Hist Assoc; Church of England Record Soc; Hist Soc of the Episcopal Church, N Amer Conf on British Stud; Sixteenth Century Stud Conf; Soc for Reformation Res. **RESEARCH** Liturgy & identity in English church; sixteenth & seventeenth centuries; English reformation; women & relig; image of Charles I. **SELECTED PUBLICATIONS** Auth, The Sovereignties of Body and Soul: Women's Political and Religious Actions in the English Civil war, Women and Sovereignty, Edinburgh Univ Press, 91; art, Spiritual and Sacred Publique Actions: The Book of Common Prayer and the Understanding of Worship in the Elizabethan and Jacobean Church of England, Religion and the English People, 1500-1640: New Voices, New Perspectives, Sixteenth Century Stud, 98; rev, Katherine L French's, The Parish in English Life, 1400-1600, Sixteenth Century J, 98. **CONTACT ADDRESS** Dept of History, SW Tx St Univ, San Marcos, TX, 45333. **EMAIL** sa06@swt.edu

ARONOFF, MYRON J.
PERSONAL Born 03/01/1940, Kansas City, MO, m, 1962, 2 children **DISCIPLINE** ANTHROPOLOGY **EDUCATION** Miami Univ, BA, 62; UCLA, MA, 65, PhD, 76; Manchester Univ, PhD, 69. **CAREER** Res fel, Manchester Univ, 65-69; lectr, 70-73, sr lectr, 73-76, assoc prof, 76-77, Tel Aviv Univ; assoc prof, 77-81, prof, 81-90, prof II of political science & anthropology, 90-, Rutgers Univ. **HONORS AND AWARDS** SSRC-UK 1969-71; Ford Found, 72-73; ACLS & SSRC, 82-83; Neth Inst Advan Stud fel, 74-75 & 96-97. **MEMBERSHIPS** Int Union Anthrop & Ethnol (vpres 93-2003); Am Polit Sci Asn; Am Anthrop Asn; Asn Polit & Legal Anthrop (pres 85-87); Asn Israel Stud (pres 85-87). **RESEARCH** Political culture; collective identity-ethnicity & nationalism; literature & politics; politics of espionage; Israeli culture & politics; Israel-Palestinian relations. **SELECTED PUBLICATIONS** Auth, Power and Ritual in the Israel Labor Party, M E Sharpe, 93; coauth, Explaining Domestic Influences on Current Israeli Foreign Policy: The Peace Negotiations, The Brown Jour World Affairs, 96; The Peace Process and Competing Challenges to the Dominant Zionist Discourse, The Middle East Peace Process, SUNY Press, 98; Domestic Determinants of Israeli Foreign Policy: The Peace Process from the Declaration of Principles to the Oslo II Interim Agreement, The Middle East and the Peace Process: The Impact of the Oslo Accords, Univ Press Fla, 98; auth The Spy Novels of John le Carre: Balancing Ethics and Politics, St Martins, 99. **CONTACT ADDRESS** Political Studies Dept, Rutgers Univ, Hickman Hall-Douglas Campus, PO Box 270, New Brunswick, NJ, 08903-0270. **EMAIL** maronoff@rci.rutgers.edu

ARONSON, ELLIOT
PERSONAL Born 01/09/1932, Revere, MA, m, 1954, 4 children **DISCIPLINE** SOCIAL PSYCHOLOGY **EDUCATION** Brandeis Univ, BA 54; Wesleyan Univ, MA 56; Stanford Univ, PhD 59. **CAREER** Harvard Univ, asst prof, 59-62; Univ Minnesota, prof, 62-66; Univ Texas Austin, prof, 66-74; Univ Cal Santa Cruz, prof, 74-. **HONORS AND AWARDS** AAAS Dist Res Awd; APA Dist Res Awd; SESP Dist Res Awd; 3 Dist Teaching Awd, APA, UCSC most Fav Teacher, U of T; Donald Campbell Awd; Prof of the Year CASE; Guggenheim Fel; Gordon Allport Prize; Dist Sci-Lect APA; Dist Sci Career Awd; Bernhard Dist Vis Prof Williams Coll **MEMBERSHIPS** APA; APS; SPSSI; SESP; AAAS Fel. **RESEARCH** Social influence; prejudice reduction; cognitive dissonance. **SELECTED PUBLICATIONS** Auth, Cooperation in the Classroom: The Jigsaw Method, coauth, NY, Longman, 97; Social Psychology: The Heart and the Mind, coauth, NY, Harper Collins 94, 2nd ed, Longman 97, 3rd ed forthcoming, 99; Social Psychology: Vol 1,2,3, coauth, London, Elgar Ltd, 93; Age of Propaganda, coauth, NY, W H Freeman & Co, 92; Dissonance Hypocrisy and the Self Concept, in: Cognitive Dissonance Theory: Revival Revisions and Controversies, by E. Harmon-Jones and J. Mills, Wash DC, Amer Psych Assoc, 98 in press; The experimental method in social psychology, coauth, in: The Handbook of Social Psychology, eds, G. Lindzey D. Gilbert and S. Fiske, NY Random House, 98; The giving away of psychology--and condoms, APS Observer, 97; When Exemplification Fails: Hypocrisy and the motive for self-integrity, coauth, JPSP, 97; The theory of cognitive dissonance: The evolution and vicissitudes of an idea, in: The Message of Social Psychology, eds, C. McCarty and S. A. Haslam, London, Blackwell, 97; On Baseball and Failure, Dialogue, 95. **CONTACT ADDRESS** Dept of Psychology, Univ of California, Santa Cruz, 136 Tree Frog Lane, Santa Cruz, CA, 95060. **EMAIL** elliot@cats.ucsc.edu

ARONSON, JAY RICHARD
PERSONAL Born 08/26/1937, New York, NY, m, 1959, 3 children **DISCIPLINE** ECONOMICS **EDUCATION** Clark Univ, AB, 59, PhD, 64; Stanford Univ, MA, 61. **CAREER** Asst prof, Worcester Polytech Inst, 61-65; asst prof to assoc prof Economics, 65-73, prof Economics, 73-84, Master of Taylor Residential Col, 84-88, DIR MARTINDALE CTR STUDY PVT ENTERPRISE & WILLIAM L CLAYTON PROF BUS & ECON, LEHIGH UNIV, 80-; Rockefeller fel, Stanford Univ, 59-61; hon fel, 62, vis lectr Clark Univ, 64-66; vis scholar, 73, Fulbright scholar, 78 & 96, vis scholar, 91, HON PROF, DEPT ECONOMICS, 96-99, Univ York. **HONORS AND AWARDS** Lindback Award, 68, Stabler Award, 74, Deming Lewis Award, 84, Hillman Serv Award, 86, Lehigh Univ. **MEMBERSHIPS** Int Bus Asn; Asn Can Studies US; Fulbright Alumni Asn; Public Choice Soc; Royal Econ Soc; Nat Tax Asn; Am Fin Asn; Am Econ Asn. **SELECTED PUBLICATIONS** coauth "Inequality Decomposition Analysis and the Gini Coefficient Revisited," Econ Jour, 93; "Redistributial Effect and Unequal Income Tax Treatment," Econ Jour, 94; "Decomposing the Gini Coefficient to Reveal Vertical, Horizontal and Reranking Effects of Income Taxation," Nat Tax Jour, 94; Non equivalence in a Ferderalism: Dual Tax Shares, Flypaper Effects and Leviathan, Public Choice, 96; ed Management Policies in Local Government Finance, ICMA, Wash, 96. **CONTACT ADDRESS** Dept of Economics, Lehigh Univ, Bethlehem, PA, 18015. **EMAIL** JRA1@lehigh.edu

ARONSON, JONATHAN
DISCIPLINE INTERNATIONAL RELATIONS **EDUCATION** Stanford Univ, PhD. **CAREER** Prof, Univ of Southern CA. **RESEARCH** International intellectual property protection; how the globalization of telecommunications networks is transforming international financial activities. **SELECTED PUBLICATIONS** Auth, Money and Power: Banks and the World Monetary System, Sage, 77; Debt and the Less Developed Countries, Westview, 79 & Trade in Services: Case for Open Markets, Amer Enterprises Inst, 84; coauth, Trade Talks: America Better Listen, Coun For Rel(s), 85; When Countries Talk: Trade in Telecommunication Services, Ballinger, 88; Changing Networks: Mexico's Telecommunications Options, UCSD, 89 & Managing the World Economy: The Consequences of Corporate Alliances, Coun For Rel(s), 93. **CONTACT ADDRESS** Annenberg School for Commun, Univ of Southern California, University Park Campus, Los Angeles, CA, 90089. **EMAIL** admitusc@usc.edu

ARRINGTON, PAMELA GRAY
PERSONAL Born 02/28/1953, Montgomery, AL, m **DISCIPLINE** PSYCHOLOGY **EDUCATION** Spelman Coll, BA 1974; The Univ of MI, MA 1975; George Mason Univ, DA 1987, PhD, 1993. **CAREER** Talladega Coll, counselor 1976-

77; Northern VA Comm Coll, counselor 1977-80, coord of affirmative action & grants develop 1980-88; BOWIE STATE UNIV, HUMAN RESOURCE DEVEL, PROF 1988-. **HONORS AND AWARDS** Honor Scholarship Spelman Coll 1972-74; Psi Chi Spelman College 1974; Graduate Scholarship Univ of MI 1-74-75; Pi Lambda Theta 1975; Leaders for the 80's FIPSE/Maricopa Colleges 1983; Phi Delta Kappa 1983; Grad Rsch Asst & Scholarship George Mason Univ 1984-86; Faculty Fellow, Dept of Defense, Office of the Secretary of Defense, Civilian Personnel Policy, 1989-91. **MEMBERSHIPS** Mem ASTD, OD; HRD Professors Network, Washington Metro Area; American Assn of Univ Prof; dir, Natl Retention Project, Amer Assn of State Colleges and Universities, 1993-; Alpha Kappa Alpha Sorority. **CONTACT ADDRESS** Human Resource Devt, Bowie State Univ, Dept of Behavioral Sciences & Human Services.

ARSENAULT, JOSEPH G.
PERSONAL Born 04/19/1952, Abram's Village, PE, Canada **DISCIPLINE** HISTORY CONSULTANT **EDUCATION** Univ Moncton, BSocSci, 74; Univ Laval, MA, 79. **CAREER** Cult animateur, Soc Saint-Thomas d'Aquin, 77-79; coordr, Acad Hist Cult Proj, 79-82; vis prof, Acadian stud, Univ PEI, 82-86; HOST, BONJOUR ATLANTIQUE, RADIO-CANADA, 86-; CONSULTANT, ACADIAN HIST. **HONORS AND AWARDS** Prix France-Acadie; Prix Champlain. **MEMBERSHIPS** L'Ordre des francophones d'Amerique; Ordre de la Pleiade; PEI Acadian Hist Soc (pres, 82-84); PEI Mus Heritage Found (bd mem, 80-86); Acadian Mus (bd mem, 81-85). **RESEARCH** Acadian history and folklore studies. **SELECTED PUBLICATIONS** Auth, Complaintes acadiennes de l'Ile-du-Prince-Edouard, 80; auth, Courir la Chandeleur, 82; auth, Les Acadiens de l'Ile 1720-1980, 87; auth, Par un dimanche au soir, 93. **CONTACT ADDRESS** PO Box 2230, Charlottetown, PE, C1A 8B9.

ARTHUR, ALAN
DISCIPLINE HISTORY OF MEDIEVAL AND REFORMATION EUROPE **EDUCATION** Alberta Univ, BA; Univ Toronto, MA; Emory Univ, PhD. **CAREER** Assoc prof. **RESEARCH** Early modern France. **SELECTED PUBLICATIONS** Auth, Popular Religion in France, Encycl of the Reformation, Oxford UP, 95. **CONTACT ADDRESS** Dept of Hist, Brock Univ, 500 Glenridge Ave, St Catharines, ON, L2S 3A1. **EMAIL** aarthur@spartan.ac.BrockU.CA

ARTIBISE, ALAN F.J.
PERSONAL Born 01/23/1946, Dauphin, MB, Canada **DISCIPLINE** URBAN/SOCIAL HISTORY **EDUCATION** Univ Man, BA, 67; Univ BC, PhD, 72. **CAREER** Lectr, hist & Can stud, Cariboo Col(Kamloops), 71, chmn soc sci & coordr Can stud prog, 73-75; head, W Can sect hist div, Can Mus Civilization, 75-76; fac mem to prof hist, Univ Victoria, 76-82; prof hist & dir, Inst Urban Stud, Univ Winnipeg, 83-88; sch dir, 88-93, PROF COMMUNITY & REGIONAL PLANNING, UNIV BC, 88-. **HONORS AND AWARDS** Man Hist Soc Medal; Award Merit Can Hist Asn; Award Merit Am Asn State & Local Hist; Award Merit Asn Can Stud USA; Excellence Planning Award, Planning Inst BC; Media Club Can Award; Marie Tremaine Medal Bibliog Soc Can. **MEMBERSHIPS** Asn Can Stud (pres, 82-86); Pacific Rim Coun Urban Develop; Can Reg Sci Asn; Can Hist Asn; Can Fedn Hum. **SELECTED PUBLICATIONS** Auth, Winnipeg: A Social History of Urban Growth, 75; auth, Winnipeg: An Illustrated History, 77; auth, The Canadian City: Essays in Social and Urban History, 77, 2nd ed, 84; auth, Western Canada Since 1870: A Bibliography and Guide, 78; auth, The Usable Urban Past, 79; auth, Town and City: Aspects of Western Canadian Urban Development, 81; auth, Canada's Urban Past: A Bibliography and Guide to Urban Studies, 81; auth, Shaping the Canadian Urban Landscape, 82; auth, Power and Place: Canadian Urban Development in the North American Context, 86; auth, Canadian Regional Development: The Urban Dimension, 89; auth, The Pacific Fraser Region: Towards 2010, 91; ed-in-chief, Urban Hist Rev/Revue d'histoire urbaine, 75-88; assoc ed, Prairie Forum; assoc ed, America: Hist & Life; assoc ed, Urban Affairs Quart; assoc ed, Public Works Mgt & Policy; assoc ed, Can J Urban Res; assoc ed, J Urban Affairs; gen ed, Hist Can Cities series. **CONTACT ADDRESS** Sch Comm & Reg Planning, Univ of British Columbia, 6333 Memorial Rd, Vancouver, BC, V6T 1Z2.

ASANTE, MOLEFI KETE
PERSONAL Born 08/14/1942, Valdosta, GA, m **DISCIPLINE** AFRICAN-AMERICAN STUDIES **EDUCATION** Southwestern Christian Coll, AA 1962; Oklahoma Christian Coll, BA 1964; Pepperdine Univ, MA 1965; UCLA, PhD 1968. **CAREER** CA State Polytechnic Coll, instr 1967; CA State Univ Northridge, instr 1968; Purdue Univ, asst prof 1968-69; Pepperdine Univ, visit prof 1969; Univ of CA LA, asst prof 1969-71; CA State Univ, visit prof 1971; Univ of CA LA, dir Center for Afro-Amer Studies 1970-73, assoc prof speech 1971-73; FL State Univ Tallahassee, visit assoc prof 1972; State Univ of NY Buffalo, prof communication dept; Center for Positive Thought Buffalo, curator; Univ of Ibadan, Univ of Nairobi, external examiner 1976-80; Zimbabwe Inst of Mass Communications, fulbright prof; Howard Univ, visiting prof 1979-80; Temple Univ Dept of African-American Studies, prof, currently. **MEMBERSHIPS** Spec in Black Rhetoric County Probation Dept LA 1969-; mem Intl Soc for Gen Semantics; Intl Assn for Symbolic Analysis; Intl Comm Assn; Western Speech Assn; Central State Speech Assn; So Speech Assn; Natl Assn for Dramatic & Speech Arts; ed bds Nigerian Journal of Political Economy, Afrodiaspora, Afrique Histoire, Africa and the World, Urban African Quarterly, Journal of African Civilization; contributing writer for Buffalo Challenger, Philadelphia New Observer, Philadelphia Tribune; UNESCO reviewer for scholarly books 1985; consultant Zimbabwe Ministry of Information and Telecommunications; Intl Scientific Comm of FESPAC 1986-87 Senegal; chairperson, IMHOTEP 1987-; president, Natl Council for Black Studies, 1988-; vice president, African Heritage Studies Assn 1989-. **SELECTED PUBLICATIONS** Author of 40 books; consulting editor for books; bd editors Black Man in Am; editorial assoc "The Speech Teacher"; editor "Journal of Black Studies"; auth, The Afrocentric Idea 1987; Afrocentricity, 1987; Kemet, Afrocentricity and Knowledge, 1990; Historical and Cultural Atlas of African-Americans, 1991; African American History: A Journey of Liberation, 1995; Love Dance, 1996; African Intellectual Heritage, 1996; African American Names, 1998. **CONTACT ADDRESS** Dept African-Am Studies, Temple Univ, Gladfelter Hall 025-26, Philadelphia, PA, 19122.

ASH, STEPHEN V.
DISCIPLINE HISTORY **EDUCATION** Tennessee Univ, PhD. **CAREER** Assoc prof. **RESEARCH** Civil War. **SELECTED PUBLICATIONS** Auth, When the Yankees Came: Conflict and Chaos in the Occupied South, 1861-1865, Univ NC; Middle Tennessee Society Transformed, 1860-1870: War and Peace in the Upper South, LA State Univ. **CONTACT ADDRESS** Dept of History, Knoxville, TN, 37996.

ASHANIN, CHARLES B.
PERSONAL Born 11/15/1920, Montenegro, Yugoslavia, m, 1953, 4 children **DISCIPLINE** RELIGION HISTORY **EDUCATION** Church Col, Yugoslavia, AB, 43; Univ Glasgow, BD, 52, PhD, 55. **CAREER** Asst prof relig, Univ Col Ghana, 55-60; from assoc prof to prof relig & philos, Allen Univ, 60-65; prof, Claflin Univ, 65-67; assoc prof early church hist, 67-76, PROF EARLY CHURCH HIST, CHRISTIAN THEOL SEM, 76-; Guest scholar, Princeton Theol Sem, 57; vis scholar & Lilly fel, Harvard Divinity Sch, 64-65; assoc ed, The Logas, 68-; fel, Woodbrooke Col, Eng, 73-74; mem, Patristic Cong Am Acad Relig. **MEMBERSHIPS** Am Soc Church Hist; Orthodox Theol Soc Am. **RESEARCH** Roman Empire and Christian Church in the IV century; history of Christian humanism from the beginning until AD 1536; philosophy of religion; religion and culture; Emperor Constantine and his age. **SELECTED PUBLICATIONS** Auth, Cultural and Existential Aspects of Religious Language, J Relig Thought, 65-66; Ethics of Eastern Orthodox Church, In: Dictionary of Christian Ethics, Westminster, 67; The Church Historian in Dialogue, Encounter, winter 68; The Black Heroes of the Philadelphia Plague in 1793, In: Religion in Pluralistic Society, E J Brill, Leiden, 76; Theology of Liberation: European Frontier, Encounter, winter 77; Backgrounds of Early Christianity, with E. Ferguson, Church History, Vol 64, 95. **CONTACT ADDRESS** Christian Theol Sem, 1000 W 42nd St, Indianapolis, IN, 46208.

ASHBY, LEROY
DISCIPLINE TWENTIETH CENTURY AMERICAN HISTORY **EDUCATION** Univ Md, PhD, 66. **CAREER** Prof, Washington State Univ. **HONORS AND AWARDS** WSU President's Fac Excellence Award in Instruction, 83; CASE prof of the Yr for the State of Wash, 90 & 93. **SELECTED PUBLICATIONS** Auth, The Spearless Leader: Senator Borah and the Progressive Movement in the 1920's, Univ Ill Press, 72; Saving the Waifs: Reformers and Dependent Children, Temple UP, 84; William Jennings Bryan: Champion of Democracy, Twayne, 87; Fighting the Odds: The Life of Senator Frank Church, WSU Press, 94 & Endangered Children: Dependency, Neglect and Abuse in American History, Twayne, 97. **CONTACT ADDRESS** Dept of History, Washington State Univ, 301 Wilson Hall, PO Box 644030, Pullman, WA, 99164-4030. **EMAIL** ashby@wsu.edu

ASHER, ROBERT
PERSONAL Born 10/01/1944, New York, NY, m, 1968, 1 child **DISCIPLINE** LABOR & SOCIAL HISTORY **EDUCATION** City Col New York, BA, 66; Harvard Univ, AM, 67; Univ MN, PhD(hist), 71. **CAREER** Asst prof, 71-77, ASSOC PROF HIST, UNIV CT, 77-. **MEMBERSHIPS** Orgn Am Historians; Labor Historians. **RESEARCH** Industrial accidents and workmen's compensation; workers and technological change. **SELECTED PUBLICATIONS** Auth, German Workers in Industrial Chicago, 1850-1910--A Comparative Perspective, with H Keil and J. B. Jentz, Labor Hist, vol 34, 93; Urban Revolt--Ethnic Politics in the 19th-Century Chicago Labor-Movement, with E. L. Hirsch, Labor Hist, vol 34, 93; Behind the Wheel at Chrysler--The Iacocca Legacy, with D. P. Levin, MI Hist Rev, vol 22, 96; Race and Labor in Western Copper--The Fight for Equality, 1896-1918, P. J. Mellinger, J of Am Hist, vol 83, 96. **CONTACT ADDRESS** Dept Hist, Univ CT, Storrs, CT, 06268.

ASHLEY, SUSAN A.
PERSONAL Born 09/27/1943, Portland, OR, m, 1967, 2 children **DISCIPLINE** MODERN EUROPEAN HISTORY **EDUCATION** Carleton Col, BA, summa cum laude, 65; Columbia Univ, MA, 67, PhD, Columbia Univ, 73; Europ Inst, cert, 73. **CAREER** Instr, Hist, 70-73; vist asst Prof, Denver Univ, Grad School of Intl Studies, 73; asst prof hist, CO Col, 73-79, assoc prof hist, CO Col, 79-86; Academic Director, Assoc Col of the Midwest Florence and London-Florence Progs, Florence Italy, 84-85, Visiting Prof, 91-92; Ch, Hist dept, CO Col, 88-97; Prof of Hist, CO Col, 86-; Carlton Prof of the Soc Sci, CO Col, 94-97. **HONORS AND AWARDS** Phi Beta Kappa; Best Unpubl Manuscript Award, Society for Italian Hist Studies, 73; Carlton Prof Soc Sci, 94-97; School Dist Exemplary Award, 93, 95, 97; Award of Merit, Western Society for French Hist, 90; Mellon Faculty Develop Grants, CO Col, 79, 81, 83, 84, 87, 98; Research Grant, CO Col, 71, 79, 88, 90, 97; Ford For Area Fellow, 68-71; President's Fellow, CO Univ, 66-67; Woodrow Wilson Fellow, 65-66. **MEMBERSHIPS** AHA; FHS; SIHS; CONGRIP; Soc Ital Hist Studies; Pres, Western Society for French Hist, 97-98; Vice Pres and Pres Elect, Western Society for French Hist, 96-97; Governing Council and Sect, Western Society for french Hist, 86-96. **RESEARCH** Late 19th-20th century parliamentary politics in France and Italy. **SELECTED PUBLICATIONS** Auth, The Parliamentary Politics of the French Right, Proc Soc Fr Hist, fall 74; The Failure of Gambetta's Grand Ministere, Fr Hist Studies, spring 75; Ministries and Majorities: France, 1879-1902, Proceedings of the Western Society for French Hist, IX, 82; End of the Century Crises, Proceedings of the Western Society for French Hist, X, 83; The Radical Left in Parliament, 1879-1902, IX, 84; Allain-Targe, Brisson, Dupuy, Casimir-Perier, Scheurer-Kestner, Deputies of the Third Republic, Dict of the Third Republic, Greenwood Press, 85. **CONTACT ADDRESS** Dept Hist, Colorado Col, 14 E Cache La Poudre, Colorado Springs, CO, 80903-3294. **EMAIL** sashley@ColoradoCollege.edu

ASMIS, ELIZABETH
DISCIPLINE CLASSICS **EDUCATION** Univ Toronto, BA, 62; Yale Univ, MA, 66, PhD, 70. **CAREER** Lectr, McGill Univ, 63-65; res asst, British Museum, 66-68; asst prof, Cornell Univ, 70-79; Assoc prof, Univ Chicago, 79-94; Prof, Univ Chicago, 94-. **HONORS AND AWARDS** Woodrow Wilson Fel; Phi Beta Kappa Fel; NEH Fel., Ed, Clas Philol. **SELECTED PUBLICATIONS** Auth, Epicurus' Scientific Method, Cornell Univ Press, 84; auth, Asclepiades Rediscovered?, Class Philol, 93; auth, Philodemus on Censorship, Moral Utility, and Formalism in Poetry, Philodemus and Poetry: Poetic THeory and Practice in Lucretius, Philodemus and Horace, 95; auth, Epicurean Semiotics, Knowledge Through Signs, Ancient Semiotic Theoris and Practices, 95; The Stoics on Women, Ancient Philos and Feminism, 96. **CONTACT ADDRESS** Dept of Classics, Univ Chicago, 1050 E 59th St, Chicago, IL, 60637. **EMAIL** e-asmis@uchicago.edu

ASSELIN, OLIVIER
DISCIPLINE MODERN AND CONTEMPORARY ART **EDUCATION** Univ de Montreal, Univ de Paris VIII, doctorate, 86; McGill Univ, PhD, 86-90. **CAREER** Dept Art Hist, Concordia Univ **RESEARCH** Canadian contemporary art and in XVIIIth-century aesthetics and art theory. **SELECTED PUBLICATIONS** Pub(s), articles and rev(s), periodicals (Parachute, Protee, Trois, La recherche photographique, 24 images, Jeu; co-ed, Fictions supremes. La question du site dans l'esthetique de Diderot; De la curiosite. Petite anatomie d'un regard; auth, L'art philosophique, Definitions de la culture visuelle III, Proc of the conf Art et philos, Montreal, Musee d'art contemporain, 98; The Sublime: the Limits of Vision and the Inflation of Commentary, Theory Rules: Art as Theory ¤ Theory and Art, Toronto, YYZ Bk(s), Univ Toronto Press, 96. **CONTACT ADDRESS** Dept Art Hist, Concordia Univ, Montreal, 1455 de Maisonneuve W, Montreal, PQ, H3G 1M8.

ASTER, SIDNEY
PERSONAL Born 05/24/1942, Montreal, PQ, Canada **DISCIPLINE** HISTORY **EDUCATION** McGill Univ, BA, 63, MA, 65; London Sch Econ, Univ London, PhD, 69. **CAREER** Lectr, Univ Glasgow, 69-70; prin res asst to Sir Martin Gilbert, Winston Churchill Official Biogr, 69-70; prin res asst to former Romanian min, V.V. Tilea, 70-73; prin res asst to Baron Salter of Kidlington, 72-75; vis assoc prof, Concordia Univ, 75; asst prof, 76-80, assoc prof, 80-91, PROF HISTORY, UNIV TORONTO, 91-, acting assoc dean hum, 96-97. **HONORS AND AWARDS** Lt Gov Gold Medal Hist (Que), 63; Que govt fels, 64-68; Leverhulme Trust fel, 73; Twenty-Seven Fedn Award, 76. **SELECTED PUBLICATIONS** Auth, 1939: The Making of the Second World War, 73; auth, Les Origines de la Seconde Guerre Mondiale, 74; auth, Anthony Eden, 76; auth, British Foreign Policy 1918-1945: A Guide TO Research Materials, 91; ed, A.P. Young, The 'X' Documents, The Secret History of Foreign Office Contacts with the German Resistance 1937-1939, 74; ed, The Second World War as a National Experience, 81; ed, A.P. Young, Die X-Dokumente: Die geheimen Kontakte Carl Goerdelers mit der britischen Regierung, 1938/1939, 89. **CONTACT ADDRESS** Erindale Col, Univ of Toronto, Mississauga, ON, L5L 1C6. **EMAIL** saster@credit.erin.utoronto.ca

ASTOUR, MICHAEL CZERNICHOW
PERSONAL Born 12/17/1916, Kharkov, Russia, m, 1952 **DISCIPLINE** ANCIENT HISTORY, SEMITIC STUDIES **EDUCATION** Univ Paris, Lic es Lett, 37; Brandeis Univ, PhD(Mediter studies), 62. **CAREER** Asst prof Europ lang, Brandeis Univ, 60-65, Mediter studies, 63-65; assoc prof, 65-69, PROF ANCIENT HIST, SOUTHERN IL UNIV, EDWARDSVILLE, 69-, Vis prof, Univ NC, Chapel Hill, 69-70; Am Philos Soc grant, 72; assoc fel, Am Res Inst, Turkey, 72. **MEMBERSHIPS** Corresp mem Inst Antiq & Christianity; Am Name Soc; AHA; Am Orient Soc; Soc Bibl Lit. **RESEARCH** History, geography and civilization of the ancient Near East; western Semitic lit and mythology; Greco-Semitic connections. **SELECTED PUBLICATIONS** Auth, Place Names, In: Ras Shamra Parallels, vol 2, Pont Bibl Inst, Rome, 75; Continuite et changement dans la toponymie de la Syrie du Nord, In: La Toponymie Antique, Univ Strasbourg & E J Brill, Leiden, 77; Tall-Al-Hamidya, vol 2, with S. Eichler and M. Wafler, and D. Warburton, J of the Am Oriental Soc, vol 113, 93; The Hurrians, with G. Wilhelm, J of Near Eastern Studies, vol 53, 94; The Cities of Seleukid Syria, with J. D. Granger, J of the Am Oriental Soc, vol 114, 94; Place-Names from the Elba Tablets (Italian), with A. Archi, P. Piacentini, and F. Pomponio, J of the Am Oriental Soc, vol 117, 97. **CONTACT ADDRESS** Dept of Hist Studies, Southern IL Univ, Edwardsville, IL, 62026.

ATHANASSAKIS, APOSTOLOS N.
DISCIPLINE CLASSICAL LINGUISTICS, GREEK POETRY **EDUCATION** Univ Pa, PhD, 65. **CAREER** PROF, CLASS LING, UNIV CALIF, SANTA BARBARA. **SELECTED PUBLICATIONS** Transl, introd, text, Via Sancti Pachomii, Scholars' Press, 75; Transl, introd, comment, The Homeric Hymns, Johns Hopkins Univ Press, 76; Transl, text, The Orphic Hymns, Scholar's Press, 77; Transl, introd, Hesiod: Theogony, Works and Days, Shield, Johns Hopkins Univ Press, 88; ed, Essays on Hesiod, Vol I, Ramus 21, 92; Essays on Hesiod, Vol II, Ramus 21, 93. **CONTACT ADDRESS** Dept of Classics, Univ Calif, Santa Barbara, CA, 93106-7150. **EMAIL** gmangold@humanitas.ucsb.edu

ATKESON, E.B.
PERSONAL Born 12/06/1929, Newport News, VA, m, 1954 **DISCIPLINE** MILITARY STRATEGY **EDUCATION** US Military Acad, BS 51; Syracuse Univ, MEA 64; US Army Comm Gen Staff College, 63; US Army War College, 69. **CAREER** US Army 51-84; Harvard Univ Cen Intl Affs, Fell 73-74; US Army War College, Dep Comm 75-76; US Army Europe, Dep Ch of Staff Intell, 78-80; Nat Intell coun, mem 82-84. **HONORS AND AWARDS** Beta Gamma Sigma Sch Awd; Us Army Dist Ser Medal; CIA Dist Ser Medal; many other Milt Awds. **MEMBERSHIPS** IISS; ACUS; ASSOC US ARMY; ASSOC FORMER INTELL OFFICERS. **RESEARCH** Foreign Military forces and strategy **SELECTED PUBLICATIONS** Auth, The Final Argument of Kings: Reflections on the Art of War, Hero Books 88; The Powder Keg: An Intelligence Officers Guide to Military Forces in the Middle East 1996-2000, Nova Pub, 96, over 100 articles in journals and newspapers. **CONTACT ADDRESS** 202 Vassar Place, Alexandria, VA, 22314. **EMAIL** atkeson@ ix.netcom.com

ATKIN, MURIEL ANN
PERSONAL New York, NY **DISCIPLINE** RUSSIAN & IRANIAN HISTORY **EDUCATION** Sarah Lawrence Col, BA, 67; Yale Univ, MPhil, 71, PhD(hist), 76. **CAREER** Asst prof, Univ TX, San Antonio, 76-80; ASST PROF HIST, GEORGE WASHINGTON UNIV, 80-. **MEMBERSHIPS** Am Asn Advan Slavic Studies; Middle East Studies Asn; Soc Iranian Studies. **RESEARCH** Russo-Iranian relations; Russia's empire; Russian Moslems. **SELECTED PUBLICATIONS** Auth, The Strange Death of Ibrahim Khalil Khan of Qarabagh, Iranian Studies, 79; The Pragmatic Diplomacy of Paul I: Russia's Relations with Asia, 1796-1801, Slavic Rev, 3/79; Russia and Iran 1780-1828, Univ MN Press, 80; The Kremlin and Khomeini, Wash Quart, spring 81; Land-Use and Management in the Upland Demesne of the Delancy-Estate of Blackburnshire c. 1300, Agricultural Hist Rev, vol 42, 94. **CONTACT ADDRESS** Hist Dept, George Washington Univ, 2035 H St N W, Washington, DC, 20052-0001.

ATKINS, E. TAYLOR
PERSONAL Born 05/04/1967, Murray, KY, m, 1991, 1 child **DISCIPLINE** HISTORY **EDUCATION** Univ AR, Fayetteville, BA, 89; Univ IL, Urbana-Champaign, AM, 92, PhD, 97. **CAREER** Vis asst prof of Hist, Univ IA, spring 97; univ affiliate prof, Univ AR, summer 97; ASST PROF, NORTHERN IL UNIV, 97-. **HONORS AND AWARDS** Andrew W. Mellon fel in the Humanities, 90-96; Fulbright fel, 93-95; Northeast Asia Council res grant, 98. **MEMBERSHIPS** Asn Asian Studies; Soc for Ethnomusicology. **RESEARCH** Modern Japanese hist; popular culture; jazz. **SELECTED PUBLICATIONS** Auth, Nipponism in Japanese Painting, 1937-45, The Wittenberg Rev 1.1, 90; The War on Jazz, or Jazz Goes to War: Toward a New Cultural Order in Wartime Japan, positions: east asia cultures critique 6.2, fall 98; Jammin' on the Jazz Frontier: The Japanese Jazz Community in Interwar Shanghai, Japanese Studies 19.1, forthcoming May 99; Can Japanese Sing the Blues? Japanese Jazz and the Problem of Authenticity, Japan Pop: Inside the World of Japanese Popular Culture, ed Tim Craig, forthcoming; entries for Baker's Biographical Dictionary of Jazz, ed Lewis Porter, Schirmer Books, forthcoming Sept 99. **CONTACT ADDRESS** Dept of Hist, No Illinois Univ, Dekalb, IL, 60115. **EMAIL** etatkins@niu.edu

ATKINS, ROBERT
DISCIPLINE HISTORY **EDUCATION** Univ Ca, BS, MA, PhD. **CAREER** Assoc prof. **RESEARCH** Philosophy; social change theory and practice; public policy; organizational management; law; environmental issues; therapeutic intervention with children; gender studies; racism in American culture. **SELECTED PUBLICATIONS** Auth, pubs on philosophical and legal issues; political commentary and production of children's radio programming; political-jurisprudential analyses of Supreme Court opinions. **CONTACT ADDRESS** Union Inst, 440 E McMillan St., Cincinnati, OH, 45206-1925.

ATKINS, STEPHEN E.
PERSONAL Born 01/29/1941, Columbia, MO, m, 1966, 2 children **DISCIPLINE** POLITICAL SCIENCE, LIBRARY SCIENCE **EDUCATION** Univ Missouri, Columbia, BA, 63, MA, 64; Univ Iowa, PhD, 76, MA, 83. **CAREER** Monograph cataloger, Library, Univ Iowa, 74-89; polit sci subject specialist, Library, Univ Ill, Urbana-Champaign, 83-89; head, collection dev, 89-97, Asst Univ Librn, 97- Texas A & M Univ. **HONORS AND AWARDS** Phi Eta Sigma; Peace Award, ALA, 92; **MEMBERSHIPS** ALA; ACRL; LAMA. **RESEARCH** International security issues; arms control and disarmament; terrorism; atomic energy; academic library history. **SELECTED PUBLICATIONS** Auth, The Academic Library in the American University, ALA, 91; auth, Terrorism: A Reference Handbook, ABC-CLIO, 92; auth, A Historical Encyclopedia of Atomic Energy, Greenwood, 99. **CONTACT ADDRESS** 716 Royal Adelaide Dr, College Station, TX, 77845. **EMAIL** s-atkins@tamu.edu

ATLAS, JOHN WESLEY
PERSONAL Born 08/15/1941, Lake Providence, LA, m **DISCIPLINE** EDUCATION **EDUCATION** Grambling Coll, BS 1963; Wayne State Univ, MEd 1968, EdD 1972. **CAREER** LA Schools, music teacher 1963-65; Detroit Public Schools, music teacher 1965-67, guidance counselor 1967-70, asst prin 1970-72; Gov State Univ, prof 1972-73; Oakland Univ, assoc prof 1973-. **MEMBERSHIPS** Mem Amer Personnel & Guidance Assn; mem Assn for Non-White Concerns in Personnel & Guidance; mem Omega Psi Phi Frat; Topical Conf on Career Educ for Handicapped Indiv 1979. **SELECTED PUBLICATIONS** "Consulting, Affecting Change for Minority Students" Jour of Non-White Concerns in Pers & Guidance Wash, DC 1975; publ "Effects of Crystal & Bolles on Vocational Choice" Jour of Emp Counsel Wash, DC 1977; publ "Career Planning Need of Unemployed Minority Persons" Jour of Emp Counseling Wash, DC 1978; book chap "The Role of Counseling & Guidance in Facilitating Career Educ Needs of Handicapped". **CONTACT ADDRESS** Sch of Human & Educ Serv, Oakland Univ, Rochester, MI, 48309.

ATTREED, LORRAINE C.
DISCIPLINE HISTORY **EDUCATION** Univ NMex, Albuquerque, BA, 76; Univ York, Eng, MA, 80; Harvard Univ, AM, 81, PhD, 84. **CAREER** Assoc prof, 92- & asst prof, 86-92, Holy Cross Col; lectr, 84-85 & tchg fel/tchg asst, 81-86, Harvard Univ; freelance consult on acquisition of rare manuscripts, private NY collectors, 81-87. **HONORS AND AWARDS** Fac fel, 97; Hewlett-Mellon grant, 96; res and publ grant, Rome, Italy; elected fel, Royal Hist Soc Eng, 95; 8 res and publ grants, Holy Cross Col, 87-93; Nat Endowment for the Humanities Travel to Collections grant, 92; Batchelor Ford Summer fac fel, Holy Cross Col, 88; American Bar Foundation and National Endowment for the Humanities fel, 86; Krupp Found fel, 82; Sheldon Memorial Trust awd, Univ York, 79; Marshall Scholar to Univ York, 77, 2 yrs; Phi Beta Kappa, Univ NMex chap, 76 & Phi Alpha Theta, honor soc hist, 75. **MEMBERSHIPS** Elected gen sec, New Eng Medieval Conf, 97-98, 5 year term; mem, plan comt and session ch for conf Pages Past and Present: Commun Arts from the Middle Ages to the Internet, Higgins Armory Mus, Worcester, 98; mem, selection comt, William Schallek Mem Grad Fel, 97-98, 95-96, 94-95, 93-94, 92-93 & 91-92; elected pres, New Eng Medieval Conf, 95-96, 94-95; mem, plan comt, Medievalism conf 10th annual meeting, Higgins Armory Mus, 95; elected VP, New Eng Medieval Conf, and co-organizer 94 21st annual meeting, Higgins Armory Mus, 93-94; mem, Best Book in Non-N Amer Urban Hist prize comt, Urban Hist Asn, 93-94; reader medieval entries, David Pinkney Prize of the Soc for Fr Hist Stud, Best Bk publ 91, 92-93; treas, New Eng Hist Asn, 91-92; mem, Urban Hist Asn comt to awd prize for best article in urban hist publ 90, 91-92. **RESEARCH** Medieval Europe, 500-1500; England, medieval and early modern; Renaissance Europe; Medieval France; all in fields of political, social, institutional, urban and constitutional. **SELECTED PUBLICATIONS** Auth, The York House Books, 1461-1490, 2 vols, London and Gloucester, Eng, and Wolfeboro, NH: Alan Sutton Publ, 91; Poverty, Payments, and Fiscal Policies in English Provincial Towns, in Portraits of Medieval Living: Essays in Memory of David Herlihy, Ann Arbor: Univ Mich Press, 96; The Politics of Welcome - Ceremonies and Constitutional Development in Later Medieval English Towns, in City and Spectacle in Medieval Europe, Minneapolis, Univ Minn Press, 94 & Arbitration and the Growth of Urban Liberties in Late Medieval England, J Brit Stud, 31, 92; coauth, Lessons in the Dark: Teaching the Middle Ages with Film, AHA Perspectives 35 1, 97; contribur, AHA Guide to Historical Literature, 3rd ed, 2 vols, NY: Oxford UP, 95; rev(s), Fictions of Advice: The Literature and Politics of Counsel in Late Medieval England, in The Bryn Mawr Medieval Review, 96; The Wars of the Roses: A Review Essay, in Albion, 28, 96; Growing Up in Medieval London: The Experience of Childhood in History, in J Interdisciplinary Hist, 26, 95; Women, Work, and Life Cycle in a Medieval Economy, in Speculum, 69, 94; English and French Towns in Feudal Society: A Comparative Study, in Speculum, 69, 94; The King's Mother: Lady Margaret Beaufort, Countess of Richmond and Derby, in Speculum, 69, 94 & The Hundred Years' War: Trial by Battle, in Medievalia et Humanistica, 21, 94. **CONTACT ADDRESS** Dept of History, Col of the Holy Cross, Worcester, MA, 01610-2395. **EMAIL** lattreed@holycross.edu

ATTREP, ABRAHAM M.
DISCIPLINE HISTORY **EDUCATION** La Col, BA, 55; Tulane Univ, MA, 58; Univ GA, PhD, 72. **CAREER** Tchr, Sulphur High Sch, 58-59; hist instr, Millsaps Col, 59-61; instr, Alexandria High Sch, 61-62; instr, 62-66, asst prof hist, 68-72, assoc prof hist, 72-78, prof hist, La Tech Univ, 78-; tchg asst, Univ GA, 66-68. **HONORS AND AWARDS** Tchg Award, Amoco Found, 86-87. **RESEARCH** Medieval hist, Renaissance and Reformation, Europ soc and intellectual hist. **SELECTED PUBLICATIONS** Auth, St. Ephrem the Syrian (306 A.D.--373 A.D.) A Voice for Our Times?, Jour Orthodox Life and Thought, 95; The Teacher and His Teachings Chrysostom's Homeletic Approach as seen in Commentaries on the Johannine Gospel, St Vladimir's Theol Quart, 94; 'A State of Wretchedness and Impotence': A British View of Constantinople, Int Jour Mid East Studies, 78; The White Lie, Southern Federation of Syrian-Lebanese American Clubs, 76; A Lenten Incident, The Orthodox Observer, 76; Eastern Orthodoxy Language and Love, The Living Church, 74; Muslim World, 67. **CONTACT ADDRESS** Dept of Hist, Louisiana Tech Univ, PO Box 3178, Ruston, LA, 71272.

AUERBACH, JEROLD STEPHEN
PERSONAL Born 05/07/1936, Philadelphia, PA, 4 children **DISCIPLINE** MODERN AMERICAN HISTORY **EDUCATION** Oberlin Col, BA, 57; Columbia Univ, MA, 59, PhD, 65. **CAREER** Lectr hist, Queens Col, NY, 64-65; asst prof, Brandeis Univ, 65-71; from asst prof to assoc prof, 71-77, prof hist, Wellesley Col, 77-, Chmn Dept, 80-85; lib arts fel law & hist, Law Sch, Harvard Univ, 69-70; Sr Fulbright lectr, Tel-Aviv Univ, 74-75; vis scholar, Law Sch, Harvard Univ, 78-85. **HONORS AND AWARDS** Am Coun Learned Soc grant, 66; Am Philos Soc grant, 69-; Soc Sci Res Coun fac res grant, 69-70; Nat Endowment for Humanities grant, 69-70; Pelzer Award, Orgn Am Historians, 64.Guggenheim fel, 74-75; NSF grant, 79-82; NEH Fel, 85-86, 90-91. **MEMBERSHIPS** Am Jewish Hist Soc. **RESEARCH** Social history of legal institutions; modern America; Jewish history. **SELECTED PUBLICATIONS** Auth, Labor and Liberty, 66 & American Labor: The Twentieth Century, 69, Bobbs; Unequal Justice, 76 & Justice Without Law?, Oxford Univ, 83; Rabbis and Lawyers, Ind, 91; Jacob's Voices, S Ill, 96. **CONTACT ADDRESS** Dept of Hist, Wellesley Col, 106 Central St, Wellesley, MA, 02181-8204. **EMAIL** jauerbach@wellesley.edu

AUGER, REGINALD
PERSONAL Born 04/03/1955, Quebec, PQ, Canada **DISCIPLINE** ARCHAEOLOGY/HISTORY **EDUCATION** Univ Montreal, BS, 78; Memorial Univ Nfld, MA, 83; Univ Calgary, PhD, 89. **CAREER** PROF ARCHAEOLOGY, LAVAL UNIV. **MEMBERSHIPS** CELAT (Interdisc stud); Can Archaeol Asn; Soc Am Archaeol; Soc Hist Archaeol; Asn canadienne francaise pour l'avancement des sciences. **RESEARCH** Arctic prehistory; contact between Inuit & Europeans in Labrador. **SELECTED PUBLICATIONS** Auth, Labrador Inuit and Europeans in the Strait of Belle isle, 91; co-ed, Ethnicity and Culture, 87. **CONTACT ADDRESS** Dept of History, Laval Univ, Ste-Foy, PQ, G1K 7P4. **EMAIL** reginald.auger@celat.ulaval.ca

AUGUSTINOS, GERASIMOS
PERSONAL Born 10/18/1939, Syracuse, NY, m, 1966, 2 children **DISCIPLINE** EASTERN EUROPEAN HISTORY **EDUCATION** Syracuse Univ, AB, 62; IN Univ, Bloomington, MA, 64, PhD(hist), 71. **CAREER** Asst prof, 71-76, ASSOC PROF HIST, UNIV SC, 77-. **MEMBERSHIPS** Am Asn Advan Slavic Studies; Mod Greek Studies Asn. **RESEARCH** Southeast Europe and Eastern Mediterranean; comparative nationalism; modern Greece. **SELECTED PUBLICATIONS** Auth, The dynamics of modern Greek nationalism: The great idea and the Macedonian problem, 73 & Consciousness and history: Nationalist critics of Greek Society, 77, East Europ Quart; The Greek Minority of Istanbul and Greek-Turkish Relations 1918-1974, with A. Alexandris, Am Hist Rev, Vol 99, 94; Greece, 1981-89-The Populist Decade, with R. Clogg, Slavonic and East European Rev, Vol 73, 95; Shattered Eagles-Balkan Fragments, with T. J. Winnifrith, Slavonic and East European Rev, Vol 74, 96;

Russian Society and the Greek Revolution, with T. C. Prousis, Slavic Rev, Vol 55, 96; Review of Prousis Book on Russian Society and the Greek Revolution, A Rejoinder, Slavic Rev, Vol 56, 97; Who Are the Macedonians, with H. Poulton, Am Hist Rev, Vol 102, 97. **CONTACT ADDRESS** Dept of Hist, Univ of SC, Columbia, SC, 29208.

AULT, BRADLEY A.
DISCIPLINE CLASSICS **EDUCATION** IN Univ, BA; MA; PhD. **CAREER** Asst prof, present, SUNY Buffalo. **HONORS AND AWARDS** Commr Inst CoopScholar, Univ MN; Horstmann fellow, Freie Universitat Berlin; Fulbright fellow, Am Schl Class Studies Athens., Blegen Res Fellow, Vassar Col. **RESEARCH** Class archaeol, Ancient-Medieval art hist. **SELECTED PUBLICATIONS** Auth, publ about ancient Greek agricultural practice and Roman metalwork. **CONTACT ADDRESS** Dept Classics, SUNY Buffalo, 712 Clemens Hall, Buffalo, NY, 14260.

AURAND, HAROLD, JR.
PERSONAL Born 11/29/1963, Bellefonte, PA, s **DISCIPLINE** HISTORY **EDUCATION** Penn St Univ, BA, 86; Univ Minn, MA, 89, PhD, 98. **CAREER** Instr, 92-97, asst prof, 92-, Penn St. **RESEARCH** Early Amer politics, sports hist. **CONTACT ADDRESS** 119 North St, Apt 1A, Port Carbon, PA, 17965.

AURAND, HAROLD WILSON
PERSONAL Born 06/24/1940, Danville, PA, m, 1962, 2 children **DISCIPLINE** AMERICAN LABOR HISTORY **EDUCATION** Franklin & Marshall Col, BA, 62; Pa State Univ, University Park, MA, 63, PhD(Hist), 69. **CAREER** From instr to asst prof, 64-72, assoc prof Hist, PA State Univ, Hazelton, 72-. **HONORS AND AWARDS** Amoco Found Outstanding Teaching Award, 80. **MEMBERSHIPS** Orgn Am Historians. **RESEARCH** American labor history, 1867 to 1920. **SELECTED PUBLICATIONS** Auth, the Workingmen's Benevolent Association, Labor Hist, 66; The Anthracite Strike of 1887, Pa Hist, 68; Diversifying the Economy of the Anthracite Regions, 1880-1900, Pa Mag Hist & Biog, 70; From the Molly Maguires to the United Mine Workers, Temple Univ, 71; Social Motivation of the Anthracite Mine Workers: 1901-1920, Labor Hist, Summer 77; The Anthracite Miner; An Occupational Analyis, Pa Mag Hist & Biog, 80. **CONTACT ADDRESS** Pennsylvania State Univ, Highacres, Hazleton, PA, 18201-1202. **EMAIL** hwa1@psu.edu

AUSMUS, HARRY JACK
PERSONAL Born 06/14/1937, Lafollette, TN, m, 1963, 2 children **DISCIPLINE** EUROPEAN INTELLECTUAL HISTORY, HISTORIOGRAPHY **EDUCATION** E TN State Univ, BA, 59, MA, 63; Drew Univ, BD, 63; OH State Univ, PhD(hist), 69. **CAREER** PROF HIST, SOUTHERN CT STATE COL, 67-. **MEMBERSHIPS** AHA; Soc Reformation Res. **RESEARCH** Modern European intellectual history; historigraphy; philosophy of history. **SELECTED PUBLICATIONS** Auth, Schelling on History, 1841, CT Rev, 72; Schopenhauer and Christianity, IL Quart, 74; Schopenhauer's View of History: A Note, Hist & Theory, 76; Schopenhauer's Philosophy of Language, Midwest Quart, 77; Nietzsche and Eschatology, J Relig, 10/78; The Polite Escape: On the Myth of Secularyation, OH Univ Press, 82; Nothing But History-Reconstruction and Extremity After Metaphysics, with D. D. Roberts, Am Hist Rev, Vol 102, 97. **CONTACT ADDRESS** Dept of Hist, Southern CT State Col, 501 Crescent St, New Haven, CT, 06515-1330.

AUSTEN, RALPH ALBERT
PERSONAL Born 01/09/1937, Leipzig, Germany, m, 1967 **DISCIPLINE** AFRICAN & IMPERIAL HISTORY **EDUCATION** Harvard Univ, AB, 58, PhD(hist), 66; Univ Calif, Berkeley, MA, 60. **CAREER** Asst prof hist, NY Univ, 65-67, asst prof hist, Univ Chicago, 67-74, assoc dir, Civilization Course Mat Prog, 77-80, ASSOC PROF HIST, UNIV CHICAGO, 74-, DIR, MASTER ARTS PROG SOCIAL SCI, 78-; Rockefeller Found exchange fel, Univ Ibadan, 69-70; Fulbright prof, Univ Yaounde, 72-73; Soc Sci Res Coun fel, Europe, Cameroon, 72-73; NSF fel, 75. **MEMBERSHIPS** Tanzania Hist Soc; Hist Soc Nigeria; AHA; African Studies Asn; Int African Inst. **SELECTED PUBLICATIONS** Auth, Abushiri et la Lutte Contre La Domination Allemande en Tanzanie, in Charles Andre Julien et al, Les Africains, Vol 1, 77; Slavery Among Coastal Middlemen: The Duala of Cameroon, in Suzanne Miers and Igor Kopytoff, Slavery in Africa: Historical and Anthropological Perspectives, 77; Duala vs Germans in Cameroon: Economic Dimensions of a Political Conflict, Revue Francaise d'Historire d'Outre-Mer, Vol 4, 77; coauth (with C F Holmes), Usukuma in Historical Perspective: Traditional Society and the Colonial Experience, Studies in Third World Societies, Vols 3 & 4, 78; The Transsaharan Slave Trade: A Tentative Census, in The Uncommon Market: Essays in the Economic History of the Atlantic Slave Trade, 79; The Islamic Red Sea Slave Trade: An Effort at Quantification, Proceedings of the Fifth International Conference on Ethiopian Studies, 79; African Commerce Without Europeans: The Development Impact of Trade in the Pre-Modern Era, Kenya Hist Rev, Vol 6, No 1 & 2; Islam in African History, in Cyriac Pullapilly, Islam in the Contemporary World, 80. **CONTACT ADDRESS** Univ of Chicago, 5828 S University Ave, Chicago, IL, 60637-1539. **EMAIL** wwb3@midway.uchicago.edu

AUSTENSEN, ROY ALLEN
PERSONAL Born 05/31/1942, Berwyn, IL, m, 1966, 3 children **DISCIPLINE** MODERN HISTORY **EDUCATION** Concordia Col, IL, BS, 63; Univ IL, Urbana, MA, 64, PhD(hist), 69. **CAREER** Instr hist, Univ IL, Urbana, 68-69; asst prof, 69-75, ASSOC PROF HIST, IL STATE UNIV, 75-, Nat Endowment for Humanities fel, 82-83. **HONORS AND AWARDS** Best Article award, Conf Group Cent Europ Hist, 80; W Dee Halverson Prize, Western Asn Ger Studies, 81. **MEMBERSHIPS** AHA; Conf Group Cent Europ Hist; Soc Hist Educ; Western Asn Ger Studies. **RESEARCH** European diplomatic history; Austrian history. **SELECTED PUBLICATIONS** Auth, Count Buol and the Metternich Tradition, In: Austrian History Yearbook, 73-74; History and the Humanities: An Integrative Approach, In: The Social Studies, 9-10/75; Felix Schwarzenberg: Realpolitiker or Metternichian?, In: Mitteilugen des Osterreichischen Staatsarchivs, 77; Austria and the Stuggle for Supremacy in Germany, 1848-1864, J Modern Hist, 6/80; Mother-Tongue and Fatherland-Language and Politics in German, with M. Townson, German Studies Rev, Vol 17, 94; From the Aehrenthal Legacy-Letters and Documents on Austrian-Hungarian Domestic and Foreign-Policy 1885-1912, German, with S. Wank and F. Fellner, Slavic Rev, Vol 55, 96. **CONTACT ADDRESS** Dept of Hist, Illinois State Univ, Normal, IL, 61761.

AUSTERN, LINDA
PERSONAL Born 02/20/1957, Pittsburgh, PA, m **DISCIPLINE** MUSICOLOGY **EDUCATION** Univ Pittsburgh, BA, 77; Univ Chicago, PhD, 84. **CAREER** Cornell Univ, vis fel, 84-86; Allegheny Col, vis asst prof, 86-87; Univ New Haven, vis asst prof, 87-88; Radcliffe Col, Harvard Univ, Bunting fel, 88-89; Univ of Notre Dame, asst prof, 89-95; Univ Notre Dame, assoc prof, tenure, 95; Univ Iowa, vis assoc prof, 97; Folger Shakespeare Libr NEH long-term fel, 97-98 Newberry Libr, 87; Scholar-in-Residence, 98-99. **HONORS AND AWARDS** Newberry Libr Short-Term Resident Fel, 87 Andrew W Mellon Fel to Harvard Univ, 88-89 (turned down); Fel, Bunting Inst of Radcliffe Col, 88-89; Am Council of Learned Societies Travel Grant, 90; Folger Shakespeare Libr NEH Fel, 97-98; NEH Fel for Col Teachers, 97-98; ACLS Fel, 98; Brit Acad Vis Fel, 98. **MEMBERSHIPS** Am Musicol Soc; Int Musicol Soc; Renaissance Soc Am; Royal Musical Asn; Shakespeare Asn Am; Soc for Emblem Studies; Soc for 17th-Century Music; Soc for the Study of Early Mod Women; **RESEARCH** Music, gender and sexuality; music in early mod England; 17th-century opera; music in early mod science and medicine; emblematics; cult criticism of European & N Am musics; Shakespearean drama. **SELECTED PUBLICATIONS** 'Alluring the Auditorie to Effeminacie:' Music and the Idea of the Feminine in Early Modern England, Music & Letters 74, 93; Music and the English Controversy Over Women, in Cecilia Reclaimed: Feminist Perspectives on Gender and Music, ed Susan Cook and Judy Tsou, Univ Ill Press, 94; 'No Women Are Indeed': The Bouy Actor as Vocal Seductress in English Renaissance Drama, in Embodied Voices: Female Vocality in Western Culture, ed Leslie Dunn & Nancy Jones, Cambridge Univ Press, 94; 'The Conceit of the Minde': Music, Medicine and Mental Process in Early Modern England, Irish Musical Studies 4, 96; 'Foreign Conceits and Wand'ring Devices': The Erotic as Exotic, in The Exotic in Western Music, ed Jonathan Bellman, Northeastern Univ Press, 98; Nature, Culture, Myth and the Musician in Early Modern England, J Am Musicol Soc 51, 98; 'For, Love's a Good Musician': Performance, Audition and Erotic Disorders in Early Modern Europe, in Musical Quarterly, 98; 'No Pill's Gonna Cure My Ill': Erotic Melancholy and Traditions of Musical Healing in the Modern West, in Musical Healing in Cultural Contexts, ed Penelope Gouk, Ashgate Publ, 98; Musical Treatments for Lovesickness: The Early Modern Heritage, in Music as Medicine: The History of Music Therapy Since Antiquity, Variorum/Scolar Press, 98; The Siren, the Muse, and the God of Love: Music and Gender in Seventeenth-Century English Emblem Books, J Musicol Res; My Mother Musicke, in Mothers and Others: The Caregiver Figure in Early Modern Europe, ed Naomi Miller and Naomi Yavneh. **CONTACT ADDRESS** Newberry Libr, 60 West Walton St, Chicago, IL, 60610-3380. **EMAIL** austern@calumet.purdue.edu

AUSTIN, GAYLE M.
DISCIPLINE THEATRE HISTORY **EDUCATION** CUNY, PhD. **CAREER** Instr, Hunter Col; instr, Univ SC; assoc prof, Ga State Univ; exec dir, Southeast Playwrights Proj, 87-89. **SELECTED PUBLICATIONS** Auth, The Madwoman in the Spotlight: Plays of Maria Irene Fornes, in Making a Spectacle, Univ Mich Press, 89; The Exchange of Women and Male Homosocial Desire in Miller's 'Death of a Salesman' and Hellman's 'Another Part of the Forest,' in Feminist Rereadings of Modern American Drama, Fairleigh Dickinson UP, 89; Feminist Theories for Dramatic Criticism, Univ Mich Press, 90; Resisting the Birth Mark: Subverting Hawthorne in a Feminist Theory Play, in Upstaging Big Daddy: Directing Theater as if Gender and Race Matter, Univ Mich Press, 93. **CONTACT ADDRESS** Georgia State Univ, Atlanta, GA, 30303. **EMAIL** jougma@panther.gsu.edu

AUSTIN, J. NORMAN
PERSONAL Born 05/20/1937, Anshun, China, s **DISCIPLINE** CLASSICS **EDUCATION** Univ of Toronto, BA, 58; Univ of Calif, MA, 60, PhD, 65 **CAREER** Lect, 64-65, Oakland Univ MI; Asst Prof, 65-66, Univ S CA; Assoc Prof, 66-76, Univ of CA; Aurelio Prof, 76-78, Boston Univ; Prof, 78-80, Univ MA Amherst **HONORS AND AWARDS** John S Guggenheim Fel, 74-75; Jnr Fel, Center for Hellenic Studies, 68-69 **MEMBERSHIPS** Am Philol Assoc; Am Assoc of Univ Profs **RESEARCH** Homer; Archaic Greek Culture & Literature; Comparative Literature **SELECTED PUBLICATIONS** Auth, Archery at the Dark of the Moon Poetic Problems in Homer's Odyssey, Univ of CA Press, 75 **CONTACT ADDRESS** Dept of Classics, Univ of AZ, 2939 E Third St, Tucson, AZ, 85716. **EMAIL** naustin@u.arizona.edu

AUSTIN, JUDITH
PERSONAL Born 06/18/1940, San Diego, CA **DISCIPLINE** UNITED STATES HISTORY **EDUCATION** Duke Univ, BA, 61; Columbia Univ, MA, 63. **CAREER** Ed, Teachers Col Press, Columbia Univ, 62-66; RES HISTORIAN & ARCHIVIST, ID STATE HIST SOC, 67-, ED, ID YESTERDAYS, 76-. **MEMBERSHIPS** Western Hist Asn; Orgn Am Historians; Forest Hist Soc; Am Asn State & Local Hist; AHA. **RESEARCH** Western United States; United States political and social. **SELECTED PUBLICATIONS** Auth, Joseph Thing, In: Mountain Men and Fur Trade of the Far West, Vol 9, Arthur Clark; coauth, Case Study of Federal Expenditures on a Water and Related Land Resources Project: Boise Project, Idaho and Oregon, Idaho Water Resource Bd and Idaho Water Resources Res Inst, 74; Desert, Sagebrush, and the Pacific Northwest, In: The Pacific Northwest: A Region in Myth and Reality, OR State Univ (in prep). **CONTACT ADDRESS** 1621 Martha St, Boise, ID, 83706.

AUSTIN, SCOTT
PERSONAL Born 03/10/1953, New York, NY **DISCIPLINE** ANCIENT PHILOSOPHY **EDUCATION** Yale Univ, BA, 74; Univ Tex at Austin, PhD, 79. **CAREER** Asst prof, Texas A&M Univ, 88-91 to assoc prof, 91-. **HONORS AND AWARDS** App vis fel, Princeton Univ, 99-2000; Golden Key Honor Soc, Tex A&M Asn of Former Students Fac Distinguished Tchg Awd, 95; Univ Honors Prog Awd to develop new course, 90; Univ Mini-grant, 89; Dept Res Grant, 89; Fulbright Fel, to Christ's Col, Cambridge, 83-84, Dining Rights at Christ's Col; Danforth Fel, 75-79. **SELECTED PUBLICATIONS** Auth, Parmenides: Being, Bounds, Logic, Yale UP, 86; Genesis and Motion in Parmenides: B8 l2-l3, Harvard Stud in Classical Philos 87, 83; Parmenides and Ultimate Reality, Ultimate Reality and Meaning 7, 84; The Paradox of Socratic Ignorance, Philosophical Topics 15, 87 & Parmenides' Reference, Classical Quart, 90. **CONTACT ADDRESS** Dept of Philosophy, Texas A&M Univ, 309E Bolton Hall, College Station, TX, 77843-4237. **EMAIL** s-austin@tamu.edu

AUSTIN, WILLIAM WEAVER
PERSONAL Born 01/18/1920, Lawton, OK, m, 1942, 2 children **DISCIPLINE** MUSIC **EDUCATION** Harvard Univ, AB, 39, AM, 40, PhD, 51. **CAREER** Asst prof, Univ Va, 46-47; from asst prof to prof music, 47-69, GOLDIN SMITH PROF MUSICOL, CORNELL UNIV, 69- **HONORS AND AWARDS** E J Dent Prize, 67; Otto Kinkeldey Award, 67. **MEMBERSHIPS** Am Musicol Soc; Col Music Soc (pres, 60-62); Soc Ethnomusicol; Music Educ Nat Conf; Int Musicol Soc. **RESEARCH** 20th century music; American music. **SELECTED PUBLICATIONS** Auth, Music in the 20th century, Norton, 66; ed, New Looks at Italian Opera, Cornell Univ, 68; Claude Debussy: Prelude to L'Apres-midi d'un faune, Norton, 70; auth, Ives and histories, Cong Report, Ges Musikforsch, 71; Susanna, Jeanie and the Old Folks at Home: The Songs of Stephen C Foster From His Time to Ours, Macmillan, 75; Neue musik, Musik in Geschichte u Gegenwart, Suppl, 77; transl, Carl Dahlhaus, Esthetics of Music, Cambridge, 82; auth, Debussy, Wagner and Others, Nineteenth Century Music, 82. **CONTACT ADDRESS** Dept of Music, Cornell Univ, Lincoln Hall, Ithaca, NY, 14853.

AUTEN, ARTHUR
DISCIPLINE HISTORY **EDUCATION** Case Western Reserve Univ, BA, MA, PhD. **CAREER** Prof, Hartford Univ. **SELECTED PUBLICATIONS** Auth, Western Civilization, 97; American History, 97; ed, Readings in Western Civilization, 96. **CONTACT ADDRESS** History Dept, Univ of Hartford, 200 Bloomfield Ave, West Hartford, CT, 06117.

AVAKUMOVIC, IVAN
PERSONAL Born 08/22/1926, Belgrade, Yugoslavia, m, 1957, 1 child **DISCIPLINE** MODERN HISTORY, POLITICAL SCIENCE **EDUCATION** Cambridge Univ, BA, 47, MA, 52; Univ London, MA, 54; Oxford Univ, DPhil(soc sci), 58. **CAREER** Asst lectr polit, Aberdeen Univ, 57-58; from asst prof to assoc prof polit sci & int rels, Univ Man, 58-63; from assoc prof to prof polit sci, 63-69, PROF HIST, UNIV BC, 69-, Can Coun leave fel, 68-69; Killam Sr Fel, Killam Found, 76-77. **MEMBERSHIPS** AHA; Am Asn Advan Slavic Studies; Am Polit Sci Asn; Can Hist Asn. **RESEARCH** Movements of social dissent; East European politics and history; international relations. **SELECTED PUBLICATIONS** Coauth, The Anarchist Prince--A Biographical Study of Peter Kropotkin, Boardman, London & NY, 50; auth, History of the Communist

Party of Yogoslavia, Aberdeen Univ, Vol I, 64; coauth The Doukhobors, Oxford, Toronto & NY, 68; auth, Mihailovic Prema Nemackim Dokumentima, Nase Delo, London Eng, 69; The Communist Party in Canada: A History 75 & Socialism in Canada: A Study of the CCF-NDP in Federal and Provincial Politics, 78, McClelland & Stewart; Distant Friends-The United-States-And-Russia, 1763-1867, with N. E. Saul, Russian History-Histoire Russe, Vol 20, 93. **CONTACT ADDRESS** Dept of Hist, Univ of BC, Vancouver, BC, V6T 1W5.

AVALOS, HECTOR
PERSONAL Born 10/08/1958, Nogales, Mexico, m, 1979 **DISCIPLINE** ANTHROPOLOGY **EDUCATION** Univ Ariz, BA, 82; Harvard Div School, MTS, 85; Harvard Univ, PhD, 91. **CAREER** Carolina Minor postdoc fel, 91-93, Univ of NC; Asst Prof, 93-98, Assoc Prof, Dir Latino Stud, Iowa State Univ. **HONORS AND AWARDS** Prof of the Year, Early Excell research Awd. **MEMBERSHIPS** SBL, AAR. **RESEARCH** History of medicine, science & religion **SELECTED PUBLICATIONS** Auth, Illness and Health Care in the Ancient Near East, The role of The Temple in Greece, Mesopotamia and Israel, in: Harvard Semitic Monographs, Atlanta Scholars Press, 95; Daniel 9: 24-25 and Mesopotamian Temple Rededications, in: J of Biblical Lit, 98; Can Science Prove that Prayer Works? in: Free Inquiry, 97; The Gospel of Lucas Gavilan as Postcolonial Biblical Exegesis, in: Semeia, 96; A Ladino Version of the Targum of Ruth, in: Estudios Biblicos, 96; Ancient Medicine, In Case of Emergency Contact Your Local Prophet, in: Bible Review, 95; The Biblical Sources of Columbus's Libro de las profecias, in: Traditio, 94. **CONTACT ADDRESS** Religious Studies Program, Iowa State Univ, 402 Catt Hall, Ames, IA, 50011. **EMAIL** havalos@iastate.edu

AVERY, HARRY COSTAS
PERSONAL Born 04/09/1930, Philadelphia, PA, m, 1962, 4 children **DISCIPLINE** CLASSICS **EDUCATION** Univ PA, AB, 53; Univ IL, MA, 56; Princeton Univ, PhD, 59. **CAREER** Instr Greek, Bryn Mawr Col, 59-61; from asst prof to assoc prof classics, Univ TX, Austin, 61-67; PROF CLASSICS & CHMN DEPT, UNIV PITTSBURGH, 67-, Jr fel, Ctr Hellenic Studies, 63-64; chmn adv coun, Comt Sch Class Studies, Am Acad Rome, 70-73, trustee, 75-78; vis res prof Greek hist & lit, Am Sch Class Studies Athens, 71-72, mem exec comt, Managing Comt, 72-76. **HONORS AND AWARDS** Bromberg Award, Univ TX, 66. **MEMBERSHIPS** Am Philol Asn; Soc Promotion Hellenic Studies; Archaeol Inst Am. **RESEARCH** Greek history and literature; Roman history. **SELECTED PUBLICATIONS** Auth, Euripides' Heracleidai, 71 & Herodotus' Picture of Cyrus, 72, Am J Philol; Herodotus 6.112.2, Trans Am Philol Asn, 72; Themes in Thucydides' Account of the Sicilian Expedition, Hermes, 73; Sophocles' Political Career, Historia, 73; The Three Hundred at Thasos, 411 BC, Class Philol, 78; A Lost Episode in Caesar Civil War, Hermes-Zeitschrift Fur Klassische Philologie, Vol 121, 93; Glaucus, A God, 'Iliad' Zeta-128-143 & Homer, Hermes-Zeitschrift Fur Klassische Philologie, Vol 122, 94. **CONTACT ADDRESS** Dept of Classics, Univ of Pittsburgh, Pittsburgh, PA, 51260.

AVERY, KEVIN J.
PERSONAL Born 09/19/1950, Jersey City, NJ, s, 2 children **DISCIPLINE** HISTORY OF NINETEENTH-CENTURY AMERICAN ART **EDUCATION** Columbia Univ, PhD, 95. **CAREER** Assoc Curator, Dept of Am Paintings and Sculpture, Metropolitan Museum of Art; adjunct asst prof, Dept of Art, Hunter Col, CUNY. **HONORS AND AWARDS** Chester Dale Fel, Metropolitan Museum of Art, 83-84; Andrew Mellon Fel, MMA, 84-85; Whiting Fel, Columbia Univ, 87-88. **MEMBERSHIPS** Col Art Asn; Historians of Nineteenth-Century Art. **RESEARCH** Hudson River School landscape painting; Frederic E. Church; Sanford R. Gifford; Thomas Cole; panorama painting. **SELECTED PUBLICATIONS** Auth, American Drawings in the Metropolitan Museum of Art, Volume I: Catalogue of Works by Artists born between 1738 and 1835, Metropolitan Museum of Art, forthcoming; American Tonalism, Am Tonalism from the Metropolitan Museum of Art, Montclair Art Museum, 99; Movies for Manifest Destiny: The Moving Panorama Phenomenon in America, Panorama of Bunyan's Pilgrim's Progress, Montclair Art Museum, 99; Church's Great Picture: The Heart of the Andes, Metropolitan Museum of Art, 93; Picturing the Frontier: the Panorama Phenomenon in America, Sehsuct ¤The Desire to Seel, Kunst-und Ausstellungshalle der Bundesrepublik Deutschland, 93. **CONTACT ADDRESS** Dept of Am Paintings and Sculpture, Metropolitan Mus of Art, 1000 Fifth Ave, New York, NY, 10028.

AVERY-PECK, ALAN J.
PERSONAL Born 06/26/1953, Chicago, IL, m, 1981, 2 children **DISCIPLINE** HISTORY OF RELIGION; JUDAISM **EDUCATION** Brown Univ, PhD, 81. **CAREER** Dir, Jewish studies, Tulane Univ, 81-93; KRAFT-HIATT PROF IN JUDAIC STUDIES, COL OF THE HOLY CROSS, 93-. **MEMBERSHIPS** AAR/SBL **RESEARCH** Rabbinic Judaism. **SELECTED PUBLICATIONS** Auth, Rhetorical Argumentation in Early Rabbinic Pronouncement Stories, in Vernon K. Robins, ed, The Rhetoric of Pronouncement, Semia: An Experimental Journal for Biblical Criticism, vol 64, 93; Judaism, with Jacob Neusner, in The Reader's Adviser, 14th ed, vol 4: The Best of Philosophy and Religion, R. R. Bowker, NJ, 94; The Mishnah, Tosefta, and the Talmuds: The Problem of Text and Context, in Jacob Neusner, ed, Handbuch der Orientalistik Judaistik: Judaism in Late Antiquity, Part One, The Literary and Archaeological Sources, E. J. Brill, Leided, 94; The Talmud of Babylonia, An American Translation, vol V, Tractatae Rosh Hashanah, Brown Judaic Studies: Scholars Press, Atlanta, 95; The Politics of the Mishnah in its Contemporary Context, in J. Neusner, ed, Religion and Political Order: Politics in Classical and Contemporary Christianity, Islam and Judaism, Atlanta, Scholars Press, 96; The Exodus in Jewish Faith: The Problem of God's Intervention in History, in the Annual of Rabbinic Judaism, vol 1, Brill, 98; ed, with Jacob Neusner, Where We Stand: Issues and Debates in the Study of Ancient Judaism, vol 1, Handbuch der Orientalistik, E. J. Brill, Leiden, 98; ed, The Annual of Rabbinic Judaism: Ancient, Medieval, and Modern, vol 1, E. J. Brill, Leiden, 98. **CONTACT ADDRESS** Dept of Relig Studies, Col of the Holy Cross, Box 17, Worchester, MA, 01610-2395. **EMAIL** AAvery@Holycross.edu

AVINS, STYRA
PERSONAL New York, NY, m, 2 children **DISCIPLINE** CELLO; SOCIAL SCIENCES **EDUCATION** City Col of NY, BA, 59; Juilliard Sch of Music, BS, 59; Manhattan Sch of Music, MS, 63. **CAREER** Mem, Seoul Symphony, Am Symphony Orchestra, NY City Opera Orchestra, 60-69; fac mem, United Nations Int Sch, 80-90; mem of Queens Symphony Orchestra, 80-; assoc prof, Drew U. Grad Sch, 95-. **HONORS AND AWARDS** Royal Philharmonic Soc Award, High Commendation, 98. **MEMBERSHIPS** Am Brahms Soc; Violoncello Soc; Am Musicological Soc; Johannes Brahms Gesellschaft Int. Vereinigung e.V.; Oesterreichische Brahms Gesellschaft; AF of M Fedn of Musicians, Local 802. **RESEARCH** Documents relating to life and work of Johannes Brahms and his circle; Women musicians in the Brahms circle; Sir Georg Henschel and his American, English and German careers; 19th century performance practice as it relates to the music of Brahms. **SELECTED PUBLICATIONS** Auth, Brahms the Cellist, in Newsletter of the Violoncello Soc, summer and fall, 92; A Jolly End to My Summer: Gustav Wendt and the Clarinet Sonatas, in Newsletter of the Am Brahms Soc, vol. IX, 199?; The Young Brahms: Another View, Newsletter of the Am Brahms Soc, vol. XI, no. 2, 93; An Undeniable Gift, in The Strad Mag, Oct. 96; Johannes Brahms: Life and Letters, 97. **CONTACT ADDRESS** The Graduate Sch, Drew Univ, Madison Ave, Madison, NJ, 07940. **EMAIL** savins@drew.edu

AVOTINS, IVARS
PERSONAL Born 11/16/1931, Riga, Latvia, m, 1967 **DISCIPLINE** CLASSICS **EDUCATION** Univ Toronto, BA, 59; Harvard Univ, PhD, 68. **CAREER** Lectr, asst prof, Univ W Ontario, 62-66; asst prof, Univ Calif, Berkeley, 68-70; assoc prof, prof, Univ W Ontario, 70- . **RESEARCH** Epicurus and Lucretius; the second Sophistic; Greek legal language in the Roman Empire. **SELECTED PUBLICATIONS** Auth, Index to the Lives of the Sophists of Philostratus, 78; Index in Eunapii, 83; On the Greek of the Code of Justinian, 89; On the Greek of the Novels of Justinian, 92. **CONTACT ADDRESS** Dept of Classical Studies, Univ of Western Ontario, London, ON, N6A 3K7.

AVRECH BERKMAN, JOYCE
DISCIPLINE HISTORY **EDUCATION** Yale Univ, PhD, 67. **CAREER** Prof, Univ MA Amherst. **HONORS AND AWARDS** Distinguished Tchr Awd, 80; Prof of the Year Awd, 89. **RESEARCH** Brit hist. **SELECTED PUBLICATIONS** Auth, The Healing Imagination of Olive Schreiner: Beyond South African Colonialism, Univ Mass, 93; co-ed, African American Women and the Vote 1837-1965, Univ MA, 97. **CONTACT ADDRESS** Dept of Hist, Univ Massachusetts Amherst, Mass Ave, Amherst, MA, 01003.

AVRICH, PAUL HENRY
PERSONAL Born 08/04/1931, Brooklyn, NY, m, 1954, 2 children **DISCIPLINE** HISTORY **EDUCATION** Cornell Univ, AB, 52; Columbia Univ, AM, 59, PhD, 61. **CAREER** Vis asst Prof, 61-62 & 63-64, Wesleyan Univ; vis assoc prof, 66, vis prof, 81, Columbia Univ; instr to assoc prof, 60-70, prof, 70-82, dist prof hist, 82-, Queens Col, NY. **HONORS AND AWARDS** Amer Coun Learned Socs 7 Soc Sci Res Coun Slavic Stud Grant 62; Amer Philos Soc res grant, 64; Guggenheim fel, 67-68; NEH sr fel, 72-73; Amer Coun of Learned Soc Fel, 82-83; co-win Philip Taft Labor Hist Award 84; NEH fel, 89-90. **MEMBERSHIPS** AHA; Am Assn Advan Slavic Studies; Orgn Am Historians. **RESEARCH** Modern Russian history; anarchism; revolutionary movements. **SELECTED PUBLICATIONS** Auth, The Russian Anarchists, Princeton, 70; auth, Russian Rebels 1600-1800, Schocken, 72; ed, The Anarchists in the Russian Revolution, Cornell Univ, 73; auth, An American Anarchist: The Life of Voltairine de Cleyre, The Modern School Movement, Princeton, 80; auth, The Haymarket Tragedy, Princeton, 84; auth, Anarchisty Portraits, Princeton, 88; auth, Sacco and Vanzetti: The Anarchist Background, Princeton, 91; auth, Anarchist Voices: An Oral History of Anarchism in America, Princeton, 95. **CONTACT ADDRESS** 425 Riverside Dr, New York, NY, 10025. **EMAIL** paulavr@aol.com

AXELRAD, ALLAN M.
PERSONAL Born 07/15/1941, Washington, DC, 2 children **DISCIPLINE** AMERICAN STUDIES, HISTORY **EDUCATION** Univ CA, Riverside, BA, 65, MA, 65; Univ PA, MA, 69, PhD(Am civilization), 74. **CAREER** Lectr Am studies, Skidmore Col, 72-73; asst prof Am studies, Sacred Heart Col, 73-75; lectr hist, Calif Polytech State Univ, San Luis Obispo, 75-76; lectr, 76-80, ASSOC PROF AM STUDIES, CA STATE UNIV, FULLERTON, 76-, Consult, Nat Am Studies Fac, 74-75. **MEMBERSHIPS** Am Studies Asn; Orgn Am Historians; AHA. **RESEARCH** Pretwentieth-century American cultural history. **SELECTED PUBLICATIONS** Auth, Ideology and Utopia in the Works of Ignatius Donnelly, Am Studies, 71; History and Utopia: A Study of the World View of James Fenimore Cooper, Norwood, 78; The Protagonist of the Protestant Ethic: Max Weber's Ben Franklin, Rendezvous, 78; The Order of the Leatherstocking Tales: D H Lawrence, David Noble, and the Iron Trap of History, Am Lit, 82. **CONTACT ADDRESS** Dept of Am Studies, California State Univ, Fullerton, Fullerton, CA, 92634.

AXTELL, JAMES LEWIS
PERSONAL Born 12/20/1941, Endicott, NY, m, 1963, 2 children **DISCIPLINE** HISTORY **EDUCATION** Yale Univ, BA, 63; Cambridge Univ, PhD(hist), 67. **CAREER** Asst prof hist, Yale Univ, 66-72; assoc prof, Sarah Lawrence Col, 72-75; vis prof, Northwestern Univ, Ill, 77-78; PROF HIST, COL WILLIAM & MARY, 78-, Kenan prof hum, 86-; Res fel hist, Social Sci Res Coun, 65-66; Morse Jr Fac res fel, Yale Univ, 69-70; res fel, Nat Endowment Humanities, 75-77, 86, 92; res fel, J S Guggenheim Found, 81-82; res fel Am Coun Learned Socs, 87. **HONORS AND AWARDS** Outstanding Fac, Va State Counc High Educ, 88; Loyola-Mellon Hum Aw, 92; Fleming Lecturer Southern Hist, LSU, 96. **MEMBERSHIPS** AHA; Orgn Am Historians; Am Soc Ethnohistory; Champlain Soc; Haklyut Soc; Colonial Soc Mass; mass His Soc; Soc Am Historians; French Colonial His Soc; Soc for the Hist of Discoveries. **RESEARCH** History of Colonial North America; ethnohistory of Indian-white relations; history of Am higher education. **SELECTED PUBLICATIONS** The Educational Writings of John Locke: A Critical Edition with Introduction and Notes, Cambridge Univ Press, 68; The School upon a Hill: Education and Society in Colonial New England, Yale Univ Press, 74; Indian Missions: A Critical Bibliography, Newberry Libr Ctr Hist Am Indian, 78; The Indian Peoples of Eastern America: A Documentary History of the Sexes, Oxford Univ Press, 81; The European and the Indian: Essays in the Ethnohistory of Colonial North America, Oxford Univ Press, 81; The Invasion Within: The Contact of Cultures in Colonial North America, Oxford Univ Press, 85; After Columbus: Essays in the Ethnohistory of Colonial North America, Oxford Univ Press, 88; Beyond 1492: Encounters in Colonial North America, Oxford Univ Press, 92; The Indians' New South: Cultural Change in the Colonial Southeast, LSU, 97; The Pleasures of Academia: A Celebration and Defense of Higher Education, Nebraska Univ Press, 98. **CONTACT ADDRESS** Dept of Hist, Col of William and Mary, Williamsburg, VA, 23187-8795. **EMAIL** jlaxte@facstaff.wm.edu

AZZARA, CHRISTOPHER D.
DISCIPLINE MUSIC **EDUCATION** George Mason University, BM; Eastman Sch Music, MM, PhD. **CAREER** Prof, Hartt Sch Music, 91-. **RESEARCH** Improvisatio; instrumental music education; jazz studies-piano arranging; measurement and evaluation in music; music learning theory; music technology, & music learning. **SELECTED PUBLICATIONS** Auth, Creativity In Improvisation; Jump Right In: The Instrumental Series; ed, Concert Selections for Winds and Percussion. **CONTACT ADDRESS** Hartt Sch Music, Univ Hartford, 200 Bloomfield Ave, West Hartford, CT, 06117.

AZZOLINA, DAVIS S
PERSONAL Born 05/22/1957, East Orange, NJ, s **DISCIPLINE** FOLKLORE **EDUCATION** Univ Penn, BA, 78, MA, 91, PhD, 96; Columbia Univ, MS, 79; **CAREER** Ref asst, 78-79, Butler Libr, Columbia Univ; ref-col devel libr, Fondren Lib, Rice Univ; ref libr, 82-86, Eisenhower Library, John Hopkins Univ; adj asst prof, 97-, Univ Penn; ref libr, 86-, Van Pelt Libr, Univ Penn. **RESEARCH** Folklore, gay studies, Mormonism **CONTACT ADDRESS** Reference Libr, Univ of Pennsylvania, 3420 Walnut St, Philadelphia, PA, 19104.

B

BABBITT, BEATRICE C.
DISCIPLINE LEARNING DISABILITIES; MATHEMATICS DISABILITIES; ASSISTIVE TECHNOLOGY **EDUCATION** UCLA, PhD, 86. **CAREER** Assoc prof, dir, technol related grant, coordr, grad prog, dir, tchr educ, Univ Nev, Las Vegas. **SELECTED PUBLICATIONS** Auth, Hypermedia: Making the mathematics connection, Intervention in Schl and Clinic, 93; Cross-disciplinary training in assistive technology, Proc of the 10th Annual Int Technol and Persons with Disabilities Conf, Calif State Univ, Northridge, 95; coauth, Using hypermedia to improve the mathematics problem-solving skills of

students with learning disabilities, J of Learning Disabilities, 29, 96. **CONTACT ADDRESS** Dept of Spec Educ, Univ Nev, Las Vegas, 4505 Maryland Pky, Las Vegas, NV, 89154-3014. **EMAIL** babbitt@nevada.edu

BABCOCK, ROBERT
PERSONAL Born 10/17/1958, Marion, IN, m, 1979, 2 children **DISCIPLINE** CLASSICS **EDUCATION** CSU, BA 78; Duke Univ, MA 81, 83 PHD **CAREER** Asst Prof, 84-86, Miss St Univ; Asst Prof, 87, Bucknell Univ; Cur/Lect, 87, Yale Univ **HONORS AND AWARDS** Alexander von Humbolt Fellow, 84; Comite Internationale de Paleographielitve, 98 **MEMBERSHIPS** Am Philolol Assoc; Medieval Acad of Am; Am Soc of Papyrologists **RESEARCH** Classical Transmission **SELECTED PUBLICATIONS** Coauth, Learning from the Greeks, New Haven, 94; Auth, The Rosenthal Collection of Printed Books with Manuscript Annotations, New Haven, 97; Auth, The Luxeuil Prophets and the Gallican Liturgy, Scriptorium 47, 93, 52-5 **CONTACT ADDRESS** Dept of Papyrologists, PO Box 208240, New Haven, CT, 06520-8240. **EMAIL** robert.babcock@yale.edu

BABCOCK, ROBERT HARPER
PERSONAL Born 12/19/1931, Cincinnati, OH, m, 1955, 6 children **DISCIPLINE** AMERICAN & CANADIAN HISTORY **EDUCATION** State Univ NY, Albany, AB, 53, MA, 57; Duke Univ, PhD(hist), 70. **CAREER** Teacher Am hist, Guilderland Sr High Sch, 57-66; instr, Duke Univ, 68-69; from asst prof to assoc prof hist, Wells Col, 69-75, chmn dept, 72-74; actg chmn, 79, ASSOC PROF HIST, UNIV ME, ORONO, 75-, Consult, Nat Endowment for Humanities, 75-. **HONORS AND AWARDS** Albert B Corey Prize, Can & Am Hist Asns, 76. **MEMBERSHIPS** AHA; Can Hist Asn; Orgn Am Historians; Asn Can Studies US; Atlantic Asn Historians.. **RESEARCH** Late 19th & 20th century American history; Canadian social and economic history; Canadian-American relations. **SELECTED PUBLICATIONS** Contrib, The Influence of the United States on Canadian Development: Eleven Case Studies, Duke Univ, 72; auth, Gompers in Canada, Univ Toronto, 74; Economic Development in Portland and Saint John During the Age of Iron and Steam, 1850-1914, Am Rev Can Studies, spring 79; Samuel Gompers et les travailleurs quebecois, 1900-1914, In: Le mouvement ouvrier au Quebec, Boreal Press, 80; Will You Walk-Yes, Well Walk- Popular Support for a Street Railway Strike in Portland, Maine, Labor Hist, Vol 35, 94; Dictionary of Canadian Biography, Vol 13, with R. Cook, Acadiensis, Vol 25, 95; Where the Fraser-River Flows-The Industrial Workers of the World in British-Columbia, with M. Leier, Labor Hist, Vol 36, 95. **CONTACT ADDRESS** Dept of Hist, Univ of ME, Orono, ME, 04473.

BABCOCK, WILLIAM SUMMER
PERSONAL Born 06/18/1939, Boston, MA, m, 1960, 2 children **DISCIPLINE** CHURCH HISTORY **EDUCATION** Brown Univ, AB, 61; Yale Univ, MA, 65, PhD(relig studies), 71. **CAREER** From instr to asst prof, 67-77, ASSOC PROF CHURCH HIST, PERKINS SCH THEOL, SOUTHERN METHODIST UNIV, 77-, Am Coun Learned Socs studies fel, 73-74. **MEMBERSHIPS** Am Soc Church Hist; Mediaeval Acad Am; NAm Patristics Soc; Am Cath Hist Asn. **RESEARCH** Augustine; Latin Patristics; history of Christian theology. **SELECTED PUBLICATIONS** Auth, Grace, Freedom and Justice: Augustine and the Christian Tradition, summer 73 & Patterns of Roman Selfbood: Marcus Aurelius and Augustine of Hippo, fall 74, Perkins Sch Theol J; Augustine's Interpretation of Romans (AD 394-396), Augustinian Studies 19, 79; Agustin y Ticonio: sobre la appropriacion latina de Pablo, Augustinus, 7-12/81; Art and Architecture, Christian, In: Abingdon Dict of Living Religions, 81; Is There Only One True Religion or Are There Many, with S. M. Ogden, Theology Today, Vol 50, 94. **CONTACT ADDRESS** Perkins Sch of Theol, Southern Methodist Univ, Dallas, TX, 75275.

BABER, CEOLA ROSS
PERSONAL Born 11/30/1950, Selma, Alabama, m **DISCIPLINE** EDUCATION **EDUCATION** CA State Univ Sacramento, BA 1972; Stanford Univ, MA 1975; Purdue Univ, PhD 1984. **CAREER** Sequoia Union HS Dist, teacher 1974-78; Tuskegee Univ, project coord/instructor 1979-80; Purdue Univ, rsch assoc 1980-81, dir/asst prof 1984-89; Univ of North Carolina-Greensboro, School of Education, asst assoc prof 1989-. **HONORS AND AWARDS** UNCG Alumni Teaching Excellence Awd, Jr Faculty Recipient, 1993; Consortium of Doctors, Distinguished Women of Color Awd, 1991. **MEMBERSHIPS** American Educational Research Association; National Association of Multicultural Education; National Council for Social Studies; Phi Delta Kappa; Kappa Delta Pi; Delta Kappa Gamma International Education Society; advisory council, People of America Foundation, 1996-; editorial bd, Theory and Research in Social Education, 1996-. **CONTACT ADDRESS** Univ of North Carolina-Greensboro, PO Box 26171, Greensboro, NC, 27402-6171. **EMAIL** baberca@dewey.uncg.edu

BABER, LUCKY LARRY
PERSONAL Born 04/16/1949, Ackerman, MS **DISCIPLINE** SOCIOLOGY **EDUCATION** Grand Valley State College, BS, 1972; Central Michigan University, MA, 1975; Bowling Green State University, PhD, 1978. **CAREER** Saginaw Big Brothers, asst director, 1972-73; Delta College, instructor, 1973-74; Buena Vista High School, teacher, 1974-75; Lincoln University, Dept Soc, asst professor/chairman, beginning 1978; Goldey Beacon College, College of Arts & Sciences, professor. **MEMBERSHIPS** Vice chairman, bd of fellows, Center for Studying Soc Welfare and Community Development, 1979-80; chairman, Bowling Green Chapter, Alpha Kappa Delta, 1977-78. **CONTACT ADDRESS** Col of Arts & Sciences, Goldey-Beacom Col, 4701 Limestone Rd, Wilmington, DE, 19808-1927.

BABROW, AUSTIN S.
DISCIPLINE SOCIAL INFLUENCE AND RESEARCH METHODS **EDUCATION** Univ Ill, PhD, 86. **CAREER** Assoc prof, Purdue Univ. **SELECTED PUBLICATIONS** Auth, Communication and Problematic Integration: Milan Kundera's Lost Letters, The Book of Laughter and Forgetting, 95; coauth, Communication and problematic integration in end-of-life decisions: Dialysis decisions among the elderly; Health Communication; Theorizing health communication, Communication Studies; Social support messages and the management of uncertainty in the experience of breast cancer: An application of problematic integration theory, Commun Monogr, 96. **CONTACT ADDRESS** Dept of Commun, Purdue Univ, 1080 Schleman Hall, West Lafayette, IN, 47907-1080. **EMAIL** ababrow@sla.purdue.edu

BABSON, JANE F.
PERSONAL Born 08/17/1925, Leitchfield, KY, m, 1954, 2 children **DISCIPLINE** ART & ART HISTORY **EDUCATION** Mt Holyoke, BA (art hist); Univ IL, Champaign, MFA. **CAREER** Former member of the staff of the Corcoran Gallery of Art, Washington, DC; Professional Printmeaker, Artitist and Photographer; founder, The Winstead Press LTD, 86-. **MEMBERSHIPS** Soc of Architectural Hist; Company of Military Historians; Nat Trust for Historic Preservation; The Ephemera Soc, London; IL Hist Soc; Am Crafts Coun. **RESEARCH** A... of Sir Jacob Sysleur and his art; Am Colonial forts; res on early colonial America. **SELECTED PUBLICATIONS** Auth, The Architecture of Early Illinois Forts, IL Hist Soc J, spring 68, from book Some Early Types in the Northwest Territory, 1679-1832, IL Hist Soc Lib, 67; The Epsteins, A Family Album, Taylor-Hall Pub, 84. **CONTACT ADDRESS** 202 Slice Dr, Stamford, CT, 06907.

BACCHIOCCHI, SAMUELE
PERSONAL Rome, Italy **DISCIPLINE** THEOLOGY AND CHURCH HISTORY **EDUCATION** Newbold Col, Eng, BA; Andrews Univ, BD, MA; Pontifical Gregorian Univ, Ital, PhD, summa cum laude, 74. **CAREER** Prof, Andrews Univ. **HONORS AND AWARDS** Gold medal, Pope Paul VI. **SELECTED PUBLICATIONS** Auth, Immortality or Resurrection? A Biblical Study on Human Nature and Destiny; From Sabbath to Sunday: A Historical Investigation of the Rise of Sunday Observance in Early Christianity; Divine Rest for Human Restlessness: A Theological Study of the Good News of the Sabbath for Today; The Sabbath in the New Testament. Answers to Questions; God's Festivals in Scripture and History, Vol I: The Spring Festivals; God's Festivals in Scripture and History, Vol 2: The Fall Festivals; Wine in the Bible: A Biblical Study on the Use of Alcoholic Beverages; The Advent Hope for Human Hopelessness. A Theological Study of the Meaning of the Second Advent for Today; Women in the Church: A Biblical Study on the Role of Women in the Church; Christian Dress and Adornment; Hal Lindsey's Prophetic Jigsaw Puzzle: Five Predictions that Failed!; The Time of the Crucifixion and the Resurrection; The Marriage Covenant: A Biblical Study on Marriage, Divorce, and Remarriage. **CONTACT ADDRESS** Andrews Univ, Berrien Springs, MI, 49104-0180.

BACHARACH, JERE L.
PERSONAL Born 11/18/1938, New York, NY, m, 1962, 2 children **DISCIPLINE** ISLAMIC HISTORY **EDUCATION** Trinity Col, CT, BA, 60; Harvard Univ, MA, 62; Univ MI, PhD(hist), 67. **CAREER** Asst prof, 67-73, assoc prof, 73-82, PROF HIST, UNIV WA, 82-, Chmn res & training comt, Mid E Studies Asn, 77-; prin investigator, NEH Mus & Hist Orgn award, 77-79; ed, MESA Bull, 78-. **MEMBERSHIPS** AHA; Am Orient Soc; Mediaeval Acad Am; Am Numis Soc; Mid E Studies Asn N Am. **RESEARCH** Medieval Islamic political, economic and numismatic history. **SELECTED PUBLICATIONS** Auth, A Near East Studies Handbook, Univ WA, rev ed, 76; co-ed, The Warp and Weft of Islam, Henry Art Gallery, 78; Symbols of Islam, 82; Laqab For a Future Caliph, The Case of the Abbasid Al-Mahdi, J of the Am Oriental Soc, Vol 113, 93; The Caliphate in the West-An Islamic Institution in the Iberian Peninsula, with D. J. Wasserstein, Speculum-A J of Medieval Studies, Vol 70, 95; Al-Almin Designated Successor-The Limitations of Numismatic Evidence, J of the Am Oriental Soc, Vol 116, 96. **CONTACT ADDRESS** Dept of Hist, Univ of WA, Seattle, WA, 98105.

BACHRACH, BERNARD S.
PERSONAL Born 05/14/1939, New York, NY **DISCIPLINE** MEDIEVAL HISTORY **EDUCATION** Queens Col, NY, BA, 61; Univ CA, Berkeley, MA, 62, PhD(medieval hist), 66. **CAREER** Lectr Hist, Queens Col, NY, 66-67; from asst prof to assoc prof, 67-75, assoc dir, Prog Jewish Studies, 76-80, PROF HIST, UNIV MN, MINNEAPOLIS, 75-, ADJ PROF ANCIENT STUDIES & RELIG STUDIES, 80-, McKnight award Europ hist, 68; Am Coun Learned Socs res grant, 73-74; co-ed, Medieval Prosopography. **MEMBERSHIPS** AHA; Mediaeval Acad Am; Soc Antiquaires de l'Ouest; Asn Medieval Historians of Mid-West. **RESEARCH** Medieval Europe. **SELECTED PUBLICATIONS** Auth, Charles Martel, the Stirrup, Mounted Shock Combat and Feudalism, Study Medieval & Renaissance Hist, 70; ed, The Medieval Church: Success or Failure, Holt, 72; auth, Merovingian Military Organization, 72 & A History of the Alans in the West, 73, Univ MN; ed & transl, The Liber Historiae Francorum, Coronado, 73; A Reassessment of Visigothic Jewish Policy, Am Hist Rev; auth, Early Medieval Jewish Policy, Univ MN, 77; ed & transl, Jews in Barbarian Europe, Coronado, 77; auth, Fortifications and Military Tactics, Technol & Cult, 79; Montjoie-et-Saint-Denis-Paris and St-Denis as the Origins of the Spiritual Center of Gaul (French), with A. Lombardjourdan, Speculum-A J of Medieval Studies, Vol 67, 92; Sociobiology and Human Social Behavior-Reply, J of Interdisciplinary Hist, Vol 23, 93; Medieval Seige Warfare-A Reconnaissance-A Review-Essay, J of Military Hist, Vol 58, 94; Anthropologists and Early-Medieval History-Some Problems, Cithara-Essays in the Judeo-Christian Tradition, Vol 33, 94; Terrence J. Daly Comment on Medieval Seige Warfare-Reply, J of Military Hist, Vol 58, 94; Feifs and Vassals-The Medieval Evedence Reinterpreted, with S. Reynolds, Albion, Vol 27, 95; Roman Defeat, Christian Response, and the Literary Construction of the Jew, with D. M. Olster, Speculum-A J of Medieval Studies, Vol 71, 96; Medieval Source Identification and Citations (French), J. Berlioz, Speculum- A J of Medieval Studies, Vol 71, 96; Medieval Diplomatics (French), with O. Guyotjeannin, J. Pycke, and B. M. Tock, Speculum-A J of Medieval Studies, Vol 71, 96; Arms, Armies and Fortifications in the 100 Years War, with A. Curry and M. Hughes, Historian, Vol 59, 96; Phantoms of Remembrance-Memory and Oblivion at the End of the First Millennium, with P. J. Geary, J of Interdisciplinary Hist, Vol 27, 96; Warfare Under the Anglo-Norman Kings, 1066-1135, with S. Morillo, Int Hist Rev, Vol 18, 96; Knights and Warhorses-Military Service and the English Aristocracy Under Edward III, with A. Ayton, J of Military Hist, Vol 60, 96; Family Power in Southern Italy-The Duchy-og-Gaeta and Its Neighbors, 850-1139, with P. Skinner, J of Interdisciplinary Hist, Vol 27, 97; King Alfred the Great, with A. P. Smith, J of Military Hist, Vol 61, 97; Neglected Heroes-Leadership and War in the Early-Medieval Period, with T. L. Gore, Speculum-A J of Medieval Studies, Vol 72, 97; Medieval Warfare Source Book, Vol 1, Warfare in Western Christendom, with D. Nicolle, Int Hist Rev, Vol 19, 97. **CONTACT ADDRESS** Dept of Hist, Univ of MN, 267 19th Ave S, Minneapolis, MN, 55455-0499.

BACON, HELEN HAZARD
PERSONAL Born 03/09/1919, Berkeley, CA **DISCIPLINE** CLASSICAL LANGUAGES & LITERATURE **EDUCATION** Bryn Mawr Col, BA, 40, PhD(classics), 55. **CAREER** Instr Greek & English, Bryn Mawr Col, 46-48, instr Greek, 48-49; instr classics, Woman's Col, 51-52; from instr to assoc prof, Smith Col, 53-61; assoc prof, 61-65, PROF CLASSICS, BARNARD COL, COLUMBIA UNIV, 65-, Mem, Col Bd Latin Comt, 61-64; Am Asn Univ Women Founders fel, 63-64; mem fac, Bread Loaf Sch English, Vt, summers 66, 68, 73 & 75; scholar-in-residence, Am Acad in Rome, 68-69; Blegen Distinguished vis res prof, Vassar, fall 79; consult Latin lang & scholar, Comt Physicians Overseeing Translation of 16th Century Latin Medieval Text, 73-. **HONORS AND AWARDS** DLitt, Middlebury Col, 70. **MEMBERSHIPS** Am Philol Asn; Archaeol Inst Am. **RESEARCH** Greek tragedy; Plato; ancient romances. **SELECTED PUBLICATIONS** Auth, Socrates crowned, Va Quart Rev, 59; Barbarians in Greek Tragedy, Yale Univ, 61; The Shield of Eteocles, Arion, 64; Woman's Two Faces: Sophocles' View of Woman's Relation to the Tragedy of Oedipus and His Family, Sci & Psychoanal, 66; co-transl, Aeschylus' Seven against Thebes, Oxford Univ, 73; auth, In- and Out-door Schoolings Robert Frost and the Classics, Am Scholar, 74; For Girls: From Birches to Wild Grapes, Yale Rev, 77; Aeschylus and Early Tragedy, In: Ancient Writers: Greece, Scribner's, 82; The Chorus in Greek Life and Drama, Arion-A Journal of Humanities and the Classics, Vol 3, 95. **CONTACT ADDRESS** Dept of Greek & Latin, Barnard Col, New York, NY, 10027.

BACON, MARDGES
PERSONAL Born 07/04/1944, Plainfield, NJ, m, 1990, 4 children **DISCIPLINE** ART & ARCHITECTURE **EDUCATION** Univ Del, BA, 66; Univ Mich, MA, 68; Brown Univ, PhD, 78. **CAREER** Res asst, ed asst, 68-69, Fogg Art Museum, Harvard Univ; instr, fine arts, 69-70, Tufts Univ; admin, chmn, orient prog, ed stud guide, 70-71, Boston Col; proj dir, 76-78, NEH Interpretive Prog Soc, Preserv of New Eng Antiq, Boston; lectr, 77, MIT; asst prof, 78-84, Trinity Col; assoc prof, 85-88, prof, 88-, art & archit, Northeastern Univ. **HONORS AND AWARDS** Trinity Col grantee, 79, 81, 82, 85, 87; Guggenheim fel, 87-88; Northeastern Univ grantee, 91, 92. **MEMBERSHIPS** Soc for Preserv of New Eng Antiq; Amer Stud Assn; Col Art Assn. **SELECTED PUBLICATIONS** Auth, Ernest Flagg: Beaux-Arts Architect and Urban Reformer, 86. **CON-**

TACT ADDRESS Dept of Art and Architecture, Northeastern Univ, 239 Ryder Hall, Boston, MA, 02115. **EMAIL** mbacon@lynx.new.edu

BADASH, LAWRENCE
PERSONAL Born 05/08/1934, Brooklyn, NY, 2 children **DISCIPLINE** HISTORY OF SCIENCE **EDUCATION** Rensselaer Polytech Inst, BS (physics), 56; Yale Univ, PhD(hist of sci), 64. **CAREER** Instr Hist of Sci, Yale Univ, 64-65, res assoc, 65-66; asst prof, 66-73, assoc prof, 73-79, prof Hist of Sci, Univ Calif, Santa Barbara, 79-, consult, Am Chem Soc, 61, Time-Life Publ, Inc, 63 & Gen Res Corp, 68; NATO fel, 65-66; NSF res grants, 65-66 & 69-72; mem adv bd, Reactor Hist Proj, Rand Corp, 75-77; mem adv bd, inst Appropriate Technol, Univ Calif, 77-79; dir summer seminar on Global Security and Arms Control, Univ Calif, 83, 86; instr, Cen of Postgrad Studies, Dubrovnik, 86, 87, 96; vis prof Meiji Gakuin Univ, Yokohama, 93. **HONORS AND AWARDS** Fel, US European Summer School on Global Security and Arms Control. Univ Sussex, 87; fell, Amer Physical Soc, 87; fell, Summer Seminar on East-West Sec Probs, Moscow State Institute of International Affairs, 89. **MEMBERSHIPS** Hist Sci Soc; AAAS; Fedn Am Sci; WCoast Hist of Sci Soc. **RESEARCH** History of modern physics, especially radioactivity and nuclear physics; development of military and civilian uses of nuclear energy. **SELECTED PUBLICATIONS** Auth, Radioactivity before the Curies, Am J Physics, 2/65; How the newer alchemy was received, Sci Am, 8/66; Rutherford, Boltwood, and the age of the earth: The origin of radioactive dating techniques, Proc Am Philos Soc, 6/68; ed, Rutherford and Boltwood, Letters on Radioactivity, Yale Univ, 69; Rutherford Correspondence Catalog, Am Inst Physics, 74; auth, The completeness of 19th century science, Isis, 3/72; Radioactivity in America: Growth and decay of a science, Johns Hopkins, 79; ed, Reminiscences of Los Alamos, 1943-1945, Reidel, 80; Kapitza, Rutherford, and the Kremlin, Yale Univ, 85; Scientists and the Development of Nuclear Weapons, Humanities Press, 95. **CONTACT ADDRESS** Dept of History, Univ of California, Santa Barbara, 552 University Rd, Santa Barbara, CA, 93106-0001. **EMAIL** badash@humanitas.ucsb.edu

BADGER, REID
PERSONAL Born 07/31/1942, Salt Lake City, UT, m, 1965, 2 children **DISCIPLINE** AMERICAN STUDIES **EDUCATION** US Naval Acad, BS, 64; Syracuse Univ, MSS, 74, PhD, 75. **CAREER** Prof, 74-98 dir, program in Amer Studies, 75-80, asst dean, Coll of Arts and Sci, 80-83, 98- prof emeritus of American Studies, Univ of AL. **MEMBERSHIPS** Amer Studies Assoc; Amer Historical Assn; Organization of Amer Historians; Ctr for Black Music Research **RESEARCH** American Culture **SELECTED PUBLICATIONS** auth, A Life in Ragtime: A Biography of James Reese Europe, Oxford Univ Press, 95; auth, Pride without Prejudice: The Day New York Drew No Color Line, Prospects: A Journ of Amer Cultural Studies, 91; A Military Band Whose Exotic Beat Led Them All, New York Newsday, May 15, 95; The Jazz King, The Baltimore Sun, Feb 1, 98. **CONTACT ADDRESS** Amer Studies Program, Univ of Alabama, University, AL, 35486.

BADIAN, ERNST
PERSONAL m, 1950, 2 children **DISCIPLINE** ANCIENT GREEK & ROMAN HISTORY **EDUCATION** Univ NZ, BA, 44, MA, 45 & 46; Oxford Univ, BA, 50, MA, 54, DPhil, 56; Victoria Univ, Wellington, LitD, 62. **CAREER** Jr lectr classics, Victoria Univ Wellington, 47-48; asst lectr classics & ancient hist, Univ Sheffield, 52-54; lectr classics, Univ Durham, 54-65; prof ancient hist, Univ Leeds, 65-69; prof classics & hist, State Univ NY Buffalo, 69-71; prof hist, 71-82, JOHN MOON CABOT PROF HIST, HARVARD UNIV, 82-, De Carle lectr, Univ Otago, NZ, 69; Todd lectr, Univ Sydney, 69; Louise Taft Semple lectr, Univ Cincinnati, 70; Am Coun Learned Soc fel, 72-73; Leverhulme fel, Brit Acad, 73; Suther prof classics, Univ Calif, 73; ed, Am J Ancient Hist 76-; corresp mem, Ger Archaeol Inst. **MEMBERSHIPS** Fel Brit Acad; corresp mem Austrian Acad Sci; fel Am Acad Arts & Sci; Am Numismatic Soc; Asn Ancient Historians. **RESEARCH** Alexander the Great; Roman republic. **SELECTED PUBLICATIONS** Auth, Foreign Clientelae (264-70 BC), Oxford Univ, 58; Studies in Greek and Roman History, 64 & ed & contribr, Ancient Society and Institutions, 66, Blackwell, Oxford; ed, Polybius, Washington Sq, 66; auth, Roman Imperialism in the Late Republic, 68 & Publicans and Sinners, 72, Blackwell-Cornell Univ; contribr var class & hist jour & collections; ed, Ronald Syme, Roman Papers (2 Vols), Oxford Univ, 79; The Legend of the Legate Who Lost His Luggage & The Career of Gaius Cato, According to Cicero 'In Verrem' 2, 4, 22 and Modern Scholarship, Historia-Zeitschrift Fur Alte Geschichte, Vol 42, 93. **CONTACT ADDRESS** Dept of Hist, Harvard Univ, Robinson Hall, Cambridge, MA, 02138-3800.

BAER, JUDITH A.
PERSONAL Born 04/05/1945, New York, NY **DISCIPLINE** POLITICAL SCIENCE **EDUCATION** Univ Chicago, PhD, 74. **CAREER** Asst prof, SUNY Albany, 76-83; asst prof to assoc prof, Calif State Polytech Univ, 85-88; assoc prof, to prof, Texas A&M Univ, 88- . **HONORS AND AWARDS** Fel, Woodrow Wilson Int Ctr for Scholars, 95-96; roving Fulbright sr lectr, Turkey, 97-98. **MEMBERSHIPS** Am Polit Sci Asn; Pi Sigma Alpha. **RESEARCH** Public law; feminist theory. **SELECTED PUBLICATIONS** Auth, Women in American Law, 2d ed, Holmes & Meier, 96; auth, Our Lives before The Law: Constructing a Feminist Jurisprudence, Princeton, forthcoming. **CONTACT ADDRESS** Dept of Political Science, Texas A&M Univ, College Station, TX, 77843-4348. **EMAIL** j_baer@tamu.edu

BAGBY, WESLEY MARVIN
PERSONAL Born 06/15/1922, Albany, GA **DISCIPLINE** HISTORY **EDUCATION** Univ NC, AB, 43, MA, 45; Columbia Univ, PhD(hist), 53. **CAREER** Instr hist, Pfeiffer Jr Col, 45-46, Wake Forest Col, 46-48, Univ TN, 49-51 & Univ Md, 51-52; teacher, High Schs, Md, 53-56; actg chmn dept, 62-63, from instr to assoc prof, 56-68, PROF HIST, WVA UNIV, 68-, Fulbright lectr US hist, Grad Sch Am Studies, Tamkang Col & Fu Re Jem Univ, Taiwan, 75-76. **MEMBERSHIPS** AHA; AAUP; Soc Historians of Am Foreign Rels. **RESEARCH** Recent American history; American diplomatic history. **SELECTED PUBLICATIONS** Auth, Woodrow Wilson, a Third Term and the Solemn Referendum, Am Hist Rev; The Smoke Filled Room and the Nomination of Warren G Harding, Miss Valley Hist Rev; The Harding Election: Wilson Repudiated, In: History of the First World War, Vol 8, Purnell, London, 71; An Identification and Classification of America's Historic Foreign Policies, Tamkang J, Taiwan, 76; The Women's Liberation Movement, In: American Studies, Acad Sinica, Taiwan, 76; United States Foreign Policy in Transition, Proc of Sec Tamkang Am Studies Conf, Taiwan, 77; Uncertain Partners-Stalin, Mao, and the Korean-War, with S. N. Goncharov, J. W. Lewis, and L. T. Xue, J of Am Hist, Vol 81, 95; A Revolutionary War-Korea and the Transformation of the Postwar World, with W. J. Williams, J of Am Hist, Vol 81, 95. **CONTACT ADDRESS** Dept of Hist, West Virginia Univ, P O Box 6303, Morgantown, WV, 26506-6303.

BAGNALL, ROGER SHALER
PERSONAL Born 08/19/1947, Seattle, WA, m, 1969, 2 children **DISCIPLINE** GREEK PAPYROLOGY, ANCIENT HISTORY. **EDUCATION** Yale Univ, BA, 68; Univ Toronto, MA, 69, PHD(class studies), 72. **CAREER** Asst prof classics, Fla State Univ, 72-74; asst prof Greek & Latin, 74-79, assoc prof to prof Classics & Hist, Columbia Univ, 74-; mem bd, Scholars Press, 77-85; pres, Egyptological Sem of NY, 81-83; vis prof, Univ Florence, 81. **HONORS AND AWARDS** Am Coun Learned Soc grant-in-aid, 75; Am Coun Learned Soc study fel, 76-77; Am Philos Soc grant-in-aid, 80; Guggenheim fel, 90-91; Fel, Am Numismatic Soc; Assoc Academie Royale des Sciences; des Lettres et des Beaux-Arts de Relgique. **MEMBERSHIPS** Am Soc Papyrologists (secy-treas, 74-79); Am Philol Asn (secy-treas, 79-85); Asn pour les Etudes Grecques; Egypt Exploration Soc; Asn Ancient Historians. **RESEARCH** Greek papyri; social and economic history of the late Roman Egypt; Hellenistic social and economic history. **SELECTED PUBLICATIONS** Coauth, Ostraka in the Royal Ontario Museum (2 vols), Samuel Stevens, Toronto, 71-76; auth, Ptolemaic Foreign Correspondence in Tebtunis Papyrus 8, J Egyptian Archaeol, 75; The Administration of the Ptolemaic Possessions, Brill, Leiden, 76; coauth, Ostraka in Amsterdam Collections, Terra, Zutphen, 76; auth, The Florida Ostraka: Documents from the Roman Army in Upper Egypt, Duke Univ, 76; Bullion Purchases and Landholding in the Fourth Century, Chronique d'Egypt, 77; coauth, The Chronological Systems of Byzantine Egypt, Terra, Zutphen, 78; Columbia Papyri VII, Scholars Press, 78; auth, Egypt in Late Antiquity, Princeton, 93; coauth, Demography of Roman Egypt, Cambridge, 94; auth, Reading Papyri, Writing Ancient History, Routledge, 95. **CONTACT ADDRESS** Columbia Univ, 1130 Amsterdam Ave, Rm 606, New York, NY, 10027-6900. **EMAIL** baguall@columbia.edu

BAIGELL, MATTHEW
DISCIPLINE AMERICAN ART **EDUCATION** Univ Pa, PhD. **CAREER** Prof II, Rutgers, The State Univ NJ, Univ Col-Camden. **RESEARCH** American art. **SELECTED PUBLICATIONS** Auth, Reflections on/of Richard Estes, in Art Criticism 8, no 2, 93; Barnett Newman's Stripe Paintings and Kaballah: A Jewish Take, in American Art 8, 94; Jewish-American Artists and the Holocaust, Rutgers UP, 97; coauth, Soviet Dissident Art: Interviews after Perestroika, Rutgers UP, 95. **CONTACT ADDRESS** Dept of Art Hist, Rutgers, The State Univ NJ, Univ Col-Camden, Voorhees Hall, 71 Hamilton St, New Brunswick, NJ, 08903. **EMAIL** baigell@rci.rutgers.edu

BAILEY, ADRIENNE YVONNE
PERSONAL Born 11/24/1944, Chicago, IL **DISCIPLINE** EDUCATION **EDUCATION** Mundelein Coll, BA 1966; Wayne State Univ, MEd 1968; Northwestern Univ, PhD 1973. **CAREER** Chicago Bd of Educ, Deneen Elementary School, teacher Social Studies, English, French, Math 1966-67; So Shore YMCA, Chicago, neighborhood youth corps supvr 1967; Circle Maxwell YMCA, Chicago, program coordinator 1967-68; Detroit Bd of Educ, substitute teacher 1968-69; Gov Office of Human Resources, Chicago, educ coord 1969-71; Northwestern Comm Educ Proj, Northwestern Univ, univ coord 1972-73; Chicago Comm Trust, Chicago, sr staff assoc 1973-81; College Bd NY, vice pres acad affairs 1981-. **HONORS AND AWARDS** Merit Award, NW Alumni Assn 1981; Diamond Jubilee Recognition, Phi Delta Kappa 1981; Certificate of Recognition, Phi Delta Kappa NW Univ Chapter 1980; Salute IL Serv, Federal Savings & Loan Bank 1980; Meritorious Serv Award, Educ Commission of the State NAEP 1980; Human Relations Award, IL Educ Assn 1980; attendance at White House Celebration for the Signing of S210 Creating a Dept of Educ, 1979; Kizzy Award for Outstanding Contributions in Educ 1979; Outstanding Achievement Award in Educ, YWCA of Metro Chicago 1978; Distinguished Serv Award, Ed Commission of the State 1977; 1 of 10 Outstanding Young Citizens Award, Chicago Jaycees 1976; Community Motivation Award HU MA BE Karate Assoc 1975; 1 of 10 Outstanding Young Persons Award, IL Jaycees 1975; 1of 10 Outstanding Black Women in AmAward, Operation PUSH 1975; Commencement Speaker Mundelein Coll 1975; Image Award for Outstanding Contributions in Field of Educ, League of Black Women 1974; Recognition Award, Black Achiever of Indust YMCA of Metro Chicago 1974; TTT Fellowship, Northwestern Univ 1971-73; MDEA Inst in French, Univ of ME 1966; Special Service Award, Natl Alliance of Black School Educators, 1987. **MEMBERSHIPS** Gov Educ Adv Comm 1983-87, Natl Comm on Secondary Schooling for Hispanics 1983-85, Educ & Career Devel Advisory Comm Natl Urban League 1982-, visiting comm Grad School of Educ Harvard Univ 1977-83; advisory panel Phi Delta Kappa Gallup Poll of the Publics Attitudes Toward Public Educ 1984; policy comm School of Educ Northwestern Univ 1983-; bd of trustees Hazen Found, New Haven CT, 1977-87; bd of trustees So Educ Found, Atlanta GA, 1983-; Natl Task Force on State Efforts to Achieve Sex Equity 1980-83, chmn advisory comm Council on Found Internship & Fellowship Program for Minorities & Women 1980-82; adv comm Inst for Educ Finance & Govt Stanford Univ 1980-85; bd of dir Assn of Black Found Exec 1975-87; IL State Bd of Educ 1974-81, pres1978-79; Natl Assn of State Bds of Educ; commiss 1981, steering comm 1974-79, exec comm 1977-75, 1978-79 Educ Commiss of the States; Natl Assessment of Educ Program Policy Comm 1976-80; task force Desegregation Strategies Project 1976-81; bd of dir Council on Foundations 86; META 86; editorial bd, The Kappan (Phi Delta Kappan); Governor's Advisory Comm on Black Affairs, NY, co-chair, Educ sub-Committee 1986-; bd of dir The Negro Ensemble, NY, 1987-; bd of trustees Marymount Coll 1988-89; bd of trustees The Foundation Center 1989-. **SELECTED PUBLICATIONS** Auth, "Comm Coll Capability Project," IL Bd of Higher Educ 1972; "Citizens in Public Ed in Chicago" Citizen Action in Educ 1976; "Agenda for Action" Educ Leadership 1984; "Top 100 Black Business & Professional Women," Dollars & Sense Magazine, 1985. **CONTACT ADDRESS** Acad Affairs, The Col Board, 45 Columbus Ave, New York, NY, 10023.

BAILEY, BETH
DISCIPLINE AMERICAN STUDIES **EDUCATION** Univ Chicago, PhD, 86. **CAREER** Assoc prof, Univ NMex; bd od eds, Am Stud and Pacific Hist Rev. **HONORS AND AWARDS** Grant, ACLS, NEH; Ann Whitney Olin scholar, Columbia Univ, 91-94; Sr Fulbright Lectureship, Indonesia, 96. **RESEARCH** American cultural history; popular culture. **SELECTED PUBLICATIONS** Auth, From Front Porch to Back Seat: Courtship in 20th Century America, 88; coauth, The First Strange Place: The Alchemy of Race and Sex in WWII Hawaii, 92. **CONTACT ADDRESS** Univ NMex, Albuquerque, NM, 87131.

BAILEY, CHARLES RANDALL
PERSONAL Born 02/07/1938, Plain City, OH, m, 1970, 2 children **DISCIPLINE** MODERN EUROPEAN HISTORY & HISTORY OF EDUCATION **EDUCATION** OH Univ, BA, 60; Univ Chicago, MA, 62, PhD(hist), 68. **CAREER** Instr hist, Juniata Col, 62-63; asst prof, 67-78, ASSOC PROF HIST, STATE UNIV NY COL GENESEO, 78-, Nat Endowment for Humanities fel, Univ NC, Chapel Hill, 78-79. **MEMBERSHIPS** AHA; Soc Fr Hist Studies. **RESEARCH** Eighteenth-century French education. **SELECTED PUBLICATIONS** Auth, French Secondary Education, 1763-1790: The Secularization of Ex-Jesuit Colleges, Am Philos Soc, 78; Municipal colleges: Small-town Secondary Schools in France Prior to the Revolution, Fr Hist Studies, 82; Speculative Freeemasonry and the Enlightenment-A Study of the Craft in London, Paris, Prague and Vienna, with R. W. Weisberger, European Hist Quart, Vol 25, 95. **CONTACT ADDRESS** Dept of Hist, State Univ NY Col, 1 College Cir, Geneseo, NY, 14454-1401.

BAILEY, COLIN B.
PERSONAL Born 10/20/1955, London, England **DISCIPLINE** ART HISTORY **EDUCATION** Brasenose Col, BA, 78; Sorbonne, Univ de Paris, dipl art hist, 82-83; Oxford Univ, MA, DPhil, 85. **CAREER** Asst cur, Europ painting & sculpture, Philadelphia Mus Art, 85-89; cur, Europ painting & sculpture, 89-90, sr cur, Kimbell Art Mus (Ft Worth, TX), 90-94; CHIEF CURATOR, NATIONAL GALLERY CANADA, 95-; vis prof, Univ Pa, 88; vis prof, Bryn Mawr Col, 89; Paul Mellon sr vis fel, Nat Gallery Art, Washington, 94. **HONORS AND AWARDS** Vasari Award, Dallas Mus Art, 93; Chevalier de l'ordre des arts et lettres. **RESEARCH** European painting. **SELECTED PUBLICATIONS** Auth, The First Painters of the King, 85; auth, The Loves of the Gods: Mythological Painting from Watteau to David, 92; auth, Renoir's Portraits, 97; coauth,

Masterpieces of Impressionism & Post-Impressionism, 89. **CONTACT ADDRESS** National Gallery of Canada, 380 Sussex Dr, Box 427, Sta A, Ottawa, ON, K1N 9N4.

BAILEY, DONALD ATHOLL
PERSONAL Born 02/24/1940, Rochester, MN, m, 1963, 2 children **DISCIPLINE** EUROPEAN HISTORY **EDUCATION** Univ Sask, BA, 62; Oxford Univ, Hons, 64, MA, 68; Univ MM, Minneapolis, PhD(hist), 73. **CAREER** Instr hist, Univ Sask, 64-65; lectr, Carleton Col, 66-67; from instr to asst prof, 69-77, ASSOC PROF HIST, UNIV WINNIPEG, 77-, Part-time instr, Mennonite Brethren Col Arts, 81. **MEMBERSHIPS** Soc Fr Hist Studies; Can Hist Asn; Western Soc Fr Hist. **RESEARCH** France at the time of Cardinal Richelieu; life of Michel de Marillac, 1563-1632. **SELECTED PUBLICATIONS** Auth, Les Pamphlets de Mathieu de Morgues (1582-1670): Bibliographie des Ouvrages Disponibles dans les Bibliotheques Parisiennes et Certaines Bibliotheques des Etats-Unis, Revue Fransaise d'Historie du Livre, No 18, 41-86, 1-3/78; Les Pamphlets des Associes Polemistes de Mathieu de Morgues: Marie de Medicis, Gaston d'Orleans et Jacques Chanteloube, Une Bibliographie des Fonds des Bibliotheques de paris et des Etats-Unis, Revue Francaise d'histoire du Livre, No 27, 229-70, 4-6/80; The Pamphlets of Mathieu de Morgues, Marie de Medicis, Gaston d'Orleans and Jacques Chanteloube: A Bibliography of Holdings in Selected Belgian Libraries, Archives et Bibliotheques de Belgique/Archief-en Bibliotheekwezen in Belgie, 12/80; Les Recueils de Mathieu de Morgues: Une Bibliogrpahie des Collections aux Bibliotheques de Paris, Revue Francaise d'Histoire du Livre; Civic Politics in the Rome of Urban VIII, with L. Nussdorfer, Urban Hist Rev, Vol 23, 95; The Miracle of Laon-Reasonable, Unreasonable, Apocalyptic and Political Elements in Various Accounts of the Miracle of Laon 1566-1578 (French), with I. Backus, Sixteenth Century J, Vol 26, 95. **CONTACT ADDRESS** Dept of Hist, Univ of Winnipeg, Winnipeg, MB, R3B 2E9.

BAILEY, FREDERICK GEORGE
PERSONAL Born 02/24/1924, United Kingdom, m, 1949, 2 children **DISCIPLINE** SOCIAL ANTHROPOLOGY **EDUCATION** Manchester, PhD. **CAREER** Emer, Univ Cal San Diego; Guggenheim fel, 77. **HONORS AND AWARDS** S C Roy Memorial Gold Medal distinguished services to anthrop in India. **MEMBERSHIPS** Am Acad Arts Sci. **RESEARCH** Micro-politics; India; Peasants. **SELECTED PUBLICATIONS** Auth The Kingdom of Individuals, Cornell Univ Press, 94; The Witch-Hunt, Cornell Univ Press, 94; The Civility of Indifference, Cornell Univ Press, 96; The Need ofr Enemies, Cornell Univ Press, 98. **CONTACT ADDRESS** Dept of Anthropology, Univ Calif San Diego, La Jolla, CA, 92093. **EMAIL** fbailey@UCSD.edu

BAILEY, JACKSON HOLBROOK
PERSONAL Born 09/22/1925, Portland, ME, m, 1949, 4 children **DISCIPLINE** MODERN JAPANESE HISTORY **EDUCATION** Earlham Col, AB, 50; Univ WI, AM, 51; Harvard Univ, PhD, 59. **CAREER** From asst prof to assoc prof, 59-69, PROF HIST, EARLHAM COL, 67-, Dir Asian studies prog, Earlham & Antioch Cols, 59-63; vis asst prof, Antioch Col, 60-63; dir, US Off Educ Ctr for EAsian Lang & Area Studies, 65-73; consult, US Off Educ on Int Educ Act, 66-67; Fulbright res fel, Inst Humanistic Sci, Univ Kyoto, 67-68; mem adv comt to Ambassador, Japan Found, 72-75; dir ctr EAsian studies, Great Lakes Cols Asn, 73-76; dir intro course pub TV on Japanese cult & hist, Univ Mid-Am, Lincoln, Nebr, 75-78; mem nat bd consult, Nat Endowment for Humanities. **MEMBERSHIPS** AHA; Asn Asian Studies; Midwest Conf Asian Affairs (vpres, 66-67, pres, 67-68). **RESEARCH** Modern Japanese Political History, Meiji Period; East Asian History; History of Modern China. **SELECTED PUBLICATIONS** Auth, Prince Saionji and the popular rights movement, J Asian Studies, 11/61; ed, Japan and Korea Sect, Asia: A Guide to Paperbacks, rev ed, Asia Soc, 68; auth, The Origin and Nature of the Genro, In: Vol 6, 65, Studies on Asia, Univ NE; ed, Listening to Japan, Praeger, 73; ed, Japan: The Living Tradition, 76 & Japan the Changing Tradition, 78, Univ Mid-Am; Antiquity in Japanese History, with J. P. Mass, Histiorian, Vol 55, 93; Servants, Shophands, and Laborers in the Cities of Tokugawa, Japan, with G. P. Leupp, Historian, Vol 56, 94. **CONTACT ADDRESS** Dept of Hist, Earlham Col, Richmond, IN, 47374.

BAILEY, JOHN WENDELL
PERSONAL Born 04/02/1934, Richmond, VA, m, 1959, 2 children **DISCIPLINE** AMERICAN HISTORY **EDUCATION** Hampden Sydney Col, BS, 59; Univ MD, MA, 61; Marquette Univ, PhD(hist), 74. **CAREER** Asst prof hist, Allegany Col, 61-66; asst prof, 67-74, ASSOC PROF HIST, CARTHAGE COL, 74-, CHAIRPERSON DEPT, 77-. **MEMBERSHIPS** Western Hist Asn; Orgn Am Historians; AHA; Southern Hist Asn; Western Am Lit Asn. **RESEARCH** Western military frontier; Western American literature. **SELECTED PUBLICATIONS** Auth, The McNeill Rangers and the capture of General Crook and Kelley, Md Hist Mag, 67; The presidential election of 1900 in Nebraska: McKinley over Bryan, Nebr Hist, 73; contribr, Kenosha County in the 20th Century, Kenosha County Bicentennial Comn, 76; auth, General Alfred Terry and the Decline of the Sioux, 1866-1890, Greenwood, 79; contribr, Kenosha retrospective, Kenosha County Bicentennial Comn, 81; Tellowstone Command-Colonel Nelson A. Miles and the Great Sioux War, 1877-1878, with J. A. Greene, Int Hist Rev, Vol 15, 93; Tales Never Told Around the Campfire-True Stories of Frontier America, with M. Dugan, Western Hist Quart, Vol 24, 93; Nelson Miles and the Twilight of the Frontier Army, with R. Wooster, J of Military Hist, Vol 58, 94; Strategic Deception in the Second World War-British Intelligence Operations Against the German High Command, with M. Howard, Historian, Vol 59, 97. **CONTACT ADDRESS** Dept of Hist, Carthage Col, 2001 Alford Park Dr, Kenosha, WI, 53140-1994.

BAILEY, STEPHEN
PERSONAL Born 04/04/1939, Chicago, IL, m, 1966, 3 children **DISCIPLINE** MODERN EUROPEAN HISTORY **EDUCATION** Univ Chicago, BA, 60, PhD, 66. **CAREER** Asst prof, 65-71, assoc prof, 71-79, prof hist, 79-, Dir, Florence Prog, Assoc Cols of Midwest, 77-78, assoc dean, Knox Coll, 85-. **MEMBERSHIPS** AHA. **RESEARCH** Germany during World War I; literature and politics under Napoleon III. **SELECTED PUBLICATIONS** Art, The Berlin Strike of January 1918, Central European History, Vol XII, Vol 2, 6/80. **CONTACT ADDRESS** Dept of History, Knox Col, 2 E South St, Galesburg, IL, 61401-4938. **EMAIL** sbailey@know.edu

BAILEY, TERENCE
DISCIPLINE MUSIC **EDUCATION** Univ Wash, PhD, 68. **CAREER** Prof **HONORS AND AWARDS** Fel, Royal Soc Can. **RESEARCH** Ambrosian chant; music and Liturgy of the Latin Church; medieval modal theory; musical paleography; text/music relationships in the Middle Ages and Renaissance. **SELECTED PUBLICATIONS** Auth, Ambrosianischer Gesang, 96; Antiphon and Psalm in the Ambrosian Office, Inst Mediaeval Music, 94; An Ancient Psalmody without Antiphons in the Ambrosian Ferial Office, 93; Word Painting and the Romantic Interpretation of Chant, Inst Medieval Music, 90; Milanese Melodic Tropes, Jour Plainsong Mediaeval Music Soc, 90; The Ambrosian Cantus, Inst Medieval Music, 87; Commemoratio Brevis, Univ Ottawa, 79. **CONTACT ADDRESS** Dept of Music, Western Ontario Univ, London, ON, N6A 5B8. **EMAIL** tbailey@julian.uwo.ca

BAILEY, VICTOR
PERSONAL Born 08/14/1948, Keighley, United Kingdom, d **DISCIPLINE** HISTORY, BRITISH **EDUCATION** Univ Warwick, BA, 69; Univ Cambridge, Mphilo, 70; Univ Warwick, PhD, 75. **CAREER** Cen Crimino Res, Oxford res off; Worchester Col, Oxford univ, fel, 78; Univ Hull, lectr, 83; Univ Kansas, prof, 88-. **HONORS AND AWARDS** Hon Res fel, Univ Hull. **MEMBERSHIPS** AHA; North Am Conf Brit Stud. **RESEARCH** Hist Mod Brit; Hist Eng Crim Law Admin. **SELECTED PUBLICATIONS** English Prisons, Penal Culture and the Abatement of Imprisonment, 1895-1922, J Brit Stud, 97; The Fabrication of Deviance, Dangerous Classes and Criminal Classes in Vict England, in: R Malocclusion and J Rule, eds, Protest the Survival: The Historical Experience, Essays for E P Thompson, The New Press, 93; This Rash Act: Suicide Across the Life Cycle In the Victorian City, Stanford Univ Press, 98. **CONTACT ADDRESS** Dept Hist, Univ Kansas, 3001 Woscoe Hall, Lawrence, KS, 66045. **EMAIL** vbailey@falcon.cc.ukans.edu

BAILLY, JACQUES A.
PERSONAL Born 01/28/1966, Salt Lake City, UT **DISCIPLINE** CLASSICS **EDUCATION** Brown Univ, BA, 88; Cornell Univ, PhD, 97. **CAREER** Lectr, Colby Col, 96-97; lectr, 97-98, asst prof, 98- , Univ Vermont. **HONORS AND AWARDS** Fulbright award, 88-90; Jakob K Javits Scholarship, 91-95. **MEMBERSHIPS** APA. **RESEARCH** Ancient philosophy; philology. **CONTACT ADDRESS** Dept of Classics, Vermont Univ, 481 Main St, Burlington, VT, 05401.

BAILY, SAMUEL LONGSTRETH
PERSONAL Born 05/09/1936, Philadelphia, PA, m, 1960, 3 children **DISCIPLINE** LATIN AMERICAN HISTORY **EDUCATION** Harvard Univ, BA, 58; Columbia Univ, MA, 63; Univ PA, PhD(Latin Am hist), 64. **CAREER** Asst prof hist, 64-68, assoc dir, Latin Am Inst, 67-70, grad adv hist, 70-71, dir, Rutgers Jr Yr Mex, 74-75, assoc prof hist, 68-78, PROF HIST, RUTGERS UNIV, 78-, CHMN UNDERGRAD EDUC, DEPT HIST, 81-, Am Friends Serv, Mex, 58-59; prog dir, Cambridge Neighborhood House, 59-60; dir, NDEA Summer Inst, Latin Am Hist, Rutgers Univ, 67, Soc Sci Res Coun fel, 68; Am Philos Soc grant, 73 & 80; chmn, Chile-Rio Plata Group, Conf Latin Am Hist, 77-78. **MEMBERSHIPS** AHA; Latin Am Studies Asn; Am Ital Hist Asn. **RESEARCH** Twentieth century Argentina; Italian immigration in the Western Hemisphere; labor history in Latin America. **SELECTED PUBLICATIONS** Auth, The Italians and Organized Labor in the United States and Argentina: 1880-1910, Int Migration Rev, summer 67; The Italians and the Development of Organized Labor in Argentina, Brazil and the United States, 1880-1914, J Social Hist, winter 69; ed, Nationalism in Latin America, Knopf, 71; co-ed, Perspective on Latin America, Macmillan, 74; auth, The United States and the Development of South America, Watts, 76; Role of the Press and the Assimilation of Italians in Buenos Aires and Sao Paulo, Int Migration Rev, fall 78; Marriage Patterns and Immigrant Assimilation in Buenos Aires, Hisp Am Hist Rev, 2/80; Chain Migration of Italians to Argentina, Studi Emigrazione, spring 82; Crossings-The Great Transatlantic Migrations, 1870-1914, with W. Nugent, Hispanic Am Hist Rev, Vol 74, 94; Frontier Development-Land, Labor, and Capital on the Wheatlands of Argentina and Canada, 1890-1914, with J. Adelman, J of Interdisciplinary Hist, Vol 27, 96. **CONTACT ADDRESS** Dept of Hist, Rutgers Univ, P O Box 5059, New Brunswick, NJ, 08903-5059.

BAILYN, BERNARD
PERSONAL Born 09/10/1922, Hartford, CT, m, 1952 **DISCIPLINE** HISTORY **EDUCATION** Williams Col, MA, BA, 45; Harvard Univ, MA, 47, PhD(hist), 53. **CAREER** Instr educ, 53-54, from asst prof to prof hist, 54-66, ed-in-chief, John Harvard Libr, 62-70, Winthrop prof hist, 66-81, ADAMS UNIV PROF, HARVARD UNIV, 81-, Co-ed, Perspectives Am Hist, 67-77; Trevelyan lectr, Cambridge, 71. **HONORS AND AWARDS** Robert H Lord Award, 67; Bancroft & Pulitzer Prizes in Hist, 68; Nat Bk Award in Hist, 75., LHD, Lawrence Univ, 67, Bard Col, 68, Clark Univ, 75, Yale Univ, 76 & Grinnell Col, 79; LittD, Williams Col, Mass, 69, Rutgers Univ & Fordham Univ, 76. **MEMBERSHIPS** Am Hist Soc (pres, 81); Nat Acad Educ; Royal Hist Soc; Am Philos Soc; Am Acad Arts & Sci. **SELECTED PUBLICATIONS** Ed, Pamphlets of the American Revolution, Vol 1, 65 & auth, Ideological Origins of the American Revolution, 67, Harvard Univ; Origins of American Politics, Knopf, 68; co-ed, The Intellectual Migration, Europe and America 1930-1960, Harvard Univ, 69; Law in American History, Little, 72; auth, The Ordeal of Thomas Hutchinson, Harvard Univ, 74; coauth, The Great Republic, Heath, 77; co-ed, The Press and the American Revolution, Am Antiquarian Soc, 80; Jefferson and the Ambiguities of Freedom, Proceedings of the Am Philos Soc, Vol 137, 93; Sometimes an Art, Never a Science, Always a Craft, A Conversation with Bernard Bailyn, William and Mary Quart, Vol 51, 94; To Make America-European Immigration in the Early Modern Period, with I. Altman and J. Horn, J of Am Ethnic Hist, Vol 13, 94; The American Revolution in Indian Country-Crisis and Diversity in Native American Communities, with C. G. Calloway, NY Rev of Books, Vol 42, 95; Saints in Slippers & Louis Tucker History of the Massachusetts Historical Society, New England Quart-A Historical Revue of New England Life and Letters, Vol 70, 97. **CONTACT ADDRESS** Dept Hist, Harvard Univ, Cambridge, MA, 02138.

BAILYN, LOTTE
PERSONAL Born 07/17/1930, Vienna, Austria, m, 1952, 2 children **DISCIPLINE** SOCIAL PSYCHOLOGY **EDUCATION** Swarthmore Col, BA, 51; Harvard Univ, MA, 53, PhD, 56. **CAREER** Res assoc, Grad Sch of Educ, Harvard, 56-57; instr, Dept Econ and Soc Sci, MIT, 57-58; res assoc, 58-64, lectr, 63-67, Dept Soc Rel, Harvard Univ; from res assoc to sr lectr, prof, Sloan Sch of Mgt, MIT, 69-91, T. Wilson Prof, 91-; vis scholar, Dept Social and Econ Stud, Imperial Col of Sci and Technol, London, 82, scholar in res, Rockefeller Found Study and Conf Ctr, Bellagio, Italy, 83; vis univ fel, Dept of Mgt Studies, Univ Auckland, NZ, 84; vis scholar, Univ Cambridge, 86-87; acad vis, Mgt School, Imperial Col of Sci Technol and Med, London, 91, 95; Matina S Horner distinguished vis prof, Radliffe Col, 95-97. **HONORS AND AWARDS** Phi Beta Kappa; listed, Who's Who in America. **MEMBERSHIPS** Acad Mgt; Am Psych Asn; Am Psych Soc; Am Sociol Asn. **SELECTED PUBLICATIONS** Coauth, Living with Technology: Issues at Mid-Career, MIT Press, 80; coauth, Working with Careers, Columbia Univ, 84; auth, Breaking the Mold: Women, Men, and Time in The New Corporate World, Free Press, 93. **CONTACT ADDRESS** Sloan School of Management, Massachusetts Inst of Tech, E52-585, Cambridge, MA, 02139. **EMAIL** lbailyn@mit.edu

BAIRD, BRUCE C.
PERSONAL Born 11/22/1956, New Orleans, LA, m, 1987 **DISCIPLINE** HISTORY **EDUCATION** Texas A & M Univ, BS, 77; Col Wm & Mary, MA, 90; Univ Fla, PhD, 95. **CAREER** Adj asst prof, Univ Fla, 95-96; ASST PROF HIST, UNIV ALA, HUNTSVILLE, 97-; H-SHEAR book rev ed, 97-. **HONORS AND AWARDS** Ohio State Univ fel 96-97; Jacob K. Javits fel, 94-95. **MEMBERSHIPS** AHA; So Hist Asn; Soc Historians Early Am Rep. **RESEARCH** Early Am South **SELECTED PUBLICATIONS** Auth, Necessity and the Perverse Supply of Labor in Pre- Clasical British Political Economy, Hist Pol Econ 29.3, fall 97; auth, The Social Origins of Dueling in Virginia, In Lethal Imagination: Violence and Brutality in American History, NY Univ Press, forthcoming. **CONTACT ADDRESS** Dept of History, Univ of Alabama, Huntsville, 409 Roberts Hall, Huntsville, AL, 35899. **EMAIL** bairdb@email.uah.edu

BAIRD, DAVID
PERSONAL Born 07/08/1939, Oklahoma City, OK, m, 1961, 2 children **DISCIPLINE** HISTORY **EDUCATION** George Wash Univ, AA, 59; Univ Cent Okla, BA, 61; Univ Okla, MA, 65, PhD, 69. **CAREER** Tchg asst, Univ OK, 66-68; asst, assoc prof, Univ AR, 68-78; prof, prof, dept hd, OK State Univ, 78-84; prof, OK State Univ, 84-88; Howard A. White prof, Pepperdine, 88-; Fulbright lectr, Univ Canterbury, New Zealand, 91;

vis prof, Ger, 92-93 ch, Adv Coun Am Hist Assn, 92-93;; ch, 94-. **HONORS AND AWARDS** Cert Merit, OK State Hist Preservation Off, 91; grant, OK Found Hum, 97. **MEMBERSHIPS** Mem, Prog Commun, 86-87; Mem Commun, 92-93; Commun on Ethnicity, 97-. **SELECTED PUBLICATIONS** Auth, The Quapaw Indians: A History of the Downstream People, Norman: Univ Okla P, 80; A Creek Warrior for the Confederacy: The Autobiography of Chief G. W. Grayson, Norman: Univ Okla Press, 88; The Quapaws, Chelsea House, 89; coauth,The Story of Oklahoma, Univ Okla Press, 94; Oklahoma: The Stories of the State and Its People, Univ OK Press, 98. **CONTACT ADDRESS** Dept of Hum and Tchr Educ, Pepperdine Univ, 24255 Pacific Coast Hwy, Malibu, CA, 90263. **EMAIL** dbaird@pepperdine.edu

BAIRD, JAY WARREN
PERSONAL Born 07/01/1936, Toledo, OH, m, 1958, 3 children **DISCIPLINE** MODERN EUROPEAN & GERMAN HISTORY **EDUCATION** Denison Univ, BA, 58; Columbia Univ, MA & PhD(mod hist), 66. **CAREER** Instr hist western civilization, Stanford Univ, 63-65; asst prof mod Europe, Pomona Col, 65-67; from asst prof to assoc prof, 67-75, PROF MOD EUROPE & GER, MIAMI UNIV, 75-, Nat Endowment for Humanities fel, 69-70; Am Philos Soc grant, 71; ed consult, Can Rev Hist Nationalism, 73-; mem nat screening bd, Fulbright-Hays Fel, Ger, 75-77; consult, Nat Endowment for Humanities, 76-, Nat Found Jewish Cult, 81. **MEMBERSHIPS** AHA; Conf Group Cent Europe Hist; Conf Group on German Politics; Am Asn Advan Humanities. **RESEARCH** Third Reich; Nazi propaganda; German film. **SELECTED PUBLICATIONS** Auth, The Nazi Propaganda Campaign of 1945, J Hist Deuxieme Guerre Mondiale, 69; The Myth of Stalingrad, J Contemp Hist, London, 70; ed, From Nurenberg to My Lai, Heath, 72; auth, The Mythical World of Nazi War Propaganda: 1939-1945, Univ MN, 74; L'expert en Bolshevisme du Dr Goebbels, J Hist Deuxieme Mondiale, 10/74; The World of Charlemagne, Forum Press, 77; Das Politische Testament Julius Streichers, Vierteljahrshefte fur Zeitgeschichte, 78; Nazi Film Propaganda and the Soviet Union, Film & Hist, 81; Germans Against Nazism-Nonconformity, Opposition, and Resistance in the Third Reich-Essays in Honor of Peter Hoffman, with F. R. Nicosia and L. D. Stokes, Central European Hist, Vol 25, 92; A Uniformed Reichstag-History of False Representation (German), with P. Hubert, Am Hist Rev, Vol 98, 93; Hitler Muse-The Political Aesthetics of the Poet and Playwright Eberhard Wolfgang Moller, German Studies Rev, Vol 17, 94; The Beautiful Guise of the 3rd Reich-Fascination and Violence of Fascism (German), with P. Reichel, Am Hist Rev, Vol 99, 94; Art, Ideology, and Economics in Nazi Germany-The Reich Chambers of Music, Theater, and the Visual Arts, with A. E. Steinweis, Am Hist Rev, Vol 100, 95; National-Socialist Cultural Policy, with G. R. Cuomo, German Studies Rev, Vol 19, 96; Art as Politics in the Third Reich, with J. Petropoulos, German Studies Rev, Vol 19, 96; Students in the Third Reich (German), with M. Gruttner, Am Hist Rev, Vol 102, 97. **CONTACT ADDRESS** Dept of Hist, Miami Univ, 500 E High St, Oxford, OH, 45056-1602.

BAIRD, KEITH E.
PERSONAL Born 01/20/1923 **DISCIPLINE** AFRICAN-AMERICAN STUDIES **EDUCATION** Columbia University, BS, 1952; Union Graduate School, PhD, 1982. **CAREER** Hunter College, professor/director, Afro-American studies, 1969-70; Hofstra University, professor of humanities, 1970-73; SUNY at Old Westbury, professor of humanities, 1973-75; SUNY at Buffalo, assoc prof of anthropology, 1975-; Clark Atlanta University, Dept of Social Sciences, professor, currently. **HONORS AND AWARDS** Travel Seminar Grant, Ford Foundation, 1969; publication, Names from Africa, Johnson Publishing Co, 1972; Summer Scholarship Grant, US GOR Friendship Comm, University of Jena, 1981. **MEMBERSHIPS** Assoc fellow, Center for Afro-American Studies, Atlanta University, 1973-; SUNY Chancellor's Task Force on Afro Studies, 1984; consult on Gullah Lang, Sea Island Center, 1977; pres emeritus, New York African Studies Assn; assoc ed, Freedomways; ed bd, Journal of Black Studies, African Urban Quarterly. **CONTACT ADDRESS** Dept of Social Sciences, Clark Atlanta Univ, 223 James Brawley SW, Atlanta, GA, 30314-4358.

BAIRD, WILLIAM DAVID
PERSONAL Born 07/08/1939, Oklahoma City, OK, m, 1961, 2 children **DISCIPLINE** AMERICAN HISTORY **EDUCATION** Cent State Univ, OK, BA, 63; Univ OK, MA, 65, PhD(hist), 69. **CAREER** Asst hist, Univ OK, 66-68; from asst prof to assoc prof hist, Univ AR, Fayetteville, 68-77, prof hist, 77-78; PROF HIST & DEPT HEAD, OK STATE UNIV, 78-, Am Philos Soc grantee, 71. **MEMBERSHIPS** Western Hist Asn; Orgn Am Historians. **RESEARCH** American Indian; 19th century medicine in America. **SELECTED PUBLICATIONS** Auth, Peter Pitchlynn: Chief of the Choctaws, Univ OK, 72; The Osage People, 72, The Choctaw People, 73, The Chickawaw People, 74 & The Quapaw People, 75, Indian Tribal Series; ed, Years of Discontent: Dr Frank L James in Arkansas, 1877-78, Memphis State Univ, 77; Medical Education in Arkansas, 1879-1978, Memphis State Univ, 79; The Quapan Indians: A History of the Downstream People, Univ OK, 80; A Naturalist in Indian Territory-The Journals of S. W. Woodhouse, 1849-50, with J. S. Tomer and M. J. Brodhead, J of Am Hist, Vol 81, 94; The Lance and the Shield-The Life and Times of Siting Bull, with R. M. Utley, Western Hist Quart, Vol 25, 94; The Osage-An Ethnohistorical Study of Hegemony on the Prairie Plains, with W. H. Rollings, J of Am Hist, Vol 80, 94; The American West and the Nixon Presidency, 1969-1974, J of the West, Vol 34, 95; Indian Territory and the United States, 1866-1906-Courts, Governments, and the Movement for Oklahoma Statehood, with J. Burton, Pacific Hist Rev, Vol 6, 97. **CONTACT ADDRESS** Dept Hist, Oklahoma State Univ, Stillwater, OK, 74078.

BAJPAI, SHIVA GOPAL
PERSONAL Born 07/02/1923, Balhemau, India, m, 1967, 1 child **DISCIPLINE** SOUTH ASIAN HISTORY **EDUCATION** Banaras Hindu Univ, BA, 55, MA, 57; Univ London, PhD(Indian Hist), 67. **CAREER** Asst prof Hist, Hindu Degree Col, Gorakhpur Univ, 57-58; lectr, Banaras Hindu Univ, 58-68; res assoc Hist Geog & Cult, S Asia Hist Atlas Proj, Univ Minn, Minneapolis, 67-70; asst prof, 70-74, assoc prof, 74-78, prof Hist, Calif State Univ, Northridge, 78-, dir coord Asian Studies Prog, 73-, ed consult, Can Rev Study Nationalism, Univ of PEI, 73. **MEMBERSHIPS** Asn Asian Studies; Am Orient Soc. **RESEARCH** Intellectual history of classical and medieval South Asia; political idealogies and practices; regions and regionalism in ancient and early medieval history of South Asia; India's cultural relations with China and Southeast Asia in the classical period. **SELECTED PUBLICATIONS** Auth, Chingiz Khan, the Mongol World Conqueror, 66, Chiang Kai Shek, 66 & Jonaraja, The Poet-Historian of Medieval Kashmir, 67, Hindi Encycl, Vols IV & V; Concept of neutrality and non-alignment in the post-Kautiliyan political thought in India, Actes XXIX Cong Int des Orientalists, L'Asiatheque, Paris, 76; coauth, A Historical Atlas of South Asia, Univ Chicago, 78. **CONTACT ADDRESS** Dept of History, California State Univ, Northridge, 18111 Nordhoff St, Northridge, CA, 91330-8200. **EMAIL** sbajpai@csun.edu

BAK, JANOS M.
PERSONAL Born 04/25/1929, Budapest, Hungary, m, 1951, 3 children **DISCIPLINE** MEDIEVAL HISTORY **EDUCATION** Eotvos Lorand Univ, Budapest, MA, 50; Univ Gottingen, Dr Phil(hist), 60. **CAREER** Instr hist, Acad Commerce, Budapest, 53-56; Brit Coun scholar, St Anthony's Col, Oxford, 60-62; asst, Univ Marburg, 63-66; asst prof, Univ Del, 66-68; ASSOC PROF HIST, UNIV BC, 68-, Ger Res Asn res scholar, 62-64; vis prof, Univ Kassel, 80. **MEMBERSHIPS** Am Asn Study Hungarian Hist; Conf Group Social & Admin Hist: Mediaeval Acad Am; Mediaeval Asn Pac; Int Comt Hist Paul Asn; Int Asn Hungarian Studies. **RESEARCH** Medieval central Europe; constitutional history; social history. **SELECTED PUBLICATIONS** Auth, Konigtum und Stande in Ungarn im 14-16, Jahrhundert, Steiner Verlag, Wiesbaden, 73; Medieval symbology of the state: P E Schramm's contribution, Viator, 4: 33-63, 73; ed, The German Peasant War of 1525, F Cass, Eng, 77; auth, Serfs and Serfdom: Words and Things, Rev of the F Braudel Ctr, 4: 3-18; co-ed (with Bela K Kiraly), From Hunyadi to Rakoczi: War and Society in Late Medieval and Early Modern Hungary, Brooklyn, NY, 82; co-ed (with Gy Litran), Socialism and Social Science: Selected Works of Ervin Szabo, Routledge & Kegan Paul; London, 82; Decreta Regni Hungariae-Laws and Decrees of Hungary, 1458-1490 (Latin and German), F. Dory, ed, Hisorisches Jahrbuch, Vol 113, 93; The 2 Cities-Medieval Europe, 1050-1320, with M. Barber, Histoire Sociale, Vol 27, 94; East-Central Europe in the Middle Ages, 1000-1500, with J. W. Sedlar, Speculum-A J of Medieval Studies, Vol 71, 96. **CONTACT ADDRESS** Dept of Hist, Univ of BC, Vancouver, BC, V6T 1W5.

BAKER, DONALD G.
PERSONAL Born 02/16/1932, Elgin, IL, d, 1 child **DISCIPLINE** AMERICAN STUDIES **EDUCATION** Univ Denver, BA, 53; Syracuse Univ, MA, 58, PhD, 61. **CAREER** Asst prof Am studies & govt & dir Am studies prog, Skidmore Col, 59-64; dir soc sci div, 64-71, assoc prof, 64-68, prof polit sci & am studies, Southhampton Col, Long Island Univ, 68-; Ford grant fac supvr, NY State Grad Legis Internship Prog, Columbia Univ, Hunter Col & Syracuse Univ, 60-64; adj prof polit sci, Grad Sch Pub Affairs, State Univ NY, 62-63; lectr progs, Peace Corps, 63-66, consult, 64-65; sr res fel race rels, Ctr Inter-Racial Studies, Univ Rhodesia, Salisbury, 75-76; sr res fel develop studies, Ctr Applied Soc Sci, Univ Zimbabwe, Salisbury, 80, sr assoc mem, St. Antony's Coll, Oxford Univ, 79-80 and 85-86; assoc res fel, Southern African res prog, Yale Univ, 92-93; vis res fel, sociol, Victoria Univ, New Zealand, 93. **MEMBERSHIPS** Am Studies Assn; Am Polit Sci Assn; Can Assn Am Studies; Assn Can Studies US. **RESEARCH** Comparative studies of race and ethnicity; problems of development in Third World countries. **SELECTED PUBLICATIONS** Co-ed, The Autobiography of James Monroe, Syracuse Univ, 59; co-ed, Postwar America: The Search for Identity, Glencoe, 69; ed, Politics of Race: Comparative Studies, Saxon House/Heath, Eng, 75; auth, Race, Ethnicity and Power: A Comparative Study, Routledge & Kegan Paul, 83. **CONTACT ADDRESS** Div of Soc Sci, Long Island Univ, 239 Montauk Hwy, Southampton, NY, 11968-4198.

BAKER, JAMES FRANKLIN
PERSONAL Born 05/17/1943, Houston, TX, m, 1963, 2 children **DISCIPLINE** UNITED STATES HISTORY **EDUCATION** Univ Houston, BA, 65; Tulane Univ, MA, 67, PhD, 70. **CAREER** Instr Hist, Xavier Univ La, 69-70; asst prof, 70-76, assoc prof, 76-80, prof Hist, Univ Central Okla, 80-. **MEMBERSHIPS** Soc Historians Am Foreign Rels. **RESEARCH** United States foreign relations; United States 20th century. **CONTACT ADDRESS** Dept of History & Geography, Univ of Central Oklahoma, 100 N University Dr, Edmond, OK, 73034-5209.

BAKER, JEAN HARVEY
PERSONAL Born 02/09/1933, Baltimore, MD, m, 1953, 4 children **DISCIPLINE** AMERICAN HISTORY **EDUCATION** Goucher Col, AB, 61; Johns Hopkins Univ, MA, 64, PhD, 71. **CAREER** Instr hist, Col Notre Dame, Md, 65-69; asst prof, 69-76, assoc prof hist, Goucher Col, 76, Am Coun Learned Socs fel, 77-78. **MEMBERSHIPS** Orgn Am Historians; Women Historians. **RESEARCH** Am polit hist; Civil War and Reconstruction; women's hist. **SELECTED PUBLICATIONS** Auth, Politics of Continuity, 73 & Ambivalent Americans, 77, Johns Hopkins Univ; Affairs of Party, Cornell Univ Press, 82; Mary Todd Lincoln: A Biography, W.W. Norton, 87; The Stevensons: Biography of an American Family, W.W. Norton, 95. **CONTACT ADDRESS** Dept of Hist, Goucher Col, 1021 Dulaney Vlly Rd, Baltimore, MD, 21204-2780. **EMAIL** jbaker@goucher.edu

BAKER, JOSEPH WAYNE
PERSONAL Born 06/26/1934, Zion, IL **DISCIPLINE** REFORMATION & RENAISSANCE HISTORY **EDUCATION** Western Baptist Col, BA, 57; Talbot Theol Sem, BD, 61; Pepperdine Col, BA, 62; Univ IA, MA, 64, PhD(hist), 70. **CAREER** Instr hist, OH State Univ, 65-68; from instr to asst prof, 68-76, ASSOC PROF HIST, UNIV AKRON, 76-, Am Philos Soc grant, 72. **MEMBERSHIPS** Am Soc Reformation Res; AHA; Sixteenth Century Studies Conf (treas, 76-77); Am Soc Church Hist. **RESEARCH** The Reformation; the Reformed tradition; Puritanism. **SELECTED PUBLICATIONS** Auth, Populist themes in the fiction of Ignatius Donnelly, Am Studies, 73; Heinrich Bullinger and the Idea of Usury, Sixteenth Century J, 74; In Defense of Magisterial Discipline: Bullinger's Tractatus de Excommunicatione of 1568, In: Heinrich Bullinger 1504-1575, Gesammelte Aufs,tze zum 400 Todestag Erster Band, Leben und Werk, Vol VII, Z?richer Beitr,ge zur Reformationsgeschichte, Theol Verlag, Zurich, 75; Das Datum von Bullingers Antwort an Johannes Burchard, In: Zwingliana, Vol XIV, 76; co-ed, The Western Intellectual Tradition (2 vols), Kendall-Hunt, 78; auth, Heinrich Bullinger and the Covenant: The Other Reformed Tradition, OH Univ Press, 80; The Theology of History and Apologetic Historiography in Heinrich Bullinger-Truth in History, with A. A. Garciaarchilla, Sixteenth Century J, Vol 24, 93; John Calvin 'Doctrine of the Christian Life', with J. H. Leith, Church Hist, Vol 62, 93; Doorkeepers at the House of Righteousness, Heinrich Bullinger and the Zurich Clergy, 1535-1575, with P. Biel, Sixteenth Century J, Vol 24, 93; Always Among Us-Images of the Poor in Zwingli Zurich, with L. P. Wandel, Church Hist, Vol 62, 93; Zwingli-An Introduction to His Thought, with W. P. Stephens, Church Hist, Vol 64, 95; Between Reformed Scholasticism and Pan-Protestantism, Jean-Alphonse Turetin, 1671-1737 and Enlightened Orthodoxy at the Academy of Geneva, with M. I. Klauber, Am Hist Rev, Vol 100, 95; Johann Sturm on Education-The Reformation and Humanist Learning, with L. W. Spitz and B. S. Tinsely, Sixteenth Century J, Vol 27, 96. **CONTACT ADDRESS** Dept of Hist, Univ of Akron, 302 Buchtel Mall, Akron, OH, 44325-0002.

BAKER, KEITH M.
PERSONAL Born 08/07/1938, Swindon, WL, England, m, 2 children **DISCIPLINE** HISTORY **EDUCATION** Peterhouse, Cambridge, BA, 60; Univ London, PhD, 64. **CAREER** Instr, Reed Col, 64-65; Asst Prof to Prof Hist, Univ Chicago, 65-89; Vis Assoc Prof, Yale Univ, 74; Prof Hist, 88-, J.E. Wallace Sterling Prof Humanities, Stanford Univ, 92-, Anthony P. Meier Family Prof and Dir, Stanford Humanities Ctr, 95-; French Revolution Bicentennial Prof, UCLA, 89. **HONORS AND AWARDS** Col Prize for Hist, Peterhouse, Cambridge, 60; Title of Schol of the Col, Peterhouse, Cambridge, 60; Fulbright Travel Grant, 60-61; Teaching Assistantship, Cornell Univ, 60-61; Ministry Educ State Studentship (U.K.), 61-64; Res Fel, Inst Hist Res, Univ London, 63-64; NEH Fel Jr Fac, 67-68; Univ Chicago Inland Steel Fel, 69; Am Coun Learned Soc Study Fel, 72-73; Univ Chicago Press Laing Prize, 75; Am Philos Soc Grant-in-Aid, 76; Guggenheim Fel, 79; Fel, Ctr Advanced Study Behavioral Sci, Stanford, 86-87; Elected Chevalier dans L'Ordre des Palmes Acad, 88; Vis Fel, Clare Hall, Cambridge, 94; Vis Fel, Max Planck Inst fur Geschichte, Gottingen, 94. **RESEARCH** Problems of intellectual history; history of political culture. **SELECTED PUBLICATIONS** Auth, Condorcet. From Natural Philosophy to Social Mathematics,Univ Chicago Press, 75; ed & contribr, Report of the Commission on Graduate Education, Univ of Chicago Record, 82; ed, The Old Regime and the French Revolution, Univ Chicago Press, 87; The French Revolution and the Creation of Modern Political Culture. vol. 1, The Political Culture of the Old Regime, Pergamon Press, 87; transl, Condorcet, Raison et politique, Hermann, 88; auth, In-

venting the French Revolution. Essays on French Political Culture in the Eighteenth Century, Cambridge Univ Press, 90; ed, The French Revolution and the Creation of Modern Political Culture. vol 4, The Terror, Pergamon Press, 94; author of numerous articles and other publications. **CONTACT ADDRESS** Mariposa House, Stanford Humanities Ctr, 546 Salvatierra Walk, Stanford, CA, 94305-8630. **EMAIL** kbaker@leland.stanford.edu

BAKER, MELVA JOYCE
PERSONAL Born 11/17/1939, Baca County, CO **DISCIPLINE** UNITED STATES & WOMEN'S HISTORY **EDUCATION** Univ Colo, Boulder, BA, 61; Univ Calif, Santa Barbara, MA, 70, PhD(hist), 78. **CAREER** Teacher hist & English, Boulder, CO & Ventura, CA, 61-68; res asst & reader, Univ CA, Santa Barbara, 68-69, teaching asst hist, 70-74, lectr, 75-77; vis asst prof, KS State Univ, 79-80; DIR EDUC SERV, INFO SERV, ABC-CLIO, 80-, Proj coordr, Neighborhood Youth Corps, Dept Labor, 70-71; instr, Santa Barbara City Col, 77-78. **MEMBERSHIPS** Am Hist Asn; Orgn Am Historians; Western Asn Women Historians; Asn Bibliog Hist. **RESEARCH** American popular culture; American women's history; research methodologies. **SELECTED PUBLICATIONS** Auth, Images of Women in Film: The War Years, 1941-1945, Univ Microfilms Int Res Press, 81. **CONTACT ADDRESS** PO Box 621, Summerland, CA, 93067.

BAKER, PAUL R.
PERSONAL Born 09/28/1927, Everett, WA, m, 1972, 1 child **DISCIPLINE** AMERICAN STUDIES & HISTORY **EDUCATION** Stanford Univ, AB, 49; Columbia Univ, MA, 51; Harvard Univ, PhD, 60. **CAREER** Instr hist, CA Inst Technol, 60-62, asst prof hum, 62-63; lectr hist, Univ CA, Riverside, 63-64; lectr, Univ OR, 64-65; assoc prof, 65-78, res grant, 66, 74, 75, prof hist, NY Univ, 78-, dir, grad prog Am Civilization, 72-92, Consult & panelist, Nat Endowment for Hum, 74. **HONORS AND AWARDS** Mary C. Turpie Prize of the Am Studies Asn for excellence in tchg, administration, and Advisement; NJ Literary Hall of Fame. **MEMBERSHIPS** Am Studies Asn; Orgn Am Historians; Soc Archit Historians; Victorian Soc Am. **RESEARCH** Am intellectual hist; Am painting and archit; Am cult hist. **SELECTED PUBLICATIONS** Ed, Views of Society and Manners in America, Harvard Univ, 63; auth, Lord Byron and the American in Italy, Keats-Shelley J, winter 64; The Fortunate Pilgrims: Americans in Italy, 1800-1860, Harvard Univ, 64; ed, The Atomic Bomb: The Great Decision, Holt, 68, Holt-Dryden, 2nd rev ed, 76; gen ed, American Problem Studies Series, Holt-Dryden, 41 Vols, 69-; coauth, The American Experience, Sadlier (5 vols), 76-79; auth, Richard Morris Hunt, Mass Inst Technol, 80; Auth, Stanny: The Gilded Life of Stanford White, 89. **CONTACT ADDRESS** Dept of Hist, New York Univ, 53 Washington Sq, New York, NY, 10012. **EMAIL** prb2@is.nyu.edu

BAKER, RICHARD ALLAN
PERSONAL Born 03/18/1940, Stoneham, MA, m, 1963, 2 children **DISCIPLINE** POLITICAL HISTORY **EDUCATION** Univ Mass, Amherst, BA, 62; Mich St Univ, MA, 65; Columbia Univ, MS, 68; Univ Maryland, PhD, 82. **CAREER** Instr hist, Holy Apostles Sem, Cromwell, Conn, 65-67; ref lib Amer hist, Lib Cong, Wash, DC, 68-70; dir res US Govt policy, Govt Res Corp, 70-75; dir, Senate Hist off, US Senate, Wash, DC, 75-. **HONORS AND AWARDS** Beta Phi Mu; Phi Kappa Phi, Joseph Towne Wheeler Award, 68; Ralph W Hidy Award, 86. **MEMBERSHIPS** Orgn Am Hist; AHA; Soc Hist Am Foreign Rels; Southern Hist Assn; APSA; Natl Coun of Pub Hist; Soc for Hist in Fed Govt **RESEARCH** United States Congressional history; American political history; historical bibliography. **SELECTED PUBLICATIONS** Ed, Proceedings, Conference on the Research Use and Disposition of Senators' Papers, 78, Govt Printing Off, OAH Mag of Hist, sum, 98; auth, Managing Congressional Papers: A Senate View, Am Archivist, 7/78; The Records of Congress: Opportunities and Obstacles in the Senate, Pub Hist, sum 80; auth, Conservation Politics: The Senate Career of Clinton P. Anderson, NMex, 85; auth, The Senate of the United States: A Bicentennial History, Krieger, 88; auth, Exploring Legislative Ethics, Plenum, 85; auth, The United States Senate, Readers' Comp to Amer Hist, Houghton Mifflin, 91; auth, Research Opportunities in the Records of the United States Senate, Western Hist Q 24, 93; auth, Legislative Power over Appointments and Confirmations, Encycl of Amer Legislative Sys 3, Scribners, 94; auth, The United States Congress Responds to Judicial Review, Constitutional Justice Under Old Constitutions, Kluwer Law, 95 **CONTACT ADDRESS** US Senate, Hist Office, Washington, DC, 20510-7108. **EMAIL** Richard_Baker@sec.senate.gov

BAKER, RONALD LEE
PERSONAL Born 06/30/1937, Indianapolis, IN, m, 1960, 2 children **DISCIPLINE** FOLKLORE **EDUCATION** IN State Univ, Terre Haute, BS, 60, MA, 61; IN Univ, Bloomington, PhD(folklore), 69. **CAREER** Instr English, Univ IL, Urbana, 63-65; teaching assoc, English & Folklore, IN Univ, Ft Wayne, 65-66; from instr to assoc prof, 66-76, prof English, IN State Univ, Terre Haute, 76-, chemn dept, 80-; Vis lectr English, Univ IL, Urbana, 72-73; vis assoc prof folklore, IN Univ, Bloomington, 75, vis prof, 78; ed, Midwestern Folklore, 75-. **HONORS AND AWARDS** Res/Creativity Award, IN State Univ, 90; fel, Am Folklore Soc, 96. **MEMBERSHIPS** Am Folklore Soc; Am Name Soc; MLA; Hoosier Folklore Soc. **RESEARCH** American folklore; narrative folklore; folklore and literary relations; namelore; Indiana folklore. **SELECTED PUBLICATIONS** Auth, Folklore in the Writings of Rowland E Robinson, Bowling Green Univ, 73; coauth, Indiana Place Names, IN Univ, 75; auth, Hoosier Folk Legends, IN Univ, 82; Jokelore: Humorous Folktales from Indiana, IN Univ, 86; French Folklife in Old Vincennes, ICTE/HFS, 89; ed, The Study of Place Names, ICTE/HFS, 91; auth, From Needmore to Prosperity: Hoosier Place Names in Folklore and History, IN Univ, 95. **CONTACT ADDRESS** Dept of English, Indiana State Univ, 210 N 7th St, Terre Haute, IN, 47809. **EMAIL** ejrlb@root.indstate.edu

BAKER, THOMAS H.
PERSONAL Born 10/14/1933, Houston, TX, m, 1955, 2 children **DISCIPLINE** AMERICAN HISTORY **EDUCATION** TX A&M Univ, BA, 55; Univ TX, MA, 63, PhD(hist), 65. **CAREER** Assoc prof hist, MS State Col Women, 63-68; spec res assoc, Oral Hist Prog, Univ TX, Austin, 68-69; assoc prof, 69-76, assoc vice chancellor, 73-81, PROF HIST, UNIV AR, LITTLE ROCK, 76-, Mem bd dir, Inst Politics & Govt, 73-77. **MEMBERSHIPS** Orgn Am Historians; Southern Hist Asn; Ark Hist Asn (pres, 81-82). **RESEARCH** History of American South; 20th century United States history. **SELECTED PUBLICATIONS** Auth, The Early Newspaper of Memphis, Tennessee, 1827-1860, W Tenn Hist Soc Papers, 63; Refugee Newspaper: the Memphis Daily Appeal, 1862-1865, J Southern Hist, 8/63; Yellowjack: the Yellow Fever Epidemic of 1878 in Memphis, Tennessee, Bull Hist Med, 68; The Memphis Commercial Appeal: The History of a Southern Newspaper, LA State Univ, 71; 1st Movers and the Growth of Small Industry in Northeastern Italy, Comparative Studies in Society and History, Vol 36, 94; Fulbright-A Biography, with R. B. Woods, AR Hist Quart, Vol 55, 96; A Matter of Black-and-White-The Autobiography of Ada Louise Sipuelfisher, with Al Sipuelfisher and D. Goble, AR Hist Quart, Vol 55, 96; Beyond Batholomew-The Portland Area History, with R. Dearmondhuskey, AR Hist Quart, Vol 56, 97. **CONTACT ADDRESS** Dept of Hist, Univ of AR, Little Rock, AR, 72204.

BAKER, THOMAS LINDSAY
PERSONAL Born 04/22/1947, Cleburne, TX, m, 1990, 2 children **DISCIPLINE** HISTORY **EDUCATION** Texas Tech Univ, BA, 69, MA, 72, PhD, 77. **CAREER** Res assoc, Hist of Engineering Prog, Texas Technol Univ, 70-75, 77; Fulbright lectr Tech Univ Wroclaw Poland, 75-77; cur of Agr & Technol, Panhandle-Plains Hist Mus, 78-87; cur of Hist, Fort Worth Mus Sci & Hist, 87-89; asst prof, Dept Mus Studies, Baylor Univ, 89-97; dir, Texas Heritage Mus, Hill Col, 97-. **HONORS AND AWARDS** Coral H Tullis, 80; Kate Broocks Bates Award, 80; Ralph Coats Roe Medal, 87; Cert Commendation Am Asn State & Loc Hist, 93. **MEMBERSHIPS** Orgn Am Hist; Am Asn of Mus; Int Molinological Soc; W Hist Asn; Texas State Hist Asn; Nat Trust for Hist Preserv; Soc SW Arch; W Writers of Am. **RESEARCH** History of Texas and the American West; History of engineering and technology; Social and cultural history of the United States. **SELECTED PUBLICATIONS** Auth The First Polish Americans: Silesian Settlements in Texas, Texas A & M Univ Press, 79; A Field Guide to American Windmills, Univ Okla Press, 85; Adobe Walls: The History and Archeology of the 1874 Trading Post, Texas A & M Univ Press, 86; Lighthouses of Texas, Texas A & M Univ Press, 91; The WPA Oklahoma Slave Narratives, Univ Okla Press, 98. **CONTACT ADDRESS** PO Box 507, Rio Vista, TX, 76093. **EMAIL** TLBAKER@hillcollege.hill-college.cc.tx.us

BAKER, WILLIAM JOSEPH
PERSONAL Born 01/28/1938, Chattanooga, TN, m, 1961, 2 children **DISCIPLINE** ENGLISH & INTELLECTUAL HISTORY **EDUCATION** Furman Univ, BA, 60; Southeast Sem, BD, 63; Cambridge Univ, PhD(hist), 67. **CAREER** Asst prof hist, Eastern TN State Univ, 66-67; asst prof hist & chmn dept hist & polit sci, Tusculum Col, 67-69; Bailey lectr hist, Univ NC, Charlotte, 70; asst prof, 70-73, assoc prof, 73-82, PROF HIST, UNIV ME, ORONO, 82-, Am Philos Soc res grant, 69-70 & 77; lectr, Duke Univ, 81. **MEMBERSHIPS** AHA; Conf Brit Studies; NAm Soc Sport Hist. **RESEARCH** Victorian England; Anglo-American history; sports history. **SELECTED PUBLICATIONS** Auth, Hurrell Froude and the Reformers, J Ecclesiastical Hist, 7/70; Charles Kingsley on the Crimean War: A Study in Chauvinism, Southern Humanities Rev, summer 70; Julius Charles Hake: A Victorian Interpreter of Luther, S Atlantic Quart, winter 71; ed, America Perceived: A View from Abroad in the 19th Century, Pendulum, 74; auth, Historical Meaning in Mother Goose, J Popular Cult, winter 76; The Making of a Working-Class Football Culture in Victorian England, J Social Hist, winter 79; Beyond Port and Prejudice: Charles Lloyd of Oxford, 1784-1829, Univ Maine, 81; ed (with John M Carroll), Sports in Modern America, River City; Reading Football-How the Popular Press Created an American Spectacle, with M. Oriard, Rev in Am Hist, Vol 22, 94; Big-Time Football at Harvard, 1905-The Diary of Coach Bill Reid, with R. A. Smith, Rev in Am Hist, Vol 22, 94; Shake Down the Thunder-The Creation of Notre-Dame Football, with M. Sperber, Rev in Am Hist, Vol 22, 94; Sportswriter-The Life and Times of Grantland Rice, with C. Fountain, Rev in Am Hist, Vol 22, 94. **CONTACT ADDRESS** 42 Grant St, Bangor, ME, 04401.

BAKER, WILLIAM M.
PERSONAL Born 11/10/1943, Toronto, ON, Canada **DISCIPLINE** HISTORY **EDUCATION** Univ Toronto, BA, 66; Carleton Univ, MA, 67; Univ Western Ont, PhD, 72. **CAREER** Asst prof, 70-75, chmn, 75-78, 89-91, assoc prof, 75-84, assoc dean, hum, 79-80, PROF HISTORY, UNIV LETHBRIDGE, 84-; vis prof Can stud, Hokkaigakuen Univ, Japan, 82. **MEMBERSHIPS** Can Hist Asn; Hist Soc Alta; Lethbridge Hist Soc. **SELECTED PUBLICATIONS** Auth, Timothy Warren Anglin, 1822-1896, 77; Lethbridge: Founding the Community to 1914, 92; coauth, A Preliminary Guide to Archival Sources Relating to Southern Alberta, 79; ed, Pioneer Policing in Southern Alberta, 93; co-ed Weddings, Work & War, 94. **CONTACT ADDRESS** Dept of History, Univ of Lethbridge, 4401 University Dr, Lethbridge, AB, T1K 3M4. **EMAIL** baker@hg.uleth.ca

BAKERMAN, JANE SCHNABEL
PERSONAL Born 07/04/1931, Gary, IN, m, 1971 **DISCIPLINE** AMERICAN LITERATURE, POPULAR CULTURE **EDUCATION** Hanover Col, AB, 53; Univ IL, MA, 59. **CAREER** Teacher English, William A Wirt High Sch, Gary, Ind, 53-57; assoc prof, WV Wesleyan Col, 59-64; ASSOC PROF ENGLISH, IN STATE UNIV, 64-, Consult, Guide to Am Women Writers, Frederick Ungar Publ, 77- & Twentieth Century Crime and Mystery Writers, St James Press, 80. **MEMBERSHIPS** AAUP; MLA; Popular Cult Asn; Nat Women's Studies Asn; NCTE. **RESEARCH** American literature; feminist studies; mystery-detective fiction. **SELECTED PUBLICATIONS** Contribr to numerous journals, 72-; Pioneering on the Yukon 1892-1917, with A. Degraf and R. S. Brown, Western Am Lit, Vol 28, 94. **CONTACT ADDRESS** Dept of English & Jour, Indiana State Univ, Terre Haute, IN, 47809.

BAKEWELL, PETER
DISCIPLINE HISTORY **EDUCATION** Cambridge Univ, BA, 65, MA, 68, PhD, 69. **CAREER** Prof **HONORS AND AWARDS** Herbert Eugene Bolton Prize, Conf Lat Am Hist, 73; Mexican Reg Hist Medal, Banco Nacional de Mexico, 88. **RESEARCH** Spanish American colonial history. **SELECTED PUBLICATIONS** Auth, Silver Mining and Society in Colonial Mexico: Zacatecas, 1546-1700; Miners of the Red Mountain: Indian Labor in Potosi, 1545-1650; Silver and Entrepreneurship in Seventeenth-Century Potosi: The Life and Times of Antonio Lopez de Quiroga; A History of Latin America: Empires and Sequels, 1450-1930. **CONTACT ADDRESS** Dept History, Emory Univ, 221 Bowden Hall, 561 Kilgo Cir, Atlanta, GA, 30322-1950. **EMAIL** pbakewe@emory.edu

BAKKEN, GORDON MORRIS
PERSONAL Born 01/10/1943, Madison, WI, m, 1964, 2 children **DISCIPLINE** AMERICAN HISTORY, LAW **EDUCATION** Univ WI-Madison, BS, 66, MS, 67, PhD(Am hist), 70, JD, 73. **CAREER** From asst prof to assoc prof Am hist, 69-76, PROF HIST, CA STATE UNIV, FULLERTON, 76-, DIR FAC AFFAIRS & RECORDS, 74-, Penrose Fund/Am Philos Soc fel, 74. **MEMBERSHIPS** AHA; Orgn Am Historians; Western Hist Asn. **RESEARCH** American legal history. **SELECTED PUBLICATIONS** Auth, To Reclaim a Divided West-Water, Law, and Public Policy, 1848-1902, with D. J. Pisani, Pacific Northwest Quart, Vol 84, 93; Founding the Far West-California, Oregon, and Nevada, 1840-1890, with D. A. Johnson, California Hist, Vol 72, 93; Workingmen in San Francisco, 1880-1901, with J. Tygiel, Reviews in Am Hist, Vol 21, 93; Montana Frontier Lawyer-A Memoir, with L. L. Callaway, Pacific Northwest Quart, Vol 84, 93; No Duty to Retreat-Violence and Values in American History and Society, with R. M. Brown, Montana-The Magazine of Western Hist, Vol 43, 93; In the Floating Arm, F. C. Mills on Intinerant Life in California, 1914, with G. R. Woirol, Reviews in Am Hist, Vol 21, 93; Flooding the Courtrooms-Law and Water in the Far-West, with M. C. Miller, Pacific Hist Rev, Vol 63, 94; Thirst for Growth-Water Agencies as Hidden Government in California, with R. Gottlieb and M. Fitzsimmons, Montana-The Magazine of Western Hist, Vol 44, 94; A Germ of Goodness-The California State Prison System, 1851-1944, with S. Bookspan, Am J of Legal Hist, Vol 38, 94; Rugged Justice-the 9th Circuit Court of Appeals and the American West, 1891-1941, with D. C. Frederick, Am J of Legal Hist, vol 39, 95; Then to the Rock Let Me Fly-Luther Bohanon and Judicial Activism, with J. Weaver, Great Plains Quart, Vol 15, 95; The First Duty-A History of the US District Court of Oregon, with C. M. Buan, Am J of Legal Hist, Vol 39, 95; Federal Justice in Western Missouri-The Judges, The Cases, The Times, with L. H. Larsen, Am Hist Rev, Vol 101, 96; Railroad Crossing-Californians and the Railroad, 1850-1910, with W. Deverell, Montana-The Magazine of Western Hist, Vol 46, 96; 3 Frontiers-Family, Land and Society in the American West, 1850-1900, with D. L. May, Historian, Vol 58, 96; Making Law, Order, and Authority in British Columbia, 1821-1871, with T. Loo. Pacific Northwest Quart, Vol 87, 96; Neither Wolf Nor Dog-American Indians, Environment, and Agrarian Change, with D. R. Lewis, Montana-The Magazine of Western Hist, Vol 46, 96; Law and the Great Plains-Essays on the Legal History of the Heartland, with J. R. Wunder, Historian, Vol 59, 97; Lewis Cass and the Politics of Moderation, with

W. C. Klunder, MI Hist Rev, Vol 23, 97. **CONTACT ADDRESS** Off of Dir Fac Affairs & Records, California State Univ, Fullerton, Fullerton, CA, 92634.

BALCER, JACK MARTIN
PERSONAL Born 11/09/1935, Newark, NJ **DISCIPLINE** ANCIENT HISTORY & ARCHEOLOGY **EDUCATION** Montclair State Col, BA, 57; Univ Mich, MA, 58, PhD, 64. **CAREER** Asst prof hist, Denison Univ, 64-65; asst prof hist, Ind Univ, Bloomington, 65-71; assoc prof, 71-80, prof hist, 80-, Ohio State Univ; numismatist, Archaeological Expedition, Malyan, Iran, 76. **HONORS AND AWARDS** NEH grant, 67; Danforth teaching associateship, 68-70. **MEMBERSHIPS** Am Numis Soc; Archaeol Inst Am; Assn Ancient Historians. **RESEARCH** Athenian and Persian Empires; Greek history, archaeology and numismatics. **SELECTED PUBLICATIONS** Art, Erich Friedrich Schmidt, Achaemenid History, 91; art, ancient Epic Conventions in the Bisitun Text, Achaemenid History, 94; art, Herodotus, The Early State, Lydia, Historia, 94; art, The Liberation of Ionia: 478 B C, Historia, 97. **CONTACT ADDRESS** Dept of History, Ohio State Univ, 230 W 17th Ave, Columbus, OH, 43210-1361. **EMAIL** balcer.1@osu.edu

BALDWIN, JOHN WESLEY
PERSONAL Born 07/13/1929, Chicago, IL, m, 1954, 4 children **DISCIPLINE** HISTORY **EDUCATION** Wheaton Col, BA, 50; PA State Univ, MA, 51; Johns Hopkins Univ, PhD(hist), 56. **CAREER** From instr to asst prof hist, Univ MI, 56-61; assoc prof medieval hist, 61-66, PROF HIST, JOHNS HOPKINS UNIV, 66-, Guggenheim & Howard fels, 60-61; Am Coun Learned Soc fel, 65-66; Fulbright res fel, 65-66; Nat Endowment for Humanities sr fel, 72-73. **MEMBERSHIPS** AHA; fel Medieval Acad Am; Soc Fr Hist Studies; foreign mem Royal Danish Acad Sci & Letters; Comn Int de Diplomatique. **RESEARCH** Medieval history; medieval France; intellectual history of the 12th and 13th centuries. **SELECTED PUBLICATIONS** Auth, Medieval Theories of the Just Price, Am Philos Soc, 59; Philip Augustus and the Norman Church, Fr Hist Studies, 69; Masters, Princes, and Merchants: The Social Views of Peter the Chanter and His Circle (2 vols), Princeton Univ, 70; The Scholastic Culture of the Middle Ages, 1000-1300, Heath, 71; ed, Universities in Politics: Case Studies from the Late Middle Ages and Early Modern Period, Johns Hopkins Univ, 72; The Rise of Administrative Kingship: Henry I and Philip Augustus, Am Hist Rev, 78; Contributions a l'etude des finances de Philippe Auguste, Bibliotheque de l'Ecole des Chartes, 80; La Decennie Decisive: Les Annees, 1190-1230 Dans Le Regue de Philippe Auguste, Rev Hist, 82; The Study of Chivalry-Resources and Approaches, H. Chickering and T. H. Seiler, eds, Speculum-A J of Medieval Studies, Vol 67, 92; Coronations-Medieval and Early Modern Monarchic Ritual- J. M. Bak, ed, Speculum- A J of Medieval Studies, Vol 68, 93; Albertanus-of-Brescia-The Pursuit of Happiness in the Early 13th-Century, with J. M. Powell, Am Hist Rev, Vol 98, 93; Philip-Augustus (French), with G. Sivery, Speculum-A J of Medieval Studies, Vol 69, 94; Economics in the Medieval Schools-Wealth, Exchange, Value, Money and Usury According to the Paris Theological Tradition, 1200-1350, with O. Langholm, Speculum-A J of Medieval Studies, Vol 69, 94; The Crisis of the Ordeal & A Contextualization of the Controversy Through 13th-Century Literary Texts-Literature, Law, and Religion Around AD-1200, J of Medieval and Renaissance Studies, Vol 24, 94; Meanings of Sex Differences in the Middle Ages-Medicine, Science, and Culture, with J. Cadden, J of the Hist of Sexuality, Vol 5, 94; Parish Schools-Thomas-of-Chobham and the Advancement of Preaching at the Beginnings of the 13th-Century (French), with F. Morenzoni, J of Ecclesiastical Hist, Vol 48, 97; Fortuna, Money, and the Sublunar World-12th-Century Ethical Poetics and the Satirical Poetry of the Carmina Burana, with T. M. S. Lehtonen, Am Hist Rev, Vol 102, 97; Death and the Prince-Memorial Preaching Before AD 1350, with D. L. Davray, J of Religion, Vol 77, 97; The Image of the Jongleur in Northern France Around 1200, Speculum-A J of Medieval Studies, Vol 72, 97. **CONTACT ADDRESS** Dept of Hist, Johns Hopkins Univ, 3400 N Charles St, Baltimore, MD, 21218-2680.

BALJON, NEIL
PERSONAL Born 09/08/1949, Oeastgeest, Netherlands, m, 1989, 2 children **DISCIPLINE** ARCHITECTURE **EDUCATION** Delft Tech Univ, MA, 75, PhD, 93. **CAREER** Urban designer, 77-82; systems analyst, 82-89; writer, 89- . **MEMBERSHIPS** Soc Archit Historians; Am Soc Aesthet. **RESEARCH** Eighteenth and nineteenth century architectural writings; design theory; architectural aesthetics. **SELECTED PUBLICATIONS** Auth, The Structure of Architectural Theory: A Study of Some Writings by Gottfried Semper, John Ruskin, and Christopher Alexander, Delft Technical, 93; auth, Design Justifications as an Instance of Modal Logic, or of Rhetoric, in Design Stud, 96; auth, Interpreting Ruskin: The Argument of The Seven Lamps of Architecture and The Stones of Venice, in J of Aesthet and Art Criticism, 97; auth, As Architecture, in Architecture and Civilization, Rodopi, 99. **CONTACT ADDRESS** 111 Tudor Rd, Ithaca, NY, 14850-6327. **EMAIL** ARB20@cornell.edu

BALL, ROBERT J.
PERSONAL Born 11/04/1941, New York, NY **DISCIPLINE** CLASSICS **EDUCATION** Queens Col, BA, 62; Tufts Univ, MA, 63; Columbia Univ, PhD(class), 71. **CAREER** Asst prof, 71-76, assoc prof, 76-83, prof class, Univ Hawaii, 83-. **HONORS AND AWARDS** Excellence in Teaching Award, Am Philol Asn; Regents' Medal for Excellence in Teaching, Univ Hawaii. **MEMBERSHIPS** Am Philol Asn. **RESEARCH** Latin poetry; Latin pedagogy; history of classical scholarship. **SELECTED PUBLICATIONS** Auth, Tibullus the Elegist: A Critical Survey, Vandenhoeck & Ruprecht, 83; ed, The Classical Papers of Gilbert Highet, Columbia Univ Press, 83; Reading Classical Latin: A Reasonable Approach (2nd ed), McGraw-Hill, 97; Reading Classical Latin: The Second Year (2nd ed), McGraw-Hill, 98; The Unpublished Lectures of Gilbert Highet, Peter Lang Pub, 98. **CONTACT ADDRESS** Dept Europ Lang & Lit, Univ Hawaii, 1890 E West Rd, Honolulu, HI, 96822-2318. **EMAIL** rball@hawaii.edu

BALL, SUSAN
PERSONAL Born 05/25/1947, Pasadena, CA, m, 1983, 1 child **DISCIPLINE** ART **EDUCATION** Yale Univ, PhD, 78. **CAREER** Asst prof, Univ Delaware, 78-81; asst treas Chase Manhattan Bank, 82-85; dir, Govt & Found Affairs, Art Inst Chicago, 85-86; exec dir, Col Art Asn, 86- . **MEMBERSHIPS** Coll Art Asn; Am Asn of Mus. **RESEARCH** Late nineteenth, early twentieth century European art and architecture. **SELECTED PUBLICATIONS** Auth, Rossetti and the Double Work of Art, 79; Andre Derain, 80; Ozenfaut and Purism, 81. **CONTACT ADDRESS** Col Art Association, 275 7th Ave, New York, NY, 10001. **EMAIL** sball@collegeart.org

BALLARD, ALLEN BUTLER, JR.
PERSONAL Born 11/01/1930, Philadelphia, PA, d **DISCIPLINE** HISTORY **EDUCATION** Kenyon Clg, BA 1952; Harvard Univ, MA, PhD 1961. **CAREER** City Coll of NY, asst prof, assoc prof 1961-69; City Univ of NY, dean of faculty 1969-76; professor emeritus, 1986, professor of history, SUNY-Albany, 1986-. **HONORS AND AWARDS** Ford Fndtn, Natl Humanities Cntr, Moton Ctr Grants; Fulbright Schlr; Phi Beta Kappa 1952. **SELECTED PUBLICATIONS** "The Education of Black Folk" Harper & Row, 1974; "One More Days Journey" McGraw-Hill 1984. **CONTACT ADDRESS** History, SUNY, Albany, 1400 Washington Ave, Albany, NY, 12222.

BALLOT, MICHAEL
PERSONAL Born 01/08/1940, New York, NY, m, 1963, 3 children **DISCIPLINE** BUSINESS ADMINISTRATION **EDUCATION** Cornell Univ, BME, 62; Univ Santa Clara, MBA, 65; Stanford Univ, MA, 68, PhD, 73. **CAREER** Engineer, 62-64, Lockheed Missiles & Space; mfg eng, 64-64, Beckman Instruments; Asst Prof econ, 68-71, Cal State U; Asst, Assoc, Prof, 71-, Univ Pacific. **HONORS AND AWARDS** Stanford U Fel. **MEMBERSHIPS** AEA; IRRA; DSI; SCS; AAPSS. **RESEARCH** Labor Mgmt Relations; Comparative IR; Forecasting for Business. **SELECTED PUBLICATIONS** Auth, British Labor Relations and the Law, Labor L J96; Auth, Labor Relations in Russia and Eastern Europe, Labor and L J95; coauth, Where will all the Workers Go? Chinese Labor Relations in Transition, Labor L J, 95; coauth, Labor Relations in Pacific Asia's Four Little Tigers, Govt Union Rev, 95; coauth, The Iron Rice Bowel: Labor Turmoil in China, Research & Practice in Human Resource Mgmt, 95. **CONTACT ADDRESS** Eberhardt Sch of Business, Univ of Pacific, Stockton, CA, 95211. **EMAIL** mballot@uop.edu

BALTZER, REBECCA
DISCIPLINE MEDIEVAL MUSIC **EDUCATION** Boston Univ, PhD. **CAREER** Prof; act, Medieval Stud prog; vis prof, Princeton Univ, 96. **MEMBERSHIPS** Current treas & past VP, Amer Musicol Soc. **RESEARCH** Medieval music, espec that of the Notre-Dame School and Ars Antiqua; notation; hist of theory; codicology; liturgy and liturgical books of medieval Paris. **SELECTED PUBLICATIONS** Ed, vol 5, critical edition of the Magnus liber organi, Monaco, 95; co-ed, The Union of Words and Music in Medieval Poetry, Tex, 91 & The Divine Office in the Latin Middle Ages, Oxford, 98. **CONTACT ADDRESS** School of Music, Univ of Texas at Austin, 2613 Wichita St, Austin, TX, 78705.

BAMBACH, CHARLES
DISCIPLINE HISTORY **EDUCATION** Univ Mich, PhD, 87. **CAREER** Assoc prof. **RESEARCH** Hermeneutics; contemporary continental philosophy; 19th and 20th century European intellectual history and philosophy. **SELECTED PUBLICATIONS** Auth, Heidegger, Dilthey, and the Crisis of Historicism, Cornell, 95; The Genesis of Heidegger's Being and Time, Am Cath Philos Quart, 95; Phenomenological Res as Destruktion: The Early Heidegger's Reading of Dilthey, Philos Today, 93; The Six Great Themes in Western Metaphysics, Mod Age, 95; Hermeneutics and the Life World, Psychohis Rev, 92. **CONTACT ADDRESS** Dept of History, Texas Univ, Richardson, TX, 75083-0688. **EMAIL** cbambach@utdallas.edu

BANES, RUTH A.
PERSONAL Born 07/07/1950, Rochester, NY, m, 1975 **DISCIPLINE** AMERICAN STUDIES **EDUCATION** Univ NM, BA, 72, PhD(Am studies), 78. **CAREER** Asst prof English, Elon Col, NC, 78-79; vis asst prof, 79-80, ASST PROF AM STUDIES, UNIV SOUTH FL, 80-. **MEMBERSHIPS** Am Studies Asn; Am Cult Asn. **RESEARCH** American autobiography; social intellectual history and historiography; regionalism in American culture. **SELECTED PUBLICATIONS** Auth, Southern Women in Country Songs, J Regional Cult, winter 82; The Exemplary Self: Autobiography in Eighteenth Century American, Biography; Ante-bellum Slave Narratives as Social History: Self and Community in the Struggle Against Slavery, J Am Cult; contribr, Loretta Lynn, Dolly Parton & Southern Autobiography, In: Encycl of Southern Culture; Images of the South-Constructing a Regional Culture on Film and Video, with K. G. Heider, Southern Cultures, Vol 1, 95. **CONTACT ADDRESS** Dept of Am Studies, Univ of S FL, 4202 Fowler Ave, Tampa, FL, 33620-9951.

BANKER, JAMES RODERICK
PERSONAL Born 04/29/1938, Plattsburgh, NY, m, 1961, 2 children **DISCIPLINE** ITALIAN RENAISSANCE, HISTORY OF THE MIDDLE AGES **EDUCATION** Taylor Univ, AB, 61; Boston Univ, MA, 62; Univ Rochester, PhD(Ital Renaissance hist), 71. **CAREER** From instr to asst prof, 67-76, ASSOC PROF ITAL HIST, NC STATE UNIV, 76-, Nat Endowment for Humanities scholar death in Mid Ages, 76-77. **MEMBERSHIPS** AHA; Renaissance Soc Am; Medieval Acad. **RESEARCH** Death in the Middle Ages and Renaissance; Medieval and Renaissance rhetoric; grief and consolation in the Italian Renaissance. **SELECTED PUBLICATIONS** Auth, Giovanni di Bonandrea and Civic Society, Manuscripta, 74; Ars Dictaminis and Rhetorical Textbooks at the Bolognese University, Medievali & Humanistica, 74; Mourning a Son: Childhood and Paternal Love in the Consolateria of G Manetti, Hist Childhood Quart, 76; Albertanus of Brescia-The Pursuit of Happiness in the Early 13th-Century, with J. M. Powell, Cath Hist Rev, Vol 79, 93; A Legal and Humanistic Library in Borgo-San-Sepolcro in the Middle of the 15th-Century, Rinascimento, Vol 33, 93; Episcopal Power and Florentine Society, AD 1000-1320, with G. W. Dameron, Speculum-A J of Medieval Studies, Vol 68, 93; The Cult of Remembrance and the Black Death-6 Renaissance Cities in Central Italy, with S. K. Cohn, Cath Hist Rev, Vol 79, 93; The Formation of a Medieval Church-Ecclesiastical Change in Verona 9509-1150, with M. C. Miller, Speculum-A J of Medieval Studies, Vol 70, 95; A New World in a Small Place-Church and Religion in the Diocese of Rieti, 1188-1378, with R. Brentano, Am Hist Rev, Vol 100, 95; A Moral Art-Grammar, Society, and Culture in Trecento Florence, with P. F. Gehl, Cath Hist Rev, Vol 82, 96; Piety and Charity in Late Medieval Florence, with J. Henderson, Cath Hist Rev, Vol 82, 96. **CONTACT ADDRESS** Dept of Hist, No Carolina State Univ, Raleigh, NC, 27604.

BANKER, MARK T.
PERSONAL Born 02/04/1951, Oakridge, TN, m, 1976, 1 child **DISCIPLINE** HISTORY **EDUCATION** Warren Wilson Col, NC, BA hist, 71; Univ VA, MAT hist, 75; Univ New Mexico, PhD, 87. **CAREER** Warren Wilson Col, teaching intern, 74-76; Menaul School, NM, teacher us hist, dean stud, 76-83; Univ NM, instr, 86, grad asst 83-86; Albuquerque Academy, NM, teacher us hist, 86-87; Webb School Knoxville, TN, hist teacher, 87-. **HONORS AND AWARDS** Warren Wilson Col Schls Medal 70, 71, 72, 73; Who's Who in Am Col Univ; Warren Wilson Cll Awd for excell in Hist Pol Sci; Magna Cum Laude, Warren Wilson; Dorothy Woodward Found Gnt; Most Influential Teacher, 90, 91, 92, 94, 98; Nat Endow for the Humanities/Readers Digest Awd; Distg Ser Awd, Warren Wilson Alumni Asn. **MEMBERSHIPS** OAH; WHA; Presby Hist Soc; East TN Hist Soc; Appalachian Stud Asn. **SELECTED PUBLICATIONS** Of Missionaries Multiculturalism and Mainstream Malaise: Historical Insights into the Presbyterian Predicament, 97; Beyond the Melting Pot & Multiculturalism: Insights into American Culture Politics from Southern Appalachian Studies Conference, Boone NC, 98; Mountain Vistas: Insights into the Rural-urban Encounter and American culture Politics form Southern Appalachia and Hispanic New Mexico, 97; Warren Wilson College: A Centennial Portrait, with Reuben A Holden, NC 94, numerous articles and pub. **CONTACT ADDRESS** Webb School Knoxville, 9800 Webb School Dr, Knoxville, TN, 37923.

BANKS, JAMES ALBERT
PERSONAL Born 09/24/1941, Marianna, AR, m **DISCIPLINE** EDUCATION **EDUCATION** Chicago City College, AA, 1963; Chicago State University, BE, 1964; Michigan State University, MA, 1967, PhD, 1969. **CAREER** Joilet Illinois Public Schools, teacher, 1965; Francis W Parker School, teacher, 1965-66; University of Michigan, visiting prof of education, summer 1975; The British Academy, UK, visiting lecturer, 1983; Monash University, Australia, visiting prof of education, 1985; University of Washington-Seattle, assoc prof, 1971-73, professor of education, 1973-, chairman, dept of curriculum & instruction, 1982-87, College of Education, professor, currently. **HONORS AND AWARDS** Golden Key Natl Honor Society, honorary member, 1985; Distinguished Scholar/Researcher

on Minority Education, American Education Research Assn, 1986. **MEMBERSHIPS** Natl Defense Education Act; Spencer fellow, Natl Academy of Education, 1973-76; Natl fellow, W K Kellogg Foundation, 1980-83; Rockefeller Foundation Fellowship, 1980; bd of dirs, Social Science Education Consortium, 1976-79; bd dir, Assn for Supervision & Curriculum Development, 1976-80; Natl Council for the Social Studies, vice president, 1980, president elect, 1981, president, 1982, bd of dirs, 1980-84. **SELECTED PUBLICATIONS** We Americans, Our History and People, two vol, 82; Teaching Strategies for the Social Studies, 4th ed, 90; co-auth, Multicultural Education in Western Societies, 86; Teaching Strategies for Ethnic Studies, 4th ed, 87; Multiethnic Education Theory and Practice, 2nd ed, 88; March Toward Freedom: A History of Black Americans, 78; co-auth, Multicultural Education: Issues and Prespectives, 89. **CONTACT ADDRESS** Col of Education, DQ-12, Univ of Washington, Seattle, WA, 98195-0001.

BANKS, WILLIAM MARON, III
PERSONAL Born 09/22/1943, Thomasville, GA **DISCIPLINE** EDUCATION **EDUCATION** Dillard Univ, B 1963; Univ of KY, Doctorate 1967. **CAREER** Attebury Job Corps Center, supr counselor & psychol 1967; Howard Univ, counselor psychol 1967-70, dept chairperson 1972-75; Univ of CA at Berkeley, prof 1970-, provost, 1988-89. **HONORS AND AWARDS** Summer Scholars Awd US Civil Serv Commn; Univ of CA Regents Fellowship; Instructional Improve Grant; American Book Award, 1996. **MEMBERSHIPS** Mem Soc for Psychol Study of Soc Issues; Soc for Study of Soc Problems; Amer Personnel & Guid Assn; chairperson Univ of CA Afro-Amer Studies Consortium 1979-81; Assn of Black Psychologists. **SELECTED PUBLICATIONS** articles monographs on effects of racial differences in psychotherapy & counseling; auth, "Black Intellectuals." **CONTACT ADDRESS** Univ of California, 682 Barrows, Berkeley, CA, 94720. **EMAIL** bilbankssociety@rates.berkeley.edu

BANNER, LOIS W.
DISCIPLINE HISTORY **EDUCATION** Columbia, PhD, 70. **CAREER** Prof; past ch, Prog for the Study of Women and Men; past ch, Dept Hist, Univ Southern Calif. **MEMBERSHIPS** Pres, Conf Gp in Women's Hist, 79-81; pres, Amer Stud Asn, 86-88; pres, Pacific Coast Branch, AHA, 91-93. **RESEARCH** Women and Gender; Social; Popular Culture. **SELECTED PUBLICATIONS** Auth, In Full Flower: Aging Women, Power and Sexuality, Knopf, 92; American Beauty, Knopf, 83, paperback Univ Chicago; Elizabeth Cady Stanton: A Radical for Woman's Rights, Little, Brown, 79; Women in Modern America: A Brief History, Harcourt Brace, 74; co-ed, Clio's Consciousness Raised: New Perspectives on the History of Women, Harper and Row, 74. **CONTACT ADDRESS** Dept of History, Univ Southern Calif, University Park Campus, Los Angeles, CA, 90089. **EMAIL** lbanner@usc.edu

BANNING, LANCE
PERSONAL Born 01/24/1942, Kansas City, MO, m, 1964, 1 child **DISCIPLINE** HISTORY **EDUCATION** Univ of Mo at Kans City, BA, 64; Wash Univ, MA, PhD, 71. **CAREER** Lectr, Exec Dir of Am Civilization Prog, Brown Univ, 71-73; DIR OF UNDERGRAD STUDIES, 78-80, DIR OF GRAD STUDIES, 80-84, ASST PROF TO PROF OF HIST, UNIV OF KY, 73-; John Adams prof, Univ of Groningen, The Netherlands, spring, 97. **HONORS AND AWARDS** NEH Fel for Younger Humanists, 74-75; Guggenheim Fel, 79-80; Univ Res Prof, Ky, 84-85; Nat Humanities Center Fel, 86-87; Center for the Hist of Freedom, Wash Univ, Fel, 91; Fulbright Distinguished Chair Awd, 97. **SELECTED PUBLICATIONS** Auth, Jefferson and Madison: Three conversations from the Founding, Madison House, 95, 96; The Sacred Fire of Liberty: James Madison and the Founding of the Federal Republic, Cornell Univ Press, 95; Political Economy and the Creation of the Federal Republic, Devising Liberty: Preserving and Creating Freedom in the New Am Republic, Stanford Univ Press, 95; The Republican Interpretation: Retrospect and Prospect published jointly in Am Antiquarian Soc Proceedings and in The Republican Synthesis Revisited: Essays in Honor of George Athan Billias, Univ Press of Va, 92. **CONTACT ADDRESS** 204 Cromwell Way, Lexington, KY, 40503.

BANNING, LANCE G.
PERSONAL Born 01/24/1942, Kansas City, MO, m, 1964, 1 child **DISCIPLINE** HISTORY **EDUCATION** Univ of Mo, BA, 64; Washington Univ, MA, PhD, 71. **CAREER** Lectr, Brown Univ, 71-73; from asst prof to prof, Univ of Ky, 73- ; core fac mem, NEH Summer Inst for Elementary and Secondary Tchrs, 84; ed and adv bds, Va Mag of Hist and Biog, 84-87; Jour of the Early Repub, 85-89; S.H.E.A.R., 86-89; lectr, Monticello-Stratford Hall Summer Sem for Tchrs, 87, Summer Inst for the James Madison Fels, 93. **HONORS AND AWARDS** NEH fel, 74-75; Guggenheim fel, 79-80; Univ Res prof, 84-85; Nat Hums Ctr fel, 86-87, Ctr for the Hist of Freedom fel, 91, Fulbright Disting. Ch Award, 97. **SELECTED PUBLICATIONS** Auth, The Jeffersonian Persuasion: Evolution of a Party Ideology, 78; After the Constitution: Party Conflict in the New Republic, 89; The Republican Interpretation: Retrospect and Prospect, Am Antiquarian Soc Procs, CII, 92, and The Republican Synthesis Revisited: Essays in Honor of George Athan Billias, ed M.M. Klein et al., 92; The Jeffersonians: First Principles, Democrats and the Am Idea: A Bicentennial Appraisal, ed P.B. Kovler, 92; Political Economy and the Creation of the Federal Republic, Devising Liberty: Preserving and Creating Freedom in the New Am Repub, ed D.T. Konig, 95; Jefferson and Madison: Three Conversations from the Founding, 95; The Sacred Fire of Liberty: James Madison and the Founding of the Federal Republic, 95. **CONTACT ADDRESS** Dept of History, Univ of Kentucky, Lexington, KY, 40506. **EMAIL** banning@uky.campus.mci.net

BANNON, CYNTHIA J.
DISCIPLINE CLASSICAL STUDIES **EDUCATION** Harvard Univ, BA, 84; Univ Mich, PhD, 91. **CAREER** Asst prof. **RESEARCH** Roman law; Latin prose style and grammar; rhetoric; history. **SELECTED PUBLICATIONS** Auth, The Brothers of Romulus, Princeton, 97. **CONTACT ADDRESS** Dept of Classical Studies, Indiana Univ, Bloomington, 300 N Jordan Ave, Bloomington, IN, 47405.

BARANY, GEORGE
PERSONAL Born 04/12/1922, Budapest, Hungary, m, 1949 **DISCIPLINE** HISTORY **EDUCATION** Univ CO, MA, 58, PhD, 60. **CAREER** From asst prof to assoc prof, 60-69, PROF HIST, UNIV DENVER, 69-, Am Philos Soc res grant, 61; Am Coun Learned Soc res grants, 63, 66-67 & 70-71; study grant, Grad Sch Int Rels, Univ Denver, 66-67, Fac Res Fund res grant, 67-68. **MEMBERSHIPS** AHA; Am Asn Advan Slavic Studies; Am Asn Study Hungarian Hist; Western Slavic Asn. **RESEARCH** History of the Austro-Hungarian Empire; Hungarian-American relations; East European history. **SELECTED PUBLICATIONS** Auth, chaps, In: The Immigrants' Influence on Wilson's Peace Policies, Univ Ky, 67; Stephen Szechenyi and the Awakening of Hungarian Nationalism, 1791-1841, Princeton Univ, 68; Nationalism in Eastern Europe, Univ WA, 69; Hoping Against Hope: The Enlightened Age in Hungary, Am Hist Rev, 4/71; Die Habsburgermonarchie, 1848-1918, Austrian Acad, Vienna, 73-; Jews and Non-Jews in Eastern Europe, Keter, Jerusalem, 74; East Central European Perceptions of Early America, De Ridder, Holland, 77; Exile and Social Thought-Hungarian Intellectuals in Germany and Austria, 1919-1933, with L. Congdon, Slavic Rev, Vol 53, 94. **CONTACT ADDRESS** Dept Hist, Univ Denver, Denver, CO, 80210.

BARBER, ELIZABETH J. WAYLAND
PERSONAL Born 12/02/1940, Pasadena, CA, m, 1965 **DISCIPLINE** ARCHAEOLOGY, LINGUISTICS **EDUCATION** Bryn Mawr Col, BA, 62; Yale Univ, PhD, 68. **CAREER** Res assoc, Princeton Univ, 68-69; LECTR TO FULL PROF, OCCIDENTAL COL, 70-. **HONORS AND AWARDS** NEH Grants, 72, 74, & 93; J Guggenheim Memorial Fel, 79-80; Wenner-Gren ACLS Haynes grants; book prizes from Amer Hist Asn, 93, Costume Soc, 92 & 95. **MEMBERSHIPS** Archaeol Inst of Am; Linguistic Soc of Am; Textile Soc of Am; Costume Soc of Am; LACUS; CIETA. **RESEARCH** Prehistoric archaeology and languages of Southern & Eastern Europe; decipherment; ancient textiles, costumes, & rituals. **SELECTED PUBLICATIONS** Auth, The Mummies of Urumchi, W.W. Norton, 99; auth, Women's Work-The First 20,000 Years, W.W. Norton, 94; auth, Prehistoric Textiles, Princeton Univ Press, 91; auth, Archaeological Decipherment, Princeton Univ Press, 74; auth, On the Origins of the Vily/Rusalki, Varia on the Indo-European Past, 97; auth, Minoan Women and the Challenge of Weaving for Home, Trade, and Shrine, Texnh: Craftsmen, Craftswomen and Craftsmanship in the Aegean Bronze Age, 97; auth, Textiles of the Neolithic through Iron Ages, The Oxford Encycl of Archaeol in the Near East, 97; auth, On the Antiquity of East European Bridal Clothing, Dress, 94; auth, The Peplos of Athena, Goddess and Polis: The Panathenaic Festival in Ancient Athens, Princeton, 92. **CONTACT ADDRESS** 1126 N. Chester Ave., Pasadena, CA, 91104. **EMAIL** barber@oxy.edu

BARBER, MARYLIN J.
DISCIPLINE HISTORY **EDUCATION** Queen's Univ, BA, MA; Univ London, PhD. **CAREER** Assoc prof. **RESEARCH** Female immigration to Canada. **SELECTED PUBLICATIONS** Auth, "Immigrant Domestic Servants in Canada," Can Hist Assn Booklet, Canada's Ethnic Groups Series, 91; The Servant Problem in Manitoba, 1896-1930, First Days, Fighting Days: Women in Manitoba Hist, Can Plains Res Ctr, 87; Domestic Servants in the 20th Century Ontario Kitchen, Consuming Passions, The Ontario Hist Soc, 90; The Fellowship of the Maple Leaf Teachers, The Anglican Church and the World of W Can 1820-1970, Can Plains Res Ctr, 91; The Motor Caravan Mission: Anglican Women Workers in the New Era, Women Within the Christian Church in Canada , Univ Toronto Press, 95. **CONTACT ADDRESS** Dept of Hist, Carleton Univ, 1125 Colonel By Dr, Ottawa, ON, K1S 5B6. **EMAIL** marilyn_barber@carleton.ca

BARBERA, ANDRE
PERSONAL Born 05/24/1950, New London, CT, m, 1970, 3 children **DISCIPLINE** MUSICOLOGY **EDUCATION** Wesleyan Univ, BA, 74; Univ NC, PhD, 80. **CAREER** Tutor, St John's Col, Annapolis, 1990- . **HONORS AND AWARDS** The Am Counc of Learned Soc Grant, 87; Nat Endow Human Grant, 83, 86, 87; Newberry Library Grant, Chicago, 78. **MEMBERSHIPS** Am Musicol Soc. **RESEARCH** History of jazz; history of music theory; non-Euclidean geometry. **SELECTED PUBLICATIONS** Republic 530C - 531C: Another Look at Plato and the Pythagoreans, Am Jour Philology 102, 81, 395-410; Interpreting an Arithmetical Error in Boethius's De Institutione Musica, iii 14-16, Arch int d'hist des sciences 31, 81, 26-41; Octave Species, Jour Musicol 3, 84, 229-241; The Consonant Eleventh and the Expansion of the Musical Tetractys: A Study of Ancient Pythagoreanism, Jour Mus Theory 28, 84, 191-223; Placing Sectio canonis in Historical and Philosophical Contexts, Jour Hellenic Stud 104, 84, 157-161; Recent Studies in Ancient Music and Ancient Music Theory, Jour Am Musicol Soc 43, 90, 353-367; Music Theory and its Sources: Antiquity and the Middle Ages, Univ Notre Dame Press, 90; The Euclidean Division of the Canon: Greek and Latin Sources, Univ Nebr Press, 91; New and Revived Approaches to Text Criticism in Early Music Theory, Jour Musicol 9, 91, 57-73; George Gershwin and Jazz, The Gershwin Style, Oxford Univ Press, 98; **CONTACT ADDRESS** St John's Col, Annapolis, MD, 21404. **EMAIL** c-barbera@sjca.edu

BARBOUR, HUGH
PERSONAL Born 08/07/1921, Peking, China, m, 1959, 3 children **DISCIPLINE** CHURCH HISTORY **EDUCATION** Harbard Univ, AB, 42; Union Theol Sem, NY, BD, 45; Yale Univ, PhD(relig), 52. **CAREER** Pastor, Congregational Church, Coventry, CT, 45-47; instr Bible & relig, Syracuse Univ, 47-49; instr Bible, Wellesley Col, 50-53; from asst prof to assoc prof relig, 53-67, PROF RELIG, EARLHAM COL, 67-, Mem gov bd, Nat Coun Churches, 72-. **MEMBERSHIPS** Soc Bibl Theol; Soc Bibl Lit. **RESEARCH** Theological writings of William Penn. **SELECTED PUBLICATIONS** Auth, The Quakers in Puritan England, Yale Univ, 64; Step by Step in Reading the Old Testament, Asn Press, 64; Programmed teaching for Old Testament, Relig Educ, 11-12/67; Protestant Quakerism, 71 & The God of peace, 72, Quaker Relig Thought; co-ed, Early Quaker Writings, 1650-1700, Eerdmans, 73; Margaret Fell and the Rise of Quakerism, with B. Y. Kunze, J of Relig, Vol 76, 96; Gentle Invaders-Quaker Women Educators and Racial Issues During the Civil-War and Reconstruction, with L. B. Selleck, Church History, Vol 66, 97. **CONTACT ADDRESS** 1840 SW E St., Richmond, IN, 47374.

BARDAGLIO, PETER W.
PERSONAL Born 04/25/1953, Hartford, CT, m, 1983, 3 children **DISCIPLINE** HISTORY **EDUCATION** Brown Univ, AB, 75; Stanford Univ, MA, 78; Stanford Univ, PhD, 87. **CAREER** Visiting lectr, Univ Md at Col Pk, fall 95, 81-83; visiting prof in Amer studies, Univ Exeter, 94-95; instr, 83-87, asst prof, 87-93, assoc prof, 93-, Elizabeth Conolly Todd Distinguished assoc prof, sep 95-, Goucher Col. **HONORS AND AWARDS** Who's Who in the East, 99-00; Who's Who in the East; Outstanding Educ of the Year, Md Asn of Higher Educ, May, 98; James Rawley prize, Orgn of Amer Hist, 96; Who's Who Among America's Teachers, 96, 98; Caroline Doebler Bruckerl Award for Outstanding Teaching, may, 94; Nat Endow for the Humanities summer stipend, 92; Littleton-Griswold Res grant, Amer Hist Asn, 89-90; Award for outstanding teaching in soc sci, May, 88. **MEMBERSHIPS** Amer Hist Asn; Orgn of Amer Hist; Southern Hist Asn; Amer Soc for Legal Hist; Amer Studies Asn; Southern Asn for Women Hist. **RESEARCH** Race, gender, and the law in the 19th century South; History of childhood. **SELECTED PUBLICATIONS** Auth, Reconstructing the Household: Families, Sex and the law in the Nineteenth-Century South, Chapel Hill, Univ NC Press, 95; article, Rape and the Law in the Old South: Calculated to Excite Indignation in Every Heart, Jour of Southern Hist, 60, 749-72, nov, 94; article, The Children of Jubilee: African-American Childhood in Wartime, Divided Houses: Gender and the Civil War, NY, Oxford Univ Press, 213-29, 92; article, An Outrage Upon Nature: Incest and the Law in the Nineteenth-Century South, In Joy and in Sorrow: Women, Family and Marriage in the Victorian South, 1830-1900, NY, Oxford Univ Press, 32-51, 91. **CONTACT ADDRESS** Goucher Col, 1021 Dulaney Valley Rd., Baltimore, MD, 21204. **EMAIL** pbardagl@goucher.edu

BARKAN, ELLIOTT ROBERT
PERSONAL Born 12/15/1940, Brooklyn, NY, m, 1968, 2 children **DISCIPLINE** AMERICAN HISTORY, ETHNIC STUDIES **EDUCATION** Queens Col, NY, BA, 62; Harvard Univ, MA, 64, PhD(hist), 69. **CAREER** Instr hist, Pace Col, 64-68; from asst prof to prof, 68-74, FULL PROF HIST, CA STATE COL, SAN BERNARDINO, 74-, Consult, Los Angeles City Sch Syst, 73-74; Calif State Univ Soc Sci Res Council's Field Inst fel, 82-83; vis prof, Summer Inst, Amerika House, Falkenstein, West Germany, 78. **MEMBERSHIPS** AHA; Orgn Am Historians; Econ Hist Asn; Am Sociol Asn; Immigration Hist Soc. **RESEARCH** Comparative American ethnic history; pre-Civil War American political history. **SELECTED PUBLICATIONS** Auth, Diplomatic History of the United States, Monarch, 66; ed, Edmund Burke on the American Revolution, Harper, 66; auth, The Emergence of a Whig Persuasion: Conservatism, Democratism, and the New York State Whigs, NY Hist, 10-71; James Barbour (1775-1842), In: Encyclopedia of Southern History, 76; Proximity and Commuting Immigration, In: American Ethnic Revival, 77; French Canadian Americans, In: Harvard Encyclopedia of American Ethnic Groups, 80; The

Price of Equality: Comparative American Ethnic History, Prentice-Hall; coauth (with Nikolas Khokhlov), Socio Economic Data Indices of Naturalization Patterns in the United States, A Theory Revisited, Ethnicity, 6/80; Race, Religion, and Nationality in American Society-A Model of Ethnicity-From Contact to Assimilation-Response, J of Am Ethnic Hist, Vol 14, 95; The White Peril-Foreign Relations and Asian Immigration to Australia and North-America, 1919-1978, with S. Brawley, J of Am Hist, Vol 82, 95; Peopling Indiana-The Ethnic Experience, with R. M. Taylor and C. A. McBirney, J of Am Hist, Vol 84, 97. **CONTACT ADDRESS** Dept of Hist, California State Univ, San Bernardino, 5500 University Pky, San Bernardino, CA, 92407-7500.

BARKER, JOHN W.
PERSONAL Born 10/07/1933, Brooklyn, NY, m, 1998, 2 children **DISCIPLINE** MEDIEVAL HISTORY **EDUCATION** Brooklyn Col, BA, 55; Rutgers Univ, MA, 56, PhD, 61. **CAREER** Teaching asst, Rutgers Univ, 57-59; instr, Brooklyn Col, 58-59; jr fel, Dumbarton Oaks, 59-62; vis prof, Inst for Res in the Humanities, Univ of Wis, 64-65; vis prof, Inst for Advanced Study, Princeton Univ, 78-79; asst to assoc prof, 67; prof of hist, 70-96, Prof Emeritus, Univ of Wis, 96-. **HONORS AND AWARDS** Phi Beta Kappa, 55; prize for Outstanding Lit Achievement, Coun for Wis Writers, 67; Guggenheim Fel, 74-75. **MEMBERSHIPS** Medieval Academy; Byzantine Studies Conf; Midwest Medieval Conf; Soc for the Study of the Crusades and the Latin East. **RESEARCH** Byzantine history & civilization; Venetian history & civilization; crusades; music & western cultural history. **SELECTED PUBLICATIONS** Auth, Justinian and the Later Roman Empire, Univ of Wis Press, 66; Manuel II Palaeologus (1391-1425): A Study in Late Byzantine Statesmanship, Rutgers Univ Press, 69; The Monody of Demetrios Kydones on the Zealot Rising of 1345 in Thessaloniki, Essays in Memory of Basil Laourdas, Thessaloniki, 75; Miscellaneous Genoese Documents on the Levantine World of the Late Fourteenth and Early Fifteenth Centuries, Essays in Honor of Peter Charanis, 79; Byzantium and the Display of War Trophies: Between Antiquity and the Venetians, TO EAA, 93. **CONTACT ADDRESS** History Dept, Univ of Wisconsin, Humanities Bldg, Madison, WI, 53706. **EMAIL** jwbarker@facstaff.wisc.edu

BARKER, NANCY NICHOLS
PERSONAL Born 12/26/1925, Mt Vernon, NY, m, 1950 **DISCIPLINE** MODERN EUROPEAN HISTORY **EDUCATION** Vassar Col, BA, 46; Univ PA, MA, 47, PhD, 55. **CAREER** Asst instr, Univ PA, 48-49; instr, Univ DE, 49-50; lectr mod Europ hist, 55-67, from asst prof to assoc prof hist, 67-72, PROF HIST, UNIV TX, AUSTIN, 72-, TX Res Inst res grant, 67-68. **HONORS AND AWARDS** Gilbert Chinard Prize for Bk on Franco-Am Rels, 72; Summerfield G Roberts Award for Bk on Repub of Tex, 72. **MEMBERSHIPS** AHA; Soc Fr Hist Studies. **RESEARCH** Nineteenth century Europe; France in the New World; French Revolution. **SELECTED PUBLICATIONS** Auth, France, Austria and the Mexican Venture, 1861-1864, Fr Hist Studies, fall 63; Austria, France and the Venetian Question, J Mod Hist, 6/64; Distaff Diplomacy: The Empress Eugenie and the Foreign Policy of the Second Empire, Univ TX, Austin & London, 67; co-ed & contribr, Diplomacy in an Age of Nationalism: Essays in Honor of Lynn Marshall Case, Martinus Nijhoff, The Hague, 71; ed & transl, Recognition, Rupture and Reconciliation, Vol I, In: The French Legation in Texas, TX Hist Asn, 71; auth, From Texas to Mexico: An Affairiste at Work, Southwestern Hist Quart, 7/71; ed & transl, Mission Miscarried, Vol II, In: The French Legation in Texas, TX Hist Asn, 73; Let Them Eat Cake-The Mythical Marie Antoinette and the French Revolution, Historian, Vol 55, 93. **CONTACT ADDRESS** Dept of Hist, Univ of TX, Austin, TX, 78712.

BARKER, ROSANNE M.
DISCIPLINE HISTORY **EDUCATION** Univ Calif, Santa Barbara, BA, MA, PhD. **CAREER** Asst prof, Sam Houston State Univ, 92-. **RESEARCH** History of women, native americans, colonial america. **SELECTED PUBLICATIONS** Auth, Small Town Progressivism: Pearl Chase and Female Activism in Conservation in Santa Barbara, California, Southern Calif Quart. **CONTACT ADDRESS** Dept of History, Sam Houston State Univ, Huntsville, TX, 77341.

BARKER, THOMAS M.
PERSONAL Born 08/26/1929, Minneapolis, MN, m, 1955, 2 children **DISCIPLINE** MODERN HISTORY **EDUCATION** Carleton Col, BA, 51; Harvard Univ, AM, 52; Univ MN, PhD, 57. **CAREER** Asst prof hist, Glassboro State Col, 58-62; asst prof, Western IL Univ, 62-63; assoc prof, 63-68, PROF HIST, STATE UNIV NY ALBANY, 68-, State Univ NY Res Found fels & grants, 64-67; Am Philos Soc grants, 68, 75; Int Res & Exchange Bd grants, 70-71 & 76-77; Nat Endowment Humanities transl prog, 79. **MEMBERSHIPS** Inter-univ Sem Armed Forces & Soc; War & Soc East Cent Europe Res Proj; Soc For Slovene Studies; Inter-univ Ctr Europ Studies; Am Asn Study Hungarian Hist. **RESEARCH** German and Austrian history, 17th-20th centuries, especially social and military history. **SELECTED PUBLICATIONS** Auth, Double Eagle and Crescent: Vienna's Second Turkish Siege and its Historical Setting, State Univ NY, 67; ed, transl, Frederick the Great and the Making of Prussia, Holt, 71; auth, The Military Intellectual and Battle: Raimondo Montecuccoli and the Thirty Years War, State Univ NY, 74; The Slovene Minority of Carinthia, 82 & Army, Aristocracy, Monarchy: Essays on War, Society and Government in Austria, 1618-1780, In: Social Science Monographs, 82, Columbia; Oss and the Yugoslav Resistance, 1943-1945, with K. Ford, J of Military Hist, Vol 57, 93; The Uskoks of Senj-Piracy, Banditry and the Holy War in the 16th-Century Adriatic, with C. W. Bracewell, J of Military Hist, Vol 57, 93; Kirk Ford Comment on Thomas M. Barker, Book Review-Reply, J of Military Hist, Vol 58, 94; Gubbins and Soe, with P. Wilkinson and J. B. Ashley, J of Military Hist, Vol 58, 94; Cambridge Illustrated History of Warfare, with G. Parker, J of Military Hist, Vol 60, 96; The Military Revolution-Military Innovation and the Rise of the West, 1500-1800, with G. Parker, J of Military Hist, Vol 61, 97. **CONTACT ADDRESS** Dept of Hist, State Univ of NY, 1400 Washington Ave, Albany, NY, 12222.

BARKER, WENDY
DISCIPLINE FINE ARTS AND HUMANITIES **EDUCATION** AR State Univ, BA, MA; Univ CA at Davis, PhD. **CAREER** Prof; taught at, Univ CA at Davis & AR State Univ; Rockefeller Foun Residency, Bellagio Stud and Conf Ctr, 94; organized, ch & presented, papers on panels on var Am writers at Mod Lan Asn meetings. **HONORS AND AWARDS** Mary Elinore Smith Poetry Prize, ed(s) of The Am Scholar, 91; won the Ithaca House Poetry Series competition, 90; NEA fel, 86; 3 UTSA Fac Res Awd(s);UTSA President's Distinguished Achievement Awd for Tchg Excellence. **RESEARCH** Creative writing-poetry; 19th and 20th-century Am lit; 20th-century Brit poetry; lit by women; poetry; mod poetry. **SELECTED PUBLICATIONS** Auth, bk of poems, Winter Chickens, Corona Publ Comp, 90; Let the Ice Speak, Ithaca House Bks, Greenfield Rev Press, 91; Lunacy of Light: Emily Dickinson and the Experience of Metaphor, Southern IL UP, 87; co-ed, a collection of essays on the poetry of Ruth Stone, The House Is Made of Poetry, Southern IL UP, 96; Eve Remembers, Aark Arts Publ, London, 96; Way of Whiteness, Goblin Market Publ, 97. **CONTACT ADDRESS** Col of Fine Arts and Hum, Univ Texas at San Antonio, 6900 N Loop 1604 W, San Antonio, TX, 78249.

BARKER, WILLIAM SHIRMER, II
DISCIPLINE CHURCH HISTORY **EDUCATION** Princeton Univ, BA, 56; Cornell Univ, MA, 59; Covenant Theol Sem, BD, 60; Vanderbilt Univ, PhD, 70. **CAREER** Instr, Covenant Col, 58-64; asst prof, 64-70; assoc prof, dean of fac, 70-72; assoc prof, dean of fac, Covenant Theol Sem, 72-77; assoc prof, pres, 77-84; prof, Westminster Theol Sem, 87-. **SELECTED PUBLICATIONS** Ed, Presbyterian Jour, 84-87; auth, Puritan Profiles: 54 Influential Puritans at the Time When the Westminster Confession of Faith Was Written; The Hemphill Case, Benjamin Franklin, and Subscription to the Westminster Confession, Amer Presbyterians, 91. **CONTACT ADDRESS** Westminister Theol Sem, PO Box 27009, Philadelphia, PA, 19118.

BARKER-BENFIELD, GRAHAM JOHN
PERSONAL Born 05/28/1941, London, England, m, 1987, 1 child **DISCIPLINE** HISTORY **EDUCATION** Trinity Col, BA Hons, 63; Univ CA, Los Angeles, PhD, 68. **CAREER** Asst prof hist, Am Univ, 69-72; vis asst prof, Lewis & Clark Col, 72-74; asst prof Am studies, 74-75, asst prof, 75-78, ASSOC TO FULL PROF HIST, STATE UNIV NY, ALBANY, 78-, NEH & Shelby Cullom Davis Ctr fel hist, Princeton Univ, 77-78. **HONORS AND AWARDS** Univ Award for Excellence in Teaching, State Univ NY, Albany, 92; The Chancellor's Award for Excellence in Teaching, SUNY, 92., MA, Trinity Col. **MEMBERSHIPS** AHA; Orgn Am Historians; Brit Soc 18th Century Studies. **RESEARCH** American social hist, hist of sex roles, British hist of sex roles. **SELECTED PUBLICATIONS** Auth, The Spermatic Economy: A Nineteenth Century View of Sexuality, summer 72 & St Martin's rev ed, In: The American Family in Social-Historical Perspective, 73; Anne Hutchinson and the Puritan Attitude Toward Women, Feminist Studies, fall 72; Sexual Surgery in Late Nineteenth Century America, Int J Health Serv, 75 & Random, In: Seizing Our Bodies, 78; The Horrors of the Half Known Life: Male Attitudes Toward Women and Sexuality in Nineteenth Century America, Harper & Row, 76; Female Circumcision, Women & Health, spring 76; Mother-Emancipator: The Meaning of Jane Addam's Sickness and Cure, J Family Hist, winter 79; Weir Mitchell and the Woman Question: Gender and Therapy, Quart J Ideology, fall 81; Mary Wollstonecraft's Depression and Diagnosis: The Relation Between Sensibility and Women's Susceptibility to Nervous Disorders, Psychohistory Rev, 85; Mary Wollstonecraft: Eighteenth Century Common Wealth Woman, J of the Hist of Ideas, 89; The Culture of Sensibility: Sex and Society in Eighteenth-Century Britain, Univ of Chicago Press, 92; Portraits of American Women, ed with C. Clinton,. St. Martin's, 91, rev ed Oxford Univ Press, 98; Sex and Sensibility, in The Age of Romanticism and Revolution: An Oxford Companion to British Culture, ed 1, McCalman, Oxford Univ Press, 99. **CONTACT ADDRESS** Dept of Hist, State Univ NY, 1400 Washington Ave, Albany, NY, 12222-1000.

BARKIN, KENNETH
PERSONAL Born 07/16/1939, Brooklyn, NY, 2 children **DISCIPLINE** MODERN GERMAN HISTORY **EDUCATION** Brooklyn Col, BA, 60; Brown Univ, PhD, 66. **CAREER** Asst prof mod hist, Brandeis Univ, 65-68; from asst prof to assoc prof, 68-76, prof mod hist, Univ of Calif, Riverside, 76-; Mem adv comt, Coun Int Educ, 76-79; Ed, Central Europ Hist, 91-. **HONORS AND AWARDS** Biannual Prize for Best Article, Conf Group Cent Europ Hist, 69-70, 82-83. **MEMBERSHIPS** AHA; Conf Group Cent Europ. **RESEARCH** Economic and educational history of nineteenth century Germany. **SELECTED PUBLICATIONS** Auth, The Controversy Over German Industrialization, Univ Chicago, 70; A case study in comparative history: Populism in Germany and America, in The State of American History, Quadrangle, 70; Conflict and concord in Wilhelmian social thought, Cent Europ Hist, 3/72; Germany's Path to Industrial Maturity, Laurentian Univ Rev, 6/73; Autobiography and history, Societas, spring 76; Amerikanische ver offentlichungen zur modernen deutschen sozial-und Wirtschaftsgeschichte, Geschichte und Gesellschaft, 78; From uniformity to pluralism: German historical writing since World War I, Ger Life & Lett, winter 81; Preussens Schulen sind besser, in Hilfe, Schule, Berlin, 81. **CONTACT ADDRESS** Dept of Hist, Univ of Calif, 900 University Ave, Riverside, CA, 92521-0001.

BARLOW, K. RENEE
DISCIPLINE ANTHROPOLOGY, ARCHAEOLOGY, BEHAVIORAL ECOLOGY **EDUCATION** Brigham Young Univ, BS, 84; Univ Utak, MA, 93, PhD, 97, **CAREER** Mus asst, Brigham Young Univ Mus Peoples and Cultures, 81- 83; Archaeologist, Salt Lake City, 85-90; archaeologist, Northwest Archaeol Consult, Seattle, 96; adj instr, Univ Utah/princ investigator, Univ Archeol Ctr, 93-98; cur collect, Edge of the Cedars Mus, Utah State Div Pks & Rec, 98-. **CONTACT ADDRESS** Edge of the Cedars State Park, PO Box 788, Blanding, UT, 84511. **EMAIL** NRDPR.rbarlow@state.ut.us

BARLOW, WILLIAM
DISCIPLINE RADIO PRODUCTION, HISTORY OF BROADCASTING **EDUCATION** Univ Southern Calif, PhD. **CAREER** Prof. **RESEARCH** World music. **SELECTED PUBLICATIONS** Auth, bk and numerous publ on, history of Black music and radio. **CONTACT ADDRESS** School of Communications, Howard Univ, 2400 Sixth St NW, Washington, DC, 20059.

BARLOW, WILLIAM B.
PERSONAL Born 02/25/1943, Fort Rucker, AL, d **DISCIPLINE** EDUCATION **EDUCATION** San Francisco State University, BA, 1968; University of California at Santa Cruz, MA, 1974, PhD, 1983. **CAREER** Mount Vernon College, assistant professor, 1976-80; HOWARD UNIVERSTIY, PROFESSOR, 1980-. **HONORS AND AWARDS** Schomburg, NEH Fellowship, 1991-92; University of Mississippi, NEH Fellowship, 1986. **MEMBERSHIPS** Union of Democratic Communication, steering committee, 1977-; International Association for Study of Popular Music, steering committee, 1989-; International Association for Mass Communication Research, 1986-. **SELECTED PUBLICATIONS** From Cakewalks to Concert Halls, 1992; co-author with Jan Dates, Split Image: African-Americans in the Mass Media, 1990; Looking Up at Down: The Emergence of Blues Culture, 1989. **CONTACT ADDRESS** Department of Radio/TV/Film, Howard Univ, Washington, DC, 20059.

BARMAN, JEAN
PERSONAL Born 08/01/1939 **DISCIPLINE** HISTORY/EDUCATION **EDUCATION** Macalester Col, BA, 61; Harvard Univ, MA, 63; Univ Calif Berkeley, MLS, 70; Univ BC, EdD, 82. **CAREER** PROF, EDUCATIONAL STUDIES, UNIV BC. **HONORS AND AWARDS** Can Hist Educ Asn Founders' Prize, 89, 92-93; Can Hist Asn Reg Hist Prize, 92; UBC Alumni Prize Soc Sci, 92; Killam res fel, 92-93; UBC Killam Tchg Prize, 96. **MEMBERSHIPS** Can Hist Asn. **SELECTED PUBLICATIONS** Auth, The West beyond the West: A History of British Columbia, 91, rev 96; co-ed, British Columbia Local Histories: A Bibliography, 91; co-ed, Contemporary Canadian Childhood and Youth: A Bibliography, 92; co-ed, History of Canadian Childhood and Youth: A Bibliography, 92; co-ed, First Nations Education in Canada: The Circle Unfolds, 95; co-ed, Children, Teachers and Schools in the History of British Columbia, 95. **CONTACT ADDRESS** Educ Studies Dept, Univ BC, Vancouver, BC, V6T 1Z4. **EMAIL** jean.barman@ubc.ca

BARMAN, LAWRENCE
PERSONAL Born 06/09/1932, Maryville, MO **DISCIPLINE** INTELLECTUAL HISTORY **EDUCATION** St Louis Univ BA, 56; Fordham Univ, MA, 60; Cambridge Univ, PhD, 70. **CAREER** St Louis Univ, 1970-present. **HONORS AND AWARDS** APS Gnt; Nancy McNeir Ring Awd; Danforth Fel; Outstanding Teacher Hum. **MEMBERSHIPS** AAR **RESEARCH** The Modernist Crisis In Catholicism; Baron Friedrich von Hugel. **SELECTED PUBLICATIONS** Auth, Baron Friedrich von Hugel and the Modernist Crisis in England, Cambridge, 72; The Letters of Baron Friedrich von Hugel and Prof Norman Kemp Smith, Fordham, 81; The Modernist as Mystic:

Baron Friedrich von Hugel, Zeitschrift fur Neuers Theologiegeschichte, 97; and several other major articles. **CONTACT ADDRESS** 4501 Lindell Blvd, St. Louis, MO, 63108.

BARMAN, RODERICK JAMES
PERSONAL Born 01/16/1937, Radlett, England, m, 1963, 2 children **DISCIPLINE** LATIN AMERICAN HISTORY **EDUCATION** Cambridge Univ, BA, 59; Univ CA, Berkeley, MA, 65, PhD(hist), 70. **CAREER** Vis asst prof hist, State Univ NY Albany, 70-71; asst prof Hisp & Ital studies, 71-78, ASSOC PROF HIST, UNIV BC, 78-, Can Coun res grant, 73-78; contrib ed, Handbk of Latin Am Studies, 76-. **HONORS AND AWARDS** Conf on Latin Am Hist prize, 77. **MEMBERSHIPS** Soc Latin Am Studies, England; Can Asn Latin Am Studies; AHA; Conf Latin Am Hist; Latin Am Studies Asn. **RESEARCH** Social and political structure of 19th century Brazil; education in the Empire of Brazil. **SELECTED PUBLICATIONS** Auth, The Forgotten Journey: Georg Heinrich Langsdorff and the Russian Imperial Scientific Expedition to Brazil, 1821-1829, Terrae Incognitae: Annals Soc Hist Discoveries, 71; Justiniano Jose da Rocha e a Conciliacao Como se escreveu Acao; reacao; transacao, Revista do Inst Hist e Geog Brasileiro, 73; A New World Nobility: The Role of Titles in Imperial Brazil, In: University of British Columbia Hispanic Studies, Tamesis, London, 74; coauth, The Role of the Law Graduate in the Political Elite of Imperial Brazil, J Interam Studies & World Affairs, 76; auth, Politics on the Stage: The Latin Brazilian Empire as dramatized by Franca Junior, Luso-Brazilian Rev, 77; coauth, Prosopography by Computer: The Development of a Database, Hist Methods Newslett, 77; auth, The Brazilian Peasantry Reexamined: The Implications of the Quebra-Quilo Revolt, 1874-75, Hisp Am Hist Rev, 77; coauth, The Prosopography of the Brazilian Empire, Latin Am Res Rev, 78; Popular Organization and Democracy in Rio-de-janeiro-A Tale of 2 Favelas, with R. Gay, Hispanic Am Hist Rev, Vol 76, 96; Policing Rio-de-Janeiro-Repression and Resistance in a 19th-Century City, with T. H. Holloway, Am Hist Rev, Vol 101, 96. **CONTACT ADDRESS** Dept of Hist, Univ of BC, Vancouver, BC, V6T 1W5.

BARNARD, VIRGIL JOHN
PERSONAL Born 11/05/1932, Wichita, KS, m, 1954, 3 children **DISCIPLINE** HISTORY **EDUCATION** Oberlin Coll, BA, 55; Univ Chicago, MA, 57; PhD, 64. **CAREER** Instr, Hist, Ohio State Univ, 60-64; asst prof, Oakland Univ, 64-67; assoc prof, Oakland Univ, 67-71; prof, Oakland Univ, 71-97; PROF EMER, HIST, OAKLAND UNIV, 97-. **MEMBERSHIPS** Am Hist Asn; Org Am Hist; AAUP **RESEARCH** US History, 1945-present; US labor history. **SELECTED PUBLICATIONS** Walter Reuther and the Rise of Auto Workers; From Evangelicalism to Progressivism at Oberlin College; assoc edr, Children and Youth in America: A Documentary History. **CONTACT ADDRESS** Dept Hist, Oakland Univ, Rochester, MI, 48063. **EMAIL** Barnard@oakland.edu

BARNES, JAMES JOHN
PERSONAL Born 11/16/1931, St. Paul, MN, m, 1955, 2 children **DISCIPLINE** ENGLISH & MODERN EUROPEAN HISTORY **EDUCATION** Amherst Col, BA, 54; Oxford Univ, BA, 56, MA 61; Harvard Univ, PhD, 60. **CAREER** Instr hist, Amherst Col, 59-62; from asst prof to assoc prof, 62-76, prof hist, Wabash Col, 76-, Amherst Col res grant, 61-62; Soc Sci Res Coun res grant-in-aid, 62-63 & 70; Am Coun Learned Soc res grant, 64-65; Am Philos Soc res grant 64-65. **HONORS AND AWARDS** Phi Beta Kappa, 54; Rhodes Scholar, 54-56; Woodrow Wilson Fel, 56-67; D H L Col of Wooster, 76; Fulbright Scholar, 78; Distinguished Alumni, St Paul Acad & Summit Sch, 89; Hon Alumnus, Wabash Col, 94 **MEMBERSHIPS** AHA; Conf Brit Studies; Southern Historians Asn; Bibli Soc Engl. **RESEARCH** Eng and mod Europ soc and economic hist; lit taste since 1800; nineteenth century Anglo-Am rel. **SELECTED PUBLICATIONS** Auth, Free Trade in Books: A Study of the London Book Trade Since 1800, Clarendon, Oxford, 64; Edward Lytton Bulwer and the publishing firm of Harper and Brothers, Am Lit, 3/66; Clio's blind disciples: Parkman, Prescott and Thierry, Am Oxonian, 4/69; Galignani and the publication of English books in France, Bibliog Soc England, 12/70; Authors, Publishers, and Politicians: The Quest for an Anglo-American Copyright Agreement, 1815-1854, Routledge Univ, London, 74 & Ohio State Univ, 74; Mein Kampf in Britain 1930-39, Weiner Libr Bull, Vol XXVII, 74; co-auth, Hitler's Mein Kampf in Britain & America, 1930-39; Cambridge Univ Press, 80; co-auth, James Vincent Murphy, Translator and Interpreter of Fascist Europe, 1880-1946, Univ Press Am, 87; co-auth, Private & Confidential: Letters from British Ministers in Washington to Their Foreign Secretaries in London, 1845-47, Susquehanna Univ Press, 93. **CONTACT ADDRESS** Dept of Hist, Wabash Col, PO Box 352, Crawfordsville, IN, 47933-0352. **EMAIL** barnesj@wabash.edu

BARNES, KENNETH C.
PERSONAL Born 04/24/1956, Conway, AR, m, 1978, 2 children **DISCIPLINE** HISTORY **EDUCATION** Duke Univ, PhD, 85. **CAREER** Assoc Prof, 92-, Univ Cen AR; Asst Prof, 91-92, Univ S MS; Asst, Assoc Prof, 82-91, Concordia Univ IL. **HONORS AND AWARDS** Fulbright Fel; NEH Fel; DAAD. **SELECTED PUBLICATIONS** Auth, Who Killed John Clayton?: Political Violence and the Emergence of the New South 1861-1893, Durham NC, Duke Univ Press, 98; Nazism Liberalism and Christianity: Protestant Social Thought in Germany and Great Britain 1925-1937, Lexington KY, Univ Press of KY, 91. **CONTACT ADDRESS** Dept History, Univ Central Arkansas, 210 Donaghey Rd, Conway, AR, 72035. **EMAIL** kennethb@mail.uca.edu

BARNES, THOMAS GARDEN
PERSONAL Born 04/29/1930, Pittsburgh, PA, m, 1955, 4 children **DISCIPLINE** HISTORY **EDUCATION** Harvard Univ, AB, 52; Oxford Univ, DPhil, 55. **CAREER** From asst prof to assoc prof hist, Lycoming Col, 56-60; lectr, 60-61, from asst prof to prof hist, 61-74, PROF HIST & LAW, UNIV CALIF, BERKELEY, 74-, Am Acad Arts & Sci grant, 58; Huntington Libr grant, 60; Am Coun Learned Soc fel, 62; ed, Pub Rec Off, 63-; proj dir, Am Bar Found Anglo-Am Legal Hist Proj, 65-86; Guggenheim fel, 71; historian, Centennial Hist Hastings Col Law, 73-78; co-chair, Canadian stu prog, Univ of Calif, Berkeley 82-; chair, ed board, legal class lib, 82-. **HONORS AND AWARDS** Alexander Prize, Royal Hist Soc, 58. **MEMBERSHIPS** Selden Soc; fel Royal Hist Soc. **RESEARCH** English legal history; Tudor-Stuart England; Court of Star Chamber, 1596-1641; early Canadian legal history. **SELECTED PUBLICATIONS** Auth, Somerset assize orders, 1629-1640, Somerset Rec Soc, 59; auth, Clerk of the Peace in Caroline Somerset, 61; auth, Somerset 1625-1640, 61; coauth, The European World: A History, 66; co-ed, A Documentary History of Europe, 72; auth, Hastings College of the Law: The First Century, 78. **CONTACT ADDRESS** Sch of Law, Univ of California, Berkeley, 454 Boalt Hall, Berkeley, CA, 94720-7200.

BARNES, TIMOTHY DAVID
PERSONAL Born 03/13/1942, Yorkshire, England, m, 1965, 3 children **DISCIPLINE** CLASSICS, HISTORY **EDUCATION** Oxford Univ, BA, 64, MA, 67, DPhil, 70. **CAREER** Jr res fel classics, Queen's Col, Oxford, 66-70; from asst prof to assoc prof, Univ Col, Toronto, 70-76; assoc chmn grad studies, 79-83, PROF CLASSICS UNIV TORONTO, 76-. **HONORS AND AWARDS** Conington Prize, Oxford Univ, 74. **MEMBERSHIPS** Am Philol Asn; Can Class Asn; Am Soc Papyrologists; Am Asn Ancient Historians; Soc Promotion Roman Studies. **RESEARCH** Roman history; early Christianity; patristics. **SELECTED PUBLICATIONS** Auth, The Conversion of the Roman Aristocracy in Prudentius 'Contra Symmachum', Phoenix-The J of the Classical Asn of Canada, Vol 45, 91; Handbook of Classical Latin Literature, Vol 5, Restoration and Renewal, 284-374 AD (German), with R. Herzog and P. L. Schmidt, Phoenix-The J of the Classical Asn of Canada, Vol 45, 91; The Greek City From Homer to Alexander, with O. Murray and S. Price, Urban Hist Rev, Vol 21, 93; Augusta Helena-The Mother of Constantine the Great and the Legend of Her Finding of the True Cross, with J. W. Drijvers, J of Ecclesiastical Hist, Vol 44, 93; Marcellinus Ammianus and His World & An Investigation of the Historical Melieu of the Later Roman Empire, Classical Philol, Vol 88, 93; The City in the Greek and Roman World, with E. J. Owens, Urban Hist Rev, Vol 21, 93; How the Holy Cross Was Found-From Event to Medieval Legend, with S. Borgehammar, J of Ecclesiastical Hist, Vol 44, 93; Christianizing the Roman Empire and the Pagan Resistance (German), with P. Thrams, J of Theological Studies, Vol 44, 93; Augustine "Confessions', Vol 1, Introduction and Text, Vol 2, Commentary on Books 1-7, Vol 3, Commentary on Books 8-13 (English and Latin), with J. J. O'Donnell, ed, ed-commentator, Classical Philol, Vol 89, 94; Understanding Tertullian-26 Studies on the Author and His Works, 1955-1990 (French), with R. Braun, J of Theological Studies, Vol 45, 94; Statistics and the Conversion of the Roman Aristocracy, J of Roman Studies, Vol 85, 95; Prosopography and Social History-Studies on the Methodology and the Possibility for Knowledge in the Prosopography of the Imperial Period-The Koln Colloquium, November 24-26, 1991 (German), with W. Eck, J of Roman Studies, Vol 85, 95; Falschung and Forgery, Historia Zeitschrift Fur Alte Geschichte, Vol 44, 95; The Mediterranean World in Late Antiquity AD 395-600, with A. Cameron, Phoenix-The J of the Classical Asn of Can, Vol 49, 95; The Later Roman Empire, AD 284-430, with A. Cameron, Phoenix-The J of the Classical Asn of Can, Vol 49, 95; The 'Martyrdom of Pionius', The Bishop of Smyrna (French), L. Robert, ed, J of Theological Studies, Vol 46, 95; Christian Intolerance in Confrontations with Pagans (Italian), with P. F. Beatrice, J of Ecclesiastical Hist, Vol 46, 95; Barbarians and Politics at the Court of Arcadius, with A. Cameron, J. Long, and L. Sherry, Classical Philol, Vol 90, 95; Athanasius of Alexandria, 'Life of Anthony' (French), G. M. J. Bartelink, ed, J of Theological Studies, Vol 46, 95; Research in Ancient Latin Historiography (Italian), with G. Zecchini, Aevum-Rassegna di Scienze Storiche Linguistiche e Filologiche, Vol 70, 96; The Crimes of Basil of Ancyra & The Exercise of Jurisdiction in Civil Cases Between Christian in the Roman Judicial System After Constantibe Episcopalis Audientia, J of Theological Studies, Vol 47, 96; Religion and Authority in Roman Carthage from Augustus to Constantine, with J. B. Rives, J of Theological Studies, Vol 47, 96; Public Disputation, Power, and Social Order in Late Antiquity, with R. Lim, Am Hist Rev, Vol 101, 96; Women and Law in Late Antiquity, with A. Arjava, J of Theological Studies, Vol 48, 97; Athanasius and the Politics of Asceticism, with D. Brakke, J of Ecclesiastical Hist, Vol 48, 97; The Late Roman Army, with P. Southern and K. R. Dixon, Am Hist Rev, Vol 102, 97; The 'Ecclesiastical History' of Sozomenus (German), with G. C. Hansen and J. Bidez, J of Ecclesiastical Hist, Vol 48, 97; The 'Ecclesiastical History' of Theodorus Anagnostes (German), J of Ecclesiastical Hist, Vol 48, 97; The 'Ecclesiastical History' of Socrates (German), with G. C. Hansen and M. Sirinian, J of Ecclesiastical Hist, Vol 48, 97. **CONTACT ADDRESS** Dept of Classics, Univ Toronto, 16 Hart House Circle, Toronto, ON, M5S 1A1.

BARNES, TIMOTHY MARK
PERSONAL Born 04/27/1942, Los Angeles, CA, 2 children **DISCIPLINE** EARLY AMERICAN HISTORY **EDUCATION** Univ NMex, BA, 65, MA, 66, PhD(Hist), 69. **CAREER** Asst Am Hist, Univ NMex, 65-67; asst prof, Univ Albuquerque, 68; assoc prof, 69-80, prof Am Hist, Calif Poly State Univ, San Luis Obispo, 80-, Distinguished teacher, Calif Poly State Univ, 77-78. **MEMBERSHIPS** Orgn Am Historians. **RESEARCH** Loyalists of the American Revolution. **SELECTED PUBLICATIONS** Auth, Loyalist newspapers of the American Revolution: Bibliography and biography, Proc Am Antiquarian Soc, 4/74; Moral Allegiance: John Witherspoon & Loyalist Recautatise in Loyalist Community in North American, Greenwood Press, 90; Loyalist Discourse and the Moderation of the American Revolution in Stephen Lucus, ed, Discourse in and Revolutionary Era, Michigan State University Press, 98. **CONTACT ADDRESS** Dept of History, California Polytech State Univ, 1 Grand Ave, San Luis Obispo, CA, 93407-0001. **EMAIL** tbarnes@calpoly.edu

BARNES ROBINSON, SUSAN
DISCIPLINE ART HISTORY **EDUCATION** UCLA, BA, MA; Michigan Univ, PhD. **CAREER** Prof. **HONORS AND AWARDS** Fulbright fel, Italy. **RESEARCH** 20th century American and European Art **SELECTED PUBLICATIONS** Auth, Giacomo Balla: Divisionism and Futurism, Smithsonian, 96; Mabel Dwight: a catalogue raisonne of the lithographs, Smithsonian, 96. **CONTACT ADDRESS** Dept of Art and Art History, Loyola Marymount Univ, 7900 Loyola Blvd, Los Angeles, CA, 90045. **EMAIL** srobinso@popmail.lmu.edu

BARNETT, LOUISE
DISCIPLINE AMERICAN LITERATURE, NATIVE AMERICAN LITERATURE **EDUCATION** Univ NC, BA; Bryn Mawr, MA, PhD **CAREER** Prof Eng, Rutgers, The State Univ NJ, Univ Col-Camden. **RESEARCH** 19th Century American Culture. **SELECTED PUBLICATIONS** Auth, The Ignoble Savage: American Literary Racism; Touched by Fire: the Life, Death, and Mythic Afterlife of George Armstrong Custer; Authority and Speech: Language, Society, and Self in the American Novel. **CONTACT ADDRESS** Dept of Lit in Eng, Rutgers, The State Univ NJ, Univ Col-Camden, Murray Hall 010, New Brunswick, NJ, 08903. **EMAIL** lk_barnett@acad.fandm.edu

BARNETT, RICHARD CHAMBERS
PERSONAL Born 04/27/1932, Davenport, FL, m, 1957, 2 children **DISCIPLINE** MODERN HISTORY **EDUCATION** Wake Forest Col, BA, 53; Univ NC, PhD, 63. **CAREER** Instr social studies, Gardner-Webb Col, 56-68; from instr to assoc prof, 61-76, chmn dept, 68-75, prof hist, Wake Forest Univ, 76-98, PROF EMER, 98-. **MEMBERSHIPS** Conf Brit Studies; AHA. **RESEARCH** Sixteenth century English administrative history. **SELECTED PUBLICATIONS** Auth, Place, Profit, and Power: The Household of William Cecil, Lord Burghley, Univ NC, 69. **CONTACT ADDRESS** 2130 Royall Dr, Winston-Salem, NC, 27106. **EMAIL** barnetrc@WFU.edu

BARNETT, SUZANNE WILSON
PERSONAL Born 06/01/1940, Columbus, OH, m, 1969 **DISCIPLINE** CHINESE HISTORY **EDUCATION** Muskingum Col, BA, 61; Harvard Univ, AM, 63, PhD(hist, E Asian lang), 73. **CAREER** Vis asst prof hist, Univ VA, 73; asst prof, 74-79, assoc prof, 79-85, prof hist, Univ Puget Sound, 85-, Robert G Albertson Prof, 98-2000; dir, Henry Luce Found Proj on Chinese-Am Interaction, Harvard Univ, 77-79. **MEMBERSHIPS** AHA (coun, 92-95); Asn Asian Studies (bd dir, 79-82). **RESEARCH** Conceptual change in late imperial China; Protestant missions in China; educational innovation. **SELECTED PUBLICATIONS** Auth, Silent Evangelism: Presbyterians and the Mission Press in China, J Presbyterian Hist, winter 71; Protestant expansion and Chinese views of the West, Mod Asian Studies, 4/72; contrib, article, In: Reform in Nineteenth Century China, Harvard Univ, 76; co-ed and contrib, chapter in Christianity in China: Early Protestant Missionary Writings, Harvard Univ, 85; Foochow's Academics: Public Ordering and Expanding Education in the Late Nineteenth Century, Bull Inst Med Hist, June 87. **CONTACT ADDRESS** Dept Hist, Univ Puget Sound, 1500 N Warner St, Tacoma, WA, 98416-0033. **EMAIL** sbarnett@ups.edu

BARNEY, STEPHEN ALLEN
PERSONAL Born 10/10/1942, Rocky Mount, NC, m, 1962, 2 children **DISCIPLINE** ENGLISH LITERATURE, MEDIEVAL STUDIES **EDUCATION** Univ Va, BA, 64; Harvard Univ, PhD(English), 69. **CAREER** From asst prof to assoc prof English, Yale Univ, 68-78; PROF ENGLISH, UNIV CA, IR-

VINE, 79-, Morse fel allegory, Yale Univ, 72-73; Am Coun Learned Soc fel Medieval Latin, 76; Nat Endowment Humanities fel Medieval Latin, 79-81; vis assoc prof English, Univ VA, 78. **HONORS AND AWARDS** Elliott Prize, Mediaeval Acad Am, 74. **MEMBERSHIPS** MLA; Mediaeval Acad Am; Early English Text Soc; New Chaucer Soc. **RESEARCH** Chaucer; Medieval Latin allegorical dictionaries; textual criticism. **SELECTED PUBLICATIONS** Auth, The Plowshare of the Tongue, Mediaeval Studies, 73; An Evaluation of the Pardoner's Tale, In: T-C Interpretations of the Pardoner's Tale, 73; Word-Hoard, Yale Univ, 77; Allegories of History, Allegories of Love, Archon Bks, 79; Chaucer's Troilus: Essays in Criticism, Archon Books, 80; Suddeness and Process in Chaucer, Chaucer Rev, 82; Visible Allegory, Harvard English Studies, 82; Ordo-Paginis, The 'Gloss' on 'Genesis 38', South Atlantic Quart, Vol 91, 92; The Life of Geoffrey Chaucer-A Critical Biography, with D. Pearsall, Notes and Queries, Vol 40, 93; Oxford Guides to Chaucer 'Troilus and Criseyde', with B. Windeatt, Notes and Queries, Vol 40, 93; Geoffrey Chaucer, with V. B Richmind, Speculum-A J of Medieval Studies, Vol 69, 94. **CONTACT ADDRESS** Univ CA Irvine, Irvine, CA, 92717.

BARNEY, WILLIAM LESKO
PERSONAL Born 02/02/1943, Kingston, PA, m, 1967, 2 children **DISCIPLINE** AMERICAN HISTORY **EDUCATION** Cornell Univ, BA, 64; Columbia Univ, MA, 65, PhD(Am hist), 71. **CAREER** Asst prof US hist, 71-75, Trenton St Col; assoc prof, 75-82, prof, 82-, Univ NC Chapel Hill. **HONORS AND AWARDS** NEH fel, 77; Fulbright Sr Lectr Univ Genva, 87. **MEMBERSHIPS** AHA; Orgn Amer Hist; Southern Hist Assn. **RESEARCH** Antebellum South; Civil War. **SELECTED PUBLICATIONS** Auth, Road to Secession, Praeger, 72; auth, The Secessionist Impulse, Princeton Univ, 74; auth, Flawed Victory: A New Perspective on the Civil War, Praeger, 75 & Univ Press Am, 80; auth, Passage of the Republic, CD Health, 87; coauth, The American Journey, Prentice Hall, 97. **CONTACT ADDRESS** 407 Westwood Dr, Chapel Hill, NC, 27516. **EMAIL** wbarney@email.uhc.edu

BARNHART, MICHAEL ANDREW
PERSONAL Born 06/08/1951, Hanover, PA, m, 1978, 1 child **DISCIPLINE** HISTORY **EDUCATION** Harvard, PhD, 80. **CAREER** Prof of History, SUNY-Stony Brook, 80-. **MEMBERSHIPS** SHAFR; AHA; OAH; AAS. **RESEARCH** US-Japan relations, 20th century. **SELECTED PUBLICATIONS** Auth, Japan's Economic Security and the Origins of the Pacific War, The J of Strategic Studies 4, June 81; Planning the Pearl Harbor Attack: A Study in Military Politics, Aerospace Hist 29, Dec 82; Japan's Drive to Autarky, Japan Examined, eds Harry Wray and Hilary Conroy, Univ HI Press, 83; Japanese Intelligence before the Pacific War: Best Case Analysis, Knowing One's Enemies: Intelligence Assessment Before the Two World Wars, ed Ernest R May, Princeton Univ Press, 84; ed, Congress and United States Foreign Policy: Controlling the Use of Force in the Nuclear Age, SUNY Press, 87; auth, Japan Prepares for Total War: The Search for Economic Security, 1919-1941, Cornell Univ Press, 87; Hornbeck was Right: The Realist Approach to American Foreign Policy toward Japan, Pearl Harbor Reexamined, eds Hilary Conroy and Harry Wray, Univ HI Press, 90; Nihon rikugun no shinchitsujokoso to kaisen kettei ¤The Imperial Army's New Order and Japan's Decision for War,| Taiheiyo senso ¤The Pacific War, ed Hosoya Chihiro, Homma Nagayo, Akira Iriye, and Hatano Sumio, Univ Tokyo Press, 93; The Incomplete Alliance: America and Japan after World War II, Diplomatic Hist 18, fall 93; Japan and the World Since 1868, Edwin Arnold Books Ltd, 95; Driven By Domestics: American Relations with Japan and Korea, 1900-1945, Pacific Passage: The Study of American-East Asian Relations on the Eve of the Twenty-First Century, ed Warren I Cohen, Columbia Univ Press, 96; The Origins of World War II in Asia and the Pacific, Diplomatic Hist 20, spring 96. **CONTACT ADDRESS** Dept of History, SUNY, Stony Brook, Stony Brook, NY, 11794. **EMAIL** HistorianB@col.com

BARNHILL, GEORGIA BRADY
PERSONAL Born 12/08/1944, Mount Kisco, NY, m, 1987 **DISCIPLINE** HISTORY **EDUCATION** Wellesley Col, BA, art hist, 66. **CAREER** Readers Svcs Dept, 68-69, Amer Antiq Soc; Andrew W. Mellon Curator, Graphic Arts, 69-, Amer Antiq Soc. **HONORS AND AWARDS** APS fels, 86; Bibl Soc Amer, 86; Huntington Lib Soc, 93; Maurice Rickards Award Ephemera Soc. **MEMBERSHIPS** AAS; Print Coun of Amer; Colonial Soc of Mass; Grolier Club; Amer Hist Print Collectors Soc; Sonneck Soc; Amer Printing Hist Assn, Col Art Assn, ARLIS. **RESEARCH** History of Amer prints & illustrated bks. **SELECTED PUBLICATIONS** Ed, Prints of New England, Worcester: Amer Antiq Soc, 91; auth, Political Cartoons of New England 1812-1861, Amer Antiq Soc, 91; auth, FOC Darley's Illustrations for Southern Humor, Graphic Arts & the South, Univ Ark Press, 93; auth, Extracts from the Journals of Ethan A Greenwood': Portrait Painter and Museum Proprietor, Proc of Amer Antiq Soc, vol 103, 93; auth, Illustrations of the Adirondacks in the Popular Press, Adirondack Prints & Printmakers, Adirondack Mus & Syracuse Univ Press, 98; auth, Political Cartoons at the American Antiquarian Society, Inks, vol 2, 95; auth, Pictorial Histories of the United States, Visual Rsrcs, vol 11, 95; auth, Wild Impressions: The Adirondackson Paper, Adirondack Mus, 95; coauth, Early American Lithography: Images to 1830, Boston Athenaeum, 97; co-ed, The Cultivation of Artists in Nineteenth-Century America, Amer Antiq Soc, 97. **CONTACT ADDRESS** 157 Robinson Rd, Oakham, MA, 01068. **EMAIL** gbb@mwa.org

BARNHILL, JOHN HERSCHEL
PERSONAL Born 03/02/1947, Walnut Ridge, AR, d, 1 child **DISCIPLINE** HISTORY **EDUCATION** Okla St Univ, PhD, 81. **CAREER** Instr, 77-81, Okla St Univ; asst dir, 81-82, 45th Infantry Div Mus, OK; videotape archiv, 82-84, OK Dept of Lib; hist, engg & instl div, 84-85, Tinker AFB; prog analysts, 85-, DISA Area Command, OK City. **HONORS AND AWARDS** Phi Alpha Theta, 73-74; Phi Theta Kappa, 77-81; Phi Kappa Phi, 81-; LeRoy Fischer Award, 81; Outstanding Young Men of Amer, 81; Dist Alumnus, Corpus Christi St Univ, 83; Air Force Org Excel Awards, 84-85, 86-87, 88-89, 90, 92-93; Who's Who in South & Southwest, 91; Air Force Assn Beacon of Freedom Award, 91; Who's Who in World, 94; Joint Meritorious Unit Award, 96. **RESEARCH** Non-mainstream relig movements; roles of minority groups in Amer society. **SELECTED PUBLICATIONS** Art, Civil Rights in Utah: The Mormon Way, J of West XXV, 86; art, Triumph of Will: The Coal Strike of 1899-1903 in Indian Territory, Chronicles of OK, LXI, 83; art, Civil Rights in the 1940's: The Fair Employment Practices Commission, Brooks Hays, and the Arkansas Plan, Negro Hist Bull, LV, 82; art, The Way West: The California Road, Red River Valley Hist Rev, VI, 81; art, Digging Coal: Conflict or Conciliation? The English Strike of 1893 and the American Strike of 1894, OK St Hist Rev, II, 81; art, With 'All' Deliberate Speed: Desegregation of the Public Schools in Oklahoma City and Tulsa, 1954-1972, Red River Valley Hist Rev, VI, 81; art, The Punitive Expedition Against Pancho Villa: The Forced Motorization of the American Army, Mil Hist of Texas & The Southwest XIV, 78; auth, From Surplus to Substitution: Energy in Texas, Amer Press, 83. **CONTACT ADDRESS** DISA Area Command, 8705 Industrial Blvd, Tinker AFB, OK, 73145. **EMAIL** jbarnhil@okc.disa.mil

BAROLSKY, PAUL
PERSONAL Born 07/13/1941, Paterson, NJ, m, 1966, 2 children **DISCIPLINE** ART HISTORY, LITERARY CRITICISM **EDUCATION** Middleburg Col, BA, 63; Harvard Univ, MA, 64, PhD(Art hist), 69. **CAREER** Asst prof, Cornell Univ, 68-69; ASSOC PROF ART HIST, UNIV VA, 69-. **RESEARCH** Italian Renaissance art; history of art criticism. **SELECTED PUBLICATIONS** Auth, Toward an Interpretation of One Pazzi Chapel, J One Soc Archit Historians, 73; Infinite Jest: Wit and Humor in Italian Renaissance Art, Univ MO Press, 78; Daniele da Volterra: A Catalogue Raisonne, Garland, 79; Walter Patev's Renaissance, VA Quart, 82; Cellini, Vasari, and the Marvels of Malady & Benvenuto Cellini 'Autobiography', Sixteenth Century J, Vol 24, 93; Andrea Del Castagno and His Patrons, with J. R. Spencer, Renaissance Quart, Vol 46, 93; The Painter Who Almost Became a Cheese & Paolo Ucello, VA Quart Rev, Vol 70, 94; Lord Byron, Strength-Romantic Writing and Commercial Society, with J. Christensen, VA Quart Rev, Vol 70, 94; Fables of Art, VA Quart Rev, Vol 71, 95; A Very Brief History of Art From Narcissus to Picasso, Classical J, Vol 90, 95; The Visionary Experience of Renaissance Art, Word & Image, Vol 11, 95; Johannes Vermeer, with A. K. Wheelock, VA Quart Rev, Vol 72, 96; Flesh and the Ideal-Winckelman and the Origins of Art History, with A. Potts, Classical J, Vol 91, 96; The Fable of Failure in Modern Art, VA Quart Rev, Vol 73, 97. **CONTACT ADDRESS** Dept of Art, Univ of VA, 102 Fayerweather, Charlottesville, VA, 22903.

BARON, CAROL K.
PERSONAL New York, NY, w, 1963, 2 children **DISCIPLINE** MUSIC **EDUCATION** Graduate Ctr of the City Univ of NY, PhD, 87. **CAREER** Adjunct lectr, York Col, 74-75; adjunct lectr, Hunter Col, 78-80; adjunct prof, Adelphi Univ, 80-82; exec dir, Bach Area Group Asn, Bach Aria Festival and Inst at the Univ Stony Brook, 80-97. **HONORS AND AWARDS** Travel grant, American Council of Learned Societies; Alfred P. Sloan Fel; ASCAP Deems Taylor Award. **MEMBERSHIPS** Am Musicology Soc; Soc for Music Theory; Sonneck Soc. **RESEARCH** Music of Charles Ives; late 19th century/early 20th century American culture; music of J.S. Bach; religious trends in 17th and early 18th century Germany. **SELECTED PUBLICATIONS** Auth, Dating the Music of Charles Ives: Facts and Fictions, in Perspectives of New Music 28, 90; auth, Meaning in the Music of Charles Ives, in Metaphor - A Musical Dimension, Australian Studies in the History, Philosophy and Social Studies of Music, 91; auth, George Ives's Essay on Music Theory: An Introduction and An Annotated Edition, in American Music, 92; auth, Larry Starr. A Union of Diversities: Style in the Music of Charles Ives, in Notes, 93; auth, At the Cutting Edge: Three American Theorists at the End of the Nineteenth Century, in International Journal of Musicology 2, 93; auth, What Motivated Charles Ives's search for Time Past, in The Musical Quart 78/2, 94. **CONTACT ADDRESS** 321 Melbourne Rd, Great Neck, NY, 11021. **EMAIL** cbaron@ccmail.sunysb.edu

BARON, JAMES
PERSONAL Born 11/21/1942 **DISCIPLINE** CLASSICAL STUDIES **EDUCATION** Catholic Univ Am, AB, 64; Univ Minn, MA, 67, PhD, 72. **CAREER** Tchg asst, 66-69; tchg assoc, 69-70, Univ Minn; asst prof, Macalester Col, St Paul, Minn, 70-71; asst prof, Concordia Col, Moorehead, Minn, 70-71; asst prof, Col William and Mary in Va, 71-76; assoc prof, 76- & ept ch, 83-89 & 91-92. **RESEARCH** Augustan poetry; classical tradition in film; Scandinavian literature. **SELECTED PUBLICATIONS** Auth, Drag Humor in Aristophanes Comedies, Class Asn Mid W and S, 90; Direct Address to the Audience in the Films of Ingmar Bergman: A Classical Device Radically Transformed, Inaugural Meeting Int Soc for the Class Tradition, Boston, 91; The Orpheus Myth in the Early Films of Ingmar Bergman, CAMWS Southern Sect Meeting, Richmond, 92; Horatii Carmina I.37.17-20: Citus Venator: Homo aut Canis, Class Asn Mid W and S, Atlanta Georgia, 94; Bergman's Cries and Whispers, a Masterpiece of Classical Architecture, Soc Advancement for Scand Study, Davenport, 94; Alliteration and Other Sound Effects in Seneca's Tragedies, Class Asn Mid W and S, Southern Section, Chapel Hill, NC, 94; Willa Cather's Alexandra Bergson: Aeneas on the Nebraska Prairie, Class Asn Mid W and S, Omaha, 95 & A Child of Soil Reads Catullus, Horace, and Vergil, Amer Philol Asn, San Diego, 95; rev, Persona: the Transcendent Image, Scand Stud, vol 60, 98. **CONTACT ADDRESS** Dept of Classical Studies, Col of William and Mary, Morton Hall, PO Box 8795, Williamsburg, VA, 23187-8795. **EMAIL** jrbaro@facstaff.wm.edu

BARON, SAMUEL HASKELL
PERSONAL Born 05/24/1921, New York, NY, m, 1949, 3 children **DISCIPLINE** HISTORY **EDUCATION** Cornell Univ, BS, 42; Columbia Univ, MA, 48, PhD, 52. **CAREER** Instr hist, Univ TN, 48-53; vis lectr, Northwest Univ, 53-54; vis asst prof, Univ MO, 54-55 & Univ NE, 55-56; from asst prof to prof, Grinnell Col, 56-66; prof, Univ CA, San Diego, 66-72; ALUMNI DISTINGUISHED PROF HIST, UNIV NC, CHAPEL HILL, 72-, Fel E Asian Studies, Harvard Univ, 58-59; Am Philos Soc res grant, 63; Inter-Univ travel grant fel, 63-64; Am Coun Learned Soc fels, 64-71; Int Res & Exchange Bd fel, 70; Guggenheim Mem Found fel, 70-71; pres, Conf Slavic & East Europ Studies, 75; Nat Endowment for Humanities fel, 76. **MEMBERSHIPS** AHA; Am Asn Advan Slavic Studies; AAUP. **RESEARCH** Russian social and intellectual history. **SELECTED PUBLICATIONS** Auth, Plekhanov: The Father of Russian Marxism, 63 & The Travels of Olearius in Seventeenth Century Russia, 67, Stanford Univ; contribr, Revisionism: Essays in the History of Marxist Ideas, Allen & Unwin, 62; co-ed, Windows on the Russian Past, Essays on Soviet Historiography Since Stalin, Am Asn Advan Slavic Studies, 77; auth, Muscovite Russia: Collected Essays, Variorum, 80; Great Scholar-Teachers, Klyuchevskii, Pascal, Torke, Intro, Russian Hist, Vol 21, 94; An Obsession With History-Russian Writers Confront the Past, with A. B. Wachtel, Am Hist Rev, Vol 100, 95; The Founding of Russia Navy-Peter-the-Gret and the Azov Fleet, 1688-1714, with E. J. Phillips, Russian Rev, Vol 55, 96. **CONTACT ADDRESS** Dept of Hist, Univ of NC, Chapel Hill, NC, 27514.

BARR, CHESTER ALWYN
PERSONAL Born 01/18/1938, Austin, TX, m, 1961, 2 children **DISCIPLINE** HISTORY **EDUCATION** Univ of Tex, BA, 59, MA, 61, PhD, 66. **CAREER** Asst prof, Purdue Univ, 66-69; from assoc prof to prof, Tex Tech Univ, 69- ; chair, Dept of Hist, Tex Tech Univ, 78-85. **HONORS AND AWARDS** Tullis Prize, Tex State Hist Asn, 71; Fel, Tex State Hist Asn, 72; President's Excellence in Tchg Award, 87., President's Acad Achievement Award, Texas Tech Univ, 92. **MEMBERSHIPS** Am Hist Asn, Org of Am Hist; Southern Hist Asn; Tex State Hist Asn; Tex Coun for the Hum. **RESEARCH** African American history; Civil War history; Southern military, polit and social history. **SELECTED PUBLICATIONS** Auth, Polignac's Texas Brigade, 64; Reconstruction to Reform: Texas Politics, 1876-1906, 71; Black Texans: A History of African Americans in Texas, 1528-1995, 73; Texans in Revolt: The Battle for San Antonio, 1835, 90; numerous articles and book chapters. **CONTACT ADDRESS** Dept of History, Texas Tech Univ, Lubbock, TX, 79409. **EMAIL** nbarr@hub.ofthe.net

BARR, DAVID LAWRENCE
PERSONAL Born 04/24/1942, Belding, MI, m, 1966, 3 children **DISCIPLINE** BIBLICAL STUDIES, HISTORY OF RELIGIONS **EDUCATION** Ft Wayne Bible Col, BA, 65; FL State Univ, MA, 69, PhD, 74. **CAREER** Consult relig pub educ, Relig Instr Asn, 67-71; instr relig, FL A&M Univ, 72-74; asst prof, Univ Northern IA, 74-75; asst prof, 75-80, assoc prof, 80-88, prof relig, Wright State Univ, 88, Chmn, Relig Dept, Wright State Univ, 80-86, Dir, Honors Prog 87-94. **HONORS AND AWARDS** Pres, Eastern Grt Lakes Bible Soc; Pres, Mideast Honors Asn; Phi Kappa Phi; Pres Fac. **MEMBERSHIPS** Soc Bibl Lit; Cath Bibl Asn, Am Acad Relig. **RESEARCH** Apocalypse of John; Narrative analysis; Soc world of early Christianity. **SELECTED PUBLICATIONS** Co-ed (with Nicholas Piediscalzi), The Bible in American Education, a centennial volume prepared for the Soc of Bibl Lit, Fortress Press and Scholars Press, 82; New Testament Story: An Introduction, Wadsworth Publ Co, 87, 2nd ed, 95; Co-ed (with Linda Bennett Elder and Elizabeth Struthers Malbon), Biblical and Humane:

A Festschrift for John Priest; Tales of the End: A Narrative Commentary on the Book of Revelation, Polebridge Press, 98. **CONTACT ADDRESS** Dept of Relig, Wright State Univ, 3640 Colonel Glenn, Dayton, OH, 45435-0002. **EMAIL** dbarr@wright.edu

BARRETT, ANTHONY ARTHUR
PERSONAL Born 07/30/1941, Worthing, England **DISCIPLINE** CLASSICS **EDUCATION** Univ Durham, BA, 63; Univ Newcastle, BA, 64; Univ Toronto, MA, 65, PhD(classics), 68; Oxford Univ, dipl class archaeol, 74. **CAREER** Lectr Classics, Carleton Univ, 65-66; asst prof, 68-73, ASSOC PROF CLASSICS, UNIV BC, 73-. **MEMBERSHIPS** Class Asn Can (secy, 71-73); Humanities Asn Can; Royal Astron Soc; fel, Soc Antiquaries; Archeol Inst Am. **RESEARCH** Roman history; Romano-British archaeology; Latin literature. **SELECTED PUBLICATIONS** Auth, The Authorship of the Culex, Latomus, 70; Catullus 52 and the Consulship of Vatinius, Trans Am Philol Asn, 72; Sohaemus, King of Emesa and Sophene, Am J Philol, 77; Gaius' Policy in the Bosporus, Trans Am Philol Asn, 77; coauth, The Oxford Brygos cup: A New Interpretation, J Hellenic Studies, 78; auth, The Literary Classics in Roman Britain, 78 & The Career of Cogidubnus, 79, Britannia; The Epigrams of Janus Pannonius, Corvina Press, Budapest, 82; Claudius, with B. Levick, Phonix--The J of the Classical Asn of Canada, Vol 46, 92; Flavius Josephus, 'Death of an Emperor', trans with an intro and commentary, English and Greek, with T. P. Wiseman, Translator-Commentator, Classical Review, Vol 42, 92; An Historical and Historiographical Commentary on Suetonius 'Life of C. Caligula', with D. W. Hurley, Phoenix--The J of the Classical Asn of Canada, Vol 49, 95. **CONTACT ADDRESS** Dept of Classics, Univ of BC, Vancouver, BC, V6T 1W5.

BARRETT, BARNABY B.
DISCIPLINE CLINICAL PSYCHOLOGY, EDUCATIONAL AND CLINICAL SEXOLOGY **EDUCATION** Harvard Univ, PhD, 76; Inst Advanced Study of Human Sexology, DHS, 94. **CAREER** Dir, Midwest Inst of Sexology; prof, Wayne State Univ. **RESEARCH** Sexuality; Psychoanalytic Psychology; Anthropology; Cultural Studies. **SELECTED PUBLICATIONS** Auth, Psychoanalysis and The Postmodern Impulse, 93. **CONTACT ADDRESS** 7480 Greenwich East, Bloomifield Hills, MI, 48301-3920.

BARRETT, DAVID P.
DISCIPLINE HISTORY **EDUCATION** Univ Toronto, BA, MA, MP; London Univ, PhD. **RESEARCH** Republican China **SELECTED PUBLICATIONS** Auth, Ideological Foundations of the Wang Jingwei Regime: Rural Pacification, the New Citizens' Movement, and the Great East Asia War, 93. **CONTACT ADDRESS** History Dept, McMaster Univ, 1280 Main St W, Hamilton, ON, L8S 4L9.

BARRETT, JAMES R.
DISCIPLINE HISTORY **EDUCATION** Univ Ill Chicago, AB; Univ Warwick, England, MAUniv; Pittsburgh, PhD, 81. **CAREER** Asst prof, NC State Univ, 81-84; asst prof to prof & dept.ch, Univ Ill Urbana Champaign, 84-. **RESEARCH** U.S. ,comparative working-class history and class; race; ethnicity in twentieth-century U.S. social history; Current research interests focus on the social and ideological bases of labor radicalism and the mentalities of immigrant workers. **SELECTED PUBLICATIONS** Auth, Unity and Fragmentation: Class, Race, and Ethnicity on Chicago's South Side, 1900-1922, J Social Hist, 84; Work and Community in The Jungle: Chicago's Packinghouse Workers, 1894-1922, Univ Ill, 87; Americanization from the Bottom Up: Immigration and the Remaking of the Working Class in the United States, 1880-1930, J Am Hist, 92. **CONTACT ADDRESS** History Dept, Univ Ill Urbana Champaign, 52 E Gregory Dr, Champaign, IL, 61820. **EMAIL** jrbarret@uiuc.edu

BARRETT, MICHAEL BAKER
PERSONAL Born 10/12/1946, Honululu, HI, m, 1969, 1 child **DISCIPLINE** MODERN GERMAN & MILITARY HISTORY **EDUCATION** The Citadel, BA, 68; Univ MA, MA, 69, PhD, 77. **CAREER** Lectr, Univ MA, 75-76; instr, 76-78, asst prof, 78-82, ASSOC PROF HIST, THE CITADEL, 82-. **MEMBERSHIPS** AHA; Conf Group Cent Europ Hist; Am Mil Inst; Southern Hist Asn. **RESEARCH** Weimar Republic-Third Reich military; Weimar Republic police. **SELECTED PUBLICATIONS** Ed, Proc of The Citadel Symposium on Hitler and the National Socialist Era, 82. **CONTACT ADDRESS** Hist Dept, The Citadel, 171 Moultrie St, Charleston, SC, 29409-0002. **EMAIL** barrettm@citadel.edu

BARRON, HAL S.
PERSONAL Born 12/29/1951, Louisville, KY, m, 1977, 1 child **DISCIPLINE** AMERICAN HISTORY **EDUCATION** Oberlin Col, AB, 73; Univ Pa, MA, 76, PhD(Hist), 80. **CAREER** Instr, 799-80; asst prof, 80-85; assoc prof, 85-91; full prof History, Harvey Mudd Col, 91-; dept chmn, 93-98; mem grad fac History, Claremont Grad Univ, 81-; visit assoc prof Waseda Univ, Tokyo, Japan, 89-90; HEH sen fell, 93; Newberry Library, NEH fel, 86-87; NEH Sum Stipend, 92; Huntington Library, Haynes Found fell, 88; Haynes Found Sum res fell, 86; NEH Sum Stipend, 82. **HONORS AND AWARDS** Carstensen Award agr hist, 81; Arnold & Lois S Graves Award, 82. **MEMBERSHIPS** Orgn Am Historians; Social Sci Hist Asn, Exec Comm, 97-; Am Hist Soc; convener Rural History network 80-92, prog comm, 87; Agr Hist Soc, exec comm, 94-97. **RESEARCH** Rural history; social history. **SELECTED PUBLICATIONS** Auth, A case for Appalachian demographic history, Appalachian J, 77; coauth (with Walter M Licht), Labor's men: A collective biography of union officialdom during the New Deal years, Labor Hist, 78; auth, The impact of rural depopulation on the local economy: Chelsea, Vt, 1840-1900, Agr Hist, 80; Outstanding in His Field: Perspectives on American Agriculture in Honor of Wayne D Rasmussen, Ames, Iowa State Univ Press, 93; Mixed Harvest: The Second Great Transformation in the Rural North, 1870-1930, Chapel Hill, UNC Press, dual edition, 97. **CONTACT ADDRESS** Dept of Humanities & Social Sci, Harvey Mudd Col, 301 E 12th St, Claremont, CA, 91711-5990. **EMAIL** Hal_Barron@HMC.EDU

BARSTOW, ANNE LLEWELLYN
PERSONAL Born 06/22/1929, Jacksonville, FL, m, 1952, 3 children **DISCIPLINE** MEDIEVAL & WOMEN'S HISTORY **EDUCATION** Univ FL, BA, 49; Columbia Univ, MA, 64, PhD(medieval hist), 78. **CAREER** Asst prof, 70-79, ASSOC PROF MEDIEVAL HIST, STATE UNIV NY, COL OLD WESTBURY, 79-, Lectr, Relig Dept, NY Univ, 70-73 & Episcopal Divinity Sch, 78. **MEMBERSHIPS** Am Acad Relig; AHA; Inst Res Hist; Feminist Theol Inst. **RESEARCH** Late medieval radical female mysticism: Joan of Arc; history of compulsory celebacy laws for priesthood; the churches' attitudes towards clergy wives. **SELECTED PUBLICATIONS** Auth, Early Goddess Religions, In: An Introductin to the Religion of the Goddess, Seabury Press, 82; Anglican Clergy Wives after the Reformation, In: Women in New Worlds, Vol II, Abingdon Press, 82; Married Priests and the Reforming Papacy: The Eleventh-Century Debates, 82 & Joan of Arc and Radical Mysticism, Edwin Mellen Press; Womens Lives in Medieval Europe-A Sourcebook, E. Amt, ed, Church Hist, Vol 63, 94; The Albigensian Crusades, with J. R. Strayer and C. Lansing, Church Hist, Vol 63, 94; Ways of Lying-Dissimulation, Persecution, and Conformity in Early Modern Europe, with P. Zagorin, Am Hist Rev, Vol 99, 94; Backlash & Excerpts From the Speeches to 1992 Republican National Convention on the Nature, Manifestations and Effects of the Feminist Movement in the Last 30 Years, J of Feminist Studies in Religion, Vol 10, 94; Confession and Community in 17th-Century France-Catholic and Protestant Coexistence in Aquitaine, with G. Hanlon, Church Hist, Vol 64, 95; Women Religious-The Founding of English Nunneries After the Norman Conquest, with S. Thompson, Church Hist, Vol 64, 95; The Oldest Vocation-Christian Motherhood in the Middle Ages, with C. W. Atkinson, Church Hist, Vol 64, 95; Growing Up in Medieval London-The Experience of Childhood in History, with B. A. Hanawalt, Church Hist, Vol 64, 95; From Virile Woman to Womanchrist-Studies in Medieval Religion and Literature, with B. Newman, Church Hist, Vol 65, 96; The Law of the Father-Patriarchy in the Transition From Feudalism to Capitalism, with M. Murray, Am Hist Rev, Vol 102, 97. **CONTACT ADDRESS** 606 W 122 St, New York, NY, 10027.

BARTEL, LEE R.
PERSONAL Born 04/04/1948, Steinbach, MB, Canada **DISCIPLINE** MUSIC EDUCATION **EDUCATION** Univ Man, BA, 73, MEd, 84; Brandon Univ, BMus, 75; Univ Ill, PhD, 88. **CAREER** High sch & univ mus tchr, 69-76; prof & mus dept ch, Steinbach Bible Col, 75-85; dir develop, 86-87, ASSOC PROF & CHAIR MUSIC EDUCATION, UNIV TORONTO, 87-, founder & dir, Can Mus Educ Res Ctr, 89-. **MEMBERSHIPS** Am Educ Res Asn; Can Univ Mus Soc; Int Soc Mus Educ; Mus Educ Nat Conf; Ont Mus Educ Asn. **SELECTED PUBLICATIONS** Coauth, A Guide to Provincial Music Curriculum Documents since 1980, 93; coauth, Get Into Guitar, 73; ed, A College Looks Forward, 87; ed, Research Perspectives on Music Education (monograph ser); ed, Can J Res Mus Educ, 93-. **CONTACT ADDRESS** Music Educ Div, Univ of Toronto, Toronto, ON, M5S 1A1.

BARTH, GUNTHER
PERSONAL Born 01/10/1925, Duesseldorf, Germany, m, 1960, 4 children **DISCIPLINE** AMERICAN & URBAN HISTORY **EDUCATION** Univ OR, BA, 55, MA, 57; Harvard Univ, PhD(hist), 62. **CAREER** Tutor hist, Harvard Col, 60-62; from instr to assoc prof, 62-71, PROF HIST, UNIV CA, BERKELEY, 71-, Guggenheim fel, 68-69; Fulbright prof, Univ Cologne, 70-71. **MEMBERSHIPS** AHA; Orgn Am Historians. **RESEARCH** Social and cultural history; urban society in comparative perspective; immigration. **SELECTED PUBLICATIONS** All Quiet in the Yamhill, Univ Ore, 59; Bitter Strength, Harvard Univ, 64; Metropolism and Urban Elites in the Far West, In: The Age of Industrialism in America, Free Press, 68; Instant Cities, 75 & City People, 80, Oxford Univ; Performing Beethoven, with R. Stowell, Music and Letters, Vol 78, 97. **CONTACT ADDRESS** Dept of Hist, Univ of CA, Berkeley, CA, 94720.

BARTHOLOMEW, JAMES RICHARD
PERSONAL Born 06/30/1941, Hot Springs, SD **DISCIPLINE** JAPANESE HISTORY; HISTORY OF SCIENCE **EDUCATION** Stanford Univ, BA, 63, MA, 64, PhD(hist), 72. **CAREER** Asst prof, 71-77, from assoc prof to prof Japanese Hist, Ohio State Univ, 77-91; Nat Endowment for Humanities fel, 76-77; Nat Science Found, 85-86; vis fel, Sch Hist Studies, Inst Advan Study, Princeton, NJ, 76-; Fulbright Fel, 95-96. **MEMBERSHIPS** AHA; Asn Asian Studies; Hist Sci Soc. **RESEARCH** Modern Japanese history; history of Japanese science. **SELECTED PUBLICATIONS** Japanese culture and the problem of modern science, In: Science and Values, Humanities, 74; Why was there no scientific revolution in Tokugawa Japan? Japanese Studies Hist Sci, No 15, 76; Japanese modernization and the Imperial Universities, 1870-1920, J Asian Studies, 78; Science, Bureaucracy and Freedom in Meiji and Talsho Japan, In: Dimensions of Conflict in Modern Japan, 82; The formation of Science in Japan: Building a Research Tradition, Yale Univ Press, 1989, paperback, 93. **CONTACT ADDRESS** Dept of History, Ohio State Univ, 230 W 17th Ave, Columbus, OH, 43210-1361. **EMAIL** bartholomew.5@osu.edu

BARTLET, ELIZABETH C.
DISCIPLINE MUSIC **EDUCATION** Univ Chicago, PhD. **CAREER** Musicol prof, Duke Univ. **SELECTED PUBLICATIONS** Auth, publ(s) on 18th and 19th century French opera; music during the French Revolution. **CONTACT ADDRESS** Dept of Music, Duke Univ, Mary Duke Biddle Music Bldg, Durham, NC, 27706. **EMAIL** mecb@duke.edu

BARTLETT, IRVING HENRY
PERSONAL Born 02/02/1923, Springfield, MA, m, 1944 **DISCIPLINE** AMERICAN SOCIAL & INTELLECTUAL HISTORY **EDUCATION** Ohio Wesleyan Univ, BA, 48; Brown Univ, MA, 49, PhD(Am civilization), 52. **CAREER** Lectr Am Civilization, US Info Serv, Pakistan, 52-53; asst prof, RI Col Educ, 53-54 & Mass Inst Technol, 54-60; pres, Cape Cod Community Col, 60-64; prof hist, Carnegie-Mellon Univ, 64-80; Kennedy prof am Civilization, 80-93, EMER PROF AM STUD, 94- , UNIV MASS. **HONORS AND AWARDS** Vchm bd trustees, Community Col, Allegheny County, 64-71; Guggenheim fel, 66-67; Dorrance vis prof hist, Trinity Col, Conn, 71-72; Charles Warren Fel, Charles Warren Ctr Studies Am Hist, Harvard Univ, 78-79. **MEMBERSHIPS** AHA; Am Studies Asn. **RESEARCH** American social and intellectual history; biography. **SELECTED PUBLICATIONS** Auth, From Slave to Citizen: The Story of the Negro in Rhode Island, Providence Urban League, 53; Bushnell, Cousin and Comprehensive Christianity, J Relig, 4/57; ed, William Ellery Channing: Unitarian Christianity and Other Essays, Bobbs, 57; auth, Wendell Phillips, Brahmin Radical, Beacon, 61; The American Mind at the Mid-Nineteenth Century, Crowell, 67; coauth, New History of the United States, Holt, 69; Daniel Webster, 78 & Wendell and Ann Phillips, 80, Norton; auth, John C. Calhoun, 93. **CONTACT ADDRESS** 47 Bradley Hill Rd, Hingham, MA, 02043. **EMAIL** vkbihb@aol.com

BARTLETT, KENNETH ROY
PERSONAL Born 11/28/1948, Toronto, ON, Canada, m, 1971 **DISCIPLINE** RENAISSANCE & MEDIEVAL EUROPEAN HISTORY **EDUCATION** Univ Toronto, BA, 71, MA, 72, PhD(medieval studies), 78. **CAREER** Asst to the pres, 79-80, ASST PROF HIST, UNIV TORONTO, 78-, EXEC ASST TO VPRES INST REL, 80-, Chmn, Toronto Renaissance & Reformation Colloquium, 81. **MEMBERSHIPS** Can Soc Renaissance Studies (secy-treas, 80-82 & pres, 82-84); Renaissance Soc Am; Medieval Acad Am; AHA; Can Soc Ital Studies. **RESEARCH** Cultural and intellectual relations between England and Italy in the 16th century; English travellers and residents in Italy during the Renaissance; espionage and secret operatives in the 16th century. **SELECTED PUBLICATIONS** Auth, The Decline and Abolition of the Master of Grammar: An Early Victory of Humanism at the University of Cambridge, Hist Educ, 77; The Misfortune That is Wished For Him: The Exile and Death of Edward Courtenay, 8th Earl of Devon, Can J Hist, 79; A Misdated Letter of Roger Ascham, Notes & Queries, 79; co-ed, A Catalogue of Humanist Editions of the Classics in the CRRS Library, CRRS, 79; The Strangeness of Strangers: English Impressions of Italy in the 16th Century, Quaderni d'Italianistica, 80; The English Exile Community in Italy and the Political Opposition to Queen Mary I, Albion, 81; The Household of Francis Russell, 2nd Earl of Bedford, in Venice, 1555, Medieval Prosopography, 81; The Role of the Marian Exiles in the Parliaments of Elizabeth, In: History of Parliament Trust: The House of Commons, 1558-1603, HMSO, London, 82; Gardens and Gardening in Papal Rome, with D. R. Coffin, Quaderni D Italianistica, Vol 13, 92; Machiavelli in the Florentine Historiography-On the History of a Literary Genre (Italian), with A. Matucci, Quaderni D Italianistica, Vol 13, 92; Lorenzo De Medici-Studies (Italian), with G. C. Garfagnini, Quaderni D Italianistica, Vol 14, 93; Garden and Grove-The Italian Renaissance Garden in the English Imagination, 1600-1750, with J. D. Hunt, Renaissance and Reformation, Vol 17, 93; Englishmen Abroad, Being an Account of Their Travels in the 17th-Century, with R. Munter and C. L. Grose, Renaissance and Reformation, Vol 17, 93; Philosophy, Science, and Religion in England, 1640-1700, with R. Kroll, R. Ashcraft, and P. Zagorin, Cath Hist Rev, Vol 80, 94; After Machiavelli-Rewriting and the

Hermeneutic Attitude, with B. J. Godorecci, Sixteenth Century J, Vol 26, 95; Renaissance Florence-Society, Culture and Religion, with G. A. Brucker, Sixteenth Century J, Vol 28, 97. **CONTACT ADDRESS** Victoria Col, Univ Toronto, Toronto, ON, M5S 1A1.

BARTLETT, RICHARD ADAMS
PERSONAL Born 11/23/1920, m, 1945, 4 children **DISCIPLINE** UNITED STATES HISTORY **EDUCATION** Univ CO, BA, 42, PhD, 53; Univ Chicago, MA, 47. **CAREER** Instr hist, Agr & Mech Col, TX, 45-52; info librn, legis ref serv, Libr Cong, 53-55; dir FL State Univ Col Prog, Tyndall Air Force Base, 55-57; from asst prof to assoc prof, 57-67, PROF HIST, FL STATE UNIV, 67-, Assoc ed, J Libr Hist, 66-74; sr historian, hist Great Plains, Univ Mid-Am, 76. **HONORS AND AWARDS** Spur Award, Western Writers Am, 62. **MEMBERSHIPS** AHA, Orgn Am Historians; Western Hist Asn; Southern Hist Asn. **RESEARCH** The westward movement; conservation. **SELECTED PUBLICATIONS** Auth, Great Surveys of the American West, Univ OK, 62; ed, The Gilded Age: America, 1865-1900, Addison-Wesley, 69; auth, Nature's Yellowstone, Univ NM, 74; The New Country, Oxford Univ, 74; contribr, The Great Plains Experience: A Cultural History, Univ Mid-Am, 78; coauth, Freedom's Trail, Houghton; Josiah Royce From Grass Valley to Harvard, with R. V. Hine, Montana-The Magazine of Western History, Vol 43, 93; Creating the West-Historical Interpretations, 1890-1990, with G. D. Nash, J of the West, Vol 33, 94; George Montague Wheeler-The Man and the Myth, with D. O. Dawdy, Montana-The Magazine of Western Hist, Vol 45, 95; Death in Yellowstone-Accidents and Foolhardiness in the First National Park, with L. H. Whittlesey, J of the West, Vol 35, 96; Yellowstone Ski Pioneers-Peril and Heroism on the Winter Trail, with P. Schullery, J of the West, Vol 36, 97; Kinship With the Land-Regionalist Thought in Iowa, 1894-1942, with E. B. Burns, Pacific Hist Rev, Vol 66, 97; Wind Energy in America-A History, with R. W. Righter, Pacific Hist Rev, Vol 66, 97; Ghost Grizzlies-Does the Great Bear Still Haunt Colorado, with D. Petersen, J of the west, Vol 36, 97. **CONTACT ADDRESS** Dept of Hist, Florida State Univ, Tallahassee, FL, 32306.

BARTLETT, ROBERT V.
PERSONAL Born 05/02/1953, Portland, IN, m, 1973, 2 children **DISCIPLINE** POLITICAL SCIENCE **EDUCATION** BA 74; MPA 76; PhD 84. **CAREER** IN Univ, res assoc 79-82; TX Tech Univ asst prof 82-85; Purdue Univ asst prof 85-89, assoc prof 89. **HONORS AND AWARDS** Univ Canterbury and Lincoln Univ NZ, Fulbright Sch 90; Lincoln Univ Vis Sch 92; Trinity Col, Dublin, Fulbright Sch. **MEMBERSHIPS** APSA; ASEH; PSO; Intl Assn for Impact Assess. **RESEARCH** Environmental Politics and Safety **SELECTED PUBLICATIONS** Environmental Policy: Transnational Issues and National Trends, ed with Lenten K Caldell, Westport Ct, Quorum Books, 97; Environment as a Focus for Public Policy, ed with James N Gladden, Essays by Lynton K Caldwell, Coll Stn, TX, TX A&M Univ Press, 95; From Rationality to Reasonableness in Environmental Administration: Moving Beyond Proverbs, with Walter F Barber, Journal of Management History, forthcoming, 99; numerous other articles and bks. **CONTACT ADDRESS** Dept of Polit Sci, Purdue Univ, West Lafayette, IN, 47907.

BARTLEY, NUMAN V.
PERSONAL Born 10/29/1934, Ladonia, TX, m, 1968 **DISCIPLINE** AMERICAN HISTORY **EDUCATION** E TX State Col, BS, 55; N TX State Univ, MA, 61; Vanderbilt Univ, PhD(recent Am hist), 68. **CAREER** From instr to assoc prof hist, GA Inst Technol, 64-72; assoc prof, 72-76, PROF HIST, UNIV GA, 76-, Consult & area studies dir, Westinghouse VISTA Training Prog, 67-69; sr res fel, Inst Southern Hist, Johns Hopkins Univ, 69-70; vis scholar, Inter-Univ Consortium Polit Res, Univ MI, 71; fel, Woodrow Wilson Int Ctr Scholars, Washington, DC, 72. **HONORS AND AWARDS** Chastain Award, Southern Polit Sci Asn, 76. **MEMBERSHIPS** Orgn Am Historians; Southern Hist Asn; Southern Polit Sci Asn. **RESEARCH** South; Recent United States. **SELECTED PUBLICATIONS** Auth, The Rise of Massive Resistance: Race and Politics in the South During the 1950's, LA State Univ, 69; From Thurmond to Wallace: Political Tendencies in Georgia, 1948-1968, Johns Hopkins, 70; coauth, Southern Politics and the Second Reconstruction, Johns Hopkins, 75; auth, Voters and Party Systems, Hist Teacher, 75; The South and Sectionalism in American Politics, J Politics, 76; coauth, A History of Georgia, Univ GA, 77; co-ed, Southern Elections: County and Precinct Data, 1950-1972, LA State Univ, 78; The Creation of Modern Georgia, Univ GA, 82; Politics in the New South-Republicanism, Race, and Leadership in the 20th-Century, with R. K. Scher, Am Hist Rev, Vol 98, 93; Agenda for Reform-Winthrop Rockefeller as Governor of Arkansas, 1967-71, with C. K. Urwin, Southwestern Hist Quart, Vol 97, 93; Strom Thurmond and the Politics of Southern Change, with N. Cohodas, Am Hist Rev, Vol 99, 94; Social-Change and Sectional Identity, J of Southern Hist, Vol 61, 95; Conflict of Interests-Organized Labor and the Civil Rights Movement in the South, 1954-1968, with A. Draper, J of Am Hist, Vol 82, 95. **CONTACT ADDRESS** Dept of Hist, Univ of GA, Athens, GA, 30602.

BARTLEY, RUSSELL HOWARD
PERSONAL Born 03/03/1939, Glen Ridge, NJ, m, 1963, 1 child **DISCIPLINE** MODERN HISTORY **EDUCATION** Colgate Univ, BA, 61; Middlebury Col, MA, 62; Stanford Univ, MA, 65, PhD(hist), 71. **CAREER** Instr, 69-71, ASST PROF HIST, UNIV WI-MILWAUKEE, 71-, Nat Endowment for Humanities fel, 73. **MEMBERSHIPS** AHA; Am Asn Advan Slavic Studies; Conf Latin Am Hist; MLA. **RESEARCH** Modern Latin American history; Soviet historiography of Latin America. **SELECTED PUBLICATIONS** Auth, On Scholarly Dialogue: The Case of United States and Soviet Latin Americanists, Latin Am Res Rev, 70; A Decade of Soviet Scholarship in Brazilian History: 1958-1968, Hist Am Hist Rev, 70; coauth, Latin America in Basic Historical Collections: A Working Guide, Hoover Inst, 72; The Diplomacy of Simon Bolivar (Russian), with A. N. Glinkin, Hispanic Am Hist Rev, Vol 72, 92. **CONTACT ADDRESS** Dept of Hist, Univ of Wisconsin, Milwaukee, WI, 53201.

BARTON, CARLIN
DISCIPLINE HISTORY **EDUCATION** Univ CA, PhD, 84. **CAREER** Assoc prof, Univ MA Amherst. **RESEARCH** Ancient hist. **SELECTED PUBLICATIONS** Auth, Roman The Sorrows of the Ancient Romans; The Gladiator and the Monster, Princeton, 93; Savage Miracles, The Redemption of Lost Honor and the Sacramentum of the Gladiator and the Martyr, Representations, 94; All Things Beseem the Victor, Gender Rhet, 94. **CONTACT ADDRESS** Dept of Hist, Univ Massachusetts Amherst, Mass Ave, Amherst, MA, 01003.

BARTON, H. ARNOLD
PERSONAL Born 11/30/1929, Los Angeles, CA, m, 1960 **DISCIPLINE** EUROPEAN HISTORY **EDUCATION** Pomona Col, BA, 53; Princeton Univ, PhD(hist), 62. **CAREER** Lectr hist, Univ Alta, 60-61, asst prof, 61-63; asst prof, Univ CA, Santa Barbara, 63-70; assoc prof, 70-75, PROF HIST, SOUTHERN IL UNIV, CARBONDALE, 75-, Publ grant, Swed State Humanistic Res Coun, 73; ed, Swed Pioneer Hist Quart, 74-; Nat Endowment for Humanities fel, 76; Elected mem, Royal Soc Humanistic Studies as Uppsala, Sweden. **MEMBERSHIPS** AHA; Soc Advan Scand Studies; Swed Pioneer Hist Soc; Swed Emigrant Inst. **RESEARCH** Scandinavia, early modern; Europe, 18th century; Scandinavian emigration history. **SELECTED PUBLICATIONS** Auth, Sweden and the War of American Independence, William & Mary Quart, 7/66; The Origins of the Brunswick Manifesto, Fr Hist Studies, fall 67; Gustav III of Sweden and the Enlightenment, 18th Century Studies, 72; Late Gustavian autocracy in Sweden, Scand Studies, No 46, 74; Count Hans Axel von Fersen, Twayne, 75; Letters from the Promised Land, Univ Minn, 75; Gustav III of Sweden and the East Baltic, J Baltic Studies, No 7, 76; The Search for Ancestors, Southern IL Univ Press, 79; Let Us Be Finns-Essays on History, with M. Klinge, Scandinavian Studies, Vol 65, 93; Hilma Angeredstrandberg and the Swedish Americans Appearance in Swedish Literature, Vol 66, 94; Gode-Dronning-Sophie Magdalene, Sweden Crown Princess, Queen and Queen Dowager (Danish), with G. Hartmann, Scandinavian Studies, Vol 66, 94; Transplanted Swedishness-Cultural Self-Assertion and Ethnic Consciousness in the Swedish-American Yearbook 'Prarieblomman', 1900-1913 (Swedish), with B. Svensson, Scandinavian Studies, Vol 67, 95; The Folk of the Parish-Rural Estates in Savolax, Finland, 1790-1850 (Swedish), with A. M. Astrom, Scandinavian Studies, Vol 67, 95; Pioneer Cross-Swedish Settlements Along the Smoky Hill Bluffs, with T. N. Holmquist, J of Am hist, Vol 81, 95; Where Have the Scandinavian-Americanists Been, J of Am Ethnic Hist, Vol 15, 95; Gustav III- A Crowned Democrat (French), with C. Nordmann, Scandinavian Studies, Vol 67, 95; Iter-Scandinavicum-Foreign Travelers Views of the Late 18th-Century North, Scandinavian Studies, Vol 68, 96; The Minds of the West-Ethnocultural Evolution in the Rural Middle West, 1830-1917, with J. Gjerde, Am Hist Rev, Vol 102, 97. **CONTACT ADDRESS** Dept of Hist, Southern IL Univ, Carbondale, IL, 62901-4300.

BARTON, MARCELLA BIRO
PERSONAL Bedford, OH, m, 2 children **DISCIPLINE** EARLY MODERN EUROPEAN HISTORY **EDUCATION** Univ CA, BA, 70; Univ Akron, MA, 73; Univ Chicago, PhD(hist), 81. **CAREER** Instr hist, CA State Univ, 78-79; ASST PROF HIST, RIO GRANDE COL/COMMUNITY COL, OH, 80-. **MEMBERSHIPS** AHA; Am Soc Church Hist; Am Cath Hist Asn; OH Acad Hist. **RESEARCH** Intellectual, religious and social history with an emphasis on Britain and modern Europe; impact on the Americas of Britain and Europe. **SELECTED PUBLICATIONS** Auth, Saint Teresa of Avila: Did She Have Epilepsy?, Cath Hist Rev, 10/82; Algernon Sidney and the Restoration Crisis, 1677-1683, with J. Scott, Church History, Vol 63, 94; The Pillars of Priesthood Shaken-The Church-of-England and its Enemies 1600-1730, with J. A. I. Champion, Vol 64, 95; Events That Changed the World in the 20th-Century, with F. W. Thackeray and J. E. Finding, Historian, Vol 58, 96; **CONTACT ADDRESS** Univ Rio Grande, 4201 Springdale Rd, Rio Grande, OH, 45674.

BARTON, MIKE ALAN
PERSONAL Born 09/30/1940, Wichita, KS, m, 1964, 1 child **DISCIPLINE** THEATRE HISTORY, DRAMATIC LITERATURE **EDUCATION** Kans State Teachers Col, BA, 61, MS, 66; Ind Univ, PhD(theatre hist), 71. **CAREER** Prof actor, New York City, 61-62; instr speech, Kans State Teachers Col, 65-66; instr theatre, Univ Omaha, 66-68; asst, Ind Univ, Bloomington, 68-71; prof Theatre, Drake Univ, 71-. **RESEARCH** Nineteenth century theatre history; film history. **SELECTED PUBLICATIONS** Auth, Silent films: High camp or genuine art, Advance, 11/72; Aline Bernstein, In: Notable American Women, Harvard Univ, 78. **CONTACT ADDRESS** Dept of Theatre Arts, Drake Univ, 2507 University Ave, Des Moines, IA, 50311-4505. **EMAIL** mike.barton@drake.edu

BARTSCH, SHADI
PERSONAL Born 03/17/1966, London, England, m, 1996 **DISCIPLINE** LATIN LITERATURE OF THE EARLY EMPIRE, CULTURAL THEORY AND INTERPRETATION, HISTORY OF CLASSICAL RHETORIC, THE ANCIENT NOVEL. **EDUCATION** Princeton Univ, BA (summa cum laude), 87; Harvard Univ, in PhD prog, 87-89, then as exchange scholar at the Univ CA, Berkeley, 88-89; Univ CA, Berkeley, MA, Latin, 89, PhD (Classics), 92. **CAREER** Acting asst prof, Classics and Rhetoric, Univ CA, Berkeley, 91-92, asst prof, 92-95, assoc prof, 95-98; vis assoc prof, Classics, Univ Chicago, Jan-June, 98, prof, Classics and the Committee on the History of Culture, Univ Chicago, July 98-; ed bd, Representations, 97-98; ed bd, Classical Philology, 98-. **HONORS AND AWARDS** Mellon fel in the Humanities, Harvard Univ, 87-89; Berkeley fel, Univ CA, Berkeley, 89-91; Richardson Prize for Trans into Latin, Univ CA, Berkeley, 90; Honorary P S Allen Junior Res fel, Corpus Christi, Oxford, 90; Humanities Res fel, Univ CA, Berkeley, 95-96; George Walsh Memorial Lecturer, Univ Chicago, 98. **MEMBERSHIPS** APA; adv committee for APA 1998; adv committee for ICAN 2000; co-ordinator, Workshop on Ancient Societies, Univ Chicago, 98-99. **SELECTED PUBLICATIONS** Auth, Decoding the Ancient Novel: The Reader and the Role of Description in Heliodorus and Achilles Tatius, Princeton Univ Press, 89; Actors in the Audience: Theatricality and Doublespeak from Nero to Hadrian, Harvard Univ Press, 94; Ideology in Cold Blood: A Reading of Lubcan's Civil War, Harvard Univ Press, 98; review, V Rudich, Dissidence and Literature under Nero: The Prince of Rhetoricization, in the Times Literary Supp, March 27, 98; Ars and the Man: The Politics of Art in Vergil's Aeneid, Classical Philology, forthcoming 98; Saints, Stoics, Specularity: A Genealogy of the Exemplum in the Latin West, forthcoming in Zeitschrift fur Antike und Christentum, 99; The Philosopher as Narcissus: Knowing Oneself in Classical Antiquity, forthcoming in Robert S Nelson, ed, Seeing as Others Saw: Visuality Before and Beyond the Renaissance, Cambridge Univ Press, 99; ed with Tom Sloan, Oxford Encyclopedia of Rhetoric, Oxford Univ Press, forthcoming; auth, The Cult of the Trope: Hermeneutics and the Classics in the Middle Ages, Princeton Univ Press, forthcoming; The Mirror of Philosophy: Specularity, Sexuality, and Self-Knowledge in the Roman Empire, forthcoming; numerous other articles, reviews, papers, and publications. **CONTACT ADDRESS** Dept of Classics, Univ of Chicago, 1010 E 59th St, Chicago, IL, 60637. **EMAIL** sbartsch@midway.uchicago.edu

BARUA, PRADEEP P.
DISCIPLINE SOUTH HISTORY **EDUCATION** Univ Ill, Urbana-Champaign, PhD, 95. **CAREER** Olin Post-Doctoral fel & lectr, Yale Univ, 95-96; instr, Univ Nebr, Kearney. **RESEARCH** Comparative colonialism. **SELECTED PUBLICATIONS** Auth, Ethnic Conflict in the Military of Developing Nations a Comparative of India and Nigeria, Armed Forces & Soc, Vol 19, No 1, 92; Inventing Race: The British and the Martial Races of India, The Historian, Vol 58, No 1, 95. **CONTACT ADDRESS** Univ Nebr, Kearney, Kearney, NE, 68849. **EMAIL** BARUAP@UNK.EDU

BARYOSEF, O.
PERSONAL Born 08/29/1937, Jerusalem, m **DISCIPLINE** ARCHAEOLOGY; PREHISTORY OF THE MIDDLE EAST & EURASIA **EDUCATION** BA, 63, MA, 65, PhD, 70, Hebrew Univ. **CAREER** Prof, 79-88, Hebrew Univ; prof, 88-, Harvard Univ. **MEMBERSHIPS** AAA; SAS; GSA. **RESEARCH** Human evolution; Climatic changes; Prehistory of Eurasia. **SELECTED PUBLICATIONS** Co-auth, Evidence for the Use of Fire at Zhoukoudian, China, 98; auth, On the Nature of Transitions: the Middle to Upper Paleolithic and the Neolithic Revolution, Cambridge Archaeol Jour, 8, 2, 141-177, 98; auth, The Natufian Culture in the Levant, Threshold to the Origins of Agriculture, Evolutionary Anthrop, 6, 5, 159-177, 98; co-ed, Neanderthals and Modern Humans in Western Asia, Plenum, 98; auth, Symbolic Expressions in Later Prehistory in the Levant - Why Are So Few?, Beyond Art: Pleistocene Image and Symbol, 161-187, Memoirs of the Calif Acad of Sci, San Francisco, 97; auth, The Middle/Upper Paleolithic Transition: A View from the Eastern Mediterranean, The Last Neanderthals, the First Anatomically Modern Humans, 79-94, Fundacio Catalana per la Recerca: Taragona, 96; auth, Modern Humans, Neanderthals and the Middle/Upper Paleolithic Transition in Western Asia, The Lower and Middle Paleolithic, Colloquium X: The Origins of Modern Humans, XIIIe IUPPS Congress, Forli, Edizioni, A.B.A.C.O., 175-190, 96; co-auth, Another

Look at the Levantine Aurignacian In: Colloquium XI, The Late Aurignacian, sect 6, the Upper Paleolithic, XIII IUPPS Congress, Forli, ABACO edizioni, 139-150, 96; auth, The Impact of Late Pleistocene-Early Holocene Climatic Changes on Humans in South-Western Asia In: Humans at the End of the Ice Age, Plenum Press, 61-78, 96; co-auth, The Dating of the Upper Paleolithic Layers in Kebara Cave, Mt Carmel, Jour of Archaeol Sci, 23, 297-306, 96; co-ed, Seasonality and Sedentism: Archaeological Perspectives from Old and New World Sites, Peabody Mus Bull 6, Harvard Univ; co-ed, The Definition and Interpretation of Levallois Technology, Prehist Press, 95; co-ed, Late Quaternary Chronology and Paleoclimates in the Eastern Mediterranean. Radiocarbon, Amer Sch of Prehist Res, Peabody Mus, Harvard Univ, 94. **CONTACT ADDRESS** Peabody Museum, Harvard Univ, 11 Divinity Av., Cambridge, MA, 02138. **EMAIL** obaryos@fas.harvard.edu

BARZUN, JACQUES
PERSONAL Born 11/30/1907, Creteil, France **DISCIPLINE** HISTORY **EDUCATION** Columbia Univ, AB, 27, MA, 28, PhD, 32. **CAREER** From instr to prof hist, Columbia Univ, 29-67, dean grad faculties, 55-58, dean faculties & provost, 58-67, Univ prof & adv arts, 67-75; LIT ADV, SCRIBNER'S, 75-, Fel, Coun Learned Soc, 33-34; extraordinary fel, Churchill Col, Cambridge; Mellon lectr, Nat Gallery Art, 73; dir, Macmillan Co, Peabody Inst Music & Art & Coun Basic Educ. **HONORS AND AWARDS** Silver Medal, Royal Soc Arts, 72; French Legion of Honor. **MEMBERSHIPS** Am Inst Arts & Lett (pres, 72-75 & 77-78); fel Royal Soc Arts; AHA. **RESEARCH** History of modern European thought and culture; the French race. **SELECTED PUBLICATIONS** Auth, Classic, Romantic and Modern, 61; Science: The Glorious Entertainment, 64, The American University, 68 & coauth, A Catalogue of Crime, 71, Harper; auth, Berlioz and the Roman Century, Columbia Univ, 69; coauth, The Modern Researcher, Harcourt, 70; auth, On Writing, Editing and Publishing, 71 & ed, Hector Berlioz: Evenings With the Orchestra, 73, Univ Chicago; The Press and the Prose & Content, Grammar and Linguistics of Broadcast News, Am Scholar, Vol 63, 94; Psychotherapy Awry & Response to Paul McHugh Article on the Lozano-Beanbayog Case, Am Scholar, Vol 63, 94; Attitudes and Assumptions & A Reply to Benjamin Fortson Commentary on the Article, The Press and the Prose, Am Scholar, Vol 64, 95; Is Music Unspeakable & The Fear of Talking About a Musical Performance, Am Scholar, Vol 65, 96. **CONTACT ADDRESS** 597 Fifth Ave, New York, NY, 10017.

BASCH, NORMA
PERSONAL Norwich, CT **DISCIPLINE** AMERICAN HISTORY, LAW **EDUCATION** Columbia Univ, BA, 56; New York Univ, PhD(Am civilization), 79. **CAREER** ASST PROF HIST, RUTGERS UNIV, 79-. **MEMBERSHIPS** AHA; Orgn Am Historians; Am Studies Asn; Soc Historians Early Am Repub. **RESEARCH** Women's history; cultural history; legal history. **SELECTED PUBLICATIONS** Auth, Invisible Women: The Legal Fiction of Marital Unity in Antebellum America, Feminist Studies, 79; In the Eyes of the Law: Women, Marriage and Property in 19th Century New York, Cornell Univ Press, 82; Marriage, Morals, and Politics in the Election of 1828, J of Am Hist, Vol 80, 93; Girls Lean Back Everywhere-The Law on Obscenity and the Assult on Genius, with E. Degrazia, Am Hist Rev, Vol 98, 93; Untitled, J of Am Hist, Vol 81, 94; Inheritance and Family Life in Colonial New York City, with D. E. Narrett, Reviews in Am Hist, Vol 23, 95; Private Acts in Public Places-A Social History of Divorce in the Formative Era of American Family Law, with R. H. Chused, J of Am Hist, Vol 82, 95; Redeconstructing the Household-Families, Sex, and the Law in the 19th-Century South, with P. W. Bardaglio, Reviews in Am Hist, Vol 24, 96. **CONTACT ADDRESS** Dept Hist, Rutgers Univ, Newark, NJ, 07102.

BASDEN, B.H.
PERSONAL Born 02/10/1940, Coeur d'Alene, IN, m, 1962, 2 children **DISCIPLINE** EXPERIMENTAL PSYCHOLOGY **EDUCATION** NCSB, PhD, 69. **CAREER** Prof, 73-, Cal State Univ. **MEMBERSHIPS** APA; APS; PS. **RESEARCH** Human Memory. **SELECTED PUBLICATIONS** Coed, Directed Forgetting: A contrast of methods and interpretations, in: JM Goldberg, C MacLeod, eds, Intl Forgetting: Interdisciplinary Approaches, Lawrence Erlbaum Pub, 98; coauth, Laboratory Experiences in Introductory Psychology, Dubuque IA, Kendall-Hunt Pub, 97; coauth, Study Guide to accompany, Psychology, Forth Edition, by Roedier, Capaaldi, Paris, Polivy, LA, West Pub, 96; Directed Forgetting: A further comparison of the list and item methods, Memory, 96; coauth, Retrievalinhibition in directed forgetting and posthypnotic amnesia, Intl J Clinical and Exper Hypnosis, 94; coauth, Cross language priming in word fragment completion, J Memory and Lang, 94; coauth, A comparison of group and individual remembering: Does group participation disrupt retrieval?, J Exper Psychol, Learning Mem Cognition, 97. **CONTACT ADDRESS** Dept Psychology, California State Univ, Fresno, Fresno, CA, 8019. **EMAIL** barbb@csafresno.edu

BASIL, JOHN DURYEA
PERSONAL Born 01/19/1934, Shanghai, China, m, 1960, 4 children **DISCIPLINE** MODERN RUSSIAN HISTORY **EDUCATION** Univ WA, PhD(Russ hist), 66. **CAREER** Asst prof hist, LA State Univ, New Orleans, 66-68; ASSOC PROF HIST, UNIV SC, 68-. **MEMBERSHIPS** Am Asn Advan Slavic Studies. **RESEARCH** Russian Revolution of 1917; Russian church history. **SELECTED PUBLICATIONS** Auth, Russia and the Bolshevik Revolution, Russ Rev, 1/68; Orthodox Church in 1917, Church Hist, 12/78; Pobedonostsev, Konstantin, Petrovich & An Examination of the Changing Political and Religious Relationships Between Church and State in Late Imperial Russia-An Argument for a Russian State Church, Church Hist, Vol 64, 95; Swiss Theologians in Czarist Russia 1700-1917-Emigration and the Everyday Life in Russia of Clergymen and Their Wives (German), with H. Schneider, Slavic Rev, Vol 55, 96; The Price of Prophecy-Orthodox Churches on Peace, Freedom, and Security, with A. F. C. Webster, Church Hist, Vol 65, 96; Politics and Religion in Central and Eastern Europe-Traditions and Transitions, with W. H. Swatos, Church Hist, Vol 65, 96; **CONTACT ADDRESS** Dept of Hist, Univ of SC, Columbia, SC, 29208.

BASS, FLOYD L.
PERSONAL Born 08/11/1921, Sullivan, Indiana, m **DISCIPLINE** EDUCATION **EDUCATION** Indiana State Univ, BS 1948, MS 1950; Univ of CO-Boulder, EdD 1960. **CAREER** LeMoyne Coll, dean 1960-63; AL State Univ, dean 1963-64; CCNY, admin intern w/pres 1964-65; NC Central Univ, prof of educ 1965-68; The Univ of CT, prof of educ 1968-. **HONORS AND AWARDS** Ellis L Phillips Fellow; UNCF Fellow; John Jay Whitney Fellow; Thirty third Degree United Supreme Council AASR Freemasonry PHA Inc 1987. **MEMBERSHIPS** Dir The Ctr for Black Studies Univ of CT 1969-; pres Northeastern Chap CT Affiliate ADA 1982-84; pres Willimantic Rotary Club 1983-85; grand historian Grand Encampment Knights Templar 1985,87; pres CT Order of High Priesthood 1985,86; accreditation team mem NCATE 1983,84,85,86,87.

BASS, GEORGE FLETCHER
PERSONAL Born 12/09/1932, Columbia, SC, m, 1960, 2 children **DISCIPLINE** CLASSICAL & NAUTICAL ARCHEOLOGY **EDUCATION** Johns Hopkins Univ, MA, 55; Univ PA, PhD(class archaeol), 64. **CAREER** Res asst class archaeol, univ mus, 62-62, res assoc, 63-64, asst prof, univ, 64-68, ASSOC PROF CLASS ARCHAEOL, UNIV PA, 68-, Vis scholar archaeol, St John's Col, Cambridge, 69-70; pres, Inst Nautical Archaeol, 73-; alumni prof anthrop, TX A&M Univ, 80-. **HONORS AND AWARDS** John Oliver La Gorce gold medal, Nat Geog Soc. **MEMBERSHIPS** Archaeol Inst Am. **SELECTED PUBLICATIONS** Auth, Mycenaean and Protogeometric Tmbs in the Halicarnassos Peninsula, Am J Archaeol, 67: 353-361; ed, Underwater Ecavations at Yassi Ada: A Byzantine Shipwreck, Archaologischer Anzeiger, 62; Smithsonian Twentieth-Century Treasury of Science, Simon & Schuster, 66; auth, Archaeology Under Water, Praeger, New York & Thames & Hudson, London, 66; Cape Gelidonya: A Bronze Age Shipwreck, Am Philos Soc, 67; ed, A History of Seafaring Based on Underwater Archaeology, Thamas & Hudson, London & Walker, New York, 72; auth, Archaeology Beneath the Sea, Walker, 76; The Ancient Harbor and Anchorage at Dor, Israel, with S. A. Kingsley and K. Raveh, Biblical Archaeologist, Vol 60, 97. **CONTACT ADDRESS** Inst Nautical Archaeol, TX A & M Univ, College Station, TX, 77843.

BASSETT, WILLIAM W.
PERSONAL Born 12/18/1932, Peoria, IL, m, 1973, 3 children **DISCIPLINE** LAW; LEGAL HISTORY **EDUCATION** S.T.L. St. Mary of the Lake (IL), MA, 58; Gregorian Univ (Rome), JCD, 65; Cath Univ Am (Wash), JD, 72. **CAREER** Asst to assoc prof, 67-73, Cath Univ Am, 67-73; scholar in res, 73-74, Ludwig-Maximilians Universitat (Munich); vis prof 82-83, Univ Calif; PROF LAW, 74-, UNIV SAN FRANCISCO, 74-. **MEMBERSHIPS** Seldom Soc; Canon Law Soc Am; Asn Iuris Cononici Int; Am Soc Legal Hist **RESEARCH** Law of Religious Organizations; Legal History. **SELECTED PUBLICATIONS** California Commmunity Property Law, Bancroft Witness, 95; Religious Organizations and the Law, West, 98. **CONTACT ADDRESS** School of Law, Univ of San Francisco, 2150 Fulton St., San Francisco, CA, 94117. **EMAIL** Bassettw@usfca.edu

BAST, ROBERT
DISCIPLINE HISTORY **EDUCATION** Univ Ariz, PhD. **CAREER** Asst prof. **RESEARCH** Early modern Europe; early modern Germany; history of the Reformation. **SELECTED PUBLICATIONS** Auth, Honor your Fathers: Catechisms and the Emergence of Patriarchal Ideology in Germany C. 1400-1600, 97. **CONTACT ADDRESS** Dept of History, Knoxville, TN, 37996.

BATALDEN, STEPHEN KALMAR
PERSONAL Born 05/23/1945, Minneapolis, MN, m, 1970, 2 children **DISCIPLINE** HISTORY **EDUCATION** Augsburg Col, BA, 67; Univ MN, MA, 72, PhD(Russian hist), 75. **CAREER** Instr hist, Augsburg Col, 69-70; asst prof, Grambling State Univ, 75-76; asst prof, 76-81, ASSOC PROF HIST, AZ TATE UNIV, 81-. **MEMBERSHIPS** AHA; Am Asn Advan Slavic Studies; Modern Greek Studies Asn. **RESEARCH** Russian intellectual and church history; Greco-Slavic relations. **SELECTED PUBLICATIONS** Auth, Notes from a Leningrad Manuscript: Eugenios Voulgaris' Autograph List of His Own Works, Ho Eranistes, Athens, Greece, 77; Catherine II's Greek Prelate: Eugenios Voulgaris in Russia, 1771-1806, Columbia Univ Press, 82; Christianity and the Arts in Russia, with W. C. Brumfield and M. M. Velimirovic, Russian Rev, Vol 54, 95; Religious and Secular Forces in Late Czarist Russia--Essays in Honor of Donald W. Treadgold, with C. E. Timberlake, Slavic Rev, Vol 54, 95. **CONTACT ADDRESS** Dept Hist, Arizona State Univ, Tempe, Tempe, AZ, 85281.

BATES, DONALD G.
PERSONAL Born 03/18/1933, Windsor, ON, Canada **DISCIPLINE** HISTORY OF MEDICINE **EDUCATION** Univ Western Ont, MD, 58, BA, 60; Johns Hopkins Univ, PhD, 75. **CAREER** Intern, Victoria Hosp, 58-60; NIH fel, Inst Hist Med, Johns Hopkins Univ, 60-62; instr to assoc prof, 62-75, ch, 66-82, 87-88, COTTON-HANNAH PROF HIST MED, DEPT SOCIAL STUD MED, McGILL UNIV, 75-. **MEMBERSHIPS** Am Asn Hist Med; Am Asn Advan Sci; Can Soc Hist Med; Soc Social Hist Med. **SELECTED PUBLICATIONS** Auth, Thoughts on Peace and Security, 85-87; ed, Knowledge and the Scholarly Medical Traditions, 95. **CONTACT ADDRESS** Dept of Social Stud Med, McGill Univ, 3655 Drummond St, Montreal, PQ, H3G 1Y6.

BATESON, MARY C.
PERSONAL Born 12/08/1939, New York, NY, m, 1960, 1 child **DISCIPLINE** ANTHROPOLOGY **EDUCATION** Radcliffe Col, BA, 60; Harvard Univ, PhD, 63. **CAREER** Instr, Harvard Univ, 63-66; asst to assoc prof, Ateneo de Manila Univ, 66-68; sr res fel, Brandeis Univ, 68-69; assoc prof, Northeastern Univ, 69-71; vis lectr, Univ Tehran, 72-74; vis prof, Northeastern Univ, 74-75; prof, Damavand Col, 75-77; dean of social sci and humanities, Univ Northern Iran, 77-79; vis scholar, Harvard Univ, 79-80; prof, Amherst Col, 80-86; vis prof, Spelman Col, 96; Guggenheim fel, 87-88, fieldwork in Israel, 89, Clarence J. Robinson prof, 87-, George Mason Univ. **MEMBERSHIPS** Amer Anthrop Asn; Lindisfarne Asn; Authors Guild, PEN. **SELECTED PUBLICATIONS** Auth, Being Alone/Being On Your Own, 33 Things Every Girl Should Know, spring, 98; auth, In Praise of Ambiguity, Educ, Info and Tranformation, Prentice-Hall, 97; auth, Enfolded Activity and the Concept of Occupation, Occupational Sci: The Emerging Discipline, FA Davis Co, 96; auth, The New Older Woman: A Dialogue for the Coming Century, Celestial Arts Press, 96; foreward, A Mythic Life: Learning to Live Our Greater Story, HarperCollins, 96; auth, Learning From Others, Sun and Shadow, 96; auth, A Spade With Which to Dig: Valuing Human Occupations, Dalhousie Rev, 95; auth, Social Diversity: An Anthropologist's Perspective on Being Human, Holistic Resource Mgt Quart, 95; auth, Holding Up the Sky Together, Civilzation, 95; auth, Commitment in a Time of Change, Armenian Women in a Time of Change, AIWA Press, 95; auth, On the Naturalness of Things, How Things Are: A Science Tool-Kit for the Mind, William Morrow and Co Inc, 95; auth, Democracy, Ecology and Participation, Democracy, Education and the Schools, Jossey-Bass, 95; foreward, Media Anthropology: Informing Global Citizens, Bergin and Garvey, 94; auth, Peripheral Visions: Learning Along the Way, HarperCollins, chapt VII, Learning As Coming Home, Holistic Educ Rev, 94. **CONTACT ADDRESS** 47 Depot St., Hancock, NH, 03449. **EMAIL** mcatb@ibm.net

BATINSKI, EMILY E.
DISCIPLINE LATIN EPIC, ROMAN HISTORIANS, SILVER AGE LITERATURE **EDUCATION** Univ Colo, PhD, 83. **CAREER** Assoc prof Classics, dept ch, univ fac senate, univ coun on acad prog abroad, La State Univ. **RESEARCH** Silver Age Roman epic; Latin lyric; Roman historians; genre theory. **SELECTED PUBLICATIONS** Auth, Lucan's Catalogue of Caesar's Troops: Paradox and Convention, in Class J; Word-patterning in the Latin Hendecasyllable, in Latomus. **CONTACT ADDRESS** Dept of For Lang and Lit, Louisiana State Univ, 222 Prescott Hall, Baton Rouge, LA, 70803. **EMAIL** Batinski@Homer.Forlang.lsu.edu

BATTICK, JOHN FRANCIS
PERSONAL Born 04/12/1932, North Haven, CT, m, 1956, 3 children **DISCIPLINE** MARITIME HISTORY, EARLY MODERN EUROPE **EDUCATION** Boston Univ, BA, 58, MA, 59, PhD(hist), 67. **CAREER** Instr hist & govt, Mass Bay Community Col, 62-64; asst prof hist, 64-73, ASSOC PROF, UNIV ME, ORONO, 73-, Vis prof hist, Bangor Theol Sem, 69-79; Am Philos Soc grant, 72. **RESEARCH** Cromwellian naval and diplomatic history; demographic history of seafaring communities. **SELECTED PUBLICATIONS** Auth, Richard Rooth's Journal of the Western Design, 1654-55, Jamaica J, 12/71; Cromwell's Imperial Vision: A Revaluation of the Western Design, Barbados Mus & Hist Soc, J, 5/72; Cromwell's Diplomatic Blunder...The Western Design and the Anglo-French Alliance of 1657, Albion, winter 73; William Lockhart's First Audience as Ambassador to the Court of Louis XIV, Bull Inst Hist Res, 5/74; coauth, Much Ado About Oliver, Hist Today, 6/74; Night Boat to England, 1815-1900, with E. L. Dunbaugh, New England Quart--A Historical Review of New England Life and Letters, Vol 66, 93. **CONTACT ADDRESS** Dept Hist, Univ ME, Orono, ME, 04469.

BAUER, ARNOLD JACOB
PERSONAL Born 04/11/1931, 1 child **DISCIPLINE** HISTORY **EDUCATION** Univ Americas, BA, 56; Univ CA, Berkeley, PhD(hist), 69. **CAREER** PROF HIST, UNIV CA, DAVIS, 70-. **RESEARCH** History of Spanish America; Chile; rural history. **SELECTED PUBLICATIONS** Auth, The Church and Spanish American Agrarian Structure, Americas, 71; Chilean Rural Labor in the 19th Century, Am Hist Rev, 71; Chilean Rural Society from the Spanish Conquest to 1930, Cambridge Univ, 75; The Bethlehemites in Buenos-Aires-Convent, Economy, and Society 1748-1822 (Spanish), with C. A. Mayo, Hispanic Am Hist Rev, Vol 72, 92; A Bucaneers Atlas-Basil Ringrose, 'South Sea Waggoner', with D. Howse and N. J. W. Thrower, Hispanic Am Hist Rev, Vol 73, 93; Domestic and Foreign Finance in Modern Peru, 1850-1950-Financing Visions of Develoment, with A. W. Quiroz, J of Economic Hist, Vol 53, 93; The Andes and Mesopotamia-Cultures and Societies (French), with R. Thiercelin, Hisp Am Hist Rev, Vol 73; 93; Haciendas and Ayullus-Rural Society in the Bolivian Andes in the 18th and 19th Centuries, with H. S. Klein, Am Hist Rev, Vol 99, 94; Mirages of Transition-The Peruvian Altiplano, 1780-1930, with N. Jacobsen, J of Economic Hist, Vol 54, 94; Coercion and Market-Silver Mining in Colonial Potosi, 1692-1826, with E. Trandeter, J of Economic Hist, Vol 54, 94; Colonialism and Science-Saint Domingue in the Old Regime, with J. E. McClellan, Hispanic Am Hist Rev, Vol 74, 94; Civilizing Mission, Exact Sciences and French Overseas Expansion, 1830-1940, with L. Pyenson, Hispanic Am Hist Rev, Vol 75, 95; Frontier Development-Land, Labor, and Capitol on the Wheatlands of Argentina and Canada, 1890-1914, with J. Adelman, Am Hist Rev, Vol 101, 96; Rolando Mellaferojas, 1929-1995, Hispanic Am Hist Rev, Vol 76, 96; The Economic History of Latin America Since Independence, with V. Bulmerthomas, Hispanic Am Hist rev, Vol 76, 96. **CONTACT ADDRESS** Dept Hist, Univ CA, Davis, CA, 95616-5200.

BAUER, HENRY H.
PERSONAL Born 11/16/1931, Vienna, Austria, m, 1986, 2 children **DISCIPLINE** CHEMISTRY **EDUCATION** Univ Sydney, Bsc, 51, Msc, 52, PhD, 56. **CAREER** Univ Sydney, 58-56; Univ Mich 65-66; assoc-full prof, Chem, Unvi KY, 66-78; dean, Arts & Sci, Va Polytechnic Inst & State Univ, 78-86' PROF, CHEM, SCI STUD, Va POLYTECHNIC INST & STATE UNIV, 86-. **MEMBERSHIPS** Soc Scientific Exploration; Va Asn Scholars; Nat Asn Scholars **RESEARCH** Pop misconceptions related to science; Pseudo-science; scientific anomalies. **SELECTED PUBLICATIONS** "Two Kinds of Knowledge: Maps and Stories," Jour Scientific Exploration, 95; "Velikovsky's Place in the History of Science," Skeptic, 95; "Cryptozoology," Encyclopedia of the Paranormal, 96; "The Anti-Science Phenomenon in Science & Technology Studies," Sci Stud, 96; "A Consumer's Guide to Science Punditry," Science Today: Problem or Crisis?, Routledge, 97; "Students Who Don't Study," Inside Laboratory Management, 97. **CONTACT ADDRESS** Va Polytechnical Inst & State Univ, Blacksburg, VA, 24061-0247. **EMAIL** hhbauer@vt.edu

BAUER, JOSEPH P.
PERSONAL Born 11/03/1945, New York, NY, m, 1969, 2 children **DISCIPLINE** ANTITRUST & TRADE REGULATION LAW **EDUCATION** Univ Pa, BA, 65; Law Sch Harvard Univ, JD, 69. **CAREER** Instr law, Sch Law, Univ Mich, 72-73; prof law, Sch Law, Univ Notre Dame, 73-, assoc dean, 85-88, 91, 96; vis prof law, Sch Law, Univ NC, 81-82; summer teaching, Univ Bridgeport, 84; Univ Innsbruck, 94; dir, Notre Dame's Law School's Year Abroad Program in London, England, 75-76, 89-90. **HONORS AND AWARDS** Co-winner Teacher of the Year Award, 77; Winner, Teacher of the Year Award, 81; Special Pres Award, Univ Notre Dame, 96. **MEMBERSHIPS** Am Bar Asn, ABA Antitrust Sect **RESEARCH** Antitrust; civil procedure; trade regulation; intellectual property; conflict of laws; business associations; appellate advocacy; administrative law. **SELECTED PUBLICATIONS** Coauth, Corporate antitrust audit--establishing a document retention program, Practical Lawyer, 73 & Barrister, 74; auth, Professional activities and the antitrust laws, Notre Dame Lawyer, 75; Challenging conglomerate mergers under section 7 of the Clayton Act: Today's law and tomorrow's legislation, Boston Univ Law Rev, 78; Per se illegality of concerted refusals to deal: A rule ripe for reexamination, Columbia Law Rev, 79; A simplified approach to tying arrangements: A legal and economic analysis, Vanderbilt Law Rev, 80; Government Enforcement Policy of Clayton Act Section 7: Carte Blanche For Conglomerate Mergers?, 71 Cal Law Rev, 83; coauth, Antitrust Exemptions for Private Requests for Governmental Action: A Critical Analysis of the Noerr-Pennington Doctrine, 17 UC-Davis Law Rev, 84; auth, A Federal Law of Unfair Competition: What Should Be the Reach of Section 43 (a) of the Lanham Act?, 31 UCLA Law Rev, 84; multiple other articles to various Journals thru 96; coauth and contribr to Kintner's Federal Antitrust Law Treatise, vol I - XI, with annual supplements annually since 85. **CONTACT ADDRESS** Sch of Law, Univ of Notre Dame, Notre Dame, IN, 46556.

BAUGH, DANIEL ALBERT
PERSONAL Born 07/10/1931, Philadelphia, PA, m, 1955, 3 children **DISCIPLINE** BRITISH HISTORY **EDUCATION** Univ Pa, AB, 53, AM, 57; Cambridge Univ, PhD, 61. **CAREER** From instr to asst prof hist, Princeton Univ, 61-69; assoc prof, 69-82, PROF HIST, CORNELL UNIV, 82-, Soc Sci Res Coun grant-in-aid, 66-67; NEH fel, 77-78. **MEMBERSHIPS** Fel Royal Hist Soc; AHA; Econ Hist Soc; Soc Nautical Res; Mid Atlantic Conf Brit Studies (pres, 92-94). **RESEARCH** British administrative history; British social and economic history 1660-1890; British naval history; European maritime history. **SELECTED PUBLICATIONS** Auth, British Naval Administration in the Age of Walpole, Princeton, 65; The cost of poor relief in Southeast England, 1790-1834, Econ Hist Rev, 75; Naval Administration 1715-1750, Navy Record Soc, 77; Great Britain's Blue-Water Policy, 1689-1815, Intl Hist Rev, 88; Maritime Strength and Atlantic Commerce: the Uses of a Grand Marine Empire, in An Imperial State at War, 94; The Eighteenth Century Navy as a National Institution, 1690-1815, in Oxford Illustrated History of the Royal Navy. **CONTACT ADDRESS** Dept of Hist, Cornell Univ, Mcgraw Hall, Ithaca, NY, 14853-4601.

BAUM, DALE
PERSONAL Born 03/14/1943, Jersey City, NJ **DISCIPLINE** UNITED STATES & LATIN AMERICAN HISTORY **EDUCATION** Georgetown Univ, BA, 65; Univ MN, MA, 72, PhD(hist), 78. **CAREER** ASST PROF AM HIST, TX A&M UNIV, 78-. **MEMBERSHIPS** Am Hist Asn; Orgn Am Historians; Social Sci Hist Asn. **RESEARCH** Civil War and reconstruction; American voting behavior. **SELECTED PUBLICATIONS** Auth, The New Day in North Dakota: The Nonpartisan League and the Politics of Negative Revolution, NDak Hist, spring 73; Retorica y realidad en el Mexico dominononico--ensayo de interpretacion de su historia politica, Hist Mexicana, 7-9/77; coauth, Class and Party in the Secession Crisis: Voting Behavior in the Deep South, 1856-1860, J Interdisciplinary Hist, winter 78; auth, Know-nothingism and the Republican Majority in Massachusetts: The Political Realignment of the 1850's, J Am Hist, 3/78; Noisy but Not Numerous: The Revolt of the Massachusetts Mugwumps, The Historian, 2/79; The Irish Vote and Party Politics in Massachusetts, 1860-1876, Civil War Hist, 6/80; Ethnic Conflict and Machine Politics in San Antonio, 1892-1899, J of Urban Hist, Vol 19, 93; Tunnel Vision, ABA J, Vol 79, 93; Chicanery and Intimidation in the 1869 Texas Gubernatorial Race, Southwestern Hist Quart, Vol 97, 93; Butte, America & Montana Boomtown, Am Heritage, Vol 48, 97. **CONTACT ADDRESS** Dept of Hist, Tex A&M Univ, 1 Texas A and M Univ, College Station, TX, 77843.

BAUMANN, CAROL EDLER
PERSONAL Born 08/11/1932, Plymouth, WI, m, 1959, 2 children **DISCIPLINE** INTERNATIONAL RELATIONS **EDUCATION** BA Univ of WI-Madison, 54; PhD-LSE, Univ of London, 57. **CAREER** Dir Emeritus Inst of Workd Affairs, Prof Emeritus, Dept Poli Sci, Dir Intl Studies and Prog, Univ of WI-Milwaukee, 82-88; Deputy Asst Sec for Assessments and Res, Bureau of Intelligence and Res, Dept of State, 79-81; Chm Intl Rel Major, Univ of WI_Milwaukee, 62-79. **HONORS AND AWARDS** Phi Beta Kappa; Phi Kappa Phi; Phi Eta Sigma; Marshall Scholar; Hon Woodrow Wilson Fel. **MEMBERSHIPS** China Council of the Asia Soc,Inc; Comm on Atlantic Studies; North Am Chair, Council on Foreigh Rel NY; Intl Studies Assoc; Natl Comm on US-China Rel; Natl Council of World Affairs Org; Pres, Bd of Dir, VP, Natl Univ Continuing Edu Assoc; Soc for Citizen Edu in World Affairs Pres. **SELECTED PUBLICATIONS** Auth, Program Planning about World Affairs, The American Forum for Global Education, NY, 91; ed, Europe in NATO: Deterrence, Defense, and Arms Control, Praeger, NY, 87; auth, The Diplomatic Kidnappings, Martinus-Nijhoff, The Hague, 73; ed, Western Europe: What Path to Integration, DC Heath & Co, Boston, 67; co-auth, Great Decisions, 68, Institute of World Affairs, Milwaukee, WI, 69; auth, Political Co-Operation in NATO, National Security Studies Group, Univ WI, Madison, 60. **CONTACT ADDRESS** Inst World Affairs, Uni Wisconsin, Milwaukee, WI, 53201. **EMAIL** cbaumann@excel.net

BAUMLER, ALAN
DISCIPLINE HISTORY **EDUCATION** N Ill Univ; BA, 87; Univ Ill, MA, 90, PhD, 97. **CAREER** Lectr, Univ Ill, 93; Sangamon State Univ, 95; asst prof, Piedmont Col, 95-. **HONORS AND AWARDS** Ill-Tamkang fel, 89, 92-93; FLAS, 90-92, Resident Scholar, Nanking, China, 1994; Internet proj reviewer, Longman Press; ed, NEH Journey to the West Website. **RESEARCH** China, Japan, early modern Europe. **SELECTED PUBLICATIONS** Rev, Edward L. Dreyer, China at War 1901-1949, China Infor, 96; auth, Playing with Fire: The Nationalist Government and Popular Anti-Opium Agitation in 1927-1928, Republican China 21:1, 95. **CONTACT ADDRESS** Dept of Hist, Piedmont Col, 165 Central Ave., PO Box 10, Demorest, GA, 30535. **EMAIL** dprice@piedmont.edu

BAUR, JOHN EDWARD
PERSONAL Born 02/19/1922, Chicago, IL **DISCIPLINE** UNITED STATES HISTORY **EDUCATION** Univ CA, AB, 45, AM, 47, PhD, 51. **CAREER** Ed asst, Pac Hist Rev, 49-53; instr hist, Los Angeles County Mus, 54-64; from asst prof to assoc prof, 64-71, PROF HIST, CA STATE UNIV, NORTHRIDGE, 71-, Researcher, Ducommun Metals & Supply Co, 52; lectr hist, Univ CA, Los Angeles, 54, 57, 59-60, teacher, exten div, 57-66; asst pub off, Huntington Libr, 54. **MEMBERSHIPS** Western Hist Asn. **RESEARCH** California history, 1850-1900; the Trans-Mississippi west, 1800-1900; Mexico and the Caribbean area, 1800-1900. **SELECTED PUBLICATIONS** Auth, Health Seekers of Southern California, 1870-1900, Huntington Libr, 59; Christmas on the American Frontier, Caxton, 61; Dogs on the Frontier, Naylor, 64; contribr, The Rumble of California Politics, Wiley, 70 & Encyclopedia of Latin America, 73; auth, Growing Up with California: A History of California's Children, Western Am Studies Series, 78; contribr, five articles, In: Biographical Dictionary of American Mayors, 1820-1980, Greenwood Press, 81; The Final Voyage of the Central-America, 1857, with N. E. Klare, Paific Hist Rev, Vol 62, 93; Henry E. Huntington and the Creation of Southern California, with W. B. Friedricks, Thech and Culture, Vol 34, 93. **CONTACT ADDRESS** Dept of Hist, California State Univ, Northridge, Northridge, CA, 91330.

BAUSUM, HENRY S.
PERSONAL Born 02/19/1924, Annapolis, MD, m, 1947, 2 children **DISCIPLINE** HISTORY **EDUCATION** Univ MD, BA, 49; Boston Univ, AM, 51; Univ Chicago, PhD(hist), 63. **CAREER** Assoc prof hist, Carson-Newman Col, 56-64; assoc prof, 64-80, PROF HIST, VA MIL INST, 80-, Vis assoc prof, Univ VA, 67-68. **MEMBERSHIPS** AAUP; AHA; Va Soc Hist Teachers (pres-elect, 77-79); Va Soc Sci Asn. **RESEARCH** Historiography; early modern European history; contemporary world history. **SELECTED PUBLICATIONS** Auth, Alternative to Pax Americana, World Affairs, 9/67; Edenic Images of the Western World: A Reappraisal, SAtlantic Quart, autumn 68; co-ed, Teaching History Today, Monthly Column in AHA Newsletter, 74-; The History of War & Symposium, Panel 1, Intro, J of Military Hist, Vol 57, 93; The 'Bombing of Auschwitz Re-Examined'-Comment, J of Military Hist, Vol 61, 97. **CONTACT ADDRESS** George C. Marshall Lib, VA Mil Inst, Lexington, VA, 24450.

BAXTER, COLIN FRANK
PERSONAL Born 02/17/1942, Harrow, England **DISCIPLINE** BRITISH & MODERN EUROPEN HISTORY **EDUCATION** E TN State Univ, BSc, 61; Univ GA, MA, 63, PhD(hist), 65. **CAREER** Asst prof hist, Furman Univ, 65-71; ASST PROF HIST, E TN STATE UNIV, 71-. **MEMBERSHIPS** AHA; Soc Nautical Res.. **RESEARCH** Nineteenth century British naval history. **SELECTED PUBLICATIONS** Auth, Lord Palmerston: Panic-monger or Naval Peacemaker, Soc Sci, autumn 72; The Duke of Somerset and the Creation of the British Ironclad Navy, 1859-66, Mariner's Mirror, 8/77; Hidden Ally-The French Resistance, Special Operations, and the Landings in Southern France, 1944, with A. L. Funk, Am Hist Rev, Vol 100, 95; The Hardest Victory-RAF Bomber Command in the Second World War, with D. Richards, Historian, Vol 59, 97. **CONTACT ADDRESS** Dept of Hist, East Tennesee State Univ, Johnson City, TN, 37601.

BAXTER, DOUGLAS CLARK
PERSONAL Born 09/20/1942, Flint, MI, m **DISCIPLINE** EARLY MODERN EUROPEAN & FRENCH HISTORY **EDUCATION** Wayne State Univ, AB, 64; Univ WI, MA, 66; Univ MN, PhD, 71. **CAREER** From instr to asst prof, 69-76, assoc prof hist, OH Univ, 76. **HONORS AND AWARDS** Phi Beta Kappa, 64. **MEMBERSHIPS** AHA; Soc Fr Hist Studies; Western Soc Fr Hist. **RESEARCH** Seventeenth & eighteenth century French hist; soc-institutional hist; mil hist. **SELECTED PUBLICATIONS** Auth Louvois, Francois-Michel Le Tellier, Encycl Britannica, 73; Servants of the Sword: French Intendants of the Army, 1630-70, Univ Ill, 76; Pension Expectations of the French Military Commis, In: Adapting to Condition. War and Society in the Eighteenth Century, Univ Ala, 86; First Encounters, Bourbon Princes Meet Their Brides: Ceremony, Gender, and Monarchy, Proceedings of the Western Soc for Fr Hist, vol 22, Univ Calif-Riverside, 95; articles on Asiento, Madame de Maintenon, Philip V, and Princesse des Ursins, In: The Treaties of the War of Spanish Succession: An Historical and Critical Dictionary, Greenwood, 95. **CONTACT ADDRESS** Dept of Hist, Ohio Univ, Athens, OH, 45701-2979. **EMAIL** dbaxter2@ohiou.edu

BAXTER, HAROLD J.
DISCIPLINE INTERDISCIPLINARY STUDIES **EDUCATION** Houghton Col, BA, 66; Evangelical Sch Theol, BD, 69; Eastern Baptist Sem, ThM, 71; Old Dominion, MA, 80; FL State Univ, PhD, 83. **CAREER** Relig, Trinity Int Univ. **SELECTED PUBLICATIONS** Auth, Shadows and Fog. **CONTACT ADDRESS** Trinity Int Univ, 2065 Half Day Road, Deerfield, IL, 60015.

BAXTER, STEPHEN BARTOW
PERSONAL Born 03/08/1929, Boston, MA, m, 1953, 6 children **DISCIPLINE** HISTORY **EDUCATION** Harvard Univ, BA, 50; Cambridge Univ, PhD, 55. **CAREER** Instr hist, Dartmouth Col, 54-57; vis asst prof, Univ MO, 57-58; from asst prof to assoc prof, 58-66, prof, 66-74, alumni distinguished prof, 68-69, KENAN PROF HIST, UNIV NC, CHAPEL HILL, 75-, Guggenheim fels, 59-60 & 73-74; sr ed, Studies in Brit Hist & Cult, 75-; Clark Libr Prof, Univ CA, Los Angeles, 77-78; dir, Nat Endowment for Humanities postdoctoral sem, 78-79.

MEMBERSHIPS AHA; fel Royal Hist Soc; Mediaeval Acad Am; Conf Brit Studies. **RESEARCH** English administrative and constitutional history. **SELECTED PUBLICATIONS** Auth, Development of the Treasury, 1660-1702, Harvard Univ, 57; The Struggle for a New Order in England: Cromwell's Search for Lawful Government, 1647-58, In: Major Crises in Western Civilization, Harcourt, 65; Recent writings on William III, J Mod Hist, 9/66; William III, Longmans, Green, 66; Basic Documents of English History, Houghton, 69; The Age of Personal Monarchy in England, In: Eighteenth Century Studies Presented to Arthur M Wilson, Univ Press New Eng, 72; A Comment on Clayton Roberts Perspective, Albion, Vol 25, 93; The Augustan Court- Queen Anne and the Decline of Court Culture, with R. O. Bucholz, Am Hist Rev, Vol 100, 95; Holland and the Dutch-Republic in the 17th-Century-The Politics of Particularism, J. L. Price, Am Hist Rev, Vol 101, 96. **CONTACT ADDRESS** Dept of Hist, Univ of NC, Chapel Hill, NC, 27514.

BAYLEN, JOSEPH OSCAR
PERSONAL Born 02/12/1920, Chicago, IL, m, 1979, 2 children **DISCIPLINE** HISTORY **EDUCATION** Northern Ill Univ, BEd, 41; Emory Univ, MA, 47; Univ NMex, PhD, 49. **CAREER** Asst prof soc sci, Ga State Teachers Col, 49-50; from asst prof to assoc prof Europ hist, NMex Highlands Univ, 50-54; prof hist & head div soc sci, Delta State Teachers Col, 54-57; prof Europ hist, Miss State Univ, 57-61 & Univ Miss, 61-66; prof, 66-68, head dept, 66-78, Regents prof hist, 68-83, emeritus, 83- , Georgia State Univ; Vis asst prof, Univ Md overseas prog, Europe, 52-53: vis assoc prof, Agnes Scott Col, 53; Southern Fel Found grant-in-aid, Eng, 55; Am Philos Soc grant, France, 56 & UK, 65-66; Guggenheim fel, UK & USSR, 58-59; Am Coun Learned Soc res grant, 60; Fulbright lectr, Univ Wales, 61-62; mem & chmn, Nat Fulbright Screening Comt Hist, 62-65; mem, Inst Advan Study, Princeton Univ, 66-67; consult, NDEA Insts Hist, US Off Educ, 66-67; vis prof, Tulane Univ, 66 & 68; consult, Nat Endowment for Humanities, 69-; mem, Regional Arch Comt, Region IV, Fed Govt, 70-73; Fulbright-Hays sr lectr hist, York Univ, 72-73. **HONORS AND AWARDS** Most Distinguished Alumni Award, N Ill Univ, 76; Distinguished Prof Award, Ga State Univ, 79, 80; Hugh McCall award for distinguished achievement in hist stud, 82; fel Royal Hist Soc; fel, Royal Commonwealth Soc. **MEMBERSHIPS** AHA; Southern Hist Asn; N Am Conf Brit Studies; Southern Conf British Studies (pres, 77-79); European Movement; Travellers Club; London Press Club; Phi Kappa Phi; Omicron Delta Kappa; Phi Alpha Theta; Pi Gamma Mu; Kappa Delta Pi; Phi Kappa Tau. **RESEARCH** Modern European history; British history, 1870-1914, especially journalism and diplomacy of that period; Anglo-Russian relations, 1870-1914. **SELECTED PUBLICATIONS** Co-ed, Dreyfusards and the foreign press: The Syndicate and the Daily News, February-March 1898, Fr Hist Studies, 72; The new journalism in late Victorian Britain, Australian J Polit & Hist, 72; coauth, Col P R Faymonville and the Red Army, 1934-43, Slavic Rev, 76; Adm Kolchak's Mission to the US, Sept 10-Nov 9, 1917, Mil Affairs, 76; contribr, Dict of Labor Biog, Vol IV, Macmillan, 77; Emily Hobhouse's peace mission, 1916, J Contemp Hist, 78; contribr, Encycl of Russian and Soviet History, Vol IX, Acad Press, 78; co-ed, Biographical Dict of Modern British Radicals, 3 vol, Harvester, 79-88; contribur, Biographical Dictionary of Internationalists, 83; co-ed, The 1890's: An Encyclopedia of British Literature, Art and Culture, 83; contribur, British Literary Magazines, 84; contribur, Biographical Dictionary of Peace Leaders, 85; contribur, Victorian Britain: An Encyclopedia, 88; contribur, Biographical Dictionary of American Journalism, 89; contribur, Encyclopedia of the British Press, 92; contribur, Dictionary of Literary Biography, British Publishing Houses, 1881-1965, 92; co-ed, Twentieth Century Britain: An Encyclopedia, 95; co-ed, Shaping the Collective Memory, Government and International Historians through Two World Wars, 96; co-ed, A Journalism Reader, 97. **CONTACT ADDRESS** 45 Saffrons Ct, Eastbourne, ., BN21 1DY.

BAYLEY, C.C.
PERSONAL Born 03/05/1907, Congleton, England, m, 1936, 2 children **DISCIPLINE** HISTORY **EDUCATION** Univ Manchester, BA, 28, MA, 29; Univ Chicago, PhD, 38. **CAREER** Lectr, Univ Toronto, 31; asst prof, Colorado Col, 32; univ fel, Univ Chicago, 35; fac mem, 35, EMER KINGSFORD PROF & PROF HISTORY, McGILL UNIV. **HONORS AND AWARDS** Guggenheim fel, 48; Can Coun sr fel, 66; Killam fel, 70; fel, Royal Soc Can, 61. **SELECTED PUBLICATIONS** Auth, The Formation of the German College of Electors, 49; auth, War and Society in Renaissance Florence, 61; auth, Mercenaries for the Crimea: The German, Swiss and Italian Legions in British Service 1854-1856, 77. **CONTACT ADDRESS** 3610 McTavish St, No 34, Montreal, PQ, H3A 1Y2.

BAYLOR, MICHAEL G.
DISCIPLINE EARLY MODERN EUROPEAN HISTORY **EDUCATION** PhD; Stanford University. **CAREER** Prof, Lehigh Univ **HONORS AND AWARDS** Dir, Sci and Technol Soc Prog. **RESEARCH** Social and cultural history of Reformation Germany. **SELECTED PUBLICATIONS** Co-auth, Technology and Values in American Civilization, in Context: History and the History of Technology; New Worlds, New Technologies, New Issues; ed, The Radical Reformation:Basic Writings of Thomas M?ntzer. **CONTACT ADDRESS** Lehigh Univ, Bethlehem, PA, 18015.

BAYNTON, DOUGLAS C.
PERSONAL Born 04/26/1953, NJ, m, 1997 **DISCIPLINE** HISTORY **EDUCATION** W Or Univ, BS, 86; Univ Iowa, PhD, 93. **CAREER** Vis asst prof to asst prof, 94-, Univ Iowa. **HONORS AND AWARDS** Smithsonian Inst Postdoctoral Fel, Nat Museum of Amer Hist, 97-98; Obermann Center for Adv Stud, Univ Iowa, Res Seminar Fel, 97; Irving T Zola Emerging Scholar Award, Soc for Disabilities Stud, 96. **MEMBERSHIPS** Amer Hist Assoc; Amer Stud Assoc; Org of Amer Hist; Soc for Disability Stud; Amer Sign Lang Teachers Assoc. **RESEARCH** Amer cultural hist; hist of disability. **SELECTED PUBLICATIONS** Auth, Forbidden Signs: American Culture and the Campaign Against Sign Language, Univ Chicago Press, 96; art, Out of Sight: The Suppression of American Sign Language, Multilingual America: Transnationalism, Ethnicity, and the Languages of American Literature, NYU Press, 98; art, Disability: A Useful Category of Historical Analysis, Disability Stud Quart, 97; art, Savages and Deaf-Mutes: Evolutionary Theory and the Campaign Against Sign Language in the Nineteenth Century, Deaf History Unveiled: Interpretations From the New Scholarship, Scarecrow Press, 99; art, A Silent Exile on this Earth: The Metaphorical Construction of Deafness in the Nineteenth Century, The Disability Stud Reader, 97. **CONTACT ADDRESS** Dept of History, Univ Iowa, 280 SH, Iowa City, IA, 52242. **EMAIL** douglas-baynton@uiowa.edu

BAYOR, RONALD HOWARD
PERSONAL Born 03/14/1944, New York, NY, m, 1966, 2 children **DISCIPLINE** AMERICAN HISTORY, URBAN-ETHNIC STUDIES **EDUCATION** City Col New York, BA, 65; Syracuse Univ, MA, 66; Univ PA, PhD(hist), 70. **CAREER** Grad asst hist, Syracuse Univ, 66; grad asst humanities, Univ PA, 66-67; from instr to asst prof Am hist, St John's Univ, 69-73; asst prof, 73-77, assoc prof, 77-82, PROF HIST, GA INST TECHNOL, 83-, Vis asst prof, NY Univ, 72 & Lehman Col, 73; consult, Urban Inst, 73-74; consult, New York Ctr Visual Hist, 79; ed, J Am Ethnic Hist, 80-; senior advisor/editor, Greenwood Press Series, The New Americans. 94-; special ed, Transaction Publishers Book Series on Ethnic Studies, 94-; consultant, museum exhibit, Creating Community: The Jews of Atlanta, 92-95. **HONORS AND AWARDS** Nat Endowment for the Humanities Fellowship, 92-93; Am Hist Asn Albert J. Beveridge Grant for Research in the History of the Western Hemisphere, 86; GA Tech Outstanding Teacher of the Year Award, 83; GA Tech School of Social Science, Excellence in Teaching Award, 90; Distinguished Service Award, Immigration History Soc, 92; John S. Donnelly, Sr Prize for best book in history and social sciences, Am Conference for Irish Studies, 97 for co-edited book The New York Irish; Outstanding Book Award, Gustavus Myers Center for the Study of Human Rights in North America, for Race and the Shaping of Twentieth-Century Atlanta. **MEMBERSHIPS** AHA; Orgn Am Historians; Am Ital Hist Asn; Immigration Hist Soc; Am Jewish Hist Soc; Urban Hist Asn; H-Ethnic; H-Urban; Southern Hist Asn. **RESEARCH** History of cities; ethnic and racial groups in cities. **SELECTED PUBLICATIONS** Auth, Italians, Jews and Ethnic Conflict, Int Migration Rev, winter 72; The Transplanted Americans, Immigrants in an Urban World & The Darker Side of Urban Life, Slums in the City, In: Cities in Transition, Nelson-Hall, 74; Italians and Jews in New York: The La Guardia Elections, Proc Am Ital Hist Asn, 74; Neighbors in Conflict: The Irish, Germans, Jews and Italians of New York City, 1929-1941, Johns Hopkins Univ, 78; Ethnic Residential Patterns in Atlanta, 1880-1940, Ga Hist Quart, winter 79; ed, Neighborhoods in Urban America, Kennikat Press, 82; co-auth, Engineering the New South: Georgia Tech, 1885-1985, Univ GA Press, 85; Changing Neighborhoods: Ethnic and Racial Succession in the Urban North and South, in From Melting Pot to Multiculturalism, ed, Valeria Lerda, Bulzione Editore, 90; Reform Mayors and Urban Politics: New York and Chicago, a review essay, J of Urban Hist, Nov 91; The Twentieth-Century Urban South and the Atlanta Experience, GA Hist Quart, 75, fall 91; Race and City Services: The Shaping of Atlanta's Police and Fire Departments, Atlanta Hist, 36, fall 92; The Civil Rights Movement as Urban Reform: Atlanta's Black Neighborhoods and a New Progressivism, GA Hist Quart 77, summer 93; Fiorello LaGuardia: Ethnicity and Reform, Harlan-Davidson, 93; Historical Encounters: Intergroup Relations in a Nation of Nations, The Annals of the Am Academy of Political and Social Sciences, Nov 93; co-ed, The New York Irish, Johns Hopkins Univ Press, 96; Race and the Shaping of Twentieth-Century Atlanta, Univ of NC Press, 96; The Changing South, J of Policy Hist, 9, 2, 97. **CONTACT ADDRESS** School of History, Technology, and Society, Georgia Inst of Tech, 685 Cherry St., Atlanta, GA, 30332. **EMAIL** RB2@prism.gatech.edu

BAYS, DANIEL HENRY
PERSONAL Born 03/27/1942, Berrien Springs, MI, m, 1967, 2 children **DISCIPLINE** MODERN CHINESE & EAST ASIAN HISTORY **EDUCATION** Stanford Univ, AB, 64; Univ MI, Ann Arbor, MA, 67, PhD(hist), 71. **CAREER** Asst prof, 71-76, ASSOC PROF HIST, UNIV KS, 76-, Nat Endowment for Humanities fel, 73; Fulbright res fel, Repub China, 77-78. **MEMBERSHIPS** AHA; Asn Asian Studies; Soc Ch'ing Studies; Soc Study Chinese Relig. **RESEARCH** Chinese politics, 1895-1911; early 20th century Sino-foreign relations; Christianity in China, 1860-1915. **SELECTED PUBLICATIONS** Auth, Agrarian Reform in Kwangtung, 1950-1953, MI Papers in Chinese Studies, 69; The Nature of Provincial Political Authority in Late Ch'ing Times, Mod Asian Studies, 70; The Chinese Government and the Revolutionary Students in Japan after 1900, J Asian Hist, 73; Missionaries and Reform Institutions in Modern China, Mod Asian Studies, 75; contribr, Chang Chih-tung After the 100 Days, In: Reform in Nineteenth Century China, Harvard Univ, 76; auth, China Enters the Twentieth Century, Univ MI, 78; Christianity and the Chinese Sectarian Tradition, Ch'ing-shih wen-t'i, 82; Popular Religious Movements in China and US in the 19th Century, Fides et Historia, 82; All Under Heaven- Chinese Tradition and Christian Life in the Peoples Republic of China, with A. Hunter and D. Rimmington, J of Church and State, Vol 36, 94; Sowing the Seeds of Change-Chinese Students, Japanese Teachers, 1895-1905, with P. Harrell, Am Hist Rev, Vol 99, 94. **CONTACT ADDRESS** Dept of Hist, Univ of KS, Lawrence, KS, 66045-0001.

BAZARGAN, SUSAN
DISCIPLINE ART HISTORY **EDUCATION** DePauw Univ, BA,68; Univ WA, MA, 79, PhD, 84. **CAREER** Part-time Instr, Mashad Univ , 69-78; Tchg Asst, Univ WA, 80-82; Predoctoral Tchg Ass, Univ WA, 82-84; Acting asst prof, Univ WA, 84-95; Assoc prof, Eastern IL Univ, 85-93; Prof, Eastern IL Univ, 93-. **HONORS AND AWARDS** Robert Heilman Award; Jessie J. Atkinson Award, 79; Robert Heilman Dissertation Award, 84; EIU Pres Summer Res Awards, 85, 89; EIU Fac Excellence Award Res, 90; EIU Fac Res Award, 94; NEH Independant Study Grant, 95;, Assoc ed, Works & Days. **MEMBERSHIPS** Virginia Woolf Soc; James Joyce Found, ACIS; SCE; MLA. **SELECTED PUBLICATIONS** Auth, Oxen of the Sun': Maternity, Language and History, James Joyce Quart, 85; The Headings in 'Aeolus': Cinematographic View, James Joyce Quart, 86; Monologue as Dialogue: Molly Bloom's 'History' as Myriorama, Socio-Hist Dimensions Lit & Arts, 87; Representation and Ideology in "The Real Thing", Henry James Rev, 91; Mapping Gibralter: Colonialism, Time, and Narrative in "Penelope', Molly Blooms: A Polylogue on 'Penelope', 94. **CONTACT ADDRESS** Eastern Illinois Univ, 600 Lincoln Ave, Charleston, IL, 61920-3099. **EMAIL** cfsxb@eiu.edu

BAZILLION, RICHARD J.
PERSONAL Born 02/25/1943, Saint John, NB, Canada, m, 1965, 2 children **DISCIPLINE** MODERN EUROPEAN HISTORY **EDUCATION** Boston Univ, BA, 96; Harvard Univ, MAT, 66, PhD, 70, MALS, 78. **CAREER** Librn, Algoma Univ Col, 80-90; dir libr svc, Brandon Univ, 90-95; prof, dean libr & Infor svc, Winona St Univ, 95- . **HONORS AND AWARDS** Dankstipendium, 68-69. **MEMBERSHIPS** Amer Libr Assoc; Assoc of Col & Res Libr. **RESEARCH** Industrialization in nineteenth century kingdom of Saxony; architecture of acad libr bdlg. **SELECTED PUBLICATIONS** Auth, State Bureaucracy and the Modernization Process in the Kingdom of Saxony, 1840-1861, German Hist, UK, 95; Building Virtual and Spatial Libraries for Distance Learning, Cause/Effect, 95; Teaching on the Web and in the Studio Classroom, Syllabus, 98; coauth, Academic Libraries as High-Tech Gateways: A Guide to Design and Space Decisions, Amer Libr Assoc, 2000. **CONTACT ADDRESS** Library, Winona State Univ, PO Box 5838, Winona, MN, 55987. **EMAIL** rbazillion@winona.msus.edu

BEALE, DAVID OTIS
PERSONAL VA, m, 3 children **DISCIPLINE** CHURCH HISTORY, THEOLOGY **EDUCATION** Bob Jones Univ, BA, 73, MA, 75, PhD(church hist), 80. **CAREER** Grad asst hist & church hist, 73-78, prof Church Hist, Theology & Bible, Bob Jones Univ, 78-. **HONORS AND AWARDS** Certificate of Award, Society for the Advancement and Preservation of Fundamental Studies of the Christian Faith, 95. **MEMBERSHIPS** Society for the Advancement and Preservation of Fundamental Studies. **RESEARCH** Historical Theology; Church Fathers; Colonial American churches; American Christianity since 1800; Baptist History; continued on-site research in British Isles and Holland tracing roots of Puritans, Pilgrims, Methodists, and Baptists. **SELECTED PUBLICATIONS** Auth, A Pictorial History of Our English Bible, Bob Jones Univ Press, 82; In Pursuit of Purity: American Fundamentalism Since 1950, Bob Jones Univ Press, 86; Ancient Attitudes towards Abortion, 1/82; A Family Travel and Tour Guide: Role of Protestant Churches in Early American History, 7-8/82; Fundamentalism: Past and Present, 10/82; The Purgatory Myth, 1/83; Francis Makemie: Champion of Religious Liberty, 5-6/83; Peter Muhlenberg: from the Pulpit to the Battlefield, 7-8/83; Lessons from the Catacombs, 12/83; The Pilgroms and God's Providence, 11/84; The Log College, 3/85; Faith for Family; The Revelation of Jesus Christ, Rev 19:1-21, Bibl Viewpoint, 11/82. **CONTACT ADDRESS** Relig Dept, Bob Jones Univ, 1700 Wade Hampton, Greenville, SC, 29614-0001. **EMAIL** Beale_BookSearch@compuserve.com

BEAME, EDMOND MORTON
PERSONAL Born 05/05/1931, New York, NY, m, 1952, 2 children **DISCIPLINE** RENAISSANCE & REFORMATION HISTORY **EDUCATION** Cornell Univ, BA, 52; Univ IL, Ph-

D(hist), 57. **CAREER** Lectr hist, Univ Toronto, 58-62; asst prof, 62-66, ASSOC PROF HIST, McMASTER UNIV, 66-. **MEMBERSHIPS** AHA; Renaissance Soc Am; Am Soc Reformation Res. **RESEARCH** Reformation religious thought and political theory; Italian Renaissance theatre. **SELECTED PUBLICATIONS** Auth, The Limits of Toleration in Sixteenth Century France, Studies Renaissance, 67; co-ed, The Comedies of Ariosto, Univ Chicago, 75; The Politiques and the Historians, J of the History of Ideas, Vol 54, 93. **CONTACT ADDRESS** Dept of Hist, McMaster Univ, 1280 Main St W, Hamilton, ON, L8S 4L9.

BEAN, JOHN MALCOLM WILLIAM
PERSONAL Born 08/25/1928, Bridgend, United Kingdom **DISCIPLINE** MEDIEVAL & ENGLISH HISTORY **EDUCATION** Oxford Univ, BA, 49, PhD(hist), 52. **CAREER** Asst lectr hist, Univ Manchester, 56-59, lectr, 59-67; chmn dept, 73-80, PROF HIST, COLUMBIA UNIV, 68-, Am Coun Learned Soc fel, 76-77. **MEMBERSHIPS** Fel Royal Hist Soc; Mediaeval Acad Am; Econ Hist Soc. **RESEARCH** English history in late middle ages. **SELECTED PUBLICATIONS** Auth, The Estates of the Percy Family, 1416-1537, Clarendon, 58; The Decline of English Feudalism, 1215-1540, Univ Manchester, 68; The Origins of Peasant Servitude in Medieval Catalonia, with P. Freedman, Labor Hist, Vol 34, 93. **CONTACT ADDRESS** Columbia Univ, 622 Fayerweather Hall, New York, NY.

BEANBLOSSOM, RONALD EDWIN
PERSONAL Born 11/24/1941, Des Moines, IA, m, 1965, 2 children **DISCIPLINE** HISTORY OF MODERN PHILOSOPHY **EDUCATION** Morningside Col, BA, 64; Union Theol Sem, NY, BD, 67; Univ Rochester, PhD(philos), 71. **CAREER** Asst prof philos, Northern Ill Univ, 70-77; Univ Chaplain, Ohio Northern Univ, 79-; assoc prof Philos & relig, Ohio Northern Univ, 82-87; chemn dept Philos & relig, 88-91; prof Philos & relig, 87-. **HONORS AND AWARDS** Sara A Ridenour Endowed Chair for Humanities, 89-90. **MEMBERSHIPS** Am Philos Asn. **RESEARCH** British empiricism; theories of perception; problems of knowledge; Quarterly, 88; Natural Reason: Essays in Honor of Joseph Norio Uemura, Hamline, 92; Reid and Hume, On the Nature of Belief, Reid Studies, 98. **SELECTED PUBLICATIONS** Auth, Walton on rational action, Mind, 71; Thomas Reid's Inquiry & Essays, LLA, 75; Russel's indebtedness to Reid, Monist, 78; A new foundation for human scepticism, Philos Studies, 76. **CONTACT ADDRESS** Dept of Philos & Relig, Ohio Northern Univ, 525 S Main St, Ada, OH, 45810-1555.

BEARDSLEY, EDWARD HENRY
PERSONAL Born 05/18/1935, Jacksonville, FL, m, 1960, 3 children **DISCIPLINE** UNITED STATES HISTORY, HISTORY OF SCIENCE & MEDICINE **EDUCATION** Univ FL, BChE, 53; Univ WI, MS, 63, PhD(hist), 66. **CAREER** Tech sales, Rohm & Haas Co, 58-60; asst prof Am hist, 66-70, dean freshmen, 73-75, ASSOC PROF AM HIST, UNIV SC, 70-. **HONORS AND AWARDS** Willia, B Hesseltine Award, WI Mag Hist, 67; Distinguished Teaching Award, Univ SC, 70. **MEMBERSHIPS** Orgn Am Historians. **RESEARCH** History of American medicine and public health; history of American science. **SELECTED PUBLICATIONS** Auth, The Rise of the American Chemistry Profession, Univ FL, 64; An Industry Revitalized, WI Mag Hist, 65; Hrry L Russell and Agricultural Science in Wisconsin, Univ WI, 69; The American Scientist as Social Activist, Isis, 73; Allied Against Sin: American and British Responses to VD, Med Hist, 76; Doctors to the Barricades, Bull Hist Med, 77; Secrets Between Friends, Social Studies Sci, 77; Medical Research Exchange Between Russia and West in WWII, Med Hist, 78; The History of American Sci & Med, Info Sources Hist Sci & Med, 82; Voegelin on the Idea of Race-An Analysis of Modern European Racism, with T. W. Heilke, Isis, Vol 84, 93; Science with Practice- C. E. Bessey and the Maturing of American Botany, with R. A. Overfield, Agricultural Hist, Vol 68, 94; The Cold War and American Science-The Military-Industrial-Academic Complex at MIT and Stanford, with S. W. Leslie, Vol 57, 95; Patronage, Practice, and the Culture of American Science, with Bache, Alexander, Dallas and the United States Coast Survey, with H. R. Slotten, Reviews in Am Hist, Vol 24, 96. **CONTACT ADDRESS** Dept of Hist, Univ of SC, Columbia, SC, 29208.

BEARDSMORE, BARRY
DISCIPLINE HISTORY OF THE FRENCH LANGUAGE **EDUCATION** Univ Brit Columbia, PhD. **RESEARCH** Old and Middle French romance. **SELECTED PUBLICATIONS** Auth, Ysaie le Triste: a Tale of Two Heroes, Zeitschrift fur romanische Philologie, 89; About the Seventieth of the Cent Nouvelles Nouvelles, Romania 110, 89; Les elements epiques dans le roman, Ysaie le Triste, Memorias de la Real Academia de Buenas Letras de Barcelona, 90. **CONTACT ADDRESS** Dept of French, Victoria Univ, PO Box 3045 STN CSC, Victoria, BC, V8W 3P4. **EMAIL** bfb@uvvm.uvic.ca

BEARSS, EDWIN COLE
PERSONAL Born 06/26/1923, Billings, MT, m, 1958, 3 children **DISCIPLINE** AMERICAN MILITARY HISTORY **EDUCATION** Georgetown Univ, BS, 49; IN Univ, MA, 55. **CAREER** Historian, Vicksburg Nat Mil Park, 55-58; regional res historian, 58-66, historian, Div Hist, 66-72, SUPVRY HISTORIAN HIST PRESERV, EAST DENVER SERV CTR, SOUTHEAST REGION, NAT PARK SERV, 72-, Mem, Civil War Centennial Comn, 58-60. **HONORS AND AWARDS** Super Performance Awards, Nat Park Serv, 58, 66 & 67; Harry S Truman Award, Kansas City Civil War Round Table, 61. **MEMBERSHIPS** Fel Col Mil Hist. **RESEARCH** American Civil War; American revolution; recent presidents, especially Hoover, Eisenhower and Johnson. **SELECTED PUBLICATIONS** Coauth, Fort Smith: Little Gibraltar on the Arkansas, Univ OK, 69; ed, A Southern Record, 70 & Memoirs of the First Missouri Confederate Brigade: Anderson, 72, Morningside; A Louisiana Confederate: Diary of Felix Pierre Poche, LA State Univ, 72; auth, General John Hunt Morgan's second Kentucky raid, Register, 4/73; contribr, A History of Mississippi, Univ & Col MS, 73; auth, The Battle of Brice's Crossroads, Morningside, 79; coauth (with A M Gibson), Fort Smith: Little Gibraltar on the Arkansas, 79; The Civil War in the American West, with A. M. Josephy, Pacific Hist Rev, Vol 62, 93; Pea Ridge-Civil War Campaign in the West, with W. L. Shea and E. J. Hess, J of Am Hist, Vol 81, 94. **CONTACT ADDRESS** 1126 17th St S, Arlington, VA, 22202.

BEATIE, BRUCE A.
PERSONAL Born 03/04/1935, Oakland, CA, m, 1990 **DISCIPLINE** MEDIEVAL, FOLK, AND POPULAR LITERATURE **EDUCATION** Univ Calif, Berkeley, AB, 59; Univ Colo, MA, 60; Harvard Univ, PhD(comp lit), 67. **CAREER** Asst prof Ger, Univ Colo, 64-67, asst prof Ger & comp lit, 67-68; assoc prof, Univ Rochester, 68-70; chmn, Dept Mod Lang, 70-77, Prof Ger,Cleaveland State Univ, 77-88, Prof Comp & Medieval Studies, 89-. **HONORS AND AWARDS** Nat Endowment for Humanities younger scholar fel, 70. **MEMBERSHIPS** Midwest MLA; AAUP. **RESEARCH** Medieval comparative literature; popular and traditional narrative; folklore. **SELECTED PUBLICATIONS** Auth, Arthurian films and Arthurian texts: problems of reception and comprehension, Arthurian Interpretations, Spring 88; Arthur C. Clarke and the alien encounter: The background of Childhood's End, Extrapolation, Spring 89; E.E. Smith, In: Twentieth Century Science Fiction Writers, 3rd ed, St. James, 91; The broken quest: the Perceval romances of Chretien de Troyes and Eric Rohmer, In: The Arthurian Revival: Essays on Form, Tradition, and Transformation, Garland, 92; coauth, Reflected images in two Mexican poems of 1957: Piedra de sol by Octavio Paz and Misterios gozosos by Rosario Castellanos, Revista / Review Interamericana 26, 96; author of several other articles. **CONTACT ADDRESS** Dept of Mod Lang, Cleveland State Univ, 1983 E 24th St, Cleveland, OH, 44115-2440. **EMAIL** b.beatie@popmail.csuohio.edu

BEAU, BRYAN LE
DISCIPLINE HISTORY **EDUCATION** NY Univ, PhD. **CAREER** Dept ch, prof, Creighton Univ, 83-; cord, Amer Stud Prog & John C. Kenefick fac ch in Human. **HONORS AND AWARDS** Creighton Cole Art and Sci Dean's awds for Excellence in Tchg, Svc and Res. **RESEARCH** Pre-Civil War; US cultural, especially religious, history. **SELECTED PUBLICATIONS** Publ on res interest. **CONTACT ADDRESS** Dept of History, Creighton Univ, 2500 California Plaza, Omaha, NE, 68178. **EMAIL** blbeau@creighton.edu

BEAUDOIN-ROSS, JACQUELINE
PERSONAL Born 08/15/1931, Montreal, PQ, Canada **DISCIPLINE** HISTORY **EDUCATION** McGill Univ, BA, 52, MA, 75. **CAREER** CURATOR, COSTUME & TEXTILES, McCORD MUSEUM CANADIAN HISTORY, 79-; lectr, Concordia Univ, 80-81; lectr, McGill Univ, 86. **SELECTED PUBLICATIONS** Coauth, Costume in Canada: An Annotated Bibliography, 84; coauth, Costume in Canada: The Sequel, 91; coauth, Form and Fashion: Nineteenth Century Montreal Dress, 92; coauth, Daring Deco-Styles and Lifestyles, 95; contribur, The Canadian Encyclopedia, 85; contribur, Encyclopedia of the North American Colonies, 93. **CONTACT ADDRESS** McCord Mus, 690 Sherbrooke St W, Montreal, PQ, H3A 1E9.

BEAUDRY, MARY CAROLYN
PERSONAL Born 11/25/1950, Great Lakes, IL **DISCIPLINE** HISTORICAL ARCHEOLOGY, ANTHROPOLOGY **EDUCATION** Col William & Mary, BA, 73; Brown Univ, MA, 75, PhD(anthrop), 80. **CAREER** ASST PROF ARCHAEOL, BOSTON UNIV, 80-, Dir, Ft Christanna Archaeol Proj, Brunswick County Hist Soc Inc, 79-. **MEMBERSHIPS** Soc Hist Archaeol; Soc Am Archaeol; Asn Field Archaeol; Soc Post-Medieval Archaeol; Vernacular Archit Forum. **RESEARCH** Historical archaeology, especially 17th century Anglo-America; vernacular architecture and material culture studies; folk taxonomies of early Anglo-America derived from documentary analysis. **SELECTED PUBLICATIONS** Auth, Worth its Weight in Iron: Categories of Material Culture in Early Virginia Probate Inventories, Archaeol Soc Va Quart Bull, Vol 33, No 1; A Preliminary Study of Ceramics in York County, Virginia, Inventories, 1730-1750, Conf Hist Site Archaeol Papers, Vol 12, 78; Insult and Slander in Seventeenth Century Virginia, Folklore & Folklife Va, 1: 42-51; Spoons from the Burr's Hill Collection, Studies Anthrop & Material Cult, 80; Fort Christanna: Frontier Trading Post of the Va Indian Company, In: Forgotton Places & Things, Ctr Anthrop Studies, 82; coauth, Filling in Round Pond: Refuse Disposal in Post-revolutionary Boston, Northeast Hist Archaeol, 82; Vessel Typology in Historical Archaeology: The Potomac Typological System, Hist Archaeol, Vol 17, No 1; Public Aesthetics Versus Personal Experience-Worker Health and Well-Being in 19th-Century Lowell, Massachusetts, Hist Archaeol, Vol 27, 93; Ethnicity and the American Cemetery, with R. E. Meyer, J of Am Hist, Vol 81, 94; Under the Boardwalk in Quebec City-French and English, with P. Beaudet, Hist Archaeol, Vol 28, 94; Percy, Wharram, Deserted Medieval Village, with M. Beresford and J. Hurst, J of Field Archaeol, Vol 21, 94; A Chesapeake Family and Their Slaves-A Study in Historical Archaeology, with A. E. Yentsche, Antiquity, Vol 69, 95; Hisrorical Archaeology of the Chesapeake, with P. A. Shackel and B. Little, Antiquity, Vol 69, 95; **CONTACT ADDRESS** Dept of Archaeol, Boston Univ, Boston, MA, 02215.

BEAUMONT, ROGER A.
PERSONAL Born 10/02/1935, Milwaukee, WI, m, 1974, 2 children **DISCIPLINE** HISTORY **EDUCATION** Univ WI, BS, 57, MS, 60; KS State Univ, PhD(hist), 73. **CAREER** Asst to dir, Ctr Advan Study Orgn Sci, Univ WI-Milwaukee, 65-67; instr hist, Univ WI-Oshkosh, 68-69; from asst prof to assoc prof, Ctr Advan Study Orgn Sci, Univ WI-Milwaukee, 70-74; assoc prof, 74-79, prof hist, Tex A&M Univ, 79-. **MEMBERSHIPS** Am Mil Inst; Inter-Univ Sem Armed Forces & Soc; US Naval Inst; Science Fiction & Fantasy Writers of Am. **RESEARCH** Modern military history. **SELECTED PUBLICATIONS** Auth, Military Elites, Bobbs-Merrill, 74; co-ed, War in the Next Decade, Univ Ky & Macmillan, UK, 74; auth, Sword of the Raj, Bobbs-Merrill, 77; Nerves of War, AFCEA Press, 86; Elite Forces and Special Operations, Greenwood, 88; Joint Military Operations, Greenwood, 94; War Chaos and History, Praeger, 95; four res monographs, 85 book chapters and articles. **CONTACT ADDRESS** Dept Hist, Texas A&M Univ, College Station, TX, 77843. **EMAIL** rabeaum@acs.tamu.edu

BEAVER, DANIEL R.
PERSONAL Born 09/23/1928, Hamilton, ON, Canada, m, 1952, 2 children **DISCIPLINE** AMERICAN HISTORY **EDUCATION** Heidelberg Col, AB, 51; Univ Cincinnati, MA, 54; Northwestern Univ, PhD, 62. **CAREER** From instr to assoc prof, 58-70, prof Hist, Univ Cinncinati, 70-, Mershon fel, 64-65; lect, 71-73, Harold K Johnson prof, US Army Mil Hist Inst, US Army War Col, 83-84; Distinguished Vis Scholar, US Army Ctr Mil Hist, 85-87. **MEMBERSHIPS** AHA; Orgn Am Hist; Asn Mil Hist. **RESEARCH** Diplomatic and military history. **SELECTED PUBLICATIONS** Auth, Newton D Baker and the American War Effort 1917-1919, Univ Nebr, 66; Some Pathways in Modern History, Wayne State Univ, 68; War and Society in the Seventeenth Century, Some Dimensions of Military History, US Army War Col, 72; The Problem of Military Supply, War Business and American Society, Kennikat, 77; Ideas and Policy: The War Department Wheeled Vehicle Program 1920-1940, Mil Aff Fall 83; Logistics in John E Vessup (ed) Encycl of the Am Mil, Scribner's, 94. **CONTACT ADDRESS** Dept Hist, Univ Cincinnati, PO Box 210373, Cincinnati, OH, 45221-0373. **EMAIL** BEAVERD@email.uc.edu

BEAVER, DONALD DE BLASIIS
PERSONAL Born 07/16/1936, New York, NY, m, 1962, 2 children **DISCIPLINE** HISTORY OF SCIENCE **EDUCATION** Harvard Col, AB, 58; Yale Univ, PhD(hist of sci), 66. **CAREER** Asst prof hist of sci & phys sci, Univ Mo, Kansas City, 66-70,; asst prof hist of sci, Franklin & Marshall Col, 70-71; assoc prof, 71-84, PROF HIST OF SCI, WILLIAMS COL, 85-, Univ Mo, Kansas City fac res grant, 67-68 & asst prof res grant, 68; vis fel hist sci, Yale Univ, 77-78. **MEMBERSHIPS** AAAS; Hist Sci Soc; Midwest Junto Hist Sci; Soc Social Study Sci **RESEARCH** History of science in America; social history of science. **SELECTED PUBLICATIONS** Coauth, Collaboration in an invisible college, Am Psychologist, 11/66; auth, Altruism, patriotism, and science: Scientific journals in the early republic, Am Studies, spring 71; The Smithsonian origin of the Royal Society Catalogue of Scientific Papers, Sci Studies, 72; Reflections on the natural history of eponymy and scientific law, Social Studies Sci, No 6, 2/76; Studies in Scientific Collaboration: Vol I, The Professional Origins of Scientific Co-Authorship, Vol II, Scientific Co-Authorship, Research Productivity and Visibility in the French Elite, 1799-1830, Vol III, Professionalization and the Natural History of Modern Scientific Co-Authorship, Scientometrics 1, 78-79. **CONTACT ADDRESS** Dept of the Hist of Sci, Williams Col, 880 Main St, Williamstown, MA, 01267-2600. **EMAIL** dbeaver@williams.edu

BECK, GUY
PERSONAL Born 08/03/1948, New York, NY, m, 1979 **DISCIPLINE** HISTORY OF RELIGION **EDUCATION** Syracuse Univ, PhD, MA; Univ FL, MA. **CAREER** Vis Asst Prof, 97-99, College of Charleston; Asst Prof, 95-97, Loyola Univ; act Asst Prof, 90-95, LSU. **HONORS AND AWARDS** Fulbright Schshp; AIIS SR Res Fel. **MEMBERSHIPS** AAR; SE. **RESEARCH** Sacred sound, Hindu Music; Phenomenology of Ethno musicology. **SELECTED PUBLICATIONS** Auth, Seven invited entries for Encarta Encyclopedia on CD-ROM by

Microsoft Inc, including, Om, Bhagavata Purana, Sutra, Mudra, Prayer Wheel, Satori, Ahura Mazda, forthcoming; auth, Religious Music of Northern Areas, in: Garland Encyc of World Music: South Asia Volume, Alison Arnold, ed, forthcoming; Bhajan/Devotional Music, Music Festivals and Music Academies, for the Encyc of Hinduism, forthcoming; auth, Devotional Hymns from Sanskrit, in: Religions In India, DS Lopez Jr ed, Princeton Univ Press, 95; Fire in the Atman: Repentance in Hinduism, in: Repentance: A Comparative Perspective, Amitai Etzioni, David Carney, ed, Lanham MD, Rowman and Littlefield, 97. **CONTACT ADDRESS** Col of Charleston, 14 Glebe St, Charleston, SC, 29424. **EMAIL** beckg@cofc.edu

BECK, JAMES HENRY
PERSONAL Born 05/14/1930, New York, NY, m, 1956, 1 child **DISCIPLINE** HISTORY OF ART **EDUCATION** Oberlin Col, BA, 52; NY Univ, MA, 54; Columbia Univ, PhD (art hist), 63. **CAREER** Asst prof art hist, Univ AL, Tuscaloosa, 58-59 & AZ State Univ, 59-60; from instr to assoc prof, 61-71, Prof Art Hist, Columbia Univ, 71-, Fels, Instr Advan Studies, 67, Villa I Tatti, Harvard Univ, 67-68 & 72, Guggenheim Found, 73-74 & Nat Endowment for Hum, 81-82. **MEMBERSHIPS** Col Art Asn; Medieval Soc Am; Renaissance Soc Am. **RESEARCH** Italian art of the 14th, 15th and 16th centuries. **SELECTED PUBLICATIONS** Auth, Mariano di Jacopo detto il Taccola, Il Polifilo, Milan, 69; Jacopo della Quercia e suo portale a Bologna, Edizioni Alfa, Bologna, 70; Michelangelo: A Lesson in Anatomy, Viking, 75; Raphael Library of Great Painters, Abrams, 76; Masaccio: The Documents, Villa I Tatti, 78; Leonardo's Rules of Painting, Viking Press, 79; Italian Renaissance Painting, Harper, 81. **CONTACT ADDRESS** Dept of Art History, Columbia Univ, 2960 Broadway, New York, NY, 10027-6900. **EMAIL** JHB3@Columbia.edu

BECK, ROGER L.
PERSONAL Born 01/11/1937, London, England **DISCIPLINE** CLASSICS **EDUCATION** New Col, Oxford Univ, BA, 61; Univ Ill, MA, 63, PhD, 71. **CAREER** Lectr, Univ Man, 63-64; lectr, Univ Col, Univ Toronto, 64-65; asst prof, 68 to PROF CLASSICS, ERINDALE COL, UNIV TORONTO. **MEMBERSHIPS** Class Asn Can (secy 77-79); Am Philol Asn. **RESEARCH** Petronius and the ancient novel; the cult of Mithras. **SELECTED PUBLICATIONS** Auth, Planetary Gods in the Mysteries of Mithras, 88; rev ed, 78-81, assoc ed, Phoenix, 82-86. **CONTACT ADDRESS** Erindale Col, Univ Toronto, Toronto, ON, M5S 1K7.

BECKER, MARJORIE R.
DISCIPLINE LATIN AMERICAN HISTORY **EDUCATION** Duke, BA, 74, MA, 80; Yale Univ, MA, 83, MPhil, 83, PhD, 88. **CAREER** Prof, Univ Southern Calif, 87-.. **RESEARCH** Cultural invention, race; gender; ethnicity,;class; spiritual life; socialism; liberalism; national states. **SELECTED PUBLICATIONS** Auth, Virgin on Fire: Lazaro Cardenas, Michoacan Peasants, & the Invention of the Mexican Revolution, Berkeley, 95, rep, 96; Torching La Purisima, Dancing at the Altar: The Construction of Hegemony in Revolutionary Michoacan, 1934-1940, in Joseph &Nugent, Everyday Forms of State Formation: Revolution & the Negotiation of Rule in Modern Mexico, Duke, 94; Cardenistas, Campesinos and The Weapons of the Weak: The Limits of Everyday Resistance in Michoacan, Mexico, 1934-1940, in Peasant Stud 16, 89; Black & White and Color: Cardenismo & the Search for a Campesino Ideology, in comp Stud Soc and Hist 29, 87; Lazaro Cardenas & the Mexican Counter-Revolution: The Struggle over Culture in Michoacan, 1934-1940, **CONTACT ADDRESS** Dept of History, Univ Southern Calif, University Park Campus, Los Angeles, CA, 90089. **EMAIL** mrbecker@bcf.usc.edu

BECKER, MARVIN BURTON
PERSONAL Born 07/20/1922, Philadelphia, PA, m, 1944, 2 children **DISCIPLINE** MEDIEVAL & RENAISSANCE HISTORY **EDUCATION** Univ PA, BS, 46, Am, 47, PhD, 50. **CAREER** Teacher hist, Lincoln Prep Sch, 45-50; asst prof medieval hist, Univ AR, 50-52; asst prof hist, Baldwin-Wallace Col, 52-57; assoc prof hist, Western Reserve Univ, 57-63; prof, Univ Rochester, 63-73; chemn dept, 77-79, prof hist, Univ Mich, Ann Arbor, 73-; asst, Univ PA, 47-48; Fulbright res fel, Italy, 53-55 & Guggenheim mem fel, 56-57; Am Philos Soc fels, 61-62; Am Coun Learned Soc fel, Harvard Ctr Renaissance Studies, Florence, Italy, 63-64; prof, Johns Hopkins Univ, 66-67, sr fel, Inst Humanities, 66-67; fel, Inst Advan Studies, Princeton Univ, 68-69; vis prof hist, Univ Toronto, 71; vis prof hist, Univ AZ, 80. **HONORS AND AWARDS** Deputazione de Storia Patria per la Toscana. **MEMBERSHIPS** AHA; Mediaeval Acad Am; Renaissance Soc Am. **RESEARCH** Social, economic, cultural hist Italy. **SELECTED PUBLICATIONS** Auth, Church and State in Florence on the Eve of the Renaissance, Mediaeval Acad; Florence in Transition, Johns Hopkins Univ, Vol I, 67, Vol II, 68; An Essay on the Novi Cives and Florentine Politics, Mediaeval Studies, 62; Florentine Popular Government, 1343-48, Proc Am Philos Soc, 62; Medieval Italy, IN Univ, 81; Civility and Society in Western Europe, 1300-1600, IN Univ, 88; The Emergence of Civil Society in the 18th Century, IN Univ, 94. **CONTACT ADDRESS** Dept Hist, Univ Mich, 435 S State St, Ann Arbor, MI, 48109-1003.

BECKER, PETER WOLFGANG
PERSONAL Born 09/06/1929, Munich, Germany **DISCIPLINE** MODERN EUROPEAN HISTORY **EDUCATION** N TX State Univ, BA, 60; Stanford Univ, MA, 61, PhD(hist), 71. **CAREER** Instr hist, San Jose State Col, 65-66; from instr to asst prof, 66-76, asst chmn, 76-78, ASSOC PROF HIST, UNIV SC, 76-, ASST CHMN, 82-. **MEMBERSHIPS** AHA; Southern Hist Asn. **RESEARCH** Modern German history. **SELECTED PUBLICATIONS** Transl, Franzen, History of the Church, Herder, 69; History of the Church, Vol V: Reformation and Counter Reformation, 80, History of the Church, Vol VII: Church Between Revolution and Restoration, 81 & History of the Church, Vol VIII: Church in the Age of Liberalism, 81, Seabury; The Politics of Progressive Education-The Odenwaldschule in Nazi Germany, with D. Shirley, J of Interdiciplinary Hist, Vol, 25, 95. **CONTACT ADDRESS** Dept of Hist, Univ of SC, Columbia, SC, 29208.

BECKER, ROBERT ARTHUR
PERSONAL Born 06/09/1943, Brooklyn, NY, 3 children **DISCIPLINE** AMERICAN HISTORY **EDUCATION** St Lawrence Univ, BA, 65; Univ Wis-Madison, MA, 67, PhD(Hist), 71. **CAREER** Vis lectr Am Hist, Univ Ill, Urbana-Champaign, 70-71; asst prof, 71-80, assoc prof Am Hist, LA State Univ, Baton Rouge, 80-. **HONORS AND AWARDS** Phi Beta Kappa. **MEMBERSHIPS** Orgn Am Historians. **RESEARCH** American revolution, 1763-1789; American Colonial South. **SELECTED PUBLICATIONS** Asst ed, Documentary History of the First Federal Elections, I Univ Wis, 74; auth, Revolution and reform: an interpretation of Southern taxation, 1763-1783, William & Mary Quart, 7/75; Salvs populi suprema lex: Public order and South Carolinas' debtor laws, 1783-1787, SC Hist Mag, 1/79; Revolution, Reform and the Politics of American Taxation, 1763-1783, La State Univ Press, 80. **CONTACT ADDRESS** Dept of History, Louisiana State Univ, Baton Rouge, LA, 70803-0001. **EMAIL** rbecker@whflemming.hist.lsu.edu

BECKER, SEYMOUR
PERSONAL Born 09/15/1934, Rochester, NY, m, 1957, 2 children **DISCIPLINE** MODERN HISTORY **EDUCATION** Williams Col, AB, 56; Harvard Univ, AM, 58, PhD(Russ Hist), 63. **CAREER** From instr to assoc prof, 62-86, assoc prof Hist, Rutgers Univ, 86-, exchange scholar, Moscow State Univ, 67-68; Russian Academy of Sciences, 84, 88. **MEMBERSHIPS** AHA; Am Asn Advan Slavic Studies; Assn for Study of Nationalities. **RESEARCH** Social and political history of Russia, 1861-1917; Russian imperial policy, 1861-1917. **SELECTED PUBLICATIONS** Auth, Russia's Protectorates in Central Asia: Bukhara and Khiva, 1865-1924, Harvard Univ, 68; contribr, The Nationality Question in Soviet Central Asia, Praeger, 73; contrib, Russian colonial Expansion to 1917, Mansell Publ. Ltd, 88; Central Asia: Its Strategic Importance and Future Prospects, St Martin's, 94. **CONTACT ADDRESS** Dept of History, Rutgers Univ, PO Box 5059, New Brunswick, NJ, 08903-5059. **EMAIL** sbecker@mail.idt.net

BECKER, SUSAN D.
DISCIPLINE HISTORY **EDUCATION** Case Western Reserve, PhD. **CAREER** Assoc prof. **SELECTED PUBLICATIONS** Auth, The Origins of the Equal Rights Amendment: American Feminism Between the Wars, Greenwood; coauth, Discovering the American Past: A Look at the Evidence, Houghton Mifflin. **CONTACT ADDRESS** Dept of History, Knoxville, TN, 37996.

BECKER, WILLIAM HENRY
PERSONAL Born 03/28/1943, New York, NY, m, 1965, 2 children **DISCIPLINE** AMERICAN BUSINESS & ECONOMIC HISTORY **EDUCATION** Muhlenberg Col, BA, 64; Johns Hopkins Univ, PhD, 69. **CAREER** Asst prof, Univ MD Baltimore County, 69-73, assoc prof, 73-80; vis assoc prof, 80-82, assoc prof, 82-83, prof hist, George Washington Univ, 83-; Vis Prof Hist, Johns Hopkins Univ, 96 & Nat Univ Singapore, 98. **HONORS AND AWARDS** Newcomen Award, Outstanding Bk Bus Hist, 79-82. **MEMBERSHIPS** AHA; Orgn Am Historians; Econ Hist Asn; Econ Hist Asn; Bus Hist Conf. **RESEARCH** Hist of business; comp business hist; business-government rel. **SELECTED PUBLICATIONS** Auth, The Dynamics of Business-Government Relations: Industry and Exports, 1893-1921, Univ Chicago Press, 82; co-ed (with Samuel F Wells), Economics and Diplomacy: An Assessment of American Diplomacy Since 1789, Columbia Univ Press, 84; gen ed, The Encyclopedia of American Business History & Biography, 9 vol, Broccoli Clark Layman, 86-92. **CONTACT ADDRESS** Dept of Hist, George Washington Univ, 2035 H St N W, Washington, DC, 20052. **EMAIL** whbecker@gwu.edu

BECKER-SLATON, NELLIE FRANCES
PERSONAL Born 08/31/1921, Providence, Rhode Island, m, 1950 **DISCIPLINE** EDUCATION **EDUCATION** NY Univ, BS Occup Therapy 1946; CA State Clge at Los Angeles, Tchrs Credential 1952; Pepperdine Univ, MA 1975; Claremont Grad Schl, PhD 1988. **CAREER** Hines VA Hosp in Chicago IL, Sawtelle VA Hosp in Los Angeles CA, occup therapist 1947-50; CA Eagle, family edit 1948-51; Pittsburgh Courier, contrib writer 1951-52; LA Unified Sch Dist Reg D, multicultural adult educ tchr 1972-77; Frances Blend School for Visually Handicapped, sci coord 1973-75; Westminster Elem Sch, multicultural coord 1978-79; Walgrove Elem Sch and Charnock Elem Sch, intgrtn coord 1979-80; LA Unified Sch Dist, educ prof writer; Westminster Elementary, 1980-. **HONORS AND AWARDS** Resolution comm work LA City Cncl 1985; Women of the Year LA Sentinel Newspaper 1962; author writers award Our Authors Study Club 1966; comm work Natl Assc for coll Women; Sci Authors Radio Station KDAY 1965; comm work Westminster Presb 1973; Senate Resolution State of California 199. **MEMBERSHIPS** Dir Comm Sci Workshops 1960-69; former pres Intl Scribbles West 1960-65; Chap 587 Council for Excep Children; former bd mem LA Reading Assn; Amer Folklore Soc; LA CA Genealogical Soc; EDUCARE; Linguistics Soc of Amer; Alpha Kappa Alpha Sor; co-founder Doctoral Support Group 1982; mem Western Folklore Soc, NAPPS and SCC-LYP; Afro-Amer Genealogical Soc of Southern California; Los Angeles Urban League; co-founder, pres Association of Pan African Doctoral Scholars 1981-92; Daughters of American Revolution; Hollywood Chapter of California, 1996 . **SELECTED PUBLICATIONS** author Bacteria and Viruses Prentice Hall; author On My Own Harcourt Brace-Jovanovich. **CONTACT ADDRESS** LA Unified Schl Dist, 1010 Abbot Kinney Blvd, Venice, CA, 90291.

BECKERMAN, PAUL
PERSONAL Born 08/23/1948, Denver, CO, m, 1983, 1 child **DISCIPLINE** ECONOMICS **EDUCATION** Princeton Univ, PhD 79. **CAREER** World Bank, 88-; Federal Reserve Bank, 85-88. **RESEARCH** Economics of Development; Stabilization. **CONTACT ADDRESS** World Bank, 1818 H St., N W, Washington, DC, 20433. **EMAIL** pbeckerman@worldbank.org

BECKERMAN DAVIS, BARBARA
DISCIPLINE EUROPEAN HISTORY, 16TH CENTURY URBAN FRANCE HISTORY **EDUCATION** CUNY, Uptown, BA; Univ CA, Berkeley, MA, PhD. **CAREER** Assoc prof, Antioch Col. **HONORS AND AWARDS** NEH inst, 91 NEH sem, 95. **RESEARCH** Poor relief institutions and the poor in Toulouse. **SELECTED PUBLICATIONS** Articles appeared in Hist Reections/Reexions historiques (91) and Fr Hist (93); she reviews for the 16th Century J, Cath Hist J, and J of Mod Hist. **CONTACT ADDRESS** Antioch Col, Yellow Springs, OH, 45387.

BECKHAM, STEPHEN DOW
PERSONAL Born 08/31/1941, Coos Bay, OR, m, 1967, 2 children **DISCIPLINE** AMERICAN WEST, NATIVE AMERICANS, UNTED STATES HISTORY **EDUCATION** Univ Ore, BA, 64; Univ Calif, Los Angeles, MA, 66, PhD(hist), 69. **CAREER** Lectr hist, Long Beach State Univ, 68-69; assoc prof, Linfield Col, 69-76; assoc prof, 77-81, prof hist, Lewis & Clark Col, 81-92, PAMPLIN PROF HIST, LEWIS & CLARK COL, 92-; Nat Endowment for Humanities res grant to write & narrate six TV progs for CBS & Ore Educ Broadcasting, 71-72; consult, US Forest Serv, US Bur Land Mgt, US Army Corps Engineers, US Coast Guard, Ore Dept Transp, Ore State Parks; expert witness, US Dept of Justice, Ore Dept of Justice, Karuk Tribe of Calif, Cow Creek Ban of Umpqua Tribe of Indians, Chinook Indian Tribe, Cowlitz Indian Tribe; adv Comt Hist Preserv, State of Ore, 77-; bd adv, Nat Trust Hist Preserv, Washington, DC, 77-85, bd, John & LaRee Caughey Found, 79-, bd, Ore Hist Soc, 94-. **HONORS AND AWARDS** Asher Distinguished Teaching Award, Am Hist Asn, 95; Ore Prof of the Year, Counc Advance and Support of Higher Educ, 92-93; Sears-Roebuck Found Teaching Excellence and Campus Leadership Award, Lewis & Clark Col, 90. **MEMBERSHIPS** AHA; Western Hist Asn **RESEARCH** Indian-white relations; history of Pacific Northwest and Calif **SELECTED PUBLICATIONS** Auth, Requiem for a People: The Rogue Indians and the Frontiersmen, Univ Okla, 71, Ore State Univ Press, 91; The Simpsons of Shore Acres, Arago, 71; Coos Bay: The Pioneer Period, 1851-1890, Arago, 73; The Indians of Western Oregon: This Land Was Theirs, Arago, 77; You May Have Someting There: Identifying Historical Cultural Resources in the Pacific Northwest, USDA Forest Service, 78; Land of the Umpqua: A History of Douglas County, Oregon, Doug Co Comnr, 87; Lewis & Clark College, Trustees of Lewis & Clark Col, 91; Many Faces: An Anthology of Ore Autobiography, Ore State Univ Press, 93; Seventy-Five Years at Building: Hoffman Construction Company, Hoffman Corp, 95; Hist of Western Ore Since 1846, vol 7, Northwest Coast, Handbook of North Am Indians, Smithsonian Inst, 90; History Since 1846, vol 12, Plateau, Handbookd of North Am Indians, Smithsonian Inst, 98. **CONTACT ADDRESS** Dept of Hist, Lewis & Clark Col, 0615 SW Palatine Hill Rd, Portland, OR, 97219-7879. **EMAIL** beckham@lclark.edu

BECKWITH, JOHN
PERSONAL Born 03/09/1927, Victoria, BC, Canada **DISCIPLINE** HISTORY OF MUSIC **EDUCATION** Victoria Col, 44-45; Royal Conserv Music, 45-50; Univ Toronto, MusB, 47, MusM, 61. **CAREER** Lectr, 55-61, asst prof 61-66, assoc prof, 66-70, dean, 70-77, Prof Music, Univ Toronto (RETIRED), 70-90; dir, Inst Can Music, 84-90; assoc ed, Can Music J, 57-62. **HONORS AND AWARDS** Can Music Coun Annual medal, 72; MusD (honoris causa), Mt Allison Univ, 74; Univ Toronto

Sesquicentennial Award, 77; MusD (honoris causa), McGill Univ, 78; Can Music Coun Composer Year, 85; mem, Order Can, 87; Richard S. Hill Award, US Music Libr Asn, 90; Toronto Arts Award, 94; Mus D (honoris causa), Univ Guelph, 95; diplome d'honneur, Can Conf Arts, 96. **MEMBERSHIPS** Can Musical Heritage Soc; Toronto Musicians Asn; Can League Composers; Sonneck Soc Am Music. **SELECTED PUBLICATIONS** Auth, Music Papers, 97; ed, Canadian Composers study ser, 75-90; ed, The Canadian Musical Heritage, vol 5, Hymn Tunes, 86, vol 18, Oratoria and Cantata Excerpts, 95; co-ed, The Modern Composer and His World, 61; co-ed, Contemporary Canadian Composers, 75; co-ed, Musical Canada, 88; contribur, Dictionary of Contemporary Music, 74; Can consult & contribur, The New Grove, 80; contribur & exec bd mem, Encyclopedia of Music in Canada, 81, 93. **CONTACT ADDRESS** Fac of Music, Univ of Toronto, Toronto, ON, M5S 1A1.

BEDESKI, ROBERT E.
PERSONAL Born 11/03/1937, Detroit, MI **DISCIPLINE** POLITICAL SCIENCE/ASIAN STUD/HISTORY **EDUCATION** Univ Calif Berkeley, BA, 64, MA, 65, PhD, 69. **CAREER** Asst prof, Ohio State Univ, 69-73; asst prof, 73-75, assoc prof, Carleton Univ, 75-89; PROF POLITICAL SCIENCE, UNIV VICTORIA, 89-; vis prof, Meiji Univ (Tokyo), 93-94. **HONORS AND AWARDS** Nat Defense Foreign Lang fel in Japanese, 65-67; sr res fel, Ctr Chinese Stud, Univ Calif Berkeley, 67-69; Social Sci Res Coun grant contemporary China, 71-72; SSHRC leave grant, 80-81; Japan Found res fel, 80-81; Pacific Cultur Found grant 82-83; Bilateral Exchange Grant SSHRC & Chinese Acad Soc Sci, 83-84, 86; res fel, Kyungnam Univ Inst Far Eastern Stud (Korea), 88; res fel, Int Cultur Soc Korea, 90; Japan Found fel, 93-94. **MEMBERSHIPS** Can Soc Chinese Stud (bd dir); Can Polit Sci Asn; Can Asian Stud Asn; Int Polit Sci Asn; Can Inst Strategic Stud; Japanese Stud Asn Can (pres 95-96). **SELECTED PUBLICATIONS** Auth, State-Building in Modern China: The Kuomintang in the Prewar Period, 81; auth, The Fragile Entente: the 1978 Japan-China Peace Treaty in a Global Context, 83; auth, The Transformation of South Korea: Reform and Reconstitution in the Sixth Republic Under Roh Tae Woo 1987-93, 94; ed, Confidence Building in the North Pacific: New Approaches to the Korean Peninsula, 96. **CONTACT ADDRESS** Dept of Political Science, Univ of Victoria, Victoria, BC, V8W 2Y2.

BEDFORD, HAROLD
PERSONAL Born 10/31/1929, Toronto, ON, Canada **DISCIPLINE** RUSSIAN & EAST EUROPEAN STUDIES **EDUCATION** Univ Toronto, BA, 51, MA, 52; Univ London, PhD, 56. **CAREER** Lectr, 55-59, asst prof, 59-64, assoc prof, 64-75, prof Slavic lang & lit, ctr Russian & E European stud, 75-95, PROF EMER, UNIV TORONTO, 95-. **MEMBERSHIPS** Can Friends Finland. **SELECTED PUBLICATIONS** Auth, The Seeker: D.S. Merezhkovskiy, 75. **CONTACT ADDRESS** Ctr Russian & East European Studies, Univ of Toronto, Toronto, ON, M5S 1A1.

BEDFORD, HENRY F.
PERSONAL Born 06/21/1931, Oskaloosa, IA, m, 1952, 4 children **DISCIPLINE** AMERICAN HISTORY **EDUCATION** Amherst Col, BA, 52; Univ WI, MA, 53; Univ MA, PhD(hist), 65. **CAREER** Chmn dept hist, 66-69, dean fac, 69-73, vprin, 79-82, MEM FAC HIST, PHILLIPS EXETER ACAD, 57-, Nat comt, Scholastic Aptitude Test, 77-81. **MEMBERSHIPS** AHA; Orgn Am Historians; New Eng Hist Asn. **RESEARCH** American socialism; American labor history; nineteenth century American history. **SELECTED PUBLICATIONS** Auth, The Union Divides, 63 & From Versailles to Nuremberg, 69, Macmillan; Socialism and the Workers in Massachusetts, 1886-1913, Univ MA, 66; coauth, The Americans: A Brief History, 72, 76 & 80 & Trouble Downtown, 78, Harcourt Brace Jovanovich; Wolf Creek Station-Kansas Gas and Electric Company in the Nuclear Era, with C. Miner, J of Am Hist, Vol 81, 95. **CONTACT ADDRESS** Dept of Hist, Phillips Exeter Acad, Exeter, NH, 03833.

BEDFORD, STEVEN M.
PERSONAL Born 10/03/1953, Norfolk, VA, m, 1986, 2 children **DISCIPLINE** HISTORY **EDUCATION** Columbia Univ PhD 94. **CAREER** Fitzgerald Halliday Inc, principle planner 98-; TAMS Consultants Inc, assoc 95-98; Trinity Col, freelance vis and adj positions, 85-93. **MEMBERSHIPS** SAH; US/ICOMOS: Ntl Council **RESEARCH** Architectural history, military and coldwar. **SELECTED PUBLICATIONS** Auth, The Dictionary of Art, forthcoming; John Russell Pope, Architect of Empire, NY Rizzoli 98; John Russell Pope Christopher Grant Lafarge and Palmer and Hornbostel IN: Mackay, Baker, Traynor eds, Long Island Country Houses and Their Architects, 1860-1940, NY Norton 97; Managing Travel in Connecticut: 100 Years of Progress, CT Dept of Trans 95. **CONTACT ADDRESS** Dept of History, Fordham Univ, 409 Sand Brook Rd, PO Box 7, Middlebury, CT, 06762. **EMAIL** bedford@aol.com

BEDOS-REZAK, BRIGITTE
PERSONAL Born 06/03/1953, Paris, France, m, 1980 **DISCIPLINE** HISTORY **EDUCATION** Ecole nationale de Chartes, Paris, Sorbonne, 77 **CAREER** Curator, Ctr Dept Seals, Nat Archive France, 77-80; vis curator/Mellon fel, dept Medieval art, Metrop Mus Art, 82-87; adj assoc prof, State Univ NY, Stony Brook, 85-87; dir, summer sem col teach, NEH, 87; vis assoc prof, 87-89, assoc prof, 89-94, dir grad stud, 90-93, PROF HIST, UNIV MD, COL PK, 94; aff prof, Jos & Rebecca Meyerhoff Ctr Jewish Stud, Univ Md, 95-; vis prof, Ecole Hautes Etudes Scis Soc, Paris, 95; mem Sch Hist Stud, Inst Adv Stud, Princeton, 96-97. **HONORS AND AWARDS** Univ Md, Col Pk, grad res bd, summer res award; NEH fel Ind Study, Res. **MEMBERSHIPS** NEH grant rev; ed bd, Historical Reflections/Reflexions historiques, 93-; rev, Cornell Univ Press; Medieval Acad Am; AHA; Apices; Asn Archivistes France; Columbia Univ Sem Medieval Stud; Int Ctr Medieval Art; Majestas; Medieval Acad Am; Soc l'Ecole Chartes; Soc Fr Hist Stud; Soc fr d'heraldique, sigillographic; Soc Nat Antiquaires France. **RESEARCH** Medieval civilization; hist anthro Middle Ages; medieval pol hist; medieval Fr soc, cult hist; medieval diplomatics, sigillography; Latin, old Fr paleography; women's stud medieval hist. **SELECTED PUBLICATIONS** Ed, contr, Polity and Place: Regionalism in Medieval France, Historical Reflection/Reflexions historiques, 19:2, 93; auth, Form and Order in Medieval France, Studies in Social and Quantitative Sigillography, Various, 93; Elements de semiotique medievale. Le cas des sceaux, L'Atelier du medieviste, forthcoming; auth, Form as Social Process, and Towards a Cultural Biography of the Gothic Cathedral: Reflections on History and Art History, in Artistic Integration in Gothic Buildings, Univ Toronto Press, 95; auth, Seals and Sigillography, Medieval France: An Encyclopedia, Garland, 95; auth, Montmorency, Lexicon des Mittelalters, vol 6, Artemis and Winkler, 93; auth, Secular Administration, Medieval Latin Studies: An Introduction and Bibliographical Guide, and Anthology of Medieval Latin, Catholic Univ Am Press, 97. **CONTACT ADDRESS** Dept of History, Univ of Maryland, College Park, MD, 20742. **EMAIL** bb54@umail.umd.edu

BEEBE, RALPH KENNETH
PERSONAL Born 02/14/1932, Caldwell, ID, m, 1953, 3 children **DISCIPLINE** AMERICAN HISTORY **EDUCATION** George Fox Col, AB, 54; Linfield Col, MEd, 55; Univ OR, MA, 69, PhD(curric & instr), 72. **CAREER** Dean of men, George Fox Univ, 55-57; teacher hist, Willamette High Sch, Eugene, OR, 57-66 & Churchill High Sch, Eugene, OR, 66; assoc prof, 74-80, prof 80-97, prof hist emer, George Fox Univ, 97-. **HONORS AND AWARDS** John Hay Fellow, summer 62; NEH Summer Seminars for Col Teachers, 76, 81; Christian Col Consortium travel/study grants, 86, 87; Northwest Yearly Meeting of Friends Church Social Service Award, 96; George Fox Univ John Woolman Peacemaking Award, 97. **MEMBERSHIPS** NEA; Orgn Am Historians; Friends Hist Asn; Conference on Faith and History; Asn for Preservation of Civil War Sites; Nat Museum of Civil War Medicine. **RESEARCH** 19th Century United States; inquiry teaching of history; Quaker history; Middle East. **SELECTED PUBLICATIONS** Auth, A Garden of the Lord: A History of Oregon Yearly Meeting of Friends Church, Barclay, 68; The Worker and Social Change: The Pullman Strike of 1894, Heath, 70; Thomas Jefferson, the Embargo and the Decision for Peace, Addison-Wesley, 72; coauth, Waging Peace, A study in Biblical Pacifism, Barclay Press, 80, 81; War Tax Concerns, 1986: Blessed are the Peacemakers, A Palestinian Christian in the Occupied West Bank, 90; auth, A History of George Fox College, Barclay, 91. **CONTACT ADDRESS** George Fox Univ, 414 N Meridan St, Newberg, OR, 97132-2625. **EMAIL** rbeebe@georgefox.edu

BEECHER, MAUREEN URSENBACH
PERSONAL Born 03/19/1935, Calgary, AB, Canada **DISCIPLINE** COMPARATIVE LITERATURE, WESTERN HISTORY **EDUCATION** Brigham Young Univ, BSc, 58; Univ UT, MA, 66, PhD(comp lit), 73. **CAREER** Res historian & ed western hist, Church of Jesus Christ Latter-Day Saints, 72-80; ASSOC PROF ENGLISH & RES HISTORIAN, BRIGHAM YOUNG UNIV, PROVO, UT, 80-. **HONORS AND AWARDS** John Whitmer Hist Asn Award, 78. **MEMBERSHIPS** AHA; Western Hist Asn; Mormon Hist Asn; Asn for Mormon Lett. **RESEARCH** History of women in America; history of Mormon women; literature of the Mormon movement. **SELECTED PUBLICATIONS** Auth, Three Women and the Life of the Mind, UT Hist Quart, winter 75; Letters From the Frontier: Commerce, Nauvoo and Salt Lake City, J of Mormon Hist, 75; Past and Present: Some Thoughts on Being a Mormon Woman, Sunstone, 76; Under the Sunbonnets: Mormon Women with Faces, BYU Studies, summer 76; contribr, The Oft-crossed Border: Canadians in Utah, In: The Peoples of Utah, Utah State His Soc, 76; contribr, Eliza R Snow, In: Mormon Sisters, Emmeline, 77; auth, The Eliza Enigma: The Life and Legend of Eliza R Snow, Dialogue: J Mormon Thought, reprinted in, Sister Saints, spring 78; contribr, Women in Twentieth Century Utah, In: Utah's History, Brigham Young Univ, 78; Tryed and Purified as Gold & 19th-Century Reminiscences and Diaries of Latter-Day Saints-Mormon Womens Lives, Brigham Young Univ Studies, Vol 34, 94; On Being Mormon in Canada and Canadian in Utah-Personal Essay, Brigham Young Univ Studies, Vol 36, 97. **CONTACT ADDRESS** Brigham Young Univ, Provo, UT, 84602.

BEECHERT, EDWARD D.
PERSONAL Born 06/10/1920, Hawthorne, CA, m, 1950, 3 children **DISCIPLINE** UNITED STATES ECONOMIC HISTORY, LATIN AMERICAN DEVELOPMENT **EDUCATION** Univ CA, Berkeley, MA, 50, PhD, 57. **CAREER** Instr hist, MX City Col, 53; instr hist & econ, Modesto Jr Col, 55-57; instr hist, Ventura Col, 57-60; asst prof soc sci, Sacramento State Col, 60-63; from asst prof to assoc prof hist, Univ HI, Hilo Campus, 63-66; assoc prof, St Mary's Col, CA, 66-68; assoc prof, 68-73, PROF HIST, UNIV HI, 73-, COORDR, PAC REGIONAL ORAL HIST PROG, 70-, Grant archaeol of Dos Pueblos, Samuel Mosher Found, 56-57; grant, Inst Am Hist, 64; staff mem Negro in Am econ, Inst Am Hist, Univ Calif, 65; grant for Hutchison Plantation Paper, Nat Arch, 76; Nat Endowment for Humanities grant, 77-78. **MEMBERSHIPS** Econ Hist Asn; Orgn Am Historians; Oral Hist Asn. **RESEARCH** Industrialization in developing areas; trade unions and economic development. **SELECTED PUBLICATIONS** Auth, The Gap Between Planning Goals and Achievements, Inter-Am Econ Rev, 6/66; Writing the History of Hawaiian Trade Unions, 67, coauth, American Trade Union Movement, 70, ed, History of the Honolulu Typographical Union, 70 & auth, A History of Local 5 (hotel workers), 70, Univ HI; Racial Divisions and Labor Organizing in Hawaii, Southwest Labor Hist Conf, 3/77; Labor Relations in Hawaii, 1850-1937, Univ CA, 80; The Filipino in the ILWU Philippines Study Association, Univ MI; Organizing Asian-American Labor-The Pacific Coast Canned Salmon Industry, 1870-1942, with C. Friday, Pacific Hist Rev, Vol 64, 95. **CONTACT ADDRESS** Dept of Hist, Univ of HI, Honolulu, HI, 96822.

BEER, FRANCIS A.
PERSONAL Born 02/05/1939, New York, NY, m, 1965, 3 children **DISCIPLINE** POLITICAL SCIENCE **EDUCATION** Harvard Univ, AB, 60; Berkeley Univ, MA, 63, PhD, 67. **CAREER** Asst Prof to Assoc Prof, Dept Govt, Univ Tex, 67-75; Prof Polit Sci, Univ Colo, 75-. **HONORS AND AWARDS** Undergrad Scholarship, Harvard Col, 57-58; Fulbright Fel, Fondation nationale des sciences politiques, Paris, 65-66; Doctoral Fel, Mershon Prog Educ Nat Security, Ohio State Univ, 66-67; Postdoctoral Schol, Inter-University Consortium for Polit Res, Univ Mich, 78; Fulbright Res Prof, John F. Kennedy Inst, Cath Univ, The Netherlands, 71; Vis Fel, Ctr Int Studies, Univ Cambridge, 82; Univ Colo, Col Arts & Sci, Dean's Writing Prize for Best Article, 87; Outstanding Prof, Univ Colo, Int Affairs Prog, 97; recipient of numerous grants. **MEMBERSHIPS** Am Polit Sci Asn; Int Polit Sci Asn; Int Soc Polit Psychol; Int Soc Study Europ Ideas; Int Soc Study Argumentation; Int Studies Asn. **SELECTED PUBLICATIONS** Auth, Integration and Disintegration in NATO: Processes of Alliance Cohesion and Prospects for Atlantic Community, Ohio State Univ Press, 69; Alliances: Latent War Communities in the Contemporary World, Holt, Rinehart, Winston, 70; The Political Economy of Alliances: Benefits, Costs, and Institutions in NATO, Sage, 75; How Much War in History: Definitions, Estimates Extrapolations, and Trends, Sage, 75; Peace Against War: The Ecology of International Violence, W. H. Freeman, 91; co-ed, Post-Realism: The Rhetorical Turn in International Relations, Mich State Univ Press, 96; author of numerous articles and other publications. **CONTACT ADDRESS** Political Science Dept, Univ Colo, Boulder, CO, 80309. **EMAIL** beer@spot.colorado.edu

BEERS, BURTON FLOYD
PERSONAL Born 09/13/1927, Chemung, NY, m, 1952, 2 children **DISCIPLINE** MODERN HISTORY **EDUCATION** Hobart Col, AB, 50; Duke Univ, MA, 52, PhD, 56. **CAREER** From instr to assoc prof, 55-66, Prof Hist, NC State Univ, 66-96, Fel, East Asian Studies, Harvard Univ, 59-60; Fulbright vis lect, Nat Taiwan Univ, 66-67; mem, Nat Adv Bd, China Coun, 78-81; Chief Exec ed, NC State Hum Pubs, 93-96; Prof Emer, 97-. **HONORS AND AWARDS** Phi Beta Kappa, Phi Kappa Phi, Alumni Distinquished Prof, NC State Univ, 70; Alexander Quarles Holladay Medal for Excellence, NC State Univ, 92; Medal for Excellence, Hobart, 94; NC Council for Soc Stud, 97; Watauga Medal, 98. **MEMBERSHIPS** AHA; Asn Asian Studies; Southern His Asn; Soc Hist Am For Rels, NC Literary and Hist Asn; World Hist Asn. **RESEARCH** Amer Far East policy; mod E Asia; world hist and geog. **SELECTED PUBLICATIONS** Auth, Vain Endeavor: Robert Lansing's Attempts to End the American Japanese Rivalry, Duke Univ, 62; China in Old Photographs, Scribner's, 78; coauth, The Far East: A History of the Western Impact and the Eastern Response, 1830-1965, 66-75; The Far East: A History of Western Impacts and Eastern Responses, 1830-1975, Prentice-Hall, 75; contribr, American East Asian Relations, Harvard Univ, 72;World History: Patterns of Civilization 1st-6th eds, 83-93; Chiliying: Life on a Chinese Commune, NCSU Col of Ed, 79; NCSU: A Pictorial history, 86; Teaching History and the Social Studies, Greenwood Publishing Group, 93; contribr, North Carolina Biographical Dictionary, UNC Press, 94; co-auth, Japan and Korea: Regional Studies Series, Globe Books, 93; Globe Fearon Historical Case Studies: The Vietnam War, 97. **CONTACT ADDRESS** 629 S Lakeshore Dr, Raleigh, NC, 27607. **EMAIL** Burtbeers@aol.com

BEETH, HOWARD
PERSONAL Born 02/05/1942, Petersburg, VA, s, 1 child **DISCIPLINE** U.S. HISTORY **EDUCATION** Temple Univ, BA, 66, MA, 68; Univ Houston, PhD, 84. **CAREER** Assoc prof, hist, Tex Southern Univ, Houston, 88-98. **HONORS AND AWARDS** School-of-the-Year Award, Tex Southern Univ, 92

MEMBERSHIPS SWestern Hist Asn (pres 95-96); Am Hist Asn; Friends Hist Asn; NC Friends Hist Soc. **RESEARCH** Southern history; African-American history; urban history. **SELECTED PUBLICATIONS** Co-ed, Black Dixie: Afro-Texan History and Culture in Houston, Tex A&M Univ Press, 92; auth, Historiographical Developments in Early North American Quaker Studies, The Southern Friend, 91; auth, A Black Elite Agenda in the Urban South: The Call for Political Change and Racial Economic Solidarity in Houston during the 1920's, Essays in Econ and Business Hist 10, 92; auth, How to Resist? Reformism vs. Communism in Houston's Black Press during the 1920s, Bringing the World Together: Proceedings of the Nat Asn African Am Studies, 96. **CONTACT ADDRESS** Dept Hist, Tex Southern Univ, 3100 Cleburne Ave, Houston, TX, 77004. **EMAIL** aashobeeth@tsu.edu

BEHRENDS, FREDERICK
PERSONAL Born 08/10/1934, Wilmington, NC **DISCIPLINE** MEDIEVAL HISTORY **EDUCATION** Belmont Abbey Col, AB, 58; Univ NC, MA, 60 PhD, 62. **CAREER** Asst prof hist, Univ SC, 61-62; asst prof, 62-67, assoc prof, 67-77, PROF HIST, UNIV NC, CHAPEL HILL, 77-. **MEMBERSHIPS** Mediaeval Acad Am. **RESEARCH** Fulbert of Chartres; France and Germany in the tenth and eleventh centuries. **SELECTED PUBLICATIONS** Letters and Poems of Fulbert of Chartres, Oxford, 76; Germany-France-the Birth of 2 Peoples (German), with C. Bruhl, Speculum-A J of Medieval Studies, Vol 69, 94. **CONTACT ADDRESS** 229 Severin St, Chapel Hill, NC, 27514.

BEIK, WILLIAM
DISCIPLINE HISTORY **EDUCATION** Haverford Col, BA, 63; Harvard Univ, MA, 66; PhD, 69. **CAREER** Prof **HONORS AND AWARDS** Herbert Baxter Adams Prize, Am Hist Assn. **RESEARCH** Early modern French social and institutional history. **SELECTED PUBLICATIONS** Auth, Absolutism and Society in Seventeenth-Century France: State Power and Provincial Aristocracy in Languedoc; Urban Protest in Seventeenth-Century France: the Culture of Retribution; co-ed, New Approaches to European History (series), Cambridge UP. **CONTACT ADDRESS** Dept History, Emory Univ, 221 Bowden Hall, 561 Kilgo Cir, Atlanta, GA, 30322-1950. **EMAIL** wbeik@emory.edu

BEINFELD, SOLON
PERSONAL Born 07/20/1934, New York, NY **DISCIPLINE** MODERN EUROPEAN HISTORY **EDUCATION** NY Univ, AB, 54; Harvard Univ, AM, 56, PhD(hist), 61. **CAREER** Asst prof, 61-70, ASSOC PROF HIST, WASH UNIV, 70-. **MEMBERSHIPS** AHA. **RESEARCH** Modern European history, especially France, Germany and diplomacy. **SELECTED PUBLICATIONS** Auth, Dimensions of the Holocaust-The Number of Jewish Victims Under National-Socialism (German), with W. Benz, Jahrbucher Fur Geschite Osteuropas, Vol 41, 93. **CONTACT ADDRESS** Washington Univ, St Louis, MO, 63130.

BEISNER, ROBERT L.
PERSONAL Born 03/08/1936, Lexington, NE, m, 1976, 2 children **DISCIPLINE** AMERICAN HISTORY **EDUCATION** Univ Chicago, MA, 60, PhD(hist), 65. **CAREER** Instr soc sci, Univ Chicago, 62-63; instr hist, Colgate Univ, 63-65; from asst prof to assoc prof, 65-71, Prof Hist, American Univ, 71-98, Chmn, 81-90, EMERITUS, 98-; Nat Endowment for Humanities Younger Scholar's fel, 68-69. **HONORS AND AWARDS** Nevins Prize, Soc Am Historians, 66; John H Dunning Prize, AHA, 68. **MEMBERSHIPS** Orgn Am Historians; Soc Am Historians; Soc Historians of Am Foreign Rels; Acad Polit Sci. **RESEARCH** United States diplomatic history; Dean Acheson. **SELECTED PUBLICATIONS** Auth, Twelve Against Empire: The Anti-Imperialists, 1898-1900, McGraw, 68; From the Old Diplomacy to the New, 1865-1900, Am Hist Ser, Harlan Davidson, Inc, 75, 2nd ed, 86; History and Henry Kissinger, Diplomatic History, fall 90; Patterns of Peril: Dean Acheson Joins the Cold Warriors, 1945-46, Diplomatic Hist, summer 96; Dean Acheson's Alger Hiss, Weekly Standard, 12/2/96. **CONTACT ADDRESS** 3851 Newark St, NW, Washington, DC, 20016-3026.

BELFIORE, ELIZABETH STAFFORD
PERSONAL Born 06/21/1944, Austin, TX **DISCIPLINE** CLASSICAL LANGUAGE, PHILOSOPHY **EDUCATION** Barnard Col, AB, 66; Univ Calif, Los Angeles, MA, 74, PhD(classics), 78. **CAREER** Asst prof, Scripps Col, 79-80, asst prof to assoc prof 80-93, PROF CLASSICS UNIV MINN, 93-. **HONORS AND AWARDS** ACLU 85-86. **MEMBERSHIPS** Am Philol Asn; Class Asn MidWest & South; Women's Class Caucus; Soc Ancient Greek Philos **RESEARCH** Ancient philosophy; Greek tragedy. **SELECTED PUBLICATIONS** Auth, A Theory of Imitation in Plato's Republic, TAPA, 84; Wine and Catharsis of the Emotions in Plato's Laws, CQ, 86; Tragic Pleasures: Aristotlean Plot and Emotion, Princeton, 92; Xenia in Sophocles' Philoctetes, CJ, 94; Harming Friends: Problematic Reciprocity in Greek Tragedy, In: Reciprocity in Ancient Greece, Oxford, 98. **CONTACT ADDRESS** Dept of Classical & Near East Studies, Univ of Minn, 9 Pleasant St SE, Minneapolis, MN, 55455-0194. **EMAIL** esb@maroon.tc.umn.edu

BELISLE, JEAN
DISCIPLINE ART HISTORY **EDUCATION** Univ de Paris IV, PhD, 83. **CAREER** Dept Art Hist, Concordia Univ **HONORS AND AWARDS** Award, Quebec Sci Tchr(s) Assn. **RESEARCH** Canadian art, industrial archaeology and sculpture. **SELECTED PUBLICATIONS** Co-auth, La sculpture traditionelle au Quebec, Di L'omme, 96; auth, A propos d'un bateau a vapeur, HMH, 94. **CONTACT ADDRESS** Dept Art Hist, Concordia Univ, Montreal, 1455 de Maisonneuve W, Montreal, PQ, H3G 1M8.

BELL, ANDREW J.E.
DISCIPLINE HISTORY **EDUCATION** Stanford Univ, PhD, 94. **CAREER** Asst prof,Columbia Col Columbia. **SELECTED PUBLICATIONS** Auth, pubs on Ancient Greece and Rome, and Ancient Mediterranean. **CONTACT ADDRESS** History Dept, Univ Nev Las Vegas, 4505 Md Pky, Las Vegas, NV, 89154.

BELL, BARBARA MOSALLAI
PERSONAL Born 11/19/1937, Indianapolis, IN, m, 1975, 3 children **DISCIPLINE** PSYCHOLOGY **EDUCATION** PhD 63, MA 59, Univ of Tehran. **CAREER** Prof Psychol Univ of Iran, Therapist, Private Practice, Houston, Writer. **MEMBERSHIPS** Writer's Guild of Las Vegas, Intl Wonens Writers Guild. **RESEARCH** Psychol-in most all fields. **SELECTED PUBLICATIONS** Auth of,The Peacock Princess, 95; True Story of my Life in Iran. **CONTACT ADDRESS** 3001 Lake East Dr Apt 1137, Las Vegas, NV, 89117. **EMAIL** B. Bell26846@AOL.com

BELL, DIANE
PERSONAL Born 06/11/1943, Melbourne, Australia, d, 2 children **DISCIPLINE** ANTHROPOLOGY **EDUCATION** Frankstons Tchr Col, Victoria, TPTC, 61; Monash Univ, Victoria, BA, 76; Australian Nat Univ, PhD, 81. **CAREER** Henry R Luce Prof Relig, Econ Develop & Soc Justice, Holy Cross Col, 89-98; dir Womens Stud Prog & Prof Anthrop, George Wash Univ, 99-; finalist Staley Award. **MEMBERSHIPS** Am Anthrop Asn; Am Acad Relig; Australian Anthrop Soc; Australian Inst Aboriginal & Torres Straits Is Stud. **RESEARCH** Indigenous peoples; Land rights; Law reform; Feminist theory and practice; Human rights; Comparative religion. **SELECTED PUBLICATIONS** Auth Daughters of the Dreaming, Univ Minn Press, 93; coed Gendered Fields: Women, Men & ethnogr aphy, Routledge, 93; coed Radically Speaking: Feminism Reclaimed, Spinifex Press, 96; Ngarrindjeri Wurruwarrin: A World that is, was, and will be, Spinifex Press, 98. **CONTACT ADDRESS** 43 Burncoat Lane, Leicester, MA, 01524. **EMAIL** dbell@gwu.edu

BELL, JAMES BRUGLER
PERSONAL Born 04/17/1932, St. Paul, MN, m, 1957, 4 children **DISCIPLINE** HISTORY **EDUCATION** Univ MN, Minneapolis, BA, 55; Episcopal Theol Sch, MDiv, 61; Balliol Col, Oxford, DPhil (mod hist), 64. **CAREER** Instr hist, OH State Univ, 64-67; vis lectr, Col Wooster, 67; res fel & lectr, Princeton Univ, 67-69; DIR & LIBRN, NEW ENG HIST GENEAL SOC, 73-, Nat Hist Publ Comn fel, 67-68; chmn, Commonwealth MA Arch Adv Comn, 74-; comnr, MA Hist Comn, 74-78. **MEMBERSHIPS** Orgn Am Historians; AHA; fel Soc Antiquaries; Am Antiquarian Soc. **RESEARCH** Eighteenth century American and English history. **SELECTED PUBLICATIONS** Contribr, Charles P McIlvaine, In: For the Union: Ohio Leaders in the Civil War, OH State Univ, 68; Anglican Clergy in Colonial America Ordained by Bishops of London, Proc Am Antiq Soc, 73; Anglican Quilldrivers in Eighteenth Century America, Hist Mag Protestant Episcopal Church, 74; auth, Portraits at the New England Historic Genealogical Society, 11/76 & Furniture at the New England Historic Genealogical Society, 5/78, Antiques Mag; contribr, Richard Rush: Spokesman for the Administration, July 4, 1812, Colonial Soc Mass, 78; Searching for Your Ancestors, Family Hist Rec Bk, 81; Waiting for Mario, The Esopositos, Joyce, and Beckett, Eire-Ireland, Vol 30, 95. **CONTACT ADDRESS** New England Historical Genealogical Society, Newbury St, Boston, MA, 02116.

BELL, JOHN D.
DISCIPLINE HISTORY **EDUCATION** Princeton Univ, PhD. **CAREER** Prof, Univ MD Baltimore County . **RESEARCH** Russ and East Europ hist. **SELECTED PUBLICATIONS** Auth, Peasants in Power and The Bulgarian Communist Party from Blagoev to Zhivkov; pubs on Bulgaria and its history; co-auth, Bulgaria's Road from Dictatorship to Democracy. **CONTACT ADDRESS** Dept of Hist, Univ MD Baltimore County, Hilltop Circle, PO Box 1000, Baltimore, MD, 21250. **EMAIL** bell@umbc2.umbc.edu

BELL, JOHN P.
DISCIPLINE HISTORY **EDUCATION** Tulane Univ, PhD, 68. **CAREER** Prof. **SELECTED PUBLICATIONS** Auth, Crisis in Costa Rica: the 1948 Revolution. **CONTACT ADDRESS** Dept of History, Indiana Univ-Purdue Univ, Fort Wayne, 2101 Coliseum Blvd, Fort Wayne, IN, 46805. **EMAIL** bellj@smtplink.ipfw.edu

BELL, KATIE ROBERSON
PERSONAL Born 06/14/1936, Birmingham, AL, m **DISCIPLINE** EDUCATION **EDUCATION** AL State Coll, BS 1956, EdS 1977; Wayne State Univ, MSLA 1973; Univ of AL, PhD 1982. **CAREER** Tuskegee Inst HS, librarian 1956-59; Parker HS, asst librarian 1959-70, librarian 1970-73; AL State Univ, asst ref lib 1973-74, coord of user serv 1974-75, coord lib educ 1975-; So AL Reg Inserv Educ Ctr, dir 1985; AL STATE UNIV, PROF OF LIB EDUC 1985-. **HONORS AND AWARDS** Cert of Honor Birmingham Classroom Teachers Assoc 1970; Educator of the Year Area of Instructional Leadership/ Univ of AL 1981; Identification of Activities in Staff Capstone Journal 1982; Development Progs for Secondary Educ Teachers. **MEMBERSHIPS** Consultant ESAA Task Force ASU & Mobile Sch System 1979-82; Comm Tutorial Prog/ Links Inc 1982-84; evaluator Natl Council for the Accreditation of Teacher Educ 1983-; bd mem pres elect AL Instructional Media Assoc 1984-; counselor Nu Epsilon Chap Kappa Delta Pi 1984-; evaluator S Assn of Schs & Colls 1985-; bd mem Montgomery Comm Council of the United Way 1985-; area director, The Links, Inc., southern area director, 1991-94. **CONTACT ADDRESS** Library Educ, Alabama State Univ, 915 S Jackson St, Montgomery, AL, 36195.

BELL, LELAND V.
PERSONAL Born 03/02/1934, Johnson City, NY, m, 1961, 2 children **DISCIPLINE** AMERICAN CIVILIZATION, MODERN EUROPEAN HISTORY **EDUCATION** Wayne State Univ, AB, 58; PA State Univ, AM, 61; WV Univ, PhD(hist), 68. **CAREER** Instr hist, Jr Col Kansas City, 62-64; asst prof, West Liberty State Col, 64-66; instr, WV Univ, 67-68; PROF HIST, CENT STATE UNIV, OH, 68-, Adj prof, Sch Community Educ, Wittenberg Univ, 70-71, Wright State Univ, 73, Union Grad Sch, 73, Univ Dayton, 76 & Antioch Col, 76; proj dir, OH Prog Humanities, 79-80. **HONORS AND AWARDS** Outstanding Educr of Am, 74-75. **MEMBERSHIPS** AHA; Am Asn Hist Med; Cheiron; Orgn Am Historians. **RESEARCH** Intellectual history; history of mental health, history of technology. **SELECTED PUBLICATIONS** In Hitler's Shadow, The Anatomy of American Nazism, Kennikat, 73; The Failure of Nazism in America: the German American Bund, 1936-1941, Polit Sci Quart, 70; Death in the Technocracy, J Human Rels, 70; Violence in Contemporary American Art, IL Quart, 73; Treating the Mentally Ill, From Colonial Times to the Present, Praeger, 80 Colonial Psychiatry and the African Mind, with J. McCullock, Int J of African Historical Studies, Vol 29, 97. **CONTACT ADDRESS** PO Box 271, Yellow Springs, OH, 45387.

BELL, REVA PEARL
PERSONAL Born 08/17/1925, Marshall, TX, m **DISCIPLINE** EDUCATION **EDUCATION** Bishop Coll, BS 1947; TX Christian Univ, MEd 1965; TX Woman's Univ, PhD 1980. **CAREER** Ft Worth Public Schools, teacher, curriculum writer, curriculum content analyst, head teacher early childhood learning center; SW Educ Devel Lab, curriculum coord; TX Christian Univ, instructor. **HONORS AND AWARDS** Concepts & lang prog co-author SW Educ Devel Lab 1974; Getting Started co-author Natl Educ Lab Publishers 1975; Natl Sic Found Grant N TX State Univ. **MEMBERSHIPS** Consult SW Educ Devel Lab; consult Indian & Migrants Div OCD; consult Early Childhood Parent Prog; treas/bd of dirs Winnie-the-Pooh Day Care Ctr 1978-79; day care ctr educ chairperson task force Amer Heart Assn 1979-; Curriculum Guide for Early Childhood Ft Worth Pub Schs 1972. **CONTACT ADDRESS** Texas Christian Univ, 2900 S University Dr, Fort Worth, TX, 76129.

BELL, RUDOLPH MARK
PERSONAL Born 11/05/1942, New York, NY, m, 1964, 2 children **DISCIPLINE** SOCIAL & CULTURAL HISTORY **EDUCATION** Queens Col, NY, BA, 63; City Univ New York, PhD, 69. **CAREER** From instr to asst prof, 68-73, assoc prof, 73-80, prof hist, Rutgers Univ, 80-, Fulbright-Hays lectr, Univ Genoa, 71-72. **MEMBERSHIPS** AHA. **RESEARCH** Italy; sixteenth-century Europe. **SELECTED PUBLICATIONS** Auth, Party and Faction in American Politics: The House of Representatives, 1789-1801, 73; "The Transformation of a Rural Village, Istria, 1870-1972, Journal of Social History, spring 74; Fate and Honor, Family and Village: Demographic and Cultural Change in Modern Rural Italy, Univ Chicago, 79; coauth, Saints and Society, Univ Chicago, 83; auth, Holy Anorexia, Univ Chicago, 85; auth, How To Do It, Univ Chicago, 99. **CONTACT ADDRESS** Dept of History, Rutgers Univ, 16 Seminary Pl, New Brunswick, NJ, 08901-1108. **EMAIL** rbell@rci.rutgers.edu

BELL, SUSAN GROAG
PERSONAL Czechoslovakia **DISCIPLINE** HISTORY OF WOMEN **EDUCATION** Stanford Univ, AB, 64; Univ Santa Clara, MA, 70. **CAREER** Adj lectr, Univ Santa Clara, 71-81; LECTR HIST, STANFORD UNIV, 82-, Affiliated scholar, Ctr Res on Women, Stanford Univ, 78-. **MEMBERSHIPS** AHA; Conf British Studies; Coord Comt Women in the Hist Profession; Western Asn Women Historians; Garden Hist Soc. **RESEARCH** European and British women's intellectual history; history of women as gardeners; history of women and literacy. **SELECTED PUBLICATIONS** Auth, Johann Eberlin von

G?nzburg's Wolfaria, Church Hist, 67; co-ed, Second Careers for Women: A View from the San Francisco Peninsula, Stanford, 71; auth, Discovering Women's History Through Art in the Classroom, The Hist Teacher, 73; Women: From the Greeks to the French Revolution, Wadsworth Publ Co, 73 & Stanford Univ Press, 80; Christine de Pizan, 1364-1430: Humanism and the Problem of a Studious Woman, Feminist Studies, 76; Lady Warwick: Aristocrat, Socialist Gardener, San Jose Studies, 82; Medieval Women Bookowners: Arbiters of Lay Piety and Ambassadors of Culture, Signs: J of Women in Culture and Soc, 82; coauth, Women, the Family and Freedom: 1750-1950; The Debate in Documents, 2 Vols, Stanford Univ Press; The Womens Movements in the United States and Britain from the 1790's to the 1920's, with C. Bolt, Albion, Vol 26, 94. **CONTACT ADDRESS** Ctr for Res on Women, Stanford Univ, 1 Stanford Universit, Stanford, CA, 94305-1926.

BELL, WILLIAM DUDLEY
PERSONAL Born 03/13/1931, Macon, MS, m, 1960, 2 children **DISCIPLINE** UNITED STATES HISTORY **EDUCATION** MS State Univ, BA, 53, BS, 58, MA, 62; LA State Univ, PhD(hist), 73. **CAREER** Assoc prof hist, Athens Col, 65-73; asst prof, 73-76, ASSOC PROF HIST, MERIDIAN BR, MI STATE UNIV, 76-, COORD LIB ARTS PROG, 73-, Adv, Ala Hist Comn, 66-. **MEMBERSHIPS** Southern Hist Asn; Am Asn State & Local Hist. **RESEARCH** United States 19th century; Civil War and Reconstruction; Ku Klux Klan; Mississippi military history. **SELECTED PUBLICATIONS** Auth, Edward James, Smithsonian, Vol 25, 94. **CONTACT ADDRESS** Dept of Hist, Mississippi State Univ, Hwy 19 N, Meridian, MS, 39301.

BELL, WILLIAM GARDNER
PERSONAL Born 10/29/1914, New York, NY, m, 1947, 1 child **DISCIPLINE** MILITARY HISTORY **CAREER** Assoc ed, Armored Cavalry J, 47-50; ed, Armor Mag, 50-53; mil historian, Off Chief Mil Hist, US Dept Army, 56-59, br & div chief, 59-62; MIL HISTORIAN, US ARMY CTR MIL HIST, 63-, Ed, Dept Army Hist Summary, 69-74, contribr, 75-78. **MEMBERSHIPS** AHA, Western Hist Asn; Western Lit Asn; US Comn Mil Hist; Soc Hist in Fed Govt. **RESEARCH** Army-Indian frontier campaigns; Snake River Basin; Western art. **SELECTED PUBLICATIONS** Auth, Society and Journal of the Mounted Arm, Armor Mag, 58; Frontier Lawman, Am West, 64; The Snake: A Noble and Various River, Potomac Corral, Westerners, 69; contribr, American Military History, Off Chief Mil Hist, US Army, 69; John Gregory Bourke: A Soldier-Scientist on the Frontier, Potomac Corral, Westerners, 78; Quarters One: The United States Army Chief of Staff's Residence, Fort Myer, Va, US Army Ctr Mil Hist, 81; A Rebirth of Classic Western Art, Southwest Art, 82; Secretaries of War and Secretaries of the Army: Portraits and Biographical Sketches, US Army Ctr Mil Hist, 82; Commanding Generals and Chiefs of Staff: Portraits and Biographical Sketches, US Army Ctr Mil Hist; My Interest Lays Toward the Horse-Canadian-Born Author, Artist, and Horseman, Will James Changed His Name, His Country, and His Language to Follow His Dream of Becoming a Genuine American Cowboy, Am Hist, Vol 31, 96. **CONTACT ADDRESS** US Army Ctr of Mil Hist, 1000 Independence Ave SW, Washington, DC, 20314.

BELL CHAMBERS, MARJORIE
DISCIPLINE HISTORY **EDUCATION** Mt. Holyoke Col, BA; Cornell Univ, MA; Univ NMex, PhD. **CAREER** Prof. **RESEARCH** Contemporary American history; Soviet and Chinese studies; European history; social, intellectual, and women's History; history of art. **SELECTED PUBLICATIONS** Auth, pubs about women's striving for equal opportunity and citizenship. **CONTACT ADDRESS** History Dept, Union Inst, 440 E McMillan St, Cincinnati, OH, 45206-1925.

BELLAMY, DONNIE DUGLIE
PERSONAL Born 09/13/1938, Jacksonville, NC, m, 1959, 2 children **DISCIPLINE** POLITICAL SCIENCE, AMERICAN HISTORY **EDUCATION** NC Cent Univ, AB, 62, MA, 64; Univ Mo-Columbia, PhD, 70. **CAREER** Instr soc sci, Lincoln Univ, Mo, 63-64; instr soc sci, 64-67, from asst prof to assoc prof hist, 67-75, chmn dept hist, 73-, chmn div soc sci, 74-, prof hist, 75, Regents prof hist, 81-, Fort Valley State Col. **HONORS AND AWARDS** Ford Found fel hist, 68-70. **MEMBERSHIPS** Southern Hist Assn; Assn Study Afro-Am Life & Hist; Gd Assn of Historians. **RESEARCH** Education of Blacks; slavery; Antebellum. **SELECTED PUBLICATIONS** Art, Legal Status of Black Georgians during the Colonial and Revolutionary Eras, Journal of Negro History; auth, Light in the Valley: A Pictorial History of Fort Valley State College Since 1985, Donning Company Publishers, 96; auth, From Slavery to Freedom: A Pictorial History of Shish Missionary Baptist Church Since 1863, Donning Company Publishers, 98. **CONTACT ADDRESS** Fort Valley State Univ, 1005 State Univ Dr, Box 4456, Fort Valley, GA, 31030-3298.

BELLAMY, EVERETT
PERSONAL Born 12/29/1949, Chicago, Illinois, d **DISCIPLINE** EDUCATION **EDUCATION** University of Wisconsin, BS, 1972, MS, 1974; Cleveland State University, JD, 1980; Cleveland-Marshall College of Law. **CAREER** University of Wisconsin, graduate assistant; Cleveland State University, coordinator of student activities; Charles Hamilton Houston Pre-Law Institute, instructor and assistant executive director; Georgetown University Law Center, assistant dean, adjunct professor. **HONORS AND AWARDS** Honors Cert, Montgomery County, MD, 1996. **MEMBERSHIPS** National Bar Association, 1986-; American Bar Association, 1984-; National Conference of Black Lawyers, DC Chapter, chairperson, 1981-83; Phi Alpha Delta Law Fraternity International, 1980-. **SELECTED PUBLICATIONS** "The Status of the African American Law Professors," 1990; "Academic Enhancement and Counseling Programs," 1991; Where We Stand: African American Law Professors Demographies, 1992. **CONTACT ADDRESS** Law Ctr, Georgetown Univ, 600 New Jersey Ave, Ste 304, Washington, VT, 20001.

BELLEGARDE-SMITH, PATRICK
PERSONAL Born 08/08/1947, Spokane, WA **DISCIPLINE** AFRICAN HISTORY **EDUCATION** Syracuse Univ, BA 1968; The Amer Univ, MA, PhD 1977. **CAREER** Howard Univ Dept of Romance Languages, lecturer 1977; Bradley Univ Inst of Intl Studies, assoc prof 1978-86; The Univ of WI-Milwaukee, prof of Dept of Africology, 1986-. **MEMBERSHIPS** Amer Association of University Professors; African Studies Association, Association of Caribbean Studies; National Council for Black Studies; National Conf of Black Political Scientists; Association of Caribbean Historians; Latin Amer Studies Assn. **SELECTED PUBLICATIONS** Auth, "In the Shadow of Powers, Dantes Bellegarde in Haitian Social Thought" Atlantic Highlands, Humanities Press 1985; "Haiti: The Breached Citadel," Westview Press 1990; "Fragments of Bone: African Religions in the Americas," Univ Press of Florida, 1999. **CONTACT ADDRESS** Dept of Africology, Univ of Wisconsin, PO Box 413, Milwaukee, WI, 53201. **EMAIL** pbs@uwm.edu

BELLESILES, MICHAEL A.
DISCIPLINE HISTORY **EDUCATION** Univ Calif Santa Cruz, BA, 75; Univ Calif Irvine, PhD, 86. **CAREER** Assoc prof **RESEARCH** Early American history, focusing on the Revolution; the early Republic; constitutional law; origins of American gun culture. **SELECTED PUBLICATIONS** Auth, Revolutionary Outlaws: Ethan Allen and the Struggle for Independence on the Early American Frontier. **CONTACT ADDRESS** Dept History, Emory Univ, 221 Bowden Hall, 561 Kilgo Cir, Atlanta, GA, 30322-1950. **EMAIL** mbelles@emory.edu

BELLINZONI, ARTHUR J.
PERSONAL Brooklyn, NY **DISCIPLINE** HISTORY AND PHILOSOPHY OF RELIGION **EDUCATION** Princeton Univ, AB; Harvard Univ, MA, PhD. **CAREER** PROF RELIG, DIR PLANNED AND LEADERSHIP GIVING, WELLS COL **HONORS AND AWARDS** Exxon Educational Found Travel Grant for study in Israel; Ruth and Albert Koch Prof of Humanities, Wells Coll **MEMBERSHIPS** Soc Bibl Lit; Am Acad Relig; Am School Orient Res; Novi Testamenti Studiorum Soc. **RESEARCH** Old Testament; New Testament; Second Century; Middle East; Major Gift Fund Development. **SELECTED PUBLICATIONS** The Sayings of Jesus in the Writings of Justin Martyr, Brill; Intellectual Honesty and Religious Commitment, Fortress Press; The Two Source Hupothesis: A Critical Appraisal, Mercer University Press; The Influence of the Gospel of Matthew on Christian Literature Before Saint Irenaeus, Mercer Univ Press; "The Source of the Agraphon in Justin Martyr's Dialogue with Trypho 47:5," in Virgilae Christianae. **CONTACT ADDRESS** PO Box 5, Aurora, NY, 13026.

BELLMAN, JONATHAN
PERSONAL Born 08/15/1957, Fresno, CA, m, 1 child **DISCIPLINE** MUSICOLOGY **EDUCATION** Univ Calif,BA,79; Univ Ill,MM,82; Stanford Univ,DMA,90. **CAREER** Asst prof, Univ Richmond, 90-92; assoc prof, Univ N Colo, 93-. **RESEARCH** Music style; Hungarian-Gypsy music; Musical exoticism; Chopin; 19th-century music; Piano performance practices; Rock music. **SELECTED PUBLICATIONS** Auth, The Style Hongrois in the Music of Western Europe, 93; ed, The Exotic in Western Music, 98, Northeastern Univ. **CONTACT ADDRESS** School of Music, Univ Northern Colo, Greeley, CO, 80639. **EMAIL** jdbellm@bentley.unco.edu

BELLOT, LELAND JOSEPH
PERSONAL Born 12/10/1936, Port Arthur, TX, m, 1958, 2 children **DISCIPLINE** HISTORY **EDUCATION** Lamar State Col, BA, 58; Rice Inst, MA, 60; Univ Tex, Austin, PhD(hist), 67. **CAREER** From asst prof to assoc prof hist, 64-74, PROF HIST & DEAN HUMANITIES & SOC SCI, CALIF STATE UNIV, FULLERTON, 74- **MEMBERSHIPS** AHA; Conf Brit Stud. **RESEARCH** Modern British history, 18th century; Anglo Amer history; comparative slavery. **SELECTED PUBLICATIONS** Auth, Wild Hares and Red Herrings, A Case-Study of Estate Management in the 18th-Century English Countryside, Huntington Libr Quart, Vol 0056, 93. **CONTACT ADDRESS** California State Univ, Fullerton, Fullerton, CA, 92634.

BELLUSH, BERNARD
PERSONAL Born 11/15/1917, New York, NY, m, 1947, 2 children **DISCIPLINE** HISTORY **EDUCATION** City Col New York, BSS, 41; Columbia Univ, MA, 43, PhD(hist), 51. **CAREER** Tutor, Hunter Col, 46-49; asst prof, 51-61, assoc prof & sub-chmn dept, 61-68, PROF HIST, CITY COL NEW YORK, 68-, Lectr, Ballard Sch, YWCA, 50-53; Am Philos Soc grants, 59-60 & 62; lectr, Teachers Col, Columbia Univ, 60, vis assoc prof, 64-66; lectr, Cooper Union, 61; Fulbright prof, State Univ Utrecht, 66-67 & 70-71; mem nat bd, Am for Democratic Action, 71-, NY State chmn, 71-73. **MEMBERSHIPS** AHA; Orgn Am Historians; Am Civil Liberties Union. **RESEARCH** Franklin D Roosevelt and the New Deal area; John G Winant, governor of New Hampshire; Robert P Bass and the Progressive Era. **SELECTED PUBLICATIONS** Auth, Goy Vey Response to Simurda,Stephen Article on Handler, Evelyn, Lingua Fr, Vol 0003, 93. **CONTACT ADDRESS** Dept of Hist, City Col, CUNY, Convent Ave at 138th St, New York, NY, 10031.

BELSLEY, DAVID A.
PERSONAL Born 05/24/1939, Chicago, IL, m, 1961, 2 children **DISCIPLINE** ECONOMICS; ECONOMETRICS **EDUCATION** Haverford Col, BA, 61; Mass Inst of Tech, PhD, 65. **CAREER** Asst Prof, 65-66, 66-69, Assoc Prof, 69-74, Prof, 74-, Boston Col. **HONORS AND AWARDS** Grad Honors, Haverford Col, 65; Phi Beta Kappa; Grad Fellow, NSF, 61-65; Fellow, J of Econometrics, 88; Adv Coun, Soc for Computational Econ. **MEMBERSHIPS** Am Econ Asn; Soc for Computational Econ. **RESEARCH** Computational economics & econometrics. **SELECTED PUBLICATIONS** Ed, Computational Techniques for Econometrics and Economic Analysis, Kluwer Acad Pub, 94; auth, Assessing the Value of Zero-Padding when Testing for Serial Correlation Using Artificial Regressions, Computational Econ & Stat at the Certosa, 9, 181-198, 96; Auth, Computational Economics in Geneva, vol 1, 10, 97, vol 2 , forthcoming. **CONTACT ADDRESS** 33 Bolton Rd, Newtonville, MA, 01260-2130. **EMAIL** belsley@bc.edu

BELTMAN, BRIAN WILLIAM
PERSONAL Born 10/05/1945, Orange City, IA **DISCIPLINE** AMERICAN HISTORY **EDUCATION** Northwestern Col, Iowa, BA, 67; Univ Wis-Madison, MA, 69, PhD(hist), 74. **CAREER** Res historian immigration, State Hist Soc Wis, 74-75; asst prof hist, Hamilton Col, 75-76, Dartmouth Col, 76-77 & Ariz State Univ, 77-78; res historian rural hist, Univ Mid-Am, 78-79; asst prof, 79-80, LECTR HIST, UNIV SC, 80-, Legal specialist, SC Elec & Gas Co, 80- **MEMBERSHIPS** Orgn Am Historians. **RESEARCH** Rural social history; agricultural history; Amer West. **SELECTED PUBLICATIONS** Auth, Born in the Country in a Hist of Rural America, J of Southern Hist, Vol 0063, 97. **CONTACT ADDRESS** Univ S Carolina, 3623 Yale Ave, Columbia, SC, 29208.

BELZ, HERMAN JULIUS
PERSONAL Born 09/13/1937, Camden, NJ, m, 1961, 2 children **DISCIPLINE** AMERICAN NINETEENTH CENTURY & CONSTITUTIONAL HISTORY **EDUCATION** Princeton Univ, AB, 59; Univ Wash, MA, 63, PhD(hist), 66. **CAREER** From asst prof to assoc prof, 66-77, univ res bd grant, 68, PROF HIST, UNIV MD, COLLEGE PARK, 77-; Am Philos Soc grant, 72; Am Bar Found legal hist merit res fel, 72-73; Guggenheim fel, 80-81; Project 87 fel, 80-81; academic advisor, James Madison Memorial Fel Found. **HONORS AND AWARDS** Beveridge Award, AHA, 66. **MEMBERSHIPS** AHA; Orgn Am Historians; Am Soc Legal Hist; Southern Hist Asn. **RESEARCH** Constitutionalism and political action; the legitimacy of Supreme Court decision making; secession, revolution, and social contract theory in Am political thought. **SELECTED PUBLICATIONS** Auth, Changing Conceptions of Constitutionalism in the Era of World War Two and the Cold War, J Am Hist, 12/72; The New Orthodoxy in Reconstruction Historiography, Rev Am Hist, 3/73; New Left Reverberations in the Academy: The Anti-pluralist Critique of Constitutionalism, Rev Polit, 4/74; The Freedmen's Bureau Act of 1865 and the Principle of No Discrimination According to Color, Civil War Hist, 9/75; Protection of Personal Liberty in Republican Emancipation Legislation of 1862, J Southern Hist, 8/76; Race, Law, and Politics in the Struggle for Equal Pay during the Civil War, Civil War Hist, 9/76; A New Birth of Freedom: The Republican Party and Freedmen's Rights 1861-1866, Greenwood, 76; Emancipation and Equal Rights: Politics and Constitutionalism in the Civil War Era, Norton, 78; coauth, The American Constitution: Its Origins and Development, W. W. Norton, 91; Equality Transformed: A Quarter Century of Affirmative Action, Transaction Pubs, 91; Abraham Lincoln, Constitutionalism and Equal Rights in the Civil War Era, Fordham Univ Press, 98. **CONTACT ADDRESS** Dept of Hist, Univ of MD, College Park, MD, 20742-0001. **EMAIL** hb5@umail.umd.edu

BEN-ATAR, DORON
DISCIPLINE AMERICAN HISTORY **EDUCATION** Columbia Univ, PhD. **CAREER** Assoc prof, Fordham Univ. **RESEARCH** Psychohistory. **SELECTED PUBLICATIONS** Auth, The Origins of Jeffersonian Commercial Policy and Diplomacy, 93; Alexander Hamilton's Alternative Technology Piracy and the Report on Manufactures, William and Mary Quart 52, 95; Private Friendship and Political Harmony?, Rev(s) Amer Hist, 96. **CONTACT ADDRESS** Dept of Hist, Fordham Univ, 113 W 60th St, New York, NY, 10023.

BEN-GHIAT, RUTH
PERSONAL Born 05/17/1960, Evanston, IL, s **DISCIPLINE** HISTORY **EDUCATION** UCLA, BA, 81; Brandeis Univ, PhD, 91. **CAREER** Asst prof, Univ NC at Charlotte, 91-95; asst prof, Fordham Univ, 95-98; assoc prof, 98- . **HONORS AND AWARDS** Fulbright Res Fel (Italy); postdoctoral fel, Getty Res Inst for Hist of Art and Humanities; fel from APS; NEH. **MEMBERSHIPS** AHA; AAIS; Asoc for Study Modern Italy; Soc for Ital Hist Studies. **RESEARCH** Twentieth century Italian culture and politics; Cold War. **SELECTED PUBLICATIONS** Auth, Envisioning Modernity: Desire and Discipline in the Italian Fascist Film, Critical Inquiry, 96; auth, Der Faschismus, das Screiben und die Strategien der Erinnerung, Der Italienische Fil Zwischen Faschismus und Demokratie, 97; auth, Language and the Construction of National Identity in Fascist Italy, The European Legacy, 97; auth, Liberation: Film and the Flight from the Italian Past, 1945-50, Italian Fascism: History, Memory and Representation, forthcoming; Fascist Modernities: Italy, 1922-45, forthcoming. **CONTACT ADDRESS** Dept. of History, Fordham Univ, 441 E. Fordham Rd., Bronx, NY, 10458. **EMAIL** benghiat@murray.fordham.edu

BENARDETE, SETH GABRIEL
PERSONAL Born 04/04/1930, New York, NY, m, 1960 **DISCIPLINE** CLASSICS **EDUCATION** Univ Chicago, BA, 49, MA, 53, PhD, 55. **CAREER** Teaching intern Greek & humanities, St John's Col, Md, 55-57; jr fel, Harvard Univ, 57-60; asst prof Greek & Latin, Brandeis Univ, 60-65; assoc prof, 65-76, prof classics, NY Univ, 76-, vis lectr philos, Grad Fac, New Sch Social Res, 65-; Nat Endowment for Humanities sr fel, 72. **RESEARCH** Greek poetry and philosophy. **SELECTED PUBLICATIONS** Transl, Aeschylus II,The Persians and The Suppliant Maidens, Univ Chicago, 56; Herodotean Inquiries, M Nijhoff, 69; The Being of the Beautiful, Univ Chicago, 84; The Rhetoric of Morality & Philosophy, Univ Chicago, 91; Socrates Second Sailing, Univ Chicago, 89; The Tradegy & Comedy of Life, Univ Chicago, 93; The Bow & the Lyre, Rauman & Littlefield, 97; Sacred Transgressions, St Augustine's Press, 98. **CONTACT ADDRESS** Dept of Classics, New York Univ, 25 Waverly Pl, New York, NY, 10003-6701.

BENARIO, HERBERT W.
PERSONAL Born 07/21/1929, New York, NY, m, 1957, 2 children **DISCIPLINE** CLASSICS **EDUCATION** City Col New York, BA, 48; Columbia Univ, MA, 49; Johns Hopkins Univ, PhD(classics), 51. **CAREER** Instr Greek & Latin, Columbia Univ, 53-58; asst prof classics, Sweet Briar Col, 58-60; from asst prof to assoc prof, 60-67, chmn dept, 68-73 & 76-78, Prof Classics, Emory Univ, 67-, Mem Latin achievement test comt, Col Entrance Exam Bd, 63-66; fel, Southeastern Inst Medieval & Renaissance Stud, 65; consult, Nat Endowment for Humanities, 71 & 72; Am Coun Learned Soc fel, 78. **HONORS AND AWARDS** Ovation from Class Asn Midwest & South, 79. **MEMBERSHIPS** Am Philol Asn; Vergilian Soc Am (pres, 80-82); Class Soc Am Acad Rome (pres, 65); Archaeol Inst Am; Class Asn Midwest & South (pres, 71-72). **RESEARCH** Latin literature; Roman history; Roman monuments and topography. **SELECTED PUBLICATIONS** Auth, Christians and Pagans in Roman Britain, Classical World, Vol 0086, 92; Roman Papers, Vol 6, Vol 7, Classical J, Vol 0087, 92; Tacitus and Commotus in 'Ann 13.56'/, Historia-Zeitschrift Fur Alte Geschichte, Vol 0043, 94; Roman Towns in Britain, Classical World, Vol 0087, 94; Tacitus and Commotus in 'Ann 13.56'/, Historia Zeitschrift Fur Alte Geschichte, Vol 0043, 94; Recent Work on Tacitus 1984-1993, Classical World, Vol 0089, 95; Camws the Classical Assoc of the Middle West andSouth--the 9th Decade, Classical J, Vol 0091, 96; Academic Tributes to 97, Classical J, Vol 0093, 97. **CONTACT ADDRESS** Dept of Classics, Emory Univ, Atlanta, GA, 30322.

BENDER, HENRY V.
PERSONAL Born 05/23/1945, Teaneck, NJ, m, 1973, 3 children **DISCIPLINE** CLASSICS **EDUCATION** Fordham Univ, BA, 67; Pa State Univ, MA, 68; Rutgers Univ, PhD, 87. **CAREER** Adjunct assoc prof, Rutgers Univ, 93-95; St. Joseph's Univ, 84-; Villanova Univ, 85-. **HONORS AND AWARDS** Fulbright fel, 84. **MEMBERSHIPS** Am Philos Asn; Vergilian Soc. **RESEARCH** Augustan art; Archaeology; Greek archaeology; Topography of Ancient Greece and Rome; Computers and the classics. **SELECTED PUBLICATIONS** Auth, A Horace Reader, 98; Catullus for the A.P., 96; auth, "De Habitu Vestis: Clothing in the Aeneid," 94; "Princeps and Cosmos in Augustan Rome," 92. **CONTACT ADDRESS** 1116 Harvest Rd, Cherry Hill, NJ, 08002. **EMAIL** hbender@hill.org

BENDER, MARVIN LIONEL
PERSONAL Born 08/18/1934, Mechanicsburg, PA, m, 1956, 2 children **DISCIPLINE** LINGUISTICS, ANTHROPOLOGY **EDUCATION** Dartmouth Col, BA, 56, MA, 58; Univ Tex, Austing, PhD(ling), 68. **CAREER** Master math, Adisadel Col, Cape Coast, Ghana, 59-60; res assoc, Educ Res Coun, Greater Cleveland, 60-62; asst prof math, Haile Selassie Univ, 62-65; proj specialist ling, Ford Found 68-69; asst prof math, Haile Selassie Univ, 69-70; vis asst prof ling, Stanford Univ, 70-71; asst prof, 71-76, ASSOC PROF ANTHROP, SOUTHERN ILL UNIV, CARBONDALE, 76-, Ford Found consult, EAfrica, 69-70; prin investr, NSF grant, 73-75; ed, Nilo-Sahelian Newsletter. **MEMBERSHIPS** Ling Soc Am; fel Am Anthrop Asn; Am Fed Teachers. **RESEARCH** Comparative and historial linguistics; descriptive and theoretical linguistics; Afroasiatic and Ethiopian languages; Nilo-Sahelian languages. **SELECTED PUBLICATIONS** Auth, Nubians and the Nubian Language in Contemporary Egypt in A Case of Cultural and Linguistic Contact, J of Pidgin and Creole Lang(s), Vol 0008, 93; Nominal and Verbal Plurality in Chadic, Word--J of the Int Ling Assoc, Vol 0044, 93; Toward A Typology of European Languages, Word-J of the Int Ling Assoc, Vol 0044, 93; A Concise Introduction to Syntactic Theory the Government Binding Approach, Word--J of the Int Ling Assoc, Vol 0045, 94; Language and Soc in Africa in the Theory and Practice of Sociolinguistics, Word-J of the Int Ling Assoc, Vol 0046, 95; English-Kanuri Dictionary in English, Kanuri, Word-J of the Int Ling Assoc, Vol 0047, 96; Loan Verbs in Maltese - A Descriptive and Comparative Study, J of Pidgin and Creole Lang(s), Vol 0012, 97. **CONTACT ADDRESS** Dept Foreign Languages & Liter, Southern Ill Univ, Carbondale, IL, 62901.

BENDER, MELVIN E.
PERSONAL Born 03/15/1953, Elgin, IL, m, 1975, 5 children **DISCIPLINE** HISTORY **EDUCATION** Central Baptist Col, AA, 77; Univ Central Ark, MA, 86, BSE, 79; Univ Memphis, PhD, 97. **CAREER** From asst prof to assoc prof, 79-, Central Baptist Col; adj prof, 96-, Univ Central Ark. **HONORS AND AWARDS** Who's Who Among Am Teachers, 95, 97; Academic Excellence Award, 89, Central Baptist Col; Award for Best Church Hist, 95, Ark Hist Asn. **MEMBERSHIPS** Ark Hist Asn, Ark Asn of Col Hist Teachers; Phi Alpha Theta; Friends of Nat Hist Day; Civil War Trust. **SELECTED PUBLICATIONS** Auth, Prison Experiences and Treatment of Officers Captured at Arkansas Post, 81; auth, History in the Bible College Curriculum, 89; auth, Founding of Central Baptist College, 95; auth, A Small School with a Big Heart, 92. **CONTACT ADDRESS** 1501 College Ave, Conway, AR, 72032. **EMAIL** dbender@admin.cbc.edu

BENDER, NATHAN E.
DISCIPLINE ANTHROPOLOGY, LIBRARY SCIENCE **EDUCATION** Ohio State Univ, BA, 80; Univ Wash, MA, 83; Kent State Univ, MLS, 86. **CAREER** Princ Investigator/Dir, Piatt Park Archeol Proj, 84-85; libr Western Hist Collections, Univ Okla, 86-89; Head, spec collections, Mont State Univ Librs, 89-94; curator, head spec collections, WV Univ Librs, 94-97; curator, McCracker REs Libr, Buffalo Bill Hist Ctr, 97-. **CONTACT ADDRESS** McCracker Research Library, 720 Sheridan Ave, Cody, WY, 82414. **EMAIL** nbender@wavecom.net

BENDER, THOMAS
PERSONAL Born 04/18/1944, San Mateo, CA, 2 children **DISCIPLINE** AMERICAN HISTORY **EDUCATION** Univ Santa Clara, BA, 66; Univ Calif, Davis, MA, 67, PhD(hist), 71. **CAREER** Asst prof hist & urban anal, Univ Wis-Green Bay, 71-74; from asst prof to assoc prof hist, 74-77, Samuel Rudin prof Hum, 77-82, UNIV PROF OF HUM AND PROF OF HIST, 82- , CTR FOR ADVANCED STUD NY UNIV; DIR, INT, 96- ; Dean for Hum, 95-98. **HONORS AND AWARDS** Frederick Jackson Turner Prize, Orgn Am Historians, 75; Assoc mem, Columbia Univ Sem on the City, 76-; fel, NY Inst Humanities, 76-86; ed, Intellectual History Group, Newsletter, 78-; Guggenheim fel, 80-81; adv ed, New Studies in Am Intellectual & Cultural Hist, Johns Hopkins Univ Press, 81- ; Soc Am Historians, elected 83; Rockefeller Hum Fel, 84-85; Getty scholar, 92-93; fel, Am Acad Arts and Sci, 94. **MEMBERSHIPS** AHA; Orgn Am Historians; Am Studies Asn; PEN; Writer's Guild. **RESEARCH** American social and intellectual history; intellectuals; cities. **SELECTED PUBLICATIONS** Auth, Toward an Urban Vision, 75; auth, Community and Social Change in America, 78; co-auth, The Making of American Society, 78; auth, New York Intellect, 87; auth, Intellect and Public Life, 93; co-ed, American Academic Disciplines in Transformation, 98; contrib, The Urban University and Its Identity, 98; contrib, The Transformation of Humanistic Studies in the Twenty-First Century, 98; contrib, Cities and Citizenship, 98. **CONTACT ADDRESS** Dept of History, New York Univ, New York, NY, 10012.

BENDER, TODD K.
PERSONAL Born 01/08/1936, Stark County, OH, m, 1958, 2 children **DISCIPLINE** ENGLISH, CLASSICAL LANGUAGES **EDUCATION** Kenyon Col, BA, 58; Stanford Univ, PhD(class lang & English), 62. **CAREER** Instr English, Stanford Univ, 61-62; instr, Dartmouth Col, 62-63; asst prof, Univ Va, 63-65; assoc prof, 65-73, PROF ENGLISH, UNIV WIS, MADISON, 73-, Am Coun Learned Soc grant-in-aid, Oxford Univ, 63 & fel, Bibliot Nat, Paris, 65-66; Am Philos Soc grant, Paris, 69; vis prof, World Campus Prog, 73; Fulbright lectr, Univ Athens, Greece, 78-79. **MEMBERSHIPS** MLA. **RESEARCH** Nineteenth century English and European literature; Homeric Greek; computational linguistics. **SELECTED PUBLICATIONS** Auth, Conrad,Joseph and the Fictions of Skepticism, Anq--A Quart J of Short Articles Notes and Rev(s), Vol 0006, 93; Conrad Existentialism, Anq--A Quart J of Short Articles Notes and Rev(s), Vol 0006, 93; Hopkins in A Literary Biography, 19th-Century Lit, Vol 0049, 94; Representing Modernist Texts in Editing As Interpretation, Engl Lang Notes, Vol 0031, 94; The Invention of the West in Conrad, Joseph and the Double-Mapping of Europe and Empire, Clio--A J of Lit Hist and the Philos of Hist, Vol 0025, 96; Hopkins Against Hist, Clio--A J of Lite Hist and the Philos of Hist, Vol 0026, 97. **CONTACT ADDRESS** Dept of English, Univ of Wis, Madison, WI, 53706.

BENDERSKY, JOSEPH WILLIAM
PERSONAL Born 07/30/1946, Carbondale, PA **DISCIPLINE** MODERN EUROPEAN & MODERN GERMAN HISTORY **EDUCATION** City Col New York, BA, 69; Mich State Univ, MA, 70, PhD(German hist), 75. **CAREER** Instr humanities, Mich State Univ, 74-75; asst prof German hist, Marquette Univ, 75-76; instr, 76-79, asst prof, 79-82, ASSOC PROF GERMAN HIST, VA COMMONWEALTH UNIV, 82- **MEMBERSHIPS** Southern Hist Asn; Conf Group for Cent Europ Hist. **RESEARCH** Political and legal theory of Carl Schmitt; Weimar and Nazi Germany; history of German conservatism. **SELECTED PUBLICATIONS** Auth, Frick,Wilhelm in the Legalist of the Unconstitutional State, Amer Hist Rev, Vol 0099, 94; Hitler As Philosophe in Remnants of the Enlightenment in National-Socialism, Amer Hist Rev, Vol 0101, 96. **CONTACT ADDRESS** Dept of Hist, Va Commonwealth Univ, Box 2001, Richmond, VA, 23284-9004.

BENDINER, KENNETH PAUL
PERSONAL Born 06/06/1947, New York, NY, m, 1974, 3 children **DISCIPLINE** ART **EDUCATION** Univ Mich, BA, 69; Columbia Univ, PhD, 79. **CAREER** Instr, 77-78, Vassar Col; asst prof, 78-79, Wellesley Col; asst prof, 79-80, Columbia Col; assoc prof, prof, 85-99, Univ Wisc - Milwaukee. **RESEARCH** 19th & 20th century art, esp victorian painting, Matisse. **CONTACT ADDRESS** Art History, Univ of Wisconsin, Milwaukee, PO Box 413, Milwaukee, WI, 53201. **EMAIL** bendiner@uwm.edu

BENEDICT, MICHAEL LES
PERSONAL Born 03/18/1945, Chicago, IL, m, 1968 **DISCIPLINE** AMERICAN & LEGAL CONSTITUTIONAL HISTORY, CIVIL WAR RECONSTRUCTION **EDUCATION** Univ Ill, Urbana-Champaign, BA, 65, MA, 67; Rice Univ, PhD(hist), 71. **CAREER** Asst prof, 70-75, assoc prof, 75-81, prof Hist, Ohio State Univ, 81-, Nat Endowment for Humanities Younger Humanist fel, 73-74; vis mem, Inst Advan Study, Princeton Univ, 74; Guggenheim Mem Found fel, 77-78; fel, Woodrow Wilson Int Ctr Scholars, 79; Fulbright sr lectr, Japan, 82-83. **MEMBERSHIPS** Southern Hist Asn; Orgn Am Historians; Am Soc Legal Hist; Soc Sci Hist Asn. **RESEARCH** American Civil War and Reconstruction; American legal and constitutional history. **SELECTED PUBLICATIONS** Auth, The Impeachment and Trial of Andrew Johnson, 73 & A Compromise of Principle: Congressional Republicans and Reconstruction, 1863-1869, 74, Norton; The Fruits of Victory: Alternatives in Restoring the Union, Lippincott, 75; rev ed 86; The Blessings of Liberty: A Concise History of the Constitution of the United States, Heath, 95; Preserving Federalism: Reconstruction and the Waite Court, Super Ct Rev, 78; Southern Democrats in the Crisis of 1876-1877: A Reconsideration of Reunion and Reaction, J Southern Hist, 11/80. **CONTACT ADDRESS** Dept of History, Ohio State Univ, 230 W 17th Ave, Columbus, OH, 43210-1361. **EMAIL** benedict.3@osu.edu

BENEDICT, PHILIP JOSEPH
PERSONAL Born 08/20/1949, Washington, DC, m, 1970, 2 children **DISCIPLINE** EARLY MODERN EUROPEAN HISTORY **EDUCATION** Cornell Univ, BA, 70; Princeton Univ, MA, 72, PhD(hist), 75. **CAREER** Vis asst prof hist, Cornell Univ, 75-76; asst prof, Univ Md, College Park, 76-78; from asst prof to assoc prof, 78-92, PROF HIST, BROWN UNIV, 92-. **HONORS AND AWARDS** Nancy Lyman Roelker Prize, awarded by the Sixteenth Century Studies Conf for: Rouen's Foreign Trade in the Age of the Religious Wars (1560-1600), (see Publications), 85; Nancy Lyman Roelker Prize, awarded by the Sixteenth Century Studies Conf for: Faith, Fortune and Social Structure in Seventeenth-Century Montpellier, (see Publications), 97. **MEMBERSHIPS** AHA; Soc Fr Hist Studies; Am Soc Reformation Res. **RESEARCH** Reformation and society; French wars of religion; urban history. **SELECTED PUBLICATIONS** Auth, The Saint Bartholomew's Massacres in the Provinces, The Hist J, XXI, 78; Rouen During the Wars of Religion, Cambridge Univ Press, 81; Rouen's Foreign Trade in the Age of the Religious Wars (1560-1600), The J of Europ Economic Hist, XIII, 84; Bibliotheques protestantes et catholiques ... Metz au XVIIe siecle, Annales: Economies Societes, Civilisations, no 2, 85; Towards the Comparative Study of the Popular Market for Art: The Ownership of Paintings in Seventeenth-Century Metz, Past and Present, 109, 85; ed and contribr, Cities and Social Change in Early Modern France, Unwin Hyman, 89; auth, The Huguenot Population of France, 1600-1685: The Demographic Fate and Customs of a Religious Minority, Transactions of the Am Philos Soc, 91; auth, Of Marmites and Martyrs: Images and Polemics in the Wars of Religion, In: The French Renaissance in Prints, exhibition catalogue, 94; Un roi, une loi, deux fois: Parameters for the History of Catholic-Reformed Coexistence in France, 1555-1685, In: Tolerance and Intolerance in the European Reformation, Cambridge Univ Press, 96; Faith,

Fortune and Social Structure in Seventeenth-Century Montpellier, Past and Present, 152, 96. **CONTACT ADDRESS** Dept of Hist, Brown Univ, Providence, RI, 02912-9127. **EMAIL** Philip_Benedict@brown.edu

BENJAMIN, ROGER
DISCIPLINE ART HISTORY **CAREER** Sr lectr, Sch of Fine Arts, Classics and Archaeology, Univ of Melbourne; res fel, Ctr Cross-Cult Res, Australian Natl Univ. **RESEARCH** French Orientalist painting; Vietnamese painint; contemporary Aboriginal art. **CONTACT ADDRESS** Dept of Education, Australian National Univ. **EMAIL** Roger.Benjamin@anu.edu.au

BENKO, STEPHEN
PERSONAL Born 06/13/1924, Budapest, Hungary, m, 1952, 4 children **DISCIPLINE** RELIGION, ANCIENT HISTORY **EDUCATION** Reformed Theol Sem Budapest, BD, 47; Univ Basel, PhD(relig), 51. **CAREER** Res fel, Divinity Sch, Yale Univ, 53-54; instr, Sch Theol, Temple Univ, 57-59 & lectr, Grad Sch Philos & Relig, 59-61; prof Bibl studies & patristics, Conwell Sch Theol, 60-69; PROF ANCIENT HIST, CALIF STATE UNIV, FRESNO, 69-. **MEMBERSHIPS** Am Hist Asn; Am Philol Asn; Am Soc Church Hist; Soc Bibl Lit. **RESEARCH** Ancient church history; ecumenical relations. **SELECTED PUBLICATIONS** Auth, Education, Culture and the Arts Transylvanian Cultural Hist, Hungarian Quart, Vol 0035, 94. **CONTACT ADDRESS** Dept of Hist, California State Univ, Fresno, Fresno, CA, 93740.

BENN, CARL E.
PERSONAL Born 03/04/1953, Toronto, ON, Canada **DISCIPLINE** MILITARY HISTORY **EDUCATION** Univ Toronto, BA, 80, MDiv, 83; York Univ, PhD, 95. **CAREER** Hist interp, Toronto Hist Bd, 71-75; sr hist interp, Borough Etobicoke, 75-80; cur collections, Regional Municipality Waterloo, 83-85; CUR MILITARY HISTORY, TORONTO HISTORICAL BOARD, 85-; Tchr (part-time), Univ Toronto, 90-. **MEMBERSHIPS** Ont Mus Asn; Ont Hist Soc. **SELECTED PUBLICATIONS** Auth, The King's Mill on the Humber, 79; auth, The Battle of York, 84; auth, Historic Fort York 1793-1993, 93; auth, The Iroquois in the War of 1812, 98. **CONTACT ADDRESS** Toronto Historical Board, 205 Yonge St, Toronto, ON, M5B 1N2.

BENNET, JOEL F.
DISCIPLINE LAW OFFICE MANAGEMENT **EDUCATION** Brown Univ, AB, 68; Georgetown Univ Law Ctr, JD, 72. **CAREER** Adj fac; trial atty, Fed Trade Commission's Bureau of Consumer Protection; assoc, Stein, Mitchell & Mezines, 75-76; partner, Bennet, Deso, Greenberg & Thomas, 81-84. **SELECTED PUBLICATIONS** Publ on var aspects of, private practice; ed, Flying Solo: A Survival Guide for the Solo Lawyer, 2nd ed, Am Bar Assoc(s) Section on Econ of Law Practice, 94. **CONTACT ADDRESS** School of Law, Univ of District of Columbia, 4200 Connecticut Ave Northwest, Washington, DC, 20008.

BENNETT, DAVID HARRY
PERSONAL Born 01/22/1935, Syracuse, NY, m, 1961, 2 children **DISCIPLINE** AMERICAN HISTORY **EDUCATION** Syracuse Univ, AB, 56; Univ Chicago, AM, 58, PhD(hist), 63. **CAREER** Lectr hist, Univ Chicago, 58-60; instr Am studies, 61-63, asst prof hist & Am studies, 63-70, assoc prof, 70-80, PROF HIST & CHMN DEPT, SYRACUSE UNIV, 80- **MEMBERSHIPS** AHA; Orgn Am Historians. **RESEARCH** Recent Amer history; Amer studies. **SELECTED PUBLICATIONS** Auth, Religion and the Racist Right in the Origins of the Christian Identity Movement, Amer Hist Rev, Vol 0101, 96; Forging New Freedoms in Nativism, Education, and the Constitution, 1917-1927, J of Amer Hist, Vol 0083, 96; The Populist Persuasion in An American History, Amer Hist Rev, Vol 0101, 96. **CONTACT ADDRESS** Syracuse Univ, 320 Berkeley Dr, Syracuse, NY, 13210.

BENNETT, EDWARD MOORE
PERSONAL Born 09/28/1927, Dixon, IL, m, 1950, 1 child **DISCIPLINE** AMERICAN HISTORY **EDUCATION** Butler Univ, BA, 52; Univ Ill, MA, 56, PhD(Am diplomatic hist), 61. **CAREER** Teaching asst, Univ Ill, 56-60; instr Am hist, Agr & Mech Col Tex, 60-61; from asst prof to assoc prof Am & Russ hist, 61-71, PROF HIST, WASH STATE UNIV, 71-, Participant, Ford Found Community Sem, 65; pres, Pac-Eight Conf Coun, 72-73. **HONORS AND AWARDS** Outstanding Fac Award, Wash State Univ, 79. **MEMBERSHIPS** AHA; Orgn Am Historians; AAUP; Soc Hist Am Foreign Rels. **RESEARCH** Russian-Amer diplomacy, especially the 1930's; Amer diplomatic history; Amer Far Eastern relations 1932-1941. **SELECTED PUBLICATIONS** Auth, Fdr and His Contemporaries in Foreign Perceptions of An Amer President, Amer Hist Rev, Vol 0098, 93; Davies, Joseph, E in Envoy to the Soviets, Amer Hist Rev, Vol 0100, 95; Working With 7 Year Old to 12 Year Old Children Who Stutter in Ideas For Intervention in the Public-Schools, Lang Speech and Hearing Services in Sch(s), Vol 0026, 95; the Vulnerability of Empire, Amer Hist Rev, Vol 0100, 95. **CONTACT ADDRESS** Dept of Hist, Washington State Univ, 323 Wilson Hall, Pullman, WA, 99164.

BENNETT, JAMES D.
PERSONAL Born 08/02/1926, Calhoun, KY, m, 1951 **DISCIPLINE** HISTORY **EDUCATION** Centre Col Ky, BA, 47; Tex Christian Univ, MA, 54; Vanderbilt Univ, PhD(hist), 68. **CAREER** Asst, Tex Christian Univ, 53-54; from instr to asst prof US Hist, San Antonio Col, 54-59; assoc prof, 59-69, PROF US HIST, WESTERN KY UNIV, 69- **MEMBERSHIPS** Southern Hist Asn; Orgn Am Historians; Western Hist Asn. **RESEARCH** Urban history; trans-Mississippi west; Tennessee Valley Authority. **SELECTED PUBLICATIONS** Auth, That Damned Cowboy in Roosevelt, Theodore and the Amer West, 1883-1898, J West, Vol 0032, 93. **CONTACT ADDRESS** Dept of Hist, Western Kentucky Univ, Bowling Green, KY, 42101.

BENNETT, JUDITH MACKENZIE
PERSONAL Born 01/12/1951, Neptune, NJ **DISCIPLINE** EUROPEAN WOMEN'S & MEDIEVAL HISTORY **EDUCATION** Mt Holyoke Col, AB, 73; Univ Toronto, MA, 74, PhD(medieval studies), 81; Pontifical Inst Mediaeval Stud, MSL, 78. **CAREER** ASST PROF HIST, UNIV NC, CHAPEL HILL, 81-. **MEMBERSHIPS** AHA; Coord Comt Women in Hist Profession. **RESEARCH** Marriage and the family in medieval Europe; women's work; medieval peasantry. **SELECTED PUBLICATIONS** Auth, Medieval peasant marriage: An examination of marriage license fines in the Liber Gersumarum, In: Pathways to Medieval Peasants, Pontifical Inst Mediaeval Stud, Toronto, 81. **CONTACT ADDRESS** Dept of Hist, Univ NC, Chapel Hill, NC, 27514.

BENNETT, NORMAN ROBERT
PERSONAL Born 10/31/1932, Marlboro, MA, 2 children **DISCIPLINE** AFRICAN, WINE & PORTUGUESE HISTORY **EDUCATION** Tufts Univ, AB, 54; Fletcher Sch Law, MA, 56; Boston Univ, PhD, 61. **CAREER** From instr to asst prof African hist, 60-67, assoc prof, 67-70, PROF HIST, BOSTON UNIV, 70-98, PROF EMER, 98-; Am Philos Soc fel, 66; ed, African Studies Asn Bull, 66-70 & Int J Hist African Studies, 68-; vis scholar, Eduardo Mondlane Univ, Mozambique, 77. **HONORS AND AWARDS** Ford Found African Scholar, 58-60; Smith-Mundt lectr, Kivukoni Col, Tanganyika, 62-63 **MEMBERSHIPS** AHA; African Studies Asn (pres, 81); Tanzania Soc; Acad Royale des Sci d'Outre-Mer, Belgium. **RESEARCH** African history; Portuguese history; Wine history. **SELECTED PUBLICATIONS** ed, Leadership in Eastern Africa, 68, From Zanzibar to Ujiji: The Journal of Arthur W Dodgshun, 69, Stanley's Dispatches to the New York Herald, 1871-1872, 1874-1877, 70 & co-ed, The Central African Journal of L J Procter, 1860-1864, 71, Boston Univ; auth, Mirambo of Tanzania, Oxford Univ, 71; ed, The Zanzibar Letters of E D Ropes, Jr, 1882-1892, Boston Univ African Studies Ctr, 73; auth, Africa and Europe from Roman Times to the Present, Africana, 75; A History of the Arab State of Zanzibar, Methuen, Inc, 78; Arab Versus European Diplomacy & War in 19th Century East Central Africa, Africana, 86. **CONTACT ADDRESS** African Studies Ctr, Boston Univ, 270 Bay State Rd, Boston, MA, 02215-1403. **EMAIL** bennet-1@idt.net

BENNETT, Y. ALEKSANDRA
DISCIPLINE HISTORY **EDUCATION** Univ Windsor, BA, MA; McMaster Univ, PhD. **CAREER** Assoc prof. **RESEARCH** Peace, religion, war and society in twentieth-century Britain. **SELECTED PUBLICATIONS** Auth, A Question of Responsibility and Tactics: Vera Brittain and Food Relief for Occupied Europe, 1941-1944, The Pacifist Impulse in Historical Perspective, Toronto UP, 96. **CONTACT ADDRESS** Dept of Hist, Carleton Univ, 1125 Colonel By Dr, Ottawa, ON, K1S 5B6. **EMAIL** bennett@ccs.carleton.ca

BENSEL, RICHARD F.
PERSONAL Born 11/13/1949, Pendleton, OR, m, 1979, 1 child **DISCIPLINE** POLITICAL SCIENCE **EDUCATION** Univ Chicago, Ba, 71; Cornell Univ, PhD, 78. **CAREER** Instr, 77-78, asst prof, 78-82, Texas A&M Univ; asst prof, Univ Texas, Dallas, 82-84; ass prof and prof, Grad Fac, New School for Soc Res, 84-93; prof, Cornell Univ, 93- . **HONORS AND AWARDS** Mark H Ingraham Prize, 84. **MEMBERSHIPS** Am Polit Sci Asn; Am Hist Asn; Social Sci Hist Asn; Economic Hist Asn; Org of Am Hist; Agr Hist Asn; AAAS. **RESEARCH** Political development in America; history of Congress; theories of political economy. **SELECTED PUBLICATIONS** Auth, Sectionalism and American Political Development, 1880-1980, Wisconsin, 84; auth, Yankee Leviathan: The Origins of Central State Authority in America, 1859-1877, Cambridge, 90; auth, Congress, Sectionalism, and Public Policy Formation since 1870, in Silbey, ed, Encyclopedia of the American Legislative System, Scribner's, 94; auth, Confederate Cabinet, in Current, ed, Encyclopedia of the Confederacy, Simon & Schuster, 93; auth, Sectionalism, in Bacon, ed, Encyclopedia of the United States Congress, Simon & Schuster, 94. **CONTACT ADDRESS** Government Dept, Cornell Univ, McGraw Hall, Ithaca, NY, 14853. **EMAIL** rfb2@cornell.edu

BENSON, JACK LEONARD
PERSONAL Born 06/25/1920, Kansas City, MO, m, 1954 **DISCIPLINE** CLASSICAL ARCHAEOLOGY **EDUCATION** Univ Mo, BA, 41; Ind Univ, MA, 47; Univ Basel, Switz, PhD, 52. **CAREER** Instr, Yale Univ, 52-53; res assoc class archaeol, Univ Mus, Univ Pa, 53; assoc prof classics, Univ Miss, 58-61; vis assoc prof art, Princeton Univ, 60-61; assoc prof, Wellesley Col, 61-64; prof Ancient Art, 65-85, prof emeritus, 85-, Univ Mass, Amherst; Res assoc, Univ Mus, Univ Pa, 54-85; Fulbright res scholar & Guggenheim fel, 56-58; mem, Brit Sch Archaeol, Jerusalem, 57-75; Am Philos Soc Penrose Fund fel, 61; mem, Inst Advan Study, Princeton Univ, 55, 64-65 & 70; Am Coun Learned Soc fel, 65; guest prof, Univ Freiburg, 76. **MEMBERSHIPS** Archaeol Inst Am; Class Asn New England. **RESEARCH** Theory of period setting in Greek art; archaic Greek vases; Cypriote archaeology. **SELECTED PUBLICATIONS** Coauth, Corinth, vol XV pt 3, The Potters' Quarter: The Corinthian Pottery, Princeton, 84; auth, Earlier Corinthian Workshops, Amsterdam, 89; auth, The Inner Nature of Greek Art, 92; auth, CVA Fascicule 29, Univ Mus Fascicule II: Corinthian Pottery, Penn, 95. **CONTACT ADDRESS** Art History Dept, Univ of Mass, Amherst, MA, 01003. **EMAIL** jlb@vgernet.net

BENSON, KEITH RODNEY
PERSONAL Born 07/22/1948, Portland, OR, m, 1980 **DISCIPLINE** HISTORY **EDUCATION** Whitworth Col, BA, 70; Ore State Univ, MA, 73, PhD(biol sci), 79. **CAREER** Instr biol, Whitworth Col, 77-78; asst prof, Pac Lutheran Univ, 79-81; ASST PROF BIOMEDICAL HIST, UNIV WASH, 81- **MEMBERSHIPS** Sigma Xi; Hist Sci Soc. **RESEARCH** Hist of marine biology; development of Amer science; evolution theory. **SELECTED PUBLICATIONS** Auth, Dohrn,Anton in A Life For Science, Hist and Philos of the Life Sciences, Vol 0014, 92; Experimental Ecology on the Pacific Coast in Shelford, Victor and His Search For Appropriate Methods, Hist and Philos of the Life Sciences, Vol 0014, 92; Experimental Ecology on the Pacific Coast in Shelford, Victor and His Search For Appropriate Methods, Hist and Philos of the Life Sciences, Vol 0014, 92; Reading the Shape of Nature in Comparative Zoology At the Agassiz Museum, Hist and Philos of the Life Sciences, Vol 0014, 92; Dohrn, Anton in A Life For Science, Hist and Philos of the Life Sciences, Vol 0014, 92; Reading the Shape of Nature in Comparative Zoology At the Agassiz-Museum, Hist and Philos of the Life Sciences, Vol 0014, 92; Making Sex in Body and Gender From the Greeks to Freud, Hist and Philos of the Life Sciences, Vol 0015, 93; Making Sex in Body and Gender From the Greeks to Freud, Hist and Philos of the Life Sciences, Vol 0015, 93; Sovereign Oceanographers, Hist and Philos of the Life Sciences, Vol 0017, 95; Sovereign Oceanographers, Hist and Philos of the Life Sciences, Vol 0017, 95; Styles of Scientific Thought in the German Genetics Community, 1900-1933, Annals of Sci, Vol 0052, 95; Styles of Scientific Thought in the German Genetics Community, 1900-1933, Annals of Sci, Vol 0052, 95; To Make A Spotless Orange in Biological-Control in California, J of Amer Hist, Vol 0084, 97. **CONTACT ADDRESS** Dept Med Hist & Eth, Univ of Wash, SB-20, Seattle, WA, 98195.

BENSON, LEGRACE
PERSONAL Born 02/23/1930, Richmond, VA, w, 1952, 3 children **DISCIPLINE** ART; PHILOSOPHY; PERCEPTUAL PSYCHOLOGY **EDUCATION** Meredith Coll, AB, 51; Univ Georgia Athens, MFA, 56; Cornell Univ, PhD, 74. **CAREER** Asst prof, Cornell Univ, 68-71; assoc prof/assoc dean for special programs, Wells Coll, 71-77; assoc dean, SUNY-Empire State Coll, 77-80; coordinator of arts, humanities and communications study, center for distance learning, SUNY-Empire State Coll, 81-92. **HONORS AND AWARDS** Empire State Coll Excellence in Scholarship, 92. **MEMBERSHIPS** Natl Coalition of Independent Scholars; Haitian Studies Assn; Coll Art Assn; Latin Amer Studies Assn; Arts Council African Studies Assn; African Studies Assn; Canadian Assn Latin Amer and Caribbean Studies. **RESEARCH** Arts and Culture of Haiti; adult distance learning **SELECTED PUBLICATIONS** Auth, The Utopian Vision in Haitian Painting, Callaloo, Spring 92; Journal of Caribbean Studies, Observations on Islamic Motifs in Haitian Visual Arts, Winter 92/Spring 93; The Arts of Haiti Considered Ecologically, Paper for Culture Change and Technology in the Americas conference, Nov 95; Three Presentations of the Arts of Haiti, Journal of Haitian Studies, Autumn 96; Habits of Attention: Persistence of Lan Ginee in Haiti, in The African Diaspora African Origins and New-world Self-fashioning, 98; How Houngans Use the Light from Distant Stars; Muslim and Breton Survivals in Haitian Voudou Arts, 99; The Artists and the Arts of Haiti in Their Geographical and Conversational Domains, 99. **CONTACT ADDRESS** 314 E. Buffalo St., Ithaca, NY, 14850-4227. **EMAIL** LeGraceBenson@clarityconnect.com

BENSON, ROBERT LOUIS
PERSONAL Born 08/21/1925, Portland, OR **DISCIPLINE** HISTORY **EDUCATION** Univ Calif, BA, 50; Princeton Univ, MA, 53, PhD(hist), 57. **CAREER** Res asst, Inst Advan Study, 52-53; instr hist, Barnard Col, Columbia Univ, 56-59; from asst prof to prof, Wesleyan Univ, 59-75, PROF HIST, UNIV CALIF, LOS ANGELES, 74-, Vis assoc prof, Cornell Univ, 61-62; Am Coun Learned Soc fel, 64-65; vis prof, Free Univ Berlin, 73-74; Inst Advan Study fel, 77. **MEMBERSHIPS** Mediaeval Acad Am; AHA. **SELECTED PUBLICATIONS** Auth, The Bishop Elect: A Study in Medieval Ecclesiastical Office, Princeton Univ, 68; Plenitudo potestatis: Evolution of a formula from Gregory IV to Gratian, Studia Gratiana, 67. **CONTACT ADDRESS** Dept of Hist, Univ Calif, Los Angeles, CA, 90024.

BENSON, WARREN S.
PERSONAL Born 08/23/1929, Chicago, IL, m, 1953, 2 children **DISCIPLINE** HISTORY OF EDUCATION **EDUCATION** NW Col, BA, 52; Dallas Theol Sem, ThM, 56; SW Baptist Theol Sem, MRE, 57; Loyola Univ Chicago, PhD, 75. **CAREER** Min of Education, Winnetka Bible Church, 57-62; Min of Youth & Education, First Covenant Church, Minn, 62-65; Min of Education, Lake Ave Congregational Church, Pasedena, 65-69; Assoc prof, Christian Education, Dallas Theol Sem, 74-78; asst prof, Christian Education, Trinity Evangelical Divinity School, Deerfield, 70-74 & 78-. **HONORS AND AWARDS** Distinguished Prof of Christian Education (NAPCE) **MEMBERSHIPS** N Amer Prof Christian Education; Asn Prof & Res Relig Educ **SELECTED PUBLICATIONS** Coauth, A History and Philosophy of Christian Education, Moody Press; coed, Youth Education in the Church, Moody Press; The Complete Book of Youth Ministry, Moody Press; auth, Leading the Church in Education, Word Publishing. **CONTACT ADDRESS** Trinity Evangelical Divinity School, 2065 Half Day Rd., Deerfield, IL, 60015.

BENT, MARGARET
PERSONAL Born 12/23/1940, St. Albans, England, 2 children **DISCIPLINE** MUSICOLOGY **EDUCATION** Cambridge Univ, BA, 62, MusB, 63, MA, 65, PhD, 69. **CAREER** Lectr music, Goldsmiths' Col, Univ London, 72-75; Ziskind vis prof, 75-76, prof, Brandeis Univ, 76-81; PROF MUSIC, PRINCETON UNIV, 81-, Dir, Nat Endowment for Humanities summer sem, 79 & 81. **HONORS AND AWARDS** Dent medal, 79. **MEMBERSHIPS** Am Musicol Soc; Medieval Acad Am; Renaissance Soc Am. **RESEARCH** Late-medieval music, notation and manuscript studies; compositional and performance problems. **SELECTED PUBLICATIONS** Auth, Discarding Images in Reflections on Music and Culture in Medieval France, Early Mus, Vol 0021, 93; Mensuration and Proportion Signs in Origin and Evolution, Early Mus, Vol 0021, 93; Editing Early Music in the Dilemma of Translation, Early Music, Vol 0022, 94; Accidentals, Counterpoint and Notation in Aaron Aggiunta to the 'Toscanello in Musica', J of Musicol, Vol 0012, 94; 15th Century and 16th-Century Manuscripts of Polyphonic Music, J of the Amer Musicolog Soc, Vol 0048, 95; the Early Use of the Sign O With a Line Through It Its Pedigree and Significance As An Indicator of Proportion Or Mensuration, Early Mus, Vol 0024, 96; Facsimiles of the Squarcialupi Ms and Other Sources, Early Mus Hist, Vol 0015, 96; Walker, Thomas, 1936-95--Obituary, Early Mus, Vol 0024, 96. **CONTACT ADDRESS** Univ Oxford All Souls Col, Oxford, ., OX1 4AL.

BENTLEY, JERRY HARRELL
PERSONAL Born 12/09/1949, Birmingham, AL, m, 1972 **DISCIPLINE** EUROPEAN AND RENAISSANCE HISTORY **EDUCATION** Univ Tenn, BA, 71; Univ Minn, MA, 74, PhD (hist), 76. **CAREER** Asst prof, 76-82, ASSOC PROF HIST, UNIV HAWAII, 82- **MEMBERSHIPS** Renaissance Soc Am; Am Soc Reformation Res; AHA. **RESEARCH** Renaissance Europe; Renaissance humanism; politics and culture. **SELECTED PUBLICATIONS** Auth, The European Opportunity, 16th Century Jour, Vol 0028, 97; Scientific Aspects of European Expansion, 16th Century Jour, Vol 0028, 97; The Globe Encircled and the World Revealed, 16th Century Jour, Vol 0028, 97; Technology and European Overseas Enterprise--Diffusion, Adaptation and Adoption, 16th Century Jour, Vol 0028, 97; Historiography of Europeans in Africa and Asia, 16th Century Jour, Vol 0028, 97; An Island for Itself Economic Development and Social Change on Late Medieval Sicily, Renaissance Quart, Vol 0048, 95; Establishing Exceptionalism--Historiography and Colonial America, 16th Century Jour, Vol 0028, 97; World History, Am Hist Rev, Vol 0101, 96; The Global Opportunity, 16th Century J , Vol 0028, 97; The Continuity of Feudal Power--The Caracciolo Di Brienza in Spanish Naples, Renaissance Quart, Vol 0046, 93; Merchant Networks in the Modern World, 16th Century Jour, Vol 0028, 97. **CONTACT ADDRESS** Dept of Hist, Univ of Hawaii, 2530 Dole St, Honolulu, HI, 96822-2303.

BENTON, CATHERINE
DISCIPLINE HISTORY OF RELIGION **EDUCATION** Columbia Univ, PhD, 91. **CAREER** LECTR, RELIG, LAKE FOREST COL, 87-. **CONTACT ADDRESS** Dept of Relig, Lake Forest Col, 555 N Sheridan Rd, Lake Forest, IL, 60045. **EMAIL** benton@lfc.edu

BERCUSON, DAVID JAY
PERSONAL Born 08/31/1945, Montreal, PQ, Canada, m, 1966, 1 child **DISCIPLINE** CANADIAN HISTORY **EDUCATION** Sir George Williams Univ, BA, 66; Univ Toronto, MA, 67, PhD (hist), 71. **CAREER** Asst prof, 71-80, PROF HIST, UNIV CALGARY, 80- **MEMBERSHIPS** Can Hist Asn. **RESEARCH** Canadian labor history; Middle East military history; Canadian diplomatic history. **SELECTED PUBLICATIONS** Auth, Which Reminds Me--A Memoir, Can Hist Rev, Vol 0078, 97; Seeing Canada Whole--A Memoir, Can Hist Rev, Vol 0078, 97; Eisenhower and the German Pows--Facts Against Falsehood, Can Rev Am Stud, Vol 0023, 93; Reaction and Reform--The Politics of the Conservative Party Under Bennett, R. B., 1927-1938, Pac Northwest Quart, Vol 0084, 93. **CONTACT ADDRESS** Dept of Hist, Univ of Calgary, Calgary, AB, T2N 1N4.

BERG, GERALD MICHAEL
PERSONAL Born 06/29/1946, New York, NY, m **DISCIPLINE** HISTORY **EDUCATION** Univ Calif, Berkeley, BA, 69, PhD, 75. **CAREER** From asst prof to prof History, Sweet Briar Col, 75-; Nat Endowment Hum fel, 82; Fulbright fel 89-90. **MEMBERSHIPS** AHA; African Studies Asn. **RESEARCH** Madagascar; civic religion; ideology. **SELECTED PUBLICATIONS** Auth, The myth of racial strife and Merina Kinglists, History in Africa, 77; Royal ritual in 19th century Imerina, Madagascar in History, Found Malagasy Studies, 80; Some Words about Merina Historical Literature, The African Past Speaks, Dawson, 80; Riziculture and the Founding of Monarchy in Imerina, J African Hist, Vol 22, 289-308; The Sacred Musket, Comp Studies in Soc and History, (27/2) 85; Sacred Acquisition, J African Hist, (29) 88; Writing Ideology, Hist in Africa, (22) 95; Virtue and Fortuna..., Hist in Africa (23) 96; Radama's Smile, Hist in Africa (25) 98. **CONTACT ADDRESS** Dept Hist, Sweet Briar Col, Box 8, Sweet Briar, VA, 24595-0008. **EMAIL** gberg@sbc.edu

BERGE, DENNIS EUGENE
PERSONAL Born 09/17/1930, Elbow Lake, MN, m, 1961 **DISCIPLINE** US HISTORY **EDUCATION** San Diego State Univ, AB, 55, MA, 58; Univ Calif, Berkeley, PhD (hist), 65. **CAREER** From asst prof to assoc prof, 63-70, chmn dept, 70-74, PROF HIST, SAN DIEGO STATE UNIV, 70- **MEMBERSHIPS** Western Hist Asn; Orgn Am Historians. **RESEARCH** United State expansionism; Mexican War. **SELECTED PUBLICATIONS** Auth, Cushing at Zuni--The Correspondence and Journals of Cushing, Frank, Hamilton, 1879-1884, J West, Vol 0032, 93. **CONTACT ADDRESS** Dept of Hist, San Diego State Univ, San Diego, CA, 92182.

BERGEN, DORIS
PERSONAL Born 10/19/1960, Saskatoon, Canada, m, 1998 **DISCIPLINE** HISTORY OF MODERN EUROPE **EDUCATION** Univ Saskatchewan, BA, 82; Univ Alberta, MA, 84; Univ N Carolina, Chapel Hill, PhD, 91. **CAREER** Asst prof, Univ Vermont, 91-96; asst prof, 96-98, assoc prof, 98- , Univ Notre Dame. **HONORS AND AWARDS** DAAD grant, 98; fel, German Marshall Fund, 98; Charles H Revson Fel, Ctr for Advanced Holocaust Stud, US Holocaust Mem Mus, 98. **MEMBERSHIPS** Am Hist Asn; German Stud Asn; Berkshire Conf of Women Hist. **RESEARCH** Religion; ethnicity and gender in National Socialist Germany; Holocaust; World War II; German military chaplains; ethnic Germans in Eastern Europe. **SELECTED PUBLICATIONS** Auth, The Nazi Concept of Volksdeutsche and The Exacerbation of Antisemitism in Eastern Europe, 1939-1945, J of Contemp Hist, 94; auth, Catholics, Protestants, and Anti-Jewish Christianity in Nazi Germany, Cent Europ Hist, 94; auth, Nazi Christians and Christian Nazis: The German Christian Movement in National Socialist Germany, in Rubenstein, ed, What Kind of God: Essays in Honor of Richard L. Rubenstein, Univ Press of Am, 95; auth, Twisted Cross: The German Christian Movement in the Third Reich, Univ No Carolina Press, 96; auth, Germany Is Our Mission--Christ Is Our Strength!: The Wehrmacht Chaplaincy and the German Christian Movement, Church Hist, 97; auth, What God Has Put Asunder, Let No Man Join Together: Overseas Missions and the German Christian View of Race, in Tobler, ed, Remembrance, Repentance, Reconciliation: The 25th Anniversary Volume of the Annual Scholars' Conference on the Holocaust and the Churches, Univ Press of America, 98; auth, The Volksdeutschen, World War II, and the Holocaust, in Bullivant, ed, Germany and Eastern Europe, 1870-1996: Cultural Identities and Cultural Differences, Walter De Gruyter, 98. **CONTACT ADDRESS** Dept of History, Univ of Notre Dame, 219 O'Shaughnessy Hall, Notre Dame, IN, 46556-0368. **EMAIL** Doris.L.Bergen.4@nd.edu

BERGER, BENNET MAURICE
PERSONAL Born 05/01/1926, New York, NY, m, 1981, 4 children **DISCIPLINE** SOCIOLOGY **EDUCATION** Hunter Col, BA, 50; Univ Cal Berk, PhD, 58. **CAREER** Univ IL, Urbana, Asst Prof, Assoc Prof, 59-63; Univ Cal Davis, Assoc Prof, Prof, 63-73; Univ Cal San Diego, Prof, Prof Emer, 73-91. **HONORS AND AWARDS** NIMH Grant, 70-73; NEH fel, 81-82. **MEMBERSHIPS** Am Sociol Asn. **RESEARCH** Youth, culture, theory. **SELECTED PUBLICATIONS** An Essay On Culture; Authors of Their own Lives, ed, 90; Re Survival of a Counterculture, 81; Looking For America, 71. **CONTACT ADDRESS** Univ Calif San Diego, Dept Sociology, San Diego, CA, 92037. **EMAIL** bberger@ucsd.edu

BERGER, CARL
PERSONAL Born 01/28/1925, Chicago, IL **DISCIPLINE** AMERICAN HISTORY **EDUCATION** Univ Iowa, AB, 49; Drake Univ, MA, 51. **CAREER** Reporter and asst city ed, Des Moines Register, Iowa, 49-53; historian, US Army, Japan, 53-55, Tech Serv Corps, Washington, DC, 56-57, writer-analyst, spec opers res off, Am Univ, 57-59; historian, 1st Strategic Aerospace Div, Vandenberg AFB, Calif, 59-61, Cambridge Res Labs, Bedford, Mass, 61-62 and hq, Washington, DC, 62-69, CHIEF HIST DIV, OFF AIR FORCE HIST, HQ, US DEPT AIR FORCE, WASHINGTON, DC, 69- **MEMBERSHIPS** AHA; Orgn Am Historians. **RESEARCH** Far Eastern history; the Jacksonian period. **SELECTED PUBLICATIONS** Auth, Source Studies on Ockeghem, Johannes Motets, Musiktheorie, Vol 0007, 92; Haydn Farewell Symphony and the Idea of Classical Style-Through Composition and Cyclic Integration in his Instrumental Music, Musiktheorie, Vol 0009, 94; Stevens, Wallace, The Plain Sense of Things, Mod Philol, Vol 0092, 94; Musical Form Theory in the Context of National Traditions of the 17th Century--The Lamento from Biber, Heinrich, Ignaz, Franz Rosenkranzsonate Nr. 6, Acta Musicologica, Vol 0064, 92; Poetry of Mourning--The Modern Elegy from Hardy to Heaney, Mod Philol, Vol 0095, 97; Wagner Das Rheingold, Musikforschung, Vol 0048, 95; Biber, Heinrich, Franz 1644-1704--Music and Culture in Salzburg During the High Baroque Period, Musikforschung, Vol 0048, 95; pour Doulz Regard--A Newly Discovered Manuscript Page with French Chansons from the Beginning of the 15th Century, Archiv Musikwissenschaft, Vol 0051, 94; Opera Incerta--Authenticity as a Problem of Complete Musicological Editions, Musikforschung, Vol 0046, 93; An Analysis of Rabanus Maurus Views on Atonality and Tradition--Webern, Anton Vier Stucke fur Geige und Klavier, Op.7, Archiv Musikwissenschaft, Vol 0053, 96; music, Musiktheorie, Vol 0008, 93; Sound and Structure of 13th Century English Polyphonic Compositions--Interchange of Parts in the Worcester Fragments, Musikforschung, Vol 0047, 94; Sicilian Contrafacta--The Unity of Music and Lyrics in 13th Century Sicilian and Siculo Tuscan Music and Poetry, Musikforschung, Vol 0046, 93; The Granddaughters Archive--Dove, Rita Thomas and Beulah, Western Hum Rev, Vol 0051, 97; Corpus Troporum, Vol 7, Tropes Du Sanctus, Musikforschung, Vol 0046, 93; Stevens, Wallace, The Plain Sense of Things, Mod Philol, Vol 0092, 94; Reading as Poets Read,, Philos Lit, Vol 0020, 96; The Monographic Songs in the Roman de Fauvel, Musikforschung, Vol 0046, 93; Macahut Mass--An Introduction, Musiktheorie, Vol 0007,92; The Rondeau Ay Las Quant Je Pans in the Lucca Codex, Musikforschung, Vol 0048, 95; Quadruplum and Trimplum Parisian Organum--A Collection of Plainchants, Musikforschung, Vol 0048, 95; The Man with Night Sweats, Raritan Quart Rev, Vol 0013, 93; Foundations of Medieval Music, Mus, Vol 0049, 95. **CONTACT ADDRESS** 927 Clintwood Dr, Silver Spring, MD, 20902.

BERGER, CARL
PERSONAL Born 02/25/1939, The Pas, MB, Canada **DISCIPLINE** HISTORY **EDUCATION** Univ Man, BA, 61; Univ Toronto, MA, 62, PhD, 67. **CAREER** PROF HISTORY, UNIV TORONTO. **HONORS AND AWARDS** Gov Gen's Award Non-fiction 77 **MEMBERSHIPS** Royal Soc Can **SELECTED PUBLICATIONS** Auth, The Sense of Power: Studies in the Ideas of Canadian Imperialism 1867-1914, 70; The Writing of Canadian History, 76; Science, God and Nature in Victorian Canada, 83. **CONTACT ADDRESS** Dept of History, Univ of Toronto, Toronto, ON, M5S 3G3.

BERGER, DAVID
PERSONAL Born 06/24/1943, Brooklyn, NY, m, 1965, 3 children **DISCIPLINE** JEWISH HISTORY **EDUCATION** Yeshiva Col, BA, 64; Columbia Univ, MA, 65, PhD(hist), 70. **CAREER** Instr Jewish hist, Yeshiva Col, 68-70; asst prof, 70-75, assoc prof, 76-80, PROF HIST, BROOKLYN COL & GRAD CTR, CITY UNIV NEW YORK, 81-. **HONORS AND AWARDS** John Nicholas Brown Prize of the Medieval Academy of Am, 83; Fel, Am Acad Jewish Res. **MEMBERSHIPS** Asn Jewish Studies (pres, 97-); AHA; Mediaeval Acad Am; Am Acad Jewish Res. **RESEARCH** Medieval Jewish history; intellectual history of the Jews, Jewish-Christian relations; Messianism. **SELECTED PUBLICATIONS** Auth, Gilbert Crispin, Alan of Lille and Jacob ben Reuben: a study in the transmission of medieval polemic, Speculum, 1/74; The Jewish-Christian Debate in the High Middle Ages: A critical edition of the Nizzahon Vetus with an introduction, translation, and commentary, Jewish Public Soc Am, 79, softcover ed, Aronson, 96; Miracles and the Natural Order in Nahmanides, in Rabbi Moses nahmanides, 83; Mission to the Jews and Jewish-Christian contacts in the polemical literature of the high Middle Ages, Am Hist Rev, 86; Some ironic consequences of Maimonides' rationalistic messianism, Maimonidean Studies, 91; co-auth, Judaism's Encounter with Other Cultures: Rejection or Integration?, Aronson, 97; ed, History and Hate: the Dimensions of anti-semitism, Jew Publ Soc Am, 86. **CONTACT ADDRESS** Dept of Hist, Brooklyn Col, CUNY, Brooklyn, NY, 11210-2813. **EMAIL** dvbbc@cuynyvm.cuny.edu

BERGER, GORDON
DISCIPLINE HISTORY **EDUCATION** Yale Univ, PhD, 72. **CAREER** Prof, Univ Southern Calif. **RESEARCH** Modern Japanese history; history of Japanese politics in the 20th century. **SELECTED PUBLICATIONS** Auth, Politics and Militarism in the 1930s"; Parties Out of Power in Japan. **CONTACT ADDRESS** East Asian Studies Center, Univ Southern Calif, University Park Campus, Los Angeles, CA, 90089.

BERGER, HENRY WEINBERG
PERSONAL Born 07/12/1937, Frederick, MD, m, 1966, 2 children **DISCIPLINE** UNITED STATES HISTORY **EDUCATION** Ohio State Univ, BA, 59; Univ Wis, MS, 61, PhD(Hist) 66. **CAREER** From instr to asst prof Hist, Univ Vt, 65-70; asst prof, 70-72, assoc prof Hist, Wash Univ, 72-, fac res grant, 68-69; Nat Endowment for Humanities jr fel, 72-73; vis prof

Hist, Concordia Univ, 75-76; consult, Mo Comt, Nat Endowment for Humanities, 77-78; Alfred P Sloan Found grant, 81, 83; chmn Jewish Studies, Washington Univ, 81-84; chmn Jewish and Near Eastern Studies, 84-89, Washington Univ. **MEMBERSHIPS** Orgn Am Historians; Phi Beta Kappa, Soc for Historians of Am Foreign Relations. **RESEARCH** United States foreign relations, especially in the 20th century; United States labor history. **SELECTED PUBLICATIONS** Contribr, Senator Robert A Taft dissents from military escalation, In: Cold War Critics, Quadrangle, 71; Crisis diplomacy in the 1930's, In: From Colony to Empire, Wiley, 72; auth, Warren Austin in China, 1916-1917, Vt Hist, Fall 72; Bipartisanship, Senator Taft and the Truman Administration, Polit Sci Quart, Summer 75; Unions and empire: Organized labor and American corporations abroad, Peace & Change, Spring 76; Ed and Commentator, Amllian Appleman Williams Reader: Selections from His Major Historical Writings, Ivan R Dee, 92. **CONTACT ADDRESS** Dept of History, Washington Univ, 1 Brookings Dr, Box 1062, St. Louis, MO, 63130-4899. **EMAIL** hwberger@artsci.wustl.edu

BERGER, IRIS

PERSONAL Born 10/12/1941, Chicago, IL, 2 children **DISCIPLINE** AFRICAN & WOMEN'S HISTORY **EDUCATION** Univ Mich, BA, 63; Univ Wis, MA, 67, PhD(African hist), 73. **CAREER** Kaaga Elementary School, Meru, Kenya, 63; Kenya-Israel Sch of Social Work, Machakos, Kenya, adult educ, 64-65; Machakos Girl's High Sch, head hist teacher, 64-65; Res Assoc, Makerere Univ, Uganda, 70; Res Assoc, Univ of Dar es Salaam, Tanzania, 70; Adj lectr hist, State Univ NY Oneonta, 72-75, 76-79; asst prof, Wellesley Col, 75-76; Dewar Chair Lectr in Non-Western Hist, 77-78; Res Assoc African Hist, Boston Univ, 79-83; from Vis Asst Prof to Assoc Prof, 81-93, Prof of Hist, Africana and Women's Studies, State Univ of NY, Albany, 93-, Dir, Women's Studies Prog, 81-84, Dir, Grad Studies, Hist Dept, 96-97; Dir, Inst for Res on Women, 91-95; Pres, African Studies Asn, 95-96. **HONORS AND AWARDS** Nat Endowment for Humanities fel, 79-80, 86-87; Soc Sci Res Coun res fel, 80-81; Annual book award from the Academie Royale des Sciences d'Outre Mer, Brussels, to: Religion and Resistance: East African Kingdoms in the Precolonial Period, 82; The Rockefeller Found, Res Fel, 87; ACLS, Int Travel Award, Summer 90, Summer 95; Soc Sci Res Coun, Joint Comt on African Studies, Res Fel, Fall 90; Ford Found, Individual Award, 91; Distinguished Africanist Award, NY African Studies Asn, 97; recipient of numerous grants, research awards, graduate and undergraduate awards. **MEMBERSHIPS** African Studies Asn; Nat Women's Studies Asn. **RESEARCH** Women, work and trade unions in South Africa; women and industrialization--comparative perspectives. **SELECTED PUBLICATIONS** Contribr, East African Culture History, Syracuse Univ, 76; Women in Africa: Studies in Social and Economic Change, Stanford Univ Press, 76; The African Past Speaks, Dawson Publ Co, 80; auth, Religion and Resistance: East African Kingdoms in the Precolonial Period, Mus Royal Afrique Cent, 81; ed, Women and Class in Africa, Holmes and Meier/Africana Publ Co, 86; auth, Threads of Solidarity: Women in South African Industry, 1900-1980, Ind Univ Press/James Currey, 92; coauth, Women in Africa: Restoring Women to History, Ind Univ Press (forthcoming, 98); auth of numerous journal articles and review essays. **CONTACT ADDRESS** History Dept, State Univ of NY, Albany, 1400 Washington, Albany, NY, 12222-1000. **EMAIL** IB344@cnsvax.albany.edu

BERGER, MARK LEWIS

PERSONAL Born 12/02/1942, Brooklyn, NY, m, 1969, 2 children **DISCIPLINE** MIDDLE PERIOD OF AMERICAN HISTORY **EDUCATION** Queens Col, NY, BA, 64; City Univ New York, PhD, 72. **CAREER** Asst prof, 69-80, prof hist, Columbus Col, 80-. **MEMBERSHIPS** AHA; Orgn Am Historians; Southern Hist Assn. **RESEARCH** Pre-Civil War era. **SELECTED PUBLICATIONS** Auth, The Revolution in the New York Party Systems, 1840-1860, Kennikat. **CONTACT ADDRESS** Dept of History, Columbus State Univ, 4225 University Ave, Columbus, GA, 31907-5645. **EMAIL** berge_mark@colstate.edu

BERGER, MARTIN

DISCIPLINE ART HISTORY **EDUCATION** Yale Univ, PhD. **CAREER** Prof, Northwestern Univ **RESEARCH** Construction of gender and race; 19th century painting.. **SELECTED PUBLICATIONS** Auth, Man Made: Thomas Eakins and the Construction of Victorian Manhood, Univ Calif Press; essays on, 19th-century Am painting. **CONTACT ADDRESS** Dept of Art History, Northwestern Univ, 1801 Hinman, Evanston, IL, 60208.

BERGER, MARTIN EDGAR

PERSONAL Born 11/22/1942, Columbus, OH, m, 1965, 3 children **DISCIPLINE** MODERN EUROPEAN HISTORY **EDUCATION** Columbia Univ, BA, 64; Univ Pittsburgh, MA, 64, PhD(hist), 69. **CAREER** Asst prof, 69-77, from assoc prof to prof Hist, Youngstown State Univ, 77-. **MEMBERSHIPS** AHA; Study Group Int Labor & Working Class Hist; Conf Group Cent Europ Hist. **RESEARCH** Socialist movement; fascism; modern Germany. **SELECTED PUBLICATIONS** Auth, Engels, Armies, and Revolution: The Revolutionary Tactics of classical Marxism, Archon, 77. **CONTACT ADDRESS** Dept of History, Youngstown State Univ, One University Plz, Youngstown, OH, 44555-3452. **EMAIL** meberger@cc.ysu.edu

BERGER, PATRICE

DISCIPLINE HISTORY OF OLD REGIME EUROPE AND FRANCE **EDUCATION** Univ Chicago, PhD, 72. **CAREER** Assoc prof, dir, Honors prog, Univ Nebr, Lincoln. **HONORS AND AWARDS** Acad of Distinguished Tchr; Chancellor's Award for Exemplary Serv to Stud, 92; Outstanding Tchg and Instruct Creativity Award, 95. **RESEARCH** Biography of Louis de Pontchartrain. **SELECTED PUBLICATIONS** Published several articles on 17th century France. **CONTACT ADDRESS** Univ Nebr, Lincoln, 634 Oldfat, Lincoln, NE, 68588-0417. **EMAIL** pberger@unlinfo.unl.edu

BERGERON, PAUL H.

PERSONAL Born 02/08/1938, Alexandria, LA, m, 1968, 3 children **DISCIPLINE** HISTORY **EDUCATION** La Col, BA, 60; Vanderbilt Univ, MA, 62, PhD(hist), 65. **CAREER** From instr to assoc prof hist, Vanderbilt Univ, 65-72; assoc prof, 72-80, PROF HIST, UNIV TENN, KNOXVILLE, 80-; Ed, The Papers of Andrew Johnson, 87-. **MEMBERSHIPS** Orgn Am Historians; Southern History Asn. **RESEARCH** United States middle period, 1787-1865; political history of the Jacksonian era, 1830-60; Southern history. **SELECTED PUBLICATIONS** Co-ed, Correspondence of James K Polk, Vanderbilt Univ, Vols I & II, 69-72; auth, Paths of the Past, Tennessee, 1770-1970, Univ Tenn Press, 79; Antebellum Politics in Tennessee, Univ Press Ky, 82; The Presidency of James K. Polk, Univ Press Kans, 87; ed, The Papers of Andrew Johnson, Vol 8-14, Univ Tenn Press, 89-97. **CONTACT ADDRESS** Dept of History, Univ of Tennessee, Dunford Hall, Knoxville, TN, 37996-4065. **EMAIL** bergeron@utk.edu

BERGMAN, ROBERT P.

PERSONAL Born 05/17/1945, Bayonne, NJ, m, 1971, 1 child **DISCIPLINE** ART **EDUCATION** Rutgers Univ, BA, 66; Princeton Univ, MA, 69; Princeton Univ, PhD, 72 **CAREER** Assist prof, Univ Rochester, 71-72; assist prof, Princeton Univ, 72-76; assist prof, Harvard Univ, 76-81; assoc prof, Harvard Univ, 81-93; adjunct prof, John Hopkins Univ, 93-; dir, Cleveland Museum Hist Art **HONORS AND AWARDS** Junior Fel; Fulbright Fel (Rome); Rome Prize Fel **MEMBERSHIPS** Col Art Assoc; Amer Assoc Museums; Med Acad Amer **RESEARCH** Medieval Art and Architecture; Museums and Society **SELECTED PUBLICATIONS** Coauth, Vatican Treasures, Cleveland, 98; "The Culture of His Kingdom." Jrnl Soc Archit Historians, 98; Santa Maria de Olearia in Maiori, I: Architettura e affreschi, Centro di Cultura e storia Amalfitana, 95 **CONTACT ADDRESS** Cleveland Mus of Art, 11150 East Blvd., Cleveland, OH, 44106-1797. **EMAIL** bergman@cma-oh.org

BERGQUIST, JAMES MANNING

PERSONAL Born 02/01/1934, Council Bluffs, IA, m, 1969, 2 children **DISCIPLINE** UNITED STATES HISTORY **EDUCATION** Univ Notre Dame, BA, 55; Northwestern Univ, MA, 56, PhD(hist), 66. **CAREER** Instr hist, Coe Col, 61-63; from instr to asst prof, 63-69, assoc prof hist, 69-86, prof hist, Villanova Univ, 86-. **HONORS AND AWARDS** NEH Summer Fel, 67, 77, 80. **MEMBERSHIPS** AHA; Orgn Am Historians; Am Asn State & Local Hist; Immigration Hist Soc; Am Studies Asn; SHEAR; AAUP; Balch Inst for Thnic Studies, Philadelphia, 88-. **RESEARCH** Am soc hist; immigration; hist of old Northwest. **SELECTED PUBLICATIONS** Auth, The Oregon Donation Act and the National Land Policy, Ore Hist Quart, 3/57; People and Politics in Transition: The Illinois Germans, 1850-1860, In: Ethnic Voters and the Election of Lincoln, Univ Nebr, 71; The Forty-Eighters and the Politics of the 1850s, In: Germany and America, Brooklyn Col Press, 80; Tracing the origins of a midwestern culture, Ind Mag Hist, 3/82; German Communities and American Cities, J. Am Ethnic Hist, fall 84; The Concept of Nativism in Historical Study, Am Jewish Hist, 12/86; German Americans, Multiculturalism in the U.S., Greenwood, 92; The German American Press, The Ethic Press in the U.S., Greenwood, 87; ed, Immigration History Newsletter, 96-. **CONTACT ADDRESS** Dept of History, Villanova Univ, 845 E Lancaster Ave, Villanova, PA, 19085. **EMAIL** BERGQUIST@ucis.vill.edu

BERGQUIST, PETER

PERSONAL Born 08/05/1930, Sacramento, CA, m, 1956, 2 children **DISCIPLINE** MUSICOLOGY **EDUCATION** Mannes Col Music, NY, BS, 58; Columbia Univ, MA, 60, PhD, 64. **CAREER** From asst prof to assoc prof, 64-73, prof music, Sch Music, Univ OR, 73-95, Emer, 95. **HONORS AND AWARDS** Ersted Distinguished Tchg Award, Univ OR, 73; Fulbright Sr Res Grant, Germany, 85; DAAD study grant, 92; ACLS travel grant, 95; NEH publ grant, 94-98. **MEMBERSHIPS** Am Musicol Soc; Col Music Soc; Music Libr Asn; AAUP; Soc Music Theory. **RESEARCH** Renaissance music and music theory; Late Romantic music, Schenkerian analysis. **SELECTED PUBLICATIONS** Auth, Mode and Polyphony around 1500: Theory and practice, Vol I, Music Forum, 67; transl, Pietro Aaron, Toscanello in Musica, (1523, 1529), Colo Col Music, 70; auth, The first movement of Mahler's Symphony No 10: An analysis and examination of the sketches, Vol V, Music Forum, 80; eight articles on 16th century music and musicians, In: New Grove's Dictionary of Music and Musicians, 80; The poems of Orlando di Lasso's Prophetiae Sibylarum and their sources, J Am Musicol Soc, Vol 32, 79; ed, Orlando di Lasso, two motet cycles on readings from the Prophet Job, In: Recent Researches in the Music of the Renaissance, 83; ed, Orlando di Lasso, The Seven Penitential Psalms and Laudate Dominum de caelis, In: Recent Researches/Renaissance, 90; Orlando di Lasso Nunc dimittis-Vertonungen, Musik in Bayern, 86; Why did Orlando di Lasso not publish his posthumous motets?, Festschrift fur Horst Leuchtmann, Tutzing, Hans Schneider, 93; The anonymous propers in Munich Mss 32 and 76: Are they previously unknown works by Orlando di Lass, Acta Musicologica, 93; ed, Orlando di Lasso, Samtliche Werke neue Reihe, vol 22, Lamentationes Jeremiae Prophetae, 92, vol 23, Offizien und Messproprien, 93, vol 24, Musik fur die Officia, 93, vol 25, Litaneien und Falsibordoni, 93; The modality of Lasso's compositions in A Minor, Orlando di Lasso in der Musikgeschichte, Verl der Bayer Akad der Wissensch, 96; ed, Orlando di Lasso, The Complete Motets, In: Recent Researches/Renaissance, 1995-; 8 vol; ed, Orlando Di Lasso Studies, Cambridge Univ Press, 99. **CONTACT ADDRESS** Sch of Music, Univ of OR, Eugene, OR, 97403-1205. **EMAIL** pberg1@darkwing.uoregon.edu

BERGREN, ANN L.T.

DISCIPLINE CLASSICAL PHILOLOGY **EDUCATION** Wellesley Col, BA, 61-65; Univ Iowa, MA, 65-68; Harvard Univ, PhD, 68-73. **CAREER** Tchg fel, Harvard Univ, 71; instr, Wellesley Col, 72; asst prof, Princeton Univ, 72-79; summer vis asst prof, Univ Iowa, 73; vis asst prof, Stanford Univ, 76; vis prof, Harvard Univ, 93; adj prof, South Calif Inst of Arch, 87-; PROF, CLASS, UCLA, 79-. **HONORS AND AWARDS** Fel(s), Ctr Hellenic Stud, 76-77; Amer Coun of Learned Soc, 84; Chicago Inst for Arch and Urbanism, 89-90; Hum Res Inst, Univ Calif-Irvine, 91; Hon(s) Collegium Fac Recognition award, 86; distinguished tchg award, Univ Calif, LA, 88; award for excellence in the tchg of classics, Amer Philol Assn, 88., Ed bd(s), Amer Philol Assn, 80-84; Helios, Jour of the Class Assn of the Southwestern US, 79-82; Univ Calif Publ in Class Stud, 83-88. **RESEARCH** Architecture. **SELECTED PUBLICATIONS** Auth, "Letter to Jennifer Bloomer on Architecture and the Feminine," ANY Architecture New York, "Architecture and the Feminine: Mop-Up Work," 94; "The (Re)Marriage of Penelope and Odysseus," Architecture Gender Philosophy, Assemblage, A Critical Jour of Arch and Design Cult 21, 93. **CONTACT ADDRESS** Dept of Classics, Univ Calif, PO Box 951436, Los Angeles, CA, 90095-1436.

BERINGER, RICHARD E.

PERSONAL Born 12/29/1933, Madison, WI, m, 1964, 2 children **DISCIPLINE** HISTORY **EDUCATION** Lawrence Col, BA, 56; Northwestern Univ Evanston Il, MA, 57, PhD, 66. **CAREER** Teaching asst, 60-62, Northwestern Univ; personnel off, 57-60, USAF; instr, 63-64, Wisc St Univ; asst prof, 65-69, Calif St Univ Hayward; assoc prof, to prof, grad faculty, dept chair, prof emeritus, 70-99, Univ ND. **HONORS AND AWARDS** Phi Beta Kappa, Magna Cum Laude, Lawrence Col, 56; Nat Hist Publ & Records Comm Fel, 69-70; Jefferson Davis Award, 73, 87; Charles Sackett Sydnor Award, 73; Rev Elmer & Min West Outstanding Faculty Award, 87; Chester Fritz Distinguished Professorship, 88; Fulbright Travel Award, Germany, 94. **MEMBERSHIPS** S Hist Assoc; Hist Soc. **RESEARCH** U S Civil War era; nineteenth century U S mil hist. **SELECTED PUBLICATIONS** Vis coed, auth of intro, The Papers of Jefferson Davis, La St Univ Press, 83; coauth, Why the South Lost the Civil War, Univ Ga Press, 86, 88; rev, American Against Itself, rev of Battle Cry of Freedom: The Civil War Era, NY Rev of Books, 88; auth, Jefferson Davis's Pursuit of Ambition: The Attractive Features of Alternative Decisions, Civil War Hist, 92; art, Confederate Identity and the Will to Fight, On the Road to Total War: The American Civil War and the German Wars of Unification, 1861-1871, Cambridge Univ Press, 96. **CONTACT ADDRESS** Dept of History, Univ ND, Univ Station, Box 8096, Grand Forks, ND, 58202. **EMAIL** beringer@plains.nodak.edu

BERKELEY, EDMUND

PERSONAL Born 04/01/1937, Charlottesville, VA, m, 2 children **DISCIPLINE** HISTORY **EDUCATION** Univ of the South, BA, 58; Univ Va, MA, 61. **CAREER** Asst archv, Va State Lib, 61-63; from sr asst to acting cur, 65-65, asst prof & Cur of Manuscripts, 70-76, assoc prof & univ archv, 76-87, agency records adminr, 79- , dir special collections, 87-94, Univ Archv & Coordr, Special Collections Digital Ctr, 95- , Univ Va. **HONORS AND AWARDS** Phi Beta Kappa; fel, Soc of Am Archv, 76; fel, Va Ctr for Hum and Public Policy, 88. **MEMBERSHIPS** Albemarle Co Hist Soc; Asn for Documentary Editing; Bibliog Soc of Univ Va; Book Arts Press; Mid-Atlantic Regional Arch Conf; Mid-West Archv Conf; Soc of Am Archv; Soc of Ga Archv; Va Asn of Gov Arch and Records Adminr; Va Hist Soc. **SELECTED PUBLICATIONS** Ed, Robert Carter as Agricultural Administrator: His Letters to Robert Jones, 1727-1729, Va Mag of Hist and Biog, 93; auth, The Great War Exhibit at the University of Virginia Library, in Dictionary of Literary Biography Year Book 1993, Gale, 94; auth, Linton R. Massey, in Rosenblum, ed, American Book Collectors and Bibliographers, Second Series, Gale, 97. **CONTACT ADDRESS**

Special Collections Dept, Univ Virginia Library, Charlottesville, VA, 22903-2498. **EMAIL** eb2c@virginia.edu

BERKEY, JONATHAN P.
PERSONAL Born 12/05/1959, Northampton, MA, m, 1988, 2 children **DISCIPLINE** HISTORY **EDUCATION** Williams, BA, 81; Princeton, MA, 86, PhD, 89. **CAREER** Asst Prof Relig, Mt Holyoke Col, 90-93; Asst Prof Hist, Davidson Col, 93-96; Assoc Prof, 96-. **HONORS AND AWARDS** Fulbright/IIE, 86-87; NEH Fellow, 92-93. **MEMBERSHIPS** Inst for Adv Stud, 94-95; Mid E Stud Asn. **RESEARCH** Medieval Islamic History. **SELECTED PUBLICATIONS** auth, The Transmission of Knowledge in Medieval Cairo: A Social History of Islamic Education, Princeton Press, 92; auth, Tradition, Innovation and the Social Construction of Knowledge in the Medieval Islamic Near East, Past & Present, 146, 38-65, 95; auth, Women in Medieval Islamic Society, Women & Medieval Culture, Garland Pub, forthcoming; auth, Popular Preaching and Religious Authority in the Medieval Islamic Near East, Univ Wa Press, (in press). **CONTACT ADDRESS** Dept Hist, Davidson Col, Davidson, NC, 28036. **EMAIL** joberkey@davidson.edu

BERKIN, CAROL RUTH
PERSONAL Born 10/01/1942, Mobile, AL, m, 1970, 2 children **DISCIPLINE** AMERICAN HISTORY **EDUCATION** Barnard Col, AB, 64; Columbia Univ, MA, 66, PhD(Am hist), 72. **CAREER** Mem ed staff, Papers of Alexander Hamilton, 64-65; lectr, Columbia Univ, 69 & Hunter Col, City Univ New York, 69-70; asst prof, 72-75; assoc prof, 75-79, PROF HIST, BARUCH COL, CITY UNIV NEW YORK, 79-, PROF, GRAD CTR, CUNY, 80-. **HONORS AND AWARDS** Bancroft Dissertation Award, Columbia Univ, 72; Am Coun Learned Socs study fel, 78-79. **MEMBERSHIPS** AHA; Orgn Am Historians; Soc Am Historians; Am Studies Asn; Am Soc 18th Century Studies; Coord Comt Women in Hist Profession. **SELECTED PUBLICATIONS** Auth, Jonathan Sewall: Odyssey of an American Loyalist, Columbia Univ, 74; Within the Conjurer's Circle: Women in Colonial America, Gen Learning, 74; co-ed, Women of America: A History, Houghton-Mifflin, 79; auth, Private Woman, Public Woman: The contradictions of Charlotte Perkins Gilman, In: The Women of America, 79, Houghton-Mifflin; co-ed, Women, War and Revolution, Holmes-Meier, 79; auth, First Generations: Women in Colonial America, Hill & Wang, 96; co-ed, Women's Voices, Women's Lives: Documents in Early American History, Northeastern Univ Press, 98. **CONTACT ADDRESS** CUNY, Baruch Col, 17 Lexington Ave, New York, NY, 10010-5518. **EMAIL** Berkin@aol.com

BERKLEY, GERALD WAYNE
PERSONAL Born 09/02/1942, Oklahoma City, OK, m, 1968, 1 child **DISCIPLINE** ASIAN HISTORY **EDUCATION** Okla City Univ, BA, 69; Univ Hawaii, MA, 71; Univ Hong Kong, PhD (hist), 77. **CAREER** Dir gen English, New Asia Col, Chinese Univ Hong Kong, 71-75; instr Far Eastern hist, Ark State Univ, 76-77; asst prof Asian hist, Univ Md, College Park, 77-78; asst prof, Va Polytech Inst & State Univ, 78-79; asst prof, 79-82, ASSOC PROF ASIAN HIST, AUBURN UNIV, MONTGOMERY, 82- **MEMBERSHIPS** Asn Asian Studies. **RESEARCH** Peasant revolution in China in the 1920's; missionaries from Alabama who served in China. **SELECTED PUBLICATIONS** Auth, Indo China in the 1940s and 1950s, J Asian Hist, Vol 0028, 94; After Tet--The Bloodiest Year in Vietnam, J Asian Hist, Vol 0028, 94; Radicalism and the Origins of the Vietnamese Revolution, J Asian Hist, Vol 0027, 93; Dragons Entangled Indo China and the China Vietnam War, J Asian Hist, Vol 0027, 93; Vietnam at the Crossroads, J Asian Hist, Vol 0028, 94. **CONTACT ADDRESS** Hist Dept, Auburn Univ, Montgomery, AL, 36193.

BERKMAN, JOYCE A.
PERSONAL Born 11/20/1937, San Jose, CA, m, 1962, 2 children **DISCIPLINE** HISTORY, WOMEN'S STUDIES **EDUCATION** Univ Calif, Los Angeles, BA, 58; Yale Univ, MA, 59, PhD, 67. **CAREER** Instr, Conn Col, 62-63; instr, 66-68, asst prof, 68-80, ASSOC PROF HIST, UNIV MASS, 80-; Danforth Found assoc, 75. **HONORS AND AWARDS** Distinguished Teacher Award, Univ Mass, 80. **MEMBERSHIPS** Am Hist Assoc; Berkshire Orgn Women Historians; Conf Brit Historians; Northeast Victorian Studies Asn; New Eng Hist Asn; Nat Women's Studies Asn. **RESEARCH** 19th and 20th century British and American women's history; African-American women's history; Victorian social and intellectual history; historical methodology. **SELECTED PUBLICATIONS** Auth, The Healing Imagination of Olive Schreiner: Beyond South African Colonialism, Univ Mass Press, 89; co-ed, African American Women and the Vote, Univ mass Press, 97 **CONTACT ADDRESS** Univ of Mass, Amherst, MA, 01003-0002. **EMAIL** jberkman@history.umass.edu

BERKOWITZ, EDWARD D.
PERSONAL Born 01/11/1950, Passaic, NJ, m, 2 children **DISCIPLINE** HISTORY **EDUCATION** Princeton Univ, AB, 72; Northwestern Univ, MA, 73, PhD, 76. **CAREER** Asst prof, Univ Ma, Boston, 77-80; dir to assoc prof, Brandeis Univ, Waltham, Ma, 82-89; chair to prof, dir, George Washington Univ, Washington, DC, 89- . **HONORS AND AWARDS** Ed bd

member, J of Policy Hist; assoc ed & book rev ed, J of Disability Policy Stud; ed bd member, J of Gerontology-Soc Sci; ed bd member, Soc Insurance Update; founding member, Nat Acad of Soc Insurance; Mary Switzer Scholar, 84., Robert Wood Johnson Found Faculty Fel, Health Care Fin, Johns Hopkins Med Inst, 87-88. **MEMBERSHIPS** Amer Hist Assoc, Org of Amer Hist; Soc Sci Hist Assoc. **RESEARCH** History & public policy; soc welfare policy, hist of Soc Sec; disability policy; hist of med care; the presidency. **SELECTED PUBLICATIONS** Auth, Disabled Policy: America's Programs for the Handicapped--A Twentieth Century Fund Report, Cambridge Univ Press, 87, 89; America's Welfare State: From Roosevelt to Reagan, Johns Hopkins Press, 91; Mr. Social Security: The Life of Wilbur J. Cohen, Univ Press Ks, 95; To Heal A Nation: A History of the Institute of Medicine, Nat Acad Press, 98; coauth, Group Health Association: A Portrait of a Health Maintenance Organization, Temple Univ Press, 88. **CONTACT ADDRESS** Dept of History, George Washington Univ, Washington, DC, 20052.

BERLANSTEIN, LENARD RUSSELL
PERSONAL Born 11/29/1947, Brooklyn, NY **DISCIPLINE** EUROPEAN HISTORY **EDUCATION** Univ Mich, BA, 69; Johns Hopkins Univ, MA, 71, PhD, 73. **CAREER** Asst prof, 73-79, assoc prof, 79-86, PROF HISTORY, UNIV VA, 86-. **MEMBERSHIPS** AHA; Soc Fr Hist Studies. **RESEARCH** French social and cultural history. **SELECTED PUBLICATIONS** Auth, The Advocates of Toulouse in the Eighteenth Century, 1750-1793, Johns Hopkins Univ, 75; The Working People of Paris, 1871-1914, Johns Hopkins Univ Press, 86; Big Business and Industrial Conflict in Nineteenth Century France, Univ Calif Press, 91. **CONTACT ADDRESS** Dept of Hist, Univ of Va, 1 Randall Hall, Charlottesville, VA, 22903-3284. **EMAIL** lrb@virginia.edu

BERLIN, ADELE
PERSONAL Born 05/23/1943, Philadelphia, PA, m, 2 children **DISCIPLINE** ANCIENT NEAR EASTERN STUDIES **EDUCATION** Univ Pa, PhD, 76. **CAREER** Robert H Smith prof of Hebrew Bible, Univ MD. **HONORS AND AWARDS** Guggenheim fel; ACLS fel; NEH translation fel; fel, Am Academy of Jewish Res. **MEMBERSHIPS** Soc of Biblical Lit; Asn for Jewish Studies; Am Oriental Soc. **RESEARCH** Biblical literature. **SELECTED PUBLICATIONS** Auth, Zephaniah, Anchor Bible; The Dynamics of Biblical Parallelism; Poetics and Interpretation of Biblical Narrative. **CONTACT ADDRESS** Dept of English, Univ of Maryland, Col Park, College Park, MD, 20742. **EMAIL** aberlin@deans.umd.edu

BERLIN, ANDREA MICHELLE
DISCIPLINE HELLENISTIC AND ROMAN CERAMICS, HELLENISTIC AND ROMAN NEAR EAST, ARCHAEOLOG **EDUCATION** Univ Mich, AB, 76; Univ Chicago, AM, 79; Univ Mich, PhD, 88. **CAREER** Instr, Univ Mich, 81-84; instr, Hebrew Univ, Jerusalem, 85; lectr, George Washington Univ, 88; lectr, Univ Va, 89; lectr, Univ Md, 90; adj asst prof, Georgetown Univ, 94-95; asst prof, Univ Minn, Twin Cities, 97-. **HONORS AND AWARDS** Samuel H Kress fel, Am Sch of Orient Res & Albright Inst of Archaeol, Jerusalem, 84-85; Fulbright-Hays jr res fel, Greece, 85-86; Homer A and Dorothy B Thompson fel, Am Sch of Class Stud, Athens, 86-87; Grad Col Scholar Award, Univ Ill, Urbana-Champaign, 93-94; jr fel, Ctr for Hellenic Stud, Wash, 96-97; Shelby White-Leon Levy fel, 97-98. **RESEARCH** Persian, Hellenistic, and Roman pottery. **SELECTED PUBLICATIONS** Auth, Excavations at Tel Anafa, vol II, i. The Persian, Hellenistic, and Roman Plain Wares, J of Roman Archaeol Suppl Ser vol 10.2, 97; From Monarchy to Markets: The Phoenicians in Hellenistic Palestine, Bull of Am Sch of Orient Res 306: 75-88, 97; Between Large Forces: Palestine in the Hellenistic Period, Bibl Archaeol 60.1: 2- 57, 97. **CONTACT ADDRESS** Dept of Class & Near Eastern Stud, Univ Minn, Twin Cities, Minneapolis, MN, 55455. **EMAIL** aberlin@tc.umn.edu

BERLIN, I.
PERSONAL Born 05/27/1941, New York, NY, m, 1963, 2 children **DISCIPLINE** HISTORY **EDUCATION** Univ Wis, PhD. **CAREER** Prof, Univ Md, 83-, Actg Dean Undergrad Studies, Univ Md, 92-94, Actg Dean Col Arts & Humanities, 95-96; Ford Found Lectr, Ctr Study Southern Cult, Univ Miss, 86; Bi-Centennial Fulbright Prof, Ctr Recherche sur l'Histoire des Etats-Unis, Univ Paris VII, 87; William B. Cardozo Vis Prof, Yale Univ, 99. **HONORS AND AWARDS** Thomas Jefferson Prize, Soc Hist Fed Govt, 85; J. Franklin Jameson Prize, Am Hist Asn, 85; Founders Award, Confederate Mem Lit Soc, 85; Distinguished Teacher-Scholar, Univ Md, 90-91; Thomas Jefferson Prize, Soc Hist Fed Govt, 90; The State's Outstanding Fac Mem, Md Asn Higher Educ, 91; Distinguished Fac Res Fel, Univ Md, 91-92; Abraham Lincoln Prize, Lincoln and Soldiers Inst, for Free at Last, 94; Founders Award, Valentine Museum, for The Wartime Genesis of Slavery, 95; Fel, Res Ctr Soc Sci, Inst Advanced Studies, Australian Nat Univ, 98; William Percy Award, SEast Eighteenth-Century Studies Asn, 1996; Daughters of Colonial War Prize, 96; Douglass Adair Prize, 98. **MEMBERSHIPS** Soc Sci Hist Asn; Southern Hist Asn; Org Am Hist; Am Hist Asn; Columbia Seminar on Econ Hist; Comt on Race & Ethnicity; Int Sociol Asn; Europ-Am Studies Asn;

Milan Group Am Hist. **RESEARCH** American history. **SELECTED PUBLICATIONS** Co-ed, The Slaves' Economy: Independent Production by Slaves in the New World, Cass, 91; Culture and Cultivation: Labor and the Shaping of Slave Life in the Americas, Univ Va Press, 93; coauth, Slaves No More: Three Essays on Emancipation and the Civil War, Cambridge Univ Press, 92; Free At Last: A Documentary History of Slavery, Freedom, and the Civil War, New Press, 92; Families and Freedom: A Documentary History of African-American Kinship in the Civil War Era, New Press, 97; We Were Slaves: Memories of Slavery and Freedom in America, New Press, 98; Many Thousands Gone: The First Two Centuries of African-American Slavery in mainland North America, Harvard Univ Press, 98; Freedom's Soldiers: The Black Military Experience and the Civil War, Cambridge Univ Press (forthcoming 98). **CONTACT ADDRESS** History Dept, Univ of Maryland, College Park, MD, 20742. **EMAIL** ib3@umail.umd.edu

BERLIN, NETTA
DISCIPLINE LATIN AND GREEK LANGUAGE AND LITERATURE **EDUCATION** Wellesley Col, BA, 84; Univ MI, MA, 88, PhD, 93. **CAREER** Asst prof, 93-, Tulane Univ. **RESEARCH** Epic poetry, mythology, ancient literary criticism. **SELECTED PUBLICATIONS** Auth, War and Remembrance: Aeneid 12.554-60, and Aeneas' Memory of Troy, Amer Jour Philol 119, 98. **CONTACT ADDRESS** Dept of Class Stud, Tulane Univ, 6823 St Charles Ave, New Orleans, LA, 70118. **EMAIL** nberlin@mailhost.tcs.tulane.edu

BERLIN, ROBERT HARRY
PERSONAL Born 10/24/1946, Pittsburgh, PA, m, 1971 **DISCIPLINE** AMERICAN AND MILITARY HISTORY **EDUCATION** Rockford Col, BA, 68; Univ Calif, Santa Barbara, PhD (hist), 76. **CAREER** Instr hist, Allan Hancock Community Col, 76-79; vis assoc prof mil hist, 79-81, ASSOC PROF MIL HIST, US ARMY COMMAND AND GEN STAFF COL, 81-, Vis asst prof hist Am Revolution, Mansfield State Col, 76; lectr, Continuing Educ Div, Santa Barbara City Col, 76. **MEMBERSHIPS** Orgn Am Historians; Am Mil Inst; fel Inter-Univ Sem on Armed Forces & Soc; Soc Hist Fed Govt. **RESEARCH** American military history; American Revolution. **SELECTED PUBLICATIONS** Auth, US Marines in the Persia -Gulf, 1990-1991--With he 1st Marine Division in Desert Shield and Desert Storm, Pub Hist, Vol 0017, 95; Infamous Day--Marines at Pearl Harbor, 7 December 1941, Pub Hist, Vol 0017, 95; 1st Offensive--The Marine Campaign for Guadalcanal, Pub Hist, Vol 0017, 95; United States Marines in Vietnam--The War that Would Not End, 1971-1973, Pub Hist, Vol 0017, 95. **CONTACT ADDRESS** 1716 Miami St, Leavenworth, KS, 66048.

BERLO, JANET CATHERINE
DISCIPLINE ART HISTORY **EDUCATION** Yale Univ, PhD, 80. **CAREER** Prof & Susan B. Anthony ch Gender and Women's Stud. **HONORS AND AWARDS** Sr res grant, J. Paul Getty Found, 94-96; fel col tchr(s), Nat Endowment for the Humanities, 94; fac res grant, Can Govt, 94; presidential awd excellence tchg, Univ MO, 94 & Summer grant, Am Philos Soc, 89. **RESEARCH** North Am Indian art hist; mus studies; arts of the colonial encounter; Pre-Columbian art and archaeol. **SELECTED PUBLICATIONS** Auth, Plains Indian Drawings 1865-1935: Pages from a Visual History, NY, Abrams Press, 96; Ed, Art and Ideology at Teotihuacan, WA, Dumbarton Oaks Res Ctr, 93; The Early Years of Native American Art History: The Politics of Scholarship and Collecting, Univ WA Press, 92; co-ed, Arts of Africa, Oceania and the Americas: Selected Readings, Prentice Hall Co, 92. **CONTACT ADDRESS** Dept of Art and Art Hist, Univ of Rochester, 601 Elmwood Ave, Ste. 656, 421 Morey , Rochester, NY, 14642. **EMAIL** brlo@uhura.cc.rochester.edu

BERMAN, HYMAN
PERSONAL Born 02/20/1925, New York, NY, m, 1950 **DISCIPLINE** HISTORY **EDUCATION** City Col New York, BS, 48; Columbia Univ, PhD (hist), 56. **CAREER** Instr Hist, Brooklyn Col, 57-60; asst prof Am thought, Mich State Univ, 60-61; from asst prof to assoc prof hist, 61-61, dir soc sci prog, 68-71, PROF HIST AND DIR EXP COURSES PROG, UNIV MINN, MINNEAPOLIS, 71-, Vis lectr, Osmania Univ, India, 64; mem screening comt, Woodrow Wilson Fel Found, 66-; vis prof, Univ Calif, Berkeley, 67-68. **MEMBERSHIPS** AHA; Immigration Hist Group (exec secy, 67); Orgn Am Historians; Labor Historians. **RESEARCH** US labor; immigration and social history. **SELECTED PUBLICATIONS** Auth, A Restriction on the Shape of Proto Algonquian Nouns, Int J Am Ling, Vol 0058, 92; Nuclear Roles in the Post Cold War World, Wash Quart, Vol 0020, 97; The Declining Utility of Nuclear Weapons Wash Quart, Vol 0020, 97; Insecure Prosperity Small Town Jews in Industrial America, 1890-1940, J Am Hist, Vol 0083, 97. **CONTACT ADDRESS** Dept of Hist, Univ of Minn, 267 19th Ave S, Minneapolis, MN, 55455-0499.

BERMAN, WILLIAM C.
PERSONAL Born 01/09/1932, Cleveland, OH, m, 1962, 2 children **DISCIPLINE** MODERN AMERICAN HISTORY **EDUCATION** Ohio State Univ, BA, 54, MA, 59, PhD (hist), 63. **CAREER** Asst prof hist, Calif State Col, 63-65 and Univ Louisville, 65-68; assoc prof, 68-73, PROF HIST, UNIV TO-

RONTO, 73-, Can Coun res grant, 70-73. **MEMBERSHIPS** Orgn Am Historians. **RESEARCH** Recent American political history; post 1945 American foreign policy. **SELECTED PUBLICATIONS** Auth, The Politics of Rage--Wallace, George, The Origins of the New Conservatism, and the Transformation of American Politics, Am Hist Rev, Vol 0102, 97; Fighting the Odds--The Life of Senator Church, Frank, Am Hist Rev, Vol 0100, 95; Turning Right in the 60s--The Conservative Capture of the Gop, Revs Am Hist, Vol 0024, 96; Goldwater, Barry, Revs Am Hist, Vol 0024, 96. **CONTACT ADDRESS** Dept of Hist, Univ of Toronto, Toronto, ON, M5S 1A1.

BERNARD, J.W.
PERSONAL Born 06/27/1951, Portsmouth, NH, m, 1984, 1 child **DISCIPLINE** MUSIC EDUCATION **EDUCATION** Harvard Univ, BA 72; Yale Univ, PhD 77. **CAREER** Univ Washington, prof 87-; previously at Yale Univ and Amherst College, 22 years teaching experience. **HONORS AND AWARDS** Morse Fel; Young Sch Awd; Paul Sacher Foun. **MEMBERSHIPS** SMT; AMS. **RESEARCH** Theory and analysis of 20th century music; the history of music theory 1700 to present. **SELECTED PUBLICATIONS** Auth, Music Theory in Concept and Practice, con't ed, Rochester, Univ Rochester Press, 97; Elliot Carter: Collected Essays and Lectures, ed, Rochester, Rochester Univ Press, 97; Listening to Zappa, in: Contemporary Music Rev, spec issue, eds, John Covach and Walter Everett, 99; Tonal Traditions in Art Music since 1960, in:: The Cambridge Hist of Amer Music, ed, Dave Nicholls, Cambridge Univ Press, 98; Chord Collection and Set in Twentieth-Century Theory, in: Music Theory in Concept Practice, ed, Dave Nicholls, Cambridge Univ Press, 98; Poem as Non-Verbal Text: Elliot Carter's Concerto for Orchestra and St John Perse's Vents, in: Analytical Strategies and Musical Interp, eds, Craig Ayrey, Mark Everist, Cambridge Univ Press, 96; Elliot Carter and the Modern Meaning of Time, The Musical Quart, 95; Theory Analysis and the Problem of Minimal Music, in: Concert Music Rock and Jazz Since 1945: Essays and Analytical Studies, eds, Elizabeth W. Marvin, Richard Hermann, Rochester, Univ Rochester Press, 95. **CONTACT ADDRESS** Dept off Music, Washington Univ, Seattle, WA, 98195. **EMAIL** jbernard@u.washington.edu

BERNARD, PAUL PETER
PERSONAL Born 07/05/1929, Antwerp, Belgium, m, 1949, 3 children **DISCIPLINE** HISTORY **EDUCATION** Univ Denver, AB, 48; Univ Colo, MA, 52, PhD (hist), 55. **CAREER** Instr French, Univ Colo, 55; from instr to assoc prof hist, Colo Col, 55-68; PROF HIST, UNIV ILL, URBANA-CHAMPAIGN, 68-, Ford Found pub affairs fel, Austria, 60-61; assoc, Ctr Advan Study, Univ Ill, 71-72 and 79-80; Nat Endowment for Humanities sr fel, 75-76. **MEMBERSHIPS** AHA. **RESEARCH** Hussite movement; Joseph II of Austria; Austrian enlightenment. **SELECTED PUBLICATIONS** Auth, Kaunitz and the Renversement Des Alliances--Studies on the Foreign Policy Concepts of Kaunitz, Wenzel, Anton, Eng Hist Rev, Vol 0110, 95; Kaunitz and Enlightened Absolutism, 1753-1780, Eng Hist Rev, Vol 0110, 95; Joseph II, Int Hist Rev, Vol 0017, 95; The City and the Crown--Vienna and the Imperial Court 1600-1740, Am Hist Rev, Vol 0099, 94. **CONTACT ADDRESS** Dept of Hist, Univ of Ill, Urbana, IL, 61801.

BERNARDO, FELIX MARIO
PERSONAL Born 02/07/1934, Waterbury, CT, m, 1979, 2 children **DISCIPLINE** SOCIOLOGY **EDUCATION** Univ CT, BA (Sociology), 61; FL State Univ, PhD (Sociology & Anthropology, High Honors and Distinction), 65. **CAREER** Asst prof Sociology and Rural Sociology, Washington State Univ, 65-69; assoc prof Sociology, 69-73, assoc chair, 72-77, prof Sociology, Univ FL, 73-, dept chair, 85-91; ed, J of Marriage and the Family, 75-81, assoc ed, 72-75, 82-85; assoc ed, Int J of Sociology of the Family, 70-92; assoc ed, The Family Coordinator, 71-75; assoc ed, Social Forces, 76-79; assoc ed, Death education, 79-86; assoc ed, J of Aging Studies, 86-; consult ed, Death studies, 86-92; ed adv bd, Population Res and Policy Rev, 80-90, Sage Family Studies Abstracts, 81-, Sociological Inquiry, 91-. **HONORS AND AWARDS** Phi Beta Kappa, Phi Kappa Phi, Univ CT; Alpha Kappa Delta, FL State Univ; Arthur Peterson Award in Death Education, 86; One of Ten Family Sociologist in America, recognition by NCFR, 87; One of Top Publishers of Family Studies in refereed professional journals from 80-87, Univ NE, 88; nominated for Pres, Southern Sociol Soc, 88; Certificate of Recognition, Nat Coun on Family Relations, 88; nominated for Pres, Nat Coun on Family Relations, 89; nominated for Assoc Dean, CLAS, 95; recognized as "Very Important Professor," Career Resource Center, 90; nominated, Publications Vice-Pres, Nat Coun on Family Relations, 95; awarded fel status, Gerontological Soc of Am, 92; selected to be included in Profiles in Gerontology: Biographical Dictionary of Sociology; invited by Pres, Japanese Sociol Soc, to visit Japan to consult with faculty in Tokyo Metropolitan Inst; listing found in many bibliographical directories. **MEMBERSHIPS** Am Sociol Asn (sec, Family Section); Nat Coun on Family Relations (Section chmn; chair, Pub Bd Chair, Strategic Planning Comm); Southern Sociological Soc (Section chair; Chmn, Fl Membership Comm, Chair, Program Comm); Gerontological Soc of Am, fel; Southeastern Coun on Family Relations (Chair, Nomination's Comm); FL Coun on Family Relations (Pres). **SELECTED PUBLICATIONS** Auth, Scientific Norms and Research Publication: Issues and Professional Ethics, in Roma S Hanks, Linda K Matocha, and Marvin B Sussman, eds, Publishing in Journals on the Family: Essays on Publishing, Haworth Press, 93; Scholarly Publication: A Career Retrospective, in Roma S Hanks, Linda K Matocha, and Marvin B Sussman, eds, Publishing in Journals on the Family: Essays on Publishing, Haworth Press, 93; Widowhood, in David Levison, ed, Encyclopedia of Marriage and the Family, Macmillan, 95; Cohabitation, in David Levison, ed, Encyclopedia of Marriage and the Family, Macmillan, 95; with Constance L Shehan and Felix M Bernardo, Exercising Authority in the Undergraduate Classroom: Assisting the Novice Teacher in Achieving a Balance Between Cuidance and Control, Family Science Rev, vol 11, no 1, Feb 98; ed, Family Privacy, special issue, J of Family Issues, vol 19, no 1, Jan 98; Family Privacy: Issues and Concepts, J of Family Issues, 118, vol 19, no 1, Jan 98; and numerous other books, articles and other publications. **CONTACT ADDRESS** Dept of Sociology, Univ of Florida, Gainsville, FL, 32611.

BERNSTEIN, BARTON JANNEN
PERSONAL Born 09/08/1936, New York, NY, m, 1967 **DISCIPLINE** AMERICAN HISTORY **EDUCATION** Queens Col, AB, 57; Harvard Univ, PhD, 64. **CAREER** Mem fac soc sci, Bennington Col, 63-65; asst prof hist, 65-68, assoc prof, 68-82, PROF HIST, STANFORD UNIV, 82-, Am Coun Learned Soc grant-in-aid, 64-65; Charles Warren fel, Harvard Univ, 67-68; Harry S Truman Inst fel, 67-68; fel, Ctr Advan Studies, Univ Ill, Urbana, 70-71 and Comt Res Int Studies grant, 74; adv ed, Little, Brown and Co, 70-73; Hoover Inst peace fel, 74-75; Nat Endowment for Humanities fel, 77-78; Ford Found fel, 80. **HONORS AND AWARDS** Goldstein Prize in Civil War Hist, 58; Dean's Teaching Award, Stanford Univ, 77; Koontz Prize, Pac Hist Rev, 78. **MEMBERSHIPS** AHA; Orgn Am Historians; Conf Peace Res Hist; Soc Hist & Am Foreign Rels. **RESEARCH** Twentieth century American history; history of the cold war; American social history and foreign policy. **SELECTED PUBLICATIONS** Auth, Understanding the Atomic Bomb and the Japanese Surrender--Missed Opportunities, Little Known Near Disasters and Modern Memory, Dipl Hist, Vol 0019, 95; Seizing the Contested Terrain of Early Nuclear History--Stimson, Conant, and Their Allies Explain the Decision to Use the Atomic Bomb, Dipl Hist, Vol 0017, 93; The Challenge of National Security--A Skeptical View, Dipl Hist, Vol 0017, 93. **CONTACT ADDRESS** Dept of Hist, Stanford Univ, Stanford, CA, 94305-1926.

BERNSTEIN, GAIL LEE
PERSONAL Born 02/22/1939, Brooklyn, NY **DISCIPLINE** JAPANESE HISTORY **EDUCATION** Barnard Col, Columbia Univ, BA, 59; Radcliffe Col, MA, 61; Harvard Univ, PhD(hist), 68. **CAREER** From asst prof to assoc prof, 67-84, Prof Orient Studies, Univ Ariz, 84-; Ed, J Asian Studies, 78-83. **HONORS AND AWARDS** John K Fairbank Award East Asian Hist, Am Hist Asn, 77; Asn for Asian Studies Distinguished Lectr on Japan, 94. **MEMBERSHIPS** Asn Asian Studies. **RESEARCH** Modern Japanese intellectual and social history. **SELECTED PUBLICATIONS** Auth, Japanese Marxist, A Portrait of Kawakami Hajime, Harvard Univ Press, 76; Women in Rural Japan, In: Women in Changing Japan, Westview Press, 76; The Early Japanese Socialists, the Russian Revolution and the Problem of Dogmatism, Studies in Comparative Communism, 76; coauth (with Yasve Aoki Kidd), Child bearing in Japan, In: An Anthropology of Childbearing, F A Davis Co, 81; auth, Harvko's World, A Japanese Farm Woman and Her Community, Stanford Univ Press, 83, rev ed, 96; Women in the Silk Reeling Industry in Nineteenth-Century Japan, In: Japan and the World, St Martin's Press, 88; co-ed, Japan and the World, St Martin's Press, 88; auth, Recreating Japanese Women, Univ Calif Press, 91. **CONTACT ADDRESS** Dept of Hist, Univ of Ariz, Tucson, AZ, 85721-0001. **EMAIL** gail-bernstein@ns.arizona.edu

BERNSTEIN, IVER
DISCIPLINE HISTORY **EDUCATION** Brown Univ, BA, 77; Yale Univ, MA, 79, Mphil, 82, PhD, 85. **CAREER** Act instr, Yale Univ, 82; Adj asst prof, NY Univ, 84; Vis asst prof, Univ Chicago, 85-86; Asst prof to prof, Washington Univ, 86. **HONORS AND AWARDS** Nat Endowment Hum stipend, 87; Am Coun Learned Societies, 87-88; Hist Soc Pa & Library Comp fel Recent Recipients Ph.D. Phil fel, 90; Mayer Fund fel, Huntington Library, 93; Am Coun Learned Societies fel, 95-96. **SELECTED PUBLICATIONS** Co-Auth, Work, Family And Class Values In The Nineteenth Century, International Labor And Working Class History, 81; Expanding The Boundaries The Political: Workers And Political Change In The Nineteenth Century, International Labor And Working Class History, 87; What Did The New York City Draft Rioters Think They Were Doing?, The Rise Am Capitalism, NY Hist Soc, 89; The New York City Draft Riots: Their Significance For Am Society And Politics In The Age The Civil War, Oxford Univ Profess, 90; Moral Perspective And The Cycles Jacksonian History, Jour Policy Hist, 94. **CONTACT ADDRESS** Washington Univ, 1 Brookings Dr, St. Louis, MO, 63130.

BERNSTEIN, JOANNE G.
DISCIPLINE HISTORY OF ART **EDUCATION** Univ Pa, BA, 62; NY Univ, MA, 64, PhD, 72. **CAREER** Prof; Mills Col, 89-. **RESEARCH** Italian Renaissance art; women in European art and society. **SELECTED PUBLICATIONS** Auth, Patronage, Autobiography, and Iconography: the Facade of the Colleoni Chapel, In Giovanni Antonio Amadeo: Scultura e Architettura del suo tempo, Milan: Cisalpino, 93; The Female Model and the Renaissance Nude: Durer, Giorgione, and Raphael, Artibus et Historiae, XIII, 92; Work in progress: problems in methodology, and The Portal of the Medici Bank in Milan, In Verrocchio and Late Quattrocento Italian Sculpture, Florence: Le Lettere, 92; Milanese and Antique Aspects of the Colleoni Chapel: Site and Symbolism, Arte Lombarda, 100, 92; rev, Janice Shell, Grazioso Sironi, Giovanni Antonio Amadeo, Documents / I documenti, in Arte Lombarda, 94-95, 90; Restauro della Cappella Colleoni: Primi Ritrovamenti, Arte Lombarda, 92-93, 90. **CONTACT ADDRESS** Dept of Art, Mills Col, 5000 MacArthur Blvd, Oakland, CA, 94613-1301. **EMAIL** jobern@mills.edu

BERNSTEIN, JOHN ANDREW
PERSONAL Born 03/25/1944, Boston, MA **DISCIPLINE** MODERN EUROPEAN INTELLECTUAL HISTORY **EDUCATION** Harvard Univ, AB, 66, AM, 67, PhD(hist), 70. **CAREER** Asst prof, 70-79, assoc prof, 79-88, PROF HIST, UNIV DEL, 89-. **RESEARCH** Eighteenth through twentieth century ethical thought. **SELECTED PUBLICATIONS** Ed, Select Sermons of Benjamin Whichcote, Scholar's Facsimiles and Reprints, 77; auth, Shaftesbury's Identification of the Good with the Beautiful, Eighteenth-Century Studies, spring 77; Adam Ferguson and the Idea of Progress, Studies in Burke and His Times, spring 78; Shaftesbury, Rousseau and Kant, Fairleigh Dickinson, 80; Ethics, Theology and the Original State of Man: An Historical Sketch, Anglican Theol Rev, spring 79; Nietzsche's Moral Philosophy, Faircloth Dickinson, 87; Progress and the Quest for Meaning, Faircloth Dickinson, 87. **CONTACT ADDRESS** Dept of Hist, Univ Del, Newark, DE, 19711. **EMAIL** John Bernstein@mvs.udel.edu

BERNSTEIN, JOHN ANDREW
PERSONAL Born 03/25/1944, Boston, MA **DISCIPLINE** MODERN EUROPEAN INTELLECTUAL HISTORY **EDUCATION** Harvard Univ, AB, 66, AM, 67, PhD(hist), 70. **CAREER** Asst prof, 70-79, assoc prof, 79-88, PROF HIST, UNIV DEL, 89-. **RESEARCH** Eighteenth through twentieth century ethical thought. **SELECTED PUBLICATIONS** Ed, Select Sermons of Benjamin Whichcote, Scholar's Facsimiles and Reprints, 77; auth, Shaftesbury's Identification of the Good with the Beautiful, Eighteenth-Century Studies, spring 77; Adam Ferguson and the Idea of Progress, Studies in Burke and His Times, spring 78; Shaftesbury, Rousseau and Kant, Fairleigh Dickinson, 80; Ethics, Theology and the Original State of Man: An Historical Sketch, Anglican Theol Rev, spring 79; Nietzsche's Moral Philosophy, Faircloth Dickinson, 87; Progress and the Quest for Meaning, Faircloth Dickinson, 87. **CONTACT ADDRESS** Dept of Hist, Univ Del, Newark, DE, 19711. **EMAIL** John Bernstein@mvs.udel.edu

BERNSTEIN, LAWRENCE F.
PERSONAL Born 03/25/1939, New York, NY, m, 1965 **DISCIPLINE** MUSICOLOGY **EDUCATION** Hofstra Univ, BS, 60; NY Univ, PhD (musicol), 69. **CAREER** From instr to asst prof music and humanities, Univ Chicago, 65-70; assoc prof, 70-80, PROF MUSIC, UNIV PA, 80- **MEMBERSHIPS** Am Musicol Soc; Int Musicol Soc; Music Libr Asn; AAUP. **RESEARCH** French secular music of the Renaissance; eighteenth century symphony; stylistic analysis. **SELECTED PUBLICATIONS** Auth, Ma Bouche Rit Et Mon Coeur Pleure--A Chanson A 5 Attributed to Josquin Desprez, J Musicol, Vol 0012, 94. **CONTACT ADDRESS** Dept of Music, Univ of Pa, Philadelphia, PA, 19174.

BERROL, SELMA CANTOR
PERSONAL Born 06/07/1924, New York, NY, m, 1948, 2 children **DISCIPLINE** AMERICAN HISTORY **EDUCATION** Hunter Col, BA, 45; Columbia Univ, MA, 46; City Univ NY, PhD (hist), 67. **CAREER** Instr hist, Hunter Col, 46-49; teacher social studies, NY City High Sch, 49-55; lectr hist, Queens Col, City Univ NY, 67-68; asst prof hist, 68-73, assoc prof, 73-77, asst dean lib arts, 72-79, PROF HIST, BARUCH COL, CITY UNIV NEW YORK, 77- **HONORS AND AWARDS** Distinguished Teaching Award, Baruch Col, 82. **MEMBERSHIPS** AHA; Orgn Am Historians; Immigration Hist Soc; Am Jewish Hist Soc; Yivo Inst Jewish Studies. **RESEARCH** American immigration history; New York City history; public schools. **SELECTED PUBLICATIONS** Auth, Streets--A Memoir of the Lower East Side, J Am Hist, Vol 0083, 96; The Luckiest Orphans--A History of the Hebrew Orphan Asylum of New York, J Am Hist, Vol 0080, 93. **CONTACT ADDRESS** Dept Hist, Baruch Col, CUNY, New York, NY, 10010.

BERRY, J. DUNCAN
PERSONAL Born 12/14/1959, OH, m, 1989, 1 child **DISCIPLINE** HISTORY OF ART AND ARCHITECTURE **EDUCATION** Col Wooster, BA, 82; Brown Univ, AM, 85; PhD, 89. **CAREER** Adj prof, Roger Williams Univ, 86-87; adj prof, RI Sch of Design, 86-90; adj prof, Brown Univ, 89-90. **HONORS AND AWARDS** Fulbright scholar, Univ Vienna, 87-88; Irex scholar, Tech Univ Dresden, 88; dissertation fel, Inst for Int Studies, 88-89. **MEMBERSHIPS** Soc of Archit Hist. **RE-**

SEARCH Architectural theory; German/Austrian/Swiss/ French architecture 1500-1900; architectural drawings and fantasies; history of ideas; Freemasonry. **SELECTED PUBLICATIONS** Auth, Pamet Cottage: An Updated Truro Retreat, Cape Cod Home, 97; auth, Reaping what is Soane, The New Criterion, 97; auth, A Richardson Round-up, The New Criterion, 98; auth, A Vibrant Tetonic Strain, The New Criterion, 98; auth, Heinrich Hubsch, Encyclopedia of Aesthetics, forthcoming. **CONTACT ADDRESS** PO Box 727, Harwich Port, MA, 02646. **EMAIL** duncanb@capecod.net

BERRY, LEE ROY, JR.
PERSONAL Born 11/05/1943, Lake Placid, FL, m **DISCIPLINE** HISTORY **EDUCATION** Eastern Mennonite College, BA, 1966; University of Notre Dame, PhD, 1976; Indiana University Bloomington, School of Law, JD, 1984. **CAREER** Cleveland Public Schools, teacher, 1966-68; Goshen College, professor, 1969-79, leader, study serv trimester, 1979-80, Dept of History & Government, associate professor, 1980-. **HONORS AND AWARDS** John Hay Whitney Fellow, 1970-71; Natl Fellowships Fund Felow, 1975-76. **MEMBERSHIPS** General Board, Mennonite Ch; chairman, High Aim Committee, member, Relief & Service Committee, Mennonite Board of Missions; Peace Sect, Mennonite Central Committee. **CONTACT ADDRESS** Dept of History & Government, Goshen Col, S Main St, Goshen, IN, 46526-4795.

BERS, VICTOR
PERSONAL Born 08/30/1944, Providence, RI, m, 1966, 2 children **DISCIPLINE** CLASSICS **EDUCATION** Chicago Univ, AB, 66; Oxford Univ, BA, 68; Harvard Univ, PhD, 72. **CAREER** Lectr to prof, 72-, Yale Univ. **MEMBERSHIPS** APA **RESEARCH** Greek literature; Greek stylistics; Greek history. **SELECTED PUBLICATIONS** Auth, Enallage and Greek Style, Leiden, 74; auth, Greek Poetic Syntax in the Classical Age, New Haven, 84; auth, Speech in Speech: Studies in Incorporated Oration Recta in Attic Drama and Oratory, Langham, MD, 97. **CONTACT ADDRESS** Dept of Classics, Yale Univ, Box 08266, New Haven, CT, 06520-8266. **EMAIL** victor.bers@yal.edu

BERTHOLD, RICHARD M.
PERSONAL Born 01/22/1946, San Francisco, CA, m **DISCIPLINE** CLASSICAL HISTORY **EDUCATION** Stanford Univ, BA, great distin, 67; Cornell Univ, MA, 69, PhD, 71. **CAREER** Cornell Univ, pt lectr, 71-72; Univ New Mexico, asst prof, 72-85, assoc prof, 85-; Faculty Advisor, Cam Librit, 96-, Am-Arab Anti-discrim comm, 96-, col repub, 96-, Iranian hum rts org, 92-93, Weregamers guild, 90-94, Regular Columnist for UNM LOBO, 82-91, 92-; numerous other Univ serv positions. **HONORS AND AWARDS** Republic of Rome, Avalon Hill Games, with Robert Haines, 90, Award for Best Pre-20th Century Board Game, Res Publica Romana, french ver, 94., New Mex Humanities Council, accepted and pub 3 essays in sev NM newspapers. **SELECTED PUBLICATIONS** Monograph on Marathon, Hear, O Israel, a Novel about Moses, Three Hour Video Documentary on the Greeks, in progress; Game Simulation of Weimar Republic politics, in progress; Rhodes in the Hellenistic Age, Ithaca, 84; Dare to Struggle: The History and Society of Greece, seeking pub; Day of the Long Night: A Palestinian Refugee Remembers the Nakba, Albuquerque Journal, 98; many numerous reviews and articles. **CONTACT ADDRESS** Dept History, Univ New Mexico, Albuquerque, NM, 87131.

BERTHRONG, DONALD JOHN
PERSONAL Born 10/02/1922, La Crosse, WI, m, 1942, 2 children **DISCIPLINE** US HISTORY **EDUCATION** Univ Wis, BS, 46, MS, 47, PhD (hist), 52. **CAREER** Instr Am hist, Univ Kansas City, 51-52; from asst prof to prof, Univ Okla, 52-64, chmn dept hist, 66-70; HEAD DEPT HIST, PURDUE UNIV, LAFAYETTE, 70-, Consult, US Dept Justice, 57-64; Fulbright lectr, Univ Hong Kong, 65-66. **HONORS AND AWARDS** Award of Merit, Am Asn State and Local Hist, 64. **MEMBERSHIPS** AHA; Orgn Am Historians; AAUP; Western Hist Asn. **SELECTED PUBLICATIONS** Auth, The Battle of Beecher Island and the Indian War of 1867-1869, J Am Hist, Vol 0081, 94; Adventures on the Western Frontier, Am Indian Cult Res Jour, Vol 0019, 95; Lakota and Cheyenne--Indian Views of the Great Sioux War, 1876-1877, Am Indian Cult Res Jour, Vol 0019, 95; The Dispossession of the American Indian, 1887-1934, Southwestern Hist Quart, Vol 0096, 93; Pawnee Passage--1870-1875, Pac Hist Rev, Vol 0061, 92. **CONTACT ADDRESS** Dept Hist, Purdue Univ, West Lafayette, IN, 47907.

BERTMAN, STEPHEN
PERSONAL Born 07/20/1937, New York, NY, m, 1968, 2 children **DISCIPLINE** CLASSICS; HUMANITIES **EDUCATION** NY Univ, BA, 59; Brandeis Univ, MA, 60; Columbia, PhD, 65. **CAREER** Asst prof, Fla State Univ, 63-67; Prof, Univ Windsor, 67-. **HONORS AND AWARDS** Phi Beta Kappa; Eta Sigma Phi; Alumni Award Exc, Univ Teaching, Univ Windsor. **MEMBERSHIPS** Amer Philol Asn; Archeol Inst Amer; Class Asn Mid W & S; World Future Soc; Soc Psychol Study Soc Issues. **RESEARCH** The impact of time and speed on cultural values and memory. **SELECTED PUBLICATIONS** auth, Art and the Romans, 75; The Conflict of Generations in Ancient Greece and Rome, 76; Doorways Through Time: The Romance of Archaelogy, 86; Hyperculture: The Human Cost of Speed, 98; Cultural Amnesia: America's Future and the Crisis of Memory, 99. **CONTACT ADDRESS** 5459 Piccadilly Circle N, West Bloomfield, MI, 48322.

BERTOLONI MELI, DOMENICO
DISCIPLINE HISTORY OF SCIENCE **EDUCATION** Pavia Univ, BA, 83; Cambridge Univ, PhD, 88. **CAREER** Assoc prof. **RESEARCH** 18th century mathematics and mechanics; medicine in the Scientific Revolution. **SELECTED PUBLICATIONS** Auth, Equivalence and Priority: Newton Versus Leibniz, Including Leibniz's Unpublished Manuscripts on the "Principia", Oxford, 93; The Relativization of Centrifugal Force, Isis, 90; Public Claims, Private Worries: Newton's Principia and Leibniz's Theory of Planetary Motion, 91; Guidobaldo dal Monte and the Archimedean Revival, Nuncius, 92; The Emergence of Reference Frames and the Transformation of Mechanics in the Enlightenment, 93; co-auth, Sphaera Mundi, 94; ed, Marcello Malpighi, Anatomist And Physician, Olschki, 97. **CONTACT ADDRESS** Dept of History and Philosophy of Science, Indiana Univ, Bloomington, 300 N Jordan Ave, Bloomington, IN, 47405. **EMAIL** dbmeli@indiana.edu

BERTON, PETER
DISCIPLINE INTERNATIONAL RELATIONS **EDUCATION** Columbia Univ, PhD, 56. **CAREER** Prof emer,Univ Southern Calif. **RESEARCH** International relations of Asia and the Pacific; US foreign policy in Asia; Japanese political parties. **SELECTED PUBLICATIONS** Auth, The Psychological Dimension of Japanese Negotiating Behavior; Japan and Russia in the Post-Cold War Era. **CONTACT ADDRESS** East Asian Studies Center, Univ Southern Calif, University Park Campus, Los Angeles, CA, 90089.

BERTRAND, CHARLES L.
DISCIPLINE MODERN EUROPEAN HISTORY **EDUCATION** Univ Wis, PhD. **CAREER** Assoc prof, 67-. **SELECTED PUBLICATIONS** Ed, Revolutionary Situations in Europe, 1917-1922: Germany, Italy, Austria-Hungary; auth, articles on Italian revolutionary syndicalism, the Italian trade union movement and Italian anarchism. **CONTACT ADDRESS** Dept of Hist, Concordia Univ, Montreal, 1455 de Maisonneuve W, Montreal, PQ, H3G 1M8.

BERUBE, MAURICE R.
PERSONAL Born 05/24/1933, Portland, ME, s, 3 children **DISCIPLINE** EDUCATION **EDUCATION** Fordham Col, BA, 54; New York Univ, MA, 65; Union Grad School, 75, PhD. **CAREER** Teacher, 60-64, ed & teacher, Union Grad School, 68-76; Queens Col, 68-76; Old Dominion Univ, 79-. **HONORS AND AWARDS** Va Cultural Laureate; Univ & Col Outstanding Teacher, Old Dominion Univ; Eminent Scholar; listed in Who's Who in Am Ed. **MEMBERSHIPS** Am Ed Res Asn. **RESEARCH** Educational history; policy. **SELECTED PUBLICATIONS** Auth, American School Reform, 94; American Presidents and Education, 91; Teacher Politics, 88; Education and Poverty, 84; The Urban University in America, 78. **CONTACT ADDRESS** Dept of Education Leadership, Old Dominion Univ, 330 Wl Brambleton, Norfolk, VA, 23508. **EMAIL** MBerube@odu.edu

BERWANGER, EUGENE H.
PERSONAL Born 06/08/1929, Calumet City, IL, m, 1967, 2 children **DISCIPLINE** HISTORY **EDUCATION** Il St Univ, BA, 51, MA, 52; Univ Il Urbana, PhD, 64. **CAREER** Teacher, Maine Twp High School, Des Plaines, Il, 54-60; asst prof, Il Col, 64-67; prof, Co St Univ Ft. Collins, 67- . **HONORS AND AWARDS** Fulbright Scholar, Italy, 83-84; Dickerson Award, Univ Il, 67; Oliver Pennock Award, Co St Univ, 83; John N. Stern Distinguished Prof, Co St Univ, 91., Chair, Hist Dept, Co St Univ, 91-98 **MEMBERSHIPS** Org of Amer Hist; S Hist Assoc; Soc of Hist for the Early Republic. **RESEARCH** Antebellum US; civil war & reconstruction. **SELECTED PUBLICATIONS** Auth, My Diary North and South, Alfred A Knopf, 87; The Civil War Era: Historical Viewpoints, Harcourt Brace, 93; The British Foreign Service and the American Civil War, Univ Press Ky, 94. **CONTACT ADDRESS** Dept of History, Colorado State Univ, Fort Collins, CO, 80523. **EMAIL** eberwanger@vines.colostate.edu

BEST, GARY DEAN
PERSONAL Born 09/18/1936, Estherville, IA, m **DISCIPLINE** HISTORY **EDUCATION** Univ Hawaii, Manoa, BA, 68, MA, 69, PhD(Hist), 73. **CAREER** Asst prof, Sophia Univ, Japan, 73-74; asst prof, 75-78, assoc prof, 79-82, prof Hist, Univ Hawaii, HILO, 82-, Am-E Asian rel fel Hist, AHA, 73-74; Fulbright scholar Hist, Japan, 74-75; Nat Endowment of Humanities fel, 82-83; vis scholar, Hoover Inst, 83. **MEMBERSHIPS** Orgn Am Historians. **RESEARCH** Twentieth century United States political history; United States diplomatic history. **SELECTED PUBLICATIONS** Witch Hunt in Wise County: The Persecution of Edith Maxwell, Praeger, 93; The United States in the Pacific: Private Interests and Public Policies with Donald D Johnson, Praeger, 94; Herbert Hoover: The Elder Statesman, Norton, in prep. **CONTACT ADDRESS** Dept of History, Univ of Hawaii, 200 W Kawili St, Hilo, HI, 96720-4091. **EMAIL** gbest@hawaii.edu

BEST, HENRY
DISCIPLINE HISTORY **EDUCATION** Laval Univ, BA, MA, PhD. **CAREER** Prof. **HONORS AND AWARDS** Dir, Fondation Germain Lemieux; dir, Musee franco-ontarien de Folklore. **SELECTED PUBLICATIONS** Auth, The Scot in New France, Scottish Colloquium Proceedings, Guelph, 71; art, L'Etat culturel du Canada a la cession, Revue de l'Universite Laval, 61. **CONTACT ADDRESS** Dept of History, Laurentian Univ, 935 Ramsey Lake Rd, Sudbury, ON, P3E 2C6.

BEST, JUDITH A.
PERSONAL Chicago, IL **DISCIPLINE** POLITICAL SCIENCE **EDUCATION** Cornell Univ, PhD, 71. **CAREER** Dist Teach Prof Pol Sci, SUNY, Cortland, 84-. **HONORS AND AWARDS** NY Chanc Awd Excell Teaching, 77; Am High Edu & Carnegie Found, Salute for Edu Leadershp, 86. **MEMBERSHIPS** Bd Editors, Pres Stud Quart, Cent for the Study of the Pres. **RESEARCH** Elect Col, Pol Theory, Found Period. **SELECTED PUBLICATIONS** The Choice of the People?, Debating the Electoral College, Rowman and Littlefield, 96; The Mainstream of Western Political Thought, Univ Free Press, 97; National Representation for the District of Columbia, 84. **CONTACT ADDRESS** SUNY Cortland, Dept Political Science, Cortland, NY, 13045.

BETANCOURT, PHILIP PAUL
PERSONAL Born 10/17/1936, Los Angeles, CA, m, 1959, 2 children **DISCIPLINE** ART HISTORY, CLASSICAL ARCHAEOLOGY **EDUCATION** Southwest Mo State Univ, BS, 59; Wash Univ, St Louis, MA, 67; Univ Pa, PhD (class archaeol), 70. **CAREER** Asst prof, 70-74, assoc prof, 75-78, PROF ART HIST, TEMPLE UNIV, 78-, Vis lectr class archaeol, Univ Pa, 76-; res assoc Bronze Age archaeol, Univ Mus, Univ Pa, 77- **MEMBERSHIPS** Archaeol Inst Am; Col Art Asn. **RESEARCH** Aegean prehistory. **SELECTED PUBLICATIONS** Auth, An Unpublished Minoan Stone Quarry from Eastern Crete, Am J Archeol, Vol 0100, 96; Investigations at the Amnissos Cave, Am J Archeol, Vol 0098, 94; Excavations at Chrysokamino, Crete, 1996, Am J Archaeol, Vol 0101, 97. **CONTACT ADDRESS** Dept of Art Hist, Temple Univ, 1301 Cecil B Moore, Philadelphia, PA, 19122-6029.

BETT, RICHARD
PERSONAL Born 07/10/1957, London, England, m, 1986 **DISCIPLINE** CLASSICS AND PHILOSOPHY **EDUCATION** Oxford Univ, BA, 80; UC Berkley, PhD, 86. **CAREER** Asst Prof, Univ TX, 86-91; Asst Prof, 91-94; Assoc Prof, 94-, Sec Appt in Classics, 96-. **HONORS AND AWARDS** Fel Center for Hellenic Stud, Washington DC 94-95. **MEMBERSHIPS** APA; Soc for Ancient Greek Phil; North Amer Nietzsche Soc **RESEARCH** Ancient Greek philosophy, especially Greek skepticism. **SELECTED PUBLICATIONS** Art, Scepticism and Everyday Attitudes in Ancient and Modern Philosophy, Metaphilosophy, 93; art, What Did Pyrrho Think about the Nature of the Divine and the Good, Phronesis, 94; art, Aristocleson Timon on Pyrrho the Text it Logic and its Credibility, Oxford Stud in Ancient Phil, 94; auth, Sextus Against the Ethicists Scepticism, Relativisim or Both, Apeiron, 94; art, Hellenistic Essays Translated, Papers in Hellenistic Phil, 96; Entries in Encyl of Class Philos, 97. **CONTACT ADDRESS** Dept of Philosophy, Johns Hopkins Univ, Gilman Hall, Baltimore, MD, 21218-2890. **EMAIL** bett_r@jhunix.hcf.jhu.edu

BETTINGER, ROBERT L.
PERSONAL Born 05/08/1948, Berkeley, CA, m, 1969, 1 child **DISCIPLINE** ANTHROPOLOGY **EDUCATION** Univ Calif, BA, PhD, 75. **CAREER** Asst prof, 75-79, assoc prof, 79-80, NYU; asst prof, 80-82, assoc prof, 82-88, prof, 88-, Univ Calif, Davis. **HONORS AND AWARDS** Dist fac award, 92; dist alumni award, 94, Univ Calif Riverside. **MEMBERSHIPS** Soc Amer Anthropology **RESEARCH** Prehistory; hunter-gatherers; evolutionary theory. **SELECTED PUBLICATIONS** Art, Doing Great Basin Archaeology Recently: Coping with Variability, J of Archaeol Res, NY Plenum, 93; coauth, Prehistoric Settlement Categories and Settlement Systems in the Alashan Desert of Inner Mongolia, PRC J Anthrop Archaeol, 94; auth, How, When, and Why Numic Spread, Across the West: Human Population Movement and the Expansion of the Numa, Univ Utah Press, 94; auth, Prehistory of the Crooked Creek area, Crooked Creek Guidebook, Univ Calif White Mountain Res Station Pub, 94; coauth, The Numic Spread: a Computer Simulation, Amer Antiquity, 95; coauth, Simulating the global human expansion in the late Pleistocene, J Archaeol Science, 95; coauth, Settlement Patterns Refected in Assemblages from the Pleistocene/Holocene Transition in North Central China, J Archaeol Science, 95; coauth, Serum albumin phenotypes at Stillwater: Implications for Population History in the Great Basin, Antropol Papers Amer Museum of Nat Hist, 95; coauth, Style, Function and Cultural Evolutionary Processes, Darwinian Archaeol, Plenum, 96; coauth, The State of Evolutionary Archaeology: Evolutionary Correctness or the Search for the Common Ground, Darwinian Archaeol, Plenum, 96; coauth, Central Place Models of Acorn and Mussell Processing, J Archaeol Science, 97; coauth, Evolutionary Implications of Metrical Variation in Great Basin Projectile Points, Rediscovering Darwin: Evolutionary Theory & Archaeol Explanation, Archaeol Papers Amer Anthropol Assn, 97; coauth, New Dates for

the North China Mesolithic, Antiquity, 97; auth, Cultural, Human, and Historical Ecology in the Great Basin: Fifty Years of Ideas about Ten Thousand Years of Prehistory, Advances in Hist Ecology, Columbia Univ Press, 98; auth, A Hunter-Gatherer Landscape: Southwest Germany in the Late Paleolithic and Mesolithic, Plenum, 98. **CONTACT ADDRESS** Dept of Anthropology, Univ of California Davis, Davis, CA, 95616. **EMAIL** rlbettenger@ucdavis.edu

BETTS, RAYMOND FREDERICK
PERSONAL Born 12/23/1925, Bloomfield, NJ, m, 1956, 3 children **DISCIPLINE** HISTORY **EDUCATION** Rutgers Univ, AB, 49; Columbia Univ, MA, 50, PhD, 58; Univ Grenoble, France, D'Univ(hist), 55; Univ Paris, cert, 55. **CAREER** From Instr to asst prof hist, Bryn Mawr Col, 56-61; from asst prof to prof, Grinnell Col, 61-71; PROF HIST, UNIV KY, 71-98, dir, Honors Prog, 78-90, founding dir Gains Ctr for Hum, 83-98. **HONORS AND AWARDS** Assoc Cols, Midwest-Ford Found res fel, 66-67; consult, Nat Endowment for Humanities, 72-75; co-ed Fr Colonial Hist Studies, 76-80; Camargo Found res fel, 80; chm, Ky Humanities Coun, 81- ; distinguished prof,Univ Ky, 85; Outstanding Ky Hum Award, Ky Hum Coun, 89; Chancellor's Award for Excellence in Tchg, 90; Acorn Award for Outstanding Excellence in Service and Commitment to Tchg, Ky Advocates of Higher Educ, 92. **MEMBERSHIPS** Fr Colonial Hist Studies; Soc Fr Hist Studies; Ky Hum Coun, chm 81-82; Nat Hum and Liberal Arts Fac. **RESEARCH** Modern European, French Colonial and Modern African history. **SELECTED PUBLICATIONS** Auth, Assimilation and Association in French Colonial Theory, 1890-1914, Columbia Univ, 61; ed, The Scramble for Africa, Heath, 66, 2nd ed, 72; auth, Europe Overseas; Phases of Imperialism, Basic Bks, 68, contribr, From the Ancient Regime to the Popular Front, Columbia Univ, 69, ed, The Ideology of Blackness, Heath, 71; auth, The False Dawn: European Imperialism in the Nineteenth Century, Univ Minn, 75; Tricouleur: A Brief History of French Colonial Empire, Gordon & Cremonsei, 78; Europe in Retrospect: A Brief History of the Last Two Hundred Years, Heath, 79; auth, Uncertain Dimensions: Western Overseas Empire in the Twentieth Century, Minnesota, 85; auth, France and Decolonization, Macmillan, 91; auth, Decolonization, Routledge, 98. **CONTACT ADDRESS** Dept of History, Univ Ky, Lexington, KY, 40506.

BETTS, RICHARD KEVIN
PERSONAL Born 08/15/1947, Easton, PA, m, 1987, 3 children **DISCIPLINE** GOVERNMENT **EDUCATION** Harvard Univ, BA, 69, MA, 71, PhD, 75. **CAREER** Lectr, Harvard Univ, Govt, 75-76; res assoc, Brookings Inst, 76-81,sr fel, 81-90; adj lectr, Johns Hopkins School Advanced Int Stud, 78-85; vis prof, Harvard Univ, 85-88; Johns Hopkins, 88-90; PROF, POLIT SCI, DIR, INST WAR & PEACE STUD, COLUMBIA UNIV, 90-. **MEMBERSHIPS** Am Polit Sci Asn; Int Inst Strategis Stud; Coun For Relations; Int Stud Asn; Consortium Stud Intell **RESEARCH** War; Strategy; National Security; Military Affairs; International relations; Intelligence Analysis. **SELECTED PUBLICATIONS** Military Readiness: Concepts, Choices, Consequences, Brookings Inst, 95; edr, Conflict After the Cold War: Arguments on Causes of War and Peace, MacMillan/Allyn & Bacon, 94. **CONTACT ADDRESS** Inst War & Peace Stud, Columbia Univ, 420 W 118th St, New York, NY, 10027. **EMAIL** rkb4@columbia.edu

BEYEA, MARION
PERSONAL Saint John, NB, Canada **DISCIPLINE** ARCHIVIST **EDUCATION** Univ NB, BA, 67. **CAREER** Manuscript archiv, Arch Ont, 67-75; archiv, Anglican Ch Can, 75-78; PROV ARCHIVIST, PROV ARCH NB 78-. **MEMBERSHIPS** Can Coun Archv; Asn Can Archv; Coun Archv NB; Anglican Diocese Fredericton. **SELECTED PUBLICATIONS** Auth, The Professional Associations and the Formation of the Canadian Archival System in Janus, 87; auth, Technology, Industry and the Archival Heritage, Possibilities and Needs in Janus, 92; ed, Archives Bulletin, 73-75. **CONTACT ADDRESS** Prov Archives of New Brunswick, PO Box 6000, Fredericton, NB, E3B 5H1. **EMAIL** marionb@gov.nb.ca

BEYER, DAVID W.
PERSONAL Born 10/03/1949, Sioux Falls, SD, s **DISCIPLINE** MUSIC EDUCATION **EDUCATION** North Tex State Univ, MME, 72. **CAREER** Independent scholar, bibl chronol, unaffiliated, San Diego/Newport Beach, Calif. **MEMBERSHIPS** Soc of Bibl Lit. **RESEARCH** Biblical chronology; Josephus studies. **SELECTED PUBLICATIONS** Auth, Josephus Reexamined: Unraveling the Twenty-second Year of Tiberius, Chronos Kairos Christos II, Vardaman, Mercer Univ Press, 98; auth, Finegan's Reliance on Early Manuscript Discoveries of Beyer, 284, 292, 301, Handbook of Biblical Chronology, Hendrickson Publ, 98. **CONTACT ADDRESS** 204 N. El Camino Real E-401, Encinitas, CA, 92024.

BHAGUE, GERARD
DISCIPLINE MUSIC, LATIN AMERICAN MUSIC, ETHNOMUSICOL **EDUCATION** Tulane Univ, PhD. **CAREER** Prof; Virginia Murchison Regents prof; ed, Lat Am Music Rev; ch, Music Dept, 80-89. **HONORS AND AWARDS** Helped develop, grad prog in ethnomusicol; founder & ed, Lat Am Music Rev, 80-. **MEMBERSHIPS** Former pres, Soc for Ethnomusicol & ed, its J, 70s. **RESEARCH** Musical traditions of Latin Am and the Span Caribbean. **SELECTED PUBLICATIONS** Publ on, var aspects of Lat Am music. **CONTACT ADDRESS** School of Music, Univ of Texas at Austin, 2613 Wichita St, Austin, TX, 78705.

BIANCHI, ROBERT S.
PERSONAL Born 11/30/1943, New York, NY, m, 1998, 1 child **DISCIPLINE** ART HISTORY **EDUCATION** New York Univ, Inst of Fine Arts, PhD, 96. **CAREER** Cur, Dept of Egyptian Class and Ancient Middle Eastern Art, Brooklyn Mus of Art, 76-91; dir acad and cur aff, Broughton Int, Inc, St. Petersburg, Fla, 96- . **HONORS AND AWARDS** Scholar, Am Sch of Class Stud, Athens, 69; Fulbright-Hayes scholar, 77; J. Clawson Mills fell, Metropolitan Mus of Mod Art, 92-93. **MEMBERSHIPS** Archaeol Inst Am; Am Res Ctr in Egypt. **RESEARCH** Ancient glass; women of antiquity. **SELECTED PUBLICATIONS** Auth, Nana Tokatah: En Apxn Hn Aeyko, Corfu, Antonia Havani Contemp Art, 96; auth, Alexander the Great: The Exhibition, Docent Manual, St. Petersburg, Fla, 96; auth, Raneferef's Carnelian, in van Dijk, ed, Essays on Ancient Egypt in Honour of Herman te Velde, Groningen, 97; auth, Egipcios-Soberanos de la tierra negra, Estrella 8, 98; auth, A Memphite Plaque of Athena, in Bible Lands Museum Jerusalem. Sixth Anniversary Dinner in Honor of Museum Founder Dr. Elie Borowski, Jerusalem, 98; auth, A Question of Political Identity: Nicholas II's Dilemma, Del Hum Forum, Newsl, 98; auth, Egito Milenario: Vida Cotidiana en la Epoca de Los Faraones, Fundacio, 98; auth, Egipte Mil lenair: Vida Quotidiana en l'Epoca Dels Faraons, Fundacio, 98; auth, Nicholas and Alexandra: The Last Imperial Family of Tsarist Russia, Curriculum Guide for Educators and Docents, Broughton Int, 98. **CONTACT ADDRESS** 522 Valley Vista Blvd, Lewiston, ID, 83501. **EMAIL** drbob04@ibm.net

BIDDLE, TAMI DAVIS
PERSONAL m, 1 child **DISCIPLINE** HISTORY **EDUCATION** Lehigh Univ, BA, 81; Yale Univ, PhD, 95. **CAREER** Asst prof, Duke Univ. **RESEARCH** Hist of air warfare, particularly strategic bombing; law of war; hist of the Cold War. **SELECTED PUBLICATIONS** Auth, Rhetoric and Reality in Air Warfare: the Evolution of British and American Thinking about Strategic Bombing 1914-1945; British and American Approaches to Strategic Bombing: Their Origins and Implementation in the World War II Combined Bomber Offensive, Jour Strategic Studies, 95. **CONTACT ADDRESS** Dept of Hist, Duke Univ, Carr Bldg, Durham, NC, 27706. **EMAIL** tbiddle@acpub.duke.edu

BIEBER, JUDY
DISCIPLINE BRAZIL & LATIN AMERICA HISTORY **EDUCATION** Johns Hopkins Univ, PhD, 95. **CAREER** Asst prof, Univ NMex; ed bd, Colonial Lat Am Hist Rev. **RESEARCH** 19th-century Brazil. **SELECTED PUBLICATIONS** Auth, Slavery and Social Life: Attempts to Reduce Free People to Slavery in the Sertao Mineiro, Brazil, 1850-1871, Journal of Latin American Studies, 26, 94. **CONTACT ADDRESS** Univ NMex, Albuquerque, NM, 87131.

BIETENHOLZ, PETER GERARD
PERSONAL Born 01/07/1933, Basel, Switzerland, m, 1958, 3 children **DISCIPLINE** RENAISSANCE AND REFORMATION HISTORY **EDUCATION** Univ Basel, PhD (hist, Ital lit), 58. **CAREER** Res fel hist, Warburg Inst, Univ London, 58-59; lectr, Univ Khartoum, 59-63; from asst prof to assoc prof, 63-70, head dept, 74-77, PROF HIST, UNIV SASK, 70-, Ed, Can J Hist-Ann Can Hist, 67; Swiss Nat fund sci Res and Can Coun grants; mem exec comt, Collected Works of Erasmus, Univ Toronto Press, 68- 74; res fel, Harvard Inst Ital Renaissance Studies, Florence, 69-70. **MEMBERSHIPS** Can Hist Asn; Renaissance Soc Am; Soc Reformation Res. **RESEARCH** Intellectual history of the 14th-16th centuries; history of the printed book. **SELECTED PUBLICATIONS** Auth, Erasmus, the Preceptor of Europe, Sixteenth Century Jour, Vol 0027, 96; Patristic Scholarship--The Edition of St Jerome, Cath Hist Rev, Vol 0079, 93; Rabelais and the Challenge of the Gospel, Bibl Hum Renaissance, Vol 0055, 93; Collected Works of Erasmus, Vol 33--Adages Iii, 1 Iiv, 100, Renaissance Reformation, Vol 0018, 94; Collected Works of Erasmus, Vol 10--The Correspondence of Erasmus, Letter 1356 to Letter 1534, Renaissance Reformation, Vol 0018, 94; Erasmus--A Critical Biography, Europ Hist Quart, Vol 0024, 94; Erasmus, Lee and the Correction of the Vulgate--The Shaking of the Foundations, Bibliotheque D Humanisme Et Renaissance, Vol 0055, 93; Language and Truth--Studies Offered to Margolin, Jean, Claude by his Colleagues, Collaborators, Pupils, and Friends, Renaissance Reformation, Vol 0019, 95; Concerning the Review of Historia and Fabula, Myths and Legends in Historical Thought from Antiquity to the Modern Age, Sixteenth Century Jour, Vol 0027, 96; Collected Works of Erasmus, Vol 10--The Correspondence of Erasmus, Letter 1356 to Letter 1534, Renaissance Reformation, Vol 0018, 94. **CONTACT ADDRESS** Dept of Hist, Univ of Sask, Saskatoon, SK, S7N 0W0.

BIGGS, ANSELM
PERSONAL Born 01/11/1914, Pocahontas, VA **DISCIPLINE** HISTORY **EDUCATION** Belmont Abbey Col, Ab, 36; Cath Univ Am, MA, 46, PhD(hist), 49. **CAREER** Instr Latin, 40-48, PROF HIST, BELMONT ABBEY COL, 48-, CHMN DEPT, 76-, Mem, Am Benedictine Acad, 47- **MEMBERSHIPS** Am Cath Hist Asn; Mediaeval Acad Am; AHA. **RESEARCH** Spain in the Middle Ages; medieval papacy; England in the Middle Ages. **SELECTED PUBLICATIONS** Auth, Diego Gelmirez: First Archbishop of Compostela, Cath Univ Am, 49; transl, History of the Catholic Church, Herthing, & Handbook of Church History, Vols II, III, IV, V, and X, Verlag Herder, 68. **CONTACT ADDRESS** Belmont Abbey Col, 100 Belmont Mt Holly, Belmont, NC, 28012-1802.

BIGGS, ROBERT DALE
PERSONAL Born 06/13/1934, Pasco, WA **DISCIPLINE** ASSYRIOLOGY **EDUCATION** Eastern Wash State Col, BA, 56, Johns Hopkins Univ, PhD(Assyriol), 62. **CAREER** Res assoc Assyriol, Orient Inst, 63-64, from asst prof to assoc prof, 64-72, Prof Assyriol, Univ Chicago, 72-, Fel, Baghdad Sch, Am Schs Orient Res, 62-63; assoc ed, Assyrian Dictionary, 64-; ed, J Near Eastern Studies, 71- **MEMBERSHIPS** Am Orient Soc; Archaeol Inst Am. **RESEARCH** Babylonian and Assyrian languages; Sumerian language. **SELECTED PUBLICATIONS** Auth, The Abu Salabikh tablets: A preliminary survey, J Cuneiform Studies, 66; Semitic names in the Fara Period, Orientalia, 67; SA ZI GA: Ancient Mesopotamian Potency Incantations, J J Augustin, 67; An esoteric Babylonian commentary, Rev Assyriologie, 68; coauth, Cuneiform Texts from Nippur: The Eighth and Ninth Seasons, Univ Chicago, 69; auth, Inscriptions from al-Hiba-Lagash: The First and Second Seasons, 76 & co-ed, Seals and Sealing in the Ancient Near East, 77, Undena, Malibu; coauth, Nippur II: The North Temple and Sounding E, Univ Chicago, 78. **CONTACT ADDRESS** Orient Inst, Univ of Chicago, 1155 E 58th St, Chicago, IL, 60637-1540. **EMAIL** r-biggs@uchicago.edu

BIGGS, SHIRLEY ANN
PERSONAL Born 03/09/1938, Richmond, VA, m **DISCIPLINE** EDUCATION **EDUCATION** Duquesne U, BEd 1960; Univ of SC, MEd 1972; Univ of Pittsburgh, EdD 1977. **CAREER** Pittsburgh Public School, teacher, 1961-68; Benedict Coll, instructor, 1968-72, reading specialist consultant, 1972-; Univ of Pittsburgh, faculty in school of educ, 1974-, asso prof, asst dean for student affairs 1986-, director of affirmative action, minority affairs, 1989-. **HONORS AND AWARDS** honored for literacy research activities by the Pittsburgh City Council 1986; editor Innovative Learning Strategies, 1989-90; Intl Reading Assn, 1989-90. **MEMBERSHIPS** Pres Gerald A Yoakam Reading Cncl 1978-79; chmn research div Pittsburgh Literacy Coalition 1984-; mem Intl Reading Assoc 1973-; mem Nat Reading Conference; director of research Coalition for the Advancement of Literacy Pittsburgh, 1985-; chair College Reading Improvement Group, International Reading Association, 1990-; chair, Pittsburgh Peace Institute, 1997-; Natl Conference on Research in Language and Literacy. **SELECTED PUBLICATIONS** Auth, "The Plight of Black Males in American Schools: Separation May not be the Answer;" auth, "Building on Strengths: Closing the Literacy Gap;" auth, "African American Adult Reading Performance: Progress in the Face of Problem;" ed, Journal of College Literacy and Learning (formerly Forum for Reading); co- auth, Administrators Reference Manual: Bridging Assessment and Instruction, 1998; "Minority Student Retention: A Framework for Discussion and Decision-making," 98; co-auth, Students Self Questioning and Summarizing, 84; Co-auth, Reading to Achieve, Strategies for Adult Coll; 83. **CONTACT ADDRESS** Sch of Education, Univ of Pittsburgh, 5TO1 Forbes Quandrangle, Pittsburgh, PA, 15260.

BIGHAM, DARREL EUGENE
PERSONAL Born 08/12/1942, Harrisburg, PA, m, 1965, 2 children **DISCIPLINE** UNITED STATES HISTORY **EDUCATION** Messiah Col, BA, 64; Univ Kans, PhD, 70. **CAREER** Asst instr US hist, Univ Kans, 68-70; co-dir regional arch proj, 72-75, from Asst Prof to Prof, 70-89, Distinguished Prof Hist, Univ Southern Ind, Evansville, 89-, Dir, Historic Southern Ind, 86-; Exec dir, Leadership Evansville, 76-79. **HONORS AND AWARDS** Paul Harris Fel, Evansville Rotary Club, 92; Rotarian of the Decade, 97. **MEMBERSHIPS** AHA; Orgn Am Historians; AASLH; NCSS. **RESEARCH** Recent American social and intellectual history; religion in American history; state and local history. **SELECTED PUBLICATIONS** Auth, From the Green Mountains to the Tombigbee: Henry Hitchcock in territorial Alabama, 1817-1819, Ala Rev, 7/73; Charles Leich and company: A note on the dilemma of German Americans during World War I, Ind Mag Hist, 6/74; The Black family in Evansville and Vanderburgh County, Indiana, in 1880, 6/79 & Work, residence, and the origins of the Black ghetto in Evansville, 1865-1900, 12/80, Ind Mag Hist; Reflections on a heritage: The German Americans of southwest Indiana, ISUE, 80; War as obligation in the thought of American Christians, 1898-1900, Peace & Change, winter 81; The Black family in Evansville and Vanderburgh County: A 1900 post-script, Ind Mag Hist, 6/82; contribr, Their Infinite Variety: Essays on Indiana Politicians, Ind Hist Bur, 82; We Ask Only a Fair Trial: A History of the Black Community of Evansville, Indiana, Ind Univ Press, 87; An Evansville Album, Ind Univ

Press, 88; contribr, Always a River, Ind Univ Press, 91; auth, Towns and Villages of the Lower Ohio, Univ Press Ky, 98. **CONTACT ADDRESS** Dept of Hist, Univ Southern Ind, 8600 University Blvd, Evansville, IN, 47712-3591. **EMAIL** dbigham.ucs@smtp.usi.edu

BILHARTZ, TERRY D.
DISCIPLINE HISTORY **EDUCATION** Dallas Baptist Univ, BS; Emory Univ, MA; George Washington Univ, PhD. **CAREER** Prof, Sam Houston State Univ, 79; vis fel, Australian Nat Univ, 91-. **RESEARCH** American religion, historiography and philosophy of history. **SELECTED PUBLICATIONS** Auth, Urban Religion and the Second Great Awakening: Church and Society in Early National Baltimore, Fairleigh Dickinson UP, 86; Francis Asbury's America: An Album of Early American Methodism, 84; co-ed, Constructing the American Past. **CONTACT ADDRESS** Dept of History, Sam Houston State Univ, Huntsville, TX, 77341.

BILLIAS, GEORGE ATHAN
PERSONAL Born 06/26/1919, Lynn, MA, m, 1948, 3 children **DISCIPLINE** AMERICAN HISTORY **EDUCATION** Bates Col, AB, 48; Columbia Univ, MA, 49, PhD, 58. **CAREER** From instr to assoc prof Am hist, Univ Maine, 54-62; assoc prof Am colonial hist, 62-66, PROF AM HIST, CLARK UNIV, 66-, Guggenheim Mem Found fel, 61-62; Am Coun Learned Soc fel, 68-69; mem coun, Inst Early Am Hist and Cult, Col William and Mary, 68-71; mem heritage comt, Am Revolution Bicentennial Comn, 72- **MEMBERSHIPS** AHA; Manuscript Soc; Am Antiq Soc. **RESEARCH** Maritime history of the US ; American military history. **SELECTED PUBLICATIONS** Auth, Knight, Russell, Wallace--Proceedings of the American Antiquarian Society, Vol 0104, 94; Privileged Person, William Mary Quart, Vol 0052, 95; A Culture of Rights, The Bill of Rights in Philosophy, Politics and Law, 1791-1991, William And Mary Quart, Vol 0050, 93; My Intellectual Odyssey, Proc Am Antiq Soc, Vol 0102, 92. **CONTACT ADDRESS** Dept of Hist, Clark Univ, Worcester, MA, 01610.

BILLINGS, WILLIAM M.
DISCIPLINE HISTORY **EDUCATION** William & Mary, AB, 62; Pitt, AM, 63; N Ill Univ, PhD, 68. **CAREER** Asst prof-prof, Univ New Orleans, 68-78; res prof, 88; prof, Univ New Orleans, 94- . **HONORS AND AWARDS** Phi Beta Kappa; Am Bar Found Fel, 82; Weddell Lectr, Va Hist Soc, 88; LS Fac Found Fel, 87; VHS Mellon Found Fel, 89, 92. **MEMBERSHIPS** Va Hist Soc; La Hist Asoc; Southern Hist Asoc; Am Asoc of Law Libr; British-Irish Asoc of Law Librns. **RESEARCH** Early American law; 17th century Virginia; documentary editing, 19th century law. **SELECTED PUBLICATIONS** Auth, Vignettes of Jamestown, Va Cavalcade, 95; co-ed with Judith Kelleher Schafer, An Uncommon Experience: Law and Judicial Institutions in Louisiana, 1803-2003, 97; auth, The Return of Sir William Berkeley, Va Cavalcade, 98; auth, The Papers of Sir William Berkeley, 1605-1677, forthcoming; auth, Councils, Assemblies, and Courts of Judicature: The General Assembly of Virginia, 1619-1699, forthcoming. **CONTACT ADDRESS** History Dept, Univ of New Orleans, New Orleans, LA, 70148. **EMAIL** wmbilin@uno.edu

BILLINGTON, JAMES H.
PERSONAL Born 06/01/1929, Bryn Mawr, PA, m, 1957, 3 children **DISCIPLINE** EUROPEAN HISTORY **EDUCATION** Princeton Univ, BA, 50; Oxford Univ, DPhil, 53. **CAREER** From instr to asst prof hist and gen educ, Harvard Univ, 57-62, res fel, Russian Res Ctr, 58-59; asst prof hist, 62-64, Hodder fel, Coun Humanities, 61-62, prof, 64-75, DIR, WOODROW WILSON INT CTR SCHOLARS, PRINCETON UNIV, 73-, Fulbright res prof, Univ Helsinki, 60-61; Guggenheim fel, 60-61; guest prof, Univ Leningrad, 61; exchange prof, Univ Moscow, 64 and Inst Hist, Soviet Acad Sci, Moscow, 66-67, chmn bd foreign scholar, Fulbright Prog, 71-73; historian-host, Humanities Film Forum, Nat Pub TV, 73-74. **HONORS AND AWARDS** LittD, Lafayette Col, 81, LeMoyne Col, 82. **MEMBERSHIPS** AHA; Am Asn Advan Slavic Studies; Coun Foreign Rels; PEN Club. **RESEARCH** Russian history, especially cultural and intellectual history of 17th and 19th to 20th centuries; general European history. **SELECTED PUBLICATIONS** Auth, The Intellectual and Cultural Dimensions of International Relations--Present Ironies and Future Possibilities, J Arts Mgt Law Soc, Vol 0022, 92; The Church in the World, Conflict and Hope in the Russian Orthodox Christian Renewal, Theol Today, Vol 0052, 95; Libraries, The Library of Congress, and the Information Age, Daedalus, Vol 0125, 96. **CONTACT ADDRESS** Woodrow Wilson Int Ctr Scholars Smithsonian Inst B, Washington, DC, 20560.

BILLINGTON, MONROE
PERSONAL Born 03/04/1928, m, 1951, 3 children **DISCIPLINE** HISTORY **EDUCATION** Okla Baptist Univ, BA, 50; Univ Okla, MA, 51; Univ Ky, PhD (hist), 55. **CAREER** From instr to prof hist, Univ SDak, 55-66; prof, Univ Toledo, 66-68; head dept, 68-75, PROF HIST, N MEX STATE UNIV, 68-, News ed, Historian, 60-70; vis Fulbright prof, Univ Vienna, 62-63. **MEMBERSHIPS** Orgn Am Historians; Southern Hist Asn. **RESEARCH** Twentieth century US history; the American South; the Negro and civil rights. **SELECTED PUBLICATIONS** Auth, Black Soldiers in Jim Crow Texas, J Am Hist, Vol 0082, 96; Berg Wozzeck, Opera, Vol 0044, 93; Sondheim Passion, Opera, Vol 0047, 96; Nunn in Opera, Opera, Vol 0045, 94; Catholic Clergymen, Roosevelt, Franklin, D. and the New Deal, Cath Hist RevVol 0079, 93; Poppy Baby Doll, Opera, Vol 0044, 93. **CONTACT ADDRESS** Dept of History, New Mexico State Univ, Las Cruces, NM, 88001.

BILLOWS, RICHARD A.
DISCIPLINE ANCIENT GREEK AND ROMAN HISTORY **EDUCATION** Oxford Univ, BA, 78; Univ Calif-Berkeley, PhD, 85. **CAREER** Assoc **RESEARCH** Greek epigraphy **SELECTED PUBLICATIONS** Auth, Antigonos the One-Eyed and the Creation of the Hellenistic State, 90; Kings and Colonists: Aspects of Macedonian Imperialism, 95. **CONTACT ADDRESS** Dept of Hist, Columbia Col, New York, 2960 Broadway, New York, NY, 10027-6902.

BILMES, JACK
PERSONAL Born 08/09/1940, New York, NY, m, 1963, 1 child **DISCIPLINE** ANTHROPOLOGY **EDUCATION** Brandeis Univ, BA, 61; Yale Univ, MA, 68; Stanford Univ, PhD, 74. **CAREER** Visiting asst prof, 73-75, asst prof, 75-81, assoc prof, 81-90; prof, 90-present, Univ HI. **MEMBERSHIPS** Amer Anthropological Assn; Intl Pragmatics Assn. **RESEARCH** Social interaction; Thailand; Bali **SELECTED PUBLICATIONS** Auth, Negotiation and Compromise: A Microanalysis of a Discussion in the Federal Trade Commission, The Discourse of Negotiation: Studies of Language in the Workplace, 95; Constituting Silence: Life in the World of Total Meaning, Semiotica, 94, trans and reprinted in Reseaux, 96; Problems and Resources in Analyzing Thai Language Data, Journal of Pragmatices, 96; Being Interrupted, Language In Society, 97; Questions, Answers, And The Organization Of Talk In The 1992 Vice Presidential Debate: Fundamental Considerations, Research In Language And Social Interaction, 99. **CONTACT ADDRESS** Dept of Anthropology, Univ HI, Honolulu, HI, 96822. **EMAIL** bilmes@hawaii.edu

BILODEAU, LORRAINE
PERSONAL Born 12/09/1935, Holyoke, MA **DISCIPLINE** ELEMENTARY EDUCATION; RELIGIOUS EDUCATION; LIBRARY SCIENCE AND INFORMATION **EDUCATION** Catholic Teachers Col; BS, 69; Fairfield Univ, MA, 75; Dominican Univ, MLS, 88. **CAREER** Tchr, Rhode Island Catholic Sch; DRE dir, St. Leo the Great; librn, dir, Anna Maria Col. **MEMBERSHIPS** ALA; NEACRL; CLA; NECLA. **RESEARCH** Geneology and icons. **CONTACT ADDRESS** Mondor-Eagen Library, Anna Maria Col, Paxton, MA, 01612-1198. **EMAIL** lbilodeau@annamaria.edu

BILSKY, LESTER JAMES
PERSONAL Born 12/20/1935, St. Louis, MO, m, 1960, 3 children **DISCIPLINE** CHINESE HISTORY **EDUCATION** Wash Univ, BA, 56; Univ Wash, Seattle, PhD(hist), 71. **CAREER** Instr hist, Univ Akron, 62-71; asst prof, 72-76, assoc prof, 76-81, prof hist, Univ Ark, Little Rock, 81-, chm dept, 80-86, 98-. **MEMBERSHIPS** Asn Asian Studies; Soc Study Early China; Southwest Conf Asian Studies. **RESEARCH** Ancient China, especially religious history and environmental history. **SELECTED PUBLICATIONS** Auth, The State Religion of Ancient China, Orient Cult Serv, Taipei, 75; ed, Historical Ecology: Essays on Environment and Social Change, Kennikat Press, 80. **CONTACT ADDRESS** Dept of Hist, Univ of Ark, 2801 S University Ave., Little Rock, AR, 72204-1000. **EMAIL** ljbilsky@ualr.edu

BILSON, MALCOLM
DISCIPLINE MUSIC **EDUCATION** Vienna State Acad, Reifezeugnis, 59; Paris, Licena Libre, Ecole Normale de Musique, 60; Urbana, DMA, 68; Bard Col, Hon Doct, 91. **CAREER** Frederick J. Whiton prof; **HONORS AND AWARDS** Fulbright fel, Vienna, 57-59; Harriet Hale Woolley fel, Paris, 59-60. **MEMBERSHIPS** Amer Musicol Soc; Early Music Am; ed bd, Early Mus Mag London; ed bd, Piano and Keyboard Mag, US; Amer Acad Arts and Sci. **RESEARCH** Music of the late 18th and early 19th centuries; performance practice; problems of notation and execution; instruments; aesthetics. **SELECTED PUBLICATIONS** Auth, Beethoven and the Piano, Clavier Magazine, Vol 22, 83; Execution and Expression in Mozart's Sonata in E-flat, K. 282, Early Music Mag, 92; Do We Know How to Read Urtext Editions, Piano and Keyboard Mag, 95. **CONTACT ADDRESS** Dept of Music, Cornell Univ, 104 Lincoln Hall, Ithaca, NY, 14853. **EMAIL** mb68@cornell.edu

BILSTEIN, ROGER EUGENE
PERSONAL Born 01/19/1937, Hyannis, NE, m, 1964, 2 children **DISCIPLINE** HISTORY OF TECHNOLOGY **EDUCATION** Doane Col, BA, 59; Ohio State Univ, MA, 60, PhD (recent US), 65. **CAREER** Asst prof recent US, Wis State Univ-Whitewater, 65-69, assoc prof hist technol, 69-72; asst prof technol and aero hist, Univ Ill, Urbana, 72-74; assoc prof, 74-79, PROF TECHNOL, AERO HIST AND RECENT US, UNIV HOUSTON, CLEAR LAKE CITY, 79-, Sr res assoc, Res Inst, Univ Ala, Huntsville, 70-72; vis scholar aerospace hist, Nat Air and Space Mus, Smithsonian Inst, 77-78; consult, Epic of Flight series, Time and Life, Inc, 80-82. **HONORS AND AWARDS** Writing Awards, Aviation and Space Writers Asn, 75, 80 and 82; Goddard Essay Award, Am Inst Astronaut, 77; Manuscript Award, An Inst Aeronaut and Astronaut, 79. **MEMBERSHIPS** Soc Hist Technol; Orgn Am Historians; Aviation and Space Writers Asn; Air Force Hist Found. **RESEARCH** History of aviation and space flight; technology since 1900; social, political and diplomatic history of the US since 1900. **SELECTED PUBLICATIONS** Auth, Building the B 29, Tech Cult, Vol 0038, 97; Courage and Air Warfare--The Allied Aircrew Experience in the 2nd World War, Tech Cult, Vol 0038, 97; From Colony to Commonwealth--The Rise of the Aerospace Industry in the West, J W, Vol 0036, 97; The Rise of the Gunbelt--The Military Remapping of Industrial America, Southwestern Hist Quart, Vol 0097, 94; **CONTACT ADDRESS** Dept of Hist, Univ Houston at Clear Lake City, 2700 Bay Area Blvd, Houston, TX, 77058-1025.

BINDER, FREDERICK MELVIN
PERSONAL Born 06/19/1931, Chelsea, MA, m, 1964, 1 child **DISCIPLINE** AMERICAN HISTORY **EDUCATION** Boston Univ, BS, 53; Columbia Univ, MA, 54, EdD(Am hist), 62. **CAREER** Asst prof US hist, Ball State Univ, 62-65; from asst prof to prof Am educ hist, City Col New York, 65-74, chmn dept social and psychol found, 68-72; assoc dean fac, 74-79, PROF HIST, COL STATEN ISLAND, CITY UNIV NEW YORK, 74-, Dir NDEA US Hist Inst, Ball State Univ, 65 and City Col New York, 67. **MEMBERSHIPS** AHA; Orgn Am Historians; Hist Educ Soc; Am Studies Asn. **RESEARCH** American educational, social and intellectual history; the age of the common school, 1830-1865; race and ethnicity in American educational history. **SELECTED PUBLICATIONS** Auth, Gateway to the Promised Land--Ethnic Cultures in New York Lower East Side, Am Jewish Hist, Vol 0084, 96. **CONTACT ADDRESS** Col of Staten Island, CUNY, Staten Island, NY, 10301.

BINDON, KATHRYN
PERSONAL Toronto, ON, Canada **DISCIPLINE** HISTORY **EDUCATION** Sir George Williams Univ, BA, 71; Queen's Univ MA, 73, PhD, 79. **CAREER** Lectr, 78-80, asst prof, 80-83, prin, Sch Community & Pub Affairs, 81-84, Concordia Univ; assoc prof, 83, assoc prof, 87-91, Mt St Vincent Univ; PRIN & PROF HISTORY, SIR WILFRED GRENFELL COL, 91-. **HONORS AND AWARDS** Woodrow Wilson Fel, 71-72; R. Samuuel McLaughlin Scholar, Queen's Univ, 71-72; Sir John A. Macdonald Grad Fel, 72-74. **MEMBERSHIPS** Can Hist Soc; Champlain Soc; Nova Scotia Coun Higher Learning; Gov Gen Can Stud Conf. **SELECTED PUBLICATIONS** Auth, Canada at War, 1914-1918, 79; coauth, Newfoundland: More Canadian Than British, But Longer Getting There in Higher Education in Canada: Different Systems, Different Perspectives. **CONTACT ADDRESS** Sir Wilfred Grenfell Col, Univ of Newfoundland, Cornerbrook, NF, A2H 2PN. **EMAIL** kbindon@beothuk.swgc.mun.ca

BINFORD, HENRY C.
PERSONAL Born 05/02/1944, Berea, Ohio, m **DISCIPLINE** HISTORY **EDUCATION** Harvard Univ, AB 1966, PhD 1973; Univ of Sussex England, MA 1967. **CAREER** Northwestern Univ, asst prof 1973-79, assoc prof 1979-. **MEMBERSHIPS** Dir Business and Professional People for the Public Interest 1985-; mem Sigma Pi Phi 1985-; editorial board, Chicago Reporter, 1988-. **SELECTED PUBLICATIONS** Author, The First Suburbs, Univ of Chicago Press, 1985. **CONTACT ADDRESS** Northwestern Univ, Evanston, IL, 60208.

BING, J. DANIEL
DISCIPLINE HISTORY **EDUCATION** Univ Ind, PhD. **CAREER** Assoc prof. **RESEARCH** Greece history. **SELECTED PUBLICATIONS** Auth, pubs on Sumerian and Babylonian literature, Assyrian, Persian and early Hellenistic imperial policy in southeast Anatolia, and Athenian political-military development. **CONTACT ADDRESS** Dept of History, Knoxville, TN, 37996.

BINGHAM, EDWIN RALPH
PERSONAL Born 01/21/1920, Denver, CO, m, 1952, 2 children **DISCIPLINE** HISTORY **EDUCATION** Occidental Col, AB, 41, MA, 42; Univ Calif, Los Angeles, PhD, 51. **CAREER** From instr to assoc prof, 49-63, PROF HIST, UNIV ORE, 64-, Ford Found advan educ grant, Yale Univ, 54-55; sr Fulbright lectr, Mysore Univ, India, 78-79. **MEMBERSHIPS** Am Studies Asn; Orgn Am Historians; AHA; Western Hist Asn. **RESEARCH** Cultural and intellectual history; history of the American West. **SELECTED PUBLICATIONS** Auth, The Big Empty--Essays on Western Landscapes as Narrative, Pac Hist Rev, Vol 0064, 95; Cather, Willa and the Myth of American Migration, Pac Hist Rev, Vol 0066, 97; Mountain Medicine, Ore Hist Quart, Vol 0094, 93; The Columbia, Ore Hist Quart, Vol 0094, 93. **CONTACT ADDRESS** 1805 Longview St, Eugene, OR, 97403.

BINION, RUDOLPH
PERSONAL Born 01/18/1927, New York, NY, m, 1952 **DISCIPLINE** HISTORY **EDUCATION** Columbia Col, BA, 45, PhD, 58. **CAREER** Instr hist, Rutgers Univ, 55-56; instr hum,

Mass Inst Technol, 56-59; from asst prof to assoc prof hist, Columbia Univ, 59-67; prof hist, Brandeis Univ, MA, 67, Coun Res Soc Sci res grant, Columbia Univ, 60; Am Coun Learned Soc fel, 61; Deutscher Akademischer Austauschdienst fel, 81. **HONORS AND AWARDS** Clarke F Ansley Award, Columbia Univ, 58; George Louis Beer Prize, AHA, 60; medal, Col de France, 80. **MEMBERSHIPS** International Psychohistorical Asn. **RESEARCH** Mod Europ polit, thought and cult, psychohist. **SELECTED PUBLICATIONS** Defeated Leaders, the Political Fate of Caillaux, Jouvenel and Tardieu, Columbia Univ, 60; Frau Lou: Nietzsche's Wayward Disciple, Princeton Univ, 68; Hitler Among the Germans, Elsevier, 76; Soundings, Psychohistory Press, 81; Introduction a la psychohistoire, Pressses Univ France & Col Frane, 82; After Christianity, Logbrigde-Rhodes, 86; Love Beyond Death: The Anatomy of a Myth in the Arts, NYU, 93; Freud uber Aggression und Tos, Picus, 95; Sounding the Classics: From Sophacles to Thomas Mann, Greenwood, 97. **CONTACT ADDRESS** Dept of Hist, Brandeis Univ, 415 South St, Waltham, MA, 02254-9110. **EMAIL** binion@brandeis.edu

BIRCH, BRUCE CHARLES
PERSONAL Born 12/03/1941, Wichita, KS, m, 1962, 2 children **DISCIPLINE** OLD TESTAMENT, ANCIENT NEAR EASTERN STUDIES **EDUCATION** Southwestern Col, BA, 62; Southern Methodist Univ, BD, 65; Yale Univ, MA, 67, MPhil, 68, PhD, 70. **CAREER** Asst prof relig, Iowa Wesleyan Col, 68-70; asst prof Bible & relig, 70-71, Erskine Col; assoc prof Old Testament, 71-77, prof Old Testament, 77-, dean, 98-, Wesley Theol Sem; Chmn Nat Intersem Coun, 64-67; mem bd dir, Washington Int Col, 71-74; dir & chmn bd, Int Prog Human Resources Develop, 75-; res fel, Asn Theol Schs, 77-78; vis prof, Sch Theol, summer 82, Claremont. **MEMBERSHIPS** Soc Bibl Lit: Am Acad Relig. **RESEARCH** Deuteronomic history; Biblical theology; Biblical ethics. **SELECTED PUBLICATIONS** Auth, Let Justice Roll Down: Old Testament, Ethics, and Christian Life, Westminster, 91; auth, Hosea, Joel, Amos: Westminster Bible Companion, Westminster, 97; auth, 1 and 2 Samuel: The New Interpreter's Bible, v.2, Abingdon, 98. **CONTACT ADDRESS** Wesley Theol Sem, 4500 Mass Ave N W, Washington, DC, 20016-5632. **EMAIL** otbruce@aol.com

BIRCHETTE, WILLIAM ASHBY, III
PERSONAL Born 05/09/1942, Newport News, VA, s **DISCIPLINE** EDUCATION **EDUCATION** St Augustine's College, BA 1964; VA State Univ, MEd 1973; Univ of VA, EdD 1982. **CAREER** Wilson City Public Schools; Delaware Tech & Community College; Banneker Jr HS, principal, DC Public Schools; Hampton Univ, instructor; asst to reg supt, DC Public Schools; Magruder Middle School, principal 1983-87; Reservoir Middle School, principal 1988-90; Vasguard Middle School, VA Dept of Education, principal, 1989; Southern Vance High School, Vance County Schools, principal, 1990-92; Isle of Wight County Schools, assistant superintendent for instruction, 1992-97; Spotsylvania County Schools, supervisor English, language arts, 1998-. **HONORS AND AWARDS** Outstanding Leadership Awd 1978; Citizen Involvement in Education 1980; Charles Stewart Mott Fellow 1980; Education Fellow Univ of VA; Principal, Vanguard Middle School, VA Dept of Education 1987; Author, "Guidelines for Middle Schools in Virginia," (VASSP Journal) 1988; Contributions (Executive Educator) 1988; Twenty-Five Outstanding High Schools, NC Dept of Ed, principal, 1991. **MEMBERSHIPS** Phi Delta Kappa; ASCD; Natl Comm Educ Assn; VA Comm Educ Assn; advisory bd Hampton Roads Boys Club; bd of directors Youth Programs-Mall Tennis Club; Omega Psi Phi; member NAACP; pres Peninsula Council of Urban League; pres, PTPA; An Achievable Dream, bd of dirs. **CONTACT ADDRESS** Spotsylvania County Schools, 6717 Smith Station Rd, Spotsylvania, VA, 22553.

BIRD, HAROLD WESLEY
PERSONAL Born 08/23/1937, Nottingham, England, m, 1962, 2 children **DISCIPLINE** ANCIENT HISTORY AND LITERATURE **EDUCATION** Cambridge Univ, BA, 60, dipl, 61, MA, 64; McMaster Univ, MA, 63; Univ Toronto, PhD (Greek and Roman hist), 72. **CAREER** Head Latin Dept, Salt Fleet High Sch, Ont, 63-64; from lectr to asst prof classics, Univ NB, 64-67; from asst prof to assoc prof, 69-75, PROF CLASSICS, UNIV WINDSOR, 75-, HEAD, DEPT CLASS AND MOD LANG, 82- **MEMBERSHIPS** Class Asn Can; Am Asn Ancient Historians. **RESEARCH** Roman imperial history; history of the late Roman Republic; Roman historiography. **SELECTED PUBLICATIONS** Auth, Julian and Aurelius Victor--Did Victor Receive the Governorship of Pannonia Secunda for Writing De Caesaribus, Latomus, Vol 0055, 96. **CONTACT ADDRESS** Dept of Class Studies, Univ of Windsor, Windsor, ON, N9B 3P4.

BIRELEY, ROBERT LEE
PERSONAL Born 07/26/1933, Evanston, IL **DISCIPLINE** EARLY MODERN EUROPEAN HISTORY **EDUCATION** Loyola Univ, Chicago, AB, 56, MA, 63; Hochschule Sankt Georgen, Frankfurt, STL, 65; Harvard Univ, PhD, 72. **CAREER** Instr hist, St Ignatius High Sch, Cleveland, 58-61; instr, 71-72, asst prof, 72-76, assoc prof, 76-82, prof hist, Loyola Univ, Chicago, 82, adv ed, Cath Hist Rev, 79-; mem, Inst for Advanced Study, Princeton, 86-86. **HONORS AND AWARDS** Nat Endowment for Hum fel, Rome, Vienna, Brno, Czech & Gyor, Hungary, 72-73; Am Coun Learned Soc res fel, 79; Guggenheim fel, 83; NEH Sr Res Fel, 86-87; Fel, Nat Hum Ctr, Research Triangle Parl, NC, 98-99. **MEMBERSHIPS** AHA; Am Cath Hist Asn; Ren Soc Am; Am Soc Reformation Res; 16th Century Studies Conf. **RESEARCH** Early mod Catholicism; Thirty Years War; Hist of the Jesuits; early mod polit thought. **SELECTED PUBLICATIONS** Auth, Maximilian von Bayern, Adam Contzen, S J, und die Gegen reformation in Deutschland 1624-1635, Vandenhoeck & Ruprecht, G"ttingen, 75; The Peace of Prague (1635) and the Counterreformation in Germany, J Mod Hist, 76; Religion and Politics in the Age of Counterreformation, Univ NC Press, 81; The Counter-Reformation Prince. Antimachiavellianism or Catholic Statecraft in Early Modern Europe, Univ NC Press, 90; The Thirty Years' War as Germany's Religious War, In: Krieg und Politik, 1618-1648, Kolloquien 8, 88; Confessional Absolutism in the Habsburg Lands in the Seventeenth Century, In: State and Society in Early Modern Austria, Purdue Univ Press, 94; Scholasticism and Reason of State, In: Aristotelismo politico e ragion di stato, Centro di Studi sul pensiero politico, Studi e Testi 4, 95; Neue Orden, Katholische Reform, und Konfessionalisierung, In: Die katholische Konfessionalisierung, Aschendorff, 95. **CONTACT ADDRESS** Dept of Hist, Loyola Univ, 6525 N Sheridan Rd, Chicago, IL, 60626-5385. **EMAIL** rbirele@orion.it.luc.edu

BIRKNER, MICHAEL J.
PERSONAL Born 03/26/1950, Teaneck, NJ, m, 1979, 3 children **DISCIPLINE** HISTORY **EDUCATION** Gettysburg Col, BA, 72; Univ Va, MA, 73, PhD, 81. **CAREER** Vis asst prof, Univ Ky, 79-81; assoc ed, Dartmouth Col, 81-83; ed, Concord Monitor, 83-85; asst prof, Millersville Univ, 85-89; from assoc to prof to chemn, Gettysburg Col, 89-. **HONORS AND AWARDS** John A. Booth Prize, New Jersey Hist Society; NEH Summer Fel, 89; Cert of Commendation, Am Asn of State and Local Hist, 95., Phi Beta Kappa, 72; Thomas Jefferson Fel, 72-74. **MEMBERSHIPS** AHA; OAH **RESEARCH** American political history **SELECTED PUBLICATIONS** Coed, The Governor's of New Jersey, 82; auth, Samuel L. Southard: Jeffersonian Whig, 84; coed, Correspondence of Daniel Webster, 1850-1852, 86; auth, A Country Place No More: The Transformation of Bergenfield, New Jersey 1894-1994, 94; ed, James Buchanan and the Political Crisis of the 1850s, 96. **CONTACT ADDRESS** Dept of History, Gettysburg Col, Gettysburg, PA, 17325. **EMAIL** mbirkner@gettysburg.edu

BIRN, DONALD S.
PERSONAL Born 08/11/1937, New York, NY, m, 1964, 2 children **DISCIPLINE** MODERN HISTORY **EDUCATION** Union Col, NY, AB, 59; Columbia Univ, MA, 60, PhD(hist), 64. **CAREER** Foreign serv officer, US Info Serv, Madras, India, 64-66; asst prof, 66-81, ASSOC PROF HIST, STATE UNIV NY ALBANY, 81-, Fel, Richardson Inst for Conflict and Peace Res, London, 73-74. **MEMBERSHIPS** Conf on Brit Studies; AHA; Conf Peace Res in Hist. **RESEARCH** Twentieth century Europe; modern Britain; British cultural propaganda. **SELECTED PUBLICATIONS** Auth, Fantasy, The Bomb, and the Greening of Britain in Romantic Protest, 1945-1980, Am Hist Rev, Vol 0101, 96; Britain and Italy, 1943-1949 in The Decline of British Influence, Am Hist Rev, Vol 0102, 97. **CONTACT ADDRESS** Dept of Hist, State Univ NY, Albany, NY, 12054.

BIRN, RAYMOND F.
PERSONAL Born 05/10/1935, New York, NY **DISCIPLINE** MODERN EUROPEAN HISTORY **EDUCATION** NY Univ, BA, 56; Univ IL, MA, 57, PhD (hist), 61. **CAREER** From instr to assoc prof, 61-72, head dept, 71-78, prof hist, Univ OR, 72-; Am Coun Learned Soc & Am Philos Soc grants-in-aid, 63-64; Fulbright res fel, France, 68-69; adv ed, Eighteenth-Century Studies, 73-; fel, Nat Endowment for Humanities, 76-77, 87-88; fel, Center for the Hist of Freedoms, 92; prof Ecole des Hautes Etudes en Sciences Sociales, 92. **MEMBERSHIPS** AHA; Soc Fr Hist Studies; Am Soc 18th Century Studies. **RESEARCH** Eighteenth century France; the French press and book trade before 1789. **SELECTED PUBLICATIONS** Auth, Pierre Rousseau and the Philosophes of Bouillon, Inst et musee Voltaire, Switz, 64; Le Journal des Savants sous L'Ancien Regime, J Savants, 1-3/65; The French Language Press and the Encyclopedie, 1750-1759, Studies Voltaire & 18th Century, 67; The Profits of Ideas: Privileges en librairie in 18th century France, Eighteenth Century Studies, 2/71; Livre et societe after ten years: Formation of a Discipline, Studies Voltaire & 18th Century, 76; Crisis, Absolutism, Revolution: Europe 1648-1789/91, Dryden, 77, 2nd ed rev, Harcourt Brace J Vanovido, 92; Le livre ancien Francais dans la recherche Nord-Americaine, Rev Francaise d'Histoire du Livre, 78; La Contrabande et la Saisie de Livres a l'Aube du Siecle des Lumieres, Rev d'Histoire moderne et contemporaine, 1/81; auth, Book Production and Censorship in France, 1700-1715, in Books and Soc in Hist, 83; ed, The Printed Word in the 18th Century, Eighteenth-Century Studies, 84; auth, Malesherbes and the Call for a Free Press, in Revolution in Print: The Press in France, 1770-1800, 89; La Clandestinite aux Frontieres: Boillon, in Histoire de l'edition francaise, vol II, 90; Publishing and Censorship, in The Blackwell Companion to the Enlightenment, 92; Rousseau et ses Editeurs, Revue d'histoire moderne et contemporaine, 1/93; Freedom of Religion and Liberty of Expression, in The French Idea of Freedom, 94; Rousseau Senza Frontiere, Rivista storica italiana, 3/95; Enciclopedismo, in Illuminismo: Dizionarie Storico, 97; Les Deuvres completes de Rousseau sous l'Ancien Regime, Annales de la Societe Jean-Jacques Rousseau, 97. **CONTACT ADDRESS** Dept Hist, Univ Ore, Eugene, OR, 97403-1205. **EMAIL** rbirn@oregon.uoregon.edu

BIRNBAUM, LUCIA CHIAVOLA
PERSONAL Born 01/03/1924, Kansas City, MO, m, 1946, 3 children **DISCIPLINE** HISTORY **EDUCATION** Univ Calif, Berkeley, PhD. **CAREER** Res assoc, 83-85, Women's Ctr; res assoc, 90-96, dept hist, Univ Calif; affil scholar, 87-94, Inst Res & Gender, Stanford Univ; vis scholar, 84, 95, Grad Theol Union Berkley; instr, 94-, Women's Spirituality, Calif Inst of Integral Stud; 98- Italian Res & Stud Prog, Ctr of Western Europe Stud. **RESEARCH** Cultural history **CONTACT ADDRESS** 349 Gravatt Dr., Berkeley, CA, 94705-1503. **EMAIL** cowari@aol.com

BIRNBAUM, NORMAN
PERSONAL Born 07/21/1926, New York, NY, 2 children **DISCIPLINE** POLITICAL SCIENCE, SOCIAL SCIENCE **EDUCATION** Williams Col, BA, 47; Harvard Univ, PhD, 58. **CAREER** Lectr, London School of Econ and Polit Sci, 53-59; fel, Nuffield Col, Oxford Univ, 59-64; vis prof, Univ Strasbourg, 64-66; prof, Grad Fac of Political and Soc Sci, New School for Social Res, 66-68; prof, Amherst Col, 68-79; mellon Prof Hum, 79-81, Univ Prof, 81- , Georgetown Univ Law Center. **HONORS AND AWARDS** Guggenheim Found fel; mem, Inst for Advanced Study; vis scholar, Giovanni Agnelli Found; vis fel, Wissenschaftskolleg; dir d-Etudes Associe, Ecole des Hautes Etudes en Sciences Sociales; Fulbright Distinguished Chair, Univ Bologna; founding ed board, New Left Review, London, 59; ed board, Partisan Rev, 71-83; ed board, The Nation, 76- . **RESEARCH** Modern industrial society; modern social movements; religion and society. **SELECTED PUBLICATIONS** Auth, Crisis of Industrial Society, 69; auth, Toward A Critical Sociology, 71; auth, The Radical Renewal, 88; auth, Searching for the Light, 93. **CONTACT ADDRESS** Law Ctr, Georgetown Univ, 600 New Jersey Ave NW, Washington, DC, 20001. **EMAIL** birnbaum@law.georgetown.edu

BISHOP, C. JAMES
PERSONAL Born 11/09/1935, Loretto, PA, m, 1959, 4 children **DISCIPLINE** HISTORY **EDUCATION** Clarion State Col, BS, 61; Ohio Univ, MA, 64; Univ Wis, Madison, MA, 66; Univ Va, PhD, 72. **CAREER** Asst prof, Winthrop Col, 64-67; lectr, Kans State Univ, 68-69; PROF ASIAN HIST, MANCHESTER COL, 69-; Fulbright Scholar hist, US Educ Found in India, 67-68; NEH grant hist of socialism, Duke Univ, 67-67 & 77. **MEMBERSHIPS** AHA, Am Asn Asian Studies. **RESEARCH** Social and political structure and history of South and Southeast Asia, particularly Modern India, 1857-1947. **SELECTED PUBLICATIONS** Auth, The Chinese Laborer in Malaya 1900-1922, Univ Singapore, 72; coauth, The Indian World, Forum Press, 77. **CONTACT ADDRESS** Dept Hist, Manchester Col, 601 E College Ave, N Manchester, IN, 46962-1226.

BISHOP, OLGA B.
PERSONAL Born 06/24/1911, Dover, NB, Canada **DISCIPLINE** LIBRARY & INFO SCI/HISTORY **EDUCATION** Mt Allison Univ, BA, 38, MA, 51, LLD, 71; Carleton Univ, BPubAdmin, 46; Univ Mich, AMLS, 52, PhD, 62. **CAREER** Can civil serv, 40-46; asst & gen librn, 46-54, med librn, Univ Western Ont, 54-65; assoc prof, 65-70, prof, 70-77, PROF EMER, UNIV TORONTO FAC LIBRARY & INFORMATION SCI, 77-. **HONORS AND AWARDS** Marie Tremaine Medal in Can Bibliog, 81; CASLIS Award, 81; Ont Col Univ Asn Merit Award, 87. **MEMBERSHIPS** Can Libr Asn; Can Asn Col Univ Librs; Ex Libris Asn; Ont Libr Asn; Ont Asn Col Univ Librs; Inst Prof Libr Ont; Can Asn Univ Tchrs; Med Libr Asn; Bibliog Soc Can; Ont Hist Soc; Asn Can Stud; Heritage Can. **SELECTED PUBLICATIONS** Auth, Publications of the Governments of Nova Scotia, Prince Edward Island, New Brunswick 1758-1952, 57; auth, Publications of the Government of the Province of Canada 1841-1867, 63; auth, Publications of the Government of Ontario 1867-1900, 76; auth, Bibliography of Ontario History 1867-1976: Cultural, Economic, Political, Social, 80; auth, Canadian Official Publications, 81; auth, Publications of the Province of Upper Canada and of Great Britain relating to Upper Canada 1791-1840, 84; ed, Growing to Serve, A History of Victoria Hospital, London, Ontario, 85; ed, North Talbot Road, Westminster Township, 86; ed, Glanworth, Westminster Township, 87; ed, Westminster Township Southeast of the Thames, 88; comp, History of the English Speaking Union of Canada: London and Western Ontario Branch 1967-87, 90. **CONTACT ADDRESS** 62 Thornton Ave, London, ON, N5Y 2Y3.

BISMANIS, MAIJA
PERSONAL Riga, Latvia **DISCIPLINE** ART HISTORY **EDUCATION** Univ BC, BA, MA, 68; Univ Nottingham, PhD, 74; Oriel Col, Oxford, post-doc, 74-76. **CAREER** Educ & Res curator, Vancouver Art Gallery, 68-70; PROF UNIV REGINA 70-. **HONORS AND AWARDS** Heritage Award, City Regina,

82. **MEMBERSHIPS** Univ Art Asn Can; Int Ctr Medieval Art; Medieval Soc Am; Soc Archit Hists. **SELECTED PUBLICATIONS** Auth, Canada Collects: the Middle Ages; auth, The English Medieval Timber Roof: A Handbook of Types; auth, Medieval Sculpture in Canadian Collections. **CONTACT ADDRESS** Dept of Art History, Univ Regina, 3737 Wascana Pkwy Dr, Regina, SK.

BISSON, THOMAS N.
PERSONAL Born 03/30/1931, New York, NY, m, 1962, 2 children **DISCIPLINE** HISTORY **EDUCATION** Haverford Col, BA, 53; Princeton Univ, MA, 55, PhD, 58. **CAREER** Instr, Amherst Col, 57-60; asst prof, Brown Univ, 60-65; assoc prof, Swarthmore Col, 65-67; from assoc prof to prof, Univ of Calif, Berkeley, 67-87; prof, Harvard Univ, 87-. **HONORS AND AWARDS** J.S. Guggenheim Mem Fel, 64-65; Univ of Calif Res Comt Fels for the Hums, 68-69, 76, 80; Am Philos Soc, Grants-in Aid, 69, 78; Inst for Advan Study, Princeton, vis mem, 71-72; Nat Endowment for the Hums, sen fel, 75-76; Am Coun of Learned Socs, sen fel, 79-80; All Souls Col, Oxford, vis fel, 83-84; Fulbright Fel for West European Studies, 83-84; W. Channing Cabot Fel in the Fac of Arts and Scis, Harvard Univ, 89-90. **MEMBERSHIPS** Medieval Acad of Am; Am Acad of Arts and Scis; Reial Academia de Bones Lletres; Brit Acad; Royal Hist Soc; Institut d'Estudis Catalans; Am Philos Soc; AHA. **RESEARCH** Medieval history: power and cultural change, tenth to thirteenth centuries. **SELECTED PUBLICATIONS** Auth, Assemblies and Representation in Languedoc in the Thirteenth Century, 64; Medieval Representative Institutions: Their Origins and Nature, 73; Conservation of Coinage: Monetary Exploitation and its Restraint in France, Catalonia and Aragon (c.A.D. 1000-c.1225), 79; Fiscal Accounts of Catalonia under the Early Count-Kings (1151-1213), 84; The Medieval Crown of Aragon: a Short History, 86; Medieval France and her Pyrenean neighbours: studies in early institutional history, 89; The war of the two Arnaus: a memorial of the broken peace in Cerdanya, in Miscellania en homenatge al P. Agusti Altisent, 91; Utilia perniciem operantur: forme et objet dans le Memorial del'eveque Aldebert III de Mende, in Histoire et société. Melanges offerts a Georges Duby, 92; The 'Feudal revolution, in Past and Present, 142, 94; Medieval lordship, in Speculum 1xx, 95; Cultures of Power: Lordship, Status, and Process in Twelfth-Century Europe, 95; The politicising of west European societies (c.1175-c.1225), in Georges Duby.L'ecriture de l'histoire, 96; The origins of the Corts of Catalonia, in Parliaments, Estates and Representation 16, 96; Els origens de l'impost sobre la moneda a Catalunya: una reconsideracio, in Acta historica et archaelogica mediavalia 16-17, 96; 'State-building' in the medieval Crown of Aragon, in XV Congreso de Historia de la Corona de Aragon. Actas tomo1. El poder real en la Corona de Aragon (Siglos XIV-XVI), 96; In memoriam: Georges Duby, in French Politics & Society, 15:1, 97; The Feudal revolution': Debate: Reply, in Past & Present, 155, 97; L'Impuls de Catalunya: recerques sobre l'epoca dels primers comtes-reis (vers 1140-vers 1225), 97; Tormented Voices: Power, Crisis and Humanity in Rural Catalonia, 1140-1200, 98. **CONTACT ADDRESS** Dept of History, Harvard Univ, 213 Robinson Hall, Cambridge, MA, 02138. **EMAIL** tnbisson@fas.harvard.edu

BIZZARRO, TINA W.
PERSONAL Media, PA, m, 1977, 2 children **DISCIPLINE** HISTORY OF ART **EDUCATION** Univ Pittsburgh, BA, 71; Bryn Mawr Col, PhD(hist art), 85. **CAREER** Assoc prof, 85-, chair, Arts Division, 85-, Rosemont Coll. **HONORS AND AWARDS** Phi Beta Kappa **MEMBERSHIPS** Col Art Asn; Am Asn Univ Women; Soc Architectural Historians; Del Valley Medieval Asn. **RESEARCH** History of criticism; medieval architecture. **SELECTED PUBLICATIONS** Auth, Romanesque Architectural Criticism: A Prehistory, Cambridge Univ Press, 93. **CONTACT ADDRESS** 511 N. Wynnewood Ave., Narbeth, PA, 19072. **EMAIL** tbizzarro@rosemont.edu

BJERKEN, XAK
DISCIPLINE MUSIC **EDUCATION** Univ Calif at Los Angeles, BA, 89; Peabody Conserv Music, MM, 91, DMA, 94. **CAREER** Lectr. **HONORS AND AWARDS** Second place, Harrison Winter Concerto Competition, Peabody Conserv, 92; Winner of all undergrad performance awards, Univ Calif, Los Angeles, 86-89; Dean's Gold Medal., Founding mem, Florestan Trio now Taliesin Trio, 95 & Third Millenium Music, 94. **RESEARCH** 20th-century music; Messiaen and post-WWII Eastern Europeans. **SELECTED PUBLICATIONS** Auth, Chopin's Harmony, Preston-Whitelaw, Ltd, 95; CD-ROM discussing Chopin's harmony, with over 50 excerpts from his piano music. **CONTACT ADDRESS** Dept of Music, Cornell Univ, 104 Lincoln Hall, Ithaca, NY, 14853. **EMAIL** xb10@cornell.edu

BLACK, BRIAN C.
PERSONAL Born 08/08/1966, Ahoona, PA, m, 1994, 2 children **DISCIPLINE** AMERICAN STUDIES **EDUCATION** Gettysburg Col, BA, 88; NY Univ, MA, 91; Univ Kansas, PhD, 96 **CAREER** Lctr, Wilson Col, 95-97; lctr, Harrisburg Area Comm Col, 96-97; visiting asst prof, Gettysburg Col, 94-97; visiting asst prof, Skidmore Col, 97- **HONORS AND AWARDS** NEH Fel, 96; Beeke-Levy Res Fel, 97; Skidmore Col Faculty Development Grant, 98 **RESEARCH** Environmental History; 19th & 20th Centuries **SELECTED PUBLICATIONS** Auth, "PETROLIA: The Landscape of Pennsylvania's Oil Boom, 1859-1872," Johns Hopkins Univ, forthcoming; auth, "A Triumph of Individualism," Pa Hist, forthcoming; auth, "Organic Planning: Ecology and Design in Landscape of the Tennessee Valley Authority, 1930-1945," Environmentalism in Landscape Architecture, 98 **CONTACT ADDRESS** Dept Amer Studies, Skidmore Col, Saratoga Springs, PA, 12866. **EMAIL** bcblack@skidmore.edu

BLACK, EUGENE CHARLTON
PERSONAL Born 12/15/1927, Boston, MA, m, 1983, 5 children **DISCIPLINE** MODERN EUROPEAN HISTORY **EDUCATION** Col William & Mary, AB, 48; Harvard Univ, AM, 54, PhD, 58. **CAREER** From instr to prof, 58-69, SPRINGER PROF HIST, BRANDEIS UNIV, 71-; Vis prof, Boston Univ, 69. **HONORS AND AWARDS** Mazer Fellow, 83, 86, 90; Tauber Fellowship, 83; APS grant, 85, 87; Sacher Fellowship, 86; NEH Grant, 87; Guest Fellow, Wolfson Col, Oxford, 88; Who's Who in America, 87-; Who's Who Among American Teachers, 98-. **MEMBERSHIPS** AHA; Hist Asn UK; Conf Brit Studies; fel Royal Hist Soc; Econ Hist Soc Atheneeum. **RESEARCH** Transition from voluntarism to collectivism; feminism and liberalism; diplomacy of minority rights in Eastern Europe, 1914-1930; universal Judaism and the Republican tradition; modern British social history. **SELECTED PUBLICATIONS** Auth, The Association: British Extraparliamentary Political Organization, 1769-1793, Harvard Univ, 63; Posture of Europe, 1815-1940: Readings in European Intellectual History, Dorsey, 64; European Political History, 1815-70: Aspects of Liberalism, 67, British Politics in the Nineteenth Century, 69 & Victorian Culture and Society, 73, Harper; Feminists, Liberalism, and Morality: The Unresolvable Triangle, Fawcett Libr Papers, 81; Social Politics of Anglo-Jewry, 1880-1920, 88. **CONTACT ADDRESS** Dept of Hist, Brandeis Univ, Mailstop 036, Waltham, MA, 02454. **EMAIL** blackec@brandeis.edu

BLACK, J. LAURENCE
DISCIPLINE HISTORY **EDUCATION** Mount Allison Univ, BA; Boston Univ, MA; McGill Univ, PhD. **CAREER** Prof. **RESEARCH** Russian and Soviet Education. **SELECTED PUBLICATIONS** Auth, Into the Dustbin of History: The USSR from August Coup to Commonwealth, 1991, Gulf Breeze, Fla: Acad Intl Press, 93; Skovoroda as Teacher: The Image as Model, Hyrhorij Savyc Skovoroda, An Anthology of Critical Articles, Can Inst Ukrainian Stud Press, Univ Toronto Press, 94; "Canada in the Soviet Mirror: English-Canadian Literature in Soviet Translation," Jour Can Stud/Rev d'etudes canadiennes 30:2, 95; Canada in the Russian Mirror: The 'Canada Card' in Russian politics and Foreign policy, 1802-1860, Occasional Paper No 4, Ctr for Res on Can-Russ Rel(s), 95. **CONTACT ADDRESS** Dept of Hist, Carleton Univ, 1125 Colonel By Dr, Ottawa, ON, K1S 5B6. **EMAIL** larry_black@carleton.ca

BLACK, NAOMI
PERSONAL Born 02/13/1935, Newcastle-upon-Tyne, England **DISCIPLINE** POLITICAL SCIENCE/HISTORY **EDUCATION** Cornell Univ, AB, 55; Yale Univ, MA, 57, PhD, 64. **CAREER** Instr, polit sci, Brown Univ, 63-64; instr, govt, Ind Univ, 64-65; asst prof, 65-71, assoc prof, 71-84, PROF POLITICAL SCIENCE, YORK UNIV, 85-. **SELECTED PUBLICATIONS** Auth, Social Feminism, 89; coauth, Canadian Women: A History, 88, 2nd ed, 96. **CONTACT ADDRESS** Dept of Political Science, York Univ, 4700 Keele St, North York, ON, M3J 1P3.

BLACK, SHIRLEY JEAN
PERSONAL Born 04/20/1935, Tulsa, OK **DISCIPLINE** MODERN EUROPEAN HISTORY, FRENCH HISTORY **EDUCATION** Univ Okla, BA, 67, MA, 69, PhD(hist), 74. **CAREER** ASST PROF HIST, TEX AandM UNIV, 73-, Ed adv hist, Military Affairs, 76-79. **MEMBERSHIPS** Soc Fr Hist Studies; Western Soc Fr Hist (secy, 78-81); AHA; Fr Colonial Hist Soc. **RESEARCH** Napoleon III and the French intervention in Mexico; nineteenth century French diplomatic history. **SELECTED PUBLICATIONS** Auth, Napoleon-III and the Stoffel-Affair, J of Mil Hist, Vol 0057, 93; Maximilian Lieutenant - A Personal History of the Mexican Campaign, 1864-67, J of Mil Hist, Vol 0059, 95. **CONTACT ADDRESS** Dept of Hist, Tex AandM Univ, College Station, TX, 77843.

BLACK, WESLEY O.
PERSONAL m, 2 children **DISCIPLINE** YOUTH EDUCATION **EDUCATION** Hardin - Simmins Univ, BM, 68; Southwestern Baptist Theol Sem, MA, 75, PhD, 85. **CAREER** Assoc prof, Southwestern Baptist Theol Sem, 83-. **HONORS AND AWARDS** Min Youth, Ctr Baptist Church, 70-71; First Baptist Church, Duncan, 73-81; North Side Baptist Church, 75-81; youth consult, Baptist Sunday Sch Bd, 81-83. **MEMBERSHIPS** N Amer Prof Christian Edu; Youth Ministry Educator's Forum; Baptist Rel Edu Assn Southwest; S Baptist Rel Edu Assn. **SELECTED PUBLICATIONS** Auth, Introduction to Youth Ministry, Holman, 91. **CONTACT ADDRESS** Sch Theol, Southwestern Baptist Theol Sem, PO Box 22000, Fort Worth, TX, 76122-0418. **EMAIL** wob@swbts.swbts.edu

BLACK, JR, KENNETH
PERSONAL Born 01/30/1925, Norfolk, VA, m, 1948, 2 children **DISCIPLINE** INSURANCE **EDUCATION** Univ NC, BA, 48, MS, 51; Univ Pa, PhD, 53. **CAREER** Instr, Univ Pa, 52-53; Lecturer, Swiss Insurance Training Ctr, 67; Ch, Dept of Insurance, Ga State Univ, 53-69; Dean, Col of Bus Admin, Ga State Univ, 59-92; Holder, CV Starr Ch of Int Insurance, Ga State Univ, 84-92; Regents' Prof Emeritus of Insurance & Dean Emeritus, Ga State Univ. **HONORS AND AWARDS** Phi Beta Kappa, Univ NC, 46; Order of the Golden Fleece, Univ NC, 48; Beta Gamma Sigma, Ga State Univ, 61; Kenneth Black Jr Special Lib Collection in Risk & Insurance, Old Dominion Univ, 5/78; Solomon S Huebner Gold Medal, The Am Col, 85; Kenneth Black Jr Ch of Insurance, Ga State Univ, 88; 1st Ann Distinguished Svc Award, Life Insurers Conf, 90; Kenneth Black Jr Wing dedicated in Gregg Hall Conf Ctr, Am Col, 6/92; Dr Kenneth Black Jr Distinguished Service Award est by Int Insurance Soc, Inc, 92; Laureate, Insurance Hall of Fame, Int Insurance Soc, Inc, Tokyo, Japan, 93., Pres Commission on RR Retirement, V Ch, 71-72. **MEMBERSHIPS** Southern Risk & Insurance Asn; Am Risk & Insurance Asn; Soc of Chartered Property & Casualty Underwriters; Alpha Kappa Psi; Am Soc of CLU & ChFC; Risk & Insurance Management Soc, Inc. **RESEARCH** Int Risk & Insurance/Life Insurance. **SELECTED PUBLICATIONS** Co-auth, Human Behavior and Life Insurance, rev ed, Ga State Univ Bus Press, 93; co-auth, Life Insurance, 12th ed, Prentice-Hall, Inc, 94; auth, The Social Value of Life Insurance, Insurance Soc of ROC, Proceedings, Taipei, Taiwan, 1/95; co-auth, Property and Liability Insurance, 4th ed, Prentice-Hall, Inc, 96; auth, The Future of the Life Insurance Business, J of the Am Soc of CLU & ChFC, vol L, no 1, 1/96. **CONTACT ADDRESS** Dept of Risk Mgt & Insurance, Georgia State Univ, PO Box 4036, Atlanta, GA, 30302-4036. **EMAIL** inskbj@langate.gsu.edu

BLACKBURN, GEORGE MCCOY
PERSONAL Born 05/05/1926, Bloomington, IN, m, 1952, 5 children **DISCIPLINE** AMERICAN HISTORY **EDUCATION** State Univ NY Albany, BA, 47; Ind Univ, MA, 50, PhD(hist), 56. **CAREER** Teacher social studies, Alpena Community Col, 55-58; asst prof hist, Ferris Inst, 58-59; from asst prof to assoc prof, 59-67, assoc dean arts and sci, 70-76, chmn dept, 76-82, PROF HIST, CENT MICH UNIV, 67- **MEMBERSHIPS** AHA; Orgn Am Historians. **RESEARCH** Civil War; Reconstruction; demographic history. **SELECTED PUBLICATIONS** Auth, Unequal Opportunity on a Mining Frontier - the Role of Gender, Race, and Birthplace, Pac Hist Rev, Vol 0062, 93. **CONTACT ADDRESS** Dept of Hist, Central Michigan Univ, Mt Pleasant, MI, 48859.

BLACKFORD, MANSEL GRIFFITHS
PERSONAL Born 05/12/1944, Seattle, WA, m, 1966, 2 children **DISCIPLINE** HISTORY **EDUCATION** Stanford Univ, BA, 66; Univ Wash, MA, 67; Univ Calif, Berkeley, PhD(hist), 72. **CAREER** Asst prof, 72-78, ASSOC PROF HIST, OHIO STATE UNIV, 79-, Fulbright lectr, Japan, 80-81. **MEMBERSHIPS** Bus Hist Conf; Econ Bus Hist Soc; Western Hist Asn. **RESEARCH** Business history; history of American West. **SELECTED PUBLICATIONS** Auth, Silverado - Bush,Neil and the Savings-and-Loan Scandal, J of the W, Vol 0032, 93; Silver,Harold,F., Western Inventor, Businessman, and Civic Leader, Western Hist Quart, Vol 0024, 93; Cargill - Trading the Worlds Grain, J of Econ Hist, Vol 0053, 93; Platt-Brothers-and-Company - Small Business In American Manufacturing, New Eng Quart-A Hist Rev of New Eng Life and Letters, Vol 0067, 94; Long,George,S - Timber Statesman, Am Hist Rev, Vol 0100, 95; Wellsprings of Achievement - Cultural and Economic-Dynamics In Early-Modern England and Japan, Technol and Cult, Vol 0038, 97; Competition Policy In America, 1888-1992 - History, Rhetoric, Law, J of Am Hist, Vol 0083, 97. **CONTACT ADDRESS** Dept of Hist, Ohio State Univ, 230 W 17th Ave, Columbus, OH, 43210-1361.

BLACKMAR, ELIZABETH
DISCIPLINE UNITED STATES HISTORY **EDUCATION** Smith Univ, BA, 72; Harvard Univ, PhD, 81. **CAREER** Prof. **RESEARCH** Social and urban history. **SELECTED PUBLICATIONS** Auth, Manhattan for Rent 1785-1850, 89; co-auth, The Park and the People: A History of Central Park, 92. **CONTACT ADDRESS** Dept of History, Columbia Col, New York, 2960 Broadway, New York, NY, 10027-6902.

BLACKWELL, FREDERICK WARN
PERSONAL Born 09/09/1936, Spokane, WA, m, 1 child **DISCIPLINE** SOUTH ASIAN CULTURE, HISTORY **EDUCATION** WA State Univ, BA, 58, MA, 60; Univ WI, MA, 65, PhD(SAsian lang & lit), 73. **CAREER** Asst prof hist, WA State Univ, 69-72, asst prof English, 70-72, asst prof foreign lang & lit, 72-76, univ ombudsman, 79-81, assoc prof Foreign Lang & Lit, 76-90, assoc prof hist, WA State Univ, 90-, dir East & South Asia Program, 80-93; Exec comt, Indian Studies Asn, 77-80 & Philol Asn Pac Coast, 78-81; educ consult, Educ Resources Ctr, New Delhi, 80; assoc ed, J SAsian Lit, 81-. **RESEARCH** Literature of and about India, in English; concepts of M. K. Gandhi; journals of Lewis Thompson; translation of contemporary Hindi writers. **SELECTED PUBLICATIONS** Auth, Comment on Mohan Rakesh and Socialist Realism,

SAsia Ser Occas Paper, 74; Four Plays of Nissim Ezekiel, J SAsian Lit, 76; Experiences of Teaching South Asian Literature to Non-Asians, SAsia Perspectives, 77; ed, Feminine Sensibility and Characterization Issue, J SAsian Lit, Vol 13, No 3 & 4; auth, Perception of the Guru in the Fiction of Ruth Prawer Jhabvala, J Indian Writing English, 77; Krishna Motifs in the Poetry of Sarojini Naidu and Kamala Das, 78 & coauth, Mohan Rakesh's Lahrom Ke Rajhans and Ashvagosha's Saundarananda, 78, J SAsian Lit; auth, In Defense of Kaikeyi and Draupadi, Indian Lit, 78; co-ed, English Poetry by Indians, 88; co-ed, Letters from Chittagong, 92. **CONTACT ADDRESS** History, Washington State Univ, PO Box 644030, Pullman, WA, 99164-4030. **EMAIL** blackwel@wsu.edu

BLACKWELL, FRITZ
DISCIPLINE SOUTH ASIA AND WORLD HISTORY **EDUCATION** Univ Wis, PhD, 73. **CAREER** Assoc prof, Wash State Univ. **SELECTED PUBLICATIONS** Assoc ed, J of South Asian Lit; co-ed a vol, Ind poetry and a collection of Amer letters from East Pakistan; publ in, Ariel; South Asia in Rev; Asiaweek; J South Asian Lit & Indian Lit. **CONTACT ADDRESS** Dept of History, Washington State Univ, 301 Wilson Hall, PO Box 644030, Pullman, WA, 99164-4030. **EMAIL** blackwel@wsu.edu

BLAINE, BRADFORD BENNETT
PERSONAL Born 05/29/1930, Cedar Rapids, IA, m, 1954, 2 children **DISCIPLINE** MEDIEVAL HISTORY **EDUCATION** Stanford Univ, BA, 52, MA, 54; Univ Calif, Los Angeles, PhD, 66. **CAREER** Asst dean men, Stanford Univ, 53-54; asst dean men, Univ Ore, 54-56; teaching asst hist, Univ Calif, Los Angeles, 59-62; instr, Fullerton Col, 62-64; prof hist, Scripps Col, 64-; prof emeritus, 98. **MEMBERSHIPS** AHA; Soc Hist Technol; Mediaeval Acad Am; Medieval Assn Pac; Int Molinological Soc. **RESEARCH** Medieval technology; 7th century Europoe. **SELECTED PUBLICATIONS** Auth, Enigmatic Water-Mill, Lynn White Festschrift, Univ Calif, 74; art, Technology and the Muses, Humanitas-Essays in Honor of Ralph Ross, Scripps Col, 77; art, Mills: Wind and Water, Dictionary of the Middle Ages, Am Coun Learned Socs, Charles Scribner's Sons, 82; art, Mills and Milling, Medieval France: An Encyclopedia, Garland Publishing, 95. **CONTACT ADDRESS** Dept of History, Scripps Col, 586 W 11th St, Claremont, CA, 91711. **EMAIL** bblaine@scripps.edu

BLAIR, JOHN GEORGE
PERSONAL Born 12/03/1934, Brooklyn, NY, m, 1961, 1 child **DISCIPLINE** ENGLISH, AMERICAN STUDIES **EDUCATION** Brown Univ, AB, 56, PhD(English, Am lit), 62; Columbia Univ MA, 57. **CAREER** Part-time instr English, RI Sch Design, 58-62; from instr to assoc prof, Oakland Univ, 62-70; PROF ENGLISH, UNIV GENEVA, 70-, Fulbright lectr Am lit, Univ Strasbourg, 67-68. **MEMBERSHIPS** MLA; Am Studies Asn; Europ Am Studies Asn; Swiss Asn Univ Teachers English; Swiss Asn Am Studies. **RESEARCH** American literature and civilization, especially cross-cultural studies and structuralism. **SELECTED PUBLICATIONS** Auth, American Drama, Text and Video, and the Relationship Between the Printed-Text and the Changes introduced in Different Adaptations, Including a Master-List of Plays Which Have Been Adapted for Film or Television, Am Stud Int, Vol 0034; Change and Cultures - Reality Presumptions in China and the West, New Lit Hist, Vol 0024, 93; Love and Theft, Blackface Minstrelsy and the American Working-Class, Am Quart, Vol 0047, 95. **CONTACT ADDRESS** Dept of English, Univ of Geneva, Ch-1211, Geneva, ..

BLAISDELL, CHARMARIE JENKINS
PERSONAL Born 01/23/1934, Philadelphia, PA, m, 1953, 2 children **DISCIPLINE** HISTORY **EDUCATION** Boston Univ, AB, 55; Tufts Univ, MA, 64, PhD(hist), 69. **CAREER** Asst prof hist, Boston Col, 70-71; asst prof, 71-77, ASSOC PROF HIST, NORTHEASTERN UNIV, 77-. **HONORS AND AWARDS** Elliott Lectr, Pittsburgh Theol Sem, 10/81. **MEMBERSHIPS** AHA; Soc Fr Hist Studies; Coord Comt Women in Hist Prof; Am Soc Reformation. **RESEARCH** Early modern France; Italian Reformation; social and intellectual history, 1350-1815. **SELECTED PUBLICATIONS** Auth, Women Who Would Be Kings - Female Rulers in the 16th-Century, 16th Century J, Vol 0023, 92; Conversini-Da-Ravenna,Giovanni - Dialog Between Giovanni and a Letter, Church Hist, Vol 0062, 93; Women of the Renaissance, Church Hist, Vol 0062, 93; The Life, Early Letters and Eucharistic Writings of Peter-Martyr, Church Hist, Vol 0063, 94; A History of Women in the West, Vol 3 - Renaissance and Enlightenment Paradoxes, 16th Century J, Vol 0025, 94; Women on the Margins - 3 17th-Century Lives, Church Hist, Vol 0065, 96; Beneath the Cross - Catholics and Huguenots in 16th-Century Paris, Church Hist, Vol 0065, 96. **CONTACT ADDRESS** Northeastern Univ, Boston, MA, 02115.

BLAKE, J. HERMAN
PERSONAL Born 03/15/1934, Mt. Vernon, NY, m **DISCIPLINE** SOCIOLOGY **EDUCATION** NY Univ, BA 1960; Univ CA, MA 1965, PhD 1973. **CAREER** Univ CA, asst prof 1966-70, assoc prof 1970-74; UCSC, prof 1974-84; Oakes Coll UCSC, founding provost 1972-84; Tougaloo Coll, pres 1984-87. **HONORS AND AWARDS** Named among Top 100 Emerging Young Leaders in Higher Educ Amer Council of Educ 1978. **MEMBERSHIPS** Mem Amer Sociol Assn, Population Assn of Amer, Pacific Sociol Assn; bd trustee Save the Children Fedn; bd trustee Penn Comm Serv Fellowships Woodrow Wilson 1960, John Hay Whitney 1963; mem Population Council 1964; Danforth Found 1964; Rockefeller Found 1965; Ford Found 1970. **SELECTED PUBLICATIONS** Co-author "Revolutionary Suicide" 73. **CONTACT ADDRESS** Dept Sociology, Swarthmore Col, Swarthmore, PA, 19081.

BLAKE, STEPHEN
DISCIPLINE SOUTH ASIAN AND MIDDLE EASTERN HISTORY **EDUCATION** Dartmouth Col, BA; Univ Chicago, MA, PhD. **CAREER** History, St. Olaf Col. **SELECTED PUBLICATIONS** Auth, Shanjahanabad: The Soverign City in Mughal India, 1639-1739, Cambridge Univ Press, 91; Indian paperback ed, Found Books, 93. **CONTACT ADDRESS** St Olaf Col, 1520 St Olaf Ave, Northfield, MN, 55057. **EMAIL** blake@stolaf.edu

BLAKE MCHAM, SARAH
DISCIPLINE ITALIAN RENAISSANCE ART **EDUCATION** NY Univ, PhD. **CAREER** Prof, ch, dept Art Hist, Rutgers, The State Univ NJ, Univ Col-Camden. **RESEARCH** Social and political context of painting and sculpture of the Venetian Empire and of Florence, especially patronage and religious practices. **SELECTED PUBLICATIONS** Auth, Donatello's Tomb of Pope John XXII, in Life and Death in Fifteenth-Century Florence, eds Rona Goffen, Marcel Tetel, and Ronald Witt, Duke UP, 89; Donatello's High Altar in the Santo, Padua, in Verrocchio and Late Quattrocento Sculpture, ed Steven Bule, et al, Casa Editrice Le Lettere, 92; The Cult of St. Anthony of Padua, in Sancta, Sanctus, Studies in Hagiography, Ctr for Medieval and Early Renaissance Stud, 94; Donatello's Judith and Holofernes, in Companion to the Making of Western Art, Routledge, 95; The Chapel of St. Anthony at the Santo and the Development of Venetian Renaissance Sculpture, Cambridge UP, 94; Florentine Public Sculpture, in Looking at Italian Renaissance Sculpture, Cambridge UP, 98; ed, Looking at Italian Renaissance Sculpture, Cambridge UP, 98. **CONTACT ADDRESS** Dept of Art Hist, Rutgers, The State Univ NJ, Univ Col-Camden, Voorhees Hall, 71 Hamilton St, New Brunswick, NJ, 08903. **EMAIL** mcham@rci.rutgers.edu

BLAKELY, ALLISON
PERSONAL Born 03/31/1940, Clinton, AL, m, 1968, 2 children **DISCIPLINE** HISTORY **EDUCATION** Univ Ore, BA, 62; Univ Calif, Berkeley, MA, 64, PhD, 71. **CAREER** Instr, Stanford Univ, 70-71; from Asst Prof to Assoc Prof, 71-87, prof hist, Howard Univ, 87-. **HONORS AND AWARDS** Andrew Mellon fel humanities, Aspen Inst Humanities Studies, 76-77; Fulbright-Hays Res Fel, 85-86; Am Book Award, 88; Phi Beta Kappa Soc Senator, 94-2000. **MEMBERSHIPS** AHA; Am Asn Advan Slavic Studies; World Hist Asn; Am Asn Neth Studies. **RESEARCH** Modern Russia; comparative populism; African Diaspora. **SELECTED PUBLICATIONS** Auth, The Dynamics of Revolutionary Populism in Russian and American Society, Studia Africana, spring 78; The Making of Populist Revolution in Russia 1900-1907, in Latin American Populism in Comparative Perspective, Univ NMex Press, 82; Russia and the Negro: Blacks in Russian History and Thought, Howard Univ Press, 86; American Influences on Russian Reformist Thought in the Era of the French Revolution, The Russ Rev, 10/93; Blacks in the Dutch World: The Evolution of Racial Imagery in a Modern Society, Ind Univ Press, 94. **CONTACT ADDRESS** Dept of Hist, Howard Univ, 2400 6th St NW, Washington, DC, 20059-0002. **EMAIL** ablakely@fac.howard.edu

BLAKEY, GEORGE THOMAS
PERSONAL Born 08/25/1939, Beattyville, KY, m, 1970 **DISCIPLINE** UNITED STATES HISTORY **EDUCATION** Berea Col, BA, 61; Vanderbilt Univ, MA, 62; IN Univ, Bloomington, PhD, 69. **CAREER** From instr to asst prof, 67-73, assoc prof, 73-81, prof hist, IN Univ East, 81, Eli Lilly fac res fel, 75-76. **MEMBERSHIPS** Orgn Am Historians. **RESEARCH** The New Deal and Progressivism in the US; IN hist. **SELECTED PUBLICATIONS** Auth, Ham that never was: 1933 Emergency Hog Slaughter, Historian, 11/67; Historians on the Home Front, Univ KY, 70; Calling a boss a boss, NY Hist, 4/79; Hard Times and New Deal in KY, Univ Press Ky, 86; Wendell Willkie as a Hoosier, In: Wendell Willkie: Essays, IN Univ Press, 92; Battling the Great Depression on Stage in IN, IN Mag Hist, 3/94. **CONTACT ADDRESS** Dept of Hist, Indiana Univ, East, 2325 Chester Blvd, Richmond, IN, 47374-1220. **EMAIL** gblakey@indiana.edu

BLANCHARD, PETER
DISCIPLINE LATIN AMERICAN HISTORY **EDUCATION** Univ Toronto, BA, 67; Univ London, PhD(hist), 75. **CAREER** Asst prof, 75-82, ASSOC PROF HIST, UNIV TORONTO, 82-. **MEMBERSHIPS** Can Asn Latin Am and Caribbean Studies. **RESEARCH** Peruvian labor history; abolition of Peruvian slavery. **SELECTED PUBLICATIONS** Auth, Coercion and Market - Silver Mining in Colonial Potosi 1692-1826, J of Lat Am Stud, Vol 0026, 94; Paying the Price of Freedom - Family and Labor Among Limas Slaves, 1800-1854, Labor Hist, Vol 0036, 95; Agents of Their Own Freedom - Slaves in Lima and the Disintegration of Slavery 1821-1854, Am Hist Rev, Vol 0100, 95; Slavery and Beyond - the African Impact on Latin-America and the Caribbean, Hisp Am Hist Rev, Vol 0076, 96. **CONTACT ADDRESS** Dept Hist, Univ Toronto, Toronto, ON, M5S 1A1.

BLAND, LARRY IRVIN
PERSONAL Born 08/20/1940, Indianapolis, IN, m, 1962, 2 children **DISCIPLINE** US DIPLOMATIC HISTORY **EDUCATION** Purdue Univ, West Lafayette, BS (Physics), 62; Univ WI-Madison, MA, 68, PhD, 72. **CAREER** Product engineer & computer systems analyst, 62-67, P R Mallory Capacitor Co, Indianapolis, In; College Hist teacher: Gaston Col, Dallas, NC, 71-76, Belmont Abby Col, NC, 75-76; documentary ed, George C Marshall Found, Lexington, VA, 77-. **HONORS AND AWARDS** NEH College Teaching Fel, Univ IL, 76-77. **MEMBERSHIPS** Soc for Historians of Am Foreign Relations; Soc for Military Hist; Org of Am Historians; Asn for Documentary Editing. **RESEARCH** World War II; George C Marshall. **SELECTED PUBLICATIONS** Auth, Assoc ed, The J of Military Hist, 88-; ed, George C Marshall Interviews and Reminiscences for Forrest C Pogue: Transcripts and Notes, 1956-67, 91; auth, Fully the Equal of the Best: George C Marshall and the Virginia Military Institute, 96; ed, The Papers of George Catlett Marshall, Johns Hopkins Univ Press, vols 1-4, 81-96; auth, George C Marshall, intro essay in George C Marshall, Soldier of Peace, Smithsonian Inst, 97; ed, George C Marshall's Mediation Mission to China, December 1945-January 1947, 98; auth, George C Marshall: The Truman Doctrine and the Marshall Plan, in Eugene T Rossides, ed, The Truman Doctrine of Aid to Greece: A Fifty-Year Retrospective, Academy of Political Science and the Am Hellenic Inst Found, 98. **CONTACT ADDRESS** George C. Marshall Research Found., Drawer 1600, Lexington, VA. **EMAIL** blandli@vmi.edu

BLAND, SIDNEY RODERICK
PERSONAL Born 10/31/1936, Caroleen, NC, m, 1962, 2 children **DISCIPLINE** WOMEN'S HISTORY, AMERICAN HISTORY **EDUCATION** Furman Univ, BA, 59; Univ Md, College Park, MA, 61; George Washington Univ, PhD(Am civilization), 72. **CAREER** Asst prof, 65-72, assoc prof, 72-81, PROF HIST, JAMES MADISON UNIV, 81-, Co-chmn, Am Studies Comt, 73-; grant, Am Philos Soc, 81. **RESEARCH** Militancy in the woman suffrage movement in the early twentieth century; women in Southern history; late 19th-early 20th century American history. **SELECTED PUBLICATIONS** Auth, Pankhurst,Sylvia - From Artist to Antifascist, Hist, Vol 0055, 93; Dearest Chums and Partners - Harris, Joel, Chandler Letters to His Children - A Domestic Biography, J of Southern Hist, Vol 0061, 95. **CONTACT ADDRESS** Dept of Hist, James Madison Univ, Harrisonburg, VA, 22801.

BLANK, DAVID L.
DISCIPLINE CLASSICS **EDUCATION** Yale Univ, BA, 74; Amer Sch of Class Stud, 74-75; Princeton Univ, MA, 77; Univ Bonn, grad stud, 77-78; Princeton Univ, PhD, 80. **CAREER** Vis asst prof, UCLA, 80-82; asst prof, UCLA, 82-86; lehrauftrag, Freie-Univ Berlin, 89; assoc prof, UCLA, 86-95; PROF, CH, UCLA, 95-. **HONORS AND AWARDS** ITT-Fulbright fel, Greece, 74-75; Paul Elmer More fel, Princeton, 75-76, 78-79; Deutscher Akademischer Austauschdienst Stipendium, Ger, 77-78; Whiting res fel, Princeton, 79-80; Alexander-von-Humboldt fel, Berlin, 88-89. **SELECTED PUBLICATIONS** Auth, "Analogy, Anomaly, and Apollonius," Companions to Ancient Thought, 3: Philos of Lang, Cambridge 94; "Philodemus on the Technicity of Rhetoric, Philodemus On Poetry," Oxford, 94; "Diogenes of Babylon and the Kritikoi in Philodemus: A Preliminary Suggestion," Cronache Ercolanesi 20, 93; "Stop or Spirant: A Note on the Division of Nonvocal and Semivocal Elements," Glotta 94; Rev, Stefania N. Pieri, Platone. Gorgia, Ancient Philos, 94; Catherine Atherton, The Stoics on Ambiguity, Philos Rev, 94; Ammonius, Commentary on On Interpretation, Vol 1, London, Duckworth, 95. **CONTACT ADDRESS** Univ Calif, PO Box 951436, Los Angeles, CA, 90095-1436.

BLANKE, RICHARD
PERSONAL Born 07/08/1940, Pasadena, CA, m, 3 children **DISCIPLINE** MODERN EUROPEAN HISTORY **EDUCATION** San Fernando Valley State Col, BA, 63; Univ Calif, Berkeley, MA, 64, PhD(hist), 70. **CAREER** Asst prof, 69-74, ASSOC PROF HIST, UNIV MAINE, ORONO, 74-. **MEMBERSHIPS** AHA; Am Asn Advan Slavic Studies. **RESEARCH** Modern German and Polish history; nationalism. **SELECTED PUBLICATIONS** Auth, Provincial Prussia, Can Slavonic Papers-Revue Canadienne Des Slavistes, Vol 0034, 92; The Volksdeutsche-Selbstschutz in Poland 1939-40, Slavic Rev, Vol 0053, 1994; Lower Silesia from Nazi Germany to Communist Poland, 1942-49, Am Hist Rev, Vol 0100, 95; The 2 Germanies, 1945-1990 - Problems of Interpretation, Ger Stud Rev, Vol 0018, 95; Germany and Poland from 1918/19 to 1925, Slavic Rev, Vol 0055, 96; Reptile Journalism - the Official Polish-Language Press under the Nazis, 1939-1945, Am Hist Rev, Vol 0102, 97. **CONTACT ADDRESS** Dept of Hist, Univ of Maine, Orono, ME, 04473.

BLANTZ, THOMAS E.
PERSONAL Born 06/18/1934, Massillon, OH **DISCIPLINE** AMERICAN HISTORY **EDUCATION** Univ Notre Dame, AB, 57, MA, 63; Gregorian Univ, STB, 59, STL, 61; Columbia Univ, PhD, 68. **CAREER** From Asst Prof to Assoc Prof, 68-94, prof hist, Univ of Notre Dame, 94-, Univ Archivist, 69-78. **MEMBERSHIPS** Orgn Am Historians; AHA; Cath Hist Asn. **RESEARCH** Recent American history; American political and social history. **SELECTED PUBLICATIONS** Auth, Francis Haas and Minneapolis truckers strike in 1934, Minn Hist, 70; Francis Haas: priest and government servant, Cath Hist Rev, 1/72; The librarian as archivist, Cath Libr World, 74; Justice through organization, Social Thought, 77; A Priest in Public Service: Francis J. Haas and the New Deal, Univ Notre Dame Press, 82; George N. Shuster: On the Side of Truth, Univ Notre Dame Press, 93. **CONTACT ADDRESS** Dept of Hist, Univ of Notre Dame, 219 Oshaugnessy Hall, Notre Dame, IN, 46556. **EMAIL** Thomas.E.Blantz.1@nd.edu

BLASI, ANTHONY J.
PERSONAL Born 04/13/1946, Dayton, OH **DISCIPLINE** SOCIOLOGY **EDUCATION** St Edward's Univ, BA (history), 68; Univ of Notre Dame, MA (sociology), 71, PhD (sociology), 74; Univ of St. Michael's Col, Toronto, MA (Biblical studies), 84; Regis Col and Univ of Toronto, ThD (Religous ethics), 86. **CAREER** Asst prof sociology, Univ of Louisville, KY, 76-78; assoc prof and chair sociology, Daemen Col, New York, 78-80; asst prof sociol, Univ HI at Hilo, 86-90; assoc prof sociol, Muskingum Col, OH, 90-94; assoc prof Sociol, TN State Univ, 94-. **HONORS AND AWARDS** William Rainey Harper Award, Muskingum Col. **MEMBERSHIPS** Am Sociol Asn; Southern Sociol Asn; Asn for the Sociol of Religion; Soc for the Scientific Study of Religion; Religous Res Asn. **RESEARCH** Sociology of religion. **SELECTED PUBLICATIONS** Auth, A Phenomenological Transformation of the Social Scientific Study of Religion, Peter Lang, 85; Moral Conflict and Christian Religion, Peter Lang, 88; Making Charisma: The Social Construction of Paul's Public Image, Transaction, 91; Office Charisma in Early Christian Ephesus, Sociology of Religion, 95; Social Fundamentalism in Today's Society, in Luigi Tomasi, ed, Fundamentalism and Youth in Europe, Franco Angeli, 95; A Sociology of Johannine Christianity, Edwin Mellon Press, 96; Fundamental Versus Influential Factors in Regional Identities, in Luigi Tomasi, ed, The Local Community, A Sociological Interpretation of European Localism, Franco Angeli, 96; The Social Process of Opera, Reflections Occasioned by the Centennary of Falstaff, in Fabio B Dasilva and David L Brunsma, eds, All Music Essays on the Hermeneutics of Music, Avebury, 96; Marginalization and Martydom: Social Context of Ignatius of Antioch, Listening, J of Religion and Culture, 97. **CONTACT ADDRESS** Dept of Sociol, Tennessee State Univ, Nashville, TN, 37209-1561. **EMAIL** ablasi@vol.com

BLASSINGAME, JOHN W.
PERSONAL Born 03/23/1940, Covington, GA **DISCIPLINE** HISTORY **EDUCATION** Ft Valley State College, BA, 1960; Howard University, MA, 1961; Yale University, PhD, 1971 **CAREER** Yale University, lecturer, 1970-71, asst professor, 1971-72, acting chairman, Afro-American Studies Dept, 1971-72, assoc professor, 1972-74, History Dept, professor, 1974-. **MEMBERSHIPS** Phi Alpha Theta; Assn Behavioral Social Sciences; Assn Study Afro-American Life & History; Southern & American Historical Assn, 1974-; orgn, American Historian; adv bd, Afro-American Bicentennial Corp, 1971-; bd, Centre Internationale de Recherches Africaines, 1971-; American Historical Assn, rev bd, 1972-73; ed bd, Reviews of American History, 1973-; Journal of Negro History, 1973-; executive council, Assn for the Study Afro-American Life & History, 1973-; chairman, program com, Organization of American Historians, 1974. **SELECTED PUBLICATIONS** Contrib ed, Black Scholar, 1971-; numerous articles and books. **CONTACT ADDRESS** Dept of History, Yale Univ, PO Box 1504a, New Haven, CT, 06520.

BLATT, SIDNEY JULES
PERSONAL Born 10/15/1928, Philadelphia, PA, m, 1951, 3 children **DISCIPLINE** PSYCHOLOGY **EDUCATION** Univ of Chicago, PhD, 57. **CAREER** PROF, YALE UNIV, 60-. **HONORS AND AWARDS** Sigmund Freud Prof, Zachs Prof of Art Hist, Hebrew Univ, 88-89; Fulbright Sr Res Fel, 88-89; Bruno Klopfer Award for Distinquished Res Contributions. **MEMBERSHIPS** Asn of Medical School Profs of Psychol; Am Psychol Asn; Distinguished Res Contriburs. **RESEARCH** Mental representations and their role in personality development; psychopathology and the therapeutic process. **SELECTED PUBLICATIONS** Co-ed, The Self in Emotional Distress: Cognitive and Psychodynamic Perspectives, Guilford Press, 93; coed, Depression and the Self, In Session: Pyschotherapy in Practice, John Wiley & Sons, 97; coauth, Therapeutic Change: An Object Relations Perspective, Plenum, 94; coauth, The Prediction of Therapeutic Response to the Long-term Extensive Treatment of Seriously Disturbed Young Adults, Psychotherapy Res, 95; coauth, Developmental Lines, Schemas, and Archtypes, Am Psychol, 95; coauth, Differential Vulnerability of Dependency and Self-criticism Among Disadvantaged Teenages, J of Res on Adolescence, 95; coauth, Relatedness and Self Definition: A Dialectic Model of Personality Development, Development and Vulnerabilities in Close Relationships, Lawrence Erlbaum Assocs, 96; coauth, Precursors of Relatedness and Self-definition in Mother-Infant Interaction, Pschoanalytic Perspectives on Developmental Psychol, APA, 96; coauth, A Psychodynamic Approach to the Diagnosis of Psychopathology, Making Diagnosis Meaningful, APA Press, 98; coauth, Attachment Styles and Parental Representations, J of Personality & Soc Psychol, 98. **CONTACT ADDRESS** Depts of Psychol and Psychiat, Yale Univ, 25 Park St, New Haven, CT, 06519. **EMAIL** sidney.blatt@yale.edu

BLAU, JUDITH R.
PERSONAL Born 09/27/1942, Elansius, MI, m, 1968, 2 children **DISCIPLINE** SOCIOLOGY **EDUCATION** Univ Chicago, BA, 64, MA, 67; Northwestern Univ, PhD, 72; **CAREER** Asst Prof to Assoc Prof, State Univ NY - Albany, 78-88; Prof, 88-97, Gillian T. Cell Prof, Univ NC - Chapel Hill, 97-. **MEMBERSHIPS** Am Sociol Asn; Int Sociol Asn; Southern Sociol Soc. **RESEARCH** Education; art; organization. **SELECTED PUBLICATIONS** Auth, Left-Brain v. Right-Brain Mistakes, Mistakes Social Scientists Make, St. Martin's Press, 95; The Toggle Switch of Institutions: Religion and Art in the U.S. in the Nineteenth and Early Twentieth Century, Soc Forces, 96; coauth, Black and White Students in Two-Year Colleges, Thought & Action. Spring 96; Second-Order Cultural Effects of Civil Rights on Southern Nonprofit Organizations, Nonprofit & Voluntary Sector Quart 25, 96; auth, Organizations as Overlapping Jurisdictions Restoring Reason in Organizational Accounts, Admin Sci Quart, 96; coauth, Historically Black Organizations in the Nonprofit Sector, Nonprofit and Voluntary Sector Quart, 96; The Duality of Church and Faith, Sociol Perspectives 4, 97. **CONTACT ADDRESS** Univ N. Carolina, Hamilton Hall, CB# 3210, Chapel Hill, NC, 27599-3210. **EMAIL** judith_blau@unc.edu

BLAZEKOVIC, ZDRAVKO
PERSONAL Born 05/13/1956, Zagreb, Croatia **DISCIPLINE** MUSICOLOGY **EDUCATION** Acad Mus, Zagreb, Croatia, BA, 80, MA, 83; City Univ NY, MPhil, 91, PhD, 97. **CAREER** Editor, RILM Abstracts of Mus Lit, NY, 87- ; Assoc dir, 91-98, dir, 98- , Res Ctr Mus Iconography; Ed, RIdIM/RCMI newsletter, 89-97, Art in Mus, 98- ; US Corresp, Hrvatsko Slovo, 96- ; Area ed, Die Musik in Geschichte und Gegenwart, 2nd ed, Kassel, Ger, 95- ; res asst, Inst Musicol Res, Croatian Acad Sci and Arts, 81. **MEMBERSHIPS** Int Asn Mus Libr, Archives and Document Ctr; Int Musicol Soc; Croatian Musicol Soc; Int Coun Trad Mus. **RESEARCH** History of Croatian music; music iconography; music in medieval astrological thoughts; social history of music. **SELECTED PUBLICATIONS** Music in Zagreb between Croatian, Hungarian and Austrian politics, Hist Euro Ideas XVI/4-6, 93; Horns in a Bag, or, Disparity of Parallel Musical Histories among the South Slavs, The Consortium on Revolutionary Europe, 1750-1850: Proceedings, 1992. Talahasee, Fla State Univ; Inst on Napoleon and the French Rev, 93, 107-116; Franz von Suppe und Dalmatien, Studien zur Musikwissenschaft XLIII 94, 249-268; Political Implications of the Croatian Opera in the Nineteenth-Century, Music Cultures in Contact: Convergences and Collisions, Sydney, Gordon and Breach, Currency Press, 94, 48-58; Due musicisti nella Pannonia del primo Ottocento: Djuro Arnold e Johann Petrus Haibel, Danubio: Una civilta musicale. VI: Croazia, Serbia, Bulgaria, Romania, Monfalcone: Teatro Communale, 94, 47-64; Salonsko Kolo: Dance of Nineteenth-Century Croatian Ballrooms, Dance res: The jour Soc for Dance Res XII/2, 94, 114-126; Origins of Modern Croatian Music, 1770-1830, Jour Croatian stud XXXIV-XXXV, 93-94, 75-97; Coauth, European Fiction Facts or Music, Hist of Euro Ideas XX/1-3, Jan 95, 461-467; Coauth, Jakob Petrus Haibel (1762-1826) and His Sixteen Newly-Discovered Masses from Djakovo, Off-Mozart: Musical culture and the Kleinmeister of Central Europe, 1750-1820, Zagreb, Hrvatsko muzikolosko drustvo, 95, 67-75; Music autographs in the Nikola Udina Algarotti Collection in Zagreb (circa 1740-1838), Current musicol 57, 95, 127-164; Indian decans, Arabic interpretations, European images, European iconography east and west: Selected papers of the Szeged international conference June 9-12, 1993, Leiden, E.J. Brill, 96, 225-235; Jugoslavien, Die Musik in Geschichte und Gegenwart: Allgemeine Enzyklopodie der Musik, Sachteil 4, Kassel, Barenreiter, Stuttgart: Metzler, 96; Anonymous vs. onymous, or When will Croatian musicology remember an unknown composer, Studia musicologica Academiae Scientiarum Hungaricae XXXVII/2-4, 96, 217-230; Orgelbildung: Kroatien und Montenegro, Die Musik in Geschichte und Gegenwart: Allgemeine Enzyklopadie der Musik, Sachteil 7, Kassel, Barenreiter; Stuttgart: Metzler, 97; Ed, Music and Politics in Post-Communist Europe, The European Legacy: Toward New Paradigms II/1, Mar 97, 133-159; Coauth, Serbien und Montenegro, Die Musik in Geschichte und Gegenwart: Allgemeine Enzyklopadie der Musik, Sachteil 8, Kassel: Barenreiter; Stuttgart: Metzler, 98; The shadow of politics on the north Croatian music of the nineteenth century, Music, politics, and war: Views from Croatia, Zagreb: Zavod za etnologiju and folklore res, 98, 65-78. **CONTACT ADDRESS** City Univ, 33 W 42nd St, New York, NY, 10036. **EMAIL** zblazeko@email.gc.cuny.edu

BLECKER, ROBERT A.
PERSONAL Born 11/17/1956, Philadelphia, PA, m, 1982, 2 children **DISCIPLINE** ECONOMICS **EDUCATION** Stanford Univ, PhD 87, MA 83; Yale univ, BA 78. **CAREER** Am Univ, prof econ 98, assoc prof 92-98, asst prof 85-92. **HONORS AND AWARDS** Fulbright Schl; NSF Fell. **MEMBERSHIPS** AEA; Union of Radical Political Econ **RESEARCH** Intl Econ; macroeconomics; polit econ. **SELECTED PUBLICATIONS** Fundamentals of U S Foreign Trade Policy, co auth Stephen D Cohen, Joel R Paul, Boulder, Westview, 96; U S Trade Policy and Global Growth: New Directions in the Intl Economy, ed Armonk, NY, ME Sharpe Inc, 96; Kaleckian Macro Models for Open Economies, in: Foundations of Intl Econ, ed by John Y Harvey Johan Deprez, London, Routledge, forthcoming; Policy Implications of the International Saving-Investment Correlation, in: The Macroeconomics of Finance, Saving and Investment, ed by Robert Pollin, Ann Arbor, Univ MI Press, 97. **CONTACT ADDRESS** Dept of Economics, American Univ, Washington, DC, 20016. **EMAIL** blecker@american.edu

BLEDSTEIN, ADRIEN
PERSONAL Born 03/04/1939, Los Angeles, CA, m, 1959, 2 children **DISCIPLINE** HISTORY; ENGLISH **EDUCATION** Univ California at Los Angeles, BA, 60; Teaching Certificate, 61. **CAREER** KAM Isiah Israel Congregation, Chicago, 30 years. **MEMBERSHIPS** SBL; Chicago Soc for Biblical Research **RESEARCH** Bible and ancient near Eastern lit. **SELECTED PUBLICATIONS** Auth, Was Eve Cursed (Or Did a Woman Write Genesis), Bible Review, 93; Are Women Cursed in Genesis 3.16, A Feminist Companion to Genesis, 93; Binder, Trickster, Heel and Hairy-man: Re-reading Genesis 27 as a Trickster Tale Told by a Woman, A Feminist Companion to Genesis, 93; Is Judges a Woman's Satire of Men Who Play God, A Feminist Companion to Judges, 93; Female Companionships: If the Book of Ruth Were Written by a Woman, A Feminist Companion to Ruth, 93; Dr. Tamar, Bible Review, 95; Tamar and the Coat of Many Colours, A Feminist Companion to Samuel and Kings II, forthcoming. **CONTACT ADDRESS** 5459 S. Hyde Pk. Blvd., Chicago, IL, 60615-5801. **EMAIL** ajb@mcs.net

BLEDSTEIN, BURTON J.
PERSONAL Born 07/05/1937, Los Angeles, CA, m, 1959, 2 children **DISCIPLINE** AMERICAN INTELLECTUAL AND SOCIAL THOUGHT **EDUCATION** Univ Calif, Los Angeles, BA, 59; Princeton Univ, MA, 63, PhD(hist), 67. **CAREER** Asst prof, 67-77, ASSOC PROF HIST, UNIV ILL, CHICAGO CIRCLE, 77-, Nat Endowment for Humanities fel, 72-73; fel, Nat Humanities Inst, Univ Chicago, 77-78. **MEMBERSHIPS** Orgn Am Historians; Am Studies Asn; AHA. **RESEARCH** American social thought and culture in the 19th and 20th centuries. **SELECTED PUBLICATIONS** Auth, Architects of Charleston, Miss Quart, Vol 0045, 92; The Quest For Authority and Honor in the American Professions, 1750-00, Am Hist Rev, Vol 0098, 93; The Definition of a Profession - the Authority of Metaphor in the History of Intelligence-Testing, 1890-30, Rev in Am Hist, Vol 0022, 94; The True Professional Ideal in America - a History, J of Interdisciplinary Hist, Vol 0025, 95; Patricians, Professors, and Public-Schools - the Origins of Modern Educational-Thought in America, J of Am Hist, Vol 0082, 95; Huntington,Henry,Edwards - a Biography, Am Hist Rev, Vol 0101, 96. **CONTACT ADDRESS** Dept of Hist, Univ of Ill at Chicago Circle, Box 4348, Chicago, IL, 60680.

BLEE, K.M.
DISCIPLINE SOCIOLOGY **EDUCATION** Univ Wisc, PhD, 82. **CAREER** Prof of sociol, dir of women's studies, assoc dean of col of art and sci, Univ Ky, 81-96; prof of sociol and hist and dir of women's studies, Univ Pittsburgh, 96-. **RESEARCH** Gender; Racism; Politics. **SELECTED PUBLICATIONS** Auth, No Middle Ground, NY Univ Press, 98; auth, Women of the Klan, Univ Calif Press, 91. **CONTACT ADDRESS** Univ of Pittsburgh, 2603 FQ, Pittsburgh, PA, 15260. **EMAIL** kblee@pitt.edu

BLESSINGTON, FRANCIS CHARLES
PERSONAL Born 05/21/1942, Boston, MA, m, 2 children **DISCIPLINE** ENGLISH LITERATURE, CLASSICS **EDUCATION** Boston Col, AB, 63; Northeastern Univ, MA, 66; Brown Univ, PhD, 72, AM, 73. **CAREER** From instr to asst prof, 69-75, assoc prof English, prof English, 84-, Northeastern Univ, 75-. **MEMBERSHIPS** MLA. **RESEARCH** Milton; Renaissance English literature; classics. **SELECTED PUBLICATIONS** Auth, Euripides: The Bacchae and Aristophanes: The Frogs, Crofts Classics, 93; Review of The New Oxford Book of Seventeenth-Century Poetry, ed Alastair Fowler, The Scriblerian, 93; Review of Roger Pooley's English Prose of the Seventeenth Century: 1590-1700, The Scriblerian, 94. **CONTACT ADDRESS** Dept English, Northeastern Univ, Boston, MA, 02115.

BLETHEN, H. TYLER
DISCIPLINE HISTORY **EDUCATION** Bowdoin Col, BA, 67; Univ N Carolina, Chapel Hill, MA, 69, Phd, 72. **CAREER** From asst prof to full prof, 72- , dir, Mountain Heritage Ctr, 85- , actg head, Dept of Hist, 81-82, Western Carolina Univ. **HONORS AND AWARDS** Hist Soc N Carolina; Phi Kappa Phi; Phi Alpha Theta. **MEMBERSHIPS** Appalachian Consortium; Appalachian Stud Asn; Carolinas Symp on Brit Stud; N Am Conf on Brit Stud; N Carolina Lit and Hist Soc; S Conf on Brit Stud; S Hist Asn. **RESEARCH** History of Southern Appalachia;

early Stuart Britain. **SELECTED PUBLICATIONS** Auth, A Mountain Heritage: The Illustrated History of Western Carolina University, Western Carolina Univ, 89; ed, Diversity in Appalachia: Images and Realities, v 5 of J of the Appalachian Stud Asn, 93; co-ed, Ulster and North America: Transatlantic Perspectives on the Scotch-Irish, Alabama, 97; coauth, From Ulster to Carolina: The Migration of the Scotch-Irish to Southwestern North Carolina, North Carolina Archives and History, 98. **CONTACT ADDRESS** Dept of History, Western Carolina Univ, Cullowhee, NC, 28723. **EMAIL** blethen@wcu.edu

BLEWETT, MARY H.
PERSONAL Born 12/17/1938, St. Louis, MO **DISCIPLINE** RECENT UNITED STATES HISTORY **EDUCATION** Univ Mo, BA, 60; MA, 61; PhD (hist), 65. **CAREER** From asst to assoc prof, 65-76; PROF HIST, UNIV LOWELL, 76-. **RESEARCH** Truman administration; municipal reform in textile cities of Massachusetts; sex and class in shoe industry. **SELECTED PUBLICATIONS** Auth, Religion and the Working-Class in Antebellum America, Jour Soc Hist, Vol 0030, 96; Women of the Commonwealth--Work, Family, and Social-Change in 19th-Century Massachusetts, Labor Hist, Vol 0037, 96; Dishing It Out--Waitresses and Their Unions in the 20th-Century, Int Rev Soc Hist, Vol 0037, 92; Transforming Womens Work--New-England Lives in the Industrial-Revolution, Jour Soc Hist, Vol 0029, 95; A Very Social Time--Crafting Community in Antebellum New-England, Jour Interdisciplinary Hist, Vol 0026, 96. **CONTACT ADDRESS** Dept of Hist, Univ of Lowell, Lowell, MA, 01854.

BLICKSILVER, JACK
PERSONAL Born 05/16/1926, New York, NY, m, 1948, 3 children **DISCIPLINE** ECONOMICS AND BUSINESS HISTORY **EDUCATION** Queens Col, NY, BA, 48; Northwestern Univ, MA, 53, PhD(hist), 55. **CAREER** Instr soc sci, S State Tchr's Col, SDak, 53-55; from asst prof to assoc prof, 55-61, PROF, GA STATE UNIV, 61-. **MEMBERSHIPS** AHA; Mem, Nat Educ-Indust Adv Coun, Lincoln Educ Found, 75-; Am Econ Asn; Econ Hist Asn; Southern Hist Asn; Orgn Am Historians. **SELECTED PUBLICATIONS** Auth, Southwest Virginias Railroad--Modernization And The Sectional Crisis, Jour Econ Hist, Vol 0055, 95. **CONTACT ADDRESS** Dept of Econ, Georgia State Univ, Atlanta, GA, 30303.

BLIER, SUZANNE PRESTON
PERSONAL Born 10/22/1948, Burlington, VT, m, 1969 **DISCIPLINE** ART HISTORY; AFRICAN STUDIES **EDUCATION** Univ Vt, BA, 73; Columbia Univ, MA, 76, MPhil, 76, PhD, 81. **CAREER** Res asst primitive art, Metropolitan Mus of Art, 79-81; Mellon asst prof Art Hist, Northwestern Univ, 81-, Cur, primitive slide collection, Columbia Univ, 73-75, adj lectr, 79; vis lectr, Vassar Col, 79-81; consult, Am Mus of Natural Hist, 80-81; vis asst prof, Univ Ill, Chicago Circle, 82. **MEMBERSHIPS** Col Art Asn; Soc Archit Historians; African Studies Asn; Am Soc Aesthetics. **RESEARCH** African art; Archaeoastronomy; Vernacular architecture. **SELECTED PUBLICATIONS** Auth, Beauty and the beast & creative/destructive, In: African Art as Philosophy, Interbook, 74; Beauty and the Beast, A Study in Contrasts, Tribal Arts Gallery, 76; African Art as Theatre: The Mount Collection, Vassar Col, 80; Africa's Cross River: Art of the Nigerian-Cameroon Border Redefined, L Kahan Gallery, 80; House, heart and the soul in Tamerma, Crafts Int, 81; The dance of death: Notes on the architecture and staging of Tamberma funeral performances, Res 2, Harvard Univ, Peabody Mus, 81. **CONTACT ADDRESS** Dept of Art History, Northwestern Univ, Evanston, IL, 60201.

BLIQUEZ, LAWRENCE J.
PERSONAL Born 06/12/1941, Des Moines, IA, m, 1969, 2 children **DISCIPLINE** CLASSICS **EDUCATION** St Mary's Coll Calif, BA, 63; Stanford Univ, MA, 65; PhD, 68. **CAREER** Asst prof, San Francisco State Coll, 66-69; asst prof Univ Wash Seattle, 69-77; assoc prof, 77-85; prof, Univ Wash Seattle, 85-. **HONORS AND AWARDS** Jr Fel, Center for Hellenic Studies, 77-78; Distinguished Teaching Award, Univ Wash, 77-78. **MEMBERSHIPS** APA; AIP; Soc for Ancient Med. **RESEARCH** Greek and Roman Minor Objects, surgical instruments. **SELECTED PUBLICATIONS** Auth, Roman Surgical Instruments and Other Minor Objectsin the Nat Archaeol Museum of Naples, 94. **CONTACT ADDRESS** Dept of Classics, Univ of Wash, Box 353110, Seattle, WA, 98195. **EMAIL** lbliquez@u.washington.edu

BLISS, FRANCIS ROYSTER
PERSONAL Born 06/07/1919, Big Stone Gap, VA, m, 1943, 3 children **DISCIPLINE** LATIN, GREEK **EDUCATION** Bowdoin Col, AB, 40; Univ NC, PhD(Latin), 51. **CAREER** From instr to asst prof classics, Colby Col, 48-55; assoc prof, Western Reserve Univ, 55-66; assoc prof classics, UNIV VT, 66-70, PROF, 70-79. **MEMBERSHIPS** Class Asn Mid W & S; Class Asn New England; Soc Ancient Greek Philos; Vergilian Soc; Am Philol Asn. **RESEARCH** Literary imitation, cultural history. **SELECTED PUBLICATIONS** Auth, Roman law and Romand citizenship, Law in a Troubled World, W Reserve Univ, 59; The Plancus ode, Trans & Proc Am Philol Assn, 60; A rogues' gallery, Class Outlook, 63; Unity of Odyssey Eight, Bucknell Rev, 68. **CONTACT ADDRESS** RFD 1, Box 240, New Vineyard, ME, 04956.

BLISS, JOHN W.M.
PERSONAL Born 01/18/1941, Leamington, ON, Canada **DISCIPLINE** HISTORY **EDUCATION** Univ Toronto, BA, 62; MA, 66, PhD, 72. **CAREER** Tchg asst, Harvard Univ, 67-68; mem Gov Coun Univ, 75-78; PROF HISTORY, UNIV TORONTO. **HONORS AND AWARDS** F-X Garneau Medal & Sir John A Macdonald Prize, Can Hist Asn; Univ BC Medal Can Biog; City Toronto Book Award; Toronto Hist Bd Award Merit; Jason Hannah Medal, Royal Soc Can; Wm H Welch Medal, Am Asn Hist Med. **MEMBERSHIPS** Royal Soc Can **SELECTED PUBLICATIONS** Auth, A Living Profit: Studies in the Social History of Canadian Business 1883-1911, 74; A Canadian Millionaire: The Life and Business Times of Sir Joseph Flavelle, Bart, 78; The Discovery of Insulin, 82; Banting: A Biography, 84; Northern Enterprise: Five Centuries of Canadian Business, 87; Plague: A Story of Smallpox in Montreal, 91; Right Honourable Men: The Descent of Canadian Politics from Macdonald to Mulroney, 94. **CONTACT ADDRESS** History of Medicine, Univ of Toronto, 88 College St, Toronto, ON, M5G 1L4.

BLISS, KATHERINE
DISCIPLINE HISTORY **EDUCATION** Univ Chicago, PhD, 96. **CAREER** Asst prof, Univ MA Amherst. **RESEARCH** Latin Am hist; mod Mex. **SELECTED PUBLICATIONS** Auth, publ(s) on experience and soc mobilization of poor women in revolutionary Mexico City. **CONTACT ADDRESS** Dept of Hist, Univ Massachusetts Amherst, Mass Ave, Amherst, MA, 01003.

BLISS, ROBERT M.
PERSONAL Born 04/30/1943, Portland, OR, m, 1966, 2 children **DISCIPLINE** HISTORY **EDUCATION** Univ Pa, BA, 65; Univ Wis,Madison, MA, 67, PhD, 83. **CAREER** Wis Res Fel, Linacre Col, Oxford Univ, 69-70; lect to sen lect, hist, Lancaster Univ, 70-97; principal, Grizedale Col, Lancaster Univ, 78-93; dir Am Stud, 92-97; DEAN PIERRE LACLEDE HONORS, ASSOC PROF, HIST, UNIV MO, 97-. **HONORS AND AWARDS** Dist Bk Award, Soc Colonial Wars, NY, 93; res fel, Newberry Library, 81; Lancaster Univ Res Fund, 84-85; John Carter Brown Library, 91. **MEMBERSHIPS** Org Am Hist; Inst Early Am Hist & Cult; Hist Asn (UK); British Asn for Am Stud. **RESEARCH** Anglo-Am politics and culture 1550-1700. **SELECTED PUBLICATIONS** Auth, Revolution and Empire: English Politics and the American Colonies in the Seventeenth Century, 90,93; 'Paradigms Lost? British-Amican Colonial History and the Encyclopedia of the North Amican Colonies,' in Jour of Am Stud 29, 95. **CONTACT ADDRESS** Pierre Laclede Honors Col, Univ Missouri, St. Louis, 8001 Natural Bridge Rd, St. Louis, MO, 63121. **EMAIL** rmbliss@umsl.edu

BLOCK, DANIEL I.
PERSONAL Born 05/22/1943, Borden, SK, Canada, m, 1966, 2 children **DISCIPLINE** SEMITICS, CLASSICAL HEBREW **EDUCATION** Univ Liverpool, England, PhD. **CAREER** Prof Old Testament Interp, S Baptist Theol Sem, 95-; prof Old Testament, Bethel Theol Sem, 83-95; prof Old Test, Providence Col, Manitoba, Canada. **HONORS AND AWARDS** DAAD scholar; Canada coun awd, 78-80. **MEMBERSHIPS** Soc Bibl Lit; inst Bibl res; Evangelical Theol Soc. **RESEARCH** Deuteronomy; Judges; Family Issues in Ancient Israel. **SELECTED PUBLICATIONS** Auth, Ezekiel 1-24, Ezekiel 25-28, in New International Commentary on the Old Testament, Eerdmans, 97, 98. **CONTACT ADDRESS** Dept of Old Testament, S Baptist Theological Sem, 2825 Lexington Rd, Louisville, KY, 40280. **EMAIL** diblock@aol.com

BLOCK, GEOFFREY
PERSONAL Born 05/07/1948, Oakland, CA, m, 1982, 2 children **DISCIPLINE** MUSIC HISTORY **EDUCATION** UCLA, BA 70; Harvard Univ, MA, 73, PhD, 79. **CAREER** The Thacher Sch, Dir of Music, 77-80, Univ of Puget Sound, 80-present, prof of Music Hist. **HONORS AND AWARDS** Fulbright Fel 75-76, Washington Commission for the hum: Inquiring Mind Scholar 85-87, National Endowment for the Hum, 90-91, Univ of Puget Sound Regester Lectr, 99, General Ed, Yal Broadway Masters. **MEMBERSHIPS** Am Musicological Soc Sonneck Soc. **RESEARCH** Beethoven Mozart Ives Am musical theater. **SELECTED PUBLICATIONS** Enchanted Evenings: The Broadway Musical from Show Boat to Sondheim, Oxford Univ Press, 97; Ives: Piano Sonata No. 2 (Concord, MA, 1840-1860), Cambridge Univ Press, 96); co-ed, Charles Ives and the Classical Tradition, New Haven: Yal Univ Press, 96; Charles Ives, A Biobibliography, Greenwood Press, 88; Articles in Ives Studies, Cambridge Univ Press, 98; Journal of the Royal Musical Association, 96; The Journal of Musicology, 93; Mozart-Jahrbuch 91, 92; Beethoven's Compositional Process, Univ of NE, 91; The Opera Quarterly, 90; The Musical Quarterly, 89; Beethoven Essays, Harvard Univ Press, 84. **CONTACT ADDRESS** Music Dept, Univ of Puget Sound, 1500 N. Warner, Tacoma, WA, 98416. **EMAIL** Block@ups.edu

BLOCK, JOYCE
PERSONAL Born 12/29/1951, New York, NY, m, 1984, 2 children **DISCIPLINE** PSYCHOLOGY **EDUCATION** Grad Cen, CVNY, PhD, 82. **CAREER** Clinical Psychol, 82; Post Doct Fellow, Psychol, Penn State Med Cen, 85; Asst Prof, Notre Dame Univ, St Mary's Col. **MEMBERSHIPS** Am Psychol Asn **SELECTED PUBLICATIONS** Motherhood as Metamorph, Dutton, 90; Family Myths, Simon & Schuster, 94. **CONTACT ADDRESS** 300 North Michigan St, South Bend, IN, 46601.

BLODGETT, RALPH EDWARD
PERSONAL Born 11/05/1941, Goodland, KS, m, 1966, 2 children **DISCIPLINE** AMERICAN HISTORY **EDUCATION** Univ Colo, Boulder, BA, 64, MA, 69, PhD, 71. **CAREER** Teacher hist, Mapleton Publ Schs, Denver, 64-67; teaching asst US hist, Univ CO, 69-71; asst prof hist, Lenior Rhyne Col, 71-72; asst prof, 72-75, assoc prof, 75-79, PROF HIST, CAMERON UNIV, 79-. **MEMBERSHIPS** Orgn Am Historians; Inst Early Am Hist & Cult. **RESEARCH** American colonial and Revolutionary War era; US diplomatic history; Western US--history and development. **SELECTED PUBLICATIONS** Auth, The Colorado Territorial Board of Immigration, CO Mag, CO State Hist Soc, 69. **CONTACT ADDRESS** Dept of Hist, Cameron Univ, 2800 Gore Blvd, Lawton, OK, 73505-6377.

BLOMQUIST, THOMAS W.
PERSONAL Born 03/03/1931, St. Paul, MN, m, 1963, 2 children **DISCIPLINE** MEDIEVAL EUROPEAN AND ITALIAN HISTORY **EDUCATION** Dartmouth Col, BA, 53; Univ Minn, MA, 59, PhD(hist), 66. **CAREER** From instr to asst prof, 65-71, ASSOC PROF, N ILL UNIV, 71-. **HONORS AND AWARDS** Am Coun Learned Socs fel, 70-71. **MEMBERSHIPS** Mediaeval Acad Am; Soc Ital Hist Studies; Econ Hist Soc. **RESEARCH** Medieval Italian social and economic history. **SELECTED PUBLICATIONS** Auth, The Reconstruction Of An Italian City-Republic--Speculum-Jour Medieval Stud, Vol 0072, 97. **CONTACT ADDRESS** Dept of Hist, No Illinois Univ, 1425 W Lincoln Hwy, De Kalb, IL, 60115-2825.

BLOOM, ALEXANDER
PERSONAL Born 10/10/1947, Los Angeles, CA, d, 2 children **DISCIPLINE** AMERICAN HISTORY **EDUCATION** Univ Calif, Santa Cruz, BA, 68; Boston Col, MA, 73, PhD, 79. **CAREER** Asst prof, prof, 80-, Wheaton Col. **MEMBERSHIPS** AHA; Orgn Amer Hist; AAUP; Amer Stud Assn. **RESEARCH** American intellectual history; American radicalism; 20th century American political history. **SELECTED PUBLICATIONS** Auth, Prodigal Sons: The New York Intellectuals and Their World, Oxford Press, 84; auth, Takin' It To The Streets, Oxford Univ Press, 95. **CONTACT ADDRESS** History Dept, Wheaton Col, 26 E Main St, Norton, MA, 02766-2322. **EMAIL** abloom@wheatonma.edu

BLOOM, JOHN PORTER
PERSONAL Born 12/30/1924, Albuquerque, NM, m, 1954, 3 children **DISCIPLINE** AMERICAN HISTORY **EDUCATION** Univ NMex, AB, 47; George Washington Univ, AM, 49; Emory Univ, PhD, 56. **CAREER** Instr soc sci, NGa Col, 50-51; assoc prof hist, Brenau Col, 52-56; from instr to asst prof Am hist, Univ Tex, El Paso, 56-60; staff historian, Nat Park Serv, 60-64; ed, Territorial Papers US & sr specialist Western hist, Nat Arch, Washington, DC, 64-80; dir, Holtatherton Pac Ctr W Stud & Ed; PAC HISTORIAN, UNIV PAC, 81-; rev ed, Ariz and West, 60-63; prog chmn, Conf Hist Western Am, 61 & 71, secy pro-tem & mem organizing comt, 61-62. **MEMBERSHIPS** Western Hist Assn (secy-treas, 62-67, vpres, 72-73, pres, 73-74); Orgn Am Historians; S Hist Assn; Am Assn State & Local Hist; AHA. **RESEARCH** Trans-Mississippi West, American territorial system, American southwest. **SELECTED PUBLICATIONS** Auth, Volunteers--The Mexican-War Jour, 2nd-Pennsylvania-Infantry, Jour So Hist, Vol 0059, 93; Essays in 20th-Century New-Mexico History, Jour W, Vol 0036, 97; Contemp New-Mex, 1940-1990, Jour W, Vol 0035, 96; Presbyterian Missions And Cultural Interaction in the Far Southwest, 1850-1950, Jour W, Vol 0034, 95; The Wilderness of the Southwest, Quest for Desert Bighorn Sheep and Adventures with the Havasupai and Seri Indians, Jour W, Vol 0035, 96; Seeing-The-Elephant, Mag W Hist, Vol 0047, 97.

BLOOMER, JENNIFER A.
PERSONAL Born 11/13/1951, Knoxville, TN, m, 1990, 3 children **DISCIPLINE** ARCHITECTURAL HISTORY, THEORY AND CRITICISM **EDUCATION** Georgia Inst Technol, PhD, 89; Georgia Inst Technol, MA, 81; Mount Holyoke Col, AB, 73 **CAREER** Prof, Iowa State Univ, 98-; assoc prof, Iowa State Univ, 91-98; asst prof, Univ Flor, 88-91; instr, Georgia Tech Univ, 82-88 **HONORS AND AWARDS** Distinguished Visting Critic, Yale Univ, 95; Ruth & Norman Moore Lectr, Washington Univ, 94; Eva Maddox Lectr, Univ Illinois Chicago, 92; Annual Discourse, Royal Inst British Architects, 92; Swanson Lectr, Cranbrook Acad Art, 90 **MEMBERSHIPS** Soc Archit Historians; Ed Boards: Archit New York, Assemblage, Space and Culture **RESEARCH** Architecture and Literature; Architecture and Hypertextuality; Critical Theory **SELECTED PUBLICATIONS** The Longing for Gravity, Academy Editions, 97; "Nature Morte," Architect: Reconstructing Her Practice, MIT, 96; "The Matter of the Cutting Edge," Desiring Practices, Black Dog, 96; Architecture and the Text: The (S)crypts of Joyce and Piranesi, Yale Univ, 93 **CONTACT ADDRESS** Dept Archit, Iowa State Univ, Ames, IA, 50011. **EMAIL** jbloomer@iastate.edu

BLOOMER, W. MARTIN
DISCIPLINE CLASSICS **EDUCATION** BA, 82; MA, 83; MPhil, 84; Yale Univ, PhD, 87. **CAREER** Asst prof, Stanford Univ. **RESEARCH** Latin lit; ancient rhetoric; ancient historiography. **SELECTED PUBLICATIONS** Auth, Valerius Maximus and the Rhetoric of the New Nobility, 92; The Superlative Nomoi of Herodotus's Histories, 93; A Preface to the History of Declamation: Whose Speech? Whose History?, 96; Latinity and Literary Society at Rome, 97. **CONTACT ADDRESS** Stanford Univ, Bldg 20, Main Quad, Stanford, CA, 94305.

BLOXAM, M. JENNIFER
DISCIPLINE MUSIC **EDUCATION** Yale Univ, PhD. **CAREER** Assoc prof, Williams Col, 86. **HONORS AND AWARDS** NEH; Martha Baird Rockefeller Fund & Fulbright Found. **RESEARCH** Exegesis and narrative in medieval and Renaissance music and the arts; musical borrowing; compositional process; the cultural context of music. **SELECTED PUBLICATIONS** Publ on late medieval plainsong and sacred polyphony, J Amer Musicological Soc, Early Mus Hist, J Musicol; Plainsong in the Age of Polyphony, Cambridge, 92; Hearing the Motet, Oxford, 96; Continuities and Transformations in Musical Culture, 1450-1500, Oxford, 96; publ on, Haydn in The Haydn Yearbk; contribur, to the new ed of Musik in Geschichte und Gegenwart, rev ed, The New Grove Dictionary of Music and Musicians. **CONTACT ADDRESS** Music Dept, Williams Col, Williamstown, MA, 01267.

BLUE, FREDERICK J.
PERSONAL Born 04/18/1937, Staten Island, NY, m, 1962, 2 children **DISCIPLINE** AMERICAN HISTORY **EDUCATION** Yale Univ, AB, 58; Univ Wis, MS, 62, PhD(hist), 66. **CAREER** From asst prof to assoc prof, 64-75, prof hist, Youngstown State Univ, 75-. **MEMBERSHIPS** Orgn Am Historians; Soc Historians Early Am Repub. **RESEARCH** Pre-Civil War political history; Ohio; 19th century American West. **SELECTED PUBLICATIONS** Auth, The Ohio Free Soilers and Problems of Factionalism, Ohio Hist, winter-spring 67; The Free Soilers: Third Party Politics, 1848-1854, Univ Ill, 73; Chase and the Governorship: A Stepping Stone to the Presidency, Ohio Hist, summer 81; A Reformer for all Seasons, in The Pursuit of Public Power: Political Culture in Ohio, 1787-1861, co-authored with Robert McCormick, Kent State Univ, Ohio, 94; Charles Sumner and the Conscience of the North, Harlan Davidson, 94; The Poet and the Reformer: Longfellow, Sumner and the Bonds of Male Friendship, 1837-1874, Journal of the Early Republic, summer, 95. **CONTACT ADDRESS** Dept of History, Youngstown State Univ, One University Plz, Youngstown, OH, 44555-0002. **EMAIL** fr020601@ysub.ysu.edu

BLUESTONE, DANIEL
DISCIPLINE ARCHITECTURAL HISTORY **EDUCATION** Harvard Univ, BA, 75; Univ Chicago, PhD, 84. **CAREER** Assoc prof. **HONORS AND AWARDS** Int Bk Awd, 91; Nat Hist Preservation Bk Prize, 91. **RESEARCH** Nineteenth century American architecture and urbanism. **SELECTED PUBLICATIONS** Auth, Constructing Chicago, 91; **CONTACT ADDRESS** Dept of Architectural History., Virginia Univ, Charlottesville, VA, 22903. **EMAIL** dblues@virginia.edu

BLUM, ALBERT A.
PERSONAL Born 04/05/1924, New York, NY, m, 1949, 2 children **DISCIPLINE** HISTORY **EDUCATION** City Col NY, BS, 47; Columbia Univ, MA, 48, PhD, 53. **CAREER** Labor hist, Office of Chief of Mil Hist, Washington DC, 51-53; lect, Queens Col, Brooklyn Col, 54-56; labor rel, Natl Industrial Conf Bd, 56-58; asst prof, NYU, 57-58; asst prof, Cornell Univ, 58-59; assoc prof, Am Univ, 59-60; res assoc, Int Labour Off, Geneva, 66-67; Fulbright res prof, Danish Natl Inst for Soc Res, and lectr Univ Copenhagen, 68; Exec sec, Natl Acad Sci, 73-74; prof, chm, Sch of Labor and Ind Rel, Michigan St Univ, 60-74; dean, prof, Stuart School of Bus Adm, Ill Inst Tech, 78-82; George Wilson prof Int Mgt, Univ of the Pacific, 82-84; prof, chm, Int Bus Dept, Am Univ of Paris, 87-89; vis prof, Univ Witwatersrand, 91-92; vis prof, Helsinki Sch of Bus Admin and Econ, 93; guest prof, Aalborg Univ, 96; prof, New Mex State Univ, 85- . **HONORS AND AWARDS** Phi Beta Kappa; Soc Sci Res Council National Security Program Grant, 58-59; Res Fulbright, Denmark, 67-68; Dept Labor Res Grant, 74-76; Lyndon B Johnson Found Grant, 75-76. **MEMBERSHIPS** Int Ind Rel Asoc. **RESEARCH** Labor history; international labor; negotiation and conflict management. **SELECTED PUBLICATIONS** Auth, Drafted or Deferred: Practices Past and Present, Univ Michigan, 67; ed, Teacher Unions and Associations: A Comparative Study, Univ Ill, 69; co-auth, White Collar Workers, Random, 71; auth, A Brief History of the American Labor Movement, Am Hist Assoc, 72; auth of numerous articles. **CONTACT ADDRESS** Dept of Management, New Mexico State Univ, Dept 3DJ, PO Box 30001, Las Cruces, NM, 88003. **EMAIL** ablum@nmsu.edu

BLUM, GEORGE PAUL
PERSONAL Born 02/05/1932, Kibartai, Lithuania, m, 1961, 2 children **DISCIPLINE** MODERN EUROPEAN HISTORY **EDUCATION** Hamline Univ, BA, 56; Univ Minn, MA, 58, PhD(mod Ger hist), 62. **CAREER** From asst prof soc sci to prof, Raymond Col, 62-77, prof hist, Raymond-Callison Col, 77-80; PROF HIST, UNIV PAC, 80-, CHAIR DEPT, 91-; Nat Endowment for Humanities young scholar, 67-68. **MEMBERSHIPS** AHA; AAUP; Conf Group Cent Europ Hist; Conf Group Ger Politics; Ger Studies Asn **RESEARCH** Modern German and European history; social democracy. **SELECTED PUBLICATIONS** Contrib, Research Guide to European Historical Biography, Beacham, 92-93; Statesmen Who Changed the World, Greenwood, 93; Events That Changed the World in the Twentieth Century, Greenwood, 95; Auth, The Rise of Fascism in Europe, Greenwood, 98. **CONTACT ADDRESS** Dept. of History, Univ of the Pacific, 3601 Pacific Ave, Stockton, CA, 95211-0197. **EMAIL** gblum@uop.edu

BLUMBERG, ARNOLD
PERSONAL Born 05/09/1925, Philadelphia, PA, m, 1954, 3 children **DISCIPLINE** MODERN EUROPEAN HISTORY **EDUCATION** Univ Pa, PhD, 52. **CAREER** Assoc prof, 58-64, prof, hist, 64-, prof emer, 87- Towson Univ; found sum res grant, 61; abstractor, Hist Abstr, 63-80; ed consult, Am Hist Rev, The Hist and the Pacific Coast Hist Rev. **HONORS AND AWARDS** Amer Philos Soc Johnson res fund grant, 66; res grants, Towson Univ. **MEMBERSHIPS** AHA; Soc Hist Studies; Southern Hist Assn; AAUP. **RESEARCH** French second empire; Italian unification; diplomatic history; mid-19th century British and Prussian consular correspondence at the Israel State Archives in Jerusalem. **SELECTED PUBLICATIONS** Auth, The Diplomacy of the Mexican Empire, 1963-1867, Amer Philos Soc, 71; auth, A View from Jerusalem, 1849-1858, Fairleigh Dickinson Univ/Assoc Univ Press, 80; auth, Zion Before Zionism, 1838-1880, Syracuse Univ Press, 86; auth, A Carefully Planned Accident; The Italian War of 1859, Susquehanna Univ Press/Assoc Univ Press, 90; auth, Great Leaders, Great Tyrants? Contemporary Views of the World Rulers Who Made History, Greenwood Press, 95; auth, A History of Israel, Greenwood Press, 98. **CONTACT ADDRESS** Dept of History, Towson Univ, Linthicum Hall, 119c, Baltimore, MD, 21204. **EMAIL** ablumberg@towson.edu

BLUMENFELD, DAVID
DISCIPLINE HISTORY OF MODERN PHILOSOPHY, METAPHYSICS, ETHICS, ANALYTIC PHILOSOPHY **EDUCATION** Univ Calif, Berkeley, PhD, 66. **CAREER** Prof, assoc dean, Hum, Ga State Univ. **SELECTED PUBLICATIONS** Author of over twenty-five articles, including two recent ones in The Cambridge Companion to Leibniz, and an article on free will in Am Philos Quart. Editor of Proceedings from Ga State Univ Conference on Human Freedom. **CONTACT ADDRESS** Georgia State Univ, Atlanta, GA, 30303. **EMAIL** phlddb@panther.gsu.edu

BLUMENSHINE, GARY B.
DISCIPLINE HISTORY **EDUCATION** Northwestern Univ, BA; Univ Ill, PhD. **CAREER** Prof. **RESEARCH** Medieval Europe history; Roman history; historiography. **SELECTED PUBLICATIONS** Ed, Liber Alcuini Contra Haeresim, 80. **CONTACT ADDRESS** Dept of History, Indiana Univ-Purdue Univ, Fort Wayne, 2101 Coliseum Blvd, Fort Wayne, IN, 46805. **EMAIL** blumensh@smtplink.ipfw.edu

BLUMIN, STUART
PERSONAL Born 03/29/1940, Miami, FL, m, 1965, 2 children **DISCIPLINE** HISTORY **EDUCATION** Univ PA, BS, 62, MA, 63, PhD, 68. **CAREER** Asst prof Am studies, Skidmore Col, 67-69; asst prof hist, Mass Inst Technol, 69-73; asst prof, 74-77, assoc prof, 77-87, prof hist, Cornell Univ, 87-, Res fel, Charles Warren Ctr Studies in Am Hist, Harvard Univ, 71-72; vis lectr, Brandeis Univ, 72. **HONORS AND AWARDS** NEH Fel Univ Tchr(s), 87-88, 97-98; Kerr Prize (NYSHA), 75; Urban Hist Asn Best Book Prize, 89; Binkley-Stepehnson Prize (OAH), 97. **MEMBERSHIPS** AHA; Orgn Am Historians; Urban Hist Asn. **RESEARCH** Am soc hist; the Am city. **SELECTED PUBLICATIONS** Auth, The Historical Study of Vertical Mobility, Hist Methods Newsletter, 68; Mobility and Change in Ante-Bellum Philadelphia, In: Nineteenth-Century Cities: Essays in the New Urban History, Yale Univ, 69; Residential Mobility in the Nineteenth-Century City, In: The Peoples of Philadelphia, Temple Univ, 73; Rip Van Winkle's Grandchildren: Family and Household in the Hudson Valley, 1800-1860, J Urban Hist, 75; Church and Community: A Case Study of Lay Leadership in Nineteenth-Century America, New York Hist, 75; The Urban Threshold: Growth and Change in A Nineteenth-Century American Community, Univ Chicago, 76; Black Coats to White Collars: Economic Change, Nonmanual Work, and the Social Structure of Industrializing America, In: Small Business in American Life, Columbia Univ, 80; The Short Season of Sharon Springs: Portrait of Another New York, Cornell Univ, 80; The Emergence of the Middle Class: Social Experience in the American City, Cambridge, 89; ed, New York by Gas-Light and Other Urban Sketches by George G Foster, Calif, 90; The Social Implications of American Economic Development, In: The Cambridge Economic History of the United States, Cambridge, 99; co-auth (with Glenn C Altschauler), Rude Republic: Americans and Their Politics in the Nineteenth Century, Princeton, 99. **CONTACT ADDRESS** Dept of Hist, Cornell Univ, Mcgraw Hall, Ithaca, NY, 14853-0001. **EMAIL** smb5@cornell.edu

BLUSTEIN, BONNIE ELLEN
PERSONAL Born 04/17/1951, Middletown, CT **DISCIPLINE** HISTORY OF SCIENCE & MEDICINE **EDUCATION** Harvard Univ, AB, 73; Univ Pa, PhD(hist & sociol sci), 79. **CAREER** Asst prof hist, Univ Louisville, 79-81; RESEARCHER, MUS SCI & INDUST, 81- **MEMBERSHIPS** Hist Sci Soc; Am Asn Hist Med; Cheiron Soc. **RESEARCH** History of neurosciences; social relations of science and medicine; history of American science and technology. **SELECTED PUBLICATIONS** Auth, Madness and Social Representations--Living With The Mad In One French Community, Isis, Vol 0084, 93; Fits and Starts--A Genealogy of Hysteria in Modern France, Isis, Vol 0084, 93; To the Ends of the Earth--Womens Search for Education in Medicine, Jour of Interdisciplinary Hist, Vol 0024, 94; Women, Health, and Science 1900-1991--Works on Women in the Section-Hist-Med-Sci Lib Univ Granada, Isis, Vol 0085, 94; Final Solutions--Biology, Prejudice, And Genocide, Isis, Vol 0085, 94; The Retreat of Scientific Racism--Changing Concepts of Race in Britain and the United-States Between the World-Wars, Isis, Vol 0085, 94; Madness and Social Representations--Living with the Mad in One French Community, Isis, Vol 0084, 93; Fits And Starts--A Genealogy of Hysteria in Modern France, Isis, Vol 0084, 93; The Retreat of Scientific Racism--Changing Concepts of Race in Britain and the United-States Between The World-Wars, Isis, Vol 0085, 94; Inhibition--History and Meaning in the Sciences of Mind and Brain, Jour Interdisciplinary Hist, Vol 0025, 95. **CONTACT ADDRESS** Dept Hist, Univ Louisville, Louisville, KY, 40208.

BOATWRIGHT, MARY T.
PERSONAL Born 04/16/1952, VA, m, 1981, 2 children **DISCIPLINE** CLASSICS **EDUCATION** Stanford Univ, BA, 73; Univ per Stranieri Perugia, Laurea voto ottimo, 74; Univ of Mich, MA, 75, PhD, 80. **CAREER** ICCS, grad Asst, 76-77, Duke Univ; A W Mellon Asst Prof, Asst Prof, Assoc Prof, Prof, Chmn dept Classics 79-, ICCS Rome; A W Mellon Prof in charge, 92-93. **HONORS AND AWARDS** Phi Beta Kappa, Borso di Studio, Duke Endowment Awd Excellence in Teaching, G A & E G Howard Found Fel, NEH Fel. **MEMBERSHIPS** APA, AIA, SPRS, AAH, SFAAR. **RESEARCH** Social & cultural history during the Imperial Roman period, Roman women, Roman cities. **SELECTED PUBLICATIONS** Auth, Hadrian and the Cities of the Roman Empire, Princeton Univ Press, forthcoming; co-ed, The Shapes of City Life in Rome and Pompeii, Essays in Honor of L Richardson Jr on the Occasion of his Retirement, Caratzas, forthcoming; auth, Hadrian and the City of Rome, Princeton Univ Press, 97; auth, Imperial Women of the Early Second Century A C, Amer J of Philology, 91; Hadrian and Italian Cities, Chiron, 89. **CONTACT ADDRESS** Dept of Classical Studies, Duke Univ, Durham, NC, 27708-0103. **EMAIL** tboat@acpub.duke.edu

BOBER, PHYLLIS PRAY
PERSONAL Born 12/02/1920, Portland, ME, 2 children **DISCIPLINE** ARCHAEOLOGY, HISTORY OF ART **EDUCATION** Wellesley Col, BA, 41; NY Univ, MA, 43, PhD(fine arts), 46. **CAREER** Instr art, Wellesley Col, 47-49, lectr & cur mus, 51-54; res assoc, Inst Fine Arts, NY Univ, 54-73, assoc prof, Univ Col, 67-70, prof, 70-73, chmn, Dept Fine Arts, 67-73, DEAN GRAD SCH ARTS & SCI, BRYN MAWR COL, 73-, In charge census of antique works of art known to Renaissance artists, Warburg Inst, Univ London, 49-, planning grant, Archit Ecol, 71; panelist educ progs, Nat Endowment for Humanities, 72-, mem, Nat Bd Consult, 74-; bd mem, Grad Record Exam, 76-80, exec comt chmn, Serv Comt, 77-80, pres, Asn Pa Grad Deans, 77-78; adj prof fine arts, New York Univ, 81-82. **MEMBERSHIPS** Am Inst Archaeol; Col Art Asn Am; Victorian Soc in Am; Am Mycol Asn; Northeast Asn Grad Schs (pres-elect, 77-78, pres, 79-80); Renaissance Soc Am. **RESEARCH** Relationships between Renaissance and antique art; late antique art and thought; history of city planning. **SELECTED PUBLICATIONS** Auth, Sculptures in Rome Palazzo-Albertoni-Spinola and the Paluzzi and Altieri Collections--Italian, Amer Jour Archaeol, Vol 0101, 97; The Antiquarian and the Myth of Antiquity--The Origins of Rome in Renaissance Thought, Amer Jour Archaeol, Vol 0099, 95. **CONTACT ADDRESS** 29 Simpson Rd, Ardmore, PA, 19003.

BOBINSKI, GEORGE SYLVAN
PERSONAL Born 10/24/1929, Cleveland, OH, m, 1953, 2 children **DISCIPLINE** LIBRARY/INFORMATION SCIENCE, HISTORY **EDUCATION** Case Western Univ, BA, 51, MLS, 55; Univ of Mich, MA, 61, PhD, 66. **CAREER** Ref asst, Cleveland Pub Libr, 54-55; asst dir, Royal Oak Pub Libr, 55-59; dir of libraries, SUNY Col at Cortland, NY, 60-67; asst dean/assoc prof, Sch of Libr Sci, Univ of Ky, 67-70; DEAN and PROF, SCH of INFOR AND LIBR STUDIES, UNIV at BUFFALO, 70-. **HONORS AND AWARDS** Beta Phi Mu Int Libr Sci Hon Soc; Fulbright Sch Lectr, Univ of Warsaw, 77; Vis Sch, Jagiellonian Univ-Krakow, 92, 97; Meritorious Medal, 97. **MEMBERSHIPS** Am Libr Asn; Asn for Libr and Infor Sci Educ. **RESEARCH** History of Libraries; Library Education; Comparative Librarianship-Poland. **SELECTED PUBLICATIONS** auth, Carnegie Libraries: Their History and Impact on American Public Library Developments, ALA, 69; auth, Dictionary of American Library Biography, Libraries Unlimited, 78; auth, "The Golden Age of American Librarianship 1945-1970," Wilson Libr Bull, 84; ed, "Current and Future Trends in Library

and Information Science, " Libr Trends; auth, "Carnegie Libraries: Their Current and Future Status," Public Libraries, 92; "Libraries in the Democratic Process," Jagiellonian Press, 95. **CONTACT ADDRESS** Sch of Infor and Libr Studies, State Univ of NY, Buffalo, NY, 14260. **EMAIL** bobinski@acsu.buffalo.edu

BOCK, PHILIP K.
PERSONAL Born 08/26/1934, New York, NY, m, 1976, 3 children **DISCIPLINE** SOCIAL ANTHROPOLOGY **EDUCATION** Harvard Univ, PhD, 62. **CAREER** Asst prof to prof emer, Univ New Mexico, 62-92. **HONORS AND AWARDS** Woodrow Wilson Fel; Harvard Univ Fel; Danforth Fel; NSF and NEA awds; Univ New Mexico Pres Prof, 85-90. **MEMBERSHIPS** Am Anthrop Asn; Soc for Psychol Anthrop. **RESEARCH** Social anthropology; musicology; cognitive psychology; Shakespeare and Elizabethan culture. **SELECTED PUBLICATIONS** Auth, Shakespeare and Elizabethan Culture, Schocken, 84; auth,The Formal Content of Ethnography, International Museum of Cultures, 86; auth, Rethinking Psychological Anthropology, Freeman, 88; ed, and auth two chap, Handbook of Psychological Anthropology, Greenwood, 94. **CONTACT ADDRESS** Univ of New Mexico, Albuquerque, NM, 87131. **EMAIL** pbock@unm.edu

BOCK, ROBERT L.
PERSONAL Born 09/05/1925, Macksville, KS, d, 4 children **DISCIPLINE** POLITICAL SCIENCE **EDUCATION** Univ Kansas, AB, 48, BA, 53; Washburn, JD, 53; Amer Univ, PhD, 60. **CAREER** Prof, WNEC/Springfield, 68-. **MEMBERSHIPS** A Political Science Assn **CONTACT ADDRESS** 66 Holly St, Springfield, MA, 01151.

BOCK-WEISS, CATHERINE C.
DISCIPLINE ART HISTORY **EDUCATION** Cath Univ Am, MFA, 57; Univ CA, PhD, 77. **CAREER** Instr, Univ WI; prof, 77-. **HONORS AND AWARDS** Grant for res in Fr, Univ CA, LA Arts Coun. **SELECTED PUBLICATIONS** Auth, Henri Matisse and Neo-Impressionism, 1898-1908; Henri Matisse: A Guide to Research, 94. **CONTACT ADDRESS** Dept of Art Hist, Sch of the Art Inst of Chicago, 37 S Wabash Ave, Chicago, IL, 60603.

BODDEWYN, JEAN J.
PERSONAL Born 02/03/1929, Brussels, Belgium, m, 1979, 3 children **DISCIPLINE** MANAGEMENT AND STRATEGY, BUSINESS AND SOCIETY, AND MARKETING **EDUCATION** Univ Louvain, Belgium, commercial eng, 51; Univ Ore, MBA, 52; Univ Wash, PhD, Bus Admin. **CAREER** Galeries Anspach, Belgian dept store, market res and systems anal, 52-55; Jantzen Inc, time and motion study, 55-57; Univ Portland Ore, asst prof bus admin, 57-64; NY Univ, full prof of intl bus, 64-73; Baruch Col CUNY, full prof of intl bus, 73-. **HONORS AND AWARDS** Fulbright scholar, 51-52; fel, Acad of Mgt, 74; fel, Acad of Intl Bus, 80; fel, Intl Acad Mgt, 81. **MEMBERSHIPS** Acad Intl Bus; Acad Mgt; Europ Intl Bus Acad; Intl Asn for Bus and Soc. **RESEARCH** International regulation and self-regulation of advertising; International standardization of marketing policies; Political behavior of business firms at home and abroad. **SELECTED PUBLICATIONS** Auth, Global Perspectives on Advertising Self-Regulation, Westport, CT, Quorum Books, 92; Advertising Self-Regulation and Outside Participation: A Multinational 12-country Comparison, Westport, CT, Quorum Books, 88; papers in prof jour, American Marketing in the European Union: Standardization's Uneven Progress in 1973-1993, with Robert Grosse, Europ Jour of Marketing, 29, 12, 23-42, 95; The Legitimacy of International-Business Political Behavior, The Intl Trade Jour, 9, 1, 143-161, spring, 95; International-Business Political Behavior: New Theoretical Dimensions, with Th. J. Brewer, Acad of Mgt Rev, 19, 1, 119-143, 94; articles, Cigarette Advertising Bans and Cigarette Consumption: The Flawed Policy Connection, Intl Jour of Advert, 13, 4, 325-345, 94; The Taxation of Advertising: A Review of Current Issues, Jour of Current Issues & Res in Advert, 16, 1, 1-13, spring, 94; chapters in books, Is International Business a Distinct Field of Inquiry?, in B. Toyne and D. W. Nigh, International Business: Institutions and the Dissemination of Knowledge, Columbia, SC, Univ SC Press, 17-23, 97; The Conceptual Domain of International Business: Territory, Boundaries, and Levels, in B. Toyne and D. W. Nigh, International Business Inquiry: An Emerging Vision, Columbia, SC, Univ SC Press, 50-61, 101-102, 97; Political Resources and Markets in International Business: Beyond Porter's Generic Strategies, in A. M. Rugman and A. Verbeke, Global Competition: Beyond the Three Generics, Research in Global Strategic Management, vol 4, Greenwich, CT, JAI Press, 83-99, 93. **CONTACT ADDRESS** 372 Fifth Ave., Apt 9K, New York, NY, 10018.

BODE, FREDERICK AUGUST
PERSONAL Born 12/12/1940, Geneva, IL, m, 1971, 1 child **DISCIPLINE** HISTORY **EDUCATION** Univ Calif, Los Angeles, BA, 62; Yale Univ, MA, 63, PhD(hist), 69. **CAREER** Instr hist, Univ NC, Chapel Hill, 67-70; asst prof, 70-73, ASSOC PROF HIST, CONCORDIA UNIV, 73- **MEMBERSHIPS** AHA; Orgn Am Historians; Southern Hist Asn; Econ Hist Asn. **RESEARCH** United States social history, antebellum United States south. **CONTACT ADDRESS** Dept of Hist, Concordia Univ, Montreal, Montreal, PQ, H3G 1M8.

BODEL, JOHN
PERSONAL Born 01/25/1957, Sharon, CT, m, 1979, 2 children **DISCIPLINE** CLASSICS **EDUCATION** Princeton Univ, BA, 78; Univ Mich, MA, 79, PhD, 84. **CAREER** Asst dir, 83, co dir, 91, 95, Am Acad Rome; asst prof to assoc prof, 84-92; Harvard Univ; vist asst prof, Brown Univ, 92-93; dir to assoc prof to chemn to prof, 94-, Rutgers Univ. **HONORS AND AWARDS** NEH Res Fel, 93; Fel, 82-83, trustee, 99-01, Am Acad Rome; Pres, Am Society of Greek and Latin Epigraphy, 98-00; Dir, US Epigraphy Project, 95-. **RESEARCH** Latin epigraphy; Latin literature; Roman history. **SELECTED PUBLICATIONS** Auth, Roman Brick Stamps in the Kelsey Museum, 83; auth, Graveyards and Groves: A Study of the Lex Lucerina, 94; auth, art, Chronology and Succession 2: Notes on Some Consular Lists on Stone, 95; auth, art, Monumental Villas and Villa Monuments, 97; coauth, Greek and Latin Inscriptions in the USA: A Checklist, 97. **CONTACT ADDRESS** Dept of Classics, Rutgers Univ, 131 George St, New Brunswick, NJ, 08901-1414. **EMAIL** bodel@rci.rutgers.edu

BODLING, KURT A.
DISCIPLINE HISTORICAL THEOLOGY, LIBRARY SCIENCE **EDUCATION** Concordia Col, AA, 74; Concordia Sen Col, BA, 76; Concordia Sem, MDiv, 80, MST, 86; Univ Ill, MS; Fordham Univ, PhD cand. **CAREER** Ref, res asst, 81-86; asst dir, ref svcs, 86-87, Concordia Hist Inst; free-lance ed, Concordia Pub, 88-89; assoc lib, Winterthur Mus, 90-91; dean, spiritual life, 95-96, COL ARCH, 93- , asst prof, 91-98, ASSOC PROF, RELIG, 98-, DIR LIBR SVCS, 91-, CONCORDIA COL. **CONTACT ADDRESS** 214 Midland Ave, Tuchahoe, NY, 10707-4308.

BODNAR, JOHN EDWARD
PERSONAL Born 05/19/1944, m, 1968, 2 children **DISCIPLINE** AMERICAN SOCIAL HISTORY, PUBLIC HISTORY **EDUCATION** John Carroll Univ, BA, 66 MA, 68; Univ Conn, PhD, 74. **CAREER** Chief historian, Pa Hist Mus Comn, 71-81; Assoc Prof, 81-85, prof hist, Ind Univ, 85-, Chair, Dept Hist, 97-; Adj Prof Am studies, Pa State Univ, Middletown, 74-80; selected speaker, Int Hist Congr, Bucharest, 80. **HONORS AND AWARDS** Res grant Rockefeller Found, 75 & Am Coun Learned Soc, 76; Beveridge grant, AHA, 81; Guggenheim Fel, 83-84; Fulbright Chair, Europ Univ Inst, Florence, Italy, 94. **MEMBERSHIPS** Orgn Am Historians; Immigration Hist Soc; AHA. **RESEARCH** American immigration and labor history; public history. **SELECTED PUBLICATIONS** Ed, Ethnic Experience in Pennsylvania, Bucknell Univ, 73; auth, Materialism and Morality: Slavic Americans and Education, J Ethnic Studies, 76; Immigration and Modernization: Slavic Peasants in Industrial America, J Soc Hist, 76; Immigration and Industrialization: Ethnicity in an American Mill Town, Univ Pittsburgh, 77; Migration, Kinship and Urban Adjustment: Blacks & Poles in Pittsburgh, J Am Hist, 79; Immigration, Kinship, and the Rise of Working-Class Realism, J Social Hist, 80; coauth, Lives of Their Own: Blacks, Italians, and Poles in Pittsburgh, Univ Ill, 82; Workers' World: Kinship, Community and Protest in an Industrial Society, Johns Hopkins, 82; auth, The Transplanted: A History of Immigrants in Urban America, Ind, 85; Remaking America: Public Memory, Commemoration, and Patriotism, Princeton, 92; ed, Bonds of Affection: Americans Define Their Patriotism, Princeton, 96; auth, Generational Memory in an American Town, J Interdisciplinary Hist, 96. **CONTACT ADDRESS** Dept of Hist, Indiana Univ, Bloomington, Bloomington, IN, 47405. **EMAIL** bodnar@indiana.edu

BOEGEHOLD, ALAN
PERSONAL Born 03/21/1927, Detroit, MI, m, 1954, 2 children **DISCIPLINE** CLASSICS **EDUCATION** Univ MI, AB, 50; Harvard Univ, AM, 54, PhD, 58. **CAREER** Instr, asst prof dept classics, Champaign-Urbana, 57-60; from asst prof to prof dept classics, Brown Univ, 60; dir summer session Amer Sch Classical Studies Athens, 63, 64, 74, 80, vis prof, 68-69; dir Ancient studies program Brown Univ, 85-91, chmn dept classics, 66-71, acting chmn, 73-74; visiting lectr hist Harvard Univ, 67; visiting prof classics Yale Univ, 71, Univ CA, Berkeley, 78; mem com to evaluate dept classics Swarthmore Coll, 72, Univ VA, 82, 88, coms humanities and hist Yale Univ Coun, 82-87; interim pres, vp and sec Nargansett Soc Archaeol Inst Am; vice chmn mng com Am Sch Classical Studies,85-90, chmn, 90-. **HONORS AND AWARDS** Thomas Day Seymour fel Amer Sch Classical Studies Athens, 55-56; Rsch fel, 74-75; Rsch fel Agora Excavations, 80-81; Charles Eliot Norton fel Amer Sch Classical Sudies Athens; Howard fel, 56-57; grantee Amer Coun Learned Socs, 80-81. **MEMBERSHIPS** Active ACLU; Amnesty Internat; Providence Athenaeum; Mass Audubon Soc; Common Cause **SELECTED PUBLICATIONS** Ed, Athenian Identity and Civic Ideology, 93; auth, ed, Agora XXVIII, Law Courts at Athens, 95 **CONTACT ADDRESS** Dept of Classics, Brown Univ, 48 College Hill St, Providence, RI, 02912-9079.

BOEGER, PALMER HENRY
PERSONAL Born 03/27/1919, Plymouth, WI, m, 1957, 2 children **DISCIPLINE** UNITED STATES & MODERN EUROPEAN HISTORY **EDUCATION** Univ Wis, BS, 41, PhM, 42, PhD(hist), 53. **CAREER** Instr US & mod Europ hist, Exten Div, Univ Wis, 48-49, Exten Ctr, Milwaukee, 49-51; assoc prof US hist, 53-57, prof hist, E Cent State Col, 57-, chemn dept hist & govt, 62-; US Nat Park Service ranger/interpretor, summers, 69-94. **MEMBERSHIPS** Orgn Am Historians; Southern Hist Asn. **RESEARCH** United States Civil War army supply; the war and American industrial development; teaching history via television. **SELECTED PUBLICATIONS** Auth, Hardtack and burned beans, Civil War Hist, 3/58; The great Kentucky hog swindle, J Southern Hist, 2/62; General Burnside's Knoxville Packing Project, E Tenn Hist Soc Publ, 63; From Platt NP to Chickasaw NRA, Western Heritage Press, 87. **CONTACT ADDRESS** Dept of History, East Central Univ, 1100 E 14th St, Ada, OK, 74820-6999.

BOEHLING, REBECCA
DISCIPLINE HISTORY **EDUCATION** Univ WI Madison, PhD. **CAREER** Assoc prof, Univ MD Baltimore County. **RESEARCH** Europ hist; Ger Am rel(s); Ger women in the postwar era. **SELECTED PUBLICATIONS** Auth, A Question of Priorities: Democratic Reforms and Economic Recovery in Postwar Germany. **CONTACT ADDRESS** Dept of Hist, Univ MD Baltimore County, Hilltop Circle, PO Box 1000, Baltimore, MD, 21250. **EMAIL** boehling@research.umbc.edu

BOERSMA, HANS
PERSONAL Born 05/03/1961, Urk, Netherlands, m, 1984, 5 children **DISCIPLINE** HISTORICAL SOCIETY **EDUCATION** State Univ of Utrecht, ThD, 93. **CAREER** Pastor, 94-98. **HONORS AND AWARDS** MTh, Univ of Utrecht with high honors. **MEMBERSHIPS** SBL; ETS; Calvin Theol Soc. **RESEARCH** History of Doctrine, Justification, Historical Jesus, Worldview Studies. **SELECTED PUBLICATIONS** Auth, The Life of Jeremiah, Eating God's Words, Study Guide, RevelationSeries, Grand Rapids, CRC Pub, 98; The Weak and the Strong, Koinwnja, 95; A Hot Pepper Corn: Richard Baxter's Doctrine of Justification in Its Seventeenth-Century Context of Controversy, Zoetermeer: Boekencentrum, 93; review, The Origins of the Federal Theology in Sixteenth-Century Reformation Thought, by David A. Weir, Evangelical Quarterly, 93, Jesus and the Victory of God, Christian Origins and the Question of God, by NT Wright, Calvin Theo J, 97; Clavinism, Authentic Calvinism, A Clarification, by Alan C. Clifford, Westminster Theo J, 96. **CONTACT ADDRESS** 20571 49A Ave, Langley, BC, V3A 5T. **EMAIL** boersma@universe.com

BOGGER, TOMMY L.
PERSONAL Born 05/07/1944, Williamsburg, VA, 1 child **DISCIPLINE** SOUTHERN & AFRO-AMERICAN HISTORY **EDUCATION** Norfolk State Col, BA, 68; Carnegie-Mellon Univ, MA, 69; Univ Va, PhD(hist), 76. **CAREER** From instr to asst prof, 69-76, ASSOC PROF HIST, NORFOLK STATE COL, 76- **MEMBERSHIPS** Asn Study Afro-Am Life & Hist; Southern Hist Asn. **RESEARCH** The free Black community; Black families. **SELECTED PUBLICATIONS** Auth, Witness To Injustice, Jour of So Hist, Vol 0063, 97. **CONTACT ADDRESS** Norfolk State Col, 2401 Corprew Ave, Norfolk, VA, 23504-3993.

BOGIN, RUTH
PERSONAL New York, NY **DISCIPLINE** AMERICAN HISTORY **EDUCATION** Univ Wis, BA, 41; Sarah Lawrence Col, MA, 65; Union Grad Sch, PhD(Am hist), 78. **CAREER** Assoc hist, Sarah Lawrence Col, 65-70; ADJ PROF HIST, PACE UNIV, 65-, Vis asst prof, NY Univ, summer, 80; res fel, Nat Endowment for Humanities, 80-81. **MEMBERSHIPS** Inst Res Hist; Orgn Am Historians; AHA; Am Studies Asn; Soc Historians Early Am Repub. **RESEARCH** History of the American Revolutionary era; history of women, particularly black women; egalitarianism. **SELECTED PUBLICATIONS** Auth, Race and Revolution, William and Mary Quart, Vol 0051, 94. **CONTACT ADDRESS** 3 Brook Lane, Great Neck, NY, 11023.

BOGUE, ALLAN G.
PERSONAL Born 05/12/1921, London, ON, Canada, m, 1950, 3 children **DISCIPLINE** AMERICAN HISTORY **EDUCATION** Univ Western Ont, BA, 43, MA, 46; Cornell Univ, PhD, 51. **CAREER** Lectr econ & hist & asst librn, Univ Western Ont, 49-52; from asst prof to prof hist, Univ Iowa, 52-64, chmn dept, 59-63; prof hist, 64-68, chmn dept, 72-73, FREDERICK JACKSON TURNER PROF HIST, UNIV WIS-MADISON, 68-, Soc Sci Res Coun fel, 55 & 66; mem hist adv comt, Math Soc Sci Bd, 65-71; Scand-Am Found Thord-Gray lectr, 68; Guggenheim fel, 70; mem, Coun Inter-Univ Consortium Polit Res, 71-73; vis prof hist, Harvard Univ, 72; dir, Soc Sci Res Coun, 73-76; Sherman Fairchild distinguished fel, Calif Inst Technol, 75. **HONORS AND AWARDS** LLD, Univ Western Ont, 73; DFil, Univ Uppsala, 77. **MEMBERSHIPS** Agr Hist Soc (pres, 63-64); Orgn Am Historians (pres, 82-83); AHA; Econ Hist Asn (pres, 81-82); Soc Sci Hist Asn (pres, 77-78). **RESEARCH** Nineteenth century American economic and political history; the American West. **SELECTED PUBLICATIONS** Auth, Fundamental Development of the Social-Sciences--Rockefeller Philanthropy and the US Soc-Sci Res Coun, Jour Interdisciplinary Hist, Vol 0026, 95; Americans--A Collision of Histories, Jour Interdisciplinary Hist, Vol 0028, 97; Designing Social Inquiry--Sci Inference In Qualitative Res, Jour Interdisciplinary Hist, Vol 0026, 96; Dry Farming In The Northern Great-Plains, Years Of Readjustment, 1920-1990--

Hargreaves,Mwm, W Hist Quart, Vol 0024, 93; The Senate, 1789-1989--Addresses on the History of the United-States-Senate, Vol 2, Pub Hist, Vol 0017, 95; Agricult Hist, Agricult Hist, Vol 0067, 93; Under Western Skies-Nature and History in the American-West, Pacific Hist Rev, Vol 0062, 93; The End of American Exceptionalism--Frontier Anxiety From the Old West to the New-Deal, Pacific Hist Rev, Vol 0063, 94; The Senate, 1789-1989--Addresses on the History of the United-States-Senate, Vol 1, Pub Historian, Vol 0017, 95; The Significance of the History Of The American West--Postscripts and Prospects, W Hist Quart, Vol 0024, 93; Trails--Toward a New Western History, Pacific Northwest Quart, Vol 0084, 93; Quantitative Methods For Historians--A Guide to Research, Data, And Statistics, Jour Amer Hist, Vol 0080, 94; Atlas of Historical County Boundaries, Jour Amer Hist, Vol 0081, 95; Atlas of Historical County Boundaries--Mississippi, Jour Amer Hist, Vol 0081, 95; Quantitative Studies In Agrarian History, Jour Econ Hist, Vol 0054, 94; Old-West, New-Wes--Quo-Vadis, Pacific Hist Rev, Vol 0065, 96. **CONTACT ADDRESS** Univ Wis, 1914 Vilas Ave, Madison, WI, 53711.

BOHNSTEDT, JOHN WOLFGANG
PERSONAL Born 02/22/1927, Berlin, Germany, m, 1948, 2 children **DISCIPLINE** HISTORY **EDUCATION** Mich State Col, BA, 50; Univ Minn, MA, 52, PhD(hist), 59. **CAREER** Instr Europ hist, Univ SDak, 55-56; from instr to assoc prof, 56-68, PROF HIST, CALIF STATE UNIV, FRESNO, 68-, Am Philos Soc res grant, Harvard Univ, 65; res grants, Calif State Univ, Fresno, 65-67. **HONORS AND AWARDS** Distinguished Teaching Award, Fresno State Col, 66. **MEMBERSHIPS** AHA. **RESEARCH** History of Germany in the nineteenth and twentieth centuries; global aspects of European history in the nineteenth and twentieth centuries; German ideas concerning the Turkish menace in the Reformation era. **SELECTED PUBLICATIONS** Auth, The Infidel Scourge of God: The Turkish Menace as Seen by German Pamphleteers of the Reformation Era, Am Philos Soc, 68. **CONTACT ADDRESS** Dept of History, California State Univ, Fresno, 5340 N Campus Dr, Fresno, CA, 93740-0021. **EMAIL** john_bohnstedt@csufresno.edu

BOHSTEDT, JOHN HOWARD
PERSONAL Born 09/28/1943, Des Moines, IA, m, 1988, 2 children **DISCIPLINE** MODERN BRITISH HISTORY **EDUCATION** Cornell Col, BA, 64; Oxford Univ, BA, 66, MA, 70; Harvard Univ, PhD(mod hist), 72. **CAREER** Leverhulme vis fel, Stirling Univ, Scotland, 72-73; asst prof hist, Harvard Univ, 73-79; Asoc Prof Hist, Univ Tenn, 79-, Assoc Head Hist Dept, 93-; Interviewer, Grad Fel Prog, Danforth Found, 75-80. **HONORS AND AWARDS** Rhodes Scholarships; Phi Beta Kappa; Vis Fel, Dept Econ Hist, Univ Liverpool; LR Hesler Award for Excellence in Teaching and Service; Am Coun of Learned Soc, Grant in aid, 80; Harry Frank Guggenheim Res Grant, 88-89; Convenor, Res Planning Group, Coun for Europ Studies, Columbia Univ, grant, 92-95; Brit Acad Vis Fel, Summer 93; Principal Investigator, NEH Collaborative Res Grant, 93-96: Social Protest and the Politics of Provisions in Britain, France, Germany, 1750-1850; Alexander von Humboldt-Stiftung grant, 94-97. **MEMBERSHIPS** AHA; Econ Hist Soc; Soc Sci Hist Asn. **RESEARCH** Riots; popular culture; labor history. **SELECTED PUBLICATIONS** Auth, The politics of riot and food relief in England during the Industrial Revolution, Proc of the Tenth Consortium on Revolutionary Europe, 80; contribr, An Atlas of Rural Protest in England, 1549-1800, Croom Helm, 82; auth, Riots and Community Politics in England and Wales 1790-1810, Harvard Univ Press, 83; coauth, The Diffusion of Riots: The Patterns of 1766, 1795, and 1801 in Devonshire, J Interdisciplinary Hist, Summer 88; auth, Gender, Household, and Community Politics: Women in English Riots, 1790-1810, Past and Present, 8/88; The Myth of the Feminine Food Riot: Women as Proto-Citizens in English Community Politics, 1790-1810, In: Women and Politics in the Age of Democratic Revolution, Univ Mich Press, 90; More than One Working Class: Protestant-Catholic Riots in Edwardian Liverpool, In: Popular Politics, Riot, and Labour: Essays in Liverpool History 1790-1940, Liverpool Univ Press, 92; The Moral Economy and the Discipline of Historical Context, J Soc Hist, Winter 92; The Dynamics of Riots: Escalation and Diffusion/Contagion, In: The Dynamics of Aggression: Biological and Social Processes in Dyads and Groups, Lawrence Erlbaum Assoc, 94; The Pragmatic Economy, The Politics of Provisions, and the 'Invention' of the Food Riot Tradition in 1740, In: Festschrift, Macmillan (forthcoming 98). **CONTACT ADDRESS** Dept of History, Univ of Tennessee, 915 Volunteer Blvd, Knoxville, TN, 37996-4065.

BOIRE, GARY
DISCIPLINE EARLY ROMAN IMPERIAL HISTORY **EDUCATION** Loyola, BA; McMaster, MA, PhD. **CAREER** Prof **SELECTED PUBLICATIONS** Auth, Morley Callaghan: Literary Anarchist, 94; Tribunalations: George Ryga's Postcolonial Trial Play; Inside Out: Prison Theatre from Australia, Canada, and New Zealand; Wide-Wasting Pest: Social History in The Vanity of Human Wishes; Canadian Twink: Surviving the Whiteouts. **CONTACT ADDRESS** Dept of English, Wilfrid Laurier Univ, 75 University Ave W, Waterloo, ON, N2L 3C5. **EMAIL** gboire@mach1.wlu.cas

BOKER, HANS J.
PERSONAL Born 03/30/1953, Dalhausen, Germany, m, 1994 **DISCIPLINE** ART HISTORY **EDUCATION** Univ Saarbrucken, PhD, 79. **CAREER** Univ Hanover Germany, asst prof, 82-88; Ruhr-Universitat Bocham Germany, prof, 88-89; McGill Univ, prof, 89-. **MEMBERSHIPS** SAH, SFd'A **RESEARCH** Medieval Architecture. **SELECTED PUBLICATIONS** Auth, Idensen: Architekur und Ausmalung einer romanischen Hofkapelle, Berlin: Gebr Mann, 95; coauth, Respiciendo et prospiciendo: Allegories of Architecture and Sculpture on the Frontispieces of Leoni's Editions of Palladio and Alberti, in; Architecture and the Emblem, Montreal: McGill- Queens Univ Press, forthcoming; auth, Cologne Cathedral, Intl Dict Architects and Architecture, Bd 2: Architecture, ed. R. van Vynckt, Chicago: St James Press, 93; auth, The Bishops Chapel at Hereford and the Question of Architectural Copies in the Middle Ages, Gesta, 98; auth, Per Grecos Operarios: Die Bartholomauskapelle in Paderborn und ihr Byzantinisches Vorbild, Niederdeutsche Beitrage zur Kunstgeschichte, 97; auth, Ein heiliger Georg aus Soest? Zur Deutung der Patroklusstatue in Munster, Soester Zeitschrift, 96. **CONTACT ADDRESS** Dept of Art History, McGill Univ, 853 Sherbrooke St W, Montreal, PQ, H3A 2T6. **EMAIL** boker@leacock.lan.mcgill.ca

BOKINA, JOHN
PERSONAL Born 01/06/1948, Chicago, IL, m, 1982, 1 child **DISCIPLINE** POLITICAL THEORY **EDUCATION** Univ Ill-Chicago, AB, 70; MA, 72; Univ Ill-Urbana, PhD, 79. **CAREER** Vis asst prof, inst, asst prof, Univ Detroit, 76-81; Honors Prog Dir, 77-80; asst prof, asoc prof, prof, Univ Tex, 82- . **HONORS AND AWARDS** Pi Sigma Alpha - Polit Sci Asoc Fac Member of the Year, 80-81; NEH Fel for Col Teachers, 81-82; UTPA Distinguished Fac Achievement Awards, 86, 97. **MEMBERSHIPS** PSA; Int PSA; Midwest PSA; Am Hist Asoc; Caucus for New Polit Sci; Conf Group on German Pol; Found of Pol Theory Group; German Studies Asoc. **RESEARCH** History of modern and contemporary political theory; politics of art and mass culture. **SELECTED PUBLICATIONS** Auth, Holocaust at Mount Carmel, Telos, 95; auth, Eros and Revolution: Henze's Bassarids, The Europ Legacy, 96; auth, Viennese Hysteria-Clinical and Operatic, Vienna: The World of Yesterday, 1889-1914, 97; auth, Opera and Politics: From Monteverdi to Henze, 97; auth, Herbert Mancuse, 99. **CONTACT ADDRESS** 303 Austin Blvd., Edinburg, TX, 78539. **EMAIL** JB83E8@panam.edu

BOLCHAZY, LADISLAUS J.
PERSONAL Born 06/07/1937, Slovakia, m, 1965, 1 child **DISCIPLINE** CLASSICS AND PHILOSOPHY **EDUCATION** St. Joseph's Col & Sem, NY, BA, philos, 63; NY Univ, MS, classics, 67; SUNY Albany, PhD, classics, 73. **CAREER** Latin/eng, Iona Prep, 64-65; Latin/eng, Sacred Heart High Sch, 62-64; instr, Siena Col, 66-67; asst prof, La Salette Col and Sem, 71-75; visiting asst prof, Millersville State Univ, 75-76; visiting asst prof, Loyola Univ of Chicago, 76-77; adjunct prof, Loyola Univ of Chicago, 79-; pres, Bolchazy-Carducci Publ Inc. **HONORS AND AWARDS** NEH summer inst, ancient hist, Univ Mich, 77; NEH summer sem, Sophocles and Thucydides, Cornell Univ, 76; teaching fel, State Univ of NY Albany, 67-71; res grants, Loyola Univ, spring and summer, 77. **MEMBERSHIPS** Amer Philol Asn. **RESEARCH** History of ethical & theological concepts; Stylometric analysis of language. **SELECTED PUBLICATIONS** Auth, Hospitality in Antiquity, Ares Publ, Chicago, 96; auth, A Concordance to Ausonius, George Olms, Hildesheim, 83; auth, The Coin-Iscriptions and Epigraphical Abbreviations of Imperial Rome, Ares Publ, 78; auth, A Concordance to the Utopia of St. Thomas More, Georg Olms, Hildesheim, 78; auth, Hospitality in Early Rome, Ares Publ, Chicago, 77. **CONTACT ADDRESS** Ladislaus J. Bolchazy, PhD, Bolchazy-Carducci Publishers, Inc., 1000 Brown St., No 101, Unit 101, Wauconda, IL, 60084. **EMAIL** classics@bolchazy.com

BOLES, JOHN BRUCE
PERSONAL Born 10/20/1943, Houston, TX, m, 1967, 2 children **DISCIPLINE** UNITED STATES HISTORY **EDUCATION** Rice Univ, BA, 65; Univ Va, PhD(hist), 69. **CAREER** From asst prof to prof, Towson State Col, 69-71; vis assoc prof, Rice Univ, 77-78; assoc prof, 78-80, prof hist, Tulane Univ, 80-81; PROF HIST, RICE UNIV, 81-, Bk rev ed, Md Hist Mag, 71-; ed, 75-77; Nat Endowmwnt for Humanities fel Anthrop, Johns Hopkins Univ, 76-77; actg ed, J Southern Hist, 77-78; assoc ed, J Southern Hist, 81- **MEMBERSHIPS** Orgn Am Historians; Southern Hist Asn. **RESEARCH** United States religious and cultural history; Southern history; US slavery. **SELECTED PUBLICATIONS** Auth, The New Southern History, Miss Quart, Vol 0045, 92; Taking Up Serpents--Snake Handlers of E Ky, Amer Hist Rev, Vol 0102, 97; Under Their Own Vine and Fig Tree--The African-American Church in the South, 1865-1900, Civil War Hist, Vol 0041, 95; Early American Methodism, Pa Mag Hist and Biog, Vol 0117, 93.ü **CONTACT ADDRESS** Dept of Hist, Rice Univ, New Orleans, LA, 70118.

BOLGER, FRANCIS W.P.
PERSONAL Born 07/08/1925, Stanley Bridge, PE, Canada **DISCIPLINE** HISTORY **EDUCATION** St Dunstan's Univ, BA, 47; Univ Montreal, STL, 51; Univ Toronto, MA, 56, PhD, 59. **CAREER** Diocese Charlottetown, 51-; assoc pastor, St. Dunstan's Basilica, Charlottetown, 51-53; prof, St. Dunstan's Univ, 59-69; prof, 69-94, PROF EMER HISTORY, UNIV PEI, 94-; chaplain, Air Force Reserve, 54-60; USSO Off, RCAF, 60-67. **HONORS AND AWARDS** Islander Year, 74; Award excellence tchg, Univ PEI, 86-87; PEI Model Educ Prize, 90; mem, Order Can, 95; Int Rotary Paul Harris fel, 97., O. Roman Cath priest, 1951 **MEMBERSHIPS** Can Cath Hist Asn (pres, 64, pres-gen, 65); PEI rep, Hist Sites & Monuments Can, 66-78, 90-; chmn, Lucy Maud Montgomery Found Bd, 80. **RESEARCH** PEI history & literature; L.M. Montgomery. **SELECTED PUBLICATIONS** Auth, PEI and Confederation 1863-1873, 64; auth, The Years Before Anne, 74; coauth, Spirit of Place, 82; coauth, Memories of the Old Home Place, 84; ed, Canada's Smallest Province, 73; co-ed, My Dear Mr. M.: Letters of L.M. Montgomery to G.B. Macmillan, 80. **CONTACT ADDRESS** Dept of History, Univ of Prince Edward Island, Charlottetown, PE, C1A 1A1.

BOLIN, JOHN SEELYE
PERSONAL Born 09/20/1943, Ft Bragg, NC, m, 1965, 1 child **DISCIPLINE** DRAMATIC LITERATURE, THEATRE HISTORY **EDUCATION** Kalamazoo Col, BA, 65; Univ MI, Ann Arbor, MA, 65, PhD, 70. **CAREER** Asst prof theatre, 70, prof eng & theatre ,Berea Col, 70, dir repertory theatre festival, 81-83, Assoc dean Gen Educ, 89-94, Dean Fac, 98-; Mellon Found, Berea Col, Sabbatical fel, 77-78. **HONORS AND AWARDS** Kellog Nat Fel, 83-86; Canadian Embassy, Fac Res Grant, 94-95. **MEMBERSHIPS** AAUP; William Morris Soc; Asn Canadian Studies in U S; Midwestern Asn canadian Studies; KY Hum Coun, bd mem,, Asn Am Col and Univ, 94-98. **RESEARCH** Theatre aesthetics; theatre hist; criticism of drama. **SELECTED PUBLICATIONS** Auth, var rev & articles on Canadian Theatre and drama. **CONTACT ADDRESS** Dept of Eng, Berea Col, 101 Chestnut St, Berea, KY, 40404-0003. **EMAIL** john_bolin@berea.edu

BOLL, MICHAEL MITCHEL
PERSONAL Born 03/03/1938, Antigo, WI, m, 1960, 2 children **DISCIPLINE** SOVIET & MODERN EUROPEAN HISTORY **EDUCATION** Univ Wis-Madison, BS, 61, MS, 65, PhD(soviet hist), 70. **CAREER** Instr Soviet hist, Ripon Col, 66-68; Soviet analyst, Radio Free Europe, Munich, 68-69; foreign serv officer soviet affairs, US Info Agency, Washington DC, 70; asst prof, 70-74, assoc prof, 75-80, PROF SOVIET HIST, SAN JOSE STATE UNIV, 80- **MEMBERSHIPS** Am Asn Advan Slavic Studies; AHA. **RESEARCH** The militia and Red Guard in the Russian revolutions; the evolution of Soviet policy toward East Europe in the 70's; contemporary Soviet foreign affairs. **SELECTED PUBLICATIONS** Auth, Buildup--The Politics of Defense in the Reagan Era, Amer Hist Rev, Vol 0098, 93. **CONTACT ADDRESS** Dept of Hist, San Jose State Univ, 1 Washington Sq, San Jose, CA, 95192-0001.

BOLLAND, O. NIGEL
PERSONAL Born 09/18/1943, Great Britain, m, 1966, 2 children **DISCIPLINE** SOCIOLOGY **EDUCATION** Hull, BA, 66; McMaster, MA, 67; Hull, PhD, 76. **CAREER** Res fel, Inst of Soc and Econ Res, Univ West Indies, Jamaica, 68-72; PROF, COLGATE UNIV, 72- . **HONORS AND AWARDS** NEM Fellowship, 94. **MEMBERSHIPS** Soc for Caribbean Studies; Caribbean Studies Asoc; Asoc of Caribbean Hist. **RESEARCH** Colonialism and labor in the Caribbean and Central America. **SELECTED PUBLICATIONS** auth, Belize: A New Nation in Central America, 86; Colonialism and Resistance in Belize: Essays in Historical Sociology, 88; Colonialism y resistencia en Belice: Ensayos de sociologia historia, 92; On the March: Labour Rebellions in the British Caribbean, 1934-39, 95; Struggles for Freedom: Essays on Slavery, Colonialism, and Culture in the Caribbean and Central America, 97. **CONTACT ADDRESS** Dept of Sociology and Anthropology, Colgate Univ, Hamilton, NY, 13346. **EMAIL** nbolland@mail.colgate.edu

BOLSTER, W. JEFFREY
DISCIPLINE HISTORY **EDUCATION** Johns Hopkins Univ, PhD. **CAREER** Asst prof, Univ NH, 91. **HONORS AND AWARDS** NEH fel; Nat Mus of Am Hist fel, Smithsonian; Paul Cuffe fel, Mystic Seaport Mus; Binkley-Stephenson Award, JAH; Louis Pelzer Mem Award, JAH; Hortense Cavis Shepherd prof, UNH, 95-98. **RESEARCH** African-American seafaring. **SELECTED PUBLICATIONS** Auth, 'To Feel Like a Man': Black Seamen in the Northern States, 1800-1860, J of Am Hist 76, 90; An Inner Diaspora: Black Sailors marking Selves, in Through a Glass Darkly: Reflections on Self in Early America, eds, Ronald Hoffman, et al, Omohundro Inst of Early Am Hist and Cult 97; Black Jacks: African American Seamen in the Age of Sail, 97. **CONTACT ADDRESS** History Dept., Univ NH, Durham, NH, 03824. **EMAIL** jbolster@christa.unh.edu

BOLSTERLI, MARGARET JONES
PERSONAL Born 05/10/1931, Watson, AR, 2 children **DISCIPLINE** ENGLISH, CULTURAL HISTORY **EDUCATION**

Univ Ark, BA, 53; Wash Univ, MA, 53; Univ Minn, PhD(English), 67. **CAREER** Asst prof English, Augsburg Col, 67-68; PROF ENGLISH, UNIV ARK, 68-, Nat Endowment Humanities Younger Humanist Award, 70-71; Ark Endowment Humanities grant, 80-81. **MEMBERSHIPS** MLA; SCent Mod Land Asn; Am Asn State & Local Hist. **RESEARCH** Nineteenth century Britain; the American south; women's studies. **SELECTED PUBLICATIONS** Auth, Porter,Katherine,Anne and Texas, Mod Fiction Stud, Vol 0038, 92; An Interview with Bolsterli,Margaret,Jones, Ark Hist Quart, Vol 0055, 96; Warren,Robert,Penn And The American Imagination--Mod Fiction Stud, Vol 0038, 92. **CONTACT ADDRESS** Dept of English, Univ of Ark, Fayetteville, AR, 72701.

BOLT, BRUCE A.
PERSONAL Born 02/15/1930, Australia, m, 1957, 4 children **DISCIPLINE** APPLIED MATH **EDUCATION** Univ Sydney, New Eng Univ Col, Aust, BSc honors, 52; Univ Sydney, Aust, MSc, 55, PhD, 59, DSc, 72. **CAREER** Univ California, Berkley, dept geol geophys, prof seism, 63-92, emeritus, 93-, dept civl eng, 88-92, dir seism stns, 63-89, chmn grad counc, 80-82, chmn, earthquake prepdns, 76-80, seismic rev comm, 88-91; Chancellors emerg pre task force, Univ Cal Berk, 90-; V ch Acad sen 92,93-, ch, acad sen, 93-; Univ Armenia, Yerevan, vis prof, 92; Cal Acad Sci, br trus, 81-92, pres, 82-85; Seismic Safety Comm, Commissioner, 78-93. **HONORS AND AWARDS** Ful Res sch, 60; fel, Am geophy unio, 67; fel, cal acad sci, 72; mem, us ant acad eng, 78; overseas fel, Churchill Col, 80; assoc royal astron soc, 87; fel medal, cal acad sci, 89; Harold Jefferies lectr, RASL, 91; Berkeley cit and fel, Univ Cal, Berk, 96. **MEMBERSHIPS** The Faculty Club, Pres, UCB; CUREe. **RESEARCH** Seismology; sci est **SELECTED PUBLICATIONS** Peak Strong Motion Attenuation Relations for Horizontal and Vertical Ground Displacements, J Earthquake Eng, with N J Gregor, 97; Discrimination of a Seismic Source Doublet in the Northridge, California Earthquake of 17 January 1994, with N J Gregor, J Seis, 97; From Earthquake Acceleration to Seismic Displacement, The Fifth Mallet_milne Lectr, SECD, John Wiley and Sons, 96; Earthquakes, W H Freeman, 87, rev 3d ed, 95; Seismic Wave Slowness-Vector Estimation from Broad-Band Array Data, Geo J Intl, with S J Chiou, 93. **CONTACT ADDRESS** Dept Geology Geophysics, Univ California, Mc Cone Hall, Berkeley, CA, 94720. **EMAIL** boltuc@socrates.berkely.edu

BOLT, ERNEST C., JR.
DISCIPLINE HISTORY **EDUCATION** Furman Univ, BA, 58; Univ GA, MA, 63, PhD, 66. **CAREER** Samuel Chiles Mitchell-Jacob Billikopf prof, 82-88 & reapp, 88 and 94, Univ Richmond; Univ Richmond, 66-; Furman Univ, 65 & 68; grad tchg asst, Univ GA, 61-66; consul on Boatwright Mem Libr, Univ Richmond, 69-74; dir, 4 proj Dept Hist, 84-87; ch, Dept Hist, 83-89 & interim ch, 66; dir, Univ Richmond Self-Study, 96-98. **HONORS AND AWARDS** Grant & co-dir, Libr-Fac Partnership Prog, 73-78, Nat Endowment Hum and the Coun on Libr Rsrc(s); Frederick Jackson Turner awd, 74; mem, Phi Kappa Phi; Phi Alpha Theta; Omicron Delta Kappa & Phi Beta Delta; Who's Who in the South and Southwest and Contemp Authors. **MEMBERSHIPS** Act dir, Va Baptist Hist Soc, 75-79; AHA, Southern Hist Asn, 73-74; Orgn Am Historians; Soc for Historians Am For Rel; Conf on Peace Res in Hist; past VP and sec local chap, AAUP; exec comt and pres several terms, VA Baptist Hist Socy; pres, Richmond Oral Hist Asn 76-78 & exec coun, Friends of Boatwright Mem Libr. **RESEARCH** Am diplomatic hist, 1919 to 1941 and since 1945; Am peace movement hist; Am biog; Vietnam War. **SELECTED PUBLICATIONS** Auth, Isolation, Expansion, and Peace: American Foreign Policy Between the Wars, chap 8, American Foreign Relations: A Historiographical Review, Greenwood Press, 81; Reluctant Belligerent: The Career of Louis L. Ludlow, chap 11, Their Infinite Variety: Essays on Indiana Politicians, Indiana Hist Bureau, 82; William McClannahan: Early Virginia Bi-Vocational Minister and His Family, The Virginia Baptist Register, 97; Samuel Chiles Mitchell 1864-1948, in Biog Dictionary of Internationalists, Greenwood Press, 83; rev(s) in, J Amer Hist, 75; J Southern Hist, 77, 95; Amer Hist Rev, 79, 84, 87, 89, 90; Hist Tchr, 83, 84, 86 & Histy: Rev(s) New Bk(s), 97. **CONTACT ADDRESS** Dept of Hist, Univ of Richmond, 28 Westhampton Way, Richmond, VA, 23173.

BOLT, ROBERT
PERSONAL Born 08/16/1930, Grand Rapids, MI, m, 1952, 5 children **DISCIPLINE** AMERICAN HISTORY **EDUCATION** Calvin Col, AB, 52; Univ Mich, AM, 53; Mich State Univ, PhD(hist), 63. **CAREER** Asst hist, Mich State Univ, 60-62; asst prof Am hist, Ill State Univ, 62-65; assoc prof, 65-73, PROF HIST, CALVIN COL, 73- **MEMBERSHIPS** AHA; Orgn Am Historians. **RESEARCH** Biographical study of Donald M Dickson; twentieth century American history; local history. **SELECTED PUBLICATIONS** Auth, Apologia--The Screenplay for Lean 'Lawrence of Arabia, Cineaste, Vol 0021, 95. **CONTACT ADDRESS** Dept of Hist, Calvin Col, Grand Rapids, MI, 49506.

BOLTON, LISSANT
DISCIPLINE CULTURAL HISTORY **EDUCATION** PhD **CAREER** Vis fel, Ctr Cross-Cult Res, Australian Natl Univ, 98. **RESEARCH** Women's cultural art; Vanuatu. **CONTACT ADDRESS** Dept of Education, Australian National Univ. **EMAIL** Lissant.Bolton@anu.edu.au

BOLTON, SIDNEY CHARLES
PERSONAL Born 04/18/1943, Brooklyn, NY, m, 1965, 3 children **DISCIPLINE** AMERICAN HISTORY **EDUCATION** St Lawrence Univ, BA, 66; Univ Wis-Madison, MA, 68, PhD(hist), 73. **CAREER** Asst prof hist, Ill State Univ, 70-73; asst prof, 73-77, ASSOC PROF HIST, UNIV ARK, LITTLE ROCK, 77- **MEMBERSHIPS** Orgn Am Historians. **RESEARCH** American colonial society; Anglicanism; South Carolina. **SELECTED PUBLICATIONS** Auth, The Arkansas Delta--Land of Paradox, W Hist Quart, Vol 0025, 94; Benevolence Among Slaveholders--Assisting the Poor in Charleston, 1670-1860, Jour So Hist, Vol 0061, 95; Shadows Over Sunnyside--An Arkansas Plantation in Transition, 1830-1945, W Hist Quart, Vol 0025, 94; The Arrogance of Faith--Christianity and Race in America from the Colonial-Era to the 20th-Century, Jour Sci Stud Rel, Vol 0032, 93; The Angelical Conjunction--The Preacher-Physicians of Colonial New-England, Jour Sci Stud Rel, Vol 0032, 93; Black Dixie--Afro-Texan History and Culture in Houston, Ark Hist Quart, Vol 0052, 93. **CONTACT ADDRESS** Dept of Hist, Univ of Ark, 33rd & University, Little Rock, AR, 72204.

BOMBERGER, E. DOUGLAS
PERSONAL Born 11/15/1958, Lancaster, PA, m, 1982, 2 children **DISCIPLINE** HISTORICAL MUSICOLGY **EDUCATION** Univ of MD-Col Park, PhD, 91, Univ of NC-Chapel Hill, MM, 83, Goshen IN Col, BA, 81. **CAREER** Univ of HI-Manoa assoc prof, 98-, asst prof, 94-98 Ithaca Col asst prof, 92-94 Sweet Briar Col lectr, 89-90, Goshen Col asst prof, 83-87. **HONORS AND AWARDS** Deutscher Akademischer Austauschdienst fel, 90-91 Irving Lowens Student Research in Music Award, 88 Dean's Fel, Univ of MD, 87-89. **MEMBERSHIPS** Am Musicological Soc, ch, Capital Chapter, 93-94; Col Music Soc Sonneck Soc for Am Music Am Liszt Soc. **RESEARCH** Am and Ger music of the late 19th century hist and lit of the piano. **CONTACT ADDRESS** Univ of HI at Manoa, 2411 Dole Street, Honolulu, HI, 96822. **EMAIL** EDB@hawaii.edu

BOND, GERALD ALBERT
PERSONAL Born 03/15/1944, Rochester, NY, m, 1966, 2 children **DISCIPLINE** FRENCH AND GERMAN LANGUAGE, MEDIEVAL HISTORY **EDUCATION** William Col, BA, 65; Tufts Univ, MA, 66; Yale Univ, PhD(Medieval studies), 73. **CAREER** Instr Ger, 70-73, asst prof French & Ger, 73-78, ASSOC PROF FRENCH & GERMAN, 78- **HONORS AND AWARDS** Younger humanist fel, Mellon Found, 76; Camargo Found fel, 77. **MEMBERSHIPS** Medieval Acad; MLA; Int Courtly Lit Soc. **RESEARCH** Medieval lyric poetry; courtly love; game and literature. **SELECTED PUBLICATIONS** Auth, The Game of Love, Troubadour Wordplay, Romance Philol, Vol 0048, 94; The Envy of Angels--Cathedral Schools and Social Ideas in Medieval Europe, Speculum- Jour Medieval Stud, Vol 0071, 96. **CONTACT ADDRESS** Dept of Foreign Lang Lit & Ling, Univ of Rochester, Rochester, NY, 14627.

BOND, GORDON CREWS
PERSONAL Born 11/17/1939, Ft Myers, FL, m, 1974, 2 children **DISCIPLINE** MODERN EUROPEAN HISTORY **EDUCATION** Fla State Univ, BS, 62, MA, 63, PhD(hist), 66. **CAREER** Asst prof hist, Univ Southern Miss, 66-67; asst prof, 67-76, ASSOC PROF HIST, AUBURN UNIV, 76- **MEMBERSHIPS** AHA; Soc Fr Hist Studies; Belg Soc Napoleonic Studies. **RESEARCH** The French Revolution and Napoleon. **SELECTED PUBLICATIONS** Auth, British Strategy In The Napoleonic War, 1803-15, Jour Military Hist, Vol 0057, 93; Napoleon Conquers Austria, The 1809 Campaign For Viena, Historian, Vol 0059, 97. **CONTACT ADDRESS** Dept of Hist, Auburn Univ, Auburn, AL, 36830.

BONE, QUENTIN
PERSONAL Born 09/03/1918, Bond Co, IL **DISCIPLINE** MODERN EUROPEAN AND ENGLISH HISTORY **EDUCATION** Univ Ill, Urbana, AB, 40, MA, 41, PhD(hist), 54. **CAREER** Teacher social studies, Sorento High Sch, 41-42; master, DeVeaux Sch, 46-48; teacher, East Peoria Community High Sch, 48-52; asst prof hist, Fairmont State Col, 54-55; PROF HIST, IND STATE UNIV, TERRE HAUTE, 55- **MEMBERSHIPS** AHA. **RESEARCH** Seventeenth and nineteenth century English history. **SELECTED PUBLICATIONS** Auth, An Old Radical and His Brood, Notes And Records Of The Royal Society Of London, Vol 0050, 96; Pittrivers, The Life And Archaeological Work Of Pittrivers,Augustus,Henry,Lane,Fox, Notes And Records Of The Royal Society Of London, Vol 0049, 95; Sir Bowring,John, 1792-1872--Aspects of His Life and Career, Notes and Records of the Royal Society of London, Vol 0050, 96. **CONTACT ADDRESS** 2524 N 10th St, Terre Haute, IN, 47804.

BONEY, FRANCIS NASH
PERSONAL Born 11/10/1929, Richmond, VA, m, 1959, 2 children **DISCIPLINE** AMERICAN HISTORY **EDUCATION** Hampden-Sydney Col, BS, 52; Univ Va, MA, 60, PhD (hist), 63. **CAREER** Asst prof hist, Murray State Col, 62-63 and Univ Ga, 63-65; from asst prof to assoc prof, Wash State Univ, 65-68; assoc prof, 68-72, PROF HIST, UNIV GA, 72-, Am Philos Soc grants, 72, 73 and 79. **MEMBERSHIPS** Southern Hist Asn. **RESEARCH** American Civil War; antebellum South; American Middle Period, 1800-1877. **SELECTED PUBLICATIONS** Auth, Andersonville the Last Depot, J Am Hist, Vol 0082, 95; For the Sake of my Country--The Diary of Ward, W.W., 9th Tennessee Cavalry, Morgans Brigade, CSA, Va Mag Hist Biog, Vol 0102, 94; The Georgia Gold Rush-Twenty Niners, Cherokees, and Gold Fever, Am Hist Rev, Vol 0099, 94. **CONTACT ADDRESS** Dept of Hist, Univ of Ga, Athens, GA, 30602.

BONFANTE, LARISSA
PERSONAL 1 child **DISCIPLINE** ETRUSCAN STUDIES, ROMAN HISTORY **EDUCATION** Barnard Col, BA, 54; Univ Cincinnati, MA, 57; Columbia Univ, PhD (archaeol), 66. **CAREER** Instr classics, Douglass Col, Rutgers Univ, 63; from instr to asst prof, 63-69, assoc prof, 69-78, PROF CLASSICS and CHMN DEPT, NY UNIV, 78-, Assoc prof classics, City Univ New York Consortium Classics, 69-; instr adv studies, Washington State Col, 80. **MEMBERSHIPS** Archaeol Inst Am; Inst Etruscan and Ital Studies. **RESEARCH** Etruscan studies; Roman history; Latin language and literature. **SELECTED PUBLICATIONS** Auth, The Naked Goddess--Iconography and Interpretation of Unclothed Female Figures in Early Greek Art, Am J Archaeol, Vol 0099, 95; Variations on Antiquity--New Exhibitions of Class Art, Archaeol, Vol 0050, 97; Pallottino, Massimo, 1909-1995, Am J Archaeol, Vol 0100, 96; The Archaeology of Ancient Sicily Archael, Vol 0046, 93. **CONTACT ADDRESS** Dept of Classics, New York Univ, 25 Waverly Pl, New York, NY, 10003.

BONNER, MARY WINSTEAD
PERSONAL Born 04/20/1924, Nash Co, NC, m, 1956 **DISCIPLINE** EDUCATION **EDUCATION** St Pauls University, BS (cum laude) 1946, LhD, 1979; VA State University, MS 1952; New York Univ 1953-67; Southern Univ 1953, 1954; OK State Univ, EdD 1968; Univ of KS, Post Doct 1974; Univ of California Berkeley 1974; Instde Fililogia Satillo Mexico, further study 1984. **CAREER** Greensville Cty VA, instr 1946-52; So Univ, instr 1952-57; St Louis Publ Schools, instr 1957-64; OK State Univ, grad asst 1965-66; USC, vstg prof 1968; Norfolk State Coll, vstg prof 1971-73; Emporia State Univ, professor, professor emeritus 1986. **HONORS AND AWARDS** European Tour England, Belgium, Holland, Germany, France, Switzerland 1983; tour of Soviet Union & Warsaw Poland 1974, Spain 1976, Mexico 1979, Venezuela 1981, Caribbean 1986; Hall of Fame Sigma Gamma Rho; Cert of Achievement in Spanish Emporia State Univ 1978; languages Spanish, French, Russian; Outstanding Aluma St Pauls Coll 1979, 1984; creation of Bonner-Bonner Lecture Series, Emporia State Univ; Emporia State Univ, Ruth Schillinger Award, 1998. **MEMBERSHIPS** Mem Sigma Gamma Rho, Amer Assn of Univ Women, Natl Council of Negro Women, natl Spanish Hon Soc, Sigma Delta Pi 1979, International Platform Assn, Panel of American Women, KS Children's Service League, Retired Teachers Assn; asst dir, ast district coordinator 1989-90, editor state newsletter 1991-92, Hospital Auxiliaries of Kansas; secretary, Emporia Retired Teachers Assn 1988-89; bd of dirs, Societas Docta; mem, Lyon County Board of Corrections 1990-91; mem, Lyon County Planning Committee 1991-92. **CONTACT ADDRESS** Emporia State Univ, 1200 Commercial St, Emporia, KS, 66801.

BONNER, ROBERT ELLIOTT
PERSONAL Born 06/06/1938, Covina, CA, m, 1962, 2 children **DISCIPLINE** EARLY MODERN HISTORY **EDUCATION** Univ Wyo, BA, 61; Univ Ore, MA, 63; Univ Minn, PhD(Hist), 68. **CAREER** From instr to asst prof, 67-74, assoc prof Hist, Carlton Col, 74-81; prof Hist, 82-. **MEMBERSHIPS** Am Studies Assoc, Western Hist Assn. **RESEARCH** Am West **CONTACT ADDRESS** Dept of American Studies, Carleton Col, 1 N College St, Northfield, MN, 55057-4044. **EMAIL** RBonner@Carleton.edu

BONNER, THOMAS NEVILLE
PERSONAL Born 05/28/1923, Rochester, NY, 2 children **DISCIPLINE** HISTORY **EDUCATION** Univ Rochester, AB, 47, MA, 49; Northwestern Univ, PhD, 52. **CAREER** Acad dean, William Woods Col, 51-54; Fulbright prof Am civilization, Univ Mainz, 54-55; from assoc prof to prof hist, Univ Omaha, 55-62; legis asst, Sen George McGovern, 62-63; prof hist and chmn dept, Univ Cincinnati, 63-68, vpres and provost, 67-71; prof hist and pres, Univ NH, 71-74; pres and chancellor, Union Col, 74-78; pres, 78-82, DISTINGUISHED PROF HIST, WAYNE STATE UNIV, 82-, Guggenheim Mem fels, 58-59, 64-65. **MEMBERSHIPS** AHA; Orgn Am Historians. **RESEARCH** Recent American history; history of medicine; American intellectual history. **SELECTED PUBLICATIONS** Auth, Making a Medical Living--Doctors and Patients in the English Market for Medicine, 1720-1911, Soc Hist Med, Vol 0008, 95; Yellow-Fever and Public-Health in the New South,

Hist, Vol 0055, 93; Order out of Chaos--Billings, John, Shaw and America Coming of Age, Isis, Vol 0086, 95; Frontier Doctor--Beaumont, William, America First Great Medical Scientist, J Am Hist, Vol 0083, 97; Order Out of Chaos--Billings, John, Shaw and America Coming of Age, Isis, Vol 0086, 95; Science at Harvard-University--Historical Perspectives, J Am Hist, Vol 0079, 93; Making a Medical Living--Doctors and Patients in the English Market for Medicine, 1720-1911, Soc Hist Med, Vol 0008, 95. **CONTACT ADDRESS** 838 Mackenzie, Detroit, MI, 48202-3919.

BONO, BARBARA JANE
PERSONAL Born 08/08/1948, Poughkeepsie, NY, m, 1970, 1 child **DISCIPLINE** ENGLISH LITERATURE, HISTORY OF IDEAS **EDUCATION** Fordham Univ, AB, 70; Brown Univ, PhD (English), 78. **CAREER** Instr, 75-78, ASST PROF ENGLISH, UNIV MICH, ANN ARBOR, 78- **MEMBERSHIPS** MLA; Renaissance Soc Am. **RESEARCH** Renaissance intellectual history; English and comparative literature; genre criticism. **SELECTED PUBLICATIONS** Auth, Medicine and Shakespeare in the English Renaissance, Lit Med, Vol 0012, 93; The Birth of Tragedy--Tragic Action in Julius Caesar, Engl Lit Renaissance, Vol 0024, 94 **CONTACT ADDRESS** Dept of English, Univ of Mich, Ann Arbor, MI, 48109.

BONOMI, PATRICIA UPDEGRAFF
PERSONAL Born 01/16/1928, Longview, WA, m, 1953, 2 children **DISCIPLINE** EARLY AMERICAN HISTORY **EDUCATION** Univ Calif, Los Angeles, BA, 48; NY Univ, MA, 63; Columbia Univ, PhD (hist), 70. **CAREER** Lectr Am hist, Lehman Col, 67-70, vis asst prof, 70; from asst prof to assoc prof, 70-78, PROF AM HIST, NY UNIV, 78-, Mem, Columbia Univ Sem Early Am Hist and Cult, 70-; Am Coun Learned Socs fel, 73-74; Guggenheim fel, 76-77; Rockefeller Found Humanities fel, 79-80; vis fel, Shelby Cullom Davis Ctr, Princeton Univ, 79-80. **MEMBERSHIPS** AHA; Inst Early Am Hist and Cult; Orgn Am Historians. **RESEARCH** Political, social and religious history. **SELECTED PUBLICATIONS** Auth, Making the Empire Work--London and American Interest Groups, 1690-1790, William Mary Quart, Vol 0050, 93; Cornbury, Lord Redressed--The Governor and the Problem Portrait, William and Mary Quart, Vol 0051, 94; Memorandum McGiffert, Michael Retirement from William and Mary Quart, William and Mary Quart, Vol 0054, 97; Forming American Politics--Ideals, Interests, and Institutions in Colonial New-York and Pennsylvania, William and Mary Quart, Vol 0052, 95; Pedlar in Divinity--Whitefield, George and the Transatlantic Revivals, 1737-1770 J American Hist, Vol 0081, 95; Contested Boundaries--Itinerancy and the Reshaping of the Colonial American Religious World, J Ecclesiastical Hist, Vol 0047, 96; Contested Boundaries--Itinerancy and the Reshaping of the Colonial American Religious World J Ecclesiastical Hist, Vol 0047, 96; The Myth of American Individualism--The Protestant Origins of American Political Thought Am Hist Rev, Vol 0101, 96. **CONTACT ADDRESS** Dept of Hist, New York Univ, 19 University Pl, New York, NY, 10003.

BOORSTIN, DANIEL JOSEPH
PERSONAL Born 10/01/1914, Atlanta, GA, m, 1941, 3 children **DISCIPLINE** HISTORY **EDUCATION** Harvard Univ, AB, 34: Oxford Univ, BA, 36, BCL, 37; Yale Univ, JSD, 40. **CAREER** Instr hist and lit, Harvard and Radcliffe Cols, 38-42; instr legal hist, Law Sch, Harvard Univ, 39-42; asst prof hist, Swarthmore Col, 42-44; from assoc prof to prof, Univ Chicago, 44-64, Preston and Sterling Morton distinguished prof Am hist, 64-69; LIBRN OF CONG, CONG LIBR, 75-, Barrister-at-law, Inner Temple, London, England, 37-; Fulbright vis prof, Univ Rome, 50-51; Walgreen lectr Am civilization, Univ Chicago, 52; ed, Am hist, Encycl Britannica, 52-55; consult, Soc Sci Res Ctr, Univ PR, 55; vis prof, Kyoto Univ, 57; State Dept lectr, Turkey, Iran, Nepal, India and Ceylon, 59-60, India, Pakistan and Iceland, 74, Philippines, Thailand, Malaysia, India and Egypt, 75; first holder, Chair of Am Hist Sorbonne, 61-62; Pitt prof, Cambridge Univ and fel, Trinity Col, 64-65; mem, Am Revolution Bicentennial Comm, 66-70 and Indust Govt Spec Task Force on Travel, 68; trustee, Colonial Williamsburg, 68-; lectr, William W Cook Lect Ser, Univ Mich, 72; trustee, Am Film Inst, 72-76, John F Kenneddy Ctr Performing arts, 75-, Woodrow Wilson Int Ctr Scholars, 75- and Nat Humanities Ctr, 77-78; Shelby and Kathry Davis lectr, Grad Inst Int Studies, Geneve, 73-74; mem, Comn Critical Choices for Am, 73-75; mem adv bd, Morris and Gwendolyn Cafritz Found, 76-; mem, Japan-US Friendship Comn, 78-; mem, Carl Albert Cong Res and Studies Ctr, 79-; mem, pres task force, Arts and Humanities, 81. **HONORS AND AWARDS** Bancroft Prize, Columbia Univ, 59; Frances Parkman Prize, Soc Am Historians, 66; Pulitzer Prize for Hist, 74; Dexter Prize, 74., 18 hon degrees from various cols and univs. **MEMBERSHIPS** AHA; Orgn Am Historians; Am Antiq Soc; Am Acad Arts and Sci; Am Studies Asn (pres, 69-71). **RESEARCH** American history; intellectual and social history; world history. **SELECTED PUBLICATIONS** Auth, From Empire to Community--The Late 20th Century Emergence of Invisible Communities of Science, Technology, Consumption, and The Arts--The Role of the Discoveries Port Stud, Vol 0008, 92. **CONTACT ADDRESS** 3541 Ordway St NW, Washington, DC, 20016.

BOOTH, ALAN R.
PERSONAL Born 03/20/1934, Manchester, NH, m, 1956, 3 children **DISCIPLINE** AFRICAN HISTORY **EDUCATION** Dartmouth Col, AB, 56; Boston Univ, MA, 62, PhD (hist), 64. **CAREER** Asst prof hist, 64-68, dir African studies, 66-73, chmn dept, 75-80, ASSOC PROF HIST, OHIO UNIV, 68-, Ohio Univ Fund grant, 64-65; lectr African hist, Foreign Serv Inst, 65; Am Philos Soc grant, 65; Fulbright fel, 65-66; US Off Educ grant, Lesotho Field Proj, 67; consult, African Studies Ctr, Cent State Univ, 67-68; consult, Choice. **HONORS AND AWARDS** Outstanding Grad Fac Award, Ohio Univ, 77. **MEMBERSHIPS** AHA; African Studies Asn. **RESEARCH** Role of Lord Selborne in South Africa and the protectorates; American role in South Africa, 19th and 20th centuries; labour migrations in southern Africa. **SELECTED PUBLICATIONS** Auth, Black Mountain--Land, Class and Power in the Eastern Orange Free State, 1880s to 1980s, Am Hist Rev, Vol 0098, 93; The Strange Death of the Liberal Empire--Lord Selborne in South-Africa, Am Hist Rev, Vol 0102, 97; A Biographical Register of Swaziland to 1902, Intl J African Hist Stud, Vol 0029, 96; Power and Resistance in an African Society--The Ciskei Xhosa and the Malting of South-Africa, Am Hist Rev, Vol 0100, 95. **CONTACT ADDRESS** Dept of Hist, Ohio Univ, Bentley Hall, Athens, OH, 45701.

BORAH, WOODROW
PERSONAL Born 12/23/1912, Utica, MS, m, 1945, 2 children **DISCIPLINE** HISTORY **EDUCATION** Univ Calif, Los Angeles, AB, 35, MA, 36, PhD, 40. **CAREER** Instr, Scl Pub Affairs & Hist, Princeton Univ, 41-42; from asst prof to prof speech, Univ Calif, Berkeley, 48-62, prof hist, 48-80., Guggenheim fels, 51-52 & 58-59; Soc Sci Coun fel, 65-66. **HONORS AND AWARDS** Gold Medal, Fray Bernardino de Sahagun, Inst Nac de Antropologia e Hist, Mexico, 71; Steel Medal of Hist Merit, Captain Alonso de Leon, Soc Nuevoleonesa de Hist, Geog y Estadistica, Monterrey, 72. **MEMBERSHIPS** AHA; AAUP; Sociedad Mexicana de Antropologia. **RESEARCH** Social and economic history of Latin America, especially Colonial Mexico; Historical Demography. **SELECTED PUBLICATIONS** Auth, New Spain's Century of Depression, 51, Early Trade and Navigation Between Mexico and Peru, 54, coauth, Aboriginal Population of Central Mexico on the Eve of the Spanish Conquest, 63 & Essays in Population History (3 vols), 71-78, Univ Calif. **CONTACT ADDRESS** Dept of History, Berkeley, CA, 94720.

BORELLI, JOHN
PERSONAL Born 07/19/1946, Oklahoma City, OK, m, 1970, 3 children **DISCIPLINE** HISTORY OF RELIGIONS, THEOLOGY **EDUCATION** Fordham Univ, PhD, 76. **CAREER** Instr, Dept Theology, Fordham Univ, Bronx, NY, 75-76; Prof Religious Studies, Col Mount St Vincent, Riverdale, NY, 76-87; dir, Interreligous Relations, Nat Conference of Catholic Bishops, 87-. **HONORS AND AWARDS** Phi Beta Kappa, St. Louis Univ, 68. **MEMBERSHIPS** Consultor, Pontifical Coun for Interreligous Dialogue, Vatican; Int Buddhist-Christian Theological Encounter Group; Exec Coun, World Conference on Religion and Peace, USA; adv bd, Monastic Interreligous Dialogue; Am Academy of Religion; Soc for Buddhist-Christian Studies; Soc for Hindu-Christian Studies. **RESEARCH** Interreligous relations; theology of religions; the Hindu tradition; Yoga and meditation. **SELECTED PUBLICATIONS** Auth, Children of Abraham: Muslim-Christian-Jewish Relations, Mid-Stream 34, 2, April 95; The 1994 International Buddhist-Christian Theological Encounter, with Judith Simmer-Brown, Buddhist-Christian Studies, 15, 95; Interreligous Relations, Annual report, 1994, Pro Dialogo, Bul of the Pontifical Coun for Interreligous Dialogue, 89, 95; The Goal and Fruit of Catholic-Muslim Dialogue, The Living Light, Dept of Ed, US Cath Conference, 32, 2, winter 95; Talking With Muslims, Faith Alive, Cath News Service, Feb 96; Indispensable Resources on the Christian East and Other Important Books, Ecumenical Trends, 25, 6, June 96; Jesus Christ's Challenge to World Religions: A Response, The Continuing Challenge of Jesus Christ to the World, a Symposium on the Coming of the Third Millenium and the Jubilee Year 2000, sponsored by the NCCB Subcommittee on the Millenium, Sept 7-8, 96, Proceedings; The Virgin Mary in the Breadth and Scope of Interreligious Dialogue, Marian Spirituality and Interreligous Dialogue, Marian Studies, 47, 96; Introductory Address for Imam Warith Deen Mohammed, Living City, Oct, 97; The Catholic Church and Interreligous Dialogue, in Vatican II: The Continuing Agenda, ed by Anthony J Cernera, Sacred Heart Univ Press, 97; Religous Pluralism in India and the Mission of the Church, Periodic Paper #4, US Cath Mission Asn, in Mission Update 6, 4, Dec 97; Interreligous Relations, 1996, Annual Report, Pro Dialogo, Bul of the Pontifical Coun for Interreligious Dialogue, 96, 97; Islamic-Catholic Relations in the USA: Activities of the National Conference of Catholic Bishops (1996) and Recent Developments, Islamochristiana 23, 97; ed with John H Erickson, The Quest for Unity, Orthodox and Catholics in Dialogue, St Vladimir's Seminary Press/US Cath Conf, 96. **CONTACT ADDRESS** Interreligious Relations, 3211 Fourth St NE, Washington, DC, 20017. **EMAIL** seiamail@nccbuscc.org

BOREN, HENRY C.
PERSONAL Born 02/10/1921, Pike Co, IL, m, 1942, 1 child **DISCIPLINE** ANCIENT HISTORY **EDUCATION** Southwest Mo State Col, AB, 49; Univ Ill, MA, 50, PhD, 52. **CAREER** Instr English and hist, Southwest Mo State Col, 52-54; instr hist, Univ Nebr, 55; asst prof, Southern Ill Univ, 55-60; assoc prof, 60-67, PROF HIST, UNIV NC, CHAPEL HILL, 67-, SECY FAC, 69-, Nat Endowment for Humanities sr fel and scholar in residence, Am Acad Rome, 67-68; consult-panelist, Nat Endowment for Humanities, 76- **MEMBERSHIPS** AHA; Am Philol Asn; Am Numis Soc; Archaeol Inst Am; Soc Promotion Roman Studies. **RESEARCH** Roman Republic; economic and social history; numismatics. **SELECTED PUBLICATIONS** Auth, Coins of the Roman-Empire, Class World, Vol 0086, 92; Cicero and the Roman-Republic, Hist, Vol 0056, 94. **CONTACT ADDRESS** Dept of Hist, Univ of NC, Chapel Hill, NC, 27514.

BORG, DANIEL RAYMOND
PERSONAL Born 08/01/1931, Tracy, MN, m, 1959, 4 children **DISCIPLINE** MODERN HISTORY **EDUCATION** Gustavus Adolphus Col, BA, 53, Yale Univ, MA, 57, PhD (hist), 63. **CAREER** From instr to asst prof, 61-66, ASSOC PROF HIST, CLARK UNIV, 66-, CHMN DEPT, 69-72, 77-, Nat Endowment for Humanities fel, 68. **MEMBERSHIPS** AHA. **RESEARCH** Modern German history; political attitudes of German Protestants in the Weimar Republic. **SELECTED PUBLICATIONS** Auth, A History of Christianity in Germany--Religion, Politics and Society from the End of the Enlightenment to the Mid 20th Century, Church Hist, Vol 0065, 96; The Varieties of Protestantism in Nazi Germany--5 Theopolitical Positions, Church Hist, Vol 0063, 94; The Catholic Church in the Free City of Danzig 1920-1933--Catholicism Between Libertas and Irredenta, Am Hist Rev, Vol 0099, 94; A History of Christianity in Germany--Religion, Politics and Society from the End of the Enlightenment to the Mid-20th Century, Church Hist, Vol 0065, 96; The Politics of Conversion--Missionary Protestantism and the Jews in Prussia 1728-1941, Am Hist Rev, Vol 0101, 96. **CONTACT ADDRESS** Dept of Hist, Clark Univ, Worcester, MA, 01610.

BORG, DOROTHY
PERSONAL Born 09/04/1902, Elberon **DISCIPLINE** HISTORY, PUBLIC LAW **EDUCATION** Wellesley Col, AB, 23; Columbia Univ, MA, 31, PhD (pub law and govt), 46. **CAREER** Res assoc Am-Chinese rels, Inst Pac Rels, 38-59; res assoc, EAsian Res Ctr, Harvard Univ, 59-61; SR RES ASSOC, AM FAR EAST POLICY, EAST ASIAN INST, COLUMBIA UNIV, 62-, Lectr, Peking Univ, 47-48. **HONORS AND AWARDS** Bancroft Prize Hist, 65. **MEMBERSHIPS** AHA; Asn Asian Studies, Acad Polit Sci.. **SELECTED PUBLICATIONS** Auth, Social Protestantism in the 20th Century--History of the Inner Mission 1914-1945, J Mod Hist, Vol 0064, 92. **CONTACT ADDRESS** 22 Riverside Dr, New York, NY, 10023.

BORN, JOHN D.
DISCIPLINE COLONIAL AMERICAN HISTORY; AMERICAN REVOLUTION AND THE EARLY REPUBLIC **EDUCATION** Univ Tex, BA, 52; Univ Houston, MA, 58; Univ Nmex, PhD, 63. **CAREER** Asst graduate dean; grad co-ord, hist dept, 78-; assoc prof-. **HONORS AND AWARDS** Summer and Academic yr grants, NEH. **SELECTED PUBLICATIONS** Co-auth, History of the United States With Topics and Readings in United States History With Topics, Vol. II, 96; contribu, Soc Sci Perspectives Jour, Psychohist Rev, Jour Miss Hist, Jour Ala Hist, Wichita State Univ Stud. **CONTACT ADDRESS** Dept of Hist, Wichita State Univ, 1845 Fairmont, Wichita, KS, 67260-0062.

BORNE, LAWRENCE ROGER
PERSONAL Born 01/08/1939, Indianapolis, IN **DISCIPLINE** UNITED STATES HISTORY **EDUCATION** Xavier Univ, Ohio, BS, 59, MA, 66; Univ Colo, Boulder, PhD, 70. **CAREER** Instr hist, Univ Colo, 68-70; asst prof, 70-73, assoc prof, 73-81, prof hist, Northern Ky Univ, 81-, NDEA fel, 66-69; mem adv bd, League of Kentucky Property Owners. **MEMBERSHIPS** Western Hist Asn. **RESEARCH** Western tourism; communism in the United States; conservation. **SELECTED PUBLICATIONS** Auth, The Wootton Land and Fuel Company, 1905-1910, Colo Mag, summer 69; auth, Triumph to Disaster: Colonel James A Ownbey, Colo Mag, fall 71; art, The Cowboy and Dude Ranching, Red River Valley Hist Rev, spring 75; contribr, The Cowboys: Six-Shooters, Songs and Sex, Univ Okla, 76; auth, Recreation, Government and Freedom, World Res INK, 8/77; auth, Dude Ranches and the Development of the West, J of the West, 7/78; contribr, Sports and Recreation in the West, Sunflower Univ Press, 78; auth, Welcome to My West, I.H. Larom: Dude Rancher, Conservationist, Collector, Buffalo Bill Hist Ctr, 82; auth, Western Railroads and the Dude Ranching Industry, The pacific Hist, 86; auth, Dude Ranching in the Rockies, Montana: The Magazine of Western Hist, 88. **CONTACT ADDRESS** 2945 Wild Rose Dr, Edgewood, KY, 41017. **EMAIL** bornel@nku.com

BORNSTEIN, DANIEL
PERSONAL Born 09/10/1950, New Haven, CT, m, 1998, 1 child **DISCIPLINE** MEDIEVAL AND RENAISSANCE HISTORY **EDUCATION** Oberlin Col, BA, 72; Univ Chicago, MA, 77; PhD, 85. **CAREER** Asst prof and fel, Mich Soc of Fel,

Univ Mich, 83-86; lectr, Univ Calif San Diego, 86-89; vis prof, Univ Degli Studi di Milano, Milan, Italy, 97; vis prof, Cent Europ Univ, Budapest, Hungary, 97; asst prof, 89-94, assoc prof, 94-, dir relig studies, 96-, Texas A&M Univ. **HONORS AND AWARDS** Fel and grants, Nat Endowment for the Humanities, 89-90, 93, 95; grants-in-aid, Amer Philos Soc, 90, 96, 98; grant Gladys Krieble Delmas Found, 96. **MEMBERSHIPS** AHA; RSA; MAA; ASCH. **RESEARCH** Religious Culture of Medieval and Early Modern Europe, espec Italy. **SELECTED PUBLICATIONS** Auth, Spiritual Kin and Domestic Devotions, Gender and Society in Renaissance Italy, ed Judith C. Brown and Robert C. Davis, London and New York, Longman, pp 173-192, 98; Parish Priests in Late Medieval Cortona: The Urban and Rural Clergy, Quaderni di Storia Religiosa, 4, pp 165-193, 97; Dominican Friar, Lay Saint: The Case of Marcolino of Forli, Church Hist, 66, pp 252-267, 97; Priests and Villagers in the Diocese of Cortona, Ricerche Storiche, 27, pp 93-106, 97; Le donne di Giovanni Dominici: un caso nella recezione e trasmissione dei messaggi religiosi, Studi medievali, ser 3, 36, pp 355-361, 95; Le Conseil des Dix et le controle de la vie religieuse a Venise a la fin du Moyan Age, La religion civique a l'epoque medievale et modern (Chretiente et Islam), Rome, Ecole Francaise de Rome, pp 187-200, 95; Corporazioni spirituali: proprieta delle confraternite e pieta dei laici, Ricerche de storia sociale e religiosa, 48, pp 77-90, 95; Violenza al corpo di una santa: fra agiografia e pornografia, Quaderni medievali, 39, pp 31-46, June, 95; The Uses of the Body: The Church and the Cult of Santa Margherita da Cortona, Church Hist, 62, pp 163-177, 93; Giovanni Dominici, the Bianchi, and Venice: Symbolic Action and Interpretive Grids, Jour Medieval and Renaissance Studies, 23, pp 143-171, 93. **CONTACT ADDRESS** History Dept, Texas A&M Univ, College Station, TX, 77843. **EMAIL** d-bornstein@tamu.edu

BOROWSKI, ODED
PERSONAL Born 08/26/1939, Israel, m, 1964, 2 children **DISCIPLINE** BIBLICAL ARCHAEOLOGY; BIBLICAL STUDIES **EDUCATION** Wayne State Univ, BA, 70; Univ Mich, PhD, 79. **CAREER** Ch, Dept of Near Eastern and Judaic Lang and Lit, Emory Univ, 88-91; INSTRUCT, ASST PROF, ASSOC PROF, EMORY UNIV, 77- . **HONORS AND AWARDS** Annual Professor, AIAR in Jerusalem, 95-96; Memorial Foundation for Jewish Culture, 94-95. **MEMBERSHIPS** Israel Explor Soc; Am Sch of Oriental Res; Soc for Bibl Lit; Nat Asoc of Prof of Hebrew. **RESEARCH** Ancient agriculture; ancient animal use; remote sensing and GPS in araeology; the Iron Age in Syria-Palestine. **SELECTED PUBLICATIONS** auth, The Pomegranate Bowl from Tell Halif, Israel Explor Jour, 95; Viticulture, Dictionary of Judaism in the Biblical Period, 96; auth, A Penetrating Look: An Experiment in Remote Sensing at Tell Halif, Retrieving the Past: Essays on Archaeological Research and Methodology in Honor of Gus W. Van Beek, 96; Food Storage, Granaries and Silos, Irrigation, The Oxford Encyclopedia of Near Eastern Archaelogy, 96; auth, Every Living Thing: The Daily Use of Animals in Ancient Israel, 98. **CONTACT ADDRESS** Dept of MES, Emory Univ, S310 Callaway Center, Atlanta, GA, 30322. **EMAIL** oborows@emory.edu

BORSTELMANN, THOMAS
PERSONAL Born 04/29/1958, Durham, NC, m, 1988, 2 children **DISCIPLINE** HISTORY **EDUCATION** Stanford Univ, BA, 80; Duke Univ, MA, 86, PhD, 90. **CAREER** Visiting asst prof, Duke Univ, 91; ASST PROF, 91-97, ASSOC PROF, 97-, CORNELL UNIV. **HONORS AND AWARDS** Stuart Bernath Book Prize, Hist of Am Foreign Relations, 94; Robert & Helen Appel Fel, Cornell Univ, 98. **MEMBERSHIPS** Org of Am Historians; Am Hist Asn; Soc for Hist of Am Foreign Relations. **RESEARCH** Twentieth Century United States; U.S. foreign relations; the Cold War; race relations. **SELECTED PUBLICATIONS** Auth, Apartheid's Reluctant Uncle: The United States and Southern Africa in the Early Cold War, Oxford Univ Press, 93; auth, A World of Color: Race Relations and American Foreign Policy Since 1945, forthcoming. **CONTACT ADDRESS** Dept of Hist, Cornell Univ, Ithaca, NY, 14853. **EMAIL** borsel@dreamscape.com

BORZA, EUGENE N.
PERSONAL Born 03/03/1935, Cleveland, OH **DISCIPLINE** ANCIENT HISTORY **EDUCATION** Baldwin-Wallace Col, AB, 57; Univ Chicago, AM, 62, PhD (hist), 66. **CAREER** Asst prof, 64-71, assoc prof hist, 71-81, PROF ANCIENT HIST, PA STATE UNIV, UNIVERSITY PARK, 81-, Archaeol Inst Am Olivia James traveling fel, 70-71; Am Coun Learned Socs-Nat Endowment for Humanities travel grant, 73 and 77; mem managing comt, Am Sch Class Studies Athens, 75-; nat lectr, Archaeol Inst Am, 76-; hist consult, Nat Gallery Art; Am Philos Soc res grant, 79. **MEMBERSHIPS** AHA; Am Philol Asn; Archaeol Inst Am; Asn Ancient Historians. **RESEARCH** Alexander the Great; Macedonia; the classical tradition. **SELECTED PUBLICATIONS** Auth, The Tomb of Lyson and Kallikles--A Painted Macedonian Tomb, Am J Archaeol, Vol 0099, 95. **CONTACT ADDRESS** Dept of Hist, Pennsylvania State Univ, University Park, PA, 16802.

BOSKIN, JOSEPH
PERSONAL Born 08/10/1929, Brooklyn, NY, m, 1955, 3 children **DISCIPLINE** AMERICAN HISTORY, SOCIAL CULTURAL HISTORY **EDUCATION** State Univ NY, BS, 51; NY Univ, MA, 52; Univ Minn, PhD, 59. **CAREER** Instr hist, State Univ Iowa, 59-60; assoc prof hist & Am studies, Univ Southern Calif, 60-69; co-dir, Urban Studies Prog, 77-81, prof hist, Boston Univ, 69-, Tozer Found res award, 59; Univ Southern Calif res grant, 61-63; consult, Gov Comn on Los Angeles riot, 65-66; US Comn Civil Rights, 71-72; vis prof, Univ Calif, San Diego, 67-68; NIMH study grant, 68-69; vis prof, Univ Calif, Los Angeles, 70-71; dir, Inst Law & Urban Studies, 70-71; Russell Sage Found fel, 76-77. **HONORS AND AWARDS** Outstanding Teacher Award, Univ Southern Calif, 62 & 67; Emmy Award for NBC TV ser, The Afro-American in American Culture, 68; Danforth Found Assocs Award, 81. **MEMBERSHIPS** AHA; Orgn Am Historians; Popular Cult Asn; Am Humor Asn. **RESEARCH** Recent social and cultural American history; Afro-American history; popular culture. **SELECTED PUBLICATIONS** Auth, Goodbye, Mr Bones, NY Times Mag, 5/1/66; ed & contribr, The Revolt of the Urban Ghettos, Annals Acad Polit & Soc Sci, 3/69; auth, Sambo: The National Jester in the Population Culture, In: The Great Fear, 70 & co-ed & contribr, Seasons of Rebellion, 71, Holt; auth, Aftermath of an Urban Crisis: Watts, In: Social Theory and Ethnic Conduct, Wiley, 72; ed & contribr, Urban Racial Violence in the Twentieth Century, Glencoe, 69 & 76; auth, Into Slavery: Racial Decisions in the Virginia Colony, Lippincott, 76; Humor and Society, Boston Pub Libr, 78; auth, Rebellious Laughter: People's Humor in American Culture, Syracuse Univ Press, 97; The Humor Prism in 20th Century America, Wayne State Univ Press, 97. **CONTACT ADDRESS** Dept of Hist, Boston Univ, 226 Bay State Rd, Boston, MA, 02215-1403. **EMAIL** JBoskin@bu.edu

BOTHWELL, ROBERT S.
PERSONAL Born 08/17/1944, Ottawa, ON, Canada **DISCIPLINE** HISTORY **EDUCATION** Univ Toronto, BA, 66; Harvard Univ, AM, 67, PhD, 72. **CAREER** Tchg fel, Harvard Univ 68-70; lectr 70, asst prof 72, assoc prof 75, PROF HISTORY, UNIV TORONTO, 81-; vis fel Woodrow Wilson Int Ctr Scholars 97-98. **HONORS AND AWARDS** Corey Prize, Can & Am Hist Asns 80 **SELECTED PUBLICATIONS** Auth, The World of Lester Pearson 78; Eldorado: Canada's National Uranium Company 1984; A Short History of Ontario 86; Years of Victory 87; Nucleus 88; Loring Christie 88; Laying the Foundations 91; Canada & the United States 92; Canada & Quebec 95; coauth, CD Howe: A Biography 79; Canada Since 1945, 81, 2nd ed, 89; The Great Brain Robbery 84; Canada 1900-1945, 87; Pirouette, 90; The Petrified Campus, 97; co-ed Policy By Other Means, 72; The In-Between Time, 75. **CONTACT ADDRESS** Dept of History, Univ of Toronto, Toronto, ON, M5S 3G3. **EMAIL** bothwell@chass.utoronto.ca

BOTJER, GEORGE
DISCIPLINE EUROPEAN HISTORY, ECONOMIC GEOGRAPHY AND THIRD WORLD HISTORY **EDUCATION** NY Univ, BS, 59, MA, 61; FL State Univ, PhD, 73. **CAREER** Prof, Univ of Tampa . **SELECTED PUBLICATIONS** Auth, A Short History of Nationalist China 1919-1949, Putnam, 80; Sideshow War: A History of the Italian Campaign, 1943-45, Tex A&M UP, 96. **CONTACT ADDRESS** Dept of Hist, Univ of Tampa, 401 W. Kennedy Blvd, Tampa, FL, 33606-1490.

BOTSTEIN, LEON
PERSONAL Born 12/14/1946, Zurich, Switzerland, m, 2 children **DISCIPLINE** HISTORY **EDUCATION** Univ Chicago, BA, 67; Harvard Univ, AM, 68, PhD, 85. **CAREER** Teaching Fel and Non-Resident Tutor, Harvard Univ, 68-69; Lectr, Boston Univ, 69; Special Asst to the Pres Bd Educ, City of New York, 69-70; Pres, Franconia Col, 70-75; Vis Fac, Manhattan Sch Music, 86; Vis Prof, Vienna, 88; Ed, The Musical Quart, 92-; Artistic Dir, Am Russ Youth Orchestra, 95-; Music Dir, Am Symphony Orchestra, 92-; Pres, Simon's Rock Col of Bard, 79-; Leon Levy Prof Arts & Humanities, Bard Col, 75-, Pres, 75-. **HONORS AND AWARDS** Howell Murray Alumni Award, Univ Chicago, 67; Woodrow Wilson Fel, 67; Danforth Found Fel, 67; Sloan Found Urban Fel, 69; Annual Award, Nat Conf Christians and Jews, 75; Rockefeller Fel, Aspen Inst Humanistic Studies, 75; Honorary Doctorate Humane Letters, Cedar Crest Col, 80; Professional Achievement Award, Univ Chicago Alumni Asn, 84; Honorary Doctorate Humane Letters, Salisbury State Univ, 88; Fel, Am Acad Arts & Sci, 93-; Nat Arts Club Gold Medal, 95; Centennial Medal, Harvard Grad Sch Arts & Sci, 96; Honorary Doctorate Humane Letters, Western Conn State Univ, 97. **RESEARCH** Jewish Culture. **SELECTED PUBLICATIONS** Auth, Hearing is Seeing: Thoughts on the History of Music and the Imagination, The Musical Quart, 95; Music and Ideology: Thoughts on Bruckner, The Music Quart, 96; The Future of the Orchestra, The Music Quart, 96; Realism Transformed: Franz Schubert and Vienna, The Cambridge Companion to Schubert, Cambridge Univ Press, 97; The Demise of Philosophical Listening: Haydn in the 19th Century, Haydn and His World, Princeton Univ Press, 97; Brahms the performer, editor and collector, BBC Proms, BBC Radio 3 Publ, 97; Jefferson's Children: Education and the Promise of American Culture, Doubleday, 97; Music and Its Public: Habits of Listening and the Crisis of Musical Modernism in Vienna, 1870-1914, Univ Chicago Press (forthcoming); author of numerous other articles and chapters. **CONTACT ADDRESS** Bard Col, Annandale-on-Hudson, NY, 12504.

BOTTIGHEIMER, KARL S.
PERSONAL Born 03/19/1937, Louisville, KY, m, 1960, 2 children **DISCIPLINE** BRITISH HISTORY **EDUCATION** Harvard Univ, AB, 58; Univ Wis, MA, 59; Univ Calif, Berkeley, PhD (hist), 65. **CAREER** Instr hist, Univ Calif, Berkeley, 63-64; from instr to asst prof, 64-70, ASSOC PROF HIST, STATE UNIV NY STONY BROOK, 70-, Nat Endowment for Humanities jr scholar, 69; vis reader hist, Univ Sussex, 70-71; Guggenheim fel, 73-74. **MEMBERSHIPS** AHA; Conf Brit Studies; Econ Hist Soc; Am Comt Irish Studies; fel Royal Hist Soc. **RESEARCH** Early modern Britain, 1485-1714; early modern Europe; Ireland. **SELECTED PUBLICATIONS** Auth, The Outbreak of the Irish Rebellion of 1641, Am Hist Rev, Vol 0100, 95; Ireland from Independence to Occupation, 1641-1660, Albion, Vol 0028, 96; Religion, Law and Power--The Making of Protestant Ireland, 1660-1760, Am Hist Rev, Vol 0099, 94; Civil-War and Restoration in the 3 Stuart Kingdoms--The Career of Macdonnell, Randal, Marquis of Antrim, 1609-1683, Am Hist Rev, Vol 0099, 94. **CONTACT ADDRESS** Dept of Hist, State Univ of NY, Stony Brook, NY, 11790.

BOTTOMS, BETTE L.
PERSONAL m **DISCIPLINE** PSYCHOLOGY **EDUCATION** Randolph-Macon Woman's Col, Lynchburg, VA, BA, 86; Univ Denver, MA, 89; SUNY, Buffalo, PhD, 92. **CAREER** Asst prof, 92-96, assoc prof, Dept of Psychology, Univ IL, Chicago, 97-, assoc chairperson, 97-. **HONORS AND AWARDS** Am Psychol/Law Soc First Place Dissertation Award, 93; UIC-Amoco Silver Circle Teaching Excellence nomination, 96, Award, 97; UIC Teaching Recognition Prog Award, 97; UIC Teaching Excellence Award, 98; Saleem Shah Early Career Award, 98; numerous research and travel grants, 90-98. **MEMBERSHIPS** Phi Beta Kappa; Sigma Xi; Psi Chi; APA; Midwestern Psychol Asn; Soc for Applied Res in Memory and Cognition; Soc for the Psychological Study of Social Issues; Am Psychol/Law Soc; Am Professional Soc on the Abuse of Children; Int Soc for the Prevention of Child Abuse and Neglect; Children's Healthcare is a Legal Duty, Inc. **SELECTED PUBLICATIONS** Auth, with P R Shaver, G S Goodman, and J J Qin, In the Name of God: A Profile of Religion-Related Child Abuse, J of Social Issues, 51, 95; with B M Schwartz-Kenney, and G S Goodman, Techniques for Improving Children's Person Identification Accuracy, Child Maltreatment, 1, 96; with C A Carter and M Levine, Linguistic and Socio-Emotional Influences on the Accuracy of Children's Reports, Law and Human Behavior, 20, 96; with P R Shaver and G S Goodman, An Analysis of Ritualistic Child Abuse Allegations, Law and Human Behavior, 20, 96; with G S Goodman, International Perspectives on Child Witnesses: An Introduction to the Issues, Criminal Justice and Behavior, 23, 96; with K R Diviak and S L Davis, Jurpor's Reactions to Satanic Ritual Abuse Allegations, Child Abuse and Neglect, 21, 97; with S L Davis, The Creation of Satanic Ritual Abuse, J of Social and Clinical Psychology, 16, 97; with J J Qin, G S Goodman, and P R Shaver, Repressed Memories of Ritualistic and Religion-Related Child Abuse, in S J Lynn & K McConkey, eds, Truth in Memory, Guilford, 98; ed, with G S Goodman, International Perspectives on Child Abuse and Children's Testimony: Psychological Research and Law, Sage, 96; numerous other publications, several forthcoming. **CONTACT ADDRESS** Dept of Psychology, Univ of Illinois, Chicago, 1007 West Harrison St, Chicago, IL, 60607-7131. **EMAIL** bbottoms@uic.edu

BOTZENHART-VIEHE, VERENA
DISCIPLINE EUROPEAN HISTORY, GREEK SOCIETY, WESTERN CIVILIZATION **EDUCATION** Univ Tulsa, BA, 74; Univ Calif, Santa Barbara, MA, 75, PhD, 80. **CAREER** 1977-78 Pres, Hist Grad Stud Assn, Univ Calif, 77-78; tchg asst, Univ Calif, 75-78; adjunct prof, Youngstown State Univ, 86-90; assist prof, 90; fac consult, Princeton, 94-; assoc prof, 96-. **HONORS AND AWARDS** Sullins award, Univ Tulsa, 74; grant, Sem Fur Politische Bildung in Munich, 88-93; fac develop grant, Univ Chicago, 91; Silver memorial scholar, 89; President's grant, Univ Calif, 83. **MEMBERSHIPS** Mem, President's Admissions Task Force. **SELECTED PUBLICATIONS** Auth, George Bancroft, Notable U.S. Ambassadors 1775-1995: A Biographical Dictionary, Greenwood Press, 96. Andrew White, Notable U.S. Ambassadors 1775-1995: A Biographical Dictionary, Greenwood Press, 96; rev(s), Origins of a Spontaneous Revolution: East Germany, 1989, by Karl Dieter Opp, Peter Voss, and Christiane Gern, History, Rev of New Bk(s), 96; The End of an Era? Europe 1945-1990s, by Antonio Varsori, Hist Rev of New Bk(s), 96; The Cold War-A History, by Martin Walker, Hist Rev of New Bk(s), 95; James B. Conant: Harvard to Hiroshima and the Making of the Nuclear Age, by James G. Hershberg, The Historian, 94; Chester Bowles: New Dealer in the Cold War, by Howard B Schaffer, Hist Rev(s) of New Bk(s), 94. **CONTACT ADDRESS** Rel, Hist, Philos, Classics Dept, Westminster Col, New Wilmington, PA, 16172-0001. **EMAIL** verenabv@westminster.edu

BOUCHARD, CONSTANCE BRITTAIN
PERSONAL Born 05/17/1948, Syracuse, NY, m, 1970 **DISCIPLINE** MEDIEVAL HISTORY **EDUCATION** Middlebury Col, AB, 70; Univ Chicago, AM, 73, PhD 76. **CAREER** Prof hist, Univ Akron, 90- . **HONORS AND AWARDS** NEH Fellow, 82; John Simon Guggenheim Mem Fellow, 95. **MEMBERSHIPS** Medieval Acad Am; Am Hist Assoc; Ohio Acad Hist; Soc French Hist; Catholic Hist Asn. **RESEARCH** Medieval history, especially relations between nobility and the church. **SELECTED PUBLICATIONS** Strong of Body, Brave and Noble: Chivalry and Society in Medieval France, Cornell Univ Press, 98; The Cartulary of Flavigny, Medieval Acad, 91; Holy Entrepreneurs: Cistercians, Knights, and Economic Exchange in Twelfth-Century Burgundy, Cornell Univ Press, 91; Life and Society in the West: Antiquity and the Middle Ages, HBJ, 88; Sword, Miter, and Cloister: Nobility and the Church in Burgundy, 980-1198, Cornell Univ Press, 87. **CONTACT ADDRESS** Univ of Akron, Dept of History, Akron, OH, 44325-1902. **EMAIL** CBouchard@UAkron.edu

BOUCHER, PHILIP P.
PERSONAL Born 07/22/1944, Hartford, CT, m, 1989, 3 children **DISCIPLINE** HISTORY **EDUCATION** Univ COnn, PhD, 74 **CAREER** Inst, Univ NC, Charlotte, 73-74; asst prof, 74-80, assoc prof, 80-89, PROF, UNIV ALA, HUNTSVILLE, 89-. **HONORS AND AWARDS** Dist Prof Hist, 96; res grant, 92, Fr Col Hist Soc Alf Andrew Heggoy Prize, 92. **MEMBERSHIPS** Fr Colonial Hist Sco; Am Hist Soc; Asn Caribbean Historians. **RESEARCH** Fr colonial hist, esp Caribbean during Old Regime. **SELECTED PUBLICATIONS** Auth, Cannibal Encounters: Europeans and Island Caribs 1491- 1763, Johns Hopkins Univ Press, 92; co-auth, Gabriel Debien, Chronique bibliographique de l'histoire des Antilles francaise, Bul soc d'hist Guadelopue 59; auth, Proceedings of the Fifteenth Annual Meeting of the French Colonial Historical Society, Univ Press Am, 91 (also twelfth ann meet, 88, and thirteenth, fourteenth ann meet, 90); auth, Why Island Caribs Loved the French and Hated the English, Proceedings of the Eighteenth Meeting of the French Colonial Historical Society, 93, repr in Actes de Colloque France-Amerique, 97; auth, W. J. Eccles' France in America from a Caribbeanist Perspective, Br J Can Stud 11, no 1, 96. **CONTACT ADDRESS** Dept of History, Univ of Alabama, Huntsville, 409 Roberts Hall, Huntsville, AL, 35899. **EMAIL** boucherp@email.uah.edu

BOUDREAU, JOSEPH A.
PERSONAL Born 12/23/1934, San Francisco, CA, m, 1961, 3 children **DISCIPLINE** CANADIAN HISTORY **EDUCATION** Univ Calif, Los Angeles, BA, 56, MA, 58, PhD(Hist), 65. **CAREER** Lectr hist, Univ BC, 61-62; asst prof, Univ Alta, Calgary, 62-66; from asst prof to assoc prof, 66-75, PROF HIST, SAN JOSE STATE UNIV, 75-, Nat Endowment for Humanities fel, Yale, 81; Can govt enrichment grant, 82-83. **HONORS AND AWARDS** Mem & chair, Corey Prize Comt, Am Hist Asn, 95-98. **MEMBERSHIPS** Am Hist Asn; Can Hist Asn; Asn Can Studies in US **RESEARCH** Canadian, Australian and New Zealand history. **SELECTED PUBLICATIONS** Auth, Western Canada's enemy aliens in World War I, Alta Hist Rev, winter, 64; Alberta, In: Canadian Annual Review for 1963, 64, 65 & 66, Univ Toronto, 64-67; Interning Canada's enemy aliens, Canadian Hist Mag, 9/74; Alberta, Aberhart and Social Credit, Holt, 75; The medium and the message of Wm Aberhart, Am Rev Can Studies, spring 78; Social credit Reconsidered, in: The Man on the Spot, 95. **CONTACT ADDRESS** Dept of Hist, San Jose State Univ, 1 Washington Sq, San Jose, CA, 95192-0001. **EMAIL** jboudrea@pacbell.net

BOURDON, ROGER J.
PERSONAL Born 05/08/1937, St. Paul, MN, m, 1967, 3 children **DISCIPLINE** UNITED STATES HISTORY **EDUCATION** Loyola Univ, Calif, BS, 59; Univ Calif, Los Angeles, MA, 61, PhD(US Hist), 65. **CAREER** Asst prof US Hist, Wichita State Univ, 56-67 & Marquette Univ, 67-68; from asst prof to assoc prof, 68-75, prof US Hist, Mary Washington Col, Univ VA, 75-, bicentennial lect ser Campus & Community, 75; chmn fac Welfare Comt, Mary Washington Col, 76-77. **HONORS AND AWARDS** Simpson Award for Excellence in Teaching, 89. **MEMBERSHIPS** Inst Early Am Hist & Cult AHA; Western Hist Asn; Orgn Am Hist. **RESEARCH** Westward expansion; colonial United States history. **CONTACT ADDRESS** Dept of History, Mary Washington Col, 1301 College Ave, Fredericksburg, VA, 22401-5300. **EMAIL** rbourdon@mwc.edu

BOURGUIGNON, ERIKA EICHHORN
PERSONAL Born 02/18/1924, Vienna, Austria, m, 1950 **DISCIPLINE** ANTHROPOLOGY **EDUCATION** Queens Coll, BA, 45; Univ Conn, grad study, 45; Northwestern Univ, PhD, 51. **CAREER** Instr, Ohio State Univ, 49-56; asst prof, Ohio state Univ, 56-60; assoc prof, Ohio State Univ, 60-66; prof, Ohio State Univ, 66-90; act ch, Anthrop, 71-72; PROF EMER, OHIO STATE UNIV, 90-. **MEMBERSHIPS** Am Anthrop Asn; Ctrl State Anthrop Soc; Ohio Acad Sci; World Psychiat Asn; Am Ethnol Soc; Antrop Soc for Psychol; Phi Beta Kappa; Sigma Xi **SELECTED PUBLICATIONS** Edr, Margaret Mead: The Anthropologist in America-Occasional Papers in Anthropology, Ohio State Univ, 86. **CONTACT ADDRESS** Dept Anthrop, Ohio State Univ, 124 W 17th Ave, Columbus, OH, 43210-1316.

BOUWSMA, WILLIAM JAMES
PERSONAL Born 11/22/1923, Ann Arbor, MI, m, 1944, 4 children **DISCIPLINE** HISTORY **EDUCATION** Harvard Univ, AB, 43, AM, 47, PhD, 50. **CAREER** From instr to assoc prof hist, Univ Ill, 50-57; from assoc prof to prof, Univ Calif, Berkeley, 57-69, chmn dept, 66-67, vchancellor acad affairs, 67-69; prof hist, Harvard Univ, 69-71; SATHER PROF HIST, UNIV CALIF, BERKELEY, 71-, CHMN DEPT, 81-, Guggenheim fel and Fulbright res fel, Italy, 59-60; fel, Ctr advan Studies Behav Sci, 63-64; Nat Humanities Inst, New Haven, fel, 76-77. **MEMBERSHIPS** AHA (pres, 78); Am Soc Reformation Res (pres, 63); Renaissance Soc Am; fel Am Acad Arts and Sci; fel Am Philos Soc. **SELECTED PUBLICATIONS** Auth, Wondrous in his Saints--Counterreformation Propaganda in Bavaria, Church Hist, Vol 0064, 95; Wondrous in his Saints--Counterreformation Propaganda in Bavaria, Church Hist, Vol 0064, 95; Voracious Idols and Violent Hands--Iconoclasm in Reformation Zurich, Strasbourg, and Basel, J Mod Hist, Vol 0068, 96; The Contribution of Roelker, Nancy to French Historical Studies, Fr Hist Stud, Vol 0018, 94; Machiavellian Rhetoric--From The Counterreformation to Milton, A Hist Rev, Vol 0101, 96; An Italian Renaissance Sextet--6 Tales in Historical Context, J Interdisciplinary Hist, Vol 0028, 97; The Civilization of Europe in the Renaissance, Am Hist Rev, Vol 0101, 96; Calvin and the Consolidation of the Genevan Reformation, J Mod Hist, Vol 0068, 96. **CONTACT ADDRESS** Dept of Hist, Univ of Calif, Berkeley, CA, 94720.

BOWDEN, HENRY WARNER
PERSONAL Born 04/01/1939, Memphis, TN, m, 1962, 2 children **DISCIPLINE** HISTORY, RELIGION **EDUCATION** Baylor Univ, AB, 61; Princeton Univ, AM, 64, PhD (relig), 66. **CAREER** From instr to asst prof, 64-71, asst dean col, 69-71, assoc prof, 71-79, PROF RELIG, DOUGLASS COL, RUTGERS UNIV, 79- **MEMBERSHIPS** Am Soc Church Hist; Orgn Am Historians. **RESEARCH** Historiographical studies, chiefly in the United States; religion of American Indians and missionary activities by Europeans. **SELECTED PUBLICATIONS** Auth, Native and Christian--Indigenous Voices on Religious Identity in the United States and Canada, Am Indian Cult Res J, Vol 0021, 97; Historians of the Christian Tradition--Their Methodology and Influence on Western Thought, Church Hist, Vol 0066, 97; Missionary Conquest--The Gospel and Native American Cultural Genocide, Church Hist, Vol 0064, 95; Historians of the Christian Tradition--Their Methodology and Influence on Western Thought, Church Hist, Vol 0066, 97 Choctaws and Missionaries in Mississippi, 1818-1918, Am Hist Rev, Vol 0102, 97; Converting the West--A Biography of Whitman, Narcissa, Pac Hist Rev, Vol 0061, 92. **CONTACT ADDRESS** Dept of Relig Douglass Col, Rutgers Univ, P O Box 270, New Brunswick, NJ, 08903-0270.

BOWDEN, JAMES HENRY
PERSONAL Born 10/28/1934, Louisville, KY, d, 3 children **DISCIPLINE** AMERICAN STUDIES, RELIGION **EDUCATION** Univ Louisville, MA, 59; Univ MN, Minneapolis, PhD, 70; Louisville Presbyterian Theol Sem, MA, 87. **CAREER** Instr Eng, Univ KY, 60-61, Univ MT, 62-64 & Colgate Univ, 65-66; from Instr to Assoc Prof, 66-80, Prof English, 80-98, Prof Emeritus, Ind Univ SE, 98-, Chmn Hum Div, 80-85; Assoc Dir, Am Studies Ctr, Warsaw, 85-86; Prof, Institut Teknologi Mari, Malaysia, 89-91. **HONORS AND AWARDS** Nat Endowment for the Humanities summer fel, Univ MI, 77; fel, Bread Loaf Writers Conf, 80. **RESEARCH** Relig in Am life; imaginative writing; theories of humor. **SELECTED PUBLICATIONS** Auth, The bland leading the bland, New Oxford Rev, 77; Go purple, West Branch, 77; The grief of Terry Magoo, Great River Rev, 77; The Bible and other Novels, Cresset, 78; Don't Lose This, It's My Only Copy, Col English, 79; ICU, Thornleigh Rev, 82; Conwell Lives, New Oxford Rev, 82; Peter DeVries, A Critical Study, G K Hall, 83. **CONTACT ADDRESS** Dept of Hum, Indiana Univ, Southeast, 4201 Grant Line Rd, New Albany, IN, 47150-2158. **EMAIL** jhbowden@iusmail.ius.indiana.edu

BOWEN, LYNNE E.
PERSONAL Born 08/22/1940, Indian Head, SK, Canada **DISCIPLINE** HISTORY **EDUCATION** Univ Alta, BS, RN, 63; Univ Victoria, MA, 80. **CAREER** Victorian Order Nurses, 63-64; vis guest lectr, various univ, 80-; Maclean Hunter Lectr, Univ BC, 92-. **HONORS AND AWARDS** Eaton's BC Bk Award, 83; Can Hist Asn Reg Cert Merit, 83, 92; BC Lt-Gov Award Writing Hist, 87; Hubert Evans Non-fiction Prize, BC Bk Awards, 92. **MEMBERSHIPS** Writer's Union Can; BC Fedn Writers; Nanaimo Harbourfront Ctr Soc; Nanaimo Hist Soc; Int PEN. **SELECTED PUBLICATIONS** Auth, Boss Whistle: The Coal Miners of Vancouver Island Remember, 82; auth, Three Dollar Dreams, 87; auth, The Dunsmuirs of Nanaimo, 89; auth, Muddling Through: The Remarkable Story of the Barr Colonists, 92; auth, Those Lake People, 95. **CONTACT ADDRESS** 4982 Fillinger Cr., Nanaimo, BC, V9V 1J1.

BOWER, BEVERLY LYNNE
PERSONAL Born 09/10/1951, Washington, DC, m **DISCIPLINE** EDUCATION **EDUCATION** Univ of KS, BS Ed 1973; Emporia State Univ, MLS 1980; Florida State University, Tallahassee, FL, PhD, 1992. **CAREER** Lansing Jr High School, reading teacher 1973-74; Chillicothe HS, French/English teacher 1974-75; Dept of Defense Dependent Schools, French/English teacher 1975-80; Pensacola Jr Coll, librarian 1980-84; Pensacola Jr Coll, dir lrc serv 1985-92; University of SC, College of Education, asst professor, 1993-96; FLORIDA STATE UNIV, COLLEGE OF EDUCATION, ASST PROF, 1997-. **HONORS AND AWARDS** Natl Achievement Scholar; Leaders Program, Amer Assn of Women in Community & Junior Colleges, 1989; Florida State University Fellowship, 1990-91; USC Mortar Board Outstanding Teacher Award, 1994. **MEMBERSHIPS** Sec West FL Library Assn 1981-83; mem ALA-JMRT Minorities Recruitment Comm 1982-83, FL Library Assn, community college caucus chair/chair-elect 1986-88; FL Assn of Comm Coll, regional dir 1987; chapter president, Florida Assn of Community Colleges, 1988; bd of directors, YWCA Pensacola, 1989-91; AAWCC, founding chapter president; AAWCC, 1990-96; ASHE, 1991-; CSCC, bod, 1998; FSU Hardee Ctr, bd of governors, 1997-. **CONTACT ADDRESS** Col of Educ, Florida State Univ, Tallahassee, FL, 32306.

BOWERS, RICHARD HUGH
PERSONAL Born 07/30/1937, Onawa, IA, m, 1960, 2 children **DISCIPLINE** MEDIEVAL HISTORY **EDUCATION** Miss State Univ, BA, 59, MA, 60 PhD(hist), 65. **CAREER** Asst prof hist, Univ Southwestern La, 65-66; assoc prof, 66-76, HONORS PROF HIST, UNIV SOUTHERN MISS, 76-, ASSOC DIR HONS COL, 57- **MEMBERSHIPS** Mediaeval Acad Am; AHA; Selden Soc. **RESEARCH** Economic history of Medieval England; development of the royal household in England. **SELECTED PUBLICATIONS** Auth, England and the German Hanse, 1157-1611--A Study of Their Trade and Commercial Diplomacy, Speculum- Jour Medieval Stud, Vol 0069, 94; The Commercialization of English Society, 1000-1500, Speculum- Jour Medieval Stud, Vol 0070, 95; The Commercialization of English Society, 1000-1500, Speculum- Jour Medieval Stud, Vol 0070, 95; England and the German Hanse, 1157-1611--Study of Their Trade and Commercial Diplomacy, Speculum- Jour Medieval Stud, Vol 0069, 94. **CONTACT ADDRESS** Southern Station, Box 135, Hattiesburg, MS, 39401.

BOWERS, WILLIAM LAVALLE
PERSONAL Born 06/09/1930, Mason City, IA, m, 1954, 4 children **DISCIPLINE** HISTORY **EDUCATION** Univ Northern Iowa, BA, 55, MA, 58; Univ Iowa, PhD, 68. **CAREER** From instr to assoc prof, 62-76, PROF HIST, BRADLEY UNIV, 76- **MEMBERSHIPS** AAUP; AHA; Orgn Am Hist. **RESEARCH** American social history; agricultural history. **CONTACT ADDRESS** Bradley Univ, 1314 Schneblin Ct, Peoria, IL, 61604.

BOWERSOCK, GLEN WARREN
PERSONAL Born 01/12/1936, Providence, RI **DISCIPLINE** HISTORY, CLASSICS **EDUCATION** Harvard Univ, AB, 57; Oxford Univ, BA, 59, MA & DPhil, 62. **CAREER** Lectr ancient hist, Oxford Univ, 61-62; from instr to assoc prof classics, Harvard Univ, 62-69, prof classics, 69-80, chmn, Dept Hist, 72-77, assoc dean fac arts & sci, 77-80; PROF HIST STUDIES, INST ADVAN STUDY, PRINCETON, 80-, Consult, Educ Serv Inc, 64 & Nat Endowment for Humanities, 71-; mem, Int Colloquium Classics in Educ, 64-66; vis lectr, Oxford Univ, 66; sr fel, Ctr for Hellenic Studies, Washington, DC, 76-; syndic, Harvard Univ Press, 77-81. **MEMBERSHIPS** Fel Am Acad Arts & Sci; corresp mem Ger Archaeol Inst; Soc Prom Roman Studies; Soc Prom Hellenic Studies; Am Philol Asn. **RESEARCH** Greek history; Roman history; pre-Islamic Arabia. **SELECTED PUBLICATIONS** Auth, The New Cavafy, Unfinished Poems 1918-1932, Amer Scholar, Vol 0065, 96; Rostovtzeff and Harvard--English, Russian, Philologus, Vol 0140, 96; Egypt in Late-Antiquity, Jour of Interdisciplinary Hist, Vol 0026, 95; Antonine Literature, Gnomon-Kritische Zeitschrift fur die Gesamte Klassische Altertumswissenschaft, Vol 0064, 92; Performance and Partisans at Aphrodisias in the Roman and Late Roman Periods--A Study Based on Inscriptions from the Current Excavations at Aphrodisias in Caria, Gnomon-Kritische Zeitschrift fur die Gesamte Klassische Altert; Wagner, Opera News, Vol 0061, 96. **CONTACT ADDRESS** Hist Studies Dept, Inst for Advanced Studies, Princeton, NJ, 08540.

BOWKER, WILBUR F.
PERSONAL Born 02/18/1910, Ponoka, AB, Canada **DISCIPLINE** LAW (HISTORY) **EDUCATION** Univ Alta, BA, 30, LLB, 32, LLD, 72; Sterling Fel, Yal Law Sch, 52-53; Univ Minn, LLM, 53. **CAREER** Law pract, Edmonton, 32-42; Can Army, 42-45; prof law, Univ Alta, 45-75(RETIRED), dean law, 48-68; dir, Alta Law Reform Inst, 68-75. **HONORS AND AWARDS** KC, 51; hon bencher, Law Soc Alta, 76; hon prof law, Univ Calgary, 77; hon mem, Can Bar Asn, 79 (pres award, 89); Justice Medal, Can Inst Admin Justice, 89; OC, 90. **MEMBERSHIPS** Can Asn Law Tchrs (pres, 56). **SELECTED PUBLICATIONS** Auth, Consolidation of Fifty Years of Legal Writings 1938-1988, 89. **CONTACT ADDRESS** 10925 85 Ave, Edmonton, AB, T6G 0W3.

BOWLER, PETER JOHN
PERSONAL Born 10/08/1944, Leicester, England, m, 1966, 2 children **DISCIPLINE** HISTORY OF SCIENCE, HISTORY

OF IDEAS **EDUCATION** King's Col, Cambridge, BA, 66; Univ Sussex, MSc, 67; Univ Toronto, PhD(hist of sci), 71. **CAREER** Asst prof hist of sci, Univ Toronto, 71-72; lectr hist, Univ Sains Malaysia, 72-75; asst prof hist, Univ Winnipeg, 75-79; lectr hist of sci, Queens Univ Belfast, 79- **MEMBERSHIPS** Hist Sci Soc; Can Soc Hist & Philos Sci; Brit Soc Hist Sci. **RESEARCH** History of evolutionary theories; social and religious implications of science; history of science in Canada. **SELECTED PUBLICATIONS** Auth, The Founders of Evolutionary Genetics--A Centenary Reappraisal, Brit Jour Hist Sci, Vol 0027, 94; The Social-History of British Anthropology, 1885-1945, Brit Jour Hist Sci, Vol 0026, 93; Theory Change In Science--Strategies from Mendelian Genetics, Annals of Sci, Vol 0050, 93; Evolution By Association-History of Symbiosis, Annals Sci, Vol 0053, 96; Nature Lost--Natural-Science and the German Theological Traditions of the 19th-Century, Hist and Philos Life Sci, Vol 0016, 94; Biology Takes Form--Animal Morphology and the German Universities, 1800-1900, Annals Sci, Vol 0053, 96; A Calendar of the Correspondence of Darwin,Charles, 1821-1881--With Supplement, Annals of Sci, Vol 0052, 95; Darwin, Soc History Of Medicine, Vol 0005, 1992; An Agenda for Antiquity--Osborn, Henry, Fairfield and Vertebrate Paleontology at the American-Museum-of-Natural-History, 1890-1935, Brit Jour Hist Sci, Vol 0026, 93; Darwin, Darwinism, Evolutionism--French, Brit Jour Hist Sci, Vol 0026, 93; Are the Arthropoda a National Group--An Episode in the History of Evolutionary Biology, Jour Hist Biol, Vol 0027, 94; The Founders of Evolutionary Genetics--Centenary Reappraisal, Brit Jour Hist Sci, Vol 0027, 94; Huxley,Julian--Biologist and Statesman of Science, Annals of Sci, Vol 0052, 95; Evolution by Association--History of Symbiosis, Annals Sci, Vol 0053, 96; Darwinism and Society, Brit Jour Hist Sci, Vol 0026, 93; Dawson,John,William--Faith, Hope, and Science, Amer Hist Rev, Vol 0102, 97; Victorian Values--The Life And Times Of Lankester,Edwin, Notes and Records of the Royal Society of London, 93; A Calendar of the Correspondence of Darwin, Charles, 1821-1881--With Supplement, Annals of Sci, Vol 0052, 95; Transforming Traditions in American Biology, 1880-1915, Brit Jour Hist Sci, Vol 0025, 92; Are the Arthropoda a National Group--An Episode in the History of Evolutionary Biology, Jour Hist Biol, Vol 0027, 94; Darwinism and Society--French, Brit Jour Hist Sci, Vol 0026, 93; Cultures Of Natural-History, Annals of Sci, Vol 0053, 96; Darwin and After Darwin--History of the Hypothesis of Natural-Selection, Brit Jour Hist Sci, Vol 0026, 93; The Social-History of British Anthropology, 1885-1945, Brit Jour Hist Sci, Vol 0026, 93; Huxley--The Devils Disciple, Hist Philos Life Sci, Vol 0017, 95; Huxley--The Devils Disciple, Hist and Philos Life Sci, Vol 0017, 95; The Correspondence of Darwin,Charles, Vol 9, Hist and Philos Life Sci, Vol 0017, 95; An Agenda for Antiquity--Osborn, Henry, Fairfield and Vertebrate Paleontology at the American-Museum-of-Natural-History, 1890-1935, Brit Jour Hist Sci, Vol 0026, 93; Biology Takes Form--Animal Morphology and the German Universities, 1800-1900, Annals of Sci, Vol 0053, 96; Darwin, Darwinism, Evolutionism--French, Brit Jour Hist Sci, Vol 0026, 93; History of the Concept of Recapitulation--Ontogeny and Phylogenesis in Biology and the Human-Sciences--French, Brit Jour Hist Sci, Vol 0028, 95; The Meaning of Evolution--The Morphological Construction and Ideological Reconstruction of Darwin Theory, Biol and Philos, Vol 0008, 93; Ideology and the History of Science, Biol and Philos, Vol 0008, 93; Darwin, Soc Hist Med, Vol 0005, 92; Transforming Traditions in American Biology, 1880-1915, Brit Jour Hist Sci, Vol 0025, 92; History of the Concept of Recapitulation--Ontogeny and Phylogenesis in Biology and the Human-Sciences--French, Brit Jour Hist Sci, Vol 0028, 95; Victorian Values--The Life and Times of Lankester, Edwin, Notes and Records of the Royal Society of London, Vol 0047, 93; The Correspondence of Darwin, Charles, Vol 9--1861, Hist and Philos Life Sci, Vol 0017, 95; Huxley,Julian--Biologist and Statesman of Science, Annals of Sci, Vol 0052, 95; Antievolution--A Readers Guide to Writings Before and After Darwin, Annals Sci, Vol 0051, 94; Antievolution--A Readers Guide to Writings Before and After Darwin, Annals Sci, Vol 0051, 94; Nature Lost--Natural-Science and the German Theological Traditions of the 19th-Century, Hist and Philos Life Sci, Vol 0016, 94; Cultures of Natural-History, Annals Sci, Vol 0053, 96; Theory Change in Science--Strategies from Mendelian Genetics, Annals of Sci, Vol 0050, 93; Darwin and After Darwin--History of the Hypothesis of Natural-Selection--French, Brit Jour Hist Sci, Vol 0026, 93. **CONTACT ADDRESS** Dept Hist, Queens Univ, Belfast, ..

BOWLING, KENNETH R.
PERSONAL Born 09/12/1940, Baltimore, MD, 1 child **DISCIPLINE** EARLY AMERICAN HISTORY **EDUCATION** Dickinson Col, BA, 62; Univ Wis-Madison, MA, 64, PhD(hist), 68. **CAREER** Proj assoc hist, 67-70, Nat Endowment for Humanities bicentennial fel, 70-71, asst prof hist, Inst Environ Studies, Univ Wis-Madison, 71-74; MEM STAFF, FIRST FED CONG PROJ, GEORGE WASHINGTON UNIV, 75-, Am Philos Soc res grant, 77. **HONORS AND AWARDS** Charles Thomson Prize, Nat Archives, 76. **RESEARCH** Late 18th century American politics; American reactions to the environment; cultural ecology. **CONTACT ADDRESS** George Washington Univ, 1323 E Wilson St, Madison, WI, 53703.

BOWMAN, JEFFREY A.
DISCIPLINE HISTORY **EDUCATION** Carleton Col, BA, 88; Yale Univ, MA, 92; Mphil, 94; PhD, 97. **CAREER** Asst prof, Kenyon Coll, 97-; Fel, Yale Univ, 90-94; tchg asst, Yale Univ, 93-94; instr, Yale Summer Lang Inst, 94-96; fel, John F. Enders, 95; instr, Yale Univ, 95; Whiting Found Diss fel, 95-96; Bourses Chateaubriand, 95-96; Yale Univ Diss Fel, 96-97; asst prof, Kenyon Col, 97-. **HONORS AND AWARDS** Sterling Prize for Outstanding Entering Grad Students, Yale Univ, 90-92; res grant, Prog for Cult Coop, 93; res grant, Am Hist Assoc Bernadotte E. Schmitt, 93. **RESEARCH** European history. **SELECTED PUBLICATIONS** Auth, Do Neo-Romans Curse? Land, Law, and Ritual in the Midi (900-1100), Viator 28, 97; Sicilian Identity and the Middle Ages (1000-1300), Sicilia Bella: The Other Side of Italy, proceedings of a symposium at the Museo ItaloAmericano, 96. **CONTACT ADDRESS** Dept of Hist, Kenyon Col, Gambier, OH, 43022. **EMAIL** bowmanj@kenyon.edu

BOWMAN, JOYE L.
DISCIPLINE HISTORY **EDUCATION** UCLA, PhD, 80. **CAREER** Prof, Univ MA Amherst. **RESEARCH** Hist of Portuguese Africa. **SELECTED PUBLICATIONS** Auth, Ominous Transition: Commerce and Colonial Expansion in the Senegambia and Guinea 1857-1919, 97; publ(s) on Guinea-Bissau; African Affairs. **CONTACT ADDRESS** Dept of Hist, Univ Massachusetts Amherst, Mass Ave, Amherst, MA, 01003.

BOWMAN, L.M.
DISCIPLINE GREEK TRAGEDY; HELLENISTIC POETRY **EDUCATION** Univ Toronto, BA, 81; Univ Brit Col, MA, 86; UCLA, PhD, 94. **CAREER** Asst prof, 92. **RESEARCH** Women in antiquity. **SELECTED PUBLICATIONS** Auth, Interview with David Halperin, Favonius 3, 91; Klytaimnestra's Dream: Prophecy in Sophokles' Elektra, Phoenix 51, 97. **CONTACT ADDRESS** Dept of Greek and Roman Studies, Victoria Univ, PO Box 1700 STN CSC, Victoria, BC, V8W 2Y2. **EMAIL** lbowman@uvic.ca

BOWMAN, SHEARER DAVIS
DISCIPLINE HISTORY **EDUCATION** Univ Virginia, BA, 71; MA, 76, PhD, 86, Univ California-Berkeley. **CAREER** Asst Prof, Hampden-Sydney Col, VA, 84-86; Asst Prof, 86-93, Assoc Prof, 93-, Univ Texas-Austin **CONTACT ADDRESS** Dept of History, Univ of Texas, Austin, Austin, TX, 78712-1163. **EMAIL** s.bowman@mail.utexas.edu

BOWSER, BENJAMIN P.
PERSONAL Born 08/20/1946, New York, NY, m, 1 child **DISCIPLINE** SOCIOLOGY **EDUCATION** Franklin & Marshall Col, BA, 68; Cornell Univ, PhD, 76. **CAREER** Asst Prof, SUNY, 72-75; Asst Dean of Grad Sch, Cornell Univ, 75-72; Dir, Minority Educ Ofce, W Interstate Commission Higher Educ, Boulder, Colo, 82-83; Dir, Black Student Aff, Santa Clara Univ, 83-85; Asst to Dir, Infor Tech Svcs, Stanford Univ, 85-86; Res Dir, Bayview Hunters Pt Found, 90-91; Prof Sociol & Soc Svcs, Calif State Univ, Hayward, 86-. **HONORS AND AWARDS** Rockefeller Found Dissertation Res Fellow, 72; Soc Sci Asn Honor, 82; Vis Res Schol, Ind Univ of Pa, 84; For Contribution to Higher Educ in Santa Clara Valley, 87; Meritorious Perf & Prof Promise, Calif State Univ, 90; James H Nakano Citation for Outstanding Sci Paper, 95; Outstanding Prof of the Yr, Calif State Univ, Hayward, 96; Pres Distinguished Fellow, Franklin & Marshall Col, 97. **RESEARCH** Sociology. **SELECTED PUBLICATIONS** Co-auth, Confronting Diversity Issues on Campus, Sage, 93; co-auth, Intersecting Epidemics--Crack Cocaine Use and HIV Infection Among Inner-City Young Adults, New England J of Med, 331, 1422-1427, 94; ed, Racism and Anti-Racism in World Perspective, Sage, 95; co-auth, Personal Reflections on WEB DuBois: The Person, Scholar, and Activist, WEB DuBois: The Scholar as Activist, vol 9, JAI Press, 96; auth, African American Men as Injection Drug Users: An Application of Alienation Theory to Addiction and Treatment, The J of Res on Minority Affairs, 6:1, 85-101, 96; co-auth, Impacts of Racism on White Americans, Sage, 2nd ed, 96. **CONTACT ADDRESS** Dept of Sociol & Soc Services, California State Univ, Hayward, 3103 Meiklejohn Hall, Hayward, CA, 94542. **EMAIL** bbowser@csuhayward.edu

BOWSKY, MARTHA WELBORN
PERSONAL Born 07/17/1950, High Point, NC, m, 1986, 2 children **DISCIPLINE** CLASSICAL STUDIES **EDUCATION** Univ of Michigan, Ann Arbor, PhD, 83; Univ of NC, Chapel Hill, MA, 74, BA, 72. **CAREER** Asst, Assoc, Prof, 84-, Univ of the Pacific Coast; Vis Asst Prof, 83-84, Univ of Cal, Davis. **HONORS AND AWARDS** Who's Who Among Amer Tchr; Amer Philos Soc; HEH Trave to Collections; Amer Philos Soc. **MEMBERSHIPS** Assoc Intl d'Epigraphie Grecque et Latine; Amer Philological Assoc; Archaeol Inst Amer; Assoc of Ancient Hist; CA Classical Assoc. **RESEARCH** Epigraphy; Ancient Hist; Women's Gender Stud. **SELECTED PUBLICATIONS** Auth, An Atticizing Stele from Western Crete, Zeitschrift fur Papyrologie und Epigraphik 118, 97; Knossos and Campania: the Critical Connection, Preliminary Publication of the Eleventh International Congress of Greek and Latin Epigraphy, 97; Roman Crete: No Provincial Backwater, Proceedings of the Seventh International Cretological Congress, Rethymnon, Crete, 95; Eight Inscriptions from Roman Crete, Zeitschrift fur Papyrologie und Epigraphik, 95; Cretan Connections: The Transformation of Hierapytna, Cretan Studies, 95; Portrait of a Polis: Lato pros Kamara in the Late Second Century B.C., Hesperia, 89. **CONTACT ADDRESS** 824 Burr St, Davis, CA. **EMAIL** MWBowsky@vmsl.cc.uop.edu

BOWSKY, WILLIAM MARVIN
PERSONAL Born 04/16/1930, New York, NY, 2 children **DISCIPLINE** MEDIEVAL HISTORY **EDUCATION** NY Univ, BA, 52; Princeton Univ, MA, 53, PhD, 57. **CAREER** Instr hist, Princeton Univ, 56-57 & Univ Ore, 57-58; from asst prof to prof, Univ Nebr, 58-67; PROF HIST, UNIV CALIF, DAVIS, 67-, Asst, Inst Advan Studies, 56-57; res grants, Am Coun Learned Soc, 60 & Am Philos Soc, 61; Soc Sci Res Coun & Guggenheim fels, 63-64; fel, Accad Senese degli Intronati; fel, Deputazione di Storia Patria per la Toscana. **HONORS AND AWARDS** Dr, Univ Siena. **MEMBERSHIPS** AHA; fel Mediaeval Acad Am; Renaissance Soc Am; Medieval Asn Pac; Soc Ital Hist Studies. **RESEARCH** Italian history; institutional history; urban history. **SELECTED PUBLICATIONS** Auth, City Spaces--Siena and the Sienese Region 13th-14th Century-French, Speculum-Jour Medieval Stud, Vol 0072, 97; Territorial Organization in 13th-Century and 14th-Century Italy and Germany-Ital, Speculum-Jour Medieval Stud, Vol 0071, 96; The Other Tuscany--Essays in the History of Lucca, Pisa, and Siena during the 13th, 14th, and 15th Centuries, Renaissance Quart, Vol 0050, 97; The Laity in the Middle-Ages--Religious Beliefs and Devotional Practices, Speculum-Jour Medieval Stud, Vol 0070, 95; City Spaces--Siena and the Sienese Region 13th-14th Century--French, Speculum-Jour Medieval Stud, Vol 0072, 97; Territorial Organization in 13th-Century and 14th-Century Italy and Germany-Ital, Speculum-Jour Medieval Stud, Vol 0071, 96; The Laity in the Middle-Ages--Religious Beliefs and Devotional Practices, Speculum-Jour Medieval Stud, Vol 0070, 95. **CONTACT ADDRESS** Dept of Hist, Univ of Calif, Davis, CA, 95616.

BOYAJIAN, JAMES CHARLES
PERSONAL Born 10/26/1949, Fresno, CA **DISCIPLINE** MODERN EUROPEAN AND LATIN AMERICAN HISTORY **EDUCATION** Univ Calif, Santa Barbara, BA, 71; Univ Calif, Berkeley, MA, 72, PhD(hist), 78. **CAREER** Lecter urban hist, Univ Calif, Berkeley, 79; res fel hist, Fundacao Calouste Gulbenkian, Lisbon, 79-80; RES & WRITING, 81- **MEMBERSHIPS** AHA; Soc Span & Portuguese Hist Studies; Conf Group Mod Portugal. **RESEARCH** Iberian social and economic history; Iberian overseas expansion and trade; Iberian Inquisitions. **SELECTED PUBLICATIONS** Auth, Untitled, Amer Hist Rev, Vol 0099, 94; Spanish Monetary-Policy in the Spanish-American Colonies, 1750-1808--Concepts and Measures Within the Framework of Bourbon Reform Policies-German, Amer Hist Rev, Vol 0099, 94. **CONTACT ADDRESS** 7349 S Cherry Ave, Fresno, CA, 93725.

BOYD, BARBARA WEIDEN
PERSONAL Born 03/31/1952, Bronx, NY, m, 1980, 1 child **DISCIPLINE** CLASSICAL STUDIES **EDUCATION** Manhattanville Col, BA, 74; Univ Mich, MA, 76. PhD, 80. **CAREER** Asst prof to prof, Bowdoin Col, 80- . **HONORS AND AWARDS** NEH Fel, 87-88. **MEMBERSHIPS** Am Philol Asn; Vergilian Soc; Class Asn of the Midwest & South; Class Assn of New England. **RESEARCH** Latin poetry, Vergil and Ovid; Augustan Rome; Republican Roman literature and society. **SELECTED PUBLICATIONS** Auth, Cydonea mala: Virgilian Word-Play and Allusion, in Harvard Studies in Class Philol, 83; auth, Tarpeia's Tomb: A Note on Propertius 4.4, in Am J of Philol, 84; auth, Parva seges satis est: The Landscape of Tibullan Elegy in 1.1. and 1.10, in Transactions of the Am Philol Asn, 84; auth, the Death of Corinna's Parrot Reconsidered: Poetry and Ovid's Amores, in the Class J, 87; auth, Propertius on the Banks of the Eurotas, in Class Q, 87; auth, Virtus Effeminata and Sallust's Sempronia, in Transactions of the Am Philol Asn, 97; auth, Non Hortamine Longo: An Ovidian "Correction of Virgil, in Am J of Philol, 90; auth, Vergil's Camilla and the Traditions of Catalogue and Ecphrasis, in Am J of Philol, 92; auth, Non enarrabile textum: Ecphrastic Trespass and Narrative Ambiguity in the Aeneid, in Vergilius, 95; auth, Bibliography for Ovid's Amores and Metamorphoses, in Teacher's Guide to Advanced Placement Courses in Latin, 95; auth, Changes in the 1999 Advanced Placement Examinations in Latin (Vergil and Latin Literature), in Class Outlook, 97; auth, Ovid's Literary Loves: Influence and Innovation in the Amores, Univ Michigan Pr, 97; auth, Pallas and Turnus: Selections from Vergil, Aeneid Books 10 and 12, Bolchazy-Carducci, 98. **CONTACT ADDRESS** Dept of Classics, Bowdoin Col, Brunswick, ME, 04011. **EMAIL** bboyd@bowdoin.edu

BOYD, CARL
PERSONAL Born 03/27/1936, Philadelphia, PA **DISCIPLINE** MILITARY HISTORY **EDUCATION** Ind Univ, Bloomington, AB, 62, AM, 63; Univ Calif, Davis, PhD, 71. **CAREER** Instr hist, Henderson St Col, 63-64; instr, asst prof, 69-75, Ohio St Univ; asst prof, assoc prof, prof, 75-85, eminent scholar, 94-, Louis I Jaffe Prof, Col of Arts & Letters, 95-, Old Dominion Univ; vis scholar, 87-89, US Army Ctr Mil Hist; vis, 93, Inst Advan Stud, Princeton; vis prof, 95, 96, Kitakyushu Univ, Japan; Scholar in res, 96-97, Natl Sec Agency. **HONORS AND AWARDS** Amer Philos Soc res grant, 90; Huntington

Fel, Mariners' Museum, 96; Charles O & Elisabeth C Burgess Fac Res & Creativity Award, 98. **MEMBERSHIPS** AHA; Int Naval Res Orgn; Amer Comt Hist Second World War; US Naval Inst; Amer Mil Inst. **RESEARCH** War studies; naval history; modern German and Japanese military strategy and policy. **SELECTED PUBLICATIONS** Art, Exaltation and Hindsight: Tojo's Reflections upon Parting with Lieutenant Colonel Kenworthy, A Man Bearing the Spirit of an Ancient Samurai, Mintclair J Soc Sci & Humanities, fall 74; auth, Attacking the Indianapolis: A Re-examination, Warship Int, 76; art, The Role of Hiroshi Oshima in the Preparation of the Anti-Comintern Pact, J Asian Hist, 77; contribr, The Japanese Submarine Force and the Legacy of Strategic and Operational Doctrine Developed between the World Wars, Selected Papers from The Citadel Conference on War and Diplomacy, Citadel, 79; auth, The Extraordinary Envoy: General Hiroshi Oshima and Diplomacy in the Third Reich, 1934-1939, Univ Press Am, 80; auth, The Berlin-Tokyo Axis and Japanese Military Initiative, Modern Asian Studies, UK, 81; art, New Documentation for the Study of the Second World War, Microform Rev, fall 81; contribr, The Magic Betrayal of Hitler, Selected Papers from the Citadel Symposium on Hitler and the National Socialist Era, Citadel, 82; auth, Hitler's Japanese Confidant: General Oshima Hiroshi and MAGIC Intelligence, 1941-1945, Univ Press KS, 93; auth, American Command of the Sea through Carriers, Codes, and the Silent Service, Mariners' Museum, 95; coauth, The Japanese Submarine Force and World War II, Naval Inst Press, 95. **CONTACT ADDRESS** Dept of History, Old Dominion Univ, Norfolk, VA, 23529-0091. **EMAIL** CBOYD31480@aol.com

BOYD, CAROLYN PATRICIA
PERSONAL Born 06/01/1944, San Diego, CA, m, 1975, 1 child **DISCIPLINE** SPANISH HISTORY **EDUCATION** Stanford Univ, AB, 66; Univ Wash, MA, 69, PhD, 74. **CAREER** Instr, 73-74, asst prof, 74-79, assoc prof, 79-95, prof hist, Univ TX, Austin, 95, ch, 94-, Am Coun Learned Soc grant hist, 77-78, 85; Am Philos Soc grant hist, 78-79. **HONORS AND AWARDS** Phi Beta Kappa, Phi Alpha Theta. **MEMBERSHIPS** Soc Span & Port Hist Studies; AHA; Coun for Europ Studies. **RESEARCH** Mod Span hist, polit and cult; civil-mil rel; hist of educ; nationalism. **SELECTED PUBLICATIONS** Auth, The Anarchists and Education in Spain, 1868-1909, J Mod Hist, 76; Praetorian Politics in Liberal Spain, Univ NC, 79; Responsibilities and the Second Spanish Republic, European Hist Quart, 84; Las reformas militares, Historia general de Espana y America, vol 17, 86; La politica pretoriana en el reinado de Alfonso XIII, Alianza Editorial, 90; Historia Patria: Politics, History and National Identity in Spain, 1875-1975, Princeton, 97. **CONTACT ADDRESS** Dept of Hist, Univ of Texas, Austin, TX, 78712-1026. **EMAIL** cpboyd@mail.utexas.edu

BOYER, HORACE CLARENCE
PERSONAL Born 07/28/1935, Winter Park, Florida, m **DISCIPLINE** MUSIC **EDUCATION** Bethune-Cookman College, BA, 1957; Eastman School of Music, University of Rochester, MA, 1964, PhD, 1973. **CAREER** Monroe High School, instructor 1957-58; Poinsett Elementary School, instructor, 1960-63; Albany State College, asst professor, 1964-65; University of Central Florida, asst professor, 1972-73; University of Massachusetts Amherst, Dept of Music, professor, 1973-. **HONORS AND AWARDS** Ford Foundation Fellow, Eastman School of Music, 1969-72; curator, Natl Museum of American History, Smithsonian, 1985-86; United Negro College Fund, Distinguished Scholar-at-Large, Fisk University, 1986-87. **MEMBERSHIPS** Vice Pres, A Better Chance, 1980-82; editorial board, Black Music Research Journal, 1980-83; vice president, Gospel Music Assn, 1983-84. **CONTACT ADDRESS** Dept of Music, Univ of Massachusetts at Amherst, Amherst, MA, 01003-0041.

BOYER, JOHN WILLIAM
PERSONAL Born 10/17/1946, Chicago, IL, m, 1968, 3 children **DISCIPLINE** EUROPEAN HISTORY **EDUCATION** Loyola Univ, Chicago, BA, 68; Univ Chicago, MA, 69, PhD, 75. **CAREER** Lectr western civilization, 73-74, from Instr Europ Hist to Prof Modern Hist, 74-95, Martin A. Ryerson Distinguished Service Professor of History, Univ Chicago, 95-, Dean of the Col, 92-; Assoc Ed, 78-80, Co-ed, J Mod Hist, 80-; Christensen Vis Fel, St Catherine's Col, Oxford Univ, 83. **HONORS AND AWARDS** Foreign Area Fel, Am Coun Learned Soc & Soc Res Coun, 70-72; Grant-in-Aid, Am Coun Learned Soc, 76, 82; Spencer Found Res Awards, 77, 80, 82; Theodor Krner Prize, 78; Alexander von Humboldt fel, 80-81; John Gilmary Shea Prize, Am Cath Hist Asn, for: Political Radicalism in Late Imperial Vienna, 82; NEH Sr Res Fel, 83-84; Res Grant, Lilly Found, 88; Ludwig Jedlicka Memorial Prize, for: "Culture and Political Crisis in Vienna", 96. **MEMBERSHIPS** Am Hist Asn. **RESEARCH** Austrian and Ger hist; relig and polit in mod Europ hist; comp Europ and Am polit hist. **SELECTED PUBLICATIONS** Auth, Catholic priests in lower Austria, Proc Am Philos Soc, 74; A J P Taylor and the art of modern history, 77 & Freud, marriage and late Viennese liberalism, 78, J Mod Hist; Karl Lueger and Viennese Jewry, Leo Baeck Inst Yearbk, 81; Political Radicalism in Late Imperial Vienna, Univ Chicago Press, 81; Verderungen im politischen Leben Wiens, Jahrbuch des Vereins fuer Geschichte der Stadt Wien, 80-81; co-ed, Nineteenth Century Europe. Liberalism and its Critics, Univ Chicago Press, 87; Twentieth Century Europe, Univ Chicago Press, 87; auth, Some Reflections on the Problem of Austria, Germany, and Mitteleuropa, Central Europ Hist, 89; Culture and Political Crisis in Vienna: Christian Socialism in Power, 1879-1918, Univ Chicago Press, 95; ed, The Aims of Education, Col of the Univ Chicago, 97. **CONTACT ADDRESS** Dept of Hist, Univ of Chicago, 1126 E 59th St, Chicago, IL, 60637-1476. **EMAIL** jwboyer@midway.uchicago.edu

BOYER, LEE R.
DISCIPLINE HISTORY **EDUCATION** Univ Notre Dame, PhD. **CAREER** Prof, Eastern Michigan Univ, 70-. **RESEARCH** US, native american. **SELECTED PUBLICATIONS** Auth, US Indians: A Brief History. **CONTACT ADDRESS** Dept of History and Philosophy, Eastern Michigan Univ, 701 Pray-Harrold, Ypsilanti, MI, 48197.

BOYER, MARJORIE NICE
PERSONAL Born 11/16/1912, Pelham, MA, m, 1935, 4 children **DISCIPLINE** MEDIEVAL HISTORY **EDUCATION** Ohio State Univ, AB, 33; Columbia Univ, MA, 34, PhD, 58. **CAREER** Lectr hist, Brooklyn Col, 56-66 & Univ Kans, 66; asst prof, 67-71, assoc prof, 72-78, PROF HIST, YORK COL, 79- **MEMBERSHIPS** AHA; Mediaeval Acad Am; Renaissance Soc Am; Soc Hist Technol; Soc Hist Paris & l'Ile-de-France. **RESEARCH** History of travel, technology and bridges in medieval France. **SELECTED PUBLICATIONS** Auth, The Art of Medieval Technolog--Images of Noah the Shipbuilde, Amer Hist Rev, Vol 0098, 93. **CONTACT ADDRESS** Dept of Hist, York Col, CUNY, 150-14 Jamaica Ave, Jamaica, NY, 11432.

BOYER, PAUL S.
PERSONAL Born 08/02/1935, Dayton, OH, m, 1962, 2 children **DISCIPLINE** AMERICAN INTELLECTUAL HISTORY & CULTURAL HISTORY **EDUCATION** Harvard Univ, AB, 60, MA, 61, PhD, 66. **CAREER** Asst ed, Notable Am Women, Harvard, 63-67; from asst prof to assoc prof, 67-75, prof hist, Univ MA, Amherst, 75-80, chmn dept, 78-80; prof hist, Univ WI-Madison, 80-, Merle Curti prof, 85; dir, Inst for Res in the Humanities, 93. **HONORS AND AWARDS** Guggenheim Mem Found fel, 73-74; Rockefeller Hum fel, 82-83; Nat Bk Award nom, 75; John H Dunning Prize, Am Hist Asn, 74; Banta Award, Wis Lib Asn, 93. **MEMBERSHIPS** AHA; Orgn Am Historians; Am Antiq Soc (elected mem, 84); Soc of Am Hist (elected mem, 90); MA Hist Soc (elected mem, 97); Am Acad Arts and Sci (elected mem, 97). **RESEARCH** Nuclear weapons in Am thought and cult; prophetic belief in Am popular relig; Am intellectual hist overview survey. **SELECTED PUBLICATIONS** Auth, Purity in Print: The Vice Society Movement and Book Censorship in America, Scribner's, 68; Asst ed, Notable Am Women, 3 vols, Harvard Univ Press, 71; Co-auth, Salem Possessed: The Social Origins of Witchcraft, Harvard Univ Press, 74; Urban masses and Moral Order in America, 1820-1920, Harvard Univ Press, 78; By the Bomb's Early Light: American Thought and Culture at the Dawn of the Atomic Age, Pantheon, 85, Univ of NC Press, 95; When Time Shall Be No More: Prophecy Belief in Modern American Culture, Harvard Univ Press, 92; Fallout: A Historian Reflects on America's Half-Century Encounter with Nuclear Weapons, Ohio State Univ Press, 98; Promises to Keep: The U S Since World War II, 2nd ed, Houghton Mifflin, 98; The American Nation, Holt, Rinehart & Winston, 98; Co-auth, The Enduring Vision: A History of the American People, 4th ed, Houghton Mifflin, 99; Ed-in-chief, Oxford Companion to United States History, Oxford Univ Press, 2000. **CONTACT ADDRESS** Inst Res in the Hum, Washburn Observatory Univ Wisconsin-Madison, 1401 Observatory Dr, Madison, WI, 53706-1483. **EMAIL** psboyer@facstaff.wisc.edu

BOYER, RICHARD
PERSONAL Los Angeles, CA **DISCIPLINE** LATIN AMERICAN HISTORY **EDUCATION** Westmont Col, BA, 59; Univ Wash, MA, 62; Univ Conn, PhD(hist), 73. **CAREER** Teacher hist, Lakeside Sch, 63-67 & 71-72; from instr to asst prof, 72-77, ASSOC PROF HIST, SIMON FRASER UNIV, 77- **MEMBERSHIPS** AHA; Conf Latin Am Hist; Can Asn Latin Am Studies. **RESEARCH** Social history of New Spain in the 17th century; urban history of Latin America. **SELECTED PUBLICATIONS** Auth, Old-Norse Images of Women, Cahiers de Civilisation Medievale, Vol 0040, 97; Women in Old-Norse Society, Cahiers de Civilisation Medievale, Vol 0040, 97; Riots in the Cities--Popular Politics and the Urban-Poor in Latin-America, 1765-1910, Urban Hist Rev, Vol 0025, 97; Urban Space and Housing in Mexico-City-Spanish, Hisp Amer Hist Rev, Vol 0073, 93; Negotiating Calidad--The Everyday Struggle for Status in Mexico, Hist Archaeol, Vol 0031, 97; The Secret History of Gender--Women, Men, and Power in Late Colonial Mexico, Hisp Amer Hist Rev, Vol 0077, 97; The Adaptation of Oriental Imagery in Norse Fornaldarsogu-- Materials Adding a New Dimension to the Study of Old-Norse Literature-German, Cahiers de Civilisation Medievale, Vol 0038, 95; Peasant and Nation, the Making of Postcolonial Mexico and Peru, Intl Hist Rev, Vol 0018, 96; The Myth of the North, Etudes Germaniques, Vol 0050, 95; The Protean Muse of Danish Poet Rifbjerg,Klaus, Europe-Rev Lit Mensuelle, Vol 0074, 96; Swedish Letters--Swedish Lit, Europe-Rev Lit Mensuelle, Vol 0072, 94; Guatemala in the Spanish Colonial Period, Hisp Amer Hist Rev, Vol 0075, 95; Laxness,Halldor-The Novel--An Introduction-German, Etudes Germaniques, Vol 0052, 97; Trotzig,Brigitta, On The Other Side of Darkness, Europe-Rev Lit Mensuelle, Vol 0072, 94; Pilgrims, Miracles and Everyday Life--Forms of Behavior in Scandinavia During the Middle-Ages-12th-Century to the 15th-Century-German, Vol 0038, 95; Medieval Iceland--Society, Sagas and Power, Cahiers de Civilisation Medievale, Vol 0036, 93. **CONTACT ADDRESS** Dept of Hist, Simon Fraser Univ, Burnaby, BC, V5A 1S6.

BOYLAN, ANNE MARY
PERSONAL Born 04/09/1947, Thurles, Ireland **DISCIPLINE** UNITED STATES HISTORY **EDUCATION** Mundelein Col, BA, 68; Univ Wis-Madison, MA, 70, PhD(US hist), 73. **CAREER** Vis asst prof hist, Univ Minn, 73-76, lectr, Univ NMex, 76-77; lectr, Univ Tex, El Paso, 77-79; VIS LECTR, UNIV NMEX, 79-, Res grant, Auburn Theological Sem, 74; teaching consult, Pueblo Teacher Educ Prog, Univ NMex, 76-77; Nat Endowment Humanities summer stipend, 79. **MEMBERSHIPS** Orgn Am Historians; Irish-Am Cult Inst; Western Asn Women Historians. **RESEARCH** History of American religion; history of the family; history of women. **SELECTED PUBLICATIONS** Auth, Ahead of Her Time--Kelley, Abby and the Politics Of Antislavery--Sterling, Am Hist Rev, vol 0098, 93; The Transformation of Charity in Postrevolutionary New-England--Wright, William Mary Quarterly, vol 0050, 93; Ladies, Women and Wenches--Choice and Constraint in Antebellum Charleston and Boston--Pease, J Soc Hist, vol 0026, 93; The Womens Movements in the United-States and Britain From the 1790s to the 1920s--Bolt, J Am Hist, vol 0081, 94; Keepers of the Covenant--Frontier Missions and the Decline of Congregationalism, 1774-1818--Rohrer, William Mary Quarterly, vol 0053, 96; Moralists and Modernizers--America Pre-Civil War Reformers--Mintz, J Southern Hist, vol 0063, 97; Pilgrim Path--The 1st Company of Women Missionaries to Hawaii--Zwiep, Am Hist Rev, vol 0098, 93; Women Against Women--American Anti-Suffragism, 1880-1920--Camhi, J Am Hist, vol 0083, 96; The Home, Heaven, and Mother Party--Female Anti-Suffragists in the United-States, 1868-1920--Jablonsky, J Am Hist, vol 0083, 96. **CONTACT ADDRESS** Univ Delaware, Newark, DE, 19718.

BOYLE, JOHN HUNTER
PERSONAL Born 10/06/1930, Huron, SD, m, 1958, 2 children **DISCIPLINE** HISTORY OF EAST ASIA **EDUCATION** Georgetown Univ, BS, 53; Harvard Univ, MA, 58; Stanford Univ, PhD(hist), 68. **CAREER** Assoc prof, 68-74, PROF HIST, CALIF STATE UNIV, CHICO, 74-, Fulbright grant for asst ed, Japan Interpreter, Tokyo, 69-70. **MEMBERSHIPS** Asn Asian Studies; AHA; Pac Area Intercol Coun Asian Studies. **RESEARCH** History of Sino-Japanese War, 1937-45. **SELECTED PUBLICATIONS** Auth, The Way of the Heavenly Sword--The Japanese Army in the 1920s--Humphreys, Am Hist Rev, vol 0101, 96. **CONTACT ADDRESS** Dept Hist, California State Univ, Chico, Chico, CA, 95929.

BOYLE, KEVIN
DISCIPLINE HISTORY **EDUCATION** Univ Detroit, BA, 82; Univ Michigan , MA, 84, PhD, 90. **CAREER** Asst Prof, 90-94, Univ Toledo; Asst Prof, 94-97, Assoc Prof, 97-, Univ Massachusetts. **CONTACT ADDRESS** Dept of History, Univ of Massachusetts, Amherst, Amherst, MA, 01003. **EMAIL** kboyle@history.umass.edu

BOZEMAN, THEODORE DWIGHT
PERSONAL Born 01/27/1942, Gainesville, FL, m, 1974 **DISCIPLINE** RELIGION, HISTORY **EDUCATION** Fla Presby Col, BA, 64; Union Theol Sem, New York, BD, 68; Union Theol Sem, Richmond, ThM, 70; Duke Univ, PhD, 74. **CAREER** From instr to asst prof, 74-78, from assoc prof to prof Am Relig Hist, Univ Iowa, 78-88; sr assoc mem, St. Antony's Coll, Oxford, 83-84. **MEMBERSHIPS** Am Soc Church Hist; Orgn Am Historians; Am Acad Relig; Southern Hist Assn. **RESEARCH** American religious history; history American religious thought; English and American Puritonism. **SELECTED PUBLICATIONS** Auth To Live Ancient Lives, The Primitivist Dimension in Puritonism, University of North Carolina, 88. **CONTACT ADDRESS** Sch of Relig, Univ of Iowa, 308 Gilmore Hall, Iowa City, IA, 52242-1376. **EMAIL** d-bozeman@uiowa.edu

BRABANT, JOZEF M.
PERSONAL Born 11/05/1942, Hasselt, Belgium, m, 2 children **DISCIPLINE** ECONOMICS **EDUCATION** Yale Univ, PhD 73, MPhil 68, MA 67; Cath Univ, Louvain Belgium, 65, Tchr-(s), Math, Economics and Thomistic Philo Degrees, with Distinction or Great Distinction. **CAREER** United Nations Secretariat, Dept of Econ and Soc Affairs, NY, 75-98-; Isituto Univ Europeo, Italy, vis prof, 87. **HONORS AND AWARDS** Bel Nat Found Sci Res Fellow; Sch of Econ Warsaw Fel; Fulbright-Hays Gnt; Yale Fellow; Belgian Fellowships. **RESEARCH** Eastern Europ Planning. **SELECTED PUBLICATIONS** The 1996 IGC, in: The Europ Union, ed, Boulder CO, Rowman and Littlefield, 99 forthcoming; Managing Globalization, One Europe Mag, forthcoming; The Implications of Widening and

Third Countries, in: The Euro Union, ed, Boulder Co, Rowman and Littlefield, 99 forthcoming; Eastern Europe and the World Trade Organization, in: Eastern Europe and the World Economy, ed by Iliana Zloch-Christy, Chelt, Northampton, MA, Edward Elgar, 98; numerous articles, conf papers, rev. **CONTACT ADDRESS** United Nations, DC 2108, New York, NY, 10163-0020. **EMAIL** brabant@un.org

BRACKENRIDGE, ROBERT DOUGLAS
PERSONAL Born 08/06/1932, Youngstown, OH, m, 1954, 5 children **DISCIPLINE** HISTORY, CHURCH HISTORY **EDUCATION** Muskingum Col, BA, 54; Pittsburgh Theol Sem, BD, 57, ThM, 59; Glasgow Univ, PhD(church hist), 62. **CAREER** Pastor, Cross Rd United Presby Church, 58-60; from asst prof to assoc prof, 62-72, Prof Relig, Trinity Univ, Tex, 72-, Assoc, Danforth Found, 72- **HONORS AND AWARDS** Thornwell Award, 68; Piper Prof, Minnie Stevens Piper Found, 73; Distinguished Serv Award, Presby Hist Soc, 81. **MEMBERSHIPS** Presby Hist Soc (pres, 76-); Am Soc Church Hist; Am Acad Relig; Scottish Church Hist Soc. **SELECTED PUBLICATIONS** Auth, Power From on High--The Development of Mormon Priesthood--Prince, Rev Relig Res, vol 0037, 96; Dictionary of Scottish Church History and Theology--Cameron, Church Hist, vol 0064, 95; Dictionary of Scottish Church History and Theology--Cameron, Church Hist, vol 0064, 95; A History of Memphis-Theological-Seminary of the Cumberland-Presbyterian-Church, 1852-1990--Ingram, Am Presbyterians J, vol 0071, 93; A Contest of Faiths, Missionary Women and Pluralism in the American Southwest--Yohn, Am Presbyterians J, 96. **CONTACT ADDRESS** Dept of Relig, Trinity Univ, San Antonio, TX, 78287.

BRACKETT, DAVID
DISCIPLINE MUSIC HISTORY **EDUCATION** Univ CA Santa Cruz, BA; New Engl Conservatory, MM; Cornell Univ, DMA. **CAREER** Fac, Univ MI and Cornell Univ, vis asst prof, present. **HONORS AND AWARDS** Scholar/awds/fellows from Meet the Composer, Yaddo Artist's Colony, Pittsburgh New Music Festival, Cornell Coun Performing Arts, Cornell Univ, New Engl Conservatory., Performances by the Soc Composers, Pittsburgh New Music Festival, Syracuse Soc New Music, Cornell Contemporary Chamber Players, and Chiron New Music. Commissions by the Harpur Jazz Ensemble and Binghamton Univ Theater Dept; sec/treas, US branch Int Assoc Study Pop Music (IASPM). **MEMBERSHIPS** US branch Int Assoc Study Pop Music (IASPM). **RESEARCH** Compos; non-Western music; hist of popular music. **SELECTED PUBLICATIONS** Auth, Interpreting Popular Music, Cambridge UP, 95; articles/revs in The Journal Am Musicol Soc, Pop Music, Am Music, The Stanford Hum Rev, The Musical Quart, and Critical Quart. **CONTACT ADDRESS** Dept Music, SUNY Binghamton, PO Box 6000, Binghamton, NY, 13902-6000.

BRADBURY, MILES L.
PERSONAL Born 06/16/1938, Sioux City, IA **DISCIPLINE** AMERICAN HISTORY **EDUCATION** Harvard Univ, AB, 60, AM, 61, PhD(hist), 67. **CAREER** ASST PROF HIST, UNIV MD, COLLEGE PARK, 67- **RESEARCH** Early American and American church history. **SELECTED PUBLICATIONS** Auth, Frontier Faiths--Church, Temple, and Synagogue in Los Angeles, 1846-1888--Engh, Am Jewish Hist, vol 0082, 94. **CONTACT ADDRESS** Dept of Hist, Univ of Md, College Park, MD, 20742-0001.

BRADDOCK, ROBERT COOK
PERSONAL Born 05/31/1939, Mt Holly, NJ, m, 1962, 2 children **DISCIPLINE** ENGLISH & EARLY MODERN EUROPEAN HISTORY **EDUCATION** Middlebury Col, AB, 61; Northwestern Univ, MA, 63, PhD(hist), 71. **CAREER** From instr to asst prof, 70-75, chmn dept, 76-78, 96-98, assoc prof to prof Hist, Saginaw Valley State Univ, 75-. **HONORS AND AWARDS** Dist Fac Award, State Univ Mich, 91; Fel of Early Mod Studies, Sixteenth Century Studies Conf, 98. **MEMBERSHIPS** AHA; Renaissance Soc Am; Conf Brit Studies. **RESEARCH** Administrative history especially early modern Europe; the court in Tudor-Stuart England; office holding. **SELECTED PUBLICATIONS** Auth, The Character and Composition of the Duke of Northumberland's Army, Albion VI, 74; The Rewards of Office-Holding in Tudor England, J Brit Studies XIV, 75; J. H. Plumb and the Whig Tradition, In: Recent Historians of Great Britain, Iowa State Univ Press, 90; contribr, Historical Dictionary of Tudor England, Greenwood Press, 91. **CONTACT ADDRESS** Dept of Hist, Saginaw Valley State Univ, 7400 Bay Rd, University Center, MI, 48710-0001. **EMAIL** rcbrad@svsu.edu

BRADFORD, JAMES CHAPIN
PERSONAL Born 04/07/1945, Detroit, MI, m, 1964, 2 children **DISCIPLINE** AMERICAN NAVAL & MILITARY HISTORY **EDUCATION** Mich State Univ, BA, 67, MA, 68; Univ Va, PhD(hist), 76. **CAREER** Res asst, Thomas Jefferson Mem Found, 72-73; asst prof hist, US Naval Acad, 73-81; ASST PROF HIST, TEX A&M UNIV, 81-, Ed, The Papers of John Paul Jones, 78-; mem, Int Comn Maritime Hist, 80-; bk rev ed, J Early Repub, 80- **MEMBERSHIPS** AHA; Orgn Am Historians; NAm Soc Oceanic Hist; Soc Historians of Early Am Repub; Asn Documentary Editing. **RESEARCH** Naval history of the age of sail; local government in Virginia, 1750-1820; early American history. **SELECTED PUBLICATIONS** Auth, Mad Jack--The Biography of Percival, John, Captain, Usn, 1779-1862--Long, Am Neptune, vol 0054, 94; The Commissioned Sea Officers of the Royal Navy, 1600-1815--Syrett, Am Neptune, vol 0057, 97; Admiral Porter, David, Dixon--The Civil War Years--Hearn, Am Neptune, vol 0057, 97; Admiral Moffett, William, A Architect of Naval Aviation--Trimble, Am Hist Rev, vol 0100, 95. **CONTACT ADDRESS** Dept of Hist, Tex A&M Univ, College Station, TX, 77801.

BRADFORD, RICHARD HEADLEE
PERSONAL Born 04/14/1938, Waynesburg, PA, m, 1966 **DISCIPLINE** AMERICAN HISTORY **EDUCATION** Pa State Univ, BA, 62; Ind Univ, MA, 64, PhD(hist), 73. **CAREER** Instr hist, St Louis Jr Col Dist, 64-66; teaching assoc, Ind Univ, 66-68; from asst prof to prof Hist, WVa Univ Inst Technol, 68-. **HONORS AND AWARDS** Phi Alpha Theta Best First Book Award, 81; Am Philos Soc research grant, 82; WVa Writers Asn 1st Prize Dramatic Writing for Knight, Death, and the Devil, 89; WVa Humanities Coun Fel, 97. **RESEARCH** American history. **SELECTED PUBLICATIONS** Auth, Religion and Politics: Alfred E Smith and the 1928 Presidential Primary in West Virginia, WVa Hist, 4/75; And Oregon Rushed Home, Am Neptune, 10/76; John F Kennedy and the 1960 Presidential Primary in West Virginia, S Atlantic Quart, spring 76; That prodigal son: Philo McGiffin and the Chinese Navy, 1885-1894, Am Neptune, 7/78; The Virginius Affair, Colo Assoc Univ Press, 80, 81; The Spanish Problem in American Politics, In: La Republique Imperialiste, Univ De Provence, 87; coauth, An American Family on the American Frontier, Rinehart, 94. **CONTACT ADDRESS** Dept of Hist, West Virginia Univ Inst of Tech, 405 Fayette Pike, Montgomery, WV, 25136-2436. **EMAIL** rhbrad@wvit.wvnet.edu

BRADFORD SMITH, ELIZABETH
DISCIPLINE WESTERN MEDIEVAL ART AND ARCHITECTURE **EDUCATION** Inst Fine Arts, NY, MA, PhD; lisc, Univ Strasbrg, France. **CAREER** Assoc prof, Pa State Univ, 82-. **RESEARCH** Structure of French Romanesque and Italian Gothic architecture. **SELECTED PUBLICATIONS** Auth, Medieval Art in America; patterns of Collecting, Palmer Museum, 1800-1940; arts, Romanesque sculpture in France, England and the Low Countries. **CONTACT ADDRESS** Pennsylvania State Univ, 201 Shields Bldg, University Park, PA, 16802. **EMAIL** exs11@psu.edu

BRADLEY, JAMES R.
PERSONAL Born 03/28/1935, Philadelphia, PA, d, 4 children **DISCIPLINE** CLASSICS **EDUCATION** Trinity Col, BA, 57; Harvard Univ, MA, 59, PhD, 68. **CAREER** Instr, Hobart & William Smith Col, 59-61; asst prof, Univ NC Chapel Hill, 67-70; asst prof, 70-74, assoc prof, 74-, Trinity Col. **MEMBERSHIPS** Amer Philol Asn; Archaeol Inst of Amer. **RESEARCH** Latin & Greek literature; Classical civilization; Classical tradition. **SELECTED PUBLICATIONS** Auth, The Elegies of Sulpicia: An Introduction and Commentary, New Eng Class Newsletter and Jour, XXII, 159-164, May, 95; rev, Apuleius, Cupid and Psyche, New Eng Class Newsletter and Jour, XIX, May, 92; auth, Chinese New Year: Four Centuries Ago, New Eng Class Newsletter and Jour, XIX, 26-27, Dec, 91; auth, The Sources of Cornelius Nepos, Selected Lives, Garland Publ, 91; auth, All the Tea in China, Class Outlook, 68, Fall, 90; auth, Ovid, Ars 1.39-40: Making Tracks - Speed, Ritual or Art, Class World, 83, 100-101, 89; rev, Ars Amatoria I, New Eng Class Newsletter, XIV, Oct, 86. **CONTACT ADDRESS** Classics Dept., Trinity Col, 300 Summit St., Hartford, CT, 06106. **EMAIL** james.bradley@mail.trincoll.edu

BRADLEY, JAMES ROBERT
PERSONAL Born 03/28/1935, Philadelphia, PA, d, 4 children **DISCIPLINE** CLASSICS **EDUCATION** Trinity Col, CT, BA, 57; Harvard Univ, MA, 59, PhD(class philol), 68. **CAREER** Instr classics, Hobart & William Smith Cols, 60-62; asst prof, Univ NC, 67-70; asst prof, 70-74, assoc prof classics, Trinity Col, CT, 74-. **MEMBERSHIPS** Am Philol Asn; Archaeol Inst Am. **RESEARCH** Greek and Latin literature; classical civilization. **SELECTED PUBLICATIONS** Auth, The Sources of Cornelius Nepos: Selected Lives, NY and London, Garland Pub, 91. **CONTACT ADDRESS** Dept Classics, Trinity Col, 300 Summit St, Hartford, CT, 06106-3186. **EMAIL** james.bradley@mail.trincoll.edu

BRADLEY, KEITH RICHARD
PERSONAL Born 04/30/1946, Oldswinford, England, m, 1976, 3 children **DISCIPLINE** ANCIENT HISTORY, CLASSICAL LANGUAGES **EDUCATION** Sheffield Univ, BA, 67, MA, 68; Oxford Univ, BLitt, 75. **CAREER** Asst prof, Johns Hopkins Univ, 72-77; vis asst prof, Stanford Univ, 77-80; ASST PROF CLASSICS & ANCIENT HIST, UNIV VICTORIA, 80- **MEMBERSHIPS** Soc Prom Roman Studies; Am Philol Asn; Am Asn Ancient Historians; Class Asn Can. **RESEARCH** Roman social history; Roman historiography. **SELECTED PUBLICATIONS** Auth, Slaves And Freedmen in Roman Society Under the Empire--A Selection of Texts With Translations--German, Greek And Latin, vol 0068, 96; Suetonius, 'Lives Of Galba, Otho And Vitellius', Latomus, vol 0055, 96. **CONTACT ADDRESS** Dept of Classics, Univ of Victoria, Victoria, BC, V8W 2Y2.

BRADLEY, OWEN
DISCIPLINE HISTORY **EDUCATION** Cornell Univ, PhD. **CAREER** Asst prof. **RESEARCH** Modern European cultural and intellectual history. **SELECTED PUBLICATIONS** Auth, Joseph de Maistre: Sacred Violence and Modern Social Theory, Univ Nebr. **CONTACT ADDRESS** History Dept, Knoxville, TN, 37996.

BRAEMAN, JOHN
DISCIPLINE 20TH CENTURY AMERICAN HISTORY **EDUCATION** Johns Hopkins Univ, PhD, 60. **CAREER** Prof, Univ Nebr, Lincoln; vis scholar, Bowling Green State Univ, 95; instr, Univ Hannover, Ger, 97. **RESEARCH** The Supreme Court and its civil liberties rulings. **SELECTED PUBLICATIONS** Auth, Albert J. Beveridge: American Nationalist, Univ Chicago Press, 71; Before The Civil Rights Revolution: The Old Court and Individual Rights, Greenwood Press, 88. **CONTACT ADDRESS** Univ Nebr, Lincoln, 643 Oldfat, Lincoln, NE, 68588-0417. **EMAIL** jbraeman@unlinfo.unl.edu

BRAISTED, WILLIAM REYNOLDS
PERSONAL Born 03/14/1918, Washington, DC **DISCIPLINE** HISTORY **EDUCATION** Stanford Univ, AB, 39; Univ Chicago, AM, 40, PhD, 50. **CAREER** Res analyst, Mil Intel Serv, 44-46; Ford Found grant, 52; Fulbright grant, Japan, 55; assoc prof, 58-66, PROF HIST, UNIV TEX, AUSTIN, 66-, Mershon Found grant, 60; Am Coun Learned Soc fel, 67-68; vis prof, US Naval Acad, 77-78. **RESEARCH** Far Eastern history; United States Navy in the Far East. **SELECTED PUBLICATIONS** Auth, American Merchant Ships on the Yangtze, 1920-1941--Grover, Pacific Hist Rev, vol 0063, 94; Kinkaid of The Seventh-Fleet--A Biography of Admiral Kinkaid, Thomas,C., US Navy--Wheeler, J Am Hist, vol 0084, 97; Thailand and Japan Southern Advance, 1940-1945, Hist, vol 0057, 95; 100 Years of Sea Power--The Us-Navy, 1890-1990, Am Neptune, vol 0056, 96; Japan 1st Modern War--Army and Society in the Conflict With China, 1894-1895, J Military Hist, vol 0060, 96. **CONTACT ADDRESS** Dept of Hist, Univ of Tex, Austin, TX, 78712.

BRAND, CHARLES MACY
PERSONAL Born 04/07/1932, Stanford, CA, m, 1954, 2 children **DISCIPLINE** MEDIEVAL HISTORY **EDUCATION** Stanford Univ, AB, 53; Harvard Univ, AM, 54, PhD, 61. **CAREER** Teaching fel, Harvard Univ, 58-61, vis fel, Dumbarton Oaks Res Libr, 61-62, 88; asst prof hist, San Francisco State Col, 62-64; from asst prof to assoc prof, 64-76; pro hist, Bryn Mawr Col, 76-; Fulbright res fel, Greece, 68-69; gov bd, Byzantine Studies Conf, 81-84; Guggenheim Fel, 72-73. **MEMBERSHIPS** AHA; Mediaeval Acad Am. **RESEARCH** Byzantine history; relations between Byzantium and the West. **SELECTED PUBLICATIONS** Auth, Byzantines and Saladin, 1185-1192: opponents of the third crusade, Speculum, 4/62; Byzantium Confronts the West, 1180-1204, Harvard Univ, 68; translr, John Kinnamos, Deeds of John and Manuel Comnenus, Columbia Univ, 76. **CONTACT ADDRESS** Dept of History, Bryn Mawr Col, 101 N Merion Ave, Bryn Mawr, PA, 19010-2899.

BRANDIMARTE, CYNTHIA A.
DISCIPLINE AMERICAN CIVILIZATION **EDUCATION** Univ Texas, PhD, 80 **CAREER** Dir Cult Resources, Tex Pks, Wildlife Dept, 92-97; asst prof, Southwest Tex State Univ, 97-. **CONTACT ADDRESS** Southwest Texas State Univ, 601 Univ Dr, San Marcos, TX, 78666-4615.

BRANDT, BEVERLY K.
PERSONAL Born 08/26/1951, Evanston, IL, s **DISCIPLINE** ARCHITECTURE **EDUCATION** Univ Mich, BFA, 73; Mich State Univ, MA, 77; Boston Univ, PhD, 85 **CAREER** Vis Instr, Ore State Univ, 77-78; Instr, Mich State Univ, 78-80; Asst Prof, Iowa State Univ, 84-87; Asst Prof, 87-92, Fac Affiliate, 94-96, Assoc Prof with tenure, Ariz State Univ, 92-, Dir, Herberger Ctr for Design Excellence, 92-95. **HONORS AND AWARDS** Kappa Omicron Nu; Burlington Resources Found Fac Achievement Award for excellence in teaching, 91; Fel, Ariz Wakonse Conf on Teaching, 92; Lincoln Fel, Joan & David Lincoln Ctr for Ethics, ASU's Col Bus, 96; Fac of the Year award, Student Asn Interior Designers, Ariz State Univ, 98; recipient of numerous grants. **MEMBERSHIPS** Soc Archit Hist; Int Interior Design Asn; Am Soc Interior Designers; Decorative Arts Soc; William Morris Soc. **RESEARCH** History of interior design, ancient to the present; history of decorative arts in interiors, ancient to the present; history of textiles in interiors, ancient to the present; design criticism. **SELECTED PUBLICATIONS** Auth, "Introduction", "Afterword", and chapters on "Interior Design" and "Architecture", The Encyclopedia of Arts & Crafts: The International Arts Movement 1850-1920, EP Dutton/Headline, 89; The Critic and the Evolution of Early-Twentieth-Century American Craft, The Ideal Home. The History of Twentieth-Century American Craft, 1900-1920, Harry N. Abrams, Inc, 93; Foreword, Innovation and Derivation: The Contribution of L & JG Stickley to the Arts and Crafts Movement, The Craftsman Farms Found, 95; One Who Has Seen More and Knows More: The Design Critic and the Arts and Crafts, The Substance of Style: Perspectives on the American Arts and Crafts Movement, The Henry Francis du Pont Winterthur Museum, 96; Overview: Gustave Stickley's Craftsman

Magazine, The Craftsman on CD-ROM, Interactive Bureau, 98; author of numerous articles and other publications. **CONTACT ADDRESS** College of Architecture & Environmental Design, Arizona State Univ, Tempe, Tempe, AR, 85287-2105. **EMAIL** beverly.brandt@asu.edu

BRANHAM, JOAN R.
DISCIPLINE ART HISTORY **EDUCATION** Fla State Univ, BA, 83, MA, 85; Diplome d-etudes francaises, 86; Grad Inst, Lib Arts, Emory Univ, PhD, 93. **CAREER** Fel, Getty Ctr Hist Art, Hum, 93-94; fel, Ecole Pratique des Hautes Etudes, Sorbonne, 94-95; ASSOC PROF, ART HISTORY, PROVIDENCE COL, PRESENTLY. **CONTACT ADDRESS** Dept of Art & Art Hist, Providence Col, Providence, RI, 02918-0001. **EMAIL** jbranham@providence.edu

BRANSON, SUSAN
DISCIPLINE HISTORY **EDUCATION** Northern Ill Univ, PhD, 94. **CAREER** Asst prof. **RESEARCH** U.S. women's history; 18th and 19th century; U.S. early republic. **SELECTED PUBLICATIONS** Auth, Women and the Family Economy in the Early Republic: The Case of Elizabeth Meredith, Jour Early Repub, 96; Beyond Respectability: the Female World of Love and Crime in Nineteenth-Century Philadelphia, 96. **CONTACT ADDRESS** Dept of History, Richardson, TX, 75083-0688. **EMAIL** sbranson@utdallas.edu

BRATTON, TIMOTHY L.
PERSONAL Born 04/21/1947, Cleveland, OH, m, 1975, 3 children **DISCIPLINE** HISTORY & POLITICAL SCIENCE **EDUCATION** Baldwin-Wallace College, BA, 69; Mich St Univ, MA, 71; Bryn Mawr Col, PhD, 79. **CAREER** Instr, 80-82, Villanova Univ; asst prof to assoc prof to prof, chair, 97-, Jamestown Col. **HONORS AND AWARDS** Prof of the Year, 85-86; Burlington Northern Found Faculty Achievement Award, 88; Nat Sci Found Grant, 94. **MEMBERSHIPS** Mediaeval Acad Amer; Amer Hist Assoc, Amer Assoc Hist of Medicine; Paleopathology Assoc; Planetary Soc. **RESEARCH** Hist epidemiology, hist of medicine, hist of astronomy. **SELECTED PUBLICATIONS** Rev, Doctor Bernard de Gordon, J of Hist of Medicine & Allied Sci, 82; art, Jamestown Mounds Project: Vol 2, Skeletal Biology, Paleopathology Newsletter, 87; art, The Birth of the Hospital in the Byzantine Empire, J of Hist of Medicine & Allied Sci, 87; coauth, A Catalogue of the Manuscripts and Archives of the Library of the College of Physicians of Philadelphia, Univ Pa Press, 83; auth, The Identity of the New England Indian Epidemic of 1616-19, Bull of Hist of Medicine, 88; auth, Pre-Columbian Native American Diseases, Or Soc Stud, 97. **CONTACT ADDRESS** 6006 College Ln, Jamestown, ND, 58405. **EMAIL** bratton@acc.jc.edu

BRAUDE, BENJAMIN
DISCIPLINE HISTORY; RELIGION **EDUCATION** Harvard Univ, hist, BA, 67, MA, 75, PhD, 78. **CAREER** Affil, Ctr for Middle Eastern Studies, Harvard Univ, 67-; assoc dir and res assoc, Intl Sem-Conf on Minorities in the Middle East, Prog in Near Eastern Studies, Princeton Univ, 77-78; asst prof, dept of hist, Boston Col, 78-84; adjunct lectr, dept of theol, Boston Col, 79-; assoc prof, dept of hist, Boston Col, 84-; book rev ed, Mod Arab, Turkish, and Ottoman Hist and Polit Sci, Middle East Studies Asn Bull, 84-87; dir, Comt on Middle Eastern Studies, Boston Col, 86-; res assoc, dept of relig, Smith Col, 89-; **HONORS AND AWARDS** George W. Dillaway fel, 67-68; Sinclair Kennedy fel, 68; NDFL fel, 67-68, 68-69; Smith fel, 69-74; Bowdoin prize competition hon mention, 76-77; fel, Res Gp on Jewish World after 1492, Inst for Adv Studies, Hebrew Univ, Jerusalem, 91-92; res grant, Sassoon Intl Ctr for the Study of Antisemitism, 94-97; res grant, Lucius N. Littauer Found, 97. **MEMBERSHIPS** AHA; MESA; AJS. **RESEARCH** Middle Eastern, European, American and Jewish history, particularly issues of race and ethnicity. **SELECTED PUBLICATIONS** Article, Les Contours Indecis d'Une Nouvelle Geographie, Cahiers de Sci et Vie, no 44, 45-53, Apr, 98; article, The Sons of Noah and the Construction of Ethnic and Geographical Identities in the Medieval and Early Modern Periods, William and Mary Quart, 3rd series, vol 54, 103-142, Jan, 97; article, Burckhardt, Jean Louis, I, 427, Burton, Richard, I, 430, Canning, Stratford, I, 442-443, Dickson, Harold Richard Patrick, II, 569-570, Donme, II, 577-578, Doughty, Charles, II, 579, Lawrence, Thomas Edward, III, 1082, Millet System, III, 1224-1226, Minorities, III, 1229-1231, Palgrave, William Gifford, III, 1425, Pelly, Lewis, III, 1440, Philby, Harry St. John Bridger, III, 1461-1462, Thesiger, Wilfrid, IV, 1767, Encycl of the Mod Middle East, NY, 96; article, Mandeville's Jews among Others, Pilgrims and Travellers to the Holy Land, Proceedings of the Seventh Annual Symposium of the Philip M. and Ethel Klutznick Chair in Jewish Civilization, Omaha, 141-168, 96; article, Les Contes Persans de Menasseh Ben Israel: Polemique, Apologetique et Dissimulation a Amsterdam au xvii Siecle, Annales Hist, Sci Sociales, 49, 1107-1138, Sept-Oct, 94. **CONTACT ADDRESS** Dept. of History, Boston Col, Chestnut Hill, MA, 02467. **EMAIL** braude@bc.edu

BRAUER, CARL MALCOLM
PERSONAL Born 09/13/1945, Jersey City, NJ, m, 2 children **DISCIPLINE** HISTORY **EDUCATION** Rutgers Univ, New Brunswick, BA, 68, Harvard Univ, MA, 69, PhD(hist), 73. **CAREER** Vis asst prof hist, Univ Mo-Columbia, 73-74; vis asst prof, Brown Univ, 74-75; asst prof hist, Univ Va, 75-81; RES FEL, INST POLITICS, KENNEDY SCH GOVT, HARVARD UNIV, 82-, Nat Endowment Humanities res fel, 78-79; Charles Warren Ctr Studies Am Hist fel, 78-79. **MEMBERSHIPS** Orgn Am Historians. **RESEARCH** Recent American history; history of public policy; public history. **SELECTED PUBLICATIONS** Auth, Calculating Visions--Kennedy, Johnson, And Civil-Rights--Stern, J Am Hist, vol 0079, 93. **CONTACT ADDRESS** 3 Dean St, Belmont, MA, 02178.

BRAUER, JERALD
PERSONAL Born 09/16/1921, Fond du Lac, WI, m, 1945, 3 children **DISCIPLINE** HISTORY OF CHRISTIANITY **EDUCATION** Carthage Col, AB, 43; Northwestern Lutheran Theol Sem, BD, 45; Univ Chicago, PhD, 48. **CAREER** Instr church hist & hist Christian thought, Union Theol Sem, NY, 48-50; from asst prof to prof church hist, 50-69, dean federated theol fac, 55-60, dean divinity sch, 60-70, Prof Hist Christianity, Univ Chicago, 69-, Naomi Shenstone Donnelley Prof, 69-, Kessler lectr, Hamma Divinity Sch & Wittenberg Col, 54; Merrick lectr, Ohio Wesleyan, 58; mem bd dirs, Rockefeller Theol Fel Prog & Inst Advan Pastoral Studies; trustee, Carthage Col; pres bd theol educ, Lutheran Church in Am, 62-68; deleg observer, Vatican Coun II, session 3, 64, session 4, 65; vis lectr, Univ Tokoyo & Kokagokuin Univ, 66; consult, NY State Dept Educ, 70-; vis fel, Ctr Studies Democratic Insts, 72 & 74; pres bd gov, Int House, 73-; Am Asn Theol Schs grant; fel, Ctr Policy Study, 74-79; Nat Endowment for Humanities fel, 77-78; chmn bd, Coun Relig & Int Affairs, 79- **HONORS AND AWARDS** DD, Miami Univ, 56; LLD, Carthage Col, 57; STD, Ripon Col, 61; LHD, Gettysburg Col, 63. **MEMBERSHIPS** Am Soc Church Hist (pres, 60). **RESEARCH** Puritanism influence in the United States and England; revivalism; religion in America. **SELECTED PUBLICATIONS** Auth, Paying the Words Extra--Religious Discourse in The Supreme-Court of the United-States--Sullivan, Int Rev Hist Relig, vol 0043, 96; Paying the Words Extra--Religious Discourse in the Supreme Court of the United States--Sullivan, Numen Int Rev Hist Relig, vol 0043, 96. **CONTACT ADDRESS** Divinity Sch, Univ of Chicago, 207 Swift Hall, Chicago, IL, 60637.

BRAUER, KINLEY
DISCIPLINE HISTORY **EDUCATION** Univ Rochester, BA, 57; Univ Calif, PhD, 63. **CAREER** Lectr, Oxford Univ, 76-77; vis prof, Univ Munich, 87; dir, Ctr for Austrian Studies, 88-89; dir, Intl Relations Prog, 93-94; Fulbright prof, Univ of Graz, 94-95; prof, Univ Minn Twin Cities. **HONORS AND AWARDS** McKnight Foundation Humanities Awd, 67. **RESEARCH** History of American-foreign relations; Pre-Civil War period. **SELECTED PUBLICATIONS** Auth, pubs on history of American foreign relations; ed, Austria in the Age of the French Revolution, 90. **CONTACT ADDRESS** History Dept, Univ of Minnesota, Twin Cities, 614 Social Sciences Tower, 267 19th Ave. S, Minneapolis, MN, 55455. **EMAIL** braue001@tc.umn.edu

BRAUS, IRA
DISCIPLINE MUSIC **EDUCATION** Oberlin Conservatory, BM; State Univ NY, MM; Harvard Univ, PhD. **CAREER** Taught at SUNY Oneonata, New England Conserv of music, Baters College; Prof, Hartt Sch Music, 97-. **SELECTED PUBLICATIONS** Auth, pubs in The History and Psychology of Music. **CONTACT ADDRESS** Hartt Sch Music, Univ Hartford, 200 Bloomfield Ave, West Hartford, CT, 06117.

BRAUTIGAM, DEBORAH
DISCIPLINE INTERNATIONAL DEVELOPMENT **EDUCATION** Ohio Wesleyan Univ, BA; Tufts Univ, MALD, PhD. **CAREER** Prof, Am Univ, 94-. **HONORS AND AWARDS** Res fel; UN, Res fel, World Bank; U.S; Res fel, Agency Int Develop. **RESEARCH** Political economy of foreign aid and economic reform. **SELECTED PUBLICATIONS** Contribur, Asian Industrialization: Lessons for Africa. MacMillan, 95; The Changing Politics of NGOs and African States, Praeger, 94. **CONTACT ADDRESS** American Univ, 4400 Massachusetts Ave, Washington, DC, 20016.

BRAY, R. MATTHEW
DISCIPLINE HISTORY **EDUCATION** Univ Manitoba, BA, MA; York Univ, PhD. **CAREER** Prof. **RESEARCH** Hist of Can Copper Co. **SELECTED PUBLICATIONS** Co-ed, Reappraisals in Canadian History: Post-Confederation, Toronto, 96; co-ed, Reappraisals in Canadian History: Pre-Confederation, Toronto, 96. **CONTACT ADDRESS** Dept of History, Laurentian Univ, 935 Ramsey Lake Rd, Sudbury, ON, P3E 2C6.

BRECKENRIDGE, JAMES
PERSONAL Born 06/30/1935, St. Louis, MO, m, 1969, 2 children **DISCIPLINE** HISTORY OF RELIGIONS, CHURCH HISTORY **EDUCATION** Biola Col, BA, 57; Calif Baptist theol Sem, BD, 60; Univ Southern Calif, MA, 65, PhD(relig), 68. **CAREER** Lectr church hist & world relig hist, Am Baptist Sem the West, 67-74; ASSOC PROF HIST RELIG, BAYLOR UNIV, 74-, Lectr philos, Calif State Polytech Univ, 69-74. **MEMBERSHIPS** Am Acad Relig. **SELECTED PUBLICATIONS** Auth, Pelagius, Evangel Quart,70; Julian and Athanasius, theology, 73; Augustine and the Donatists, Foundations, 76; Religion and the problem of death, J Dharma, 79. **CONTACT ADDRESS** Dept of Relig, Baylor Univ, Waco, TX, 76703.

BREEN, TIMOTHY HALL
PERSONAL Born 09/05/1942, Cincinnati, OH, m, 1963, 2 children **DISCIPLINE** HISTORY, AMERICAN CULTURE **EDUCATION** Yale Univ, BA, 64, MA, 66, PhD(hist), 68. **CAREER** Asst prof hist, Yale Univ, 68-70; assoc prof hist, 70-75, dir Am cult prog, 75-79, PROF HIST, NORTHWESTERN UNIV, 75-, Am Coun Learned Socs res fel, 71 & Guggenheim res fel, 75; mem, inst Adv Study, 79; Bellagio-Rockefeller Ctr, scholar, 81. **MEMBERSHIPS** Inst Early Am Hist & Cult. **RESEARCH** Colonial America; American cultural history; social and cultural anthropology. **SELECTED PUBLICATIONS** Auth, Narrative of Commercial Life, Consumption Ideology, and Community on the Eve of the American-Revolution, William and Mary Quart, Vol 0050, 93; The Refinement of America in Persons, Houses, Cities, J Southern Hist, Vol 0060, 94; The Power of Commerce in Economy and Governance in the 1st British Empire, J Econ Hist, Vol 0055, 95; The Combing of History, J interdisciplinary Hist, Vol 0027, 96; Ideology and Nationalism on the Eve of the American Revolution, J Amer Hist, Vol 0084, 97; Cooper, William Town in Power and Persuasion on the Frontier of the Early American Republic, Amer Lit, Vol 0069, 97. **CONTACT ADDRESS** Dept of Hist, Northwestern Univ, Evanston, IL, 60201.

BREIHAN, JOHN R.
PERSONAL Born 08/24/1947, St. Louis, MO, m, 1970, 3 children **DISCIPLINE** MODERN ENGLISH HISTORY; 20TH CENTURY AMERICAN HISTORY; AVIATION HISTORY. **EDUCATION** Princeton Univ, AB, 69; Univ Cambridge, PhD, 78. **CAREER** Asst instr hist, Mercer County Community Col, 69-70; prog dir, Regional Conf Hist Agencies, 77; Assoc Prof to Prof Hist, Loyola Col, 77-. Chair, Dept Hist, 83-87; Assoc dir, Fac Inst Writing Across the Curric, Md Writing Prof, 81-82; co-dir, Empirical Rhetoric II writing prog, Loyola Col, 82-87. **HONORS AND AWARDS** Loyola Col summer research grants, 80, 86, 91; sabbatical grant, 88-89, 96-97; Merit Awards for teaching and service, Loyola Col, 82, 83, 96; NEH Summer Inst in Writing Across the Curriculumn, 81; NEH, program implementation grant for Empirical Rhetoric II, cross-curricular writing program at Loyola Col, 82-87; Md Hist Trust, Md Humanities Coun, Nat Trust for Historic Preservation: grant funding for Past and Future of a Planned Suburb: Community Hist and Community Planning for Middle River (Md); Baltimore County Landmarks Preservation Comn, Award for Excellence in Historic Preservation, 96; Verville Fel in Aviation Hist, Smithsonian Inst, 96-97. **MEMBERSHIPS** Nat Trust Hist Preserv; Soc Military Hist; Soc Hist Technol. **RESEARCH** The reform of British government administration during the fifty years between the American War and the Reform Act of 1832; writing in college history courses; historic preservation and local history; history of aircraft industry and effects on city planning. **SELECTED PUBLICATIONS** Auth, The Addington party and the Navy in British politics, 1801-1806, in New Aspects of Naval History, US Naval Inst Press, 81; The abolition of Sinecures, 1782-1834, Proc Consortium on Revolutionary Europe, 81; William Pitt and the Commission on Fees, 1785-1801, The Hist J 27, 84; coauth, Thinking and Writing in College: A Naturalistic Study in Four Disciplines, NCTE, 91; Martin Aircraft 1909-1960, Thompson/Narkiewicz, 95. **CONTACT ADDRESS** Dept of Hist, Loyola Col, 4501 N Charles St, Baltimore, MD, 21210-2694. **EMAIL** breihan@loyola.edu

BREINES, PAUL
PERSONAL Born 04/16/1941, New York, NY, m, 1964, 2 children **DISCIPLINE** MODERN HISTORY **EDUCATION** Univ Wis-Madison, BA, 63, MA, 67, PhD(hist), 72. **CAREER** Asst prof soc sci, Boston Univ, 71-74; asst prof hist, 74-80, ASSOC PROF HIST, BOSTON COL, 80-, DIR GRAD STUDIES, 80-, Book rev ed, Telos, 69-; contrib ed, theory & Soc, 77-. **RESEARCH** Social theory; Marxism: intellectuals. **SELECTED PUBLICATIONS** Auth, Moments of Decision in Political History and the Crises of Radicalism, Amer Hist Rev, Vol 0098, 93; The Frankfurt School in Its History, theories, and Political Significance, Amer Hist Rev, Vol 0101, 96. **CONTACT ADDRESS** Dept of Hist, Boston Col, 140 Commonwealth Ave, Chestnut Hill, MA, 02167.

BREINES, WINIFRED
PERSONAL New York, NY, 2 children **DISCIPLINE** SOCIOLOGY; WOMEN'S STUDIES **EDUCATION** Univ Wisconsic, BA; Cornell Univ, MCP; Brandeis Univ, PhD **CAREER** Prof, Northeastern Univ, 80- **RESEARCH** Social Movements; Postwar America; Gender; Race; Women's Studies **SELECTED PUBLICATIONS** The Great Refusal: Community and Organization in the New Left, Rutgers Univ; Young, White, and Miserable: Growing Up Female in the Fifties, Beacon **CONTACT ADDRESS** Dept Soc, Northeastern Univ, Boston, MA, 02115.

BREISACH, ERNST ADOLF
PERSONAL Born 10/08/1923, Schwanberg, Austria, m, 1945, 2 children **DISCIPLINE** HISTORY **EDUCATION** Univ Vienna, PhD(hist), 46; Dr rer oec, Vienna Sch Econ, 50. **CAREER** Prof hist & geog, Realsch, Vienna, 46-52; assoc prof hist, Olivet Col, 53-57; PROF HIST, WESTERN MICH UNIV, 57-, Fulbright fel & UN off Educ grant, 51-52; fel, Am Philos Soc, 65. **MEMBERSHIPS** Renaissance Soc Am; AHA. **RESEARCH** History of Renaissance and Reformation; theory of history; historiography. **SELECTED PUBLICATIONS** Auth, Reconstruction of History in Critique of Historical Rationality, Pt 2, Amer Hist Rev, Vol 0098; History of Historiography as the theory of History, Amer Hist Rev, Vol 0098, 93; World Historians and their Goals in 20th Century Answers to Modernism, Clio, Vol 0024, 94. **CONTACT ADDRESS** Western Michigan Univ, 228 W Ridge Circle, Kalamazoo, MI, 49008.

BREIT, FREDERICK JOSEPH
PERSONAL Born 03/19/1936, Chicago, IL, m, 1957, 3 children **DISCIPLINE** RUSSIAN & MODERN EUROPEAN HISTORY **EDUCATION** Roosevelt Univ, BA, 63; Duke Univ, MA, 66, PhD, 72. **CAREER** Asst prof, 67-74, assoc prof hist, Whitman Col, 75-, Nat Endowment for Hum fel, 77-78. **MEMBERSHIPS** Am Comt Study World War II; AHA. **RESEARCH** International communism.. **SELECTED PUBLICATIONS** Auth, Concerning the Origins of World War I, In: Problems in European History, Moore Pub Co. **CONTACT ADDRESS** Dept of Hist, Whitman Col, 345 Boyer Ave, Walla Walla, WA, 99362-2083. **EMAIL** breitfj@whitman.edu

BREIT, PETER K.
DISCIPLINE HISTORY **EDUCATION** Univ CO, BA; Univ MA, MA, PhD. **CAREER** Prof, Univ Hartford. **HONORS AND AWARDS** Distinguished Serv Awd; Oscar and Shoshana Trachtenberg Awd; Roy E. Larsen Awd; **MEMBERSHIPS** Northeastern Polit Sci Asn. **RESEARCH** Europ polit and hist; Holocaust studies. **SELECTED PUBLICATIONS** Auth, Culture as Authority: US Cultural Influences in Germany 1945-1949; International Relations; Alliances; Postwar Alliances; The Encyclopedia Americana; The Christian Response to the Holocaust; Military Occupation as an Instrument of National Policy; War and Morality. **CONTACT ADDRESS** Hist Dept, Univ Hartford, Bloomfield Ave, PO Box 200, W Hartford, CT, 06117. **EMAIL** moore@uhavax.hartford.edu

BREIT, WILLIAM LEO
PERSONAL Born 02/13/1933, New Orleans, LA, s **DISCIPLINE** ECONOMICS **EDUCATION** Univ Tx, BA, 55, MA, 56; Mich State Univ, PhD, 61. **CAREER** ADJUNCT SCHOLAR, AM ENTERPRISE INST FOR PUBLIC POLICY RES, 77-; E.M. STEVENS DISTINGUISHED PROF OF ECONOMICS, TRINITY UNIV, 83-. **HONORS AND AWARDS** Distinguished Alumni Award, Mich State Univ, 98; Phi Beta Kappa. **MEMBERSHIPS** Am Economic Asn; Mystery Writers of Am; Southern Economic Asn; Southwestern Social Sci Asn; Mont Pelerin Soc. **RESEARCH** History of economic thought; antitrust economics. **SELECTED PUBLICATIONS** Auth, Stone, Sire John Richard N., An Encycl of Keynesian Economics, Edward Elgar, 97; coauth, Discrimination and Diversity: Market and Non-Market Settings, Public Choice, 95; A Deadly Indifference, Carrol & Graf, 95, Princeton Univ Press, 98; The Academic Scribblers, Princeton Univ Press, 98; The Antitrust Casebook: Milestones in Economic Regulation, The Dryden Press, 96; The Yeager Mystique: The Polymath as Teacher, Scholar and Colleague, Eastern Economic J, spring 96; Reputation versus Influence: The Evidence from Textbook References, Eastern Economic J, fall 97; co-ed, Lives of the Laureates: Thirteen Nobel Economists, MIT Press, 95 & 97. **CONTACT ADDRESS** Dept of Economics, Trinity Univ, 715 Stadium Dr., San Antonio, TX, 78212-7200.

BREITMAN, RICHARD D.
PERSONAL Born 03/27/1947, Hartford, CT, 2 children **DISCIPLINE** HISTORY **EDUCATION** Yale Univ, BA, 69; Harvard Univ, MA, 71, PhD, 75. **CAREER** From Asst Prof to Assoc Prof, 76-85, Prof Hist, Am Univ, 85-, Chair, Hist Dept, 95-97; co-ed, 94-95, ed-in-chief, Holocaust and Genocide Studies, 95-98; mem ed bd, J Contemp Hist, 94-98. **HONORS AND AWARDS** Phi Beta Kappa, Yale Univ; Graduation Honors, Summa cum Laude, Yale Univ; Fel, Woodrow Wilson Int Ctr for Schol, 87; Merit of Distinction Award, Ctr for Holocaust Studies, anti-Defamation League, for: Breaking the Silence; Fraenkel Prize for Contemp Hist, for: The Architect of Genocide. **MEMBERSHIPS** AHA. **RESEARCH** Europ Socialism: twentieth-century Germany; Am Refugee Policy and Europ Jews, 1933-1945. **SELECTED PUBLICATIONS** Auth, German Socialism and Weimar Democracy, Univ NC Press, 81; coauth, Breaking the Silence, Simon & Schuster, 86, multiple international editions, revised Am Paperback ed: Breaking the Silence: The German Who Exposed the Final Solution, Univ Press New England, 94; American Refugee Policy and European Jewry, 1933-1945, Ind Univ Press, 88; auth, The Architect of Genocide: Himmler and the Final Solution, Alfred A. Knopf, 91, & multiple international editons; Official Secrets: What the Nazis Planned, What the British and Americans Knew, Farrar, Straus, and Giroux (forthcoming Fall 98); author of numerous journal articles. **CONTACT ADDRESS** Dept of Hist, American Univ, 4400 Massachusetts Ave NW, Washington, DC, 20016-8200. **EMAIL** rbreit@american.edu

BREMER, FRANCIS JOHN
PERSONAL Born 01/26/1947, New York, NY, m, 1968, 3 children **DISCIPLINE** AMERICAN HISTORY **EDUCATION** Fordham Univ, BA, 68; Columbia Univ, MA, 69, PhD, 72. **CAREER** Adj instr, 69-70, Fordham Col; lectr, 70-71, Richmond Col, CUNY; intr, 71-72, asst prof, 72-76, assoc prof, 76-77, tenured, 76, dir, Hum Enrich Prog, 73-76, dir, Hist Cooperative Ed, 76-77, Thomas More Col; assoc prof, 77-80, prof, 80-, reg dir, 79-81, 85-89, Natl History Day, grad coord, hist, 81-85, dir, Applied History Prog, 82-, chmn, 92, dept Econ, Millersvile Univ; co-dir, NEH sum sem, 94-95. **HONORS AND AWARDS** Herbert H Lehman Fel, 68; Woodrow Wilson Found Dis Fel, 70. **MEMBERSHIPS** Orgn Am Historians. **RESEARCH** 17th century trans-Atlantic Puritanism; anthropological approaches to Colonial America. **SELECTED PUBLICATIONS** Co-ed, Research Guide to Pennsylvania History, Greenwood, 93; ed, Puritanism: TransAtlantic Perspectives on a 17th Century Anglo-American Faith, Mass Hist Soc, 93; auth, The Growth of Puritanism, Christian Hist, 94; auth, Shaping New Englands: Puritan Clergymen in 17th Century England and New England, Twayne, 94; auth, Congregationalist Communion: Clerical Friendship in the Anglo-American Puritan Community, 1610-1690, Northeastern Univ Press, 94; auth, The Puritan Experiment: New England Society from Bradford to Edwards, Univ Press New England, 95; auth, Puritans in the Pulpit: Center Stage in the Theater of God's Judgement, Hist Today, 95; auth, The Heritage of John Winthrop: Religion along the Stour Valley, 1548-1630, New England Quart, 97; coauth, The Boxford Lecture in 1620, Suffolk Rev, 98. **CONTACT ADDRESS** History Dept, The Winthrop Papers, Millersville Univ, Pennsylvania, Millersville, PA, 17551. **EMAIL** fbremer@marauder.millersv.edu

BREMER, WILLIAM WALLING
PERSONAL Born 01/08/1942, Chicago, IL, d **DISCIPLINE** UNITED STATES HISTORY **EDUCATION** Stanford Univ, BA, 64; Univ Wis, MA, 66; Stanford Univ, PhD, 73. **CAREER** Instr, 69-72, chmn dept, 75-76, 79-82, 86-89, 96-97, from assoc prof to prof hist, 82-98, Lawrence Univ. **HONORS AND AWARDS** New York State Historical Society of Wisconsin, 84; Award of Merit of State Historical Society of Wisconsin, 84; Excellent Teaching Award, Lawrence University, 94. **MEMBERSHIPS** Orgn Am Historians; AHA; Am Hist Assn Social Welfare Hist Group; Am Studies Assn. **RESEARCH** Twentieth-century United States history; United States social welfare history. **SELECTED PUBLICATIONS** Art, Along the American Way: The New Deal's Work Relief Programs For The Unemployed, J Am Hist, 75; art, Into The Grain: Golf's Ascent In American Culture, J am Cult, 81; auth, Depression Winters: New York Social Workers and the New Deal, 84; auth, A Little Ways Ahead: The Centennial History of Thilmany Pulp & Paper Company, Caukauna, Wisconsin, 83. **CONTACT ADDRESS** Dept of History, Lawrence Univ, 115 S Drew St, Appleton, WI, 54912-0599.

BREMNER, ROBERT HAMLETT
PERSONAL Born 05/26/1917, Brunswick, OH, m, 1950, 2 children **DISCIPLINE** AMERICAN HISTORY **EDUCATION** Baldwin-Wallace Col, AB, 38; Ohio State Univ, AM, 39, PhD, 43. **CAREER** From instr to assoc prof Am hist, 46-60, prof hist, 60-80, EMER PROF HIST, OHIO STATE UNIV, 80-, NATO res fel, 61; Soc Sci Res Coun fel, 63; Huntington Libr fel, 63; res assoc, Charles Warren Ctr, Harvard Univ, 66-69 & res ed, Child & State Proj, 67-73; sr fel, Nat Endowment for Humanities, 73-74. **MEMBERSHIPS** AHA; Soc Welfare Hist Group. **RESEARCH** American social and intellectual history; history of social welfare. **SELECTED PUBLICATIONS** Coauth & ed, Change and Continuity in Modern America, Ohio State Univ, 64 & 68; auth, Octavia Hill system of housing management in United States, Soc Serv Rev, 65; Impact of Civil War on philanthropy and social welfare, Civil War Hist, 66; auth & ed, Essays on History and Literature, Ohio State Univ, 66; auth, Anthony Comstock, in: Traps for the Young, Harvard Univ, 67; ed, Children and Youth in America (3 vols), Harvard Univ, 70-74; auth, Public Good, Knopf, 80; coauth & ed, Reshaping America, Ohio State Univ, 82. **CONTACT ADDRESS** Dept of Hist, Ohio State Univ, 33 Orchard Drive, Worthington, OH, 43085.

BRENK, FREDERICK EUGENE
PERSONAL Born 07/18/1929, Milwaukee, WI **DISCIPLINE** GREEK & ROMAN CLASSICS **EDUCATION** Marquette Univ, BA, 51; St Louis Univ, MA, 58; Univ Ky, PhD(hist), 71; Cambridge Univ, MLitt, 71. **CAREER** Asst prof classics, Marquette Univ, 71-80; Vis Lectr, Boston Col & Tufts Univ, 80-. **MEMBERSHIPS** Am Philol Soc; Class Asn Midwest & South; Vergilian Soc; Am Acad Relig. **RESEARCH** Greek and Roman literature; Greek and Roman religion. **SELECTED PUBLICATIONS** Auth, Ideas Religiosas En Plutarco-De-Queronea, the 3rd Int Symp on Plutarch, Univ-De-Oviedo, Gnomon Kritische Zeitschrift fur die Gesamte Klassische Altertumswissenschaft, Vol 0064, 92; Mackenzie, Roderick, A.F. 1911-1994, in Memoriam, Biblica, Vol 0075, 94; What are the Gospels in a Comparison With Greco Roman Biography, Gnomon Kritische Zeitschrift fur die Gesamte Klassische Altertumswissenschaft, Vol 0066, 94; Plutarco E La Religione', the 4th Convegno Plutarcheo Italiano on the theme of Plutarch and Religion, Gnomon Kritische Zeitschrift fur die Gesamte Klassische Altertumswissenschaft, Vol 0068, 96. **CONTACT ADDRESS** Pontifical Biblical Inst, Via Pilotta 25, Rome, ., I-00187.

BRENNAN, MARY ALETHEA
PERSONAL Born 06/11/1909, Larksville, PA **DISCIPLINE** PHILOSOPHY CLASSICS **EDUCATION** Col Mt St Vincent, BA, 30; Cath Univ Am, MA, 44, PhL, 48, PhD(philos), 50; Univ Freiburg & Univ Dublin, 62. **CAREER** Instr chem & math, Cathedral High Sch, New York, NY, 34-35, chem, 35-41, head dept, 41-43; instr chem & Latin, 44-45, asst prof Latin, 45-47, from instr to assoc prof philos, 50-76, ADJ ASSOC PROF PHILOS, COL MT ST VINCENT, 76- **MEMBERSHIPS** Am Philos Soc; Am Cath Philos Asn; Metaphys Soc Am; Cath Class Asn (pres, 43-44). **RESEARCH** Science, especially chemistry. **SELECTED PUBLICATIONS** Auth, Religion, Law, and Power, the Making of Protestant Ireland, 1660-1760, Albion, Vol 0025, 93; Neither Kingdom Nor Nation in the Irish Quest For Constitutional-Rights, 1698-1800, Albion, Vol 0027, 95. **CONTACT ADDRESS** Dept of Philos, St Josephs Coll, Mt View, CA, 94039.

BRENNAN, TIMOTHY J.
PERSONAL Born 12/26/1952, Washington, DC, d **DISCIPLINE** ECONOMICS **EDUCATION** Univ Wis, PhD, 78. **CAREER** Economist, Antitrust div, US Dept Justice, 78-98; Assoc prof Pul Policy, Commun (s), and Econ (s), Grad Sch Arts and Sci, George Washington Univ, 86-89; Gilber White fel, resources for the futures, Wash, DC, 95; sr Econ Industrial org and reg, coun Econ Adv (s), Exec Office Pres, Wash DC, 96-97; sr fel, res for the futures, Wash DC, 95- ; Prof Policy Sci and Econ (s), Univ Md, 93- . **HONORS AND AWARDS** Gilbert White fel, res for the futures, Wash DC; Wis Alumni res found grad fel: Math, 74-75, Econ (s), 76-77, doct diss Econ (s), 77-78; Valedictorian, Univ Md, Dec 73; Who's Who in the East, 92-95; Dept Justice merit awd, 82, 84; Dept Justice Antitrust Div awd of merit, 85. **MEMBERSHIPS** Amer Econ (s) Assn; Amer Philos Assn; Amer Bar Assn; Amer Law Econ (s) Assn; Assn Pub Policy Analysis and Mgt; Assn Environ Res Econ (s); Indust org soc; Assn Ed Jour and Mass Commun; Broadcast Ed Asn; Assn Soc Econ; Hist Econ Soc; Assn Evolutionary Econ (s); S Econ Assn. **RESEARCH** Ethics and public policy; First Amendment policy; regulation, antitrust, intellectual property law; methodology of economics. **SELECTED PUBLICATIONS** Auth, A Methodological Assessment of Multiple Utility frameworks, in The Philosophy and Methodology of Economics, Aldershot, Edward Elgar, 93, vol 1, 405-424; The Futility of Multiple Utility, Economics and Philosophy, 9,1, 93, 155-164; Copyright, Property, and the Right to Deny, Chicago-Kent Law Rev, 68,2, 93, 675-714; Comparing the Costs and Benefits of Diversification by Regulated Firms, Jour Regulatory Econ, 6, 2, 94, 115-136; Economic Theory in Industrial Policy: Lessons from U.S. vs AT&T, Res in the Hist Econ Thought and Methodology, 11, 94, 49-72; Talking to One's Selves: The Social Science of Jon Elster, Jour Communication, 44, 1, 94, 73-81; Markets, Information, and Benevolence, Econ and Philos, 10, 2, 94, 151-168; Game Theory and the First Amendment: Strategic Implications of Freedom of the Press, in Toward a Competitive Telecommunication Industry: Selected Papers from the 1994 Telecommunications Policy Research Conference, New York, Lawrence erlbaum, 95, 309-331; Does the Theory Behind U.S. v AT&T Still Apply Today?, Antitrust Bulletin, 40, 3, 95, 455-482; Remote sensing Satellites and Privacy: a Framework for Policy Assessment, Jour of Law, Computers, and Artificial Intel, 4, 3, 95, 233-248; Ed, Symposium: Recent Competition Issues in Telecommunications, Antitrust Bulletin, 40, 3, 95; Balancing Present Costs and Future Benefits, in National Res Counc, Financing Tomorrow's Infrastructure: Challenges and Issues, Washington, National Acad Press, 96, 7-20; Does the theory Behind U.S. v AT&T Still Apply Today?, in The Internet and Telecommunications Policy: Selected Papers from the 1995 Telecommunications Policy Research Conference, New York, Lawrence Erlbaum, 96, 13-33; Additional Considerations in the Electricity Competition Debate, in Natl Res Coun, Competition in the electricity Industry: Emerging Issues, Opportunities and Risks for Facility Operators, Washington, Natl Acad Press, 96; Is Cost-of Service Regulation Worth the Cost?, Intl Jour Econ Bus, 3, 1, 96, 25-42; Methodology-Abstract Philosophy or Criticism of Diminishing Returns, Res in Hist Econ Thought and Method, 14, 96, 329-342; Making Sense of the Telecommunications Act of 1996, Industrial and Corp Change, 5, 96, 941-961; A Shock to the System: Restructuring America's Electricity Industry, Wash DC, Resources for the Future, 96; Die okonomische Analyse des Rechts aus philosopher Sicht: Gesellschaftspolitsche Ziele im Kontext des Rechts, in effiziente Verhaltenssteuerung und Kooperation im Zivilrecht, Tubingen, Mohr Siebeck, 97, 283-309; Stranded Costs, Takings, and the Law and Economics of Implicit Contracts, Jour Regulatory Econ, 11, 97, 41-54; Technology and Coordination: Antitrust Implications of Remote Sensing Satellites, Antitrust Bulletin, 42, 97, 477-502; Industry Parallel Interconnection Agreements, Info Econ and Policy, 9, 97, 133-149; American Democratic Institutions and Social Values, in Democracy, Social Values, and Pub Policy, Westport, CT, Greenwood, 98, 37-55. **CONTACT ADDRESS** Dept of Economics, Univ of Maryland, 1000 Hilltop Cir, Baltimore, MD, 21250. **EMAIL** brennan@umbc2.umbc.edu

BRENNEMAN, WALTER L.
PERSONAL Born 12/05/1936, Harrisburg, PA, m, 1963, 6 children **DISCIPLINE** HISTORY OF RELIGION **EDUCATION** Gettysburg Col, BA; Univ Chicago, BA; Union Inst, PhD. **CAREER** Prof relig, Univ Ver, 68- . **MEMBERSHIPS** Am Acad Relig; Am Comt Irish Stud. **RESEARCH** Irish Celtic religion; Irish Celtic Christianity; phenomenological method. **SELECTED PUBLICATIONS** Auth, Spirals: A study in Symbol, Myth and Ritual, Univ Press Am, 78; coauth, The Seeing Eye: Hermeneutical Phenomenology in the Study of Religion, Penn State, 82; coauth, Crossing the Circle at the Holy Walls of Ireland, Univ Press of Vir, 95. **CONTACT ADDRESS** HLR32, PO Box 760, Montpelier, VT, 05602. **EMAIL** wbrennem@zoo.uvm.edu

BRENNER, LOUIS
PERSONAL Born 06/19/1937, Memphis, TN, m, 1959, 2 children **DISCIPLINE** AFRICAN HISTORY **EDUCATION** Univ Wis, BS, 59; Columbia Univ, MA, 64, PhD(hist), 68. **CAREER** ASST PROF HIST & FAC MEM, AFRICAN STUDIES CTR, BOSTON UNIV, 67-80. **MEMBERSHIPS** AHA; African Studies Asn. **RESEARCH** West African history, especially the Lake Chad Basin; history of Sufism in West Africa. **SELECTED PUBLICATIONS** Auth, Sage Philosophy in indigenous Thinkers and Modern Debate on African Philosophy, Bull Sch Oriental and African Stud Univ London, Vol 0056, 93; Parables and Fables in Exegesis, Textuality, and Politics in Central-Africa, Bull School Oriental and African Stud Univ London, Vol 0057, 94; The Hermeneutics of African Philosophy in Horizon and Discourse, Bull Sch Oriental and African Stud Univ London, Vol 0059, 96; African Philosophy in Search of Identity, Bull Sch Oriental and African Stud Univ London, Vol 0059, 96. **CONTACT ADDRESS** 46 Craftsman Rd, Brookline, MA, 02167.

BRENTANO, ROBERT
PERSONAL Born 05/19/1926, Evansville, IN, m, 1956, 3 children **DISCIPLINE** MEDIEVAL HISTORY **EDUCATION** Swarthmore Col, BA, 49; Oxford Univ, DPhil, 52. **CAREER** From instr to assoc prof, 52-65, chmn dept, 75-78, PROF HIST, UNIV CALIF, BERKELEY, 65-, Fulbright fel, Italy, 56-57; Am Coun Learned Soc fel, 60-61; Guggenheim fel, 65-66 & 78-79; Nat Endowment for Humanities fel, 72-73. **HONORS AND AWARDS** Haskins Medal, Mediaeval Acad Am, 70; John Gilmary Shea Prize, Am Cath Hist Asn, 70; Howard R Marraro Prize, AHA, 75. **MEMBERSHIPS** Mediaeval Acad Am; Royal Hist Soc; Conf Brit Studies; Soc Ital Hist Studies. **RESEARCH** English Medieval history; Italian ecclesiastical history; writing of history in the 19th century. **SELECTED PUBLICATIONS** Auth, The Papal Monarchy in the Western Church from Ad1050 to Ad1250, Speculum--J Medieval Stud, Vol 0067, 92; the Papal Monarchy in the Western Church from Ad1050 to Ad1250, Speculum--J Medieval Stud, Vol 0067, 92; Urban Spaces and Habitats from 10th Century Rome to the End of the 13th-Century, Speculum--J Medieval Stud, Vol 0068, 93; Urban Spaces and Habitats from 10th-Century Rome to the End of the 13th-Century, Speculum--J Medieval Stud, Vol 0068, 93; Episcopal Power and Florentine Society, Church Hist, Vol 0063, 94; Church and City, 1000-1500 in Essays in Honor of Brooke, Christopher, Cath Hist Rev, Vol 0080, 94; Episcopal Power and Florentine Society, Church Hist, Vol 0063, 94. **CONTACT ADDRESS** Dept of Hist, Univ of Calif, 3229 Dwinelle Hall, Berkeley, CA, 94720.

BRESLAW, ELAINE
DISCIPLINE HISTORY **EDUCATION** Univ Md, PhD. **CAREER** Vis prof. **RESEARCH** Early American history. **SELECTED PUBLICATIONS** Auth, Reluctant Witch: A Woman Named Tituba, Univ NY, 96. **CONTACT ADDRESS** Dept of History, Knoxville, TN, 37996.

BRESLIN, THOMAS ALOYSIUS
PERSONAL Born 05/23/1944, Philadelphia, PA, m, 1977, 2 children **DISCIPLINE** HISTORY & INTERNATIONAL RELATIONS **EDUCATION** Fordham Univ, BA, 68; Univ Va, MA, 69, PhD, 72. **CAREER** Asst prof hist, 76-77, asst prof & assoc dean, 77-82, assoc prof int rels & dir div sponsored res & training, FL Int Univ, 81, assoc prof Intl rels and Dir Div Sponsored Research and training, 82-93; asst vice pres, acad Affairs, 85-87; Assoc Vice Ores, Acad affairs, 85-86; vice provost, 87-96; vice pres, research and grad studies, 96-; Fac Fulbright adv, FL Int Univ, 77-82; mem adv bd, Univ Presses FL, 80-; consult, Global Educ Prog, FL Dept Educ, 79-80; board mem, Center for Health tech, Miami, 91-97. **MEMBERSHIPS** Soc Historians Am Foreign Rels; Assoc Asian Studies; Authors Guild. **RESEARCH** US diplomatic hist; mod China; Roman Cath Church. **SELECTED PUBLICATIONS** Coauth, State of Danger: Childhood Lead Paint Poisoning in Massachusetts, Mass Advocacy Ctr, 74; auth, Roman Catholic Mission to China: Victim of Religious Myopia, Holy Cross Quart, 6/75; Trouble Over Oil: America, Japan, and the Oil Cartel, 1934-35, Bull Concerned Asian Scholars, 7-9/75; coauth, Brainwashing and Managed Group Experiences: Converging New Techniques, Reason Papers, fall 75; auth, Mystifying the Past: Establishment Historians and the Origins of the Pacific War, Bull Concerned Asian Scholars, 10-12/76; China, American Catholicism, and the Missionary, Pa State Univ Press, 80; coauth, An Ordinary Relationship: American Opposition to Republican Revolution in China, FIU and U Presses of FL, 86; auth, The Administration of International Education at Florida International University in Backman, Approaches to International Education, Macmillan, 84. **CONTACT ADDRESS** Div Sponsored Res & Training, Florida Intl Univ, 1 FIU U Park, Miami, FL, 33199-0001. **EMAIL** breslint@fiu.edu

BRESLOW, BOYD
PERSONAL Born 09/08/1937, Lincoln, NE **DISCIPLINE** HISTORY **EDUCATION** Univ NE, BA, 59, MA 63; OH State Univ, PhD, 68. **CAREER** From instr to asst prof hist, Univ AZ, 67-71; asst prof, 71-81, prof hist, FL Atlantic Univ, 81-, Am Philos Soc grant, 70. **MEMBERSHIPS** Mediaeval Acad Am; Conf Brit Studies; Haskins Soc; AHA; London Rec Soc. **RESEARCH** Medieval Eng constitutional, admin and urban hist. **SELECTED PUBLICATIONS** Auth, The social status and economic interests of Richer de Refham, Lord Mayor of London, J Medieval Hist, 12/77; Ambiguities of political loyalties in Edwardian England, The case of Richer de Refham, Medieval Prosopography, 85; London merchants and the origins of the House of Commons, Medieval Prosopography, 89. **CONTACT ADDRESS** Dept of Hist, Florida Atlantic Univ, PO Box 3091, Boca Raton, FL, 33431-0991. **EMAIL** breslow@fau.edu

BRESLOW, MARVIN A.
PERSONAL Born 01/09/1936, Lincoln, NE **DISCIPLINE** HISTORY **EDUCATION** Univ Nebr, BA, 57; Harvard Univ, MA, 58, PhD(hist), 63. **CAREER** From instr to asst prof, 62-68, ASSOC PROF HIST, UNIV MD, COLLEGE PARK, 68-, Consult Elizabethan hist, Educ Serv, inc, 65-67; fel, Folger Shakespeare Libr, 66. **MEMBERSHIPS** AHA; Conf Brit Studies. **RESEARCH** Puritanism; political thought. **SELECTED PUBLICATIONS** Auth, Exile and Kingdom, History and Apocalypse in the Puritan Migration to America, Albion, Vol 0024, 92; Cromwellian Foreign-Policy, Amer Hist Rev, Vol 0101, 96. **CONTACT ADDRESS** Dept of His, Univ of Md, College Park, MD, 20742-0001.

BRETON, RAYMOND J.
PERSONAL Born 08/19/1931, Montmartre, SK, Canada **DISCIPLINE** SOCIAL/POPULATION HISTORY **EDUCATION** Univ Man, BA, 52; Univ Chicago, MA, 58; Johns Hopkins Univ, PhD, 61. **CAREER** Res dir, Soc Res Gp, Montreal, 57-64; prog dir, Inst Res Pub Policy, 76-81; dir, grad stud soc, 81-85, PROF SOCIOLOGY, UNIV TORONTO; William Lyon MacKenzie King Prof Can Stud, Harvard Univ, 96-97. **HONORS AND AWARDS** Samuel S. Fels fel, 60-61; Can Coun leave fel, 72-73, 81-82; sr res fel, Statistics Can, 87-88; sr Connaught fel soc sci, 88-89; Outstanding Contrib Award, Can Soc & Anthrop Asn, 90; DL (honoris causa), Univ Guelph, 94. **MEMBERSHIPS** Royal Soc Can **SELECTED PUBLICATIONS** Auth, Academic and Social Factors in Career Decision-Making: A Study of Canadian Secondary School Students, 72; auth, The Governance of Ethnic Communities: Political Structures and Processes in Canada, 91; auth, Why Meech Lake Failed: Lessons in Canadian Constitutionmaking, 92; coauth, The Social Impact of Changes in Population Size and Composition: An Analysis of Reactions to Patterns of Immigration, 74; coauth, Cultural Boundaries and the Cohesion of Canada, 80; coauth, Why Disunity: An Analysis of Linguistic and Regional Cleavages in Canada, 80; coauth, The Illusion of Difference: Realities of Ethnicity in Canada and the United States, 94; ed, Aspects of Canadian Society, 74; ed, Ethnic Identity and Equality: Varieties of Experience in a Canadian City, 90; ed, Can Rev Soc Anthrop, 73-76. **CONTACT ADDRESS** Dept of Sociology, Univ of Toronto, 203 College St, 5th Fl, Toronto, ON, M5T 1P9. **EMAIL** rbreton@chass.utoronto.ca

BRETT, PHILIP
PERSONAL Born 10/17/1937, Edwinstowe, United Kingdom **DISCIPLINE** MUSIC **EDUCATION** BA, Cambridge 58, BMUS 61, MA, 62, PhD, 65. **CAREER** King's Col, fel, 63-66, asst lectr, 64-66; Univ of CA, Dean, 66-91,asst prof, 66-71, asst prof, 71-78, Univ of CA, Riverside, 78-91. **HONORS AND AWARDS** Royal Insurance Company Fel and Fulbright Travel Awd; The Archibald Davison Medal for Musicology (Harriet Cohen International Music Awards), 71-72; Am Council of Learned Soc Fel, 80; The Noah Greenberg Award of the Am Musicological Soc, 80-82; Project Dir, The Byrd Edition, National Endowment for the Hum 84-86; Bd of the Am Musicological Soc, 85; Distinguished vis prof, Univ of Alberta, 85-91; Grammy nomination in the Best Class Choral Perfomance, 96; The Gay and Lesbian Study Group of the Am Musicological Soc Inst Philip Brett Award, 97; BBC Proms lectr The Britten Era. **MEMBERSHIPS** Am Musicological Soc, Royal Musical Assoc, Soc for Ethnomusicology. **RESEARCH** Eng music, textual criticism and ed, gay studies and queer theory, perfomativity. **SELECTED PUBLICATIONS** Ed, Benjamin Britten: Peter Grimes, Cambridge Univ Press, 83; ed, Queering the Pitch: The New Gay and Lesbian Musicology; Crusing the Performative:Interventions into the Representation of Ethnicity, Nationality, and Sexuality, IN Univ Press, 95. **CONTACT ADDRESS** Univ of California, Riverside, CA, 92521-0325. **EMAIL** pbrett@mail.ucr.edu

BRETT-SMITH, SARAH
DISCIPLINE ART HISTORY **EDUCATION** Yale Univ, PhD, 82. **CAREER** Assoc prof, Rutgers Univ. **HONORS AND AWARDS** Hon Men Victor Turner Prize, Soc Hum Anthro, 95; Arts Coun African Studies Asn, 93-95; Arnold J Rubin awd outstanding bk African Art. **RESEARCH** Bamana (Bambara) sculpture: gender and art making; the symbolism of Bamana, Dogon, Malinke, Minianka, Senufo and Bobo textiles; surrealism and primitive art. **SELECTED PUBLICATIONS** Auth, The Mouth of the Komo, Res: Anthropology and Aesthetics, 97; The Artfulness of M'Fa Jigi: An Interview with Nyamaton Diarra, Univ Wis, 96; The Making of Bamana Sculpture: Creativity and Gender, Cambridge UP, 94; Bamanakan ka Gelen or The Voice of the Bamana is Hard, Art Tribal, Musee Barbier-Mueller, 87; The Poisonous Child, Res: Anthropology and Aesthetics, 83; Symbolic Blood: Cloths for Excised Women, RES: Anthro Aesthetics), 82. **CONTACT ADDRESS** Dept of Art Hist, Rutgers Univ/Rutgers Col, Hamilton St., New Brunswick, NJ, 08903. **EMAIL** brettsmi@rci.rutgers.edu

BRETTELL, CAROLINE B.
PERSONAL Born 06/11/1950, Montreal, PQ, Canada, m, 1973 **DISCIPLINE** ANTHROPOLOGY **EDUCATION** Yale Univ, BA 71; Brown Univ, MA 72, PhD 78. **CAREER** Brown Univ, tech asst 71-74; Univ TX, instr 77-78, Res assoc 79-80; Univ IL vis asst prof 81; De Paul Univ, instr 82; Loyola Univ, lectr vis asst 83-87; The Newberry Library, Res assoc proj dir 84-88; S Meth Univ, vis assoc prof 88-91, assoc prof 91-93, dir womens stud 89-94, prof anthropo 93-, chair dept anthropo 94. **HONORS AND AWARDS** Alice Palmer Fellowship, declined; Lichtstern Fell; NEH; Newberry Lib Fell; Nat Res Ser Awd; Gulbenkian Foun Fell; Soc Sci Res Fell; Woodrow Wilson Foun doc Fell; CA Coun Doc Fell; Univ Fell Brown; John Chester Adams Cup Yale; numerous research grants. **MEMBERSHIPS** Coun Euro Stud; SSHA; Soc Span Portug Hist Stud; Amer Ethnological Soc; AAA. **RESEARCH** Relig, migration, immigration, gender issues. **SELECTED PUBLICATIONS** Zoe: Writing a Mother's Life in Journalism, Wilmington, Scholarly Resources, in Press; Gender and Health: An International Perspective, ed with Carolyn Sargent, Prentice Hall, 96; When They Read What We Write: The Politics of Ethnography, ed vol, Westport CT, Bergin and Garvey, Greenwood 93; Fieldwork in the Archives: Methods and Sources in Historical Anthropology, in: H Russell Bernard, ed, Handbook of Mthods In Anthropology, Altamira Press, 98; Historical Perspectives on Infant Mortality in Northwestern Portugal, in: Small Wars: The Cultural Politics of Childhood, Nancy Scheper-Hughs and Carolyn Sargent, eds, Berkeley, Univ Of CA Press, 98; numerous bks, chapters and articles. **CONTACT ADDRESS** Dept of Anthrop, Southern Methodist Univ, Dallas, TX, 75275. **EMAIL** cbrettel@mail.smu.edu

BRETTSCHNEIDER, MARLA
PERSONAL Born 05/16/1965, New York, NY **DISCIPLINE** POLITICS **EDUCATION** SUNY, Binghamton, BA, 86; NYU, MA, 88, PhD, 93. **CAREER** Asst prof, 93-96, Bloomsburg Univ; asst prof, 96-, Univ NH. **HONORS AND AWARDS** Gustavus Meyers Human Rights Award. **MEMBERSHIPS** APSA; AJS; SWIP; AAR; APA. **RESEARCH** Democratic theory; feminist theory; multicultural theory; Jewish politics. **SELECTED PUBLICATIONS** Auth, Cornerstones of Peace: Jewish Identity Politics & Democratic Theory, Rutgers, 96; auth, The Narrow Bridge: Jewish Views on Multiculturalism, Rutgers, 96; auth, Race, Gender, & Class: Jewish Persp, 98. **CONTACT ADDRESS** Univ of New Hampshire, Durham, NH, 03824.

BRICELAND, ALAN VANCE
PERSONAL Born 04/17/1939, Baltimore, MD, m, 1962, 2 children **DISCIPLINE** AMERICAN HISTORY **EDUCATION** Col William & Mary, AB, 61; Duke Univ, MA, 63, PhD, 65. **CAREER** Asst prof hist, N TX State Univ, 65-66; asst prof, 66-74, assoc prof hist, VA Commonwealth Univ, 74. **MEMBERSHIPS** AHA; Orgn Am Historians; Southern Hist Asn; AAUP; Soc Hist Early Am Repub. **RESEARCH** South side Virginia in mid 17th century; frontier Alabama: 1800-1805; Virginia ratifying conviction of 1788. **SELECTED PUBLICATIONS** Auth, Daniel McCalla, 1746-1809: New Side Revolutionary and Jeffersonian, J Presby Hist, fall 78; The Search for Edward Bland's New Britain, Va Mag Hist & Biog, 4/79; Land, Law, and Politics on the Tombigbee Frontier, 1804, Ala Rev, 4/80; The Group-Task Approach: Developing Analytical Skills in the United States History Survey, The Hist Teacher, 2/81; Westward from Virginia: The Exploration of the Virginia-Carolina Frontier, 1650-1710, Univ Press Va, 87; 1788: The Year of Decision: Virginia's Ratification of the U.S. Constitution, Va Dept Educ: Soc Studies Prog, 89; British Exploration of the United States Interior 1707-1804, In: The Exploration of North America, vol II, Univ Nebr Press, 97; North America: Inland from the East Coast, 1607-1769, In: The Times Atlas of World Exploration, HarperCollins Publ, 91; Batts and Fallam Explore the Backbone on the Continent, In: Appalachian Frontiers: Settlement, Society & Development in the Preindustrial Era, Univ Press KY, 91. **CONTACT ADDRESS** Dept of Hist, Virginia Commonwealth Univ, Box 2001, Richmond, VA, 23284-9004. **EMAIL** abricela@atlas.vcu.edu

BRIDENTHAL, RENATE
PERSONAL Born 06/13/1935, Germany **DISCIPLINE** MODERN EUROPEAN HISTORY, WOMEN'S HISTORY **EDUCATION** City Col New York, BA, 60; Columbia Univ, MA, 61, PhD(hist), 70. **CAREER** Lectr hist, Borough Manhattan Community Col, 66-67; lectr, 67-74, asst prof, 74-80, assoc prof 80-86, PROF HIST, BROOKLYN COL, 86-, Ed, Sci & Soc, 72- **HONORS AND AWARDS** PSC-BHE res award, 80; Intl Res and Exchanges Bd, 83; NEH, 83-84; Fulbright, 83-84 (declined). **MEMBERSHIPS** AHA; Coord Comt Women Hist Profession; Berkshire Conf Women Historians; Phi Beta Kappa **RESEARCH** Modern European history, with emphasis on Germany, especially women in the Weimar Republic and their position in the labor force. **SELECTED PUBLICATIONS** Auth, The greening of Germany: 1848: Karl Grun's true socialism, Sci & Soc, 71; Was there a Roman Homer? Niebuhrs thesis and its critics, Hist & Theory, 72; Beyond Kinder, Kuche, Kirche: Weimar women at work, Cent Europ Hist, 73; The dialectics of production and reproduction in history, Radical Am, 3-4/76; co-ed, Becoming Visible: Women in European History, Houghton, 77; auth, Critique of family history, Feminist Studies, spring 79; The family: The view from the room of her own, In: Rethinking the Family: Some Feminist Questions, Longmans, 82; Class struggle around the hearth: Women and domestic service in the Weimar Republic, In: Towards the Holocaust: Anti-Semitism and Fascism in the Weimar Republic, Greenwood, 83; co-ed & contrb, When biology became destiny: Women in Weimar and Nazi Germany, Monthly Rev, 84; Women and the Conservative Mobilization Of The Countryside in Weimar Republic, in: Between Reform, Reaction, and Resistance: Studies in the History of German Conservativism from 1789 to the Present, Berg, 93; co-ed, Becoming Visible: Women in European History, 3rd ed, Houghton, 98. **CONTACT ADDRESS** Dept of Hist, Brooklyn Col, CUNY, 2900 Bedford Ave, Brooklyn, NY, 11210-2889. **EMAIL** RBriden1@juno.com

BRIDENTHAL, RENATE
PERSONAL Born 06/13/1935, Germany **DISCIPLINE** MODERN EUROPEAN HISTORY **EDUCATION** City Col New York, BA, 60; Columbia Univ, MA, 61, PhD(hist), 70. **CAREER** Lectr hist, Borough Manhattan Community Col, 66-67; lectr, 67-74, asst prof, 74-80, assoc prof, 80-86, prof, 86-, Brooklyn Col, Ed, Sci & Soc, 72- **HONORS AND AWARDS** PSC-BHE res award, 80; Int Res and Exch Bd, NEH, Fulbright.. **MEMBERSHIPS** Phi Beta Kappa; Berkshire Conf of Women Historians; AHA; Coord Comt Women Hist Profession; Berkshire Conf Women Historians. **RESEARCH** Modern European history, with emphasis on Germany, especially women in the Weimar Republic and their position in the labor force. **SELECTED PUBLICATIONS** Auth, The greening of Germany: 1848: Karl Grun's true socialism, Sci & Soc, 71; Was there a Roman Homer? Niebuhrs thesis and its critics, Hist & Theory, 72; Beyond Kinder, Kuche, Kirche: Weimar women at work, Cent Europ Hist, 73; The dialectics of production and reproduction in history, Radical Am, 3-4/76; co-ed, Becoming Visible: Women in European History, Houghton, 77; auth, Critique of family history, Feminist Studies, spring 79; The family: The view from the room of her own, In: Rethinking the Family: Some Feminist Questions, Longmans, 82; Class struggle around the hearth: Women and domestic service in the Weimar Republic, In: Towards the Holocaust: Anti-Semitism and Fascism in the Weimar Republic, Greenwood, 83; co-ed, Becoming Visible: Women in European History, Houghton, 98; co-ed, contrib, When Bioligy Became Destiny: Women in Weimar and Nazi Germany, Mon Rev, 84; co-ed, contrib, Women and the Conservative Mobilization of the Countryside in the Weimar Republic, Between Reform, Reaction, and Resistance: Studies in the History of German Conservatism from 1789 to the Present, Berg, 93. **CONTACT ADDRESS** Dept of Hist, Brooklyn Col, CUNY, 2900 Bedford Ave., Brooklyn, NY, 11210-2889. **EMAIL** rbriden1@juno.com

BRIDGES, ROGER DEAN
PERSONAL Born 02/10/1937, Marshalltown, IA, m, 1960, 3 children **DISCIPLINE** UNITED STATES HISTORY **EDUCATION** Univ Northern Iowa, BA, 59, MA, 63; Univ Ill, Urbana-Champaign, PhD(hist), 70. **CAREER** Teacher-librn, Jr High Sch, Keokuk, Iowa, 59-62; asst soc sci, Univ Northern Iowa, 62-63 & hist, Univ Ill, Urbana-Champaign, 63-68; asst prof, Univ SDak, 68-69; Nat Hist Publ Comn fel, Ulysses S Grant Asn & vis adj lectr hist, Southern Ill Univ, Carbondale, 69-70; dir res, ill state hist libr, 70-, head librn, 77-, LECTR HIST, ILL STATE UNIV, 74-. **MEMBERSHIPS** AHA; Orgn Am Hist; Southern Hist Asn; Asn Doc Editing. **RESEARCH** United States Civil War and Reconstruction history; Illinois history; Afro-American history. **SELECTED PUBLICATIONS** Auth, An Oral History of Lincoln,Abraham in Nicolay, John,G. interviews and essays, J Southern Hist, Vol 0063, 97. **CONTACT ADDRESS** Illinois State Historical Libr, Old State Capitol, Springfield, IL, 62706.

BRIDWELL, R. RANDAL
DISCIPLINE ADMIRALTY, LEGAL HISTORY, AND CONFLICTS **EDUCATION** Midwestern Univ, BA, 67; Southern Methodist Univ, JD, 70; Harvard Univ, LLM, 71. **CAREER** Strom Thurmond prof, Univ of SC. **SELECTED PUBLICATIONS** Publ on, legal hist and admiralty issues. **CONTACT ADDRESS** School of Law, Univ of S. Carolina, Law Center, Columbia, SC, 29208. **EMAIL** Randall@law.law.sc.edu

BRIEGER, GERT HENRY
PERSONAL Born 01/05/1932, Hamburg, Germany, m, 1955, 3 children **DISCIPLINE** HISTORY OF MEDICINE **EDUCATION** Univ Calif, Berkeley, AB, 53; Univ Calif, Los Angeles, MD, 57; Harvard Univ, MPh, 62; Johns Hopkins Univ, PhD, 68. **CAREER** Asst prof hist med, Sch Med, Johns Hopkins Univ, 66-70; assoc prof, Duke Univ, 70-75; PROF HIST MED, UNIV CALIF, SAN FRANSISCO, 75-. **MEMBERSHIPS** Hist Sci Soc; AHA; Orgn Am Historians; Am Asn Hist Med (vpres, 78-80, pres, 80-82). **RESEARCH** History of American medicine; 19th and 20th century history of medical education. **SELECTED PUBLICATIONS** Auth, Yellow Fever and Public Health in the New South, Tech and Culture, Vol 0034, 93; Yellow Fever and Public Health in the New South, Tech and Culture, Vol 0034, 93; Surgery and Society in Peace and War, Orthopedics and the Organization of Modern Medicine 1880-1948, Soc Hist Mede, Vol 0007, 94; Surgery and Society in Peace and War, Orthopedics and the Organization of Modern Medicine 1880-1948, Soc Hist Med, Vol 0007, 94; The Western Medical Tradition, 800 BC to AD 1800, Soc Hist Med, Vol 0009, 96; The Western Medical Tradition, 800 BC to AD 1800, Soc Hist Med, Vol 0009, 96. **CONTACT ADDRESS** Sch Med, Johns Hopkins Univ, 3400 N Charles St, Baltimore, MD, 21218.

BRIGGS, CHARLES L.
PERSONAL Born 04/08/1953, Albuquerque, NM, m, 1996, 2 children **DISCIPLINE** ANTHROPOLOGY **EDUCATION** Colo Col, BA, 74; Univ Chicago, MA, 78, PhD, 81. **CAREER** Asst prof to prof, anthrop, chemn dept 90-94, Vassar Col, 80-95; Andrew W. Mellon Fac Fel in Hum, Comm on Degrees in Folklore and Mythology, 83-84; vis asst prof, SUNY Albany, anthrop, 86; lectr, Dept Folklore, Univ Penn, 89; vis assoc prof and acting chemn, Dept Perf Stud, NY Univ, 91-92; prof ethnic stud, Univ Calif, San Diego, 95- . **HONORS AND AWARDS** Phi Beta Kappa; tuition fel, 75-76; training fel, NIMH, 76-79; James Mooney Award, So Anthrop Soc, 78; Mellon Fac Fel, 83-84; fel, NEH, 89-90; Chicago Folklore Prize, 89; fel, Am Folklore Soc Fellows, 90; fel, John Simon Guggenheim Mem Found, 94-95; fel Woodrow Wilson Int Ctr for Scholars, 97-98. **MEMBERSHIPS** Am Anthrop Asn; Am Ethnolog Soc; Am Folklore Soc; Am Stud Asn; Int Pragmatics Asn; Latin Am Indian Lit Asn; Latin Am Stud Asn; Ling Soc of Am; NY Folklore Soc; Soc for Cult Anthrop; Soc for Ling Anthrop; Soc for Stud of the Indigenous Lang of the Am. **SELECTED PUBLICATIONS** Coauth, Hispano Folklore of New Mexico: The Lorin W. Brown Federal Writers' Project Manuscripts, Univ New Mexico, 78; auth, The Wood Carvers of Cordova, New Mexico: Social Dimensions of an Artistic Revival, Univ Tenn, 80; auth, Learning How to Ask: A Sociolinguistic Appraisal of the Role of the Interview in Social Science Research, Cambridge, 86; co-ed, Land, Water, and Culture: New Perspectives on Hispanic Land Grants, Univ New Mexico, 87; auth, Competence in Performance: The Creativity of Tradition in Mexicano Verbal Art, Univ Penn, 88; co-ed, The Lost Gold Mine of Juan Mondragon: A Legend of New Mexico Performed by Melaquias Romero, Univ Az, 90; ed, Disorderly Discourse: Narrative, Conflict, and Social Inequality, Oxford, 96. **CONTACT ADDRESS** Dept of Ethnic Studies, Univ of California, San Diego, 9500 Gilman Dr, La Jolla, CA, 92093-0522. **EMAIL** clbriggs@weber.ucsd.edu

BRIGGS, J.M.
DISCIPLINE HISTORY OF SCIENCE, EARLY MODERN EUROPE, AND HISTORY THROUGH SCIENCE FICTIO **EDUCATION** Columbia Univ, PhD, 62. **CAREER** Dept Hist, Univ of RI **RESEARCH** Sci, technol and cult. **SELECTED PUBLICATIONS** Publ on, effects of industrial pollution in 18th century Fr. **CONTACT ADDRESS** Dept of Hist, Univ of RI, 8 Ranger Rd, Ste. 1, Kingston, RI, 02881-0807.

BRIGGS, WARD W.
PERSONAL Born 11/26/1945, Riverside, CA, s **DISCIPLINE** CLASSICS **EDUCATION** Wash & Lee Univ, AB, 67; Univ of NC, MA, 69, PhD, 74. **CAREER** Instr, Univ of SC, 73-74; from asst prof to prof, Univ of SC, 75- ; Carolina disting. prof of Classics and L. Fry Scudder prof of hum, 96- ; Mel Hill disting. prof, Hobart & Wm. Smith Colleges, 92-93. **MEMBERSHIPS** Am Philol Asn; Class Asn of Middle West and South, Am Class League. **RESEARCH** Hist of Class Scholarship; Latin lit of the Golden Age. **SELECTED PUBLICATIONS** Auth, Narrative and Simile, 79; Concordantia in Varronis Libros De Re Rustica, 83; Concordantia in Catonis Librum De Agri Cultura, 84; Soldier and Scholar: The Southern Papers of Basil Lanneau Gildersleeve, 88; coed, Basil Lanneau Gildersleeve: An American Classicist, 86; Classical Scholarship: A Biog Encycl, 90; The Roosevelt Lects of Paul Shorey (1913-1914), 98; ed, The Letters of Basil Lanneau Gildersleeve, 87; Selected Classical Papers of Basil Lanneau Gildersleeve, 92; Biog Dictionary of North American Classicists, 94; Greek Authors, Dictionary of Lit Biog, vol 176, 97; Ancient Roman Auths, Dictionary of Lit Biog, 98. **CONTACT ADDRESS** Dept of French and Classics, South Carolina Univ, Columbia, SC, 29208. **EMAIL** wardbriggs@sc.edu

BRIGHAM, JOHN
PERSONAL Born 08/27/1945, San Francisco, CA, m, 1982, 2 children **DISCIPLINE** POLITICAL SCIENCE **EDUCATION** Univ Calif Berkeley, BA, 67; Univ W Madison, MA, 69; Univ Calif Santa Barbara, PhD, 75. **CAREER** Vis prof, Univ Chicago, Syracuse, SUNY-Albany, CSU Chico; Prof, Political Science Dept, Univ Mass Amherst, 76-. **HONORS AND AWARDS** Fel Int Inst Sociol Law; Trustee, Law & Soc Asn. **MEMBERSHIPS** APSA; Law Soc Asn. **RESEARCH** Law; Social movements; Gender; Property. **SELECTED PUBLICATIONS** Auth, Property and the Politics of Entitlement, Temple Univ Press, 90; The Constitution of Interests: Beyond the Politics of Rights, NY Univ Press, 96; The Other Countries of American Law, Social Identities: Jour for the Study of Race, Nation and Cult, 96; Institutional Authority and Political Momentum: Constitutional Equal Protection in American Politics, Critic of Auth, Institutions Series: Horizons of Justice, Peter Lang Publ, 96; Law in Politics: Struggles Over Property and Public Space on New York Citys Lower East Side, Law and Social Inquiry, 96; From the Matz Patrol to the Free Speech Movement, States, Citizens and Questions of Significance, Peter Lang, 97; Staates, Citizens and Questions of Significance: Proceedings of the Tenth Roundtable on Law and Semiotics, Peter Lang, 97. **CONTACT ADDRESS** Political Science Dept, Univ Mass, Amherst, MA, 01003. **EMAIL** brigham@polsci.umass.edu

BRIGHT, DAVID F.
PERSONAL Born 04/13/1942, Winnipeg, MB, Canada, m, 2 children **DISCIPLINE** CLASSICS **EDUCATION** Univ Manitoba, BA, 62; Univ Cincinnati, MA, 63 PhD, 67. **CAREER** Univ Manitoba, inst, 61-62; Univ Cincinnati, tchg fel, 63-67; Williams Col, asst prof, 67-70; Univ IL asst prof, assoc prof, prof, ch classics, acting dir, sch Hum, chemn dept classics, dir prog comp lit, acting dean, 70-89; Iowa State Univ, prof, dean of coll lib arts & sci, 89-91, Emory Univ, prof, vpres arts & sci, dean Emory col, 91-. **HONORS AND AWARDS** Skuli Johnson Gold Medal, Univ Man Gold medallist, Woodrow Wilson Fel, Can Council Res fel, Semple Trav fell, Univ Cinci res fel, Elected Society of Fel, Amer Acad Rome, Delmas Found Schl, Phi Beta Kappa **MEMBERSHIPS** APA, CAMW&S, Vergilian Soc., AAHE **RESEARCH** Latin poetry; literature of late antiquity and early mediaeval literature. **SELECTED PUBLICATIONS** Auth, Haec mihi fingebam: Tibullus in His World, Leiden: Brill, 78; auth, Elaborate Disarray: The Nature of Statius' Silvae, Meisenheim, 80; auth, Classical Texts and their Traditions, Studies in Honor of C.R. Trahman, ed., D.F. Bright & E.S. Ramage, Chico CA: Scholars Press, 84; auth, The Miniature Epic in Vandal Africa, Norman: Univ Oklahoma Press, 87; Theory and Practice in the Vergilian cento, IL Class Stud, 84; auth, The Chronology of the Poems of Dracontius, Classica et Mediaevalia, forthcoming. **CONTACT ADDRESS** Dept of Classics, Emory Univ, N404 Callaway Center, Atlanta, GA, 30322. **EMAIL** dbright@emory.edu

BRILLIANT, RICHARD
PERSONAL Born 11/20/1929, Boston, MA, m, 1951, 4 children **DISCIPLINE** HISTORY OF GREEK & ROMAN ART **EDUCATION** Yale Univ, BA, 51, MA, 56, PhD(art hist), 60; LLB, Harvard Univ, 54. **CAREER** From asst prof to prof hist of art, Univ Pa, 62-70; prof art hist, Columbia Univ, 70-; Anna S. Garbedian prof in the Humanities (Columbia), 90-; dir, Italian Academy for Advanced Studies in America at Columbia, 96-99; Fulbright grant, Italy, 57-59; Am Acad Rome fel, 60-62; Guggenheim fel, 67-68; vis Mellon prof fine arts, Univ Pittsburgh, 71; Nat Endowment Humanities sr fel, 72-73; vis Lincei prof, Scuola Normale Superiore, Pisa, 74, 80, & 88; ed in chief, The Art Bulletin, 91-94. **MEMBERSHIPS** Corresp mem, Ger Archaeol Inst; Col Art Asn; Am Numis Soc; Archaeol Inst Am; Soc Prom Hellenic Studies. **RESEARCH** Greek and Roman art and archaeology; theory in the historiography of art; the city of Rome, antiquity to the early Renaissance. **SELECTED PUBLICATIONS** Auth, Gesture and Rank in Roman Art, Conn Acad, 63; The Arch of Septimius Severus in the Roman Forum, Am Acad Rome, 67; Arts of the Ancient Greeks, McGraw, 73; Roman Art, Phaidon, 74; Pompeii: AD 79, The Treasure of Rediscovery, 79; Visual Narratives, Cornell, 84; Portraiture, Harvard, 91; Commentaries on Roman Art, London, 94; Facing the New World, NY, 97. **CONTACT ADDRESS** Dept of Art Hist & Archaeol, Columbia Univ, 2960 Broadway, New York, NY, 10027-6900.

BRINK, JAMES EASTGATE
PERSONAL Born 02/28/1945, Santa Fe, NM, m, 1968, 1 child **DISCIPLINE** HISTORY **EDUCATION** Univ Kans, BA, 67; Univ Wash, MA, 70, PhD(hist), 74. **CAREER** Asst prof to assoc prof hist, Tex Tech Univ, 76-; interim vice pres for Enrollment of Management, 97; vice provost, 98. **MEMBERSHIPS** AHA; Int Comn Hist Representative & Parliamentary Inst; Soc Reformation Res; Western Soc French Hist. **RESEARCH** Representative institutions of early modern Europe; the estates general of Languedoc: sixteenth century political and social history. **SELECTED PUBLICATIONS** Auth, A Tax Loop-Hole in the Sixteenth Century, Western French Hist, 76; Les Etats de Languedoc de 1515-1560, Annales du Midi, 7-9/76; The Case for Provincial Autonomy: The Estates of Languedoc, 1515-1560, Legis Studies Quart, Vol 3, 437-446. **CONTACT ADDRESS** Office of the Provost, Tex Tech Univ, Box 42019, Lubbock, TX, 79409-0001. **EMAIL** jsjeb@ttacs.ttu.edu

BRINKLEY, ALAN
PERSONAL Born 06/02/1949, Washington, DC, m, 1989, 1 child **DISCIPLINE** HISTORY **EDUCATION** Princeton, AB, 71; Harvard Univ, PhD, 79. **CAREER** Asst prof, history, MIT, 78-82; asoc prof, history, Harvard Univ, 82-88; prof, history, CUNY Grad Sch, 88-91; prof, history, Columbia Univ 91-98; Allan Nevins Prof of Hist, 98- . **HONORS AND AWARDS** Am Book Awd, Hist, 83. **RESEARCH** Twentieth century U.S. history. **SELECTED PUBLICATIONS** Auth, Voices of Protest: Huey Long, Father Coughlin, and the Great Depression, Knopf, 82; auth, The End of Reform: New Deal Liberalism in Recession and War, Knopf, 95; auth, The Unfinished Nation: A Concise History of the American People, Knopf, 97; auth, Eyes of the Nation: A Visual History of the United States, Knopf, 97; auth, New Federalist Papers, Norton, 97; auth, American History: A Survey, McGraw-Hill, 98; auth, Liberalism and its Discontents, Harvard, 98. **CONTACT ADDRESS** Dept of History, Columbia Univ, New York, NY, 10027. **EMAIL** ab65@columbia.edu

BRINKLEY, GEORGE A.
PERSONAL Born 04/20/1931, Wilmington, NC, m, 1959, 1 child **DISCIPLINE** INTERNATIONAL RELATIONS, RUSSIAN AND EAST EUROPEAN STUDIES **EDUCATION** Davidson Col, BA, 53; Columbia Univ, MA, 55, PhD, 64. **CAREER** Instr, Columbia Univ, 57-58; Instr to prof emer, 58-91, dir, 69-87, Prog of Soviet and East European Stud, Univ of Notre Dame. **HONORS AND AWARDS** Phi Beta Kappa, 52; Ford Found Fel, 54-57; Beer Prize, Am Hist Asn, 67; Fel Coun on For Rel, 68. **MEMBERSHIPS** Am Asn for Advan of Slavic Stud. **RESEARCH** Soviet/Russian government and foreign relations. **SELECTED PUBLICATIONS** Auth, The Volunteer Army and Allied Intervention in South Russia, 1917-1921, Univ Notre Dame Pr, 66. **CONTACT ADDRESS** 19539 Cowles Ave, South Bend, IN, 46637.

BRINKMAN, JOHN ANTHONY
PERSONAL Born 07/04/1934, Chicago, IL, m, 1970, 1 child **DISCIPLINE** ANCIENT NEAR EASTERN HISTORY **EDUCATION** Loyola Univ, AB, 56, AM, 58; Univ Chicago, PhD, 62. **CAREER** From asst prof to assoc prof, 64-70; chmn, Dept Near Eastern Lang & Civilizations, 69-72; dir, Orient Inst, 72-81; PROF, MESOPOTAMIAN HISTORY, ORIENT INST, UNIV CHICAGO, 70-, CHARLES H. SWIFT DISTINGUISHED SERV PROF, 84- , CHMN DEPT NEAR EASTERN LANG & CIVS, HARVARD, 95- ,Am Coun Learned Soc fel, 63-64; annual prof, Am Schs Orient Res, Baghdad, 68-69, chmn Baghdad sch comt, 71, chmn exec comt, 73-75; res fel, Am Res Inst Turkey, 71; mem vis comt, Dept Near Eastern Lang & Lit, Harvard Univ, 73-80; Nat Endowment for Humanities sr fel, 73-74; cur tablet collection, Orient Inst, 77; ed, Chicago Assyrian Dict, 77- **MEMBERSHIPS** Am Orient Soc; Brit Inst Persian Studies; Brit Inst Archaeol Ankara; Brit Sch Archaeol Iraq; Deutsche Orient Ges. **RESEARCH** Political history of Babylonia; Assyrian historiography; ancient Oriental numismatics. **SELECTED PUBLICATIONS** Auth, A political history of post-Kassite Babylonia, Pontif Bibl Inst, 68; Foreign relations of Babylonia from 1600 to 625 BC, Am J Archaeol, 72; Comments on the Nassouhi Kinglist and the Assyrian Kinglist tradition, Orientalia, 73; Sennacherib's Babylonian problem: An interpretation, J Cuneiform Studies, 73; Materials and Studies for Kassite History, Vol I, Orient Inst, Univ Chicago, 76; Prelude to Empire, 84. **CONTACT ADDRESS** Oriental Inst, Univ of Chicago, 1155 E 58th St, Chicago, IL, 60637-1540. **EMAIL** j-brinkman@uchicago.edu

BRINKMAN, JOHN T.
DISCIPLINE HISTORY OF RELIGION **EDUCATION** Fordham Univ, PhD, 88. **CAREER** Inst of Asian Stud, St John's Univ, 89-97. **MEMBERSHIPS** AAAS; AAR. **RESEARCH** Ecological dimension of world religion; East Asian thought; history of religions with refined focus in the sequence; Japan; Chiina; India; **SELECTED PUBLICATIONS** Auth, The Simplicity of Dogen, Eastern Buddhist, 94; auth, Harmony, Attribute of the Sacred and Phenomenal in Aquinas and Kukai, Buddhist-Christian Stud, 95; auth, The Simplicity of Nichiren, Eastern Buddhist, 95; auth, Simplicity: A Distinctive Quality of Japanese Spirituality, Peter Land, 96; auth, Cosmology and Consciousness, Buddhist-Christian Studies, 98; auth, The Kyoto Protocol and Exigent Ecological Vision, Int Shinto Found Symp Proc, 98-99. **CONTACT ADDRESS** 2 Darthouth Rd, Shoreham, NY, 11786.

BRINKS, HERBERT JOHN
PERSONAL Born 05/25/1935, IL, m, 1957, 2 children **DISCIPLINE** HISTORY **EDUCATION** Calvin Col & Sem, AB, 57; Univ Mich, MA, 61, PhD, 65. **CAREER** Res asst, Mich Hist Collection, Univ Mich, 61-62; from instr to assoc prof, 62-71, PROF HIST, CALVIN COL, 71- CUR COLONIAL COLLECTION, 62-, Consult, Immigration Sources Proj, Univ Mich, 75-; Earhart Found fel, 76-77. **MEMBERSHIPS** Orgn Am Hist. **RESEARCH** Dutch-American immigration and Americanization. **SELECTED PUBLICATIONS** Auth, The Myth of the West in America as the Last Empire, J Amer Hist, Vol 0082, 95. **CONTACT ADDRESS** Dept of Hist, Calvin Col, Grand Rapids, MI, 49506.

BRISCO, THOMAS V.
PERSONAL m, 2 children **DISCIPLINE** BIBLICAL BACKGROUNDS AND ARCHAELOLOGY **EDUCATION** Ouachita Baptist Univ, BA, 69; Southwestern Baptist Theol Sem, MDiv, 73; Southwestern Baptist Theol Sem, PhD, 81; advan stud, Cambridge Univ, 86. **CAREER** Tchg fel, Southwestern Baptist Theol Sem, 75-76; instr, Ouachita Baptist Univ, 77-80; instr, 80-82; asst prof, 82-90; assoc prof, 90-; assoc dean, Spec Masters Degrees. **HONORS AND AWARDS** David Meier Intl Stud League Award, Southwestern Baptist Theol Sem, 74; Outstanding Young Men of Am, 78, 79; Who's Who Among Students in Amer Univ(s) and Col(s), 76; Who's Who Among Biblical Archaeol., Interim pastor, Kingsland Baptist Church, 96-97; First Baptist Church, 95-96; First Baptist Church, Humble, 94-95; Intl Baptist Church, 93; First Baptist Church, Arkadelphia, 92-93; VP, Amer Sch(s) Oriental Res, 82-83; president, 83-84; VP, Nat Assn Baptist Prof(s) Rel, 91; pres, 92. **SELECTED PUBLICATIONS** Auth, Biblical Illustrator, Baptist Sunday Sch Bd, 79; Intl Standard Bible Encycl, Eerdmans, 88; contrib, Holman Bible Dictionary, Broadman & Holman, 91. **CONTACT ADDRESS** Sch Theol, Southwestern Baptist Theol Sem, PO Box 22000, Fort Worth, TX, 76122-0418. **EMAIL** tvb@swbts.swbts.edu

BRISTOW, EDWARD
DISCIPLINE JEWISH HISTORY **EDUCATION** Yale Univ, PhD. **CAREER** Dean, prof, Fordham Univ. **HONORS AND AWARDS** Grants, NEH; Am Philos Soc. **RESEARCH** Mod Britain. **SELECTED PUBLICATIONS** Auth, Profit-Sharing, Socialism and Labor Unrest, Essays in Anti-Labor Hist, 75; Vice and Vigilance: Purity Movements in Britain Since 1700, Rowan and Littlefield, 78; Prostitution and Prejudice: The Jewish Fight Against White Slavery, 1875-1939, Clarendon Press, 82; Individualism Versus Socialism in Britain, 1880-1914, Garland Publ, 87. **CONTACT ADDRESS** Dept of Hist, Fordham Univ, 113 W 60th St, New York, NY, 10023.

BRITSCH, R. LANIER
PERSONAL Born 11/16/1938, Provo, UT, m, 1961, 6 children **DISCIPLINE** HISTORY **EDUCATION** BYU, BA, 63, MA, 64; Claremont Grad Univ, PhD, 67. **CAREER** From instr to asst prof to assoc prof to prof, 66-, vp, academics, BYU, Hawaii Campus, 86-90; dir, David M. Kennedy Ctr, 91-97. **HONORS AND AWARDS** Nat Defense Foreign Lang Fel, 65-66; Fel, Blaisdell Inst, 66; Fulbright-Hays Summer Sem, 68; BYU Res Grant, 73; LDS Church Historians Grant, 74; Prof Development Leave, 78, 95, 97, 98. **MEMBERSHIPS** Mormon Hist Asn. **RESEARCH** History of the Church of Jesus Christ of Latter-day Saints in Asia and the Pacific; Christian mission history in Asia. **SELECTED PUBLICATIONS** Auth, Unto the Islands of the Sea: A History of the Latter-day Saints in the Pacific, 86; auth, Moramona: The Mormon in Hawaii, 89; auth, From the East: The History of the Latter-day Saints in Asia, 1851-1996, 98; auth, art, Faithful, Good, Virtuous, True: Pioneers in the Philippines, 98; auth, art, Mormon Intruders in Tonga: The Passport Act of 1922, 98. **CONTACT ADDRESS** Dept of History, Brigham Young Univ, Provo, UT, 84602. **EMAIL** rlb23@email.byu.edu

BRITTAIN, JAMES EDWARD
PERSONAL Born 05/20/1931, Mills River, NC, m, 1973 **DISCIPLINE** HISTORY OF SCIENCE & TECHNOLOGY **EDUCATION** Clemson Univ, BS, 57; Univ Tenn, MS, 58; Case Western Reserve Univ, MA, 68, PhD(hist), 70. **CAREER** Asst prof elec eng, Clemson Univ, 59-66; asst prof hist, Ga inst Technol, 69-72; res fel, Smithsonian inst, 72-73; ASSOC PROF HIST, GA INST TECHNOL, 73-, Asst ed, Technol & Cult, 74-75, assoc ed, 76-77; chmn, inst Elec & Electronics Comn, 78-79. **HONORS AND AWARDS** Usher Award, Soc Hist Technol, 71. **MEMBERSHIPS** Soc Hist Technol; Hist Sci Soc; inst Elect & Electronics Engrs; Soc indust Archaeol; Royal Soc Arts. **RESEARCH** History of electrical science and technology; history of technology in the American south. **SELECTED PUBLICATIONS** Auth, Across Fortunes Tracks in A Biography of Kenan, William, Rand Jr, J Amer Hist, Vol 0084, 97. **CONTACT ADDRESS** Sch Soc Sci Ga inst Technol, Atlanta, GA, 30332.

BRITTON, ALLEN PERDUE
PERSONAL Born 05/25/1914, Elgin, IL, m, 1938 **DISCIPLINE** MUSIC **EDUCATION** Univ Ill, BS, 37, MA, 39; Univ Mich, PhD(musicol), 49. **CAREER** Teacher, pub schs, ind, 38-41; instr music, Eastern Ill State Col, 41-43; dean, 69-79, PROF MUSIC, UNIV MICH, ANN ARBOR, 49-, EMER DEAN SCH MUSIC, 79-, Ed, J Music Educ Nat Conf, 53-73; assoc dean sch music, Univ Mich, Ann Arbor, 60-68; mem overseas tours comt, United Serv Orgn-Dept Defense, 62-72; mem exec comt, Mus Am Music, 67-; mem bd trustees, interlochen Ctr Arts, 73-; ed, Am Music, 79-; mem bd dir, Univ Mich Musical Soc, 74- **MEMBERSHIPS** Am Musicol Soc; Am Studies Asn; Music Educ Nat Conf (pres, 60-62, vpres, 62-64); Sonneck Soc. **RESEARCH** Early American music. **SELECTED PUBLICATIONS** Auth, Easy instructor, 1798-1831, J Res Music Educ; Music in Early American public education, Nat Soc Study Educ, 58; Singing school movement in the United States, Cong Report, Int Musicol Soc, 61. **CONTACT ADDRESS** Sch of Music, Univ of Mich, Ann Arbor, MI, 48109.

BROAD, DAVID B.
PERSONAL Born 10/30/1946, Brooklyn, NY, m, 1989, 2 children **DISCIPLINE** SOCIOLOGY **EDUCATION** Univ Houston, BS, 71, MA, 73; Regents Col, BA, 78; Canisius Col, MS, 88; State Univ NY at Buffalo, PhD, 86. **CAREER** Instr, Buffalo State Col, 77-84; asst prof, Canisius Col, 84-87; assoc prof, Adams State Col, 87-89; prof, William Penn Col, 89-91; prof, Tenn State Univ, 91-98; dean, Elgin Commun Col, 98-. **HONORS AND AWARDS** Tchr Year, 97, Tenn State Univ; Gold Medal, 87, Empire State Games. **MEMBERSHIPS** Am Social Asn; Popular Culture Asn. **RESEARCH** American class structure; popular culture. **SELECTED PUBLICATIONS** Auth, art, The Parent Trap: A Myth of the Reunited Self, 95; auth, art, The Social Register: Directory of America's Upperclass, 96; coed, Student, Self and Society: Stories From the Lives of Learners, 96; auth, art, Sheena, Queen of the Jungle: White Goddess of the Dumont Era, 97; auth, art, Annie Oakley: Women, Legend and Myth, 98. **CONTACT ADDRESS** Elgin Comm Col, Elgin, IL, 60123. **EMAIL** dbroad@elgin.cc.il.us

BROAD, ROBIN
DISCIPLINE POLITICAL ECONOMY AND INTERNATIONAL DEVELOPMENT **EDUCATION** Williams Col, BA; Princeton Univ, MA, PhD. **CAREER** Prof, Am Univ. **HONORS AND AWARDS** Grants, John D. and Catherine T. MacArthur Found, Asn Asian Studies; Coun For Rel., Int econ, Carnegie Endowment Int Peace, U.S. House Representatives, U.S. Dept Treasury. **SELECTED PUBLICATIONS** Coauth, Plundering Paradise: The Struggle for the Environment in the Philippines, Univ Calif Press, 93; Auth, Unequal Alliance: The World Bank, the International Monetary Fund, and the Philippines,Univ Calif Press, 88. **CONTACT ADDRESS** American Univ, 4400 Massachusetts Ave, Washington, DC, 20016.

BROCK, KAREN L.
DISCIPLINE JAPANESE ART HISTORY **EDUCATION** Profinceton Univ, PhD. **CAREER** Hist, Washington Univ. **HONORS AND AWARDS** Japan Found Prof Fel. **SELECTED PUBLICATIONS** Auth, The Shogun's 'Painting Match' Monumenta Nipponica, 95; Do Not Hang Me in the Center; Ed, Living Bodies:The Japanese Buddhist Icon in its Monastic Context. A study Kasuga devotion at Kozanji. **CONTACT ADDRESS** Washington Univ, 1 Brookings Dr, St. Louis, MO, 63130. **EMAIL** YMatsusaka@ wellesley.edu

BROCK, PETER DE BEAUVOIR
PERSONAL Born 01/30/1920, Guernsey Channel Is, United Kingdom **DISCIPLINE** HISTORY **EDUCATION** Univ Oxford, MA, 48, DPhil, 54; Univ Cracow, PhD, 50. **CAREER** Asst prof, Univ Alta, 58-60; assoc prof, Columbia Univ, 61-66; prof, 66-85, PROF EMER HISTORY, UNIV TORONTO, 85-. **HONORS AND AWARDS** Dlit(hon), Univ Toronto, 91. **MEMBERSHIPS** Can Asn Slavists; Czek Hist Conf; Peace Hist Soc; Polish Inst Arts Sci Am. **SELECTED PUBLICATIONS** Auth, Twentieth Century Pacifism, 70; auth, Pacifism in Europe to 1914, 72; auth, Nationalism and Populism in Partitioned Poland, 73; auth, The Slovak National Awakening, 76; auth, Polish Revolutionary Populism, 77; auth, The Roots of War Resistance, 81; auth, The Mahatma and Mother India, 83; auth, The Military Question in the Early Church, 88; auth, The Quaker Peace Testimony 1660 to 1914, 90; auth, Freedom from War, 91; auth, Freedom from Violence, 91; auth, Folk Cultures and Little Peoples, 92; auth, Breve historia del pacifismo, 97; ed, Records of Conscience, 93; ed, Testimonies of Conscience from the Soviet Union to the War Resisters' International 1923-1929, 97; co-ed, The Czech Renascence of the Nineteenth Century, 70. **CONTACT ADDRESS** Dept of History, Univ Toronto, Toronto, ON, M5S 3G3.

BRODHEAD, GARRY
DISCIPLINE MUSIC THEORY **EDUCATION** Univ Pa, BA; Univ Ind, MM, PhD. **CAREER** Prof. **SELECTED PUBLICATIONS** Auth, pubs on qualitative time and structure in music. **CONTACT ADDRESS** Dept of Music History, Theory and Composition, Ithaca Col, 100 Job Hall, Ithaca, NY, 14850. **EMAIL** gbrodhea@ithaca.edu

BRODHEAD, MICHAEL JOHN
PERSONAL Born 11/20/1935, Abilene, KS, m, 1969, 2 children **DISCIPLINE** HISTORY **EDUCATION** Univ Kans, BA, 59, MA, 62; Univ Minn, PhD(hist), 67. **CAREER** Cur Kans Collection, Univ Kans Libr, 65-67; asst prof hist, 67-71, assoc prof, 71-79, PROF HIST, UNIV NEV, RENO, 79-. **MEMBERSHIPS** Orgn Am Historians; Western Hist Asn; Am Soc Environ Hist; Coun Am Mil Past. **RESEARCH** Natural history; exploration and travel; populism. **SELECTED PUBLICATIONS** Auth, Women in the Field in America Pioneering Women Naturalists, Pacific Hist Rev, Vol 0061, 92; Iwo Jima in Monuments, Memories and the American Hero, J Mil Hist, Vol 0057, 93; Fremont, John, Charles in Character as Destiny, J the West, Vol 0034, 95; The United States Army Signal Service and Natural History in Alaska, 1874-1883, Pacific Northwest Quart, Vol 0086, 95; Owen, Richard in Victorian Naturalist, Env Hist, Vol 0001, 96; Land Grants and Lawsuits in Northern New Mexico, J the West, Vol 0035, 96; Adventures of a Frontier Naturalist in the Life and Times of Dr Lincecum,Gideon, Env Hist, Vol 0001, 96; Naturalist, Env Hist, Vol 0001, 96. **CONTACT ADDRESS** Cent Plains Reg, National Archives, 2312 Bannister Rd, Kansas City, MO, 64131.

BRODMAN, JAMES WILLIAM
PERSONAL Born 12/09/1945, Rochester, NY, m, 1980, 1 child **DISCIPLINE** HISTORY **EDUCATION** Canisius Col, BA, 67; Univ Va, MA, 69, PhD(hist), 74. **CAREER** Asst prof, 72-78, ASSOC PROF HIST, UNIV CENT ARK, 78- **MEMBERSHIPS** Medieval Acad Am; Am Acad Res Historians on Medieval Spain. **RESEARCH** Spanish redemptionist orders; Medieval ransoming; Medieval Spanish charity. **SELECTED PUBLICATIONS** Auth, Christianity and Islam--Captivity and Liberation in the Name of God--Time of innocent-Ii After 1187, Cath Hist Rev, Vol 0080, 94; The Church and the Origins of the Modern State in Castile 1369-1480, Speculum--J Medieval Stud, Vol 0070, 95; The Church and the Origins of the Modern State in Castile 1369-1480, Speculum--J Medieval Stud, Vol 0070, 95; The Learned King in the Reign of Alfonso X of Castile, Amer Hist Rev, Vol 0100, 95; Religion and Society in Spain, C.1492, Cath Hist Rev, Vol 0083, 97. **CONTACT ADDRESS** Dept of Hist, Univ Cent Ark, Conway, AR, 72035.

BRODY, DAVID
PERSONAL Born 06/05/1930, Elizabeth, NJ, m, 1955, 2 children **DISCIPLINE** HISTORY **EDUCATION** Harvard Univ, AB, 52, MA, 53, PhD, 58. **CAREER** Instr hist, Northeastern Univ, 58-59; res assoc labor mgt hist, Harvard Univ, 59-61; asst prof hist, Columbia Univ, 61-65; assoc prof, Ohio State Univ, 65-67; PROF HIST, UNIV CALIF, DAVIS, 67-, Soc Sci Res Coun fac fel, 66-67; vis prof US labor hist, Warwick Univ, 72-73; Fulbright sr lectr, Moscow State Univ, 75; sr fel, Nat Endowment for Humanities, 78-79. **MEMBERSHIPS** AHA; Orgn Am Hist; Labor Hist Asn. **RESEARCH** American labor, social and economic history. **SELECTED PUBLICATIONS** Auth, The Wages of Whiteness in Race and the Making of the American Working Class, J Interdisciplinary Hist, Vol 0024, 93; Getting Work in Philadelphia, 1840-1950, J Amer Hist, Vol 0080, 93; The incorrectness of the New Labor History, Pacific Hist Rev, Vol 0062, 93; Reconciling the Old Labor History and the New, Pacific Hist Rev, Vol 0062, 93; Sources of Stability and Seeds of Subversion in Brody,David and the Making of the New Labor History, Labor Hist, Vol 0034, 93; Steel City in A Docudrama in 3 Acts, Labor Hist, Vol 0034, 93; American Cool in Constructing A 20th-Century Emotional Style, J Amer Culture, Vol 0018, 95; The Politics of Pensions in A Comparative-Analysis of Britain, Canada, and the United States, 1880-1940, J interdisciplinary Hist, Vol 0026, 95; Heroes of Unwritten Story in the Uaw, 1934-39 , Labor Hist, Vol 0036, 95. **CONTACT ADDRESS** Dept of Hist, Univ of Calif, Davis, CA, 95616.

BROESAMLE, JOHN JOSEPH
PERSONAL Born 02/10/1941, Long Beach, CA, m, 1963, 2 children **DISCIPLINE** UNITED STATES HISTORY **EDUCATION** Univ of the Pac, BA, 64; Columbia Univ, MA, 65, PhD (hist), 70. **CAREER** Assoc dean, Sch Social & Behav Sci, 73-76, from asst prof to assoc prof, 68-75, Prof Hist, CA State Univ, Northridge, 75-, Danforth Assoc, 81- **HONORS AND AWARDS** Woodrow Wilson fel, Woodrow Wilson Dissertation fel, 64-67; CA State Univ , Northridge Distinguished Teaching award, 73; CA State Univ, Northridge Scholarly Pub Award, 91. **MEMBERSHIPS** AHA; Orgn Am Hist; Academy of Political Science; Soc for Hist of the Gilded Age and Progressive Era; AAUP. **RESEARCH** Twentieth century United States political and cultural history. **SELECTED PUBLICATIONS** Auth, The Struggle for Control of the Federal Reserve System, 1914-1917, Mid-Am, 10/70; William Gibbs McAdoo: A Passion for Change, 1863-1917, Kennikat, 73; The Democrats from Bryan to Wilson, In: The Progressive Era, Syracuse Univ, 74; Reform and Reaction in Twentieth Century American politics, Greenwood, 90; Suddenly a Giant: A History of California State University, Northridge, Santa Susana, 93; History: Cross-cultural Perspectives, in: Cross-cultural Perspectives in the Curriculum, Chandler & Sharpe, 86; William Gibbs McAdoo and the Hopeless Candidacy Syndrome, in Statesman Who Were Never President, Univ Press Am, 97. **CONTACT ADDRESS** Dept Hist, California State Univ, Northridge, 18111 Nordhoff St, Northridge, CA, 91330-8250.

BROMAN, PER F.
PERSONAL Born 07/26/1962, Norrkoping, Sweden, m, 1997 **DISCIPLINE** MUSICOLOGY **EDUCATION** Ingesund Col Mus, MA, 87; Royal Col Mus, Stockholm, Post-grad Dipl in Mus Theory, 92; McGill Univ, Montreal, MA, 98; Univ Gothenburg, PhD, 99. **CAREER** Res Fellow, Univ Gothenburg, Fac Mus, 97- ; Asst prof, Lulea Univ Tech, Sweden, Sch Mus, 93-; Lect, Orebro Univ, Sweden, Sch Mus, 91-93; Asst prof, Swedish Conserv in Jakobstad, Finland, 87-88; Ed, Internet publ, STM-Online, 98- ; Mem, ed board for ex tempore: A Journal of Compositional and Theoretical Research in Music, 97- . **HONORS AND AWARDS** Carl-Allan Moberg Musicol Award, 96. **MEMBERSHIPS** Am Musicol Soc; Soc Mus Theory; Col Mus Soc; Swedish Musicol Soc. **RESEARCH** Aesthetics; Historiography of Western Art Music; Scandinavian Art Music. **SELECTED PUBLICATIONS** Jan Sandstrom and Modernism, Nutida Musik, 37/4, 94, 51-58; Emperor's New Clothes: Performance Practice in the Late Twentieth Century, Journal of Swedish Musicological Society, 76-77, 94-95, 31-53; Paleomodernism, Neomodernism, Postmodernism and the Musical Life in Montreal, Nutida Musik, 38/3, 95, 3-13; A Musicological Debacle, Nutida Musik, 38/1, 95, 79-82; Richard Wagner's Die Meistersinger in Nurnberg: A Hidden anti-Semitic Plan? OV-Revyns Arsbok 1995-96, Stockholm, Operavannerna, 96, 20-22; Darmstadt on memory lane, Nutida Musik, 39, 2-3, 96, 82-84; Camp, Irony, (Neo) Avantgarde: Three Readings of the Gloria Movement from Sven-David Sandstrom's High Mass, Nutida Musik, 39, 2-3, 96, 33-38; Richard Wagners Antisemitism was also Apparent in his Operas, Svenska Dagbladet, May 14, 96; The Russian Folk Music's Importance for Stravinsky, Oxford Univ Press, 96, Svenska Dagbladet, Sept 18, 97; I am no longer sure what MUSIC, New Questions Demand New Answers: Recent Approaches in Musicology, Nutida Musik, 40/1, 97, 4-14; Pluralistic Perception, Token Musics, and Canon Formations: Memoirs from Darmstadt 1996, In the Plural: Institutions, Pluralism and Critical Self-Awareness in Contemporary Music, Copenhagen, Dept Musicol, Univ Copenhagen, 97, 49-53; The Compositions of Bengt Hambraeus, Crosscurrents and Counterpoints: Offerings in Honor of Bengt Hambraeus at 70, 255-66; The Writings of Bengt Hambraeus: A Selective Bibliography, Crosscurrents and Counterpoints: Offerings in Honor of Bengt Hambraeus at 70, 267-280; Countries, Stockholm, Kungl Musikaliska Akademien, 97, Nutida Musik, 41/2, 98, 48-54; Ed-in-chief, Crosscurrents and Counterpoints: Offerings in Honor of Bengt Hambraeus at 70, Gothenburg, Univ of Gothenburg, 98; The Idea of the Authentic Performance Is a Chimera, Svenska Dagbladet, Jan 29, 98. **CONTACT ADDRESS** Univ of Gothenburg, Lulea Univ of Technology, 669 Potomac Ave, Apt 8, Buffalo, NY, 14222. **EMAIL** per.broman@mh.luth.se

BRONNER, EDWIN BLAINE
PERSONAL Born 09/02/1920, Yorba Linda, CA, m, 1946, 4 children **DISCIPLINE** HISTORY **EDUCATION** Whittier Col, BA, 41; Haverford Col, MA, 47; Univ Pa, PhD(hist), 52. **CAREER** From instr to assoc prof hist, Temple Univ, 47-62; PROF HIST & CUR QUAKER COLLECTION, HAVERFORD COL, 62-, LIBRN, 69-, Am Philos Soc grant, 68; coun mem, Region 3 Arch Adv Coun, Nat Arch & Rec Serv, 72-74, Nat Endowment for Humanities grant, 81. **MEMBERSHIPS** Conf Early Am Hist; Orgn Am Historians; Friends Hist Asn (pres, 70-72); Friends Hist Soc (pres, 70); Conf Peace Res in Hist. **RESEARCH** Quaker history; early Pennsylvania history; William Penn. **SELECTED PUBLICATIONS** Auth, Holme,Thomas, 1624-1695 in Surveyor General of Pennsylvania, J Amer Hist, Vol 0080, 94; Piety and Tolerance in Pennsylvania German Religion, 1700-1840, J Amer Hist, Vol 0083, 96. **CONTACT ADDRESS** The Libr Haverford Col, Haverford, PA, 19041.

BRONNER, SIMON J.
PERSONAL Born 04/07/1954, Haifa, Israel, m, 1998 **DISCIPLINE** AMERICAN STUDIES **EDUCATION** St Univ NY, BA, 74, MA, 77; Ind Univ, PhD, 81. **CAREER** Asst prof, Pa St Univ, 81-84; assoc prof, 85-88; prof, 88-91; DISTINGUISHED PROF, AMER STUDIES, PA ST UNIV, 1991-; vis prof, Univ Cal, 91; Fulbright prof, Osaka Univ, 96-97; vis prof, Harvard, 97; dir, Amer Studies Prog, 87-96, dir, Ctr Penn Culture Studies, 90-96, 98- . **HONORS AND AWARDS** Dickinson Col Memorial Award, 74; Amer Folklore Soc Fels Award, 80 & 81; James A. Jordon Memorial Award for Teaching Excellence, 85; Chicago Folklore Prize, 86; Jon Ben Snow Found Prize, 87; Regional Coun of Hist Socs Award of Merit, 88; Peter and Iona Opie Prize, 90; Wayland Hand Prize, 94; Penn-German Soc Award of Merit, 96; Penn St Harrisburg Excellence in Res Award, 98; NY St Scholar Incentive Award, 71-74; NY St Regents Scholar, 71-74 NY St Coun on the Arts Fel, 74-75; Rockefeller Found Grad Fel, 78-81; NEH Res Fel, 84., Opie Prize Comm, 88; chmn Foodways Sect, 79-80, chmn, History Sect, 85-96, Amer Folklore Soc; chmn, Folklore Fels Prize Comm, 95; Ralph Henry Gabriel Prize Comm, 95 fel, Amer Folklore Soc, 94- . **MEMBERSHIPS** Amer Studies Assn; Amer Folklore Soc; Org Amer Historians; Soc Folklore Studies; Penn Hist Assn. **RESEARCH** Folklore; material culture; ethnicity; industrial era. **SELECTED PUBLICATIONS** Ed, Folklore Forum 79; ed, Material Culture 83-86; ed, Folklore Historian, 83-89; ed, American Folk Art: A Guide to Sources, Garland, 84; ed, American Material Culture and Folklife series, UMI Res, 84-90; co-ed, Folk Art and Art Worlds, UMI Res, 86; ed, Folklife Studies from the Gilded Age: Object, Rite and Custom in Victorian America, UMI Res, 88; ed, Consuming Visions: Accumulation and Display of Goods in Amer, 1880-1920, WW Norton, 89; coed, Folk Art and Art Worlds, Utah St Univ, 92; ed, American Material Culture and Folklife, Utah St Univ, 92; ed, Creativity and Tradition in Folklore: New Directions, Utah St Univ, 92; ed, Pennsylvania Traditions, 94-96; ed, Material Worlds series, Univ Ky, 1996-; assoc ed, Jewish Folklore and Ethnology Review, 96-; auth, Chain Carvers: Old Men Crafting Meaning, Univ Ky, 85; auth, American Folklore Studies: An Intellectual History, Univ Kans, 86; auth, Grasping Things: Folk Material Culture and Mass Society in America, Univ Ky, 86; auth, Old-Time Music Makers of New York State, Syracuse Univ, 87; auth, American Children's Folklore, August House, 88; auth, Piled Higher and Deeper: The Folklore of Campus Life, August House, 90; auth, Piled Higher and Deeper: The Folklore of Student Life, August House, 95; auth, The Carver's Art: Crafting Meaning from Wood, Univ Ky, 96; auth, Popularizing Pennsylvania: Henry W Shoemaker and the Progressive Uses of Folklore and History, Penn St, 96; auth, Following Tradition: Folklore in the Discourse of American Culture, Utah St Univ, 98. **CONTACT ADDRESS** American Studies Prog, Pennsylvania State Univ, 777 W Harrisburg Pike, Middletown, PA, 17057-4898. **EMAIL** sjb2@psu.edu

BROOK, BARRY SHELLEY
PERSONAL Born 11/01/1918, New York, NY, m, 1958, 2 children **DISCIPLINE** MUSICOLOGY **EDUCATION** City Col New York, BSS, 39; Columbia Univ, MA, 42; Univ Paris, DUniv, 59. **CAREER** Tutor music, 45-47, from instr to assoc prof, 48-66, PROF MUSICOL, QUEENS COL, NY, 66-; EXEC OFF, PHD PROG IN MUSIC, CITY UNIV NEW YORK, 67-, Ford Found fel, 54-55; Fulbright res scholar, 58-59; adv ed col music, Holt, Rinehart & Winston, inc, 60-; mem, Nat Screening Comt, Fulbright awards in musicol, 60-63; Guggenheim fels, 61-62 & 66-67; Univ Club Educ Found res grant, 62; vis prof, Grad Sch Arts & Sci, NY Univ, 64-65; inst Musicol, Sorbonne, 67-68; Nat Endowment for Humanities grant to estab computerized bibliog of music lit, 67-68; ed, RILM Abstr, 67-; Martha Baird Rockefeller & Am Coun Learned Soc grants for RILM proj, 68; mem, Music Adv Screening Comt Sr Fulbright Awards, 68-70; chmn, Comn Mixte, Repertoire int Iconographie Musicale, 72- **HONORS AND AWARDS** Publ Award, Nat Ctr Sci Res, 62; Dent Medal, Royal Musical Asn, 65; Chevalier, Order of Arts & Lett, France, 72. **MEMBERSHIPS** Am Musicol Soc; int Musicol Soc; Fr Musicol Soc; Belgian Musicol Soc; Royal Musical Asn. **RESEARCH** Music and aesthetics of the classical period; sociology of music; computer applications in musicology. **SELECTED PUBLICATIONS** Auth, On Reprinting Music and Books About Music in then and Now, Fontes Artis Musicae, Vol 0039, 92; The Symphonie Concertante in Its Musical and Sociological Bases/, Int Rev Aesthet and Sociol Mus Vol 0025, 94. **CONTACT ADDRESS** Ctr Mus Res & Documentat, Graduate Sch and Univ Ctr, CUNY, 50 Central Park West, New York, NY, 10021.

BROOKE, JOHN L.
PERSONAL Born 08/19/1953, Pittsfield, MA, m, 1979, 2 children **DISCIPLINE** AMERICAN HISTORY **EDUCATION** Cornell Univ, BA, 76; Univ Penn, MA, 77, PhD, 82. **CAREER** Vis asst prof, Amherst Col, 82-83; asst prof, 83-89, assoc prof, 89-97, prof, 97- Tufts Univ. **HONORS AND AWARDS** Charles Warren fel, Harvard Univ, 86-87; Am Coun of Learned Soc fel, 90-91; Orgn of Am Hist Merle Curtis Award for Intellectual Hist, 91; Natl Hist Soc Book Prize, 91; New England Hist Asn Book Award, 95; Soc of Hist of the Early Am Republic Book Prize, 95; Bancroft Prize, Columbia Univ, 95; NEH Fel for Ind Study and Res, 97-98; Guggenheim Fel, 97-98. **MEMBERSHIPS** Am Antiq Soc; Am Hist Assoc; Asn of Am Univ Prof; Orgn of Am Hist; Mass Hist Soc; New England Hist Asn; Soc for Hist of the Early Am Republic. **SELECTED PUBLICATIONS** Auth, The Heart of the Commonwealth: Society and Political Culture in Worcester County, Massachusetts, 1713-1861, Cambridge Univ Pr, 89; auth, The Refiner's Fire: The Making of Mormon Cosmology, 1644-1844, Cambridge, 94; auth, The True Spiritual Seed: Sectarian Religion and the Persistance of the Occult in Eighteenth-Century New England, in Benes, ed, Wonders of the Invisible World: 1600-1900, Boston Univ, 95; auth, Ancient Lodges and Self-Created Societies: Freemasonry and the Public Sphere in the Early Republic, in Hoffman, ed, The Beginnings of the Extended Republic: The Federalist Era, Univ Va, 96; auth, Reason and Passion in the Public Sphere: Habermas and the Cultural Historians, J of Interdisciplinary Hist, 98; auth, Press, Party, and Public Sphere in the United States, 1790-1840, in Kelly, ed, The History of the Book in America, v.2, forthcoming. **CONTACT ADDRESS** Dept of History, Tufts Univ, Medford, MA, 02155. **EMAIL** jbrooke@emerald.tufts.edu

BROOKER, JEWEL SPEARS
PERSONAL Born 06/13/1940, Jenkins, KY, m, 1962, 2 children **DISCIPLINE** MODERN BRITISH & AMERICAN LITERATURE **EDUCATION** Stetson Univ, BS, 62; Univ Fla, MA, 64; Univ SFla, PhD(English), 76. **CAREER** Lectr English, Univ Tampa, 68-71 & Univ SFla, 78-80; fel English, Yale Univ, 80-81; PROF LIT, ECKERD COL, 81-. **HONORS AND AWARDS** Nat Endowment for Humanities fel, 80, 87; Sears-Roebuck Found Teaching Excellence and Campus Leadership Award, 89-90; SAMLA Prize, best scholarly essay, SAtlantic Mod Lang Asn, 93-94; grants from Knight Found, Liberty Fund, Fla Endowment for the Humanities. **MEMBERSHIPS** MLA; Int Asn Philos & Lit; Am Asn Advan Humanities. **RESEARCH** T S Eliot; T E Hulme and Irving Babbitt. **SELECTED PUBLICATIONS** Auth and ed, Approaches to Teaching Eliot's Poetry and Plays, Mod Lang Asn, 88; ed, The Placing of T.S. Eliot, Univ Mo Press, 91; coauth, Reading The Waste Land: Modernism and the Limits of Interpretation, Univ Mass Press, 90; auth, Mastery and Escape: T.S. Eliot and the Dialectic of Modernism, Univ Mass Press, 94; ed, Conversations with Denise Levertov, Univ Press of Miss, 98; T.S. Eliot and Our Turning World, Macmillan (forthcoming 98); author of numerous essays and reviews in scholarly journals. **CONTACT ADDRESS** Letters Collegium, Eckerd Col, 4200 54th Ave S, Saint Petersburg, FL, 33711-0000. **EMAIL** jsbrooker@aol.com

BROOKS, E. BRUCE
PERSONAL Born 06/23/1936, Akron, OH, m, 1964, 1 child **DISCIPLINE** CHINESE HISTORY **EDUCATION** Oberlin

Conserv Music, MusB, 58; Univ Wash, PhD(Chinese lang & lit), 68. **CAREER** Lectr Chinese, Harvard Univ, 67-68, instr, 68-69, asst prof, 69-73, lectr, 73-74; ASST PROF CHINESE HIST, SMITH COL, 74-78; pres, Sinfac Minor, 68-80., Nat Endowment for Humanities res grant, 71-72; Am Coun Learned Socs, 76-77. **HONORS AND AWARDS** Waring Prize, Western Reserve Acad, 80. **RESEARCH** Prosody; stylistics; evolution of thought. **SELECTED PUBLICATIONS** Auth, Iron and Steel in Ancient-China, ISIS, Vol 0087, 96. **CONTACT ADDRESS** 39 Hillside Rd, Northampton, MA, 01060.

BROOKS, E. WILLIS
PERSONAL Kingston, RI, m, 1960, 2 children **DISCIPLINE** HISTORY **EDUCATION** Dartmouth Col, AB, 58; Stanford Univ, MA, 62, PhD(hist), 70. **CAREER** Dep chmn, Comt Travel Grants, ind Univ, 66-68; lectr hist, 68-70, asst prof, 70-79, ASSOC PROF HIST, UNIV NC, CHAPEL HILL, 79- **HONORS AND AWARDS** Tanner Award, Univ NC, 73. **MEMBERSHIPS** AHA; Am Asn Advan Slavic Studies; Southern Conf Slavic Studies. **RESEARCH** Modern Russian history. **SELECTED PUBLICATIONS** Auth, 1812-1814--Secret Correspondence of Bagration, P.I., Personal Letters of Raevskii, N.N., Notes of Vorontsov, M.S., Diaries of Russian Army officers from the Collection of the State-Historical-Museum, Slavic Rev, Vol 0053; The Legacy of History in Russia and the New States of Eurasia, Slavic Rev, Vol 0054, 95. **CONTACT ADDRESS** Univ NC, 475 Hamilton Hall 070A, Chapel Hill, NC, 27514.

BROOKS, GEORGE E.
PERSONAL Born 04/20/1933, Lynn, MS, m, 1985, 4 children **DISCIPLINE** HISTORY **EDUCATION** Dartmouth Col, Ab 57; Boston Univ, MA 58, PhD 62. **CAREER** IN Univ, asst prof 62-68, assoc prof 68-75, prof 75-; Vis Prof, Shandong Univ, China 85; Univ Zimbabwe 84; Tufts Univ 69. **HONORS AND AWARDS** Bost Univ Fell; Phi Alpha Theta; Ford Found Fell; 8 Facul Res Gnts; Herman Frederic Lieber Awd; NEH; Fulbright Fell; ACLS Fell. **MEMBERSHIPS** ASA; AHA; LSA; MANSA; WHA. **SELECTED PUBLICATIONS** Climate and History in West Africa: in: Transformations in Africa, ed, Graham Connah, Leichester Univ Press, 98; Teaching a Non-Centric World History Course, in: The Aspen World History Handbook, ed George E Brooks, Dik A Daso, Marilynn Hitchens, Heidi Roupp, Denver, World Hist Assn, 94; Reports of Chimpanzee Natural History, Including Tool Use in 16th and 17th Century Sierra Leone, with Jeanne M Sept, Intl Journal of Primatology, 94; Getting Along Together: World History Perspectives for Living in the Twenty-First Century, forthcoming; Samuel Hodges Jr: American Trader and Counsul in the Cape Verde Islands. **CONTACT ADDRESS** Dept of Hist, Indiana Univ, Bloomington, 1615 East University St, Bloomington, IN, 47405. **EMAIL** BROOKSG@ucs.indiana.edu

BROOKS, ROBIN
PERSONAL Born 05/28/1927, Moscow, USSR, m, 1950, 2 children **DISCIPLINE** AMERICAN HISTORY **EDUCATION** Brooklyn Col, BA, 57; Univ Rochester, PhD(hist), 64. **CAREER** From instr to asst prof hist, Rochester inst Technol, 61-64; asst prof, Calif State Col, Hayward, 64-65; from asst prof to assoc prof, 65-73, PROF HIST, SAN JOSE STATE UNIV, 73-, Fulbright-Hays lectr Am hist, Univ india, 75-76; mem, inst Early Am Hist & Cult, Williamsburg, Va. **MEMBERSHIPS** Am Studies Asn; Orgn Am Hist. **RESEARCH** American studies; environmental studies; United States social history. **SELECTED PUBLICATIONS** Auth, Storm Over Mono in the Mono Lake Battle and the California Water Future, Env Hist, Vol 0002, 97. **CONTACT ADDRESS** Dept of Hist, San Jose State Univ, San Jose, CA, 95192.

BROOKSHIRE, JERRY HARDMAN
PERSONAL Born 10/17/1943, Athens, GA, m, 1968, 2 children **DISCIPLINE** MODERN EUROPEAN & BRITISH HISTORY **EDUCATION** Univ Ga, AB, 65; Vanderbilt Univ, MA, 67, PhD, 70. **CAREER** Mil historian, US Mil Acad, 70-72; asst prof, 72-80, assoc prof hist, Mid Tenn State Univ, 80-86; actg chemn hist, 91-92; pres facil senate, 98-99. **MEMBERSHIPS** AHA; Southern Hist Assn; Conf Brit Studies; Soc Study Labour Hist. **RESEARCH** British Labour Party history. **SELECTED PUBLICATIONS** Auth, Clement Attlee, Manchester University Press, 95; auth, The National Council of Labour, 1921-1946, Albion, 98. **CONTACT ADDRESS** Dept of History, Middle Tennessee State Univ, Murfreesboro, TN, 37132-0001. **EMAIL** jbrookshire@mtsu.edu

BROSS, JAMES BEVERLEY
PERSONAL Born 11/21/1938, Knoxville, TN, m, 1959, 4 children **DISCIPLINE** RELIGION; HISTORY **EDUCATION** Cent Wesleyan Col, AB, 59; Univ Ill, MA, 65; Univ Iowa, PhD(relig), 72. **CAREER** Teacher math, Tenn Pub Schs, 59-60, 62-63 & All Tribes Indian Mission Sch, 60-62; instr, Southern Wesleyan Univ, 63-64; asst prof, Iowa Wesleyan Col, 65-68; teacher, Iowa Publ Schs, 72-73; Prof Relig, Southern Wesleyan Univ, 73-. **MEMBERSHIPS** Wesleyan Theol Soc; Am Soc Church Hist; Conf Faith & Hist; Evangelical Theol Soc. **RESEARCH** Puritanism in England; American religion. **CONTACT ADDRESS** Southern Wesleyan Univ, P O Box 1020, Central, SC, 29630-1020. **EMAIL** jbbross@hotmail.com

BROTHERS, THOMAS
DISCIPLINE MUSIC **EDUCATION** Univ CA Berkeley, PhD. **CAREER** Musicol prof, Duke Univ. **RESEARCH** Music of the 14th, 15th and 16th centuries; African-Am music; jazz. **SELECTED PUBLICATIONS** Auth, publ(s) on Medieval and Renaissance music. **CONTACT ADDRESS** Dept of Music, Duke Univ, Mary Duke Biddle Music Bldg, Durham, NC, 27706. **EMAIL** tdb@duke.edu

BROUGHTON, THOMAS ROBERT SHANNON
PERSONAL Born 02/17/1900, Corbetton, ON, Canada, m, 1931, 2 children **DISCIPLINE** CLASSICS, ANCIENT HISTORY **EDUCATION** Univ Toronto, AB, 21, MA, 22; Johns Hopkins Univ, PhD (Latin), 28. **CAREER** Instr Greek, Amherst Col, 26-27; assoc Latin, Bryn Mawr Col, 28-30, from assoc prof to prof, 30-65; Paddison prof class, 65-70, EMER PROF CLASSICS, UNIV NC, CHAPEL HILL, 70-, Vis prof, Johns Hopkins Univ, 38-40; Guggenheim fel, 45-46; Fulbright res grant, Italy, 51-52; prof in charge, Sch Classical Studies, Am Acad Rome, 59-61; vpres, int Fed Soc Classical Studies, 59-69; mem comt res libr, Am Coun Learned Soc, 67; ann mem, inst Advan Studies, 71-72. **HONORS AND AWARDS** Award, Am Philol Asn, 53., LLD, Johns Hopkins Univ, 69, Univ Toronto, 71 & Univ NC, Chapel Hill, 74. **MEMBERSHIPS** Am Acad Arts & Sci; AHA; Archaeol inst Am (hon vpres, 53-58); Am Philol Asn (pres, 54); Class Asn Can. **RESEARCH** Economic history of Rome; provinces of the Roman Empire; Roman constitutional history and politics. **SELECTED PUBLICATIONS** Auth, Dionysus and the History of Archaic Rome, Classical J, Vol 0088, 93. **CONTACT ADDRESS** Dept of Classics, Univ of No Carolina, Murphey Hall, Chapel Hill, NC, 27514.

BROUSSARD, RAY F.
PERSONAL Born 04/22/1926, Lafayette, LA, m, 1951, 3 children **DISCIPLINE** LATIN AMERICAN HISTORY **EDUCATION** Southwestern La Inst, BA, 49; Univ Tex, MA, 52, PhD, 59. **CAREER** Head dept foreign lang, Southwest Tex Jr Col, 52-55; instr hist, Howard County Jr Col, 55-57; dir, Bi-Nat Ctr, Cartagena, Colombia, 59-61; asst prof hist, Miss State Univ, 62-66; Assoc Prof Hist, Univ Ga, 66-, Consult on Colombia, Spec Oper Res Off, Am Univ, 62-63; univ fel, Portuguese Inst, Univ Tex, 63. **MEMBERSHIPS** AHA; Conf Latin Am Hist; Southeastern Conf Latin Am Studies; Nat Social Sci Asn. **RESEARCH** Caribbean defense, Armada de Barlovento; Mexican reform; American West, Mexican-Texas relations. **SELECTED PUBLICATIONS** Auth, "John Quitman and the Lopez Expedition," Journal of Mississippi History, 66; San Antonio During the Texas Republic, Monogr 18, Southwestern Studies, Tex Western Press, 67; Comonfort: Misunderstood Reformer, WGa Col Study Soc Sci, 67; "Juarez, Vidaurri and Comonfort's Return from Exile," Hispanic American History Review, 69; auth, "Bautista Antonelli: Architect of Caribbean Defense," The Historian, 88. **CONTACT ADDRESS** Dept of History, Univ of Georgia, Athens, GA, 30602-0001. **EMAIL** raybruce@arches.uga.edu

BROWDER, GEORGE C.
PERSONAL Born 03/14/1939, Baltimore, MD, m, 1959, 3 children **DISCIPLINE** MODERN EUROPEAN HISTORY **EDUCATION** Univ Wis-Madison, PhD, 68. **CAREER** ASST PROF TO PROF, DEPT HIST, STATE UNIV NY-FREDONIA, 68-. **HONORS AND AWARDS** SUNY Chancellor's Award for Excellence in Teaching, 74; Kasling Lectr, SUNY-Fredonia, 97; Revson Fel, Inst for Advan Holocaust Studies, US Mem Holocaust Mus, 98. **MEMBERSHIPS** Am Hist Asn; Conf Group on Central Europ Hist; World War II Studies Asn; NY State Asn of European Hist; German Studies Assoc; German Hist Soc; Int Gesellschaft fur Geschichtsdidaktik; Arbeitskreis Geschichte der Nachrjchtendienste e V. **RESEARCH** German detective police and national security agencies, 1920-45; the Holocaust perpetrators; teaching-learning methodology and assessment in higher education. **SELECTED PUBLICATIONS** Auth, The Foundations of the Nazi Police State: The Formation of SIPO and SD, 90, Univ Press Ky; auth, "Captured German and Other Nations' Documents in the Osoby Archive Moscow," Central Europ Hist, 91; auth, "Update on the Captured Docuements in the Former Osoby Archive, Moscow," Central Europ Hist, 93; auth, "Non-Context Specific Assessment," The History Teacher, Aug 94; auth, Index of RG 15. 007M, Files of the Reichssicherheitshauptant, held by the Main Commission for the Investigation of Crimes against the Polish Nation, 95, US Holocaust Mem Research Inst; auth, Hitler's Enforcers: The Gestapo and the SS Security Service in the Nazi Revolution, 96, Oxford Univ Press; auth, "The Gestapo," "Kripo," "The Security Police," and "Security Service of the SS," in Encyclopedic History of Modern Germany, 98, Garland Publishing Inc. **CONTACT ADDRESS** Dept of History, SUNY, Fredonia, Fredonia, NY, 14063. **EMAIL** browder@fredonia.edu

BROWER, DANIEL ROBERTS
PERSONAL Born 01/09/1936, m, 1959, 3 children **DISCIPLINE** HISTORY **EDUCATION** Carleton Col, BA, 57; Columbia Univ, MA, 59, PhD, 63. **CAREER** Instr, Bowdoin Col, 62-63; asst prof, Oberlin Col, 63-68; prof, Univ CA-Davis, 68-. **MEMBERSHIPS** Am Asn for Advancement of Slavic Studies; Am Hist Asn; World Hist Soc. **RESEARCH** Russian empire; comparative colonialism. **SELECTED PUBLICATIONS** Auth, The New Jacobins: The French Communist Party and the Popular Front, Cornell Univ Press, 68; Training the Nihilists: Education and Radicalism in Tsarist Russia, Cornell Univ Press, 75; The Russian City between Tradition and Modernity, 1850-1900, Univ CA Press, 90; The Penny Press and Its Readers, in S Frank and M Steinberg, eds, Cultures in Flux: Lower Class Values, Practices, and Resistance in Late Imperial Russia, Princeton Univ Press, 94; Imperial Russia and Its Orient: The Renown of Nikolai Przhevalsky, The Russian Rev, v 53, July 94; Kyrgyz Nomads and Russian Pioneers: Colonization and Ethnic Conflict in the Turkestan Revolt of 1916, Jahrbucher fur Geschichte Osteuropas, v 44, 96; Russian Roads to Mecca: Religious Tolerance and Muslim Pilgrimage in the Russian Empire, Slavic Rev, v 55, fall 96; Islam and Ethnicity: Russia Colonial Policy in Turkestan, in Russia's Orient: Imperial Borderlands and Peoples, ed Daniel Brower & Edward Lazzerini, IN Univ Press, 97; Russia'a Orient: Imperial Borderlands and Peoples, 1700-1914, co-ed with Edward Lazzerini, IN Univ Press, 97; The World in the Twentieth Century: From Empires to Nations, 4th ed, Prentice-Hall, 99. **CONTACT ADDRESS** Dept of History, Univ of California, Davis, Davis, CA, 95616. **EMAIL** drbrower@ucdavis.edu

BROWN, A. PETER
PERSONAL Born 04/30/1943, Chicago, IL, m, 1968, 1 child **DISCIPLINE** HISTORICAL MUSICOLOGY **EDUCATION** Northwestern Univ, BME, 65, MM, 66, PhD(music), 70. **CAREER** Asst prof music, Univ Hawaii, 69-74; assoc prof, 74-81, PROF MUSICOL, IND UNIV, SCH MUSIC, 81-, Am Coun Learned Soc fel Ordonez, 72-73; Guggenheim Found fel haydn, 78-79. **MEMBERSHIPS** Am Musicol Soc; int Musicol Soc; Music Libr Asn; Nat Acad Rec Arts & Sci. **RESEARCH** Viennese music 1730-1830; history of orchestral music; Joseph Haydn. **SELECTED PUBLICATIONS** Auth, The Rise of Musical Classics in 18th Century England in A Study in Canon, Ritual, and Ideology, Amer Hist Rev, Vol 0098, 93; Opera Incerta, Complete Musicological Editions and their integrity, Notes, Vol 0049, 93; Communications Response to Temperley Review of the Brown-And-Schnepel Edition of Haydn 'Creation', Notes, Vol 0049, 93; Musical Settings of Hunter,Anne Poetry--from National Song to Canzonetta, J Amer Musicolog Soc, Vol 0047, 94; Walking Through Different Groves With Sir George, Amer Scholar, Vol 0064, 95. **CONTACT ADDRESS** Sch of Music, Indiana Univ, Bloomington, Bloomington, IN, 47401.

BROWN, ALAN S.
PERSONAL Born 04/23/1922, Detroit, MI, m, 1950, 3 children **DISCIPLINE** HISTORY **EDUCATION** Univ Mich, AB, 49, MA, 50, PhD, 53. **CAREER** instr, Univ Mich, 53-54 & Kent State Univ, 54-55; from asst prof to assoc prof, 55-63, PROF HIST, WESTERN MICH UNIV, 63- **MEMBERSHIPS** Orgn Am Hist; AHA. **RESEARCH** American Revolution; American Colonial and Revolutionary eras; Michigan. **SELECTED PUBLICATIONS** Auth, Payoffs in the Cloakroom in the Greening of the Michigan Legislature, 1938-1946, Mich Hist Rev, Vol 0022, 96; The Emerging Midwest in Upland Southerners and the Political Culture of the Old Northwest, 1787-1861, Mich Hist Rev, Vol 0022, 96; Aphrodite and the Pandora Complex, Classical Quart, Vol 0047, 97. **CONTACT ADDRESS** Western Michigan Univ, 1201 Oliver St, Kalamazoo, MI, 49008-3805.

BROWN, BEATRICE S.
PERSONAL Born 07/14/1950, Louisville, Kentucky, s **DISCIPLINE** PSYCHOLOGY **EDUCATION** Addis Ababa Univ, psychology, Ethiopia, 1990-; Cornell Univ, Cooperative Nutrition Program, PhD Doctoral/Elected Research Visiting Faculty Member, certificate, 1991; Postgraduate Ctr for Mental Health, New York, certificate, 1995. **CAREER** City Coll, City Univ, NY, adjunct prof, 1990-; Upper Manhattan Mental Health Ctr, children day treatment unit dir, 1989-91; Jewish Board of Family & Children Svcs, residential treatment facility girls unit dir, 1994-; Central Brooklyn Coordinating Council Inc, mental health unit psychologist, 1997-. **HONORS AND AWARDS** American Psychological Assn, Full Membership Status, 1995; Black Psychologists Assn, 1998. **MEMBERSHIPS** BSB Wholistic Psychological Center, Inc, founder, dir, CEO, 1997. **CONTACT ADDRESS** PO Box 172, Mt Vernon, NY, 10552.

BROWN, BLANCHE RACHEL
PERSONAL Born 04/12/1915, Boston, MA, m, 1938 **DISCIPLINE** HISTORY OF ART **EDUCATION** NY Univ, BFA, 36, MA, 38, PhD, 67; cert, Univ Paris, 37. **CAREER** Lectr hist of art, Metropolitan Mus Art, 42-66; assoc prof, 67-73, prof hist of art, NY Univ, 73-85, EMERITA, 85-. **HONORS AND AWARDS** Assoc, Univ Sem Class Civilization, Columbia Univ, 71; Nat Endowment for Humanities fel, 76-77; John Simon Guggenheim Mem Found fel, 78-79. **MEMBERSHIPS** Archaeol Inst Am; Col Art Asn Am; fel Am Numismatic Soc. **RESEARCH** Hellenistic art. **SELECTED PUBLICATIONS** Auth, Ptolemaic Paintings and Mosaics, Archaeol Inst Am, Col Art Asn Am, 57; Five Cities, Doubleday, 64 & Anchor, 66; Anticlassicism in Greek Sculpture of the 4th Century BC, Archaeol Inst Am Col Art Asn Am Monogr Ser, 73; Questions about the Late Hellenistic Period, In: Art Studies for an Editor, NY, 75;

The Iliad to Me, In: De Ilias Van Homerus, Antwerp, Galerie de Zwarte Panter, 76; Out of the Ashes: Glowing Treasures of Pompeii, NY Times Mag, 4/78 & Reader's Digest, 2/79; Deinokrates and Alexandria, Bulletin Am Soc Papyrologists, Vol XV, 78; Novelty, Ingenuity, Self-Aggrandisement, Ostentation, Extravagance, Gigantism and Kitsch in the Art of Alexander the Great and His Successors, In: Art the Ape Of Nature: Studies in Honor of HW Janson, Abrams, 81; Styles in the Alexander Portraits on the Coins of Lysimachos, Coins Culture and History: Studies in Honor of Bluma Trell, Wayne State Univ Press, 81; auth, Royal Portraits in Sculpture and Coins: Pyrrhos and the Successors of Alexander the Great, Peter Lang, 95; "Alexander the Great as Patron of the Arts," in The Fire of Hephaistos, Harvard Univ Press, 96. **CONTACT ADDRESS** 15 W 70 St, New York, NY, 10023.

BROWN, DEE ALEXANDER
PERSONAL Born 02/28/1908, LA, m, 1934, 2 children **DISCIPLINE** AMERICAN HISTORY **EDUCATION** George Washington Univ, BLS, 37; Univ Ill, MS, 52. **CAREER** Libr asst, US Dept Agr, 34-45; tech librn, US War Dept, 45-48; librn agr, Univ Ill, Urbana, 48-72, RETIRED., Ed, Agr Hist, Agr Hist Soc, 56-58. **MEMBERSHIPS** Am Libr Asn; Soc Am Historians; Authors Guild. **RESEARCH** American Civil War; American western frontier. **SELECTED PUBLICATIONS** Auth, Grierson's Raid, Univ Ill, 54; The Bold Cavaliers, Lippincott, 59; Fort Phil Kearny, Putnam, 62; The Galvanized Yankees, Univ Ill, 63; The Year of the Century, Scribner, 66; Bury My Heart at Wounded Knee, 71, the Westerners, 74 & Hear that Lonesome Whistle Blow, 74, Holt, Rinehart. **CONTACT ADDRESS** 7 Overlook Dr, Little Rock, AR, 72207.

BROWN, DENNIS T.
DISCIPLINE MUSIC **EDUCATION** Boston Univ, BM; Univ Mich, MM, PhD. **CAREER** Assoc prof. **SELECTED PUBLICATIONS** Auth, pubs in Music Edu J, Annual Jazz Rev, Percussive Notes, Instrumentalist, and Nat Asn Jazz Edu Res Papers. **CONTACT ADDRESS** Music and Dance Dept, Univ of Massachusetts, Amherst, 720 Massachusetts Ave, Amherst, MA, 01003.

BROWN, DOROTHY M.
PERSONAL Born 12/23/1932, Baltimore, MD **DISCIPLINE** HISTORY **EDUCATION** Coll of Notre Dame Maryland, BA, 54; Georgetown Univ, MA, 59, PhD, 62. **CAREER** Asst Prof, 59-66, interim pres, 96-97, Coll of Notre Dame Maryland; Asst Prof, Assoc Prof, Prof, 66-, interim provost, 98-99, Georgetown Univ. **MEMBERSHIPS** AHA, OAH, ASA. **RESEARCH** 20th century American society & culture, history of American women. **SELECTED PUBLICATIONS** Co-auth, The Poor Belong to Us, Catholic Charities and American Welfare, Cambridge Harvard Univ Press, 97; auth, Setting a Course, American Women in the 1920s, Boston Twayne/G K Hall, 87; Mabel Walker Willebrandt, A Study in Power Loyalty and Law, Knoxville Univ of Tenn Press, 84. **CONTACT ADDRESS** Dept of History, Georgetown Univ, Washington, DC, 20057. **EMAIL** browndo@gunet.georgetown.edu

BROWN, FRANK
PERSONAL Born 05/01/1935, Gallian, Alabama, m **DISCIPLINE** EDUCATION **EDUCATION** AL State Univ, BS 1957; OR State Univ, MS 1962; Univ of CA at Berkeley, MA 1969, PhD 1970; Harvard University, Institute for Educational Management, fellow, 1988. **CAREER** NY State Commiss on Ed, assoc dir, 1970-72; Urban Inst CCNY, dir 1971-72; Cora P Maloney Coll SUNY Buffalo, dir 1974-77; SUNY Buffalo, prof 1972-83; Univ of NC Chapel Hill, School of Ed, dean 1983-90; Institute for Research in Social Science, Chapel Hill, NC, dir, educational research policy studies project, 1990-; Cary C Boshamer, professor of education, 1990-; University of California, Berkeley, CA, visiting scholar, 1990-91. **HONORS AND AWARDS** Grad Fellowship OR State Univ 1961-62; Grad Fellowship Univ of CA Berkeley 1968-70; Rockefeller Found Scholars Awd 1979-80; Langston Hughes Inst Award, Outstanding Service & Leadership; SUNY Buffalo Special Award, Achievement in Research, Teaching & Service; Tar Heel of the Week, Raleigh News & Observer; Amer Educ Research Assn Award, Dedicated Service & Leadership; numerours other awards; Publ 5 books, monographs & 90 articles; Fellow, Harvard Univ Institute for Educational Management 1988; Book Series Editor, Educational Excellence, Diversity, and Equity, Corwin Press, 1991-. **MEMBERSHIPS** Rho Lambda Chapter of Alpha Phi Alpha Fraternity, Buffalo, New York, president, 1977-78; Western New York Black Educators Association and the National Urban Education Conference, co-founder, 1975-83; State University of New York at Buffalo; Black Faculty Association, co-founder, 1972; Buffalo Urban League, board of directors, 1978-81; Langston Hughes Institute-Black Cultural Center for Western New York and Buffalo, board of directors, 1978-83; Buffalo School Desegregation Case, Federal District of Western New York, consultant and researcher, 1976-83; vice pres Div A of American Ed Research Assn 1986-88; bd of dirs, American Assn of Colleges of Teacher Education 1988-92; board of directors, National Organization for Legal Problems in Education, 1990-93. **CONTACT ADDRESS** Dir, Educ Research, Univ of North Carolina at Chapel Hill, Manning Hall, CB #3355, Chapel Hill, NC, 27599-3355.

BROWN, IRA VERNON
PERSONAL Born 08/14/1922, Albemarle Co, VA, m, 1955, 1 child **DISCIPLINE** HISTORY **EDUCATION** George Washington Univ, AB, 41; Univ Va, AM, 42; Harvard Univ, AM, 43; PhD, 46. **CAREER** From instr to assoc prof, 47-60, PROF AM HIST, PA STATE UNIV, 60-, Fund for Advan of Educ fel, 52-53. **HONORS AND AWARDS** Brewer Prize, Am Soc Church Hist, 49. **MEMBERSHIPS** AHA; Orgn Am Historians. **RESEARCH** American social and cultural history; the formative period, 1776-1828; abolition and feminism. **SELECTED PUBLICATIONS** Auth, Women of the Antislavery Movement in the Weston Sisters, Amer Hist Rev, Vol 0101, 96; The Abolitionists and the South, 1831-1861, Amer Hist Rev, Vol 0101, 96. **CONTACT ADDRESS** Pennsylvania State Univ, 104 Davey Lab, University PK, PA, 16802.

BROWN, JENNIFER S.H.
PERSONAL Born 12/30/1940, Providence, RI **DISCIPLINE** HISTORY **EDUCATION** Brown Univ, AB, 62; Harvard Univ, AM, 63; Univ Chicago, PhD, 76. **CAREER** Asst prof, Collby Col, N Ill Univ, Univ Ind, 66-82; vis distinguished prof Can stud, Univ Alta, 82; assoc prof, 82-88, PROF HISTORY, UNIV WINNIPEG, 88-, dir, Ctr Rupert's Land Stud, 97-; Woodrow Wilson fel, 62-63; publs ed, Middle Am Res Inst, Tulane Univ, 75-82; res fel, Newberry Libr Chicago, 82; gen ed, Rupert's Land Record Soc, 86-. **HONORS AND AWARDS** Phi Beta Kappa Honor Soc; hon men, Sir John A. Macdonald Prize. **MEMBERSHIPS** Man Record Soc; Champlain Soc **RESEARCH** First Nations history **SELECTED PUBLICATIONS** Auth, Strangers in Blood: Fur Trade Company Families in Indian Country, 80; coauth, The Orders of the Dreamed: George Nelson on Cree and Northern Ojibwa Religion and Myth, 88; ed, The Ojibwa of Berens River, Manitoba: Ethnography into History, 92; co-ed, The New Peoples: Being and Becoming Metis in North America, 85; co-ed, Reading Beyond Words: Contexts for Native History, 96; contribur, Dictionary of Canadian Biography; contribur, Canadian Encyclopedia. **CONTACT ADDRESS** Dept of History, Univ of Winnipeg, 515 Portage Ave, Winnipeg, MB, R3B 2E9. **EMAIL** jennifer.brown@uwinnipeg.ca

BROWN, JERRY WAYNE
PERSONAL Born 02/24/1936, Frederick, OK, m, 1958, 1 child **DISCIPLINE** RELIGION, HISTORY **EDUCATION** Harvard Univ, AB, 58; Eastern Baptist Theol Sem, BD, 61; Univ Pa, MA, 61; Princeton Univ, MA, 63, PhD(relig), 64. **CAREER** Teaching fel relig, Princeton Univ, 63-64; asst prof, Bowdoin Col, 64-69, actg chmn dept, 64-65, resident prof, Sr Ctr, 65-66, dean students, 66-69; ASSOC PROF HIST, RIDER COL 69-, VPRES ACAD AFFAIRS, 70-;, PROVOST, 75-. **RESEARCH** Religion in America. **SELECTED PUBLICATIONS** The Rise of Biblical Criticism in American, 1800-1870, Wesleyan Univ, 69. **CONTACT ADDRESS** Dept of Hist, Rider Col, Lawrenceville, NJ, 08648.

BROWN, JOHN ANDREW
PERSONAL Born 07/17/1945, Birmingham, Alabama, m, 1993 **DISCIPLINE** EDUCATION **EDUCATION** Daniel Payne College, AA, 1965; Columbia University, 1966; Dartmouth College, 1966; Miles College, BA, 1967; Yale University Divinity School, MDiv, 1970, STM, 1972. **CAREER** Yale Univ Divinity Sch, assoc prof 1970-73; Trinity Coll Hartford, asst prof rel/dir ICS prog 1973-76; CT Coll New London, vstg prof rel 1974-75;The Coll of New Rochelle at NY, theol sem adj prof rel 1980-; Audrey Cohen College, prof/adm, 1979-93, adjunct prof of business ethics, 1988-93, special asst to the vice pres/dir of staff development, 1991-93; Miles Coll, adjunct prof of history, 1994-; Lawson State Community Coll, adjunct prof of history, philosophy and religion, 1994-; Univ of Alabama at Birmingham, consultant, 1994. **HONORS AND AWARDS** Carnegie Fellowship Columbia Univ 1966; Richard Allen Awd; Rockefeller Protestant Fellowship Theological Education 1967-70; Oliver E Daggett Prize Yale Corp 1969; Research Fellowship Yale Univ 1971-72; mem Pi Gamma Mu; Fellowship UTS Black Econ Develop Fund 1976; Biog sketch in Yale Univ 1985 Alumni Directory; The College of New Rochelle, en Years of Outstanding Teaching and Contributions to the College, 1989, Award for Fourteen Years of Outstanding Teaching and Service to the College, 1993; Audrey Cohen College, Crystal Award, 1991; Phi Theta Kappa Inc, Alpha Epsilon Gama Chapter, Award for Outstanding Service, 1996. **MEMBERSHIPS** Consultant Trinity Coll 1973, Manchester Comm Coll1976; educ admin Bronx Extension Site-Coll for Human Serv 1986-; mem NY Urban League, Alpha Phi Alpha,NAACP, ASALH, Yale Alumni Associates of Afro-Americans, AAUP. **CONTACT ADDRESS** Professor, Social Science Dept, Lawson State Community Col, 3060 Wilson Rd, Birmingham, AL, 35221.

BROWN, JONATHAN CHARLES
PERSONAL Born 10/02/1942, Fond du Lac, WI, m, 1965, 1 child **DISCIPLINE** ECONOMIC HISTORY **EDUCATION** Univ Wis, Madison, BA, 66; Univ Ariz, MA, 68; Univ Tex, Austin, PhD(hist), 76. **CAREER** Lectr hist, Univ Calif, Santa Barbara, 76-77; LECTR HIST, UNIV CALIF, LOS ANGELES, 77-. **MEMBERSHIPS** AHA; Conf Latin Am Hist; Econ Hist Asn; Can Econ Asn. **RESEARCH** Argentina; Latin American economic history; Venezuela. **SELECTED PUBLICATIONS** Auth, Dynamics and autonomy of a traditional marketing system: Buenos Aires, 1810-1860, Hisp Am Hist Rev, 76; A nineteenth century Argentine cattle empire, Agr Hist, 78; The genteel tradition of nineteenth century Colombian culture, Americas, 78; A Socioeconomic History of Argentina, Cambridge Univ, 79. **CONTACT ADDRESS** Dept of Hist, Univ of Calif, Los Angeles, CA, 90024.

BROWN, JONATHAN M.
PERSONAL Born 07/15/1939, Springfield, MA, m, 1966 **DISCIPLINE** ART HISTORY **EDUCATION** Dartmouth Col, AB, 60; Princeton Univ, MFA, 63, PhD(art hist), 64. **CAREER** From instr to assoc prof art hist, Princeton Univ, 65-73; assoc prof, 73-77, actg dir, 73-75, DIR, INST FINE ARTS, NY UNIV, 75-, PROF ART HIST, 77-. **HONORS AND AWARDS** A K Porter Prize, Art Asn Am, 70; Nat Endowment for Humanities fel, 78-79. **MEMBERSHIPS** Art Asn Am. **RESEARCH** Spanish art of the 17th century. **SELECTED PUBLICATIONS** Auth, Hieroglyphs of death and salvation: The decoration of the Church of the Hermandad de la Caridad, Seville, Art Bull, 9/70; co-ed, Sources and Documents in the History of Art: Italy and Spain 2600-2750, Princeton-Hall, 70; auth, Jusepe de Ribera: Prints and Drawings, 73, Murillo and His Drawings, 76 & Images and Ideas in 17th Century Spanish Painting, 78, Princeton Univ. **CONTACT ADDRESS** Inst of Fine Arts, New York Univ, 1 E 78 St, New York, NY, 10021.

BROWN, KENDALL H.
DISCIPLINE ASIAN ART **EDUCATION** Yale Univ, PhD, 94. **CAREER** Asst prof, Univ Southern Calif. **RESEARCH** Japanese art in the 20th century; Asian art history. **SELECTED PUBLICATIONS** Auth, The Politics of Reclusion: Painting and Power in Momoyama Japan, Hawai'i, 97; Shin-hanga: New Prints in Modern Japan, Los Angeles Co Mus Art, 96 & Light In Darkness: Women in Japanese Prints of Early Showa 1926-1945, Fisher Gallery, 96. **CONTACT ADDRESS** Col of Letters, Arts and Sciences, Univ Southern Calif, University Park Campus, Los Angeles, CA, 90089.

BROWN, KENDALL WALKER
PERSONAL Born 01/14/1949, American Fork, UT, m, 1974, 2 children **DISCIPLINE** LATIN AMERICAN HISTORY **EDUCATION** Brigham Young Univ, BA, 73; Duke Univ, MA, 75, PhD, 79. **CAREER** Vis prof Span Am hist, Univ Fed de Santa Catarina, Brazil, 79-81; vis asst prof Latin Am hist, Univ NC, Charlotte, 81-82; asst prof Latin Am Hist, Hillsdale Col, 82-. **MEMBERSHIPS** AHA; Conf Latin Am Hist; Latin Am Studies Asn. **RESEARCH** Economic history of Colonial Spanish America; prices in Viceregal Peru; commerce and trade in Southern Brazil. **SELECTED PUBLICATIONS** Auth, A Evolucao da Vinicultura em Arequipa, 1550-1800, Estudos Ibero-Americanos, 80; A documentacao da real hacienda como fonte para a historia economica da America Espanhola, Memorias da II Semana de Hist, 81; co-ed, Peru, In: Royal Treasuries of the Spanish Empire in America, Vol 1, Duke Univ Press, 82. **CONTACT ADDRESS** Dept of History and Political Science, Hillsdale Col, Hillsdale, MI, 49242.

BROWN, KENNETH
PERSONAL Born 03/05/1943, Chicago, IL, 2 children **DISCIPLINE** BIBLE, THEOLOGY, HISTORY **EDUCATION** Asbury Theol Sem, BA Theol, 66; Mdiv 76; Drew Univ, PhD, 88. **CAREER** Pastor/Minister, 66-; Prof, Vennard Coll, 76-79. **MEMBERSHIPS** Amer Acad Rel; ATLA; Wesleyan Theol Soc; Christian Holiness Partnership. **RESEARCH** Camp Meeting History; History of the Holiness Movement; Biographical Studies. **SELECTED PUBLICATIONS** Auth, Holy Ground, Too, The Camp Meeting Family Tree, Hazleton, Holiness Archives, 98. **CONTACT ADDRESS** 243 S Pine St, Hazleton, PA, 18201. **EMAIL** cmbooks@ptdprolog.net

BROWN, KENNETH LEE
PERSONAL Born 06/15/1933, Wichita, KS, m, 1960, 3 children **DISCIPLINE** PEACE STUDIES, RELIGION **EDUCATION** McPherson Col, AB, 55; Bethany Theol Sem, BD, 58; Duke Univ, PhD, 65. **CAREER** From instr to assoc prof, 61-73, Prof Relig & Philos, Manchester Col, 73-, Lilly Endowment Open Fel, Fel of Reconciliation, Inst for World Order, NYC, 78-79; dir, Peace Studies Inst & Prog in Conflict Resolution, 80. **MEMBERSHIPS** Am Acad Relig; Am Soc Christian Ethics. **RESEARCH** Soc ethics; polit philos; pacifism. **SELECTED PUBLICATIONS** Ed, Bull of the Peace Studies Inst, 80-; Auth, Christian's relationship to the state, In: Six Papers on Peace, Brethren, 69; The flow children, In: Life Styles, Scott, 71. **CONTACT ADDRESS** Peace Studies Inst, Manchester Col, 601 E College Ave, N Manchester, IN, 46962-1226. **EMAIL** klbrown@manchester.edu

BROWN, KRISTEN M.
DISCIPLINE 19TH CENTURY GERMAN PHILOSOPHY, ANCIENT PHILOSOPHY **EDUCATION** Stanford Univ, BA; Vanderbilt Univ, MA, PhD. **CAREER** Dept Philos, Millsaps Col **SELECTED PUBLICATIONS** Publ on, Embodiment and Feminine Other in Nietzsche & Form as Logos in Aristotle's Metaphysics Z and Politics. **CONTACT ADDRESS** Dept of Philosophy, Millsaps Col, 1701 N State St, Jackson, MS, 39210. **EMAIL** brownkm@okra.millsaps.edu

BROWN, LESLIE
PERSONAL Born 12/02/1954, New York, NY, s **DISCIPLINE** HISTORY **EDUCATION** Duke Univ, PhD, 97. **CAREER** ASST PROF, UNIV OF MO AT ST. LOUIS. **MEMBERSHIPS** AHA; OAH; CCWH; NWSA. **RESEARCH** African American women. **CONTACT ADDRESS** Dept of Hist, Univ of Missouri at St. Louis, St. Louis, MO, 63121. **EMAIL** slbrown@umsl.edu

BROWN, MARILYN
DISCIPLINE ART HISTORY **EDUCATION** Birmingham-S Col, BA, 72; Yale Univ, MA, 74, Mphil, 75, PhD, 78. **CAREER** Lecturer, Yale Univ, 77; vis asst prof, ReedCol, 77-78; asst prof, Univ CA, 78-79; asst prof, Tulane Univ, 79-85; grad coord, 93-94; 95-96; 97-98; prof, 95-. **HONORS AND AWARDS** Summer stipend, NEH, 79; grant, ACLS, 82; grant-in-aid, ACLS, 87, 88, 89., Vis Arts Comm,Contemp Arts Ctr, 85-86; fel selection comm, ACLS, 91-92; bd trustees, New Orleans Mus Art, 1996-; bd dir(s), Col Art Assn Am, 97-01. **SELECTED PUBLICATIONS** Auth, Two Generations of Abstract Painting, Alice Trumbull Mason, Emily Mason, NY Eaton House, 82; Gypsies and Other Bohemians, The Myth of the Artist in Nineteenth-Century France, UMI Res Press, Avant-Garde Series, 85; The Degas-Musson Family Papers, An Annotated Inventory, Tulane Univ Lib, 91; Degas and the Business of Art: A Cotton Office in New Orleans, Penn State Press/ CAA Monogr, 94. **CONTACT ADDRESS** Dept of Art, Tulane Univ, 6823 St Charles Ave, New Orleans, LA, 70118.

BROWN, MARK M.
DISCIPLINE ART; ARCHITECTURAL HISTORY **EDUCATION** Macalester Col, BA, 80; State Univ NY, MA, 83; Univ Pittsburgh, PhD, 95. **CAREER** Historian, Hist Am Engineering Record, Nat Park Service, 89-92, 96-97; Asst Prof Art Hist & Curator, Earlham Col, 97-. **HONORS AND AWARDS** H.B. du Pont Fel, 94; Henry Luce Found/ACLS Doctoral Dissertation Fel in Am Art, 94-95. **MEMBERSHIPS** Col Art Asn; Soc Archit Hist; Vernacular Archit Forum; Soc Industrial Archeol; Soc Hist Technol. **RESEARCH** Interdisciplinary approaches to diverse themes of architecture, urbanism, structural systems, and cultural landscapes; especially: American steel industry, bridges. **SELECTED PUBLICATIONS** Coauth, The History of the Duquesne Club, Duquesne Club, 89; auth, Nineteenth-Century Cable-Stayed Bridges in Texas, ¤Proceedings¦, Fifth Annual Hist Bridges Conf, 97; Technology and the Homestead Steel Works: 1879-1945, Canal History and Technology Proceedings, Canal Hist and Technol Press, 92; The Cathedral of Learning: Concept, Design, Construction, Univ Art Gallery, Univ Pittsburgh, 87, 2nd printing, 95. **CONTACT ADDRESS** Art Dept, Earlham Col, Richmond, IN, 47374. **EMAIL** brownma1@earlham.edu

BROWN, MARY ELLEN
PERSONAL Born 01/06/1939, Vicksburg, MS, d, 2 children **DISCIPLINE** FOLKLORE **EDUCATION** Mary Baldwin Col, BA, 60; Univ Pa, MA, 63; PhD, 68. **CAREER** Teaching fel, Univ Pa, 62-63; asst prof, Ind State Univ, 70-72, 74-79; assoc prof 79-85; prof, 85-97; dir, Inst for Advan Study, Ind Univ, 98- . **HONORS AND AWARDS** ACLS Grant-in-Aid, 79; Ind Univ sr fac fel, 91-92; Fulbright Res UK, 98. **MEMBERSHIPS** Asoc for Scottish Lit Study; Am Folklore Soc; Ballad Comn-Societie Int d'ethnologie et de folklore; Int Soc for Folk Narrative Res. **RESEARCH** Relationships between oral and written literature; ballads; historical ethnology; Scotland. **SELECTED PUBLICATIONS** auth, Burns, The Eighteenth Century British Poets: The Dictionary of Literary Biography, 91; auth, The Mechanism of the Ancient Ballad; William Motherwell's Explanation, Oral Tradition, 96; auth, Mr. Child's Scottish Mentor, Ballads into Books: The Legacy of F.J. Child, 97; auth, Old Singing Women and the Canons of Scottish Balladry and Song, A History of Scottish Women's Writing, 97; ed with Bruce Rosenberg, Encyclopedia of Folklore and Literature, 98. **CONTACT ADDRESS** 818 S. Stull Ave., Bloomington, IN, 47401. **EMAIL** brown2@indiana.edu

BROWN, MICHAEL FOBES
PERSONAL Born 07/06/1950, Syracuse, NY **DISCIPLINE** CULTURAL ANTHROPOLOGY **EDUCATION** Princeton Univ, BA, 72; Univ of Mich, PhD, 81. **CAREER** LAMBERT PROF OF ANTHROPOLOGY & LATIN AM STUDIES, WILLIAMS COL, 80-. **HONORS AND AWARDS** Smithsonian fel, 83; NEH fel, 88; Weatherhood Scholar, School of Am Res, 93. **MEMBERSHIPS** Am Anthropological Asn; Am Ethnological Soc. **RESEARCH** Religion; human ecology; social movements; cultural/intellectual property. **SELECTED PUBLICATIONS** Auth, Tsewa's Gift: Magic and Meaning in an Amazonian Society, Smithsonian Inst Press, 86; auth, Facing the State, Facing the World: Amazonia's Native Leaders and the New Politics of Identity, L'Homme, 93; auth, On Resisting Resistance, Am Anthropologist, 96; auth, The Channeling Zone: American Spirituality in an Anxious Age, Harvard Univ Press, 97; auth, Can Culture Be Copyrighted?, Current Anthropology, 98; auth, The New Alienists: Healing Shattered Selves at Century's End, Paranoia Within Reason, Univ of Chicago Press, 98; coauth, War of Shadows: The Struggle for Utopia in the Peruvian Amazon, Unis of Calif Press, 91. **CONTACT ADDRESS** Dept of Anthropology & Sociology, Williams Col, Williamstown, MA, 01267-2606. **EMAIL** mbrown@williams.edu

BROWN, MICHAEL G.
PERSONAL Born 03/31/1938, Scranton, PA **DISCIPLINE** HUMANITIES & HEBREW **EDUCATION** Harvard Col, BA, 60; Columbia Univ, MA, 63; Jewish Theol Sem, MHL, 66, rabbi, 68; State Univ NY Buffalo, PhD, 76. **CAREER** PROF HUMANTIIES & HEBREW, YORK UNIV, 68-, dir, Ctr Jewish Stud, 95-; chair Can stud, vis assoc prof, Hebrew Univ (Jerusalem), 80-82; vis assoc prof, Univ Toronto, 83-84; vis assoc prof, Univ Calif San Diego, 85, 88; fel, Am-Holy Land stud proj, 85-87. **HONORS AND AWARDS** DD (Hon), Jewish Theol Sem, 94 **MEMBERSHIPS** Dir, Asn Hebrew Schs; dir, Can Jewish Hist Soc; Can Sem Zionist Thought; Asn Jewish Stud; Rabbinical Assembly; Toronto Bd Rabbis. **SELECTED PUBLICATIONS** Auth, Jew or Juif? Jews, French Canadians, and Anglo-Canadians 1759-1914, 87; auth, The Israeli-American Connection: Its Roots in the Yishuv 1914-1945, 96; ed, Approaches to Antisemitism: Context and Curriculum, 94. **CONTACT ADDRESS** Dept of Humanities, York Univ, 4700 Keele St N, North York, ON, M3J 1P3.

BROWN, MURRAY
PERSONAL Born 07/04/1929, Alden, NY, m, 1954, 1 child **DISCIPLINE** ECONOMICS **EDUCATION** Univ Buff, BA, 52; Grad fac The New Sch, PhD, 56. **CAREER** Prof, SUNY, Buff, 67-; res assoc, Cen econo stud, 64-84; Prof econo George Wash Univ, 62-65; Asst prof, Univ Penn, 56-61. **HONORS AND AWARDS** Fulbright, 87; Guggenheim fel, 66; Ford Fac fel, 62. **MEMBERSHIPS** AEA **RESEARCH** Coalition formation; game theory **SELECTED PUBLICATIONS** Essays in Modern Capitol Theory, ed with Kazuo Sato, Paul Zarembka, N Holl, NY, 76; many numerous articles in books and journals. **CONTACT ADDRESS** 80 Fairlawn Rd, Amherst, NY, 14260. **EMAIL** mbrown@acsu.buffalo.edu

BROWN, NORMAN D.
PERSONAL Born 06/28/1935, Pittsburgh, PA, m, 1966, 2 children **DISCIPLINE** AMERICAN, SOUTHERN & TEXAS HISTORY **EDUCATION** IN Univ, BA, 57; Univ NC, Chapel Hill, MA, 59, PhD, 63. **CAREER** From instr to asst prof, 62-69, assoc prof, 69-83, prof hist, Univ TX, Austin, 83-84, Barbara White Stuart Centennial prof TX hist, 84. **HONORS AND AWARDS** Fel, TX State Hist Asn; Hon life mem, TX State Hist Asn; Earl R Davis Award for Contrib to TX Conf Hist; UDC's Jefferson Davis Medal; John Bell Hood Award, Hill Col Conf Hist Symposium. **MEMBERSHIPS** Soc Historians Early Am Repub; Orgn Am Hist; Southern Hist Asn; TX State Hist Asn; Soc of Civil War Hist; Civil War Round Table Assoc. **RESEARCH** The Whig Party; Civil War and Reconstruction; TX polit, 1921-1938. **SELECTED PUBLICATIONS** Auth, A Union Election in Civil War North Carolina, NC Hist Rev, autumn 66; Edward Stanly: First Republican Candidate for Governor of California, Calif Hist Soc Quart, 9/68; Daniel Webster and the Politics of Availability, Univ Ga, 69; Edward Stanly: Whiggery's Tarheel Conqueror, Univ Ala, 74; Dan's the Man, Me for Ma, and Lynch is a Cinch: The Gubernatorial Election of 1926 in Texas, WTex Hist Asn Year Bk, 79; ed, One of Cleburne's Command: The Civil War Reminiscences and Diary of Capt Samuel T Foster, Granbury's Texas Brigade, CSA, Univ Tex Press, 80; ed, Journey to Pleasant Hill: The Civil War Letters of Captain Elijah P Petty, Walker's Texas Division, CSA, Inst Texan Cult, 82; Hood, Bonnet, and Little Brown Jug: Texas Politics, 1921-1928, Tex A&M Univ Press, 84; A Brief History of Walker's Texas Division, In: Joseph P Blessington's Campaigns of Walker's Texas Division, 1875, reprint, Austin, State House Press, 94. **CONTACT ADDRESS** Dept of Hist, Univ of Texas, Austin, TX, 78712-1026.

BROWN, OLA M.
PERSONAL Born 04/07/1941, Albany, GA, s **DISCIPLINE** EDUCATION **EDUCATION** Albany State Coll, BS 1961; Univ of GA, MEd 1972, EdS 1973, EdD 1974. **CAREER** Thomas County Schools, Thomasville GA, teacher, 1961-67; Dougherty County Schools, Albany GA, teacher, 1967-71; Univ of GA Athens, grad asst, 1972-74; Valdosta State Coll GA, prof of educ 1974-91; Dept Head, Early Childhood and Reading Education, 1980-90; dept head, professor emerita, currently. **HONORS AND AWARDS** Educ Instr of Yr Student GA Assn of Educ (VSC) 1975; WH Dennis Meml Awd Albany State Coll 1976; Ira E Aaron Reading Awd S Central GA Council of IRA 1977. **MEMBERSHIPS** Mem Phi Delta Kappa Educ Frat 1975-; recording sec GA Council of Intl Reading Assn 1977-79; treas GA Assn of Higher Educ (GAE Affl) 1977-80; mem Amer Assn of Univ Prof 1977-80; vice pres 1979-80, pres 1980-81 GA Council of Intl Reading Assn; state coordinator Intl Reading Assn 1988-91. **CONTACT ADDRESS** Dept Head, Valdosta State Univ, 1500 N Patterson St, Valdosta, GA, 31698.

BROWN, PETER B.
DISCIPLINE RUSSIAN, SOVIET, EASTERN EUROPEAN HISTORY **EDUCATION** Stanford Univ, BA; Univ Chicago, MA, PhD. **CAREER** Instr, RI Col. **RESEARCH** 14th-18th century Russian soc hist; comp Medieval and Early Mod hist; late Imperial-early Soviet economic hist. **SELECTED PUBLICATIONS** Auth, Anthropological Perspective and Early Muscovite Court Politics, Russian Hist; Muscovy, Poland, and the Seventeenth-Century Crisis, The Polish Rev; ed, Studies and Essays on the Soviet and Eastern European Economies. **CONTACT ADDRESS** Rhode Island Col, Providence, RI, 02908.

BROWN, RICHARD CARL
PERSONAL Born 04/09/1919, Logan, OH, m, 1946 **DISCIPLINE** HISTORY **EDUCATION** Ohio State Univ, BSc 47; Colgate Univ, MA, 48; Univ Wis, PhD(Am hist), 51. **CAREER** Instr social studies, Colgate Univ, 47-48; from instr to prof, 52-77, Distinguished serv prof, 77-79, EMER PROF HIST, STATE UNIV NY, COL BUFFALO, 79-. **MEMBERSHIPS** AHA; Am Studies Asn; Orgn Am Hist. **RESEARCH** American social and intellectual history; immigration and ethnicity. **SELECTED PUBLICATIONS** Auth, Human Side of American History, Ginn, 62; coauth, United States of America: A History for Young Citizens, 63 & The American Achievement, 66, Silver Burdett; Man in America, Gen Learning Corp, 73; auth, Let Freedom Ring, 76; Social Attitudes of American Generals, Arno Press, 79. **CONTACT ADDRESS** 521 Boone Trail, Danville, KY, 40422.

BROWN, RICHARD DAVID
PERSONAL Born 10/31/1939, New York, NY, m, 1962 **DISCIPLINE** AMERICAM COLONIAL HISTORY, 1600-1763; AMERICAN REVOLUTION, 1763-1790 **EDUCATION** Oberlin Col, AB, 61; Harvard Univ, AM, 62, PhD, 66. **CAREER** Vis prof hist & Fulbright lectr, Univ Toulouse, 65-66; asst prof, Oberlin Col, 66-71; assoc prof, 71-75, head dept hist, 74-80, PROF EARLY AM HIST, UNIV CONN, 75-, Soc Sci Res Coun fel, 70-71; fel, Charles Warren Ctr, Harvard Univ, 70-71; Nat Endowment for Humanties fel, Am Antiq Soc, 77-78 & 85 & 92-93; Ctr Histo of Freedom fel, 90-91; John Simon Guggenheim fel, 98-99. **HONORS AND AWARDS** Charles F Montgomery Prize, 86; Fac Excellence Award Res, Univ Conn, 91. **MEMBERSHIPS** Orgn Am Hist; AHA; Am Antiquarian Soc. **RESEARCH** Colonial-Revolutionary and early national history; social history; communications in early America, 1700-1865. **SELECTED PUBLICATIONS** Auth, Confiscation and disposition of Loyalists' estates in Suffolk County, Massachusetts, William & Mary Quart, 10/64; Revolutionary Politics in Massachusetts: The Boston Committee of Correspondence and the Towns: 1772-1774, Harvard Univ, 70; Emergence of urban society in rural Massachusetts, 1760-1820, J Am Hist, 3/74; Modernization: A Victorian climax, Am Quart, 12/75; The founding fathers of 1776 and 1787: A collective view, William & Mary Quart, 7/76; Modernization: The Transformation of American Life, Hill & Wang, 76; Massachusetts: A Bicentennial History, Norton, 78; Knowledge is Power: The Diffusion of Information in Early America, 1700-1865, Oxford Univ Press, 89; The Idea of an Infromed Citizenry in the Early Republic, Devising Liberty: Perserving and Creating Freedom in the New American Republic, Stanford Univ Press, 95; The Strength of a People: The Idea of an Informed Citizenry in American, 1650-1870, Univ N C Press, 96. **CONTACT ADDRESS** Dept of Hist, Univ of Conn, Storrs, CT, 06268.

BROWN, RICHARD FARGO
PERSONAL Born 09/20/1916, New York, NY, m, 1941, 1 child **DISCIPLINE** ART HISTORY **EDUCATION** Bucknell Univ, AB, 40; Harvard Univ, MA, 47, PhD, 52. **CAREER** Teaching fel, Harvard Univ, 47-49; res & lectr fine arts, Frick Collection, 49-54; vis prof, Harvard Univ, 54; chief cur art, Los Angeles County Mus, 55-62, dir, Los Angeles Art Mus, 62-66; DIR, KIMBELL ART FOUND, 66-. **HONORS AND AWARDS** Order of Arts & Lett, France, 63., DLit, Bucknell Univ, 67. **MEMBERSHIPS** Art Asn Am (pres, 61-); Mus Dir Asn (secy-treas, 62, pres, 70-72); Nat Coun Arts; Am Asn Mus. **RESEARCH** History and criticism of art; 19th century French painting; history of painting media and techniques. **CONTACT ADDRESS** Kimbell Art Mus, 3333 Camp Bouie Blvd, PO Box 9440, Ft Worth, TX, 76107.

BROWN, RICHARD HARVEY
PERSONAL Born 05/12/1940, New York, NY, m, 1967, 1 child **DISCIPLINE** SOCIOLOGY **EDUCATION** Univ Calif, Berkeley, BA, 61; Columbia Univ, MA, 65; Univ Calif, San Diego, PhD, 73. **CAREER** Visiting instr, New Sch Social Research, 68; lecturer, Univ Calif, San Diego, 71-72; prof, Univ Maryland, College Park, 75-. **MEMBERSHIPS** Amer Sociol Assn; Speech Commun Assn. **RESEARCH** Relations between language, knowledge, and power; relations between global capitalism, postmodern culture, and democratic practice. **SELECTED PUBLICATIONS** Auth, A Poetic for Sociology: Toward a Logic of Discovery for the Human Sciences, 89; auth, Social Science as Civic Discourse: Essays on the Invention, Uses, and Legitimization of Social Theory, 89; auth, Society as Text: Essays on Reason, Rhetoric and Reality, 92; auth, Toward Democratic Sciences, 98; coauth, America in Transit: Culture, Capitalism and Democracy in the United States, 99. **CONTACT ADDRESS** Dept of Sociology, Univ of Maryland, College Park, MD, 20742-1315. **EMAIL** rbrown@bss1.umd.edu7

BROWN, RICHARD HOLBROOK
PERSONAL Born 09/25/1927, Boston, MA **DISCIPLINE** HISTORY **EDUCATION** Yale Univ, BA, 49, MA, 52, PhD(hist), 55. **CAREER** From instr to asst prof hist, Univ Mass, 55-62; assoc prof, Northern Ill Univ, 62-64; dir, Amherst Proj, Amherst & Hampshire Cols & Newberry Libr, 64-73; DIR RES & EDUC, NEWBERRY LIBR, 73-, Andrew Mellon fel, Univ Pittsburgh, 60-61; mem bd dirs, Soc Sci Educ Consortium, 73-79, pres, 75-77; mem, Nat Endowment for Humanities Bd Con-

sults, 77-; chmn, Teaching Resource Group, Nat Coord Comt for Prom Hist, 77-80. **HONORS AND AWARDS** Egleston Hist Prize, Yale Univ, 55. **MEMBERSHIPS** AHA; Orgn Am Historians; Nat Coun Social Studies. **RESEARCH** Pre-Civil War American history and the South; Jackson-Van Buren era; history education. **SELECTED PUBLICATIONS** Auth, The Hero and the People: The Meaning of Jacksonian Democracy, Macmillan, 63; History and the new social studies, Saturday Rev, 10/66; The Missouri crisis, slavery, and the politics of Jacksonianism, South Atlantic Quart, winter 66. **CONTACT ADDRESS** 880 N Lake Shore Dr Apt 16E, Chicago, IL, 60611.

BROWN, RICHMOND F.
DISCIPLINE LATIN AMERICA AND THE CARIBBEAN, SOCIAL HISTORY **EDUCATION** Spring Hill Col, BA; Tulane Univ, MA, PhD. **CAREER** Asst prof, Univ Kans, 89-90; Asst Prof, Univ South Al, 90-. **SELECTED PUBLICATIONS** Auth, Juan Fermin de Aycinena: Central American Colonial Entrepreneur, 1729-1796, Norman, Univ Okla Press, 97; Profits, Prestige, and Persistence: Juan Fermin de Aycinena and the Spirit of Enterprise in the Kingdom of Guatemala, Hisp Amer Hist Rev 75, 95 & Charles Lennox Wyke and the Clayton-Bulwer Formula in Central America, 1852-1860, The Americas 47, 91. **CONTACT ADDRESS** Dept of History, Univ South Alabama, 379 Humanities, Mobile, AL, 36688-0002. **EMAIL** rbrown@jaguar1.usouthal.edu

BROWN, ROBERT C.
PERSONAL Born 10/14/1935, Rochester, NY **DISCIPLINE** HISTORY **EDUCATION** Univ Rochester, BA, 57; Univ Toronto, MA, 58, PhD, 62. **CAREER** Asst prof, Univ Calgary, 61-64; asst prof, 64-66, assoc prof, 66-70, PROF HISTORY, UNIV TORONTO, 70-, dir grad stud, 72-73, assoc dept chair, 74-77, assoc dean grad stud, 81-85, acting dean, 85, vice dean arts & sci, 87-92, dept chair, 92-; sr fel, Massey Col, 87-; vice pres 88-91, pres 91-94, Acad II, Royal Soc Can. **HONORS AND AWARDS** Izaak Walton Killam sr res scholar; SSHRC leave grant. **MEMBERSHIPS** Can Hist Asn (coun, 64-67, 78-82, vice-pres, 78-79, pres, 79-80); Am Hist Asn, Can Inst Advan Res. **RESEARCH** Canadian history **SELECTED PUBLICATIONS** Auth, Canada's National Policy 1883-1900, 64; auth, Robert Laird Borden: A Biography, vol 1 75, vol 2 80; coauth, Canada Views the United States, 66; coauth, Confederation to 1949, 66; coauth, The Canadians 1867-1967, 67; coauth, Canada 1896-1921, 74; coauth, Twentieth Century Canada, 83; coauth, Nation: Canada Since Confederation, 90; ed, The Illustrated History of Canada, 87; ed, Histoire Generale du Canada, 88. **CONTACT ADDRESS** Dept of History, Univ of Toronto, Toronto, ON, M5S 1A1.

BROWN, ROBERT CRAIG
PERSONAL Born 10/14/1935, Rochester, NY, m, 1960, 3 children **DISCIPLINE** CANADIAN HISTORY **EDUCATION** Univ Rochester, BA, 57; Univ Toronto, MA, 58, PhD(hist), 62. **CAREER** Asst prof hist, Univ Calgary, 61-64; from asst prof to assoc prof, 64-70, dir, Grad Studies, Dept Hist, 72-73, assoc chmn, Dept Hist, 74-77, PROF HIST, UNIV TORONTO, 70-, ASSOC DEAN SCH GRAD STUDIES, 81-, Can Coun grants, 62, 63, 65, 73; ed, Can Hist Rev, 68-73; sr res scholar, Izaak Walton Killam Scholar, 77-78. **MEMBERSHIPS** AHA; Can Hist Asn (pres, 80). **RESEARCH** Canadian-American relations; Canadian history. **SELECTED PUBLICATIONS** Auth, Canada's National Policy, 1883-1900, Princeton Univ, 64; co-ed, Confederation to 1949, Prentice-Hall, Can, 66; coauth, Canada Views the United States, Wash Univ, 67; co-ed, The Canadians, 1867-1967, Macmillan, Can, 67; auth, Canada in North America, In: Twentieth Century: American Foreign Policy, Ohio State Univ, 71; Political leadership in Canada during World War I, In: War and Society in North America, Nelson, 71; coauth, Canada, 1896-1921: A Nation Transformed, McClelland & Stewart, 74; auth, Robert Laird Borden, A Biography, 1854-1914, Vol I, 75 & Vol II, 80, Macmillan, Can; The American Response to Canada since 1776 - Stewart,GT/, Canadian Hist Rev, Vol 75, 1994; Canada and the United-States - Ambivalent Allies - Thompson,JH, Randall,SJ/, Canadian Hist Rev, Vol 77, 1996. **CONTACT ADDRESS** Dept of Hist, Univ of Toronto, Toronto, ON, M5S 1A1.

BROWN, ROBERT WARREN
DISCIPLINE HISTORY **EDUCATION** Univ NC, Chapel Hill, AB, 69; Marshall Univ, MA, 71; Duke Univ, MA, 73, PhD, 79. **CAREER** Lectr, Univ Md, Heidelberg, Germany, 75-76; Lehrbeauftragter, Universitat Munster, Munster, Germany, 76-77; instr, Duke Univ, 77-78; instr NC St Univ, 78-79; asst prof to prof, dept chair, Univ NC, Pembroke, 79- . **HONORS AND AWARDS** Univ NC Pembroke's Outstanding Teacher Award, 97 **MEMBERSHIPS** Amer Hist Assoc; Col Art Assoc; Assoc of Hist of Nineteenth-century Art; Soc for French Hist Stud; W Soc for French Hist; Soc for Hist Educ; consortium on Revolutionary Europe, Assoc of Hist in NC. **RESEARCH** Nineteenth-century France; Germany during the Nazi era; history & topography of Paris; townscape painting; preservation of historical monuments. **SELECTED PUBLICATIONS** Auth, Paris 1900: Exposition universelle, Historical Dictionary of the World's Fairs and Expositions, 1851-1988, Greenwood Press, 90; Albert Robida's Vieux Paris Exhibit: Art and Historical Recreation at the Paris World's Fair of 1900, year Book of Interdisciplinary Studies in the Fine Arts, Edwin Mellen Press, 91; The London Diorama, Landscape Painting, 1780-1803, & Topographical and Travel Prints, 1780-1830, Encyclopedia of Romanticism: Culture in Britain, Garland Publ Inc, 92; Topography, The Dictionary of Art, Macmillan Publ Co, 96; Horst Wessel Song, The Encyclopedia of Propaganda, M. E. Sharpe, 97; ed, book rev ed, Journal of the Association of Historians in North Carolina, 91- . **CONTACT ADDRESS** Dept of History, Univ of NC Pembroke, PO Box 1510, Pembroke, NC, 29372-1510. **EMAIL** rwb@papa.uncp.edu

BROWN, RONALD CONKLIN
PERSONAL Born 04/25/1945, Brownwood, TX, m, 1969 **DISCIPLINE** UNITED STATES NATIONAL HISTORY **EDUCATION** Wabash Col, AB, 67; Univ Ill, Urbana, AM, 68, PhD(hist), 75. **CAREER** Instr, 75-78, asst prof, 78-81, ASSOC PROF US HIST, SOUTHWEST TEX STATE UNIV, 81-, UNIV ARCHIVIST, 79-, & DIR HON PROG, 80-. **MEMBERSHIPS** AHA; Orgn Am Historians; Western Hist Asn; Nat Col Hon Coun. **RESEARCH** Trans-Mississippi West; labor; historiography. **SELECTED PUBLICATIONS** Auth, Dedication to Fred A Shannon, Ariz and the West, spring 78; Hard-Rock Miners: The Intermountain West, 1860-1920, Tex A&M Press, 79; Beacon on the Hill: Southwest Texas State University, 1903-1978, Southwest Tex, 79. **CONTACT ADDRESS** Dept of Hist, Southwest Tex State Univ, 601 University Dr, San Marcos, TX, 78666-4685.

BROWN, RONALD PAUL
PERSONAL Born 03/19/1938, Ravenna, OH, m **DISCIPLINE** HISTORY **EDUCATION** Univ of Akron, BS, history & govt, 1967, MS, counseling & guidance, 1969, PhD, counselor educ, 1974. **CAREER** Univ of Akron, coord of dev serv & student adv 1969-74; Cuyahoga Co Bd of Mental Retardation, dir of habilitation serv 1974-80; Co of Summit, admin asst 1981-84; Kent State Univ, asst to the dean for minority & women affairs 1984-87; Kent State Univ Ashtabula Campus, asst dean and asst prof of counselor educ 1987-92, assistant professor of Pan African Studies/dir of multicultural affairs, 1992-98; JOPARO, OWNER currently. **HONORS AND AWARDS** Chmn of the Educ Comm Eta Tau Lambda 1982-84; Outstanding Serv Awd Eta Tau Lambda 1983; chairman Univ of Akron's Black Alumni 1984; Key to the City of Ashtabula Ohio, 1990; Developed African American Speaker Series, Ashtabula Campus, 1990; NAACP, Ashtabula Chapter, Man of the Year, 1991, 1995. **MEMBERSHIPS** Univ of Akron Alumni Council 1978-81; bd of trustees Cuyahoga Valley Mental Health 1982-84; Natl Cert Counselor Natl Bd for Certified Couns Inc 1984; bd of trustees St Paul AME Church 1978-; Alpha Phi Alpha, 1982-; board of directors Alpha Homes Inc 1982-; chap sec Natl Old Timers Inc 1984-87; treasurers Black Alumni Assoc 1987-; vice pres, Comm Action Council Ashtabula OH; adv board member Ashtabula Salvation Army; dir Community Resource Economic Comm Ashtabula, Home Safe Inc, bd of trustees 1990, adv bd, 1992; Private Industry Council Advisory Board, 1990, vice pres, Jobs for Ohio's Graduates, president, 1992; Goodwill Industries, bd of advisors. **SELECTED PUBLICATIONS** "The Joys and Pain of Brotherhood: A Neophyte Expressed Himself" Alpha Newsletter 1983. **CONTACT ADDRESS** PO Box 9301, Akron, OH, 44305-9301.

BROWN, SALLIE
DISCIPLINE HISTORY **EDUCATION** Ga State Univ, PhD. **CAREER** Asst prof. **HONORS AND AWARDS** E. Merton Coulter Awd; Leroy Collins Prize. **MEMBERSHIPS** Fla Hist Asn. **RESEARCH** United States history; modern South; civil rights. **SELECTED PUBLICATIONS** Auth, Standing Against Dragons: Three Southern Lawyers in the Era of Fear 1945-1965, 98; Federal Anti-Communism and the Segregationist South: From New Orleans to Atlanta 1954-1958, Ga Hist Quarterly, 96. **CONTACT ADDRESS** History Dept, Florida Atlantic Univ, 777 Glades Rd, Boca Raton, FL, 33431. **EMAIL** rinaldi@acc.fau.edu

BROWN, SCOTT KENT
PERSONAL Born 10/01/1940, Murray, UT, m, 1966, 4 children **DISCIPLINE** EARLY CHRISTIAN HISTORY & LITERATURE **EDUCATION** Univ Calif, Berkeley, BA, 67; Brown Univ, PhD (Bibl studies), 72. **CAREER** Asst prof, 71-76, ASSOC PROF ANCIENT SCRIPTURE, BRIGHAM YOUNG UNIV, 76-, Mem, Inst Ancient Studies, Brigham Young Univ, 73-; corresp mem, Inst Antiquity & Christianity, Calif, 73-. **MEMBERSHIPS** Soc Bibl Lit. **RESEARCH** New Testament; New Testament apocrypha. **SELECTED PUBLICATIONS** Auth, James the Just and the question of Peter's leadership in the light of new sources, In: Sperry Lectr Series, Brigham Young Univ, 73; The book of Lehi: A lost record?, spring 74 & The Apocalypse of Peter (CG VII, 3): A translation, spring 74, Brigham Young Univ Studies; Masada + Excavations and Discoveries from the World of the New-Testament - Herod Fortress and the Zealots Last Stand - a Brigham-Young-University forum address, Brigham Young Univ Studies, Vol 36, 1997. **CONTACT ADDRESS** Dept of Ancient Scripture, Brigham Young Univ, Joseph Smith Bldg, Provo, UT, 84602-0002.

BROWN, SIDNEY DEVERE
PERSONAL Born 01/29/1925, Douglass, KS, m, 1948, 4 children **DISCIPLINE** HISTORY **EDUCATION** Southwestern Col, BA, 47; Univ Wis, MA, 50, PhD(hist), 53. **CAREER** From instr to assoc prof hist, Okla State Univ, 52-66, prof 66-71; PROF EAST ASIAN HIST, UNIV OKLA, 71-, Ford Found fel, Japan, 56-57; ed, Studies Asia, Univ Nebr, 62, 67; vis prof, Univ Ill, Urbana-Champaign, 68-69; Am Philos Soc Grant travel & res in Japan, 71; Japan Found fel, Tokyo Univ, 77-78. **MEMBERSHIPS** AHA; Asn Asian Studies; Japan Soc; Midwest Conf Asian Affiars (pres, 59-60); Southwest Conf Asian Studies (pres, 78). **RESEARCH** Meiji leaders in Japan's modernization. **SELECTED PUBLICATIONS** Auth, Okubo Toshimochi: Meiji economic policies, J Asian Studies, 2/62; Okubo and the first home ministry bureaucracy, In: Japan's Modern Leadership, Univ Ariz, 66; contribr, Political assassination in Early Meiji Japan: the plot against Okubo, In: Meiji Japan's Centennial, Univ Kans, 71; Shidehara Kijuro: The Diplomacy of the Yen, In: Diplomacy in Crisis, Clio Press, 74; The Self-Image of an Early Meiji Statesman: Through the Diary of Kido Takayoshi, Selected Papers on Asia, Vol I, 197-207; 'Seijoki No Kikoenai Heya' - Levy,IH/, World Lit Today, Vol 67, 1993; 'Youth' and Other Stories - Ogai,M, Rimer,JT, ed/, World Lit Today, Vol 69, 1995; Saigo,Takamori - The Man Behind the Myth - Yates,CL/, Monumenta Nipponica, Vol 51, 1996; On Familiar Terms - A Journey Across Cultures - Keene,D/, World Lit Today, Vol 70, 1996; **CONTACT ADDRESS** Dept of Hist, Room 406 Univ of Okla, 455 W Lindsey St, Norman, OK, 73069.

BROWN, SPENCER HUNTER
PERSONAL Born 06/10/1928, Knoxville, TN, m, 1951, 1 child **DISCIPLINE** HISTORY **EDUCATION** Univ Ill, BA, 54, MA, 55; Northwestern Univ, PhD(African hist), 64. **CAREER** Teacher, Carl Sandburg High Sch, 55-56, chmn dept social studies, 56-59; from asst prof to assoc prof hist, 62-71, PROF HIST, WESTERN ILL UNIV, 71-, CHMN DEPT, 76-, Gen ed, J Developing Areas, 65-76, bus mgr, 77-. **MEMBERSHIPS** African Studies Asn; AHA. **RESEARCH** Social history of Lagos, Nigeria, 1852-1886. **SELECTED PUBLICATIONS** Auth, British Army Surgeons Commissioned 1840-1909 with West-Indian West-African Service - A Prosopographical Evaluation/, Med Hist, Vol 37, 1993; Public-Health in United-States and West-African Cities, 1870-1900/, Hist, Vol 56, 1994; Colonialism on the Cheap - A Tale of 2 English Army Surgeons in Lagos, Rowe,Samuel and Simpson,Frank, 1862-1882/, Int J African Hist Studies, Vol 27, 1994. **CONTACT ADDRESS** Dept of Hist, Western Illinois Univ, 1 University Cir, Macomb, IL, 61455-1390.

BROWN, STEWART JAY
PERSONAL Born 07/08/1951, Oak Park, IL, m, 1972, 2 children **DISCIPLINE** MODERN BRITISH & EUROPEAN HISTORY **EDUCATION** Univ Ill, Urbana, BA, 73; Univ Chicago, MA, 74, PhD(hist), 81. **CAREER** Head, Foreign Newspaper Microfilm Proj, Ctr Res Libr, 78-79; asst to dean, Col Arts & Sci, Northwestern Univ, 80-82, lectr hist, 81-82; ASST PROF HIST, UNIV GA, 82- **MEMBERSHIPS** Am Hist Asn; Conf on Brit Studies; Am Soc Church Hist; Scottish Church Hist Soc. **RESEARCH** Modern Scottish and Irish & nineteenth century British social and religious history; history of the British Empire. **SELECTED PUBLICATIONS** Auth, The disruption and urban proverty: T Chalmers and the West Port in Edinburgh 1844-47, Records of the Scottish Church Hist Soc, 78; Thomas Chalmers and the Godly Commonwealth in Scotland, Oxford Univ Press, 82. **CONTACT ADDRESS** Dept of Hist, Univ of Georgia, Athens, GA, 30602-0001.

BROWN, WALLACE
PERSONAL Born 11/20/1933, Edmonton, AB, Canada, m, 1957 **DISCIPLINE** MODERN HISTORY **EDUCATION** Oxford Univ, BA, 57, MA, 62; Univ Nebr, MA, 59; Univ Calif, Berkeley, PhD(Am hist), 64. **CAREER** Asst prof Am hist, Univ Alta, 63-64 & Eng hist, Brown Univ, 64-67; assoc prof, 67-70, PROF AM HIST, UNIV NB, FREDERICTON, 70-, Can Coun leave fel, 73-74. **MEMBERSHIPS** AHA; Orgn Am Historians; Can Hist Soc. **RESEARCH** Anglo-American history in the eighteenth century. **SELECTED PUBLICATIONS** Auth, George L Miller and the struggle over Nebraska statehood, Nebr Hist, 12/60; Negroes and the American Revolution, Hist Today, 8/64; The King's Friends, Brown Univ, 65; Viewpoints of a Pennslvania Loyalist, Pa Mag Hist & Biog, 10-67; The Good Americans, Morrow, 69; The American Loyalists in Jamaica/, J Caribbean Hist, Vol 26, 1992; Plunder, Profit, and Paroles, a Social-History of the War of 1812 in Upper-Canada - Sheppard,G/, J Mil Hist, Vol 58, 1994; While the Women only Wept - Loyalist Refugee Women - Pottermackinnon,J/, J Am History, Vol 81, 1994; Governor Wentworth,John and the American-Revolution - The English Connection - Wilderson,PW/, Am Hist Rev, Vol 100, 1995; Some Recent Books on Late 18th-Century Atlantic Canada/, Acadiensis, Vol 24, 1995; 'Muriel 1969', Callaloo, Vol 19, 1996; Loyalists and Community in North-America - Calhoon,RM, Barnes,TM, Rawlyk,GA/, William and Mary Quart, Vol 53, 1996. **CONTACT ADDRESS** Dept of Hist, Univ of NB, Fredericton, NB, E3B 5A3.

BROWN, WELDON AMZY
PERSONAL Born 01/29/1911, Cycle, NC, m, 1933, 1 child **DISCIPLINE** RECENT & AMERICAN REVOLUTIONARY HISTORY **EDUCATION** Dartmouth Col, BA, 33; Univ NC, Chapel Hill, MA, 34, PhD(hist), 36. **CAREER** Dir, Decatur Ctr, Univ Ala, 36-38; instr hist & polit sci, Univ Ala, Tuscaloosa, 38-39; from asst prof to assoc prof, 39-57, prof hist, Va Polytech Inst & State Univ, 57-79; RETIRED. **MEMBERSHIPS** Orgn Am Hist. **RESEARCH** Colonial, Revolutionary and contemporary history. **SELECTED PUBLICATIONS** Auth, The Howe Peace Commission of 1776, NC Hist Rev, 4/36; Empire or Independence: A Study in the Failure of Reconciliation, 1774-1783, La State Univ, 41 & Kennikat, 66; The Common Cause--Collectivism: Menace or Challenge, 49 & Democracy: Man's Great Opportunity, 49, North River; Prelude to Disaster: The American Role in Vietnam, 1940-1963, 75 & The Last Chopper: The Denouement of the American Role in Vietnam, 1963-1975, 76, Kennikat. **CONTACT ADDRESS** 804 S Main St, Blacksburg, VA, 24060.

BROWN., JAMES SEAY, JR.
PERSONAL Born 11/12/1944, Boston, MA, m, 1966, 3 children **DISCIPLINE** EUROPEAN HISTORY **EDUCATION** TN Technological Univ, BA (Hist), 66; Vanderbilt Univ, MA (Hist), 68, PhD (European Hist), 71. **CAREER** FULL-TIME TEACHING, DEPT OF HIST AND PHILOS, SAMFORD UNIV, 71-. **HONORS AND AWARDS** Buchanon Teaching Award, Samford Univ. **MEMBERSHIPS** Southern Hist Asn; AL Folklife Asn; Southern Conference on Slavic Studies. **RESEARCH** Nationalism. **SELECTED PUBLICATIONS** Ed, Up Before Daylight: Life Histories from the Alabama Writer's Project, 1938-1939, Univ AL Press, 82, 97. **CONTACT ADDRESS** Samford Univ, Box 292206, Birmingham, AL, 35229. **EMAIL** jsbrown@samford.edu

BROWNE, GARY L.
PERSONAL Born 09/21/1939, Lansing, MI, m, 1984, 1 child **DISCIPLINE** HISTORY **EDUCATION** Univ Mich, BA, 62, MA, 65; Wayne St Univ, PhD, 73. **CAREER** Ed, 78-86, Maryland Historical Mag; assoc prof, 76-, Univ Maryland. **RESEARCH** Amer Business & social hist; Amer, 18th & 19th century; Maryland hist. **CONTACT ADDRESS** Dept of History, Univ of Maryland, Baltimore County, Baltimore, MD, 21250. **EMAIL** browne@umbc.edu

BROWNE, GARY LAWSON
PERSONAL Born 09/21/1939, Lansing, MI, 1 child **DISCIPLINE** AMERICAN HISTORY **EDUCATION** Univ Mich, BA, 62; Wayne State Univ, MA, 65, PhD(hist), 73. **CAREER** Instr hist, Wayne State Univ, 72-73, asst prof, 73-75; asst prof, 76-81, ASSOC PROF HIST, UNIV MD, BALTIMORE, 81-, Ed, Md Hist Mag, 77- & Md Mag Genealogy, 77- **MEMBERSHIPS** Orgn Am Historians; Southern Hist Asn; AHA. **RESEARCH** American early republic; business history; Maryland history. **SELECTED PUBLICATIONS** Auth, Business Innovation and Social Change: The career of Alexander Brown after the War of 1812, Md Hist Mag, fall 74; The Panic of 1819 in Baltimore, In: Law, Society, and Politics in Early Maryland, Johns Hopkins Univ, 77; Baltimore in the Nation, 1789-1861, Univ NC Press, 80; Cultural Conservatism and the Industrial Revolution: The case of Baltimore, 1776-1860, Continuity, 1/81. **CONTACT ADDRESS** Dept of Hist, Univ of Maryland, Baltimore, MD, 21228. **EMAIL** browne@umbc.edu

BROWNING, C.R.
PERSONAL Born 05/22/1944, Durham, NC, m, 1970, 2 children **DISCIPLINE** MODERN EUROPEAN HISTORY **EDUCATION** Oberlin Col, BA 67; Univ Wisconsin Madison, MA 68, PhD 75. **CAREER** Allegheny Col PA, instr 69-71; Pacific Lutheran Univ, all ranks, 74-; Univ N Carolina Chapel Hill, Frank Porter Graham Dist Prof, 99-. **HONORS AND AWARDS** Woodrow Wilson Fel; DAAD; Humboldt; Fulbright; Inst Adv Stud Princeton and Hebrew U; Schhapior Sr Sch in Res US Holocaust Mem Museum. **MEMBERSHIPS** AHA; GSA; Holocaust Edu Found. **RESEARCH** Holocaust; Nazi Germany; Second World War. **SELECTED PUBLICATIONS** Auth, Der Weg zur Endlosung, Entscheidungen und Taeter, Bonn 98; The Path to Genocide, NY 92; Ordinary Men: Reserve Police Battalion 101 and the Final Solution in Poland, NY 92; Fateful Months: Essays on the Emergence of the Final Solution, NY 85. **CONTACT ADDRESS** Pacific Lutheran Univ, Tacoma, WA, 98447.

BROWNING, DANIEL C.
PERSONAL Born 10/26/1956, Albany, GA, m, 1982, 2 children **DISCIPLINE** ARCHAEOLOGY; BIBLICAL BACKGROUNDS **EDUCATION** Univ Alabama Huntsville, BSE, 80; MDiv, 84, PhD, 88, Southwestern Baptist Theological Seminary. **CAREER** Instr, Texas Christian Univ, 87-89; Teaching Fel, 85-87, Adjunct Instr, 87-89, Southwestern Baptist Theological Seminary; Instr, 88-90, Tarrant County Jr. Col; Asst Prof, 90-93, Assoc Prof, 93-, William Carey Col. **HONORS AND AWARDS** Endowment for Biblical Research/American Schools of Oriental Research Travel Grant, 84; Research Fel, Albright Inst of Archaeological Research, Jerusalem, 88; Outstanding Faculty Member 95/96, William Carey Col (Student Govt Assoc Award), 96; Teaching Excellence Grants William Carey Col, 93-97. **MEMBERSHIPS** Amer Schools of Oriental Research; Israel Exploration Soc; Soc of Biblical Lit. **RESEARCH** Biblical backgrounds; culture of New Testament times; archaeological field work **SELECTED PUBLICATIONS** Auth, Land of Goshen, Biblical Illustrator 19, 93; The Other Side of the Sea of Galilee, Biblical Illustrator, 20, 94; Standards of Greatness in the First Century, Biblical Illustrator 21, 95; Coauth, Of Seals and Scrolls, Biblical Illustrator 22, 96; Auth, The Strange Search for the Ashes of the Red Hefer, Biblical Archaeologist, 96; The Hill Country is not Enough for Us: Recent Arcaheology and the Book of Joshua, Southwestern Journal of Theology, 98; Jesus as Carpenter, Biblical Illustrator, 98; Iron Age Loom Weights from Timnah, Tell Batash (Timnah) II: The Finds from the Iron Age II, forthcoming. **CONTACT ADDRESS** William Carey Col, Hattiesburg, MS, 39401. **EMAIL** browning@wmcarey.edu

BROWNING, REED ST. CLAIR
PERSONAL Born 08/26/1938, New York, NY, m, 1 child **DISCIPLINE** HISTORY **EDUCATION** Dartmouth Col, BA, 60; Yale Univ, PhD, 65. **CAREER** Amherst Col, 64-67; Kenyon Col, instr to asst prof, 67-86, asst prof to prof provost, 86-94, act pres, 89. **HONORS AND AWARDS** Fulbright Scholarship; NEH summer stipend; dir NEH summer sem for school teachers; Jacob Javits Fel Board. **MEMBERSHIPS** Ohio Acad Hist, Hist Soc, Soc for Am Baseball Res. **RESEARCH** 18th-century Britain; 18th-century Europe; baseball hist. **SELECTED PUBLICATIONS** The Duke of Newcastle, 75; Political and Constitutional Ideas of the Court Whigs, 82; The War of the Austrian Succession, 94. **CONTACT ADDRESS** Kenyon Col, Gambier, OH, 43022. **EMAIL** browninr@kenyon.edu

BROWNING COLE, EVE
DISCIPLINE ANCIENT GREEK PHILOSOPHY, FEMINIST THEORY, ETHICS, CLASSICAL STUDIES **EDUCATION** Univ Fla, BA, 73; Univ Calif, San Diego, PhD; 79. **CAREER** Instr, Univ Denver; instr, Ohio State Univ; assoc prof, 84-, ch, Environ Stud adv bd, Univ Minn, Duluth. **RESEARCH** Ancient Greek philosophy; ethics. **SELECTED PUBLICATIONS** Auth, Philosophy and Feminist Criticism, Paragon, 93; coed, Explorations in Feminist Ethics: Theory and Practice, Ind UP, 88. **CONTACT ADDRESS** Univ Minn, Duluth, Duluth, MN, 55812-2496.

BROWNLEE, GERALDINE DANIELS
PERSONAL East Chicago, IN, m, 1957 **DISCIPLINE** EDUCATION **EDUCATION** West VA State Coll, BA (cum laude) 1947; Univ of IL, grad 1949-50; Univ of MI, grad 1950; Chicago Teachers Coll, grad 1955; Univ of Chicago, MST 1967, PhD 1975; IN Univ, post-doctoral study, american council on education, fellow, 1978-79. **CAREER** Cook Co IL, Dept of Pub Welfare, adv caseworker 1950-55; Chicago Public Sch, elem sch teacher 1955-66; Univ of Chicago, staff assoc 1968-70; University of Chicago, Ford Found Training & Placement Prog, coord 1969-70; University of Chicago, asst dir trainer of tchr trainers prog 1970-71; Univ of IL, Coll of Educ, asst dean, asst prof 1971-74; Park Forest IL Sch Dist, dir title VII proj 1975-76; Univ of IL, associate professor emerita, 1990; DePaul University, Urban Teacher Corps, director, office of provost, specail asst, 1990-91. **HONORS AND AWARDS** Fifteenth Annual Distinguished Research Award, from Assn of Teacher Educators: Beautiful People Award, Chicago Urban League, 1989; Outstanding Achievement Award in the Field of Education, YWCA of Metropolitan Chicago, 1990. **MEMBERSHIPS** Consul US Off of Educ; consul Pk Forest Sch Dist 163; Amer Educ Res Assn; Natl Soc for the Study of Educ; Amer Assn for Higher Educ; Alpha Kappa Alpha; Amer Assn of Univ Women; Links Inc; Education Network; International vice pres Pi Lambda Theta Honor Assn for Professionals in Educ; Assn for Supervision and Curriculum Devel, 1988-89; Assn of Teacher Educ; 1982-88; chairperson, Chicago Urban League Education Advisory Comm, 1983-90; bd of dirs, Chicago Urban League, 1984-90; Chicago United Way Allocations, comm, 1992-97; Metropolitan Chicago YWCA, bd of dirs, vice pres, 1991-97. **SELECTED PUBLICATIONS** The Role of Teacher Career Stages and Professional Develop Practices in Determining Rewards and Incentives in Teaching 1987; co-auth, Parent-Teacher Contacts and Students Learning, A Research Report, The Journal of Educ Rsch 1981; Characteristics of Teacher Leaders" Educational Horizons, 1979; reprint in the Practising Administrator (Australia) 1980; Teachers Who Can, Lead, Alpha Delta Kappan, 1980; Research & Evaluation of Alternative Programs for High School Truants," 1988, 1989.

BROWNMILLER, SARA N.
PERSONAL Born 03/11/1952, San Antonio, TX, m, 1975, 2 children **DISCIPLINE** POLITICAL SCIENCE **EDUCATION** Incarnate Word Col, BA, 74; Univ of AZ, MLS, 78 **CAREER** Ref Librn, 79-82, Univ of N IA; Cent Ref Librn, 82-87, Univ of AZ, Coord, 87-89, 89-94, Prof, 94-, Univ of OR **HONORS AND AWARDS** Beta Phi Mu; IAC **MEMBERSHIPS** Am Lib Asn **RESEARCH** Women's studies **SELECTED PUBLICATIONS** Coauth, Index to Women's Studies Anthologies: Research Across the Disciplines, 1980-1984, Boston: GK Hall, 94; Index to Women's Studies Anthologies: Research Across the Disciplines, 1985-1989, Boston: GK Hall, 96 **CONTACT ADDRESS** Libr Sys Dept, Univ of Oregon, Eugene, OR, 97403-1299. **EMAIL** snb@darkwing.uoregon.edu

BROYLES, MICHAEL
DISCIPLINE MUSIC HISTORY, HISTORY **EDUCATION** Austin Coll, BA, 61; Univ Texas at Austin, MA, 64, PhD, 76. **CAREER** Prof, mus, Univ Maryland Baltimore; PROF, MUS & AM HIST, PENN STATE UNIV. **MEMBERSHIPS** Am Antiquarian Soc **SELECTED PUBLICATIONS** Auth, A Yankee Musician in Europe: The European Journals of Lowell Mason, UMI Research Press, 90; auth, "Music and Class Structure in Antebellum Boston," Jour of the Am Mus Soc, 91; auth, "Music of the Highest Class": Elitism and Populism in Antebellum Boston, Yale Univ Press. 92. **CONTACT ADDRESS** Sch of Mus, Pennsylvania State Univ, University Park, PA, 16802. **EMAIL** meb11@psu.edu

BRUCE, D.D.
PERSONAL Born 04/11/1946, Dallas, TX, m, 1967, 1 child **DISCIPLINE** AMERICAN CIVILIZATION **EDUCATION** Univ Pa, PhD, 71. **CAREER** Asst prof, Univ Calif, Irvine; assoc prof, 76-81; prof, 81- . **HONORS AND AWARDS** James Mooney Award, Southern Anthrop Soc, 73; Fulbright lectr in Am lit, Szeged, Hungary, 87-88. **RESEARCH** 19th century U.S. history; African-American intellectual/cultural history. **SELECTED PUBLICATIONS** Auth, And They All Sang Hallelujah: Plain-Folk Camp-Meeting Religion, 1800-1845, 74; auth, Violence and Culture in the Antebellum South, 79; auth, The Rhetoric of Conservatism: The Virginia Convention of 1829-30 and the Conservative Tradition in the South, 82; auth, Black American Writing from the Nadir: The Evolution of a Literary Tradition, 1877-1915, 89; auth, Archibald Grimke: Portrait of a Black Independent, 93. **CONTACT ADDRESS** History Dept, Univ of California, Irvine, Irvine, CA, 92697-3275. **EMAIL** ddbruce@uci.edu

BRUCE, ROBERT VANCE
PERSONAL Born 12/19/1923, Malden, MA **DISCIPLINE** HISTORY **EDUCATION** Univ NH, BS, 45; Boston Univ, AM, 47, PhD(hist), 53. **CAREER** Instr hist & math, Univ Bridgeport, 47-48; master hist, Lawrence Acad, 48-51; from instr to assoc prof, 55-66, prof hist, 66-85, PROF EMER, 84- BOSTON UNIV. **HONORS AND AWARDS** Guggenheim Mem fel, 57-58; vis assoc prof hist, Univ Wis, 62-63; Henry E Huntington Libr fel, 66; Pulitzer Prize History, 88. **MEMBERSHIPS** AAAS; AHA; Orgn Am Hist; Soc Am Hist. **RESEARCH** American Civil War; United States history, 1846-1897; history of American science and technology. **SELECTED PUBLICATIONS** Auth, Lincoln and the Tools of War, Bobbs,56; 1877: Year of Violence, Bobbs,59; Chap, In: Abraham Lincoln: A New Portrait, Putnam, 59; Chap, In: Lincoln for the Ages, Doubleday, 60; contribr, Nineteenth Century American Science: A Reappraisal, Northwestern Univ, 72; auth, Bell: Alexander Graham Bell and the Conquest of Solitude, Little, 73; Packaging the Past, J Interdisciplinary Hist, winter 76; Lincoln and the Riddle of Modern Death, Louis Warren Libr, 81; auth, The Launching of Modern American Science, Knopf, 87; chap, in Lincoln the War President, Oxford, 92; chap, In Feeding Mars, Westview, 93; chap, in War Comes Again, Oxford, 95. **CONTACT ADDRESS** Dept of History, Boston Univ, 226 Bay State Rd, Boston, MA, 02215.

BRUCKER, GENE ADAM
PERSONAL Born 10/15/1924, Cropsey, IL, m, 1949, 3 children **DISCIPLINE** HISTORY **EDUCATION** Univ Ill, AB, 47, MA, 48; Oxford Univ, BLitt, 50; Princeton Univ, PhD(hist), 54. **CAREER** From instr to assoc prof, 54-64, prof, 64-80, SHEPARD PROF HIST, UNIV CALIF, BERKELEY, 80-, Guggenheim fel, 60-61; Am Coun Learned Soc fel, 64-65; fel, Inst Advan Studies, Princeton Univ, 68-69. **RESEARCH** Renaissance Italian history; history of Florence. **SELECTED PUBLICATIONS** Auth, Renaissance Florence, Wiley, 69; ed, The Society of Renaissance Florence, Harper, 72; auth, The Civic World of Early Renaissance Florence, Princeton Univ, 77; Ecclesiastical Courts in 15th-Century Florence and Fiesole/, Mediaeval Studies, Vol 53, 1991; The Criminal-Law System of Medieval and Renaissance Florence - Stern,LI/, Renaissance Quart, Vol 48, 1995; The 'Consulte e Pratiche' of the Florentine Republic 1498-1505 - Italian - Fachard,D, ed/, Renaissance Quart, Vol 48, 1995; Charity and State in Late Renaissance Italy - The Monte-de-Pieta of Florence - Menning,CB/, Renaissance Quart, Vol 48, 1995; Institutional Legislation and Documents from the Florentine Republic, 1494-1512, Vol 1 - 2-December,1494 to 14-February,1497 - Italian - Cadoni,G, Ed/, Speculum- a J Medieval Studies, Vol 71, 1996; Lucca 1439-1494 - The Reconstruction of an Italian City-Republic - Bratchel,ME/, J Interdisciplinary Hist, Vol 27, 1997. **CONTACT ADDRESS** Dept of Hist, Univ of Calif, Berkeley, CA, 94720.

BRUEGMANN, ROBERT
PERSONAL Born 05/21/1948, Chicago, IL, s **DISCIPLINE** HISTORY OF ARCHITECTURE **EDUCATION** Principia Col, BA, 70; Univ Pa, PhD, 76. **CAREER** Phil Col Art, lectr, 76-77; Univ Ill Chicago, asst prof, 77-83; assoc prof, 83-93; dir Preservation Prog, 77-83; Dir Grad Study, 87-90; prof, 94- . **HONORS AND AWARDS** Teaching fel, Univ Pa, 72-74; Head Teaching fel, Univ Pa, 73-74; Penfield Scholar in Diplomacy, Int Affaris and Belles lettres, 73-74; Founder's Award, Soc of Archit Hist, 78; Univ Ill Chicago, fac summer fel, 80; NEH fel, 83-84; Graham Found for Advan Studies in the Arts,

85; Sr fel, Temply Hoyne Bell Ctr for the Study of Am Archit, Columbia Univ, 89-90; fel, Inst for the Human, Univ Ill Chicago, 92-93; scholar, Great Cities Inst, Univ Ill Chicago, 98-99; Spro Kostof Award, Soc of Archit Hist, 98. **MEMBERSHIPS** Int Planning Hist Soc; Nat Trust for Hist Preserv; Soc of Archit Hist; Metrop Planning Coun, Chicago; Chicago Archit Club; Vernacular Archit Forum. **RESEARCH** Modern and contemporary architecture, urbanism, planning and landscape; contemporary urban built evironment and urban sprawl. **SELECTED PUBLICATIONS** Auth, Benicia: Portrait of an Early California Town: An Architectural History, 1846 to the Present, 80; auth, Holabird & Roche/Holbird & Root, Catalog of Work 1910-1940, 91; ed, Modernism at Mid-Century: The Architecture of the United States Air Force Academy, 94; auth, The Architects and the City: Holabird and Roche of Chicago 1880-1918, 97. **CONTACT ADDRESS** Art History M/C 201, Univ of Illinois at Chicago, 935 W. Harrison St., Chicago, IL, 60607. **EMAIL** bbrueg@uic.edu

BRUHN, JOHN GLYNDON
PERSONAL Born 04/27/1934, Norfolk, NE **DISCIPLINE** SOCIOLOGY **EDUCATION** Univ Nebr, BA, 52-56, MA, 56-58; Yale Univ, PhD, 58-61; Harvard Grad Sch Edu, MLE, 97. **CAREER** Resr, Nebr Sch Med, 58; resr, Yale Univ, Conn Dept Mental Health, 58-59; instr, Sociol, South Conn Coll, 60-61; res couns, Yale Univ, 61; resr sociol, Dept Psychol Med, Univ Edinburgh, Scotland, 61-62; instr, Med Sociol, Unik Okla, 62-63; asst prof, Dept Psych & Behav Sci, Univ Olla, 63-64;asst prof, Prevent Med & Public Health, Univ Okla Med Ctr, 64-67; clin investr, Okla Med Res Found, 65-67; assoc prof, Sociol Med, Univ Okla Med Ctr, 67-72; assoc prof, Human Ecol, Sch Health, Univ Okla Med Ctr, 67-69; prof & ch, Dept Human Ecol, Sch Health, Univ Okla Med Ctr, 69-72; assoc dean, Univ Tx Med Br-Galveston, 72-81; prof, Prevent Med & Commun Health, Univ Tx Med Ctr, 71-91; dean, Sch Allied Health Sci, Univ Tx Med Br, 81-91; vpres, Acad Affs & Res, Univ Tx -El Paso, 91-95; prof, Coll Nurs & Health Sci, Univ Tx-El Paso, 91-95; adj prof, Mgt & Policy Sci, Univ Tx Health Sci Ctr, 91-95; PROVOST, DEAN, PROF, SOCIOL, SCH BEHAV SCI & EDUC, PENN STATE HARRISBURG, 95-. **RESEARCH** Organizational behavior; organizational ethics. **SELECTED PUBLICATIONS** Coauth, Managing Boundaries in the Health Professions, Charles C Thomas, 93; coauth, Perspectives on Life-Threatening Illness for Allied Health Professionals, Haworth Press, 93; coauth, Clinical Sociology: An Agenda for Action, Plenum Publ, 96; co-edr, Border health: Challenges for the United States and Mexico, Garland Publ, 97. **CONTACT ADDRESS** School Behavioral Sciences & Educ, Pennsylvania State Univ, 777 W Harrisburg Pike, Olmstead B, Middletown, PA, 17057. **EMAIL** jgb5@psu.edu

BRUMBERG, JOAN JACOBS
PERSONAL Born 04/29/1944, Mt Vernon, NY, m, 1972, 1 child **DISCIPLINE** AMERICAN HISTORY **EDUCATION** Univ Rochester, BA, 65; Boston Col, MA, 71; Univ Va, PhD, 78. **CAREER** Vis asst prof, State Univ NY, Binghamton, 78-79; from asst prof to prof, 79-96, Stephen H. Weiss Presidential Fel and prof hist, Cornell Univ, 96-. **HONORS AND AWARDS** Fel, Charles Warren Ctr, Harvard Univ, 82-83; fel, Rockefeller Found, 84-85; Berkshire Book Prize, 88; John Hope Franklin Prize, 89; Watson Davis Prize, 89; Basker Memorial Prize, 89; fel, NEH, 90-91; fel, John Simon Guggenheim Found, 91-92; fel, OAH Japanese Am Studies Asn, 97; fel, Am Col Obstetricians & Gynecologists, 91; fel, Soc Am Hist, 98-. **MEMBERSHIPS** Orgn Am Historians; Berkshire Womens Hist Conf; ASA; AAHM. **RESEARCH** Nineteenth century social and cultural history of the United States; history of women, childhood, and the family; history of medicine. **SELECTED PUBLICATIONS** Auth, Mission for Life: The Judson Family and American Evangelical Culture, The Free Press, 80, NY Univ Press pb, 84; coauth, Women in the professions: A research agenda for American historians, in Rev Am Hist, 6/82; auth, Zenanas and Girlless villages: The ethnology of American evangelical women, 1870-1910, in J Am Hist, 9/82; Chlorotic girls, 1870 to 1920: An historical perspective on female adolescence, in Child Develop, 12/82; Fasting Girls: The Emergence of Anorexia Nervosa as a Modern Disease, Harvard Univ Press, 88 (selected for numerous book prizes); The Body Project: An Intimate History of American Girls, Random House, 97; auth numerous articles and book reviews. **CONTACT ADDRESS** Dept of Human Development, Cornell Univ, Martha Van Rensselaer Hall, Ithaca, NY, 14853-0001. **EMAIL** jjb10@cornell.edu

BRUMFIELD, WILLIAM CRAFT
PERSONAL Born 06/28/1944, Charlotte, NC **DISCIPLINE** RUSSIAN LITERATURE & ART HISTORY **EDUCATION** Tulane Univ, BA, 66; Univ Calif, Berkeley, MA, 68, PhD(Slavic lang), 73 **CAREER** Vis lectr Russ lit, Univ Wis-Madison, 73-74; asst prof Russ lit, Harvard Univ, 74-79; ASST PROF RUSS LIT, TULANE UNIV, 81-, Res dir, ACTR Moscow, 79-80. **MEMBERSHIPS** Am Asn Advan Slavic Studies; Am Asn Teachers Slavic East Europ Lang; MLA. **RESEARCH** Ideology in the Russian novel of the 1860's; Dostoevsky and the French Enlightenment; Russian architectural history. **SELECTED PUBLICATIONS** Auth, Sleptsov redvius, Calif Slavic Studies, 76; Bazarov and Rjazanov: The romantic archetype in Russian nihilism, Slavic East Europ J, winter 77; Petersburg: the imperial design, 11/78, Harvard Mag; Therese philosophe and Dostoevsky's Great Sinner, Comp Lit, summer 80; Ukrainian Churches: Kiev and Chernihiv, Harvard Ukrainian Fund, 81; The Soviet Union: Post-war architecture and planning, Bull Atomic Scientists, 3/82; Le-Corbusier and the Mystique of the USSR - Theories and Projects for Moscow 1928-1936 - Cohen,JL/, Am Hist Rev, Vol 98, 1993; Architecture and Ideology in Eastern-Europe during the Stalin Era - An Aspect of Cold-War History - Aman,A/, Slavic Rev, Vol 53, 1994; Moscow and Leningrad, A Topographical Guide to Russian Cultural History, Vol 1, Buildings and Builders, Vol 2, Writers, Painters, Musicians and their Gathering Places - Ward,CA/, Slavic Rev, Vol 54, 1995; The Church-of-Christ-the-Savior in Moscow - Russian - Kirichenko,EI/, Slavic Rev, Vol 55, 1996; A History of St. Petersburg - French - Berelowitch,W, Medvedkova,o/, Slavic Rev, Vol 56, 1997; The Development of Medieval Church Architecture in the Vologda Region of the Russian North/, Architect Hist, Vol 40, 1997. **CONTACT ADDRESS** Dept of Ger & Slavic Lang, Tulane Univ, 6823 St Charles Ave, New Orleans, LA, 70118-5698.

BRUMMETT, PALMIRA
DISCIPLINE HISTORY **EDUCATION** Univ Chicago, PhD. **CAREER** Assoc prof. **RESEARCH** Ottoman history. **SELECTED PUBLICATIONS** Auth, Ottoman Seapower and Levantine Diplomacy in the Age of Discovery, NY State Univ. **CONTACT ADDRESS** Dept of History, Knoxville, TN, 37996.

BRUNDAGE, JAMES A.
PERSONAL Born 02/05/1929, Lincoln, NE, d, 6 children **DISCIPLINE** HISTORY **EDUCATION** Univ Nebraska, BA, 50, MA, 51; Fordham Univ, PhD, 55. **CAREER** Lectr, 53-55, Fordham Univ; Asst Prof, 57-60, Univ Wisconsin Milwaukee; Assoc Prof, Prof, Ahmanson-Murphy Dist Prof hist, 60 to 89-, Univ Kansas; Courtesy Prof law, 90-. **HONORS AND AWARDS** Guggenheim Fel; Fulbright Fel Spain; NEH Fel. **MEMBERSHIPS** RHS; MAA; ASLH; CLSA; AHA; ACHA. **RESEARCH** History of Medieval Law; Canon Law; Roman Law; Ius Commune; History of Universities; History of the Crusades. **SELECTED PUBLICATIONS** Auth, Obscene and Lascivious: Behavior Obscenity in Canon Law, in: Obscenity: Social Control and Artistic Creation in the European Middle Ages, ed, Jan M Ziolkowski, Cultures Beliefs and Traditions: Medieval and Early Modern Peoples, Leiden Brill, 98; auth, Taxation of Costs in Medieval Cononical Courts, in: Forschungen zur Reichs-Papst und Landesgeschichte: Peter Herde zum 65, Geburtstag, ed, Karl Borchardt, Enno Bunz, Stuttgart, Anton Hiersemann, 98; The Calumny Oath and Ethical Ideals of Canonical Advocates, in: Proceedings of the Ninth Intl Congress of Medieval Canon Law, ed, Peter Landau, Joers Mueller, Vatican City, BAV, 97; coed, Handbook of Medieval sexuality, NY, Garland, 96; Medieval Canon Law, London, Longmans, 95; auth, Sex Law and Marriage in the Middle Ages, London, Variorum, 93. **CONTACT ADDRESS** 1102 Sunset Dr, Lawrence, KS, 66044-4548. **EMAIL** jabrun@kuhub.cc.ukans.edu

BRUNER, EDWARD M.
PERSONAL Born 09/28/1924, New York, NY, m, 1948, 2 children **DISCIPLINE** ANTHROPOLOGY **EDUCATION** Univ Chicago, PhD 54; OH State Univ, MA 50, BA 48. **CAREER** Yale Univ, asst prof 54-60; Center for Advanced Study, Fell 60-61; Univ IL, assoc prof, 61-94; prof emeritus 94. **HONORS AND AWARDS** Campus Awd for Tchg; Pres, AES; pres, SHA. **MEMBERSHIPS** AAA; SHA; AES; SCA. **RESEARCH** Tourism, culture change, interpretive anthropology, Indonesia. **SELECTED PUBLICATIONS** Tourism in Ghana: The Representation of Slavery and the Return of the Black Diaspora, Amer Anthro; 96; Tourism in the Balinese Borderzone, In Displacement, Diaspora and Geographies of Identity, ed, Smadar Lavie and Ted Sewdenburg, Durham, Duke Univ Press, 96; Maasai on the Lawn: Tourist Realism in East Africa, with Barbara Kirshenblatt-Gimblett, Cultural Anthropology, 94; numerous publications. **CONTACT ADDRESS** Dept of Anthrop, Univ Illinois, 607 South Mathews, Urbana, IL, 61801. **EMAIL** ebruner@uiuc.edu

BRUNO, JAMES EDWARD
DISCIPLINE EDUCATION; ECONOMICS; ENGINEERING **EDUCATION** UCLA, PhD, 68. **CAREER** PROF EDUCATION, UCLA **HONORS AND AWARDS** EUCLAN Res Award **MEMBERSHIPS** AERA; ORSA **RESEARCH** Temporal orientation and human behavior; Decision analysis-operations research; Information referenced testing and assessment. **SELECTED PUBLICATIONS** coauth, Item Banking: Interactive Testing and Self Assessment, Springer-Verlag, Berling, 93; auth Time in the lifetime of a Teacher: Educational Leadership in an Era of Time Scarcity, Corwin Press, 97. **CONTACT ADDRESS** Dept of Education, UCLouisiana, 1032A Moore Hall, Los Angeles, CA, 90095. **EMAIL** jbruno@ucla.edu

BRUNVAND, JAN HAROLD
PERSONAL Born 03/23/1933, Cadillac, MI, m, 1956, 4 children **DISCIPLINE** FOLKLORE **EDUCATION** Mich State Univ, BA, 55, MA, 57; Ind Univ, PhD, 61. **CAREER** Asst prof English, Univ Idaho, 61-65; assoc prof, Southern Ill Univ, 65-66; assoc prof, 66-71, PROF ENGLISH, UNIV UTAH, 71-, Fulbright grant & Guggenheim Found fel, Romania, 70-71, Int Res & Exchanges Bd grant, Romania, 73-74 & 81; ed, J Am Folklore, 76-80. **MEMBERSHIPS** Am Folklore Soc. **RESEARCH** The folktale; Romanian folklore; American folklore. **SELECTED PUBLICATIONS** Auth, A Dictionary of Proverbs and Proverbial Phrases From Books Published by Indiana Authors Before 1890, Ind Univ, 61; The folktale origin of The Taming of the Shrew, Shakespeare Quart, autumn 66; The Study of American Folklore, Norton, 68, 2nd ed, 78; A Guide For Collectors of Folklore in Utah, Univ Utah, 71; The study of Romanian folklore, J Folklore Inst, 72; Folklore: A Study and Research Guide, St Martins, 79; Readings in Am Folklore, 79 & The Vanishing Hitchhiker: American Urban Legends and Their Meanings, 81, Norton; Creativity and Tradition in Folklore - New Directions - Bronner,SJ/, Western Folklore, Vol 53, 1994. **CONTACT ADDRESS** Dept of English, Univ of Utah, Salt Lake City, UT, 84112.

BRUSH, STEPHEN GEORGE
PERSONAL Bangor, ME, m, 1960, 2 children **DISCIPLINE** HISTORY OF SCIENCE **EDUCATION** Harvard Univ, AB, 55; Oxford Univ, DPhil, 58. **CAREER** NSF fel physics, Imp Col, Univ London, 58-59; physicist, Lawrence Radiation Lab, Univ Calif, Livermore, 59-65; res assoc educ, Harvard Proj Physics, Harvard Univ, 65-68, lectr physics & hist sci, 66-68; assoc prof, 68-71, PROF, DEPT HIST & INST PHYS SCI & TECHNOL, UNIV MD, COLLEGE PARK, 71-; Prin investr res grants, NSF, 65-; adv ed, Isis, 79-. **HONORS AND AWARDS** Pfizer Award, Hist Sci Soc, 77; Distinguished Univ Prof of Hist of Sci, 95. **MEMBERSHIPS** Hist Sci Soc; Am Phys Soc; AAAS; Am Hist Asn. **RESEARCH** History of modern physical science, especially geophysics and astrophysics. **SELECTED PUBLICATIONS** Auth, Kinetic Theory (3 vols), Pergamon, New York, 65, 66 & 72; ed, Resources for the History of Physics, 72 & co-ed, History in the Teaching of Physics, 72, Univ New England; coauth, Introduction to Concepts and Theories in Physical Science, Addison-Wesley Publ Co, 73; auth, The Kind of Motion We Call Heat: A History of the Kinetic Theory of Gases in the 19th Century, North-Holland, 76; The Temperature of History; Phases of Science & Culture in the 19th Century, Burt Franklin, 78; Statistical Physics and the Atomic Theory of Matter from Boyle and Newton to Landau and Unsager, 83; A History of Modern Planetary Physics, 96. **CONTACT ADDRESS** Dept of Hist, Univ of Md, College Park, MD, 20742-0001. **EMAIL** brush@ipst.umd.edu

BRUSTER, DOUGLAS
DISCIPLINE FINE ARTS AND HUMANITIES **EDUCATION** Univ NE, BA; Harvard Univ, MA, PhD. **CAREER** Asst prof; taught at, Harvard Univ & Univ Chicago. **RESEARCH** Shakespeare and early mod drama; poetry of early mod Engl; 20th-century drama and film; critical theory. **SELECTED PUBLICATIONS** Auth, Drama and the Market in the Age of Shakespeare, Cambridge UP, 92; publ on, lit and cult of early mod Engl. **CONTACT ADDRESS** Col of Fine Arts and Hum, Univ Texas at San Antonio, 6900 N Loop 1604 W, San Antonio, TX, 78249.

BRUZELIUS, CAROLINE
DISCIPLINE ART HISTORY **EDUCATION** Yale Univ, PhD. **CAREER** Hist, Duke Univ. **HONORS AND AWARDS** Duke Alumni Distinguished Tchg Award, 85. **RESEARCH** Gothic archit and sculpture in France and Italy. **SELECTED PUBLICATIONS** Auth, The Thirteenth Century Church at Saint Denis; The Architecture of the Cistercians in the Early Thirteenth Century. **CONTACT ADDRESS** Dept of Art and Art Hist, Duke Univ, East Duke Building, Durham, NC, 27706.

BRYAN, JESSE A.
PERSONAL Born 06/15/1939, Red Springs, North Carolina, m, 1950 **DISCIPLINE** EDUCATION **EDUCATION** Johnson C Smith Univ, Undergrad Degree 1964; Univ of GA, Grad Studies 1964; Temple Univ, MEd 1968; Univ of Toledo, PhD 1977. **CAREER** Admissions Glassboro State Coll, numerous positions & assoc dir 1969-70; Student Field Experience Office Univ of Toledo, admin asst 1970-71; Univ of Toledo, dir upward bound 1971-73; Bloomsburg Univ, dir center for acad devel 1973-87, dir, Dept of Dev Instr, beginning 1987, retired. **HONORS AND AWARDS** Special Recognition Ed Opportunity Ctr, Ctr for Acad Devel; Two Advisory Awards Third World Cultural Soc; Advisory Award Kappa Alpha Psi Lambda Alpha; Vol Leader Awd Young Men's Christian Assoc; special award from former students. **MEMBERSHIPS** Mem Kappa Alpha Psi Fraternity 1961-; mem Phi Delta Kappa 1972-; dir Act 101 Program 1973-; mem Act 101 Exec Comm 1973-83; Black Conf on Higher Educ 1973-; mem Western Reg of Act 101 1978-; mem Kiwanis Intl 1979-; pres Equal Educ Oppor Program 1980-. **CONTACT ADDRESS** Professor Emeritus, Bloomsburg Univ of Pennsylvania, Waller Administration Bldg Room #14, Bloomsburg, PA, 17815.

BRYANT, BUNYAN I.
PERSONAL Born 03/06/1935, Little Rock, Arkansas, m, 1993 **DISCIPLINE** EDUCATION **EDUCATION** Eastern MI Univ, BS, 1958; Univ of MI, Social Work, MSW, 1965; Univ of MI, Education, PhD, 1970. **CAREER** Univ of MI, School of Natu-

ral Resources & Environment, prof. **HONORS AND AWARDS** MLK Dreamkeeper Award, Distinguished Leadership to the Environmental Justice Movement Award; Environmental Justice Advisory Council, Recognition Award. **MEMBERSHIPS** League of Conservation, bd mem; USEPA Clean Air Act, advisory comm. **SELECTED PUBLICATIONS** Author/editor, Environmental Justice: Issues, Policies & Solutions, 1995; Race & the Indicence of Environmental Hazards, Westview Press, Baulder, 1992. **CONTACT ADDRESS** Professor, Univ of MI School of Natural Resources & Environment, 430 E University, Dana Bldg, Rm 1536, Ann Arbor, MI, 48109.

BRYSON, WILLIAM HAMILTON
PERSONAL Born 07/29/1941, Richmond, VA **DISCIPLINE** ENGLISH & AMERICAN LEGAL HISTORY **EDUCATION** Hampden-Sydney Col, BA, 63; Harvard Univ, LLB, 67; Univ Va, LLM, 68; Cambridge Univ, PhD, 72. **CAREER** Max Planck Inst grant, Frankfurt, 72-73; prof law, Univ Richmond, 73-. **HONORS AND AWARDS** Yorke Prize, Cambridge Univ, 73; Am Coun Learned Soc fel, 80. **MEMBERSHIPS** Fel Royal Hist Soc; Selden Soc; Am Soc Legal Hist; Medieval Acad Am. **RESEARCH** English legal history (particularly the history of equity); Virginia legal institutions; Virginia civil procedure. **SELECTED PUBLICATIONS** Auth, Dict of Sigla and Abbreviations to and in Law Books Before 1607, Hein, 96; ed, Legal Education in Virginia, 1779-1979, Univ Press Va, 82; ed, Sir John Randolph's King's Bench Reports, Hein, 96. **CONTACT ADDRESS** Law School, Univ of Richmond, 28 Westhampton Way, Richmond, VA, 23173-0002.

BUCCELLATI, GIORGIO
PERSONAL Born 02/08/1937, Milano, Italy, m, 1966 **DISCIPLINE** HISTORY OF MESOPOTAMIA & SYRIA **EDUCATION** Cath Univ Sacred Heart, Milan, Phil Dr (hist), 58; Fordham Univ, MA, 60; Univ Chicago, PhD(Orient lang), 65. **CAREER** Instr hist, Loyola Univ, Ill, 63-65; from asst prof to prof, 65-76, DIR, INST ARCHAEOL, UNIV CALIF, LOS ANGELES, 76-, Epigrapher Cuneiform texts, Orient Inst, Chicago, 62-63 & 66-67; Am Sch Orient Res fel, Bagdad, 62-63; Univ Calif Humanities Inst fel, 66 & 68; co-dir archeol exped, Korucu Tepe, Turkey, 68-72; vis prof Assyriol, Pontif Bibl Inst, Rome, 72; dir, Old Babylon Ling Anal Proj, 72-; gen ed, Monographic Journals of the Near East, Undena Publ, 74; dir, Joint Exped to Terga, Syria, 76- **MEMBERSHIPS** Am Orient Soc; AHA; Soc Bibl Lit; Cath Bibl Asn Am; Soc Am Archaeol. **RESEARCH** Political institutions of Syria and Mesopotamia; archaeology of Mesopotamia; Akkadian linguistics. **SELECTED PUBLICATIONS** Auth, Cities and Nations of Ancient Syria, Univ Rome, 67; An interpretation of the Akkadian stative, J Near Eastern Studies, 68; coauth, Cuneiform Texts from Nippur, Orient Inst, Chicago, 69; auth, On the use of Akkadian infinitive after sha or construct state, J Semitic Studies, 72; Tre saggi sulla sapienza Mesopotamia, Oriens Antiquus, 72; ed, Approach to the Study of the Ancient Near East, Pontif Bibl Inst Rome, 73; auth, Terga preliminary report, Vol 10, 80; co-ed, The Shape of the Past, 81; Urkesh, the first Hurrian Capital/, Bibl Archaeol, Vol 60, 1997. **CONTACT ADDRESS** Dept New Eastern Lang, Univ Calif, Los Angeles, CA, 90024.

BUCHANAN, DONNA A.
DISCIPLINE MUSIC **EDUCATION** Beloit Col, BA; Univ TX, PhD. **CAREER** Asst prof, 97-, Univ IL at Chicago. **RESEARCH** Musical styles of Bulgaria; music as symbolic commun; music in aesthetic syst; music and power rel(s); music and cosmology; and music and soc identity. **SELECTED PUBLICATIONS** Auth, Performing Democracy: Bulgarian Music and Musicians in Transition, 97; pubs in Ethnomusicology. **CONTACT ADDRESS** Dept of Music, Univ Illinois Urbana Champaign, E Gregory Dr, PO Box 52, Champaign, IL, 61820. **EMAIL** buchana1@uiuc.edu

BUCHANAN, HARVEY
PERSONAL Born 09/18/1923, New Haven, CT **DISCIPLINE** HISTORY, ART HISTORY **EDUCATION** Yale Univ, BA, 44, MA, 48, PhD(hist), 53. **CAREER** From instr to assoc prof, 52-64, head dept humanities & soc sci, 63-68, assoc dean humanities & fine arts, 68-71, dean, 71-72, provost, 72-77, PROF HIST, CASE WESTERN RESERVE UNIV, 64-, PROF HUMANITIES, 77-, Relief worker, Am Friends Serv Comt, Normandy, Ger & Palestine, 45-49; Fulbright scholar, Crose Inst, Naples, Italy, 49-51; mem Nat Bd Consults, Nat Endowment for Humanities, 75-. **HONORS AND AWARDS** Ordre des Palmes Academiques, Fr Govt, 75. **MEMBERSHIPS** AHA; Am Soc Reformation Res; Renaissance Soc Am; Ancient Hist Soc, Naples. **RESEARCH** The enlightenment of Italy; Luther and the Turks; Renaissance political thought. **CONTACT ADDRESS** Mather Hall, Case Western Reserve Univ, Cleveland, OH, 44106.

BUCHOLZ, ARDEN
PERSONAL Born 05/14/1936, Chicago, IL, m, 1962, 2 children **DISCIPLINE** HISTORY **EDUCATION** Dartmouth Col, AB, 58; Univ Vienna, Dipl, 60; Univ Chicago, AM, 65, PhD, 72. **CAREER** INSTR TO PROF OF HIST, STATE UNIV NY-BROCKPORT, 70-; Co-dir, SUNY Prog, Brunel Univ, 87-88; teacher of hist, Latin School of Chicago, 65-70; Teacher of English, Staples High School, Conn, 64; Teacher of English, Amerika Orta Okulu, Talas-Kayseri, Turkey, 58-60. **HONORS AND AWARDS** SUNY Chancellor's Award for Excellence in Teaching, 77. **MEMBERSHIPS** Am Hist Asn **RESEARCH** Modern German military hist. **SELECTED PUBLICATIONS** Auth, reviews in Am Hist Rev, Jour of Modern Hist, Militaergeschichtliche Mitteilungen, Tech and Culture, Jour of World Hist; auth, articles in Research Guide to European Biography, Encyclopedia of Nationalism, Oxford Companion to American Military History, American National Biography, Oxford Companion to Military History. **CONTACT ADDRESS** 13510 Roosevelt Hwy, Waterport, NY, 14571. **EMAIL** abucholz@acspr1.acs.brockport.edu

BUCK, DAVID D.
PERSONAL Born 12/31/1936, Denver, CO, m, 1964, 2 children **DISCIPLINE** CHINESE HISTORY **EDUCATION** Stanford Univ, AB, 58, PhD, 71; Harvard Univ, MA, 60. **CAREER** Instr, 69-71, asst prof, 72-76, chmn dept, 78-81, assoc prof hist, Univ WI-Milwaukee, 77-88; prof , Univ WI-Milwaukee, 88-;Assoc Dir, Center Intl Studies, 91-; Dir, inst World affairs, 97-; Dir, Inter-Univ Prog Chinese Lang Studies, Taipei, 71-72. **MEMBERSHIPS** AHA; Asn Asian Studies. **RESEARCH** Chinese soc hist; late Ch'ing and Republican periods. **SELECTED PUBLICATIONS** Auth, China and Containment of Ethnonationlism: Global Convulsions, SUNY Press, 97; Pearl Buck in Search of Am: The Several Worlds of Pearl Buck, Greenwood, 94; ed, Ethnic and Cultural Nationalism in Asia, Jnl of Asian Studies, 94; Universalism and Relativism in Asian Studies, Jnl of Asian Studies, 92; Recent Chinese Studies of the Boxer Movement, ME Sharpe, 86; Urban Change in China, Univ WI, 78. **CONTACT ADDRESS** Inst World Affairs, Univ of Wisconsin, Milwaukee, 3271 N Lake Dr, Milwaukee, WI, 53211. **EMAIL** davebuck@uwm.edu

BUCK, HARRY MERWYN
PERSONAL Born 11/18/1921, Enola, PA, m, 1943, 2 children **DISCIPLINE** HISTORY OF RELIGIONS **EDUCATION** Albright Col, AB, 42; Evangel Sch Theol, MDiv, 45; Univ Chicago, PhD, 54. **CAREER** Pastor, Evangel United Brethren Church, Md, 42-46, Pa, 46-49; from instr to asst prof Bibl hist, 51-59, assoc prof Bible & relig, 59-68, prof Relig Studies, Wilson Col, 68-; consult, New Testament Greek Text Proj, Am Bible Soc, 55; mem, East-West Philosophers Conf, Honolulu, Hawaii, 59; comt lectionary study, Int Greek New Testament Proj, 59-; seminar Indian Civilization, Hyderabad, India, 61; managing ed, J Am Acad Relig, 61-73; chmn, Am Textual Criticism Sem, 60-62; fac training fel, Am Inst Indian Studies & hist relig fel, Soc Relig Higher Educ, 65-66; partic fel, Int Conf-Sem on Tamil Studies, Univ Malaya, 66; ed, Anima, 74-. **MEMBERSHIPS** Am Acad Relig; Soc Bibl Lit; Soc Study New Testament; Asn Asian Studies; Int Soc Study Relig. **RESEARCH** Epic literature of South Asia; function of sacred tradition; methodology in the history of religions. **SELECTED PUBLICATIONS** Co-ed, Religious Traditions and the Limits of Tolerance, Anima, 88; auth, Rama in Buddhist Cultures, 95; art, Beyond Walls, Fences, and Interreligious Dialogue, J of Ecumenical Stories, 97; auth, Beware the Self Evident, Dharma World, 98. **CONTACT ADDRESS** 1053 Wilson Ave, Chambersburg, PA, 17201.

BUCK, ROBERT J.
PERSONAL Born 07/05/1926, Vermilion, AB, Canada **DISCIPLINE** CLASSICS **EDUCATION** Univ Alta, BA, 49; Univ Kentucky, MA, 50; Univ Cincinnati, PhD, 56. **CAREER** Asst prof, Univ Kentucky, 55-60; assoc prof, 60-66, head dept, 64-72, prof, 66-91, PROF EMER CLASSICS, UNIV ALTA, 91-; mng comt, Am Sch Classical Stud (Athens), 61-83. **HONORS AND AWARDS** Fel, Can Inst Rome, 76. **MEMBERSHIPS** Can Mediter Inst; Can Archaeol Inst Athens; Class Asn Can. **RESEARCH** Greek history; Greek and Roman archaeology. **SELECTED PUBLICATIONS** Auth, A History of Boetia, 79; coauth, The Excavations of San Giovanni di Ruoti, vol I 93, vol II 96. **CONTACT ADDRESS** Classics Dept, Univ of Alberta, Edmonton, AB, T6G 2E5.

BUCKLAND, ROSCOE LAWRENCE
PERSONAL Born 07/28/1918, Blackfoot, ID, m, 1941, 2 children **DISCIPLINE** ENGLISH, AMERICAN CIVILIZATION **EDUCATION** Univ Idaho, BA & MA, 48; State Univ Iowa, PhD(Am civilization), 55. **CAREER** Instr English, Wash State Col, 48-51; from asst prof to prof, Long Beach State Col, 55-70, chmn dept, 60-68; chmn dept, 70-78, PROF LIB STUDIES, WESTERN WASH UNIV, 70-, Asst, Univ Iowa, 52-55; lectr, Workers Educ Asn & Nat Arts Coun, Sydney, Australia, 68-69. **MEMBERSHIPS** Am Studies Asn; Brit Asn Am Studies; Am Cult Asn; Western Lit Asn; Am Folklore Asn. **RESEARCH** Australian and American frontier literature; American folklore; 19th century popular culture. **SELECTED PUBLICATIONS** Auth, Harte,Bret - Scharnhorst,G/, Studies in Short Fiction, Vol 30, 1993; On the Oregon Trail - Nichols,J/, Western Am Lit, Vol 29, 1994; Varieties of Hope - An Anthology of Oregon Prose - Dodds,GB/, Pacific Northwest Quarterly, Vol 85, 1994; Mark-Twain and the Art of the Tall-Tale - Wonham,HB/, Studies in Short Fiction, Vol 31, 1994; Kanaka - The Untold Story of Hawaiian Pioneers in British-Columbia and the Pacific-Northwest - Koppel,T/, Western Am Lit, Vol 30, 1995; The Island of California - A History of the Myth - Polk,DB/, Western Am Lit, Vol 31, 1996. **CONTACT ADDRESS** Dept of Lib Studies, Western Washington Univ, Bellingham, WA, 98225.

BUCKLER, JOHN
DISCIPLINE GREEK HISTORY **EDUCATION** Univ Louisville, AB, 67; Am School of Classical Studies, Athens, 70-71; Harvard Univ, MA, 68, PhD(hist), 73. **CAREER** Vis lectr, 73-75, asst prof, 75-80, assoc prof, 80-89, prof hist, Univ IL, 90-; Alexander von Humboldt fel, Univ Munich, 84-86. **HONORS AND AWARDS** Am Coun Learned Soc, 83; Am Philos Soc, 83; Deutscher Akademischer Austauschdienst, 84; Alexander von Humboldt Found, 84-. **MEMBERSHIPS** Am Ancient Hist. **RESEARCH** Greek history; fourth century BC; Greek topopography, Greek diplomatic and military hist. **SELECTED PUBLICATIONS** Auth, Theban Treaty Obligations in IG II2 40, Historia, 71; Dating the peace of 375/4 BC, Greek, Roman, & Byzantine Studies, 71; A Second Look at the Monument of Chabrias, Hesperia, 72; coauth, The Wrong Salamis?, Rheinisches Mus Philol, 75; auth, The Thespians at Leuktra, Wiener Studien, 77; Plutarch and the Fate of Antalkidas, Greek, Roman, & Byzantine Studies, 77; Land and Money in the Spartan Economy, Res Econ Hist, 77; Plutarch on the Trials of Pelopidas and Epameinondas (369 BC), Class Philol, 78; The Alleged Achaian Arbitration after Leuktra, Symbolae Osloenses, 78; The Theban Hegemony, 371-362 BC, 80; Philip II and the Sacred War, 89; coauth, A History of Western Societies, 6 eds, A History of World Socities, 5 eds, Boiotika: Vortrage vom 5, Int Bootien-Kolloquium, 89; William Abbott Oldfather, Encyclopedia of Classical Scholars, 90; Plutarch and Autopsy, Aufstieg und Niedergang der romischen Welt, 91; Il Federalismo in Grecia e in America, Federazione e federalismo nell'Europa antica, 94; co-ed, Of the Athenian Government, George Grote Reconsidered, 96; Philip's Designs on Greece, Transitions to Empire, 96; Helikon and Klio, La Montagne des Muses, 96; 56 articles in American Historical Association's Guide to Historical Literature, 3rd ed, 95; 28 articles, The Oxford Classical Dictionary, 3rd ed, 96; 6 articles, Encyclopedia of Greece and the Hellenic Tradition, 99; and more than 50 other articles. **CONTACT ADDRESS** Dept Hist, Univ Illinois, 810 S Wright St, Urbana, IL, 61801-3611. **EMAIL** jbuckler@uxl.cso.uiuc.edu

BUCKLEY, THOMAS HUGH
PERSONAL Born 09/11/1932, Elkhart, IN, m, 5 children **DISCIPLINE** HISTORY **EDUCATION** Ind Univ, AB, 55, MA, 56, PhD, 61. **CAREER** From instr to prof hist, Univ SDak, 60-71; chmn dept, 71-81, chmn fac humanistic studies, 74-81, PROF HIST, UNIV TULSA, 71-, Assoc Dean of the Graduate Sch, 95-; vis prof hist, Ind Univ, 69-71; ed, Research and Roster Guide, Soc Historians Am Foreign Rels, 80-83. **HONORS AND AWARDS** Denver Sch Int Rels res fel, 64-65; Stanford Univ fel, 68-69; Best First Bk by Hist Award, Phi Alpha Theta, 71; Fulbright, Univ Western Australia, 86. **MEMBERSHIPS** Orgn Am Hist; AHA; Soc Hist Am Foreign Rels. **RESEARCH** American policy; American East Asian policies; national defense and national security since 1939. **SELECTED PUBLICATIONS** Auth, The United States and the Washington Conference, 1921-1922, Univ Tenn, 70; ed, Challenge Was My Master, Univ Tulsa, 79; contribr, Guide to US Foreign Relation Since 1700, Clio, 82; auth, Walter Helmerich, Independent Oilman, Okla, 82; contribr, Treaty Ratification, St. Martin's Press, 91; Encyclopedia of Arms Control and Disarmament, Scribner's, 92; The Washington Conference; The Politics of Arms control, Cross, 94; **CONTACT ADDRESS** Dept of History, Univ of Tulsa, 600 S College, Tulsa, OK, 74104-3126.

BUCKNER, PHILLIP ALFRED
PERSONAL Born 06/04/1942, Toronto, ON, Canada, m, 1969 **DISCIPLINE** CANADIAN HISTORY, BRITISH IMPERIAL HISTORY **EDUCATION** Univ Toronto, BA, 65; Univ London, PhD(hist), 69. **CAREER** Lectr, 68-69, asst prof, 69-79, PROF HIST, UNIV NB, FREDERICTON, 80-, Ed, Acadiensis: J Hist Atlantic Region, 70-74; mem, Can Hist Asn-Am Hist Asn Coord Comt, 73- **MEMBERSHIPS** Can Hist Asn; Can Asn Univ Teachers. **RESEARCH** Nineteenth century British imperial history. **SELECTED PUBLICATIONS** Auth, Governors and Settlers - Images of Authority in the British Colonies, 1820-1860 - Francis,M/, Int Hist Rev, Vol 15, 1993. **CONTACT ADDRESS** Dept Hist, Univ of NB, Fredericton, NB, E3B 5A3.

BUDDS, MICHAEL
PERSONAL IL **DISCIPLINE** MUSIC HISTORY AND LITERATURE **EDUCATION** Knox Col; Univ Iowa, PhD. **CAREER** Assoc prof & coordr, Music Hist and Lit; actv, Col Music Soc, Ed, annual proc, mem Bd Dir, CMS Publ Inc, mem ed bd Col Music Symp, Bibliographies and Monographs in Amer Music & CMS Reports; ed, publ series Monographs and Bibliographies in Amer Music. **RESEARCH** American music; history of African-American music; music in Victorian England. **SELECTED PUBLICATIONS** Auth, monograph Jazz in the Sixties, 2nd ed, 90; coauth, sourcebk Rock Recall: Readings in American Popular Music from the Emergence of Rock and Roll to the Demise of the Woodstock Nation, 93; ed, Source Readings in American Choral Music, 96; contribur, The New Grove Dictionary of American Music, the New Grove Dictionary of Jazz, Women & Music: A History. **CONTACT ADDRESS** Dept of Music, Univ of Missouri-Columbia, 140 Fine Arts Bldg, Columbia, MO, 65211. **EMAIL** musicmjb@showme.missouri.edu

BUEL, RICHARD (VAN WYCK)
PERSONAL Born 07/22/1933, Morristown, NJ, m, 1992, 1 child **DISCIPLINE** HISTORY **EDUCATION** Amherst Coll, Amherst, MA, 55, BA: Harvard Univ, Cambridge, MA, 57, Phd 62. **CAREER** Asst Prof, Wesleyan Univ, 62-69; Asoc Prof, Wesleyan Univ, 69-75; Full Prof Wesleyan Univ, 75. **HONORS AND AWARDS** PBIC; ACLS Fac Fellowships 67-68, 74-75, NEH fellowships, 71-72, 85, Guggenheim Fellowship, 86; Chauks Warren Fellowship, 67-68; John Couta Brown Library Fellowship, 86. **MEMBERSHIPS** Amer Hist Assoc; Organization of Amer Hist; Amer Hist and Culture Soc for Hist, at Ke Eovly Amer Rep; CT Academy of Arts and Sci; Soc for Ke Study at CT Hist. **RESEARCH** Revolutionary Amer 1730-1830. **SELECTED PUBLICATIONS** Scanning the Revolution, 72; Dear Liberty, 80; The Way of Duty, 84; In Iran 98. **CONTACT ADDRESS** Dept of Hist, Wesleyan Univ, Middleton, CT, 06457. **EMAIL** Rbucl@Wesleyan.edu

BUELOW, GEORGE JOHN
PERSONAL Born 03/31/1929, Chicago, IL **DISCIPLINE** MUSICOLOGY **EDUCATION** Chicago Musical Col, BM, 50, MM, 51; NY Univ, PhD, 61. **CAREER** Instr music hist, Chicago Conserv Music, 59-61; assoc prof, Univ Calif, Riverside, 61-68; prof & chmn dept, Univ Ky, 68-69; prof music, coord chmn dept & dir grad studies, Rutgers Univ, New Brunswick, 69-77; PROF MUSICOL, IND UNIV, BLOOMINGTON, 77-; Am ed, Acta Musicologica, 67-86; mem exec comt, The New Grove Dict Music & Musicians, 6th ed, 72-80; fac res fel, Rutgers State Univ, 74-75; gen ed, Studies in Musicol, Univ Microfilms Res Press, 77-90; co-chmn, Int Johann Mattheson Symp, Wolfenbuttel, Ger, 81; co-ed, New Mattheson Studies, Cambridge Univ Press, 83; ed comt, Documenta musicologica, 81-. **HONORS AND AWARDS** Fulbright scholar, Univ Hamburg, 54-55; Guggenheim fel, 67; The "Martin Bernstein" Lectr, NYU, 85. **MEMBERSHIPS** Am Musicol Soc; Int Musicol Soc; Gesellschaft fur Musikforschung; Am Bach Soc (pres 87-91); Am Handel Soc (vpres 89-91); Soc 17th Century Music. **RESEARCH** Baroque music and performance practices; the history of opera; the music of Richard Strauss. **SELECTED PUBLICATIONS** Ed & auth, Music and Society--The Late Baroque, Macmillan, 93; The Italian Influence in Heinichen's Der General-Bass in der Composition, Basler Jahrbuch fur Historische Musikpraxis 18, Amadeus, Basel, 94; co-ed, Musicology and Performance, Essays of Paul Henry Lang, Yale, New Haven, 97; author of numerous other articles and publications. **CONTACT ADDRESS** Sch of Music, Indiana Univ, Bloomington, 1 Indiana University, Bloomington, IN, 47405.

BUENKER, JOHN D.
PERSONAL Born 08/11/1937, Dubuque, IA, m, 1962, 5 children **DISCIPLINE** UNITED STATES HISTORY **EDUCATION** Loras Col, BA, 59; Georgetown Univ, MA, 62, PhD, 64. **CAREER** Instr hist, Prince George's Community Col, 62-65; asst prof, Eastern Ill Univ, 65-70; assoc prof, 70-73, dir ethnic studies, Ctr Multicult Studies, 77-81, 88-91, prof hist, Univ of Wis Parkside, 73-, Vis Prof, Holy Redeemer Col, 73-85; Vis Prof, Univ Wis-Madison, 86-87. **HONORS AND AWARDS** William Adee Whitehead Award, NJ Hist Soc, 70; Harry E Pratt Award, Ill State Hist Soc, 71; John Simon Guggenheim Found fel, 75-76; Newberry Libr fel, 79; Univ Wis-Parkside Award for Excellence in Schol Activity, 89; Wis CASE Prof of the Year, 90-91; SEastern Wis Educ Hall of Fame, 91; Fel, Univ Wis System Ctr for Res in the Humanities, 91-92. **MEMBERSHIPS** Orgn Am Hist; Immigration Hist Soc; Urban Hist Asn; Soc Hist of the Gilded Age and Progressive Era; Nat Coun for Hist Educ; Kappa Delta Pi; Phi Kappa Delta. **RESEARCH** Immigration, urban; the progressive era. **SELECTED PUBLICATIONS** Auth, The Urban Political Machine and the Seventeenth Amendment, J Am Hist, 69; The Progressive Era: Search for a Synthesis, Mid-Am, 69; The Politics of Resistance, New England Quart, 6/74; Urban Liberalism and Progressive Reform, Norton, 77; coauth, Progressivism, Schenkman, 77; co-ed, Immigration and Ethnicity: Guide to the Information Sources, 77, Progressive Reform: Guide to the Information Sources, 80 & Urban History: Guide to the Information Sources, 81, Gale Res Co; auth, The Income Tax and the Progressive Era, Garland, 85; co-ed, Historical Dictionary of the Progressive Era, Greenwood, 88; Multiculturism in the U.S., Greenwood, 92; Those United States, Harcourt Brace, 98; auth, Wisconsin The Progressive Era, Univ Wis Press, 98; Invention City, Racine Heritage Museum, 98. **CONTACT ADDRESS** Dept of Hist, Univ of Wis Parkside, Box 2000, Kenosha, WI, 53141-2000. **EMAIL** buenker@uwp.edu

BUETTINGER, CRAIG
PERSONAL Born 01/20/1951, Cincinnati, OH **DISCIPLINE** AMERICAN HISTORY **EDUCATION** Johns Hopkins, BA, 73; Northwestern Univ, MA, 77, PhD, 82. **CAREER** Asst prof, 83-92, assoc prof, 92-96, prof, 96- , Jacksonville Univ. **MEMBERSHIPS** AHA. **RESEARCH** Nineteenth-century U.S. social history. **SELECTED PUBLICATIONS** Auth, Economic Inequality in Early Chicago, 1849-1850, in J of Soc Hist, 78; auth, The Rise and Fall of Hiram Pearson: Mobility on the Urban Frontier, in Chicago Hist, 80; auth, Antivivisection and the Charge of Zoophil-Psychosis in the Early Twentieth Century, in The Historian, 93; auth, Sarah Cleghorn, Antivivisection, and the Victorian Sensitivity about Pain and Cruelty, in Vermont Hist, 94; auth, Women and Antivivisection in Late Nineteenth-Century America, in J of Soc Hist, 97. **CONTACT ADDRESS** Dept of History, Jacksonville Univ, Jacksonville, FL, 32211. **EMAIL** cbuetti@ju.edu

BUETTNER, BRIGITTE
DISCIPLINE ART HISTORY **EDUCATION** Maitrise Paris-X Nanterre, PhD. **CAREER** Dir, JYA Prog, Hamburg, Ger, 97-98. **RESEARCH** Late medieval art, particularly secular art produced within the context of court cult. **SELECTED PUBLICATIONS** Auth, Boccaccio's, Des cleres et nobles femmes: Systems of Signification in an Illuminated Manuscript, Col Art Asn Monograph Ser, Univ WA Press, 96. **CONTACT ADDRESS** Dept of Art, Smith Col, Hillyer Hall 316, Northampton, MA, 01063. **EMAIL** bbuettner@julia.smith.edu

BUFFORD, RODGER K.
PERSONAL Born 12/23/1944, Santa Rosa, CA, m, 1968, 2 children **DISCIPLINE** PSYCHOLOGY **EDUCATION** Kings Col, BA, 66; Univ Illinois, MA, 70; PhD, 71. **CAREER** Asst prof, 71-76, Amer Univ; chmn, dept of psychology, 76-77 Huntington Col; part-time inst,77-81, dept of counseling and psychological stud, Georgia St Univ; assoc prof, 77-81, dir of clinical training, 80-81, psychological stud inst; psychologist, 80-82, Atlanta Counseling Center; psychologist, 82-, Western Psychological and Counseling Svc; assoc prof, 82-86, prof & chmn, 86-90, div of clinical psychology, Western Conservative Baptist Sem; prof & chmn, grad school of clinical psychology, 90-95, prof, & dir of research and integration, George Fox Univ; **HONORS AND AWARDS** Exemplary Paper in Humility Theology for 1997 Award in Religion and the Human Behavioral Sciences, John Templeton Found; Templeton Found Award - 1993 Call for Papers in Humility Theology Program. **MEMBERSHIPS** Who's Who in the World, 84-98; Who's Who in Med and Healthcare, 97-98; Who's Who in Science and Eng, 96-97; Who's Who in the West, 84-99; Who's Who among Human Svc Prof, 85; Who's Who in Frontier Science and Tech, 84-85; Who's Who in the South an Southwest, 77-78; Who's Who among Students, 65-66; Amer Men and Women of Science, 95-96; Personalities of the South, 75-76; Who's Who Among Students in Amer Col and Univ. **RESEARCH** Theoretical and empirical integration of psychology and Christian faith, including empirical psychology of religion, and esp empricial investigation of spiritual wellbeing and maturity, spiritual interventions in psychotherapy, and spiritual outcomes of psychotherapy. **SELECTED PUBLICATIONS** Art, The Human Reflex: Behavioral Psychology in Biblical perspective, Harper and Row, 81; art, Counseling and the Demonic, Word Books, 88; coauth, Norms for the Spiritual Well-being Scale, Jour of Psych and Theol, 91; art, Reflections on Christian counseling, CAPS W Newsletter 19, 92; art, Looking Over the Horizon: Presidential reflections, CAPS W Newsletter 20, 93; art, Faith that Hurts, CAPS W Newsletter 19, 93; coauth, Effects of Cognitive-Behavioral Marriage Enrichment On Marital Adjustment Of Church Couples, Jour of Psych and Theol 24, 96; art, Managed Care; What good is it? OPA Newsgram, 96; art, The Scientist as Christian or Atheist, Persp on Science & Christian faith 48, 96; art, Consecrated Counseling: Reflections on the Distinctives of Christian Counseling, Jour of Psych and Theol 25, 97; art, Personal Knowledge and Truth: A Response to Sorenson's Leper Metaphor, Internet Pub, Christian Asn for Psychol Stud, 97; coauth, Evolutionary Psychology: A Paradigm Whose Time May Come, Persp on Science and Christian Faith 50, 98. **CONTACT ADDRESS** Grad School of Clinical Psychology, George Fox Univ, 414 N. Meridian, Newberg, OR, 97132-2697. **EMAIL** rbufford@georgefox.edu

BUJA, MAUREEN
PERSONAL Born 10/30/1958, Pittsburgh, PA, m **DISCIPLINE** MUSICOLOGY **EDUCATION** Univ of IL, Urbana-Champaign, BA, 80; Univ of NC, Chapel Hill , MA, 82, PhD, 95; Columbia Univ MPHIL, 87. **CAREER** Professional managing ed, Stagebill, 97. **MEMBERSHIPS** MLA, IAML, AMS, RMA. **RESEARCH** Renaissance printing, Italian madrigals. **SELECTED PUBLICATIONS** Bks Vincenzo Ruffo The Italian Madrigal in the Sixteenth Century, vol 26, NY Garland Publ, 89, Introduction and Edition, Vincenzo Ruffo, Italian Renaissance Poetry, A First-Line Index to Petrarch, Ariosto, Tasso and Others, var articles, Essays in Honour of Donald Mitchell on His 70th Birthday. **CONTACT ADDRESS** Stagebill, 140 East 65th Str., New York, NY, 10023. **EMAIL** mebuja@stagebill.com

BUKEY, EVAN BURR
PERSONAL Born 04/24/1940, Cincinnati, OH, m, 1963, 2 children **DISCIPLINE** HISTORY **EDUCATION** Ohio Wesleyan Univ, BA, 62; The Ohio State Univ, MA, 64, PhD, 69. **CAREER** Grad Assoc, The Ohio State Univ, 64-66, 68-69; INSTR, 69-70, ASST PROF, 70-75, ASSOC PROF, 75-86, DIR OF EUROPEAN STUDIES, 91-93, PROF, UNIV OF ARK, 86-; vis fel, Wolfson Col, Univ of Cambridge, 93-94. **HONORS AND AWARDS** Master teacher awd, Fulbright Col, 97; fulbright fel, Univ of Goettingen, 66-67. **MEMBERSHIPS** German Studies Asn; Confr Group Central European Hist; Am Hist Asn; The Hist Soc; Phi Alpha Theta; Delta Phi Alpha; Golden Key. **RESEARCH** Central Europe; Austrian and German Nazism; World War II. **SELECTED PUBLICATIONS** Auth, Hitler's Austria: Popular Sentiment in the Nazi Era 1938-1945, Univ of NC Press, 99; Patenstadt des Fuhrers. Eine Politik-und Sozialgeschichte von Linz 1908-1945, Campus Verlag, 93; Hitler's Hometown: Linz, Austria, 1908-1945, Ind Univ Press, 86; Great Men and the Twentieth Century, The Hist J, 96; Nazi Rule in Austria: A Review Essay, Austrian Hist Yearbook, 92. **CONTACT ADDRESS** History Dept, Univ of Arkansas, Old Main 416, Fayetteville, AR, 72701. **EMAIL** ebukey@comp.uark.edu

BUKEY, EVAN BURR
PERSONAL Born 04/24/1940, Cincinnati, OH, m, 1963, 2 children **DISCIPLINE** MODERN EUROPEAN HISTORY **EDUCATION** Ohio Wesleyan Univ, BA, 62; Ohio State Univ, MA, 64, PhD(hist), 69. **CAREER** Asst prof, 69-75, ASSOC PROF HIST, UNIV ARK, FAYETTEVILLE, 75-, Am Philos Soc grant, 75. **MEMBERSHIPS** AHA; Conf Group Cent Europ Hist; Conf Group Ger Polit; Western Asn Ger Studies. **RESEARCH** Particularism and local history; Austrian national socialism; German and Austrian Marxism. **SELECTED PUBLICATIONS** Auth, The exile government of King George V of Hanover, 1866-1918, Can J Hist, 70; The Guelph party in imperial Germany, 1866-1918, Historian, 72; Arkansas after the war: From the journal of Frederick Gerstaecker, Ark Hist Quart, 73; The Nazi party in Linz, Austria, 1919-39: A sociological perspective, Ger Studies Rev, 78; From Prejudice to Persecution - A History of Austrian Anti-Semitism - Pauley,BF/, Ger Studies Rev, Vol 16, 1993; The Origins of the Cold-War in Europe - International Perspectives - Reynolds,D/, Hist J, Vol 39, 1996; Allies at War - The Soviet, American, and British-Experience, 1939-1945 - Reynolds,D, Kimball,WF, Chubarian,AO/, Hist J, Vol 39, 1996; A World at Arms - A Global History of World-War-2 - Weinberg,GL/, Hist J, Vol 39, 1996. **CONTACT ADDRESS** Dept of Hist, Univ of Ark, Fayetteville, AR, 72701-1202.

BULL, ROBERT JEHU
PERSONAL Born 10/21/1920, Harrington, DE, m, 1959 **DISCIPLINE** CHURCH HISTORY, ARCHAEOLOGY **EDUCATION** Randolph-Macon Col, BA, 43; Duke Univ, BD, 46; Yale Univ, MA, 51, PhD, 56. **CAREER** Instr philos, Colgate Univ, 54-55; from instr to assoc prof, 55-70, field supvr, Drew Univ-McCormick Archaeol Exped, Jordan, 56-57, 60-62, 64, PROF CHURCH HIST, DREW UNIV, 70-, DIR, INST ARCHAEOL RES, 68-, Mem, Hazen Theol Discussion Group; Am Asn Theol Sch fel, Univ Utrecht, 59-60; Am Sch Orient Res, Jordan, 66-67; field supvr, Wooster Exped, Pella, 66; dir, Tell er Ras Exped, 66, 68; vpres, Comm Arch & Hist, United Methodist Church, 68; dir, Am Sch Orient Res, Jerusalem, 70-71, Joint Exped Khirbet Shemac, 1970 & Joint Exped Caesarea, 71; res prof, William Foxwell Albright Inst Archaeol Res, 74. **MEMBERSHIPS** Am Soc Church Hist; Am Sch Orient Res; Albright Inst Archaeol Res; Nat Lectr Archaeol Inst Am. **RESEARCH** Patristics; Palestinian archaeology; early American Methodist history. **SELECTED PUBLICATIONS** Auth, The Making of Our Tradition, Westminster, 67; coauth, The sixth campaign at Balatah, Bull Am Sch Orient Res, 4/68; The excavation of Tell er Ras, Bull Am Sch Orient Res, 4/68; The excavation of Tell er Ras on Mt Gerigim, Bibl Archaeologist, 5/68; Towards a Corpus Inscriptonum Latinarum Britannecarum in Palestina, Blestine Exploration Quart, 70; Tell er Ras, The Pottery, 71 & Tell er Ras, The Coins, 71, Smithsonian; co-ed, Eaesarea, The Preliminary Reports, Vol I, Harvard Univ, 74; auth, The Gold Coin Hoard at Caesarea + Ancient Numismatic Studies/, Bibl Archaeol, Vol 56, 1993; Caesarea and King Herod Magnificent City Plan/, Am J Archaeol, Vol 100, 1996. **CONTACT ADDRESS** Dept of Hist, Drew Univ, Madison, NJ, 07940.

BULLARD, MELISSA MERIAM
PERSONAL Born 03/12/1946, Berkeley, CA, m, 1969 **DISCIPLINE** HISTORY **EDUCATION** Duke Univ, AB, 67; Cornell Univ, MA, 69, PhD(hist), 77. **CAREER** ASST PROF HIST, UNIV NC, CHAPEL HILL, 77-. **HONORS AND AWARDS** Best unpubl manuscript in Ital hist, Soc Ital Hist Studies, 77. **MEMBERSHIPS** Renaissance Soc Am; Soc Ital Hist Studies; AAUP Res Italian and Mediterranean history of the early modern period. **SELECTED PUBLICATIONS** Auth, Mercatores Romanam Curiam Sequentes in the early sixteenth century, J Medieval & Renaissance Studies, 76; The Cost of Empire - The Finances of the Kingdom of Naples in the Time of Spanish Rule - Calabria,A/, Renaissance Quarterly, Vol 46, 1993; Civic Politics in the Rome of Urban-VIII - Nussdorfer,L/, Am Hist Rev, Vol 99, 1994; Heroes and their Workshops + An Analysis of the Increase in Private Consumption of the Arts in 15th-Century Italy - Medici Patronage and the Problem of Shared Agency/, J Medieval and Renaissance Studies, Vol 24, 1994; Wealth and the Demand for Art in Italy, 1300-1600 - Goldthwaite,RA/, Am Hist Rev, Vol 99, 1994; Michelangelo at San-Lorenzo - The Genius as Entrepreneur - Wallace,WE/, Am Hist Rev, Vol 100, 1995; The Elect Nation - The Savonarolan Movement in Florence, 1494-1545 - Hay,D, Trapp,JB/, J Mod Hist, Vol 68, 1996. **CONTACT ADDRESS** Dept of Hist, Univ of NC, Chapel Hill, NC, 27514.

BULLARD, TRUMAN
DISCIPLINE MUSIC **EDUCATION** Haverford Col, BA, 60; Harvard Univ, MA, 63; Univ Roch, Eastman Sch Music, PhD,

71. **CAREER** Music teach, Lakeside School, Seattle, WA, 63-65; Inst, 65, asst prof, 67, assoc prof, 71, PROF, 81-, DICKINSON COL; ADJ PROF MUSICOL, EASTMAN SCH MUSIC, 87-. **CONTACT ADDRESS** Music Dept, Dickinson Col, Carlisle, PA, 17013-2896. **EMAIL** bullardt@dickinson.edu

BULLIET, RICHARD
DISCIPLINE MIDDLE EASTERN HISTORY **EDUCATION** Harvard Univ, BA, 62, PhD, 67. **CAREER** Prof. **RESEARCH** The social and institutional history of Islamic countries. **SELECTED PUBLICATIONS** Auth, The Patricians of Nishapur: a Study in Medieval Islamic Hist, 72; The Tomb of the Twelfth Imam, 72; The Camel and the Wheel, 75; The Gulf Scenario, 84; The Sufi Fiddle, 91; Islam: the View from the Edge, 94. **CONTACT ADDRESS** Dept of Hist, Columbia Col, New York, 2960 Broadway, New York, NY, 10027-6902.

BULLION, JOHN LEWIS
PERSONAL Born 10/23/1944, Washington, DC, m, 1976, 2 children **DISCIPLINE** HISTORY **EDUCATION** Stanford Univ, BA, 66; Univ of Tex at Austin, MA, 68, PhD, 77. **CAREER** Instr of Hist, Southwest Tex State Univ, 74-78; CHEMN, 91-96, ASST PROF TO PROF, UNIV OF MO-COLUMBIA, 78-. **HONORS AND AWARDS** Phi Beta Kappa, 66; Colonial Dames Commemorative Awd for Best Masters Thesis or Doctoral Dissertation in The Southeastern United States, 68; Univ of Mo Curators' Publication Awd, 83; Am Military Inst Distinguished Article Awd, 88; Burlington Northern Foundation Faculty Achievement Awd for Significant and Meritorious Tchg in the Univ of Mo System, 90. **MEMBERSHIPS** Am Hist Asn; Am Soc of Eighteenth-Century Studies; North Am Coun of British Studies. **RESEARCH** British politics and the American Revolution; race relations in early Twentieth-Century Mo. **SELECTED PUBLICATIONS** Auth, A Great and Necessary Measure: George Grenville and the Genesis of the Stamp Act, 82; Securing the Peace: Lord Bute, the plan for the army, and the origins of the American Revolution, Lord Bute: Essays in Reinterpretation, 88; Security and Economy: The Bute Administration's Plans for the American Army and Revenue, William and Mary Quart, 88; British Ministers and American Resistance tot he Stamp Act, October-December, 1765, William and Mary Quart, 92; George III on Empire 1783, William and Mary Quart, 94; George, be a King! The Relationship between Princess Augusta and George III, Hanoverian Britain and Empire, 98. **CONTACT ADDRESS** Dept of Hist, Univ of Missouri, Columbia, 101 Read Hall, Columbia, MO, 65211. **EMAIL** histjb@showme.missouri.edu

BULLOCK, STEVEN C.
DISCIPLINE HISTORY **EDUCATION** Houghton Coll, BA, 78; State Univ NY-Binghamton, MA, 80; Brown Univ, AM, 82, PhD, 86. **CAREER** ASSOC PROF, HIST, WORCESTER POLYTECH INST **MEMBERSHIPS** Am Antiquarian Soc **SELECTED PUBLICATIONS** Auth, "According to Their Rank: Masonry and the Revolution, 1775-1792", in Heredom: The Transaction of the Scottish Rite Society, IV, 95; auth, Revolutionary Brotherhood: Freemasonry and the Transformation of the American Social Order, 1730-1840, IEAHC and Univ NC Press, 96; auth, "Review Essay - Initiating the Enlightenment?: Recent Works on European Freemasonry," Eighteenth-Century Life, 20, 96. **CONTACT ADDRESS** 2 Eagle Terr, Worcester, MA, 01602. **EMAIL** sbullock@wpi.edu

BULLOUGH, WILLIAM ALFRED
PERSONAL Born 01/03/1933, CA **DISCIPLINE** URBAN HISTORY **EDUCATION** Univ Calif, Santa Barbara, BA, 55, MA, 67, PhD(hist), 70. **CAREER** Teacher, Calif Pub Schs, 57-65; asst prof, 70-74, assoc prof, 74-79, PROF HIST, CALIF STATE UNIV, HAYWARD, 79-. **MEMBERSHIPS** Orgn Am Historians; AHA; Western Hist Asn. **RESEARCH** Urban institutional history; western municipal politics; California history. **SELECTED PUBLICATIONS** Auth, It is better to be a country boy: The lure of the country in urban education in the Gilded Age, Historian, 2/73; The steam beer handicap: Chris Buckley and the San Francisco municipal election of 1896, Calif Hist Quart, fall 75; Hannibal versus the blind boss: The Junta, Chris Buckley and democratic reform politics in San Francisco, Pac Hist Rev, 5/77; The Blind Boss and His City: Christopher Augustine Buckley and Nineteenth Century San Francisco, Univ Calif Press, 79; Shadowcatchers - A Directory of Women in California Photography Before 1901 - Palmquist,PE/, Calif Hist, Vol 70, 1991; The Evolution of Political Protest and the Workingmens-Party-of-California - Shumsky,NL/, Pac Hist Rev, Vol 62, 1993. **CONTACT ADDRESS** Dept of Hist, California State Univ, Hayward, Hayward, CA, 94542.

BULLOUGH JR, ROBERT V.
PERSONAL Born 02/12/1949, Salt Lake City, UT, m, 1976, 4 children **DISCIPLINE** EDUCATIONAL STUDIES; HISTORY **EDUCATION** Univ of Utah, BS, 71, MEd, 73; Ohio State Univ, PhD, 76. **CAREER** Prof, Educ Stud, Univ of Utah, 76-. **HONORS AND AWARDS** Phi Beta Kappa; Phi Kappa Phi, 71; AACTE Outstanding Writing Award, 97. **MEMBERSHIPS** Am Educ Res Asn; Prof of Curriculum; Phi Delta Kappa. **RESEARCH** Teacher development; curriculum studies; lives of children. **SELECTED PUBLICATIONS** Auth, Trends in teacher education reform in America: A personal perspective, Teacher Educators' Annual Handbook, Queensland Univ of Tech, 87-97, 93; co-auth, Becoming a Student of Teaching: Methodologies for Exploring Self and School Context, Garland Publishing Inc, 95; auth, Professorial dreams and mentoring: A personal view, Teachers and mentors: Profiles of distinguished 20th century professors of education, Garland Publishing Inc, 257-267, 96; auth, Becoming a teacher: Self and the social location of teacher education, Int Handbook of Tchrs and Tchng, Kluwer Acad Publishers, 87-148; auth, Practicing theory and theorizing practice in teacher education, Purposes, passion, & pedagogy in teacher education, The Falmer Press, 13-21, 97; co-auth, First year teacher--after eight years: An inquiry into teacher development, Tchrs Col Press, 97; auth, Musing on life writing: Biography and case studies in teacher education, Writing educational biography: Adventures in qualitative research, Garland Publishing, 19-32, 98. **CONTACT ADDRESS** 413 4th Ave, Salt Lake City, UT, 84103. **EMAIL** bbullough@gse.utah.edu

BUMSTED, JOHN M.
PERSONAL Born 12/12/1938, White Plains, NY **DISCIPLINE** CANADIAN & NORTH AMERICAN HISTORY **EDUCATION** Tufts Col, BA, 59; Brown Univ, PhD(hist), 65. **CAREER** Instr hist, Tufts Col, 63-65; asst prof, Simon Fraser Univ, 65-67 & McMaster Univ, 67-69; assoc prof, Simon Fraser Univ, 69-75, prof hist, 75-80; PROF HIST, UNIV MANITOBA, 80-, Assoc dir, Can Studies Prog, Simon Fraser Univ, 79-80; gen ed, Selkirk Papers Publ Proj, 80-; actg gen ed, Man Rec Soc, 82. **MEMBERSHIPS** Orgn Am Historians; Can Hist Asn; Can Asn Am Studies; fel Pilgrim Soc. **RESEARCH** Early Canadian history. **SELECTED PUBLICATIONS** Ed, Documentary Problems in Canadian History (2 vols), Irwin-Dorsey, 69; The Great Awakening: The Beginnings of Evangelical Pietism in America, Blaisdell, 70; auth, Henry Alline, 1748-1781, Univ Toronto Press, 71; ed, Canada Before Confederation: Essays and Interpretations, Irwin-Dorsey, 72, rev ed, 79; coauth, What Must I Do to Be Saved? The Great Awakening in Colonial America, Dryden Press, 76; auth, The People's Clearance: Scottish Emigration to British North America, 1770-1815, Univ Edenburgh & Univ Man Presses, 82; co-ed, The Journal of Alexander Walker, 1786, Douglas & McIntyre, 82; coauth, In the Shadow of the Law - Divorce in Canada, 1900-1939 - Snell,JG/, Can Hist Rev, Vol 74, 1993; 19th-Century Cape-Breton - A Historical Geography - Hornsby,SJ/, Am Hist Rev, Vol 98, 1993; Sojourners in the Sun - Scottish Migrants in Jamaica and the Chesapeake, 1740-1800, J Am Hist, Vol 81, 1994; Encyclopedia of the North-American Colonies, William and Mary Quart, Vol 52, 1995; Europeans on the Move - Studies on European Migration, 1500-1800 - Canny,N/, J Am Hist, Vol 82, 1995; Scottish Emigration to Colonial America, 1607-1785 - Dobson,D/, J Am Hist, Vol 82, 1995. **CONTACT ADDRESS** St John's Col, Univ Manitoba, Winnipeg, MB, R3T 2M5.

BUNGE, WILFRED F.
PERSONAL Born 11/21/1931, Caledonia, MN, m, 1963, 2 children **DISCIPLINE** RELIGION, CLASSICAL LANGUAGES **EDUCATION** Luther Col, BA, 53; Luther Theol Sem, BTh, 58; State Univ Iowa, MA, 55; Harvard Univ, ThD(New Testament), 66. **CAREER** Instr Relig & Classics, Luther Col, 56-57; instr Greek, Luther Theol Sem, 57-58; asst prof Relig & Classics & actg head Dept Relig, 62-69, assoc prof Relig, 69-74, registrar, 72-79, prof Relig, Luther Col, 74-, head dept, 79-87; Bk ed, Dialog, 66-70, asst prof, St John's Univ, Minn, 67-68. **MEMBERSHIPS** Soc Bibl Lit; Am Asn Col Registr & Admin Off; corresp mem Inst Antiq & Christianity. **RESEARCH** Ecumenical Christian dialogue; Greco-Roman religions; Apuleius. **SELECTED PUBLICATIONS** Auth, Critical method and the New Testament, In: Theological Perspectives, Luther Col, 64; transl, God's righteousness in Paul, the Bultmann School of Biblical interpretation: New directions?, 65 & Paul and Nascent Catholicism, Distinctive Protestant and Catholic themes reconsidered, 67, J Theol & Church, Harper Torchbk; coauth (with John Bale), The word and words: Liberal education of the clergy, Dialog, Spring 80; Warmly Weston: A Luther College Life, Decorah: Luther College Press, 98. **CONTACT ADDRESS** Dept of Classics & Relig, Luther Col, 700 College Dr, Decorah, IA, 52101-1045. **EMAIL** bungewil@luther.edu

BUNI, ANDREW
PERSONAL Born 06/12/1931, Manchester, NH, m, 1960, 4 children **DISCIPLINE** AMERICAN NEGRO HISTORY **EDUCATION** Univ NH, BA, 58, MA, 59; Univ Va, PhD(hist), 65. **CAREER** From asst prof to assoc prof hist, Mary Washington Col, Univ Va, 64-68; ASSOC PROF HIST, BOSTON COL, 68- **MEMBERSHIPS** AHA; Soc Am Hist; Southern Hist Asn; Asn Study Negro Life & Hist. **RESEARCH** Negro in American history; Negro press in the 20th century. **SELECTED PUBLICATIONS** Auth, The Negro in Virginia Politics, 1902-1965, Univ Va, 67; Robert L Vann and the Pittsburgh Courier, Univ Pittsburgh, 74. **CONTACT ADDRESS** Dept Hist, Boston Col, Chestnut Hill, MA, 02167.

BUNTROCK, DANA
DISCIPLINE ARCHITECTURE **EDUCATION** Tulane Univ, BA, 81; The Univ MI, MA Architecutre, High Distinction, May, 88, MA, Urban Planning, Dec, 88. **CAREER** Visit Asst Prof, Carnegie Mellon Univ, 89-91; Visit Academic, Univ of Adelaide S. Australia, 94; Asst Prof, Univ Ill at Chicago, 94-; Research Assoc, Univ of Tokyo, 98. **HONORS AND AWARDS** Henry Adams Certificate, Marion Sarah Parker Mem Prize. **MEMBERSHIPS** Assn of Collegiate Schs of Architecture; Assn for Asian Studies, Patron; Ctr for the Study of the Practice of Architecture, sustaining member. **SELECTED PUBLICATIONS** coauth, The Use of Tradition in Japanese Architecture, Identity, Tradition, and Built Form: The Role of Culture in Planning and Development, Dec 96; Collaborative Production: Building Opportunities in Japan, Journal of Architectural Education, May 97; Japanese Building Production: Four Models of Design Development and Delivery, Oct 98. **CONTACT ADDRESS** 1242 North Lake Shore Dr. #17N, Chicago, IL, 60610. **EMAIL** dana@uic.edu

BURCKEL, NICHOLAS C.
PERSONAL Born 08/15/1943, Evansville, Ind, m, 1969 **DISCIPLINE** UNITED STATES HISTORY **EDUCATION** Georgetown Univ, BA, 65; Univ Wis-Madison, MA, 67, PhD(hist), 71. **CAREER** Asst archivist, Univ Wis-Madison, 71-72; DIR, ARCH & AREA RES CTR, UNIV WIS-PARKSIDE, 72-, EXEC ASST TO CHANCELLOR, 75- **HONORS AND AWARDS** Cert Commendation, Am Asn State & Local Hist, 78. **MEMBERSHIPS** AHA; Orgn Am Historians; Soc Am Archivists; Midwest Arch Conf; Am Asn State & Local Hist. **RESEARCH** Progressivism, Wisconsin history; archival administration. **SELECTED PUBLICATIONS** Auth, From Beckham to McCreary: The progressive record of Kentucky governors, Regist Ky Hist Soc, 10/78; co-ed, Govenor Albert B White and the beginning of progressive reform, 1901-05, WVa Hist, fall 78; auth, Business archives in a university setting: Status and prospect, Col & Res Libr, 5/80; co-ed, Progressive Reform, Gale, 80; Kenosha Retrospective: A Biographical Approach, Kenosha County, 81; auth, A O Stanley and progressive reform, 1902-1919, Regist Ky Hist Soc, spring 81; Govenor Austin Lane Crothers and progressive reform in Maryland, 1908-1912, Md Hist Mag, summer 81; Publicizing progressivism: William M O Dawson, WVa Hist, spring-summer 81. **CONTACT ADDRESS** 2422 West Lawn Ave, Racine, WI, 53405.

BURFORD, JIM
PERSONAL Born 07/25/1945, Vancouver, WA, m, 1972, 2 children **DISCIPLINE** STUDIO ARTS **EDUCATION** Univ Or, BS, 71; Carnegie Mellon Univ, MFA, 78. **CAREER** Instr, Duquesne Univ, 77-78; instr, Carnegie Mellon Univ, 77-78; instr, N Va Commun Col, 78; instr, Md Col, 98- ; Assoc prof, Mt Vernon Col, 78- . **HONORS AND AWARDS** Who's Who, 92-93; guest lectr, Hirshhorn Museum, 93-95; Cert of Merit, 95-96; Faculty Develop Grant, 96-97; guest artist lectr, 98. **RESEARCH** Exhibitions of painting & drawings **CONTACT ADDRESS** 3222 First Rd N, Arlington, VA, 22201.

BURG, BARRY RICHARD
PERSONAL Born 08/02/1938, Denver, CO **DISCIPLINE** BRITISH IMPERIAL & UNITED STATES HISTORY **EDUCATION** Univ Colo, BA, 60, PhD(hist), 67; Western State Col Colo, MA, 63. **CAREER** From asst prof hist to assoc prof Am hist, 67-77, PROF HIST, ARIZ STATE UNIV, 77-, DIR, HON PROG, 78-, Fac res Award, Ariz State Univ, 68, 70 & 73; Ford Found fel Adams Papers, 69-70; res grant, Shell Oil Found, 76; consult, Time-Life Bks, The Seafarers Libr, 77. **HONORS AND AWARDS** Symposium Award, Nat Endowment for Humanities, 77. **MEMBERSHIPS** AHA; Asn Caribbean Historians; Western Soc Sci Asn; Orgn Am Historians. **RESEARCH** Seventeenth-century England and America; the Caribbean; history of deviant behavior. **SELECTED PUBLICATIONS** Auth, The Autograph Trade and Documentary Editing, Manuscripts, 70; ed, A Letter of R Mather to Cleric in Old England, William & Mary Quart, 72; auth, The Cambridge Platform, Church Hist, 74; Legitimacy and Authority of Pirate Commanders, Am Neptune, 77; Richard Mather of Dorchester, Univ Ky, 77; Ho Hum, Another Work of the Devil, J Homosexuality, 80/81 & Historical Perspectives on Homosexuality, Stein & Day, 82; Richard Mather: The Writer in the Old and New Worlds, G K Hall, 82; Sodomy and the Pirate Tradition, NY Univ, 82; The Forgotten Trade - Comprising the Log of the Daniel and Henry of 1700 and Accounts of the Slave-Trade from the Minor Ports of England, 1698-1725 - Tattersfield,N/, Am Neptune, Vol 54, 1994; Tattoo Designs and Locations in the Old United-States-Navy/, J Am Cult, Vol 18, 1995; Romantic Longings - Love in America, 1830-1980 - Seidman,S/, Hist, Vol 57, 1995; On the Sources of Patriarchal Rage - The Commonplace Books of Byrd,William and Jefferson,Thomas and the Gendering of Power in the 18th-Century - Lockridge,KA/, J Hist Sexuality, Vol 5, 1995; Iron Men, Wooden Women - Gender and Seafaring in the Atlantic World, 1700-1920 - Creighton,MS, Norling,L/, J Am Hist, Vol 84, 1997; **CONTACT ADDRESS** Dept of Hist, Arizona State Univ, Tempe, Tempe, AZ, 85281.

BURGER, MARY WILLIAMS
PERSONAL North Little Rock, AR **DISCIPLINE** EDUCATION **EDUCATION** University of Arkansas, BA (magna cum laude), 1959; Colorado State University, MA, English lit, 1961; Washington University, PhD, modern literature, 1973; Harvard University, certified in education management, 1978. **CA-**

REER Lincoln University, instructor, English, 1961-66; University of Missouri, instructor, asst professor, English, 1966-69, 1973-75; University of Maryland, asst provost/asst vice pres, 1975-84; Tennessee State University, vice pres for academic affairs, professor, English, starting 1984; CALIFORNIA STATE UNIVERSITY SACRAMENTO, VICE PRES FOR ACADEMIC AFFAIRS, currently. **MEMBERSHIPS** Consultant, Natl Education Assn, 1973; reviewer, Middle States Assn of Colleges & Schools, 1974-75; consultant, Urban Behavioral Research Assn, 1974-79; consultant, Midwest Center for EEO, 1974-75; Alpha Kappa Mu; Alpha Kappa Alpha; Phi Kappa Phi; Sister Cities of Baltimore-Garnga Liberia; College Language Assn; State Planning Committee ACE/NIP. **SELECTED PUBLICATIONS** Black Viewpoint, New American Library, 1971; Ford Foundation Fellow, Washington University, 1972-73; Images of Black Women Sturdy, Black Bridges, Doubleday, 1979; Improving Opportunity for Black Students, NAFEO Proceedings, 1983; Sister Cities, Intl TAP Grant, Gbarnga Liberia, 1983. **CONTACT ADDRESS** California State Univ, Sacramento, 6000 J St, Sacramento, CA, 95819-2605.

BURGESS, JONATHAN
PERSONAL Born 04/17/1960, Baltimore, MD, m, 1988, 2 children **DISCIPLINE** CLASSICS **EDUCATION** Univ Toronto, PhD, 95. **CAREER** Asst prof, classics, Univ Toronto, 95-. **HONORS AND AWARDS** Gov Gen Gold Medal, Univ Toronto, 95. **MEMBERSHIPS** APA; CAC; CAAS. **RESEARCH** Early Greek epic; mythology. **SELECTED PUBLICATIONS** Auth, The Death of Achilles, forthcoming. **CONTACT ADDRESS** Dept of Classics, Toronto Univ, 97 St George St, Toronto, ON, M5S 1A1. **EMAIL** jburgess@class.utoronto.ca

BURGGRAAFF, WINFIELD J.
PERSONAL Born 05/21/1940, Brooklyn, NY, m, 1966 **DISCIPLINE** HISTORY **EDUCATION** Hope Col, AB, 61; Univ NMex, PhD(Latin Am hist), 67. **CAREER** Asst prof, 66-72, ASSOC PROF HIST, UNIV MO-COLUMBIA, 72-, Actg dir, Div Inter-Am Studies, Univ NMex, 70. **HONORS AND AWARDS** Cur Publ Award, Cur of Univ Mo, 72. **MEMBERSHIPS** AHA; Conf Latin Am Hist; Latin Am Studies Asn. **RESEARCH** Modern Venezuelan history; the Latin American military; oil politics in Latin America. **SELECTED PUBLICATIONS** Auth, The military origin of Venezuela's 1945 revolution, Caribbean Studies, 10/71; The Venezuelan Armed Forces in Politics, Univ Mo, 72; El ocaso de una era, Bol Hist, 9/72; Andeanism and Anti-Andeanism in Twentieth-Century Venezuela, The Americas, 7/75; co-ed, El petroleo en Venezuela: Una bibliografia, Edicionex Centauro, 77; Rank and Privilege, The Military and Society in Latin-America - Rodriguez,La/, Hisp Am Hist Rev, Vol 75, 1995; Venezuela - The Political-Economy of Oil - Boue,JC/, Hisp Am Hist Rev, Vol 76, 1996; The Dynamics of Domination - State, Class, and Social-Reform in Mexico, 1910-1990 - Brachetmarquez,V/, J West, Vol 35, 1996. **CONTACT ADDRESS** Dept of Hist, Univ of Mo, Columbia, MO, 65201.

BURKE, ALBIE
PERSONAL Born 03/21/1932, Rugby, ND, m, 1960, 2 children **DISCIPLINE** AMERICAN CONSTITUTIONAL & LEGAL HISTORY **EDUCATION** Univ Chicago, BA, 58, MA, 65, PhD, 68. **CAREER** Assoc prof, 72-77, prof hist, Calif State Univ, Long Beach, 77-. **MEMBERSHIPS** Am Civil Liberties Union; Orgn Am Historians; Am Soc Legal Hist. **SELECTED PUBLICATIONS** Auth, Federal regulation of congressional elections in Northern cities 1871-94, Am J Legal Hist, 1/70; ed, The Hist Teacher, 79-85. **CONTACT ADDRESS** Dept Hist, California State Univ, Long Beach, 1250 N Bellflower, Long Beach, CA, 90840-0001.

BURKE, COLIN B.
DISCIPLINE HISTORY **EDUCATION** WA Univ, PhD. **CAREER** Assoc prof, Univ MD Baltimore County . **RESEARCH** 19th-century Am hist; hist of computing and computers; hist of information policy. **SELECTED PUBLICATIONS** Auth, American Collegiate Populations: A Test of the Traditional View; Information and Secrecy: Vannevar Bush; Ultra; Other Memex. **CONTACT ADDRESS** Dept of Hist, Univ MD Baltimore County, Hilltop Circle, PO Box 1000, Baltimore, MD, 21250. **EMAIL** burke@research.umbc.edu

BURKE, MARTIN J.
DISCIPLINE HISTORY **EDUCATION** City Coll NY, AB, 73; Univ Mich, AM, 77, PhD, 87. **CAREER** LECT, HIST, UNIV COLL, GALWAY, IRELAND **MEMBERSHIPS** Am Antiquarian Soc **SELECTED PUBLICATIONS** Auth, "Mathew Carey and the Vindicia Hibernicae," in The Literature of Politics and the Politics of Literature, RoDoPi, 94; auth, "A German Academic in the Wilderness: Francis Lieber and the Higher Learning in America," in The Fate of Liberal Education, Open Court, 95; auth, The Conundrum of Class: Public Discourse on the Social Order in America, Univ Chicago Press, 95. **CONTACT ADDRESS** Sch of Hist Stud, Inst for Advanced Studies, Olden Lane, Princeton, NJ, 08540.

BURKE, MICHAEL E.
DISCIPLINE LATIN AMERICAN HISTORY **EDUCATION** Holy Cross Col, AB, 64; Duke Univ, MA, 67, PhD, 71. **CAREER** Assoc prof; dir, Villanova Hon(s) Prog, 82-93; founding pres, Villanova Phi Beta Kappa Chap. . **HONORS AND AWARDS** Sears-Roebuck Found Awd; Danforth Tchg Assoc; NEH, Brazil. **RESEARCH** Colonial Latin America; Mexico; Cultural & religious diversity; Reform and Revolution; Comparative Colonialism. **SELECTED PUBLICATIONS** Auth, The Royal College of San Carlos: Surgery and Spanish Medical Reform in the Eighteenth Century Enlightenment, Duke Univ Press, 77; Mexico's New Prisons, Corrections Today, 81; Mexico, Hippocrene Press, 92; Mexico como 'el otro', Vertebracion, 97; ed, dir, Signpost Biographies; articles on, colonial Latin American medicine, 20th century Mexico, teaching. **CONTACT ADDRESS** Dept of History, Villanova Univ, 800 Lancaster Ave., Villanova, PA, 19085-1692. **EMAIL** mburke@email.vill.edu

BURKE, SARA Z.
DISCIPLINE HISTORY **EDUCATION** McMaster Univ, BA, MA; Carleton Univ, PhD. **CAREER** Asst prof. **RESEARCH** Coeducation in Canada **SELECTED PUBLICATIONS** Auth, Seeking the Highest Good: Social Service and Gender at the University of Toronto 1888-1937, Univ Toronto, 96; art, Science and Sentiment: Social Service and Gender at the University of Toronto, 1888-1910, Jour Can Hist Asn, 93. **CONTACT ADDRESS** Dept of History, Laurentian Univ, 935 Ramsey Lake Rd, Sudbury, ON, P3E 2C6.

BURKETT, RANDALL KEITH
PERSONAL Born 10/23/1943, Union City, IN, m, 1965 **DISCIPLINE** RELIGION, HISTORY **EDUCATION** Am Univ, AB, 65; Harvard Divinity Sch, MTS, 69; Univ Southern Calif, PhD(social ethics), 75. **CAREER** Admin asst curric develop, Univ Southern Calif, 72-73; assoc dir spec studies, 73-77, assoc coordr grants & res, 76-79, DIR SPEC STUDIES, COL OF HOLY CROSS, 77-, COORDR GRANTS & RES, 79-, Lectr, Ctr Exp Studies; ed, Afro-Am Relig Hist Group Newsletter, Am Acad of Relig, 76-; Nat Endowment for the Humanities fel, 79-80. **MEMBERSHIPS** Am Acad Relig; Am Soc Church Hist; Asn for Study Afro-Am Life & Hist. **RESEARCH** Afro-American religious history. **SELECTED PUBLICATIONS** Auth, Black Redemption: Churchmen Speak for the Garvey Movement, Temple Univ, 78; co-ed, Black Apostles: Afro-American Clergy Confront the Twentieth Century, G K Hall, 78; auth, Garveyism as a Religious Movement: The Institutionalization of a Black Civil Religion, Scarecrow, 78. **CONTACT ADDRESS** Off of Spec Studies, Col of the Holy Cross, Worcester, MA, 01610.

BURKHARDT, RICHARD W.
DISCIPLINE HISTORY **EDUCATION** Harvard Univ, PhD, 72. **CAREER** Prof, Univ Ill Champaign Urbana. **RESEARCH** Scientific and social dimensions of animal behavior studies from 1800 and the present and the social and cultural history of zoos. **SELECTED PUBLICATIONS** Auth, The Spirit of System: Lamarck and Evolutionary Biology, Harvard, 95; Charles Otis Whitman, Wallace Craig, and the Biological Study of Behavior in America, 1898-1924, Univ Pa, 88; Le comportement animal et l'ideologie de domestication chez Buffon et les ethologistes modernes, Buffon, 88; Actes du Colloque international pour le bicentenaire de la mort de Buffon, Vrin, 92. **CONTACT ADDRESS** History Dept, Univ Ill Urbana Champaign, 52 E Gregory Dr, Champaign, IL, 61820.

BURKHOLDER, MARK A.
PERSONAL Born 09/03/1943, Chicago, IL, 2 children **DISCIPLINE** HISTORY **EDUCATION** Muskingum Col, BA, 65; Univ Or, MA, 67; Duke Univ, PhD, 70. **CAREER** Acad assoc to assoc v pres, Univ Mo, 83-84; asst dean to assoc dean to chair, asst prof to assoc prof to prof, Univ Mo St Louis, 70- . **HONORS AND AWARDS** Phi Beta Kappa; Phi Kappa Phi; Phi Alpha Theta; Chancellor's Award for Excellence in Svc, 97; Edwin Lieuwin Award; Hubert Herring Award for Best Book. **MEMBERSHIPS** Amer Hist Assoc; Conf on Latin Amer Hist; Rocky Mountain Coun of Latin Amer Stud; Pac Coast Coun of Latin Amer Stud, Soc for Spanish & Portuguese Hist Stud. **RESEARCH** Bureaucracy in eighteenth-century Spain & Spanish Amer **SELECTED PUBLICATIONS** Auth, Latin American Colonial Era, in Latin American Military History: An Annotated Bibliography, Garland Press, 93; Honest Judges Leave Destitute Heirs: the Price of Integrity in Eighteenth-Century Spain, in Virtue, Corruption, and Self-Interest: Political Values in the Eighteenth Century, Lehigh Univ Press, 94; coauth, Colonial Latin America, Oxford Univ Press, 90, 94, 98; ed, Latin American to 1800, in The American Historical Association's Guide to Historical Literature, Oxford Univ Press, 95; Administrators of Empire Latin America to 1800, Ashgate Publ Ltd, 98. **CONTACT ADDRESS** Dept of History, Univ Mo St. Louis, St. Louis, MO, 63121. **EMAIL** hismburk@jinx.umsl.edu

BURKINSHAW, ROBERT K.
DISCIPLINE CANADIAN HISTORY **EDUCATION** Vancouver Bible Col, BTh; UBC, BA; Univ Waterloo, MA; UBC, PhD, 88. **CAREER** Assoc prof and chemn. **RESEARCH** Evangelicalism in Western Canada espec B.C; Bible school movement in Canada; religious, social and ethnic signifigance. **SELECTED PUBLICATIONS** Auth, Pilgrims in Lotus Land: Conservative Protestantism in British Columbia, 1917-1981, Montreal & Kingston: McGill-Queen's UP, 95. **CONTACT ADDRESS** Dept of History and Political Science, Trinity Western Univ, 7600 Glover Rd, Langley, BC, V2Y 1Y1. **EMAIL** burkinsh@twu.ca

BURKMAN, THOMAS
PERSONAL Born 01/28/1944, Philadelphia, PA, m, 1982, 4 children **DISCIPLINE** HISTORY, MODERN JAPAN **EDUCATION** Univ MI, PhD, 75. **CAREER** Instr, Colby Col, 75-76; assoc prof of hist, Old Dominion Univ, 76-91; vis assoc prof, Hamilton Col, 92-93; dir of Asian Studies, SUNY at Buffalo, 94-. **HONORS AND AWARDS** Fulbright scholar, 78. **MEMBERSHIPS** Asn for Asian Studies; Soc of Peace Hist; Conf on Faith and Hist. **RESEARCH** 20th century Japan; East Asian int relations. **SELECTED PUBLICATIONS** Ed, The Occupation of Japan: Arts and Culture, The MacArthur Memorial, 88; auth, Reflections on the Occupation's Grassroots and the Eight Symposia, in W Nimmo, ed, The Occupation of Japan: The GrassRoots, 92; The Geneva Spirit, in John F Howes, ed, Nitobe Inazo: Japan's Bridge Across the Pacific, Westview Press, 95; Japanese trans, 97; Japan and the League of Nations: An Asian Power Confronts the European Club, in World Affairs, summer 95; The Immigration Act of 1924: The Limits of American Progressivisn, in Miwa Kimitada, ed, 1924-nen Amerika Shinminho no kokusai kankyo to Nihon no taio, Tokyo, 96. **CONTACT ADDRESS** Asian Studies, SUNY, Buffalo, 636 Baldy Hall, Buffalo, NY, 14260-1040. **EMAIL** burkman@acsu.buffalo.edu

BURLING, ROBBINS
PERSONAL Born 04/08/1926, Minneapolis, MN, m, 1951, 3 children **DISCIPLINE** ANTHROPOLOGY & LINGUISTICS **EDUCATION** Yale Univ, BA, 50; Harvard Univ, PhD, 58. **CAREER** From instr to asst prof anthrop, Univ Pa, 57-63; assoc prof, 63-67, Prof Anthrop & Ling, Univ Mich, Ann Arbor, 67-; Fulbright Found lectr, Rangoon, Burma, 59-60; fel, Ctr Advan Studies Behav Sci, 63-64; Guggenheim Found fel, 71-72; vis prof, Univ Gothenburg, Sweden, 79-80; Fulbright Found Lectr, Skillong, India, 96-97. **MEMBERSHIPS** Am Anthrop Asn; Ling Soc Am; Asn Asian Studies. **RESEARCH** Anthropology; linguistics. **SELECTED PUBLICATIONS** Auth, Rengsanggri, Family and Kinship in a Garo Village, Univ Pa, 63; Hill Farms and Padi Fields, Prentice-Hall, 65; Man's Many Voices, 70 & English in Black and White, 73, Holt; The Passage of Power, Acad Press, 74; Sounding Right, Newbury House, 82; Learning a Field Language, Univ Mich Press, 84; Patterns of Language, Acad Press, 92; The Strong Women of Modhupur Dhaka, Univ Press Ltd, 97. **CONTACT ADDRESS** Dept of Anthrop, Univ of Mich, 500 S State St, Ann Arbor, MI, 48109-1382. **EMAIL** rburling@umich.edu

BURLINGAME, MICHAEL A.
DISCIPLINE HISTORY **EDUCATION** Princeton Univ, BA; John Hopkins Univ, PhD. **CAREER** Prof; Conn Col, 68-; past Woodrow Wilson fel and Fulbright schol. **HONORS AND AWARDS** Abraham Lincoln Asn awd. **MEMBERSHIPS** Treas, Conn Asn Scholars; National Asn Scholars. **RESEARCH** US History; Civil War; Abraham Lincoln; Psychohistory. **SELECTED PUBLICATIONS** Auth, The Inner World of Abraham Lincoln, Univ Ill Press, 94; An Oral History of Abraham Lincoln, Southern Ill UP, 96. **CONTACT ADDRESS** Dept of History, Connecticut Col, 270 Mohegan Ave, Box 5426, New London, CT, 06320. **EMAIL** mabur@conncoll.edu

BURMAN, THOMAS
DISCIPLINE HISTORY **EDUCATION** Univ Toronto, PhD. **CAREER** Assoc prof. **RESEARCH** Medieval history. **SELECTED PUBLICATIONS** Auth, Religious Polemic and the Intellectual History of the Mozarabs 1050-1200, E.J. Brill, 94; pubs on Jewish-Christian-Muslim social, religious, and intellectual relations in Europe and the Middle East. **CONTACT ADDRESS** Dept of History, Knoxville, TN, 37996.

BURNELL, DEVIN
DISCIPLINE ART HISTORY **EDUCATION** Smith Col, BA, 61; Boston Univ, MA, 66; Univ Chicago, PhD, 76. **CAREER** Instr, Univ Ill; vis assoc prof, 77. **HONORS AND AWARDS** Unendowed grants, Univ Chicago; res fel, Ford Foundation; res grant, Amer Assn Univ Women; grant-in-aid, Am Coun of Learned Soc(s). **SELECTED PUBLICATIONS** Pub(s), var prof papers and articles on 18th and 19th century Europ art. **CONTACT ADDRESS** Dept of Art Hist, Sch of the Art Inst of Chicago, 37 S Wabash Ave, Chicago, IL, 60603.

BURNER, DAVID B.
PERSONAL Born 05/10/1937, Cornwall, NY, m, 1958, 2 children **DISCIPLINE** HISTORY, LITERATURE **EDUCATION** AB Hamilton Col, 58; PhD Columbia Univ, 65. **CAREER** Colby Col, 62-63; Oakland Univ, 63-67; SUNY, Stony Brook, 67-. **HONORS AND AWARDS** Guggenheim Fellowship; NYS Excellence Award; Natl Hum Found. **MEMBERSHIPS** ASA; OAH; AHA. **RESEARCH** 20th century Am Poli. SE-

LECTED PUBLICATIONS Making Peace with the 60s, Princeton Univ Press, 96; John F Kennedy and a New Generation, Little Brown, 89; Herbert Hoover: A Public Life, Alfred A Rucpt, 68; The Polotics of Provincialism: The Democratic Party in Transition, 1918-1932. **CONTACT ADDRESS** Dept Hist, State Univ of NY, Stony Brook, NY, 11794. **EMAIL** DBBurner@AOL.com

BURNETT, AMY
DISCIPLINE EARLY MODERN EUROPE HISTORY **EDUCATION** Univ Wis, Madison, PhD, 89. **CAREER** Assoc prof, Grad Ch, Univ Nebr, Lincoln, 97-. **RESEARCH** The Protestant Reformation in Basel. **SELECTED PUBLICATIONS** Auth, The Yoke of Christ: Martin Bucer and Christian Discipline, 16th Century J, 94. **CONTACT ADDRESS** Univ Nebr, Lincoln, 626 Oldfat, Lincoln, NE, 68588-0417. **EMAIL** ab@unlinfo.unl.edu

BURNETT, ANNE PIPPIN
PERSONAL Born 10/10/1925, Salt Lake City, UT, m, 1960, 2 children **DISCIPLINE** CLASSICS **EDUCATION** Swarthmore Col, BA, 46; Columbia Univ, MA, 47; Univ Calif, Berkeley, PhD(ancient hist & classics), 53. **CAREER** Instr classics, Vassar Col, 57-58; asst prof, 61-66, assoc prof, 67-69, PROF CLASSICS & CHMN DEPT, UNIV CHICAGO, 70-, Am Asn Univ Women traveling fel, Am Sch Class Studies Athens, 56-57; fel, Am Acad Rome, 58-59; grant, Am Philos Soc, 59-60; Am Coun Learned Soc fel, 68-69. **RESEARCH** Greek tragedy; Greek lyric poetry; Greek history. **SELECTED PUBLICATIONS** Auth, Helena Euripides: Wege der Forschung, Bd 89, Darmstadt, 68; Euripides' Ion, Prentice-Hall, 70; Catastrophe Survived, Clarendon, Oxford Univ, 71; Medea's revenge, Class Philol, 73; Curse and dream in Aeschylus' Septem, Greek, Roman & Byzantine Studies, 74; The Psychoanalytic-Theory of Greek Tragedy - Alford,CF/, Am J Philol, Vol 115, 1994; Hekabe the Dog + Euripides 'Hekabe'/, Arethusa, Vol 27, 1994. **CONTACT ADDRESS** Dept of Classics Div of Humanities, Univ of Chicago, Chicago, IL, 60637.

BURNETT, DAVID G.
PERSONAL Born 10/01/1940, Lincoln, England **DISCIPLINE** CURATOR **EDUCATION** Univ London, Birkbeck Col, BA 65; Courtauld Inst Art, MA, 67, PhD, 73. **CAREER** Lectr hist art, Univ Bristol, 67-70; assoc prof art hist, 70-80, dept chair, 74-77, 78-79, Carleton Univ; curator, Art Gallery Ont, 80-84; dir, Drabinsky Gallery, 90. **HONORS AND AWARDS** Can Coun grants, 74, 80 **MEMBERSHIPS** Univ Art Asn; Asn Univs & Cols Scholar Bd; Int Asn Art Critics. **RESEARCH** Canadian art **SELECTED PUBLICATIONS** Auth, Alex Colville, 83; auth, Town, 86; auth, Anton Cetin, 86; auth, Jeremy Smith, 88; auth, Cineplex Odeon: The First Ten Years, A Celebration of Contemporary Canadian Art, 89; auth, Masterpieces of Canadian Art from the National Gallery of Canada, 90; coauth, Contemporary Canadian Art, 83. **CONTACT ADDRESS** 601-10 Tichester Rd, Toronto, ON, M5P 3M4.

BURNETT, DONALD L.
PERSONAL Born 10/01/1946, Pocatello, ID, m, 1969, 2 children **DISCIPLINE** ECONOMICS **EDUCATION** Harvard Col, AB 68; Univ Chicago, JD, 71; Univ Va, LLM, 90. **CAREER** Law clerk to Chief Justice, Idaho Supreme Court, 71-72; asst atty general, State of Idaho, 72-74; private practice, 75-81; judge, Idaho Court of Appeals, 82-90; dean, Louis D. Brandeis School of Law, Univ of Louisville, 90-. **HONORS AND AWARDS** Pres, Idaho State Bar , 81. **MEMBERSHIPS** Idaho State Bar; Louisville Bar Assn; Am Bar Assn; Kentucky Ctr for Public Issues; Judge Advocate General's Corps, U.S. Army Reserve. **RESEARCH** Judiciary and judicial administration; law and economic theory; health law and policy; environmental law and policy. **SELECTED PUBLICATIONS** Auth, "Subject of Native American Law", in Harvard Journal on Legislation, 72; auth, "Subject of Water Law", in Idaho Law Review, 85; auth and ed, Idaho Appellate Handbook, 86, 90; auth, Remand, Am Bar Assn, 86-90; auth, "Subject of Legal Education", in Kentucky Bench & Bar, 96. **CONTACT ADDRESS** Louis D. Brandeis School of Law, Univ of Louisville, Louisville, KY, 40292. **EMAIL** don.burnett@louisville.edu

BURNETT, STEPHEN G.
PERSONAL Born 10/06/1956, Madison, WI, m, 1981, 3 children **DISCIPLINE** HEBREW; SEMITIC STUDIES **EDUCATION** BA, 78, MA, 83, PhD, 90 Univ Wisc Madison. **CAREER** Visiting prof, hist & Judaic studies, 93-96, lectr, hist, classics and Judaic studies, 96-, Univ Neb Lincoln. **HONORS AND AWARDS** Friends of the Univ Wisc libr grant-in-aid, 98; res grant, Amer Philos Soc, 95, Frank S. Elizabeth D. Brewer prize, Amer Soc of Church Hist, 94. **MEMBERSHIPS** Asn of Jewish Studies; Asn of Jewish Libr; Sixteenth Century Studies Conf. **RESEARCH** Christian Hebrew scholarship; Christian-Jewish relations in early modern Europe. **SELECTED PUBLICATIONS** Auth, From Christian Hebraism to Jewish Studies: Johannes Buxtorf (1564-1629) and Hebrew Learning in the Seventeenth-Century, Studies in the History of Christian Thought, vol 68, Leiden, E. J. Brill, 96; article, From Israel to Germany: A Conference Report, Judaic Studies Newsletter, Univ Neb Lincoln, 97-98; article, The Regulation of Hebrew Printing in Germany, 1555-1630: Confessional Politics and the Limits of Jewish Toleration, 329-348, Infinite Boundaries: Order, Disorder, and Reorder in Early Modern German Culture, Sixteenth Century Jour Publ, 98; article, Jews and Anti-Semitism in Early Modern Germany: A Review Article, Sixteenth Century Jour, 27/4, 1057-1064, 96; article, Hebrew Censorship in Hanau: A Mirror of Jewish-Christian Coextistence in Seventeenth Century Germany, 199-222, The Expulsion of the Jews: 1492 and After, Garland Studies in the Renaissance, vol 2, 94; article, Buxtorf Family Papers, 71-88, Die Handschriften der Universitat Basel: Die hebraische Handschriften, Verlag der Universitatsbibliothek, 94. **CONTACT ADDRESS** Dept. of History, Univ of Nebraska, 612 Old Father Hall, Lincoln, NE, 68588-0327. **EMAIL** sburnett@unlinfo.unl.edu

BURNETT, STEPHEN G.
PERSONAL Born 10/06/1956, Madison, WI, m, 1981, 3 children **DISCIPLINE** HISTORY **EDUCATION** Univ of Wis-Madison, BA, 78, MA, 83, PhD, 90; Trinity Evangelical Divinity School, MA, 82. **CAREER** VIS ASST PROF, LECTR, UNIV OF NEBR-LINCOLN, 93-. **HONORS AND AWARDS** Grant in Aid, Friends of the Univ of Wisconsin Libries, 98. **MEMBERSHIPS** Asn for Jewish Studies; Asn of Jewish Libries; Sixteenth Century Studies Confr; Fruhe Neuzeitliche Interdiziplinar. **RESEARCH** Christian-Jewish relations in early modern Germany. **SELECTED PUBLICATIONS** Auth, From Christian Hebraism to Jewish Studies: Johannes Buxtorf (1564-1629) and Hebrew Learning in the Seventeenth-Century, E.J. Brill, 96; The Regulation of Hebrew Printing in Germany 1555-1630: Confessional Politics and the Limits of Jewish Toleration, Infinite Boundaries: Order, Disorder, and Reorder in Early Modern German Culture, Sixteenth Century J Pub, 98; Jews and Anti-Semitism in Early Modern Germany: A Review Article, Sixteenth Century J, 96; Hebrew Censorship in Hanau: A mirror of Jewish-Christian Coexistence in Seventeenth Century Germany, The Expulsion of the Jews: 1492 and After, Garland, 94; Distorted Mirrors: Antonius Margaritha, Johann Buxtorf and Christian Ethnographies of Judaism, Sixteenth Century J, 94. **CONTACT ADDRESS** Dept of Hist, Univ of Nebraska, 612 Old Father Hall, Lincoln, NE, 68588-0327. **EMAIL** sburnett@unlinfo.unl.edu

BURNETTE, RAND
PERSONAL Born 08/10/1936, Evansville, IN, m, 1958, 3 children **DISCIPLINE** HISTORY **EDUCATION** Wabash Col, AB, 58; Univ Wis, Madison, MS, 59; Ind Univ, PhD, 67. **CAREER** Instr, Carthage Col, 62-63; asst to assoc to PROF, HISTORY, MACMURRAY COL, 63-; CHAIR, 74-77, 80-83, 86-89, 92-. **HONORS AND AWARDS** Phi Alpha Theta; Outstanding Educator Am, 75; fel, Hermon Dunlap Smith Ctr Hist Cartography, Newberry Libr, 90; fel, Early Mod Stud, 98., NEH Inst, 80, 88, 91, 93; NEH Summer Seminar, 84. **MEMBERSHIPS** Am Hist Asn; Org Am Hist; Soc Hist Discoveries; Sixteenth Cent Stud Conf; Renaissance Soc Am; Soc Reformation Res; Indiana Hist Soc; Ill St Hist Soc; His Soc Pa; Communal Stud Asn; Am Soc 18th Century Stud; Am Asn Univ Prof. **RESEARCH** Early Am hist; hist cartography; hist of Am animation. **SELECTED PUBLICATIONS** Auth, "British Rule and American Settlement 1765-1818" in A Guide to the History of Illinois, 91; "So You Want to Teach a Mickey Mouse Course: An Undergraduate Course in the History of Animation," Teaching History: A Jour of Methods, 17, 92. **CONTACT ADDRESS** Dept of History, MacMurray Col, 447 E. Colege, Jacksonville, IL, 62650. **EMAIL** rburnett@mac.edu

BURNHAM, JOHN CHYNOWETH
PERSONAL Born 07/14/1929, Boulder, CO, m, 1957, 4 children **DISCIPLINE** UNITED STATES HISTORY **EDUCATION** Stanford Univ, BA, 51, PhD, 58; Univ Wis, MA, 52. **CAREER** Actg instr hist, Stanford Univ, 56; lectr, Claremont Men's Col, 56-57; actg instr hist, Stanford Univ, 57-58, instr, 58; fel, Found Fund Res Psychiat, 58-61; asst prof hist, San Francisco State Col, 61-63; from asst prof to assoc prof, 63-69, PROF HIST, OHIO STATE UNIV, 69-, Fulbright lectr, Univ Melbourne, 67 & Univs Tasmania & New England, Australia, 73; Tallman vis prof hist & psychol, Bowdoin Col, 82. **MEMBERSHIPS** AHA; Orgn Am Historians; Am Asn Hist Med; Am Studies Asn; Hist Sci Soc. **RESEARCH** History of psychiatry; history of American medicine, science, and society. **SELECTED PUBLICATIONS** Auth, Psychoanalysis and American Medicine, 1894-1918: Medicine, Science, and Culture, Int Univ, 67; ed, Science in America: Historical Selections, Holt, 71; coauth, Progressivism, Schenkman, 77; auth, Jellife: American Psychoanalyst and Physician, Chicago, 83; How Superstition Won and Science Lost: Popularizing Science and Health in the United States, Rutgers, 87; Paths into American Culture: Psychology, Medicine, and Morals, Temple, 88; Bad Habits: Drinking, Smoking, Taking Drugs, Gambling, Sexual Misbehavior, and Swearing American History, NY Univ, 93. **CONTACT ADDRESS** Dept Hist, Ohio State Univ, 230 W 17th Ave, Columbus, OH, 43210-1367. **EMAIL** burnham.2@osu.edu

BURNHAM, PATRICIA
DISCIPLINE AMERICAN HISTORY PAINTING AND AMERICAN LANDSCAPE ART **EDUCATION** Boston Univ, PhD, 84. **CAREER** Sr lectr & lectr, Univ TX, 88-. **HONORS AND AWARDS** Curated, exhibition of Bernstein's work, Philadelphia Mus Judaica. **RESEARCH** 20th century Ashcan painter Theresa Bernstein. **SELECTED PUBLICATIONS** Co-ed, Redefining American History Painting, Cambridge UP. **CONTACT ADDRESS** Dept of Art and Art Hist, Univ of Texas at Austin, 2613 Wichita St, ART 3.404, Austin, TX, 78705.

BURNIM, MELLONEE VICTORIA
PERSONAL Born 09/27/1950, Teague, TX, m **DISCIPLINE** MUSICOLOGY **EDUCATION** Northern Texas State University, BM (cum laude), music education, 1971; University of Wisconsin Madison, MM, African music ethnomusicology, 1976; Indiana University, PhD, ethnomusicology, 1980. **CAREER** Delay Middle School, director of choral music, 1971-73; University of Wisconsin, research asst, 1973, academic advisor, 1973; Indiana University Bloomington, Afro-American Choral Ensemble, director, 1976-82, Opera Theater, choral director, 1976, 1980, Dept of Afro-American Studies, professor, currently. **HONORS AND AWARDS** Full Music Scholarship, NTSU, 1969-71; Natl Defense Foreign Language Fellow in Arabic, University of Wisconsin, 1973-74; fellow, Natl Fellowships Fund, University of Wisconsin & Indiana Unviersity, 1973-78; Eli Lilly Postdoctoral Teaching Fellow, 1984; alternate, Natl Research Council Postdoctoral Fellowship, Washington DC, 1984. **MEMBERSHIPS** Musical director, WTUI Bloomington, "Contemporary Black Gospel Music," 1979; Alpha Lambda Delta, 1968; Sigma Alpha Iota, NTSU, 1969; chapter vice pres, Mortar Board, NTSU, 1970-71; Pi Kappa Lambda, 1971. **SELECTED PUBLICATIONS** Musical director, video tapes 2-30 minutes, "The Life & Works of Undine S Moore," Afro-American Arts Institute, Indiana University, 1979. **CONTACT ADDRESS** Dept of Afro-American Studies, Indiana Univ, Bloomington, Bloomington, IN, 47405-1101.

BURNS, CAROL J.
PERSONAL Born 11/24/1954, IA, ., m, 1989, 1 child **DISCIPLINE** ARCHITECTURE **EDUCATION** Yale Col, BA, 80; Yale School of Architecture, M.Arch, 83 **CAREER** Asst prof, Harvard, 87-92; asst Chair Archit Dept, Harvard, 92-94; assoc prof, Harvard, 92- **HONORS AND AWARDS** Graham Found Grant, 88; Milton Grant, 90; ALA Education Honors, 96 **MEMBERSHIPS** Ed board, Jrnl Archit Education, 96-99; Commissioner Education, Boston Soc Archit, 96-98; MA Dept Housing & Community Development **RESEARCH** American Housing and Settlement Patterns; Architectural Design Theory **SELECTED PUBLICATIONS** "Re: Visions of Findings on Architecture's Way Forward," Jrnl Archit Education, 98; "Review of Building Community," Jrnl Archit Planning Res, 98; "Land as a Commodity of Limited Supply," Thresholds 4, 98 **CONTACT ADDRESS** 42 Union Park, Boston, MA, 02118. **EMAIL** cb@taymacbur.com

BURNS, CHESTER RAY
PERSONAL Born 12/05/1937, Nashville, TN, m, 1962, 2 children **DISCIPLINE** HISTORY OF MEDICINE, AMERICAN HISTORY **EDUCATION** Vanderbilt Univ, BA, 59, MD, 63; Johns Hopkins Univ, PhD, 69. **CAREER** Asst prof hist of med, 69-71, James Wade Rockwell asst prof, 71-74, dir div, 69-74, assoc dir, Inst Med Humanities, 74-80, James Wade Rockwell assoc prof, 75-79, James Wade Rockwell prof hist of med & mem, inst med humanities, 79-, Asst prof, Dept Prev Med & Community Health, Univ Tex Med Br, 74-75; from assoc prof to prof, 75-79; assoc, Univ Tex Grad Sch Biomed Sci Galveston, 74-77, mem, 77-; consult, Nat Ctr Health Servs Res, 76-78; Nat Bd Consult, Nat Endowment for Humanities, 78-. **HONORS AND AWARDS** Philos Soc TX, 97 **MEMBERSHIPS** Am Assn Hist Med; Hist Sci Soc; AHA; Orgn Am Hist; Assn Am Med Col. **RESEARCH** History of medical ethics and philosophy; history of American medicine; history of medical education. **SELECTED PUBLICATIONS** Art, The Development of Hospitals in Galveston Druing the Nineteenth Century, Southwestern Historical Quarterly, 93; auth, Thirty-three biographical essays for the New Handbook of Texas, Texas State Historical Association, 96; auth, Eight non-biographical essays for the New Handbook of Texas, Texas State Historical Association, 96; auth, Philosophy of Medicine and Bioethics: A Twenty-Year Retrospective and Critical Appraisal, Dordrecht: Kluwer Academic Publishers, 97. **CONTACT ADDRESS** Inst for the Med Humanities Univ of Tex Med Br, 301 University Blvd, Galveston, TX, 77550-2708. **EMAIL** cburns@utmb.edu

BURNS, MICHAEL
PERSONAL Born 12/30/1947, New York, NY, m, 1986, 1 child **DISCIPLINE** HISTORY **EDUCATION** Univ Calif Los Angeles, BA, 76; Yale Univ, PhD, 81. **CAREER** Acting instr, Yale Univ, 79-80; PROF, Mount Holyoke Coll, 81-. **HONORS AND AWARDS** Best Book Award, Phi Alpha Theta; Prix Lecache; Woodrow Wilson Int Center for Scholars Fel; Fulbright; Rockefeller; Tocqueville Award. **MEMBERSHIPS** Am Hist Asn. **RESEARCH** Modern Europe; Modern France. **SELECTED PUBLICATIONS** Auth, Disturbed Spirits: minority rights and New World Orders 1919 and 1990, New European Orders, 96; France and the Dreyfus Affair, 98. **CONTACT ADDRESS** Dept of History, Mount Holyoke Col, South Hadley, MA, 01075. **EMAIL** mburns@mtholyoke.edu

BURNS, SARAH
DISCIPLINE AMERICAN ART **EDUCATION** Univ Ill, PhD. **CAREER** Prof. **RESEARCH** Social history of American art; popular prints; consumer culture; gender studies. **SELECTED PUBLICATIONS** Auth, Pastoral Inventions: Rural Life in Nineteenth-Century American Art and Culture, Temple, 89; Inventing the Modern Artist: Art and Culture in Gilded Age America, Yale, 96. **CONTACT ADDRESS** Dept of History and Art, Indiana Univ, Bloomington, 300 N Jordan Ave, Bloomington, IN, 47405. **EMAIL** burnss@indiana.edu

BURNS, THOMAS
DISCIPLINE HISTORY **EDUCATION** Wabash Col, BA, 67; Univ Mich, MA 68, PhD, 74. **CAREER** Samuel Candler Dobbs Prof History. **HONORS AND AWARDS** Co-dir, archaeol excavations, Passau-Haibach/Manching, Germany and Babarc, Hungary. **RESEARCH** Ancient and early medieval history; barbarian invasions of the Roman Empire and the resultant barbarian kingdoms. **SELECTED PUBLICATIONS** Auth, The Ostrogoths: Kingship and Society; A History of the Ostrogoths; Barbarians within the Gates of Rome; coauth, Rome and the Barbarians as Seen in Coinage. **CONTACT ADDRESS** Dept History, Emory Univ, 221 Bowden Hall, 561 Kilgo Cir, Atlanta, GA, 30322-1950. **EMAIL** histsb@emory.edu

BURNSTEIN, DANIEL
DISCIPLINE AMERICAN HISTORY, WESTERN CIVILIZATION **EDUCATION** Univ TX, Austin, BA, 73; Tulane Univ, MSW, 80; Rutgers Univ, Doctorate, 92. **CAREER** Instr, Seattle Univ. **MEMBERSHIPS** Am Asn for the Hist of Med; AHA; Orgn of Am Hist; Nat Asn of Soc Workers; Urban Hist Asn. **SELECTED PUBLICATIONS** Auth, Progressivism and Urban Crisis: The New York City Garbage Workers' Strike of 1907, J of Urban Hist 16, 90; Rev of The Sanitarians: A History of American Public Health, by John Duffy, ISIS 82, 91; The Vegetable Man Cometh: Political and Moral Choices in Pushcart Policy in Progressive Era New York City, NY Hist 77, 96. **CONTACT ADDRESS** Seattle Univ, Seattle, WA, 98122-4460. **EMAIL** danielbu@seattleu.edu

BURRELL, BARBARA
DISCIPLINE CLASSICAL ARCHAEOLOGY **EDUCATION** NY Univ, AB, 73; Harvard Univ, MA, 75, PhD, 80. **CAREER** Tutor, NY Univ, 75; Tchg Fel, Harvard Univ, 78-80; Asst prof, Univ Pa, 81-83; Vis Lecturer, Johns Hopkins Univ, 87; Asst prof, Swarthmore Col, 84-90; Lecturer, Hebrew Union Col, 92-; Assoc Res Prof, Univ Cincinnati, 91-. **HONORS AND AWARDS** Magna cum laude, 73; Phi beta Kappa, 73; Fel Am Numismatic Soc, 74; Norton Fel, 75-76; Fel Royal Numismatic Soc, 77; May Isabel Sibley Fel, 77-78; Eugene Lang Fel, 88-89. **SELECTED PUBLICATIONS** Coauth, Notes on some Archaeological Contexts, Greek, Roman and Islamic Coins from Sardis, Archaeological Exploration of Sardis, 81; auth, Neokoroi, Harvard Studies in Classical Philol, 85; coauth, Uncovering Herod's Seaside Palace, Biblical Archaeol Rev, 93; auth, Two Inscribed Columns from Caesarea Maritima, Zeitschrift fur Papyrologie und Epigraphik, 93; auth, Palace to Praetorium: The Romanization of Caesarea, Caesarea Maritima: a Retrospective After Two Milennia, 96. **CONTACT ADDRESS** Dept of Classics, Univ Cincinnati, PO Box 0226, Cincinnati, OH, 45210-0226. **EMAIL** parkerhn@ucbeh.san.uc.edu

BURRISON, JOHN A.
PERSONAL Born 10/11/1942, Philadelphia, PA, s **DISCIPLINE** FOLKLORE **EDUCATION** Penn St Univ, BA, 64; Univ Penn, MA, 66, PhD, 73. **CAREER** Prof, dir, folklore cur, Georgia St Univ. **RESEARCH** Folklore, US Southern British Isles, specialization in folk pottery **CONTACT ADDRESS** Dept of English, Georgia State Univ, Univ Plaza, Atlanta, GA, 30308-3083.

BURROUGHS, CHARLES
DISCIPLINE ART HISTORY **EDUCATION** Univ London, PhD, 75. **CAREER** Assoc prof/dir Ctr Medieval/Renaissance Studies. **HONORS AND AWARDS** Assoc ed, Mediaevalia. **RESEARCH** Italian Renaissance art: archit and urban design, landscape, visual cult. **SELECTED PUBLICATIONS** Auth, Alberti e Roma in Joseph Rykwert, 94; Absolutism and the Rhetoric of Topography: Streets in the Rome of Sixtus V in Zeynep Celik in Streets: Critical Perspectives on Public Space, 94; The Building's Face and the Herculean Paradigm: Agendas and Agency in Roman Renaissance Architecture, Res: Anthrop Aesthetics, 93; Hieroglyphs in the Street: Architectural Emblematics and the Idea of the Facade in Early Sixteenth-Century Palace Design in Architecture and the Emblem, AMS. **CONTACT ADDRESS** SUNY Binghamton, PO Box 6000, Binghamton, NY, 13902-6000. **EMAIL** cburrou@binghamton.edu

BURSTEIN, ANDREW
DISCIPLINE HISTORY **EDUCATION** Columbia Univ, ABA, 74; Univ Mich, MA, 75; Univ VA, PhD, 94. **CAREER** ASST PROF, HIST, UNIV N IOWA **MEMBERSHIPS** Am Antiquarian Soc **SELECTED PUBLICATIONS** Auth, The Inner Jefferson: Portrait of a Grieving Optimist, Univ Va Press, 95. **CONTACT ADDRESS** Dept of Hist, Univ of N Iowa, Cedar Falls, IA, 50614.

BURSTEIN, L. POUNDIE
DISCIPLINE MUSIC THEORY **EDUCATION** CUNY, PhD. **CAREER** Prof; taught at, Mannes Col. **RESEARCH** Schenkerian theory. **SELECTED PUBLICATIONS** Publ on music of, Haydn, Beethoven & Schubert, in Musical Quart, Theory and Practice & J Music Theory. **CONTACT ADDRESS** Dept of Music, Hunter Col, CUNY, 695 Park Ave, New York, NY, 10021.

BURTON, DAVID HENRY
PERSONAL Born 08/04/1925, Oil City, PA **DISCIPLINE** HISTORY **EDUCATION** Univ Scranton, BSS, 49; Georgetown Univ, MA, 51, PhD, 53. **CAREER** Instr soc sci, St Joseph's Col, Pa, 53-55; asst prof hist, Duquesne Univ, 55-56; from asst prof to assoc prof, 56-62, prof hist, St Joseph's Col, PA, 62-, Vis lectr Am hist, Georgetown Univ, 54; English-Speaking Union Winston Churchill traveling fel, 72. **HONORS AND AWARDS** Themis Award for Contributions to the Study of Law, 80; Tengelmann Award for Distinguished Research and Teaching, 96; Earhart Fel, 85, 95. **MEMBERSHIPS** AHA; Am Cath Hist Asn; Orgn Am Historians; English-Speaking Union. **RESEARCH** American intellectual history, 19th and 20th centuries; British interpretations of American history; Oliver Wendell Holmes, Jr. **SELECTED PUBLICATIONS** Auth, Theodore Roosevelt: Confident Imperialist, Univ Pa, 69; Theodore Roosevelt: A Biography, Twayne, 72; Theodore Roosevelt and his English Correspondents, Am Philos Soc, 73; ed, American History--British Historians, Nelson-Hall, 76; Holmes-Sheehan Correspondence, Kennikat, 76; The Friendship of Justice Holmes and Canon Sheehan, Harvard Libr Bull, 4/77; Oliver Wendell Holmes, Jr, Twayne, 80; Progressive Masks, Univ of Del Press, 82; Clara Barton In The Service of Humanity, Greenwood, 95; Theodore Roosevelt American Politician, Fairleigh Dickinson Univ Press, 97; Taft, Holmes and the 1920s Court, Fairleigh Dickinson Univ Press, 98. **CONTACT ADDRESS** Dept of History, St. Joseph's Col, 5600 City Ave, Philadelphia, PA, 19131-1376.

BURTON, J.D.
PERSONAL Born 05/28/1959, Mankato, MN **DISCIPLINE** HISTORY OF EDUCATION **EDUCATION** St Olaf Coll, BA, 81; Univ Chicago, MA, 85; Coll of William & Mary, MA, 89; PhD, 96. **CAREER** Res Assoc, De Paul Univ, 85-88; Sr Res Asoc, Asoc Dir Inst Plan Res, De Paul Univ91-92; Dir Inst Plan Res, De Paul Univ, 92-94; Dir, Mgt Support De Paul Univ, 94-96; dir acad support De Paul Univ, 96-. **MEMBERSHIPS** Orgn of Am Historians; Hist of Educ Soc; Soc Sci Hist Asn; Asn for the Stduy of Hist Educ. **RESEARCH** History of Education; History of Higher Education; Colonial New England. **SELECTED PUBLICATIONS** Auth, Crimson Missionaries: Harvard College and the Robert Boyle trust, The New England Quart, 94; Harvard Tutors: The Beginning of an Academic Profession, Hist of Higher Educ Annual, 96; Philanthropy and the Origins of Educational Cooperation: Harvard College, the Hopkins Trust and the Cambridge Grammar School, The Hist of Educ Quart, 97; coauth, Data Linking: A Model of Student Outcomes Assessment, A Collection of Papers on Self-Study and Institutional Improvement, 94; Faculty Vitality in the Comprehensive University: Changing Context and Concerns, Res and Higher Educ, 96; From Retention to Satisfaction: New Outcomes for Assessing the Freshmen Experience, Res in Higher Educ, 96. **CONTACT ADDRESS** DePaul Univ, 2320 N Kennore Ave, Chicago, IL, 60614. **EMAIL** jburton@wppost.depaul.edu

BURTON, JOAN
PERSONAL Columbia, MO, m **DISCIPLINE** CLASSICAL STUDIES **EDUCATION** BA, 75, MA, 78, CPhil, 83, PhD, 88, Univ Calif, Berkeley. **CAREER** Actg instr, tchg assoc, classics, Univ Calif, Berkeley, 79-86; actg instr, classics, Univ Calif, Santa Cruz, 88; asst prof, 88-94, assoc prof, 94-, classics, chemn and assoc prof, comp lit, 98-, Trinity Univ. **HONORS AND AWARDS** Phi Beta Kappa, 74; dept citation class lang, 75; chancellor's fel, classics, 77-78, 80-81; John Rogers Fac Fel, 90-92. **MEMBERSHIPS** APA; Byzantine Stud Conf; Women's Class Caucus. **RESEARCH** Greek and Roman literature and culture; women's studies. **SELECTED PUBLICATIONS** Auth, The Function of the Symposium Theme in Theocritus' Idyll, Greek Roman, and Byzantine Stud, 92; auth, Why the Ancient Greeks Were Obsessed with Heroes and the Ancient Egyptians Were Not, Class Bull, 93; auth, Theocritus' Urban Mimes: Mobility, Gender and Patronage, Univ Calif, 95; auth, Women's Commensality in the Ancient Greek World, Greece and Rome, 98. **CONTACT ADDRESS** Dept of Classical Studies, Trinity Univ, 715 Stadium Dr, San Antonio, TX, 78212-7200.

BURTON, ORVILLE VERNON
PERSONAL Born 04/15/1947, Royston, GA, m, 1980, 5 children **DISCIPLINE** AMERICAN HISTORY **EDUCATION** Furman Univ, BA, 69; Princeton Univ, MA, 71, PhD(hist), 76. **CAREER** Instr hist, Mercer County Community Col, 71-72; asst master admin, dean Woodrow Wilson Residential Col, Princeton Univ, 72-74; instr, 74-75, asst prof, 75-82, assoc prof, 82-89, PROF HIST AND SOCIOL, 89- Univ Il; senior res sci and head, Initiative for Soc Sci and Hum, Nat Ctr for Supercomputing Applications, Univ Ill, 94- . **HONORS AND AWARDS** Grants-in-aid, 77-78; Humanities fel, Rockefeller Found, 77-78; acad humanist consult, Ill State Comt Bread for the World, 77-78; consult-evaluator, Nat Endowment for Humanities Workshop, Univ Miss, 80; Nat Endowment for Humanities res fel, summer 82; Phi Beta Kappa, 86; Nat Hum Ctr, 94; Pew Found, 96; NEH Educ Technol Grant, 97; Partnership Ill Award, 98. **MEMBERSHIPS** AHA; Orgn Am Historians; Southern Hist Asn; Social Sci Hist Asn; Conf Faith & Hist; Assoc for the Study of AFro American Hist and Life; So Asn for Women Hist; Soc Sci Computing Asn; H-Net; Nat Adv Bd, Alan Lomax's Global Jukebox: Giving Voice to the Human Species; Abraham Lincoln Hist Digitization Project; Univ Ill Press Bd. **RESEARCH** United States southern history; race relations; family; community; religion; agrarian society; voting rights. **SELECTED PUBLICATIONS** Auth, Teaching Historians with Databases, Hist Microcomputer Rev, 93; contrib, Encyclopedia of the Confederacy, Simon and Schuster, 93; contribur, Encyclopedia of Social History, Garland, 94; contrib, Encyclopedia of African American Culture and History, Macmillan, 96; contribur, Reader's Guide to American History, Fitzroy Dearborn, 97; contrib, Walking Integrity: Benjamin Elijah Mays: Mentor to Generations, Scholars, 96; auth, Edgefield South Carolina: Home to Dave the Potter, In: I Made This Jar: The Life and Works of the Enslaved African-American Potter, Dave, McKissick Museum, 98. **CONTACT ADDRESS** Dept of History, Univ of Illinois at Urbana-Champaign, 810 S Wright S, Urbana, IL, 61801-3611.

BURTON, WILLIAM LESTER
PERSONAL Born 09/20/1928, Moundsville, WV, m, 1958, 2 children **DISCIPLINE** UNITED STATES HISTORY **EDUCATION** Bethany Col, WVa, AB, 49; Univ Wis, MS, 52, PhD, 58. **CAREER** Instr hist, high sch, Va, 49-50; from asst prof to assoc prof, 57-68, chmn dept, 69-76, PROF HIST, WESTERN ILL UNIV, 68-, Acad coordr, Independent Travel Study Prog. **MEMBERSHIPS** AHA; Orgn Am Hist. **RESEARCH** Social and intellectual history; recent United States history; teaching of history. **SELECTED PUBLICATIONS** Auth, First Wisconsin railroad commission, Wis Mag Hist, 62; Revolution and American mythology, Midwest Quart, 63; Illinois in the age of exploration, Study Ill Hist, 66; A Descriptive Bibliography of Civil War Manuscripts in Illinois, Northwestern Univ, 66; ed, A Manual for History Teachers, Ill Off Pub Instr, 67; auth, Illinois: A Student's History of the Prairie State, Panoramic, 68; coauth, Exploring Regions Near and Far, 77 & Exploring Regions of the Western Hemisphere, 77, Follett; auth, Hard Marching Every Day - The Civil-War Letters of Fisk,Wilbur, 1861-1865 - Rosenblatt,E, Rosenblatt,R/, J Am Hist, Vol 80, 1993; Partisans and Progressives - Private Interest and Public-Policy in Illinois, 1870-1922 - Pegram,TR/, Hist, Vol 55, 1993; Rally Round the Flag - Chicago and the Civil-War - Karamanski,TJ/, Civil War Hist, Vol 40, 1994; Fire Within, A Civil-War Narrative from Wisconsin - Trask,KA/, Civil War Hist, Vol 42, 1996; **CONTACT ADDRESS** Dept of Hist, Western Illinois Univ, Macomb, IL, 61455.

BUSCH, BRITON COOPER
PERSONAL Born 09/05/1936, Los Angeles, CA, m, 1958, 2 children **DISCIPLINE** MODERN EUROPEAN & MIDDLE EASTERN HISTORY **EDUCATION** Stanford Univ, AB, 58; Univ Calif, Berkeley, MA, 60, PhD(mod Europ hist), 65. **CAREER** From instr to assoc prof, 63-73, prof hist, 73-78, WILLIAM R KENAN JR PROF, COLGATE UNIV, 78-, CHMN DEPT, 80-, Nat Endowment for Humanities fel, 68; Soc Sci Res Coun fel, 69. **MEMBERSHIPS** AHA; Mideast Inst; fel Am Asn Mideast Studies; Royal Soc Asian Affairs; NAm Soc Oceanic Hist. **RESEARCH** Maritime history; nineteenth and twentieth century Middle East and India. **SELECTED PUBLICATIONS** Auth, Mr-Bligh Bad Language - Passion, Power and Theater on the Bounty - Dening,G/, Am Neptune, Vol 53, 1993; United-States Trade with China 1784-1814 + Introductory-Remarks with Tables Listing American Vessels at China/, Am Neptune, Vol 54, 1994; The New Maritime History of Devon, Vol 1, From Early Times to the Late 18th-Century - Duffy,M, Fisher,S, Greenhill,B, Starkey,DJ, Youings,J/, Am Neptune, Vol 55, 1995; The New Maritime History of Devon, Vol 2, From the Late 18th-Century to the Present - Duffy,M, Fisher,S, Greenhill,B, Starkey,DJ, Youings,J/, Am Neptune, Vol 55, 1995; Log of Logs - A Catalog of Logs, Journals, Shipboard Diaries, Letters and all Forms of Voyage Narratives, 1788 to 1993, for Australia and New-Zealand and Surrounding Oceans, Vol 2 - Nicholson,I/, Am Neptune, Vol 55, 1995; Whaling and History - Perspectives on the Evolution of the Industry - Basberg,BL, Ringstad,JE, Wexelsen,E/, Am Neptune, Vol 55, 1995; Quarterdeck and Bridge - 2 Centuries of American Naval Leaders - Bradford,JC/, Am Neptune, Vol 57, 1997; author of numerous other articles. **CONTACT ADDRESS** Dept Hist, Colgate Univ, 13 Oak Dr, Hamilton, NY, 13346-1379.

BUSE, DIETER KURT
PERSONAL Born 09/15/1941, Soldau, Germany, m, 1961, 2 children **DISCIPLINE** MODERN HISTORY **EDUCATION** Univ Alta, BA, 64; Univ Ore, MA, 66, PhD(hist), 72. **CAREER** From lectr to asst prof, 69-75, ASSOC PROF HIST, LAURENTIAN UNIV, 75-, Ed, Laurentian Univ Rev, 71-73, Can Coun res grant, 73; Alexander von Humboldt-Stiftung res fel, Bonn, 75-77; Social Sci Res Coun res grant, 81. **MEMBERSHIPS** AHA. **RESEARCH** Modern German 1870-1933;

socialism and social movements; industrialization, comparative. **SELECTED PUBLICATIONS** Auth, Ebert and the coming of World War I, Int Rev Social Hist, 68; German revolutions, Dalhousie Rev, 72; Ebert and the German crisis 1917-1920, Cent Europ Hist, 72; ed, Aspects of Imperial Germany, Spec Issue Laurentian Univ Rev, 73; Parteiagitation and Wahlkreisvertretung, Verlag Neue Gesellschaft, Bonn, 75; Bibliographic annotations on German Nationalism, In: Canadian Review of Studies in Nationalism, 74, 78 & 81; Economic interest and lobbying, Early Weimar Repub Hist J, 81; Urban and National Identity - Bremen, 1860-1920/, J Soc Hist, Vol 26, 1993; Unitarianism and South-German Self-Awareness - Weimar-Coalition and Social-Democratic-Party in the Reich Reform Discussions of 1918-1933 - German - Heimers,MP/, Am Hist Rev, Vol 99, 1994; The SPD - Proletarian Party, National Party, Quota Party - Development of Social-Democracy from the Weimar-Republic to German Unification - German - Losche,P, Walter,F/, J Mod Hist, Vol 67, 1995; The Brown Plague - Travels in Late Weimar and Early Nazi Germany - Guerin,D/, Arachne, Vol 3, 1996. **CONTACT ADDRESS** Dept of Hist, Laurentian Univ, 935 Ramsey Lake Rd, Sudbury, ON, P3E 2C6.

BUSH, JOHN M.
DISCIPLINE HISTORY **EDUCATION** Ark Tchr Col, BSE, 60; MS State Univ, MA, 62, PhD, 64. **CAREER** Tchr, Benton Jr High Sch, 60-61; tchg asst, MS State Univ, 62-62; instr Am hist, Ark Polytech inst, 64-65; assoc prof hist, 65-69, prof hist, La Tech Univ, 69-. **MEMBERSHIPS** Am Hist Asoc; La Hist Asoc; N La Hist Asoc. **RESEARCH** Hist of the late 19th century; recent Am hist; diplomatic hist. **SELECTED PUBLICATIONS** Auth, The Tensas Gazette: A Brief Sketch, N La Hist Asoc Jour, 74; Hale Boggs in Dic La Biog, La Hist Asoc, 88. **CONTACT ADDRESS** Dept of Hist, Louisiana Tech Univ, PO Box 3178, Ruston, LA, 71272.

BUSH-BROWN, ALBERT
PERSONAL Born 01/02/1926, West Hartford, CT, m, 1948, 4 children **DISCIPLINE** HISTORY OF ART & ARCHITECTURE **EDUCATION** Princeton Univ, AB, 47, MFA, 49, PhD, 58. **CAREER** Instr art & archaeol, Princeton Univ, 49-50; lectr, Lowell Inst, 52; asst prof, Western Reserve Univ, 53-54; asst prof archit, Mass Inst Technol, 54-58, assoc prof archit & exec off, 58-62; pres, RI Sch Design, 62-68; Bemis vis prof, Mass Inst Technol, 68-69; vis prof & dir coun urban & regional studies, State Univ NY Buffalo, 68-69, vpres facilities planning, 68-71; CHANCELLOR LONG ISLAND UNIV, 71-, Prof, exten course, Harvard Univ, 56-61; ed archit & planning, Encycl Brittanica, 55; ed, J Archit Educ, 57-61; adv ed, J Aesthet & Art Criticism, 58-61; Benjamin Duke Lectr, Duke Univ, 63; mem, Nat Coun Arts, 65-70; spec consult to secy, Dept Housing & Urban Develop, 68; mem bd trustees, Comn Independent Cols & Univs, 73; managing dir, Metrop Opera Asn, New York & dir, Recording for the Blind, 76-79. **HONORS AND AWARDS** LLD, Emerson Col, 64; HHD, Providence Col, 66; DFA, Mercy Col, 76. **MEMBERSHIPS** Soc Archit Hist; Col Art Asn Am; Nat Coun Art in Educ. **RESEARCH** College and university architecture; architectural criticism; urban studies. **SELECTED PUBLICATIONS** Auth, The honest arrogance of Frank Lloyd Wright, Atlantic Monthly, 59; The architectural polemic, J Aesthet & Art Criticism, 12/59; Louis Sullivan, Braziller, 60; coauth, The Architecture of America: A Social Interpretation, Little, 61; Books, Bass Barnstable, Gt Marshes Press, 67; introd, The Architecture of the United States, New England and the Mid-Atlantic States, Doubleday/Mus Mod Art, Vol I, 81. **CONTACT ADDRESS** Long Island Univ, Greenvale, NY, 11548.

BUSHMAN, CLAUDIA
DISCIPLINE HISTORY **EDUCATION** Wellesley Coll, AB, 56; Brigham Young Univ, MA, 63, PhD, 78. **CAREER** ADJ PROF, HIST, COLUMBIA UNIV **MEMBERSHIPS** Am Antiquarian Soc **SELECTED PUBLICATIONS** Auth, America Discovers Columbus: How an Italian Explorer Became and American Hero, Univ Press of New England, 92; auth, Mormon Sisters: Women in Early Utah, Emmeline Press, 76, and Olympus Publ, 80. **CONTACT ADDRESS** 456 Riverside Dr, 10A, New York, NY, 10027.

BUSHMAN, RICHARD
DISCIPLINE UNITED STATES HISTORY **EDUCATION** Harvard Univ, BA, 55, PhD, 61. **CAREER** Prof. **SELECTED PUBLICATIONS** Auth, Joseph Smith and the Beginnings of Mormonism, 84; King and People in Provincial Massachusetts, 85; The Refinement of America: Persons, Houses, Cities, 92. **CONTACT ADDRESS** Dept of History, Columbia Col, New York, 2960 Broadway, New York, NY, 10027-6902.

BUSHNELL, DAVID
PERSONAL Born 05/14/1923, Philadelphia, PA, m, 1945, 3 children **DISCIPLINE** HISTORY **EDUCATION** Harvard Univ, BA, 43, PhD(hist), 51. **CAREER** Res analyst, Off Strategic Serv & US Dept State, 44-46; from instr to asst prof hist, Univ Del, 49-56; historian, US Air Force Missile Develop Ctr, 56-61, chief hist div, Off Aerospace Res, 61-63; assoc prof, 63-68, PROF HIST, UNIV FLA, 68-, Contrib ed, Handbook Latin Am Studies, 56-. **MEMBERSHIPS** Conf Latin Am Hist; Latin Am Studies Assn; corresp mem Colombian Acad Hist. **RESEARCH** Nineteenth century Colombia and Argentina. **SELECTED PUBLICATIONS** Auth, Protestants, Liberals, and Freemasons - Societies of Ideas and Modernism in Latin-America, 19th-Century - Spanish - Bastian,JP/, Hisp Am Hist Rev, Vol 72, 1992; Bello and Bolivar, Poetry and Politics in the Spanish-American Revolution - Cussen,A/, Hisp Am Hist Rev, Vol 74, 1994; Sarmiento, Author of a Nation - Halperin-donghi,T/, Hisp Am Hist Review, Vol 75, 1995; Latin-American Federalisms, Mexico/Brazil/Argentina - Spanish - Carmagnani,M/, Americas, Vol 52, 1995; Between Legitimacy and Violence - Colombia, 1875-1994 - Spanish - Palacios,M/, Hisp Am Hist Rev, Vol 76, 1996; The Rhythm of Leisure and Pleasures in Bogota - Spanish - Peralta,V/, Hisp Am Hist Rev, Vol 76, 1996; Irregular War in South-America, 18th-Century 19th-Century - An Essay of Comparative Social-History of Spain and New Granada - Spanish - Perez,EO/, Hisp Am Hist Rev, Vol 77, 1997. **CONTACT ADDRESS** Dept of Hist, Univ of Fla, Gainesville, FL, 32601.

BUSSANICH, JOHN
DISCIPLINE GREEK PHILOSOPHY, MEDIEVAL PHILOSOPHY, PHILOSOPHY OF RELIGION, COMPARATIVE **EDUCATION** Stanford Univ, BA, 72, PhD, 82. **CAREER** Assoc prof, Univ NMex. **SELECTED PUBLICATIONS** Auth, The One and its Relation to Intellect in Plotinus: A Commentary on Selected Texts, Brill, 88; Plotinus' Metaphysics of the One, in The Cambridge Companion to Plotinus, ed, Lloyd P Gerson, Cambridge UP, 96; coed, Ancient Philosophy. **CONTACT ADDRESS** Univ NMex, Albuquerque, NM, 87131.

BUTLER, JEFFREY ERNEST
PERSONAL Born 09/27/1922, Cape Province, South Africa, m, 1947, 3 children **DISCIPLINE** MODERN HISTORY **EDUCATION** Rhodes Univ, S Africa, BA, 47; Oxford Univ, MA, 56, DPhil, 63. **CAREER** Staff tutor delegacy extramural studies, Oxford Univ, 53-57; vis asst prof govt, Boston Univ, 57-58, res assoc hist govt, 58-64; PROF HIST, WESLEYAN UNIV, 64-, Lectr hist, Wellesley Col, 60-64. **MEMBERSHIPS** Fel African Studies Asn; AHA. **RESEARCH** British liberal colonial policy, particularly South Africa; African political organizations; South African politics. **SELECTED PUBLICATIONS** Auth, The Liberal Party and the Jameson Raid, Clarendon, Oxford, 68; Petty Offenses, Serious Consequences - Multiple Petty Offenses and the 6th Amendment Right to Jury Trial/, Mich Law Rev, Vol 94, 1995. **CONTACT ADDRESS** Dept of Hist, Wesleyan Univ, Middletown, CT, 06457.

BUTLER, JON
PERSONAL Born 06/04/1940, Fort Smith, AK, m, 1970, 2 children **DISCIPLINE** HISTORY **EDUCATION** Univ Minnesota BA 64, PhD 72. **CAREER** Yale Univ prof of Amer studies, history and religious studies, 85 to 98-; Univ Illinois, Chicago, asst prof to prof, hist, 75-85; California State Col, asst prof, hist, 71-75. **HONORS AND AWARDS** Beveridge Prize of AHA for Best Book in Amer Hist: Awash in a Sea of Faith; Outler Prize; Theodore Saloutos Prize; Gilbert Chinard Prize. **MEMBERSHIPS** AHA; ASA; OAH; ASCH **RESEARCH** Colonial and religious Amer history. **SELECTED PUBLICATIONS** Auth, Religion in American History: A Reader, co-ed Harry S Stout, NY 97; Awash in a Sea of Faith: Christianizing the American People, Cambridge MA, Harvard Univ Press, 90; The Christianization of Modern America, Kirchliche Zeitgeschichte, 98; Protestant Success in the New American City, 1870-1920, The Anxious Secrets of Rev Walter Laidlaw PhD, IN: Harry S. Stout and Darryl G. Hart, eds, New Directions in American Religious History, NY Oxford Press 97; Coercion, Miracle, Reason: Rethinking Religion in the Revolutionary Age, in: Religion in the Revolutionary Age, ed Ronald Hoffman, Char VA, Univ Press Of VA 94. **CONTACT ADDRESS** American Studies Program, Yale Univ, PO Box 208236, New Haven, CT, 06520-8236. **EMAIL** jon.butler@yale.edu

BUTLER, LEE HAYWARD, JR.
PERSONAL Born 02/15/1959, Harrisburg, PA, m **DISCIPLINE** PSYCHOLOGY **EDUCATION** Eastern Baptist Sem, Mdiv, 86; Princeton Sem, ThM, 88; Drew Univ, MPhil, 92; PhD, 94. **CAREER** Asst prof, Lancaster Theol Sem, 91-96; Chicago Theol Sem, 96-. **MEMBERSHIPS** AAR; Soc for the Study of Black Relig; Asn of Black Psychologists. **RESEARCH** Psychology; Religion; Identity formation; Healing traditions. **CONTACT ADDRESS** Chicago Theol Sem, 5757 S University Ave, Chicago, IL, 60637-5213. **EMAIL** lhbutler@compuserve.com

BUTLER, LESLIE
DISCIPLINE HISTORY **EDUCATION** Univ of Rochester, BA, 91; Yale Univ, Phil, 94; PhD, 97. **CAREER** VIS ASST PROF, HIST, REED COLL **MEMBERSHIPS** Am Antiquarian Soc **RESEARCH** James Russell Lowell **CONTACT ADDRESS** History Dept, Reed Col, 3203 SE Woodstock Blvd, Portland, OR, 97202.

BUTLER, REBECCA BATTS
PERSONAL Norfolk, VA **DISCIPLINE** EDUCATION **EDUCATION** Temple U, DEd 1965; Temple U, MEd 1958; Glassboro State Coll, BS 1942. **CAREER** Camden Public Schools, elementary teacher 1937-51, supvr of guidance 1966-68, dir adult comm prog 1969-74; Camden Secondary School, teacher 1951-59; NJ State Dept of Educ, 1968-69; Glassboro State Coll, adj prof; Organized Lincoln School for Unwed Mothers Camden City, director. **SELECTED PUBLICATIONS** "Protraits of Black Role Models In The History of Southern New Jersey"; "My Thoughts I Write," 1990. **CONTACT ADDRESS** 15 Eddy Pl, Cherry Hill, NJ, 08002.

BUTOW, ROBERT J.C.
PERSONAL Born 03/19/1924, San Mateo, CA, m, 1950, 1 child **DISCIPLINE** HISTORY **EDUCATION** Stanford Univ, PhD(hist), 53. **CAREER** Res fel, Ctr Int Studies, Princeton Univ, 53-54, res assoc, 57-60, from instr to asst prof, 54-60; assoc prof, 60-66, PROF HIST, UNIV WASH, 66-, MEM FAC, SCH INT STUDIES, 60-, Rockefeller Found & Soc Sci Res Coun res fel, Japan, 56-57; mem, Inst Advan Studies & Rockefeller Found grant int rels res, 62-63; Guggenheim Mem Found fel, 65-66 & 78-79. **MEMBERSHIPS** Asn Mem Inst Advan Study; Soc Hist Am Foreign Rel. **RESEARCH** Japanese-American relations. **SELECTED PUBLICATIONS** Auth, Japan's Decision to Surrender, Stanford Univ, 54 & 67; The Hull-Nomura Conversations: A Fundamental Misconception, Am Hist Rev, 7/60; Tojo and the Coming of the War, Princeton Univ, 61 & Stanford Univ, 69; Backdoor Diplomacy in the Pacific: The Proposal for a Konoye-Roosevelt Meeting, 1941, J Am Hist, 6/72; The John Doe Associates: Backdoor Diplomacy for Peace, 1941, Stanford Univ, 74; The FDR Tapes: Secret Recordings Made in the Oval Office of the President in the Autumn of 1940, Am Heritage, 2-3/82; Marching Off to War on the Wrong Foot, The Final Note Tokyo Did Not Send to Washington/, Pac Hist Rev, Vol 63, 1994; How Roosevelt Attacked Japan at Pearl-Harbor - Myth Masquerading as History/, Prologue-Quarterly of the National Archives, Vol 28, 1996. **CONTACT ADDRESS** Sch of Int Studies, Thomson Hall DR-05 Univ of Wash, Seattle, WA, 98195.

BUTSCHER, EDWARD
PERSONAL Born 09/30/1938, Flushing, NY, m, 1976 **DISCIPLINE** MODERN BRITISH & AMERICAN LITERATURE **EDUCATION** Queens Col, BA, 63; Long Island Univ, MA, 70. **CAREER** TEACHER ENGLISH, JOHN BOWNE, 71-, Ed, Univ Rev, 67-73; ed mem, NY Poets Cooperative, 73-81; contrib ed, Home Planet News, 76-; bd mem, Cross-Cult Commun, 76-; mem fac English, New Sch Social Res, 76-78; instr poetry, C W Posts Poetry Ctr, 78-80. **MEMBERSHIPS** MLA; Authors' Guild; Cross-Cult Commun; Poets & Writers; Poetry Soc Am. **RESEARCH** Twentieth century British and American poetry; American literature (literary biography); contemporary British and American novel. **SELECTED PUBLICATIONS** Auth, The Fictive World of Aiken,Conrad - A Celebration of Consciousness - Seigel,CF/, Am Lit, Vol 66, 1994; The Western Canon - The Books and School of the Ages - Bloom,H/, Ga Rev, Vol 49, 1995; Hopper,Edward - An Intimate Biography - Levin,G/, Ga Rev, Vol 51, 1997; author of other articles and reviews. **CONTACT ADDRESS** 84-01 Main St, Jamaica, NY, 11435.

BUTTS, MICHELLE TUCKER
PERSONAL Born 12/22/1952, Clarksville, TN, d **DISCIPLINE** HISTORY **EDUCATION** Austin Peay State Univ, BA, 73, MA, 74; Univ of Nmex, PhD, 92. **CAREER** Adj instr, Santa Fe Community Col, 83-84; adj instr, Albuquerque Tech-Voc Inst, 87-88; adj instr, Hopkinsville Community Col, Univ of Kent, 91-92; ASST PROF OF HIST, AUSTIN PEAY STATE UNIV, 93-99. **MEMBERSHIPS** Org of Am Hist; Western Hist Asn; Southern Asn of Women Hist. **RESEARCH** Religious history; Galvanized Yankees; Native America; Western History; Civil War History. **CONTACT ADDRESS** Dept of Hist and Philos, Austin Peay State Univ, Clarksville, TN, 37044. **EMAIL** ButtsMT@APSU01.APSU.EDU

BYMAN, SEYMOUR DAVID
PERSONAL Born 10/26/1934, Chicago, IL, m, 1956, 3 children **DISCIPLINE** RELIGIOUS HISTORY **EDUCATION** Univ Ill, Urbana, BA, 56; Roosevelt Univ, MA, 67; Northwestern Univ, PhD(hist), 71. **CAREER** Asst prof, 70-75, assoc prof, 75-78, PROF HIST, WINONA STATE UNIV, 78-, Assoc, Inst Psychohistory, 77-78. **MEMBERSHIPS** AHA. **RESEARCH** Martyrology. **SELECTED PUBLICATIONS** Auth, Tudor death stands, Moreana, 73; Suicide and alienation: Martyrdom in Tudor England, Psychoanal Rev, 74; Guilt and martyrdom: The case of John Bradford, Harvard Theol Rev, 75; A defense of psychohistory, 78 & Child raising and melancholia in Tudor England, 78, J Psychohistory; Ritualistic acts and compulsive behavior: The pattern of sixteenth century martyrdom, Am Hist Rev, 78; Humanities and the Law School Experience, J of Legal Educ, 85; The Perils of Psychohistory, J of Psychohistory, 88. **CONTACT ADDRESS** Dept of History, Winona State Univ, P O Box 5838, Winona, MN, 55987-0838. **EMAIL** sbyman@vax2.winona.msus.edu

BYNUM, CAROLINE WALKER
PERSONAL Born 05/10/1941, Atlanta, GA, m, 1983, 1 child **DISCIPLINE** HISTORY, MEDIEVAL EUROPE **EDUCATION** Univ MI, BA, 62; Harvard Univ, PhD, 69. **CAREER**

Asst prof, Harvard Univ, 69-74, assoc prof, 74-76; assoc prof and prof, Univ WA, Seattle, 76-88; prof, Columbia Univ, NYC, 88-, Morris and Alma Schapiro chair in History, 90-. **HONORS AND AWARDS** Berkshire Prize, for Best Historical Article Written by a Woman, 85; MacArthur Fel, July 86-July 91; Nelson Prize for best article, Renaissance Soc of Am, 87; fel, Medieval Academy of Am, 89; Philip Schaff prize of the ASCH/AHA for the best book in any field of Church History, for Holy Feast, Holy Fast; Trilling Prize for the Best Book by a Columbia Faculty Member, 92, for Fragmentation and Redemption, given by the Am Academy of Religion, 92; Ralph Waldo Emerson Prize of Phi Beta Kappa given for the best book of the year on "the intellectual and cultural condition of man," 95, for Resurrection of the Body; Jacques Barzun Prize for the best work in cultural history, given by the Am Philos Soc for Resurrection of the Body, 96; Presidential Award for Outstanding teaching, Columbia Univ, May, 97; six honorary degrees. **MEMBERSHIPS** Am Hist Asn; Medieval Academy of Am; Am Soc of Church History; Am Cath Hist Asn; Am Academy of Relig; Am Soc for the Study of Relig (86); Am Academy of Arts and Sciences (93); Am Philos Soc (95). **RESEARCH** The religious and intellectual history of medieval Europe, ca 500-ca 1500; escatology; hagiography; women's religious movements; mysticism; the history of science; scholasticism. **SELECTED PUBLICATIONS** Auth, Jesus as Mother: Studies in the Spirituality of the High Middle Ages, Univ CA Press, 82; Gender and Religion: On the Complexity of Symbols, ed Caroline Bynum, Stevan Harrell, and Paula Richman, Beacon Press, 86; Holy Feast and Holy Fast: The Religious Significance of Food to Medieval Women, Univ CA Press, 87; Fragmentation and Redemption: Essays on Gender and the Human Body in Medieval Religion, Urzone Pubs, 91; The Resurrection of the Body in Western Christianity, 200-1336, Columbia Univ Press, 95; Why All the Fuss About the Body? A Medievalist's Perspective, Critical Inquiry 22, autumn 95; Wonder, The Am Hist Rev 102 1, Feb 97; Metamorphosis, or Gerald and the Werewolf, Speculum 73, Oct 98. **CONTACT ADDRESS** History Dept, Columbia Univ, Fayerweather Hall, MC 2546, New York, NY, 10027.

BYNUM, DAVID ELIAB
PERSONAL Born 01/26/1936, Louisville, KY, m, 1966, 2 children **DISCIPLINE** EASTERN EUROPEAN ORAL LITERATURE **EDUCATION** Harvard Univ, AB, 58, Am, 62, PhD(Slavic lang & lit), 64. **CAREER** From instr to asst prof Slavic & gen educ & asst cur, Harvard Univ, 64-72, cur, Milman Parry Collection oral lit, 72-78, lectr oral lit, 73-78; prof mod lang & chmn dept, The Citadel, 80-82; PROF MOD LANG & DEAN COL ARTS & SCI, CLEVELAND STATE UNIV, 82-, Consult, subcomt E Cent & Southeast Europ studies & mem adv comt libr needs, Am Coun Learned Soc, 67-72; assoc bibliogr, MLA, 67-, exec comt, div anthrop approaches to lit, 78-82, deleg assembly, 80-82; chmn bd tutors in folklore & mythology, Harvard Univ, 68-77, managing ed, Publ Milman Parry Collection, 73-, exec officer, Ctr Study Oral Traditions, 74-78, mem, Standing Comt African Studies, 74-78, tutor folklore & myth, John Winthrop House, 77-80; prin investr, Nat Endowment for Humanities Prog Dev Grant, 72-74; Guggenheim fel, 79-80; chmn, Comt to Rev Daniel Lib, 81-. **MEMBERSHIPS** MLA; Am Folklore Soc; Am Asn Advan Slavic Studies; Am Asn Southern European Studies; Comp Lit Asn. **RESEARCH** Oral traditions; narrative; East European literatures. **SELECTED PUBLICATIONS** Auth, The generic nature of oral epic poetry, Genre, 69; Thematic sequences and transformation of character in oral narrative tradition, Rev Philol, 70; ed, Serbocroatian Heroic Songs, Harvard Univ, Vol 4, 74, Vol 6, 79 & Vol 14, 80; auth, Child's legacy enlarged: Oral literary studies at Harvard since 1856, Harvard Libr Bull, 74; The Daemon in the Wood: A Study of Oral Narrative Patterns, Harvard Univ, 78; The bell, the drum, Milman Parry, and the time machine, Chinese Lit, 79; Myth and ritual: Two faces of tradition, Festschrift for Albert Bates Lord, 81; Formula, theme and critical method, Can-Am Slavic Studies, 81; The Singer of Tales in Performance - Foley,JM/, Slavic and East Europ J, Vol 40, 1996; The Singer of Tales in Performance - Foley,JM/, Slavic and East Europ J, Vol 40, 1996. **CONTACT ADDRESS** Dept Mod Lang, Cleveland State Univ, 1983 E 24th St, Cleveland, OH, 44115-2440.

BYRE, CALVIN S.
PERSONAL Born 11/22/1947, Appleton, MN, m, 1972 **DISCIPLINE** CLASSICAL LANGUAGES AND LITERATURES **EDUCATION** Univ Minn, BA, 69; Univ Chicago, PhD, 76; Rosary Col, MALS, 85. **CAREER** Asst prof/head of ref, Roosevelt Univ, 86-90; asst prof of bibliog and adjunct asst prof of classics, Univ Okla, 90-96; assoc prof of bibliog and adjunct assoc prof of classics, Univ Okla, 96-. **HONORS AND AWARDS** Phi Beta Kappa; Robert V. Cram Memorial Scholar in Classics, Univ Minn; Ford four-year fel, Univ Chicago. **MEMBERSHIPS** Amer Philol Asn; Classical Asn of the Middle West and South. **RESEARCH** Greek epic; Literary criticism. **SELECTED PUBLICATIONS** Auth, Suspense in the Phaeacian Episode of Apollonius' Argonautica, Ill Class Studes, 22, 65-73, 97; auth, On the Departure from Pagasae and the Passage of the Plactae in Apollonius/ Argonautica, Mus Helveticum, 54, 106-114, 97; auth, The Killing of Apsyrtus in Apollonious Rhodius' Argonautica, Phoenix, 50, 3-16, 96; auth, Distant Encounters: The Prometheus and Phaethon Episodes in Apollonius' Argonautica, Amer Jour of Philol, 117, 275-283, 96; auth, The Rhetoric of Description in Odyssey, 9.116-41, Odysseus and the Goat Island, Class Jour, 89, 357-367, 94; auth, On the Description of the Harbor of Phorkys and the Cave of the Nymphs, Odyssey, 13.96-112, Amer Jour of Philol, 115, 1-13, 94; auth, Narration, Description, and Theme in the Shield of Achilles, Class Jour, 88, 33-42, 92; auth, The Narrator's Addresses to the Narratee in Apollonius Rhodius' Argonautica, Transactions of the Amer Philos Asn, 121, 215-227, 91; auth, Penelope and the Suitors before Odysseus: Odyssey, 18.158-303, Amer Jour of Philol, 109, 159-173, 88; auth, Per aspera (et arborem) ad astra. Ramifications of the Allegory of Arete in Quintus Smyrnaeus Posthomerica, 5, 49-68, Hermes, 110, 184-195, 82. **CONTACT ADDRESS** 1727 Bryant Cir., Norman, OK, 73026. **EMAIL** cbyre@ou.edu

BYRNE, FRANK LOYOLA
PERSONAL Born 05/12/1928, Hackensack, NJ, m, 1962, 2 children **DISCIPLINE** UNITED STATES HISTORY **EDUCATION** NJ State Col, Trenton, BS, 50; Univ Wis, MS, 51, PhD(hist), 57. **CAREER** Instr hist, La State Univ, 57-58; from asst prof to assoc prof, Creighton Univ, 58-66; assoc prof, 66-68, chmn, Grad Prog Hist, 69-72, PROF HIST, KENT STATE UNIV, 68-, Mem, Nebr Civil War Centennial Comn, 60-65; Wis Civil War Centennial Comn res grant, 62-63; Am Philos Soc res grant, 65; Kent State Univ fac res grant, 67, 69, 72. **MEMBERSHIPS** AHA; Orgn Am Hist; Southern Hist Asn. **RESEARCH** Civil War; temperance movement; Reconstruction. **SELECTED PUBLICATIONS** Auth, Libby Prison: A Study in Emotions, J Southern Hist, 11/58; Prophet of Prohibition: Neal Dow and His Crusade, 61 & ed, The View From Headquarters: Civil War Letters of Harvey Reid, 65, Wis State Hist Soc; auth, A Terrible Machine: General Neal Dow's Military Government on the Gulf Coast, Civil War Hist, 3/66; compiler, Prisons and Prisoners of War, In: Civil War Books: A Critical Bibliography, La State Univ, Vol I, 67; co-ed, Haskell of Gettysburg: His Life and Civil War Papers, Wis State Hist Soc, 70; ed, Bound to See the President: A Michigan Private Calls on Lincoln, Mich Hist, 7-8/79; auth, Libby Prison, Salisbury Prison, In: Encyclopedia of Southern History, La State Univ, 79; The Sultana Tragedy - America Greatest Maritime Disaster - Potter,JO/, Civil War History, Vol 38, 1992; Civil-War Prisons and Escapes - A Day-to-Day Chronicle - Denney,RE/, Civil War Hist, Vol 40, 1994; Andersonville - The Last Depot - Marvel,W/, Civil War Hist, Vol 41, 1995; Recollected Words of Lincoln,Abraham - Fehrenbacher,DE, Fehrenbacher,V/, Civil War History, Vol 43, 1997. **CONTACT ADDRESS** Dept of Hist, Kent State Univ, Kent, OH, 44242.

BYRNES, JOSEPH FRANCIS
PERSONAL Born 10/25/1939, Waterbury, CT, m, 2 children **DISCIPLINE** HISTORY OF CHRISTIANITY; MODERN EUROPEAN HISTORY **EDUCATION** De Montfort Col BA, 66; Univ Notre Dame, MA, 67; Univ Chicago, MA, 74, PhD(relig & psychol), 76. **CAREER** From Asst Prof to Prof Relig Studies, 77-88, Prof History, Okla State Univ, 88-. **HONORS AND AWARDS** Fel, Inst for the Med Humanities, Univ Tex Med Branch, 80-81; Fel, Inst for the Advanced Study of Relig, Univ Chicago, 81-82; Southwestern Bell Res Fel, OSU, 89; NEH Travel Grant, 84, 91; Okla Found for the Humanities Res Grant, 90, 92, 94, 96. **MEMBERSHIPS** Am Acad Relig; Soc for Fr Hist Studies; Western Soc for Fr Hist; Am Soc of Church Hist; Cath Hist Soc. **RESEARCH** Religion and nationalism in modern France; Priests of the French Revolution. **SELECTED PUBLICATIONS** Auth, The Virgin of Chartres, Fairleigh Dickinson Univ Press, 81; The Psychology of Religion, Free Press, 84; Chateaubriand and Destutt de Tracy, Church Hist, 91; Christianity, in Rel World, Macmillan, 93; Revolutionary Festivals under the Directory, Church Hist, 94; Emile M¤le (1862-1954), Cath Hist Rev, 97. **CONTACT ADDRESS** Dept of History, Oklahoma State Univ, Stillwater, OK, 74078-0002. **EMAIL** byr6620@okway.okstate.edu

BYRNES, ROBERT FRANCIS
PERSONAL Born 12/30/1917, Waterville, NY, m, 1942, 7 children **DISCIPLINE** HISTORY **EDUCATION** Amherst Col, AB, 39; Harvard Univ, AM, 40, PhD, 47. **CAREER** From asst prof to assoc prof hist, Rutgers Univ, 46-53; dir, Mid-Europ Studies Ctr, NY, 54-56; prof hist, 56-67, chmn dept, 58-65, dir, Russ & E Europ Inst, 59-62, dir, Int Affairs Ctr, 65-67, dir, Russ & E Europ Inst, 71-76, DISTINGUISHED SERV PROF HIST, IND UNIV, BLOOMINGTON, 67-, Vis lectr, Swarthmore Col, 46-48; Rutgers Res coun grant, 47-48, 50-51; Soc Sci Res Coun grant-in-aid, 48, fel, 60; Rockefeller Found sr fel, Russ Inst, Columbia Univ, 48-50; mem, Inst Advan Studies, 50; Guggenheim fel, 50; chmn, Inter-Univ Comt, 58-69; secy, Joint Comt Slavic Studies, Am Coun Learned Soc-Soc Sci Res Coun, 58-61; Am Coun Learned Soc fel, 62-63; hon mem, Polish Inst Arts & Sci Abroad, 62-; vis scholar, Inst Hist, Soviet Acad Sci, 63, 78; consult, US Dept Health, Educ & Welfare, 64-; hist ed, JB Lippincott & Co, 64-70; trustee, Alverno Col, 67-76, chmn bd, 72-76; trustee, Boston Col, 69-73; actg ed, Am Hist Rev, 76-77; Netherlands Inst Advan Study fel, 76-77. **HONORS AND AWARDS** Presidential Bicentennial Medallion, Boston Col, 76; Sesqui-centennial Award, St Louis Univ, 78; Nat Acad Sci distinguished scholar exchange prog, China, 81., DHL, Amherst Col, 64; LLD, Coe Col, 64; DLitt, St Mary's Col, 67. **MEMBERSHIPS** AHA; Am Cath Hist Asn (pres, 61); Soc Fr Hist Studies; Am Asn Advan Slavic Studies (pres, 78-79); Midwest Slavic Conf (pres, 77-78). **RESEARCH** Conservatism in modern Europe, especially in France and Russia; anti-Semitism in Modern France; Christian democrats in modern France. **SELECTED PUBLICATIONS** Auth, Bibliography of American Publications on East-Central Europe, 1945-1957, 59 & coauth, The Second Soviet-Yugoslav Dispute, 59, Ind Univ; The United States and Eastern Europe, Prentice-Hall, 67; auth, Pobedonostsev: His Life and Thought, Ind Univ, 68; Russia in Eastern Europe: Hegemony Without Security, Foreign Affairs, Vol VI, 71; Soviet & American Academic Exchanges, 1958-1975, Ind Univ, 76; ed, Communal Families in the Balkans: The Zadruga, Univ Notre Dame, 76; auth, Awakening American Education to the World: The Role of Archibald Cary Coolidge, Univ Notre Dame, 82; The Shape of the New Europe - Treverton,GF/, Slavic Rev, Vol 53, 1994; Klyuchevskii,V.O., Teacher + The Greatest Historian of Russia, 1841-1911/, Russ Hist-Histoire Russe, Vol 21, 1994; The Survey Course That Became a Classic Set - Kliuchevskiis Course of Russian History/, J Mod Hist, Vol 66, 1994; Soviet-Foreign-Policy in Transition - Kanet,RE, Miner,DN, Resler,TJ/, Slavic Rev, Vol 54, 1995; Russia and Europe - An End to Confrontation - Malcolm,N/, Slavic Rev, Vol 54, 1995. **CONTACT ADDRESS** Dept of Hist, Indiana Univ, Bloomington, Bloomington, IN, 47401.

C

CABAN, PEDRO
DISCIPLINE POLITICAL ECONOMY OF COLONIALISM IN PUERTO RICAN, POLITICS AND COMPARATIVE **EDUCATION** City Col NY, BA; Columbia Univ, PhD. **CAREER** Assoc prof, dir, Puerto Rican and Lat Am Stud Prog, Fordham Univ; assoc prof, Rutgers, State Univ NJ, Livingston Col, 90-; ed bd, Latin Am Res Rev; bd dir, 85-91, chemn, 87-89, Inst for Puerto Rican Policy. **HONORS AND AWARDS** Fel, Ford Found; fel, Rockefeller Found. **MEMBERSHIPS** Lat Am Stud Asn. **RESEARCH** The nature of economic change and the role of the state in Puerto Rico during the post World War II era. **SELECTED PUBLICATIONS** Numerous reviews and articles on the political economy of Puerto Rico and US-Puerto Rico relations. **CONTACT ADDRESS** Dept of Puerto Rican & Hisp Carib Stud, Rutgers, State Univ NJ, Livingston Col, Tillett Hall 237, Livingston, NJ, 50011. **EMAIL** caban@rci.rutgers.edu

CAFFERTY, PASTORA SAN JUAN
PERSONAL Born 07/29/1940, Cienfuegos, Cuba, w **DISCIPLINE** HISTORY **EDUCATION** St. Bernard Col, BA, 62; George Washington Univ, MA 66, PhD, 71. **CAREER** Inst, Sacred Heart Acad, 62-64; inst, George Washington Univ, 67-69; spec asst to the Sec Transp, 69-70; spec asst to General Asst Sec, HUD, 70-71; sr study dir, Nat Opinion Res Ctr, 75-70, res assoc 80-88, Nat Opinion Res Ctr; asst prof, 71-76, assoc prof, 76-85, PROF, SCH OF SOCIAL SERV ADMIN, UNIV CHICAGO, 76- . **HONORS AND AWARDS** Wall St. J fel, 62; Smithsonian Res fel, 66-67; White House fel 69-70; Operation PUSH Woman of the Year, 75; Founder's Day Award, 76; Outstanding Achievement Award YWCA, 79; Dr of Humane Letters, honoris causa, Columbia Col, 87; Outstanding Achievement Award, Girl Scouts of Amer, 89; Comm of 100, Hull House Assn, 89. **RESEARCH** Language and culture; race and ethnicity; politics and governance. **SELECTED PUBLICATIONS** Coauth, Youth and the Environment: Report to the White House, GPO, 70; auth, Chicago's Spanish-Speaking Population: Selected Statistics, Chicago Dept Develop & Planning, 73; auth, LaPolacion Hispana de Chicago, Chicago Dept Develop & Planning, 73; coauth, Diverse Society: Implication for Social Policy, Nat Assn of Social Workers, 76; coauth, Selected Bibliography on Ethnicity and Social Policy: Health Care Delivery to Meet the Changing Needs of the American Family, DHEW, 78; coauth, Politics of Language: The Dilemma of Bilingual Education for Puerto Ricans, Westview, 81; coauth, Backs Against the Wall: Urban-Oriented Colleges and Universities with the Urban Poor and Disadvantaged, Ford Found, 83; coauth, The Dilemma of Immigration in America: Beyond the Golden Door, Transaction-Rutger Univ, 83; auth, Chicago Project: A Report on Civic Life in Chicago, Crain's Business, 87; coauth, Hispanics in the USA: A New Social Agenda, Transaction-Rutger Univ, 4th ed., 94. **CONTACT ADDRESS** Sch of Social Serv Admin, Univ of Chicago, 969 E 60th St, Chicago, IL, 60637.

CAFFREY, MARGARET M.
DISCIPLINE AMERICAN STUDIES **EDUCATION** Univ Texas, PhD 86. **CAREER** Memphis State Univ, asst prof, 88-93; Univ Memphis, assoc prof, 93-. **HONORS AND AWARDS** Facu Res Gnt; Outstnd Young Res Awd; Critics Choice Awd. **MEMBERSHIPS** SHA; ASA; OAH; Southern Asn Womens Historians. **RESEARCH** Am Women; cultural hist. **SELECTED PUBLICATIONS** Ruth Benedict: Stranger in this Land. **CONTACT ADDRESS** Dept History, Univ Memphis, Memphis, TN, 38152. **EMAIL** MCAFFREY@mocha.memphis.edu

CAHAN, DAVID
DISCIPLINE HISTORY OF SCIENCE **EDUCATION** Johns Hopkins Univ, PhD, 80. **CAREER** Prof, Univ Nebr, Lincoln.

HONORS AND AWARDS NEH fel, 94-96; vis fel, Ctr de la Recherche en Hist des Sci et des Techniques, Paris, Fr, 97. **RESEARCH** 19th century German scientist Hermann von Helmholtz. **SELECTED PUBLICATIONS** Auth, An Institute for an Empire: The Physikalisch-Technische Reichsanstalt, 1871-1918, Cambridge UP, 89. **CONTACT ADDRESS** Univ Nebr, Lincoln, 629 Oldfat, Lincoln, NE, 68588-0417. **EMAIL** dcahan@unlinfo.unl.edu

CAHILL, JANE
DISCIPLINE CLASSICAL MYTHOLOGY **EDUCATION** Leicester Univ, Eng, BA, 70; Univ W Ontario, MA, 71; Univ Brit Columbia, PhD, 76. **CAREER** Assoc prof **RESEARCH** Mythology and storytelling; history of words. **SELECTED PUBLICATIONS** Auth, Her Kind: Stories of Women from Greek Mythology, Broadview Press, 95. **CONTACT ADDRESS** Dept of Classics, Univ of Winnipeg, 515 Portage Ave, Winnipeg, MB, R3B 2E9. **EMAIL** cahill-j@s-h.uwinnipeg.ca

CAIDEN, GERALD E.
PERSONAL Born 02/06/1936, London, England, m, 1960, 2 children **DISCIPLINE** PUBLIC ADMINISTRATION, POLITICAL SCIENCE **EDUCATION** London School of Economics & Political Sci, PhD, 59. **CAREER** Australian Nat Univ, 61-66; Hebrew Univ, 66-68; Univ of Calif at Berkeley, 68-71; Haifa Univ, 71-75; Univ Southern Calif, 75-. **RESEARCH** International public administration; public policy; public ethics; administrative reform. **SELECTED PUBLICATIONS** Over 25 books and monographs, and over 220 refereed articles. **CONTACT ADDRESS** School of Public Admin, Univ of Southern Calif, Los Angeles, CA, 90089-0041. **EMAIL** caiden@usc.edu

CAINE, STANLEY PAUL
PERSONAL Born 02/11/1940, Huron, SD, m, 1964, 3 children **DISCIPLINE** AMERICAN HISTORY **EDUCATION** Macalester Col, BA, 62; Univ Wis-Madison, MS, 64, PhD(hist), 67. **CAREER** Asst prof hist, Lindenwood Cols, 67-71 & DePauw Univ, 71-77; PROF HIST & V PRES ACAD AFFAIRS, HANOVER COL, 77- **MEMBERSHIPS** Orgn Am Historians; Nat Humanities Fac. **RESEARCH** Late 19th century American history; early 20th century America. **SELECTED PUBLICATIONS** Auth, Roosevelt,Theodore--A Life, Historian, Vol 0056, 93. **CONTACT ADDRESS** Hanover Col, Hanover, IN, 47243.

CAIRNS, HUGH A.C.
PERSONAL Born 03/02/1930, Galt, ON, Canada **DISCIPLINE** LAW/POLITICAL SCIENCE/HISTORY **EDUCATION** Univ Toronto, BA, 53, MA, 57; St. Antony's Col, Oxford Univ, Dphil, 63. **CAREER** Instr to prof, polit sci, 60-95, chmn, 73-80, PROF EMER, UNIV BC, 95-; vis prof, Memorial Univ Nfld, 70-71; vis prof, Can stud, Univ Edinburgh, 77-78; vis prof, Can stud, Harvard Univ 82-83; Brenda and David McLean ch Can stud, 93-95; John Willis vis prof law, Univ Toronto, 95-96; PROF AND LAW FOUNDATION OF SASK CHAIR, COLLEGE OF LAW, UNIV OF SASKATCHEWAN, 97-. **HONORS AND AWARDS** Gold Medal Polit Sci & Econ, 53; Queen's Silver Jubilee Medal, 77; Pres Medal Univ Western Ont, 77; Molson Prize Can Coun, 82; Killam res fel, 89-91; Gov Gen Int Award Can Stud, 94; DLaws(hon), Carleton Univ, 94; DLaws(hon), Univ Toronto, 96; DLaws(hon), Univ BC, 98. **MEMBERSHIPS** Can Polit Sci Asn (pres, 76-77); Int Polit Sci Asn (mem coun, 76-79). **SELECTED PUBLICATIONS** Auth, Prelude to Imperialism: British Reactions to Central African Society 1840-1890, 65; coauth, A Survey of the Contemporary Indians of Canada: Economic, Political and Educational Needs and Policies, vol 1, 66; coauth, Constitution, Government and Society in Canada: Selected Essays by Alan C. Cairns, 88; coauth, Disruptions: Constitutional Struggles from the Charter to Meech Lake, 91; coauth, Charter versus Federalism: The Dilemmas of Constitutional Reform, 92; coauth, Reconfigurations: Canadian Citizenship and Constitutional Change, 95. **CONTACT ADDRESS** 1866 Main Mall, Vancouver, BC, V6T 1Z1.

CAIRNS, JOHN C.
PERSONAL Born 04/27/1924, Windsor, ON, Canada **DISCIPLINE** HISTORY **EDUCATION** Univ Toronto, BA, 45, MA, 47; Cornell Univ, PhD, 51. **CAREER** Instr, Univ N Carolina, 51-52; lectr to prof, 52-89, PROF EMER HISTORY, UNIV TORONTO; vis prof, Cornell Univ, 62; vis prof, Stanford Univ, 68. **MEMBERSHIPS** Am Hist Asn; Soc Fr Hist Stud. **RESEARCH** Modern French history; international history; historiography. **SELECTED PUBLICATIONS** Auth, France, 65; coauth, The Foundations of the West, 63; ed, The Nineteenth Century, 65; ed, Contemporary France, 78. **CONTACT ADDRESS** 706-20 Avoca Ave, Toronto, ON, M4T 2B8.

CALDER, LENDOL
PERSONAL Born 11/19/1958, Beaumont, TX, m, 1990, 2 children **DISCIPLINE** HISTORY **EDUCATION** Univ Tex, BA, 80; Univ Chicago, MA, 86, PhD, 93. **CAREER** Asst prof, Univ Wash, 92-93; asst prof, Colby-Sawyer Col, 93-96; asst prof, Augustana Col, 96-. **HONORS AND AWARDS** Phi Beta Kappa, 79; Charles Kennedy Award, 96, Econ bus Hist Society. **MEMBERSHIPS** Org Am Hist **RESEARCH** Consumer culture; the sixties; US social and cultural history. **SELECTED PUBLICATIONS** Auth, Financing the American Dream: A Cultural History of Consumer Credit, 99. **CONTACT ADDRESS** Dept of History, Augustana Col, 639 38th St, Rock Island, IL, 61201. **EMAIL** hicalder@augustana.edu

CALDER, WILLIAM M.
PERSONAL Born 09/03/1932, Brooklyn, NY **DISCIPLINE** CLASSICS **EDUCATION** Harvard Col, BA, 54, MA, 56; Univ of Chicago, PhD, 58. **CAREER** Harvard Col, ta, 55-56; Univ of Chicago, ta, 57-58; Columbia Univ, instr, asst prof, assoc prof, prof, 58-76; Univ of Colorado Boulder, prof, 76-88; Univ of Illinois Urbana, prof of classics & literature 88-. **HONORS AND AWARDS** Erfurt Acad of Sci, Elected For Mem; Ger Acad Sci, Heinrich Medallion; Univ of IL Urbana, A. O. Beckman Award, Neubukow's Heinrich Schliemann Medallion, Alexander von Humbolt Prize Winner **MEMBERSHIPS** SPHS London, SPRS London, CAE&W, EES, TM Gesell, ICC, ASGLE, AIA, APA, AAH, CAMS, GSA, ANS. **RESEARCH** Classic Greek hist; Greek and Roman pagan; hist of class scholar; 19th and 20th cent in Eng, Ger, and US. **SELECTED PUBLICATIONS** Co-auth, Philology and Philosophy: The Letters of Hermann Diels to Theodor and Heinrich Gomperz, Hildesheim, 95; Lieber Prinz: Der Breifwechsel zwischen Hermann Diels und Ulrich von Wilamowitz-Moellendorf ,1869-1921, Hildesheim 95; Sed serviendum officio... The Correspondence Between Ulrich von Wilamowitz-Moellendorff and Eduard Norden 1892-1931, Hildesheim, 97; Men in their Books: Studies in the Modern History of Classical Scholarship, Hidesheim, 98. **CONTACT ADDRESS** Dept of Classics, Univ of Illinois, Urbana-Champaign, 609 W Delaware Ave, Urbana, IL, 61801. **EMAIL** wmcalder@uiuc.edu

CALDWELL, L.K.
PERSONAL Born 11/21/1913, Montezuma, IA, m, 1940, 2 children **DISCIPLINE** HISTORY, GOVERNMENT **EDUCATION** Univ Chicago, PhB, 34 PhD, 43; Harvard Univ, MA, 38; Western Mich Univ, LLD, 77. **CAREER** Dir Res, Council of State Governments, 44-47; prof polit sci, Syracuse Univ, 47-53; co-dir, Public Admin Inst for Turkey and Middle East, United Nations, 53-54; vis prof, Univ Calif, Berkeley, 54-55; prof Polit Sci & Public and Environ Affairs, Indiana Univ, 55- . **HONORS AND AWARDS** UN Global 500, 91; John Gaus Award, Am Polit Sci Asn, 96; Natural Rsrc Coun Award, 97; Hon Life Member, Int Asn of Impact Assessment; fel, Am Asn for Advanc of Sci; fel, Nat Acad of Public Admin; fel, Royal Soc of the Arts. **MEMBERSHIPS** Am Polit Sci Asn; Am Soc for Public Admin; Asn for Polit and Life Sci. **RESEARCH** Public policy, law, and administration; policy for science, technology, and the environment. **SELECTED PUBLICATIONS** Coauth, Policy for Land: Law and Ethics, Rowman and Littlefield, 93; auth, Environment as a Focus for Public Policy, Texas A & M, 95; co-ed, Environmental Policy: Transnational Issues and National Trends, Quorum, 96; auth, International Environmental Policy, 3d ed, Duke, 96; auth, Scientific Assumptions and Misplaced Certainty in Natural Resources and Environmental problem-Solving, in Lemons, ed, Scientific Uncertainty and Environmental Problem-Solving, Blackwell, 96; auth, Implications for a World Economy for Environmental Policy and Law, in Dasgupta, ed, The Economics of Transnational Commons, Oxford, 97; auth, The national Environmental Policy Act: Agenda for the Future, Indiana, 98; auth, The Concept of Sustainability: A Critical Approach, in Lemons, Ecological Sustainability and Integrity; Concepts and Approaches, Kluwer Academic, 98. **CONTACT ADDRESS** School of Public and Environmental Affairs, Indiana Univ, Bloomington, Bloomington, IN, 47405. **EMAIL** lkcaldwe@indiana.edu

CALDWELL, M. MILFORD
PERSONAL Born 02/20/1928, SC, m **DISCIPLINE** EDUCATION **EDUCATION** SC State Coll, BS 1949; SC State Coll, MS 1950; OH State U, PhD 1959; OH State U, Post Doctoral Fellow. **CAREER** DE State Coll, prof of educ; Elizabeth City State Univ, prof of educ 1961-62; OH State Univ, asst prof of educ 1959-61. **MEMBERSHIPS** Pres Assn of Coll & Sch of Educ in State Univ & Land-Grant Colls; past pres DE Acad of Sci; mem Am Assn of Higher Edn; gov comm of Vocational Edn; mem Century Club YMCA; NAACP; Phi Alpha Theta; Gamma Sigma Delta; Phi Delta Kappa. **CONTACT ADDRESS** 1200 N Dupont Hwy, Dover, DE, 19901.

CALDWELL, RONALD JAMES
PERSONAL Born 07/02/1943, Pensacola, FL, m, 1966, 2 children **DISCIPLINE** MODERN EUROPEAN HISTORY **EDUCATION** Fla State Univ, BS, 65, MA, 66 PhD(hist), 71, M.L.I.S., Univ Al, 88. **CAREER** Instr hist, Orlando Jr Col, 66-68; assoc prof hist, Jacksonville State Univ, 71-, prof of hist, 83-. **MEMBERSHIPS** AHA; Southern Hist Asn; Soc Fr Hist Studies. **RESEARCH** Political history of the French Revolution. **SELECTED PUBLICATIONS** The Era of the French Revolution: A Bibliography of the History of Western Civilization, 1789-1799, 85; The Era of Napolean: A Bibliography of the History of Western Civilization, 1799-1815, 91. **CONTACT ADDRESS** Dept of Hist, Jacksonville State Univ, 700 Pelham Rd N, Jacksonville, AL, 36265-1602. **EMAIL** rcaldwel@jsucc.jsu.edu

CALDWELL, SARAH
PERSONAL Born 09/18/1957, Berkeley, CA, m, 1 child **DISCIPLINE** ANTHROPOLOGY **EDUCATION** Univ Calif, Berkeley, BA, 87, MA, 88, PhD, 95. **CAREER** Asst prof, anthrop and relig, Univ Mich, Ann Arbor, 95-98; asst prof, relig, Calif State Univ, Chico, 98- . **HONORS AND AWARDS** NEH Younger Scholars Prog, 86; Univ medal for most distinguished grad sr, Univ Calif, Berkeley, 87; Javits grad fel, 87-91; Fulbright-Hays fel, 92; Ruth C. Boyer Prize, 93; diss writing fel, 93-94; Robert Stoller Found prize, 95; Mich Soc of Fel, postdoc fel, 95-98. **MEMBERSHIPS** Am Acad Relig; Am Anthrop Asn; Am Asn of Univ Women; Am Ethnol Soc; Asn for Asian Stud; Asn for the Psychoanalysis of Culture and Soc; Soc for Psychol Anthrop; Soc for Tantric Stud. **RESEARCH** South Asia; Hinduism; performance; folklore; anthropology of religion; ritual; gender and sexuality; feminist psychoanalysis; cognition; abuse and trauma. **SELECTED PUBLICATIONS** Auth, Geza Roheim's Theory of the Dream Origin of Myth, Psychoanalytic Stud of Soc, 88; auth, Ghagavati: Ball of Fire, in Hawley, ed, Devi: Goddesses of India, Univ Calif, 96; contribur, Claus, ed, South Asian Folklore: An Encyclopedia, Garland, in press; auth, The Bloodthirsty Tongue and the Self-Feeding Breast: Homosexual Fellatio Fantasy in a South Indian Ritual Tradition, in Vaidyanathan, ed, Vishnu on Freud's Desk: A Hunduism and Psychoanalysis Reader, Oxford, in press; auth, Transcendence and Culture: Anthropologists Theorize Religion, Relig Stud Rev, 99; auth, Waves of Beauty, Rivers of Blood: Constructing the Goddess' Body in Kerala, in Pintchmann, ed, In Search of Mahadevi: Constructing the Identity of the Hindu Great Goddess, SUNY, 99; auth, On Terrifying Mother: Sexuality, Violence, and Worship of the Goddess Kali in Kerala, Delhi: Oxford Univ, 99. **CONTACT ADDRESS** Dept of Religious Studies, California State Univ, Chico, Chico, CA, 95929-0740. **EMAIL** scaldwell@csuchico.edu

CALHOON, ROBERT M.
PERSONAL Born 10/03/1935, Pittsburgh, PA, m, 1966 **DISCIPLINE** AMERICAN HISTORY **EDUCATION** Wooster Col, BA, 58; Western Reserve Univ, MA, 49, PhD, 64. **CAREER** Jr high sch teacher, Ohio, 59-60; from instr to assoc prof, 64-74, prof hist, Univ Nc, Greensboro, 74-; vis asst prof hist, Univ Conn, 66-67. **HONORS AND AWARDS** Fel, Duke-Univ NC Prog Humanities, 69-70; Nat Endowment Humanities res grant, 75. **MEMBERSHIPS** AHA; Orgn Am Historians; Southern Hist Assn. **RESEARCH** Early American political and intellectual history; the American Revolution; religion and cultural change in the south, 1750-1840. **SELECTED PUBLICATIONS** Auth, The Loyalists in Revolutionary America, 1760-1781, 73; auth, Revolutionary America: An Interpretive Overview, Harcourt, 76; ed, Religion and the American Revolution in North Carolina, NC Div Archives & Hist, 76; auth, A Troubled Culture: North Carolina in the New Nation, Writing North Carolina History, 79. **CONTACT ADDRESS** Dept of History, Univ of North Carolina, 1000 Spring Garden, Greensboro, NC, 27412-0001.

CALHOUN, DANIEL FAIRCHILD
PERSONAL Born 06/21/1929, Bridgeport, CT, m, 1952, 3 children **DISCIPLINE** MODERN HISTORY **EDUCATION** Williams Col, AB, 50; Univ Chicago, MA, 51, PhD(hist), 59. **CAREER** From instr to assoc prof, 56-66, PROF HIST, COL WOOSTER, 66- **MEMBERSHIPS** AHA. **RESEARCH** Russian history; Anglo-Soviet relations. **SELECTED PUBLICATIONS** Auth, Paths Not Taken--Brit Labor and International-Policy in the 1920s, Amer Hist Rev, Vol 0101, 96; National Crisis and National Government--Brit Politics, the Economy and Empire, 1926-1932, Jour Econ Hist, Vol 0053, 93; Britain Confronts the Stalin Revolution--Anglo-Soviet Relations and the Metro-Vickers Crisis, Amer Hist Rev, Vol 0102, 97. **CONTACT ADDRESS** Dept of Hist, Col of Wooster, Wooster, OH, 44691.

CALHOUN, LEE A.
PERSONAL Born 08/16/1947, Mobile, AL **DISCIPLINE** SOCIOLOGY **EDUCATION** Univ Toledo, BA 1969; Notre Dame, MA 1971; Univ MI, MA 1972; Univ of MI, PhD Candidate. **CAREER** Herring-Guerden Assoc, S Bend IN, consultant 1971; Dept of Sociology Notre Dame, teacher asst 1971; Dept of Sociology Univ MI, teaching fellow 1972; Afram Assoc, Ann Arbor MI, owner 1972; Howard Univ, lectr 1973-. **MEMBERSHIPS** Mem Am Acad Polit & Social Sci; inst Soc Ethics Life Sci; Am Soc Pub Adminstrn; Nat conf Black Polit Scintists; Univ Toledo Alumni Assn; Notre Dame Alumni Assn Alpha Kappa Delta; Sociology Honor Soc; NASSPAA Fellowship 1971-73; fellowship Univ MI 1972. **CONTACT ADDRESS** Dept Polit Sci, Howard Univ, Washington, DC, 20059.

CALKINS, KENNETH ROY
PERSONAL Born 02/19/1935, Detroit, MI, m, 1966, 3 children **DISCIPLINE** MODERN EUROPEAN HISTORY **EDUCATION** Haverford Col, BA, 57; Univ Chicago, MA, 58, PhD(hist), 66. **CAREER** From instr to asst prof hist, Lake Forest Col, 63-67; asst prof, 67-75, assoc prof, 75-81, PROF HIST, KENT STATE UNIV, 81-, Nat coun, AAUP, 81-84. **MEMBERSHIPS** AHA. **RESEARCH** Late 19th and 20th century German and Austrian history; the development of European Socialism. **SELECTED PUBLICATIONS** Auth, Marxist Intel-

lectuals and the Working-Class Mentality in Germany, 1887-1912, Amer Hist Rev, Vol 0100, 95. **CONTACT ADDRESS** Dept of Hist, Kent State Univ, Kent, OH, 44240.

CALKINS, ROBERT GILMER
PERSONAL Born 12/29/1932, Oakland, CA, m, 1962, 3 children **DISCIPLINE** HISTORY OF ART **EDUCATION** Princeton Univ, AB, 55; Harvard Univ, MA, 62, PhD, 67. **CAREER** Assoc prof, 66-80, chmn dept, 76-81, PROF HIST OF ART, CORNELL UNIV, 80-, Am Coun Learned Soc grant-in-aid, 73; Am Philos Soc grant-in-aid, 80. **MEMBERSHIPS** Col Art Asn Am; Mediaeval Acad Am; Int Ctr Medieval Art. **RESEARCH** Fifteenth century manuscript illumination; Medieval architecture; Flemish painting. **SELECTED PUBLICATIONS** Auth, A Medieval Treasury, Medieval Art Exhib Catalogue, Cornell Univ, 10/68; Medieval and Renaissance Illuminated Manuscripts in the Cornell University Library, Cornell Libr J, 5/72; Stages of Execution: Procedures of Illumination as Revealed in an Unfinished Book of Hours, Gesta, 78; Parallels Between Inculabula and Manuscripts from the Circle of the Master of Catherine of Cleves, Oud Holland, 78; Distribution of Labor: The Illuminators of the Hours of Catherine of Cleves and Their Workshop, Trans of Am Philos Soc, 79; Monuments of Medieval Art, E P Dutton, 79; An Italian in Paris: The Master of the Brussels Initials and His Participation in the French Book Industry, Gesta, 81; auth The Question of the Origins of the Master of Catherine of Cleves, Masters and Miniatures: Proceedings of the Congress on Medieval Manuscript Illumination in the Northern Netherlands, 92; Pictorial Emphases in Early Biblical Manuscripts, The Bible in the Middle Ages: Its Influence on Literature and Art, Medieval and Renaissance Texts and Studies, 92; Narrative in Image and Text in Medieval Illuminated Manuscripts, Medieval Perspectives, 92; Secular Objects and Their Implications in Early Netherlandish Painting, Art into Life: Collected Papers from the Kresge Art Museum Symposia, Mich State Univ Press, 95; The Cathedral as Text, Hum, 95; Medieval Architecture in Western Europe from AD 300 to 1500, Oxford Univ Press, 98. **CONTACT ADDRESS** Dept Hist of Art, Cornell Univ, Goldwin Smith Hall, Ithaca, NY, 14850. **EMAIL** rgc1@cornell.edu

CALLAHAN, DANIEL FRANCIS
PERSONAL Born 11/28/1939, Boston, MA **DISCIPLINE** MEDIEVAL & CHURCH HISTORY **EDUCATION** St John's Sem, Mass, BA, 62; Boston Col, MA, 66; Univ Wis-Madison, PhD(hist), 68. **CAREER** Asst prof, 68-77, ASSOC PROF MEDIEVAL HIST, UNIV DEL, 77-, Am Coun Learned Soc grant, 82. **MEMBERSHIPS** Mediaeval Acad Am; AHA; Am Cath Hist Asn. **RESEARCH** The church in France, 750-1050; Medieval pilgrimages. **SELECTED PUBLICATIONS** Auth, The Diocese of Arras From Ad1093 Up to the 14th-Century--Research on Religious Life in the North of France During the Middle-Ages, Cath Hist Rev, Vol 0082, 96; Ademar-of-Chabannes, Millennial Fears and the Development of Western Anti-Judaism-An Examination of the Role of the Apocalypse in Late 10th-Century European Communities andiIts Effect on Jewish-Christian Relations, Jour Ecclesiastical Hist; The Archive and Possessions of the Abbey-of-Saint-Victor in Paris, Speculum-Jour Medieval Stud, Vol 0068, 93. **CONTACT ADDRESS** Dept of Hist, Univ of Del, Newark, DE, 19711.

CALLAHAN, RAYMOND ALOYSIUS
PERSONAL Born 11/30/1938, Trenton, NJ, m, 1964, 2 children **DISCIPLINE** MODERN BRITISH HISTORY **EDUCATION** Georgetown Univ, AB, 61; Harvard Univ, MA, 62, PhD(hist), 67. **CAREER** From asst prof to assoc prof, 67-76, PROF HIST, UNIV DEL, 76- **MEMBERSHIPS** AHA; Conf Brit Studies; Am Comt Hist Second World War; Am Comt Irish Studies. **RESEARCH** Modern Britain; British empire; Second World War. **SELECTED PUBLICATIONS** Auth, D-Day, June 6, 1944--The Climactic Battle of World-War-II, Rev(s) Amer Hist, Vol 0023, 95; D-Day--Piercing the Atlantic Wall, Rev(s) Amer Hist, Vol 0023, 95. **CONTACT ADDRESS** Dept of Hist, Univ of Del, 401 KOF, Newark, DE, 19711.

CALLAHAN, WILLIAM JAMES
PERSONAL Born 01/22/1937, Winchester, MA **DISCIPLINE** EARLY MODERN EUROPEAN HISTORY **EDUCATION** Boston Col, AB, 58; Harvard Univ, AM, 59, PhD(hist), 64. **CAREER** From asst prof to assoc prof, 65-75, PROF HIST, UNIV TORONTO, 75- **MEMBERSHIPS** Soc Span-Port Hist Studies; Can Hist Asn. **RESEARCH** Early modern and 18th century Spain. **SELECTED PUBLICATIONS** Auth, A Century of Social Catholicism in Europe, 1891-1991, Church Hist, Vol 0066, 97; Regalism, Liberalism and General Franco, Cath Hist Rev, Vol 0083, 97; Church and Society of Saragossa in the Mid 1700s--Pastoral Visit of Anoa, D., Francisco to his Archdiocese 1745-1749-Spanish, Cath Hist Rev, vol 0079, 93; Llorete, J.A., A Model of the Bourgeoisie--His Life and Work Until His Exile in France 1756-1813-Spanish, Cath Hist Rev, Vol 0079, 93; Sexuality in the Confessional--A Sacrament Profaned, Cath Hist Rev, Vol 0083, 97; Passional Culture--Emotion, Religion, and Society in Southern Spain, Church Hist, Vol 0062, 93; A Century of Social Catholicism in Europe, 1891-1991-Spanish, Church Hist, Vol 0066, 97; The Crisis of the 17th-Century in Europe and Latin-America-French, Amer Hist Rev, Vol 0100, 95. **CONTACT ADDRESS** Dept of Hist, Univ of Toronto, Toronto, ON, M5S 1A1.

CALLAWAY, ANITA
DISCIPLINE FINE ARTS **EDUCATION** Univ Sydney, Australia, PhD, 96. **CAREER** Res fel, Ctr Cross-Cult Res, Australian Natl Univ. **HONORS AND AWARDS** Grantee, Visions Australia research and development, 95. **RESEARCH** Australian art;, children's book illustrations. **SELECTED PUBLICATIONS** Contrib auth, The Dictionary of Australian Artists: Painters, Sketchers, Photographers and Engravers to 1870, Oxford Univ, 92; contrib auth, Heritage: The Australian Women's Art Book, Fine Arts Press, 95. **CONTACT ADDRESS** Dept of Education, Australian National Univ. **EMAIL** Anita.Callaway@anu.edu.au

CALLON, GORDON
PERSONAL Born 08/11/1945, Arvida, PQ, Canada, m, 1985 **DISCIPLINE** MUSIC **EDUCATION** MMA, McGill Univ, 71, BMUS, 89; DMA Univ of WA at Seattle, 84. **CAREER** Acadia Univ, 78-present: Assoc prof 84, Acadia Univ, 95-98: Dir, Sch of Music, Acadia Univ, 91-92,94-95: Actg Dir, Sch of Music Vancouver Community Col , found fac mem at VCC, Courtenay Youth Music Centre, summers 74-75; Univ of WA, 71-73 tchg asst: McGill Univ, 69-70, tchg asst. **HONORS AND AWARDS** Acadia Univ: Tchg Innovation Grant; 93-94, mem of group receiving award for develop of music/lang multimedia computer stations in teh lang lab; SSHRC Conference Grant; SSHRC General Grants 84-85, 91-92, Spring 93; Autumn 93; Research Fund Grants 89-90, 90-91, 93-94; Harvey T. Reid Summer Study Awards: 82,83. Canadian Music Centre: accepted as Assoc Composer, August 74; CBC/Canada Council Awards for Young Composers: Award Winner, 73-74; Univ of British Columbia: HR MacMillan Family Fel, 73-74: Univ of WA, Canada Council Doctoral Fel, 71-72, 72-73, offered 73-74, 76-77; McGill Univ Scholarship, 66-67, 67-68; Fac of Music Scholarships, 66-69; Gold Medal of the Minister of Educ, 69, Graduate Fac Spec Scholarship, 69-70; JW McConnell Memorial Fel, 70-71; Canada Council Arts Bursary 70-71, Southern IL Univ, mem, Phi Eta Sigma Hon Fraternity; Dean's List. **MEMBERSHIPS** Royal Musical Assoc. **RESEARCH** 17th Century Eng vocal music; computer applications in music, pedag applications of online research. **SELECTED PUBLICATIONS** Research & Publ: Nicholas Lanier: The Complete Works Ed by Gordon J. Callon; Hereford, Engl: Severinus Press, 94, Music 2223: Baroque Music (An Anthology of Baroque Music), Acadia Univ, 97; Quarterly Journal of Music Library Assoc LIII 2, 96, Songs with Theorbo by Charles Colman and his Comteporaries in Oxford, Bodleian Library MS Broxbourne 84.9 and London, Lambeth Palace Library, Journal of the Lute Society of American, XXIV,The Complete Vocal Music of William Lawes 1602-1645. **CONTACT ADDRESS** Acadia Univ, Wolfville, NS, B0P 1X0. **EMAIL** gcallon@ns.sympatico.ca

CAMARGO, MARTIN
DISCIPLINE MEDIEVAL ENGLISH LITERATURE, HISTORY OF ENGLISH, AND HISTORY OF RHETORIC **EDUCATION** Univ Ill, PhD, 78. **CAREER** Prof. **HONORS AND AWARDS** ACLS; Fulbright & Humboldt Found fel; Gold Chalk awd, 93. **SELECTED PUBLICATIONS** Auth, Middle English Verse Love Epistle, Niemeyer, 91 & Medieval Rhetorics of Prose Composition, Medieval& Renaissance Texts & Stud, 95. **CONTACT ADDRESS** Dept of English, Univ of Missouri-Columbia, 309 University Hall, Columbia, MO, 65211.

CAMERON, ALAN
PERSONAL Born 03/13/1938, Windsor, England, m, 1961, 2 children **DISCIPLINE** CLASSICAL PHILOLOGY, BYZANTINE STUDIES **EDUCATION** Oxford Univ, BA, 61, MA, 64. **CAREER** Lectr Latin, Univ Glasgow, 61-64, Bedord Col, Univ London, 64-71 & Kings Col, 72-76; ANTHON PROF LATIN, COLUMBIA UNIV, 77- **HONORS AND AWARDS** N H Baynes Prize, London Univ, 67; J Conington Prize, Oxford Univ, 68; fel, British Acad, 75. **MEMBERSHIPS** Soc Roman Studies; Am Philol Asn; fel Am Acad Arts & Sci. **RESEARCH** Latin literature; Roman history; Byzantine history and literature. **SELECTED PUBLICATIONS** Auth, Gender in Performance--The Presentation of Difference in the Performing Arts, Theatre Res Intl, Vol 0019, 94; Just Another Fucking Mystery at Sea, Meanjin, Vol 0055, 96; The Life of Stephen, Saint of the Monastery of Mar-Saba-Italian-Leontius-Of-Damascus, Heythrop Jour-Quart Rev Philos And Theol, Vol 0035, 94; Egypt in Late-Antiquity, NY Rev Of Bk(s), Vol 0042, 95; The Roman Near-East, 31-Bc-337-Ad, NY Rev Bk(s), Vol 0042, 95; The Byzantine Church--Between Power and Spirit 313-1204-French, Rev Belge Philol Et D Hist, Vol 0072, 94; On the Date of John-Of-Gaza, Class Quart, Vol 0043, 93; Byzantines and Jews- Some Recent Work on Early Byzantium, Byzantine and Modern Greek Studies, Vol 0020, 96; Transforming Womens Work--New-England Lives in the Industrial-Revolution, Labor Hist, Vol 0036, 95; Themistius and the Imperial Court-Oratory, Civic Duty, and Paideia from Constantius to Theodosius, Amer Hist Rev, Vol 0102, 97; Genre and Style in Callimachus, Transactions Amer Philol Assn, Vol 0122, 92; The Origenist Controversy--The Cultural Construction of an Early-Christian Debate, Scottish Jour Theol, Vol 0050, 97; Ancient Anagrams/, American Journal Of Philology, Vol 0116, 1995; Holy City, Holy Places--Christian Attitudes to Jerusalem and the Holy-Land in the 4th-Century, Heythrop Jour-Quart Rev Philos and Theol, Vol 0034, 93. **CONTACT ADDRESS** Columbia Univ, 2960 Broadway, New York, NY, 10027-6900.

CAMERON, CHRISTINA S.R.
PERSONAL Born 03/15/1945, Toronto, ON, Canada **DISCIPLINE** HISTORY OF ARCHITECTURE **EDUCATION** Univ Toronto, BA, 67; Brown Univ, MA, 70; Laval Univ, PhD, 83 **CAREER** Guest lectr, Concordia Univ, 75-78; DIR GEN, NAT HIST SITES, PARKS CAN, CAN HERITAGE, 87-; ADJ PROF ART HISTORY Carleton Univ, 91-. **MEMBERSHIPS** Gov, Royal Can Geog Soc; ed bd, J Can Art Hist. **SELECTED PUBLICATIONS** Auth, Second Empire Style in Canadian Architecture, 80; Vieux-Quebec: son architecture interieure, 86; Charles Baillairge: Architect, 89. **CONTACT ADDRESS** Nat Hist Sites, Parks Can, Ottawa, ON, K1A 0M5.

CAMERON, JAMES D.
DISCIPLINE HISTORY **EDUCATION** Univ Prince Edward Island, BA, 81; BEd, 81; Acadia Univ, MA, 85; Queen's Univ, PhD, 90. **CAREER** Lectr. **SELECTED PUBLICATIONS** Auth, pubs about Canadian higher education, Canadian congregations of women religious, and Celtic fiddle music. **CONTACT ADDRESS** History Dept, St Francis Xavier Univ, Antigonish, NS, B2G 2W5. **EMAIL** jdcamero@stfx.ca

CAMERON, JAMES REESE
PERSONAL Born 08/27/1929, Columbus, OH, m, 1950, 2 children **DISCIPLINE** HISTORY **EDUCATION** Eastern Nazarene Col, AB, 51; Boston Univ, MA, 52, PhD, 59. **CAREER** Instr hist, 51-55; asst prof to assoc prof, 55-64, prof, 64-, Eastern Nazarene Col. **MEMBERSHIPS** AHA; Mediaeval Acad Am; Conf Brit Studies; fel Pilgrim Soc. **RESEARCH** English constitutional history; history of the Middle Ages; Massachusetts local history. **SELECTED PUBLICATIONS** Auth, Frederick William Maitland and the History of English Law, Greenwood, 77; auth, The Public Career of Josiah Quincy, 1802-1882, Quincy Coop Bank, 62; art, The Christian Perspective and The Teaching of Political Science, J Am Sci Affil, 66; auth, New Beginnings: Quincy and Norfolk County, Massachusetts, Quincy Hist Soc, 66; auth, Eastern Nazarene College: The First Fifty Years, 1900-1950, Nazarene Publ House, 68; auth, Church on the Campus, Wollaston Church of the Nazarene, 72; auth, Economic Life, Quincy, 350 Years, City of Quincy, Mass, 74; ed, Calendar of the papers of General Joseph Palmer, 1716-1788, Quincy Hist Soc, 78; auth, Semper Fidelis: The Life of James R. McIntyre, ENC Press, 90; auth, The Spirit Makes the Difference: Eastern Nazarene College, 1948-98, ENC Press, 00. **CONTACT ADDRESS** Dept of History, Eastern Nazarene Col, 23 E Elm Ave, Quincy, MA, 02170. **EMAIL** cameronj@enc.edu

CAMFIELD, THOMAS M.
DISCIPLINE HISTORY **EDUCATION** Univ Tex at Austin, BA, PhD; Univ Calif Berkeley, MA. **CAREER** Sr tenured prof, Sam Houston State Univ, 69-; **RESEARCH** American social and intellectual history, late 19th and early 20th-century america. **SELECTED PUBLICATIONS** Auth, The American Psychological Association and World War I, in The American Psychological Association: A Historical Perspective, 93; rev, A Can or Two of Worms: Virginia Bernhard and the Historiography of Early Virginia, 1607-1610, J Southern Hist, 94; co-ed, Exploring United States History. **CONTACT ADDRESS** Dept of History, Sam Houston State Univ, Huntsville, TX, 77341.

CAMP, RICHARD
PERSONAL Born 03/31/1936, Yankton, SD, m, 1963 **DISCIPLINE** MODERN EUROPEAN HISTORY **EDUCATION** Goshen Col, BA, 58; Columbia Univ, MA, 60, PhD(hist), 65. **CAREER** Asst prof Europ hist, Goshen Col, 62-65; PROF HIST & COORDR INTERDISCIPLINARY HUMANITIES PROG, CALIF STATE UNIV, NORTHRIDGE, 65- **MEMBERSHIPS** AHA; Soc Italian Hist Studies; AAUP; Conf Group Women's Hist. **RESEARCH** Italy in the 19th and 20th centuries; social and intellectual history of modern Europe; women in Italy and Europe since 1815. **SELECTED PUBLICATIONS** Auth, The Catholic-Church And Secularization-Italian, Cath Hist Rev, Vol 0080, 94; Annaratone, Angelo 1844-1922--States of Prefects in Liberal Italy-Italian, Amer Hist Rev, Vol 0097, 92. **CONTACT ADDRESS** Dept of Hist, California State Univ, Northridge, Northridge, CA, 91324.

CAMP, ROBERT C.
PERSONAL Born 07/22/1935, Milwaukee, WI, m, 1958, 2 children **DISCIPLINE** ENGINEERING, LOGISTICS **EDUCATION** Cornell Univ, BCR, 59, MBA, 60; Pa State, PhD, 73. **CAREER** Trans engr, Mobil Oil, 60-64; dist engr, DuPont, 64-69; logistics mgr, Xerox, 72-95, PRINCIPAL, BEST PRACTICES INST. **MEMBERSHIPS** Coun Logistics Mgt **RESEARCH** Best practice sourcing, exchange & adoption **SELECTED PUBLICATIONS** Coauth, "Benchmarking Applied to Health Care," Jour on Qual Improvement of the Joint Comn, 94; auth, Business Process Benchmarking: Finding and Implementing Best Practices, ASQC Qual Press, 95; Global Cases in Benchmarking: Best Practices from Organizations Around the World, ASQ Qual Press, 98. **CONTACT ADDRESS** Best Practice Inst, 625 Panorama Trail, Ste 1-200, Rochester, NY, 14625-2432. **EMAIL** rcampbpi@worldnet.att.net

CAMP, RODERIC A.
PERSONAL Born 02/19/1945, Colfax, WA, m, 1966, 2 children **DISCIPLINE** GOVERNMENT **EDUCATION** George Washington Univ, BA, 66, MA, 67; Univ Ariz, PhD, 70. **CAREER** Asst to Assoc to Prof, Polit Sci, Cent Univ of Iowa, 70-91, Ch 73-76, 80-82, 85-91, Asst Dean, 78; Ch, Polit Sci Dept, Tulane Univ, 93-96; Adjunct Fellow, Ctr for Strategic & Int Stud, 98-; Prof of Govt, Claremont McKenna Col, 98-. **HONORS AND AWARDS** Winfield Scott Blaney Fellow in Int Aff, GW Univ, 66-67; NEH Grant, 79, 82, Fellow, 77, 81, 91; Tinker Mex Policy Stud Fellow, Mexico, 93, 94, 95, 96; Hewlett Foundation Award, Latin Am Dem, 98-99. **MEMBERSHIPS** NE Coun of Latin Am Stud (Exec Coun 90-98); MidW Polit Sci Asn; N Cent Coun of Latin Americanists (pres 83-84); AHA; LASA. **RESEARCH** Latin Am history. **SELECTED PUBLICATIONS** Auth, Generals in the Palacio, the Military in Modern Mexico, Oxford Univ Press, 92; auth, Who's Who in Mexico Today, 2nd ed, Westview Press, 93; auth, The Successor, A Political Thriller, Univ NMex Press, 93; auth, Mexican Political Biographies, 1935-1993, 3rd ed, Univ Tex Press, 95; Political Recruitment Across Two Centuries, Mexico, 1884-1991, Univ Tex Press, 95; auth, Politics in Mexico, Democratizing Authoritarianism, Oxford Univ Press, 2nd ed, 96; auth, Crossing Swords, Politics and Religion in Mexico, Oxford Univ Press, 97. **CONTACT ADDRESS** Dept of Govt, Claremont McKenna Col, Claremont, CA, 91711.

CAMPBELL, BALLARD C.
PERSONAL Born 11/30/1940, Orange, NJ, m, 1988, 3 children **DISCIPLINE** AMERICAN HISTORY **EDUCATION** Northwestern Univ, BA, 62; Northeastern Univ, MA, 64; Univ Wisc, Madison, PhD, 70. **CAREER** Inst, 69-70, Asst Prof, 70-76, Assoc Prof, 76-82, Prof, 82-, Dept Hist, NorthEastern Univ. **HONORS AND AWARDS** Fellow, Charles Warren Ctr, 76-77; Fellow, Am Coun of Learned Soc, 82. **MEMBERSHIPS** AHA; OAH; Soc Sci Hist Asn; Econ Hist Asn. **RESEARCH** American governmental history; economic & business history. **SELECTED PUBLICATIONS** Auth, Federalism and American Legislatures, Encyclopedia of the American Legislative System, Charles Scribner Sons, I, 71-88, 94; auth, The Growth of American Government: Governance from the Cleveland Era to the Present, Ind Univ Press, 95; auth, Public Policy and State Government, The Gilded Age: Essays on the Origins of Modern America, Schol Res Inc, 309-329, 96; auth, Tax Revolts and Political Change, J of Policy Hist, 10, 153-178, 98; ed, contributor, The Challenges of Change: American Lives, 1870-1920, Schol Res, 99. **CONTACT ADDRESS** Dept Hist, Northeastern Univ, 360 Huntington Ave, Boston, MA, 02115. **EMAIL** campbell@neu.edu

CAMPBELL, DAVID A.
PERSONAL Born 08/14/1927, Killywhan, Scotland, m, 1956, 3 children **DISCIPLINE** CLASSICS **EDUCATION** Glasgow Univ, MA, 48; Oxford Univ, BA, 53, MA, 67. **CAREER** Asst to sr lectr, Univ Bristol, 53-71; vis asst prof, Univ Toronto, 59-60; vis prof, Univ Texas Austin, 69-70; prof, 71-93, ch, 72-77, PROF EMER CLASSICS, UNIV VICTORIA, 93-. **MEMBERSHIPS** Am Philol Asn; Class Asn Can; Class Asn Pac NW; Class Asn Can W. **SELECTED PUBLICATIONS** Auth, Greek Lyric Poetry, 67, 2nd ed 82; auth, The Golden Lyre: The Themes of the Greek Lyric Poets, 83; auth, Greek Lyric, vols 1-5, 82-93; contribur, The Cambridge History of Classical Literature, vol 1, 85;Auth, The Fragments of Mimnermus--Text and Commentary, Jour Class Assn Can, Vol 0049, 95.. **CONTACT ADDRESS** 6154 Patricia Bay Hwy, Victoria, BC, V8Y 1T2.

CAMPBELL, JOAN
PERSONAL Born 06/22/1929, Berlin, Germany, m, 1954, 4 children **DISCIPLINE** MODERN EUROPEAN HISTORY, GERMAN HISTORY **EDUCATION** Radcliffe Col, BA, 50; Oxford Univ, MA, 52; Queen's Univ, Ont, PhD(hist), 75. **CAREER** ASST PROF HIST, UNIV TORONTO, 77- **MEMBERSHIPS** AHA; Can Hist Asn. **RESEARCH** German Werkbund; the idea of Arbeitsfreude (joy in work). **SELECTED PUBLICATIONS** Auth, At the Turn of a Civilization--Jones, David and Modern Poetics, Rel & Lit, Vol 0027, 95; At the Turn of a Civilization--Jones, David and Modern Poetics, Rel & Lit, Vol 0027, 95; The Language of Gender and Class--Transformation in the Victorian Novel, Intl Fiction Rev, Vol 0024, 97; New Women, New Novels--Feminism and Early Modernism, Intl Fiction Rev, Vol 0019, 92; Country Parsons, Country Poets--Hebert,George and Hopkins, Gerard, Manley as Spiritual Autobiographers, Rel and Lit, Vol 0026, 94; The Concept of Work--Ancient, Medieval, and Modern, Amer Hist Rev, Vol 0099, 94; Visions of Modernity--American Business and the Modernization of Germany, Amer Hist Rev, Vol 0101, 96; Labor and Power in the Iron-And-Steel-Industry--Industrial and Labor-Relations in the German and American Iron-and-Steel-Industry from the 1860s to the 1930s-Ger, Amer Hist Rev, Vol 0100, 95; Protecting Motherhood--Women and the Family in the Politics of Postwar West-Germany, Labor Hist, Vol 0035, 94. **CONTACT ADDRESS** 43 Cross St, Dundas, ON, L9H 2R5.

CAMPBELL, JOHN COERT
PERSONAL Born 10/08/1911, New York, NY **DISCIPLINE** EASTERN EUROPEAN HISTORY **EDUCATION** Harvard Univ, AB, 33, AM, 36, PhD, 40. **CAREER** Instr polit sci, Univ Louisville, 40-41; Rockefeller fel, 41-42; div asst, US Dept State, 42-46; ed, Coun Foreign Rels, 46-49; officer-in-chg Balkan Affairs, US Dept State, 49-52 & Nat War Col, 52-53; mem policy planning staff, US Dept State, 53-55; dir polit studies & sr res fel, Coun Foreign Rels, 55-78; CONSULT & ADV, US DEPT STATE, 63-, Consult, US Dept State, 63-67 & 68-, mem policy planning coun, 67-68; mem joint comt Slavic studies, Am Coun Learned Soc--Soc Sci Res Coun, 65-67; vis lectr, Columbia Univ, 68; consult, Brookings Inst, 72-73. **MEMBERSHIPS** Int Studies Asn; Am Asn Advan Slavic Studies; Mideast Inst (vpres, 67-77); Mideast Studies Asn; AHA. **RESEARCH** United States foreign relations; Balkan history; Middle East studies. **SELECTED PUBLICATIONS** Auth, Moscow and the Middle-East--Soviet-Policy Since the Invasion of Afghanistan, Russian Rev, Vol 0052, 93; Beacons in the Night--With the Oss and Tito Partisans in Wartime Yugoslavia, Jour Amer Hist, Vol 0081, 94; Yugoslavias Bloody Collapse--Causes, Course and Consequences, Amer Hist Rev, Vol 0101, 96; Nationalism and Federalism in Yugoslavia, 1962-1991, 2nd Edition, Amer Hist Rev, Vol 0098, 93. **CONTACT ADDRESS** 220 S Main St, Cohasset, MA, 02025.

CAMPBELL, JOHN POLLOCK
PERSONAL Born 06/03/1933, New Milns, Scotland **DISCIPLINE** MODERN HISTORY **EDUCATION** Glasgow Univ, MA, 55; Yale Univ, MA, 59 PhD(hist), 61. **CAREER** Asst prof, 62-68, ASSOC PROF HIST, McMASTER UNIV, 68- **MEMBERSHIPS** AHA; Orgn Am Historians. **RESEARCH** United States foreign policy in 20th century; military history since 1914. **SELECTED PUBLICATIONS** Auth, A British Plan to Invade England, 1941, Jour Military Hist, Vol 0058, 94; The Year of D-Day--The 1944 Diary of Admiral Ramsay, Bertram, War In Hist, Vol 0002, 95. **CONTACT ADDRESS** 479 Dundurn St S, Hamilton, ON, L8P 4M2.

CAMPBELL, MARY SCHMIDT
PERSONAL Born 10/21/1947, Philadelphia, PA, m, 1968 **DISCIPLINE** ART HISTORY **EDUCATION** Swarthmore Coll, BA English Lit 1969; Syracuse Univ, MA art history 1973, PhD, 1982. **CAREER** Syracuse University, Syracuse, NY, lecturer; Nkumbi Intl Coll, Kabwe, Zambia, instr, 1969-71; Syracuse New Times, writer, art editor, 1973-77; Everson Museum, curator, guest curator, 1974-76; The Studio Museum in Harlem, exec dir, 1977-87; New York City Department of Cultural Affairs, New York, commissioner, 1987-91; TISCH SCHOOL, DEAN, 1991-. **HONORS AND AWARDS** Ford Fellow, 1973-77; Rockefeller Fellowship in the Humanities, 1985; Municipal Art Society Certificate, 1985; Candace Award, 100 Black Women, 1986; consultant to the Ford Foundation as part of their mid-decade review; lectures on American & African-American Art, The Studio Museum in Harlem and the issues involved in the Institutionalization of Diverse Cultures and Public Policy and the Arts; City College, NY, Honorary Doctorate, 1992. **MEMBERSHIPS** Chair, Student Life Committee, Swarthmore College Board of Managers, 1991-; member, Visiting Committee on Fine Arts, Harvard College Board of Overseers, 1991-93; chair, Advisory Committee for African American Institutional Study, Smithsonian Institute, 1989-91; advisory board member , Barnes Foundation, 1991-; fellow, Institute for Humanities, New York University, 1989-. **SELECTED PUBLICATIONS** Author, Black American Art & Harlem Renaissance, 1987; author of numerous articles on Black American art. **CONTACT ADDRESS** Tisch Sch of the Arts, New York Univ, 721 Broadway, New York, NY, 10003.

CAMPBELL, RANDOLPH BLUFORD
PERSONAL Born 11/16/1940, Charlottesville, VA, m, 1962, 2 children **DISCIPLINE** UNITED STATES HISTORY **EDUCATION** Univ Va, BS, 61, MA, 63, PhD(hist), 66. **CAREER** Instr hist, Va Polytech Inst, 63-64; asst prof, 66-69, assoc prof, 69-77, 66-67, PROF HIST, N TEX STATE UNIV, 77- **HONORS AND AWARDS** H Bailey Carroll Award, Tex State Hist Asn, 70; Ramsdell Award, Southern Hist Asn, 75. **MEMBERSHIPS** Soc Sci Hist Asn; Orgn Am Historians; Southern Hist Asn. **RESEARCH** United States history, especially the period from the revolution to the Civil War; antebellum Texas. **SELECTED PUBLICATIONS** Auth, Southern Slavery and the Law, 1619-1860, Southwestern Hist Quart, Vol 0100, 96; The Inner Jefferson--Portrait of a Grieving Optimist, Miss Quart, Vol 0050, 97; One South or Many--Plantation Belt and Upcountry in Civil-War Era Tennessee, Amer Hist Rev, Vol 0101, 96; The Freedmens Bureau and Black Texans, Jour Amer Hist, Vol 0080, 93; The Papers of Johnson, Andrew, Southwestern Hist Quart, Vol 0099, 95; Reconstruction in Mclennan-County, Texas 1865-1876, Prologue-Quart Nat Arch, Vol 0027, 95; Empire of Bones--A Novel of Houston, Sam and the Texas Revolution, Historian, Vol 0056, 93; Carpetbagger Rule in Reconstruction Texas--An Enduring Myth, Southwestern Hist Quart, Vol 0097, 94; The Cartwrights of San-Augustine--3 Generations of Agricultural Entrepreneurs in 19th-Century Texas, Agricult Hist, Vol 0068, 94; The Cartwrights of San-Augustine--Generations of Agricultural Entrepreneurs in 19th-Century Texas, Agricult Hist, Vol 0068, 94; Sword of San-Jacinto--A Life of Houston, Sam, Historian, Vol 0056, 93; Houston,Sam--A Biography of the Father of Texas, Historian, Vol 0056, 93; The Burden of Local Black-Leadership During Reconstruction--A Research Note, Civil War Hist, Vol 0039, 93. **CONTACT ADDRESS** Dept of Hist, No Texas State Univ, Denton, TX, 76201.

CAMPBELL, STUART LORIN
PERSONAL Born 04/15/1938, Whittier, CA, m, 1960, 1 child **DISCIPLINE** MODERN & FRENCH HISTORY **EDUCATION** Univ Ore, BA, 59, MA, 61; Univ Rochester, PhD, 69. **CAREER** Instr hist, Ore State Univ, 65-66; asst prof, 66-71, assoc prof, 71-79, prof, 79-80, Hagar Prof Hum, Alfred Univ, 81-; Chief Ed, Hist Reflections/Reflexions Historiques, 91-. **HONORS AND AWARDS** Col Ctr Finger Lakers res grant, 72-73; NEH fel, 82-83. **MEMBERSHIPS** AHA; Soc Fr Hist Studies; Soc Mod Hist. **RESEARCH** Historiography of the French Second Empire; political and social history of the French Second Republic; 20th century French political-intellectual. **SELECTED PUBLICATIONS** Auth, The Second Empire Reconsidered: A Study in French Historiography, Rutgers Univ, 78. **CONTACT ADDRESS** Div of Human, Studies Alfred Univ, 26 N Main St, Alfred, NY, 14802-1222. **EMAIL** fcampbell@bigvax.alfred.edu

CAMPBELL, TED A.
PERSONAL Born 09/03/1953, Beaumont, TX, m, 1975, 2 children **DISCIPLINE** CHURCH HISTORY **EDUCATION** Univ N Tex, BA, 76; Oxford Univ, BA/MA, 79; SMU, PhD, 84 **CAREER** Visiting lctr, Methodist Thelog School, 84-85; asst prof, Duke Divinity, 85-93; prof, Wesley Theolog Seminary, 93 **MEMBERSHIPS** AAR; ASCH; World Methodist Hist Soc **RESEARCH** Wesleyan Studies; History of Christian Doctrine **SELECTED PUBLICATIONS** Auth, Christian Confessions, Westminister John Knox Press, 96; auth, John Wesley and Christian Antiquity, Kingsword Bks, 91; **CONTACT ADDRESS** Wesley Theol Sem, 4500 Massachussettes, Washington, DC, 20016. **EMAIL** tcamp@clark.net

CAMUS, RAOUL F.
PERSONAL Born 12/05/1930, Buffalo, NY, m, 1963, 3 children **DISCIPLINE** MUSIC **EDUCATION** Queens Col, CUNY, BA, 52; Columbia Univ, MA, 56; New York Univ, PhD, 69. **CAREER** Teacher of orchestral music, Newtown High School, 59-62; teacher of orchestral music, Queens Village Jr High School, 62-65; dir of bands, Martin Van Buren High School, 65-70; Adjunct Lectr, 69-70, Asst Prof, 70-75, Assoc Prof, 75-79, Prof, 79-95, Dept Chair, 83-86, Prof Emeritus, Queensborough Community Col, CUNY, 95-. **HONORS AND AWARDS** Queens Coun on the Arts Certificate of Appreciation, 75; PSC-CUNY Res award, 79-80, 80-81, & 86; Nat Endowment for the Humanities Fel, 79-80 & 82-83; Queens Col Choral Soc Silver Jubilee Award, 84; Distinguished Service Award, The Sonneck Soc for Am Music, 94; Fulbright Vis Prof, 95. **MEMBERSHIPS** Am Musicological Soc; Asn of Concert Bands; Col Band Dir Nat Asn; Int Military Music Soc; Int Soc for the Promotion and Investigation of Band Music; The Sonneck Soc; World Asn of Symphonic Bands and Ensembles. **RESEARCH** American music; wind bands; military music. **SELECTED PUBLICATIONS** Auth, American Wind and Percussion Music Vol 12: Three Centuries of American Music, G.K. Hall & Co, 92; Military Music of the American Revolution, Univ of NC Press, 76, Integrity Press, 93; Military Music in the United States Army Prior to 1834, Univ Microfilms, 69; Military Music and the Roots of the American Band Movement, New England Music: The Public Sphere 1600-1900, Boston Univ, 98; The American School Band Movement, Kongressbericht Mainz 1996, Alta Musica, Hans Schneider, 98; Some New Tools in Early American Band Research, Kongressbericht Abony/Ungarn 1994 Alta Musica, Hans Schneider, 96; Early American Wind and Cermemonial Music 1636-1836: Phase 2 of the National Tune Index, Notes, 96; The Early American Wind Band: Hautboys, Harmonies, and Janissaries, The Wind Ensemble and its Repertoire, Univ of Rochester Press, 94; Some Nineteenth-Century Band Journals, Festschrift zum 60. Geburtstag von Wolfgang Suppan, Hans Schneider, 93. **CONTACT ADDRESS** Dept of Music, Queensborough Comm Col, CUNY, Bayside, NY, 11364. **EMAIL** rcamus@cuny.campus.mci.net

CANNADINE, DAVID
DISCIPLINE MODERN BRITISH HISTORY **EDUCATION** Cambridge Univ, PhD, 72; Oxford Univ, PhD, 75. **CAREER** Moore Collegiate prof. **RESEARCH** Biography of Andrew Mellon. **SELECTED PUBLICATIONS** Auth, Lords and Landlords: the Aristocracy and the Towns, 1774-1967, 80; The Pleasures of the Past, 89; The Decline and Fall of the British Aristocracy, 90; G M Trevelyan: a Life in History, 92; Aspects of Aristocracy: Grandeur and Decline, Mod Britain, 94. **CONTACT ADDRESS** Dept of Hist, Columbia Col, New York, 2960 Broadway, New York, NY, 10027-6902.

CANNING, PAUL
PERSONAL Born 01/10/1947, m, 1987, 3 children **DISCIPLINE** HISTORY **EDUCATION** Univ Washington, BA 69; Univ Connecticut, MA 71; Univ Washington, 79. **CAREER** Gunzaga Univ, instr, 76-77, vis prof 82; Marymont Col, vis prof, 83-84; Univ Connecticut, asst prof, assoc prof, 85 to 89-.

MEMBERSHIPS AHA; NACBS; ACIS. **RESEARCH** Modern Britain, Modern Ireland and Modern Africa. **SELECTED PUBLICATIONS** Auth, British Policy Towards Ireland, Oxford, Clarendon Press of OUP, 85. **CONTACT ADDRESS** Dept of History, 85 Lawler Rd, West Hartford, CT, 06117.

CANNISTRARO, PHILIP VINCENT
PERSONAL Born 11/13/1942, New York, NY **DISCIPLINE** MODERN ITALIAN HISTORY **EDUCATION** NY Univ, BA, 65, MA, 66, PhD(hist), 70. **CAREER** Instr hist, NY Univ, 69-70; from asst prof to assoc prof, 70-78, PROF HIST, FLA STATE UNIV, 78-, Am ed, Storia Contemporanea, 72-; mem, Columbia Univ Sem Mod italy, 73-; Fulbright sr fel, Rome 77-78. **MEMBERSHIPS** Soc Ital Hist Studies; AHA; Am Ital Hist Asn. **RESEARCH** Italian history; history of fascism; Italian-Americans and fascism. **SELECTED PUBLICATIONS** Auth, A History of Italian Fascism in the United-States 1921-1929, Storia Contemporanea, Vol 0026, 95; The Legend of Mutilated Victory--Italy, The Great-War and the Paris-Conference, 1915-1919, Storia Contemporanea, Vol 0025, 94. **CONTACT ADDRESS** Dept of Hist, Florida State Univ, Tallahassee, FL, 32306.

CANNON, DONALD QUAYLE
PERSONAL Born 12/24/1936, Washington, DC, m, 1960, 5 children **DISCIPLINE** AMERICAN COLONIAL HISTORY **EDUCATION** Univ Utah, BA, 61, MA, 62; Clark Univ, PhD(hist), 67. **CAREER** Asst prof Am hist, Univ Maine, Portland, 67-73; assoc prof, 73-80, PROF CHURCH HIST & DOCTRINE, BRIGHAM YOUNG UNIV, 80-, Mem, Inst Early Am Hist & Cult, Va. **MEMBERSHIPS** AHA. **RESEARCH** History of geography; early history of the Mormon Church. **SELECTED PUBLICATIONS** Auth, The Story of the Latter-Day-Saint, Brigham Young Univ Stud, Vol 0033, 93; Kingdom on the Mississippi Revisited--Nauvoo in Mormon History, Brigham Young Univ Stud, Vol 0036, 97. **CONTACT ADDRESS** Dept of Church Hist, Brigham Young Univ, Joseph Smith Bldg, Provo, UT, 84602-0002.

CANTELON, PHILIP LOUIS
PERSONAL Born 11/07/1940, Ft Wayne, IN **DISCIPLINE** AMERICAN AND PUBLIC HISTORY **EDUCATION** Dartmouth Col, AB, 62; Univ Mich, Ann Arbor, AM, 63; Ind Univ, Bloomington, PhD(hist), 71. **CAREER** Master hist, Howe Mil Sch, 63-65; lectr, Williams Col, 68-69, asst prof, 69-77, dir oral hist proj, 73-77; prof Am hist & civilization, Kyushu & Seinan Gakuin Univs, 78-79; SR PARTNER, C&W ASSOCS/HIST CONSULTS, 79-; PRES, HIST ASSOCS INC, 80-, Speechwriter/ed, Off Secy, US Dept Housing & Urban Develop, 74-75; Fulbright-Hays sr lectr, US Educ Comn, Japan, 77; exec secy, Nat Coun Pub Hist, 81-; hist consult, Dept Energy, Consol Edison Co, Tex Instruments & State NMex. **MEMBERSHIPS** AHA; Orgn Am Historians; Oral Hist Asn; Soc Hist in Fed Govt (secy-treas, 79-81); Nat Coun Pub Hist. **RESEARCH** Recent American history, 1933 to the present; oral history. **SELECTED PUBLICATIONS** Auth, The Origins of Microwave Telephony--Waves of Change, Tech and Cult, Vol 0036, 95; The Origins of Microwave Telephony--Waves of Change, Tech and Cult, Vol 0036, 95; The Atomic-Energy Commission Under Nixon--Adjusting to Troubled Times, Jour Amer Hist, Vol 0081, 94. **CONTACT ADDRESS** Hist Associates Inc, 18903 Smoothstone Way Suite 5, Rockville, MD.

CANTOR, LOUIS
DISCIPLINE HISTORY **EDUCATION** Duke Univ, PhD, 63. **CAREER** Prof. **SELECTED PUBLICATIONS** Auth, A Prologue to the Protest Movementand Wheelin' on Beale: How WDIA Memphis became the Nation's First All-Black Radio Station and Created the Sound that Changed America. **CONTACT ADDRESS** Dept of History, Indiana Univ-Purdue Univ, Fort Wayne, 2101 Coliseum Blvd, Fort Wayne, IN, 46805.

CANTOR, MILTON
DISCIPLINE HISTORY **EDUCATION** Columbia Univ, PhD, 54. **CAREER** Prof, Univ MA Amherst. **SELECTED PUBLICATIONS** Auth, Max Eastman, 70; The Divided Left: American Radicalism in the Twentieth Century, 78; ed, American Working Class Culture,79; co-ed, Sex, Class and the Women Worker, 77; Documents of American History, 89. **CONTACT ADDRESS** Dept of Hist, Univ Massachusetts Amherst, Mass Ave, Amherst, MA, 01003.

CANTOR, NORMAN FRANK
PERSONAL Born 11/19/1929, Winnipeg, MB, Canada, m, 1957, 2 children **DISCIPLINE** MEDIEVAL & ENGLISH LEGAL HISTORY, HISTORICAL SOCIOLOGY **EDUCATION** Univ Man, BA, 51; Princeton Univ, MA, 53, PhD, 57. **CAREER** From instr to asst prof hist, Princeton Univ, 55-60; vis prof, Johns Hopkins Univ, 60; from assoc prof to prof, Columbia Univ, 60-66; prof, Brandeis Univ, 66-68, Leff prof, 68-70; chmn dept, State Univ NY, Binghamton, 70-74, distinguished prof hist, 70-76, provost for grad studies, 75-76, vpres acad affairs, 75-76; vchancellor acad affairs & prof hist, Ill-Chicago Circle, 76-78; dean fac arts & sci, 78-81, prof hist, 78-81, PROF HIST & SOCIOL, NEW YORK UNIV, 81-; Can Coun fel, 60; Am Coun Learned Soc fel, 60; consult, Bar Asn NYC, 63-67; consult, Encycl Britannica, 64-65; consult, Life mag, 66-68; vis prof, Brooklyn Col, 72-73, Adelphi Univ, 87; Fulbright prof, Tel Aviv, 87-88; consult, NEH 73, 89-91. **HONORS AND AWARDS** Nat Book Critics Circle Nomination, 91; NY Public Libr Award, 97; Fel Royal Hist Soc, 74., LLD, Univ Winnipeg, 73. **MEMBERSHIPS** AHA; AAUP. **RESEARCH** Medieval cultural history; legal history; comparative European history. **SELECTED PUBLICATIONS** Inventing the Middle Ages, Morrow, 91; Civilization of the Middle Ages, HarperCollins, 93; The Sacred Chain, HarperCollins, 94; Medieval Lives, HarperCollins, 94; The Medieval Reader, 95; The Jewish Experience, HarperCollins, 95; The American Century, HarperCollins, 97; Imagining the Law, HarperCollins, 97. **CONTACT ADDRESS** Dept Hist, New York Univ, 53 Washington Sq S, New York, NY, 10012-4556.

CANTRELL, GREGG
PERSONAL Born 06/20/1958, Sweetwater, TX, m, 1997, 2 children **DISCIPLINE** HISTORY **EDUCATION** Tx A&M Univ, BBA, 79, MBA, 80, PhD, 88 **CAREER** Asst prof to assoc prof, Sam Houston St Univ, 88-98; Rupert N. Richardson Prof, Hardin-Simmons Univ, 98- . **HONORS AND AWARDS** Tullis Mem Award, Tx St Hist Assoc, 94; Phi Alpha Theta Book Award, 94; Fel, Nat Endow for the Humanities, 94-95; Carroll Award, Tx St Hist Assoc, 96; Res Fel, Clements Center for SW Stud, S Methodist Univ, 96-97. **MEMBERSHIPS** Tx St Hist Assoc; S Hist Assoc; E Tx Hist Assoc; W Hist Assoc. **RESEARCH** Hist of the Amer south; the southwest; Tx. **SELECTED PUBLICATIONS** Auth, Southerner and Nativist: Kenneth Rayner and the Ideology of Americanism, NC Hist Rev, 92; Sam Houston and the Know-Nothings: A Reappraisal, SW Hist Quart, 93; The Partnership of Stephen F. Austin and Joseph H. Hawkins, SW Hist Quart, 95; Kenneth and John B. Rayner and the Limits of Southern Dissent, Univ of Il Press, 93; Stephen F. Austin: Empresario of Texas, Yale Univ Press, 99. **CONTACT ADDRESS** Dept of History, Hardin-Simmons Univ, Box 16125, Abilene, TX, 79698-6125. **EMAIL** greggc@hsutx.edu

CANTRILL, DANTE
DISCIPLINE AMERICAN STUDIES **EDUCATION** Univ Wash, PhD, 76. **CAREER** Prof. **RESEARCH** History of ideas. **SELECTED PUBLICATIONS** Auth, Adam's Apple. **CONTACT ADDRESS** Dept of English and Philosophy, Idaho State Univ, Pocatello, ID, 83209. **EMAIL** cantdant@isu.edu

CANUP, JOHN
DISCIPLINE HISTORY **EDUCATION** Univ Georgia, AB, 73; Univ Hawaii-Manoa, MA, 75; Univ N Carol at Chapel Hill, PhD, 86. **CAREER** ASST PROF, HIST, TEXAS A&M UNIV **MEMBERSHIPS** Am Antiquarian Soc **SELECTED PUBLICATIONS** Auth, Out of the Wilderness, Wesleyan Univ Press, 90; Drem Castles, Viking, 99; Andrew Deutsch, London, 66; El Escorial, Newsbreak Books, 71; The Cry of Sodom Enquired Into, Procs of AAS 98, 88; Cotton Mather and Criolian Degeneracy, Early Am Lt 24, 89. **CONTACT ADDRESS** Dept of Hist, Texas A & M Univ, College Station, TX, 77843-4236.

CAPE, ROBERT W.
DISCIPLINE CLASSICS **EDUCATION** Uniz Ariz, BA, 83, MA, 85; UCLA, MA, 88, PhD, 91. **CAREER** Vis asst prof, Skidmore Col, 91-94; asst prof, Austin Col, 94-98; assoc prof, Austin Col, 98-. **HONORS AND AWARDS** Dir of Gender Studies, Austin Col, 95-. **MEMBERSHIPS** Am Philol Assoc; Nat Commun Assoc; Am Class League; Int Soc for the Hist of Rhet; Class Assoc of the Mid W & S. **RESEARCH** Cicero; ancient rhetoric; Roman literatukre & society; women in antiquity. **SELECTED PUBLICATIONS** Auth, The Rhetoric of Politics in Cicero's Fourth Catilinarian, Am J of Philol, 116.2, 155-177, 95; auth, Persuasive History: Roman Rhetoric and Historiography, Roman Eloquence: Rhetoric in Society and Literature, Routledge, 212-228, 97; auth, Roman Women in the History of Rhetoric and Oratory, Listening to Their Voices: The Rhetorical Activities of Historical Women, Univ SC Press, 112-132, 97. **CONTACT ADDRESS** Dept of Class & Mod Lang, Austin Col, Ste 61653, Sherman, TX, 75090-4440. **EMAIL** rcape@austinc.edu

CAPRON, ALEXANDER M.
PERSONAL Born 08/16/1944, Hartford, CT, m, 1989, 4 children **DISCIPLINE** ECONOMICS & HISTORY, LAW **EDUCATION** Swarthmore Col, BA, 66; Yale Law Sch, LLB, 69. **CAREER** USC Law School **HONORS AND AWARDS** Fellow, Am Asn for Advan of Sci; Hon Fellow, Am Col of Legal Med. **MEMBERSHIPS** Inst Med; Nat Acad Sci; Int Asn of Bioethics; Am Soc of Law, Med, & Ethics (past pres). **RESEARCH** Ethical & social issues in medical & the life sciences. **CONTACT ADDRESS** USC Law School, Univ Southern Calif, Los Angeles, CA, 90089-0071. **EMAIL** acapron@law.usc.edu

CAPSHEW, J. H.
PERSONAL Born 10/14/1954, Indianapolis, IN, m, 1984, 3 children **DISCIPLINE** HISTORY OF SCIENCE **EDUCATION** Ind Univ, BA, 79; Univ Pa, AM, 82; PhD, 86. **CAREER** Res assoc, Univ Md, 86-89; asst prof, Ind Univ, 90-96; assoc prof, Ind Univ, 96-. **HONORS AND AWARDS** Joan Cahalin Robinson Prize, Soc for the Hist of Technol, 86; Mellon Grad Fel, Univ Pa, 85-86; nat Sci Found Grad Fel, 80-84; Phi Beta Kappa, 79. **MEMBERSHIPS** Cheiron Soc; Forum for Hist of Human Sci; Forum for the Hist of Sci in Am; Hist of Sci Soc; Soc for Social Studies of Sci; Soc for the Hist of Technol; Ind Hist Soc; Am Asn of Univ Prpfs. **RESEARCH** Disciplinary and cultural history of psychology; History of education; Historiography; Biography. **SELECTED PUBLICATIONS** Auth, The Yale Connection in American Psychology: Philanthropy, War, and the Emergence of an Academic Elite, in The Development of the Social Sciences in the United States and Canada: The Role of Philanthropy, 98; Psychology on the March: Science, Practice, and Professional Identity in America, 1929-1969, 98. **CONTACT ADDRESS** Dept of History and Philosophy of Science, Indiana Univ, Bloomington, Bloomington, IN, 47401. **EMAIL** jcapshew@indiana.edu

CAPUTI, JANE
PERSONAL Born 10/27/1953, Brooklyn, NY **DISCIPLINE** HISTORY AND LIBRARY SCIENCE **EDUCATION** Boston Col, BA, 74; Simmons Col, MA, 77; Bowling Green State Univ, PhD, 82. **CAREER** Prof, Amer Studies, Univ Nmex, 95-97; prof, women's studies, Fla Atlantic Univ, 97-. **HONORS AND AWARDS** Emily Toth Award, for The Age of Sex Crime, 88; Honorable Mention, Carl Bode Award, Amer Culture Asn, for The New Founding Fathers: The Lore and Lure of the Serial Killer, 91; Kathleen Gregory Klein Award, Popular Culture Asn, for American Psychos: The Serial Killer in Contemporary Fiction, 92. **RESEARCH** New spiritualities; Violence against women; Popular culture. **SELECTED PUBLICATIONS** Auth, Unthinkable Fathering: Connecting Incest and Nuclearism, Hypatia: A Journal of Feminist Philosophy, vol 9, no 2, 102-122, 94; auth, American Psychos: The Serial Killer in Contemporary Fiction, Jour of Amer Culture, 16, no 4, 101-112, 93; auth, The Heart of Knowledge: Nuclear Themes in Native American Thought and Literature, Amer Indian Culture and Res Jour, 14, no 4, 1-27, 92; auth, Gossips, Gorgons & Crones: The Fates of the Earth, Bear and Co, 93; co-auth, Websters' First New Intergalactic Wickedary of the English Language, Beacon Press, Boston, 87; auth, The Age of Sex Crime, Bowling Green State Univ Popular Press, Bowling Green, Oh, 87. **CONTACT ADDRESS** Women's Studies, Florida Atlantic Univ, Boca Raton, FL, 33431. **EMAIL** jcaputi@fau.edu

CAPWELL, CHARLES
DISCIPLINE MUSIC **EDUCATION** Brown Univ, MA; Harvard Univ, PhD. **CAREER** Assoc prof, 77-, Univ IL Urbana Champaign. **RESEARCH** Music of India; music of Indonesia. **SELECTED PUBLICATIONS** Auth, The Music of the Bauls of Bengal; pubs on contemp and hist aspects of the music of India. **CONTACT ADDRESS** Dept of Music, Univ Illinois Urbana Champaign, E Gregory Dr, PO Box 52, Champaign, IL, 61820. **EMAIL** capwell@uiuc.edu

CARBY, HAZEL V.
PERSONAL Born 01/15/1948, Oakhampton, England, m, 1982 **DISCIPLINE** AFRICAN-AMERICAN STUDIES **EDUCATION** Birmingham University, Center for Contemporary Cultural Studies, PhD, 1984. **CAREER** Wesleyan University, associate professor, 1982-89; YALE UNIVERSITY, PROFESSOR, 1989-. **CONTACT ADDRESS** African-American Studies, Yale Univ, PO Box 3388, Yale Station, New Haven, CT, 06520.

CARDAMONE, DONNA
PERSONAL Born 11/16/1937, Utica, NY, m, 1978, 1 child **DISCIPLINE** MUSICOLOGY **EDUCATION** Wells Coll, AB, 59; Harvard Univ, MA, 64, PhD, 72. **CAREER** FULL PROF, 80-, UNIV MINN, 69-; Fullbright Scholar; Am Coun Learned Soc Fel; Am Philos Soc Res Grant. **HONORS AND AWARDS** Am Asn Univ Women Diss Award **MEMBERSHIPS** Am Musicol Soc; Int Musicol Soc; Renaissance Soc Am; Soc Ital di Musicol. **RESEARCH** 16th century Italian music; Music patronage in early modern Italy; Music printing in 16th century Italy; Women musicians in early modern Italy; Editing early music. **SELECTED PUBLICATIONS** auth The Prince and Princess of Salerno and the Spanish Viceroy: Popular Songs of Exile, Revista de musicologia, 93; The Prince of Salerno and the Dynamics of Oral Transmission in Songs of Political Exile, Acta Musicologica, 95; Lifting the Protective Veil of Anonymity: Woman as Composer-Performers, ca. 1300-1566, Women Composers: Music Through the Ages, Prentice Hall Int, 96; Orlando di Lasso and Pro-French Factions in Rome, Jaarboek van de Alamire Found, Antwerp, 96; The Salon as Marketplace in the 1550's: Patrons and Collectors of Orlando di Lasso's Secular Music, Orlando di Lasso Stud, Cambridge Univ Press. **CONTACT ADDRESS** School of Music, Univ of Minn, 2106 Fourth St, S, Ferguson H, Minneapolis, MN, 55455. **EMAIL** jacks001@tc.umn.edu

CARDOSO, JOAQUIN JOSE
PERSONAL Born 08/20/1932, Mahoning Township, PA, 3 children **DISCIPLINE** UNITED STATES HISTORY **EDUCATION** Pa State Teachers Col, BS, 58; Lehigh Univ, MA, 59; Univ Wis-Madison, PhD(hist), 67. **CAREER** Instr English,

Parkland High Sch, Orefield, Pa, 58-60; instr econ, social & hist, Madison West High Sch, Wis, 60-62; instr Am Hist, San Bernardino High Sch, Calif, 62-65; asst prof Am Hist, Chico State Col, 65-68; assoc prof, 68-72, PROF AM HIST, STATE UNIV NY COL BUFFALO, 73-, State Univ NY Res Found fels, 71 & 73; ed consult, World Mag, 73-75. **MEMBERSHIPS** Orgn Am Historians; AHA; Southern Hist Asn; Can Am Studies Asn. **RESEARCH** Canadian-United States relations; political and economic history of mid-19th century United States; South/Civil War Reconstruction. **SELECTED PUBLICATIONS** Auth, Portrait of an Abolitionist--A Biography of Stearns, George, Luther, 1809-1867, Jour Amer Hist, Vol 0083, 97. **CONTACT ADDRESS** Dept of Hist, State Univ of NY, 1300 Elmwood Ave, Buffalo, NY, 14222-1095.

CARDOZA, ANTHONY L.
DISCIPLINE HISTORY **EDUCATION** Princeton Univ, PhD. **CAREER** Hist, Loyola Univ. **HONORS AND AWARDS** Howard R. Marraro prize. **RESEARCH** Modern Italian soc and Polit history. **SELECTED PUBLICATIONS** Auth, Agrarian Elites and Italian Fascism, Princeton UP, 82; The Long Goodbye: The Landed Aristocracy in Northwestern Italy, 1880-1930, Europ Hist Quart 23, 93. **CONTACT ADDRESS** Fine Arts Dept, Loyola Univ, Chicago, 6525 N. Sheridan Rd., Chicago, IL, 60626. **EMAIL** acardoz@orion.it.luc.edu

CARELESS, JAMES M.S.
PERSONAL Born 02/17/1919, Toronto, ON, Canada **DISCIPLINE** HISTORY **EDUCATION** Univ Toronto, BA, 40; Harvard Univ, AM, 41, PhD, 50. **CAREER** Sheldon Trav fel, Harvard Univ, 42-43; lectr to assoc prof, 45-59, chmn, 59-67, prof 59-84, PROF EMER HISTORY, UNIV TORONTO, 84-; dir, Ont Heritage Found, 75-81; chmn, Ont Hist Stud Ser, 82-93. **HONORS AND AWARDS** Tyrrell Medal Can Hist, 62; Gov Gen Award non-fiction, 64; Cruickshank Medal Ont Hist Soc, 68; sr res fel, Australian Nat Univ, 78; Order Ont, 87. **MEMBERSHIPS** Multicultural Hist Soc, 76-88; Hist Sites & Monuments Bd Can, 80-85; Can Hist Asn (pres, 67-68); Ont Hist Soc (pres, 59). **RESEARCH** Canadian history **SELECTED PUBLICATIONS** Auth, Canada: A Story of Challenge, 53; auth, Brown of the Globe, vol 1 59, vol 2 63; auth, The Union of the Canadas, 67; auth, Rise of Cities in Canada, 78; auth, Toronto to 1918, 84; auth, Frontier and Metropolis, 89; auth, Ontario: A Celebration of Heritage, vol 1 91, vol 2 92; auth, Canada: A Celebration of Heritage, vol 1 94, vol 2 95; coauth, The Pioneers, 69; coauth, Colonist and Canadiens, 71; coauth, Aspects of 19th Century Ontario, 74; coauth, Pre-Confederation Premiers, 80. **CONTACT ADDRESS** 121 Ranleigh St, Toronto, ON, M4N 1X2.

CAREY, JAMES CHARLES
PERSONAL Born 04/01/1915, Bancroft, NE **DISCIPLINE** HISTORY **EDUCATION** Nebr State Teachers Col, AB, 37; Univ Colo, AM, 40, PhD, 48; Univ San Marcos, Peru, cert, 42. **CAREER** Dir, Col Am Deleg Callao, Peru, 41-45; instr, Univ Colo, 46-48; assoc prof, 48-54, PROF HIST KANS STATE UNIV, 54-, Dir, Pub Libr, Callao, Peru; chief party, USAID/Southwest Alliance Latin Am, Univ Santa Maria Antigua, CZ, 68-69. **RESEARCH** Latin American history; United States colonial history; Yucatan in the 20th century. **SELECTED PUBLICATIONS** Auth, Setting the Virgin on Fire--Cardenas, Lazaro, Michoacan Peasants, and the Redemption of the Mexican-Revolution, Hisp Amer Hist Rev, Vol 0077, 97; Indigenous Rulers--An Ethnohistory of Town Government in Colonial Cuernavaca, Jour West, Vol 0032, 93; How the West Was Also Won--An Account of the Family Of Omaha Chief Laflesche, Joseph Iron-Eye, Jour W, Vol 0035, 96. **CONTACT ADDRESS** Dept of Hist, Kansas State Univ, Manhattan, KS, 66502.

CAREY, PATRICK W.
PERSONAL Born 07/02/1940, m, 2 children **DISCIPLINE** RELIGIOUS STUDIES; HISTORY OF AMERICAN RELIGION **EDUCATION** St John's Univ, BA, 62; St John's Sem, M Div, 66; Union Theol Sem, STM, 71; Fordham Univ, PhD, 75. **CAREER** Asst prof, St Peter's Col, 75-76; Elisabeth Seton Col, 76; Carleton Col, 76-77; Gustavus Adolphus, 77-78; from asst prof to assoc prof, Marquette Univ, 78-. **MEMBERSHIPS** Am Acad of Rel; Am Soc of Church Hist; U.S. Cath. Hist Soc; Am Cath. Hist Asn; Am Cath. Hist Soc of Philadelphia; Col Theol Soc; Cath. Theol Soc of Am. **RESEARCH** Hist of Am Rel. **SELECTED PUBLICATIONS** Auth, Orestes A. Brownson: Selected Writings, 91; The Roman Catholics, 93; The Roman Catholics in America, 96; Orestes A. Brownson: A Bibliography, 1826-1876, 96; Ontologism in American Catholic Thought, 1840-1900, Revue d'Histoire Ecclesiastique 91/3-4, 96; Catholicism, Encycl of the United States in the Twentieth Century, ed S. I. Kutler et al, 96; After Testem Benevolentiae and Pascendi, Catholic Southwest: A Jour of History and Culture 7, 96; ed, The Pastoral Letters of the United States Catholic Bishops, vol 6, 1989-1997, 98; coed, Theological Education in the Catholic Tradition: Contemporary Challenges, 97. **CONTACT ADDRESS** Dept of Theology, Marquette Univ, 100 Coughlin Hall, PO Box 1881, Milwaukee, WI, 53233-2295. **EMAIL** careyp@csd.mu.edu

CARGILL, JACK
PERSONAL Born 05/19/1941, TX, d, 1 child **DISCIPLINE** HISTORY/ANCIENT HISTORY **EDUCATION** Univ Tex, Austin, BA, 63, MA, 66; Univ Calif, Berkeley, PhD, 77. **CAREER** Lect, vis, asst prof, 65-66, 75-80; asst to Prof History, Rutgers Univ, 81-. **MEMBERSHIPS** Am Philological Asn; Asn Ancient Historians. **RESEARCH** Ancient Greece, Rome, Near East; Greek Epigraphy. **SELECTED PUBLICATIONS** Auth, Handbook for Ancient History Classes, Regina Books, 97; auth, Athenian Settlements of the Fourth Century B.C., Leiden, 95; auth, The Second Athenian League: Empire or Free Alliance? Univ Calif Press, 81; auth, The Decree of Aristoteles: Some Epigraphical Details, Ancient World 27, 96; auth, David in History: A Secular Approach, Judaism 35, 86; auth, Demosthenes, Aischines, and the Crop of Traitors, Ancient World 5, 82. **CONTACT ADDRESS** Dept Hist, Rutgers Univ, New Brunswick, NJ, 08903. **EMAIL** jcargill@rci.rutgers.edu

CARLEBACH, MICHAEL L.
DISCIPLINE HISTORY **EDUCATION** Colgate Univ, AB, 67; Fla State Univ, MA, 80; Brown Univ, PhD, 88. **CAREER** Asst prof, hist, PROF COMM & AM STUD, UNIV MIAMI **MEMBERSHIPS** Am Antiquarian Soc **SELECTED PUBLICATIONS** Auth, The Origins of Photojournalism in America, Smith Inst Press, 92; auth, Art and Propaganda: The Photograhy Project of the Farm Security Administration, Jour of Decorative and Propaganda Arts 8, 88; coauth, Farm Security Administration Photographs of Florida, Univ Fla Press, 93; American Photojournalism Comes of Age, Smith Inst Press, 97. **CONTACT ADDRESS** Sch of Comm, Univ of Miami, PO Box 248127, Coral Gables, FL, 33124. **EMAIL** mcarleba@umiami.ir.miami.edu

CARLETON, MARK THOMAS
PERSONAL Born 02/07/1935, Baton Rouge, LA, m, 1963, 3 children **DISCIPLINE** HISTORY OF LOUISIANA AND THE SOUTH **EDUCATION** Yale Univ, AB, 57; Stanford, Univ, MA, 64, PhD(US hist), 70. **CAREER** From instr to asst prof, 65-73, ASSOC PROF US HIST, LA STATE UNIV, BATON ROUGE, 73-, Mem, Gov Coun of Econ Adv, State of La, 73-; mem exec comt, La Comt for Humanities, 78-81. **HONORS AND AWARDS** Cert Commendation, Am Asn State & Local Hist, 73. **MEMBERSHIPS** Southern Hist Asn. **RESEARCH** Late 19th century United States. **SELECTED PUBLICATIONS** Auth, Acadian to Cajun--Transformation of a People, 1803-1877, Jour Amer Hist, Vol 0081, 94; Prisons and the American Conscience--History of United-States Federal Corrections, Amer Jour Legal Hist, Vol 0037, 93. **CONTACT ADDRESS** Dept of Hist, Louisiana State Univ, Baton Rouge, LA, 70803.

CARLISLE, RODNEY
PERSONAL Born 10/10/1936, Hempstead, NY, m, 1959, 2 children **DISCIPLINE** UNITED STATES HISTORY **EDUCATION** Harvard Univ, Ab, 58; Univ Calif, Berkeley, MA, 62, PhD(hist), 65. **CAREER** Instr hist, Merritt Col, 64-66; asst prof, 66-73 dir dept urban univ, 69-71, chmn dept, 73-80, 92 & 97, PROF HIST, RUTGERS UNIV, CAMDEN, 80-, Pres fac senate, Rutgers Univ, Camden, 77-78; vis scholar, Dept Energy, 79-80; sr assoc, Hist Assoc Inc, 81-. **RESEARCH** Maritime history; Political biography of W R Hearst; Afro-American history **SELECTED PUBLICATIONS** Auth, W R Hearst and the American Newspaper Guild: A Test of New Deal Labor Legislation, Labor Hist, winter 69; Prologue to Liberation, A History of Black People in America, Appleton, 72, 2nd ed, Univ Press Am, 79; Black Nationalism, an Integral Tradition, Black World, 2/73; W R Hearst--A Fascist Reputation Reconsidered, J Quart, spring 73; The Roots of Black Nationalism, Kennikat, 75; Hearst and the New Deal, Garland, 78; The American Century Implemented: Stettinius and the Liberian Flag of Convenience, Bus Hist Rev, summer 80; Sovereignty For Sale: The Origins and Evolution of the Panamanian and Liberian Flags of Convenience, Naval Inst Press, 81; Bartlesville Energy Research Center: The Federal Government in Petroleum Research, 1918-1983, U S Dept Energy, 85; Powder and Propellants: Energetic Materials at Indian Head, Maryland, 1890-1990, GPO, 90; Production Reactors: An Outline Overview 1944-1988, U S Dept of Energy, 10/92; Probabilistic Risk Assessment in New Production Reactors: Background and Issues to 1991, U S Dept of Energy, 10/92; Management of the U S Navy Research and Development Centers, Naval Hist Center, 96; Supplying the Nuclear Arsenal: American Production Reactors, 1942-1992, Johns Hopkins Univ Press, 96; A Guide to Writing the Longer Piece, Serenus Press, 97; The Relationship of Science and Technology, A Bibliographic Guide, Naval Hist Center, 97; Navy RDT&E Planning in an Age of Transition: A Survey Guide to Contemporary Literature, Naval Hist Center, 97; Probabilistic Risk Assessment in Nuclear Reactors: Engineering Success, Public Relations Failure, Technology and Culture, winter 97. **CONTACT ADDRESS** Dept of Hist, Rutgers Univ, 311 N 5th St, Camden, NJ, 08102-1461. **EMAIL** carlisle@crab.rutgers.edu

CARLS, ALICE
PERSONAL Born 06/14/1950, Mulhouse, France, m, 1977, 3 children **DISCIPLINE** HISTORY **EDUCATION** Univ of Paris IV-Sorbonne, France, BA, 70; MA, 72; BA,73; Univ of Paris I-Sorbonne, France, PhD, 76. **CAREER** Eastern European correspondent, Ctr for Public Justice, Washington, DC, 81-98; from asst prof to assoc prof, Univ of Tenn at Martin, 92-; assoc prof and chemn, Dept of Hist and Polit Sci, Univ of Tenn at Martin, 97- ; ed adv, Asn for Public Justice/Ctr for Public Justice, Washington, DC, 98-. **HONORS AND AWARDS** Who's Who in the South and Southwest, 93, 96, 97, 99; Who's Who in America, 94; Who's Who among Polish-Americans, 95; Who's Who in American Education, 95; Int Scholar Award Nominee, Univ of Tenn at Martin, 95; Who's Who in Polish America, 96; Who's Who in the World, 96; Who's Who among America's teachers, 97; Int Authors and Writers Who's Who, 97. **MEMBERSHIPS** Phi Kappa Phi; UN Asn of the U.S.; Phi Alpha Theta; Phi Delta Phi; Polish-Am Hist Asn; Polish Inst of Arts and Scis; Am Asn for the Advancement of Slavic Studies; AHA; Ctr for Public Justice; Southern Asn for Slavic Studies; Southern Hist Asn. **RESEARCH** Polish cultural history **SELECTED PUBLICATIONS** Auth, La Ville Libre de Dantzig en crise ouverte. 24-X-1938 - 1-IX-1939 - Politique et diplomatie, 82; Of Two Minds, in Public Justice Report, vol. 16, no. 5, 93; The Clash of Civilizations: Samuel Huntington a Prophet?, in Background Paper #93:4, 93; Ksiegarnia Polska--Librairie Polonaise. 160 years of Polish Presence in Paris, in Polish Rev, vol. XXXIX, no. 3, 94; The Dilemna of European Security: Back to the Future?, in Public Justice Report, March-Apr, 96; transl, La cavalier polonais, 91; La vie qu'il faut choisir, 92; Echapper a ma tombe, 95; Une mouche dans ma soupe, 98. **CONTACT ADDRESS** Dept of History, Univ of Tennessee Martin, 59 Lesa Dr, Jackson, TN, 38305. **EMAIL** accarls@utm.edu

CARLSEN, JAMES CALDWELL
PERSONAL Born 02/11/1927, Pasco, WA, m, 1949, 4 children **DISCIPLINE** SYSTEMATIC MUSICOLOGY **EDUCATION** Whitworth Col, Wash, BA, 50; Univ Wash, MA, 58; Northwestern Univ, (music), 62. **CAREER** Teacher, Almira Pub Schs, 50-53 & Portland pub Schs, 53-54; assoc prof music theory & band dir, Whitworth Col, Wash, 54-63; assoc prof music theory & music educ, Univ conn, 63-67; PROF SYST MUSICOL & MUSIC EDUC, UNIV WASH, 67-, Secy, Music Educ Res Coun, 68-70, chmn, 70-72; Fulbright-Hays Comn sr researcher, Staatliches Inst Musikforschung 73-74. **MEMBERSHIPS** Music Educ Nat Conf; Am Educ Res Asn; Int Soc Music Educ. **RESEARCH** Aural perception training; aural perception of music as a function of expectancy; physiologic effects of music. **SELECTED PUBLICATIONS** Auth, The Need to Know, 1994 Sr-Researcher-Award Acceptance Address, Jour Res Mus Edu, Vol 0042, 94. **CONTACT ADDRESS** Sch of Music, Univ of Wash, Seattle, WA, 98195.

CARLSON, ANDREW RAYMOND
PERSONAL Born 08/19/1934, Ludington, MI, m, 1959, 2 children **DISCIPLINE** MODERN EUROPEAN HISTORY **EDUCATION** Western Mich Univ, BA, 60, MA, 61; Mich State Univ, PhD(mod Europ hist), 68. **CAREER** Asst prof hist, Eastern Ky Univ, 67-70; asst prof soc sci, Ferris State Col, 70-73; ASST PROF SOC SCI, WESTERN MICH UNIV, 73-75; Archivist Probate, Ct, Kalamazoo County, Mich, 76- **MEMBERSHIPS** AHA: Inst Contemp Hist, English; Study Group Europ Labor & Working Class Hist; Hist Comn Berlin. **RESEARCH** European labor and working class history; European diplomatic history 1890-; modern Germany history. **SELECTED PUBLICATIONS** Auth, The German Reich in the South-Pacific 1900-1921--An Examination of the Experiences of Various Cultures-Ger, Amer Hist Rev, Vol 0102, 97; The Outbreak of the First-World-War--Strategic-Planning, Crisis Decision-Making and Deterrence Failure, Ger Stud Rev, Vol 0019, 96; Development for Exploitation--German Colonial Policies in Mainland Tanzania, 1884-1914, Ger Stud Rev, Vol 0020, 97; The Neglected War--The German South-Pacific and the Influence of World War-I, Amer Hist Rev, Vol 0102, 97; Ambassador Sackett, Frederic and the Collapse of the Weimar-Republic, 1930-1933--The United-States and Hitler Rise to Power, Ger Stud Rev, Vol 0018, 95; Justice of the Genesis of War, Ger Stud Rev, Vol 0018, 95. **CONTACT ADDRESS** Western Michigan Univ, Kalamazoo, MI, 49008.

CARLSON, ARVID JOHN
PERSONAL Born 09/12/1928, East Tawas, MI, m, 1950, 2 children **DISCIPLINE** EARLY MODERN EUROPEAN HISTORY **EDUCATION** Univ Mich, AB, 50, AM, 51; Princeton Univ, AM, 58, PhD, 62. **CAREER** Instr social studies, Emory-at-Oxford, 51-55; Danforth teacher grant, 55-56; assoc prof hist, Wofford Col, 58-61; assoc prof, 62-65, PROF HIST & BASIC STUDIES, AUSTIN COL, 65-, CHMN HUMANITIES, 67-, ASSOC DEAN COL, 71- **MEMBERSHIPS** AHA: Am Soc Church Hist; Conf Brit Studies. **RESEARCH** Elizabethan history; influence of Puritanism on early Elizabethan bishops, Reformation studies, effect of Martin Buber and reformed theology in general; higher education, impact of change on liberal arts education. **SELECTED PUBLICATIONS** Auth, The Sign of the Golden Grasshopper--A Biography of Sir Gresham, Thomas, Sixteenth Century Jour, Vol 0027, 96; Mundus-Muliebris--The World of Women Reviled and Defiled C.195-Bc and 1551-Ad and Other Things, Sixteenth Century Jour, Vol 0024, 93; The English-Civil-War--A Contemporary Account, Vol 1, 1625-1639, Sixteenth Century Jour, Vol 0028, 97. **CONTACT ADDRESS** Dept of Hist, Austin Col, Sherman, TX, 95090.

CARLSON, LEWIS H.
PERSONAL Born 08/01/1934, Muskegon, MI, m, 1960, 2 children **DISCIPLINE** RECENT AMERICAN HISTORY **EDUCATION** Univ Mich, BA, 57, MA, 62; Mich State Univ, PhD(hist), 67. **CAREER** Asst prof hist, Ferris State Col, 65-68; asst prof hist, 68-80, prof hist and dir of Am studies, Western Mich Univ, 80-. **HONORS AND AWARDS** Western Mich Univ Alumni Award, 72. **MEMBERSHIPS** Asn Popular Cult. **RESEARCH** Oral history and popular culture. **SELECTED PUBLICATIONS** Co-auth, with George Colburn, In Their Place: White America Defines Her Minorities, John Wiley & Sons, 71;auth, Energy and the Way We Live, The Humanist's Guide to Energy, 79; co-auth, with John J. Fogarty, Tales of Gold: Olympic Stories as Told by Those Who Lived Them, Chicago: Contemporary Books, 87; writer and producer, Images in Black and White: a Documentary Film on Racial Images in Popular Culture, 88; co-auth, with Frank Unger, Amerika - der gespaltene Traum (America the Fragmented Dream), Berlin: Aufbau Verlag, Berlin, 92; with James Ferreira, Beyond the Red, White, and Blue: A Student's Introduction to American Studies, Dubuque, Iowa: Kendall/Hunt, 93; with Frank Unger, Highland Park oder Stadt der Zukunft (Highland Park: City of the Future?), Berlin: Aufbau Verlag, 94; with Kevin Vichcales, American Popular Culture at Home and Abroad, Kalamazoo, Mi: New Issues Press, 96; with Norbert Haase, Warten auf Freiheit: Deutsche und Amerikanische Kriegsgefangene des Zweiten Weltkrieges Erzahlen (Waiting for Freedom: An Oral History of World War II German and American Prisoners of War, Berlin: Aufbau Verlag, 96; auth, We Were Each Other's Prisoners: An Oral History of World War II American and German Prisoners of War, NY: Basic Books, 97, and writer and co-producer of over 100 educational tapes since 1974. **CONTACT ADDRESS** Dept of Hist, Western Michigan Univ, 1201 Oliver St, Kalamazoo, MI, 49008-3805. **EMAIL** lewis.carlson@wmich.edu

CARLSON, ROBERT E.
PERSONAL Born 01/22/1922, Johnstown, PA, m, 1946, 2 children **DISCIPLINE** HISTORY **EDUCATION** Univ Pittsburgh, AB, 43, MA, 50, PhD(hist), 55. **CAREER** Lectr & instr hist, Univ Pittsburgh at Johnstown, 47-49, from lectr to asst prof, Univ Pittsburgh, 49-61; Prof Hist, West Chester Univ, 61-84; Prof Emer, 84-. Am Coun Learned Soc & Am Philos Soc grants, 60-61; Am Philos Soc grant, 69. **HONORS AND AWARDS** Distinguished prof hist, West Univ, 79. **MEMBERSHIPS** AAUP; AHA. **RESEARCH** Hist of Am and Brit railways; Chester County hist. **SELECTED PUBLICATIONS** Auth, British railroads and engineers and the beginnings of American railroad development, Bus Hist Rev, 60; The Pennsylvania Improvement Society and its promotion of canals and railroads, 1824-1826, Pa Hist, 7/64; The Liverpool and Manchester Railway Project 1821-1831, David & Charles, Newton Abbot, Devon & Kelley, NY, 69; Chester County Pennsylvania Bibliography, KNA Press, 81; Dictionary of Chester County Biography, 82. **CONTACT ADDRESS** 1343 W Baltimore Pike, Media, PA, 19063.

CARLSON, ROY L.
PERSONAL Born 06/25/1930, Bremerton, WA **DISCIPLINE** ARCHAEOLOGY/ART **EDUCATION** Univ Wash, BA, 52, MA, 55; Univ Ariz, PhD, 61. **CAREER** Asst prof, Univ Colo, 61, field dir, 4th Nubian Exped, 65; asst prof to prof, 66-95, dept ch, 71-79, 84-89, PROF EMER ARCHAEOLOGY, SIMON FRASER, UNIV, 95-. **HONORS AND AWARDS** Smith-Wintemberg Award, Can Archaeol Asn, 95. **MEMBERSHIPS** Can Archaeol Asn; Soc Am Archaeol; Am Indian Art Stud Asn; Am Asn Advan Sci. **SELECTED PUBLICATIONS** Auth, Basket Maker III Sites Near Durango, Colorado, 63; auth, Eighteenth Century Navajo Fortresses of the Gobernador District, 65; auth, White Mountain Red Ware, 70; auth, Teachers' Manual for Early Indian Cultures of North America, 73; auth, Indian Art Traditions of the Northwest Coast, 83. **CONTACT ADDRESS** Dept of Archaeol, Simon Fraser Univ, Burnaby, BC, V5A 1S6.

CARLTON, DAVID L.
PERSONAL Born 01/06/1948, Spartanburg, SC, s **DISCIPLINE** HISTORY **EDUCATION** Amherst Col, BA, 70; Yale Univ, MA, MPhil, 74, PhD, 77. **CAREER** Vis asst prof, Tex Tech Univ, 79-80; lectr in Hist, Coastal Carolina Col, 81-82; ASST PROF OF HIST, 83-89; ASSOC PROF, VANDERBILT UNIV, 89-. **HONORS AND AWARDS** NEH Fel, 80-81; Fel, Nat Humanities Center, 94-95. **RESEARCH** History of the American South; Industrialization. **SELECTED PUBLICATIONS** Auth, Mill and Town in South Carolina, 1880-1920, La State Univ Press, 82; The Revolution From Above: The National Economy and the Beginnings of Industrialization in North Carolina, J of Am Hist, 90; Paternalism and Southern Textile Labor: A Historiographical View, Race, Class, and Community in Southern Labor Hist, Univ of Ala Press, 94; coauth, Capital Mobilization and Southern Industry, 1880-1920: The Case of the Southern Piedmont, J of Economic Hist, 89; co-ed, Confronting Southern Poverty in the Great Depression: The Report on Economic Conditions of the South and Supplementary Documents, Bedford Books of St. Martin's Press, 96. **CONTACT ADDRESS** 2307 Belmont Blvd, Nashville, TN, 37212. **EMAIL** david.l.carlton@vanderbilt.edu

CARMACK, NOEL A.
PERSONAL Born 11/21/1967, Paso Robles, CA, m, 1990, 1 child **DISCIPLINE** ART/ILLUSTRATION **EDUCATION** Utah State Univ, BFA, 93, MFA, magna cum laude, 97. **CAREER** Pres lib, 94-, Utah State Univ; Conservator, 91-94, archive Asst, 89-91, Spec Collections. **HONORS AND AWARDS** Mountain W Cen Reg Stud Fel; Liquitex Excel Art Prod Gnt; W Mont Timmons Awd; Liquitex Excel Art Univ Awd; George B and Marie Eccles Caine Art Schsp; CVHS Hist Preser Awd; SMA, Awd of Merit; 3rd PL Eccles Comm Art Cent Blk/Wht Competition. **MEMBERSHIPS** MHA; CAA; CIA; GB; ULA; UASAL. **RESEARCH** Art, preservation, conservation, collections mgmt; American culture and religious history with emphasis in Mormon experience. **SELECTED PUBLICATIONS** Auth, Before the Flapper Girl: John Held Jr's Utah Beginnings, UT Historical Qtly, forthcoming; A Memorable Creation: The Life and Art of Effie Marquess Carmack, BYU Studies, 97-98; One of the Most Interesting Seeneries that can be Found in Zion: Philo Dibble's Panorama, and Museum, Nauvoo J, 98; Conservation Note: Selection for Preservation: A Few Considerations, Con Inter-Mountain Archv News Letter, 98; Portrait of a Lady Rediscovered?, Marginalia, 97; Saving the Serials: Preserving Mass Culture at the Utah State Univ Libraries, Archv Prod News, 97; The Yellow Ochre Club: B Forthcoming; Larson and the Pioneer Trail Art Tour 1936, UT Hist Qtly, 97; Of Prophets and Pale Horses: Joseph Smith Benjamin West and the American Millenarian Tradition, Dialogue, J Mormon Thought, 96; Labor in the Construction of the Logan Temple, 1877-18884, J Mormon History, 96; A Note on Nauvoo Theater, BYU Studies, 94; The Seven Ages of Thomas Lyne: A Tragedian Among the Mormons, John Whitmer Hist Assoc, 94; The Identification of Rare and Popular Serials for Preservation, Popular Culture in Libraries, forthcoming; Down Memory Lane: The Autobiography of Effie Marquess Carmack, USU Press, currently editing, forthcoming. **CONTACT ADDRESS** Special Collections and Archives, Utah State Univ, 3000 Old Main Hill, Logan, UT, 84322-3000. **EMAIL** noecar@ngw.lib.usu.edu

CARMACK, ROBERT M.
PERSONAL Born 02/24/1934, AZ, m, 1981, 5 children **DISCIPLINE** ANTHROPOLOGY **EDUCATION** Univ Calif, LA, BA, 60, MA, 62, PhD, 65. **CAREER** Asst Prof, Ariz State Univ, 64-66; Asst Prof, Univ Calif, San Diego, 67-70; Prof, SUNY, 70-. **HONORS AND AWARDS** SUNY Pres Excellence. **MEMBERSHIPS** AA; CIHMA; Inst Meso-American Stud. **RESEARCH** Political anthropology; Central America, Mayan Studies. **SELECTED PUBLICATIONS** Co-ed, Historia Antigua de America Central: Del Poblamiento a la Conquista, FLASCO, 93; ed, Soplos del viento en Buenos Aires: La antropoliogia de un canton brunca de Costa Rica, Univ de Costa Rica, 94; auth, Rebels of Highland Gautemala, Univ Okla Press, 95; co-ed, The Legacy of Mesoamerica: History and Culture of a Native American Civilization, Prentice Hall, 95; auth, Introduction to Cultural Anthropology: A World Systems Approach, McGraw-Hill, 95; Historia social de los K'ichee, Cholsamaj, 98. **CONTACT ADDRESS** Dept Anthrop, SUNY, 1400 Washington Ave, Albany, NY, 12222. **EMAIL** rcarmack@csc.albany.edu

CARMAN, CHARLES
DISCIPLINE ART HISTORY **EDUCATION** Johns Hopkins Univ, PhD. **CAREER** Fac, SUNY Buffalo. **HONORS AND AWARDS** Summer Research in Italy Awd, UUP. **RESEARCH** Italian Renaissance and Baroque Art; 18th Century Europ Art. **SELECTED PUBLICATIONS** Auth, Images of Dignity in Italian Renaissance Art. **CONTACT ADDRESS** Dept Art, SUNY Buffalo, 202 Center for the Arts, Buffalo, NY, 14260-6010.

CARMICHAEL, ANN GRAYTON
PERSONAL Born 08/28/1947, Roanoke, VA, d, 1 child **DISCIPLINE** HISTORY OF MEDICINE **EDUCATION** DePauw Univ, BA, 69; Duke Univ, MD, 78, PhD, 78. **CAREER** Indiana Univ, asst prof, assoc prof, 79-. **MEMBERSHIPS** AAHM, AHA, HSS, RSA. **RESEARCH** Hist of infectious diseases; hist medicine; renaissance Italy. **CONTACT ADDRESS** Dept of History, Indiana Univ, Bloomington, 742 Ballantine Hall, Bloomington, IN, 47405. **EMAIL** carmicha@indiana.edu

CARMICHAEL, PETER S.
DISCIPLINE CIVIL WAR AND RECONSTRUCTION **EDUCATION** PA State Univ, PhD. **CAREER** Hist Dept, Western Carolina Univ **SELECTED PUBLICATIONS** Auth, Lee's Young Artillerist: William R. J. Pegram, 95. **CONTACT ADDRESS** Western Carolina Univ, Cullowhee, NC, 28723.

CARNEAL, THOMAS WILLIAM
PERSONAL Born 04/08/1934, Plattsmouth, NE, 1 child **DISCIPLINE** UNITED STATES URBAN & ECONOMIC HISTORY **EDUCATION** Univ Mo-Kansas City, BA, 63, MA, 66. **CAREER** Instr hist, Kemper Mil Acad, 65-68; asst prof, 68-80, assoc prof hist, 80-, chemn, hist humanities & philos dept, Northwest Mo State Univ, 93-, dir Missouriana Collection, 69-, Dir, Patee House Mus, 70-73; grant humanities, 77-80 & Dept Interior-Mo Off Hist Preserv grant, 78-79, 79-80 & 80-81. **MEMBERSHIPS** Orgn Am Historians; Econ Hist Asn; AAUP. **RESEARCH** Urban problems; Missouri urban and economic problems. **SELECTED PUBLICATIONS** Auth, Issac Miller House, St Joseph, 79; Caleb Burns House, Maryville, 79; Walnut Inn, Tarkio, 80; Fenton House, Buchanan County, 80; Slatten Thousand Acres, Bethany, 80; Delaney House, 80 & Mathias House, 80, DeKalb County; Jessie James House, 80 & American Electric Company, 80, St Joseph. **CONTACT ADDRESS** Dept of History, Missouri State Univ, 800 University Dr, Maryville, MO, 64468-6015. **EMAIL** tcarneal@mail.nwmissouri.edu

CARNES, MARK C.
PERSONAL Born 11/17/1950, Pocatello, ID, m, 1976, 1 child **DISCIPLINE** HISTORY **EDUCATION** Harvard Univ, BA, 74; Columbia Univ, PhD, 82. **CAREER** Gen ed, Am National Biography; asst prof, 82-89, assoc prof, 89-92, PROF HIST, BARNARD COL, COLUMBIA UNIV, 92-. **MEMBERSHIPS** OAH, AHA, Soc Am Historians **RESEARCH** Am social hist **SELECTED PUBLICATIONS** various **CONTACT ADDRESS** Dept Hist, Barnard Col, 606 W 120th St, New York, NY, 10027. **EMAIL** mc422@columbia.edu

CAROLI, BETTY BOYD
PERSONAL Born 01/09/1938, Mt Vernon, OH, m, 1966 **DISCIPLINE** AMERICAN HISTORY **EDUCATION** Oberlin Col, BA, 60; Univ Pa, MA, 61; NY Univ, PhD(Am civilization), 72. **CAREER** Instr speech, State Univ NY Brockport, 61-63; teacher English as second lang, British Col, Sicily & English Sch, Rome, Italy, 64-65; lectr debate, Queens Col, 65-66; instr, 66-78, PROF HIST, KINGSBOROUGH COMMUNITY COL, 78-95. **MEMBERSHIPS** Am Ital Hist Asn (secy, 78-82); Immigration Hist Soc. **RESEARCH** American women's history; immigration history. **SELECTED PUBLICATIONS** Auth, Italian Repatriation From the United States, 1900-1914, Ctr Migration Studies, 73; co-ed, The Italian Immigrant Woman in North America, Multicult Hist Soc, 78; coauth, Today's Immigrants: Their Stories, Oxford Univ Press, 81; contrib, Images: A Photographic History of Italian Americans, Ctr Migration Studies, 81; Rhetoric of Protest and Reform, Ohio Univ Press, 80; auth, First Ladies, Oxford, 87, expanded ed, 95; auth, Immigrants Who Returned Home, Chelsea, 90; auth, Inside the White House, Doubleday, 92, expanded ed, 99; auth, America's First Ladies, Doubleday, 96; auth, The Roosevelt Women, Basic, 98. **CONTACT ADDRESS** 30 Fifth Ave, New York, NY, 10011. **EMAIL** bbckb@aol.com

CARP, E. WAYNE
PERSONAL Born 08/02/1946, New York, NY, s **DISCIPLINE** HISTORY **EDUCATION** Univ of CA, Berkeley, PhD, 81, MA, 73, AB, 72 **CAREER** Prof, 98-, Chair, 95-, Assoc Prof, 92-98, Asst Prof, 86-92, Pac Luth Univ; Visit Asst Prof, 84-85, Univ of WA **HONORS AND AWARDS** Univ Faculty Excel Awd, 98, Grad cum laude, 72 **MEMBERSHIPS** Am Hist Asn; Orgn of Am Historians **RESEARCH** Hist of adoption **SELECTED PUBLICATIONS** Auth, Family Matters: Secrecy and Disclosure in the History of Adoption, Harvard Univ Press, 98; To Starve the Army at Pleasure, Univ of NC Press, 84 **CONTACT ADDRESS** Dept of History, Pac Lutheran Univ, Tacoma, WA, 98447. **EMAIL** carpw@plu.edu

CARPENTER, JOEL A.
PERSONAL Born 02/02/1952, South Haven, MI, m, 1978, 2 children **DISCIPLINE** HISTORY **EDUCATION** Calvin Col, BA, 74; Johns Hopkins, MA, 77, PhD, 84. **CAREER** Vis instr, 76-77, Calvin Col; res asst, 77-78, Johns Hopkins; asst prof, 78-83, Trinity Col, IL; asst to assoc prof, 83-89, Wheaton Col; admin to dir, 83-89, Inst for Study of Am Evangelicals; dir, 89-96, Relig Prog, Pew Charitable Trusts; provost, 96-, Calvin Col. **HONORS AND AWARDS** Honors scholar, Calvin Col; Lilly Fel, Johns Hopkins Univ; Earthen Vessels: yrs best, 91, Int Bul of Missionary Res; Revive Us Again: 98 Christianity Today bk award. **MEMBERSHIPS** Am Hist Asn; Am Soc of Church Hist; Conf on Faith and Hist. **RESEARCH** Am relig and cult hist; evangel & fundamentalist Christianity; foreign missions. **SELECTED PUBLICATIONS** Co-ed, Twentieth-Century Evangelicalism: A Guide to the Sources, Garland, 80; co-ed, Making Higher Education Christian: The History and Mission of Evangelical Colleges in America, Eerdmans, 87; ed, Fundamentalism in American Religion, a 45-volume repr ser, Garland, 88; co-ed, Earthen Vessels: American Evangelicals and Foreign Missions, 1880-1980, Eerdmans, 90; auth, Revive Us Again: The Reawakening of American Fundamentalism, Oxford Univ Press, 97. **CONTACT ADDRESS** Provost's Office, Calvin Col, 3201 Burton St SE, Grand Rapids, MI, 49546. **EMAIL** jcarpent@calvin.edu

CARPENTER, JOSEPH, II
PERSONAL Born 07/21/1937, Aliceville, AL, m **DISCIPLINE** AFRICAN-AMERICAN STUDIES **EDUCATION** MATC, AA 1965; Marquette U, BA 1967; Fisk U, 1968-69; Marquette U, PhD 1970; Univ of IA, Post Doctorate 1972. **CAREER** Univ of WI, prof Afro-Educ, soc research 1972-. **HONORS AND AWARDS** Distinguished Christian Fellowship Award for Comm Serv 1973; distinguished political serv Award 1974. **MEMBERSHIPS** Dir Carthage Coll 1970-72; asst prof Lehman Coll Bronx Summer 1971; NEA Fellow Marquette Univ 1968-70; chmn City of Milwaukee Bd of Election

Commr; chmn bd dir Northcott Youth Serv Bur for Prevention of Juvenile Delinq; chmn Univ of WI Afro-am Stud Comm Rel Comm; exec bd mem Social Studies Council of WI; consult State of NJ Dept of Ed; mem Phi Delta Kappa; alpha Psi Alpha; Milwaukee Frontiers Internat; bd dir Nat Council for Black Child Develop Inc. **SELECTED PUBLICATIONS** numerous articles **CONTACT ADDRESS** Dept of Afro Am Studies, Univ of Wisconsin, Milwaukee, WI, 53201.

CARPENTER, T.H.
PERSONAL Born 07/07/1944, Eugene, OR, m **DISCIPLINE** CLASSICAL ARCHAEOLOGY **EDUCATION** Johns Hopkins Univ, BA, 66; Harvard Univ, MTS, 71; Oxford Univ, D Philos, 83. **CAREER** Teacher, Groton Sch, Groton, MA, 71-76; teacher and admr, St. Stephen's Sch, Rome, Italy, 76-80; chief res, Beazley Archive Ashmolean Mus, Oxford, England, 82-86; prof, Va Polytechnic Inst and State Univ, 86-97; prof, Oh Univ, Athens, Oh, 97-. **MEMBERSHIPS** Amer Philol Asn; Archaeol Asn of Amer; Col Art Asn. **RESEARCH** Ancient Greek vase painting; Greek iconography (archaic and classical); Ancient Greek religion. **SELECTED PUBLICATIONS** Auth, Dionysian Imagery in Fifth Century Athens, Oxford Univ Press, Clarendon, 97; auth, Masks of Dionysus, Cornell Univ Press, 93; auth, Art and Myth in Ancient Greece, Thames and Hudson, World of Art Series, 91; auth, Beazley Addenda, Additional References to ABV, ARV and Paralipomena, 2nd ed, Oxford Univ Press for the Brit Acad, 89; auth, Dionysian Imagery in Archaic Greek Art, Oxford Univ Press, Clarendon, 86; auth, Summary Guide to the Corpus Vasorum Antiquorum, Oxford Univ Press for the Brit Acad, 84; co-auth, Mythology, Greek and Roman, Independent Sch Press, 77; article, Nymphs, not Maenads, Amer Jour of Archaeol, 99, 314, 95; article, A Symposium of Gods, In Vino Veritas, Oxford, 145-63, 95; article, The Terrible Twins in Sixth Century Attic Art, Apollo, Origins and Influences, Univ Ariz Press, 61-79, 94; article, Harmodios and Apollo in Fifth Century Athens. What's in a Pose?, in J. Oakley ed. Athenian Potters and Painters, American School of Classical Studies, Athens, 97. **CONTACT ADDRESS** Classics Dept., Ohio Univ, Ellis Hall, Athens, OH, 45701. **EMAIL** carpentt@ohiou.edu

CARR, AMELIA J.
PERSONAL Born 04/22/1955, Columbus, OH **DISCIPLINE** ART HISTORY **EDUCATION** Ohio State Univ, BA, 76; Northwestern Univ, PhD, 84. **CAREER** Lectr, Northwestern Univ, 82; asst prof, 82-87, dir, prog in Greece and Turkey, Lake Forest Col, 85; asst prof, 87-94, dir, summer prog in Fr, 90, assoc prof, 94-, dir, Women's Stud prog, Allegheny Col, 96-. **SELECTED PUBLICATIONS** Auth, Narrative Pictorial Cycles of the Renaissance and Baroque. **CONTACT ADDRESS** Allegheny Col, Meadville, PA, 16335.

CARR, DAVID RANDOLPH
PERSONAL Born 08/03/1942, San Francisco, CA, m, 1965 **DISCIPLINE** MEDIEVAL HISTORY **EDUCATION** Colo State Univ, BA, 64; Univ Nebr-Lincoln, MA, 68, PhD(hist), 71. **CAREER** Asst prof Hist, Univ South Fla, 71-80; assoc prof Hist, 80-. **MEMBERSHIPS** AHA; Medieval Acad Am; Soc Ital Hist Studies; Wiltshire Record Society, Haskins Society, American Society for Legal History. **RESEARCH** Medieval urban history, especially Italy and England; philosophy of history, social history (medieval, Renaissance, Reformation). **SELECTED PUBLICATIONS** Auth, History and Its Uses: A Guide for Studying History, Omniprint, 74; coauth, The process of criticism in interpretive sociology and history, Human Studies, 78; auth, The prince and the city: Ideology and reality in the thought of Marsilius of Padua, Medioevo rivista di storia della filos medievale, 81; Marsilius of Padua: The use and image of history in Defensor Pacis, Altro Polo, 82; From Pollution to Prostitution: Supervising the Citizens of Fifteenth-Century Salisbury, Southern History: A Review of the History of Southern England, 97; Salisbury City First General Entry Book, Wiltshire Record Society, Devizes, 99, forthcoming; Judaism in Christendom, in Blackwell Companion to Judaism, ed Jacob Nuesner & Alan Avery-Peck, London, Blackwell, 99, forthcoming. **CONTACT ADDRESS** Dept of History, Univ of South Florida, 140 7th Ave S, St. Petersburg, FL, 33701-5016. **EMAIL** carr@bayflash.stpt.usf.edu

CARR, DEREK COOPER
PERSONAL Born 02/26/1944, Darlington, England, m, 1970, 1 child **DISCIPLINE** HISPANIC AND MEDIEVAL STUDIES **EDUCATION** Univ Newcastle, Eng, BA, 65, dipl educ, 66; Univ BC, PhD(Romance studies), 72. **CAREER** Lectr Span, 72-74, asst prof, 74-79, ASSOC PROF SPAN, UNIV BC, 79-, CHMN DEPT, 81- **MEMBERSHIPS** Can Asn Hispanists; MLA; Int Asn Hispanists. **RESEARCH** Medieval & Renaissance Spanish literature; Don Enrique de Villena (1384-1434); editing medieval texts. **SELECTED PUBLICATIONS** Auth, The Poets Art--Literary-Theory in Castile C. 1400-60, Mod Lang Rev, Vol 0088, 93; Letters and Society in 15th-Century Spain--Studies Presented to Russell, P.E. on his 80th Birthday, Mod Lang Rev, Vol 0092, 97; Think and Talk Spanish, Can Mod Lang Rev-Rev Can Des Lang Vivantes, Vol 0050, 94; The Poets Art --Literary-Theory in Castile C.1400-60, Mod Lang Rev, Vol 0088, 93; Letters and Society in 15th-Century Spain--Studies Presented to Russell,P.E. on his 80th Birthday, Mod Lang Rev, Vol 0092, 97; The Debate Over Restoring Historical Instruments, Early Mus, Vol 0022, 94. **CONTACT ADDRESS** Dept of Hisp & Ital Studies, Univ BC, Vancouver, BC, V6T 1W5.

CARR, GRAHAM
DISCIPLINE MODERN NORTH AMERICAN CULTURAL HISTORY **EDUCATION** Queen's Univ, BA, MA; Univ Maine, PhD. **CAREER** Assoc prof. **RESEARCH** Relationship between public history and social memory in contemporary Canadian society. **SELECTED PUBLICATIONS** Pub(s), on culture and free trade, literary history, and historiography. **CONTACT ADDRESS** Dept of Hist, Concordia Univ, Montreal, 1455 de Maisonneuve W, Montreal, PQ, H3G 1M8. **EMAIL** gcarr@vax2.concordia.ca

CARR, LOIS GREEN
PERSONAL Born 03/07/1922, Holyoke, MA, m, 1963, 1 child **DISCIPLINE** AMERICAN COLONIAL & LEGAL HISTORY **EDUCATION** Swarthmore Col, AB, 43; Radcliffe Col, AM, 44; Harvard Univ, PhD(hist), 68. **CAREER** Asst ed, Alfred A Knopf, Inc Col Dept, 51-52; jr archivist, Hall of Rec Comn, Annapolis, 56-64; adj prof hist, Univ Md, 82- ; HISTORIAN, HISTORIC ST MARY'S CITY COMN, MD, 67-, adv bd, McNeil Ctr for Early Am Stud, 81- ; sr adj scholar, Md State Archv, 88- ; proj dir, Am Asn for State and Local Hist grant, 88-89; sr hist, Md Hist Trust, 89- ; pres, Econ Hist Asn, 90-91; publ comt, Md Hist Soc, 90- ; Bd of Trustees, Charles Carroll House of Annapolis, 94- ; Md Hum Coun, 98- . **HONORS AND AWARDS** Phi Beta Kappa; Vis prof hist, St Mary's Col Md, 70; co-prin investr, Nat Sci Found grant, 72-73 & Nat Endowment for Humanities grant, 76-79; fel, Regional Econ Hist Res Ctr, Eleutherian Mills-Hagley Found, 79-80; coun mem, Inst Early Am Hist & Cult, 80-82; mem, Res Div, AHA, 80-82; sr res assoc, Nat Endowment for Humanities grant, 81-83; co-winner, Md Hist Soc Book Prize, 93; co-winner, Econ Hist Asn Alice Hanson Jones Prize, 94; co-winner, Eisenberg Prize for Excellence in the Hum, Md Hum Coun, 96. **MEMBERSHIPS** AHA; Orgn Am Historians; Econ Hist Asn; Soc Sci Hist Asn.; So Hist Asn; Am Soc for Legal Hist. **RESEARCH** Colonial Chesapeake society and economy; local government and the courts of colonial Maryland; social analysis of communities. **SELECTED PUBLICATIONS** Auth, The Metropolis of Maryland: A Comment on Town Development Along the Tobacco Coast, Md Hist Mag, summer 74; coauth, Maryland's Revolution of Government, 1689-1692, Cornell Univ, 74; The Planter's Wife: The Experience of White Women in Seventeenth Century Maryland, William & Mary Quart, 10/77; auth, The Development of the Maryland Orphan's Court, 1654-1715, In: Law, Society and Politics in Early Maryland, Johns Hopkins Univ Press, 77; The Foundations of Social Order: Local Government in Colonial Maryland, In: Town and County: Essays on the Structure of Local Government in the American Colonies, Wesleyan Univ Press, 78; coauth, Immigration and Opportunity: The Freedman in early Colonial Maryland, In: The Chesapeake in the Seventeenth Century: Essays on Anglo-American Society and Politics, Univ NC Press, 79; Inventories and the Analysis of Wealth and Consumption Patterns in St Mary's County, Maryland, 1658-1777, Hist Methods, spring 80; The Lords Baltimore and the Colonization of Maryland, In: Maryland in a Wider World, Wayne State Univ Press, 82; auth, Robert Cole's World: Agriculture and Society in Early Maryland, North Carolina, 91; auth, Emigration and the Standard of the Living: The Seventeenth Century Chesapeake, in J of Econ Hist, 92; co-auth, Changing Life Styles and Consumer Behavior in the Colonial Chesapeake, In: Of Consuming Interests: Styles of Life in the Eighteenth Century, Univ Pr of Va, 94; auth, Wealth and Welfare in the Colonial Chesapeake, William and Mary Q, 99. **CONTACT ADDRESS** Maryland State Archives, 350 Rowe Blvd, Annapolis, MD, 21401.

CARR, MICHAEL HAROLD
PERSONAL Born 05/26/1935, Leeds, England, m, 1961, 1 child **DISCIPLINE** GEOLOGY **EDUCATION** London, BSc, 56; Yale, PhD, 60. **CAREER** Res assoc, Univ W Ontario, 60-62; GEOLOGIST, US GEOL SURV, 62-. **HONORS AND AWARDS** NASA Medal Except Sci Achievement, 77; Dept Interior Distinguished Serv Award, 88; Geol Soc Am Gilbert Award, 93; Natl Air & Space Mus Lifetime Achievement Award, 94. **MEMBERSHIPS** Am Asn Advanced Sci; Geol Soc Am; Am Geophys Soc **RESEARCH** Planetary Science **SELECTED PUBLICATIONS** The Surface of Mars, Yale; Water on Mars, Oxford. **CONTACT ADDRESS** US Geol Survey, Menlo Park, CA, 94025. **EMAIL** carr@asthnl.wr.usgs.gov

CARRAHER, CHARLES E.
PERSONAL Born 05/08/1941, Des Moines, IA, m, 1998, 8 children **DISCIPLINE** HISTORY OF SCIENCE **EDUCATION** Sterling Col, BS, 63; Univ Mo, Kansas City, PhD; 67. **CAREER** Instr, Univ SD, 67-68; asst prof, Univ SD, 68-70; assoc prof, Univ SD, 70-73; chair, sci div, Univ SD, 71-74; prof, Univ SD, 73-76; prof and chair, dept chem, Wright State Univ, 76-84; prof and chair, Wright State Univ, 83-85; prof, chem, dean, Col of Sci, Fla Atlantic Univ, 85-95; prof, chem, assoc dir, Fla Ctr for Environ Studies, 95-. **HONORS AND AWARDS** Florida award, 92; Saltarilli Sigma Xi award, 92; Who's Who in Amer, 92; Who's Who in the South and South-west, 90; Intl Leaders in Achievement, 88; Who's Who in Tech, 88; Men of Achievement, 87; Intl Leaders in Achievement, 87; Intl Dir of Distinguished Leadership, 89; Outstanding Alumni, Sterling Col, 88; Who's Who in Frontier Sci and Tech, 83; Comunity Leaders of Amer, 82; Who's Who in Tech Today, 81; Who's Who in Tech Today, 80; Community Leaders of Amer, 80; Dir of Distinguished Amer, 80; Personalities of the West and Midwest, 78; Intl Who's Who in Community Svc, 78; Personalities of Amer, 78; Men of Achievement, 78; Men and Women of Distinction, 78; Notable Amer, 76; Amer Men and Women of Sci, 76; Amer Men of Sci, 76; Community Leaders and Noteworthy Amer, 76; Dir of Intl Bio, 75; Intl Scholar Dir, 74; Who's Who in Amer Midwest, 74; Outstanding Young Men of Amer, 71, 78; Alpha Xi, 63-65; Who's Who Among Students in Amer Univ and Col, 63; Kelsey Scholar, 60-63. **CONTACT ADDRESS** Florida Atlantic Univ, Boca Raton, FL, 33431. **EMAIL** carraher@fau.edu

CARRASCO, GILBERT P.
DISCIPLINE IMMIGRATION LAW AND POLICY; CONSTITUTIONAL LAW; CIVIL RIGHTS LITIGATION **EDUCATION** Univ San Diego, BA, 75; Univ Santa Clara, JD, 78; Georgetown Univ Law Ctr, LLM, 79. **CAREER** Vis prof, Univ San Diego Sch Law; Seton Hall Sch Law; legis dir, Equal Justice found, 79; consult, Migrant Legal Aid Prog, Inc, 79; trial atty, US Dept Justice, Civil Rights Div, 80-84; dir atty, Nat Ctr Immigrants' Rt(s), 84-85; dir atty, Legal Aid Soc, 85-86; Nat dir, Immigration Serv, US Cath Conf, 86-88. **HONORS AND AWARDS** Hon mem, Order of the Coif., Pres, Pa Hisp Bar Assn. **MEMBERSHIPS** Mem, Hisp Nat Bar Assn; Latin Amer Law Stud Assn; UNHCR. **RESEARCH** Civil rights and immigration. **SELECTED PUBLICATIONS** Co-auth, Civil Rights Litigation, 95; Immigration and Nationality Law: Cases and Materials, 91, 92; auth, Latinos in the United States: Invitation and Exile,The New Nativism, 96. **CONTACT ADDRESS** Willamette Univ, 900 State St, Salem, OR, 97301. **EMAIL** carrasco@law.vill.edu

CARRIGAN, DAVID O.
PERSONAL Born 11/30/1933, New Glasgow, NS, Canada **DISCIPLINE** HISTORY **EDUCATION** St Francis Xavier Univ, BA, 54; Boston Univ, MA, 55; Univ Maine, PhD, 66. **CAREER** Asst prof, 57-61, assoc prof & dept ch, Xavier Col, St Francis Xavier Univ, 61-67; assoc prof, Wilfrid Laurier Univ, 67-68; prin & dean arts, King's Col, Univ Western Ont, 68-71; pres, 71-79, PROF HISTORY, ST MARY'S UNIV, 79-. **MEMBERSHIPS** Am Hist Asn. **SELECTED PUBLICATIONS** Auth, Canadian Party Platforms 1867-1968, 68; auth, Crime and Punishment in Canada, A History, 91; auth, Juvenile Delinquency in Canada, 97. **CONTACT ADDRESS** Dept of History, St Mary's Univ, Halifax, NS, B3H 3C3.

CARRIKER, ROBERT C.
PERSONAL Born 08/18/1940, St. Louis, MO, m, 1963, 3 children **DISCIPLINE** AMERICAN HISTORY **EDUCATION** St Louis Univ, BS, 62, AM, 63; Univ OK, PhD, 67. **CAREER** From asst prof to prof hist, Gonzaga Univ, 67, Henry E Huntington Libr fels, 69 & 71; Am Philos Soc grant, 70; vis lectr Am Indian hist, AZ State Univ, 71-72. **HONORS AND AWARDS** Burlington Northern Scholar of the Year, 85, 96. **MEMBERSHIPS** Western Hist Asn; Orgn Am Historians. **RESEARCH** Frontier and Western Am hist; Southwestern mil frontier; Am Indians. **SELECTED PUBLICATIONS** Fort Supply: Indian Territory, Univ OK, 70, 2nd ed, 90; Kalispel people, Indian Tribal Series, 73; ed, An Army Wife on The Frontier, Univ UT, 75; ed, Microfilm Edition IN Lang Collection, 76; Microfilm Edition Alaska Missions Collection, 80; Microfilm Edition Pacific Northwest Tribes Missions Collection, 86; Father Peter John De Smet: Jesuit in the West, 95; Bk rev ed, Columbia, Mag of Northwest Hist, 87. **CONTACT ADDRESS** Dept of Hist, Gonzaga Univ, 502 E Boone Ave, Spokane, WA, 99258-0001. **EMAIL** carriker@gonzaga.edu

CARRILLO, ELISA ANNA
PERSONAL Born 01/03/1922, Brooklyn, NY **DISCIPLINE** HISTORY **EDUCATION** St Joseph's Col, AB, 43; Fordham Univ, AM, 45, PhD, 53. **CAREER** Prof hist, 45-79, ACAD DEAN, MARYMOUNT COL, NY, 79-, Consult, Col Proficiency Exam Prog, State Educ Dept, NY, 64-77; mem, Columbia Univ Fac Sem Mod Italy, 66-. **MEMBERSHIPS** AHA; Am Cath Hist Asn; Soc Ital Hist Studies; AAUP; Berkshire Conf Women Historians. **RESEARCH** Modern European history; Italian and Russian history. **SELECTED PUBLICATIONS** Auth, The Catholic-Church in the Crisis of Italy 1943-1948-French, Cath Hist Rev, Vol 0079, 93. **CONTACT ADDRESS** Dept of Hist, Marymount Col, 100 Marymount Ave, Tarrytown, NY, 10591-3796.

CARRINGTON, LAUREL
DISCIPLINE MEDIEVAL AND EARLY MODERN EUROPE **EDUCATION** Wellesley, BA; Cornell, PhD. **CAREER** History, St. Olaf Col. **SELECTED PUBLICATIONS** Articles: The Erasmus of Rotterdam Society Yearbook; Archiv fur Reformationsgeschichte. **CONTACT ADDRESS** St Olaf Col, 1520 St Olaf Ave, Northfield, MN, 55057. **EMAIL** carrington@stolaf.edu

CARROLL, BRET E.
DISCIPLINE HISTORY **EDUCATION** Emory, BA, 83; Cornell Univ, MA, 88, PhD, 91. **CAREER** VIS ASST PROF, HIST, UNIV TEXAS ARLINGTON **MEMBERSHIPS** Am Antiquarian Soc **RESEARCH** Religion **SELECTED PUBLICATIONS** Religion and Masuclinity in Antebellum America **CONTACT ADDRESS** Dept of Hist, Univ of Texas at Arlington, PO Box 19529, Arlington, TX, 76019-0529.

CARROLL, CHARLES FRANCIS
PERSONAL Born 10/05/1936, Cambridge, MA, m, 1970, 1 child **DISCIPLINE** AMERICAN HISTORY **EDUCATION** Boston Col, AB, 59, MA, 61; Brown Univ, PhD(hist), 70. **CAREER** Instr hist,62-63, 66-68 & Univ RI, 65-66; asst prof, assoc prof, 68-74, prof, 74-, chmn, Dept Hist, Univ Mass, Lowell **MEMBERSHIPS** Colonial Soc of Mass; Orgn Am Hist; Am Hist Assn; Soc for Hist of Tech. **RESEARCH** Colonial history of New England; American Colonial history; American economic history. **SELECTED PUBLICATIONS** Auth, Timber Economy of Puritan New England, Brown Univ, 73; The Forest Society of New England, America's Wooden Age, Sleepy Hollow Restorations, 74; contrib, 3 chap on Chelmsford, Mass, Cotton Was King, NH Publ Co. 76; contrib, 4 art, Encycl of Am Forest & Conservation Hist, Free Press, Macmillan Pub, 83; auth, Empirical Technology and the Early Industrial Development of Lowell, Continuing Revolution: A History of Lowell, Mass, Lowell Hist Soc, 91; auth, The Human Impact on the New England Landscape, Thoreau's World and Ours: A Natural Legacy, No Am Press, 93. **CONTACT ADDRESS** Box 172, Harvard, MA, 01451. **EMAIL** Charles_Carroll@uml.edu

CARROLL, FRANCIS MARTIN
PERSONAL Born 01/31/1938, Cloquet, MN, m, 1963, 1 child **DISCIPLINE** AMERICAN & IRISH HISTORY **EDUCATION** Carleton Col, BA, 60; Univ Minn, MA, 62; Dublin Univ, PhD(hist), 70. **CAREER** Instr English, SDak State Univ, 62-64; vis instr hist, Kalamazoo Col, 67-68; asst prof, 69-74, ASSOC PROF HIST, ST JOHN'S COL, UNIV MAN, 74-, ASSOC HEAD DEPT, 82-, Dean studies, St John's Col, Univ Man, 76-78; vis scholar, Columbia Univ Law Sch, 80. **MEMBERSHIPS** Am Comt Irish Studies; Am Hist Asn; Forest Hist Soc; Orgn Am Historians; Soc Historians Am Foreign Rels. **RESEARCH** Anglo-Irish-American relations (twentieth century); Anglo-Canadian-American relations (nineteenth century); international law, American international lawyers. **SELECTED PUBLICATIONS** Auth, Blockaders, Refugees, and Contrabands--Civil-War On Florida Gulf-Coast, 1861-1865, Intl History Rev, Vol 0016, 94; Congress and Us Military Aid to Britain--Interdependence and Dependence, 1949-56, Jour Amer Hist, Vol 0083, 96; The Sims Incident--Irish-Americans and Social Tensions in the 1920s, Prologue-Quart Nat Arch, Vol 0025, 93; The War Correspondents--The American-Civil-War, Intl Hist Rev, Vol 0016, 94; History and the Shaping of Irish Protestantism, Historian, Vol 0059, 97; Irish America and the Ulster Conflict, 1968-1995, Intl Hist Rev, Vol 0018, 96; Ireland and the League-Of-Nations, 1914-1946--International-Relations, Diplomacy, and Politics, Intl Hist Rev, Vol 0019, 97; From Cape-Charles to Cape-Fear--The North-Atlantic Blockading Squadron During the Civil-War, Intl Hist Rev, Vol 0016, 94; The Passionate Canadians--The Historical Debate About the Eastern Canadian-American Boundary, New Eng Quart- Hist Rev New Eng Life and Letters, Vol 0070, 97; Private and Confidential--Letters from British Ministers in Washington to the Foreign-Secretaries in London, 1844-67, Intl Hist Rev, Vol 0016, 94; Union in Peril--The Crisis Over British Intervention in the Civil-War, Intl Hist Rev, Vol 0016, 94; Trial by Friendship--Anglo-American Relations, 1917-1918, Jour Amer Hist, Vol 0081, 94; The Irish Constitutional Tradition, Responsible Government and Modern Ireland, 1792-1992, Eire-Ireland, Vol 0030, 95; The Passionate Canadians--The Historical Debate About the Eastern Canadian-American Boundary, New Eng Quart-Hist Rev New England Life and Letters, Vol 0070, 97. **CONTACT ADDRESS** St John's Col Univ of Man, Winnipeg, MB, R3T 2M5.

CARROLL, JOHN MARTIN
PERSONAL Born 03/29/1943, Providence, RI, m, 1969, 1 child **DISCIPLINE** UNITED STATES AND DIPLOMATIC HISTORY **EDUCATION** Brown Univ, AB, 65; Providence Col, MA, 67; Univ Ky, PhD(hist), 73. **CAREER** Instr hist, Berkeley Sch, Fla, 67-69; asst prof, 72-80, ASSOC PROF HIST, LAMAR UNIV, 80-, Ed, The Lamar J of the Humanities, 74- **HONORS AND AWARDS** Regents Teaching Award, Lamar Univ, 74. **MEMBERSHIPS** AHA; Orgn Am Historians; Soc Historians Am Foreign Rels; Southern Hist Asn. **RESEARCH** Twentieth-century American history; American diplomatic history. **SELECTED PUBLICATIONS** Auth, Stagg-University--The Rise, Decline, and Fall of Big-Time Football in Chicago, Historian, Vol 0059, 97; American Merchant Ships on the Yangtze, 1920-1941, Historian, Vol 0056, 93; Walker,Fleet Divided Heart--The Life of Baseballs First Black Major-League, Jour Amer Hist, Vol 0083, 96; Bowles,Chester--New Dealer in the Cold-War, Historian, Vol 0057, 95. **CONTACT ADDRESS** Lamar Univ, 3825 Holland Dr, Beaumont, TX, 77707.

CARROLL, ROSEMARY F.
PERSONAL Born 10/15/1935, Providence, RI, s **DISCIPLINE** HISTORY **EDUCATION** Univ of IA, JDD, 83; Rutgers Univ, PhD, 68; Wesleyan Univ, MA, 62; Brown Univ, BA, 57 **CAREER** Prof, 84-, Assoc Prof, 75-84, Asst Prof, 71-75, Coe Col; Visit Asst Prof, 70-71, Denison Univ; Asst Prof, 68-70, Notre Dame col **HONORS AND AWARDS** Phi Kappa Phi, 67; Univ Fel, 66-67 **MEMBERSHIPS** Am Bar Asn; IA St Bar Asn **RESEARCH** US Legal Hist **CONTACT ADDRESS** Dept of History, Coe Col, Cedar Rapids, IA, 52402. **EMAIL** rcarroll@coe.edu

CARROLL, WARREN HASTY
PERSONAL Born 03/24/1932, Minneapolis, MN, m, 1967 **DISCIPLINE** CATHOLIC HISTORY **EDUCATION** Bates Col, BA, 53; Columbia Univ, MA, 54, PhD(hist), 59. **CAREER** Instr hist, Ind Univ, 57-58; asst command historian, Sec Air Force, US Strategic Air Command, 60-61; admin asst, Calif State Senator John G Schmitz, 67-70, legis asst, 70-72; dir, Christian Commonwealth Inst, 73-75; Pres, Christendom Col, 77-85, Contrib ed, Triumph Mag, 73-75; trustee, Seton Sch, Manassas, 76-. **MEMBERSHIPS** Fel Catholic Scholars. **RESEARCH** Church history in the broadest sense; history of the Spanish-speaking peoples; history of modern revolutionary movements, since 1789. **SELECTED PUBLICATIONS** Auth, Law: The Quest for Certainty, Am Bar Asn J, 1/63; The West come to Judgment, Triumph, 5/72; Philip II versus William Cecil: The Cleaving of Christendom, Faith & Reason, winter 75-76; coauth, Reasons for Hope, Christendom Col Press, 78; auth, The dispersion of the Apostles: Overview, Peter, spring 81, The Dispersion of the Apostles: Thomas, summer 81 & The Dispersion of the Apostles: St Jude and the Shroud, fall 81, Faith & Reason; 1917: Red Banners, White Mantle, Christendom Publ, 81; Our Lady of Guadalupe and the Conquest of Darkness, 83; The Founding of Christendom , 85; The Guillotine and the Cross, 86; The Building of Christendom, 87; Isabel of Spain, the Catholic Queen, 91; The Glory of Christendom, 93; The Rise and Fall of the Communist Revolution, 95; The Last Crusade, 96. **CONTACT ADDRESS** Christendom Col, 134 Christendom Dr, Box 87, Front Royal, VA, 22630-6534. **EMAIL** Warren.h.carroll@trincomm.org

CARRUBBA, ROBERT W.
DISCIPLINE LATIN LITERATURE, NEO-LATIN STUDIES **EDUCATION** Princeton, PhD. **CAREER** VP, Acad Aff; prof, Fordham Univ. **SELECTED PUBLICATIONS** Auth, The Epodes of Horace: A Study in Poetic Arrangemen, 69; Englebert Kaempfer's Exotic Pleasures: Fascicle III, Curious Scientific and Medical Observations, 96. **CONTACT ADDRESS** Dept of Class Lang and Lit, Fordham Univ, 113 W 60th St, New York, NY, 10023.

CARSON PASTAN, ELIZABETH
DISCIPLINE WOMEN'S VOICES AND IMAGES OF WOMEN IN JAPANESE ART **EDUCATION** Brown Univ, PhD, 86. **CAREER** Emory Univ. **SELECTED PUBLICATIONS** Joint auth, Stained Glass in American Collections before 1700, 89; Edouard Manet and the Execution of Maximillian. **CONTACT ADDRESS** Emory Univ, Atlanta, GA, 30322-1950. **EMAIL** jmeye03@emory.edu

CARTER, BARBARA LILLIAN
PERSONAL Born 06/20/1942, Mexia, Texas, s **DISCIPLINE** EDUCATION **EDUCATION** Fisk Univ, AB 1963; Brandeis Univ, MA 1967, PhD 1972; Harvard Univ Inst of Educ Mgmt, attended 1984. **CAREER** Federal City College, asst prof 1969-72, assoc provost and assoc prof 1972-77; Univ of District of Columbia, assoc vice pres and prof 1977-80, vice pres for academic affairs 1980-81; Spelman Coll, vice pres for academic affairs and dean 1981-, acting dean 1986-87. **HONORS AND AWARDS** Woodrow Wilson Fellow 1963; Phi Beta Kappa 1963; Fellow Natl Inst of Mental Health 1964-67; Aspen Institute for Humanistic Studies Fellowship 1981. **MEMBERSHIPS** Mem Amer Sociological Assoc 1969-; bd dirs YWCA of Atlanta 1982-; bd dirs United Way of Atlanta 1985-, Public Broadcast Assoc 1985-; bd trustees Atlanta Coll of Art 1986-; bd of trustees Chatham Coll. **SELECTED PUBLICATIONS** Coauth, "Protest, Politics and Prosperity" 1978. **CONTACT ADDRESS** Vice Pres for Academic Afrs, Spelman Col, 350 Spelman Ln SW, Atlanta, GA, 30314.

CARTER, DAN T.
DISCIPLINE HISTORY **EDUCATION** Univ SC, BA, 62; Univ Wis, MA, 64; Univ NC, PhD, 67. **CAREER** Prof **HONORS AND AWARDS** Anisfield Wolfe Awd; 2 times Jules Landry Prize; Lillian Smith Awd; Bancroft Prize; Avery Craven Prize, Organ Am Hist; Robert F. Kennedy Bk Awd; Seltzer Prize. **RESEARCH** Southern history. **SELECTED PUBLICATIONS** Auth, Scottsboro: A Tragedy of the American South; When the War Was Over: the Failure of Self-Reconstruction in the South, 1865-1867; Politics of Rage: George Wallace, the Rise of the New Conservatism and the Transformation of American Politics; From George Wallace to Newt Gingrich: Race in the Conservative Counterrevolution, 1963-1994. **CONTACT ADDRESS** Dept History, Emory Univ, 221 Bowden Hall, 561 Kilgo Cir, Atlanta, GA, 30322-1950. **EMAIL** dcarter@emory.edu

CARTER, DAVID G., SR.
PERSONAL Born 10/25/1942, Dayton, OH **DISCIPLINE** EDUCATION **EDUCATION** Central State Univ, BS 1962-65; Miami Univ, MEd 1967-68; The OH State Univ, PhD 1969-71. **CAREER** Dayton City Schools, 6th grade tchr 1965-68, asst prin 1968-69, elem prin 1969-70, unit facilitator 1970-71; Dayton Publ Schools, serv unit dir (dist supt) 1971-73; Wright State Univ, adj prof 1972; Penn State Univ, asst prof dept of educ admn 1973-75, assoc prof dept educ admn 1975-77; Univ of CT, assoc prof dept educ admin 1977-79, prof dept educ admn 1980-, assoc dean/sch educ 1977-82, assoc vice pres acad affairs 1982-; Univ of CT, Storrs, CT, assoc vice pres academicaffairs, 1982-88; Eastern CT State Univ, Willimantic, CT, president 1988-. **HONORS AND AWARDS** NAACP, Roy Wilkins Civil Rights Award, 1994; Connecticut American Legion Dept, 39th Americanism Award, 1994; Inducted into the Donald K Anthony Achievement Hall of Fame, 1993; Central State University, Wilberforce, OH, 1993; Selected Young Man of the Year Dayton Jr C of C 1973. **MEMBERSHIPS** Commission's Division III NCAA, chair, 1994-97; Urban League of Greater Hartford, bd of dirs, 1994-97; Consult Professional Devel Assoc 1979-80; consult Milwaukee Pub Schools 1980; consult Syracuse Univ Research Corp 1976; consult PA Dept of Educ 1973-77; consult So Ea Delco Sch Dist 1973-83; consult Booz-Allen and Hamilton Inc 1972-73; bd trustees Dayton Museum of Natl Hist 1973; mem Centre Cnty Mental Hlth and Mental Retardation Adv Bd 1974-76; mem Adv Cncl to the Bd of Mental Health for Program Dev 1977-80; mem Governor's Task Force on Jail and Prison Overcrowding 1980; bd dir New Engl Reg Exch 1981-; corporator Windham Meml Comm Hosp 1982; trustee Windham Meml Comm Hosp 1984; dir Windham Healthcare Sys Inc 1984; mem Phi Delta Kappa; mem Amer Educ Rsch Assn; mem NAACP; mem Pi Lambda Theta; mem Phi Kappa Phi; bd dir Natl Organiz on LegalProbl in Education 1980-83; ed bd Journal of Eduquity and Leadership 1980; mem Good Samaritan Mental Health Adv 1968-73. **SELECTED PUBLICATIONS** Auth, "Students Rights and Responsibilities, Challenge or Revolt" Penn School Master Journal for Secondary Principals 1974; auth, "Implications of Teacher Performance Appraisal" The Penn School Master 1975; co-auth, "Minority Students, Ability Grouping and Career Development" Journal of Black Studies with Frank Brown and J John Harris, 1978; auth, "Race, Language and Sex Discrimination" in A Digest of Supreme Court Decisions Affecting Education, 1978. **CONTACT ADDRESS** Eastern Connecticut State Univ, 83 Windham St, Willimantic, CT, 06226-2295.

CARTER, EDWARD C., II
PERSONAL Born 01/10/1928, Rochester, NY, m, 1975, 4 children **DISCIPLINE** AMERICAN HISTORY, AMERICAN LANDSCAPE, CALIFORNIA **EDUCATION** Univ Penn, AB, 54, MA, 56; Bryn Mawr Col, PhD, 62. **CAREER** Vis lect, hist, Univ of PA, 62-64; chemn, dept of hist, St. Stephen's Sch, Rome, 65-69; prof, hist, Catholic Univ Am, 69-80; ed-in-chief, Papers of Benjamin Henry Latrobe, Baltimore, 70-95; adj prof, hist, Univ of Penn, 80- ; librn, Am Philos Soc, 80- . **HONORS AND AWARDS** Elected Am Philos Soc, 83 and Am Antiq Soc, 87; 7 NEH grants; 12 NHPRC grants, 2 NSF grants; Huntington Lib Fel, 89; English-Speaking Union Ambassador Book Awd; 2 APS res grants; ACLS grant-in-aid. **RESEARCH** Creation of American landscape; California history; Philadelphia. **SELECTED PUBLICATIONS** Co-ed, Enterprise and Entrepreneurs in Nineteenth and Twentieth Century France, Johns Hopkins, 76; co-ed, Beyond Confederation: Origins of the Constitution and American National Identity, Univ of North Carolina Pr, 87; auth, One Grand Pursuit: A Brief History of the American Philosophical Society's First 250 Years, 1743-1993, Am Philos Soc, 93; ed-in-chief, The Papers of Benjamin Henry Latrobe, 10 vols, Yale, 95; ed, Surveying the Record: North American Scientific Exploration to 1930, Am Philos Soc, 98. **CONTACT ADDRESS** 105 South Fifth St, Philadelphia, PA, 19106. **EMAIL** ecarter@mail.sas.upenn.edu

CARTER, GUY C.
PERSONAL Born 02/21/1951, Austin, TX, m, 1994, 2 children **DISCIPLINE** HISTORICAL THEOLOGY **EDUCATION** Univ St. Thomas, BA, 73; Marquette Univ, MA, 80; Lutheran Sch Theol, MDiv, 86; Marquette Univ, PhD, 87. **CAREER** Pastor, Evangel Lutheran Abbey of St. Boniface, hamelin, Ger, 89-91; pastor, Grace Evangel Lutheran Church, NJ, 92-94; pastor, Trinity Evangel Lutheran Church, NJ, 94-89; adj lectr, St. Peter's Col, 92-98, asst prof, 98- . **HONORS AND AWARDS** Magna cum Laude, 73; Arthur J. Schmitt Doctoral Fel, 81-82, 82-83. **MEMBERSHIPS** Am Acad Relig; Soc of Bibl Lit; Int Bonhoeffer Soc for Arch & Res. **RESEARCH** Historical theology of the German Church struggle, 1933-45; Holocaust studies. **SELECTED PUBLICATIONS** Auth, "Walter A. Maier," Twentieth Century Shapers of American Ppular Religion, Greenwood, 89; co-ed, "Bonhoeffer's Ethics," Kok Pharos, 91; auth, "Evangelische Theologie und ihre Didaktik," Damit wir einander mahe sind, Haensel-Hohenhausen, 98. **CONTACT ADDRESS** Theology Dept, St. Peter's Col, 2641 Kennedy Blvd, Jersey City, NJ, 07306. **EMAIL** gcemc@earthlink.net

CARTER, JANE B.
DISCIPLINE CLASSICAL ARCHAEOLOGY **EDUCATION** Mount Holyoke Col, AB, 70; Univ VA, MA, 71; Har-

vard Univ, PhD, 84. **CAREER** Assoc prof, Tulane Univ. **SELECTED PUBLICATIONS** Auth, Greek Ivory-Carving in the Orientalizing and Archaic Periods, Garland Publ Inc, 85; Ancestor Cult and the Occasion of Homeric Performance, The Ages of Homer, Univ Tex Press, 95; Thiasos and Marzeah: Ancestor Cult in the Age of Homer, From Pasture to Polis: Art in the Age of Homer, Univ Mo Press, 97; co-ed, The Ages of Homer, Univ Tex Press, 95; Egyptian Bronze Jugs from Crete and Lefkandi, Jour Hellenic Stud, 98. **CONTACT ADDRESS** Dept of Class Stud, Tulane Univ, 6823 St Charles Ave, New Orleans, LA, 70118. **EMAIL** jcarter@mailhost.tcs.tulane.edu

CARTER, JEFFREY D.R.
PERSONAL Born 04/18/1963, Boston, MA, m, 1996 **DISCIPLINE** THE HISTORY OF RELIGIONS; THE RELIGIONS OF AFRICA **EDUCATION** Univ of Chicago, PhD, 97 **CAREER** Vis asst prof, Davidson Col, 97-98; vis asst prof, Univ S Carolina, 98-99. **HONORS AND AWARDS** Fulbright Dissertation Fel Nigeria; Pre-dissertation Fel Soc Sci Res Coun Nigeria; Inst Advan Study Relig Chicago. **MEMBERSHIPS** Amer Acad Relig **RESEARCH** Comparative religions; Indigenous religious traditions; Religions of Africa; Methods & theories in the study of religion. **SELECTED PUBLICATIONS** rev, Prey into Hunter: The Politics of Religious Experience, Jour Relig, 93; rev, The Social Control of Religious Zeal: A Study of Organizational Contradictions, Jour Relig, 95; rev, A History of Christianity in Africa: From Antiquity to the Present, Jour Relig, 97; Religion and Politics in Nigeria: A Study of Middle Belt Christianity, Jour Relig, 97; auth, Description is not Explanation: A Methodology of Comparison, Method & Theory in the Study of Religion, 98. **CONTACT ADDRESS** Dept of Religious Studies, Univ S Carolina, Columbia, SC, 29208. **EMAIL** carterj@garnet.cla.sc.edu

CARTER, JOHN ROSS
PERSONAL Born 06/22/1938, Baytown, TX, m, 1960 **DISCIPLINE** HISTORY OF RELIGIONS, BUDDHIST STUDIES **EDUCATION** Baylor Univ, BA, 60; Southern Baptist Theol Sem, BD, 63; Univ London, MTh, 65; Harvard Univ, PhD(hist relig), 72. **CAREER** Asst prof, 72-80, assoc prof relig, Colgate Univ, 80-, Dir, Fund Study Great Relig & Chapel House, Colgate Univ, 74-. **MEMBERSHIPS** Am Acad Relig; Asn Asian Studes. **RESEARCH** History of religion; Buddhist studies. **SELECTED PUBLICATIONS** Auth, Dhamma: Western Academic and Sinhalese Buddhist Interpretations, Hokuseido Press, Tokyo, 78; ed, Religiousness in Sri Lanka, Marga Inst, Colombo, 79; co-ed, Religiousness in Yoga by T K V Desikachar, Univ Press Am, 80. **CONTACT ADDRESS** Colgate Univ, 13 Oak Dr, Hamilton, NY, 13346-1379.

CARTER, JOSEPH COLEMAN
PERSONAL Born 12/23/1941, New York, NY, 3 children **DISCIPLINE** CLASSICAL ARCHAEOLOGY, CLASSICS **EDUCATION** Amherst Col, BA, 63; Princeton Univ, MA, 67, PhD, 71. **CAREER** Asst prof, 71-76, prof class & class Archaeol, Univ TX Austin; Class Archaeol, Univ TX, Nat Endowment for Humanities younger humanist fel, 73-74; Am Coun Learned Soc fel, 79. **MEMBERSHIPS** Soc Promot Hellenic Studies; Archaeol Inst Am; Soc Promotion Roman Studies; Inst per la Storia della Magna Precia. **RESEARCH** Excavation & research of Greek colonies on the Black Sea; Archaeological excavation, survey and research in Greek colonial S Italy. **SELECTED PUBLICATIONS** Auth, Relief sculpture from the Necropolis of Taranto, 74 & The Tomb of the Sire, 78, Am J Archaeol; The Sculpture of Taras, Philadelphia, 75; auth, The Chora of Metaponto: The Necropoleis, 97. **CONTACT ADDRESS** Dept of Class, Univ of Texas, Austin, TX, 78712-1026. **EMAIL** j.carter@mail.utexas.edu

CARTER, JUDY L.
PERSONAL Born 06/07/1942, McCormick, South Carolina, m, 1968 **DISCIPLINE** EDUCATION **EDUCATION** Paine College, Augusta, GA, BA, 1967; Augusta College, Augusta, GA, MEd, 1976; University of South Carolina, Columbia, SC, EdD, 1981. **CAREER** Richmond County Bd of Ed, Augusta, GA, teacher, 1967-76; Paine College, Augusta, GA, instructor, 1976-80; University of South Carolina, Aiken, SC, dir of student teaching, 1980-84; Paine College, Augusta, GA, chair, div of education, 1984-. **HONORS AND AWARDS** Teacher of the Year, Paine College, 1979-80; Graduate Advisor of the Year, Alpha Kappa Alpha Sorority Inc, 1988; Minority Teacher Recruitment Project, Consortium for the Advancement of Private Higher Education, 1988-90; Outstanding Community Leader, Wrights Enterprise, 1990. **MEMBERSHIPS** Vice-president, Alpha Kappa Alpha Sorority Inc, 1985-87; president, The Augusta Chapter of Links Inc, 1986-89; chairperson, Georgia Advisory Council, 1988-89; director, Bush Faculty Development Program, 1988-; site coordinator, Ford Teacher-Scholar Program, 1990-; member, Georgia Assn of Colleges for Teacher Education, 1985- **CONTACT ADDRESS** Paine Col, 1235 15th St, Augusta, GA, 30910-2799.

CARTER, K. CODELL
PERSONAL Born 12/27/1939, Salt Lake City, UT, m, 1965, 2 children **DISCIPLINE** HISTORY **EDUCATION** Univ Utah, BS, 63, MA, 64; Cornell Univ, PhD, 68. **CAREER** Asst prof, Rutgers Univ, 67-73; prof, Brigham Young Univ, 73-. **MEMBERSHIPS** Am Philos Asn; Am Asn Hist Medicine; Royal Society Medicine. **RESEARCH** History of medicine. **SELECTED PUBLICATIONS** Auth, Essays of Robert Koch, 87; auth, art, The Development of Pasteur's Concept of Disease Causation and the Emergence of Specific Causes in Nineteenth-Century Medicine, 91; auth, Childbed Fever: A Scientific Biography of Ignaz Semmelweis, 94; auth, art, Toward a Rational History of Medical Science, 95; auth, art, Causes of Disease and Causes of Death, 97. **CONTACT ADDRESS** Brigham Young Univ, 3196 JKHB, Provo, UT, 84602. **EMAIL** codell_carter@byu.edu

CARTER, MARION ELIZABETH
PERSONAL Washington, DC **DISCIPLINE** EDUCATION **EDUCATION** Wellesley College; Howard University, MA; Middlebury College, MA; Georgetown University, MS; Catholic University, PhD; Georgetown University, PhD. **CAREER** Wellesley College, visiting prof; Gordon College, prof; Teachers College, prof; Howard University, instructor; Barber Scotia College, instructor; Wiley College, assoc prof; University of La Gaguna, lecturer; American Language Institute of Georgetown University, teacher; St Mary University Nova Scotia, lecturer. **HONORS AND AWARDS** Intl Biog Ctrt; Buena Aires Conv Award; Agnes Meyer Award; AATSP Award, Spain; Directory of Amer Scholars; Fulbright Award Spain; placque, Lifetime Bd of Governors, American Biographical Inst, Intl Hall of Leaders, IBC Book of Dedications. **MEMBERSHIPS** Natl Assn of Foreign Student Affairs; mem Le Droit Park Civic Assn; mem Smithsonian Inst; past sec, Amer Assn of Teachers of Spanish & Portuguese; mem AAUP, AAUW, IBC, ABI; trustee, World University; elected mem, Order of International Fellowship.

CARTER, MARVA GRIFFIN
PERSONAL Born 06/04/1947, Cleveland, Ohio, m, 1969 **DISCIPLINE** MUSIC **EDUCATION** Boston Conservatory of Music, BM, 1968; New England Conservatory of Music, MM, 1970; Boston Univ, MA, 1975; Univ of Illinois, PhD, 1988. **CAREER** Boston Univ, administrative assistant, Afro-American Studies Program, 1970-71, coordinator of freshman/sophomore seminars, 1972-73; Simmons College, coordinator of Afro-Am studies program, 1973-77; Clark Atlanta Univ, adjunct assoc prof of music, 1988-89; Ebenezer Baptist Church, organist and music coord, 1982-92; Morris Brown Coll, coordinator of music, 1988-93; Georgia State Univ, asst director, School of Music, 1993-95, asst prof of music hist & lit, currently. **HONORS AND AWARDS** Miss Texas High, poise, 1964; Winner of piano award, 1964; Smithsonian Institution Research Fellow, 1983. **MEMBERSHIPS** American Musicological Society, cultural diversity and the committee on the publication of American music, 1973-77, 1993-; Sonneck Society for American Music, nominating committee, education committee and cultural diversity committee, 1973-77, 1993-; Center for Black Music Research, associate mem, 1993-; Society for Ethnomusicology, 1973-77, 1993-; Young Audiences of Atlanta, board member, ed comm, 1992-94; Atlanta Symphony Action Committee for Black Audience Development, 1992-94. **SELECTED PUBLICATIONS** First African American to receive the PhD in musicology from the Univ of Illinois, 1988; Roland Hayes, Expresser of the Soul in Song, Black Perspective in Music, pp 189-220, Fall, 1977; Articles published in Black Women in the US and Notable Black American Women; musical biography on Will Marion Cook, forthcoming. **CONTACT ADDRESS** Asst Director of the School of Music, Unversity Plaza, Rm 117, Atlanta, GA, 30303.

CARTER, NANCY CORSON
PERSONAL Born 03/28/1943, Williamsport, PA, m, 1967, 1 child **DISCIPLINE** AMERICAN & WOMEN'S STUDIES **EDUCATION** Susquehanna Univ, BA, 65; Univ Iowa, MA, 68, PhD(Am Civics), 72. **CAREER** Dir, Learning Resources Ctr, 74-76, asst prof Am Studies, 76-78, asst prof Lit & Humanities, 78-79, asst prof Lit & Creative Writing, Eckerd Col, 79-; prof Humanities, 91; fel, Cross-Disciplinary Inst, Summer, 75 & Inst Ecumenical & Cult Res, St John's Univ, Fall, 77; Fla Corresp, Art Voices/South, 78-82; poet-in-schs, Pinellas County Arts Coun, 81. **HONORS AND AWARDS** Dana Fellow, Southeastern Consortium Humanities Program, Emory Univ, 89-90; Visiting Prof, Duke Univ School of the Environment, 95-96. **MEMBERSHIPS** Soc Values Higher Educ; Am Studies Asn; Southeast Women's Studies Asn; MLA. **RESEARCH** Writings of Doris Lessing, especially mythical and evolutionary aspects; interdisciplinary approaches to theme and process of the spiritual journey; psycho-historical, mythical and spiritual ramifications of Jean Houston's work. **SELECTED PUBLICATIONS** Contribr poems, Survivor's Box, Possum Press, 77; 1970's images of the machine and the garden: Kosinski, Crews & Pirsig, Soundings: An Interdisciplinary J, 78; Artist profiles for Florida artists issue: Beckett, Crane, Hodgell, Rigg, Art Voices/South, 79; Demeter & Persephone in Margaret Atwood's novels: Mother-daughter transformations, J Anal Psychol, 10/79; coauth, Spirit of Eve: The Art of Marion Beckeet (videotape), produced on WEDU, 81; Journey toward wholeness: A meditation on Doris Lessing's The Memoirs of a Survivor, J Evolutionary Psychol, 8/81; Dragon Poems, Lewiston/Queenston/Lampeter: Mellen Poetry Press, 93. **CONTACT ADDRESS** Lett Collegium Eckerd Col, 4200 54th Ave S, St. Petersburg, FL, 33711-4744. **EMAIL** carternc@eckerd.edu

CARTER, PAUL ALLEN
PERSONAL Born 09/03/1926, New Bedford, MA, m, 1962, 4 children **DISCIPLINE** AMERICAN HISTORY **EDUCATION** Wesleyan Univ, BA, 50; Columbia Univ, MA, 51, PhD(hist), 54. **CAREER** Lectr hist, Columbia Univ, 54-55; actg asst prof, Cornell Univ, 55; asst prof, Univ Md, 55-56; from asst prof to assoc prof, Univ Mont, 56-62; vis assoc prof hist, Smith Col, 62-63; vis lectr, Univ Calif, Berkeley, 63-64; vis assoc prof, Univ Mass, 64-65; vis assoc prof relig, Amherst Col, 65-66; from assoc prof to prof, Northern Ill Univ, 66-73; PROF HIST, UNIV ARIZ, 73-, Hist consult, Nat Pub Radio, DC, 77-79. **RESEARCH** American intellectual and religious history; 20th century American history; history of American science fiction. **SELECTED PUBLICATIONS** Auth, The Social-Gospel in Black-and-White--American Radical Reform, 1885-1912, Church Hist, Vol 0062, 93; Protestantism and Social Christianity, Church Hist, Vol 0063, 94; Soul in Society--The Making and Renewal of Social Christianity, Church Hist, Vol 0065, 96; Oxnam, G.Bromley--Paladin of Liberal Protestantism, Jour Amer Hist, Vol 0080, 94; Soul in Society--The Making and Renewal of Social Christianity, Church History, Vol 0065, 96. **CONTACT ADDRESS** Dept of Hist, Univ of Ariz, Tucson, AZ, 85721.

CARTWRIGHT, DAVID TODD
PERSONAL Born 04/10/1952, Kansas City, MO, m, 1976, 2 children **DISCIPLINE** HISTORY **EDUCATION** Univ Kansas, BA, 74; Rice Coll, PhD, 79. **CAREER** Fac assoc, Univ Tex Sc Publ Health, Epid, 78-79; asst clin prof, Commun Med, Univ Conn Health Ctr, 81-88; asst prof, Hist, Univ Hartford, 79-85; assoc prof, Hist, Univ Hartford, 85-88; prof, Hist, Univ North Fla, 88-98, DIST PROF, UNIV NORTH FLA, HIST ARTS & SCI, 98-. **MEMBERSHIPS** AHA, OAH, AAHM **RESEARCH** Social, legal, & medical History; Drug use & violence **SELECTED PUBLICATIONS** Violent Land: Single Men and Social Disorder from the Frontier to the Inner City, Harvard Univ Press, 96. **CONTACT ADDRESS** Dept Hist, Univ North Fla, 4567 St Johns Bluff Rd S, Jacksonville, FL, 32224-2645. **EMAIL** dcourtwr@unf.edu

CARTWRIGHT, JOSEPH HOWARD
PERSONAL Born 05/16/1939, Nashville, TN, m, 1959, 2 children **DISCIPLINE** AMERICAN HISTORY **EDUCATION** Murray State Univ, BS & MA, 62; Vanderbilt Univ, MA, 68, PhD, 73. **CAREER** From asst prof to assoc prof, 70-81, prof hist and dept chmn, 81-91, dean, Col Humanities, Murray State Univ, 91-. **MEMBERSHIPS** Orgn Am Historians; Southern Hist Asn. **RESEARCH** Southern United States history: reconstruction, race relations, politics. **SELECTED PUBLICATIONS** Auth, Black legislators in Tennessee in the 1880s: a case study in Black political leadership, in Tenn Hist Quart, fall 73; The Triumph of Jim Crow: Race Relations in Transition in Tennessee, Univ Tenn, 76. **CONTACT ADDRESS** Dept of Hist, Murray State Univ, 1 Murray St, Murray, KY, 42071-3310. **EMAIL** Joseph.Cartwright@MurrayState.edu

CASDORPH, PAUL DOUGLAS
PERSONAL Born 09/05/1932, Charleston, WV, m, 1972 **DISCIPLINE** AMERICAN HISTORY **EDUCATION** Univ Tex, Austin, BA, 60, MA, 61; Univ Ky, EdD, 70. **CAREER** Social worker, Tex Dept of Pub Welfare, 62-66; instr sociol & hist, 66-71, from asst prof to assoc prof hist, 71-77, PROF HIST, WVA STATE COL, 77-, Lectr, WVa Univ, 71-72; instr, Morris Harvey Col, 71-73; lectr, WVa Col Grad Studies, 72-73. **MEMBERSHIPS** Southern Hist Asn. **RESEARCH** Southern Republicanism; the Bull Moose or progressive politics; American politics and education. **SELECTED PUBLICATIONS** Auth, Army Surveillance in America, 1775-1980, Historian, Vol 0056, 93; The Draft, 1940-1973, Historian, Vol 0056, 94; Lees Terrible Swift Sword--From Antietam to Chancellorsville, An Eyewitness History, Jour Amer Hist, Vol 0080, 93. **CONTACT ADDRESS** W VA Univ, 1413 Alexander Pl, Charleston, WV, 25314.

CASEBIER, ALLAN
PERSONAL Born 10/01/1934, Los Angeles, CA, m, 1994 **DISCIPLINE** PHILOSOPHY; HISTORY **EDUCATION** UCLA, MA, 64; Michigan, PhD, 69. **CAREER** Philos Prof, USC, IL; CINEMA/TELEVISION, USC, MIAMI, FL. **HONORS AND AWARDS** Fulbright, India, 82. **MEMBERSHIPS** Amer Philos Assoc; Amer Soc for Aesthetics; Soc for Cinema Studies. **RESEARCH** Aesthetics; ethics; ontology; film hist. **SELECTED PUBLICATIONS** Auth, Film Appreciation, NY: Harcourt Brace Jovanovich, 76; Social Responsibilities of the Mass Media, Washington, DC: Univ Press Amer, 78; The Phenomenology of Japanese Cinema, Quart Rev Film & Video, 90; Film and Phenomenology, NY: Cambridge Univ Press, 91; Phenomenology and Aesthetics, Encyclopedia of Aesthetics, Oxford Univ Press, 97; A Phenomenology of Motion Picture Experience, Film and Philosophy, vol 4, 98; The Japanese Aesthetic, Journal of Comparative Lit and Art, fall 98; Theorizing the Moving Image, Film and Philos, vol 5, 99; Representation: Cultural Representations and Signifying Practices, World Communication, winter 99; Critical Communication, manuscript in progress. **CONTACT ADDRESS** 5825 SW 35th St., Miami, FL, 33155. **EMAIL** casebier@umiami.ir.miami.edu

CASEY, JOHN DUDLEY
PERSONAL Born 01/18/1939, Worcester, MA, m, 1982, 4 children **DISCIPLINE** HISTORY, LAW, AND LITERATURE **EDUCATION** Harvard Coll, BA; Harvard Law School, LLB; Univ of Iowa, MFA. **CAREER** Prof of English, Univ of Va, 72-92. **HONORS AND AWARDS** Nat Board Award for Fiction, 89. **MEMBERSHIPS** P.E.N. **SELECTED PUBLICATIONS** Auth, The Half-life of Happiness, 98; auth, Supper at the Black Pearl, 95; auth, Spartina, 89; auth, Testimony & Demeanor, 79; auth, An American Romance, 77. **CONTACT ADDRESS** Dept of English, Univ of Virginia, Bryant Hall, Charlottesville, VA, 22904.

CASH, PHILIP
PERSONAL Born 01/28/1931, South Portland, ME, m, 1962 **DISCIPLINE** AMERICAN COLONIAL AND MEDICAL HISTORY **EDUCATION** Gorham State Teachers Col, BS, 53; Boston Col, MA, 55, PhD(hist), 68. **CAREER** Chmn dept, 63-72, PROF HIST, EMMANUEL COL, MASS, 60-, CHMN DEPT, 82- **MEMBERSHIPS** AAUP; AHA; Am Asn Hist Med; Am Inst Hist Pharm; Int Soc Hist Med. **RESEARCH** Anglo-American colonial medical and military history; American medical history. **SELECTED PUBLICATIONS** Auth, Science and the Founding-Fathers--Science in the Political Thought of Jefferson, Franklin, Adams, and Madison, New Eng Quart-Hist Rev of New Eng Life and Letters, Vol 0069, 96; Living in the Shadow of Death--Tuberculosis and the Social Experience of Illness in American History, New Eng Quart-Hist Rev of New Eng Life and Letters, Vol 0069, 96; How Like An Angel Came I Down--Conversations With Children on the Gospels, Parabola-Myth Tradition and the Search for Meaning, Vol 0018, 93; Science and the Founding-Fathers--Science in the Political Thought of Jefferson, Franklin, Adams, and Madison, New Eng Quart Historical Rev of New Eng Life and Letters, Vol 0069, 96; Healing the Republic-- The Language of Health and the Culture of Nationalism in 19th-Century America, New Eng Quart Hist Rev of New Eng Life and Letters, Vol 0068, 95; Healing the Republic--The Language of Health and the Culture of Nationalism in 19th-Century America, New England Quart Hist Rev of New Eng Life and Letters, Vol 0068, 95. **CONTACT ADDRESS** Dept Hist, Emmanuel Col, Massachusetts, Boston, MA, 02115.

CASHDOLLAR, CHARLES DAVID
PERSONAL Born 10/24/1943, Pittsburgh, PA, m, 1968 **DISCIPLINE** UNITED STATES HISTORY **EDUCATION** Indiana Univ Pa, BS, 65; Univ Pa, MA, 66, PhD(hist), 69. **CAREER** Instr hist, Univ Pa, 69; from asst prof to assoc prof, 69-77, PROF HIST, INDIANA UNIV PA, 77- **MEMBERSHIPS** AHA; Orgn Am Historians; Am Soc Church Hist; Am Studies Asn. **RESEARCH** Nineteenth Century American religious thought. **SELECTED PUBLICATIONS** Auth, God and History--Aspects of British Theology, 1875-1914, Amer Hist Rev, Vol 0099, 94; Reviving the Ancient Faith--The Story of Churches of Christ in America, Amer Hist Rev, Vol 0102, 97. **CONTACT ADDRESS** Dept of Hist, Indiana Univ of Pennsylvania, Indiana, PA, 15701.

CASPER, SCOTT E.
DISCIPLINE HISTORY **EDUCATION** Princeton Univ, AB, 86; Yale Univ, MA, MPhil, 90, PhD, 92. **CAREER** ASSOC PROF, HIST, UNIV NEVADA RENO **HONORS AND AWARDS** Theron Rockwell Field prize, Yale Univ. **MEMBERSHIPS** Am Antiquarian Soc **SELECTED PUBLICATIONS** Auth, Constructing American Lives: The Cultural History of Biography in Nineteenth-Century America, Yale, 92; auth, "The Two Lives of Franklin Pierce: Hawthorne, Political Culture, and the Literary Market," Am Lit Hist 5, 93; auth, "An Uneasy Marriage of Sentiment and Scholarship: Elizabeth F. Ellet and the Domestic Origins of American Women's History," Jour Women's Hist 4, 92; auth, "Defining the National Pantheon: The Making of Houghton Mifflin's Biographical Series, 1880-1900," in Reading Books: Essays on the Material Text and Literature in America, Amherst, 97. **CONTACT ADDRESS** Dept of Hist/308, Univ of Nevada, Reno, NV, 89557. **EMAIL** casper@scs.unr.edu

CASS, MICHAEL MCCONNELL
PERSONAL Born 07/01/1941, Macon, GA, m, 1965, 2 children **DISCIPLINE** AMERICAN LITERATURE & HISTORY **EDUCATION** University of the South, BA, 63; Emory Univ, PhD(Am Studies), 71. **CAREER** From instr to asst prof, 69-76, from assoc prof to prof Interdisciplinary Studies, Mercer Univ, 76-84; chmn, Lamar Mem Lec Comm, 92. **MEMBERSHIPS** SAtlantic Mod Lang Assn; Soc for the Study of Southern Lit. **RESEARCH** Southern literature; southern culture. **SELECTED PUBLICATIONS** Auth, Charles C Jones Jr and the lost cause, Ga Hist Quart, Summer 71; The South Will Rise Again, Anniversary & October Poem (poems), Southern Rev, Autumn 74; foreword to Lewis P Simpson's The Dispossessed Garden: Pastoral and History in Southern Literature, 74 & to Walter L Sullivan's A Requiem for the Renaissance: The State of Fiction in the Modern South, 75, Univ Ga Press; Joshua & Coming Back to Poetry (poems), World Order, Summer 75; At Home in the Dark, The Fairest Lass in All Christendom & The Lonesome End (poems), Southern Rev, Spring 77; Georgia Preacher (poem), Christian Century, 10/4/78; Survivors (poem), Christianity & Lit, Winter 79; The Writer in the Postmodern South, Athens, 91; to Jack Temple Kirby, The Counter-Cultural South, Athens, 96. **CONTACT ADDRESS** Dept of English, Mercer Univ, 1400 Coleman Ave, Macon, GA, 31207-0003. **EMAIL** cass_mm@mercer.edu

CASSAR, GEORGE H.
DISCIPLINE HISTORY **EDUCATION** McGill Univ, PhD. **CAREER** Prof, Eastern Michigan Univ. **HONORS AND AWARDS** Fac awd for res and pub. **RESEARCH** Modern Europe, military. **SELECTED PUBLICATIONS** Auth, Kitchener: Architect of Victory; Asquith as War Leader; Beyond Courage; The Tragedy of Sir John French. **CONTACT ADDRESS** Dept of History and Philosophy, Eastern Michigan Univ, 701 Pray-Harrold, Ypsilanti, MI, 48197.

CASSEDY, JAMES HIGGINS
PERSONAL Born 10/11/1919, Gloversville, NY, m, 1949, 2 children **DISCIPLINE** AMERICAN HISTORY **EDUCATION** Middlebury Col, AB, 41; Brown Univ, AM, 50, PhD, 59. **CAREER** Personnel officer, US Vet Admin, 46-48; instr employ pract & placement officer, Northeastern Univ, 48-49; dir, Haitian-Am Inst, Port-au-Prince, 51-53, Burma Inst, Rangoon, 53-55 & Pakistan-Am Cult Ctr, Karachi, 60-62; exec secy, Hist Life Sci Study Sect, Nat Inst Health, 62-66, dep chief Europ off, Paris, 66-68; HISTORIAN, NAT LIBR MED, 68-, Instr Am hist, Williams Col, 59-60; Garrison lectr, Am Asn Hist Med, 78; Sigerist lectr, Yale Univ, 82. **MEMBERSHIPS** AHA; Am Asn Hist Med; Hist Sci Soc; Am Studies Asn; Orgn Am Historians. **RESEARCH** History of statistics and demography; history of American medicine and science; American social and intellectual history. **SELECTED PUBLICATIONS** Auth, Duffy,John, 1915-1996--In-Memoriam, Bulletin Hist Med, Vol 0070, 96; Doctors, Politics and Society--Historical Essays, Soc Hist Med, Vol 0007, 94; The Gifts of Civilization--Germs and Genocide in Hawaii, Amer Hist Rev, Vol 0100, 95; The Angelical Conjunction--The Preacher-Physicians of Colonial New-England, Jour Amer Hist, Vol 0080, 93; Medical Journals and Medical Knowledge--Historical Essays, Soc Hist Med, Vol 0006, 93; Sentinel for Health--A History of the Centers-for-Disease-Control, Public Historian, Vol 0015, 93; Farmcarts to Fords--A History of the Military Ambulance, 1790-1925, Amer Hist Rev, Vol 0099, 94. **CONTACT ADDRESS** Hist of Med Div, National Libr of Med, 8600 Rockville Pike, Bethesda, MD, 20209.

CASSELL, P.G.
PERSONAL Born 06/05/1959, Orange, CA, m, 1988, 3 children **DISCIPLINE** ECONOMICS **EDUCATION** Stanford Univ, BA, JD, 81. **CAREER** Prof 92-, Univ Utah; E Dist VA Asst Us Att, 88-91; US Dept Justice Att Gen, Assoc deputy, 86-88; law clerk, 85-86, Justice W E Berger; law clerk, 84-85, Judge A Scalia. **HONORS AND AWARDS** Order of the Coif. **RESEARCH** Criminal Justice; Rights of Crime Victims. **SELECTED PUBLICATIONS** Coauth, Handcuffing the Cops: A Thirty Year Perspective on Miranda, Effects on Law Enforcement, Stanford L Rev 98; auth, Miranda, Negligible Effect on Law Enforcement: Some Skeptical Observations, Harv J L & Pub 97; The Costs of the Miranda Mandate: A Lesson in the Dangers of Inflexible Prophylactic, Supreme Court Inventions, AZ St L J 96; co auth, Police Interrogation in the 1990's: An Empirical Study of the Effects of Miranda, UCLA L Rev, 96; auth, All Benefits No Costs: The Grand Illusion of Miranda, Defenders, Northwestern U L Rev, 96; Miranda's Social Costs: An Empirical Reassessment Northwestern L Rev, 96; Search and Seizure Law in Utah: The Irrelevance of the Antipolygamy Raids, BYU L Rev 95; Balancing the Scales of Justice: The Case For and the Effects Of Utah's Victim Rights Amendment, Utah L Rev 94; The Rodney King Trials and the Double Jeopardy Clause: Some Observations on Original Meaning and the ACLU's Schizophrenic Views of the Dual Sovereign Doctrine, UCLA L Rev, 94. **CONTACT ADDRESS** College of Law, Univ Utah, Salt Lake City, UT, 84112.

CASSELS, ALAN
PERSONAL Born 02/20/1929, Liverpool, England, m, 1961, 2 children **DISCIPLINE** MODERN EUROPEAN HISTORY **EDUCATION** Oxford Univ, BA, 52, MA, 56; Univ Mich, PhD(europ diplomatic hist), 61. **CAREER** Teaching fel, Univ Mich, 52-54 & 57-58; vis lectr hist, Sweet Briar Col, 56-57; instr, Trinity Col, Conn, 59-62; asst prof, Univ Pa, 62-67; assoc prof, 67-71, PROF HIST, McMASTER UNIV, 71-, Vis asst prof, Haverford Col, 63-64; Can Coun fel, 73-74 & 80-81; adv bd, Can J Italian Studies, 81- **HONORS AND AWARDS** Soc Ital Hist Studies Essay Prize, 62. **MEMBERSHIPS** Soc Ital Hist Studies (vpres, 78-79); Interuniv Ctr Europ Studies; Am Comt Hist of Second World War; AHA. **RESEARCH** Twentieth century European diplomatic history; fascism. **SELECTED PUBLICATIONS** Auth, A Disobedient Faithful Follower--Grandi, Dino from the Palazzo-Chigi to the 25th-of-July, Intl Hist Rev, Vol 0016, 94; Genoa, Rapallo, and European Reconstruction in 1922, Intl Hist Rev, Vol 0014, 92; A Nation Banished--Italian Armistice of September 1943-Ital, Amer Hist Rev, Vol 0100, 95; Italian Fascists on Trial, 1943-1948, Amer Hist Rev, Vol 0098, 93; The Crisis of Liberal Italy-- Monetary and Financial Policy, 1914-1922, Amer Hist Rev, Vol 0100, 95; Britain and Italy, 1943-1949--The Decline of British Influence, Intl Hist Rev, Vol 0019, 97; The Faces of Fraternalism--Nazi Germany, Fascist Italy, and Imperial Japan, Intl Hist Rev Vol 0014, 92. **CONTACT ADDRESS** Dept of Hist, McMaster Univ, 1280 Main St W, Hamilton, ON, L8S 4M4.

CASSIDAY, JULIE A.
DISCIPLINE RUSSIAN **EDUCATION** Stanford Univ, MA, 90; Stanford Univ, PhD, 95. **CAREER** Asst prof, Williams Col, 94-. **HONORS AND AWARDS** ACTR-ACCELS Travel Grant to Moscow, on US Infor Agency, Bureau of Educ & Cult Aff, Reg Scholar Exchange Fel, 96. **RESEARCH** 19th-Century Russian Literature; Russian Theater and Drama; Revolutionary Cultural Studies. **SELECTED PUBLICATIONS** Auth, The Enemy on Trial: Early Soviet Courts on Stage and Screen. **CONTACT ADDRESS** Center for Foreign Languages, Literatures and Cult, Williams Col, Williamstown, MA, 01267. **EMAIL** Julie.A.Cassiday@williams.edu

CASSIDY, DAVID C.
PERSONAL Born 08/10/1945, Richmond, VA **DISCIPLINE** HISTORY OF SCIENCE **EDUCATION** Rutgers Univ, BA, 67, MS, 70; Purdue Univ, PhD, 76. **CAREER** Res fel, Univ Calif. Berkeley, 76-77; Humboldt fel, Univ. Stuttgart, Germany, 77-80; asst prof, Univ Regensburg, Germany, 80-83; assoc ed, Einstein Papers, Princeton and Boston, 83-90; from assoc prof to prof, Hofstra Univ, 90-. **HONORS AND AWARDS** Sci Writing Award, Am Inst Physics, 93; Fel, Am Physical Soc, 94; Pfizer Award, Hist of Sci Soc, 95; Hon Dr Sci, Purdue Univ, 97. **MEMBERSHIPS** Hist of Sci Soc; Am Phys Soc; NY Acad of Scis, Ed Board, Phys in Perspective. **RESEARCH** Hist of German Physics, espec 18th and 20th centuries, biographies of Albert Einstein and Werner Heisenberg, science education. **SELECTED PUBLICATIONS** Auth, Meteorology in Mannheim, The Palatine Meteorological Society 1781-1795, Sudhoffs Archiv, 69, 85; Uncertainty: The Life and Science of Werner Heisenberg, 92; Werner Heisenberg--Die deutsche Wissenschaft und das Dritte Reich, Naturwissenschaft und Technik in der Geschichte, Helmuth Albrecht, ed, 93; Controlling German Science I: U.S. and Allied Forces in Germany, 1945-1947, Historical Studies in the Physical and Biological Sciences, 24, 94; Einstein and Our World, 95; Introduction to reprint of Samuel Goudsmit, Alsos: The Failure of German Science, 95; German Scientists and the Nazi Atomic Bomb, Dimensions: A Jour of Holocaust Studies, 10/2, 96; Controlling German Science II: U.S. and Allied Forces in Germany, 1945-1947, Historical Studies in the Physical and Biological Sciences, 26, 96; Reading Gothic German Print and Manuscript, 98. **CONTACT ADDRESS** Dept of Natural Science, Hofstra Univ, Hempstead, NY, 11549.

CASSIDY, JAMES G.
DISCIPLINE HISTORY OF SCIENCE **EDUCATION** St Anselm Col, BA, 79; St John's Sem, MATheol, 84; Univ Toronto, MA, 87; Univ PA, MA, 89; Univ PA, PhD, 91. **CAREER** Fac, 85-87; to asst prof, 91-, St Anselm Col. **RESEARCH** Develop of sci and sci educ in Am hist, with particular interest in the role of the federal government as a patron of sci in the Gilded Age and Progressive Era; develop of the US Geological and Geographical Survey in the immediate post-Civil War decades; develop of the Marine Hospital Service. **SELECTED PUBLICATIONS** Auth, Monastic Silence and Solitude as Supports of Prayer in the Teaching of Pope Paul VI, Am Benedictine Rev, 87; George Frederic Matthew--Invertebrate Paleontologist, Geoscience Canada, 88. **CONTACT ADDRESS** St Anselm Col, 100 Saint Anselm Dr, Manchester, NH, 03102-1310. **EMAIL** jcassidy@anselm.edu

CASSIDY, JANE W.
PERSONAL Born 05/29/1956, Palestine, TX, m, 1988, 1 child **DISCIPLINE** MUSIC **EDUCATION** Hartt Col of Music at the Univ of Hartford, BME, 78; Fla State Univ, MME, 85; Fla State Univ, PhD, 88. **CAREER** Music specialist, Putnum Public Schs, 78-84; GTA, Fla State Univ, 84-88; asst prof, Louisiana State Univ, 88-94; assoc prof, Louisiana State Univ, 94-present. **HONORS AND AWARDS** Phi Delta Kappa; Pi Kappa Lambda; Alpha Chi. **MEMBERSHIPS** Music Educators Nat Conf; Am Music Therapy Asn; Coun for Exceptional Children. **RESEARCH** Musical development and learning among children; music for special populations; teacher effectiveness. **SELECTED PUBLICATIONS** Auth, A comparison between student's self-observation and instructor observation of teacher intensity behaviors,Bull of the Coun for Res in Music Educ, 115, 93; auth, Effects of various sightseeing strategies on nonmusic majors' pitch accuracy,Jour of Res in Music Educ, 41, 93; coauth, The effect of music listening on physiological responses of premature infants in the NICU,Jour of Music Therapy, 22, 95; coauth, Verbal and operant responses of young children to vocal versus instrumental song performances, Jour of Res in Music Educ, 44, 97; coauth, Effects of music with video on responses of nonmusic majors: An exploratory study in Jour of Res in Music Educ, 44, 97; coauth, Nonmusic Majors' cognitive and affective responses to performance and programmatic music videos, Jour of Res in Music Educ, 35, 98; coauth, Presentation of aural stimuli to newborn and premature infants: An audiological perspective, in Jour of Music Therapy, 35, 98. **CONTACT ADDRESS** Sch of Music, Louisiana State Univ, Baton Rouge, LA, 70803. **EMAIL** jcassid@lsu.edu

CASSON, LIONEL
PERSONAL Born 07/22/1914, New York, NY, 2 children **DISCIPLINE** ANCIENT HISTORY **EDUCATION** NY Univ, AB, 34, AM, 35, PhD, 39. **CAREER** From instr to assoc prof, 36-59, Prof Classics, Washington Square Col, NY UNIV, 59-, Guggenheim fels, 52-53 & 59-60; dir summer session, Am Acad Rome, 63-66; Nat Endowment for Hum sr fel, 67-68 dir, Nat Endowment for Hum, summer seminar in Classics, 78; Andrew W Mellon prof class studies, Am Acad Rome, 81-82. **MEMBERSHIPS** Am Philo Asn; Archaeol Inst Am; Am Soc Papyrologists. **RESEARCH** Greek and Roman maritime hist; papyrology; hist of naval technol. **SELECTED PUBLICATIONS** Auth, Six Plays of Plautus, Anchor, 63; Illustrated History of Ships and Boats, Doubleday, 64; Ancient Egypt, Time-Life, 65; The Plays of Menander, NY Univ, 71; Daily Life in Ancient Rome, Horizon Bks, 75; Periphus Maris Erythraei, 89; The Ancient Mariners, Princeton Univ, 91; Ships and Seamanship in the Ancient World, 3rd ed, John Hopkins Univ, 95; Travel in the Ancient World, 2nd ed, John Hopkins Univ, 94. **CONTACT ADDRESS** 100 Bleecker, New York, NY, 10012.

CAST, DAVID JESSE DALE
PERSONAL Born 01/08/1942, London, England, m **DISCIPLINE** ART HISTORY **EDUCATION** Oxford Univ, BA, 65; Columbia Univ, MA, 67, PhD, 70. **CAREER** Asst/assoc prof, Yale Univ, 70-80; ASSOC PROF, BRYN MAWR COLL, 81-. **MEMBERSHIPS** Coll Art Asn; Royal Soc Arts; Renaissance Soc Am **RESEARCH** Renaissance art; British painting. **CONTACT ADDRESS** Bryn Mawr Col, 244 Thomas, Bryn Mawr, PA, 19010. **EMAIL** dcast@brynmawr.edu

CASTELLANI, VICTOR
PERSONAL Born 02/14/1947, Brooklyn, NY, m, 1976, 2 children **DISCIPLINE** CLASSICS **EDUCATION** Fordham Univ, BA, 68; Princeton Univ, PhD, 71. **CAREER** Adj lectr, classics, Fordham Univ, 70-71; instr, 71-72, asst prof, 72-80, assoc prof, 80- , chemn 81-85, 89-98, Dept of Lang and Lit, Univ Denver. **HONORS AND AWARDS** Horace Acad, 65; Classic Prize, 66; Phi Beta Kappa, 67; Columbia Tchrs Col Book Award, 67; NDEA, Princton fel, 68; Woodrow Wilson fel, 68; pres, Rocky Mtn MLN, 84; Award for Outstanding Support, 93. **MEMBERSHIPS** Am Class League; Archaeol Inst Am; APA; Class Asn of Middle West and South; Pacific Ancient and Modern Lang Asn; Pro-Riesling Verein, Trier, Ger; Rocky Mountain MLA. **RESEARCH** Greek and Latin literature, especially epic and drama; ancient religion; comparative literature, especially narrative poetry, Dante, and drama, Ibsen; art and literature. **SELECTED PUBLICATIONS** Auth, Captive Captor Freed: The National Theater of Ancient Rome, Drama: Beitrage zum antiken Drama und seiner Rezeption, 95; auth, Flesh or Fish or What? Euripides' Orestes, Didaskalia: Ancient Theater Today, 95; auth, Athena and Friends: One Among the Greek Religions, in Dillon, ed, Religion in the Ancient World: New Themes and Approaches, Hakkert, 96; auth, Europa, Euripides, and the Differentiation of Europe, Jour of the Int Soc for the Study of European Ideas, 96; auth, Regulated European Wine: A View From Middle America, and, Classics at a Small University, Selected Proceedings of the 5th International Conference on ISSEI, 96; auth, After Stormy Seas Calm Once More I See: Reconciliation and Re-Moralization in Euripides, Jour of the Int Soc for Stud of European Ideas, 97; auth, Melpomene Polias: Athenian Tragedy and Politics in the Later Fifth Century, in Hillard, ed, Ancient History in a Modern University, vol 1, Eerdmans, 98. **CONTACT ADDRESS** Dept of Languages and Literatures, Univ of Denver, Denver, CO, 80208-2662. **EMAIL** vcastell@du.edu

CASTELLANO, CHARLENE
DISCIPLINE RUSSIAN **EDUCATION** Cornell Univ, PhD. **CAREER** Languages, Carnegie Mellon Univ. **SELECTED PUBLICATIONS** Auth, Making Sense of Synesthesia and The Synesthetics of Apocalypse in Andrey Bely's Petersburg, New Rev, 93; The Mystery Play in Andrey Bely's Dramaturgy and Prose, Canadian-American Slavic Studies, 95; Andrey Bely's Memories of Fiction, in Autobiographical Statements in Twentieth-Century Russian Literature, princeton Univ Press, 98. **CONTACT ADDRESS** Carnegie Mellon Univ, 5000 Forbes Ave, Pittsburgh, PA, 15213.

CASTENELL, LOUIS ANTHONY, JR.
PERSONAL Born 10/20/1947, New York, NY, m **DISCIPLINE** EDUCATION **EDUCATION** Xavier Univ of LA, BA Educ 1968; Univ of WI Milwaukee, MS Educ Psych 1973; Univ of IL, PhD Educ Psych 1980. **CAREER** Univ of WI-Milwaukee, academic adv 1971-74; Xavier Univ, dir alumni affairs 1974-77, asst prof 1980-81, dean grad sch; UNIV OF CINCINNATI, DEAN, COLLEGE OF EDUCATION, currently. **HONORS AND AWARDS** Craig Rice Scholarship Xavier Univ 1968; Fellowship Univ of IL 1977-78; Fellowship Natl Inst of Mental Health 1978-80; over 15 published works on aspects of educ; American Educational Studies Association, Critic's Choice Awards, 1993; Presidential Award, Networking Together Inc, 1996. **MEMBERSHIPS** Editorial Boards, Journal of Curriculum Theorizing 1990-95; reviewer, Journal of Teacher Education; reviewer, Journal of Educational Foundations, Educ Task Force Urban League 1984; chair Human Rights and Academic Freedom AERA 1985-86; consultant Sch of Educ 1980-; bd mem Ronald McDonald House of Louisiana, 1987; board member, NAACP; Children Museum of Cincinnati, board member. **CONTACT ADDRESS** Col of Educ, Univ of Cincinnati, ML002, Cincinnati, OH, 45215.

CASTILLO, ED
PERSONAL Born 08/25/1947, San Jacinto, CA, d, 2 children **DISCIPLINE** AMERICAN ANTHROPOLOGY, U.S. HISTORY **EDUCATION** Univ Calif, Riverside, BA, 69; Univ Calif, Berkeley, MA, 74, PhD, 77. **CAREER** Prof & dept chmn, Native Am Stud, 72- , Univ Calif, Berkeley, Univ Calif, Santa Cruz, Sonoma State Univ. **HONORS AND AWARDS** Outstanding Fac of the Year, 74; Fac Meritorious Performance Award, 89-90; Award for Academic Excellence, 98; listed in Who's Who, 99. **MEMBERSHIPS** Am Indian Hist Soc; Am Hist Soc, Pacific Branch; Am Indian and Alaskan Native Prof Asn. **RESEARCH** California Indian history; North American Indian history. **SELECTED PUBLICATIONS** Auth, History of the Impact of Euro-American Exploration and Settlement on the Indians of California, and, Recent Secular Movements Among California Indians, 1900-1973, in Handbook of North American Indians, v.8, California, Smithsonian Inst, 78; coauth, A Bibliography of California Indian History, Ballena, 78; contribur, The Missions of California: A Legacy of Genocide, American Indian Historical Society, 87; auth, The Ethnography and History of the California Indians, in Champagne, ed, The Native North American Indian Almanac, Gale, 94; auth, The Language of Race Hatred, in Bean, ed, The Ohlone Past and Present: Native Americans of the San Francisco Bay Region, Ballen, 94; coauth, Indians, Franciscans and Spanish Colonization: The Impact of Franciscan Missionaries on the Indians of California, Univ New Mexico, 95; auth, Mission Indian Federation: Protecting Tribal Soverignty, 1919-1967, in Davis, ed, The Encyclopedia of Native Americans in the 20th Century, Garland, 95; auth, California Overview, in Encyclopedia of Native American Tribes, Gale, 98; auth, The Indians of Southern California, Bellerophon, 98. **CONTACT ADDRESS** Sonoma State Univ, 1501 E Colati Blvd, Rohnert Park, CA, 94928.

CASTILLO CRIMM, CAROLINA
DISCIPLINE HISTORY **EDUCATION** Univ Miami, Florida, BA; Tex Tech Univ, MA; Univ Tex-Austin, PhD. **CAREER** Asst prof, Sam Houston State Univ, 92-. **RESEARCH** Latin America, Texas and the Southwest. **SELECTED PUBLICATIONS** Auth, Founding Families: The Mexican-Americans of Victoria, South Tex Stud, 92. **CONTACT ADDRESS** Dept of History, Sam Houston State Univ, Huntsville, TX, 77341.

CASTRICANO, JODEY
DISCIPLINE CULTURAL STUDIES **EDUCATION** Simon Fraser, BA, MA; British Columbia, PhD. **CAREER** Asst Prof **SELECTED PUBLICATIONS** Auth, If a Building Is a Senctence, So Is A Body: Kathy Acker's Empire of the Senseless and Postcolonial Gothic; Rude Awakenings--or, What happens When a Lesbian Reads the Hieroglyphics of Sleep in Djuna Barnes Nightwood; West Coast Line, 94. **CONTACT ADDRESS** Dept of English, Wilfrid Laurier Univ, 75 University Ave W, Waterloo, ON, N2L 3C5. **EMAIL** jcastric@mach1.wlu.ca

CATANIA, ANTHONY CHARLES
PERSONAL Born 06/22/1936, New York, NY, m, 1962, 2 children **DISCIPLINE** PSYCHOLOGY **EDUCATION** Columbia Col, AB (NY State Regents Scholarship, Phi Beta Kappa, Highest Honors with Distinction in Psychology), 57; Columbia Univ, MA, 58; Harvard Univ, PhD (Psychology), 61. **CAREER** Teaching asst, Columbia Col, 56-58; res tech, Bell Telephone Labs, summer 58; res fel in Psychol, Harvard Univ, 60-62; Sr Pharmacologist, Smith Kline and French Labs, 62-64; asst prof, 64-66, assoc prof, 66-69, prof and dept chair, Univ Col of Arts and Science, New York Univ, 69-73; prof, Univ of MD, Baltimore County, 73-; prof fel, Univ Wales, 86-87, vis res fel, 89-; vis prof, Keio Univ, Yokyo, Japan, July 92. **HONORS AND AWARDS** Nat Science Found fel, 58-60; British Coun fel, 86; James McKeen Cattell Sabbatical Award, 86-87; Fulbright Sr Res fel (US-UK), 86-87; Outstanding contrib to Behavior Analysis, Northern CA Asn for Behavior Analysis, 90; Outstanding Scientific Contributions to Psychology Award, MD Psychol Asn, 93; The Don F Hake Basic/Applied Res Award, div 25 of the Am Pyschol Asn, 98; Master lect, Animal Learning and Behavior, Am Psychol Asn, 98. **MEMBERSHIPS** Soc for the Experimental Analysis of Behavior (Pres, 66-67, 81-83; bd of dirs, 66-74, 78-86, 87-95, 97-2005); Am Psychol Asn (Fellow, div 3, 25, 28; Distinguished vis prog, Div 25, Experimental Analysis of Behavior, prog co-chair, 76, pres, 76-79, exec comm, 81-84, Pres elect, 96-98); Eastern Psychol Asn; Asn for Behavioral Analysis (pres, 81-84, chair pub bd, 91-95; Language Origins Soc (prog chair, 96 Annual Meeting, bd of dird, 97); Am Psychol Asn (charter member and fel); Phi BetaKappa; Psychonomic Soc; Sigma Xi. **RESEARCH** Analysis of behavior; experimental psychology; psychology of learning; language and verbal behavior. **SELECTED PUBLICATIONS** Ed, Contemporary Research in Operant Behavior, Scott Foresman, 68, Spanish ed, Editorial Trillas, 80; ed with T A Brigham, Handbook of Applied Behavior Analysis: Social and Instructional Processes, Irvington, 78; ed with S Harnad, The Seelction of Behavior: the Operant Behaviorism of B F Skinner, Cambridge Univ Press, 88; auth with E Shimoff and B A Matthews, Psychology on a Disk, Version 4-0, Columbia, MD: CMS Software, 92; with B A Matthews and E Shimoff, Sociology on a Disk, Version 4-0, Columbia, MD: CMS Software, 92; ed with P N Hineline, Variations and Selections: An Anthology of Reviews from the Journal of the Experimental Analysis of Behavior, Bloomington, IN: Soc for the Experimental Analysis of Behavior, 96; with B A Matthews and E Shimoff, Behavior on a Disk: Version 4-0, Columbia, MD: CMS Software, 97; auth, Learning, 4th ed, Prentice-Hall, 98; numerous other publications (about 175 in all). **CONTACT ADDRESS** Dept of Psychology, Univ of Maryland, Baltimore County, 1000 Hilltop Circle, Baltimore, MD, 21250. **EMAIL** Catania@umbc.edu

CATTO, BONNIE
PERSONAL Born 04/19/1951, Boston, MA, m, 1975 **DISCIPLINE** CLASSICS **EDUCATION** Mt Holyoke Col, AB, 73; Univ Penn, MA, 76, PhD, 81. **CAREER** Vis lectr, Univ Mass Amherst, 78; instr, 78-81, asst prof, 81-87, assoc prof, 87-88, Mt Holyoke Col; vis assoc prof, Middleburg Col, 88-89; assoc prof, 89-97, prof, 97-, classics, Assumption Col. **HONORS AND AWARDS** Fully funded sabbatical, Assumption Col, 95-96; Sloan Found grant, 86; Phi Beta Kappa; Mary Lyon Scholar; Sarah Williston scholar. **MEMBERSHIPS** Amer Philol Asn; Archaeol Inst of Amer; Classical Asn of New England; Vergilian Soc; Pioneer Valley Classical Asn; Classical Asn of Mass. **RESEARCH** Lucretius; Ancient science; Vergil; Lyric & Elegiac poetry; Greek tragedy. **SELECTED PUBLICATIONS** Rev, Lucy Hutchinson's Translation of Lucretius: De Rerum Natura, The New England Classical Jour, 98; auth, Lucretius. Selections from De Rerum Natura, Bolchazy-Carducci Publ, 98; auth, Lucretian Light: Bacon's Debt to Lucretius and Epicurus, New England Classical Jour, 98; auth, The Wedding of Peleus and Thetis, Athenaze Newsletter, 97; auth, Selections from Lucretius' De Rerum Natura, The Classical Asn of New England, Short Greek and Latin Texts for Students, 96; rev, Musical Design in Sophoclean Theater, The New England Classical Jour, 96; auth, Duals, Athenaze Newsletter, 94; **CONTACT ADDRESS** Dept of Foreign Languages, Assumption Col, 500 Salisbury St., Worcester, MA, 01615. **EMAIL** bcatto@eve.assumption.edu

CAUGHEY, JOHN L.
DISCIPLINE ETHNOGRAPHY AND AMERICAN STUDIES **EDUCATION** Harvard Col, BA, 63; Univ PA, MA, 67, PhD, 70. **CAREER** Am Stud Dept, Univ Md **RESEARCH** Ethnographic, comp investigation of contemp cult as syst of meaning. **SELECTED PUBLICATIONS** Auth, Imaginary Social Worlds: A Cultural Approach, Univ Nebr Press, 84; On the Anthropology of America, Epilogue to Symbolizing America, Univ Nebr Press, 86; Gina as Steven: The Social and Cultural Dimensions of a Media Relationship, Visual Anthrop Rev, Special issue on Culture/Media, 94; Imaginary Social Relationships, Media Jour: Reading and Writing About Popular Culture, Allyn and Bacon, 95; Personal Identity on Faanakkar, Pieces of The Personality Puzzle: Readings in Theory and Research, W W Norton and Co, 97. **CONTACT ADDRESS** Am Stud Dept, Univ MD, Col Park, College Park, MD, 20742. **EMAIL** jc29@umail.umd.edu

CAVAGLIERI, GIORGIO
PERSONAL Born 08/01/1911, Venice, Italy, w, 1942 **DISCIPLINE** ARCHITECTURAL ENGINEERING **EDUCATION** Superior School of Engineering, Doctor Arch Engineering, Milan, ITA, 32; Superior School, of Architecture, Specialized City Planning, Rome ITA, 35. **CAREER** Own office, Milan, Italy, & instr City Planning at Superior Schools of Engineering & Architecture, Milan, Italy, 34-39; to US, 39; draftsman NY and Baltimore, MD, 39-43; US Army, ETO, 43-45; own office, NY City, 46-; adjunct prof, Pratt School of Architecture, 56-71; vis prof and lect, Lawrence Inst of Architecture, Detroit, MI, & Columbia Univ School of Architecture. **HONORS AND AWARDS** Gold Medal, NY Architectural League, 56; fel, AIA, 65; Medal of Honor, NY Chapter AIA, 90; Presidential Citation, AIA, 90; Nat Academician, Nat Academy of Design. **MEMBERSHIPS** Nat Inst of Architectural Ed (pres, 56-58); NY Municipal Art Soc (pres, 62-64); Fine Art Federation (pres, 70-72, 74-76); NY Chapter AIA (pres, 70-71); NY Victorian Soc (pres, 74-76). **RESEARCH** Historic preservation; urban design. **SELECTED PUBLICATIONS** Auth, Landmark Buildings for Uses of Today, Empire State Architect, Sept/Oct, 67; Design in Adaptive Reuse, Hist Preservation, Jan/March 74; Review of La Citta american dalla guerra civile al New Deal, by Ciucci, Dal Co, et al, J of the Soc of Architectural Hist, Oct 74; Large Scale Preservation Projects, Preservation and Building Codes, Nat Trust for Hist Preservation, 74; Plus Factors of Old Buildings, Economic Benefits of Preserving Old Buildings, Nat Trust for Historic Preservation, 76; On Restoring Historic Residential Properties for Institutional Use, Saving Large Estates, Soc for the Preservation of Long Island Antiquities, 77; The Harmony That Can't Be Dictated, Old and New Architecture: Design Relationship, Nat Trust for Historic Preservation, 80; The Past is Present--the Adaptive Reuse of 19th Century Buildings, Around the Square, 1830-1890: Essays on Life, Letters and Architecture, NY Univ, 82; Review of New York 1930: Architecture and Urbanism Between the Two World Wars, by Robert A M Stern, Gregory Gilmartin, Thomas Mellins, Citizens Housing and Planning Council of New York Book News,

June 89; Review of The Meissenhofsiedlung: Experimental Housing Built for the Deutscher Werkbund: Stuutgart, 1927, by Karin Kirsch, Citizens Housing and Planning Council of New York Book News, Sept 90; An Architect's View of 'Appropriateness,' District Lines, News and Views of the Historic Districts Council, vol 7, no 2, 3, 4, 92. **CONTACT ADDRESS** 250 West 57th St, Ste 2016, New York, NY, 10107.

CAVE, ALFRED A.
PERSONAL Born 02/08/1935, Albuquerque, NM, m, 1950, 2 children **DISCIPLINE** AMERICAN HISTORY **EDUCATION** Linfield Col, BA, 57; Univ Fla, MA, 59, PhD, 61. **CAREER** Instr soc sci, Univ Fla, 59-61; instr hist, City Col New York, 61-62; from asst prof to assoc prof, Univ Utah, 62-73, dir honors prog, 65-67, assoc dean col lett & sci, 67-68, dean col humanities, 68-73; DEAN COL ARTS & SCI, UNIV TOLEDO, 73- **MEMBERSHIPS** Southern Hist Asn; Orgn Am Historians. **RESEARCH** The Jackson era; Southern history. **SELECTED PUBLICATIONS** Auth, Why Was the Sagadahoc Colony Abandoned--An Evaluation of the Evidence, New Eng Quart-Hist Rev of New Eng Life and Letters, Vol 0068, 95; Historic Contact--Indian People and Colonists in Todays Northeastern United-States in the 16th Through 18th Centuries, New England Quart-Hist Rev of New Eng Life and Letters, Vol 0070, 97; The Failure of the Shawnee Prophets Witch-Hunt, Ethnohist, Vol 0042, 95. **CONTACT ADDRESS** Off of the Dean Col of Arts & Sci, Univ of Toledo, 2801 W Bancroft St, Toledo, OH, 43606-3390.

CAVER, CHRISTINE
DISCIPLINE FINE ARTS AND HUMANITIES **EDUCATION** Univ TX at San Antonio, BA; Univ TX at Austin, MA, PhD. **CAREER** Asst prof; taught at, Univ TX at Austin. **RESEARCH** Contemp Am fiction. **SELECTED PUBLICATIONS** Publ on res interest. **CONTACT ADDRESS** Col of Fine Arts and Hum, Univ Texas at San Antonio, 6900 N Loop 1604 W, San Antonio, TX, 78249.

CAVINESS, MADELINE H.
PERSONAL Born 03/27/1938, London, England, m, 1962, 2 children **DISCIPLINE** ART HISTORY **EDUCATION** Newnham Col, Cambridge Univ, BA, 59; Harvard Univ, PhD, 70. **CAREER** Prog organizer, British Council, 59-60; asst to librarian, Harry Elkins Widener Rare Book Collection, Harvard Univ, 62-63; res asst, Paintings Dept, Boston Museum of Fine Arts, 63; instr, Art Dept, Wellesley Col, 70-71; Radcliff Inst Fel, Harvard Univ, 70-72; asst prof, Tufts Univ, 72-75; assoc prof, Tufts Univ, 76-81; chair, Fine Arts Dept, 75-82, 88-90; Mary Richardson prof, Dept of Art and the Hist of Art, Tufts Univ, 87-; Benjamin Sonnenberg vis prof, Inst of Fine Arts, NY Univ, 91; Robert Sterling Clark vis prof, Williams Col/Clark Art Inst, 96. **HONORS AND AWARDS** Haskins Medal of the Medieval Academy; Fel of Art Medieval Academy; Fel of the Soc of Antiquaries of London; Honorary Phi Beta Kappa. **MEMBERSHIPS** Medieval Academy of Am; Corpus Vitrearum Int Board; Corpus Vitrearum Committee for the USA; Am Council of Learned Societies; Col Art Asn of Am; Census of Am Stained Glass, Governing Board; Int Ctr for Medieval Art. **RESEARCH** Feminist critique of medieval art history. **SELECTED PUBLICATIONS** Auth, "Patron or Matron? A Capetian Bride and a Vade Mecum for her Marriage Bed", in Speculum68, 93, auth, "Introduction: The Corpus Vitrearum Project", in Stained Glass: Conservation of Monumental Stained and Painted Glass, 93; coauth, "Women in Medieval Art and Literature", in Medieval Feminist Newsletter 15, 93; auth, "The politics of conservation and the role of the Corpus Vitrearum in the preservation of stained glass windows", in XXVIII, Internationaler Kongress fr Kunstgeschichte, Berlin, III, 94; auth, "Learning from Forest Lawn", in Speculum 69, 94; auth, "Artistic Integration in Early Gothic Churches: A Postmodern Construct?" in Artistic Integration in Gothic Churches, Univ Toronto Press, 95; auth, "A Feminist Reading of the Hours of Jeanne d'Evreux", in Japan and Europe in Art History: Papers of the Colloquium of the Comite International d'Histoire de l'Art, 95; auth, "Anchoress, Abbess and Queen: Donors and Patrons or Intercessors and Matrons?", in Women's Literary and Artistic Patronage in the Middle Ages, Univ of Ga Press, 96; auth, Stained Glass Windows, Tournhout: Brepols, 96; Paintings on Glass: Studies in Romanesque and Gothic Monumental Art, Variorum, 97. **CONTACT ADDRESS** Department of Art & Art History, Tufts Univ, 11 Talbot Ave., Medford, MA, 02155. **EMAIL** mcavines@emerald.tufts.edu

CAWELTI, JOHN GEORGE
PERSONAL Born 12/31/1929, Evanston, IL, m, 1955, 5 children **DISCIPLINE** AMERICAN CIVILIZATION, MODERN & CONTEMPORARY LITERATURE **EDUCATION** Oberlin Col, BA, 51; State Univ Iowa, MA, 56, PhD(Am civilization), 60. **CAREER** From instr to asst prof humanities, Univ Chicago, 57-64, assoc prof English & humanities, 64-68, prof, 68-80, chmn comt gen studies in humanities, 70-75; PROF ENGLISH, UNIV KY, 80- **MEMBERSHIPS** Am Studies Asn; Popular Cult Asn. **RESEARCH** Study of popular culture; literature and culture; American literature. **SELECTED PUBLICATIONS** Auth, Popular Culture, Jour Pop Cult, Vol 0030, 96; Fiction, Crime and Empire--Clues to Modernity and Postmodernism, Quart Jour Short Articles Notes and Rev(s), Vol 0008, 95; What Rough Beast, New Westerns, Quart Jour Short Articles Notes and Rev(s), Vol 0009, 96; The Ethos of Romance at the Turn-Of-the-Century, Nineteenth-Century Lit, Vol 0049, 95; Who Named Franklin Autobiography, Quart Jour Short Articles Notes and Rev(s), Vol 0008, 95; Murder At The Mla, Quart Jour Short Articles Notes and Rev(s), Vol 0008, 95. **CONTACT ADDRESS** Dept of English, Univ of Ky, 500 S Limestone St, Lexington, KY, 40506-0003.

CAZEAUX, ISABELLE
PERSONAL Born 02/24/1926, New York, NY **DISCIPLINE** MUSICOLOGY **EDUCATION** Hunter Col, BA, 45; Smith Col, MA, 46; Ecole normale de musique, Paris, Licence d'Enseignement, 50; Conserva Toire national de musique, Paris, Premiere medaille, 50; Columbia Univ, PhD, 61. **CAREER** Music & phoneorecords cataloguer, New York Pub Libr, 1957-63; Lectr, A.C. Dickerman Prof, Bryn Mawr col, 63-92; Musicology Fac, Manhattan Sch Mus, 1969-82; vis prof, Rutgers Univ, Douglass Col, 78. **HONORS AND AWARDS** Libby van Arsdale Prize for Music, Hunter Col, 54; Fel, Smith Col, Columbia Univ, Inst Int Educ, 1941-59; grant from Martha Baird Rockefeller Fund Music, 1971-71; grant from Herman Goldman Foundation, 1980. **MEMBERSHIPS** Am Musicological Soc, Societe Francaise de Musicologie; Intl Musicological Soc, Mus Libr Asn, Nat Opera Assoc, Societe Theolphile Gautier. **RESEARCH** French music: Renaissance & La Belle Epoque **SELECTED PUBLICATIONS** Auth, French Music in the Fifteenth and Sixteenth Centuries, Blackwell, Praeger, 75; Trans, The Memoirs of Philippe de Commynes, Univ SC Press, 69-73; co-ed, Anthologie de la chanson parisienne au XVI siecle; One Does not Defend the Sum: Some Notes on Peladan and Wagner, Norton, 84. **CONTACT ADDRESS** 415 East 72nd St., #5FE, New York, NY, 10021.

CEBULA, JAMES E.
PERSONAL Born 07/28/1942, Dupont, PA, m, 1965, 2 children **DISCIPLINE** AMERICAN LABOR, POLITICAL, & URBAN HISTORY **EDUCATION** Univ Cincinnati, PhD(hist), 72. **CAREER** Teacher hist, Delaware Valley High Sch, Pa, 63-64; from instr to asst prof, 68-77, assoc prof hist, Raymond Walters Col, Univ, Cinncinnati, 77-. **MEMBERSHIPS** AHA; Orgn Am Historians, Ohio Academy of History. **RESEARCH** National and state politics; labor history. **SELECTED PUBLICATIONS** Auth, Kennedy Heights: A Fragmented Hilltop Suburb, Cincinnati Hist Soc Bull, 7/76; Glory and Despair, Challenge and Change, a History of the Molders Union, Cincinnati Int Molders Union, 8/76; James M. Cox: Journalist and Politician, NY: Garland Publishing, 85; James Cebula and James Wolfe, eds, Rhyme and Reason: Molders Portey from Sylvies to the Great Depression, Cincinnati: Sylvies Soc, 85. **CONTACT ADDRESS** Dept of Hist, Univ of Cincinnati, 9555 Plainfield Rd, Cincinnati, OH, 45236-1007. **EMAIL** James.cebula@uc.edu

CECIRE, ROBERT C.
DISCIPLINE CHURCH HISTORY **EDUCATION** Wheaton Col, BA; Gordon Divinity Sch, BD; Univ Kans, MA, PhD. **CAREER** Adj prof, Bethel Col; Anoka-Ramsey Community Col; vis lectr, Univ Kans; lectr, Gordon Col; asst prof, Wiinebrenner Theol Sem, 97-; dir, Theol Stud. **MEMBERSHIPS** Mem, Soc Biblical Lit; Conf on Faith and History; Nat Hist Honor Soc. **SELECTED PUBLICATIONS** Rev(s), Jour Evangel Theol Soc; Res Publica Litterarum; pub, article on Encratism, Res Publica Litterarum. **CONTACT ADDRESS** Winebrenner Theol Sem, 701 E Melrose Ave, PO Box 478, Findlay, OH, 45839.

CEDERBERG, HERBERT RENANDO
PERSONAL Born 08/11/1933, Spokane, WA, m, 1955, 2 children **DISCIPLINE** COLONIAL HISTORY; ECONOMIC HISTORY **EDUCATION** Univ Calif, Berkeley, AB, 59, MA, 63, PhD(hist), 68. **CAREER** From asst prof to prof US colonial hist, 66-78, admin dir minority serv off, 72-73, PROF HIST, UNIV WIS-RIVER FALLS, 78-; guest prof, Univ Minn, 75-76; Chair, Bd of Dir of Jobs Now Coalition, 98-. **HONORS AND AWARDS** Wis State Legis res fels, 68-69, 75-76; Nat Endowment for Humanities fel in residence, 77. **MEMBERSHIPS** AHA; Inst Early Am Hist & Cult; Hakluyt Soc. **RESEARCH** Economic analysis of early settlement in colonial America; colonial art history; probate and inventory records in 17th and 18th century Massachusetts. **SELECTED PUBLICATIONS** Auth, An Economic Analysis of English Settlement in North America 1583-1635, Arno, 77. **CONTACT ADDRESS** Dept of History, Univ of Wisconsin, 410 S 3rd St, River Falls, WI, 54022-5013. **EMAIL** herbert.cederberg@uwrf.edu

CELL, JOHN W.
PERSONAL 3 children **DISCIPLINE** HISTORY **EDUCATION** Duke Univ, BA, 57, PhD, 65. **CAREER** Prof, Duke Univ. **RESEARCH** Brit Empire Commonwealth. **SELECTED PUBLICATIONS** Auth, British Colonial Administration in the Mid-Nineteenth Century: The Policy-Making Process, 70; By Kenya Possessed: The Correspondence of Norman Leys and J.H. Oldham, 76; The Highest Stage of White Supremacy: The Origins of Segregation in South Africa and the American South, 82; Hailey: A Study in British Imperialism 1872-1969, 92. **CONTACT ADDRESS** Dept of Hist, Duke Univ, Carr Bldg, Durham, NC, 27706. **EMAIL** jcell@acpub.duke.edu

CELMS, PETER
DISCIPLINE HISTORY **EDUCATION** Duke Univ, AB, MA; Union Grad Sch, PhD. **CAREER** Prof, 62-; **HONORS AND AWARDS** Woodrow Wilson fel; Danforth fel, Fulbright Scholar; NEH Fel. **RESEARCH** German historiography since late 18th century, Friedrich Mienecke. **SELECTED PUBLICATIONS** Area: Wilhelmian Germany. **CONTACT ADDRESS** Wittenberg Univ, Springfield, OH, 45501-0720.

CENKNER, WILLIAM
PERSONAL Born 10/25/1930, Cleveland, OH **DISCIPLINE** HISTORY OF RELIGIONS **EDUCATION** Providence Col, AB, 54; Pontif Fac Theol, STL, 59; Fordham Univ, PhD(hist relig), 69. **CAREER** Assoc prof hist, 69-80, ASSOC PROF HISTRELIG & RELIG EDUC, CATH UNIV AM, 80-, Chauncey Stillman Found res grant, 69; mem, Nat Coun Relig & Pub Educ, 72-; assoc ed, Col Theol Soc, 73- **MEMBERSHIPS** Col Theol Soc (pres, 78-80); Am Acad Relig; Asn Asian Studies. **RESEARCH** Encounter of world religions; religion and education; Sankaracarya's. **SELECTED PUBLICATIONS** Auth, Theology After Vedanta--An Experiment in Comparative Theology, Theol Stud, Vol 0054, 93; The Asrama System--The History and Hermeneutics of a Religious Institution, Theol Stud, Vol 0056, 95; World Religions in America--An Introduction, Horizons, Vol 0023, 96. **CONTACT ADDRESS** Sch of Relig Studies, Catholic Univ of America, 620 Michigan Ave NE, Washington, DC, 20064-0002.

CENSER, JACK R.
DISCIPLINE HISTORY **EDUCATION** Duke Univ, BA, 68; Johns Hopkins Univ, MA, 71, PhD, 73. **CAREER** Fel, Metro Ctr, Johns Hopkins Univ, 73-74; asst prof, Col Charleston, 74-77; asst to PROF HIST, 77-, CHAIR, 95-, GEORGE MASON UNIV. **CONTACT ADDRESS** Dept of History, George Mason Univ, Fairfax, VA, 22030. **EMAIL** jcenser@smu.edu

CERILLO, AUGUSTUS
DISCIPLINE HISTORY AND POLITICAL SCIENCE **EDUCATION** Northwestern Univ, PhD. **CAREER** Adj prof; full-time fac, CA State Univ at Long Beach. **HONORS AND AWARDS** Outstanding prof, CA State Univ at Long Beach. **RESEARCH** Hist since the Civil War; urban hist; hist of the involvement of Evangelicals in Am politics. **SELECTED PUBLICATIONS** Auth, Reform in New York City: A Study of Urban Progressivism; co-ed, Salt and Light: Evangelical Political Thought in Modern America. **CONTACT ADDRESS** Dept of Hist and Polit Sci, Southern California Col, 55 Fair Dr., Costa Mesa, CA, 92626.

CHALFANT, WILLIAM Y.
PERSONAL Born 10/03/1928, Hutchinson, KS, m, 1956, 2 children **DISCIPLINE** HISTORY; LAW **EDUCATION** Univ Kans, AB, 50; Univ Mich, Juris Dr, 56. **CAREER** Atty at Law, Branwe, Chalfant, & Hill, 56-. **HONORS AND AWARDS** Various. **MEMBERSHIPS** Kans Bar Asn; Am Bar Asn; SW Bar Asn; W Hist Asn; Santa Fe Trail Asn. **RESEARCH** Spanish Entrada on Western Plains; military history of Southern Plains; Plains Indians. **SELECTED PUBLICATIONS** Auth, Cheyennes and Horse Soldiers, Univ Okla Press, 89; auth, Without Quarter, Univ Okla Press, 91; Dangerous Passage, Univ Okla Press, 94; Cheyennes at Darkwater Creek, Univ Okla Press, 97. **CONTACT ADDRESS** Branwe, Chalfant & Hill, 411 First Nat Ctr, PO Box 2027, Hutchinson, KS, 67504-2027.

CHALK, FRANK
DISCIPLINE HISTORY **EDUCATION** Univ Wis, BS, MS, PhD. **CAREER** Instr, Tex A & M Univ; Fulbright prof, Univ Ibadan, Nigeria; assoc prof. **RESEARCH** History of genocide and humanitarian intervention, modern American foreign policy. **SELECTED PUBLICATIONS** Coauth, The History and Sociology of Genocide: Analyses and Case Studies; pub(s), chapters in various bk(s) and articles, Can Jour of African Stud; Holocaust and Genocide Stud. **CONTACT ADDRESS** Dept of Hist, Concordia Univ, Montreal, 1455 de Maisonneuve W, Montreal, PQ, H3G 1M8. **EMAIL** drfrank@alcor.concordia.ca

CHALLENER, RICHARD DELO
PERSONAL Born 01/15/1923, Pittsburgh, PA, m, 1947, 3 children **DISCIPLINE** HISTORY **EDUCATION** Princeton Univ, AB, 47; Columbia Univ, AM, 48, PhD(hist), 52. **CAREER** From instr to assoc prof, 49-64, asst dean, 57-61, assoc dean, 61-66, chmn dept hist, 70-71 & 73-77, PROF HIST, PRINCETON UNIV, 64-, Mem, Col Entrance Exam Bd Advan Placement Comt, 58-61; vis prof, Johns Hopkins Univ, 67-68. **MEMBERSHIPS** AHA; Am Mil Inst. **RESEARCH** American diplomatic and military history since 1861; modern French history. **SELECTED PUBLICATIONS** Auth, The Navy in The Post-Cold-War World--The Uses and Value of Strategic Sea-Power, Intl Hist Rev, Vol 0018, 96; Napoleon-III and the Stoffel Affair, Amer Hist Rev, Vol 0100, 95. **CONTACT ADDRESS** Dept of Hist, Princeton Univ, Princeton, NJ, 08544.

CHAMBERLAIN, GORDON BLANDING
PERSONAL Born 06/10/1939, New York, NY, m, 1964, 2 children **DISCIPLINE** MODERN JAPANESE HISTORY

EDUCATION Yale Univ, BA, 60; Univ Calif, Berkeley, MA, 5 65, PhD(hist), 72. **CAREER** Lectr hist, Leland Stanford Jr Univ, 71; asst prof, Macalester Col, 73-76; ASST PROF, ORE STATE UNIV, 76-80. **MEMBERSHIPS** Asn Asian Studies; AHA. **RESEARCH** Pre-1914 Japanese foreign policy. **SELECTED PUBLICATIONS** Auth, Ashoka Dream--Historical Background to the Opera Based on the Life of the 3rd-Century-Bc Indian Warrior-King, Opera News, Vol 0062, 97. **CONTACT ADDRESS** 1915 NW Arthur, Corvallis, OR, 97330.

CHAMBERLAIN, MICHAEL
DISCIPLINE HISTORY **EDUCATION** Univ of California, Berkeley, PhD, 92. **CAREER** Acting Asst Prof, 89-91, Stanford Univ; Asst Prof, 92-97, Assoc Prof, 97-, Univ Of Wisconsin, Madison. **RESEARCH** Medieval Islamic social & cultural history, comparative history. **SELECTED PUBLICATIONS** Auth, Knowledge and Social Practice in Medieval Damascus, Cambridge, UK, 94. **CONTACT ADDRESS** 455 N Park St, #4118, Madison, WI, 53706. **EMAIL** mchamber@facstaff.wisc.edu

CHAMBERLIN, EUGENE KEITH
PERSONAL Born 02/15/1916, Gustine, CA, m, 1940, 5 children **DISCIPLINE** HISTORY **EDUCATION** Univ Calif, BA, 39, MA, 40, PhD(hist), 49. **CAREER** From instr to asst prof hist, Mont State Univ, 48-54; from asst prof to prof, San Diego City Col, 54-58; PROF HIST, SAN DIEGO MIRAMAR COL, 78-, Lectr Univ Calif, Los Angeles, exten, 64-66; lectr, San Diego State Col, 67-67; lectr & coord hist lectr, Univ Calif, San Diego, exten, 66-67; lectr Mex & Mex Am hist in Southwest, San Diego Community Cols-TV Col, 69-77. **MEMBERSHIPS** AHA; Pac Coast Conf Latin Am Studies; Conf Latin Am Hist; Asoc Cult las Califs, US & Mex; AAUP. **RESEARCH** American southwest; Mexico; Mexican northwest and American southwest interrelationships. **SELECTED PUBLICATIONS** Auth, Antigua California--Mission and Colony on the Peninsular Frontier, 1697-1768, Pacific Hist Rev, Vol 0064, 95; Modest Fortunes--Mining in Northern Baja-California, Pacific Hist Rev, Vol 0063, 94. **CONTACT ADDRESS** 3033 Dale St, San Diego, CA, 92104.

CHAMBERS, HENRY EDMUND
PERSONAL Born 08/27/1941, Detroit, MI, m, 1967, 2 children **DISCIPLINE** HISTORY **EDUCATION** Xavier Univ, Ohio, AB, 63, MA, 64; Ind Univ, Bloomington, PhD(ancient hist), 68. **CAREER** From Asst Prof to Assoc Prof, 67-80, PROF ANCIENT HIST, CALIF STATE UNIV, SACRAMENTO, 80-. **MEMBERSHIPS** Am Inst Archaeol; AHA; Asn Ancient Historians. **RESEARCH** Ancient Near East, Greece and Rome. **CONTACT ADDRESS** Dept of History, California State Univ, Sacramento, 6000 J St, Sacramento, CA, 95819-2694. **EMAIL** hchamber@csus.edu

CHAMBERS, JOHN W.
PERSONAL Born 00/00/1936 **DISCIPLINE** HISTORY **EDUCATION** Temple Univ, BS, 58; San Francisco State Col, MA, 65; Columbia Univ, PhD(hist), 73. **CAREER** Asst prof, Barnard Col, Columbia Univ, 72-82; ASST PROF, RUTGERS UNIV, 82-, Newspaper reporter & TV newswriter/producer, 58-65; dir res, In Pursuit of Liberty (TV prog ser), 75-77; Andrew W Mellon grant, 79; Rockefeller humanities fel, 81-82; Fulbright lectr, Univ Rome, spring, 82; Albert J Beveridge grant, Am Hist Asn, 82. **HONORS AND AWARDS** Barnard Col Outstanding Teacher Award, 75. **MEMBERSHIPS** Am Hist Asn; Conf Peace Res Hist (pres, 75-77); Orgn Am Historians. **RESEARCH** Military history; foreign policy; twentieth century United States history. **SELECTED PUBLICATIONS** Auth, The Peace Progressives and American Foreign-Relations, Jour Amer Hist, Vol 0082, 95; All Quiet on the Western Front--The Antiwar Film and the Image of the 1st-World-War, Hist Jour Film Radio and Television, Vol 0014, 94; Rich Relations--The American Occupation of Britain, 1942-1945, Amer Hist Rev, Vol 0101, 96; War, Film and History--Introduction, Hist Jour Film Radio and Television, Vol 0014, 94. **CONTACT ADDRESS** 549 Riverside Dr, New York, NY, 10027.

CHAMBERS, MORTIMER HARDIN
PERSONAL Born 01/09/1927, Saginaw, MI, m, 1973, 3 children **DISCIPLINE** CLASSICAL PHILOLOGY **EDUCATION** Harvard, AB, 49, PhD, 54; Oxford, MA, 55. **CAREER** Instr, classics, Harvard, 54-55; asst prof, history and Greek, Univ Chicago, 55-58; asst prof, assoc prof, prof History, UCLA, 58-. **HONORS AND AWARDS** Rhodes Scholarship; Fulbright Scholarship. **MEMBERSHIPS** Am Hist Asn; Am Philol Asn. **RESEARCH** Greek history; history of classical scholarship. **SELECTED PUBLICATIONS** Auth, Aristotle's History of Athenian Democracy, with J Day, Berkeley-Los Angeles, 62; Polybius, selections trans, ed, E Badian, New York, 66; The Western Experience, with four coauthors, New York, 74, ed 7, 98; Aristotelis Athenaion Politeia, Leipzig, 86, ed 2, 94; Georg Busolt, His Career in His Letters, Leiden, 90; Aristotle, Staat der Athener, Berlin-Darmstadt, 90; George Grote's History of Greece, in: George Grote Reconsidered, Hildescheim, 96; Athen's Alliance with Egesta in the Year of Antiphon, with R Galluci-P Spanos, Zeitschrift fur Papyrologie und Epigraphik 83, 90; The Reception of Gibbon in the New World, in: Imperium Romanum, Festschrift for Karl Christ, Stuttgart, 98. **CONTACT ADDRESS** Dept of History, Univ of California, Los Angeles, Los Angeles, CA, 90024-1473. **EMAIL** chambers@history.ucla.edu

CHAMBERS, SARAH
DISCIPLINE HISTORY **EDUCATION** Univ Wis Madison, PhD, 92. **CAREER** Asst prof, 98-. **RESEARCH** Eighteenth- and nineteenth-century social, cultural, and legal history. **SELECTED PUBLICATIONS** Auth, From Subjects to Citizens: Honor, Gender and Politics in Arequipa, Peru, 1780-1854, Penn State Univ; 'To the company of a man like my husband; no law can compel me': Women's Strategies against Domestic Violence in Arequipa, Peru, 1780-1850, J Women's Hist. **CONTACT ADDRESS** History Dept, Univ of Minnesota, Twin Cities, 614 Social Sciences Tower, 267 19th Ave. S, Minneapolis, MN, 55455. **EMAIL** chamb023@tc.umn.edu

CHAMPLIN, EDWARD JAMES
PERSONAL Born 06/03/1948, New York, NY, m, 1972, 2 children **DISCIPLINE** ANCIENT HISTORY **EDUCATION** Univ Toronto, BA, 70, MA, 72; Oxford Univ, DPhil(Literae Humaniores), 76. **CAREER** Instr, 75-76, asst prof, 76-81, assoc prof, 81-86, PROF CLASSICS, 86-, COTSEN PROF HUMANITIES PRINCETON UNIV, 87-; MASTER OF BUTLER COL PRINCETON UNIV, 95-. **HONORS AND AWARDS** Alexander von Humboldt fel, Heidelberg Univ, 84-85; Fowler Hamilton fel, Christ Church, Oxford Univ, 89-91; Resident in Classics, Am Academy in Rome, 94; corresponding member, German Archaeological Inst, 91-. **MEMBERSHIPS** Am Philol Asn; Class Asn Can; Asn Ancient Historians; Soc Prom Roman Studies. **RESEARCH** Roman history; Roman law; Latin literature. **SELECTED PUBLICATIONS** Auth, Fronto and Antonine Rome, Harvard Univ, 80; Final Judgments, CA Univ, 91; ed, Cambridge Ancient History vol X, 96. **CONTACT ADDRESS** Dept Classics, Princeton Univ, 104 East Pyne, Princeton, NJ, 08544. **EMAIL** champlin@princeton.edu

CHAN, LOREN BRIGGS
PERSONAL Born 09/10/1943, Palo Alto, CA **DISCIPLINE** AMERICAN HISTORY **EDUCATION** Stanford Univ, AB, 65, AM, 66; Univ Calif, Los Angeles, MA, 67, CPhil, 69, PhD(hist), 71. **CAREER** Lectr hist, San Fernando Valley State Col, 70-71; lectr, 71-72, asst prof, 72-76, ASSOC PROF HIST, SAN JOSE STATE UNIV, 76-, Partic, Workshop in hist, Danforth Found, 75; adj lectr mod Chinese hist, Univ Santa Clara, 77-78. **MEMBERSHIPS** AHA; Orgn Am Historians; Am Studies Asn; Western Hist Asn; Chinese Hist Soc Am. **RESEARCH** United States, 1900-1940; Nevada, 1864-1940; Chinese-Americans, 1920-1950. **SELECTED PUBLICATIONS** Auth, Letters from the Nevada Frontier--Correspondence of Oddie, Tasker,L. 1898-1902, Jour Amer Hist, Vol 0081, 94; The Silver State--Nevadas Heritage Reinterpreted, Pacific Hist Rev, Vol 0062, 93. **CONTACT ADDRESS** Dept of Hist, San Jose State Univ, San Jose, CA, 95192.

CHANCELLOR, JAMES D.
PERSONAL Born 11/23/1944, St. Louis, MO, m, 1969, 2 children **DISCIPLINE** HISTORY OF RELIGION, ISLAM **EDUCATION** Duke Univ, PhD, 88. **CAREER** Assoc prof Relig, 85-89, Col Baptist Univ; dean, prof Rel, Col Christian Univ, 89-92; assoc prof Rel, S Bapt Theol Sem, 92- . **MEMBERSHIPS** AAR **RESEARCH** New Religious Movements; The Family **SELECTED PUBLICATIONS** Auth, The Night of the Cross, The Dividing Edge, Fall, 91; Christ and Religious Pluralism, Rev and Expositor, vol 91, no 4, Fall, 94; Religion in the Middle East, in Introduction to Missions, Broadman and Holman Publ, 98. **CONTACT ADDRESS** Dept of Religion, S Baptist Theological Sem, 2825 Lexington Rd, Louisville, KY, 40280. **EMAIL** jchancellor@sbts.edu

CHANDLER, JOAN
DISCIPLINE HISTORY **EDUCATION** Univ Tex, PhD, 72. **CAREER** Prof. **RESEARCH** Sport in culture; U.S. popular culture; southwestern U.S. history and literature. **SELECTED PUBLICATIONS** Auth, Television and National Sport: The United States and Britain, Univ Ill, 88; Camping for Life: Transmission of Values at a Girls' Summer Camp, Hall, 81; American Televised Sport: Business as Usual, Bucknell, 85; Sport as TV Product: A Case Study of Monday Night Football, Univ Ill, 91. **CONTACT ADDRESS** Dept of History, Richardson, TX, 75083-0688. **EMAIL** jchandlr@utdallas.edu

CHANDLER, ROBERT JOSEPH
PERSONAL Born 07/31/1942, Salt Lake City, UT, m, 1975, 2 children **DISCIPLINE** AMERICAN HISTORY **EDUCATION** Earlham Col, BA, 64; Univ Calif, Riverside, MA, 66, PhD(hist), 78. **CAREER** PUB RELATIONS OFFICER & SR RES SPECIALIST, HIST DEPT, WELLS FARGO BANK, 78-. **MEMBERSHIPS** Orgn Am Historians. **RESEARCH** Civil war; California and the west; journalism. **SELECTED PUBLICATIONS** Auth, Spreading the News--The American Postal System from Franklin to Morse, New Eng Quart-Hist Rev of New Eng Life and Letters, Vol 0070, 97; In the Van--Spiritualists As Catalysts for the California Womens Suffrage Movement, Calif Hist, Vol 0073, 94; A San-Francisco Scandal--The California of Gordon, George, Calif Hist, Vol 0074, 95; Spreading the News--The American Postal System From Franklin To Morse, New Eng Quart-Hist Rev of New Eng Life and Letters, Vol 0070, 97; Integrity Amid Tumult, Wells-Fargo-And-Cos Gold-Rush Banking, Calif Hist, Vol 0070, 91; The Other California--The Great-Central-Valley in Life and Letters, Jour W, Vol 0032, 93; Newhall, Henry, Mayo and His Times--A California Legacy, Pacific Northwest Quart, Vol 0084, 93; Patterson,Tom--Colorado Crusader For Change, Jour W, Vol 0036, 97. **CONTACT ADDRESS** 4625 Stillwater Ct, Concord, CA, 94521.

CHANDLER, THEODORE ALAN
PERSONAL Born 09/19/1949, St. Louis, MO **DISCIPLINE** EDUCATION **EDUCATION** Northwest MO State Univ, BS 1973; Southern IL Univ Edwardsville, MA 1980; Univ of FL, PhD 1986. **CAREER** Cleveland HS, secondary teacher 1976-79; New Student Life-SIU Edwardsville, consul 1980; SIU Edwardsville, grad teaching asst 1979-80; Univ of FL, grad teaching asst 1980-83; Sex Equity in Voc Ed, project asst 1983; FL KEYS COMM COLL, prof & ea/co coord 1983-90, ARTS & SCIENCES DIVISION, CHAIRMAN, 1990-. **HONORS AND AWARDS** Top Ranked Paper Competitive FL Speech Comm Assn 1982; Outstanding Young Men of Amer Jaycees 1984; Teaching Excellence Awds SIU-E, 1980, Univ of FL, 1983; Outstanding Faculty Member Phi Theta Kappa 1989-90. **MEMBERSHIPS** Mem FL Speech Comm Assn 1981-; mem Speech Comm Assn 1980-; mem Southern Speech Comm Assn 1981-; mem FL Assn of Equal Oppor Profs 1983-; mem Tennessee Williams Fine Arts Ctr Founders Soc, Key West, 1985-; board of directors Helpline Inc, secretary 1992-93, president 1993-94; AIDS Help Inc, volunteer, 1988-93. **CONTACT ADDRESS** Arts & Sci Div, Florida Keys Comm Col, 5901 W College Rd, Key West, FL, 33040.

CHANDLER, VICTORIA
PERSONAL Born 04/17/1950, Athens, GA **DISCIPLINE** HISTORY **EDUCATION** Univ GA, AB, 70, MA, 71; Univ VA, PhD(hist), 79. **CAREER** Asst prof hist, Col William & Mary, 76-77; asst prof, Ferrum Col, 77; instr, Old Dominion Univ, 78; asst prof, 78-83, assoc prof, 83-89; prof hist GA Col & State Univ, 89-; fel, NEH, Inst Teaching Medieval Civilization, summer 81 & Am Philos Soc, summer 82; Fulbright Western European Res grant, 83; NEH Travel to Collections grant, 85; Am Philos Soc Res grant, 87; Newberry Library Short Term fel, 89. **HONORS AND AWARDS** GA Col Distinguished Graduate Fac Publication Awards, 86, 88, 91. **MEMBERSHIPS** AHA; Medieval Acad Am; Southeastern Medieval Asn; Charles Homer Haskins Soc (exec sec, 82-); N Am Conf on British Studies. **RESEARCH** Anglo-Norman biography aristocracy; monastic history; food history. **SELECTED PUBLICATIONS** Auth, The Role of the Southeastern Indians in the Civil War, Working Papers Sociol & Anthrop, 72; Intimations of Authority: Notes on Three Anglo-Norman Countesses, in Social Studies Quart, 78; Politics and Piety: Influences on Charitable Donations during the Anglo-Norman Period, Revue Benedictine, 80; Ada de Warenne, Queen Mother of Scotland (c 1123-1178), Scottish Hist Rev, 81; Historical Revision and the English Monarchs: The Case of William II and his Barons, in Social Studies Quart, 80; A Proposal for a Dictionary of Anglo-Norman Biograpghy, with C A Newman and D S Spear, Medieval Prosopography, 5 #2, fall 84; Family Histories: An Aid in the Study of the Anglo-Norman Aristocracy, Medieval Prosopography, 6 #2, fall 85; The Last of the Montgomerys: Roger the Poitevin and Arnulf, Hist Res, 62 #147, Feb 89; Gundrada de Warenne and the Victorian Gentleman Scholars, Southern Hist, 12, 90; The Wreck of the White Ship: A Mass Murder Revealed?, in The Final Argument: The Imprint of Violence on Society in Medieval and Early Modern Europe, ed Donald J Kagay and L J Andrew Villalon, Boydell Press, 98; William de Warenne III, Earl of Surrey and Reginald de Warenne for The New Dictionary of National Biography, Oxford Univ Press, forthcoming. **CONTACT ADDRESS** Dept of History and Geography, Georgia Col, Milledgeville, GA, 31061. **EMAIL** vchandl@mail.gac.peachnet.edu

CHANDRA, VIPAN
PERSONAL Born 01/20/1940, Rawalpindi, India, m, 1969, 1 child **DISCIPLINE** ASIAN HISTORY & POLITICS **EDUCATION** Agra Univ, India, BA, 59, MA, 61; Harvard Univ, MA, 71, PhD, 77. **CAREER** Lectr pol sci, Meerut Col, India, 61-65; lectr Hindi, Hanguk Univ Foreign Studies, Seoul, 66-68; prof East Asian hist, Wheaton Col, 77-, Coordr Asian studies, Wheaton Col, 78-; consult, Harvard Law Sch, 80. **MEMBERSHIPS** Asn Asian Studies. **RESEARCH** Modern Korean and Japanese history. **SELECTED PUBLICATIONS** Auth, An Outline Study of Korea's Advancement Society, 74 & Korea's First Proposal for a National Assembly, 75, in Occasional Papers on Korea, Soc Sci Res Coun & Am Coun Learned Soc; The Concept of Popular Sovereignty: The Case of So Chael-p'il and Yun Ch'i-ho, Korea J, Seoul, 4/81; The Korean Enlightenment: A Reexamination, Korea J, 5/82; Imperialism, Resistance and Reform in Late 19th-Century Korea: Enlightenment and the Independence Club, Inst E Asian Studies, Univ Calif, 88. **CONTACT ADDRESS** Dept of Hist, Wheaton Col, 26 E Main St, Norton, MA, 02766-2322. **EMAIL** vipan_chandra@wheaton.ma.edu

CHANEY, WILLIAM ALBERT
PERSONAL Born 12/23/1922, Arcadia, CA **DISCIPLINE** MEDIEVAL HISTORY **EDUCATION** Univ CA, Berkeley, AB, 43, PhD, 61. **CAREER** From asst prof to assoc prof, 52-66, George McKendree Steele assoc prof, 62-66, chmn dept hist, 67-71, 95-96; George McKendree Steele prof hist, Lawrence Univ, 66-, Lectr, MI State Univ, 58; Am Coun Learned Soc grant-in-aid, 66-67; Royal Soc of Arts fel, 77. **MEMBERSHIPS** AHA; MLA; Am Soc Church Hist; Mediaeval Acad Am; Archaeol Inst Am. **RESEARCH** Anglo-Saxon Engl; medieval rulership, sacred space. **SELECTED PUBLICATIONS** Auth, Grendel and the Gifstol: A legal view of monsters, PMLA, 62, Aethelberht's code and the king's number, Am J Legal Hist, 62; A Louisiana planter in the Gold Rush, La Hist, 62; Anglo-Saxon Church dues, Church Hist, 63; The economics of ruler-cult in Anglo-Saxon law, J Brit Studies, 65; Paganism to Christianity in Anglo-Saxon England: In: Early Medieval Society, Appleton, 67; The Cult of Kingship in Anglo-Saxon England: The Transition from Paganism to Christianity, Univ Calif & Manchester Univ, 70; Eleven articles in New Catholic Encycl, Schafer Williams: A Memoir in In Iure Veritas: Studies in Canon Law in Memory of Schafer Williams, univ on cin col law, 91. **CONTACT ADDRESS** Dept of Hist, Lawrence Univ, 115 S Drew St, Appleton, WI, 54911-5798.

CHANG, DAE HONG
PERSONAL Born 01/09/1928, Nara, Japan, m, 1964, 2 children **DISCIPLINE** SOCIAL SCIENCE, POLITICAL SCIENCE **EDUCATION** Mich State Univ, BA, Polit Sci, 57, MA, 58, PhD, Soc Sci, 62. **CAREER** Statistical analyst, Sec State, State of Mich, 58-61; grad & tchg asst, Soc Sci, Mich State Univ, 61-62; asst prof, Soc & Anthrop, Olivet Coll, 62-66; asst prof, Soc, Northern Ill Univ, 66-69; prof & ch, Soc & Anthrop, Univ Wis, 69-75; PROF & CH, ADMIN & JUSTICE, WICHITA STATE UNIV, 75-; ch, Asian Stud Prog, Wichita State Univ, 87-. **SELECTED PUBLICATIONS** Juvenile Delinquency and Juvenile Justice: Comparative and International Perspective, Acorn Press, 95; "Organized Crime in South Korea," Comparative Criminal Justice: Traditional and Nontraditional Systems of Law and Control, Waveland press, 96; "Drug and Punishment: An International Survey," International Journal of Comparative and Applied Criminal Justice, 93; "International Judicial Cooperation in Criminal Matters," International Journal of Comparative and Applied Criminal Justice, 94; "A New Form of International Crime: The Human Organ Trade," International Journal of Comparative and Applied Criminal Justice, 95. **CONTACT ADDRESS** Crim Justice, Hugo Wall Sch Urban & Public Affairs, Wichita State Univ, Wichita, KS, 67260-0135. **EMAIL** dchang@twsuvm.uc.twsu.edu

CHANNELL, DAVID
DISCIPLINE HISTORY **EDUCATION** Case Western Reserve Univ, PhD, 75. **CAREER** Prof. **RESEARCH** History of science, technology and medicine; philosophy of science and technology; 18th to 20th century European intellectual history; 19th century British history. **SELECTED PUBLICATIONS** Auth, The Vital Machine: A Study of Technology and Organic Life, Oxford, 91; The History of Engineering Science, Garland, 89; Scottish Men of Science-W.J.M. Rankine, F.R.S.E., F.R.S., Scotland's Cult Heritage, 86. **CONTACT ADDRESS** Dept of History, Richardson, TX, 75083-0688. **EMAIL** channell@utdallas.edu

CHANZIT, GWEN
DISCIPLINE EUROPEAN MODERN ART **EDUCATION** Univ Iowa, PhD, 84. **CAREER** Experience-cur, Herbert Bayer Coll and Archiv; assoc cur, Denver Art Mus; sr lectr-. **SELECTED PUBLICATIONS** Auth, Herbert Bayer and Modernist Design in America, UMI Res Press, 87; The Herbert Bayer Collection and Artchive at the Denver Art Musema, Denver Art Mus, 88. **CONTACT ADDRESS** Dept of Art and Art Hist, Univ Denver, 2199 S Univ Blvd, Denver, CO, 80208.

CHAPMAN, H. PERRY
DISCIPLINE ART HISTORY **EDUCATION** Swarthmore Col, BA, 75; Princeton Univ, MFA, 78; PhD, 83. **CAREER** Instr, Swarthmore Col, 81; lectr, Amer Univ, 82; instr, 82-83; asst prof, 83-89;assoc prof, 89-96; dept assoc ch, 91-93;prof, 96. **HONORS AND AWARDS** Kress fel, Princeton Univ, 79; gen res grant, Univ Del, 89, 84, 92; res grant, Am Philos Soc, 84; stipend, NEH, 85; supplemental funds grant, Univ Del, 86, 88; publ grant, Getty Grant Prog, 90; fel, Woodrow Wilson Intl Ctr for Scholars, 90-91; fel, NEH, Univ tchr(s), 93-94., Gst cur, Nat Gallery of Art, Wash, DC, 96. **MEMBERSHIPS** Mem, Amer Assn Netherlandic Stud; Col Art Assn; Historians of Netherlandish Art. **SELECTED PUBLICATIONS** Auth, Rembrandt's Self-Portraits: A Study in Seventeenth-Century Identity, Princeton Univ Press, 90; Rembrandt's burgerlijk Self-Portraits, Leids Kunsthistorisch Jaarboek 89, The Hague, 90; Jan Steen's Household Revisited, Simiolus, 91; Persona and Myth in Houbraken's Life of Jan Steen, The Art Bulletin, 93. **CONTACT ADDRESS** Dept of Art Hist, Univ Delaware, 162 Ctr Mall, Newark, DE, 19716. **EMAIL** pchapman@udel.edu

CHAPPELL, DAVID L.
PERSONAL Born 03/28/1959, Chicago, IL, s **DISCIPLINE** HISTORY **EDUCATION** Yale Univ, BA, 82; Univ Rochester, NY, PhD, 92. **CAREER** Pre-dr fel, 89-90, Frederick Douglass Inst, Univ Rochester; lectr, 91, SUNY; asst prof, 91-92, Hartwick Col, NY; asst prof, 92-97, assoc prof, 98-, Univ Arkansas; **RESEARCH** Amer intellectual & cultural hist; African-Amer hist, southern hist. **SELECTED PUBLICATIONS** Auth, Inside Agitators: White Southerners in the Civil Rights Movement,Johns Hopkins, 94; Diversity within a Racial Group: White Little Rock in the School Crisis of 1957-1958, Ark Hist Quarterly, 95. **CONTACT ADDRESS** History Dept, Univ of Arkansas, Old Main 416, Fayetteville, AR, 72701. **EMAIL** dchappel@comp.uark.edu

CHAPPELL, DAVID WELLINGTON
PERSONAL Born 02/03/1940, St. John, NB, Canada, 2 children **DISCIPLINE** HISTORY OF RELIGIONS **EDUCATION** Mt Allison Univ, BA, 61; McGill Univ, BD, 65; Yale Univ, PhD(Chinese Buddhism), 76. **CAREER** Teaching asst world relig, Yale Univ, 70-71; actg asst prof Chinese relig, Univ Hawaii, 71-77; asst prof, Univ Toronto, 77-78; asst prof, 78-80, Prof Chinese Relig, Univ Hawaii, Manoa, 85- **MEMBERSHIPS** Asn for Asian Studies; Am Acad Relig; Soc Study Chinese Relig; NAm Soc Buddhist Studies; Soc for Buddhist-Christian Stu. **RESEARCH** Formation of Chinese Buddhism; Buddhist-Christian comparisons. **SELECTED PUBLICATIONS** Auth, Introduction to the T'ien-t'ai ssu-chiao-i, Eastern Buddhist, 5/76; A perspective on the Pure Land Doctrine of T'ien-t'ai Chih-i (538-597), (in Japanese), Taisho Daigaku Bukkyo gaku, 76; coed & contribr article, In: Buddhist and Taoist Studies (Vol I), Univ Hawaii, 77; contribr, Early Ch'an in China and Tibet, 82; ed, T'ien-t'ai Buddhism, Dai-ichi-Shobo, 83; auth, Pure Land Buddhism: History, Culture and Doctrine, Univ Calif, 97.Pure Land Buddhism: History, Culture and Doctrine, Univ Calif, 97. **CONTACT ADDRESS** Dept of Relig, Univ of Hawaii, 2530 Dole St, Honolulu, HI, 96822-2303. **EMAIL** dwchap@hawaii.edu

CHAPPLE, C.K.
PERSONAL Born 09/04/1954, Medina, NY, m, 1974, 2 children **DISCIPLINE** HISTORY OF RELIGION **EDUCATION** SUNY Stony Brook, BA, 76; Fordham Univ, MA, 78, PhD, 80. **CAREER** Prof, 85-, Loyola Marymont Univ; Lectr, 80-85, SUNY Stony Brook; Asst Dir, 80-85, Inst Adv Stud Wld Rel. **HONORS AND AWARDS** 2 NEH Fels; Lily Gnt; College Fel; Chilton Ch Awd; Gannett Schlshp; IAAPEA Res Awd; CWHE Appre Certif; Grant Devel Gnt. **MEMBERSHIPS** AAR; AA; AIIS. **RESEARCH** Yoga Traditions; Jainism; Hinduism; Buddhism. **SELECTED PUBLICATIONS** Ed, Ecological Prospects: Scientific Religious and Aesthetic Perspectives, Albany, SUNY Press, 94, Intl edition, Delhi, Indian Books Cen, 95; auth, Nonviolence to Animals Earth and Self in Asian Traditions, Albany, NY, SUNY Press, 93, Intl edition, Delhi, Indian Books Cen, 95; ed, Jesuit Tradition in Education and Missions, Scranton, U of Scranton Press, 93; Haribhadra's Analysis of Patanjala and Kula Yoga in the Yogadrstisamuccaya, in: Open Boundaries: Jain Communities and Cultures in Indian History, ed, John E Cort, Albany, SUNY Press, 98; India: The Land of Plentitude, Satya, 98; Animals in the Buddhist Birth Stories, in: Buddhism and Ecology: The Interconnection of Dharma, and Deeds, ed, Mary Evelyn Tucker, Duncan Ryuken Williams, Cambridge MA, Harv Univ Cen Stud Of World Rel, 97; Renouncer Traditions Of India: Jainism and Buddhism, in: Ananya: A Portrait of India, ed, S Sn Sridhar, Nirmal K Mattoo, NY, Assoc of Indians in Amer, 97. **CONTACT ADDRESS** Dept Theol Studies, Loyola Marymount Univ, 7900 Loyola Blvd, Los Angeles, CA, 90045. **EMAIL** cchapple@lmumail.lmu.edu

CHAPUT, DONALD
PERSONAL Born 12/19/1933, Houghton County, MI, m, 1960, 2 children **DISCIPLINE** UNITED STATES HISTORY **EDUCATION** Northland Col, BA, 57; Mich State Univ, MA, 58. **CAREER** Instr hist, Elgin Community Col, 64-66; ed & chief, Mich Hist Comn, 66-71; SR CUR HIST, NATURAL HIST MUS, LOS ANGELES, 72-, US consult, Dict Can Biog, 66- **MEMBERSHIPS** Orgn Am Historians. **RESEARCH** Exploration; military; mining. **SELECTED PUBLICATIONS** Auth, In Search of Silver and Gold--Cashman, Nellie, Miner and Philanthropist in the Late 1800s, Amer Hist, Vol 0030, 96; Brothers on the Santa-Fe and Chihuahua Trails-- Glasgow, Edward, James and Glasgow , William, Henry 1846-1848, Pacific Hist Rev, Vol 0064, 95. **CONTACT ADDRESS** Hist Div Natural Hist, Mus Exposition Park, Los Angeles, CA, 90001.

CHARLESWORTH, MICHAEL
DISCIPLINE 19TH-CENTURY EUROPEAN PAINTING AND PHOTOGRAPHY **EDUCATION** Univ Manchester, MA; Univ Kent at Canterbury, Engl, PhD. **CAREER** Asst prof; Univ TX, 93-; taught at, Kent & Univ SC. **RESEARCH** Panoramic representation of landscape. **SELECTED PUBLICATIONS** Ed, 3-vol bk, The English Garden: Literary Sources and Documents, 93; contrib chap, gothic architecture and the picturesque movement to The Politics of the Picturesque, 94; auth, series of essays on 19th century photography. **CONTACT ADDRESS** Dept of Art and Art Hist, Univ of Texas at Austin, 2613 Wichita St, FAB 1.112, Austin, TX, 78705.

CHARLTON, THOMAS LEE
PERSONAL Born 12/18/1936, Helena, AR, m, 1959, 2 children **DISCIPLINE** HISTORY **EDUCATION** Baylor Univ, BA, 59; Univ Tex, Austin, MA, 61, PhD(hist), 69. **CAREER** From instr to assoc prof hist, San Antonio Col, 62-70; asst prof, 70-75, ASSOC PROF HIST, BAYLOR UNIV, 75-, Dir, Baylor Univ Prog Oral Hist, 70-; ed, Oral Hist Asn Newsletter, 75-; mem, Bd Rev, Tex, Nat Regist Hist Places, 77- **MEMBERSHIPS** Oral Hist Asn; Orgn Am Historians; Western Hist Asn; Am Asn Univ Prof. **RESEARCH** Oral history; Texas history; recent United States history. **SELECTED PUBLICATIONS** Auth, Always Bet on the Butcher--Nelson, Warren and Casino Gaming, 1930s-1980s, W Hist Quart, Vol 0026, 95; Profiles in Power--20th-Century Texans in Washington, W Hist Quart, Vol 0025, 94. **CONTACT ADDRESS** Dept of Hist, Baylor Univ, Box 228, Waco, TX, 76703.

CHARTIER, YVES
DISCIPLINE HISTORY OF MUSIC **EDUCATION** Univ Ottawa, BA, MA; Univ Paris, DU. **CAREER** Prof, Univ Ottawa. **RESEARCH** Musicology (Middle Ages, Renaissance), aesthetics. **SELECTED PUBLICATIONS** Auth, L'Oeuvre musicale d'Hucbald de Saint-Amand, Mont real-Paris, Editions Bellarmin-Vrin, 94; Clavis opervm Hvcbaldi Elnonensis, Jour of Medieval Latin 4, 95; Les outils du musicologue, Dubuque, 91; coauth, Glossaire de Musique, Toronto, 90; ed, Georges MIGOT, Douze hymnes liturgiques, Paris, 87. **CONTACT ADDRESS** Dept of Music, Univ Ottawa, 70 Laurier Ave, PO Box 450, Ottawa, ON, K1N 6N5.

CHASE, JAMES S.
DISCIPLINE HISTORY **EDUCATION** Univ Chicago, PhD. **CAREER** Prof. **RESEARCH** United States political parties; early national period. **SELECTED PUBLICATIONS** Auth, Democratizing the Old Dominion: Virginia and the Second Party System, 1824-1861 (rev), 98; DeWitt Clinton and the Rise of the People's Men (rev), Am Hist Rev, 97; Character Above All: Ten Presidents from FDR to George Bush (rev), Ark Hist Rev, 97; The Presidency of Andrew Jackson (rev), Hist Rev New Brooks, 94; The 1992 Presidential Election in the South (rev), Ark Hist Quarterly, 94. **CONTACT ADDRESS** History Dept, Univ of Arkansas, Fayetteville, 406 Old Main, Fayetteville, AR, 72701. **EMAIL** jchase@comp.uark.edu

CHASE, PHILANDER DEAN
PERSONAL Born 03/10/1943, Eikin, NC, m, 1971 **DISCIPLINE** AMERICAN HISTORY **EDUCATION** NC State Univ, BA, 65; Duke Univ, MA, 68, PhD(hist), 73. **CAREER** Nat Hist Publ & Rec Comn fel, Papers George Washington, 73-74; asst ed, 74-89, assoc ed, 89-98, EDITOR, PAPERS OF GEORGE WASHINGTON, ALDERMAN LIBR, UNIV VA, CHARLOTTESVILLE, 98-. **HONORS AND AWARDS** Philip M Hamer Award, Soc Am Archivists, 78; Distinguished Alumnus Award, Col of Humanities and Social Sciences, NC State Univ, 94. **MEMBERSHIPS** AHA; Southern Hist Asn; Asn Doc Ed; Inst Early Am Hist & Cult. **RESEARCH** American Revolution; 18th century military history. **SELECTED PUBLICATIONS** Auth, A la recherche de l'esprit et de l'ame de la Revolution Americaine, Annales Hist Revolution Fr, Vol 48, 76; co-ed, The Diaries of George Washington, Univ Press VA (6 vols), 76-79; co-ed, The Papers of George Washington: Colonial Series (10 vols), Univ Press VA, 83-95; ed, The Papers of George Washington: Revolutionary War Series (7 vols to date), Univ Press VA, 85-; auth, Years of Hardships and Revelations: The Convention Army at the Albemarle Barracks, 1779-1781, Mag of Albemarle County Hist, 41, 83; A Stake in the West: George Washington as Back Country Surveyor and Landowner, in Warren R. Hofstra, ed, George Washington and the Virginia Back Country, Madison, WI: Madison House, 97. **CONTACT ADDRESS** Alderman Libr, Univ of Virginia, Charlottesville, VA, 22903-2498. **EMAIL** pdc7m@virginia.edu

CHASE, WILLIAM JOHN
PERSONAL Born 09/04/1947, Glen Cove, NY, m, 1972, 2 children **DISCIPLINE** SOVIET HISTORY **EDUCATION** Lafayette Col, BA, 69; Boston Col, MA, 73, PhD, 79. **CAREER** Instr, Boston Col, 76-79; asst prof hist, Univ Pittsburgh, 79-85; assoc prof, 85-; co-dir, Russ Archive Series, 91-; dir, Russ Pub Proj, 90; ed, Carl Beck Papers Russ & East Europ studies, 82-; dir, Cen for Russ and Eur Studies, Univ of Pittsburgh, 89-91. **HONORS AND AWARDS** Nat Coun for Soviet & East European Res grants, 83, 84, 85, 92, 95; NEH-84; SSRC, 91; IREX, 90; ACLS, 81; Sr Fel, Harriman Inst for Adv Stud of Sov Union, Columbia Univ, 82; Distinguished Teaching Award, 84; **RESEARCH** Soviet social and labor history; collective biographical study of Soviet national, regional and local political leaders, 1917-1941. **SELECTED PUBLICATIONS** Co-ed, Rossiiskii Gosudarstvennyi Arkhiv Ekonomiki, Putevodital, Vol 1, Moscow, 94. **CONTACT ADDRESS** Dept of History, Univ of Pittsburgh, 3p38 Forbes Quad, Pittsburgh, PA, 15260-0001. **EMAIL** bchase@vms.cis.pitt.edu

CHASSEN-LOPEZ, FRANCIE R.
PERSONAL Born 07/04/1947, New York, NY, 1 child **DISCIPLINE** HISTORY **EDUCATION** Vassar Col, BA, 69; Univ Nac Autonoma Mexico, MA, 75, PhD, 86. **CAREER** Prof,

Univ Autonoma, Estado Mexico, 77-78, 80-81; assoc prof, Univ Nac Autonoma Mexico, Mexico City, 76-81; assoc prof, Univ Autonoma Metropolitana, Ixtapalapa, 81-86; vis instr, Fla Int Univ, 86-87; vis instr, Fla Atlantic Univ, 86-88; asst prof, 88-91, ASSOC PROF, 91-; act dir Lat Am Stud Prog, Univ Ky, 97; ed bd, Guchachi Reza, 96-. **HONORS AND AWARDS** Gabino Berreda Meda acad exc, Univ Nac Autonoma Mexico, 88; PRONAES grant res reg Hist, 84-86; Univ Ky res fund grant, 89; NEH summer inst, 92; Univ Ky grant, 94, 96. **MEMBERSHIPS** Conf Lat Am Hist; Lat Am Stud Asn; Rocky Mountain Counc Lat Am Stud; Midwest Asn Lat Am Stud; Phi Alpha Theta; Vassar Alumni Asn. **SELECTED PUBLICATIONS** Co-auth, Diccionario Historico de la Revolucion en Oaxaca, Univ Autonoma Benito Juarez Oaxaca and Inst Estatal Educ Pub Oaxaca, 97; co-auth, La Revolucion en Oaxaca 1900-1930, Mins Adm Pub Oaxaca, 85, Consejo Nac Cult, Artes, 93; auth, Capitalismo o comunalismo: Cambio y Continuidad en la Tenencia de la Tierra en la Oaxaca Profirista, in El Porfiriato: Sintesis y Perspectivas, Univ Iberoamericana, 98; auth, Dona Juana Cata Romero, in Forjando Matrias. Las mujeres y la Historia Mexicana, Univ Calif Press and Col Mex, forthcoming; auth, Maderismo or Mixtec Empire? Class and Ethnicity in the Mexican Revolution (Costa Chica of Oaxaca, 1911) The Americas, 55:1, Jul 98; auth, El Ferrocarril Nacional de Tehuantepec, Acervos 10, Oct/Dec 98; auth, Cheaper than Machines: Women in Agriculture in Porfirian Oaxaca, in Creating Spaces, Shaping Transitions: Women of the Mexican Countryside, 1850-1990, Univ Az, 94, Sp trans, 96. **CONTACT ADDRESS** Dept of History, Univ of Kentucky, 1715 Patterson Off, Lexington, KY, 40506-0027. **EMAIL** frclopz@pop.uky.edu

CHASTAIN, CATHERINE

DISCIPLINE ART HISTORY **EDUCATION** Rhodes Col, BA, 90; Emory Univ, MA, 93, PhD, 98. **HONORS AND AWARDS** Res fel(s), 93, 96. **SELECTED PUBLICATIONS** Publ, articles, essays in the field of American Modernism, Oxford Univ Press22,Woman's Art Jour. **CONTACT ADDRESS** Art Dept, Piedmont Col, 165 Central Ave., PO Box 10, Demorest, GA, 30535. **EMAIL** cgoldsle@piedmont.edu

CHASTAIN, JAMES G.

PERSONAL Born 03/15/1939, Chickasha, OK, m, 1965, 2 children **DISCIPLINE** MODERN EUROPEAN HISTORY **EDUCATION** Harvard Univ, BA, 61; Univ Okla, MA, 66, Ph-D(hist), 67. **CAREER** Asst prof, 67-72, ASSOC PROF HIST, OHIO UNIV, 72- **MEMBERSHIPS** AHA; Soc Fr Hist Studies; Conf Group Cent Europ Hist; Western Soc Fr Hist. **RESEARCH** Modern French history; modern German history; 19th century revolutions. **SELECTED PUBLICATIONS** Auth, German History 1770-1866, Historian, Vol 0057, 95; From the Vienna--Congress to the Paris-Congress-England, the German Question and the Balance of Power 1815-1856, Amer Hist Rev, Vol 0097, 92. **CONTACT ADDRESS** Athens, OH, 45701-2979.

CHATFIELD, E. CHARLES

PERSONAL Born 03/11/1934, Philadelphia, PA, m, 1957, 2 children **DISCIPLINE** HISTORY **EDUCATION** Monmouth Col, BA, 56; Vanderbilt Univ, MA, 58, Phd, 65; Univ of Chicago, postdoctoral work, 66. **CAREER** Vis prof, hist, Gustavus Adlphus Col, 74; vis prof, hist, Univ of Toledo, 87-88; PROF, HIST, WITTENBERG UNIV, 61- . **HONORS AND AWARDS** Named to endowed chair: H. Orth Hirt Prof of Hist, 98; Hon PhD, Monmouth Col, 95; Danforth Fel, 56-65; Warren Kuehl Prize of the Soc for Hists of Am For Policy for an Am Ordeal; Publ Prize of the Ohio Acad of Hist For Peace and Justice: Pacifism in Am, 72. **MEMBERSHIPS** Am Hist Asn; Ohio Acad of Hist; Peace Hist Soc; Int Peace Res Asn. **RESEARCH** History of peace and antiwar movements, in U.S. and twentieth century; history of internationalism. **SELECTED PUBLICATIONS** Coauth, An American Ordeal: The Antiwar Movement of the Vietnam Era, Syracuse Univ Pr, 90; auth, The American Peace Movement: Ideals and Activism, Syracuse Univ Pr, 92; co-ed, Peace/Mir: An Anthology of Historic Alternatives to War, Syracuse Univ Pr, 94; co-ed, Transnational Movements and Global Politics: Solidarity Beyond the State, Syracuse Univ Pr, 1997; co-ed, Peace Movements and Political Cultures, Tenn Univ Pr, 88. **CONTACT ADDRESS** Wittenberg Univ, PO Box 720, Springfield, OH, 45501-0720. **EMAIL** echatfield@wittenberg.edu

CHAUSSE, GILLES

PERSONAL Born 06/06/1931, Montreal, PQ, Canada **DISCIPLINE** THEOLOGY/CHURCH HISTORY **EDUCATION** Univ Montreal, MA, 58, PhD, 73. **CAREER** Prof hist, Col Jean-de-Brebeuf Montreal, 69-85; PROF D'HISTOIRE DE L'EGLISE, FACULTE DE THEOLOGIE, UNIV MONTREAL, 86-. **HONORS AND AWARDS** Collaborateur a l'Institut historique de la Compagnie de Jesus a Rome; recipiendaire du Merite Diocesain 'Monseigneur Ignace Bourger', 86. **MEMBERSHIPS** Societe Canadienne d'Histoire de l'Eglise catholique **SELECTED PUBLICATIONS** Auth, Jean-Jacques Lartigue, premier eveque de Montreal, 80; coauth, Les Ultramontains canadiens-francais, 85; coauth, Le Christianisme d'ici a-t-il un avenir?, 88; coauth, L'Image de la Revolution francaise au Quebec 1789-1989, 89; coauth, Quebec, terre d'Evangile: les defis de l'evangelisation dans la culture contemporaine, 91; coauth, Montreal 1642-1992, 92; coauth, Dictionnaire Biographique du Canada, tomes 4-8; coauth, A Concise History of Christianity in Canada, 96. **CONTACT ADDRESS** Fac de Theologie, Univ Montreal, CP 6128, Succ Centre Ville, Montreal, PQ, H3C 3J7. **EMAIL** chausseg@magellan.umontreal.ca

CHAVALAS, MARK W.

DISCIPLINE HISTORY **EDUCATION** Univ Calif Los Angeles, PhD, 88. **CAREER** Instr, Univ Wis, 89-; Prof, Univ Wis, 98-. **HONORS AND AWARDS** NEH Summer Sem, Cornell, 98; NEH Summer Inst, Univ Ariz, 96; NEH Summer Inst, Brown, 95. **MEMBERSHIPS** Am Oriental Soc; Am Schs of Oriental Res; Archeol Inst of Am; Soc of Bibl Lit. **RESEARCH** Ancient Near East history; archaeology; Biblical studies; classical studies. **SELECTED PUBLICATIONS** Co-ed, New Horizons in the Study of Ancient Syria, 92; Ed, Emar: The History, Religion, and Culture of a Syrian Town in the Late Bronze Age, 96; Co-ed, Crossing Boundaries and Linking Horizons: Studies in Honor of Michael C. Astour on his 80th Birthday, 97; Co-ed, Syro-Mesopotamia and the Bible, 99. **CONTACT ADDRESS** Dept of History, Univ of Wisconsin, La Crosse, La Crosse, WI, 54601. **EMAIL** chavalas@mail.uwut.edu

CHEAL, CATHERYN LEDA

PERSONAL Born 04/11/1951, Mich **DISCIPLINE** CLASSICAL ARCHEOLOGY, NUMISMATICS **EDUCATION** Univ Mich, BS, 73; Brown Univ, PhD(class archaeol), 78. **CAREER** Teaching asst to assoc Latin & archaeol, Brown Univ, 76-78; instr hist archit, Roger Williams Col, 77-79; LECTR CLASSICS & ART HIST, CALIF STATE UNIV, NORTHRIDGE 81-. **MEMBERSHIPS** Am Inst Archaeol. **RESEARCH** Greek sculpture. **SELECTED PUBLICATIONS** Auth, The Myth of the Goddess--Evolution of an Image, Class World, Vol 0088, 95; Looking at Greek Vases, Class World, Vol 0086, 93. **CONTACT ADDRESS** 1343 Erringer Rd, Simi Valley, CA, 93065.

CHEATHAM, CARL W.

PERSONAL Born 08/04/1940, Lincoln, AR, m, 1961, 4 children **DISCIPLINE** MODERN CHURCH HISTORY **EDUCATION** Harding Univ, BA, 62; Harding Graduate Sch, MTh, 65; Vanderbilt, MA, 79, PhD, 82. **CAREER** Prof, Faulkner Univ, 81-. **MEMBERSHIPS** Am Soc Church Hist; AAR; SBL; ETS. **RESEARCH** Restoration History **CONTACT ADDRESS** Faulkner Univ, 5345 Atlanta Hwy, Box 110, Montgomery, AL, 36109. **EMAIL** ccheatha@faulkner.edu

CHECK, ED

DISCIPLINE ART HISTORY **EDUCATION** Univ WI, Milwaukee, BFA, 80, MS, 87, PhD, 96. **CAREER** Lectr, McPherson Col-Milwaukee Ctr, 89; tchg asst, 89-95, lectr, Univ WI, Madison, 95; asst prof, TX Tech Univ, 96-; rev bd mem, J of Gender Issues in Art and Educ. **HONORS AND AWARDS** Frederick M Logan scholar, Univ WI, 93. **MEMBERSHIPS** Nat Art Educ Asn; TX Art Educ Asn; US Soc for Educ through Art; Col Arts Asn; Gay and Lesbian Spec Interest Gp; Southern Poverty Law Ctr; Lubbock Arts Alliance. **RESEARCH** Gender (masculinity) and sexuality; cult criticism. **SELECTED PUBLICATIONS** Auth, Queers, art and education, in M. Zurmuehlen, ed, Working Papers In Art Education, Univ Iowa, 92; Letter to the editor, Art Educ, 47 (2), 6-7, 94; My Self-Education as a Gay Artist, Dissertation Abstracts Int, 57-07A, 96; coauth, Living the discourses, J of Soc Theory in Art Educ, 17, 38-68, 97; ed, The Caucus Newsletter: Newsletter of the Caucus on Social Theory and Art Education, 93-94. **CONTACT ADDRESS** Texas Tech Univ, Lubbock, TX, 79409-5015. **EMAIL** a5dms@ttuvm1.ttu.edu

CHEETHAM, MARK A.

DISCIPLINE ART **EDUCATION** Univ Toronto, BA; MA; Univ London, PhD. **RESEARCH** Art theory. **SELECTED PUBLICATIONS** Auth, Alex Colville: The Observer Observed, ECW, 94; The Rhetoric of Purity: Essentialist Theory & the Advent of Abstract Painting, Cambridge, 91; Remembering Postmodernism: Trends in Recent Canadian Art, Oxford, 91; coauth, Disturbing Abstraction: Christian Eckart, 96; co-ed, Theory Between the Disciplines: Authority/Vision/Politics, Michigan, 90. **CONTACT ADDRESS** Dept of Visual Arts, Western Ontario Univ, London, ON, N6A 5B8.

CHEN, CHING-CHIH

PERSONAL Born 05/24/1937, Taoyuan, Taiwan, m, 1965, 2 children **DISCIPLINE** EAST ASIAN HISTORY **EDUCATION** Tunghai Univ, Taiwan, BA, 60; Harvard Univ, MA, 65, PhD(hist & EAsian lang), 73. **CAREER** Teaching asst polit sci, Tunghai Univ, Taiwan, 61-63; asst prof, 69-77, ASSOC PROF HIST, SOUTHERN ILL UNIV, EDWARDSVILLE, 77- **MEMBERSHIPS** AHA; Asn Asian Studies. **RESEARCH** History of Japanese colonial expansion; history of Sino-Japanese relations; history of Taiwan. **SELECTED PUBLICATIONS** Auth, Bamboo Stone--The Evolution of a Chinese Medical Elite, Historian, Vol 0058, 95. **CONTACT ADDRESS** Dept of Hist Studies, Southern Ill Univ, 6 Hairpin Dr, Edwardsville, IL, 62026-0001.

CHEN, JEROME

PERSONAL Born 10/02/1921, Chengdu, China **DISCIPLINE** HISTORY **EDUCATION** Southwest Assoc Univs China, MA, 43; Nankai Inst Econ China, 45; Univ London, PhD, 56. **CAREER** Lectr, Yenching Univ, Peking, 45-47; lectr, hist, Univ Leeds, 63-71; distinguished res prof hist, York Univ, 71-87, PROF EMER, YORK UNIV, 87-; vis prof, Univ Kansas, 70; vis prof, Australian Nat Univ, 71; vis prof, Univ Adelaide, 74; vis prof, Univ Kyoto, 78; vis prof, Keio Univ, 91; vis prof, Univ Vienna, 92. **RESEARCH** Chinese history. **SELECTED PUBLICATIONS** Auth, Mao and the Chinese Revolution, 65; auth, Mao: Great Lives Observed, 70; auth, China and the West, 79; auth, The Nationalist Era in China, 92; auth, The Highlanders of Central China, 92. **CONTACT ADDRESS** Dept of History, York Univ, Downsview, ON, M3J 1P3.

CHENG, WEIKUN

DISCIPLINE HISTORY **EDUCATION** Johns Hopkins Univ, PhD. **CAREER** Vis asst prof, SUNY Oswego. **RESEARCH** Mod China; mod Japan; Chinese soc and cult hist. **SELECTED PUBLICATIONS** Auth, The Challenge of the Actresses: Female Performers and the Cultural Alternatives in the Early Twentieth-Century Beijing and Tianjin, in Modern China, 96; The Politics of Headdress: Agitations Regarding the Queue in the Beginning and the End of Qing China in Hair in Asian Cultures: Context and Change, SUNY Albany P, 96. **CONTACT ADDRESS** Dept Hist, SUNY Oswego, 423 Mahar Hall, Oswego, NY, 13126.

CHENG-CHI HSU, GINGER

DISCIPLINE CHINESE ART AND CULTURE **EDUCATION** Univ Calif-Berkeley, PhD. **CAREER** PROF, ART HIST, UNIV CALIF, RIVERSIDE. **SELECTED PUBLICATIONS** Auth, "Anhui Merchant Culture and Patronage," Shadows of Mt Huang, 81; Merchant Patronage of the Eighteen Century Yangchow Painting, 89; Zheng Xie's Price List: Paintings as a Source of Income, Yangzhou, 91; The Drunken Demon Queller, 96; Incarnations of the Blossoming Plum, 96. **CONTACT ADDRESS** Dept of Art Hist, Univ Calif, 1156 Hinderaker Hall, Riverside, CA, 92521-0209.

CHERNOW, BARBARA A.

PERSONAL Born 04/18/1948, New York, NY, m, 1981 **DISCIPLINE** AMERICAN HISTORY **EDUCATION** Hunter Coll, CUNY, BA, 68; Columbia Univ, MA, 69, PhD, 74. **CAREER** Assoc edr, 69-76; ref edr, MacMillan Publ Co, 77-82; PRES, CHERNOW EDIT SERVS, 82-. **MEMBERSHIPS** Soc Women Geog; Womens City Club of NY **RESEARCH** Early national period of American history **SELECTED PUBLICATIONS** Co-edr, The Columbia Encyclopedia 5th ed, Columbia Univ Press/Houghton Mifflin, 93. **CONTACT ADDRESS** Chernow Editorial Services, 1133 Broadway, New York, NY, 10010. **EMAIL** bchernow@chernow.com

CHERNY, ROBERT WALLACE

PERSONAL Born 04/04/1943, Marysville, KS, m, 1967, 1 child **DISCIPLINE** AMERICAN HISTORY **EDUCATION** Univ NE, BA, 65; Columbia Univ, MA, 67, PhD(hist), 72. **CAREER** Instr Am hist, 71-72, asst prof, 72-77, assoc prof, 77-81, PROF AM HIST, SAN FRANCISCO STATE UNIV, 81-, Chair, 87-92, 95; Vis assoc prof, Univ NE-Lincoln, 80, vis prof, 82. **HONORS AND AWARDS** Vis Res Scholar, Univ Melbourne, 97; Distinguished Fulbright Lect, Moscow State Univ, 96; fel, Nat Endowment for the Humanities, 92-93. **MEMBERSHIPS** AHA; Orgn Am Historians; Southwest Labor Studies Asn (pres, 82-86); Am Hist Asn, Pacific Coast Branch: Council, 91-94; Soc Hist of the Gilded Age and the Progressive Era, pres, 95-96. **RESEARCH** United States political, labor, and urban history, 1877-1945; US West, especially CA. **SELECTED PUBLICATIONS** Auth, Isolationist voting in 1940: A statistical analysis, Nebr Hist, 71; Anti-imperialism on the middle border, 1898-1900, Midwest Rev, 79; Populism, Progressivism and the Transformation of Nebraska Politics, 1885-1915, Univ NE Press, 81; Lawrence Goodwyn and Nebraska Populism: A review essay, Gt Plains Quart, summer 81; Willa Cather and the Populists, Gt Plains Quart, 83; A Righteous Cause: The Life of William Jennings Bryan, Little, Brown, 85, reprint, Univ OK Press, 94; coauth, San Francisco, 1865-1932: Politics, Power, and Urban Development, Univ CA Press, 86; auth, Democratic Party in the Era of William Jennings Bryan, Democrats and the Am Idea, Center for Nat Policy Press, 92; City Commercial, City Beautiful, City Practical: The San Francisco Visions of Willliam Ralston, James Phelan, and Michael O'Shaughnessy, CA Hist, 95; coauth, Making America: A History of the United States, Houghton Mifflin, 95, 2nd ed, 99;auth, The Making of a Labor Radical: Harry Bridges, 1901-1934, Pacific Hist Rev, 95; William Jennnings Bryan and the Historians, NE Hist, 96; American Politics in the Gilded Age, 1868-1900, Harlan Davidson, 97. **CONTACT ADDRESS** Dept of Hist, San Francisco State Univ, 1600 Holloway Ave, San Francisco, CA, 94132-1740. **EMAIL** cherny@sfsu.edu

CHERRY, CHARLES L.

PERSONAL Born 07/30/1942, Baltimore, MD, m, 1968 **DISCIPLINE** ENGLISH LITERATURE, HISTORY OF PSYCHIATRY **EDUCATION** Loyola Col, Md, BA, 64; Univ NC, Chapel Hill, MA, 66, PhD(English), 68. **CAREER** Asst English, Univ NC, 65-68; asst prof, 68-77, dir honors prog, 72-77, assoc prof, 77-80, prof English, Villinova Univ, 80-; assoc acad vp, 79-94; chemn, English dept, 96-; Commun consult, fed govt & ins indust, 71-; Am Coun Educ fel & asst to pres of Univ Pa, 77-78; Cooper-Woods travel study grant, 77; Am Coun Educ fel, 77-78; Lilly Found fel hist of sci, 80; T Wistar Brown fel, Haverford Col, 82-83; A Quiet Haven: Quakers Moral Treatment and Asylum Reform, Fairleigh Dickinson Univ Press, 89. **MEMBERSHIPS** Nat Col Honors Coun; MLA; NCTE; Quaker Hist Soc. **RESEARCH** History of psychiatry; nineteenth century British literature; written communication. **SELECTED PUBLICATIONS** Auth, The apotheosis of desire: Dialectic and image in The French Revolution, Visions of the daughters of Albion, and the Preludium to America, Xavier Univ Studies, 7/69; William Blake and Mrs Grundy: Suppression of Visions of the daughters of Albion, Blake Newslett, 8/70; coauth, Contemporary Composition, Prentice-Hall, 70; One approach to a course in the methods of teaching composition, English Educ, 73; coauth, Write up the Ladder: A Communications Text, Goodyear, 76; auth, Friends Asylum, Morgan Hinchman, and moral insanity, Quaker Hist, spring 78; Scalpels and swords: The surgery of contingency planning, Educ Rec, fall 78; The southern retreat: Thomas Hodgkin and Archille-Louis Foville, Med Hist, London, 7/79. **CONTACT ADDRESS** Dept of English, Villanova Univ, 845 E Lancaster Ave, Villanova, PA, 19085. **EMAIL** ccherry@email.vill.edu

CHERRY, PAUL
PERSONAL Born 06/17/1934, Memphis, TN, m, 1963 **DISCIPLINE** MUSICOLOGY **EDUCATION** Duke, AB, 56; Eastman, MM, 58; Univ Colo, PhD, 80. **CAREER** Prof Mus, 37 yrs. **HONORS AND AWARDS** Outstanding Tchr. **MEMBERSHIPS** Am Musicol Soc; Mus Union. **RESEARCH** Music of Darius Milhaud. **SELECTED PUBLICATIONS** Le Train bleu, rev of Darius Milhaud's ballet performed in Paris, Nov, 93; Etudes sur des themes liturgiques cu Comtat-Venaissin: A Hidden Mahzor in an Unknown String Auartet by Darious Milhaud; Two 'Unknown' String Quartets by Darius Milhaud; A Cornucopia of Quartets: The String Quartets of Darius Milhaud; Ten Seconds to a Terrific Tone; Helpful Hints for the High Register, Clarinet Pedagocical articles. **CONTACT ADDRESS** Univ of South Dakota, Vermillion, SD, 57069. **EMAIL** pcherry@usd.edu

CHERU, FANTU
DISCIPLINE AFRICAN AND DEVELOPMENT STUDIES **EDUCATION** Colo Col, BA; Portland State Univ, MS, PhD. **CAREER** Prof, Am Univ. **HONORS AND AWARDS** Consult, UN. **SELECTED PUBLICATIONS** Auth, The Financial Implications of Divesting from South Africa: A Review of the Evidence; Underdevelopment and Unemployment in Kenya, Int Jour African Hist Studies, 88; The Silent Revolution in Africa: Debt, Development and Democracy, Zed Press, 89: Ethiopia: Options for Rural Development, Zed Press, 90, The Not So Brave New World: Rethinking Regional Integration in Post-Apartheid Southern Africa, Bradlow Occasional Paper Series 92. **CONTACT ADDRESS** American Univ, 4400 Massachusetts Ave, Washington, DC, 20016.

CHESSON, MICHAEL B.
DISCIPLINE HISTORY **EDUCATION** Col Wm & Mary, AB, ; Harvard Univ, PhD, 78. **CAREER** Teach fel, Harvard, 75-78; asst, 78-82, assoc, 82-96, PROF HIST, 96-, CHAIR DEPT HIST, 96-98, UNIV MASS, BOSTON. **CONTACT ADDRESS** Dept of History, Univ of Massachusetts, Boston, McCormack Hall, 100 Morrissey Blvd, Boston, MA, 02125-3393. **EMAIL** omohundro@aol.com

CHESTNUT, DENNIS EARL
PERSONAL Born 05/17/1947, Green Sea, South Carolina **DISCIPLINE** EDUCATION, PSYCHOLOGY **EDUCATION** East Carolina Univ, BA Psych & Soc 1965-69, MA Clinical Psych 1971; Univ of utah, Doc Prog Clin Psy 1971-74; NY Univ, PhD Comm Psych 1982. **CAREER** Camden Co MH Ctr, psychological consul 1974-75; Neuse Mental Health Ctr, qual assurance consult 1975-77; Medgar Evers Coll CUNY, instr psychology 1979-81; East Carolina Univ, asst prof psychol 1974-, prof of psychol. **HONORS AND AWARDS** Outstanding Sr Dept of Sociology E Carolina Univ 1969; NIMH Fellow Univ Utah 1971-74; NIMH Fellow NY Univ 1978; NEH Summer Stipend for study of Southern Black Culture 1982. **MEMBERSHIPS** Pres Young People's Holiness Assoc United Pentecostal Holiness Churches of Amer Inc; Alpha Phi Alpha Frat; natl treas Assoc of Black Psychologists 1983-84; organizational liaison Assoc for Humanistic Psychology 1983-84; s regional rep Assoc of Black Psychologists 1984-85; mem at large bd of dirs Assn for Humanistic Psychology 1984-85; reg rep NC Group Behavior Soc 1981-; vice bishop United Pentecostal Holiness Churches of Amer 1981-; pastor Mt Olive Holiness Church Tabor City NC 1984-; treas NC Assoc Black Psychologists; mem Pitt Cty Mental Health Assoc; pres NC Chap Assoc Black Psychologists 1986-87; dir Minority Affairs Assoc for Humanistic Psychology 1986-; co-chmn Natl Black Family Task Force of the Assoc of Black Psychologists. **CONTACT ADDRESS** Prof of Psychology, East Carolina Univ, Greenville, NC, 27834.

CHESTNUT, PAUL IVAR
PERSONAL Born 06/07/1939, Charleston, SC **DISCIPLINE** AMERICAN HISTORY **EDUCATION** Duke Univ, AB, 61, PhD(Am hist), 74; Yale Univ, BD, 64. **CAREER** Asst cur of manuscripts for reader serv, Perkins Libr, Duke Univ, 72-78; ASST STATE ARCHIVIST, VA STATE LIBRARY, 78-, Adj fac, Va Commonweatlh Univ, 80-81. **MEMBERSHIPS** Soc Am Archivists; Nat Asn State Archives & Records Adminr; Am Asn State & Local Hist. **RESEARCH** American religious and social history; archives administration. **SELECTED PUBLICATIONS** Auth, The Archival Imagination--Essays in Honor of Taylor, Hugh,A., Public Historian, Vol 0016, 94. **CONTACT ADDRESS** 221 N 25th St, Richmond, VA, 23223.

CHEYETTE, FREDRIC LAWRENCE
PERSONAL Born 01/13/1932, New York, NY, m, 1957, 3 children **DISCIPLINE** MEDIEVAL HISTORY **EDUCATION** Princeton Univ, AB, 53; Harvard Univ, MA, 55, PhD, 59. **CAREER** From instr to asst prof Hist, Stanford Univ, 59-61; asst prof, Oberlin Col, 62-63; from asst prof to assoc prof, 63-74, prof Hist, Amherst Col, 74-, Nat Endowment Humanities grant, 77-78; book rev, Speculum, 78-. **HONORS AND AWARDS** Webb-Smith Essay Prize, Univ Tex-Arlington, 77; A H Cole Prize, Econ Hist Asn, 77; Auggenheim fell, 83-84. **MEMBERSHIPS** Medieval Acad. **SELECTED PUBLICATIONS** Auth, Lordship and Community in Medieval Europe, Holt, 68; Origins of European villages, J Econ Hist, 77; The invention of the state, Walter P Webb Mem Lect (12), 78. **CONTACT ADDRESS** Dept of History, Amherst Col, Amherst, MA, 01002-5003. **EMAIL** flcheyette@amherst.edu

CHIARENZA, CARL
PERSONAL Rochester, NY **DISCIPLINE** ART HISTORY **EDUCATION** Roch Inst Tech, BFA, 57, MS, 59; Boston Univ, AM, 64; Harvard Univ, PhD, 73. **CAREER** Ch/dir/prof, Art Hist, Boston Univ, 64-86; ARTIST, ART HIST, & CRITIC, FANNY KNAPP ALLEN PROF, ART HIST, UNIV ROCH. **CONTACT ADDRESS** Dept Art & Art Hist, Univ Roch, Morey Hall 424, Rochester, NY, 14627. **EMAIL** ccrz@db1.cc.rochester.edu

CHILDS, ELIZABETH C.
PERSONAL Born 07/05/1954, Denver, CO, m, 1987, 1 child **DISCIPLINE** ART HISTORY **EDUCATION** Wake Forest Univ, BA, Art Hist & Anthrop, 76; Columbia Univ, MA, 80, PhD, 89. **CAREER** Intern/ consult/ lectr, Metro Museum Art, 76-82; curat consult, Peggy Guggenheim Coll, Venice, 84-85; res assoc, Contemp Am Art, Solomon R Guggenheim Museum, 87-91; asst prof, Art Hist, SUNY-Purchase Coll, 87-92; asst prof, Wash Univ, 93-98; ASSOC PROF, ART HIST & ARCHAEOL, WASH UNIV, 98-. **RESEARCH** Art & censorship; Nineteenth century French painting; Photography; Printmaking; Eroticism in modern art. **SELECTED PUBLICATIONS** In Search of Paradise: Painting and Photography in Tahiti, 1880-1910, Univ Calif Press, forthcoming; edr, Suspended License: Censorship and the Visual Arts, Univ Wash Press, 97; Making the News: Modernity and the Mass Press in Nineteenth-Century France, Univ Mass Press, 98. **CONTACT ADDRESS** Dept Art Hist & Archaeol, Wash Univ, One Brookings Dr, Campus Box 1189, St Louis, MO, 63130. **EMAIL** ecchilds@artsci.wustl.edu

CHILDS, FRANCINE C.
PERSONAL Born 0208, Wellington, Texas, s **DISCIPLINE** EDUCATION **EDUCATION** Paul Quinn Coll, BS 1962; East TX State Univ, MEd 1970, EdD 1975. **CAREER** Wiley Coll, dean of students 1970-72; East TX State Univ, part-time project dir special svcs/full time doctorial student 1972-74; Ohio Univ, prof afro-amer studies 1974-85, chair/prof afro-amer studies 1985-. **HONORS AND AWARDS** Paul Quin Coll Outstanding Alumni 1982; Individual Witness for Peace & Justice Awd 1985; OU Higher Educ Mgmt Develop Prog 1985-86; Outstanding Black Alumni Awd 1986; Fulbright Hays Scholarship 1986; Peace Corp Black Educator of Year, 1988-89; Anna Cooper Presidential Award, 1992; Phenomenal Woman Award, 1996; Marcus Foster Distinguished Educators Award, 1996; Ohio University Honorary Alumni Award, 1997. **MEMBERSHIPS** Local pres & advisor OH Univ Chap NAACP 1971-; mem League of Women Voters 1977-; educ chair OH Conf of Branches NAACP 1978-; natl coord Booker T Washington Alumni Assoc 1982-; prayer coord Athens Christian Women Club 1984-86; workshop leader Ohio Bapt Women Aux Convention 1985-; local conf host and progcomm Natl Cncl on Black Studies 1987; National Alliance of Blk School Education; Mt Zion Baptist Ch, assoc pastor, currently. **CONTACT ADDRESS** Prof African Amer Studies, Ohio Univ, 302 Lindley, Athens, OH, 45701.

CHINNICI, JOSEPH PATRICK
PERSONAL Born 03/16/1945, Altadena, CA **DISCIPLINE** HISTORY THEOLOGY **EDUCATION** San Luis Rey Col, BA, 68; Grad Theol Union, MA, 71; Franciscan Sch Theol, MDiv, 72; Oxford Univ, DPhil(hist, theol), 76. **CAREER** ASST PROF CHURCH HIST, FRANCISCAN SCH THEOL, 75- & ASST PROF, GRAD THEOL UNION, 75-, Univ Notre Dame travel grant, 78. **MEMBERSHIPS** AHA; Am Cath Hist Asn; US Cath Hist Soc. **RESEARCH** Church and the Enlightenment; American Catholicism; American religious history. **SELECTED PUBLICATIONS** Auth, The French Disease--The Catholic-Church and Radicalism in Ireland, 1790-1800, Amer Hist Rev, Vol 0101, 96. **CONTACT ADDRESS** Franciscan Sch of Theol, 1712 Euclid Ave, Berkeley, CA, 94709-1294.

CHIPMAN, DONALD EUGENE
PERSONAL Born 11/19/1928, Hill City, KS, m, 1955, 2 children **DISCIPLINE** LATIN AMERICAN HISTORY **EDUCATION** Ft Hays Kans State Col, AB, 55, MS, 58; Univ NMex, PhD(hist), 62. **CAREER** Teacher pub sch, Kans, 55-57; asst prof, Ft Hays Kans State Col, 62-64; assoc prof, 64-67, PROF HIST, NTEX STATE UNIV, 67-, Am Coun Learned Soc grant-in-aid, 63-64; ed hist gen, Handbk Latin Am Studies, 73-; Am Philos Soc grant-in-aid, 76. **MEMBERSHIPS** Latin Am Studies Asn; Conf Latin Am Hist. **RESEARCH** Mexican history. **SELECTED PUBLICATIONS** Auth, The Desoto Chronicles--The Expedition of Desoto,Hernando to North-America, 1539-1543, Volume 1, Southwestern Hist Quart, Vol 0097, 94; San-Antonio De Bexar--A Community on New-Spain Northern Frontier, Amer Hist Rev, Vol 0101, 96; The Desoto Chronicles--The Expedition of Desoto, Hernando to North-America, 1539-1543, Volume 2, Southwestern Hist Quart, Vol 0097, 94; Flags Along the Coast--Charting the Gulf-Of-Mexico, 1519-1759, Southwestern Hist Quart, Vol 0099, 95; Depineda, Alonso, Alvarez and The Rio-De-Las-Palmas--Scholars and the Mislocation of a River, Southwestern Hist Quart, Vol 0098, 95; Tejano Origins in 18th-Century San-Antonio, Hisp Amer Hist Rev, Vol 0072, 92; Tejanos and Texas Under the Mexican Flag, 1821-1836, Amer Hist Rev, Vol 0101, 96; The Dominguez-Escalante Journal, Southwestern Hist Quart, Vol 0099, 95; Spanish Observers and the American-Revolution, 1775-1778, Southwestern Hist Quart, Vol 0097, 93; To the Royal Crown Restored--The Journals of Don Vargas, Diego, De, New-Mexico, 1692-1694, Hisp Amer Hist Rev, Vol 0077, 97; Along Ancient Trails--The Mallet Expedition of 1739, Jour Amer Hist, Vol 0083, 96. **CONTACT ADDRESS** Dept of Hist, No Texas State Univ, PO Box 310650, Denton, TX, 76203-0650.

CHMIELEWSKI, WENDY E.
PERSONAL Born 11/06/1955, United Kingdom, s **DISCIPLINE** US HISTORY **EDUCATION** State Univ NY, BING, PhD 89, MA 81; Goucher Col, BA 77. **CAREER** Swathmore Col, Curator, Peace Collection, 88, lectr, peace studies 94. **MEMBERSHIPS** Peace Hist Soc; Communal Stud Asn. **RESEARCH** Women in intentional communities; women in 19th century peace movement **SELECTED PUBLICATIONS** Binding Themselves the Closer to Their Own Peculiar Duties: Gender and Women's Work for Peace, 1818-1860, Peace and Change, 95; Mid the Din a Dove Appeared: Women's Work in the Nineteenth-Century Peace Movement, in: Over Here, 97. **CONTACT ADDRESS** Swathmore Col Peace Collection, Swathmore Col, 500 College Av, Swathmore, PA, 19081. **EMAIL** wchmiel1@swathmore.edu

CHO, JOANNE M.
DISCIPLINE MODERN EUROPEAN AND GERMAN HISTORY **EDUCATION** Univ Chicago, MA, 84; Univ Calif, Los Angeles, BA, 83; Univ Chicago, PhD, 93. **CAREER** Asst prof, William Paterson Col, 95-; asst prof, Hope Col, 92-; tchg intern, Univ Chicago, 88-89; res asst, Univ Chicago, 84-90; acad serv, World Hist Comt, William Paterson Col, 95-96; fac adv to freshmen, Hope Col, 93-; AP Reader in Europ His, 94; Hope Col Rep, Midwest Fac Sem, Univ Chicago; Professionalization in the Mod World, 92; Pierre Bourdieu, 92. **HONORS AND AWARDS** DAAD post-doctoral res fel, Univ Tubingen, 95; Summer res grant, Hope Col, Mich, 94; Knight Found Grant, Hope Col, Mich, 93; Dissertation fel, Inst fur europaische Geschichte, Mainz, Ger, 91-92; Progetto Federico II, Int Workshop, Trani, Italy, 91; Awd, Ger Hist Inst & the Stiftung Volkswagenwerk, Herzog August Bibliothek in Wolfenbuttel, Ger, 90; Awd, Atlantic Coun of the US for a study-tour of NATO, 89; DAAD fel(s), Univat Regensburg, Ger, 87, Univat Mannheim, Ger, 86 & Univ Calif, Berkeley, 84; grad fel(s), Univ Chicago, 85-88. **MEMBERSHIPS** AHA, Ger Stud Asn; Ernst Troeltsch Gesellschaft. **RESEARCH** Mod European and German History; The Idea of Europeanism; German Liberalism; Ernst Troeltsch; Weimar Culture; The image of Asia in Mod Germany and Europe. **SELECTED PUBLICATIONS** Auth, The Crisis of Historicism and Troeltsch's Europeanism, Hist Europ Ideas, 95. **CONTACT ADDRESS** Dept of History, William Paterson Col, 300 Pompton Rd., Wayne, NJ, 07470. **EMAIL** jcho@frontier.wilpaterson.edu

CHOE, YONG-HO
PERSONAL Born 06/13/1931, Kyongsan, Korea, m, 1966, 2 children **DISCIPLINE** ASIAN HISTORY **EDUCATION** Univ Ariz, BA, 61; Univ Chicago, AM, 63, PhD(hist), 71. **CAREER** Res assoc Korean hist, EAsia Res Ctr, Harvard Univ, 68-70; asst prof, 70-77, ASSOC PROF HIST, UNIV HAWAII, MANOA, 77- **HONORS AND AWARDS** Phi Beta Kappa **MEMBERSHIPS** Asn Asian Studies; Korean Hist Asn; Acad Asn Koreanology Japan. **RESEARCH** Civil service examinations in traditional Korea; social structure in traditional Korea. **SELECTED PUBLICATIONS** Auth, Sino-Korean relations, 1866-1876: A study of Korea's tributary relationship to China, Asea Yon'fu, 3/66; Commoners in early Yi Dynasty civil examinations, J Asian Studies, 74; History in North Korea, J East &

West Studies, 5/76; The Civil Examinations & the Social Structure in Early Yi Korea, 87; co-ed, Sourcebook of Korean Civilisation, 2 vols, 93, 96; auth, Sources of Korean Tradition, 97. **CONTACT ADDRESS** Dept of History, Univ of Hawaii, Manoa, 2530 Dole St, Honolulu, HI, 96822-2303. **EMAIL** choeyh@hawaii.edu

CHOKSY, JAMSHEED K.
PERSONAL m, 1 child **DISCIPLINE** NEAR EASTERN, IRANIAN, INDIAN, CENTRAL EURASIAN AND MEDIEVAL STUDIES **EDUCATION** Columbia Univ, AB, 85; Harvard Univ, PhD, 91. **CAREER** Tchg Fel, 88, Jr Fel, 88-91, Harvard Univ; Vis Asst Prof, Stanford Univ, 91-93; Mem School of Hist Stud, Inst for Adv Stud, Princeton, 93-94; Asst Prof, 93-97, Assoc Prof, 97-98, Dir, UnderGrad Stud, 95-, Adj Assoc Prof, Grad Fac, 93-, Indiana Univ . **HONORS AND AWARDS** Andrew W. Mellon Found Fel, Stanford Univ, 91-93; NEH Fel at the Inst for Advanced Stud, Princeton, 93-94; Indiana Univ Outstanding Jr Fac Awd, 95-96; Amer Acad of Rel Ind Res Grant, 95-96; John Simon Guggenheim Mem Found Fel, 96-97. **RESEARCH** History; Religions, Archaeology, and Languages of the Near East and Inner Asia; Indian, Iranian, and Islamic Stud; History of Religions; Numismatics. **SELECTED PUBLICATIONS** Purity and Pollution in Zoroastrianism: Triumph Over Evil, Univ of TX Press, 89; Gesture in Ancient Iran and Central Asia I: The Raised Hand, Acta Iranica, 90; Gesture in Ancient Iran and Central Asia II; Proskynesis and the Bent Forefinger, Bul of the Asia Inst, 90; Conflict, Coexistence, and Cooperation: Muslims and Zoroastrians in Eastern Iran During the Medievel Period, The Muslim World, 90; An Emissary from Akbar to Abbas I: Inscriptions, Texts, and the Career of Amir Muhammad Masum al-Bhakkari, Jou of the Royal Asiatic Soc, 91; Doctrinal Variation with Zoroastrianism: The Notion of Dualism, Proced of the Sec Intl Congress of the K.R. Cama Oriental Inst, 96; Aging, Death, and the Afterlife in Zoroastrianism, How Different Rel View Death and Afterlife, 98. **CONTACT ADDRESS** Indiana Univ, Bloomington, Dept of Near East Lang, Goodbody H, Bloomington, IN, 47405. **EMAIL** jchoksy@indiana.edu

CHOLDIN, MARIANNA TAX
PERSONAL Born 02/26/1942, Chicago, IL, m, 1962, 2 children **DISCIPLINE** RUSSIAN AND SOVIET STUDIES **EDUCATION** Univ Chicago, BA, 62, MA, 67, PhD(librarianship), 79. **CAREER** Slavic bibliogr, Mich State Univ, 67-79; Slavic Bibliogr, Univ Ill Urbana-Champaign, 69-, RES DIR, RUSS & EAST EUROP CTR, UNIV ILL URBANA-CHAMPAIGN, 80-, dept affil, Grad Sch Libr & Info Sci, 80-; mem, exec comt, Midwest Slavic Conf, 81-84. **MEMBERSHIPS** Am Asn Advan Slavic Studies; Am Libr Asn; Midwest Slavic Conf. **RESEARCH** Russian and Soviet censorship; Russian bibliography; Russian history, culture and literature. **SELECTED PUBLICATIONS** Auth, Censorship in Soviet Literature, 1917-1991, Slavic Rev, Vol 0056, 97; Russian Libraries in Transition--An Anthology of Glasnost Literature, Slavic Rev, Vol 0051, 92. **CONTACT ADDRESS** Univ Ill, 1111 S Pine St, Champaign, IL, 61820.

CHOMSKY, AVIVA
DISCIPLINE HISTORY **EDUCATION** Univ Calif, Berkeley, BA, 82; Univ Calif, Berkeley, MA, 85; Univ Calif, Berkeley, PhD, 90. **CAREER** Teaching asst, Spanish Dept, Univ Calif, Berkeley, 85-87; teaching asst, Hist Dept, Univ Calif, Berkeley, 97-90; asst prof, Bates Col, 90-97; assoc prof, Salem State Col, 97-present. **HONORS AND AWARDS** Best Book Prize, New England Coun of Latin Am Studies; Fac Res Assoc, Inst for Health and Social Justice; Cuban Studies Travel Grant, Johns Hopkins Univ; vis scholar, Harvard Univ; Univ Fla Ctr for Latin Am Studies Library Travel Grant; Bates Col Mellon Professional Leave Grant; Bates Col McGinty Fac Res Grant; Bates Col Mellon Summer Res Grant; Bates Col Lincoln and Gloria Ladd Fac Res Grant; Mabelle McLeod Lewis Memorial Fund Dissertation Grant; Soc of Women Geographers Fel; Ctr for Latin Am Studies/Tinker Found Grant; Univ Calif Berkeley Hist Dept Outstanding Teaching Award; Comite Conjunto Hispano-Norteamericano para la Cooperacion Cultural y Educativa Cooperative Res Grant; Departmental Citation, Dept of Spanish and Portuguese, Univ Calif, Berkeley. **MEMBERSHIPS** Asn of Caribbean Historians; AHA; Latin Am Labor Hist Group; Latin Am Studies Asn; New England Council on Latin Am Studies; New England Historical Asn. **SELECTED PUBLICATIONS** Auth, West Indian Workers in Costa Rican Radical and Nationalist Ideology, 1900-1950, in The Americas: A Quarterly Review of Inter-American Cultural History 51:1, 94; auth, Labor in Coasta Rica's Gold Mines, 1900-1940, in Journal of Third World Studies XI:2, 94; auth, Recent Historiography of Cuba, in Latin American Research Review 29:3, 94; auth,Afro-Jamaican Traditions and Labor Organizing on United Fruit Company Plantations in Costa Rica, 1910, in Journal of Social History 28:4, 95; auth, West Indian Workers and the United Fruit Company in Costa Rica, 1870-1940, Louisiana State Univ Press, 96. **CONTACT ADDRESS** Dept of History, Salem State Col, Salem, MA, 01970. **EMAIL** achomsky@salem.mass.edu

CHRISLOCK, C. WINSTON
PERSONAL Born 11/08/1940, Owatonna, MN, m, 1965, 2 children **DISCIPLINE** MODERN HISTORY **EDUCATION** Univ Minn, Minneapolis, BA, 62; Ind Univ, Bloomington, MA, 64 PhD(hist), 71. **CAREER** Instr hist, Augsburg Col, 64-65; assoc, Ind Univ, Bloomington, 65-67; asst prof, Calif State Univ, Northridge, 68-73; asst prof, 72-80, from assoc prof to prof hist, Univ St Thomas, 80-91, prof hist, 91-; travelling prof, Nat Humanities Ser, Woodrow Wilson Found, 70, consult, 71; Nat Endowment for Humanities grant, 75-76. **MEMBERSHIPS** AHA; Am Asn Advan Slavic Studies. **RESEARCH** Modern Czechoslovak political, cultural and social history. **SELECTED PUBLICATIONS** Coauth, A more perfect union, an annotated bibliography, Nat Humanities Ser, 72; Charles Jonas: Czech National Liberal, Wisconsin Bourbon Democrat, Balch Press-Associated University Presses, 93, Cranbury, NJ. **CONTACT ADDRESS** Dept of History, Univ of St. Thomas, 2115 Summit Ave, St. Paul, MN, 55105-1096. **EMAIL** cwchrislock@stthomas.edu

CHRISMAN, MIRIAM USHER
PERSONAL Born 05/20/1920, Ithaca, NY, m, 1943, 2 children **DISCIPLINE** EARLY MODERN SOCIAL HISTORY **EDUCATION** Smith Col, AB, 41, MA, 55; Am Univ, MA, 48; Yale Univ, PhD(hist), 62. **CAREER** Res asst, Nat Planning Asn, 43-46; teacher, Tenacre Sch, Mass, 46-47, Bryn Mawr Sch, Md, 47-49 & Northampton Sch Girls, Mass, 49-59; instr hist, Smith Col, 55-57; from instr to assoc prof, 62-71, PROF HIST, UNIV MASS, AMHERST, 71- **MEMBERSHIPS** AHA; Am Soc Reformation Res (pres, 76-77); Sixteenth Century Studies Conf. **RESEARCH** Renaissance and Reformation; early modern social and intellectual history; early modern urban history. **SELECTED PUBLICATIONS** Auth, Blood and Belief--Family Survival and Confessional Identity Among the Provincial Huguenot Nobility, Church Hist, Vol 0064, 95; Always Among Us--Images of the Poor in Zwingli Zurich, Renaissance Quart, Vol 0045, 92. **CONTACT ADDRESS** Hist Dept, Univ of Mass, Amherst, MA, 01003.

CHRIST, MATTHEW R.
DISCIPLINE CLASSICAL STUDIES **EDUCATION** Carleton Col, BA, 82; Princeton Univ, PhD, 87. **CAREER** Asst prof. **RESEARCH** Greek Historiography; Athenian rhetoric and law; Athenian social history. **SELECTED PUBLICATIONS** Auth, Herodotean Kings and Historical Inquiry, 94; Liturgy Avoidance and Antidosis in Classical Athens, 90. **CONTACT ADDRESS** Dept of Classical Studies, Indiana Univ, Bloomington, 300 N Jordan Ave, Bloomington, IN, 47405.

CHRISTENSEN, CARL C.
PERSONAL Born 02/15/1935, Chicago, IL, m, 1960, 3 children **DISCIPLINE** RENAISSANCE & REFORMATION HISTORY **EDUCATION** State Univ Iowa, BA, 60; Ohio State Univ, MA, 61, PhD(hist), 65. **CAREER** From instr to asst prof, 65-70, assoc prof, 70-78, PROF HIST, UNIV COLO, BOULDER, 78-, Fac fel, Univ Colo, Boulder, 71; vis lectr hist, Univ Kent at Canterbury, 75-76. **MEMBERSHIPS** Am Soc Reformation Res; Sixteenth Century Studies Conf. **RESEARCH** Reformation and art in Germany. **SELECTED PUBLICATIONS** Auth, Municipal patronage and the crisis of the arts in Reformation Nuernberg, Church Hist, 6/67; D?rer's Four Apostles and the dedication as a form of Renaissance art patronage, Renaissance Quart, 67; Luther's theology and the uses of religious art, Lutheran Quart, 70; Iconoclasm and the preservation of ecclesiastical art in Reformation Nuernberg, Arch Reformations-Ges, 70; The Reformation and the decline of German art, Cent Europ Hist, 9/73; Patterns of iconoclasm in the early Reformation: Strasbourg and Basel, In: The Image and the Word: Confrontations in Judaism, Christianity and Islam, Scholars Press, 77; Art and the Reformation in Germany, Wayne State Univ, 79; Five biographical essays, In: The Holy Roman Empire: A Dictionary Handbook, Greenwood Press, 80; Reformation and Art, In: Reformation Europe: A Guide to Research, Ctr for Reformation Res, 82; John of Saxony's Diplomacy, 1529-1530: Reformation or Realpolitik?, The Sixteenth Century J 15, 84; Princes and Propaganda: Electoral Saxon Art of the Reformation, Sixteenth Century Journal Publ, Inc, 92; Art, In: The Oxford Encyclopedia of the Reformation, Oxford Univ Press, 96. **CONTACT ADDRESS** Dept of Hist, Univ of Colo, Box 234, Boulder, CO, 80309-0234.

CHRISTENSEN, JOHN E.
DISCIPLINE SPECIAL EDUCATION AND COMMUNICATION DISORDERS **EDUCATION** Dana Col, BS; Univ Nebr, Omaha, MS; Univ Kans, PhD. **CAREER** Asst prof, 80-86, dir, Speech-Lang-Hearing prog, 83-88, assoc prof, 86-, ch, dept Spec Educ & Commun Disorders, Univ Nebr, Omaha, 88-. **RESEARCH** Pre-referral practices. **SELECTED PUBLICATIONS** Coauth, Policy Issues Concerning Public School Choice and Special Education Programs, Case In Point: J of Coun of Adminr, 6(1), 91. **CONTACT ADDRESS** Univ Nebr, Omaha, 60th & Dodge Sts, Kayser Hal, Omaha, NE, 68182-0054. **EMAIL** jechrist@unomaha.edu

CHRISTENSEN, KERRY A.
DISCIPLINE CLASSICS **EDUCATION** Swarthmore Col, BA, 81; Princeton Univ, MA, 83; PhD, 93. **CAREER** Classics Dept, Williams Col **RESEARCH** Greek social and political history of the archaic era; Greek and Roman civic identity and models of leadership; ancient historiography; Greek cult and ritual. **SELECTED PUBLICATIONS** Auth, The Theseion: a Slave Refuge at Athens, Amer J Ancient Hist 9, 84; Solon's Mania: Forms of Public Discourse in Archaic Athens, Bryn Mawr Classics Colloquia, Bryn Mawr Col, 87-88; Kleisthenes, Ajax, and the Athenian Incorporation of Salamis, APA/AIA Annual Meeting, Atlanta, 94. **CONTACT ADDRESS** Classics Dept, Williams Col, Stetson Hall D28, Williamstown, MA, 01267. **EMAIL** kchriste@williams.edu

CHRISTENSEN, MICHAEL
DISCIPLINE THEOLOGY; RELIGIOUS STUDIES; HISTORICAL THEOLOGY **EDUCATION** Point Loma Col, BA, 77; Yale Univ Divinity School, MA, 81; M.Phil, 95, PhD, 97, Drew Univ. **CAREER** Asst Prof, 97-, Dir of Doctor of Ministry Program, 95-, Drew Univ. **HONORS AND AWARDS** John Wesley Fel, 93-97; Will Herberg Merit Scholarship, Drew Univ, 93-96; Crossroads Scholar Program (research stipend for writing public policy monograph on nuclear issues in former Soviet Union), 94-96; Research Fel, Newark Project, 94-95; Recipient of the Helen Le Page and William Hale Chamberlain Prize awarded for the PhD Dissertation that is singularly distinguished by creative thought and excellent prose style, 97; Recipient of the Martin Luther King Jr. and Abraham Joshua Heschel Humanitarian Award for Spirituality and Social Justice, 98; Research Fel, Senior Research Scholar for Russia, The Princeton Project on Youth, Globalization and the Church, 98-01. **MEMBERSHIPS** Amer Acad of Religion; Phi Delta Lamba Honor Soc; The Patristic Soc; Soc for the Study of Eastern Orthodoxy and Evangelicalism; Charles Williams Soc. **RESEARCH** Theology and Culture; Russian Eschatology; Spirituality **SELECTED PUBLICATIONS** Auth, C.S. Lewis on Scripture, 79 (reprinted 96), Coauth, Children of Chernobyl: Raising Hope from the Ashes, 93; Auth, AIDS Ministry and the Article of Death: A Wesleyan Pastoral Theological Perspective, Catalyst, 95; Theosis and Sanctification: John Wesley's Reformulation of a Pastoric Doctrine, Wesleyan Theological Journal, 96; Evangelical-Orthodox Dialogue in Russia, The Journal of Ecumenical Studies, 96; Evangelism, Ecumenism and Mission, Religion in Eastern Europe, 96; The World after Chernobyl: Social Impact and Christian Response, Crossroads Monograph Series on Faith and Public Policy, 97. **CONTACT ADDRESS** Drew Univ, 12 Campus Dr., Madison, NJ, 07940. **EMAIL** mchriste@drew.edu

CHRISTENSON, ALLEN J.
PERSONAL Born 08/21/1957, Sherman Oaks, CA, m, 1980, 3 children **DISCIPLINE** ART HISTORY **EDUCATION** Brigham Young Univ, BS, 80; UCLA, DDS, 84; Univ Tx Austin, MA, 96, PhD, 98. **CAREER** Instr, Merced Col, 85-90; instr to asst prof, Brigham Young Univ, 90- . **MEMBERSHIPS** CAA; AAA. **RESEARCH** Maya ethnology, art history **SELECTED PUBLICATIONS** Auth, Bare Bones and the Divine Right of Kings: The Carved Femurs of Chiapa de Corzo, Mexico, Univ of Tx Austin, 96; Prehistory of the K'iche'an People of Highland Guatemala, Univ of Tx, 96; The World Tree of the Ancient Maya, BYU Stud, 97; Sealing the Mountain of the Ancients: The Altarpiece of Santiago Atitlan, Univ Tx Austin, 98; Popol Vuh, BYU Press, 99. **CONTACT ADDRESS** 2975 N Iroquois Dr, Provo, UT, 84604. **EMAIL** allen_christenson@byu.edu

CHRISTIAN, GARNA
PERSONAL Born 01/06/1935, Houston, TX, m, 1958, 2 children **DISCIPLINE** HISTORY **EDUCATION** Mex City Col, BA, 59; Texas W Col, MA, 61; Texas Tech Univ, PhD, 77. **CAREER** S Texas Jr Col, 62-73; prof of History, Univ Houston-Downtown, 74-; E Texas Hist Asn Ottis Lock Award Excellence Tchg, 85. **HONORS AND AWARDS** T R Fehrenback Award Texas Hist Comn; State & local Hist Asn; Hum Rights Found. **MEMBERSHIPS** Texas State Hist Asn; E Texas Hist Asn; S Conf Afro-Am Cult. **RESEARCH** Texas history; Black history; Music history. **SELECTED PUBLICATIONS** Black Soldiers in Jim Crow Texas 1899-1917, Texas A&M Univ Press, 95; articles on black military in Texas, country music, and jazz. **CONTACT ADDRESS** Univ Houston-Downtown, One Main St, Houston, TX, 77002. **EMAIL** Christian@DT3.DT.UH.EDU

CHRISTIANSON, ERIC HOWARD
PERSONAL Born 11/24/1946, Peoria, IL, 1 child **DISCIPLINE** HISTORY **EDUCATION** Univ Southern Calif, AB, 68, AM, 70, PhD(hist), 76. **CAREER** Instr, 75-76, ASST PROF HIST, UNIV KY, 76- **MEMBERSHIPS** Am Assoc Hist Med; Soc Social Studies Sci; Am Soc Eighteenth Century Studies. **RESEARCH** History of science and medicine post-1700; quantitative methods; United States social history. **SELECTED PUBLICATIONS** Auth, Medical Protestants--The Eclectics in American Medicine, Isis, Vol 0086, 95; Surgeons, Smallpox, and the Poor--History of Medicine and Social Conditions in Nova-Scotia, 1749-1799, Amer Hist Rev, Vol 0100, 95. **CONTACT ADDRESS** Dept of Hist, Univ Ky, 500 S Limestone St, Lexington, KY, 40506-0003.

CHRISTIANSON, GALE EDWARD
PERSONAL Born 06/29/1942, Charles City, IA **DISCIPLINE** MODERN HISTORY, HISTORY OF SCIENCE **EDUCATION** Univ IA, BA, 64; Univ Northern IA, MA, 66; Carnegie-Mellon Univ, DA, 71. **CAREER** Instr hist, Northern IA Area Community Col, 66-69 & Carnegie-Mellon Univ, 69-71; asst prof, 71-75, assoc prof, 75-80, prof hist, IN State Univ, 80, IN State Univ Fac Res Comt res grants, 72 & 73; Am Philos Soc res grant, 72-73, Am Coun of Learned Soc grant, 84, Am Inst of Physics grant, 91, Nat Endowment for the Hum summer stipend, 91, Fletcher Jones Foun fel: The Huntington Lib, 91, John Simon Guggenheim Mem Fel, 92. **HONORS AND AWARDS** Distinguished Prof, Col Arts & Sci, IN State Univ, 87, First Place Award: Prof Papers, Nineteenth Annual Dakota Hist Conf, 88, Loren Eiseley Medal, 95, Science Writing Award, Rockwell Int, 97. **MEMBERSHIPS** AHA; AAUP; Hist of Sci Soc. **SELECTED PUBLICATIONS** Auth, This Wild Abyss: The Story of the Men who Made Modern Astronomy, The Free Press/Macmillan, 78; In the Presence of the Creator: Isaac Newton and His Times, The Free Press/Macmillan, 84; Fox at the Wood's Edge: A Biography of Loren Eiseley, Henry Holt, 90; Writing Lives is the Devil! Essays of a Biographer at Work, Archon Books, 93; Edwin Hubble: Mariner of the Nebulae, Farrar, Straus and Giroux, 95; Isaac Newton and the Scientific Revolution, Oxford Univ Press, 96 **CONTACT ADDRESS** Dept of Hist, Indiana State Univ, 210 N 7th St, Terre Haute, IN, 47809-0002. **EMAIL** Higalee@ruby.indstate.edu

CHRISTIANSON, JOHN ROBERT
PERSONAL Born 01/21/1934, Mankato, MN, m, 1964, 1 child **DISCIPLINE** SCANDINAVIAN HISTORY **EDUCATION** Mankato State Col, BA, 56; Univ Minn, Minneapolis, MA, 59 PhD(hist), 64. **CAREER** Asst prof hist, Univ SDak, 64-66; vis asst prof, Univ Minn, Minneapolis, 66-67; assoc prof, 67-72, PROF HIST, LUTHER COL, IOWA, 72-, CHMN DEPT, 67-, Asst dir, Norweg-Am Mus, 69-; exec bd mem, Norweg-Am Hist Asn, 71-; Am Coun Learned Socs fel & George C Marshall Mem Fund in Denmark grant, 73-74; mem, 16th Century Studies Coun, 76- **MEMBERSHIPS** AHA; Soc Advan Scand Studies; Am-Scand Found; Norweg-Am Hist Asn. **RESEARCH** Tycho Brahe; 16th century Denmark; Scandinavian population movements. **SELECTED PUBLICATIONS** Auth, Vanderschardt, Johan, Gregor--Sculptor Associated with Maximilian-II, The Danish Court and Brahe, Tycho - Ger, Scandinavian Stud, Vol 0067, 95; The Cultural Landscape During 6000 Years in Southern Sweden--The Ystad Project, Scandinavian Stud, Vol 0069, 97; Nordic Science in Historical-Perspective--, Isis, Vol 0086, 95; Norway--A History From the Vikings to Our Own Times, Scandinavian Stud, Vol 0069, 97; The Renaissance of the Goths in 16th-Century Sweden--Magnus, Johannes and Magnus, Olaus as Politicians and Historians, Scandinavian Stud, Vol 0065, 93; Brahe, Tyge--Danish, Scandinavian Stud, Vol 0068, 96; Scandinavia in the European World-Economy, Ca.1570-1625--Some Local Evidence of Economic-Integration, Scandinavian Stud, Vol 0068, 96. **CONTACT ADDRESS** Dept of Hist, Luther Col, Decorah, IA, 52101.

CHRISTIE, JEAN
PERSONAL Manila, Philippines, m, 2 children **DISCIPLINE** UNITED STATES HISTORY **EDUCATION** Columbia Univ, PhD(Am hist), 63. **CAREER** Lectr hist, Brooklyn Col, 55-58 & 59-60; instr, Vassar Col, 59; lectr, Hunter Col, 60-62 & Bronx Community Col, 62-63; lectr, 63-64, from asst prof to assoc prof, 64-75, prof, 75-77, EMER PROF HIST, FAIRLEIGH DICKINSON UNIV, TEANECK CAMPUS, 77-, Fairleigh Dickinson Univ fac res grant, 77-78. **MEMBERSHIPS** Berkshire Conf Women Historians; Conf Group on Women's Hist; AHA; Orgn Am Historians; Conf Peace Res in Hist. **RESEARCH** Conservation movement; women in the 1920's. **SELECTED PUBLICATIONS** Auth, Machine-Age Ideology--Social Engineering and American Liberalism, 1911-1939, Tech and Cult, Vol 0036, 95; Steinmetz-- Engineer and Socialist, Tech and Cult, Vol 0034, 93. **CONTACT ADDRESS** Fairleigh Dickinson Univ, 34 Bellingham Ln, Great Neck, NY, 11023.

CHRISTMAN, CALVIN LEE
PERSONAL Born 07/12/1942, Lakewood, OH, m, 1968, 2 children **DISCIPLINE** UNITED STATES HISTORY **EDUCATION** Dartmouth Col, AB, 64; Vanderbilt Univ, MA & MAT, 66; OH State Univ, PhD, 71. **CAREER** Instr hist, Mid TN State Univ, 66-68 & OH State Univ, 71-72; assoc prof hist & govt, William Penn Col, 72-76; prof, Mountain View Col, 76-77; prof hist, Cedar Valley Col, 77-, vis assoc prof, Univ IA, spring, 76; vis assoc prof, Univ North TX, 91-92. **HONORS AND AWARDS** Outstanding Educr Am, Outstanding Educrs Am, Washington DC, 74; Who's Who Among Am(s) Tchr(s), 94, 94, 96 & 97; Who's Who in the South and Southwest, 95. **MEMBERSHIPS** Inter-Univ Sem Armed Serv & Soc; Soc Historians Am For Rel; Soc for Mil Hist; World War Two Studies Assoc. **RESEARCH** Am mil hist; World War II and postwar defense policy; historiography. **SELECTED PUBLICATIONS** Auth, The Chaco War: A tentative bibliography of its diplomacy, Americas, 7/69; Charles A Beard, Ferdinand Eberstadt and America's postwar security, Mid-Am, 7/72; Donald Nelson and the army: Personality as a factor in civil-military relations during World War II, Mil Affairs, 10/73; contribr, A Guide to the Sources of United States Military History, Archon, 75; coauth, Doctoral dissertations in military affairs, Mil Affairs, 2/78, Diplomatic History, spring 79, spring 80, spring 81 & spring 82; contribr, A Guide to the Sources of United States Military History: Supplement I, Archon, 81; Co-ed, War and the Southwest, series, Univ North Tex Press; Contribur & auth, Franklin D Roosevelt and the Craft of Strategic Assessment, In: Calculations: Net Assessment and the Coming of World War II (Williamson Murray & Allan Millett, ed), The Free Press, 92; Ed, America at War, Naval Inst Press, 95; Ed, Lost in the Victory: Reflections of American War Orphans of World War II, Univ North Tex Press, 98. **CONTACT ADDRESS** Dept of Liberal Arts, Cedar Valley Col, 3030 N Dallas Ave, Lancaster, TX, 75134-3799. **EMAIL** cchristman@ollie.dcccd.edu

CHU, JONATHAN M.
DISCIPLINE HISTORY **EDUCATION** Univ Penn, AB, 67; Univ Hawaii, MA, 69; Univ Wash, PhD, 78; Yale Univ, MS, Law, 83. **CAREER** ASSOC PROF, HIST, UNIV MASS BOSTON **MEMBERSHIPS** Am Antiquarian Soc **SELECTED PUBLICATIONS** Auth, "Historiographical Developments in Early American Quakerism: A Reply," So Friend, Fall, 91; auth, "Debt Litigation & Shay's Rebellion," in Debt to Shay's, Univ Va Press, 92; "Does History Begin at Jamestown and Plymouth?," OAH Mag of Hist, Fall, 96; auth, "Debt and Taxes: Public Finance and Private Economic Behavior in Post-Revolutionary Massachusetts," in Massachusetts Historical Society Studies in American History and Culture. **CONTACT ADDRESS** Dept of Hist, Univ of Mass-Boston, 1000 Morrissey Blvd, Boston, MA, 02125. **EMAIL** chuj@umbsky.cc.umb.edu

CHU, PAO-CHIN
PERSONAL Born 08/05/1928, Ho-pei, China, m, 1961, 2 children **DISCIPLINE** CHINESE HISTORY **EDUCATION** Nat Taiwan Univ, BA, 54; Univ PA, MA, 62, PhD, 70. **CAREER** Interpreter Eng-Chinese, Combat Air Command, Chinese Air Force, 55-57; asst prof, 67-70, assoc prof, 71-81, prof Chinese hist, San Diego State Univ, 82-, dir, Center for Asian Studies, 81-84, dir, China Studies Inst, 88-90, 95-96. **MEMBERSHIPS** AHA; Asn Asian Studies. **RESEARCH** Diplomatic hist of Republican China, 1912-1949; hist of the Chinese Communist Party, 1919-1949. **SELECTED PUBLICATIONS** The Impact of External War: The Demise of Chiang's China, In: Civil Wars in the Twentieth Century (Robin Higham, ed), Univ KY, 72; V K Wellington Koo: Diplomacy of Nationalism, In: Diplomats in Crisis: The Coming of the Pacific War (E Bennett and R D Burns, ed), Clio Press, 74; From Paris Peace Conference to Manchurian Incident: The Diplomacy of Resistance Against Japan (Hilary Conroy and Alvin Coox, ed), Clio Press, 78; V K Wellington Koo: A Case Study of China's Diplomat and Diplomacy of Nationalism, 1912-1966, Chinse Univ Hong Kong Press, 81; Yen Hui-ch'ing, In: Biographical Dictionary of Modern Peace Leaders (Harold Josephson, ed), Greenwood Press, 85; The American View of China, 1957-1982: the Personal Experience of a China-born Sinologist, In: America Views China: American Images of China Then and Now (Jonathan Goldstein, Jerry Israel, Hilary Conroy, ed), Assoc Univ Presses, 91; Sheng Hsuan-huai and the Self-Protection of the Southeastern Provinces during the Boxer Movement, In: Yi-he-tuan yun-dong yu jin-dai Zhongguo she-hui guo-je xue-so tao-lung hui lung-wen-je (Collected Papers of the Int Conf on Boxer Movement and the Modern Chinese Society), Jinan, Qi-lu Press, 92. **CONTACT ADDRESS** Dept of Hist, San Diego State Univ, 5500 Campanile Dr, San Diego, CA, 92182-0002.

CHU, PETRA
PERSONAL Born 10/15/1942, Zeist, Netherlands, m, 1971, 4 children **DISCIPLINE** ART HISTORY **EDUCATION** Diplome superieur du Cours de civilisation Francaise, 60-61; Utrecht Univ, doctoraal, 61-67; Columbia Univ, PhD, 67-72. **CAREER** Res, Institut Neerlandais, 65-72; vis prof, Princeton Univ, 90-92; prof, Seton Hall Univ, 72-. **HONORS AND AWARDS** Institute for Advanced Study, Princeton, 90; Wheatland Found, 90; John Simon Guggenheim Memorial Found, 91; Nat Endowment, 94; Jane and Morgan Whitney Art Hist Fel, 94-95. **SELECTED PUBLICATIONS** Auth, French Realism and the Dutch Masters, 74; auth, Courbet in Perspective, 77; auth, Dominique Vivant Denon, 85; auth, The Letters of Gustave Courbet, 92; auth, The Popularization of Images, 94. **CONTACT ADDRESS** Dept of Art and Music, Seton Hall Univ, 400 S Orange Ave, South Orange, NJ, 07079-2697. **EMAIL** chupetrt@shu.edu

CHU, PETRA TEN-DOESSCHATE
PERSONAL Born 10/15/1942, Zeist, Netherlands, m, 1972, 4 children **DISCIPLINE** ART HISTORY **EDUCATION** Sorbonne, Paris, Diplome superieur du Cours de civilsation francaise, 60-61; Utrecht Univ, Doctoral degree, 61-67; Columbia Univ, PhD, 67-72. **CAREER** PROF, DEPT OF ART AND MUSIC, 72-, DEPT CHAIR, SETON HALL UNIV, 79-98; visiting prof, Princeton Univ, 90-92. **HONORS AND AWARDS** Jane and Morgan Whitney Art Hist Fel, Metropolitan Museum of Art, 94-95; Nat Endowment/Humanities Res Grant, 86-88, & 94; John Simon Guggenheim Memorial Found Pub Grant, 91; Translation Grant, Wheatland Found, 90; Guggenheim Fel, 86-87; Grant, New Jersey Dept of Higher Ed, 85; ZWO Pub Grant, 74; Seton Hall Univ Res Grants, 73, 81, 82, 84, & 92; Columbia Univ Noble Fel, 67-71. **RESEARCH** French nineteenth-century painting (Realism/Courbet); Dutch seventeenth-century painting. **SELECTED PUBLICATIONS** Auth, Frank Buchser im Kontext, Frank Buchser 1828-1890, 90 & 96; auth, Bound by a Shared Heritage: The Interplay Between Dutch and French Landscape Painting during the Nineteenth Century, Langs Velden en Wegen: De Verbeelding van het landschap in de 18e 19e eeuw, 97; auth, Pop Culture in the Making: The Romantic Craze for History, The Popularization of Images: Visual Culture under the July Monarchy (1830-1848), Princeton Univ Press, 94; auth, Emblems for a Modern Age: The Still Lifes of Vincent van Gogh, The Object as Subject: Studies in the Interpretation of Still Life, Princeton Univ Press, 96; La Correspondance de Gustave Courbet, Nouvelles approches de l'epistolair. Lettres d'artistes, archives, et correspondances, Honore Champion, 96; auth, Directeur vs Amateur: The Public and Private Collections of Dominique Vivant Denon, Patrocinio, Collecion y Circulacion de las Artes, Universidad Nat Autonoma de Mex, 98. **CONTACT ADDRESS** Dept of Art and Music, Seton Hall Univ, South Orange, NJ, 07079. **EMAIL** chupetrt@shu.edu

CHU, SAMUEL C.
PERSONAL Born 03/25/1929, China, m, 1957, 3 children **DISCIPLINE** EAST ASIAN HISTORY **EDUCATION** Dartmouth Col, AB, 51; Columbia Univ, MA, 53, PhD, 58. **CAREER** Res asst China, Human Rels Area Files, Yale Univ, 55-58; asst prof hist, State Univ NY Col New Paltz, 58 & Bucknell Univ, 58-60; assoc prof, Univ Pittsburgh, 60-69; PROF HIST & DIR E ASIAN PROG, OHIO STATE UNIV, 69-, Vis assoc prof hist, Univ Mich, 57-58; Fulbright res grant, Formosa, 61-62; Soc Sci Res Coun exchange scholar, Formosa, 65-66; Am Coun Learned Socs sr res fels, 74-75; mem US solid state physics deleg to China, Nat Acad Sci, 75. **MEMBERSHIPS** Nat Comt US-China Rels; Asia Soc; Asn Asian Studies; AHA; AAUP. **RESEARCH** Modern Chinese history; institutional history; Japanese history. **SELECTED PUBLICATIONS** Auth, China in World-History, Historian, Vol 0058, 96. **CONTACT ADDRESS** Dept of Hist, Ohio State Univ, Columbus, OH, 43210.

CHUDACOFF, HOWARD PETER
PERSONAL Born 01/21/1943, Omaha, NE, m, 1967 **DISCIPLINE** UNITED STATES HISTORY **EDUCATION** Univ Chicago, BA 65, MA 67, PhD 69. **CAREER** Vis asst prof, Univ Cincinnati, 69-70; from asst to prof, hist, 70-92, Brown Univ, now Univ Prof & Prof of History, 92- . **MEMBERSHIPS** Am Hist Asn; Orgn of Am Hist; Urban Hist Asn. **RESEARCH** United States urban and social history. **SELECTED PUBLICATIONS** Auth, How Old Are You? Age Consciousness in American Culture, Princeton, 89; coauth, A People and a Nation, 3d through 6th ed, 90, 94, 97, 20000; Houghton Mifflin; auth, Major Problems in American Urban History, Heath, 93; coauth, The Evolution of American Urban Society, 4th ed, 93, 5th ed, 99, Prentice-Hall; auth, The Age of the Bachelor: Creating an American Subculture, Princeton, 99. **CONTACT ADDRESS** 84 Cole Ave, Providence, RI, 02906. **EMAIL** Howard_Chudacoff@Brown.edu

CHUNG, SUE FAWN
PERSONAL Los Angeles, CA, m, 1980, 2 children **DISCIPLINE** CHINESE & JAPANESE HISTORY **EDUCATION** Univ CA, Los Angeles, BA, 65; Harvard Univ, AM, 67; Univ CA, Berkeley, PhD, 75. **CAREER** Lectr, San Francisco State Univ, 71-73; tchg asst, Univ CA, Berkeley, 71-73; asst prof, 75-79, assoc prof hist, Univ NV, Las Vegas, 79. **HONORS AND AWARDS** Distinguished Nevadan, NV Hum Comt, 96; Rita Abbey Tchg Award, UNLV Col Lib Arts, 98. **MEMBERSHIPS** AHA; Asn Asian Studies; Asn Asian Am Studies; Org Am Hist. **RESEARCH** Empress Dowager Ci Xi (1835-1908); Chinese in Nevada; governor-general Liu Kunyi. **SELECTED PUBLICATIONS** Auth, The image of the Empress Dowager Tz'u-hsi, In: Reform in Nineteenth Century China, Harvard Univ Press, 76; Their Changing World: Chinese Women on the Comstock, In: Comstock Women: The Other Side of Bonanza, Nev Univ Press, 97; Fighting for Their American Rights: A History of the Chinese American Citizens Alliance, In: Claiming America: Constructing Chinese American Identities during the Exclusion Era, Temple Univ Press, 98; auth of numerous other works. **CONTACT ADDRESS** Dept of Hist, Univ of NV, Las Vegas, PO Box 455020, Las Vegas, NV, 89154-5020. **EMAIL** chung@nevada.edu

CHURCHER, BETTY
DISCIPLINE CULTURAL HISTORY **CAREER** Dir, Art Gallery of West Austral and Natl Gallery, Canberra; res assoc, Ctr Cross-Cult Res, Australian Natl Univ. **RESEARCH** Art education; Australian art. **SELECTED PUBLICATIONS** Auth, The Museum of Modern Art, New York, 1933-1943: The Influence of Its Exhibitions Program on the Work of Jackson Pollock & Arshile Gorky, Courtauld Inst of Art, 97. **CONTACT ADDRESS** Dept of Education, Australian National Univ. **EMAIL** Betty.Churcher@anu.edu.au

CHURCHILL, FREDERICK BARTON
PERSONAL Boston, MA **DISCIPLINE** HISTORY OF BIOLOGY **EDUCATION** Harvard Univ, AB, 55, PhD(hist of sci), 67; Columbia Univ, MA, 61. **CAREER** Lectr, 66-67, asst prof, 67-70, assoc prof, 70-80, PROF HIST & PHILOS OF SCI,

IND UNIV, BLOOMINGTON, 80-, Ed, Mendel Newsletter, 76- **MEMBERSHIPS** AAAS; Hist Sci Soc; Am Asn Hist Med. **RESEARCH** History of biology. **SELECTED PUBLICATIONS** Auth, The Discovery of Meiosis and the Centorsome by Vanbeneden, Edouard-- French, Hist and Philos of the Life Sci, Vol 0018, 96; Styles of Scientific Thought--The German Genetics Community 1900-1933, Soc Hist of Med, Vol 0008, 95. **CONTACT ADDRESS** Dept of Hist & Philos of Sci, Indiana Univ, Bloomington, Bloomington, IN, 47401.

CHUSID, MARTIN
PERSONAL Born 08/19/1925, Brooklyn, NY, m, 1952, 1 child **DISCIPLINE** MUSIC HISTORY **EDUCATION** Univ Calif, Berkeley, AB, 50, AM, 55, PhD, 61. **CAREER** From instr to asst prof music hist, Univ Southern Calif, 59-63; assoc prof music, 63-68, chmn dept, 67-70, assoc dean grad sch arts & sci, 70-72, PROF MUSIC, NY UNIV, 68-, DIR, AM INST VERDI STUDIES, 76-, Am Coun Learned Socs sr fel, 74; mem screening comt music, Sr Fulbright-Hays Awards, 75-78, chmn, 77-78; Nat Endowment for Humanities grants, 77 & 77-79. **HONORS AND AWARDS** DHL, Centre Col Ky, 77. **MEMBERSHIPS** Am Musicol Soc; Int Musicol Soc; Int Music Libr Asn; Am Inst for Verdi Stud; Beethoven Soc; Am Schubert Inst. **RESEARCH** Music of Verdi, Schubert and Mozart. **SELECTED PUBLICATIONS** Auth, Schubert's overture for string quintet and Cherubini's overture to Faniska, J Am Musicol Soc, 62; Schubert's cyclic compostions of 1824, Acta Musicol, 64; The significance of D minor in Mozart's dramatic music, Mozart-Jahrbuch 1965-66, 67; auth & ed, Schubert's Symphony in B Minor (Unfinished): Essays in History and Analysis, a Critical Edition, Norton, 68, 2nd ed, 71; ed, Franz Schubert Streichquintette, Streichquartette vol.1, Neue Schubert-Ausgabe, Barenreiter, Ser VI, Vols II & III, 71 & 78; auth, Rigoletto and Monterone: A Study in Musical Dramaturgy, Report XI Congr, Int Musicol Soc, 72, Hansen, 74; A Catalog of Verdi's Operas, Boonin, 74; co-ed, A Verdi Companion, Norton, 79; ed, Rigoletto, the works of Guisseppe Verdi, 83; Verdi's Middle Period, Univ Chicago 97. **CONTACT ADDRESS** Dept of Music, New York Univ, 24 Waverly Pl, New York, NY, 10003-6757. **EMAIL** mc4@is6.nyu.edu

CHYET, STANLEY F.
DISCIPLINE AMERICAN JEWISH HISTORY **EDUCATION** Brandeis Univ; Hebrew Union Col, PhD, 60. **CAREER** Prof; ordained, HUC-JIR, Cincinnati, 57; fac, HUC-JIR, Cincinnati, 60-; fac, HUC-JIR, Los Angeles, 76-. **SELECTED PUBLICATIONS** Pub(s), Amer Jewish history and liturature translations of 20th Century Israeli Poetry. **CONTACT ADDRESS** Hebrew Union College-Jewish Institute Of Religion, Univ Southern Calif, University Park Campus, Los Angeles, CA, 90089.

CIENCIALA, ANNA M.
PERSONAL Born 11/08/1929, Gdansk, Poland **DISCIPLINE** EUROPEAN DIPLOMATIC HISTORY WITH EMPHASIS ON POLAND **EDUCATION** Univ Liverpool, BA, 52; McGill Univ, MA, 55; Ind Univ, PhD(mod Europ hist), 62. **CAREER** Lectr Europ & Russ hist, Univ Ottawa, 61-62; Instr, Univ Toronto, 62-65; from asst prof to assoc prof, 65-71, PROF E EUROP & RUSS HIST, UNIV KANS, 71-; res dir, Kans Studies Poznan, 71; mem, Kosciuszko Found, Polish Inst Arts & Sci. **HONORS AND AWARDS** Res grants, Univ Kans, 65-68, 70 & 72, Fulbright-Hays NDEA fac fel, 68-69; other grants and fellowships from NEH, IREX, ACLS, Lawrence, Ks, Kosciuszko Found, Univ Kans. **MEMBERSHIPS** Am Asn Advan Slavic Studies; Polish Am Hist Asn; AAUP; Polish Inst Arts & Sci Am; Joseph Pilsudski Inst Am. **RESEARCH** European history 1914-1945; modern East European history. **SELECTED PUBLICATIONS** Auth, Poland and the Western powers, 1938-1938, Univ Toronto, 68; co-ed, Sir James Headlam-Morley, a memoir of the Paris Peace Conference 191 9, London, 72; coauth, From Versailles to Locarno. Keys to Polish Foreign Policy, 1919-1925, Lawrence, Ks, 84; ed, annotated version of: Jozef Beck, Polska Polityka Zagraniczna, 1926-1939, (Polish Foreign Policy, 1926-1939), Paris, 90; author of numerous of articles in U.S., German, and Polish professional journals. **CONTACT ADDRESS** Dept of Hist, Univ of Kans, Lawrence, KS, 66045-0001. **EMAIL** Annac@eagle.cc.ukans.edu

CIFELLI, EDWARD M.
PERSONAL Born 04/28/1942, Newark, NJ, m, 1966, 2 children **DISCIPLINE** AMERICAN STUDIES **EDUCATION** Rutgers Univ, BA, 64; Tex Tech Univ, MA, 67; NYU, MA, 70 PhD, 77. **CAREER** Lectr, Rutgers Univ, 67-69; prof, County Col Morris, 69-. **HONORS AND AWARDS** Tchg Excellece Award, 98, NISOD; Outstanding Acad Book Award, 99, Choice Magazine. **RESEARCH** Colonial American studies and twentieth century American poetry. **SELECTED PUBLICATIONS** Auth, David Humphreys, 82; auth, art, Ciardi, John (Anthony), 94; auth, art, John Ciardi, Birth of a Poet, 96; auth, art, John Ciardi and the Italian American Question, 97; auth, John Ciardi: A Biography, 97. **CONTACT ADDRESS** 147 Merriam Ave, Newton, NJ, 07860. **EMAIL** ecifelli@webspan.net

CIMBALA, PAUL A.
DISCIPLINE AFRICAN-AMERICAN HISTORY **EDUCATION** Emory Univ, PhD. **CAREER** Assoc prof, Fordham Univ. **HONORS AND AWARDS** Ed, Fordham UP. **MEMBERSHIPS** Mem, Adv Coun Lincoln Prize, Gettysburg Col. **SELECTED PUBLICATIONS** Auth, The Black Abolitionist Papers, vol 2: Canada, 1830-1865, Univ NC 86; Against the Tide: Women Reformers in American Society, 96; Historians and Race: Autobiography and the Writing of History, 96; American Reform and Reformers: A Biog Dictionary, 96; Under the Guardianship of the Nation: The Freedmen's Bureau and the Reconstruction of Georgia, 1865-1870, 97; co-ed,The Freedmen's Bureau and Reconstruction: Interpretive Essays on an Organization and its Failure, 98. **CONTACT ADDRESS** Dept of Hist, Fordham Univ, 113 W 60th St, New York, NY, 10023.

CIMBALA, STEPHEN J.
DISCIPLINE POLITICAL SCIENCE **EDUCATION** BA, PA State Univ, 65; MA, 67; Phd, 69, Univ of WI. **CAREER** Prof of Political Sci, Delaware County, 86-; Assoc Prof of Political Sci, PA State Univ, Delaware County, 73-86; Asst Pfor of Political Sci, State Univ of NY, Stony Brook NY, 69-73; Asst Dean for Undergraduate Studies, State Univ of NY, Stony Brook NY, 71-73; Chief Acad Officer, 73-81; Acting Chief Acad Officer, PA State Univ Delaware County, 87-88. **HONORS AND AWARDS** Milton S. Eisenhower Award for Distinguished Teaching, PA State Univ, 95; Consult expert U S, AVDA Strategy Analysis Grp IVI/ITA. **SELECTED PUBLICATIONS** Auth, The Past and Future of Nuclear Deterrence, Praeger Publ, 98; The Politics of Warfare: The Great Powers in the Twentieth Century, Univ Park PA Penn State Press, 97; Collective Insecurity: U S Defense Policy and the New World Disorder, Greenwood Press, 95; U S Military Strategy and the Cold War Endgame London, Frank Cass Publ 95; Military Persuasion: Deterrence and Provocation in Crisis and War, Univ Park PA Penn State Press, 94; U S Nuclear Strategy in the New World Order, Paragon House, 93; Clinton and Post-Cold War Defense, Praeger Publ 96. **CONTACT ADDRESS** Pennsylvania State Univ, Delaware County, 118 Vairo Library, Media, PA, 19063-5596. **EMAIL** sjc@psu.edu

CIMPRICH, JOHN V.
PERSONAL Born 06/26/1949, Middletown, OH, m, 1985 **DISCIPLINE** HISTORY **EDUCATION** Thomas More Col, AB, 71, Oh St Univ, MA, 73, PhD, 77. **CAREER** Lectr, Oh St Univ, 77-79; instr to vis asst prof, SE Mo St Univ, 80-85; lectr to prof to dept chair, Thomas More Col, 91- . **HONORS AND AWARDS** Phi Alpha Theta His Honor Soc Faculty Adv Res Grant, 97; Nat Hist Public & Records Comm Fel, 79-80., AB, Magna Cum Laude, 71; Humanities Col Grad Res Award Runner-up, 77. **MEMBERSHIPS** Org of Amer Hist; Phi Alpha Theta Honor Soc in Hist; World Hist Assoc. **RESEARCH** Civil War Period of US hist. **SELECTED PUBLICATIONS** Coed, Fort Pillow Revisited: New Evidence about an Old controversy, Civil War History, 82; Dr. Fitch's Report on the Fort Pillow Massacre, Tennessee Hist Quart, 83; coauth, The Fort Pillow Massacre: A Statistical Note, J of Amer Hist, 89; auth, Slavery's End in Tennessee, 1861-1865, Univ Al Press, 85; A Critical Moment and Its Aftermath for George H. Thomas, in The Moment of Decision: Biographical Essays in American Character and Regional Identity, Greenwood Press, 94. **CONTACT ADDRESS** Dept of History, Thomas More Col, Crestview Hills, KY, 41017. **EMAIL** cimpricj@thomasmore.edu

CIOCHON, RUSSELL L.
PERSONAL Born 03/11/1948, Altadena, CA, m, 1986 **DISCIPLINE** ANTHROPOLOGY **EDUCATION** Univ Calif Berkeley, MA, 74, PhD 86. **CAREER** Lectr, Univ North Carolina, Charlotte, 78-81; res paleontol, Univ Calif, Berkeley, 82-83; res assoc, Inst Human Origins, Berkeley, 83-85; res assoc, SUNY Stony Brook, 85-86; asst prof, Univ Iowa, 87-90, assoc prof, 90-96, prof, 96- , ch, Dept of Anthrop, Univ Iowa. **HONORS AND AWARDS** Res grant Smithsonian Foreign Currency Prog, 78; Leakey Found, 87. **MEMBERSHIPS** AAAS, Am Anthrop Asn; Am Asn Phys Anthrop; Soc Syst Biol; Phi Beta Kappa. **SELECTED PUBLICATIONS** Ed, Human Evolution Source Book, 93; auth/ed, Integrative Paths to the Past, 94; auth, Evolution of the Cercopithecoid Forelimb, 93; co-ed, Oxford Series in Human Evolution, 95- . **CONTACT ADDRESS** Dept of Anthropology, Univ of Iowa, 114 Macbride Hall, Iowa City, IA, 52242-1322. **EMAIL** rciochon@blue.weeg.uiowa.edu

CITINO, ROBERT M.
DISCIPLINE HISTORY **EDUCATION** Univ Ind, PhD. **CAREER** Prof, Eastern Michigan Univ. **RESEARCH** Europe, Germany Europe, military. **SELECTED PUBLICATIONS** Auth, Armored Forces: A History and Sourcebook; The Evolution of Blitzkrieg Tactics. **CONTACT ADDRESS** Dept of History and Philosophy, Eastern Michigan Univ, 701 Pray-Harrold, Ypsilanti, MI, 48197.

CITRON, HENRY
PERSONAL Born 01/15/1937, Philadelphia, PA, m, 1963, 2 children **DISCIPLINE** HISTORY, POLITICAL SCIENCE **EDUCATION** Temple Univ, BA, 60, MA, 61, NY Univ, PhD, 76. **CAREER** Substitute teacher, Philadelphia Pub Sch, 60-61; instr hist, Moravian Col, Bethlehem, Pa, 61-63; teacher social studies, Glen Cove High Sch, Glen Cove, NY, 63-65; dean students & group leader hist dept, Pa State Univ, Monaca, 65-68; prof hist & chemn dept Hist & Polit Sci, County Col Morris, 68-. **MEMBERSHIPS** AHA, Community Col Social Sci Asn: Eastern Community Col Social Sci Asn. **RESEARCH** Study of the arguments of interest groups which opposed federal aid to education from 1949-1965. **SELECTED PUBLICATIONS** Auth: Some recent discoveries at the Ohioview Archaeological Site, Ohio Archaeologist, 2/66; The Discovery of the Bakery at Old Economy, Pa Hist Comn, 68; Technology and New Teaching Techniques, Community Col Social Sci Conf, Dallas, 11/74; The End of History, Eastern Community Col Social Sci Conf, Princeton, 75; Search for the Czar: Russian Oral History, Kentucky Hist Comn, Frankfort, 3/76; "The American Reaction to the Boxer Rebellion," Community College Social Science Review, winter 76. **CONTACT ADDRESS** County Col of Morris, 214 Center Grove Rd, Randolph, NJ, 07869-2086. **EMAIL** hank360@intercoll.net

CIVIL, MIGUEL
PERSONAL Born 05/07/1926, Sabadell, Spain, 2 children **DISCIPLINE** ASSYRIOLOGY, LINGUISTICS **EDUCATION** Univ Paris, PhD, 58. **CAREER** Res assoc Assyriol, Univ Pa, 58-63; from asst prof to assoc prof Near Eastern Lang & civilizations & ling, 63-70, Prof Near Eastern Lang & Civilizations & Ling, Univ Chicago, 70-, Mem ed bd, Chicago Assyrian Dict, 67-; dir d'etudes associe etranger, Sorbonne, 68-70; ed, Materials for the Sumerian Lexicon, 68- **MEMBERSHIPS** Am Orient Soc; Am Sch Orient Res. **RESEARCH** Sumerian grammar and literature; anthropology of Mesopotamia; lexicography. **SELECTED PUBLICATIONS** Auth, Prescriptions medicales Sumeriennes, Rev D'Assyriol, 60; The message of Lu-dingirra, J Near Eastern Studies, 64; Notes on Sumerian lexicography, J Cuneiform Studies, 66; coauth, Vol IX, Materials for the Sumerian Lexicon, 67 & auth, Vol XIII-XIV, 71, Pontificio Inst Biblico, Rome. **CONTACT ADDRESS** Oriental Institute Univ, Univ of Chicago, 1155 E 58th St, Chicago, IL, 60637-1540.

CLAASSEN, CHERYL
PERSONAL Born 07/24/1953, Syracuse, NY, 1 child **DISCIPLINE** ANTHROPOLOGY **EDUCATION** Univ Ark, BA, BSW, 75; Harvard Univ, PhD, 82. **CAREER** Archaeol, State of NC, 79-80; dir, Seasonality Lab, Center for Archaeol Res and Development, Peabody Museum, Harvard Univ, 81-82; Charles Phelps Taft postdoctoral res fel, Univ Cincinnati, 82-83; vis prof, Anthropology, Universidad de las Americas, 90-91; asst to assoc prof, anthropology, 83-94, PROF OF ANTHROPOLOGY, APPALACHIAN STATE UNIV, 94-; RES ASSOC, CENTER FRO AM ARCHAEL, 95-. **HONORS AND AWARDS** Certificate of Commendation, Am Asn for State & Local Hist; NSF grant, 85, 87, & 93; Am Philos Soc Grant, 87. **MEMBERSHIPS** Soc for Am Archaeol; Southeastern Archaeol Conf. **RESEARCH** Gender; sociology of archaeology; shells; symbolic landscapes, Eastern U.S. **SELECTED PUBLICATIONS** Auth, Shells for the Archaeologist, Cambridge Univ Press, 98; Black and White Women at Irene: A Revised View, Where We've Been: Early Women Archaeologists in the Southeast, Univ of Fl Press, 98; Washboards, Pigtoes, and Muckets: Historic Musseling in the Mississippi Watershed, Hist Archaeol, 94; Looking for Gender in Appalachian Prehistory, Archaeol of Appalachia, NY State Museum Monographs in Archaeol, 98; Challenges in Gendering Southeastern Prehisotry, Gender and Southeastern Prehistory, 98; Changing Venue: Proposals About Women's Lives in Prehistoric North America, Women in Prehistory: North Am and Mesoamerica, Univ of Pa Press, 97; Social Organization of the Shell Mound Archaic, The Middle and Late Archaic in the Southeastern U.S., Univ of Fl Press, 96; Research Problems with Shell from Shell Mound Archaic Sites, Of Caves in Shell Mounds, Univ of Ala Press, 96; coauth, Women in the Ancient Americas: Archaeologists, Gender, and the Making of Prehistory, Women in Prehistory: North Am and Mesoamerica, Univ of Pa Press, 97; co-ed, Women in Prehistory: North America and Mesoamerica, Univ of Pa Press, 97; ed, Dogan Point: An Archaic Shell-Matrix Site on the Hudson, Archaeol Services, 95; Women in Archaeology, Univ of Pa Press, 94; Exploring Gender Through Archaeology, Prehist Press, 92. **CONTACT ADDRESS** Dept of Anthropology, Appalachian State Univ, Boone, NC, 28608.

CLACK, JERRY
PERSONAL Born 07/22/1926, New York, NY **DISCIPLINE** CLASSICS **EDUCATION** Univ Pittsburgh, PhD 62, MA 58; Princeton Univ, BA 46. **CAREER** Duquesne Univ, prof 68-; The March of Dimes Pittsburgh, dir 53-68; US Delegation to UNESCO, prog officer 46-67. **MEMBERSHIPS** APA; CAAS; PCA; CAP. **RESEARCH** Hellenistic poetry; Augustan literature. **SELECTED PUBLICATIONS** Auth, The Poems of Meleager, 94; The APA and Regional Associations: Transactions of the American Philological Association, 93. **CONTACT ADDRESS** Dept of Classic, Duquesne Univ, Pittsburgh, PA, 15282. **EMAIL** clack@duq2.cc.duq.edu

CLADER, LINDA
PERSONAL Born 02/11/1946, Evanston, IL, m, 1991 **DISCIPLINE** CLASSICAL PHILOLOGY; HOMILETICS **EDUCATION** Carleton Col, AB, 68; Harvard Univ, AM, 70, PhD, 73;

Church Divinity School of Pacific, M Div, 88. **CAREER** Instr to full prof Classical languages, Carleton Col, 72-90; asst to assoc prof, homiletics, Church Divinity School Pacific, 91-. **HONORS AND AWARDS** Phi Beta Kappa, 68. **MEMBERSHIPS** AAR/SBL; Acad Homiletics **RESEARCH** Liturgical preaching; Myth; Homer. **SELECTED PUBLICATIONS** Auth, Preaching the Liturgical Narratives: The Easter Vigil and the Language of Myth, Worship, 98. **CONTACT ADDRESS** Church Divinity Sch of the Pacific, 2451 Ridge Rd, Berkeley, CA, 94709. **EMAIL** Lclader@cdsp.edu

CLAGETT, MARSHALL
PERSONAL Born 01/23/1916, Washington, DC, m, 1946, 3 children **DISCIPLINE** MEDIEVAL HISTORY **EDUCATION** George Washington Univ, AB, 37, AM, 38; Columbia Univ, PhD, 41. **CAREER** Instr hist & hist sci, Columbia Univ, 46-47; from asst prof to prof hist sci, Univ Wis, 47-64, dir inst res humanities, 59-64; PROF HIST SCI, INST ADVAN STUDY, 64-, Guggenheim fels, 46, 50-51; Nat Sci Found grant, Rome & London, 55-56. **HONORS AND AWARDS** LLD, George Washington Univ, 69; LHD, Univ Wis, 74. **MEMBERSHIPS** Hist Sci Soc (pres, 62-64); fel Mediaeval Acad Am; fel Am Acad Arts & Sci; Am Philos Soc; Int Acad Hist Sci. **RESEARCH** Ancient and medieval science and mathematics. **SELECTED PUBLICATIONS** Auth, Sarton Medal Citation, Isis, Vol 0084, 93. **CONTACT ADDRESS** Inst for Advan Study, Princeton, NJ, 08540.

CLANTON, ORVAL GENE
PERSONAL Born 09/14/1934, Pittsburg, KS, m, 1959, 2 children **DISCIPLINE** UNITED STATES HISTORY **EDUCATION** Kans State Col, Pittsburg, BS, 59, MS, 61; Univ Kans, PhD(US hist), 67. **CAREER** Teacher, high sch, Colo, 60-62; from instr to asst prof US hist, Tex A&M Univ, 66-68; asst prof, 68-71, assoc prof, 71-78, prof Emeritus, US Hist, Wash State Univ, 78-. **MEMBERSHIPS** AHA; Orgn Am Historians. **RESEARCH** Populism and progressivism; Gilded Age; the Congressional Populist delegations. **SELECTED PUBLICATIONS** Auth, Mary Elizabeth Lease: Intolerant Populist?, Kans Hist Quart, summer 68; Kansas Populism: Ideas and Men, Univ Press of Kans, 69; A Rose by Any Other Name: Kansas Populism and Progressivism, fall 69 & coauth, G C Clemens: The Sociable Socialist, winter 74, Kans Hist Quart; Populism, Progressivism and Equality: The Kansas Paradigm, Agr Hist, 7/77; Multiple entries, The Readers Encyclopedia of the American West, T Y Crowell, 77; Populism: The Humane Preference in America, 1890-1900, Twayne Pub, 91; Congressional Populism and the Crisis of the 1890's, Univ Press of Kansas, 98. **CONTACT ADDRESS** Dept of Hist, Wash State Univ, P O Box 644030, Pullman, WA, 99164-4030. **EMAIL** geno@iea.com

CLAPPER, MICHAEL
DISCIPLINE ART HISTORY **EDUCATION** Swarthmore Coll, BA, 87; Washington Univ, MFA, 89; Northwestern, PhD, 97. **CAREER** ASST PROF, ART HIST, SKIDMORE COLL **MEMBERSHIPS** AM Antiquarian Soc **SELECTED PUBLICATIONS** Auth, "Art, Industry and Education in Prang's Chromolithograph Company, " Procs of the AAS, 105:1, April, 95; auth, "The Chromo and the Art Museum: Popular and Elite Art Institutions in Late Nineteenth-Century America," in Not at Home: The Suppression of Domesticity in Modern Art and Architecture, 33-47. **CONTACT ADDRESS** Dept of Art & Art Hist, Skidmore Coll, 815 North Broadway, Saratoga Springs, NY, 12866-1632.

CLARDY, JESSE V.
PERSONAL Born 02/15/1931, Olney, TX, m, 1964 **DISCIPLINE** RUSSIAN AND MODERN CHINESE HISTORY **EDUCATION** Tex A&I Univ, BS & MS, 60; Univ Mich, PhD(hist), 61. **CAREER** PROF HIST, UNIV MO-KANSAS CITY, 64-. **MEMBERSHIPS** Am Asn Advan Slavic Studies; Asn Slavic & East Europ Studies. **SELECTED PUBLICATIONS** Auth, Political-Culture in Vienna and Warsaw, Ger Stud Rev, Vol 0015, 92. **CONTACT ADDRESS** Dept Hist, Univ Mo-Kansas City, 5100 Rockhill Rd, Kansas City, MO, 64110-2499.

CLARK, ANDREW
DISCIPLINE WEST AFRICAN HISTORY **EDUCATION** Mich State Univ, PhD, 90. **CAREER** Prof, Univ NC, Wilmington. **RESEARCH** Slavery and its demise in West Africa. **SELECTED PUBLICATIONS** Published articles in the J of African Hist, Slavery and Abolition, Oral Hist Rev, J of 3rd World Stud, Can J of African Stud and the Int J of African Hist Stud. He is co-author of Historical Dictionary of Senegal. **CONTACT ADDRESS** Univ N. Carolina, Wilmington, 227 Morton Hall, Wilmington, NC, 28403-3297. **EMAIL** clarka@uncwil.edu

CLARK, ANNA
DISCIPLINE MODERN BRITAIN HISTORY, EUROPEAN WOMEN'S HISTORY, HISTORY OF SEXUALITY, MOD **EDUCATION** Rutgers Univ, PhD, 87. **CAREER** Assoc prof, Univ NC, Charlotte. **HONORS AND AWARDS** N Am Conf on Brit Stud Prize in the Hum. **RESEARCH** Gender and Politics in late 18th and Early 19th Century Britain; domesticity and the Poor Laws in the 19th Century. **SELECTED PUBLICA-**

TIONS Auth, The Struggle for the Breeches: Gender and the Making of the British Working Class, Univ Calif Press. **CONTACT ADDRESS** Univ N. Carolina, Charlotte, Charlotte, NC, 28223-0001.

CLARK, CHARLES EDWIN
PERSONAL Born 04/28/1929, Brunswick, ME, m, 1952, 4 children **DISCIPLINE** AMERICAN HISTORY **EDUCATION** Bates Col, AB, 51; Columbia Univ, MS, 52; Brown Univ, PhD(Am civilization), 66. **CAREER** Reporter, Providence Jour & Evening Bull, RI, 56-61; asst prof hist, Southeastern Mass Technol Inst, 65-67; from asst prof to prof, 67-97, chmn dept, 77-80, EMERITUS PROF HIST, UNIV NH, 98-, James H. Hayes and Claire Short Hayes Chair in the Humanities, 93-97; researcher, Prog Loyalist Studies & Publ, 71. **HONORS AND AWARDS** Nat Endowment Arts & Humanities fel, 68; Henry E Huntington fel, 72; Am Coun Learned Soc fel, 73-74; Daniels fel, Am Antiquarian Soc, 80; Commonwealth Fel, Col of William and Mary, 90. **MEMBERSHIPS** AHA; Asn Inst Early Am Hist & Culture; OAH. **RESEARCH** Intellectual and cultural history of early America; regional history of northern New England; eighteenth-century English and American journalism. **SELECTED PUBLICATIONS** Coauth, New England's Tom Paine: John Allen and the Spirit of Liberty, William & Mary Quart, 10/64; auth, Science, Reason and an Angry God: The Literature of an Earthquake, New Eng quart, 9/65; A Test of Religious Liberty: The Ministry Land Case in Narragansett, 1668-1752, J Church & State, 69; The Eastern Frontier: The Settlement of Northern New England, 1610, 1763, Knopf, 70; Maine during the Colonial Period: A Bibliographical Guide, Maine Hist Soc, 74; Maine: A Bicentennial History, Norton, 77; History, literature, and Belknap's social happiness, Hist NH, Vol XXXV, 1-22; coauth, The Measure of Maturity: The Pennsylvania Gazettem 1728-1765, William and Mary Quart, 3rd ser, XLVI, 89; auth, Metropolis and Province in Eighteenth-Century Press Relations: The Case of Boston, J Newspaper and Periodical Hist, Autumn 89; The Newspapers of Provincial America, Am Antiquarian Soc Proceedings, 100, 90; Boston and the Nurturing of Newspapers, New Eng Quart LXIV, 91; The Public Prints: The Newspaper in Anglo-American Culture, 1665-1740, Oxford, 94; The Meetinghouse Tragedy: An Episode in the Life of a New England Town, Univ Press of New Eng, 98. **CONTACT ADDRESS** 2 Thompson Ln, Durham, NH, 03824. **EMAIL** ceclark@christa.unh.edu

CLARK, CHRISTOPHER F.
DISCIPLINE HISTORY **EDUCATION** Univ Warwick, BA, 74; Harvard Univ, MA, 75, PhD, 82. **CAREER** Lect, hist, York; PROF, HIST, UNIV WARWICK. **HONORS AND AWARDS** Frederick Jackson Turner Award **MEMBERSHIPS** Am Antiquarian Soc **RESEARCH** Rural Mass, 1790-1860. **SELECTED PUBLICATIONS** Auth, "The Truck System in 19th-Century New England: An Interpretation," in Merchant Credit and Labour Strategies, Acadiensis Press, 90; auth, The Roots of Rural Capitalism: Western Massachusetts 1780-1860, Cornell Univ Press, 90; "Economics and Culture: Opening Up the Rural History of the Early American Northeast, " Am Quart, June, 91; auth, "Work and Labor in Rural Massachusetts: The Connecticut Valley, 1750-1820,: in Travail et Loisir dans les Societes Pre-Industrielles, Presses Universitaires de Nancy, 91; auth, "Social Structure and Manufacturing Before the Factory: Rural New England, 1750-1830," in The Workplace Before the Factory, Cornell Univ Press, 93; auth, "Agrarian Societies and Economic Development in Nineteenth-Century North America," in Development and Underdevelopment in America, de Gruyter, 93; The Communities Movement: The Radical Challenge of the Northampton Association, Cornell Univ Press, 95; "The Consequences of the 'Market Revolution' in the American North," in The Market Revolution: Social Culture and Religious Expression, Univ Press Va, 96; auth, "Rural America and the Transition to Capitalism," Jour of the Early Repub, June, 96. **CONTACT ADDRESS** Dept of Hist, Univ of Warwick, Coventry, ., CV4 7AL. **EMAIL** c.clark@warwick.ac.uk

CLARK, GEOFFREY W.
DISCIPLINE HISTORY **EDUCATION** Wesleyan Univ, BA, 81; Princeton Univ, MA, 87, PhD, 93. **CAREER** Asst prof **RESEARCH** Early modern British history; social and economic history of Augustan England; cultural history of financial speculation. **SELECTED PUBLICATIONS** Auth, Betting on Lives: Providence, chance, and the culture of life insurance in England 1695-1775. **CONTACT ADDRESS** Dept History, Emory Univ, 221 Bowden Hall, 561 Kilgo Cir, Atlanta, GA, 30322-1950. **EMAIL** gclark@emory.edu

CLARK, HUGH R.
DISCIPLINE HISTORY AND EAST ASIAN STUDIES **EDUCATION** Univ Pa, PhD. **CAREER** Prof Hist and E Asian Stud, ch, dept Hist, Ursinus Col. **HONORS AND AWARDS** Laughlin Prof Achievement Award, Ursinus Col; grant, Chiang Ching-kuo Found, NEH, Comt for Scholarly Res in China. **RESEARCH** Middle period Chinese history. **SELECTED PUBLICATIONS** Auth, Community, Trade, and Networks: Southern Fujian Province from the 3rd to the 13th Centuries. **CONTACT ADDRESS** Ursinus Col, Collegeville, PA, 19426-1000.

CLARK, JOHN GARRETSON
PERSONAL Born 05/26/1932, Somerville, NJ, m, 1954, 3 children **DISCIPLINE** AMERICAN HISTORY, ECONOMIC HISTORY **EDUCATION** Park Col, AB, 54; Univ Kans, MA, 60; Stanford Univ, PhD(hist), 63. **CAREER** From instr to assoc prof hist, Univ Kans, 63-69; res assoc, State Geol Surv Kans, 69-71; assoc chmn, 73-77, PROF HIST, UNIV KANS, 71-, Asn State & Local Hist res grant-in-aid, 65-66; Nat Endowment for Humanities fel, 68; Am Philos Soc grant, 69-70; Coun Econ Hist grant, 69-70; vis scholar, US Dept of Energy, 77-78. **HONORS AND AWARDS** Manuscript Award, Agr Hist Soc, 66. **RESEARCH** Community studies; United States economic history from the 18th to the 20th centuries; energy use in United States. **SELECTED PUBLICATIONS** Auth, Wolf-Creek-Station--Kansas-Gas-and-Electric-Company in the Nuclear Era, W Hist Quart, Vol 0025, 94; Containing the Atom--Nuclear-Regulation in a Changing Environment, 1963-1971, Pub Historian, Vol 0016, 94; Wind Energy in America-A History, Environ Hist, Vol 0002, 97; The International Petrochemical Industry, Econ Hist Rev, Vol 0046, 93; Beyond Interdependence-- The Meshing of the Worlds Economy and the Earths Ecology, Diplomatic Hist, Vol 0021, 97; Environmental Diplomacy-- Negotiating More Effective International Agreements, Diplomatic Hist, Vol 0021, 97; The Greening of Machiavelli--The Evolution of International Environmental Politics, Diplomatic Hist, Vol 0021, 97; International Environmental-Policy, 1st Edition, Diplomatic Hist, Vol 0021, 97; Biosphere Politics-- A New Consciousness for a New Century, Diplomatic Hist, Vol 0021, 97; Global Environmental Politics, 1st Edition, Diplomatic Hist, Vol 0021, 97; Global Ecology--A New Arena of Political-Conflict, Diplomatic Hist, Vol 0021, 97; Clean Cheap Heat-The Development of Residential Markets for Natural-Gas in the United-States, Jour Econ Hist, Vol 0053, 93; Reclaiming Paradise--The Global Environment Movement, Diplomatic Hist, Vol 0021, 97. **CONTACT ADDRESS** Dept of Hist, Univ of Kans, Lawrence, KS, 66044.

CLARK, JOHN RICHARD
PERSONAL Born 06/11/1947, Dayton, OH, m, 1 child **DISCIPLINE** CLASSICAL LANGUAGES, MEDIEVAL LATIN **EDUCATION** Univ Cincinnati, BA, 69; Cornell Univ, MA, 71, PhD, 74. **CAREER** Asst prof, Univ Pa, 75-79; Asst Prof, 80-86, Assoc Prof Class, Medieval & Palaeography, Fordham Univ, 86-. **MEMBERSHIPS** Am Philol Asn; Medieval Acad Am. **RESEARCH** Marsilio Ficino's De vita(1489); medieval Latin love lyric; Plautus. **SELECTED PUBLICATIONS** Auth, Structure and symmetry in the Bacchides of Plautus, Transactions of the Am Philol Asn, 76; Two ghost editions of Marsilio Ficino's De vita, Papers of the Bibliog Soc of Am, 79; Teaching Medieval Latin, Class J, 79; Word play in Plautus' Amphitruo, Class Philol, 80; Marsilio Ficino among the alchemists, Class Bull, 83; coauth, Marsilio Ficino: Three Books on Life: A Critical Edition and Translation with Introduction & Notes, SUNY, 89; auth, Platonianus es, non Plautinianus (Jerome Ep. 22.30), CW, 84; The Traditional Figure of Dina and Abeland's First Planetus, Proceeds of PMR Conf, 82; Roger Bacon and the Composition of Marsilio Ficino's De vita longa, J Warburg & Courtauld Inst, 86; Love & Learning in the Metamorphosis Golye Episcopi, MJ, 86. **CONTACT ADDRESS** Dept of Class, Fordham Univ, 441 E Fordham Rd, Bronx, NY, 10458-5191. **EMAIL** clark@murray.fordham.edu

CLARK, LINDA LOEB
PERSONAL Born 09/18/1942, Syracuse, NY **DISCIPLINE** MODERN FRENCH AND EUROPEAN HISTORY **EDUCATION** Duke Univ, BA, 64; Univ NC, Chapel Hill, PhD(mod Europ hist), 68. **CAREER** Asst prof hist, Shepherd Col, 69-70; asst prof, 70-72, ASSOC PROF HIST, MILLERSVILLE STATE COL, 72-, Nat Endowment for Humanities fel in residence for col teachers, 75-76; res fel, Bunting Inst, Radcliffe Col, 79-80. **MEMBERSHIPS** AHA; Soc Fr Hist Studies. **RESEARCH** Social Darwinism in France; primary education in France. **SELECTED PUBLICATIONS** Auth, An Unknown Factor in the Social-Sciences--The Foundation-Alexis-Carrel, 1941-1945-French, Amer Hist Rev, Vol 0099, 94; The Public Eye--A History of Reading in Modern France, 1800-1940, Jour Mod Hist, Vol 0066, 94; Centuries of Tutoring--A History of Alternative Education in America and Western-Europe, Amer Hist Rev, Vol 0098, 93; The Light Infantry Soldiers of the Republic--Labor Inspection Until 1914--German, Jour Soc Hist, Vol 0029, 96. **CONTACT ADDRESS** Dept of Hist, Millersville Univ, Pennsylvania, Millersville, PA, 17551.

CLARK, MALCOLM CAMERON
PERSONAL Born 01/24/1930, Washington, DC, m, 1972 **DISCIPLINE** AMERICAN & EUROPEAN HISTORY **EDUCATION** George Washington Univ, BA, 53, MA, 59; Georgetown Univ, PhD(hist), 70. **CAREER** From asst prof to assoc prof, 66-75, chmn dept, 72-75, prof Hist, 75-95, DISTINGUISHED PROF EMERITUS COL CHARLESTON, 95-. **HONORS AND AWARDS** SC Hist Soc: pres, 82-85, ed bd, 68-98, chmn, 76-98, Mary Elizabeth Prior Award, 96. **MEMBERSHIPS** AHA; Orgn Am Historians; Southern Hist Asn. **RESEARCH** American colonial history; American economic history. **SELECTED PUBLICATIONS** Auth, Federalism at high tide: the election of 1796 in Maryland, Md Hist Mag, 9/66; The birth of an enterprise: Baldwin locomotive, 1831-1842, Pa Mag Hist & Biog, 10/66. **CONTACT ADDRESS** Dept of Hist, Col of Charleston, 66 George St, Charleston, SC, 29424-0001.

CLARK, MICHAEL DORSEY
PERSONAL Born 11/05/1937, Baltimore, MD, m, 1965, 2 children **DISCIPLINE** AMERICAN INTELLECTUAL HISTORY **EDUCATION** Yale Univ, BA, 59; Univ NC, MA, 62, PhD(hist), 65. **CAREER** Asst prof US hist, 64-70, ASSOC PROF HIST, UNIV NEW ORLEANS, 70- **MEMBERSHIPS** Am Studies Asn. **RESEARCH** Late nineteenth century American thought; American loyalism in the Revolutionary War; American religious history. **SELECTED PUBLICATIONS** Auth, Gender in America, Proteus, Vol 0010, 93; The American Encounter with Buddhism, 1844-1912--Victorian Culture and the Limits of Dissent, Amer Hist Rev, Vol 0098, 93; More English than the English--Cavalier and Democrat in Virginia Historical Writing, 1870-1930, Jour Amer Stud, Vol 0027, 93. **CONTACT ADDRESS** Dept of Hist, Univ of New Orleans Lakefront, New Orleans, LA, 70122.

CLARK, RAYMOND JOHN
PERSONAL Born 07/08/1941, Bristol, England, m, 1964, 3 children **DISCIPLINE** CLASSICS **EDUCATION** Univ Exeter, BA, 63, cert educ, 64, PhD(classics), 70. **CAREER** Assoc prof, 69-80, PROF CLASSICS, MEM UNIV NFLD, 80-, Can Coun leave fel, 76-77. **MEMBERSHIPS** Class Asn Can (vpres, 80-82); Vergilian Soc Am; Virgil Soc Eng; Am Philol Soc; Brit Class Asn. **RESEARCH** Greek and Latin epic, especially Homeric and Vergilian; classical religion, mythology and folklore, especially mortuary; pre-Socratic philosophy. **SELECTED PUBLICATIONS** Auth, Peter-of-Eboli, De Balneis Puteolanis--Manuscripts from the Aragonese-Scriptorium in Naples, Traditio-Stud in Ancient and Medieval Hist Thought and Rel, Vol 0045, 90; Giles-of-Viterbo on the Phlegraean-Fields--A Vergilian View, Phoenix-Jour Class Assn Can, Vol 0049, 95. **CONTACT ADDRESS** Dept of Classics, Memorial Univ of Newfoundland, St John's, NF, A1C 5S7.

CLARK, SANZA BARBARA
PERSONAL Born 07/03/1940, Cleveland, Ohio, d **DISCIPLINE** EDUCATION **EDUCATION** Kent State Univ, BA 1967; Duquesne Univ, MA 1970; Howard Univ, CAS 1980; Univ of IL, PhD 1985. **CAREER** Univ of Pittsburgh, Swahili instructor 1969-72; Tanzanian Min of Natl Educ, educ officer IIA 1972-78; University of Illinois, statistical consultant, 1980-83; OH State Univ, Swahili instructor 1983-84; Cleveland State Univ, assoc prof educ/rsch 1985-. **HONORS AND AWARDS** Mem Phi Delta Kappa Professional Soc; mem Phi Kappa Phi Honor Soc; Guide-Formulas-Hypothesis Testing Univ of IL 1982; Effects-Parental Educ & Sch on Ach Univ of IL 1985; Ed Refugees in Tanzania Comp & Intl Educ Soc 1986; Honoree, Outstanding African-American Women, 1996; Queen Mother Award, Excellence in Service & Community, 1996. **MEMBERSHIPS** Pres Orchard Family Housing Council 1981-83; pres Parents for Quality Educ 1986-87; chmn, Mali Yetu Alternative Educ School 1988-; trustee, Center for Human Services, 1989-91. **SELECTED PUBLICATIONS** "African-American Research," The State of Black Cleveland, 1989; "Persistence Patterns of African-American College Students," Readings on the State of Education in Urban America, 1991; "An Analysis of African-American First Year College Student Attitudes & Attrition Rates," Journal of Urban Education, 1992; "The Great Migration," Mali Yetu, 1993; "The Schooling of Cultural and Ethnic Subordinate Groups," Comparative Education Review, 1993; "Rediscovering Our Roots in Ghana, Africa," Mali Yetu, 1995. **CONTACT ADDRESS** Cleveland State Univ, Cleveland, OH, 44115.

CLARK, TERRY NICHOLS
PERSONAL Born 11/26/1940, Chicago, IL **DISCIPLINE** SOCIOLOGY **EDUCATION** Bowdoin Col, BA, 62; Columbia Univ, MA, 65, PhD, 67. **CAREER** Asst prof, 66-71, assoc prof, 71-85, prof, 85-, chmn, Sociology Program, 89-, Univ of Chicago; Sr Study Dir, Nat Opinion Res Ctr, 74-; vis assoc prof, Yale Univ, 72; vis scholar, Centre Universitaire Internat Paris, 65, 69; Brookings Instr, 75; Coord Fiscal Austerity and Urban Innovation Project US and World; Dir Comparative Study Community Decision-making, Univ of Chicago, 67-; chmn, Comm on Community Res and Devel Soc for Study Social Problems, 70-71; vis res, Urban Inst Pub Fin Group WA Summer 70; consul to Office Policy Devel and Res HUD, WA, summer 75. **MEMBERSHIPS** Amer Sociology Asn; Intl Sociology Asn; The Tocqueville Soc. **SELECTED PUBLICATIONS** Auth, A Mayors Financial Management Handbook, 82; coauth, City Money Political Processes Fiscal Strain and Retrenchment, 83; coauth, Policy Responsiveness and Fiscal Strain in 51 American Communities A Manual for Studying City Politics Using the MORC Permanent Community Sample, 83; auth, Coping with Urban Austerity Research in Urban Policy, 84. **CONTACT ADDRESS** Univ of Chicago, 1126 East 59th St, 326 Soc Sci Bldg, Chicago, IL, 60637.

CLARK, VEVE A.
PERSONAL Born 12/14/1944, Jamaica, New York **DISCIPLINE** EDUCATION **EDUCATION** Univ of CA Berkeley, PhD; Queens Coll NY, MA; Univ de Nancy France, Cert d'Etudes Superieures; Queens Coll NY, BA. **CAREER** Univ of CA Berkeley, lecturer 1974-79; Tufts Univ, assoc prof 1980-90; Univ of California, Berkeley, associate professor, 1991-. **HONORS AND AWARDS** Natl Endowment for the Arts Grants for Maya Deren Proj & Katherine Dunham Proj 1980-81; Merrill Ingram Found Writing Grant for Deren Proj 1982; Mellon Faculty Rsch Awd Tufts Univ 1983-84; co-editor The Legend of Maya Deren, Film Culture NY 1985; Gussenheim Fellow, 1987; Brown University Fellow, Rites and Reason and Univ Massachusetts, Boston, MA, 1988. **MEMBERSHIPS** Archivist The Katherine Dunham Fund 1977-; coord Africa & The New World Program at Tufts Univ 1981-; bd mem Fenway Comm Devel Corp 1981-83. **CONTACT ADDRESS** Univ of California Berkeley, 660 Barrows Hall, Berkeley, CA, 94720-2572.

CLARK, WALTER
PERSONAL Born 08/23/1952, Minneapolis, MN, m, 1 child **DISCIPLINE** MUSICOLOGY **EDUCATION** Univ California Los Angeles, PhD, 92 **CAREER** Prof Musicology, Univ Kansas, 93- **HONORS AND AWARDS** Fulbright to West Germany, 84-86; Del Amo Endowdowment Res Grant, 90-91; Res Grant, Prog Cult Coop between Spain's Ministry of Culture and U.S. universities, 95-96 **MEMBERSHIPS** Amer Musicol Soc; Sociedad Espanola de Musicolgia; Soc Ethnomusicology; Col Music Soc **RESEARCH** Music of Spain and Latin America, 1800 to present **SELECTED PUBLICATIONS** Isaac Albeniz: Portrait of a Romantic, Oxford, 98; Isaac Albeniz: A Guide to Research, Garland, 98 **CONTACT ADDRESS** Dept Music Dance, Univ Kansas, 452 Murphy Hall, Lawrence, KS, 66045. **EMAIL** wclark@lark.cc.ukans.edu

CLARK KROEGER, CATHERINE
DISCIPLINE CLASSICAL AND MINISTRY STUDIES **EDUCATION** Bryn Mawr Col, AB; Univ Minn, MA, PhD. **CAREER** Instr Hamilton Col; Univ Minn; adj assoc prof, Gordon-Conwell Theol Sem, 90-. **HONORS AND AWARDS** Chaplain, Hamilton Col; founding organizer, Christians for Biblical Equality. **MEMBERSHIPS** Mem, Amer Acad Rel; Soc Biblical Lit; Evangel Theol Soc. **RESEARCH** Women in ancient religion and human sexuality and biblical mandate. **SELECTED PUBLICATIONS** Co-ed, The Goddess Revival. **CONTACT ADDRESS** Gordon-Conwell Theol Sem, 130 Essex St, South Hamilton, MA, 01982.

CLARKE, DUNCAN
DISCIPLINE U.S. FOREIGN AND NATIONAL SECURITY POLICY **EDUCATION** Clark Univ; AB; Cornell Univ, JD; Univ Va, PhD. **CAREER** Prof, Am Univ. **HONORS AND AWARDS** Ten Best Professors, Am Univ; Tchg/schol yr, Scool of Int Serv. **SELECTED PUBLICATIONS** Auth, American Defense and Foreign Policy Institutions Harper and Row, 89; Send Guns and Money: Security Assistance and United States Foreign Policy, Praeger, 97. **CONTACT ADDRESS** American Univ, 4400 Massachusetts Ave, Washington, DC, 20016.

CLARKE, JAMES ALEXANDER
PERSONAL Born 07/04/1925, Jacksonville, Florida, m, 1946 **DISCIPLINE** EDUCATION **EDUCATION** Morehouse Coll, attended 1946-47; Johnson C Smith Univ, BS 1949; NC A&T State Univ, MS 1954; Columbia Univ, MA 1963; Univ of NC-Chapel Hill, EdD 1976. **CAREER** Kannapolis City Schools, teacher 1949-51; Rowan Co Schools, principal 1951-56; Charlotte-Mecklenburg Schools, principal & program dir 1956-72; Asheville City Schools, assoc supt 1972-77; NC Dept of Public Instruction, state dir 1977-82; Halifax County Schools, superintendent 1982-86 (retired); part-time, coll professor. **HONORS AND AWARDS** First black associate superintendent in NC; first black superintendent of Halifax County Schools; The Order of the Long Leaf Pine presented by Gov James Hunt of NC 1982; Educ Service Awd Phi Beta Sigma Frat 1984; Distinguished Alumni Awd Natl Assn of Equal Oppor in Higher Educ 1985; Outstanding Educ Leadership Award, Phi Beta Sigma, 1989; Distinguished Service Chapter of Phi Beta Sigma Fraternity, 1990; Hall of Fame, National Alliance of Black School Educators, 1996. **MEMBERSHIPS** Pres Div of Superintendents NC Dist VIII 1975-76; dir exec bd Natl Alliance of Black School Educators 1976-82; mem bd dirs Natl Community Educ Assoc 1980-82; deacon Martin St Baptist Church Raleigh 1980-; regional dir SE Region of Phi Beta Sigma Frat Inc 1981-84; mem AASA, NCASA, NCAE, NSBA, Sigma Pi Phi Frat, NASSP, NAACP; NC state & area 3 housing coord, AARP, 1988-94; AARP Association, state director NC: deacon Martin Street Baptist Church, Raleigh, NC, 1982-; natl dir of educ, Phi Beta Sigma 1987-91.

CLARKE, JAMES W.
PERSONAL Born 02/16/1937, Elizabeth, PA, m, 1983, 2 children **DISCIPLINE** POLITICAL SCIENCE **EDUCATION** Washington and Jefferson Col, BA, 62; Pennsylvania State Univ, MA, 64, PhD, 68. **CAREER** Asst and assoc prof, Florida State Univ, 67-71; prof, Univ Arizona, 71- . **HONORS AND AWARDS** Burlington Northern Found Award for Excellence in Tchg, 87; Fulbright scholar, 99. **MEMBERSHIPS** Am Polit Sci Asn. **RESEARCH** Race and public policy; violent crime and political order. **SELECTED PUBLICATIONS** Auth, American Assassins: The Darker Side of Politics, Princeton, 82; auth, Last Rampage: The Escape of Gary Tison, Houghton Mifflin, 88, updated ed, Univ Arizona, forthcoming; auth, On Being Mad or Merely Angry: John W. Hinckley, Jr. and Other Dangerous People, Princeton, 90; auth, The Lineaments of Wrath: Race, Violent Crime, and American Culture, Rutgers, 98. **CONTACT ADDRESS** Univ of Arizona, 313 Social Sciences Bldg, Tucson, AZ, 85721. **EMAIL** jclarke@u.arizona.edu

CLARKE, JOHN
DISCIPLINE ART HISTORY **EDUCATION** Yale Univ, PhD. **CAREER** Prof; Univ TX at Austin, 80-; critic, contemp art. **MEMBERSHIPS** VP & pres-elect, Col Art Asn Am. **RESEARCH** Ancient Roman art. **SELECTED PUBLICATIONS** Auth, Roman Black-and-White Figural Mosaics, 79 & res in Italy at the archaeological sites of Pompeii, Torre Annunziata, Herculaneum, and Ostia Antica between 80-89, and in 91 Houses of Roman Italy 100 BC-AD 250: Ritual, Space, and Decoration was publ; publ in, Arts Mag and Art in Am. **CONTACT ADDRESS** Dept of Art and Art Hist, Univ of Texas at Austin, 2613 Wichita St, FAB 2.114, Austin, TX, 78705.

CLARKE, JOHN R.
PERSONAL Born 01/25/1945, Pittsburgh, PA **DISCIPLINE** HISTORY OF ART **EDUCATION** AB, Georgetown Univ, 67; MA, 69; PhD, Yale Univ, 73. **CAREER** Asst Prof Univ Mich, 73-74; Asst Prof, Univ Calif, San Diego, 74-75; Asst Prof, Yale Univ, 75-80; Asst to Full Prof Univ TX, Austin, 80-. **HONORS AND AWARDS** Phi Beta Kappa; Fulbright-Hays Fel; NEH Grant; Res, Am Acad in Rome; ACLS Grants; APS Grants. **MEMBERSHIPS** Col Art Assoc; Bd Dir, Sec, VP, Pres, Archeol Inst Am. **RESEARCH** Hist of Greek and Roman Art; Ancient Mosiacs; Ancient Painting; Constr of Gender and Sexuality in Greece and Rome; Cultural Studies; Contemporary Am Art. **SELECTED PUBLICATIONS** Looking at Lovemaking: Construction of Sexuality in Roman Art-100BC_AD 250, Berkeley Univ CA Press, 98; The Houses of Roman Italy, 100BC_AD 250: Ritual, Space, and Decoration, Berkeley, Univ California Press, 91; Roman Blac and White Figura Mosaics, Monograph XXVX Archeol Inst of Am and the Col Art Assoc, NY Univ Press, 79; Romam Ancient, In Encylopedia of Interior Design, 2 vols, Ed, by Joanna Banham, 1079-1084, Fitzroy Dearborn Pub, 97; Just Like Us: Cultural Constructions of Sexuality and Race in Roman Art, The Art Bulletin 78, 4, 96; Landscape Paintings in the Villa Oplontis, Journal of Roman Archaelolgy 9, 96. **CONTACT ADDRESS** Dept Art and Art Hist, Univ Texas, Austin, TX, 78712-1285. **EMAIL** j.clarke@mail.utexas.edu

CLARKE, WILLIAM M.
DISCIPLINE GREEK AND ROMAN MYTHOLOGY, ROMAN EPIC **EDUCATION** Univ NC, PhD, 72. **CAREER** Assoc prof Classics, pres, Phi Beta Kappa, La State Univ. **RESEARCH** Greek poetry. **SELECTED PUBLICATIONS** Auth, The Manuscript of Straton's Musa puerilis, in GRBS 4, 76; Jewish Table Manners in the Cena Trimalcionis, in CJ 3, 92. **CONTACT ADDRESS** Dept of For Lang and Lit, Louisiana State Univ, 241 A Prescott Hall, Baton Rouge, LA, 70803.

CLARY, DAVID ALLEN
PERSONAL Born 09/05/1946, Lafayette, IN, m, 1966, 1 child **DISCIPLINE** HISTORY, HISTORIC PRESERVATION **EDUCATION** Ind Univ, AB, 68; Univ Tex, MA, 70. **CAREER** Historian, Nat Park Serv, Ft Davis Nat Hist Site, 68-70 & Nat Park Serv, Wash, 70-74; regional historian, Nat Park Serv, Midwest Region, Omaha, Nebr, 74-76; chief historian, US Forest Serv, Washington, DC, 76-; PRIN, DAVID A CLARY & ASSOCS, BLOOMINGTON, IND, 79-, NDEA Title IV fel hist, Univ Tex, 68-70; coordr environ & protection activities, Off Archaeol & Hist Preserv, 72-74; partner, Architect Perservation Consults, 79- **HONORS AND AWARDS** Special Achievement Awards, Nat Park Serv, 71, 73 & 76. **MEMBERSHIPS** Orgn Am Historians; Western Hist Asn; Asn Preserv Technol; Forest Hist Soc; Soc Hist Archeol. **RESEARCH** United States history; military history; historic preservation. **SELECTED PUBLICATIONS** Auth, The History of Engineering in the Forest-Service, A Compilation of History and Memoirs, 1905-1989, Public Historian, Vol 0015, 93; In A Dark Wood--The Fight Over Forests and the Rising Tyranny of Ecology, Environ Hist, Vol 0002, 97. **CONTACT ADDRESS** David A Clary & Associates, Worthington, IN.

CLASTER, JILL NADELL
PERSONAL Born 05/14/1932, New York, NY, 1 child **DISCIPLINE** ANCIENT & MEDIEVAL HISTORY **EDUCATION** NY Univ, AB, 52, MA, 54; Univ PA, PhD, 59. **CAREER** Teaching asst, Univ PA, 55-57; from instr to asst prof hist, Univ KY, 59-62; asst prof classics, 63-64, asst prof medieval hist, 64-67, dir, Master Arts Liberal Studies Prog, 76-78, actg dean, Col Arts & Sci, 78, assoc prof, 67-83, PROF HIST, NY UNIV, 84-; Dean, Washington Sq & Univ Col, 79-86; dir, Center for Near Eastern Studies, NYU, 91-96. **MEMBERSHIPS** AHA; Archaeol Inst Am; Mediaeval Acad Am; Classical Asn Atlantic States. **RESEARCH** Social and intellectual late Roman and medieval history; the classical tradition in the Middle Ages. **SELECTED PUBLICATIONS** Auth, Anthenian Democracy: Triumph or Travesty?, Holt, 67; The Medieval Experience 300-1400, NY Univ Press & Columbia Univ Press, 81. **CONTACT ADDRESS** Dept of Hist, New York Univ, 53 Washington Sq. S, New York, NY, 10012. **EMAIL** jill.claster@nyu.edu

CLAUSEN, MEREDITH L.
PERSONAL Born 06/10/1942, Hollywood, CA, w, 1967 **DISCIPLINE** ARCHITECTURAL HISTORY **EDUCATION** Univ Cal Berk, PhD 75, MA 72; Scripps College, BA. **CAREER** Univ Washington prof 79-. **HONORS AND AWARDS** Graham Foun Ad Stud; Mellon Fell; Res Professorshp Awd; NEH; Fulbright-Hays Fel; J Paul Getty Gnt., Available on the Web,http://www.washington.edu/ark2/Cities/Building Archive, digitized images for academic use throughout the univ and prof comm. **MEMBERSHIPS** SAH; FA; AIA. **RESEARCH** 20TH Cent Architecture; Amer architecture. **SELECTED PUBLICATIONS** Auth, Craig Ellwood, the Art Center College of Design: Shattering the Image, Casabella, 98; Pietro Belluschi, Modern American Architect, MIT Press, 94; Spiritual Space, The Religious Architecture of Pietro Belluschi, U of W Press, 92; The Michael Graves Portland Building and Its Problems, coauth, Architronic, 97; Essays on Art Dans La Rue, Department Store, Pietro Belluschi, Frantz Jourdain, Shopping Malls, in: Dictionary of Art, Macmillam Pub, London, 96; in progress, The Pan Am Building and the Demise of Modernism. **CONTACT ADDRESS** Dept of Aritectural History, Washington Univ, 4332 Thackeray Place NE, Seattle, WA, 98105. **EMAIL** mlc@washington.edu

CLAYMAN, DEE LESSER
PERSONAL New York **DISCIPLINE** CLASSICAL PHILOLOGY **EDUCATION** Wellesley Col, BA, 67; Univ Pa, MA, 69, PhD(classics), 72. **CAREER** Asst prof classics, Brooklyn Col, 72-77, assoc prof, 78-81, PROF CLASSICS, BROOKLYN COL & GRAD CTR, CITY UNIV NEW YORK, 82-, Grants-in-aid, Am Philos Soc, 75 & Am Coun Learned Soc, 78. **MEMBERSHIPS** Am Philol Asn; Asn Lit & Ling Computing; Asn Computational Linguistics. **RESEARCH** Greek poetry; computer-assisted stylometry; history of literary criticism. **SELECTED PUBLICATIONS** Auth, Trends and Issues in Quantitative Stylistics, Transactions of the Amer Philol Assn, Vol 0122, 92. **CONTACT ADDRESS** Dept of Classics, Brooklyn Col, CUNY, Brooklyn, NY, 11210.

CLAYSON, S. HOLLIS
DISCIPLINE ART HISTORY **EDUCATION** Wellesley Col, BA, 68; Univ Calif Los Angeles, MA 75, PhD, 84. **CAREER** Instr, Calif Inst Arts, 74-76; instr, Schiller Col, 77-78; asst prof, Wichita State Univ, 78-82; asst prof, Univ Ill Chicago, 84-85; vis assoc prof, Univ Chicago, 96; from vis asst prof to asst prof to assoc prof, Northwestern Univ, 82-. **HONORS AND AWARDS** Edward A. Dickson Support Fel in Hist Art, 75-77; US Dept Educ FIPSE Grant, 82; Lilly Endowment Post-Dr Award, 85-86; ACLS Res Fel, 87-88, 90-91; Univ Res Grants Comm Northwestern Univ Res Award, 88, 90, 93; CIRA Northwestern Univ Fel, 90-91, 91-92; AAUW Educ Found Am Fel, 94-95; Sr Fel Ctr Hum Northwestern Univ, 94-95; UCLA Distinguished Tchg Asst Award Honor Mention, 74-75; Fac Honor Roll, Assoc Student Govt List Outstanding Instructors, Northwestern Univ, 83-84, 86-87, 87-88, 92-93, 94, 96-97; Award Outstanding Tchg, Col Arts Sci, Northwestern Univ, 87; Col Art Asn, Distinguished Tchg Art Hist Award Jr Prof, 90; Charles Deering McCormick Prof Tchg Excellence, Northwestern Univ, 93-94, 95-97; Carnegie Found Advan Tchg US Prof Year Prg, Northwestern Univ nominee, 94, 95; Lake Park High Sch Educ Found Distinguished Alumna Award, 94. **RESEARCH** Nineteenth century European art concentrating on painting and printmaking in France; women and visual representation; sexual identity and cultural representation; feminist and gender theory; artistic identity and practice in the Franco-Prussian War; Orientalism; post-ethnographic physiognomy in Edgar Degas' later work. **SELECTED PUBLICATIONS** Auth, Painted Love: Prostitution in French Art of the Impressionist Era, 91; coauth, Quaecumque sunt vera? Revising the Intro Course at Northwestern University, Art Jour, Fall, 95; auth, Materialist Art History and its Points of Difficulty, Range Critical Perspectives: Art Hist, The Art Bull, Sept, 95; auth, A Wintry Masculinity: Art, Soldiering and Gendered Space in Paris Under Siege, Nineteenth-Century Contexts, 98. **CONTACT ADDRESS** Dept of Art History, Northwestern Univ, 244 Kresge Hall, Evanston, IL, 60208. **EMAIL** shc@nwu.edu

CLAYTON, JAMES L.
PERSONAL Born 07/28/1931, Salt Lake City, UT, m, 1957, 7 children **DISCIPLINE** ECONOMIC & LEGAL HISTORY **EDUCATION** Univ Utah, BA, 58; Cornell Univ, PhD(Econ Hist), 64. **CAREER** Case officer, Cent Intel Agency, 57-58; instr Hist, Hamilton Col, 62-63; from instr to assoc prof, 63-71, dir honors prog, 67-70, prof Hist, Univ Utah, 71-, dean, grad school, 78-86; provost, 86-90; vis asst prof, Dartmouth Col, 66-67; mem, Coun Grad Schs, US, 78-84. **HONORS AND AWARDS** Distinguished Teaching Award, Univ Utah, 66; Minn Hist Soc Solon J Buck Prize, 67; Distinguished Hon Prof, Univ Utah, 77; Univ Prof, 77-78; Phi Kappa Phi; Phi Beta Kappa. **MEMBERSHIPS** Western Asn Grad Schs (pres, 82); GRE Board, 82-87. **RESEARCH** Economic and social impact of war since 1945; Economic Consequence of Debt; American economic history; legal history. **SELECTED PUBLICATIONS** Coauth, American Civilization: A Documentary History, W C Brown, 66; auth, The growth and economic significance of the American fur trade, Minn Hist, Winter 66; ed, The Economic Impact of the Cold War, In: Forces in Am Growth series, Harcourt, 70; auth, The fiscal cost of the Cold War to the United States: the first 25 years, 1947-1971, Western Polit Quart, 9/72; The fiscal limits of the warfare-welfare state, Western Polit Quart, 76; A comparison of defense and welfare spending in the US and the UK, J Biol & Social Welfare, 77; A Farewell to the Welfare State, Univ Utah Press, 76; Does Defense Beggar Welfare?, Nat Strategy Info Ctr, 79. **CONTACT ADDRESS** Univ of Utah, 217 Carlson Hall, Salt Lake City, UT, 84112-0311.

CLAYTON, LAWRENCE A.
DISCIPLINE COLONIAL LATIN AMERICA **EDUCATION** Tulane Univ, PhD. **CAREER** Univ Ala **HONORS AND AWARDS** Two Fulbright Awards., Dir Grad Studies Hist; Dir, Latin Am Studies Prog. **SELECTED PUBLICATIONS** Auth, Los astilleros de Guayaquil colonial 78; The Bolivarian Nations, 84; Alabama and the Borderlands: From Prehistory to Statehood, 85; Grace, W. R. Grace & Co., The Formative Years, 1850-1930, 85; The Hispanic Experience in North America: Sources for Study in the United States, 92; The DeSoto Chronicles, 93. **CONTACT ADDRESS** Univ AL, Box 870000, Tuscaloosa, AL, 35487-0000. **EMAIL** lclayton@ua1vm.ua.edu

CLEGERN, WAYNE MCLAUCHLIN
PERSONAL Born 11/25/1929, Edmond, OK, m, 1954, 2 children **DISCIPLINE** LATIN AMERICAN HISTORY **EDUCATION** Univ Okla, AB, 51, MA, 54; Univ Calif, PhD, 59. **CAREER** From asst prof to prof hist, La State Univ, New Orleans, 59-69, actg chmn dept, 62-63, chmn dept, 63-65; PROF HIST, COLO STATE UNIV, 69-, Fel, Inst Caribbean Studies, Univ PR, 66; Orgn Am States fel, 77. **MEMBERSHIPS** AHA; Conf Latin Am Hist (secy-treas, 63). **RESEARCH** Political change in late 19th century; middle American History; rise of Third World. **SELECTED PUBLICATIONS** Auth, Central-America, 1821-1871--Liberalism Before Liberal Reform, Americas, Vol 0052, 96; Guatemalan Politics--The Popular Struggle for Democracy, Americas, Vol 0051, 95; Rural Guatemala, 1760-1940, Americas, Vol 0053, 96. **CONTACT ADDRESS** Dept of Hist, Colorado State Univ, Fort Collins, CO, 80523-0001.

CLEMENS, DIANE SHAVER
PERSONAL Born 09/05/1936, Cincinnati, OH, m, 1960, 1 child **DISCIPLINE** DIPLOMATIC HISTORY **EDUCATION** Univ Cincinnati, BA & BS, 58, MA, 60; Univ Calif, PhD(hist), 66. **CAREER** Instr hist, Santa Barbara City Col, 60-62; lectr, Boston Univ, 64-66; asst prof, Mass Inst Technol, 66-72; ASSOC PROF HIST, UNIV CALIF, BERKELEY, 72-, Lectr Ger, Univ Hawaii & asst to dean, East-West Ctr, 60-61; travel grants, Moscow, 67-68 & Budapest, 68; Old Dominion fel, 69. **MEMBERSHIPS** Peace Res Soc; AHA; Am Asn Advan Slavic Studies; Soc Historians of Am Foreign Rels; Orgn Am Historians. **RESEARCH** Soviet-American diplomacy; the Cold War; 19th and 20th century European and American diplomacy. **SELECTED PUBLICATIONS** Auth, Allies at War--The Soviet, American, and British-Experience, 1939-1945, Jour Amer Hist, Vol 0082, 95. **CONTACT ADDRESS** Dept of Hist, Univ of Calif, 3229 Dwinelle Hall, Berkeley, CA, 94720-2551.

CLEMENT, PRISCILLA FERGUSON
PERSONAL Born 01/12/1942, Long Beach, CA, m, 1964, 3 children **DISCIPLINE** AMERICAN HISTORY **EDUCATION** Stanford Univ, BA, 63, MA, 64; Univ Pa, PhD(hist), 77. **CAREER** Instr hist, Santa Ana Col, 64-66; instr, 66-78, ASST PROF HIST, PA STATE UNIV, DELAWARE COUNTY CAMPUS, 67-, Reviewer, Nat Endowment for Humanities, 80-; referee, Pa Mag Hist & Biog, 81- **MEMBERSHIPS** Orgn Am Historians; Conf Group Women's Hist; Social Welfare Hist Group; Berkshire Conf. **RESEARCH** Children and poverty in 19th century America; welfare and poverty in America, colonial times to the present; juvenile delinquency. **SELECTED PUBLICATIONS** Auth, Prisons and the American Conscience--A History of United-States Federal Corrections, Jour Amer Hist Vol 0080, 93; On The Edge--A History of Poor Black-Children and Their American Dreams, Jour Amer Hist, Vol 0081, 95; Moralists and Modernizers--America Pre-Civil War Reformers, Amer Hist Rev, Vol 0102, 97. **CONTACT ADDRESS** Delaware Cty Campus, Pennsylvania State Univ, Media, PA.

CLEMENTS, BARBARA EVANS
PERSONAL Born 05/26/1945, Richmond, VA **DISCIPLINE** RUSSIAN HISTORY **EDUCATION** Univ Richmond, BA, 67; Duke Univ, MA, 69, PhD, 71. **CAREER** Asst prof, 71-78, assoc prof, 78-86, PROF HIST, UNIV AKRON, 86-; Am Coun Learned Soc-Soc Sci Res Coun grant Soviet studies, 72-73. **HONORS AND AWARDS** NEH grants, 88, 93. **MEMBERSHIPS** AHA; Am Asn Advan Slavic Studies. **RESEARCH** Russian Revolution; Russian woman's movement; early Soviet history. **SELECTED PUBLICATIONS** Auth, Emancipation through Communism: The ideology of A M Kollontai, Slavic Rev, 6/73; Kollontai's contribution to the workers' opposition, Russ Hist, 75; Aleksandra Kollontai: Libertine or feminist?, Reconsideration Russ Revolution, 76; Bolshevik Feminist: The Life of Aleksandra Kollontai, Ind Univ Press, 79; Bolshevik women: The first generation, in Women in Eastern Europe and The Soviet Union, Praeger, 80; Working-class and peasant women in the Russian Revolution, 1917-1923; Signs, winter 82; The enduring kinship of the Baba and the Bolshevik women, Soviet Union, 85; The birth of the new Soviet woman, in Bolshevik Culture: Experiment and Order in the Russian Revolution, Ind Univ Press, 85; The impact of the Civil War on women and family relations, in Party, State, and Society in the Russian Civil War, Ind Univ Press, 89; Images of women: Views from the discipline of history, in Foundations for a Feminist Restructuring of Academic Disciplines, Harrington Park Press, 90; co-ed, Russia's Women: Accommodation, Resistance, Transformation, Univ Calif Press, 91; The Utopianism of the Zhenotdel, Slavic Rev, fall 92; Daughters of Revolution: A History of Soviet Women, Harlan Davidson, 94; Women in Russia: Images and realities, in Reemerging Russia: Search for Identity, Simon and Schuster, 95; Bolshevik Women, Cambridge Univ Press, 97; Women and the gender question, in Critical Companion to the Russian Revolution, Arnold, 97. **CONTACT ADDRESS** Dept of Hist, Univ of Akron, Akron, OH, 44325-1902. **EMAIL** bclements@uakron.edu

CLEMENTS, KENDRICK ALLING
PERSONAL Born 02/07/1939, Rochester, NY, m, 1964, 2 children **DISCIPLINE** AMERICAN HISTORY AND DIPLOMACY **EDUCATION** Williams Col, BA, 60; Univ Calif, Berkeley, MA, 61, PhD(hist), 70. **CAREER** From Instr to asst prof, 67-73, asst head dept, 72-73, ASSOC PROF HIST, UNIV SC,., Fulbright lectureship, US Dept State, 77-78. **MEMBERSHIPS** Orgn Am Hist; Southern Hist Asn; Soc Historians Am Foreign Policy. **RESEARCH** American foreign policy; environmental history; Canadian history. **SELECTED PUBLICATIONS** Auth, The Papers of Wilson,Woodrow, Va Mag Hist and Biog, Vol 0102, 94; The Presidents Man--Crowley, Leo and Roosevelt, Franklin in Peace and War, Jour Amer Hist, Vol 0083, 96; The Myth of the Modern Presidency, Jour Amer Hist, Vol 0082, 95; Herbert-Hoover-National-Historic-Site Cultural Landscape Report--Land-and-Community-Associates, Pub Historian, Vol 0019, 97; The St-Francis-Dam Disaster Revisited, Calif Hist, Vol 0075, 96. **CONTACT ADDRESS** Dept of Hist, Univ of SC, Columbia, SC, 29208.

CLENDENNING, JOHN
PERSONAL Born 10/12/1934, Huntington, WV, 2 children **DISCIPLINE** AMERICAN LITERATURE & CIVILIZATION **EDUCATION** Calif State Univ, Los Angeles, BA, 57; Univ Iowa, MA, 58, PhD, 62. **CAREER** From instr to PROF ENGLISH, CA STATE UNIV, NORTHRIDGE, 60-, INTERIM ASSOC DEAN, 97-98, chmn dept, 73-79; Am Coun Learned Soc study fel, 64-65 & fel, 68-69; Wesleyan Univ Ctr Advan Studies jr fel, 64-65; Guggenheim fel, 71-72; lectureship, Fulbright-Hays/Univ Athens, 77-78; mem delegate assembly, Mod Lang Asn, 78-80; pres, Stephen Crane Soc, 94-96. **HONORS AND AWARDS** Jerome Richfield Scholar, 96-97; Outstanding Prof, 96-97. **MEMBERSHIPS** MLA; Stephen Crane Soc. **RESEARCH** Philosophical themes in literature; American poetry. **SELECTED PUBLICATIONS** Auth, Cummings, comedy and criticism, Colo Quart, summer 63; Time, doubt and vision: Emerson and Eliot, Am Scholar, winter 66-67; Introd to Josiah Royce's The Feud of Oakfield Creek, 70; Letters of Josiah Royce, Univ Chicago, 70; The Life and Thought of Josiah Royce, Univ WI, 85; Stephen Crane and His Biographies, Am Lit Realism, 95. **CONTACT ADDRESS** Dept of English, California State Univ, Northridge, 18111 Nordhoff St, Northridge, CA, 91330-8200. **EMAIL** john.clendenning@csun.edu

CLIFFORD, DALE LOTHROP
PERSONAL Born 09/18/1945, Knoxville, TN **DISCIPLINE** HISTORY **EDUCATION** Vanderbilt Univ, BA, 66; Univ Tenn, MA, 68, PhD(hist), 75. **CAREER** Asst prof, 72-81, ASSOC PROF HIST, UNIV NORTH FLA, 81-. **MEMBERSHIPS** AHA; Soc Fr Hist Studies; Western Soc Fr Hist; Coord Comt Women Hist Profession. **RESEARCH** French National Guard; direct democracy in the French Revolutionary tradition. **SELECTED PUBLICATIONS** Auth, The French Revolutionary-Wars, 1787-1802, Jour Military Hist, Vol 0061, 97. **CONTACT ADDRESS** Dept of Hist, Univ N Fla, Jacksonville, FL, 32216.

CLIFFORD, GERALDINE JONCICH
PERSONAL Born 04/17/1931, San Pedro, CA **DISCIPLINE** HISTORY OF AMERICAN EDUCATION **EDUCATION** Univ Calif, Los Angeles, AB, 54, MEd, 57; Columbia Univ, EdD(hist educ), 61. **CAREER** Lectr hist & soc found educ, Univ Calif, Santa Barbara, 61-62; from asst prof to assoc prof educ, 62-72, res & travel grant, 63, assoc dean, Sch Educ, 76-80, chmn, Dept Educ, 78-81, PROF HIST EDUC, UNIV CALIF, BERKELEY, 72-, Guggenheim fel, 65-66; humanities res fel, 73-74 & 81-82; Rockefeller Humanities fel, Rockefeller Found, 77-78. **MEMBERSHIPS** AHA; Am Studies Asn; Hist Educ Soc (pres, 76-77); Am Educ Studies Asn; Am Educ Res Asn (vpres, 73-75). **RESEARCH** Autobiographical sources in the history of American education; women in educational history; nineteenth century American schools and colleges. **SELECTED PUBLICATIONS** Auth, Degrees of Equality--The American-Association-of-University-Women and the Challenge of 20th-Century Feminism, Amer Hist Rev, Vol 0102, 97; Intimate Communities--Representation and Social Transformation in Womens College Fiction, 1895-1910, Jour Amer Hist, Vol 0084, 97. **CONTACT ADDRESS** Sch of Educ, Univ of Calif, 1501 Tolman Hall, Berkeley, CA, 94720-1671.

CLIFFORD, JOHN GARRY
PERSONAL Born 03/22/1942, Haverhill, MA **DISCIPLINE** AMERICAN DIPLOMATIC HISTORY **EDUCATION** Williams Col, BA, 64; Ind Univ, MA, 65, PhD(hist), 69. **CAREER** Teaching asst hist, Ind Univ, 65-67; instr, Univ Tenn, 68-69; asst prof polit sci, Univ Conn, 69-72; vis assoc prof hist, Dartmouth Col, 72-73; ASSOC PROF POLIT SCI, UNIV CONN, 73-, Nat Endowment for Humanities younger humanist fel, 72. **HONORS AND AWARDS** Frederick Jackson Turner Award, Orgn Am Historians, 71. **MEMBERSHIPS** AHA; Soc Historians Am Foreign Rels. **RESEARCH** Biography of Grenville Clark; Selective Service Act of 1940; early Cold War; United States-Britain relations, 1945-1956. **SELECTED PUBLICATIONS** Auth, The Juggler--Roosevelt, Franklin as Wartime Statesman, Diplomatic Hist, Vol 0017, 93; Behind the Throne--Servants of Power to Imperial Presidents, 1898-1968, Jour Military Hist, Vol 0058, 94; American Visions of Europe--Roosevelt, Franklin,D., Kennan, George,F., and Acheson, Dean,G., Jour Interdisciplinary Hist, Vol 0027, 96; In the Shadow of War--The United-States Since the 1930s, Jour Military Hist, Vol 0061, 97. **CONTACT ADDRESS** Univ Connecticut, Storrs, CT, 06269.

CLIFFORD, NICHOLAS R.
PERSONAL Born 10/12/1930, Radnor, PA, m, 1957, 4 children **DISCIPLINE** MODERN HISTORY **EDUCATION** Princeton Univ, AB, 52; Harvard Univ, AM, 57, PhD (hist), 61. **CAREER** Instr humanities, Mass Inst Technol, 61-62; instr hist, Princeton Univ, 62-66; asst prof, 66-68, assoc prof, 68-76, chmn dept, 71-76, prof hist, 76-85, col prof, 85-93, vpres acad affairs and provost, 79-85, dean, E Asian Summer Lang Sch, 73-81, emeritus prof, 93- Middlebury Col. **MEMBERSHIPS** Am Hist Asn; Asn Asian Studies. **RESEARCH** China and the West; early 20th century. **SELECTED PUBLICATIONS** Auth, Retreat from China: British policy in the Far East, 1937-1941, Longmans, Green & Univ Wash, 67; auth, Urban Nationalism and the Defense of Foreign Privilege, Univ Mich, 79; auth, Spoilt Children of Empire: Westerners in Shanghai and the Chinese Revolution of the 1920s, Univ Press of New England, 91; auth, House of memory, Ballantine, 94. **CONTACT ADDRESS** 125 Sherman Ln, New Haven, CT, 05472. **EMAIL** clifford@panther.middlebury.edu

CLINE, CATHERINE ANN
PERSONAL Born 07/27/1927, West Springfield, MA **DISCIPLINE** HISTORY **EDUCATION** Smith Col, AB, 48; Columbia Univ, MA, 50; Bryn Mawr Col, PhD, 57. **CAREER** Instr hist, St Mary's Col, Ind, 53-54; from asst prof to prof, Notre Dame Col Staten Island, 54-68; assoc prof, 68-73, PROF HIST, CATH UNIV AM, 73-. **MEMBERSHIPS** AHA; Conf Brit Studies; Am Cath Hist Asn. **RESEARCH** Twentieth century England. **SELECTED PUBLICATIONS** Auth, Labor at War--France and Britain, 1914-1918, Jour Mod Hist, Vol 0066, 94; Defending the Empire--The Conservative Party and British Defense Policy, 1899-1915, Jour Mod Hist, Vol 0066, 94; Contemporary British History 1931-1961-- Politics and the Limits of Policy, Albion, Vol 0025, 93; Labors War--The Labor-Party During the World-War-2, Amer Hist Rev, Vol 0099, 94; Political-Change and the Labor-Party, 1900-1918, Jour Mod Hist, Vol 0066, 94; The Politics of Continuity--British Foreign-Policy and the Labor Government, 1945-46, Amer Hist Rev, Vol 0100, 95. **CONTACT ADDRESS** Dept of Hist, Catholic Univ of America, Washington, DC, 20064.

CLINE, ERIC
DISCIPLINE ANCIENT HISTORY **EDUCATION** Dartmouth Col, AB, 82; Yale Univ, MA, 84; Univ Pa, PhD, 91. **CAREER** Adj Asst prof, Col Sequoias, 92-94; Instr, Fresno City Col, 92-94; Adj Asst prof, Calif State Univ, 92-94; Adj Asst Prof, Miami Univ Ohio, 94-97; Adj Res Ast Prof, Univ Cincinnati, 94-97; Lecturer & Vis Ast Prof , Xavier Univ, 94-97; Lecturer & Postdoctoral Tchg Fel, Stanford Univ, 97-98. **HONORS AND AWARDS** Kress Found INSTAP, AIA, & Semple Fund Conf Grants; Fulbright Sch; ASOR/EBR Summer Res Grant; AIA Olivia James Traveling Fel; INSTAP Publ Subvention. **SELECTED PUBLICATIONS** Auth, Sailing the Wine-Dark Sea: International Trade and the Late Bronze Age Aegean, Tempus Reparatum, 94; auth, Amenhotep III: Perspectives on his Reign, Univ Mich Press, 97. **CONTACT ADDRESS** Univ Cincinnati, 3433 Ruther Ave, Cincinnati, OH, 45220. **EMAIL** Clinee@ucbeh.san.uc.edu

CLINE, PETER KNOX
PERSONAL Born 03/04/1942, La Crosse, WI, d **DISCIPLINE** MODERN BRITISH HISTORY **EDUCATION** Univ Wis-Madison, BA, 64; Stanford Univ, MA, 65, PhD(Brit hist), 69. **CAREER** Actg asst prof hist, Univ Wash, 67; asst prof, Univ Calif, Davis, 68-76; asst prof, 76-80, assoc prof, 80-83, PROF HIST, EARLHAM COL, 83-, assoc acad dean, 88-90; Regional coordr of Hist Day, Nat Endowment for Humanities, 77-; Humanities Develop grant, Earlham Col, 77. **MEMBERSHIPS** AHA; Conf Brit Studies; Soc Studies Labour Hist **RESEARCH** Nineteenth and 20th century British commercial policy; British imperialism; European politics since 1789; gay and lesbian studies. **SELECTED PUBLICATIONS** Auth, Reopening the case of Lloyd George and the postwar transition 1918-19, J Brit Studies, 11/70; Eric Geddes: Experiment with businessmen in Lloyd George's coalition governments 1915-1922, in: Essays in Anti-Labour History, Macmillan, London, 74; The Problem Of Economic Recovery, 1915-1919, in: War and the State, The Transformation of British Government, 1914-1919, Geo Allen & Unwin, London, 82. **CONTACT ADDRESS** Earlham Col, 801 National Rd W, Richmond, IN, 47374-4095. **EMAIL** peterc@earlham.edu

CLINTON, KEVIN
PERSONAL Born 09/29/1942, New York, NY, m, 1970, 2 children **DISCIPLINE** CLASSICS **EDUCATION** Boston Col, BA, 64; Johns Hopkins Univ, PhD, 69. **CAREER** Asst Prof Classics, St Louis Univ, 69-70; from Asst Prof to Assoc Prof, 70-81, Prof Classics, Cornell Univ, 81, Chmn Dept, 77-83; Vis Prof, Univ Calif-Berkeley, 86; mem, Inst for Advanced Study, 87-88. **HONORS AND AWARDS** Am Coun Learned Soc fel, 75; Soc for Humanities fel, Cornell Univ, 76-77; spec res fel, Am Sch Class Studies, Athens, 83-84; Guggenheim Fel, 87-88; corresponding member, Ger Archaeol Inst. **MEMBERSHIPS** Am Philol Asn; Archaeol Inst Am. **RESEARCH** Greek relig, lit and institutions. **SELECTED PUBLICATIONS** Auth, Inscriptions from Eleusis, Arkhaiologike Ephemeris, 71; Apollo, Pan and Zeus, avengers of vultures: Agamemnon, 55-9, Am J Philol, 74; The Sacred Officials of the Eleusinian Mysteries, Am Philos Soc, 74; The Hymn to Zeus, Traditio, 79; A Law in the City Eleusinion Concerning the Mysteries, 80 & The Nature of the Late Fifth-Century Revision of the Athenian Law Code, Suppl 19, 80, Hesperia; Myth and Cult: The Iconography of the Eleusinian Hysterics, Stockholm, 92. **CONTACT ADDRESS** Dept of Class, Cornell Univ, 120 Goldwin Smith, Ithaca, NY, 14853-0001.

CLINTON, RICHARD LEE
PERSONAL Born 09/20/1938, Cookeville, TN, m, 1986, 2 children **DISCIPLINE** POLITICAL SCIENCE **EDUCATION** Vanderbilt Univ, BA, 60, double MA, 64; Univ of NC at Chapel Hill, PhD, 71. **CAREER** Asst prof, Univ of NC at Chapel Hill, 71-76; assoc prof to prof, Ore State Univ, 76-98. **HONORS AND AWARDS** Fulbright sr lectureship, Lima, Peru, 82-83, & 97; A.J. Hanna Distinguished Visiting Prof, Rollins Col, 90, 93, 94, & 95; master teacher, Col of Liberal Arts, Ore State Univ, 95-97. **MEMBERSHIPS** Latin Am Studies Asn. **RESEARCH** Population & development policies. **SELECTED PUBLICATIONS** Auth, Grassroots Development Where No Grass Grows: Small-scale Development Efforts on the Peruvian Coast, Studies in Comparative Int Development, 91; auth, The Demographic Erosion of Development Efforts in Latin America: 1960-2000, Population Growth in Latin Am and U.S. Nat Security, Allen & Unwin Inc, 86; auth, Poblacion y Desarrollo en el Peru, Universidad de Lima, 85; auth, Does Ecological Risk Assessment Fit into Democracy?, Human and Ecological Risk Assessment, 95; auth, Latin America in Comparative Perspective: New Approaches to Methods and Analysis, Hispanic Am Hist Rev, 97. **CONTACT ADDRESS** Dept of Political Sci, Oregon State Univ, Corvallis, OR, 97331-6246. **EMAIL** richard.clinton@orst.edu

CLOTHEY, FREDERICK WILSON
PERSONAL Born 02/29/1936, Madras, India, m, 1962, 4 children **DISCIPLINE** HISTORY OF RELIGIONS **EDUCATION** Aurora Col, BA & BTh, 57; Evangel Theol Sem, BD, 59; Univ Chicago, MA, 65, PhD(hist relig), 68. **CAREER** Dir youth work, Advent Christian Gen Conf, 59-62; from instr to asst prof relig Boston Univ, 67-77; Assoc Prof Hist Relig, Univ Pittsburgh, 77-, Chmn Dept Relig Studies, 78-88; 95-98, Resident coordr, Great Lakes Cols Asn Year in India Prog, 71-72; producer & dir films, Yakam: A Fire Ritual in South India, spring 73, Skanda-Sasti: A Festival of Conquest, fall 73 & Pankuni Uttiram: A Festival of Marriage, spring 74. **HONORS AND AWARDS** Fulbright fel, 78, 82, 91, 98; AIIS Fellow 66-67, 81, 85, 91, 94. **MEMBERSHIPS** Am Acad Relig; Soc Indian Studies; Conf Indian Relig; Soc Sci Study Relig; Asn Asian Studies. **RESEARCH** Religion in South India; nature of myth, symbol, ritual; ethnic religion in America. **SELECTED PUBLICATIONS** Auth, The many faces of Murukan: The history and meaning of a South Indian God, Mouton, The Hague, 78; contribr, Chronometry, cosmology and the festival calendar of the Murukan Cultus, In: Interludes: Festivals of South India and Sri Lanka, Manohar Bks, 82; "Sasta-Aiyanar-Aiyappan: The God as prism of social History," Images of Man: Relgion and Historical Process in South Asia, 82; The construction of a temple in an American city & The acculturation process, In: Rythm & Intent: Ritual Studies from South India, Blackie & Son, 82; auth, Quiscence and passion: The vision of Arunakiri, Tamil Mystic Austin and Winfield, 1996; Rhythm & intent: Ritual studies from South India, Blackie & Son, 82; ed, Experiencing Siva: Encounters with a Hindu Deity, Manohar Bks, 82; Images of man: Religion and historical process, New Era Publ, 82. **CONTACT ADDRESS** Dept of Relig Studies, Univ of Pittsburgh, 2604 Cathedral/Learn, Pittsburgh, PA, 15260-0001. **EMAIL** clothey+@pitt.edu

CLOUSE, ROBERT G.
PERSONAL Born 08/26/1931, Mansfield, OH, m, 1955, 2 children **DISCIPLINE** EARLY MODERN EUROPEAN HISTORY **EDUCATION** Bryan Col, BA, 54; Grace Theol Sem, BS, 57; Univ Iowa, MA, 60, PhD(hist), 63. **CAREER** Assoc prof, 63-72, PROF HIST, IND STATE UNIV, TERRE HAUTE, 72-, Fel, Folger Shakespeare-Libr, Washington, DC, 64; grant, Penrose Rund, Am Philos Soc, 68; grants, Newberry Libr, 72, Lilly Libr, 76 & Nat Endowment for Humanities, 77. **MEMBERSHIPS** AHA; Am Soc Church Hist; Renaissance Soc Am.. **RESEARCH** Millennial thought in early modern Europe; Calvinism before the Age of reason; the rise of Pietism. **SELECTED PUBLICATIONS** Auth, The Protestant Evangelical Revival, Amer Hist Rev, Vol 0099, 94; The Formation of Hell--Death and Retribution in the Ancient and Early-Christian Worlds, Amer Hist Rev, Vol 0100, 95; Atheism from the Reformation to the Enlightenment, Church Hist, Vol 0064, 95. **CONTACT ADDRESS** Dept of Hist, Indiana State Univ, 210 N 7th St, Terre Haute, IN, 47809-0002.

CLOVER, FRANK M.
PERSONAL Born 05/05/1940, Denver, CO, w, 1965, 2 children **DISCIPLINE** ANCIENT HISTORY **EDUCATION** Univ of Chicago, PhD, 66. **CAREER** Prof of Hist and Classics, Univ Wis, Madison, 78-. **HONORS AND AWARDS** Netherlands Inst for Advanced Study, 91 & 94. **MEMBERSHIPS** Soc for Promotion of Roman Studies; Asn pour l'Antiquite Tardive. **RESEARCH** Roman empire; hellenistic age. **SELECTED PUBLICATIONS** Auth, The Late Roman West and the Vandals, Variorum, 93. **CONTACT ADDRESS** History Dept, Univ of Wisconsin at Madison, 455 N Park St., Madison, WI, 53706. **EMAIL** fmclover@facstaff.wisc.edu

CLOWSE, CONVERSE DILWORTH
PERSONAL Born 04/15/1929, Burlington, VT, m, 1964, 2 children **DISCIPLINE** AMERICAN HISTORY **EDUCATION** Univ Vt, BA, 51, MA, 53; Northwestern Univ, PhD(hist), 63. **CAREER** Admin asst sales, Procter & Gamble Co, Boston & Cincinnati, 55-57; from instr to asst prof, 62-69, ASSOC PROF HIST, UNIV NC, GREENSBORO, 69-. **MEMBERSHIPS** AHA; Orgn Am Historians. **RESEARCH** American Colonial history; American economic history. **SELECTED PUBLICATIONS** Auth, Mcgillivray, Lachlan Indian Trader--The Shaping of the Southern Colonial Frontier, Jour So Hist, Vol 0059, 93. **CONTACT ADDRESS** Dept of Hist, Univ of NC, Greensboro, NC, 27412.

CLULEE, NICHOLAS H.
PERSONAL Born 02/13/1945, Oak Park, IL, m, 1973, 2 children **DISCIPLINE** RENAISSANCE & REFORMATION HISTORY **EDUCATION** Hobart Col, BA, 66; Univ Chicago, MA, 68, PhD(hist), 73. **CAREER** From instr to asst prof, 71-76, chemn, dept of hist, 97-, prof hist, Frostburg State Univ, 85-; dir, Mod Humanities Inst, 92-. **MEMBERSHIPS** AHA; Renaissance Soc Am; Hist Sci Soc. **RESEARCH** Renaissance and natural philosophy; history of science. **SELECTED PUBLICATIONS** Auth, John Dee's mathematics and the grading of compound qualities, Ambix, 11/71; Astrology, magic and optics: Facets of John Dee's early natural philosophy, Renaissance Quart, 77; John Dee's natural philosophy: Between Science and Religion, Routledge, 88. **CONTACT ADDRESS** Dept of History, Frostburg State Univ, Frostburg, MD, 21532-1715. **EMAIL** n.clulee@tre.fsu.umd.edu

CLYMER, KENTON JAMES
PERSONAL Born 11/17/1943, Brooklyn, NY, m, 1967, 1 child **DISCIPLINE** UNITED STATE DIPLOMATIC HISTORY **EDUCATION** Grinnell Col, AB, 65; Univ MI, MA, 66, PhD, 70. **CAREER** Asst prof, 70-75, assoc prof, 75-82, Prof US Hist, Univ TX, El Paso, 82-; Fulbright prof, Silliman Univ, Phillipines, 77-78, Univ Indonesia, 90-91; George Bancroft Prof, Univ Gottingen, Germany, 92-93; Ch, Dept. Hist, Univ TX, El Paso, 84-85, 93-96; Assoc provost, TX Int Educ Consortium Prog, Malaysia, 86. **HONORS AND AWARDS** NEH summer stipends, 83, 98; Am Philos Soc, 72, 76, 81; Indo-US Subcomn on Educ and Cult, 87; Distinguished Res Award, UTEP, 94. **MEMBERSHIPS** Orgn Am Historians; AHA; Soc Historians Am For Rel(s); AAS. **RESEARCH** The US and Cambodia. **SELECTED PUBLICATIONS** Auth, John Hay: The Gentleman as Diplomat, Univ MI, 75; Protestant Missionaries in the Phillippines, 1893-1916: An Inquiry into the American Colonial Mentality, Univ Ill, 86; Quest for Freedom: The United States and India's Independence, Columbia Univ Press, 95; ed, The Vietnam War: It's History, Literature, and Music, TX Western Press, 98. **CONTACT ADDRESS** Dept Of US Hist, Univ of Texas, 500 W University Ave, El Paso, TX, 79968-0532. **EMAIL** kclymer@utep.edu

COAKLEY, THOMAS M.
PERSONAL Born 05/25/1929, Hamilton, OH **DISCIPLINE** BRITISH HISTORY **EDUCATION** Miami Univ, AB, 51; Univ Minn, Minneapolis, MA, 53, PhD(hist), 59. **CAREER** Asst prof hist, St John's Col, Man, 58-63; asst prof, 63-68, ASSOC PROF HIST, MIAMI UNIV, 68-. **MEMBERSHIPS** AHA: Conf Brit Studies. **RESEARCH** Tudor and Stuart England: Office patronage of Robert Cecil, first Earl of Salisbury; George Calvert, first Lord Baltimore. **SELECTED PUBLICATIONS** Auth, Hunters and Poachers--A Social and Cultural History of Unlawful Hunting in England, 1485-1640, Historian, Vol 0057, 94. **CONTACT ADDRESS** Dept of Hist, Miami Univ, Oxford, OH, 45056.

COALE, SAMUEL CHASE
PERSONAL Born 07/26/1943, Hartford, CT, m, 1972, 1 child **DISCIPLINE** ENGLISH, AMERICAN CIVILIZATION **EDUCATION** Trinity Col, Conn, AB, 65; Brown Univ, Am & PhD, 70. **CAREER** Instr Eng, 68-71, asst prof, 71-76, assoc prof, 76-81, asst dean, 78-80, prof eng & Am lit, Wheaton Col, 81, Co-Ch, Am hist & lit, 70, Wheaton res & travel grant, Wordsworth-Coleridge Conf, Engl, 72; Fulbright sr lectureship, Aristotelian Univ, Greece, 76-77, Universidade Federal de Minas Gerais, Brazil, 94; lectr, Engl, 72 & 96, Ann Poznan Am Cult Sem, Poland, 77, 78 & 79, India and Pakistan, 81, Sweden, 81, Czechoslovakia, 83-89, Israel and Egypt, 87, Pakistan, 90 & 93, Brazil, 90, Ygoslavia, 91, India, 94; Nat Endowment for Hum fel, 81-82. **HONORS AND AWARDS** A Howard Meneely Prof Hum, Wheaton, 98. **MEMBERSHIPS** MLA; Northeast Mod Lang Asn; Hawthorne Soc; Poe Soc; Knight of Mark Twain. **RESEARCH** Mod Am lit; 19th century Am lit; Engromantic poets. **SELECTED PUBLICATIONS** Auth, Faulkner and the Southern Imagination, Grammata, Greece, 77; John Cheever, Ungar, 77; Hawthorne's American Notebooks: Contours of a haunted mind, Nathaniel Hawthorne J, 78; The Marble Faun: A frail structure of our own rearing, Essays in Lit, 80; Anthony Burgess, Ungar, 81; A Quality of Light: The fiction of Paul Theroux, Critique, 81; An interview with Anthony Burgess, In: The Ludic loves of Anthony Burgess, Mod Fiction Studies, 81; Into the Farther Darkness: The Manichean pastoralism of John Gardner, In: Critical Essys on John Gardner, Southern Ill Univ Press, 82; Didion's Disorder: An American Romancer's Art, Critique, 84; Paul Theroux, Twayne, 87; William Styron Revisited, Twayne, 91; The Scarlet Letter as Icon, ATQ, 92; Hawthorne's Black Veil: From Image to Icon, CEA Critic, 93; Red Noses, The Black Death, and AIDS: Cycles of Despair and Disease, Ill, 93; Spiritualism and Hawthorne's Romance: The Blithedale Theater as False Consciousness, Literature and Belief, 94; The Resurrection of Bullet Park: John Cheever's Curative Spell, Greenwood, 94; The Romance of Mesmerism: Hawthorne's Medium of Romance, Studies in the Am Renaissance, 94; Hillerman and Cross: The Re-Invention and Mythic (Re)-Modeling of the Poplar Mystery, Clues, 95; The Dark Domain of James Lee Burke: Mysteries within Mystery, Clues, 97; Mesmerism and Hawthorne: Mediums of American Romance, Alabama, 98; Blood Rites (a novel), Commonwealth, 98. **CONTACT ADDRESS** Dept of Eng & Am Lit, Wheaton Col, 26 E Main St, Norton, MA, 02766-2322. **EMAIL** samcoale@aol.com

COBB, WILLIAM HENRY
PERSONAL Born 04/19/1938, Little Rock, AR, m, 1961, 2 children **DISCIPLINE** FRENCH HISTORY **EDUCATION** Univ Ark, Fayetteville, AB, 60, MA, 62; Tulane Univ, PhD(hist), 70. **CAREER** Instr hist, Memphis State Univ, 62-65; asst prof, Zavier Univ, La, 67-69; ASST PROF HIST, E CAROLINE UNIV, 69-. **MEMBERSHIPS** Soc Fr Hist Studies. **RESEARCH** Reign of Louis XIII: French political institutions and diplomatic history; Arkansas history. **SELECTED PUBLICATIONS** Auth, Rebel Against Injustice--The Life of Ohare, Frank,P., Ark Hist Quart, Vol 0056, 97. **CONTACT ADDRESS** Dept of Hist, East Carolina Univ, Greenville, NC, 27834.

COBEN, STANLEY
PERSONAL Born 08/06/1929, Flushing, NY, m, 1951, 2 children **DISCIPLINE** UNITED STATES HISTORY **EDUCATION** Univ Southern Calif, BA, 54; Columbia Univ, MA, 59, PhD(hist), 61. **CAREER** Lectr hist, Hunter Col, 60-62, asst prof, 62-64; asst prof, Princeton Univ, 64-67; assoc prof, 67-68, PROF HIST, UNIV CALIF, LOS ANGELES, 68-, Mem Am hist adv comt, NY State Bd Higher Educ, 64-66; Soc Sci Res Coun fac res fel, 67-68; vis prof hist, Univ Calif, Berkeley, 71; Am Philos Soc fel, 72, Guggenheim Mem Found fel, 72-73; Woodrow Wilson Int Ctr for Scholars fel, 74-75; mem, Univ Calif Liason Comt, Educ Progs, 77- **MEMBERSHIPS** AHA; Orgn Am Historians; Am Studies Asn; Econ Hist Asn. **RESEARCH** Twentieth century United States history: American nativism and race relations; American culture. **SELECTED PUBLICATIONS** Auth, Steel Valley Klan--The Ku-Klux-Klan in Ohio Mahoning Valley, Jour Soc Hist, Vol 0028, 94; The Invisible Empire in the West, Jour Soc Hist, Vol 0028, 94; Citizen Klansmen--The Ku-Klux-Klan in Indiana, 1921-1928, Jour Soc Hist, Vol 0028, 94. **CONTACT ADDRESS** Dept of Hist, Univ of Calif, Los Angeles, CA, 90024.

COBLE, PARKS
DISCIPLINE HISTORY OF EAST ASIA **EDUCATION** Univ Ill, Urbana, PhD, 75. **CAREER** Prof, Univ Nebr, Lincoln; ed bd, 20th Century China; assoc-in-res, Fairbank Ctr for E Asian Res, Harvard Univ. **HONORS AND AWARDS** Distinguished Tchg Award, Univ Nebr, Lincoln, 90. **RESEARCH** The Japanese occupation of China during the World War II. **SELECTED PUBLICATIONS** Auth, The Shanghai Capitalists and the Nationalist Government, 1927-1937, Harvard E Asian Monogr Ser, 80; Facing Japan: Chinese Politics and Japanese Imperialism, 1931-1937, Harvard E Asian Monogr Ser, 91. **CONTACT ADDRESS** Univ Nebr, Lincoln, 622 Oldfat, Lincoln, NE, 68588-0417. **EMAIL** pcoble@unlinfo.unl.edu

COBURN, THOMAS BOWEN
PERSONAL Born 02/08/1944, New York, NY, d, 2 children **DISCIPLINE** HISTORY OF RELIGION **EDUCATION** Princeton Univ, AB, 65; Harvard Univ, MTS, 69, PhD(comp relig), 77. **CAREER** Teaching fel relig, Phillips Acad, 65-66; instr math & physics, Am Community Sch, Lebanon, 66-67; from Instr to Prof, 74-90, Charles A. Dana Prof Rel Studies, St Lawrence Univ, 90-, Vice Pres St Lawrence Univ and Dean of Acad Affairs, 96-. **HONORS AND AWARDS** Sr res fel, Am Inst Indian Studies, 81-82; Nat Endowment for Humanities fel, 82. **MEMBERSHIPS** Am Orient Soc; Am Acad Relig; Asn Asian Studies; Asia Network. **RESEARCH** South Asian religion, especially the literature and mythology of popular religion in India; goddesses; methods in comparative study. **SELECTED PUBLICATIONS** Auth, Religion departments in liberal arts colleges: An inquiry, Ctr Study World Relig, Harvard Univ Bull, summer 77; Consort of none, Sakti of all: The vision of the Devi-Mahatmya, In: The Divine Consort: Radha and the Goddesses of India, Berkeley Res Publ, 1982, rev ed, 95; The Crystallization of the Goddess Tradition: The Sources and Context of the Devi-Mahatmya, Motilal Banarsidass, New Delhi, 84; The Conceptualization of Religious Change and the Worship of the Great Goddess, St Lawrence Univ, 80; Rethinking Scripture, SUNY Press, repr 89; Encountering the Goddess: A Trans. of the Devi-Mahatmya and a Study of Its Interpretation, State Univ of NY Press, 91; guest ed, Education About Asia, 2/97; author of numerous other journal articles. **CONTACT ADDRESS** Vice Pres and Dean of Acad Affairs, St Lawrence Univ, Canton, NY, 13617-1499. **EMAIL** tcob@ccmaillink.stlawu.edu

COCHRAN, CHARLES LEO
PERSONAL Born 05/03/1940, Salisbury, MD, m, 1966, 4 children **DISCIPLINE** POLITICAL SCIENCE **EDUCATION** Mount St Mary's Coll, BS; Niagara Univ, MA; Tufts Univ, PhD. **CAREER** Asst prof, Johns Hopkins Univ, 66-70; assoc prof, Johns Hopkins Univ, 70-75; ch, Johns Hopkins Univ, 86-90; ADJ PROF, JOHNS HOPKINS UNIV, 84-. **RESEARCH** Public policy; political economy. **SELECTED PUBLICATIONS** Coauth, Public Policy: Perspectives & Choices, McGraw-Hill, 95. **CONTACT ADDRESS** Dept Polit Sci, US Naval Acad, Annapolis, MD, 21402. **EMAIL** ccochran@nadn.navy.mil

COCHRAN, ROBERT
DISCIPLINE FOLKLORE **EDUCATION** Univ Toronto, PhD. **CAREER** English and Lit, Univ Ark. **HONORS AND AWARDS** Dir, Ctr Ark & Regional Studies. **SELECTED PUBLICATIONS** Auth, Vance Randolph: An Ozark Life, Ill, 85; Samuel Beckett: A Study of the Short Fiction, G K Hall, 91; A Mountain Life: Walter Williams of Newton County, Ark, 92; Unable to Sleep, The Father Fills Page After Page, Quart, 91; Deliberate Valediction: Williams' 'Pictures from Brueghel', Tenn Quart, 94; Our own Sweet Sounds: A popular History of Arkansas Music, Ark, 96. **CONTACT ADDRESS** Univ Ark, Fayetteville, AR, 72701.

COCHRAN, SHERMAN
DISCIPLINE HISTORY **EDUCATION** Yale Univ, BA, 62, MA, 67, PhD, 75. **CAREER** Asst prof, 73-79; assoc prof, 79-86; prof, 86-. **SELECTED PUBLICATIONS** Auth, Big Business in China: Sino-Foreign Rivalry in the Cigarette Industry 1890-1930, Cambridge, 80; coauth, One Day in China: May 21 1936, Yale, 83. **CONTACT ADDRESS** Dept of History, Cornell Univ, Ithaca, NY, 14853-2801. **EMAIL** sgc11@cornell.edu

COCHRAN, THOMAS CHILDS
PERSONAL Born 04/29/1902, Brooklyn, NY **DISCIPLINE** HISTORY **EDUCATION** NY Univ, BS, 23, AM, 25; Univ Pa, PhD, 30; Cambridge Univ, MA, 65. **CAREER** From instr to prof hist, NY Univ, 27-50; prof, 50-68, Benjamin Franklin prof, 68-72, EMER BENJAMIN FRANKLIN PROF HIST, UNIV PA, 72-, Mem historiography comt, Soc Sci Res Coun, 43-64, exec comt, 62-65; co-ed jour, Econ Hist Asn, 45-50, ed, 50-55; chmn & pres, Nat Records Mgt Coun, 48-50; vis lectr, Harvard Univ, 48-49; sem assoc, Columbia Univ, 49-; dir, Nat Bur Econ Res, 49-52; mem adv comt, Eleutherian-Milla-Hagley Found, 62-69; Pitt prof, Cambridge Univ, 65-66; fel, St Anthony's Col, Oxford Univ, 70; sr fel, Eleutherian Mills Libr, 73-74, 77-; Robert Lee Bailey prof, Univ NC, Charlotte, 73-74; guest ed, Am Hist Rev, 73-74. **HONORS AND AWARDS** LLD, Univ Pa, 72; LittD, Rider Col, 76. **MEMBERSHIPS** AHA (Pres, 72-); Am Acad Arts & Sci; Am Philos Soc; Orgn Am Historians (vpres, 64-65, pres, 65-66); Econ Hist Asn (secy-treas, 42-46, pres, 58-60). **RESEARCH** American social and economic history; the cultural approach to history. **SELECTED PUBLICATIONS** Auth, The Culture of Technology--An Alternative View of the Industrial-Revolution in the United-States, Science in Context, Vol 0008, 95. **CONTACT ADDRESS** Dept Hist, Univ Penn, Philadelphia, PA, 19104.

COCKFIELD, JAMIE HARTWELL
PERSONAL Born 06/20/1945, Charleston, SC **DISCIPLINE** HISTORY **EDUCATION** Univ SC, BA, 67, MA, 68; Univ Va, PhD, 72. **CAREER** Prof, Mercer Univ, 72- **MEMBERSHIPS** Amer Assoc Adv Slavic Stud; S Conf of Slavic Stud. **RESEARCH** Reign of Nicholas II; late nineteenth-early twentieth century Amer. **SELECTED PUBLICATIONS** Auth, Dollars and Diplomacy, Duke Univ Press, 81; With Snow on Their Boots, St. Martin's Press, 98. **CONTACT ADDRESS** 117 Huntington Pl, Macon, GA, 31210.

COCKRELL, DALE
DISCIPLINE MUSIC **EDUCATION** Univ Ill, BM, 71; MM, 83: PhD, 78 **CAREER** Asst prof, mus, Middlebury Coll; Bottoms prof mus, Wm & Mary Coll; PROF MUSICOL, BLAIR SCH MUS, VANDERBILT UNIV **HONORS AND AWARDS** Irving Lowens Award in Am Mus, 89. **MEMBERSHIPS** Am Antiquarian Soc **SELECTED PUBLICATIONS** Auth, "The Hutchinson Family: 1841-45, or The Origins of Some Yankee Doodles," Inst for Stud in Am Mus Newsltr, vol XII/I, 82; auth, articles in The New Grove Dictionary of Music in America, 86; auth, "Of Gospel Hymns, Minstrel Shows, and Jubilee Choirs: Toward Some Black African Musics," Am Mus, 87; ed, Excelsior, Journals of the Hutchinson Family Singers, 1842-46, 89; coauth, History of Western Music, 91; auth, Il Pescaballo and Ten Nights in a Barroom, Nineteenth Century American Music Theatre, no 8, 94; auth, "Jim Crow: Demon of Disorder," Am Mus 14/2, 96; auth, "Callithumpans, Mummers, Maskers, and Minstrels: Blackface in the Streets of Jacksonian American," Theater Annual 49, 96; auth, "Hutchinson Family Singers," in Encycl of New Eng Cult, forthcoming; auth, "Demons of Disorder: Early Blackface Minstrels and Their World," Cambridge Studies in American Theatre and Drama, No. 8, 97; auth, "Popular Music in the United States: 1820- 1880," in The Universe of Music: A World History, vol 10, forthcoming; auth, "Popular Music of the Parlor and Stage," Garland Encyclopedia of World Music, vol 8: North Am volume, forthcoming; auth, "Nineteenth Century Popular Music," The Cambridge History of American Music, forthcoming. **CONTACT ADDRESS** Blair Sch of Mus, Vanderbilt Univ, Nashville, TN, 37212. **EMAIL** cockrell@ctrvax.vanderbilt.edu

COCKS, GEOFFREY C.
PERSONAL Born 11/13/1948, New Bedford, MA, m, 1971, 1 child **DISCIPLINE** HISTORY **EDUCATION** Occidental Col, BA 70; UCLA, MA 71, PhD 75. **CAREER** Occidental Col, inst 74-75; Albion Col, asst prof, assoc prof, prof, 75-; UCLA, vis asst prof, 80; Albion Col, Royal G. Hall Prof, 94-. **HONORS AND AWARDS** Phi Beta Kappa; Outstanding Jr Fac Mem; Honor Prog Sch Tchg Awd; 3 NEH; 2 DAAD; NIH; Fulbright Fel. **MEMBERSHIPS** AHA **RESEARCH** Modern Germany; Hist of Psychotherapy; Medicine; Health Nazi Germany. **SELECTED PUBLICATIONS** Auth, Treating Mind and Body: Essays in the History of Science, Professions and Society Under Extreme Conditions, New Bruns NJ, Transaction, 98; Psychotherapy in the Third Reich: The Goring Institute, New Bruns NJ, Transaction, 97; Medicine and Modernity: Public Health and Medical Care in Nineteenth and Twentieth Century Germany, coed, Cambridge, CUP, 96; The Goring Institute: Context and Contents of the History of Psychiatry, in: Power and Knowledge: Perspectives in the History of Psychiatry, ed Matthias Weber, Munich, 98; Teaching Undergraduates Psychohistory, Clio's Psych, 97; The Old as New: the Nuremberg Doctor's Trial and Medicine in Modern Germany, in: Medicine and Modernity, co-ed, 96. **CONTACT ADDRESS** Dept of History, Albion Col, 611 East Porter St, Albion, MI, 49224. **EMAIL** gcocks@albion.edu

CODELL, JULIE
PERSONAL Born 09/19/1945, Chicago, IL, 1 child **DISCIPLINE** ART **EDUCATION** Vassar Col, BA, 67; Univ Mich, MA, 68; Ind Univ Bloomington, MA, 75, PhD, 78. **CAREER** Prof, 79-90, Univ Mt; dir, 91-, Az St Univ. **HONORS AND AWARDS** NEH Summer Stipend, 88; NEH Fel, 93; Yale British Art Center Fel, 94. **MEMBERSHIPS** Res Soc for Victorian Per; CAA; HBA; MLA; INCS. **RESEARCH** 19th cent British art; literature; early modernism; critical theory; film. **SELECTED PUBLICATIONS** Art, The Public Image of Victorian Artists: Family Biographies, J Pre-Raphaelite St, 96; auth, The Artist Colonized: Holman Hunt's 'Bio-History', Masculinity, Nationalism & The English School, Re-framing the Pre-Raphaelites, Scolar, 96; art, Charles Fairfax Murray and the Pre-Raphaelite Academy: Writing and Forging the Artistic Field, Collecting the Pre-Raphaelites, Scolar, 97; art, Ford Madox Brown, Carlyle, Macaulay, Bakhtin: The Pratfalls and Penultimates of History, Art Hist, 98; coed, Orientalism Transposed: The Impact of the Colonies on British Culture, 98. **CONTACT ADDRESS** Sch of Art, Arizona State Univ, Tempe, Tempe, AZ, 85287-1505. **EMAIL** Julie.Codell@asu.edu

CODY, MARTIN LEONARD
PERSONAL Born 08/07/1941, Peterborough, England, m, 1980, 4 children **DISCIPLINE** ZOOLOGY, MATH **EDUCATION** Univ Edinburgh, MA, 63; Univ Pa,PhD, 66. **CAREER** Asst prof, Zool, Univ Calif, LA, 66-72; PROF, BIOL, UNIV CALIF, LA, 72- **MEMBERSHIPS** Am Soc Natur; Ecol Soc Am; Cooper Ornith Soc **RESEARCH** Community ecology; Birds & plants. **SELECTED PUBLICATIONS** Monitoring Breeding Bird Populations in Grand Teton National Park," Univ Wy Nat Park Ser Res Center, 94; "Short-Term Evolution of Reduced Dispersal in Island Plant Populations," J Ecol, 96; "Long-Term Studies of Vertebrate Communities," Acad Press, 96; "An

Introduction to Neotropical Species Diversity," Diversity & Conser in Neotropics, 97; Birds of North America: California Thrasher Toxostoma Redivivum, 97; Birds of North America: Crissal Thrasher Toxostoma Redivivum, 98; "Assembly Rules in Plant and Bird Communities," Assembly Rules in communities, 98. **CONTACT ADDRESS** Dept Biol, Univ Calif, Los Angles, CA, 90024. **EMAIL** mlcody@ucla.edu

COFFEY, JOAN L.
DISCIPLINE HISTORY **EDUCATION** Barat Col, BA; Univ Colo, MA, PhD. **CAREER** Asst prof, Sam Houston State Univ, 90-. **RESEARCH** France and southern Europe, world history. **SELECTED PUBLICATIONS** Auth, French Labor Law and the Christian Corporation at Val des Bois, 1840-1914, Hist Reflections. **CONTACT ADDRESS** Dept of History, Sam Houston State Univ, Huntsville, TX, 77341.

COFFIN, DAVID ROBBINS
PERSONAL Born 03/20/1918, New York, NY, m, 1947, 4 children **DISCIPLINE** HISTORY OF ART **EDUCATION** Princeton Univ, AB, 40, MFA, 47, PhD(hist of art), 54. **CAREER** Instr fine arts, Univ Mich, 47-49; lectr art & archaeol, 49-54, from asst prof to assoc prof, 54-60, Marquand prof, 66-70, chmn dept, 64-70, PROF ART & ARCHAEOL, PRINCETON UNIV, 60-, H C BUTLER PROF HIST OF ARCHIT, 70-, Ed-in-chief, Art Bull, 59-62; Am Coun Learned Socs fel, 63-64; Guggenheim Found fel, 72-73. **MEMBERSHIPS** Col Art Asn; Soc Archit Hist (treas, 69-70); Renaissance Soc Am. **RESEARCH** History of Renaissance and Baroque architecture; history of Italian Renaissance art. **SELECTED PUBLICATIONS** Auth, Rome and the Studium-Urbis--Urban Space and Culture from the 15th to the 17th Centuries--Proceedings of a Convention, June 7-10, 1989-Italian, Cath Hist Rev, Vol 0079, 93; Il-Gran-Cardinale--Farnese, Alessandro, Patron of the Arts, Cath Hist Rev, Vol 0079, 93; Architecture in the Culture of Early Humanism--Ethics, Aesthetics, and Eloquence 1400-1470, Amer Hist Rev, Vol 0098, 93; The House of Gold--Building a Palace in Medieval Venice, Amer Hist Rev, Vol 0099, 94. **CONTACT ADDRESS** Dept of Arts & Archaeol, Princeton Univ, Princeton, NJ, 08540.

COFFMAN, EDWARD M.
PERSONAL Born 01/27/1929, Hopkinsville, KY, m, 1955, 3 children **DISCIPLINE** AMERICAN HISTORY **EDUCATION** Univ Ky, ABJ, 51, MA, 55, PhD, 59. **CAREER** From instr to asst prof hist, Memphis State Univ, 57-61; from asst prof to assoc prof hist, 61-68, PROF HIST, UNIV WISMADISON, 68-, Am Philos Soc grant, 60; res assoc, G C Marshall Found, 60-61; Nat Security Study Group grant-in-aid, 63; vis Dwight D Eisenhower prof, Kans State Univ, 69-70; mem adv comt, Off Chief Mil Hist, Dept Army, 72-76; mem, Nat Hist Publ Comn, 72-76; Guggenheim fel, 73-74; dir, US Comn on Mil Hist; vis prof US Mil Acad, 77-78; Harmon lectr, US Air Force Acad, 76. **MEMBERSHIPS** AHA; Am Mil Inst; Orgn Am Historians; Southern Hist Asn. **RESEARCH** American history, especially military and social history; the life of Gen Peyton C March; the United States in World War I. **SELECTED PUBLICATIONS** Auth, Lejeune--A Marines Life, 1867-1942, Jour Amer Hist, Vol 0079, 93; The American 15th-Infantry-Regiment in China, 1912-1938--A Vignette in Social-History, Jour Military Hist, Vol 0058, 94; Fort-Meade and the Black-Hills, Jour W, Vol 0033, 94; Blood Brothers--A Short History of the Civil-War, Jour So Hist, Vol 0060, 94; The Brownsville Raid, Jour W, Vol 0033, 94; Miles, Nelson and the Twilight of the Frontier Army, Jour Amer Hist, Vol 0081, 94. **CONTACT ADDRESS** Dept of Hist, Univ of Wis, Madison, WI, 53706.

COFFTA, DAVID J.
DISCIPLINE CLASSICAL PHILOLOGY **EDUCATION** Adjunct assoc prof, Canisius Col. **MEMBERSHIPS** APA; CAMWS. **SELECTED PUBLICATIONS** Auth, Programmatic Synthesis in Horace, Odes 3 13 in Collection Latomus, forthcoming; Programme and Persona in Horace Odes 1 5, in Eranos, forthcoming. **CONTACT ADDRESS** Classics Dept, Canisius Col, 2001 Main St, Buffalo, NY, 14208. **EMAIL** cofftad@canisius.edu

COFIELD, ELIZABETH BIAS
PERSONAL Born 01/21/1920, Raleigh, NC, m **DISCIPLINE** EDUCATION **EDUCATION** Hampton Inst, BS; Columbia U, MA; diploma in adminstrn & supervision. **CAREER** Wade County Bd of Commrs, Juan Medford co commr 1972; Shaw Univ, prof of educ. **MEMBERSHIPS** Elected to Raleigh Sch Bd 1969-72. **CONTACT ADDRESS** Education, Shaw Univ, 118 E South St, Raleigh, NC, 27602.

COHEN, ADA
DISCIPLINE ART HISTORY **EDUCATION** Brandeis Univ, BA; Harvard Univ, MA, PhD. **CAREER** Assoc prof, Dartmouth Col. **RESEARCH** Greek large-scale painting and mosaic in the late Classical/early Hellenistic periods; ancient art and gender. **SELECTED PUBLICATIONS** Auth, The Alexander Mosaic: Stories of Victory and Defeat, Cambridge UP, 97; Portrayals of Abduction in Greek Art: Rape or Metaphor? in Sexuality in Ancient Art, Cambridge UP, 96; Alexander and Achilles: Macedonians and 'Mycenaeans,' in The Ages of Homer, Univ Tex P, 95. **CONTACT ADDRESS** Dartmouth Col, 3529 N Main St, Ste. 207, Hanover, NH, 03755. **EMAIL** ada.cohen@dartmouth.edu

COHEN, ALVIN PHILIP
PERSONAL Born 12/12/1937, Los Angeles, CA, 2 children **DISCIPLINE** CHINESE PHILOLOGY & CULTURAL HISTORY **EDUCATION** Univ Calif, Berkeley, BS, 60, MA, 66, PhD(Orient Lang), 71. **CAREER** Lectr Orient Lang, Univ Calif, Davis, 70-71; asst prof, 71-77, assoc prof Chinese, Univ Mass, Amherst 77-83; actg bibliogr Orient Collection, Univ Mass, Amherst, 71-. **HONORS AND AWARDS** Fulbright-Hays Fel, 68-69; China and Inner Asia Council of the Assoc for Asian Studies grant, 95-97. **MEMBERSHIPS** Am Orient Soc; Chinese Lang Teachers Asn; Soc Study Chinese Relig; Assn for Asian Studies. **RESEARCH** Chinese historiography; Chinese folk religion. **SELECTED PUBLICATIONS** Auth, A bibliography of writings contributory to the study of Chinese folk religion, J Am Acad Relig, 75; Grammar Notes for Introductory Classical Chinese, Chinese Materials Ctr, 75, 2nd ed, 80; Humorous anecdotes in Chinese historical texts & Notes on a Chinese workingclass bookshelf, J Am Orient Soc, 76; Coercing the rain deities in ancient China, Hist Relig, 78; ed, Selected Works of Peter A Boodberg, Univ Calif, Berkeley, 79; Legend, Lore and Religion in China, Chinese Materials Ctr, 79. **CONTACT ADDRESS** Asian Lang Dept, Univ of Massachusetts, Amherst, MA, 01003-0002.

COHEN, GARY BENNETT
PERSONAL Born 10/26/1948, Los Angeles, CA **DISCIPLINE** HISTORY **EDUCATION** Univ Southern Calif, BA, 70; Princeton Univ, MA, 72, PhD(hist), 75. **CAREER** Instr, Princeton Univ, 74-76; asst prof, 76-82, assoc prof, Univ Okla, 82-95; res fel, dept hist, Princeton Univ, 78, Fulbright Hays & Int Res & Exchange Bd, 82. **MEMBERSHIPS** AHA; Conf Group Cent Europ Hist; Social Sci Hist Asn. **RESEARCH** Social history of modern Central and East Central Europe; Bohemian lands and Austria; European ethnic minorities. **SELECTED PUBLICATIONS** Auth, Jews in German Society: Prague 1860-1914, Cent Europ Hist, 3/77; Recent research on Czech nation-building, J Mod Hist, 12/79; The Politics of Ethnic Survival: Germans in Prague, 1861-1914, Princeton Univ Press, 81; Education and Middle-class Society in Imperial Austria 1848-1918, Purdue Univ Press, 96. **CONTACT ADDRESS** Dept of History, Univ of Oklahoma, 455 W Lindsey St, Norman, OK, 73019-2000. **EMAIL** gcohen@ou.edu

COHEN, GEORGE MICHAEL
PERSONAL Born 09/24/1931, Brookline, MA, m, 1964, 2 children **DISCIPLINE** ART HISTORY **EDUCATION** Harvard Univ, AB, 55, AM, 58; Boston Univ, PhD, 62. **CAREER** Asst prof art hist, Mass Col Art, 63-68; assoc prof, C W Post Col, Long Island Univ, 68-69 & Newark State Col, 69-70; prof art hist, Hofstra Univ, 70. **MEMBERSHIPS** Col Art Asn Am; AAUP; Appraisers Asn Am; Authors Guild. **RESEARCH** Am art. **SELECTED PUBLICATIONS** Auth, The paintings of Charles Sheeler, 59 & The lithographs of Thomas Hart Benton, 62, Am Artist; A History of American Art, Dell, 71; American impressionism, Ford Motor Co, 72; An art historical discovery and its importance to personal property appraisal, 6/75 & Interest and rise in market valuation of 19th century American genre painting, 12/77, Valuation; Outlines of art history, Univ Col Tutors, 77; Essentials of Art History & Essentials, J Am Art. **CONTACT ADDRESS** Fine Arts Dept, Hofstra Univ, 113 Calkins Hall, Hempstead, NY, 11549-0000.

COHEN, JEFFREY A.
PERSONAL Born 04/17/1952, Boston, MA **DISCIPLINE** HISTORY OF ARCHITECTURE **EDUCATION** Univ Pa, PhD, 91. **CAREER** Tchg fel, dept art hist, Univ Pa, 75-77; archit draftsman and surveyor, Univ Mus Exped, Cyrene, Libya, summers, 78-79; instr, art dept, Muhlenberg Col, Allentown, Pa, fall 79; res, surveyor, and photographer, Philadelphia Hist Sites Surv, Clio Grp Inc, Phildelphia, 77-80; lectr, archit dept, Drexel Univ, Philadelphia, sept 77-dec 80; asst ed for archit hist, The Papers of Benjamin Henry Latrobe, Md Hist Soc, feb 81-jan 86; assoc ed for archit hist, The Papers of Benjamin Henry Latrobe, Md Hist Soc, feb 86-sep 94; consult, Marianna Thomas Archit, Philadelphia, jul 93-dec 94; lectr, hist of art dept, Univ Pa, sep-dec 93; adjunct prof, archit dept, Drexel Univ, sept-dec 95; dir of res, archit arch, Univ Pa, may 95-; adjunct instr, MA prog in hist preserv, Goucher Col, Baltimore, Md, jun-dec 96; lectr, Growth and Structure of Cities dept, Bryn Mawr Col, jan 95; dir, Digital Media and Visual Resource Ctr, Bryn Mawr Col, jan 97-. **HONORS AND AWARDS** Robert Smith fel, Carpenters' Co of the City and County of Philadelphia, 92; Andrew W. Mellon fel, Amer Philos Soc, 89; Charles E. Peterson fel, Athenaeum of Philadelphia, 89-91; Dept Kress Found Fel, Univ Pa, 88-89; Dean's Scholar, Univ Pa, 88; Mellon Grad Fel, Univ Pa, 82-83; Dept Kress Found Fel, Univ Pa, 81-82; Victorian Soc Summer Sch Scholarship, 77; Rockefeller Found travel grant, 77; Nat Merit Scholarship, 70-74. **MEMBERSHIPS** Soc of Archit Hist, Philadelphia Chap, vpres, 96-98, pres, 98-; Soc of Archit Hist, nat, Educ Comt, 96-; Soc of Archit Hist, nat, Elect Comt, 95-; chair, 98-. **SELECTED PUBLICATIONS** Auth, with Charles B. Brownell, The Architectural Drawings of Benjamin Henry Latrobe, 2 vol, New Haven, Yale Univ Press, 95; auth, Accommodation and Redefinition in the Twentieth Century, in Norman Johnston, Eastern State Penitentiary: Crucible and Good Intentions, Philadelphia, Philadelphia Mus of Art, 80-99, 94; Building a Discipline: Early Institutional Settings for Architectural Education in Philadelphia, 1804-1890, Jour of the Soc of Archit Hist, 53, 139-83, jun 94; Rowhouse Heaven, ed Kenneth Finkel, Philadelphia Almanac and Citizens' Manual, Philadelphia, 100, 94; coauth, with George E. Thomas and Michael J. Lewis, Frank Furness: The Complete Works, NY, Princeton Archit Press, 91, expanded and corrected in rev ed, 96; assoc ed, The Correspondence and Miscellaneous Papers of Benjamin Henry Latrobe, vol 2, 1805-10, New Haven, Yale Univ Press, 86; vol 3, 1811-20, New Haven, Yale Univ Press, 88; coauth, with James F. O'Gorman, George E. Thomas and G. Holmes Perkins, Drawing Toward Building: Philadelphia Architectural Graphics 1732-1986, Philadelphia, Univ Pa Press, 15-116, 151-53, 86; asst ed, The Correspondence and Miscellaneous Papers of Benjamin Henry Latrobe, vol 1, 1784-1804, ed John C. Van Horne and Lee W. Formwalt, New Haven, Yale Univ Press, 84. **CONTACT ADDRESS** Rhys Carpenter Library A5, Bryn Mawr Col, 101 N. Merion Av., Bryn Mawr, PA, 19010-2899. **EMAIL** jcohen@brynmawr.edu

COHEN, JEREMY
PERSONAL New York, NY, m, 1977, 1 child **DISCIPLINE** JEWISH AND MEDIEVAL HISTORY **EDUCATION** Columbia Univ, AB, 74; Jewish Theol Sem Am, BHL, 74; Cornell Univ, MA, 76, PhD(hist), 78. **CAREER** Instr Jewish hist, Cornell Univ, 77-78, asst prof, 78-81 & coordr prog Jewish studies, 78-81; MELTON CHAIR JEWISH HIST, OHIO STATE UNIV, 82-, Fac fel, Soc for Humanities, Cornell Univ, 80-81. **MEMBERSHIPS** AHA; Medieval Acad Am; Asn Jewish Studies. **RESEARCH** Judaism and Christianity: comparative cultural history; anti-semitism; history of western religious traditions. **SELECTED PUBLICATIONS** Auth, Kentucky, Amer Jewish Arch, Vol 0046, 94; Political Liberalism, Mich Law Rev, Vol 0092, 94; Alfonsi,Petrus and His Medieval Readers, Amer Hist Rev, Vol 0100, 95. **CONTACT ADDRESS** Dept Hist, Ohio State Univ, Columbus, OH, 43210.

COHEN, JOEL ALDEN
PERSONAL Born 09/06/1938, Providence, RI, 2 children **DISCIPLINE** AMERICAN HISTORY **EDUCATION** Univ RI, BA, 60; Univ Conn, MA, 62, PhD, 67. **CAREER** From instr to asst prof, 65-73, assoc prof, 73-79, prof hist, Univ RI, 79-; Ed, RI Hist, 70-75. **HONORS AND AWARDS** Univ of RI Teaching in Excellence Award, 78 **RESEARCH** Colonial America; social and political history of the American Revolution; Rhode Island history. **SELECTED PUBLICATIONS** Auth, Rhode Island Loyalism and the American Revolution, 10/68; art, Democracy in Revolutionary Rhode Island: A Statistical Analysis, 2 & 5/70; art, Molasses to Muskets-Rhode Island 1763-1775, 11/75, RI Hist; coauth, Rule, Rhode Island (play), 76. **CONTACT ADDRESS** Dept of History, Univ of Rhode Island, Kingston, RI, 02881.

COHEN, JUDITH
PERSONAL Born 12/09/1949, Montreal, PQ, Canada **DISCIPLINE** MUSIC/HISTORY **EDUCATION** McGill Univ, BA, 71; Concordia Univ, BFA, 75; Univ Montreal, MA, 80, PhD, 89; Univ Toronto BEd, 96. **CAREER** Pres, Can Soc Traditional Mus, 93-97; ADJ GRAD FAC MUS, YORK UNIV. **HONORS AND AWARDS** Can Coun grants; SSHRCC grants. **MEMBERSHIPS** Iberian Ethnomusicol Soc; Europ Sem Ethnomusicol; Folklore Stud Asn Can; Int Coun Traditional Mus. **SELECTED PUBLICATIONS** Auth, Sonography of Judeo-Spanish Song in Jewish Folklore & Ethnol Rev, 93; auth, Women's Role in Judeo-Spanish Song in Active Voices, 95; auth, Pero la voz es muy educada in Hommage H.V. Sophia, 96. **CONTACT ADDRESS** 751 Euclid Ave, Toronto, ON, M6G 2V3.

COHEN, LESTER H.
DISCIPLINE HISTORY **EDUCATION** UCLA, BA, 66; Yale Univ, MA, 72; PhD, 74. **CAREER** ASSOC PROF, HIST, PURDUE UNIV **MEMBERSHIPS** Am Antiquarian Soc **RESEARCH** Am Liberalism, 1780-1820 **CONTACT ADDRESS** Dept of History, Purdue Univ.

COHEN, MARJORIE G.
PERSONAL Born 02/17/1944, Franklin, NJ **DISCIPLINE** POLITICAL SCIENCE/WOMEN'S STUDIES **EDUCATION** Iowa Wesleyan Col, BA, 65; NY Univ, MA, 69; York Univ, PhD 85. **CAREER** Lectr, 71-82, prof, York Univ, 84-86; prof, Ont Inst Stud Educ, 86-91; Ruth Wynn Woodward Endowed Prof, 89-90; CHAIR, WOMEN'S STUD & PROF POLITICAL SCIENCE & WOMEN'S STUD, SIMON FRASER UNIV, 91-. **HONORS AND AWARDS** Marion Porter Prize Feminist Res, 85; York Univ Fac Grad Stud Dissertation Prize, 85; Laura Jamieson Bk Prize, 89. **MEMBERSHIPS** Ed bd, Can Forum, 77-85; ed bd, Labour/Le Travail, 91-94; Nat Action Comt Status Women. **SELECTED PUBLICATIONS** Auth, Free Trade and the Future of Women's Work: Manufacturing and Service Industries, 87; auth, Women's Work, Markets and Economic Development in Nineteenth Century Ontario, 88; coauth, Cana-

dian Women's Issues, Vol I, Strong Voices 93, Vol II, Bold Visions, 95. **CONTACT ADDRESS** Dept of Women's Stud, Simon Fraser Univ, Burnaby, BC, V5A 1S6. **EMAIL** mcohen@sfu.ca

COHEN, MARTIN AARON
PERSONAL Born 02/10/1928, Philadelphia, PA, m, 1953 **DISCIPLINE** JEWISH HISTORY AND THEOLOGY **EDUCATION** Univ Pa, BA, 46, MA, 49; Hebrew Union Col, Ohio, BHL, 55, MAHL, 57, PhD(Jewish hist), 60. **CAREER** Asst instr Roman lang, Univ Pa, 46-48, instr, 48-50; instr, Rutgers Univ, New Brunswick, 50-51; instr Jewish hist, Jewish Inst Relig, Hebrew Union Col, Ohio, 60-62; from asst prof to assoc prof, 62-69, PROF JEWISH HIST, JEWISH INST RELIG, HEBREW UNION COL, NY, 69-, Nat chaplain, Am Vets World War II & Korea, 61-62; vis lectr, Antioch Col, 61-62; vis prof, Temple Univ, 63-65 & Hunter Col, 73-74; chmn, Nat Comt Jewish-Cath Rels Anti-Defamation League, B'rith, 76- **HONORS AND AWARDS** Chadabee Award for Outstanding Achievement, Nat Fedn Temple Brotherhoods, 76. **MEMBERSHIPS** Am Jewish Hist Soc; Cent Conf Am Rabbis; Soc Bibl Lit; Am Acad Relig; Am Soc Sephardic Studies (pres, 76-66). **RESEARCH** General Jewish history; Sephardic history; Jewish theology. **SELECTED PUBLICATIONS** Auth, The Sephardic Phenomenon--The Story of Sephardic Jews in the America and Their Subsequent Universalization Through Diaspora-A Reappraisal, Amer Jewish Archv, Vol 0044, 92. **CONTACT ADDRESS** Jewish Inst of Relig, Hebrew Union Col, 40 W 68th St, New York, NY, 10023.

COHEN, MIRIAM J.
PERSONAL Born 11/16/1950, Chicago, IL, m, 1974, 2 children **DISCIPLINE** HISTORY **EDUCATION** Univ of Rochester, AB, 71; Univ of Mich, MA, 73, PhD, 78. **CAREER** INSTR, 77-78, ASST PROF, 78-85, ASSOC PROF, 86-92, PROF, 92-, CHEMN, DEPT OF HIST, VASSAR COL, 96-99. **HONORS AND AWARDS** Phi Beta Kappa, 71; Ford Fel, ACLS, 87-88; Woodrow Wilson Nat Fel in Women's Studies, 75-76. **MEMBERSHIPS** Am Hist Asn; Org of Am Historians; Soc Sci Hist Asn; Coord Comt on Women in the Hist Profession; Berkshire Confr of Women Historians. **SELECTED PUBLICATIONS** Coauth, Politics, Unemployment and Citizenship: Unemployment Policy in England, France and the United States 1890-1950, Citizenship, Identity and Soc Hist, Cambridge Univ Press, 96; coauth, Work, School and Reform: A Comparison of Birmingham, England and Pittsburgh USA: 1900-1950, Int Labor and Working Class Hist, 91; The Politics of Gender and the Making of the Welfare State: A Comparative Perspective, J of Soc Hist, 91; auth, Workshop to Office: Two Generations of Italian Women in New York 1900-1950, Cornell Univ Press, 93. **CONTACT ADDRESS** Dept of Hist, Vassar Col, 124 Raymond Ave, Box 711, Poughkeepsie, NY, 12604-0711. **EMAIL** Cohen@vassar.edu

COHEN, MYRON L.
PERSONAL Born 06/24/1937, Jersey City, NY, m, 1996 **DISCIPLINE** ANTHROPOLOGY **EDUCATION** Columbia Col NY, BA 58; Columbia Univ, MA 63, PhD 67. **CAREER** Columbia Univ, lectr, asst prof, assoc prof, prof 66 to 97-. **HONORS AND AWARDS** Sr Sch Res Fell 2; Chiang China-kuo Foun Fell; Henry Luce Foun. **MEMBERSHIPS** FAAA; RAI; AAS **RESEARCH** Family organization; social organ; political organ; econ culture; religion; China; East Asia. **SELECTED PUBLICATIONS** Auth, Asia Case Studies in the Social Sciences: A Guide for Teaching, Armonk NY, M E Sharpe 92; House United, House Divided: The Chinese Family in Taiwan, NY, CUP 76; Commodities and Contracts In Late Imperial China: Economic Culture in a Qing-Period South Taiwan Community, in: Locating Capitalism in Time and Space: Global restructuring Power and Identity, ed, David L. Nugent, Berkeley CA, UCP forthcoming; North China Rural Families: Changes During the Communist era, Etudes Chinoises, Bull Assoc Fran, forthcoming; State and Society Under Qing 1644-1911, in: Asia in Western and World History: A Guide for Teaching, eds, Ainslie T. Embree Carol T. Gluck, Armonk NY, M E Sharpe 97; The Hakka or Guest People: Dialect as a Sociological Variable in Southeastern China, in: Guest People Hakka Identity in China and Abroad, ed, Nicole Constable, Seattle, UWP 96. **CONTACT ADDRESS** Dept of Anthropology, Columbia Univ, New York, NY, 10027. **EMAIL** mlc5@columbia.edu

COHEN, NAOMI WIENER
PERSONAL Born 11/13/1927, New York, NY, m, 1948, 2 children **DISCIPLINE** AMERICAN HISTORY **EDUCATION** Hunter Col, BA, 47; Sem Col Jewish Studies, BHL, 48; Columbia Univ, MA, 49, PhD(hist), 55. **CAREER** Asst prof, 62-67, assoc prof, 68-72, PROF HIST, HUNTER COL, 73-. **MEMBERSHIPS** AHA; Orgn Am Historians; Am Jewish Hist Soc; Asn Jewish Studies; Conf Jewish Social Studies. **RESEARCH** History of the United States in the twentieth century; American Jewish history. **SELECTED PUBLICATIONS** Auth, A Scapegoat in the New Wilderness--The Origins and Rise of Anti-Semitism in America, Jour Interdisciplinary Hist, Vol 0026, 96. **CONTACT ADDRESS** Dept of Hist, Hunter Col, CUNY, 695 Park Ave, New York, NY, 10021.

COHEN, NORMAN SONNY
PERSONAL Born 06/30/1933, Washington, DC, m, 1957, 2 children **DISCIPLINE** UNITED STATES HISTORY **EDUCATION** George Washington Univ, AB, 58; Pa State Univ, MA, 60; Univ Calif, Berkeley, PhD(Hist), 66. **CAREER** Instr US & English Hist, Purdue Univ, 64-65; instr, Ind Univ, 65-66; asst prof, 66-70, from assoc prof to prof Hist, Occidental Col, 70-82; ret Emeritus status. **HONORS AND AWARDS** The Robert Glass Prof Am Hist. **MEMBERSHIPS** AHA; Orgn Am Historians. **RESEARCH** American Revolution; class conflict and crowd action in early America; the Confederation period. **SELECTED PUBLICATIONS** Auth, The Philadelphia election riot 1742, Pa Mag Hist & Biog, 7/68; ed, Civil Strife in America, Dryden, 72. **CONTACT ADDRESS** Dept of History, Occidental Col, 1600 Campus Rd, Los Angeles, CA, 90041-3314.

COHEN, PATRICIA CLINE
DISCIPLINE HISTORY **EDUCATION** Univ Chicago, BA, 68; Univ Calif, Berkeley, PhD, 77. **CAREER** Assoc prof, asst prof to PROF, HIST, & ACTG DEAN HUM, UNIV CALIF SANTA BARBARA **MEMBERSHIPS** Am Antiquarian Soc **SELECTED PUBLICATIONS** Auth, "Statistics and the State: Changing Social Thought and the Emergence of a Quantitative Mentality in America, 1790-1820," Will & Mary Quar 3d ser, 38, 81; A Calculating People: The Spread of Numeracy in Early America, 82; "The Helen Jewett Murder: Gender, Licentiousness and Violence in Antebellum America," NWSA Jour, 90; "The Early (and soon broken) Marriage and Statistics: Boston, 1839," Hist Methods, 90; "Safety and Danger: Women on American Public Transport, 1750-1850," in Gendered Domains: Beyond the Public-Private Dichotomy in Women's History, 92; "Unregulated Youth: Masculinity and Murder in the 1830s City," Radical Hist Rev 52, 92; "Reckoning with Commerce: Numeracy in 17th and 18th Century America," in Consumption and the World of Goods, 93; "Doing Women's History at the American Antiquarian Society," Procs of the AAS 103, 93; "The Mystery of Helen Jewett: Romantic Fiction and the Eroticization of Violence," Legal Stud Forum, 93; "Ministerial Misdeeds: Bishop Onderdonk's Trial for Sexual Harassment in the 1840's," The Jour of Women's Hist 7, 95; The American Promise, 97; The Murder of Helen Jewett, 98. **CONTACT ADDRESS** Coll of Lett & Sci, Univ of Calif at Santa Barbara, Cheadle Hall, Santa Barbara, CA, 93106. **EMAIL** cohen@humanitas.ucsb.edu.

COHEN, PAUL ANDREW
PERSONAL Born 06/02/1934, New York, NY, 4 children **DISCIPLINE** CHINESE HISTORY **EDUCATION** Univ Chicago, BA, 55; Harvard Univ, MA, 57, PhD(E Asian hist), 61. **CAREER** Vis lectr hist, Univ Mich, 62-63; asst prof, Amherst Col, 63-65; assoc prof, 65-71, Edith Stix Wasserman Prof Asian Studies, Wellesley Col, 71-, ASSOC, E ASIAN RES CTR, HARVARD UNIV, 65- **MEMBERSHIPS** Asn Asian Studies; Soc Ch'ing Studies; AHA; AAUP. **RESEARCH** Nineteenth century Chinese history. **SELECTED PUBLICATIONS** Auth, Cultural China, Some Definitional Issues, Philos E and W, Vol 0043, 93; Fairbank, John, King May 24, 1907, September 14, 1991--In-Memoriam, Proc Amer Philos Soc, Vol 0137, 93; China and the American-Dream--A Moral Inquiry, Amer Hist Rev, Vol 0101, 96. **CONTACT ADDRESS** Dept of Hist, Wellesley Col, 106 Central St, Wellesley, MA, 02181-8204.

COHEN, RONALD DENNIS
PERSONAL Born 08/03/1940, Los Angeles, CA, m, 1965, 2 children **DISCIPLINE** HISTORY OF AMERICAN EDUCATION **EDUCATION** Univ Calif, Berkeley, BA, 62; Univ Minn, Minneapolis, MA, 64, PhD(Am colonial hist), 67. **CAREER** Asst prof Am hist, Hartwick Col, 67-69; fel, Macalester Col, 69-70; asst prof to prof hist, Ind Univ NW, 70-98. **MEMBERSHIPS** Orgn Am Historians; Hist Educ Soc (past pres and mem board of dir, 96-98); Sonneck Soc; Hist of Am Communism (vice-pres, 98-99). **RESEARCH** History of education in the United States; History of popular music in the United States. **SELECTED PUBLICATIONS** Coauth, The Paradox of Progressive Education: The Gary Plan and Urban Schooling, Kennikat, 79; Gary: A Pictorial History, Donning Co, 83; auth, Children of the Mill: Schooling and Society in Gary, Indiana, 1906-1960, Ind Univ Press, 90; ed, Wasn't That a Time!: First-hand Accounts of the Folk Music Revival, Scarecrow Press, 95; co-prod, Songs for Political Action: Folk Music, Topical Songs and the American Left, 1926-1954, Bear Family Records, 96; co-ed, Moonlight in Duneland: The Illustrated Story of the Chicago South Shore and South Bend Railroad, Ind Univ Press, 98; ed, Red Dust and Broadsides: The Autobiography of Sis Cunningham and Gordon Friesen, Univ Mass Press, 99; co-ed, Folk Music and Musicians, book series, Scarecrow Press; auth and coauth of numerous articles and other publications. **CONTACT ADDRESS** Indiana Univ, Northwest, 3400 Broadway, Gary, IN, 46408-1101. **EMAIL** rcohen@iunhaw1.iun.indiana.edu

COHEN, SHELDON S.
DISCIPLINE HISTORY **EDUCATION** NY Univ, PhD. **CAREER** Hist, Loyola Univ. **RESEARCH** American history. **SELECTED PUBLICATIONS** Auth, Thomas Wren: Portsmouth's Patron of American Liberty, Portsmouth Papers, 91; Yankee Sailors in British Gaols; Prisoners of War at Forton and Mill, 1777-1783, Univ Delaware Press, 95. **CONTACT ADDRESS** Fine Arts Dept, Loyola Univ, Chicago, 6525 N. Sheridan Rd., Chicago, IL, 60626. **EMAIL** scohen@wpo.it.luc.edu

COHEN, STEPHEN P.
DISCIPLINE POLITICAL SCIENCE **EDUCATION** Univ Chicago, BA, MA, Univ Wisconsin, PhD. **CAREER** Sr fel, Foreign Policy Studies, Brookings Inst; prof hist and polit sci, & dir of Program in Arms Control, Disarmament and Int Security, Univ Illinois, Urbana; Public Policy Planning staff, US Dept of State. **HONORS AND AWARDS** Scholar in residence, Ford Found, New Delhi. **RESEARCH** India; Pakistan; South Asian security and proliferation issues. **SELECTED PUBLICATIONS** Ed, Nuclear Proliferation in South Asia, 90; ed, South Asia after the Cold War: International Perspectives, 93; auth, Brasstacks and Beyond: Perception and Management of Crisis in South Asia, 95; auth, The Pakistan Army, 2d ed, 98; auth, Every Fifth Person: Perception of War and Peace in South Asia, forthcoming. **CONTACT ADDRESS** The Brookings Inst, 1775 Massachusetts Ave NW, Washington, DC, 20036.

COHEN, THOMAS VANCE
PERSONAL Born 12/19/1942, Norfolk, VA, m, 1967, 2 children **DISCIPLINE** SOCIAL HISTORY **EDUCATION** Mich Univ, BA, 64; Harvard Univ, PhD(hist), 74. **CAREER** LECTR TO ASSOC PROF HIST, YORK UNIV, TORONTO, 69-. **RESEARCH** Social origins, career patterns and opinions of Jesuits of sixteenth century; social anthropology of the honour ethic in Mediterranean Europe. **SELECTED PUBLICATIONS** Auth, The War of the Fists--Popular-Culture and Public Violence in Late Renaissance Venice, Jour Soc Hist, Vol 0028, 95; Binding Passions--Tales of Magic, Marriage, and Power at the End of the Renaissance, Jour Soc Hist, Vol 0028, 95; Mad Blood Stirring--Vendetta and Factions in Friuli During the Renaissance, Jour Soc Hist, Vol 0027, 94. **CONTACT ADDRESS** York Univ, 4700 Keele St, Downsview, ON, M3J 1P3.

COHEN, WARREN I.
PERSONAL Born 06/20/1934, Brooklyn, NY, m, 1988, 2 children **DISCIPLINE** HISTORY **EDUCATION** Columbia Col, AB, 55; Fletcher Schl Law & Diplomacy, AM, 56; Univ Wash, PhD, 62. **CAREER** Lectr, 62-63, Univ Calif, Riverside; asst prof to prof, 63-93, Mich St Univ; dist univ prof, 93-, Univ Maryland. **RESEARCH** Intl rels, esp Amer-E Asian. **CONTACT ADDRESS** Dept of History, Univ of Maryland, Baltimore County, Baltimore, MD, 21250. **EMAIL** wcohen@umbc2.umbc.edu

COHEN, WILLIAM
PERSONAL Born 06/27/1936, Los Angeles, CA, 3 children **DISCIPLINE** UNITED STATES & URBAN HISTORY **EDUCATION** Brooklyn Col, BA, 57; Columbia Univ, MA, 60; NY Univ, PhD, 68. **CAREER** Lectr US hist, Hunter Col, 65-68; res assoc Negro in the cities, Ctr Urban Studies, Univ Chicago, 68-71; from Asst Prof to Assoc Prof, 71-88, prof hist, Hope Col, 88; Vis asst prof, Univ Ill, Chicago, 68-69. **HONORS AND AWARDS** Nat Endowment for Hum fel, 80-81; Francis Butler Simkins Award for best first bk in southern hist in the past two years, Southern Hist Asn, for: At Freedom's Edge, 93. **MEMBERSHIPS** AHA; Orgn Am Historians; Southern Hist Asn. **RESEARCH** Reconstruction; agricult labor in the South; Black hist. **SELECTED PUBLICATIONS** Auth, Thomas Jefferson and the Problem of Slavery, J Am His, 12/69; Riots, Racism and Hysteria: The Response of Federal Investigative Officials to the Race Riots of 1919, Mass Rev, summer 72; Negro Involuntary Servitude in the South, 1865-1940, J Southern Hist, 2/76; Black Immobility and Free Labor: The Freedmen's Bureau and the Relocation of Black Labor, 1865-1868, Civil War Hist, 9/84; The Great Migration as a Lever for Social Change, In: Black Exodus: The Great Migration from the American South, Univ Miss Press, 91; At Freedom's Edge: Black Mobility and the Southern White Quest for Racial Control, 1861-1915, La State Univ Press, 91. **CONTACT ADDRESS** Dept Hist, Hope Col, 137 E 12th St, Holland, MI, 49423-3698. **EMAIL** cohen@hope.edu

COHEN, WILLIAM B.
PERSONAL Born 05/02/1941, Jakobstad, Finland, m, 1964, 2 children **DISCIPLINE** MODERN EUROPEAN HISTORY **EDUCATION** Pomona Col, BA, 62, Stanford Univ, PhD(hist),68. **CAREER** Instr mod Europe & France, Northwestern Univ, 66-67; lectr mod Europe, 67-68, asst prof mod Europe & France, 68-70, ASSOC PROF MOD EUROPE & FRANCE, IND UNIV, BLOOMINGTON, 70-, NDEA fel & Foreign Area fel, 68; Nat Endowment for Humanities grant, 71-72. **MEMBERSHIPS** AHA; Soc Fr Hist Studies. **RESEARCH** French racial thought; colonial history; modern Europe; French social history. **SELECTED PUBLICATIONS** Auth, The Colonial Experience in African Literature--French, Intl Jour African Hist Stud, Vol 0029, 97; Western Expansion and Imperialism from the 18th-Century to 1914--French, Intl Jour African Hist Stud, Vol 0029, 97; A Centenary, 1885-1985--Europe Relations with Africa and the Controversies Surrounding the Commemoration--French, Intl Jour African Hist Stud, Vol 0027, 94; French-Speaking West-Africa--Colonizers and Colonized, C.1860-1960--French, Intl Jour African Hist Stud, Vol 0027, 94; Civi-

lizing Mission--Exact Sciences and French Overseas Expansion, 1830-1940, Jour Interdisciplinary Hist, Vol 0026, 95; The Marseilles Colonial Trade--The Crisis of 1929-French, Intl Jour African Hist Stud, Vol 0026, 93; Nature, the Exotic, and the Science of French Colonialism, Jour Interdisciplinary Hist, Vol 0026, 96; Curing Their Ills--Colonial Power and African Illness, Jour Mod Hist, Vol 0066, 94; Finland and the Holocaust, Holocaust and Genocide Stud, Vol 0009, 95; There are No Slaves in France--The Political-Culture of Race and Slavery in the Ancien-Regime, Jour Interdisciplinary Hist, Vol 0028, 98; Imperial Identities--Stereotyping, Prejudice and Race in Colonial Algeria, Amer Hist Rev, Vol 0101, 96; France and Decolonization, 1900-1960, Intl Hist Rev, Vol 0015, 93; Disorienting Encounters--Travels of a Moroccan Scholar in France, 1845-1846, Intl Jour African Hist Stud, Vol 0029, 96. **CONTACT ADDRESS** Dept of Hist, Indiana Univ, Bloomington, Bloomington, IN, 47401.

COHN, BERNARD SAMUEL
PERSONAL Born 05/13/1928, Brooklyn, NY, m, 1950, 4 children **DISCIPLINE** ANTHROPOLOGY, HISTORY **EDUCATION** Univ Wis, BA, 49; Cornell Univ, PhD(anthrop), 54. **CAREER** Res assoc anthrop, Univ Chicago, 56-57; fel hist, Rockefeller Found, 57-59; asst prof, Univ Chicago, 59-60; assoc prof anthrop, Univ Rochester, 60-64; assoc prof, 64-67, chmn dept anthrop, 69-71, PROF ANTHROP & HIST, UNIV CHICAGO, 67-, Guggenheim fel, 64-65; vis prof, Univ Mich, 66-67; fel, Ctr Advan Study Behav Sci, 67-68; Richards lectr, Univ Va, 65; Am Coun Learned Soc-Soc Sci Res Coun fel, Comt Southern Asia, 73-74; Am Inst Indian Studies fel, 74-75; NSF grant, 75-77. **MEMBERSHIPS** Am Anthrop Asn; Asn Asian Studies; Royal Anthrop Inst; Am Soc Ethnohist; AHA. **RESEARCH** History of South Asia; comparative colonial systems; representations of authority in colonial India. **SELECTED PUBLICATIONS** Auth, The Sepoy and the Raj--The Indian Army, 1860-1940, Intl Hist Rev, Vol 0017, 95. **CONTACT ADDRESS** Dept of Anthrop, Univ of Chicago, Chicago, IL, 60637.

COKER, WILLIAM SIDNEY
PERSONAL Born 07/18/1924, Des Moines, IA, m, 1944, 4 children **DISCIPLINE** LATIN AMERICAN AND UNITED STATES HISTORY **EDUCATION** Univ Okla, BA, 59, PhD(Mex hist), 65; Univ Southern Miss, MA, 62. **CAREER** From asst prof to assoc prof Latin Am hist, Univ Southern Miss, 66-69; assoc prof, 69-74, PROF LATIN AM HIST, UNIV W FLA, 74-. **MEMBERSHIPS** Latin Am Studies Asn; Southeastern Conf Latin Am Studies; Southern Hist Asn; Soc Hist Discoveries. **RESEARCH** Spain in the Old Southwest and the Floridas; Mexico; United States-Latin American relations. **SELECTED PUBLICATIONS** Auth, Indians, Settlers, and Slaves in a Frontier Exchange Economy--The Lower Mississippi Valley Before 1783, Jour So Hist, Vol 0059, 93; Spanish Bluecoats--The Catalonian Volunteers in Northwestern New-Spain, 1767-1810, Jour W, Vol 0032, 93. **CONTACT ADDRESS** Fac Hist, Univ WFla, Pensacola, FL, 32504.

COLANTUONO, ANTHONY
PERSONAL Born 05/05/1958, Somerville, NJ, m, 1993, 1 child **DISCIPLINE** ART HISTORY **EDUCATION** Rutgers Univ, BA, 80; Johns Hopkins Univ, MA, 82, PhD, 87. **CAREER** vis asst prof, 86-88, Kenyon Col; vis asst prof, 88-89, Wake Forest Univ; asst prof, 89-90, Vanderbilt Univ; assoc prof, 90-, Univ Maryland Col. **RESEARCH** 16th & 17th century Italian, French & Spanish art. **CONTACT ADDRESS** Dept of Art History & Archaeology, Univ of Maryland, College Park, MD, 20742-1335. **EMAIL** ac65@umail.umd.edu

COLATRELLA, CAROL
DISCIPLINE CULTURAL STUDY OF NINETEENTH- AND TWENTIETH-CENTURY AMERICAN AND EUROPEAN L **EDUCATION** Rutgers Univ, PhD, 87. **CAREER** Assoc prof, exec dir, Soc for Lit & Sci, Ga Inst of Technol. **RESEARCH** Herman Melville's fictions. **SELECTED PUBLICATIONS** Auth, Evolution, Sacrifice, and Narrative: Balzac, Zola, and Faulkner; coed, Cohesion and Dissent in America. **CONTACT ADDRESS** Sch of Lit, Commun & Cult, Georgia Inst of Tech, Skiles Cla, Atlanta, GA, 30332. **EMAIL** carol.colatrella@lcc.gatech.edu

COLBERT, THOMAS BURNELL
PERSONAL Born 09/23/1947, Carroll, IA, m, 1978, 1 child **DISCIPLINE** HISTORY **EDUCATION** Univ Iowa, BA, 69, MA, 75; Oklahoma St Univ, PhD, 82. **CAREER** Vis instr, 79-80, Huron Col, SD; tchng asst, 75-79, 80-81, Oklahoma St Univ; instr, 81-87, chmn, social sci dept, 88-92, chmn social sci & physical ed, 92-96, prof, 92-, Marshalltown Comm Col. **RESEARCH** Amer Indian hist; political hist; 19th century rural western & midwestern hist. **CONTACT ADDRESS** 1707 Olson Way, Marshalltown, IA, 50158. **EMAIL** tcolbert@iavalley.cc.ia.us

COLBURN, DAVID RICHARD
PERSONAL Born 09/29/1942, Providence, RI, m, 1966, 3 children **DISCIPLINE** HISTORY AND SOCIAL SCIENCES **EDUCATION** Providence Col, AB, 64, MA, 65; Univ NC, PhD(hist), 71. **CAREER** Asst prof hist, East Carolina Univ, 71-72; ASSOC PROF HIST, UNIV FLA, 72-, Consult, Pa Ethnic Heritage Proj, 76-77; ed consult, Fla Hist Quart, 76- **HONORS AND AWARDS** Teacher of the Year, Univ Col, Univ Fla, 77; Social Sciences Publication Award, Dept Social Sci, Univ Fla, 77. **MEMBERSHIPS** Southern Hist Asn; Orgn Am Historians; Am Acad Polit Sci. **RESEARCH** Twentieth century American history; the Civil Rights Movement; American politics in the twentieth century. **SELECTED PUBLICATIONS** Auth, Crusaders in the Courts--How a Dedicated Band of Lawyers Fought for the Civil-Rights Revolution, Rev(s) Amer Hist, Vol 0023, 95; Inside Agitators--White Southerners in the Civil-Rights-Movement, Rev(s) Amer Hist, Vol 0023, 95; Race in America--The Struggle for Equality, Rev(s) Amer Hist, Vol 0023, 95; The Civil-Rights Era--Origins and Development of National Policy, 1960-1972, Jour Amer Ethnic Hist, Vol 0012, 93; New Directions in Civil-Rights Studies, Jour So Hist, Vol 0059, 93; The Color of Their Skin--Education and Race in Richmond, Virginia, 1954-89, Jour Amer Hist, Vol 0080, 93. **CONTACT ADDRESS** Dept of Hist, Univ Fla, P O Box 117320, Gainesville, FL, 32611-7320.

COLBY-HALL, ALICE MARY
PERSONAL Born 02/25/1932, Portland, ME, m, 1976 **DISCIPLINE** MEDIEVAL FRENCH LITERATURE **EDUCATION** Colby Col, BA, 53; Middlebury Col, MA, 54; Columbia Univ, PhD, 62. **CAREER** Teacher high sch, Maine, 54-55; teacher French, Gould Acad, Bethel, Maine, 55-57; lectr, Columbia Univ, 59-60; from instr to assoc prof Romance Studies, 62-75, Prof Romance Studies, Cornell Univ, 75-. **HONORS AND AWARDS** Fulbright grant, 53-54; NEH Fel, 84-85; recipient, Medaille des Amis d'Orange, 85; Chevalier des Arts et Lettre, French Govt, 97. **MEMBERSHIPS** Mediaeval Acad Am; MLA; Soc Rencesvals; Int Arthurian Soc; Acad de Vaucluse; Les Amis d'Orange; Soc Guilhem IX. **RESEARCH** Chretien de Troyes; the style of medieval French literary texts; William cycle epics. **SELECTED PUBLICATIONS** Auth, The Portrait in 12th Century French Literature: An Example of the Stylistic Originality of Chretien de Troyes, Droz, 65; In Search of the Lost Epics of the Lower Rhone Valley, Olifant, 80/81; Frustration and Fulfillment: The Double Ending of the Bel Inconnu, Yale Fr Studies, 84; William of Orange in the Canso de la Crosada, Magister Regis: Studies in Honor of Robert Earl Kaske, 86; L'Heraldique au service de la linguistique: le cas du cor nier de Guillaume, Au carrefour des routes d'Europe: la chanson de geste, 87; Guillaume d'Orange sur un noveau sceau medieval de l'abbaye de Gellone et la vache pie de Chateauneuf-de-Gadagne, Etudes sur l'Herault, 93. **CONTACT ADDRESS** Dept of Romance Studies, Cornell Univ, Goldwin Smith Hall, Ithaca, NY, 14853-3201. **EMAIL** amc12@cornell.edu

COLE, BRUCE
PERSONAL Born 08/02/1938, Cleveland, OH, m, 1962, 2 children **DISCIPLINE** ART HISTORY **EDUCATION** Western Reserve Univ, BA, 62; Oberlin Col, MA, 64; Bryn Mawr Col, PhD(art hist), 69. **CAREER** Asst prof art hist, Univ Rochester, 69-73; assoc prof, 73-77, prof art hist, Ind Univ, 77-, distinguished prof, 88; Nat Endowment for Humanities fel art hist, 72; Guggenheim Foundation fel, 76; Am Coun Learned Soc fel, 81. **RESEARCH** Italian Renaissance. **SELECTED PUBLICATIONS** Auth, Old and new in the early Trecento, Klara Steinweg-In Memoriam, 73; Some Sinopie by Taddeo Gaddi Reconsidered, Pantheon, 76; Giotto and Florentine Painting 1280-1375, Harper & Row, 76; Agnolo Gaddi, Oxford Univ, 77; Italian Maiolica from Midwestern Collections, Ind Univ Art Mus, 77; Musaccio and the Art of Early Renaissance Florence, Ind Univ Press, 80; Sienese Painting From Its Origins to the Fifteenth Century, 80 & The Renaissance Artist at Work, 82, Harper & Row; Pieio deua Francesca, Harper Colllins, 92; Siotto, The Scrovegni Chapel, Brazilier, 93; Studies in de Histoy of Italian Art, Pindar Press, 96; Titian and Venetian Painting, Westview Press, 98. **CONTACT ADDRESS** Dept of History and Art, Indiana Univ, Bloomington, 300 N Jordan Ave, Bloomington, IN, 47405. **EMAIL** coleb@indiana.edu

COLE, DONALD BARNARD
PERSONAL Born 03/31/1922, Lawrence, MA, m, 1949, 4 children **DISCIPLINE** HISTORY **EDUCATION** Harvard Univ, AB, 43, AM, 47, PhD, 57. **CAREER** Instr hist, 47-71, chmn dept, 61-66, dean, 75-80, PROF HIST, PHILLIPS EXETER ACAD, 71-, Consult, US Off Educ, 65-66; vis prof, Univ Calif, Los Angeles, 67-78; mem vis comt hist, Harvard Univ, 68-71; Am Coun Learned Soc grant-in-aid, 70-71; mem adv comt, Papers of Martin Van Buren, 71-; mem admin bd, Papers of Andrew Jackson, 72- **HONORS AND AWARDS** Yale Sec Sch Teaching Award, 65; Kidger Award, New Eng Hist Teachers Asn, 68. **MEMBERSHIPS** AHA; Orgn Am Historians. **RESEARCH** American immigration history; Jackson period in American history; biography of Martin Van Buren. **SELECTED PUBLICATIONS** Auth, The Jacksonian Promise--America, 1815-1840, Jour Amer Hist, Vol 0083, 96; Clinton,Dewitt and the Rise of the Peoples Men, Jour Early Repub-lic, Vol 0017, 97. **CONTACT ADDRESS** Phillips Exeter Acad, Tan Lane, Exeter, NH, 03833.

COLE, MARY HILL
PERSONAL Born 07/24/1957, Richmond, VA **DISCIPLINE** HISTORY **EDUCATION** James Madison Univ, BA, 79; Univ Va, MA, 82, PhD, 85. **CAREER** Asst prof hist, Wilson Col, 85-87; asst to ASSOC PROF, MARY BALDWIN COL, 87-. **HONORS AND AWARDS** Outstadning Teach Award, Mary Baldwin Col, 89; Alpha Lambda Delta, Freshman Teach Award, 92, 93; NEH Summer Inst, 91; Omicron Delta Kappa, 94., Phi Kappa Phi, 79; Governor's Fel, Univ Va, 80,79. **MEMBERSHIPS** Am Hist Asn, Folger Shakespeare Libr. **RESEARCH** 16th century English political hist. **SELECTED PUBLICATIONS** Auth, "James II and the Royal Bounty," in Essays in History XXVII, 83; "The Ceremonial Dialogue of Elizabeth and her Civic Hosts," in Ceremony and Text in the Renaissance, 96. **CONTACT ADDRESS** History Dept, Mary Baldwin Col, Staunton, VA, 24401. **EMAIL** mhcole@mbc.edu

COLE, RICHARD G.
PERSONAL Born 11/24/1934, Sioux Falls, SD, m, 1962, 4 children **DISCIPLINE** EUROPEAN HISTORY **EDUCATION** Eastern NMex Univ, BA, 56; Iowa State Univ, MA, 58; Ohio State Univ, PhD, 63. **CAREER** Instr hist, Ohio State Univ, 63-64; from asst prof to assoc prof, 64-74, actg chmn dept, 73-74, prof hist, Luther Col, Iowa, 74-, Dept Head, 86-98. **HONORS AND AWARDS** Fel inst res, Univ Wis, 66-67; Deutsche Forschungsgemeinschaft award to participate in reformation pamphlet conference, Tuebingen, Ger, 80; Fulbright Summer Seminar Award, Bonn and Berlin, Germany, 88; named Fel of Early Mod Studies, Sixteenth-Century Studies Coun, 98. **MEMBERSHIPS** AHA; Am Soc Reformation Res. **RESEARCH** Renaissance and reformation; modern Europe; sixteenth century Germany. **SELECTED PUBLICATIONS** Auth, European attitudes toward non-western peoples in sixteenth century French and German pamphlets, in Yearbook Am Philos Soc, 70; Sixteenth century travel books as a source of European attitudes toward non-white and non-western culture, Proc Am Philos Soc, 2/72; Dynamics of printing in the sixteenth century, in The Social History of the Reformation, Ohio State Univ, 73; The reformation in print, Arch Reformation Hist, 75; The Reformation Pamphlet and Communication Processes, In: Flugschriften als Massenmedium der Reformationzeit, Stuttgart: Klett-Cota, 81; Pamphlet Woodcuts in the Communication Processes of Reformation Germany, in Pietas et Societas: New Trends in Reformation Social History, Forum Press, 85; Humanists and Professors Encounter the New World in the Age of Discovery, in Platte Valley Rev, 92; The Interface of Academic and Popular Medicine in the Sixteenth Century, in J Popular Culture, Spring 93. **CONTACT ADDRESS** Dept of Hist, Luther Col, 700 College Dr, Decorah, IA, 52101-1045. **EMAIL** coler@martin.luther.edu

COLE, ROBERT
PERSONAL Born 08/24/1939, Harper, KS, m, 1990, 1 child **DISCIPLINE** HISTORY **EDUCATION** Ottawa Univ, BA; Kans State Univ, MA; Claremont Grad Univ, PhD. **CAREER** Prof of Hist, Utah State Univ, 70-. **HONORS AND AWARDS** Hon Lecturer Award, USU, 92, 94; HAST Col Res of the Yr, 93; elected Fellow of Royal Hist Soc, 94. **MEMBERSHIPS** N Am Conf on Brit Stud; West Conf on Brit Stud (co-founder & 1st pres). **RESEARCH** Modern Brit propaganda in war; film hist. **SELECTED PUBLICATIONS** Auth, A.J.P. Taylor: The Traitor Within the Gates, Macmillan, 93; auth, Traveller's History of Paris, Windrush, 2nd ed, 94; auth, Good Relations: Irish Neutrality and the Propaganda of John Betjeman, 1941-1943, Eire-Ireland, vol 30, no 4, 96. **CONTACT ADDRESS** Dept of Hist, Utah State Univ, Logan, UT, 84322-0710. **EMAIL** rcole@hass.usu.edu

COLE, TERRENCE M.
DISCIPLINE TWENTIETH CENTURY AMERICA **EDUCATION** Univ WA, PhD, 83. **CAREER** Univ Alaska **HONORS AND AWARDS** Usibelli Award. **SELECTED PUBLICATIONS** Auth,The Cornerstone on College Hill, Univ Alaska Press, 94; Crooked Past: The History of A Frontier Mining Camp, Univ Alaska Press 91; Nome: City of the Golden Beaches, Alaska Geog Soc, 84. **CONTACT ADDRESS** Univ AK Fairbanks, PO Box 757480, Fairbanks, AK, 99775-7480. **EMAIL** fftmc@aurora.alaska.edu

COLE, THOMAS RICHARD
PERSONAL Born 03/15/1949, New Haven, CT, m, 1972, 1 child **DISCIPLINE** AMERICAN HISTORY **EDUCATION** Yale Univ, BA, 71; Wesleyan Univ, MA, 75; Univ Rochester, PhD(hist), 81. **CAREER** ASST PROF MED HUMANITIES, UNIV TEX, MED BR, 82- **MEMBERSHIPS** Orgn Am Historians; Gerontol Soc. **RESEARCH** Aging and culture. **SELECTED PUBLICATIONS** Auth, Framing Disease--Studies in Cultural History, Jour Amer Hist, Vol 0080, 93. **CONTACT ADDRESS** Inst for Med Humanities, Univ of Tex, 301 University Blvd, Galveston, TX, 77550-2708.

COLE, WAYNE S.
PERSONAL Born 11/11/1922, Manning, IA, m, 1950, 1 child **DISCIPLINE** AMERICAN DIPLOMATIC HISTORY **EDUCATION** Iowa State Teachers Col, BA, 46; Univ Wish, MS, 48, PhD(hist), 51. **CAREER** Instr social studies, Bedford High Sch, Iowa, 46-47; from instr to asst prof hist, Univ Ark, 50-54;

asst prof, Iowa State Col, 54-56; from assoc prof to prof, Iowa State Univ, 56-65; PROF HIST, UNIV MD, COLLEGE PARK, 65-, Vis asst prof, Iowa State Col, 52-53; Fulbright lectr, Univ Keele, 62-63; fel, Woodrow Wilson Int Ctr Scholars, 73; Nat Endowment for Humanities fel, 78-79. **MEMBERSHIPS** Orgn Am Historians; Soc Historians Am; Foreign Rels (pres, 73). **RESEARCH** History of American foreign relations; American isolationism; Roosevelt and the isolationists. **SELECTED PUBLICATIONS** Auth, Selling War--The British Propaganda Campaign Against American Neutrality in World-War-II, Jour Amer Hist, Vol 0082, 95; The United-States and the Cold-War in the High North, Amer Hist Rev, Vol 0098, 93. **CONTACT ADDRESS** Dept of Hist, Univ of Md, College Park, MD, 20743.

COLEMAN, JOHN E.
PERSONAL Born 04/23/1940, Vancouver, BC, Canada **DISCIPLINE** CLASSICAL ARCHEOLOGY, GREEK **EDUCATION** Univ BC, BA, 61; Univ Cincinnati, PhD(classics), 67. **CAREER** Asst prof classics, Univ Colo, 67-69; lectr classical archaeol, Bryn Mawr Col, 69-70; asst prof, 70-74, ASSOC PROF CLASSICS, CORNELL UNIV, 74-, Dir, Excavations at Elean Pylos, Greece, 68 & Cornell Excavations at Alambra, Cyprus, 76- **MEMBERSHIPS** Archaeol Inst Am; Am Sch Class Studies Athens. **RESEARCH** Classical archaeology; Aegean archaeology; Cypriot archaeology. **SELECTED PUBLICATIONS** Auth, Early Aegean History, 2nd Series--Research Report 1975-1993 I--The Neolithic in Greece Excluding Crete and Cyprus-German, Amer Jour Archaeol, Vol 0101, 97; Halai, 1992-1993, Amer Jour Archaeol, Vol 0098, 94. **CONTACT ADDRESS** Dept of Classics, Cornell Univ, 120-A Goldwin Smith, Ithaca, NY, 14853-0001.

COLEMAN, RONALD GERALD
PERSONAL Born 04/03/1944, San Francisco, California, s **DISCIPLINE** HISTORY **EDUCATION** Univ of UT, BS Sociology 1966, PhD History 1980; CA State Univ Sacramento, CA teaching certificate secondary 1968, MA Social Science 1973. **CAREER** General Mills Inc, grocery sales rep 1966-67; San Francisco Unified Sch Dist, faculty teacher social studies phys ed 1968-70; Sacramento City Coll, faculty instructor social science 1970-73; Univ of UT, dir of Afro-Amer studies 1981-, coord of ethnic studies 1984-; CA State Univ Haywood, visiting prof Afro-Amer studies 1981; Univ of UT, prof of history, Diversity and Faculty Development, associate vice president 1989-. **HONORS AND AWARDS** Phi Kappa Phi 1979; Merit Society for Distinguished Alumni George Washington High School; University of Utah, Hatch Price Award for Distinguished Teaching, 1990. **MEMBERSHIPS** Consultant UT State Cultural Awareness Training Prog 1974-76; consultant UT State Bd of Educ 1981; consultant UT State Historical Soc 1981; mem UT Endowment for the Humanities 1982-88; commissioner Salt Lake City Civil Service Comm 1983-; chairperson Salt Lake City Branch NAACP Educ Comm 1984-85; mem UT Chapter American Civil Liberties Union 1989-; mem Salt Lake Sports Advisory Board 1990-. **SELECTED PUBLICATIONS** "Blacks in Pioneer Utah 1847-1869" UOMOJA Scholar/Journal of Black Studies 1979; "Blacks in Utah History: An Unknown Legacy" The Peoples of Utah 1976; "The Buffalo Soldiers, Guardians of the Uintah Frontier 1886-1901" Utah Historical Quarterly 1979; Martin Luther King Jr: Apostle of Social Justice, Peace and Love pamphlet printed for Univ of Utah Martin Luther King Jr Comm 1985 **CONTACT ADDRESS** Professor of History, Univ of Utah, Salt Lake City, UT, 84112.

COLETTA, PAOLO E.
PERSONAL Born 02/03/1916, Plainfield, NJ, m, 1940, 3 children **DISCIPLINE** UNITED STATES HISTORY **EDUCATION** Univ Mo, BS, 38, MA, 39, PhD(Brit hist), 42. **CAREER** Instr Am hist, Univ Mo, 40-42 & SDak State Col, 46; instr soc sci, Stephens Col, 42-43 & Univ Louisville, 46; from instr to asst prof hist, 46-55, assoc prof, 58-63, PROF HIST, US NAVAL ACAD, 63-, Fulbright sr lectr Am hist, Univ Genoa, 71. **MEMBERSHIPS** AHA; Orgn Am Historians: Am Mil Inst; Nav Inst; Southern Hist Asn. **RESEARCH** Recent United States history; naval history. **SELECTED PUBLICATIONS** Auth, Launching the Doolittle Raid on Japan, April 18, 1942, Pacific Hist Rev, Vol 0062, 93; A Selectively Annotated-Bibliography of Naval Power in the American-Civil-War, Civil War Hist, Vol 0042, 96; Moffet, William,A. and His Disastrous Dirigibles--The Rear Admiral and His Promotion of Nonrigid Airships, Amer Neptune, Vol 0056, 96; Macarthur Ultra Codebreaking and the War Against Japan, 1942-1945, Pacific Hist Rev, Vol 0063, 94. **CONTACT ADDRESS** Dept of Hist, US Naval Acad, Annapolis, MD, 21402.

COLISH, MARCIA L.
PERSONAL Born 07/27/1937, Brooklyn, NY **DISCIPLINE** HISTORY **EDUCATION** Smith Col, BA, 58; Yale Univ, MA, 59, PhD, 65. **CAREER** Instr, Skidmore Col, 62-63; instr, Oberlin Col, 63-65; from asst prof to prof, Oberlin Col, 65-; lectr, Case Western Reserve Univ, 66-67; chemn, Dept of Hist, Oberlin Col, 73-74, 78-81, 85-86. **HONORS AND AWARDS** Phi Beta Kappa, 58; Hazel Edgerly Prize, Smith Col, 58; Samuel S. Fels Fel, Yale Univ, 61-61; Grants for res and travel, Oberlin Col, 63, 66, 72, 74, 77, 79, 84, 85, 89, 98; Res Status App, Oberlin Col, 68-69, 89-90; Nat Endowment for the Hums, Younger Scholar Fel, 68-69, Sen Fel, 81-82; Vis Scholar, Am Acad in Rome, 68-69; ACLS Travel Grants, 74, 87; Fel Inst for Res in the Hums, Univ of Wis, 74-75; Fel, Nat Hums Ctr, 81-82; Vis Scholar, Harvard Univ, fall term, 82; Vis Scholar, Weston Sch of Theol, fall term, 82; Mem, Sch for Hist Studies, Inst for Advan Study, 86-87; Fel, Medieval Acad of Am, 88-; J.S. Guggenheim Fel, 89-90; Vis Fel, Yale Univ, 89-90; Wilbur Cross Medal, Yale Grad Sch Alumni Asn, 93; NEH Summer Sem, Univ of Calif, 93; Fel, W. Wilson Ctr, 94-95; Rockefeller Found Writing Residency, Bellagio, 95; Haskins Medal, Medieval Acad of Am, 98; Travel Grant, Am Philos Soc, 98. **MEMBERSHIPS** AHA; Medieval Acad of Am; Midwest Medieval Conf; Medieval Asn of the Midwest; Renaissance Soc of Am; Central Renaissance Conf; Am Asn of Univ Profs; Societe Internationale Pour l'Etude de Philosophie Medievale; Int Soc for the Classical Tradition; Ohio Hums Coun. **SELECTED PUBLICATIONS** Auth, The Mirror of Language: A Study in the Medieval Theory of Knowledge, 83; The Stoic Tradition from Antiquity to the Early Middle Ages, I: Stoicism in Classical Latin Literature, 90; The Stoic Tradion from Antiquity to the Early Middle Ages, II: Stoicism in Latin Christian Thought through the Sixth Century, 90; Habitus Revisited: A Reply to Cary Nederman, in Traditio 48, 93; Intellectual History, in The Past and Future of Medieval Studies, ed. J. Van Engen, 94; Peter Lombard, 2 vols., 94; From the Sentence Collection to the Sentence Commentary and the Summa: Parisian Scholastic Theology, 1130-1215, in Manuels, programmes de cours et techniques d'enseignement dans les universites medievales, ed. J. Hamesse, 94; The Development of Lombardian Theology, 1160-1215, in Centres of Learning and Location in Pre-Modern Europe and the Near East, ed. J.E. Drijvers and A.A. MacDonald, 95; Medieval Europe: Church and Intellectual History, in AHA Guide to Hist Lit, 3rd ed, 95; Early Scholastic Angelology, in Recherches de theologie ancienne et medievale 62, 95; Christological Nihilianism in The Second Half of the Twelfth Century, in Recherches de theologie ancienne et medievale 63, 96; The Virtuous Pagan: Dante and the Christian Tradition, in The Unbounded Community: Papers in Christian Ecumenism in Honor of Jaroslav Pelikan, ed W. Caferro and D.G. Fisher, 96, The Sentence Collection and the Education of Professional Theologians in the Twelfth Century, in The Intellectual Climate of the Early Univ: Essays in Honor of Otto Gruendler, ed N. Van Deusen, 97; Medieval Foundations of the Western Intellectual Tradition, 400-1400, 97; Peter Lombard, in Routledge Dictionary of Philos, ed. E. Craig, 98. **CONTACT ADDRESS** Dept of History, Oberlin Col, Oberlin, OH, 44074. **EMAIL** fcolish@oberlin.edu

COLL, BLANCHE D
PERSONAL Born 12/26/1916, Baltimore, MD **DISCIPLINE** AMERICAN AND SOCIAL HISTORY **EDUCATION** Johns Hopkins Univ, BS, 43, MA, 48. **CAREER** Historian Labor hist, Hist Div, US Maritime Comn, 46-48 & Am mil hist, Engr Hist Div, US Dept Army, 48-60; historian social welfare hist, Social & Rehab Serv, 64-77, chief, planning & eval br, Off Child Support Enforcement, Hew, 77-79; RES & WRITING, 79- **HONORS AND AWARDS** Sustained Superior Performance Award, US Army Corps Engrs, 59. **MEMBERSHIPS** Orgn Am Historians; Soc Hist Fed Govt. **RESEARCH** Social Welfare; labor and military history. **SELECTED PUBLICATIONS** Auth, Improving Poor People--The Welfare-State, the Underclass, and Urban-Schools as History, Jour Econ Hist, Vol 0056, 96. **CONTACT ADDRESS** Dept of Health & Human Services, 314 Massachusetts Ave NE, Washington, DC, 20002.

COLLARD, ELIZABETH
PERSONAL Born 10/20/1917, Sawyerville, PQ, Canada **DISCIPLINE** HISTORY **EDUCATION** Univ Toronto, 37-38; Mt Allison Univ, BA, 39; Univ Maine 40. **CAREER** Tchr, St. Helen's Sch, 40-42; educ ed, The Montreal Gazette, 42-47; lectr, hist ceramics, Univ Ottawa, 84-89; lectr, hist ceramics, McGill Univ, 86, 88; consult ceramics, Can Mus Civilization, Ottawa; hon cur ceramics, McCord Mus Can Hist, Montreal. **HONORS AND AWARDS** Order Can, 87 **MEMBERSHIPS** Eng Ceramic Circle; Wedgewood Soc Eng. **SELECTED PUBLICATIONS** Auth, Nineteenth Century Pottery and Porcelain in Canada, 67, rev 84; auth, The Potters' View of Canada: Canadian Scenes on Nineteenth Century Earthenware, 83; auth, Victorian Pottery and Porcelain in the Canadian Home, 84; contribur, Book of Canadian Antiques, 74; contribur, English Pottery and Porcelain, 80; contribur, The Canadian Encyclopedia; contribur, Dictionary of Canadian Biography. **CONTACT ADDRESS** 400 Stewart St, Apt 1609, Ottawa, ON, K1N 6L2.

COLLIE, MICHAEL J.
PERSONAL Born 08/08/1929, Eastbourne, England **DISCIPLINE** ENGLISH/HISTORY OF SCIENCE **EDUCATION** St Catharine's Col, Cambridge Univ, MA, 56. **CAREER** Asst prof, Univ Man, 57; lectr, Univ Exeter, 61; assoc prof, Mt Allison Univ, 62; prof Eng, 65-90, dept ch, 67-69, dean grad stud, 69-73, PROF EMER, YORK UNIV, 90-. **MEMBERSHIPS** Int Asn Univ Profs Eng; Mod Hum Res Asn; Bibliog Soc; Bibliog Soc Am; Asn Can Univ Tchrs Eng (pres, 68-69); Can Bibliog Soc; Soc Hist Sci; Geol Soc Am; Geol Soc London; Edinburgh Bibliog Soc. **SELECTED PUBLICATIONS** Auth, George Borrow Eccentric, 82; auth, George Borrow: A Bibliographical Study, 84; auth, George Gissing: A Bibliographical Study, 85; auth, Henry Maudsley: Victorian Psychiatrist, 88; auth, Huxley at Work, 91; auth, Murchison in Moray: the Geologist on Home Ground, 95; auth, George Gordon: A Catalogue of His Scientific Correspondence, 96. **CONTACT ADDRESS** Winters Col, York Univ, North York, ON, M3J 1P3.

COLLIER-THOMAS, BETTYE
PERSONAL Born 02/18/1941, Macon, GA, m, 1963 **DISCIPLINE** HISTORY **EDUCATION** Allen Univ, BA, 63; Atlanta Univ, MA, 66; George Wash Univ, 74. **CAREER** Instr, 66-69, Dir of Hon, 69-71, Howard Univ; lectr, 71-74, asst prof, 74-76, Univ Maryland; spec consul, 77-81, Natl Endowment for Hum; founding exec dir, 77-89, Bethune Mus & Archives; assoc prof, 89-97, prof, 98-, dir, Ctr for African Am Hist & Cult, 89-97, Temple Univ. **HONORS AND AWARDS** Ford Found Fel; Southern Fel Fund Grant; Atlanta Univ Pres Scholar; Mark Schaeffer Award Hist; Am Asn of Univ Women's Award Scholar; Delta Sigma Theta Award Scholar; Alpha Kappa Mu Natl Honor Soc; Howard Univ Res Grant; Who's Who in Am Col and Univ; Who's Who in Black Am; Lilly Endow multi-yr grant; Septima Poinsett Clark Award, Alpha Kappa Alpha Sorority, 98; Mary McLeod Bethune Award, Phil Coun of Natl Council of Negro Women, 94; Conservation Svc Award, U S Dept of Interior, 94; Carlton Qualey Award, best article, J of Am Ethnic Hist, Immigration Hist Soc, 95; Black Women in Sisterhood for Action, 95 Dist Black Women. **MEMBERSHIPS** AHA; Asn for Stud of Afro-AM Hist & Cult; Org of Am Hist; Asn of Black Women Hist; Southern Hist Asn. **RESEARCH** Amer soc & intel hist; African Am hist; women; relig & popular cult. **SELECTED PUBLICATIONS** Auth, Uncovering Methodist History, African-Am Relig: Res Problems Resources for the 1990s, 92; auth, Harvey Johnson and the Brotherhood of Liberty, From Reconstruction to the Great Migration, Garland Press, 91; auth, Amy Jacques Garvey, Notable Black Am Women, Gale Res, 96; auth, Race, Class and Color: The African American Discourse on Identity, J of Am Ethnic Hist, vol 14, 94; auth, Minister and Feminist Reformer: The Life of Florence Spearing Randolph, This Far by Faith: Readings in African-Am Women's Relig Biog, Routledge Press, 96; auth, Frances Ellen Watkins Harper: Abolitionist and Feminist Reformer, 1825-1911, Afro-Am Women and the Vote, 1937-1965, Univ Mass Press, 97; co-ed, Vindicating the Race: Contributions to African American Intellectual History, J of Negro Hist, 96. **CONTACT ADDRESS** Ctr for Afro-Am Hist & Cult, Temple Univ, 13th St and Cecil B Moore Ave, Philadelphia, PA, 19122. **EMAIL** bcollier@astro.temple.edu

COLLIN, RICHARD H.
PERSONAL Born 03/04/1932, Philadelphia, PA, m, 1969 **DISCIPLINE** CULTURAL AND RECENT AMERICAN HISTORY **EDUCATION** Kenyon Col, AB, 54; NY Univ, PhD(Am civilization), 66. **CAREER** Asst prof, 66-71, ASSOC PROF HIST, UNIV NEW ORLEANS, 71-, Am Philos Soc res grant, 67; columnist, New Orleans States-Item, 70- **MEMBERSHIPS** AHA; Orgn Am Historians; Am Studies Asn. **RESEARCH** Theodore Roosevelt and the Progressive Era; American cultural and social history. **SELECTED PUBLICATIONS** Auth, Impressionists in Britain, Intl Hist Rev, Vol 0018, 96; Impressionism for England, Courtauld, Samuel as Patron and Collector, Intl Hist Rev, Vol 0018, 96; The Last Years of the Monroe-Doctrine, 1945-1993, Jour Military Hist, Vol 0060, 96; From 16 to 60--Memoirs of a Collector, Amer Quart, Vol 0046, 94; Great French Paintings from the Barnes-Collection, Impressionism, Postimpressionism, and Early-Modern, Amer Quart, Vol 0046, 94; Freer--A Legacy of Art, Amer Quart, Vol 0046, 94; The United-States in Central-America, 1860-1911--Episodes of Social Imperialism and Imperial Rivalry in the World-System, Jour So Hist, Vol 0059, 93; American Salons--Encounters with European Modernism, 1885-1917, Intl Hist Rev, Vol 0015, 93; Crucible of Empire--The Spanish-American War and Its Aftermath, Amer Neptune, Vol 0055, 95; Symbiosis Versus Hegemony, New Directions in the Foreign-Relations Historiography of Roosevelt, Theodore and Taft, William, Howard, Diplomatic Hist, Vol 0019, 95; In August Company, the Collections of the Pierpont-Morgan-Library, Amer Quart, Vol 0046, 94; Splendid Legacy--The Havemeyer-Collection, Amer Quart, Vol 0046, 94; Panama and the United-States--The Forced Alliance, Pacific Hist Rev, Vol 0062, 93. **CONTACT ADDRESS** Dept of Hist, Univ of New Orleans, Lakefront St, New Orleans, LA, 70122.

COLLINS, DEREK B.
PERSONAL Born 08/24/1965, Washington, DC, m, 1990, 2 children **DISCIPLINE** COMPARATIVE LIT/CLASSICS; FOLKLORE & MYTHOLOGY **EDUCATION** Univ CA, Los Angeles, MA, 91; Harvard Univ, PhD, 97. **CAREER** ASST PROF CLASSICS, UNIV TEXAS AT AUSTIN, 97-. **HONORS AND AWARDS** Nat Academy of Sciences, Ford Found, Doctoral Dissertation fel, 9/96--6/97. **MEMBERSHIPS** Am Philos Asn; Classical Asn of the Middle West and South; Am Folklore Soc. **RESEARCH** Greek lit; comparative lit (German); witchcraft. **SELECTED PUBLICATIONS** Trans, Greek selections in the Appendix to Claude Calame, The Craft of Poetic Speech in Ancient Greece, Cornell Univ Press, 95; auth, The Myth and Ritual of Ezili Freda in Hurston's Their Eyes Were Watching God, Western Folklore 55, 96; trans with J. Orion, Claude Calame, Young Women's Choruses in Ancient Greece: Their Morphology, Religious Role, and Social Func-

tions, Lanham, MD, Rowman & Littlefield Pubs, 97; auth, Fatum, in the Dictionaire International des Termes Litteraitres, gen ed, Jean-Marie Grassin, A. Francke-Berne, Saur-Vg Pub, Berne, Munich, Paris, New York, 97; On the Aesthetics of the Deceiving Self in Nietzsche, Pindar, and Theognis, Nietzsche-Studien 26, 97; Review of Jacob Rabinowitz, The Rotting Goddess: The Origin of the Witch in Classical Antiquity, Scholia 7 (ns), 16, 98; Immortal Armor: The Concept of Alke in Archaic Greek Poetry, Lanham, MD, Rowman & Littlefield Pubs, 98; Hesiod and the Divine Voice of the Muses, Arethusa, forthcoming, 99. **CONTACT ADDRESS** Dept of Classics, Univ Texas at Austin, 123 Waggener Hall, Austin, TX, 78712-1181. **EMAIL** dbcollins@mail.utexas.edu

COLLINS, ELIZABETH F.
PERSONAL Born 08/23/1942, d, 3 children **DISCIPLINE** POLITICAL THEORY **EDUCATION** Univ Calif, Berkeley, PhD, 91. **CAREER** Assoc prof, philos and Southeast Asian stud, Ohio Univ. **CONTACT ADDRESS** Dept of Philosophy, Ohio Univ, 51 Fairview Dr, Athens, OH, 45701. **EMAIL** collinse@ohiou.edu

COLLINS, ELLIOTT
PERSONAL Born 03/18/1943, Eastman, GA, m, 1967 **DISCIPLINE** POLITICAL SCIENCE **EDUCATION** Univ of DE, BA 1966; New York Univ, MPA 1971; Drew Univ, Madison, NJ, MA, political science, 1983; NYU, American Studies, PhD. **CAREER** Passaic Cty Community College, president, 1991-96, interim president, 1990-91, dean of academic services, 1986-89, dean of students, 1979-86; Upsala College, East Orange, NJ, coordinator of science enrichment program, 1976-77; Upsala Coll, Drew Univ, lecturer political science 1974-; Upsala Coll, asst dean for acad counseling 1976-77; Upsala Coll, affirmative action officer 1974-77; Educ Opportunity Fund Program Upsala Coll, dir and coordinator 1970-76; City of E Orange NJ, asst city planner 1969; Passaic (NJ) County Community College, Paterson, NJ, Professor, History and Political Science, 1996-. **HONORS AND AWARDS** Alpha Phi Alpha Scholarship 1962-64; Young Man of the Year Unity Club Wilmington DE 1965; Martin Luther King Scholarship 1968-70. **MEMBERSHIPS** Vp United Way & Community Serv Council 1971-75; vice pres bd of dir Rotary Club of E Orange NJ 1971-72; bd of trustees Family Servs & Child Guidance Center 1975-76; board of directors, Opportunities Industrialization Center, 1987-95; board of directors, Paterson YMCA, 1983-87; board of trustees, Passaic-Clifton YMCA, 1989-93; United Way of Passaic Valley, board of directors, 1992-95; Inner City Christian Action for Housing Inc, board of trustees, 1992-96; North Jersey Regional Chamber of Commerce, 1991-95; Greater Paterson Chamber of Commerce, 1991-95; Passaic Valley Council Boy Scouts of America, executive board member, 1992-95. **CONTACT ADDRESS** College Blvd, Paterson, NJ, 07509.

COLLINS, ELSIE
PERSONAL Durham, NC, d **DISCIPLINE** EDUCATION **EDUCATION** DE St Coll, BA 1945; Columbia U, MA 1952; Union Grad Sch, PhD 1977. **CAREER** Trenton State Coll, asst prof 1971-; Trenton, NJ, asst dir of COP 1971; Natl Teachers Corp, Trenton NJ, team leader 1968-71; Core Curr Jr High School, Trenton NJ, teacher 1961-62, 1964-68, demonstration teacher 1965-68; Trenton State Coll, supvr summer semester for teachers 1965-75; Dover DE Jr & Sr High Schools, teacher 1945-59; Beth Jacob Jewish High School New York City, teacher 1960-61; Consult Serv & In-serv Workshops Trenton; Teahcer Educ NJ State Dept Higher Educ 1967-72; Afro-Amer Studies 1969-76; Urban Educ Curriculum Spec 1972-. **HONORS AND AWARDS** Valedictorian high sch schlrship high honor DE St Coll; scholarship student of music Tchrs Coll Columbia Univ 1950-57; soloist St Paul United Meth Ch Trenton 1967-; publ "Poverty & the Poor" 1968; contributed to Devl of Urban Educ Series Prob of Amer Soc 1966-68; special award World Who's Who of Women in Educ 1977-78; Internatl Artists & Fellows of Distinction 1980. **MEMBERSHIPS** Mem Community Leaders & Noteworthy Am 1979; mem Doctorate Assn of NY Educators 1980; mem Amer Assn Univ Women 1954-60; current membrshp New Jersey HistSoc Am Assn Negro Mus; NAACP; Urban Leag Couns of Soc Studies NEA NJEA Poverty Law Ctr AKA Assn for Superv & Curriculum Devel. **CONTACT ADDRESS** Trenton State Col, 371 Education Bldg, Trenton, NJ, 08625.

COLLINS, JACQUELIN
PERSONAL Born 12/27/1933, Kenaston, SK, Canada, m, 1961, 2 children **DISCIPLINE** BRITISH HISTORY **EDUCATION** Rice Univ, BA, 56, MA, 59; Univ Ill, PhD(hist), 64. **CAREER** Asst prof, 62-66, ASSOC PROF HIST, TEX TECH UNIV, 66-. **MEMBERSHIPS** AHA; AAUP; Conf Brit Studies. **RESEARCH** Seventeenth century England; 16th and 17th century Scotland. **SELECTED PUBLICATIONS** Auth, The English Civil-War, Albion, Vol 0024, 92; Historical Dictionary of Tudor England, 1485-1603, Albion, Vol 0024, 92; Powle,Stephen of Court and Country, Memorabilia of a Government Agent for Elizabeth-I, Chancery Official, and English Country Gentleman, Albion, Vol 0026, 94. **CONTACT ADDRESS** Dept of Hist, Tex Tech Univ, Lubbock, TX, 79409-0001.

COLLINS, JAMES M.
DISCIPLINE POSTMODERNISM, CULTURAL THEORY **EDUCATION** Univ Iowa, PhD. **CAREER** Instr, Univ Notre Dame. **HONORS AND AWARDS** Mellon fel. **RESEARCH** Cultural life in the '90s. **SELECTED PUBLICATIONS** Auth, Uncommon Cultures: Popular Culture and Postmodernism; coed, Film Theory Goes to the Movies. **CONTACT ADDRESS** Univ Notre Dame, Notre Dame, IN, 46556.

COLLINS, PATRICIA HILL
PERSONAL Born 05/01/1948, Philadelphia, PA, m **DISCIPLINE** AFRICAN-AMERICAN STUDIES **EDUCATION** Brandeis Univ, AB 1969, PhD 1984; Harvard Univ, MAT 1970. **CAREER** Harvard UTTT Program, teacher/curriculum spec 1970-73; St Joseph Community School, curriculum specialist 1973-76; Tufts Univ, dir African Amer Ctr 1976-80; UNIV OF CINCINNATI, assoc prof of African-American Studies 1987-94, PROF, 1994-, assoc prof of Sociology 1988-. **HONORS AND AWARDS** Career Woman of Achievement Award, YWCA of Cincinnati, 1993. **MEMBERSHIPS** Chair Minority Fellowship Program Comm 1986-1989; mem Amer Sociological Assn; vp Great Rivers Girl Scouts Council 1992-94. **SELECTED PUBLICATIONS** C Wright Mills Award for "Black Feminist Thought," 1990. **CONTACT ADDRESS** African-American Studies, Univ of Cincinnati, ML 370, Cincinnati, OH, 45221.

COLLINS, ROBERT MAURICE
PERSONAL Born 12/29/1943, Kearny, NJ **DISCIPLINE** AMERICAN HISTORY **EDUCATION** Jersey City State Col, BA, 67; Columbia Univ, MA, 68; Johns Hopkins Univ, PhD, 75. **CAREER** Asst prof, NC State Univ, 75-80; ASSOC PROF AM HIST, UNIV MO-COLUMBIA, 80-, Vis prof, Univ Manchester, 82-83. **MEMBERSHIPS** Orgn Am Historians; AHA. **RESEARCH** Public policy; business-government relations; political history. **SELECTED PUBLICATIONS** Auth, New Deals--Business, Labor, and Politics in America, 1920-1935, Jour Econ Hist, Vol 0055, 95; Operation Crossroads--The Atomic Tests at Bikini--Atoll , Historian, Vol 0057, 95; The Economic-Crisis of 1968 and the Waning of the American Century, Amer Hist Rev, Vol 0101, 96; Losing Time--The Industrial-Policy Debate, Amer Hist Rev, Vol 0098, 93; Contrived Competition--Regulation and Deregulation in America, Amer Hist Rev, Vol 0100, 95; Regulation in the White-House--The Johnson Presidency, Amer Hist Rev, Vol 0100, 95. **CONTACT ADDRESS** Dept Hist, Univ Mo, 310 Watson Pl, Columbia, MO, 65211-0001.

COLLINS, ROBERT O.
PERSONAL Born 04/01/1933, Waukegan, IL, m, 1974, 3 children **DISCIPLINE** AFRICAN HISTORY **EDUCATION** Dartmouth Col, BA, 54; Balliol College, Oxford Univ, AB, 56, MA, 60; Yale Univ, MA, 58, PhD, 59. **CAREER** From instr to asst prof Hist, Williams Col, 59-65; dir UC Santa Barbara Washington Cen; assoc prof, 65-69, prof Hist, Univ Calif, Santa Barbara, 69-94; prof Emeritus, 94; dean Grad Div, 70-80, lectr, Univ Mass, Pittsfield, 60-61 & Shiloah Ctr, Tel-Aviv Univ, 73; vis asst prof, Columbia Univ, 62; Soc Sci Res Coun fel, 62 & 68; chmn, Herskovits Prize Comt, 71-73; consult, Sudan Govt & High Exec Coun Southern Sudan Regional Govt, 75-; mem comt, Coun Grad Schs, 76-. **HONORS AND AWARDS** Order of Sciences, Arts and Art-Gold Class, Democratic Republic of the Sudan, 80; Senior Associate Member, St Antony's College, 81, 87, 89; Who's Who in American, the West, American Authors, American Scholars, Contemporary Authors, International Dictionary of Scholars in the Third World, International Authors and Writers. **MEMBERSHIPS** AHA; African Studies Asn; Conf Brit Studies. **RESEARCH** African history; history of Sudan and East Africa. **SELECTED PUBLICATIONS** Auth, King Leopold, England, and the Upper Nile, 1898-1909, Yale Univ, 68; ed, Problems in African history, Prentice-Hall, 68; An Arabian diary, Univ Calif, 69; The partition of Africa, Wiley, 69; Problems in the History of Colonial Africa, Prentice-Hall, 70; auth, Europeans in Africa, Knopf, 71; African History: Test and Readings, Random, 71; Land beyond the rivers: The Southern Sudan, 1898-1918, Yale Univ, 71.; Historical Problems of Imperial Africa, Markus Wiener, 94; Problems in Modern Africa, Markus Wiener, 96. **CONTACT ADDRESS** Dept of History, Univ of California, Santa Barbara, 552 University Rd, Santa Barbara, CA, 93106-0001. **EMAIL** rcollins@humanitas.ucsb.edu

COLLINS, VICKI
DISCIPLINE HISTORY OF RHETORIC **EDUCATION** Wake Forest Univ, BA, 67; Duke Univ, MA, 68; Auburn Univ, PhD, 93. **CAREER** Engl, Oregon St Univ. **RESEARCH** 18th & 19th century Brit lit. **SELECTED PUBLICATIONS** Auth, Personality Type and Collaborative Writing. Collaborative Technical Writing: Theory and Practice Asn Tchrs Technical Writing, 89. **CONTACT ADDRESS** Oregon State Univ, Corvallis, OR, 97331-4501. **EMAIL** vcollins@orst.edu

COLMAN, GOULD P.
PERSONAL Born 04/30/1926, Medina, NY, m, 1957, 2 children **DISCIPLINE** AGRICULTURAL ORAL HISTORY **EDUCATION** Cornell Univ, BA, 51, MA, 53, PhD(Am hist), 62. **CAREER** Asst archivist, Cornell Univ, 53-55; instr Am hist, Storm King Sch, 56-59; col historian, NY State Col Agr, 61-63, dir, Oral Hist Proj, 63-65, prog in oral hist, 67-71, chmn dept manuscripts & univ arch, 71-79, UNIV ARCHIVIST, CORNELL UNIV, 71-, Res specialist, Dept Rural Sociol. **MEMBERSHIPS** Agr Hist Soc; Oral Hist Asn (vpres, 68, pres, 69-70); Orgn Am Historians; Soc Am Arch; Rural Sociol Soc. **RESEARCH** Institutional studies; oral history techniques; archives administration. **SELECTED PUBLICATIONS** Auth, The Agrarian Origins of American Capitalism, NY Hist, Vol 0075, 94. **CONTACT ADDRESS** John M Olin Libr, Cornell Univ, Ithaca, NY, 14853.

COLOMBO, JOHN R.
PERSONAL Born 03/24/1936, Kitchener, ON, Canada **DISCIPLINE** CANADIAN STUDIES **EDUCATION** Univ Toronto, BA, 59, Sch Grad Stud, 60. **HONORS AND AWARDS** Centennial Medal, 67; Award Merit, Ont Libr Asn, 77; Philips Info Syst Lit Award, 85. **MEMBERSHIPS** ACTRA; PEN. **SELECTED PUBLICATIONS** Auth, Colombo's Canadian References, 76; auth, The Poets of Canada, 78; auth, Other Canadas, 79; auth, Great Moments in Canadian History, 84; auth, Canadian Literary Landmarks, 84; auth, Mysterious Canada, 88; auth, The Dictionary of Canadian Quotations, 91; auth, Close Encounters of the Canadian Kind, 94; auth, Ghost Stories of Ontario, 95; co-transl, Some Hungarian Poets, 95; gen ed, The Canadian Global Almanac, 92-. **CONTACT ADDRESS** 42 Dell Park Ave, Toronto, ON, M6B 2T6. **EMAIL** jrc@inforamp.net

COLTON, GLENN
DISCIPLINE MUSICOLOGY **EDUCATION** Memorial Univ Newfoundland, BM; McMaster Univ, MA; Univ Victoria, PhD. **CAREER** Dept Lang, Lakehead Univ **RESEARCH** Canadian music, nineteenth and twentieth-century music. **SELECTED PUBLICATIONS** Ed, Coulthard's second piano sonata; pub(s), numerous articles for, Can Univ Mus Rev; Fermata; Intl Alliance for Women in Mus Jour. **CONTACT ADDRESS** Dept of Lang, Lakehead Univ, 955 Oliver Rd, Thunder Bay, ON, P7B 5E1. **EMAIL** Glenn.Colton@lakeheadu.ca

COLTON, JOEL
PERSONAL Born 08/23/1918, New York, NY, m, 1942, 2 children **DISCIPLINE** MODERN HISTORY **EDUCATION** City Col New York, AB, 37, MS, 38; Columbia Univ, AM, 40, PhD, 50. **CAREER** Lectr, Columbia Univ, 46-47; from instr to prof, hist, Duke Univ, 47-74, chmn dept, 67-74, chmn acad coun, 71-72; dir for humanities, Rockefeller Found, 74-81; PROF HIST, DUKE UNIV, 82-, Guggenheim fel, 57-58; Rockefeller Found fel, 61-62; chmn, Europ Hist Advan Placement Comt, Col Entrance Exam Bd, 67-70; Nat Endowment for Humanties sr fel, 70-71. **HONORS AND AWARDS** Bk Award, Mayflower Soc, 67. **MEMBERSHIPS** AHA; fel Am Acad Arts & Sci; Southern Hist Assoc; Soc Fr Hist Studies (vpres 72-73). **RESEARCH** Modern and contemporary history; modern France; history of social thought. **SELECTED PUBLICATIONS** Auth, Lost Comrades--Socialists of the Front Generation 1918-1945, Amer Hist Rev, Vol 0099, 94; Choice and Democratic Order--The French Socialist-Party, 1937-1950, Amer Hist Rev, Vol 0101, 96; Loucheur, Louis and the Shaping of Modern France, 1916-1931, Amer Histl Rev, Vol 0100, 95; Stanzione, Massimo-- Complete Works-Italian, Renaissance Quart, Vol 0050, 97. **CONTACT ADDRESS** 215 East 68th, New York, NY, 10021.

COLVIN, WILLIAM E.
PERSONAL Born 05/27/1930, Birmingham, AL, m, 1956 **DISCIPLINE** AFRICAN-AMERICAN STUDIES **EDUCATION** AL State Univ, BS 1951; IN Univ, MS 1960; Academic Affairs Conf of Midwestern Univs, Cert of Administration; IL State, EdD 1971. **CAREER** Stillman Coll, Department of Art, chair 1958-69; Illinois State Univ, dir of ethnic studies 1974-78, prof of art 1971-91; EASTERN ILLINOIS UNIV, PROFESSOR OF ART, 1987-, CHAIR AFRO-AMERICAN STUDIES, 1991-. **HONORS AND AWARDS** Rockefeller Fellow 1973-74; Phelps-Stokes Fund Grant 1973; publs exhibitions in field; Martin Luther King BLM Normal Human Relations 1983; Outstanding Artist in the Field AL State Univ 1985; Outstanding Service Awd IL Committee on Black Concerns in Higher Educ 1985; Fulbright Lecture/Rsch Fulbright Brazil 1981-85; univ grant to Belize for research, 1989. **MEMBERSHIPS** Elected rep to US/Brazilian Mod Art Soc 1981-; dir career program IL Comm on Black Concerns in Higher Educ 1983-; mem Natl Conf of Artists; mem Natl Art Educ Assn; mem Phi Delta Kappa Hon Soc in Educ. **CONTACT ADDRESS** Eastern Illinois Univ, Charleston, IL, 61920.

COMACCHIO, CYNTHIA
DISCIPLINE CANADIAN SOCIAL HISTORY **EDUCATION** Glendon, BA; York, MA; Univ Guelph, PhD. **CAREER** Prof **SELECTED PUBLICATIONS** Auth, Nations are Built of Babies, McGill-Queen's Univ Press, 93; **CONTACT ADDRESS** Dept of History, Wilfrid Laurier Univ, 75 University Ave W, Waterloo, ON, N2L 3C5. **EMAIL** ccomacch@mach1.wlu.ca

COMAROFF, JEAN
PERSONAL Born 07/22/1946, Edinburgh, Scotland, m, 1967, 2 children **DISCIPLINE** ANTHROPOLOGY **EDUCATION** Cape Town, BA; London Sch of Econ, PhD. **CAREER** Asst Prof, Univ Chicago, 79-87; Prof, 87-96; Bernard E & Ellen C Sunny Distinguished Science Prof & Ch, 96. **HONORS AND AWARDS** Gordon Lainy Prize, Best Book; teaching awards. **MEMBERSHIPS** African Stud Asn; Am Anthrop Asn. **RESEARCH** Ritual, body; medicine; colonialism & history in Southern Africa (Tswana peoples). **SELECTED PUBLICATIONS** Auth, Body of Power, Spirit of Resistance: The Culture and History of a South African People, Univ Chicago Press, 85; co-auth, Of Revelation and Revolution: Christianity, Colonialism, and Consciousness in South Africa, Univ Chicago Press, 91, vol II, 97; co-auth, Ethnography and the Historical Imagination, Westview Press, 92; co-ed, Modernity and its Malcontents: Ritual and Power in Africa, Univ Chicago Press, 93; co-ed, Civil Society, Moral Community and Public Sphere in Africa, in press. **CONTACT ADDRESS** Dept of Anthrop, Univ Chicago, 1126 E 59th St, Chicago, IL, 60637. **EMAIL** jeancom@uchicago.edu

COMBS, JERALD A.
PERSONAL Born 04/19/1937, Long Beach, CA, m, 1958, 2 children **DISCIPLINE** UNITED STATES HISTORY **EDUCATION** Univ Calif, Santa Barbara, BA, 58, Los Angeles, Ph-d(hist), 64. **CAREER** Assoc prof, 64-73, PROF HIST, CALIF STATE UNIV, SAN FRANCISCO, 73-. **MEMBERSHIPS** AHA; Conf Early Am Hist; Soc Hist Am Foreign Rel. **RESEARCH** United States diplomacy and Revolutionary and Federalist Eras. **SELECTED PUBLICATIONS** Auth, American Diplomats in the Netherlands, 1815-50, Jour Amer Hist, Vol 0081, 94; The Cambridge History of American Foreign-Relations, Vol 2, The American Search for Opportunity, 1865-1913, Amer Hist Rev, Vol 0099, 94; The Emerging Nation--A Documentary History of the Foreign-Relations of the United-States Under the Article-of-Confederation, 1780-1789, William and Mary Quart, Vol 0054; The Cambridge History of American Foreign-Relations, Vol 1, The Creation of a Republican Empire, 1776-1865, Amer Hist Rev, Vol 0099, 94; The Cambridge History of American Foreign-Relations, Vol 4, America in thehe Age of Soviet Power, Amer Hist Rev, Vol 0099, 94. **CONTACT ADDRESS** Dept of History, California State Univ, San Francisco, 1600 Holloway Ave, San Francisco, CA, 94132-1740.

CONACHER, DESMOND J.
PERSONAL Born 12/27/1918, Kingston, ON, Canada **DISCIPLINE** CLASSICS **EDUCATION** Queen's Univ, BA, 41, MA (Classics), 42; Univ Chicago, PhD (Greek Lang & Lit), 50; LLD(hon), Dalhousie Univ, 92; DLitt(hon), Univ Victoria, 93; LLD(hon), Queen's Univ, 95; LLD(hon), Univ Sask, 97. **CAREER** Lectr, Dalhousie Univ, 46-47; asst prof to assoc prof, Univ Sask, 47-58; assoc prof to prof, 58-84, dept head, 66-72, PROF EMER CLASSICS, TRINITY COL, UNIV TORONTO, 84-, mem, sch grad stud, 84-90. **HONORS AND AWARDS** Fel, Royal Soc Can, 76. **MEMBERSHIPS** Class Asn Can; Am Philol Asn. **RESEARCH** Greek tragedy; Euripides; Aeschylus. **SELECTED PUBLICATIONS** Auth, Euripedean Drama, 67; auth, Aeschylus' 'Prometheus Bound': A Literary Study, 80; auth, Aeschylus' 'Oresteia': A Literary Commentary, 87; auth, Euripides' 'Alcestis': with Introduction, Translation and Commentary, 88; contribur, Sources of Dramatic Theory, vol 1, 91; contribur, Aeschylus: The Earlier Plays and Related Studies, 96. **CONTACT ADDRESS** Trinity Col, Univ of Toronto, Toronto, ON, M5S 1H8.

CONACHER, JAMES BLENNERHASSET
PERSONAL Born 10/31/1916, Kingston, ON, Canada, m, 1943, 2 children **DISCIPLINE** HISTORY **EDUCATION** Queen's Univ, Can, BA, 38, MA, 39; Harvard Univ, PhD(hist), 49. **CAREER** From lectr to assoc prof hist, 46-63, chmn dept, 72-78, PROF HIST, UNIV TORONTO, 63-, Joint ed, Can Hist Rev, 49-56; gen ed, Champlain Soc, 52-62; vis prof, Univ Notre Dame, 65-66. **MEMBERSHIPS** Can Hist Asn (pres, 74-75), Conf Brit Studies; fel Royal Hist Soc. **RESEARCH** Modern British history; Victorian party politics. **SELECTED PUBLICATIONS** Auth, British Policy in the Anglo-American Enlistment Crisis of 1855-1856, Proc Amer Philos Soc, Vol 0136, 92; The Crimean-War--British Grand-Strategy, 1853-56, Eng Hist Rev, Vol 0108, 93. **CONTACT ADDRESS** Dept of Hist, Univ of Toronto, Toronto, ON, M5S 1A1.

CONDON, RICHARD HERRICK
PERSONAL Born 05/29/1935, Lewiston, ME, m, 1957, 3 children **DISCIPLINE** BRITISH HISTORY **EDUCATION** Bates Col, AB, 56; Brown Univ, AM, 57, PhD(hist), 62. **CAREER** Instr hist, Kent State Univ, 60-64; asst prof, State Univ NY Col Oneonta, 64-65; from asst prof to assoc prof, 65-68, PROF HIST, UNIV MAINE, FARMINGTON, 68-, CHMN DEPT, 69- **MEMBERSHIPS** AHA; Hist Asn, England. **RESEARCH** British 18th and 19th century social reform. **SELECTED PUBLICATIONS** Auth, Politics of Conscience--A Biography of Smith, Margaret, Chase, New Eng Quart, Hist Rev New Eng Life and Letters, Vol 0069, 96. **CONTACT ADDRESS** Dept of Hist, Univ of Maine, 86 Main St, Farmington, ME, 04938-1990.

CONGDON, KRISTIN G.
PERSONAL Born 10/09/1948, Boston, MA, m, 1970 **DISCIPLINE** ART-ART EDUCATION, FOLKLORE, ART HISTORY **EDUCATION** PhD Univ of Oregon, 83; MS IN Univ, 72; BA Valparaiso Univ, 70. **CAREER** Prof of Art, Univ of Central FL, Orlando, Coordinator AA Hist Prog 88-present; Asst Prof, AA Edu Bowling Green State Univ,OH, 84-87. **HONORS AND AWARDS** Natl Art Edu Assoc, Zeigfeld Award, Res of the Year Award, Southeastern Region's Natl Art Edu Assoc Higher Edu Div Natl Art Educator of the Year Award, NAEA Barkan Award. **MEMBERSHIPS** Am Folklore Assoc, Col Art Assoc, Intl Soc for Edu through AA, Natl Art Edu Assoc, Woman's Caucus for AA. **RESEARCH** Commun AAS Soc Eco, Feminist& AA Criticism, Folklore At/Traditional AA, Art and Eco multi-cultural Edu. **SELECTED PUBLICATIONS** Review ed,: Indigenous Teaching(Webb-based Pub) 98-present; Member, Review Bd, The Journal of Gender Issues in Art and Education, 96-present; Outside Review Ed, Aouthern Folklore, 93-95; Member Ed Advisory Bd, Studies in Art Education, 91-95; Journal of Multi-cultural and Cross-cultural Research in Art Education, 87-present; Asst Ed: Journal of Social Theory and Art Education, 90-91; Browne, R Browne P, Congdon, KG et al, The Encyclopedia of Popular Culture in the United States, NY ABC-CLIO Publishing Co, in press. **CONTACT ADDRESS** Col of Arts and Sci, Univ of Central FL, Orlando, FL, 32816. **EMAIL** kcongdon@pegasus.cc.ucf.edu

CONGDON, LEE W.
PERSONAL Born 08/11/1939, Chicago, IL, m, 1967, 2 children **DISCIPLINE** HISTORY **EDUCATION** Wheaton Col, BA, 61; Northern Ill Univ, MA, 67, PhD, 73. **CAREER** Encycl Britannica, ed asst, 65, writer, 67-68; Asst Prof, Assoc Prof, Prof, James Madison Univ, 72-. **HONORS AND AWARDS** Fulbright-Hayes Fac Res Abroad Prog, Hungary, 77-78; Sch of Hist Stud, Inst for Adv Stud, Princeton, 81-82. **MEMBERSHIPS** Am Asn for the Stud of Hungarian Hist. **RESEARCH** Modern European intellectual history; history of Hungary. **SELECTED PUBLICATIONS** Auth, The Young Lukacs, Univ NC Press, 83; auth, Exile and Social Thought: Hungarian Intellectuals in Germany and Austria, 1919-1933, Princeton Univ Press, 91. **CONTACT ADDRESS** Dept of Hist, James Madison Univ, Harrisburg, VA, 22807. **EMAIL** congdolw@jmu.edu

CONKIN, PAUL K.
PERSONAL Born 10/25/1929, Chuckey, TN, m, 1954, 3 children **DISCIPLINE** HISTORY **EDUCATION** Milligan Col, BA, 51; Vanderbilt Univ, MA, 53, PhD, 57. **CAREER** Asst prof, Univ SW La, 57-58; asst prof to prof, Univ Md, 59-67; prof, Univ Wi Madison, 67-79; distinguished prof, Vanderbilt Univ, 79- . **MEMBERSHIPS** Amer Hist Assoc; Org Amer Hist; S Hist Assoc. **RESEARCH** Amer intellectual & recent US philos of hist **SELECTED PUBLICATIONS** Auth, the Southern Agrarians, Univ Tn Press, 88; Cane Ridge: America's Pentecost, Univ Wi Press, 91; The Four Foundations of American government: consent, Limits, Balance, and Participation, Harlan Davidson, 94; The Uneasy Center: Reformed Christianity in Antebellum America, Univ NC Press, 95; American Originals: Homemade Varieties of Christianity, Univ NC Press, 97; When All the gods Trembled: Darwinism, scopes, and American Intellectuals, Roman & Littlefield, 98. **CONTACT ADDRESS** 1609-B Vanderbilt, Nashville, TN, 37235. **EMAIL** conkinPK@CTRUAX.vanderbilt.edu

CONLEY, CAROLINE A.
PERSONAL Born 01/29/1958, Savannah, GA **DISCIPLINE** HISTORY **EDUCATION** Duke Univ, BA, 75, PhD, 84; Univ of Chicago, MA, 76. **CAREER** Instr, Duke Univ, 84-85; ASST PROF, 85-91, ASSOC PROF, 91-, DIR OF GRAD STUDIES IN HIST, UNIV OF ALA AT BIRMINGHAM, 93-. **HONORS AND AWARDS** NEH Fel, 91; LaPrade Fel, Duke Univ. **MEMBERSHIPS** AHA; NACBS; ACIS. **RESEARCH** Crime and violence in Brit and Irish hist. **SELECTED PUBLICATIONS** Auth, The Unwritten Law: Criminal Justice in Victorian Kent, Oxford Univ Press, 91; Irish Criminal Records, 1865-1892, Eire-Ireland, 93; No Pedestals: Women and Violence in Late nineteenth-Century Ireland, J of Soc Hist, 95; Melancholy Accidents: The Meaning of Violence in Post-Famine Ireland, Lexington Books, 98; The Agreeable Recreation of Fighting, J of Soc Hist, 99. **CONTACT ADDRESS** Dept of Hist, Univ Alabama, Birmingham, Birmingham, AL, 35294-3350. **EMAIL** muirne@uab.edu

CONLEY, PATRICK THOMAS
PERSONAL Born 06/22/1938, New Haven, CT, m, 1962, 5 children **DISCIPLINE** AMERICAN HISTORY, CONSTITUTIONAL LAW **EDUCATION** Providence Col, AB, 59; Univ Notre Dame, MA, 61, PhD(hist), 70; Suffolk Univ, JD, 73. **CAREER** PROF HIST, PROVIDENCE COL, 63-, Spec asst to Congressman Robert O Tiernan, RI, 67-74; secy, RI Constitutional Convention, 73; chmn, RI Bicentennial Comn/Found, 74-; trustee, Bicentennial Coun of the 13 Original States, 77-. **MEMBERSHIPS** AHA; Orgn Am Historians. **RESEARCH** Rhode Island history; American ethnic history; constitutional history. **SELECTED PUBLICATIONS** Auth, Brotherly Love--Murder and Politics of Prejudice in 19th-Century Rhode-Island, New Eng Quart-Hist Rev New Eng Life and Letters, Vol 0068, 95. **CONTACT ADDRESS** Dept of Hist, Providence Col, Providence, RI, 02918.

CONLIN, JOSEPH R.
PERSONAL Born 01/07/1940, Philadelphia, PA **DISCIPLINE** AMERICAN HISTORY **EDUCATION** Villanova Univ, AB, 61; Univ Wis, MA, 62, PhD(hist), 66. **CAREER** Instr hist, Univ Wis, Fox Valley, 64-65; instr, Rider Col, 65-66; asst prof soc sci, Manhattan Community Col, 66-67; asst prof, 67-80, PROF HIST, CALIF STATE UNIV, CHICO, 80-, Vis lectr Am social hist, Univ Warwick, 71 & 76-77; vis prof, Univ Calif, Davis, 72-73. **MEMBERSHIPS** Aha; Orgn Am Historians; Soc Studies Labour Hist; Pac Northwest Labor Hist; Southwest Labor Studies Asn. **RESEARCH** American social history; American labor history; late 19th century United States. **SELECTED PUBLICATIONS** Auth, This Emigrating Company--The 1844 Oregon-Trail Journal of Hammer, Jour W, Vol 0032, 93. **CONTACT ADDRESS** 1406 Bidwell Ave, Chico, CA, 95926.

CONLON, FRANK FOWLER
PERSONAL Born 11/06/1938, Omaha, NE, m, 1972 **DISCIPLINE** HISTORY OF INDIA **EDUCATION** Northwestern Univ, Evanston, AB, 60; Univ Minn, Minneapolis, MA, 63, PhD(hist), 69. **CAREER** Asst prof, 68-75, ASSOC PROF HIST, UNIV WASH, 75-, Sr fel, Am Inst Indian Studies, 71 & 77-78, chmn bd, 82-83; Asia rev ed, Journal Asian Studies, 78-80. **MEMBERSHIPS** Asn Asian Studies; AHA; Bharata Itihasa Samshodak Mandal. **RESEARCH** Modern India; social history of India; Maharashtra and west coast. **SELECTED PUBLICATIONS** Auth, Marathas, Marauders, and State Formation in 18th-Century India, Jour Amer Oriental Soc, Vol 0116, 96; The New Cambridge History of India, Vol 2, Pt 4, The Marathas 1600-1818, Amer Hist Rev, Vol 0100, 95; In the Absence of God - the Early Years of an Indian Sect--A Translation of Smrtisthal with an Introduction, Jour Amer Oriental Soc, Vol 0115, 95; The Unification and Division of India, Historian, Vol 0055, 93. **CONTACT ADDRESS** Dept of Hist, Univ of Wash, Seattle, WA, 98195.

CONNELL-SZASZ, MARGARET
DISCIPLINE WESTERN AMERICA, INDIAN HISTORY **EDUCATION** Univ NMex, PhD, 72. **CAREER** Instr, Univ Exeter, Eng; instr, Univ Aberdeen, Scottland; prof, Univ NMex. **HONORS AND AWARDS** D'Arcy McNickle Ctr fel; Spencer Found grant. **RESEARCH** History of American education; Scottland. **SELECTED PUBLICATIONS** Auth, Education and the American Indian, The Road to Self-Determination, 74, 77; Between Indian and White Worlds: The Cultural Broker, 94. **CONTACT ADDRESS** Univ NMex, Albuquerque, NM, 87131.

CONNELLY, OWEN
PERSONAL Born 01/24/1929, Morganton, NC **DISCIPLINE** MODERN EUROPEAN HISTORY **EDUCATION** Univ NC, PhD, 60. **CAREER** Instr hist, Univ NC, 56-60; instr, Duke Univ, 60-61; from asst prof to assoc prof, Univ NC, Greensboro, 61-67; assoc prof, 67-68, PROF HIST, UNIV SC, 68-. **MEMBERSHIPS** AHA; Soc Fr Hist Studies; Soc Mod Hist, France; Inst Napoleon. **RESEARCH** French Revolution and Napoleon. **SELECTED PUBLICATIONS** Auth, The Wars of Napoleon, Intl Hist Rev, Vol 0018, 96; The Military History of France, Vol 2, from 1715 to 187--French, Jour Military Hist, Vol 0057, 93; With Musket, Cannon and Sword--Battle Tactics of Napoleon and His Enemies, Jour Military Hist, Vol 0060, 96; On The Fields of Glory--The Battlefields of the 1815 Campaign, Intl Hist Rev, Vol 0019, 97; Napoleon Last Victory and the Emergence of Modern War, Intl Hist Rev, Vol 0017, 95; War, Revolution and the Bureaucratic State--Politics and Army Administration in France, 1791-1799, Jour Military Hist, Vol 0061, 97; Soldiers of Napoleon Kingdom of Italy--Army, State and Society, 1800-1815, Jour Military Hist, Vol 0060, 96; Bonaparte,Napoleon and the Legacy of the French-Revolution, Historian, Vol 0058, 95. **CONTACT ADDRESS** Dept of Hist, Univ of SC, Columbia, SC, 29208.

CONNELLY, OWEN S.
PERSONAL Born 01/24/1929, Morganton, NC, m, 1965, 3 children **DISCIPLINE** HISTORY; MODERN EUROPEAN **EDUCATION** Wake Forest, BS, 48; UNC-Chapel Hill, PhD, 60. **CAREER** Tchr, Duke Univ, UNC-Greensboro, Univ Kentucky; Assoc prof, 67, prof, 68-93, McKissick Dial Prof, 93- , Univ S Carolina, 67- ; US Army ranger; chr Europ Sect, SHA, 82; Bd Dir Consortium Revolutionary Europ, 71- . **MEMBERSHIPS** Soc d'Hist Mod; Inst Napoleon; Soc Mil Hist; Asn Mem Inst for Advan Study. **RESEARCH** French Revolution; Napoleonic era; Military history. **SELECTED PUBLICATIONS** Auth, The Gentle Bonaparte...Joseph, Napoleon's Elder Brother, 68; The Epoch of Napoleon, 72 & 78; ed, Historical Dictionary of Napoleonic France, 85; auth, Napoleon's Satellite Kingdoms, 65 & 69 & 90; Blundering to Glory: Napoleon's Military Campaigns, 87 & 90 & 99; The French Revolution and Napoleonic Era, 79 & 91 & 99. **CONTACT ADDRESS** History Dept, Univ S Carolina, 221 Gambrell, Columbia, SC, 29208. **EMAIL** Owen-Connelly@sc.edu

CONNER, VALERIE JEAN
PERSONAL Born 10/23/1945, Jennings, LA, m **DISCIPLINE** HISTORY **EDUCATION** Loyola Univ, BA, 67; Univ VA, MA, 69, PhD, 74. **CAREER** Res staff local govt, style &

drafting, La Const Conv, 73-74; asst prof, 74-81, assoc prof Am hist, FL State Univ, 82. **MEMBERSHIPS** Orgn Am Historians. **RESEARCH** US polit, economic, and soc hist: 1890-1940. **SELECTED PUBLICATIONS** Auth, The Mothers of the Race in World War I: The National War Labor Board and Women in Industry, Labor Hist, Vol 21, winter 80; The National War Labor Board in 1918-1919: Stability and Social Justice in the Voluntary State, Univ NC Press, 83. **CONTACT ADDRESS** Florida State Univ, 600 W College Ave, Tallahassee, FL, 32306-1096. **EMAIL** vconner@mailer.fsu.edu

CONNOLLY, JOY P.T.
PERSONAL Born 04/07/1970, Lowell, MA **DISCIPLINE** CLASSICS **EDUCATION** Princeton Univ, AB, 91; Univ of Pa, MA; PhD, 97. **CAREER** Asst Prof, Univ Wash, 97-. **HONORS AND AWARDS** Dean's Scholar Award, Univ Pa; Center for the Humanities Res Fel, 98; Endowment for Excellence Aw, 97-98; **MEMBERSHIPS** Am Philol Asn; Class Asn of Atlantic States; Class Asn of the Pacific Northwest. **RESEARCH** Greek and Latin Literature of the Empire; Feminist Theory. **SELECTED PUBLICATIONS** Auth, Mastering Corruption: Constructions of Identity in Roman Oratory; Women and Slaves in Class Culture: Differential Equations, 98. **CONTACT ADDRESS** Dept of Classics, Univ of Wash, Seattle, WA, 98195-3110. **EMAIL** jptc@u.washington.edu

CONNOLLY, THOMAS J.
PERSONAL Born 03/01/1954, Fargo, ND, m, 1982, 1 child **DISCIPLINE** ANTHROPOLOGY/ARCHAEOLOGY **EDUCATION** Univ Oregon, PhD, 86 **CAREER** Research div dir, State Mus Anthrop, Univ Oregon, 86- **MEMBERSHIPS** Soc Amer Archaeol; Soc Calif Archaeol; Assoc Ore Archaeologist; Plains Archaeol Soc **RESEARCH** Archaelogy of Western North America **SELECTED PUBLICATIONS** "Radiocarbon Evidence Relating to Northern Great Basin Basketry Chronology." Jour Calif & Gt Brit Anthrop, 98; "Newberry Crater: A Ten-Thousand-Year Record of Human Occupation and Environmental Change in the Basin-Plateau Borderlands." Univ Utah Anthro Papers; "Oregon Wet Site Basketry: A Review of Structural Type." Contribution to the Archaeology of Oregon, 95-97 **CONTACT ADDRESS** Dept Anthro, Univ Oregon, Eugene, OR, 97403. **EMAIL** connolly@darkwing.uoregon.edu

CONNOR, CAROLYN
DISCIPLINE CLASSICS **EDUCATION** NY Univ, PhD. **CAREER** Prof, Univ NC, Chapel Hill. **RESEARCH** Byzantine art and civilization. **SELECTED PUBLICATIONS** Auth, Art and Miracles in Medieval Byzantium: The Crypt at Hosios Loukas and Its Frescoes, Princeton UP, 91; New Perspectives on Byzantine Ivories, Gesta, Vol 30, 91; Hosios Loukas as a Victory Church, Greek, Roman and Byzantine Stud, Vol 33, 92; coauth, The Life and Miracles of Saint Luke of Steiris, A Translation and Commentary, Hellenic Col Orthodox Press, 94. **CONTACT ADDRESS** Univ N. Carolina, Chapel Hill, Chapel Hill, NC, 27599. **EMAIL** clconnor@email.unc.edu

CONNOR, WALTER ROBERT
PERSONAL Born 07/30/1934, Worcester, MA, m, 1968, 2 children **DISCIPLINE** CLASSICAL STUDIES **EDUCATION** Hamilton Coll, BA, 56; Princeton Univ, PhD, 61. **CAREER** Instr, 60-63, Univ MI; jr fel, 63-64, Ctr Hellenic Studies; asst prof, 64-70, assoc prof, 70-72, prof, 72-89, Princeton Univ; prof, 89-present, Duke Univ; pres and dir, 89-present, Natl Humanities Ctr. **HONORS AND AWARDS** Phi Beta Kappa, Woodrow Wilson, Danforth, ACLS, and NEH fels; Fulbright fel, Univ Coll, Oxford, 56-57, Howard Behrman Award for Distinguished Achievement in Humanities, 86; LHD, Hamilton and Knox Colleges; Fel, Amer Acad Arts Sciences and Amer Phil Soc.. **MEMBERSHIPS** Howard Behrman Awar for Distinguished Achievement in the Humanities, 86; LHD Hamilton Coll, 91; fel, Amer Acad of Artist Sciences, 92-; LHD Knox Coll, 93; fel, American Philosphical Soc, 96-. **RESEARCH** Ancient Greek hist and lit **SELECTED PUBLICATIONS** Auth, The New Politicians of Fifth Century Athens, 71, reissued 92; Thucydides, 87; coauth, The Life and Miracles of Saint Luke of Steiris, 94; Theses and His City, Religion and Power in the Ancient Greek World, 96; Festival and Democracy, Democratie athenienne et Cultrue, 96. **CONTACT ADDRESS** National Humanities Ctr, 7 Alexander Dr, Res Triangle Pk, NC, 27709. **EMAIL** connor@ga.unc.edu

CONRAD, DAVID
PERSONAL Born 03/25/1939, Spokane, WA, m **DISCIPLINE** AFRICAN HISTORY **EDUCATION** Univ of London, School of Oriental and African Studies, PhD, 81. **CAREER** Lectr, San Francisco State Univ, 71-72, 79; Research Prof, State Univ of NY-Buffalo, Subang Jaya, Malaysia, 88-90; Asst Prof, State Univ of NY-Oswego, 85-92; Assoc Prof, State Univ of NY-Oswego, 93-present; Visiting Prof, Ecole des Hutes Etudes en Sciences Sociales, 99 **HONORS AND AWARDS** Natl Endowment for the Humanities Translations Grant, 84-85; Fulbright Senior Research Grant, 93-94; SUNY-Oswego President's Award for Scholarly Achievement, 97. **MEMBERSHIPS** Mande Studies Assoc; African Studies Assoc; West African Research Assoc. **RESEARCH** Precolonial west African kingdoms; oral epic and tradition; influence of Islam in sub-Saharan west Africa, Mande history and culture, traditional Mande religion. **SELECTED PUBLICATIONS** Auth, Journal of African History, A Town Called Dakajalan: The Sunjata Tradition and the Question of Ancient Mali's Capital, 94; auth, Status and Identiy in West Africa: Nyamakalaw of Mande, Blind Man Meets Prophet: Oral Tradition, Islam, and fune Identity, Indiana Univ Press, Bloomington, 95; auth, In Search of Sunjata: The Mande Epic as History, Literature and Performance, Mooning Armies and Mothering Heroes: Female Power in Mande Epic Tradition, Indiana Univ Press, 98; auth, Segu Maana Bamanakan Na: Bamana Language Edition of the Epic of Segu, Univ of Wis African Stud Prog, Madison, 98; auth, The Songhay Empire, Frankiln Watts, NY, 98. **CONTACT ADDRESS** History Dept, SUNY Coll Oswego, Oswego, NY, 13126. **EMAIL** dconrad@oswego.edu

CONRAD, GLENN RUSSELL
PERSONAL Born 09/03/1932, New Iberia, LA, m, 1955, 4 children **DISCIPLINE** MODERN FRENCH AND FRENCH COLONIAL HISTORY **EDUCATION** Georgetown Univ, BS, 53, MA, 59. **CAREER** Instr hist, Univ Southwestern La, 58-62; asst prof, Southern State Col, 63-64; instr, 65-70, asst prof, 70-76, ASSOC PROF HIST, UNIV SOUTHWESTERN LA, 76-, DIR CTR LA STUDIES, 73-, Ed, La Hist, La Hist Asn, 73; Adminr, Revue de Louisiane. **MEMBERSHIPS** Southern Hist Asn; Fr Hist Soc; Fr Soc Overseas Hist. **RESEARCH** Nineteenth century France; French Louisiana colonial history; local history. **SELECTED PUBLICATIONS** Auth, A History of French Louisiana, Vol 2, Years of Transition, 1715-1717, Jour So Hist, Vol 0060, 94. **CONTACT ADDRESS** Ctr for La Studies, Univ of Southwestern, La Lafayette, LA, 70501.

CONRAD, MARGARET R.
PERSONAL Born 12/14/1946, Bridgewater, NS, Canada **DISCIPLINE** HISTORY/WOMEN'S STUDIES **EDUCATION** Acadia Univ, BA, 67; Univ Toronto, MA, 68, PhD, 79. **CAREER** Ed, Clark, Irwin Publ, 68-69; lectr to assoc prof, 69-87, PROF HISTORY, ACADIA UNIV, 87-; adj prof, Dalhousie Univ, 91-; Nancy Rowell Jackman Chair Women's Stud, Mt St Vincent Univ, 96-98. **HONORS AND AWARDS** Fel, Royal Soc Canada, 95. **MEMBERSHIPS** Asn Can Stud; Can Hist Asn; Can Res Inst Advan Women; Can Women's Stud Asn; Planter Stud Ctr. **RESEARCH** History of Atlantic Canada. **SELECTED PUBLICATIONS** Auth, Recording Angels, 83; auth, George Nowlan: Maritime Conservative in National Politics, 86; coauth, Twentieth Century Canada, 74; coauth, Women at Acadia University: The First Fifty Years 1884-1934, 83; coauth, No Place Like Home: The Diaries and Letters of Nova Scotia Women 1771-1938, 88; coauth, History of the Canadian Peoples, 2 vols, 93, 2nd ed 97; supv ed, New England Planters in Maritime Canada, 93; ed, They Planted Well, 88; ed, Making Adjustments: Change and Continuity in Planter Nova Scotia, 91; ed, Intimate Relations, 95; co-ed, Atlantis: A Women's Stud J, 75-85; co-ed, Can Hist Rev, 97-. **CONTACT ADDRESS** History Dept, Acadia Univ, Wolfville, NS, B0P 1X0. **EMAIL** margaret.conrad@acadiau.ca

CONRAD, RUDOLPH
DISCIPLINE MEDIEVAL ART HISTORY **EDUCATION** UCLA, PhD. **CAREER** PROF, ART HIST, UNIV CALIF, RIVERSIDE. **HONORS AND AWARDS** Fel(s), Guggenheim; J Paul Getty; Mellon. **RESEARCH** Social history of art. **SELECTED PUBLICATIONS** Auth, "The Things of Greater Importance": Bernard of Clairvaux's Apologia and the Medieval Attitude Toward Art, Philadelphia 90; Artistic Change at St-Denis: Abbot Suger's Program and the Early Twelfth-Century Congroversy over Art, Princeton, 90; Violence and Daily Life: Reading, Art, and Polemics, Citeaux Moralia in Job, Princeton, 97. **CONTACT ADDRESS** Dept of Arh Hist, Univ Calif, 1156 Hinderaker Hall, Riverside, CA, 92521-0209. **EMAIL** crudolph@ucrac1.ucr.edu

CONSER, WALTER H., JR.
PERSONAL Born 04/04/1949, Riverside, CA, m, 1986, 3 children **DISCIPLINE** AMERICAN RELIGIOUS HISTORY **EDUCATION** Univ Calif Irvine, BA, 71; Brown Univ, MA, 74, PhD, hist, 81. **CAREER** James A. Gray fel in relig, Univ NC Chapel Hill, 82-84; adjunct facul, Univ San Francisco, 85; vis asst prof to asst prof, 85-89, assoc prof, 89-94, chemn, 92-98, prof relig, 94-, Univ NC Wilmington; fel, Albert Einstein Inst for Nonviolent Alternatives, 84-87; vis prof, JF Kennedy Inst for North Amer Studies, Free Univ Berlin, 90; prof, hist, Univ NC Wilmington, 95-. **MEMBERSHIPS** Amer Acad of Relig; Amer Hist Asn. **SELECTED PUBLICATIONS** Auth, Religious Diversity and American Religious History, Univ Ga Press, 97; auth, God and the Natural World: Religion and Science in Antebellum America, Univ SC Press, 93; co-ed, Experience of the Sacred: Readings in the Phenomenology of Religion, Brown Univ Press, 92; auth, James Marsh and the Germans, New Eng Quart, 86; auth, Conservative Critique of Church and State, Jour of Church and State, 83; auth, John Ross and the Cherokee Resistance Campaign, Jour of Southern Hist, 78; auth, Cherokee Reponses to the Debate Over Indian Origins, Amer Quart, 89; co-auth, Cherokees in Transition, Jour of Amer Hist, 77. **CONTACT ADDRESS** Dept. of Philosophy and Religion, Univ of North Carolina at Wilmington, 601 S. College Rd., Wilmington, NC, 28403.

CONSTANCE, JOSEPH
PERSONAL Born 04/16/1952, Montaul, MA, m, 1982, 2 children **DISCIPLINE** HISTORY, LIBRARY SCIENCE **EDUCATION** St. Michael's Col, BA (magna cum laude), 76; Univ VT, MA (Hist), 79; SUNY, Albany, MLS, 83; Boston Univ, PhD Candidate, 95-. **CAREER** Archivist and curator of Manuscripts, Soc of St. Edmund, Burlington, VT, 78-80; archivist and curator of Special Collections, Middle GA Hist Soc, Macon, 80-81; Univ archivist and curator of Rare Books, GA State Univ, Atlanta, 83-87; Head, Archives and Manuscripts Dept, John J. Burns Library of Special Collections, Chestnut Hill, MA, 87-90; COLLEGE LIBRARIAN, SAINT ANSELM COL, MANCHESTER, NH, 90-. **SELECTED PUBLICATIONS** Auth, Time Management for Archivists, with Robert C. Dinwiddie in Provenance, fall 85; book reviewer for Library Journal, 83-. **CONTACT ADDRESS** Geisel Library, Saint Anselm Col, 87 St. Anselm Dr., Manchester, NH, 03102-1323.

CONSTANTELOS, DEMETRIOS J.
PERSONAL Born 07/27/1927, Spilia, Messenia, m, 1954, 4 children **DISCIPLINE** BYZANTINE HISTORY **EDUCATION** Holy Cross Orthodox Theol Sch, BA, 58; Princeton Theol Sem, ThM, 59; Rutgers Univ, MA, 63, PhD(hist), 65. **CAREER** Tchng asst hist, Rutgers Univ, 61-62; from asst prof to assoc prof, Hellenic Col, 65-71; prof, 71-86, Charches Cooper Townsend Dist Prof, hist & relig stud, 86-, Richard Stockton Col, , Ed, Greek Orthodox Theol Rev, 66-71; vis lectr, Boston Col, 67-68; mem, Anglican-Orthodox Theol Consult, 68-& Orthodox-Cath Theol Consult, 69-; pres, Orthodox Theol Soc Am, 69-71; mem, Natl Comm Byzantine Studies, 73-. **MEMBERSHIPS** Mediaeval Acad Am; Am Soc Church Hist; Mod Greek Studies Assn. **RESEARCH** Byzantine civilization; Greek orthodox theology; ecclesiastical history. **SELECTED PUBLICATIONS** Auth, Byzantine Philanthropy and Social Welfare, Rutgers Univ, 68, 2nd ed, Aristide D Caratzas Publ, 91; contribr, Southeastern Europe: A Guide to Basic Publications, Univ Chicago, 69; auth, Kyros Panopolites, Rebuilder of Constantinople, Greek-Roman and Byzantine Studies, 71; The Moslem conquests of the Near East as revealed in the Greek sources, Byzantion, 72; ed, Encyclicals and Documents of the Greek Archdiocese (1922-1972), Patriarchal Inst, 76; contribr, The Oxford Annotated Apocrypha, Oxford Univ, 77; ed, Orthodox Theology and Diakonia: Trends and Prospects, Hellenic Col Press, 81; auth, Understanding the Greek Orthodox Church, Seabury, 82, 3rd ed,Hellenic Col Press, 98; auth, Poverty, Society and Philanthropy in the Late Mediaeval Greek World, Aristide D Caratzas, Publ, 92; auth, The Greeks: Their Heritage and its Value Today, Hellenic Col Press, 96; contr, The Parallel Apocrypha, Oxford Univ, 97; auth, Christian Hellenism: Essays and Studies in Continuity and Change, Caratzas: Melissa Media Assn, 98. **CONTACT ADDRESS** Dept of Arts & Humanities, Richard Stockton Col New Jersey, Pomona, NJ, 08240.

CONSTANTINOU, CONSTANTIA
DISCIPLINE MUSICOLOGY, LIBRARY SCIENCE **EDUCATION** CUNY, Queens College, BA, 87, MA, 91, MLS, 95. **CAREER** Asst, Avery Fisher Center for Multimedia, 91-92, ref assoc, 93, bibliog spec, 93, Elmer Bobst Libr, NY Univ; asst prof, act dir multimedia & elect svcs, CUNY, LaGuardia Community College, 95-96; dir, Arrigoni Libr, Iona Col, 96. **CONTACT ADDRESS** 36-54 Forest Ave, #3-R, Ridgewood, NY, 11385. **EMAIL** cconstantinou@iona.edu

CONTOSTA, DAVID RICHARD
PERSONAL Born 02/03/1945, Lancaster, OH, m, 1984, 3 children **DISCIPLINE** UNITED STATES INTELLECTUAL HISTORY **EDUCATION** Miami Univ, OH, AB, 67, MA, 70, PhD, 73. **CAREER** Prof Hist, Chestnut Hill Col, 74-, Fulbright fel, 72. **MEMBERSHIPS** AHA; Am Studies Asn. **RESEARCH** Henry Adams. **SELECTED PUBLICATIONS** Auth, Henry Adams and the American Experiment, Little, Brown & Co, 80; Rise to World Power: Selected Letters of Whitelaw Reid, 1895-1912, Am Philos Soc, 86; America in the Twentieth Century: Coming of Age: HarperCollins, 88; A Philadelphia Family: The Houstons and the Woodwards of Chestnut Hill, Univ Penn Press, 88; Suburb in the City: Chestnut Hill, Philadelphia, 1850-1990, Ohio State Univ Press, 92; Henry Adams and His World, Am Philos Soc, 93; The Private Life of James Bond, Sutter House, 93; Villanova University, 1842-1992: American-Catholic-Augustinian, Penn State Press, 95; Philadelphia's Progressive Orphanage: The Carson Valley School, Penn State Press, 95. **CONTACT ADDRESS** Dept of Hist, Chestnut Hill Col, 9601 Germantown Ave, Philadelphia, PA, 19118-2693. **EMAIL** contosta@msn.com

CONTRENI, JOHN JOSEPH
PERSONAL Born 08/31/1944, Savannah, GA, m, 1986, 6 children **DISCIPLINE** MEDIEVAL HISTORY **EDUCATION** St Vincent Col, BA, 66; Mich State Univ, MA, 68, PhD, 71. **CAREER** From asst prof to assoc prof, 71-82, prof hist, Purdue Univ, West Lafayette, 82-, asst dean, Sch Humanities, Soc Sci, & Educ, 81-85, interim head, Dept For Lang & Lit, 83-85, head, Dept Hist, 85-97; co-ed, French Hist Studies, 92-. **HONORS AND AWARDS** Excellence in Graduate Teaching Citation, Mich State Univ, 71; Grant, Summer Sem Paleography, Univ Chicago, 73; Am Philos Soc grant, 73 & 76; Nat Endowment for Humanities summer grant, 75; Am Coun Learned Soc study

fel, 77-78; Liberal Arts Excellence in Teaching Award, Purdue Univ, West Lafayette, 81; John Nicholas Brown Prize for "The Cathedral School of Laon...", Medieval Acad Am, 82; Liberal Arts Educational Excellence Award, Purdue Univ, West Lafayette, 90; recipient of numerous research grants. **MEMBERSHIPS** AHA; Mediaeval Acad Am; Soc Prom Eriugenian Studies (Dublin). **RESEARCH** Carolingian renaissance; early medieval intellectual and cultural history; the liberal arts; education in the Middle Ages; Latin manuscripts and Palaeography. **SELECTED PUBLICATIONS** Transl, Pierre Riche, Education and culture in the Barbarian West, Sixth Through Eighth Centuries, Univ SC, 76; auth, The Cathedral School of Laon from 850 to 930: Its Manuscripts and Masters, Arbeo Gesellschaft, Munich, 78; co-ed, Religion, Culture and Society in the Early Middle Ages: Studies in Honor of Richard E. Sullivan, Western Mich Univ Press, 87; auth, Carolingian Learning, Masters and Manuscripts, Collected Studies Series, CS 363, Variorum, 92; coauth, Glossae Divinae Historiae: The Biblical Glosses of John Scottus Eriugena, Millennio Medievale 1, Testi 1, SISMEL: Edizioni del Galluzzo, 97; author of numerous journal articles, review essays, and book chapters. **CONTACT ADDRESS** Dept of Hist, Purdue Univ, West Lafayette, IN, 47907-1358. **EMAIL** contreni@purdue.edu

CONVERSE, HYLA STUNTZ
PERSONAL Born 10/31/1920, Lahore, Pakistan, m, 1951, 2 children **DISCIPLINE** HISTORY OF RELIGIONS, SOUTH ASIAN LITERATURE **EDUCATION** Smith Col, BA, 43; Union Theol Sem, BD, 49; Columbia Univ, PhD(hist of relig), 71. **CAREER** Relief & rehab worker, Eglise Reforme France, 45-48; dir student work, Judson Mem Church, New York, 52-55; dir lit & study, Nat Student Christian Fed, 57-63; asst prof Asian relig & humanities, 68-78, chmn humanities fac, 73-78, assoc prof, 78-80, PROF ASIAN RELIG & HUMANITIES, OKLA STATE UNIV, 80-, Fulbright res fel, India, 74-75; Am Inst Pakistan Studies fel, 78-79. **MEMBERSHIPS** Am Orient Soc; Bhandarkar Oriental Res Inst. **RESEARCH** Religions of South Asia; literature of South Asia; arts of South Asia. **SELECTED PUBLICATIONS** Auth, An Ancient Sudra Account of the Origins of Castes, Jour Amer Oriental Soc, Vol 0114, 94. **CONTACT ADDRESS** Dept Relig Studies, Oklahoma State Univ, Stillwater, OK, 74074.

CONWAY, JOHN F.
PERSONAL Born 11/19/1943, Moose Jaw, SK, Canada **DISCIPLINE** SOCIOLOGY/HISTORY **EDUCATION** Univ Sask, BA, 66, MA, 68; Simon Fraser Univ, PhD, 79; Univ Regina Bilingal Ctr, 86-87; Laval Univ Fr Lang, 87. **CAREER** Lectr to assoc prof, 71-84, dept head, 76-81, PROF SOCIOL, UNIV REGINA, 84-; vis prof, Can stud, Univ Edinburgh, 81-82. **MEMBERSHIPS** Writers' Union Can; ACTRA; Can Sociol & Anthrop Asn; Asn Can Stud; Can Civil Liberties Asn. **SELECTED PUBLICATIONS** Auth, The Recrudescence of Western Canadian Separatist Sentiment, 82; auth, The Place of the Prairie West in the Canadian Confederation, 82; auth, The West: The History of a Region in Confederation, 83, 2nd ed, 94; auth, The Canadian Family in Crisis, 90, 2nd ed, 93, 3rd ed, 97; auth, Debts to Pay: English Canada and Quebec from the Conquest to the Referendum, 92, 2nd ed, Debts to Pay: A Fresh Approach to the Quebec Question, 97; auth, Des comptes a rendre: le Canada anglais et le Quebec, de la Conquete a l'Accord Charlottetown, 95. **CONTACT ADDRESS** Dept of Sociology, Univ of Regina, Regina, SK, S4S 0A2. **EMAIL** conwayj@leroy.cc.uregina.ca

CONWAY, JOHN S.
PERSONAL Born 12/31/1929, London, England **DISCIPLINE** HISTORY **EDUCATION** Cambridge Univ, BA, 52; MA, 55, PhD, 56. **CAREER** Asst prof, Univ Man, 55-57; asst prof, 57-64, assoc prof, 64-69, prof, 69-95, PROF EMER HISTORY, UNIV BC, 95-; moderator, Asn Contemp Church Hist, 95-. **HONORS AND AWARDS** Queen's Jubilee Medal, 77 **RESEARCH** Church history **SELECTED PUBLICATIONS** Auth, The Nazi Persecution of the Churches 1933-45, 68, reissued 97. **CONTACT ADDRESS** Dept of History, Univ of British Columbia, Vancouver, BC, V6T 1Z1.

CONWAY, MELISSA
DISCIPLINE MEDIEVAL STUDIES **EDUCATION** Yale Univ, PhD, 94. **CAREER** Cur, Wash D.C., 91-; codir, Union Manuscript Computer Catalogue, De Ricci Census Update Project, 96-. **MEMBERSHIPS** Medieval Acad Am; Am Libry Asn; Am Inst Conservation. **RESEARCH** Manuscripts and early printing **CONTACT ADDRESS** 25705 Horado Ln, Moreno Valley, CA, 92551-1985. **EMAIL** drmconway@aol.com

CONWELL, DAVID
PERSONAL Born 01/13/1959, Philadelphia, PA, m, 1992, 2 children **DISCIPLINE** CLASSICAL STUDIES **EDUCATION** Trinity Col, BA, 82; Univ Pa, PhD, 92. **CAREER** Instr, Baylor School, 95-. **HONORS AND AWARDS** NEH Teacher Exchange Fel, 97. **MEMBERSHIPS** Archaeol Inst of Am; Am Philol Asn; Classical Asn of the Midwest and South. **RESEARCH** Archaeology of Cyprus, Greece, and Italy; Ancient fortifications; Art history. **SELECTED PUBLICATIONS** Auth, "The White Poros Wall on the Athenian Pnyx: Character and Context," in The Pnyx in the Hist of Athens, 96; "Rediscovering the Athenian Long Walls," in Am School of Class Studies Newsletter, 95; "Topography and Toponyms between Athens and Piraeus," in J of Ancient Topography, 93. **CONTACT ADDRESS** 1112 Crown Point Rd W, Signal Mountain, TN, 37377.

COOK, BERNARD ANTHONY
PERSONAL Born 07/11/1941, Meridian, MS, m, 1966, 2 children **DISCIPLINE** MODERN EUROPEAN AND GERMAN HISTORY **EDUCATION** Notre Dame Sem, BA, 63; St Louis Univ, MA, 66, PhD(hist), 70. **CAREER** Instr hist, Northern Mich Univ, 68; from instr to asst prof, 68-74, ASSOC PROF HIST, LOYOLA UNIV, LA, 74-. **MEMBERSHIPS** AHA. **RESEARCH** Socialist movement; labor history. **SELECTED PUBLICATIONS** Auth, The Origins of the Wars of German Unification, Jour Military Hist, Vol 0057, 93; The Origins of the Italian Wars of Independence, Jour Military Hist, Vol 0057, 93; The War in Italy, 1943-1945--A Brutal Story, Jour Military Hist, Vol 0059, 95. **CONTACT ADDRESS** Dept of Hist, Loyola Univ, 6363 St Charles Ave, New Orleans, LA, 70118-6195.

COOK, BLANCHE WIESEN
PERSONAL Born 04/20/1941, New York, NY **DISCIPLINE** UNITED STATES HISTORY **EDUCATION** Hunter Col, BA, 62; Johns Hopkins Univ, MA, 64, PhD(hist), 70. **CAREER** Hampton Inst, 63; instr hist, Stern Col, Yeshiva Univ, 64-67; assoc prof, 69-80, DIST PROF HIST, JOHN JAY COL CRIMINAL JUSTICE, & GRAD CTR 80-, Mem, Fac Sem Am Civilization, Columbia Univ, 70-; consult, World Law Fund-Inst Int Order, 71-76; co-chairwoman, Coord Comt of Women in Hist Prof, New York, 72-73; co-chairwoman, Freedom Info Off, Orgn Am Hist, 80-82. **MEMBERSHIPS** AHA; Orgn Am Hist; Am Studies Asn; Conf Peace Res in Hist (exec secy, 70-73, vpres, 76-78). **RESEARCH** Violence; war and peace; women. **SELECTED PUBLICATIONS** Sr ed, Garland Lib on War and Peace (360 vol reprint ser), Garland, 70-73; co-ed & contribr, Past--Imperfect, Knopf, 73; The Woman's Peace Party: Collaboration and Non-Cooperation in World War I, J Peace & Change, 72; Democracy in Wartime, Am Studies J, 72; contribr, American Peace Movements, Schocken, 73; auth, Female Support Networks and Political Activism, Chrysalis, Autumn 77; contribr, The D D Eisenhower Library: The Manuscript Fiefdom at Abilene, AHA-PAH-SAA, 77; ed, Crystal Eastman on Women & Revolution, Oxford Univ, 10/78; The Declassified Eisenhower: A Divided Legacy of Peace & Political Warfare, Doubleday, 81; Eleanor Roosevelt, Vol I, Viking-Penguin, 92; Eleanor Roosevelt, Vol II, Spring 99. **CONTACT ADDRESS** John Jay Col of Criminal Justice, CUNY, 445 W 59th St, New York, NY, 10019.

COOK, ERWIN
PERSONAL Born 04/27/1957, Edinburgh, Scotland, 1 child **DISCIPLINE** CLASSICS **EDUCATION** Univ Calif, Berkeley, MA, 85, PhD, 90. **CAREER** Asst prof, Univ Texas, Austin, 90-93, 94-96; vis assoc prof, 93-94, assoc prof, 97- , Johns Hopkins. **MEMBERSHIPS** Am Philol Asn; Classical Asn of the Midwest and South. **RESEARCH** Epic poetry, Greek religion, mythology, archaic Greek history. **SELECTED PUBLICATIONS** Auth, A Note on the Text of Sextus Empiricus, Adv. Math, Hermes, 91; auth, Ferrymen of Elysium and the Homeric Phaeacians, J of Indo-European Stud, 92; auth, Some Remarks on Odyssey 3.2 16-38, Class Philol, 94; auth, The Odyssey in Athens: Myths of Cultural Origins, Cornell, 95; auth, rev, Homer: His Art and His World, by Latacz, Bryn Mawr Class Rev, 96; auth, Heroism, Suffering and Change, Proceedings of a Conference Sponsored by the Smithsonian Institution and the Society for the Preservation of the Greek Heritage, 98. **CONTACT ADDRESS** Dept of Classics, Univ Texas, 123 WAG, Austin, TX, 78212. **EMAIL** efcook@mail.utexas.edu

COOK, NOBLE DAVID
PERSONAL Born 04/18/1941, Gary, IN, m, 1975, 3 children **DISCIPLINE** HISTORY **EDUCATION** Univ Florida, BA, 62, MA, 64; Univ Texas, PhD, 73. **CAREER** Fulbright Prof, 74, 84, Catholic Univ Peru; vis prof, 89-90, Yale Univ; instr, prof, 69-92, Univ Bridgeport; prof, 92-, chmn, 95-98, Florida Intl Univ. **RESEARCH** Colonial Hispanic Amer, early modern Spain. **CONTACT ADDRESS** Dept of History, Florida Intl Univ, Miami, FL, 33199-0001. **EMAIL** cookn@fiu.edu

COOK, PHILIP C.
DISCIPLINE HISTORY **EDUCATION** La State Univ, BA, 56; La Tech Univ, MA, 66; Univ GA, PhD, 68. **CAREER** Instr hist, La Tech Univ, 63-64; tchg asst, Univ Ga, 64-67; asst prof hist, NE La Univ, 67 69; assoc prof hist, 69-87, prof-hist, La Tech Univ, 87-. **MEMBERSHIPS** La Hist Rec Adv Comn; Southern Hist Asoc; La Hist Asoc; N La Hist Asoc; Southwestern Hist Asoc. **RESEARCH** Louisiana hist; mod Europ hist. **SELECTED PUBLICATIONS** Auth, Louisiana: A Political History in Cartoon and Narrative, Dean. La Hist,96; End of the Land: A South Carolina Family on the Louisiana Frontier, Shreveport Times, 94; The Foreign French: Immigration into Ninteenth Century Louisiana, Vol I, 1820-1837, Brasseaux. La Hist, 92; The Roads and Trails of Early North Louisiana, N La Geneal Soc Jour, 88; The Pioneer Preachers of the North Louisiana Hill Country, N La Hist Asoc Jour, 83; A Case Study of Functional Preservation The Kidd-Davis House of Ruston, N La Hist Asoc Jour, 78. **CONTACT ADDRESS** Dept of Hist, Louisiana Tech Univ, PO Box 3178, Ruston, LA, 71272.

COOK, ROBERT FRANCIS
PERSONAL Born 10/24/1944, Atlanta, GA **DISCIPLINE** MEDIEVAL FRENCH LANGUAGE & LITERATURE **EDUCATION** King Col, AB, 65; Vanderbilt Univ, MA, 68, PhD(-French), 70; Univ Pittsburgh, MS, 75. **CAREER** Asst prof French, Univ Pittsburgh, 69-75; assoc Prof French, 75-91, FULL PROF, UNIV VA, 91-. **MEMBERSHIPS** MLA; Am Asn Teachers Fr; Mediaeval Acad Am; Int Arthurian Soc; Soc Rencesvals. **RESEARCH** The chansons de geste; textual criticism. **SELECTED PUBLICATIONS** Auth, Les manuscrits de Baudouin de Sebourc, Romania, 70; ed, Le batard de Bouillon, chanson de geste, Droz-Minard, 72; coauth, Le deuxieme Cycle de la Croisade, Droz, 72; auth, Foreign language study and intellectual power, ADFL Bull, 5/77; coauth, The Legendary Sources of Flaubert's Saint Julien l'Hospitalier, Univ Toronto, 77; coauth, Chanson d'Antioche, Chanson de geste, 80; Aucassin et Nicolete, a Critical Bibliography, 82; The Sense of the Song of Roland, 87. **CONTACT ADDRESS** Dept of French, Univ of Virginia, 302 Cabell Hall, Charlottesville, VA, 22903. **EMAIL** rfc@virginia.edu

COOK, WARREN LAWRENCE
PERSONAL Born 07/29/1925, Spokane, WA, m, 1963 **DISCIPLINE** LATIN AMERICAN HISTORY **EDUCATION** Univ San Marcos, Peru, BA, 50; Yale Univ, MA, 57, PhD, 60. **CAREER** From asst prof to assoc prof hist, 60-70, chmn dept soc sci, 67-68, PROF HIST & ANTHROP, CASTLETON STATE COL, 70-. **HONORS AND AWARDS** Bolton Prize, Conf Latin Am Hist, 74., Dlitt, Univ San Marcos, Peru, 55. **MEMBERSHIPS** AHA; Conf Latin Am Hist; Soc Hist Discoveries; Epigraphic Soc. **RESEARCH** Andean history and anthropology; Spanish explorations in North America, especially in the Pacific Northwest; ancient lithic culture of New England. **SELECTED PUBLICATIONS** Auth, The Roots of Country-Music, Amer Heritage, Vol 0046, 95. **CONTACT ADDRESS** Dept of Hist, Castleton State Col, Castleton, VT, 05735.

COOK, WILLIAM ROBERT
PERSONAL Born 12/27/1943, Indianapolis, IN **DISCIPLINE** MEDIEVAL HISTORY, HISTORY OF CHRISTIANITY **EDUCATION** Wabash Col, AB, 66; Cornell Univ, MA, 70, PhD(medieval hist), 71. **CAREER** Asst prof hist, 70-77, ASSOC PROF HIST, STATE UNIV NY COL GENESEO, 77-, Nat Endowment for Humanities fel in residence, Harvard Univ, 76-77; adj prof lit, Attica Correctional Facil, 80 & 81; adj prof relig studies, Siena Col, NY, 81. **MEMBERSHIPS** AHA; Mediaeval Acad Am; Am Soc Church Hist; Am Friends Bodley; Dante Soc Am. **RESEARCH** Medieval Franciscanism; Monasticism; Siena, Italy. **SELECTED PUBLICATIONS** Auth, Aurora, Their Last Utopia--Oregon Christian Commune, 1856-1883, Ore Hist Quart, Vol 0095, 94. **CONTACT ADDRESS** Dept of Hist, State Univ of NY Col, 1 College Cir, Geneseo, NY, 14454-1401.

COOK, JR, THEODORE F.
DISCIPLINE JAPANESE HISTORY **EDUCATION** Trinity Col, BA, 69; Univ London, MA, 70; Princeton Univ, PhD, 87. **CAREER** Assoc prof, William Paterson Col, 88-; for res fel, Defense Res Inst, Japan Defense Agency, Tokyo, 95; sr res fel, Inst for Soc Sci Res, Tokyo Univ, 94-95; sr res fel, Japan, 94-95; adj assoc prof, NY Univ, 93-94; dir, Japanese Hist and Cult Curric, , Univ Calif San Diego & Japan Performing Arts Ctr Prog, Higashi-Tonami Gun, Toyama Prefecture, Japan, 88-93; sr res fel, Inst Soc Sci Res, Tokyo Univ, 88-89; lectr, Univ Calif San Diego, 87-88; lectr, Merrill Col, Univ Calif Santa Cruz, 87; doctoral cand, Princeton Univ, 84-87; mil and polit anal, Off E Asian Anal, Cent Intel Agency, Washington, DC, 81-84; sponsored lectr, Far E Div, Univ Md, 77-81; for res fel, Inst Soc Sci Res, Tokyo Univ, 77-78 & 75-76; Summer Workshop in Quantitative Methods for Historians, Princeton Univ, 74; asst intr, Princeton Univ, 73-74. **HONORS AND AWARDS** Nat Endowment for the Humanities Res fel, Col Tchr(s) Div, 94-95; NJ State Fac fel, Rutgers Ctr for Hist Anal, Rutgers Univ, 94-95; Nobel Res fel, Norwegian Nobel Inst, 94; Nat Endowment for the Humanities, Summer Stipend, NEH Small Col Div, 93; Japan Found, Int Conf Awd, William Paterson Col, 91; tes travel grant Northeast Asia Coun, Asn Asian Stud, 91; NEH Travel to Collections Grant for Japan, Nat Endowment for the Humanities, 90; Prof fel for Res in Japan, Japan Foundation, 88-89; Univ Calif San Diego fel, 87; Dissertation Res Fel for Res in Japan, Japan Found, 77-78; Fulbright-Hays Dissertation Res Abroad fel, 75-76; Princeton Summer Workshop in Quantitative Methods Grant, 74; Nat Defense Educ Act Title IV fel, Princeton Univ, 73-74; Nat Defense For Lang Title VI fel, Princeton Univ, 72-73; Princeton Univ Korean Stud Travel Grant, 72; Inter-Univ Ctr in for Japanese Lang Stud in Tokyo Grant, 71-72; Princeton Univ grade fel, 70-72; Meade Prize in Hist, Trinity Col, 69. **MEMBERSHIPS** Ch, Columbia Univ Sem on Mod Japan, 91-93 & exec comt, 91-; Int-Univ Sem on Armed Forces & Soc; Gunjishi Gakkai, Mil Hist Asn Japan; Mil Hist Asn US; World War Two Stud Asn & the Comte Int d'Hist de la Deuxieme Guerre Mondiale; NY Mil Aff Symp; AHA; Asn Asian Stud; Asn Japanese Stud; Int House of Japan; Japan Soc NY; Asia Soc NY; Assoc Inst for Global Conflict and Coop, Univ Calif & the Nuclear Hist Prog, Sch Publ Aff, Univ Md. **RESEARCH** War and society in Japan, a study of modern Japanese history from the prospective of war and society. **SELECTED PUBLICATIONS** Auth, Heishi to kokka, heishi to

shakai: Y"bei sekai e Nihon no Sanny- The Soldier and the State, Soldiers and Society: Japan Joins the Western World, Nihon Kin-Gendaishi, A Hist of Mod and Contemporary Japan, vol 2: Shihonshugi to Jiy-shugim Capitalism and Liberalism, Tokyo: Iwanami Sh"ten, 93; The Merchant Seaman's Tale, MHQ: The Quart J of Mil Hist, 93; Tokyo: December 8, 1941; Dawn of a New War, MHQ: The Quart J of Mil Hist, 91; Cataclysm and Career Rebirth: The Imperial Military Elite, Work and Lifecourse in Japan, Albany: SUNY Press, 83; rev(s) J Japanese Stud & J Asian Stud; in, Rev in Hist; Armed Forces and Soci; Naval War Col Rev;coauth, Japan at War, An Oral History, NY: The New Press, 92. **CONTACT ADDRESS** Dept of History, William Paterson Col, 300 Pompton Rd., Wayne, NJ, 07470. **EMAIL** cooktf@frontier.wilpaterson.edu

COOKE, JACOB ERNEST
PERSONAL Born 09/23/1924, Aulander, NC, m, 1956 **DISCIPLINE** HISTORY **EDUCATION** Columbia Univ, PhD, 55. **CAREER** Instr hist, Columbia Univ, 52-55, asst prof, 60-61; prof & head dept, Carnegie Inst technol, 61-62; MacCRACKEN PROF HIST, LAFAYETTE COL, 62-, Assoc ed, Papers of Alexander Hamilton, 55-72; assoc, sem, Columbia Univ, 67-72, vis prof, univ, 68-69; Guggenheim fel, 68-69; Nat Endowment for Humanities fel, 72-73; Nat Humanities Ctr fel, 81; resident scholar, Bellagio Study and Conf Ctr, spring 82. **MEMBERSHIPS** AHA; Orgn Am Historians. **RESEARCH** American history, 1763-1815; United States constitutional history; American history, post World War II. **SELECTED PUBLICATIONS** Auth, When Illness Strikes the Leader--The Dilemma of the Captive King from George-III to Reagan,Ronald, Jour Interdisciplinary Hist, Vol 0025, 95; Historian by Happenstance--One Scholars Odyssey, William and Mary Quart, Vol 0052, 95. **CONTACT ADDRESS** Lafayette Col, 172 Shawnee Ave, Easton, PA, 18042.

COOKE, JAMES JEROME
PERSONAL Born 08/02/1939, Baltimore, MD, m, 1961, 4 children **DISCIPLINE** NORTH AFRICAN, MILITARY, & FRENCH HISTORY **EDUCATION** MS Col, BA, 65, MA, 66; Univ GA, PhD(hist), 69. **CAREER** Asst prof, 69-73, assoc prof, 73-79, PROF HIST, UNIV MS, 79-. **HONORS AND AWARDS** Order of the Academic Palms, Knight, Min of Educ, Fr Govt, 75. **MEMBERSHIPS** Western Front Asn; fel, Royal Hist Soc; League of WWI Aviation Historians. **SELECTED PUBLICATIONS** Auth, New French Imperialism: The Third Republic Colonial Expansion, 1880-1910, 73 & A Dict of Modern French History, 1789-1962, 75, Newton Abbot, England & David & Charles; coauth, Through Foreign Eyes: Western Attitudes Toward North Africa, Univ Press Am, 81; auth, The Old South in the Crucibles of War, Univ Press MS, 83; 100 Miles From Bagdad, 93; The Rainbow Division in the Great War, 1917-1919, 94; The US Air Service in the Great War, 1917-1919, 96; Pershing and His Generals: Command and Staff in the AEF, Praeger Pub, 97. **CONTACT ADDRESS** Dept of Hist, Univ of MS, General Delivery, University, MS, 38677-9999. **EMAIL** jjcooke@olemiss.edu

COOKE, NYM
DISCIPLINE MUSIC **EDUCATION** Harvard Univ, BA, 74; Univ Mich, MA, 80, PhD, 90. **CAREER** Libr asst, music lib, Harvard Univ; LECT, MUS HIST AND MUS, HOLY CROSS **MEMBERSHIPS** Am Antiquarian Soc **RESEARCH** Mus in New Eng, 1720-1780 **SELECTED PUBLICATIONS** "Itinerant Yankee Singing Masters in the Eighteenth Century," in Itinerancy in New England and New York, (Dublin Sem for New Eng Folklife, Ann Procs,) 84; "American Psalmodists in Contact and Collaboration, 1770-1820," PhD diss, Univ of Mich, 90; "William Billings in the District of Maine, 1780," Am Mus 9, 91; Timothy Swan: Psalmody and Secular Songs, 97; "Sacred Music to 1800," in The Cambridge History of American Music, forthcoming **CONTACT ADDRESS** 290 Wine Road, New Braintree, MA, 01531-1604. **EMAIL** nym@tiac.net

COOLEY, TIMOTHY
PERSONAL Born 10/15/1962, Norfolk, VA **DISCIPLINE** ETHNOMUSICOLOGY **EDUCATION** Wheaton Conserv Music, Wheaton Col (Ill), B Mus, 85; Northwestern Univ, M Music, 87; Brown Univ, PhD, 99. **CAREER** Adjunct Instr, Rhode Island Col, 95-98; Lectr, Univ Cal, 98-. **HONORS AND AWARDS** Wilk Prize for Res in Polish Music, 97, for Authentic Troupes and Inauthentic Tropes; Polish Music Reference Center, Univ S Cal-Los Angeles; Graduate Fel, 97, Brown Univ, 97; James T Koetting Prize, 96, for Authenticity on Trial in Polish Contest Festivals; Northeast Chapter, Soc for Ethnomusicol Int Res and Exchanges Board: Individual Advanced Res Fel in Eastern Europ Studies, Poland, 94-95; Am Council of Learned Societies: Predissertation Travel Grant Program in Eastern European Studies, Poland, 1992, East European Language Training Grant, Poland, 1993; Polish Am Teachers Asn: Summer Sessions Scholarship, Jagiellonian Univ, Poland, 1993; Kosciuszko Found: Summer Sessions Scholarship, Jagiellonian Univ, Krakow, Poland, 1992, 2) Study Abroad Scholarship, Inst of Art, Polish Acad of Sciences, Warsaw, Poland, 1994, 3) Dissertation writing grant, 95-96; Pi Kappa Lambda, 87; Presser Scholar; Wheaton Col Conservatory, 84-85; Nat Asn of Teachers of Singing, First Place, performance competition, 84. **MEMBERSHIPS** Soc for Ethnomusicol; Am Musicol Soc; Int Coun for Traditional Music; Am Folklore Soc. **RESEARCH** Music cult Eastern Europe, Middle East, Oceania, Multicult Am, Ethnicity. **SELECTED PUBLICATIONS** Music of the Polish Tatra Mountain Gorale in Chicago, forthcoming; Am Musical Atlas, ed Jeff Todd Titon, Schirmer Books; United States of America, European-Am music, Polish, forthcoming, Janice Kleeman; In The New Grove Dictionary of Music and Musicians, rev ed; Macmillan; Authentic Troupes and Inauthentic Tropes, 98; Polish Music J, Online, 1(1), Univ S Cal; Shadows in the Field: An Introduction, 97; co-ed, In Shadows in the Field: New Perspectives for Fieldwork in Ethnomusicology, Oxford Univ Press; co-ed, Shadows in the Field: New Perspectives for Fieldwork in Ethnomusicology, 97, Oxford Univ Press; Dance, Ritual, and Music, 95; asst ed, Warsaw: Inst of Art, Polish Acad of Sciences; Fire in the Mountains: Polish Mountain Fiddle Music, v1, The Karol Stoch Band. CD with extensive notes, Shanachie Entertainment Corp, 97; Fire in the Mountains: Polish Mountain Fiddle Music, v2; The Great Highland Bands, CD with extensive notes, Shanachie Entertainment Corp, 97; Polish Village Music: Historic Polish-American Recordings 1927-1933, CD song transcriptions and translations, Arhoolie Productions, Inc, 95. **CONTACT ADDRESS** Dept of Music, Univ of California, Santa Barbara, Santa Barbara, CA, 93106-6070.

COOLIDGE, ROBERT TYTUS
PERSONAL Born 03/30/1933, Boston, MA, m, 1960, 3 children **DISCIPLINE** MEDIEVAL HISTORY **EDUCATION** Harvard Univ, AB, 55; Univ Calif, Berkeley, MA 57; Oxford Univ, BLitt, 66. **CAREER** Asst prof, 63-68, ASSOC PROF HIST, CONCORDIAN UNIV, 68-. **MEMBERSHIPS** AHA; Mediaeval Acad Am; Am Cath Hist Asn; Can Hist Asn; fel Royal Hist Soc. **RESEARCH** Medieval ecclesiastical and intellectual history; medieval French history; political role of the church, 850-1050 AD. **SELECTED PUBLICATIONS** Auth, The Formation of a Medieval Church--Ecclesiastical Change in Verona, Ad950-1150, Church Hist, Vol 0064, 95; History of Christianity, From its Beginnings to Present-Day, Vol 4--Bishops, Monks and Emperors 610-1054-Ad-French, Church Hist, Vol 0066, 97. **CONTACT ADDRESS** Dept of Hist, Concordia Univ, Montreal, Montreal, PQ, H4B 1R6.

COOMBS, FRANK ALAN
PERSONAL Born 09/26/1938, Belleville, KS, m, 1961, 2 children **DISCIPLINE** RECENT UNITED STATES HISTORY **EDUCATION** Univ Kans, BA, 60; Univ Ill, MA, 64, PhD(Hist), 68. **CAREER** Asst prof, 68-73, assoc prof Hist, Univ Utah, 73-, vis prof, Univ Hawaii, Hilo, 77-78. **MEMBERSHIPS** AHA; Orgn Am Historians. **RESEARCH** The New Deal; American politics; Truman and Eisenhower eras. **SELECTED PUBLICATIONS** Auth, The impact of the new deal on Wyoming politics, In: The New Deal, Vol 2, The State and Local Levels, Ohio State Univ Press, 75; Twentieth-century western politics, In: Historians and the American West, Univ of Nebraska Press, 83; Congressional opinion and war relocation, 43, In: Japanese Americans from Relocation to Redress, Univ of Utah Press, 86. **CONTACT ADDRESS** Dept of History, Univ of Utah, 380 S 1400 E Rm 211, Salt Lake City, UT, 84112-0311. **EMAIL** ACoombs@lrc.hum.utah.edu

COOMBS, ROBERT H.
PERSONAL Born 09/16/1934, Salt Lake City, UT, m, 1958, 7 children **DISCIPLINE** SOCIOLOGY **EDUCATION** Univ Utah, MS, 58, MS, 59; Washington State Univ, PhD, 64. **CAREER** Instr, 63-64 and asst prof, 64-66, sociol, Iowa State Univ; asst prof, 66-68, assoc prof, 68-70, sociol, Wake Forest Univ; res specialist, Calif Dept Mental Hygiene, 70-73; from assoc res sociol to prof is residence at highest level, UCLA Neuropsychiatric Inst/Dept of Psychiat and Biobehavioral Sci, 70- . **HONORS AND AWARDS** Phi Kappa Phi; Alpha Kappa Delta; NSF fel, 62, 63; US Congress Citation for Exemplary Project, 75, 76; delegat, White House Conf on Children and Youth, 78; Kappa Delta Pi; Sigma Xi; fel, AAAS, 91; fel, Am Psychol Soc, 91; award for Excellence in Educ, 92; distinguished Faculty Educ Award, 92; fel, Am Asn of Applied and Preventive Psychol, 94. **MEMBERSHIPS** Am Sociol Asn; Int Sociol Asn; World Federation for Mental health; AAAS; World Federation for Medical Educ; Am Pshchol Soc; Am Asn of Applied and Preventive Psychol; Am Psychotherapy Asn. **RESEARCH** Professional socialization in medicine; substance abuse. **SELECTED PUBLICATIONS** Coauth, Handbook of Drug Abuse Prevention: A Comprehensive Strategy to Prevent the Abuse of Alcohol and Other Drugs, Allyn & Bacon, 95; auth, Drug-Impaired Professionals, Harvard Univ, 97; auth, Surviving Medical School, Sage, 98; auth, Cool Parents/Drug-Free Kids, Center Press, forthcoming; auth, Handbook on Addiction Recovery Tools and Programs, forthcoming; auth, Women Surgeons: Breaking the Sex Barriers, forthcoming; coauth, Seasons of Marriage: A Thirty-Year Developmental Study of Physicians' Wives, forthcoming. **CONTACT ADDRESS** School of Medicine, Univ of California, 760 Westwood Plz, Los Angeles, CA, 90024-1759. **EMAIL** rcoombs@npih.medsch.ucla.edu

COON, DAVID L.
DISCIPLINE EARLY AMERICA HISTORY **EDUCATION** Univ Ill Urbana, PhD, 72. **CAREER** Assoc prof, Washington State Univ. **HONORS AND AWARDS** Burlington Northern Fac Achievement Award, 88. **RESEARCH** George Washington's Mount Vernon slave community and a general survey of American agricultural history. **SELECTED PUBLICATIONS** Auth, The Development of Market Agriculture in South Carolina, 89. **CONTACT ADDRESS** Dept of History, Washington State Univ, 301 Wilson Hall, PO Box 644030, Pullman, WA, 99164-4030. **EMAIL** coond@wsu.edu

COON, LYNDA L.
DISCIPLINE HISTORY **EDUCATION** Univ Va, PhD. **CAREER** Assoc prof. **RESEARCH** Medieval European history. **SELECTED PUBLICATIONS** Auth, Sacred Fictions: Holy Women and Hagiography in late Antiquity, Univ Pa, 97; co-ed, That Gentle Strength: Historical Perspectives on Women and Christianity, Univ Va, 90. **CONTACT ADDRESS** History Dept, Univ of Arkansas, Fayetteville, 509 Old Main, Fayetteville, AR, 72701. **EMAIL** llcoon@comp.uark.edu

COONEY, TERRY ARNOLD
PERSONAL Born 06/20/1948, Presque Isle, ME, m, 1974, 2 children **DISCIPLINE** UNITED STATES HISTORY **EDUCATION** Harvard Univ, BA, 70; State Univ NY, Stony Brook, MA, 71, PhD(hist), 76. **CAREER** ASST PROF HIST, UNIV PUGET SOUND, 76-, Nat Endowment Humanities fel, 80-81. **MEMBERSHIPS** AHA; Orgn Am Historians. **RESEARCH** Literary radicalism in the twentieth century; American cultural values; liberalism. **SELECTED PUBLICATIONS** Auth, Renewing The Left--Politics, Imagination, and the New-York Intellectuals, Amer Hist Rev, Vol 0102, 97; Remaking America--Public Memory, Commemoration, and Patriotism in the 20th-Century, Pacific Northwest Quart, Vol 0084, 93. **CONTACT ADDRESS** Dept of Hist, Univ Puget Sound, 1500 N Warner St, Tacoma, WA, 98416-0005.

COONS, RONALD EDWARD
PERSONAL Born 07/24/1936, Elmhurst, IL **DISCIPLINE** MODERN EUROPEAN HISTORY **EDUCATION** DePauw Univ, AB, 58; Harvard Univ, AM, 59, PhD(hist), 66. **CAREER** Asst prof, 66-72, assoc prof, 72-79, PROF HIST, UNIV CONN, 79-, Am Coun Learned Soc study grant, 74; Am Philos Soc res grant, 74; Nat Inst Health res grant, 79. **MEMBERSHIPS** AHA; Conf Group Cent Europ Hist; Verein fur geschichte der Stadt Wien, Vienna, Austria. **RESEARCH** Modern European history; nineteenth-century Austrian political history; history of Vienna. **SELECTED PUBLICATIONS** Auth, The City and the Crown--Vienna and the Imperial-Court, 1600-1740, Historian, Vol 0056, 94. **CONTACT ADDRESS** Dept Hist, Univ Conn, U-103, Storrs, CT, 06268.

COOPE, JESSICA
DISCIPLINE MEDIEVAL EUROPEAN HISTORY **EDUCATION** Univ Calif, Berkeley, PhD, 88. **CAREER** Assoc prof, Undergrad Ch, Univ Nebr, Lincoln. **HONORS AND AWARDS** Distinguished Tchg Award, Univ Nebr, Lincoln, 98. **RESEARCH** Medieval Spain. **SELECTED PUBLICATIONS** Auth, The Martyrs of Cordoba: Community and Family Conflict in an Age of Mass Conversion, Univ Nebr Press, 95. **CONTACT ADDRESS** Univ Nebr, Lincoln, 625 Oldfat, Lincoln, NE, 68588-0417. **EMAIL** jcoope@unlinfo.unl.edu

COOPER, ALLAN D.
PERSONAL Born 04/13/1952, Oklahoma City, OK, m, 1980, 2 children **DISCIPLINE** POLITICAL SCIENCE **EDUCATION** Univ Okla, BA, 74; Univ Wis, MA, 76; Atlanta Univ, PhD, 81. **CAREER** From asst prof to assoc prof to chemn, 81-93, St Augustines Col; from assoc prof to prof to chemn, 93-, Otterbein Col. **HONORS AND AWARDS** Am Counc Learned Societies, res grant, 94; Fulbright-Hays Res Award, 92; NEH Stud Awards, 84, 87, 91, 93; Am Polit Science Asn, Res Award, 89. **MEMBERSHIPS** Am Polit Science Asn; African Stud Asn; Asn Concerned Africa Scholars; Asn Third World Stud. **RESEARCH** Politics of Namibia and Southern Africa. **SELECTED PUBLICATIONS** Auth, US Economic Power and Political Influence in Namibia, 1700-1982, 82; ed, Allies in Apartheid: Western Capitalism in Occupied Namibia, 88; auth, The Occupation of Namibia: Afrikanerdom's Attack on The British Empire, 91; auth, art, Namibia in Joel Krieger, 93; auth, art, State Sponsorship of Women's Rights and Implications for Patriarchism, 97. **CONTACT ADDRESS** Dept of History and Political Science, Otterbein Col, One Otterbein, Westerville, OH, 43081. **EMAIL** acooper@otterbein.edu

COOPER, CRAIG
DISCIPLINE GREEK; ROMAN **EDUCATION** Univ Alberta, BA, 83; Univ Brit Columbia, MA, 85, PhD, 92. **CAREER** Asst prof **RESEARCH** Greek historiography; Athenian law; Athenian orators and rhetoric. **SELECTED PUBLICATIONS** Auth, Hyperides and the Trial of Phryne, Phoenix 49, 95. **CONTACT ADDRESS** Dept of Classics, Univ of Winnipeg, 515 Portage Ave, Winnipeg, MB, R3B 2E9. **EMAIL** craig.cooper@uwinnipeg.ca

COOPER, DONALD B.
PERSONAL Born 08/20/1931, Columbus, OH, m, 1957, 3 children **DISCIPLINE** LATIN AMERICAN HISTORY **EDUCATION** Ohio State Univ, BA, 57; Univ Tex, MA, 58, PhD, 63. **CAREER** Asst prof Latin Am hist, Okla State Univ, 61-63; from asst prof to assoc prof, Tulane Univ, 63-69; PROF LATIN AM HIST, OHIO STATE UNIV, 69-, Nat Libr Med & Commonwealth Fund spec res fels, Brazil, 67-68. **MEMBERSHIPS** AHA; Latin Am Studies Asn; Conf Latin Am Hist. **RESEARCH** Medical and social history of Latin America, especially 19th and 20th century Brazil and 18th century Mexico. **SELECTED PUBLICATIONS** Auth, Secret Judgments of God--Old-World Disease in Colonial Spanish-America, Amer Hist Rev, Vol 0098, 93; Healing the Masses, Cuban Health Politics at Home and Abroad, Hisp Amer Hist Rev, Vol 0075, 95. **CONTACT ADDRESS** Dept of Hist, Ohio State Univ, Columbus, OH, 43210.

COOPER, FREDERICK A.
DISCIPLINE GREEK AND ROMAN ART, GREEK ARCHITECTURE **EDUCATION** Yale Univ, AB, 59; Univ Pittsburg, MA, 62; Univ Pa, PhD, 70. **CAREER** Prof, Univ Minn, Twin Cities. **HONORS AND AWARDS** CLA Distinguished Tchr Awards, Univ Minn, 72-73, 89-90; Guggenheim fel, 79-80; Morse-Minn Alumni Award, 91; Excellence in Undergrad Tchg Award, Archaeol Inst of Am, 96. **RESEARCH** Medieval architecture. **SELECTED PUBLICATIONS** Auth, The Temple of Zeus at Nemea: The Reconstruction Project, 83; coauth, Dining in Round Buildings, in Sympotika, ed, O Murray, 90; Satellite Spectral Data and Archaeological Reconnaissance in Western Greece, in Applications of Space-Age Technology in Anthropology, eds, C Behrens and L Sever, 91; The Quarries of Mt. Taygetos in the Peloponessos, Greece, in Marble in Ancient Greece and Rome: Geology, Quarries, Commerce, Artifacts, ed, N Herz and M Waelkens, 92; The Temple of Apollo Bassitas, 92-97. **CONTACT ADDRESS** Dept of Class and Near Eastern Stud, Univ Minn, Twin Cities, Minneapolis, MN, 55455. **EMAIL** coope002@maroon.tc.umn.edu

COOPER, GAIL
PERSONAL Born 03/20/1954, Visalia, CA, m, 1988 **DISCIPLINE** HISTORY **EDUCATION** Univ Calif, Santa Barbara, PhD, 87. **CAREER** Asst prof, 87-96, assoc prof, 96-, Lehigh Univ. **MEMBERSHIPS** Soc History Tech; Amer Hist Assn. **RESEARCH** History of technology; Japanese industrialization; technology and gender. **SELECTED PUBLICATIONS** Auth, Air-conditioning America: Engineers and the Controlled Environment, 1900-1960, 98; auth, "Love, War, and Chocolate: Gender and the American Candy Industry, 1890-1930," in His and Hers: Gender, Consumption, and technology, 98. **CONTACT ADDRESS** Dept of History, Lehigh Univ, 9 W Packer Ave, Bethlehem, PA, 18015. **EMAIL** gc05@lehigh.edu

COOPER, JERROLD STEPHEN
PERSONAL Born 11/24/1942, Chicago, IL, 3 children **DISCIPLINE** ASSYRIOLOGY **EDUCATION** Univ Calif, Berkeley, AB, 63, AM, 64; Univ Chicago, PhD(Assyriol), 69. **CAREER** Asst prof, 68-74, assoc prof, 74-79, prof Near Eastern Studies, Johns Hopkins Univ, 79-, Co-ed, J Cuneiform Studies, 72-89. **MEMBERSHIPS** Am Orient Soc; Am Schools of Oriental Res. **SELECTED PUBLICATIONS** Auth, The Return of Ninurta to Nippur, Pontif Bibl Inst, 78; Symmetry and repetion in Akkadian narrative, J Am Orient Soc, 78; Apodotic death and the historicity of historical omens, Mesopotamia, Vol 8, 80; Studies in Mesopotamian Lapidary Inscription, Vol I & II, J Cuneiform Studies & Rev'd Assyriologie, 80; The Curse of the Agade, Johns Hopkins Press, 82; ed, Mesopotamian Civilizations, 87-; auth, Reconstructing History from Ancient Sources: The Lagash-Umma Border Conflict, Malibu, Udena Publ, 87; auth, Sumerian and Akkadian royal Inscriptions Vol.1: Presargonic Inscriptions, New Haven, Am Oriental Soc, 86; co-ed, The Study of the Ancient Near East in the 21st Century: The WF Albright Centenary Conference, Eisenbrauns, 96; auth, Paradigm and Propaganda: The Dynasty of Akkade in the 21st Century BC, Akkad, the First World Empire: Structure, Ideology, Traditions, ed. M. Liverani, 11-23, 93; Magic and M(is)use: Poetic Promiscuity in Mesopotamian Ritual, Mesopotamian Poetic Language: Sumerian and Akkadian, Styx Publ, 47-57, 96. **CONTACT ADDRESS** Dept of Near Eastern Studies, Johns Hopkins Univ, 3400 N Charles St, Baltimore, MD, 21218-2680. **EMAIL** anzu@jhu.edu

COOPER, JERRY MARVIN
PERSONAL Born 11/25/1939, Three Rivers, MI, m, 1966, 1 child **DISCIPLINE** AMERICAN HISTORY **EDUCATION** Western Mich Univ, BA, 65; Univ Wis-Madison, MA, 68, PhD(Am hist), 71. **CAREER** Asst prof, 71-77, assoc prof Am Hist, Univ Mo-St Louis, 77-. **MEMBERSHIPS** Orgn Am Historians; Soc of Military History; Society for Historians of American Foreign Relations. **RESEARCH** American military history; 20th century American history. **SELECTED PUBLICATIONS** Auth, The Wisconsin National Guard in the Milwaukee riots of 2886, Wis Mag Hist, fall 71; National Guard reform, the Army, and the Spanish-American war: the view from Wisconsin, Mil Affairs, 2/78; The Army and Civil Disorder: Federal Military Intervention in American Labor Disputes, Greenwood Press, 80; Citizens As Soldiers: A History of the North Dakota National Gueard, North Dakota State U. Press, 86; The Militia and National Guard In America Since Colonial Times: A Research Guide, Greenwood Press, 93; The Rise of the National Guard: Evolution of the American Militia, 1865-1920, University of Nebraska Press, 97. **CONTACT ADDRESS** Dept of History, Univ of Missouri, St. Louis, 8001 Natural Bridge, St. Louis, MO, 63121-4499.

COOPER, PATRICIA ANN
PERSONAL Born 08/29/1949, VA **DISCIPLINE** HISTORY **EDUCATION** Wittenberg Univ, BA, 71; Univ of Md, MA, 74, PhD, 81. **CAREER** Historian, Service Employees Int Union, 82-83; asst prof, 83-88, assoc prof, Drexel Univ, 88-93,; ASSOC PROF, UNIV OF KY, 93-. **HONORS AND AWARDS** Postdoctoral fel, Smithsonian Inst, 81-82; fel, Hagley Museum & Libr, 89; res comt Awd, Univ of Ky, 93-94. **MEMBERSHIPS** AHA; OAH; Berkshire Confr of Women Historians; Labor & Working Class Hist Asn; Oral Hist in the Mid-Atlantic Region; Coord Coun on Women in the Historical Profession. **RESEARCH** U.S. industrial history; race, gender, class and U.S. history; U.S. women's history; U.S. working class history; U.S. cultural history. **SELECTED PUBLICATIONS** Auth, Once a Cigar Maker: Men, Women and Work Culture in American Cigar Factories 1900-1919, Univ of Ill Press, 87; A Masculinist Vision of Useful Labor: Popular Thinking on Women and Work in the United States 1830-1940, Ky Law J, 95-96; The Faces of Gender: Work and Work Relations at Philco 1928-1938, Work Engendered: Toward a New Hist of Am Labor, Cornell Univ Press, 91; What This Country Needs is a Good Five-Cent Cigar: The Mechanization of Cigar Manufacturing, Tech and Culture, 88. **CONTACT ADDRESS** Dept of Hist, Univ of Kentucky. **EMAIL** pacoop@pop.uky.edu

COOPER, SANDI E.
PERSONAL Born 05/11/1936, New York, NY, m, 1967, 2 children **DISCIPLINE** MODERN HISTORY **CAREER** Grad asst hist,59-60, NY Univ; instr,61-65, lectr, 66-67, Douglass Col, Rutgers Univ; asst prof, 67-71, assoc prof, 71-79, prof hist, div soc sci, chmn, 94-98, Univ Fac Senate, Col Staten Island, Grad Schl - CUNY; Natl co-pres, Coord Comt Women in Hist Profes, 71-73; pres, Berkshire Conf Women Historians, 79-81. **HONORS AND AWARDS** NEH; USIP Fels. **MEMBERSHIPS** AHA; Soc Hist Studies, France; Peace Hist Soc; Inst Res Hist. **SELECTED PUBLICATIONS** Auth, Patriotic Pacifism: Waging War on War in Europe 1815-1914, Oxford, 91; auth, of 30 introd & ed, Garland Library of War and Peace, Garland, 71-76; ed, Biographical Dictionary of Modern Peace Leaders, Greenwood (in prep). **CONTACT ADDRESS** Dept of History, Col of Staten Island, CUNY, Staten Island, NY, 10301. **EMAIL** Sansi@cunyum.cuny.edu

COOPER, WILLIAM
PERSONAL Born 10/22/1940, Kingstree, SC, m, 1962, 2 children **DISCIPLINE** HISTORY **EDUCATION** Princeton Univ, AB, 62; Johns Hopkins Univ, PhD, 66. **CAREER** Asst prof, 68-70, Assoc prof, 70-78, prof 78-89, dean, graduate sch, 82-89, Boyd prof, 89-, Louisiana State Univ. **MEMBERSHIPS** Amer Hist Assn; Organization of Amer Historian; Southern Historical Assn. **RESEARCH** Amer Hist; Hist of the South (19th century) **SELECTED PUBLICATIONS** auth, The Conservative Regime: South Carolina 1877-1890, LSU Press, 91; coauth, The American South: A History, McGraw Hill, NY, 96; coauth, Writing the Civil War: The Quest to Understand, Univ S. Carolina Press, 98. **CONTACT ADDRESS** Dept of History, Louisiana State Univ, Baton Rouge, LA, 70803.

COOX, ALVIN DAVID
PERSONAL Born 03/08/1924, Rochester, NY, m, 1954, 1 child **DISCIPLINE** MODERN HISTORY AND MILITARY AFFAIRS **EDUCATION** NY Univ, AB, 45; Harvard Univ, AM, 46, PhD(Fr mil), 51. **CAREER** Sr historian, Oper Res Off, Johns Hopkins Univ, 49-54; vis prof mod hist, Shiga Nat Univ, Japan, 54-55; defense historian, Japanese Res Div, US Army, 55-57; analyst nat defense, US Air Force, 57-63; mem fac mod hist, Far E Div, Univ Md, 63-64; from asst prof to assoc prof, 64-69, dir, Ctr Asian Studies, 66-79, PROF HIST, SAN DIEGO STATE UNIV, 69-, Lectr hist & govt, Far E Div, Univ Calif, 54-56; lectr, Far E Div, Univ Md, 56-63; Rockefeller Found res grants, 61-63; San Diego State Univ Found fac res grants, 65-82. **HONORS AND AWARDS** Cert of Commendation, Air Univ Inst Technol, 72; Trustee Outstanding Prof Award, Calif State Univ Syst, 73. **MEMBERSHIPS** AHA; Asn Asian Studies; Am Mil Inst; Int House Japan. **RESEARCH** Modern French military doctrine; modern Japanese military history; Japanese versus Soviet Russian military confrontations. **SELECTED PUBLICATIONS** Auth, Tennozan--The Battle of Okinawa and the Atomic-Bomb, Jour Amer Hist, Vol 0081, 95. **CONTACT ADDRESS** Dept of Hist, San Diego State Univ, San Diego, CA, 92182.

COPE, ESTHER SIDNEY
PERSONAL Born 09/09/1942, West Chester, PA **DISCIPLINE** ENGLISH AND EUROPEAN HISTORY **EDUCATION** Wilson Col, BA, 64; Univ Wis, MA, 65; Bryn Mawr Col, PhD(hist), 69. **CAREER** Instr hist, Ursinus Col, 68-70, asst prof, 70-75; asst prof, 75-77, assoc prof, 77-81, PROF HIST, UNIV NEBR-LINCOLN, 81-. **MEMBERSHIPS** Conf Brit Studies (rec secy, 77-81); AHA; Int Comn Study Rep & Parliamentary Inst; fel Royal Hist Soc. **RESEARCH** Political history of early Stuart England. **SELECTED PUBLICATIONS** Auth, Loyalty and Locality--Popular Allegiance in Devon During the English-Civil-War, Sixteenth Century Jour, Vol 0026, 95; The Personal Rule of Charles, Amer Hist Rev, Vol 0099, 94. **CONTACT ADDRESS** Dept of Hist, Univ of Nebr, Lincoln, NE, 68588.

COPELAND, HENRY JEFFERSON
PERSONAL Born 06/13/1936, Griffin, GA, m, 1958, 2 children **DISCIPLINE** MODERN EUROPEAN HISTORY **EDUCATION** Baylor Univ, AB, 58; Cornell Univ, PhD, 66. **CAREER** Instr hist, Cornell Univ, 65-66; from asst prof to assoc prof, 66-74, assoc dean, 69-74, dean fac, 74-77, Pres, Col Wooster, 77-95, prof hist, 74-99. **MEMBERSHIPS** AHA; Soc Fr Hist Studies. **RESEARCH** Fourth Republic of France. **CONTACT ADDRESS** Dept of History, 1189 Beall Ave, Wooster, OH, 44691-2363.

COPELAND, ROBERT M.
PERSONAL Born 05/12/1943, Hendersonville, NC **DISCIPLINE** EDUCATION **EDUCATION** Livingstone Coll, BS, 1964; Oregon State Univ, MS, 1971; Oregon State Univ, PhD, 1974. **CAREER** Coll of Liberal Arts & Sciences, Univ of IL, assoc dean, 1986-96, asst dean, 1974-86; exc and senior assoc dean, 1996-; Oregon State Univ, teacher, counselor, 1971-74; Ebenezer Ave School Rock Hill SC, teacher, 1968-70; Sunset Park School, Rock Hill, SC, teacher, coach, 1964-68. **HONORS AND AWARDS** fellow, Natl Science Found, 1970-71, Ford Found, 1971-72, Natl Fellowships Fund, 1972-74; Pres, Natl Assn of Acad Affairs Administrators 1987. **MEMBERSHIPS** Mem, Natl Science Teacher's Assn, Natl Educ Assn, Assn for Educ of Teachers of Sci, Urbana Council Comm for Training of Teachers of Science, Alpha Phi Alpha, Phi Delta Kappa Hon Soc, Amer Coll Personnel Assn, Assn for Council & Devel; member, National Academic Advisory Association, 1988-. **CONTACT ADDRESS** Col Liberal Arts and Scis, Univ of Illinois, Urbana-Champaign, 702 S Wright Street, Urbana, IL, 61801.

COPELAND, ROBERT M.
PERSONAL Born 01/30/1945, Douglas, WY, m, 1966, 3 children **DISCIPLINE** MUSICOLGY **EDUCATION** Geneva Col, BS, 66; Univ of Cincinnati, MMus, 70, PhD, 74. **CAREER** Mid-Am Nazarene Col, asst prof to prof, 71-81; Geneva Col, actg div hd, 80-81, 81-; prof of music and ch, dept of music, 77 vis lectr in music hist, Univ of KS, 83 vis prof of church music, reformed presbyterian theol seminary. **HONORS AND AWARDS** Fac Excellence in Scholarship Award, 83-84 and 94-95 NDEA Fel, 68-71 NEH Summer Seminar, Univ of KS, 78. **MEMBERSHIPS** Am Musicological Soc; Sonneck Soc for Am Music; Soc for Ethnomusicology, Am Choral Dir Assoc; Am Assoc of Univ Profs. **RESEARCH** Am sacred music of the 18th-19th century; Parlor songs : Psalmody of the Refomation ; music historiography; music and musicians in fiction; the Holocaust and the arts. **SELECTED PUBLICATIONS** Sing Up: Learning Music for Worship, Pittsburgh, 73; Spare No Exertions, Pittsburgh, 86 Isaac Baker Woodbury, NJ, 95; Chapters in: Museums, Humanities and Educated Eyes, 82; Metrical Psalmody of the Covenanters, St. Louis, 77; articles, Musical Quarterly, Col Music Symposium; American Music; Notes; Christian Scholars Review, Reformed Worship. **CONTACT ADDRESS** Dept of Music, Geneva Col, 3200 Col Ave, Beaver Falls, PA, 15010. **EMAIL** rmc@geneva.edu

COPLE JAHER, FREDERICK
DISCIPLINE HISTORY **EDUCATION** Harvard Univ, PhD, 61. **CAREER** Prof, Univ Ill Urbana Champaign **RESEARCH** American social; intellectual; and cultural history. **SELECTED PUBLICATIONS** Auth, Doubters and Dissenters, Free, 64; The Urban Establishment, Univ Ill, 82; A Scapegoat in the New Wilderness, Harvard, 94. **CONTACT ADDRESS** History Dept, Univ Ill Urbana Champaign, 52 E Gregory Dr, Champaign, IL, 61820. **EMAIL** f-jaher@uiuc.edu

COPP, JOHN T.
PERSONAL Born 10/28/1938, Ottawa, ON, Canada **DISCIPLINE** HISTORY **EDUCATION** Sir George Williams Col, BA, 59; McGill Univ, MA, 62. **CAREER** Lectr, Loyola Col & McGill Univ, 63-70; lectr, Sir George Williams Col & Concordia Univ, 70-75; fac mem, 75-81, PROF HISTORY, WILFRID LAURIER UNIV, 81-, ch hist, 82-95, co-dir, Laurier Ctr Mil Strategic & Disarmament Stud; vis prof, Univ Victoria, 71-72; vis prof, Univ Ottawa, 71-73. **HONORS AND AWARDS** C.P. Stacey Bk Award, 90, 92. **RESEARCH** Canadian social, labor and military history. **SELECTED PUBLICATIONS** Auth, The Anatomy of Poverty: The Condition of the Working Class in Montreal 1897-1929, 74; auth, The Brigade: The Fifth Canadian Infantry Brigade 1939-1945, 92; auth, A Canadian's Guide to the Battlefields of Normandy, 94; auth, No Price Too High, 95; coauth, Maple Leaf Route, 5 vols, 82-88; coauth, Battle Exhaustion: Soldiers and Psychiatrists in the Canadian Army 1939-1945, 90. **CONTACT ADDRESS** Dept of History, Wilfrid Laurier Univ, Waterloo, ON, N2L 3C5.

COPPA, FRANK JOHN
PERSONAL Born 07/18/1937, New York, NY, m, 1965, 2 children **DISCIPLINE** MODERN EUROPEAN HISTORY **EDUCATION** Brooklyn Col, BA, 60; Cath Univ, MA, 62, PhD, 66. **CAREER** Lectr hist, Brooklyn Col, 64; from instr to asst prof, 65-70, res grants on Italy, 67 & 69, assoc prof, 70-79, PROF HIST & CHMN DEPT, ST JOHN'S UNIV, NY, 79-; Assoc, Sem on Studies in Mod Italy, Columbia Univ, 71-80; chmn, 80-82; mem, Nat Comt of USA Bicentennial--The Italian Contrib, 75-76 & Inst Storia Risorgimento Ital. **HONORS AND AWARDS** Generoso Pope Scholarship, 56; Knights of Columbus Fel, 60-64; Fulbright Grant to Italy, 64-65; Grant by the US Ed Found in BEL, 65; Univ Grants, summers of 67 and 69; Faculty Research Award, 74; NEH, Sr div grant, summer 77; grants from the Italian Ministry of Foreign Affairs and the Banca Commerciate Italiana, Int Conference on Post-War Italy at Columbia Univ, 89. **MEMBERSHIPS** AHA; Am Cath Hist Asn, exec coun, 91-; Soc Ital Hist Studies; NY State Asn European Hist; Instituto per la storia del Risorgimento; Columbia Sem on Modern Italy, sec, 76-77, chair, 80-81; Interuniversity Center for European Studies. **RESEARCH** Modern European history 1800 to present; modern Italian history; relations between church and state in Italy; examination of counter-Risorgimento with emphasis on Pope Pius IX and his Secretary of State Cardinal Giacomo Antonelli; Giovanni Giolitti, Italian Prime Minister dominating Italian political life from 1901-1914. **SELECTED PUBLICATIONS** Co-ed, Modern From Vienna to Vietnam: War and Peace in the Modern World, with B. Bast and W. Griffin, Dubuque: W. C. Brown, 69; auth, Economics and Politics in the Giolittian Age, Cath Univ Am, DC, 71; Camillo di Cavour, Twayne Pubs, 73; co-ed, Cities in Transition: From the Ancient World to Urban America, with P. Dolce, Nelson-Hall, 74;ed, Religion in the Making of Western Man, NY: St John's Univ Press, 74; ed, The Immigrant Experience in America, with T. Curran, Boston and NY: Twayne Pubs, 76; auth, Giolitti e I Cattolici nell Italia Liberale, 1904-1914, Rassegna Storica del Risorgimento, 7-9/77; Pope Pius IX: Crusader in a Secular Age, Twayne, 79; ed, Screen and Society: The Impact of Television upon Aspects of Contemporary Civilization, Nelson-Hall, 79; auth, Papal Rome in 1848: From Reform to Revolution, Proc Consortium Revolutionary Europ, 79; Pope Pius IX, Twayne Pubs, Boston, 79; Cardinal Giacomo Antonelli: An Accommodating Personality in the Politics of Confrontation, Biog, Vol II, No 4, fall 79; Pessimism and Traditionalism in the Personality and Policies of Pio Nono, J Italian Hist, Vol II, No 2, autumn 79; Francesco Saverio Nitti: Early Critic of the Treaty of Versailles, Risorgimento, No II, 80; ed, Technology in the Twentieth Century, co-ed by R. Harmond, Kendall-Hunt Pub Co, 83; ed, Dictionary of Modern Italian History, Westport, CT: Greenwood Press, 85; ed, Studies in Modern Italian History: From the Risorgimento to the Republic, NY and Berne: Peter Lang, 86; ed, Italian History: An Annotated Bibliography, NY: Greenwood Press, 90; Cardinal Giacomo Antonelli and Papal Politics in European Affairs, SUNY, 90; The Origins of the Italian Wars of Independence, Longman, London/NY, 92; many scholarly articles and presentations of papers at professional meetings, and many radio and television shows. **CONTACT ADDRESS** Dept of Hist, St John's Univ, 8150 Utopia Pky, Jamaica, NY, 11439-0002. **EMAIL** coppaf@stjohns.edu

CORAL, LENORE
DISCIPLINE MUSIC **EDUCATION** Univ Chicago, MA; Univ London, PhD. **CAREER** Music librn and adj ptof. **HONORS AND AWARDS** Citation, Music Libr Asn, 91; spec ach awd, Music Libr Asn, 95. **MEMBERSHIPS** Past pres, Music Libr Asn; pres, US Branch, Int Asn Music Libr, Arch and Doc Centre; dir, US-RILM Off. **RESEARCH** History of publishing and disseminating music. **SELECTED PUBLICATIONS** Auth, Towards the Bibliography of British Book Auction Catalogues, Papers of the Bibliog Soc Am, v.89/4, 95; Evaluating the Conspectus Approach: Problems and Alternatives, in Collection Assessment in Music Libr, Canton, MA: Music Libr Asn, 94; Music Librarianship, in Careers in Music Librarianship, Canton, MA: Music Lib Asn, 90. **CONTACT ADDRESS** Dept of Music, Cornell Univ, 104 Lincoln Hall, Ithaca, NY, 14853. **EMAIL** lfc1@cornell.edu

CORAZZO, NINA
DISCIPLINE ART HISTORY **EDUCATION** IN Univ, BA, 69; MA, 71; Phd, 77. **CAREER** Assoc prof, Valparaiso Univ. **HONORS AND AWARDS** Hellenic Laurel Outstanding Tchg, 96 and 97. **SELECTED PUBLICATIONS** Auth, The Enclosed Garden (hortus conclusus) as Sign of the Virgin Mary in Paradise by the Upper Rhine Master, c. 1410, Semiotics, 97; Women and Monocles, Semiotics, 97; Two studies of Art History: The Virgin Mary as Enclosed Garden and The Construction of Masculine Evil: Francois-Eduard Cibot's 'The Fallen Angels,' 1833; Remembering and Dis-membering: Agatha's Breast, Semiotics, 94; The Construction of Sexual Difference: The Representation of Woman as the Deadly Sin Gluttony, Semiotics, 93; The Collapse of Time: Baubo's Obscene Display and Magritte's painting 'Le Viol', Semiotics, 94; The Unnatural Woman in 18th Century France: Charlotte Corday and the femme homme in Literate Women and French Revolution of 1789. **CONTACT ADDRESS** Valparaiso Univ, 1500 E Lincoln Way, Valparaiso, IN, 46383-6493. **EMAIL** ncorazzo@exodus.valpo.edu

CORBEILL, ANTHONY
DISCIPLINE CLASSICAL LANGUAGES AND LITERATURE **EDUCATION** Univ MI, AB, 83; Univ CA, Berkeley, MA, 85, PhD, 90. **CAREER** Assoc prof, Univ KS. **HONORS AND AWARDS** APA fel, Thesaurus Linguae Latinae, Ger, 90-91; Rome Prize fel, Am Acad Rome, 94-95., Adv coun, AAR; contrib, TOCS-IN. **MEMBERSHIPS** Mem, Am Philol Assn; CAMWS; Am Class League; Soc of Fellows Am Acad Rome; outsanding acad book, Controlling Laughter. Polit Humor in the Late Roman Republic, Princeton, 97. **RESEARCH** Latin lit and Roman cult hist. **SELECTED PUBLICATIONS** Auth, Controlling Laughter. Political Humor in the Late Roman Republic, Princeton, 96; Deviant Diners in Roman Political Invective, Roman Sexualities, Princeton, 98. **CONTACT ADDRESS** Dept of Class, Univ Kansas, Admin Building, Lawrence, KS, 66045.

CORBETT, WILLIAM P.
PERSONAL Born 11/19/1948, Clarion, PA, m, 1983, 2 children **DISCIPLINE** HISTORY **EDUCATION** Clarion State Col, BS, 70; Univ SD, MA, 76; OK State Univ, PhD, 82. **CAREER** US Navy, 70-74; Tchr, Clarion-Limestone Sch, 75-; Grad Tchg Fel, OK State Univ, 76-80; instr, 80-88, dir, N OK Col, 86-88; from asst prof to assoc prof to chemn, 88-, Northeastern State Univ. **HONORS AND AWARDS** Pi Gamma Mu; Phi Alpha Theta; Gilbert Fite Award; Homer L. Knight Award; Albert Pike Award; Jefferson Davis Award; Muriel H Wright Award. **MEMBERSHIPS** Western Hist Asn; OK Hist Soc, chair, Historic Sites Committee, member, Indian Heritage Committee. **RESEARCH** State and local history. **SELECTED PUBLICATIONS** Auth, Oklahoma Passage: The Telecourse Study Guide; "Men, Mud, and Mules: The Good Roads Movement in Oklahoma"; "Peerless Princess of the Best Country: Early Years of Tonkawa"; "They Hired Every Farmer in the Country: Establishing the Prisoner of War Camp at Tonkawa," in The Chronicles of OK. **CONTACT ADDRESS** Dept of History, Northeastern State Univ, 600 N Grand Ave, Tahlequah, OK, 74464. **EMAIL** corbett@cherokee.nsuok.edu

CORBIN SIES, MARY
DISCIPLINE AMERICAN CULTURE/HISTORY **EDUCATION** MI State Univ, BA, 74; Univ MI, MA, 77, PhD, 87. **CAREER** Dir, grad stud; assoc prof; affil fac mem, women's stud dept; mem, Hist Preservation fac. **RESEARCH** Archit. **SELECTED PUBLICATIONS** Auth, God's Very Kingdom on the Earth: The Design Program for the American Suburban Home, 1877-1917, Mod Arch in Am: Visions and Revisions, Iowa State UP, 91; Toward a Performance Theory of the Suburban Ideal, 1877- 1917, Perspectives in Vernacular Architecture IV, Univ Mo Press, 91; Planning the American City Since 1900, (Johns Hopkins UP, 96; George W. Maher's Planning and Architecture, An Inquiry Into the Ideology of Arts & Crafts Design, The Substance of Style: New Perspectives on the Amer Arts and Crafts Movement, Winterthur Mus, 96; Paradise Retained: An Analysis of Persistence in Planned, Exclusive Suburbs, 1880-1980, Planning Perspectives 12, 97. **CONTACT ADDRESS** Am Stud Dept, Univ MD, Col Park, College Park, MD, 20742. **EMAIL** ms128@umail.umd.edu

CORDASCO, FRANCESCO
PERSONAL Born 11/02/1920, New York, NY, m, 1942, 2 children **DISCIPLINE** AMERICAN EDUCATIONAL HISTORY **EDUCATION** Columbia Univ, BA, 44; NY Univ, MA, 45, PhD(sociol), 59. **CAREER** Assoc prof English, Long Island Univ, 46-53; prof educ, Fairleigh Dickinson Univ, 53-58; prof, Seton Hall Univ, 58-63; prof educ, 63-89, PROF EMER EDUC, 89- ,MONTCLAIR STATE COL, 63- ; Educ consult, Migration Div, Commonwealth of PR, 61-71; vis prof educ, NY Univ, summer, 62; consult, US Off of Educ, 67-70; vis prof educ, Univ of PR, summer, 69 & City Univ New York, 72-73. **HONORS AND AWARDS** Order of Merit, Repub of Italy, 76; Brotherhood Award, Nat Conf Christians & Jews, 67. **MEMBERSHIPS** Am Sociol Asn; Am Asn Hist Professors; Hist Educ Soc; British Sociol Asn; Immigration Hist Soc. **RESEARCH** American ethnic communities; immigrant children in American schools. **SELECTED PUBLICATIONS** Auth, Brief History of Education, Littlefield, Adams, 63, rev ed, 70 & 76; Jacob Riis Revisited: Poverty & the Slum, Doubleday, 68; Education in the Urban Community, Am Book Co, 69; Minorities & American City, David McKay, 70; Shaping of American Graduate Education, Rowman & Littlefield, 72; School in the Social Order, Intext, 73; Italian Community & Its Language in United States, Rowman & Littlefield, 75; Bilingual Schooling in the United States, McGraw-Hill, 76; Italian Mass Emigration, Rowman & Littlefield, 80; American Medical Imprints, 1820-1910, Rowman & Littlefield, 85; Immigrant Woman in North American, Scarecrow/Grolier, 85; The Puerto Rican Community, Scarecrow/Grolier, 82; The New American Immigration, Garland Publ, 87; Dictionary of American Immigration History, Scarecrow/Grolier, 90; Theodore Besterman: Bibliographer & Editor, Scarecrow/Grolier, 92. **CONTACT ADDRESS** 6606 Jackson St, West New York, NJ, 07093.

CORDELL, DENNIS DALE
PERSONAL Born 01/01/1947, St. Louis, MO **DISCIPLINE** HISTORY **EDUCATION** Yale Univ, BA, 68; Univ Wis, MA, (History) 72, PhD, 77; Maitrise es-Science, (Demography), 87. **CAREER** Assoc prof, Dept Demog, Univ Montreal, 89-; chmn, Dept History, prof History, 95, South Methodist Univ, Dallas; assoc dean Gen Ed, 97. **HONORS AND AWARDS** Univ Research Coun, Southern Methodist Univ, Travel Grant, 95; Int Migration Proj, Social Science Research Coun, Planning Grant, 96; American Philosophical Soc Award, 96. **MEMBERSHIPS** African Studies Asn; AHA; Western Asn Africanists; Southern Africanists Asn; Comt Concerned Africanist Scholars. **RESEARCH** History of Equatorial Africa; Islamic Africa; Trans-Saharan slave trade. **SELECTED PUBLICATIONS** Coauth, Sara Madjingaye: Guide pour L-Etude Orale de la Langue, US Peace Corps, 69; auth, Throwing knives in Equatorial Africa: A distribution study, BaShiru, 73; A History of the Central African Republic, US Peace Corps, 75; Research resources in Chad and the Central African Republic, Hist Africa, 75; coauth, Southern Africa films: A selected listing of 16mm socio-political films, African Studies Newslett, 76; auth, Eastern Libya, Wadai and the Sanusiya: A Tariqa and a trade route, J African Hist, 77; Population, reproduction, societes, Perspectives et enjeux de demographie sociale, Melanges en lhonneur de Joel Gregory, Montreal: Les presses de lUniversite de Montreal, 93; Hoe and Wage: A Social History of a Circular Migration System in West Africa, 1900-1975, Doulder, San Francisco and London: HarperCollins/Westview Press, 96, with Joel W Gregory and Victor Piche. **CONTACT ADDRESS** Dept of History, Southern Methodist Univ, PO Box 750176, Dallas, TX, 75275-0176.

CORDERY, SIMON
PERSONAL Born 07/08/1960, London, England, m, 1992, 1 child **DISCIPLINE** LEGAL AND SOCIAL HISTORY **EDUCATION** Northern Ill Univ, Ba, 82; Univ of York, MA, 84; Univ of Tex at Austin, PhD, 95. **CAREER** Res asst, Am Hist Asn, 85-88; instr, Louisburg Col, 92-94; INSTR, MONMOUTH COL, 94-. **HONORS AND AWARDS** NEH summer stipend, 98. **MEMBERSHIPS** AHA; NACBS; RLHS; LHS. **RESEARCH** Modern British labor and social history; the history of mutualism. **SELECTED PUBLICATIONS** Auth, Joshua Hobson 1810-1876, Dictionary of Labour Bio, Macmillan, 87; Joshua Hobson and the Business of Radicalism, Bio: An Interdisciplinary Quart, 88; Friendly Societies and the Discourse of Respectability in Britain 1825-1875, J of British Studies, 95; Friendly Societies and the British Labour Movement Before 1914, J of the Asn of Historians in NC, 95; Mutual Benefit Societies in the United States: A Quest for Protection and Identity, Social Security Mutualism: The Comparative Hist of Mutual Benefit Societies, Peter Lang, 96. **CONTACT ADDRESS** Hist Dept, Monmouth Col, 700 E Broadway, Monmouth, IL, 61462. **EMAIL** simon@monm.edu

CORDERY, STACY A. ROZEK
PERSONAL Born 05/22/1961, Saqinaw, MI, m, 1992, 1 child **DISCIPLINE** HISTORY **EDUCATION** Univ of Tex, BA, 83, MA, 86, PhD, 92. **CAREER** Vis asst prof, East Carolina Univ, 92-94; ASST PROF OF HIST & COORD OF WOMEN'S STUDIES, 94-98, ASSOC PROF OF HIST & COORD OF WOMEN'S STUDIES, MONMOUTH COL, 95-. **HONORS AND AWARDS** Prof of the Year, 97 & 98. **MEMBERSHIPS** AHA; SHQAPE; WHOM; Theodore Roosevelt Asn. **RESEARCH** Gilded age; progressive era; women; the Roosevelt family. **SELECTED PUBLICATIONS** Auth, Gertrude Vanderbilt Whitney, Women in World Hist, Yorkin Pub, 98; Juliette Gordon Low, Women in World Hist, Yorking Pub, 98; Alice Roosevelt Longworth, The Biographical and Genealogical Directory of the Roosevelt Family, 97; Alice Roosevelt Longworth, Am Nat Bio, Oxford Univ Press, 98; Helen H. Taft, Am Nat Bio, Oxford Univ Press, 98. **CONTACT ADDRESS** Dept of Hist, Monmouth Col, 700 E Broadway, Monmouth, IL, 61462. **EMAIL** stacy@monm.edu

CORDOVA, CARLOS E.
PERSONAL Born 03/30/1965, San Miguel, El Salvador, m, 1997 **DISCIPLINE** GEOGRAPHY **EDUCATION** Natl Autonomous Univ MEX, BA, 88, MA, 91; Univ TX, PhD, 97. **CAREER** Asst prof, OK Univ, 97. **HONORS AND AWARDS** ED Farmer Fel, 93-94; Univ TX Dissertation Grant Fel, 94-95. **MEMBERSHIPS** Amer Schs of Oriental Research **RESEARCH** Geomorphology; Soils; Geoarchaeology **CONTACT ADDRESS** Dept of Geography, Oklahoma State Univ, 225 Scott Hall, Stillwater, OK, 74078. **EMAIL** cordova@okway.okstate.edu

CORKIN, JANE
PERSONAL Boston, MA **DISCIPLINE** ARCHIVIST/PHOTOGRAPHY **EDUCATION** Queen's Univ, BA, 71. **CAREER** Asst, David Mirvish Gallery, 72-78; OWNER, JANE CORKIN GALLERY 79-; consult, Nat Archs, Ottawa, 85; Adv, Sloane Museum, London, Eng, 88. **HONORS AND AWARDS** Women Who Make A Difference, 93; Toronto Branch Award, Queen's Univ Alumni Asn, 95. **MEMBERSHIPS** Asn Int Photography Art Dealers; Power Plant Contemp Art Gallery; AGO; Art Bank. **SELECTED PUBLICATIONS** Auth, Twelve Canadians, Contemporary Canadian Photography, 81; auth, Margaret Bourke-White, Photographs, 88. **CONTACT ADDRESS** Jane Corkin Gallery, 179 John St, Ste 302, Toronto, ON, M5T 1X4.

CORNELIUS, JANET DUITSMAN
PERSONAL Born 01/20/1938, Danville, IL, m, 1956, 4 children **DISCIPLINE** HISTORY **EDUCATION** Univ Ill, Urbana-Champaign, BA, 68, MA, 69, PhD(hist), 77. **CAREER** Instr soc sci, Danville Jr Col, 69-77; asst prof Am hist, Univ Ill, Urbana-Champaign, 77-78; CHMN SOC SCI DEPT, DANVILLE JR COL, 82-, Fel col teachers, Nat Endowment Humanities, 80-81. **MEMBERSHIPS** Orgn Am Historians; Southern Hist Asn; AHA; Community Col Social Sci Asn; Community Col Humanities Asn. **RESEARCH** Southern religion and slavery; comparative slave systems; family in antebellum United States. **SELECTED PUBLICATIONS** Auth, Sapelos People--A Long Walk Into Freedom, Jour So Hist, Vol 0061, 95; The Abolitionist Sisterhood--Womens Political-Culture in Antebellum America, Jour Amer History, Vol 0082, 1995 **CONTACT ADDRESS** Dept of Hist, Univ of Ill, 309 Gregory Hall, Urbana, IL, 61801.

CORNELL, PAUL G.
PERSONAL Born 09/13/1918, Toronto, ON, Canada **DISCIPLINE** HISTORY **EDUCATION** Univ Toronto, BA, MA, PhD. **CAREER** Lectr to prof hist, Acadia Univ, 49-60; dept ch, 60-68, prof hist, 60-85, dean arts, 70-73, acting vice pres, 72, hon archivist, 77-85, PROF EMER, UNIV WATERLOO, 94-; **HONORS AND AWARDS** Fel, Royal Soc Can; Cruickshank medal, 78. **MEMBERSHIPS** Can Hist Asn (ed, Report, 53-56); Ont Hist Soc (pres, 73-74) **RESEARCH** Canadian history **SELECTED PUBLICATIONS** Auth, The Alignment of Political Groups in the Province of Canada, 62; auth, The Great Coalition, 67, repr 71; coauth, Canada: Unity in Diversity, 67, Fr transl 71; co-ed, Ontario Hist, 63-78. **CONTACT ADDRESS** 202 Laurier Pl, Waterloo, ON, N2L 1K8.

CORNELL, SAUL A.
DISCIPLINE HISTORY **EDUCATION** Amherst, BA, 82; Univ Sussex, 81; Univ of Penn, MA, 83, PhD, 89. **CAREER** Andrew W Mellon Fellow, Univ Penn; current, ASST PROF, HIST, OHIO STATE UNIV **MEMBERSHIPS** Am Antiquarian Soc **RESEARCH** Antifederalists **SELECTED PUBLICATIONS** Auth,"Observations on the 'Late Remarkable Revolution in Government:' Samuel Bryan and Aedanus Burke's Unpublished History of the Ratification Struggle in Pennsylvania," Penn Mag of Hist & Biog, 88; "The Changing Historical Fortunes of the Anti-Federalists," Northwestern Law Rev, 89; "Aristocracy Assailed: The Ideology of Backcountry Anti- Federalism," Jour of Am Hist 76, 90; "Politics of the Middling Sort: The Bourgeois Radicalism of Abraham Yates, Melancton Smith and the New York Antifederalists," in New York in the Age of the Constitution, 92; "Early American History in a Post-Modern Age," Will & Mary Quar 50, 93; The Other Founders: Anti-Federalism and the Dissenting Tradition in America, forthcoming. **CONTACT ADDRESS** Dept of History, Ohio State Univ. **EMAIL** cornell.14@osu.edu

CORNISH, DUDLEY TAYLOR
PERSONAL Born 01/11/1915, Carmel, NY, m, 1946, 1 child **DISCIPLINE** AMERICAN HISTORY **EDUCATION** Univ Rochester, AB, 38; Univ Colo, AM, 47, PhD(hist), 49. **CAREER** From asst prof to assoc prof, 49-56, chmn, Dept Soc Sci, 59-61, chmn, Dept Hist, 66-78, PROF HIST, PITTSBURG STATE UNIV, 58-, Ed-in-chief, Midwest Quart, 59-67; guest lectr, US Army Command & Gen Staff Col, Ft Leavenworth, Kans, 77 & 78, John F Morrison prof mil hist, 78-79; guest lectr, US Army Mil Hist Inst, 82. **HONORS AND AWARDS** Commander's Award Civilian Serv, Dept Army, 79. **MEMBERSHIPS** Am Mil Inst; Orgn Am Historians; Southern Hist Asn; Am Asn State & Local Hist; US Naval Inst. **RESEARCH** American Civil War; American military history; United States naval history. **SELECTED PUBLICATIONS** Auth, From Cape-Charles to Cape-Fear--The North-American Blockading Squadron During the Civil-War, Civil War Hist, Vol 0040, 94; New-Mexico Buffalo Soldiers, 1866-1900, Southwestern Hist Quart, Vol 0096, 93. **CONTACT ADDRESS** Dept of Hist, Pittsburg State Univ, 1701 S Broadway St, Pittsburg, KS, 66762.

CORNWALL, PETER G.
DISCIPLINE MODERN JAPAN **EDUCATION** Univ MI, PhD, 70. **CAREER** Univ Alaska **SELECTED PUBLICATIONS** Ed, Alaska's Rural Development. **CONTACT ADDRESS** Univ AK Fairbanks, PO Box 757480, Fairbanks, AK, 99775-7480. **EMAIL** fyhist@aurora.alaska.edu

CORNWALL, ROBERT D.
PERSONAL Born 03/03/1958, Los Angeles, CA, m, 1983, 1 child **DISCIPLINE** HISTORICAL THEOLOGY **EDUCATION** Northwest Christian Col, BS, 80; Fuller Theol Sem, M Div, 85, PhD, 91. **CAREER** Dir of the Lib, 92-94, William Carey Int Univ; vis asst prof of Church Hist, 94-95, Fuller Theol Sem; assoc prof Theol, 95-97, Manhattan Christian Col; pastor, First Christian Church, Santa Barbara, CA, 98-. **HONORS AND AWARDS** Winner, Land O' Lakes Essay Competition, Shaw Hist Library, 91. **MEMBERSHIPS** North Am Conf of Brit Stud; Am Acad of Relig; Am Soc of Church Hist. **RESEARCH** Anglicanism 17th & 18th century; church-state issues; Nonjurors; Jacobites; Sacramental Theol. **SELECTED PUBLICATIONS** Auth, Visible and Apostolic: The Constitution of the Church in High Church Anglican and Non-Juror Thought 1688-1745, Univ DE Press, 93; auth, The Later Non-Jurors and the Theological Basis of the Usages Controversy, Anglican Theol Rev, 75, 93; auth, The Church and Salvation: An Early Eighteenth-Century High Church Anglican Perspective, Anglican and Episcopal History, 62, 93; auth, Advocacy of the Independence of the Church from the State in Eighteenth Century England: A Comparison of a Nonjuror and a Nonconformist View, Enlightenment and Dissent, 12, 93; auth, The Crisis in Disciples of Christ Ecclesiology: The Search for Identity, Encounter 55, 94; auth, Unity, Restoration, and Ecclesiology: Why the Stone-Campbell Movement Divided, J of Relig Stud, 19, 95; auth, The Ministry of Reconciliation: Toward a Balanced Understanding of the Global Mission of the Christian Church (Disciples of Christ), Lexington Theol Sem Quart, 30, 95; auth, Education for Ministry in the Augustan Age: A Comparison of the Views of Gilbert Burnet and George Bull and Their Implications for the Modern Church, Anglican Theol Rev, 78, 96; auth, The Scandal of the Cross: Self-Sacrifice, Obedience, and Modern Culture, Encounter 58, 97; ed, Gilbert Burnet, Discourse of the Pastoral Care, Edwin Mellon Press, 97; auth, The Agricultural Revolution: An Interpretive Essay, in Events that Changed the World in the Eighteenth Century, Greenwood Press, 98. **CONTACT ADDRESS** First Christian Church, 1905 Chapala St, Santa Barbara, CA, 93101. **EMAIL** bobcornwall@juno.com

CORRIGAN, JOHN
DISCIPLINE RELIGION; AMERICAN STUDIES **EDUCATION** Univ of Chicago, PhD; 82 **CAREER** Asst prof, rel stud, Univ Va; current, PROF, AM STUD, ARIZ STATE UNIV **MEMBERSHIPS** Am Antiquarian Soc **RESEARCH** 18th century religion **SELECTED PUBLICATIONS** Auth, The Hidden Balance: Religion and the Social Theories of Charles Chauncy and Jonathan Mayhew, 87; auth, The Prism of Piety: Catholic Congregational Clergy at the Beginning of the Enlightenment, 91; auth, "Habits from the Heart: The American Enlightenment and Religious Ideas about Emotion and Habit," Jour of Rel 73, 93; Jews, Christians, Muslims, 97; coauth, Religion in America, 98. **CONTACT ADDRESS** 15236 N 6th Cir, Phoenix, AZ, 85023. **EMAIL** john.corrigan@asu.edu

CORRIGAN, KATHLEEN
DISCIPLINE ART HISTORY **EDUCATION** UCLA, BA, MA, PhD. **CAREER** Assoc prof, Dartmouth Col. **RESEARCH** Medieval manuscript illumination; Byzantine monasticism; Byzantine icons. **SELECTED PUBLICATIONS** Auth, Visual Polemics in the Ninth-Century Byzantine Psalters, Cambridge UP, 92; var articles on Byzantine icons and ivories. **CONTACT ADDRESS** Dartmouth Col, 3529 N Main St, Ste. 207, Hanover, NH, 03755. **EMAIL** kathleen.corrigan@dartmouth.edu

CORRIGAN, VINCENT
PERSONAL Born 03/28/1945, Pittsburgh, PA, m, 1971, 2 children **DISCIPLINE** MUSICOLOGY **EDUCATION** Indiana Univ, PhD, 80 **CAREER** Prof, 73-. **MEMBERSHIPS** Am Musicol Soc; Medieval Acad of Am; Hagiography Soc. **RESEARCH** Medieval polyphony; music of troubadours and trouveres; early liturgies; harpsichord performance. **SELECTED PUBLICATIONS** Modal Transmutation in the 13th Century, Essays in Honor of Hans Tischler, ed David Halperin, Orbis Musicae Vol. XII, pp. 83-106; Music and Pilgrimage, The Pilgrimage to Compostela in the Middle Ages, ed Maryjane Dunn and Linda Kay Davidson, Garland Publ, 96; Modal Rhythm and the Interpretation of Trouvere Song, The Cultural meliue of the Troubadours and Trouveres, ed, Nancy Van Deusen, Musicol Studies LXII/1. Ottawa, Inst of Medieval Music, 94. **CONTACT ADDRESS** Col Musical Arts, Bowling Green State Univ, Bowling Green, OH, 43403. **EMAIL** vcorrig@bgnet.bgsu.edu

CORRIN, JAY PATRICK
PERSONAL Born 12/18/1943, Duluth, MN, m, 1967 **DISCIPLINE** MODERN EUROPEAN HISTORY **EDUCATION** Mich State Univ, BA, 66; Univ Hawaii, MA, 68; Boston Univ, PhD(hist mod Europe), 76. **CAREER** Teacher English, Misurata Prep School, Libya N Africa, 68-69; asst prof hist, Col Lib Arts, 76-77, ASST PROF SOCIAL SCI, COL BASIC STUDIES, BOSTON UNIV, 77-. **MEMBERSHIPS** AHA; New Eng Hist Asn; Chesterton Soc. **RESEARCH** British intellectual and social history. **SELECTED PUBLICATIONS** Auth, Reinhold,Hans,Anscar--Liturgical Pioneer and Antifascist, Cath Hist Rev, Vol 0082, 96. **CONTACT ADDRESS** Col of Basic, Studies Boston Univ, 755 Commonwealth Ave, Boston, MA, 02215-1401.

CORTES, CARLOS ELISEO
PERSONAL Born 04/06/1934, Oakland, CA, m, 1978, 1 child **DISCIPLINE** MEXICAN-AMERICAN AND LATIN AMERICAN HISTORY **EDUCATION** Univ Calif, Berkeley, BA, 56; Columbia Univ, MS, 57; Am Inst Foreign Trade, BFT, 62; Univ N Mex, MA, 65, PhD(hist), 69. **CAREER** Actg asst prof hist, 68-69, asst prof, chmn Latin Am studies & asst to VChancellor Acad Affairs, 69-72, assoc prof hist, 72-76, PROF HIST, UNIV CALIF, RIVERSIDE, 78-, CHMN CHICANO STUDIES, 72-79., Consult, US Comn Civil Rights, 71, Intergroup Human Rels Comn Ore Bd Educ, 72, Teacher Corps, 73, Calif Dept Educ, 73, Soc Sci Educ Consortium, 75- & Ford Found; Nat Endowment for Humanities Educ Prog grant, 71-72; fac mem, Nat Humanities, 76-; adv comn, Youth Educ for Citizenship, Am Bar Asn, 80- **HONORS AND AWARDS** Hubert Herring Mem Award, Pac Coast Counc Latin Am Studies, 74; Distinguished Teaching Award, Univ Calif, Riverside, 76; Eleanor Fishburn Award, Wash Ed Press Asn, 77; Distinguished Calif Humanist Award, Calif Coun Humanities, 80. **MEMBERSHIPS** AHA; Western Hist Asn; Latin Am Studies Asn; Nat Counc Social Studies; Nat Asn Chicano Studies. **RESEARCH** History of Brazil; comparative ethnic history; multicultural education. **SELECTED PUBLICATIONS** Auth, My History, Not Yours--The Formation of Mexican-American Autobiography, Amer Hist Rev, Vol 0100, 95. **CONTACT ADDRESS** Dept of Hist, Univ Calif, Riverside, CA, 92521.

COSGROVE, RICHARD A.
PERSONAL Born 02/26/1941, Jersey City, NJ, m, 1963, 4 children **DISCIPLINE** MODERN BRITISH HISTORY **EDUCATION** Holy Cross Col, BS, 62; Univ Calif, Riverside, MA, 63, PhD(Hist), 67. **CAREER** Asst prof, 67-72, from assoc prof to prof Hist, Univ Ariz, 72-98. **MEMBERSHIPS** Conf Brit Studies. **RESEARCH** Nineteenth and 20th century British history; British legal history. **SELECTED PUBLICATIONS** Auth, The Rule of Law: A V Dicey, Victorian Jurist, Univ NC Press, 80; Our Lady the Common Law: An Anglo-American Legal Community, 1870-1930, NYU Press, 87; Scholars of the Law: English Jurisprudence from Blackstone to Hart, NYU Press, 96. **CONTACT ADDRESS** Dept of History, Univ of Arizona, Tucson, AZ, 85721-0001.

COSTA, GUSTAVO
PERSONAL Born 03/21/1930, Rome, Italy, m, 1963, 1 child **DISCIPLINE** ITALIAN, HISTORY **EDUCATION** Univ Rome, DPhilos, 54. **CAREER** Asst hist of mod & contemporary philos, Univ Rome, 57-60; lectr Ital, Univ Lyon, 60-61; from instr to assoc prof, 61-72, chmn dept, 73-76, PROF ITAL, UNIV CALIF, BERKELEY, 72-, Ist Ital Studi Storici, Naples fel, 54-57; French & Belg govt grants, 56; Am Philos Soc grant, 67; Nat Endowment for Humanities fel, 70-71; consult Centro del Lessico Intellettuale Europeo, Univ Rome, 76-77; Guggenheim Mem Found fel, 76-77; ed staff, Romance Philology, Forum Italicum & Nouxelles de la Republique des Lettress. **MEMBERSHIPS** AHA; MLA; AATI; Renaissance Soc Am; Am Soc Aesthet. **RESEARCH** Literary criticism; history; philosophy. **SELECTED PUBLICATIONS** Auth, Legislation and Reform in 18th-Century Trent--Barbacovi,Francesco,Vigilio Between Absolutism and Enlightenment-Italian, Amer Hist Rev, Vol 0099, 94; Alfieri, Romantic Irony and the French-Revolution, Rev des Etudes Italiennes, Vol 0038, 92; The Undivine Comedy--Detheologizing Dante, Romance Philol, Vol 0048, 94; The Worlds of Petrarch, Romance Philol, Vol 0050, 96; Tasso le Jerusalem Delivree--Gerusalemme Liberata-French and Italian, Italica, Vol 0069, 92; Foscolo,Ugo Europe--A Journey from the Sublime to Romantic Humor, Symposium-Quart Jour Mod Lit, Vol 0047, 93. **CONTACT ADDRESS** Dept of Ital, Univ of Calif, Berkeley, CA, 94720.

COSTELLO, DONALD PAUL
PERSONAL Born 08/04/1931, Chicago, IL, m, 1952, 6 children **DISCIPLINE** AMERICAN STUDIES, DRAMA & FILM **EDUCATION** DePaul Univ, AB, 55; Univ Chicago, MA, 56, PhD, 62. **CAREER** Instr, Roosevelt Univ, 57-60 & Chicago City Jr Col, 58-59; from instr to assoc prof, 60-71, prof English, Univ Notre Dame, 71-, chmn Am studies & commun arts, 79-, soc relig higher educ fel, 64-65; consult, Educ Assoc, Inc for Proj Upward Bound, Wash, DC, 66-; consult/panelist, Nat Endowment for Humanities Lit & Fine Arts Panel, 77-. **MEMBERSHIPS** Soc Values Higher Educ; MLA. **RESEARCH** American literature; modern drama; cinema. **SELECTED PUBLICATIONS** Auth, The Language of The Catcher in the Rye, Am Speech, 10/59; art, Graham Greene and the Catholic Press, Renaissance, autumn 59; art, The Structure of the Turn of the Screw, Mod Lang Notes, 4/60; art, The Serpent's Eye: Shaw and the Cinema, Univ Notre Dame, 65; contribr, Black Man as Victim: The Drama of LeRoi Jones, Five Black Writers, New York Univ, 70; art, Counter-culture to Anti-culture: Woodstock, Easy Rider, and A Clockwork Orange, The Rev Polit, 10/72; art, Tennessee Williams' Fugitive Kind, Mod Drama, 5/72; art, Fellini's Road, Univ Notre Dame, 82. **CONTACT ADDRESS** Dept of English, Univ of Notre Dame, 356 Oshaugnessy Hall, Notre Dame, IN, 46556.

COSTIGLIOLA, FRANK CHARLES
PERSONAL Born 11/01/1946, Spring Valley, NY, 3 children **DISCIPLINE** HISTORY **EDUCATION** Hamilton Col, BA, 68; Cornell Univ, PhD(hist), 73. **CAREER** Asst prof, 72-80, assoc prof History, Univ RI, 80-84, prof 85-, prof Univ Conn, 98-, Nat endowment for Humanities fel, 77. **MEMBERSHIPS** AHA, Orgn Am Historians. **RESEARCH** Formation of meaning in the Cold War. **SELECTED PUBLICATIONS** Auth, The establishment of the First World Bank 1929-1930 J Am Hist, 72; The US and the reconstruction of Germany in the 1920's, Bus Hist Rev, 77; Anglo-American financial rivalry in the 1920's, J Econ Hist, 77; Awkward Dominion, 84; Col Alli-

ance, 92; Kennan's Formation of the Cold War, J Am Hist, 97; Tropes of Gender and Potuology in Western Alliance Pip Hist, 97. **CONTACT ADDRESS** Dept of Hist, Univ Conn, Storrs, CT, 06269. **EMAIL** costig@uconnvm.uconn.edu

COTE, JOANNE
PERSONAL Montreal, PQ, Canada **DISCIPLINE** MUSEUM STUDIES **EDUCATION** Univ Quebec Montreal, BA, 79; John F. Kennedy Univ, San Francisco, MA, 87. **CAREER** Asst Registr, Collections Mgmt Svs, Montreal Mus Fine Arts, 79-84; mgr Mus Move & Proj Coordr, Bldg Expansion & Reno Proj, McCord Mus Can Hist, 88-92, head, special proj, 92, head, Educ Svs & Cultural Prog, 94-96. **HONORS AND AWARDS** Joy Feinberg Scholar, 87. **MEMBERSHIPS** Can Mus Asn; Int Coun Mus. **SELECTED PUBLICATIONS** Auth, Moving A Museum: Nightmare or Opportunity, in MUSE, 90. **CONTACT ADDRESS** Museum Studies, Univ Montreal, Montreal, PQ.

COTHREN, MICHAEL W.
DISCIPLINE ART HISTORY **EDUCATION** Vanderbilt Univ, BA, 73; Colombia Univ, MA, 74; PhD, 80. **CAREER** Prof, Swarthmore Col. **HONORS AND AWARDS** Consult curator, Glencairn Mus (Bryn Athyn, PA); pres, Am Corpus Vitrearum; bd dir, Int Ctr Medieval Art. **RESEARCH** Medieval art. **SELECTED PUBLICATIONS** Auth, Restaurateurs et createurs de vitraux a la cathedrale de Beauvais dans les annees 1340, Revue de l'art, 96; Replacing the Survey at Swarthmore, Art Jour, 95; A propos de trois panneaux du musee de Picardie provenant de l'ancienne vitrerie de la cathedrale de Beauvais in Groupe d'Etude des Monuments et Oeuvres d'art de l'Oise et du Beauvaisis, Bulletin, 95; Who is the Bishop in the Virgin Chapel of Beauvais Cathedral?, Gazette des Beaux Arts, 95; Is the 'Tete Gerente' from Saint-Denis?, Jour Glass Studies, 93. **CONTACT ADDRESS** Swarthmore Col, Swarthmore, PA, 19081-1397. **EMAIL** mcothre1@cc.swarthmore.edu

COTMAN, JOHN W.
PERSONAL Born 03/02/1954, Springfield, MA, d, 1 child **DISCIPLINE** POLITICAL SCIENCE **EDUCATION** Univ Colo, BA, 77; Boston Univ, MA, 87, PhD, 92. **CAREER** Inst, Howard Univ, 90-91; Vis Schol, Am Univ, 94-95; Asst Prof, Polit Sci, 91-96, Assoc Prof, 96-, Howard Univ. **HONORS AND AWARDS** Ford Found Postdoctoral Fellow, 94-95, Doctoral Fellow, 87-88; Ctr for Adv Stud in Behavioral Sci, Fellow nomination, 94; Howard Univ, travel Grant, 94, Fac Res Grants, 92/93, 93/94, 95/96, 96/97, 97/98; Boston Univ Grad Dissertation Fellow, 90; Fulbright Grant for PhD Res, 88-89; Dr. Martin Luther King, Jr Fellow, 84-87; Phi Beta Kappa. **MEMBERSHIPS** AM Polit Sci Asn; Carib Stud Asn; Ctr for Cuban Stud; Int Polit Sci Asn; Latin Am Stud Asn; Mid Atl Coun on Latin Am Stud; New England Coun of Latin Am Stud. **RESEARCH** Political science. **SELECTED PUBLICATIONS** Auth, The Gorrion Tree: Cuba & the Grenada Revolution, Peter Lang Pub, 93; auth, Cuba and Caribbean Integration, Govt & Polit, 1:3, 8-10, 93; auth, Cuba and the Caribbean: The Last Decade, Cuba: New Ties to a New World, Rienner Pubs, 93; auth, Hand Carry Important Documents, Mistakes that Social Scientists Make, St Martin's Press, 100, 96; auth, A Tale of Two Exhibits: Hiroshima, the Enola Gay, and Official History, Govt & Polit, 2:1, 14-21, 98; auth, Grenada: The New JEWEL Revolution, Encycl of Polit Revolutions, Congressional Quart Books, forthcoming; auth, Caribbean Convergence: Cuba and CARICOM Relations through 1995, 21st Cent Policy Rev, forthcoming, 98. **CONTACT ADDRESS** Dept of Polit Sci, Howard Univ, PO Box 849, Washington, DC, 20059-2345. **EMAIL** jcotman@fac.howard.edu

COTRONEO, ROSS RALPH
PERSONAL Born 07/24/1930, Lewiston, ID, m, 1962, 1 child **DISCIPLINE** AMERICAN HISTORY **EDUCATION** Univ Idaho, BS, 59, MA, 62, PhD(hist), 66. **CAREER** Asst prof hist, Valley City State Col, 63-66; from asst prof to assoc prof, 66-76, PROF HIST, WESTERN ORE STATE COL, 76-, CHMN, DEPT SOC SCI, 79-. **MEMBERSHIPS** Orgn Am Historians; Western Hist Asn. **RESEARCH** Land grant history of the Northern Pacific Railway. **SELECTED PUBLICATIONS** Auth, Railroad Signatures Across the Pacific-Northwest, Pacific Hist Rev, Vol 0064, 95. **CONTACT ADDRESS** Dept of Hist, Western Oregon Univ, Monmouth, OR, 97361.

COTT, NANCY FALIK
PERSONAL Born 11/08/1945, Philadelphia, PA, m, 1969, 2 children **DISCIPLINE** HISTORY **EDUCATION** Cornell Univ, BA, 67; Brandeis Univ, PhD, 74. **CAREER** Instr hist, Wheaton Col, 71, Clark Univ, 72 & Wellesley Col, 73-74; asst prof, 75-79, assoc prof hist Am studies, Yale Univ, 79-81, prof, 81-91; Fel, law & hist, Harvard Law School, 78-79; Stanley Woodward Prof, 91-; Rockefeller Found Hum fel, 78-79; Guggenheim, 85; NEH, 93-94; Radcliffe res scholar, 82, 97. **MEMBERSHIPS** OHA; Am Studies Asn; Coord Comt Women Hist Profession; AHA. **RESEARCH** Women and gender hist in USA. **SELECTED PUBLICATIONS** Ed, Root of Bitterness: Documents of the History of American Women, E P Dutton, 72; auth, Young Women in the 2d Great Awakening in New England, Feminist Studies, 75; Divorce and the Changing Status of Women in 18th-Century Massachusetts, William & Mary Quart, 76; 18th-Century Family and Social Life Revealed in Massachusetts Divorce Records, J Social Hist, 76; The Bonds of Womanhood: Women's Sphere in New England, 1780-1835, Yale Press, 77; Passionlessness: An Interpretation of Victorian Sexual Ideology, Signs, 78; co-ed, A Heritage of Her Own, Simon & Schuster, 79; The Grounding of Modern Feminism, Yale, 1987; A Womens Making History: Mary Ritter Beard Through Her Letters, Yale Press, 91. **CONTACT ADDRESS** American Studies Prog, Yale Univ, PO Box 208236, New Haven, CT, 06520-8236.

COTTER, JOHN LAMBERT
PERSONAL Born 12/06/1911, Denver, CO, m, 1941, 2 children **DISCIPLINE** HISTORICAL ARCHEOLOGY, ANTHROPOLOGY **EDUCATION** Univ Denver, BA, 34, MA, 35; Univ Pa, PhD(anthrop), 59. **CAREER** Supvr, Archaeol Surv Ky, 38-40; archaeologist, US Nat Park Serv, 40-77; res & writing, 77-, Adj assoc prof Am Civilization, Univ Pa, 60-79, ASSOC CUR, AM HIST ARCHAEOL, UNIV MUS, 70-79, EMER ASSOC CUR, 79-; ed, Bibliog Hist Archaeol. **HONORS AND AWARDS** J A Mason Award, Archaeol Soc Pa, 74; D E Finley Award, Nat Trust for Hist Preserv, 78. **MEMBERSHIPS** Fel Am Anthrop Asn; fel AAAS; Soc Prof Archaeologists; Archaeol Inst Am; Soc Hist Archaeol (pres, 66-67). **RESEARCH** Archaeology of historical American sites and their conservation; archaeology of prehistoric American sites, and conservation. **SELECTED PUBLICATIONS** Auth, Historical Archaeology of the Chesapeake, Pa Mag Hist and Biog, Vol 0119, 95; You Can Take It with You, Archaeol, Vol 0048, 95; Whats the Point, Archaeol, Vol 0050, 97; The Triumph of Fossil Homo, Archaeol, Vol 0047, 94; An Unsinkable Story, Archaeol, Vol 0050, 97; Antique Archaeologists, Archaeol, Vol 0050, 97. **CONTACT ADDRESS** Univ Museum, 34th & Spruce Sts, Philadelphia, PA, 19174.

COTTLE, THOMAS J.
PERSONAL Born 01/22/1937, Chicago, IL, m, 1964, 3 children **DISCIPLINE** PSYCHOLOGY; SOCIOLOGY **EDUCATION** Harvard Univ, BA; Univ Chicago, MA, PhD. **CAREER** Boston Univ, prof 90-; Harvard Med Sch, lectr 75-90; Harvard Univ, asst prof, asst chemn; Amherst Col, vis prof; Wesleyan Univ, vis prof; Boston Univ, lectr; Columbia Col, vis prof; Radcliffe Inst, instr; Duquesne Univ, dist vis prof. **HONORS AND AWARDS** Young Psychologist Awd; Guggenheim Fel; Pioneer Fel; Nat Bdcst Tele Awd; Amer Can Soc Awd; PA Awd; Emmy Awds; Gabriel Awd; Tom Phillips Awd; Cit Par Choice Awd; Derose/Hinkhouser Awd; Amer Women Rad/TV Awd; MA Alli Mentally Ill., Presently a regular contributor to Midday News, WCVB-TV, ABC, Boston; actively appearing on: The Tom Cottle Show; Tom Cottle Up Close; Tom Cottle Soap Box; Good Morning America; Today Show; 20/20; John Davidson Show; Hour Magazine; David Suskind Show; NOVA, PBS; Kids Are People Too; Charlie Rose Show; The Human Experience; Face The Nation; Shattered Glory; Goodday; The Morning Show. **SELECTED PUBLICATIONS** Auth, Private Lives and Public Accounts; A Family Album; Busing; Children in Jail; Children's Secrets; Hidden Survivors; The Voices of School; Time's Children; Like Fathers Like Sons; Barred From School; Perceiving Time; The Abandoners; The Present of things Future, coath; Getting Married, coauth; Black Children White Dreams; Black Testimony; et al. **CONTACT ADDRESS** School of Education, Boston Univ, 605 Commonwealth Ave, Boston, MA, 02215. **EMAIL** tcottle@bu.edu

COTTRELL, JACK WARREN
PERSONAL Born 04/30/1938, Scott County, KY, m, 1958, 3 children **DISCIPLINE** HISTORY OF DOCTRINE **EDUCATION** Cincinnati Bible Coll, AB, 59, ThB, 60; Univ Cincinnati, AB, Philos, 62; Westminster Theol Sem, MDiv, 65; Princeton Theol Sem, PhD, 71. **CAREER** Stud instr, Cincinnati Bible Coll, 59-62; PROF, THEOL, CINCINNATI BIBLE SEM, 67-. **MEMBERSHIPS** Evan Theol Sem **SELECTED PUBLICATIONS** Auth, Feminism and the Bible: An Introduction to Feminism for Christians, Coll Press, 92; auth, Gender Roles and the Bible: Creation, the Fall, and Redemption. A Critique of Feminist Biblical Interpretation, Coll Press, 94; Faith's Fundamentals: Seven Essentials of Christian Belief, Standard Publ, 95; TheCollege Press NIV Commentary: Romans, Volume 1, Coll Press, 96; auth, The College Press NIV Commentary: Romans, Volume 2, Coll Press, 98. **CONTACT ADDRESS** Jack Cottrell, 2700 Glenway Ave, Cincinnati, OH, 45204. **EMAIL** Jack.Cottrell@cincybible.edu

COUCH, LEON W., III
PERSONAL Born 09/01/1970, Gainesville, FL, s **DISCIPLINE** MUSIC THEORY & ORGAN **EDUCATION** Organ Performance, MM, 95; ABD DMA Organ, PhD Theory. **CAREER** Asst prof Music **HONORS AND AWARDS** Various. **MEMBERSHIPS** Soc Music Theory; Am Musicol Soc; Int Computer Music Asn; Am Guild Organists. **RESEARCH** Performance & Theory; Pedagogy. **CONTACT ADDRESS** Luther Col, 612 1/2 Heivly St, Decorah, IA, 52101-1313. **EMAIL** couchlw@email.uc.edu

COUDERT, ALLISON P.
PERSONAL Born 12/02/1941, New York, NY, m, 2 children **DISCIPLINE** HISTORY **EDUCATION** Vassar Col, BA, 63; Univ London, Warbird Inst, PhD. **CAREER** Assoc prof, Ariz St Univ. **MEMBERSHIPS** AHA; AAR; AJS; Renaissance Soc of Am; Int Soc for Intellectual Hist; Authors Guild; PEN. **RESEARCH** The relation between religion and science in early modern history; women's hist. **SELECTED PUBLICATIONS** Auth, Alchemy: The Philosopher's Stone, Wildwood House, 80, Shambhala, 80; co-ed, The Politics of Gender in Early Modern Europe vol xii Sixteenth Century Essays & Studies, Sixteenth Century J Pubs, 89; co-ed, Playing With Gender: A Renaissance Pursuit, Univ Ill Press, 91; co-ed, transl, & intro, The Principles of the Most Ancient and Modern Philosophy, of Anne Conway's Principia Philosophiae Antiquissimae & Recentissimae, Amsterdam, 1690, Cambridge Texts in the History of Philosophy, Cambridge Univ Press, 96; auth, Leibniz and the Kabbalah, Kluwer Acad Pubs, 95; auth, The Impact of the Kabbalah in the Seventeenth Century: The Life and Thought of Francis Mercury van Helmont, E. J. Brill, 98; co-ed, Leibniz, Mysticism and Religion, Kluwer, 98. **CONTACT ADDRESS** Dept of Relig Studies, Arizona State Univ, Tempe, Tempe, AZ, 85287-3104. **EMAIL** allison.coudert@asu.edu

COUGHTRY, JAY
DISCIPLINE HISTORY **EDUCATION** Univ Wis Madison, PhD, 78. **CAREER** Assoc prof, Univ Nev Las Vegas. **RESEARCH** Colonial and early national US history; social history; Afro-American history. **SELECTED PUBLICATIONS** Auth, The Notorious Triangle: Rhode Island and the African Slave Trade, 1700-1807, 81. **CONTACT ADDRESS** History Dept, Univ Nev Las Vegas, 4505 Md Pky, Las Vegas, NV, 89154.

COULET DU GARD, RENE
PERSONAL Born 12/29/1919, Saint-Denis-du Sig, Algeria, m, 1940, 5 children **DISCIPLINE** ROMAN LANGUAGES **EDUCATION** Univ PA, MS, 63; Univ Besancon, PhD(lit), 66. **CAREER** Prin, Ecole d'Apprentissage, Morocco, 46-52; teacher, high sch, NY, 53-57 & Kimberton Sch, Pa, 57-62; teacher French, Ursinus Col, 62-63; asst prof French & Span, West Chester State Col, 63-66; from asst prof to assoc prof, 66-80, Prof French, Univ Del, 80-, Ed, Thursday Page, Maroc Press, Morocco, 47-52; foreign corresp, Echos Monde Roman Inedit, Morocco, 52-55. **HONORS AND AWARDS** Adventure Novel Prize, Soc Arts et Let Algeria, 52; Poetry Award, Acad Jeux Floraux Tunisia, 53; Chevalier, Soc Philanthropique at Culturelle France, 66, Commandeur, 68; Chevalier, Palmes Academiques, 67, Officier, 77; Medaille d'argent, Concours Lit: Acad Int Lutece, Paris, 73; Medaille d'OR Concours Litteraire, Acad Int Lutece, Paris, 74; Prix d'Hist Maritime, Soc Arts et Lettres Acad Bordeaux, France, 80; Prix de la Langue Francaise, Acad Francaise, 80. **MEMBERSHIPS** Am Asn Tchrs Fr; Soc des Gens Lett et auteurs France. **RESEARCH** Eighteenth and 19th century French lit; origin of French geog names in the US. **SELECTED PUBLICATIONS** Auth, L'Arithmosophie de Gerard de Nerval, Ed Deux Mondes, 72; Reine (novel), Ed La Revue Mod, Paris, 73; The Handbook of French Place Names in the USA, Ed Des Deux Mondes, 74 & 77; La France Contemporaine de 1900 a 1976, 76 & L-Oiseau de feu (poetry), 76, Slavuta, Can; Le fruit defendu (poetry), Ed Chantecler, France, 76; Pleure pas P'tit Bonhomme (novel), Ed Du Vent, France, 77; The Handbook of AmCounties, Parishes and Independent Cities, Ed Deux Mondes, 81; Dictionary of Spanish Place Names in the USA, 5v; auth, L'Epopee Algerienne, Ed des Deux Mondes, 97; auth, Eglantine, Ed des Deux Mondes; auth, Vie et Mort des Indiens d'Amerique du Nord, Ed France-Empire; auth, La Rage, Ed des Deux Mondes. **CONTACT ADDRESS** PO Box 251, Elkton, MD, 21921.

COULTER, HARRIS L.
PERSONAL Born 10/08/1932, Baltimore, MD, 4 children **DISCIPLINE** MEDICAL HISTORY **EDUCATION** Yale Univ, Columbia Univ, PhD, 69. **CAREER** Medical historian, lectr, and analyst of medical practice, 72-94. **HONORS AND AWARDS** Centenary Gold Medal, Academica Medico-Homeopatica de Barcelona; Hahnemann Prize, Belgian Fac of Homeopathy; honors at the 39th Congress of the Int Homeopathic Medical League. **MEMBERSHIPS** NIH Workshop on Alternative Medicine; Ad Hoc Advisory Panel of the Office of Alternative Medicine, 93. **SELECTED PUBLICATIONS** Auth, Divided Legacy Vol IV: Twentieth Century Medicine: The Bacteriological Era; The Controlled Clinical Trial: an Analysis; Vaccination, Social Violence, and Criminality; AIDS and Syphilis: the Hidden Link; Homeopathic Science and Modern Medicine; Divided Legacy Vol II: The Origins of Modern Western Medicine: J.B. Van Helmont to Claude Bernard; Divided Legacy Vol I: The Patterns Emerge: Hippocrates to Paracelus; Divided Legacy Vol III The Conflict Between Homeopathy and the American Medical Association and Homeopathic Influences in Nineteenth-Century Allopathic Therapeutics; Homeopathic Medicine; coauth, DPT: A Shot in the Dark. **CONTACT ADDRESS** 237 W 11th St, New York, NY, 10014.

COUNTRYMAN, EDWARD
DISCIPLINE AMERICAN HISTORY **EDUCATION** Manhattan, BA, 66: Cornell Univ, MA, 67, PhD, 71. **CAREER** Sr Lect, Warwick; PROF, AM HIST, S METH UNIV **MEMBERSHIPS** Am Antiquarian Soc **SELECTED PUBLICATIONS** Auth, A People in Revolution: The American Revolution and

Political Society in New York, 81; auth, The People's American Revolution, 84; auth, The American Revolution, 85; contribur, The British Film Institute Companion to the Western,88; coauth, vol 1, Who Built America, 89; auth, "The Uses of Capital in Revolutionary America: The Case of the New York Loyalist Merchants," Will & Mary Quar, 92; auth, "To Secure the Blessings of Liberty: Language, Capitalism and the Revolution," in Beyond the American Revolution, 93; auth, "Indians, the Colonial Order, and the Social Significance of the American Declaration," Will & Mary Quar, 96; America: A Cousin of Histories, 96; coauth, A New History of New York State, forthcoming. **CONTACT ADDRESS** Dept of Hist, S Methodist Univ, Dallas, TX, 75275-0176. **EMAIL** ecountry@mail.smu.edu

COUNTRYMAN, L. WM
PERSONAL Born 10/21/1941, Oklahoma City, OK **DISCIPLINE** CLASSICS, NEW TESTAMENT **EDUCATION** Univ of Chicago, BA, 62, MA, 74, PhD, 77; Grand Theol Sem, STB, 65 **CAREER** Lect, 74-76, Univ of Chicago; Asst Prof, 76-79, SW Mission St Univ; Asst Prof, 79-83 TX Christ Univ; Prof, 83-pres, Church Div Sch of the Pac **HONORS AND AWARDS** Phi Beta Kappa **MEMBERSHIPS** Soc of Bibl Lit; Assoc of Anglican Bibl Schols; Soc for Study of Christian Spirituality **RESEARCH** Spirituality; Sexual Orientation **SELECTED PUBLICATIONS** Auth, The Rich Christian in the Church of the Early Empire, Edwin Mellen Press, 80; Auth, The Mystical Way in the Fourth Gospel, Crossing Over into God, Fortress Press, 87; Living on the Border of the Holy: The Priesthood of Humanity and the Priesthoods of the Church, Morehouse Publ, 99; Forgiven and Forgiving, Morehouse Publ, 98 **CONTACT ADDRESS** Church Divinity Sch of the Pacific, 2451 Ridge, Berkeley, CA, 94709. **EMAIL** bcountryman@cdsp.edu

COURTEMANCHE, REGIS ARMAND
PERSONAL Born 05/05/1933, Scranton, PA, m, 1967, 7 children **DISCIPLINE** BRITISH & NAVAL HISTORY **EDUCATION** St John's Univ, BA, 59, MA, 62; London Sch Econ, PhD, 67. **CAREER** Instr hist, Delehanty High Sch, 61-64; assoc prof, 67-77, Prof Hist, CW Post Col, Long Island Univ, 77-, Mem bd, Educ Reviewer, Inc, 72. **RESEARCH** Nineteenth century Brit hist. **SELECTED PUBLICATIONS** Auth, The Royal Navy and the end of William Walker, Historian, 5/68; Home and history, Designer, 10/71; An American at the London School of Economics, Univ Bookman, summer 73; No Need of Glory, the British Navy in American Waters, 1860-64, Naval Inst, 77. **CONTACT ADDRESS** Dept of Hist, Long Island Univ, C.W. Post, 720 Northern Blvd, Greenvale, NY, 11548-1300.

COURTENAY, WILLIAM JAMES
PERSONAL Born 11/05/1935, Neenah, WI, m, 1967, 2 children **DISCIPLINE** MEDIEVAL HISTORY **EDUCATION** Vanderbilt Univ, AB, 57; Harvard Univ, STB, 60, PhD, 67. **CAREER** Instr hist, Stanford Univ, 65-66; from asst prof to assoc prof, 66-71, PROF HIST, UNIV WIS-MADISON, 71-, Nat Endowment for Humanities younger scholar award, 68-69; vis prof, Inst Res Humanities, Univ Wis, 72-73; Humboldt fel, Tubingen, Ger, 75-76 & 79-80; Guggenheim fel, 80. **MEMBERSHIPS** Fel Mediaeval Acad Am; Am Soc Church Hist; Int Soc Study Mediaeval Philos. **RESEARCH** Intellectual history of the high and late Middle Ages. **SELECTED PUBLICATIONS** Auth, Scholastic Humanism and the Unification of Europe, Vol-I--Foundations, Cath Hist Rev, Vol 0083, 97; Teaching and Learning Latin in 13th-Century England, Vol 1, Texts, Vol 2, Glosses, Vol 3, Indexes, Amer Hist Rev, Vol 0098, 93; Between Pope and King--The Rise of National Monarchies, the Papacy, and the Shaping of Public-Opinion in Late-Medieval France--The Parisian Letters-Of-Adhesion of 1303, Speculum-Jour Medieval Stud, Vol 0071, 96; Klenkok,Johannes--A Friars Life C.1310-1374, Speculum-Jour Medieval Stud, Vol 0070, 95; Universities in the Middle-Ages, Speculum-Jour Medieval Stud, Vol 0070, 95; Northern English Books, Owners, and Makers in the Late-Middle-Ages, Amer Hist Rev, Vol 0102, 97; The Rationale I-IV of Durandus,William--Latin, English, Jour Ecclesiastical Hist, Vol 0048, 97; Intellectuals in the Middle-Ages, Jour Interdisciplinary Hist, Vol 0026, 96; Megenberg 2nd-Hand--Studies on Redaction-B of the Buch-Von-Den-Naturlichen-Dingen-German, Isis, Vol 0086, 95. **CONTACT ADDRESS** Dept of Hist, Univ of Wis, Madison, WI, 53706.

COURTNEY, EDWARD
PERSONAL Born 03/22/1932, Belfast, Ireland, m, 1962, 2 children **DISCIPLINE** CLASSICS **EDUCATION** Trinity College Dublin, BA, 54; Christ Church Oxford, MA, 57. **CAREER** Lectr, reader, 55-77, Christ Church Oxford; Prof 77-82, Univ London King's College; Prof, 82-93, Stanford Univ; Gildersleeve Prof, classics, 93-, Univ Virginia. **MEMBERSHIPS** APA; CAMW&S; CAV. **RESEARCH** Latin language and literature; Textual criticism and transmission of texts. **SELECTED PUBLICATIONS** Auth, Commentary on the Satires of Juvenal, 80; The Poems of Petronius, 91; The Fragmentary Latin Poets, 93; Musa Lapidaria, 95, texts edited; Valerius Flaccus, Argonantica, 70; coauth, Ovid, Fasti, 78, 4th edition, 97; auth, Juvenal, Satires, 84; Statins, Silvae, 90. **CONTACT ADDRESS** 1500 West Pines Dr, Charlottesville, VA, 22901. **EMAIL** EC4S@virginia..edu

COUTENAY, LYNN
PERSONAL Born 07/08/1943, Nashville, TN, d, 2 children **DISCIPLINE** ENGLISH; HISTORY; ART HISTORY **EDUCATION** Vassar Coll, BA, 65; MA, PhD, 79, Univ of WI-Madison. **CAREER** Visiting lectr, University of WI-Madison; lectr, sr lectr, 84-96, asst prof, 96-, University of WI-Whitewata. **HONORS AND AWARDS** Fel in humanities, Newberry Library, 90-91; NEH Cooperative Project Grant, 91; Honorary Fel in Art hist, 94-97; elected Fel of the Soc of Antiquaries (members by invitation only), 95; Who's Who Among America's Teachers, Natl Honor Students' nomination, 96; University of WI System Fel: Inst for research in the humanities, 98-99 **MEMBERSHIPS** Soc of Antiquairies; ICMA; AVISTA; CAA; Vernacular Architecture Group; RAI; AIA (USA). **RESEARCH** Medieval Architecture; historic carpentry; Roman architecture; late medieval social and cultural hist; hist of technology. **SELECTED PUBLICATIONS** Auth, The Westminster Hall Roof: A New Archaeological Source, British Archaeological Association Journal, 90; Architectural Technology up to the Scientific Revolution: The Art and Structure of Large-scale Buildings, 93; Scale and Scantling: Technological Issues in large-scale Timberwork of the High Middle Ages, in Technology and Resource Use in Medieval Europe, Cathedrals, the Mills, and Mines, Dec 97; The Engineering of Gothic Cathedrals, Studies in the History of Civil Engineering, Dec 11, 1997. **CONTACT ADDRESS** 3100 Lake Mendota Dr., #504, Madison, WI, 53705. **EMAIL** hcourte@facstoff.wise.edu

COUTTS, BRIAN E.
DISCIPLINE HISTORY, LIBRARY AND INFORMATION SCIENCE **EDUCATION** La State Univ, MLS, 83, Phd, 81. **CAREER** Hist bibliog, Fondren Libr, Rice Univ, 84-86; Coord, Collection Dev. Western Ky Univ, 87-90; PROF, HEAD, DEPT LIBRARY PUB SVCS, WESTERN KY UNIV, 91-. **HONORS AND AWARDS** Western Ky Univ, Distinguished Research, 91, 94. **MEMBERSHIPS** ALA, ACRL, La Hist. **RESEARCH** Colonial La hist, reference books publishing, hsitory of Belize. **SELECTED PUBLICATIONS** Auth, Belize, Clio Press, 93; auth, Reference Sources in History, 90; auth, Best Reference Sources of 1998, Libr J, Apr 15, 99; auth, Best Reference Websites of 1998, Libr J, apr 15, 99; auth, The Reference Revolution:Wired for the 90s, Libr J, Nov 15, 97; auth, Central America: From Civil Wards to Tourist Mecca, Libr J, Mar 1, 97. **CONTACT ADDRESS** Dept Libr Pub Svcs, Western Kentucky Univ, 1 Big Beaver Red Way, Bowling Green, KY, 42101-3576. **EMAIL** brian.coutts@wku

COUVARES, F.G.
PERSONAL Born 03/26/1948, Brooklyn, NY, m, 1969, 1 child **DISCIPLINE** HISTORY **EDUCATION** Univ Pittsburg, BA, 69; Univ of Michigan, MA, 74, PhD, 80 **CAREER** Asst prof, 80-83, Clark Univ; dean of new students, 96-present, Amherst Coll, prof of hist and Amer studies, 83-present. **HONORS AND AWARDS** Amherst coll Lazerowitz lect grants: NEH, Getty, Amherst coll **MEMBERSHIPS** Amer hist assoc; org of Amer historians; Amer studies assoc **RESEARCH** US social and cultural hist; hist of popular culture; hist of censorship and civil liberties **SELECTED PUBLICATIONS** Guest editor and contributor, Hollywood, censorship, and American Culture, special issue of American Quarterly, Hollywood, Main Stree, and the Church: Trying to Censor the Movie befor the Production Code, 92; auth, The Good Censor: Race, Sex, and Censorship in the Early Cinema, Yale Journal of Criticism, 94; ed and contributor, Movie Censorship and American Culture, Smithsonian, 96; Hollywood and the Politcs of Culture, review essay, American Quarterly, 98. **CONTACT ADDRESS** History Dept., Amherst Col, Amherst, MA, 01002. **EMAIL** fgcouvares@amherst.edu

COVERT, JAMES THAYNE
PERSONAL Born 04/20/1932, Cimarron, KS, m, 1952, 6 children **DISCIPLINE** ENGLISH AND MODERN EUROPEAN HISTORY **EDUCATION** Univ Portland, BA, 59; Univ Ore, MA, 61, PhD(hist), 67. **CAREER** From instr to assoc prof hist, 61-71, chmn dept, 67-72, PROF HIST, UNIV PORTLAND, 71-, Danforth assoc, 70- **HONORS AND AWARDS** Standard Oil Calif Leadership Award, 57; Nat Asn Manufacturers' Presidential Award, 58; Am Red Cross Recognition Award for Vol Serv, 64; Culligan Fac Award, 68 & Distinguished Prof Award, 77, Univ Portland. **MEMBERSHIPS** AHA; Am Cath Hist Asn; Conf Brit Studies. **RESEARCH** Victorian and Edwardian England and England in the twentieth century; social, intellectual, political and especially, education history; history of the University of Portland. **SELECTED PUBLICATIONS** Auth, Victorian Feminists, Historian, Vol 0056, 94. **CONTACT ADDRESS** Dept of Hist, Univ of Portland, Portland, OR, 97203.

COVIN, DAVID LEROY
PERSONAL Born 10/03/1940, Chicago, IL, m, 1965, 2 children **DISCIPLINE** POLITICAL SCIENCE **EDUCATION** Univ Illinois, Urbana-Champaign, 62; Colorado Univ, MA, 66; Washington State Univ, PhD, 70. **CAREER** Asst prof, 70-75, assoc dean, general studies, 72-74, assoc prof, 75-79, prof govt and Pan African Studies, 79-, acting dir, 79-81, dir, 86-, Pan African Studies, prof govt and ethnic studies, Calif State Univ-Sacramento, 86-. **HONORS AND AWARDS** Cooper-Woodson Coll Medal of Freedom, 98; John C. Livingston Annual Distinguished Faculty Lecturer, 92; Meritorious Performance Award, CSU Sacramento, 88. **MEMBERSHIPS** Natl Conf Black Polit Sci; Natl Coun Black Studies; Western Polit Sci Assn. **RESEARCH** Black politics in U.S.; social movements; Afro-Brazilian politics. **SELECTED PUBLICATIONS** Auth, "Henry Dumas: The Writer as Teacher," special summer ed, Black Literature Forum, 88; auth, "Pan Africanism in the Caribbean," Journal of Pan African Studies, vol 1, 88; auth, "The Walk," in The Griot, 88; auth, "On Resituating Identities, the Politics of Race, Ethnicity, and Culture," in Ethnic Studies Review, vol 19, 98; auth, "Wither Goeth Black Nationalism: The Case of the MNU in Bahia," National Political Science Review, spring 98. **CONTACT ADDRESS** Pan African Studies, California State Univ, Sacramento, 6000 J St, Sacramento, CA, 95819-6013. **EMAIL** covindl@csus.edu

COWAN, RICHARD O.
PERSONAL Born 01/24/1934, Los Angeles, CA, m, 1958, 6 children **DISCIPLINE** CHURCH HISTORY **EDUCATION** Occidental Col, BA, 58; Stanford Univ, MA, 59, PhD, 61. **CAREER** Asst prof religious instr, 61-65, assoc prof history religion, 65-71, prof history religion, Brigham Young Univ, 71-; Danforth Fel, 58. **HONORS AND AWARDS** Phi Beta Kappa, 57. **MEMBERSHIPS** Mormom Hist Asn. **RESEARCH** Latter-day Saint history and theology. **SELECTED PUBLICATIONS** Coauth, Mormonism in the Twentieth Century 64, auth, The Doctrine and Covenants: Our Modern Scripture, 67, Temple Building Ancient and Modern, 71 & coauth, The Living Church, 74, Brigham Young Univ; Church in the Twentieth Century, 85; Doctrine and Covenants: Our Modern Scripture, 84; Temples to Dot the Earth, 89; Joseph Smith and the Doctrine and Covenants, 92; California Saints, 96; LDS Church History Encyclopedia, (pending). **CONTACT ADDRESS** Brigham Young Univ, 270L Joseph Smith Bldg, Provo, UT, 84602. **EMAIL** richard_cowan@byu.edu

COWAN, RUTH SCHWARTZ
PERSONAL Born 04/09/1941, Brooklyn, NY, m, 1968, 3 children **DISCIPLINE** HISTORY OF SCIENCE AND TECHNOLOGY **EDUCATION** Barnard Col, AB, 61; Univ Calif, Berkeley, MA, 64; Johns Hopkins Univ, PhD(hist sci), 69. **CAREER** From instr to asst prof, 67-74, ASSOC PROF HIST, STATE UNIV NY STONY BROOK, 74-, NIH grad res asst, Johns Hopkins Univ, 65-66; vis asst prof hist, Princeton Univ, 72-73; NSF res grant, 75-77 & 79-80. **MEMBERSHIPS** Hist Sci Soc; Soc Hist Technol; AAAS. **RESEARCH** History of biology; history of technology; women's history. **SELECTED PUBLICATIONS** Auth, Whose Science-Whose Knowledge--Thinking from Womens Lives, Soc Stud Sci, Vol 0025, 95; Descartes Legacy--A Theme Issue on Biomedical and Behavioral Technology, Tech and Cult, Vol 0034, 93; Lifting the Veil--The Feminine Face of Science, Soc Stud Sci, Vol 0025, 95; Daughters of the Shtetl--Life and Labor in the Immigrant Generation, Jour Amer Ethnic Hist, Vol 0012, 93; Technology Is to Science as Female as to Male--Musings on the History and Character of Our Discipline, Tech and Cult, Vol 0037, 96; Mothers and Daughters of Invention--Notes for a Revised History of Technology, Isis, Vol 0087, 96. **CONTACT ADDRESS** Dept of Hist, State Univ of NY, 100 Nicolls Rd, Stony Brook, NY, 11794-0002.

COWARD, HAROLD G.
PERSONAL Born 12/13/1936, Calgary, AB, Canada **DISCIPLINE** RELIGION/HISTORY **EDUCATION** Univ Alta, BA, 58, BD, 67, MA, 69; McMaster Univ, PhD, 73. **CAREER** Prof, Univ Calgary, 73-92, head relig stud, 76, 79-83, assoc dean hum, 77, dir, univ press, 81-83; dir, Calgary Inst Hum, 80-92; DIR, CENTRE FOR STUDIES IN RELIGION AND SOCIETY & PROF HISTORY, UNIV VICTORIA, 92-. **HONORS AND AWARDS** Fel, Royal Soc Can **MEMBERSHIPS** Pres, Can Soc Stud Relig, 84-86; pres, Shastri Indo-Can Inst, 86-88; pres, Can Corp Stud Relig, 87-90; pres, Can Fedn Hum, 90-91. **RESEARCH** Eastern religions; Hindu thought & religion; religious pluralism. **SELECTED PUBLICATIONS** Auth, Bhartrhari, 76; auth, Sphota Theory of Language, 80; auth, Jung and Eastern Thought, 85; auth, Pluralism: Challenge to World Religions; auth, Sacred Word and Sacred Text: Scripture in the World Religions, 88; auth, Hindu Ethics: Purity, Euthanasia and Abortion, 88; Derrida and Indian Philosophy, 90; coauth, Psychological Epistemology, 78; coauth, Humanities in Alberta, 84; coauth, Philosophy of the Grammarians, 90; coauth, Mantra: Hearing the Divine in India, 91; ed, Mystics and Scholars, 77; ed, Revelation in Indian Thought, 77; ed, Religion and Ethnicity, 78; ed, Humanities in the Present Day, 79; ed, Scholarly Communication, 80; ed, Calgary's Growth: Bane or Boon? 81; ed, Ethical Issues in the Allocation of Health Care Resources, 82; ed, Studies in Indian Thought, 82; ed, Religions in Contact and Change, 83; ed, The Role of the Modern Union, 85; ed, Modern Indian Responses to Religious Pluralism, 87; ed, Silence, Sacred and the Word, 88; ed, Readings in Eastern Religions, 88; ed, Hindu-Christian Dialogue, 89; ed, Privacy, 89; ed, The Future of Fossil Fuels, 91; ed, Derrida and Negative Theology, 92; ed, Reflections on Cultural Policy, 93; ed, Aging and Dying: Legal, Scientific and Religious Challenges, 93; ed, Anger in Our City: Youth Seeking Meaning, 94; ed, Population, Consumption and the Environment, 95; ed, Life After Death in World Religions, 97. **CONTACT ADDRESS** Ctr for Stud in Relig & Society, Univ of Victoria, Victoria, BC, V8W 3P4. **EMAIL** csrs@uvic.ca

COWDEN, JOANNA DUNLAP
PERSONAL Born 02/09/1933, Woburn, MA, d, 4 children **DISCIPLINE** NINETEENTH CENTURY AMERICAN HISTORY **EDUCATION** Radcliffe Col, AB, 55; Trinity Col, Conn, MA, 65; Univ Conn, PhD(hist), 75. **CAREER** Prof 19th Century Am Hist, Calif State Univ, Chico, 76-. **MEMBERSHIPS** Orgn Am Historians; AHA; Western Assn of Women Historians. **RESEARCH** Study of Civil War and Reconstruction politics. **SELECTED PUBLICATIONS** Co-ed, Slavery in America: Theodore Weld's American Slavery as It Is, F E Peacock, 72. **CONTACT ADDRESS** Dept of History, California State Univ, Chico, 101 Orange St, Chico, CA, 95929-0001. **EMAIL** jcowden@oavax.csuchico.edu

COWING, CEDRIC BRESLYN
PERSONAL Born 07/29/1926, Pasadena, CA, m, 1963, 1 child **DISCIPLINE** AMERICAN HISTORY **EDUCATION** Stanford Univ, AB, 48, AM, 51; Univ Wis, PhD(hist), 55. **CAREER** Actg instr hist, Univ Calif, Santa Barbara, 55-57; from asst prof to assoc prof, 57-68, PROF HIST, UNIV HAWAII, MANOA, 68-. **HONORS AND AWARDS** Annual Award, Am Studies Asn, 68. **MEMBERSHIPS** Orgn Am Historians; Am Studies Asn; Am Soc Church Hist. **RESEARCH** Social and religious history. **SELECTED PUBLICATIONS** Auth, Keepers of the Covenant--Frontier Missions and the Decline of Congregationalism, 1774-1818, Amer Hist Rev, Vol 0102, 97. **CONTACT ADDRESS** Dept of Hist, Univ of Hawaii at Manoa, Honolulu, HI, 96822.

COX, CAROLINE
PERSONAL Born 11/23/1954, Scotland, m **DISCIPLINE** HISTORY **EDUCATION** Univ Calif, Berkeley, AB, 90, MA, 93, PhD, 97. **CAREER** Asst prof, 98-, Univ Pacific. **RESEARCH** Early Amer, Native Amer, Africa Amer. **CONTACT ADDRESS** Dept of History, Univ of the Pacific, Stockton, CA, 95211. **EMAIL** ccox@uop.edu

COX, HAROLD E.
PERSONAL Born 06/27/1931, Lynchburg, VA, m, 1956 **DISCIPLINE** HISTORY **EDUCATION** Wm & Mary Col, AB, 51; Univ Va, MA, 54, PhD, 58. **CAREER** Asst prof, Temple Univ, 56-63; assoc, 63-69, PROF HIST, 69-, WILKES UNIV. **RESEARCH** Hist tech, industrial revolution in U.S. **SELECTED PUBLICATIONS** Co-auth, A Concise Historical Atlas of Eastern Europe, St Martin's Press, 96. **CONTACT ADDRESS** Wilkes Univ, Box 11, Wilkes Barre, PA, 18766.

COX, JOSEPH W.
PERSONAL Born 05/26/1937, Hagerstown, MD, m, 1963, 3 children **DISCIPLINE** EARLY AMERICAN HISTORY, HIGHER EDUCATION **EDUCATION** Univ Md, BA, 59, PhD(hist), 67. **CAREER** Asst hist, Univ Md, 60-64; assoc dean English, hist & soc sci, Towson State Univ, 69-72, dean eve col & summer session, 72-75, dir fac develop, 75-77, prof hist, 64-81, vpres acad affairs & dean univ, 77-81; VPRES ACAD AFFAIRS, NORTHERN ARIZ UNIV, 81-, Consult on col governance, Bd Trustees, Md State Cols, 68; consult on fac teaching awards, Pa State Dept Educ, 76-78. **MEMBERSHIPS** Am Asn Higher Educ; AAUP. **RESEARCH** Early American history; Maryland history; history of higher education; cultural philanthropy in 19th century America; the Historical Society movement. **SELECTED PUBLICATIONS** Auth, The Great Road--The Building of the Baltimore and Ohio, The Nations 1st Railroad, 1828-1853, Jour So Hist, Vol 0061, 95. **CONTACT ADDRESS** Dept of History, No Arizona Univ, Flagstaff, AZ, 86001.

COX, KEVIN R.
PERSONAL Born 03/22/1939, Warwick, England, m, 1965, 2 children **DISCIPLINE** GEOGRAPHY **EDUCATION** Cambridge Univ, BA, 61; Univ of Ill, MA, 63, PhD, 67. **CAREER** Asst prof, Ohio State Univ, 65-68; assoc prof, Ohio State Univ, 68-71; PROF, OHIO STATE UNIV, 71-; distinguished vis prof, Reading Univ, 95-. **HONORS AND AWARDS** Asn of Am Geog Honors Award, 85; Distinguished Res Sch Award, Ohio State Univ, 97. **MEMBERSHIPS** Asn of Am Geog **RESEARCH** Politics of local economic development; Geographic thought; South Africa. **SELECTED PUBLICATIONS** auth, "The Local and the Global in the New Urban Politics: A Critical Reconstruction Society and Space," 93; auth, "Concepts of Space, Understanding in Human Geography, and Spatial Analysis," Urban Geog, 95; auth, "Globablization, Competition, and the Politics of Local Economic Development," Urban Studies, 95; auth, "Period and Place, Capitalist Development, and the Flexible Specialization Debate," Kluwer Press, 96; auth, "Governance, Urban Regime Analysis and the Politics of Local Economic Development," Sage Prod, 97; auth, "Globalization and Workers'Struggles in the Late Twentieth Century," Geographies of Economies, 97; auth, "Spaces of Dependence, Spaces of Engagement and the Politics of Scale, or: Looking for Local Politics, Polit Geog, 98; ed, Spaces of Globalization: Reasserting the Power of the Local, Guilford Press, 97. **CONTACT ADDRESS** Dept of Geog, Ohio State Univ, 7179 Lorine Ct, Columbus, OH, 43235. **EMAIL** kcox@geography.ohio-state.edu

COX, SHARON G.
PERSONAL 3 children **DISCIPLINE** ART **EDUCATION** Mercer Univ, BA, 82; Univ Georgia, MFA, 83. **CAREER** Lectr, art, Mercer Univ, 83-85; asst prof, journalism, Jackson State Univ, 87-89; asst prof journalism, Lynchburg Col, 89-91; head, Art Dept, Jamestown Col, 92- . **HONORS AND AWARDS** Outstanding Citizen, Warner Robins, GA, 69; Outstanding Student, hum div, Macon Jr Col, 80; press awards for newspaper work. **MEMBERSHIPS** CAA; AAUW; SPJ; Ga Press Assoc; Asia Soc. **RESEARCH** Native American pigment sites in the Dakotas. **CONTACT ADDRESS** Jamestown Col, 6003 College Ln, Box 1559, Jamestown, ND, 58402. **EMAIL** cox@jc.edu

COX, THOMAS C.
DISCIPLINE HISTORY **EDUCATION** Princeton Univ, PhD, 80. **CAREER** Assoc prof, Univ Southern Calif. **RESEARCH** Grasshopper Plague in the Trans-Mississippi West, 1874-1878. **SELECTED PUBLICATIONS** Auth, Blacks in Topeka, Kansas, 1865-1915: A Social History, La State, 82. **CONTACT ADDRESS** Dept of History, Univ Southern Calif, University Park Campus, Los Angeles, CA, 90089. **EMAIL** tcox@bcf.usc.edu

COX, THOMAS RICHARD
PERSONAL Born 01/16/1933, Portland, OR, m, 1954, 4 children **DISCIPLINE** AMERICAN HISTORY **EDUCATION** Ore State Univ, BS, 55; Univ Ore, MS, 59, PhD(hist), 69. **CAREER** Teacher, Pub High Schs, 56-63; from asst prof to assoc prof hist, 67-74, PROF US HIST, SAN DIEGO STATE UNIV, 74-, Fulbright prof, Kyushu Univ & Seinan Gakuin Univ, Japan, 75-76; Forest Hist Soc vis fel, Univ Calif, Santa Cruz, 79-80. **HONORS AND AWARDS** Max Savelle Prize, 65; Emil & Kathleen Sick Lect-Bk Award, 74; Theodore Blegen Award, Forest Hist Soc, 74. **MEMBERSHIPS** Orgn Am Historians; Agr Hist Soc (pres, 78-80); Forest Hist Soc; Western Hist Asn; Asn Asian Studies. **RESEARCH** Forest and conservation history; late 19th and early 20th century United States history; Asian-American relations. **SELECTED PUBLICATIONS** Auth, Environment and Experience--Settlement Culture in 19th-Century Oregon, Pacific Hist Rev, Vol 0063, 94; Who Controls Public Lands--Mining, Forestry, and Grazing Policies, 1870-1990, Jour Amer Hist, Vol 0083, 97; Closing the Lumbermans Frontier-Oregon-The Far Western Pine Country, Jour W, Vol 0033, 94; Ruetten, Richard,T, Montana, Mag W Hist, Vol 0046, 96; Fashioning Australia Forests, Environ Hist, Vol 0002, 97; Before the Casino, Scrugham, James,G., State-Parks, and Nevadas Quest for Tourism, West Hist Quart, Vol 0024, 93; Frontier Enterprise Versus the Modern-Age--Herrick,Fred and the Closing of the Lumbermans Frontier, Pacific Northwest Quart, Vol 0084, 93; Origins of the National Forests--A Centennial Symposium, West Hist Quart, Vol 0025, 94. **CONTACT ADDRESS** Dept of Hist, San Diego State Univ, 5500 Campanile Dr, San Diego, CA, 92182-0002.

COYLE, J. KEVIN
PERSONAL Born 04/25/1943, Iroquois Falls, ON, Canada, s **DISCIPLINE** EARLY CHRISTIAN HISTORY **EDUCATION** Univ of Ottawa, BA, BPh, 63; Catholic Univ of Amer, BTh, LTh, 65 and 67; Univ de Fribourg en Suisse, DTh, 79. **CAREER** Lectr, 76-79, Asst Prof, 79-84, Assoc Prof, 84-87, Full Prof, 87-, Universite Saint-Paul, Ottawa. **MEMBERSHIPS** Canadian Soc of Patristic Studies; North Amer Patristic Soc; Intl Assoc for Patristic Studies; Intl Assoc of Manichaean Studies; Societe quebecoise pour l etude de las religion; Soc of Biblical Lit. **RESEARCH** History of early Christianity; Latin Palaeography; Development of Christian Thought; Manichaeism **SELECTED PUBLICATIONS** Auth, De moribus ecclesiae catholicae: Augustin chretien a Rome, De moribus ecclesiae catholicae et de moribus Manichaeorum: De quantitate animae, 91; Mary Magdalene in Manichaeism, Le Museon, 91; Augustine's Millenialism Reconsidered, Charisteria Augustiniana Iosepho Oroz Reta dicata, 93; Recent Reviews on the Origins of Clerical Celibacy, Logos, 93; Hands and the Impositions of Hands in Manichaesim, Pegrina Curiositas: Eine Reise durch den orbis antiquus. Zu Ehren von Dirk van Damme, 94; Early Monks, Prayer and the Devil, Prayer and Spirituality in the Early Church, 98. **CONTACT ADDRESS** St. Paul Univ, 223 Main St., Ottawa, ON, K1S 1C4. **EMAIL** JKCOYLE@AIX1.UOTTAWA.CA

CRABTREE, LOREN WILLIAM
PERSONAL Born 09/02/1940, Aberdeen, SD, m, 1961, 3 children **DISCIPLINE** HISTORY; ASIAN STUDIES **EDUCATION** Univ Minn, BA, 61, MA, 65, PhD(hist), 69. **CAREER** Instr hist, Bethel Col, St Paul, Minn, 65-67; from instr to assoc prof, 67-85, PROF HIST, COLO STATE UNIV, 85-, Dean, Col Liberal Arts, 91-97, Provost, 97-. **HONORS AND AWARDS** Nat Endowment for Humanities Younger Humanist fel, 73-74. **MEMBERSHIPS** Asn Asian Studies; AHA; Asia Soc; Conf Faith & Hist; Western Soc Sci Asn. **RESEARCH** Chinese history, 1900-1937; rural development in Asia; Christian missions in China and India. **SELECTED PUBLICATIONS** Auth, The papers of the National Federation of Settlements, Soc Serv Rev, 66; Communism and the Chinese cultural tradition, Int Quart, 68; coauth, Descriptive Inventories of Collections in the Social Welfare Archives Center, Greenwood, 70; From Mohensodaro to Mao: Perspectives on reaching Asian civilization, Hist Teacher, 73; auth, New perspectives on Sino-American relations, 73 & coauth, Interpreting Asia to Americans, 74, Rocky Mountain Soc Sci J; auth, Seeing red in China: Missouri Synod missionaries and the Chinese Revolution, 1913-30, Selected Papers on Asia, 76; coauth, The Lion and the Dragon: An Introduction to the Civilizations of India and China, J Weston Walch, 79. **CONTACT ADDRESS** Off of the Provost, Colorado State Univ, Fort Collins, CO, 80523-0001. **EMAIL** 1crabtree@vines.colostate.edu

CRAFT, JR., GEORGE S.
PERSONAL Born 12/13/1942, Atlanta, GA, w, 5 children **DISCIPLINE** HISTORY **EDUCATION** Univ Notre Dame, AB, 64; Oxford Univ, BA, 66; Stanford Univ, PhD, 71. **CAREER** PROF, CA STATE UNIV, SACRAMENTO, 1970-. **RESEARCH** Modern France, culture, history, and film. **SELECTED PUBLICATIONS** Auth, The Emergence of National Sentiment in French Lorraine, 1871-1889, Third Republic/ Troisieme republique, no 2, 76; California State University, Sacramento: The First Forty Years, 1947-1987, 87. **CONTACT ADDRESS** Dept of Hist, California State Univ, Sacramento, Sacramento, CA, 95819. **EMAIL** gcraft@csus.edu

CRAIG, ALBERT MORTON
PERSONAL Born 12/09/1927, Chicago, IL, m, 1953, 3 children **DISCIPLINE** JAPANESE HISTORY **EDUCATION** Northwestern Univ, BS, 49; Harvard Univ, PhD, 59. **CAREER** Instr hist, Univ MA, 57-59; from instr to asst prof Japanese hist, 59-63, assoc prof hist, 63-67, assoc dir, E Asian Res Ctr, 70-76, prof Hist, Harvard Univ, 67-, dir, Yenching Inst, 76-87, HARVARD-YENCHING PROF HIST, 89-99; Fulbright res prof & Am Coun Learned Soc grant, Kyoto Univ, 62-63; Guggenheim fel, 67-68; fellow, Pembroke Col, Oxford Univ, 95; vis prof, Inst of Social Science, Tokyo Univ, 96; Burns vis prof, Univ HI, 97. **MEMBERSHIPS** Asn Asian Studies; Hist Soc Japan. **RESEARCH** Modern Japanese thought; comparative studies of Asian development, society and religion, Meiji restoration. **SELECTED PUBLICATIONS** Auth, Choshu in the Meiji Restoration, Harvard Univ, 61; coauth, East Asia the Modern Transformation, Houghton, 65; co-ed, Personality in Japanese History, Univ CA, 70; coauth, East Asia: Tradition and Transformation, 73 & Japan: Tradition and Transformation, 78, Houghton; Japan, A Comparative View, Princeton Univ Press, 80; Heritage of World Civilization (with others), Prentice Hall, 86, 90, 94, 97. **CONTACT ADDRESS** Dept of Hist, Harvard Univ, Robinson Hall, Cambridge, MA, 02138-3800. **EMAIL** acraig@fas.harvard.edu

CRAIG, CHRISTOPHER P.
DISCIPLINE CLASSICAL STUDIES **EDUCATION** Oberlin Col, BA, 74; Univ NC, PhD, 79. **CAREER** Instr, Stockley Inst, 83-84; Tchg fel, Univ NC, 78-79; instr, Univ Ca, 79-80; asst prof, 80-86; assoc prof, 86-. **HONORS AND AWARDS** Dir, Vergilian Soc Am, 85-93. **MEMBERSHIPS** Am Philol Asn; Archaeol Inst Am; Class Asn Middle W and S; Am Class League; Vergilian Soc Am; Tennessee Lang Tchr Asn; Tennessee Class Asn; Int Soc Hist Rhet; Am Soc Hist Rhet; Speech Commun Asn. **RESEARCH** Classical rhetoric and oratory; Cicero. **SELECTED PUBLICATIONS** Auth, Cicero's Strategy of Embarrassment in the Speech for Plancius, Am Jour Philol, 90; Form as Argument in Cicero's Speeches, Scholars, 93; Three Simple Questions for Teaching Cicero's First Catilinarian Oration, Class Jour, 93; Teaching Cicero's Speech for Caelius: What Enquiring Minds Want to Know, Class Jour, 95. **CONTACT ADDRESS** Dept of Classics, Knoxville, TN, 37996. **EMAIL** ccraig@utk.edu

CRAIG, GORDON ALEXANDER
PERSONAL Born 11/26/1913, Glasgow, Scotland **DISCIPLINE** HISTORY **EDUCATION** Princeton Univ, AB, 36, AM, 39 PhD, 41. **CAREER** Instr hist, Yale Univ, 39-41; from instr to prof, Princeton Univ, 41-61; prof, 61-69, J E WALLACE STERLING PROF HUMANITIES, STANFORD UNIV, 69-, Vis prof, Columbia Univ, 47-48, 49-50; fel, Ctr Advan Study Behav Sci, 56-57; prof mod hist, Free Univ, Berlin, 62-; mem soc sci adv bd, US Arms Control & Disarmament Agency, 64-70; mem, US Air Force Acad Adv Coun, 68-71. **HONORS AND AWARDS** Historians Prize, City of M¤nster, Westphalia, 81., LittD, Princeton Univ, 70; Blitt, Oxford Univ, 38. **MEMBERSHIPS** AHA (pres, 82); AAAS; Am Philos Soc. **RESEARCH** German history; modern diplomacy; military history. **SELECTED PUBLICATIONS** Auth, Goebbels--Mastermind of the Third-Reich, NY Rev Bk(s), Vol 0043, 96; The Rape-of-Europa--The Fate of Europe Treasures in the Third-Reich and the Second-World-War, NY Rev Bk(s), Vol 0041, 94; German Unification in the European Context, NY Rev Bk(s), Vol 0041, 94; The Lost Museum--The Nazi Conspiracy to Steal the Worlds Greatest Works-Of-Art, NY Rev Bk(s), Vol 0044, 97; The 1st-World-War, a Complete History, NY Rev Bk(s), Vol 0042, 95; The Spoils of World-War-2--The American Militarys Role in the Stealing of Europe Treasures, NY Rev Bk(s), Vol 0041, 94; The Rush to German Unity, NY Rev Bk(s), Vol 0041, 94; Victory Must Be Ours--Germany in the Great-War, 1914-1918, NY Rev Bk(s), Vol 0042, 95; The Hitler of History, NY Rev Bk(s), Vol 0044, 97; Nazi Germany and the Jews, Vol 1, the Years of Persecution, 1933-1939, NY

Rev Bk(s), Vol 0044, 97; Confronting the Nazi Past--New Debates on Modern German History, NY Rev Bk(s), Vol 0044, 97; Goebbels and Der-Angriff, NY Rev Bk(s), Vol 0041, 94; Goebbels, NY Rev Bk(s), Vol 0041, 94; The Spoils of War--World-War-II and Its Aftermath--The Loss, Reappearance, and Recovery of Cultural Property, NY Rev Bk(s), Vol 0044, 97; The Wages of Guilt--Memories of War in Germany and Japan, NY Rev Bk(s), Vol 0041, 94; Semper, Gottfried--Architect of the 19th-Century, NY Rev Bk(s), Vol 0043, 96; Beyond the Wall--Germany Road to Unification, NY Rev Bk(s), Vol 0041, 94; Hitler 30 Days to Power--January 1933, NY Rev Bk(s), Vol 0044, 97; Goebbels, Joseph--A National-Socialist--German, NY Rev Bk(s), Vol 0041, 94; Journals 1954-1955--German, NY Rev Bk(s), Vol 0043, 96; Mann,Thomas--A Life, NY Rev Bk(s), Vol 0043, 96; Letters on Dark Times--The Correspondence of Arendt, Hannah and Jaspers,Karl, NY Rev Bk(s), Vol 0040, 93; Hitler Willing Executioners--Ordinary Germans and the Holocaust, NY Rev Bk(s), Vol 0043, 96; Mann,Thomas--Eros and Literature, NY Rev Bk(s), Vol 0043, 96; The Origins of Nazi Genocide--From Euthanasia to the Final-Solution, NY Rev Bk(s), Vol 0042, 95; Mann,Thomas--A Biography-German, NY Rev Bk(s), Vol 0043, 96; Founder--A Portrait of the First Rothschild and His Time, NY Rev Bk(s), Vol 0044, 97; Bound Upon a Wheel of Fire--Why So Many German Jews Made the Tragic Decision to Remain in Nazi Germany, NY Rev Bk(s), Vol 0043, 96; Speer,Albert--His Battle with Truth, NY Rev Bk(s), Vol 0042, 95; Wilhelm-II and the Germans--A Study in Leadership, Jour Interdisciplinary Hist, Vol 0024, 93; The Politics of Memory--Looking for Germany in the New Germany, NY Rev Bk(s), Vol 0043, 96; Nazi Germany--A New History, NY Rev Bk(s), Vol 0042, 95; From Court Jews to the Rothschilds--Art, Patronage, and Power, 1600-1800, NY Rev Bk(s), Vol 0044, 97; Gilbert,Felix, May 21, 1905, February 14, 1991--In-Memoriam, Proc Amer Philos Soc, Vol 0137, 93; On the Origins of War and the Preservation of Peace, NY Rev Bk(s), Vol 0042, 95. **CONTACT ADDRESS** Dept of Hist, Stanford Univ, Stanford, CA, 94305.

CRAIG, JOHN ELDON

PERSONAL Born 07/23/1941, Sherbrooke, PQ, Canada, m, 1975 **DISCIPLINE** MODERN EUROPEAN HISTORY/ COMPARATIVE EDUCATION **EDUCATION** Bowdoin Col, AB, 62; Stanford Univ, AM, 63, PhD, 73. **CAREER** Actg instr hist, Stanford Univ, 67; actg asst prof, Univ Va, 67-73; asst prof, 75-81, assoc prof, Educ, Univ Chicago, 81-. **MEMBERSHIPS** AHA; Conf Group Cent Europ Hist; Soc Fr Hist Studies; Soc Sci Hist Asn; Int Sociol Asn. **RESEARCH** Modern European social history; educational expansion in developed and developing countries. **SELECTED PUBLICATIONS** Auth, Maurice Halbwachs a Strasbourg, Rev Fr Sociol, Vol 20, 273-292; "On the Development of Educational Systems," American Journal of Education, 89; The Expansion of Education, Rev Res in Educ, 9: 151-213; Die Durkheim-Schule und die Annales, Gerschichte der Soziologie, Suhrkamp (4 vols), 3: 298-322; Higher Education and Social Mobility in Germany, 1850-1930, The Transformation of Higher Learning, 1850-1930, Klett-Cotta, 82; coauth (with N. Spear), Explaining Educational Expansion: An Agenda for Historical and Comparative Research, & Rational Actors, Group Processes, and the Development of Educational Systems, The Sociology of Educational Expansion, Sage, 82; auth, Scholarship and Nation Building: The Universities of Strasbourg and Alsatian Society, 1870-1939, Univ Chicago Press, 84. **CONTACT ADDRESS** Dept of Educ, Univ of Chicago, 5835 Kimbark Ave, Chicago, IL, 60637-1684. **EMAIL** j-craig@uchicago.edu

CRAIG, ROBERT M.

PERSONAL Born 05/29/1944, St. Louis, MO, m, 1975, 1 child **DISCIPLINE** ARCHITECTURURAL HISTORY **EDUCATION** Principia Col, BA, 66; Univ Ill, MA, 67; Cornell Univ, PhD (hist archit), 73. **CAREER** Instr, Meremac Jr Col, 67-68; instr, Principia Col, 72-73; asst prof, Ga Inst Tech, 73-78, assoc prof, 78-. **HONORS AND AWARDS** Donaghey Dist Lectr, 93; Who's Who in Sci and Engg. 92, 95; Who's Who in the World, 94; Men of Achievement, 93, 94; Who's Who in Am Educ, 90, 92. **MEMBERSHIPS** SAH; SESAH; SECAC; NCSA; SCA; SEASECS; PCAS/ACAS. **RESEARCH** Nineteenth and twentieth century American and English architecture; Bernard Maybeck; art deco; arts and crafts movement; garden history. **SELECTED PUBLICATIONS** Auth, Is Atlanta Losing Its Early Modern Heritage?, in Atlanta Hist, 95; auth, Atlanta Architecture:Art Deco to Modern Classic, Gretna, 95; auth, Functional Sculpture: The early work of Julian H. Harris, SECAC Rev, 96; auth, Atlanta's Moderne Diner Revival: History, Nostalgia, Youth and Car Culture, in On the Culture of the American South, Stud in Am/Popular Culture, 96; auth, Edwin Lutyens, Frank Lloyd Wright, Gustav Stickley, essays in Encyclopedia of Interior Design, 97; coauth, John Portman: An Island on an Island, L'Arca'Edizioni, 97. **CONTACT ADDRESS** College of Architecture, Georgia Inst of Tech, Atlanta, GA, 30332-0155. **EMAIL** rob.craig@arch.gatech.edu

CRAIS, CLIFTON C.

PERSONAL Born 04/04/1960 **DISCIPLINE** AFRICAN HISTORY **EDUCATION** Univ of Md, BA, 82; Johns Hopkins Univ, MA, 84; PhD, 88; Mellon Fac Sem on Post-Modernism, Kenyon Col, 88. **CAREER** Visiting Sch, Rhodes Univ, 85; visiting instr, Kenyon Col, 87-88; visiting asst professor, Univ of Cape Town, 88-89; res asst, Univ of Cape Town, 88-89; Post-Doc Res Fel, Univ of Cape Town, 88, 89; ch, African and African-Am Studies Comm, 90-91; ch, Kenyon Sem, 90-96; ch, African-Am Hist Search Comm, 90-91; visiting assoc, Univ of Cape Town, 89, 91; Univ res scholar, Rhodes Univ, 92; Univ res scholar, Rhodes Univ, 92; asst prof, 88-93; assoc prof, Kenyon Col, 93-; visiting assoc prof, Stanford Univ 95; ch, Fac Aff Comm, 96-97. **HONORS AND AWARDS** Full Tuition Scholar, Johns Hopkins Univ, 82-88; tchg fel, 83-84; grad fel, 85,Kenan spec tchg fel, 87; Fulbright full fel, 84-85; fac devel grants, Kenyon Col, 88, 91, 92; Univ Res Fel, Rhodes Univ, 92; ACLS Fel,-In-Aid, 93; fac devel grant, Stanford Univ, 94-5; fel, Stanford Hum Center, 95; fel, Stanford Univ, 94-95; Spring Quarter, 1995; panels ch, African Studies Assoc, 97; ch, Fac Aff Comm, Kenyon Col, 96-98; ch, Kenyon Col, 95-98. **MEMBERSHIPS** World Hist Assoc, 93-4; Inst of Histl Res, Univ of London, 85-86; Inst of Commonwealth Studies, Sch of Oriental and African Studies, 85-94; Ctr for African Studies, 84-95; Ctr for African Studies, 84-95; Am Hist Assoc, 88-. **RESEARCH** Pre-colonial, colonial and contemporary Africa, slavery and emancipation. **SELECTED PUBLICATIONS** Auth, White Supremacy and Black Resistance in Pre-Industrial South Africa: The Making of the Colonial Order in the Eastern Cape, 1770-1865, Cambridge Univ Press, 92, Witwatersrand Univ Press, 92; Breaking the Chains: Slavery and its Legacy in Nineteenth-Century South Africa, Witwatersrand Univ Press, 94; Representation and the Politics of Identity in South Africa: An Eastern Cape Example, Intl Jour of African Hist Studies, 92; Rev of Carolyn Hamilton, The Mfecane Aftermath, Intl Jour of African Hist Studies, 97; Rev of E. Eldredge and F. Morton, Slavery in South Africa: Captive Labor on the Dutch Frontier, Jour of Soc Hist, 97. **CONTACT ADDRESS** Dept of Hist, Kenyon Col, Gambier, OH, 43022. **EMAIL** Crais@kenyon.edu

CRAMER, OWEN CARVER

PERSONAL Born 12/01/1941, Tampa, FL, m, 1962, 4 children **DISCIPLINE** CLASSICS **EDUCATION** Oberlin Col, AB, 62; Univ Tex, Austin, PhD(Greek), 73. **CAREER** From instr to prof Classics, Colo Col, 65-, M C Gile Chair, 77-. **HONORS AND AWARDS** Phi Beta Kappa, Hon Woodrow Wilson Fel, 62. **MEMBERSHIPS** Am Philol Asn; Class Asn Mid W & S; Am Comparative Lit Asn; Mod Greek Studies Asn. **RESEARCH** Early Greek literature. **SELECTED PUBLICATIONS** Auth, Ulysses the Good?, TAPA, 74; Speech and Silence in the Iliad, Class J, 76. **CONTACT ADDRESS** Dept of Classics, Colorado Col, 14 E Cache La Poudre, Colorado Springs, CO, 80903-3294. **EMAIL** ocramer@ColoradoCollege.edu

CRAMER, RICHARD S.

PERSONAL Born 10/08/1928, Bandon, OR, m, 1950, 3 children **DISCIPLINE** UNITED STATES HISTORY **EDUCATION** Univ OR, BS, 50, MS, 52; Stanford Univ, PhD, 60. **CAREER** Instr western civilization, Stanford Univ, 60-61; from asst prof to assoc prof US hist, 61-70, prof hist, CA State Univ, San Jose, 70-96, Col Found res grant, 62. **MEMBERSHIPS** AHA; Orgn Am Historians; Pac Coast Br AHA; Southern Hist Asn; Soc for Historians for the Early Republic. **RESEARCH** The ante-bellum South; 19th century Am polit hist; 19th century, Anglo-Am soc and intellectual rel(s). **SELECTED PUBLICATIONS** Auth, British magazines and the Oregon question, Pac Hist Rev, 11/63; Ole P Balling: Painter of Civil War heroes, Am Scand Rev, summer 66; coauth, Portraits of Nobel Peace Prize Laureates, Abelard, 69 & American Humor and Humorists (2 vols), Spartan Bk Store, 70-71. **CONTACT ADDRESS** Dept of Hist, California State Univ, San Jose, 1 Washington Sq, San Jose, CA, 95192-0001.

CRANE, CONRAD C.

PERSONAL Born 01/22/1952, Wilkes-Barre, PA, m, 1979, 2 children **DISCIPLINE** AMERICAN HISTORY; MILITARY HISTORY **EDUCATION** U.S. Military Acad, BS, 74; Stanford Univ, MA, 83, PhD, 90. **CAREER** From asst prof to prof, U.S. Mil Acad, 83- ; also Army off, 74- . **HONORS AND AWARDS** John Alexander Hottell III Award for Mod Hist, U.S. Mil Acad, 74; West Point Chap Phi Kappa Phi Award for Schol, U.S. Mil Acad, 86; 3rd place, Douglas MacArthur Mil Leadership Writing Competition, U.S. Army Command and Gen Staff Col, 91; several Mil Awards. **MEMBERSHIPS** Hon Soc of Phi Kappa Phi; Air Defense Artillery Asn; Soc for Mil Hist; Hon Soc of Phi Alpha Theta; WWII Studies Asn; Hist Soc. **RESEARCH** Airpower; The World Wars; 20th century Mil Hist; Men in battle. **SELECTED PUBLICATIONS** Coauth, The Prudent Soldier, The Rash Old Fighter, and the Walking Whiskey Keg: The Battle of Valverde, New Mexico, 13-21 February 1862, 87; auth, Bombs, Cities, and Civilians: American Airpower Strategy in World War II, 93; Twilight of the Superfortresses: Strategic Airpower in the Korean War, 97; A Clarion of Thunderclaps and Hurricanes: The Search for Victory Through Airpower in Europe, World War II in Europe: The Final Year, ed Charles F. Brower, IV, 97; Eagle Over the Sun: The Air War Against Japan and the End of the War in the Pacific, World War II in Asia and the Pacifiic and the Post-War World, ed Loud Lee, 98; Raiding the Beggar's Pantry: The Search for Airpower Strategy in the Korean War, The Jour of Mil Hist, 99. **CONTACT ADDRESS** Dept of History, U.S. Military Academy, West Point, NY, 10996-1793. **EMAIL** kc5318@usma.edu

CRANE, CONRAD CHARLES

PERSONAL Born 01/22/1952, Wilkes-Barre, PA, m, 1979, 2 children **DISCIPLINE** MILITARY HISTORY **EDUCATION** U.S. Military Acad, BS, 74; Stanford Univ, MA, 83, PhD, 90. **CAREER** U.S. Army officer, 74- ; from asst prof to prof, hist, 83-99, U.S. Mil Acad. **HONORS AND AWARDS** John A. Hotell III Award for modern history, 74; Phi Kappa Phi Award for Scholarship, 86., Graduate of U.S. Army War Col & U.S. Army Command and General Staff Col. **MEMBERSHIPS** Soc for Mil Hist; Hist Soc; World War II Studies Asn; Phi Kappa Phi; Phi Alpha Theta. **RESEARCH** Airpower; Twentieth Century warfare and wars; experience of combat; American Civil War. **SELECTED PUBLICATIONS** Co-ed, rev WWI vol of The West Point Atlas of American Wars, Holt, 97; auth, Twilight of the Superfortresses: Strategic Airpower in the Korean War, Inst for Security Stud, 97; auth, A Clarion of Thunderclaps and Hurricanes; The Search for Victory Through Airpower in Europe, in Brower, ed, World War II in Europe: The Final Year, St Martin's, 98; auth, Eagle Over the Sun: The Air War Against Japan and the End of the War in the Pacific, in Lee, ed, World War II in Asia and the Pacific and the War's Aftermath, with General Themes: A Handbook of Literature and Research, Greenwood, 98; auth, Raiding the Beggar's Pantry: The Search for Airpower Strategy in the Korean War, J of Mil Hist, 99; auth, American Airpower Strategy in Korea, 1950-1953, Kansas, 99. **CONTACT ADDRESS** Dept of History, U.S. Military Academy, West Point, NY, 10996-1793. **EMAIL** kc5318@usma.edu

CRANE, DIANA

PERSONAL Born 04/05/1933, Toronto, ON, Canada, m, 1965, 1 child **DISCIPLINE** SOCIOLOGY **EDUCATION** Columbia Univ, PhD, 64. **CAREER** Asst prof sociology, Yale Univ, 64-68; Asst to assoc prof, Johns Hopkins Univ, 68-72; assoc to full prof sociology, Univ Penn, 73-. **HONORS AND AWARDS** Guggenheim fel, 74-75; Inst Adv Study, 76-77; Fulbright Res Award, 87-88. **MEMBERSHIPS** Am Sociol Asn **RESEARCH** Sociology of culture, art, media, and popular culture. **SELECTED PUBLICATIONS** Auth, Invisible Colleges: Diffusion of Knowledge in Scientific Communities, Univ Chicago Press, 72; The Sanctity of Social Life: Physicians Treatment of Critically Ill Patients, Russell Sage Found, 75; The Transformation of the Avant-Garde: The New York Art World, 1940-1985, Univ Chicago Press, 87; The Production of Culture: Media and Urban Arts, Sage, 92; ed, The Sociology of Culture: Emerging Theoretical Perspectives, Basil Blackwell, 94. **CONTACT ADDRESS** Dept of Sociology, Univ of Pennsylvania, 113 McNeil, Philadelphia, PA, 19104-6299. **EMAIL** craneher@sas.upenn.edu

CRANE, ELAINE F.

PERSONAL Born 07/23/1939, New York, NY, m, 1960, 2 children **DISCIPLINE** AMERICAN HISTORY **EDUCATION** Cornell Univ, BA, 61; NY Univ, MA, 73, PhD(Am hist), 77. **CAREER** Asst ed, Papers Robert Morris, 76-77, Papers William Livingston, 77-78; asst prof Hist, 78-83, assoc prof, 84-91, PROF HIST, FORDHAM UNIV, 91-. **HONORS AND AWARDS** Soc of Am Archivists, 92. **MEMBERSHIPS** Orgn Am Historians. **RESEARCH** Colonial and revolutionary history; women's history. **SELECTED PUBLICATIONS** Auth, A Dependent People: Newport, Rhode Island in the Revolutionary Era, NY: Fordhan Univ Press, 85; ed, The Diary of Elizabeth Drinker, 3 vols, Boston: Northeastern Univ Press, 91; auth, Ebb Tide in New England: Women, Seaports, and Social Change 1630-1800, Boston: Northeastern Univ Press, 98. **CONTACT ADDRESS** Dept of Hist, Fordham Univ, 501 E Fordham Rd, Bronx, NY, 10458-5191. **EMAIL** ecrane@murray.fordham.edu

CRANK, JOE N.

DISCIPLINE SPECIAL EDUCATION; SCHOOL PSYCHOLOGY **EDUCATION** Southern Ill Univ, BA; Ill State Univ, MS; Univ Kans, PhD. **CAREER** Coordr, schl psychol prog, Univ Nev, Las Vegas. **SELECTED PUBLICATIONS** Auth, Decisions, decisions, decisions: Solving personal problems, Intervention in Schl and Clinic, 23, 88; Surface Counseling Instructors Manuel, Ctr for Res and Learning, KU, 95; coauth, A self-instructional surface-counseling program: Development and validation, Learning Disabilities, 1 (3), 90; Visual depictions as information organizers for enhancing achievement of students with learning disabilities, Learning Disabilities Res and Pract, 8 (3), 93; Surface Counseling, Edge Enterprises, 95. **CONTACT ADDRESS** Dept of Spec Educ, Univ Nev, Las Vegas, 4505 Maryland Pky, PO Box 453014, Las Vegas, NV, 89154-3014. **EMAIL** crank@nevada.edu

CRAPOL, EDWARD PAUL

PERSONAL Born 09/29/1936, Buffalo, NY **DISCIPLINE** UNITED STATES HISTORY **EDUCATION** State Univ NY, Buffalo, BS, 60; Univ Wis-Madison, MS, 64, PhD(hist), 68. **CAREER** Instr hist, Wis State Univ, Eau Claire, 66-67; from asst prof to assoc prof, 67-78, PROF HIST, COL WILLIAM & MARY, 78-, CHMN, 81-, Exchange prof, Am hist, Univ Exeter, Eng, 76-77. **MEMBERSHIPS** AHA; Orgn Am Historians; Soc Historians Am Foreign Rels. **RESEARCH** The foreign policy of the Tyler administration, 1841-1845; Anglo-American relations and the Cold War, 1945-1947. **SELECTED PUBLI-**

CATIONS Auth, An Unwanted War--The Diplomacy of the United-States and Spain Over Cuba, 1895-1898, Amer Hist Rev, Vol 0098, 93; Gendered States--Feminist Re-Visions of International-Relations Theory, Diplomatic Hist, Vol 0018, 94. **CONTACT ADDRESS** Dept of Hist, Col of William and Mary, Williamsburg, VA, 23185.

CRAVEN, WAYNE
DISCIPLINE AMERICAN PAINTING AND SCULPTURE **EDUCATION** Columbia Univ, PhD. **CAREER** Prof. **SELECTED PUBLICATIONS** Publ, Cat of Amer Portraits, NY Hist Soc, Yale, 74; Sculpture in America from the Colonial Period to the Present, Del Univ Press, 84; Colonial American Portraiture, Cambridge, 86; American Art: History and Culture, Brown and Benchmark, 93. **CONTACT ADDRESS** Dept of Art Hist, Univ Delaware, 162 Ctr Mall, Newark, DE, 19716. **EMAIL** Wayne.Craven@mvs.udel.edu

CRAVENS, HAMILTON
PERSONAL Born 08/12/1938, Evanston, IL, d, 2 children **DISCIPLINE** AMERICAN HISTORY, HISTORY OF SCIENCE, MEDICINE, AND TECHNOLOGY **EDUCATION** Univ WA, BA, 60, MA, 62; Univ IA, PhD, 69. **CAREER** Teaching asst hist, Univ WA, 60-62; teaching asst, Univ IA, 62-64, instr, 64-65; instr, OH State Univ, 65-68; from instr to asst prof, 68-69, asst prof, 69-73, assoc prof, 73-80, PROF, IA STATE UNIV, 80-; Vis asst prof hist, Univ MD, College Park, 71-72; consult, Soc for Research in Child Development, 80-83, Rand Corp, 81, Distinguished Senior Lecturer, German Fulbright Prog, Goettingen Univ, 88-89, Distinguished Senior Lecturer, German Fulbright Prog, Bonn Univ and Cologne Univ, summer sem, 97. **HONORS AND AWARDS** Ford Foundation Fellow, 60-61, Univ WA, Univ IA Fellow, 64-65; Charles M Gates Mem Award, WA St Hist Soc, 66; NEH Summer Stipend, 73; Bicentennial Award, Nat Sci Teachers Asn, 76; NSF Grants, 78, 79, 80-83; Vis Fellow, Hoover Institution, 86; Fellow, Stanford Humanities Center, 86; George Bancroft Prof of Am Hist, Goettingen Univ, GER, 88-89; Fellow, Davis Humanities Center, Univ CA, Davis, 90-92; Vis Scholar, Hist, Univ CA, Berkeley, 90-92; J. William Fulbright Distinguished Prof Am Studies, Bonn and Cologne Univs, 97; Vis Scholar, Max Planck Institut fuer Geschichte, Goettingen, GER, 97. **MEMBERSHIPS** AHA; ASA; Hist Sci Soc; OAH; MAASA. **RESEARCH** Am intellectual hist; American cultural hist; the hist of Am science, medicine, and technology. **SELECTED PUBLICATIONS** Auth, The Triumph of Evolution: American Scientists and the Heredity-Environment Controversy, 1900-1941, Univ PA, 78; ed, Ideas in America's Cultures: From Republic to Mass Society, IA State Univ Press, 82; auth, Child-Saving in the Age of Professionalism, 1915-1930, in J. Hawes and N. R. Hiner, eds, American Childhood, Greenwood, 85; History of the Social Sciences, in S. G. Kohlstedt and M. G. Rossiter, eds, Historical Writing on American Science, Johns Hopkins Univ Press, 86; The Triumph of Evolution. The Heredity-Environment Controversy, 1900-1941, paper ed, Johns Hopkins Univ Press, 88; Before Head Start. The Iowa Station and America's Children, Univ NC Press, 93; co-auth and co-ed, Technical Knowledge in America, Science, Medicine, and Technology in America since 1800, Univ AL Press, 96; auth, Scientific racism in Modern America, 1870's-1990's, Prospects, 21, 96; co-auth and co-ed, Health Care Policy in Contemporary America, PA State Univ Press, 97; co-auth, History in an Ahistorical World, Teachers College Record, 98. **CONTACT ADDRESS** Dept of Hist, Iowa State Univ, Ames, IA, 50011-1202. **EMAIL** hcravens@iastate.edu

CRAWFORD, JOHN S.
DISCIPLINE ANCIENT ART AND ARCHAEOLOGY **EDUCATION** Harvard Univ, PhD. **CAREER** Prof. **SELECTED PUBLICATIONS** Auth, The Byzantine Shops at Sardis, Harvard, 89. **CONTACT ADDRESS** Dept of Art Hist, Univ Delaware, 162 Ctr Mall, Newark, DE, 19716. **EMAIL** jstephens@udel.edu

CRAWFORD, MICHAEL JOHN
PERSONAL Born 06/03/1950, St. Louis, MO, m, 1982 **DISCIPLINE** AMERICAN AND BRITISH HISTORY **EDUCATION** Washington Univ, AB, 71, AM, 72; Boston Univ, PhD(hist), 78. **CAREER** Vis asst prof Am hist, Tex Tech Univ, 78-80; Nat Hist Publ & Rec Comn fel, Adams Papers, 80-81; HISTORIAN, NAVAL HIST CTR, 82- **MEMBERSHIPS** AHA; Asn Doc Ed; Soc Hist Fed Govt. **RESEARCH** Religion in early modern America and Britain; political culture in early modern America and Britian; early United States Naval history. **SELECTED PUBLICATIONS** Auth, Contested Boundaries--Itinerancy and the Reshaping of the Colonial American Religious World, Amer Hist Rev, Vol 0101, 96; The Golden Rock--An Episode of the American War of Independence 1775-1783, Amer Neptune, Vol 0057, 97; Pedlar in Divinity, Whitefield,George and the Transatlantic Revivals, 1737-1770, William and Mary Quart, Vol 0052, 95. **CONTACT ADDRESS** Naval History Ctr Washington Navy Yard, Washington, DC, 20374.

CRAWFORD, RICHARD
DISCIPLINE MUSIC **EDUCATION** Univ Mich, BM, 58, MM, 59, PhD, 65. **CAREER** Asst prof, mus, Univ Mich; current, PROF, MUS, GLENN MCCEOCH COLL **HONORS AND AWARDS** Vincent H. Duckles Award; Otto Kinkeldey Award for Musical Excellence; Irving Lowens Award of the Sonneck Society for American Music. **MEMBERSHIPS** Am Antiquarian Soc **SELECTED PUBLICATIONS** Auth, Andrew Law: American Psalmodist, 68; auth, William Billings of Boston, 75; auth, The Core Repertory of Early American Pslamody, 84; co-ed & contribur, A Celebration of American Music, 90; auth, American Sacred Music Imprints, 1698-1810: A Bibliography, 90; coauth, Jazz Standards on Record, 1900-1942, 92; auth, The American Musical Landscape, 93; ed-in-chief, Music of the United States of America. **CONTACT ADDRESS** 1158 Baldwin St, Ann Arbor, MI, 48104.

CRECELIUS, DANIEL
PERSONAL Born 01/15/1937, St. Louis, MO, m, 1963 **DISCIPLINE** MODERN MIDDLE EASTERN HISTORY **EDUCATION** CO Col, BA, 59; Princeton Univ, MA, 62, PhD, 67. **CAREER** From asst prof to assoc prof, 64-73, prof mid east hist, CA State Univ, Los Angeles, 73-, Ch, Dept Hist, 80-83, actg chair, summer 86; Vis lectr, UCLA, 66-67; Vis prof, CO Col, 10/90; Vis prof, Cairo Univ, 1/92-2/92; Trustees Scholarship, CO Col, 55-59; Esden Award, Outstanding Student in Soc Sci, CO Col, 59; Dunniway Prize, Outstanding Student in Hist, CO Col, 59; Woodrow Wilson Nat Fel, Princeton Univ, 59-60; Ford Found Foreign Area Traineeship, Princeton Univ, 60-61; Princeton Univ Near East Fel, 61-62; Five Universities' summer grant for intensive study of Arabic, Univ MI, 60; Princeton Univ summer grant for intensive study of Arabic at Princeton Univ, 61; Fulbright award, Al-Azhar Univ, Cairo, 62-63; Nat Defense For Lang Award, Am Univ of Beirut, 63-64; Am Res Center grant, Egypt, WAQF archives, 68-69, summer 72, summer 79; Soc Sci Res Counc grant, joint res London and Paris, ulama in Cairo and Damascus in 18th Century, 73; Am Phil Soc summer res grant, Cairo, Shari'ah court archives, 75 and 80; Fulbright award, joint res on Acehnese royal decrees, Australia, Indonesia, and Malayasia; CA State Univ, Los Angeles Found, 18th century Egyptian hist, 79 and 81; Nat Endowment for Hum, transl al-Jabarti's Aja'ib al-Athar fi al-Tarajim wa al-Akhbar, 80-82; Nat Endowment for Hum grant, archival res on late 18th Century Egyptian hist, London, Paris, Vienna, and Cairo, 83-84; Am Res Center summer grant, archival res, late 18th Centry Egyptian hist, Egypt, 84; Am Res Center summer grant, annotated transl of manuscript of Ahmad Katkhuda Azaban al-Damurdashi, Egypt, 87; Nat Endowment for the Hum Travel to Collections summer grant, Cairo's Nat Libr, 87; CA State Univ, Los Angeles Found, mini-grant, manuscript of Ahmad Katkhuda Azaban al-Damurdashi, 87; Am Philo Soc summer grant, al-Damurdashi's manuscript, Cairo, 89; CA State Univ, Los Angeles, mini-grant, annotated transl of al=damurdashi's al-Durrah al-Musanah, 90; Sch of Natural Sci and Soc Sci, CA State Univ, Los Angeles, and Fulbright/Cairo, int conf on Arabic Manuscript Sources for 18th Century Egyptian Hist, 90; Fulbright sr scholar area award, Istanbul and Cairo, 91-92; Nat Endowment for Hum, Travel to Collections summer grant, Cairo, 92; Fulbright Found, Cairo, grant to publ selected papers of the Int Conf on Soc and Econ Hist of Ottoman Egypt, 92; Fulbright Inst award, 95-96; Fulbright collaborative res award, edit and annotate Shaykh al-Rajabi's Ta'rikh al-Wazir Muhammad Ali Basha, 95-96; CA State Univ, Los Angeles, Sch of Natural and Soc Sci summer mini-grant, Cairo, 95; Am Res Center, Eqypt, res Egyptian archives, 96; Fulbright award, Int Conf on Econ and Soc Hist of Ottoman Egypt, Cairo, 96. **HONORS AND AWARDS** CA State Univ, Los Angeles, Outstanding Prof Award, 74; Meritorius Service Award, 84, 85, 86, 87, 88 & 89. **MEMBERSHIPS** MidE Inst; Am Asn MidE Studies; Turkish Studies Assoc; Nat Geog Soc. **RESEARCH** Eighteenth to twentieth century Egyptian hist; mod Arab polit; Acehnese sarakatas. **SELECTED PUBLICATIONS** Auth, Al-Azhar in the Revolution, Middle East Jour, winter 66, reprint, Schools in Transition: Essays in Comparative Education (Erwin H Epstein and Andreas Kazamais), 68; Al-Azhar, In: Encyclopedia Americana, 67; Die religion im Dienste des islamischen Staatssozialismus in Aegypten, Bustan, 67; Waqf Archives in the U A R, Newsletter of the Am Res Center in Egypt, 10/69; Report on Research in Cairo's Archives, Bull of the Am Res Center in Eqypt, 5/15/70; Al-Azhar: A Millenium of Faithfulness to Tradition, Mid East, 4/70; The organization of Waqf documents in Cairo, IJMES, 71; Emergence of the Shaykh al-Azhar as the pre-eminent religious leader in Egypt, Colloque Int sur l-Hist du Caire, 72; Nonideological Responses of the Egyptian Ulama to Modernization, In: Scholars, Saints and Sufis (Nikki Keddie, ed), Berkeley and Los Angeles, 72; The Course of Secularization in Modern Egypt, In: Religion and Political Modernization (Donald E Smith, ed), New Haven, 74; Sa'udi-Egyptian Relations, Int Studies, 75; Co-auth (with Anahid Crecelius), An Egyptian Battalion in Mexico: 1863-1867, Der Islam, 2/76; The waqfiyah of Muhammad Bey Abu al-Dhabab, JARCE, 78 & 79; A Reputed Acehense Sarakata of the Jamal al-Layl Dynasty, JMBRAS, 79; The Course of Secularism in Modern Egypt, In: Islam and Development (John Esposito, ed), Syracuse, 80; Co-auth (with Edward A Beardow), Another Acehnese Sarakata, Proceedings of the Third Int Symposium on Asian Studies, Hong Kong, 81; Archival Sources for Demographic Studies of the Middle East, In: The Islamic Middle East, 700-1900: Studies in Economic and Social History (A L Udovitch, ed), Princeton, 81; The Roots of Modern Egypt: A Study of the Regimes of Ali Bey al-kabir and Muhammad Bey Abu al-Dhahab, 1760-1775, Minneapolis and Chicago, 81, Juthur Misr al-Haditha, Arabic transl, Cairo, 85; Des Incidences de cas du waqf dans trois cours du Caire (1640-1802), Jour Econ and Soc Hist of the Orient, 86; Unratified Commercial Treaties between Egypt and England and France, 1773-1794, Revue d'Histoire Maghrebine, 6/85; Egypt's Reawakening Interest in Palestine during the Regimes of Ali Bey al-Kabir and Muhammad Bey Abu al-Dhahab, 1760-1775, In: Palestine in the Late Ottoman Period: Political, Social and Economic Transformation (David Kushner, ed), Jerusalem, 86; The Attempt by Greek Catholics to Control Egypt's Trade with Europe in the Second Half of the Eighteenth Centruy, In: La vie sociale dans les provinces arabes a l'epoque ottomane (Abdeljelil Temimi, ed), Zaghouan, 88; Russia's Relations with mamluk Beys of Egypt, 1770-1798, In: A Way Prepared, Essays on Islamic culture in Honor of Richard Bayly Winder (Farhad Kazemi and R D McChesney, ed), New York, 88; A Source for al-Jabarti's History, Newsletter of the Am Res Center in Egypt, spring 89; Ahmad Shalabi ibn Abd al-Ghani and Ahmad Katkhuda Azaban al-Damurdashi: Two Sources for al-Jabarti's Aja'ib al-Athar fi 'l-Tarajim wa 'l-Akhbar, In: Eighteenth Century Egypt: The Arabic Manuscript Sources (Daniel Crecelius, ed), Claremont, 90; The Importance of Qusayr in the Late Eighteenth Century, JARCE, 90; Masadir T'rikh al-Jabarti fi Awakhir al-Qarn al-Sabi Ashar wa Awa'il al-Qarn al-Thamin Ashar (Sources for al-Jabarti's History of the Latter Part of the 17th Century and the Early 18th century), al-Majallah al-Ta'rikhiyah al-Maghribiyah, 7/90; Al-Hudud al-Siyasiyyah li al-Bayt al-Mamluki (The Political Parameters of the Maluk Faction), Majallat Kulliyyat al-Adab, Jami'at Zagazig, 90; Co-auth (with Butrus Abd al-Malik), A Late Eighteenth Century Egyptian Waqf Endowed by a Sister of the Maluk Shaykh al-Balad Muhammad Bey Abu al-Dhahab, Arab Hist Rev for Ottoman Studies, 1/90; Ed, Al-Damurdashi's Chronicle of Egypt, 1688-1755, Leiden, 91; The Waqf of Muhammad Bey Abu al-Dhahab in Historical Perspective, Int Jour of Middle East Studies, 2/91; Makhtutat al-Durrah al-Musanah fi Akhbar al-Kinanah li al-Amir Ahmad al-Damurdashi katkhuda Azaban, Cairo, 92; Ed, Fihris Waqfiyyat al-Asr al-Uthmani al-Mahfudhah bi Wizarat al-Awqaf wa Dar al-Watha'iq al-ta'rikhiyya al-Qawmiyyah bi al-Qahirah (Index of Waqfiyyat from the Ottoman Period Preserved in the Ministry of Awqaf and the Dar al-Watha'ig in Cairo), Dar al-Nahdah al-Arabiyyah, Cairo, 92; Co-ed (with Hamza Abd al'Aziz Badr and Daniel Crecelius), A Short Manuscript History of the Career of Murad Bey, al-Maktabah al-Arabiyyah, Cairo, 92; Co-auth (with Hamza Abd al-Aziz Badr), The Waqfs of Shahin Ahmad Agha, Annales Islamologiques, 92; Co-ed (with Fa'uf Abbas and Daniel Crecelius), Abhath Nadwah ta'rikh Misr al-Iqtisadi wa al-Ijtima i fi al-Asr al-Uthmani: 1517-1798, Majallat Kulliyyat al-Adab, jami at al-Qahirah, 2/93; Co-auth (with Hamza Abd al-Azia Badr), An Egyptian Grain Shipment of 1763 to the Imperial Pantry in Istanbul, JARCE, 93, Arabic transl, Shuhnat Ghilal Misriyyah illa al-Ki9lar al-Sultani bi Istanbul: 1763, Al-Mu'arrikh al Misri, 1/93; Hawliyat Awqaf Dumyat fi Awakhir al-Qarn al-Thamin Ashar, Majallat Kulliyyat al-Adab, Jami'at al-Qahirah, 2/93; Co-auth (with Hamza Abd al-Aziz Badr), The Awqaf of al-Hajj Bahir Agha in Cairo, Annales Islamologiques, 93; Co-auth, (with Hamza Abd al-Aziz Badr), The Awqaf of Hasan Bey al-Jiddawi, Arab Hist Rev for Ottoman Studies, 8/94; Co-auth (with Hamza Abd al-Aziz Badr), French Ships and Their Cargoes Sailing between Damiette and Ottoman Ports, 1777-1781, Jour Econ and Soc Hist of the Orient, 94; An Austrian Attempt to Develop the Red Sea Trade Route in the Late Eighteenth Century, Middle Eastern Studies, 4/94; Shaykh Abd al-Rahman ibn Hasan al-Jabarti's Aja'ib al-Athar fi al-Tarajim wa al-Akhbar, annotated transl (with Butrus Abd al-Malik), Franz Steiner Verlag, Stuttgart, 94; Guest ed & contr, Introduction, Jour Econ and Soc Hist of the Orient, 8/95; Co-auth (with Hamza Abd al-Aziz Badr), The Waqfiyya of the Two Hammams in Cairo Known as al-Sukkariyya, In: Le waqf dans l'espace islamique (Randi Deguilhem, ed), Damascus, 95; Co-auth (with Hamza Adb al-Aziz Badr), The Usurpation of Waqf Revenues in Sixteenth Century Damiette, JARCE, 95; Co-auth (with Hamza Abd al-Azia Badr), An Agreement between the Ulama and the Mamluk Amirs in 1795: A Test of the Accuracy of Two Contemporary Chronicles, In: Dirasat fi Ta'rikh Misr al-Iqtisadi wa al-Ijtima i fi al-Asr al-Uthmani (Daniel Crecelius, Hamza Badr, and Husam al-Din Isma'il, ed), Dar al-Afaq al-Arabi, Cairo, 97; Co-ed (with Hamza Badr and Husam al-Din Ismail), Dirasat fi Ta'rikh al-Iqtisadi wa al-Ijtima i fi al-Asr al-Uthmani, dar al-Afaq al-Arabi, Cairo, 97; Co-ed (with Hamza Badr and Husam al-Din Ismail), ta-rikh al-Wazir Muhammad Ali Basha li al-Shaykh Khalil ibn Ahmad al-Rajabi, Dar al-Afaq al-Arabi, Cairo, 97. **CONTACT ADDRESS** Dept of Hist, California State Univ, Los Angeles, 5151 Rancho Castilla, Los Angeles, CA, 90032-4202. **EMAIL** dcrecel@calstatela.edu

CREGIER, DON MESICK
PERSONAL Born 03/28/1930, Schenectady, NY, m, 1965 **DISCIPLINE** BRITISH AND AMERICAN HISTORY **EDUCATION** Union Col, NY, AB, 51; Univ Mich, MA, 52. **CAREER** Asst instr govt, Clark Univ, 52-54; instr hist & polit sci, Univ Tenn, 56-57; from instr to asst prof, Baker Univ, 58-61; asst prof, Keuka Col, 62-64; vis asst prof hist, St John's Univ, 64-65; sr fel hist & polit sci, Mary Hopkins Col, 65-66; asst prof hist, St Dunstan's Univ, 66-68, assoc prof, 68-69; ASSOC PROF HIST, UNIV PRINCE EDWARD ISLAND, 69-, Can Coun fel, 72-73; abstractor, Am Bibliog Ctr, Santa Barbara, Calif, 78- **MEMBERSHIPS** AHA; Conf Brit Studies; Hist

Asn, Eng; Am Polit Sci Asn; Asn Contemporary Hist; hon mem, Mark Twain Soc. **RESEARCH** Nineteenth and 20th century British, Irish and American history. **SELECTED PUBLICATIONS** Auth, The Age of Upheaval--Edwardian Politics, 1899-1914, Albion, Vol 0028, 96; Lloydgeorge, David--A Political Life--Organizer of Victory 1912-1916, Amer Hist Rev, Vol 0099, 94. **CONTACT ADDRESS** Dept of Hist, Univ of Prince Edward Island Charlottetown, PE, C1A 4P3.

CRESSON, BRUCE COLLINS
PERSONAL Born 10/27/1930, Lenoir, NC, m, 1955, 2 children **DISCIPLINE** RELIGION, ARCHEALOGY **EDUCATION** Wake Forest Col, BA, 52; Southeastern Baptist Theol Sem, BD, 55, ThM, 56; Duke Univ, PhD(relig), 64. **CAREER** Instr Hebrew, Southeastern Baptist Theol Sem, 62-63; instr relig, Duke Univ, 63-66; assoc prof, 66-77, PROF RELIG, BAYLOR UNIV, 77-, Mem, excavation staff, Aphek-Antipatris, 74-76, Wendeh, 77; dir, excavation to Tel Dhalia, 78- **MEMBERSHIPS** Am Sch Org Res; Soc Bibl Lit. **RESEARCH** Edom; history of Old Testament and intertestamental period in its world setting; Biblical archaeology. **SELECTED PUBLICATIONS** Auth, Ammon, Moab and Edom--Early States-Nations of Jordan in the Biblical Period, Biblical Archaeol, Vol 0059, 96. **CONTACT ADDRESS** Dept of Relig, Baylor Univ, Waco, TX, 76703.

CRESSY, DAVID
DISCIPLINE HISTORY **EDUCATION** Cambridge Univ, BA, 67, MA, 71, PhD, 73. **CAREER** Vis, assoc prof, hist, Claremont Grad Sch; current, PROF HIST, CALIF STATE UNIV LONG BEACH **MEMBERSHIPS** Am Antiquarian Soc **SELECTED PUBLICATIONS** Auth, Literacy and the Social Order: Reading and Writing in Tudor and Stuart England, 80; auth, "The Environment for Literacy: Accomplishment and Context in Seventeenth-Century England and New England," in Literacy in Hist Perspective, 83; auth "Kinship and Kin: Interaction in Early Modern England," 86; auth, Coming Over: Migration and Communication between England and New England, 1620-1720, 87; auth, Bonfire and Bells: National Memory and the Protestant Calendar in Elizabethan and Stuart England, 90; auth, "De la Fiction dans les archives? Ou le Monstre de 1569," Annales ESC, 93; auth, "Purification, Thanksgiving and the Churching of Women in Post Reformation England," Past & Pres, 93; auth, "Literacy in Context: Meaning and Measurement in Early Modern England," in Consumption and the World of Goods, 93; auth, Birth, Marriage and Death: Ritual, Religion on the Life Cycle in Tudor and Stuart England, 97. **CONTACT ADDRESS** 231 W 6th St, Claremont, CA, 91711.

CREW, SPENCER R.
PERSONAL Born 01/07/1949, Poughkeepsie, NY, m, 1971 **DISCIPLINE** CURATOR **EDUCATION** Brown Univ, Providence RI, AB, 1967-71; Rutgers Univ, New Brunswick NJ, MA, 1971-73; Rutgers Univ, New Brunswick NJ, PhD, 1973-79. **CAREER** Univ of MD Baltimore County, Catonsville MD, assistant professor, 1978-81; Smithsonian Institution, Natl Museum of Amer History, Washington DC, historian 1981-87; Natl Museum of Amer History, curator 1987-89; Natl Museum of Amer History, chair, Dept of Social and Cultural History 1989-91, deputy director, 1991-92, acting director, 1992-94; director, 1994. **HONORS AND AWARDS** Curator for exhibition "Field to Factory: Afro-American Migration 1915-1940"; Osceola Award, Delta Sigma Theta Sorority, Inc 1988; co-curator: "Go Forth and Serve: Black Land Grant Colleges Enter a Second Century," 1990, "African American Images in Postal Service Stamps," 1992; **MEMBERSHIPS** Program chairperson, 1985-86, executive bd member, 1986-90, Oral History in the Mid-Atlantic Region; mem Oral History Assn 1988-; 2nd vice pres African Amer Museums Assn, 1988-91; program co-chairperson, Oral History Assn 1988; commissioner (bd mem), Banneker-Douglass Museum, 1989-93; editorial board mem, Journal of Amer History, 1989-93; program chairperson, African Amer Museums Assn, 1989; senior youth group coordinator, St John Baptist Church, 1989, co-editor, Newsletter for the American Historical Assn, 1990-; trustee, Brown Univ, 1995-; mem of bd Amer Assn of Museums, 1995-98. **SELECTED PUBLICATIONS** Author of booklet Field to Factory: Afro-American Migration 1915-1940, 1987; author, Black Life in Secondary Cities: A Comparative Analysis of the Black Communities of Camden and Elizabeth, NJ, 1860-1920, 1993. **CONTACT ADDRESS** Natl Museum of American History, Smithsonian Inst, Rm 5112, Washington, DC, 20560.

CREWS, DANIEL A.
PERSONAL Born 10/17/1956, Lawrenceburg, TN, m, 1975, 1 child **DISCIPLINE** HISTORY **EDUCATION** Univ N Ala, BA, 77; Memphis State Univ, MA, 79; Auburn Univ, PhD, 84. **CAREER** Asst prof, Okla Baptist Univ, 84-87; asst to ASSOC PROF, HIST, CENTRAL MISSOURI STATE UNIV, 87-; edit bd, Med Studies, 90-; gen ed, Bull, Soc Span & Port Hist Stud, 89-. **HONORS AND AWARDS** Invited lectr, Spanish fac, Oxford Univ, 99., Phi Kappa Phi **MEMBERSHIPS** Soc Span, Port Hist Stud **RESEARCH** Span humanism, diplomacy of Charles V, imperial ideology. **SELECTED PUBLICATIONS** Auth, "Vives: Edicions Princeps," bk rev in The 16th Cent J, 95; auth, "Uprising of the Comuneros," and "The Defeat of the Spanish Armada," in Chron Eur Hist, 97. **CONTACT ADDRESS** History Dept, Central Missouri State Univ, Wood 136E, Warrensburg, MO, 64093.

CRIBIORE, RAFFAELA
PERSONAL Born 03/27/1948, Varese, Italy, m, 1970, 2 children **DISCIPLINE** CLASSICS **EDUCATION** Universita Cattolica Milan, BA, 72; M Philos, 90; Columbia Univ, PhD, 93. **CAREER** Lectr, High School A Mosso Italy, 72-76; Scuola D'Italia NY, 79-85; tchg asst, Columbia Univ, 86-89; preceptor, 90; instr, 96, 97; res assoc, Columbia Univ, 96-; assoc curator of Papyri Rare Book and Manuscripts Library, 94-. **HONORS AND AWARDS** President's Fel, 86-89; Polychronis Fel, 89-90, Bd Dir of the Am Soc of Papyrologists, 95-98; Vis Comm to the Grad Fac of Political and Soc Sci, New School for Soc Res, 94-96. **RESEARCH** Greek and Latin Education; Greek Literature; Papyrology. **SELECTED PUBLICATIONS** Auth, Writing, Teachers, and Students in Graeco-Roman Egypt, 96. **CONTACT ADDRESS** 17 Sutton Pl, New York, NY, 10022. **EMAIL** rc141@columbia.edu

CRIM, ALONZO A.
PERSONAL Born 10/01/1928, Chicago, IL, m **DISCIPLINE** EDUCATION **EDUCATION** Roosevelt Coll, BA 1950; Univ of Chicago, MA 1958; Harvard Univ, EdD 1969. **CAREER** Chicago Pub Schs, teacher 1954-63, supr 1968-69; Whittier Elem Sch, principal 1963-65; Adult Educ Ctr, 1965; Wendell Phillips HS, 1965-68; Compton Union HS, 1969-70; Compton Unified Sch Dist, 1970-73; Atlanta Pub Sch, 1973-88; GA State Univ, prof, beginning 1988; Spelman College, prof, currently. **HONORS AND AWARDS** Eleanor Roosevelt Key Awd Roosevelt Univ 1974; Vincent Conroy Awd Harvard Grad Sch 1970; Distingushed Educators Awd Teacher's Coll Columbia Univ 1980; Father of the Year Awd in Educ SE Region of the US 1981; Honor of the Yr Awd in Patriotism Military Order of World Wars 1981; Hon life mem IL Congress of Parents and Teachers 1982; One of North Amer 100 Top Execs The Executive Educator magazine 1984; Big Heart Awd GA Special Olympics 1985; The Golden Staff Awd GA State Univ; Volunteer of the Year YMCA of Metro Atlanta; Horace Mann Bond Cup Fort Valley Coll 1985; Abe Goldstein Human Relations Awd Anti-Defamation League 1985; Distinguished Public Relations Awd GA Chap of the Public Relations Soc of Amer 1986; hon DL degree Newberry Coll, hon doctor of public serv degree Gettysburg Coll, Honorary Degree Georgetown Univ; Honorary Degree Princeton Univ; Honorary Degree Harvard Univ; Honorary Degree Tuskege Univ; Honorary Degree Columbia Univ. **MEMBERSHIPS** Mem various offices and committees, Amer Assn Sch Admin; Natl Alliance Black Sch Superintendents; Natl Alliance Black Sch Educ; Harvard Grad Sch Educ; Jr Achievement Gr Atlanta; So Council Intl & Pub Affairs; Educ Prog Assn Amer; GA Council Economic Educ; Amer Cancer Soc; GA Assn Sch Superintendents; Atlanta YMCA; Natl EdD Prog Educ Leaders; Rotary Club; Atlanta Council for Intl Visitors; Atlanta Area Scout Council's Expo; Phi Beta Kappa; life mem NAACP; mem Amer Assn of Sch Administrators; mem Kappa Alpha Psi, Kappa Boule, Phi Delta Kappa. **CONTACT ADDRESS** Education Dept, Spelman Col, Box 360, 350 Spelman Ln, Atlanta, GA, 30314.

CRIMANDO, THOMAS
DISCIPLINE HISTORY **EDUCATION** St John Fisher Col; BA; Univ Rochester, MA, PhD. **CAREER** Adj lectr. **RESEARCH** Renaissance and Reformation Europe; Modern Europe. **SELECTED PUBLICATIONS** Auth, Two French Views of the Council of Trent, 88; Biographical Sketch of Bruce Cotton, Oxford, 98. **CONTACT ADDRESS** Dept of History, State Univ NY Col Brockport, Brockport, NY, 14420. **EMAIL** tcrimando@acspr1.acs.brockport.edu

CRIMP, DOUGLAS
DISCIPLINE ART HISTORY AND VISUAL AND CULTURAL STUDIES **EDUCATION** CUNY, PhD, 94. **CAREER** Prof, Univ of Rochester. **SELECTED PUBLICATIONS** Auth, On the Museum's Ruins, Cambridge: MIT Press, 93 & AIDS Demo Graphics, Seattle: Bay Press, 90; co-ed, How Do I Look Queer Film and Video, Seattle: Bay Press, 91; ed, AIDS: Cultural Analysis/Cultural Activism, Cambridge: MIT Press, 88. **CONTACT ADDRESS** Dept of Art and Art Hist, Univ of Rochester, 601 Elmwood Ave, Ste. 656, 424 Morey , Rochester, NY, 14642. **EMAIL** crmp@db1.cc.rochester.edu

CRIPPS, THOMAS
PERSONAL Born 09/17/1932, m, 1954, 3 children **DISCIPLINE** AMERICAN HISTORY **EDUCATION** Towson State Col, BS, 54; Univ Md, MA, 57, PhD(hist), 67. **CAREER** Asst prof hist, Pembroke State Col, 57-58; asst prof hist & soc sci & chmn soc sci div, Harford Jr Col, 58-61; asst prof 61-67, assoc prof hist, 67-68, PROF HIST MORGAN STATE UNIV, 68-, COORDR GRAD PROG POPULAR CULT, 73-, Lectr, Univ Md, 63 & Johns Hopkins Univ, 67-68; consult Negro hist, Westinghouse Learning Corp & Md Educ TV Comn, 67-68; Am Philos Soc study grant cinema in Europ arch, 67 & 72; co-producer, writer & host, 30 show ser & talk shows, Westinghouse Broadcasting Co, 68-69; vis prof Afro-Am hist, Stanford Univ, 69-70, Am Coun Learned Soc fel, 71-72; Rockefeller Found fel humanities & Woodrow Wilson Int Ctr for Scholars fel, 75-76; Am Coun Learned Soc & Nat Humanities Ctr fel, 80-81, Nat Endowment for Humanities grant, 82. **HONORS AND AWARDS** Charles Thomson Prize Essay, 82. **MEMBERSHIPS** AHA; Am Film Inst; Brit Film Inst; Popular Cult Asn; Int Asn AV Media Hist Res. **RESEARCH** Black history; cinema history; popular culture. **SELECTED PUBLICATIONS** Auth, From Harlem to Hollywood, The Struggle for Racial and Cultural Democracy, 1920-1943, West Hist Quart, Vol 0024, 93; Statements by Educators Library-of-Congress Hearings, Los-Angeles, New-York-City, and Washington, Dc, March 1996, Hist Jour Film Radio and TV, Vol 0016, 96; Mickey-Mouse History and Other Essays on American Memory, Labor Hist, Vol 0038, 97; Love and Theft--Blackface Minstrelsy and the American Working-Class, Labor Hist, Vol 0035, 94; Historical Truth--An Interview with Burns, Ken, Amer Hist Rev, Vol 0100, 95; A White Scholar and the Black-Community, 1945-1965--Essays and Reflections, Jour So Hist, Vol 0060, 94; On the Real Side--Laughing, Lying, and Signifying--The Underground Tradition of African-American Humor that Transformed American Culture, from Slavery to Pryor, Richard, Amer Hist Rev, Vol 0100, 95; Revisioning History--Film and the Construction of a New Past, Amer Hist Rev, Vol 0101, 96; Blackface, White-Noise--Jewish Immigrants in the Hollywood Melting-Pot, Jour Amer Hist, Vol 0083, 97. **CONTACT ADDRESS** 1714 Bolton St, Baltimore, MD, 21217.

CRISCENTI, JOSEPH THOMAS
PERSONAL Born 08/07/1920, Detroit, MI **DISCIPLINE** HISTORY **EDUCATION** Univ Detroit, PhB, 42; Harvard Univ, MA, 47, PhD(hist), 56. **CAREER** From instr to asst prof, 55-62, ASSOC PROF LATIN AM HIST, BOSTON COL, 62-, Chmn comt, James Alexander Robertson Mem Prize, 62 & 72; Am Philos Soc grant, 63; mem, Exec Comt, Conf Latin Am Hist, 63-64; consult, Cooperative Res Inst Collection, Asn Col & Res Libr, 71-72; mem, Regional Liaison Comt, Latin Am Studies Asn, 73-; judge Domingo Faustino Sarmiento Prize Comt, Argentine Embassy, 75; chmn, Comt on Chile Rio de la Plata Studies, Conf Latin Am Hist, 75-76. **HONORS AND AWARDS** James Alexander Robertson Mem Prize, 61. **MEMBERSHIPS** Latin Am Studies Asn; AHA; Conf Latin Am Hist; New England Coun Latin Am Studies (secy-treas, 72-). **RESEARCH** National period of Argentina and Uruguay; economic aspects of foreign policy of Brazil in the 19th century; bibliographical guide to the travel literature of Argentina, Urguay and Paraguay, 1810-1910. **SELECTED PUBLICATIONS** Auth, Rediscovering a Continent--Spanish, Americas, Vol 0052, 96. **CONTACT ADDRESS** Dept of Hist, Boston Col, Chestnut Hill, MA, 02167.

CRISP, JAMES ERNEST
PERSONAL Born 05/28/1946, Wichita Falls, TX, m, 1968, 1 child **DISCIPLINE** HISTORY **EDUCATION** Rice Univ, BA, 68; Yale Univ, MPh, 71, PhD(hist), 76. **CAREER** Instr, 72-76, ASST PROF HIST, NC STATE UNIV, 76-. **MEMBERSHIPS** AHA. **RESEARCH** American expansion; race relations; the Republic of Texas. **SELECTED PUBLICATIONS** Auth, Writing Western History--Essays on Major Western Historians, Sothwestern Hist Quart, Vol 0096, 93; Inherit the Alamo--Myth and Ritual at an American Shrine, So Cult(s), Vol 0002, 95; Tejanos and Texas Under the Mexican Flag, 1821-1836, Jour So Hist, Vol 0062, 96; Houston, Sam Speechwriters--The Grad Student, the Teenager, the Editors, and the Historians, Southwestern Hist Quart, Vol 0097, 93; The Alamo Remembered--Tejano Accounts and Perspectives, Southwestern Hist Quart, Vol 0100, 96; The Little Book That Wasnt There--The Myth and Mystery of the Delapena Diary, Southwestern Hist Quart, Vol 0098, 94; Freedom on the Border--The Seminole Maroons in Florida, the Indian-Territory, Coahuila, and Texas, So Cult(s), Vol 0001, 95. **CONTACT ADDRESS** Dept of Hist, No Carolina State Univ, Raleigh, NC, 27650.

CRIST, LYNDA LASSWELL
PERSONAL Born 11/03/1945, Bay City, TX, m, 1977 **DISCIPLINE** SOUTHERN AMERICAN HISTORY **EDUCATION** Rice Univ, BA, 67, MA, 69; Univ Tenn, Knoxville, PhD(hist), 80. **CAREER** Asst ed, 73-76, assoc ed, 76-79, ED, PAPERS OF JEFFERSON DAVIS, 79-. **MEMBERSHIPS** Southern Hist Soc; Orgn Am Historians; Asn Doc Ed; Am Asn State & Local Hist. **RESEARCH** Jefferson Davis; Mississippi history; American art and architecture. **SELECTED PUBLICATIONS** Auth, A Users Guide to the Official Records of the American-Civil-War, Jour So Hist, Vol 0060, 94; Civil-War Battlefields and Landmarks--A Guide to the National-Park Sites, Jour So Hist, Vol 0063, 97; The American Heritage New History of the Civil-War, Jour So Hist, Vol 0063, 97; The Civil-War in Books--An Analytical Bibliography, Jour So Hist, Vol 0063, 97; The Battlefields of the Civil-War, Jour So Hist, Vol 0063, 97; A Womans Civil-War--A Diary, with Reminiscences of the War, from March, 1862, Va Mag Hist and Biography, Vol 0101, 93; The Confederate Republic--A Revolution Against Politics, Miss Quart, Vol 0049, 96; Lion of the South--General Hindman, Thomas, Jour So Hist, Vol 0060, 94; Guide to Civil-War Books--An Annotated Selection of Modern Works on the War Between the States, Jour So Hist, Vol 0063, 97. **CONTACT ADDRESS** Rice Univ, Houston, TX, 77251.

CRISTI, RENATO
DISCIPLINE INTELLECTUAL IMPACT OF SCIENCE IN CANADA **EDUCATION** Toronto, PhD, 80. **CAREER** Prof **SELECTED PUBLICATIONS** Coauth, El pensamiento conservador en Chile: Seis ensayos, Santiago: Editorial Universi-

taria, 92; Auth, Le liberalisme conservateur: Trois essais sur Schmitt, Hayek et Hegel, 93; Carl Schmitt and Authoritarian Liberalism: Strong State, Free Economy, U of Wales P, 98. **CONTACT ADDRESS** Dept of Philosophy, Wilfrid Laurier Univ, 75 University Ave W, Waterloo, ON, N2L 3C5. **EMAIL** rcristi@mach1.wlu.ca

CRITCHLOW, D.T.
PERSONAL Born 05/18/1948, Pasadena, CA, m, 1978, 2 children **DISCIPLINE** HISTORY **EDUCATION** Univ Cal Berk, PhD 78, MA 72; San Francisco State Univ, BA 70. **CAREER** St Louis Univ, prof 91-97; Univ Notre Dame, asst prof, assoc prof, 83-91; Univ Dayton, asst prof, 81-83. **HONORS AND AWARDS** Fulbright Fel; Woodrow Wilson Fel; NEH Fel; U of Warsaw vis prof; Woodrow Wilson Intl guest sch; Brookings Inst guest sch; USIA Dist Lectr. **RESEARCH** Hist of Amer pub policy; Amer business hist. **SELECTED PUBLICATIONS** Auth, Intended Consequences: Birth Control Abortion and the Federal Government in Modern America, Oxford Univ Press, in press, 99; Studebaker: The Life and Death of an American Auto Company: Studebaker 1852-1963, IN Univ Press, 96; With Us Always: Private Charity and Public Welfare in Historical Perspective, co-ed, Lantham MD, Rowman and Littlefield, 98; America: A Concise History, coauth, Belmont CA, Wadsworth Pub, 93; The Politics of Abortion and Birth Control in Historical Perspective, ed, Univ Pk PA, PSUP, 96; A History of United States, a five vol hist incl essays by Polish and Amer scholars, Warsaw Poland, Polish Acad Press, 95; Innovation in the Classroom: Teaching Policy History, The History Teacher, 99; Birth Control Population Control and Family Planning: An Overview, Jour of Policy Hist, 95; reviews, What's In and What's Out, Revs in Amer Hist, 97. **CONTACT ADDRESS** Dept of History, St Louis Univ, St Louis, MO, 63103. **EMAIL** dcritchlow@compuserve.com

CRITCHLOW, DONALD T.
DISCIPLINE AMERICAN PUBLIC POLICY AND BUSINESS **EDUCATION** Saint Louis Univ, PhD. **CAREER** Eng Dept, St. Edward's Univ **HONORS AND AWARDS** Ed, Jour Policy Hist. **SELECTED PUBLICATIONS** Auth, Studebaker: The Life and Death of an American Corporation; The Brookings Institution, 1916-1952: Expertise and the Public Interest in a Democratic Society; Coauth, America!: A Concise History; Ed, Socialism in the Heartland: The Midwestern Experience; Politics of Population: Birth Control and Abortion in Modern America; Coed, Poverty and Public Policy in Modern America; Federal Social Policy: The Historical Dimension. **CONTACT ADDRESS** St Edward's Univ, 3001 S Congress Ave, Austin, TX, 78704-6489.

CROCE, LEWIS HENRY
PERSONAL Born 12/21/1933, Washington, DC **DISCIPLINE** AMERICAN HISTORY **EDUCATION** Univ Md, BA, 64, MA, 65, PhD(hist), 68. **CAREER** From asst prof Am hist to assoc prof, 68-77, PROF HIST, MANKATO STATE UNIV, 77-, Sr lectr hist, Univ London, 72-73; res grants, Henry E Huntington Libr & Harry S Truman Libr Inst, 77; adj fac, Princeton Univ, summer 81; prof, US Military Acad, summer 82. **MEMBERSHIPS** AHA; Orgn Am Historians; Southern Hist Asn. **RESEARCH** United States, 1815-1877; Abraham Lincoln; American Civil War. **SELECTED PUBLICATIONS** Auth, Sykes Regular Infantry Division, 1861-1864--A History of Regular United-States Infantry Operations in the Civil-Wars Eastern Theater, Civil War Hist, Vol 0039, 93. **CONTACT ADDRESS** Mankato State Univ, 734 Marsh St, Mankato, MN, 56001-4490.

CROCE, PAUL JEROME
PERSONAL Born 06/28/1957, Washington, DC, m, 1985, 2 children **DISCIPLINE** AMERICAN STUDIES **EDUCATION** Georgetown Univ, BA, 79; Brown Univ, MA, 81, PhD, 87. **CAREER** Vis Prof, 85-87, Georgetown Univ; Vis Asst Prof, 87-89, Rollins Col; Asst Prof, 89-95, Assoc Prof, 95-, Chmn, 97-, Stetson Univ. **HONORS AND AWARDS** NEH Grants, 89 & 95. **MEMBERSHIPS** AHA; OAH; ASA; AAR; Cheiron; HSS; Historical Soc; Intellectual History Group **RESEARCH** American cultural & intellectual history; history of philosophy; religion; science; William James. **SELECTED PUBLICATIONS** Science andReligion in the Era of William James Volume 1 Eclipse of Certainty 1820-1880, Univ of NC Press, 95; From Virtue to Morality Republicanism in the Texts and Contexts of William James, Jour of Amer Stud of Turkey, 95; The Scientific Education of William James, Hist of the Human Sciences, 95; Polarizing America The Erosion of Mass Culture, An Amer Mosaic Rethinking Amer Cult Stud, 96; Intellectual Historians in the Academic Public Square, Intel Hist Newsletter, 96; Science and the Moral Religion of William James, Bulletin of the Honors Prog, 96; Accommodation vs Struggle, DuBois Ency, 97; Probabilistic Darwinism Louis Agassiz vs Asa Gray on Science Religion and Certainty, Jour of Rel Hist, 98; Between Spiritualism and Science William James on Religion and Human Nature, Jour for the Hist of Modern Theol, 97-98. **CONTACT ADDRESS** Stetson Univ, Box 8274, Deland, FL, 32720-3756. **EMAIL** pcroce@stetson.edu

CROCKER, RICHARD LINCOLN
PERSONAL Born 02/17/1927, Roxbury, MA, m, 1948, 3 children **DISCIPLINE** HISTORY OF MUSIC **EDUCATION** Yale Univ, BA, 50, PhD(music), 57. **CAREER** From instr to asst prof music, Yale Univ, 55-62; from asst prof to assoc prof, 63-71, PROF MUSIC, UNIV CALIF, BERKELEY, 71-, Morse fel, Yale Univ, 60-61; Humanities Inst res fel, 67; Guggenheim fel, 69-70; Humanities Res fel, 73. **HONORS AND AWARDS** Alfred Einstein Mem Prize, Am Musicol Soc, 67. **MEMBERSHIPS** Am Musicol Soc. **RESEARCH** Early Medieval music, sequences. **SELECTED PUBLICATIONS** Auth, The Service-Books of the Royal-Abbey-Of-Saint-Denis--Images of Ritual and Music in the Middle-Ages, Speculum-Jour Medieval Stud, Vol 0069, 94; Western Plainchant--A Handbook, Speculum-Jour Medieval Stud, Vol 0070, 95; Tropes in Beneventan Chant, Vol 1--Tropes of the Proper of the Mass From Southern Italy, Ad1000-1250, Speculum-Jour Medieval Stud, Vol 0071, 96. **CONTACT ADDRESS** Dept of Music, Univ of Calif, Berkeley, CA, 94720.

CROFTS, DANIEL WALLACE
PERSONAL Born 06/25/1941, m, 1966, 2 children **DISCIPLINE** AMERICAN HISTORY **EDUCATION** Wabash Col, BA, 63; Yale Univ, MA, 64, PhD(hist), 68. **CAREER** Asst prof hist, Dickinson Col, 68-69 & NY Univ, 69-72; lectr hist & Afro-Am studies, Yale Univ, 72-74; ASST PROF HIST, TRENTON STATE COL, 75-, Nat Endownment for Humanities res fel, 74-75. **RESEARCH** Nineteenth century American political and social history. **SELECTED PUBLICATIONS** Auth, The Origins of Southern Sharecropping, Rev(s) Amer Hist, Vol 0023, 95; The Work of Reconstruction--From Slave to Wage Laborer in South-Carolina, 1860-1870, Rev(s) Amer Hist, Vol 0023, 95; Lincolns Loyalists--Union Soldiers from the Confederacy, Jour Amer Hist, Vol 0080, 93; Rayner,Kenneth and Rayner, John,B. and the Limits of Southern Dissent, Amer Hist Rev, Vol 0099, 94; The Confederate-Republic--A Revolution Against Politics, Amer Hist Rev, Vol 0100, 95; Arguing About Slavery--The Great Battle in the United-States-Congress, Rev(s) Amer Hist, Vol 0025, 97. **CONTACT ADDRESS** 1373 Butternut Dr, Southampton, PA, 18966.

CROMLEY, ELIZABETH
PERSONAL NJ, w, 2 children **DISCIPLINE** ART **EDUCATION** Univ Penn, BA, 63; New York Univ, MA, 66; City Univ of New York, PhD, 82 **CAREER** Lectr Art Dept, Bronx Comm Col, 74-75; lectr, Archit & Art Hist, City College, City Univ New York, 72-80; visit assoc prof, Univ Calif Berkeley, 87; asst prof Archit Hist, SUNY, 80-86, assoc prof Archit Hist, SUNY, 86-92; prof Archit Hist, SUNY, 92-96; chair & prof Art & Archit, Northeastern Univ, 97- **HONORS AND AWARDS** Mary Wahington Col Hist Presev Prize, 96; Nat Endowment Humanities Fel, 94; Abbot Lowell Cummings Award, 92; Nat Endowment Humanities Fel, 90-91; Benno Forman Fel, 88 **MEMBERSHIPS** Vernacular Archit Forum; Soc Archit Historians; Amer Studies Assoc **RESEARCH** American Architecture; **SELECTED PUBLICATIONS** Auth, Internal Affairs, a History of American Domestic Space, Cornell, forthcoming; co-ed, Shaping Communities: Pespectives in Vernacular Architecture, Univ Tenn, 97; auth, "The First House," Intersight, 97 **CONTACT ADDRESS** Dept Art & Architecture, Northeastern Univ, 239 Ryder Hall, Boston, MA, 02115. **EMAIL** ecromley@lynx.neu.edu

CROMWELL, WILLIAM C.
DISCIPLINE INTERNATIONAL RELATIONS OF WESTERN EUROPE **EDUCATION** Emory Univ; BA; Am Univ, MA, PhD. **CAREER** Prof, Am Univ. **RESEARCH** Foreign policy of foreign powers. **SELECTED PUBLICATIONS** Auth, The United States and the European Pillar, St. Martin's Press, 92. **CONTACT ADDRESS** American Univ, 4400 Massachusetts Ave, Washington, DC, 20016.

CRONAN ROSE, ELLEN
DISCIPLINE HISTORY **EDUCATION** Univ Mass Amherst, PhD, 74. **CAREER** Prof, Univ Nev Las Vegas. **SELECTED PUBLICATIONS** Auth, pubs on Contemporary Women Writers, particularly Doris Lessing and Margaret Drabble. **CONTACT ADDRESS** History Dept, Univ Nev Las Vegas, 4505 Md Pky, Las Vegas, NV, 89154.

CRONIN, JAMES E.
PERSONAL Born 09/14/1947, Boston, MA, 2 children **DISCIPLINE** COMPARATIVE HISTORY **EDUCATION** Brandeis Univ, PhD, 77. **CAREER** Asst prof, Univ Wis-Milwaukee, 76-80; assoc prof, 80-84; prof, 84-86; prof, Boston Col, 86- ; dept chemn, 92-97; facul assoc, Center for Europ Studies, Harvard Univ, 97- . **HONORS AND AWARDS** NEA fel, 81; German Marshall Fund, 86. **MEMBERSHIPS** Am Hist Asoc; North Am Conf on British Studies. **RESEARCH** Labor history; politics in Great Britain; Cold War. **SELECTED PUBLICATIONS** Auth, Power, Secrecy and the British Constitution: Vetting Samuel Beer's Treasury Control, Twentieth Century British Hist, 92; auth, Neither Exceptional nor Peculiar: Towards the Comparative Study of Labor in Advanced Society, Int Rev of Social Hist, 92; auth, The Historical Margaret Thatcher, The Lady is not for Turning: An Assessment of Margaret Thatcher's Decade in Power, 1979-90, 94; auth, Britain: Steady Hands, Unsteady Course?, Current Hist, 94; auth, The World the Cold War Made: Order, Chaos and the Return of History, 96. **CONTACT ADDRESS** Dept Hist, Boston Col, Chestnut Hill, MA, 02167. **EMAIL** croninj@bc.edu

CROOKS, JAMES BENEDICT
PERSONAL Born 09/27/1933, Paterson, NJ, m, 1958, 2 children **DISCIPLINE** AMERICAN HISTORY **EDUCATION** Yale Univ, BA, 57; Johns Hopkins Univ, MA, 62, PhD(hist), 64. **CAREER** Contract worker, Conn Gen Life Ins Co, 57-59; vis lectr hist, Univ Col, Dublin, 64-66; asst prof & chmn dept, Hollins Col, 66-72; PROF HIST, CHMN DEPT & ASST DEAN COL ARTS & SCI, UNIV N FLA, 72-. **MEMBERSHIPS** AHA; Orgn Am Historians; Am Studies Asn. **RESEARCH** Progressive era in American history; urban history. **SELECTED PUBLICATIONS** Auth, The Promise of Paradise--Recreational and Retirement Communities in the United-States since 1950, Jour Amer Hist, Vol 0082, 95; Florida--A Short History, Jour Amer Hist, Vol 0081, 94; Language Death, Language Genesis, and World-History, Jour World Hist, Vol 0006, 95. **CONTACT ADDRESS** Dept of Hist, Univ of NFla, Jacksonville, FL, 32216.

CROSBY, ALFRED W.
PERSONAL Boston, MA, 1983 children **DISCIPLINE** HISTORY **EDUCATION** AMT Harvard, AB, 56; Berton Univ, PhD, 61 **CAREER** Albion Coll; Ohio St; San Fernando Valley St; Washington St Univ; Univ Texas, 97- **HONORS AND AWARDS** Phi Beta Kappa; bk prize, 1986, AMT Harvard, AB, 56; Berton Univ, PhD, 61 **MEMBERSHIPS** Amer Hist Soc; World Hist Soc; Environ Hist Soc; Amer Acad Arts Sci **RESEARCH** Environmental and World history **SELECTED PUBLICATIONS** Auth, Ecological Imperialism: The Biological Expansion of Europe, 900-1900 **CONTACT ADDRESS** Dept Hist, Univ Texas, Amer Studies, 303 Garris, Austin, TX.

CROSBY, EDWARD WARREN
PERSONAL Born 11/04/1932, Cleveland, OH, m, 1956 **DISCIPLINE** AFRICAN-AMERICAN STUDIES **EDUCATION** Kent State Univ, BA 1957, MA 1959; Univ of KA, PhD 1965. **CAREER** Educ Resources Inst Inc E St Louis, vice pres program devel 1968; Experiment in Higher Educ SIU, dir of educ 1966-69; Inst for African Amer Affairs Kent State Univ, dir 1969-76; Univ of WA, dir Black Studies Program 1976-78; Kent State Univ, assoc prof 1969-94, chm, dept of Pan-African Studies, 1976-94; Network for Educ Devel & Enrichment, Kent OH, vp, 1988-. **HONORS AND AWARDS** Hon Leadership Award Omicron Delta Kappa 1976; Hon mem Alpha Kappa Mu; **MEMBERSHIPS** Resident consult Regional Council on Intl Educ; Faculty Inst on the Black World 1970-72; consult Peat Marwick Mitchell & Co 1971-72; pres NE OH Black Studies Consortium 1974; pres OH Consortium for Black Studies 1980-; former board member, Harriet Tubman, African American Museum 1985-. **SELECTED PUBLICATIONS** Publ The Black Experience, "An Anthology" 1976; published "Chronology of Notable Dates in the History of Africans in the Am & Elsewhere" 1976; publ "The Educ of Black Folk, An Historical Perspective" The Western Journal of Black Studies 1977; publ "The African Experience in Community Devel" Two Vols 1980; Your History, A Chronology of Notable Events 1988. **CONTACT ADDRESS** Kent State Univ, Rm 117, Center of Pan-African Culture, Kent, OH, 44242.

CROSBY, MARGAREE SEAWRIGHT
PERSONAL Born 11/21/1941, Greenville, South Carolina, m, 1963 **DISCIPLINE** EDUCATION **EDUCATION** South Carolina State University, BS, 1963; Clemson University, MEd, 1973; University of Massachusetts/Amerst, EdD, 1976. **CAREER** School District of Greenville County, headstart tchr, summers, 1965, 1966, elementary tchr, 1964-68, reading resource tchr, 1968-74; University of Massachusetts, teaching asst, CUETEP coordinator, 1974-76; University of South Carolina, Spartanburg, asst professor, 1976-77; Clemson University, associate professor, 1977-. **HONORS AND AWARDS** SC Pageant, 1992 SC Women Achievement Award, The First Award, 1992; Fifty Most Influential Black Women of South Carolina, 1992; Greenville News/Hayward Mall, Order of the Jessamine Award, 1991; American Association of University Women, Women in History Who Make a Difference, 1982; Greenville Middle School, Outstanding Educator and Service Award, 1992; Regional Positive Image Award, 1993; International Citizen of the Year, Omega Psi Phi Fraternity Inc, 1994, Cleveland, OH; Appointed Woman of Achievement, South Carolina Governor's Office, 1994. **MEMBERSHIPS** National Association of Black Educators, 1991-; National Association of Black Reading and Language Arts Educators; Greenville Hospital System Board of Trustees, chairperson, nominating committee, 1991-97; Governor's Blue Ribbon Committee on Job Training, 1985; SC Council of International Reading Association, board of directors, chairperson, conf pro comm, 1992; Sunbelt Human Advancement Resources, Project RISE advisory board, 1988-; Clemson University, university self study committee, 1986; Affirmative Action Committee; Elementary Curriculum Committee, chairperson, 1992, department head search committee, 1985, faculty search committee, chairman, 1988. **SELECTED PUBLICATIONS** Groomed and trained over 1500 young men and ladies for presentation to society in Debu-

tante Cotillion, AKA, Beautillion (Jack & Jill), 1968-; trained and developed over 500 AFDC mothers for gainful employment in the hospitality sector, 1984-88; principal investigator, A Survey of Principal Attitudes Toward Ability Grouping/Tracking in the Public School of So St, 1991; coordinator, Multi-Cultural Enhancement Project, 1992; "Cooperative Learning," "Alternatives to Tracking and Ability Grouping," Natl Council for Teachers of English and the Natl Dropout Prevention Center. **CONTACT ADDRESS** College of Education, Tillman Hall, Clemson Univ, PO Box 340709, Clemson, SC, 29634-0001.

CROSBY, TRAVIS L.
DISCIPLINE BRITISH HISTORY; MODERN EUROPEAN HISTORY **EDUCATION** Univ Tex, BA; Johns Hopkins Univ; PhD. **CAREER** Hist, Wheaton Col. **RESEARCH** Psychological studies of British politicians. **SELECTED PUBLICATIONS** Auth, Two Mr. Gladstones: A Study in Psychology and History, Yale UP, 97. **CONTACT ADDRESS** Dept of Hist, Wheaton Col, 26 East Main St, Norton, MA, 02766. **EMAIL** tcrosby@wheatonma.edu

CROSS, DOLORES E.
PERSONAL Born 08/29/1938, Newark, NJ, d **DISCIPLINE** EDUCATION **EDUCATION** Seton Hall University, South Orange Newark, NJ, BS, 1963; Hofstra University, Hempstead, NY, MS 1968; The University of Michigan, Ann Arbor, MI, PhD, 1971. **CAREER** Northwestern University, Evanston, IL, assistant professor in education & director of master of arts in teaching, 1970-74; Claremont Graduate School, Claremont CA, assoc prof in education & dir of teacher education, 1974-78; City University of New York, New York, NY, vice chancellor for student aff & spec programs, 1978-81; New York State Higher Education Service Corp, Albany, NY, president, 1981-88; University of Minnesota, Minneapolis, MN, associate provost & assoc vice pres for acad affairs, 1988-90; Chicago State University, Chicago, IL, president, 1990-97; MORRIS BROWN COLLEGE, PRESIDENT, 1998-. **HONORS AND AWARDS** Honorary Doctorate of Law, Skidmore College, 1988; Honorary Doctorate of Law, Marymount Manhattan, 1984; John Jay Award, New York State Commission of Independent Colleges and Universities, 1989; NAACP, Muriel Silverberg Award, New York, 1987; Honorary Doctorate, Hofstra University, Elmhurst College. **MEMBERSHIPS** Member, Women Executives in State Government; advisory board member, Assn of Black Women in Higher Education; member, NAACP; member, American Educational Research Assn, 1990-; vice chr, American Association for Higher Education; vice chr, Campus Compact, Senior Consultant South Africa Project. **CONTACT ADDRESS** The GE Fund, 3135 Easton Turnpike, Fairfield, CT, 06431.

CROSS, GARY
DISCIPLINE HISTORY **EDUCATION** Wahs State Univ, BA, 68; Harvard, MDiv, 73; Univ Wis, PhD, 77. **CAREER** PROF HIST, PA STATE, 90. **CONTACT ADDRESS** Dept of History, Pennsylvania State Univ, University Park, PA, 16802. **EMAIL** gsc2@psu.edu

CROSS, MICHAEL SEAN
PERSONAL Born 10/14/1938, Toronto, ON, Canada **DISCIPLINE** CANADIAN HISTORY **EDUCATION** Univ Toronto, BA, 60, MA, 61, PhD(Can hist),68. **CAREER** Asst prof hist, Univ Calgary, 64-66; asst prof, Carleton Univ, 66-68; from asst prof to assoc prof, Univ Toronto, 68-75, managing ed, Can Forum, 73-75; chmn dept, 78-80, PROF HIST, DALHOUSIE UNIV, 75-, Assoc ed, Can Hist Rev, 68-72, ed, 73-77; dean men, Victoria Univ, 69-73; Can Coun Leave fel, 72-73; gen ed, Champlain Soc, 72-75 & Social Hist Can Ser, 72-; Can Coun res grant, 77-78; Dalhousie Univ res grant, 80-81. **MEMBERSHIPS** Can Hist Asn. **RESEARCH** Canadian social history; history of violence in Canada. **SELECTED PUBLICATIONS** Auth, The Upper Ottawa-Valley to 1855, Can Hist Rev, Vol 0073, 92. **CONTACT ADDRESS** Dept of Hist, Dalhousie Univ, Halifax, NS, B3H 3J5.

CROSS, ROBERT DOUGHERTY
PERSONAL Born 01/21/1924, Grinnel, IA, m, 1951, 2 children **DISCIPLINE** HISTORY **EDUCATION** Harvard Univ, AB, 47, AM, 51, PhD(hist), 55. **CAREER** From instr to asst prof hist, Swarthmore Col, 52-59; assoc prof, Columbia Univ, 59-64, prof & chmn dept, 64-67; prof hist & pres, Hunter Col, 67-69; pres, Swarthmore Col, 69-72; dean fac arts & sci, 72-74, PROF HIST, 72-, ASST DEAN ARTS & SCI, 81-. **HONORS AND AWARDS** DHL, Villanova Univ, 68 & St Mary's Univ, Md, 71; LLD, Univ, Pa, 70. **MEMBERSHIPS** AHA; Am Studies Asn. **RESEARCH** American church history; social history of the 20th century; immigration history. **SELECTED PUBLICATIONS** Auth, Critics on Trial--An Introduction to the Catholic Modernist Crisis, Amer Hist Rev, Vol 0101, 96; Church and Age Unite--The Modernist Impulse in American-Catholicism, Amer Hist Rev, Vol 0098, 93. **CONTACT ADDRESS** Univ of Va, 218 Randall Hall, Charlottesville, VA, 22903.

CROSTHWAITE, JANE FREEMAN
PERSONAL Born 11/07/1936, Salisbury, NC, m, 1964 **DISCIPLINE** AMERICAN RELIGIOUS HISTORY **EDUCATION** Wake Forest Univ, BA, 59; Duke Univ, MA, 62, PhD(relig), 72. **CAREER** Asst dean women & instr philos, Wake Forest Univ, 62-64; head corp rec, Harvard Bus Sch Libr, 64-65q instr English, Queens Col, NC, 69-72, registr, 72-74, assoc prof relig, 74-76; lectr philos & relig, Univ NC, Charlotte, 76-79; ASST PROF RELIG, MOUNT HOLYOKE COL, 79-. **MEMBERSHIPS** Am Acad Relig; MLA; Church Hist Soc. **RESEARCH** American religious history; Emily Dickinson; women in American religion. **SELECTED PUBLICATIONS** Auth, Spiritual Spectacles--Vision and Image in Mid-19th-Century Shakerism, Jour Interdisciplinary Hist, Vol 0026, 95; The Carmelite Adventure--Dickinson, Clare,Joseph Journal of the Trip To America and Other Documents, Church Hist, Vol 0063, 94. **CONTACT ADDRESS** Dept of Relig, Mount Holyoke Col, 50 College St, South Hadley, MA, 01075-1461.

CROUCH, DORA POLK
PERSONAL Born 02/15/1931, Ann Arbor, MI, 7 children **DISCIPLINE** ARCHITECTURAL AND URBAN HISTORY **EDUCATION** Univ Calif, Los Angeles, BA & MA, 65, PhD(art hist), 67. **CAREER** Asst prof art hist, San Francisco State Univ, 69-70; vis asst prof archit hist, Univ Calif, Berkeley, 70-71; lectr art hist, Univ Calif, Los Angeles, 71-72; asst prof, Calif State Univ, Dominguez Hills, 72-75; ASSOC PROF ARCHIT HIST, RENSSELAER POLYTECH INST, 75-, Ed newslett, Soc Archit Historians, 77-80; fel, Ctr Advan Study, Nat Gallery Art, 80-81. **MEMBERSHIPS** Soc Archit Historians; Col Art Asn; Am Inst Archeol. **RESEARCH** Urban history especially Spanish colonial; ancient Greek water systems; Palmyra. **SELECTED PUBLICATIONS** Auth, Geological Differences in Ancient Water-Supply--Syracuse and Agrigento, Amer Jour Archaeol, Vol 0101, 97. **CONTACT ADDRESS** Sch of Archit, Rensselaer Polytech Inst, Troy, NY, 12181.

CROUCH, TOM DAY
PERSONAL Born 02/28/1944, Dayton, OH, m, 1963, 3 children **DISCIPLINE** AMERICAN HISTORY, HISTORY OF TECHNOLOGY **EDUCATION** Ohio Univ, BA, 66; Miami Univ, MA, 68; Ohio State Univ, PhD(hist), 76. **CAREER** Dir educ, Ohio Hist Soc, 69-70; dir, Ohio Am Revolution Bicentennial Comn, Ohio Hist Soc, 72-74; CUR AERONAUT, NAT AIR & SPACE MUS, SMITHSONIAN INST, 74-, Adj prof, Dept Hist, Univ Md, 76-; mem, Am Inst Aeronaut & Astronaut Hist Comt, 76-; Distinguished Lectr, Am Inst Aeronaut & Astronaut, 78-79. **HONORS AND AWARDS** Hist Award, Am Inst Aeronaut & Astronaut, 76. **RESEARCH** History of technology; history of aeronautics; United States social and cultural history. **SELECTED PUBLICATIONS** Auth, The Dream Machines--An Illustrated History of the Spaceship in Art, Science and Literature, Tech and Cult, Vol 0035, 94; Local Hero--Montgomery, John, Joseph and the First Winged Flight in America, Jour W, Vol 0036, 97; The Dream Machines--An Illustrated History of the Spaceship in Art, Science and Literature, Tech and Cult, Vol 0035, 94; Triumph at Kitty-Hawk--The Wright Brothers and Powered Flight, Pub Historian, Vol 0017, 95. **CONTACT ADDRESS** Aeronautics Dept Natl Air and Sp, Smithsonian Inst, Washington, DC, 20560.

CROUSE, MAURICE ALFRED
PERSONAL Born 02/15/1934, Lincolnton, NC, m, 1958, 3 children **DISCIPLINE** AMERICAN COLONIAL HISTORY **EDUCATION** Davidson Col, BS, 56; Northwestern Univ, MA, 57, PhD(hist), 64. **CAREER** Asst Am hist, Northwestern Univ, 60-61; from asst prof to assoc prof, 62-72, PROF HIST, MEMPHIS STATE UNIV, 72-. **MEMBERSHIPS** AHA; Orgn Am Historians. **RESEARCH** Provincial South Carolina; early American civilization; methods of historical research. **SELECTED PUBLICATIONS** Auth, A Quest for Glory--Major General Robert Howe and the American-Revolution, NY Hist, Vol 0074, 93. **CONTACT ADDRESS** 1595 Wheaton St, Memphis, TN, 38117.

CROUTER, RICHARD
PERSONAL Born 11/02/1937, Washington, DC, m, 1960, 2 children **DISCIPLINE** HISTORY OF THEOLOGY **EDUCATION** Occidental Col, AB, 60; Union Theol Sem, BD, 63, ThD, 68. **CAREER** From instr to asst prof 67-73, assoc prof, 73-79, prof relig, Carleton Col, 79-, John M. and Elizabeth Musser Prof of Religious Studies, 97-, Univ Toronto, 72-73; Am Coun Learned Soc fel, 76-77; sr Fulbright scholar, Univ Marburg, 76-77, 91-92. **MEMBERSHIPS** Am Soc Church Hist; Am Acad Relig; Hegel Soc Am. **RESEARCH** History of Christian thought; Schleiermacher, Hegel, Kierkegaard. **SELECTED PUBLICATIONS** Auth, Michael Novak and the study of religion, J Am Acad Relig, 3/72; H Richard Niebuhr and stoicism, J Relig Ethics, 2/74; Hegel and Schleiermacher at Berlin: A many-sided debate, J Am Acad Relig, 3/80; Rhetoric and substance in Schleiermacher's revision of The Christian Faith, 1821-1822, J Relig, 7/80; ed and trans, Friedrich Schleiermacher, On Religion: Speeches to its Cultured Despisers, Cambridge: Cambridge Univ Press, 88, 96. **CONTACT ADDRESS** Dept of Relig, Carleton Col, 1 N College St, Northfield, MN, 55057-4044. **EMAIL** rcrouter@carleton.edu

CROUTHAMEL, JAMES L.
PERSONAL Born 01/29/1931, Lansdale, PA, 3 children **DISCIPLINE** AMERICAN HISTORY **EDUCATION** Franklin & Marshall Col, BA, 52; Univ Rochester, PhD, 58. **CAREER** Instr hist, Ill Col, 56-58 & Pa State Univ, 58-60; from asst prof to assoc prof, 60-69, PROF HIST, HOBART & WILLIAM SMITH COLS, 69-. **MEMBERSHIPS** Orgn Am Historians; Southern Hist Asn; Soc Hist Early Am Repub. **RESEARCH** History of newspapers; American politics, 1828-1860; history of New York. **SELECTED PUBLICATIONS** Auth, The Astonishing Scripps--The Turbulent Life of America Lord,Penny,Press, Jour Amer Hist, Vol 0080, 93; Gentleman of the Press--The Life and Times of an Early Reporter, Ralph,Julian of the Sun, NY Hist, Vol 0073, 92; Buchanan,James and the Political Crisis of the 1850s, NY Hist, Vol 0077, 96; The Sun Shines for All--Journalism and Ideology in the Life of Dana,Charles,A., NY Hist, Vol 0075, 94; Froth and Scum--Truth, Beauty, Goodness and the Ax Murder in America 1st Mass Medium, NY Hist, Vol 0075, 94. **CONTACT ADDRESS** Dept of Hist, Hobart & William Smith Cols, Geneva, NY, 14456.

CROUTHER, BETTY JEAN
PERSONAL Born 03/02/1950, Carthage, Mississippi, d **DISCIPLINE** ART **EDUCATION** Jackson State Univ, BS (Summa Cum Laude) 1972; Univ of MS, MFA 1975; Univ of MO Columbia, PhD 1985. **CAREER** Lincoln Univ, asst prof of art 1978-80; Jackson State Univ, asst prof of art 1980-83; Univ of MS, assoc prof of art history 1983-. **HONORS AND AWARDS** University of Missouri, Superior Graduate Achievement Award, 1985; Stanford University, J Paul Getty Postdoctoral Fellowship, 1986; participant in Fulbright Group Studies program, India, 1989; Southeastern Coll Art Conference, Award for Excellence in Teaching, 1994. **MEMBERSHIPS** College Art Assn; Southeastern College Art Conference; Natl Art Ed Assn; MS Art Ed Assn; Phi Kappa Phi Honor Society; Kappa Pi International Honorary Art Fraternity; Pi Delta Phi Honorary Fraternity; University of Mississippi, University Museum, friends of the museum. **SELECTED PUBLICATIONS** Juried exhibition, "Images '84," The Mississippi Pavilion, Louisiana World Exposition, 1984; contributor, exhibition catalogue "Dean Cornwell, Painter As Illustrator," Museum of Art and Archaeology Univ of MO-Columbia 1978; co-moderator with Dr Joanne V Hawks in enrichment program "Uniting Generations Together/The Search for Meaning," 1984; author, "Deciphering the Mississippi River Iconography of Frederick Oakes Sylvester," MUSE, vol 20, pp 81-9, 1986; reader for Jacob K Javit's Fellowship Fund, U S Department of Education 1989-90; invited papers: "Diversity in Afro-American Art," University of Missouri, Columbia, 1990; "Iconography of a Henry Gudgell Walking Stick," Southeastern College Art Conference, Memphis, 1991; "Iconography in the Art of Contemporary African-Americans: Lawrence A Jones and Roger Rice," James A Porter Colloquium, Howard University, 1992; "Marriage and Social Aspiration in the Art of Rembrandt," Mississippi Museum of Art, 1992; "Images of Peace and African Heritage in the Art of Lawrence A Jones," Southeastern College Art Conference, Birmingham, AL, 1992; Betty J Crouther, "Iconography of a Henry Gudgell Walking Stick," SECAC REVIEW, p 187-91, 1993; Southeastern College Art Conference, New Orleans, LA, "The Hand as a Symbol for African American Artists," 1994. **CONTACT ADDRESS** Univ of Mississippi, University, MS, 38677.

CROW, JEFFREY JAY
PERSONAL Born 05/29/1947, Akron, OH, m, 1979, 1 child **DISCIPLINE** AMERICAN HISTORY **EDUCATION** Ohio State Univ, BA, 69; Univ Akron, MA, 72; Duke Univ, PhD(hist), 74. **CAREER** Historian, NC Bicentennial Comt, NC Div Archives & Hist, 74-76; hist publ ed, 76-82, ADMINR, DIV ARCHIVES & HIST, HIST PUBL SECT, NC, 82-. **HONORS AND AWARDS** Best article in 1980 award, William & Mary Quart, 81. **MEMBERSHIPS** Orgn Am Historians; Southern Hist Asn. **RESEARCH** Colonial and revolutionary South; Afro-American history; New South. **SELECTED PUBLICATIONS** Auth, Settle,Thomas Jr, Reconstruction, and the Memory of the Civil-War, Jour So Hist, Vol 0062, 96; Tyron,Willian and the Course of Empire--A Life in British Imperial Service, William and Mary Quart, Vol 0050, 93. **CONTACT ADDRESS** 129 Bonnell Ct, Cary, NC, 27511.

CROWDER, CHRISTOPHER M. D.
PERSONAL Born 09/26/1922, Weybridge, England, m, 1951, 3 children **DISCIPLINE** MEDIEVAL HISTORY **EDUCATION** Oxford Univ, BA & MA, 48, DPhil, 53. **CAREER** Asst hist, Aberdeen Univ, 50-53; lectr, Queen's Univ, Belfast, 53-66; assoc prof, 66-69, assoc dean grad studies, 76-80, PROF HIST, QUEEN'S UNIV, ONT, 69-, Vis mem, Inst Adv Study, Princeton Univ, 80-81. **MEMBERSHIPS** Fel Royal Hist Soc; Ecclesiastical Hist Soc; Medieval Acad Am. **RESEARCH** Conciliar history of late Middle Ages; Papal administration in the fifteenth century. **SELECTED PUBLICATIONS** Auth, The History of Christianity from Its Origins to the Present, Vol 6--A Time of Trials 1274-1449--French, Speculum-Jour Medieval Stud, Vol 0068, 93; The Reforms of the Council-of-Constance 1414-1418, Jour Ecclesiastical Hist, Vol 0046, 95; Nicholas-Of-Cusa--The Catholic Concordance, Jour Ecclesiastical Hist, Vol 0048, 97; The Reforms of the Council-Of-Constance 1414-

1418, Jour Ecclesiastical Hist, Vol 0046, 95. **CONTACT ADDRESS** Dept of Hist, Queen's Univ, Kingston, ON, K7L 3N6.

CROWE, DAVID M.
DISCIPLINE HISTORY **EDUCATION** Univ Georgia, PhD, 74. **CAREER** Prof, 77-, Elon Col. **CONTACT ADDRESS** Dept of History, Elon Col, 3505 Henderson Rd, Greensboro, NC, 27410. **EMAIL** crowed@numen.elon.edu

CROWE, MICHAEL J.
DISCIPLINE HISTORY **EDUCATION** Univ Notre Dame, BS, 58; Univ Wis, PhD, 65. **CAREER** Prof. **RESEARCH** History of astronomy; physics and mathematics. **SELECTED PUBLICATIONS** Auth, Modern Theories of the Universe from Herschel to Hubble, 94; The Extraterrestrial Life Debate and Nineteenth-century Religion, 94; A History of the Extraterrestrial Life Debate, 97; Extraterrestrial Intelligence, 97. **CONTACT ADDRESS** History and Philosophy of Science Dept, Univ of Notre Dame, Notre Dame, IN, 46556. **EMAIL** Michael.J.Crowe.1@nd.edu

CRUIKSHANK, KENNETH
DISCIPLINE HISTORY **EDUCATION** Carleton Univ, BA; York Univ, MA, PhD. **RESEARCH** Hist of business; development of the administrative state in Canada and the United States. **SELECTED PUBLICATIONS** Auth, Close Ties: Railways, Government and the Board of Railway Commissioners, 1851-1933. **CONTACT ADDRESS** History Dept, McMaster Univ, 1280 Main St W, Hamilton, ON, L8S 4L9.

CRUMBLEY, DEIDRE H.
PERSONAL Born 12/12/1947, Philadelphia, PA, s **DISCIPLINE** ANTHROPOLOGY: RELIGION & CULTURE **EDUCATION** Temple Univ, BA, 70; North Western, MA, 84, PhD, 89; Harvard, MTS. **CAREER** Jr res fel, 82-84, African Studies Dept; Univ of Ibadan Nigeria West Africa, 82-86; jr lectr, 84-86, Arecheology & Anthropology; Rollins Col, 88-91, Anthropology; Univ FL, Anthropology, 91-98; asst prof, 98, NC State Univ, Africana Studies, Multidisciplinary Studies Div. **HONORS AND AWARDS** Lilly Fel, 79; Fuebrigher Hays, 85; Ford Post doc fel, 91. **MEMBERSHIPS** Amer Anthropological Assn; Amer Acad Religion; **RESEARCH** Religion and change in Africa and the African disapora **SELECTED PUBLICATIONS** Auth, West African Journal of Archeology & Anthropology, vol 16, Ibadan, Nigeria, 88; Impurity and Power: Women in Aladura churches, Africa, 92; Even a Woman: Sex Roles and Mobility in an Aldura Hierarchy, Sept 14, 1998 **CONTACT ADDRESS** Africana Studies/Div of Multidisciplinary Studies, No Carolina State Univ, Raleigh, NC, 27695-7107. **EMAIL** deidre_crumbley@ncsu.edu

CRUMMEY, DONALD E.
DISCIPLINE HISTORY **EDUCATION** Univ London, PhD, 67. **CAREER** Prof, Univ Ill Urbana Champaign **RESEARCH** History of east and southern Africa since the eighteenth century. **SELECTED PUBLICATIONS** Auth, Abyssinian Feudalism?, 80; Family and Property Amongst the Amhara Nobility, J African Hist, 83; Banditry, Rebellion, and Social Protest in Africa, James Currey and Heinemann Edu Bk, 86. **CONTACT ADDRESS** History Dept, Univ Ill Urbana Champaign, 52 E Gregory Dr, Champaign, IL, 61820. **EMAIL** dcrummey@uiuc.edu

CRUMMEY, ROBERT OWEN
PERSONAL Born 04/12/1936, New Glasgow, NS, Canada, m, 1980 **DISCIPLINE** RUSSIAN HISTORY **EDUCATION** Univ Toronto, BA, 58; Univ Chicago, PhD(hist), 64. **CAREER** Asst prof hist, Univ Ill, 64-65; from asst prof to assoc prof hist, Yale Univ, 65-74; assoc prof, 74-79, PROF HIST, UNIV CALIF, DAVIS, 79-. **MEMBERSHIPS** Am Asn Advan Slavic Studies. **RESEARCH** Russian history of the 16th and 17th centuries, especially institutional and social history. **SELECTED PUBLICATIONS** Auth, Sources of Boyar Power in the 17th-Century--The Descendants of the Upper Oka Serving Princes, Cahiers du Monde Russe, Vol 0034, 93; The Reforms of Peter-The-Great--Progress Through Coercion in Russia, Amer Hist Rev, Vol 0099, 94; Old-Belief as Popular Religion--New Approaches, Slavic Rev, Vol 0052, 93. **CONTACT ADDRESS** Dept of Hist, Univ of Calif, Davis, CA, 95616.

CRUMP, GAIL BRUCE
PERSONAL Born 04/05/1942, Kirksville, MO **DISCIPLINE** MODERN BRITISH & AMERICAN LITERATURE **EDUCATION** NE Mo State Col, BA & BSEd, 64; Univ Ark, Fayetteville, MA, 65, PhD(English), 69. **CAREER** Asst prof, 69-76, assoc prof to prof English, Cent Mo State Univ, 76-. **HONORS AND AWARDS** Nat Endowment for Humanities jr scholars grant, 76. **MEMBERSHIPS** MLA; AAUP; D H Lawrence Soc NAm; Soc Study Midwestern Lit; NCTE; Western Lit Asn; Popular Cult Asn. **RESEARCH** Modern British and American fiction; modern drama; literature and film. **SELECTED PUBLICATIONS** Ed, Doctoral dissertations on D H Lawrence, 1931-1968: A bibliography, 70, auth, Gopher Prairie Or papplewick? The Virgin and the Gipsy, as Film, 71 & Women in Love: Novel and Film, 71, D H Lawrence Rev; Wright Morris's One Day, Mid America, 76; D H Lawrence and the Immediate Present, D H Lawrence Rev, 77; The Novels of Wright Morris, Univ Nebr, 78; The Universe as Murder Mystery: Tom Stoppard's Jumpers, Contemp Lit, 79; auth, Transformations of Reality in R. M. Koster's Tinieblan Novels, Critique, 83; Art and Experience in Stoppard's The Real Thing, In: Tom Stoppard: A Casebook, 88; Lawrence's Rainbow and and Russell's Rainbow, D H Lawrence Rev, 89; Wright Morris: Author in Hiding, Western Am Lit, 90. **CONTACT ADDRESS** Dept of English, Central Missouri State Univ, Warrensburg, MO, 64093-8888. **EMAIL** gbc8696@cmsu2.cmsu.edu

CRUMP, GARY ALLEN
PERSONAL Born 04/05/1942, Kirksville, MO, m, 1972 **DISCIPLINE** GREEK & ROMAN HISTORY **EDUCATION** Northeast Mo State Teachers Col, BS & AB, 64; Univ Ill, Urbana, MA, 66, PhD(class hist), 69. **CAREER** Asst prof, 68-75, assoc prof hist, State Univ, Baton Rouge, 75-97. **MEMBERSHIPS** AHA; Soc Promotion Roman Studies; Am Asn Ancient Historians. **RESEARCH** Late Roman military history; Roman imperial propaganda. **SELECTED PUBLICATIONS** Auth, Ammianus and the late Roman army, Historia, 73; Ammianus Marcellinus as a military historian, Historia Einzelschriften, 75.

CRUNDEN, ROBERT M.
PERSONAL Born 12/23/1940, Jersey City, NJ, d, 3 children **DISCIPLINE** HISTORY **EDUCATION** Yale Col, BA (magna cum laude), 62; Harvard Univ, PhD, 67. **CAREER** ASST PROF TO FULL PROF, UNIV OF TEX AT AUSTIN, 67-; bicentennial prof of Am Studies, Univ of Helsinki, 76-77 & 91-92; sr fulbright lectr in hist, La Trobe Univ, 78; vis prof of English, Wuerzburg Univ, 79 & 82; dir, Am Studies Res Centre, Hyderabad, India, 82-84. **HONORS AND AWARDS** H.G. Porthan Prize, Finnish Hist Asn, 91; Western Hist Asn Awd for best essay, 70; Ohioana Awd for best bio, 69. **MEMBERSHIPS** Finnish Acad; Am Hist Asn; Org of Am Historians; Fin Hist Soc. **RESEARCH** American culture 1885-1941, especially in the arts and letters. **SELECTED PUBLICATIONS** Auth, American Salons: Encounters with European Modernism, 1885-1917, Oxford Univ Press, 93; A Brief History of American Culture, Finnish Historical Soc, 90, Paragon House, 94; Ministers of Reform: The Progressives' Achievement in American Civilization, 1889-1920, Basic Books, 82, Univ of Ill Press, 84; ed, Traffic of Ideas between India and America, South Asia Books, 85; coed, New Perspectives on America and South Asia, South Asia Books, 84. **CONTACT ADDRESS** Hist Dept, Univ of Texas, Austin, TX, 78712. **EMAIL** rmcrunden@mail.utexas.edu

CRUZ TAURA, GRACIELLA
DISCIPLINE HISTORY **EDUCATION** Univ Miami, PhD. **CAREER** Assoc prof. **MEMBERSHIPS** Am Hist Asn; Cuban Studies Asn; Latin Am Studies Asn. **RESEARCH** Latin American intellectual history; Cuban and Cuban American Studies; women's history. **SELECTED PUBLICATIONS** Auth, Annexation and National Identity: The Issues of Cuba's Mid-Nineteenth Century Debate, 97; Women's Rights and the Cuban Constitution of 1940, 94; co-ed, Outside Cuba/Fuera de Cuba: Contemporary Cuban Visual Artists, 89. **CONTACT ADDRESS** History Dept, Florida Atlantic Univ, 777 Glades Rd, Boca Raton, FL, 33431. **EMAIL** rinaldi@acc.fau.edu

CSIKSZENTMIHALYI, MIHALY
PERSONAL Born 09/29/1934, Fivme, Italy, m, 1961, 2 children **DISCIPLINE** PSYCHOLOGY **EDUCATION** Univ Chicago, PhD, 64. **CAREER** Chr Dept Sociology & Anthropology, Lake Forest, IL, 64-69; PROF & CHR, DEPT PSYCHOLOGY, UNIV CHICAGO, 70-; fel, Am Acad Art Sci, Am Acad Educ, Hungarian Acad Sci. **RESEARCH** Psychology of creativity; Enjoyment; Cultural evolution. **SELECTED PUBLICATIONS** Flow=The Psychology of Optimal Experience, 90; The Evolving Self, 93; Creativity, 96; Finding Flow, 97. **CONTACT ADDRESS** Dept of Psychology, Univ Chicago, 5848 S Univ Ave, Chicago, IL, 60637. **EMAIL** miska@ccp.uchicago.edu

CUDJOE, SELWYN REGINALD
PERSONAL Born 12/01/1943, s **DISCIPLINE** AFRICAN STUDIES **EDUCATION** Fordham Univ, BA 1969, MA 1972; Cornell Univ, PhD 1976. **CAREER** Fordham Univ, instructor 1970-72; Ithaca Coll, adjunct asst prof 1973-75; Ohio Univ, assoc prof 1975-76; Harvard Univ, asst prof 1976-81; Wellesley Coll, Marion Butler McLean, Professor in the History of Ideas, prof, African studies. **HONORS AND AWARDS** NEH Fellowship, 1991-92, 1997-98; American Council of Learned Societies Fellowship 1991-92; Senior Fellow, Society for the Humanities, Cornell University 1992; Visiting Fellow, WEB DuBois Institute for African-American Research, Harvard University 1991; Visiting Scholar, African-American Studies Department, Harvard University 1992-97. **SELECTED PUBLICATIONS** Resistance and Caribbean Literature, Ohio Univ Press 1980; Movement of the People Calaloux, 1983; A Just and Moral Society Calaloux, 1984; VS Naipaul: A Materialist Reading, Univ of Mass Press, 1988; Caribbean Women Writers: Essays from the First International Conference, Calaloux & University of Mass Press, 1990; ed, Eric E Wiilliams Speaks, 1993; co-ed, CLR James: His Intellectual Legacies, 1995; ed, Maxwell Philip, EmmanueL Appadocca, Univ of Massachusetts, 1997. **CONTACT ADDRESS** Africana Studies, Wellesley Col, Wellesley, MA, 02181.

CUFF, ROBERT DENNIS
PERSONAL Born 05/02/1941, Peterborough, ON, Canada, m, 1964, 3 children **DISCIPLINE** MODERN AMERICAN HISTORY **EDUCATION** Univ Toronto, BA, 63; Princeton Univ, PhD(hist), 66. **CAREER** Instr Am hist, Princeton Univ, 66-67; asst prof mod Am hist, Univ Rochester, 67-69; from asst prof to assoc prof Am hist, 69-78; PROF HIST, YORK UNIV, 78-, Mem adv bd, Bus Hist Rev, 71-74; Killam sr res fel, 73; fel, Charles Warren Ctr, Harvard Univ, 73-74; vis fel hist, Johns Hopkins Univ, 77-78; Quest scholar, Woodrow Wilson Int Ctr, 82. **HONORS AND AWARDS** Newcomen Award, 70. **MEMBERSHIPS** Orgn Am Historians; Can Hist Asn; Can Asn Am Studies. **RESEARCH** Business-government relations; public policy; Canadian-American relations. **SELECTED PUBLICATIONS** Auth, The Development of Postwar Canadian Trade-Policy--The Failure of the Anglo-European Option, Intl Hist Rev, Vol 0016, 94; The Wilson Administration and the Shipbuilding Crisis of 1917--Steel Ships and Wooden Steamers, Pacific Northwest Quart, Vol 0084, 93; From the Outside in--World-War-II and the American State, Intl Hist Rev, Vol 0019, 97. **CONTACT ADDRESS** Dept of Hist, York Univ, 4700 Keele St, Downsview, ON, L3J 1P3.

CUFFEY, KENNETH H.
PERSONAL Born 04/21/1956, Bloomington, IN, m, 1980, 4 children **DISCIPLINE** BIBLICAL STUDIES, OLD TESTAMENT **EDUCATION** Drew Univ, PhD, 87. **CAREER** Coll pastor, Ind, 81-83; adj fac, Trinity Divinity School, 87-94; Alliance Theol Sem, 87-94; Drew Univ, 87-94; pastor, Wyckoff NJ, 88-94; Scholar, Dir, Christian Studies Center, Ill, 94-. **MEMBERSHIPS** Soc of Bibl Lit; Inst for Bibl Res. **RESEARCH** Coherence in Old Testament/Hebrew Bible Book; Hebrew Wisdom Literature. **CONTACT ADDRESS** 1711 S Vine St, Urbana, IL, 61801-5831. **EMAIL** klcuffey80@aol.com

CULBERT, DAVID H.
PERSONAL Born 07/07/1943, San Antonio, TX, m, 1979 **DISCIPLINE** AMERICAN HISTORY **EDUCATION** Oberlin Col, BA, 66; Oberlin Conservatory of Music, BMus, 66; Northwestern Univ, PhD, 70. **CAREER** Asst Prof, Yale Univ, 70-71; Asst Prof to Prof, La State Univ, 71-. **HONORS AND AWARDS** NDEA Title IV Fellow, MidWestern, 66-70; Phi Beta Kappa; Pi Kappa Lambda; Fellow, Wilson Ctr for Sch, Smithsonian, 76-77; Nat Hum Inst, Yale Univ, 77-78; Kellogg Nat Fellow, 81-84; Vis Fellow, Inst for Adv Stud, Princeton, 95. **MEMBERSHIPS** Am Hist Asn; Org Am Hist; IAMHIST; SHAFR; ASA. **RESEARCH** Mass media & propaganda. **SELECTED PUBLICATIONS** Auth, News for Everyman: Radio and Foreign Affairs in Thirties America, Greenwood Press, 76; auth, Mission to Moscow, Univ Wisc Press, 80; ed-in-chief, Film and Propaganda in America: A Documentary History, 5 vols, Greenwood Press, 90-93; co-ed, World War II: Film and History, Oxford Univ Press, 96; ed, Historical Journal of Film, Radio, and Television, Oxford Univ Press, 92-; auth, Television's Visual Impact on Decision-making in the USA, 1968, J of Contemp Hist, vol 33, no 3, 419-50, 7/98. **CONTACT ADDRESS** Dept of Hist, Louisiana State Univ, Baton Rouge, LA, 70803. **EMAIL** culbert@whfleming.hist.lsu.edu

CULHAM, PHYLLIS
PERSONAL Born 06/22/1948, Junction City, KS, m, 1969, 1 child **DISCIPLINE** ANCIENT HISTORY, CLASSICAL LITERATURE **EDUCATION** Univ Kans, BA, 70; State Univ NY Buffalo, MA, 72, PhD, 76. **CAREER** Lectr classics, Univ Calif, Irvine, 75-77; asst prof hist, Univ Ill, Chicago, 77-79; from Asst Prof to Assoc Prof, 79-91, prof hist, US Naval Acad, 91-. **HONORS AND AWARDS** NEH Curriculum Grant, 94. **MEMBERSHIPS** Asn Ancient Historians; Am Philol Asn. **RESEARCH** Roman bureaucratic history; Latin epigraphy. **SELECTED PUBLICATIONS** Auth, Classics: A Discipline and Profession in Crisis, 89; Seneca's on Favors, 95. **CONTACT ADDRESS** Dept of Hist, US Naval Acad, Annapolis, MD, 21402. **EMAIL** culham@nadn.navy.mil

CULLEY, JOHN JOEL
PERSONAL Born 11/13/1938, Clovis, NM **DISCIPLINE** AMERICAN HISTORY **EDUCATION** Univ NMex, BA, 61, MA, 62; Univ Va, PhD(hist), 67. **CAREER** Teaching asst, Univ Va, 63-65 & 66-67; asst prof, 67-72, ASSOC PROF US HIST, WEST TEX STATE UNIV, 72-. **MEMBERSHIPS** Southern Hist Asn; Orgn Am Historians; Western Hist Asn. **RESEARCH** Recent United States history; United States cultural & social; southern history. **SELECTED PUBLICATIONS** Auth, A Troublesome Presence--World-War-II Internment of German Sailors in New-Mexico, Prologue-Quart National Archv, Vol 0028, 96; Plains Farmer--The Diary of Deloach, William,G. 1914-1964, Jour So Hist, Vol 0059, 93. **CONTACT ADDRESS** Dept of Hist, West Texas A&M Univ, 2501 4th Ave, Canyon, TX, 79016-0001.

CUMINGS, BRUCE
PERSONAL Rochester, NY, m, 3 children **DISCIPLINE** POLITICAL SCIENCE **EDUCATION** Columbia Univ, PhD, 75. **CAREER** Asst prof, polit sci, Swarthmore Col, 75-77; Assoc prof, prof, int stud, Univ Washington, 77-87; prof East Asian and int hist, Univ Chicago, 87-94; John Evans Prof Int Hist and Polit, Northwestern Univ, 94-97; Norman and Edna Freehling

Prof, hist, Univ Chicago, 97-. **HONORS AND AWARDS** John Fairbank Book Award, Am Hist Asn, 83; Quincy Wright Book Award, Int Stud Asn, 92., Principal hist consult, Thames Television/PBS documentary, Korea: The Unknown War. **MEMBERSHIPS** Asn for Asian Stud; Am Hist Asn; Am Polit Sci Asn. **RESEARCH** Modern Korean history; United States - East Asian relations; international political economy; American foreign relations. **SELECTED PUBLICATIONS** Auth, Origins of the Korean War, Princeton, 81, 90; auth, War and Television, Verso, 92; Korea's Place in the Sun: A Modern History, Norton, 97; auth, Parallax Visions: American-East Asian Relations at Century's End, Duke, forthcoming. **CONTACT ADDRESS** Dept of History, Univ of Chicago, 1126 E 59th St, Chicago, IL, 60637. **EMAIL** Bcumings@midway.uchicago.edu

CUMMINGS, ANTHONY M.
PERSONAL Born 05/03/1951, Worcester, MA **DISCIPLINE** MUSICOLOGY **EDUCATION** BA, Williams Col, 73; MA, Princeton Univ, 73; PhD, 80. **CAREER** Lectr in Music, Princton Univ, 79-81, 82-83, 85-88; Dean of Admission, Princeton Univ, 83-88, Fulbright Scholar, Univ of Florence, 88-89, National Endowment for the Hum and Robert Lehman Found Fel, Villa I Tatti, The Harvard Univ Center for Italian Renaissance Studies, Florence, 89-90; Research Assoc, The Andrew W. Mellon Found, 90-92, Assoc prof of Music, Tulane Univ, and Dean of Tulane Col, 92-. **HONORS AND AWARDS** Fulbright Scholar, Univ of Florence, 88-89, National Endowment for the Hum and Robert Lehman Found Fel, Villa I Tatti, The Harvard Univ Center for Italian Renaissance Studies, Florence, 89-90; Trustee, Williams Col, 86-91; serve by invitation as rev of manuscripts for the Jour of Royal Musical Assoc, acad yr 90-91 and Renaissance Quarterly, 96-97; mem of a promotion and tenure commit at Haverford Col, 94-95, rev of proposals for funding from the National Endowment for the Hum, 95-96. **MEMBERSHIPS** Am Musicological Soc, Col Board, National Assoc of Col Admissions Counselors, Renaissance Soc of Am. **RESEARCH** Italian Renaissance hist and music, electronic infor tech. **SELECTED PUBLICATIONS** Madrigal Origins: Francesco de Layolle, Philippe Verdelot, and the Florentine Cultural Elite; The Motet, 1520-1640, The New Oxford History of Music, vol IV, Oxford Univ Press; Music in Reniassance Cities and Courts: Studies in Honor of Lewis Lockwood; co-ed Harmonie Park Press, 96; Mouton's and Palestrinas Sequence-Motet; A Conference on the Motet of the Middle Ages and Renaissance, Feb 13,-14, 1994, Washington Univ in St Louis Univ Libraries and Scholarly Commun: A Study Prepared for the Andrew W. Mellon Found, with William G. Bowen, Richard H. Ekman, Laura O Lazarus, and Marcia L. Witte: Music for Medici Festivals, 1512-1537, Princeton Essays on the Arts, Princeton Univ Press, 92; Gian Maria Giudeo, Sonatore del Liuto, and the Medici, Fontes Artis Musicae, Gulio de Medici's Music Bks, Early Music History, The Florentine Carnival of 1513, rev of Bernhard Meier, The Modes of Classical Vocal Polyphony, transl by Ellen S. Beebe, Broude Brothers Limited, 88; in Music and Letters, The Transmission of Some Josquin Motets, Journal of the Royal Musical Assoc, Ghiselin, and Alfonso II of Naples, with Allan W. Atlas, The Journal of Musicology, Collaborated on the production of the CD Musica a Firenze al tempo di Lorenzo il Magnifico (Music in Florence at the Time Lorenzo the Magnificent). **CONTACT ADDRESS** Tulane Univ, New Orleans, LA, 70118-5698.

CUMMINGS, CRAIG
DISCIPLINE MUSIC THEORY **EDUCATION** Univ Ind, PhD. **CAREER** Assoc prof. **MEMBERSHIPS** Col Music Soc; Soc Music Theory. **SELECTED PUBLICATIONS** Auth, pubs on Schenkerian analysis, history of music theory, and music theory pedagogy. **CONTACT ADDRESS** Dept of Music History, Theory and Composition, Ithaca Col, 100 Job Hall, Ithaca, NY, 14850. **EMAIL** cummings@ithaca.edu

CUMMINGS, RAYMOND L.
PERSONAL Born 11/06/1922, Baltimore, MD, m, 1950, 3 children **DISCIPLINE** MODERN EUROPEAN HISTORY **EDUCATION** Villanova Univ, BA, 48; Georgetown Univ, MA, 52; Univ Pa, PhD(hist), 64. **CAREER** Assoc prof, 49-69, PROF HIST, VILLANOVA UNIV, 69-. **MEMBERSHIPS** AHA; Soc Fr Hist Studies; Soc Ital Hist Studies; Cath Hist Asn. **RESEARCH** European diplomatic history, 19th century: the Risorgimento; French history, 19th century. **SELECTED PUBLICATIONS** Auth, Crime, Disorder and the Risorgimento--The Politics of Policing in Bologna, Cath Hist Rev, Vol 0082, 96. **CONTACT ADDRESS** Villanova Univ, Villanova, PA, 19085.

CUMMINGS, RICHARD M.
PERSONAL Born 03/23/1938, New York, NY, m, 1965, 2 children **DISCIPLINE** POLITICAL SCIENCE **EDUCATION** Princeton Univ, BA 59; Columbia Univ, JD, 62; Cambridge Univ, MLitt, 65, PhD, 89. **CAREER** Prof, Pace Univ School of Law, 87-95; prof, John Marshall Law Sch, 95-98. **HONORS AND AWARDS** Buchanan Prize, polit, Princeton Univ. **MEMBERSHIPS** PEN Am Ctr; Natl Asn Scholars. **RESEARCH** Political sciences; history. **SELECTED PUBLICATIONS** Auth, Proposition Fourteen: A Secessionist Remedy, Grove, 81; auth, The Pied Piper: Allard K. Lowenstein and the Liberal Dream, Grove, 85; ed and intro, Nine Scorpions in a Bottle: Great Judges and Cases of the Supreme Court by Max Lerner, Arcade, 95. **CONTACT ADDRESS** PO Box 349, Bridgehampton, NY, 11932. **EMAIL** cummings01@earthlink.net

CUMMINS, LIGHT TOWNSEND
PERSONAL Born 04/23/1946, Derby, CT, m, 1977, 2 children **DISCIPLINE** HISTORY **EDUCATION** Southwest Texas State Univ, BS, 68, MA, 72; Tulane Univ, PhD, 77. **CAREER** Abraham Baldwin Agricultural Col, 76-78; vis asst prof, Tulane Univ, 82; Austin Col, 78- , Guy M. Bryan, Jr. Prof of History, 86- . **HONORS AND AWARDS** Fulbright scholar, 74-76; NEH Summer Seminar, 79; Danforth Assoc, 81- ; Rice Univ Sem Fel, 84; Sid Richardson Grants, 80, 82, 84-85; Columbus Quincentennial Prize, 86; NEH Sum Sem, 89; Sid Richardson Sabbatical Grant, 91-92; Francisco Bouligny Prize, Louisiana Hist Asn, 93. **MEMBERSHIPS** Texas State Hist Asn; AHA; So His Asn; SW Hist Asn; Publ Comm, Social Sci Q; LA Hist Asn; Conf on Latin Am Hist. **RESEARCH** Southeastern Spanish Borderlands; The Old Southwest; Anglo-Spanish rivalry in the eighteenth century Gulf Coast and lower Mississippi Valley; colonial Texas. **SELECTED PUBLICATIONS** Co-ed, A Guide to the History of Louisiana, Greenwood, 82; co-ed, A Guide to the History of Texas, Greenwood, 88; auth, Spanish Observers and the American Revolution, 1775-1783, Louisiana State Univ, 92; coauth, Louisiana: A History, 3d ed, Harlan Davidson, 96; co-ed, Spanish Borderlands History: A Sourcebook and Interviews with Scholars, Texas A&M, forthcoming. **CONTACT ADDRESS** Dept of History, Austin Col, 900 N Grand Ave, Ste 61606, Sherman, TX, 75090-4440. **EMAIL** lcummins@penelope.austinc.edu

CUMMINS, VICTORIA HENNESSEY
PERSONAL Born 03/10/1951, Yonkers, NY, m, 1975 **DISCIPLINE** LATIN AMERICAN AND EUROPEAN HISTORY **EDUCATION** Univ Md, BA, 72; Tulane Univ, MA, 74, PhD(hist), 79. **CAREER** Instr hist, Abraham Baldwin Agr Col, 77-78; ASST PROF HIST, AUSTIN COL, 78- **MEMBERSHIPS** Conf Latin Am Hist; Southern Hist Asn; Am Hist Asn; Latin Am Studies Asn; Southwestern Conf Latin Am Studies. **RESEARCH** Catholic church in colonial Mexico and Peru; bureaucracies in colonial Mexico and Peru; imperial policy in the Spanish Empire. **SELECTED PUBLICATIONS** Auth, An Evil Lost to View--An Investigation of Post-Evangelization Andean Religion in Mid-Colonial Peru, Colonial Latin Amer Hist Rev, Vol 0005, 96. **CONTACT ADDRESS** Austin Col, 900 N Grand Ave, Sherman, TX, 75090-4400.

CUNNIFF, ROGER LEE
PERSONAL Born 10/29/1932, Stonewall, CO, m, 1959, 4 children **DISCIPLINE** LATIN AMERICAN AND BRAZILIAN HISTORY **EDUCATION** Univ Northern Colo, BA, 54, MA, 58, Univ Tex, Austin, PhD(hist), 70. **CAREER** Teacher social studies, Riverton High Sch, Wyo, 58-59 & Hana Sch, Maui, Hawaii, 59-61; teaching asst hist, Univ Tex, Austin, 62-65; asst prof, 67-72, assoc prof, 72-80, PROF HIST OF BRAZIL, SAN DIEGO STATE UNIV, 80-. **MEMBERSHIPS** AHA: Conf Latin Am Hist; Latin Am Studies Asn; Pac Cost Coun Latin Am Studies (pres, 73). **RESEARCH** Social history of northeast Brazil; history of natural disasters; history of education in Latin America. **SELECTED PUBLICATIONS** Auth, With Broadax and Firebrand--The Destruction of the Brazilian Atlantic Forest, Hisp Amer Hist Rev, Vol 0076, 96. **CONTACT ADDRESS** Dept of Hist, San Diego State Univ, 5500 Campanile Dr, San Diego, CA, 92182-0002.

CUNNINGHAM, JAMES J.
PERSONAL Born 04/19/1938, Pittsburgh, PA, m **DISCIPLINE** EDUCATION **EDUCATION** BS, 1964; MA, 1967; EdS, 1969; DEd, 1971. **CAREER** Elementary school teacher, 1964-66; Washington DC, counselor, prin 1966-68; Fed City Coll, Washington DC, 1968-71; Assoc Cont Res & Analysis Inc, Washington DC, consultant 1969; Fed City Coll, dir of admissions 1971; HEW/DE, Washington DC, consultant 1971; Moton Consortium on Adm & Financial Aid, co-dir 1971-72; TX Southern Univ, dean of students, prof of educ 1972-74; Mankato State Coll, Mankato MN, vice pres student servs, prof of educ 1974; TX Southern Univ Houston, special asst to the pres 1986, prof of graduate educ, vice pres institutional advancement. **MEMBERSHIPS** Mem Natl Assn for Higher Edn; Personnel Guidance Assn; Assn of Coll Adm Counselors; DC Couns Assn; Elem Classroom Tchrs Assn; Natl Tchrs Assn; TX Personnel Serv Adminstrs; MN State Coll Student Assn; MN Student Serv Adminstrn; NAACP. **CONTACT ADDRESS** Graduate Education, Texas So Univ, Houston, TX, 77004.

CUNNINGHAM, NOBLE E., JR.
PERSONAL Born 07/25/1926, Evans Landing, IN, m, 1954 **DISCIPLINE** HISTORY **EDUCATION** Duke Univ, PhD 52, MA 49; Univ Louisville, BA 48. **CAREER** Univ Missouri CO, assoc prof , prof, chemn, 64-74, Byler Dist Prof, 80-81, Frederick A Middlebush Prof 86-88; curators prof hist 88-97, Curators' Prof Emer 97-. **HONORS AND AWARDS** Phi Beta Kappa; Guggenheim Fel; Outstanding Prof; NHPC Gnt; 2 NEH Fel; APS Penrose Gnt; Thomas Jefferson Awd; Chancellors Awd; Fac Alum; Thomas Jefferson Mem Foun Medal; MO Conf on Hist Awd; Awd for Schly Excellence. **MEMBERSHIPS** AHS' OAH; SHA; SHER. **SELECTED PUBLICATIONS** Auth, The Presidency of James Monroe, Lawrence, Univ Press of Kansas, 96; Popular Images of the Presidency: From Washington to Lincoln, Columbia, Univ of MO Press, 91; In Pursuit of Reason: The Life of Thomas Jefferson, Baton Rouge, LA State Univ Press, 87. **CONTACT ADDRESS** Dept of History, Univ of Missouri, Columbia, MO, 65211.

CUNNINGHAM, SARAH GARDNER
DISCIPLINE HISTORY AND RELIGION **EDUCATION** Princeton Univ, BA, 79; Union Theol Sem, MDiv, 89, PhD, 84. **CAREER** Macmillan Lib Ref, Simon and Schuster Acad Ref, 94-98; Marymont Sch, upper Sch History, 98-. **MEMBERSHIPS** AAR; AHA; ASCH. **RESEARCH** US Religious History; Hist of Christianity; Gender Studies. **CONTACT ADDRESS** 1735 York Ave, #6C, New York, NY, 10128. **EMAIL** sarah_cunningham@marymont.kiz.ny.us

CUNNINGHAM, WILLIAM DEAN
PERSONAL Born 08/09/1937, Kansas City, MO, d **DISCIPLINE** EDUCATION **EDUCATION** Univ of KS, BA 1959; Univ of TX, MLS 1962, PhD 1972. **CAREER** Federal Aviation Agency, chief library serv 1965-67; Topeka Public Library, head adult serv 1967-68; US Dept of Educ, program officer 1968-71; Howard Univ, dir univ libraries 1970-73; Univ of MD Coll of Library & Information Services, asst prof 1973-. **HONORS AND AWARDS** Citations from Dept of Education, FAA, ASALA. **MEMBERSHIPS** Mem Amer Library Assn 1970-, Assn for the Study of Afro-Amer Life and History 1974-; bd dirs Soul Journey Enterprises 1974-; mem Natl Black Heritage Council 1984-. **SELECTED PUBLICATIONS** Auth, Blacks in Performing Arts; co-auth, Black Guide to Washington. **CONTACT ADDRESS** Col of Library & Info Serv, Univ of Maryland, College Park, MD, 20742.

CUNO, KENNETH M.
PERSONAL Born 01/04/1950, Syracuse, NY, m, 1986, 2 children **DISCIPLINE** HISTORY **EDUCATION** Lewis & Clark Col, BA, hist, 72; Univ Calif Los Angeles, MA, hist, 77, PhD, hist, 85. **CAREER** Vis asst prof, Amer Univ in Cairo, 85-90; asst prof, 90-96, assoc prof, 96-, Univ Ill Urbana-Champaign. **HONORS AND AWARDS** SSRC res fel, 99; Fulbright Sr Res fel, 98-99; US Info Agency, US speaker and specialist grant, 98; vis res scholar, Amer Univ Cairo, 94, 96; fel, Ctr for Advan Study, UIUC, 94-95; fel, Amer Res Ctr in Egypt, 94; honorable mention, Albert Hourani Book Prize, Middle East Studies Asn, 93; humanities released time award, 93; teachers rated excellent by students, UIUC, 90, 94; outstanding teacher, AUC Student Union, 87, 89; soc sci res coun intl doctoral res fel, 81-82; Fulbright-Hays dissertation res abroad fel, 80-81; fel, Ctr for Arabic Studies, 79-80; fel, Amer Res Ctr in Egypt, 79-80. **MEMBERSHIPS** Amer Hist Asn; Middle East Studies Asn of North Amer; Amer Res Ctr in Egypt; Ctr for Middle Eastern Studies at Univ of Chicago; Soc Sci Hist Asn; Turkish Studies Asn. **RESEARCH** Pre-modern and modern family history. **SELECTED PUBLICATIONS** Auth, A Tale of Two Villages: Family, Property, and Economic Activity in Rural Egypt in the 1840s, land, Settlement and Agriculture in Egypt from Pharaonic to Modern Times, Oxford Univ Press, 98; auth, Ideology and Juridical Discourse in Ottoman Egypt: the Uses of the Concept of Irsad, Islamic Law and Soc, 98; co-auth, The Census Registers of Nineteenth-Century Egypt: A New Source for Social Historians, Brit Jour of Middle Eastern Studies, 97; auth, Migrants, Islam, Refugees and Behind the Veil, Imagining the Twentieth Century, Univ Ill Press, 97; auth, In Memoriam (Ronald C. Jennings), Turkish Studies Asn Bull, 96; auth, Joint Family Households and Rural Notables in Nineteenth-Century Egypt, Intl Jour of Middle East Studies, 95; auth, Was the Land of Ottoman Syria Miri or Milk? An Examination of Juridical Differences within the Hanafi School, Studia Islamica, 95; auth, The Origins of Private Ownership of Land in Egypt: a Reappraisal, The Modern Middle East: a Reader, Univ Calif Press, 94. **CONTACT ADDRESS** Dept. of History, Univ of Illinois, 309 Gregory Hall, 810 S. Wri, Urbana, IL, 61801. **EMAIL** k-cuno@uiuc.edu

CUNSOLO, RONALD S.
PERSONAL Born 05/03/1923, New York, NY **DISCIPLINE** MODERN EUROPEAN HISTORY **EDUCATION** NY Univ, BA, 49, PhD(hist), 62; Univ Chicago, MA, 56. **CAREER** Permanent substitute hist, Brooklyn Col, 62-63; from instr to assoc prof, 63-71, chmn dept hist & polit sci, 66-73, PROF HIST, NASSAU COMMUNITY COL, 71-, Assoc, Sem Mod Ital Hist, Columbia Univ, 70-, chmn, 73-74; chmn Sem Studies Mod Italy, 74-75; exec secy, Matteotti Int Symp, Columbia Univ, 75-78. **HONORS AND AWARDS** Great Teacher Award, State Univ NY, 81-82. **MEMBERSHIPS** AHA; Acad Polit Sci; Soc Ital Hist Studies. **RESEARCH** Modern Italian history; nationalism; imperialism. **SELECTED PUBLICATIONS** Auth, Nationalists and Catholics in Giolittian Italy--An Uneasy Collaboration, Cath Hist Rev, Vol 0079, 93. **CONTACT ADDRESS** Nassau Comm Col, Garden City, NY, 11530.

CUPPO CSAKI, LUCIANA
PERSONAL Born 05/30/1941, Trieste, Italy **DISCIPLINE** CLASSIC LANGUAGES **EDUCATION** Univ of Heidelberg, BA, Univ of Kansas, MA, 70; Fordham Univ, MA, 85, PhD, 95.

CAREER Instr, 77-83, Penn Valley Comm Coll; Frances Schwartz Fel, 86-87, Amer Numismatic Society; teach fel, 83-87, Fordham Univ; Lectr, 86-88, Mount St Mary's Coll; inst & dept head Classics, 89-92, Manhattanville Coll, Purchase; teacher of Latin, 91-98, CUNY Graduate School; adj Prof, 95-, SUNY Westchester & Albany. **MEMBERSHIPS** APA **RESEARCH** Late antiquity early medieval history, medieval & classical latin, palaeography manuscript studies. **SELECTED PUBLICATIONS** Auth, Roma magistra historiae, The Year 680 as caput saeculi in Cas 641 in Melanges offerts au Pere L E Boyle a l'occasion de son 75e anniversaire, in: Beatus Cassiodorus, Vivarium Scyllacense, 97; Contra Voluntatem fundatorum, il monasterium Vivariense di Cassiodoro dopo il 575, in Acta of the XIII International Cogress for Christian Archaeology, Rome/Split, 96; La catacomba di S Domittilla come centro di culto e pellegrinaggio nel sesto secolo ed alto Medioevo, in: Akten des XII, Internationalen Kongresses fur Christliche Archaologie, Munster, 95; The Copper Coinage of Theodahad, a Reappraisal, in: Proceedings of the XIth International Numismatic Congress, ed, T Hackens, Louvain-la-Neuve, 93. **CONTACT ADDRESS** 24 Pecoho Rd, Lake Peekskill, NY, 10537. **EMAIL** vivario@geocities.com

CURD, MARTIN VINCENT
PERSONAL Born 04/25/1951, Luton, United Kingdom, m, 1975 **DISCIPLINE** HISTORY & PHILOSOPHY OF SCIENCE **EDUCATION** Univ Cambridge, BA, 72; Univ Pittsburgh, MA, 74, PhD, 78. **CAREER** Instr hist & philos sci, Univ Pittsburgh, 75-77; Mellon instr humanities & philos, Vanderbilt Univ, 77-78; Asst Prof, 78-84, Assoc Prof Philos, Purdue Univ, 84-. **MEMBERSHIPS** Am Philos Asn; Philos Sci Asn. **RESEARCH** Scientific revolution; direction of time; logic of scientific discovery. **SELECTED PUBLICATIONS** Auth, The Logic of Discovery: An Analysis of Three Approaches, in Scientific Discovery, Logic and Rationality: Proceedings of the First Leonard Conf, D Reidel, Dordrecht, Holland, 80; The Rationality of the Copernican Revolution, PSA, 82; coauth, Professional Responsibility For Harm, Kendall/Hunt Publ Co, 84; Principles of Reasoning, St. Martin's Press, 89; auth, Argument and Analysis: An Introduction to Philosophy, West, 92; coauth, Philosophy of Science: The Central Issues, W.W. Norton, 98. **CONTACT ADDRESS** Dept of Philos, Purdue Univ, LAEB - 1360, West Lafayette, IN, 47907-1360. **EMAIL** curd@purdue.edu

CURD, PATRICIA
DISCIPLINE ANCIENT PHILOSOPHY, ETHICS **EDUCATION** Pittsburgh, PhD. **CAREER** Assoc prof, Purdue Univ. **SELECTED PUBLICATIONS** Published papers on the Presocratics and on the development of Plato's metaphysics. **CONTACT ADDRESS** Dept of Philos, Purdue Univ, 1080 Schleman Hall, West Lafayette, IN, 47907-1080.

CURET, LUIS ANTONIO
PERSONAL Born 10/20/1960, San Juan, PR, m, 1990, 2 children **DISCIPLINE** ANTHROPOLOGY/ARCHAEOLOGY **EDUCATION** Arizona State Univ, PhD, 92. **CAREER** Asst prof, Gettysburg Col, 93-96; asst prof, Univ of Colorado, Denver, 96- . **HONORS AND AWARDS** Res awd, Univ Colorado, 98. **MEMBERSHIPS** Soc for Am Archaeol; Sigma Xi Sci Soc; Int Asoc Caribbean Archaeol; Asociacion Puertorriquencia de Antropologos y Arqueologos. **RESEARCH** Caribbean and Mesoamerica; complex societies. **SELECTED PUBLICATIONS** Auth, Ceramic Production Areas and Regional Studies: An Example From La Mixtequilla, Veracruz, Mexico, in J of Field Archaeol, 93; auth, Prehistoric Demographic Changes in the Valley of Maunabo, Puerto Rico: A Preliminary Report, in Proc of the 14th Int Cong for Caribbean Archaeol, 93; coauth, Post classic Changes in Veracruz, Mexico, Ancient Mesoamerica, 94; auth, Ideology, Chiefly Power, and Material Culture: An Example from the Greater Antilles, Latin Am Antiq, 96; auth, Technological Changes in Prehistoric Ceramics from Eastern Puerto Rico: An Exploratory Study, in J of Archaeol Sci, 97; auth, New Formulae for Estimating prehistoric Populations for Lowland South America and the Caribbean, in Antiquity, 98; coauth, Poder e ideologia: el control del simbolismo en los cacicazgos tempranos de Puerto Rico, Historia y Sociedad, 98; coauth, Mortuary Practices, Social Development and Ideology in Precolumbian Puerto Rico, Latin Am Antiq, in press; coauth, Informe Preliminar del Proyecto Arqueologico del Centro Indigena de Tibes, Ponce, Puerto Rico, in Proc of the 16th Int Cong for Caribbean Archaeol, in press. **CONTACT ADDRESS** Dept of Anthropology, Univ of Colorado, Denver, Campus Box 103, PO Box 173364, Denver, CO, 80217-3364. **EMAIL** lcuret@carbon.cudenver.edu

CURL, DONALD WALTER
PERSONAL Born 10/07/1935, East Liberty, OH **DISCIPLINE** UNITED STATES HISTORY **EDUCATION** Ohio State Univ, BScEd, 57, MA, 58, PhD (Hist), 64. **CAREER** Instr Hist, Kent State Univ, 62-64; from asst prof to assoc prof, 64-71, chmn dept, 69-75, 90-92, 94-98; prof Hist, Fla Atlantic Univ, 71-. **HONORS AND AWARDS** Cert of Commendation, Am Asn State & Local Hist, 71; Award for best article in Florida Hist Quarterly, 93; Award of Merit, Am Assn State & Local Hist, 96. **MEMBERSHIPS** AHA. **RESEARCH** United States social and intellectual history; Florida history; political party history. **SELECTED PUBLICATIONS** Auth, The Senate Rejects, Ohio Hist, summer 67; Murat Halstead, In: For the Union, Ohio State Univ, 68; ed, Pioneer Life in Southeast Florida, Univ Miami, 70; auth, An American reporter and the Franco-Prussian War, Jour Quart, Fall 72; The pioneer cook in SE Florida, Boca Raton Hist Soc, 75; Murat Halstead and the Cincinnati Commercial, Univ Fla, 80; Joseph Urban's Palm Beach Architecture, FL Hist Quarterly, April 93; Palm Beach County: In a Class by Itself, ed, Copperfield, 98; The Florida Architecture of F Burrall Hoffman, Jr, 1882-1980, FL Hist Quarterly, Spring 98. **CONTACT ADDRESS** Dept of History, Florida Atlantic Univ, PO Box 3091, Boca Raton, FL, 33431-0991. **EMAIL** curld@fau.edu

CURNOW, KATHY
DISCIPLINE AFRICAN AND AFRICAN-AMERICAN ART HISTORY **EDUCATION** PA State Univ, BA, 76; IN State Univ, MA, 80, PhD, 83. **CAREER** Instr, Univ PA; Lincoln Univ; Univ Arts, NTA TV Col, Nigeria; assoc prof, 80-. **HONORS AND AWARDS** NEH grant; Fulbright; Soc Sci Res Coun grant. **RESEARCH** Fiction writing. **SELECTED PUBLICATIONS** Publ, art Benin Kingdom; Itsekiri; Nupe of Nigeria; articles, Benin's ideal man, Art Jour; Benin's Ague Festival, African Arts; dwarf figures from Benin, exhib cat, Linz, Austria. **CONTACT ADDRESS** Dept of Art, Cleveland State Univ, 83 E 24th St, Cleveland, OH, 44115.

CURRAN, BRIAN A.
DISCIPLINE ANCIENT EGYPT AND EGYPTIAN ANTIQUITIES IN ITALIAN RENAISSANCE ART AND CULTU **EDUCATION** Mass Coll Art, BFA; Univ Mass, MA; Princeton Univ, MA, PhD. **CAREER** 84-90, Museum of Fine Arts, Boston; Tchg fel, Columbia Univ, 96-97; asst prof, Pa State Univ, 97-;. **HONORS AND AWARDS** Fel, Am Acad, Rome; fel, Bibliotheca Hertziana, Rome. **MEMBERSHIPS** Dept Egyptian & Ancient Near Eastern Art, Museum of Fine Arts, Boston **SELECTED PUBLICATIONS** Articles, Art Bull; Jour Warburg & Courtauld Insts; Words & Image.. **CONTACT ADDRESS** Pennsylvania State Univ, 201 Shields Bldg, University Park, PA, 16802. **EMAIL** bac18@psu.edu

CURRAN, DANIEL JOHN
PERSONAL Born 10/27/1932, Brooklyn, NY **DISCIPLINE** HISTORY **EDUCATION** Manhattan Col, BA, 52; Fordham Univ, MA, 53, PhD (hist), 62. **CAREER** Assoc prof, 58-72, PROF HIST, KING'S COL, PA, 72-. **MEMBERSHIPS** AHA; Am Cath Hist Asn; Orgn Am Historians; Am Asn Slavic Studies. **RESEARCH** American contemporary political history; modern Russian history. **SELECTED PUBLICATIONS** Auth, Polk, Politics and Patronage--The Rejection of Woodward, George,W. Nomination to the Supreme-Court, Pa Mag Hist and Biog, Vol 0121, 97. **CONTACT ADDRESS** Dept of Hist, King's Col, 133 N River St, Wilkes Barre, PA, 18711-0801.

CURRAN, LEO C.
DISCIPLINE CLASSICS **EDUCATION** Oxford Univ, MA, 58; Yale Univ, PhD, 61. **CAREER** Fac, 67-; to assoc prof emer, present, SUNY Buffalo. **HONORS AND AWARDS** Chancellor's Awd Excel Tchg, 80., Found assoc ed, Arethusa. **RESEARCH** Software for computer analysis of Latin lit and for Latin instruction. **SELECTED PUBLICATIONS** Auth, Identification of Latin Poets by Sound, Syllecta Classica 2, 90; Identification of Latin Poets by Sound II, Syllecta Classica 3, 91. **CONTACT ADDRESS** Dept Classics, SUNY Buffalo, 712 Clemens Hall, Buffalo, NY, 14260. **EMAIL** lccurran@acsu.buffalo.edu

CURRAN, ROBERT EMMOTT
PERSONAL Born 05/23/1936, Baltimore, MD, m, 1998 **DISCIPLINE** HISTORY **EDUCATION** Col of Holy Cross, AB, 58; Fordham Univ, MA, 65; Yale Univ, PhD, 74. **CAREER** Instr to asst prof to assoc prof to prof, 72-, Georgetown Univ. **MEMBERSHIPS** Amer Hist Assoc; Org of Amer Hist; Amer Stud Assoc; Amer Catholic Hist Assoc; S Hist Assoc; Immigration Hist Assoc; Amer Soc of Church Hist. **RESEARCH** US religions; education; US South. **SELECTED PUBLICATIONS** Auth, The Bicentennial History of Georgetown University, 93; auth, The Jesuits as Educators in Anglo-America in Jesuit Encounters in the New World: Jesuit Chroniclers, Geographers, Educators and Missionaries in the Americas, 1549-1767, Jesuit Hist Inst, 97; art, Christianity: Roman Catholicism, Encyclopedia of Slaver, 99. **CONTACT ADDRESS** History Dept, Georgetown Univ, Washington, DC, 20057. **EMAIL** currane@GUNET.GEORGETOWN.EDU

CURRAN, THOMAS F.
DISCIPLINE US CIVIL WAR **EDUCATION** Univ Notre Dame, PhD. **CAREER** Hist Dept, St Edward's Univ **HONORS AND AWARDS** Managing ed, Jour Policy Hist. **SELECTED PUBLICATIONS** Articles: Civil War Hist; Jour Church & State. **CONTACT ADDRESS** St Edward's Univ, 3001 S Congress Ave, Austin, TX, 78704-6489.

CURRAN, THOMAS J.
PERSONAL Born 10/03/1929, Brooklyn, NY, 2 children **DISCIPLINE** AMERICAN HISTORY **EDUCATION** Manhattan Col, AB, 48; Columbia Univ, MA, 51, PhD, 63. **CAREER** Instr hist, Manhattanville Col Sacred Heart, 55-56; from instr to asst prof, 56-65, assoc prof Hist, St John's Univ, NY, 65-, Acad coordr, Nat Broadcasting Co-TV & consult, Columbia Broadcasting Syst-TV, 71-. **MEMBERSHIPS** AHA; Am Cath Hist Asn; Orgn Am Historians. **RESEARCH** Nineteenth century American history--know nothing movement. **SELECTED PUBLICATIONS** Auth, Assimilation and nativism, Int Migration Rev, spring 66; Seward and the know-nothings, 4/67 & ed, The diary of Henry Van Der Lyn, spring 71, NY Hist Soc Quart; auth, Xenophobia and Immigration, 76 & co-ed, Immigrant in American History, 77, Twayne. **CONTACT ADDRESS** Dept of History, St. John's Univ, 8150 Utopia Pky, Jamaica, NY, 11439-0002.

CURRENT, RICHARD NELSON
PERSONAL Born 10/05/1912, Colorado City, CO, m, 1937, 2 children **DISCIPLINE** AMERICAN HISTORY **EDUCATION** Oberlin Col, AB, 34; Fletcher Sch Law, AM, 35; Univ Wis, PhD, 39. **CAREER** Instr soc sci, Md State Teachers Col, Salisbury, 38-42; asst prof hist & polit sci, Rutgers Univ, 42-43; asst prof hist, Hamilton Col, 43-44; prof, Northern Mich Col Educ, 44-45; assoc prof, Lawrence Col, 45-47; Morrison prof Am hist, Mills Col, 47-50; from assoc prof to prof hist, Univ Ill, 50-55; prof hist & polit sci & head dept Woman's Col, Univ NC, 55-60; prof hist, Univ Wis, Madison, 60-66; DISTINGUISHED PROF HIST, UNIV NC, GREENSBORO, 66-, Lectr, Doshisha Univ, 58; lectr, Am specialist prog, India & Fulbright Lectr, Univ Munich, 59; Harmsworth prof, Oxford Univ, 62-63; lectr, India, 65, 67-68, Chile & Arg, 65, Australia & Europe, 66, Japan, Taiwan & Philippines, 67, Chile & Ecuador, 68. **HONORS AND AWARDS** Bancroft Prize, Columbia Univ, 56; Banta Award, Wis Libr Asn, 77., MA, Oxford Univ, 62. **MEMBERSHIPS** AHA; Orgn Am Historians; Soc Am Historians; Southern Hist Asn (pres, 74-75). **RESEARCH** American diplomatic history; American political biography; the Civil War and Reconstruction. **SELECTED PUBLICATIONS** Auth, Foote,Shelby--Novelist and Historian, Jour So Hist, Vol 0059, 93. **CONTACT ADDRESS** 1805 Brookcliff Dr, Greensboro, NC, 27408.

CURREY, CECIL B.
PERSONAL Born 11/29/1932, Clarks, NE, m, 1952, 3 children **DISCIPLINE** EARLY AMERICAN AND MILITARY HISTORY **EDUCATION** Ft Hays Kans State Col, AB, 58, MA, 59; Univ Kans, PhD(hist), 65. **CAREER** Asst prof Am hist, Nebr Wesleyan Univ, 65-67, assoc prof, 67; assoc prof, 67-69, PROF COLONIAL, US MILITARY & REVOLUTION AM HIST, UNIV S FLA, TAMPA, 69-, S & H Lectureship Found grants, 67, 68.. **MEMBERSHIPS** Evangel Theol Soc; AHA; Orgn Am Historians. **RESEARCH** The career of Benjamin Franklin; Dutch colonization in the New World; Puritan theology and culture. **SELECTED PUBLICATIONS** Auth, Guerrilla Warfare--A Historical, Biographical, and Bibliographical Sourcebook, Jour Military Hist, Vol 0061, 97; Franklin,Benjamin in American Thought and Culture-1790-1990s, Amer Hist Rev, Vol 0101, 96. **CONTACT ADDRESS** Dept of Hist, Univ of SFla, 4202 Fowler Ave, Tampa, FL, 33620-9951.

CURRY, LAWRENCE H., JR.
PERSONAL Born 02/04/1935, Anderson, SC, m, 1994, 3 children **DISCIPLINE** HISTORY **EDUCATION** Univ SC, BS, 57, MA, 59; Duke Univ, PhD, 71. **CAREER** From instr to asst prof to assoc dean, 68-, Univ Houston. **HONORS AND AWARDS** Univ Houston Tchg Excellence, 77, 97. **MEMBERSHIPS** Am Hist Asn; Southern Hist Asn. **RESEARCH** Recent US history **CONTACT ADDRESS** Dept of History, Univ of Houston, Houston, TX, 77204-3785. **EMAIL** lcurry@uh.edu

CURRY, LEONARD PRESTON
PERSONAL Born 03/23/1929, Cave City, KY, m, 1959, 2 children **DISCIPLINE** UNITED STATES HISTORY **EDUCATION** Western Ky State Col, AB, 51; Univ Ky, MA, 56, PhD, 61. **CAREER** From instr to asst prof hist, Memphis State Univ, 58-62; from asst prof to assoc prof, 62-69, PROF HIST, UNIV LOUISVILLE, 69-, Am Philos Soc res grants, 62, 72 & 76; vis asst prof, Univ Maine, 64-65; vis assoc prof, Univ Md, 68-69; vis res assoc, Smithsonian Inst, 70-71; mem, Adv Comt Ky Arch & Rec Comn, 72-; fac res grants, 63, 66, 67 & 73-81; Am Coun Learned Socs res grant, 76; mem, Ky Comn Pub Doc, 76-; consult, Nat Endowment for Humanities, 76, 77, 78 & 81; Southern Regional Educ Bd res grant, 81. **MEMBERSHIPS** AHA; Orgn Am Historians; Southern Hist Asn. **RESEARCH** United States history, 1820-1877; urban development in the United States, 1800-1850; United States congressional history. **SELECTED PUBLICATIONS** Auth, A History of Black in Kentucky, Vol 1, from Slavery to Segregation, 1760-1891, Jour Amer Hist, Vol 0081, 95; Yankee Merchants and the Making of the Urban West--The Rise and Fall of Antebellum St-Louis, Amer Hist Rev, Vol 0097, 92; Free People of Color--Inside the African-American Community, Amer Hist Rev, Vol 0099, 94. **CONTACT ADDRESS** Dept of Hist, Univ of Louisville, 2301 S 3rd St, Louisville, KY, 40292-2001.

CURRY, RICHARD ORR
PERSONAL Born 01/26/1931, White Sulphur Springs, WV, m, 1953, 4 children **DISCIPLINE** UNITED STATES HISTORY **EDUCATION** Marshall Univ, BA, 52, MA, 56; Univ Pa, PhD(hist), 61. **CAREER** Instr Europ hist, Morris Harvey Col, 59-60; instr US hist, Pa State Univ, 60-62; vis asst prof, Univ Pittsburgh, 62-63; from asst prof to assoc prof, 63-71, PROF US HIST, UNIV CONN, 71-, Am Asn State & Local Hist grant, 64; Soc Relig Higher Educ & Harvard Divinity Sch fel, 65-66; Am Philos Soc grant, 67 & 70. **HONORS AND AWARDS** Haynes Lectr, 74; US Int Commun Agency Lectr, Philippines, 78 & Australia, 81; Fulbright Lectr, 81; Charles Hill Moffat Lectr, 82. **MEMBERSHIPS** Orgn Am Historians; Southern Hist Asn; Am Studies Asn. **RESEARCH** Nineteenth century United States social political and intellectual history. **SELECTED PUBLICATIONS** Auth, The New Individualists--The Generation After the Organization-Man, Jour Amer Hist, Vol 0080, 93; Untitled, Jour Amer Hist, Vol 0082, 95. **CONTACT ADDRESS** Dept of Hist, Univ of Conn, Storrs, CT, 06268.

CURTIN, N.J.
PERSONAL Born 07/01/1952, Reedsburg, WI **DISCIPLINE** HISTORY **EDUCATION** Univ of Wisconsin-Madison, BA 76, MA 80, PhD 88. **CAREER** Fordham Univ, asst prof to prof, 88 to 98-. **MEMBERSHIPS** AHA; Amer Conf for Irish Studies; North Amer Conf for British Studies **RESEARCH** Modern Ireland, nationalism, republicanism and gender. **SELECTED PUBLICATIONS** Auth, Eire-Ireland: An Interdisciplinary Jour of Irish Studies, co-ed, 96-; The United Irishmen: Popular Politics in Ulster and Dublin, 1791-1798, Oxford Clarendon Press 94, ppbk 98; Matilda Tone and Virtuous Republican Femininity, Women in '98 ed Daire Keogh, 98; Radicals and Rebels: The United Irishmen in County Down, in Down Hist and Soc, ed Lindsay Proudfoot, 97; forthcoming, A Perfect Liberty: The Irish Whigs, 1789-1797, in Political Discourse in Early Modern Ireland, eds W. G. Boyce, R. R. Eccleshall, V. Geoghegan, London Macmillan; Reclaiming Gender: Transgressive Identities in Modern Ireland, co-ed Marilyn Cohen, NY St Martins press. **CONTACT ADDRESS** Dept of History, Fordham Univ, Bronx, NY, 10458. **EMAIL** curtin@murray.fordham.edu

CURTIN, PHILIP DE ARMOND
PERSONAL Born 05/22/1922, Philadelphia, PA, m, 1957, 3 children **DISCIPLINE** HISTORY **EDUCATION** Swarthmore Col, AB, 48; Harvard Univ, MA, 49, PhD, 53. **CAREER** From instr to asst prof hist, Swarthmore Col, 53-56; from asst prof to prof, Univ WI Madison, 56-70, chmn, Prog Comp World Hist, 59-75,chmn, Dept African Languages and Lit, 63-64, 65-66; mem, African Studies Prog, 61-66, Melville J Herskovits prof, 70-75, co-dir res prog in African econ hist, 71-75; Prof Hist, Johns Hopkins Univ, 75-82, HERBERT BAXTER ADAMS PROF OF HIST, 82-; Ford Found African area training fel, 58-59; US-African Leader Exchange Prog fac exchange travel grant, 62-63; mem joint comt African studies Soc Sci Res Coun-Am Coun Learned Socs, 63-73, chmn, 71-73; Guggenheim fel, 66 & 80; mem coun, Soc Sci Res Coun, 67-71; Nat Endowment for Humanities sr fel, 68-69;chmn, Prog Atlantic Studies in Hist and Culture, 76-79; Univ of Hawaii, John A. Burns Distinguished Vis Prof of Hist, spring semester, 88; Univ MN, Union Pacific Vis Prof, spring semester, 90. **HONORS AND AWARDS** Phi Beta Kappa, 48; Ford Fellowship, 58-59; United States-South Africa Leader Exchange Program Fellowship, 62-63; Guggenheim Fellowship, 66, 80; Robert Livingston Schuyler Prize, 66; Sr Fellowship, NEH, 68-69; MacArthur Prize Fellowship, 83-88; Phi Beta Kappa Assoc, 83; Presented with Africans in Bondage, ed Paul Lovejoy, essays in honor of Philip D. Curtain, by African Studies Program, Univ WI, Oct 86; Doctor of Humane Letters, Swarthmore Col, 87; Welch Medal from the Am Assoc for the Hist of Medicine, 92; Distinguished Africanist Award, 92. **MEMBERSHIPS** AHA, pres 83; African Studies Asn (pres, 70-71); Int Cong Africanists (vpres, 69-73); Am Anthrop Asn; Econ Hist Asn; Am Philos Asn. **RESEARCH** African history; Caribbean history; world history. **SELECTED PUBLICATIONS** Auth, Two Jamaicas, Harvard Univ, 55; The Image of Africa, 64, Africa Remembered, 67, The Atlantic Slave Trade: A Census, 69 & ed & Contrib, Africa and the West, 69, Univ WI; coauth, Africa and Africans, Natural Hist, 71; auth, Economic Change in Pre-Colonial Africa, Univ WI, 75; coauth, African History, Little, 78; Cross-Cultural Trade in World History, NY, Cambridge Univ Press, 84; Death by Migration: Europe's Encounter with the Tropical World in the Nineteenth Century, NY, Cambridge Univ Press, 89; The Rise and Fall of the Plantation Complex: Essays in Atlantic History, NY, Cambridge Univ Press, 90; Why People Move: Migration in African History, Waco, Tx: Baylor Univ Press, 95.; contrib ed to: Current History, 55-59, Jnal of African Hist, 60-76, Jnal of African Studies, 74-, African Economic Hist, 75-, Social Science Hist, 76-, Am Hist Rev, 77-80, Hist in Africa, 74-, J of Economic Hist, 75-78, Plantation Soc, 78-. **CONTACT ADDRESS** Dept of Hist, Johns Hopkins Univ, 3400 N Charles St, Baltimore, MD, 21218-2680. **EMAIL** curtinpd@aol.com

CURTIS, JAMES C.
PERSONAL Born 07/12/1938, Evanston, IL, m, 1961, 2 children **DISCIPLINE** AMERICAN HISTORY **EDUCATION** Carleton Col, BA, 59; Northwestern Univ, MA, 66, PhD (Am hist), 67. **CAREER** Asst prof, Univ Tex, Austin, 67-70; assoc prof, 70-76, PROF HIST & AM STUDIES, UNIV DEL, 76-, Nat Endowment for Humanities fel, 73-74. **HONORS AND AWARDS** Excellence in Teaching Award, Univ Del, 76. **MEMBERSHIPS** AHA; Orgn Am Historians. **RESEARCH** Jacksonian politics; the history of the 19th century Presidency; history and media. **SELECTED PUBLICATIONS** Auth, Image as Artifact--The Historical-Analysis of Film and Television, Jour So Hist, Vol 0059, 93. **CONTACT ADDRESS** Dept of Hist, Univ of Del, Newark, DE, 19711.

CURTIS, ROBERT I.
PERSONAL Born 10/17/1943, Waycross, GA, m, 1976, 1 child **DISCIPLINE** ANCIENT HISTORY **EDUCATION** Univ Maryland, PhD 78. **CAREER** Univ Georgia, asst prof, assoc prof, prof, 78 to 98-; Univ of Leeds, vis prof 97. **HONORS AND AWARDS** Outstanding Honors Prof, 91 **MEMBERSHIPS** AIA; ISCT; AAH **RESEARCH** Roman social and econ history; Roman food and drink; Pompeii and Herculaneum. **SELECTED PUBLICATIONS** Auth, Garum and Salsamenta: The Production and Commerce of Materia Medica, Leiden, E. J. Brill, 91; Confederate Classical Textbooks: A Lost Cause? In: The Intl Jour for the Classical Tradition, 97; The Bingham School and Classical Education in North Carolina, 1793-1873, The North Carol Hist Rev, 96. **CONTACT ADDRESS** Dept of Classics, Univ of Georgia, Park Hall, Athens, GA, 30602-6203. **EMAIL** ricurtis@arches.uga.edu

CURTIS, SUSAN
PERSONAL Born 07/09/1956, Red Oak, IA, m, 1992 **DISCIPLINE** HISTORY **EDUCATION** Graceland Coll, BA, 77; Univ Mo-Columbia, MA, 81, PhD, 86. **CAREER** Asst prof, Fla Int Univ, 86-89; asst prof, Purdue Univ, 89-94; ASSOC PROF, PURDUE UNIV, 94-. **MEMBERSHIPS** Org Am Historians; Am Stud Asn; Am Hist Asn; Am Soc Church Hist; John Whitmer Hist Asn **RESEARCH** American Cultural History; American Religious History. **SELECTED PUBLICATIONS** "Scott Joplin and Sedalia: The King of Ragtime in the Queen City of Missouri," Gateway Heritage, 94; Dancing to a Black Man's Tune: A Life of Scott Joplin, Columbia: Univ Mo Press, 94; The First Black Actors on the Great White Way, Columbia: Univ Mo Press, 98. **CONTACT ADDRESS** Dept Hist, Purdue Univ, West Lafayette, IN, 47907-1358.

CUSHING, JAMES T.
DISCIPLINE HISTORY **EDUCATION** Loyola Univ, BS, 59; Northwestern Univ, MS, 60; Univ Iowa, PhD, 63. **CAREER** Prof. **RESEARCH** History and philosophy of quantum physics. **SELECTED PUBLICATIONS** Auth, Underdetermination, Conventionalism, and Realism, 93; Why Local Realism?, 93; A Bohmian Response to Bohr's Complementarity, 94; Hermeneutics, Underdetermination and Quantum Mechanics, 94; Bohmian Mechanics and Quantum Theory: An Appraisal, 96; co-ed, Quantum Mechanics: Historical Contingency and the Copenhagen Hegemony, 94. **CONTACT ADDRESS** History and Philosophy of Science Dept, Univ of Notre Dame, Notre Dame, IN, 46556. **EMAIL** Cushing.1@nd.edu

CUSICK, SUZANNE G.
DISCIPLINE MUSIC HISTORY **EDUCATION** Univ NC, PhD. **CAREER** Dept Music, Va Univ **RESEARCH** Feminist criticism; cultural history of 16th and 17th century European music; early opera; 19th century American popular music. **SELECTED PUBLICATIONS** Auth, Of Women, Music, and Power: A Model from Seicento Florence, Univ Ca, 93; Gendering Modern Music: Thoughts on the Monteverdi-Artusi Controversy, Jour Am Musicol Soc; 93; Thinking from Women's Lives: Francesca Caccini after 1627, 93; Feminist Theory, Music Theory, and the Mind-Body Problem, 93; 'And not one lady failed to shed a tear': Arianna's Lament and the Construction of Modern Womanhood, 94. **CONTACT ADDRESS** Dept of Music, Virginia Univ, Charlottesville, VA, 22903. **EMAIL** sgc5u@virginia.edu

CUTCLIFFE, STEPHEN HOSMER
PERSONAL Born 01/17/1947, Melrose, MA, m, 1980 **DISCIPLINE** SCIENCE, TECHNOLOGY & SOCIETY; HISTORY OF TECHNOLOGY **EDUCATION** Bates Col, AB, 68; Lehigh Univ, MA, 73, PhD(hist), 76. **CAREER** Admin asst, Sci, Technol & Soc Prog, 76-81, dir, Sci, Technol & Soc Prog, 88-, ed, Science, Technology and Society Newsletter, 77-. **MEMBERSHIPS** Orgn Am Historians; Soc Hist Technol; Nat Assn for Sci, Technol, and Soc. **RESEARCH** Technology and society; history of technology. **SELECTED PUBLICATIONS** Coauth, Technology and Values in American Civilization Detroit, Gale Res, 80; Responsibility and the technological process, Technol in Society, spring 80; auth, Colonial Indian policy as a measure of rising imperialism: New York and Pennsylvania, 1700-1755, Western Pa Hist Mag, 7/81; coauth, Technology and Values in American Civilization, Gale Research, 80; co-ed, In Context: History and the History of Technology-Essays in Honor of Melvin Kranzberg, Research in Technol Studies, vol 1, Lehigh Univ Press, 89; co-ed, New Worlds, New Technologies, New Issues, Research in Technol Studies, vol 6, Lehigh Univ Press, 92; co-ed, Technology and the West and Technology and American History, Univ Chicago Press, 97; The Emergence of STS as an Academic Field, Research in Philosophy and Technology 9, 287-301, 89; The Warp and Woof of Science and Technology Studies in the United States, Education, 352, 391-91, Spring 93. **CONTACT ADDRESS** Lehigh Univ, 9 W Packer Ave, Bethlehem, PA, 18015-3081. **EMAIL** shc0@lehigh.edu

CUTLER, ANTHONY
PERSONAL Born 02/18/1934, London, England, m, 1961, 2 children **DISCIPLINE** ART HISTORY **EDUCATION** Cambridge Univ, BA, 55, MA, 60; Emory Univ, PhD, 63. **CAREER** Instr humanities, Morehouse Col, 60-63; asst prof fine arts, 63-67, Emory Univ; assoc prof, 67-74, prof art hist, 74-, PA State Univ, Univ Park; Rockefeller res scholar, Inst Hist Studies, Naples, Italy, 56; Brit Coun Scholar, Univ Belgrade, 62; Am Numis Soc grant-in-aid, 63; vis assoc prof archit hist, 69, Univ Calif, Berkeley; Gennadeion fel, Am Sch Classical Studies, Athens, 70-71; fel, Dumbarton Oaks Ctr for Byzantine Studies, 75-76; consult, NEH, 76-; Am Coun Learned Soc, grant-in-aid, 81; sr res scholar, Corpus Christi Col, 82-83. **HONORS AND AWARDS** Choices list of Outstanding Academic Books of 1994; American Society of Eighteenth-Century Studies Fellow, Houghton Library, Harvard University, 94-95; Visiting Fellow, Princeton Univ, 95; Francois Ier medal, Coll de France, Paris, 95; Paul Mellon Sen Fel, Cen; vis fel, Princeton Univ, Spring, 95. **MEMBERSHIPS** Soc Am Archaeol; Mediaeval Acad Am; Col Art Assn; Byzantine Studies Conf; Francois Ier Medal, College de France, Paris, 95. **RESEARCH** Byzantine art history, especially late antique and early Christian ivories. manuscript illumination, mosaic and fresco painting. **SELECTED PUBLICATIONS** Auth, The Hand of the Martes, Craftsmanship Ivory and Society in Byzantium, Princeton University Press, 94. **CONTACT ADDRESS** Dept of Art Hist, Pennsylvania State Univ, Univ Park, 229 Arts Bldg, University Park, PA, 16802-2901. **EMAIL** axcb@psu.edu

CUTLER III, WILLIAM W.
DISCIPLINE HISTORY OF AMERICAN EDUCATION, AMERICAN URBAN HISTORY **EDUCATION** Cornell Univ, PhD. **CAREER** Assoc prof Hist and Educ Policy Stud, Temple Univ; guest lectr, Univ Algiers, 89. **HONORS AND AWARDS** The best article, Am Quart, 72. **RESEARCH** The hist of the home-school relationship in Am since the middle of the 19th century; the material cult of Am educ. **SELECTED PUBLICATIONS** Auth, Status, Values and the Education of the Poor: The Trustees of the New York Public School Society, 1805-1853, Am Quart, 72; Continuity and Discontinuity in the History of Childhood and the Family: A Reappraisal, Hist of Educ Quart, 86; Cathedral of Culture: The Schoolhouse in American Educational Thought and Practice since 1820, Hist of Educ Quart, 89; Symbol of Paradox in the New Republic: Classicism in the Design of Schoolhouses and Other Public Buildings in the United States, 1800-1860, in Aspects of Antiquity in the History of Education, F-P. Hager, et al, eds, 92; In Search of Influence and Authority: Parents and the Politics of the Home-School Relationship in Philadelphia and Two of its Suburbs, 1905-1035, Pa Hist, 96; co-ed, The Divided Metropolis: Social and Spatial Dimensions of Philadelphia, 1800-1975, 80. **CONTACT ADDRESS** Temple Univ, Philadelphia, PA, 19122. **EMAIL** wcutler@vm.temple.edu

CUTRER, THOMAS W.
PERSONAL Born 05/01/1947, Spring Creek, LA, m, 1978, 2 children **DISCIPLINE** HISTORY **EDUCATION** La St Univ, BA, 69, MA, 74; Univ Tx, PhD, 80. **CAREER** Curator, Univ Tx Inst of Texan Cultures, 80-82; res assoc, Univ Tx, 82-90; asst prof to assoc prof to prof, Az St Univ, 90- . **HONORS AND AWARDS** General L. Kemper Williams Prize, La Hist Soc, best book, 84; La Liter Award, La Libr Assoc, best book, 84; Summerfield G. Roberts Award, sons of the Republic of Tx, best book, 93; listed in Contemporary Authors, 69-70. **RESEARCH** Nineteenth century US mil hist; Amer South. **SELECTED PUBLICATIONS** Auth, Parnassus on the Mississippi: The Southern Review and the Baton Rouge Literary Community, 1935-1942, La St Univ Press, 84; Ben McCulloch and the Frontier Military Tradition, Univ NC Press, 93; ed, Longstreet's Aide: The Civil War Letters of Major Thomas J. Goree, Univ Press of Va, 95; coed, Brothers in Gray: The Civil War Letters of the Pierson Family, La St Univ Press, 97. **CONTACT ADDRESS** Col of Arts & Sci, Arizona State Univ, West, 4701 W Thunderbird Rd, PO Box 37100, Phoenix, AZ, 85069-7100. **EMAIL** cutrer@asu.edu

CUTTER, DONALD C.
PERSONAL Born 01/09/1922, Chico, CA, m, 1945, 9 children **DISCIPLINE** HISTORY **EDUCATION** Univ Calif, Berkeley, AB, 43, MA, 47, PhD, 50. **CAREER** Inst of Hist, San Diego St Col, 50-51; asst prof, 51-56, assoc prof, 56-61, prof, 61-62, Univ of So Calif; prof, 62-82, prof emeritus, 82-, Univ N Mex; O'Connor Prof, Spanish Colonial Hist of Texas & S W, 82-88, prof emeritus, 88-, St Mary's Univ. **RESEARCH** Spanish SW; Spanish naval explor; Amer Indian legal status. **SELECTED PUBLICATIONS** Auth, Changing Tides--Twilight and Dawn In the Spanish Sea, 1763-1803, Pacific Hist Rev, Vol 0066, 97; Malaspina,Alejandro--Impossible America-Spanish, Pacific Hist Rev, Vol 0064, 95; The Red Captain--The Life of Oconor, Hugo, Commandant-Inspector of New-Spain, NMex Hist Rev, Vol 0071, 96; The Discovery of San-Francisco-Bay--

Spanish and English, Calif Hist, Vol 0072, 93; The Pueblo Revolt of 1680--Conquest and Resistance in 17th-Century New-Mexico, Jour W, Vol 0036, 97; Hail, Columbia--Gray, Robert, Kendrick, John and the Pacific Fur Trade, Pacific Hist Rev, Vol 0064, 95; They Are Coming--The Conquest of Mexico, Jour W, Vol 0034, 95. **CONTACT ADDRESS** 2508 Harold Pl. NE, Albuquerque, NM, 87106. **EMAIL** d-cutter@unm.edu

CUTTER, PAUL F.
DISCIPLINE MUSIC HISTORY AND LITERATURE **EDUCATION** UCLA, BA; Harvard, MA; Princeton, MFA, PhD. **CAREER** Prof Mus, ch, Mus Hist and Lit, assoc dir, grad stud, TX Tech Univ. **HONORS AND AWARDS** TX Tech's President's Excellence in Tchg Award, 88. **SELECTED PUBLICATIONS** Publ bks and articles on subjects ranging from Gregorian Chant to music in pioneer West Texas. **CONTACT ADDRESS** Texas Tech Univ, Lubbock, TX, 79409-5015. **EMAIL** mspfc@ttacs.ttu.edu

CUTTLER, CHARLES DAVID
PERSONAL Born 04/08/1913, Cleveland, OH, 1 child **DISCIPLINE** HISTORY OF ART **EDUCATION** NY Univ, PhD(art hist), 52. **CAREER** Asst art hist, Ohio State Univ, 35-37; asst prof, Mich State Univ, 47-57; assoc prof hist of art, 57-65, res prof, 65-66, 75-76 & 82, PROF HIST OF ART, UNIV IOWA, 65-, Sr Fulbright fel, Belgium, 65-66; consult, Nat Endowment for Humanities, 73-; guest lectr Europe, 66 & 76 & Japan, 79. **MEMBERSHIPS** Col Art Asn Am; Renaissance Soc Am; Mediaeval Acad Am; Midwest Art Hist Soc (pres, 73-77). **RESEARCH** Medieval art; late medieval art. **SELECTED PUBLICATIONS** Auth, Holbein Inscriptions, Sixteenth Century Jour, Vol 0024, 93. **CONTACT ADDRESS** Sch of Art & Art Hist, Univ of Iowa, Iowa City, IA, 52242.

CVORNYEK, BOB
DISCIPLINE AFRICAN-AMERICAN, LABOR HISTORY **EDUCATION** Univ Del, BA; Columbia Univ, MPhil, PhD. **CAREER** Instr, RI Col. **RESEARCH** 19th-20th century African-Am and labor. **SELECTED PUBLICATIONS** Coed, A Documentary History of the Black Worker: From the AFL-CIO Merger to the Present. **CONTACT ADDRESS** Rhode Island Col, Providence, RI, 02908.

CYR, MARY
PERSONAL Fargo, ND **DISCIPLINE** MUSIC/HISTORY **EDUCATION** Univ Calif, BA, 68, MA, 70, PhD, 75. **CAREER** Prof, McGill Univ, 76-92, dir grad studs, 91-92; PROF & CHAIR, MUSIC, UNIV GUELPH 92-. **HONORS AND AWARDS** Noah Greenberg Award Excellence, Am Musicological Soc. **MEMBERSHIPS** Can Univ Music Soc; Early Music Soc; Am Musicological Soc. **SELECTED PUBLICATIONS** Auth, Performing Baroque Music, 92; auth, Violin Playing in Late Seventeenth-Century England: Baltzar, Matteis and Purcell in Performance Practice Review 8:1, 95. **CONTACT ADDRESS** Dept of Music, Univ of Guelph, Guelph, ON, N1G 2W1. **EMAIL** mcyr@arts.uoguelph.ca

CYRUS, CYNTHIA
PERSONAL Born 09/02/1963, Seattle, WA, m, 1995, 2 children **DISCIPLINE** MUSIC **EDUCATION** Pomona Col, BA, 84; Univ NC Chapel Hill, MA, 87, PhD, 90. **CAREER** Vis asst prof, Univ Rochester, 91-92; vis asst prof, SUNY Stony Brook, 92- 94; asst prof, Vanderbilt Univ, 94- . **HONORS AND AWARDS** Univ Post-doctoral Fel, Oh St Univ, 90-91; Vanderbilt Univ Res Coun Grants, 95, 96; Distinguished Leadership Award, 97. **MEMBERSHIPS** Amer Musicol Soc; Int Machant Soc; Renaissance Soc; Medieval Acad. **RESEARCH** Medieval & Renaissance musical literacy; women & music; musical modeling in the 15th-16th centuries. **SELECTED PUBLICATIONS** Auth, Rereading Absence: Women in Medieval and Renaissance Music, Col Music Symp, 98; Women Owners and Women Readers: The Circulation of Music Books in the Late Medieval and Early Modern Eras, forthcoming; Obsessed with Death in Freiburg, Sewanee Medieval Stud, forthcoming. **CONTACT ADDRESS** Blair School of Music, Vanderbilt Univ, 2400 Blakemore Ave, Nashville, TN, 37212. **EMAIL** cynthia.cyrus@vanderbilt.edu

CZUMA, STANISLAW
DISCIPLINE ART OF INDIA AND SOUTHEAST ASIA **EDUCATION** Jagiellon Univ, BA, MA; Univ Mich, PhD, 69. **CAREER** Art, Case Western Univ. **HONORS AND AWARDS** Paderewski Found; National Defense; Ford Found; Am Inst Indian Studies; Am Philos Soc; George P. Bickford grant; Andrew W. Mellon grant. **SELECTED PUBLICATIONS** Articles, Bull Cleveland Mus Art. **CONTACT ADDRESS** Case Western Reserve Univ, 10900 Euclid Ave, Cleveland, OH, 44106. **EMAIL** czuma@cma-oh.org

D

D'AGOSTINO, PETER R.
PERSONAL Born 12/22/1962, New York, NY, s **DISCIPLINE** RELIGIOUS STUDIES; HISTORY **EDUCATION** Brown Univ, BA, 80-84; Univ Chicago, MA, 86-87; Univ Chicago, PhD, 87-93 **CAREER** Visiting asst prof, Univ Ill, 94-95; asst prof Relig Studies & History, Stonehill Col, 95 **HONORS AND AWARDS** PEW Grant for Relig in Amer History, 98-99; Fulbright Jr Fac Res Fel, 96; Jr Fel, Univ Chic, 91-92; Giovanni Agnelli Found Italian Amer Studies Fel, 90-91; John T. McNeil Fel, 88-89 **MEMBERSHIPS** Orgn Amer Historians; Immigration History Soc; Amer Italian Historical Assoc; Amer Cath Historical Assoc; Amer Soc Church History; Amer Acad Relig **RESEARCH** U.S. Immigration History; U.S. Religious History; U.S. Society, 1877-1945; Modern Italy **SELECTED PUBLICATIONS** "The Sacraments of Whiteness: Racial Ambiguity and Religious Discipline Among Italians in Urban America," Religion and the City, forthcoming; "Urban Restructuring and the Religious Adaptation: Cardinal Joseph Bernardin of Chicago (1982-1995)," Public Religion and Urban Transformation, NY Univ Pr, forthcoming; "The Crisis of Authority in American Catholicism: Urban Schools and Cultural Conflict," Records of the American Catholic Historical Association of Philadelphia, forthcoming **CONTACT ADDRESS** 22 Bradbury St, Allston, MA, 02134. **EMAIL** pdagostino@stonehill.edu

D'ALLAIRE, MICHELINE
PERSONAL Born 04/23/1938, Montreal, PQ, Canada **DISCIPLINE** HISTORY **EDUCATION** Univ Montreal, BA, MA; Univ Ottawa, PhD. **CAREER** Prof, 65-86, PROF TITULAIRE D'HISTOIRE, UNIV OTTAWA, 86-. **RESEARCH** Canadian history; Quebec history; socio-religious history. **SELECTED PUBLICATIONS** Auth, Talon, 70; auth, L'Hopital-General du Quebec 1692-1764, 71; auth, Sans Soleil, 76; auth, Martei et declin d'une famille noble, 80; auth, Vingt ans de crise chez les religieuses 1960-1980, 82; auth, Les dats des communautes de femmes au Canada francais, aux XVIIe et XVIIIe siecles, 86. **CONTACT ADDRESS** History Dept, Univ of Ottawa, 155 Seraphim Marion, Ottawa, ON, K1N 6N5.

D'ARMS, JOHN H.
PERSONAL Born 11/27/1934, Poughkeepsie, NY, m, 1961, 2 children **DISCIPLINE** CLASSICAL PHILOLOGY **EDUCATION** Princeton Univ, AB, 56; New College, Oxford, BA (Literae Humaniores), 59; Harvard Univ, PhD (Classical Philol), 65. **CAREER** Chmn, dept classical studies, Univ MI, 72-75, 76-77, 80-85; dir, Am Academy in Rome and A W Mellon Prof, School of Classical Studies, 77-80; dean, Horace H Rackham School of Graduate Studies, Univ MI, 85-95, prof history, 86-97, Vice Provost for Academic Affairs, 90-95, G F Else Prof Humanities, Univ MI, 95-97; adjunct prof Classics and History, Columbia Univ, 97-; pres, AM Coun of Learned Societies, 97-. **HONORS AND AWARDS** Phi Beta Kappa, Princeton Univ, 56; Princeton Univ, Keasbey Scholar, 56; Honorary Woodrow Wilson fel, 56; Fulbright fel, Univ Rome, 61-62; Am Coun Learned Societies fel, 71-72; fel, John Simon Guggenheim Memorial Found, 75-76; vis member, School of Historical Studies, Inst for Advanced Study, Princeton, 75-76; corresponding member, German Archaeological Inst, Rome, 80-; Distinguished Faculty Achievement Award, Univ MI, 82; fel, Am Academy of Arts and Sciences, 92-; Centennial Medal, Am Academy in Rome, 95; Presidential Medal for Outstanding Service, Univ MI, 95; member, Am Philos Soc, 98; Docteur Honoris Causa (honorary), Univ Montreal, 98. **MEMBERSHIPS** Archaeolog Inst of Am; Am Hist Asn; Soc for the Promotion of Roman Studies (England); Am Philol Asn. **RESEARCH** Roman social, cultural, and economic history; Roman historiography; Latin epigraphy; Roman art, architecture, and archaeology; Latin prose and poetry. **SELECTED PUBLICATIONS** Auth, Romans on the Bay of Naples: A Social and Cultural Study of the Villas and their Owners from 150 BC to AD 400, Harvard Univ Press, 70; co-ed with E C Kopff, Roman Seaborne Commerce: Studies in Archaeology and History (Memoirs of the Am Academy in Rome), 80; auth, Commerce and Social Standing in Ancient Rome, Harvard Univ Press, 81; Control, Companionship, and Clientela: some Social Functions of the Roman Communal Meal, Echos du Monde Classique, N S 3, 84; The Roman Convivium and the Idea of Equality, in O Murray, ed, Sympotica: A Symposium on the Symposium, Claredon Press, Oxford, 90; Slaves at Roman Convivia, in W J Slater, ed, Dining in a Classical Context, Univ MI Press, 91; Heavy Drinking and Drunkenness in the Roman World: Questions for Historians, in O Murray, ed, In Vino Veritas, British School at Rome, 95; Funding Trends in the Academic Humanities, 1970-1995: Reflections on the Stability of the System, in A Kernan, ed, What's Happened to the Humanities, Princeton Univ Press, 97. **CONTACT ADDRESS** American Council of Learned Societies, 228 E 45th St, New York, NY, 10017-3398.

D'ELIA, DONALD JOHN
PERSONAL Born 06/16/1933, Jersey City, NJ, m, 1957, 4 children **DISCIPLINE** AMERICAN HISTORY **EDUCATION** Rutgers Univ, BA, 56, MA, 57; Pa State Univ, PhD, 65. **CAREER** Teaching asst hist, Pa State Univ, 59-61; from asst prof to assoc prof social studies, Bloomsburg State Col, 61-65; assoc prof, 65-71, prof hist, SUNY New Paltz, 71-; Boyd Lee Spahr lect Americana, Dickinson Col, 66; fac res fel, State Univ NY, 68, 74. **MEMBERSHIPS** Am Catholic Hist Asn; Fellowship Catholic Scholars. **RESEARCH** Early American scientific and religious thought; American intellectual history; the American Revolution. **SELECTED PUBLICATIONS** Auth, Dr Benjamin Rush and the Negro, J Hist Ideas, 7/69; auth, Dr Benjamin Rush, David Hartley, and the Revolutionary Uses of Psychology, Proc Am Philos Soc, 4/70; auth, Jefferson, Rush and the Limits of Philosophical Friendship, Proc Am Philos Soc, 10/73; auth, Benjamin Rush: Philosopher of the American Revolution, Trans Am Philos Soc, 74. **CONTACT ADDRESS** Dept of History, SUNY, New Paltz, New Paltz, NY, 12561.

D'EVELYN, MARGARET M.
PERSONAL Born 08/23/1948, Brookline, MA, m, 1970, 1 child **DISCIPLINE** HISTORY OF ART **EDUCATION** Princeton Univ, PhD 94. **CAREER** Author **RESEARCH** 15th, 16th century illustrated architectural books; art and architecture of renaissance. Venice **SELECTED PUBLICATIONS** Auth, Venice as Vitruvius's City in Daniele Barbara's Commentaries, Studi Venezian, 96. **CONTACT ADDRESS** 48 Pratt St, Providence, RI, 02906. **EMAIL** mdevelyn@mailexcite.com

DAHLSTRAND, FREDERICK CHARLES
PERSONAL Born 07/22/1945, Corry, PA, m, 1989, 1 child **DISCIPLINE** AMERICAN HISTORY **EDUCATION** Thiel Col, Ba, 67; Univ KS, MPhil, 76, PhD, 77. **CAREER** From Asst Prof to Assoc Prof Hist, Assoc Dean, OH State Univ, Mansfield, 78. **HONORS AND AWARDS** Univ Distinguished Tchg Award, 83. **MEMBERSHIPS** AHA; Orgn Am Historians. **RESEARCH** Am transcendentalism; impact of sci and technol on Am thought. **SELECTED PUBLICATIONS** Auth, Amos Bronson Alcott: An Intellectual Biography, Fairleigh-Dickinson Univ Press, 82. **CONTACT ADDRESS** Dept of Hist, Ohio State Univ, 1680 University Dr, Mansfield, OH, 44906-1547. **EMAIL** dahlstrand.1@osu.edu

DAILY, JONATHAN
PERSONAL Born 05/07/1958, Port Chester, NY, m, 1989, 2 children **DISCIPLINE** HISTORY **EDUCATION** Universite de Montreal, BA, 83; Georgetown Univ, MA, 86; Harvard Univ, AM, 87, PhD, 92. **CAREER** Tutor, 88-92, Senior Thesis Adv, 91-92, Harvard Univ; lectr to asst prof to assoc chemn, Univ Ill, 92-. **HONORS AND AWARDS** HF Guggenheim Res Grant, 95-96. **MEMBERSHIPS** Am Assoc Adv Slavic Stud. **RESEARCH** Political, institutional, and legal history of late Imperial Russia and early Soviet history. **SELECTED PUBLICATIONS** Auth, art, On the Significance of Emergency Legislation in Late Imperial Russia, 95; auth, Autocracy under Siege: Security Police and Opposition in Russia, 1866-1905, 98. **CONTACT ADDRESS** Dept of History, Univ of Illinois, Chicago, UH 913, Chicago, IL, 60607-7109. **EMAIL** daly@uic.edu

DAIN, NORMAN
PERSONAL Born 10/05/1925, Brooklyn, NY, m, 1950, 1 child **DISCIPLINE** AMERICAN HISTORY **EDUCATION** Brooklyn Col, BA, 53; Columbia Univ, MA, 57, PhD, 61. **CAREER** Res asst psychiat, Med Col, Cornell Univ, 58-61; from instr to assoc prof, 61-68, PROF AM HIST, RUTGERS UNIV, NEWARK, 68-, Mem ed staff, Hist Behav Sci Newslett, 60-65; Rutgers Univ Res Coun fac fels, 66-67 & 71-72; Soc Sci Res Coun grant-in-aid, 63-65; mem ed bd, J Hist Behav Sci, 65-81; NIH res grant, 66-69; sem assoc, Columbia Univ, 66-; res assoc, Med Col, Cornell Univ, 68-76, adj prof, 76- **MEMBERSHIPS** AHA; Am Asn Hist Med; Orgn Am Historians; Int Soc Hist Behav & Soc Sci; AAUP. **RESEARCH** American intellectual history; history of psychiatric thought; social history of the United States. **SELECTED PUBLICATIONS** Auth, Feeble-Minded in Our Midst--Institution for the Mentally-Retarded in the South 1900-1940, Amer Hist Rev, Vol 0102, 97; Moonlight, Magnolias, and Madness--Insanity in South-Carolina from the Colonial Period to the Progressive-Era, Jour So Hist, Vol 0063, 97. **CONTACT ADDRESS** Dept of History, Rutgers Univ, Newark, NJ, 07102.

DALE, WILLIAM S.A.
PERSONAL Born 09/18/1921, Toronto, ON, Canada **DISCIPLINE** ART HISTORY **EDUCATION** Univ Toronto, BA, 44, MA, 46; Harvard Univ, PhD, 55; Courtauld Inst, London Univ, 48-50. **CAREER** Staff, 50-57, asst dir, 61-66, dep dir, Nat Gallery Can, 66-67; curator, Art Gallery Toronto, 57-59; dir, Vancouver Art Gallery, 59-61; prof 67-87, dept ch, 67-75, 85-87, PROF EMER VISUAL ARTS, UNIV WESTERN ONT, 87-; res fel, Dumbarton Oaks Res Libr, Washington, 56-57. **MEMBERSHIPS** Arts & Letters Club Toronto; Col Art Asn Am; Medieval Acad Am; Royal Soc Arts; Int Ctr Medieval Art; Univ Art Asn Can. **SELECTED PUBLICATIONS** Contribur, Apollo; contribur, Art Bull; contribur, Brit Mus Yearbk; contribur, Burlington Mag; contribur, Can Art; contribur, RACAR; contribur, Speculum. **CONTACT ADDRESS** 1517 Gloucester Rd, London, ON, N6G 2S5.

DALES, RICHARD C.
PERSONAL Born 04/17/1926, Akron, OH, m, 1950, 2 children **DISCIPLINE** HISTORY **EDUCATION** Univ Rochester, BA, 49; Univ Colo, MA, 52, PhD, 55. **CAREER** Instr hist, NDak Agr Col, 54-55; from instr to assoc prof, Lewis & Clark Col, 55-64; assoc prof, 64-66, PROF HIST, UNIV SOUTHERN CALIF, 66-, Am Coun Learned Soc fel, 60-61; vis assoc prof, Univ Southern Calif, 62-63; mem, Inst Advan Studies, 66-67; Am Philos Soc fel, 68. **MEMBERSHIPS** Medieval Acad Am. **RESEARCH** Medieval intellectual history; history of science. **SELECTED PUBLICATIONS** Auth, Glossae Super Genesim-Prolog and Chapters 1-3--Latin, Isis, Vol 0084, 93; The Beginnings of Western Science--The European Scientific Tradition in Philosophical, Religious, and Institutional Context, 600bc to Ad1450, Amer Hist Rev, Vol 0098, 93. **CONTACT ADDRESS** Dept of Hist, Univ of Southern Calif, Los Angeles, CA, 90007.

DALEY, BRIAN EDWARD
PERSONAL Born 01/18/1940, Orange, NJ **DISCIPLINE** HISTORICAL THEOLOGY, CHRUCH HISTORY **EDUCATION** Fordham Univ, BA, 61; Oxford Univ, BA, 64, MA, 67, DPhil(theol), 79; Loyola Sem, PhL, 66; Hochschule Sankt Georgen, Frankfurt, Lic theol, 72. **CAREER** Instr classics, Fordham Univ, 66-67; ASST PROF HIST THEOL, WESTON SCH THEOL, 78-, Ed, Traditio, 78-; trustee, Le Moyne Col, 79- **MEMBERSHIPS** Asn Int Etudes Patristiques; Am Soc Church Hist; Soc Values Higher Educ; Am Asn Rhodes Scholars. **RESEARCH** Greek patristic theology; history of spirituality; Neoplatonism. **SELECTED PUBLICATIONS** Auth, Position and Patronage in the Early-Church--Distinguishing Between Personal or Moral Authority and Canonical or Structural Jurisdiction in the Early-Christian Community and Civil-Society--The Original Meaning of Primacy-Of-Honor, Jour Theol; Regnum-Caelorum--Patterns of Future Hope in Early Christianity, Jour Theol Stud, Vol 0045, 94; Apollo as a Chalcedonian--Tracing the Trajectory of a Christian Oracle and Christological Apologia--A New Fragment of a Controversial Work From Early 6th-Century Constantinople, Traditio-Stud Ancient and Medieval Hist Thought and Rel. **CONTACT ADDRESS** Dept of Hist Theol, Weston Jesuit Sch of Theol, Cambridge, MA, 02138.

DALLEK, ROBERT
PERSONAL Born 05/16/1934, Brooklyn, NY, m, 1965 **DISCIPLINE** AMERICAN DIPLOMATIC HISTORY **EDUCATION** Univ Ill, BA, 55; Columbia Univ, MA, 57, PhD(hist), 64. **CAREER** Lectr hist, City Col New York, 58-60; instr, Columbia Univ, 60-64; from asst prof to assoc prof, 64-73, PROF HIST, UNIV CALIF, LOS ANGELES, 73-, Humanities Inst fel, Univ Calif, Los Angeles, 69, vchmn dept, 70-73; Guggenheim fel, 73-74; sr fel, Nat Endowment for Humanities, 76-77; Rockefeller Found fel humanities, 81-82. **HONORS AND AWARDS** Bancroft Prize, 80. **MEMBERSHIPS** AHA; Orgn Am Historians; Soc Hist Am Foreign Relat. **RESEARCH** Franklin D Roosevelt's diplomacy. **SELECTED PUBLICATIONS** Auth, Johnson,Lyndon and Vietnam--The Making of a Tragedy, Diplomatic Hist, Vol 0020, 96; The American Presidency--An Intellectual History, Rev(s) in Amer Hist, Vol 0022, 94. **CONTACT ADDRESS** Dept of Hist, Univ of Calif, Los Angeles, CA, 90024.

DALLIN, ALEXANDER
PERSONAL Born 05/21/1924, Berlin, Germany, 3 children **DISCIPLINE** HISTORY, POLITICAL SCIENCE **EDUCATION** City Col New York, BS, 46; Columbia Univ, MA, 47, PhD(hist), 53. **CAREER** Prof int rels, Columbia Univ, 65-69; PROF HIST & POLIT SCI, STANFORD UNIV, 71-, Dir Russ Inst, Columbia Univ, 62-67; consult, US Govt, 62-70; sr res fel, Hoover Inst, Stanford Univ, 71-78. **HONORS AND AWARDS** G L Beer Prize, AHA, 57. **MEMBERSHIPS** Am Asn Advan Slavic Studies; AHA; Nat Coun Soviet & East Europ Res; Western Slavic Studies. **RESEARCH** Modern Russian history; Soviet foreign policy; international communism. **SELECTED PUBLICATIONS** Auth, The End of Communist Power--Anti-Corruption Campaigns and Legitimation Crisis, Slavic Rev, Vol 0053, 94; The Gulag at War--Stalins Forced Labor System in the Light of the Archives, Amer Hist Rev, Vol 0101, 96; The Great Exodus--The Russian Emigration and its Centers 1917 to 1941--German, Slavic Rev, Vol 0055, 96; A World at Arms--A Global History of World-War-II, Intl Hist Rev, Vol 0017, 95; Autopsy on an Empire--The American Ambassadors Account of the Collapse of the Soviet-Union, Amer Hist Rev, Vol 0102, 97. **CONTACT ADDRESS** 607 Cabrillo Ave, Stanford, CA, 94305.

DALSTROM, HARL A.
PERSONAL Born 04/11/1936, Omaha, NE **DISCIPLINE** UNITED STATES HISTORY **EDUCATION** Munic Univ Omaha, BA, 58, MA, 59; Univ Nebr, PhD(hist), 65. **CAREER** Instr hist, 63-65, from asst prof to assoc prof, 65-74, chmn dept, 71-75, PROF HIST, UNIV NEBR, OMAHA, 74-. **MEMBERSHIPS** Orgn Am Historians; Southern Hist Asn; Western Hist Asn; Agr Hist Soc. **RESEARCH** Recent American history; state and local history. **SELECTED PUBLICATIONS** Auth, An Unspeakable Sadness--The Dispossession of the Nebraska Indians, West Hist Quart, Vol 0027, 96; The Changing Image of the City--Planning for Downtown Omaha, 1945-1973, Great Plains Quart, Vol 0013, 93; Fort-Meade and the Black-Hills, Pacific Northwest Quart, Vol 0084, 93; Law and the Great-Plains--Essays on the Legal History of the Heartland, Mich Hist Rev, Vol 0022, 96. **CONTACT ADDRESS** Dept of Hist, Univ of Nebr, 6001 Dodge St, Omaha, NE, 68182-0002.

DALTON, KATHLEEN MARY
PERSONAL Born 11/18/1948, Martinez, CA, m, 1981 **DISCIPLINE** AMERICAN HISTORY AND STUDIES **EDUCATION** Mills Col, AB, 70; Johns Hopkins Univ, MA, 75, PhD(Am hist), 79. **CAREER** Instr hist, Hartford Col for Women, 76, Nat Cathedral Sch, 73-74 & 78-79; adj prof hist & Am studies, Am Univ, 79-80; INSTR HIST & SOC SCI, PHILLIPS ACAD, 80-, Consult, Nat Geog Soc, 79-80; assoc ed, Psychohist Rev, 81- **MEMBERSHIPS** Orgn Am Historians; AHA; Coord Comt Women in Hist Profession; Am Studies Asn; Group for Use of Psychol in Hist. **RESEARCH** American social, intellectual and cultural history; Theodore Roosevelt and his America; sex roles in recent United States history. **SELECTED PUBLICATIONS** Auth, Ives,Charles--My Fathers Song--A Psychoanalytic Biography, Amer Hist Rev, Vol 0098, 93; The Inner World of Lincoln,Abraham, Amer Hist Rev, Vol 0101, 96; Icons of Democracy--American Leaders as Heroes, Aristocrats, Dissenters, and Democrats, Jour Interdisciplinary Hist, Vol 0025, 95. **CONTACT ADDRESS** Phillips Acad, 137 Main St, Andover, MA, 01810.

DALY, JOHN P.
DISCIPLINE HISTORY **EDUCATION** Univ VA, BA, 86; Rice Univ, MA, PhD 93. **CAREER** Am hist instr, Univ St Thomas, 90-94; col instr, Univ Houston, 91-92; Am hist instr, Tex Southern Univ, 93-94; relig and hist instr, Rice Univ, 92-95; hist adj, Univ Houston, 94-95; vis asst prof, Austin Col, 95-96; asst prof, La Tech Univ, 96-. **HONORS AND AWARDS** Barbara Field Kennedy Award in Am Hist, 93. **RESEARCH** Am hist; Am intellectual and cult hist; southern hist. **SELECTED PUBLICATIONS** Auth, Redeeming America, Jour of Southern Hist, 95; Henry Hughes and Proslavery, Jour of Southern Hist, 95; Virtue is Power: Sectionalism, Slavery, and the Moral Culture of Antebellum America, 1830-1865, Univ Ky. **CONTACT ADDRESS** Dept of Hist, Louisiana Tech Univ, PO Box 3178, Ruston, LA, 71272.

DALY, LAWRENCE JOHN
PERSONAL Born 02/07/1938, Middletown, OH, m, 1960, 4 children **DISCIPLINE** HISTORY **EDUCATION** Xavier Univ, Ohio, AB, 60, MA, 61; Loyola Univ, III, PhD(hist), 70. **CAREER** From instr to asst prof, 65-72, asoc prof hist, Bowling Green State Univ, 72- **MEMBERSHIPS** Soc Prom Roman Studies; Asn Ancient Historians. **RESEARCH** Late Roman Empire; the pagan opposition; imperial ideology. **SELECTED PUBLICATIONS** Auth, Themistius' Plea for Religious Tolerance, Greek Roman & Byzantine Studies, 71; The Mandarin and the Barbarian: Themistius' Response to the Gothic Challenge, 72 & Verginius at Vesontio: The Incongruity of the Bellum Neronis, 75, Historia; Themistius' Concept of Philanthropia, Byzantion, 75; Varro Murena, cos 23 BC: (magistratu motus) est, Historia, 78. **CONTACT ADDRESS** Dept of Hist, Bowling Green State Univ, 1001 E Wooster St, Bowling Green, OH, 43403-0001. **EMAIL** ldaly@bgnet.bgsu.edu

DALY, WILLIAM M.
PERSONAL Born 12/27/1920, Great Barrington, MA, m, 1947, 3 children **DISCIPLINE** HISTORY **EDUCATION** Boston Col, BA, 42, MA, 47; Brown Univ, PhD, 55. **CAREER** From instr to assoc prof, 47-71, PROF HIST, BOSTON COL, 71-, Vis assoc prof hist, Brown Univ, 60; fac res fel, Boston Col, 61-62; Am Coun Learned Soc fel, 68-69. **MEMBERSHIPS** Mediaeval Acad Am; AHA. **RESEARCH** Early Medieval France, especially political and social thought; Medieval English constitutional history. **SELECTED PUBLICATIONS** Auth, Clovis--A Portrayal of the First Frankish King of Gaul Through Primary and Secondary Source Material--How Barbaric, How Pagan, Speculum-A Jour Medieval Stud, Vol 0069, 94. **CONTACT ADDRESS** Dept of Hist, Boston Col, Chestnut Hill, MA, 02167.

DALZELL, ALEXANDER
PERSONAL Born 05/08/1925, Belfast, Northern Ireland **DISCIPLINE** CLASSICS **EDUCATION** Trinity Col (Dublin), BA, 50, MA, 53, BLitt, 56. **CAREER** Lectr, Kings Col, Univ London, 51-53; lectr, Univ Sheffield, 53-54; lectr to prof, 54-88, dean arts, 68-73, vice provost, 72-79, acting provost, 73, 79, PROF EMER, TRINITY COL, UNIV TORONTO, 88-. **MEMBERSHIPS** Class Asn Can (pres 80-82); Am Philol Asn (mem publ comt), 81-84. **SELECTED PUBLICATIONS** Auth, The Criticism of Didactic Poetry, 96; contribur, Correspondence of Erasmus, vols 10 & 11, 92, 93; assoc ed/ed, Phoenix, 60-71; ed bd, Collected Works of Erasmus. **CONTACT ADDRESS** 344 Saunders St, Fredericton, NB, E3B 1N8.

DANBOM, DAVID BYERS
PERSONAL Born 03/29/1947, Denver, CO, m, 1971, 2 children **DISCIPLINE** AMERICAN HISTORY **EDUCATION** CO State Univ, BA, 69; Stanford Univ, MA, 70, PhD, 74. **CAREER** Prof Am hist, ND, State Univ, 74, Assoc ed, NDak Inst Regional Studies, 81-92. **HONORS AND AWARDS** Fargo Chamber of Commerce Distinguished Prof, 90; CASE ND Prof of the Year, 1990; NDSU Fac Lectr, 98. **MEMBERSHIPS** Orgn Am Historians; Agr Hist Soc. **RESEARCH** Progressivism; rural and agricultural hist; ND hist. **SELECTED PUBLICATIONS** Auth, The Resisted Revolution: Urban America and the Industrialization of Agriculture, 1900-1930, Iowa State Univ Press, 79; The World of Hope: Progressives and the Struggle for an Ethical Public Life, Temple Univ Press, 87; Our Purpose Is to Serve: The First Century of the North Dakota Agricultural Experiment Station, NDIRS, 90; Born in the Country: A History of Rural America, Johns Hopkins Univ press, 95. **CONTACT ADDRESS** Dept of Hist, No Dakota State Univ, PO Box 5075, Fargo, ND, 58105-5075. **EMAIL** danbom@plains.nodak.edu

DANBY, JUDD G.
PERSONAL Born 10/11/1966, New York, NY **DISCIPLINE** MUSIC COMPOSITION AND THEORY **EDUCATION** Rutgers Univ, BMus, 88; Univ Ill at Urbana-Champaign, MMus, 92; Univ Ill at Urbana-Champaign, AMusD, 98 **CAREER** Vis lectr music, Univ Ill at Urbana-Champaign, 95-97; vis prof music, Wabash Col, 98-. **MEMBERSHIPS** Am Music Ctr; Am Soc for Aesthetics; Broadcast Music, Inc.; Col Music Soc; Soc for Electro-Acoustic Music in the U.S.; Soc of Composers, Inc. **RESEARCH** Pitch-class set theory; twelve-tone/serial theory; Schenkerian analysis; the notion of form in music; perception and musical experience. **SELECTED PUBLICATIONS** Auth, Mirrors, for percussion quartet, Media Press; auth, The Piano's Stuck, for solo piano, Soundout Digital Press. **CONTACT ADDRESS** Fine Arts Center, Wabash Col, 301 W. Wabash, Crawford, IN, 47933. **EMAIL** danbyj@wabash.edu

DANIEL, CLETUS EDWARD
PERSONAL Born 12/26/1943, Salinas, CA, m, 1976, 2 children **DISCIPLINE** HISTORY **EDUCATION** San Jose State Univ, BA, 67, MA, 69; Univ Washington, PhD, 72. **CAREER** Vis asst prof, hist, Univ Wash, 73; asst prof, 73-79, assos prof, 79-88, prof, 88 -, Sch Indus and Labor Rel, Cornell Univ. **HONORS AND AWARDS** Magna cum laude; Phi Beta Kappa; Woodrow Wilson Diss Fel, 71-72; NEH Fel, 74-75; ILR Excellence in Teaching Award, 79-80, 82-83; Univ Paramount Prof for Tchg Excellence, 92-93. **MEMBERSHIPS** Ed Bd, Labor History; ed consult NY State Labor Legacy Project. **SELECTED PUBLICATIONS** Auth, The ACLU and the Wagner Act: An Inquiry into the Depression-Era Crisis of American Liberalism, ILR Press, 81; auth, Bitter Harvest: A History of California Farmworkers, 1870-1941, Cornell, 81; auth, Cesar Chavez, in Dubofsky, ed, Labor Leaders in Industrial America, Univ Ill, 87; auth, Cesar Chavez and the Unionization of California Farm Workers, in Nash, ed, Retracing the Past: Readings in the History of the American People, v.2, 2d ed, Harper & Row, 90; auth, Chicano Workers and the Politics of Fairness: The FEPC in the Southwest, 1941-1945, Univ Texas, 91; auth, Cesar Chavez and California Farm Workers, in Cornford, ed, Working People of California, Univ Calif, 95; auth, Communist Involvement in Agricultural Labor Struggles, in Chan, ed, Major Problems in California History: Documents and Essays, Houghton Mifflin, 97; auth, Cesar Chavez and the Unionization of California Farm Workers, in Weisner, ed, American Lives, McGraw-Hill, forthcoming. **CONTACT ADDRESS** School of Industrial and Labor Relations, Cornell Univ, Ithaca, NY, 14853.

DANIEL, HERSHEY
PERSONAL Born 02/12/1931, New York, NY, m, 1965, 2 children **DISCIPLINE** INTERDISCPLINARY STUDIES **EDUCATION** Cooper Union, BS, 53; Univ Tenn, PhD, 61. **CAREER** PROF, UNIV CINCINNATI, 62-. **HONORS AND AWARDS** Fulbright fel, 75 & 91; Tau Beta Pi teaching award, 70 & 72, 1st place, Cincinnati Eds Assn fiction writing, 75; Clinical Research Award, Amer Soc **MEMBERSHIPS** Int Soc for Systems Sciences; Amer Aging Assn; Amer Inst Chemical Engineers; Am Soc Bariatric Physicians. **RESEARCH** Aging, Evolving Systems, Living humans and Inanimate corporations and the universe. **SELECTED PUBLICATIONS** Ed, Chemical Engineering in Medicine and Biology, Plenum, 67; auth, In God We Trust, Vantage, 67; ed, Blood Oxygenation, Plenum, 70; auth, Everyday Science, Doubleday, 71; Transport Analysis, Plenum, 73; Lifespan and Factors Affecting It, CC Thomas, 74; A New Age-Scale for Humans, Lexington Books, 80; Must We Grow Old: From Pauling to Prigogine to Toynbee, Basal Books, 84; Diagnosing and Organizational Bureaucracy, Basal Books, 84; Entropy, Infinity, and God, Basal Books, 97. **CONTACT ADDRESS** 726 Lafayette Ave., Cincinnati, OH, 45220-1053.

DANIEL, MARCUS L.
DISCIPLINE HISTORY **EDUCATION** Cambridge Univ, BA, 84; Princeton Univ, MA, 89, PhD, 97. **CAREER** ASST PROF, HIST, UNIV HAWAII MANOA **MEMBERSHIPS** Am Antiquarian Soc **SELECTED PUBLICATIONS** Auth, "Ribaldry and Billingsgate: Popular Journalism and Political Culture in the Early Republic, 97. **CONTACT ADDRESS** Dept of Hist, Coll of Arts & Human, Univ of Hawaii, 2530 Dole St, Honolulu, HI, 96822. **EMAIL** mdaniel@hawaii.edu

DANIEL, PETE
PERSONAL Born 11/24/1938, Rocky Mount, NC **DISCIPLINE** SOUTHERN UNITED STATES AND AGRICULTURAL HISTORY **EDUCATION** Wake Forest Univ, BA, 61, MA, 62; Univ Md, College Park, PhD(hist), 70. **CAREER** Instr hist, Univ NC, Wilmington, 63-66; asst ed, Booker T Washington Papers, Univ Md, 69-70; Nat Endowment for Humanities fel Afro-Am hist, Johns Hopkins Univ, 70-71; asst prof, Univ Tenn, Knoxville, 71-73, assoc prof, 73-78, prof, 78; FEL, WOODROW WILSON INT CTR SCHOLARS, 79-, Vis prof hist, Univ Mass, Boston, 74-75; Nat Endowment for Humanities Independent Study res fel, 78-79; consult, US Dept Educ, 81 & Smithsonian Inst, 81. **HONORS AND AWARDS** Louis Pelzer Prize, Orgn Am Historians, 70. **MEMBERSHIPS** Orgn Am Historians; AHA; Southern History Asn. **RESEARCH** United States Southern history; agricultural history. **SELECTED PUBLICATIONS** Auth, Rhythm of the Land, Agricult Hist, Vol 0068, 94. **CONTACT ADDRESS** Natl Museum Amer Hist, Smithsonian Inst, Div Agr and Nat Resour, Washington, DC, 20560.

DANIEL, WILBON HARRISON
PERSONAL Born 09/25/1922, Lynchburg, VA, m, 1950, 1 child **DISCIPLINE** AMERICAN HISTORY **EDUCATION** Lynchburg Col, BA, 44; Vanderbilt Univ, BD, 46, MA, 47; Duke Univ, PhD(Am hist, Am Christianity), 57. **CAREER** Teacher hist, Va Intermont Col, 47-54; from instr to assoc prof, 56-69, chmn dept, 69-74, prof, 69-80, WILLIAM BINFORD VEST PROF HIST, UNIV RICHMOND, 80-. **MEMBERSHIPS** AHA; Southern Hist Asn; Orgn Am Historians. **RESEARCH** Civil War period; American church history; 19th century United States. **SELECTED PUBLICATIONS** Auth, Religion in the South--A Review of 7 Recent Books, Miss Quart, Vol 0050, 97; Toward Peacemaking--Presbyterians in the South and National-Security, 1945-1983, Miss Quart, Vol 0049, 96; Longstreet,James the Confederacys Most Controversial Soldier--A Biography, Historian, Vol 0057, 94; What Happened to the Southern Baptist Convention, A Memoir of the Controversy, Miss Quart, Vol 0047, 94; Chancellorsville, 1863--The Souls of the Brave, Civil War Hist, Vol 0040, 94. **CONTACT ADDRESS** Dept of Hist, Univ Richmond, Richmond, VA, 23173.

DANIELL, JERE ROGERS
PERSONAL Born 11/28/1932, Millinocket, ME, m, 1969, 5 children **DISCIPLINE** HISTORY **EDUCATION** Dartmouth Col, BA, 55; Harvard Univ, PhD, 64. **CAREER** Asst prof, 64-69, assoc prof, 69-74, prof hist, 74- , Class of 1925 Prof, 84- , Dartmouth Col. **HONORS AND AWARDS** Who's Who in Am, 85- ; New Hampshire Notables, 86. **MEMBERSHIPS** Colonial Soc Mass; Thetford, Vt Hist Soc; NH Hist Soc; New Hampshire Bicentennial on the U.S. Constitution. **RESEARCH** Early American history; history of New England. **SELECTED PUBLICATIONS** Auth, Frontier and Constitution: Why Grafton County Delegates Voted 10-1 for Ratification, Hist New Hampshire, 90; auth, A Sense of Place: Lobstermen, Milltowns and Witchcraft Shape New England Still, Dartmouth Alumni Mag, 90; contribur, Doan, ed, Indian Stream Republic: Settling a New England Frontier, 1785-1842, Univ Press of New England, 97; contribur, Encyclopedia of New England Culture, forthcoming. **CONTACT ADDRESS** Dept of History, Dartmouth Col, Hanover, NH, 03755. **EMAIL** jere.r.daniell@dartmouth.edu

DANIELS, BRUCE C.
PERSONAL Born 08/27/1943, Baldwin, NY **DISCIPLINE** HISTORY **EDUCATION** Syracuse Univ, AB, 64; Univ Conn, MA, 67, PhD, 70. **CAREER** PROF HISTORY, UNIV WINNIPEG, 70-. **HONORS AND AWARDS** Award merit, Am Asn State Local Hist, 90; Homer Babbidge Award, 90. **SELECTED PUBLICATIONS** Auth, Connecticut's First Family, 75; auth, Town and Country, 78; auth, The Connecticut Town, 79; auth, Dissent and Conformity on Narragansett Bay, 83; auth, Power and Status in the American Colonies, 86; auth, The Fragmentation of New England, 89; auth, Puritans at Play, 95; ed, Can Rev Am Stud, 77-86; assoc ed, Am Nat Biogr, 91-. **CONTACT ADDRESS** Dept of History, Univ of Winnipeg, Winnipeg, MB, R3B 2E9.

DANIELS, DOUGLAS HENRY
PERSONAL Born 10/12/1943, Chicago, IL, m, 1987, 3 children **DISCIPLINE** HISTORY **EDUCATION** Univ Chicago, BA 64; Univ Cal Berk, Ma and PhD, 69 and 75. **CAREER** Univ Texas, asst prof 75-78; Univ Cal Santa Barb, prof 79-. **HONORS AND AWARDS** Fulbright fel; Mellon fel; Ford fel; NEH **MEMBERSHIPS** OAH; ASAALA **RESEARCH** Hist of Jazz; urban hist; photography; E African pop music. **SELECTED PUBLICATIONS** Auth, Pioneer Urbanites: A Social and Cultural History of Black San Francisco, ed et al; Peoples of Color in the American West; Charlemagne Peralte and the First American Occupation of Haiti, by George Michael. **CONTACT ADDRESS** Dept of Black Studies, Univ of California, Santa Barbara, Santa Barbara, CA, 93106-3150. **EMAIL** daniels@aleshaw.ucsb.edu

DANIELS, R.V.
PERSONAL Born 01/04/1926, Boston, MA, m, 1945, 4 children **DISCIPLINE** HISTORY **EDUCATION** Harvard Univ, AB 45, MA 47, PhD 51. **CAREER** Univ Vermont, chmn 64-69, prof 58-88, prof emer 88-. **HONORS AND AWARDS** Guggenheim fel; Kennan Inst fel; LLD Honors **MEMBERSHIPS** AAASS; CAS; VAAS **RESEARCH** Russian hist politics since 1917. **SELECTED PUBLICATIONS** Auth, The End of the Communist Revolution, Routledge, 93; A Documentary History of Communism, ed, Univ Press New Eng, 94; Soviet Communism from Reform to Collapse, ed, DC Health, 95; The Stalin Revolution, ed, Houghton Mifflin, 97; Russia's Transformation, Rowman Littlefield, 97. **CONTACT ADDRESS** Dept of History, Vermont Univ, 195 South Prospect St, Burlington, VT, 05401. **EMAIL** rdaniels@zoo.uvm.edu

DANKER, DONALD FLOYD
PERSONAL Born 10/07/1922, Riverton, NE, m, 1946, 2 children **DISCIPLINE** AMERICAN HISTORY **EDUCATION** Univ Nebr, BS, 48, MA, 49, PhD, 55. **CAREER** Prof Am hist & polit sci, York Col, 49-51; instr Am hist, Univ Nebr, 55-63; asst prof US hist, Washburn Univ Topeka, 63-64; historian, Nebr State Hist Soc, 64-67; assoc prof, 67-71, PROF HIST, WASHBURN UNIV TOPEKA, 71-, Archivist, Nebr State Hist Soc, 52-63; mem, Kans Hist Sites Bd Rev, 71-77. **MEMBERSHIPS** Orgn Am Historians; Western Hist Asn. **RESEARCH** Western history. **SELECTED PUBLICATIONS** Auth, The Ghost-Dance Religion and the Sioux Outbreak of 1890, Jour W, Vol 0032, 93; Eyewitness at Wounded-Knee, Jour W, Vol 0032, 93; Lakota Recollections of the Custer Fight--New Sources of Indian Military History, Jour W, Vol 0032, 93. **CONTACT ADDRESS** Dept of Hist, Washburn Univ, Topeka, KS, 66621.

DANYSK, CECILIA
DISCIPLINE HISTORY **EDUCATION** Concordia Univ, Montreal, BA, 78; McGill Univ, Montreal, MA, 81, PhD, 91. **CAREER** Lectr, Dept Hist, Univ Alberta, Can, 86-88; Lectr, Dept Hist & Can Stud Prog, Trent Univ, Can, 88-91; Asst prof, Dept Hist & Can Stud, Dalhousie Univ, Can, 91-96; ASST PROF, DEPT HIST & CAN-AM PROG, W WASH UNIV, 96-. **HONORS AND AWARDS** Res fel Can Plains Res Ctr, Univ Regina, Can, 94; Soc Sci & Hum Res Coun Can grant, 93-97. **MEMBERSHIPS** Can Hist Asn; Asn Can Stud; Can Comm Labour Hist; Can Comm Women's Hist; Asn Atlantic Hist; Women in AB & SK Hist; Soc Soc Stud; Asn Can Stud in US, Am Hist Asn. **RESEARCH** Western Canadian rural, labour and social history; Current research project on Bonanza Farming in Prairie Canada, 1880-1930. **SELECTED PUBLICATIONS** Auth, No Help for the Farm Help: The Farm Placement Plans of the 1930's in Prairie Canada, Prairie Forum, 94; Recreating the Pluralism of the Past, Teaching Women's History: Challenges and Solutions, Athabasca Univ, 95; When Agribusiness Failed: The Qu'Appelle Valley Farming Company, 1882-1889, Rural Res in Hum & Soc Sci II: Proceedings of the Second Annual Colloquium of Rural Res Ctr, Nova Scotia Agr Col, 95; Hired Hands: Labour and the Development of Prairie Agriculture, 1880 to 1930, Oxford Univ Press, 95; A Bachelor's Paradise: Homesteaders, Hired Hands and the Construction of Masculinity, Making Western Canada: Essays on European Colonization and Settlement, Garamond Press, 96; 'James Speakman' and 'Edwin Carswell' Dictionary of Can Biog, Volume XIV, 1911-1920, Univ Toronto Press, 98. **CONTACT ADDRESS** Hist Dept, W. Washington Univ, Bellingham, WA, 98225-9056. **EMAIL** danysk@cc.wwu.edu

DANZER, GERALD A.
DISCIPLINE HISTORY **EDUCATION** Concordia Col, BS, 59; MA, 61, PhD, 67, Northwestern Univ. **CAREER** Chr, Council for Effective Teaching and Learning, Univ Illinois, 92-94; Prof and Dir of MA program for teachers of history, 67-, Univ Illinois. **CONTACT ADDRESS** Dept of History, Univ of Illinois, Chicago, 601 S Morgan St, Chicago, IL, 60607. **EMAIL** gdanzer@uic.edu

DANZIGER, EDMUND J.
PERSONAL Born 02/10/1938, Newark, NJ, m, 1961, 2 children **DISCIPLINE** HISTORY **EDUCATION** Col of Wooster, BA, 60; Univ Ill, MA, 62, PhD, 66. **CAREER** Dist Teach Prof, Bowling Green State Univ, 66-. **MEMBERSHIPS** Western Hist Asn; Org of Am Hist. **RESEARCH** American & Canadian Indian History. **SELECTED PUBLICATIONS** Auth, United States Indian Policy during the Late Nineteenth Century: Change and Continuity, Hayes Hist J, vol 12, 27-39, Fall 92; auth, Conflict, Cooperation, and Accomodation Along the Great Lakes Frontier, NW Ohio Quart, vol 65, 129-33, summer 93; auth, Self-Determination, Native Am in the 20th cent, an Encycl, Garland Publishing, Inc, 223-25, 94; auth, Native American Resistance and Accomodations in the Late Nineteenth Century, The Gilded Age: Essays on the Origins of Modern America, Schol Resources, Inc., 163-84, 95; co-auth, Taking Hold of the Tools: Post-Secondary Education for Canada's Walpole Island First Nation, 1965-1994, Can J of Native Stud, 16(no 2), 229-46, 96; Auth, A People Living Apart: Indians of the Great Lakes, 1855-1900, Univ Mich Press, (in press). **CONTACT ADDRESS** Dept Hist, Bowling Green State Univ, Bowling Green, OH, 43403. **EMAIL** edanzig@bgnet.bgsu.edu

DARDEN, LINDLEY
PERSONAL Born 12/17/1945, New Albany, MS **DISCIPLINE** PHILOSOPHY AND HISTORY OF SCIENCE **EDUCATION** Southwestern at Memphis, BA, 68; Univ Chicago, AM, 69, SM, 72, PhD, 74. **CAREER** Asst prof, 74-78, ASSOC PROF PHILOS AND HIST, UNIV MD, COLLEGE PARK, 78-, NSF grant, 78-80; Am Coun Learned Soc fel, 82. **MEMBERSHIPS** Philos Sci Asn; Hist Sci Soc; AAAS. **RESEARCH** Theory construction in science; emergence of new fields in biology. **SELECTED PUBLICATIONS** Auth, Discovery and Explanation in Biology and Medicine, Stud Hist and Philos Sci, Vol 0027, 96; Discovering Complexity--Decomposition and Localization as Strategies in Scientific-Research, Bioln and Philos, Vol 0012, 97. **CONTACT ADDRESS** Dept of Philos, Univ of Md, College Park, MD, 20783.

DARDESS, JOHN WOLFE
PERSONAL Born 01/17/1937, Albany, NY, m, 1967, 1 child **DISCIPLINE** PREMODERN CHINESE HISTORY **EDUCATION** Georgetown Univ, BS, 58; Columbia Univ, PhD(-Chinese), 68. **CAREER** Asst prof, 66-72, assoc prof, 72-79, prof Hist, Univ Kans, 79-, Am Coun Learned Soc/Soc Sci Res Coun grant, 71-72. **MEMBERSHIPS** Assn Asian Studies. **RESEARCH** Yuan Dynasty, 1271-1368; Ming Dynasty, 1368-1644; political and social history. **SELECTED PUBLICATIONS** Conquerors and Confucians, Columbia Univ, 73; Confucianism and Autocracy, Univ Calif Press, 82; A Ming Society, Univ Calif Press, 96. **CONTACT ADDRESS** Dept of History, Univ of Kansas, Lawrence, KS, 66045-2130.

DARLING, LINDA T.
PERSONAL Born 02/16/1945, s **DISCIPLINE** HISTORY **EDUCATION** Univ of Conn, BA, 67; Univ of Chicago, MAT, 73, MA, 80, PhD, 90. **CAREER** Asst prof, 89-96, ASSOC PROF OF HIST, UNIV OF ARIZ, 96-. **HONORS AND AWARDS** Am Coun of Learned Soc Fel; Outstanding Fac member, Mortar Board and Golden Key Honor Societies. **MEMBERSHIPS** Am Hist Asn; Middle East Studies Asn; Turkish Studies Asn. **RESEARCH** Ottoman Empire; admin and govt; taxation and political relations; Lyria and Lebanon in the Ottoman period; world hist. **SELECTED PUBLICATIONS** Auth, Rethinking Europe and the Islamic World in the Age of Exploration, The J of Early Modern Hist, 98; Ottoman Provincial Treasuries: The Case of Syria, Arab Hist Rev for Ottoman Studies, 97; Ottoman Fiscal Administration: Decline or Adaptation, The J of European Economic Hist, 97; Revenue Raising and Legitimacy: Tax Collection and the Central Finance Department in Capitulations, Oxford Encycl of the Modern Islamic World, Oxford Univ Press, 95; Ottoman Politics through British Eyes: Paul Rycaut's The Present State of the Ottoman Empire, The J of World Hist, 94; The Finance Scribes and Ottoman Politics, Decision Making in the Ottoman Empire, Thomas Jefferson Univ Press and Univ Press of Am, 93. **CONTACT ADDRESS** Dept of Hist, Univ of Arizona, Tucson, AZ, 85721. **EMAIL** ldarling@u.arizona.edu

DAUBE, DAVID
PERSONAL Born 02/08/1909, Freiburg im Breisgau, Germany, d, 3 children **DISCIPLINE** ROMAN LAW, BIBLICAL STUDIES **EDUCATION** Univ Gottingen, DrJur, 32; Cambridge Univ, PhD, 35; Oxford Univ, MA & DCL, 55. **CAREER** Fel, Caius Col, Cambridge, 38-46, lectr law, univ, 46-51; prof jurisp, Univ Aberdeen, 51-55; Regius prof civil law, Oxford Univ & fel, All Souls Col, 55-70; PROF LAW & DIR ROBBINS COLLECTION, UNIV CALIF, BERKELEY, 70-, Rockefeller award, 61-62; sr fel, Yale Univ, 62; Gifford lectr, Edinburgh, 62 & 63; Ford rotating prof polit sci, Univ Calif, Berkeley, 64; Gray lectr, Cambridge Univ, 66; hon prof law, Uiv Knostanz, 66-; Lionel Cohen lectr, Jerusalem, 70; Messenger lectr, Cornell Univ, 71; hon fel, Oxford Univ Centre Postgrad Hebrew Studies, 73- & Caius Col, 74- **HONORS AND AWARDS** Gerard lectr, Univ Calif, Irvine, 81., LLD, Univ Edinburgh, 60, Univ Leicester, 64, Cambridge Univ, 81; Dr, Univ Paris, 63; CHL, Hebrew Union Col, 71; DrJur, Univ Munich, 72. **MEMBERSHIPS** Fel Am Acad Arts & Sci; fel Brit Acad; corresp fel Acad Sci, Gottingen & Bavarian Acad Acad Sci; hon fel Royal Irish Acad; Soc Hist Ancient Law, France (pres, 57-58). **RESEARCH** Hebrew law; Old and New Testament. **SELECTED PUBLICATIONS** Auth, Judas, Calif Law Rev, Vol 0082, 94. **CONTACT ADDRESS** Sch of Law, Univ of California, Boalt Hall, Berkeley, CA, 94720.

DAUBEN, JOSEPH WARREN
PERSONAL Born 12/29/1944, Santa Monica, CA **DISCIPLINE** HISTORY OF SCIENCE & MATHEMATICS **EDUCATION** Claremont Men's Col, AB, 66; Harvard Univ, AM, 68, PhD(hist of sci), 72. **CAREER** Tutor & teaching fel hist of sci, Harvard Univ, 67-72; vis prof hist ancient sci, Clark Univ, 72; asst prof hist & hist of sci, 72-78, assoc prof, 78-81, PROF HIST OF SCI, LEHMAN COL & GRAD PROG HIST, GRAD CTR, CITY UNIV NEW YORK, 81-; mem, Inst Advan Study, Princeton, 77-78; vis prof, Columbia Univ, 79-84 & Oberlin Col, 80-81, NY Botanical Garden, 89-, NYU, 89-93, Nat Tsing-Hua Univ, Taiwan, 91, Nat Normal Univ, Taiwan 95; Guggenheim fel, 80-81; vis scholar, Harvard Univ, 81; Nat Endowment for Humanities younger humanist fel, 73-74, fel, 91-94; ACLS sr fel, 98-; ed, Historia Mathematica, 76-86. **HONORS AND**

AWARDS Mead-Swing lectr, Oberlin Col, 77 & 80; Bolzano Medal, Czech Acad Sci, 78; Lenin Medal, Univ Tashkent, USSR, 86. **MEMBERSHIPS** Fel, AAAS, NY Acad Sci; Hist Sci Soc; Int Comn Hist of Math (chmn 85-94); Sigma Xi, Phi Beta Kappa **RESEARCH** History of mathematics in the 19th century; history of science in the 16th and 17th centuries; history of philosophy from Descartes to Kant. **SELECTED PUBLICATIONS** Auth, Marat: His science and the French Revolution, Arch Int Hist Sci, 69; The Trigonometric Background to Georg Cantor's Theory of Sets, Arch Hist Exact Sci, 71; C S Peirce and American mathematics in the 19th century, Math Mag, 77; Georg Cantor and Pope Leo XIII: Philosophical and Theological Dimensions of Transfinite Set Theory, J Hist of Ideas, 77; Georg Cantor: The Personal Matrix of His Mathematics, Isis, No 69, 534-550; Georg Cantor, His Mathematics and Philosophy of the Infinite, Harvard Univ, 79; The Development of Cantorian Set Theory, in: From the Calculus to Set Theory, 1630-1910, Duckworths, London, 81; ed, Mathematical Perspectives: Essays on the History of Mathematics in Honor of Kurt R Biermann, NY Acad Press, 81. **CONTACT ADDRESS** Dept of Hist, Lehman Col, CUNY, 33 W 42nd St, New York, NY, 10036-8099. **EMAIL** jdauben@email.gc.cuny.edu

DAUGHERTY, GREGORY NEIL
DISCIPLINE DEPARTMENT OF CLASSICS **EDUCATION** Univ Richmond, BA, 70; Vanderbilt Univ, MA,75; PhD, 77. **CAREER** Instr, 76-78, asst prof, 78-84, assoc prof, 84-94, prof Class, Randolph-Macon Col, 94-; vis asst prof, Univ Richmond, 77, 91, 93; vis asst prof, Va Commonwealth Univ, 82, 85; vis assoc prof, Col William and Mary, 87. **HONORS AND AWARDS** Woodrow Wilson fel, Univ Richmond, 70; Fulbright scholar, Univ Pavia, Italy, 70-71; Thomas Branch Award for Excellence in Tchg, Randolph-Macon Col, 78, 82; Fulbright grant, Italy, 79; NEH Summer Inst on Women in Antiquity, 83, Phi Beta Kappa, 70. **MEMBERSHIPS** Secy, Richmond Soc of the Archaeol Inst of Am, 82-95; mem, Va Dept of Educ, Lat Textbk Selection Comt, 84; consult, Va Dept of Educ, Standards of Lrng for Lat, 86-87.; Mem at Large, Exec Bd of the Class Asn of Va, 87-89; ed, Prospects Newsletter of the Nat Comt on Lat and Greek, 90-96; dir, Class Essay Contest, Class Asn of Va, 90-95; exec secy, Nat Comt on Lat and Greek, 91-93; mem, Joint Comt on Class in Am Educ, Am Philol Asn, 91-94; ch, Comt on Local Arrangements, Class Asn of the Midwest and S; mem, Final Rev Bd NEH Fel Prog for For Lang Tchr K-12, 94; ch, Membership Comt, Class Asn of the Midwest and S, 94-96; pres, For Lang Asn of Va, 95-96; secy-treas, Class Asn of the Midwest and S, 96-. **SELECTED PUBLICATIONS** Auth, Rev of John E. Stambaugh, The Ancient Roman City: The Johns Hopkins Univ Press 88, Class World 84.3, 91; Rev of Walter Ellis, Alcibiades. Classical Lives, Routledge, 89, Class World 84, 91; The Cohortes Vigilum and the Great Fire of 64 AD, Class J 87.3, 92; coauth, Preparation and Training for Teachers of Latin, Class J 86, 91. **CONTACT ADDRESS** Dept of Class, Randolph-Macon Col, Ashland, VA, 23005-5505. **EMAIL** gdaugher@rmc.edu

DAVENPORT, CHRISTIAN A.
PERSONAL Born 06/04/1965, New York, NY, s **DISCIPLINE** POLITICAL SCIENCE **EDUCATION** SUNY Binghamton, MA, 1989, PhD, 1991. **CAREER** University of Houston, assistant professor, 1992-96; UNIVERSITY OF COLORADO-BOULDER, ASSOC PROF, 1996-. **HONORS AND AWARDS** National Science Foundation, Research Development Grant for Minority Scientists & Engineers, 1997; Ebony Magazine, 50 Young Leaders of Tomorrow, 1996; Malcolm X Loves Network, Keeper of the Flame Awd, 1995; National Association of African-American Honors Program, Scholarly Contributions and Leadership, 1996. **MEMBERSHIPS** American Journal of Political Science, editorial board member, 1994-; National Coalition of Blacks for Reparations in America, 1993-; Midwest Political Science Association, 1991-; American Political Science Association, 1991-; National Black Political Science Association, 1992-; Shape Cultural Ctr, instructor, 1993-95; West Dallas Detention Ctr, instructor, 1995; National Popular Culture Association, 1993-; Comparative Politics Center at Univ of Co. **SELECTED PUBLICATIONS** "Understanding Rhetoric Under The Gun," The Black Panther Party Reconsidered, 1997; "The Political and Social Relency of Malcolm X," The Journal of Politics, 1997; "Constitutional Promises and Repressive Reality," The Journal of Politics, 1996; "The Weight of the Past," Political Research Quarterly, 1996; "Multidimensional Threat Perception & State Repression," The American Journal of Political Science, 1995. **CONTACT ADDRESS** Univ of Colorado, Boulder, Ketchum Hall, Rm 106, Boulder, CO, 80309-0333. **EMAIL** christian.davenport@colorado.edu

DAVENPORT, ROBERT WILSON
PERSONAL Born 08/19/1929, Elizabeth, NJ, m, 1960, 1 child **DISCIPLINE** AMERICAN HISTORY **EDUCATION** Pomona Col, BA, 51; Univ CA, Berkeley, MA, 53; UCLA, MS, 56, PhD, 69. **CAREER** Asst jour, Univ CA, Los Angeles, 59-60; from instr to asst prof hist, 64-70, actg dean, Col Arts & Lett, 71-73, chmn dept hist, 76-78, assoc prof hist, Univ NV, Las Vegas, 70. **MEMBERSHIPS** Orgn Am Historians; Western Hist Asn. **RESEARCH** Am west; progressives; Am journalism hist. **SELECTED PUBLICATIONS** Auth, Weird note for the Vox Populi: The Los Angeles Municipal News, Calif Hist Soc Quart, 3/65; ed, Desert Heritage: Readings in Nevada History, Ginn Press, 89; Early Years, Early Workers: The Genesis of the University of Nevada, Nevada Hist Soc Quart, spring 92. **CONTACT ADDRESS** Dept of Hist, Univ of NV, PO Box 455020, Las Vegas, NV, 89154-5020. **EMAIL** davenpr1@nevada.edu

DAVID, ARTHUR LACURTISS
PERSONAL Born 04/13/1938, Chicago, IL, m **DISCIPLINE** HISTORY **EDUCATION** Lane Coll, BA 1960; Phillips Sch of Theol, BD 1963; NE U, MA 1970; ITC, MDiv 1971; Middle TN State U, Arts D 1973. **CAREER** Soc Sci Div Lane Coll, chmn; Lane Coll, prof of hist 1963-67 69-77; NE Wesleyan Univ, 1967-69; Motlow State Commn Coll, 1972-73; Lane Coll, dean, 1979-93; Prof of History, 1993-. **MEMBERSHIPS** Mem So Hist Assn; Am Hist Assn; Orgn of Am Historians; mem Pi Gamma Mu Sociol Sci, Hon Soc; Phi Alpha Theta Hist Hon Soc; Sigma Theta Epsilon Hon Soc for Clergymen; Kappa Kappa Psi Hon Band Frat; Alpha Phi Alpha Frat Inc. **SELECTED PUBLICATIONS** You Can Fool Me But You Can't Fool God, 1976; An Anthology of a Minister's Thoughts, 1977; He Touched Me, 1992. **CONTACT ADDRESS** History, Lane Col, 545 Lane Ave, Jackson, TN, 38301.

DAVIDOV, JUDITH FRYER
DISCIPLINE ENGLISH, AMERICAN STUDIES **EDUCATION** Univ Minn, BA, 61, MA, 67, PhD, 73. **CAREER** Miami Univ, Ohio, , 74-84; asst, assoc, PROF, DEPT ENG, DIR, AM STUD PORF, UNIV MASS, AMHERST, PROF, ENG, 84-; dir, grad prog Am Stud, 88-98, UNIV MASS, AMHERST. **CONTACT ADDRESS** Dept of English, Univ of Massachusetts, Bartlett Hall, Amherst, MA, 01003.

DAVIDSON, ABRAHAM A
PERSONAL Born 06/27/1935, Dorchester, MA **DISCIPLINE** HISTORY OF AMERICAN ART **EDUCATION** Harvard Univ, AB, 57; Hebrew Teachers Col, BSEd, 60; Boston Univ, AM, 60; Columbia Univ, PhD(art hist), 65. **CAREER** Vis lectr art hist, Univ Iowa, 63-64; instr, Wayne State Univ, 64-65; asst prof, Oakland Univ, 65-68; from asst prof to assoc prof, 68-75, PROF ART HIST, TYLER SCH ART, TEMPLE UNIV, 75-. **RESEARCH** Early American modernism in painting; painting of William Sydney Mount; painting of Charles Willson Peale. **SELECTED PUBLICATIONS** Auth, Utopia and Dissent--Art, Poetry, and Politics in California, Amer Hist Rev, Vol 0101, 96. **CONTACT ADDRESS** Temple Univ, Philadelphia, PA, 19122.

DAVIDSON, ROGER HARRY
PERSONAL Born 07/31/1936, Washington, DC, m, 1961, 2 children **DISCIPLINE** POLITICAL SCIENCE **EDUCATION** Univ Colo, BA, 58; Columbia Univ, PhD, 63. **CAREER** Asst prof, Govt, Dartmouth Coll, 62-68; assoc prof, Polit Sci, Univ Calif-Santa Barbara, 68-82; sr spec, Cong Res Serv, Libr Cong, 80-88; PROF, GOVT & POLIT, UNIV MD, 87-. **MEMBERSHIPS** Am Polit Sci Asn; South Polit Sci Asn; Midwest Polit Sci Asn; West Polit Sci Asn; Nat Capitol Area Pol Sci Asn **RESEARCH** US government, policies & legislature; Executive politics; National policy making. **SELECTED PUBLICATIONS** Remaking Congress, 95; Understanding the Presidency, 96; Congress and Its Members, 98. **CONTACT ADDRESS** Univ Md, 1140B Tydings Hall, College Park, MD, 20742. **EMAIL** rdavidso@bss2.umd.edu

DAVIES, CAROLE BOYCE
DISCIPLINE AFRICAN STUDIES **EDUCATION** Univ Md, BA, 71; Howard Univ, MA, 74; Univ Ibadan, PhD. **CAREER** Prof. **MEMBERSHIPS** African Lit Asn; African Studies Asn; CAFRA; MLA; Nat Women's Studies Asn; Women's Caucus African Lit Asn. **RESEARCH** Black women's writing; African American literature; comparative black literature; African literature; Caribbean oral and written literature; cross cultural feminist theory; oral tradition and written literature. **SELECTED PUBLICATIONS** Auth, Black Women, Writing, and Identity, Routledge, 94; Moving Beyond Boundaries, Univ NY, 95; Moving Beyond Boundaries, Pluto, 95; Under African Skies (rev), 97. **CONTACT ADDRESS** Dept Sciences and Arts, Florida State Univ, 11200 SW 8th St, Miami, FL, 33174. **EMAIL** cboyced@fiu.edu

DAVIES, IVOR KEVIN
PERSONAL Born 12/19/1930, Birmingham, England, m, 1966, 2 children **DISCIPLINE** PSYCHOLOGY **EDUCATION** Univ Birmingham, UK, BA, 52, MA, 54; Univ Illinois, MSc, 53; Univ Nottingham, UK, PhD, 67. **CAREER** Prof, educ, adj prof, Bus Admin, Indiana Univ. **HONORS AND AWARDS** Cadbury Prize; fel, Br Psychol Soc; fel, Col of Preceptors. **MEMBERSHIPS** Br Psychol Soc; Am Psychol Asn; Inst of Dir, UK. **RESEARCH** Strategic thinking; needs analysis and assessment; human error. **SELECTED PUBLICATIONS** Auth, Management of Learning, McGraw-Hill, 73, auth, Organization of Training, McGraw-Hill; auth, Objectives in Curriculum Design, McGraw-Hill, 76; auth, Instructional Technique, McGraw-Hill, 81. **CONTACT ADDRESS** 2447 Rock Creek Dr, Bloomington, IN, 47401. **EMAIL** davies@indiana.edu

DAVIS, ALLEN FREEMAN
PERSONAL Born 01/09/1931, Hardwick, VT, d, 2 children **DISCIPLINE** AMERICAN HISTORY **EDUCATION** Dartmouth Col, AB, 53; Univ Rochester, MA, 54; Univ Wis, PhD(Am Hist), 59. **CAREER** Instr Hist, Wayne Univ, 59-60; from asst prof to assoc prof, Univ Mo-Columbia, 60-68; prof Hist, Temple Univ, 68-; vis prof Univ Texas Austin, 83; prof, Univ of Amsterdam, 86-87. **HONORS AND AWARDS** John Adams chmn, Bode-Pearson Award; Sr fel, Am Coun Learned Soc; NEH fel, Fulbright sen fel. **MEMBERSHIPS** AHA; Orgn Am Historians; Soc Am Historians; Am Studies Asn (treas, 79-72, exec secry, 72-77). **RESEARCH** American cultural history. **SELECTED PUBLICATIONS** Co-ed, Conflict and Concensus in American History, Heath, Houghton and Mifflin, 66, 68, 72, 76, 80, 84, 86, 92, 97; auth, Spearheads for Reform, Oxford Univ, 67, Rutgers, 84; co-ed, Eighty Years at Hull House, Quadrangle, 69; auth, Introduction to Jane Addams, Spirit of youth and the city streets, Univ Ill, 72; co-ed, The Peoples of Philadelphia, Temple Univ, 73, Univ of PA, 98; auth, American Heroine: The Life and Legend of Jane Addams, Oxford Univ, 73; coauth, Generations: Your Family in Modern American History, Knopf, 74, 78 & 83; Searching for your Past, Pantheon, 78; co-auth, The American People!, Harper Collins, 86, 90, 94, Addison Wesley, Longmans, 98. **CONTACT ADDRESS** Dept of History, Temple Univ, 1114 W Berks St, Philadelphia, PA, 19122-6029.

DAVIS, AUDREY BLYMAN
PERSONAL Born 11/09/1934, Hicksville, NY, m, 1960, 2 children **DISCIPLINE** HISTORY OF SCIENCE AND MEDICINE **EDUCATION** Adelphi Univ, BS, 56; Johns Hopkins Univ, PhD(hist of sci), 69. **CAREER** Teacher biol, physics & chem, Sewanhaka High Sch, NY, 56-59; teacher biol & physics, Windsor Sch & Saugus High Sch, Mass, 61-62; consult sci educ, Sci Serv, Washington, DC, 64-66; CUR, MUS AM HIST, SMITHSONIAN INST, 67-, Curator, Smithsonian Res Found Grant, 71-72, Commonwealth Found grant, 72-73; prof, Univ Md, College Park, 73-74; prof, Univ Md, Baltimore, 82. **MEMBERSHIPS** Hist Sci Soc (secy, 82-); Am Asn Hist Med. **RESEARCH** History of biology, medicine and the technology of medicine from the 17th century to the present; history of women. **SELECTED PUBLICATIONS** Auth, Technical Knowledge in American Culture--Science, Technology and Medicine Since the Early 1800s, Annals of Sci, Vol 0054, 97; Miasma and Disease--Public-Health and the Environment in the Preindustrial Age, Tech and Cult, Vol 0034, 93; Technologies of Modern Medicine, Annals of Science, Vol 0052, 95; Epidemics and Ideas--Essays on the Historical Perception of Pestilence, Tech and Cult, Vol 0034, 93; Technical Knowledge in American Culture--Science, Technology and Medicine Since the Early 1800s, Annals of Sci, Vol 0054, 97; Cullen,William and the 18th-Century Medical World--A Bicentenary Exhibition and Symposium Arranged by the Royal-College-Of-Physicians of Edinburgh in 1990, Annals of Sci, Vol 0051, 94. **CONTACT ADDRESS** Div of Med Sci Mus Am Hist, Smithsonian Inst, Washington, DC, 20560.

DAVIS, CALVIN D.
PERSONAL Born 12/03/1927, Westport, IN **DISCIPLINE** HISTORY **EDUCATION** Franklin Col, AB, 49; Ind Univ MA, 56, PhD, 61. **CAREER** Teacher pub schs, Ind, 49-54 & Univ Sch, Ind Univ, Bloomington, 54-55; asst prof hist, Ind Cent Col, 56-57; assoc Ind Univ, 58-59; asst prof, Univ Denver, 59-62; from asst prof to assoc prof, 62-76, PROF HIST, DUKE UNIV, 76-, Consult, Nat Endowment for Humanities, 74-75. **HONORS AND AWARDS** Beveridge Award, AHA, 61. **MEMBERSHIPS** AHA; Orgn Am Historians; Southern Hist Asn; Soc Historians Am Foreign Rels. **RESEARCH** American foreign relations; American diplomacy and the Hague system; the Paris Peace Conference of 1919. **SELECTED PUBLICATIONS** Auth, Wilson,Woodrow--British Perspectives, 1912-21, Historian, Vol 0056, 93; Wilson,Woodrow, Historian, Vol 0055, 93. **CONTACT ADDRESS** Dept of Hist, Duke Univ, Durham, NC, 27706.

DAVIS, CALVIN D.
PERSONAL Born 12/03/1927, Westport, IN, s **DISCIPLINE** HISTORY **EDUCATION** Franklin Col, AB, 49; Ind Univ, BA, 56, PhD, 61. **CAREER** Tchr, 49-54, Publ Schls, Ind; US Army, 51-53; asst prof, 56-57, Ind Cent Col; assoc prof, 58-59, Univ Denver; asst prof to assoc prof, 62-76, prof, 76-96, prof emeritus, 96-, Duke Univ. **RESEARCH** WW I diplomatic hist. **CONTACT ADDRESS** Dept of History, Duke Univ, Durham, NC, 27708.

DAVIS, CARL L.
PERSONAL Born 08/27/1934, Bartlesville, OK, m, 1967, 2 children **DISCIPLINE** HISTORY, POLITICAL SCIENCE **EDUCATION** Okla State Univ, AB, 58, MA, 59, PhD(hist), 71. **CAREER** Instr hist & polit sci, 61-64, from asst prof to assoc prof hist, 74-77, PROF HIST, STEPHEN F AUSTIN STATE UNIV, 77-. **MEMBERSHIPS** AHA; Orgn Am Historians; Southern Hist Asn; Southwestern Soc Sci Asn. **RESEARCH** United States military-industrial; modern United States (since 1945) social attitudes. **SELECTED PUBLICATIONS** Auth, American Swords and Sword Makers, Civil War Hist, Vol 0041, 95. **CONTACT ADDRESS** Dept of Hist, Stephen F Austin State Univ, Box 3013, Nacogdoches, TX, 75962.

DAVIS, DANIEL CLAIR
DISCIPLINE CHURCH HISTORY **EDUCATION** Wheaton Col, AB, 53, MA, 57; Westminster Theol Sem, BD, 56; Georg-August Univ, Guttingen, ThD, 60. **CAREER** Asst prof, Olivet Col, 60-63; vis prof, asst prof, Wheaton Col, Grad Sch Theol, 63-66; prof, Westminster Theol Sem, 66-. **SELECTED PUBLICATIONS** Contrib, John Calvin: His Influence in the Western World; Challenges to Inerrancy; Inerrancy and the Church; Pressing Toward the Mark; Theonomy: A Reformed Critique. **CONTACT ADDRESS** Westminister Theol Sem, PO Box 27009, Philadelphia, PA, 19118. **EMAIL** cdavis@wts.edu

DAVIS, DAVID BRION
PERSONAL Born 02/16/1927, Denver, CO, m, 1948, 5 children **DISCIPLINE** HISTORY **EDUCATION** Dartmouth Col, AB, 50; Harvard Univ, AM, 53, PhD, 56. **CAREER** Instr hist & Ford Fund Advan Educ intern, Dartmouth Col, 53-54; from asst prof to Ernest I White prof hist, Cornell Univ, 55-69; Harmsworth prof Am hist, Oxford Univ, 69-70; prof, 69-72, Farnam prof, 72-78, STERLING PROF HIST, YALE UNIV, 78-, Guggenheim Mem fel, 58-59; Fulbright lectr, Hyderabad, India, 67; fel, Ctr Advan Studies Behav Sci, 72-73; Henry E Huntington Libr fel, 76; Nat Endowment for Humanities res grants, 79-80 & 80-81; Fulbright traveling fel, 80-81; French-Am Found Chair Am Civilization, Ecole des Hautes Etudes en Sciences Sociales, Paris, 80-81. **HONORS AND AWARDS** Anisfield-Wolf Award, 67; Nat Mass Media Award, Nat Conf Christians & Jews, 67; Pulitzer Prize, 67; Albert J Beveridge Award, AHA, 75; Bancroft Prize, Columbia Univ, 76; Nat Bk Award, Nat Inst Arts & Lett, 76; Benjamin Rush lectr, Am Psychiat Asn, 76; O Meredith Wilson lectr, Univ Utah, 78; Walter Lynwood Fleming lectr, Southern Hist, La State Univ, 79; Pierce lectr, Oberlin Col, 79., MA, Oxford Univ, 69; MA, Yale Univ, 70; LittD, Dartmouth Col, 77. **MEMBERSHIPS** AHA; Orgn Am Historians; Am Acad Arts & Sci; Soc Am Historians; Am Antiqn Soc. **RESEARCH** Intellectual history of the United States; slavery and antislavery; Anglo-American nineteenth century culture. **SELECTED PUBLICATIONS** Auth, Life in Black-And-White--Family and Community in the Slave South, NY Rev Bk(s), Vol 0044, 97; Witness for Freedom--African-American Voices on Race, Slavery and Emancipation, NY Rev Bk(s), Vol 0040, 93; Constructing Race--European-History and the Definition of Race--A Reflection, William and Mary Quart, Vol 0054, 97; Tumult and Silence at Second-Creek--An Inquiry Into a Civil-War Conspiracy, NY Rev Bk(s), Vol 0040, 93; The Age of Federalism, NY Rev Bk(s), Vol 0041, 94; Slavery and the Jews--Clarification on a Statement Made in a Recently Published Essay, NY Rev Bk(s), Vol 0042, 95; At the Heart of Slavery--Essay, NY Rev Bk(s), Vol 0043, 96; Free at Last--A Documentary History of Slavery, Freedom and the Civil-War, NY Rev Bk(s), Vol 0040, 93; The Southern Tradition--The Achievement and Limitations of an American Conservatism, NY Rev Bk(s), Vol 0042, 95; The Southern Front--History and Politics in the Cultural War, NY Rev Bk(s), Vol 0042, 95; The Slave-Trade and the Jews, NY Rev Bk(s), Vol 0041, 94; The Slaveholders Dilemma--Freedom and Progress in Southern Conservative Thought, 1820-1860, NY Rev Bk(s), Vol 0042, 95. **CONTACT ADDRESS** Dept of Hist, Yale Univ, P O Box 208301, New Haven, CT, 06520-8301.

DAVIS, DAVID D.
PERSONAL Born 08/08/1956, Boston, MA, m, 1978, 2 children **DISCIPLINE** LIBRARY SCIENCE; HISTORY **EDUCATION** Catholic Univ Am, MSLIS, MS; Simmons Col, DA. **CAREER** Publ Libr, 82-88; Corp Libr, 88-94; Copyright Clearance Ctr, 98-. **MEMBERSHIPS** SLA **RESEARCH** Service quality; copyright; electric rights management systems. **CONTACT ADDRESS** Copyright Clearance Ctr, 222 Rosewood Dr, Danvers, MA, 01923. **EMAIL** ddavis@copyright.com

DAVIS, DONALD G., JR.
PERSONAL Born 12/06/1939, San Marcos, TX, m, 1969, 3 children **DISCIPLINE** LIBRARY SCIENCE/HISTORY **EDUCATION** UCLA, BA, 61; UC Berkeley, MA, 63, MLS, 64; Univ Ill, Champaign-Urbana, PhD, 72; Austin Presbyterian Theol Sem, MA, 96. **CAREER** Libry asst, UC Berkeley, 61-64; sen ref librn, Fresno State Col, 64-68; prof, Univ Tx Austin, 71-. **HONORS AND AWARDS** Beta Phi Mu; Phi Kappa Phi; HEA Title-B Fel; Newberry Libry Fel; Am Inst Indian Stud Fel; Berner-Nash Award, Univ Ill; GLSIS; John P. Commons Tchg Fel, Univ Tex Austin. **MEMBERSHIPS** Am Hist Asn; Am Libry Asn; Asn Bibliography Hist; Am Printing Hist Asn; Conference on Faith and Hist; Nat Asn Scholars; Org Am Hist; Tex Libry Asn; Tex State Hist Asn. **RESEARCH** Hist of books and libraries; American library history; history of printing; Christian missions. **SELECTED PUBLICATIONS** Auth, art, Problems in the Life of a University Librarian: Thomas James, 1600-1620, 70; auth, art, Education for Librarianship, 76; auth, art, The Status of Library History in India: A Report of an Informal Survey and a Selective Bibliographic Essay, 89; auth, art, Destruction of Chinese Books in the Peking Siege of 1900, 97; auth, art, Arthur E. Bostwick and Chinese Library Development: A Chapter in International Cooperation, 98. **CONTACT ADDRESS** Graduate School of Library and Information Science, Univ Texas at Austin, Austin, TX, 78712-1276. **EMAIL** dgdavis@uts.cc.utexas.edu

DAVIS, EDWARD B.
PERSONAL Born 08/05/1953, Philadelphia, PA, m, 2 children **DISCIPLINE** HISTORY OF SCIENCE **EDUCATION** Drexel Univ, BS, 75; Indiana Univ Bloomington, PhD, 84. **CAREER** Vis asst prof, Dept of Hist & Philos, Vanderbilt Univ, 84-85; asst prof, 85-90, assoc prof, 90-96, Sci & Hist, prof, the history of science, 96-, Messiah Col, 85-. **HONORS AND AWARDS** Diss Year fel Charlotte W. Newcombe Found, 83-84; Nat Sci Found Res Grant, 89; Mellon fel Hum Univ Penn, 91-92; Lilly Fellows Prog Hum & Arts Summer Inst grant, 98; Scholar chr Messiah Col, 98-2000; Exemplary Papers Award Program, John M Templeton Found, 96-97; Esther L Kinsley PhD Diss Prize Ind Univ, 85. **MEMBERSHIPS** Amer Sci Affil; Hist Sci Soc **RESEARCH** Robert Boyle; Religion and science since 1650; Antievolutionism. **SELECTED PUBLICATIONS** Auth, Parcere nominibus: Boyle, Hooke, and the Rhetorical Interpretation of Descartes, Robert Boyle Reconsidered, Cambridge, 94; The Anonymous Works of Robert Boyle and the Reasons Why a Protestant Should not Turn Papist (1687), Jour Hist Ideas, 94; ed, The Antievolution Pamphlets of Harry Rimmer, Creationism in Twentieth Century America, Garland Publ, 95; auth, Fundamentalism and Folk Science Between the Wars, Relig and Amer Cult, 95; coauth, The Making of Robert Boyles Free Enquiry into the Vulgarly Receiv d Notion of Nature (1686); Early Sci Med, 96; ed, Robert Boyle A Free Enquiry into the Vulgarly Received Notion of Nature, Cambridge Texts, Cambridge Univ Press, 96; auth, Newtons Rejection of the Newtonian World View: The Role of Divine Will in Newtons Natural Philosophy, Facets of Faith and Science Vol 3: The Role of Beliefs in the Natural Sciences, Univ Press Amer, 96; Rationalism, Voluntarism, and Seventeenth-Century Science, Facets of Faith and Science Vol 3: The Role of Beliefs in the Natural Sciences, Univ Press Amer, 96. **CONTACT ADDRESS** Messiah Col, Grantham, PA, 17027. **EMAIL** tdavis@messiah.edu

DAVIS, EDWARD L.
PERSONAL Born 12/06/1943, Union Bridge, MD, m **DISCIPLINE** EDUCATION **EDUCATION** Morgan State Univ, BS 1965; OH Univ, MS 1967; Johns Hopkins Univ, MS 1973; NC State Univ, PhD 1977. **CAREER** Morgan State Univ Math Dept, instr 1970-73; Univ of Cincinnati Coll of Business, asst prof 1976-80; Atlanta Univ Graduate School of Business, assoc prof 1980-88; Clark Atlanta University, chmn decision science dept, 1988-95, Business School, acting dean, 1995-. **HONORS AND AWARDS** MD Senatorial Fellowship 1961-65; Balt Colt Found Scholarship 1961-65; So Fellowship Found 1973-76; Volunteer of the Year City of Raleigh 1974. **MEMBERSHIPS** Mem Operations Rsch Soc of Amer 1974-; mem Transport Rsch Bd 1980-; mem Alpha Phi Alpha Frat 1961-; task force mem Atlanta C of C 1982-; Operations Rsch Soc of Amer 1973-; Amer Inst for Decision Sci 1980-; Transp Rsch Bd 1980-. **CONTACT ADDRESS** Clark Atlanta Univ, James P Brawley at Fair St, Atlanta, GA, 30314.

DAVIS, ELLEN NANCY
PERSONAL Born 07/20/1937, Hackensack, NJ **DISCIPLINE** ART HISTORY, ARCHAEOLOGY **EDUCATION** St John's Col, BA, 60; Inst Fine Arts, NY Univ, PhD, 73. **CAREER** Res asst ancient art, Inst Fine Arts, NY Univ, 60-66; from lectr to asst prof, 66-78, ASSOC PROF ANCIENT ART, QUEENS COL, 78-, Nat Endowment for Humanities res grant, prin investr ancient metallurgy, 77-79. **MEMBERSHIPS** Archaeol Inst Am; New York Aegean Bronze Age Col; Anc Civilizat Sem; Am Res Ctr in Egypt; Am Sch of Class Stu, Athens; Columbia Univ Sem, Archaeology of the Mediterranean; New York Egyptological Sem. **RESEARCH** Aegean Bronze Age; ancient metallurgy. **SELECTED PUBLICATIONS** Coauth, Catalogue of Anatolian Metal Vessels, Ancient Art: The Norbert Schimmel Collection, 74; auth, The Vapheio cups: One Minoan and One Mycenean?, Art Bull, Vol 56, 74; coauth, The Classic Ideal, In: Sculpture, Newsweek: The History of Culture, NY, 75; auth, Metal Inlaying in Minoan and Mycenean Art, Temple Univ Aegean Symp, Vol I, 76; ed, Symposium on the Dark Ages, Archaeol Inst Am, NY, 77; Auth, The Vapheio Cups and Aegian Gold and Silver Ware, Garland Publ Inc, NY & London, 77; auth, Youth and the Age in the Thera Frescoes, Am Jou of Archaeology, 399-40, 86; The Cyclasic Style of the Thera Frescoes, Thera and the Aegean World III, Vol 3, Third Int Thera Congress, 214-227, 90; Art and Politics in the Aegean: The Missing Ruler, The Role of the Ruler in the Prehistoric Aegean, Aegaeum, Vol 11, 11-20, 5; The Iconography of the Thera Ship Fresco, Greek Art and Iconography, Madison, 40-54, 83. **CONTACT ADDRESS** Dept of Art, Queens Col, CUNY, 6530 Kissena Blvd, Flushing, NY, 11367-1597.

DAVIS, ELLIOT BOSTWICK
DISCIPLINE ART HISTORY **EDUCATION** Princeton Univ, AB, 84; Univ NY, MA, 85; Columbia Univ, MA, 86, MPhil, 88, PhD, 92. **CAREER** Teach asst, Harvard Univ; current, ASST CUR, DEPT DRAWINGS & PRINTS, METROPOLITAN MUSEUM ART **MEMBERSHIPS** Am Antiquarian Soc **RESEARCH** Am drawing books, 1820-1880 **SELECTED PUBLICATIONS** Auth, Training the Eye and the Hand; Fitz Hugh Lane and Nineteenth-Century Drawing Books, Cape Ann Historical Soc, 93; auth, "Fitz Hugh Lane and John B. Chapman's American Drawing Book," The Mag Antiques, 93; auth, "American Drawing Books and Their Impact on Winslow Homer," Winterthur Portfolio 31, 96; auth, "WPA Color Prints: Images from the Federal Art Project, Am Art Rev VIII, 96; auther, "American Drawing Books and Their Impact on Fitz Hugh Lane," in The Cultivation of Artists in Nineteenth-Century America, ASS, 97. **CONTACT ADDRESS** Dept of Drawings & Prints, Metropolitan Mus of Art, 1000 Fifth Ave, New York, NY, 10028.

DAVIS, GARY A.
PERSONAL Born 07/28/1938, Salt Lake City, UT, m, 1961, 3 children **DISCIPLINE** PSYCHOLOGY **EDUCATION** Univ Wisc-Madison, PhD, 65. **CAREER** Prof of Educ Psychol, Univ Wisc-Madison, 65-94. **HONORS AND AWARDS** Wilhelm Wundt Award from XXII Int Congress of Psychol, 80. **MEMBERSHIPS** APA; AERA; NAGC. **RESEARCH** Creativity; gifted education; character education. **SELECTED PUBLICATIONS** Auth, Handbook of Gifted Education, 2nd ed, 97; auth, Education of the Gifted and Talented, 4th ed, 98; auth, Creativity is Forever, 4th ed, 98. **CONTACT ADDRESS** PO Box 222, Cross Plains, WI, 53528. **EMAIL** gadavis1@facstaff.wisc.edu

DAVIS, GEORGE H.
PERSONAL Born 05/18/1938, Pittsburgh, PA, m, 1961, 2 children **DISCIPLINE** AMERICAN HISTORY **EDUCATION** Bowdoin Col, AB, 60; Univ Chicago, MAT, 62, PhD, 66. **CAREER** Lectr hist, Ind Univ, Gary, 64-65; instr, Lake Forest Col, 65-66; from Asst Prof to Assoc Prof, 66-79, prof hist, Wabash Col, 79-. **MEMBERSHIPS** AHA; Orgn Am Historians. **RESEARCH** Truman administration; urban and social history. **SELECTED PUBLICATIONS** Co-compiler, Who Was Who 1604-1896, Marquis, 64; auth, The puritan idea of success, in Present in the Past, Macmillan, 72. **CONTACT ADDRESS** Dept of Hist, Wabash Col, PO Box 352, Crawfordsville, IN, 47933-0352. **EMAIL** davisg@wabash.edu

DAVIS, GLORIA-JEANNE
PERSONAL Born 02/06/1945, Gary, IN, m **DISCIPLINE** EDUCATION **EDUCATION** Eastern KY Univ, BBA 1970, MBA 1971; IL State Univ, PhD 1986. **CAREER** Caterpillar Tractor Co, analyst/machine shop training 1974-78; Bloomington City Hall, financial advisor 1978-84; IL CENTRAL COLL, INSTRUCTOR/BUSINESS DEPT 1986-; IL STATE UNIV, UNIV AFFIRMATIVE ACTION OFFICER 1984-, ASST TO PRES FOR AFFIRMATIVE ACTION AND EQUAL OPPORTUNITY, 1988-96; MITSUBISHI MOTORS, DIR OPPORTUNITY PROGRAMS, 1996-. **HONORS AND AWARDS** Administrator of the Year Award, Black Student Union, 1987; Educ Administration & Foundations Advisory Council, Recognition Award, 1990; Administrative Professional Distinguished Service Award, Administrative Professional Staff, 1991; MacMurray Coll, NAACP, Civil Rights Award, 1994. **MEMBERSHIPS** ISU Toastmasters, pres, 1990, 1992, mem, 1989-; IL Affirmative Action Officers Assn, pres, 1986-88, mem, 1988-; Assn of Black Academic Employees, pres, 1987-89, 1990-91, mem, 1986-; ISU Recruitment & Retention Committees, chair, 1988-89, mem, 1987-96; Admini Professional Grievance Panel, elected mem, 1985-96; IL Committee on Black Concerns in Higher Educ, steering comm secretary, 1984-93, co chair annual conference, 1993, steering comm mem, 1984-96; IL State Univ Black Colleagues Assn, campus liaison, 1986-96; North Central Assn of Coll & School Self Study, mem, 1993-96; Natl Collegiate Athletic Assn Self Study, mem, 1993-96; McLean Cty AIDS Task Force, bd of dirs, 1993-. 1993-; Institute for Collaborative Solutions, bd of dirs, 1997-; Bloomington Liquor Commission, commissioner, 1997-. **CONTACT ADDRESS** Opportunity Programs, Mitsubishi, 100 N Mitsubishi Motorway, Normal, IL, 61761.

DAVIS, GORDON B.
PERSONAL Born 09/09/1930, Idaho Falls, ID, m, 1954, 4 children **DISCIPLINE** BUSINESS ADMINISTRATION **EDUCATION** Idaho State Univ, BA, BS; Stanford Univ, MBA, PhD. **CAREER** Honeywell Prof of MIS, Grad School of Mgmt, 61-, Univ of Minn; Pres, 98, AIS; vis Prof at: NYU, Euro Institute of Adv Stud in Mgmt, Nat Univ Singapore & Nanyang Univ Singapore. **HONORS AND AWARDS** Initiated first MIS Grad Program and established the Mgmt Info Sys Research Center at Univ Minn. **MEMBERSHIPS** ACM, ACPA. **RESEARCH** MIS Systems & development, information technology to improve productivity, information requirements determination. **SELECTED PUBLICATIONS** Co-auth, Management Information Systems, Conceptual Foundations, Structure and Development, 2nd ed, McGraw-Hill Book Comp, 85; co-auth, Personal Productivity with Information Technology, McGraw-Hill, 97. **CONTACT ADDRESS** Carlson School of Management, Univ of Minn, 321 19th Ave S, Minneapolis, MN, 55455. **EMAIL** gdavis@csom.umn.edu

DAVIS, GREGSON
PERSONAL Born 10/20/1940, St. John's, Antigua, m, 1980, 4 children **DISCIPLINE** CLASSICS AND COMPARATIVE LITERATURE **EDUCATION** Harvard Univ, AB, 60; Univ Cal Berkeley, PhD, 68. **CAREER** Asst prof, Stanford Univ, 69-75; assoc prof, 75-85; prof, 85-89; prof, Cornell Univ, 89-94; prof, Duke Univ, 94- . **HONORS AND AWARDS** Latin Orator, Harvard Commencement, 60; Arthur D. Cory Travelling

Fel, Harvard Univ, 61-63. **MEMBERSHIPS** Am Phil Asoc; MLA; Vergilian Soc; Caribbean Studies Asoc. **RESEARCH** Latin and Greek literature; Caribbean literature; rhetoric and poetics. **SELECTED PUBLICATIONS** Auth, Polyhymnia: The Rhetoric of Horatian Lyric Discourse, 91; auth, Desire and the Hunt in Ovid's Metamorphoses, The Burnett Lectures: A Quarter Century, 93; auth, Between Cultures: Toward a Redefinition of Liberal Education, African Studies and the Undergraduate Curriculum, 94; guest ed of spec issue, The Poetics of Derek Walcott: Intertextual Perspectives, South Atlantic Quart, 97; auth, Aime Cesaire, 97. **CONTACT ADDRESS** Dept. of Classical Studies, Duke Univ, 234A Allen Bldg., Durham, NC, 27708-0103.

DAVIS, JACK E.
DISCIPLINE HISTORY **EDUCATION** Brandeis Univ, PhD, 94. **CAREER** Asst prof, Univ Ala, Birmingham; ASST PROF HISTORY, ECkERD COL. **HONORS AND AWARDS** NEH Summer Inst, Harvard Univ, 98; N Am Soc Sport Historians, essay prize, 91. **RESEARCH** U.S. race relations, civil rights, environmental history. **SELECTED PUBLICATIONS** New Left, Revisionist, In Your Face History: Oliver Stone's Born on the Fourth of July Experience, Film and History, Oct 98; co-auth, Only in Mississippi: A Guide for the Adventurous Traveler, Quail Ridge Press, 97; Changing Places: Slave Movement in the South, The Historian 55, summer 93; Making the Cut: Racial Discrimination in Major League Spring Training, Journeys for the Junior Historian, spring/summer 93; contr, Encyclopedia of African-American Civil Rights: From Emancipation to the Present, Greenwood Press, 92; Baseball's Reluctant Challenge: Desegregating Major League Spring Training Sites, 1960-1963; Journal of Sport History 20, fall 92; Whitewash in Florida: The Lynching of Jesse James Payne and its Aftermath, Florida Historical Quarterly 63, Jan 90. **CONTACT ADDRESS** 633 Idlewild Cr, A8, Birmingham, AL, 35205.

DAVIS, JACK L.
PERSONAL Born 08/13/1950, Wooster, OH **DISCIPLINE** CLASSICS **EDUCATION** Univ Akron, BA, 72; Univ Cincinnati, PhD, 77. **CAREER** Vis Fel, Fitzwilliam Col; Carl W. Blegen Chaired Prof, Univ Cincinnati, 93-; Asst prof, Univ Ill, 77-83; Assoc prof, 84-91; Prof, 91-93. **HONORS AND AWARDS** Silver Circle award, 82; AMOCO award, 82; Univ Scholar award, 85-87; Joanne Stolaroff Cotsen Prize., James Rignall Wheeler Fel, Eugene Vanderpool Fel. **MEMBERSHIPS** Archaeol Inst Am; Future Old World Archaeol Higher Educ Commt; Am Sch Classical Studies Athens; Archaeometric laboratory comt; Wiener Laboratory; Institute for Aegean Prehistory; Archaeometry Comt; Nat Endowment Hum; Nat Hum Ctr. **SELECTED PUBLICATIONS** Co-ed, Papers in Cycladic Prehistory, UCLA, 79; auth, Period V, Meinz, 86; coauth, Landscape Archaeology as Long-Term History: Northern Keos in the Cycladic Islands, UCLA, 91. **CONTACT ADDRESS** Dept of Classics, Univ Cincinnati, PO Box 210226, Cincinnati, OH, 45210-0226. **EMAIL** jack.davis@uc.edu

DAVIS, JAMES EDWARD
PERSONAL Born 09/27/1940, Detroit, MI, m, 1966, 2 children **DISCIPLINE** HISTORY, GEOGRAPHY **EDUCATION** Wayne State Univ, AB, 62, MA, 66 Univ MI, PhD(hist), 71. **CAREER** Teacher, Dearborn Pub Schs, 62-71; assoc prof to prof hist, IL Col, 71-. **HONORS AND AWARDS** Distinguished Service Award, Ill State Historical Soc, 77. **MEMBERSHIPS** Orgn Am Historians; Soc for Hist for the Early Am Republic. **RESEARCH** The social and political history of the early National era of America; the settlement process of early America and other frontier societies; the civil war era. **SELECTED PUBLICATIONS** Auth, New Aspects of Men and New Forms of Society, the Old Northwest, 1790-1920, J Ill State Historical Soc, 8/76; Frontier America, 1800-1840: A Comparative Demographic Analysis of the Settlement Process, Arthur Clark, 77; ed, Dreams to Dust, Univ NE, 89; auth, Frontier Illinois, IN Univ Press, 99. **CONTACT ADDRESS** Dept Hist, Illinois Col, 1101 W College Ave, Jacksonville, IL, 62650-2299. **EMAIL** davis@hilltop.ic.edu

DAVIS, JOHN
DISCIPLINE ART HISTORY **EDUCATION** Cornell Univ, AB; Columbia Univ, MA, MPhil, PhD. **CAREER** Priscilla Paine Van der Poel assoc prof, Smith Col. **RESEARCH** Artists' studios; the painting of Johnson Eastman; urban cult in 19th-century NY City; Cath imagery in the Antebellum Era; Am concepts of gender and space. **SELECTED PUBLICATIONS** Auth, The Landscape of Belief: Encountering the Holy Land in the Nineteenth Century, Amer Art and Cult; coauth, Nineteenth-Century American Paintings: Collections of the National Gallery of Art, Syst Catalogue. **CONTACT ADDRESS** Dept of Art, Smith Col, Hillyer Hall 311, Northampton, MA, 01063. **EMAIL** JDAVIS@smith.edu

DAVIS, LEROY
DISCIPLINE HISTORY **EDUCATION** Howard Univ, BA, 76; Kent State Univ, MA, 78, PhD, 90. **CAREER** Assoc prof **RESEARCH** African-American history; American history; comparative education in the African Diaspora. **SELECTED PUBLICATIONS** Coauth, African Experience in Community Development: The Continuing Struggle in Africa and the Americas (v I/II); A Clashing of the Soul: John Hope and the Dilemma of African American Leadership and Black Education in the Early 20th Century. **CONTACT ADDRESS** Dept History, Emory Univ, 221 Bowden Hall, 561 Kilgo Cir, Atlanta, GA, 30322-1950. **EMAIL** ldavi04@emory.edu

DAVIS, NATALIE ZEMON
PERSONAL Born 11/08/1928, Detroit, MI, m, 1948, 3 children **DISCIPLINE** EARLY MODERN AND SOCIAL HISTORY **EDUCATION** Smith Col, BA, 49; Radcliffe Col, MA, 50; Univ Mich, PhD(hist), 59. **CAREER** Lectr hist, Brown Univ, 59-61, asst prof, 61-63; asst prof econ, Univ Toronto, 64-67, assoc prof hist, 67-71; prof, Univ Calif, Berkeley, 71-77; PROF HIST, PRINCETON UNIV, 77-, Soc Sci Res Coun fel, 62-63; vis assoc prof, Univ Calif, Berkeley, 68. **HONORS AND AWARDS** William Koren Jr Prize, Soc Fr Hist Studies, 68 & 71. **MEMBERSHIPS** Am Soc Reformation Res; AHA; Soc Fr Hist Studies; Renaissance Soc Am. **RESEARCH** Sex roles in early modern Europe; religion and society in 16th century France; popular culture. **SELECTED PUBLICATIONS** Auth, Toward Mixtures and Margins, Amer Hist Rev, Vol 0097, 92; Roelker, Nancy,Lyman--In-Memoriam, Fr Hist Stud, Vol 0018, 94. **CONTACT ADDRESS** Dept of History, Princeton Univ, Princeton, NJ, 08540.

DAVIS, NATHAN T.
PERSONAL Born 02/15/1937, Kansas City, KS, m **DISCIPLINE** ETHNOMUSICOLOGY **EDUCATION** Univ KS, BME 1960; Wesleyan U, CT, PhD Ethnomusicology. **CAREER** Club St Germain, Paris, prof debut with Kenny Clark 1963; Donald Byrd, Blue Note Club Paris, 1963; Chat Que Peche, Eric Dolphy, Paris, 1964; toured Europe with Art Blakly & New Jazz Messengers, 1965; Europe & Amer, recorded several albums as leader; total 10 LP's as leader; Belgium Radio-TV, staff composer. **HONORS AND AWARDS** Honorary Doctorate of Humane Letters, Florida Memorial College. **MEMBERSHIPS** Mem SACEM, Soc of Composers, Paris, France; co-chmn ed com Inst of Black Am Music; mem Afro-Am Bi-Cen Hall of Fame; est & created PhD degree prog in Ethnomusicology, Univ Pittsburgh; created Jazz Program at Univ Pittsburgh; created Jazz Program Paris-Am Acad Paris. **CONTACT ADDRESS** Music Dept, Univ of Pittsburgh, 5th & Belfefield, Pittsburgh, PA, 15260.

DAVIS, NATHANIEL
PERSONAL Born 04/12/1925, Boston, MA, m, 1956, 4 children **DISCIPLINE** POLITICAL SCIENCE **EDUCATION** Brown Univ, BA, 44; Fletcher School of Law and Diplomacy, MA, 47, PhD, 60. **CAREER** Third secy, Prague, 47-47; vice consul, Florence, 49-52; second secy, Rome, Moscow, 52-56; Dept of State, USSR Affairs, 56-60; first secy, Caracas, 60-62; positions within the Peace Corp, 62-65; US Min Bulgaria, 65-66; Nat Security Coun, 66-68; US Ambassador Chile, 71-73; Dir General US Foreign Service, 73-75; US Ambassador Switzerland, 75-77; State Dept Adv to Naval War Col, 77-83; Howard Univ, 62-68; Chester W Nimitz Chair of Nat Security and Foreign Affairs, US Naval War Col, 77-83; Alexander and Adelaide Hixon Chair, Harvey Mudd Col & fac Claremont Grad School, 83- . **HONORS AND AWARDS** Phi Beta Kappa; hon LLD, Brown Univ, 70; US Navy Distinguished Public Service Award, 83. **MEMBERSHIPS** Am Acad Diplomacy; Am Asn for Advanc of Slavic Stud; Am For Serv Asn; Coun on For Rel; Am Hist Asn; Acad of Polit Sci; Int Stud Asn. **RESEARCH** Religion in Russia. **SELECTED PUBLICATIONS** Contribur, Ronning, ed, Ambassadors in Foreign Policy, Praeger, 87; auth, The Last Two Years of Salvador Allende, Cornell, 85; auth, A Long Walk to Church: A Contemporary History of Russian Orthodoxy, Westview, 95. **CONTACT ADDRESS** 1783 Longwood Ave, Claremont, CA, 91711.

DAVIS, PETER
DISCIPLINE MUSIC **EDUCATION** Univ Southern CA, PhD. **CAREER** Assoc prof, Univ IL Urbana Champaign. **RESEARCH** Theatre hist; Am theatre; censorship; dramaturgy. **SELECTED PUBLICATIONS** Auth, pubs on hist of Am theatre; class theatre hist; acting and directing. **CONTACT ADDRESS** Dept of Music, Univ Illinois Urbana Champaign, E Gregory Drive, PO Box 52, Champaign, IL, 61820. **EMAIL** padavis@uiuc.edu

DAVIS, RODNEY OWEN
PERSONAL Born 07/14/1932, Newton, KS, m, 1954, 3 children **DISCIPLINE** AMERICAN HISTORY **EDUCATION** Univ Kans, BS, 54, MA, 59; Univ Iowa, PhD(hist), 66. **CAREER** From instr to assoc prof, 63-77, PROF HIST, KNOX COL, ILL, 77- **HONORS AND AWARDS** Philip Green Wright-Lombard Col Prize, 67. **MEMBERSHIPS** Orgn Am Historians; Agr Hist Soc; Western Hist Asn; Soc Historians of Early Repub; Soc Sci Hist Asn; Western Hist Asn; Soc Historians Early Am Republic. **RESEARCH** History of the American West; early United States national period; Jacksonian democracy. **SELECTED PUBLICATIONS** Auth, Homes in the Heartland--Balloon Frame Farmhouses of the Upper Midwest, 1850-1920, West Hist Quart, Vol 0025, 94; Belleville, Ottawa and Galesburg--Community and Democracy on the Illinois Frontier, West Hist Quart, Vol 0028, 97; Writing Illinois--The Prairie, Lincoln, and Chicago, Jour Eng and Ger Philol, Vol 0093, 94. **CONTACT ADDRESS** Dept of Hist, Knox Col, Galesburg, IL, 61401.

DAVIS, RONALD LEROY
PERSONAL Born 09/22/1933, Cambridge, OH **DISCIPLINE** AMERICAN CULTURAL HISTORY **EDUCATION** Univ Tex, BA, 55, MA, 57, PhD(hist), 61. **CAREER** Asst prof hist, Kans State Teachers Col (Emporia State Univ), 61-62; asst prof humanities, Mich State Univ, 62-65; from asst prof to assoc prof, 65-72, PROF HIST, SOUTHERN METHODIST UNIV, 72-; Mich State Univ All-Univ res grant, 63-64, Univ Grad Coun grant, 67-68; dir oral hist prog on performing arts, Southern Methodist Univ, 72-; dir, DeGolyer Inst Am Studies, 74-. **HONORS AND AWARDS** Phi Beta Kappa. **MEMBERSHIPS** Orgn Am Historians; Western Hist Asn. **RESEARCH** American cultural history, particularly history of American music, theater, and film. **SELECTED PUBLICATIONS** Auth, A History of Opera in the American West, Prentice-Hall, 64; Opera in Chicago, Appleton, 66; Culture on the Frontier, SW Rev, fall 68; Sopranos and Six-Guns: The Frontier Opera House as a Cultural Symbol, Am West, 11/70; ed, The Social and Cultural Life of the 1920's, Holt, 72; auth, A History of Music in American Life, Krieger Publ Co, 80-82; Hollywood Beauty: Linda Donell and the American Dream, Univ OK Press, 91; The Glamour Factory, SMU Press, 93; John Ford: Hollywood's Old Master, Univ Ok Press, 95; Celluloid Mirrors: Hollywood and American Society Since 1945, Harcourt Brace, 97; Duke: The Life and Image of John Wayne, Unvi OK Press, 98. **CONTACT ADDRESS** Dept of Hist, Southern Methodist Univ, P O Box 750001, Dallas, TX, 75275-0001.

DAVIS, THOMAS JOSEPH
PERSONAL Born 01/06/1946, New York, NY **DISCIPLINE** HISTORY **EDUCATION** SUNY at Buffalo, JD 1993; Ball State Univ, MA 1976; Columbia Univ, PhD 1974, MA 1968; Fordham Univ, AB 1967. **CAREER** Columbia Univ, instr, 1968; Southern Univ, instr 1968-69; Manhattanville Coll, dir Afro-Amer stud 1970-71; Earlham Coll, assoc/asst prof 1972-76; Howard Univ, prof/assoc prof 1977-87; State Univ of NY at Buffalo, prof, 1986-96; Arizona State Univ, prof, 1996-. **HONORS AND AWARDS** Fellow Ford Found 1971, Herbert H Lehman 1969-71; Fulbright 1972, 1994; Francis Cardinal Spellman Youth Award 1962; Newberry Library Fellow 1982; Smithsonian Inst Faculty Fellow 1983; Alpha Kappa Alpha, Gamma Iota Chapter, Educator of the Year, 1982; NY African American Inst, 1986, 1987; Amer Bar Found, Visiting Fellow, 1994-95. **MEMBERSHIPS** Bd mem New York City Council Against Poverty 1965-67; consultant Natl Endowment for Humanities 1980, Educational Testing Serv 1979-88, US Dept of Labor 1978-79; **SELECTED PUBLICATIONS** Auth, A Rumor of Revolt, Macmillian/Free Press, 1985, Univ Mass, 1990; Africans in the Americas, St Martin's Press, 1994. **CONTACT ADDRESS** Dept of History, Arizona State Univ, Tempe, Box 872501, Tempe, AZ, 85287-2501.

DAVIS, THOMAS WEBSTER
PERSONAL Born 10/03/1942, Richmond, VA, m, 1967, 1 child **DISCIPLINE** BRITISH & WORLD HISTORY **EDUCATION** Va Mil Inst, BA, 64; Univ NC, Chapel Hill, MA, 66, PhD(Brit hist), 72. **CAREER** Asst prof, 72-78, assoc prof, 78-82, PROF HIST, VA MIL INST, 82-, Am Philos Soc res grant, 74; Danforth assoc, 76-. **HONORS AND AWARDS** Who's Who Among Teachers in America **MEMBERSHIPS** World Hist Asn; AHA; Southern Conf Brit Studies **RESEARCH** Eighteenth-nineteenth century ecclesiastical history; social history. **SELECTED PUBLICATIONS** Ed, Committees for repeal of the Test and Corporation Acts, minutes 1786-90 and 1827-28, London Rec Soc, 78 **CONTACT ADDRESS** Dept of Hist, Va Mil Inst, Lexington, VA, 24450. **EMAIL** davistw@vmi.edu

DAVIS, WHITNEY
DISCIPLINE ART HISTORY **EDUCATION** Harvard Univ, PhD. **CAREER** Porf, Northwestern Univ; Lectr, Thomas Harris Lectures in History of Art, Univ Col London, 93; prof Humanities, Northwestern Univ, 93-94; tchg and res prof, Arthur Andersen Univ 94-95; dir, Alice Berline Kaplan Center for the Humanities, Northwestern Univ; Getty fel; Guggenheim fel. **SELECTED PUBLICATIONS** Auth, The Canonical Tradition in Ancient Egyptian Art, 89; Masking the Blow: The Scene of Representation in Late Prehistoric Egyptian Art, 92; Drawing the Dream of the Wolves: Homosexuality, Interpretation, and Freud's Wolf Man, 96; replications: Archaeology, Art History and Psychoanalysis, 96; Pacing the World: Construction in the Sculpture of David Rabinowitch, 96; ed, Gay and Lesbian Studies in Art History, 94. **CONTACT ADDRESS** Dept of Art History, Northwestern Univ, 1801 Hinman, Evanston, IL, 60208.

DAVIS, WINSTON
PERSONAL Born 11/05/1939, Jamestown, NY, m, 1974, 2 children **DISCIPLINE** HISTORY OF RELIGION **EDUCATION** Univ Chicago, PhD, 73. **CAREER** Wash and Lee Univ, 92-; Southwestern Univ, 83-92; Kwansei Gakuin Japan, 79-83; Stanford Univ, 73-79. **HONORS AND AWARDS** Phi Beta Kappa; NEH Fel; Dist Lectr, Univ Lectr, U of AZ. **MEMBERSHIPS** AAAR; ASSR. **RESEARCH** Max Weiber; The Ethics of Responsibility. **SELECTED PUBLICATIONS** Auth, DoJo: Magil and Exorcism in Modern Japan; Japanese Religion and Society; The Moral and Political Naturalism of Baron Kate

Hiroyuki. **CONTACT ADDRESS** Dept of Religion, Washington and Lee Univ, Lexington, VA, 24450. **EMAIL** davis.w@wlu.edu

DAVISON, JEAN MARGARET
PERSONAL Born 04/19/1922, Glens Falls, NY **DISCIPLINE** CLASSICAL LANGUAGES, ANCIENT HISTORY **EDUCATION** Univ Vt, AB, 44; Yale Univ, AM, 50, PhD(class archaeol), 57; Univ Ital Stranieri, Perugia, dipl, 60. **CAREER** Cryptanalyst, US Dept War, 44-45; foreign serv clerk, US Dept State, Athens, 45-46 & Vienna, 47-49; instr ancient hist, Latin, Greek & Greek art, 55-59, from asst prof to prof, 59-72, ROBERTS PROF CLASS LANG & LIT, UNIV VT, 72-, Am Philos Asn res grant, 67-68; mem managing comt, Am Sch Class Studies, Athens, 65, mem exec comt, 73, vis prof, 74-75. **MEMBERSHIPS** Archaeol Inst Am; Vergilian Soc Am; Class Asn New England; Am Sch Orient Res; Asn Field Archaeol. **RESEARCH** Greek Archaeology; Homeric studies; pre-Roman Italy. **SELECTED PUBLICATIONS** Auth, Vitruvius on Acoustical Vases in Greek and Roman Theaters, Amer Jour Archaeol, Vol 0100, 96. **CONTACT ADDRESS** Dept of Classics, Univ of Vt, Burlington, VT, 05401.

DAVISON, NANCY R.
DISCIPLINE AMERICAN CULTURE **EDUCATION** Smith, BA, 66; Univ Mich, MA, 73, PhD, 80. **CAREER** ARTIST, PRINTMAKER & GALLERY OWNER **MEMBERSHIPS** Am Antiquarian Soc **SELECTED PUBLICATIONS** Author, American Sheet Music Illustration: Reflections of the Nineteenth-Century, Clements Library Exhibition, 73; auth, "Andrew Jackson in Cartoon and Caricature," American Printmaking Before 1876: Fact, Fiction, and Fantasy, Lib Congress, 75; auth, "Bickham's Musical Entertainer and Other Curiosities," in Eighteenth-Century Prints in Colonial America: To Educate and Decorate, Colonial Williamsburg Found, 79; auth, E. W. Clay and the American Caricature Business, in Prints and Printmakers of New York State, 1825-1940, Syracuse Univ Press, 86; York Beach Activity Book, Blue Stocking, 96. **CONTACT ADDRESS** PO Box 1257, York Beach, ME, 03910.

DAVISON, RODERIC HOLLETT
PERSONAL Born 00/00/1916, Buffalo, NY, m, 2 children **DISCIPLINE** HISTORY **EDUCATION** Princeton Univ, AB, 37; Harvard Univ, AM, 38, PhD(hist), 42. **CAREER** Inst hist, Princeton Univ, 40-42, 46-47; from asst prof to assoc prof, 47-54, chmn dept, 60-64, 69-70, PROF HIST, GEORGE WASHINGTON UNIV, 54-, Lectr hist, Sch Advan Int Studies, Johns Hopkins Univ, 51-52 & 55-58 & Harvard Univ, 59-60; Ford fel, Fund for Advan Educ, 53-54; Soc Sci Res Coun grant, Mid East, 64-65 & 77-78; fel, Am Res Inst, Turkey, 64-65; Guggenheim fel, 70-71. **MEMBERSHIPS** AHA (treas, 74); Mid East Inst (vpres, 76-82); Mid East Studies Asn NAm (pres, 74-75); Turkish Studies Asn NAm (pres, 80-81). **RESEARCH** European diplomatic history since 1815; Ottoman and Turkish modern history; diplomacy of the Eastern question. **SELECTED PUBLICATIONS** Auth, Turkish Nationalism in the Young-Turk Era, Intl Hist Rev, Vol 0015, 93. **CONTACT ADDRESS** Dept of Hist, George Washington Univ, Washington, DC, 20052.

DAVISSON, MARY H.T.
PERSONAL Born 12/05/1952, Baltimore, MD, m, 1980, 3 children **DISCIPLINE** CLASSICS **EDUCATION** Brown Univ, AB, 74, MA, 74; Univ CA, Berkeley, PhD (Classics), 79. **CAREER** Asst prof, Univ VA, 81-83; adjunct asst prof, Loyola Col in Maryland, 84-. **HONORS AND AWARDS** Phi Beta Kappa; Sather Res assistantship, 75-76. **MEMBERSHIPS** Am Philol Asn; Classical Asn of the Middle West and South; Classical Asn of the Atlantic States; Am Classical League; Maryland Junior Classical League. **RESEARCH** Ovid; Virgil; pedagogy. **SELECTED PUBLICATIONS** Auth, Sed sum quam medico notior ipse mihi: Ovid's Use of Some Conventions in the Exile Epistles, Clasical Antiquity 2, 83; Magna Tibi Imosita Est Nostris Persona Libellis: Playwright and Actor in Ovid's Epistulae ex Ponto 3-1, Classical J 79, 84; Parents and Children in Ovid's Poems from Exile, Classical World 78, 84; Tristia 5-13 and Ovid's Use of Epistloary Form and Context, Classical J 80, 85; Quid moror exemplis?: Mythological Exempla in Ovid, Phoenix 47, 93; The Treatment of Festering Sores in Virgil, Classical World 86, 93; Mythological Exempla in Ovid's Remedia Amoris, Phoenix 50, 96; The Observers of Daedalus in Ovid, Classical World 90, 97. **CONTACT ADDRESS** Dept of Classics, Loyola Col, 4501 N Charles St, Baltimore, MD, 21210. **EMAIL** mdavisson@loyola.edu

DAVYDOV, SERGEI
DISCIPLINE RUSSIAN **EDUCATION** Charles Univ, AB; Ludwig Maximillian Univ, MA; Yale Univ, PhD. **CAREER** Prof; Middlebury Col, 88-. **RESEARCH** Literature; Alexander Pushkin; Vladimir Nabokov. **SELECTED PUBLICATIONS** Auth, Tekstymatreshki' Vladimira Nabokova, Slavistische Beitraege, Band 152, Munich: Otto Sagner, 82; The Passions of Young 'Sirin', NY Times Bk Rev, 90; Weighing Nabokov's The Gift on Pushkin's Scales, in Cult Mythologies of Russ Modernism: From the Golden Age to the Silver Age, Berkeley: Univ Calif Press, Calif Slavic Stud, 91; Pushkin i christianstvo, in Transactions of the Asn Russ¤Amer Scholars in USA, vol25, NY: 92-93 & Pushkin's Easter Triptych: 'Otcy pustynniki i zheny neporochny,'Podrazhanie italianskomu,' and 'Mirskaja vlast', in Pushkin Today, Indi UP, 93. **CONTACT ADDRESS** Dept of Russian, Middlebury Col, Middlebury, VT, 05753. **EMAIL** Davydov@Middlebury.edu

DAWSON, ANNE
DISCIPLINE ART HISTORY **EDUCATION** Brown Univ, PhD. **CAREER** Eng Dept, Eastern Conn State Univ **MEMBERSHIPS** Asn Study Conn Hist; Conn Rev; Jour Am Hist. **SELECTED PUBLICATIONS** Auth, exhib catalogues. **CONTACT ADDRESS** Eastern Connecticut State Univ, 83 Windham Street, Willimantic, CT, 06226.

DAWSON, JOHN PHILIP
PERSONAL Born 11/28/1928, Ann Arbor, MI, m, 1997, 2 children **DISCIPLINE** HISTORY **EDUCATION** Harvard Univ, PhD, 61. **CAREER** Instr, Harvard Univ, 61-64; asst prof, 64-70, assoc prof, 70-73, Stanford Univ; prof, Brooklyn Col, CUNY, 73-98. **HONORS AND AWARDS** NEH fel, 87-88. **MEMBERSHIPS** Soc des Etudes Robespierristes; Soc Hist de Paris et de l'Ile-de-France; Asn Hist Soc Rurales; Soc for French Hist Stud. **RESEARCH** French Revolution. **SELECTED PUBLICATIONS** Auth, Provincial Magistrates and Revolutionary Politics in France, 1789-1795, Harvard, 72; contribur, Aydelotte, ed, The Dimensions of Quantitative Research in History, Princeton, 72; contribur, Waldinger, ed, The French Revolution and the Meaning of Citizenship, Greenwood, 93. **CONTACT ADDRESS** 56 Seventh Ave, New York, NY, 10011. **EMAIL** Ph.Dawson@worldnet.att.net

DAY, CHARLES RODNEY
PERSONAL Born 08/06/1936, Long Beach, CA, m, 1961, 2 children **DISCIPLINE** MODERN EUROPEAN HISTORY **EDUCATION** Stanford Univ, BA, 58; Harvard Univ, MA, 59, PhD(hist), 64. **CAREER** Instr, Foothill Col, 64-66; from instr to asst prof, 66-75, ASSOC PROF HIST, SIMON FRASER UNIV, 75-, Can Coun res grant, France, 69-70; Can Coun fel, 75. **MEMBERSHIPS** Soc Fr Hist Studies. **RESEARCH** Education and Society in 19th century France. **SELECTED PUBLICATIONS** Auth, The Proletarianizing of the Fonctionnaires--Civil-Service Workers and the Labor-Movement Under the 3rd-Republic, Jour Soc Hist, Vol 0026, 93; Education for Everyone--Beyond Primary-Education and Development of Secondary-Education Under the 3rd Republic--French, Jour Soc Hist, Vol 0027, 94; Technical Workers in an Advanced Society--The Work, Careers and Politics of French Engineers, Jour Social Hist, Vol 0026, 93. **CONTACT ADDRESS** Dept of Hist, Simon Fraser Univ, Burnaby, BC, V5A 1S6.

DAY, RICHARD B.
PERSONAL Born 07/22/1942, Toronto, ON, Canada **DISCIPLINE** POLITICAL SCIENCE/HISTORY **EDUCATION** Univ Toronto, BA, 65, MA, 67, Dip REES, 67; Univ London, PhD, 70. **CAREER** Asst to assoc prof, 70-79, PROF POLITICAL SCIENCE, ERINDALE COL, UNIV TORONTO, 79-. **HONORS AND AWARDS** Killam sr res fel, 78, 79. **MEMBERSHIPS** Int Soc Study Europ Ideas; Asn Can Slavists; Can Polit Sci Asn. **SELECTED PUBLICATIONS** Auth, Leon Trotsky and the Economics of Political Isolation, 73; auth, The 'Crisis' and the 'Crash' - Soviet Studies of the West (1917-1939), 81; auth, Cold War Capitalism: The View from Moscow (1945-1975), 95; ed/transl, Selected Writings on the State and the Transition to Socialism (N.I. Bukharin); ed/transl, The Decline of Capitalism (E.A. Preobrazhensky), 85; co-ed, Democratic Theory and Technological Society, 88. **CONTACT ADDRESS** Kaneff Ctr, Erindale Campus, Univ of Toronto, Mississauga, ON, L5L 1C6. **EMAIL** rbday@credit.erin.utoronto.ca

DAY, RICHARD E.
DISCIPLINE REMEDIES, CONSUMER PROTECTION, AND INTELLECTUAL PROPERTY **EDUCATION** Univ PA, BS, 51; Univ MI, JD, 57. **CAREER** John William Thurmond ch, prof, Univ of SC. **RESEARCH** Antitrust. **SELECTED PUBLICATIONS** Publ on, antitrust law. **CONTACT ADDRESS** School of Law, Univ of S. Carolina, Law Center, Columbia, SC, 29208. **EMAIL** law0135@univscvm.csd.scarolina.edu

DAY, RONNIE
PERSONAL Born 09/20/1939, London, KY, m, 1985, 2 children **DISCIPLINE** HISTORY **EDUCATION** Cumberland Col, BA, 63; Univ Tex, MA, 65, PhD, 71. **CAREER** Prof, East Tenn State Univ, 68-. **MEMBERSHIPS** Society for Military Hist. **RESEARCH** World War II, South Pacific. **SELECTED PUBLICATIONS** Ed, South Pacific Diary: 1942-1943, 96. **CONTACT ADDRESS** East Tennessee State Univ, PO Box 70672, Johnson City, TN, 37614. **EMAIL** dayr@etsu.edu

DAY, TERENCE PATRICK
PERSONAL Born 02/02/1930, London, England, m, 1969, 3 children **DISCIPLINE** HISTORY OF RELIGIONS, BUDDHISM **EDUCATION** London Col Divinity, ALCD, 59; Univ London, BD Hons, 60; King's Col, MTh, 63, PhD(hist of relig), 66. **CAREER** Lectr philos, St John's Col, Univ Agra, India, 66-71; lectr hist of relig, Univ Nairobi, Kenya, 71-73; ASST PROF HIST OF RELIG, UNIV MANITOBA, 74- **MEMBERSHIPS** Can Soc Study Relig; Am Acad Relig; Int Asn of Buddhist Studies; Am Oriental Soc; Can Asian Studies Assoc. **RESEARCH** Iconography of religions; folk religion; modern movements in religion. **SELECTED PUBLICATIONS** Auth, The Rajneesh Papers, Stud Rel-Sciences Religieuses, Vol 0025, 96. **CONTACT ADDRESS** Dept of Relig, Univ of Manitoba, Winnipeg, MB, R3T 2N2.

DAYTON, CORNELIA H.
DISCIPLINE HISTORY **EDUCATION** Harvard-Radcliffe, AB, 79; Princeton Univ, PhD, 86 **CAREER** Assoc prof, hist, Univ Calif Irvine; current, ASSOC PROF, HIST, UNIV CONN STORRS **HONORS AND AWARDS** 1996 Homer D Babbidge Jr Award **MEMBERSHIPS** Am Antiquarian Soc **SELECTED PUBLICATIONS** Auth, Taking the Trade: Abortion and Gender Relations in an Eighteenth-Century New England Village, Will & Mary Q, 3rd Ser, 91; auth, Women Before the Bar: Gender, Law and Society in Connecticut, 1639-1789, Inst of Early Am Hist & Cult with Univ of NC Press, 95; auth, "Excommunicating the Governor's Wife: Religious Dissent in the Puritan Colonies Before the Era of Rights Consciousness," in Religious Conscience, the State, and the Law in Anglo-American History, SUNY Press, forthcoming. **CONTACT ADDRESS** Dept of Hist, Univ of Conn, 241 Glenbrook Rd, Storrs, CT, 06269-3722. **EMAIL** dayton@uconnvm.uconn.edu

DAYTON, DONALD WILBER
PERSONAL Born 07/25/1942, Chicago, IL, m, 1969 **DISCIPLINE** THEOLOGY, AMERICAN RELIGIOUS HISTORY **EDUCATION** Houghton Col, AB, 63; Yale Univ, BD, 69; Univ Ky, MS in LS, 69; Univ Chicago, PhD(Christian theol), 78. **CAREER** From asst to asst prof theol, Asbury Theol Sem, 69-72, acquisitions librn, B L Fisher Libr, 69-72; asst prof theol, North Park Theol Sem, 72-77, assoc prof, 77-80, dir, Mellander Libr, 72-80; PROF THEOL, NORTHERN BAPTIST THEOL SEM, 80-, Mem bd dir, Urban Life Ctr, 72-; bk ed, Sojourners, 75-; ed assoc, The Other Side, 75-; chmn comn social action & mem bd admin, Christian Holiness Asn, 73-; Staley lectureship, Anderson Col, 77; contrib ed, The Epworth Pulpit, 77-; fac, Sem Consortium Urban Pastoral Educ, 77- **MEMBERSHIPS** Karl Barth Soc NAm; Wesleyan Theol Soc; Am Theol Libr Asn; Am Soc Church Hist; Am Acad Relig. **RESEARCH** Theology and ethics of Karl Barth; 19th century American religious thought; holiness and Pentecostal churches. **SELECTED PUBLICATIONS** Auth, Creationism in 20th-Century America--A 10-Volume Anthology of Documents, 1903-1961, Zygon, Vol 0032, 97. **CONTACT ADDRESS** Dept of Theol, No Baptist Theol Sem, Lombard, IL, 60148.

DE BRETTEVILLE, SHEILA LEVRANT
PERSONAL Born 11/04/1940, New York, NY, m, 1965, 1 child **DISCIPLINE** HISTORY OF ART **EDUCATION** Columbia Univ B College, BA 62; Yale Univ, MFA 64. **CAREER** Cal Inst of Arts, fac 70-73, pres woman's bldg 73-80, ch Otis A&D 80-90; Yale Univ Art Sch, prof 90-. **HONORS AND AWARDS** Moore College Art Des and Cal College Art & Craft-Hon Doct. **RESEARCH** Public Art; Immigrate neighborhoods. **SELECTED PUBLICATIONS** Auth, The Architecture of the Everyday, Princeton Univ Press, 97. **CONTACT ADDRESS** Dept of Art, Yale Univ, 208270 Yale Station, New Haven, CT, 06520 82707. **EMAIL** sheila.debretteville@yale.edu

DE GIROLAMI CHENEY, LIANA
DISCIPLINE ART HISTORY **EDUCATION** Univ Miami, BA, 68, MA, 70; Boston Univ, PhD, 78. **CAREER** Asst prof, Framingham Col, 74-76; asst prof, Univ Lowell, 76-82; vis prof, York Univ, 79-86; vis prof, Emmanuel Col, 86-95; prof, Univ Lowell, 85-. **HONORS AND AWARDS** Governor's Awd, 85; Outstanding Young Woman Am Awd, 76., Pres, Asn Textual Scholar, 97-98; pres, S Cent Renaissance Asn, 98-. **MEMBERSHIPS** Asn Textual Scholar; S Cent Renaissance Asn; Div Humanities Soc Sci; Art Text Asn; Am Asn Italian Studies; British Art Hist Soc; Col Art Asn Am; Emblematic Soc; Hagiographic Soc; Master Drawings Soc; Pre Raphaelite Soc; Renaissance Soc Am. **RESEARCH** Renaissance hist and art. **SELECTED PUBLICATIONS** Auth, Readings in Italian Mannerism, Peter Lang, 97; Botticelli's Neoplatonic Images, Scripta Humanistica, 93; Symbolism of 'Vanitas' in the Arts, Literature, and Music, Edwin Mellen, 93; Medievalism and Pre-Raphaelitism, Edwin Mellen, 93. **CONTACT ADDRESS** Univ Massachusetts Lowell, One Univ Ave, Lowell, MA, 01854. **EMAIL** lianacheney@earthlink.net

DE GRAZIA, VICTORIA
DISCIPLINE CONTEMPORARY HISTORY OF WESTERN EUROPE **EDUCATION** Smith Col, BA, 68; Columbia Univ, PhD, 76. **CAREER** Prof. **SELECTED PUBLICATIONS** Auth, The Culture of Consent: Mass Organization of Leisure in Fascist Italy, 81; How Fascism Ruled Women: Italy, 1922-1945, 92; ed, The Sex of Things: Gender and Consumption, Hist Perspective, 96. **CONTACT ADDRESS** Dept of Hist, Columbia Col, New York, 2960 Broadway, New York, NY, 10027-6902.

DE LA PEDRAJA, RENE
PERSONAL Born 11/26/1951, Havana, Cuba, m, 1976, 1 child **DISCIPLINE** HISTORY **EDUCATION** Univ of Houston, BA, 73; Univ of Chicago, MA, 74, PhD, 77. **CAREER** Res prof, School of Economics, Universidad de los Andes, 76-85; asst prof, Dept of Hist, Kans State Univ, 86-89; ASST PROF, 89-92, ASSOC PROF, 92-97, PROF, 97-, DEPT OF HIST, CANISIUS COL. **HONORS AND AWARDS** Choice Outstanding Academic Boox Award, Am Libr Asn, 94. **MEMBERSHIPS** Am Hist Asn; Latin Am Studies Asn; Confr of Latin Am Hist. **RESEARCH** Business history; military history. **SELECTED PUBLICATIONS** Auth, Oil and Coffee: The Merchant Shipping of Latin America from the Imperial Era to the 1950s, Greenwood Press, 98; auth, A Historical Dictionary of the U.S. Merchant Marine and Shipping Industry: Since the Introduction of Steam, Greenwood Press, 94; auth, The Rise and Decline of U.S. Merchant Shipping in the Twentieth Century, Twayne Pub, 92; auth, Energy Politics in Colombia, Westview Press, 89; auth, Fedemetal y la industrializacion de Colombia, Op Graficas, 86; auth, Historia de la energia en Colombia 1538-1930, El Ancora Editores, 85. **CONTACT ADDRESS** Dept of Hist, Canisius Col, 2001 Main St, Buffalo, NY, 14208-1098. **EMAIL** delapedr@canisius.edu

DE LA TEJA, J.F.
PERSONAL Born 07/17/1956, Cuba, m, 1983, 2 children **DISCIPLINE** HISTORY **EDUCATION** Seton Hall Univ, BA, 79, MA, 81; Univ of Tx at Austin, PhD, 88. **CAREER** Asst archivist, 85-89, archivist, 89-91, dir of archives and records, Tex General Land Office, 90-91; ASST PROF, 91-95, ASSOC PROF, SOUTHWEST TEX STATE UNIV, 96-. **HONORS AND AWARDS** Carlos Edvardo Castaneda Service Awd, Tex Catholic Hist Soc, 97; San Antonio Conservation Soc Book Citation and Sons of the Republic of Tex Presidio La Bahia Awd; Southwest Tex State Univ Presidential Awd for Scholarly/Creative Activities, 96. **RESEARCH** Spanish borderlands, Colonial Mexico, 19th Century Texas. **SELECTED PUBLICATIONS** Auth, Spanish Colonial Texas, New Views of Borderland Hist, Univ of Nmex Press, 98; Discovering the Tejano Community in Early Texas, J of the Early Republic, 98; The Colonization and Independence of Texas: A Tejano Perspective, Myths, Misdeeds, and Misunderstandings: The Roots of Conflict in United States-Mexico Relations, Scholarly Resources, 97; Rebellion on the Frontier, Tejano Journey 1770-1860, Univ of Tex Press, 96; San Antonio de Bexar: A Community on New Spain's Northern Frontier, Univ of NMex Press, 95. **CONTACT ADDRESS** Dept of Hist, Southwest Texas State Univ, San Marcos, TX, 78666. **EMAIL** jd10@swt.edu

DE MOURA SOBRAL, LUIS
PERSONAL Born 06/24/1943, Viseu, Portugal **DISCIPLINE** ART HISTORY **EDUCATION** Coimbra Univ; Univ Louvain. **CAREER** Cur, Montreal Mus Fine Arts, 71-75; asst to assoc prof, 76-87, PROF ART HISTORY, UNIV MONTREAL, 87-, ch, 87-95. **SELECTED PUBLICATIONS** Auth, Le surrealisme portugais, 84; auth, Villalonga, les lieux du reve, 93; auth, Pintura e Poesia na Epoca Barroca, 94; auth, Do Sentido das Imagens, 96; ed, Surrealisme peripherique, 84; co-ed, Can Art Rev, 83-89. **CONTACT ADDRESS** Dept of Art History, Univ of Montreal, CP 6128, Succ Centre Ville, Montreal, PQ, H3C 3J7. **EMAIL** demoural@ere.umontreal.ca

DE PAUW, LINDA GRANT
PERSONAL Born 01/19/1940, New York, NY, 2 children **DISCIPLINE** AMERICAN HISTORY **EDUCATION** Swarthmore Col, BA, 61; Johns Hopkins Univ, PhD, 64. **CAREER** Asst prof hist, George Mason Col, Univ Va, 64-65; from asst prof to assoc prof, 66-75, PROF HIST, GEORGE WASHINGTON UNIV, 75-; ED IN CHIEF DOC HIST, FIRST FED CONG, NAT HIST PUBL COMN, 66-. **HONORS AND AWARDS** Beveridge Award, AHA, 64 **MEMBERSHIPS** AHA; Orgn Am Historians; Southern Hist Asn; Am Soc Legal Hist; Int Univ Sem Armed Forces & Soc **RESEARCH** Early American history; women and war. **SELECTED PUBLICATIONS** Auth, The Eleventh Pillar: New York State and the Federal Constitution, Cornell Univ, 66; ed, Documentary History of the First Federal Congress, Johns Hopkins Univ, 72; auth, Land of the unfree: Legal limitations on liberty in prerevolutionary America, Md Hist Mag, 73; Four traditions: Women of New York During the American Revolution, Albany, 74; Founding Mothers: Women of America in the Revolutionary era, Houghton, 75; coauth, Remember the Ladies: Women in America, 1750-1815, Viking, 76; Women in Combat: The Revolutionary War Experience, Armed Forces & Soc, winter 81; Seafaring Women, Houghton, 82; Battle Cries and Lullabies, Univ Okla, 98. **CONTACT ADDRESS** The Minerva Center, Inc., 20 Granada Rd, Pasadena, MD, 21122. **EMAIL** minervacen@aol.com

DE RIOS, MARLENE DOBKIN
PERSONAL Born 04/12/1939, New York, NY, m, 1969, 2 children **DISCIPLINE** ANTHROPOLOGY **EDUCATION** Univ Cal Riverside, PhD 72. **CAREER** Cal State Univ Fullerton, prof 69 to 98-; Univ Cal Irvine, assoc prof 87 to 98-. **HONORS AND AWARDS** Fulbright Fel; NIMH post doc Fel. **MEMBERSHIPS** AAA; APA **RESEARCH** Comparative Healing Systems; Shamanism; Latino Mental Health Issues; Hallucinogens. **SELECTED PUBLICATIONS** Auth, Amazon Healer, The Life and Times of an Urban Shaman, Bridport, England, Prism Press, 92; Hallucinogens: Cross-cultural Perspective, Albuquerque NM, U of NM press, 84, reprinted, Bridport, Eng, Prism Press, 90; Adolescent Drug Use in Cross-cultural Perspective, coauth, Jour of Drug Issues, 92. **CONTACT ADDRESS** Dept of Anthropology, California State Univ, Fullerton, Fullerton, CA, 92834. **EMAIL** mderios@fullerton.edu

DE VRIES, BERT
PERSONAL Born 03/04/1939, Netherlands, m, 1962, 4 children **DISCIPLINE** NEAR EAST HISTORY **EDUCATION** Calvin Col, BSc, 60; Calvin Theol Sem, BD, 64; Brandeis Univ, PhD(Hittite), 67. **CAREER** From asst prof to assoc prof, 67-77, PROF HIST, CALVIN COL, 77-, CHMN DEPT, 80-, Architect-survr, Heshbon Archeol Exped, 68-76; Albright fel, Am Schs Orient Res, 72; dir, Umm El-Jimal archeol exped, 72-. **MEMBERSHIPS** Am Orient Soc. **RESEARCH** Middle East archaeology. **CONTACT ADDRESS** Dept of History, Calvin Col, Grand Rapids, MI, 49506.

DE VRIES, JAN
PERSONAL Born 11/14/1943, Netherlands, m, 1968, 2 children **DISCIPLINE** HISTORY, ECONOMICS **EDUCATION** Yale, PhD, 70; Columbia Univ, BA, 65. **CAREER** Univ Calif, Berkeley, Prof, 77-, Assoc Prof 73-77; MI State Univ, Assoc Prof, 70-73. **HONORS AND AWARDS** Gugganheim fel, vis fel, All Souls Col, Oxford. **MEMBERSHIPS** Ec Hist Asn; Am Ec Asn; Soc Sci Hist Asn. **RESEARCH** European Economic Hist; Demographic Hist. **SELECTED PUBLICATIONS** The Dutch Economy in the Golden Age, 1500-1700, New Haven, Yale Univ Press, 74; The Economy of Europe in an Age of Crisis, 1600-1750, Cambridge, Cambridge Univ press, 76, Span trans, 79, Port trans, 83, Catalan trans, 93; Barges and Capitalism: Passenger Transportation in the Dutch Economy, 1632-1839, A A G Bijdragen no 21, Wageningen, The Neth, 78, reissued, Utrecht, Hes Pub 81; European Urbanization, 1500-1800, London, Methuen and Co, Cambridge MA, Harvard Univ Press 84, Span trans 87; with A M van der Woude, The First Modern Economy: Success, Failure and Perseverance of the Dutch Economy, 1500-1815, Cambridge, Cambridge Univ Press, 97, Dutch ed, Nederland, 1500-1815: De eerste ronde van modern economisch groei, Amsterdam, Uitgeverij Balans, 95; ed, with Ad van der Woude and Akira Hyami, Urbanization in History, Oxford, Oxford Univ Press, 90; with David Freedberg, Art in History, History in Art: Studies in 17th Century Dutch Culture, Chicago, Univ Chicago Press, 91. **CONTACT ADDRESS** Univ California, Dept History, Berkeley, CA, 94720. **EMAIL** devries@socrates.berkeley.edu

DEAGON, ANN FLEMING
PERSONAL Born 01/19/1930, Birmingham, AL, m, 1951, 2 children **DISCIPLINE** CLASSICS, CREATIVE WRITING **EDUCATION** Birmingham-Southern Col, BA, 50; Univ NC, MA, 51, PhD(Latin), 54. **CAREER** Asst prof classics, Furman Univ, 54-56; from asst prof to assoc prof, 56-75, prof Classics, Guilford Col, 75-92; Nat Endowment for Arts literary fel, 82. **MEMBERSHIPS** Am Philol Asn; Class Asn Midwest & S; Poetry Soc Am; Archaeological Inst Am. **SELECTED PUBLICATIONS** Auth, Poetics South, Blair, 74; Carbon 14, Univ Mass, 74; Indian Summer, Unicorn Press, 75; Women and Children First, Iron Mountain, 76; There is No Balm in Birmingham, Godine, 78; The Flood Story, Winthrop Col, 81; Habitats, Green River Press, 82; auth, The Diver's Tomb, St martins, 84; auth, The Polo Poems, Nebraska, 90. **CONTACT ADDRESS** 802 Woodbrook Dr, Greensboro, NC, 27410. **EMAIL** anndeacon@worldnet.att.net

DEAK, ISTVAN
PERSONAL Born 05/11/1926, Szekesfehervar, Hungary, m, 1959, 1 child **DISCIPLINE** MODERN EUROPEAN HISTORY **EDUCATION** Columbia Univ, MA, 58, PhD, 64. **CAREER** Instr Hist, Smith Col, 62-63; from Instr to Prof Hist, 63-93, Seth Low Prof Hist, Columbia Univ, 93-, actg dir, Inst E Cent Europe, 67-68, dir, Inst E Cent Europe, 68-78; Vis lectr, Yale Univ, 66; vis prof, Univ Calif, Los Angeles, 75 & Univ Siegen, Fed Repub of Ger, 81. **HONORS AND AWARDS** Guggenheim fel, 70-71; Fulbright-Hays travel fel, 73; Lionel Trilling Book Award, 79; Am Coun Learned Soc fel, 81; mem, Inst for Advan Study, 81; mem, Hungarian Acad Sci, 90; Wayne S. Vuchinich Book Prize, 91. **MEMBERSHIPS** Am Asn Advan Slavic Studies; Conf Group Slavic & East Europ Hist (vpres, 75-77); Mid-Atlantic Slavic Asn (pres, 77). **RESEARCH** Hist of the Habsburg Monarchy; the Central European Revolutions of 1848-1849; the army in society and polit in Central and Eastern Europe; collaboratism, resistance, and retribution in World War II Europe. **SELECTED PUBLICATIONS** Auth, Hungary, In: The European Right, a Historical Profile, 65-66 & Weimer Germany's Left-Wing Intellectuals, 68, Univ CA; The Decline and Fall of Habsburg Hungary, In: Hungary in Revolution, 1918-1919, Univ Nebr, 71; co-ed, Eastern Europe in the 1970's, Praeger, 72; Everyman in Europe: Essays in Social History, Prentice-Hall, 74 & 81; auth, An Army Divided: The Loyalty Crisis of the Habsburg Officer Corps, 1848-49, In: Jahrbuch, Univ Tel-Aviv, 79; The Lawful Revolution, Louis Kossuth and the Hungarians, 1848-49, Univ Columbia, 79; Reform Triumphant, In: The American and European Revolutions, 1776-1848, Univ Iowa, 80; Beyond Nationalism: A Social and Political History of the Habsburg Officer Corps, 1848-1918, Oxford Univ Press, 90, 91, Ger ed, 91, 93, Hungarian ed, 93, Ital ed, 94. **CONTACT ADDRESS** Inst of E Cent Europe, Columbia Univ, 420 W 118th St, New York, NY, 10027. **EMAIL** id1@columbia.edu

DEAL, J. DOUGLAS
DISCIPLINE HISTORY **EDUCATION** Harvard, AB, 71; Univ Rochester, MA, 74; PhD, 82. **CAREER** Prof, SUNY Oswego. **RESEARCH** Colonial and Revolutionary Am; slavery, the South, and the Civil War era; Am labor hist. **SELECTED PUBLICATIONS** Auth, Race and Class in Colonial Virginia: Indians, Englishmen, and Africans on the Eastern Shore During the Seventeenth Century, Garland, 93; A Constricted World: Free Blacks on Virginia's Eastern Shore, 1680-1750 in Colonial Chesapeake Society, Univ NC P. **CONTACT ADDRESS** Dept Hist, SUNY Oswego, 110 Mahar Hall, Oswego, NY, 13126. **EMAIL** deal@oswego.edu

DEAL, TERRANCE E.
PERSONAL Born 08/31/1939, m, 1975, 1 child **DISCIPLINE** EDUCATION ADMINISTRATION, SOCIOLOGY **EDUCATION** Univ LaVerne, BA, Hist, Phys Educ, 57-61; Calif State Coll-LA, MA, Educ Admin, Soc Sci, 61-66; Stanford Univ, PhD, 68-70. **CAREER** Tchr, Fremont Jun High Sch, 61-66; tchr, Pacific Grove High Sch, 66-68; admin asst to Supt Schs, Pacific Grove Unified Sch Dist, 70; prin, Community-Centered High Sch, Pacific Grove, CA, 70-71; dir, Athenian Urban Center, San Francisco, CA, 71-72; asst prof, Univ British Columbia, 73; lectr, Sch Educ, Stanford Univ, 72-76; asst prof, Admin & Policy Analysis, Stanford Univ, 76-77; assoc prof, Admin, Plan & Soc Policy, Harvard Univ, 77-83; PROF, EDUC & HUMAN DEVELOP, PEABODY COLL VANDERBILT UNIV, 83-; co-dir, Nat Center Educ Leadership, Vanderbilt/Harvard, 88-94. **MEMBERSHIPS** Mich Found Educ Leadership-Kellog Found; Center for Support of Prof Practice in Educ; Nat Bd Advisors; Round Table; Corp Family Solution; Phi Delta Kappa; Am Educ Res Asn **SELECTED PUBLICATIONS** Coauth, Becoming a Teacher-Leader: From Isolation to Collaboration, Corwin Press, 94; coauth, Becoming a School Board Member, Corwin Press, 95; coauth, Leading With Soul: An Uncommon Journey of Spirit, Jossey-Bass, 95; coauth, Reframing Organizations: Artistry, Choice, and Leadership, Jossey-Bass, 97; coauth, Corporate Celebration: Play, Purpose, and Profit at Work, Berrett-Koehler Pub, 98. **CONTACT ADDRESS** Peabody Col, Vanderbilt Univ, Box 514 Peabody, Nashville, TN, 37203.

DEAN, DAVID M.
DISCIPLINE EARLY MODERN BRITISH AND EUROPEAN HISTORY **EDUCATION** Univ Auckland, BA, MA; Univ Cambridge, PhD. **CAREER** Vis assoc prof. **RESEARCH** Political and cultural history, comparative constitutional history. **SELECTED PUBLICATIONS** Auth, Locality and Parliament: The Legislative Activities of Devon's MP's during the Reign of Elizabeth, Tudor and Stuart Devon: The Common Estate and Government, Essays Presented to Joyce Youings, Exeter, 92; Image and Ritual in the Tudor Parliament', Tudor Polit Cult, Cambridge Univ Press, 95; Law, Law-Making and Society: The Parliament of England 1584-1601, Cambridge UP, 96. **CONTACT ADDRESS** Dept of Hist, Carleton Univ, 1125 Colonel By Dr, Ottawa, ON, K1S 5B6. **EMAIL** davdean@ccs.carleton.ca

DEAN, WARREN
PERSONAL Born 10/17/1932, Passaic, NJ **DISCIPLINE** HISTORY **EDUCATION** Univ Miami, BA, 53; Univ Fla, MA, 61, PhD(hist), 64. **CAREER** Asst prof hist, Univ Tex, Austin, 65-70; assoc prof, 70-77, PROF HIST, NY UNIV, 77-, Univ Tex fel hist, 64-65; Social Sci Res Coun fel, 68-69; Guggenheim fel, 80-81. **HONORS AND AWARDS** Robertson Prize, 69. **MEMBERSHIPS** Conf Latin Am Hist; Am Soc Environ Hist. **RESEARCH** Latin America; environmental history; Brazil. **SELECTED PUBLICATIONS** Auth, Amazon Conservation in the Age of Development--The Limits of Providence, Hisp Amer Hist Rev, Vol 0074, 94; Unequal Giants--Diplomatic Relations Between the United-States and Brazil, 1889-1930, Pacific Hist Rev, Vol 0062, 93. **CONTACT ADDRESS** Dept of Hist, New York Univ, 19 University Pl, New York, NY, 10003.

DEBARDELEBEN, JOAN
PERSONAL Born 10/12/1950, Park Falls, WI **DISCIPLINE** CENTRAL/EAST EUROPEAN STUDIES **EDUCATION** Univ Wis Madison, BA, 72, MA, 74, PhD, 79. **CAREER** Asst prof, Colo State Univ, 78-80; asst prof, 80-85, assoc prof, polit sci, McGill Univ, 85-91, dir grad stud, 83-85, 89-90; assoc prof, 91-93, PROF, CARLETON UNIV, 93-, DIR INST CENTRAL/EAST EUROPEAN & RUSSIAN-AREA STUD, 92-; hon fel, Univ Wis Madison, 95-96. **MEMBERSHIPS** Can Asn Slavists (pres); Can Asn Univ Tchrs. **SELECTED PUBLICATIONS** Auth, The Environment and Marxism-Leninism: The Soviet and East German Experience, 85; auth, Soviet Politics in Transition, 92; auth, Russian Politics in Transition, 97; coauth, European Politics in Transition, 87, 92; coauth, Comparative Politics

at the Crossroads, 96; ed & coauth, To Breathe Free: Eastern Europe's Environmental Crisis, 91; co-ed & coauth, Beyond the Monolith: The Emergence of Regionalism in Post-Soviet Russia, 97; co-ed, Environmental Security and Quality After Communism, 94. **CONTACT ADDRESS** CERAS, Carleton Univ, 1125 Colonel By Dr, Ottawa, ON, K1S 5B6.

DEBLAUWE, FRANCIS
PERSONAL Born 08/01/1961, Kuurne, Belgium, m, 1989, 3 children **DISCIPLINE** ARCHAEOLOGY AND ART HISTORY **EDUCATION** Univ Cal LA, PhD, 94; Univ Leuven Belgium, Licentiaat Katholieke, 84. **CAREER** Adj doc fac, lectr, 95-, Univ Missouri; lectr, 95-97, Kansas City Art Inst. **HONORS AND AWARDS** Spec instr KCAI; Lectr St Mary's College and Univ MD. **MEMBERSHIPS** AIA; AHA; FAGDM. **RESEARCH** Mesopotamia; Ancient Near East; Archaeology; History; Spatial Analysis of Architecture. **SELECTED PUBLICATIONS** Auth, Discriminant Analysis of Selected Spatial Variables Derived from Mesopotamian Buildings of the Late Bronze Age till the Parthian Period, in: Mesopotamia Rivista di Archeologia Epigrafia e Storia Orientale Antica, 97; A Test Study of Circulation and Access Patterns in Assyrian Architecture, in: Hartmut Waetzzold, Harald Hauptmann, eds, Assyrien im Wandel der Zeiten, Recontre Assyriologique Intl, Heidelberg, 97; Spacings and Stats or a Different Method to Analyze Buildings, A Test with Mesopotamian Houses from the Late Bronze and Iron Ages, in, Akkadia, 94. **CONTACT ADDRESS** 101 E 113th Terrace, Kansas City, MO, 64114. **EMAIL** fdeblauwe@compuserve.com

DEBLY, PATRICIA
PERSONAL Canada **DISCIPLINE** MUSICOLOGY **EDUCATION** Univ of Victoria, BC, PhD, 93. **CAREER** Assoc prof, Brock Univ, 90-. **CONTACT ADDRESS** Dept of Music, Brock Univ, St. Catharines, ON, L7L 2Z4. **EMAIL** pdebly@spartan.ac.BrockU.CA

DEBO, RICHARD K.
PERSONAL Born 06/28/1938, Omaha, NE, m, 1959 **DISCIPLINE** RUSSIAN HISTORY **EDUCATION** Univ Nebr, BA, 59, MA, 61, PhD(hist), 64. **CAREER** From instr to asst prof hist, Univ Nebr, 64-66; asst prof, 66-74, assoc prof, 74-81, PROF HIST, SIMON FRASER UNIV, 81-, Corresp ed, Can-Am Slavic Studies, 67-; Can Coun leave fel, 73-74 & 80-81. **MEMBERSHIPS** AHA; Am Asn Advan Slavic Studies. **RESEARCH** Soviet foreign policy, 1917-1939. **SELECTED PUBLICATIONS** Auth, Always in Need of Credit--The Ussr and Franco-German Economic Cooperation, 1926-1929, Fr Hist Stud, Vol 0020, 97. **CONTACT ADDRESS** Dept of Hist, Simon Fraser Univ, Burnaby, BC, V5A 1S6.

DEBUYS, WILLIAM ENO
PERSONAL Born 10/30/1949, Baltimore, MD, m, 1977 **DISCIPLINE** HISTORY **EDUCATION** Univ Texas, PhD, 82; Univ Texas, MA, 80; Univ North Carolina, BA, 72; Unversite de Lyon, France, Certificat des Etudes Francaises, 70 **CAREER** Writer and conservation consultant, 86-; editor, Common Ground, bimonthly newsletter by Conservation Fund, 89-97; exec dir, North Carolina Nature Conservancy, 82-86; asst instr, Univ Texas, 80-81; writer and instr, Northern New Mexico Community Col, 75-79 **HONORS AND AWARDS** Calvin Horn Lectr, Univ New Mexico, 97; Evans Biography Award, 91; Pulitzer Prize Finalist, 91; New York Times Notable Book of the Year, 90; Distinguished Visiting Prof, New Mexico State Univ, 87; Chairman's Award, North Carolina Nature Conservancy, 87 **MEMBERSHIPS** Chairman, New Mexico Recreational Trails Advisory Board, 96-; United Way Santa Fe County Allocations Committee, 96-; Dir EarthWorks, 94-; Founding Dir, Santa Fe Conservation Trust, 93-; Chairman, Rio Grande Bosque Conservation Initiative, 91-93 **RESEARCH** Environmental History of North American West; Social//Cultural History of North American West **SELECTED PUBLICATIONS** Enchantment and Exploitation: the Life and Hard Times of a New Mexico Mountain Range, Univ New Mexico, 85; River of Traps: a Village Life, Univ New Mexico, 90; coauth, Toward a Scientific and Social Framework for Ecological-based Stewardship of Federal Lands and Waters, Elsevier, forthcoming **CONTACT ADDRESS** 1511 Don Gaspar, Santa Fe, NM, 87505. **EMAIL** wdebuys@aol.com

DECARIE, GRAEME
DISCIPLINE HISTORY **EDUCATION** Sir George Univ, BA; Acadia Univ, MA; Queen's Univ, PhD. **CAREER** Instr, Univ Prince Edward Island; Shue Yan Col, Hong Kong; Univ Groeningen; assoc prof. **RESEARCH** Prohibition in Canada. **SELECTED PUBLICATIONS** Auth, book on the history of Montreal. **CONTACT ADDRESS** Dept of Hist, Concordia Univ, Montreal, 1455 de Maisonneuve W, Montreal, PQ, H3G 1M8. **EMAIL** decarie@vax2.concordia.ca

DECI, EDWARD LEWIS
PERSONAL Born 10/14/1942, Clifton Springs, NY **DISCIPLINE** SOCIAL/PERSONALITY PSYCHOLOGY **EDUCATION** Hamilton Coll, AB, 64; Univ Pennsylvania, MBA, 67; Carnegie Mellon, MS, 69, PhD, 70. **CAREER** Faculty member, dept of psychology, Univ of Rochester, 70-present, Asst Prof, 70-76; post doctoral fel, Stanford Univ, 73-74; Assoc Prof 76-78, Prof 78-present. **HONORS AND AWARDS** Grants from Natl Sci Found; Natl Inst of Mental Health; Natl Inst of Child Health and Human Development **MEMBERSHIPS** Amer Psychological Assoc; Amer Psychological soc. **RESEARCH** Human motivation **SELECTED PUBLICATIONS** Auth, Why we do what we do, Penguin, NY, 95; coauth, Personality and Social Psychology Bulletin, Elements within the Competitive Situation that Affect Intrinsic Motivation, 96; coauth, Jrn of Personality and Social Psychology, Motivational predictors of weight loss and weight loss mmaintenance, 96, Internalization of biophysical values by medical students: a test of self determination theory, 96; coauth, Review of Educ Research, When paradigms clash: comments on Cameron and Pierce's (94) claim that rewards don't affect intrinsic motivation, 96; auth, Physchological Inquiry, Making room for self regulation: some thoughts on the linkage between emotion and behavior, 96; coauth, Learning and Individual Differences, Need satisfaction and the self regulation of learning, 96; coauth, Personality and Social Physcology Bulletin, Perceiving others as intrinsically or extrinsically motivated, 97; coauth, Development and Psychopathology, Nature and autonomy: an organizational view on the social and nuerobiological aspects of self regulation in behavior and devlopment, 97; coauth, Social Science and Medicine, Motivation underlying career choice for internal medicine and surgery, 97; coauth, Health Psychology, Autonomous Regulation and Adherence to Long term Medical Regimens in Adult Outpatients, 98; coauth, Annals of Internal Medicine, The importance of supporting autonomy in medical education, 98. **CONTACT ADDRESS** Dept of Psych, Univ of Rochester, Rochester, NY, 14627. **EMAIL** deci@psych.rochester.edu

DECKER, HANNAH S.
PERSONAL Born 03/19/1937, New York, NY, m, 1957, 2 children **DISCIPLINE** HISTORY **EDUCATION** Barnard Col, AB, 57; MA, 58, PhD, 71, Columbia Univ. **CAREER** Asst Prof/Assoc Prof/Prof, Univ Houston, 74-; Adj Asst/Assoc/Prof, Baylor Col of Medicine, 80-; Adj Mem, Houston-Galveston Pschoanalytic Inst, 94-. **SELECTED PUBLICATIONS** Auth, The Jung Cult--Origins of a Charismatic Movement, Amer Hist Rev, Vol 0101, 96; The Diary of Freud, Sigmund, 1929-1939--A Record of the Final Decade, Isis, Vol 0084, 93; In Defense of Schreber--Soul Murder and Psychiatry, Amer Hist Rev, Vol 0100, 95; Analysis Interminable--Response to Zalewski,Daniel Article on the Proposed Library-Of-Congress Freud Exhibit, Lingua Franca, Vol 0006, 96; Utopian Feminism--Womens Movements in Fin-De-Siecle Vienna, Amer Hist Rev, Vol 0099, 94; Metaphors in the History of Psychology, Cent Europ Hist, Vol 0026, 93; The Diary of Freud, Sigmund, 1929-1939--A Record of the Final Decade, Isis, Vol 0084, 93. **CONTACT ADDRESS** Dept of History, Univ of Houston, Houston, TX, 77204-3785. **EMAIL** hsdecker@jetson.uh.edu

DECKER, LESLIE EDWARD
PERSONAL Born 06/14/1930, Wellington, ME, m, 1948, 2 children **DISCIPLINE** AMERICAN HISTORY **EDUCATION** Univ Maine, BA, 51; Okla State Univ, MA, 52; Cornell Univ, PhD, 61. **CAREER** Ed, Wis Mag Hist, 56-57; asst prof hist, State Univ NY Col Potsdam, 58-61; from asst prof to assoc prof, Univ Maine, 61-69; prof, 69-75, EMER PROF HIST, UNIV ORE, 75-, Ed consult, Am hist publs, 57-; fel, Relm Found, 64-65. **MEMBERSHIPS** Orgn Am Historians; AHA; United Methodist Econ Ministry; Me chap Nat Multiple Sclerosis Soc. **RESEARCH** Peopling and politics of the trans-Mississippi country; agricultural abandonment in northern New England; economic history of the Northwest. **SELECTED PUBLICATIONS** Coauth, The anniversary publication: objectives and research, Wis Mag Hist, 57; auth, The railroads and the land office: administrative policy and the land patent controversy, 1864-1896, Miss Valley Hist Rev, 60; Railroads, Lands, and Politics: The Taxation of the Railroad Land Grants, 1864-1897, Brown Univ, 64, 66; collabr, The Torch is Passed: The United States in the Twentieth Century, Addison-Wesley, 68; auth, The great speculation, In: The Frontier in American Development: Essays in Honor of Paul Wallace Gates, Cornell Univ, 69; coauth, The Last Best Hope: A History of the United States (3 vols), 72 & co-ed, America's Major Wars: Crusaders, Critics, and Scholars (2 vols), 73, Addison-Wesley; co-auth, Place of Peace: Salem, Maine 1815-1995, forthcoming. **CONTACT ADDRESS** RFD Salem, RRI Box 884, Strong, ME, 04983. **EMAIL** lesdme@somtel.com

DECONDE, ALEXANDER
PERSONAL Born 11/13/1920, Utica, NY **DISCIPLINE** HISTORY **EDUCATION** San Francisco State Col, AB, 43; Stanford Univ, AM, 47, PhD, 49. **CAREER** Actg instr hist, Stanford Univ, 47-48; from asst prof to assoc prof, Whittier Col, 48-52; res assoc, Duke Univ, 52-53, asst prof, 53-57; assoc prof, Univ Mich, 57-61; chmn dept, 63-67, PROF HIST, UNIV CALIF, SANTA BARBARA, 61-, Pac Coast Br AHA Am hist award, 49; Soc Sci Res Coun grants, 51 & 56; Guggenheim fel, 59-60 & 67-68; Am Philos Soc grant, 63 & res grant Am diplomatic hist, 72-73; Fulbright grant, Ctr Am Studies, Rome, 64 & Fulbright-State Dept inter-country lectr Am hist & Am foreign rels, India and SE Asia, 71; fac res lectr, 67; resident scholar, Rockefeller Ctr, Bellagio, Italy, 75; State Dept lectr, Ger & Austria, 75; Italian comt Am hist lectr, Italy, 75. **MEMBERSHIPS** AHA; Orgn Am Historians; Soc Hist Am Foreign Rels (vpres, 68, pres, 69). **RESEARCH** American diplomatic and political history; inter-cultural history. **SELECTED PUBLICATIONS** Auth, Franklin,Benjamin and His Enemies, Intl Hist Rev, Vol 0019, 97; Rising Wind--Black-Americans and Us Foreign-Affairs, 1935-1960, Intl Hist Rev, Vol 0019, 97. **CONTACT ADDRESS** Dept of Hist, Univ of Calif, Santa Barbara, CA, 93106.

DECREDICO, MARY A.
PERSONAL Born 03/28/1959, Cleveland, OH, s **DISCIPLINE** US HISTORY WITH EMPHASIS ON SOUTHERN HISTORY **EDUCATION** Bucknell Univ, BA; Vanderbilt Univ, MA, PhD. **CAREER** Asst prof to assoc prof to PROF HISTORY, US NAVAL ACAD, 86-. **HONORS AND AWARDS** Jefferson Davis Award Outstanding Monogr; Meritorious Civilian Serv Medal. **MEMBERSHIPS** Am Hist Asn; S Hist Asn; Soc Civil War Hist; GA Hist Soc; VA Hist Soc; St George Tucker. **RESEARCH** Urban Confederacy **SELECTED PUBLICATIONS** Patriotism for Profit: Georgia's Urban Entrepreneurs and the Confederate War Effort, Univ NC Press, 90; Mary Boykin Chesnut: A Confederate Women's Life, Madison House, 96. **CONTACT ADDRESS** Dept of History, US Naval Acad, Annapolis, MD, 21402. **EMAIL** decredic@novell.nadn.navy.mil

DEE, JAMES HOWARD
PERSONAL Born 12/30/1943, Albany, NY, m, 1969 **DISCIPLINE** CLASSICAL LANGUAGES AND LITERATURE **EDUCATION** Univ Rochester, BA, 66; Univ Tex Austin, PhD(classics), 72. **CAREER** Asst prof, 72-79, ASSOC PROF CLASSICS, UNIV ILL CHICAGO CIRCLE, 79-, Chairperson Classics, 82-, Nat Endowment for Humanities residential fel, 77-78. **MEMBERSHIPS** Am Philol Asn; Class Asn Middle West & South; Vergilian Soc. **RESEARCH** Augustan Latin poetry; stylistic qualities in Greek and Latin epic; Roman moral and humanistic values. **SELECTED PUBLICATIONS** Auth, Greek and Egyptian Mythologies, Class Bulletin, Vol 0071, 95; The Scepter and the Spear--Studies on Forms of Repetition in the Homeric Poems, Class World, Vol 0090, 97; A Repertory of English Words with Classical Suffixes .4., Class Jour, Vol 0089, 94; The Interpretation of Order--A Study in the Poetics of Homeric Repetition, Class World, Vol 0090, 97; A Repertory of English Words with Classical Suffixes .3., Class Jour, Vol 0088, 93. **CONTACT ADDRESS** Dept of Classics, Univ of Ill, Chicago Circle, Chicago, IL, 60680.

DEERING, RONALD F.
PERSONAL Born 10/06/1929, Ford County, IL, m, 1966, 2 children **DISCIPLINE** HISTORY; NEW TESTAMENT; LIBRARY SCIENCE **EDUCATION** Georgetown Col, BA, 51; MDiv, 55, PhD, 61, Southern Baptist Theological Seminary; Columbia Univ, MSLS, 67. **CAREER** Instr, 58-61, Research Librarian, 61-67; Assoc Librarian, 67-71, Seminary Librarian, 71-95, Assoc VP for Academic Resources, Southern Baptist Theological Seminary. **HONORS AND AWARDS** Lilly Endowment Scholarship in Theological Librarianship **MEMBERSHIPS** Amer Theological Library Assoc; Amer Library Assoc; Kentucky Library Assoc; Soc of Biblical Lit; Southeastern Library Assoc; Church and Synagogue Library Assoc. **RESEARCH** Theological librarianship **CONTACT ADDRESS** Southern Baptist Theological Sem, 2825 Lexington Rd., Louisville, KY, 40280. **EMAIL** rdeering@compuserve.com

DEETER, ALLEN C
PERSONAL Born 03/08/1931, Dayton, Ohio, m, 1952, 3 children **DISCIPLINE** RELIGION, HISTORY **EDUCATION** Manchester Col, BA, 53; Bethany Theol Sem, BD, 56; Princeton Univ, MA, 58, PhD(hist Christianity), 63. **CAREER** Instr relig, 59-60, from asst prof to assoc prof, 60-72, dir, Peace Studies Inst & Prog Conflict Resolution, 67-80, assoc acad dean, 69-80, Prof Relig & Philos, Manchester Col, 72-; Adminr, Brethren Cols Abroad, 75-, Vchmn bd gov, John F Kennedy Am Haus, Marburg, 65-66; dir Brethren Cols Abroad, Univ Marburg & Univ Strasburg, 65-66; Soc Relig Higher Educ grant, 68-69; lectr, Punjabi Univ & Dibrugarh Univ, India, spring 69; exec secy, Consortium Peace Res, Educ & Develop, 71-72; consult on world order studies, various cols, univs & consortia, 71-; ed, Bull, Peace Studies Inst, Manchester Col, 71-80; spring inaugural lectr, Christian Theol Sem, Indianapolis, 72. **HONORS AND AWARDS** Hon Doctorate, Bridgewater Col. **MEMBERSHIPS** Int Studies Asn; Am Soc Church Hist; Am Acad Relig. **RESEARCH** The origins of modern radical religious and political thought; mysticism and pietism East and West, especially as related to social ethics; Tolstoyan and Gandhian political, social and religious tactics of transformation. **SELECTED PUBLICATIONS** Coauth, In His Hand, Brethren Press, 64; auth, Pietist views of the Church, Brethren Life & Thought, winter 64; Western mysticism and social concern, J Inst Traditional Cult, spring 69; Religion as a social and political force in America, Bull Ramakrishna Inst, fall 69; Toyohiko Kagawa: Mystic and Social Activist, Punjabi Univ, 70; Heirs of a Promise, Brethern Press, 72; auth, The Paradoxical Necessity of Realism and Idealism, Bull of Peace Stu Inst, 98. **CONTACT ADDRESS** Dept of Relig, Manchester Col, 601 E College Ave, N Manchester, IN, 46962-1226.

DEFLEM, MATHIEU
DISCIPLINE SOCIOLOGY, ANTHROPOLOGY **EDUCATION** Katholieke Universiteit Leuven Belgium, MA, 86; Univ Hull England, MA, 90; Univ Colo, PhD, 96. **CAREER** Vis asst prof, Kenyon Coll, 96-97; asst prof, Purdue Univ, 97-. **MEMBERSHIPS** Am Sociol Asn; Soc for the Study of Social Problems; Am Soc for Criminology; Law and Soc Asn; Acad of Criminal Justice Sci; Europ Community Studies Asn. **RESEARCH** Law and Social Control; Comparative and Historical Sociology; Sociological Theory. **SELECTED PUBLICATIONS** Auth, Law Enforcement in British Colonial Africa: A Comparative Analysis of Imperial Policing in Nyasaland, the Gold Coast, and Kenya, Police Stduies, 94; Social Control and the Theory of Communicative Action, Int J of the Sociol and Law, 94; Corruption, Law and Justice: A Conceptual Clarification, J of Criminal justice, 95; International Policing in 19th Century Europe: The Police Union of German States, 1851-1866, Int Criminal Justice Rev, 96; Surveillance and Criminal Statistics: Historical Foundations of Governmentally, Studies in Law, Politics and Society, 97; The Boundaries of Abortion Law: Systems Theory from parsons to Luhmann and Habermas, Social Forces, 98; coauth, Profit and Penalty: An Analysis of the Corrections-Commercial Complex, Crime and Delinquency, 96; The Myth of Post-National Identity: Popular Support for European Unification, Social Forces es, 96; ed, Habermas, Modernity and Law, 96. **CONTACT ADDRESS** Dept of Sociology, Purdue Univ, Stone Hall, West Lafayette, IN, 47907-1365. **EMAIL** DefleM@sri.soc.purdue.edu

DEFORD, RUTH
DISCIPLINE MUSIC HISTORY AND LITERATURE **EDUCATION** Harvard Univ, PhD. **CAREER** Prof. **RESEARCH** Music of the Renaissance. **SELECTED PUBLICATIONS** Ed vol(s) mus by, Giovanni Ferretti & Orazio Vecchi; contribur, The New Grove Dictionary of Mus and Musicians & Die Musik in Geschichte und Gegenwart; articles in, Studi musicali, Acta musicol, Mus disciplina, Early Mus Hist & J Musicol. **CONTACT ADDRESS** Dept of Music, Hunter Col, CUNY, 695 Park Ave, New York, NY, 10021.

DEGLER, CARL N.
PERSONAL Born 02/06/1921, Orange, NJ, m, 1948, 2 children **DISCIPLINE** HISTORY **EDUCATION** Upsala Coll, AB, 42; Columbia Univ, PhD, 52. **CAREER** Prof, Vassar Coll, 52068; prof, Stanford Univ, 68-90, prof, Oxford Univ, 73-74. **HONORS AND AWARDS** Pulitzer Prize, Bancroft Prize, 72; Ralph Waldo Emerson Prize, Phi Beta Kappa, 91. **MEMBERSHIPS** Am Hist Asn; Southern Hist Asn; Orgn of Am Hist. **RESEARCH** American Social History; Women's History; Southern History; History of Evolution. **SELECTED PUBLICATIONS** Auth, Neither Black Nor White; Slavery and Race Relations in Brazil and the United States, 71; The Other South; Southern Dissenters in the Nineteenth Century, 74; Affluence and Anxiety, 75; Place Over Time; The Continuity of Southern Distinctiveness, 77; The Age of Economic Revolution, 77; At Odds; Women and the Family in America from the Revolution to the Present, 80; Out of Our Past; The Forces That Shaped Modern America, 84; In Search of Human Nature; The Fall and Revival of Darwinism in American Social Thought, 91. **CONTACT ADDRESS** Stanford Univ, Stanford, CA, 94305. **EMAIL** degler@leland.stanford.edu

DEGLER, CARL NEUMANN
PERSONAL Born 02/06/1921, Orange, NJ, m, 1948, 2 children **DISCIPLINE** HISTORY **EDUCATION** Upsala Col, AB, 42; Columbia Univ, MA, 47, PhD, 52. **CAREER** Instr hist, Wash Sq Col, NY Univ, 47-50 & Adelphi Col, 50-51; lectr, City Col New York, 52; lectr, Vassar Col, 52-54, from asst prof to prof, 54-68; PROF HIST, STANFORD UNIV, 68-, Tutor, Hunter Col, 47-48; mem exam comt Am hist, Col Entrance Exam Bd, 61-66; vis prof, Grad Sch, Columbia Univ, 63-64; Am Coun Learned Soc fel, 64-65; mem exam comt, Hist Grad Rec Exam Bd, 70-72; Guggenheim fel, 72-73; Harmsworth prof, Oxford Univ, 73-74; Nat Endowment Humanities fel, 76-77; Ctr Advan Study in Behavioral Scis fel, 79-80. **HONORS AND AWARDS** Beveridge Prize, 71; Pulitzer Prize in Hist, 72; Bancroft Prize, 72; Dean's Award for Teaching, Stanford Univ, 79., LHD, Upsala Col, 69; MA, Oxford Univ, 74; LLD, Ripon Col, 76; LittD, Colgate Univ, 78. **MEMBERSHIPS** Econ Hist Asn; AHA; Orgn Am Historians (pres, 79-80); Am Studies Asn; fel Am Acad Arts & Sci. **RESEARCH** American social history; history of the American South; history of women and the family in the United States. **SELECTED PUBLICATIONS** Auth, The Temptations of Evolutionary Ethics, Amer Hist Rev, Vol 0101, 96; Rethinking Race--Boas,Franz and His Contemporaries, Jour So Hist, Vol 0063, 97; The Retreat of Scientific Racism--Changing Concepts of Race in Britain and the United-States Between the World-Wars, Jour Amer Hist, Vol 0080, 93; Race In North-America--Origin and Evolution of a Worldview, Jour Amer Hist, Vol 0081, 94; The Creationists, Jour Amer Hist, Vol 0080, 94. **CONTACT ADDRESS** Dept of Hist, Stanford Univ, Stanford, CA, 94305.

DEGROAT, JUDITH A.
PERSONAL Born 07/12/1955, Milwaukee, WI, m **DISCIPLINE** HISTORY **EDUCATION** Univ Wisc, Milwaukee, BA, 81, MA, 83; Univ Rochester, PhD, 91. **CAREER** Instr, Univ Georgia, 88-89; instr, Univ Alabama, Birmingham, 89-91; asst and assoc prof, hist, St Lawrence Univ, 91- . **HONORS AND AWARDS** Susan B. Anthony Dissertation Fel, 87-88; ACLS grant-in-aid, 92; Dean's Res Fund Grant, 94, 97. **MEMBERSHIPS** Soc for French Hist Stud; Am Hist Asn; Soc Sci Hist Asn; European Women's Stud Asn; Radical Hist Rev, ed colective. **RESEARCH** Modern France; gender; women; labor; cultural/national identities; transnational studies. **SELECTED PUBLICATIONS** Coauth, Cultural Encounters: Interdisciplinary Faculty Development for an Intercultural Core Curriculum, in 1993 Conference Proceedings of the Institute for the Study of Postsecondary Pedagogy at the State University of New York, Inst for the Stud of Postsecondary Pedagogy, 94; auth, Cultural Encounters in European History, Radical Hist Rev, 97; auth, The Public Nature of Women's Work: Definitions and Debates During the Revolution of 1848, Fr Hist Stud, 97; auth, Challenging Impoverished Curricula, Radical Hist Rev, 97. **CONTACT ADDRESS** Dept of History, St Lawrence Univ, Canton, NY, 13617. **EMAIL** jdeg@ccmaillink.stlawu.edu

DEHORATIUS, EDMUND F.
PERSONAL Philadelphia, PA **DISCIPLINE** CLASSICAL LANGUAGES **EDUCATION** Duke Univ, BA, 95. **CAREER** Tchr, Bancroft Sch, 95- , dept chemn, 89- . **HONORS AND AWARDS** MA For Lang Asn, David Taggart Clancy Prize, Chester Middlesworth Award, Duke Univ. **MEMBERSHIPS** APA, Class Asn New England; Medieval Acad Am; Renaissance Soc Am. **RESEARCH** Classical tradition; paleography; Latin literature; pedagogy. **CONTACT ADDRESS** 5 Einhorn Rd, #3, Worcester, MA, 01609-2207. **EMAIL** edehorat@bancroft.pvt.k12.ma.us

DEICHMANN EDWARDS, WENDY J.
PERSONAL Born 12/07/1957, Waterbury, CT, m, 1992, 1 child **DISCIPLINE** HISTORY **EDUCATION** Drew Univ, PhD, 91. **CAREER** Adj Prof Church History, 94-, Ashland Theo Sem. **MEMBERSHIPS** ASCH, AAR, HSUMC. **RESEARCH** Social gospel history, history of Christian missions, women in history of Christianity, Methodism. **SELECTED PUBLICATIONS** Auth, Manifest Destiny, the Social Gospel and the Coming Kingdom, Josiah Strong's Program of Global Reform, 1885-1916, in: Perspectives on the Social Gospel, Papers from the Inaugural Social Gospel Conference at Colgate Rochester Divinity School, Lewiston NY, Edwin Mellen Press, 98; Forging an Ideology for American Missions, Josiah Strong and Manifest Destiny, Curzon Press, London, and Eerdmans, Grand Rapids, 98; Domesticity with a Difference, Woman's Sphere Woman's Leadership and the Founding of the Baptist Missionary Training School in Chicago, 1881, in: Amer Baptist Qtly, 90. **CONTACT ADDRESS** 12645 Coal Bank Rd, Doylestown, OH, 33230.

DELANCEY, JULIA
DISCIPLINE ART HISTORY **EDUCATION** Univ MI, BA; Univ St Andrews, Scotland, PhD. **CAREER** Asst prof, Truman State Univ. **RESEARCH** Archival research on the pigment trade in Renaissance Italy. **SELECTED PUBLICATIONS** Auth, Quiet, Silence and Solitude: the Carthusian Order, the Certosa of Florence and Jacopo Pontormo's Passion Cycle, Inferno: St Andrews Jour Art Hist, 95; Before Michelangelo: Colour Usage in Domenico Ghirlandaio and Filippino Lippi, Apollo, 97. **CONTACT ADDRESS** Dept of Art, Truman State Univ, 100 E Normal St, Kirksville, MO, 63501-4221.

DELANEY, DAVID K.
PERSONAL Born 10/05/1957, York, PA, m, 1980, 2 children **DISCIPLINE** EARLY CHRISTIANITY **EDUCATION** Univ Va, PhD, 96. **CAREER** Lutheran pastor, St. John Lutheran Church, Roanoke VA. **MEMBERSHIPS** AAR; SBL; N Amer Patristics Soc; Amer Soc of Church Hist. **RESEARCH** History of Biblical interpretation. **CONTACT ADDRESS** St. John Lutheran Church, 4608 Brambleton Ave SW, Roanoke, VA, 24018. **EMAIL** dkd7s@ix.netcom.com

DELANEY, JEANE
DISCIPLINE LATIN AMERICA **EDUCATION** Stanford Univ, PhD, 89. **CAREER** History, St. Olaf Col. **SELECTED PUBLICATIONS** Auth, Rediscovering Spain: The Hispanismo of Manuel Galvez; Making Sense of Modernity: Changing Attitudes toward the Immigrant and the Gaucho in Turn-of-the-Century Argentina; Nation, National Identity and Immigration in Argentina, 1810-1930. **CONTACT ADDRESS** St Olaf Col, 1520 St Olaf Ave, Northfield, MN, 55057. **EMAIL** delaney@stolaf.edu

DELANEY, NORMAN CONRAD
PERSONAL Born 04/13/1932, Rockport, MA, m, 1966, 2 children **DISCIPLINE** AMERICAN AND EUROPEAN HISTORY **EDUCATION** Mass State Col, Salem, BS, 55; Boston Univ, AM, 56; Duke Univ, PhD(hist), 67. **CAREER** Missionary-teacher hist & English, Sheldon Jackson Jr Col, Alaska, 56-57; instr hist, Mass State Col, Bridgewater, 59-62; Peace Corps teacher, Osmania Univ, India, 62-64; instr, Univ Houston, 66-67; from asst prof to assoc prof, 67-73, PROF HIST, DEL MAR COL, 73-. **HONORS AND AWARDS** Mrs Simon Baruch Univ Award, United Daughters of Confederacy, 70. **MEMBERSHIPS** Asn Gravestone Studies. **RESEARCH** Civil War, Southern naval. **SELECTED PUBLICATIONS** Auth, Gray Riders of the Sea--How 8 Confederate Warships Destroyed the Unions High Seas Commerce, Amer Neptune, Vol 0053, 93; Assault and Logistics--Union Army Coastal and River Operations, 1861-1866, Amer Neptune, Vol 0056, 96; Compendium of the Confederate Armies--Fla and Ark, Jour Amer Hist, Vol 0079, 93. **CONTACT ADDRESS** 3747 Aranas St, Corpus Christi, TX, 78411.

DELANTONIO, ANDREW
DISCIPLINE MUSIC HISTORY **EDUCATION** Univ CA at Berkeley, PhD. **CAREER** Asst prof, Univ of TX at Austin. **HONORS AND AWARDS** Int prize for Musicol scholar. **RESEARCH** Musical historiography; feminist/queer theory; cult studies. **SELECTED PUBLICATIONS** Auth, doctoral dissertation on the early sonata, Libreria Musicale Italiana; publ, in Cambridge Opera J, Notes, repercussions & Il saggiatore musicale; contrib to, revised New Grove & Die Musik in Geschichte und Gegenwart, musical encycl; co-ed, archive of dissertation abstracts in Musicol on the WWW. **CONTACT ADDRESS** School of Music, Univ of Texas at Austin, 2613 Wichita St, Austin, TX, 78705.

DELEEUW, PATRICIA ALLWIN
PERSONAL Born 04/29/1950, Frankfurt, Germany, m, 1971 **DISCIPLINE** CHURCH AND MEDIEVAL HISTORY **EDUCATION** Univ Detroit, BA, 71, PhD(medieval studies), 79; Univ Toronto, MA, 72; Pontifical Inst Medieval Studies, MSL, 75. **CAREER** ASST PROF THEOL, BOSTON COL, 79-. **MEMBERSHIPS** Mediaeval Acad Am; Am Soc Church Hist. **RESEARCH** Religious social history; early medieval Germany; history of pastoral care. **SELECTED PUBLICATIONS** Auth, Hincmar-Of-Reims as Administrator of His Diocese and Ecclesiastical Province--German, Speculum-Journal of Medieval Stud, Vol 0069, 94; Medieval Handbooks of Penance--A Translation of the Principal Libri Poenitentiales and Selections from Related Documents, Church Hist, Vol 0062, 93; Background on Fulrad-De-Saint-Denis C.710-784--French, Speculum-Jour Medieval Stud, Vol 0070, 95; Faith to Creed--Ecumenical Perspectives on the Affirmation of the Apostolic Faith in the 4th-Century, Jour Ecumenical Stud, Vol 0029, 92; Luther,Martin--Faith in Christ and the Gospel--Selected Spiritual Writings, Jour Ecumenical Stud, Vol 0033, 96; Medieval Handbooks of Penance--A Translation of the Principal Libri Poenitentiales and Selections from Related Documents, Church Hist, Vol 0062, 93. **CONTACT ADDRESS** Dept of Theol, Boston Col, Chestnut Hill, MA, 02167.

DELIO, ILIA
PERSONAL Born 08/20/1955, Newark, NJ **DISCIPLINE** HISTORICAL THEOLOGY **EDUCATION** Fordham Univ, PhD 96. **CAREER** Washington Theo Union, asst prof 97-; Trinity Col CT, vis prof, 96-97. **MEMBERSHIPS** AAR; SSLB **RESEARCH** Medieval mystics; Franciscan theology **SELECTED PUBLICATIONS** Auth, The Humility of God in a Scientific World, New Theol Rev, 98. **CONTACT ADDRESS** Dept of Theology, Washington Theological Union, 6897 Laurel St, Washington, DC, 20012. **EMAIL** delio@wtu.edu

DELISLE, JEAN
PERSONAL Born 04/13/1947, Hull, PQ, Canada **DISCIPLINE** TRANSLATION STUDIES/HISTORY **EDUCATION** Laval Univ, BA, 68; Univ Montreal, LTrad, 71, MTrad, 75; Sorbonne Nouvelle (Paris), DTrad, 78. **CAREER** PROF, SCH TRNASLATION & INTERPRETATION, UNIV OTTAWA, 74-. **HONORS AND AWARDS** Can Coun schol, 76. **MEMBERSHIPS** Soc traducteurs Que, 72-92; Union ecrivains que, 87-94; Can Asn Transl Stud, 87- (pres 91-93); pres, Comt Hist Transl, 90-. **SELECTED PUBLICATIONS** Auth, L'Analyse du discours comme methode de traduction, 80; auth, Les Obsedes textuels, 83; auth, Au coeur du trialogue canadien/Bridging the Language Solitudes, 84; auth, La Traduction au Canada/Translation in Canada 1534-1984, 87; auth, The Language Alchemists, 90; auth, La Traduction raisonee, 93; coauth, Bibliographic Guide for Translators, Writers and Terminologists, 79; coauth, International Directory of Historians of Translation, 3rd ed 96; ed, L'enseignement de l'interpretation et de la traduction: de la theorie a la pedagogie, 81; ed, Les Traducteurs dans l'histoire, 95; ed, Translators Through History, 95. **CONTACT ADDRESS** Sch Transl & Interp, Univ Ottawa, Ottawa, ON, K1N 6N5. **EMAIL** jdelisle@aix1.uottawa.ca

DELONG, DAVID G.
PERSONAL Born 02/10/1939, Topeka, KS **DISCIPLINE** ARCHITECTURE **EDUCATION** Univ Kans, BArch, 62; Univ Pa, MArch, 63; Columbia Univ, PhD, 76. **CAREER** Vis Critic Archit Design, Middle East Tech Univ, 67-68; Asst Prof to Assoc Prof, Columbia Univ, 76-84, Chair, Prog Hist Preservation, 81-84; Assoc Prof, 84-87, Prof Archit, Univ Pa, 87-, Prof City & Regional Planning, 95-, Chair, Grad Group Hist Preservation, 84-96; Vis Prof, Univ Sydney, 92. **HONORS AND AWARDS** Kellogg Schol, 57-58; Summerfield Schol, Univ Kans, 59-62; Am Inst Archit Schol, 62-63; Preceptor in Archit, Columbia Univ, 71-75; Charles F. Montgomery Prize, for: Design in America, 83; Distinguished Alumnus Award, Univ Kans, 84; Vis Schol, Getty Ctr Hist Art & Humanities, 89;

Am Inst Archit Int Archit Bk Award, 92; Soc Archit Hist Bk Award, 93; Service Award, Univ Pa, 94; Am Inst Archit Int Bk Award, 96; recipient of numerous grants and fellowships. **MEMBERSHIPS** Libr Co Philadelphia; Athenaeum Philadelphia; Nat Coun Preservation Educ (Dir 81-92, VChair 89-92, Treasr 86-89); Soc Archit Hist (Dir 95-, VPres NY Chap 75-78); Asn Preservation Technol; Preservation Action; Nat Trust Hist Preservation. **SELECTED PUBLICATIONS** Auth, Eliel Saarinen and the Cranbook Tradition in Architecture and Urban Design, Design in America: the Cranbook Vision, 1925-1950, Abrams, 83; coauth, Louis I. Kahn: In the Realm of Architecture, Universe Publ, 91; ed, Wright in Hollywood: Visions of a New Architecture, Archit Hist Found & MIT Press, 94; James Gamble Rogers and the Architecture of Pragmatism, Archit Hist Found & MIT Press, 94; Working with Mr. Wright: What it was Like, Cambridge Univ Press, 95; ed & principal auth, Frank Lloyd Wright: Designs for an American Landscape, 1922-1933, Abrams, 96; Frank Lloyd Wright and the Living City, Skira, 98; author of numerous articles and other publications. **CONTACT ADDRESS** Univ of Pennsylvania, Philadelphia, PA, 19104-6311.

DELORIA, VINE, JR.
PERSONAL Born 03/26/1933, Martin, SD, m, 1958, 3 children **DISCIPLINE** HISTORY **EDUCATION** Iowa State Univ, BS, 58; Lutheran Sch Theol, MST, 63; Univ Colo Sch Law, JD, 70. **CAREER** Lectr, Western Wash Univ, 70-72; Lectr, Am Indian Cult & Res Ctr, Univ Calif - Los Angeles, 72-73; Exec Dir, Southwest Intergroup Coun, 72; Special Counsel, Native Am Rights Fund, 72; Script Writer, Indian Series, KRMA-TV, Denver, Colo, 72-74; Researcher, Am Indian Resource Assoc, 73-74; Researcher, Am Indian Resource Consult, 74-75; Vis Lectr, Pac Sch Relig, 75; Vis Lectr, New Sch Relig, 76; Vis Lectr, Colo Col, 77-78; Vis Prof, 78, Prof Law & Polit Sci, Univ Ariz, 78-90; Prof Am Indian Studies, Prof Hist, Adj Prof Law, Relis Studies, & Polit Sci, 90-. **HONORS AND AWARDS** Anisfield-Wolf Award, 70; Special Citation for We Talk, You Listen, Nat Conf Christians & Jews, 71; Hon Doctor Humane Letters, Augustana Col, 72; Indian Achievement Award, Indian Coun Fire, 72; Named one of eleven Theological Superstars of the Future, Interchurch Features, 74; Hon Doctor Letters, Scholastica Col, 76; Distinguished Alumni Award, Iowa State Univ, 77; Hon Prof, Athabasca Univ, 77; Hon Doctor Humane Letters, Hamline Univ, 79; Distinguished Alumni in Field Legal Educ, Univ Colo Sch Law, 85; Hon Doctor Humane Letters, Northern Mich Univ, 91; Senate Resolution No. 118, State of Mich, "A Resolution Honoring Vine Deloria, Jr.", 91; Lifetime Achievement Award, Mountains and Plains Booksellers Asn, 96; Non-Fiction Book of the Year Award, Colo Ctr for the Book, 96; Lifetime Achievement Award, Native Writers Am, 96. **SELECTED PUBLICATIONS** Auth, Custer Died For Your Sins: An Indian Manifesto, Macmillan, 69 (and numerous editions outside the U.S.); coauth, The Nations Within: The Past and Future of American Indian Sovereignty, Pantheon Bks, 84; auth, American Indian Policy in the Twentieth Century, Univ Okla Press, 85, 92; Indian Education in America: Eight Essays, Am Indian Sci & Engineering Soc, 91; Frank Waters: Man and Mystic, Swallow Press, 93; Red Earth, White Lies, Scribner, 95; author of numerous other publications and articles. **CONTACT ADDRESS** Univ Colo, Campus Box 234, Boulder, CO, 80309-0234. **EMAIL** vine@spot.colorado.edu

DELORME, ROLAND L.
PERSONAL Born 06/12/1937, Aberdeen, WA, 5 children **DISCIPLINE** AMERICAN HISTORY **EDUCATION** Univ Puget Sound, BA, 59; Univ PA, MA, 60; Univ CO, PhD, 65. **CAREER** Instr US hist, Skagit Valley Col, 64-66; asst prof hist & dir gen studies, 66-68, assoc prof hist, Western WA Univ, 68-, chmn hist, 71-80 and 84-89; Provost & vpres Acad Affairs, 90; Mem, Fed Regional Arch Adv Coun, 69. **RESEARCH** Twentieth century US soc and intellectual hist; 20th century Am western hist; Pacific Northwest hist. **SELECTED PUBLICATIONS** Auth, Turn-of-the-century Denver: An invitation to reform, Colo Mag, winter, 68; Colorado's mugwump interlude: The state voters' league, 1905-1906, J West, 10/68; coauth, Anti-Democratic Trends in Twentieth Century America, Addison-Wesley, 69; auth, The United States Bureau of Customs and smuggling on Puget Sound, 1851-1913, Prologue, summer 73. **CONTACT ADDRESS** Pres/Provost Office, Western Washington Univ, M/S 9033, Bellingham, WA, 98225-5996. **EMAIL** ldelorme@cms.wwu.edu

DELPH, RONALD
DISCIPLINE HISTORY **EDUCATION** Univ Mich, PhD. **CAREER** Asst prof and Honor's adv, Eastern Michigan Univ. **RESEARCH** Europe, renaissance, Europe, reformation. **SELECTED PUBLICATIONS** Publ in, J Hist Idea; Renaissance Quart; 16th-Century J. **CONTACT ADDRESS** Dept of History and Philosophy, Eastern Michigan Univ, 701 Pray-Harrold, Ypsilanti, MI, 48197.

DELZELL, CHARLES FLOYD
PERSONAL Born 03/06/1920, Klamath Falls, OR, m, 1948, 3 children **DISCIPLINE** HISTORY **EDUCATION** Univ Ore, BS, 41; Stanford Univ, AM, 43, PhD(hist), 51. **CAREER** Spec rep, Hoover Inst & War Libr, Stanford Univ, Europe, 46 & 48-49; cur Medit area collections, 47-49; asst prof hist, Univ Ha-

waii, 49-50; instr Univ Ore, 50-51; from asst prof to assoc prof, 52-61, Harvie Branscomb distinguished prof, 70-71, chmn dept, 70-73, PROF HIST, VANDERBILT UNIV, 61-; Consult Italy, Encycl Americana, 59; Borden award, Hoover Inst & Libr, Stanford Univ, 60; Soc Sci Res Coun grants, Int Cong Hist Sci, Stockholm, Sweden, 60, Int Cong Hist Europ Resistance, Milan, Italy, 61; mem exam comt advan placement in Europ hist, Col Entrance Exam Bd, Princeton Univ, 62-64, advan hist exam comt, grad rec exam, Educ Testing Serv, 66-72; Fulbright res scholar, Italy, 64-65; chmn, Am Comt on Hist 2nd World War, 72-75; Nat Endowment for Humanities sr fel, 73-74; Vanderbilt Univ centennial fel, 74-75, chmn fac senate, 76-77; res scholar, Rockefeller Found Bellagio Study and Conf Ctr, Lake Como, Italy, 78. **MEMBERSHIPS** AHA; Southern Hist Asn (secy-treas, Europ Hist sect, 61-62, vpres, 62-63, pres, 63-64); Soc Ital Hist Studies (pres, 68-69); Soc Hist Studies, France. **RESEARCH** Modern Italian history; modern European history; European historiography. **SELECTED PUBLICATIONS** Auth, Vatican Caves--Comment, NY Rev Bk(s), Vol 0040, 93; Rollier, Mario,Alberto--A Waldensian Federalist--Italian, Amer Hist Rev, Vol 0097, 92. **CONTACT ADDRESS** Dept of Hist, Vanderbilt Univ, Nashville, TN, 37235.

DEMOLEN, RICHARD LEE
PERSONAL Born 08/19/1938, Hartford, WI **DISCIPLINE** EARLY MODERN EUROPE **EDUCATION** Univ Mich, AB, 62, AM, 63, PhD(hist), 70. **CAREER** Instr hist, Crowder Col, 64-66; asst prof, Drury Col, 66-67 & Ithaca Col, 67-70; RES & WRITING, FOLGER SHAKESPEARE LIBR, 70-, Folger Shakespeare Libr fel, 69, 70 & 73; Am Philos Soc grants-in-aid, 69 & 70; Nat Endowment for Humanities younger humanist fel, 71-72; Huntington Libr fel, 73; Newberry Libr fel, 70, 73, & 76; sr Fulbright, Univ London, 74-75; ed, Erasmus Rotterdam Soc Yearbook, 80- **MEMBERSHIPS** AHA; Renaissance Soc Am; Erasmus Rotterdam Soc (secy & treas, 80-). **RESEARCH** Renaissance intellectual and cultural history; Tudor and Stuart biography. **SELECTED PUBLICATIONS** Auth, Man On His Own--Interpretations of Erasmus, C.1750-1920, Cath Hist Rev, Vol 0079, 93. **CONTACT ADDRESS** Erasmus Rotterdam Society, Ft Washington, MD, 20744.

DEMONE, HAROLD WELLINGTON
DISCIPLINE SOCIOLOGY **EDUCATION** Tufts Col, BA, 48; Tufts Univ, MA, 49; Brandeis Univ, PhD, 66. **CAREER** Instr, dept of sociology, Tufts Univ, 49-54; exec dir, NH Div on Alcoholism, State Dept of Health, 54-56; Comnr on Alcoholism, 56-59, Special Asst to the Comnr of Public Health, 59-60, Commonwealth of Mass; Exec Dir, The Medical Found Inc, 60-67; Exec Vice Pres, United Community Planning Corp, 67-77; Dean, School of Soc Work, Rutgers Univ, 77-87; Prof II, School of Social Work and Graduate Sociology Dept, Rutgers Univ, 77-92; PROF II EMERITUS, 92-; VISITING SCHOLAR, HELLER GRAD SCHOOL, BRANDEIS UNIV, 97-; LECTR, BOSTON COL GRAD SCHOOL OF SOCIAL WORK, 98-. **HONORS AND AWARDS** Alpha Kappa Delta, 51; Pi Gamma Mu, 49; Mass Asn for Mental Health Award, 66; Mass Psychological Asn Award, 66; Mass Asn for Retarded Children Award for Special Recognition, 67; Mass Public Health Asn Lemuel Shattuck Award, 75; The Joshua A. Guberman Lectr in Law and Social Policy, 86; NASW Social Work Pioneer, Nat Asn of Soc Workers, 97; Tufts Univ Alumni Asn Distinguished Service Award, 98. **MEMBERSHIPS** Nat Asn for Soc Workers, 66-; Int Coun on Soc Welfare, 78-; Coun on Soc Work Ed, 77-; Am Public Health Asn, 57-; Soc for the Study of Soc Problems, 52-; Nonprofit and Voluntary Sector Quarterly, occasional reviewer, 98-. **SELECTED PUBLICATIONS** Coauth, Alcoholism and Society, Oxford Univ Press, 62; coauth, Administrative and Planning Techniques in Human Service Organizations, Behavioral Pubs, 73; coauth, A Handbook of Human Service Organizations, Behavioral Pubs, 74; auth, Stimulating Human Services Reform, Aspen Systems Corp, 78; coauth, Social Work Past, A Twenty-five-Year History of the Graduate School of Social Work, Rutgers, 83; coauth, Services for Sale: Purchasing Health and Human Services, Rutgers Univ Press, 89; co-ed & contribur, The Privatization of Human Services Vol 1: Policy and Practice Issues, Springer Pub Company, 98; co-ed, The Privatization of Human Services Vol 1: Case Studies in the Purchase of Human Services, 98. **CONTACT ADDRESS** Graduate School of Social Work, Rutgers Univ, 536 George St, New Brunswick, NJ, 08903.

DEMOSS, DOROTHY DELL
PERSONAL Born 02/17/1942, Houston, TX **DISCIPLINE** AMERICAN AND LATIN AMERICAN HISTORY **EDUCATION** Rice Univ, BA, 63; Univ Tex Austin, MA, 66; Tex Christian Univ, PhD(hist), 81. **CAREER** Teacher social studies, Blair High Sch, Silver Spring, Md, 63-65; instr hist, Tex Woman's Univ, 66-79; teaching asst, Tex Christian Univ, 79-81; ASST PROF HIST, TEX WOMAN'S UNIV, 82-. **MEMBERSHIPS** AHA; Orgn Am Historians; Southern Hist Asn; Southern Asn Women Historians. **RESEARCH** Recent (20th century) United States history; Texas history; urban and economic history. **SELECTED PUBLICATIONS** Auth, Women and Texas History--Selected Essays, Jour So Hist, Vol 0060, 94; Pioneer Woman Educator--The Progressive Spirit Blanton, Annie,Webb, Jour So Hist, Vol 0061, 95. **CONTACT ADDRESS** Dept of Hist & Govt, Tex Woman's Univ, P O Box 425889, Denton, TX, 76204-5889.

DEMY, TIMOTHY J.
PERSONAL Born 12/06/1954, Brownsville, TX, m, 1978 **DISCIPLINE** THEOLOGY & HISTORY **EDUCATION** Tex Christian Univ, BA, 77; Dallas Theol Sem, Th M, 81, ThD, 90; Salve Regina Univ, MA, 90; Univ Tex at Arlington, MA, 94. **CAREER** Military chaplain, 81-; adj instr, Naval War Col, 96-. **HONORS AND AWARDS** Phi Alpha Theta; Outstanding Young Men in Amer; Who's Who in the South and Southwest; numerous military awards. **MEMBERSHIPS** Evang Theol Soc; Soc of Bibl Lit; Orgn of Amer Hist; Ctr for Bioethics and Human Dignity. **RESEARCH** Bioethics; The crusades; Evangelical theology; Church history. **SELECTED PUBLICATIONS** Co-auth, Basic Questions on Suicide and Euthanasia, Basic Questions on End of Life Decisions, Basic Questions on Sexuality and Reproductive Technology, Basic Questions on Alternative Medicine, Kregel Publ, 98; co-ed, Suicide: A Christian Response, Kregel Publ, 98; co-auth, Maximizing Your Marriage, Kregel Publ, 98; co-auth, Prophecy Watch, Harvest House, 98; auth, Onward Christian Soldiers? Christian Perspectives on War, The Voice, 98; auth, Suicide and the Christian Worldview, Conservative Theol Jour, 97; auth, Chaplain Walter Colton and the California Gold Rush, Navy Chaplain, 97; co-auth, The Coming Cashless Society, Harvest House, 96; auth, A Dictionary of Premillennial Theology, Kregel Books, 96; co-ed, When the Trumpet Sounds!, Harvest House, 95; auth, Blackwell's Dictionary of Evangelical Biography, Blackwells, 95; co-auth, The Rapture and an Early Medieval Citation, Bibliotheca Sacra, 95. **CONTACT ADDRESS** 7 Ellen Rd., Middletown, RI, 02842. **EMAIL** tdemy@wsii.com

DENG, FRANCIS M.
DISCIPLINE FOREIGN RELATIONS **EDUCATION** Khartoum Univ, LLB, 62; Yale Law Sch, LLM, 65, JSD, 67. **CAREER** Sr Fel, Foreign Policy Stud, Brookings Inst; Minister of State for For Aff of the Sudan; ambassador to US, Scandinavia, and Canada; human rights officer, Div of Human Rights, UN Secretariat; res assoc Woodrow Wilson Ctr. **HONORS AND AWARDS** Dist fel, Rockefeller Bros Found; Jennings Randolph Distinguished Fel, US Inst of Peace; UN Secy Gen special rep on internally displaced persons. **RESEARCH** Africa; conflict management/resolution; human rights; regional conflicts; the Sudan; internally displaced persons. **SELECTED PUBLICATIONS** Auth, War of Visions: Conflicting Identities in the Sudan, 95; coauth, Sovereignty as Responsibility; Conflict Management in Africa, 96; auth, Ethnicity: An African Predicament, Brookings Rev, 97; coauth, Masses in Flight: The Global Cirsis of Internal Displacement, 98; coauth, African Reckoning: A Quest for Good Governance, 98; coauth, The Forsaken People: Case Studies of the Internally Displaced, 98. **CONTACT ADDRESS** The Brookings Inst, 1775 Massachusetts Ave NW, Washington, DC, 20036.

DENING, GREG
DISCIPLINE CULTURAL HISTORY **CAREER** Adj prof, Ctr Cross-Cult Res, Australian Natl Univ. **RESEARCH** Cross-cultures of Pacific regions. **SELECTED PUBLICATIONS** Auth, Islands and Beaches, 81; Mr Bligh's Bad Language, 92; The Death of William Gooch ,95; Performances, 96; The Silence of the Land, pending. **CONTACT ADDRESS** Dept of Education, Australian National Univ. **EMAIL** Greg.Dening@anu.edu.au

DENNEY, COLLEEN J.
DISCIPLINE ART HISTORY **EDUCATION** La State Univ, BA, 78, MA, 83; Univ IA, PhD, 84-87; Univ MN, PhD, 90. **CAREER** Assoc prof; adj assoc prof, Women's Stud; mem, Women's Stud Resource Fac & Prof Staff; Comt on Instnl Coop Traveling Scholar, Univ MN, 86-87. **HONORS AND AWARDS** Funded projects as PI, Fac Mentor, Nat Endowment for the Hum Younger Scholars Prog, $500; funded projects as Co-PI, Nat Endowment for the Hum Implementation Grant, $250,000 given outright, $50,00 given in match. **RESEARCH** 19th century Engl and France; hist of exhibition syst. **SELECTED PUBLICATIONS** Auth, The Grosvenor Gallery: A Palace of Art in Victorian England, Yale UP, 96; Exhibitions in Artists' Studios: Francois Bonvin's 1859 Salon des Refuses, Gazette des Beaux Arts, Vol CXXII, 93; The Role of Sir Coutts Lindsay and the Grosvenor Gallery in the Reception of Pre-Raphaelitism on the Continent, IN: Pre-Raphaelitism in its European Context, Assoc UP, 95. **CONTACT ADDRESS** Dept of Art, Univ WY, PO Box 3964, Laramie, WY, 82071-3964. **EMAIL** CDENNEY@UWYO.EDU

DENNIS, DAVID B.
DISCIPLINE HISTORY **EDUCATION** UCLA, PhD, 91. **CAREER** Hist, Loyola Univ. **RESEARCH** Modern European intellectual & cultural history. **SELECTED PUBLICATIONS** Auth, Beethoven in German Politics, 1870-1989, New Hvn: Yale UP, 96; rev(s)NY Times, La Stampa Milano, Financial Times. **CONTACT ADDRESS** Fine Arts Dept, Loyola Univ, Chicago, 6525 N. Sheridan Rd., Chicago, IL, 60626. **EMAIL** dennis@orion.it.luc.edu

DENNIS, GEORGE THOMAS
PERSONAL Born 11/17/1923, Somerville, MA **DISCIPLINE** BYZANTINE HISTORY **EDUCATION** Gonzaga Univ, AB, 48; Alma Col, STL, 54; Pontif Inst Orient Studies, Rome, dipl,

60. **CAREER** Asst prof hist & theol, Loyola Univ, Los Angeles, 61-67; from adj assoc prof to assoc prof, 67-72, PROF HIST, CATH UNIV AM, 72-, Am Coun Learned Soc grant-in-aid, 62; Guggenheim Mem fel, 64-65. **MEMBERSHIPS** Mediaeval Acad Am; AHA; Am Cath Hist Asn; Am Soc Church Hist. **RESEARCH** Fourteenth century Byzantine history. **SELECTED PUBLICATIONS** Auth, Athanasius and Constantius--Theology and Politics in the Constantinian Empire, Theol Stud, Vol 0055, 94; Golden-Mouth--The Story of Chrysostom, John--Ascetic, Preacher, Bishop, Theol Stud, Vol 0057, 96; An Eyewitness to History--The Short History of Nikephoros Our Holy Father the Patriarch of Constantinople, Church Hist, Vol 0065, 96; Art and Eloquence in Byzantium, Church Hist, Vol 0065, 96; The Kingdom of Cyprus and the Crusades, 1191-1374, Church Hist, Vol 0063, 94; The Empress Theophano--Byzantium and the West at the Turn of the First Millennium, Church Hist, Vol 0066, 97; Images of the Divine--The Theology of Icons at the 7th-Ecumenical-Council, Theol Stud, Vol 0055, 94; Visual Polemics in the 9th-Century Byzantine Psalters, Church Hist, Vol 0063, 94; Rome and the Eastern Churches--A Study in Schism, Cath Hist Rev, Vol 0079, 93; Byzantium and the Crusader States 1096-1204, Cath Hist Rev, Vol 0081, 95; Constantine-VII-Porphyrogennetos--3 Treatises On Imperial Military Expeditions, Speculum-Jour Medieval Stud, Vol 0068, 93; The Twilight of Byzantium--Aspects of Cultural and Religious History in the Late Byzantine-Empire, Church Hist, Vol 0064, 95; Art and Eloquence in Byzantium, Church Hist, Vol 0065, 96; The Oxford Dictionary of Byzantium, Theol Stud, Vol 0053, 92; Greeks, Western-Europeans and Turks from Ad1054-1453--French, Speculum-Jour Medieval Stud, Vol 0069, 94; The Empire of Komnenos,Manuel,I, 1143-1180, Amer Hist Rev, Vol 0100, 95; Hesychast Monks and Bogomil Monks--Accusations of Messalianism and Bogomilism Against the Hesychasts and the Problematic Relationship Between Hesychasm and Bogomilism--Italian, Cath Hist Rev, Vol 0080, 94; The 75th-Anniversary of the Pontifical-Oriental-Institute in Rome, Proc Jubilee Celebration, 15-17-October,1992--Italian, Cath Hist Rev, Vol 0082, 96; Prophets and Emperors--Human and Divine Authority from Augustus to Theodosius, Theol Stud, Vol 0056, 95. **CONTACT ADDRESS** Catholic Univ of America, 3751 Jennifer St NW, Washington, DC, 20064.

DENNY, DON WILLIAM
PERSONAL Born 08/19/1926, Cedar Rapids, IA, m, 1953, 2 children **DISCIPLINE** HISTORY OF ART **EDUCATION** Univ Fla, BA, 59; NY Univ, MA, 61, PhD, 65. **CAREER** Instr design, Univ Fla, 54-59; instr hist of art, NY Univ, 61-62 & Princeton Univ, 62-65; from asst prof to assoc prof, 65-72, prof hist of art, Univ of Md, College Park, 72-, Nat Found for Humanities fel, 68. **RESEARCH** Medieval art and iconography. **SELECTED PUBLICATIONS** Auth, The trinity in Enguerrand Quarton's coronation of the Virgin, in Art Bull, 3/63; Simone Martini's Holy family, J Warburg & Courtauld Inst, 67; Notes on the Avignon Pieta, in Speculum, 69; Some symbols in the Arena Chapel Frescoes, in Art Bull, 73; Portal sculpture of Auxerre Cathedral, in Speculum, 76; Annunciation from the Right, Garland, 77; Historiated initials of the Lobbes Bible, in Revue Belge d'Archeologie, 77. **CONTACT ADDRESS** Dept of Art, Univ of Md, College Park, MD, 20742-0001. **EMAIL** dd18@umd.edu

DEPAUW, LINDA GRANT
PERSONAL Born 01/19/1940, New York, NY **DISCIPLINE** AMERICAN HISTORY **EDUCATION** Swarthmore Col, BA, 61; Johns Hopkins Univ, PhD, 64. **CAREER** Asst prof hist, George Mason Col, Univ Va, 64-65; from asst prof to assoc prof, 66-75, PROF HIST, GEORGE WASHINGTON UNIV, 75-; ED IN CHIEF DOC HIST, FIRST FED CONG, NAT HIST PUBL COMN, 66- **HONORS AND AWARDS** Beveridge Award, AHA, 64. **MEMBERSHIPS** AHA; Orgn Am Historians; Southern Hist Asn; Am Soc Legal Hist; Int Univ Sem Armed Forces & Soc. **RESEARCH** Early American history; women in America. **SELECTED PUBLICATIONS** Auth, Disorderly Women--Sexual Polities and Evangelicalism in Revolutionary New-England, Jour Church and State, Vol 0038, 96; Encyclopedia of the North-American Colonies, Jour Amer Hist, Vol 0081, 95. **CONTACT ADDRESS** Dept of Hist, George Washington Univ, 2035 H St N W, Washington, DC, 20052-0001.

DEPILLARS, MURRY NORMAN
PERSONAL Born 12/21/1938, Chicago, IL, m **DISCIPLINE** EDUCATION **EDUCATION** JC Wilson Coll, AA Fine Arts 1966; Roosevelt Univ, BA Art Educ 1968, MA Urban Studies 1970; PA State Univ, PhD Art Educ 1976. **CAREER** Mast Inst, Chicago comm on urban opportunity div of training 1968; Univ of IL Chicago, educ asst program asst dir 1968-71; numerous art exhibits throughout the US; VA Commonwealth Univ Richmond, dean school of art; Chicago State Univ, exec vp for planning and mgmt, currently. **HONORS AND AWARDS** Elizabeth Catlett Mora Award of Excellence Natl Conf of Artists 1977; Special Arts Awd & Art Educ Award Branches for the Arts 1980; Man of Excellence Plaque Ministry of Educ Republic of China 1980; Excellence in the Educ Preservation & Promotion of Jazz Richmond Jazz Soc 1981; Outstanding Admin Award Black Student Alliance 1982; Outstanding Achievement in the Arts Branches for the Arts 1982; Alumni Fellow Penn State Univ 1989. **MEMBERSHIPS** Bd of dir & illustrator 3rd World Press Chicago 1960-; bd of dir & art dir Kuumba Workshop Chicago 1969-; bd of dir & contributing ed Inst of Positive Educ Chicago 1970-; adv bd Journal of Negro Educ Washington 1973-; bd of dir N Amer Zone & co-chmn Upper So Region 2nd World Black & African Festival of Arts & Culture 1973-74; pres Natl Conf of Artists Richmond 1973-77; mem Intl Council of Fine Arts Deans 1976-; hmn of bd Natl Conf of Artists NY 1977; First Sino/Amer Conf on the Arts Taipei Taiwan 1980; arts commission Natl Assoc of State Univ & Land Grant Colls 1981-88; consultant Natl Endowment for the Humanities 1982-84; cons Corp of the Public Broadcasting & the Annenberg School of Communications 1983; OH Eminent Scholars Program Panel OH Bd of Regents1983-84; consult The O Paul Get-Trust 1984; Natl Endowment for the Arts Expansion Arts Program 1985-; Natl Jazz Serv Org 1985-; US Info Agency Acad Specialist to Malaysia 1985; Africobra 1985-; arts adv bd Coll Bd 1984-85; chmn, coordinator comm The Richmond Jazz Festival 1984-; art & architectural review bd Commonwealth of VA 1986-. **CONTACT ADDRESS** Exec VP, Planning and Mgmt, Chicago State Univ, 9501 S King Dr, Chicago, IL, 60628.

DEPILLIS, MARIO STEPHEN
PERSONAL Born 01/22/1926, Philadelphia, PA, m, 1952, 3 children **DISCIPLINE** AMERICAN HISTORY **EDUCATION** Univ Chicago, BA, 52, MA, 54; Yale Univ, PhD, 61. **CAREER** From instr to asst prof Am hist, Univ Mass, 58-61; vis asst prof, Univ Calif, Berkeley, 61-62; from asst prof to assoc prof, 62-75, PROF AM HIST, UNIV MASS, AMHERST, 76-, Teacher's res grants, Univ Mass, 63; Fulbright exchange prof, Univ Munich, 66-67; US State Dept lectr, Europe, 77. **HONORS AND AWARDS** Eggleston Prize, 61. **MEMBERSHIPS** AHA; Pac Coast Br AHA; Orgn Am Historians; Western Hist Asn; Mormon Hist Asn. **RESEARCH** The West in American history; Mormonism; United States social history. **SELECTED PUBLICATIONS** Auth, Science, Religion, and Mormon Cosmology, Amer Hist Rev, Vol 0099, 94. **CONTACT ADDRESS** Dept Hist, Univ Mass, Amherst, MA, 01003.

DEPUMA, RICHARD DANIEL
PERSONAL Born 05/15/1942, DuBois, PA, d, 1 child **DISCIPLINE** CLASSICAL ARCHAEOLOGY, ETRUSCOLOGY **EDUCATION** Swarthmore Col, BA, 64; Bryn Mawr Col, MA, 67, PhD(Class Archaeol), 69. **CAREER** From instr to asst prof, 68-86, prof Art Hist & Archael, Univ Iowa, 86-, Am Philos Soc fel, 70; Univ Iowa Grad Col grant, 70 & 73. **HONORS AND AWARDS** NEH, 84, 91, 93; German Arch Inst, 95. **MEMBERSHIPS** Archaeol Inst Am; Col Art Asn Am; Am Numis Soc; Soc Prom Roman Studies. **RESEARCH** Etruscan pottery and minor arts; Roman and Hellenistic mosaics; Greek vase painting. **SELECTED PUBLICATIONS** Auth, Corpus Speculorum Etruscorum USA 1, 97 and USA 2, 93; Murlo and the Etruscans, with J Small, 94; Corpus Vasorum Antiquorum: J Paul Getty Museum, fasc 6, 95. **CONTACT ADDRESS** Sch of Art & Art History, Univ of Iowa, E 100, Art Building, Iowa City, IA, 52242-1706. **EMAIL** richard-depuma@uiowa.edu

DERBY, WILLIAM EDWARD
PERSONAL Born 10/26/1925, Canton, NY, m, 1956, 7 children **DISCIPLINE** AMERICAN HISTORY **EDUCATION** Harvard Univ, AB, 47; St Lawrence Univ, MEd, 49; Univ Wis, PhD, 63. **CAREER** Teacher high schs, NY 49-51 & 5354; from asst prof to assoc prof, 57-70, PROF AM HIST, STATE UNIV NY COL GENESEO, 70-. **MEMBERSHIPS** Orgn Am Hist; AHA; Southern Hist Asn; Econ Hist Asn. **RESEARCH** American economic and urban history; Civil War and Reconstruction period; history of the Great Lakes region. **SELECTED PUBLICATIONS** Auth, A Phoenix in the Ashes--The Rise and Fall of the Koch Coalition in New-York-City Politics, Urban History Rev-Rev d Hist Urbaine, Vol 0021, 93. **CONTACT ADDRESS** Dept of History, State Univ of NY Col, Geneseo, NY, 11454.

DERDEN, JOHN K.
DISCIPLINE HISTORY **EDUCATION** Reinhardt Col, AA, 67; Univ Ga, BSEd, 69, MA, 73, PhD, 81. **CAREER** High sch teacher, 69-70; inst, 73-76, asst prof, 76-85, assoc prof, 85-90, CHAIR, SOC SCI, 90-, PROF HIST, 98-, E GA COL. **CONTACT ADDRESS** Chair, Soc Sci Div, East Georgia Col, 131 College Cr, Swainsboro, GA, 30401. **EMAIL** jderden@mail.peachnet.edu

DERFLER, LESLIE
DISCIPLINE HISTORY **EDUCATION** Columbia Univ, PhD. **CAREER** Prof. **HONORS AND AWARDS** Tchg Incentive Awd; Univ Prof Excellence Awd; Univ Distinguished Sch Awd. **RESEARCH** Modern European history; France history; socialism. **SELECTED PUBLICATIONS** Auth, An Age of Conflict: Readings in 20th Century European History, 96; Paul Lafargue and the Founding of French Marxism 1842-1882, 91; President and Parliament: A Short History of the French Presidency, 84. **CONTACT ADDRESS** History Dept, Florida Atlantic Univ, 777 Glades Rd, Boca Raton, FL, 33431. **EMAIL** rinaldi@acc.fau.edu

DERFLER, LESLIE A.
PERSONAL Born 01/11/1933, New York, NY, m, 1962, 4 children **DISCIPLINE** HISTORY **EDUCATION** City Col NY, BA, 54; Columbia Univ, MA, 57, PhD, 62. **CAREER** Instr, City Col NY, 59-62; asst prof, Carnegie-Mellon Univ, 62-68; assoc prof, Univ of Mass, 68-69; prof, Florida Atlantic Univ, 69- . **HONORS AND AWARDS** Florida Atlantic Univ Tchg Incentive and Professorial Excellence Awards; Nat Endowment for Humanities Fellowship; Koren Prize for outstanding article on French hist. **MEMBERSHIPS** Soc for French Hist Studies; Southern Hist Asn; Western Soc for French Hist. **RESEARCH** History of Socialism; Political Biography. **SELECTED PUBLICATIONS** Auth, The Dreyfus Affair: Tragedy of Errors, 63; The Third French Republic, 1870-1940, 66; Socialism Since Marx, 73; Alexandre Millerand: The Socialist Years, 77; President and Parliament. A Short History of the French Presidency, 84; An Age of Conflict: Readings in 20th Century European History, 90; Paul Lafargue and the Founding of French Marxism, 1842-1882, 91; Paul Lafargue and the Flowering of French Socialism, 1882-1911, 98. **CONTACT ADDRESS** Dept of History, Florida Atlantic Univ, Boca Raton, FL, 33432. **EMAIL** derfler@fau.edu

DERFLER, STEVEN
PERSONAL Born 12/22/1951, Columbus, OH, m, 1981, 1 child **DISCIPLINE** ARCHAEOLOGY **EDUCATION** Ind Univ, BA, 73; Univ Minn, MA, 75, PhD, 83. **CAREER** Instr, Ind Univ, 72; from teaching asst to assoc, Univ Minn, 73-78; adj fac, Tel Aviv Univ, 75-84; Metropolitan State Univ, 97-95; adj assoc prof, Univ Wis, 90-97; dir Jewish Studies, Hamline Univ, 79-93; **MEMBERSHIPS** Am Jewish Com. **RESEARCH** Archaeology; Biblical history; Comparative religions; Jewish-Christian Relations. **SELECTED PUBLICATIONS** Auth, "Its Unfair to Compare Palestinians and American Indians," 98; "Religious Freedom Amendment is Dangerous," 98; "A Night to Remember," 97; "Which will it be? Peace or Jihad?," 97; "Pluralism and the Role of Constructive Interference," 97; "Survival of Israel Depends on Celebrating Diversity," 97; "No Light at the End of This Tunnel," 96; "Collective Soul-Searching in Israel," 96; "A Democratic Experiment that Became Chaotic," 96; "Israel Comes of Age in the Democratic World," 95; "A Painful Comong of Age for Israel," 95; "A Threat to Freedom," 95; "A Cellular Phone on His Bike, Nobody's Laughing Anymore," 95; "The Pitfalls of School Vouchers," 95. **CONTACT ADDRESS** 1885 University Ave, Ste 85, St. Paul, MN, 55104. **EMAIL** 70264,1320@compuserve.com

DERR, THOMAS SIEGER
PERSONAL Born 06/18/1931, Boston, MA, m, 1956, 5 children **DISCIPLINE** SOCIAL ETHICS, AMERICAN RELIGIOUS HISTORY **EDUCATION** Harvard Univ, AB, 53; Union Theol Sem, NY, MDiv, 56; Columbia Univ, PhD, 72. **CAREER** Asst chaplain, Stanford Univ, 56-59; asst chaplain, 63-65, from asst prof to assoc prof relig, 66-76, dir, Jr Yr Int Studies, Geneva, Switz, 70-71 & 77-78, Prof Relig, Smith Col, 77-; Consult, Dept Church & Soc, World Coun Churches, Geneva, 66-, comn faith & order, 75-; mem fac, Rush Med Col, Chicago, 80-84; fel, Inst Adv Study Relig, Univ Chicago, 81. **MEMBERSHIPS** Soc Christian Ethics. **RESEARCH** Ecumenical studies; environmental ethics; med ethics. **SELECTED PUBLICATIONS** Auth, Ecology and Human Need, Westminster, 75; coauth, Church, State and Politics, The Roscoe Pound-American Trial Lawyer Found, 81; auth, Barriers to Ecumenism: The Holy See and the World Council of Churches on Social Questions, Orbis Books, 83; coauth, Believable Futures for American Protestantism, Eerdmans, 88; Creation at Risk, Eerdmans, 95; author, Environmental Ethics and Christian Humanism, Abingdon, 96. **CONTACT ADDRESS** Dept of Relig, Smith Col, Northampton, MA, 01063-0001. **EMAIL** tderr@smith.edu

DES GAGNIERS, JEAN
PERSONAL Born 02/07/1929, St. Joseph-de-la-Rive, PQ, Canada **DISCIPLINE** ARCHAEOLOGY/MUSEUM STUDIES **EDUCATION** Col Jean de Brebeuf (Montreal), BA, 49; Diplome de l'Ecole de Marine (Rimouski), 51; Univ Laval, LPh, 53; Diplome de l'Ecole du Louvre (Paris), 56. **CAREER** Laodikaia Excavations (Turkey), 61-64; Soli Excavations (Cyprus), 64-74; Trustee, Nat Mus Can, 72-79; Asst to Vice-Rector, Laval Univ, 76-94, Centre Museographique, 79-94 (RETIRED). **HONORS AND AWARDS** Mem, Royal Soc Can **SELECTED PUBLICATIONS** Auth, Fouilles de Laodicee du Lycos; auth, L'Acropole d' Athenes; auth, La ceramique chypriote a decor figure; auth, Vases et figurines de l'Age du Bronze; auth, Objets d'art grec du Louvre; auth, Soloi: dix campagnes de fouilles; auth, La conservation du patrimoine museologique du Quebec; auth, L'Ile-aux-Coudres; auth, Charlevoix, pays enchante; auth, Monseigneur de Charlevoix. **CONTACT ADDRESS** St-Joseph-de-la-rive, PQ, G0A 3Y0.

DESAI, GAURAV GAJANAN
DISCIPLINE AFRICAN AND DIASPORA STUDIES, POSTCOLONIAL LITERATURE **EDUCATION** Northwestern Univ, BA, 88; Duke Univ, PhD, 97. **CAREER** Engl, Tulane Univ. **SELECTED PUBLICATIONS** Auth, Theater as Praxis: Discursive Strategies in African Popular Theater, African Stud

Rev 33, 90; The Invention of Invention, Cult Critique 24, 93; English as an African Language, Eng Today 9, 93; Out in Africa, Genders 25, 97. **CONTACT ADDRESS** Dept of Eng, Tulane Univ, 6823 St Charles Ave, New Orleans, LA, 70118. **EMAIL** gaurav@mailhost.tcs.tulane.edu

DESAUTELS, JACQUES
PERSONAL Born 01/18/1937, Iberville, PQ, Canada **DISCIPLINE** GREEK LANGUAGE & CIVILIZATION **EDUCATION** Univ Montreal, BA, 56; Col l'Immaculee-Conception, BPh, 61; Univ Laval, LL, 64; Univ d'Aix-Marseille, DoctL, 66. **CAREER** PROF DE LANGUE, DE LITTERATURE ET DE CIVILISATION GRECQUES, UNIV LAVAL, 67-, vice-recteur, 77-82, doyen, fac des lettres, 95-. **SELECTED PUBLICATIONS** Auth, Dieux et mythes de la Grece ancienne, 88; auth, Le Quatrieme Roi mage, 93; auth, La dame de Chypre, 96. **CONTACT ADDRESS** Fac lettres, Univ Laval, Pavillon de Koninck, Quebec, PQ, G1K 7P4.

DESAUTELS, JACQUES
PERSONAL Born 01/18/1937, Iberville, PQ, Canada **DISCIPLINE** GREEK LANGUAGE & CIVILIZATION **EDUCATION** Univ Montreal, BA, 56; Col de l'Immaculee-Conception, BPh, 61; Univ Laval, LL, 64; Univ d'Aix-Marseille, DoctL, 66. **CAREER** PROF DE LANGUE, DE LITTERATURE ET DE CIVILISATION GRECQUES, UNIV LAVAL, 67-, vice-recteur, 77-82, doyen, fac des lettres, 95-. **SELECTED PUBLICATIONS** Auth, Dieux et mythes de la Grece ancienne, 88; auth, Le Quatrieme Roi mage, 93; auth, La dame de Chypre, 96. **CONTACT ADDRESS** Fac des lettres, Laval Univ, Pavillon de Koninck, Quebec, PQ, G1K 7P4. **EMAIL** Jacques.Desautels@fl.ulaval.ca

DESHMUKH, MARION F.
PERSONAL Los Angeles, CA, m, 1969, 1 child **DISCIPLINE** ART HISTORY **EDUCATION** UCLA, BA, 66; Columbia Univ, MA, 67, M.Phil, 68, PhD, 75. **CAREER** From asst prof to assoc prof, George Mason Univ, 75- , chair, Dept Hist, George Mason Univ, 84-95. **HONORS AND AWARDS** Phi Beta Kappa; President's Fel, Columbia Univ; DAAD; Am Hist Asn; J. Paul Getty Res Grant. **MEMBERSHIPS** Am Hist Asn; German Stud Asn; Southern Hist Asn; Conference group for Central European Hist; Col Art Asn. **RESEARCH** 19th and 20th century German and European cultural and art history; German impressionist painter, Max Liebermann; post-1945 arts institutions in West Germany; the intersection of visual and cultural history. **SELECTED PUBLICATIONS** Auth, art, The German War Art Collection, 96; auth, art, Politics is an Art, The Cultural Politics of Max Liebermann in Wilhelmine Germany, 96; auth, art, Cultural Migration: Arts and Visual Representation Between Americans and Germans during the 1920s and 1930s, 97; auth, art, Max Liebermann, Ein Berliner Jude, 97; coauth, art, Recovering Culture: Berlin's National Gallery and the US Occupation, 98. **CONTACT ADDRESS** Dept of Hist and Art Hist, George Mason Univ, 3G1, Fairfax, VA, 22030. **EMAIL** meshmuk@gmu.edu

DESHMUKH, MARION FISHEL
PERSONAL Los Angeles, CA, m, 1969, 1 child **DISCIPLINE** MODERN GERMAN CULTURAL HISTORY **EDUCATION** Univ Calif, Los Angeles, BA, 66; Columbia Univ, MA, 67, PhD(hist), 75. **CAREER** Lectr hist, Nassau Community Col, 68 & Brooklyn Col, 69; lectr, 69-75, asst prof, 75-80, ASSOC PROF HIST, GEORGE MASON UNIV, 80-, Dept Chair 84-95; Proposal reviewer, Nat Endowment for Humanities, 78-; lectr, US Dept State, Foreign Serv Off Inst, 79- & Smithsonian Inst, 82-. **HONORS AND AWARDS** Phi Beta Kappa, DAAD. **MEMBERSHIPS** AHA; Conf Group Cent Europ Hist; College Art Asn; Western Asn German Studies; Southern Hist Asn, Europ Sect. **RESEARCH** German art history: 1800-1914; sociology of German cultural institutions; 19th and 20th century cultural history of Europe. **SELECTED PUBLICATIONS** Auth, Max Liebermann: Observations on painting & politics in Germany, Ger Studies Rev, 5/80; German impressionist painters & World War I, Art Hist; contribr, Arts & politics in turn of the century Berlin, In: The Turn of the Century: German Literature & Art, 1890-1915, Herbert Grundmann, Bonn, 81; Berlin National Gallery after 1945, Central Euro Hist, 94. **CONTACT ADDRESS** Dept Hist, George Mason Univ, 4400 University Dr, Fairfax, VA, 22030-4444.

DESMANGLES, LESLIE GERALD
PERSONAL Born 09/28/1941, Port-au-Prince, Haiti, m, 1968, 2 children **DISCIPLINE** ANTHROPOLOGY OF RELIGION **EDUCATION** Eastern Col, BA, 64; Eastern Baptist Theol Sem, MDiv, 67; Temple Univ, PhD(anthop relig), 75. **CAREER** Instr, Eastern Col, 69-70; instr, Ohio Wesleyan Univ, 70-75 & asst prof, 75-76; asst prof, DePaul Univ, 76-78; assoc prof Relig, Trinity Col, 78-, instr, Ohio Univ, 75-76; consult, Miami Univ of Ohio, 73-74 & Hispanic Health Coun of Hartford, 81-; Nat Endowment for Humanities & Trinity Col res grant, 80; dir, Prog Intercult Studies, Trinity Col, 81-. **MEMBERSHIPS** Asn Sociol Relig; Am Acad Relig; Caribbean Studies Asn; Pres, Haitian Studies Asn. **RESEARCH** African traditional religions; Caribbean religions. **SELECTED PUBLICATIONS** Auth, African interpretations of the Christian cross in Haitian Vodun, Sociol Analysis, 76; Rites baptismaux: Symbiose du Vodou et du Catholicisme a Haiti, Concilium, 77; The way of Vodun death, J Relig Thought, 80; Vodun baptismal rites, J Inter-Denominational Theol Ctr, 81; The Faces of the Gods: Vodou and Roman Catholicism in Haiti, Univ of NC Press, 93. **CONTACT ADDRESS** Dept Relig & Intercult, Trinity Col, 300 Summit St, Hartford, CT, 06106-3186. **EMAIL** leslie.desmangles@mail.trincoll.edu

DESMOND, LAWRENCE ARTHUR
PERSONAL Born 12/07/1929, St. John, NB, Canada, m, 1959, 1 child **DISCIPLINE** MEDIEVAL CHURCH HISTORY **EDUCATION** St Thomas Univ, NB, BA, 52; Fordham Univ, MA, 54, PhD (hist), 67. **CAREER** From asst prof to assoc prof hist, St Paul's Col, Man, 59-69, dean, 74-80, ASSOC PROF HIST, UNIV MAN, 69-, Can Counc fel, 69-70. **MEMBERSHIPS** Medieval Acad Am; Can Cath Hist Asn (vpres, 68-69); Selden Soc; Am Comt Irish Studies. **RESEARCH** Medieval Cistercian history; English legal history; New Brunswick local history. **SELECTED PUBLICATIONS** Auth, ATLAS OF CISTERCIAN LANDS IN WALES - WILLIAMS,DH/, SPECULUM-A J MEDIEVAL STUDIES, Vol 68, 1993 ATLAS OF CISTERCIAN LANDS IN WALES - WILLIAMS,DH/, SPECULUM-A J MEDIEVAL STUDIES, Vol 68, 1993 **CONTACT ADDRESS** Off of Dean, St Paul's Col Univ of Man, Winnipeg, MB, R3T 2M6.

DESPALATOVIC, ELINOR MURRAY
PERSONAL Born 08/10/1933, Cleveland, OH, m, 1962, 2 children **DISCIPLINE** MODERN EUROPEAN AND EAST EUROPEAN HISTORY **EDUCATION** Columbia Univ, BA, 55, MA and cert area studies, 59, PhD (hist), 69. **CAREER** Lectr hist, Univ Mich, 62-63; res asst Southern Slavic hist, Yale Univ, 63-65; from instr to asst prof, 65-74, assoc prof, 74-79, actg chmn dept, 74, PROF HIST, CONN COL, 79-, CHMN DEPT, 80-, Am Coun Learned Soc fel, 71; Fulbright area studies fel, 72; Int Res and Exchanges Bd fel, 72 and 78-79, mem, E Europ selection comt, 73-74. **HONORS AND AWARDS** Distinguished Alumnae Award, The George Sch, Bucks County, Pa, 77. **MEMBERSHIPS** AHA; Am Asn Advan Slavic Studies; Am Asn Southeast Europ Studies. **RESEARCH** Croatian nationalism; the Illyrian Movement; the Croatian Peasant Party. **SELECTED PUBLICATIONS** Auth, The Balkan Express--Fragments from the Other Side of the War, Slavic Rev, Vol 53, 94. **CONTACT ADDRESS** Dept of Hist, Connecticut Col, 270 Mohegan Ave, New London, CT, 06320-4125.

DESSEN, CYNTHIA SHELDON
PERSONAL Born 05/14/1938, New York, NY, m, 1963, 2 children **DISCIPLINE** ROMAN LITERATURE **EDUCATION** Oberlin Col, BA, 60; Johns Hopkins Univ, MA, 62, PhD (classics), 64. **CAREER** Asst prof classics, Univ Wis, 68-69, Northwestern Univ, 70-73; Asst Prof Classics, Univ NC, Chapel Hill, 74-. **MEMBERSHIPS** Am Philol Asn. **RESEARCH** Latin literature; Roman satire; classics and English literature. **SELECTED PUBLICATIONS** Auth, The Figure of The Eunuch in Terence Eunuchus, Helios, Vol 22, 95. **CONTACT ADDRESS** Dept of Classics, Univ of NC, Chapel Hill, NC, 27514.

DETHLOFF, HENRY CLAY
PERSONAL Born 08/10/1934, New Orleans, LA, m, 1961, 2 children **DISCIPLINE** AMERICAN ECONOMIC AND SOUTHERN HISTORY **EDUCATION** Univ Tex, BA, 56; Northwestern State Col, La, MA, 60; Univ Mo, PhD (hist), 64. **CAREER** From instr to assoc prof Am hist, Univ Southwestern La, 62-69; assoc prof, 69-75, PROF HIST, TEX AM UNIV, 75-, DEPT HEAD, 80-. **MEMBERSHIPS** Southern Hist Asn; Agr Hist Asn; Econ Hist Asn. **RESEARCH** Economic history; agricultural history; Southern history. **SELECTED PUBLICATIONS** Auth,Davis, Edgar, B. and Sequences in Business Capitalism--From Shoes to Rubber to Oil - Froh, J Southern Hist, Vol 60, 94; Cinderella of the New South--A History of the Cottonseed Industry, 1855-1955, Am Hist Rev, Vol 102, 97. **CONTACT ADDRESS** Dept of Hist, Tex A and M Univ, 1 Texas A and M Univ, College Station, TX, 77843.

DETMER, HELLENA R.
DISCIPLINE CLASSICS **EDUCATION** IN Univ, BA, 72; Univ MI, PhD, 76. **CAREER** Act ch, 89;co-supvr, Elem Latin prog, 89; ch, 93-. **HONORS AND AWARDS** Mellon fel, Duke Univ, 78-79; May Brodbeck Award, 83; distinguished alumina award, Jasper High Sch, 89; pres-elect, CAMWS, 95-96., VP, CAMWS, 88-91; ch, CAMWS Col Awards Comm for transl, 90-92; ch, tchg award comm CAMWS, 94-96; exec comm, CAMWS, 94-98; pres, CAMWS, 95-96. **SELECTED PUBLICATIONS** Auth, Horace: A Study in Structure, Hildesheim, 83; A Workbook to Ayers' English Words From Latin And Greek Elements, Tucson 86; Love by the Numbers: Form and Meaning in the Poetry of Catullus, NY, 97; co-ed, Syllecta Classica 1, 89; Syllecta Classica 2, 90; Syllecta Classica 3, 92; Syllecta Classica 4, 93; Syllecta Classica 5, 94; Syllecta Classica 6, 96; The First and Last of Catullus, Syllecta Classica 5, 94; rev(s), Murgatroyd's Tibullus Elegies II, Class Outlook 74, 96; Catullus: Advanced Placement Edition, Class Outlook 75, 97; Thomspon's Catullus Rel Stud Rev, 97. **CONTACT ADDRESS** Dept of Class, Univ IA, 202 Schaeffer Hall, Iowa City, IA, 52242. **EMAIL** helena-dettmer@uiowa.edu

DETWILER, DONALD SCAIFE
PERSONAL Born 08/19/1933, Jacksonville, FL, m, 1956, 1 child **DISCIPLINE** EUROPEAN HISTORY **EDUCATION** George Washington Univ, BA, 54; Univ Gottingen, DPhil(hist), 61. **CAREER** Lectr hist, Montgomery Jr Col, Md, 62, from instr to asst prof hist, 62-65; asst prof, WVa Univ, 65-57; from asst prof to assoc prof, 67-77, PROF HIST, SOUTHERN ILL UNIV, 77-, Mem, US Comn on Mil Hist. **MEMBERSHIPS** AHA; Soc Span and Port Hist Studies. **RESEARCH** Germany; modern Spain; political and military history of the twentieth century. **SELECTED PUBLICATIONS** Auth, Germany, Hitler and World War-II--Essays in Modern German and Worldn History, J Mil Hist, Vol 61, 97. **CONTACT ADDRESS** Dept of Hist, Southern Ill Univ, Carbondale, IL, 62901-4300.

DEUTSCH, HAROLD CHARLES
PERSONAL Born 06/07/1904, Milwaukee, WI, m, 1923, 3 children **DISCIPLINE** HISTORY **EDUCATION** Univ Wis, AB, 24, AM, 25; Harvard Univ, AM, 27, PhD (French hist), 29. **CAREER** From asst prof to prof, 29-72, chmn dept, 60-66, EMER PROF HIST, UNIV MINN, MINNEAPOLIS, 72-; MEM FAC, US ARMY WAR COL, CARLISLE, PA, 74-, Soc Sci res fel, 35-36; mem, Bd Econ Warfare, 42-43; consult, Off Strategic Serv, 43-45 and Bur Europ Affairs, US Dept State, 45 and 67-72; mem civilian staff, Nat War Col, 48-50, dir Europ Studies and prof int rels, 72-74; Fulbright fel, Ger, 57-59 and 69-70; vis prof, Free Univ Berlin, 63. **MEMBERSHIPS** AHA; Am Mil Inst; Int Inst Strategic Studies; US Comn Mil Hist; Oral Hist Asn. **RESEARCH** Military opposition to Hitler; current European affairs; history of World War II. **SELECTED PUBLICATIONS** Auth, Hitler Greatest Defeat--The Collapse of Army-Group Center, June 1944, J Mil Hist, Vol 59, 95. **CONTACT ADDRESS** US Army War Col Fac, Barracks Carlisle, PA, 17013.

DEUTSCHER, IRWIN
PERSONAL Born 12/24/1923, New York, NY, m, 1950, 2 children **DISCIPLINE** SOCIOLOGY **EDUCATION** Univ Missouri, PhD, 58. **CAREER** Prof, Dir of Youth Dev Ctr, Syracuse Univ, 59-68; prof, Case Western Reserve Univ, 68-75; prof,Univ Akron, 75-84, prof emer, 84- . **HONORS AND AWARDS** Annondale Mem Medal for Distinguished Service to Indian Anthropology, 97; Am Sociol Asn Distinguished Career Awd, 97; Lee Founders Awd, Soc for the Study of Social Problems, 97; Distinguished Alumnae Awd, Univ of Missouri, 98; Lifetime Achievement Awd, Sociol Practice Asn, 98. **MEMBERSHIPS** Am Sociol Asn; Soc for Appl Sociol; Soc for the Study of Social Problems; Int Sociol Asn; District of Columbia Sociol Soc. **RESEARCH** Program evolution; reduction of ethnic violence worldwide, applied sociology. **SELECTED PUBLICATIONS** Coauth, Sentiments and Acts, Aldine/deGruyter, 93; auth, Making a Difference: The Practice of Sociology, Transaction Books, 98. **CONTACT ADDRESS** 4740 Conn Ave NW #1007, Washington, DC, 20008. **EMAIL** IrwinD@compuserv.com

DEVEAUX, SCOTT
PERSONAL Born 11/11/1954, Red Bank, NJ, m, 1981, 2 children **DISCIPLINE** MUSIC **EDUCATION** Princeton Univ, AB, 76; Univ Calif-Berkeley, MA, PhD 85. **CAREER** Vis asst prof, Humboldt State Univ, 81-82; Assoc prof, Univ Va, 83-. **HONORS AND AWARDS** Irving Lowens Award, 91; Am Book Award, for The Birth of Bebop, 98; Assoc for Recorded Sound Coll Award for Excellence, for The Birth of Bebop, 98. **MEMBERSHIPS** Am Musicol Soc; Sonneck Soc Am Mus; Soc Ethnomusicol. **RESEARCH** Jazz, American music and culture, African-American music, popular music, 20th-century music, traditional music of West Africa. **SELECTED PUBLICATIONS** Bebop and the Recording Industry: The 1942 AFM Recording Ban Reconsidered, Jour Am Musicol Soc, 41, Spring 88, 126-165; Constructing the Jazz Tradition: Jazz Historiography, Black Am Lit Forum, 25, Fall 91, 525-560; Coed, The Music of James Scott, Smithsonian Inst Press, 92; Black, Brown and Beige and the Critics, Black Mus Res Jour, 13, Fall 93, 125-146; Jazz in America: Who's Listening?, NEA Res Div Rep #31, Seven Locks Press, 95; What Did We Do to Be So Black and Blue? Mus Quart 80, Fall 96, 392-430; The Birth of Bebop: A Social and Musical History, Univ Calif Press, 97. **CONTACT ADDRESS** Univ of Virginia, 112 Old Cabell Hall, Charlottesville, VA, 22903. **EMAIL** deveaux@virginia.edu

DEVER, WILLIAM GWINN
PERSONAL Born 11/27/1933, Louisville, KY, m, 1953, 1 child **DISCIPLINE** SYRO PALESTINIAN ARCHEOLOGY **EDUCATION** Milligan Col, AB, 55; Christian Theol Sem, Ind, BD, 59; Butler Univ, MA, 59; Harvard Univ, PhD (Near Eastern lang and lit), 66. **CAREER** Sr archaeol fel, Biblical and Archaeol Sch, Hebrew Union Col, Jerusalem, 66-67, from asst prof archaeol to prof ancient Near Eastern hist and archaeol, 67-75, resident dir, 68-71; head dept, 78-81, PROF NEAR EASTERN ARCHAEOL, DEPT ORIENT STUDIES, UNIV ARIZ, 75-, Dir, Hebrew Union Col-Harvard Semitic Mus Excavations, Gezer, Israel, 66-71; dir, Hebrew Union Col Excavations, Khalit el-Ful, Hebron, 67-68 and 71; dir, W F Albright Inst Archaeol Res, Jerusalem, 71-75, trustee, 77-; Winslow lectr, Seabury Western Theol Sem, 72; dir, W F Albright Inst Excavations at Shechem, 72-73; Steloff lectr, Hebrew Univ Jerusalem,

73; Univ Ariz Found travel grants, 76 and 78; ed, Bull Am Schs Orient Res, 78-; Nat Endowment for Humanities grant, 79 and 80. **HONORS AND AWARDS** Percia Schimmel Prize, Israel Mus, 82. **MEMBERSHIPS** Am Sch Orient Res; Soc Bibl Lit; Archaeol Inst Am; Am Orient Soc. **RESEARCH** Ancient Near Eastern history in the third and second millennia BC; development of Syro-Palestinian archaeology as a modern independent discipline; relationship of archaeology to Biblical studies. **SELECTED PUBLICATIONS** Auth, The Architecture of Ancient Israel from the Prehistoric to the Persian Periods, J Am Orient Soc, Vol 113, 93; People of the Sea--The Search for the Philistines, J Am Orient Soc, Vol 114, 94; Houses and Their Furnishings in Bronze Age Palestine--Domestic Activity Areas and Artifact Distribution in the Middle Bronze Age and the Late Bronze- age, J Am Orient Soc, Vol 114, 94; Tell El Hesi--The Persian Period, J Am Orient Soc, Vol 112, 92; Excavations at the City of David 1978-1985, Vol 2--Imported Stamped Amphora Handles, Coins, Worked Bone and Ivory and Glass, J Bibl Lit, Vol 111, 92; Bab Edh Dhra--Excavations in the Cemetery Directed by Lapp, Paul, W. 1965-67, Israel Exploration J, Vol 43, 93; An Introduction to Biblical Archaeology, J Am Orient Soc, Vol 116, 96; Lower Galilee During the Iron Age, Israel Exploration J, Vol 45, 95; Ceramics, Ethnicity, and the Question of Israels Origins, Biblical Archaeol, Vol 58, 95; Subsistence, Trade, and Social Change in Early Bronze Age, J Am Orient Soc, Vol 112, 92; Burial Practices and Cultural Diversity in Late Bronze Age, Israel Exploration J, Vol 45, 95; What Remains of the House that Albright Built, Biblical Archaeol, Vol 56, 93; The Archaeology of Ancient Israel - J Biblical Lit, Vol 114, 95. **CONTACT ADDRESS** Dept Oriental Studies, Univ of Arizona, 1 University of Az, Tucson, AZ, 85721-0001.

DEVEREUX, DAVID R.
PERSONAL Born 02/06/1961, London, ON, Canada, m, 1989, 1 child **DISCIPLINE** HISTORY **EDUCATION** Univ Western Ontario, BA, 84; Dalhousie Univ, MA, 85; Univ London, PhD, 88. **CAREER** Mount Allison Univ, vis asst prof, 88-89; postdoctoral fel, social sciences/humanities, 89-91; asst prof, St John Fisher Coll, 91-96; asst prof, Canisius Coll, 96-. **MEMBERSHIPS** Amer Historical Assn; North Amer Conf British Studies. **RESEARCH** British decolonization; aviation. **SELECTED PUBLICATIONS** Auth, The Formulation of British Defense Policy Towards the Middle East 1948-56, 91. **CONTACT ADDRESS** Dept of History, Canisius Col, 2001 Main St, Buffalo, NY, 14208. **EMAIL** Derereud@canisius.edu

DEVINE, DONALD J.
PERSONAL Born 04/14/1937, Bronxville, NY, m, 1959, 4 children **DISCIPLINE** POLITICAL SCIENCE **EDUCATION** PhD, Syracuse Univ, 67. **CAREER** Assoc Prof, Univ MD 67-80; Dir, US Office of Personnel Mgt, 81-85; Adjunct Scholar, The Heritage Foundation, Columnist Washington Times, 92-. **HONORS AND AWARDS** A Symposium, New Perspective on John Locke, Univ MD, Univ Coll, Nov 76; General Res Board Faculty Res Award, 72; Dept of Government and Politics Faculty Research Support, 68; General Res Award, 68; Univ MD, Natl Sci Foundation, Doctoral Dissertation Res Award, 67; Fellowship to Maxwell School Syracus; Amer Assoc of Public Opinion Rs; Amer Political Sci Assoc; Amer Soc for Public Admin. **SELECTED PUBLICATIONS** The Attentive Public: Polyarchial Democracy, Chicago Rand McNally, 70; The Political Culture of the United States: The Mass Influence On Regime Maintenance, Little, Brown and Company, 72; Does Freedom Work? Liberty and Justice in America, Caroline House, 78; Reagan Electionomics, 1976-1984: How Reagan Ambushed the Pollster, Green Hill Publ, 91; Testoring the Tenth Amendment: The New American Federalist Agenda, Vytis, 96; Reagan's Terrible Swift Sword: Reforming and Controlling the Federa Bureaucracy, Jameson Books, 91. **CONTACT ADDRESS** 236 Forest Park PL, Ottowa, IL, 61350.

DEVINE, JOSEPH A., JR.
PERSONAL Born 06/10/1940, Philadelphia, PA, m, 1967, 3 children **DISCIPLINE** HISTORY **EDUCATION** Georgetown Univ, AB, 62; MA, 64, PhD, 68, Univ Virginia **CAREER** Prof, Stephen F. Austin State Univ **MEMBERSHIPS** AHA; OAH; SHA; TACT; ETHA **RESEARCH** Colonial America; 20th century Texas **CONTACT ADDRESS** Dept of History, Stephen F. Austin State Univ, Nacodoches, TX, 75962. **EMAIL** jdevine@sfasu.edu

DEVINE, MARY E.
DISCIPLINE POPULAR CULTURE **EDUCATION** AB, 60, PhD, 64, Loyola Univ. **CAREER** Asst Prof, Michigan State Univ, 64-69; Assoc Prof, 69-75, Prof, 75-, Salem State Col. **CONTACT ADDRESS** 28 Village St, Marblehead, MA, 01945. **EMAIL** mary.devine@salem.mass.edu

DEVINE, MICHAEL JOHN
PERSONAL Born 01/05/1945, Aurora, IL, m, 1970, 3 children **DISCIPLINE** AMERICAN HISTORY **EDUCATION** Loras Col, BA, 67, Ohio State Univ, MA, 68, PhD (hist), 74. **CAREER** Instr hist, Loras Col, 68-69; Peace Corps vol English, US Dept State, Korea, 69-70; asst prof hist, Ohio Univ, 72-74; adminr, Ohio Am Revolution Bicentennial Comn, 74-76; ASST DIR, OHIO HIST SOC, 77-, Am Philos Soc grant, 78. **MEMBERSHIPS** AHA; Am Asn Mus; Am Asn State and Local Hist; Soc Historians Am Foreign Rels. **RESEARCH** Late 19th century American political and diplomatic; Ohio history; United States-East Asian relations. **SELECTED PUBLICATIONS** Auth,US in the Pacific--Private Interests and Public Policies, 1784-1899, J Am Hist, Vol 83, 96; Credentials Required--Comment, Public Hist, Vol 17, 95. **CONTACT ADDRESS** Ohio Historical Ctr, 1982 Velma Ave, Columbus, OH, 43211.

DEW, CHARLES BURGESS
PERSONAL Born 01/05/1937, St. Petersburg, FL, m, 1968, 2 children **DISCIPLINE** AMERICAN HISTORY **EDUCATION** Williams Col, AB, 58; Johns Hopkins Univ, PhD, 64. **CAREER** Instr hist, 63-64, asst prof, 64-65, Wayne St Univ, ; asst prof, 65-68, La State Univ,; Vis assoc prof hist, 70-71, Univ Va;from assoc prof to prof, 68-78, Univ Mo-Columbia; prof hist, 78-85, Class 1956 prof Am stud, 85-96; chmn dept hist, 86-92, dir, Oakley Ctr for Hum & Soc Sci, 94-97, W. Van Alan Clark Third Century Prof in Soc Sci, Williams Col; Am Coun Learned Soc fel, 75-76. **HONORS AND AWARDS** Fletcher Pratt Award, 66; Award of Merit, Am Assn State & Local Hist, 67. **MEMBERSHIPS** AHA; Orgn Am Historians; Southern Hist Assn. **RESEARCH** Antebellum South; slavery: Civil War and Reconstruction. **SELECTED PUBLICATIONS** Auth, The Slavery Experience, Interpreting So History: Historiographical Essays in Hon of Sanford W. Higginbotham, La St Univ Press, 87; auth, Slavery and Technology in the Antebellum Southern Iron Industry: The Case of Buffalo Forge, Sci & Med in the Old South, La St Univ Press, 89; auth, Bond of Iron: Master and Slave at Buffalo Forge, Norton & Co, 94; auth, Industrial Slavery, Encycl of Slavery, Garland Pub, 97. **CONTACT ADDRESS** Dept of History, Williams Col, 880 Main St, Williamstown, MA, 01267-2600.

DEWAR, MARY
PERSONAL Born 02/13/1921, Mossley, England, m, 1944, 2 children **DISCIPLINE** MEDIEVAL AND MODERN HISTORY **EDUCATION** Oxford Univ, BA, 43, MA, 52; Univ London, PhD (medieval and mod hist), 56. **CAREER** Lectr econ and Social hist, Workers Educ Asn, Oxford Univ, 45-47; English, Maidenhead Tech Inst, 46-49; RES ASSOC HIST, UNIV TEX, AUSTIN, 63-. **RESEARCH** Tudor history. **SELECTED PUBLICATIONS** Auth, Corippus on the Wakefulness of Poets and Emperors, Mnemosyne, Vol 46, 93; Valerius Flaccus, C., Argonautica, Book 2--A Commentary, Class Rev, Vol 42, 92; Laying it on with a Trowel--The Proem to Lucan and Related Texts, Class Quart, Vol 44, 94; The Eclogues of Calpurnius Siculus, With An Introduction, Commentary, Translation and Vocabulary, Class Bull, Vol 69, 93; Sidonius Apollinaris, Carmen 22,Burgus Pontii Leontii, J Roman Stud, Vol 85, 95; Statius, Thebaid Vii--A Commentary, Gnomon-Kritische Zeitschrift fur die Gesamte Klassische Altertumswissenschaft, Vol 69, 97; Horace 2000--A Celebration--Essays for the Bimillennium, Phoenix J Class Assn Can, Vol 50, 96; The Eclogues of Calpurnius, Classical Bulletin, Vol 68, 92; Hannibal and Alaric in the Later Poems of Claudian, Mnemosyne, Vol 47, 94. **CONTACT ADDRESS** Dept of Hist, Univ Tex, Austin, TX, 78712.

DEWEY, DONALD ODELL
PERSONAL Born 07/09/1930, Portland, OR, m, 1952, 3 children **DISCIPLINE** AMERICAN HISTORY **EDUCATION** Univ OR, BA, 52; Univ UT, MS, 56; Univ Chicago, PhD, 60. **CAREER** Instr hist, Univ Chicago, 60-62; from asst prof to assoc prof, 62-70, prof hist, CA State niv, Los Angeles, 69, Dean, Sch Lett & Sci, 70-84, Dean, Sch Nat & Soc Sci, 84-96, Asst ed, Papers of James Madison, Univ Chicago, 60-61, assoc ed, 61-62; Am Philos Soc res grant, 65. **HONORS AND AWARDS** Outstanding Prof, Calif State Univ, Los Angeles, 75-76; CSLA nom for State Outstanding Prof, 89. **MEMBERSHIPS** Orgn Am Historians; AHA. **RESEARCH** US constitutional hist; James Madison; impeachment of federal judges. **SELECTED PUBLICATIONS** Coauth, The Papers of James Madison, Univ Chicago, Vols I-III, 62-63; The Continuing Dialogue, Pac Bks, Vols I & II, 63 & 64; auth, Hoosier Justice: The Journal of David McDonald, 1864-1868, Ind Mag Hist & Biog, 66; Union and Liberty, McGraw, 69; Marshall Versus Jefferson: The Political Background of Marbury v Madison, Knopf, 70; coauth, Becoming Informed Citizens: Lessons on the constitution for Junior High School Students, Regina, 88; Invitation to the Dance, RSVP, 91; The Congressional Salary Amendment: 200 Years Later, Glendale Law Rev, 91; auth, Samuel Chase, William Cushing, William Paterson in Melvin Urofsky, The Supreme Court Justices, Garland, 94; 19 Essays in Robert Rutland, James Madison and the American Nation, Simon & Schuster, 94; coauth, Becoming Informed Citizens: Lessons on the Bill of Rights for Secondary School Students, Regina, 95; Becoming Informed Citizens: Lessons on the Constitution for Secondary School Students, Regina, 95; auth, Truly the Weakest Branch: The United States Supreme Court, 1789-1803 in Roberto Martucci, Constitution & Revolution, Univ Macerata, 95; That's a Good One: Cal State LA at 50, CSULA, 97; The Federalist and Antifederalist Papers, Regina, 98. **CONTACT ADDRESS** Dept of Hist, California State Univ, Los Angeles, 5151 State University Dr, Los Angeles, CA, 90032-4202. **EMAIL** ddewey@calstatela.edu

DEWEY, TOM
DISCIPLINE 19TH AND 20TH CENTURY ART, SOUTHERN ART AND ARCHITECTURE, HISTORY OF PRINTS **EDUCATION** Univ Southern IL, BA, MA; Univ WI, Madison, PhD. **CAREER** Assoc prof, Univ MS, 76-; archv, Southern Graphics Coun, 77. **SELECTED PUBLICATIONS** Publ(s) on contemp Southern printmaking; 19th century Southern archit; the themes of horse racing, ballet, prostitution in the work of Edgar Degas and his contemp(s); the International Exhibition of Decorative and Industrial Arts, Paris 1925; critical essays on major 19th and 20th century Europ painters and archit(s), plus major Mod Movement buildings. **CONTACT ADDRESS** Univ MS, Oxford, MS, 38677.

DEWINDT, ANNE R.
PERSONAL Born 08/08/1943, m, 1969 **DISCIPLINE** MEDIEVAL STUDIES **EDUCATION** Univ Toronto, PhD, 72. **CAREER** Instr, Hist and Philos Depts, Wayne County Community Col, 72-. **MEMBERSHIPS** Am Hist Asn; Royal Hist Soc. **RESEARCH** Medieval England; social history. **SELECTED PUBLICATIONS** Auth, Redefining the Peasant Community in Medieval England: The Regional Perspective, J British Studies, 4/87; auth, Local Government in a Small Town: A Medieval Leet Jury and its Constituents, Albion, Winter 91; auth, Monks and the Town Court of Ramsey: Overlapping Communities, In: La societe rurale et les institutions gouvernementales au moyen Age, Actes du Colloque de Montreal, 5/93; auth, Witchcraft and Conflicting Visions of the Ideal Village Community, J British Studies, 10/95; auth, The Town of Ramsey: The Question of Economic Development, 1290-1523, in The Salt of Common Life: Individuality and Choice in the Medieval Town, Countryside, and Church, Essays Presented to J. Ambrose Raftis, Kalamazoo, 96. **CONTACT ADDRESS** 3446 Cambridge Rd., Detroit, MI, 48221. **EMAIL** AandE@compuserve.com

DEWINDT, EDWIN B.
DISCIPLINE HISTORY **EDUCATION** Univ Detroit, PhB; Pontifical Inst Mediaeval Stud, LMS; Univ Toronto, PhD. **CAREER** Prof, 68-. **HONORS AND AWARDS** Guggenheim fel; fel, Royal Hist Soc. **SELECTED PUBLICATIONS** Auth, ed, several bk(s) on society and law in the English Middle Ages; Royal Justice; Medieval English Countryside. **CONTACT ADDRESS** Dept of Hist, Univ Detroit Mercy, 4001 W McNichols Rd, PO BOX 19900, Detroit, MI, 48219-0900. **EMAIL** DEWINDTE@udmercy.edu

DEZEEUW, ANNE MARIE
PERSONAL Born 02/18/1947, Minneapolis, MN, m, 1984, 1 child **DISCIPLINE** MUSIC THEORY **EDUCATION** BM, Mich State Univ, 68; MA, Univ TX, Austin, 71, PhD, 83. **CAREER** Lectr, 74-77, Inst, 77-83, Asst Prof 83-84, Univ NY, Stony Brook; Asst Prof 85-91, Assoc Prof, 91-98, Prof, 98-, Univ Louisville. **MEMBERSHIPS** Soc Music Theory; Music Theory Soc NY State; Music Theory Midwest, Sec 91-94, Pres, 97-99. **RESEARCH** Tonal theory; music of the early 20th century; theory pedagogy; contemporary music. **SELECTED PUBLICATIONS** with Rebecca Jemain: An Interview with John Adams, Perspective of New Music, Vol 34, No 2, 96; Review of Nightingale version 1,4 music notation software, Notes 95; Some Notes on Teaching Score Analysis in Teacher's Guide to the Advanced Placement Course in Music Theory, ed, Kathlyn J Fujikawa, NY: College Entrance Examination Board, 93; Overall Structure and Design in a Variation Form, Journal of Music Theory Pedagogy 1, 87; With Roger E Foltz: Sight Singing: Melodic Structures in Functional Tonality, Austin, TX: Sterling Swift Publishing Co, 78; Teaching College Music Theory Classes that Include Blind Student, College Music Symposium 17 no 2, 77. **CONTACT ADDRESS** School Music, Univ Louisville, Louisville, KY, 40292. **EMAIL** amdeze01@ulkyvm.louisville.edu

DI MAIO, IRENE STOCKSIEKER
DISCIPLINE GERMAN LANGUAGE, LITERATURE AND CULTURE/HISTORY, AND FILM **EDUCATION** La State Univ, PhD, 76. **CAREER** Assoc prof Ger, A&S fac senate, univ fac senate, A&S CAPPE comt, ch, Women's and Gender stud, Delta Phi Alpha, La State Univ. **RESEARCH** Eighteenth to twentieth century German literature with focus on the nineteenth century. **SELECTED PUBLICATIONS** Auth, The Multiple Perspective in Wilhelm Raabe's Third-Person Narratives of the Braunschweig Period, J. Benjamins, 81; Reclamations of the French Revolution: Fanny Lewald's Literary Response to the Nachmaumlrz in Der Seehof, Geist und Gesellschaft. zur Rezeption der Franzoumlsiszhen Revolution, ed Eitel Timm, Munich Fink, 90; Borders of Culture: The Native American in Friedrich Gerst&aumlcker's North American Narratives, in Yearbk of Ger Am Stud 28, 93. **CONTACT ADDRESS** Dept of For Lang and Lit, Louisiana State Univ, 124 C Prescott Hall, Baton Rouge, LA, 70803.

DIACON, TODD
DISCIPLINE HISTORY **EDUCATION** Univ Wis, PhD. **CAREER** Assoc prof. **RESEARCH** Latin American history. **SELECTED PUBLICATIONS** Auth, Millenarian Vision, Capitalist Reality: Brazil's Contestado Rebellion 1912-1916, Duke. **CONTACT ADDRESS** Dept of History, Knoxville, TN, 37996.

DIAMOND, SANDER A.
PERSONAL Born 11/25/1942, New York, NY, m, 1966, 2 children **DISCIPLINE** MODERN EUROPEAN HISTORY **EDUCATION** State Univ NY Col New Paltz, AB, 64; State Univ NY Binghamton, MA, 66, PhD, 71. **CAREER** From instr to asst prof, 68-72, assoc prof, 74-78, prof hist, Keuka Col, 74-, chmn dept, 78-, Nat Endowment Humanities course develop grant, 74; vis prof hist, Hobart & William Smith Col, 76-77; vis prof hist, State Univ NY, Binghamton, 77; NEH fel, 79; Danforth teaching fel, 81-86. **MEMBERSHIPS** AHA. **RESEARCH** German history, the Nazi years; German-American diplomatic relations; study of extremist movements; historical fiction. **SELECTED PUBLICATIONS** Auth, The Nazi Movement in the United States, 1924-1941, Cornell Univ, 74; Zur Typologie de Amerikadeutschen NS-Bewegung, 75 & Aus den Papieren des Amerikanischen Botschafters in Berlin, 1922-1925, 79, Vierteljahrshefte fur Zeitgeschichte; The Bund Movement in the United States, in Germany and America: Essays on Problems of International Relations and Immigration, Brooklyn Col Press, 80; The Soul of a Nation, in Newsday, 79; Herr Hitler: Amerikas Diplomaten, Washington, und der Untergang Weimars, Droste Verlag, 85; Starik, E.P. Dutton, 89; Starik, Pinnacle Paperbacks, 90; The Red Arrow, E.P. Dutton, 92; The German Table: The Education of a Nation, DISC-US Books, Inc, 98. **CONTACT ADDRESS** Dept Hist, Keuka Col, Keuka Park, NY, 14478. **EMAIL** Sdiamond@mail.keuka.edu

DIAMOND, SIGMUND
PERSONAL Born 06/14/1920, Baltimore, MD, m, 1945, 2 children **DISCIPLINE** HISTORY, SOCIOLOGY **EDUCATION** Johns Hopkins Univ, AB, 40; Harvard Univ, PhD (US hist), 53. **CAREER** Reader-coder, Off Facts and Figures, Washington, DC, 42; head radio intel unit, Bd Econ Warfare, 42-43; int rep, United Auto Workers-Cong Indust Orgn, Mich, 43-49; from asst prof to assoc prof, 55-63, PROF SOCIOL AND HIST, COLUMBIA UNIV, 63-, Fel, Ctr Advan Studies Behav Sci, 59-60; ed, Polit Sci Quart, 63-73; sr res fel, Newberry libr, Ill, 67; vis prof, Hebrew Univ, Jerusalem, 69-70; mem panel III, comt brain sci, Nat Res Coun, 72-; Fulbright prof, Tel-Aviv Univ, 75-76; deleg, Am Coun Learned Soc, 78-80. **MEMBERSHIPS** Conf Jewish Social Studies; Inst Early Am Hist and Cult; AHA; Econ Hist Asn; Am Sociol Asn. **RESEARCH** Sixteenth and 17th century theories of human nature and social organization; comparative studies of colonization in the New World; sociology of the arts. **SELECTED PUBLICATIONS** Auth, Whos Afraid of George and Marthas Parlor, Lit Film Quart, Vol 24, 96; Mothers in the Margins--Hardy, Thomas, Lawrence,D. H., And Suffragisms Discontents, Colby Quart, Vol 32, 96; Menand Review of Hershberg Book on Conand, James,B.--A Comment, NY Rev Books, Vol 41, 94; Diamond, Sara, Womens Stud Interdisciplinary J, Vol 25, 96. **CONTACT ADDRESS** Dept of Sociol, Columbia Univ, New York, NY, 10027.

DIBABA, MAMO
DISCIPLINE SOCIAL SCIENCE **EDUCATION** BS, MA, PhD. **CAREER** Spring Arbor Col **SELECTED PUBLICATIONS** Auth, Teaching Philosophy and Style: Theory and practice from concept to application. **CONTACT ADDRESS** Spring Arbor Col, 106 E Main St, Spring Arbor, MI, 49283.

DICK, BERNARD F.
PERSONAL Born 11/25/1935, Scranton, PA, m, 1965, 2 children **DISCIPLINE** CLASSICS **EDUCATION** Univ Scranton, BA, 57; Fordham Univ, MA, 60, PhD, 62. **CAREER** Instr to assoc prof, Iona Col, 61-70; assoc prof to chair to prof, Fairleigh Dickinson Univ, 70- . **HONORS AND AWARDS** Assistantship in Classics, Fordham Univ, 57-60; outstanding scholarly book of the year, Choice, 85. **RESEARCH** Film hist & criticism. **SELECTED PUBLICATIONS** Auth, The Star-Spangled Screen: The American World War II Film, 85, 96; Radical Innocence: A Critical Study of the Hollywood Ten, 89; The Merchant Prince of Poverty Row: Harry Cohn of Columbia Pictures, 93; Billy Wilder, 96; City of Dreams: The Making and Remaking of Universal Pictures, 97. **CONTACT ADDRESS** 580 Wyndham Rd, Teaneck, NJ, 07666-2612.

DICK, ERIC L.
PERSONAL Born 11/19/1951, Brandon, MB, Canada **DISCIPLINE** HISTORY **EDUCATION** Brandon Univ, BA, 72; Univ Man, MA, 78. **CAREER** Hist, Hist Sites Planner, Cultur Rsrc Mgt Specialist, Prairie & NWT Reg, 77-92, Nat Hist Sites Directorate, 92-95, HISTORIAN, PARKS CANADA, DEPT CAN HERITAGE, WESTERN CAN SERV CTR, 96-; partner, Ronald Thomas Frohwerk, 87-; adj prof, landscape architect, Univ Man, 91-92. **HONORS AND AWARDS** Can Hist Asn Reg Hist Cert Merit, 90; Merit Award, City Winnipeg, 90; Parks Can Merit Award, 96. **RESEARCH** Canadian agricultural history & architectural history. **SELECTED PUBLICATIONS** Auth, A History of Prairie Settlement Patterns, 87; auth, Farmers "Making Good": The Development of Abernethy District, Saskatchewan 1880-1920, in Stud Archaeol, Archit Hist, 89; auth, "Pibloktoq" (Arctic Hysteria): A Construction of European-Inuit Relations? in Arctic Anthrop, 95; contribur, The Canadian Encyclopedia, 85, 88; contribur, Making Western Canada: Essays on European Colonization and Settlement, 96 **CONTACT ADDRESS** 1102-888 Hamilton St., Vancouver, BC, V6B 5W4.

DICKASON, OLIVE P.
PERSONAL Born 03/06/1920, Winnipeg, MB, Canada **DISCIPLINE** HISTORY **EDUCATION** Notre Dame Col, BA, 43; Univ Ottawa, MA, 72, PhD, 77. **CAREER** Reporter, The Leader-Post, 44-56; Globe & Mail, 56-67; chief info serv, Nat Gallery Can, 67-70; asst prof, 76-79, assoc prof, 79-85, prof, 85-92, PROF EMER HISTORY, UNIV ALTA, 92-; ADJ PROF, UNIV OTTAWA, 97-. **HONORS AND AWARDS** SSHRCC res grant, 85; Sr Rockefeller fel, 89; Sir John A. Macdonald Prize, 92; Metis Woman Year, 92; DLitt(hon), Univ NB, 93; DLitt(hon), Univ Alta, 95; Order of Can, 96; DLitt(hon), Univ Windsor, 96; LLD(hon), Univ Calgary, 96; DLitt(hon), Lakehead Univ, 97; DLitt(hon), Univ Guelph, 97; Nat Aboriginal Achievement Award, 97. **MEMBERSHIPS** Mem, Metis Nation Alta; bd mem, Nat Aboriginal Achievement Found; mem coun, Champlain Soc; Can Hist Asn; Am Soc Ethnohist; Fr Colonial Hist Soc; Soc francaise d'histoire d'outre-mer; Soc d'histoire de l'Amerique francaise. **RESEARCH** First Nations history; colonisation of the Americas **SELECTED PUBLICATIONS** Auth, Indian Arts in Canada, 72; auth, The Myth of the Savage and the Beginnings of French Colonisation in the Americas, 84; auth, Canada's First Nations: A History of Founding Peoples From Earliest Times, 92; coauth, The Law of Nations and the New World, 89. **CONTACT ADDRESS** 808-500 Laurier Ave, Ottawa, ON, K1R 5E1. **EMAIL** dickason@uottawa.ca

DICKE, THOMAS SCOTT
PERSONAL Born 11/09/1955, St. Mary's, OH, m, 2 children **DISCIPLINE** HISTORY **EDUCATION** The Ohio State Univ, PhD, 88. **CAREER** Asst Prof, Univ GA, 89-90; Asst Prof, Southwest Missouri State Univ, 90-93; Assoc Prof Southwest Missouri State Univ, 93-. **MEMBERSHIPS** Business Hist Conf. **RESEARCH** Small Bussiness; Industrialization in global context; Hist of Edu. **SELECTED PUBLICATIONS** Franchising in America, Univ of NC Press, 92. **CONTACT ADDRESS** Dept Hist, Southwest MO State Univ, 901 South National Ave, Springfield, MO, 65802-0089. **EMAIL** TomDic@Mail.SMSU.edu

DICKERMAN, EDMUND H.
PERSONAL Born 09/02/1935, Haverhill, MA, m, 1962, 1 child **DISCIPLINE** HISTORY **EDUCATION** Univ NH, BS, 57; Brown Univ, PhD (hist), 65. **CAREER** Instr hist, Conn Col, 64-65; from asst prof to assoc prof, 65-78, PROF HIST, UNIV CONN, 78-. **MEMBERSHIPS** AHA; Renaissance Soc Am; Soc Fr Hist Studies. **RESEARCH** Renaissance and reformation history of Europe; early modern history of France. **SELECTED PUBLICATIONS** Auth THE CHOICE OF HERCULES - HENRY-IV AS HERO/, HISTORICAL JOURNAL, Vol 39, 1996 **CONTACT ADDRESS** Dept of Hist, Univ of Conn, Storrs, CT, 06268.

DICKERSON, GREGORY WEIMER
PERSONAL Born 03/08/1937, Hanover, NH, m, 1967, 2 children **DISCIPLINE** CLASSICAL LANGUAGES & LITERATURE **EDUCATION** Harvard Univ, AB, 59; Princeton Univ, MA, 65, PhD, 72. **CAREER** Teaching fel classics, Phillips Acad, Andover, Mass, 59-60; secy, Am Sch Class Studies, Athens, 63-64; instr, Gilman Sch, Baltimore, 64-66; instr classics, 67-70, asst prof Greek, 70-76, assoc prof Greek, Bryn Mawr Col, 76-. **MEMBERSHIPS** Am Phil Asn. **RESEARCH** Greek drama. **SELECTED PUBLICATIONS** Auth, Aristophanes' Ranae 862: A note on the anatomy of Euripidean Tragedy, Harvard Studies Class Philol, 74; coauth, Sophocles' Women of Trachis, Oxford Univ, 78. **CONTACT ADDRESS** Dept of Greek, Bryn Mawr Col, 101 N Merion Ave, Bryn Mawr, PA, 19010-2899. **EMAIL** gdickers@brynmawr.edu

DICKIE, MATTHEW WALLACE
PERSONAL Born 11/20/1941, Edinburgh, Scotland **DISCIPLINE** CLASSICAL PHILOLOGY **EDUCATION** Univ Edinburgh, MA, 64; Univ Toronto, PhD (Greek), 72. **CAREER** Instr classics, Swarthmore Col, 67-68; asst prof, 72-78, ASSOC PROF CLASSICS, UNIV ILL, CHICAGO CIRCLE, 78-, Chmn Dept, 80-. **RESEARCH** Early Greek poetry; Greek ethics; Greek history. **SELECTED PUBLICATIONS** Auth, A Knidian Phallic Vase From Corinth, Hesperia, Vol 62, 93; A New Epigram by Poseidippus on an Irritable Dead Cretan, Bullf Am Society Papyrologists, Vol 32, 95; Baskania, Probaskania and Prosbaskania, Glotta Zeitschrift Griechische Lateinische Sprache, Vol 71, 93; Hermeias on Plato Phaedrus 238d and Synesius Dion 14.2, Am J Philol, Vol 114, 93; A New Epigram by Poseidippus on an Irritable Dead Cretan, Bull Am Soc Papyrologists, Vol 32, 95; Dioscorus and the Impotence of Envy, Bull Am Soc Papyrologists, Vol 30, 93; **CONTACT ADDRESS** Dept of Classics, Univ of Ill, Chicago Circle, Box 4348, Chicago, IL, 60680.

DICKINSON, GLORIA HARPER
PERSONAL Born 08/05/1947, New York, NY, m **DISCIPLINE** AFRICAN-AMERICAN STUDIES **EDUCATION** City Coll of NY, BA European Hist 1968; Howard Univ, MA African Studies 1970, PhD African Stud 1978. **CAREER** Camden High School Camden NJ, geography/Social studies teacher 1970-71; English Dept Trenton State Coll, instructor 1971-73; DEPT OF AFRICAN-AM STUDIES TRENTON STATE COLL, CHMN ASSOC PROF 1973-. **HONORS AND AWARDS** NEH summer fellowship for coll fac Univ of IA 1977, NY Univ School of Bus 1979, Univ of PA 1981, Princeton Univ 1984; Fac Mem of the Year Trenton State Coll 1984; Proj Dir NEH Summer Inst in African-Amer Culture Trenton State Coll 1987;Mentor of the Year, Trenton State College Minority Scholars, 1990 Blue Key Honor Society, Trenton State College, 1989. **MEMBERSHIPS** Editorial bd mem Journal of Negro History 1983-93; mem NJ Committee on The Humanities 1984-90; mem ASALH; mem ASA; mem AHSA; mem NCBS; mem NCNW; faculty advisor Zeta Sigma Chptr Alpha Kappa Alpha 1972-; contrib scholar NJ Women's Project 1984; proj dir TSC Summer Study Tours to Africa 1984-; mem NJ Historic Trust 1986-89; Alpha Kappa Alpha Sorority, chair, International Nominating Committee, 1988-92, archives comm, 1994-98; Supreme Grammateus, 1998-2000. **CONTACT ADDRESS** African-American Studies, Trenton State Col, PO Box 7718, Ewing, NJ, 08628. **EMAIL** dickinsg@tcnj.edu

DICKINSON, JOHN ALEXANDER
PERSONAL Born 08/03/1948, Toronto, ON, Canada **DISCIPLINE** HISTORY **EDUCATION** Univ Toronto, BA Hons, 70; Universite Laval, Quebec City, MA, 72; Univ Toronto, PhD (hist), 77. **CAREER** Lectr, 75-77, ASST PROF HIST, UNIV WESTERN ONT, 77-. **MEMBERSHIPS** Can Hist Asn; Institut d'Histoire de l'Amerique Francaise. **RESEARCH** New France; early modern France; North American Colonial history. **SELECTED PUBLICATIONS** Auth, Demographic Models in History, Can Hist Rev, Vol 76, 95; Monumenta Novae Franciae, Vol 4, The Great Ordeals 1638-1640, Can Hist Rev, Vol 73, 92; Anatomy of a Naval Disaster--The 1746 French Expedition to North America, Rev Hist Am Fr, Vol 51, 97; Aboriginal Ontario--Historical Perspectives on the 1st Nations, Rev Hist Am Fr, Vol 49, 95; Canadian Historians--Agents of Unity or Disunity, J Can Stud Rev Etudes Can, Vol 31, 96; The Middle Ground--Indians, Empires and Republics in the Great Lakes Region, 1650-1815, J Interdisciplinary Hist, Vol 24, 93; The Patriots and the People--The Rebellion of 1837 in Rural Lower Canada, Am Hist Rev, Vol 100, s95. **CONTACT ADDRESS** Dept of Hist, Univ Western Ont, London, ON, N6A 5B8.

DICKISON, SHEILA KATHRYN
PERSONAL Born 11/14/1942, Walkerton, ON, Canada **DISCIPLINE** CLASSICS, ANCIENT HISTORY **EDUCATION** Univ Toronto, BA, 64; Bryn Mawr Col, MA, 66, PhD (Latin and Greek), 72. **CAREER** From instr to asst prof Greek, Latin and ancient hist, Wellesley Col, 69-76; actg chmn classics, 77-78, Assoc Prof Classics, Univ Fla, 76-. **MEMBERSHIPS** Archaeol Inst Am; Am Class League. **RESEARCH** Roman historiography; ancient social history **SELECTED PUBLICATIONS** Auth, The Reasonable Approach to Beginning Greek and Latin, Class J, Vol 87, 92. **CONTACT ADDRESS** ASB-3C, Univ of Fla, 3c Arts and Sciences, Gainesville, FL, 32611-9500.

DICKS, SAMUEL EUGENE
PERSONAL Born 06/15/1935, St. Louis, MO, m, 1959, 4 children **DISCIPLINE** MEDIEVAL HISTORY, WOMEN'S HISTORY **EDUCATION** Dakota Wesleyan Univ, AB, 57; Univ SDak, AM, 58; Univ Okla, PhD (hist), 66. **CAREER** From asst prof to assoc prof, 65-67, PROF HIST, EMPORIA STATE UNIV, 75-. **MEMBERSHIPS** AHA; Renaissance Soc Am; Medieval Acad Am. **RESEARCH** Late medieval diplomacy. **SELECTED PUBLICATIONS** Auth, Go West and Grow up With the Country--An Exhibition of 19th Century Guides to the American West in the Collections of the American Antiquarian Society, J West, Vol 33, 94. **CONTACT ADDRESS** Dept of Hist, Emporia State Univ, 1200 Commercial St, Emporia, KS, 66801-5087.

DICKSON, BRUCE D., JR.
DISCIPLINE AMERICAN CULTURE, AFRICAN-AMERICAN HISTORY **EDUCATION** Univ Pa, PhD, 71. **CAREER** Dept Hist, Univ Ca **RESEARCH** African-American historians. **SELECTED PUBLICATIONS** Auth, And They All Sang Hallelujah: Plain-Folk Camp-Meeting Religion, 1800-1845, 74; Violence and Culture, Antebellum South, 79; The Rhetoric of Conservatism: The Virginia Convention of 1829-30 and the Conservative Tradition in the South, 82; Black American Writing from the Nadir: The Evolution of a Literary Tradition, 1877-1915, 89; Archibald Grimke: Portrait of a Black Independent, 93. **CONTACT ADDRESS** Dept of Hist, Univ Calif, Irvine, CA, 92697. **EMAIL** uci-cwis-support@uci.edu

DICKSON, CHARLES ELLIS
PERSONAL Born 06/13/1935, Bellevue, PA, m, 1964, 2 children **DISCIPLINE** HISTORY **EDUCATION** Ind Univ, BS, 57; Univ Pittsburgh, MA, 61; Ohio State Univ, PhD, 71. **CAREER** Assoc Prof and Fac Develop Coordr, Clark State, 89-; Asst Prof, Wright State Univ, 85-89; Fac Mem, Cottey College, 78-81; Instr, King Col, 76-77; Asst Prof, Geneva Col, 70-77. **HONORS AND AWARDS** Fulbright grant. **MEMBERSHIPS** Am Hist Asn; Ohio Acad Hist; Nat Coun for Staff, Prog and Orgn Develop. **RESEARCH** Early national political and religious history; James Monroe. **SELECTED PUBLICATIONS** John Sherman Hoyt, Dict Am Bio, NY, Charles Scribner's Sons, 77; The Election of 1816, The Election of 1820, and

Thomas Pinckney (1750-1828), in Encycl Southern Hist, La State Univ Press, 79; Prosperity Rides on Rubber Tires: The Impact of the Automobile on Minot during the 1920's, N Dak Hist: Jour Northern Plains, 53, Summer 86, 14-23; Jeremiads in the New American Republic: The Case of National Fasts in the John Adams Administration, The New Eng Quart, 60, 87, 187-207; And Ladies of the Church: The Origins of the Episcopal Congregation in Minot, North Dakota, Hist: Jour Northern Plains, 55, 88, 8-19. **CONTACT ADDRESS** Clark State Comm Col, 570 E Leffel Ln, Springfield, OH, 45501. **EMAIL** DicksonC@clark.cc.oh.us

DICKSON, JOHN H.
DISCIPLINE CHURCH MUSIC **EDUCATION** Dallas Baptist Col, BA; Baylor Univ, MM; Univ Tex, DMA; addn stud, Cambridge Univ. **CAREER** Instr, Univ Tex; Baylor Univ; assoc dean, Dr Stud, prof, S Baptist Theol Sem, 85-. **RESEARCH** Sch Church Mus and Worship. **SELECTED PUBLICATIONS** Pub(s), The Choral Jour **CONTACT ADDRESS** Sch of Church Mus and Worship, Southern Baptist Theol Sem, 2825 Lexington Rd, Louisville, KY, 40280. **EMAIL** jdickson@sbts.edu

DIEFENDORF, BARBARA BOONSTOPPEL
PERSONAL Born 12/19/1946, Oakland, CA, m, 1972 **DISCIPLINE** EUROPEAN HISTORY **EDUCATION** Univ Calif, Berkeley, AB, 68, MA, 70, PhD, 78. **CAREER** Asst prof humanities, Univ NH, 79-80; from asst to assoc prof 80-93, prof history, 93-, Boston Univ. **MEMBERSHIPS** AHA; Soc Fr Hist Studies; Sixteenth Century Studies. **RESEARCH** Sixteenth century France; wars of religion in Paris. **SELECTED PUBLICATIONS** Auth, Paris' City Councillors in the Sixteenth Century: The Politics of Patrimony, Princeton, 83; auth, Beneath the Cross: Catholics and Huguenots in Sixteenth-Century Paris, Oxford, 91; co-ed, Culture and Identity in Early Modern Europe (1500-1800), Michigan, 93. **CONTACT ADDRESS** Dept of History, Boston Univ, 226 Bay State Rd, Boston, MA, 02215-1403. **EMAIL** bdiefend@bu.edu

DIEFENDORF, JEFFRY MINDLIN
PERSONAL Born 10/19/1945, Pasadena, CA, m, 1972 **DISCIPLINE** MODERN EUROPEAN HISTORY **EDUCATION** Stanford Univ, BA, 67; Univ Calif, Berkeley, MA, 68, PhD, 75. **CAREER** Teacher hist, Stanford Univ, 73-76, lectr, 75; from Asst Prof to Assoc Prof, 76-91, prof hist, Univ NH, 91-, Dept Chair, 91-97, Sr Fac Fel, 97-. **HONORS AND AWARDS** Am Coun Learned Soc grant-in-aid, 77-78; fel, NEH, 81-82; Nat Sci Found Res Initiation Grant, 81-83; Fel, Woodrow Wilson Int Ctr for Schol, 87; Fel, Alexander von Humboldt Found, 89-90, 94; NEH Summer Fel, 94. **MEMBERSHIPS** AHA; Conf Group Cent Europ Hist; German Studies Asn; New England Hist Asn; Int Planning Hist Soc; Urban Hist Soc. **RESEARCH** Comparative urban change in Germany, Switzerland, Boston. **SELECTED PUBLICATIONS** Auth, Businessman and Politics in the Rhineland, 1789-1834, Princeton Univ Press, 80; ed, The Rebuilding of Europe's Bombed Cities, MacMillan Press/ St. Martin's Press, 90; auth, In the Wake of War: The Reconstruction of German Cities after World War II, Oxford Univ Press, 93; co-ed, America's Policy and the Reconstruction of Germany, 1945-1955, Cambridge Univ Press, 94; author of 24 journal articles and chapters. **CONTACT ADDRESS** Dept of Hist, Univ NH, Horton Soc Sci Ctr, Durham, NH, 03824-4724. **EMAIL** jeffryd@christa.unh.edu

DIERENFIELD, BRUCE JONATHAN
PERSONAL Born 07/26/1951, Waterloo, IA **DISCIPLINE** AMERICAN HISTORY **EDUCATION** St Olaf Col, BA, 73; Univ Va, MA, 77, PhD (Am hist), 81. **CAREER** Vis asst prof Am hist, Univ Ala, 81-82; WRITER, HIST ASSOCS INC, 82-. **MEMBERSHIPS** AHA; Orgn Am Historians. **RESEARCH** Legislative origins of federal energy policy; civil rights and the desegregation of Southern universities; sport, society and cultural radicalism. **SELECTED PUBLICATIONS** Auth, Chain Reaction--Expert Debate and Public Participation in American Commercial Nuclear Power, 1945-1975, Am Hist Rev, Vol 98, 93; Calculating Visions--Kennedy, Johnson, and Civil Rights, J Southern Hist, Vol 59, 93. **CONTACT ADDRESS** Hist Associates Inc, 18903 Smoothstone Way Suite 5, Gaithersburg, MD, 20879.

DIETLER, MICHAEL
PERSONAL Born 03/19/1952, Washington, DC, m, 1985 **DISCIPLINE** ANTHROPOLOGY **EDUCATION** Stanford Univ, AB, 74; Univ Calif Berkeley, MA, 76, PhD, 90. **CAREER** Asst to assoc prof, Yale Univ, 90-95; assoc prof, Univ Chicago, 95-. **MEMBERSHIPS** Amer Athrop Asn; Soc for Amer Archaeol; Europ Asn of Archaeol; Soc Prehist Fr. **RESEARCH** Archaeology of Europe (Celtic iron age); Colonialism; Material culture; Ethnoarchaeology. **SELECTED PUBLICATIONS** Auth, A tale of three sites: the monumentalization of Celtic oppida and the politics of collective memory and identity, World Archaeol, 30, 72-89, 98; Consumption, agency and cultural entanglement: theoretical implications of a Meditteranean colonial encounter, Studies in Culture Contact: Interaction, Culture Change, and Archaeology, pp 288-315, Carbondale, Univ Southern Ill Press, 98; co-auth, Habitus, techniques, style: an integrated approach to the social understanding of material culture and boundaries, The Archaeology of Social Boundaries, pp 232-263, Wash, DC, Smithsonian, 98; auth, The Iron Age in Meditteranean France: colonial encounters, entanglements, and transformations, Jour of World Prehist, 11, 269-357, 97; L'art du vin chez les Gaulois, Pour la Sci, 237, 68-74, 97; Archaeology, Encycl of Soc and Cult Anthrop, pp 45-51, London, Routledge, 96; auth, Feasts and commensal politics in the political economy: food, power, and status in prehistoric Europe, Food and the Status Quest: An Interdisciplinary Perspective, pp 87-125, Oxford, Berghahn Publ, 96; auth, Early Celtic socio-political relations: ideological representation and social competition in dynamic comparative perspective, Celtic Chiefdom, Celtic State: The Evolution of Complex Social Systems in Prehistoric Europe, pp 64-71, Cambridge, Cambridge Univ Press, 95; auth, The cup of Gyptis: rethinking the colonial encounter in Early Iron Age Western Europe and the relevance of world-systems models, Jour of Europ Archaeol, 3, 2, 89-111, 95; co-auth, Habitus et reproduction sociale des techniques: l'intelligence due style en archeologie et en ethnoarcheologie, De la prehistoire aux missiles balistiques: l'Intelligence sociale des techniques, pp 202-227, Paris, La Decouverte, 94; co-auth, Ceramics and ethnic identity: ethnoarchaeological observations on the distribution of pottery styles and the relationship between the social contexts of production and consumption, Terre cuite et societe: la ceramique, document technique, economique, culturel, XIVe Rencontre Internationale d'Archaeologie et d'Historoire d'Antibes, pp 459-472, Juan-les-Pins, Editions APDCA, 94; auth, Our ancestors the Gauls: archaeology, ethnic nationalism, and the manipulation of Celtic identity in modern Europe, Amer Anthrop, 96, 584-605, 94; auth, Quenching Celtic thirst, Archaeol, 47, 3, 44-48, 94. **CONTACT ADDRESS** Dept. of Anthropology, Univ of Chicago, 1126 E. 59th St., Chicago, IL, 60637. **EMAIL** mdietler@anthro.spc.uchicago.edu

DIETZ, HANNS-BERTOLD
DISCIPLINE MUSIC, HISTORICAL MUSICOL **EDUCATION** Univ Insbruck, PhD, 56. **CAREER** Prof, Univ of Tx at Austin. **HONORS AND AWARDS** 3 Tchg Excellence awd(s). **RESEARCH** Neapolitan opera and church music. **SELECTED PUBLICATIONS** Auth, Die Chorfuge be Georg Friedrich Handel; publ, Analecta Musicologica, Int J Musicol, J Amer Musicol Soc, Musikforschung, Notes, Pergolesi Stud; contrib to, Die Musik in Geschichte und Gegenwart, New Grove Dictionary of Music and Musicians & New Grove Dictionary of Opera. **CONTACT ADDRESS** School of Music, Univ of Texas at Austin, 2613 Wichita St, Austin, TX, 78705.

DIGGS, WILLIAM P.
PERSONAL Born 10/19/1926, Columbia, SC, m **DISCIPLINE** SOCIOLOGY **EDUCATION** Friendship Jr Coll Rock Hill SC, 1943; Morehouse College, AB 1949; Atlanta U, MA 1951; Colgate-Rochester Div Sch, BD 1955; MDiv 1972. **CAREER** Friendship Jr Coll, Rock Hill SC, instructor 1950-52; Friendship Jr Coll, instructor Sociology 1955-61; Galilee Baptist Church, York SC, pastor 1955-62; Second Baptist Church, Leroy NY, student pastor 1954-55; Benedict Coll, Columbia SC, asst prof Sociology 1964-74; Trinity Baptist Church, Florence SC & Morris Coll, Sumter SC, minister, asst prof Sociology. **HONORS AND AWARDS** Valedictorian HS class; honorary DD Friendship Jr Coll 1973; Honorary LHD Morris Coll 1973; honored by Trinity Bapt Ch Florence; recognition of dedicated service ch & community 1969; honored Zeta Phi Beta Sorority Inc; Florence outstanding leadership civic econ comm involvement 1971; citz of the yr Chi Iota Chap Omega Psi Phi Frat 1976; outst achvmt & serv Omega Psi Phi Frat 1976. **MEMBERSHIPS** Am Assn of Univ Prof; Alpha Kappa Delta Honorary Sociological Soc; pres Florence Br NAACP 1970-74; life mem NAACP; mem Community Relations Com Relations Florence, SC; chmn Community Action Agency Florence Co; mem Area Manpower Bd; mem Florence Co Bd of Health; mem trustee bd Friendship Jr Coll; mem trustee bd Morrisl Coll. **CONTACT ADDRESS** 124 W Darlington St, Florence, SC, 29501.

DIK, HELMA
DISCIPLINE CLASSICS **EDUCATION** Univ Amsterdam, PhD, 95. **CAREER** Asst prof, Univ Chicago. **HONORS AND AWARDS** Junior Fel; Fel Lexikon des fruhgriechischen Epos; Graduate fel. **SELECTED PUBLICATIONS** Auth, 'Senex: een case-study uit de oudheid', Pentecostalia, 92; auth, 'Gekloofde zinnen langs de lijn', ICG, 94; auth, 'Vrij maar niet willekeurig: Pragmatische aspecten van constituentvolgorde in twee fragmenten uit Herodotus', Lampas, 94; auth, 'Ancient Greek warfare--a case study in constituent ordering, Mouton de Gruyter, 94; auth, Word Order in Ancient Greek. A Pragmatic Account of Word Order Variation in Herodotus, Gieben, 95. **CONTACT ADDRESS** Univ Chicago, 5801 S Ellis, Chicago, IL, 60637.

DIL, NASIM
DISCIPLINE SPECIAL EDUCATION; EARLY CHILDHOOD SPECIAL EDUCATION **EDUCATION** Univ Peshawar, BA, 54; Univ Punjab, Pakistan, MA, 57; Ind Univ, Bloomington, MS, 69, PhD, 71. **CAREER** Prof, Univ Nev, Las Vegas, 77. **SELECTED PUBLICATIONS** Auth, Nonverbal communication in young children, Topics in Early Childhood Spec Educ, 4, 84; coauth, Improvement in arithmetic self-concept through combined positive reinforcement, peer interaction, and sequential curriculum, J of Sch Psychol, 9, 71; Available special education faculty positions in higher education, J of Tchr Educ and Spec Educ, 16, 93. **CONTACT ADDRESS** Dept of Spec Educ, Univ Nev, Las Vegas, 4505 Maryland Pky, Las Vegas, NV, 89154-3014.

DILLON, CLARISSA F.
PERSONAL Born 07/24/1933, Chicago, IL, d, 1 child **DISCIPLINE** POLITICAL SCIENCE; AMERICAN HISTORY; HISTORY **EDUCATION** Bryn Mawr Col, AB, 55; Univ Chicago, MA, 60; Bryn Mawr Col, PhD, 86. **CAREER** Classrom teacher, The Latin School of Chicago, grades 1, 2, 5, 6, 7, 8, 11-12; Ithan Elementary, Radnor, PA, grades 1, 4, 5, 6 (public school certification through Immaculata Col); consultant and free-lance Living History demonstrator at Historic Sites and Museums, 73-. **MEMBERSHIPS** Radnor Twp Ed Asn; PA State Ed Asn; NEA; Nat Coalition of Independent Scholars; Asn for Living History, Farms, and Agricultural Museums (ALHFAM). **RESEARCH** 18th century women's work/lives among the English in southeastern PA (demonstration/ interpretation of processes based on research findings). **SELECTED PUBLICATIONS** Auth, A Most Comfortable Dinner-18th Century Foods "to subsist a great Number of Persons at a small Expense, printed for the author, 94; To Make the Face Faire and Smooth, ALHFAM Proceedings for Annual Conference, 95; Beef--It's What's for Dinner, ALHFAM Bul, spring, 96; Barbecues, with Sandra Oliver, Food History News, spring 96; Lewd, Enormous, and Disorderly Practices: Prostitution in 18th-Century Philadelphia and Its English Background, ALHFAM Proceedings for Annual Conference, 96; Margaret Morris Burlington-NJ 1804 Gardening Memorandum, with Nancy V Webster, No 6 in Am Horticultural Series, The AM Botanist, Booksellers, Chillicothe, IL, 96; This is the Way We Wash Our Clothes, Past Masters, Newsletter, winter 98; Under the Shadow of My Wing, ALHFAM Proceedings for Annual Conference, 98; 18th-Century Dyeng in Pennsylvania, Past Masters Newsletter, summer 98. **CONTACT ADDRESS** 768 Buck Ln, Haverford, PA, 19041-1202.

DILLON, DIANE
DISCIPLINE ART HISTORY **EDUCATION** Yale Univ, PhD. **CAREER** Prof, Northwestern Univ. **RESEARCH** Gender studies, critical theory, and post-colonial studies. **SELECTED PUBLICATIONS** Writing a book about the visual culture of the World Colombian Exposition of 1893. **CONTACT ADDRESS** Dept of Art History, Northwestern Univ, 1801 Hinman, Evanston, IL, 60208.

DILLON, MERTON LYNN
PERSONAL Born 04/04/1924, Addison, MI **DISCIPLINE** AMERICAN HISTORY **EDUCATION** Mich State Norm Col, AB, 45; Univ Mich, AM, 48, PhD (hist), 51. **CAREER** Instr hist, Mich State Norm Col, 51; asst prof, NMex Mil Inst, 51-56; from asst prof to prof, Tex Tech Col, 56-65; assoc prof, Northern Ill Univ, 65-67; PROF HIST, OHIO STATE UNIV, 67-, Nat Endowment for Humanities sr fel, 73-74. **MEMBERSHIPS** AHA; Orgn Am Historians; Southern Hist Asn. **RESEARCH** Nineteenth Century United States; antislavery movement; slavery and antislavery. **SELECTED PUBLICATIONS** Auth, In Retrospect--Barnes, Gilbert, H. and Dumond, Dwight, L., Revs Am Hist, Vol 21, 93; Antiracism in United States History--The 1st 200 Years, J Southern Hist, Vol 59, 93; Witness for Freedom--African American Voices on Race, Slavery and Emancipation, African Am Rev, Vol 29, 95. **CONTACT ADDRESS** Dept of Hist, Ohio State Univ, Columbus, OH, 43210.

DILLON, WILTON STERLIN
PERSONAL Born 07/13/1923, Yale, OK, m, 1956, 1 child **DISCIPLINE** ANTHROPOLOGY **EDUCATION** BA, Univ of Calif, Berkeley, 51; PhD, Columbia Univ NY, 61; Post Graduate Studies, Univ of Paris and Univ of Leyden, 51-52. **CAREER** Info Spec, Civil Info and Edu Sec Supreme Comdr Allied Powers, Tokyo, 46-48; Lectr on Hum Sci, Hobart and William Smith Col Geneva, NY, 53-54; Letcr in Japanese Studies, Fordham Univ, MY, 54; Dir of Clearinghouse for Res in Hum Org, Soc for Applied Anthro, 63; Staff Dir Sci Org Devel Bd Natl Acad of Sci, Washington, DC, 63069; Dir of Symposia and Seminars and Intersisciplinary Studies, Smithsonian Inst, 69-. **HONORS AND AWARDS** Grant Found Res award for field work in Fance, 56; Ford Found award for field work in West Africa, 58; Excellence Award OK Baptist Univ, 89; Acheivement Award Am for Indian Opportunity, 90; Presidential Scholar Univ Alabama, Tuscaloosa. **MEMBERSHIPS** Soc for Applied Anthro Am Anthro Assoc Am Assoc for the Advan Of Sci; Inst for Psychol and Foreign Affairs; Inst for Intercultural Studies; Lit Soc of Wash; Inst for Current World Affair. **RESEARCH** Sci diplomacy; cross-cultural commun; gift exchange; Anthro of Knowledge; Kinship and Soc; Hist of Anthro. **SELECTED PUBLICATIONS** Gifts and Nations: The Obligation to Give, Receive and Repay, The Hague and Paris: Mouton 68; The Cultural Drama: Modern Idntites and Social Ferment, Dillon, Wilton S ed, Wash; Smithsonian Institution Press, 74; The Statue of Liberty Revisited: Making A Universal Symbol, Dillon, Wilton S and Lotler, Neil G, eds, Wash: Smithsonian Institution press, 93; Margaret Mead and Government:

American Anthropologist vol 82 No 2, 80; The Flow of Ideas Between Africa and America: Bulletin of the Atomic Scientists, 66; Margaret Mead: President-Elect, 74. **CONTACT ADDRESS** Smithsonian, Wash, DC, 20560. **EMAIL** MCELROYM@OP.SI.EDU

DILTS, MERVIN R.
PERSONAL Born 02/26/1938, Flemington, NJ **DISCIPLINE** CLASSICS **EDUCATION** Gettysburg Col, BA, 60; Ind Univ, MA, 61, PhD (classics), 64. **CAREER** Asst prof classics, Knox Col, 64-65 and Univ Ill, Urbana, 65-69; assoc prof, 69-79, PROF CLASSICS, NY UNIV, 79-, Am Philol Soc grant, 71; Am Coun Learned Soc grant-in-aid, 77. **MEMBERSHIPS** Am Philol Asn; Class Asn Atlantic States; Soc Textual Scholarship. **RESEARCH** Greek textual criticism; Greek codicology. **SELECTED PUBLICATIONS** Auth, Hiatus in the Orations of Aeschines, Am J Philol, Vol 115, 94. **CONTACT ADDRESS** Dept of Classics, New York Univ, 25 Waverly Pl, New York, NY, 10003-6701.

DIMAIO, MICHAEL
PERSONAL Born 06/05/1949, Providence, RI, m, 1980, 2 children **DISCIPLINE** CLASSICS **EDUCATION** Johns Hopkins Univ, BA, 70; Univ Mo, MA, 71, PhD, 77. **CAREER** Instr, Gannon Univ, 80-83; asst prof, 83-89, assoc prof, 89-97, prof, philos, Salve Regina Univ, 97-. **HONORS AND AWARDS** Dept & general honors, Johns Hopkins Univ; NDEA Title IV grant, MU; chemn, De Imperatonibus Romains, 96-97. **MEMBERSHIPS** APA; Asn of Ancient Hist. **RESEARCH** Roman history; Byzantine literature. **SELECTED PUBLICATIONS** Auth, Constan I (337-350 A.D.), Constantius II (337-361 A.D.), Constantine II (337-340 A.D.), Silvanus (355 A.D.), Nepotian (350 A.D.), Constantius I Chlorus (305-306 A.D.), De Imperatoribus Romanis: An Online Encycl of Roman Emperors, 96; ed, De Imperatoribus Romanis: An Online Encycl of Roman Emperors, 96; auth, Constantine I, Online Ref Book of Medieval Studies, 96; auth, Late Antiquity on the Internet, Late Antiquity Newsletter, 96; auth, Imago Veritatis aut Verba in Speculo: Athanasius, the Meletians and Linguistic Frontiers in Fourth Century Egypt, Shifting Frontiers in Late Antiquity, Aldershot, 96; rev, Athanasius and Constantius: Theology and Politics in the Constantinian Empire, Class World, 95; rev, Cognitio Gestorum: The Historiographic Art of Ammianus Marcellinus, Class World, 95; rev, Platonism in Late Antiquity, Class World, 94. **CONTACT ADDRESS** Dept. of Philosophy, Salve Regina Univ, Newport, RI, 02840. **EMAIL** dimaiom@salve.edu

DIN, GILBERT C.
PERSONAL Born 11/11/1932, Holtville, CA, 2 children **DISCIPLINE** COLONIAL AND MODERN LATIN AMERICAN HISTORY **EDUCATION** Univ Calif, Berkeley, AB, 57, MA, 58; Univ Madrid, PhD (hist), 60. **CAREER** Instr hist and anthrop, Imperial Valley Col, 61-65; from asst prof to assoc prof, 64-75, chmn dept, 73-80, PROF HIST, FT LEWIS COL, 75-. **MEMBERSHIPS** AHA; Conf Latin Am Hist. **RESEARCH** Eighteenth century Spanish Louisiana; medieval Spain, colonial Mexico. **SELECTED PUBLICATIONS** Auth, The 1st Spanish Instructions for Arkansas Post November 15, 1769, Ark Hist Quart, Vol 53, 94; Choctaws and Missionaries in Mississippi, 1818-1919, Ark Hist Quart, Vol 54, 95; Free Men in an Age of Servitude--3 Generations of A Black Family, Hist, Vol 56, 93; The Last Voyage of El Nuevo Constante--The Wreck and Recovery of an 18th Century Spanish Ship of the Louisiana Coast, J Southern Hist, Vol 62, 96; Tribal Wars of the Southern Plains, Pac Hist Rev, Vol 64, 95. **CONTACT ADDRESS** Dept of Hist, Fort Lewis Col, Durango, CO, 81301.

DINER, STEVEN J.
PERSONAL Born 12/14/1944, Bronx, NY, m, 1970, 3 children **DISCIPLINE** HISTORY **EDUCATION** Binghamton Univ, BA, 66; Univ Chicago, MA, 68, PhD, 72. **CAREER** Asst prof to assoc prof to prof Urban Stud, Univ DC, 72-85; prof Hist, George Mason Univ, 85-98; DEAN, FAC ARTS, SCIS, PROF HISTORY, 98-, RUTGERS, NEWARK. **MEMBERSHIPS** Am Hist Asn; Org Am Hist; Soc Hist Gilded Age & Progressive Era; Urban Hist Asn. **RESEARCH** US urban history; US immigration and ethnic history; Progressive Era; history of US higher education. **SELECTED PUBLICATIONS** Auth, "The City Under the Hill," Wash Hist 8,1, 96; auth, "Washington's Jewish Community: Separate But Not Apart," in Urban Odyssey: A Multicultural History of Washington, D.C., 96; auth, A Very Different Age: Americans of the Progressive Era, Hill & Wang, 98 **CONTACT ADDRESS** Office of Dean, Arts & Scis, Rutgers Univ, Newark, 360 Martin Luther King Jr. Blvd., Newark, NJ, 07102-1801. **EMAIL** sdiner@andromeda.rutgers.edu

DINGMAN, ROGER V.
DISCIPLINE HISTORY **EDUCATION** Harvard, PhD, 69. **CAREER** Assoc prof, Univ Southern Calif. **RESEARCH** Truman, MacArthur, and the Korean War. **SELECTED PUBLICATIONS** Auth, Power in the Pacific: The Origins of Naval Arms Limitation, 1914-1922, Chicago, 76. **CONTACT ADDRESS** Dept of History, Univ Southern Calif, University Park Campus, Los Angeles, CA, 90089. **EMAIL** dingman@mizar.usc.edu

DINKIN, ROBERT J.
PERSONAL Born 05/26/1940, Brooklyn, NY, m, 1988, 2 children **DISCIPLINE** AMERICAN HISTORY **EDUCATION** Brooklyn Col, BA, 63; Columbia Univ, MA, 64, PhD(hist), 68. **CAREER** From Asst Prof to Assoc Prof, 68-78, PROF HIST, CALIF STATE UNIV FRESNO, 78-. **MEMBERSHIPS** AHA; Orgn Am Historians; Inst Early Am Hist & Culture. **RESEARCH** Early American history; women's history. **SELECTED PUBLICATIONS** Ed, Selected Readings in Early American History, McCutchan, 69; auth, Seating the meeting-house in early Massachusetts, New Eng Quart, 70; Elections in Colonial Connecticut, Conn Hist Soc Bull, 72; Nominations in Provincial America, Historian, 73; Voting in Provincial America, Greenwood, 77; Voting in Revolutionary America, Greenwood, 82; Campaigning in America, Greenwood, 89; Before Equal Suffrage, Greenwood, 95. **CONTACT ADDRESS** Dept of Hist, California State Univ, Fresno, 5340 N Campus Dr, Fresno, CA, 93740-8019.

DINNERSTEIN, LEONARD
PERSONAL Born 05/05/1934, New York, NY, m, 1961, 2 children **DISCIPLINE** AMERICAN HISTORY **EDUCATION** City Col New York, BSS, 55; Columbia Univ, MA, 60, PhD(Am hist), 66. **CAREER** Lectr Am hist & Am govt, NY Inst Technol, 60-65; lectr hist, City Col New York, 66-67; asst prof, Fairleigh Dickinson Univ, 67-70; assoc prof to prof Am Hist, Univ Ariz, 70-, dir Judaic Studies, 93-; NEH fel, 70, 77, 78, 85, 87, 89, 91-92; dir NEH Summer Seminars for Col Teachers, 80, 83: Minorities in the Southwest, Univ Ariz. **HONORS AND AWARDS** Anisfield-Wolf Award, 69; National Jewish Book Award, 94; Myers Ctr Award for the Study of Hum Rights in Am, 94. **MEMBERSHIPS** AHA; Orgn Am Historians; Asn Jewish Hist Soc; Immigration Hist Soc. **RESEARCH** American immigration; American Jewish history; 20th century America. **SELECTED PUBLICATIONS** Auth, The Leo Frank Case, Columbia Univ, 68; co-ed, The Aliens, Appleton, 70; American Vistas, Oxford Univ, 71, 75, 79, 83, 87, 91, 95; ed, Antisemitism in the United States, Holt, 72; co-ed, Jews in the South, La State Univ, 73; Decisions and Revisions, Praeger, 75; coauth, Ethnic Americans, 77 & Natives and Strangers, 79, 89, 96, Oxford Univ; auth, America and the Survivors of the Holocaust, Columbia Univ, 82; Antisemitism in America, Oxford, 94. **CONTACT ADDRESS** Judaic Studies, Univ Ariz, 1 University of Az, PO Box 210080, Tucson, AZ, 85721-0080. **EMAIL** dinnerst@u.arizona.edu

DIONNE, E.J.
DISCIPLINE GOVERNMENT **EDUCATION** Harvard Univ, BA, 73; Oxford Univ, PhD, 82. **CAREER** Sr Fel, Govt Stud, Brookings Inst; columnist, editorial writer, reporter, Washington Post; reporter, NY Times; former corresp in Paris, Rome & Beirut. **HONORS AND AWARDS** Guest scholar, Woodrow Wilson Int Ctr. **RESEARCH** Elections; public opinion; conservative and liberal ideology; civil society; journalism. **SELECTED PUBLICATIONS** Auth, They Only Look Dead: Why Progressives Will Dominate the Next Political Era, Simon & Schuster, 96; auth, Why Civil Society? Why Now, Brookings Rev, 97; ed, Community Works: The Revival of Civil Society in America, 98. **CONTACT ADDRESS** The Brookings Inst, 1775 Massachusetts Ave NW, Washington, DC, 20036.

DIPPIE, BRIAN WILLIAM
PERSONAL Born 09/05/1943, Edmonton, AB, Canada, m, 1965 **DISCIPLINE** AMERICAN HISTORY **EDUCATION** Univ Alta, BA, 65; Univ Wyo, MA, 66; Univ Tex, Austin, PhD (Am civilization), 70. **CAREER** Asst prof, 70-75, ASSOC PROF HIST, UNIV VICTORIA, BC, 75-. **MEMBERSHIPS** Can Asn for Am Studies; Popular Cult Asn; Western Hist Asn; Western Lit Asn. **RESEARCH** American cultural history; Western American literature and art; American Indian. **SELECTED PUBLICATIONS** Auth, Hokahey--A Good Day to Die--The Indian Casualties of the Custer Fight, Montana Mag W Hist, Vol 46, 96; Government Patronage--Catlin, Stanley, and Eastman, Montana- Mag W Hist, Vol 44, 94; The Custer Autograph Album, Montana Mag W Hist, Vol 46, 96; Reflections on A Reputation, Montana Mag W Hist, Vol 47, 97; Remington, Frederic and Russell, Charles,M., Montana Mag W Hist, Vol 47, 97; Art of the American Indian Frontier, Montana Mag W Hist, Vol 43, 93; Big Eyes--The Southwestern Photographs of Schwemberger, Simeon, 1902-1908, Am Indian Cult Rsc J, Vol 17, 93; California Grandeur and Genre, Montana Mag W Hist, Vol 43, 93; Last Stand at Little Bighorn, Public Hist, Vol 15, 93; Campaigning With King, King, Charles, Chronicler of the Old Army, Am Indian Cult Rsc J, Vol 16, 92; Visions of America Since 1492, Am Indian Cult Rsc J, Vol 21, 97; Captain Crawford, Jack--Buckskin Poet, Scout, and Showman, Am Hist Rev, Vol 100, 95; Encounters With A Distant Land--Exploration and the Great Northwest, Pac Hist Rev, Vol 65, 96; First Artist of the West--Catlin, George Paintings Aad Watercolors, J West, Vol 36, 97; Prints of the West, W Hist Quart, Vol 27, 96; Art and Empire--The Politics of Ethnicity in the United States Capitol, 1815-1860, J Am Hist, Vol 80, 94; What Valor Is , Montana Maga W Hist, Vol 46, 96; Our Chiefs and Elders--Words and Photographs of Native Leaders, Montana Mag W Hist, Vol 44, 94; March of the Columns--A Chronicle of the 1876 Indian War, June 27 September 16, Montana Mag W Hist, Vol 46, 96. **CONTACT ADDRESS** Dept of Hist, Univ of Victoria, Victoria, BC, V8W 2Y2.

DIRENZO, GORDON JAMES
PERSONAL Born 07/19/1934, North Attleboro, MA, m, 1968, 3 children **DISCIPLINE** SOCIOLOGY **EDUCATION** Univ Notre Dame, BA, 56, AM, 57, PhD, 63. **CAREER** Instr, Univ Portland, 61-62; asst prof of sociology, Fairfield Univ, 62-66; assoc prof of sociology, 66-70; UNIV DEL, PROF OF SOCIOLOGY, 70-. **HONORS AND AWARDS** Fulbright-Hays Prof of Sociology, Univ Rome, 68-69, Univ Bologna, 80-81. **MEMBERSHIPS** Am Sociol Asn; Am Psychol Asn. **RESEARCH** Interaction of personality systems and social systems. **SELECTED PUBLICATIONS** Auth, Personality and Society, Simon & Shuster, 98; The Social Individual, Ginn Press, 96; Human Social Behavior, Hold, Rinehart & Winston, 90; We, the People: American Character and Social Change, Greenwood Press, 77; Personality and Politics, Doubleday and Company, 74; Personality, Power and Politics, Univ of Notre Dame Press, 67; Concepts, Theory and Explanation in the Behavioral Sciences, Random House, 66. **CONTACT ADDRESS** Dept of Sociology, Univ Del, Newark, DE, 19716.

DIRKS, NICHOLAS
DISCIPLINE SOUTH ASIAN HISTORY **EDUCATION** Wesleyan Univ, BA, 72; Univ Chicago, PhD, 78. **CAREER** Prof. **SELECTED PUBLICATIONS** Auth, The Home and the Nation: Consuming Culture and Politics in Roja, 98. **CONTACT ADDRESS** Dept of History, Columbia Col, New York, 2960 Broadway, New York, NY, 10027-6902.

DIRKS, PATRICIA
PERSONAL ON, Canada **DISCIPLINE** HISTORY **EDUCATION** Queen's Univ, BA, 63, MA, 66; Univ Toronto, PhD, 72. **CAREER** Lectr, SUNY Buffalo, 70-71; lectr to asst prof, 71-90, ASSOC PROF, BROCK UNIV 90-. **MEMBERSHIPS** Can Hist Asn; Soc Can Studs; Can Inst Int Affairs; Ont Hist Soc. **SELECTED PUBLICATIONS** Auth, Finding the Canadian Way: Origins of the Religious Education Council of Canada, in Studs Rel/Sci Rel, 87; auth, L'Action liberale nationale: A Failed Attempt to Reconcile Modernization with Tradition, 91. **CONTACT ADDRESS** History Dept, Brock Univ, St. Catherines, ON, L2S 3A1. **EMAIL** pdirks@spartan.ac.BrockU.CA

DIRLIK, ARIF
PERSONAL Born 11/23/1940, Mersin, Turkey, m, 1965, 2 children **DISCIPLINE** MODERN CHINESE HISTORY **EDUCATION** Robert Col, Istanbul, BS, 64; Univ Rochester, PhD (hist), 73. **CAREER** From instr to asst prof, 71-77, ASSOC PROF HIST, DUKE UNIV, 77-, Chairperson, Comt on East Asian Studies, 74-; dir, Triangle Univs East Asia Ctr, 75-76; vis prof, Univ Victoria, BC, summer, 80 and Univ BC, 80-81. **MEMBERSHIPS** Asn Asian Studies. **RESEARCH** Marxism in China; modern Chinese historiography; Socialist thought in China; modern Chinese political thought. **SELECTED PUBLICATIONS** Auth, The Postcolonial Aura, 3rd World Criticism in the Age of Global Capitalism, Critical Inquiry, Vol 20, 94; Dialectic of the Chinese Revolution--From Utopianism to Hedonism, Am Hist Rev, Vol 101, 96; Schoolhouse Politicians--Locality and State During the Chinese Republic, Hist, Vol 56, 94; The Genesis of Chinese Communist Foreign Policy, Am Hist Rev, Vol 102, 97; National Culture and the New Global System, J W Hist, Vol 7, 96; The Past as Legacy and Project--Postcolonial Criticism in the Perspective of Indigenous Historicism, Am Indian Cult Rsc J, Vol 20, 96; Confucius in the Borderlands, Global Capitalism and the Reinvention of Confucianism, Boundary 2, Int J Lit Cult, Vol 22, 95; Asia Pacific as Space of Cultural Production--Introduction, Boundary 2, Int J Lit Cult, Vol 21, 94; Socialism and Nationalism in the Ottoman Empire, 1876-1923, Soc Hist, Vol 20, 95; Chinese History and the Question of Orientalism, Hist Theory, Vol 35, 96; Chinese Village, Socialist State, Am Hist Rev, Vol 97, 92; Turbans and Traders--Hong-Kong Indian Communities, Hist, Vol 58, 96; Asians on the Rim--Transnational Capital and Local Community in the Making of Contemporary Asian America, Amerasia J, Vol 22, 96. **CONTACT ADDRESS** Dept of Hist, Duke Univ, Durham, NC, 27706.

DIRST, MATTHEW
PERSONAL Born 09/06/1961, Aurora, IL **DISCIPLINE** MUSICOLOGY, ORGAN, HARPSICHORD **EDUCATION** Univ Ill, BM, 83; Southern Methodist Univ, MM, 85; Stanford Univ, PhD, 96. **CAREER** Lect Harpsichord, Stanford Univ, 94-96; Lect in Mus Hist, San Jose State Univ, 95-96; Asst Prof Music, University of Houston, 96- . **HONORS AND AWARDS** Fulbright Scholar, France, 85-87; Am Guild of Organists Young Artist Compet, 90; 2nd Prize, Warsaw Int Harpsichord Comp, 93. **MEMBERSHIPS** Am Musicol Soc; Am Guild of Organists; Am Organ Inst. **RESEARCH** Bach, Bach reception, Baroque Performance Practice. **SELECTED PUBLICATIONS** Bach's French Overtures and the Politics of Overdotting, Early Mus, Feb 97. **CONTACT ADDRESS** Moores School of Music, Univ of Houston, Houston, TX, 77204-4201. **EMAIL** mdirst@uh.edu

DIUBALDO, RICHARD J.
DISCIPLINE HISTORY OF THE CANADIAN NORTH **EDUCATION** McMaster Univ, BA, MA; Univ W Ontario, PhD. **RESEARCH** Government policy and the Inuit. **SELECTED PUBLICATIONS** Pub(s), extensively on Arctic sovereignty,

Can-US relations, and Can government policy toward the Inuit; auth, Stefansson and the Canadian Arctic. **CONTACT ADDRESS** Dept of Hist, Concordia Univ, Montreal, 1455 de Maisonneuve W, Montreal, PQ, H3G 1M8.

DIVINE, ROBERT ALEXANDER
PERSONAL Born 05/10/1929, Brooklyn, NY, m, 1955, 4 children **DISCIPLINE** AMERICAN HISTORY **EDUCATION** Yale Univ, BA, 51, MA, 52, PhD (hist), 54. **CAREER** From instr to assoc rpof, 54-63, chmn dept, 63-68, prof hist, 63-81, GEORGE W LITTLEFIELD PROF AM HIST, UNIV TEX, AUSTIN, 81-, Fel, Ctr Advan Studies Behav Sci, 62-63; Albert Shaw lectr diplomatic hist, Johns Hopkins Univ, 68; Rockefeller Found humanities fel, 76-77. **MEMBERSHIPS** AHA; Orgn Am Historians; Soc Hist Am Foreign Rels (pres, 76); Am Comt Hist 2nd World War. **RESEARCH** American diplomatic history; United States since 1945; 20th century American history. **SELECTED PUBLICATIONS** Auth, The Crisis Years--Kennedy and Khrushchev, 1960-1963, Dipl Hist, Vol 18, 94; The Cuban Missile Crisis, 1962--A National Security Archive Documents Reader, Dipl Hist, Vol 18, 94; Pearl Harbor Revisited, Int Hist Rev, Vol 18, 96; Cia Documents on the Cuban Missile Crisis, 1962, Dipl Hist, Vol 18, 94; On the Brink--Americans and Soviets Reexamine the Cuban Missile Crisis, Dipl Hist, Vol 18, 94; The Missiles of October--The Declassified Story of Kennedy, John, F. and the Cuban Missile Crisis, Dipl Hist, Vol 18, 94; The Cuban Missile Revisited, Dipl Hist, Vol 18, 94; Lbj and Vietnam--A Different Kind of War, Pac Hist Rev, Vol 64, 95; The Diplomacy of the Crucial Decade--American Foreign Relations During the 1960s, J Am Hist, Vol 82, 95; Desert Storm--The Gulf War and What We Learned, Dipl Hist, Vol 19, 95; Eyeball tEyeball--Inside Story of the Cuban Missile Crisis, Dipl Hist, Vol 18, 94; From Shield to Storm High Tech Weapons, Military Strategy, And Coalition Warfare in the Persian Gulf, Dipl Hist, Vol 19, 95; The Gulf Conflict, 1990-1991--Diplomacy and War in the New World Order, Dipl Hist, Vol 19, 95; The End of the Cold War--Its Meaning and Implications, Rev Am Hist, Vol 21, 93; Presidential Lightning Rods--The Politics of Blame Avoidance, Am Hist Rev, Vol 101, 96; America and the Iraqi Crisis, 1990-1992--Origins and Aftermath, Dipl Hist, Vol 19, 95; Bush,George Vs Hussein, Saddam--Military Success--Political Failure, Dipl Hist, Vol 19, 95; The Fire This Time-United States War Crimes in the Gulf, Dipl Hist, Vol 19, 95; Bush, George War, Dipl Hist, Vol 19, 95; Desert Shield to Desert Storm--The 2nd Gulf War, Dipl Hist, Vol 19, 95; Desert Victory--The War for Kuwait/, Dipl Hist, Vol 19, 95; Storm Over Iraq--Air Power and the Gulf War, Dipl Hist, Vol 19, 95; Guardians of the Gulf--A History of America Expanding Role in the Persian Gulf, 1833-1992, Dipl Hist, Vol 19, 95; Life Under A Cloud--American Anxiety About the Atom, Am Hist Rev, Vol 99, 94. **CONTACT ADDRESS** Dept of Hist, Univ of Tex, 0 Univ of Texas, Austin, TX, 78712-1026.

DIVITA, JAMES JOHN
PERSONAL Born 01/20/1938, Chicago, Ill, m, 1964, 4 children **DISCIPLINE** MODERN EUROPEAN HISTORY **EDUCATION** DePaul Univ, BA, 59; Univ Chicago, AM, 60, PhD(hist), 72. **CAREER** From instr to assoc prof, 61-76, prof, 76-Marian Col, Ind, dept ch, 83-. **HONORS AND AWARDS** Pi Gamma Mu, Outstand Tchr. **MEMBERSHIPS** AHA; Am Cath Hist Asn; Soc Ital Hist Studies; IN Relig Hist Assn; Ital Heritage Soc of Ind; Ind German Herit Soc. **RESEARCH** Western European integration; contemporary Italy; Italian-American history; local ethnic and religious history. **SELECTED PUBLICATIONS** Auth, Ethnic Settlement Patterns in Indpls, Indpls Cathedral; auth, Histories of Assumption, Holy Rosary, Holy Trinity, St. Anthony, St. Christopher paroshes; contrib auth, Encyclopedia of Indpls and Taylor, McBirney, Peopling Ind. **CONTACT ADDRESS** Dept of Hist, Marian Col, 3200 Cold Springs Rd, Indianapolis, IN, 46222-1997. **EMAIL** jdivita@marian.edu

DIXON, LAURINDA S.
PERSONAL Born 09/04/1948, Toledo, OH, m, 1986 **DISCIPLINE** ART HISTORY **EDUCATION** Univ Cincinnati, Coll Conserv Music, BA, 70, MA, 72; Boston Univ,PhD, 80. **CAREER** Dir, Adult Educ, Ind Museum Art, 79; asst prof, John Carroll Univ, 80-81; PROF, SYRACUSE UNIV, 82-. **MEMBERSHIPS** Coll Art Asn; Am Asn Netherlandish Stud; Hist Netherlandish Art; Hermetic Text Soc; Womens Caucus for Art **RESEARCH** Northern European painting; Pre-Enlighten Medicine; Art; Music. **SELECTED PUBLICATIONS** Perilous Chastity: Women and Illness in Pre-Enlightenmnet Art and Medicine, Cornell Univ Press, 95; Nicolas Flamel, His Exposition of the Hieroglyphicall Figures 1624, English Renaissance Hermeticism Vol 2, Garland Press, 94; co-edr, The Documented Image: Visions in Art History, Syracuse Univ Press, 87; "Beware the Wandering Womb: Painterly Reflections of Early Gynecological Theory," Cancer Investigation, 94; "Some Penetrating Insights: The Imagery of Enemas in Art," Art Journal, 93. **CONTACT ADDRESS** Dept Fine Arts, Syracuse Univ, 308 Bowne Hall, Syracuse, NY, 13244-1200. **EMAIL** ldixon@mailbox.syr.edu

DIZARD, JAN
DISCIPLINE AMERICAN STUDIES **EDUCATION** Univ Chicago, PhD. **CAREER** Instr, Univ Chicago; instr, Univ Calif, Berkeley; Charles Hamilton Houston Prof Am Cult, Amherst Col, 69. **RESEARCH** Hunters and their attitudes toward politics and the environment. **SELECTED PUBLICATIONS** Wrote on race rel(s), soc conflict, the contemp Am family and on environmental issues. **CONTACT ADDRESS** Amherst Col, Amherst, MA, 01002-5000.

DJEBAR, ASSIA
DISCIPLINE MEDIEVAL HISTORY **EDUCATION** Univ Paris-Sorbonne, DES, 59. **CAREER** LSU Found Distinguished Prof, La State Univ, Dir, Ctr for Fr and Francophone Stud. **SELECTED PUBLICATIONS** Auth, La Soif, 57; Les Alouttes na(ves, 67; La Nouba des femmes du Mont Chenoua, 79; Femmes d'Alger dans leur appartemement, 80; La Zerda ou les chants d'oubli (film), 82; L'amour la fantasia, 85; Loin de M?dine,91; Le blanc d'Alg?rie, 96. **CONTACT ADDRESS** Dept of Fr Grad Stud, Louisiana State Univ, Baton Rouge, LA, 70803.

DJORDJEVIC, DIMITRIJE
PERSONAL Born 02/27/1922, Belgrade, Yugoslavia, m, 1944, 1 child **DISCIPLINE** MODERN EUROPEAN HISTORY **EDUCATION** Univ Belgrade, BA, 54, PhD (hist), 62. **CAREER** Asst hist, Hist Inst, Serbian Acad Sci, Yugoslavia, 58-63, sr staff mem, 63-69, Inst Balkan Studies, 69-70; chmn Russian area studies, 76-82, PROF HIST, UNIV CALIF, SANTA BARBARA, 70-, Mem, Yugoslav Nat Comt Hist Sci, 64-70; mem, Yugoslav Nat Comt Balkan Studies, 65-70. **MEMBERSHIPS** AHA; Am Asn Advan Slavic Studies. **RESEARCH** History of Southeast Europe in the 19th and 20th century. **SELECTED PUBLICATIONS** Auth, Yugoslavia --The Process of Disintegration, Slavic Rev, Vol 53, 94; The Development of Education in Serbia and Emergence of Its Intelligentsia 1838-1858, Slavic Rev, Vol 56, 97. **CONTACT ADDRESS** Dept of Hist, Univ of Calif, Santa Barbara, CA, 93106.

DMYTRYSHYN, BASIL
PERSONAL Born 01/14/1925, Poland, m, 1949, 2 children **DISCIPLINE** RUSSIAN HISTORY **EDUCATION** Univ Ark, BA, 50, MA, 51; Univ Calif, Berkeley, PhD, 55. **CAREER** Asst res historian, Univ Calif, Berkeley, 55-56; from asst prof to assoc prof, 56-64, PROF HIST, PORTLAND STATE UNIV, 64-, Res assoc, Columbia Univ, 56; curric consult, pub high sch, Portland, Ore, 60-62; vis prof, Univ Ill, Champaign, 64-65; Fulbright-Hays res fel, WGer, 67-68; vis prof, Harvard Univ, 71, Univ Hawaii, 76 and Hokkaido Univ, Japan, 78-79; fel, Kennan Inst, 78. **HONORS AND AWARDS** John Mosser Award, 66 and 67. **MEMBERSHIPS** AHA; Am Asn Advan Slavic Studies; Western Slavic Asn; Conf Slavic and E Europ Hist (secy, 72-75); Can Asn Slavists. **RESEARCH** Russian and modern European history; history of Eastern Europe; Russian expansion to the Pacific and America. **SELECTED PUBLICATIONS** Auth, Russian Imperialism--Development and Crisis, Russian Rev, Vol 56, 97. **CONTACT ADDRESS** Dept of Hist, Portland State Univ, Portland, OR, 97207.

DOANE, ALGER NICOLAUS
PERSONAL Born 08/16/1938, Fairfield, CA, m, 1979, 4 children **DISCIPLINE** ENGLISH & MEDIEVAL EUROPEAN LITERATURE **EDUCATION** Univ CA, Berkeley, BA, 61, MA, 63; Univ Toronto, PhD, 71. **CAREER** Lectr Eng, Victoria Univ Wellington, 65-71; asst prof, 71-77, assoc prof, 77-89, prof eng, Univ WI-Madison, 90, Am Coun Learned Soc fel, 73-74. **HONORS AND AWARDS** NEH summer stipend, 76; NEH proj grant, 94. **MEMBERSHIPS** Mediaeval Acad Am; ISAS. **RESEARCH** Old Eng poetry. **SELECTED PUBLICATIONS** Auth, Anglo Saxon Manuscripts, Orality and Texuality, 74; ed, Genesis A: A New Edition, Univ Wis, 78; The Saxon Genesis 991, 91; co-auth (with C P Posterneck) Vox Intexta: Orality and Texuality in the Middle Ages, 91; co-ed, Anglo-Saxon Manuscripts in Microfiche Facsimile. **CONTACT ADDRESS** Dept of Eng, Univ of Wisconsin, 600 North Park St, Madison, WI, 53706-1403. **EMAIL** andoane@facstaff.wisc.edu

DOBBS, BETTY JO (TEETER)
PERSONAL Born 10/19/1930, Camden, AR, m, 1953, 4 children **DISCIPLINE** HISTORY OF SCIENCE, INTELLECTUAL HISTORY **EDUCATION** Hendrix Col, BA, 51; Univ Ark, Fayetteville, MA, 53; Univ NC, Chapel Hill, PhD (hist), 74. **CAREER** Asst prof, 75-76, ASSOC PROF HIST, NORTHWESTERN UNIV, 76-, N Atlantic Treaty Orgn fel hist of sci, 74-75 and Nat Humanities Ctr, 78-79. **MEMBERSHIPS** Hist Sci Soc; Soc Hist Alchemy and Chem; Brit Soc Hist Sci; Am Chem Soc. **RESEARCH** Sir Isaac Newton; history of chemistry; history of alchemy. **SELECTED PUBLICATIONS** Auth, Newton as Final Cause and 1st Mover, Isis, Vol 85, 94; The Life of Newton, Isaac, Isis, Vol 85, 94; Newton , Isaac--Adventurer in Thought, Isis, Vol 85, 94. **CONTACT ADDRESS** Dept of Hist, Northwestern Univ, Harris Hall, Evanston, IL, 60201.

DOBSON, JOHN MCCULLOUGH
PERSONAL Born 07/20/1940, Las Cruces, NM, m, 1963 **DISCIPLINE** AMERICAN HISTORY **EDUCATION** Mass Inst Technol, BS, 62; Univ Wis, MS, 64, PhD (hist), 66. **CAREER** Asst prof hist, Chico State Col, 66-67; foreign serv off, Dept State, Washington, DC, 67-68; from asst prof to assoc prof, 68-78, PROF HIST, IOWA STATE UNIV, 78-, Historian, US Int Trade Comn, 76; Fulbright lectr, Univ Col, Dublin, 79-80. **MEMBERSHIPS** AHA; Orgn Am Historians. **RESEARCH** Nineteenth century United States history; political and diplomatic history. **SELECTED PUBLICATIONS** Auth, The Tariff Question in The Gilded Age--The Great Debate of 1888, Am Hist Rev, Vol 101, 96. **CONTACT ADDRESS** Dept of Hist, Iowa State Univ, Ames, IA, 50011-0002.

DOCKERY, DAVID S.
PERSONAL Born 10/28/1952, Tuscaloosa, AL, m, 1975, 3 children **DISCIPLINE** HISTORY; RELIGION **EDUCATION** Texas Christian Univ, MA, 86; Univ TX, PhD, 88. **CAREER** Dean & Acad VP, S Baptist Theol Sem, 88-96; pres, Union Univ, 96-. **HONORS AND AWARDS** Who's Who Relig; Who's Who Bibl Studies **MEMBERSHIPS** Soc Bibl Lit; Inst Bibl Res; Amer Acad Relig; Evangelical Theol Soc **RESEARCH** New Testament Studies; Hermeneutics; Baptist Theology. **SELECTED PUBLICATIONS** Auth, New Dimensions in Evangelical Thought, Intervarsity; Our Blessed Hope, LifeWay; Christian Scripture, Broadman & Holman; Biblical Interpretation Then and Now, Baker; auth, Ephesians, Convention; Holman Bible Handbook, Holman. **CONTACT ADDRESS** 1050 Union Univ Dr., Jackson, TN, 38305. **EMAIL** ddockery@buster.uu.edu

DODDS, DENNIS R.
PERSONAL Born 03/04/1940, OK, m, 1991, 1 child **DISCIPLINE** ARCHITECTURE; CITY PLANNING; URBAN DESIGN; ARCH. HISTORY (ISLAMIC) **EDUCATION** Ariz State Univ, B Arch, 69; Univ Pa, M Arch, 72.; MCP, 73; **CAREER** Pres, Dennis R. Dodds & Assoc. **HONORS AND AWARDS** Medal, Azerbaijan Acad of Sci and Archit; Medal, Alpha Rho Chi; AIA fel; McMillen Award for Scholar in Islamic Textiles. **MEMBERSHIPS** Soc of Archit Historians **RESEARCH** Islamic art & architecture; Early Turkish carpet weaving. **SELECTED PUBLICATIONS** Auth, Oriental Rugs in the Virginia Museum of Fine Art; auth with Murray Eiland, Jr., Oriental Rugs in Atlantic Collections. **CONTACT ADDRESS** PO Box 4312, Philadelphia, PA, 19118.

DODDS, GORDON B.
PERSONAL Born 03/12/1932, Milwaukee, WI, m, 5 children **DISCIPLINE** HISTORY **EDUCATION** Harvard, AB, 54; Univ of IL, AM, 55; Univ of WI, PhD, 58 **CAREER** Inst, Asst Prof, 58-66, Knox Col; Assoc Prof, Prof, 66-, Portland St Univ **MEMBERSHIPS** West Hist Asn **RESEARCH** Pacific NW Hist **SELECTED PUBLICATIONS** Auth, Varieties of Hope: An Anthology of Oregon Prose, OR St Univ Press, 93 **CONTACT ADDRESS** Dept of History, Portland State Univ, PO Box 751, Portland, OR, 97207-0751.

DODGE, TIMOTHY
PERSONAL Born 04/15/1957, Boston, MA **DISCIPLINE** LIBRARY SCIENCE & HISTORY **EDUCATION** Swarthmore Col, BA, 79; Columbia Univ, MLS, 80; Univ NH, MA, 82 PhD, 92. **CAREER** Librn, Univ NH, 82-84, 87-92; librn, Barry Univ, 84-87; librn, Auburn Univ, 92-. **HONORS AND AWARDS** Prof Achievement Award, 86-87, Barry Univ. **MEMBERSHIPS** Am Libr Asn; Ala Libr Asn; Asn Col & Res Librs; Ala Asn Col & Res Librs; Psi Gamma Mu; Phi Alpha Theta; Org Am Hist; NH Hist Society. **RESEARCH** Modern American history; library science. **SELECTED PUBLICATIONS** Auth, art, From Spirituals to Gospel Rap: Gospel Music Periodicals, 94; auth, art, Crime and Punishment in New Hampshire, 1812-1914, 95; auth, Poor Relief in Durham, Lee, and Madbury, New Hamshire, 1732-1891, 95; auth, art, US Department of Commerce CD-ROM Serial Databases, 96; auth art, Criminal Justice Web Sites, 98. **CONTACT ADDRESS** 1772 Lee Rd 88, Waverly, AL, 36879. **EMAIL** dodgeti@mail.auburn.edu

DOENECKE, JUSTUS D.
PERSONAL Born 03/05/1938, Brooklyn, NY, m, 1970 **DISCIPLINE** HISTORY **EDUCATION** Colgate Univ, BA, 60; Princeton Univ, MA, 62, PhD, 66. **CAREER** Instr, Colgate Univ, 63-64; Instr to Asst Prof, Ohio Wesleyan Univ, 65-69; Asst Prof to Assoc Prof, New Col, 69-75; Assoc Prof, 75-77, Prof Hist, New Col, Univ S Fla, 77-. **HONORS AND AWARDS** Phi Beta Kappa; Woodrow Wilson Nat Fel, 60; Danforth Fel, 60; Arthur S. Link Prize for Documentary Editing, Soc Hist Am For Relations, 91. **MEMBERSHIPS** Am Hist Asn; Peace Hist Soc (coun 75-79, 98-); Soc Hist Am For Relations (program co-chair 86, Link Award Comt, 92-); Am Soc Church Hist; Hist Soc Episcopal Church. **RESEARCH** American isolationism and pacifism; the gilded age. **SELECTED PUBLICATIONS** Auth, When the Wicked Rise: American Opinion-makers and the Manchurian Crisis, 1931-1933, Bucknell Univ Press, 84; Anti-Intervention: A Bibliographical Introduction to Isolationism and Pacifism from World War I to the Early Cold War, Garland, 87; In Danger Undaunted: The Anti-Interventionist Movement of 1940-1941 as Revealed in the Pa-

pers of the America First Committee, Hoover Inst Press, 90; coauth, From Isolation to War, 1931-1941, Harlan Davidson, 2nd ed, 91; auth, The Battle Against Intervention, 1939-1941, Krieger, 97. **CONTACT ADDRESS** Social Science Division, New Col of the Univ of So Florida, Sarasota, FL, 34243-2197. **EMAIL** doenecke@virtu.sar.usf.edu

DOENGES, NORMAN ARTHUR
PERSONAL Born 08/23/1926, Ft Wayne, IN, m, 1952, 3 children **DISCIPLINE** ANCIENT HISTORY, CLASSICS **EDUCATION** Yale Univ, BA, 47; Oxford Univ, BA, 49; Princeton Univ, MA, 51, PhD (classics), 54. **CAREER** Instr classics, Princeton Univ, 49-50 and 52-53; from instr to assoc prof, 55-65, chmn dept classics, 59-63, 67-71 and 78-79, chmn div humanities, 63-67, assoc dean fac, 64-66, prof-in-chg, Intercol Ctr Class Studies, Rome, Italy, 66-67, PROF CLASSICS, DARTMOUTH COL, 65-, Mem managing comt, Am Sch Class Studies; mem adv coun, Am Acad in Rome. **MEMBERSHIPS** Soc Prom Hellenic Studies; Am Philol Asn; Class Asn Can; Class Asn New Eng(secy-treas, 63-68); Asn of Ancient Historians. **RESEARCH** Greek and Roman history; Greek pseudonymic letters. **SELECTED PUBLICATIONS** Auth, Ostracism and the Boulai of Kleisthenes, Hist Zeitschrift Alte Geschichte, Vol 45, 96. **CONTACT ADDRESS** Dept of Classics, Dartmouth Col, Hanover, NH, 03755.

DOHERTY, LILLIAN E.
DISCIPLINE GREEK AND LATIN LITERATURE **EDUCATION** St Mary's Col, BA; Univ Notre Dame, MA; Univ Chicago, PhD. **CAREER** Instr, George Mason Univ; Howard Univ; asst prof, 87; assoc prof, 93-. **HONORS AND AWARDS** Affil, women's stud prog; comp lit prog. **SELECTED PUBLICATIONS** Auth, Tyro in Odyssey 11: Closed and Open Readings, Helios, 92; Gender and Internal Audiences in the Odyssey, Amer Jour of Philol, 92; Siren Songs: Gender, Audiences, and Narrators in the Odyssey, Univ Mich Press, 95; Sirens, Muses and Female Narrators in the Odyssey, The Distaff Side: Representing the Female in Homer's Odyssey, Oxford UP, 95 y **CONTACT ADDRESS** Dept of Class, Univ MD, 4229 Art-Sociology Building, College Park, MD, 20742-1335. **EMAIL** LL21@umail.umd.edu

DOLAN, JAY P.
DISCIPLINE AMERICAN RELIGIOUS HISTORY **EDUCATION** Gregorian Univ, Italy, STL, 62; Univ Chicago, PhD, 70. **CAREER** Asst prof, Univ San Francisco, 70-71; asst prof, 71-77, dir, Ctr for Stud of Am Cath, 77-93, assoc prof, 77-86, prof, Univ Notre Dame, 86-; Fulbright prof, Univ Col, Ireland, 86; vis instr, Boston Col, 91; chemn, publ ser, Notre Dame Stud in Am Cath, Univ Notre Dame Press, 77-93; publ comt, Immigration Hist Soc, 77-80; ed bd, J of Am Ethnic Hist, 80-; ed bd, Church Hist, 82-86; ed bd, Hebrew Un Co-Jewish Inst of Relig, 84-89; ed bd, Sources of Am Spirituality, publ ser, Paulist Press, 86-90; ed bd, Statue of Liberty-Ellis Island Centennial publ ser, Univ Ill Press, 86-; assoc ed, Am Nat Biogr Mid-America, 88-; assoc ed, Am Nat Biogr, 89-; ed bd, Rel and Am Cult: J of Interp, 89-; ed bd, Church Hist, 94-. **HONORS AND AWARDS** Rockefeller fel, Univ Chicago, 69-70; O'Brien Fund grant, Univ Notre Dame, 72; fac res grant, Univ Notre Dame, 73; fel, Princeton Univ, 73-74; John Gilmary Shea Award, Am Cath Hist Asn, 75; res grant, Word of God Inst, 76; Frank O'Malley Award, Univ Notre Dame, 77; fel, Am Coun of Learned Soc, 78-79; fac develop grant, Univ Notre Dame, 80; Alumnus of the Yr, Univ Chicago, 87; Emily Schossberger Award, Univ Notre Dame Press, 88; res grant Lilly Endowment, 81, 81-87, 83-84, 86-88, 90-93, 91-92. **MEMBERSHIPS** Pres, Am Soc of Church Hist, 87; pres, Am Cath Hist Asn, 95; Immigration Hist Soc; Am Acad of Relig. **SELECTED PUBLICATIONS** Auth, Patterns of Leadership in the Congregation, in James P Wind and James W Lewis, eds, American Congregations, vol 2: New Perspectives in the Study of Congregations, Univ Chicago Press, 94; Conclusion, in Jay P Dolan and Allan Figueroa Deck, SJ, eds, Hispanic Catholic Culture in the U.S., Univ Notre Dame Press, 94; The People As Well As The Prelates: A Social History of a Denomination, in R Mullin and R Richey, eds, Reimagining Denominationalism: Interpretive Essays, Oxford UP, 94; coed, Mexican Americans and the Catholic Church. 1900-1965, Univ Notre Dame Press, 94; Puerto Rican and Cuban Catholics in the U.S. 1900-1965, Univ Notre Dame Press, 94; Hispanic Catholic Culture in the U.S.: Issues and Concerns, Univ Notre Dame Press, 94. **CONTACT ADDRESS** Dept of Hist, Univ Notre Dame, Notre Dame, IN, 46556.

DOLCE, PHILIP CHARLES
PERSONAL Born 11/23/1941, New York, NY, m, 1966, 2 children **DISCIPLINE** AMERICAN HISTORY **EDUCATION** St John's Univ, NY, BA, 63; Fordham Univ, MA, 66, PhD(Am Hist), 71; Management Development Program Certificate, Harvard Univ, 91. **CAREER** Teacher hist, St Helena's High Sch, 63-66; lectr Am hist, St John's Univ, 66-68, instr, 68-71; asst prof, 71-75, assoc prof Am hist, Bergen Commun Col, 75-79, coordr Pub Media progr, 73-80, Bus mgr, J Social Hist, 70-72; Harry S Truman Libr Inst grant, 72; creator, producer & moderator of many TV & radio progs; vchairperson, Am Asn Commun Jr Cols; instr, Telecommun Consortium; exec dir, Eastern Educ Consortium; assoc, Columbia Univ Seminar on the City. **HONORS AND AWARDS** Finalist Award, Int Film and Television Festival, 87; ACE nomination, Distinguished Programming Achievement, 87; Admin Innovation and Team Leadership Award, AAU Admin, 90; First Place Award Personality Profile and Public Service Radio Reporting, N Jersey Press Club, 93; First Place Awards for Radio Feature Reporting and Sports Feature Reporting, 94; Finalist Award for Social commitment, Global Int Healthcare Commun Competition, 95; First Place Award for Sports Reporting, 96 and First Place Award Public Service Award, 97, North Jersey Press Club; Four TV Series created and produced now part of the permanent collection of Museum of Radio and Television, 97, one part of permanent collection of National Archives, 99. **MEMBERSHIPS** Oral Hist Asn; Orgn Am Historians; AHA; Ctr Study Presidency. **RESEARCH** American urban and suburban history; American presidential history. **SELECTED PUBLICATIONS** Co-ed, Cities in transition: From the Ancient World to Urban America, Nelson-Hall, 73; ed, Surburbia: The American Dream and Dilemma, Doubleday, 11/76; co-ed, Power and the Presidency, Scribner, 76; creator & producer of CBS TV ser, Paradox of power: US foreign policy, 78; Suburbia: The promised land, 79; Asia: Half the human race, 79; Metropolitan America, 80; Post industrial America: Economic strategies for the 1980's, 81; produce TV documentary The Cubans of New Jersey, 87; producer and host of Weekly WPAT radio program Suburbia: The American Dream and Dilemma, 98-97. **CONTACT ADDRESS** Dept of Soc Sci, Bergen Comm Col, 400 Paramus Rd, Paramus, NJ, 07652-1595.

DOLNIKOWSKI, EDITH W.
PERSONAL Born 07/21/1959, Pittsburgh, PA, m, 1980 **DISCIPLINE** HISTORY **EDUCATION** Coll of Wooster, BA, 81; Michigan State Univ, PhD, 84, PhD, 89. **CAREER** Asst to the Rector, 97, Priest-in-Charge, 96, Deacon, 95-96, Ministry Intern, 94-95, The Church of Our Saviour, Brookline, Massachusetts; Kellogg Fellow for Ministry in Higher Edu, 93-94, Field Edu Minister, 90-92, The Harvard-Radcliffe Episcopal Chaplaincy; Instr, 89-90, Univ of Nebraska; Instr, 88-89, Univ of Warwick, United Kingdom; Undergraduate Adviser, Dept of Hist, 85-86, Res Asst, Dept of Hist, 84-85, Graduate Tchg Asst, Dept of Hist, 81-84, Michigan State Univ. **HONORS AND AWARDS** Fulbright Res Grant; Michigan State Univ Arts and Letters Graduate Fellowship; Phi Kappa Phi; Phi Beta Kappa; Dept Honors. **MEMBERSHIPS** AMA, ASCH, Medieval Acad of Amer, AAR, Intl Medieval Sermon Studies Soc; Soc for Medieval Feminist Scholarship. **RESEARCH** Late Medieval Theology, English and Latin Sermons. **SELECTED PUBLICATIONS** Auth, Time and Memory in the Thought of Thomas Bradwardine, in: Disputatio, Vol II, Constructions of Time in the Late Middle Ages, eds, C Poster & R Utz, Northwestern Univ Press, 97; Feminine Exemplars of Reform: Women's Voices in John Foxe's Acts and Monuments, Women Preachers and Prophets through Two Millenia fo Christianit, eds, B Mayne & PJ Walker, Univ of California Press, 98; Thomas Bradwardine's Sermo epinicius: Some Reflections on it's Political, Theological and Pastoral Significance, Medieval Sermons and Society, Cloister, City, UnivTextes et etudes du moyen, 9, eds, Federation Internationale des Instituts d'Etudes Medievales, 98. **CONTACT ADDRESS** 59 Lincoln St, Natick, MA, 01760. **EMAIL** Dolnikowski@juno.com

DOLSKAYA-ACKERLY, OLGA
DISCIPLINE MUSIC HISTORY **EDUCATION** Manhattan Sch Mus, Master of Mus; Univ Kans, MS, PhD. **CAREER** Assoc prof, Univ Mo, Kansas City. **RESEARCH** The Moscow Baroque. **SELECTED PUBLICATIONS** Her publications include transcriptions of seventeenth-century Russian choral works in Monuments of Russian Sacred Music, a facsimile edition of a 17th-century collection of polyphonic songs in Russia, and articles on various aspects of Russian music. **CONTACT ADDRESS** Univ Mo, Kansas City, Kansas City, MO, 64110-2499. **EMAIL** admit@umkc.edu

DOMINGUEZ, JORGE IGNACIO
PERSONAL Born 06/02/1945, Cuba, m, 1967, 2 children **DISCIPLINE** POLITICAL SCIENCE **EDUCATION** Yale Univ, AB 67; Harvard Univ, AM 68, PhD 72. **CAREER** Harvard Univ, asst prof 72-77, assoc prof 77-79, prof 79-, Clarence Dillon Prof of Intl Aff and Dir of the Weatherhead Cen for Intl Aff at Harvard. **HONORS AND AWARDS** Harvard Coll Prof Awd; Dist Fulbright vis prof **MEMBERSHIPS** LASA; NECLAS; ICS; APSA **RESEARCH** Latin American politics, domestic and intl **SELECTED PUBLICATIONS** Democratic Politics in Latin America and the Caribbean, John Hopkins Univ Press, 98; International Security and Democracy: Latin America and the Caribbean in the Post Cold War Era, Pitts PA, Univ Pitts Press 98; From Pirates to Drug Lords: The Post Cold War Caribbean Environment, co-ed, Albany, State Univ NY Press 98; Technopolis: Freeing Politics and Markets in Latin America in the 1900s, Univ Pk, Penn State Press, 97; Democratic Transitions in Central America, with M. Lindenberg, Gainesville, Univ Press FL, 97; Constructing Democratic Governance: Latin America and the Caribbean in the 1900s, with A. Lowenthal, Baltimore, John Hop Univ Press, 96. **CONTACT ADDRESS** Weatherhead Cen for Intl Affairs, Harvard Univ, 1737 Cambridge St, Cambridge, MA, 02138. **EMAIL** jorge_dominguez@harvard.edu

DOMINICK, RAYMOND
PERSONAL Born 10/18/1945, Atlanta, GA, m, 1 child **DISCIPLINE** EUROPEAN HISTORY **EDUCATION** Univ NC, PhD, 73 **CAREER** Instr, 73-74, asst prof, 74-80, assoc prof, Univ NC, 80-92; Prof Hist,Ohio St Univ-Mansfield, 92-. **HONORS AND AWARDS** Sr Fulbright Fel, Jena, 95; Outstanding Publ Award, Ohio Hist Acad, 92; Outstanding Tchr, Mansfield, 84. **MEMBERSHIPS** Ger Stud Asn; Am Soc Environ Hist. **RESEARCH** History of the Environmental Movement. **SELECTED PUBLICATIONS** Auth, Wilhelm Liebknecht and the Founding of the German Social Democratic Party, Univ NC,82; Nascent Environmental Protection in the Second German Empire, Ger Studies Rev, 86; The Nazis and the Nature Conservationists, The Hist, 87; The Roots of the Green Movement in West Germany and the USA, Environ Rev, 88); The Environmental Movement in Germany: Prophets and Pioneers, 1871-1971, Ind Univ, 92; . **CONTACT ADDRESS** Ohio State Univ, Mansfield, 1680 University Dr., Mansfield, OH, 44906. **EMAIL** dominick.1@osu.edu

DOMINOWSKI, ROGER L.
PERSONAL Born 02/21/1939, Chicago, IL, m, 1984, 4 children **DISCIPLINE** PSYCHOLOGY **EDUCATION** DePaul Univ, BA, 60, MA, 63; Northwestern Univ, PhD, 65. **CAREER** Instr, Asst Prof, DePaul Univ, 62-66; Asst Prof, Prof, Univ Ill at Chicago, 66-. **HONORS AND AWARDS** Postdoctoral Res Fellow, Univ Aberdeen, Scotland, 72-73; Excellence in Tchng Award, Univ Ill at Chicago, 98. **MEMBERSHIPS** Am Psychol Soc; Brit Psychol Soc; Sigma Xi; Psychonomic Soc. **RESEARCH** Psychology of problem solving, reasoning, & creativity; teaching processes. **SELECTED PUBLICATIONS** Co-auth, History of research on thinking and problem solving, Thinking and Problem Solving: Handbook of Cognition and Perception, 2nd ed, Acad Press, 1-35, 94; co-auth, Insight and problem solving, The nature of Insight, MIT Press, 31-62, 95; auth, Productive problem solving, The creative cognition approach, MIT Press, 73-96, 95; co-auth, Metacognition and problem solving: A process oriented approach, J of Experimental Psychol: Learning, Memory, & Cognition, 21, 205-223, 95; auth, Verbalization and problem solving, Metacognition in educational theory and practice, 98. **CONTACT ADDRESS** Dept of Psychol, m/c 285, Univ Ill at Chicago, 1007 W Harrison St, Chicago, IL, 60617. **EMAIL** rdomin@uic.edu

DONAGHAY, MARIE
PERSONAL Born 01/10/1943, Wilmington, DE **DISCIPLINE** HISTORY **EDUCATION** Univ DE, BA, 65; Univ VA, MA, 67, PhD, 70. **CAREER** Assoc prof, Hist, Radford Col, 70-74; adjunct prof, 83-89, asst prof, 90-92, Hist, Villanova Univ; assoc prof, Hist, East Stroudsburg Univ, 92-. **MEMBERSHIPS** World Hist Asn (treas); Am Hist Asn; Soc for French Hist Studies; Southern Hist Asn. **RESEARCH** France on the eve of the French Revolution, French foreign policy; Anglo-French relations (commercial and diplomatic). **SELECTED PUBLICATIONS** Auth, Comment on a Bit of Total History: the Transfer of Technology between France and Britain during the Eighteenth Century, The Consortium on Revolutionary Europe Proceedings, 1984, Athens, GA, 86; A propos du traite commercial franco-anglais de 1786, Revue d'Histoire Diplomatique, 87; The Vicious Circle: The Anglo-French Commercial Treaty of 1786 and the Dutch Crisis of 1787, Consortium on Revolutionary Europe 1750-1850, Proceedings 1989, Tallahasse, FL, 90; The Exchange of Products of the Soil and Industrial Goods in the Anglo-French Commercial Treaty of 1786, J of European Economic Hist, 90; The French Debate on the Free Trade Treaty of 1786, in Ilaria Zilli, ed, Fra Spazio E Tempo Studi in Onori di Luigi de Rosa, Settecento E Ottocento, Naples, Italy, 95; Britain and France at the Close of the Old Regime, A Commentary, The Consortium on Revolutionary Europe, 1750-1850, selected papers, 1995, Tallahassee, FL, 95; several other publications. **CONTACT ADDRESS** History Dept, East Stroudsburg Univ of Pennsylvania, 200 Prospect St, East Stroudsburg, PA, 18301-2999.

DONAGHY, THOMAS J.
PERSONAL Born 10/20/1928, Sharon Hill, PA **DISCIPLINE** AMERICAN HISTORY **EDUCATION** Cath Univ Am, AB, 51; Univ Pittsburgh, MA, 54, PhD (hist), 60; St Charles Sem, MA, 78. **CAREER** Teacher, Cent Cath High Sch, Pa, 51-55, La Salle High Sch, 55-56 and Cent Cath High Sch, 56-61, assoc prof, 61-72, prof hist, La Salle Col, 72-79, dir summer sessions, 62-72; ACAD DEAN, ST MARY'S SEM AND UNIV, 79-. **HONORS AND AWARDS** MA, St Charles Sem, Philadelphia, 78. **MEMBERSHIPS** AHA; Am Cath Hist Asn; Lexington Group. **RESEARCH** Railway transportation, Great Britain; Colonial Philadelphia; history of educational institutions. **SELECTED PUBLICATIONS** Auth, Villanova University, 1842-1992-American Catholic Augustinian, Cath Histl Rev, Vol 83, 97. **CONTACT ADDRESS** 5450 Roland Ave, Baltimore, MD, 21210.

DONAHOE, BERNARD FRANCIS
PERSONAL Born 03/16/1932, Madison, WI **DISCIPLINE** AMERICAN POLITICAL & INTELLECTUAL HISTORY **EDUCATION** Univ Notre Dame, BA, 55, MA, 59, PhD, 65. **CAREER** Tchr hist, parochial high sch, OH, 56-57 & Ind, 57-61; master novices, St Joseph Novitiate, 64-68; asst prof, Holy

Cross Jr Col, 67-74; asst prof, 68-74, assoc prof hist, St Mary's Col, IN, 74; assoc prof hist Holy Cross Jr Col, 74. **MEMBERSHIPS** AHA; Orgn Am Historians. **RESEARCH** Polit of the New Deal; Am intellectual hist. **SELECTED PUBLICATIONS** Auth, Private Plans and Public Dangers: The Story of FDR's Third Nomination, Univ Notre Dame, 66; coauth, The congressional power to raise armies: The constitutional ratifying conventions, 1787-1788, Rev Polit, 4/71; Politics and Federal-State Programs for the Unemployed: The Case of the Indiana WPA, Humboldt J Social Relations, Vol 6, No 2; The Dictator and the Priest, Prologue, Vol 22, No 6. **CONTACT ADDRESS** Holy Cross Bros Ctr, Notre Dame, IN, 46556. **EMAIL** BDona95309@aol.com

DONAHUE, JOHN F.
DISCIPLINE CLASSICAL STUDIES **EDUCATION** Col Holy Cross, AB, 80; Univ NC at Chapel Hill, MA, 90, PhD, 96. **CAREER** Adj instr; Col William and Mary, 97; adj asst prof, Williamsburg, Va; tchg asst, Med Word Formation and Entymology, 94 & Latin, 91-93, Univ NC at Chapel Hill; Fay Sch, 86-88; UNC res ast, L'Annee Philiologique, 89-91, 94; Latin tutor, 91-93; fact checker, Amer Nat Biog, Oxford UP, 95-. **HONORS AND AWARDS** UNC Grad Sch Dissertation fel, 95; UNC Grad Sch Dept Class Travel Awd(s), 94 & Kappa Delta Pi Honor Soc, Colombia Univ, 84. **MEMBERSHIPS** Amer Philol Asn; Asn Int d'Epigraphie Grecque et Latine; Class Asn Mid W and S. **RESEARCH** Roman social history; Ancient dining; Latin inscriptions. **SELECTED PUBLICATIONS** Auth, Feasts and Females: Sex Roles, Public Recognition and Community Banquets in the Western Roman Empire, Class Asn Mid W and S, Nashville, 96; Public Banqueting in the Roman Empire: Issues for Consideration, Class Asn Mid W and S, Southern Section, Chapel Hill, 94 & Distributions of Bread During the Later Roman Empire: Some Chronological Problems, Class Asn Mid W and S, Atlanta, 94. **CONTACT ADDRESS** Dept of Classical Studies, Col of William and Mary, Morton Hall, PO Box 8795, Williamsburg, VA, 23187-8795. **EMAIL** jfdona@facstaff.wm.edu

DONAKOWSKI, CONRAD L.
PERSONAL Born 03/13/1936, Detroit, MI, m, 1961, 2 children **DISCIPLINE** HISTORY, MUSIC, RELIGION **EDUCATION** Xavier Univ, BA, 58, MA, 59; Columbia Univ, PhD, 69. **CAREER** Instr humanities, Mich State Univ, 66-69; coordr, James Madison Col, Mich State Univ, 67-72; from asst to assoc prof humanities, 69-78, prof, 78-81, prof music hist, Mich State Univ, 81-, asst dean arts & lett, 79-, Am Coun Learned Soc grant, 73. **HONORS AND AWARDS** American Revolutionary Bicentennial Article Prize, Ohio Hist Comt, 76; Rockefeller Found grants, 76 & 77. **MEMBERSHIPS** AHA; Am Soc Eighteenth Century Studies; Am Soc Church Hist; Soc Fr Hist Studies. **RESEARCH** Romanticism; enlightenment; popular culture; nonverbal communication of values; music. **SELECTED PUBLICATIONS** Auth, A Muse for the Masses: Ritual and Music in an Age of Democratic Revolution, Univ Chicago, 77. **CONTACT ADDRESS** Dept of Humanities, Michigan State Univ, 102 Music Bldg, East Lansing, MI, 48824-1043. **EMAIL** donakows@pilot.msu.edu

DONALD, DAVID HERBERT
PERSONAL Born 10/01/1920, Goodman, MS, m, 1955, 1 child **DISCIPLINE** AMERICAN HISTORY **EDUCATION** Millsaps Col, AB, 41; Univ Ill, AM, 42, PhD, 46. **CAREER** Res assoc hist, Univ Ill, 46-47; instr, Columbia Univ, 47-49; assoc prof, Smith Col, 49-51; from asst prof to prof, Columbia Univ, 51-59; prof, Princeton Univ, 59-62; prof, Johns Hopkins Univ, 62-63, Harry C Black Prof Am hist, 63-73; Charles Warren prof Am Hist, PROF EMER, 91- , HARVARD UNIV, 73-91, Prof Am Civilization, 74-91, Chr Grad Prog Am Civilization, 79-85, Vis assoc prof, Amherst Col, 50; Fulbright prof, Univ Col, NWales, Bangor, 54-55; mem, Inst Advan Studies, 57-58; George A & Eliza Gardner Howard fel, 57-58; Harmsworth prof, Oxford Univ, 59-60; Guggenheim fel, 64-65; Am Coun Learned Soc fel, 69-70; fel, Ctr Advan Studies Behav Sci, 69-70; Nat Endowment for Humanities sr fel, 71-72; gen ed, Making of Am Series & Doc Hist Am Life Series; commonwealth lectr, Univ Col London, 76. **HONORS AND AWARDS** Pulitzer Prize Biog, 61 & 88; Lincoln Prize Gettysburg Col, 96; Jefferson Davis Award, Mus Confederacy, 96., MA, Oxford Univ, 59, Harvard Univ, 73; LHD, Millsaps Col, 76; Col Charleston, 85. **MEMBERSHIPS** Orgn Am Historians; Southern Hist Asn; Soc Am Hist; AHA. **RESEARCH** The United States during the Civil War-Reconstruction Period; The Jacksonian Era; Southern history and literature. **SELECTED PUBLICATIONS** Auth, Lincoln's Herndon, 48, Lincoln Reconsidered, 56, rev ed, 61 & Charles Sumner and the Coming of the Civil War, 60, Knopf; coauth, The Civil War and Reconstruction, Heath, 61, rev ed, Little, 69; auth, The Politics of Reconstruction, 1863-1867, La State Univ, 65; Charles Sumner and the Rights of Man, Knopf, 70; coauth, The Great Republic: A History of the American People, 77 & auth, Liberty and Union, 78, DC Heath/Little-Brown; Look Homeward: A Life of Thomas Wolfe, Little-Brown, 87; Lincoln, Simon & Schuster, 95. **CONTACT ADDRESS** PO Box 6158, Lincoln Center, MA, 01773. **EMAIL** dhdonald@ix.netcom.com

DONALDSON, THOMAS
DISCIPLINE ASIAN ART HISTORY **EDUCATION** Wayne State Univ, BFA, 59, MA, 63; Case Western Reserve Univ, PhD, 73. **CAREER** Prof, Cleveland State Univ, 69-. **RESEARCH** Indian painting, Buddhist sculpt, erotic art. **SELECTED PUBLICATIONS** Auth, Hindu Temple Art of Orissa, Leiden, 85-87; Kamadeva's Pleasure Garden-Orissa, Delhi, 87; sch articles, maj intl jour(s). **CONTACT ADDRESS** Dept of Art, Cleveland State Univ, 83 E 24th St, Cleveland, OH, 44115.

DONEGAN, JANE BAUER
PERSONAL Born 09/24/1933, Brooklyn, NY, m, 1981, 2 children **DISCIPLINE** AMERICAN SOCIAL AND CULTURAL HISTORY **EDUCATION** Syracuse Univ, AB, 54, MA, 59, PhD (hist), 72. **CAREER** Teacher Am hist, Fabius Cent Sch, 55-59 and 60-62; teacher Europ hist, Deposit Cent Sch, 59-60; PROF AM HIST, ONONDAGA COMMUNITY COL, 62-, Nat Endowment for Humanities summer grant, 77; State Univ NY fac res fel, 78; Nat Endowment for Humanities fel, 80-81. **MEMBERSHIPS** Orgn Am Historians; Am Asn Hist Med; Soc Social Hist Med; Soc Historians Early Am Repub; AHA. **RESEARCH** American medical history; history of American women; American social and cultural history. **SELECTED PUBLICATIONS** Auth, Medical Protestants--The Eclectics in American Medicine, 1825-1939, Am Hist Rev, Vol 100, 95. **CONTACT ADDRESS** Dept of Soc Sci, Onondaga Comm Col, Syracuse, NY, 13215.

DONHAUSER, PETER L.
DISCIPLINE ART, ARCHITECTURAL HISTORY **EDUCATION** Vassar Col, BA, 81; Columbia Univ, MA, 89; New York Univ, PhD candidate. **CAREER** History teacher, Trinity School, New York City. **SELECTED PUBLICATIONS** Auth, A Key to Uemeer?, Artibus et Historiae, vol XIV, no 27, 93; The Encyclopedia of New York City, Yale Univ Press, 96, entries on the Metropolitan Museum of Art, Brooklyn Museum, Guggenheim Museum, and Cooper-Hewitt Museum. **CONTACT ADDRESS** 1680 York Ave, Apt 6-H, New York, NY, 10028. **EMAIL** pdonhauser@trinity.nyc.ny.us

DONLAN, WALTER
PERSONAL Born 07/30/1934, Boston, MA **DISCIPLINE** CLASSICS **EDUCATION** Harvard Col, BA, 56; Northwestern Univ, PhD, 68. **CAREER** Asst prof to prof, classics, Penn St Univ, 67-86; prof classics, Univ of Calif, Irvine, 86- . **HONORS AND AWARDS** Pres, Class Asn of the Atlantic states, 79-80. **MEMBERSHIPS** Am Philol Asn; Archaeol Inst of Am; Asn of Ancient Hist; Calif Class Asn. **RESEARCH** Early Greek literature, Greek social history. **SELECTED PUBLICATIONS** Auth, Duelling with Gifts in the Illiad: As the Audience Saw It, in Colby Q, 93; coauth, The Village Community of Ancient Greece: Neolithic, Bronze and Dark Ages, in Studi Micenei ed Egeo-Anatolici, 93; auth, Chief and Followers in Pre-State Greece, in From Political Economy to Anthropology: Situating Economic Life in Past Societies, Black Rose, 94; auth, The Homeric Economy, in A New Companion to Homeric Studies, Brill, 97; auth, The Relations of Power in the Pre-State and Early State Politics, in The Development of the Polis in Archaic Greece, Routledge, 97; auth, Political Reciprocity in Dark Age Greece: Odysseus and his Hetairoi, in Reciprocity in Ancient Greece, Oxford,, 97; coauth, Ancient Greece: A Political, Social, and Cultural History, Oxford, 99. **CONTACT ADDRESS** Dept of Classics, Univ California, Irvine, 120 Humanities Office Bldg 2, Irvine, CA, 92697. **EMAIL** wdonlan@uci.edu

DONNELLY, JOHN PATRICK
PERSONAL Born 09/23/1934, Milwaukee, WI **DISCIPLINE** HISTORY **EDUCATION** St Louis Univ, AB, 58, PhL, 59, MA, 63; St Mary's Col, Kans, STL, 67; Univ Wis-Madison, PhD (hist), 71. **CAREER** Asst prof, 71-77, ASSOC PROF HIST, MARQUETTE UNIV, 77-. **MEMBERSHIPS** AHA; Am Soc Reformation Res; Am Cath Hist Asn; Sixteenth Century Studies Conf (pres, 77). **RESEARCH** Sixteenth century Calvinist thought; Counter Reformation; early Jesuits. **SELECTED PUBLICATIONS** Auth, Contarini, Gasparo--Venice, Rome and Reform - Gleason, 16th Century J, Vol 25, 94; The Counterreformation in the Villages--Religion and Reform in the Bishopric of Speyer, 1560-1720, Church Hist, Vol 63, 94; Giambologna--Narrator of the Catholic Reformation - Gibbons,16th Century J, Vol 26, 95; Lippomano, Aloisius 1555-1557, Cath Hist Rev, Vol 81, 95; Acta Nuntiaturae Polonae, Tome Ix--Lauro, Vincenzo 1572-1578, Cath Hist Rev, Vol 82, 96; The Counterreformation in the Villages--Religion and Reform in the Bishopric of Speyer, 1560-1720, Church Hist, Vol 63, 94; The JesuitsIn Milan--Religion and Politics in the 2nd Half of the 16th Century, 16th Century J, Vol 25, 94; Galileo, Bellarmine, and the Bible, J Mod Hist, Vol 65, 93; The Letters and Instructions of Xavier, Francis, Cath Hist Rev, Vol 79, 93; The Elect Nation--The Savonarola Movement in Florence 1494-1545, 16th Century J, Vol 26, 95. **CONTACT ADDRESS** 1404 W Wisconsin Ave, Milwaukee, WI, 53233.

DONOHUE, JOHN WALDRON
PERSONAL Born 09/17/1917, New York, NY **DISCIPLINE** HISTORY & PHILOSOPHY OF EDUCATION **EDUCATION** Fordham Univ, AB, 39; St Louis Univ, MA, 44; Woodstock Col, STL, 51; Yale Univ, PhD, 55. **CAREER** Teacher high sch, NY, 44-47; from assoc prof to prof hist & philos of educ, Sch Educ, Fordham Univ, 55-70, adj prof, 77-80; Assoc Ed, America, 72- . **HONORS AND AWARDS** Mem, Society of Jesus, 39- ; ordained Roman Catholic priest, 50; Trustee, Fordham Univ, 69-77, 78-87, St Peter's Col, 80- ; St Louis Univ, 67-81. **MEMBERSHIPS** Philos Educ Soc; Nat Cath Ed Asn. **RESEARCH** Theory of Christian education; contemporary problems concerning religion and education. **SELECTED PUBLICATIONS** Auth, Work and Education, Loyola Univ, 59; Jesuit Education: An Essay on the Foundations of Its Idea, Fordham Univ, 63; St Thomas Aquinas and Education, Random, 68; Catholicism and Education, Harper, 73. **CONTACT ADDRESS** America 106 W 56th St, New York, NY, 10019.

DONOVAN, MARY ANN
PERSONAL Cincinnati, OH **DISCIPLINE** HISTORICAL THEOLOGY **EDUCATION** St Michaels, Toronto, 77 **CAREER** Prof, 94-pres, Jesuit Sch of Theol, Assoc Prof, 81-94, Assist Prof, 77-81 **HONORS AND AWARDS** Col Theology Bk Award, 98; Elizabeth Seton Medal, Distinguished Woman Theologian **MEMBERSHIPS** Cath Theol Soc of Am; Col Theology Soc; N Amer Patristics Soc; Soc for Study of Christian Spirituality **RESEARCH** History, Spirituality; Early Christianity; Women's Issues **SELECTED PUBLICATIONS** Auth, One Right Reading? A Guide to Irenaeus, Liturgical Press, 97; Auth, Sisterhood as Power, The Past and Passion of Ecclesial Women, Crossroad, 89 **CONTACT ADDRESS** Jesuit Sch of Theol, Berkeley, 1735 LeRoy Ave, Berkeley, CA, 94709. **EMAIL** mdonovan@jstb.edu

DOOLEY, HOWARD JOHN
PERSONAL Born 09/12/1944, Pittsburgh, PA, m, 1972, 2 children **DISCIPLINE** HISTORY, HUMANITIES **EDUCATION** Univ Notre Dame, AB, 66, MA, 70, PhD (hist), 76. **CAREER** Instr hist, 70-73, asst prof humanities, 73-78, dir debate, 75-80, ASSOC PROF HUMANITIES, WESTERN MICH UNIV, 78-, ASST TO DEAN INT EDUC AND PROG, 81-, CONSULT, DIV PUB PROGR, NAT ENDOWMENT HUMANITIES, 77-; TRUSTEE, MICH COUN HUMANITIES, 74-, vchair, 77-78 and 80-82. **MEMBERSHIPS** AHA; Mid E Studies Asn; Am Forensic Asn; World Future Soc. **RESEARCH** Modern Middle East; America since World War I; 20th century Europe. **SELECTED PUBLICATIONS** Auth, The Hashemites in the Modern Arab World--Essays in Honor of the Late Professor Dann, Uriel, Int Hist Rev, Vol 19, 97. **CONTACT ADDRESS** Dept of Humanities Col of Gen Studies, Western Michigan Univ, Kalamazoo, MI, 49008.

DORINSON, JOSEPH
PERSONAL Born 11/15/1936, Jersey City, NJ, m, 1968, 3 children **DISCIPLINE** HISTORY **EDUCATION** Columbia Col, BA, 58; Columbia Univ, MPhil, 76. **CAREER** Instr to prof, chair, 66-, Long Island Univ. **HONORS AND AWARDS** NY St Scholar; NY St Regents Col Teaching Fel, Scholar for study at Oslo Univ, 61; Danforth Associateship, 80-86; NEH Summer Grants, 80, 87, 89, 91; highest rank in student-faculty eval; David Newton Award for Excellence in Teaching, 88. **MEMBERSHIPS** Amer Popular Culture Assoc; DANY. **RESEARCH** Brooklyn hist; sports hist; ethnic hist; Jackie Robinson; Paul Robeson; Frank Sinatra, Jewish humor. **SELECTED PUBLICATIONS** Auth, Anyone Here A Sailor?: Popular Entertainment and the Navy with Dennis Carpenter, Brightlights Publ, 94; auth, The Enigma of Babe Ruth, Nine, 96; art, Marianne Moore & The Brooklyn Dodgers, Long Island Women: Activists and Innovators, Greenwood Press, 98; art, From Jack Johnson to Muhamad Ali: Black Heroes in American Sports, J Popular Culture, 97; art, Jackie Robinson: Man of the Times: Mentsch for All Seasons, NY Times: Newspaper in Educ Curric Guide, 97; auth, Paul Robeson: A Symposium with William Pencok, Pa Hist, 99; coauth, Jackie Robinson: Race, Sports and the American Dream, M E Sharpe, 98. **CONTACT ADDRESS** History Dept, Long Island Univ, 1 University Plaza, Brooklyn, NY, 11201. **EMAIL** jdorinso@hornet.liunet.edu

DORN, JACOB HENRY
PERSONAL Born 09/21/1939, Chicago, IL, m, 1964, 2 children **DISCIPLINE** RECENT AMERICAN HISTORY **EDUCATION** Wheaton Col, Ill, BA, 60; Univ Ore, MA, 62, PhD(hist), 65. **CAREER** From asst prof to assoc prof, 65-74, vpres fac, 77-78, PROF AM HIST, WRIGHT STATE UNIV, 74-, Dir Univ Honors Prog, 72-87. **HONORS AND AWARDS** Danforth Found assoc, 69; Outstanding Educator Am, 74; Wright State Univ Lib Arts Outstanding Teacher, 77; Ohio Acad Hist, Outstanding Teacher Award, 86; Mid-East Honors Asn Leadership Award, 88; Ohio Acad Hist, Distinguished Service Award, 97. **MEMBERSHIPS** AHA; Orgn Am Historians; Am Soc Church Hist; Conf Faith & Hist **RESEARCH** American religious history, late 19th and 20th centuries; 20th century American history, especially social and intellectual history. **SELECTED PUBLICATIONS** Auth, Washington Gladden: Prophet of the Social Gospel, Ohio State Univ, 67; Subsistence Homesteading in Dayton, Ohio, 1933-35, Ohio Hist, spring 69; co-ed, A Bibliography of Sources for Dayton, Ohio, 1850-1950, Wright State Univ, 71; auth, Sunday Afternoon: The Early Social Gospel in Journalism, New England Quart, 6/71; Religion

and the City, in: The Urban Experience: Themes in American History, Wadsworth, 73; The Rural Idea and Agrarian Realities: Arthur E. Holt and the Vision of a Decentralized American in the Interwar Years, Church Hist, 3/83; Religion and Reform in the City: the Re-thinking Chicago Movement in the 1930's, Church Hist, 9/86; Episcopal Priest and Socialist Activitist: The Case of Irwin St. John Tucker, Anglican and Episcopal Hist, 6/92; The Social Gospel and Socialism: A Comparison of the Thought of Francis Greenwood Peabody, Washington Gladden, and Walter Rauschenbusch, Church Hist, 3/93; Washington Gladden and the Social Gospel, in: American Reforms and Reformers, 95. **CONTACT ADDRESS** Dept of Hist, Wright State Univ, 3640 Colonel Glenn, Dayton, OH, 45435-0002. **EMAIL** jdorn@desire.wright.edu

DORNISH, MARGARET HAMMOND
PERSONAL Born 07/25/1934, St. Marys, PA **DISCIPLINE** HISTORY OF RELIGIONS **EDUCATION** Smith Col, AB, 56; Claremont Grad Sch, MA, 67, PhD(relig), 69. **CAREER** Teacher English, Orme Sch, 60-65; asst prof relig, 69-74, assoc prof, 74-92, prof relig & chair, relig studies, Pomona Col, 93-. **MEMBERSHIPS** Am Acad Relig; Pac Coast Theol Soc; Asn Asian Studies; Int Asn Buddhist Studies. **RESEARCH** Buddhist studies. **SELECTED PUBLICATIONS** Auth, D T Suzuki's early interpretation of Buddhism and Zen, Eastern Buddhist, 70. **CONTACT ADDRESS** Dept of Religion, Pomona Col, 551 N College Way, Claremont, CA, 91711-6319. **EMAIL** mdornish@pomona.edu

DORONDO, DAVID R.
DISCIPLINE MODERN GERMANY **EDUCATION** Oxford Univ, PhD. **CAREER** Hist Dept, Western Carolina Univ **SELECTED PUBLICATIONS** Auth, Bavaria and German Federalism: Reich to Republic, 1918-1933, 92. **CONTACT ADDRESS** Western Carolina Univ, Cullowhee, NC, 28723.

DORSETT, LYLE WESLEY
PERSONAL Born 04/17/1938, Kansas City, MO, m, 1970, 2 children **DISCIPLINE** US HISTORY **EDUCATION** Univ Mo, Kansas City, BA, 60, MA, 62; Univ Mo, Columbia, PhD (hist), 65. **CAREER** Asst prof hist, Univ Mo, St Louis, 65-66 and Univ Southern Calif, 66-68; assoc prof, Univ Mo, St Louis, 68-71 and Univ Colo, 71-72; PROF HIST, UNIV DENVER, 72-, Nat Endowment for Humanities fel, 68; Henry Haskell Distinguished Lectr, Univ Mo, Kansas City, 77-78. **HONORS AND AWARDS** W A Whitehead Award, NJ Hist, 77. **MEMBERSHIPS** AHA; Orgn Am Historians; Southern Hist Asn; Western Hist Asn; Conf Faith and Hist. **RESEARCH** Urban history; alcoholism in the 19th century; biography. **SELECTED PUBLICATIONS** Auth, Denver--Mining Camp to Metropolis, J West, Vol 33, 94. **CONTACT ADDRESS** Dept of Hist, Univ of Denver, Denver, CO, 80210.

DORSEY, CAROLYN ANN
PERSONAL Born 1008, AFRICAN-AMERICAN STUDIES, Ohio, s **DISCIPLINE** AFRICAN-AMERICAN STUDIES **EDUCATION** Kent State Univ, BS 1956, MEd 1961; Yale Univ, Danforth Fellow in Black Studies 1969-70; New York Univ, PhD 1976. **CAREER** Cleveland Public Schools, teacher 1956-62; Tabora Girls Sch, Tanzania, E Africa, teacher 1962-64; Cleveland Job Corps Ctr, social studies dept chair & teacher 1965-67; Southern IL Univ Exper in Higher Educ Prog, curriculum spec & instructor 1967-69; Yale Univ Transitional Year Program, assoc dir & teacher, 1969-70; NY Univ Inst of Afro-Amer Affairs, jr fellow 1970-74; IN State Univ, asst prof of afro-amer studies 1976-77; Univ of MO, coord of Black studies & asst prof of higher educ 1977-81, coord of Black studies & assoc prof of higher educ 1981-85, assoc prof of higher educ 1985-, dir of graduate studies, 1986-91. **HONORS AND AWARDS** Danforth Found Black Studies Fellowship yr spent at Yale Univ 1969-70; Southern Fellowship used for Dissertation Study at New York Univ 1973-74; Danforth Found Assoc 1980-86; resident participant in Summer Inst for Women in Higher Educ Admin, Bryn Mawr Coll, 1989; University of Missouri Faculty Award, 1990; University of Missouri Alumnae Anniversary Award for Contributions to the Education of Women, 1990. **MEMBERSHIPS** Stephens Coll Bd of Curators, 1981-91; Amer Assn of Higher Educ, Natl Council for Black Studies; Phi Delta Kappa; Phi Lambda Theta; Assn for the Study of Afro-American Life & History; Alpha Kappa Alpha Sorority; mem of bias panel Amer Coll Testing Program Tests 1982- & The Psychological Corp Stanford Achievement Test, 7th & 8th editions. **CONTACT ADDRESS** Univ of Missouri, 301 Hill Hall, Columbia, MO, 65211.

DORSEY, KURK
DISCIPLINE U.S. FOREIGN RELATIONS, ENVIRONMENTAL HISTORY, CANADA **EDUCATION** Yale Univ, PhD. **CAREER** Asst prof, Univ NH, 95-. **RESEARCH** U.S.-Canadian wildlife protection diplomacy, 1990-1920. **SELECTED PUBLICATIONS** Auth, Putting a Ceiling on Sealing: Conservation and Cooperation in the International Arena, Environ Hist Rev, 91; Scientists, Citizens, Statesmen: U.S.-Canadian Wildlife Protection Treaties in the Progressive Era, Diplomatic Hist, 95. **CONTACT ADDRESS** Univ NH, Durham, NH, 03824. **EMAIL** kd@hopper.unh.edu

DORSEY, LEARTHEN
DISCIPLINE HISTORY OF AFRICA **EDUCATION** Mich State Univ, PhD. **CAREER** Assoc prof Hist & Ethnic Stud, Univ Nebr, Lincoln. **RESEARCH** The colonial economic history of Rwanda. **SELECTED PUBLICATIONS** Auth, Historical Dictionary of Rwanda, Scarecrow Press, 94. **CONTACT ADDRESS** Univ Nebr, Lincoln, 615 Oldfat, Lincoln, NE, 68588-0417. **EMAIL** ldorsey@unlinfo.unl.edu

DORSEY, SCOTT W.
DISCIPLINE MUSIC **EDUCATION** Nebr Wesleyan Univ, BA; Calif State Univ, MA; Univ Iowa, PhD. **CAREER** Dir, Choral Act at Mt Union Col; past fac, Mont State Univ-Billings; Univ Northern Iowa, Cedar Falls; William Penn Col, Oskaloosa, Iowa & Vennard Col, Univ Park, Iowa; mus dir & conductor, Alliance Symphony Orchestra. **HONORS AND AWARDS** Amer Choral Directors Asn awd; appeared at, Amer Theatre Festival & before Cong US. **MEMBERSHIPS** Nat chem, Amer Choral Directors Association's Comt on Youth and Stud Act. **SELECTED PUBLICATIONS** Auth, The Choral Journal: An Index to Volumes 19-32, Amer Choral Directors Asn, 92; coauth, Up Front! Becoming the Compete Choral Conductor, EC Schirmer, Boston, 93; regular contribur, ACDA's Choral J; ed, Stud Times. **CONTACT ADDRESS** Dept of Music, Mount Union Col, 1972 Clark Ave, Alliance, OH, 44601. **EMAIL** dorseysw@muc.edu

DORWART, JEFFERY MICHAEL
PERSONAL Born 02/10/1944, Willimantic, CT, m, 1967 **DISCIPLINE** AMERICAN DIPLOMATIC HISTORY **EDUCATION** Univ Conn, BA, 65; Univ Mass, Amherst, MA, 68, PhD hist, 71. **CAREER** Asst prof, 71-79, assoc prof to prof Hist, Camden Col Arts & Sci, Rutgers Univ, 79-91. **MEMBERSHIPS** AHA. **RESEARCH** American diplomatic, military and 19th century history; naval history. **SELECTED PUBLICATIONS** Auth, Walter Quintin Gresham and East Asia, a reappraisal, Asian Forum, 73; United States Navy and the Sino-Japanese War of 1894-1895, Am Neptune, 74; The Pigtail War: American Involvement in the Sino-Japanese War, 1894-1895, Univ Mass, 75; John M B Sill and the struggle against Japanese expansion in Korea, Pac Hist Rev, 75; coauth, Bicentennial History of Camden County, New Jersey, 1886-present, Camden Cult & Heritage Comn, 76; Fort Mifflin of Philadelphia: An Illustrated History, Philadelphia, University of Pennsylvania Press, 98. **CONTACT ADDRESS** Dept of History, Rutgers Univ, 311 N 5th St, Camden, NJ, 08102-1461. **EMAIL** dorwart@craab.rutgers.edu

DOSS, SEALE
DISCIPLINE EPISTEMOLOGY, PHILOSOPHY OF NATURAL SCIENCE, HISTORY OF PHILOSOPHY, THEORY **EDUCATION** Univ TX, BA, MA; Univ CA, Berkeley, PhD. **CAREER** Prof Philos, May Bumby Severy Distinguished Serv Prof, Ripon Col. **SELECTED PUBLICATIONS** Ed, Critical Thinking as a Philosophical Movement, Ripon Col Press. **CONTACT ADDRESS** Ripon Col, Ripon, WI. **EMAIL** DossS@mac.ripon.edu

DOSTER, JAMES FLETCHER
PERSONAL Born 12/08/1912, Tuscaloosa, AL, m, 1936, 2 children **DISCIPLINE** HISTORY **EDUCATION** Univ Ala, AB, 32; Univ Chicago, AM, 36, PhD, 48. **CAREER** From instr to assoc prof, 36-62, PROF HIST, UNIV ALA, 62-, Instr, Howard Col, 44-45; Danforth Found assoc, 50-53; fel, Harvard Univ, 53-54; mem conf nature and writing of hist, Univ Kans, 55; consult Creek Nation on claims pending before Indian Claims Comn, 57-73; mem transp prize comt, Ford Motor Co, 61-64; mem fac sem, Standard Oil Co, Calif, 62; distinguished sr fel, Ctr Study Southern Hist and Cult, Univ Ala, 76-. **MEMBERSHIPS** AHA; Southern Hist Asn; Am Econ Asn; Econ Hist Orgn Am Historians. **RESEARCH** American railway history; United States history; Creek Indian Confederacy, 1740-1825. **SELECTED PUBLICATIONS** Auth, The Forgotten Centuries--Indians and Europeans in the American South, 1521-1704, J Southern Hist, Vol 62, 96; A History of the Timucua Indians and Missions, J Am Hist, Vol 83, 97; Mixing the Waters--Environment, Politics, and the Building of the Tennessee Tombigee Waterway, J Southern Hist, Vol 61, 95. **CONTACT ADDRESS** Dept of Hist, Univ of Ala, Box 1955, University, AL, 35486.

DOTSON, JOHN EDWARD
PERSONAL Born 06/12/1939, Frederick, OK **DISCIPLINE** RENAISSANCE AND MARITIME HISTORY **EDUCATION** Univ Okla, BA, 61; Univ Nebr, MA, 63; Johns Hopkins Univ, PhD (hist), 69. **CAREER** Asst prof, Concordia Univ, 67-70; ASST PROF HIST, SOUTHERN ILL UNIV CARBONDALE, 70-. **SELECTED PUBLICATIONS** Auth, Precursors of Columbus, Christopher-Piacentine Genoese Bankers and Merchants During the Middle Ages, Speculum J Medieval Stud, Vol 71, 96; Safety Regulations for Galleys Iin Mid 14th Century Genoa--Some Thoughts on Medieval Risk Management, J Medieval Hist, Vol 20, 94; Precursors of Columbus, Christopher-Piacentine Genoese Bankers and Merchants During the Middle Ages, Speculum J Medieval Stud, Vol 71, 96; A Guide to Medieval Travel the Near and Far East, 13th Century o 15th Century, Speculum J Medieval Stud, Vol 71, 96. **CONTACT ADDRESS** Dept of Hist, Southern Ill Univ, Carbondale, IL, 62901-4300.

DOTY, CHARLES STEWART
PERSONAL Born 09/08/1928, Fredonia, KS, m, 1954, 3 children **DISCIPLINE** MODERN EUROPEAN AND FRENCH HISTORY **EDUCATION** Washburn Univ, AB, 50; Univ Kans, MA, 55; Ohio State Univ, PhD (hist), 64. **CAREER** Instr hist, Kent State Univ, 61-64; asst prof, 64-67, assoc prof, 67-76, PROF HIST, UNIV MAINE, ORONO, 76-. **MEMBERSHIPS** AHA; Soc Fr Hist Studies. **RESEARCH** Comparison of French nationalism with French North American nationalism. **SELECTED PUBLICATIONS** Auth, Alsatian Emigration to the United States, 1815-1870, J Am Hist, Vol 80, 93; American Immigration--Example or Counterexample for France, J Am Hist, Vol 82, 95; The American Identity of Dantin, Louis, More Francophone American Than Franco American, Can Rev Am Stud, Vol 24, 94; Monsieur Maurras Est Ici--French Fascism in Franco American New England, J Contemporary Hist, Vol 32, 97. **CONTACT ADDRESS** 18 Sunrise Terr, Orono, ME, 04473.

DOUGAN, MICHAEL BRUCE
PERSONAL Born 02/26/1944, Burbank, CA, m, 1970 **DISCIPLINE** AMERICAN HISTORY **EDUCATION** Southwest Mo State Col, AB, 66; Emory Univ, MA, 67, PhD (hist), 70. **CAREER** Instr, 70-71, asst prof, 71-77, ASSOC PROF HIST, ARK STATE UNIV, 77-. **MEMBERSHIPS** Southern Hist Asn; Am Asn Legal Hist; Am Asn State and Local Hist. **RESEARCH** Southern history; legal history; local history. **SELECTED PUBLICATIONS** Auth, A Living History of the Ozarks J West, Vol 34, 95; Rugged and Sublime--The Civil War in Arkansas, J Southern Hist, Vol 62, 96; Entrepreneurs in the Lumber Industry--Arkansas, 1881-1963, Ark Hist Quart, Vol 55, 96; Partisans of the Southern Press--Editorial Spokesmen of the 19th Century, Ark Hist Quart, Vol 54, 95; The Impact of the Civil War and Reconstruction on Arkansas--Persistence in the Midst of Ruin, Civil War Hist, Vol 41, 95; The Lion of the SouthGeneral Hindman, Thomas, C, Civil War Hist, Vol 40, 94; The Honorable Powell, Clayton, Civil War Hist, Vol 39, 93; Ridge, John, Rollin--His Life and Works, J West, Vol 32, 93; The Battle for the Buffalo River--A 20th Century Conservation Crisis in the Ozarks, J West, Vol 35, 96; A Window on Main Street--Life Above the Corner Drug, J West, Vol 36, 97; Carpenter from Conway--Donaghey, George, Washington as Governor of Arkansas, 1909-1913, J The West, Vol 35, 96; A Connecticut Yankee in the Frontier Ozarks--The Writings Of Russell, Theodore, Pease, J West, Vol 32, 93; Territorial Ambition--Land and Society In Arkansas, 1800-1840, J Am Hist, Vol 81, 94. **CONTACT ADDRESS** P O Box 1690, Box 2607, State Univ, AR, 72467-1690.

DOUGHERTY, PATRICIA M.
PERSONAL Born 12/07/1944, CA **DISCIPLINE** MODERN EUROPEAN HISTORY **EDUCATION** Georgetown Univ, MA 79, PhD 84. **CAREER** Dominican Col SR, prof 84-. **HONORS AND AWARDS** Tchr of the Yr; NEH Fel; Fulbright Fel. **MEMBERSHIPS** ACHA; AHA; SFHS; WSFH; WAWH. **RESEARCH** France 19th century, esp July Monarchy Press; Women and religion. **SELECTED PUBLICATIONS** Auth, The French Catholic Press and the July Revolution, French History, forthcoming; Voyage sans carte: Mary Goemaere et la fondation des Soeurs dominicaines en Californie, Memoire dominicaine, 98; auth, L'Ami de la Religion, et les eveques francais sous le Concordat, 1815-1850, Rev d'hist ecclesiastique, 94; auth, The Rise and Fall of L'Ami de la Religion: History Purpose and Readership of a French Catholic Newspaper, Cath Hist Rev, 91; auth, Baudrillart Blum Freundlich Gerlier, Jeunesse ouvriere chretienne, Historical Dictionary of World War II France: The Occupation Vichy and the Resisitance, 1938-1946, ed, Bertram M. Gordon, Westport CT, Greenwood Press, 98; auth, Goemaere, Mary of the Cross, European Immigrant Women in the United State: A Biographical Dictionary, eds, Judy B. Litoff, Judith McDonnell, NY, Garland Press, 94. **CONTACT ADDRESS** Dept of History, Dominican Col, San Rafael, 50 Aracia Ave, San Rafael, CA, 94901-2298. **EMAIL** dougherty@dominican.edu

DOUGHTY, ROBERT
PERSONAL Born 11/04/1943, Tullos, LA, m, 1967, 2 children **DISCIPLINE** HISTORY **EDUCATION** Us Mil Acad, BS, 65; UCLA, MA, 72; Univ Kansas, PhD, 79. **CAREER** Instr, 72-75, assoc prof, 81-84, prof, 84-, US Mil Acad; instr, 76-79, Dept of Strategy, Command & Gen Staff Col; **RESEARCH** French military in 19th & 20th centuries **CONTACT ADDRESS** Dept of History, US Military Acad, West Point, NY, 10996. **EMAIL** kr0724@exmail.usma.edu

DOUGLAS, ANN
DISCIPLINE TWENTIETH-CENTURY AMERICAN LITERATURE **EDUCATION** Harvard Univ, BA, 64, PhD, 70; Oxford Univ, BPhil, 66. **CAREER** Instr, Princeton Univ, 70-74; prof. **HONORS AND AWARDS** Bicentennial preceptorship, Princeton Univ, 74; fel, Nat Hum Ctr, 78-79; fel, NEH, Guggenheim, 93-94; Alfred Beveridge award, Amer Hist Assn; Lionel Trilling award, Columbia Univ; Merle Curti intellectual hist award, Org Amer Historians. **SELECTED PUBLICATIONS** Auth, The Feminization of American Culture, 77; Terrible Honesty: Mongrel Manhattan in the 1920's, Farrar, Straus, 95; Little Women, Uncle Tom's Cabin, and Charlotte Temple, Penguin editions, and Word Virus, a William Burroughs anthology, 98. **CONTACT ADDRESS** Dept of Eng, Columbia Col, New York, 2960 Broadway, New York, NY, 10027-6902.

DOUGLAS, DONALD MORSE
PERSONAL Born 09/07/1924, Los Angeles, CA, m, 1943, 2 children **DISCIPLINE** EUROPEAN HISTORY **EDUCATION** Kans State Univ, BA, 61, MA, 63; Univ Kans, PhD (hist), 68. **CAREER** Asst prof, 65-75, ASSOC PROF HIST, WICHITA STATE UNIV, 75-. **MEMBERSHIPS** Western Asn German Studies. **RESEARCH** The Holocaust; Nazi Germany. **SELECTED PUBLICATIONS** Auth, The Anatomy of the Nuremberg Trials--A Personal Memoir, Hist, Vol 56, 93; The Rhetoric of Moderation--Desegregating the South During the Decade After Brown, Northwestern Univ Law Rev, Vol 89, 94; The Limits of Law in Accomplishing Racial Change--School Segregation in the Pre Brown North, Ucla Law Rev, Vol 44, 97; Race, Law and American History 1700-1990--The African American Experience, Am J Legal Hist, Vol 37, 93; Dismantling Desegregation --The Quiet Reversal of Brown V., Michigan Law Rev, Vol 95, 97. **CONTACT ADDRESS** Dept of Hist, Wichita State Univ, Wichita, KS, 67208.

DOUGLASS, MELVIN ISADORE
PERSONAL Born 07/21/1948, Manhattan, NY, s **DISCIPLINE** EDUCATION **EDUCATION** Vincinnes University, AS, 1970; Tuskegee Institute, BS, 1973; Morgan State University, MS, 1975; New York University, MA, 1977; Columbia University, EdM, 1978, EdD, 1981. **CAREER** Queensboro Society for the Prevention of Cruelty to Children Inc, child care worker, 1973-75; Public School 401-X, dean of students/teacher, 1973-75; Amistad Child Day Care Center, school age program director, 1976-77; Beck Memorial Day Care Center, administrative director, 1983-84; Department of Juvenile Justice, primary school department chair, 1984-85, ombudsman, 1985-88; John Jay College of Criminal Justice, adjunct instructor, 1988-89; STIMSON MIDDLE SCHOOL, CHAIRPERSON, BOYS TRACK HEAD COACH, 1988-; COLLEGE OF NEW ROCHELLE, INSTRUCTOR, 1993-. **HONORS AND AWARDS** Grad Scholarship Columbia Univ 1978; Kappa Delta Pi Honor Soc in Educ inducted 1978; Service Awd NY City Transit Branch NAACP 1986; Citation for Comm Serv NYS Governor Mario Cuomo 1986; Citation Awd New York City Mayor Edward Koch 1986; Citation of Honor Queens Borough Pres Claire Shulman 1986; City Council Citation Award, New York City Councilman Archie Spigner 1988; Civil Rights Award, New York City Transit Branch NAACP 1988; Black Winners: A History of Spingarn Medalists 1984; Famous Black Men of Harvard 1988; Jefferson Award, American Institute for Public Service, 1987; Omega Man of the Year Award, Nu Omicron Chapter, 1987; Cert of Ordination, Cross Roads Baptist Church, NYC, 1990; State of New York Legislative Resolution, Senator Alton R Waldon Jr, 1991; Alumni Faculty Citation Award, Vincennes University, 1991. **MEMBERSHIPS** Pres, founder Jamaica Track Club 1973-; bd of dirs Nu Omicron Chap of Omega Psi Phi Day Care Ctr 1984-; mem Prince Hall Masonry; pres bd of dirs New York City Transit Branch NAACP 1984-90; co-chairperson Educ Comm NY State Conf of NAACP 1986-89; chairperson Anti-Drug Comm Metro Council of NAACP Branches 1986-89; Jamaica East/West Adolescent Pregnancy Prevention Consortium 1986-89; basileus Nu Omicron Chap Omega Psi Phi Frat 1987-88; board of directors, Queens Council on the Arts 1983-86; bd of dirs Black Experimental Theatre 1982-; bf of dirs The United Black Men of Queens County Inc 1986-89; S Huntington Chmns' Assn, 1988-; Queens adv bd, New York Urban League, 1988-93; Amer Federation of Sch Administrators, 1988-; Council of Administrators and Supervisors, 1988-; Natl Black Child Devel Institute, 1982-; National Education Association, 1973-; community adv bd, The City of New York Dept of Correction, The Queens House of Detention for Men, 1991-94; community adv bd, Public School 40, Queens, NY, 1992-; bd of dirs Long Island Tuskegee Alumni Assn, 1986-, vp, 1987-89; bd of dirs, Dance Explosion, 1987-; area policy bd no 12, Subunit 2, 1987-; Ancient Arabic Order of Nobles of the Mystic Shrine. Licensed to preach, Calvary Bapt Ch, Jamaica NY, 1987. **SELECTED PUBLICATIONS** Written numerous publications, including: "Developing Successful Black Students," Feb 5, 1994, "Dr. Gerald W. Deas: More Than Pills," Feb 24, 1995, New York Amsterdam News; Social Studies Sixth Grade Teacher's Curriculum Guide, co-written with A. Sheppard, South Huntington School Dist, 1992. **CONTACT ADDRESS** English and Social Studies, Stimson Junior High School, Oakwood Rd, Huntington Station, NY, 11746.

DOWNEY, DENNIS B.
DISCIPLINE UNITED STATES HISTORY **EDUCATION** Fla State Univ, BA, 74, MA, 76; Marquette Univ, PhD, 81. **CAREER** Prof & actg dir, Univ Grad Stud. **HONORS AND AWARDS** Outstanding bk awd,Gustavus Myers Ctr Human Rights, 92. **MEMBERSHIPS** Org Amer Historians; AHA; Southern Hist Asn; Soc Historians of the Gilded Age and Progressive Era. **RESEARCH** US social and cultural history; society and culture, 1865-1930; race relations, esp 1865-1930; racialvViolence, esp lynching. **SELECTED PUBLICATIONS** Auth, Historical, Architectural and Archeological Survey of Duval County, Florida, State Fla, Misc Proj No 37, 81; Pennsylvania, in Microsoft Encarta, Microsoft Corp, 97; An Interview with Thomas Flanagan, Contemp Lit 35, 94; Revisionism and the Holocaust, OAH Newsl 21, 93; The Second Industrial Revolution 1865-1900, Lessons From Hist, 92, in OAH Chairs' Newsl, 92; Accidents and Incidents, Friends' Folio, 91; coauth, Industrial Pennsylvania, 1876-1919, A Guide to the History of Pennsylvania, Westport: Greenwood Press, 93; co-ed, A Guide to the History of Pennsylvania, Westport: Greenwood Press, 93; coauth, Crooked Death: Coatesville, Pennsylvania and the Lynching of Zachariah Walker, Champaign: Univ Ill Press, 91. **CONTACT ADDRESS** Dept of History, Millersville Univ, Pennsylvania, PO Box 1002, Millersville, PA, 17551-0302. **EMAIL** ddowney@mu3.millersv.edu

DOWNING, MARVIN LEE
PERSONAL Born 03/21/1937, Brownwood, TX, m, 1967, 2 children **DISCIPLINE** UNITED STATES HISTORY **EDUCATION** Wayland Baptist Col, BA, 59; Tex Christian Univ, MA, 63; Univ Okla, PhD(hist), 70. **CAREER** Instr hist, Wayland Baptist Col, 63-66; asst prof, 69-73, PROF HIST, UNIV TENN, MARTIN, 73-, Nat Endowment for Humanities, grant W Tenn Frontier, 73-74. **MEMBERSHIPS** Orgn Am Historians; Asn Asian Studies. **RESEARCH** American frontier; American agricultural history; Northwest Tennesse frontier. **SELECTED PUBLICATIONS** Auth, The PWA and the acquisition of the Fort Worth Public Library building 1933-1939, Tex Libr, fall 65; Davy Crockett in Northwest Tennessee, 75 & Christmasville and its origins, 75, River Region Monographs, Univ Tenn, Martin; coauth, Brief History of the First Baptist Church, Martin, Tennessee, First Baptist Church, 76. **CONTACT ADDRESS** Univ of Tennessee, 554 University St, Martin, TN, 38238-0002. **EMAIL** mdowning@utm.edu

DOWNS, ANTHONY
PERSONAL Born 11/21/1930, Evanston, IL, w, 1956, 5 children **DISCIPLINE** ECONOMICS **EDUCATION** Carleton Coll, BA, 52; Stanford Univ, MA; PhD, 56. **CAREER** Chemn, Real Estate Res Corp; Econ Anal, Rand Corp; Sr Fel, Brookings Inst; asst prof, Univ Chicago. **HONORS AND AWARDS** Nat Acad of Public Admin. **MEMBERSHIPS** Am Econ Asn; Am Real Estate and Urban Econ Asn; Counrs of Real Estate, Urban Land Inst. **RESEARCH** Urban affairs; real estate; housing; demographics. **SELECTED PUBLICATIONS** Auth, Stuck in Traffic, 92; New Visions for Metropolitan America, 94; A Reevaluation of Resident Rent Controls, 96; Political Theory and Public Choice: The Selected Essays of Anthony Downs, Volume One, 98; Urban Affairs and Urban Policy: The Selected Essays of Anthony Downs, Volume Two, 98. **CONTACT ADDRESS** Brookings Inst, 1775 Massachusetts Ave, Washington, DC, 20036. **EMAIL** AnthonyDowns@compuserve.com

DOWTY, ALAN K.
PERSONAL Born 01/15/1940, Greenville, OH, m, 1973, 6 children **DISCIPLINE** INTERNATIONAL RELATIONS **EDUCATION** Shimer Col, BA, 59; Univ Chicago, MA, 60; PhD, 63. **CAREER** Prof Govt & Intl Studies, Univ Notre Dame, 78-; assoc prof Govt & Intl Studies, Univ Notre Dame, 75-78; senior lctr, Hebrew Univ, 72-75; lctr, Hebrew Univ, 65-72; instr, Hebrew Univ, 64-65. **HONORS AND AWARDS** Amer Council of Learned Societies Travel Grant, 94; Twentieth Cent Fund Grant, 83-85; Quincy Wright Award, Intl Studies Assoc, 85; Res Grant, Ford Found, 77; Res Grant, Intl Crisis Behavior Res Project, 77; Res Grant, Leonard Davis Inst Intl Relations, 73-75; Resident Fel, Adlai Stevenson Inst Intl Affairs, 71-72; vis Res Fel, Univ Chi, 70-71. **MEMBERSHIPS** Amer Polit Sci Assoc; Assoc Jewish Studies; Intl Inst Strategic Studies; Intl Polit Sci Assoc; Intl Studies Assoc; Assoc Israel Studies; World Union Jewish Studies. **RESEARCH** Israel; Arab-Israeli Issues **SELECTED PUBLICATIONS** Auth, The Jewish State: A Century Later, Univ Calif Pr, 98; coauth, The Role of Domestic Politics in Isreali Peacemaking, Leonard Davis Inst for Intl Relations, 97; auth, Closed Borders: The Contemporary Assault on Freedom of Movement, Yale Univ Pr, 87; auth, Zionism's Greatest Conceit, Israel Studies, 98; auth, Israel's First Fifty Years, Current History, 97. **CONTACT ADDRESS** Dept of Government and International Studies, Univ of Notre Dame, 0313 Hesburgh Center, Notre Dame, IN, 46556. **EMAIL** dowty.1@nd.edu

DOYEL, D.
PERSONAL Born 08/24/1946, Lindsay, CA, m, 1983 **DISCIPLINE** ANTHROPOLOGY, PSYCHOLOGY AND EDUCATION **EDUCATION** BA, 69, Std Sec Credential, 70, MA, 72, Calif State Univ Chico; Univ Ariz, PhD, 77. **CAREER** Dir, Navajo Nation Archaeol Mus Div, 79-82, cons archael, 82-83, dir, Cty Phoenix Archaeol and Pueblo Grande Mus, 84-89; cons archaeol, Estrella Cult Res, 90-93; prin investr, Archaeol Consult Serv Ltd, 93-. **HONORS AND AWARDS** Outstanding Supv, Navajo Nation, 81; Who's Who in the West, 92-; Who's Who Intl, 95-. **MEMBERSHIPS** Soc Amer Archaeol, Ariz Archaeol Hist Soc, charter mem, Mus Assoc Ariz, 83; charter mem, Planetary Soc, 80; Sigma Xi, 78-. **RESEARCH** Archaeological Research (Southwest U.S.); Cultural Ecology; Southwest Ethnography; Museum Interpretation and Administration. **SELECTED PUBLICATIONS** Auth, Hohokam Exchange and Interaction, Chaco and Hohkam: Prehistoric Regional Systems in the American Southwest, ed P.L. Crown and W.J. Judge, Sch Amer Res, Santa Fe, Nmex, pp 225-252, 91; Hohokam Cultural Evolution in the Phoenix Basin, Exploring the Hohokam: Prehistoric Desert Peoples of the American Southwest, ed G.J. Gumerman, Univ Nmex Press, Albuquerque, Nmex, pp 231-278, 91; Interpreting Prehistoric Cultural Diversity in the Arizona Desert, Culture and Contact: Charles C. Di Peso's Gran Chichimeca, ed A. Woosley and J. Ravesloot, Univ Nmex Press, Albuquerque, Nmex, pp 39-64, 94; coauth, Processes of Aggregation in the Prehistoric Southwest, Themes in Southwestern Prehistory: Grand Patterns and Local Variations in Culture Change, ed G. Gumerman, Sch Amer Res, Santa Fe, Nmex, pp 109-134, 94; On Rivers and Boundaries in the Phoenix Basin, Arizona, Kiva, 8, 455-474, 93; Auth, Charles C. Di Peso: Expanding the Frontiers of American Archaeology, Amer Antiq, 59, 9-20, 94; coauth, Archaeomagnetic Dating and the Bonito Phase Chronology, Jour Archaeol Science, 21, 651-658, Acad Press Ltd, London, 94; auth, Resource Mobilization and Hohokam Society: Analysis of Obsidian Artifacts from the Gatlin Site, Kiva, 62, 45-60, 96; Ed, Anasazi Regional Organization and the Chaco System, Anthrop Papers of the Maxwell Mus, no 5, Albuquerque, Nmex, 92; The Hohokam Village: Site Structure and Organization, Amer Asn for the Advan of Science, SWARM Div, Glenwood Springs, Colo, 87. **CONTACT ADDRESS** PO Box 60474, Phoenix, AZ, 85082-0474. **EMAIL** ddoyel@doitnow.com

DOYLE, DON H.
DISCIPLINE HISTORY **EDUCATION** Univ Calif, Davis, BA, 67; Northwestern Univ, PhD, 73. **CAREER** Asst, 74-79, assoc, 79-86, PROF, 86-, VANDERBILT UNIV; vis prof, Univ Leeds, England, 97-98; Fulbright sen lectr, Univ Genoa, 95; Fulbright sen lect, Univ Rome, 91; lectr, 71-73, asst prof, 73-74, Univ Mich, Dearborn. **CONTACT ADDRESS** Vanderbilt Univ, Box 1738, Station B, Nashville, TN, 37235. **EMAIL** don.h.doyle@vanderbilt.edu

DRACHMAN, VIRGINIA GOLDSMITH
PERSONAL Born 01/12/1948, New York, NY, 2 children **DISCIPLINE** AMERICAN MEDICAL & WOMEN'S HISTORY **EDUCATION** Univ Rochester, BA, 70; State Univ NY, Buffalo, MA, 74, PhD, 76. **CAREER** Assoc prof hist med & hist women, Tufts Univ, 77, Rockefeller Found fel hist & women med movement, 77-78. **HONORS AND AWARDS** ACLS Ford, 88; NSF Law & Soc Sci, 88; NEH Summer Fel, 94. **MEMBERSHIPS** AHA; Orgn Am Historians; Am Studies Asn. **RESEARCH** Women in med. **SELECTED PUBLICATIONS** Auth, Women Lawyers & the Origins of Professional Identity in America: The Letters of the Equity Club, 1887-1890, Univ Mich Press, 94; Sisters in Law: Women Lawyers in Modern American History, Harvard Univ Press, 98; Hospital with a Heart: Women Doctors and the Paradox of Separation at the New England Hospital, 1862-1969, Cornell Univ Press, 98. **CONTACT ADDRESS** Dept of Hist, Tufts Univ, 520 Boston Ave, Medford, MA, 02155-5555. **EMAIL** drachman@tiac.net

DRAKE, FRED
PERSONAL Born 05/25/1937, Barrow in, England, m, 1963, 2 children **DISCIPLINE** NORTH AMERICAN DIPLOMATIC, NAVAL, AND MILITARY HISTORY **EDUCATION** Univ Manchester, BA, MA; Cornell Univ, PhD. **CAREER** Prof. **HONORS AND AWARDS** Great Lakes Hist prize, Cleveland State Univ, Fr-Amer Endowed Library Fund. **RESEARCH** Naval history. **SELECTED PUBLICATIONS** Auth, "The Niagara Peninsula and Naval Aspects of the War of 1812," Proc of Eighth Niagara Peninsula Hist Conf, Vanwell Press, 90; The Empire of the Seas: A Biography of Rear Admiral Shufeldt, Univ Hawaii Press. **CONTACT ADDRESS** Dept of Hist, Brock Univ, 500 Glenridge Ave, St Catharines, ON, L2S 3A1. **EMAIL** fcdrake@spartan.ac.brocku.ca

DRAKE, FRED
DISCIPLINE HISTORY **EDUCATION** Harvard Univ, PhD, 71. **CAREER** Prof, Univ MA Amherst. **SELECTED PUBLICATIONS** Auth, publ(s) on aspects of Sino-Western cult interaction; role of Western missionaries in China; pioneer photography in China; early Manchu acceptance of Chinese cult. **CONTACT ADDRESS** Dept of Hist, Univ Massachusetts Amherst, Mass Ave, Amherst, MA, 01003.

DRAKE, HAROLD ALLEN
PERSONAL Born 07/24/1942, Cincinnati, OH, m, 1969, 2 children **DISCIPLINE** ANCIENT HISTORY **EDUCATION** Univ Southern Calif, AB, 63; Univ Wis-Madison, MA, 66 and 68, PhD (ancient hist), 70. **CAREER** Lectr, 70-71, asst prof, 71-76, ASSOC PROF ROMAN HIST, UNIV CALIF, SANTA BARBARA, 76-, Nat Endowment for Humanities fel, Inst Advan Study, 76-77. **HONORS AND AWARDS** Plous Mem Award, Univ Calif, Santa Barbara, 76. **MEMBERSHIPS** Am Philol Asn; Archaeol Inst Am; Asn Ancient Historians. **RESEARCH** Late Roman empire; Constantine the Great; early Christianity. **SELECTED PUBLICATIONS** Auth, Redeeming Politics, Church Hist, Vol 65, 96; Theodosius--The Empire at Bay, Cath Hist Rev, Vol 82, 96; Augusta, Helena--The Mother of Constantine The Great and the Legend of her Finding the True Cross, Cath Hist Rev, Vol 79, 93; Eusebius, Christianity, and Judaism, Cath Hist Rev, Vol 79, 93; Constantine and Consensus, Church Hist, Vol 64, 95; The Christians and the Roman Empire, Cath Hist Rev, Vol 81, 95; Arnobius of Sicca--Religious Conflict and Competition in the Age of Diocletian, Church Hist, Vol 66, 97. **CONTACT ADDRESS** Dept of Hist, Univ of Calif, 552 University Rd, Santa Barbara, CA, 93106-0001.

DRAPER, JOAN E.
DISCIPLINE ARCHITECTURE, ARCHITECTURAL HISTORY **EDUCATION** Univ of Calif, Berkeley, BA, 69, MA, 72, PhD, 79. **CAREER** Asst prof, Mont State Univ, 76-70; asst prof, Univ of Ill at Chicago, 79-85; ASSOC PROF, UNIV OF COLO AT BOULDER & DENVER, 85-. **MEMBERSHIPS** Soc of Archit Historians; Soc of Am City & Regional Planning Hist. **RESEARCH** History of American architecture & planning, 19th and 20th centuries. **SELECTED PUBLICATIONS** Auth, John Galen Howard, Toward the Simple Life: Arts and Crafts Architects of Calif, Univ of Calif Press, 97; auth, Architectural Education and Multiculturalism, Doing Diversity, Asn of Collegiate Schools of Archit, 96; auth, Chicago: Small Parks of 1902-1903 and Park Planning in the United States, Planning the Am City: Hist, Practice and Prospects, Johns Hopkins Univ Press, 96; auth, Chicago: Planning Wacker Drive, Streets: Critical Perspectives on Public Space, Univ of Calif Press, 94; auth, Landscape Design, Oxford Companion to Am Hist, Oxford Univ Press, forthcoming; auth, Edward H. Bennett, Am Nat Bio, Oxford Univ Press and the Am Coun of Learned Socs, 98; auth, John Galen Howard, Dizionario de Architettura Contemporaneo, UTET, 97. **CONTACT ADDRESS** Archit and Planning, Univ of Colorado, EnvD Bldg, Boulder, CO, 80309.

DRAZNIN, YAFFA CLAIRE
PERSONAL Born 05/19/1922, WI, m, 1942, 2 children **DISCIPLINE** MODERN BRITISH HISTORY (VICTORIAN STUDIES) **EDUCATION** Univ Chicago, BA, 43; Univ Southern Calif, MA, 82, PhD, 85. **CAREER** Professional editor and staff writer (community activity, law enforcement, aerospace and computer hardware), 54-70; freelance magazine writer, author, 70-81; affiliated scholar, USC faculty status, SWMS program, 85-87; visiting scholars (faculty status), Dept History, Univ Chicago, 95-98. **HONORS AND AWARDS** Dr. George P. Hammond Award, Phi Alpha Theta Historical Soc, for best paper, cash award; Barbara Kanner Prize, Western Assn of Women Historians, best book, cash award, 94. **MEMBERSHIPS** Amer Hist Soc; Assn Documentary Editing; Natl Coalition Independent Scholars; Coordinating Group, Women Historians, MESNA. **RESEARCH** Victorian England, women in late 19th-century. **SELECTED PUBLICATIONS** Auth, "But What Did She Do All Day?" The Life of Middle-Class Married Women in Late-Victorian London; auth, Weep for the Fallen Women: An Olive Schreiner Mystery; auth, "My Other Self": The Letters of Olive Schreiner and Havelock Ellis, 1884-1920, 92/93; auth, book review of The Rise of Respectable Society: A Social History of Victorian Britain, 1830-1900, in The Historian, v 52, 90; auth, book review, A Mid-Victorian Feminist: Barbara Leigh Smith Bodichon, in The Historian, v 50, 88. **CONTACT ADDRESS** 5532 S Shore Dr, #14F, Chicago, IL, 60637-1990. **EMAIL** ycdrazni@midway.uchicago.edu

DREIFORT, JOHN E.
DISCIPLINE HISTORY **EDUCATION** Bowling Green State Univ, BA, 65; MA, 66; Kent State Univ, PhD, 70. **CAREER** Exec secy, Wichita Comm For Rel, 73-; affil, Coun For Rel; Amer Comm For Rel; interim VP, acad aff, 93-94; dept ch, 86-; prof-. **HONORS AND AWARDS** Pres award for achievement., Fac Senate pres, 77-78. **SELECTED PUBLICATIONS** Auth, Yvon Delbos at the Quai d'orsay: French Foreign Policy During the Popular Front, 36-38, Univ Press Kans, 73; Myopic Grandeur: The Ambivalence of French Foreign Policy toward the Far East, 1919-1945, Kent State Univ Press, 91; Reappraising the Munich Pact, Woodrow Wilson Ctr, Smithsonian Institute. **CONTACT ADDRESS** Dept of Hist, Wichita State Univ, 1845 Fairmont, Wichita, KS, 67260-0062. **EMAIL** dreifort@wsuhub.uc.twsu.edu

DREISBACH, DONALD FRED
PERSONAL Born 06/25/1941, Allentown, PA, d **DISCIPLINE** PHILOSOPHY & HISTORY OF RELIGION **EDUCATION** MA Inst Technol, BS, 63; Northwestern Univ, MA, 69, PhD, 70. **CAREER** Assoc prof, 69- 80, Prof Philos, Northern MI Univ, 80. **MEMBERSHIPS** AAUP; Am Acad Relig; Am Philos Asn; NAm Paul Tillich Soc. **RESEARCH** Philosophical theology; Paul Tillich. **SELECTED PUBLICATIONS** Auth, Paul Tillich's Herrmeneutic, J Am Acad Relig, Vol XLIII, No 1; Paul Tillich's Doctrine of Religious Symbols, Encounter, Vol 37, No 4; On the love of God, Anglican Theol Rev, Vol LIX, No 1; Circularity and consistency in Descartes, Can J Philos, Vol VIII, No 1; Agreement and obligation in the Crito, New Scholasticism, Vol LII, No 2; The unity of Paul Tillich's existential analysis, Encounter, Vol 41, No 4; On the hermeneutic of symbols: The Buri-Hardwick debate, Theologische Zeitschrift, 9-10/79; Essence, existence and the fall: Paul Tillich's analysis of existence, Harvard Theol Rev, Vol 73, No 1-2; Symbols and Salvation, Univ Press Am, 93. **CONTACT ADDRESS** Dept of Philos, No Michigan Univ, 1401 Presque Isle Av, Marquette, MI, 49855-5301. **EMAIL** ddreisba@nmu.edu

DRESCHER, SEYMOUR
PERSONAL Born 02/20/1934, Bronx, NY, m, 1955, 3 children **DISCIPLINE** HISTORY & SOCIOLOGY **EDUCATION** City Col New York, BA, 55; Univ Wis, MS, 56, PhD, 60. **CAREER** Instr hist, Harvard Univ, 60-62; from asst prof to assoc prof, 62-69, prof hist, Univ Pittsburg, 69-87, prof sociol, 73-, chairperson dept hist, 80-83, Univ Pittsburgh Int Dimensions & Soc Sci Res Coun, 68, Univ Pittsburgh Ctr Int Studies, 68 & 69-70, 92-93; vis prof, Carnegie-Mellon Univ, 73; vis prof CUNY, 87; NEH sr fel, 73-74; Woodrow Wilson Ctr Fel, 83-84; sec Europ prog Woodrow Wilson Ctr, 84-85; Am Philos Soc grant-in-aid, 75 & Am Coun Learned Soc, 76; Guggenheim Mem Found fel, 77-78; resident scholar, Bellagio Study & Conf Ctr, 80 prof hist, 87; Dean, Sem-at-Sea, 98. **MEMBERSHIPS** AHA; Soc Fr Hist Studies; NACBS; Tocqueville Soc. **RESEARCH** Modern Europe; colonial slavery and abolition; race and social change. **SELECTED PUBLICATIONS** Auth, Tocqueville and England, Harvard; auth, Dilemmas of Democracy: Tocqueville and Modernization, Univ Pittsburgh, 68; coauth, Confrontation: Paris 1968 (film), 71; auth, Le Declin du Systeme Esclavagiste Britannique et l'Abolition de la Traite, Ann-Econ, Soc, Civilizations, 3-4/76; auth, Econocide: British Slavery in the Era of Abolition, Univ Pittsburgh, 77; auth, Capitalism and Antislavery: British Mobilization in Comparitive Perspective, Oxford U Press, 87; co-ed, Anti-Slavery, Religion and Reform, Dawson/Archon, 80; auth, the Long Goodbye, Amer Hist Rev 93-94; auth Political Symbolism in Modern Europe, Trans, 82. **CONTACT ADDRESS** Dept of History, Univ of Pittsburgh, 3p32 Forbes Quad, Pittsburgh, PA, 15260-0001. **EMAIL** syd@pitt.edu

DRESSER, N.
PERSONAL Born 10/28/1931, Los Angeles, CA, m, 1951, 3 children **DISCIPLINE** ANTHROPOLOGY **EDUCATION** UCLA, MA 72; BA 70. **CAREER** Cal State Univ LA, 25 year Faculty Member, Eng Amer Studies 72-92; LA Times columnist of Multicultural Manners, and full time write of books, 92-. **HONORS AND AWARDS** John Anson Ford Awd; Smithsonian Inst Awds; NEH. **MEMBERSHIPS** AFS; CFS; ISA; CHSSC; WGA. **RESEARCH** Multicultural communication, customs and beliefs; human animal relations; vampires. **SELECTED PUBLICATIONS** Auth, Multicultural Celebrations: Today's Rules of Etiquette for Life's Special Occasions, Three Rivers Press, forthcoming 99; The Horse Bar Mitzvah, Companion Animals and Us: Exploring the Relationships Between People and Pets, Cambridge Univ Press, forthcoming 99; We Don't Ask They Don't Tell, The Intl Soc for Anthrozoology NewsL, 98; The M Word, Western Folklore, 98; Multicultural Manners: New Rules of Etiquette for a Changing Society, NY, John Wiley & Sons, 96; Korean ed 97; Vampires, American Folklore: An Encycl, Hamden CT, Garland Pub, 96; Our Own Stories: Readings for Cross-cultural Communication, 2nd ed, White Plains NY, Longman Pub, 95; The Case of the Missing Gerbil, Western Folklore, 94; Into the Light: Romania Stakes Its Claim to Dracula, The World and I, 95; First World Dracula Congress, Sky, 95; Multicultural Manners, twice mthly Los Angeles Times, Intly syn by Singer Media Corp. **CONTACT ADDRESS** Dept of English, California State Univ, Los Angeles, 5151 State Univ Dr, Los Angeles, CA, 90032. **EMAIL** norined@earthlink.net

DRESSLER, HERMIGILD
PERSONAL Born 02/03/1908, Belleville, IL **DISCIPLINE** CLASSICAL PHILOLOGY **EDUCATION** Cath Univ Am, AM, 38, PhD, 47. **CAREER** Registr, Quincy Col, 47-50, prof class lang and chmn div humanities, 50-53; from asst prof to assoc prof Greek and Latin, Cath Univ Am, 53-73, chmn dept, 71-73; PROF GREEK AND LATIN, QUINCY COL, 73-, ED DIR, FATHERS OF THE CHURCH, 75-. **MEMBERSHIPS** Ling Soc Am; Am Philol Asn; N Am Patristic Soc. **RESEARCH** Translations of papal documents; medieval Latin. **SELECTED PUBLICATIONS** Auth, Goethe Studies on the Analogy Between Color and Sound and its Validation by Modern Research, Goethe Jahrbuch, Vol 107, 90; The Principle of Polarity in Goethe Explanations of the Problem of The Major Minor Relationship as Anticipation of The Polaristic Position in Harmonic Theory, Goethe Jahrbuch, Vol 109, 92. **CONTACT ADDRESS** Dept of Greek and Latin, Quincy Col, 1831 College Ave, Quincy, IL, 62301.

DRESSLER, RACHEL
DISCIPLINE ART HISTORY **EDUCATION** Emory Univ, BA, 74; MA, 81; Columbia Univ, PhD, 93. **CAREER** Univ Albany - SUNY **HONORS AND AWARDS** Georges Lurcy Charitable & Educational Trust; Howard Hibbard Fund, 88; Fac Develop Award, 94; Fac Res Awards Prog, 96. **SELECTED PUBLICATIONS** Auth, Gary Keown at The Atlanta Art Workers' Coalition, Art Papers, 81; Duane Michals at The Atlanta Gallery of Photography, Art Papers, 81; Entries in French Romanesque Sculpture: An Annotated Bibliography, 87; Deus Hoc Vult: Visual Rhetoric at the Time of the Crusades, Medieval Encounters, 95. **CONTACT ADDRESS** Univ Albany-SUNY, 1400 Washington Ave, Albany, NY, 12222.

DREW, KATHERINE FISCHER
PERSONAL Born 09/24/1923, Houston, TX, m, 1951 **DISCIPLINE** MEDIEVAL HISTORY **EDUCATION** Rice Inst, AB, 44, AM, 45; Cornell Univ, PhD (hist), 50. **CAREER** Instr Hist, Rice Univ, 46-48; asst, Cornell Univ, 48-50; from asst prof to assoc prof, 50-63, chmn dept, 70-80, PROF HIST, RICE UNIV, 63., Guggenheim fel, 59; Fulbright seminarist, 65; ed, Rice Univ Studies, 67-81; Nat Endowment for Humanities fel, 74-75. **MEMBERSHIPS** AHA; Mediaeval Acad Am; Int Comn Hist Rep and Parliamentary Insts; Am Soc Legal Hist. **RESEARCH** Medieval legal history; medieval social and economic history. **SELECTED PUBLICATIONS** Auth, Realms of Ritual--Burgundian Ceremony and Civic Life in Late Medieval Ghent, J Interdisciplinary Hist, Vol 28, 97; European Legal History, Am J Legal Hist, Vol 38, 94; The Terrier of the Dorbec Family of Cideville Upper Normandy, 14th Century to 16th Century, Am Hist Rev, Vol 100, 95; Medieval Women--A Social-History of Women in England 450-1500, J Interdisciplinary Hist, Vol 27, 97; A New World n a Small Place--Church and Religion in the Diocese of Rieti, 1188-1378, J Interdisciplinary Hist, Vol 26, 96; Early Irish and Welsh Kinship, J Interdisciplinary Hist, Vol 25, 95. **CONTACT ADDRESS** Dept of Hist, Rice Univ, Houston, TX, 77001.

DRINKARD-HAWKSHAWE, DOROTHY
DISCIPLINE HISTORY **EDUCATION** Howard Univ, BA, 60, MA, 63; Catholic Univ Am, PhD, 74. **CAREER** Chemn, Bowie State Univ, 79-82; liaison, NEH, 83-85; chemn, 89-91, assoc dean, 92-95, dir, 93-, East Tenn State Univ. **MEMBERSHIPS** AHA, Asn for the Study of Afro-American Life and Hist. **SELECTED PUBLICATIONS** Auth, Illinois Freedom Fighters: A Civil War Saga of the 29th Infantry, United States Colored Troops, 98; auth, The Legacy of Reconstruction, 98. **CONTACT ADDRESS** Dept of History, East Tennessee State Univ, Johnson City, TN, 37604.

DRUESEDOW, JOHN E.
DISCIPLINE MUSIC **EDUCATION** IN Univ, PhD. **CAREER** Music libr dir. **RESEARCH** Music bibliog; 19th century Am music; Span Baroque; contemp Latin Am music. **SELECTED PUBLICATIONS** Auth, publ(s) on music libr res for undergraduates. **CONTACT ADDRESS** Dept of Music, Duke Univ, Mary Duke Biddle Music Bldg, Durham, NC, 27706. **EMAIL** john.druesedow@duke.edu

DRUMMOND, IAN MACDONALD
PERSONAL Born 06/04/1933, Vancouver, BC, Canada **DISCIPLINE** BRITISH AND CANADIAN ECONOMIC HISTORY **EDUCATION** Univ BC, BA, 54; Univ Toronto, MA, 55; Yale Univ, PhD (econ), 59. **CAREER** Instr econ, Yale Univ, 58-60; lectr, 60-63, asst prof, 63-65, assoc prof, 65-71, PROF ECON, UNIV TORONTO, 71-, Consult, Can Dept Labour, summer 61, Orgn Econ Coop and Develop, summer 62, Can Royal Comn on Taxation, summer 63 and Harvard Develop Adv Serv, summer 65; vis asst prof, Princeton Univ, 65; vis scholar, Australian Nat Univ, 71; vis prof, Univ Edinburgh, 75-76; vis scholar, Inst Commonwealth Studies, London, 76-77. **MEMBERSHIPS** Fel Royal Soc Can; Can Econ Asn; Royal Econ Soc; Econ Hist Soc; Econ Hist Asn. **RESEARCH** Canadian and modern British history; international economic policy. **SELECTED PUBLICATIONS** Auth, North America Without Borders--Integrating Canada, The United States, and Mexico, Can Hist Rev, Vol 74, 93; In Pursuit of World Markets, Canada Trade Pattern from 1945 to 1950, Can Hist Rev, Vol 74, 93. **CONTACT ADDRESS** Trinity Col Univ Toronto, Toronto, ON, M5S 1H8.

DRUMMOND, RICHARD HENRY
PERSONAL Born 12/14/1916, San Francisco, CA, m, 1943, 3 children **DISCIPLINE** CLASSICS **EDUCATION** UCLA, BA, 38, MA, 39; Univ Wisc, PhD, 41; Luth Theol Sem, BD, 44. **CAREER** Pastor, The Japanese Church of Christ, San Fran, 47-49; fraternal worker in Japan, 49-62; prof Christian Stud & Class Lang, 58-62, vis prof, 68-69, 76-78, & 86-87, Meiji Gakuin Univ, Tokyo; prof Ecumenical Mission & Hist of Relig, 62-85, Florence Livergood Warren Prof Comp Relig, 84-87, PROF ECUMENICAL MISSION & HIST OF RELIG EMER, 87- , UNIV DUBUQUE THEOL SEM; vis prof, Atlantic Univ, 87-89 & Old Dominion Univ, 89. **HONORS AND AWARDS** Phi Beta Kappa, 38; Outstanding Educ Am, 72 & 74; Univ fel, Univ Dubuque, 91. **SELECTED PUBLICATIONS** Auth, Missiological Lessons-From Events New and Old, Missiology, 94; A New History of Japanese Theology, Mission Studies, 94; A Broader Vision, Stud in Interreligious Dialogue, 96; A Boarder Vision: Perspectives on the Buddha and the Christ, ARE Press, 95. **CONTACT ADDRESS** Univ of Dubuque Theol Sem, 2000 University Ave, Dubuque, IA, 52001.

DUBE, JEAN-CLAUDE
PERSONAL Born 01/12/1925, Riviere-du-Loup, PQ, Canada **DISCIPLINE** HISTORY **EDUCATION** Univ Ottawa, LPhil, 46, LTheol, 50, MA, 61; Univ Paris, PhD, 66. **CAREER** Fac mem to prof, 61-90, PROF EMER HISTORY, UNIV OTTAWA, 90-; founder & first dir, Ctr de rech en hist relig du Can (St Paul Univ). **HONORS AND AWARDS** Prix litt Que (Hist), 70; fel, Royal Soc Can, 89. **MEMBERSHIPS** Soc d'Hist de France (Paris); Soc archeol de Tours; pres, Soc can d'hist de l'Eglise cath, 95-97. **SELECTED PUBLICATIONS** Auth, Claude-Thomas Dupuy, intendant de la Nouvelle-France, 69; auth, Les intendants de la Nouvelle-France, 84; auth, Les Bigot du XVIe siecle a la Revolution, 87; co-ed, Rencontres de l'historiographie francaise avec l'histoire sociale, 78. **CONTACT ADDRESS** Dept of History, Univ Ottawa, Ottawa, ON, K1N 6N5.

DUBE, THOMAS M.T.
PERSONAL Born 12/25/1938, Essexvale, Zimbabwe, m **DISCIPLINE** EDUCATION **EDUCATION** Univ of Lesotho, BA 1958; Univ of So Africa, UED 1960; CW Post Coll of Long Island U, MS 1963; Univ of Chgo, MA 1972; MI State U, MA 1974; Uof Rochester, EdD 1969; Cooley Law Sch, JD. **CAREER** Western MI Univ, asst prof Social Science; Geneva Coll PA, asst prof; Rochester NY, pre-school teacher; Ministry of African Educ, Rodesia Africa, high school teacher, elementary school teacher. **MEMBERSHIPS** Mem Rhodesian African Tchrs Assn; vol activities in Black Comm Rochester, Pittsburg, Kalamazoo; mem Assn of African Studies in Am; founder mem JairosJiri Inst for Physically-Handicapped; founder, mem, asst prin Mpopoma African Comm HS. **CONTACT ADDRESS** 337 Moore Hall, Kalamazoo, MI, 49001.

DUBERMAN, MARTIN
PERSONAL Born 08/06/1930, New York, NY **DISCIPLINE** UNITED STATES HISTORY **EDUCATION** Yale Univ, BA, 52; Harvard Univ, MA, 53, PhD, 57. **CAREER** Teaching fel, Harvard Univ, 55-57; from instr to asst prof Am hist, Yale Univ, 57-62; from asst prof to prof hist, Princeton Univ, 62-72; DISTINGUISHED PROF HIST, LEHMAN/THE GRADUATE CENTER, CUNY, 72-, founder and dir, The Center for Lesbian and Gay Studies (CLAGS), the CUNY Graduate School; Morse fel, Yale Univ, 61-62; bicentennial preceptor, Princeton Univ, 62-65; Am Coun Learned Soc grant-in-aid, 62; Rockefeller Found grant studies, Black Mountain Col, 67-68; Princeton McCosh fac fel, 68-69; var productions of plays, The Memory Bank, 70-71, Payments, New Dramatists, 71, Inner Limits, Easthampton, 71, Visions of Kerouac, Lion, 76, Back Alley, 76, Odyssey, Los Angeles, 77 & Vancouver, 78: Rockefeller fel in humanities, 76; vis Randolf Distinguished Prof, Vassar, fall 92. **HONORS AND AWARDS** Bancroft Prize, 62; Vernon Rice-Drama Desk Award, 63; Nat Acad Arts & Lett Special Award, 71; Finalist for: Nat Book Award, L.A. Times Book Award, Robert Kennedy Book Award, James Ramsey Prize, 93-94 and 97-98 Lambda Book Awards, Am Library Asn Gay and Lesbian Book Award; Runner-up in Non-fiction for the Am Library Asn Best Gay Book of the Year; Best Twenty-Five Books of the Year, The Village Voice; Best Seven Books of the Year, The Boston Globe; Winner: Manhattan Borough President's Gold Medal in Literature (88), The George Freedley Memorial Award from the New York Public Library for best book of the year, two Lambda Book Awards, Gustavus Myer Award for best books of the year, Gustavus Myers Center Award for an outstanding work on intolerance in North America (94); Public Service Award from LeGal (Asn Gay and Lesbian Lawyers), 95; Distinguished Service Award from the Asn of Gay and Lesbian Psychiatrists, 96; Public Service Award from GAYLA (Gay and Lesbian Analyists), 98; Guest of Honor, Harvard Gay and Lesbian Rev annual banquet, 98; Annual Award from the Asn of Men's Studies, 98. **MEMBERSHIPS** AHA; Orgn Am Historians; Gay Acad Union. **RESEARCH** American intellectual history; United States history, 1820-1877; history of sex roles and sexual behavior in America. **SELECTED PUBLICATIONS** Auth, Charles Francis Adams, 1807-1886, Houghton Mifflin, 60; In White America, Houghton, 64; ed, The Antislavery Vanguard, Princeton Univ, 65; auth, James Russell Lowell, Houghton Mifflin, 66; The Uncompleted Past, Random House, 69; The Memory Bank, Dial, 70; Black Mountain: An Exploration in Community, Dutton, 72; Male Armor: Selected Plays, 1968-1974, Dutton, 75; Visions of Kerouac, Little, Brown, 77; About Time: Exploring the Gay Past, Gay Presses of NY, 86, rev and enlarged 2nd ed, NAL, 91; co-ed, Hidden from History: Reclaiming the Gay and Lesbian Past, New Am Lib, 89; auth, Paul Robeson, Knopf, 89; Cures: A Gay Man's Odyssey, Dutton/NAL, 91; Mother Earth: An Epic Play on the Life of Emma Goldman, St Martins, 91; Stonewall, Dutton, 93; co-ed and intro, The CLAGS Directory of Scholars in Gay and Lesbian Studies, 94-95; gen ed, Lives of Notable Gay Men and Lesbians and Issues in Gay and Lesbian Life, Chelsea House (14 books to date); Midlife Queer, Schribner, 96, Univ WI Press (paper), 98; ed, A Queer World: The Center for Lesbian and Gay Studies Reader, NYU Press, 97; ed, Queer representations: Reading Lives, Reading Cultures, NYU Press, 97; assoc ed, J of the Hist of Sexuality, 93-; assoc ed, Masculinities: Interdisciplinary Studies on Gender, 93-; many articles and reviews. **CONTACT ADDRESS** Dept of Hist, Lehman Col, CUNY, 250 Bedford Park W, Bronx, NY, 10468-1527.

DUBIN, S.C.
PERSONAL Born 11/05/1949, Kansas City, MO **DISCIPLINE** SOCIOLOGY **EDUCATION** Univ Chicago, PhD 82, MA 76; Univ Missouri, BA 71. **CAREER** SUNY Purchase Col, lectr, asst prof, assoc prof, prof, 86 to 98-; Yale Univ, post doc fel, 83-84; Univ Chicago, post doc fel, 83. **HONORS AND AWARDS** Phi Beta Kappa; Phi Eta Sigma; NY Times Notable Book of the Year; Gustavas Myers Soc Outstanding Book. **MEMBERSHIPS** ASA **RESEARCH** Sociology of art; culture; mass media; censorship; deviant and social control; freedom of expression issues. **SELECTED PUBLICATIONS** Auth, Displays of Power: Memory and Amnesia in the American Museum, NYU Press, 99; Arresting Images, Impolitic Art, Uncivil Actions, Routledge, 92; Bureaucratizing the Muse: Public Funds and the Cultural Worker, U of Chicago Press, 87. **CONTACT ADDRESS** Social Science Division, SUNY, Purchase, Purchase, NY, 10577.

DUBOFSKY, MELVYN
PERSONAL Born 10/25/1934, Brooklyn, NY, m, 1959, 2 children **DISCIPLINE** UNITED STATES LABOR HISTORY **EDUCATION** Brooklyn Col, BA, 55; Univ Rochester, PhD, 60. **CAREER** Asst prof US hist, Northern Ill Univ, 59-67; asst prof hist, Univ Mass, Amherst, 67-69; sr lectr Am labor hist, Univ Warwick, 69-70; prof hist, Univ Wis-Milwaukee, 70-71; Fulbright sr lectr US hist, Tel Aviv Univ-Israel, 77-78; PROF HIST and SOCIOL, STATE UNIV NY, BINGHAMTON, 71-, Lectr Brooklyn Col, 58-59; grants-in-aid, Am Asn State and Local Hist, 62, Am Philos Soc, 64-65 and Am Coun Learned Soc, 65; Nat Endowment for Humanities sr fel, 73-74; adv, Am Labor Hist TV Ser, 75-. **MEMBERSHIPS** AHA; Orgn Am Historians. **RESEARCH** John L Lewis and the coal miners; labor during the Great Depression and New Deal; radicalism and trade unionism, 1870 to present. **SELECTED PUBLICATIONS** Auth, From Prairie to Prison --The Life of Social-Activist Ohare, Kate, Richards, Revs Am Hist, Vol 23, 95; The Centralia Tragedy of 1919--Smith, Elmer and the Wobblies, Revs Am Hist, Vol 23, 95; The Union Inspiration in American Politics--The Autoworkers and the Making of a Liberal Industrial Order, J Am Hist, Vol 82, 95; Wobblies, Pile Butts, and Other Heroes, Laborlore Explorations, Labor History, Vol 36, 95; Without Blare of Trumpets--Drew, Walter, the National Erectors Association, and the Open Shop Movement, 1903-1957, J Econ Hist, Vol 56, 96; Trade Union Growth and Decline--An International Study, Labor Hist, Vol 36, 95; Starting Out in the Fifties--True Confessions of a Labor Historian, Labor Hist, Vol 34, 93. **CONTACT ADDRESS** Dept of Hist, State Univ New York, Binghamton, NY, 13901.

DUCHIN, FAYE
PERSONAL Born 01/20/1944, m, 2 children **DISCIPLINE** COMPUTER SCIENCE **EDUCATION** Cornell Univ, BA, 65; Univ Grenoble & Paris; Univ Calif, Berkeley, MA, 72, PhD, 73. **CAREER** Econ, 74-77, Mathematica Inc, NJ; assoc prof, 84-86, res assoc prof, 86-87, res prof, 87-96, Wagner Schl of Public Svc; assoc res scientist, 77-80, sr res scientist, 80-96, assoc dir, 81-85, dir, 85-96, Inst for Econ Analysis, NY Univ; dean & prof, 96-, Schl of Humanities & Soc Sciences, Rensselaer Polytechnic Inst. **HONORS AND AWARDS** Boutros Boutros-Ghali Scholar for Europe/N Amer, 94-95; Fel, United Nations Univ, Tokyo, 94-, AT&T Fel, indust Ecol, 93-94 & 94-95. **MEMBERSHIPS** ISEE; AEA; AAAS; Intl Input-Output Econ Asn. **RESEARCH** Structural economics; lifestyles; technology. **SELECTED PUBLICATIONS** Auth, The Future of the Environment: Ecological Economics and Technological Change, Oxford Univ Press, 94; auth, Strategies for Environmentally Sound Economic Development, Investing in Natural Capital: The Ecological Econ Approach to Sustainability, Island Press, 94; art, Integrated Environmental-Economic Accounting, Natural Resource Accounts, and Natural Resource Management in Africa, Intl Environ Alliance, 94; art, Technological Change, Trade and the Environment, Ecological Economics, 95; art, In Honor of Wassily Leontief's 90th Birthday, Structural Change & Econ Dynamics, 95; art, The Choice of Technology and Associate Changes in Prices in the US Economy, Structural Change & Econ Dynamics, 95; auth, Ecological Economics: The Second Stage, Down to Earth: Practical Applications of Ecological Economics, 96; art, Ecological Economics: The Research Challenge, Ecological Econ Bul, 96; art, Population Change, Lifestyle and Technology: How Much Difference Can They Make?, Pop & Develop Rev, 96; auth, Structural Economics: A Strategy for Analyzing the Implications of Consumption, Environ Significant Consumption: Res Direct, Natl Acad Press, 97; auth, Life-style and Technology: How Much Difference Can They Make?, Tata Energy Res Inst, 97; auth, Global Economics, Environment, and Health, Intl Persp on Environ, Develop, Health: Toward a Sustainable World, Springer Pub, 97; art, Technology and Lifestyle, Pol Ecology, 97; art, The Far from Dismal Science, Quantum, 97; auth, Structural Economics: Measuring Changes in Technology, Lifestyles and the Environment, Island Press, 98; auth, Global Eco-Restructuring and Technological Change in the 21st Century, Eco-Restructuring: Implications for Sustainable Develop, United Nations Univ Press, 98; art, Prospects for the Recycling of Plastics in the Unites States, Structural Change and Economic Dynamics, 98. **CONTACT ADDRESS** Rensselaer Polytech Inst, 110 8th Street, Troy, NY, 12180-3590. **EMAIL** duchin@rpi.edu

DUCK, STEVE
PERSONAL Keynsham, England, m, 1987, 4 children **DISCIPLINE** PSYCHOLOGY **EDUCATION** Oxford Univ, BA, 68, MA, 72; Sheffield Univ, PhD, 71. **CAREER** Lectr, Glasgow Univ, 71-73; lectr, 73-78, sr lectr, 78-86, Univ of Lancaster; DANIEL & AMY STARCH PROF, UNIV OF IOWA, 86-. **HONORS AND AWARDS** GR Miller Book Award, SCA, 96; Fel, APA, APS, ICA, AAAPP; Berscheid-Hatfield Distinguished Mid-Career Achievement Award, INPR, 98. **MEMBERSHIPS** Int Network on Personal Relationships; Int Soc Indy Personal Relationships; Nat Commun Asn. **RESEARCH** Personal relationships; personal construct theory. **SELECTED PUBLICATIONS** Auth, Meaningful Relationships, 94; auth, Handbook of Personal Relationships, 2nd ed, Wiley, 97; auth, Human Relationships, 3rd ed, 98; auth, Relations to Others, 2nd ed, Open Univ, 99. **CONTACT ADDRESS** Commun Studies Dept, Univ of Iowa, 105-BCSB, Iowa City, IA, 52242. **EMAIL** steve-duck@uiowa.edu

DUCKER, JAMES H.
PERSONAL Born 07/24/1950, Rochester, NY **DISCIPLINE** AMERICAN HISTORY **EDUCATION** Villanova Univ, BA, 72; Univ Ill, AM, 74, PhD (hist), 80. **CAREER** HISTORIAN, BUREAU OF LAND MANAGEMENT, 81-. **MEMBERSHIPS** Orgn Am Historians. **RESEARCH** American social and Western history; Alaska History. **SELECTED PUBLICATIONS** Auth, Kusiq--An Eskimo Life from the Arctic Coast of Alaska, J West, Vol 32, 93; Inuit--Glimpses of an Arctic Past, A Indian Cult Rsrc J, Vol 21, 97; Gold Rushers North--A Census Study of the Yukon and Alaskan Gold Rushes, 1896-1900, Pac Northwest Quart, Vol 85, 94; Arctic School Teacher--Kulukak, Alaska, 1931-1933, J West, Vol 34, 95; A Hogheads Random Railroad Reminiscences, Pac Northwest Quart, Vol 88, 97; Pioneering on the Yukon 1892-1917, J West, Vol 34, 95; Out of Harms Way--Relocating Northwest Alaska Eskimos, 1907-1917, Am Indian Cult Rsrc J, Vol 20, 96; Tourism in Katmai Country--A History of Concessions Activity in Katmai National Park and Preserve, Public Historian, Vol 17, 95; Gold at Fortymile Creek--Early Days in the Yukon, J West, Vol 35, 96; Chilkoot Trail--Heritage Route to the Klondike, Public Historian, Vol 19, 97; Aleutian Echoes, J West, Vol 36, 97. **CONTACT ADDRESS** 1611 Early View Dr, Anchorage, AK, 99504.

DUCLOW, DONALD F.
PERSONAL Born 01/11/1946, Chicago, IL, m, 1970 **DISCIPLINE** ENGLISH, PHILSOSOPHY, MEDIEVAL STUDIES **EDUCATION** DePaul Univ, BA, English, philosophy, 68, MA, philosophy, 69; Bryn Mawr Coll, MA, medieval studies, 72, PhD, philosophy, 74. **CAREER** Visiting prof, philosophy, Fordham Univ, 78; asst prof of philosophy, 74-79, assoc prof of philosophy, 79-89, prof of philosophy, 89-, Gwynedd-Mercy Coll. **HONORS AND AWARDS** Mellon Fellow in the Humanities, Univ Pa, 80-81; NEH summer seminars, 87, 93. **MEMBERSHIPS** Amer Acad Religion; Medieval Acad Am; sec, Amer Cusanus Soc; Amer Assn Univ Profs; pres, Gwynedd-Mercy Coll Chap, 96-97. **RESEARCH** Medieval philosophy and religion. **SELECTED PUBLICATIONS** Auth, "Divine Nothingness and Self-Creation in John Scotus Eriugena," The Journ of Religion, vol 57, 77; "'My Suffering Is God': Meister Eckhart's Book of Divine Consolation," Theological Studies, vol 44, 83, reprinted in Classical and Medieval Literature Criticism, 93; "Into the Whirlwind of Suffering: Resistance and Transformation," Second Opinion, Nov 88; "Nicholas of Cusa," in Medieval Philosophers, vol 15, Dictionary of Literary Biography, 92; "Isaiah Meets the Seraph: Breaking Ranks in Dionysius and Eriugena?" in Eriugena: East and West, 94. **CONTACT ADDRESS** Gwynedd-Mercy Col, Gwynedd Valley, PA, 19437-0901.

DUDDEN, ARTHUR POWER
PERSONAL Born 10/26/1921, Cleveland, OH, m, 1965, 3 children **DISCIPLINE** HISTORY **EDUCATION** Wayne Univ, AB, 42; Univ Mich, AM, 47, PhD(hist), 50. **CAREER** From asst prof to assoc prof, 50-65, chm dept, 68-78, PROF EMER HIST, HUM, BRYN MAWR COL, 65-, CHMN DEPT, 81- . **HONORS AND AWARDS** Sr Fulbright res scholar, Denmark, 59-60 lectr, 92; mem screening comt, Inst Int Educ, Scandinavia, 61, 62; dist lectr, US Dept State, 63; pres, Fulbright Alumni Asn, 77-80, executive dir, 80- ; Bd Dir, Hist Soc Penn, 93- ; consult Nat Archives, 93- ; Penn Commonwealth Speaker, 91, 95; **MEMBERSHIPS** AHA; Orgn Am Historians; Am Studies Asn (treas, 68-69 & 72, exec secy, 69-72). **RESEARCH** American history, biography and humor; international relations. **SELECTED PUBLICATIONS** Ed, Woodrow Wilson and World of Today, Univ Pa, 57; The Assault of Laughter: A Treasury of American Political Humor, Barnes, 62; The United States of America: A Syllabus of American Studies (2 vols), Univ Pa, 63; Joseph Fels and the Singletax Movement, Temple Univ, 71; Pardon Us, Mr President!, a Treasury of American Political Humor, Barnes, 75; co-ed, The Fulbright Experience, 1946-1986, Rutgers, 87; ed, American Humor, Oxford, 87; auth, The American Pacific from the Old China Trade to the Present, Oxford, 92; ed, The Logbook of the Captain's Clerk: Adventures in the China Seas, Donnelley, 95. **CONTACT ADDRESS** Dept of History, Bryn Mawr Col, Bryn Mawr, PA, 19010. **EMAIL** 76511.3300@compuserve.com

DUDDEN, FAYE E.
DISCIPLINE HISTORY **EDUCATION** Cornell Univ, AB, 70; Rochester, PhD, 81. **CAREER** Asst prof, hist, Union Coll; current, PROF, HIST, COLGATE UNIV **HONORS AND AWARDS** George Freedley Mem Award **MEMBERSHIPS** Am Antiquarian Soc **RESEARCH** Women in theater, 1790-1870. **SELECTED PUBLICATIONS** Auth, Serving Women: Household Service in Nineteenth-Century America, 83; auth, "Experts and Servants, " Jour of Soc Hist, 86; "Small Town Knights," Labor Hist, 87; Women in the American Theater: Actresses and Audiences, 1790-1870, Yale Univ PRess, 94. **CONTACT ADDRESS** Dept of Hist, Colgate Univ, Hamilton, NY, 13346.

DUDGEON, RALPH T.
PERSONAL Born 11/08/1948, McKeesort, PA, m, 1973, 2 children **DISCIPLINE** MUSICOLOGY **EDUCATION** San Diego State Univ, BA, 70, MA, 72; Univ Calif, San Diego,

PhD, 80. **CAREER** Music tchr, San Diequito High Sch, 71-74; applied trumpet instr, Point Loma Col, 76; ensemble dir, Mira Costa Col, 76; dept chmn, Torrey Pines High Sch, 74-81; asst prof, Univ Tex, Dallas, 81-85; assoc prof, 85-93, prof, 94- , chemn, 97-00, State Univ New York; acting dir, cur, Streitwieser Found Trumpet Museum, 93-94; music res, consult, Musica Kremsmunster, Instrumentenmuseum, 96-; ensemble dir, Syracuse Univ, 98-. **HONORS AND AWARDS** Res Grant, Univ Calif, 79, 80; Org Res Grant, 84; Who's Who in Am Music, 85;Who's Who East,85; Pa Arts Council Grant 87; Fac Res Grant, State Univ New York, 91; Men Achievement, 93; Hon Life Membership, Tri-M Music Honor Soc,93; Crystal Trust Grant, Admin Streitwieser Found, 93-94; Mus Assesment Prog Grant, Am Asn Mus, 94. **MEMBERSHIPS** Am Fed Musicians; Am Musical Instrument Soc; Am Musicological Soc; Hist Brass Soc; Int Trumpet Guild; Nat Asn Col Wind Percussion instrs, New York State Sch Music Asn; Sonneck Soc; Streitwieser Found Trumphet Mus. **RESEARCH** Musical instruments of the 19th century & period instrument performance. **SELECTED PUBLICATIONS** Auth, art, An Interview with Edna White Chandler, 90; auth, art, Nineteenth-Century Keyed Bugle Performers: A Checklist, 92; auth, The Keyed Bugle, 93; auth, art, A Conversation with John Wallace and Trevor Herbert, 96; auth, art, The Legacy of Walter M. Smith, 98. **CONTACT ADDRESS** 5745 US Rte 11, Homer, NY, 13077. **EMAIL** dudgeonr@cortland.edu

DUDLEY, WILLIAM SHELDON
PERSONAL Born 07/14/1936, Brooklyn, NY, m, 1965, 2 children **DISCIPLINE** AMERICAN AND LATIN AMERICAN HISTORY **EDUCATION** Williams Col, BA, 58; Columbia Univ, MA, 66, PhD (hist), 72. **CAREER** Asst prof Latin Am hist, Southern Methodist Univ, 70-77; asst head res br, 77-81, HEAD RES BR, NAVAL HIST CTR, WASHINGTON NAVY YARD, 82-. **MEMBERSHIPS** Orgn Am Historians; Conf Latin Am Hist; North Am Soc Oceanic Hist; Soc Hist Federal Govt (treas); Am Military Inst. **RESEARCH** War of 1812; Brazilian history, 19th and 20th centuries. **SELECTED PUBLICATIONS** Auth, To Shining Sea--A History of the United States Navy, 1775-1991, Intl Hist Rev, Vol 15, 1993 **CONTACT ADDRESS** Naval History Ctr Washington Navy Yard, Washington, DC, 20374.

DUFF NEIMAN, FRASER
DISCIPLINE ARCHITECTURAL HISTORY **EDUCATION** Yale Univ, BA, PhD. **CAREER** Lectr. **RESEARCH** Archaeological theory; quantitative methods; historical archaeology of the Chesapeake. **SELECTED PUBLICATIONS** Auth, pubs on collapse of Classic Maya civilization, and social relations in the 17th-century Chesapeake. **CONTACT ADDRESS** Dept of Architectural History., Virginia Univ, Charlottesville, VA, 22903. **EMAIL** fn9r@virginia.edu

DUFFIN, JACALYN
PERSONAL London, ON, Canada **DISCIPLINE** HISTORY OF MEDICINE **EDUCATION** Univ Toronto, MD, 74; Sorbonne, France, DEA, 83, PhD, 85. **CAREER** Gen practice locum tenens, Come-by-Chance, NF, 77; haematology/oncology, Ont Cancer Treatment & Res Found, Thunder Bay, 80-82; Hannah Postdoc Fel Hist Med, Univ Ottawa, 85-88; consult haematologist, Kingston Gen Hospital, 88-94; HANNAH PROF HIST MEDICINE, QUEEN'S UNIV, 88-. **HONORS AND AWARDS** W.F.Connell Award Tchg Exellence, Queen's Univ, Fac Med, 92. **MEMBERSHIPS** Am Asn Hist Med; Can Fedn Hum; Can Soc Hist Med; Hist Sci Soc. **SELECTED PUBLICATIONS** Auth, In View of the Body of Job Broom: A Glimpse of the Medical Knowledge and Practice of John Rolph, in Can Bull of Med Hist, 90; auth, The Death of Sara Lovell and the Constrained Feminism of Emily Stowe, in Can Med Asn J, 92; auth, Langstaff: A Nineteenth-Century Medical Life, 93. **CONTACT ADDRESS** Dept of Medicine, Queen's Univ, Kingston, ON, K7L 3N6. **EMAIL** duffinj@post.queensu

DUFFY, JOHN JOSEPH
PERSONAL Born 04/25/1931, Charleston, SC, m, 1959, 3 children **DISCIPLINE** UNITED STATES HISTORY **EDUCATION** Col Charleston, BS, 52; Univ SC, MA, 55, PhD (hist), 63. **CAREER** Resident dir, Beaufort Regional Campus, 59-66, acad coordr Col Gen Studies, 66-67, assoc provost, Regional Campuses, 67-72, assoc prof hist and assoc vprovost, 72-77, VPRES TWO YEAR CAMPUSES AND CONTINUING EDUC, UNIV SC, 77-. **MEMBERSHIPS** Southern Hist Asn. **RESEARCH** Oral history; South Carolina politics; contemporary United States. **SELECTED PUBLICATIONS** Auth, Blood and Money , Romance Quart, Vol 44, 97; Zola--A Life, Romance Quart, Vol 44, 97; Zola Therese Raquin, 19th Century Fr Studs, Vol 23, 94; Face Value--Physiognomical Thought and the Legible Body in Marivaux, Lavater, Balzac, Gautier and Zola,19th Century Fr Studs, Vol 25, 96; Sidelines,19th Century Fr Studs, Vol 24, 95. **CONTACT ADDRESS** Univ of SC, 1626 College St, Columbia, SC, 29208.

DUFOUR, RON
DISCIPLINE COLONIAL AND REVOLUTIONARY AMERICA **EDUCATION** Merrimack Col, BA; Col William and Mary, MA, PhD. **CAREER** Instr, ch dept Hist, RI Col. **RESEARCH** Early Am, esp. soc, intellectual, cult; 20th century Am music and cult, esp. jazz, blues, rock. **SELECTED PUBLICATIONS** Auth, Modernization in Colonial Massachusetts; Colonial America **CONTACT ADDRESS** Rhode Island Col, Providence, RI, 02908.

DUGGAN, LAWRENCE GERALD
PERSONAL Born 02/18/1944, Hartford, CT, m, 1977, 1 child **DISCIPLINE** RENAISSANCE AND REFORMATION HISTORY **EDUCATION** Col of the Holy Cross, AB, 65; Harvard Univ, AM, 66, PhD (hist), 71. **CAREER** Asst prof, 70-77, ASSOC PROF HIST, UNIV DEL, 77-, Alexander von Humboldt Found fel, 76-77. **MEMBERSHIPS** Cath Hist Asn; Int Comn Study Rep and Parliamentary Inst; Past and Present Soc. **RESEARCH** Ecclesiastical and Germany history; representative institutions. **SELECTED PUBLICATIONS** Auth, Contributions to the History and Structure of the Medieval Germania Sacra - German - Crusius,I, Editor/, Speculum-A J Medieval Studies, Vol 68, 93; The German Episcopacy and the Implementation of the Decrees of the 4th Lateran Council, 1216-1245--Watchmen on the Tower, Am Hist Rev, Vol 101, 96; Noble Bondsmen--Ministerial Marriages in the Archdiocese of Salzburg,, Cath Hist Rev, Vol 82, 96; Pflug, Julius 1499-1564 and the Religious Crisis in Germany During the 16th Century--An Attempt at Biographical and Theological Synthesis, Cath Hist Rev, Vol 80, 94; The Way to the Reichstag--Studies on Changes in the Nature of Centralized Power in Germany, 1314-1410, Am Hist Rev, Vol 99, 94; Contributions to the History and Structure of the Medieval Germania Sacra, Speculum J Medieval Stud, Vol 68, 93. **CONTACT ADDRESS** Dept of Hist, Univ of Del, Newark, DE, 19711.

DUKES, JACK RICHARD
PERSONAL Born 01/21/1941, Indianapolis, IN, m, 1963, 1 child **DISCIPLINE** MODERN EUROPEAN HISTORY **EDUCATION** Beloit Col, AB, 63; Northern Ill Univ, MA, 65; Univ Ill, Urbana, PhD, 70. **CAREER** Asst prof, Macalester Col, 69-70; asst prof, 70-75, dir, Russ & E Europ Studies Prog, 72-74, Assoc Prof, 75-83, prof mod europ hist, Carroll Col, 83-, Chmn Dept, 72-96; Fel, Univ Ill, 68-69; Nat Endowment for Humanities fel in residence Ger hist, Univ Calif, Santa Barbara, 77-78; vis assoc prof Russ hist, Univ Calif, Santa Barbara, 80-81; Pres, Exec Dir-Waukesha Sister City Asn, 88. **HONORS AND AWARDS** Reader's Digest Humanitarian Award, 90; Benjamin F. Richardson Award for Excellence in Teaching, Res and Educ Innovation, Carroll Col; NEH Fel Russ Hist, St. Petersburg, USSR, 91; Distinguished Alumni Award, Beloit Col, 93; Honorary Citizenship, Kokshetan, Kayakstan, 95; Eurasia Found grants for promoting international education, 95-96, 96-97; Carroll Col Community Service Award, 98. **MEMBERSHIPS** AHA; Conf Group Cent Europ Hist; Coun Europ Studies; Western Asn Ger Studies,; Soc Historians Am Foreign Rel; Am Asn Advan Slavic Studies. **RESEARCH** Armaments policy; German history; Russian history. **SELECTED PUBLICATIONS** Coauth, Another Germany, Westview Press, 88; author of numerous articles. **CONTACT ADDRESS** Dept of Hist, Carroll Col, Wisconsin, 100 N East Ave, Waukesha, WI, 53186-5593. **EMAIL** jdukes@carroll1.cc.edu

DULEY, MARGOT I.
DISCIPLINE HISTORY **EDUCATION** Univ London, PhD. **CAREER** Prof, Eastern Michigan Univ. **RESEARCH** South Asia, history of women. **SELECTED PUBLICATIONS** Auth, Where Once Our Mothers Stood We Stand; co-ed, The Cross-Cultural Study of Women. **CONTACT ADDRESS** Dept of History and Philosophy, Eastern Michigan Univ, 701 Pray-Harrold, Ypsilanti, MI, 48197. **EMAIL** his_duley@online.emich.edu

DULLES, JOHN WATSON FOSTER
PERSONAL Born 05/20/1913, Auburn, NY, m, 1940, 4 children **DISCIPLINE** BRAZILIAN & MEXICAN POLITICAL HISTORY **EDUCATION** Princeton Univ, AB, 35; Harvard Univ, MBA, 37; Univ Ariz, BSMetE, 43, MetE, 51. **CAREER** Asst mgr ore dept, Cia Minera de Penoles, Mex, 46-48, mgr ore dept, 48-52, dir commercial div, 52-54, asst gen mgr, 54-59, exec vpres, 59; vpres, Cia de Mineracao Novalimense, Brazil, 60-62; univ prof Latin AM studies, Univ Tex, Austin, 62-, Brown-Lupton Found lectr grant, 64-66; prof hist, Univ Ariz, 66-91; mem US deleg to Inter-Am Econ & Soc Coun, Orgn Am States, Chile, 67; participant, US State Dept Consultation on Communism in Latin Am, 68; consult, Bur Intel & Res, US Dept State, 68-73. **HONORS AND AWARDS** Univ Ariz Achievement Medal, 60; Partners of Alliance Medal, Brazil 66; Theta Tau(engineering), Alumni Hall of Fame. **MEMBERSHIPS** AHA; Am Soc of the Most Verable Order of St. John of Jerusalem; Inst Hist e Geog Brasileiro; Tex Inst of Letters; Calif Inst of Int Studies. **RESEARCH** Life of Sabral Pinto; Brazilian political history, 1900-1998. **SELECTED PUBLICATIONS** Auth, Castello Branco: The Making of a Brazilian President, 78 & President Castello Branco: Brazilian Reformer, 80, Tex A&M Univ; Brazilian Communism 1935-45, Univ Texas, 83; The Sao Paulo Law School and the Anti-Vargas Resistance 1938-1945, Univ Texas, 86; Carlos Lacerda, Brazilian Crusader Vol 1, Univ Texas, 91; Carlos Lacerda Vol 2, Univ Texas, 96. **CONTACT ADDRESS** Univ of Texas, PO Box 7934, Austin, TX, 78713-7934.

DUMOND, D.E.
PERSONAL Born 03/23/1929, Childress, TX, m, 1950 **DISCIPLINE** ANTHROPOLOGY/ARCHAEOLOGY **EDUCATION** Univ New Mexico, BA, 49; Mexico City College, MA, 57; Univ Oregon, PhD, 62. **CAREER** Asst Prof, Assoc Prof, Prof, 62-94, Univ Oregon; Dir 77-96, OR State Museum; U of OR Univ Museum Nat Hist, Dir 82-96, Dir emeritus, 96-. **HONORS AND AWARDS** SSRC Fel; NEH Fel; Japan Soc Promo Sci Fel; SI Fel; Arctic Inst NA Elec Fel; AAAS Elec Fel; AAA Career Achv Awd. **MEMBERSHIPS** AAA; SAA; AAA. **RESEARCH** Archaeology and Ethnohistory of the American Arctic; Archaeology and Ethnohistory of Mexico. **SELECTED PUBLICATIONS** Auth, The Machete and the Cross: Campesino Rebellion in Yucatan, Lincoln, Univ of NE Press, 97; Poison in the Cup: The South Alaskan Smallpox Epidemic of 1835, in: Chin Hills to Chiloquin: Papers Honoring the Versatile Career of Theodore Stern, edited, Univ of Oregon Anthro Papers, 96; Holocene Prehistory of the Northernmost North Pacific, J World Prehistory, 95; co auth, Paugvik: A Nineteenth Century Native Village on Bristol Bay Southwestern Alaska, Fieldiana Anthro, Field Museum of Natural History, Chicago, 95; auth, Western Arctic Culture, a section in the article, The Arctic, Encyc Britannica, Macropaedia, 93. **CONTACT ADDRESS** Dept of Anthropology, Univ Oregon, Eugene, OR, 97403-1218. **EMAIL** ddumond@oregon.uoregon.edu

DUMONT, MICHELINE
PERSONAL Born 07/02/1935, Verdun, PQ, Canada **DISCIPLINE** HISTORY **EDUCATION** Univ Montreal, BA, 57, LL, 59; Univ Laval, DES, 64. **CAREER** Tchr, Inst Cardinal-Leger (Montreal), 59-68; PROF HISTORY, UNIV SHERBROOKE, 70-. **HONORS AND AWARDS** L'Academie I de la Soc Royale Can, 93. **MEMBERSHIPS** Institut d'histoire d'Amerique Francaise (pres, 95-97); Can Hist Asn (Coun 89-92); Soc des professeurs d'histoire du Quebec (vice-pres, 75-77). **SELECTED PUBLICATIONS** Auth, L'histoire apprivoisee, 79; coauth, Histoire des femmes au Quebec depuis quatre siecles, 82, 2nd ed 92 (Eng transl, Quebec Women: A History, 87); coauth, Les couventines, 86; coauth, Les Religieuses sont-elles feministes?, 95. **CONTACT ADDRESS** Dep d'histoire, Univ Sherbrooke, Sherbrooke, PQ, J1K 2R1.

DUNAR, ANDREW J.
PERSONAL Born 01/25/1946, Milwaukee, WI, m, 1968, 3 children **DISCIPLINE** HISTORY **EDUCATION** Northwestern Univ, BA, 68; Univ Calif, Los Angeles, MA, 74; Univ S Calif, PhD, 81. **CAREER** Asst prof, Manchester Col, 81-83; vis asst prof, Union COl, 83-84; asst prof, 84-88, assoc prof, 88-94, PROF, UNIV ALA, HUNTSVILLE, 94. **MEMBERSHIPS** OAH, AHA, Oral Hist Asn. **RESEARCH** Harry S. Truman, aerospace hist, 20th cent US society. **SELECTED PUBLICATIONS** Auth, The Truman Scnadals and the Politics of Morality, Univ Mo Press, 84, paperback, 97; co-auth, Building Hoover Dam: An Oral History of the Great Depression, Twayne Pubs, 93; co-auth, Power to Explore: The History of Marshall Space Flight Center, 1960-1990, NASA, forthcoming. **CONTACT ADDRESS** Dept of History, Univ of Alabama, Huntsville, Huntsville, AL, 35899. **EMAIL** dunara@email.uah.edu

DUNCAN, CAROL G.
DISCIPLINE ART HISTORY **EDUCATION** Univ Chicago, BA, 58, AM, 60; Columbia Univ, PhD, 68. **CAREER** Vis appointments, Univ Calif, Los Angeles, 74, Univ Calif, San Diego, 76, Univ Queensland, 85; vis Eminent Appelton Scholar, Fla State Univ, 99; vis Mellon Prof, Univ Pittsburg; 72-, Ramapo Col, NJ. **CONTACT ADDRESS** 400 Central Park W, New York, NY, 10025.

DUNCAN, RICHARD R.
DISCIPLINE HISTORY **EDUCATION** Ohio Univ, AB, 54, MA, 55; Ohio State Univ, PhD, 63. **CAREER** Instr, Kent State Univ, 61-64; asst prof, Univ Richmond, 64- 67; asst prof, 67-70, assoc prof, 70-98, PROF, GEORGETOWN UNIV. **SELECTED PUBLICATIONS** Auth, Lest We Forget, A Guide to Civil War Monuments in Maryland, Civil War Hist, Vol 42, 96; Season of Fire, The Confederate Strike on Washington, Civil War Hist, Vol 42, 96; Footprints of a Regiment--A Recollection of the 1st Georgia Regulars, 1861-1865, Civil War Hist, Vol 39, 93; Saber and Scapegoat--Stuart, J. E. B. and the Gettysburg Controversy, J Southern Hist, Vol 62, 96; A Surgeons Civil War--The Letters and Diary of Holt, Daniel, M., Civil War Hist, Vol 41, 95. **CONTACT ADDRESS** History Dept, Georgetown Univ, Washington, DC, 20057-1035.

DUNCAN, RUSSELL
DISCIPLINE HISTORY **EDUCATION** Geor South Univ, BS, 73; Valdosta State Univ, MS, 75; Univ of Geor, MA, 84, PhD, 88. **CAREER** ASST PROF, HIST, JOHN CARROLL UNIV **MEMBERSHIPS** Am Antiquarian Soc **CONTACT ADDRESS** Dept of Hist, John Carroll Univ, 20700 N Park Blvd, University Hgts, OH, 44118.

DUNDES, ALAN
PERSONAL Born 09/08/1934, New York, NY, m, 1958, 3 children **DISCIPLINE** FOLKLORE **EDUCATION** Yale Univ, BA, 55, MAT, 58; Ind Univ, Bloomington, PhD(fol-

klore), 62. **CAREER** Instr English, Univ Kans, 62-63; from asst prof to assoc prof anthrop, 63-68, prof anthrop & folklore, Univ Calif, Berkeley, 68-, Guggenheim fel, 66-67; Nat Endowment for Humanities, sr fel, 72-73. **HONORS AND AWARDS** Sigillo d'Oro (Seal of Gold), the Pitre Prize for Lifetime Achievement in Folklore, 93; Distinguished Teaching Award, 94. **MEMBERSHIPS** Am Folklore Soc; Am Anthrop Asn. **RESEARCH** Symbolism; structuralism. **SELECTED PUBLICATIONS** Auth, The Morphology of North American Indian Folktales, Acad Sci Fennica, Helsinki, 64; ed, The Study of Folklore, 65 & Mother Wit from the Laughing Barrel: Readings in the Interpretation of Afro-American Folklore, 73, Prentice-Hall; coauth, La Terra in Piazza: An Interpretation of the Palio Siena, Univ Calif Press, 75; Urban Folklore from the Paperwork Empire, Am Folklore Soc, 75; compiler, Folklore Theses and Dissertations in the United States, Univ Tex Press, 76; auth, Interpreting Folklore, Ind Univ Press, 80; coauth, The Art of Mixing Metaphors, Acad Sci Fennica, Helsinki, 81. Auth, Life is Like a Chicken Coop Ladder, Columbia Univ Press, 84; Parsing Through Customs, Univ Wisc Press, 87; Cracking Jokes, Ten Speed Press, 87; coauth, When You're Up to Your Ass in Alligators, Wayne State Univ Press, 87, auth, Folklore Matters, Univ Tenn Press, 89; coauth, Never Try to Teach a Pig to Sing, Wayne State Univ Press, 91; coauth, Sometimes the Dragon Wins, Syracuse Univ Press, 96; auth, From Game to War, Univ Press KY, 97; Two Tales of Crow and Sparrow, Rowman & Littlefield, 97. **CONTACT ADDRESS** Dept of Anthropology, Univ of Calif, 232 Kroeber Hall, Berkeley, CA, 94720-3711.

DUNKAK, HARRY MATTHEW

PERSONAL Born 04/14/1929, New York, NY **DISCIPLINE** AMERICAN HISTORY **EDUCATION** Iona Col, BA, 51; Fordham Univ, MA, 59; St John's Univ, PhD, 68. **CAREER** Teacher, Rice High Sch, NY, 52-54, Cardinal Hayes High Sch, 54-65 & Power Mem Acad, 65-66; instr, 67-69, assoc prof 69-85, asst dean, Sch Arts & Sci, 78-85, PROF HIST, IONA COL, 85-. **MEMBERSHIPS** Am Cath Hist Asn; Orgn Am Historians; AHA; Huguenot-Thomas Paine Hist Asn. **RESEARCH** The 1767-1770 non-importation agreements and the newspapers of Boston; American colonial history, especially New York in the 18th century; New York Whig politics, 1752-1769 and the role of J M Scott. **SELECTED PUBLICATIONS** Auth, Samuel Pintard, a New Rochelle loyalist, Westchester Hist Quart; The Papers of an Unheralded Irish-American Historian, Michael J O'Brien (1870-1960), in Eire - Ireland, A Journal of Irish Studies, Irish Am Cultural Inst, Morristown, NJ; The 1733 Eastchester Election, the Zenger Trial & Freedom of the Press, Westchester His, spring 88; A Colonial & Revolutionary Parish in New York: St Paul's Church in Eastchester, in Anglican & Episcopal History, 12/88; St Columbo of the Isle of Iona, Iona Mag, spring 88; The Lorillard Family of Westchester County: Tobacco, Property & Nature, Westchester Hist, summer 95; The Irish of Early Westchester County, monogr, Iona College, 94. **CONTACT ADDRESS** Dept of Hist, Iona Col, 715 North Ave, New Rochelle, NY, 10801-1890. **EMAIL** mdunkak@atgnet.com

DUNLAY, DON E.

PERSONAL Born 12/09/1928, Shreveport, LA, m, 1955, 1 child **DISCIPLINE** PSYCHOLOGY **EDUCATION** AB, Univ TN, 48; PhD, Univ MI, 55. **CAREER** Inst, Univ MI, 52; Active Duty U S Army, 54-56; Lecturer Psychol, FL State Univ; Extension for Overseas Military Personel, 55-56; Assit Prof, Univ IL, 56-59; Faculty Res Fellow Graduate Coll, 57; Res Fellow, Harvard Univ, 58; Assoc Prof, 59-64; Prof, Univ IL, 64; Affiliate, Beckman Inst, 90-. **HONORS AND AWARDS** Graduate Student Org Award for Excellence in Graduate Teaching, 74; Psi Chi Award for Excellence in Undergraduate Teaching, 84, 88; Mabel Kirkpatrick Hohenboken Award for Excellence In Teaching in Psychol, 92; William F. Prodasy Award for Distinguished Teaching in the Coll of Liberal Arts and Sci, 94. **MEMBERSHIPS** Amer Psycholo Soc Fellow; Amer Psychol Assoc Fellow Div 3 Experimental Psychol; Psychonomic Soc; Assoc for the Sci Study of Consciouseness; Soc Philos and Psycholo; Sigma Xi. **RESEARCH** Cognitive Phsychol; consciousness and non-conscious processes; intentions formation; casusal reasoning. **SELECTED PUBLICATIONS** Dulany, D E, 97; Scientific approaches to conciousness, Mahwah NJ, Lawrence Erlbaum Assoc, Dulany D E, (in press 98); Encylopedia of Psychology, Washington and NY, Amer Psychol Assoc and Oxford Univ Press, Dulany,D.E. (in press 98); Behavioral and Brain Sciences, Consciousness in theories of explicit and implicit Psychonomic Soc Chicago, 96; Ed, American Journal of Psychology, 88-; Graduate Study Committee, 94-98; Chair Livrary Committee, 95-97. **CONTACT ADDRESS** Depy of Psycholo, Univ of Illinois, Champaigh, IL, 61820. **EMAIL** ddulanyes@psych.,uiuc.edu

DUNLOP, ANNE

DISCIPLINE ART HISTORY **EDUCATION** Univ Warwick, PhD, 97. **CAREER** Dept Art Hist, Concordia Univ **HONORS AND AWARDS** Rome award, Brit Sch at Rome. **RESEARCH** Methodological and gender issues in late-medieval and early-modern art and society. **SELECTED PUBLICATIONS** Rev, articles in Art Hist and Renaissance Stud; auth, El vostro poeta, The First Florentine Printing of Dante's Commedia, RACAR XX, 93. **CONTACT ADDRESS** Dept Art Hist, Concordia Univ, Montreal, 1455 de Maisonneuve W, Montreal, PQ, H3G 1M8. **EMAIL** adunlop@alcor.concordia.ca

DUNN, DENNIS JOHN

PERSONAL Born 10/23/1942, Cleveland, OH, m, 1966, 2 children **DISCIPLINE** RUSSIAN HISTORY **EDUCATION** John Carroll Univ, BA, 66, MA, 67; Kent State Univ, PhD(Hist), 70. **CAREER** Asst Hist, John Carroll Univ, 66-67; instr, Borremeo Sem-Col, 68; instr, Cleveland State Univ, 68-69; asst prof, 73-79, prof Hist, Southwest Tex State Univ, 70-, dir Inst Studies Relig & Communism, 80-, Vis fel, London Sch Econ & Polit Sci, 75-76. **MEMBERSHIPS** Am Asn Advan Slavic Studies; Am Cath Hist Asn; AHA. **RESEARCH** Russian history; Eastern European history; church-state relations. **SELECTED PUBLICATIONS** Auth, The Disappearance of the Ukranian Uniate Church, Ukrainskii Istorik, 72; coauth, Folktales and Footprints: Stories From the Old World, Benson, 73; auth, Pre-World War II Relations Between Stalin and the Catholic Church, J Church & State, Spring 73; Stalinism and the Catholic Church during the Era of World War II, Cath Hist, Rev, 10/73; Papal-Communist Detene: Motivation, Surv, 76; Religious Renaissance in USSR, J Church & State, 77; ed, Religion and Modernization in Soviet Union, Westview, 77; auth, The Catholic Church & Soviet Government, 1939-49, Columbia Univ, 77; Caught Between Roosevelt and Stalin: American Ambassadors in Russia; Lexington's University Press of Kenturcky, 98. **CONTACT ADDRESS** Dept of History, Southwest Texas State Univ, 601 University Dr, San Marcos, TX, 78666-4685. **EMAIL** DD05@Academia.swt.edu

DUNN, DURWOOD

PERSONAL Born 11/30/1943, Chickamauga, GA **DISCIPLINE** HISTORY **EDUCATION** Univ TN, Knoxville, BA, 65, MA, 68, PhD, 76. **CAREER** Instr, Hiwassee Col, 70-74; from instr to prof to chair, 75-, TN Wesleyan Col. **HONORS AND AWARDS** Pi Beta Kappa; Phi Kappa Phi; Woodrow Wilson Nat Fel, 65; Danforth assoc, 77; Fel Independent Study and Res, 78-79, 94-95, Nat Endowment Hum; Thomas Wolfe Memorial Lit Award, 88. **MEMBERSHIPS** Am Hist Asn; Org Am Hist; Southern Hist Asn; Appalachian Studies Asn; AAUP. **RESEARCH** Tennessee state and local history; Appalachian regional history and folklore. **SELECTED PUBLICATIONS** Auth, "Mary Noailles Murfree: A Reappraisal," Appalachian Jour, 79; "Apprenticeship and Indentured Servitude in Tennessee Before the Civil War," W TN Hist Soc Publications, 82; Cades Cove: The Life and Death of A Southern Appalachian Community, 1818-1937, Univ TN Press, 88; "A Meditation on Pittman Center: An Interview with Jessie Mechem Ledford," TN Hist Quart, 91; An Abolitionist in the Appalachian South: Ezekiel Birdseye on Slavery, Capitalism, and Separate Statehood in East Tennessee, 1841-1846, Univ TN Press, 97. **CONTACT ADDRESS** PO Box 1041, Athens, TN, 37371-1041. **EMAIL** dunnd@tnwc.edu

DUNN, F.M.

PERSONAL Born 10/15/1955, Aberdeen, Scotland, m, 1986, 2 children **DISCIPLINE** CLASSICAL LITERATURE **EDUCATION** Yale Univ, BA, 76, MA, 80, PhD, 85. **CAREER** Asst Prof, Assoc Prof, 93 to 96-, UC Santa Barbara; Asst Prof, 86-93, Northwestern Univ; vis Instr, 85-86, N Carolina State Univ. **HONORS AND AWARDS** Human Res Awd; Jr Fac Fel; NEH Fel; ACLS Fel. **MEMBERSHIPS** APA **RESEARCH** Greek Drama; Narrative Theory; Latin Poetry. **SELECTED PUBLICATIONS** Auth, Tragedy's End: Closure and Innovation in Euripidean Drama, Oxford Univ Press, 96; coed, Beginnings in Classical Literature, Yale Clas Stud, Cambridge Univ Press, 92; coed, Classical Closure: Reading the End in Greek and Latin Literature, Princeton Univ Press, 97; auth, Orestes and the Urn, Mnemosyne, 98; Ends and Means in Euripides' Hercules, Classical Closure, 97; Rhetorical Approaches to Horace's Odes, Arethusa, 95; Euripides and the Rites of Hera Akraia, Greek Roman and Byzantine Stud, 94. **CONTACT ADDRESS** Dept of Classics, Univ Calif Santa Barbara, Santa Barbara, CA, 93106. **EMAIL** fdunn@humanitas.ucsb.edu

DUNN, JOE PENDER

PERSONAL Born 09/21/1945, Cape Girardeau, MO, m, 1972 **DISCIPLINE** RECENT AMERICAN HISTORY, INTERNATIONAL RELATIONS **EDUCATION** Southeast Mo State Col, BS, 67; Univ Mo-Columbia, MA, 68, PhD (hist), 73. **CAREER** Asst prof hist and polit sci, Univ Md, Europe Div, 73-77; asst prof, 77-81, ASSOC PROF HIST, CONVERSE COL, 77-. **MEMBERSHIPS** AHA; Orgn Am Historians. **RESEARCH** Recent American political and social history; national security; the Vietnam war. **SELECTED PUBLICATIONS** Auth, Thomason in Response to Morris, Donald,R. on Thomason ,John, W., Am Heritage, Vol 45, 94; Tragic Mountains--The Hmong, the Americans, and the Secret Wars for Laos, 1942-1992, J Asian Hist, Vol 28, 94; Vietnam Documents--American and Vietnam Views of the War, J Asian Hist, Vol 27, 93. **CONTACT ADDRESS** Dept of History, Converse Col, Spartanburg, SC, 29301.

DUNN, LAURA

PERSONAL Born 08/16/1960, Cincinnati, OH **DISCIPLINE** ANCIENT HISTORY **EDUCATION** Trinity Evangelical Divinity School, MA, 91; Miami Univ, PhD, 98. **CAREER** Adjunct instr, Palm Beach Community Col, 98-; Indian River Community Col, 98-. **MEMBERSHIPS** Soc of Bibl Lit. **RESEARCH** Early Christianity; Sexual relationships in the Ancient World. **SELECTED PUBLICATIONS** Auth, "A New Look at Same-Sex Relationships in 1 Cor 6:9 and 1 Tim 1:10" in J for the Critical Study of Relig, 98. **CONTACT ADDRESS** 131 Maplecrest Cir, Jupiter, FL, 33458. **EMAIL** laurad@gate.net

DUNN, PATRICK PETER

PERSONAL Born 05/05/1942, Cudahy, WI, m, 1965, 2 children **DISCIPLINE** RUSSIAN HISTORY, PSYCHOHISTORY **EDUCATION** Marquette Univ, BA, 64; Duke Univ, PhD(hist), 69. **CAREER** Asst prof hist, Duke Univ, 69-70 & Univ Wis, La Crosse, 70-74; asst prof, 74-80, assoc prof hist, Worcester Polytech Inst, 80-, Nat Endowment for Humanities younger humanist fel, 73. **MEMBERSHIPS** AHA; Am Asn Advan Slavic Studies. **RESEARCH** Russian social and intellectual history; history of childhood. **SELECTED PUBLICATIONS** Auth, Childhood of Vissarion Belinskii, Hist Childhood Quart, 12/73; contrib, History of Childhood, At com, 74; What Happened to the Hyphen in Psychohistory?, fall 74 & Intuitive and Over Forty: Barzun's Attack on the New Historians, spring 75, Book Forum; Modernization and the Family, J Psychohist, fall 76; Belinskii and Bakunin: Adolescence in Nineteenth Century Russia, spring 79 & Lithuanian Psychology and History, summer 82, Psychohist Rev. **CONTACT ADDRESS** Dept of Humanities, Worcester Polytech Inst, 100 Institute Rd, Worcester, MA, 01609-2247.

DUNN, RICHARD SLATOR

PERSONAL Born 08/09/1928, Minneapolis, MN, m, 1960, 2 children **DISCIPLINE** HISTORY **EDUCATION** Harvard Univ, AB, 50; Princeton Univ, MA, 52, PhD (hist), 55. **CAREER** Instr hist, Univ Mich, 55-57; from asst prof to assoc prof, 57-68, chmn dept, 72-77, dir Philadephia Ctr Early Am Studies, 77-80, PROF HIST, UNIV PA, 68-, Guggenheim fel, 66-67; mem coun Inst Early Am Hist and Cult, 67-69; vis prof hist, Univ Mich, 69-70; Nat Endowment Humanities fel, 74-75; mem coun Hist Soc Pa, 76-; mem Inst Adv Study, 74-75; Am Coun Learned Soc fel, 77-78; co-ed, Papers William Penn, 78-; chmn coun, Philadelphia Ctr Early Am Studies, 80-; mem, Ctr Adv Study Behav Sci, 82-83. **HONORS AND AWARDS** Jamestown Found Award, 72; Love Prize, Conf Brit Studies, 73. **MEMBERSHIPS** AHA; Royal Hist Soc Fel; Orgn Am Hist; Am Antique Soc. **RESEARCH** American colonial history; Caribbean history; Anglo-american social history, 1607-1775. **SELECTED PUBLICATIONS** Auth, Mcgiffert, Mike Edits his Journal, William Mary Quart, Vol 54, 97; Bloody Dawn--The Christiana Riot and Racial Violence in the Antebellum North, Pennsylvania Mag Hist Biography, Vol 117, 93; Astrology and the 17th Century Mind--Lilly, William and the Language of the Stars, Annals Sci, Vol 53, 96. **CONTACT ADDRESS** Dept Hist, Univ PA, Philadelphia, PA, 19104.

DUNNELL, RUTH W.

DISCIPLINE HISTORY **EDUCATION** Middlebury Col, BA, 72; Univ of Wash, MA, 75; Princeton Univ, PhD, 83. **CAREER** Postdoc res assoc, University of Wash, 83-84; instr, Roosevelt Univ, 85; visiting asst prof, Univ of Ore, 85-87; visiting for scholar, Chinese Acad of Soc Sci, 87-88; res assoc, Univ of Calif-Berkeley, 88-89; asst prof, 89-95; assoc prof, Kenyon Col, 95-. **HONORS AND AWARDS** FLAS/NDSL grants, 74-75, 76-78; Full Princeton Univ fel, 76-78, 79-80, 81-83; Andrew Mellon lang trng fel (ACLS), 83-84; IREX Emergency Support grant, 84-85; Nat Prog for Advanceded Study and Res in China Grantee, Nat Acad Sci, 87-88; Am Coun of Learned Soc Proj grant, 92; fac res grant-in-Residence, Univ of Mich, 93; Short-Term Travel grant, IREX, 93; IREX Individual Advanced Res Opportunity in Eurasia grant, 96; NEH fel for Col tchr(s) and Independent Scholars, 96-97; **MEMBERSHIPS** Assn Asian Studies; Mongolia Soc; Tibet Soc; T'ang Studies Soc. **RESEARCH** Chinese-Inner Asian political, institutional, & cultural history. **SELECTED PUBLICATIONS** Auth, The Great State of White and High: Buddhism and State Formation in Eleventh-Century Xia, Univ. of Hawaii Press, 96; The Recovery of Tangut History, Orientations 27:4, 96; Weiming (Li) Renxiao,1124-1193, Xia Biog Ser, Jour of Sung-Yuan Studies 95; Significant Peripheries: Inner Asian Perspectives on Song Studies, Jour of Sung-Yuan Studies, 94; Hsi-Hsia, The Cambridge Hist of China, Vol 6, Cambridge Univ. Press, 94; rev, Juha Janhunen, Manchuria, An Ethnic History, Jour of Sung-Yuan Studies 98; S.A.M. Adshead, Central Asia in World History, Jour of Asian Studies 94. **CONTACT ADDRESS** Dept of Hist, Kenyon Col, Gambier, OH, 43022. **EMAIL** dunnell@kenyon.edu

DUPLESSIS, ROBERT S.

PERSONAL Born 06/01/1945, New York, NY, m, 1965, 1 child **DISCIPLINE** HISTORY **EDUCATION** Williams Col, BA, 66; Columbia Univ, MA, 68, PhD, 74. **CAREER** Vis asst prof, Princeton Univ, 74; vis prof, Columbia Univ, 86-87; asst prof to prof, Swarthmore Col, 86- . **HONORS AND AWARDS** Foreign Area Fel, 70-72; Mellon Fel, 80-81; Fulbright Fel, 66-67, 85-86; Nat Endow for the Humanities Fel for Col Teachers, 96-97., Chair, Div of Soc Sci, Dept of Hist, co-chair, Women's Stud Prog, pres, Amer Assoc of Univ Prof, Swarthmore Col **MEMBERSHIPS** Amer Hist Assoc; Econ Hist Assoc; Renaissance Soc of Amer; French Colonial Hist Soc. **RESEARCH** Early modern European economic & cultural hist **SELECTED**

PUBLICATIONS Auth, Capitalism and Commercialization, in Encyclopedia of European Social History, Scribner's, forthcoming; Mercantilism, in Encyclopedia of the Renaissance, Scribner's, forthcoming; Transatlantic Textiles: European Linen in the Cloth Cultures of Colonial North American, in Linen in Europe, Oxford Univ Press, forthcoming; Circulation et appropriation des mouchoirs chez les colons et aborigenes de la Nouvelle-France aux XVIIe et XVIIIe siecles, in Le Mouchoir Dans Tous Ses Etats, Musee du Textile, Cholet, France, forthcoming; Was There A Consumer Revolution in Eighteenth Century New France?, in Proceedings of the Annual Conference of the French Colonial Historical Society, 1997, Mich St Univ Press, forthcoming. **CONTACT ADDRESS** Dept of History, Swarthmore Col, 500 College Ave, Swarthmore, PA, 19081. **EMAIL** rduples1@swarthmore.edu

DUPRE, DAN
DISCIPLINE AMERICAN HISTORY **EDUCATION** Brandeis Univ, PhD, 90. **CAREER** Assoc prof, Univ NC, Charlotte. **RESEARCH** The Old South; soc and polit hist of the early republic. **SELECTED PUBLICATIONS** Auth, Transforming the Cotton Frontier: Madison County, Alabama, 1800-1840, La State UP, 97. **CONTACT ADDRESS** Univ N. Carolina, Charlotte, Charlotte, NC, 28223-0001.

DUPREE, ANDERSON HUNTER
PERSONAL Born 01/29/1921, Hillsboro, TX, m, 1946, 2 children **DISCIPLINE** HISTORY **EDUCATION** Oberlin Col, AB, 42; Harvard Univ, AM, 47, PhD (hist), 52. **CAREER** Asst prof hist, Tex Technol Col, 50-53; res fel, Gray Herbarium, Harvard Univ, 52-54, 55-56; vis asst prof hist, Univ Calif, Berkeley, 56-58, from assoc prof to prof hist, Univ Calif, Berkeley, 58-68, asst to chancellor, 60-62; George L Littlefield prof, 68-81, EMER PROF HIST, BROWN UNIV, 81-, Fel, Ctr Advan Studies Behav Sci, 67-68; mem, hist adv comt, NASA, 64-73, hist adv comt, Atomic Energy Comn, 67-73, adv comt govt prog in behav sci, Nat Res Coun, 66-68; Smithsonian coun, 75-. **MEMBERSHIPS** AHA; Orgn Am Historians; Soc Hist Technol; Am Acad Arts and Sci (secy, 73-76); Hist Sci Soc. **RESEARCH** American social and intellectual history; history of science in America; history of science and technology. **SELECTED PUBLICATIONS** Auth, The First Nuclear Era--The Life and Times of a Technological Fixer, Isis, Vol 86, 95; The First Nuclear Era--The Life and Times of a Technological Fixer, Isis, Vol 86, 95. **CONTACT ADDRESS** Dept of Hist, Brown Univ, Providence, RI, 02912.

DURAM, JAMES C.
DISCIPLINE US CONSTITUTIONAL, LEGAL, POLITICAL, FAMILY HISTORY AND HISTORIOGRAPHY **EDUCATION** W Michigan Univ, Ba, MA; Wayne State Univ, PhD. **CAREER** Dept prelaw adv; prof-. **HONORS AND AWARDS** Fulbright fel, Intl Inst Soc Hist, Amsterdam. **RESEARCH** Uses and dynamics of constitutional argumentation. **SELECTED PUBLICATIONS** Auth, books on Norman Thomas, US Supreme Court Justice; William O. Douglas, President Dwight D Eisenhower's role in the School Segregation Cases; Biography of a Civil War Chaplain. **CONTACT ADDRESS** Dept of Hist, Wichita State Univ, 1845 Fairmont, Wichita, KS, 67260-0062.

DURDEN, ROBERT FRANKLIN
PERSONAL Born 05/10/1925, Graymont, GA, m, 1952, 2 children **DISCIPLINE** HISTORY **EDUCATION** Emory Univ, AB, 47, MA, 48; Princeton Univ, MA, 50, PhD, 52. **CAREER** Asst instr hist, Princeton Univ, 50-52; from instr to assoc prof, 52-64, chmn dept, 74-80, PROF HIST, DUKE UNIV, 65-, Fulbright prof, Am hist, Johns Hopkins Sch Int Rels, Bologna, Italy, 65-68; Fulbright prof Am hist, Monash Univ, Melbourne, Australia, 80. **HONORS AND AWARDS** LLD, Emory Univ, 81. **MEMBERSHIPS** AHA; Southern Hist Asn; Orgn Am Historians. **RESEARCH** American history. **SELECTED PUBLICATIONS** Auth, Rayner, Kenneth and Rayner, John, B. and the Limits of Southern Dissent, J Southern Hist, Vol 60, 94. **CONTACT ADDRESS** Dept of Hist, Duke Univ, Durham, NC, 27706.

DURHAM, JOSEPH THOMAS
PERSONAL Born 11/26/1923, Raleigh, NC, m **DISCIPLINE** EDUCATION **EDUCATION** Morgan State Coll, AB (honors) 1948; Temple Univ, EdM 1949; Columbia Univ, EdD 1963. **CAREER** New Lincoln School, teacher 1956-58; Southern Univ, prof 1958-60; Coppin State Coll, chmn educ 1960-63; Albany State Coll, dean & prof 1963-65; Coppin State Coll, dean of college 1965-68; IL State Univ, assoc dean educ 1968-72; Howard Univ, dean of school of educ 1972-75; Coppin State Coll Baltimore, dean of educ 1975-76; MD State Bd for Higher Educ, dir inst approval; Comm Coll of Baltimore, pres, 1985-90; Morgan State Univ, prof; COPPIN STATE COLL, LECTURER, currently. **HONORS AND AWARDS** Fellow General Educ Bd 1953-54; Fellow Danforth Found 1975; Commissioner Montgomery Co Human Relations 1983-86; Presidential Leadership Medallion, Univ of Texas, 1989. **MEMBERSHIPS** Mem Phi Delta Kappa; mem Alpha Phi Alpha; visiting prof Univ of New Hampshire 1966. **SELECTED PUBLICATIONS** "The Story of Civil Rights as Seen by the Black Church" DC Cook Publishing Co 1971. **CONTACT ADDRESS** Lecturer in Education, Coppin State Col, Baltimore, MD, 21216.

DURNBAUGH, DONALD F.
PERSONAL Born 11/16/1927, Detroit, MI, m, 1952, 3 children **DISCIPLINE** CHURCH HISTORY, MODERN EUROPEAN HISTORY **EDUCATION** Manchester Col, BA, 49; Univ Mich, MA, 53; Univ Pa, PhD (hist), 60. **CAREER** Dir, Brethren Serv Comn, Austria, 53-56; lectr Brethren hist, Bethany Theol Sem, 58; from instr to asst prof hist, Juniata Col, 58-62; assoc prof, 62-70, PROF CHURCH HIST, BETHANY THEOL SEM, 70-, Alternate serv, Brethren Serv Comn, Austria and Ger, 49-51 and 53-56; dir in Europe, Brethren Cols Abroad, 64-65; adj prof church hist, Northern Baptist Theol Sem, 68-71; assoc, Ctr Reformation and Free Church Studies, Chicago Theol Sem, 68-; Nat Endowment for Humanities res fel, 76-77. **MEMBERSHIPS** Am Soc Church Hist; Orgn Am Historians; NAm Acad Ecumenists; AHA; Am Soc Reformation Res. **RESEARCH** Modern European church history; German sectarian movements in America; Communitarian societies. **SELECTED PUBLICATIONS** Auth, Spiritual Life in Anabaptism, Church Hist, Vol 66, 97; The German Peasant War and Anabaptist Community of Goods, Church Hist, Vol 63, 94; Mennonite Entrepreneurs, Church Hist, Vol 66, 97; The German Peasant War and Anabaptist Community of Goods, Church Hist, Vol 63, 94; Spiritual Life in Anabaptism, Church Hist, Vol 66, 97; Mennonite Entrepreneurs, Church Hist, Vol 66, 97; The Writings of Philips, Dirk, J Church State, Vol 35, 93. **CONTACT ADDRESS** Bethany Theol Sem, Oak Brook, IL, 60521.

DUROCHER, RENE
PERSONAL Born 06/28/1938, Montreal, PQ, Canada **DISCIPLINE** HISTORY **EDUCATION** Univ Montreal, BA, 60, BPed, 60, LL, 65, DES Histoire, 68. **CAREER** Asst to assoc prof, York Univ, 71-74; vis prof, Univ Calgary, 72; PROF HISTORY, UNIV MONTREAL, 74-, dept ch, 84-87, dir res office, 94-; vis prof, Israel, 80. **MEMBERSHIPS** Conseil de la Sci et de la Technologie du Que, 81-86; pres, Can Hist Asn, 86-87. **SELECTED PUBLICATIONS** Coauth, Le retard du Quebec et l'inferiorite economique des Canadiens francais, 71; coauth, Histoire du Quebec contemporain 1867-1929, 79; coauth, Nouvelle histoire du Canada et du Quebec; coauth, Le Quebec depuis 1930. **CONTACT ADDRESS** Dep d'histoire, Univ Montreal, CP 6128, Succ Centre-ville, Montreal, PQ, H3C 3J7.

DVORSKY-ROHNER, DOROTHY
DISCIPLINE ART HISTORY **EDUCATION** Univ CO, BFA, MA, PhD. **CAREER** Asst prof Art, Univ NC, Asheville, 96-. **RESEARCH** The art and archit of the Ancient World. **SELECTED PUBLICATIONS** Her articles on Greek and Etruscan archit have appeared in Archaeology News and other professional jour(s). **CONTACT ADDRESS** Univ N. Carolina, Asheville, Asheville, NC, 28804-8510. **EMAIL** rtynes@unca.edu

DWYER, EUGENE JOSEPH
PERSONAL Born 09/14/1943, Buffalo, NY, m, 1969, 1 child **DISCIPLINE** CLASSICAL ARCHEOLOGY, ART HISTORY **EDUCATION** Harvard Univ, BA, 65; NY Univ, MA, 67, PhD(art hist), 74. **CAREER** Prof Art Hist, Kenyon Col, 73-. **HONORS AND AWARDS** Tatiana Warsher Award, Am Acad, Rome, 72-73. **MEMBERSHIPS** Am Numis Soc; Archaeol Inst Am; Col Art Asn. **RESEARCH** Hellenistic and Roman art; Pompeii. **SELECTED PUBLICATIONS** Auth, The Subject of Durer's Four Witches, Art Quart, 71; Augustus and the Capricorn 73 & Pompeian Oscilla Collections, 81, Romische Mitteilungen; Temporal Allegory of Tazza Farnese, Am J of Archaeol, 92; articles: Macmillan Dictionary of Art, 96; articles: Encyclopedia of Comparative Iconography, 98. **CONTACT ADDRESS** Kenyon Col, Gambier, OH, 43022-9623. **EMAIL** dwyere@kenyon.edu

DYCK, ANDREW R.
PERSONAL Born 05/24/1947, Chicago, IL, m, 1978 **DISCIPLINE** CLASSICS **EDUCATION** Univ of WI, BA; Univ of Chicago, PhD. **CAREER** Lect, Univ of Alberta, 75-76; Vis Asst Prof, UCLA, 76-77; Asst Prof, Univ MN, 78-79; Asst Prof, Prof, UCLA, 79-. **HONORS AND AWARDS** Fel, Alexander VonHumboldt-Stiftung, 81-82; Fel, Nat Endowment for Humanities, 91-92; Mem, Ints for Adv Stud, 91-92; Vis Fel, All Souls Col Oxford, 98. **MEMBERSHIPS** APA; Calif Class Asn; US Nat Com on Byzantine Studies **RESEARCH** Cicero's Philosophical Essays **SELECTED PUBLICATIONS** Epimerismi Homerici, Berlin-NY, 83-95; The Essays on Euripides and George of Pisidia and on Heliodorus and Achilles Tatius, Vienna, 86; A Commentary on Cicero, De Officiis, AA, 96; Schliemann on the Excavation of Troy: Three Unpublished Letters, Greek, Roman and Byzantine Stud, 90; Cicero the Dramaturge, Qvi Miscvit Vtile Dvlci: Festschrift Essays for Paul Lachlan MacKendrick, 98; Narrative Obfuscation, Philosophical Topoi, and Tragic Patterning in Cicero's Pro Milone, Harvard Stud in Class Philo, 98. **CONTACT ADDRESS** 405 Hilgard Ave, Los Angeles, CA, 90095-1417.

DYCK, CORNELIUS JOHN
PERSONAL Born 08/20/1921, Russia, m, 1952, 3 children **DISCIPLINE** HISTORY/HISTORICAL THEOLOGY **EDUCATION** BA, Bethel Col, N Newton KS, 53; MA Wichita State Univ, 55; BD Divinity School Univ Chicago, 59, PhD, 62. **CAREER** Prof Assoc Mennonite Seminaries, 59-89; Dir Inst of Mennonite Studies, 58-79; Exec Sec, Mennonite World Conf, 61-73. **MEMBERSHIPS** Mennonite Hist Soc, Goshen IN; Mennonitischer Geschichtsverein, Weierhof Germany; Doopsgezind Historische Kring, Amsterdam; Doc for Reformation Res; NA Soc Of Church Hist. **RESEARCH** 16th century Dutch Anabaptism. **SELECTED PUBLICATIONS** Mennonite Encyclopedia vol V ed, 90; Introduction to Mennonite History, 3rd ed, 93; Spiritual Life in Anabaptism, 95. **CONTACT ADDRESS** Associated Mennonite Biblical Sem, 3003 Benham Ave, Elkhart, IN, 46514. **EMAIL** 105152.311@compuserve.com

DYE, JAMES WAYNE
PERSONAL Born 12/22/1934, Appalachia, VA, m, 1985, 1 child **DISCIPLINE** PHILOSOPHY, HISTORY OF PHILOSOPHY **EDUCATION** Carson-Newman Col, AB, 55; New Orleans Baptist Theol Sem, BD, 58; Tulane Univ, PhD, 60. **CAREER** Teaching asst philos, Tulane Univ, 58-59; from instr to asst prof, Washington Univ, 60-66; assoc prof, 66-76, dir, Philos Inst, 67-70, prof philos, Northern Ill Univ, 76-, assoc ed, The Philos Forum, 67-70. **MEMBERSHIPS** Am Philos Asn; Soc Ancient Greek Philos; Hume Soc; S Soc Philos Psy Psychol, Pres, 94-95. **RESEARCH** Ancient Greek philosophy; philosophy of religion and culture; German idealism; Hume. **SELECTED PUBLICATIONS** Coauth, Religions of the World, Appleton, 67, Irvington, 75; auth, Denton J Snider's interpretation of Hegel, Mod Schoolman, 1/70; Unspoken philosophy: The presuppositions and applications of thought, Studium Gererale, 71; Kant as ethical naturalist, J Value Inquiry, 78; Plato's concept of causal explanation, Tulane Stud Philos, 78; Aristotle's matter as a sensible principle, Int Studies Philos, 78; Nikolai Bendyaev and his ideas on ultimate reality, J Ultimate Reality & Meaning, 79; The sensibility of intelligible matter, Int Studies Philos, 82; In Search of the Philosopher-King, Archeol News, 82; The Poetization of Science, Studies in Sci and Cult II, 86; Hume on Curing Superstition, Hume Stud, 86; Superhuman Voices and Biological Books, Hist Philos Quart, 88; A Word on Behalf of Demea, Hume Stud, 89; Demea's Departure, Hume Stud, 93. **CONTACT ADDRESS** Dept of Philosophy, No Illinois Univ, 1425 W Lincoln Hwy, De Kalb, IL, 60115-2825. **EMAIL** jdye@niu.edu

DYE, THOMAS R.
DISCIPLINE POLITICAL SCIENCE **EDUCATION** Pa State Univ, BS, 57, MA, 59; Univ of Pa, PhD, 61. **CAREER** Teacher, Univ of Pa; teacher, Univ of Wis; teacher, Univ of Ga; vis scholar, Bar-Ilan Univ; vis scholar, Brookings Inst; McKenzie prof of Gov, Fla State Univ; Pres, Lincoln Ccenter for Public Service. **HONORS AND AWARDS** Harold Lasswell Award; Donald C. Stone Award; listed in Who's Who in Am. **MEMBERSHIPS** James Madison Inst; Phi Beta Kappa; Omicron Delta Kappa; Phi Kappa Phi. **SELECTED PUBLICATIONS** Auth, The Irony of Democracy; Politics in States and Communities; Understanding Public Policy; Who's Running America?; American politics in the Media Age; power in Society; American Federalism: Competition Among Governments; Politics Economics and The Public; Politics in America, Prentice Hall/Simon & Schuster, 99; Politics in Florida, Prentice Hall/Simon & Schuster, 98. **CONTACT ADDRESS** Lincoln Ctr for Public Service, 1801 S Federal Hwy, Delray Beach, FL, 33483.

DYKE, DORIS J.
PERSONAL ON, Canada **DISCIPLINE** EDUCATION **EDUCATION** Queen's Univ, BA, 59; Univ Toronto, BEd, 61, MEd, 63; Columbia Univ & Union Theol Sem, MA, 62, EdD, 67. **CAREER** Sch tchr, Ont, 12 yrs; assoc prof, Col Ed, Univ Sask, 64-72; assoc prof, Univ Louisville, 72-73; prof & dean of educ, Dalhousie Univ, 73-77; PROF & DIR M.R.E. STUDS, EMMANUEL COL, 77-95. **HONORS AND AWARDS** Sr Res Award, ATS, 89. **MEMBERSHIPS** Can Theol Soc; Asn Prof Res Relig Educ; Royal Soc Arts; Phil Educ Soc. **SELECTED PUBLICATIONS** Auth, God's Grace on Fools, God's Pity on God in Can Women's Studs, 87; auth, Crucified Women, 91; co-ed, Education and Social Policy: Local Control of Education, 69. **CONTACT ADDRESS** Victoria Univ, 82 Admiral Rd, Toronto, ON, M5R 2L6.

DYKES, DEWITT S., JR.
PERSONAL Born 01/02/1938, Chattanooga, Tennessee, m **DISCIPLINE** HISTORY **EDUCATION** Fisk Univ, BA (Summa Cum Laude) 1960; Univ of MI, MA 1961, PhD 65. **CAREER** MI State Univ, instructor Amer Thought & Language 1965-69; Oakland Univ, asst prof of history 1969-73; Oakland Univ, dean's asst for affirmative action 1975-78, coordinator Afro-Amer studies 1975-83; Univ of SC School of Public Health, consultant 1977; Oakland Univ, assoc prof of History 1973-. **MEMBERSHIPS** African Heritage Studies Assn 1970; life mem Assn for the Study of Afro-Amer Life & History; charter mem Afro-Amer Historical & Genealogical Soc 1978; Alpha Phi Alpha Fraternity; bd of editors Detroit in Perspective, A Journal of Regional History 1978-84; vice chmn Historic Designation Advisory Bd City of Detroit 1980-82, chmn 1982-84; book review editor Journal of the Afro-Amer Historical & Genealogical Soc 1981-85; pres The Fred Hart Williams Genealogical Soc 1980-86; bd of trustees Historical Soc of MI 1983-; summer fellowship Natl Endowment for the Humanities 1985; pres Michigan Black History Network 1986-;

bd of trustees, Historical Soc of MI, 1983-89; pres, MI Black History Network, 1986-88. **SELECTED PUBLICATIONS** Published "Mary McLeod Bethune"; "Ida Gray Nelson Rollins DDS" Profiles of the Negro in Amer Dentistry 1979; "Augusta Savage;" "Jerome Cavanagh & Roman Gribbs;" "Amer Blacks as Perpetual Victims, An Historical Overview" Victimization of the Weak 1982; "The Black Population in MI, Growth, Distribution & Public Office, 1800-1983" Ethnic Groups in MI Vol 2 1983; Phi Beta Kappa, Honorary Fraternity, 1969; "The Search for Community: MI Soc and Educ, 1945-80" in MI: Visions of our Past, 1989. **CONTACT ADDRESS** Dept of History, Oakland Univ, 378 O'Dowd Hall, Rochester, MI, 48309-4401.

DYKSTRA, ROBERT R.
DISCIPLINE HISTORY & PUBLIC POLICY **EDUCATION** Univ Iowa, BA, 53, MA, 59, PhD, 64. **CAREER** PROF, HIST & PUB POLICY, STATE UNIV NY ALBANY **HONORS AND AWARDS** Benjamin F. Shambaugh Award of the State Hist Soc of Iowa; Myers Center Award; Gustivas Myers Ctr for the Study of Human Rights in N Am; Binkley-Stephenson Award of the Org of Am Hist. **MEMBERSHIPS** Am Antiquarian Soc **SELECTED PUBLICATIONS** Auth, The Cattle Towns, 68; coauth, "Serial Marriage and the Origins of the Black Stepfamily: The Rowanty Evidence," Jour of Am Hist 72, 85; "Ecological Regression Estimates: Alchemists Gold?," Soc Sci Hist 10, 86; auth, Bright Radical Star: Black Freedom and White Supremacy on the Hawkeye Frontier, Harvard Univ Press, 93; auth, "The Know Nothings Nobody Knows: Political Nativists in Antebellum Iowa, Ann of Iowa 53, 94; "Iowans and the Politics of Race in America, 1857-1880," in Iowa Hist Rd, Iowa State Univ Press, 96; "Overdosing on Dodge City," West Hist Quart 27, 96. **CONTACT ADDRESS** Dept of Hist, SUNY-Albany, Albany, NY, 12222. **EMAIL** dykstra@csc.albany.edu

DYKSTRA, ROBERT R.
DISCIPLINE HISTORY **CAREER** Ed consul; 78-, Annals of Iowa; mem ed bd, 79-82, J Am Hist; mem ed bd, 80-81, Am Stud; mem ed bd, 81-, Upper Midwest Hist; dir, 84, 7th Am Stud Sem, Am Antiquarian Soc; consult, 85, Natl Endowment Hum; res assoc 85-86, Am Antiquarian Soc; res fel, 85-86, 88-90, Natl Endowment Hum, prof, 81-, SUNY. **HONORS AND AWARDS** Binkley-Stephenson Award, Org Am Historians, 86; Myers Ctr Award, Gustavus Myers Ctr for Stud of Human Rights, N Am, 94; Shambaugh Award, St Hist Soc of Iowa, 94. **MEMBERSHIPS** Fel Soc Am Hist; Am Antiquarian Soc; Kansas St Hist Soc; St Hist Soc of Iowa. **SELECTED PUBLICATIONS** Auth, Dr Emerson's Sam: Black Iowans Before the Civil War, Palimsest, 82; auth, White Men, Black Laws: Territorial Iowans and Civil Rights, 1838-1843, Annals of Iowa, 82; auth, The Issue Squarely Met: Toward an Explanation of Iowans' Racial Attitudes, 1865-1868, Annals of Iowa, 84; coauth, Serial Marriage and the origins of the Black Stepfamily: The Rowanty Evidence, J Am Hist, 85; coauth, Doing Local History: Monographic Approaches to the Smaller Community, Am Quart, 85; auth, Ecological Regression Estimates: Alchemist's Gold? Soc Sci Hist, 86; auth, Bright Radical Star: Black Freedom and White Supremacy on the Hawkeye Frontier, Harvard Univ, 93; auth, The Know Nothings Nobody Knows: Political nativists in Antebellum Iowa, Annals of Iowa, 94; auth, Iowans and the Politics of Race in America, 1857-1880, In: Iowa History Reader, St Hist Soc of Iowa, 96; auth, Overdosing on Dodge City; Western Hist Quart, 96; auth, To Live and Die in Dodge City: Body Counts, Law and Order,a nd the Case of Kansas v. Gill, In: Lethal Imagination: Violence and Brutality in American History, NY Univ, 99; auth, Violence, Gender, and Methodology in the New Western History, Rev in Am Hist, 99. **CONTACT ADDRESS** 39 Waterford Dr, Worcester, MA, 01602.

DYSART, JANE ELLEN
PERSONAL Born 06/25/1938, Ft Worth, TX **DISCIPLINE** LATIN AMERICAN HISTORY **EDUCATION** Tex Wesleyan Col, BA, 59; Tex Christian Univ, MA, 67, PhD (hist), 72. **CAREER** Pub sch teacher English and hist, 59-68; ASST PROF LATIN AM HIST, UNIV W FLA, 71-. **MEMBERSHIPS** AHA; Western Hist Asn. **RESEARCH** Borderlands; 19th century; sociology. **SELECTED PUBLICATIONS** Auth, Dade Last Command, J Southern Hist, Vol 62, 96; Mcgillivray, Lachlan, Indian Trader--The Shaping of the Southern Colonial Frontie, J Am Hist, Vol 80, 93. **CONTACT ADDRESS** Dept of Hist, Univ of WFla, Pensacola, FL, 32504.

DYSON, MICHAEL ERIC
PERSONAL Born 10/23/1958, Detroit, MI, m, 1992 **DISCIPLINE** AFRICAN-AMERICAN STUDIES **EDUCATION** Carson-Newman, BA (magna cum laude), 1982; Princeton University, MA, 1991, PhD, 1993. **CAREER** Princeton University, Mathy College, assistant master; Hartford Seminary, faculty member; Chicago Theological Seminary, instructor, assistant professorf; Brown University, assistant professorf; Univ of NC, Professor of Comm; COLUMBIA UNIV, PROF, currently . **HONORS AND AWARDS** National Association of Black Journalists, National Magazine Award, 1992. **MEMBERSHIPS** Democratic Socialist of America. **SELECTED PUBLICATIONS** Reflecting Black: African-American Cultural Criticism, 1993; Black History Booklet, A Collection of 20 Essays; The Second Coming of Malcolm X, liner notes for RCA Records; Making Malcolm: The Myth and Meaning of Malcolm X, Oxford Univ Press, 1994; Between God and Gangsta' Rap, collection of essays, Oxford Univ Press, 1995; Race Rules: Navigating the Color Line, Addison Wesley, 1997. **CONTACT ADDRESS** Columbia Univ, New York, NY.

DYSON, ROBERT HARRIS, JR.
PERSONAL Born 08/02/1927, York, PA **DISCIPLINE** ANTHROPOLOGY; ARCHAEOLOGY **EDUCATION** Harvard College, BA magna cum laude 50; Harvard Univ, PhD 66; Univ Penn, MA hon 71. **CAREER** Univ Penn, asst prof, assoc prof, prof emer, 54-94; Univ Penn Museum, asst, assoc, curator, curator emer, 54-95, dir, dir emer, 82-94; Univ Penn Arts Sci, dean, 79-82. **HONORS AND AWARDS** R H Dyson Ch Endow, NEA; Elect Cors Mem; Elect APA; Elect Cors Mem Deutchees Arch. **MEMBERSHIPS** AIAP; AIIS; AIA; Brit Sch Arch Iraq; Brit Sch Arch Iran; Brit Sch Arch Turkey; SAA. **RESEARCH** Near Eastern and Cen Asian Arch; Pre and Protohistory. **SELECTED PUBLICATIONS** Auth, Triangle-Festoon Ware Reconsidered, Iranica Ant, in press 99; The Achaemenid Triangle Ware of Hasanlu IIIA, Anatolian Iron Ages, BIAT, 98; Hasanlu, ditto vol 2, 97; History of the Field: Archaeology in Persia, The Oxford Encycl of the Near East, OUP, 97. **CONTACT ADDRESS** Near East Laboratory, Univ of Penn Museum, Philadelphia, PA, 19104. **EMAIL** robertd@sas.upenn.edu

DYSON, STEVEN L.
DISCIPLINE CLASSICS **EDUCATION** Brown Univ, BA; Yale Univ, PhD, 63. **CAREER** Mellon prof, Intercollegiate Ctr Class Studies; Charles Eliot Norton Lectureship, Archaeolog Inst Am, 93-94; chr class dept, SUNY Buffalo, present. **HONORS AND AWARDS** Fellow, Am Coun Learned Soc; fellow, NEH;, Pres, Archaeolog Inst Am. **RESEARCH** Romanization of Sardinia; urban develop and soc hist of ancient Rome; the hist of Class archaeol. **SELECTED PUBLICATIONS** Auth, The Roman Villas of Buccino, 83; The Creation of the Roman Frontier, 85; Community and Society in Roman Italy, 92. **CONTACT ADDRESS** Dept Classics, SUNY Buffalo, 712 Clemens Hall, Buffalo, NY, 14260.

DZIEWANOWSKI, MARIAN KAMIL
PERSONAL Born 06/01/1913, Zhitomer, Russia, m, 1946, 2 children **DISCIPLINE** HISTORY **EDUCATION** Univ Warsaw, LLM, 37; French Inst, Warsaw, cert, 37; Harvard Univ, MA, 48, PhD(hist), 51. **CAREER** Res fel, Russ Res Ctr, Harvard Univ, 49-52; res assoc, Ctr Int Studies, Mass Inst Technol, 52-53; from asst prof to prof hist, Boston Col, 54-65; prof hist, Boston Univ, 65-78; PROF HIST, UNIV WIS, MILWAUKEE, 79-, Ford exchange prof, Poland, 58; Am Philos Soc res fels, 59-60; assoc Russ Res Ctr, Harvard Univ, 60-78; vis prof, Brown Univ, 61-62 & 66-67; prof int rels, Boston Univ Br Brussels & West Berlin, 72-73; vis prof, NAtlantic Treaty Orgn & Supreme Hq Allied Powers Europe, 72-73; vis prof, Grad Univ Europ Community, 79. **MEMBERSHIPS** AHA; Inst Am; Polish Inst Arts & Sci Am; Am Asn Advan Slavic Studies. **RESEARCH** Modern eastern Europe; contemporary Russia; Poland. **SELECTED PUBLICATIONS** Auth, Dualism or Trialism, Slavonic Rev, 6/60; coauth, Communist States at the Crossroads, Praeger, 65; Bibliography of Soviet Foreign Relations, Princeton Univ, 65; auth, A European Federalist, Stanford Univ, 68; Poland in the 20th Century, Columbia Univ, 77 & 79; A History of Soviet Russia, Prentice-Hall, 79-96; coauth, Communist Parties of Eastern Europe, Columbia, 80; European Federalism, Europ Univ, 82; auth, War at Any Price, Prentice-Hall, 79. **CONTACT ADDRESS** 3352 N Hackett Ave, Milwaukee, WI, 53211.

DZUBACK, MARY ANN
PERSONAL Born 03/17/1950, Chattanooga, TN, m, 1983 **DISCIPLINE** HISTORY; EDUCATION **EDUCATION** Franconia Col, BA, 74; Columbia Univ, PhD, 87. **CAREER** From asst prof to assoc prof, Wash Univ, 87-. **HONORS AND AWARDS** Rockefeller Arch Ctr grant; Spencer Found grant, Wash Univ fac res grant, Oberlin Col Arch grant. **MEMBERSHIPS** Hist of Educ Soc; Am Educ Res Asn, Am Hist Asn; Org of Am Hists; Hist of the Behavioral Scis Asn. **RESEARCH** Soc and intellectual hist of educ and higher educ; Women's hist, gender and cult. **SELECTED PUBLICATIONS** Auth, Robert M. Hutchins: Portrait of an Educator, 91; various articles. **CONTACT ADDRESS** Dept of Education, Washington Univ, 1 Brookings Dr, Campus Box 1183, St Louis, MO, 63130. **EMAIL** madzubac@artsci.wash.edu

E

EADIE, JOHN W.
PERSONAL Born 12/18/1935, Ft Smith, AR, m, 1957, 2 children **DISCIPLINE** ANCIENT HISTORY **EDUCATION** Univ Ark, BA, 57; Univ Chicago, MA, 59; Univ London, PhD (hist), 62. **CAREER** Asst prof hist, Ripon Col, 62-63; from asst prof to assoc prof, 63-73, PROF HIST, UNIV MICH, ANN ARBOR, 73-, Rackham res fel, 67-68; vis fel, Clare Hall, Cambridge Univ, 68-69; sr res, Joint Am-Yugoslavian Excavation, Sirmium, Yugoslavia, 68-72; Am Coun Learned Soc grant-in-aid, 74; humanities and arts adv to vpres for res, Univ Mich, 74-; dir, Summer Inst in Ancient Hist, Asn Ancient Historians, 77; chmn, Mich Coun for Humanities, Nat Endowment for Humanities State Coun, 77-80; dir, archaeol explor of Humayma region in southern Jordan, 82-. **MEMBERSHIPS** Asn of Ancient Historians; Soc Prom Roman Studies; AHA; Archaeol Inst Am. **RESEARCH** Roman Empire; Roman frontiers and provinces; historiography. **SELECTED PUBLICATIONS** Auth, Martyrdom and Rome, J Church State, Vol 39, 97; Information and Frontiers--Roman Foreign Relations in Late Antiquity, Am Hist Rev, Vol 100, 95; The Water Supply of Ancient Rome--A Study of Roman Imperial Administration, Am Hist Rev, Vol 98, 93; Greece, Rome, and the Bill of Rights, J Am Hist, Vol 80, 93. **CONTACT ADDRESS** Dept of Hist, Univ Mich, Ann Arbor, MI, 48109.

EAGLE, MARY
DISCIPLINE FINE ARTS **CAREER** Sr cur, Dept of Australian Art, Natl Gallery of Australia; vis fel, Ctr Cross-Cult Res, Australian Natl Univ, 97. **RESEARCH** Australian art; aboriginal art **EMAIL** Mary.Eagle@anu.edu.au

EAGLES, CHARLES W.
PERSONAL Born 09/22/1946, Spartanburg, SC, m, 1978, 2 children **DISCIPLINE** HISTORY **EDUCATION** BA, Presbyterian College, 68. **CAREER** NC State Univ, 77-80; Southeast Missouri State Univ, 80-82; Vanderbilt Univ, Univ of Mississippi, Asst Prof 83-86; Assoc Prof 86-91, Prof 91-. **HONORS AND AWARDS** Lillian Smith Award 93. **MEMBERSHIPS** Southern Historical Association; Amer Historical Association; Organization of Amer Historians; Mississippi Society. **RESEARCH** Recent US, modern South, civil rights and race relations **SELECTED PUBLICATIONS** Jonathan Daniels and Race Relations; The Evolution of a Southern Liberal 82, The Civil Rights Movement in America (ed) 86; Urban-Rural Conflict in the 1920s: A Historiographical Assessment, The Historian 49 p26-48, 86; Congressional Voting in the 1920s: A Test of Urba-Rural Conflict, Journal of American History 76, p528-34, 89; Democracy Delayed: Congressional Reapportionment and Urban-Rural Conflict in the 1920s, 90; The Mind of the South After Fifty Years, 92; Outside Agitator: Jon Daniels and the Civil Rights Movement in Alabama, 93; Is There a Southern Political Tradition?, 96. **CONTACT ADDRESS** Dept of History, Univ of Mississippi, University, MS, 38677.

EAKIN, MARSHALL C.
DISCIPLINE HISTORY **EDUCATION** Univ Kans, BA, 75, MA, 77; Univ Calif, Los Angeles, PhD, 81. **CAREER** Vis asst prof, Loyola Marymount Univ, 81-83; asst prof, 83- 89, ASSOC PROF, VANDERBILT UNIV, 89-. **CONTACT ADDRESS** Vanderbilt Univ, Box 31-B, Nashville, TN, 37235. **EMAIL** marshall.c.eakin@vanderbilt.edu

EAMON, WILLIAM
PERSONAL Born 06/05/1946, Williston, ND, m, 1967, 1 child **DISCIPLINE** HISTORY OF SCIENCE AND MEDICINE **EDUCATION** Univ Mont, BA, 68, Ma, 70; Univ Kans, PhD(hist sci), 77 **CAREER** Instr hist, Univ Miami, Coral Cables, 73-74; instr, 76-77, asst prof, 77-80, assoc prof, 80-93, PROF HIST, NMEX STATE UNIV, 94-. **MEMBERSHIPS** Hist Sci Soc; Renaissance Soc Am **RESEARCH** Renaissance science: the scientific revolution; science and popular culture. **SELECTED PUBLICATIONS** Science and the Secrets of Nature, Princeton Univ Press, 94; Cannibalism and contagion: Framing syphilis in Counter-Reformation Italy, in: Early Science and Medicine, 98. **CONTACT ADDRESS** Dept of Hist, New Mexico State Univ, PO Box 30001, Las Cruces, NM, 88003-8001. **EMAIL** weamon@nmsu.edu

EARHART, HARRY BYRON
PERSONAL Born 01/07/1935, Aledo, IL, m, 1956, 3 children **DISCIPLINE** HISTORY OF RELIGIOUS, ASIAN STUDIES **EDUCATION** Univ Chicago, BD and MA, 60, PhD, 65. **CAREER** Asst prof relig, Vanderbilt Univ, 65-66; from asst prof to assoc prof, 66-69, PROF RELIG, WESTERN MICH UNIV, 75-, Fac res fels, 68 and 73; Fulbright res grant and prof relig, Int Summer Sch Asian Studies, Ewha Womans Univ, Korea, 73; adv Far Eastern relig, Encycl Britannica; ed, Relig Studies Rev, 75-80. **MEMBERSHIPS** Am Acad Relig; Asn Asian Studies; Am Soc Study Relig. **RESEARCH** History of Japanese religion; Japanese new religions; new religious movements. **SELECTED PUBLICATIONS** Auth, Women and Millenarian Protest in Meiji Japan--Deguchi, Nao and Omotokyo, Monumenta Nipponica, Vol 48, 93. **CONTACT ADDRESS** Dept of Relig, Western Michigan Univ, Kalamazoo, MI, 49001.

EASTER, MARILYN
PERSONAL Born 01/06/1957, Oklahoma City, OK, m **DISCIPLINE** EDUCATION **EDUCATION** University of Colorado, BA; Denver University, MA, MSW; University of San Francisco, EdD. **CAREER** Marketing By Marilyn, consultant, 1979-82; General Dentistry, mktg mgr, 1982-; Amador Adult School, instructor, 1983-85; Chabot College, instructor, 1985-

87; California State Univ, instructor, 1987-91; St Mary's College, assoc prof, 1991-93; COLLEGE OF NOTRE DAME, ASSOC PROF, 1993-. **HONORS AND AWARDS** Outstanding Dissertation Award, 1993; Outstanding Student Council Leadership Award, 1992; Emmy Nominee, Affirmative Action Pro 209, 1997; NAFEO, Conference Speaker, 1998; Teacher Excellence, Key Note Speaker, 1998. **MEMBERSHIPS** College of Notre Dame, SAFE, chair, 1997-; American Soc of Training & Dev, 1993-97; Phi Delta Kappa Fraternity, 1991-; California State Teachers Association, 1994-; NAACP, 1997-; Natl Assn of Girl Scouts of Amer, 1991-95; Coll of Notre Dame, steering comm, co-chair, 1997-. **SELECTED PUBLICATIONS** The ABCs of Mktg a Successful Business, 1986; Stress and Coping Mechanism Among Female Dentists, 1991; Evaluation of Higher Education, A Case Study, 1992; Picking the Perfect School, 1993; A Triangulated Research Design for Studying Stress, 1993. **CONTACT ADDRESS** Col of Notre Dame, 1500 Ralston Ave, Belmont, CA, 94002-1997.

EASTMAN, CAROL M.
PERSONAL Born 09/27/1941, Boston, MA **DISCIPLINE** LINGUISTICS, ANTHROPOLOGY **EDUCATION** Univ Mass, BA, 63; Univ Wis, PhD (ling), 67 **CAREER** Asst prof anthrop and ling, 67-73, assoc prof, 73-79, PROF ANTHROP, UNIV WASH, 79-, Vis prof, Univ Nairobi, 79-80; ADJ PROF LING AND WOMEN STUDIES, UNIV WASH, 79-. **MEMBERSHIPS** Ling Soc Am; fel African Studies Asn; Am Anthrop Asn; Current Anthrop. **RESEARCH** Bantu linguistics and literature; Northwest Indian languages; language and culture. **SELECTED PUBLICATIONS** Auth, To the Charlottes--Dawson, George 1878 Survey of the Queen Charlotte Islands, W Hist Quart, Vol 25, 94. **CONTACT ADDRESS** Dept of Anthrop, Univ Wash, Seattle, WA, 98195.

EASTMAN, JOHN ROBERT
PERSONAL Born 06/30/1945, San Diego, CA **DISCIPLINE** HISTORY, MEDIEVAL EUROPEAN HISTORY **EDUCATION** VA Polytechnical Inst & State Univ, BA, 68; Julius-Maximilians-Universitat zu Wurzburg, PhD, 85. **CAREER** Teacher, math, Southern High School, Harwood, MD, 68-69; instr, English, Dolmetscher Inst, Wurzburg, Germany, 76-83; tourist guide, Arbeitsamt, Wurzburg, Germany, 76-85; graduate/postgraduate asst, Dept of Hist, Univ of Wurzburg, 78-82, 85; sustitute teacher, Anne Arundel Co, MD, 87-97; teacher, Latin & German, Peninsula Catholic High School, Newport News, VA, 97-; contrib to Int Medieval Bibliography, Univ of Leeds United Kingdom, 95-. **HONORS AND AWARDS** William John Bennett Memorial Scholarship, Annapolis High School, 63. **MEMBERSHIPS** Am Hist Asn; Southeastern Medieval Asn; Nat Coalition of Independent Scholars; Int Platform Asn; Am Philol Asn. **RESEARCH** Medieval scholasticism; religion; history of Germany. **SELECTED PUBLICATIONS** Auth, Editing Medieval Texts: A Modern Critical Edition of De renunciatione pape by Aegidius Romanus, Medieval Perspectives 3, 88; Giles of Rome and His Use of St Augustine in Defense of Papal Abdication, Augustiniana 38, 88; Das Leben des Augustiner-Eremiten Aegidius Romanus (c 1243-1316), Zeitschrift fuer Kirchengeschichte 100, 89; Giles of Rome and Celestine V: The Franciscan Revolution and the Theology of Abdication, Cath Hist Rev 76, 90; Papal Abdication in Later Medieval Thought, Edwin Mellon Press, 90; ed/Herausgeber, Aegidius Romanus, De Renunciatione Pape, Edwin Mellon Press, 92; auth, Giles of Rome and His Fidelity to Sources in the Context of Ecclesiological Political Thought as Exemplified in De renunciatione papae, Documentui e studi sulla tradizione filosofica medievale 3:1, 92; Relating Martin Luther to Giles of Rome: How to Proceed!, Medieval Perspectives 8, 93; Die Werke des Aegidius Romanus, Augustiniana 44, 94; Peter of Auvergne: Life, Master Regent, and the First Quodlibet of 1296, Forschungen zur Reichs-, Papst-und Landesgeschichte, Peter Herde zum 65, Geburtstag, eds, Karl Borchardt & Enno Buez, Anton Hiersemann, 98. **CONTACT ADDRESS** 11311 Winston Place, Apt B, Newport News, VA, 23602.

EASTWOOD, BRUCE STANSFIELD
PERSONAL Born 02/08/1938, Worcester, MA, m, 1958, 3 children **DISCIPLINE** HISTORY OF SCIENCE **EDUCATION** Emory Univ, AB, 59, MA, 60; Univ Wis, PhD (Grosseteste's optics), 64. **CAREER** Instr hist, Russell Sage Col, 63-64; asst prof, Ithaca Col, 64-67; asst prof hist sci, Clarkson Col Technol, 67-70; assoc prof medieval hist sci, Kans State Univ, 70-73; ASSOC PROF INTELLECTUAL HIST SCI, UNIV KY, 73-, Am Philos Soc res grant, 66-67; Nat Sci Found res grant, 66-67. **MEMBERSHIPS** Hist Sci Soc; AHA. **RESEARCH** History of optics before Newton; medieval Franciscans; 17th century physics and culture. **SELECTED PUBLICATIONS** Auth, The Liberal Arts in the Early Middle Ages 5th 9th Century--Quadrivium and Computus as Indicators for Continuity and Renewal of the Exact Sciences Between Antiquity and the Middle Ages, Isis, Vol 86, 95; The Ordering of Time--From the Ancient Computus to the Modern Computer, Speculum A J Medieval Stud, Vol 71, 96; Byrhtferth Enchiridion, Isis, Vol 88, 97; Macrobius in the Middle Ages--History of the Reception of the Commentarii in Somnium Scipionis, Isis, Vol 84, 93; Byrhtferth Enchiridion, Isis, Vol 88, 97. **CONTACT ADDRESS** Dept of Hist, Univ of Kentucky, 500 S Limestone St, Lexington, KY, 40506-0003.

EATON, RICHARD MAXWELL
PERSONAL Born 12/08/1940, Grand Rapids, MI **DISCIPLINE** HISTORY OF INDIA, ISLAMIC STUDIES. **EDUCATION** Col Wooster, BA, 62; Univ Va, Charlottesville, MA, 67; Univ Wis-Madison, PhD(hist), 72. **CAREER** Teacher Hist, Walton High Sch, WVa, 64-65; teaching asst, Univ Wis-Madison, 67-69; asst prof, 72-78, from assoc prof to prof Hist, Univ Ariz, Tuscon, 78-93; Fulbright-Hays Sr Award, fel field res Pakistan, 75-76. **MEMBERSHIPS** Asn Asian Studies; Soc Iranian Studies. **RESEARCH** History of medieval India; Islamic studies; comparative religion. **SELECTED PUBLICATIONS** Auth, The court and the dargah in the seventeenth century Deccan, Indian Econ & Social Hist Rev, Vol 10, No 1, 3/73; Sufi folk literature and the expansion of Indian Islam, Hist Religions, Vol 14, No 2, 11/74; Sufis of Bijapur, 1300-1700: Social roles of Sufis in Medieval India, Princeton Univ, 78; The Rise of Islam and the Bengal Frontier, 1204-1760, Univ of California, 93; Nonbelief and Evil, Prometheus Books, Amherst, NY, 98. **CONTACT ADDRESS** Dept of History Studies, Univ of Arizona, 1 University of Arizona, Tucson, AZ, 85721-0001. **EMAIL** reaton@u.arizona.edu

EBEL, ROLAND H.
PERSONAL Born 10/11/1928, Oak Park, IL, m, 1955, 2 children **DISCIPLINE** POLITICAL SCIENCE **EDUCATION** Wheaton Col, BA, 50; Northwestern Univ, MA, 52; Mich St Univ, PhD, 60. **CAREER** Asst prof, 60-64, Western Mich Univ; assoc prof, 64-93, assoc prof emer, 93- Tulane Univ. **HONORS AND AWARDS** Soc Sci res Coun Grant, 65-66; Natl Sci Found Grant, 73-75; Sturgis-Leavitt prize, Best Article on Latin Amer, 90. **MEMBERSHIPS** SE Coun of Latin Amer Stud. **RESEARCH** Latin Amer politics **SELECTED PUBLICATIONS** Auth, Guatemala: The Politics of Unstable Stability, Latin Amer Pol & Dev, Westview Press, 96; auth, Guillermo Ungo, Carlos Castillo Armas, Miguel Ydigoras Fuentes, Carlos Arana Osorio, Vinicio Cerezo, Francisco Villagran Kramer, Fidel Sanchez Hernandez, Carlos Humberto Romero, Oscar Osorio, Mario Mendez Montenegro, Julio Cesar Mendez Montenegro, Jose Maria Lemus, Enrique Peralta Azurdia, Juan Jose Arevalo, & Jacobo Arbenz Guzman", Encycl of Latin Amer Hist & Cult, Scribner's Sons, 98; auth, Misunderstood Caudillo: Miguel Ydigoras Fuentes and the Failure of Guatemalan Democracy, Univ Press of Amer, 98. **CONTACT ADDRESS** Dept of Political Science, Tulane Univ, New Orleans, LA, 70118.

EBER, IRENE
PERSONAL Born 12/29/1929, Halle, Germany, 2 children **DISCIPLINE** CHINESE HISTORY **EDUCATION** Pomona Col, BA, 55; Sacramento State Col, MA, 61; Claremont Grad Sch and Univ Ctr, PhD (Asian studies), 66. **CAREER** Asst prof hist, Whittier Col, 66-69; ASSOC PROF CHINESE HIST, HEBREW UNIV JERUSALEM, 69-, Soc Sci Res Coun grant, 68-69; assoc prof Chinese hist, Wesleyan Univ, 79-80. **MEMBERSHIPS** Asn Asian Studies; Am Orient Soc. **RESEARCH** Images of women in the classic Chinese novel; Ch'en Hsuching, a forgotten intellectual?; Hu Shih, 1891-1962, scholar of modern China. **SELECTED PUBLICATIONS** Auth, Translating the Ancestors, Schereschewsky, S. I. J. 1875 Chinese Version of Genesis, Bull School Oriental African Stud University London, Vol 56, 93. **CONTACT ADDRESS** Inst of Asian and African Studies, Hebrew Univ, Jerusalem, ..

EBNER, MICHAEL HOWARD
PERSONAL Born 04/22/1942, Paterson, NJ, m, 1966, 2 children **DISCIPLINE** HISTORY **EDUCATION** Univ Toledo, BA, 64; Univ Va, MA, 66, PhD, 74. **CAREER** Lectr hist, Herbert H Lehman Col, 69-72 & City Col, City Univ NY, 72-74; asst prof, 74-80, assoc prof hist, Lake Forest Col, 80-, Nat Adv Bd, Hist Teacher, 77-. **HONORS AND AWARDS** Outstanding Teaching Contrib Award, City Col New York, 73. **MEMBERSHIPS** AHA; Orgn Am Historians; Soc Hist Educ; AAUP. **RESEARCH** American urban history; American social history. **SELECTED PUBLICATIONS** Art, Experiencing Megapolis in Princeton, Journal of Urban History, 19:2, Feb 93; art, Technoburb, Inland Architect 37:1, Jan-Feb 93; art, Suburbanization, American Cities and Suburbs: An Encyclopedia ABC-Clio Press, 98. **CONTACT ADDRESS** Lake Forest Col, 555 N Sheridan Rd, Lake Forest, IL, 60045-2399. **EMAIL** ebner@lfc.edu.

ECCLES, WILLIAM JOHN
PERSONAL Born 07/17/1917, Yorkshire, England, m, 1948, 3 children **DISCIPLINE** HISTORY **EDUCATION** McGill Univ, BA, 49, MA, 51, PhD (hist), 55. **CAREER** Lectr hist, Univ Man, 53-57; from asst prof to assoc prof, Univ Alta, 57-63; PROF HIST, UNIV TORONTO, 63-, Mem, Humanities Res Coun Can, 64-66; vis prof, McGill Univ, 66-67; guest lectr, Am Univ Beirut, 67; Can Coun Killam scholar, 69-72; Connaught fel, Univ Toronto, 80-81. **HONORS AND AWARDS** Tyrrell Medal, Royal Soc Can, 79. **MEMBERSHIPS** Inst d'Hist de l'Amerique Francaise; Can Hist Asn; Soc Fr Hist Studies; Inst Early Am Hist and Cult. **RESEARCH** French colonies in America pre 1789. **SELECTED PUBLICATIONS** Auth, Parkman, Francis, Historian as Hero--The Formative Years, Can Hist Rev, Vol 75, 94; The Testimonies of Canadian and Quebecois Historians, Etudes Francaises, Vol 30, 94; The Filles Du Roi in the 17th CenturyOrphans in France, Pioneers in Canada, Can Hist Rev, Vol 74, 93; From France to New France--Founder Society and New Society - French, Rev Hist Am Fr, Vol 49, 96; Letters From New France--The Upper Country 1686-1783, Mc Hist Rev, Vol 18, 92; New France in Nort America, 16th-18th Centuries, Rev Hist Am Fr, Vol 46, 92. **CONTACT ADDRESS** Dept of Hist, Univ of Toronto, Toronto, ON, M5S 1A1.

ECHOLS, JAMES KENNETH
PERSONAL m, 2 children **DISCIPLINE** AMERICAN CHURCH HISTORY **EDUCATION** Temple Univ, BA, 73; Lutheran Theol Sem at Phil, MDiv, 77 Yale Univ, MA, 79, MPhil, 84, PhD, 89. **CAREER** Dean, Lutheran Theol Sem at Phil; pres-. **HONORS AND AWARDS** Daniel Alexander Payne awd for Ecumenical srv, African Methodist Episcopal Church, 96., Bd mem, ELCA Div for ministry; Black Lutheran Commn Develop Corporation. **MEMBERSHIPS** Mem, ELCA Delegation to Natl Coun of Churches of Christ. **SELECTED PUBLICATIONS** Pub(s), in the areas of church history, theology and Black American Lutheranism. **CONTACT ADDRESS** Dept of American Church History, Lutheran Sch of Theol, 1100 E 55th St, Chicago, IL, 60615.

ECKARDT, ALICE LYONS
PERSONAL Born 04/27/1923, Brooklyn, NY, m, 1944, 2 children **DISCIPLINE** HISTORY OF RELIGIONS **EDUCATION** Oberlin Col, BA, 44; Lehigh Univ, MA, 66. **CAREER** Lectr, 72-75, ASST PROF RELIG STUDIES, LEHIGH UNIV, 76-, Vis prof, Judaic Studies Dept, City Univ New York, 73; assoc, Rockefeller Found Grant, 75-76; Spec adv, President's Comn on the Holocaust, 79 and US Holocaust Mem Coun, 81-; vis scholar, Oxford Ctr postgrad Hebrew Studies, 82 and Cedar Crest Col, 81 and 82. **MEMBERSHIPS** Am Acad Relig; Nat Inst Holocaust; Am Professors Peace Mid East. **RESEARCH** History and theology of Jewish-Christian relations; the Holocaust, and post-Holocaust theology; sexism and world religions. **SELECTED PUBLICATIONS** Auth, The Other in Jewish Thought and History--Constructions of Jewish Culture and Identity, J Ecumenical Stud, Vol 33, 96; A Jewish Appraisal of Dialogue--Between Talk and Theology, J Ecumenical Stud, Vol 33, 96. **CONTACT ADDRESS** Beverly Hill Rd, Box 619A, Coopersburg, PA, 18036.

ECKERT, EDWARD K.
DISCIPLINE HISTORY **EDUCATION** Univ FL, PhD. **CAREER** Prof Hist and vpres Acad Affairs. **RESEARCH** US hist; the Am Civil War; mil hist; the Vietnam War. **SELECTED PUBLICATIONS** Auth, In War and Peace: An American Military History Anthology, Wadsworth , 89; "Fiction Distorting Fact:" The Prison Life, Annotated by Jefferson Davis, Mercer UP, 87; coauth, Ten Years in the Saddle: The Military Memoir of William W. Averell, Presidio, 79; The McClellans and the Grants: Generalship and Strategy in the Civil War. **CONTACT ADDRESS** St Bonaventure Univ, St Bonaventure, NY, 14778. **EMAIL** eeckert@sbu.edu

ECKHARDT, PATRICIA
PERSONAL Born 06/27/1939, Toledo, OH, m, 1961, 3 children **DISCIPLINE** ART HISTORY **EDUCATION** Lindenwood Col, BA, 61; Univ Iowa, MA, 73, MFA, 78, PhD, 90. **CAREER** Field Svc, grant manag, 77-82, St Hist Soc of Iowa; principal, 90-, Eckhardt Research. **RESEARCH** Amer Archit, 1880-1920 **CONTACT ADDRESS** 514 North Linn St, Iowa City, IA, 52245.

ECKSTEIN, A.M.
PERSONAL Born 09/13/1946, Hempstead, NY **DISCIPLINE** ANCIENT HISTORY **EDUCATION** UCLA, BA 68, MA 70; Univ Calif Berkeley, PhD 78. **CAREER** Univ N Carolina, asst prof 78-80; Univ Maryland, asst prof, assoc prof, prof 80-94-. **HONORS AND AWARDS** Woodrow Wilson Fel; svral tchrs and serv Awds UM. **MEMBERSHIPS** AHA; APA; AAAH. **RESEARCH** Roman Imperial Expansion; Hellenistic Politics; Ancient Histiography. **SELECTED PUBLICATIONS** Auth, Senate and General: Individual Decision-Making and Roman Foreign Relations, 264-194 BC, Univ Calif Press, 87; auth, Moral Vision in the Histories of Polybius, Univ Calif Press, 95; auth, Polybius Demetrius of Pharus and the Origins of the Second Illyrian War, Classical Philology, 94; auth, Glabrio and the Aetolians: A Note on deditio, Trans of the Amer Philos Assoc, 96; Physis and Nomos: Polybius the Romans and Cato the Elder, in: Peter Cartledge, Peter Garnsey, Erich Gruen, eds, Hellenistic Constructs, Univ Calif Press, 97. **CONTACT ADDRESS** Dept of History, Univ of Maryland, College Park, MD, 20742. **EMAIL** ael@umail.umd.edu

EDELMAN, DIANA
DISCIPLINE BIBLICAL STUDIES; ANCIENT SYNO-PALESTINIAN HISTORY & ARCHAEOLOGY **EDUCATION** Smith Col, AB, 75; Univ Chicago, MA, 78, PhD, 86. **CAREER** Lectr, St Xavier Univ, 90-91; assoc prof, James Madison Univ, 93-; **HONORS AND AWARDS** Grant-in-aid Amer Coun Learned Studies, 88; vis prof Ecole biblique et archeol Jerusalem, 96. **MEMBERSHIPS** Soc Bibl Lit; Amer Schools of Orient Res; Cath Bibl Asn. **RESEARCH** Ancient

Syno-Palestinian history & archaelology; Deuteronomistic history; Ancient Israelite religion; 2nd temple Judaism. **SELECTED PUBLICATIONS** Auth, King Saul in the Historiography of Judah, Journal for the Study of the Old Testament Supplement Series, 91; ed, The Fabric of History: Text, Artifact, & Israels Past, Journal for the Study of the Old Testament Supplement Series, 91; auth, You Shall Not Abhor an Edomite for He is Your Brother: Edom and Seir in History and Tradition, Archaeology and Biblical Studies, 95; The Triumph of Elohim: From Yahuisims to Judaisms, Biblical Exegesis and Theology, 95. **CONTACT ADDRESS** Dept of Philosophy & Religion, James Madison Univ, MSC 7504, Harrisonburg, VA, 22807. **EMAIL** edelmadj@jmu.edu

EDELSTEIN, MELVIN A.
PERSONAL Born 05/23/1939, New York, NY, m, 1969, 1 child **DISCIPLINE** HISTORY **EDUCATION** Univ of Chicago, BA, 60; Princeton Univ, MA, 62, PhD, 65. **CAREER** Instr in History of Western Civilization, Stanford Univ, 64-67; asst prof of hist, Herbert H. Lehman Col of CUNY, 67-73; ASSOC PROF, 73-79, PROF, 79-, CHEMN, WILLIAM PATERSON UNIV OF NEW JERSEY, 81-87. **HONORS AND AWARDS** Grant, Am Philos Soc, 69, 75, 90, & 94; summer stipend, 89, travel-to-collections grant, NEH, 90; Fulbright fel for res, 96. **MEMBERSHIPS** Am Hist Asn; Soc of French Hist Studies; Societe des Etudes Robespierristes. **RESEARCH** French revolutionary elections; French revolutionary press. **SELECTED PUBLICATIONS** Auth, La Feuille Villageoise: Communication Et Modernisation Dans Les Regions Rurales Pendant La Revolution: Comission D'Histoire Economique Et Sociale De La Revolution Francaise. Memoires Et Documents, Bibliotheque Nationale, 77; Le Comportement Electoral sous la Monarchie Constitutionnelle (1790-91): Une Interpretation Communautaire, Annales Historiques de la Revolution Francaise, 95; Participation ed Sociologie Electorales des Landes en 1790, Annales Historiques de la Revolution Francaise, forthcoming; Participation et Sociologie Electorales de l'Aisne en mai 1790 et juin 1791, AnnalesHistoriques Compiegnoises, 98; Le Militaire-Citoyen, ou le droit de vote des militaires pendant la Revolution francaise, Annales Historiques de la Revolution Francaise, 97. **CONTACT ADDRESS** Dept of Hist, William Paterson Col, 300 Pompton Rd, Wayne, NJ, 07470. **EMAIL** melvine@frontier.wilpaterson.edu

EDEN, KATHY
DISCIPLINE HISTORY OF RHETORICAL AND POETIC THEORY IN ANTIQUITY **EDUCATION** Smith, BA, 74; Stanford, PhD, 80. **CAREER** English and Lit, Columbia Univ **SELECTED PUBLICATIONS** Auth, Poetic and Legal Fiction in The Aristotelian Tradition, Princeton, 86; Hermeneutics and the Rhetorical Tradition: Chapters in the Ancient Legacy and its Humanist Reception, New Haven, 97. **CONTACT ADDRESS** Columbia Univ, 2960 Broadway, New York, NY, 10027-6902.

EDGAR, WALTER BELLINGRATH
PERSONAL Born 12/10/1943, Mobile, AL, m, 1966, 2 children **DISCIPLINE** AMERICAN HISTORY **EDUCATION** Davidson Col, AB, 65; Univ SC, MA, 67, PhD (hist), 69. **CAREER** Asst prof, 72-76, ASSOC PROF HIST, UNIV SC, 76-, Nat Hist Publ Comn, fel ed, 71-72; ed hist, SC House Comt Hist Res, 72-76; asst chmn dept hist, 79-80, dir, Inst Southern Studies, Univ SC, 80-. **MEMBERSHIPS** Orgn Am Historians; Southern Hist Asn; Am Asn State and Local Hist. **RESEARCH** South Carolina history; historic preservation; Colonial history. **SELECTED PUBLICATIONS** Auth, Harby, Isaac of Charleston, 1788-1828--Jewish Reformer and Intellectual, William Mary Quart, Vol 52, 95; Andersonville--The Last Depot, J Southern Hist, Vol 62, 96; Agriculture, Geology, and Society in Antebellum South Carolina--The Private Diary o f Ruffin, Edmund, 1843, Virginia Mag Hist Biography, Vol 101, 93. **CONTACT ADDRESS** Dept of Hist, Univ SC, Columbia, SC, 29208.

EDGEWORTH, ROBERT J.
DISCIPLINE LATIN AND GREEK LANGUAGE AND LITERATURE **EDUCATION** Univ Mich, PhD. **CAREER** Prof Classics, actg chemn, dept For Lang and Lit, La State Univ, 88-89, 92, 94. **RESEARCH** Classical epic and epistolography. **SELECTED PUBLICATIONS** Auth, The Ivory Gate and the Threshold of Apollo, in Classica et Mediaevalia 37, 86; The Colors of the Aeneid, Peter Lang, 92. **CONTACT ADDRESS** Dept of For Lang and Lit, Louisiana State Univ, 145A Prescott Hall, Baton Rouge, LA, 70803.

EDIE, CAROLYN A.
PERSONAL Born 08/09/1930, Boston, MA, m, 1960 **DISCIPLINE** HISTORY **EDUCATION** Wellesley Col, AB, 51; Univ Wis, MA, 54, PhD, 57. **CAREER** Instr hist, Hobart and William Smith Cols, 57-59, asst prof 59-61; from asst prof to assoc prof, 61-74, PROF HIST, UNIV ILL, CHICAGO CIRCLE, 74-, Am Philos Soc res grant 67; fels, Huntington Libr and Grad Col, Univ Ill, 71; Am Philos Soc grant, 74. **MEMBERSHIPS** AHA; Conf Brit Studies (rec secy, 71-73); Am Soc Legal Hist; Conf Study Soc and Polit Thought. **RESEARCH** British history, 17th century; early modern Europe. **SELECTED PUBLICATIONS** Auth, The Birth of Britain--A New Nation, 1700-1710, Albion, Vol 27, 95. **CONTACT ADDRESS** Dept of Hist, Univ of Ill Chicago Circle, Chicago, IL, 60680.

EDLUND-BERRY, INGRID E.M.
PERSONAL Born 09/18/1942, Lund, Sweden, m, 1987, 2 children **DISCIPLINE** CLASSICAL ARCHAEOLOGY; ANCIENT HISTORY **EDUCATION** Univ of Lund, SWE, FK, FM, 65, FL, 69; Bryn Mawr Col, MA, 69, PhD, 71. **CAREER** Instr, The Intercollegiate Center for Classical Studies, 71-72, asst prof, 77-78; Univ GA, vis asst prof, 73-78; vis prof, Univ MN, 82; asst prof, 78-87, assoc prof, 87-98, PROF, UNIV TX AT AUSTIN, 98-. **HONORS AND AWARDS** ACLS; Fondazione Familglia Rausing; Andrew W. Mellon Found; Alexander von Humboldt-Siftung; Univ Res Inst , Univ TX at Austin. **MEMBERSHIPS** Amer Philos Assoc; Archaeological Inst Amer; Associazone internationale di archaeologia classica; Classical Assoc of the Middle West and South; Etruscan Found; Svenska klassikerforbundet. **RESEARCH** Archaeology of ancient Italy, ancient relig. **SELECTED PUBLICATIONS** Auth, The Iron Age and Etruscan Vases in the Olcott Collection at Columbia Univ, NY, Amer Philos Soc, Transaction 70, 80; The Gods and the Place: Location and Function of Sanctuaries in the Countryside of Etruria and Magna Graecia (700-400 B. C.), Acta Instituti Romani Regni Sueciae, Stockholm, 87; Poggio Civitate (Murlo) 1966-1987: an annotated bibliography of primary and secondary publications, with the late Kyle M. Phillips, Jr, in In the Hills of Tuscany, ed, Karen B. Velluci, The Univ Museum, Univ PA, 93; The Seated and Standing Statue Akroteria from Poggio Civitate (Murlo), Giorgio Bretschneider, Rome, 92, Archaeologica, 96; numerous articles in Archaeological News, Eranos, Classical Bull, Rivista di Studi Classici, Talanta, CA Studies in Classical Antiquity, Medusa, Mededelingen van het Nederl, Historisch Instituut te Rome, Rivista di Archaeologia, Amer J of Archaeology, Vergilius, Parloa del Passato, Opuscula Romana, Acta Instituti Romani Regni Sueciae: Deliciae Fictiles, Opus mixtum, Acta Universitatis Upsaliensis: Boreas, Bollettino d'Arte, Praktika, Etruscan Studies, Kotinos. **CONTACT ADDRESS** Dept of Classics, Univ of Texas, Waggener 123, Austin, TX, 78712. **EMAIL** IEMEB@mail.utexas.edu

EDMONDS, ANTHONY OWENS
PERSONAL Born 06/11/1940, Biloxi, MS, m, 1964, 2 children **DISCIPLINE** RECENT UNITED STATES & BLACK HISTORY **EDUCATION** Yale Univ, BA, 62; Vanderbilt Univ, MA, 66, PhD, 70. **CAREER** Instr hist, Univ TN, Nashville, 68-69; from Asst Prof to Assoc Prof, 69-78, prof hist, Ball State Univ, 78. **HONORS AND AWARDS** Outstanding Tchr, Ball State Univ, 81, 91, 96; Outstanding Fac Advisor ,96. **MEMBERSHIPS** Southern Hist Asn; Orgn Am Historians; Pop Cult Asn; Soc Study For Rels. **RESEARCH** Am cult in the 1950's; sports hist; Vietnam War; higher educ. **SELECTED PUBLICATIONS** Auth, Joe Louis, Eerdmans, 73; Resources for Teaching the Vietnam War, Ctr for Soc Studies Educ, 92; The War in Vietnam, Greenwood, 98. **CONTACT ADDRESS** Dept of Hist, Ball State Univ, 2000 W University, Muncie, IN, 47306-0002. **EMAIL** 00aoedmonds@bsuvc.bsu.edu

EDMONDSON, CLIFTON EARL
PERSONAL Born 05/14/1937, Shreveport, LA, m, 1964 **DISCIPLINE** MODERN EUROPEAN HISTORY **EDUCATION** Miss Col, BA, 59; Duke Univ, MA, 62, PhD (hist), 66. **CAREER** From instr to asst prof hist, Univ NC, Chapel Hill, 62-70, Univ Res Coun fac grant, 67-69; asst prof 70-77, ASSOC PROF HIST, DAVIDSON COL, 77-. **MEMBERSHIPS** AHA; AAUP; Conf Group Cent Europ Hist; Southern Hist Asn. **RESEARCH** Central Europe; Fascism; diplomacy in 19th and 20th centuries. **SELECTED PUBLICATIONS** Auth, Austria, Germany and the Powers--International and Austrian Aspects of the Anschluss of March 1938, J Modern Hist, Vol 65, 93. **CONTACT ADDRESS** Dept of Hist, Davidson Col, Po Box 1719, Davidson, NC, 28036-1719.

EDMONSON, JAMES MILTON
PERSONAL Born 02/12/1951, Muncie, IN, m, 2 children **DISCIPLINE** HISTORY OF TECHNOLOGY **EDUCATION** Col of Wooster, BA, 73; Univ of Del, MA, 76; Univ of Del, PhD, 81. **CAREER** Curator, Dittrick Museum of Med Hist, Case Western Reserve Univ and Cleveland Med Lib Assoc, 81-; teach asst, Col Wooster, 71-72; teach asst, Univ Del, 77; Adj asst prof, Case Western Reserve University, 81-. **HONORS AND AWARDS** Hagley Fellow, 74-78; Fulbright-Hays Fellow, Paris, 78-79; Willbur Owen Sypherd Prize, Univ Del, 81; Smithsonian Inst Res Fellow, 88; FC Clark Wood Fellow, 90; Wellcome Museum Fellow, London, 92. **MEMBERSHIPS** Handerson Med Hist Soc; Ohio Acad of Med Hist; Soc Hist of Technol; Euro Asn Museums of Hist of Med Sciences; Med Museums Assoc; Am Asn Hist Med. **RESEARCH** History of American surgical instrument trade; medical patents; medical furniture; endoscopy. **SELECTED PUBLICATIONS** United States patents for medical devices: patterns of inventive activity in the nineteenth century, Proceedings of the Seventh Symposium of the European Association of Museums of History of Medical Sciences,Zurich, 94; Endoscope, in Instruments of Science: An Historical Encyclopedia, London, 97; American Surgical Instruments: An Illustrated History of Their Manufacture and a Directory of Instrument Makers to 1900, San Francisco, Norman Pub, 97. **CONTACT ADDRESS** Case Western Reserve Univ, 11000 Euclid Ave., Cleveland, OH, 44106-1714. **EMAIL** jme3@po.cwru.edu

EDMUNDS, LOWELL
PERSONAL Born 10/11/1938, Franklin, NH, m, 1966, 2 children **DISCIPLINE** CLASSICS **EDUCATION** Harvard, PhD, 70. **CAREER** Teaching asst, Classics, Berkeley, 63-64; teaching fel, Classics, Harvard, 67-69; teaching fel, Harvard summer school, 68, 69; instr Classics, Wheaton Col, 69-70; tutor, graduate asst, St John's Col, Santa Fe, NM, summers 70, 71; asst prof Classics, Harvard, 70-75; asst prof Classics, Harvard Univ Extension, 72-73; assoc prof Classics, Harvard, 75-78; assoc prof Classics, Harvard Univ Exrension, 76-80; assoc prof Classics, Boston Col, 78-83; ed, Comparative Civilizations Bul, 79082; chmn, Dept Classical Studies, Boston Col, 83; prof Classics and chmn, Johns Hopkins Univ, 83-88; member, fac ed bd, Johns Hopkins Univ Press, 83-86; member ed bd, Am J of Philol, 83-87; member, subcommittee on the Thesaurus Linguae Graecae of the Res Comm of the Am Philol Asn, 86-; chmn, Ed Adv Comm, Perseus: A New Curriculum on Ancient Greek Civilization, Harvard based, 86-92; first vice pres, Baltimore Soc of the Archaeological Inst of Am, 87-88; member, ed bd, Lexis (Univ Venice), 87-; co-dir, Coppin-Hopkins Prog in the Baltimore City Schools, 87-89; prof Classics, Rutgers Univ, 88-, dir, graduate prog in Classics, 88-90, chair, 90-96, acting dir, graduate prog in Classics, 94-96; professore a contratto, Universita degli Studi di Venezia, April 90; prof a contratto, Universita degli Studi di Trento, Nov 93; vis prof, Princeton Univ, spring 95; asst ed, Classical World, 97-. **HONORS AND AWARDS** Pushcart Prize for "Choosing Your Names," 93-94. **MEMBERSHIPS** Am Philol Asn; Int Soc for Folk Narrative Res. **RESEARCH** Greek lit; Greek mythology; Roman lit. **SELECTED PUBLICATIONS** Auth, Choosing Your Names, Raritan 11 3, winter 92, under pseudonym, Kothar wa-Khasis, reprinted in The 1993-1994 Pushcart Prize XVIII: Best of the Small Presses; Intertextuality Today, Lexis 13, 95; Theatrical Space and Historical Place in Sophocles' Oedipus at Colonus, Rowman and Littlefield, 96; Poet, Public, and Performance: Essays in Ancient Greek Literature and Literary History, ed with Robert Wallace, The Johns Hopkins Univ Press, 97; Myth in Homer, in New Companion to Homer, ed by Barry Powell and Ian Morris, Brill, April 97; The Silver Bullet: The Martini in American Civilization, Contributions in Am Studies 52, Greenwood Press, 81, 2nd ed, titled Martini Straight Up: The Classic American Cocktail, Johns Hopkins Univ Press, 98. **CONTACT ADDRESS** 440 Grant Ave, Highland Park, NJ, 08904. **EMAIL** edmunds@rci.rutgers.edu

EDSALL, NICHOLAS CRANFORD
PERSONAL Born 07/14/1936, Boston, MA **DISCIPLINE** MODERN ENGLISH HISTORY **EDUCATION** Harvard Univ, BA, 58, PhD, 66; London Sch Econ, MA, 60. **CAREER** From asst lectr to lectr hist, Univ Nottingham, 64-66; asst prof, 66-72, assoc prof Hist, 72-88, prof Hist, 88-98, PROF EMERITUS, UNIV VA, CHARLOTTESVILLE, 98-. **MEMBERSHIPS** AHA; Conf Brit Studies; AAUP. **RESEARCH** Victorian political and social history; history of homosexuality. **SELECTED PUBLICATIONS** Auth, The Antipoor Law Movement, Manchester Univ, 71; Varieties of radicalism: Attwood, Cobden and the local politics of municipal incorporation, Hist J, 73; A failed national movement: The Parliamentary and Financial Reform Association, 1848-54, Bull Inst Hist Res, 5/76; Richard Cobden, Independent Radical, Harvard Univ Press, 86. **CONTACT ADDRESS** 1924 Thomson Rd, Charlottesville, VA, 22903.

EDWARDS, DON R.
PERSONAL Born 05/26/1955, Lafayette, IN **DISCIPLINE** CLASSICS **EDUCATION** St. John's Col, BA, 78; Johns Hopkins, MS, 96; Brown Univ, PhD, 84. **CAREER** Author **RESEARCH** Philosophy **CONTACT ADDRESS** 218 East Del Ray Ave, Alexandria, VA, 22301.

EDWARDS, GEORGE CHARLES III
PERSONAL Born 12/25/1946, Rochester, NY, 4 children **DISCIPLINE** POLITICAL SCIENCE **EDUCATION** Yale, 83, PhD. **CAREER** Assoc Prof, Rensselaer Polytechnic Institute, 18 years. **HONORS AND AWARDS** Woodrow Wilson Fell; Intl Studies; Assoc Sprout Award in Intl Ecology. **MEMBERSHIPS** Am Pol Sci; Soc for Soc Studies of Sci. **RESEARCH** Wiser Steeing of Tech. **SELECTED PUBLICATIONS** The Polic-Making Process, 3rd ed, Englewood Cliffs Prentice Hall, 93; When Expert Advice Works and When it Does Not, IEEE Technology and Society Magazine, pp23-29, 97; Science, Government and the Politics of Knowledge, in Handbook of Science and Technology Sutdies, Sage, pp533-553, 95; Can Science Be More Useful In Politics? The Case of Ecological Risk Assessment, Human and Ecological Risk Assessment vol 1,pp395-406, 95; Incrementalism, Intelligent Trial-and -Error and the Future of Ploitical Decision Theory, in H. Redner ed, An Heretical Heir of the Enlightenment Westview, 93. **CONTACT ADDRESS** Rensselaer Polytech Inst, Troy, NY, 12180-3590. **EMAIL** GEDWARDS@TAMU.EDU

EDWARDS, HARRY
PERSONAL Born 11/22/1942, St. Louis, MO, m **DISCIPLINE** SOCIOLOGY **EDUCATION** San Jose State, BA 1964; Cornell U, MA 1966, PhD 1972. **CAREER** San Jose State, instructor Sociology 1966-68; Univ of Santa Clara, instructor Sociology 1967-68; Univ of CA Berkeley, asst prof So-

ciology 1970-77, assoc prof Sociology, prof Sociology. Served as consultant with producers of sports relatedprograms on NBC, CBS, ABC and PBS TV networks; sports commentary for Natl Public Radio via satellite to Washington DC; interview/ commentary prog on KPFA-Radio Berkeley CA; consulted/ appeared on camera for BBC TV (British), CBC TV (Candaian) West German TV for CBS' "60 Minutes", CNN's "Sports Focus", NBC's "Nightly News", ABC's "Sportsbeat" and "Nightline", PBS's "James Michner's World", Turner Sports Nework ESPN "SportsForum" and numerous local & relgional TV productions foing on issues relating to sports & society; participated in lecture & consulting fair at Natl Sports Inst Oslo Norway, Natl Sports Inst Moscow USSR; consultant San Francisco 49ers and Golden State Warriors. **HONORS AND AWARDS** NAACP Educ Incentive Scholarship CA State Univ 1960; Athletic Scholarship CA State Univ 1960; Woodrow Wilson Fellowship 1964; Man of Yr Awd San Francisco Sun Reporter 1968; Russwurm Awd Natl Newspaper Publishers Assoc 1968; fellowship Cornell Univ 1968; Dist Scholar in Res fall 1980 OR State Univ; Miller Scholar in Res fall 1982 Univ of IL Champaign/Urbana Charleston Gazette; Dist Scholar in Res spring 1983 Norwegian Coll of Physical Educ & Sports Oslow Norway; Dist Schlr Spring 1984 Univ of Charleston; Dist Visiting Scholar fall 1984 IN St Univ. **SELECTED PUBLICATIONS** Contributed editorials to Los Angeles Times, NY Times, San Francisco Examiner, Oakland Tribune, Chicago Sun-Times, Black Scholar, East St Louis Monitor, Milwaukee Courier, Newsday, Los Angeles Hearld Examiner, Sports Illustrated, Sports & Athletes & Inside Sports. **CONTACT ADDRESS** Sociology Dept, Univ of California, Berkeley, 410 Barrows Hall, Berkeley, CA, 94720.

EDWARDS, JAY D.

PERSONAL Born 09/05/1937, Chicago, IL, m, 1963, 1 child **DISCIPLINE** ANTHROPOLOGY **EDUCATION** Lycoming Coll, BA, sociology, 63; Tulane Univ, MA, anthrop, 65, PhD, anthrop, 70. **CAREER** Assoc grad faculty, School of Arch, full prof athrop, dir, Fred B. Kniffen Cultural Resources Lab, La State Univ. **HONORS AND AWARDS** $180,000 to conduct study of historic preservation of Whitney Plantation and planning of La's Creole Plantation Cultures, 91-93; $10,000 grant, Program for Cultural Cooperation between Spain's Ministry of Culture and the U.S.'s universities to conduct research in Spain and the Dominican Republic on the origins of Creole arch in New World, 93; $20,000 subventions, Ella West Freeman Found and Kemper and Leila Williams Found, to support the publication of Kniffen monograph, The Watercolor Paintings of Fr. Joseph M. Paret, 96. **RESEARCH** Regional specializations: Creole cultures of Louisiana, the American South, Spanish America, the West Indies, and their roots in West Africa, England, France, and Iberia; theoretical specifications: semiotics, structuralism, post-structuralism, culture theory, culture history; topical specifications: American folk and colonial cultures, material culture, oral literature, social structure, sociolinguistics. **SELECTED PUBLICATIONS** Coauth, A Creole Lexicon: Architecture, Construction and Landscape, 98; Auth, Early Creole Architecture: The LeConte Family Plantation House, Larou, Haiti, 97; Auth, Review: Jean-Paul Bourdier and Trihh T. Minh-Ha, Drawn from African Dwellings, Journal of the Society of Architectural Historians, 98. **CONTACT ADDRESS** Dept of Geography & Anthropology, Louisiana State Univ, Baton Rouge, LA, 70803. **EMAIL** gaedwa@lsu.edu

EDWARDS, LEE M.

PERSONAL Born 10/20/1937, Sydney, Australia, 1 child **DISCIPLINE** ART HISTORY **EDUCATION** Columbia Univ, PhD, 84 **CAREER** Writer, consultant **MEMBERSHIPS** Natl Coalition of Independent Scholars; Historians of Nineteenth Century Art; The Victorian Soc **RESEARCH** Victorian Painting; The Idyllists & their followers; Hubert von Herkomer **SELECTED PUBLICATIONS** Auth, numerous book and exhibition reviews since 92 for The Art Book; Sir Hubert von Herkomer, 1849-1914: A Life in Art, Scholar Press, Ashgate Publishing, Spring 99 **CONTACT ADDRESS** 1130 Park Ave, New York, NY, 10128. **EMAIL** ledwa1234@aol.com

EDWARDS, MARY

DISCIPLINE ART HISTORY **EDUCATION** Columbia Univ, MLS, BS, MA, PhD. **CAREER** Adjunct prof. **HONORS AND AWARDS** Samuel H. Kress diss fel, 82; NEH Travel to Coll(s) grant, 87. **SELECTED PUBLICATIONS** Co-auth, Wind Chant and Night Chant Sandpaintings: Studies Iconography; Source, Jour of Arch Hist, Il Santo, Bollettino del Museo Civico di Padova. **CONTACT ADDRESS** Dept of Art Hist, Pratt Inst, 200 Willoughby Ave, Brooklyn, NY, 11205.

EDWARDS, REBECCA

DISCIPLINE HISTORY **EDUCATION** Col of William and Mary, BA, 88; MA, 90, PhD, 95, Univ Virginia. **CAREER** Asst Prof, Vassar Col, 95-. **CONTACT ADDRESS** Vassar Col, 124 Raymond Ave, Box 493, Poughkeepsie, NY, 12604. **EMAIL** reedwards@vassar.edu

EDWARDS, SANDRA

DISCIPLINE MEDIEVAL PHILOSOPHY **EDUCATION** Univ Pa, PhD. **CAREER** Philos, Univ Ark **SELECTED PUBLICATIONS** Transl, St. Thomas Aquinas's Quaestiones Quodlibetales I & II, Pontifical Inst Medieval Studies, 83. **CONTACT ADDRESS** Univ Ark, Fayetteville, AR, 72701. **EMAIL** sandrae@comp.uark.edu

EDWARDS, SOLOMON

PERSONAL Born 04/02/1932, Indianapolis, IN, m **DISCIPLINE** EDUCATION **EDUCATION** IN Univ, BS 1954, MS 1969, EdD 1984. **CAREER** Arts Festival, coord 1956; IN Public Schools, teacher; Purdue Univ, assoc faculty 1971-79. **HONORS AND AWARDS** Writers Conf Poetry Awd 1953; dir New York City Dramatic Readers 1957-58; poems published 1959-77; Discussion moderator Intl Reading Assn Natl Convention 1979; educational game "Freedom & Martin Luther King" 1980. **MEMBERSHIPS** Mem Omega Psi Phi, NAACP, Phi Delta Kappa IN Univ. **SELECTED PUBLICATIONS** Auth, "What's Your Reading Attitude?" 1979; "This Day Father" 1979.

EGAN, RORY BERNARD

PERSONAL Born 02/06/1942, Sutton West, ON, Canada, m, 1970 **DISCIPLINE** CLASSICS **EDUCATION** Assumption Univ, Windsor, BA, 63; Univ Western Ont, MA, 65; Univ Southern Calif, PhD (classics), 71. **CAREER** Asst prof classics, Univ Southern Calif, 70-77; ASSOC PROF CLASSICS AND DEPT HEAD, UNIV MAN, 77-. **MEMBERSHIPS** Am Class League; Am Inst Archaeol; Am Philol Asn; Class Asn Can; Philol Asn Pac Coast. **RESEARCH** Classical mythology; Greek literature; Greek language. **SELECTED PUBLICATIONS** Auth, Stesichorus and Helen, Dallan and Columba, Class World, Vol 87, 93; Corydon Winning Words in Eclogue 7, Phoenix J Class Assn Can, Vol 50, 96. **CONTACT ADDRESS** Dept of Classics, Univ of Man, Winnipeg, MB, R3T 2N2.

EGERTON, FRANK N.

PERSONAL Born 02/06/1936, Louisburg, NC, m, 1966, 2 children **DISCIPLINE** WORLD HISTORY, HISTORY OF SCIENCE, ENV HISTORY **EDUCATION** Duke Univ, BS, 58; Univ WI-Madison, PhD, 67. **CAREER** Dept Eng, Univ Wisc-Parkside **HONORS AND AWARDS** Hunt Inst Bot Doc, 67, 68, 69 & 70; Nat Sci Found, 81; Univ WI Sea Grant Inst. **MEMBERSHIPS** Am Soc Environmental Hist **RESEARCH** History of science; environmental history. **SELECTED PUBLICATIONS** Ed, Landmarks of Botanical History, Smithsonian; Overfishing or Pollution Case History of a Controversy on the Great Lakes, Ann Arbor: Great Lakes Fishery Comn, 85. **CONTACT ADDRESS** Dept of Hist, Univ of Wisconsin, Parkside, 900 Wood Rd, Molinaro 1, PO Box 2000, Kenosha, WI, 53141-2000. **EMAIL** frank.egerton@uwp.edu

EGGENER, KEITH L.

PERSONAL Portland, OR **DISCIPLINE** ART, ARCHITECTURAL HISTORY **EDUCATION** Portland State Univ, BA, 85; Univ WA, MA, 89; Stanford Univ, PhD, 95. **CAREER** Asst prof, Art Hist, Carleton Col, Northfield, MN, 95-97; asst prof of Architecural Hist, Univ NV, Las Vegas, 97-; historic preservation consultant, Portland, OR, Charleston, SC, Las Vegas, NV, 84-; advisor, Barragan Found, Basel, Switzerland, 95-. **HONORS AND AWARDS** Samuel H Kress Found fel, 93; Sally Kress Tompkins fel, 93; Jacob K Javits fel, 93-95; Best Article of 1997, South Carolina Hist Magazine. **MEMBERSHIPS** Soc of Architectural Hist; Col Art Asn; Am Collegiate Schools of Architecture. **RESEARCH** Modern architecture in Mexico and the US; architectural photography; nationalism; melancholia. **SELECTED PUBLICATIONS** Auth, Ulama: The Game of Life and Death in Early MesoAmerica, with James A Fox, Stanford Univ Art Gallery, 94; The William Enston Home, The Vernacular Architecture of Charleston and the Low Country, 1670-1990, A Field Guide, Historic Charleston Found, 94; Maybeck's Melancholy: Architecture, Empathy, Empire, and Mental Illness at the 1915 Panama-Pacific International Exhibition, Winterthur Portfolio, winter 94; Diego Rivera's Proposal for El Pedregal, Source: Notes in the History of Art, spring 95; Expressionism and Emotional Architecture in Mexico: Luis Barragan's Collaborations with Max Cetto and Mathias Goeritz, Architectura--J of the Hist of Architecture, no 1, 95; Old Folks, New South: Charleston's William Enston Home, SC Hist Mag, July 97; Reflecting Psyche: Mirrors and Meaning at the Salon de la Princesse, hotel de Soubise, Constructing Identity: Proceedings of the 86th ACSA Annual Meeting, ACSA Press, 98; Towards an Organic Architecture in Mexico, Frank Lloyd Wright: Europe and Beyond, Anthony Alofsin, ed, Univ CA Press, 99; Past Knowing: Photography, Preservation, and Decay at the Gardens of El Pedregal, Memory and Architecture: Proceedings of the 1998 ACSA West Central Regional Conference; Image and Identity in Post-War Mexican Architecture, forthcoming; The Integration of Architecture and Landscape at the Gardens of El Pedregal, forthcoming; Barragan and Media (tentative title), essay in book on Barragan from the Vitra Design Museum, Federica Zanco, ed, forthcoming. **CONTACT ADDRESS** School of Architecture, Univ of Nevada, Las Vegas, 4505 Maryland Pkwy, Box 454018, Las Vegas, NV, 89154-4018. **EMAIL** eggenerk@nevada.edu

EGGERT, GERALD G.

PERSONAL Born 04/12/1926, Berrien Co, MI, m, 1953, 3 children **DISCIPLINE** U.S HISTORY **EDUCATION** Western Mich Univ, AB, 49; Univ Mich, AM, 51, PhD (US hist), 60. **CAREER** Teacher pub sch, Mich, 49-54; instr US hist, Univ Md, 57-60; from instr to asst prof, Bowling Green State Univ, 60-65; from asst prof to assoc prof, 65-72, PROF US HIST, PA STATE UNIV, 72-, HEAD DEPT HIST, 80-, Vis lectr, Univ Mich, 63. **MEMBERSHIPS** AHA; Orgn Am Historians. **SELECTED PUBLICATIONS** Auth, Making Iron and Steel--Independent Mills in Pittsburgh, 1820-1920, Technology and Culture, Vol 35, 94. **CONTACT ADDRESS** Dept of Hist Lib Arts, Tower Pa State Univ, University Park, PA, 16802.

EHRENREICH, N.

PERSONAL Born 05/16/1952, Topeka, KS, s, 1 child **DISCIPLINE** POLITICAL SCIENCE **EDUCATION** Yale Univ, BA 74; Univ Virginia, JD 79, LLM 82. **CAREER** Col Law, Denver Univ **MEMBERSHIPS** SALT; NLG. **RESEARCH** Feminist legal theory. **SELECTED PUBLICATIONS** Auth, Conceptualism by Any Other Name, Univ Denver L Rev, 97; The Progressive Potential in Privatization, U of Denver L Rev, 96; O.J. Simpson and the Myth of Gender/Race Conflict, U of Colorado L Rev, 96; auth, The Colonization of the Womb, Duke L Jour, 93; auth, Surrogacy as Resistance: The Misplaced Focus on Choice in the Surrogacy and Abortion Funding Contexts, DePaul L Rev, 92; auth, Wombs for Hire, Birth Power: The Case for Surrogacy, Shalev, rev, TIKKUN, 91; auth, Pluralist Myths and Powerless Men: The Ideology of Reasonableness in Sexual Harassment Law, Yale L Jour, 90. **CONTACT ADDRESS** College of Law, Univ of Denver, 1900 Olive St, Denver, CO, 80220. **EMAIL** nehrenre@mail.law.du.edu

EHRET, CHRISTOPHER

PERSONAL Born 07/27/1941, San Francisco, CA, m, 1963, 2 children **DISCIPLINE** AFRICAN HISTORY, HISTORICAL LINGUISTICS **EDUCATION** Univ Redlands, BA, 63; Northwestern Univ, Evanston, MA and cert African studies, 66, PhD (African hist), 69. **CAREER** Asst prof, 68-72, assoc prof, 72-78, PROF AFRICAN HIST, UNIV CALIF, LOS ANGELES, 78-, Ford Found grant African relig hist, 71-74; Fulbright grant, 82. **MEMBERSHIPS** Kenya Hist Soc; Hist Soc Tanzania. **RESEARCH** Development and use of linguistic evidence in historical reconstruction; eastern and southern African history; Nilotic and Cushitic historical linquistics. **SELECTED PUBLICATIONS** Auth, Kingship and State--The Buganda Dynasty, J Interdisciplinary Hist, Vol 28, 97. **CONTACT ADDRESS** Dept of Hist, Univ of Calif, Los Angeles, CA, 90024.

EICHMANN, RAYMOND

DISCIPLINE MEDIEVAL FRENCH FABLIAUX AND DRAMA **EDUCATION** Univ Ark, BA, 65; Univ Ark, MA, 67, Univ Ky, PhD, 73. **CAREER** English and Lit, Univ Ark. **HONORS AND AWARDS** Chair, dept; Chair, European Studies prog. **SELECTED PUBLICATIONS** Area: medieval French fabliaux. **CONTACT ADDRESS** Univ Ark, Fayetteville, AR, 72701.

EID, LEROY VICTOR

PERSONAL Born 12/22/1932, Cincinnati, OH, m, 1970 **DISCIPLINE** AMERICAN HISTORY **EDUCATION** Univ Dayton, BS, 53; St John's Univ, MA, 58, PhD, 61; Univ Toronto, MA, 68. **CAREER** From instr to asst prof, 61-73, assoc prof, 73-79, prof hist, Univ Dayton, 79-, chmn dept, 69-83. **RESEARCH** American Irish; Indian military history. **SELECTED PUBLICATIONS** Auth, The Colonial Scotch-Irish, Eire-Ireland, Winter, 86; auth, Irish, Scotch and Scotch-Irish, A Reconsideration, American Presbyterians: Journal of Presbyterian History, vol 64, winter, 86; auth, Their Rules of War: The Validity of James Smith's Analysis of Indian War, The Register of the Kentucky Historical Society, Winter, 86; auth A Kind of Running Fight: Indian Battlefield Tactics in the Late Eighteenth Century, The Western Pennsylvania Historical Mazagine, 88; auth, No Freight Paid So Well, in Eire-Ireland, Summer, 92; auth, American Indian Leadership, Journal of Military History 57, 93; auth, The Slaughter Was Reciprocal: Josiah Harmer's Two Defeats, 1790, Northwest Ohio Quarterly 65, Spring, 93. **CONTACT ADDRESS** Dept of History, Univ of Dayton, 300 College Park, Dayton, OH, 45469-1540. **EMAIL** E10.@checkov.hm.udayton.edu

EIDELBERG, MARTIN

DISCIPLINE BAROQUE AND ROCOCO, MODERN DECORATIVE ARTS **EDUCATION** Princeton Univ, PhD. **CAREER** Prof, Rutgers, The State Univ NJ, Univ Col-Camden. **RESEARCH** French 18th-century painting; history of modern crafts and design. **SELECTED PUBLICATIONS** Auth, Watteau in the Atelier of Gillot, in Antoine Watteau (1684 - 1721), le peintre, son temps et sa l?gende, eds Francois Moreau and Margaret Morgan Grasselli, Paris and Geneva 87; Tiffany and the Cult of Nature, in Masterworks of Louis Comfort Tiffany, Alastair Duncan, Martin Eidelberg, and Neil Harris, London and NY, 89; Myths of Style and Nationalism: American Art Pottery at the Turn of the Century, The J of Decorative and Propaganda Arts 20, 94; Watteau's Italian Reveries, in Gazette des Beaux-Arts ser 6, 126, 95; 'Dieu invenit, Watteau pinxit.' Un nouvel eclairage sur une ancienne relation, La revue de l'art 115, 97; coauth, The Dispersal of the Last Duke of Mantua's Paintings, in Gazette des Beaux-Arts ser 6, 123, 94; Watteau's Chinoiseries at La Muette, in Gazette des Beaux-Arts ser 6, 130,

97; ed, Design 1935-1965, What Modern Was; Selections from the Liliane and David M. Stewart Collection, New York, 91. **CONTACT ADDRESS** Dept of Art Hist, Rutgers, The State Univ NJ, Univ Col-Camden, Voorhees Hall, 71 Hamilton St, New Brunswick, NJ, 08903.

EIGEN, MICHAEL
DISCIPLINE PSYCHOLOGY **EDUCATION** New Sch Soc Res, PhD, 74. **CAREER** Psychologist 30 years. **MEMBERSHIPS** NPA for Psychoanalysis and post doctoral program, NYU. **SELECTED PUBLICATIONS** Auth, The Psychotic Core; The Electrified Tightrope; Psychic Deadness; Toxic Nourishment; The Psychoanalytic Mystic; Reshaping the Self; Coming Through the Whirlwind; several hundred articles. **CONTACT ADDRESS** Apt 101A, New York, NY, 10024. **EMAIL** mikeigen@aol.com

EISENSTADT, ABRAHAM S.
PERSONAL Born 06/18/1920, Brooklyn, NY, m, 1949, 3 children **DISCIPLINE** AMERICAN HISTORY **EDUCATION** Brooklyn Col, AB, 40; Columbia Univ, PhD(Brit & Am hist), 55. **CAREER** From instr to asst prof Am & Western hist, 56-64, assoc prof, 64-67, PROF HIST, BROOKLYN COL, 68-, Fulbright lectr, Johns Hopkins Univ, Bologna, Italy, 62-63; vis prof, Coun Am Studies, Rome, 63; res grant, Am Philos Soc, 65-66 & City Univ New York, 66-67; ed, Pitman Major Issues in Am Hist (6 vols), 65-73 & Crowell-AHM Ser in Am Hist (40 vols), 67-; Nat Endowment Humanities fel, 82-83. **MEMBERSHIPS** AHA; Orgn Am Historians; Am Studies Asn; Fulbright Assn. **RESEARCH** American intellectual history; American historiography; history of British-American ideas. **SELECTED PUBLICATIONS** Auth, Charles McLean Andrews: A Study in American Historical Writing, Columbia Univ, 56; ed, American History: Recent Interpretations (2 vols), Crowell, 62, 2nd ed, 70; The Craft of American History (2 vols), Harper & Row, 66; auth, The world of Andrew Carnegie, 1865-1901, Labor Hist, spring 69; The special relationship, Mass Rev, winter 77; Affirmation and anxiety: The American idea in the late 19th century, In: Main Problems in American History, Dorsey, 4th ed, 78; co-ed, Before Watergate: Problems of Corruption in American History, 78 & Political Corruption in American History: Some Further Thoughts, Brooklyn Col-Columbia, 78; auth, Reconsidering Tocqueville's Democracy in America, Rutgers, 88. **CONTACT ADDRESS** 567 First St, Brooklyn, NY, 11215. **EMAIL** ASE567@aol.com

EISENSTADT, PETER
DISCIPLINE HISTORY **EDUCATION** NY Univ; PhD,90. **CAREER** MNG ED, ENCYCLOPEDIA OF NEW YORK CITY **MEMBERSHIPS** Am Antiquarian Soc **SELECTED PUBLICATIONS** Auth, "Weather Prediction in Seventeenth-Century Massachusetts Almanacs," in Travail et Loisir dans les Societes Pre-Industrielles, 91. **CONTACT ADDRESS** 576 5th St, New York, NY, 11215.

EISENSTEIN, ELIZABETH LEWISHOHN
PERSONAL Born 10/11/1923, New York, NY, m, 1948, 3 children **DISCIPLINE** EUROPEAN HISTORY **EDUCATION** Vassar Coll, BA, 44; Radcliffe (Harvard) Univ, MA, 47, PhD, 53; Mt Holyoke Coll, hon degree, 79. **CAREER** Lectr/adj prof, Am Univ, 59-75; Alice Freeman Palmer prof, Hist, Univ Mich, 75-88; vis prof, Wolfson Coll, 90; Lyell lectr, Bodleian Libr, oxford Univ, 90; fel, Center Advanced Stud, Palo Alto Univ, 92-93; fel, Nat Human Center, Australian Nat Univ Canberra, 88, EMER PROF, UNIV MICH, 88-. **MEMBERSHIPS** Fr Hist Studies; Am Soc 18th Cent Stud; Renaissance Soc Am; Am Acad Arts & Sci; Royal Hist Soc London **RESEARCH** History of communication; Early Modern Europe intellectual history; Enlightenment & French Revolution **SELECTED PUBLICATIONS** "From the Printed Word to the Moving Image," Soc Res, 97; "The Libraire-Philosophe," Le Livre et L'Historien, 97; "The End of the Book?" Am Scholar, 95. **CONTACT ADDRESS** Dept Hist, Univ Mich, Ann Arbor, MI, 48109. **EMAIL** Eisenst@american.edu

EISENSTEIN, HESTER
PERSONAL Born 10/14/1940, New York, NY **DISCIPLINE** HISTORY **EDUCATION** Radcliffe Col, BA, 61; Yale Univ, PhD (hist), 67. **CAREER** From instr to asst prof hist, Yale Univ, 66-70; asst prof hist, 70-72, COORD EXP COL, BARNARD COL, COLUMBIA UNIV, 70-, Spivack grant, Barnard Col, Columbia Univ, 75. **MEMBERSHIPS** AHA; Nat Women's Studies Asn. **RESEARCH** History of socialism; experimental education; women's studies, especially feminist theory. **SELECTED PUBLICATIONS** Auth, Die Nataig Al Fikr of Ibnsalimassanani, Shaban--A Yemeni Health Primer of the Early 18th Century, Zeitschrift Der Deutschen Morgenlandischen Gesellschaft, Vol 146, 96. **CONTACT ADDRESS** Barnard Col, New York, NY, 10027.

EISLER, COLIN
PERSONAL Born 03/17/1931, Hamburg, Germany, m, 1961, 1 child **DISCIPLINE** HISTORY OF ART **EDUCATION** Yale Univ, BA, 52; Harvard Univ, PhD, 57. **CAREER** Cur dept prints and drawings, art gallery, and instr art hist, Yale Univ, 55-57; from asst prof to prof art hist, inst fine arts, 58-77, ROBERT LEHMAN PROF FINE ARTS, NY UNIV, 77-, Yale Univ lectr grant, Int Cong, Paris, 57; Ford lect grant, Int Cong, Bonn; fel, Inst Advan Studies, 57-58; consult, paintings dept, Metropolitan Mus Art, 58-60; Guggenheim fel, 66-67; mem vis comt, Smith Col Art Mus; Cooper-Hewitt Print and Drawing Dept; secy, Nat Comt Hist Art; visual arts consult, Renaissance Soc; Nat Endowment for Humanities sr fel, 72-73; mem bd, The Drawing Ctr and The Archit Hist Found, Am Friends Israel Mus. **MEMBERSHIPS** Drawing Soc. **RESEARCH** Western European art, 1350-1650; graphic arts, photography and decorative arts. **SELECTED PUBLICATIONS** Auth, A Study of Lorenzo Monaco, Speculum J Medieval Stud, Vol 67, 92; Giotto to Durer--Early Renaissance Painting in the National Gallery, Renaissance Quart, Vol 47, 94; The Renaissance Print, 1470-1550, Speculum J Medieval Stud, Vol 70, 95; The Renaissance Print, 1470-1550, Speculum J Medieval Stud, Vol 70, 95. **CONTACT ADDRESS** Inst of Fine Arts, New York Univ, 1 E 78th St, New York, NY, 10021.

EITELJORG, HARRISON, II
PERSONAL Born 03/04/1943, Indianapolis, IN, m, 1964, 3 children **DISCIPLINE** ARCHAEOLOGY **EDUCATION** Univ of Penn, PhD, 73. **CAREER** Vis Lectr, 77-78, Bryn Mawr Coll, Dir, 86-, Archaeology Data Archive Project, Dir, 86-, Center for the Study of Architecture. **MEMBERSHIPS** AIA, SAA, SAH, CAA, ASOR. **RESEARCH** Architecture of Classical Greece, computers in archaeology. **SELECTED PUBLICATIONS** Auth, Archiving Archaeological Data in the Next Millenium, in: CRM, 98; Review, J-F Bommelaer, Marmaria Le Sanctuaire d'Athena a Delphes, Site Monuments XVI, in: Bryn Mawr Classical Review, 98; auth, Electronic archives, in: Antiquity, 97; Where Do We Put Our Files? SAA Bulletin, 97; Archaeological Data Archive Project, in: Notes from the Center, 96; The Entrance to the Athenian Acropolis Before Mnesicles, in: Archaeological Institute of America, 94; Computer-Assisted Drafting and Design Programs for Presenting Architectural History and Archaeology, in: Hypermedia and Interactivity in Museums, Proceedings of an International Conference, ed, David Bearman, Pittsburgh Archives and Museums Informatics, 91. **CONTACT ADDRESS** Ctr for the Study of Architecture, Box 60, Bryn Mawr, PA, 19010. **EMAIL** neiteljo@brynmawr.edu

EKECHI, FELIX KAMALU
PERSONAL Born 10/30/1934, Owerri, Nigeria, m, 1966, 4 children **DISCIPLINE** AFRICAN HISTORY **EDUCATION** Univ MN, Minneapolis, BA, 63; KS State Univ, MA, 65; Univ WI-Madison, PhD, 69. **CAREER** Headmaster, St Dominic's Sch, Afara-Mbieri, Owerri, 55-56 & 57-58; asst headmaster, Cent Sch Oboro-Ogwa, 56-57; tutor hist & Igbo, Mt St Mary's Col, Azaraegbelu, 59-60; tchg asst hist, KS State Univ, 63-64; instr hist & polit sci, Alcorn Agr & Mech Col, 64-65; asst prof, 69-71, assoc prof, 71-77, prof African hist, Kent State Univ, 78-, Res Coun res fel, 73, 75 & 79; Am Philos Soc grant, 79, 82. **HONORS AND AWARDS** NEH grants, 89, 92, 96; Creative Contrib Award, KSU, 97. **MEMBERSHIPS** AHA; African Studies Asn; Hist Soc Ghana; Hist Soc Nigeria. **RESEARCH** Soc and polit hist; pre-colonial Igbo hist. **SELECTED PUBLICATIONS** Auth, Christianity and colonialism in West Africa, J African Hist, 71; Missionary Enterprise and Rivalry in Igboland, 1857-1914, Frank Cass, London, 72; The Holy Ghost Fathers in Eastern Nigeria: Observation on Missionary Strategy, African Studies Rev, 72; Traders, Missionaries and the Bombardment of Onitsha, 1879-1880, Conch Mag, 73; 1960 Response to British imperialism: The episode of Dr Stewart and the Ahiara Expedition, 1905-1916, 74 & African polygamy and Western Christian ethnocentrism, 76, J African Studies; The Missionary Career of T J Dennis in West Africa, 1893-1917, J African Relig, 78; The Igbo and Their History: The Problem of Cultural Origins, Alvana Jour Soc Sci, 82; Owerri in Transition, Owerri, 84; Tradition and Transformation in Eastern Nigeria, Kent, 89; Studies on MIssions, African Histography, 93; co-ed, African Market Women and Economic Power, Westport, 95; Gender and Economic Power: The Case of Igbo Market Women of Eastern Nigeria, African Market Women, 95; An African Initiative in Education, Educ and Develop in Africa, 98. **CONTACT ADDRESS** Dept of Hist, Kent State Univ, PO Box 5190, Kent, OH, 44242-0001. **EMAIL** fekechi@kent.edu

EKIRCH, A. ROGER
PERSONAL Born 02/06/1950, Washington, DC, m, 1988, 3 children **DISCIPLINE** HISTORY **EDUCATION** Dartmouth Col, AB, 72; Johns Hopkins Univ, MA, 74, PhD, 78. **CAREER** Inst, 77-78, asst prof, 78-82, assoc prof, 82-88, PROF, VA TECH, 88-; vis ed, Inst Early Am History & Culture, 87-88. **HONORS AND AWARDS** NEH fel, 82, 86, 92; Guggenheim fel, 98; Paul Mellon fel, Cambridge Univ, 81; fel Commoner, Peterhouse, 81. **MEMBERSHIPS** AHA; Assocs Omohundo Inst Early Am Hist and Culture. **RESEARCH** Early Am hist; British hist. **SELECTED PUBLICATIONS** Auth, Poor Carolina Politics and Society in Colonial North Carolina, 1729-1776, Univ NC Press, 81; auth, Bound for America: The Transportation of British Convicts to the Colonies, 1718- 1775, Clarendon/Oxford Univ Press, 87; auth, The North Carolina Regulators on Liberty and Corruption, 1766-1771, in Perspectives in American History, Harvard Univ, Charles Warren Ctr for Studies in Am Hist, XI, 77-78; auth, Great Britain's Secret Convict Trade to America, 1783-1784, Am Hist Rev, LXXXIX, no 5, Dec 84; auth, Bound for America: A Profile of British Convicts Transported to the Colonies, 1718-1775, Wm and Mary Q, 3d Ser, XLII, no 2, Apr 85. **CONTACT ADDRESS** Dept Hist, Virginia Tech Univ, Blacksburg, VA, 24061. **EMAIL** arekirch@vt.edu

EKSTEINS, MODRIS
PERSONAL Born 12/13/1943, Riga, Latvia **DISCIPLINE** MODERN HISTORY **EDUCATION** Univ Toronto, BA, 65; Oxford Univ, BPhil, 67, DPhil(hist), 70. **CAREER** Asst prof, 70-75, assoc prof, 75-80, PROF HIST, SCARBOROUGH COL, UNIV TORONTO, 80-, Can Coun Soc Sci and Humanities res grants, 71-72 and 74, leave fel, 81-82, res grant, 82-; Can Coun Leave fel, 76-77. **MEMBERSHIPS** AHA. **RESEARCH** Modern Germany; European liberalism; First World War. **SELECTED PUBLICATIONS** Auth, Avant Garde Florence, From Modernism to Fascism, Urban Hist Rev Rev Hist Urbaine, Vol 23, 95; All Quiet on the Western Front, Hist Today, Vol 45, 95; Adenauer, Konrad--A German Politician and Statesman in a Period of War, Revolution, and Reconstruction, Vol 1--From the German Empire to the Federal Republic, 1876-1952, Int Hist Rev, Vol 19, 97; Hist Enlightenment, Queens Quart, Vol 102, 95. **CONTACT ADDRESS** Div of Humanities, Scarborough Col Univ of Toronto, West Hill, ON, M1C 1A4.

EL-BAZ, FAROUK
PERSONAL Born 01/01/1938, Zagazig, Egypt, m, 1962, 4 children **DISCIPLINE** GEOLOGY, REMOTE SENSING **EDUCATION** Ain Shams Univ, Cairo, Egypt, B Sc, 58; MO School of Mines and Metallurgy, MS, 61; Univ MO, PhD, 64; New England Col, Henneker, NH, D Sc Honoris, 84. **CAREER** Supervisor, Lunar Science Operations, Bellcomm, Inc (NASA contractor), Washington, DC, 67-72; Res Dir, Center for Earth and Planetary Studies, Smithsonian Inst, Washington, DC, 73-82; Vice-pres for Science and Technology, Itek Optical Systems, Lexington, MA, 82-86; dir, Center for Remote Sensing, Boston Univ, Boston, MA, 86-. **HONORS AND AWARDS** NASA Exceptional Achievement Medal; Univ MO Alumni Achievement Award for Extraordinary Scientific Accomplishments; Certificate of Merit of the World Aerospace Ed Org; Arab Republic of Egypt Order of Merit-First Class; AAPG Human Needs Award. **MEMBERSHIPS** Geological Soc of Am; Am Asn for the Advancement of Science; Royal Astronomical Soc; Am Asn of Petroleum Geologists, Explorers Club; World Aerospace Ed Org; Am Soc of Photogrammetry and Remote Sensing. **RESEARCH** Interpretation of satellite images of desert regions, particularly for groundwater exploration. **SELECTED PUBLICATIONS** Auth, Origin and Evolution of the Desert, Interdisciplinary Science Reviews, Dec 88; Finding a Pharoah's Funeral Bank, Nat Geographic, April 88; The Gulf War and the Environment, co-ed with R M Makharita, Gordon and Breach, Lausanne, Switzerland, 94; Space Age Archaeology, Scientific American, Aug 97. **CONTACT ADDRESS** Center for Remote Sensing, Boston Univ, 725 Commonwealth Ave, Boston, MA, 02215. **EMAIL** farouk@bu.edu

ELAM, EARL HENRY
PERSONAL Born 12/07/1934, Wichita Falls, TX, m, 1964, 3 children **DISCIPLINE** AMERICAN HISTORY **EDUCATION** Midwest Univ, BA, 61; Tex Tech Univ, MA, 67, PhD (hist), 71. **CAREER** Instr US hist, Lubbock High Sch, Tex, 61-67; Part-time instr, Tex Tech Univ, 67-71; from asst prof to prof US hist, 71-74, dir div soc sci, 73-74, VPRES ACAD AFFAIRS, SUL ROSS STATE UNIV, 74-, Consult, Indian Claims Sect, US Dept Justice, 71-. **MEMBERSHIPS** Western Hist Asn. **RESEARCH** Indians of the southern plains and of the southwest; frontier history of the southwest; twentieth century western history. **SELECTED PUBLICATIONS** Auth,War Pony, J West, Vol 35, 96;, Noble Brutes--Camels on the American Frontier, Southwestern Hist Quart, Vol 99, 95; Portraits of the Pecos Frontier, Southwestern Hist Quart, Vol 97, 94;Lone Hunter and the Cheyennes, J West, Vol 35, 96; Lone Hunters Gray Pony, J West, Vol 35, 96. **CONTACT ADDRESS** 407 N Cockrell, Alpine, TX, 79830.

ELBERT, SARAH
PERSONAL Born 01/05/1937, New York, NY, d, 2 children **DISCIPLINE** HISTORY **EDUCATION** Cornell Univ, AB, 65, MAT, 66, MA, 68; PhD, 74. **CAREER** Res Assoc, 68-72, Vis Asst Prof, 77, Vis Assoc Prof, Cornell Univ, 81-84; Vis Asst Prof, 73-74, Asst Prof, 74-81, Assoc Prof Hist, Binghamton Univ, 81-; Vis Prof, Calif Polytechnic State Univ, 86-87; Fulbright Prof, Univ Tromso, Norway, 92-93. **HONORS AND AWARDS** NY Chancellors Award for Excellence in Teaching, 98. **MEMBERSHIPS** Am Studies Asn; Org Am Hist; Berkshire Conf Women Hist; Louisa May Alcott Soc. **RESEARCH** 19th & 20th century cultural and intellectual history in the US; Louise May Alcott; nature/culture studies. **SELECTED PUBLICATIONS** Ed, Two Little Confederates, Garland Publ, 76; The Little Colonel, Garland Publ, 76; auth, A Hunger for Home: Louisa May Alcott and Little Women, Temple Univ Press, 86; A Hunger for Home: Louise Alcott's Place in American Culture, Rutgers Univ Press, 87; Diana and Persis, In: Alternative Alcott, Rutgers Univ Press, 89; Louisa May Alcott on Race, Sex, and Slavery, Northeastern Univ Press, 97; author of nu-

merous articles, chapters, reviews, and other publications. **CONTACT ADDRESS** History Dept, State Univ of NY Binghamton, Binghamton, NY, 13901. **EMAIL** nwlostow@binghamton.edu

ELDER, ELLEN ROZANNE
PERSONAL Born 05/21/1940, Harrisburg, PA **DISCIPLINE** MEDIEVAL STUDIES **EDUCATION** Western MI Univ, AB, 62, AM, 64; Univ Toronto, PhD, 72. **CAREER** Instr hist, 68-72, prof hist & dir inst Cistercian Studies, Western MI Univ, 73; Ed Dir, Cistercian Publ, Inc, 73, Co-ed, Studies in Medieval Cult, Vols IV, V, VI & VII. **HONORS AND AWARDS** H. L.D. honoris causa, Nashotah House Theol Sem, Nashotah, WI, 95. **RESEARCH** Twelfth century Christological controversy; early Cistercian Christology. **SELECTED PUBLICATIONS** Auth, Cistercian Order, Trappistine Sisters, and Trappists, In: The Harper Encyclopedia of Catholicism, HarperSan, 95; coauth, Receiving the Vision: The Reality of Anglican-Roman Catholic Relations Today, Liturgical Press, 95; ed, The Joy of Learning and the Love of God: Essays in Honor of Jean Leclercq, Cistercian Studies Series, No 160, Cistercian Publ, 95; auth, Bernard of Clairvaux, In: The International Encyclopedia of the Church, Eerdmans, 97; Trappisten, In: Theologische Realenzyklodie. Verlag Walter de Gruyter, 99; auth and editor of numerous other publs. **CONTACT ADDRESS** Cistercian Publ, Western Michigan Univ, 1201 Oliver St, Kalamazoo, MI, 49008-3805.

ELDRED, KATHERINE O.
DISCIPLINE CLASSICS **EDUCATION** Brown Univ, BA, 89; Princeton Univ, MA, 93, PhD, 97. **CAREER** Prof, Northwestern Univ; Mellon postdoctoral fel, 97-99. **RESEARCH** Latin poetry; Roman violence; Roman cultural studies. **SELECTED PUBLICATIONS** Auth, Off With Her Head! Reading Lucan's Medusa, Bristol Univ Dept Class and Ancient Hist, 98; Telemachus Strings the Bow, in Aspects of the Hero: A Colloquium on Violence, Gender, and Self-Definition in Homer, Northwestern Univ, 98; Face/Off: Lucan's Medusa and the Gaze of Tyranny, Northwestern Univ, 98; Lucan's Medusa: Resisting Civil War, Am Philol Asn,97; All for One: the Sacrifice of Vulteius, Am Philol Asn, 96. **CONTACT ADDRESS** Dept of Classics, Northwestern Univ, 1801 Hinman, Kresge 17, Evanston, IL, 60208. **EMAIL** koeldred@nwu.edu

ELDRIDGE, DARYL
PERSONAL m, 2 children **DISCIPLINE** FOUNDATIONS OF EDUCATION **EDUCATION** Drury Col, BA, 73; Southwestern Baptist Theol Sem, MARE, 77, PhD, 85. **CAREER** Dean; prof, Southwestern Baptist Theol Sem, 84-. **HONORS AND AWARDS** J.P. Price Awards, 77; Albert G. Marsh Award, 82; Outstanding Young Men Am, 79., Min Youth and Music, FBC, 72-73; Min Edu and Youth, Parkview Baptist Church, 73-75; Min Edu and Youth, Parkview Baptist Church, 77-80; Min Edu, Tate Springs, Baptist Church, 80-84; Min Edu, Hurst Baptist Church, 91-96. **SELECTED PUBLICATIONS** Ed, Teaching Ministry of the Church, Broadman & Holman, 95; auth, Why Youth Should Study Doctrine, Equipping Youth, 90; Creative Ways to Study Doctrine, Article. Equipping Youth, 90; How Teenagers Learn at Church, Church Admin, 86. **CONTACT ADDRESS** School Edu Ministries, Southwestern Baptist Theol Sem, PO Box 22000, Fort Worth, TX, 76122-0418. **EMAIL** dre@swbts.swbts.edu

ELEY, GEOFF
PERSONAL Born 05/04/1949, Burton-on-Treat, England, 2 children **DISCIPLINE** MODERN GERMAN & EUROPEAN HISTORY **EDUCATION** Oxford Univ, BA, 70, MA, 81; Sussex Univ, DPhil(Hist), 74; Cambridge Univ, MA, 75. **CAREER** Lectr Hist, Univ Keele, 74-75; col lectr & dir Hist Studies, Emmanuel Col, Univ Cambridge, 75-79; asst prof Europ Hist, 79-81, assoc prof Europ Hist, Univ Mich, Ann Arbor, 81-, rev ed, Comp Studies Soc & Hist, 80-87; rev assoc, New Ger Critique, 81-86. **MEMBERSHIPS** Conf Group Cent Europ Hist; Coun Europ Studies; Soc Ger Historians Brit; Past & Present Soc, UK. **RESEARCH** Liberalism in German and Britain in 19th and 20th century; nationalism and popular politics; European Left from mid-19th century to the present; history & film. **SELECTED PUBLICATIONS** Auth, Defining social imperialism: Use and abuse of an idea, Social Hist, 76; Reshaping the German Right: Radical Nationalism and Political Change after Bismark, Yale Univ Press, 80; coauth, Mythen deutscher Geschichteschreibung: Die gescheiterte Grgerliche Revolution von 1848, Ullstein Materialien, 80; Why does social history ignore politics?, 80 & auth, Nationalism and social history, 81; co-ed Culture/Power/History, Princeton UP, 94; coed, Becoming National, Oxford UP, 96; ed, Society, Culture, & the State in Germany 1870-1930, U-Michigan Press, 96. **CONTACT ADDRESS** Dept of History, Univ of Michigan, Ann Arbor, MI, 48109. **EMAIL** ghe@umich.edu

ELFENBEIN, JESSICA
DISCIPLINE HISTORY **EDUCATION** Barnard Col, AB, George Washington Univ, MA; Univ Delaware, MA, PhD. **CAREER** Asst Prof, Univ Baltimore, 95-. **SELECTED PUBLICATIONS** Auth, Civics, Commerce, and Community: the History of the Greater Washington Board of Trade, 1889-1989, Kendall-Hunt Publ Co, 89; auth, Philadelphia Board of Trade, 1833-1899, Atwater Kent Museum, 95; auth, 'An Agressive Christian Enterprise': The Baltimore YMCA and the Making of Institutional Legitimacy, NY Univ Press, 96. **CONTACT ADDRESS** Univ Baltimore, 1420 N. Charles Street, Baltimore, MD, 21201.

ELIADE, MIRCEA
PERSONAL Born 03/09/1907, Bucharest, Romania, m, 1950 **DISCIPLINE** HISTORY OF RELIGIONS **EDUCATION** Univ Bucharest, MA, 28, PhD, 33. **CAREER** Asst prof metaphys, Univ Bucharest, 33-39; vis prof hist relig, Ecole des Hautes Etudes, Sorbonne, 46-49; from vis prof to prof, 56-61, DISTINGUISHED SERV PROF HIST RELIG, UNIV CHICAGO, 62-. **HONORS AND AWARDS** Dr, Yale Univ, 66. **MEMBERSHIPS** Am Soc Study Relig (pres, 63-67); Societe Asiatique; AAAS. **RESEARCH** History of religions. **SELECTED PUBLICATIONS** Auth, Initiation and Literature, Sinn Form, Vol 48, 96; Mantras, Parabola Myth Tradition Search Meaning, Vol 20, 95. **CONTACT ADDRESS** Divinity Sch, Univ Chicago, Chicago, IL, 60637.

ELKINS, JAMES
PERSONAL Born 10/13/1955, Ithaca, NY, m **DISCIPLINE** ART HISTORY **EDUCATION** Cornell Univ, BA, 77; Univ Chicago, MFA, 83, MA, 84, PhD, 84-89. **CAREER** Vis assoc prof, Northwestern Univ, 96; vis assoc prof, Univ Chicago, 96; vis assoc prof, Univ CA-Berkeley, 96; assoc prof, 89-. **HONORS AND AWARDS** PhD with hon(s), Univ Chicago, 89. **SELECTED PUBLICATIONS** Auth, The Poetics of Perspective, Cornell UP, 94; The Object Stares Back: On the Nature of Seeing, Simon and Schuster, 96; Our Beautiful, Dry, and Distant Texts: Art History as Writing, Penn State Press, 97; The Question of the Body in Mesoamerican Art, Res 26, 94; Parallel Art History / Studio Program, The Art Jour, 95; There are No Philosophic Problems Raised by Virtual Reality, Computer Graphics 28, 94; Art Criticism, The Dictionary of Art, Macmillan Publishers, 96; Visual Schemata, The Encycl of Aesthet, Garland Press, 96; Marks, Traces, Traits, Contours, Orli, and Splendores: Nonsemiotic Elements in Pictures, Critical Inquiry 21, 95; Between Picture and Proposition: Torturing Paintings in Wittgenstein's Tractatus, Visible Lang 30, 96; On the Impossibility of Close Reading: The Case of Alexander Marshack, Current Anthrop 37, 96; Art History and Images that are Not Art, The Art Bulletin 77, 95; Histoire de l'art et pratiques d'atelier, transl Why Art Historians should Draw: The Case for Studio Experience, Hist de l'art 29-30, 95; Why Are Our Pictures Puzzles? Some Thoughts on Writing Excessively, New Lit Hist 27, 96. **CONTACT ADDRESS** Dept of Art Hist, Sch of the Art Inst of Chicago, 37 S Wabash Ave, Chicago, IL, 60603. **EMAIL** j.elkins@artic.edu

ELLER, RONALD D.
PERSONAL Born 04/23/1948, Annapolis, MD, m, 1992, 3 children **DISCIPLINE** HISTORY **EDUCATION** Col Wooster, BA, 70; Univ NC, Chapel Hill, MA, 73, PhD, 79. **CAREER** Mars Hill Col, 76-85; ASSOC PROF HIST, DIR, APPALACHIAN CTR, UNIV KY, 85-. **HONORS AND AWARDS** Rockefeller Fdn Scholar, 73-76; Wm Weatherford Award, 83; Thomas Wolfe Lit Award, 82; Jim Wayne Miller Award Dist Svc, 97; W. Lyons Award Dist Pub Svc, 98; J. D. Whisman Scholar, Appalachian Reg Comt, 1999-2000. **RESEARCH** History of the South; history of Appalachia; rural dev; higher educ. **SELECTED PUBLICATIONS** Co-auth, The Rural Community College Initiative, in Creating and Benefiting From Institutional Collaborations, Jossey-Bass Pubs, 98; co-auth, Economic Development and Rural Community Colleges, Am Asn Community Cols, 98; co-auth, Access to Rural Community Colleges: Removing Barriers to Participation, Am Asn Community Cols, 98; auth, forward to Recycling Appalachia: Backtalk from an American Region, Univ Press Ky, forthcoming; auth, Lost and Found in the Promised Land: The Education of A Hillbilly, in One Hundred Years of Appalachian Visions, Berea, 97; co-auth, Kentucky Highways: Some History and Prospects for Planning, Univ Ky, 97; co-auth, Exploring and Documenting the Challenge and Opportunities Faced by Institutions Participating in the Rural Community College Initiative: A Preliminary Report of Key Findings, Am Coun Educ, Off Minorities in Higher Educ, 96; auth, forward to People, Politics and Economic Life: An Interactive Exploration of the Appalachian Region, Kendal Hunt Pubs, 96; co-auth, Kentucky Ricer Area Development District: Historic trends and Geographic Patters, Univ Ky, 96; auth, John Whisman: His Vision Was Clear, Appalachia: J Appalachian Reg Comm, 29:1, Jan/Apr 96; auth, America and Appalachia, in Perspectives of Home: The Urban Appalachian Spirit, Urban Appalachian Counc, 96; auth, John Whisman: Appalachian Vision, Appalachian Heritage, sum 95; auth, The Miner's Work, in Appalachia Inside Out, Univ Tenn Press, Knoxville, 95; **CONTACT ADDRESS** 371 Windom Ln, Nicholasville, KY, 40356. **EMAIL** eller@pop.uky.edu

ELLIOTT, B.S.
DISCIPLINE CANADIAN HISTORY **EDUCATION** Carleton Univ, BA, PhD; Univ Leicester, MA. **CAREER** Prof. **RESEARCH** English immigration, Irish Protestant immigration. **SELECTED PUBLICATIONS** Auth, Irish Migrants in the Canadas: A New Approach, McGill Queen's UP, Inst Irish Stud, 88; The City Beyond: A History of Nepean, Birthplace of Canada's Capital, 1792-1990, Corporation of the City of Nepean, 91; co-ed, The McCabe List: Early Irish in The Ottawa Valley, Ontario Genealogical Soc, 95. **CONTACT ADDRESS** Dept of Hist, Carleton Univ, 1125 Colonel By Dr, Ottawa, ON, K1S 5B6. **EMAIL** belliott@ccs.carleton.ca

ELLIOTT, BRIDGET
DISCIPLINE ART **EDUCATION** Univ Toronto, BA; Univ British Columbia, MA; Univ London, PhD. **RESEARCH** Theories of sexual difference and feminist art practices; analysis of arts institutions, critical reception and hierarchies of cultural value; theories of cultural studies and art history's relationship to film, literature, music, theatre and social history. **SELECTED PUBLICATIONS** Coauth, Women Artists and Writers: Modernist (im)positionings, Routledge, 94; Peter Greenaway: Architecture and Allegory, Academy, 97. **CONTACT ADDRESS** Dept of Visual Arts, Western Ontario Univ, London, ON, N6A 5B8.

ELLIOTT, CAROLYN S.
PERSONAL Born 02/20/1947, Glen Ridge, NJ, m, 1970, 2 children **DISCIPLINE** RELIGION AND CULTURE; HISTORY **EDUCATION** Syracuse Univ, BA, 70, MA, 73; SUNY, MLIS, 94. **CAREER** From dir to adj fac to full-time fac, 72-, Keystone Col. **HONORS AND AWARDS** Theta Chi Beta; Beta Phi Mu. **MEMBERSHIPS** Am Libr Asn; Asn Col & Res Librs; Pa Libr Asn. **RESEARCH** Religion and culture of Asia; library computing options. **SELECTED PUBLICATIONS** Auth, art, NREN Update, 1993: Washington Policy, 94. **CONTACT ADDRESS** Miller Library, Keystone Col, One College Green, La Plume, PA, 18440-0200. **EMAIL** celliott@kstone.edu

ELLIOTT, CLARK ALBERT
PERSONAL Born 01/22/1941, Ware, MA, m, 1965, 2 children **DISCIPLINE** ARCHIVES, BIBLIOGRAPHY, HISTORY OF SCIENCE **EDUCATION** Marietta Col, AB, 63; Western Reserve Univ, MSLS, 65; Case Western Reserve Univ, MA, 68, PhD(libr & info sci), 70. **CAREER** Archivist, Case Inst Technol, 64-66; asst prof libr sci, Sch of Libr Sci, Simmons Col, 69-71; assoc cur, Harvard Univ archives, 71-97; LIBRN, BURNDY LIBR, DIBNER INST FOR THE HIST OF SCI AND TECHNOL, 97- . **HONORS AND AWARDS** Rep, Joint Comt on Archives of Sci & Technol, Hist of Sci Soc, 78-83; ed, Hist of Sci in Am: News and Views, 80-87. **MEMBERSHIPS** Soc Am Archivists; New England Archivists; Hist Sci Soc; Forum for the Hist of Sci in Am, chm, 97- . **RESEARCH** History of science in America, especially scientific careers, and institutions; documentation and historiography in history of science. **SELECTED PUBLICATIONS** Auth, The Royal Society Catalogue as an Index to Nineteenth Century American Science, J of Am Soc for Info Sci, 11-12/70; Sources for the History of Science in the Harvard University Archives, Havard Libr Bull, 1/74; Experimental Data as a Source for the History of Science, Am Archivist, 1/74; A Descriptive Guide to the Harvard University Archives, Harvard Univ Libr, 74; The American scientist in Antebellum Society: A Quantitative View, Social Studies of Sci, 1/75; Biographical Dict of American Science: The Seventeenth Through the Nineteenth Centuries, Greenwood Press, 79; Citation patterns and Documentation for the History of Science: Some Methodological Considerations, Am Archivist, Spring 81; Models of the American scientist: A look at Collective Biography, Isis, 3/82; auth, Biographical Index to American Science: The Seventeenth Century to 1920, Greenwood, 90; co-ed, Science at Harvard University: Historical Perspectives, Lehigh, 92; auth, History of Science in the United States: A Chronology and Research Guide, Garland, 96. **CONTACT ADDRESS** Burndy Library, Dibner Inst for the History of Science and Tech, MIT E56-100, Cambridge, MA, 02139.

ELLIOTT, DEREK WESLEY
PERSONAL Born 10/03/1958, Nashville, TN, s **DISCIPLINE** HISTORY **EDUCATION** Harvard University, AB, 1980; University of California, Berkeley, MA, 1985; George Washington Univ, PhD, 1992. **CAREER** Smithsonian Institution, curator, 1982-92; TN STATE UNIV, ASST PROF OF HISTORY, 1992-. **HONORS AND AWARDS** Member, Robinson Prize Comm, Society for the Hist of Tech, 1991-94. **MEMBERSHIPS** American Historical Assn, 1987-; Organization of Amer Historians, 1987-; Society for the History of Technology, 1987-. **CONTACT ADDRESS** Dept of History, Tennessee State Univ, Nashville, TN, 37209.

ELLIOTT, JOHN HUXTABLE
PERSONAL Born 06/23/1930, Berkshire, England, m, 1958 **DISCIPLINE** MODERN HISTORY **EDUCATION** Cambridge Univ, BA, 52, MA & PhD, 55. **CAREER** Fel & univ lectr hist, Trinity Col, Cambridge Univ, 56-58; prof, King's Col, Univ London, 68-73; prof hist, Sch Hist Stud, Inst Advan Study, 73-90; Regins Prof of Modern Hist, Univ Oxford, 90-98; corresponding fel Royal Acad Hist, Spain; fel Brit Acad; Am Acad Arts & Sci fel, 77. **HONORS AND AWARDS** Grand Cross, Order of Alfonso X El Sabio, 88; Grand Cross Order of Isabel La Catolica, 96; Knight Bachelor, 99. **RESEARCH** Sixteenth and 17th century Spanish government and society; conquest and colonization of Spanish America. **SELECTED PUB-**

LICATIONS Auth, The Revolt of the Catalans: A Study in the Decline of Spain, 1598-1640, Cambridge Univ, 63; auth, Imperial Spain 1469-1716, Arnold, London, 63; auth, Europe Divided, 1559-1598, Collins, London, 68; co-ed, The Diversity of History: Essays in Honour of Sir Herbert Butterfield, Routledge Univ & Kegan Paul, London, 70; auth, The Old World and the New, 1492-1650, Cambridge Univ, 70; coauth, Memoriales Y Cartas del Conde Duque de Olivares, Alfaguara, Madrid, 78-80; coauth, A Palace for a King: The Buen Retiro and the Court of Philip IV, Yale Univ Press, 80; auth, The Count-Duke of Olivares, Yale, 86; auth, Spain and Its World, 1500-1700, Yale, 89. **CONTACT ADDRESS** Oriel Col, Oxford, ., OX1 GEW.

ELLIOTT, SHIRLEY B.
PERSONAL Born 06/04/1916, Wolfville, NS, Canada **DISCIPLINE** HISTORY **EDUCATION** Acadia Univ, BA, 37, MA, 39; Simmons Col (Boston), SB(LibrSci), 40; DCL(hon), Acadia Univ, 84; LLD(hon), Dalhousie Univ, 85. **CAREER** Ref asst, Brookline (Mass) Pub Libr, 40-46; asst librn, Univ RI Libr, 46-49; asst ed, Canadian Index, Can Libr Asn, 49-50; chief librn, Reg Libr, Truro(NS), 50-54; legis librn, Legis Libr NS, 54-82. **HONORS AND AWARDS** Canada 125 Medal; Atlantic Provinces Libr Asn Merit Award, 81; CASLIS Merit Award, 88. **MEMBERSHIPS** Can Fedn Univ Women; Heritage Trust NS; Royal NS Hist Soc; Bibliog Soc Can; Atlantic Provinces Libr Asn. **SELECTED PUBLICATIONS** Auth, Nova Scotia in Books 1752-1967, 67; auth, Province House, 66; auth, Nova Scotia Book of Days, 80; auth, The Legislative Assembly of Nova Scotia 1758-1983: a biographical directory, 84; auth, Nova Scotia in Books: A Quarter Century's Gleanings, 87; auth, Nova Scotia in London: a History of its Agents General 1762-1988, 88; ed & comp, Atlantic Provinces Checklist 1957-65; contribur, Dictionary of Canadian Biography. **CONTACT ADDRESS** 15 Queen St, Box 342, Wolfville, NS, B0P 1X0.

ELLIOTT, THOMAS G.
PERSONAL Born 09/12/1938, Toronto, ON, Canada, m, 1983, 1 child **DISCIPLINE** CLASSICS **EDUCATION** Harvard, PhD, 71 **CAREER** Inst Class Lang, 64-67, Trinity Col; Asst Assoc Prof, 67-98, Univ of Toronto **RESEARCH** Late Antiquity **SELECTED PUBLICATIONS** Auth, Ammianus Marcellinus and Fourth Century History, Toronto, 83; Auth, The Christianity of Constantine the Great, Scranton, 96 **CONTACT ADDRESS** Erindale Col, Mississauga, ON, M6S 4H8. **EMAIL** telliott@credit.evin.utoronto.ca

ELLIOTT, WARD EDWARD YANDELL
PERSONAL Born 08/96/1937, Cambridge, MA, m, 1969, 2 children **DISCIPLINE** POLITICAL SCIENCE **EDUCATION** Univ Va, LIB, 64; Harvard Univ, AB, 59, AM, PhD, 68. **CAREER** PROF OF GOV, 68-, BURNET C. WOHLFORD PROF OF AM POLITIC INST, CLAREMONT MCKENNA COL, 95-. **HONORS AND AWARDS** Phi Beta Kappa; Harvard Nat Scholar; NEH Fel; Distinguished Civilian Service Medal; Roy C. Crocker Prize; honorary member of CMC Class of 74. **MEMBERSHIPS** AAAS; Shakespeare Authorship Roundtable. **RESEARCH** Voting rights; transportation; population; smog policy; Shakespeare authorship. **SELECTED PUBLICATIONS** Auth, The Rise of Guardian Democracy; Greenbacks Uber Gridlock; Federal Law and Population Policy; And Then There Were None: Winnowing the Shakespeare Claimants. **CONTACT ADDRESS** Dept of Politialc Sci, Claremont McKenna Col, 850 N Columbia Ave, Claremont, CA, 91711.

ELLIS, CLYDE
PERSONAL Born 03/29/1958, Greenville, NC, m, 1990 **DISCIPLINE** HISTORY **EDUCATION** Lenoir Rhyne Col, BA 80; Univ N Carolina, MA 86; Oklahoma State Univ, PhD 93. **CAREER** Elon Col, asst prof 94-; East Cen Univ, asst prof 93-94. **HONORS AND AWARDS** Gustavus Meyers AWD., Winner of the Gustavus Meyers Book Award for Outstanding Work on Intolerance in N America. **MEMBERSHIPS** OHS; WHA. **RESEARCH** Amer Indians; Indian Edu; Cultural adaptation; ethnography **SELECTED PUBLICATIONS** Auth, To Change Them Forever: Indian Education at the Rainy Mountain Boarding School, 1893-1920, Norman, Univ Oklahoma Press, 96; She Gave us the Jesus Way: Isabel Crawford, The Kiowas and the Saddle Mountain Indian Baptist Church, intro to Kiowa: A Woman Missionary in Indian Territory, Lincoln, Univ Nebraska Press, 98; E E Dale and Tales of the Tepee, intro to Tales of the Tepee, Lincoln, Univ Nebraska Press, 98; A Gathering of Life Itself: The Kiowa Gourd Dance, in: Native Amer Values: Survival and Renewal, eds, Thomas E. Schirer, Susan Branstner, Sault Ste Marie MI, Lake Superior State Univ Press, 93; Changing Native Ways: Harrah's Casino and the Eastern Cherokees, Our State, 98; Boarding School Life at the Kiowa-Comanche Agency, 1893-1920, The Historian, 96. **CONTACT ADDRESS** Dept of History, Elon Col, PO Box 2143, Elon, NC, 27244. **EMAIL** ellisrc@elon.edu

ELLIS, EDWARD EARLE
PERSONAL Born 03/18/1926, Ft Lauderdale, FL **DISCIPLINE** THEOLOGY, HISTORY **EDUCATION** Univ Va, BS, 50; Wheaton Col, Ill, MA and BD, 53; Univ Edinburgh, PhD (Bibl studies), 55. **CAREER** Asst prof Bible and philos, Aurora Col, 56-58; asst prof New Testament interpretation, Southern Baptist Theol Sem, 58-60; from vis prof to prof Bibl Studies, 62-77, RES PROF NEW TESTAMENT, NEW BRUNSWICK THEOL SEM, 77-, Am Asn Theol Schs fel, 68-69; von Humbolt scholar, 68-69 and 75-76; lectr, Princeton Theol Sem, 74, 76, 78; Guggenheim fel, 75-76; lectr, Drew Univ, 67-68 and Univ Tubingen, 75-76; vis distinguished prof Evangel Christianity, Juniata Col, 78-79; Bye fel, Robinson Col, Cambridge Univ, 82-83; exec Comt, Soc Studies New Testament, 67-69. **HONORS AND AWARDS** DD, Wheaton Col, Ill, 82. **MEMBERSHIPS** Soc Bibl Lit (treas, 67-68); Soc Studies New Testament; Inst Biblical Res. **RESEARCH** Early Christian history and thought; Biblical studies. **SELECTED PUBLICATIONS** Auth, The Gospel of Jesus--The Pastoral Relevance of the Synoptic Problem, Interpretation J Bible Theol, Vol 50, 96; Paul and the Jewish Law--Halakha in the Letters of the Apostle to the Gentiles, Interpretation J Bible Theol, Vol 47, 93. **CONTACT ADDRESS** Dept of Bibl, Studies New Brunwick Theol Sem, New Brunswick, NJ, 08901.

ELLIS, LAURA
PERSONAL Born 12/11/1963, Albert Lea, MN, s **DISCIPLINE** MUSIC **EDUCATION** Luther Col, BA, 86; Univ Kansas, MA, 88, PhD, 91. **CAREER** Asst prof, 91-96, Univ Ozarks; chmn, Music dept, 97-, assoc prof, 96-, McMurry Univ. **RESEARCH** French organ music **CONTACT ADDRESS** 698 McMurry Station, Abilene, TX, 79697.

ELLIS, RICHARD E.
PERSONAL Born 09/07/1937, New York, NY, m, 1959, 4 children **DISCIPLINE** AMERICAN HISTORY **EDUCATION** Univ Wis-Madison, BA, 60; Univ Calif, Berkeley, MA, 61, PhD, 69. **CAREER** Teaching asst Am hist, Univ Calif, Berkeley, 61-63 & 64-65; instr hist & soc sci, Dept Hist & the Col, Univ Chicago, 65-68; from asst prof to assoc prof hist, Univ Va, 68-74; prof hist, 74-, chemn hist dept, 97-, SUNY Buffalo; John Simon Guggenheim Mem Found fel, 72-73; fel law & hist, Law Sch & fel, Charles Warren Ctr, Harvard Univ, 72-73; Nat Endowment for Humanities fel, Am Enterprise Inst, 78-79. **MEMBERSHIPS** AHA; Orgn Am Historians; Am Soc Legal Hist; Econ Hist Asn; Southern Hist Asn. **RESEARCH** Early American Constitutional and legal history; United States politics, 1776-1845; historiography. **SELECTED PUBLICATIONS** Auth, The Jeffersonian Crisis: Courts and Politics in the Young Republic, Oxford, 71; contribr, The Political Economy of Thomas Jefferson, Thomas Jefferson...The Man...His World. ..His Influence, Putnam, 73; art, John Quincy Adams, Andrew Jackson and Martin Van Buren, Response of the President to Charge of Misconduct, 74; art, United States vs Nixon: A Historical Perspective, Loyola Los Angeles Law Rev, 12/75; art, The Impeachment of Samuel Chase, American Publical Trials, Greenwood Press, 81; auth, The Union at Risk: Jacksonian Democracy, States' Rights and the Nullification Crisis, Oxford, 81; auth, The Persistence of Antifederation after 1789, Before Confederation, Chapel Hill, 87; auth, The Path Not Taken: Virginia and the Supreme Court, 1789-1821, Virginia and the Constitution, Univ Virginia, 92; auth, The Market Revolution as the Transformation of American Politics, 1801-1837, The Market Revolution in America, Univ Press of Virginia, 96. **CONTACT ADDRESS** Dept of History, SUNY, Buffalo, Park Hall, Buffalo, NY, 14260.

ELLIS, RICHARD N.
PERSONAL Born 06/06/1939, Brooklyn, NY, m, 1967 **DISCIPLINE** AMERICAN FRONTIER HISTORY **EDUCATION** Univ Colo, BA, 61, MA, 63, PhD (hist), 67. **CAREER** Asst prof, Murray State Univ, 67-68; asst prof, 68-71, assoc prof, 71-80, PROF HIST, UNIV NMEX, 80-, Asst dir and dir, Doris Duke Am Indian Oral Hist Proj, Univ NMex, 68-71; consult, Nat Park Serv, 71-72; Am Coun Learned Soc res grant, 71-72; assoc ed, Red River Valley Hist Rev, 73-; vis prof, Univ Md, 74; sr lectr, Fulbright Prog, Aarhus Univ, Aarhus, Denmark, 79; co-coordr Am Indian exhibition, Moesgaard Forhistorisk Mus, Aarhus, Denmark. **MEMBERSHIPS** AHA; Orgn Am Historians; Western Hist Asn; Am Indian Hist Soc; Am Soc Ethnohist. **RESEARCH** American Indian history; trans-Mississippi West; the Southwest. **SELECTED PUBLICATIONS** Auth, Miles, Nelson, A. and the Twilight of the Frontier Army, Southwestern Hist Quart, Vol 98, 94; The Most Promising Young Officer--A Life of Mackenzie, Ranald, Slidell, J Am Hist, Vol 81, 94; Yellowstone Command Miles, Nelson, A. and the Great Sioux War, 1876-1877, J Am Hist, Vol 80, 93; Texas, New Mexico, and the Compromise of 1850--Boundary Dispute and Sectional Crisis, J Am Hist, Vol 84, 97; Dangerous Passage--The Santa Fe Trail and the Mexican War, J Am Hist, Vol 82, 95; On Rims and Ridges--The Los Alamos Area Since 1880, Am Hist Rev, Vol 99, 94; Cochise--Chiricahua Apache Chief, Montana Mag W Hist, Vol 43, 93; By Force of Arms--The Journals of Don Diego De Vargas, New-Mexico, 1691-93, NMex Hist Rev, Vol 70, 95; Matthews, Watt of Lambshead, NMex Hist Rev, Vol 69, 94; Glory Hunter--A Biography of Connor, Patrick, Edward, Pac Hist Rev, Vol 63, 94. **CONTACT ADDRESS** Dept of Hist, Univ of NMex, Albuquerque, NM, 87131.

ELLIS, SUSAN
PERSONAL Pocatello, ID, 3 children **DISCIPLINE** ANTHROPOLOGY **EDUCATION** Univ Utah, PhD, 97. **CAREER** Heritage Col 87-; outstanding fac award; Newberry Libr fel; Templeton Found award. **MEMBERSHIPS** Am Schools Oriental Res; Near E Archaeol Soc. **RESEARCH** Pottery technology; Ethmoarchaeology; Georgraphic information systems; Palynology; Museology. **SELECTED PUBLICATIONS** Auth January 1994: Preliminary Pollen Report for 1992 Excavation Abila of the Decapolis, Jordan, Near E Archaeol Soc Bull; Household Styles and Pottery Use in Modern Egypt: Patterns for Archaeology, Am Schools Oriental Res, 94; Replication of Rammeside Pottery Styles by a Modern Egyptian Potter, Am Schools Oriental Res, 95. **CONTACT ADDRESS** 4911 Cherokee, Pocatello, ID, 83686. **EMAIL** ellis_s@heritage.edu

ELLIS, WILLIAM ELLIOTT
PERSONAL Born 01/01/1940, Danville, KY, m, 1960, 2 children **DISCIPLINE** HISTORY, SOCIAL SCIENCE **EDUCATION** Georgetown Col, AB, 62; Eastern Ky Univ, MA, 67; Univ Ky, PhD, 74. **CAREER** Instr hist, Lees Jr Col, 67-70; prof hist, Eastern Ky Univ, 70-. **MEMBERSHIPS** Southern Hist Asn. **RESEARCH** American intellectual history; southern Protestantism; evolution, education, and religion. **SELECTED PUBLICATIONS** Auth, Children, youth, and the social gospel: The reaction of Washington Gladden, Foundations, 9/80; Tenement house reform: Another episode in Kentucky progressivism, Filson Club Hist Quart, 10/81; Robert Worth Bingham and the crisis of cooperative marketing in the Twenties, Agr Hist, 1/82; Evolution, fundamentalism, and the historians: An historiographical Rev, The Historian, spring 82; A Man of Books and a Man of the People: E.Y. Mullins and the Crisis of Moderate Southern Baptist Leadership, Mercer Univ Press, 85; Patrick Henry Callahan: Progressive Catholic Layman in the American South, The Edwin Mellen Press, 89; Robert Worth Bingham and the Southern Mystique, Kent State Univ Press, 97. **CONTACT ADDRESS** Dept of Hist, Eastern Kentucky Univ, 521 Lancaster Ave, Richmond, KY, 40475-3102. **EMAIL** hisellis@acs.eku.edu

ELLISON, CURTIS WILLIAM
PERSONAL Born 10/03/1943, Jasper, AL, m, 1966, 2 children **DISCIPLINE** AMERICAN STUDIES **EDUCATION** Univ Ala, BA, 65; Univ Minn, Minneapolis, MA, 67, PhD (Am studies), 70. **CAREER** Asst prof English, 70-74, assoc prof, 74-76, dir prog Am Studies, 70-74, PROF INTERDISCIPLINARY STUDIES, MIAMI UNIV, 76-, DEAN, 80-. **MEMBERSHIPS** Am Studies Asn; MLA; Southern Hist Asn; Popular Cult Asn; Am Soc Environ Hist; Integrative Studies Asn. **RESEARCH** Methodology of culture studies; American literature; American history. **SELECTED PUBLICATIONS** Auth, Keeping Faith--Evangelical Performance in Country Music, South Atlantic Quart, Vol 94, 95. **CONTACT ADDRESS** Prog in Am Studies, Miami Univ, Oxford, OH, 45056.

ELLISON, HERBERT J.
PERSONAL Born 10/03/1929, Portland, OR, m, 1952, 2 children **DISCIPLINE** RUSSIAN HISTORY **EDUCATION** Univ Wash, BA, 51, MA, 52; Univ London, PhD, 55. **CAREER** Instr hist, Univ Wash, 55-56; asst prof, Univ Okla, 56-62; assoc prof hist and chmn Slavic and Soviet studies, Univ Kans, 62-65, prof hist, 65-68, assoc dean fac, 67-68, dir off int prog, 68-72, vprovost educ develop, 69-72, dir, Inst Comp and Foreign Area Studies, 72-78, PROF HIST, UNIV WASH, 68-, CHMN RUSS and EAST EUROP STUDIES, 78-, Travel grant, Soviet Union, 58 and res grant, 63; Am Coun Learned Soc Slavic and East Europ res grant, 66-67; mem bd and prog comt, Int Res and Exchanges Bd, 73-76. **MEMBERSHIPS** AHA; Am Asn Advan Slavic Studies (vpres, 72-75); Conf Slavic and E Europ Hist (secy, 67-69). **RESEARCH** Soviet Union; Russian agricultural history; Soviet foreign policy. **SELECTED PUBLICATIONS** Auth, Black Earth, Red Star--A History of Soviet Security Policy, 1917-1991, Am Hist Rev, Vol 98, 93; Detente in Europe--The Soviet Union and the West Since 1953, Slavic Rev, Vol 51, 92. **CONTACT ADDRESS** Sch Int Studies, Univ of Wash, DR-05, Seattle, WA, 98195.

ELLOS, JACK D.
PERSONAL Born 10/16/1941, Sulphur, OK, m, 1966, 2 children **DISCIPLINE** HISTORY **EDUCATION** Baylor Univ, BA, 63; Tulane Univ, MS, 65, PhD, 67. **CAREER** Asst prof, 67-70, assoc prof, 70-80, pfof, 80-92, chair, dept hist, Univ Del; dean, Col Lib Arts, 92-96, PROF, UNIV ALA, HUNTSVILLE, 92-. **HONORS AND AWARDS** Wm P. Lyons Master's Essay Award, 65; ACLS fel, 80; Univ Del Ctr Adv Study fels, 83-84. **MEMBERSHIPS** AHA; Soc Fr Historical Stud; So Hist Asn; Oral Hist Asn; Am Asn Hist Med. **RESEARCH** France, Third Republic; soc hist med; African-Am physicians in the South. **SELECTED PUBLICATIONS** Auth, The French Socialists and the Problem of The Peace, 1904-1914, Loyola Univ Chicago Press, 67; auth, The Early Life of Georges Clemenceau, 1841-1893, Regents Press Kans, 80; auth, The Physician-legislators of France, 1870-1914, Cambridge Univ Press, 92. **CONTACT ADDRESS** Dept of History, Univ of Alabama, Huntsville, 415 Roberts Hall, Huntsville, AL, 35899. **EMAIL** ellisj@email.auh.edu

ELLSWORTH, JAMES DENNIS
PERSONAL Born 10/25/1939, Los Angeles, CA **DISCIPLINE** CLASSICS **EDUCATION** Univ CA, Berkeley, BA, 62, PhD(classics), 71. **CAREER** From instr to asst prof clas-

sics, Univ CT, 67-73; asst prof, Southern IL Univ, Carbondale, 73-74; asst prof, 74-79, assoc prof, 79-86, prof classics, Univ Hawaii, 86-. **HONORS AND AWARDS** Dean's Award for Excellemce in Teaching, Univ Hawaii **MEMBERSHIPS** Am Philol Asn. **RESEARCH** Greek mythology; Greek pedagogy; history of classical scholarship. **SELECTED PUBLICATIONS** Auth, Ovid's Aliad (Met 12.1-13.622), Prudentia, 80; Ovid's Odyssey (Met 13.623-14.608), Mnemosyne, 88; Ovid's Aeneid Reconsidered (Met 13.623-14.608), Vergilius, 86; Reading Ancient Greek: A Reasonable Approach (2nd ed), McGraw-Hill, 97; Reading Ancient Greek: The Second Year (2nd ed), McGraw-Hill, 98. **CONTACT ADDRESS** Dept of Europ Lang & Lit, Univ of Hawaii, 1890 E West Rd, Honolulu, HI, 96822-2318. **EMAIL** ellswort@hawaii.edu

ELLSWORTH, OLIVER B.
PERSONAL Born 04/22/1940, Oakland, CA, s **DISCIPLINE** MUSICOLOGY **EDUCATION** Univ Calif, Berkeley, BA, 61; Univ Calif, Berkeley, MA, 63; Univ Calif, Berkeley, PhD, 69. **CAREER** Part-time instr, Univ Calif, 67-68; instr, Univ Colo, 69-70; asst prof, Univ Colo, 70-77; assoc prof, Univ Colo, 77-94; prof, Univ Colo, 94-. **MEMBERSHIPS** Am Musicology Soc. **RESEARCH** Translations and editions of late Medieval music theory treatises. **SELECTED PUBLICATIONS** Auth, The Berkeley Manuscript: University of California Music Library, Univ Nebraska Press, 84; auth, The Theory of Johannes Ciconia and the Revision of the Medieval Curriculum, The Influence of the Classical World on Medieval Literature, Architecture, Music and Culture: A Collection of Interdisciplinary Studies, Edwin Mellen Press, 92. **CONTACT ADDRESS** College of Music, Univ of Colorado, Campus Box 301, Boulder, CO, 80309-0301. **EMAIL** ellswort@spot.colorado.edu

ELLSWORTH, SAMUEL GEORGE
PERSONAL Born 06/19/1916, Safford, AZ, m, 1942, 2 children **DISCIPLINE** HISTORY **EDUCATION** Utah State Agr Col, BS, 41; Univ Calif, AM, 47, PhD, 51. **CAREER** From asst prof to assoc prof, 51-63, chmn dept, 66-69, PROF HIST, UTAH STATE UNIV, 63-, Ed, Western Hist Quart, 70-79. **HONORS AND AWARDS** Award of Merit, Am Asn for State and Local Hist, 74. **MEMBERSHIPS** AHA; Orgn Am Historians; Western Hist Asn. **RESEARCH** The American West; Utah; the Mormons. **SELECTED PUBLICATIONS** Auth, Men With a Mission--The Quorum of the 12 Apostles in the British Isles, 1837-1841 W Hist Quart, Vol 24, 93. **CONTACT ADDRESS** Dept Hist, Utah State Univ, Logan, UT, 84322.

ELMAN, B.A.
DISCIPLINE CHINESE HISTORY **EDUCATION** Univ Hawaii, jr yr, 66-67; Hamilton College, BA honors, 68; Inter Univ Stanford in Taiwan, lang stud, chin 73-74, in Japan, 76-77; Univ Penn, PhD 80. **CAREER** Chinese Science, editor, 92-98-; UCLA Cen of Chinese Studies, prof, dir. **HONORS AND AWARDS** NEH; Fulbright Fel; NAS Res Fell; Res/Teach Fel Japan Foun; NSC Taiwan vis prof; Ecoles des Hautes Etudes Soc Sci dir; Soc Hist Stud Princeton vis prof. **SELECTED PUBLICATIONS** Auth, The Impact of Qing Dynasty Classicism in Tokugawa Japan, in progress; A Cultural History of Modern Science in China 1850-1920; in progress; A Cultural History of Civil Examinations in Late Imperial China, UCP, 99; Classical Historiography for Chinese History: Bibliography and Exercises, published and periodically updated on the WWW since 1996; Education and Society in Late Imperial China 1600-1900, co ed, Berkeley, UCP, 94; Classicism Politics and Kinship: the Ch'ang Chou New Text School of Confucianism in Late Imperial China, Berkeley, UCP, 90, Berkeley Prize 91, Jiangsu People's Press, Chin ed, 98; From Philosophy to Philology: Social and Intellectual Aspects of Change in Late Imperial China, Cambridge, Harv Univ, Coun on E Asian Stud, 84, pbk 90, Chin Ed 95. **CONTACT ADDRESS** Dept of Chinese Studies, Univ of California, Los Angeles, Los Angeles, CA, 90024.

ELPHICK, RICHARD
DISCIPLINE SOUTH AFRICA **EDUCATION** Univ Toronto, BA; Univ Calif, MA; Yale Univ, PhD. **CAREER** Wesleyan Univ. **HONORS AND AWARDS** Assoc Ed, History & Theory. **SELECTED PUBLICATIONS** Area: South Africa. **CONTACT ADDRESS** Wesleyan Univ, Middletown, CT, 06459. **EMAIL** relphick@wesleyan.edu

ELWOOD, R. CARTER
PERSONAL Born 07/23/1935, Chicago, IL **DISCIPLINE** HISTORY **EDUCATION** Dartmouth Col, BA, 58; Columbia Univ, MA, 62, PhD, 69. **CAREER** Asst prof, Univ Alta, 68-70; asst prof to assoc prof, 68-76, PROF HISTORY, CARLETON UNIV, 76-, ch dept, 82-85; vis scholar, St Antony's Col, Oxford, 70-71, 74; vis scholar, Univ Fribourg, 77-78; vis scholar, London Sch Econ, 84-85; vis scholar, Russian Res Ctr, Harvard Univ, 91-92. **HONORS AND AWARDS** Excellence Tchg Award, 85; Marston LaFrance Fel, 87-88; Heldt Prize, Best Bk, Slavic Women's Stud, 92; Tchg Achievement Award, 95. **MEMBERSHIPS** Can Asn Slavists (pres 81-82). **SELECTED PUBLICATIONS** Auth, Russian Social Democracy in the Underground, 74; auth, Roman Malinovsky, 77; auth, Inessa Armand, 92; ed, The Russian Social Democratic Labour Party, vol 1, 74; ed, Can Slavonic Papers, 75-80; gen ed, Proceedings of the Third World Congress of Soviet and East European Studies, 15 vols, 86-89. **CONTACT ADDRESS** Dept of History, Carleton Univ, 1125 Colonel By Dr, Ottawa, ON, K1S 5B6.

EMBREE, AINSLIE THOMAS
PERSONAL Born 01/01/1921, NS, Canada, m, 1947, 2 children **DISCIPLINE** MODERN INDIAN HISTORY **EDUCATION** Dalhousie Univ, BA, 41; Pine Hill Divinity Sch, BD, 47; Union Theol Sem, NY, MA, 47; Columbia Univ, MA, 55, PhD (Brit imperial hist), 60. **CAREER** Lectr hist, Indore Christian Col, India, 48-58; from instr to assoc prof Indian hist, Columbia Univ, 58-69; prof hist, Duke Univ, 69-72; assoc dean fac int affairs, 72-78, PROF HIST, COLUMBIA UNIV, 72-, Vpres to pres, Am Inst Indian Studies, 67-73, fel, 68-69; Am Coun Learned Soc fel, 68; Nat Endowment for Humanities fel, 77; coun cult affairs, Am Embassy, India, 78-80. **MEMBERSHIPS** AHA; Asn Asian Studies (vpres and pres, 81-83); Am Orient Soc; Coun Foreign Rel. **RESEARCH** Nineteenth century Indian history; modern SAsia. **SELECTED PUBLICATIONS** Auth, The Sultanate of Aceh--Relations With the British, 1760-1824, Albion, Vol 28, 96; The Making of Early Medieval India, J Interdisciplinary Hist, Vol 27, 96; Judging the State--Courts and Constitutional Policies in Pakistan, Am Hist Rev, Vol 101, 96; Pakistan as a Peasant Utopia--The Communalization of Class Politics in East Bengal, 1920-1947, Am Hist Rev, Vol 98, 93; The Arya Samaj as a Fundamentalist Movement--A Study in Comparative Fundamentalism, J Religion, Vol 76, 96. **CONTACT ADDRESS** 54 Morningside Dr, New York, NY, 10025.

EMERICK, JUDSON
PERSONAL Born 07/03/1941, Kingston, NY, m, 1963 **DISCIPLINE** ART HISTORY **EDUCATION** Hope Col, BA, 63; Univ Mich, MA, 65; Univ Pa, PhD, 75. **CAREER** Instr, Pomona Col, 73-75; asst prof, 75-81; assoc prof, 81-97; prof, 97- . **HONORS AND AWARDS** Pennfield Scholoar, 70-71; Samuel H. Kress Found Fel, 71-73; NEH Fel, 81. **MEMBERSHIPS** Col Art Asoc; Soc of Archit Hist; Int Ctr of Medieval Art; Byzantine Studes Conf; Art Hist of Souther Cal. **RESEARCH** Late antique and early medieval art in Italy; the Corinthian order in ancient and medieval architecture; archaeology of standing walls. **SELECTED PUBLICATIONS** Co-auth with C. Davis-Weyer, The Early Sixth-Century Frescoes at S. Martino at Monti in Rome, Romisches Jahrbuch fur Kuustgeschichte, 84; auth, The Tempiettodel Clitunno near Spoleto, 98. **CONTACT ADDRESS** Dept. of Art and Art History, Pomona Col, 145 E. Bonita Ave., Claremont, CA, 91711. **EMAIL** jemerick@pomona.edu

EMERSON, ROGER LEE
PERSONAL Born 03/26/1934, Barton, VT **DISCIPLINE** THE ENLIGHTENMENT **EDUCATION** Dartmouth Col, BA, 56; Brown Univ, MA, 58; Brandeis Univ, MA, 59, PhD (hist of ideas), 62. **CAREER** Instr soc sci, Univ Minn, Minneapolis, 61-62; instr humanities, Mass Inst Technol, 62-64; asst prof, 64-66, ASSOC PROF HIST, UNIV WESTERN ONT, 66-, Fel, Inst Advan Studies Humanities, Edinburgh Univ, 71. **MEMBERSHIPS** AHA. **RESEARCH** Intellectual history of the 18th century; British social history; the Enlightenment in England, France and Scotland. **SELECTED PUBLICATIONS** Auth, An Enlightened Scot--Cleghorn, Hugh, 1752-1837, Eng Hist Rev, Vol 111, 96. **CONTACT ADDRESS** Dept Hist, Univ Western Ont, London, ON, N6A 3K7.

EMERY, TED
DISCIPLINE ITALIAN EIGHTEENTH CENTURY **EDUCATION** Trinity Col, BA; Brown Univ, MA, PhD. **CAREER** Asst prof-. **HONORS AND AWARDS** Commentator on Giacomo Casanova, Arts and Entertainment Network's biog prog. **RESEARCH** Singing and acting, scenery, costumes and dance. **SELECTED PUBLICATIONS** Auth, monograph on the opera libretti of Carlo Goldoni, Peter Lang, 91; ed, co-transl, Five Tales for the Theatre by Carlo Gozzi, Univ Chicago Press, 89. **CONTACT ADDRESS** Dept of Fr and Ital, Dickinson Col, PO Box 1773, Carlisle, PA, 17013-2896.

EMGE, STEVEN W.
PERSONAL Born 05/15/1958, Council Bluffs, IA, m, 2 children **DISCIPLINE** VOICE; MUSIC **EDUCATION** Drake Univ, BME, 80; Drake Univ, MME, 92; Univ Iowa, MA, 95; Univ Iowa, PhD, 96. **CAREER** Elementary/junior high music specialist, 86-91; instr, Univ Iowa, 92-95; instr, Coe Col, 93-95; instr, Augustana Col, 95; asst prof, Southeastern Oklahoma State Univ, 96-. **HONORS AND AWARDS** Undergraduate vocal scholarship, Drake University; graduate music educ scholarship, Drake Univ; Univ Iowa graduate teaching assistantship. **MEMBERSHIPS** National Asn of Teachers of Singing; Music Educators National Conference. **RESEARCH** Voice development; vocal pedagogy. **SELECTED PUBLICATIONS** Coauth, "Vocal Registration as it Affects Vocal Range for Seventh- and Eighth-Grade Boys", in The Journal of Research in Singing and Applied Vocal Pedagogy 18(1), 94. **CONTACT ADDRESS** Southeastern Oklahoma State Univ, 5th & University, Durant, OK, 74701-0609. **EMAIL** semge@sosu.edu

ENDELMAN, TODD MICHAEL
PERSONAL Born 11/10/1946, Fresno, CA, m, 1968, 2 children **DISCIPLINE** MODERN JEWISH AND EUROPEAN HISTORY **EDUCATION** Univ Calif, Berkeley, BA, 68; Hebrew Union Col-Jewish Inst Relig, Calif, BHL, 72; Harvard Univ, Am, 72, PhD (hist), 76. **CAREER** Asst prof Jewish hist, Yeshiva Univ, 76-79; asst prof hist, 79-81, ASSOC PROF HIST, IND UNIV, 81-, Lectr hist, Hebrew Union Col-Jewish Inst Relig, NY, 79. **HONORS AND AWARDS** Frank and Ethel S Cohen Award, Jewish Bd Coun, Nat Jewish Welfare Bd, 80; A S Diamond Mem Prize, Jewish Hist Soc England, 80. **MEMBERSHIPS** AHA; Jewish Hist Soc England; Leo Baeck Inst; Asn Jewish Studies. **RESEARCH** Anglo-Jewish history; social history of Western European Jewry; the entry of the Jews into European society, 1700-1880. **SELECTED PUBLICATIONS** Auth, Modern British Jewry, Am Hist Rev, Vol 99, 94; Jews, Idols, and MessiahsT--The Challenge from History, J Mod Hist, Vol 65, 93; Skeptics, Millenarians, and Jews, Jewish Quart Rev, Vol 83, 93; Amuel, Herbert A Political Life, J Mod Hist, Vol 67, 95; Disraeli A Biography, Am Hist Rev, Vol 100, 95; Jews, Aliens and Other Outsiders in British History, Hist J, Vol 37, 94. **CONTACT ADDRESS** Dept of Hist, Indiana Univ, Bloomington, Bloomington, IN, 47405.

ENDICOTT, STEPHEN L.
PERSONAL Born 01/05/1928, Shanghai, China **DISCIPLINE** HISTORY **EDUCATION** Univ Toronto, BA, 49, MA, 66; Sch Orient African Stud Univ London, Univ Toronto, PhD, 73. **CAREER** Journalist, Jeunesse du Monde, Hungary, 52-54; mem, Labour Progressive Party Exec, Toronto, 54-57; high sch tchr, Peel Co, Ont, 60-68; lectr to assoc prof, 72-90, SR SCHOLAR, DEPT HIST, ATKINSON COL, YORK UNIV, 90-; vis prof, Sichuan Univ (Chengdu), 80-81. **HONORS AND AWARDS** Can Coun scholar, 75-76; Killam fel, 76-78; SSHRCC fel, 83-84; Atkinson fel, 86. **RESEARCH** Chinese history. **SELECTED PUBLICATIONS** Auth, Diplomacy and Enterprise: British China Policy 1933-37, 75; auth, James G. Endicott: Rebel Out of China, 80; auth, Wen Yiuzhang Zhuan, 83; auth, Red Earth: Revolution in a Sichuan Village, 88; auth, The Red Dragon: China 1949-1990, 91. **CONTACT ADDRESS** Atkinson Col, York Univ, 4700 Keele St, North York, ON, M3J 1P3.

ENDICOTT-WEST, ELIZABETH
DISCIPLINE CHINESE HISTORY, MONGOLIAN HISTORY, EAST ASIAN HISTORY, CENTRAL ASIAN HISTO **EDUCATION** Trinity Col, AB; Yale Univ, MA; Princeton Univ, MA, PhD. **CAREER** Assoc prof, Middlebury Col, 95-. **RESEARCH** China under Mongolian rule, 13th-14th centuries; Chinese-Mongolian-Russian relations, 19th-20th centuries. **SELECTED PUBLICATIONS** Auth, Mongolian Rule in China: Local Administration in the Yuan Dynasty, Harvard UP; coauth, The Modernization of Inner Asia, M.E. Sharpe. **CONTACT ADDRESS** Dept of History, Middlebury Col, Middlebury, VT, 05753. **EMAIL** endicott@panther.middlebury.edu

ENG, ROBERT Y.
DISCIPLINE HISTORY **EDUCATION** Pomona Col, BA; Univ Calif Berkeley, MA; PhD. **CAREER** Prof,Redlands Univ. **RESEARCH** Social;economic and demographic history of modern China and Japan **SELECTED PUBLICATIONS** Auth, Land Reclamation, Merchant Wealth and Political Power in Qing and Republican China: Minglun Tang of Dongguan County, Beijing, 92; Luddism and Labor Protest Among Silk Artisans and Workers in Jiangnan and Guangdong, 1860-1930, Late Imperial China, 90; Institutional and Secondary Landlordism in the Pearl River Delta, 1600-1949, Modern China, 86; Chinese Entrepreneurs, the Government, and the Foreign Sector: The Canton and Shanghai Silk-reeling Enterprises, 1861-1932, Modern Asian Studies, 84. **CONTACT ADDRESS** History Dept, Univ Redlands, 1200 E Colton Ave, Box 3090, Redlands, CA, 92373-0999. **EMAIL** eng@uor.edu

ENGEBRETSEN, TERRY
DISCIPLINE AMERICAN STUDIES **EDUCATION** Wash State Univ, PhD, 82. **CAREER** Assoc prof. **RESEARCH** Seventeenth century American literature and culture; postmodernism. **SELECTED PUBLICATIONS** Auth, pubs in Studies in the Literary Imagination; Studies in Puritan American Spirituality. **CONTACT ADDRESS** Dept of English and Philosophy, Idaho State Univ, Pocatello, ID, 83209.

ENGEL, BARBARA
PERSONAL Born 06/28/1943, New York, NY **DISCIPLINE** RUSSIAN **EDUCATION** CCNY, BA, 65; Harvard Univ, MA, 67; Columbia Univ, PhD, 74. **CAREER** Part-time instr, Drew Univ, 72-73; adjunct lectr, CCNY, 73-74; instr, Columbia Univ, summer, 74; asst prof, Sarah Lawrence Col, 74-76; asst prof, Univ Colo, 76-82; assoc prof, Univ Colo, 82-92; prof, Univ Colo, 92-; dir, Central and Eastern Europ Studies Prog, Univ Colo, 93-95; chair, dept of hist, Univ Colo, 95-98. **HONORS AND AWARDS** Phi Beta Kappa, 65; Harvard Univ scholar, 65-66, 66-67; NY State regents fel, 65-66; NDEA Columbia Univ facul fel, 65-66, 66-67; Chancellor's writing award, Univ Colo, spring, 84; AWSS Heldt Article award, 91; Elizabeth Gee award for excellence, 93; Boulder facul assembly award, 93; Mortar Bd Sr Hon Soc, 94; AWSS Heldt prize, 96. **MEMBER-**

SHIPS AHA; AAASS; CCWH. **RESEARCH** Russian family, women; Soviet family, women. **SELECTED PUBLICA-TIONS** Co-ed, A Revolution Of Their Own: Russian Women Remember their Lives in the Twentieth Century, Westview Press, 98; auth, Between the Fields and the City: Women, Work and Family in Russia, 1861-1914, Cambridge Univ Press, 94; article, Not by Bread Alone: Subsistence Riots in Russia during World War I, Jour of Mod Hist, 69, n 4, 696-721, dec, 97; article, Les Femmes dans la Russie des Revolutions, Encycl politique et hist des femmes: Europe, Amer du Nord, Presses Univ de Fr, 433-471, 97; article, Women, Men and the Languages of Peasant Resistance, 1870-1914, Cultures in Flux: Lower Class Values, Practices and Resistance in Late Imperial Russia, Princeton Univ Press, 34-53, 94; article, Russian Peasant Views of City Life, 1861-1914, Slavic Rev, 52, no 3, 445-459, fall, 93; article, Socially Deviant Women and the Russian Peasant Community, 1861-1914, Gender Restructuring in Russian Studies, Tampere, Finland, 53-64, 93. **CONTACT ADDRESS** Dept. of History CB 234, Univ of Colorado, Boulder, CO, 80309. **EMAIL** engelb@spot.colorado.edu

ENGEL, DAVID M.
PERSONAL Born 12/11/1964, Charleston, WV, m, 1998 **DIS-CIPLINE** CLASSICS **EDUCATION** Univ Calif Berkeley, PhD **CAREER** Pa St Univ **MEMBERSHIPS** Amer Philolog Assoc; Amer Philos Assoc, Amer Inst of Archaeol. **RE-SEARCH** Ancient Greek; ancient philos; mind; lang; ethics. **CONTACT ADDRESS** Pennsylvania State Univ, 108 Weaver Bldg, University Park, PA, 16802. **EMAIL** dme8@psu.edu

ENGEL, MARTIN
PERSONAL Born 12/27/1929, Mannheim, Germany, m, 1958, 3 children **DISCIPLINE** ARTS AND HUMANITIES EDU-CATION Syracuse Univ, BA, 51, PhD, 61; Harvard Univ, MA, 53. **CAREER** Asst art hist, Syracuse Univ, 56-59, instr, 60-61; asst prof humanities, Monteith Col, Wayne State Univ, 61-62; from asst prof to assoc prof hist and fine arts, Carnegie-Mellon Univ, 62-69; sr prog officer, Arts and Humanities Prog, US Off Educ, 69-72; SR PROG OFFICER EDUC RES and DEVELOP, NAT INST EDUC, 72-; ARTS and HUMANITIES ADV, NAT INST EDUC, DEPT HEALTH, EDUC, WELFARE, 76-, Consult, Nat Endowment Humanities, 69-71 and Harcourt Brace Jovanovich, 73; adv bd, Rockefeller Brothers Fund, 80-. **MEM-BERSHIPS** Nat Art Educ Asn. **RESEARCH** Cognitive processes in the arts; education policy in arts and humanities; research management. **SELECTED PUBLICATIONS** Auth, The European Novel--History of its Poetics, Archiv Studium Neueren Sprachen Literaturen, Vol 230, 93; Aesthetics of Modernism, Archiv Studium Neueren Sprachen Literaturen, Vol 233, 96; Aesthetics of Modernism, Archiv Studium Neueren Sprachen Literaturen, Vol 233, 96; Early Realism and the Legacy of Romanticism--Myth, Dream and Fairy Tales in Immermann, Karl Works, Zeitschrift Deutsche Philologie, Vol 114, 95; The European Novel--History of its Poetics, Archiv Studium Neueren Sprachen Literaturen, Vol 230, 93; Translated Life--Rimbaud Biography in its German Translations by Klammer, Karl, Zech, Paul, and Wolfenstein, Alfred, Germanisch Romanische Monatsschrift, Vol 43, 93. **CONTACT AD-DRESS** National Inst of Educ, Washington, DC, 20208.

ENGELS, DONALD W.
PERSONAL Born 05/15/1946, Rockville Centre, NY, s **DIS-CIPLINE** HISTORY, CLASSICS **EDUCATION** Univ of Fla, Ba, 69; Univ of Tex, MA, 72; Univ of Pa, PhD, 76. **CAREER** Instr for Greek & Roman Hist, Univ of Pa, 77; vis asst prof in Hist & Classics, Brandeis Univ, 77-78; asst prof of Hist & Greek & Latin, Wellesley Col, 78-85; vis asst prof o fhist & classics, Univ of Chicago, 83; vis asst prof, Boston Col, 85-86; ASST PROF, 86-88, ASSOC PROF, UNIV OF ARK, 88-. **HONORS AND AWARDS** Tchg fel for Greek and Roman Hist, Univ of Pa, 75-76; Ford Found Archaeol Traineeship, 70; res & tchg fels, Univ of Pa, 73-76; Am Philos Soc Grant, 79; travel grant, Wellesley Col, 79; NEH summer stipend, Brown Univ, 81. **MEMBERSHIPS** Am Philol Asn; Asn of Ancient Historians; Friends of Ancient Hist; Soc for Ancient Medicine; Historical Soc. **RESEARCH** Greek and Roman history. **SE-LECTED PUBLICATIONS** Auth, Roman Corinth: An Alternative Model for the Classical City, Univ of Chicago Press, 90; Classical Cats: The Rise and Fall of the Sacred Cat, Routledge, 99; Ptolemy I, World Book Encycl, 81; The Use of Historical Demography in Ancient History, Classical Quart, 84; The Length of Eratosthenes' Stade, Am J of Philol, 85; The Classical City Reconsidered, The Eye Expanded, Berkeley, 98. **CON-TACT ADDRESS** Dept of Hist, Univ of Arkansas, Fayetteville, AR, 72701. **EMAIL** dengles@comp.uark.edu

ENGLAND, JAMES MERTON
PERSONAL Born 11/30/1915, Deepwater, MO, m, 1944, 4 children **DISCIPLINE** AMERICAN HISTORY EDUCA-TION Cent Col, Mo, AB, 36; Vanderbilt Univ, AM, 37; PhD, 41. **CAREER** Ed asst, La State Univ, 41-42; from instr to asst prof, Univ Ky, 46-48, from assoc prof hist to prof, 48-61; prog dir inst grants for sci, 61-70; exec asst to dep asst dir instnl progs, 70-71; exec asst to asst dir, 71; spec asst to dir, 71-77, HISTORIAN, NAT SCI FOUND, 77-, Ed assoc, J Southern Hist, 49-52, managing ed, 53-58; Fulbright prof, Univ Birmingham, 56-57; lectr, Salzburg Sem Am Studies, 57; vis prof Am

Civilization, sch int serv, Am Univ, 60-61. **HONORS AND AWARDS** LHD, WVa Inst Technol, 65. **MEMBERSHIPS** Southern Hist Asn; Orgn Am Historians; Am Hist Asn; AAAS. **RESEARCH** History of American education; science and federal government. **SELECTED PUBLICATIONS** Auth, To Foster the Spirit of Professionalism--Southern Scientists and State Academies of Science, J Southern Hist, Vol 59, 93. **CON-TACT ADDRESS** National Science Found, Washington, DC, 20550.

ENGLE, STEPHEN D.
DISCIPLINE HISTORY **EDUCATION** Fla State Univ, PhD. **CAREER** Assoc prof. **MEMBERSHIPS** Am Hist Asn; Southern Hist Asn; Asn German-Am. **RESEARCH** 19th century America; Civil War and reconstruction South. **SELECTED PUBLICATIONS** Auth, Yankee Dutchman: The Life of Franz Sigel, 93; Mountaineer Reconstruction: Blacks in the Political Reconstruction of West Virginia, Jour Negro Hist, 94; Don Carlos Buell, Military Philosophy, and Command Problems in the West, 95. **CONTACT ADDRESS** History Dept, Florida Atlantic Univ, 777 Glades Rd, Boca Raton, FL, 33431. **EMAIL** engle@fau.edu

ENGLISH, JOHN CAMMEL
PERSONAL Born 12/04/1934, Kansas City, MO **DISCI-PLINE** HISTORY **EDUCATION** Wash Univ, BA, 55; Yale Univ, MDiv, 58; Vanderbilt Univ, PhD (church hist), 65. **CA-REER** Asst prof hist, Stephen F Austin State Univ, 62-65; from asst prof to assoc prof, 65-68, chmn, Dept Hist and Polit Sci, 65-73, chmn, Soc Sci Div, 70-72, chmn, Humanities Div, 78-81, PROF HIST, BAKER UNIV, 68-, Fl, Summer Fac Inst South and Southeast Asia, Hamline Univ, 66; US Educ fac develop award SAsian studies, Univs Minn and Chicago, 69-70; dir, Shaping of Western Thought Prog, 77-80. **MEMBER-SHIPS** AHA; Am Soc Church Hist; Conf Brit Studies; Am Soc 18th Century Studies. **RESEARCH** European intellectual and religious history, particularly 17th and 18th century Britain; South Asian history and politics; methodology of historical research. **SELECTED PUBLICATIONS** Auth, The Mind of Locke, John--A Study of Political-Theory in its Intellectual Setting, Church Hist, Vol 64, 95; Wesley, John Conception and Use of Scripture, Church Hist, Vol 66, 97; The Mind of Locke, John--A Study of Political Theory in its Intellectual Setting, Church Hist, Vol 64, 95; Wesley, John and the Rights of Conscience Church and State, Vol 37, 95; Wesley, John Conception and Use of Scripture, Church Hist, Vol 66, 97. **CONTACT ADDRESS** PO Box 537, Baldwin, KS, 66006.

ENGS, ROBERT FRANCIS
PERSONAL Born 11/10/1943, Colorado Springs, CO, m, 1969 **DISCIPLINE** HISTORY **EDUCATION** Princeton U, AB (cum laude) 1965; Yale U, PhD History 1972. **CAREER** U Univ of PA, assoc prof history 1979-; Univ of PA, asst prof history 1972-79; Princeton U, instr history 1970-72; NJ Black History Inst NJ Dept of Educ, dir 1969-72; Coll of William & Mary, commonwealth visiting prof 1984-85; Univ of PA, Philadelphia, PA, undergraduate chair History, 1986-. **HONORS AND AWARDS** Short Term Am Grantee, US Dept of State 1971; William Penn Fellow, Moton Cntr for Ind Studies 1976-77; Freedom's First Generation, Univ of PA Press 1979; N&H Summer Fellowship, Natl Endowment of the Humanities 1980; Guggenheim Fellow 1982-83; Lindback Award for Excellence in Teaching, Univ of Pennsylvania 1988. **MEMBERSHIPS** Faculty mem/cons Nat Humanities Faculty 1972-80; adv Nat Humanities Center 1978-80; mem Orgn of Am Historians 1975-; mem Am Hist Assn 1975; mem Assn for Study of Afro-Am Life History 1975; chmn Presidents Forum Univ of PA 1985-87; member Executive Committee Alumni Council of Princeton University, 1989-91. **CONTACT ADDRESS** Univ of Pennsylvania, 3401 Walnut St, Philadelphia, PA, 19104.

ENGSTRAND, IRIS H. WILSON
PERSONAL Born 01/09/1935, Los Angeles, CA, m, 1970, 1 child **DISCIPLINE** HISTORY **EDUCATION** Univ Southern CA, BA, 56, MA, 57, PhD, 62. **CAREER** Res translr hist, Los Angeles County Mus, 59-60; instr hist, Long Beach City Col, 62-68; assoc prof, 68-74, prof hist, Univ San Diego, 74, Lectr & asst prof hist, Univ Southern CA, 62-68; Am Philos Soc fel res in Spain, 64-65; assoc prof hist, Univ CA, San Diego, 68-69; chmn, Bd Ed Consults, J San Diego Hist, 76-; Nat Endowment for Hum fel, 76; mem bd trustees, CA Hist Soc, 80; Huntington Lib fel, 89; Fulbright res scholar, Spain, 96. **HONORS AND AWARDS** Award of Merit, San Diego Hist Soc, 75-76 & Calif Hist Soc, 78; Davies Award for Fac Achievement, USD, 84; Distinguished Univ Prof, USD, 95; Am Hist Asn, pres, Pacific Coast Branch, 98-99. **MEMBERSHIPS** AHA; Latin Am Studies Asn; Western Hist Asn. **RESEARCH** Span Colonial empire; hist of sci; hist of CA. **SELECTED PUBLICATIONS** Auth, Investigacion sobre la planta maguey en Nueva Espana, Rev Indias, 63; Antonio Pineda y su Viaje Mundial, Rev Hist Militar, 64; William Wolfskill: Frontier Trapper to California Ranchero, 1798-1866, Arthur H Clark, 65; coauth, Southern California and its University: A History of USC, 1880-1964, Ward Ritchie, 69; ed & transl, Noticias de Nutka: An Account of Nootka Sound in 1792, Univ Wash, 70, rev 91; auth, Royal Officer in Baja California 1768-1770: Joaquin Velazquez de Leon, Dawson's 76; San Diego: California's Cornerstone, Con-

tinental Heritage Press, 80; Spanish Scientists in the New World: The Eighteenth Century Expeditions, Univ Wash, 81; San Diego: Gateway to the Pacific, Pioneer Publ, 92; Arizona Hispanica, Editoria Mapfre, 92; Documents for the History of California and the West, D C Heath, 92; co-auth (with Donald Cutter), Quest for Empire: Spanish Settlement in the Southwest, Fulcrum Publ, 96. **CONTACT ADDRESS** Dept of Hist, Univ of San Diego, 5998 Alcala Park, San Diego, CA, 92110-2492. **EMAIL** iris@acusd.edu

ENNS, LEONARD
DISCIPLINE MUSIC EDUCATION Northwestern Univ, MA, 75; PhD, 82. **CAREER** Assoc prof **RESEARCH** Canadian music; music theory. **SELECTED PUBLICATIONS** Auth, The Composer as Preacher, Can Mennonite Bible Col. **CON-TACT ADDRESS** Dept of Music, Conrad Grebel Col, 200 Westmount Rd, Waterloo, ON, N2L 3G6. **EMAIL** ljenns@ uwaterloo.ca

ENO, ROBERT BRYAN
PERSONAL Born 11/12/1936, Hartford, CT **DISCIPLINE** PATRISTICS, CHURCH HISTORY **EDUCATION** Cath Univ Am, BA, 58, MA, 59; Inst Cath de Paris, STD, 69. **CAREER** Asst prof, St Mary's Sem, Baltimore, 68-70; ASST PROF, 70-79, ASSOC PROF PATRISTICS, CATH UNIV AM, 79-, CHMN, DEPT CHURCH HIST, AND ASSOC CHMN, DEPT THEOL, 80-, Ed, Corpus Instrumentorum, 66-70; mem, NAT LUTHERAN-ROMAN CATH DIALOGUE, 76-; vis lectr, Princeton Theol Sem, spring, 77 and 80. **MEMBERSHIPS** NAm Patristic Soc; Asn Int des Etudes Patristiques; Am Soc Church Hist; Cath Hist Asn. **RESEARCH** Latin fathers, especially Augustine; ecclesiology; eschatology. **SELECTED PUBLICATIONS** Auth, Church, Book and Bishop--Conflict and Authority in Early Latin Christianity, Cath Hist Rev, Vol 83, 97; Historical Awareness in Augustine--Ontological, Anthropological and Historical Elements of an Augustinian Theory of History, Cath Hist Rev, Vol 80, 94; A Translation of Jerome Chronicon with Historical Commentary, Cath Hist Rev, Vol 83, 97; Desire and Delight--A New Reading of Augustine Confessions, Cath Hist Rev, Vol 79, 93; After the Apostles--Christianity in the 2nd Century, Church History, Vol 64, 95; Augustine, Arianism and Other Heresies, Cath Hist Rev, Vol 83, 97; Novitas Christiana - the Idea of Progress in the Old Church Before Eusebius, Cath Hist Rev, Vol 81, 95; Sacred and Secular--Studies on Augustine and Latin Christianity, Cath Hist Rev, Vol 83, 97; Augustine, Cath Hist Rev, Vol 83, 97; Augustine and the Catechumenate, Cath Hist Rev, Vol 83, 97; The Collection Sources Chretiennes--Editing the Fathers of the Church in the Xxth Century, Cath Hist Rev, Vol 83, 97; Chiliasm and the Myth of the Antichrist--Early Christian Controversy Regarding the Holy Land, Cath Hist Rev, Vol 80, 94; The Early Church--An Annotated Bibliography in English, Cath Hist Rev, Vol 80, 94; The Significance of the Lists of Roman Bishops in the Anti Donatist Polemic, Vigiliae Christianae, Vol 47, 93; Divine Grace and Human Agency--A Study of the Semi Pelagian Controversy, Theol Stud, Vol 57, 96; Reading the Apostolic Fathers--An Introduction, Cath Hist Rev, Vol 83, 97; After the Apostles--Christianity in the 2nd Century, Church Hist, Vol 64, 95. **CONTACT ADDRESS** Catholic Univ of America, 401 Michigan Ave NE, Washington, DC, 20017.

ENS, GERHARD J.
DISCIPLINE HISTORY **EDUCATION** Univ Manitoba, BA, MA; Univ Alberta, PhD. **CAREER** Hist, Brandon Univ. **RE-SEARCH** Nineteenth and twentieth century metis society and politics. **SELECTED PUBLICATIONS** Auth, Homeland to Hinterland: The Changing Worlds of the Red River Metis in the nineteenth century, Univ Toronto, 96; Prologue to the Red River Resistance: Pre-liminal Metis Politics and the Triumph of Riel, Jour Can Hist Asn, 94; Metis Agriculture in Red River during the Transition from Peasant Society to Industrial Capitalism: The Example of St. Francois Xavier 1835-1870, Univ Alberta, 93; co-auth, Metis Land Grants in Manitoba: A Statistical Study, 94. **CONTACT ADDRESS** History Dept, Brandon Univ, 270-18th St, Brandon, MB, R7A 6A9. **EMAIL** ens@ BrandonU.ca

ENSSLE, MANFRED JOACHIM
PERSONAL Born 03/25/1939, Stuttgart, Germany, m, 1966, 2 children **DISCIPLINE** EUROPEAN & GERMAN HISTO-RY **EDUCATION** Univ Colo, BA, 61, MA, 63, PhD(hist), 71. **CAREER** Instr, 65-70, asst prof, 71-77, assoc prof Hist, Colo State Univ, 77-87, prof Hist, 87-, vis asst prof, Univ Del, summers 71 & 77; Danforth assoc, 80-. **HONORS AND AWARDS** Fellow, Institut fur Europaishe Geschichte (Institute for European History), Mainz, Germany, 67-68, 72; Research grant, Am Philosophical Soc, 72; Nat Endowment for the Humanities Summer Seminar for College Teachers, 80; 5 Teaching awards, Colorado State Univ, 87-93. **MEMBERSHIPS** General Studies Asn. **RESEARCH** German history; 20th century Europe. **SELECTED PUBLICATIONS** Auth, Stresemann's Diplomacy Fifty Years After Locarno: Some Recent Perspectives, Hist J, 77; Stresemann's Territorial Revisionism, Germany, Belgium, and the Eupen-Malmedy Question 1919-1929, Franz Steiner Verlag, 80; The Harsh Discipline of Food Scarcity in Postwar Stuttgart, 1945-1948, German Studies Review, X, 3 (Oct 87), pp481-502; Five Theses on German Everyday Life

After World War II, Central European History 26, 1 (93), pp 1-19; Der Versorgungsalltag Stuttgerts 1945-1949, Aus Den vertraulichen stimmungs berichten der Polizeireviere, (chapter in) E. Lersch, H. Poker, and P. Suer, eds, Stuttgart in den ersten Nachkriegsjahren (Stuttgart: Klenn-Cotta, 95), pp 353-397; (with Bradley J. MacDonald), The Wrapped Reichstag, 1945: Art, Dialogic Communities and Everyday Life, Theory & Event 1, 4 (97), pp 1-19. **CONTACT ADDRESS** Dept of Hist, Colorado State Univ, Fort Collins, CO, 80523-0001. **EMAIL** menssle@vines.colostate.edu

ENTERLINE, LYNN
DISCIPLINE GENDER STUDIES, CLASSICAL, MEDIEVAL, AND EARLY MODERN LITERATURE **EDUCATION** Cornell, PhD. **CAREER** Instr, Vanderbilt Univ. **RESEARCH** Theories of rhetoric, language, and poetics from the classical period through the 17th century; contemporary intersections between feminist, queer, materialist and psychoanalytic critiques of literature and culture. **SELECTED PUBLICATIONS** Auth, The Tears of Narcissus: Melancholia and Masculinity in Early Modern Writing; The Rhetoric of the Body in Renaissance Ovidian Poetry. **CONTACT ADDRESS** Vanderbilt Univ, Nashville, TN, 37203-1727.

EPSTEIN, DAVID M.
PERSONAL Born 07/31/1930, Kansas City, MO, m, 1959 **DISCIPLINE** MODERN EUROPEAN HISTORY **EDUCATION** Univ Kansas City, BA, 55, MA, 59; Univ Nebr, PhD (hist), 67. **CAREER** Asst mod Europ hist, Univ Kansas City, 59-60; asst Western civilization, Univ Nebr, 60-62; asst prof mod Europ hist, Eastern Ky State Col, 63-67; asst prof, 67-70, ASSOC PROF HIST, UNIV TULSA, 70-, Res grants, Univ Tulsa, 68; Am Philos Soc res grant, Univ Tulsa, 74-75. **MEMBERSHIPS** AHA; Soc Fr Hist Studies; Western Soc Fr Historians. **RESEARCH** Ancient regime; the French Revolution; French naval history. **SELECTED PUBLICATIONS** Auth, Bobolink, Hudson Review, Vol 49, 97; American Dryad, Am Scholar, Vol 63, 94; After Reading Le Demon de Lanalogy, Mic Quart Rev Vol 33, 94; Collection, Hudson Rev, Vol 49, 97; The Belled Buzzard of Roxbury Mills, Am Scholar, Vol 66, 97; Phidias in Exile, Am Scholar, Vol 64, 95; The Glories, Hudson Rev, Vol 49, 97; The Inheritance, Am Scholar, Vol 64, 95. **CONTACT ADDRESS** Dept of Hist, Univ of Tulsa, Tulsa, OK, 74104.

EPSTEIN, JAMES A.
PERSONAL Born 04/13/1948, St. Louis, MO, d, 3 children **DISCIPLINE** HISTORY, BRITISH HISTORY & CULTURE **EDUCATION** Univ of Sussex, BA, 70; Univ of Birmingham, PhD, 77. **CAREER** ASST PROF, 86-90, ASSOC PROF, 90-95, PROF, VANDERBILT UNIV, 95-. **HONORS AND AWARDS** British Coun Prize in the Humanities, 95. **MEMBERSHIPS** Am Hist Asn; North Am Confr on British Studies; Soc for the Study of Labour Hist (UK). **RESEARCH** Mod Brit hist. **SELECTED PUBLICATIONS** Auth, Radical Expression: Political Language, Ritual, and Symbol in England, 1790-1850, Oxford Univ Press, 94; Our Real Constitution: Trial Defence and Radical Memory in the Age of Revolution, Rereading the Constitution, Cambridge Univ Press, 96; Turn, turn, turn: Victorian Britain's Postmodern Season, J of Victorian Culture, 96; Signs of the Social, J of British Studies, 97; coauth, The Nineteenth-Century Gentleman Leader Revisited, Soc Hist, 97. **CONTACT ADDRESS** Dept of Hist, Vanderbilt Univ, Nashville, TN, 37235. **EMAIL** epsteinj@ctrvax.vanderbilt.edu

ERENBERG, LEWIS
DISCIPLINE HISTORY **EDUCATION** Mich Univ, PhD. **CAREER** Fulbright lectr, Univ Munich, 90-91. **RESEARCH** American History. **SELECTED PUBLICATIONS** Auth, The War in American Culture, Univ Chicago Press, 96; Things to Come: Swing Bands, Bepop and the Rise of a PostwarJazz Scene, Recasting America: Culture and Politics in the Age of the Cold War, Univ Chicago Press, 89; Steppin' Out: New York City Nightlife and the Transformation of American Culture, 1890-1930, Univ Chicago Press, 84; ed, Swingin' The Dream: Big Band Jazz and The Rebirth of American Culture, Univ Chicago, 98 **CONTACT ADDRESS** Fine Arts Dept, Loyola Univ, Chicago, 6525 N. Sheridan Rd., Chicago, IL, 60626. **EMAIL** lerenbe@wpo.it.luc.edu

ERICKSON, CHARLOTTE
PERSONAL Born 10/23/1900, Oak Park, IL, m, 1952, 2 children **DISCIPLINE** HISTORY **EDUCATION** Augustana Col, BA, 45, DHumL, 77; Cornell Univ, MA, 47, PhD (hist), 52. **CAREER** Res assoc, Nat Inst Econ and Social Res, London, 52-55; from asst lectr to lectr, 55-67, sr lectr econ hist, 67-79, PROF ECON HIST, LONDON SCH ECON, 79-, Gilmore fel, Cornell Univ, 54; Guggenheim fel, 66-67; Sherman Fairchild Distinguished Scholar, Calif Inst Technol, 76-77; comt mem social and econ hist, Soc Sci Res Coun, 76-79. **MEMBERSHIPS** AHA; Orgn Am Historians; Econ Hist Asn; Hist Econ Soc; Brit Asn Am Studies (secy, 67-75); fel Royal Hist Soc. **RESEARCH** Immigration history; history of the labor movement. **SELECTED PUBLICATIONS** Auth, The European Experience of Fertility Decline--A Quiet Revolution, 1850-1970, Eng Hist Rev, Vol 111, 96; Calvinists Incorporate--Welsh Immigrants on Ohio Industrial Frontier, Economic Hist Rev, Vol 50, 97; A Century of European Migrations, 1830-1930, Economic Hist Rev, Vol 46, 93; Emigration and Immigration--The Old World Confronts the New, Vol 2, of American Immigration and Ethnicity, J Am Ethnic Hist, Vol 13, 94. **CONTACT ADDRESS** 30 Hartham Rd, London, N 7 9JG.

ERICKSON, DANIELE NATHAN
PERSONAL Born 07/30/1958, Sioux Falls, SD **DISCIPLINE** LATIN, GREEK **EDUCATION** Concordia Coll Moorhead Minn, BA, 81; Tex Tech Univ, MA, 85; Syracuse Univ, PhD, 90. **CAREER** Instr, Newport High School, 82-86; instr, The Louisiana School LA,86-93; asst prof, Univ NDak, 98-. **HONORS AND AWARDS** Grad magna cum laude, Concordia Coll, 81; Who's Who Among America's Teachers, 94. **MEMBERSHIPS** Am Philol Asn; Am Council on the Teaching of Foreign Lang; Am Classical League. **RESEARCH** Teaching of Latin and Greek; Roman History. **SELECTED PUBLICATIONS** Introduction, translation and notes, Eutropius' Compendium of Roman History, 90. **CONTACT ADDRESS** 310 Walnut St, Apt #2, Grand Forks, ND, 58201. **EMAIL** danieric@badlands.nodak.edu

ERICKSON, ERLING A.
DISCIPLINE HISTORY **EDUCATION** Luther Univ, BA, 58; ND Univ, MA, 59; IA Univ, PhD, 67. **CAREER** Prof emer, 69-, Univ Pacific. **RESEARCH** Business hist. **SELECTED PUBLICATIONS** Auth, Banking in Frontier Iowa, IA State Univ. **CONTACT ADDRESS** Hist Dept, Univ Pacific, Pacific Ave, PO Box 3601, Stockton, CA, 95211.

ERICKSON, GERALD M.
PERSONAL Born 09/23/1927, Amery, WI, m, 1951, 3 children **DISCIPLINE** CLASSICAL LANGUAGES **EDUCATION** Univ Minn, BS, 54, MA, 56, PhD (classics), 68. **CAREER** Teacher, Edina-Morningside Pub Schs, 56-65 and 66-67; vis lectr Latin, 65-66, asst prof Latin and Greek, 67-70, ASSOC PROF CLASSICS, UNIV MINN, MINNEAPOLIS, 70-, Consult classics, Am Coun Teaching Foreign Lang Annual Bibliog Foreign Lang Teaching, 69-; reader, Col Entrance Exam Bd, Advan Placement, 75-76, chief reader designate, 77, chief reader, 78. **MEMBERSHIPS** Am Class League; Class Asn Mid W and S; Am Philol Asn. **RESEARCH** Language teaching, methods and materials; madness and deviant behavior in Greece and Rome; computer based instruction for teaching vocabulary development, technical terminology and ancient Greek. **SELECTED PUBLICATIONS** Auth, Reading Classical Latin--The 2nd Year, Mod Lan J, Vol 77, 93. **CONTACT ADDRESS** Dept of Classics, Univ of Minn, 310 Folwell Hall, Minneapolis, MN, 55455.

ERICKSON, NANCY LOU
PERSONAL Born 07/14/1941, Berea, OH, m, 1964, 2 children **DISCIPLINE** HISTORY, ENGLISH **EDUCATION** Kent State Univ, BS, 61; Univ IL, Urbana, AM, 64; Univ NC, Chapel Hill, PhD(hist), 70. **CAREER** Teacher hist, Champaign Sr High Sch, IL, 63-64; teacher, Maine Twp High Sch West, Des Plaines, IL, 64-66; assoc prof to prof hist, Erskine Col, 74-, dir of institutional res, 88-; Lilly Scholar Hist, Duke Univ, 76-77. **HONORS AND AWARDS** Excellence in Teaching Award, 78; Renaissance Person of the Year, 92. **MEMBERSHIPS** Am Hist Asn; Orgn Am Historians; Coun Faith & Hist. **RESEARCH** Comparative cultures; United States-Soviet Union; national character; 17th century America. **CONTACT ADDRESS** Erskine Col, Hc 60, Due West, SC, 29639-9801. **EMAIL** nde@erskine.edu

ERICKSON, RAYMOND FREDERICK
PERSONAL Born 08/02/1941, Minneapolis, MN, m, 1982 **DISCIPLINE** MUSICOLOGY **EDUCATION** Whittier Col, BA, 63; Yale Univ, PhD(hist of music), 70. **CAREER** Actg instr music, Yale Univ, 68-70; res fel, IBM Syst Res Inst, 70-71; asst prof, 71-74, assoc prof, 74-81, prof music, 82-, dean of arts & humanities, 93-, Queens Col, NY; doctoral fac, music, CUNY Grad School, 76-; assoc fel, Pierson Col, Yale Univ, 71-; consult, Nat Endowment for Humanities, 73, prin investr grant, 73-74; dir, 13 NEH Summer Insts, Aston Magna Acad, 78-; chemn & founding dir, Aaron Copland Sch of Music, 78-81; adj prof, Sch Advan Technol, SUNY Binghamton, 82-. **HONORS AND AWARDS** Omicron Delta Kappa, Pi Delta Phi; Res Fel, IBM Systems Res Inst, 70-71; Alexander von Humboldt Found, 77-78, 84-85; NEH Res Fel, 73-74. **MEMBERSHIPS** Am Musicol Soc; Medieval Acad Am; Board of Dir, VP, 97-99, Alexander von Humboldt Asn of Am; Am Bach Soc. **RESEARCH** European and American cultural history, 17th and 18th centuries; medieval polyphony; computer applications in musicology; historical performance practice; improvisation. **SELECTED PUBLICATIONS** Auth, Music analysis and the computer, 68 & A general purpose system for computer-aided music research, 69, J Music Theory; The DARMS Project: A status report, Computers & Humanities, 75; DARMS: A Reference Manual, private publ; Musicomp '76 and the state of DARMS, Col Music Soc Symp; J S Bach, The Six Brandenbury Concertos (rec), Smithsonian Collection of Rec, 77; Musica enchiriadis and Scolica enchiriadis, Yale Univ Press, 95; ed, Schubert's Vienna, Yale Univ Press, 97. **CONTACT ADDRESS** Aaron Copland Sch of Music, Queens Col, CUNY, 6530 Kissena Blvd, Flushing, NY, 11367-1597.

ERICSON, ROBERT EDWARD
PERSONAL Born 07/19/1926, Poplar, MT, m, 1952, 3 children **DISCIPLINE** THEATRE HISTORY AND THEORY **EDUCATION** Pac Univ, BS, 51; Ind Univ, MA, 54; Univ Ore, PhD, 70. **CAREER** Grad asst theatre, Ind Univ, 53-54; asst prof, Radford Col, 54-55; instr, Columbia Basin Jr Col, 55-56; asst prof, Pac Univ, 56-60; grad asst, Univ Ore, 60-63; asst prof, Ore Col Educ, 63-64; dir univ theatre, Univ Nev, 64-70; ASSOC PROF THEATRE ARTS, BOISE STATE COL, 70-, CHMN DEPT, 71-. **MEMBERSHIPS** Am Theatre Asn; Rocky Mountain Theatre Conf. **RESEARCH** American theatre history; cinema theory and history; classical theatre. **SELECTED PUBLICATIONS** Auth, Russia and The Nis in the World Economy--East West Investment, Financing and Trade, Slavic Rev, Vol 54, 95. **CONTACT ADDRESS** 2505 Sunrise Rim, Boise, ID, 83705.

ERISMAN, FRED RAYMOND
PERSONAL Born 08/30/1937, Longview, TX, m, 1961, 1 child **DISCIPLINE** AMERICAN STUDIES & LITERATURE **EDUCATION** Rice Inst, BA, 58; Duke Univ, MA, 60; Univ Minn, Minneapolis, PhD(Am studies), 66. **CAREER** From instr to assoc prof, 65-77, actg dean, Col Arts & Sci, 70-71 & 72-73, dir honors prog, 72-74, prof English, Tex Christian Univ, 77-, Co-ed, The French-American Rev J, 76-; book rev ed, Soc Sci J, 78-82; publ ed & mem exec bd, Int Res Soc Children's Lit, 81-83; Hess fel, Univ Minn, 81; Kinnucan Arms Chair fel, Buffalo Bill Hist Ctr, 82; chrmn, dept English. **HONORS AND AWARDS** Lorraine Sherley Prof of Literature, 86; Phi Beta Kappa, 88. **MEMBERSHIPS** Am Studies Asn; MLA; Orgn Am Historians; Western Lit Asn; Popular Cult Asn. **RESEARCH** American popular literature; American regional and environmental literature; detective and suspense fiction. **SELECTED PUBLICATIONS** Auth, The environmental crisis and presentday romanticism, Rocky Mountain Soc Sci J, 73; The romantic regionalism of Harper Lee, Ala Rev, 73; Frederic Remington, Western Writers Ser, Boise State Univ, 75; Prolegomena to a theory of American life, Southern Quart, 76; Romantic reality in the spy stories of Len Deighton, Armchair Detective, 77; Jack Schaefer: The writer as ecologist, Western Am Lit, 78; Western regional writers and the uses of place, J of the West, 80; co-ed (with Richard W Etulain), Fifty Western Writers, Greenwood Press, 82; Barnboken i USA, 86; contribur, A Literary History of the American West, 87; Laura Ingalls Wilder, Western Writers Ser, 94; Updating the Literary West; 97. **CONTACT ADDRESS** Dept of English, Texas Christian Univ, Box 297270, Fort Worth, TX, 76129-0002. **EMAIL** f.erisman@tcu.edu

ERLEBACHER, ALBERT
PERSONAL Born 09/28/1932, Ulm Wurttemberg, Germany, m, 1961, 3 children **DISCIPLINE** AMERICAN HISTORY **EDUCATION** Marquette Univ, BA, 54, MS, 56; Univ Wis, PhD, 65. **CAREER** Asst prof hist, Wis State Univ, Oshkosh, 62-65; from asst prof to assoc prof, 65-77, head div humanities, 75-79, PROF HIST, DEPAUL UNIV, 77-, HEAD DIV COMMON STUDIES, 80-. **MEMBERSHIPS** Orgn Am Historians; AHA; Am Professors for Peace in Middle East. **RESEARCH** History of insurance regulation; progressive period, political and economic aspects; American foreign relations since 1900. **SELECTED PUBLICATIONS** Auth, The Party Of Lincoln, Am Heritage, Vol 45, 94. **CONTACT ADDRESS** Dept of Hist, DePaul Univ, 2323 N Seminary, Chicago, IL, 60614.

ERLMANN, VEIT
DISCIPLINE MUSIC HISTORY **EDUCATION** Berlin; Cologne, PhD, 78. **CAREER** Prof & Endowed ch; past fac, Univ Natal, Univ Chicago, Unive Witwatersrand in Johannesburg & Free Univ Berlin. **RESEARCH** Music and globalizatio; music, and the politics of broadcasting in Cameroon; critical issues concerning the role of music in late modernity. **SELECTED PUBLICATIONS** Auth, African Stars, Studies in Black South African Performance and Nightsong, Univ Chicago Press, Performance, Power and Practice in South Africa, Univ Chicago Press. **CONTACT ADDRESS** School of Music, Univ of Texas at Austin, 2613 Wichita St, Austin, TX, 78705.

ERMARTH, ELIZABETH D.
PERSONAL Born 11/30/1939, Denver, CO, m, 1977, 1 child **DISCIPLINE** CULTURAL HISTORY & THEORY **EDUCATION** Carleton Col, BA, 61; Univ Calif, Berkeley, MA, 63; Univ Chicago, PhD, 71. **CAREER** Instr, Northwestern Univ, 69-71; Adj Asst Prof, Dartmouth Col, 72-74; Asst Prof, Reed Col, 74-78; Vis Prof, Univ Stockholm, 82;Fac, Dartmouth Inst, 90-92; Vis Prof, Univ Gothenburg, 93; Asst Prof, 79-82, Assoc Prof, 82-85; Prof, 85-94, Presidential Res Prof, 91-94, Univ Md, Baltimore; Dir, Postgrad sch, Saintsbury Prof of Eng Lit, 94-. **HONORS AND AWARDS** Saintsbury Ch, Edinburgh Univ, 94-; Sr Fulbright Fellow, 92-93; Overseas Fellow, Churchill Col, 92-93; Special Res Initiative Grant, Univ Md, 92-93; Univ Md Res Initiative Grant, 87-88, Fac Fellow, 84; NEH Fellow, 80; Mellon Summer Fellow, 75, 76, 77., Ed bd of Tulsa Studies, Time and Society. **MEMBERSHIPS** Modern Lang Asn; NE Modern Lang Asn; Soc for Dada and Surrealism; Int Asn of Philos and Lit; Soc for Lit & Sci. **RESEARCH** Interdisciplinary discussion of contemporary challenges to humanist culture & to representation in art & politics & to humanist cul-

ture generally. **SELECTED PUBLICATIONS** Auth, On Having a Personal Voice, Changing Subjects: The Making of Feminist Criticism, Routledge, 93; auth, Ph(r)ase Time: Chaos Theory and Postmodern Reports on Knowledge, Time & Soc, 4:1, 91-110, 95; auth, The Novel in History, 1840-1895, Routledge, 97; auth, Realism and Concensus in the English Novel: Time, Space, and Narrative, Edinburgh Univ Press, 98. **CONTACT ADDRESS** Dept of English, Edinburgh Univ, David Hume Twr, George Sq, Edinburgh, ., EH8 934. **EMAIL** elizabeth.ermarth@ed.ac.uk

ERMARTH, HANS MICHAEL
PERSONAL Born 03/02/1944, Chicago, IL, m, 2 children **DISCIPLINE** HISTORY **EDUCATION** Wittenberg Univ, BA, 65; Univ Chicago, MA, 67, PhD(hist), 73. **CAREER** Asst prof, 71-78, assoc prof, 79-84, prof hist, 85- , Dartmouth Col. **HONORS AND AWARDS** Berman-Marshall, 84-85. **MEMBERSHIPS** AHA. **RESEARCH** Modern European intellectual history; modern Germany; theory of history. **SELECTED PUBLICATIONS** Auth, Wilhelm Dilthey: The Critique of Historical Reason, Univ Chicago, 6/78; Hermeneutics Old and New, The Monist, 4/81; ed, America and the Shaping of Germany, 1945-1955, Berg, 93. **CONTACT ADDRESS** Dept of History, Dartmouth Col, 6107 Reed Hall, Hanover, NH, 03755-3506. **EMAIL** michael.ermarth@dartmouth.edu

ERNST, ELDON G.
PERSONAL Born 01/27/1939, Seattle, WA, m, 1959, 5 children **DISCIPLINE** HISTORY **EDUCATION** Yale, PhD, 68, MA, 65; Colgate Roch, MDiv, 64; Linfield Col, BA, 61 **CAREER** Prof, 67-82 Am Bapt Sem; Prof, 82-90, Grad Theol Un; Prof, 90-pres, Am Bapt Sem **MEMBERSHIPS** Am Soc of Church Hist; Am Hist Asoc; Am Acad of Relig; Calif Historical Soc **RESEARCH** American Social Christianity; California Religious History; History of Religion in North American Pacific Region **SELECTED PUBLICATIONS** Coauth, Pilgrim Progression The Protestant Experience in California, Fithian Press, 93; Auth, Without Help or Hindrance Religious Identity in American Culture, University Press of America, Inc, 87 **CONTACT ADDRESS** 1855 San Antonio Ave, Berkeley, CA, 94707. **EMAIL** rjeernst@aol.com

ERNST, JOSEPH ALBERT
PERSONAL Born 08/19/1931, Brooklyn, NY, m, 1956, 5 children **DISCIPLINE** UNITED STATES HISTORY **EDUCATION** Brooklyn Col, BA, 56; Univ Wis-Madison, MA, 58, PhD (hist), 62. **CAREER** Instr hist, Univ Wis, 61-62, vis lectr, 67; asst prof, San Fernando Valley State Col, 62-67 and Univ Calif, Los Angeles, 67-68; assoc prof, 68-71, PROF HIST, YORK UNIV, 71-. **RESEARCH** American Revolution; economic history of colonial America. **SELECTED PUBLICATIONS** Auth, The Privileges of Independence--Neomercantilism and the American Revolution, Rev Am Hist, Vol 22, 94. **CONTACT ADDRESS** Dept of Hist, York Univ, Toronto, ON, M3J 1P3.

ERNST, ROBERT
PERSONAL Born 03/01/1915, New York, NY, m, 1950, 2 children **DISCIPLINE** MODERN HISTORY **EDUCATION** Columbia Univ, AB, 36, PhD, 47; Brown Univ, AM, 37. **CAREER** From instr to assoc prof, 46-58, PROF HIST, ADELPHI UNIV, 58-, Huntington Libr grant-in-aid, 60. **MEMBERSHIPS** AHA; Orgn Am Historians; AAUP; Immigration Hist Soc. **RESEARCH** Immigration to the United States in the nineteenth century and ethnic groups in the United States; Revolutionary and early national period of the United States; biography: Bernarr Macfadden. **SELECTED PUBLICATIONS** Auth, Low, Nicholas--Merchant and Speculator in Postrevolutionary New York, NY Hist, Vol 75, 94; Low, Issac and the American Revolution, NY Hist, Vol 74, 93; New York in the Age of the Constitution, 1775-1800, NY Hist, Vol 74, 93; Benson, Egbert, Forgotten Statesman of Revolutionary New York, NY Hist, Vol 78, 97. **CONTACT ADDRESS** Dept of Hist, Adelphi Univ, Garden City, NY, 11530.

ERRINGTON, JANE
DISCIPLINE HISTORY **EDUCATION** Trent Univ, BA; Toronto, Bed; Queen's Univ, MA, PhD. **CAREER** High School tchr; prof, dept hd, history, Royal Milit Col. **RESEARCH** History of colonial societies in North America, role of women in colonial society; life of apprentices and indentured servants in the colony in the first half of the nineteenth century. **SELECTED PUBLICATIONS** Auth, Wives and Mothers, Schhol Mistresses and Scullery Maids. **CONTACT ADDRESS** Royal Military Col Canada, PO Box 17000, Kingston, ON, K7K 7B4.

ERSHKOWITZ, HERBERT J.
DISCIPLINE AMERICAN HISTORY **EDUCATION** NY Univ, PhD. **CAREER** Prof, Temple Univ. **RESEARCH** Biog of the Philadelphia merchant, polit, and relig leader John Wanamaker. **SELECTED PUBLICATIONS** Auth, Business Attitudes toward American Foreign Policy, 1900-1914, 67; Political Behavior in the Jacksonian State Legislatures, J of Am Hist, 72; Origin of the Whig and Democratic Parties: New Jersey Politics, 1820-1837, 82; The Second Party System in New Jersey, NJ Hist, 90; History of the Philadelphia Gas Works, 92. **CONTACT ADDRESS** Temple Univ, Philadelphia, PA, 19122.

ERWIN, JOANNE
DISCIPLINE STRINGED INSTRUMENTS **EDUCATION** Univ Ill, BM, MM; Univ N Tex, PhD. **CAREER** Asst prof; act dir, Mus Edu Div, Oberlin Col, 96; pres.. **HONORS AND AWARDS** Dir, Oberlin Coll String Preparatory Prog; dir Suzuki Sch for violin and cello; founder, conductor, Symphonetta of the Northern Ohio Youth Orchestra. **MEMBERSHIPS** Pres, Ohio String Tchr(s) Assn. **SELECTED PUBLICATIONS** Contribu, Am String Tchr Jour, Suzuki Jour, Tchg Mus. **CONTACT ADDRESS** Dept of Mus, Oberlin Col, Oberlin, OH, 44074. **EMAIL** ferwin@oberlin.edu

ESCOTT, PAUL DAVID
PERSONAL Born 07/33/1947, St. Louis, MO, m, 1968, 1 child **DISCIPLINE** HISTORY **EDUCATION** Harvard Univ, BA, 69; Duke Univ, MA, 72, PhD (hist), 74. **CAREER** Asst prof, 74-79, ASSOC PROF HIST, UNIV NC, CHARLOTTE, 79-, Whitney M Young, Jr Mem Found acad fel hist, 75-76. **HONORS AND AWARDS** Mayflower Cup, 79. **MEMBERSHIPS** Southern Hist Asn. **RESEARCH** The Old South; slavery; the South in the 20th century. **SELECTED PUBLICATIONS** Auth, The Uses of Gallantry--Virginians and the Origins of Stuart, J. E. B. Historical Image, Va Mag Hist Biography, Vol 103, 95. **CONTACT ADDRESS** Dept of Hist, Univ NC, Charlotte, NC, 28223.

ESHERICK, JOSEPH WHARTON
PERSONAL Born 08/14/1942, Rose, CA, 2 children **DISCIPLINE** CHINESE HISTORY **EDUCATION** Harvard Col, BA, 64; Univ Calif, Berkeley, MA, 66, PhD (hist), 71. **CAREER** Asst prof, 71-76, ASSOC PROF CHINESE HIST, UNIV ORE, 76-. **RESEARCH** Modern Chinese history; Chinese rural society and political economy. **SELECTED PUBLICATIONS** Auth, The Amerasia Spy Case--Prelude to Mccarthyism, Rev Am Hist, Vol 25, 97. **CONTACT ADDRESS** Hist Dept, Univ of Ore, Eugene, OR, 97402.

ESKEW, HARRY LEE
PERSONAL Born 07/02/1936, Spartanburg, SC, m, 1965, 2 children **DISCIPLINE** HYMNOLOGY, AMERICAN MUSIC HISTORY **EDUCATION** Furman Univ, BA, 58; New Orleans Baptist Theol Sem, MSM, 60; Tulane Univ, PhD(musicol), 66; La State Univ, MLIS, 95. **CAREER** Assoc prof, 65-75, Prof Music Hist & Hymnol, New Orleans Baptist Theol Sem, 75-, Music Librarian, 89-; Am Asn Theol Schs fel, Univ Erlangen, 70-71; mem Baptist hymnal rev comt, Southern Baptist Sunday Sch Bd, 73-75, 89-91; ed, The Hymn Quart, Hymn Soc Am, 76-. **MEMBERSHIPS** The Hymn Soc in the U.S. and Canada; Southern Baptist Hist Soc; Southern Baptist Church Music Conf; Music Libr Asn. **RESEARCH** Church music; American folk and popular hymnody. **SELECTED PUBLICATIONS** Auth, American Folk Hymnody, Bull Hymn Soc Gt Brit & Ireland, 71; Music in the Baptist Tradition, Rev & Expositor, 72; A Cultural Understanding of Hymnody, Hymn, 72; Hymnody Kit, Part II, Convention Press, 75; coauth (with Hugh T McElrath), Sing With Understanding: An Introduction to Christian Hymnology, rev ed, Church Street Press, 95; Gospel Hymnody, Shape-note Hymnody In: The New Grove Dictionary of Music and Musicians, Macmillan, 80; coauth, Singing Baptists, Church Street Press, 94. **CONTACT ADDRESS** New Orleans Baptist Theol Sem, 3939 Gentilly Blvd., New Orleans, LA, 70126-4858. **EMAIL** heskew8141@aol.com

ESLINGER, ELLEN T.
PERSONAL Chicago, IL **DISCIPLINE** HISTORY **EDUCATION** N IL Univ, BA, 77; Univ Chicago, MA, 82, PhD, 88. **CAREER** Asst Prof, Assoc Prof, 92 to 97-, DePaul Univ; Asst Prof, 88-92, James Madison Univ. **HONORS AND AWARDS** Richard H Collins Awd; KHS Best Article. **MEMBERSHIPS** AHA; OAH; SHA; SHEAR. **RESEARCH** Southern back country, colonial period, African American History. **SELECTED PUBLICATIONS** Auth, Citizens of Zion: The Social Origins of Camp Meeting Revivalism, Univ Tenn Press, forthcoming; The Beginnings of Afro-American Christianity Among Kentucky Baptists, in: The Buzzel about Kentucky: Interpretations of the Promised Land 1750-1830, ed, Craig Friend, Lexington, Univ Press of KY, forthcoming; The Shape of Slavery on Virginia's Kentucky Frontier 1775-1800, in: Diversity and Accommodation: Essays on the Cultural Composition of the Virginia Frontier, ed, Michael Puglisi, Knoxville, Univ Tenn Press, 97; The Shape of Slavery on the Kentucky Frontier 11775-1800, Register KY Hist Soc, 94. **CONTACT ADDRESS** Dept of History, DePaul Univ, 2320 N Kenmore Ave, Chicago, IL, 60614. **EMAIL** eesline@wppost.depaul.edu

ESPOSITO, JOHN L.
PERSONAL Born 05/19/1940, Brooklyn, NY, m, 1965 **DISCIPLINE** MIDDLE EAST STUDIES **EDUCATION** St. Anthony Col, BA, 63; St. John's Univ, MA, 66; Temple Univ, PhD, 74. **CAREER** Assoc Prof and Dept Chair, 75-84, Prof Relig Studies, Col Holy Cross, 84-, Loyola Prof Middle East Studies, 91-95, Prof Islamic Studies, 87-99, Prof and Dir Ctr Int Studies, 86-93; Adj Prof Diplomacy, The Fletcher Sch Law & Diplomacy, Tufts Univ, 91-95; Prof Relig & Int Affairs, and Prof Islamic Studies, Georgetown Univ, 93-, Dir, Ctr Muslim-Christian Understanding, 93-; Vis Prof, Oberlin Col, 86; ed, The Oxford History of Islam, Oxford Univ Press, 95-. **HONORS AND AWARDS** Fac Fel, Col Holy Cross, 77, 82-83, 90-91; Vis Schol, Ctr Study World Relig, Harvard Univ, 79-80; Elected Sr. Assoc, St. Antony's Col, Oxford Univ, 82-83; NEH Interpretive Res Grant, 90-93; U.S. Inst for Peace, 92-93. **MEMBERSHIPS** Middle East Studies Asn (Pres 88-89, Bd Dir, 83-86); Am Coun Study Islamic Soc (Bd Dir 84-, VPres 86-89, Pres 89-91); Am Soc Study Relig; Middle East Inst; Int Studies Asn; Asn Asian Studies; Maghreb Studies Asn; Am Acad Relig; Coun Study Relig; Col Theol Soc. **SELECTED PUBLICATIONS** Auth, The Islamic Threat: Myth or Reality?, Oxford Univ Press, 2nd rev ed, 95; ed-in-chief, The Oxford Encyclopedia of the Modern Islamic World, 4 vols, Oxford Univ Press, 95; coauth, Islam and Democracy, Oxford Univ Press, 96; Contemporary Islamic Revival Since 1988: A Critical Survey and Bibliography, Greenwood Press, 97; auth, Political Islam: Revolution, Radicalism or Reform?, Lynne Rienner Publ, 97; coauth, Islam, Gender and Social Change, Oxford Univ Press, 97; Muslims on the Americanization Path, Schol Press (forthcoming); Religion and Global Order, Univ Wales Press (forthcoming 98); author of numerous other publications and articles. **CONTACT ADDRESS** School of Foreign Services, Georgetown Univ, Washington, DC, 20057-1052. **EMAIL** espositj@gusun.georgetown.edu

ESSIN, EMMETT M.
DISCIPLINE HISTORY **EDUCATION** Austin Col, BA, 64; Univ Tex, MA, 65, PhD, 68. **CAREER** Prof. **SELECTED PUBLICATIONS** Auth, Shave Tails and Bell Sharpes: The History of the Army Mule, Univ Nebr, 97. **CONTACT ADDRESS** Dept of History, East Tennesee State Univ, PO Box 70717, Johnson City, TN, 37614-0717. **EMAIL** EssinE@etsu.edu

ESSLINGER, DEAN ROBERT
PERSONAL Born 06/08/1942, Clifton, KS, m, 1963, 3 children **DISCIPLINE** AMERICAN URBAN & SOCIAL HISTORY **EDUCATION** Univ KS, BA, 64; Univ Notre Dame, MA, 66, PhD(hist), 72. **CAREER** Assoc prof, 68-75, prof Hist, Towson State Univ, 75-, dir Fac Develop, 77-88, assoc Dean for Faculty Develoment & Research, 88-94, assoc vice-pres for Int Education, 94-97, ASSOC VICE-PRES FOR ACADEMIC PROGRAMS, 97-; Coordr, Baltimore Hist Res Group, 76-78. **HONORS AND AWARDS** Univ Merit Award, 84-85, 87-88; President's Award for Distinguished Service to the University, 88. **MEMBERSHIPS** Orgn Am Historians; Am Studies Asn; Immigration Hist Soc; Am Asn of Higher Ed; Am Asn State Colleges and Universities;Asn Am Colleges and Universities; Int Ed Asn; NAFSA; Nat Asn State Universities and Land Grant Colleges; Board of dirs, Am Cancer Soc-Baltimore; Asn Int Education Administrators; European Int Ed Asn; Maryland Sister State Comm; Oxford Capitol Foundation Board of Trustees. **RESEARCH** Social mobility of urban populations; social history of Baltimore; social history of Friends School in Baltimore, 1784-; Baltimore immigration history. **SELECTED PUBLICATIONS** Auth, American German and Irish Attitudes Toward Neutrality, 1914-1917: A Study of Catholic Minorities, Cath Hist Rev, 7/67; Immigrants and the City: Ethnicity and Mobility in a Nineteenth-Century Midwestern Community, Kennikat, 75; Catholics and Neutrality in the Great War, 1914-1917, In: Catholics in America, 76; Friends for 200 Years:A History of Baltimore: Oldest School, MD Hist Soc and Friends School, 83; co-auth, Maryland: A History of Its People, Johns Hopkins Univ, 86; chapter in Freedom's Doors, Balch Inst, 88; chapter in Unity and Diversity: Essays on Maryland Life and Culture, Kendall/Hunt, 89. **CONTACT ADDRESS** Academic Programs, Towson Univ, Towson, MD, 21252. **EMAIL** DEsslinger@Towson.edu

ESTES, JAMES MARTIN
PERSONAL Born 10/04/1934, Hartford, MI **DISCIPLINE** MODERN HISTORY **EDUCATION** Mich State Univ, BA, 56, MA, 58; Ohio State Univ, PhD (hist), 64. **CAREER** Lectr, 62-65, asst prof, 65-69, ASSOC PROF HIST, UNIV TORONTO, 69-, Dir, Centre Reformation and Renaissance Studies, Victoria Univ, 79-. **MEMBERSHIPS** Am Soc Reformation Res. **RESEARCH** German Reformation. **SELECTED PUBLICATIONS** Auth, Humanism and Culture of Renaissance Europe, 16th Century J, Vol 28, 97. **CONTACT ADDRESS** Dept of Hist, Univ of Toronto, Toronto, ON, M5S 1A1.

ESTEVEZ, VICTOR A.
PERSONAL Born 08/23/1938, Jersey City, NJ, d, 2 children **DISCIPLINE** CLASSICAL STUDIES **EDUCATION** Fordham Univ at Shrub Oak, BA, 62, MA, 63; Fordham Prep Sch in Bronx, MA, 65; Wis Univ, PhD, 74. **CAREER** Assoc prof; Univ Mo, 75-; past dir, Undergrad Stud; dir, TA's and the elementary Latin prog; written 3 crs, Univ Independent Study; comt & panels, Status of Women, Acad Appeals, Minority Aff, Student Publ, Curric, Campus Writing Bd, Univ Grievance Panel; adv, Gay and Lesbian Alliance; 2 yrs, Columbia Human Rights Comn, on bd dir, Commun Nurseries Inc, KOPN, The Mid-Mis souri AIDS Proj, Gay/Lesbian Telephone Helpline, Columbia Cares: Fundraising for AIDS in Mid-Missouri, the Missouri Task Force for Lesbian and Gay Concerns, ch 1 yr & Nat Gay and Lesbian Task Force; fac, Fordham Prep Sch in Bronx, 63-66; fac, Catholic Univ, Wash, 66-68; full-time fac, Howard & part-time,Trinity Co, 68-69; assoc dir, Carnegie Data

Bank Proj, Nat Catholic Educ Asn, 69-70; full-time fac, Univ Houston & part-time, Rice Univ, 74; tenured in, 81; vis prof, Leicester Univ, UK, 85-86. **HONORS AND AWARDS** Laus publica & cash prize, Certamen Capitolinum XXIV, 74; distinguised crse awd, Nat Univ Cont Educ Asn; Mid-Mo Chap, ACLU, Civil Libertarian Yr awd, 93. **RESEARCH** Hellenistic poetry; Augustan poetry. **SELECTED PUBLICATIONS** Auth, Chloe and the Fawn: The Structure of Odes I 23, Helios 7, 79-80; Aeneid II and the Helen and Venus Episodes, Classical J 76, 81; Quem tu, Melpomene: The Poet's Lowered Voice C. IV 3, Emer 50, 82; Oculos ad moenia torsit: On Aeneid 4. 220, Class Philol 77, 82 & Oratio Panegyrica in Fridericum Rudolphum Solmsen. **CONTACT ADDRESS** Dept of Classical Studies, Univ of Missouri-Columbia, 309 University Hall, Columbia, MO, 65211. **EMAIL** clstudve@showme.missouri.edu

ESTHUS, RAYMOND ARTHUR
PERSONAL Born 03/17/1925, Chicago, IL, m, 1955, 2 children **DISCIPLINE** UNITED STATES DIPLOMATIC HISTORY **EDUCATION** Fla Southern Col, AB, 48; Duke Univ, MA, 51, PhD (hist), 56. **CAREER** Instr hist, Brevard Col, 54-55; from instr to asst prof, Univ Houston, 55-57; from asst prof to assoc prof, 57-66, PROF HIST, TULANE UNIV, 66-, E Asia Lang and Area Ctr fel, Yale Univ, 66-67. **MEMBERSHIPS** Asn Asian Studies; Soc Historians of Am Foreign Rels (pres, 77). **RESEARCH** History of United States Far Eastern policy. **SELECTED PUBLICATIONS** Auth, The Papers of Wilson, Woodrow, J Southern Hist, Vol 61, 95. **CONTACT ADDRESS** Dept of Hist, Tulane Univ, New Orleans, LA, 70118.

ETHINGTON, PHILIP J.
DISCIPLINE US HISTORY **EDUCATION** Univ Mich, BA, 81; Stanford Univ, PhD, 89. **CAREER** Dir, ISLA: Inf Syst for Los Angeles proj; taught at, Brandeis Univ, 89-91 and Boston Univ, 92-93; Charles Warren Center for Studies in American History fel, 91-92; Schlesinger Libr for Res on the Hist of Women in Amer fel, 92-93; taught, Harvard-Radcliffe Univ; prof, Univ Southern Calif, 93-.. **RESEARCH** Social, political, & cultural history of the US. **SELECTED PUBLICATIONS** Auth, The Public City: The Political Construction of Urban Life in San Francisco, 1850-1900, NY: Cambridge UP, 94; Toward a 'Borderlands School' for American Urban Ethnic Studies, rev of Becoming Mexican American: Ethnicity, Cluture & Identity in Chicano Los Angeles, 1900-1945, in Amer Quart, 96; Urban Constituencies, Regimes, & Policy Innovation In the Progressive Era: An Analysis of Boston, Chicago, New York City, & San Francisco, Stud in Amer Political Develop 7:2, Cambridge UP, 93; coauth, The Intellectual Legacy of the Johns Hopkins University Seminary of History & Politics: Reconsidering the Genealogy of the Social Sciences, Studies in American Political Development 8:2, Cambridge UP, 94; co-ed, Polity Forum: Institutions and Instutionalism, Polity 28: 1, 95. **CONTACT ADDRESS** Dept of History, Univ Southern Calif, University Park Campus, Los Angeles, CA, 90089. **EMAIL** philipje@mizar.usc.edu

ETHRIDGE, ROBERT WYLIE
PERSONAL Born 11/12/1940, Monroe, MI, m **DISCIPLINE** EDUCATION **EDUCATION** Western MI Univ, AB 1962, AM 1970; Univ of MI Ann Arbor, PhD 1979. **CAREER** Detroit Public Schools, teacher 1962-69; Western MI Univ, area coordinator housing 1969-72, admin asst to pres 1972-79, sec bd of trustees 1979-81; EMORY UNIV, coordinator of equal opportunity programs, 1981, asst vice pres 1982-92, ASSOCIATE VP, 1992-, ADJUNCT ASST PROF, 1982-. **HONORS AND AWARDS** Achievement Award Northern Province KAY 1961-62; Community Bldg Award Black Monitor 1985; Citation for Public Service-Kalamazoo 1979; GA Public Relations Assn 1985; 2nd annual Civil and Human Rights Award-Intl, 1988; Proclamation State of Michigan House of Representatives, 1988; Assn of Official Human Rights Agencies. **MEMBERSHIPS** Mem CUPA, NACUBO 1981-, NAACP 1981-; 2nd vice pres 1981-82, 1st vice pres 1982-84 Amer Assoc for Affirmative Action; bd mem Natl Assault on Illiteracy Program 1983-; financial subcomm United Way 1984-; pres Amer Assoc for Affirmative Action 1984-88; bd mem American Contract Compliance Assn; mem Leadership Conference on Civil rights; United Way-Health Services Council 1984-; United Way-Admissions Panel 1984-; AAAA Natl Conf Planner 1982-84; mem Natl Inst for Employment Equity 1986-; chairman of the bd, Amer Contract Compliance Assoc, 1987-89; pres, Onyx Society of Western Michigan Univ, 1989-91; president, American Assn for Affirmative Action, 1990-92; bd of dirs, Western MI Univ Alumni Assn, 1989-, vp, 1993-94, pres, 1994-96; Community Friendship Inc, bd of dirs, 1994-96, treas, 1996-97; Georgia Nursing Foundation, bd of dirs, 1994-95; WMU Onyx Society, pres, 1994-96, 1997-; 100 Black Men of Dekalb, bd of dirs, 1997-98; Leadership Atlanta, membership comm, 1997-98; Race Relations Comm, 1997-98. **CONTACT ADDRESS** Emory Univ, 110 Administration Bldg, Atlanta, GA, 30322.

ETULAIN, RICHARD W.
PERSONAL Born 08/28/1938, Wapato, WA, m, 1961, 1 child **DISCIPLINE** HISTORY **EDUCATION** NW Nazarene Col, Nampa, Id, BA, 60; Univ Or Eugene, MA, 62, PhD, 66. **CAREER** Grad asst, 63-66, Univ Or; asst prof, 66-68, NW Nazarene Col; assoc pro, 68-69f, E Nazarene Col; NHPRC Fel, 69-70, Dartmouth Col; assoc prof to prof, dept chair, 70-74, Id St Univ; prof, 79-, Univ NM; editor, 79-85, NM Hist Rev, 91; dir, 89-, Center Amer W; vis prof, 73, 78, Univ Or; vis prof, 78, UCLA; vis prof, 97, Pepperdine Univ. **HONORS AND AWARDS** HNPRC Fel, 69-70; NEH Award, 73-74; Huntington Libr Fel, 74,84; USIA lectr, 10 countries; Alumnus of the Year, NW Nazarene Col, 75; Alumni Achievement Award, Univ Or, 91; Ann Res Lectr, Univ NM, 91; W Heritage Award, 96; John Caughey Award, 96; NM End for the Humanities, Excellence in Humanities, 98., Hilliard Distinguished Prof, Univ Nv, 85; Pettyjohn Distinguished Lectr, Washington St Univ, 92. **MEMBERSHIPS** W Lit Assoc **RESEARCH** Hist & lit of Amer West; historiography; recent Amer. **SELECTED PUBLICATIONS** Coed, Religion in Modern New Mexico, 97; auth, By Grit and Grace...Women Who Made the American West, 97; auth, A Portrait of Basques in the New World, 99; auth, With Badges and Bullets: Lawmen and Outlaws in the Old West, 99; ed, Does the Frontier Experience Make American Exceptional, 99; auth, Telling Western Stories: From Buffalo Bill to Larry McMurtry, 99. **CONTACT ADDRESS** Dept of History, Univ NM, Albuquerque, NM, 87131.

EUBANK, KEITH
PERSONAL Born 12/08/1920, Princeton, NJ, m, 1951, 2 children **DISCIPLINE** MODERN EUROPEAN AND RECENT AMERICAN HISTORY **EDUCATION** Hampden-Sydney Col, BA, 42; Harvard Univ, MA, 47; Univ Pa, PhD (Europ hist), 51. **CAREER** Instr hist, Bloomfield Col, 50-53; from asst prof to prof, NTex State Univ, 54-64; PROF HIST, QUEENS COL, NY, 64-, CHMN DEPT, 67-. **MEMBERSHIPS** AHA; Southern Hist Asn. **RESEARCH** Modern European history; United States and European diplomatic history. **SELECTED PUBLICATIONS** Auth, The Cuban Missile Crisis, J Am Hist, Vol 84, 97. **CONTACT ADDRESS** Dept of Hist, Queens Col, CUNY, Flushing, NY, 11367.

EUBANKS, EUGENE E.
PERSONAL Born 06/06/1939, Meadville, PA, m **DISCIPLINE** EDUCATION **EDUCATION** Edinboro St U, BA 1963; MI St U, PhD 1972. **CAREER** University of Missouri-KC, School of Education, prof, currently, dean 1979-89; Univ of DE, prof of educ admin 1972-74; Cleveland Pub Schs, tchr & admnstr 1963-70. **HONORS AND AWARDS** Articles published: A Study of Teacher Perception of Essential Teacher Attributes, 1974; Big-City Desegregation since Detroit, 1975; Rev Jesee L Jackson & PUSH Program for Excellence in Big-City Schools, 1977. **MEMBERSHIPS** Consult Cleveland Found; consult KC Pub Schs; consult MO St Dept Edn; consult NAACP Sch Desegregation Suit in Cleveland OH; Nat Allinc Blk Sch Edctrs; Natl Conf Profs Educ Admin; Phi Delta Kappa; Am Assn of Univ Profs; NAACP; PUSH; Urban League; pres, AACTE, 1988; mem, Natl Policy Bd of Educ Admin, 1988. **CONTACT ADDRESS** Sch Educ, Univ of Missouri, Kansas City, 5100 Rockhill Rd, Kansas City, MO, 64110.

EUBANKS, RACHEL AMELIA
PERSONAL San Jose, CA, d **DISCIPLINE** MUSICOLOGY **EDUCATION** Univ of CA Berkeley, BA 1945; Columbia Univ NY, MA 1947; Pacific Western Univ, DMA 1980; Fontabl, France, Eastman Schl of Music, UCLA, USC, additional studies. **CAREER** Wilberforce Univ, chmn Music Dept 1949-50; Albany State Coll, hd of Music Dept 1947; Eubanks Conser of Music, pres, founder, 1951. **HONORS AND AWARDS** Mosenthal flwhp Columbia Univ 1946; Musicianship: Vols I II and Tapes, Symphonic Requiem, Oratorio, Trio, & others; Alpha Mu Honor Society, Univ of CA Berkley 1946; Composition Award, Natl Assn Negro Musicians 1948; Symphonic Requiem, Korean Philharmonic, Los Angeles 1982; three songs, Res Musica, Baltimore 1985; Interlude #5, National Women's Music Festival, Bloomington, Indiana, 1988. **MEMBERSHIPS** Southeast Sym Assoc; LA County Art Mus; comm Afro-American Museum 1984-; Crenshaw Chamber of Commerce; mem, Natl Guild of Piano Teachers 1959-, Intl Congress on Women in Music 1984-, Musicians Union, Local 47, 1951-, Music Teacher's Natl Assn, Natl Assn of Negro Musicians 1949-; Ethnomusicology Society; American Musicological Society. **SELECTED PUBLICATIONS** Sonata for Piano, premiered by Helen Walker-Hill, Sonneck Society, 1993; Five Interludes for Piano, Vivace Press, 1995; The First & Fifth Interludes on CD, Leonarda Records. **CONTACT ADDRESS** Eubanks Conservatory of Music, 4928 Crenshaw, Los Angeles, CA, 90043.

EULA, MICHAEL JAMES
PERSONAL Born 05/18/1957, Passaic, NJ, m, 1993, 2 children **DISCIPLINE** HISTORY, LAW **EDUCATION** Rutgers Univ, BA (cum laude), 80; Calif State Univ, MA, 83; Univ of Calif at Irvine, MA, 84, PhD, 87; Newport Univ School of Law, JD, 98. **CAREER** Teaching asst/assoc, visiting asst prof of hist, Univ of Calif at Irvine, 91; lectr in hist, Calf State Univ, 89; PROF OF HIS, EL CAMINO COL, 89-. **HONORS AND AWARDS** Nat Endowment for the Humanities Fel, 90 & 95; New Jersey Hist Comn Fel, 92; Fac Res Fel, UCLA, 93; Phi Alpha Theta Iota Kappa, Rutgers Univ, 79. **MEMBERSHIPS** Am Hist Asn; Am Italian Hist Asn. **RESEARCH** Italian Americans; social history of ideas; legal history. **SELECTED PUBLICATIONS** Auth, Cultural Identity, Foodways, and the Failure of American Food Reformers Among Ital Immigrants in New York City 1891-1897, Ital Americana, forthcoming; auth, Using Theory in the Introductory History Course: One Strategy for a Postmodern Era, The Hist Teacher, forthcoming; Langage, Time, and the Formation of Self Among Italian-American Workers in New Jersey and New York 1880-1940, Ital Americana, 97; auth, Between Peasant and Urban Villager: Italian Americans of New Jersey and New York 1880-1980. The Structures of Counter Discourse, Peter Lang, 93; auth, Cultural Continuity and Cultural Hegemony: Italian Catholics in New Jersey and New York 1880-1940, Relig, 92; auth, Thinking Historically: Using Theory in the Introductory History Classroom, The Hist Teacher, 93. **CONTACT ADDRESS** Dept of History, El Camino Col, Torrance, CA, 90506.

EVANGELIOU, CHRISTOS C.
PERSONAL Born 12/23/1946, Greece, m, 1979 **DISCIPLINE** ANCIENT GREEK PHILOSOPHY **EDUCATION** Univ Athens, Greece, BA, 69; Emory Univ, MA, 76, PhD, 79. **CAREER** Vis prof, Miss State Univ, 80-81; adj asst prof, Emory Univ, 81-84; vis prof, Appalachian State Univ, 84-85; vis scholar, Villanova Univ, 85-86; asst prof, Towson Univ, 86-90; vis prof, Central Conn State Univ, 90-91; vis scholar, NY Univ, 93-94; full prof, Towson Univ, 96- . **HONORS AND AWARDS** VP of ISNS, 97- ; Ansley-Miller Scholar, Emory, 78-79; Othon-Athena Stathatos Scholar, Athens Acad Arts Sci, Greece, 74-76. **MEMBERSHIPS** Amer Philos Assn; Amer Philolog Assn; Soc Ancient Greek Philos; Intl Soc Metaphysics; Intl Assn Greek Philos; Intl Soc Neoplatonic Stud; Intl Ctr Philos Interdisc Res; Amer Rep S African Soc Greek Philos. **RESEARCH** History of Philosophy; Metaphysics; Ethics; Classics; and Hellenic Literature. **SELECTED PUBLICATIONS** Auth, A Paradox in the Nicomachean Ethics: The Mean Which Is Extreme, Mind and Nature, IV, 79, 8-17; The Ontological Basis of Aristotle's Theory of Categories, in Studies in Neoplatonism, IV, SUNY Press, 81; Eros and Immortality in the Symposium of Plato, Diotima, XIII, 85, 199-211; Aristotle's Doctrine of Predictables and Porphyry's Isagoge, Jour of the Hist of Philos, XXIII, 85, 15-35; Alternative Ancient Interpretations of Aristotle's Categories, in Language and Realigy, Univ Athens, Greece, 85; The Aristotelianism of Averroes and the Problem of Porphyry's Isagoge, Philosophia, 15-16, 85-86, 318-331; The Problem of the Homonymy of Being in Aristotle and Pletho, in Platonism and Aristltelianism, in the series Erevnal, (in Greek) 2, Univ Athens, Greece, 87; The Aristotelian Practical Philosophy and Medicine, in Philosophy and the Sciences, (in Greek) Univ Athens, Greece, 88; The Plotinian Reduction of Aristotle's Categories, Ancient Philosophy, VII, 88, 146-162; Professor MacIntyre and the Aristotelian Tradition of Virtue: The Case of Justice, in On Justice, Proceedings of the 3rd Intl Symposium on Justice, Univ Athens, Greece, 88; Individual and Society in the Philosophy of John Dewey, in Individual and Society, Athens, Greece, 89; 'Porphyry' Criticism of Christianity and the Problem of Augustine's Platonism, Dionysius, XIII, 89, 51-70; Plotinian Platonism and the Gnostic Challenge, in Relativism, Skepticism, and Criticism, Proceedings of the Third Intl Symposium on Skepticism, Ancient Olympia, aug 90, L. Bargeliotes, ed, Univ Athens, Greece; Socratic Intellectualism and Aristotelian Criticism, in The Philosophy of Socrates, Proceedings of Intl Conference on Greek Philos, Aug 90, Athens, Greece; Plotinus' Anti-Gnostic Polemic and Porphyry, in Neoplatonism and Gnosticism, R. Wallis and J. Bregman ed, Albany, SUNY Press, 92; The Plotinian Reduction of Aristotle's Categories, in Aristotle's Ontology, A. Preus and J. Anton, ed, SUNY Press, 92; Ancient Hellenic Philosophy and the African Connection, Skepsis, IV, 94, 14-75; Aristotle's Categories and Porphyry, in Philosophia Antiqua, 48, w. Verdenius and J. Van Winden, eds, Leiden, E.J. Brill, 88, 94; When Greece Met Africa: The Genesis of Hellenic Philosophy, Inst of Global Cultural Stud, SUNY at Binghamton, 94; Plotinus on the Stoic Set of Categories, Jour of Neoplatonic Stud, II, 2, 95, 20-36; The Hellenic Philosophy: Between Europe, Asia and Africa, Inst Global Cultural Stud, SUNY at Binghamton, 97; assoc ed, Skepsis, Intl Ctr of Philos and Interdisc Res, Univ Athens, Greece; co-ed, Journal of Neoplatonic Studies, Intl Soc for Neoplatonic Stud, Dowling Col. **CONTACT ADDRESS** Dept of Philosophy, Towson Univ, Towson, MD, 21204. **EMAIL** cevangeliou@towson.edu

EVANS, DAVID C.
DISCIPLINE HISTORY **EDUCATION** Stanford Univ, BA, 61; Princeton Univ, grad study, 61-62; Stanford Univ, MA, 69, PhD, 78. **CAREER** Prof & assoc dean, Sch Arts and Sci. **SELECTED PUBLICATIONS** Ed, The Japanese Navy in World War II; In the Words of Former Japanese Naval Officers, 2nd ed, Annapolis, Naval Inst Press, 86; co-ed, KAIGUN: Strategy, Tactics and Technology in the Imperial Japanese Navy, 1887-1941, Annapolis, Naval Inst Press, 97 & Ill Winds Blow, US Naval Inst Proc 123, 97. **CONTACT ADDRESS** Dept of Hist, Univ of Richmond, 28 Westhampton Way, Ryland Hal, Richmond, VA, 23173. **EMAIL** devans@richmond.edu

EVANS, DAVID HUHN
PERSONAL Born 01/22/1944, Boston, MA, m, 1990, 2 children **DISCIPLINE** MUSIC **EDUCATION** AB, Harvard, 65; MA, 67; PhD, 76; Univ of CA, Los Angeles. **CAREER** Prof of Music, Dir of Reg Studies, Ethnomusicology, Univ of Memphis, Tchg Asst Classics, 65-68; Tchg Asst, Folklore and My-

thology, Univ of CA, Los Angeles 66-69; Lecturer in Anthro, CA State Univ, Fullerton, 69-72; Lecturer in Folklore and Hist, Univ of CA, 72-; Asst Prof Anthro, 72-76, Assoc Prof Anthro, 76-78, Univ of CA, Fullerton; Assoc Prof of Music, Memphis State Univ, 78-81. **HONORS AND AWARDS** Commencement Latin Oration; Harvard Coll, 65; Faculty Res Grant, CA State Univ, Fullerton Found, 71, 72, 78; Seed Grant to Facilitate Learning, Memphis State Univ, 78; Chicago Folklore Prize, 81-82; Univ Distinguished Res Award, Memphis State Univ, 87; Grant, Partners of the Americas for recording Venezuelan traditional music, 89, 90; Grant, Tennessee Hum Council, 98. **RESEARCH** Afro Amer Folk music, **SELECTED PUBLICATIONS** Spec Ed, New Perspectives on the Blues, American Music 14 No4, pp393-526, 96; Shane K. Bernard, Swamp Pop: Cajun and Creole Rhythm and Blues, 96; Charles Wolfe, In Close Harmony: The Story of the Louvin Brothers, 97; Guido van Rijin, Roosevelt's Blues: African-American Blues and Gospel Songs on FDR, 97; Kenneth M. Johnson, The Johnson Family Singers: We Sang for Our Supper, 97; Sebastian Danchin, Blues Boy: The Life and Music of B.B. King, 98; Blues, in Garland Encyclopedia of World Music Vol3: The United States and Canada NY Garland (in press); Beale Street, Helena, Memphis, and Mississippi Valley, in Encyclopedia of Popular Music of the World, editors Mick Gidley, David Horn, Paul Oliver and John Shepherd London Cassell (in press). **CONTACT ADDRESS** Dept of Music, Univ of Memphis, Memphis, TN, 38152. **EMAIL** dhevans@cc.memphis.edu

EVANS, DONNA BROWDER
PERSONAL Columbus, OH, d **DISCIPLINE** EDUCATION **EDUCATION** OH State Univ, BSc 1958, MS 1964, PhD 1970. **CAREER** Univ of Cincinnati, asst prof 1969-73; Univ of Maine, prof/grad dean 1973-83; Skidmore Coll, prof/chair dept of educ 1983-87, Wayne State Univ, prof/dean of educ 1987-91; UNIVERSITY OF NORTH FLORIDA, PROFESSOR/DEAN, 1991-. **MEMBERSHIPS** Mem Alpha Kappa Alpha Sor Detroit Chapt; mem Coalition of 100 Black Women Albany 1984-87; mem Amer Assoc of Univ Women Saratoga Springs 1984-87; mem Links Inc Jacksonville Chap 1987-; bd of dirs Assoc Black Educators/Profs 1985-87; bd of dirs Soroptomist Intl 1985-87; bd dir Lake George Opera Festival; bd dir Task Force Against Domestic Violence Saratoga Spngs; Sophisticates Savannah Chap 1988-, Carrousels, Detroit Chap 1988-; Junior Achievement, Jacksonville, board of directors, 1991-. **SELECTED PUBLICATIONS** Reviewer Brooks Cole Publishing Co 1980-; editorial bd Journal of Reality Therapy 1984-; publications "Success Oriented Schools in Action" 1981, "A Conversation with William Glasser" 1982, "Opening Doors to the Future Through Education" 1984, "Reality Therapy, A Model for Physicians Managing Alcoholic Patients" 1984, "Curriculum Not Either-Or", 1991. **CONTACT ADDRESS** Col of Educ & Human Svcs, Univ of No Florida, 4567 St John's Bluff Rd, Rm 2543, Jacksonville, FL, 32224.

EVANS, DORINDA
PERSONAL Born 03/05/1944, Wakefield, MA **DISCIPLINE** ART HISTORY **EDUCATION** Univ Pa, MA, 67; Courtald Inst of Art, Univ London, PhD, 72. **CAREER** Mus curator, Nat Gallery of Art, Wash, 67-69; Asst Prof, Univ Ill, 72-74; Guest Curator, Philadelphia Mus of Art, 74-75; Guest Curator, Nat Portrait Gallery, Wash, 75-78; Asst Prof, Emory Univ, 78-84; Asn Prof, 84-. **HONORS AND AWARDS** Kress Foundation Fellow, 71-72; ACLS Grant-in-aid, 85; Smithsonian Sr Post-Doctoral Fellow, 86-87; Joshua C Taylor Res Fellow, 91. **MEMBERSHIPS** Col Art Asn; Hist of Am Art; Am Soc for 18th Cent Stud; Hist of Brit Art. **RESEARCH** Late 18th & 19th century Am painting. **SELECTED PUBLICATIONS** Auth, Benjamin West and his American Students, 80; auth, Mather Brown, Early American Artist in England, 82; auth, The Genius of Gilbert Stuart, 2/99. **CONTACT ADDRESS** Art Hist Dept, Emory Univ, Atlanta, GA, 30322.

EVANS, ELLEN LOVELL
PERSONAL Born 11/17/1930, Paris, France, m, 1953, 3 children **DISCIPLINE** MODERN EUROPEAN HISTORY **EDUCATION** Swarthmore Col, BA, 51; Univ Wis, MA, 52; Columbia Univ, PhD (mod Europ hist), 56. **CAREER** From instr to asst prof, 54-68, ASSOC PROF HIST, GA STATE UNIV, 68-. **MEMBERSHIPS** AHA; Southern Hist Asn; Conf Group Cent Europ Hist. **RESEARCH** Weimar Republic in Germany, Center Party; 19th and 20th century France and Germany. **SELECTED PUBLICATIONS** Auth, German Nationalism and Religious Conflict--Ideology, Politics, 1870-1914, Am Hist Rev, Vol 101, 96; Rural Protest in the Weimar Republic--The Free Peasantry in the Rhineland and Bavaria, Am Hist Rev, Vol 99, 94; Between Class and Confession--Catholic Burgertum in Rheinland 1794-1914, Cath Hist Rev, Vol 82, 96; Christian Labor Movement in Bavaria from the World War 1 to 1933, Am Hist Rev, Vol 97, 92. **CONTACT ADDRESS** Dept of Hist, Georgia State Univ, Atlanta, GA, 30303.

EVANS, EMORY GIBBONS
PERSONAL Born 01/21/1928, Richmond, VA, m, 1953, 3 children **DISCIPLINE** AMERICAN HISTORY **EDUCATION** Randolph-Macon Col, BA, 50; Univ Va, MA, 54, PhD (Am hist), 57. **CAREER** Instr hist, Darlington Sch, 50-52; instr, Univ Md, 56-58; from instr to asst prof, Univ Pittsburgh, 58-64; from assoc prof to prof hist, Northern Ill Univ, 64-76, chmn dept, 64-76, acting vpres and provost, 75-76; PROF HIST and CHMN DEPT, UNIV MD, COLLEGE PARK, 76-, Vis prof hist, Univ Va, 70. **MEMBERSHIPS** AHA; Southern Hist Asn; Orgn Am Historians. **RESEARCH** Early American history; 18th century southern and Virginia history. **SELECTED PUBLICATIONS** Auth, A Planters Republic--The Search for Economic Independence in Revolutionary Virginia, J Southern Hist, Vol 63, 97. **CONTACT ADDRESS** Dept of Hist, Univ of Md, College Park, MD, 20742.

EVANS, HARRY B.
DISCIPLINE LATIN POETRY, ROMAN TOPOGRAPHY **EDUCATION** NC Univ, PhD. **CAREER** Prof, Fordham Univ. **SELECTED PUBLICATIONS** Auth, Publica Carmina: Ovid's Books from Exile, 83; Water Distribution in Ancient Rome: The Evidence of Frontinus, 94. **CONTACT ADDRESS** Dept of Class Lang and Lit, Fordham Univ, 113 W 60th St, New York, NY, 10023.

EVANS, JAMES A.S.
PERSONAL Born 03/24/1931, Galt, ON, Canada **DISCIPLINE** CLASSICS **EDUCATION** Univ Toronto, BA, 52; Yale Univ, MA, 53, PhD, 57. **CAREER** Prof, Univ Western Ont, 55-60; vis lectr, Victoria Col, 60-61; vis asst prof, Univ Texas Austin, 61-62; fac mem hist, McMaster Univ, 62-72; prof, 72-96, dept head, 86-93, PROF EMER CLASSICS, UNIV BC, 96-; Gertrude Smith prof, Am Sch Class Stud (Athens), 91; non-resident fac mem, Cecil Green Col, 93-94; vis prof, Univ Wash, 97; Whitehead prof, Am Sch Class Stud (Athens), 98-99. **HONORS AND AWARDS** Fel, Royal Soc Can, 92. **MEMBERSHIPS** Mng comt, Am Sch Class Stud (Athens); Class Asn Can (pres 82-84); Asn Ancient Hist (secy treas 79-82). **SELECTED PUBLICATIONS** Auth, Social and Economic History of an Egyptian Temple in Greco-Roman Egypt, 61; auth, Procopius, 72; auth, Herodotus, 82; auth, Herodotus, Explorer of the Past: Three Essays, 91; auth, The Age of Justinian: The Circumstances of Imperial Power, 96; ed, Waterloo Rev, 57-60; ed, Vergilius, 63-73; ed Polis and Imperium: Studies in Honour of Edward Togo Salmon, 74; co-ed, Studies in Medieval and Renaissance History, 77-96;. **CONTACT ADDRESS** Classics Dept, Univ of British Columbia, Buch C625, Vancouver, BC, V6T 1Z1.

EVANS, JOAN
DISCIPLINE MUSICAL LIFE IN GERMANY DURING THE FIRST HALF OF THE 20TH CENTURY **EDUCATION** Boston Univ, PhD. **CAREER** Prof **SELECTED PUBLICATIONS** Auth, Hans Rosbaud: A Bio-Bibliography. **CONTACT ADDRESS** Dept of Music, Wilfrid Laurier Univ, 75 University Ave W, Waterloo, ON, N2L 3C5.

EVANS, JOHN KARL
PERSONAL Born 02/27/1946, Los Angeles, CA, m, 1971, 2 children **DISCIPLINE** HISTORY **EDUCATION** Univ Calif Los Angeles, BA, MA; McMaster Univ, PhD, 74. **CAREER** Prof **HONORS AND AWARDS** Outstanding Academic Bk Awd, 93. **RESEARCH** Roman history. **SELECTED PUBLICATIONS** Auth, Resistance Movements in the Ancient World, Univ Tokyo; War, Women and Children in Ancient Rome, Routledge, 91. **CONTACT ADDRESS** History Dept, Univ of Minnesota, Twin Cities, 614 Social Sciences Tower, 267 19th Ave. S, Minneapolis, MN, 55455. **EMAIL** evans002@tc.umn.edu

EVANS, JOHN WHITNEY
PERSONAL Born 08/06/1931, Kansas City, MO **DISCIPLINE** UNITED STATES CHURCH HISTORY **EDUCATION** St Paul Sem, Minn, MA, 57; Cath Univ Am, MA, 58; Univ Minn, PhD (hist, philos educl, 70. **CAREER** Instr social probs, Cathedral High Sch, Minn, 58-62; chaplain and lectr psychol and educ, Univ Minn, Duluth, 66-69; coord res campus ministry, Ctr Applied Res in Apostolate, Washington, DC, 69-71; dir, Nat Ctr Campus Ministry, Mass, 71-73; CHAPLAIN AND ASST PROF HIST AND RELIG STUDIES, COL ST SCHOLASTICA, 73-, Mem comn campus ministry, Nat Cath Educ Asn, 69-73; Underwood fel, 72-73. **HONORS AND AWARDS** Cath Campus Ministry Asn Serv Award, 73. **MEMBERSHIPS** Nat Cath Educ Asn; Soc Sci Study Relig; AHA; Am Cath Hist Asn; Relig Educ Asn. **RESEARCH** History and religion in American higher education; philosophy of education; student movements. **SELECTED PUBLICATIONS** Auth, Adapting to America--Catholics, Jesuits, and Higher Education in the 20th Century, Am Hist Rev, Vol 98, 93; Fremont, John, Charles Character as Destiny, Ore Hist Quart, Vol 94, 93; The Journals of the Lewis and Clark Expedition, March 23 June 9, 1806, Vol 7, Ore Hist Quart, Vol 94, 93; In Memoriam Cruni-can, Paul, Eugene 1928-1994, Cath Hist Rev, Vol 80, 94. **CONTACT ADDRESS** Off of Chaplain, Col of St. Scholastica, 1200 Kenwood Ave, Duluth, MN, 55811-4199.

EVANS, MICHAEL J.
DISCIPLINE HISTORY **EDUCATION** Univ of Wash, BA, MA; Univ of Mich, PhD. **CAREER** Tchg asst, Univ of Wash, 1960; tchg fel, Univ of Mich, 61-65; lectr in hist, Univ of Mich, Flint, 63; instr, asst prof, assoc prof, prof, Kenyon Col, 65-; interdisciplinary affil and prof of hist, 93-. **HONORS AND AWARDS** Campus rep, ACM/GLCA Czech Prog, 1996-; ACM/GLCA exec comm, Central Europ Studies Prog 1996-; acad policy comm, 1988-90; campus sen, 1983-4, 1968-70; ch, Judicial Comm, 1982; ch, dept hist, 1973-80. **MEMBERSHIPS** Ren Soc Am; OPH Roster Hum Scholars; Am Hist Assn; Ohio Hist Soc. **RESEARCH** Machiavelli, medieval and renaissance studies. **SELECTED PUBLICATIONS** Auth, Machiavelli and Castruccio: Reflections on the Vita. Machiavelli Studies, 91; rev, Hodges, Richard: Dark Age Economics, The Origins of Towns and Trade AD 600-1000; Tagliacozzo, Giorgio, ed: Vico and Marx; Pompa, Leon, ed: Vico, Selected Writings; Merriman, John, ed: French Cities in the Nineteenth Century; Dickinson, W Calvin: James Harrington's Republic. **CONTACT ADDRESS** Dept of Hist, Kenyon Col, Gambier, OH, 43022.

EVANS, ROGER S.
PERSONAL Born 01/25/1949, Columbus, OH, m, 1974, 2 children **DISCIPLINE** CLASSICAL & HELLENISTIC GREEK; ROMAN EMPIRE REPUBLIC; BYZANTINE THRU 10TH C **EDUCATION** Columbia Union Col, BA, 76; Aandrews Theol Sem, MDiv, 79; Ohio State Univ, MA, 91, PhD, 96. **CAREER** Adj prof, History, Ohio Wesleyan Univ, 91 & 97; vis prof, Chruch History, Ecumenical Theol Sem, 98; asst prof, church history, payne theol sem, 90-. **MEMBERSHIPS** N Amer Patristic Soc; Asn Seventh-Day Adventist Hist; Andrews Univ Sem Stud; Amer Soc Church Hist; Am Soc Ancient Hist; Amer Hist Soc; Amer Acad Relig. **SELECTED PUBLICATIONS** Rev, Reading the Apostolic Fathers, Jour Early Christian Stud, Hendrickson Publ, 96; Apocalypse of Paul: a Critical Edition of Three Long Latin Versions, Jour Early Christian Stud, 97; auth, A Biblical Theology of Drinking, Min: An Int Jour for Clergy, 93; Soteriologies of Early Christianity Within the Intellectual Context of the Early Roman Empire: Barnabas and Clement of Rome as Case Studies, Dumbarton Oaks, 98. **CONTACT ADDRESS** 2945 Princeville Dr., Pickerington, OH, 43147. **EMAIL** RSE121@aol.com

EVANS, SARA M.
PERSONAL Born 12/02/1943, McCormick, SC, m, 1966, 2 children **DISCIPLINE** HISTORY **EDUCATION** Univ NC, PhD, 76. **CAREER** Prof **RESEARCH** Women's studies; twentieth-century American social history. **SELECTED PUBLICATIONS** Auth, Personal Politics: The Roots of Women's Liberation in the Civil Rights Movement and the New Left, Knopf, 79; Born For Liberty: A History of Women in America, Free, 89; co-auth, Free Spaces: The Sources of Democratic Change in America, Harper & Row, 86; Wage Justice: Comparable Worth and the Paradox of Technocratic Reform, Univ Chicago, 89. **CONTACT ADDRESS** History Dept, Univ of Minnesota, Twin Cities, 614 Social Sciences Tower, 267 19th Ave S, Minneapolis, MN, 55455. **EMAIL** s-evan@tc.umn.edu

EVANS, WILLIAM MCKEE
PERSONAL Born 09/17/1923, St. Pauls, NC, 4 children **DISCIPLINE** AMERICAN HISTORY **EDUCATION** Univ NC, AB, 48, MA, 50, PhD (US hist), 65. **CAREER** Lectr hist, Westminster Col, Utah, 62-64; asst prof, Calif Lutheran Col, 64-68; from asst prof to assoc prof, 68-77, PROF HIST, CALIF STATE POLY-TECH UNIV, 77-. **HONORS AND AWARDS** Am Asn State and Local Hist Manuscript Prize, 66. **MEMBERSHIPS** AHA; Orgn Am Historians; Southern Hist Asn. **RESEARCH** The American South; comparative race relations; comparative slavery. **SELECTED PUBLICATIONS** Auth, Cherokee Americans--The Eastern Band of Cherokees in the 20th Century, J Southern Hist, Vol 59, 93. **CONTACT ADDRESS** Dept of Hist, California State Polytech Univ, Pomona, CA, 91768.

EVANS-GRUBBS, JUDITH
PERSONAL Born 11/30/1956, Atlanta, GA, m, 1979, 1 child **DISCIPLINE** CLASSICS **EDUCATION** Emory Univ, BA, 78; Amer School of Classical Studies, 78-79; Stanford Univ, PhD, 87. **CAREER** Assoc prof Classical Studies, Sweet Briar Col, 93-98; asst prof Classical Studies, Sweet Briar Col, 87-93; Tchg Fel, Stanford Univ, 83-84, 85-87; lctr, Intercollegiate Center for Classical Studies, 84-85. **HONORS AND AWARDS** Ntl Endowment for Humanities Fel for Col Tchrs, 97-98; NEH Summer Sem for Col Tchrs, Amer Acad Rome, 95; Jessie Ball Dupont Fel, Ntl Humanities Center, 93-94; Ntl Endowment Humanities Summer Stipend, 88; Mednick Grant, Va Found Independent Colleges, 88. **MEMBERSHIPS** Amer Philoi Assoc; Amer Soc Greek & Latin Epigraphy; Amer Soc Papyrologists; Assoc Ancient Historians; Classical Assoc Middle West & South; Classical Assoc Va; N Amer Patristics Soc; Women's Classical Caucus. **RESEARCH** Marriage and Family in Ancient Roman Society; Roman Imperial Law; Slaver in Ancient Rome; Women and Gender in Antiquity. **SELECTED PUBLICATIONS** Bk rev, The Virgin and the Bride: Idealized Womanhood in Late Antiquity, Classical Philoi, 98; Law and Family in Late Antiquity: the Emperor Constantine's Marriage Legislation, Oxford Univ Pr, 95; 'Pagan' and 'Christian' Marriage: the State of the Question, Jour Early Christian Studies, 94. **CONTACT ADDRESS** Dept of Classical Studies, Sweet Briar Col, Sweet Briar, VA, 24595. **EMAIL** evansgrubbs@sbc.edu

EVERGATES, THEODORE
PERSONAL Born 09/16/1940 **DISCIPLINE** MEDIEVAL HISTORY **EDUCATION** Brown Univ, AB, 62; Johns Hopkins Univ, PhD, 71. **CAREER** Asst prof, 73-79, ASSOC PROF HIST, WESTERN MD COL, 79-; Johns Hopkins Univ fel, 71-73; Nat Endowment for Humanities fel, 75-76; Am Council Learned Soc grant, 79. **MEMBERSHIPS** AHA; Medieval Acad Am. **RESEARCH** Medieval social and economic history; history of France. **SELECTED PUBLICATIONS** Auth, The Cartulary of Saint Nicaise of Reims, Speculum J Medieval Stud, Vol 69, 94; Customary Aids and Royal Finance in Capetian France--The Marriage Aid of Philip the Fair, Am Hist Rev, Vol 99, 94; The New Knighthood--A History of the Order of the Temple, Am Hist Rev, Vol 100, 95; An Episcopal Chancery in the 12th Century--The Case of Arras, Am Hist Rev, Vol 100, 95. **CONTACT ADDRESS** Dept of Hist, Western Maryland Col, 2 College Hill, Westminster, MD, 21157-4390.

EWELL, JUDITH
PERSONAL Parksley, VA **DISCIPLINE** LATIN AMERICAN HISTORY **EDUCATION** Duke Univ, AB, 65; Univ NMex, PhD(Latin Am hist), 72. **CAREER** Asst prof, 71-77, Assoc prof hist, Col William & Mary, 77-, Orgn Am States fel Venezuelan hist, 74-75; Fulbright vis lectr, Univ Catolica Andres Bello, Caracas, Venezuela, 79-80. Prof hist 84-; Newton Family Prof hist 88-, Fullbright vis lectr, Univ Andina Simon Bolivar, Equador, 94-95. Ch, hist dept, Col of William & Mary, 91-98. **HONORS AND AWARDS** Orgn Am States Essay prize, 82; Sturgis Leavitt Award, 83; Commonwealth of VA Outstanding Faculty Award, 89; pres, conf on Latin Am hist, 92; A.B. Thomas Award, 97. **MEMBERSHIPS** AHA; Latin Am Studies Asn; Mid Atlantic Coun Latin Am Studies; Conf Latin Am Hist; Rocky Mountain Coun Latin Am Studies. **RESEARCH** Twentieth Century Venezuela; Nineteenth Century Equador. **SELECTED PUBLICATIONS** Auth, Venezuela's crucial decade: The dictatorship of Marcos Perez Jimenez, Rev Interam, fall 77; The extradition of Marcos Perez Jimenez, J Latin American Studies, England, 11/77; The Caribbean and the law of the sea, In: The Restless Carribean, Praeger, 79; Indictment of a Dictator: The Extradition of Marcos Perez Jimenez, Tex A&M Univ Press, 81; The development of Venezuelan geopolitical analysis since World War II, J Interam Studies & World Affairs, 8/82; Venezuela: A Century of Change, C. Hurst and Stanford Univ, 84; Venezuela and the United States: From Monroe's Hemisphere to Petroleum's Empire, Univ GA, 96; co-ed, The Human Tradition in Twentieth Century Latin America, Scholarly Resources, 87; The Human Tradition in Nineteenth Century Latin America, Scholarly Resources, 89; The Human Tradition in Modern Latin America, Scholarly Resources, 97. **CONTACT ADDRESS** Dept of History, Col of William and Mary, PO Box 8795, Williamsburg, VA, 23187-8795. **EMAIL** jxewel@factstaff.wm.edu

EYCK, FRANK
PERSONAL Born 07/13/1921, Berlin, Germany, m, 1955, 2 children **DISCIPLINE** MODERN HISTORY **EDUCATION** Oxford Univ, BA, 49, MA, 54, BLitt, 58. **CAREER** News subed, Brit Broadcasting Corp, 49-56; temp asst lectr mod hist, Univ Liverpool, 58-59; lectr mod Europ hist, Univ Exeter, 59-68; PROF HIST, UNIV CALGARY, 68-, Vchmn coun, Inter-Univ Ctr Post-Grad Studies, Dubrovnik, Yugoslavia, 74-. **MEMBERSHIPS** AHA; Can Hist Asn; fel Royal Hist Soc; Royal Commonwealth Soc. **RESEARCH** German history; biography; church and state diplomatic history. **SELECTED PUBLICATIONS** Auth, Word and Power--Gentz, Friedrich as a Political Writer, Cent Europ Hist, Vol 28, 95; Bismarck and Mitteleuropa, Cent Europ Hist, Vol 28,95; Rhineland Radicals--The Democratic Movement and the Revolution of 1848-1849, Am Hist Rev, Vol 97, 92; Bucher, Lothar 1817-1892--A Political Life Between Revolution and Civil Service, Cent Europ Hist, Vol 26, 93; Bureaucratic Conservatism and Modernization--Studies on the Early History of the Conservative Party in Prussia 1810-1848, Cent Europ Hist, Vol 25, 92. **CONTACT ADDRESS** Dept of Hist, Univ of Calgary, Calgary, AB, T2N 1N4.

EYCK, GUNTHER
DISCIPLINE WORLD WAR II DIPLOMACY AND COMPARATIVE FOREIGN POLICY **EDUCATION** NY Univ, PhD. **CAREER** Prof, Am Univ. **RESEARCH** Western European politics **SELECTED PUBLICATIONS** Auth, The Voice of Nations: European National Anthems and Their Authors, Greenwood Press, 95. **CONTACT ADDRESS** American Univ, 4400 Massachusetts Ave, Washington, DC, 20016.

EYER, DIANE E.
PERSONAL Born 03/21/1944, Buffalo, NY, m, 1991 **DISCIPLINE** HUMAN DEVELOPMENT **EDUCATION** Univ Pa, PhD, 88. **CAREER** Lecturer, Univ of Pa; Asst Prof, Temple Univ. **HONORS AND AWARDS** Schol & Res assistanceships. **MEMBERSHIPS** Cheiron Soc. **RESEARCH** History & sociology of psychology, especially child development. **SELECTED PUBLICATIONS** Auth, Mother-Infant Bonding: A Scientific Fiction, Yale, 92; auth, Maternal Infant Bonding: A Scientific Fiction, Human Nature, 5:1, 69-94, 94; auth, The Attachment Myth, Women, Men, and Gender: Ongoing Debates, Yale Univ Press, 96; auth, Motherguilt: How Our Culture

Blames Mothers for What's Wrong With Society, Random House, 96. **CONTACT ADDRESS** 320 Centre Ave, Newtown, PA, 18940.

EZERGAILIS, ANDREW
PERSONAL Born 12/10/1930, Latvia, m, 1957, 1 child **DISCIPLINE** RUSSIAN HISTORY, HISTORIOGRAPHY **EDUCATION** Mich State Univ, BA, 56; NY Univ, MA, 60, PhD, 68. **CAREER** Asst prof, 63-73, prof hist, Ithaca Col, 73-, Res grant, Am Coun Learned Soc, 80. **MEMBERSHIPS** AHA; Am Asn Advan Slavic Studies; Am Asn Baltic Studies. **RESEARCH** The 1917 revolution in Russia; the socialist movement; Latvian history. **SELECTED PUBLICATIONS** Auth, The bolshevization of Latvian social democracy, Can Slavic Studies, 67; Anglo-Saxonism and fascism, Yale Rev, 6/69; October insurrection in Latvia: A chronology, J Baltic Studies, winter 73; The 1917 Revolution in Latvia, Columbia Univ, 74; The 1917 Revolution in Latvia; The Latvian Impact on the Bolshevik Revolution; The Holocaust in Latvia. **CONTACT ADDRESS** Ithaca Col, 953 Danby Rd, Ithaca, NY, 14850-7002. **EMAIL** ezergail@ithaca.edu

F

FA, MAYER
PERSONAL Born 09/22/1952, Santa Cruz, CA, m, 1983, 1 child **DISCIPLINE** HISTORY **EDUCATION** Univ Southern Calif, PhD, 88. **CAREER** Adj Prof, Calif State Univ Los Angeles, 91-. **HONORS AND AWARDS** John F Kennedy Presidential Library Found grant, 89; Usia Lecture Tour-Germ 94. **MEMBERSHIPS** Ger Studies Asn; US Comm on Civil Rights. **RESEARCH** Globalization and economic power. **SELECTED PUBLICATIONS** Auth, The Opposition Years, Winston S Churchill and the Conservative Party, 1945-1951, 92; Adenauer and Kennedy: A Study in German-American Relations 1961-1963, 96. **CONTACT ADDRESS** History Dept, California State Univ, Los Angeles, Los Angeles, CA, 90032. **EMAIL** frama@earthlink.net

FABEND, FIRTH HARING
PERSONAL m, 2 children **DISCIPLINE** AMERICAN STUDIES **EDUCATION** Barnard Col, BA; New York Univ, PhD, 88. **CAREER** Independent historian. **HONORS AND AWARDS** Res grant, New Jersey Hist Comn, 85; Hendricks Manuscript Award, New Netherland Project, 89; NY State Hist Asn Annual Book Prize, 89; fel, Holland Soc, NY, 93; res grant, NJ Hist Comn, 94, 95; fel, New Netherland Project, 96. **MEMBERSHIPS** Am Hist Asn; am Soc of Church Hist; Authors Guild; Natl Coalition of Independent Scholars; Omohundro Inst of Early Am Hist and Cult. **SELECTED PUBLICATIONS** Auth, The Dutch American Farmer: A Mad Rabble or Gentlemen Standing Up for Their Rights? de Halve Maen, 90; auth, A Dutch Family in the Middle Colonies, 1660-1800, Rutgers, 91; auth, According to Holland Custome: Jacob Leisler and the Loockermans Estate Feud, de Halve Maen, 94; auth, Suffer the Little Children: Evangelical Childrearing in Reformed Dutch Households, New York and New Jersey, de Halve Maen, 95; auth, The Synod of Dort and the Persistence of Dutchness in 19th-Century New York and New Jersey, NY Hist, 96. **CONTACT ADDRESS** 54 Elston Rd, Upper Montclair, NJ, 07043. **EMAIL** fhfabend@msn.com

FABIAN, ANN
DISCIPLINE AMERICAN STUDIES, HISTORY **EDUCATION** Univ Calif at Santa Cruz, BA, 71; Yale Univ, PhD, 82. **CAREER** Assoc prof, Am stud, Yale Univ; current, VIS SCHOLAR HIST, YALE UNIV. **MEMBERSHIPS** Am Antiquarian Soc **SELECTED PUBLICATIONS** Card Sharks, Dream Books & Bucket Shops: Gambling in 19th-Century America, Cornell Univ Press, 90. **CONTACT ADDRESS** 15 Roxborough, Larchmont, NY, 10538.

FABOS, JULIUS GYULA
PERSONAL Born 04/15/1932, Marcali, Hungary, m, 1959, 3 children **DISCIPLINE** LANDSCAPE ARCHITECTURE **EDUCATION** Rutgers, Univ, BS, 61; Harvard Univ, MLA, 64; Univ Mich, PhD, 73. **CAREER** From asst prof to prof, Univ Mass, 64-97; prof emer, 98- . **HONORS AND AWARDS** Fel, ASLA, 85; hon doctorate, Univ Horticulture, Budapest, 92; Am Planning Asn Award, 94; Am Soc Landscape Arch Medalist, 97. **MEMBERSHIPS** Am Soc Landscape Arch; Coun of Educ in Landsacpe Arch. **RESEARCH** Landscape planning and greenway planning. **SELECTED PUBLICATIONS** Co-ed, Special Issue on Greenways, Landscape and Urban Planning J, 95; auth, How Can Land Use Planning Research Influence Land Use Policy Decisions? Proc ASLA, 95; co-ed, Greenways: The Beginning of an International Movement, Elsevier, 96. **CONTACT ADDRESS** 45 Canton Ave, Amherst, MA, 01002. **EMAIL** jfabos@lanp.umass.edu

FABRE, GENEVIEVE EDITH
DISCIPLINE AMERICAN STUDIES **EDUCATION** Sorbonne, PhD, 69; doctorat d'etat, 78. **CAREER** PROF, AM STUD, UNIV PARIS VII **MEMBERSHIPS** Am Antiquarian Soc **RESEARCH** Afro-Am feasts & celebrations **SELECTED PUBLICATIONS** Auth, The Restless Journey of James Agee, William Morrow, 77; auth, Drumbeats, Masks and Metaphors, Harvard Univ Press, 83; auth, "Election Day Celebrations," in Slavery in the Americas, Koningshausen & Neumann, 93; co-ed, History and Memory in African-American Culture, Oxford Univ Press, 94; ed and intro, Parcours Identitaires aux USA, Publications de la Sorbonne Nouvelle, 94; auth, "Festive Moments in Antebellum African American Culture: JonKonnu," in The Black Columbiad: Defining Moments in African-American Literature and Culture, Harvard Univ Press, 95. **CONTACT ADDRESS** 12 Square Montsouris F, Paris, ., 75014.

FABRE, MICHEL J.
DISCIPLINE AMERICAN STUDIES **EDUCATION** Sorbonne, PhD, 70. **CAREER** Prof, PROF EMER AM STUD, UNIV OF PARIS III **MEMBERSHIPS** Am Antiquarian Soc **SELECTED PUBLICATIONS** Auth, "Theophile Allain," "Caesar C. Antoine," "Couvent Institute," "Creole," "Rodolphe Desdunes," " Alice Dunbar-Nelson," "Armand Lanusse," "Les Cenelles," "PBS Pinchback," in Encyclopedia of African-American Culture and History, Macmillan, 96; auth, The World of Richard Wright, Univ Press Miss, 85; auth, From Harlem to Paris: Black American Writers In France 1840-1980, Univ Ill Press, 91; coauth, Way B(l)ack Then and Now: A Street Guide to African Americans in Paris, Universite de la Sorbonne Nouvelle, 92; coauth, An Annotated Primary and Secondary Bibliography, Greenwood Press, 92; auth, The Unfinished Quest of Richard Wright, Univ Ill Press, 93; co-ed, Conversations with Chester Himes, Univ Miss Press, 95; coauth, The French Critical Reception of African American Literature, 1840-1970: An Annotated Bibliography, Greenwood Press, 95; coauth, The Several Lives of Chester Himes, A Biography, Univ Miss Press, 97. **CONTACT ADDRESS** 12 Square Montsouris F, Paris, ., 75014.

FACKLER, HERBERT VERN
PERSONAL Born 01/23/1942, Monroe, LA, m, 1964, 2 children **DISCIPLINE** ANGLOIRISH & MODERN LITERATURE **EDUCATION** Centenary Col, LA, BA, 64; NM Highlands Univ, MA, 65; Univ NC, Chapel Hill, PhD(English), 72. **CAREER** Teaching asst English, NMex Highlands Univ, 65; instr, Centenary Col, La, 65-68; asst prof, Northwestern State Univ, LA, 69-70; asst prof, Univ Tulsa, 70-71; asst prof English & dir creative writing, 71-76, assoc prof, 76-96, PROF, UNIV SOUTHWESTERN LA, 97-; NDEA fel, Univ NC, Chapel Hill, 72; dir, Deep South Writers Conf, 80, 8, 94. **HONORS AND AWARDS** Phi Kappa Phi; Phi Eta Sigma; Sigma Tau Delta; NDEA Fellow Univ NC, Chapel Hill, 68-69; USL Found Distinguished Prof, 81; Highlands Distinguished Alumnus, 91; Assoc Samuel P. Peters Int Lit Res Center, 92. **MEMBERSHIPS** Col English Asn (treas, 72-74); SCent Mod Lang Asn; Am Comt Irish Studies; MLA; Deep South Writers Conf (dir, 80 & 81); Popular Culture Asn. **RESEARCH** Nineteenth and twentieth century British and Am literature; AngloIrish lit; mystery and detective fiction. **SELECTED PUBLICATIONS** Auth, Series of studies of Deirdre works, Eire-Ireland, spring 72; Proust and Celine, Studies, by Mem SCent Mod Lang Asn, winter 73; The Dierdre legend in Anglo-Irish lit: A prolegomenon, Univ Southwestern La Res Ser, 74; That Tragic Queen: the Deirdre in Anglo-Irish Literature, Univ Salzburg, 79; ed, Modern Irish Novel, excluding Joyce, Univ Southwestern La Res Ser, 80; Reflections on a Slender Volume, in Lawrence Durrell: Comprehending the Whole, ed, Julian Raper, et al; Dialectic in the Corpus of Robert B. Parker's Spenser Novels, Clues, 94; Spenser's New England Conscience, Colby Quart, 98; novels: The Snow Pirates, The Last Long Pass, and Virginia Creeper, Dancing Jester Press, 99. **CONTACT ADDRESS** Dept of English, Univ of Southwestern, Box 44691 USL, Lafayette, LA, 70504-8401.

FACOS, MICHELLE
DISCIPLINE NINETEENTH CENTURY EUROPEAN PAINTING AND SCULPTURE **EDUCATION** Univ NY, PhD. **CAREER** Asst prof. **RESEARCH** Romanticism; symbolism; nationalism. **SELECTED PUBLICATIONS** Auth, Nationalism and the Nordic Imagination: Swedish Painting in the 1890's, Univ Ca, 98; pubs on Scandinavian art. **CONTACT ADDRESS** Dept of History and Art, Indiana Univ, Bloomington, 300 N Jordan Ave, Bloomington, IN, 47405. **EMAIL** mfacos@indiana.edu

FAGAN, BRIAN M.
PERSONAL England, m, 2 children **DISCIPLINE** ARCHAEOLOGY **EDUCATION** Pembroke Col, BA, 59; MA, 62; PhD, 65. **CAREER** Vis assoc prof, Univ Ill, Champaign-Urbana, 66-67; prof, Univ Calif, Santa Barbara, 67- . **HONORS AND AWARDS** Guggenheim fel, 73; Lorenzini lectr, Houston Mus of Fine Arts, 88; National Sigma Xi lectr, 89; Soc of Prof Archaeol Distinguished Service Award, 96; Presidential Citation Award, Soc for Am Archaeol, 96; Public Educ Award, Soc for AM Archaeol, 97. **SELECTED PUBLICATIONS** Auth, In the Beginning; auth, People of the Earth; auth, Archaeology: A Brief Introduction; co-auth with Charles Orser, Historical Archaeology; co-auth with Chris Scarre, Ancient Civilizations, 97. **CONTACT ADDRESS** Dept. of Anthropology, Univ of Calif, Santa Barbara, CA, 93106.

FAHERTY, WILLIAM BARNABY
PERSONAL Born 12/17/1914, St. Louis, MO **DISCIPLINE** HISTORY **EDUCATION** St Louis Univ, AB, 36, AM, 38; St Mary's Col, STL, 45, PhD, 49. **CAREER** From instr to asst prof hist, Regis Col, Colo, 48-56; gen ed, Queen's Work Publ House, 56-63; ASSOC PROF, 63-68, PROF HIST, ST LOUIS UNIV, 68-, CHMN, MIDWESTERN JESUIT COMT HIST PRESERV, 71-; vis assoc prof hist and NASA grant, Univ Fla, 72-74; dir, St Stanislaus Jesuit Hist Mus, Inc, Florissant, Mo, 75. **HONORS AND AWARDS** Cath Pres Asn Nat Writing Awards, 43 and 44; Literary Award, Mo Writers Guild, 77. **MEMBERSHIPS** AHA; Am Cath Hist Asn. **RESEARCH** Saint Louis regional history; Mid-western Church history; history of America's space program. **SELECTED PUBLICATIONS** Auth, Father Desmet, Peter--Jesuit in the West, Pac Hist Rev, Vol 65, 96; Come Blackrobe--Desmet and the Indian Tragedy, Pac Hist Rev, Vol 65, 96. **CONTACT ADDRESS** St Louis Univ, 221 N Grand Blvd St, St Louis, MO, 63103.

FAHEY, DAVID MICHAEL
PERSONAL Born 05/18/1937, Ossining, NY **DISCIPLINE** BRITISH HISTORY **EDUCATION** Siena Col, NY, BA, 59; Univ Notre Dame, MA, 61, PhD(hist), 64. **CAREER** From instr to asst prof hist, Assumption Col, Mass, 63-66; asst prof, Ind Univ Northwest, 66-69; assoc prof, 69-80, prof Hist, Miami Univ, 80-, Dir Grad Studies, 82-85; dir undergrad Studies, 87, 95-98 Ed, Alcohol and Temperance History Group Newslett, 82-; Alcohol in Hist, 83-86; moderator, ATHE listserv group, 95-; pres, Alcohol and Temperance Hist Group, 86-88. **MEMBERSHIPS** North American Conf British Studies; Social Hist Soc UK; Ohio Acad of Hist; World Hist Assn. **RESEARCH** British social history; Anglo-Am temperance and fraternal societies **SELECTED PUBLICATIONS** Auth, Henry Hallam: a conservative as Whig historian, Historian, 66; R H Tawney and the sense of community, Centennial Rev, 68; Temperance and the liberal party: Lord Peel's report, 1899, J Brit Studies, 71; ed, Samuel Rawson Gardiner looks at history, home rule and empire: some Bodleian letters, 1886-1899, Proc Am Philos Soc, 71; Rosebery, the Times and the Newcastle programme, Bull Inst Hist Res, 72; coauth, The English Heritage, Forum, 78; auth, The Politics of Drink: Pressure Groups and the British Liberal Party, 1883-1908, Soc Sci, 79; Brewers, Publicans, and Working-Class Drinkers: Pressure Group Politics in Late Victorian and Edwardian England, Hist Soc, 80; ed, The Black Lodge in White America: True Reformer Browne and His Economic Strategy, Wright State UP, 94; Temperance and Racism: John Bull, Johnny Reb and the Good Templars, Univ Press of Kentucky, 96; Blacks, Good Templars and Universal Membership in Jack S Blocker, Jr and Cheryl Krasnick Warsh, eds, The Changing Face of Drink, Histoire Sociale, 97; How the Good Templars Began: Fraternal Temperance in New York State, Social History of Alcohol Review, 98. **CONTACT ADDRESS** Dept of History, Miami Univ, 500 E High St, Oxford, OH, 45056-1602. **EMAIL** faheydm@muohio.edu

FAHL, RONALD JENKS
PERSONAL Born 08/04/1942, Portland, OR, m, 1967, 2 children **DISCIPLINE** AMERICAN HISTORY **EDUCATION** Willamette Univ, BA, 64; Univ Ore, MA, 66. **CAREER** Instr hist, Eastern Ore State Col, 66-69; teaching assoc, Wash State Univ, 72-73; Bibliographer, 73-75, ED, J FOREST HIST, FOREST HIST SOC, 75-, DIR PROG DEVELOP, 80-. **MEMBERSHIPS** AHA; Orgn Am Historians; Western Hist Asn; Forest Hist Soc. **RESEARCH** Forest and conservation history; populism; American West. **SELECTED PUBLICATIONS** Auth, The National Forests of the Northern Region--Living Legacy, W Hist Quart, Vol 25, 94. **CONTACT ADDRESS** Forest Historical Society, 109 Coral St, Santa Cruz, CA, 95060.

FAHMY-EID, NADIA
PERSONAL Born 09/09/1936, Egypt **DISCIPLINE** HISTORY **EDUCATION** Univ Laval, LL, 65; McGill Univ, MA, 67; Univ Montreal, PhD, 75. **CAREER** Prof hist, Col Edouard-Montpetit, 66-69; PROF HISTOIRE, UNIV QUEBEC MONTREAL, 69-, dir du prog d'etudes avancees, 74-76. **HONORS AND AWARDS** Membre de la Societe Royale du Can, 96-; Prix Guy Fregault, Inst d'hist de l'Amerique francais; Prix des Fondateurs, Asn can d'hist de l'educ; Marion Porter Prize, Can Res Inst Advan Women; Hilda Neatby Prize, Soc d'hist Can. **MEMBERSHIPS** Ch, Can Hist Asn, 95-96. **SELECTED PUBLICATIONS** Auth, Le clerge et le pouvoir politique au Quebec, 78; coauth, Si le travail m'etait conte autrement, 87; coauth, Femmes, sante et professions. Dietetistes et physiotherapeutes au Quebec et en Ontario 1930-1980, 97; co-dir, Maitresses de maison, maitresses d'ecole, 83; co-dir, Les couventines, 86. **CONTACT ADDRESS** Dep d'histoire, Univ Quebec Montreal, CP 8888, Succ Centre-ville, Montreal, PQ, H3C 3P8.

FAHS, ALICE E.
DISCIPLINE HISTORY **EDUCATION** NY Univ, PhD, 93. **CAREER** ASST PROF, HIST, UNIV CALIF IRVINE **MEMBERSHIPS** Am Antiquarian Soc **RESEARCH** Civil War **CONTACT ADDRESS** Dept of Hist, Univ of Calif at Irvine, Irvine, CA, 92717-3275.

FAIR, JOHN DOUGLAS
PERSONAL Born 09/06/1943, Waynesboro, PA, m, 1977 **DISCIPLINE** BRITISH POLITICAL AND CONSTITUTIONAL HISTORY **EDUCATION** Juniata Col, BA, 65; Wake Forest Univ, MA, 66; Duke Univ, PhD (hist), 69. **CAREER** Instr hist, York Jr Col, 67 and Millersville State Col, 68; asst prof hist, Va Polytechnic Inst and State Univ, 69-71; asst prof, 71-75, assoc prof, 75-81, PROF HIST, AUBURN UNIV, MONTGOMERY, 81-, Vis prof hist, Univ Maine, Orono, summer, 81. **MEMBERSHIPS** AHA; Conf Brit Studies; Am Comt Irish Studies; Brit Polit Group. **RESEARCH** British political and constitutional history; Anglo-Irish history; British Empire-Commonwealth. **SELECTED PUBLICATIONS** Auth, Public and Private Doctrine--Essays in British History Presented to Cowling, Maurice, Albion, Vol 27, 95; 20th Century Britain--An Encyclopedia, Albion, Vol 28, 96; Playing The Game--Sport and British Society, 1910-45, Albion, Vol 29, 97; British Relations with the Malay Rulers from Decentralization to Malayan Independence, 1930-1957, Am Hist Rev, Vol 102, 97; Neither Kingdom nor Nation--The Irish Quest for Constitutional Rights, 1698-1800, Am Hist Rev, Vol 101, 96; Thinkers of the 20 Years Crisis--Interwar Idealism Reassessed, Int Hist Rev, Vol 18, 96; Samuel, Herbert--A Political Life, Am Hist Rev, Vol 98, 93; Boothby,Robert--A Portrait of Churchill Ally, Albion, Vol 24, 92; Taylor, A. J. P.--The Traitor Within the Gates, Am Hist Rev, Vol 100, 95; The Pursuit of Power, Albion, Vol 26, 94; Churchill--A Life, Albion, Vol 24, 92; The Irish Constitutional Tradition--Responsible Government and Modern Ireland, 1782-1992, Am Hist Rev, Vol 101, 96. **CONTACT ADDRESS** Dept of Hist, Auburn Univ, Montgomery, AL, 36117.

FAIR, THEOPOLIS
PERSONAL Born 02/03/1941, Pine Bluff, AR **DISCIPLINE** LATIN AMERICAN & BLACK HISTORY **EDUCATION** Fisk Univ, BA, 63; Columbia Univ, MA, 65; Univ Madrid, dipl hist, 65; Temple Univ, PhD(Latin Am hist), 72. **CAREER** ASSOC PROF HIST, LA SALLE UNIV, 67-. **HONORS AND AWARDS** Phi Beta Kappa; Woodrow Wilson; Fulbright. **MEMBERSHIPS** AHA; Latin Am Studies Asn **RESEARCH** Passage to and from Spain in the 16th century; Blacks in Latin America; Geraldine Farrar. **SELECTED PUBLICATIONS** Auth, The Impact of the New World on Spain, 1550-1650: Some Social Aspects, J of the Great Lake Hist Conf, Vol 2, 15-28; Asia in Latin American History, in: Asia in National & World History, 97. **CONTACT ADDRESS** Dept of Hist, La Salle Univ, 1900 W Olney Ave, Philadelphia, PA, 19141-1199. **EMAIL** fair@lasalle.edu

FAIRBAIRN, BRETT T.
PERSONAL Born 04/24/1959, Winnipeg, MB, Canada **DISCIPLINE** HISTORY **EDUCATION** Univ Sask, BA, 81; Univ Oxford, BA, 84, DPhil, 88. **CAREER** Asst to assoc prof, 86-96, PROF, UNIV SASKATCHEWAN, 96-; ed, Can J Hist, 88-95; ch, Sask Archv Bd, 97-. **HONORS AND AWARDS** Rhodes schol, 81; SSHRC doctoral fel, 84-86; SSHRC res grant, 92-95; Alexander von Humboldt fel, 97-98. **SELECTED PUBLICATIONS** Auth, Building a Dream: The Co-operative Retailing System in Western Canada, 89; auth, Democracy in the Undemocratic State: The German Reichstag Elections of 1898 and 1903, 97; coauth, Co-operatives and Community Development, 91; co-ed, Dignity and Growth, Citizen Participation in Social Change, 91. **CONTACT ADDRESS** Univ of Saskatchewan, 101 Diefenbaker Pl, Saskatoon, SK, S7N 5B8. **EMAIL** brett.fairbairn@usask.ca

FALERO, FRANK
PERSONAL Born 12/22/1937, New York, NY, m **DISCIPLINE** ECONOMICS **EDUCATION** St. Petersburg Jr Col, Fla, AA, 62; Univ South Fla, Tampa, BA, 64; Fla State Univ, Tallahassee, MS, 65; Fla State Univ, Tallahassee, PhD, 67. **CAREER** Prof, econ and finance, Calif State Univ, Bakersfield, Sept 74-; bd of dir, Ctr for Econ Educ and Res, Calif State Univ, Bakersfield, 79-; vis prof, econ and finance, Nat Sch of Finance and Mgt, Fairfield, CT, summer, 86; vis prof, Econ Inst, Univ Colo, summer, 74; dir, Ctr for Econ Educ, Calif State Univ, Bakersfield, Sep 73-Dec 79; assoc prof of econ, Calif State Univ, Bakerfield, Sep 72-Sep 74; cons, US Dept of State, Agency for Intl Develop, The Mission to Ethiopia, Jan 70-Jan 72; asst prof of econ, Va Polytechnic Inst and State Univ, Mar 67-Aug 72; Fulbright vis prof, Univ del Pacifico, Lima, Peru, Jul 68- Mar 69; res econ, Fed Reserve Bank of Richmond, Jul 67-Sep 67. **HONORS AND AWARDS** Fel, Amer Col of Forensic Exam, 97; Who's Who Worldwide, 96; arbit, Nat Futures Asn, 96; dipl, Amer Bd of Forensic Exam, 94; reg forensic econ, Amer Rehabil Econ Asn, 94; Best News Commentary, 1985, Assoc Press TV Radio Asn, Mar 85; Golden Miek, 1984, Radio-TV Newn Asn of Southern Calif, Jan 85; Best News Commentary, 1983, Calif Assoc Press TV Radio Asn, Mar 84; Dict of Intl Bio, 75; Outstanding Educ of Amer, 75; Who's Who in the US, 75; Who's Who in the West, 75; exec comt mem, N Amer Econ Studies Asn, 74-79; trustee, Calif Coun for Econ Educ, 74-79; Kazanjian Found award for the tchg of econ, 1971, hon mention, Joint Coun for Econ Educ; Alpha Kappa Psi, 68; Beta Gamma Sigma, 71; Phi Kappa Phi, 65; Delta Tau Kappa, 65; Omicron Delta Epsilon, 65; NDEA Title IV Fel, 64-67. **MEMBERSHIPS** Nat Asn of Forensic Econ, 88; Amer Acad of Econ and Financial Experts, 90; Amer Arbit Asn, 64; fel, Royal Econ Soc, 64; Amer Econ Asn, 65; Southern Econ Asn, 65; Reg Sci Asn, 65; Amer Asn for the Advan of Sci, 65. **RESEARCH** T-Bill Futures: Prediction or Reaction?; Commodity Markets: Efficient or Inefficient?; Collaborative, Competitive, and Cooperative Tele-Teaching via Teleconferencing and the Internet. **SELECTED PUBLICATIONS** Auth, Wage Loss in Wrongful Death - An Historical Analysis, Jour of Legal Econ, vol 6, no 1, spring/summer, 96; mongr, Economics 395 Interactive Study Guide, Ctr for Econ Educ and Res, Calif State Univ, Bakersfield, 97; Economics 100 Interactive Study Guide, Ctr for Econ Educ and Res, Calif State Univ, Bakersfield, 92, 94, 95, 97; Economics 201 Interactive Study Guide, Ctr for Econ Educ and Res, Calif State Univ, Bakersfield, 91, 92, 95, 97; Economics 309 Interactive Study Guide, Ctr for Econ Educ and Res, Calif State Univ, Bakersfield, 93, 94, 97; res papers, Wage Loss in Wrongful Death - A Historical Analysis, Amer Acad of Econ and Financial Experts, Law Vegas, April, 96; **CONTACT ADDRESS** Spring Valley Ranch, 40144 Balch Park Rd., PO Box 950, Springville, CA, 93265. **EMAIL** ffalero@ocsnet.net

FALK, CANDACE
DISCIPLINE HISTORY; POLITICAL THEORY **EDUCATION** Univ Chicago, BA, 69; MA, 71; Univ Calif Santa Cruz, PhD, 84. **CAREER** Intermittent fac positions, Univ Calif Berkeley, Univ Calif Santa Cruz, Stockton State Col; dir/ed, The Emma Goldman Papers, 80- . **HONORS AND AWARDS** Guggenheim fel, 98-99. **MEMBERSHIPS** Asoc Documentary Eds; Orgn of Am Historians; Am Hist Asoc. **RESEARCH** History; women's studies; labor and left social movements; intellectual and cultural history; biography. **SELECTED PUBLICATIONS** auth, Love, Anarchy, and Emma Goldman, 84; auth, Emma Goldman Papers: A Comprehensive Microfilm Edition, 91; auth with S. Cole and S. Thomas, Emma Goldman: A Guide to her Life and Documentary Sources, 95; Selected Papers of Emma Goldman, forthcoming. **CONTACT ADDRESS** Emma Goldman Papers, Univ Calif Berkeley, 2372 Ellsworth St., Berkeley, CA, 94720-6030. **EMAIL** cfalk@socrates.berkeley.edu

FALK, MARVIN W.
DISCIPLINE EUROPEAN, GERMANY **EDUCATION** Univ IA, PhD, 76. **CAREER** Univ Alaska **SELECTED PUBLICATIONS** Ed, AK, CLIO Press, 95. **CONTACT ADDRESS** Univ AK Fairbanks, PO Box 757480, Fairbanks, AK, 99775-7480. **EMAIL** ffmwf@aurora.alaska.edu

FALK, NANCY ELLEN
PERSONAL Born 09/03/1938, Bethlehem, PA, m, 1967, 2 children **DISCIPLINE** HISTORY OF RELIGIONS **EDUCATION** Cedar Crest Col, AB, 60; Univ Chicago, AM, 63, PhD(hist of relig), 72. **CAREER** Asst prof, 66-71, assoc prof, 71-79, chmn dept, 72-75, PROF RELIG, WESTERN MICH UNIV, 79-. **HONORS AND AWARDS** Fulbright, India, 84-85; AIIS sr fel, 91-92. **MEMBERSHIPS** Am Acad Relig; Asia Soc **RESEARCH** South Asian religion; women in religion. **SELECTED PUBLICATIONS** Co-ed (with Rita M Gross), Unspoken worlds: Women's religious lives in non-Western cultures, 80; auth, Women in Religion: An Annotated Bibliography of Sources in English, 1975-1992, 94. **CONTACT ADDRESS** Dept of Comp Relig, Western Michigan Univ, 1201 Oliver St, Kalamazoo, MI, 49008-3805. **EMAIL** nancy.falk@wmich.edu

FALK, STANLEY LAWRENCE
PERSONAL Born 03/11/1927, New York, NY, m, 1956, 2 children **DISCIPLINE** HISTORY, MILITARY AFFAIRS **EDUCATION** Bard Col, BA, 45; Georgetown Univ, MA, 52, PhD(hist), 59. **CAREER** Historian, Off Chief Mil Hist, US Dept Army, 49-54, 59-62, bur soc sci res, Am Univ, DC, 54-56 & hist sect, Joint Chiefs of Staff, US Dept Defense, 56-59; assoc prof nat security affairs, Indust Col Armed Forces, 62-70, prof int rels, 70-74; chief historian, US Air Force, 74-80; Dep Chief Historian, Southeast Asia, US Army Ctr Military Hist, 80-82; independent historical consult, 83- . **HONORS AND AWARDS** Phi Alpha Theta. **MEMBERSHIPS** Soc Military Hist; World War Ii Stud Asn; Soc Hist Am Foreign Rels; AHA; Orgn Am Historians; Am Jewish Hist Soc. **RESEARCH** American history; American military history; national security affairs. **SELECTED PUBLICATIONS** Auth, Bataan: The March of Death, Norton, 62; auth, Decision at Leyte, Norton, 66; auth, Human Resources for National Strength, 66, The National Security Structure, 67 & 72, The Environment of National Security, 68 & 73, Defense Military Manpower, 70 & The World in Ferment: Problem Areas for the United States, 70 & 74, Indust Col Armed Forces; Liberation of the Philippines, 71 & The Palaus Campaign, 74, Ballantine; Seventy Days to Singapore, Putnam & Hale, 75. **CONTACT ADDRESS** 2310 Kimbro St, Alexandria, VA, 22307.

FALKNER, THOMAS M.
DISCIPLINE GREEK AND LATIN LITERATURE **EDUCATION** LeMoyne Univ, AB, 69; SUNY, MA, 71, PhD, 75. **CAREER** Vis scholar Cambridge Univ, 96-97; prof; ch-. **HONORS AND AWARDS** Six different grants, NEH; fel in residence., Dit, Wooster-in-Greece prog, 84. **SELECTED PUBLICATIONS** Co-ed, Old Age in Greek and Latin Literature; auth, Euripides' Orestes, The Poetics of Old Age in Greek Epic, Lyric, and Tragedy; articles on Greek and Latin poetry,

articles on Sophoclean tragedy. **CONTACT ADDRESS** Dept of Classics, Col of Wooster, Wooster, OH, 44691. **EMAIL** tfalkner@acs.wooster.edu

FALOLA, TOYIA
PERSONAL Born 01/01/1953, m, 1981, 3 children **DISCIPLINE** HISTORY **EDUCATION** Univ of Ife, PhD, 81. **CAREER** Sr. lecturer, Univ Ife, 89; Prof, York Univ, 90; Prof, Univ TX at Austin, 91-. **HONORS AND AWARDS** Smot Fel, Cambridge, 98; Grants from the NEH, CHRC, Guggenheim, Carter Distinguished Profs, 98. **MEMBERSHIPS** Amer Hist Assoc; African Studies Assoc **RESEARCH** African economy and politics **SELECTED PUBLICATIONS** Ed, African Historiography, Longman,, London, 93; ed, Pioneer, Patriot and Pariarch: Samuel Johnson and the Yoruba People, Wisconsin-Madison: African Stud Prog, 93; co-ed, Child Health in Nigeria: the Impact of a Depressed Economy, Avebury, London, 94; co-ed, Pawnship in Africa. Debt Bondage in Historical Perspective, Westview, Colorado, 94; coauth, The Military Factor in Nigeria, Lagos and NY: Heritage and E. Mellen, 94; coauth, Religious Impact on the Nation Sate: The Nigerian Predicament, Avebury, London, 95; auth, Development Planning and Decolonization in Nigeria, Univ Press of Florida, Gainesville, 96; auth, Religious Militancy and Self-Assertion: Islam and Politics in Nigeria, Avebury, London, 96; auth, Religious Violence in Nigeria: The Crisis of Religious Politics and Secular Ideologies, Univ of Rochester Press, 98. **CONTACT ADDRESS** Dept of Hist, Univ Texas at Austin, Austin, TX, 78712. **EMAIL** Toyia.Falola@mail.utetas.edu

FANN, WILLERD REESE
PERSONAL Born 09/03/1932, Sacramento, CA, m, 1965 **DISCIPLINE** MODERN EUROPEAN HISTORY **EDUCATION** Univ Calif, Berkeley, AB, 57, MA, 59, PhD (hist), 65. **CAREER** Asst prof hist, La State Univ, New Orleans, 64-75; ASSOC PROF HIST, UNIV NEW ORLEANS, 74-. **MEMBERSHIPS** AHA; Col Mil Hist; Am Mil Inst; Conf Group on Cent Europ Hist. **RESEARCH** German history; military history. **SELECTED PUBLICATIONS** Auth, Military Conservatism--Veterans Associations and the Military Party in Prussia Between 1815 and 1848, Ger Stud Rev, Vol 15, 92. **CONTACT ADDRESS** Dept of Hist, Univ of New Orleans, New Orleans, LA, 70122.

FANNING, STEVEN
DISCIPLINE HISTORY **EDUCATION** Tex Tech Univ, BA, 68, MA, 70; Univ Minn, PhD, 77. **CAREER** Asst prof, 81-87, ASSOC PROF, 87-, ASST DEAN, COL LIB ARTS SCIES, 96-, UNIV ILL, CHICAGO, **CONTACT ADDRESS** Dept of History, Univ of Illinois, Chicago, 601 S Morgan St, Chicago, IL, 60607. **EMAIL** sfanning@uic.edu

FANT, J. CLAYTON
DISCIPLINE CLASSICAL STUDIES **EDUCATION** Williams Coll, BA, 69; Univ of Mich, PhD, 76. **CAREER** Asst Prof, 76-79, Wellesley Coll; Instr, 79-81, St Stephen's School Rome; vis Asst Prof, 81-83, Univ of Mich; Asst Prof, Assoc Prof, 84-, Univ of Akron. **HONORS AND AWARDS** Amer Acad Rome Fel. **MEMBERSHIPS** AIA, APA, ASMOSIA, Vergilian Society. **RESEARCH** Roman Archaeology **SELECTED PUBLICATIONS** Auth, Cavum Antrum Phrygiae, The Organization and Operations of the Roman Imperial Marble Quarries at Docimium, BAR Intl Series, 89; Ancient Marble Quarrying and Trade, BAR Intl Series, 88; Ideology Gift and Trade, A Distribution Model for the Roman Imperial Marbles, in: The Inscribed Economy, Production and Distribution in the Roman Empire in the Light of Instrumentum Domesticum, ed W V Harris & S Panciera, JRA, 93; The Imperial Marble Yard at Portus, in: Ancient Stones, Quarrying Trade and Provenance. Interdisciplinary Studies on Stones and Stone Technology in Europe and Near East from the Prehistoric to the Early Christian Period, ed, M Waelkens, N Herz & L Moens, 92. **CONTACT ADDRESS** Dept of Classics, Univ of Akron, 326 Olin, Akron, OH, 44325-1910. **EMAIL** cfant@uakron.edu

FANTHAM, ELAINE
PERSONAL Born 05/25/1933, Liverpool, England, w, 1958, 2 children **DISCIPLINE** CLASSICS **EDUCATION** Oxford Univ, MA, B.Litt, 57; Liverpool Univ, PhD, 62. **CAREER** Vis prof, 66-68, Indiana Univ; from asst to full Prof of Classics, 68-86, Univ Toronto; Giger Prof of Latin, Princeton Univ, 86-99. **HONORS AND AWARDS** Former vpres, Res Div, APA; trustee, Am Acad in Rome. **MEMBERSHIPS** Am Philol Asn; Class Asn of Canada; Int Soc for the Hist of Rhetoric. **RESEARCH** Latin epic; rhetoric; Roman social history; women's history. **SELECTED PUBLICATIONS** Auth, A Commentary on Lucan De Bello Civili Book 2, Cambridge, 92; co-auth, Women in the Classical World: Image and Text, Oxford, 94; auth, Roman Literary Culture: from Cicero to Apuleius, Johns Hopkins, 96; transl, The Hidden Author by Gian Biagio Conte, Berkeley, 96; transl and contribur, Ovid: Fasti Book IV, Cambridge, 96; auth, Envy and Fear the Begetters of Hate: Statius Thebaid and the Genesis of Hatred, in, Gill, ed, The Passions in Latin Literature and Thought, Cambridge, 97; auth, Occasions and Contexts of Roman Public Oratory, in Dominik, ed, Roman Eloquence, London, 97; auth, Propertius' Old New Rome, in Habinek, ed, The Roman Cultural Revolution, Cambridge, 97; auth, Allecto's First Victim, in, Vergil's Aeneid in Its Political Context, Duckworth, 98. **CONTACT ADDRESS** 28 1/2 Wiggins St, Princeton, NJ, 08540. **EMAIL** fantham@ariel.princeton.edu

FARAGHER, JOHN MACK
PERSONAL Born 08/26/1945, Phoenix, AZ, 1 child **DISCIPLINE** AMERICAN HISTORY **EDUCATION** Univ Calif, Riverside, BA, 67, MA, 70; Yale Univ, PhD (hist), 77. **CAREER** Soc worker, Dept Pub Soc Ser, Los Angeles County, 68-69; instr Am studies, Yale Univ, 75-77; asst prof hist, Univ Hartford, 77-78; ASST PROF HIST, MT HOLYOKE COL, 78-. **HONORS AND AWARDS** John Addison Porter and Fredric Beinecke Prize, Yale Univ, 77; Fredrick Jackson Turner Award, Orgn Am Historians, 80; Spec Citation, Soc Am Historians, 80. **MEMBERSHIPS** Western Hist Asn; AHA; New Eng Hist Asn; Mid Atlantic Radical Historians Asn. **RESEARCH** Sex and gender in history; Midwestern American society and culture; Antebellum America. **SELECTED PUBLICATIONS** Auth, Frontier Indiana, J Am Hist, Vol 84, 97; Under Western Skies--Nature and History in the American West, Am Hist Rev, Vol 98, 93; Past Imperfect--Fact and Truth, Am Heritage, Vol 46, 95; A Commentary on Hijiya, James, A. Article Why the West is Lost, William Mary Quart, Vol 51, 94; 3 Frontiers--Family, Land, and Society in the American West, 1850-1900, Pac Northwest Quart, Vol 87, 96; Belleville, Ottawa, and Galesburg--Community and Democracy On The Illinois Frontier, J Am Hist, Vol 84, 97; The Ohio Frontier--Crucible of the Old Northwest, 1720-1830, J Am Hist, Vol 84, 97; Under an Open Sky--Rethinking America Western Past, Am Hist Rev, Vol 98, 93; Creating the West--Historical Interpretations 1890-1990, Am Hist Rev, Vol 98, 93; An Unsettled Country--Changing Landscapes of the American West, Environmental Hist, Vol 2, 97; Writing Western History--Essays on Major Western Historians, Am Hist Rev, Vol 98, 93; All Over the Map--Rethinking American Regions, W Hist Quart, Vol 27, 96; Parkman, Francis Historian as Hero--The Formative Years, J Interdisciplinary Hist, Vol 24, 93; Trails Toward a New Western History, Am Hist Rev, Vol 98, 93; Settling the Canadian American West, 1890-1915--Pioneer Adaptation and Community Building--An Anthropological History, J Soc Hist, Vol 30, 97. **CONTACT ADDRESS** 34 Ellsworth Ave, New Haven, CT, 06511.

FARAH, CAESAR E.
PERSONAL Born 03/13/1929, Portland, OR, m, 1987, 7 children **DISCIPLINE** HISTORY, RELIGION **EDUCATION** Stanford Univ, BA, 52; Princeton Univ, MA, 55, PhD, 57. **CAREER** Pub aff asst & educ exchange attache, US Info Serv, Delhi & Karachi, 57-59; asst prof hist & Near E lang, Portland State Col, 59-63; consult US Army 62-63; asst prof hist, Los Angeles State Col, 63-64; vis prof Harvard Univ 64-65; assoc prof Near Eastern lang & lit, Ind Univ, Bloomington, 64-69; prof Middle Eastern Studies, Univ Minn, Minneapolis, 69-, Consult, spec oper res off, Am Univ, 60; cult attache's comt, Arab Embassies in Washington, DC, 61; consult, col bks div, Am Libr Asn, 64-; Ford Found grant, 66-67; guest lectr Arabic Ottoman rels, Lebanese Univ, 66 & Univ Baghdad, 67; Fulbright award, Turkey, 67-68; Am Philos Soc res grant, 70-71; guest lectr For Min Spain, Iraq, Lebanon, Iran; Min Higher Educ Saudi Arabia, Yemen, Kuwait, Qatar, Tunisia, Morocco; Syrian Acad Sci, Acad Scis Beijing; vis scholar Cambridge Univ 74; rsrc person on Middle East svc gp MN, 77; bd dir chemn Upper Midwest Consortium for Middle East Outreach, 80-; vis prof Sanaa Univ, Yemen, 84, Karl-Franzens Univ, Austria, 90, Ludwig_Maximilian Univ, Munich, 92-93; exec secy ed Am Inst Yemeni Stud 82-86; secy-gen exec bd dir Int Comt for Pre-Ottoman & Ottoman Studies, 88-; fel Res Ctr Islamic Hist, Istanbul, 93; Ctr Lebanese Stydues & St Anthony Col, Oxford, Eng, 94; vis Fulbright-Hays scholar Univ Damascus, 94. **HONORS AND AWARDS** Cert of Merit Syrian Min Higher Educ, 66-67; Stanford Univ Alumni Asn Ldr Recognition Award. **MEMBERSHIPS** Am Orient Soc; Am Asn Arabic Studies; AHA; Royal Asiatic Soc; MidE Studies Asn NAm; Asn Tchr Arabic; Turkish Studies Asn; Pi Sigma Alpha; Phi Alpha Theta. **RESEARCH** Modern Arab world, sociopolitical changes; Islamic religion and mysticism; the West and the Arab world in the 19th century. **SELECTED PUBLICATIONS** The Lebanese uprising of 1840 and the powers, J Asian Hist, 68; The Addendum in Medieval Arabic Historiography, 68; Eternal Message of Muhammad, 3rd edition, 64; Ibn-al-Najjar, Encycl of Islam, 68; Necib Pasa and the British in Syria, Archivum Ottomanicum, Budapest & Leiden, 72; Islam and revitalization, Quartet, London, 80; The quadruple alliance and proposed Ottoman reforms in Syria, 1839-41, Int J Turkish Studies II, 81; Tarikh Baghdad Ii-Ibn-al-Najjar, 80-83, 3 vols 2 edit 86; Al-Ghazali on Abstinence in Islam, 92; Decision Making in the Ottoman Empire, 92; The Road to Intervention: Fiscal Policies in Ottoman Mount Lebanon, 92; The Politics of Interventionism in Ottoman Lebanon, 2 vols, 97. **CONTACT ADDRESS** Afro-American Studies, Univ of Minnesota, Twin Cities, 267 19th Ave S, Minneapolis, MN, 55455-0499. **EMAIL** farah001@maroon.tc.umn.edu

FARAONE, CHRISTOPHER
DISCIPLINE CLASSICS **EDUCATION** Stanford Univ, PhD, 88. **CAREER** Asst prof, Va Polytech Inst & State Univ, 88-91; Asst prof, Univ Chicago, 91-93; Assoc prof, Univ Chicago, 93-. **HONORS AND AWARDS** John Simon Guggenheim Memorial Foundation Fel; Nat Endowment Hum; Jr Fel; ACLS Grant; NEH Summer Stipend; State Coun Higher Educ Va (SCHEV) Grant; Phi Beta Kappa Sch; Whiting Dissertation Fel; Stanford Grad Fel. **MEMBERSHIPS** Am Philol Asn; Clas Asn Midwest & South; Int Plutarch Soc; Soc Ancient Med; Soc Biblical Lit; Women's Clas Caucus. **SELECTED PUBLICATIONS** Auth, Talismans and Trojan Horses: Guardian Statues in Ancient Greek Myth and Ritual, Oxford Univ Press, 92, 96; auth, Ancient Greek Love Magic, Harvard Univ Press, 98; Co-ed, Magika Hiera: Ancient Greek Magic and Religion, Oxford Univ Press, 91; co-ed, Masks of Dionysus, Cornell Univ Press, 93. **CONTACT ADDRESS** Univ Chicago, 5801 S Ellis, Chicago, IL, 60637.

FARBER, JAY JOEL
PERSONAL Born 11/06/1932, Philadelphia, PA, m, 1952, 2 children **DISCIPLINE** CLASSICAL LANGUAGES AND LITERATURES **EDUCATION** Univ Chicago, BA, 52, MA, 54; Yale Univ, PhD (Greek and ancient hist), 59. **CAREER** Instr classics, Univ Chicago, 57-60; asst prof, Rutgers Univ, 60-63; assoc prof, 63-70, chmn dept, 63-79, PROF CLASSICS, FRANKLIN AND MARSHALL COL, 70-, Rutgers Univ Res Coun grants, 61 and 62; vis res assoc, Ctr Int Studies, Princeton Univ, 62-63; examnr, comt advan placement classics, Col Entrance Exam Bd, 71-74. **MEMBERSHIPS** Am Philol Asn; Am Soc Papyrologists; Class Asn Atlantic States. **RESEARCH** Greek myth; Greek tragedy; Greek political theory. **SELECTED PUBLICATIONS** Auth, The Documents from the Bar Kokhba Period in the Cave of Letters--Greek Papyri, Aramaic and Nabatean Signatures and Subscriptions, J Am Orient Soc, Vol 115, 95; Ancient Greek Alive, Classical World, Vol 89, 96. **CONTACT ADDRESS** Dept of Classics, Franklin and Marshall Col, Lancaster, PA, 17604.

FARBER, PAUL L.
PERSONAL Born 03/07/1944, New York, NY, m, 1966, 2 children **DISCIPLINE** HISTORY OF SCIENCE **EDUCATION** Univ Pittsburgh, BS, 65; Ind Univ, Bloomington, MA, 68, PhD, 70. **CAREER** Asst prof, 70-76, prof hist of sci, Ore State Univ, 76-82. **MEMBERSHIPS** Am Assn Advan Sci; Hist Sci Soc; Am Hist Assn. **RESEARCH** History of biology, especially philosophical. **SELECTED PUBLICATIONS** Auth, The Emergence of Ornithology as as Scientific Discipline: 1760-1850, Reidel, 82; auth, The Temptations of Endhetionary Ethics, University of California, 92. **CONTACT ADDRESS** Dept of Gen Hist, Oregon State Univ, 306 Milam Hall, Corvallis, OR, 97331-5104. **EMAIL** pfarber@orst.edu

FARGE, JAMES KNOX
PERSONAL Born 08/22/1938, Houston, TX **DISCIPLINE** EUROPEAN HISTORY **EDUCATION** Univ St Thomas, BA, 61; Univ Toronto, MA, 69, PhD (hist), 76. **CAREER** Instr hist, Univ St Thomas, 69-70; tutor church hist, Univ St Michael's Col, 73-75; asst prof hist, 76-80, ASSOC PROF HIST, UNIV ST THOMAS, 80-, Priest, Congregation of St Basil. **MEMBERSHIPS** Am Soc Reformation Res; Amici Thomae Morae; Cath Hist Asn; Renaissance Soc Am. **RESEARCH** University of Paris; Reformation in France; Erasmus. **SELECTED PUBLICATIONS** Auth, The Genesis of the French Reformation, 1520-1562, 16th Century J, Vol 28, 97; Soldiers of Christ--Preaching in Late Medieval and Reformation France, Cath Hist Rev, Vol 79, 93; The 5th Lateran Council 1512-17--Studies on its Membership, Diplomacy and Proposals for Reform,16th Century J, Vol 25, 94; Bouchet, Jean--La Deploration de Leglise Militante, Moreana, Vol 30, 93; Scholastic Humanism and the Unification of Europe, Vol 1, Theol Stud, Vol 57, 96. **CONTACT ADDRESS** Hist Dept, Univ St Thomas, Houston, TX, 77006.

FARIES, MOLLY
DISCIPLINE NORTHERN EUROPEAN ART **EDUCATION** Bryn Mawr Col, PhD. **CAREER** Prof. **RESEARCH** Netherlandish and German painting. **SELECTED PUBLICATIONS** Auth, Art Before Iconoclasm, 86; Northern Renaissance Paintings; The Discovery of Invention, 86. **CONTACT ADDRESS** Dept of History and Art, Indiana Univ, Bloomington, 300 N Jordan Ave, Bloomington, IN, 47405. **EMAIL** faries@indiana.edu

FARLEY, BENJAMIN WIRT
PERSONAL Born 08/06/1935, Manila, Philippines, m, 1962, 2 children **DISCIPLINE** HISTORICAL THEOLOGY, PHILOSOPHY **EDUCATION** Davidson Col, AB, 58; Union Theol Sem, Va, BD, 63, ThM, 64, ThD, 76. **CAREER** Pastor, Franklin Presby Church, 64-68 & Cove & Rockfish Presby Churches, 68-71; instr relig, Lees-McRae Col, 73-74; assoc prof to Younts Prof Bible, Religion, and Philos, Erskine Col, 74-. **HONORS AND AWARDS** Excellence in Teaching Award, Erskine Col, 77. **MEMBERSHIPS** Am Acad Refig; pres 97-99, Calvin Studies Soc. **RESEARCH** Reformation studies; philosophy of religion; literature and religion. **SELECTED PUBLICATIONS** Auth, Erskine Caldwell: Preacher's son and Southern prophet, fall 78 & George W Cable: Presbyterian Romancer, Reformer Bible Teacher, summer 80, J Presby Hist; John Calvin's Sermons on the Ten Commandments, 81 & Calvin's Treatises Against the Anabaptists and the Libertines, 82,

Baker Book House; The Hero of St Lo and Other Stories, Attic Press, 82; The Providence of God, Baker Book House, 88; Calvin's Ecclesiastical Advice, Westminster/John Knox Press, 91; In Praise of Virtue, Eerdmans, 95; Mercy Road, Cherokee Publishing Co, 86; Corbin's Rubi-Yacht, Sandlapper Press, 92. **CONTACT ADDRESS** Erskine Col, Hc 60, PO Box 595, Due West, SC, 29639-9801. **EMAIL** farley@erskine.edu

FARMER, CRAIG S.
PERSONAL Born 10/02/1961, Urbana, IL, m, 1982, 2 children **DISCIPLINE** HISTORY OF CHRISTIANITY **EDUCATION** Haverford Col, BA, 83; Univ Chicago, MA, 84; Duke Univ, PhD, 92. **CAREER** Asst prof of history and humanities, 93-98; assoc prof of hist and humanities, 98-present, Milligan Col. **MEMBERSHIPS** Amer Soc of Church Hist; Amer Acad of Relig; Medieval Acad of Amer; Sixteenth Century Studies Conf. **RESEARCH** Reformation theology; hist of biblical interpretation. **SELECTED PUBLICATIONS** Auth, Changing Images of the Samaritan Woman in Early Reformed Commentaries on John, Church History, 96; Eucharistic Exhibition and Sacramental Presence in the New Testament Commentaries of Wolfgang Musculus, Wolfgang Musculus, 97; The Gospel of John in the Sixteenth Century: The Johannine Exegesis of Wolfgang Musculus, The Oxford Studies in Historical Theology, Oxford University Press, 97. **CONTACT ADDRESS** Milligan Col, Milligan College, TN, 37682. **EMAIL** csfarmer@milligan.edu

FARMER, DAVID
PERSONAL Born 07/01/1935, Barnstable, England, m, 1978, 4 children **DISCIPLINE** POLITICAL SCIENCE, PUBLIC ADMINISTRATION **EDUCATION** London Sch Econ and Political Sci, Univ London, BS, PhD, 84; Univ Toronto, MA, 64; Univ Va, MA, 86, PhD, 89. **CAREER** Prof Political Sci and Publ Admin, Va Commonwealth Univ. **MEMBERSHIPS** Pub Admin Theory Network; Amer Soc Pub Admin. **RESEARCH** Political Philosophy; Public Administration; Philosophy of Social Science; Postmodernism. **SELECTED PUBLICATIONS** Auth, Civil Disorder Control, Public Administration Service, Chicago Il, 68; Out of Hugger-Mugger: The Case of Police Field Services, Clarke, RV, ed, Policy Effectiveness, Gower Publ, Scarborough, Eng, 80, 17-34; Thinking About Research: The Contribution of Social Science Research to Law Enforcement, Police Stud, 3, 4, 81; The Future of Local Law Enforcement: the Federal Role, Annual Editions: Criminal Justice, 81/82, Duskin Publ Group, Guildford, CT, 81, reprinted from Policy, 78 also reprinted in Annual editions, 80/81, 80; Policy Resources Allocation: Toward a Theory, Police Stud, 5, 2, 82, 34-47; Politicians, Professionals and Crime Control, Va Town and City, 5, May 84, 1-4; Crime Control: The Use and Misuse of Police Resoutces, Plenum Publ Corp, NY,84; Homicide Policy and Program Analysis: Understanding and Coping in Local Government, LAE Jour, 15, 1, Summer-Fall, 88, reprinted from Commonwealth Paper, Ctr Pub Affairs, Richmond, Va, 87; An Epidemiological Model for Crime Control, Commonwealth Paper, Ctr Pub Affairs, Richmond Va, 88; Being in Time: The Nature of Time in Light of McTaggart's Paradox, Univ Press Am, Lanham, Md, 90; Social Construction of Concepts: The Case of Efficiency, Admin Theory and Praxis, 16, 2, 94, 254-262; Bradley and McTaggart: Una Lettura Comparata, Ornella Bellini, ed, Problemi della Pedogogia, Marzorati Publ, Milan, Italy, 41, 2-3, March-June, 95, 341-355, re-publ as Bradley and McTaggart on Time, Bradley Stud, 2, 2, Fall 96, 104-116; Kill the King: Foucault and Public Administration Theory, Administrative Theory and Praxis, 17, 2, 95, 78-83; Coping with the Super-Abstract: Teaching about the Implications of Postmodernism for Public Administration, Jour Publ Admin Ed, 1, 2, 95, 90-101; John of Salisbury's Political Philosophy, McCrea Adams, ed, Survey of Social Science: Government and Politics, Pasadena, Calif, 95, 1872-1877; The Language of Public Administration: Bureaucracy, Modernity and Postmodernity, Univ Alabama Press, Univ Ala, 95; Justice, Hesitancy and the In-between, Jour Organizational Change Management, 9, 4, 96, 24-33; Remember Dionysus, Forget Ferrante, Administrative Theory and Praxis, 18, 1, April 96, 54-56, re-publ in Hugh T. Miller and Charles J. Fox, Postmodernism "Reality" and Public Administration: A Discourse, Chatelaine Press, Burke, Va, 97, 195-198; Gadflying: A Dialogue, Administrative Theory and Praxis, 18, 1, April 96, 75-78, re-publ in Hugh T. Miller and Charles J. Fox, Postmodernism Reality and Public Administration: A Discourse, Chatelaine Press, Burke, Va , 97, 161-167; The Postmodern Turn and the Socratic Gadfly, Administrative Theory and Praxis, 18, 1, April 96, 128-133; Derrida, Deconstruction and Public Administration, Amer Behavioral Scientist, 31, 1, Sept 97, 43-71; Contemporary Conceptual Space: Reading Adam Smith, Jour of Management Hist, 97; Adam Smith's Legacy, Thomas D. Lynch, ed, Handbook of Organization Theory and Management, Marcel Dekker, New York, 97, 141-164; Postmodernism and the End of Public Administration, in Abbass F. Alkhataji and Jerry Bieberman, eds, Business Research Yearbook: Global Business Perspectives, Univ Press Am, Larham, Md, 96, 628-632; Introduction: Listening to Other Voices, Publ Voices, 3, 1, July 97, 1-8; Public Administration Discourse as Play with a Purpose, Publ Voices, 3, 1, July 97, 33-51; Leopards in the Temple: Bureaucracy and the Limits of the In-Between, Administration and Soc, 29, 5, Nov 97, 507-528. **CONTACT ADDRESS** Dept of Political Science and Public Administration, Virginia Commonwealth Univ, 1110 West Ave, Richmond, VA, 23220. **EMAIL** dfarmer@vcu.edu

FARMER, EDWARD L.
DISCIPLINE HISTORY; PHILOSOPHY **EDUCATION** Stanford Univ, BA, 57; Harvard Univ, MA, 62, PhD, 68. **CAREER** Fulbright fel, Taiwan, 65-67; prof, Univ Minn Twin Cities, 68-. **HONORS AND AWARDS** Ed, Ming Studies, 75-85. **RESEARCH** Comparative early modern history; Ming institutions; social legislation. **SELECTED PUBLICATIONS** Auth, Early Ming Government: The Evolution of Dual Capitals, Harvard, 76; co-auth, Comparative History of Civilizations in Asia, 77; A World History: Links Across Time and Space, 87; ed, Encyclopedia of Asian History, 88. **CONTACT ADDRESS** History Dept, Univ of Minnesota, Twin Cities, 614 Social Sciences Tower, 267 19th Ave. S, Minneapolis, MN, 55455. **EMAIL** farme001@tc.umn.edu

FARMER, P.
PERSONAL Born 10/26/1959, North Adams, MA, m, 1997, 1 child **DISCIPLINE** ANTHROPOLOGY **EDUCATION** Harvard Univ, MD, 90, PhD, 90. **CAREER** Assoc prof, Harvard Med Schl. **HONORS AND AWARDS** MacArthur Fel, 93-98; Wellcome Medal, 92; Eileen Bashes Prize, 96. **MEMBERSHIPS** Amer Anthrop Assn; Amer Col of Internal Med; Intl Union Against Tuberculosis. **RESEARCH** AIDS, TB, Social inequalities. **SELECTED PUBLICATIONS** Auth, AIDS and Accusation, Univ Calif Press, 92; auth, Uses of Haiti, Comm Courage, 94; auth, Women, Poverty and AIDS, Common Courage, 96; auth, Infections and Inequalities, Univ Calif Press, 98; auth, Pathologies of Power, Univ Calif Press, 99. **CONTACT ADDRESS** 113 Rivers St, Cambridge, MA, 02139. **EMAIL** partnersma@aol.com

FARNSWORTH, BEATRICE
PERSONAL Born 02/03/1935, New York, NY, m, 1953, 3 children **DISCIPLINE** RUSSIAN HISTORY **EDUCATION** Ind Univ, AB, 55; Yale Univ, MA, 56, PhD, 59. **CAREER** Instr Russian Hist, Hobart and William Smith Cols, 61-64; from asst prof to assoc prof, 65-68, ASSOC PROF HIST, WELLS COL, 68-, Fel, Radcliffe Inst Independent Studies, 64-65 and 66-67; assoc, Russ Res Ctr, Harvard Univ, 64-65. **MEMBERSHIPS** AHA; Am Asn Advan Slavic Studies **RESEARCH** Russian history. **SELECTED PUBLICATIONS** Auth, Armand, Inessa--Revolutionary and Feminist, Am Hist Rev, Vol 98, 93; Peasant Icons--Representations of Rural People in Late 19th Century Russia, Russ Rev, Vol 53, 94; Between the Fields and the City--Women, Work and Family in Russia, 1861-1914, Russ Hist Histoire Russe, Vol 23, 96; Perestroika and Soviet Women, Russ Rev, Vol 53, 94. **CONTACT ADDRESS** 410 Brampton Dr, Syracuse, NY, 13214.

FARR, DAVID M.L.
PERSONAL Vancouver, BC, Canada **DISCIPLINE** HISTORY **EDUCATION** Univ BC, BA, 44; Univ Toronto, MA, 46; Oxford Univ, Dphil, 52. **CAREER** Lectr hist, Dalhousie Univ 46-47; asst prof 47, prof 61, dean of arts 63-69, PROF EMER HISTORY, UNIV TORONTO, 87-; dir, Paterson Ctr Int Prog, Carleton Univ 79-85; vis lectr, assoc prof, Univ BC, 53, 57-58; vis assoc prof, Duke Univ, 60. **MEMBERSHIPS** Can Hist Asn; Soc Sci Fedn Can; Can Inst Int Affairs **SELECTED PUBLICATIONS** Auth, The Colonial Office and Canada, 1867-1887, 55; A Church in the Glebe: St. Matthew's, Ottawa, 1898-1988, 88; coauth, Two Democracies, 63; The Canadian Experience, 69; ed Documents on Canadian External Relations, vol 1, 1909-1918, 67. **CONTACT ADDRESS** 942 Colonel By Dr, Ottawa, ON, K1S 5C9.

FARRELL, FRANK
DISCIPLINE CHURCH HISTORY **EDUCATION** Edinburgh Univ, PhD. **CAREER** Instr, Alliance Theol Sem; prof. **HONORS AND AWARDS** Founding ed, Christianity Today. **RESEARCH** Puritans. **SELECTED PUBLICATIONS** Ed-in-Chief, World Vision mag. **CONTACT ADDRESS** Dept of Church History, Reformed Theol Sem, 1015 Maitland Ctr Commons, Maitland, FL, 32751.

FARRELL, WARREN THOMAS
PERSONAL Born 06/26/1943, New York, NY **DISCIPLINE** POLITICAL SCIENCE **EDUCATION** Montclair St, BA, 65; UCLA, MA, 66; NY Univ, PhD, 74. **CAREER** Lectr, 70, Fordham Univ; instr, 70, NJ St Col; instr, 71-73, Rutgers Univ; instr, 73-74, Amer Univ; instr, 73-75, Georgetown Univ, Schl of Lib Stud; adj asst prof, CUNY; prof, 78-79, Calif Schl of Prof Psychol; prof, 79-80, San Diego St Univ; prof, 86-88, Univ Calif, Schl of Med. **HONORS AND AWARDS** Who's Who in West, 27th ed, 2000-01; White House Conf on Ed, 65; Award Outstanding Contribution, Calif Assn of Marriage & Family Therapists, 88; Hon Dr, Humane Letters, prof Schl of Psychol, San Diego CA, 85; Who's Who Among Students in Amer Col & Univ, 65; Oxford Companion to Phil, Oxford Univ Press, 95. **MEMBERSHIPS** Natl Org for Women; Children's Rights Coun; Natl Cong of Fathers & Children; Amer Coalition for Fathers & Children; Amer Bd of Sexology; Coastal Comm Found; Fathers' Rights & Equality Exchange. **RESEARCH** Politics & psychology of men & women; the women's & men's movement. **SELECTED PUBLICATIONS** Auth, The Liberated Man: Beyond Masculinity, Random House, 75, Bantam, 75, Putnam-Berkley, 93; auth, The Myth of Male Power, Simon & Schuster, 93, Putnam-Berkley, 94; auth, Why Men Are The Way They Are, McGraw-Hill, 86, Putnam-Berkley, 88. **CONTACT ADDRESS** 103 N Hwy 101, Box 220, Encinitas, CA, 92024. **EMAIL** wfarrell@cts.com

FARRER, CLAIRE RAFFERTY
PERSONAL Born 12/26/1936, New York, NY, d, 1 child **DISCIPLINE** ANTHROPOLOGY & FOLKLORE **EDUCATION** Univ CA, Berkeley, BA, 70; Univ TX, Austin, MA, 74, PhD, 77. **CAREER** Am Folklore Soc, Smithsonian Inst, Austin, TX, 73-74; res assoc, Joint Senate-House Committee on Prison reform, TX, summer 74; academic fel, Whitney M Young Memorial Found, Inc, NY, 74-75; NEA Folk Arts Prog, Washington, DC, 76-77; Weatherhead Resident fel, School of Am Res, 77-78; asst prof, anthropol, Univ IL, Urbana-Champaign, 78-85; coord of Certificate prog in Applied Anthropol and asoc prof, 85-89, prof, Anthropology, CA State Univ, Chico, 89-; vis prof, Rijksuniversiteit-Gent, Belgium, spring 90; dir, Center for Multicultural and Gender Studies, CSU-Chico, 94; exec dir/business manager, Western Folklore, CA Folklore Soc, 94-98; Hulbert Endowed chair and vis prof of Southwest Studies, Hulbert Center for Southwest Studies, the Colorado Col, Colorado Springs, CO, spring 97. **HONORS AND AWARDS** Phi Kappa Phi; Sigma Xi; Advanced Sem, School of Am Res, Santa Fe, NM, 78; Univ IL-Urbana: res bd, 79, 83, Center for Advanced Study, 82, Excellent Teacher, 80, Outstanding Teacher, 84, 85; Am Philos Soc, Phillips Fund, 82; Am Coun of Learned Socs grant, 84; CA State Univ, Chico, res, 86-88, Professional Promise Award, 87, Professional Achievement Award, 87, 93, Outstanding Prof Award, 93-94, Student Internship Service grant, 89; NEH travel grant, 88; Phi Eta Sigma, Oustanding Teacher Award, 91, hon member, 91; Golden Key Nat Honor Soc, 93, summer res fel, 95; Recipient, First Annual MAGGIE Award for Outstanding Women Leaders, 93; CHOICE Outstanding Academic Book, 93; Book, Thunder Rides a Black Horse: Mescalero Apaches and the Mythic Present, nominated for a Spur Award and a PEN literary writing award, 94; several other various res grants; listed in several honorary publications including numerous editions of Who's Who. **MEMBERSHIPS** Am Anthropological Asn; Am Ethnological Soc; Am Folklore Soc; Am Soc for Ethnohistory; Authors Guild; CA Folklore Soc; Int Soc for Archaeostonomy & Astronomy in Culture; Royal Anthropol Inst; Soc for the Anthropology of Consciousness; Soc for Cultural Anthropol; Soc for Humanistic Anthropol; Southwestern Anthropol Asn; Traditional Cosmology Soc. **RESEARCH** Ritual; ethnoastronomy; Mescalero Apaches; Whiteriver Apaches. **SELECTED PUBLICATIONS** Auth, Thunder Rides a Black Horse: Mescalero Apaches and the Mythic Present,Waveland Press, 94, 2nd ed, Waveland Press, 96; Who Owns the Words?: An Anthropological Prespective on Public Law 101-601, J of Arts, Management, Law, and Society, 94; Turning the Storm, in Bridges to Humanity: Narratives on Anthropology and Friendship, Bruce Grindal and Frank Salamone, eds, Waveland Press, 95; On Singers and Lineages: Response to Rushforth, Am Ethnologist, 95; review essay of When They Read What We Write, Caroline B Brettell, ed, On the Production of Knowledge, Hein Streefkers, and The Politics of Ethnolgraphic Reading and Writing, Henk Driessen, ed, Am Anthropol, 96; Bloed en Paarden: Culturele Evenementen in Belgie-Een Antropologische Analyse van een Vreemde Cultuur, Cultuur en Migratie, 96; numerous books, book chapters, journal and encyclopedia articles, monographs, reviews, and other publications. **CONTACT ADDRESS** Dept of Anthropol, California State Univ, Chico, Chico, CA, 95929-0400. **EMAIL** cfarrer@suchino.edu

FARRIS, W. WAYNE
DISCIPLINE HISTORY **EDUCATION** Harvard Univ, PhD. **CAREER** Prof. **RESEARCH** Early Japanese history. **SELECTED PUBLICATIONS** Auth, Population, Disease, and Land in Early Japan 645-900, Harvard; Heavenly Warriors: The Evolution of Japan's Military 500-1300, Harvard; Sacred, Texts and Buried Treasures: Issues in Historical Archaeology of Ancient Japan, Univ Hawaii, 98. **CONTACT ADDRESS** Dept of History, Knoxville, TN, 37996.

FARROW, J.G.
DISCIPLINE CLASSICS **EDUCATION** Oxford, Master of Letters, 79 **CAREER** Head class, relig stud, Haberdashers' Monmouth, Wales, 80- 86; ADJ PROF CLASS, WAYNE STATE UNIV, 88-; PROF HUM, MACOMB COMMUNITY COL, 89-. **CONTACT ADDRESS** Dept of Classics, Wayne State Univ, Manoogian Hall 430, Detroit, MI, 48101. **EMAIL** farr01J@macomb.cc.mi.us

FARTHING, JOHN L.
DISCIPLINE RELIGION AND CLASSICAL LANGUAGES **EDUCATION** Univ Tulsa, BA, 69; Duke Univ, MDiv, 74, PhD, 78. **CAREER** Prof Relig and Clas Lang, 78, ch, dept Relig, Hendrix Col. **RESEARCH** Medieval, Reformation, and Renaissance theology. **SELECTED PUBLICATIONS** Auth, Thomas Aquinas and Gabriel Biel; transl, Jean-Claude Margolin, auth, Humanism in Europe at the Time of the Renaissance. **CONTACT ADDRESS** Hendrix Col, Conway, AR, 72032.

FASOLT, CONSTANTIN
PERSONAL Born 03/18/1951, Bonn, Germany, m, 1998, 2 children **DISCIPLINE** HISTORY **EDUCATION** Beethoven-Gymnasium, Abitur, 69; Columbia Univ, MA, 76, MPhil, 78, PhD, 81. **CAREER** Preceptor in hist, 79-81, lectr in hist, 81-83, Columbia Univ; ASST PROF OF HIST, 83-90, ASSOC PROF OF HIST, 90-, UNIV OF CHICAGO; GENERAL ED OF NEW PERSPECTIVES ON THE PAST, 93-; visiting prof of hist, Univ of Va, 99-. **HONORS AND AWARDS** Pres fel, Columbia Univ, 76-79; Mellon fel, Soc of Fels in the Humanities, Columbia Univ, 81-83; res grant, Am Philos Soc, 85-86; fel, Inst for European Hist, 85-86; Soc Scis Res Grants, Univ of Chicago, 87-88, 92-93, & 98-99; summer res fel, Max-Planck-Inst for European Legal Hist, 95; fel, Nat Humanities Center, 96-97; fel, John Simon Guggenheim Memorial Found, 96-97. **MEMBERSHIPS** Am Cusanus Soc; Am Hist Asn; Asn for Core Texts & Courses; Medieval Acad of Am; Renaissance Soc of Am; Soc for Reformation Res. **RESEARCH** History of European political thought; history of historical thought. **SELECTED PUBLICATIONS** Auth, Council and Hierarchy: The Political Thought of William Durant the Younger, Cambridge Stud in Medieval Life and Thought 4th series, Cambridge Univ Press, 91; auth, Visions of Order in the Canonists and Civilians, Handbook of European Hist 1400-1600: Late Middle Ages, Renaissance and Reformation vol 2, Brill, 95; auth, William Durant the Younger and Conciliar Theory, J of the Hist of Ideas, 97; auth, A Question of Right: Hermann Conring's New Discourse on the Roman-German Emperor, Sixteenth Century J, 97; auth, Sovereignty and Heresy, Infinite Boundaries: Order, Disorder, and Reorder in Early Modern German Culture, 98. **CONTACT ADDRESS** Dept of Hist, Univ of Chicago, 1126 E 59th St., Chicago, IL, 60637. **EMAIL** icon@midway.uchicago.edu

FASS, PAULA S.
PERSONAL Born 05/22/1947, m, 2 children **DISCIPLINE** AMERICAN HISTORY **EDUCATION** Barnard Col, AB, 67; Columbia Univ, MA, 68, PhD, 74. **CAREER** Asst prof, Rutgers Univ, New Brunswick, 72-74; asst prof, 74-78, assoc prof hist, Univ CA, Berkeley , 78, Rockefeller Hum fel hist, Rockefeller Found, 76-77; Nat Endowment for Hum, 78; fel, Center for Adv Study in Behavioral Sci, Stanford, 91-92; Nat Endowment for Hum Fel, 94-95; prof hist, Univ CA, 87. **HONORS AND AWARDS** Phi Beta Kappa; Chancellor's Prof, Univ CA, Berkeley. **RESEARCH** Am soc hist; family, youth and educ in the US; Am immigration. **SELECTED PUBLICATIONS** Contribr, The writings of Richard Hofstadter, a bibliography, In: The Hofstadter Aegis, Knopf, 74; Television as cultural document: Promises and problems, In: Television as a Cultural Force, Praeger, 76; auth, The Damned and the Beautiful: American Youth in the 1920's, Oxford Univ, 77; The IQ: A Cultural and Historical Framework, Am J Educ, 8/80; Outside In: Minorities and the Transformation of American Education, Oxford Press, 89; The Leopold and the Loeb Case in American Culture, J of American Hiatory, 93; Kidnapped: Child Abduction in America, Oxford Press, 97; Parental Kidnapping: A Sign of Family Disorder; contrib to All Our Families, Oxford Press, 98. **CONTACT ADDRESS** Dept of Hist, Univ of California, 3229 Dwinelle Hall, Berkeley, CA, 94720-2551. **EMAIL** psfass@socrates.berkeley.edu

FAUE, ELIZABETH V.
PERSONAL Born 06/26/1956, Minneapolis, MN **DISCIPLINE** HISTORY **EDUCATION** Univ Minn, AB, 79, MA, 85, PhD, 87. **CAREER** Susan B. Anthony fel women's stud and hist, Univ Rochester, 88-90; asst prof, 90-93, Assoc Prof, Wayne State Univ, 93-. **HONORS AND AWARDS** Career Dev Dahir, Wayne State Univ, 95-96; Col Lib Arts teaching award, 98; Bd Gov fac rec, 92; Phi Beta Kappa, 79. **MEMBERSHIPS** AHA; Org Am Historians; Soc Sci Hist Asn. **RESEARCH** Labor, working class hist; U.S., comparative women's history, gender; political hist; 19th, 20th centuries. **SELECTED PUBLICATIONS** Auth, Community of Suffering and Struggle: Women, Men, and the Labor Movement in Minneapolis, 1915-1945, Univ NC Press, 91; ed, Gender and Labor History special issue, Labor Hist 34:2-3, Spring/Summer 93; auth, Outfoxing the Frost: Gender, Community- Based Organization, and the Contemporary American Labor Movement, Working Papers in Labor Studies No. 4, Jan 94; auth, Anti-Heroes of the Working Class, Int Rev Soc Hist 41, Dec 96; auth, Paths of Unionization: Community, Bureaucracy, and Gender in the Minneapolis Labor Movement, 1935-1945, in Work Engendered: Toward a New Labor History, Cornell Univ Press, 91; auth, Writing the Wrongs: Eva McDonald Valesh and the Political Culture of American Labor Reform, 1886-1920, Cornell Univ Press, forthcoming. **CONTACT ADDRESS** Dept Hist, Wayne State Univ, 3094 Faculty/Admn Bldg, Detroit, MI, 48202. **EMAIL** efaue@aol.com

FAUL, KARENE TARQUIN
PERSONAL Born 10/16/1934, Pittsburgh, PA, m, 1971, 2 children **DISCIPLINE** ART **EDUCATION** Notre Dame, BA, 66, MA, 68, MFA, 70. **CAREER** Assoc prof, 70-, chmn, art dept, 83-, Col of St Rose, NY. **RESEARCH** Screen printing; history of printmaking, art careers, art portfolio for col acceptance. **CONTACT ADDRESS** 432 Western Ave, Albany, NY, 12203.

FAULCON, CLARENCE AUGUSTUS, II
PERSONAL Born 08/08/1928, Philadelphia, PA, m **DISCIPLINE** MUSICOLOGY **EDUCATION** Lincoln U, 1946-48; Univ PA, BMus Ed 1950; Univ PA, MMus Ed 1952; Philadelphia Conservatory of Music, MusD in Musicolgy 1962-. **CAREER** Chairperson Sulzberger Jr Hi (Phila), music teacher, chairperson 1951-63; Cazenovia Coll (Cazenovia, NY), asst prof, chairperson 1963-68; Morgan State Univ (Balt), prof, chairperson 1968-79; Morgan State Univ, prof 1979-. **HONORS AND AWARDS** Morgan State Univ Promethan Soc Faculty Award, 1983; Intl Biographical Cong Medal of Cong, Budapest, Hungary, 1985; Afro Amer Music in Health Promotion Disease Prevention and Therapy, Montreal, Canada, Conf Natl Medical Assn 1984; recital accompanist & artist accompanist in various countries, 1982-88; accompanist, voice concert, and conducted plenary session interviews of eight delegates, International Biographical Centre Congress on Arts and Communications, Nairobi, Kenya, 1990; received IBC Silver Medal struck at the mint of the Queen of England. **MEMBERSHIPS** Delegate, Intl Biographical Centre Arts & Communication Congresses, 1981-. **CONTACT ADDRESS** Music, Morgan State Univ, Baltimore, MD, 21239.

FAULHABER, CHARLES BAILEY
PERSONAL Born 09/18/1941, East Cleveland, OH, m, 1971 **DISCIPLINE** MEDIEVAL SPANISH LITERATURE **EDUCATION** Yale Univ, BA, 63, MPhil & PhD, 69; Univ WI-Madison, MA, 66. **CAREER** Actg instr Span, Yale Univ, 68-69; from Asst Prof to Assoc Prof, 69-80, Prof Span, Univ CA, Berkeley, 80-, Chmn, Dept Span & Port, 89-94, James D. Hart Dir, The Bancroft Libr, 95-; ed, The Romance Philol, 82-, ed-in-chief, 86-87; assoc ed, Hispania, 95-98. **HONORS AND AWARDS** Prin investr, Hispanic Soc Am, Nat Endowment for Hum, 76 & 78-80; Guggenheim fel, 82-83; mem, Hisp Soc Am, 83; Ministerio de Asuntos Exteriores de Espana, beca de investigacion, 89, 95; NEH grants, 89-91, 91-93, 94-95; Quincentenary Postdoctoral Fel, Spain, 91. **MEMBERSHIPS** MLA; Assoc Int Hispanistas; Medieval Acad Am; Am Acad Res Hist Medieval Spain; Am Asn Tchr(s) Span & Port; AAUP; Asn Hisp Lit Medieval; Asn Computers and the Hum; Medieval Asn Pacific. **RESEARCH** Medieval rhetoric; computers and hum. **SELECTED PUBLICATIONS** Coauth, Normas para BOOST, Hisp Seminary of Medieval Studies, Ltd, 86; auth, Libros y bibliotecas en la Espana medieval. Una bibliografia de fuentes impresas, Research Bibliographies and Checklists, Grant & Cutler, 87; Medieval Manuscripts in the Library of the Hispanic Society of America. Documents and Letters, The Hisp Soc Am, 93; Necrology: Ruth House Webber (1918-1997), La Coronica 25.2, 97; Sobre la cultura ibrica medieval: Las lenguas vern culas y la traduccion, Actas del VI Congreso Internacional de la Asociacion Hisp nica de Literatura Medieval, Univ Alcal , 97; author numerous other articles and publ. **CONTACT ADDRESS** The Bancroft Library, Univ of California, Berkeley, CA, 94720-6000. **EMAIL** cfaulhab@library.berkeley.edu

FAULK, ODIE B.
PERSONAL Born 08/26/1933, Winnsboro, TX, m, 1959, 2 children **DISCIPLINE** SOUTHWESTERN HISTORY **EDUCATION** Tex Technol Col, BS, 58, MA, 60, PhD, 62. **CAREER** Instr southwest hist, Tex Agr and Mech Col, 62-63; asst ed, Ariz and the West, 63-67; chmn div soc sci, Ariz West Col, 67-68; from assoc prof to prof hist, 68-77 and head dept, 72-77, Okla State Univ; HISTORIAN, NAT COWBOY HALL OF FAME, OKLAHOMA CITY, 77-. **MEMBERSHIPS** AHA; Orgn Am Historians; Western Hist Asn. **RESEARCH** Southwest; Latin America. **SELECTED PUBLICATIONS** Auth, Texas Ranch Life--With Three Months Through Mexico in a Prairie Schooner, J West, Vol 32, 93; Los Comanches--The Horse People, 1751-1845, Southwestern Hist Quart, Vol 98, 94. **CONTACT ADDRESS** 418 Ramblewood Terr, Edmond, OK, 73034.

FAUSOLD, MARTIN L.
PERSONAL Born 11/11/1921, Irwin, PA, m, 1949, 4 children **DISCIPLINE** POLITICAL HISTORY **EDUCATION** Gettysburg Col, AB, 45; Syracuse Univ, PhD (polit hist Am), 53. **CAREER** From asst prof to prof, State Univ NY Col Cortland, 52-58; prof and chmn dept, 58-65, PROF HIST, STATE UNIV NY COL GENESEO, 65-, Chmn div soc sci, State Univ NY Col Geneseo, 66-69, Res Found fel and grants-in-aid, 54-79, mem joint awards coun, Res Found, 69, chmn univ awards comt, 70-77. **MEMBERSHIPS** AHA; Orgn Am Historians. **RESEARCH** American political biography; presidency of Herbert Hoover; 20th century political history. **SELECTED PUBLICATIONS** Auth, From New Day to New Deal--American Farm Policy from Hoover to Roosevelt, 1928-1933, J Southern Hist, Vol 59, 93. **CONTACT ADDRESS** Dept of Hist, State Univ of NY, Geneseo, NY, 14454.

FAUST, DREW GILPIN
PERSONAL Born 09/18/1947, New York, NY, 1 child **DISCIPLINE** AMERICAN STUDIES, AMERICAN HISTORY **EDUCATION** Bryn Mawr Col, BA, 68; Univ Pa, MA, 71, PhD, 75. **CAREER** Sr fel, 75-76, asst prof, 76-80, assoc prof am civilization, 80-84, prof, 84-88, chmn dept, 80-83, 84-86, Stanley I Sheerr Prof hist, 88-90, dir, Women's Stud, 96-, Annenberg Prof hist, 89-, UNIV PA; Soc Sci Res Coun training fel, 75; Am Coun Learned Soc grant-in-aid, 78; Nat Endowment Humanities fel, 79-80. **HONORS AND AWARDS** Spencer Found Award, 76; AACLS grant in Aid, 78; NEH Fel, indep res, 79-80; Lindback Award for Dist tchng, 82; Jules F. Landry Award, 82; assoc fel, Stanford Hum Ctr, Stanford Univ, 83-84; Prize of Soc of Hist of the Early Amer Rep, 83; Charles S Sydnor Prize of the Southern Hist Assn, 84; Amer Coun of Learned Soc Fel, 86; Guggenheim Fel, 86; Walter Lynwood Fleming Lecturer La St Univ, 87; /Soc of Amer Hist, 93; Amer Acad of Arts & Sci, 96; Ira Abrams Award for Dist tchng, Univ Pa, 96; Mothers of Invention - NY Times Notable Bk of Year, 96; Avery Craven Prize of the Org of Amer Hist, 96; Francis Parkman Prize, Soc of Amer Hist, 96. **MEMBERSHIPS** Orgn Am Historians; Southern Hist Assn. **RESEARCH** American South, American belief systems. **SELECTED PUBLICATIONS** Ed & intro, Macaria, Augusta Jane Evans, La St Univ Press, 92; auth, Introduction: Writing the War, Brokenburn: the J of Kale Stone, 1861-1868, Baton Rouge LSU, 95; auth, A Riddle of Death: Mortality and Meaning in the American Civil Wr, Fortenbaugh Lectr, 95; auth, Southern Stories: Slaveholders in Peace and War, Univ NC Press, 96. **CONTACT ADDRESS** Dept of History, Univ of Pennsylvania, Philadelphia, PA, 19104-6228. **EMAIL** dfaust@sas.upenn.edu

FAUST, NAOMI FLOWE
PERSONAL Salisbury, North Carolina, m **DISCIPLINE** EDUCATION **EDUCATION** Bennett Coll, AB; Univ of MI-Ann Arbor, MA; New York Univ, PhD. **CAREER** Public School System Gaffney SC, elem teacher; Atkins High School Winston-Salem NC, English teacher; Bennett Coll & Southern Univ Scotlandville LA, instr of English; Morgan State Univ Baltimore MD, prof of English; Greensboro Public Schools & New York City Public Schools, teacher; Queens Coll of CUNY, prof of English/Educ. **HONORS AND AWARDS** Named Teacher-Author by Teacher-Writer 1979; Certificate of Merit Cooper Hill Writers Conf; Certificate of Merit Poems by Blacks; Honored by Long Island Natl Assoc of Univ Women for High Achievement; poetry book "And I Travel by Rhythms and Words," 1990; International Poets Academy, International Eminent Poet. **MEMBERSHIPS** Mem Amer Assoc of Univ Profs, Natl Council of Teachers of English, Natl Women's Book Assoc, World Poetry Soc Intercontinental, NY Poetry Forum, NAACP. **SELECTED PUBLICATIONS** Auth, Publications "Speaking in Verse," a book of poems 1974; "Discipline and the Classroom Teacher," 1977; "All Beautiful Things," poems 1983.

FAWN CHUNG, SUE
DISCIPLINE HISTORY **EDUCATION** Univ Calif Berkeley, PhD, 75. **CAREER** Assoc prof, Univ Nevada Las Vegas. **SELECTED PUBLICATIONS** Auth, pubs on History of China, Chinese-American history, and Chinese art. **CONTACT ADDRESS** History Dept, Univ Nev Las Vegas, 4505 Md Pky, Las Vegas, NV, 89154.

FAXON, ALICIA CRAIG
PERSONAL Born 07/21/1931, New York, NY, m, 1953, 2 children **DISCIPLINE** ART HISTORY **EDUCATION** Vassar Col, BA, 52; Radcliffe Col, MA, 53; Boston Univ, BA, art hist, 75; PhD, 79. **CAREER** Lectr, 74-77, New England Schl Art & Design; asst prof, prof, 78-93, Simmons Col; ed, Rhode Island, Art New England, 93-98. **HONORS AND AWARDS** Hon degree, Simmons Col, 98; Honoree W CA, 96; Phi Beta Kappa, Vassar Col, award for art criticism, Art New England. **MEMBERSHIPS** Col Art Assn; Victorian Soc; Hist of British Art; SE Col Art Assn. **RESEARCH** Women artists; 19th century Eng & French art; Pre-Raphaelite art. **SELECTED PUBLICATIONS** Co-ed, Pre-Raphaelite Art in its European context, Assoc Univ Press, 95; auth, Dante Gabriel Rossetti, NY Abbeville, 94; auth, introduction, The Letters of Dane Gabriel and William Michael Rossetti, Ellen Clarke Bertrand Lib ed ser, Bucknell Univ, 95; ed & contr, Pilgrims & Pioneers: New England Women in the Arts, NY Midmarch, 87; auth, Jean-Louis Forain: Artist, Humanist, Realist, Wash DC: Intl Exhib Found, 82; auth, Jean-Louis Forain: A Catalogue Raisonne of the Prints, NY Garland, 82; art, Annette Messager, Art New Eng, 98; art, The Sculpture of B. Amore, Sculpture mag, 97; art, Art Collecting in Newport, Art New Eng, 97. **CONTACT ADDRESS** 2 Pond Cir, Jamaica Plain, MA, 02130.

FAY, MARY ANN
DISCIPLINE HISTORY **EDUCATION** Georgetown Univ, PhD, 93. **CAREER** Prof, Va Mil Inst, 94-; adv, Model Arab League Club; Fulbright grant, 95; NEH-Amer Res Center grant, Egypt, 96. **SELECTED PUBLICATIONS** Publ on, women in Ottoman and Islamic society. **CONTACT ADDRESS** Dept of History, Virginia Military Inst, Lexington, VA, 24450.

FAY, PETER WARD
PERSONAL Born 12/03/1924, Paris, France, m, 1957, 5 children **DISCIPLINE** EUROPEAN HISTORY, ASIAN HISTORY **EDUCATION** Harvard Univ, BA, 47; Oxford Univ, BA, 49; Harvard Univ, PhD, 54. **CAREER** Instr hist, Williams Col, 51-55; asst prof to assoc prof, 55-70, PROF HIST, CALIF INST TECHNOL, 70-, Vis prof, Indian Inst Technol, Kanpur, 64-66; Am Coun Learned Soc res grant, 77. **HONORS AND**

AWARDS Silver medal, Commonwealth Club of Calif, 76. **MEMBERSHIPS** AHA; Asn Asian Studies. **RESEARCH** Europe in Asia 19th century; Indian National Army. **SELECTED PUBLICATIONS** Auth, Inheritance of Empire--Britain, India, and the Balance of Power in Asia, Am Hist Rev, Vol 100, 95. **CONTACT ADDRESS** Div of Humanities and Soc Sci, California Inst of Tech, 1201 E California, Pasadena, CA, 91125-0002.

FEARS, J. RUFUS
PERSONAL Born 03/07/1945, Atlanta, GA, m, 1966, 2 children **DISCIPLINE** CLASSICS; HISTORY **EDUCATION** Emory Univ, BA, 66; Harvard Univ, MA, 67, PhD, 71. **CAREER** Asst Prof Classical Lang, Tulane Univ, 71-72; from Asst Prof to Prof Hist, Ind Univ, 72-86; Prof Classics and Dept Chair, Boston Univ, 86-90; Prof Classics, 90-92, G.T. and Libby Blankenship Prof Classics, Univ Okla, 92-, Dean Col Arts & Sci, 90-92. **HONORS AND AWARDS** Woodrow Wilson Fel, 66-67; Danforth Fel, 66-71; Harvard Prize Fel, 66-71; Sheldon Traveling Fel, 69-71; Fel of the Am Acad in Rome, 69-71; Howard Found Fel, 77-78; Guggenheim Fel, 76-77; Alexander von Humboldt Fel, 77-78, 80-81; Distinguished Fac Res Lectr, Ind Univ, 80; NEH Fel, 86; Woodrow Wilson Ctr Fel, 86; ACLS Fel, 86; Nat Humanities Ctr Fel, 86; Wash Univ Ctr Hist Freedom Fel, 89-90; Judah P. Benjamin Nat Merit Award, 96; 10 awards for outstanding teaching, 76-96. **MEMBERSHIPS** Phi Beta Kappa; Golden Key Nat Honor Soc; Am Philol Asn; Archaeol Inst Am; Classical Asn Middle West and South. **RESEARCH** Ancient history; history of freedom. **SELECTED PUBLICATIONS** Auth, Atlantis and the Myth of the Minoan Thalassocracy, Atlantis: Fact of Fiction, 78; Princeps A Diis Electus, 77; The Cult of Jupiter and Roman Imperial Ideology, 81; The Theology of Victory at Rome, 81; The Cult of Virtues and Roman Imperial Ideology, 81; Roman Liberty, 80; Gottesgnadentum, Reallexikon fur Antike und Christentum XI, 81; Herrscherkult, Reallexikon fur Antike und Christentum XIV, 88; Selected Writings of Lord Acton (3 vols), 85-88; Michael Rostovtzeff, Classical Scholarship: A Biographical Encyclopedia, 90; Antiquity: The Model of Rome, An Uncertain Legacy: Essays in Pursuit of Liberty, 97; Natural Law in Greece and Rome, Essays in Natural Law, 98; The Lessons of Rome for Our Own Day, Preparing America's Foreign Policy for the 21st Century, 98. **CONTACT ADDRESS** 23 Walnut Hill, Norman, OK, 73072. **EMAIL** J.R.Fears-1@ou.edu

FECHNER, ROGER JEROME
PERSONAL Born 01/20/1937, Springfield, MN, m, 1960, 2 children **DISCIPLINE** HISTORY **EDUCATION** Hamline Univ, BA, 59; Boston Univ, AM, 69; Univ Iowa, PhD, 74. **CAREER** Asst prof to assoc prof to prof, Adrian Col, 63- . **HONORS AND AWARDS** Summa Cum Laude, 59, Nat Endow for the Humanities Fel, Univ Mich, 75-76; NEH Summer Sem Fel, Univ Wi, 78, Stanford, 84., Woodrow Wilson Fel, 59-60, 62-63; Univ Iowa Fel, 61-62; Adrian Col Lilly Found Teacher Scholar, 91-94 **MEMBERSHIPS** Amer Hist Assoc; Amer Soc for Eighteenth Century Stud; Eighteenth Century Scottish Stud Soc; Int Soc for Eighteenth Century Stud; OAH. **RESEARCH** Amer & Scottish enlightenments; American Revolution; historiography; philos of hist. **SELECTED PUBLICATIONS** Auth, The Godly and Virtuous Republic of John Witherspoon, in Ideas in America's Cultures: From Republic to Mass Society, Iowa St Univ Press, 82; Adam Smith and American Academic Moral Philosophers and Philosophy in the Age of Enlightenment and Revolution, in Adam Smith: International Perspectives, St. Martin's Press, 93; Burns and American Liberty, in Love and Liberty-Robert Burns: A Bicentenary Celebration, Tuckwell Press, 94; John Witherspoon, in Routledge Encyclopedia of Philosophy, 98. **CONTACT ADDRESS** Dept of History, Adrian Col, Adrian, MI, 49221-2575. **EMAIL** rfechner@adrian.edu

FEE, ELIZABETH
PERSONAL Born 12/11/1946, Belfast, Northern Ireland **DISCIPLINE** HISTORY AND PHILOSOPHY OF SCIENCE **EDUCATION** Cambridge Univ, BA, 68, MA, 75; Princeton Univ, MA, 71, PhD (hist and philos sci), 78. **CAREER** Teaching asst hist med, Princeton Univ, 71-72; instr hist sci, State Univ NY Binghamton, 72-74; archivist, 74-78, asst prof, Sch Health Serv, 74-78, ASST PROF HIST PUBL HEALTH, SCH HYG PUBL HEALTH, JOHNS HOPKINS UNIV, 78-, Ed consult, Int J Health Serv, 79-; consult, Col Allied Health Sci, Thomas Jefferson Univ, 79-80. **MEMBERSHIPS** Am Asn Hist Med; Hist Sci Soc; AHA; Berkshire Conf Women's Hist; Am Publ Health Asn. **RESEARCH** History of public health research and practice; history of Johns Hopkins School of Hygiene and Public Health; women and science and women and health. **SELECTED PUBLICATIONS** Auth, Sexual Knowledge, Sexual Science--The History of Attitudes to Sexuality, Am Hist Rev, Vol 101, 96; The Emerging Histories of Aids--3 Successive Paradigms, Hist Philos Life Scis, Vol 15, 93; Dirt and Disease, Am Hist Rev, Vol 99, 94; The Emerging Histories of Aids--3 Successive Paradigms, Hist Philos Life Sci, Vol 15, 93. **CONTACT ADDRESS** Sch of Hygiene and Publ Health, Johns Hopkins Univ, 3400 N Charles St, Baltimore, MD, 21205.

FEELEY, MALCOLM M.
DISCIPLINE POLITICAL SCIENCE **EDUCATION** Austin Col, BA, 64; Univ Minn, MA, 62, PhD, 69. **CAREER** Asst Prof, NHU, 68-72; Res Fellow, Lecturer, Yale Univ, 72-77; Prof, Univ Wisc, 77-83; Law, Univ Calif, Berkeley, 84-. **HONORS AND AWARDS** Am Bar Asn, Silver Gavel Award, 81; Am Bar Asn Cert of Merit, 83; Claire Sanders Clements Ch, Univ Calif, 97. **MEMBERSHIPS** APSA; Law & Soc Asn. **RESEARCH** Criminal process; judicial process, law & social science. **SELECTED PUBLICATIONS** Co-auth, Judicial Policy Making & the Modern State; auth, Federalism: Our National Neurosis, UCLA; auth, Judicial Policy Making, UCLA; auth, Women & Crime: Historical Perspective, Criminal Justice Hist. **CONTACT ADDRESS** Sch of Law, Univ Calif Berkeley, Boalt Hall, Berkeley, CA, 94720. **EMAIL** mmf@uclink4.berkeley.edu

FEHL, PHILIPP P.
PERSONAL Born 05/09/1920, Vienna, Austria, m, 1945 **DISCIPLINE** HISTORY OF ART **EDUCATION** Stanford Univ, BA, 47, MA, 48; Univ Chicago, PhD (class sculpture), 63. **CAREER** Lectr humanities, Univ Col, Chicago, 50-52; instr, Univ Kansas City, 52-54; from asst prof to assoc prof art, Univ Nebr, 54-63; from assoc prof to prof hist of art, Univ NC, Chapel Hill, 63-69; PROF HIST OF ART, UNIV ILL, URBANA-CHAMPAIGN, 69-, Res fel, Warburg Inst, Univ London, 57-58; bk rev ed, Art Bull, 65-69; art Hist in residence, Am Acad Rome, 67; assoc, Ctr Advan Studies, Univ Ill, 70-71 and 81-82; fel, Nat Endowment for Humanities, 77-78; vis prof, Univ Tel Aviv, 82. **MEMBERSHIPS** Col Art Asn Am; Renaissance Soc Am; Am Soc Aesthet; Am Inst Archaeol; Int Survey Jewish Monuments (pres, 77). **RESEARCH** Renaissance painting and sculpture; history of the classical tradition in art; American art. **SELECTED PUBLICATIONS** Auth, Touchstones of Art and Art Criticism, Rubens and the Work of Junius, Franciscus, J Aesthet Educ, Vol 30, 96. **CONTACT ADDRESS** Dept of Art, Univ of Ill, Champaign, IL, 61820.

FEHRENBACH, HEIDE
DISCIPLINE HISTORY **EDUCATION** Rutgers Univ, AB, 79, PhD, 90. **CAREER** Assoc prof **HONORS AND AWARDS** Co-winner, Biennial Bk Prize, AHA Conf Group Cent Europ Hist. **RESEARCH** Modern German history; Modern European cultural history; film; gender. **SELECTED PUBLICATIONS** Auth, Cinema in Democratizing Germany: Reconstructing National Identity after Hitler; coeditor of Transactions, Transgressions, Transformations: American Culture in Western Europe and Japan (forthcoming) **CONTACT ADDRESS** Dept History, Emory Univ, 221 Bowden Hall, 561 Kilgo Cir, Atlanta, GA, 30322-1950. **EMAIL** hfehren@emory.edu

FEHRENBACHER, DON EDWARD
PERSONAL Born 08/21/1920, Sterling, IL, m, 1944, 3 children **DISCIPLINE** AMERICAN HISTORY **EDUCATION** Cornell Col, AB, 46, Univ Chicago, AM, 48, PhD, 51. **CAREER** Asst prof hist, Coe Col, 49-53; from asst prof to prof, 53-66, COE PROF HIST, STANFORD UNIV, 66-, Guggenheim fel, 59-60; Harmsworth prof Am hist, Oxford Univ, 67-68; Harrison prof hist, Col William and Mary, 73-74; Nat Endowment for Humanities fel, 75-76; Commonwealth Fund lectr, Univ Col London and Walter Lynwood Fleming lectr, La State Univ, 78. **HONORS AND AWARDS** Pulitzer Prize, 79; Seagram lectr, Univ Toronto, 81., DHL, Cornell Col, 70 and Lincoln Col, 81. **MEMBERSHIPS** AHA; Orgn Am Hists; Southern Hist Asn; Am Acad Arts and Sci; Soc Hists Early Am Repub. **RESEARCH** Nineteenth century United States; Civil War era; political and constitutional history. **SELECTED PUBLICATIONS** Auth, The Making of a Myth--Lincoln and the Vicr Presidential Nomination in 1864, Civil War Hist, Vol 41, 95. **CONTACT ADDRESS** PO Box 4024, Stanford, CA, 94305.

FEINBERG, BARBARA JANE
PERSONAL Born 06/01/1938, NY, w, 1968, 2 children **DISCIPLINE** POLITICAL SCIENCE **EDUCATION** Wellesley Col, BA, 59; Yale Univ, MA, 60, PhD, 63. **CAREER** City Col NY, lectr instr, 63-67; Brooklyn Col, vis lectr, 67-68; Seton Hall Univ, asst prof, 68-70; Hunta Col, adj asst prof, 70-73; Author of nonfiction books for children, 80-. **HONORS AND AWARDS** Wellesley Col, Durant Schl, Woodrow Wilson Prize, Phi Beta Kappa; Yale, Fellowshp. **RESEARCH** Am Hist, Biography. **SELECTED PUBLICATIONS** General Douglas MacArthur: An American Hero, Danbury Ct, Children's Press, 99; Edith Kermit Caron Roosevelt and Elizabeth Wallace Truman, Danbury CT, Children's Press, in preparation; Patricia Ryan Nixon Danbury CT Children's Press, 98; America's First Ladies, Danbury CT Children's Press, 98; Next in Line: The American Vice Presidency, Danbury Ct Children's Press, 96; many more pub books. **CONTACT ADDRESS** 535 East 86th St, New York, NY, 10028-7533.

FEINBERG, HARVEY MICHAEL
PERSONAL Born 04/17/1938, Hartford, CT, m, 1962, 2 children **DISCIPLINE** WEST AFRICAN & SOUTH AFRICAN HISTORY **EDUCATION** Yale Univ, BA, 60; Am Univ, MA, 63; Boston Univ, PhD(hist), 69. **CAREER** Arch asst, Libr Cong, 61-62; asst prof, 69-74, assoc prof, 74-79, PROF AFRICAN HIST, SOUTHERN CONN STATE UNIV, 79-. **HONORS AND AWARDS** Am Philos Soc, res fel Netherlands, summer 72 & 4-7/77, res fel South Africa, 2-6/85 & 8-11/92; postdoctoral fel, Dept Hist, Yale Univ, 76-77; vis fel, Yale Univ, 90-91; Fulbright-Hays Seminars Abroad fel, summer 91; assoc fel, South African Res Prog, Yale Univ, 93-94. **MEMBERSHIPS** African Studies Asn; Conn Acad Arts & Sci (vpres, 89-); Ghana Studies Coun; South African Hist Soc; Conn Coord Comt Promotion Hist **RESEARCH** Race and the Land: African challenges to land policy in South Africa, 1905-1936. **SELECTED PUBLICATIONS** Auth, Africans and Europeans in West Africa: Elminans and Dutchmen on the Gold Coast during the Eighteenth Century, Am Philos Soc, 89; art, The Natives Land Act of 1913 in South Africa: Politics, Race and Segregation in the Early 20th Century, Int J African Hist Studies, XXVI, 1, 93; art, South Africa and Land Ownership: What's in a deed?, in: History in Africa, 95; art, Pre-apartheid African Land Ownership and the Implication for the Current Restitution Debate in South Africa, Historia, 11/95. **CONTACT ADDRESS** Dept of Hist, Southern Conn State Univ, 501 Crescent St, New Haven, CT, 06515-1330. **EMAIL** feinberg@scsu.ctstateu.edu

FEINGOLD, HENRY L.
PERSONAL Born 02/06/1931, Germany, m, 1954, 2 children **DISCIPLINE** UNITED STATES DIPLOMACY & AMERICAN JEWISH HISTORY **EDUCATION** Brooklyn Col, BA, 53, MA, 54; NY Univ, PhD, 66. **CAREER** Tchr hist, Sec Schs, NY, 53-65; lectr, City Univ NY, 67-68; from instr to assoc prof hist, 68-76, grad ctr, 75, prof hist, Baruch Col, City Univ NY, 76-, Prof Emeritus, 98-, Dir, Jewish Resource Center, Baruch Col, CUNY; Lectr exten prog in Ger, Univ MD, 55-56; adj prof, Stern Col, Yeshiva Univ, 71-73; adj lectr, Inst Advan Study Hum Jewish Theol Inst Am, 73-76. **HONORS AND AWARDS** Leon Jolson Award for best bk on Holocaust, 77; Presidential Award for Excellence in Scholarship, Baruch Col, May 86; Lee Friedman Award in Am Jewish Hist, 94; Morim Award, Jewish Tchr(s) Asn, 95. **MEMBERSHIPS** Labor Zionist Alliance (pres, 89-92); Jewish Community Relations Coun (board of dir); World Zionist Org (gen coun); Jewish Agency for Israel (gen assembly); Am Zionist Movement (cabinet). **RESEARCH** Holocaust. **SELECTED PUBLICATIONS** Auth, The Politics of Rescue: The Roosevelt Administration and the Holocaust, 1938-1945, Rutgers Univ Press, 70; Zion in America: The Jewish Experience from Colonial Times to the Present, Twayne, 74; A Midrash on the History of American Jewry, NY State Univ Press, 82; A Time for Searching: Entering the Mainstream, 1920-1945, Johns Hopkins Univ Press, 92; Bearing Witness: How American and its Jews Responded to the Holocaust, Univ Syracuse Press, 95; Lest Memory Cease, Finding Meaning in the American Jewish Past, Univ Syracuse Press, 96. **CONTACT ADDRESS** Baruch Col, CUNY, 17 Lexington Ave, New York, NY, 10010-5518. **EMAIL** jrc@baruch.cuny.edu

FELDHERR, ANDREW
DISCIPLINE ROMAN CULTURAL STUDIES **EDUCATION** Princeton Univ, AB, 85; U C Berkeley, PhD, 91. **CAREER** Prof, Princeton Univ. **RESEARCH** Livy; Ovid; Virgil. **SELECTED PUBLICATIONS** Auth, Spectacle and Society in Livy's History. **CONTACT ADDRESS** Princeton Univ, 1 Nassau Hall, Princeton, NJ, 08544.

FELDMAN, GERALD DONALD
PERSONAL Born 04/24/1937, New York, NY, m, 1958 **DISCIPLINE** MODERN EUROPEAN HISTORY **EDUCATION** Columbia Col, BA, 58; Harvard Univ, MA, 59, PhD (hist), 64. **CAREER** From asst prof to assoc prof, 63-70, PROF HIST, UNIV CALIF, BERKELEY, 70-, Soc Sci Res Coun fac res grant, 66-67; Am Coun Learned Soc fel, 66-67 and 70-71; Guggenheim fel, 73-74; Nat Endowment for Humanities fel, 77-78; comt mem Western Europe, Soc Sci Res Coun, 74-; mem, Historische Kommission for Berlin, 80-; Lehrman fel, 81-82; German Marshal fel, 81-82; res prof, Historisches Kolleg Munchen, 82-83. **HONORS AND AWARDS** Newcomen Prize, Newcomen Soc, 76. **MEMBERSHIPS** AHA. **RESEARCH** Modern German social and economic history, European history, international relations. **SELECTED PUBLICATIONS** Auth, Freedom with Responsibility--The Social Market Economy in Germany, 1918-1963, Am Hist Rev, Vol 101, 96; Industrialists, Bankers and the Problem of Unemployment in the Weimar Republic, Cent Europ His, Vol 25, 92; Quest for Economic Empire--European Strategies of German Big Business in the 20th Century, Cent Europ Hist, Vol 29, 96; Economic Crisis and Political Collapse--The Weimar Republic 1924-1933, Historische Zeitschrift, Vol 259, 94; Germany After the 1st World War , J Soc Hist, Vol 28, 95; The Allies and the German Banks--Banking Policy After the 2nd World War in West Germany, Am Hist Rev, Vol 98, 93; Spd in the Bruning Era--Toleration or Mobilization--Maneuvering Room and Strategies of Social Democratic Politics 1930-1932, Historische Zeitschrift, Vol 258, 94; Nipperdey, Thomas 1927-1992, Cent Europ Hist, Vol 24, 91; Stinnes, Hugo and his Bankers, 1895-1914, J Ec Hist, Vol 57, 97; Paper and Iron--Hamburg Business and German Politics in the Era of Inflation, 1897-1927, Cent Europ History, Vol 30, 97; Mercedes in Peace and War--German Automobile Workers, 1903-1945, Eng Hist Rev, Vol 109, 94. **CONTACT ADDRESS** Dept of Hist, Univ of Calif, 3229 Dwinelle Hall, Berkeley, CA, 94720-2551.

FELDMAN, LOUIS H.
PERSONAL Born 10/29/1926, Hartford, CT, m, 1966, 3 children **DISCIPLINE** CLASSICS **EDUCATION** Trinity Col, BA 46, MA 47; Harvard Univ, PhD 51. **CAREER** Yeshiva College, asst prof, assoc prof, prof 55 to 66-; Yeshiva and Stern Colleges, inst 55-56; Hobart and William Smith Colleges, inst 53-55; Trinity College, inst 52-53; Hartford Seminary Foundation, inst 51-52. **HONORS AND AWARDS** Guggenheim fel; ACLS sr fel; NEH six sem; APA Awd for Excell; Judaica Ref Book Awd; Ford Foun Tchg fel; AJL fel; Inst Adv Stud Prin fel; AAJR fel **MEMBERSHIPS** APA; SBL; AJS **RESEARCH** Hellenistic Judaism, esp Josephus **SELECTED PUBLICATIONS** Auth, Studies in Josephus' Rewritten Bible, Leiden, Brill, 98; Josephus' Contra Apionem: Studies in Its Character and Context with a Latin Concordance to the Portion Missing in Greek, co-ed, Leiden, Brill, 96; Jewish Life and Thought Among Greeks and Romans: Primary Readings, coauth, Minnea, Fortress Press, 96; Studies in Hellenistic Judaism, Leiden Brill, 96; Jew and Gentile in the Ancient World: Attitudes and Interactions from Alexander to Justinian, Princeton, PUP, 93, pp 96. **CONTACT ADDRESS** Dept of Classics, Yeshiva Univ, 69-11 Harrow St, Forest Hills, NY, 11375-5151. **EMAIL** Lfeldman@ymail.yu.edu

FELIX, DAVID
PERSONAL Born 12/26/1921, New Britain, CT, m, 1966 **DISCIPLINE** MODERN HISTORY **EDUCATION** Trinity Col, Conn, BA, 42; Univ Chicago, MA, 47; Univ Paris, cert econ, Faculte de droit, 55; Columbia Univ, PhD (intel, soc & polit hist), 70. **CAREER** Reporter, Pittsburgh Sun-Tel, 47-50; info officer, US Econ Mission, Austria, 50-54; corresp, Int News Serv, Paris, 55-56; managing ed, Challenge, Mag Econ Affairs, NY Univ, 57-60; financial writer, 60-64; from instr to assoc prof, 65-74, PROF HIST, BRONX COMMUNITY COL, 74-91, GRAD CTR, CITY UNIV OF NY, 81-91, PROF EMER HIST, 91- . **HONORS AND AWARDS** Am Coun Learned Socs res grant, 70; fac res award, City Univ NY, 70 & 71; Nat Endowment Humanities sr fel, 72-73; guest lectr, London Sch Econ, 73-74; consult on grants, Nat Endowment Humanities, 75-80; dir, Global Hist Curric Proj, City Univ New York, 81-82. **MEMBERSHIPS** AHA; AEA; Royal Econ Soc. **RESEARCH** Intellectual and political history; Marxism; Keynesianism. **SELECTED PUBLICATIONS** Auth, The sense of Coexistence, Am Scholar, winter 62-63; Protest: Sacco-Vanzetti and the Intellectuals, Ind Univ, 65; Walther Rathenau and the Weimar Republic: The Politics of Reparations, John Hopkins, 71; Reparations Reconsidered with a Vengeance, Cent Europ Hist, 6/71; Walther Rathenau: The Bad Thinker and His Uses, 1/75 & Access to Germany, 4/78, Europ Studies Rev; Marx as Politician, Southern Ill Univ, 83; auth, Biography of an Idea: John Maynard Keynes and The General Theory, Transaction, 95; auth, Keynes: A Critical Life, Greenwood, 99. **CONTACT ADDRESS** 49 E 86th St, New York, NY, 10028.

FELLER, DANIEL
PERSONAL Born 10/19/1950, Washington, DC, m, 1992, 1 child **DISCIPLINE** HISTORY **EDUCATION** Reed Col, BA, 72; Univ Wi., MA, 74, PhD, 81. **CAREER** Asst prof, Northland Col, 80-83; asst ed, The Papers of Andrew Jackson, 83-86; asst to full prof, Univ Nmex, 86-. **MEMBERSHIPS** Soc for Hist of the Early Amer Repub; Orgn of Amer Hist; Asn for Doc Ed; Southern Hist Asn. **RESEARCH** American political history; Jacksonian-antebellum and Civil War eras; Old northwest. **SELECTED PUBLICATIONS** Auth, The Jacksonian Promise: America, 1815-1840, Johns Hopkins Univ Press, 95; book chapters, in Arthur M. Schlesinger, Running for President, Simon & Schuster, 94; in Jeffrey P. Brown and Andrew R. L. Cayton, The Pursuit of Public Power, Kent State Univ Press, 94; in Stanley I. Kutler, American Retrospectives: Historians on Historians, Johns Hopkins Univ Press, 95; auth, The Public Lands in Jacksonian Politics, Univ of Wis Press, 84; **CONTACT ADDRESS** Dept. of History, Univ of New Mexico, Albuquerque, NM, 87131-1181. **EMAIL** dfeller@unm.edu

FELLMAN, MICHAEL
PERSONAL Born 02/28/1943, Madison, WI **DISCIPLINE** HISTORY **EDUCATION** Univ Mich, 65; Northwestern Univ, PhD, 69. **CAREER** Asst prof to assoc prof, 68-83, PROF HISTORY, SIMON FRASER UNIV, 83-; Fulbright prof, Univ Haifa (Israel), 80-81; vis fel, Shelby Cullom Davis Ctr Hist Stud, Princeton Univ, 82-84; Marta Sutton Weeks sr res fel, 92-93, vis prof, Stanford Univ, 93. **MEMBERSHIPS** Can Asn Am Stud (pres, 81-83); Am Hist Asn; Orgn Am Hist; Southern Hist Asn. **SELECTED PUBLICATIONS** Auth, The Unbounded Frame, 73; auth, Inside War, 89; auth, Citizen Sherman, 95; coauth, Making Sense of Self, 81; co-ed, Antislavery Reconsidered, 79; ed bd, Hist Reflections, 80-91; ed bd, Middle East Focus, 84-; ed bd, Can Rev Am Stud, 92-. **CONTACT ADDRESS** Dept of History, Simon Fraser Univ, Burnaby, BC, V5A 1S6. **EMAIL** fellman@sfu.ca

FELSTINER, MARY LOWENTHAL
PERSONAL Born 02/19/1941, PA, 2 children **DISCIPLINE** COMPARATIVE HISTORY **EDUCATION** Harvard Univ, BA, 63; Columbia Univ, MA, 66; Stanford Univ, PhD, 71. **CAREER** Asst prof, 73-76, assoc prof, 76-81, prof, 81- , hist, San Francisco State Univ; vis prof Stanford Univ, 97; vis prof UC Santa Cruz, 98. **HONORS AND AWARDS** Junion Phi Beta Kappa, 62; For Area Fel, 64-66; Hubert Herring Award, 74; Am Coun Learned Soc Fel, 90; Am Hist Asn Prize in Women's Hist, 95. **MEMBERSHIPS** Am Hist Asn; Western Asn of Women Hist. **RESEARCH** Colonial Latin America; women's history; Nazi period; history of medicine. **SELECTED PUBLICATIONS** Coed & contribr, Chanzeaux: A Village in Anjou, Harvard Univ, 66; auth, Kinship politics in the Chilean independence movement, Hispanic Am Hist Rev, 2/76; auth, Family Metaphors: The Language of an Independent Revolution, Comp Stud in Soc and Hist, 83; auth, Seeing the Second Sex Through the Second Wave, Feminist Stud, 80; auth, Alois Brunner: Eichmann's Best Tool, Simon Wiesenthal Annual, 86; auth, Taking Her Life/History, Life/Lines, 88; auth, Charlotte Salomon's Inward-Turning Testimony, in, Shapes of memory, 93; auth, To Paint Her Life: Charlotte Salomon in the Nazi Era, Harper Collins, 94. **CONTACT ADDRESS** Dept of History, San Francisco State Univ, 1600 Holloway Ave, San Francisco, CA, 94132.

FELTON, CRAIG
DISCIPLINE ART HISTORY **EDUCATION** St Vincent Col, BA; Univ Pittsburgh, MA, PhD. **CAREER** Dept ch; taught at, Southern Methodist Univ & TX Christian Univ; res, Kimbell Art Mus. **HONORS AND AWARDS** Res on, Hispano-Italian painter, Jusepe de Ribera, led to the 1st exhibition of a selection of, Spagnoletto's works, and the exhibition catalogue: Jusepe Ribera, 1591-1652. **RESEARCH** Italian and Span painting of the first half of the 17th century, with an emphasis on Naples. **SELECTED PUBLICATIONS** Publ on, res interest. **CONTACT ADDRESS** Dept of Art, Smith Col, Hillyer Hall 314, Northampton, MA, 01063. **EMAIL** cfelton@sophia.smith.edu

FENTON, WILLIAM NELSON
PERSONAL Born 12/15/1908, New Rochelle, NY, m, 1936, 3 children **DISCIPLINE** ANTHROPOLOGY, ETHNOHISTORY **EDUCATION** Dartmouth Col, AB, 31; Yale Univ, PhD (anthrop), 37 Hon Degree: LLD, Hartwick Col, 68. **CAREER** Community worker among Senecas, US Indian Serv, 35-37; from instr to asst prof anthrop, St Lawrence Univ, 37-39; assoc anthropologist, Bur Am Ethnol, Smithsonian Inst, 39-43, sr ethnologist, 43-51; exec secy anthrop and psychol, Nat Acad Sci-Nat Res Coun, 52-54; asst comnr, NY State Mus and Sci Serv, NY State Educ Dept, 54-68; res prof, 68-74, distinguished prof, 74-79, EMER PROF ANTHROP, STATE UNIV NY ALBANY, 79-, Secy war comt, Smithsonian Inst, 42-44, res assoc ethnogeog bd, 43-45; mem comn lang and areal implications, Comn Armed Forces Educ Prog, Am Coun Educ, 46; trustee, Mus Am Indian, Heye Found, New York City, 76-80 and 82-; dean Iroquois Studies, 80. **MEMBERSHIPS** Am Anthrop Asn; Am Folklore Soc (pres, 59-60); Am Ethnol Soc (pres, 59); Am Soc Ethnohist (pres, 62). **RESEARCH** Iroquois studies; the Deganawidah epic of the founding of the Iroquois confederacy; Iroquois political history. **SELECTED PUBLICATIONS** Auth, The Ordeal of the Longhouse--The Peoples of the Iroquois League in the Era of European Colonization, Ethnohistory, Vol 41, 94. **CONTACT ADDRESS** Dept of Anthrop, State Univ of NY, Albany, NY, 12222.

FERERE, GERARD ALPHONSE
PERSONAL Born 07/21/1930, Cap Haitian, Haiti, m **DISCIPLINE** EDUCATION **EDUCATION** Naval Acad of Venezuela, Ensign 1953; Villanova Univ, MA 1967; Univ of PA, PhD 1974. **CAREER** Haitian Navy, naval officer 1953-58; Haiti, language teacher 1958-63; St Joseph's Univ, prof 1964-. **MEMBERSHIPS** Translator interpreter SELF 1964-; pres Coalition for Haitian Concerns 1982-; Haitian American commissioner, Pennsylvania Heritage Affairs Commission, 1991-. **CONTACT ADDRESS** St. Joseph's Univ, City Ave at 54th St, Philadelphia, PA, 19131.

FERGUSON, ARTHUS BOWLES
PERSONAL Born 10/15/1913, Canada, m, 1942 **DISCIPLINE** HISTORY **EDUCATION** Univ Western Ont, BA, 35; Cornell Univ, PhD (hist), 39. **CAREER** From instr to assoc prof, 39-60, PROF HIST, DUKE UNIV, 60-, Fund Advan Educ fel, 54-55; Guggenheim Found fel, 71-72; assoc ed, J Medieval and Renaissance Studies, 71-. **MEMBERSHIPS** AHA; Renaissance Soc Am; Conf Brit Studies; fel Royal Hist Soc. **RESEARCH** English Renaissance; late medieval English culture; historiography. **SELECTED PUBLICATIONS** Auth, Foundations of Political Economy--Some Early Tudor Views on State and Society, Albion, Vol 27, 95; Mulcaster, Richard C. 1531-1611 and Educational Reform in The Renaissance, Cath Hist Rev, Vol 79, 93; Literature and Culture in Early Modern London, Albion, Vol 28, 96. **CONTACT ADDRESS** Dept of Hist, Duke Univ, Durham, NC, 27708.

FERGUSON, CLYDE RANDOLPH
PERSONAL Born 06/03/1930, Oklahoma City, OK, m, 1954, 3 children **DISCIPLINE** AMERICAN COLONIAL AND REVOLUTIONARY HISTORY **EDUCATION** Univ Okla, BA, 55; Duke Univ, MA, 57, PhD (hist), 60. **CAREER** Instr specialist hist and govt, 60-62, coordr home studies continuing educ, 62-66, asst prof, 66-80, ASSOC PROF HIST, KANS STATE UNIV, 80-. **MEMBERSHIPS** AHA; Southern Hist Asn. **RESEARCH** Colonial America; American revolution; guerrilla warfare. **SELECTED PUBLICATIONS** Auth, On Coon Mountain--Scenes from a Childhood in the Oklahoma Hills, J West, Vol 33, 94; The Papers of Bouquet, Henry, Vol 6, J Milit Hist, Vol 60, 96; National Rifle Association Money, Firepower and Fear, J West, Vol 35, 96. **CONTACT ADDRESS** Dept of Hist, Kansas State Univ, Manhattan, KS, 66506.

FERGUSON, EUGENE S
PERSONAL Born 01/24/1916, Wilmington, DE, m, 1948, 3 children **DISCIPLINE** HISTORY OF TECHNOLOGY **EDUCATION** Carnegie Inst Technol, BS, 37, Iowa State Col, MS, 55. **CAREER** Engr, E I du Pont de Nemours and Co, 38-42; instr mech eng, Iowa State Univ, 46-48, from asst prof to assoc prof, 49-58; engr, Foote Mineral Co, 48-49; cur civil and mech eng, Smithsonian Inst, US Nat Mus, 58-61; prof mech eng, Iowa State Univ, 61-69; prof hist, Univ Del, 69-79; cur technol, Hagley Mus, Greenville, 69-79; RETIRED, Vchmn hist Am eng rec adv comt, Nat Park Serv, 72-77, chmn, 77-78. **HONORS AND AWARDS** Leonardo Da Vinci Medal, Soc Hist Technol, 77., LHD, Univ Del, 80. **MEMBERSHIPS** Soc Hist Technol (pres, 77-78); fel AAAS; Am Soc Mech Engrs; Newcomen Soc; AHA. **RESEARCH** Modern technological history. **SELECTED PUBLICATIONS** Auth, Design Paradigms--Case Histories of Error and Judgment in Engineering, Tech Cult, Vol 36, 95. **CONTACT ADDRESS** 54 Winslow Rd, Newark, DE, 19711.

FERGUSON, EVERETT
PERSONAL Born 02/18/1933, Montgomery, TX, m, 1956, 3 children **DISCIPLINE** HISTORY, PHILOSOPHY OF RELIGION **EDUCATION** Abilene Christ Univ, BA, 53, MA, 54; Harvard Univ, STB, 56, PhD, 60. **CAREER** Dean, Northeast Christ Jr Coll, 59-62; PROF, ABILENE CHRIST UNIV, 62-. **MEMBERSHIPS** North Am Patristics Soc; Am Soc Church Hist; Soc Biblical Lit; Ecclesiastical Hist Soc; Asn Int d'Etudes Patristiques; Inst Biblical Res **RESEARCH** Backgrounds Early Christianity; Early church history **CONTACT ADDRESS** Abilene Christian Univ, 609 E N 16th St, Abilene, TX, 79601. **EMAIL** Ferguson@bible.acu.edu

FERGUSON, JAMES WILSON
PERSONAL Born 10/03/1933, Muncy, PA **DISCIPLINE** EARLY MODERN EUROPEAN HISTORY **EDUCATION** Kenyon Col, AB, 55; Bryn Mawr Col, MA, 56; Princeton Univ, PhD, 61. **CAREER** Instr gen studies, Philadelphia Mus Col Art, 60-63; asst prof hist and humanities, Parsons Col, 63-66; asst prof hist and philos, Ursinus Col, 66-68; asst prof, 68-70, ASSOC PROF HIST, RUSSELL SAGE COL, 70-. **MEMBERSHIPS** AHA. **RESEARCH** Europe 1300-1700; Scottish history; history of women. **SELECTED PUBLICATIONS** Auth, Black Patie, The Life and Times of Stewart, Patrick, Earl of Orkney, Lord of Shetland , Albion, Vol 25, 93. **CONTACT ADDRESS** Box 171, Laporte, PA, 18626.

FERGUSSON, FRANCES D.
PERSONAL Born 10/03/1944, Boston, MA, m, 1988 **DISCIPLINE** ARCHITECTURAL HISTORY **EDUCATION** Wellesley Col, BA, 65; Harvard Univ, MA, 66, PhD, 74. **CAREER** Teaching Fel, Harvard Univ, 66-68; Asst Prof Art, Newton Col, 69-75, Dir Div Humanities & Fine Arts & Chair Dept Art, 72-75; Assoc Prof Art, Univ Mass - Boston, 75-82, Dir Urban Studies Prog, 78-79, Dir Am Civilization Prog, 79-80, Fac Representative to Bd Trustees, 79-80, Asst Chancellor, 80-82; Prof Art, Bucknell Univ, 82-86, Provost & VPres Acad Affairs, 82-86; Prof Art and Pres, Vassar Col, 86-. **HONORS AND AWARDS** NY State Col Teaching Fel, 65-67; Harvard Teaching Fel, 66-68; Harvard Grad Fel, 68-69; Am Asn Univ Women Fel, 70-71; Harvard Traveling Fel, 70-71; NEH Fel, 74-75; Radcliffe Inst Fel, 74-75. **RESEARCH** Late 18th - early 19th century French & English architecture; historians in architecture. **SELECTED PUBLICATIONS** Auth, Liberal Arts for the 80s, Vassar Quart, 88; Educating for a Vital Society, Vassar Quart, 89; A Commitment to Medicine and Society, Mayo Clinic Proceedings, Vol 65, 8/90; The Dilemma of Free Speech in a Diverse Society, Vassar Quart, 90; author of numerous other articles in Vassar Quarterly, and other publications. **CONTACT ADDRESS** Vassar Col, Box 43, Poughkeepsie, NY, 12604-0043. **EMAIL** fergusson@vassar.edu

FERLING, JOHN ERNIE
PERSONAL Born 01/10/1940, Charleston, WV, m, 1965 **DISCIPLINE** AMERICAN HISTORY **EDUCATION** Sam Houston State Univ, BA, 61; Baylor Univ, MA, 62; WVa Univ, PhD, 71. **CAREER** Asst prof, 65-68, Morehead State Univ; instr, 69-70, WVa Univ; assoc prof, 70-71, W Chester State Col; prof, 71-, St Univ W Ga. **RESEARCH** Colonial-revolutionary America; United States military history. **SELECTED PUBLICATIONS** Auth, John Adams: A Life, Univ Tenn Press, 92; auth, Struggle for a Continent: The Wars of Early America, Harlan Davidson Pub, 93; art, John Adams, Diplomat, Wm & Mary Quart, 51, 94; art, John Adam's Health Reconsidered, Wm & Mary Quart, 55, 98. **CONTACT ADDRESS** Dept of History, State Univ of West Georgia, Carrollton, GA, 30118. **EMAIL** jferling@westga.edu

FERN, ALAN M.
PERSONAL Born 10/19/1930, Detroit, MI, m, 1957 **DISCIPLINE** ART HISTORY **EDUCATION** Univ of Chicago, BA, 50, MA, 50, PhD, 60. **CAREER** Asst to instr to asst prof, The Col, Univ of Chicago, 52-61; curator to asst chief to chief of prints & photographs to dir of res dept to dir of special collections, Library of Congress, 61-82; Dir, Nat Portrait Gallery, Smithsonian Inst, 82-. **HONORS AND AWARDS** Fulbright scholar, 54-55; Ordre de la Couronne (Chevalier); Ordre des Arts des Letters (Chevalier); Order of the Polar Star (commander). **MEMBERSHIPS** Asn of Art Museum Dir; Col Art Asn; Print Coun of Am. **RESEARCH** History of graphic arts & photography; American art; art nouveau. **SELECTED PUBLICATIONS** Coauth, Introduction to Revisiting the White City: American Art at the 1893 World's Fair, Nat Museum of Am Art and Nat Portrait Gallery, Smithsonian Inst, 93; auth, Qu'est-ce Qu'une Bibliotheque Nat d'Art?, Bibliotheques d'Art Bulletin des Bibliotheques de France, 93; Presidential Gifts in America, The Gift as Material Culture, 95; Entries on Holger Cahill and Joseph Pennell, Dictionary of Art, 96; Leadership in Arts-Oxymorn or Opportunity, Cosmos, 97. **CONTACT ADDRESS** National Portrait Gallery, Smithsonian Inst, Washington, DC, 20560-0213. **EMAIL** afern@npg.si.edu

FERNGREN, GARY BURT
PERSONAL Born 04/14/1942, Bellingham, WA, m, 1970, 3 children **DISCIPLINE** ANCIENT HISTORY & MEDICINE **EDUCATION** Western Wash State Col, BA, 64; Univ BC, MA, 67, PhD(classics), 73. **CAREER** Instr, 70-72, asst prof, 72-78, assoc prof Ancient Hist, Ore State Univ, 78-84, prof, 84-. **HONORS AND AWARDS** National Endowment for the Humanities fellow twice, Canada Council fellow three times, Joseph J. Malone fellow (Egypt), Vice President, Int Soc of the History of Medicine, 96-97, Councillor, 97. **MEMBERSHIPS** Int Soc of the History of Medicine, Am Asn for the History of Medicine, Am Osler Soc, History of Science Soc. **RESEARCH** Social history of ancient medicine; history of medical ethics, historical relationship of religion to medicine. **SELECTED PUBLICATIONS** General ed, The History of Science and Religion in the Western Religion: An Encyclopedia (New York: Garland 99), numerous articles and chapters. **CONTACT ADDRESS** Dept of Hist, Oregon State Univ, 306 Milam Hall, Corvallis, OR, 97331-5104. **EMAIL** GFerngren@orst.edu

FERNIE, JOHN D.
PERSONAL Born 11/13/1933, Pretoria, South Africa **DISCIPLINE** ASTRONOMY/HISTORY OF SCIENCE **EDUCATION** Univ Cape Town, BS, 53, MS, 55; Ind Univ, PhD, 58. **CAREER** Lectr, Univ Cape Town, 58-61; asst prof to prof, 61-96, PROF EMER, UNIV TORONTO, 96-; Affil, Inst Hist Philos Sci Technol, 73-; dir, David Dunlap Observatory, 78-88. **MEMBERSHIPS** Royal Astron Soc Can; Int Astron Union. **SELECTED PUBLICATIONS** Auth, The Whisper and the Vision, 76. **CONTACT ADDRESS** David Dunlap Observatory, PO Box 360, Richmond Hill, ON, L4C 4Y6.

FERRARI PINNEY, GLORIA
DISCIPLINE CLASSICAL ARCHAELOGY **EDUCATION** Univ Cincinnati, PhD, 76. **CAREER** Asst prof, Wilson Col, 76-77; Lectr, Bryn Mawr Col, 71-81; Asst prof, 81-87; Assoc prof, 87-90; Prof, 90-93; Prof, Univ Chicago, 93-. **HONORS AND AWARDS** Fulbright Fel; Pew memorial Trust; Ailsa Mellon Bruce Senior Fel; Guggenheim Found; NEH grant. **SELECTED PUBLICATIONS** Auth, Il commercio dei sarcofagi asiatici, Rome, 66; Co-ed, Aspects of Ancient Greece, Allentown, 79; auth, Materiali del Museo Archeologico Nazionale di Tarquinia XI: I vasi attici a figure rosse del periodo arcaico, Rome, 88. **CONTACT ADDRESS** Dept of Art, Univ Chicago, 5540 S Greenwood Ave, Chicago, IL, 60637.

FERRELL, ROBERT HUGH
PERSONAL Born 05/08/1921, Cleveland, OH, m, 1956 **DISCIPLINE** AMERICAN HISTORY **EDUCATION** Bowling Green State Univ, BS, 46, BA, 47; Yale Univ, MA, 48, PhD, 51. **CAREER** Instr hist, Mich State Univ, 52-53; from asst prof to assoc prof, 53-61, PROF HIST, IND UNIV, BLOOMINGTON, 61-, Grants, Carnegie Found Advan Teaching, 55-56, Soc Sci Res Coun, 56 and 61-62, Smith-Mundt Act, 58-59 and Fulbright Act, 69-70. **HONORS AND AWARDS** LLD, Bowling Green State Univ, 71. **MEMBERSHIPS** Orgn Am Hists; AHA. **RESEARCH** America diplomatic history. **SELECTED PUBLICATIONS** Auth, Acheson, Dean and the Making of United States Foreign Policy, Int Hist Rev, Vol 16, 94; Truman, Harry, S--A Chance President and the New World of Superpowers, Prologue Quart Nation Arch, Vol 26, 94; The Papers of Eisenhower, Dwight, David--The Presidency, The Middle Way, Vols 14-17,Galambos, L, Vanee, D, Int Hist Rev, Vol 19, 97; Changing Differences--Women and the Shaping of American Foreign Policy, 1917-1994, Rev Am Hist, Vol 25, 97; The Mexican War J and Letters of Kirkham, Ralph, W., J West, Vol 32, 93; When Illness Strikes the Leader--The Dilemma of the Captive King, J Am Hist, Vol 81, 94; Plain Faking, Am Heritage, Vol 46, 95; Truman, Harry, S. and the War Scare of 1948--A Successful Campaign to Deceive the Nation, J Am Hist, Vol 81, 94. **CONTACT ADDRESS** Dept of Hist, Indiana Univ, Bloomington, Bloomington, IN, 47401.

FERRIN SUTTON, DANA
DISCIPLINE CLASSICS **EDUCATION** The New Sch for Soc Res, BA, 65; The Univ Wis, MA, 66, PhD, 70; postdoc, sr mem, Darwin Col, The Univ Cambridge, Eng, 72-74; postdoc res fel, The Univ Auckland, New Zealand, 74-75. **CAREER** Instr, Univ Minn, 67-68; tchg asst, Univ Wis, 68-69; lectr, Herbert Lehman Col, City Univ NY, 69-72; asst prof, Univ Ill, 75-79; asst prof, 79-81; assoc prof, 81-88; PROF, UNIV CALIF, IRVINE, 88-. **HONORS AND AWARDS** Fel, John Simon Guggenheim Memorial Found, 75-76; Adele Mellen prize, Edwin Mellen Press, 96., Grad prog dir, 80-83, 85-86, 94-96; ch, Sch Hum grants and travel comm, 84-85; act ch, dept classics, 85; dept ch, 86-94; sr admin off, S Calif Classics Res Sharing Consortium, 90-92; ch, Acad Sen, 94. **SELECTED PUBLICATIONS** Co-ed, Calif Class Assn, Laetaberis, 86-91. **CONTACT ADDRESS** Dept of Classics, Univ Calif, Irvine, CA, 92697.

FERRIS, NORMAN B.
PERSONAL Born 11/29/1931, Richmond, VA, m, 1951, 5 children **DISCIPLINE** AMERICAN HISTORY **EDUCATION** Emory Univ, PhD, 62. **CAREER** Instr hist, Emory Univ, 59-60; asst prof, Univ Southwestern La, 60-61; from asst prof to assoc prof, 62-69, PROF HIST, MID TENN STATE UNIV, 69-, Pres, Tenn Comt Humanities, 80-83. **MEMBERSHIPS** AHA; AAUP; Orgn Am Hists; Southern Hist Asn; Soc Hist Am Foreign Rel. **RESEARCH** United States diplomatic history during Civil War period. **SELECTED PUBLICATIONS** Auth, The Union, The Confederacy, and the Atlantic Rim, Int Hist Rev, Vol 18, 96; Holding the Line--The 3rd Tennesse Infantry, 1861-1864, J South Hist, Vol 62, 96. **CONTACT ADDRESS** Dept of Hist, Middle Tennessee State Univ, Box 187, Murfreesboro, TN, 37132.

FERRO, TRENTON R.
PERSONAL Born 02/08/1939, Yuma, AZ, m, 1964, 4 children **DISCIPLINE** ADULT EDUCATION **EDUCATION** Concordia Sr Col, BA, 61; Concordia Theol Sem, MDiv, 65, STM, 66; Univ Calif-Berkeley, MA, 75; Northern Ill Univ, EdD, 89. **CAREER** Inst, Northern Ill Univ, 85-87; adj prof, Nat Col Educ, 88-89; asst prof, Ball State Univ, 89-90; asst prof, 90-95, Assoc Prof, 95-, Ind Univ Penn. **HONORS AND AWARDS** Fel, Project for the Study of Adult Learning, 92. **MEMBERSHIPS** Am Asn Adult & Continuing Educ; Comn Prof Adult Educ; Relig Educ Asn; Penn Asn Adult Continuing Educ. **RESEARCH** Adult learning and development; program planning and evaluation; volunteerism; adult religious education; educational gerontology. **SELECTED PUBLICATIONS** Auth, AKC Judges Institute Instructional Design and Teaching Manual, Am Kennel Club, 91; co-ed, Proceedings of the Pennsylvania Adult and Continuing Education Research Conference, Ind Univ Pa, 94; co-ed, Proceedings of the Pennsylvania Adult and Continuing Education Research Conference, Ind Univ Pa, 95; co-ed, Proceedings of the Pennsylvania Adult and Continuing Education Research Conference, Widener Univ, 98; author of numerous articles, book chapters, and other publications. **CONTACT ADDRESS** Indiana Univ of Pennsylvania, 231 Stouffer Hall, Indiana, PA, 15705-1087. **EMAIL** trferro@grove.iup.edu

FETTER, BRUCE SIGMOND
PERSONAL Born 06/08/1938, Ashland, KY, m, 1966, 1 child **DISCIPLINE** AFRICAN HISTORY **EDUCATION** Harvard Univ, BA, 60; Oxford Univ, BPhil, 62; Univ Wis, PhD(hist), 68. **CAREER** From instr to asst prof, 67-74, from assoc prof to prof hist, Univ Wis-Milwaukee, 74-87, Fulbright sr lectr hist, Nat Univ Zaire, 72-72; res affil, Inst African Studies, Univ Zambia, 73; ed, Urbanism Past and Present, 75-; counseiller sci, Estud Africain, 81-. **HONORS AND AWARDS** Kiekhofer Teaching Award, 72; NSF Conference Award, 86-87; USIAco-PI, 94-96. **MEMBERSHIPS** African Studies Asn; AHA; Soc Sci Hist Asn; Int Union for the Sci Stu of Population, 91. **RESEARCH** Central and Southern Africa; historical demography. **SELECTED PUBLICATIONS** Coauth, Backward sloping labor supply functions and African economic development, Econ Develop & Cult Change, 68; Auth, The Luluabourg Revolt at Elisabethville, Int J African Studies, 69; L'Union Miniere du Haut-Katanga, 1920-40, la mise en place d'une sousculture totalitaire, Les Cahiers du CEDAF, Brussels, 73; African associations at Elisabethville, 1910-1935, Etudes d'Hist Africaine, 74; The Creation of Elisabethville, Hoover Inst, 76; Statistical approaches to two incidents of colonial militarianism, In: Explorations in Quantitative African History, 78; Martin Rutten: A governor from the provincial bourgeoisie, In: Rulers of the Empire, Free Press, Glenoe, 78; Colonial Rule in Africa: Readings from Primary Sources, Univ Wis Press, 79; Demography from Scanty Evidence: Central Africa in the Colonial Era, Lynne Rienner, 90. **CONTACT ADDRESS** Dept of History, Univ of Wisconsin, PO Box 413, Milwaukee, WI, 53201-0413. **EMAIL** bruf@uwm.edu

FETZER, JAMES HENRY
PERSONAL Born 12/06/1940, Pasadena, CA, m, 1977, 4 children **DISCIPLINE** HISTORY AND PHILOSOPHY OF SCIENCE **EDUCATION** Princeton Univ, AB, 62; Ind Univ, MA, 68; Ind Univ, PhD, 70. **CAREER** Asst prof, Univ Ky, 70-77; vis assoc prof, Univ Va, 77-78; vis assoc prof, Univ Cincinnati, 78-79; vis NSF res prof, Univ Cincinnati, 79-80; vis lectr, Univ NC at Chapel Hill, 80-81; vis assoc prof, New Col, Univ South Fla, 81-83; MacArthur vis distinguished prof, New Col, Univ South Fla, 83-84; adjunct prof, Univ South Fla, Fall, 84-85; vis prof, Univ Va, Spring, 84-85; res scholar, New Col, Univ South Fla, 85-86; prof, Univ Minn, Duluth, 87-96; dept chair, Univ Minn, Duluth, 88-92; dir, Master of Liberal Studies Program, Univ Minn, Duluth, 96-present; distinguished McKnight univ prof, Univ Minn, 96-present. **HONORS AND AWARDS** McKnight Endowment Fel, Univ Minn; Summer Faculty Res Fel, Univ Minn; Outstanding Res Award, Univ Minn; Lansdowne Lectr, Univ Victoria; Pres, Minn Philosophical Society; Vice-pres, Minn Philosophical Society; Medal of the Univ of Helsinki; Summer Fac Res Fel, Univ Minn; Postdoctoral Fel in Computer Sci, Wright State Univ; Postdoctoral Res Fel, Nat Sci Found; Distinguished Teaching Award, Univ Ky; Summer Fac Res Fellow, 72; Graduate Res Asst, Ind Univ; Fel of the Fac, Colombia Univ; NDEA Title IV Fel, Ind Univ; The Dickinson Prize, Princeton Univ; Magna Cum Laude, Princeton. **MEMBERSHIPS** Philos of Sci Asn; Am Philosophical Asn; Asn for Computing Machinery; Human Behavior and Evolution Society; Int Society for Human Ethnology; Am Asn of Univ Profs; Society for Machines and Mentality; Am Asn for the Advanc of Sci. **RESEARCH** Philosophy of science; computer science; artificial intelligence; cognitive science. **SELECTED PUBLICATIONS** Auth, Philosophy of Science, Paragon House Publ, 93; coauth, Glossary of Epistemology/Philosophy of Science, Paragon House Publ, 93; coauth, Glossary of Cognitive Science, Paragon House Publ, 93; ed, Foundations of Philosophy of Science, Paragon House Publ, 93; co-ed, Program Verification Fundamental Issues in Computer Science, Kluwer Academic Publ, 93; auth, Philosophy and Cognitive Science, Paragon House Publ, 96; coauth, Assassination Science: Experts Speak Out on the Death of JFK, Catfeet Press, 98, co-ed, The New Theory of Reference: Kripke, Marcusk, and Its Origins, Kluwer Academic Publ, 98. **CONTACT ADDRESS** Dept of Philosophy, Univ of Minnesota, Duluth, MN, 55812. **EMAIL** jfetzer@d.umn.edu

FEUERHAHN, RONALD R.
PERSONAL Born 12/01/1937, Cape Girardeau, MO, m, 1963, 3 children **DISCIPLINE** HISTORICAL THEOLOGY **EDUCATION** Concordia Sr Col, BA, 59; Concordia Sem, MDiv, 63; Univ Cambridge, England, MPhil, 80, PhD, 92. **CAREER** Pastor, St. David's, Cardiff, Wales, 64-70; pastor, Resurrection, Cambridge, Eng, 70-77; preceptor, Westfield House, Cambridge, England, 77-86; asst prof, 86-95, assoc prof hist theol, 95-, asst chaplain and coord musical and cultural activities, 90-92, acting dean of chapel, 98, Concordia Sem. **MEMBERSHIPS** Cambridge Theol Soc; Soc for Liturgial Stud (Gr Britain); Societas Liturgica; Luther Acad; Lutheran Missiology Soc; Am Soc of Church Hist; Luthern Hist Conf. **RESEARCH** Liturgy and worship; ecumenical movement; law and Gospel; Hermann Sasse; movements of thought (Pietism, Rationalism. **SELECTED PUBLICATIONS** Co-ed, Scripture and the Church: Selected Essays of Hermann Sasse, Concordia Seminary, 95; auth, A Bibliography of Dr. Hermann Sasse, Scarecrow, 95; auth, Hermann Sasse: Confessional Ecumenist, Lutherische Theologie und Kirche, 95; auth, Hermann Sasse-Gesetz und Evangelium in der Geshcichte, in Diestelemann, ed, Eintrachtig Lehren: Festrschrift fuer Bischof Dr. Jobst Schone, Heinrich Harms, 97. **CONTACT ADDRESS** Concordia Sem, 801 DeMun Ave, St. Louis, MO, 63105. **EMAIL** feuerhahnr@csl.edu

FEYERICK, ADA
PERSONAL Born 04/01/1928, m, 1962, 3 children **DISCIPLINE** HISTORY **EDUCATION** Douglass Col, BA, 48. **CAREER** Res, for affairs, , 50-55 Look Mag; res, pub affairs, 56-58, NBC-TV; asst ed, hist-archaeol, 58-62, Horizon Mag. **MEMBERSHIPS** Overseas Press Club; Am Oriental Soc; Am Schools of Oriental Res; Am Res Center in Egypt; Bibl Archaeol Soc of NY. **RESEARCH** Ancient Near East history/archaeology. **SELECTED PUBLICATIONS** Auth, Genesis: World of Myths and Patriarchs, NY Univ Press, 97. **CONTACT ADDRESS** 15 E Hartshorn Dr, Short Hills, NJ, 07078.

FIALA, ROBERT D.
PERSONAL Born 09/27/1938, St. Louis, MO, m, 1962, 2 children **DISCIPLINE** BRITISH, RUSSIAN & EAST ASIAN HISTORY **EDUCATION** Concordia Teachers Col, Nebr, BSEd, 60; Univ Omaha, MA, 63; Wayne State Univ, PhD (Am colonial & Brit Imperial hist), 67; Nat Endowment for the Humanities, Summer Fellwo, 89; UCLA: World of Christopher Columbus, Univ Mich, 94; Imperial China: The Qianlong Era. **CAREER** Instr, High Sch, Tex, 60-61; from asst prof to assoc prof, 65-76, prof hist, Concordia Univ, Nebr, 76-, chmn dept soc sci, 73-, vis prof hist, Tunghai Univ, Taichung, Taiwan, 75-76; summer fel, Inst Mid East, 79, Inst East Asia, Hamline Univ, 81; vis prof hist, Normal Coll of Foreign Lang, Beijing, Peoples Repub of China, 87-88; vis prof hist, Oak Hill Col, London, England, 97. **MEMBERSHIPS** AHA; Conf Brit Studies; Soc Hist Educ. **RESEARCH** George III and English politics; British Empire; British Radicalism, 17th and 18th centuries; Asian Culture and Politics. **SELECTED PUBLICATIONS** Auth, Quakers and the British monarchy: A study in Anglo-American attitudes and practices in the early 1760's, Pa Hist, 4/70; contribr, Joseph Priestley, Thomas Fyshe Palmer, William Godwin, & Beatrice Webb, In: Biographical Dict of

Modern British Radicals Since 1770, 78, 88, & Mrs Anne Hutchinson & Sir Nathaniel Rich, In: Biographical Dict of British Radicals in the Seventeenth Century, 81, Harvester; London Naval Treaty & Washington Naval Conference, Mod Japan: An Encycl of Hist, Cult, and Nationalism, Garland, 98; Numerous photographic essays on Europe and Asia. **CONTACT ADDRESS** Soc Sci Dept, Concordia Col, Nebraska, 800 N Columbia Ave, Seward, NE, 68434-1556. **EMAIL** rfiala@seward.cune.edu

FICHTNER, PAULA SUTTER
PERSONAL Born 08/13/1935, Passaic, NJ, m, 1958 **DISCIPLINE** CENTRAL EUROPEAN HISTORY, RENAISSANCE AND REFORMATION **EDUCATION** Bryn Mawr Col, BA, 57; Ind Univ, MA, 60; Univ Pa, PhD (hist), 64. **CAREER** Lectr hist, 64-66, from asst prof to assoc prof, 66-77, PROF HIST, BROOKLYN COL, 78-, Univ grants, City Univ New York, 70 and 73. **MEMBERSHIPS** Conf Group Cent Europ Hist; AHA. **RESEARCH** Habsburg monarchy; European intellectual history. **SELECTED PUBLICATIONS** Auth, Concepts of Monarchy in A SOciety Of Nobility--Semantics and Theory of one Person Rule from the Reformation to Vormarz, Vol 1, Semantics of Monarchy, Vol 2, Theory of Monarchy, J Mod Hist, Vol 68, 96; The Habsburg Monarchy, 1618-1815, Cent Europ Hist, Vol 28, 95; Sigismund, Kaiser Hus, Constance and the Turkish War, Slavic Rev, Vol 54, 95; Kleinman, Ruth, 1929-1995, Fr Hist Stud, Vol 20, 97; Crato, Johannes and the Austrian Habsburg--Reforming a Counterreformation Court,16th Century J, Vol 27, 96; German Courts in Early Modern Times, 16th Century J, Vol 28, 97; The City and the Crown--Vienna and the Imperial Court, 1600-1740, J Mod Hist, Vol 67, 95. **CONTACT ADDRESS** Dept of Hist, Brooklyn Col, CUNY, 2901 Bedford Ave, Brooklyn, NY, 11210-2813.

FICK, CAROLYN E.
DISCIPLINE HISTORY **EDUCATION** Wayne State University (Detroit), an M.A. from the University of Michigan, and a Ph.D. from Concordia **CAREER** Assoc prof. **RESEARCH** Colonial Caribbean slavery, the Haitian and French revolutions. **SELECTED PUBLICATIONS** Auth, The Making of Haiti: The Saint Domingue Revolution From Below, 90. **CONTACT ADDRESS** Dept of Hist, Concordia Univ, Montreal, 1455 de Maisonneuve W, Montreal, PQ, H3G 1M8.

FIDELER, PAUL ARTHUR
PERSONAL Born 05/16/1936, Passaic, NJ, m, 1963, 2 children **DISCIPLINE** BRITISH AND EUROPEAN HISTORY, WESTERN POLITICAL THOUGHT, WORLD PHILOSOPHIES **EDUCATION** St Lawrence Univ, BA, 58; Brandeis Univ, MA, 62, PhD(hist), 71. **CAREER** Instr, Framingham State Col, 64-68; asst prof to prof hist, 69-91, prof hist and humanities, Lesley Col, 73-; adv ed, Brit Studies Monitor. **HONORS AND AWARDS** Fel in NEH Summer Seminars and Inst, 74, 76, 77, 84, 89; Res Fel, The Folger Shakespeare Library, spring 90; Am Coun of Learned Soc Fel in Humanities Curriculum Development and Vis Schol, Harvard Univ, 92-93. **MEMBERSHIPS** AAUP; AHA; New Eng Hist Asn (pres 87-88); Am Philos Asn; Conf for the Study of Political Thought; N Am Conf on Brit Studies; NE Conf on Brit Studies (pres 91-93). **RESEARCH** Poor relief policy and political theory in early modern England; historiography and humanities methodologies; character, values, ethics, and justice in the curriculum, K-16. **SELECTED PUBLICATIONS** Auth, Christian Humanism and Poor Law Reform in Early Tudor England, Societas, fall 74; Have Historians Lost Their Perspective on the Past?, Change, Jan/Feb 84; Toward a Ccurricula of Hope: The Essential Role of Humanities Scholarship in Public School Teaching, Am Coun of Learned Soc, Occasional Paper, No. 23, 94; Rescuing Youth Culture: Cultivating Children's Natural Abilities as Philosophers, Lesley Mag, winter 94; coauth, Autobiography in the Classroom: A Triptych, Teaching the Humanities, spring 95; auth, Societas, Civitas and Early Elizabethan Poverty Relief, In: State, Sovereigns and Society: Essays in Early Modern English History, St. Martins, 98. **CONTACT ADDRESS** Humanities Faculty, Lesley Col, 29 Everett St, Cambridge, MA, 02138-2790. **EMAIL** pfideler@lesley.edu

FIDLER, ANN
DISCIPLINE HISTORY **EDUCATION** Univ of Kansas, BA, 84; Univ of Calif at Berkeley, JD, 90, PhD, 96. **CAREER** ASST PROF, HIST, OHIO UNIV **MEMBERSHIPS** Am Antiquarian Soc **SELECTED PUBLICATIONS** A Cultural History of the American Law Book, 1700-1900. **CONTACT ADDRESS** Dept of Hist, Ohio Univ, Bentley Hall, Athens, OH, 45701-2979.

FIELD, A.J.
PERSONAL Born 04/17/1949, Boston, MA, m, 1982, 2 children **DISCIPLINE** ECONOMICS **EDUCATION** Harvard Univ, BA 70; London Sch Econ, MSc 71; Univ Calif Berk, PhD 74. **CAREER** Stanford Univ, asst prof 74-82; Santa Clara Univ, assoc prof, prof, 82-88, Michel and Mary Orradre Prof 92-, actg acad vpres 86-87, actg dean 96-97. **HONORS AND AWARDS** Allen Nevins Prize; NSF Gnt; Inst Adv Stud. **MEMBERSHIPS** AEA; EHA; Phi Beta Kappa; Beta Gamma Sigma; Cliometrics Soc. **RESEARCH** Economics of technological and institutional change; macro economic history and policy; micro economics and rationality. **SELECTED PUBLICATIONS** Auth, The Telegraphic Transmission of Financial Asset Prices and Orders to Trade: Implications for Economics Growth Trading Volume and Securities Market Regulation, Research in Econ Hist, JAI Press, 98; auth, Sunk Costs Water Over the Dam and Other Liquid Parables, K. Dennis, ed, Rationality in Economics: Alternative Perspectives, Boston Kluwer-Nijhoff, 98; auth, The Relative Productivity of American Distribution, 1869-1992, Research In Econ Hist, JAI Press, 96; French Optical Telegraphy 1793-1855: Hardware Software Administration, Tech and Culture, 94; auth, Douglas North, entry in: Handbook on Institutional and Evolutionary Economics, Edward Elgar, 94. **CONTACT ADDRESS** Dept of Economics, Santa Clara Univ, 500 El Camino Real, Santa Clara, CA, 95053-0385. **EMAIL** afield@scu.edu

FIELD, DANIEL
PERSONAL Born 07/26/1938, Boston, MA, m, 1959, 2 children **DISCIPLINE** RUSSIAN AND MODERN EUROPEAN HISTORY **EDUCATION** Harvard Univ, BA, 59, MA, 62, PhD (hist), 69. **CAREER** Lectr hist, Brandeis Univ, 65-66; instr, Harvard Univ, 68-69, lectr, 69-70; asst prof, Barnard Col, Columbia Univ, 70-76; ASSOC PROF HIST, SYRACUSE UNIV, 76-, Sr fel and assoc, Russ Inst, Columbia Univ, 70-76; res fel, Russ Res Ctr, Harvard Univ, 72-73, 77-78 and 81-82; Am Coun Learned Soc grant-in-aid prog grant, 72-73; res fel, Inst Hist, Acad Sci of Moscow, 78 and 81; Fulbright-Hays fel, 78 and 81. **MEMBERSHIPS** Am Asn Advan Slavic Studies; AHA **RESEARCH** Russian serfdom; Russian intellectual history; Russian radicalism. **SELECTED PUBLICATIONS** Auth, Between the Fields and the City--Women, Work, and Family in Russia, 1861-1914, Am Hist Rev, Vol 100, 95; Making Workers Soviet--Power, Class and Identity, J Interdisciplinary Hist, Vol 27, 97; Domination and the Arts of Resistance--Hidden Transcripts, Am Hist Rev, Vol 99, 94. **CONTACT ADDRESS** Dept of Hist, Syracuse Univ, Syracuse, NY, 13210.

FIELD, EARLE
PERSONAL Born 01/14/1922, Syracuse, NY, m, 1946, 2 children **DISCIPLINE** EUROPEAN HISTORY **EDUCATION** Syracuse Univ, AB, 49, MA, 50, PhD, 54. **CAREER** Lectr hist, univ col, Syracuse Univ, 53-54; instr soc sci, State Univ NY, 54-59; from asst prof to assoc prof, 59-65, PROF HIST, CALIF STATE UNIV, NORTHRIDGE, 65-. **MEMBERSHIPS** AHA. **RESEARCH** Ancient Near East; classical civilization; Jewish history. **SELECTED PUBLICATIONS** Auth, A Toast to Vera Soloviova, Mich Quart Rev, Vol 32, 93; Variety Photoplays, Parnassus Poetry Rev, Vol 22, 97; Tea at Paul Bowles, Raritan Quart Rev, Vol 12, 93; Old Aquaintance, Mich Quart Rev, Vol 33, 94; To My Country, Mich Quart Rev, Vol 35, 96; Paris 48, Kenyon Rev, Vol 16, 94; Doing it With Mirrors, Mich Quart Rev, Vol 33, 94. **CONTACT ADDRESS** 18132 Sunburst St, Northridge, CA, 91325.

FIELD, MARK G.
PERSONAL Born 06/17/1923, Switzerland, m, 1948, 4 children **DISCIPLINE** SOCIOLOGY **EDUCATION** Harvard Col, BA, 48; Harvard Univ, MA, 50, PhD, 55. **CAREER** Assoc prof, Univ Ill, 61-62; prof, 62-88, prof emer 88- , Boston Univ; res fel & assoc, 62- , adj prof, 88- , Davis Ctr for Russ Stud, Harvard Univ. **MEMBERSHIPS** Am Sociol Asn; Am Asn Advan Slavic Stud; Soc Europeenne de Culture. **RESEARCH** Sociology of health care; health crisis in the former Soviet Union; comparative health care systems; cultural aspects of health. **SELECTED PUBLICATIONS** Ed, Success and Crisis in National Health Care Systems: A Comparative Approach, Routledge, 89; co-ed, The Political Dynamics of Physician Manpower Policy, Amsterdam, 90; coauth, Cultural Images of Health: A Neglected Dimension, Nova Science, 95; auth, The Health Crisis in the Former Soviet Union: A Report from the Post-War Zone, Soc Sci and Med, 95; coatuh, The Current State of Health Care in the Former Soviet Union: Implications for Health Care Policy and Reform, Am J of Public Health, 96; auth, Health in Russia: The Regional and National Dimensions, in Stavrakis, ed, Beyond the Monolity: The Emergence of Regionalism in Post-Soviet Russia, Woodrow Wilson Ctr, 97; coauth, From Assurance to Insurance in Russian Health Care: The Problematic Transition, Am J Pub Health, 98. **CONTACT ADDRESS** Davis Center for Russian Studies, Harvard Univ, 1737 Cambridge St, Cambridge, MA, 02138. **EMAIL** mfield@hsph.harvard.edu

FIELD, PHYLLIS FRANCES
PERSONAL Born 12/27/1946, Louisville, KY, m, 1977, 1 child **DISCIPLINE** AMERICAN HISTORY **EDUCATION** Univ Louisville, BA, 67; Cornell Univ, PhD(Am hist), 74. **CAREER** Vis asst prof, State Univ NY, Stony Brook, 74-75; asst prof, 75-80, ASSOC PROF HIST, OHIO UNIV, 81-. **MEMBERSHIPS** AHA; Orgn Am Historians; Soc Sci Hist Asn; Southern Hist Asn; Soc Hist Early Am Repub; Ohio Acad Hist. **RESEARCH** 19th century US political and social history. **SELECTED PUBLICATIONS** Auth, Republicans and Black Suffrage in New York State: The Grass Roots Response, Civil War Hist, 6/75; contribr, The History of American Electoral Behavior, Princeton Univ, 78; auth, Politics versus Principles: The Partisan Response to Bible Politics in New York State, Civil War Hist, 6/79; The Politics of Race in New York: The Struggle for Black Suffrage in the Civil War Era, Cornell Univ Press, 82; contribr, Crusaders and Compromisers: Essays on the Relationship of the Antislavery Struggle to the Antebellum Party System, Greenwood Press, 83; auth, Nineteenth-Century American Voting Studies: The New Generation, Hist Methods, 9/89; contribr, Encyclopeida of the American Legislative System, Scribner's, 1994; contribr, Political Parties & Elections in the United States, Garland, 91; contribr, American National Biography, Oxford, 98. **CONTACT ADDRESS** Dept Hist, Ohio Univ, Athens, OH, 45701-2979. **EMAIL** pfield1@ohiou.edu

FIELDS, BARBARA J.
DISCIPLINE UNITED STATES HISTORY **EDUCATION** Harvard Univ, BA, 68; Yale Univ, PhD, 78. **CAREER** Prof. **SELECTED PUBLICATIONS** Auth, Slavery and Freedom on the Middle Ground: Maryland during the Nineteenth Century, 85; Slaves No More: Three Essays on Emancipation and the Civil War, 92; Free at Last: A Documentary History of Slavery, Freedom, and the Civil War, 92; co-auth, The Destruction of Slavery, 85. **CONTACT ADDRESS** Dept of History, Columbia Col, New York, 2960 Broadway, New York, NY, 10027-6902.

FIELDS, LANNY BRUCE
PERSONAL Born 05/10/1941, Indianapolis, IN, 2 children **DISCIPLINE** EAST ASIAN HISTORY **EDUCATION** DePauw Univ, BA, 63; Univ Hawaii, Manoa, MA, 66; Ind Univ, PhD (hist), 72. **CAREER** Asst prof hist, Univ of the South, 72-73; asst prof hist, State Univ NY, Albany, 73-76, assoc prof Chinese and Russ hist, 76-78; asst prof hist, Southwest Mo State Univ, 78-79; ASSOC PROF HIST, UNIV HAWAII, HILO, 79-. **RESEARCH** Ancient Chinese history. **SELECTED PUBLICATIONS** Auth, Hsia, Wu Chu, Physician to the 1st Chin Emperor, J Asian Hist, Vol 28, 94. **CONTACT ADDRESS** Col of Arts and Sci, Univ Hawaii, Hilo, HI, 96720.

FIEMA, ZBIGNIEW
PERSONAL Born 03/07/1957, Poland, s **DISCIPLINE** ARCHAEOLOGY; ANTHROPOLOGY **EDUCATION** Univ Utah, PhD, 91 **CAREER** Assoc Instr, 86-92, Univ Utah; Visiting Prof, Univ Helsinki, Finland, 96-97; Chief Archaelogist, American Center of Oriental Research, Jordan, 92-97. **HONORS AND AWARDS** Phi Kappa Phi Honors Soc, Univ Utah **MEMBERSHIPS** Amer Schools of Oriental Research; Archaelogical Inst of Amer. **RESEARCH** Culture History of the Roman & Byzantine East; complex societies; archaelogical methodology **SELECTED PUBLICATIONS** Coauth, Report on the Petra Scrolls Project, Journal of Archaelogy, 95; Auth, Military Architecture and Defense System in Roman-Byzantine Southern Jordan. A Critical Appraisal of Recent Interpretations, Studies in the Archaeology and History of Jordan V, 95; Sr Coauth, The Petra Church Project 92-94, The Roman and Byzantine Near East: Some Recent Archaeological Research, 95; Auth, Nabataean and Palmyrene Commerce - The Mechanisms of Intensification, The Proceedings of the International Conference on Palmyra and the Silk Road, 96; Les papyri de Petra, Le Monde de la Bible, 97; Report on the Petra Church Project, American Journal of Archaeology, 97; Petra Romana et Byzantina, Petra - Antike Felsstadt zwischen Arabischer Tradition und Griechischer Norm, 97; At-Tuwan - The Development and Decline of a Classical Town in Southern Jordan, Studies in the History and Archaeology of Jordan VI, 97; Report on the Roman Street in Petra Project, American Journal of Archaeology, 98. **CONTACT ADDRESS** 1703 32nd St. NW, Washington, DC, 20007. **EMAIL** fiemaz@doaks.org

FIERCE, MILFRED C.
PERSONAL Born 07/06/1937, Brooklyn, NY **DISCIPLINE** HISTORY **EDUCATION** Wagner Coll, BA, MS; Columbia U, MA, MPhil, PhD. **CAREER** Vassar Coll, dir Black Studies 1969-71; Hunter Coll, prof, 1973-81; Brooklyn College (CUNY), professor, 1982-. **HONORS AND AWARDS** So Hist Assn recipient, NDEA 1965; EPDA 1969; delegate Intl Congress of Africanists 1973; recipient Natl Endowment for the Humanities Fellowship, City Univ of NY, 1976. **MEMBERSHIPS** Apptd exec dir Assn of Black Found Exec Inc 1976; apptd NY St Coll Proficiency Exam Com in African & Afro-Am History, fall 1976; apptd research dir Study Commn on US Policy toward South Africa 1979; mem African-Am Tchrs Assn; African Heritage Studies Assn; Assn for Study of Afro-Amer Life & History; mem Am Historical Assn; Orgn of Am Historians. **CONTACT ADDRESS** 2900 Bedford Ave, Brooklyn, NY, 11210.

FIGUEIRA, THOMAS J.
PERSONAL Born 12/30/1948, New York, NY, m, 1976, 3 children **DISCIPLINE** ANCIENT HISTORY **EDUCATION** Fordham Univ, 66-70; Bensalem Col, BA (Humanities), 70; Univ Chicago, 70-73 (Classics dept); Univ PA, PhD (Ancient History), 77. **CAREER** Teaching fel, Univ PA, 74-75; acting asst prof of Classics, Stanford Univ, 77-78; asst prof of Classics, Dickinson Col, Carlisle, PA, 78-79; asst prof of Classics and Archaeology, Rutgers Univ, 79-85, assoc prof of Classics and Ancient Hist, Rutgers Univ, 85-90; vis assoc prof of Classics, Princeton Univ, 85-86; prof of Classics and Ancient Hist (full-time, with tenure), Rutgers Univ, 91-. **HONORS AND AWARDS** Fulbright res fel to Greece, 76-77; Nat Endowment

for the Humanities, summer seminar fel, 81; res fel, Center for Hellenic Studies (Harvard Univ), Washington, DC, 92-93; Exxon Ed Found, travel grant, summer 85; Am Coun of Learned Soc, travel grant, summer 85; vis scholar, School of Historical Studies, Inst for Advanced Study, Princeton, NJ, 84-85; res fel, John Simon Guggenheim Memorial Found, 84-85. **MEMBERSHIPS** Am Philol Asn; Asn of Ancient Historians; Archaeological Inst of Am; Am Historical Asn. **RESEARCH** Ancient Greek hist and lit; social and economic hist of the ancient world; classical historiography. **SELECTED PUBLICATIONS** Auth, Aegina, Arno Press, 81-82; with G Nagy, Theognis and Megara: Poetry and the Polis, Johns Hopkins Univ Press, 85; Athens and Aigina in the Age of Imperial Colonization, Johns Hopkins Univ Press, 91; Excursions in Epichoric History, Rowman and Littlefield, 93; Khremata: Aquisition and Possession in Archaic Greece, Social Justice in the Ancient World, K D Irani and M Silver, eds, Greenwood Pub, 95; The Power of Money: Coinage and Politics in the Athenian Empire, Univ PA, 98; Attic Colonization in the Classical Period, A History of Greek Colonization, I Malkin, ed, E J Brill, forthcoming; Greek Colonization in the Classical Period, A History of Greek Colonization, I Malkin, ed, E J Brill, forthcoming; The Evolution of the Messenian Identity, in Sparta: New Pereprectives, S Hodkinson and A Powell, eds, Classical Press of Wales, forthcoming; numerous other book chapters, reviews, and articles. **CONTACT ADDRESS** Dept of Classics and Archaeology, Rutgers Univ, Box 270, New Brunswick, NJ, 08903-0270. **EMAIL** figueira@rci.rutgers.edu

FILENE, PETER GABRIEL
PERSONAL Born 01/28/1940, New York, NY, m, 1960, 2 children **DISCIPLINE** MODERN AMERICAN HISTORY **EDUCATION** Swarthmore Col, BA, 60; Harvard Univ, MA, 61, PhD (hist), 65. **CAREER** Asst prof hist, Lincoln Univ, Mo, 65-67; from asst prof to assoc prof, 65-75, PROF HIST, UNIV NC CHAPEL HILL, 75-, Fel, Charles Warren Ctr Studies Am Hist, 73. **MEMBERSHIPS** Orgn Am Hists. **RESEARCH** American social history; sex roles; multimedia techniques. **SELECTED PUBLICATIONS** Auth, Nation of Nations--A Narrative History of the American Republic, J Am Hist, Vol 79, 93; The Enduring Vision--A History of the American People, J Am Hist, Vol 79, 93; America--Past and Present, 3rd Edition, J Am Hist, Vol 79, 93; America History, J Am Hist, Vol 79, 93; A People and a Nation--A History of the United-States, J Am Hist, Vol 79, 93; American History--A Survey, 8th Edition, J Am Hist, Vol 79, 93; The Great Republic--A History of the American People, 4th Edition, J Am Hist, Vol 79, 93; The American People--Creating A Nation and A Society, 2nd Edition, J Am Hist, Vol 79, 93. **CONTACT ADDRESS** Dept of Hist, Univ of NC, Hamilton Hall, Chapel Hill, NC, 27514.

FILLER, JOHN W.
DISCIPLINE EARLY CHILDHOOD SPECIAL EDUCATION **EDUCATION** Peabody Col, PhD. **CAREER** Coordr, doctoral stud, Univ Nev, Las Vegas. **SELECTED PUBLICATIONS** Auth, A coment on inclusion: Research and Social Policy, Soc for Res in Child Develop Policy Rpt, 10, 96; coauth, Perceived importance of social skills: A survey of teachers, parents and other professionals, J of Spec Educ, 25, 91. **CONTACT ADDRESS** Dept of Spec Educ, Univ Nev, Las Vegas, 4505 Maryland Pky, Las Vegas, NV, 89154-3014. **EMAIL** jfiller@nevada.edu

FILONOWICZ, JOSEPH
DISCIPLINE HISTORY OF ETHICS, SOCIAL AND POLITICAL PHILOSOPHY **EDUCATION** Hope Col, BA; Columbia Univ, MA, MPhil, PhD. **CAREER** Assoc prof, Long Island Univ. **MEMBERSHIPS** Ch, Long Island Philos Soc. **RESEARCH** History of the ideas of the British sentimental moralists, moral philosophy, psychology of ethics, American philosophy. **SELECTED PUBLICATIONS** Wrote on ethical sentimentalism for the History of Philos Quart. **CONTACT ADDRESS** Long Island Univ, Brooklyn, NY, 11201-8423. **EMAIL** JFilonow@eagle.liunet.edu

FINAN, JOHN J.
PERSONAL Born 09/01/1925, St. Louis, MO, m, 1964, 2 children **DISCIPLINE** LATIN AMERICAN HISTORY **EDUCATION** Wash Univ, AB, 45, AM, 47; Harvard Univ, PhD(Latin Am hist), 56. **CAREER** Latin Am specialist, manuscripts div, Libr Cong, 53-55; Brown Univ President's fel, Argentina, 56-58; polit off, US Embassy, Colombia, 58-61; assoc prof, 61-69, prof & dir Latin Am Studies, 69-95, PROF EMERITUS, LATIN AM STUDIES, 95-, SCH INT SERV, AM UNIV; Vis prof, Nat War Col, 67-69 **MEMBERSHIPS** Conf Latin Am Hist (secy-treas, 63-72). **RESEARCH** Nineteenth century Argentina; Latin American foreign relations; Argentine foreign policy; moral economy of colonial Mexico. **SELECTED PUBLICATIONS** Auth, Maize in the great herbals, Chronica Botanica, 51; coauth, Diplomatic History of Latin America, La State Univ, 77. **CONTACT ADDRESS** Sch of Int Svc, American Univ, Washington, DC, 20016.

FINDLAY JR, JAMES F.
DISCIPLINE RECENT US HISTORY, AMERICAN RELIGION, AND THE CIVIL RIGHTS MOVEMENT **EDUCATION** Northwestern Univ, PhD, 61. **CAREER** Dept Hist, Univ RI **HONORS AND AWARDS** URI Res Excellence awd. **RESEARCH** Protestant churches in the Civil Rights movement. **SELECTED PUBLICATIONS** Auth, biography of Dwight L. Moody. **CONTACT ADDRESS** Dept of Hist, Univ of RI, 8 Ranger Rd, Ste. 1, Kingston, RI, 02881-0807.

FINDLEY, CARTER VAUGHN
PERSONAL Born 05/12/1941, Atlanta, GA, m, 1968, 2 children **DISCIPLINE** HISTORY; MIDDLE EASTERN STUDIES **EDUCATION** Yale Col, BA, 63; Harvard Univ, PhD, 69. **CAREER** Asst prof, 72-79, assoc prof hist, Ohio State Univ, 79-, Soc Sci Res Coun fel, 76-77, 79, 86-87, Inst Adv Study, 81-82; Fulbright-Hays Sr Res Fel, 94 & 98; vis prof, Ecole des Hautes en Sci Soc, Paris, 94; vis lect Dept Hist, Bilkent Univ, Ankara, 97. **HONORS AND AWARDS** OH Acad Publ Award and M Fuat Koprulu Book Prize Turkish Stud Assoc. **MEMBERSHIPS** Fel MidE Inst; fel MidE Studies Asn NAm; AHA; Am Oriental Soc; Comite Int pour les Etudes Pre-Ottomanes et Ottomanes; Oh Acad Hist; Turkish Stud Assoc (pres 90-92, vpres, 98-00, pres-elect, 00-02); Economic Soc Hist Found Turkey; World Hist Assoc. **RESEARCH** Ottoman history; Turkish studies; world history. **SELECTED PUBLICATIONS** Auth, Bureaucratic Reform in the Ottoman Empire: The Sublime Porte, 1789-1922, Princeton Univ, 80; Ottoman Civil Officialdom: A Social History, Princeton Univ, 89; Economic Bases of Revolution and Repression in the Late Ottoman Empire, Comparative Studies in Society and History, 86; La soumise, la subversive: Fatma Aliye, romanciere et feministe, Turcica, 95; Ebu Bekir Ratib's Vienna Embassy Narrative: Discovering Austria or Propagandizing for Reform in Istanbul, Wiener Zeitschrift fur die Kunde des Morgenlandes, 95; An Ottoman Occidentalist in Europe, 89: Ahmed Midhat Meets Madame Gulnar, 1889; Am Hist Rev, 98; coauth Twentieth-Century World, Houghton Mifflin, 98. **CONTACT ADDRESS** Dept Hist, Ohio State Univ, 230 W 17th Ave, Columbus, OH, 43210-1361. **EMAIL** findley.1@osu.edu

FINDLING, JOHN ELLIS
PERSONAL Born 03/16/1941, South Bend, IN, m, 1968, 1 child **DISCIPLINE** HISTORY OF WORLD'S FAIRS AND EXPOSITIONS, OLYMPIC MOVEMENT, U.S. DIPLOMATIC **EDUCATION** Rice Univ, BA, 63; Univ Tex, Austin, MA, 65, PhD, 71. **CAREER** Teacher English, Am Nicaraguan Sch, Managua, 65-67; from Asst Prof to Assoc Prof, 71-81, PROF HIST, IND UNIV SOUTHEAST, 81-, Chmn, Div Soc Sci, 81-87, Dir MLS Prog, 93-97. **HONORS AND AWARDS** Outstanding Res Award, Ind Univ SE, 88, 98. **MEMBERSHIPS** AHA; Soc Historians Am For Rels; NAm Soc Sport Hist; Int Soc Hist Phys Educ and Sport; Int Soc Olympic Hist. **RESEARCH** Worlds fairs and expositions; sports history. **SELECTED PUBLICATIONS** Auth, Dictionary of American Diplomatic History, 80, rev ed, 89; Close Neighbors, Distant Friends: United States-Central American Relations, 87; Historical Dictionary of World's Fairs and Expositions, 90; Chicago's Great World's Fairs, 94; Historical Dictionary of the Modern Olympic Movement, 96; author of various other edited works and articles. **CONTACT ADDRESS** Div of Soc Sci, Indiana Univ, Southeast, 4201 Grant Line Rd, New Albany, IN, 47150-2158. **EMAIL** jfindlin@iusmail.ius.indiana.edu

FINE, SIDNEY
PERSONAL Born 10/11/1920, Cleveland, OH, m, 1942, 2 children **DISCIPLINE** UNITED STATES HISTORY **EDUCATION** Western Reserve Univ, AB, 42; Univ Mich, AM, 44 PhD, 48. **CAREER** From instr to prof, 48-74, Andrew Dickson White prof hist, Univ Mich, Ann Arbor, 74-, Guggenheim fel, 57-58; fac mem Salzburg Sem Am Studies, 59; Richard Hudson res prof, Univ Mich, 63-64 & 76-77, chmn dept hist, 69-71; Nat Arch Adv Coun, 68-71. **HONORS AND AWARDS** Univ Mich Press Award, 65, 71, 85, 91; Distinguished Fac Achievement Award, Univ Mich, 69; Henry Rubel Lectr, Univ Mich, 84-85; Doctor of Letters, Wittenborg Univ, 84; Gustavus Myers Ctr for Human Rights Award, 90; Doctor of Humane Letters, DePaw Univ, 97; Doctor of Law, Univ Mass, 97. **MEMBERSHIPS** AHA; Labor Historians (pres, 69-71); Orgn Am Historians. **RESEARCH** United States history since 1876; American labor history. **SELECTED PUBLICATIONS** Auth, Anarchism and the Assassination of McKinley, Am Hist Rev, 7/55; Laissez Faire and the General-Welfare State: A Study of Conflict in American Thought 1865-1901, 56; co-ed, The American Past: Conflicting Interpretations of the Great Issues (2 vols), Macmillan, 61, 2nd ed, 65, 3rd ed, 70, 4th ed, 76; ed, Recent America: Conflicting Interpretations of the Great Issues, 62, 2nd ed, 67; auth, The Automobile Under the Blue Eagle, Univ Mich, 63; Mr Justice Murphy in World War II, J Am Hist, 6/66; Sit-Down: The General Motors Strike of 1936-1937, 69 & Frank Murphy: The Detroit Years, 75, Univ Mich; Frank Murphy: The New Deal Years, Chicago, 79; Frank Murphy: The Washington Years, 84; Violence in the Model City: The Cavanaugh Administration, Race Relations and the Detroit Riot of 1987, 89; author of numerous journal articles. **CONTACT ADDRESS** Dept of Hist, Univ of Mich, 435 S State St, Ann Arbor, MI, 48109-1003. **EMAIL** sidneyf@umich.edu

FINGARD, JUDITH
PERSONAL Born 12/21/1943, Halifax, NS, Canada **DISCIPLINE** CANADIAN HISTORY **EDUCATION** Dalhousie Univ, BA, 64; Univ London, MPhil, 67, PhD (hist), 70. **CAREER** Lectr, 67-68, asst prof, 69-73, assoc prof, 73-80, PROF HIST, DALHOUSIE UNIV, 80-, Can Coun res grants, 72-73 and 73-74, leave fel, 75-76. **MEMBERSHIPS** Can Hist Asn. **RESEARCH** Canadian social history; 19th century Atlantic provinces history. **SELECTED PUBLICATIONS** Auth, Intimate Relations--Family and Community in Planter Nova Scotia, 1759-1800, William Mary Quart, Vol 53, 96; From Sea to Rail, Black Transportation Workers and Their Families in Halifax, C. 1870-1916, Acadiensis, Vol 24, 95; The Prevention of Cruelty, Marriage Breakdown and the Rights of Wives in Nova Scotia, 1880-1900, Acadiensis, Vol 22, 93; Were Rooted Here and they Cant Pull us up--Essays in African Canadian Womens History, J Imperial Commonwealth Hist, Vol 24, 96; Politics, Shipping and the Repeal of the Navigation Laws, J Imperial Commonwealth Hist, Vol 21, 93; Toronto Girl Problem--The Perils and Pleasures of the City, 1880-1930, Can Hist Revi, Vol 77, 96. **CONTACT ADDRESS** Dept of Hist, Dalhousie Univ, Halifax, NS, B3H 3J5.

FINGER, JOHN R.
DISCIPLINE HISTORY **EDUCATION** Univ Wash, PhD. **CAREER** Prof. **RESEARCH** Indian-White relations. **SELECTED PUBLICATIONS** Auth, The Eastern Band of Cherokees 1819-1900, Univ Tennessee; Cherokee Americans: The Eastern Band of the Cherokees in the Twentieth Century, Univ Nebr. **CONTACT ADDRESS** Dept of History, Knoxville, TN, 37996.

FINIFTER, ADA WEINTRAUB
PERSONAL Born 06/06/1938, New York, NY, d **DISCIPLINE** POLITICAL SCIENCE **EDUCATION** Univ WI, PhD, 67. **CAREER** Prof, Dept of Political Science, MI State Univ, 81-; ed, Am Political Science Rev, 95-2001; **HONORS AND AWARDS** Abraham and Rebecca Sive Memorial Prize, Brooklyn Col, 59; Univ fel, Univ MI, 59-60; summer fel, Nat Science Found fellowships for graduate teaching assts, 66; grad fel, Nat Sci Found, 66-67; Nat Sci Found travel grant, 73; Am Political Science Asn Congressional fel, 73-74; vis fel, Dept of Political Science, Res School of Social Services, Australian Nat Univ, April-Dec 78; Sr scholar, Fulbright prog in Australia, Aug-Oct 78; Am Sociol Asn grant, 81; Women in Development Fac Scholar Award, 83; Excellence in Online Ed Award of Merit, Higher Ed Div, Dialog Information System, 88; Fac Developmet Award for Further Internationalizing MSU, 90; All-University Res Initiation grant, MI State Univ, 90-91; Phi Kappa Phi, 96. **MEMBERSHIPS** Am Political Science Asn; Southern Political Science Asn; Midwest Political Science Asn. **RESEARCH** Public opinion. **SELECTED PUBLICATIONS** Auth, Dimensions of Poitical Alienation, Am Political Science Rev, 64, 2, June 70; The Friendship Group as a Protective Environment for Political Deviants, Am Political Science Rev, 68, 2, June 74; with Bernard M Finifter, Part Identificetion and Political Adaptation of American Settlers in Australia, J of Politics, 51, 3, Aug 89; with Ellen Mickiewitz, Redefining the Political System of the USSR: Mass Support for Political Change, Am Political Science Rev, 86, 4, Dec 92; ed, Political Science: The State of the Discipline II, Am Political Science Asn, 93; auth with Bernard M Finifter, Pledging Allegiance to a New Flag: Citizenship Change and its Psychological Aftermath Among American Migrants in Australia, Can Rev of Studies in Nationalism, 22, 1-2, Sept 95; Attitudes Toward Individual Responsibility and Poltitical Reform in the Former Soviet Union, Am Political Science Rev, 90, 1, March 96; numerous other publications. **CONTACT ADDRESS** Dept of Political Science, Michigan State Univ, 303 South Kedzie Hall, East Lansing, MI, 48824. **EMAIL** Finifter@pilot.msu.edu

FINK, DEBORAH R.
PERSONAL Born 10/12/1944, Lincoln, NE, m, 1966, 2 children **DISCIPLINE** ANTHROPOLOGY **EDUCATION** Doane Col, Crete, NE, BA, 65; Univ NE, Lincoln, MA, 67; IA State Univ, Ames, MS, 74; Univ MN, Minneapolis, PhD, 79. **CAREER** Lect, Grinnell Col, 80; asst prof, anthropol, IA State, 80-81, adjunct prof, 83; adjunct asst prof, Women's Studies, Univ IA, 84-85; Rockefeller fel, Rural Women and Feminist Issues, 88-89; independent scholar, 89-. **HONORS AND AWARDS** Cum laude graduation, Doane Col, 65; graduate res grant, IA State, 73; MacMillan fel, Univ MN, 77; Doctoral dissertation fel, Univ MN, 78-79. **MEMBERSHIPS** Am Anthropological Asn; Central States Anthropol Asn; Soc for Applied Anthropol; Nat Coalition of Independent Scholars. **RESEARCH** Rural studies; cross-cultural study of women; labor studies. **SELECTED PUBLICATIONS** Auth, Open Country, Iowa: Rural Women, Tradition and Change, SUNY Press, 86; Agrarian Women: Wives and Mothers in Rural Nebraska 1880-1940, Univ NC Press, 92; review, All Will Yet Be Well: The Diary of Sarah Gillespie Huftalen, 1873-1952, by Suzanne L Bunkers, ND Hist, 95; review, Chasing Rainbows: A Recollection of the Great Plains, 1921-1975, by Gladys Leffler Gist, ed by James Marten, Great Plains Quart, 95; What Kind of Woman Would Work in Meatpacking, Anyway? World War II and the Road to Fair Employment, Great Plains Res, 95; World War II and Rural; Women, in IA Hist Reader, ed by Marvin Bergman, Ames: State Hist Soc of IA in assoc with IA State Univ Press, 96; Reoganizing Production: Gender and Control in Iowa Meatpacking, in Unionizing The Jungles: Labor and Community in the Twentieth-Century Meatpacking Industry, ed by Shelton

Stromquist and Marvin Bergman, Univ IA Press, 97; review, The Prairie Winnows Out Its Own, by Paula M Nelson, WI Mag of Hist, 97; review, Troublesome Creek: A Midwestern, by Jeanne Jordan and Steven Asher, H-Rural, 8, Sept 97; review, Farm Boys: Lives of Gay Men from the Rural Midwest, collected and edited by Will Fellows, Annals of IA, 97; review, A Most Comfortable Dinner-18th Century Foods to Subsist a Great Number of Persons at a Small Expense, collected by Clarissa F Dillon, The Independent Scholar, 98; review, The Danish Revolution, 1500-1800: An Ecohistorical Interpretation, by Thorkild Kjaergaard, trans by David Hohnen, H-Rural, 98; Cutting Into the Meatpacking Line: Workers and Change in the Rural Midwest, Univ NC Press, 98; several publications forthcoming; author of numerous other published works. **CONTACT ADDRESS** 222 S Russell, Ames, IA, 50010. **EMAIL** afink@iastate.edu

FINK, GARY M.
PERSONAL Born 02/04/1936, Forsyth, MT, m, 1959, 4 children **DISCIPLINE** UNITED STATES HISTORY **EDUCATION** Univ MT, BS, 60; Univ MO, MA, 64, PhD, 68. **CAREER** Asst prof hist, Mankato State Col, 68-70; assoc prof, 70-80, prof hist, GA State Univ, 80, dept ch, 84-92. **MEMBERSHIPS** AHA; Orgn Am Historians; Southern Hist Asn; Soc Sci Hist Asn. **RESEARCH** US polit hist; quantitative analysis; labor hist. **SELECTED PUBLICATIONS** Auth, Labor's Search for Political Order: The Political Behavior of the Missouri Labor Movement, 1890-1940, Univ Mo, 73; ed, Biographical Directory of American Labor Leaders, Greenwood, 74; ed, Labor Unions, 76; co-ed, Essays in Southern Labor History, Greenwood,78; auth, Prelude to the Presidency: The Political Character and Legislative Leadership Style of Governor Jimmy Carter, 80, & co-ed, Southern Workers and Their Unions, 1880-1975, 81, Greenwood; auth, The Fulton Bag and Cotton Mill Strike, 1914-1915, Univ Cornell, 93; Race, Class, and Community in Southern Labor History, Univ Ala, 94; The Carter Presidency: Policy Choices in the Post-New Deal Era, Univ Kans, 98. **CONTACT ADDRESS** Dept of Hist, Georgia State Univ, 33 Gilmer St S E, Atlanta, GA, 30303-3080. **EMAIL** hisgmf@panther.gsu.edu

FINK, WILLIAM BERTRAND
PERSONAL Born 05/11/1916, Yonkers, NY, m, 1941, 2 children **DISCIPLINE** HISTORY **EDUCATION** Wesleyan Univ, AB, 37; Columbia Univ, AM, 39, PhD (Am hist), 50. **CAREER** Teacher, Pub Schs, Md, 39-42; critic teacher, State Univ NY Col Teachers, Albany, 46-49; instr soc sci, Teachers Col, Columbia Univ, 49-51; supvr social studies, Pub Schs, NJ, 51-53; prof hist, State Univ NY Col Oneonta, 53-82, chmn, Dept Soc Sci Educ, 70-81; RETIRED, Fulbright lectr, Philippines, 61-62; surv consult, NY State Hist Trust, 67-68; vis prof, Trent Polytech, England, 78; fel, Hughes Hall, Cambridge, 78. **MEMBERSHIPS** AHA; Nat Coun Social Studies; Orgn Am Hists. **RESEARCH** New York state history; 20th century United States; social studies curriculum in secondary schools. **SELECTED PUBLICATIONS** Auth, 1939--The Lost World of the Fair, NY Hist, Vol 77, 96. **CONTACT ADDRESS** Laurens, NY, 13796.

FINKEL, ALVIN
PERSONAL Born 05/17/1949, Winnipeg, MB, Canada **DISCIPLINE** HISTORY **EDUCATION** Univ Man, BA, 70, MA, 72; Univ Toronto, PhD, 76. **CAREER** Lectr, Univ Manitoba, Univ Brandon, 74; vis lectr, Queen's Univ, 75-76; lectr, Univ Alta, 76-78; asst to assoc prof, 78-86, PROF HISTORY, ATHABASCA UNIV, 86-. **MEMBERSHIPS** Can Hist Asn **SELECTED PUBLICATIONS** Auth, Social Reform in the Thirties, 79; auth, The Social Credit Phenomenon in Alberta, 89; auth, Our Lives: Canada 1945-1996, 97; coauth, History of the Canadian Peoples, vols 1 & 2, 93, 2nd ed 97; coauth, The Chamberlain-Hitler Collusion, 97; ed, Prairie Forum, 86-95. **CONTACT ADDRESS** History Dept, Athabasca Univ, Box 10,000, Athabasca, AB, T0G 2R0.

FINKELSTEIN, BARBARA
PERSONAL Born 03/22/1937, Brooklyn, NY, m, 1959, 2 children **DISCIPLINE** AMERICAN HISTORY, HISTORY OF EDUCATION **EDUCATION** Columbia Univ, BA, 59; MA, 60; EdD, 70. **CAREER** Lectr hist educ, Brooklyn Col, 61-62; asst prof, 70-74, assoc prof, 74-83, prof, 83- , hist educ, dir, Ctr Stud Educ Policy & Human Values, 79- , Univ Md, College Park; Nat Endowment for Humanities fel, 75-76; contrib ed, J Psychohist, 77- ; Japan Soc for Promotion of Sci fel, 91-92; ser ed, Reflective Hist, Teachers Col Press, Columbia Univ, 94- ; adv bd, US Ed, Pedagogica Hist, 89- ; Int Adv Bd, Hist of Educ, 96- . **HONORS AND AWARDS** Critic's Choice Award, Am Educ Studies Asn, 81; recipient Key to the City of Osaka, 87; Am Educ Press Asn Award, 89; Distinguished Int Service Award, Univ Md, 94-95; Outstanding Woman of the Year, Univ Md, 97-98. **MEMBERSHIPS** Am Educ Studies Asn (pres, 81-82); Hist Educ Soc (pres, 98-99); Am Educ Res Asn (vpres, 89-91); Soc Res Child Develop. **RESEARCH** Family and education in historical perspective; childhood history in nineteenth century United States; learners and learning in American History; comparative cultural studies. **SELECTED PUBLICATIONS** Auth, Governing the Young: Teacher Behavior in Popular Primary Schools in Nineteenth Century United States, Taylor & Francis, 89; auth, Dollars and Dreams: Classrooms as Fictitious Message Systems, 1790-1930, Hist of Educ Q, 91; auth, Perfecting Childhood: Horace Mann and the Origins of Public Education in the United States, Biography, 91; auth, Education Historians as Mythmakers, Rev of Res in Educ, 92; auth, The Evolving Terrain of Teaching: Classroom Management in the United States, 1790-1990, in, Classroom Practices and Politics in Cross Cultural Perspective, Garland, 97; coauth, Discovering Culture in Education: An Approach to Cultural Education Program Evaluation and Design, 98; ed and contribur, Hidden Messages: Instructional Materials for Cultural Teaching and Learning, Intercultural, 98. **CONTACT ADDRESS** Dept of Educ Policy, Univ of Md, College Park, MD, 20742-0001. **EMAIL** bf6@umail.umd.edu

FINKELSTEIN, JOSEPH
PERSONAL Born 05/13/1926, Troy, NY, m, 1955 **DISCIPLINE** HISTORY **EDUCATION** Union Col, NY, BA, 46; Harvard Univ, MA, 49, PhD (hist), 52. **CAREER** Instr hist and econ, Union Col, NY, 46-48; teaching fel, Harvard Univ, 50-52; from asst prof to assoc prof, 53-63, PROF HIST and ECON and ADMIN HIST, UNION COL, NY, 63-, Fulbright grant, London, 52-53. **MEMBERSHIPS** AHA; Econ Hist Asn; Hist Asn England; Acad Int Bus, Am Arbitration Asn. **RESEARCH** American economic history; American business history; multinational companies. **SELECTED PUBLICATIONS** Auth, Relevance and Renewal at the 92nd Street Y, Dance Mag, Vol 68, 94; Humphrey, Doris and the 92nd Street Y--A Dance Center for the People, Dance Rsch J, Vol 28, 96. **CONTACT ADDRESS** Dept of Hist, Union Col, Schenectady, NY, 12308.

FINKELSTEIN, RONA
PERSONAL Born 11/07/1927, Rochester, NY, w, 1950, 2 children **DISCIPLINE** ART; PHIOSOPHY **EDUCATION** Connecticut Col, BA, 49; MA, 61, PhD, 64, Univ Rochester. **CAREER** Delaware State Col, 64-70, chairperson, 66-70; Univ Delaware, Col Parallel Program, 70-72; Exec Dir, Delaware Humanities Forum, 72-81. **MEMBERSHIPS** APA **RESEARCH** Mind-Body **CONTACT ADDRESS** 115 Sorrel Dr., Surrey Pk., Wilmington, DE, 19803. **EMAIL** rfinkel850@aol.com

FINKENBINE, ROY
PERSONAL Born 09/09/1953, Sidney, OH, m, 1982, 4 children **DISCIPLINE** HISTORY **EDUCATION** Taylor Univ, BS, 75; N Arizona Univ, MA, 76; Bowling Green State Univ, PhD, 82. **CAREER** Assoc ed, Black Abolitionist Papers Proj, Fla State Univ, 82-91; vis asst prof Hist, Murray State Univ, 91-92; asst prof Hist, Hampton Univ, 92-96; asst prof Hist, 96-98, ASSOC PROF HISTORY & DIR BLACK ABOLITIONIST ARCH, 98-, UNIV DETROIT MERCY; ed fel Nat Hist Publ 7 Rec Comn, 81-82; NEH Summer Inst Afro-Am Relig Hist, Princeton Univ, 86. **MEMBERSHIPS** Orgn Am Hist; Am Hist Asn. **RESEARCH** Black abolitionists. **SELECTED PUBLICATIONS** Coed The Black Abolitionist Papers, 1830-1865, 85-92; Witness for Freedom: African American Voices on Race, Slavery, and Emancipation, 93; auth Bostons Black Churches: Institution Centers of the Antislavery Movement, Courage and Conscience: Black and White Abolitionists in Boston, 93; Sources of the African-American Post, 97. **CONTACT ADDRESS** Dept of History, Univ Detroit Mercy, 4001 W McNichols Rd, Detroit, MI, 48219. **EMAIL** finkenre@udmercy.edu

FINLAY, ROBERT
DISCIPLINE HISTORY **EDUCATION** Univ Chicago, PhD. **CAREER** Assoc prof. **RESEARCH** Medieval and early modern European history. **SELECTED PUBLICATIONS** Auth, The Treasure-ships of Zheng He, J Hist Discoveries, 91; Portuguese and Chinese Maritime Imperialism: Camoes's Lusiads and Luo Maodeng's Voyage of the San Bao Eunuch, Comp Studies Soc Hist, 92. **CONTACT ADDRESS** History Dept, Univ of Arkansas, Fayetteville, 532 Old Main, Fayetteville, AR, 72701. **EMAIL** rfinlay@comp.uark.edu

FINLAYSON, MICHAEL G.
PERSONAL Born 10/20/1938, Melbourne, Australia **DISCIPLINE** HISTORY **EDUCATION** Univ Melbourne, BA, 59, MA, 64; Univ Toronto, PhD, 68. **CAREER** Asst to assoc prof, 68-85, PROF HISTORY, 85-, ch hist, 87-91, VICE PRES (ADMIN & HUMAN RESOURCES), UNIV TORONTO, 94-; vis fel, La Trobe Univ Melbourne, 81; vis fel, Corpus Christi Col, Cambridge, 82; vis fel, Clare Hall, Cambridge, 89. **MEMBERSHIPS** Can Hist Asn; Conf Brit Stud. **SELECTED PUBLICATIONS** Auth, Historians, Puritanism and the English Revolution, 83; co-ed, The Struggle for Power, 87. **CONTACT ADDRESS** Univ of Toronto, 27 Kings College Cir, #112, Toronto, ON, M5S 1A1.

FINLAYSON, WILLIAM D.
PERSONAL Born 03/01/1946, Toronto, ON, Canada **DISCIPLINE** ARCHAEOLOGY/HISTORY **EDUCATION** Univ Toronto, BA, 69, MA, 70, PhD, 76. **CAREER** Lectr, 73-76, vis asst prof, 76-79, adj prof, 79-82, adj assoc prof, Univ Western Ont, 95-; exec dir, 76-91, DIR GEN, LONDON MUS ARCHAEOLOGY, 91-; special lectr, 79-84, vis assoc prof, Univ Toronto, 78-79, 84-87; LAWSON PROF CAN ARCHAEOL, UNIV WESTERN ONT, 85-; dir gen, London and Middlesex Heritage Mus, 91-. **HONORS AND AWARDS** Milton Heritage Award, 92; Ralph Sherwood Conserv Award, Halton Reg Conserv Authority, 96. **MEMBERSHIPS** Ont Heritage Found; Ont Coun Archaeol. **SELECTED PUBLICATIONS** Auth, The Saugeen Culture, 76; auth, The 1975 and 1978 Rescue Excavations at the Draper Site: Introduction and Settlement Patterns, 85; coauth, What Columbus Missed!, 87; ed, Can Archaeol Asn Bull, 74-76. **CONTACT ADDRESS** London Mus of Archaeology, 1600 Attawandaron Rd, London, ON, N6G 3M6.

FINLEY, GERALD E.
PERSONAL Born 07/17/1931, Munich, Germany **DISCIPLINE** ART HISTORY **EDUCATION** Univ Toronto, BA, 55, MA, 57; Johns Hopkins Univ, PhD, 65. **CAREER** Lectr, Univ Toronto, 59-60; lectr, Univ Sask, 62-63; fac mem 63, acting/head dept, 63-72, PROF EMER HISTORY OF ART, QUEEN'S UNIV; fel, Inst Advan Stud Hum, Univ Edinburgh, 79-80. **HONORS AND AWARDS** Fel, Royal Soc Can; Brit Coun; Can Coun; SSHRCC; Can Fedn Hum. **SELECTED PUBLICATIONS** Auth, In Praise of Older Buildings, 76; auth, George Heriot 1759-1839, 79; auth, Landscapes of Memory: Turner as Illustrator to Scott, 80; auth, Turner and George IV in Edinburgh 1822, 81; auth, George Heriot: Postmaster-Painter of the Canadas, 83. **CONTACT ADDRESS** Dept of Art, Queen's Univ, Kingston, ON, K7L 3N6.

FINLEY, THOMAS JOHN
PERSONAL Born 10/29/1945, Jacksonville, FL, m, 1969, 2 children **DISCIPLINE** OLD TESTAMENT, ANCIENT SEMITIC LANGUAGES **EDUCATION** Biola Col, BA, 67, MDiv, 71; Univ Calif, Los Angeles, MA, 74, PhD, 79. **CAREER** Prof Old Testament & Semitics, Talbot Theol Sem, Biola Col, 77-. **MEMBERSHIPS** Soc Bibl Lit; Evangel Theol Soc. **RESEARCH** Old Testament biblical Hebrew, Aramaic & Akkadian languages; Studies on Joel, Amos and Obadiah. **SELECTED PUBLICATIONS** Auth, Joel, Obadiah, and Micah, Everymen Bible Commentary; Moody, 95; auth, A Bilingual Concordance to the Targum of the Prophets: Ezekiel, Brill, 98. **CONTACT ADDRESS** Talbot Theol Sem, Biola Univ, 13800 Biola Ave, La Mirada, CA, 90639-0002. **EMAIL** tom_finley@peter.biola.edu

FINN, MARGARET R.
PERSONAL Born 08/03/1916, Jersey City, NJ **DISCIPLINE** CLASSICS **EDUCATION** Col St Elizabeth, AB, 37; Fordham Univ, MA, 42, PhD, 50. **CAREER** Instr Latin, Col St Elizabeth, 37-38; teacher, St Michael's High Sch, Jersey City, NJ, 38-43; teacher Latin and math, pub high schs, Jersey City, 43-50; asst to prin, Ferris High Sch, 50-62, from vprin to prin, 62-72; coordr non-pub secular educ prog, 72-73, actg dir, 72-80, DIR ADULT EDUC, JERSEY CITY BD EDUC, 80-, Instr Latin, Seton Hall Univ, 51-54; adj asst prof, Fordham Univ, 55-69. **HONORS AND AWARDS** Women of Achievement, Jersey J, 69. **MEMBERSHIPS** Am Class League; Am Philol Asn. **RESEARCH** History of Latin paleography; medieval Latin literature. **SELECTED PUBLICATIONS** Auth, Proust, Marcel and the Neurasthenic Novel, Rev Hist Litteraire Fr, Vol 96, 96; Neurasthenia, Hysteria, Androgyny--The Goncourts and Proust, Marcel, Fr Stud, Vol 51, 97; Norpois, Father or Mentor, Rev Hist Litteraire Fr, Vol 93, 93; The Cathedral Work--Proust and Medieval Architecture, Rev Hist Litteraire France, Vol 94, 94. **CONTACT ADDRESS** 144 Erie St, Jersey City, NJ, 07302.

FINN, MARGOT C.
DISCIPLINE HISTORY **EDUCATION** Syracuse Univ, BS, 80; Columbia Univ, MA 83, MPhil, 84, PhD 87. **CAREER** Assoc prof **HONORS AND AWARDS** NACBS John Ben Snow Found Prize, 94., Ed, Jour Brit Studies. **RESEARCH** Modern British history. **SELECTED PUBLICATIONS** Auth, After Chartism: Class and Nation in English Radical Politics, 1848-1874. **CONTACT ADDRESS** Dept History, Emory Univ, 221 Bowden Hall, 561 Kilgo Cir, Atlanta, GA, 30322-1950. **EMAIL** mfinn01@emory.edu

FINN, THOMAS M.
PERSONAL Born 03/18/1927, New York, NY, m, 1968, 1 child **DISCIPLINE** PATRISTICS **EDUCATION** St. Paul's Col, AB, 56, MA, 58; Cath Univ Am, STL, 61, STD, 65. **CAREER** Chancellor Prof Relig. Col William and Mary, 73-. **HONORS AND AWARDS** Melone Fel, Coun on U.S. Arab Relations, 90; Res Fel, Inst Ecumenical and Cultural Res, 95. **MEMBERSHIPS** Am Acad Relig; Cath Bibl Asn; NAm Patristic Soc; Int Patristic Soc. **RESEARCH** Ritual in Greco-Roman antiquity, paganism, Judaism, and Christianity. **SELECTED PUBLICATIONS** Auth, Early Christian Baptism and the Catechumenate: Italy, North Africa and Egypt, Litturgical Press, 92; Early Christian Baptism and the Catechumenate: West and East Syria, Litturgical Press, 92; From Death to Rebirth: Conversion in Antiquity, Paulist Press, 97; Quodvultdeus: The Preacher and the Audience: The Homilies on the Creed, Studia Patristica 31, 97; Ritual and Conversion: The Case of Augustine, Nova & Vetera: Patristic Studies in Honor of Thomas Patrick Halton, Cath Univ Am Press, 98. **CONTACT ADDRESS** Religion Dept, Col of William and Mary, 310 Wren Building, Williamsburg, VA, 23187-8795. **EMAIL** tmfinn@facstaff.wm.edu

FINNEGAN, TERENCE ROBERT
PERSONAL Born 08/06/1961, Oak Park, IL, m, 4 children **DISCIPLINE** HISTORY **EDUCATION** Marquette Univ, BA, 83; MA, 86; Univ Ill, PhD, 93. **CAREER** Asst prof, William Paterson Col, 93-; vis prof, Nat Ctr for Supercomput Appln, Univ Ill, 94-95; postdr res assoc, Nat Ctr for Supercomput Appln(s), Univ Ill, 92-93; proj coordr, Univ Ill, Hist Census Database Proj, 91-92; asst to prin invesr, Univ Ill Hist Supercomputer Proj, 88-90; asst res, Univ Ill Lang Learning Lab, 88; co-ed, H-South, an H-Net electronic jour of US Southern Hist, 93-96; ed, Soc Sci Comput Asn Newsletter, 94-96; ed bd mem, H-MMedia, 94-96; fac affil, Univ Ill Hist Dept & Univ Ill Afro-Amer Stud Prog, 92-93 & 94-95; conf coordr, Conf on Comput for the Soc Sci, 93; VP, Hist Grad Stud Asn, 88; Hist Dept Comput Rsrc(s) Comt, 88-91; Archv, St John's Catholic Chapel & the Newman Found, Univ Ill, 88-92; grad res asst, Univ Ill, 87-89; asst prof, William Paterson Col, 93-94 & 95-96; instr, Hist Hon(s) Colloquium, Violence in America, 92; co-instr, Quantitative Methods in His, 90 & 92; asst, Family and Comm Hon(s) course, 90; tchg asst, Univ Ill, 86-87 & Marquette Univ, 84-86. **HONORS AND AWARDS** Postdoctoral fel, Nat Sci Found, CISE Inst Infrastructure Div, 92-93 & 94-95; co-investr, Nat Sci Found CISE/IRIS Div grant, 91-92; invited participant, Ctr for Documentary Stud, Duke Univ with NC Cent Univ, 91; conf fel, Wake Frst Univ, 91; Harry Frank Guggenheim Dissertation fel, 90-91; dissertation travel grant, Univ Ill, 90; Univ Ill Hist Dept fel, 89-90; Joseph L Swain Awd, Univ Ill Hist Dept, 88; Phi Kappa Phi, Univ Ill, 88; , Summer fel, Univ Ill Lang Learning Lab, 88; Summer fel, Univ Ill Soc Sci Quantitative Lab, 87; Incomplete List of Excellent Tchr(s), Univ Ill, 86; Phi Alpha Theta, Marquette Univ, 83. **RESEARCH** African-American history, Civil rights movement, comparative labor history. **SELECTED PUBLICATIONS** Auth, The Equal of Some White Men and the Superior of Others: Racial Hegemony and the 1916 Lynching of Anthony Crawford in Abbeville County, SC, The Proceedings of the SC Hist Asn, 94; coauth, Developing a Distributed Computing U.S. Census Database Linkage System, NCSA Tech Report no 027, 94; South Carolina, in Quiet Revolution in the South: The Impact of the Voting Rights Act 1965-1990, Princeton Univ Press, 94; It Ain't Broke, So Don't Fix It: The Legal and Factual Importance of Recent Attacks on Methods Used in Vote Dilution Litigation, San Francisco Law Rev, 93; The Civil War, chapter 15 of the Documents Collection that accompanies James Henretta, et al, America's Hist, vol 1, NY: Worth Publishers, 93; rev, Emancipation: The Making of the Black Lawyer, 1844-1944 in The Annals, 95; War of Another Kind: A Southern Community in the Great Rebellion, Agr Hist 65, 91. **CONTACT ADDRESS** Dept of History, William Paterson Col, 300 Pompton Rd., Wayne, NJ, 07470. **EMAIL** finnegan@frontier.wilpaterson.edu

FINNEY, BEN RUDOLPH
PERSONAL Born 10/01/1933, San Diego, CA, m, 1996, 2 children **DISCIPLINE** ANTHROPOLOGY **EDUCATION** Univ Calif Berkeley, BA, history, economics, anthropology, 55; Univ Hawaii, MA, anthropology, 59; Harvard Univ, PhD, anthropology, 64. **CAREER** Sr statistician, Kaiser Steel Corp, Industrial Engineering Dept, 56; Aviation ground officer, US Naval Reserve, active duty, 57; manufacturing analyst, General Dynamics Corp, Industrial Engineering Dept, Convair Div, mfg analyst, 56, 58; resident tutor, Harvard Coll, Lowell House, 60-61, 62-64; teaching fellow, 60-61, 62-64, visiting scholar, 79-80, Harvard Univ, Dept of Anthropology; asst prof, Univ Calif, Santa Barbara, Dept of Anthropology, 64-67; visiting fellow, New Guinea Res Unit, 67, sr res fellow, Dept Pacific History, Res School of Pacific Studies, 68-70, Australian Natl Univ; visiting scholar, Harvard Univ, Dept Anthropology, 79-80; res assoc, Bishop Museum, Dept Anthropology, 89-; bd dirs, Bernice Pauahi Bishop Museum, 93-; visiting lecturer, French Univ Pacific, 96-; chair, 94-, Dept Space & Society, Summer Session Program, visiting lecturer, 96-, Master Space Studies Program, Intl Space Univ; assoc prof, 70-73, prof, 73-, chair, 86-95, Dept of Anthropology, sr fellow, 71-72, res assoc, 72-76, Technology and Development Inst, East-West Center, (half-time appt with Univ Hawaii), Univ Hawaii. **HONORS AND AWARDS** Regent's Medal, Univ Hawaii, 97; Tsiolokovsky Medal, Tsiolokovsky State Museum of the History of Commun, 95; French Univ of the Pacific Medal, 95; Royal Inst of Navigation Bronze Medal, 94. **MEMBERSHIPS** Founding pres, Polynesian Voyaging Soc; Amer Assn for the Advancement of Sci; Intl Acad of Astronautics; Amer Anthropological Assn; Societe des Etudes Oceaniennes; Polynesian Soc; Space Studies Inst; Societe des Oceanistes; Hawaiian Acad of Sci. **RESEARCH** Experimental voyaging; humanity and space; globalization and social change. **SELECTED PUBLICATIONS** Auth, Voyage of Rediscovery: A Cultural Odyssey through Polynesia, 94; From Sea to Space, 92; "Experimental Voyaging, Oral Tradition and Long Distance Interaction in Polynesia," in Prehistoric Interaction in Oceania: an Interdisciplinary Approach, New Zealand Archaeol Assn Monograph 21, 98; "Will Space Change Humanity?" in Fundamentals of Space Life Sciences, v 2, 97; "Colonizing an Island World," in Prehistoric Settlement of the Pacific, Transactions of the American Philosophical Society, v. 86, n 86, 97; "Putting Voyaging Back into Polynesian Prehistory," in Oceanic Culture History: Essays in Honour of Roger Green, New Zealand Journal of Archaeol Special Publication, 97; coauth, Tsiolkovsky, Russian Cosmism and Extraterrestrial Intelligence," Quarterly Journal of the Royal Astronomical Society, v 36, 95; "The Other One-Third of the Globe," Journal of World History, v 5, n 2, 94. **CONTACT ADDRESS** Dept of Anthropology, Univ of Hawaii, 2424 Maile Way, Honolulu, HI, 96822. **EMAIL** bfinney@hawaii.edu

FINNEY, PAUL CORBY
DISCIPLINE HISTORY, ART & ARCHAEOLOGY, RELIGION **EDUCATION** Yale Univ, AB, 62; Maximilians Univ, Germany, 62-63; Harvard Univ, MA, PhD, 73. **CAREER** ASST PROF, ASSOC PROF, PROF, UNIV MO, ST LOUIS, 73-; area supervisor, Am Schs Oriental Res excavation Cathage, Tunisia, 75- 77; sen lectr, Hebrew Univ, Jerusalem, 79; vis lectr, Princeton Theol Sem, 83; sen assoc, Am Sch Class Stud, Athens, 87; assoc archaeologist, Gr Ministry Antiquities, 87; vis fel, Princeton Univ, 92, 95, 98, 99. **CONTACT ADDRESS** Dept of History, Univ of Missouri, 8001 Natural Bridge Rd, St. Louis, MO, 63121. **EMAIL** spcfinn@umslvma.umsl.edu

FINSON, JON WILLIAM
PERSONAL Born 11/04/1950, Chicago, IL **DISCIPLINE** MUSICOLOGY **EDUCATION** Univ Colo, Boulder, BM, 73; Univ Wis-Madison, MA, 75; Univ Chicago, PhD (musicol), 80. **CAREER** ASST PROF MUSIC, UNIV NC, CHAPEL HILL, 78-, Dir, Int Mendelssohn-Schumann Conf, 81-82. **MEMBERSHIPS** Am Musicol Soc. **RESEARCH** German music of the 19th century; American popular music. **SELECTED PUBLICATIONS** Auth, Schumann, Fantasie, Mus Letters, Vol 75, 94; Mendelssohn Studies, Mus Letters, Vol 75, 94; Mono Thematicism, Sequence and Sonata Forms in Schumann, Robert Compositions, Notes, Vol 49, 93; The American Musical Landscape, J Am Musicological Soc, Vol 48, 95; The Romantic Savage, American Indians in the Parlor, J Musicological Rsch, Vol 13, 93; Schumann, Robert Path to Symphony, Notes, Vol 51, 94; For Haar, James on His 65th Birthday, J Musicology, Vol 12, 94. **CONTACT ADDRESS** Dept of Music, Univ NC, Chapel Hill, NC, 27514.

FIREMAN, JANET RUTH
PERSONAL Born 05/09/1945, Phoenix, AZ, m, 1980 **DISCIPLINE** AMERICAN AND MEXICAN HISTORY **EDUCATION** Univ Ariz, BA, 67; Univ NMex, MA, 68, PhD (hist), 72. **CAREER** From asst prof to assoc prof hist, Calif State Univ Fresno, 71-78; ASSOC CUR SOCIAL and CULT HIST, LOS ANGELES COUNTY MUS NAT HIST, 76-, Ed consult hist, J San Diego Hist, 77- and Calif Hist, 80-. **MEMBERSHIPS** Western Hist Asn; Pac Coast Coun Latin Am Studies; AHA; Western Asn Women Hists. **RESEARCH** Spanish Southwest; Western American cultural history. **SELECTED PUBLICATIONS** Auth, The Discovery of San Francisco Bay--The Portola Expedition of 1769-1770, Pac Hist Rev, Vol 62, 93; Rogers, Will and the Ziegfeld Follies, Montana Mag W Hist, Vol 44, 94; Southern California Spanish Heritage--An Anthology, W Hist Quart, Vol 25, 94; Reagan, Ronald and the Mythic West, J West, Vol 34, 95; Land Grants and Lawsuits in Northern New Mexico, Pac Hist Rev, Vol 65, 96. **CONTACT ADDRESS** Los Angeles County Mus of Natural Hist, 900 Exposition Blvd, Los Angeles, CA, 90007.

FISCHER, BERND
DISCIPLINE HISTORY **EDUCATION** Univ Ca, PhD, 82. **CAREER** Prof. **RESEARCH** Balkans history; Ottoman Empire history. **SELECTED PUBLICATIONS** Auth, King Zog and the Struggle for Stability in Albania, 84; Kollaborationsregime in Albanien 1939-1944. **CONTACT ADDRESS** Dept of History, Indiana Univ-Purdue Univ, Fort Wayne, 2101 Coliseum Blvd, Fort Wayne, IN, 46805. **EMAIL** fischer@smtplink.ipfw.edu

FISCHER, LEROY HENRY
PERSONAL Born 05/19/1917, Hoffman, IL, m, 1948, 3 children **DISCIPLINE** AMERICAN HISTORY **EDUCATION** Univ Ill, AB, 39, AM, 40, PhD, 43. **CAREER** Res asst hist, Univ Ill, 40-43; asst prof hist, Ithaca Col, 46; from asst prof to prof, 46-72, exec secy, Col Arts and Sci Honors Prog, 59-61, OPPENHEIM REGENTS PROF HIST, OKLA STATE UNIV, 73-, Mem, Okla Civil War Centennial Comn, 58-65; Okla Chisholm Trail Centennial Comn and Tri-State Chisholm Trail Centennial Comn, 66-67; EXEC COMT AND BD DIR, OKLA HIST SOC, 66-; BD DIR, NAT INDIAN HALL OF FAME, 69-; ED CONSULT, THE WILL ROGERS PAPERS, 72-. **HONORS AND AWARDS** Nat Lit Award Competition Prize, Loyal Legion of US, 63; Okla State Univ-Okla Educ Asn Teacher of the Year, 69. **MEMBERSHIPS** AHA; Orgn Am Hists; Southern Hist Asn; Western Hist Asn; Nat Coun Soc Studies; Am Asn State and Local Hist. **RESEARCH** American Civil War and Reconstruction period; Oklahoma history. **SELECTED PUBLICATIONS** Auth, Pea Ridge--Civil War Campaign in the West, W Hist Quart, Vol 25, 94. **CONTACT ADDRESS** Dept of Hist, Oklahoma State Univ, Stillwater, OK, 74074.

FISCHER, ROGER ADRIAN
PERSONAL Born 05/08/1939, Minneapolis, MN, m, 1962, 3 children **DISCIPLINE** UNITED STATES HISTORY **EDUCATION** Univ MN, BA, 60, MA, 63; Tulane Univ, PhD, 67. **CAREER** Instr hist, Univ Southwestern La, 63-64; asst prof, Southern Univ, New Orleans Ctr, 65-67; asst prof, Sam Houston State Col, 67-69; assoc prof, Southwest MO State Col, 69-72; assoc prof, 72-80, prof hist, Univ MN, Duluth 80. **HONORS AND AWARDS** L. Kemper Williams Prize, 75; Carl Bode Award, 87. **MEMBERSHIPS** Southern Hist Asn; AHA. **RESEARCH** Hist of the Negro, the South, the Civil War and Reconstruction, Am Polit Cult. **SELECTED PUBLICATIONS** Auth, Pioneer protest: The New Orleans street-car controversy of 1867, J Negro Hist, 7/68; Racial segregation in antebellum New Orleans, Am Hist Rev, 2/69; Ghetto and gown: The birth of Black studies, Current Hist, 11/69; The Segregation Struggle in Louisiana, 1862-1877, Univ Ill, Urbana, 74; American Political Ribbons & Ribbon Badges, 1825-1981 (with Edmund B. Sullivan), Quarterman Pub, 85; Tippecanoe and Trinkets Too: Material Culture in American Presidential Campaigns, 1828-1984, Univ of Ill, 88; Them Damned Pictures: Explorations in American Political Cartoon Art, Archon, 96. **CONTACT ADDRESS** Dept of Hist, Univ of MN, 10 University Dr, Duluth, MN, 55812-2496.

FISHBACK, PRICE VANMETER
PERSONAL Born 07/08/1955, Louisville, KY, m, 1989 **DISCIPLINE** ECONOMICS **EDUCATION** Butler Univ, BA, 77; Univ of Wash, MA, 79, PhD, 83. **CAREER** Teaching asst, Univ of Wash, 77-82; economic res and forecasting, Weyerhaeuser Company, 79-80; temp asst prof, 82-83, asst prof, 83-87, assoc prof, 87-91, Univ of Ga; visitor, Univ of Tx, Austin, 87-89; ed board, J of Economic Hist, 91-94; RES ECONOMIST, 93-94, RES ASSOC, 94-, NAT BUREAU OF ECONOMIC RES; ASSOC PROF, 90-93, PROF, 93-, UNIV OF ARIZ; ED BOARD, EXPLORATIONS IN ECONOMIC HIST, 98-; TRUSTEE, 94-97, CONFR COORD, 96-, CLIOMETRICS SOC. **HONORS AND AWARDS** Phi Kappa Phi; Phi Eta Sigma; Col Prize, 96-97; Swift Teaching Award, Univ of Ga, 84; Honors Day Recognition for Outstanding Teaching, Univ of Ga, 83, 84, & 86. **MEMBERSHIPS** Am Economic Asn; Economic Hist Asn; Western Economic Asn; Cliometrics Soc; Economic Hist Soc; Nat Bureau of Economic Res. **RESEARCH** Economic history; labor economics; law and economics; applied microeconomics. **SELECTED PUBLICATIONS** Auth, Soft Coal, Hard Choices: The Economic Welfare of Bituminous Coal Miners 1890 to 1930, Oxford Univ Pres, 92; coauth, The Adoption of Workers' Compensation in the United States 1890-1930, J of Law and Economics, forthcoming; auth, Operations of Unfettered Labor Markets: Exit and Voice in American Labor Markets at the Turn of the Century, J of Economic Lit, 98; auth, The Durable Experiment: State insureance of Workers' Compensation Risk in the Early Twentieth Centruy, J of Economic Hist, 96; coauth, Precautionary Saving, Insurance, and the Origins of Workers' Compensation, J of Political Economy, 96; coauth, Did Workers Gain from the Passage of Workers' Compensation Laws?, Quart J of Economics, 95; coauth, Institutional Change, Compensating Differentials and Accident Risk in American Railroading 1892-1945, J of Economic Hist, 93. **CONTACT ADDRESS** Dept of Economics, Univ of Ariz, Tucson, AZ, 85718. **EMAIL** pfishback@bpa.arizona.edu

FISHBURN, JANET FORSYTHE
PERSONAL Born 01/18/1937, Wilkensburg, PA, m, 1958, 3 children **DISCIPLINE** AMERICAN CHURCH AND CULTURAL HISTORY **EDUCATION** Monmouth Col, BA, 58; Pa State Univ, PhD (Am relig studies), 78. **CAREER** Dir Christian educ, 1st United Presby Church, Cleveland Heights, Ohio, 58-60; Instr humanities and Am studies, Pa State Univ, 77-78; ASST PROF CHRISTIAN EDUC AND CHURCH HIST, THEOL SCH, DREW UNIV, 78-. **MEMBERSHIPS** Am Acad Relig; Asn Prof and Researchers Relig Educ; Asn Theol Sch; Asn Field Educ; Asn Prof Educ Ministry. **RESEARCH** American church history and contemporary Christian ministry; family studies and intergenerational education; theological education and contemporary Christian ministry. **SELECTED PUBLICATIONS** Auth, Cultural Diversity and Seminary Teaching, Rel Educ, Vol 90, 95; Tennent, Gilbert, Established Dissenter, Church Hist, Vol 63.95; Preacher, Sunday, Billy and Big Time American Evangelism, Am Presbyterians J Presbyterian Hist, Vol 74, 96. **CONTACT ADDRESS** Theol Sch, Drew Univ, Madison, NJ, 07940.

FISHER, ALAN WASHBURN
PERSONAL Born 11/23/1939, Columbus, OH, m, 1963, 3 children **DISCIPLINE** RUSSIAN HISTORY, TURKISH HISTORY **EDUCATION** DePauw Univ, BA, 61; Columbia Univ, MA, 64, PhD (hist), 67. **CAREER** From instr to asst prof, 66-70, assoc prof, 70-78, PROF HIST, MICH STATE UNIV, 78-, Res fel, Am Res Inst, Turkey, 69, mem, bd gov, 70-74; fel, Am Coun Learned Socs, 76-77. **MEMBERSHIPS** Mid E Studies Asn; Turkish Studies Asn. **RESEARCH** Russian-Ottoman relations; biography of Suleyman the Magnificent. **SELECTED PUBLICATIONS** Auth, The Development of the Erma Banking System--Lessons from History, Ieee Annals of the History of Computing, Vol 15, 93; Manufacturing the Erma Banking System, Ieee Annals Hist Comp, Vol 15, 93. **CONTACT ADDRESS** Dept of Hist, Michigan State Univ, 301 Morrill Hall, East Lansing, MI, 48824-1036.

FISHER, CRAIG B.
PERSONAL Born 05/10/1931, Alameda, CA **DISCIPLINE** MEDIEVAL HISTORY **EDUCATION** Univ Calif, Berkeley, BA, 52; Harvard Univ, MA, 56; Cornell Univ, PhD, 61. **CAREER** Asst prof hist, Univ Calif, Davis, 60-67, assoc prof, Conolly Col, 67-76, PROF HIST, BROOKLYN CTR, LONG ISLAND UNIV, 76-. **RESEARCH** Italy and Germany in the High Middle Ages. **SELECTED PUBLICATIONS** Auth, American sychological ssociation 1992 Ethics Code and the Validation of exual Abuse in Day Care Settings, Psych Public Policy Law, Vol 1, 95. **CONTACT ADDRESS** Dept of Hist, Long Island Univ, Brooklyn, Brooklyn, NY, 11201.

FISHER, JAMES T.
DISCIPLINE US RELIGIOUS HISTORY **EDUCATION** Rutgers Univ, PhD. **CAREER** Hist Dept, St Edward's Euniv **HONORS AND AWARDS** Managing ed, Jour Policy Hist. **SELECTED PUBLICATIONS** Auth, The Catholic Counterculture in America, 1933-1962; Dr. America: The Lives of Thomas A. Dooley. **CONTACT ADDRESS** St Edward's Univ, 3001 S Congress Ave, Austin, TX, 78704-6489.

FISHER, LOUIS
PERSONAL Born 08/17/1934, Norfolk, VA, 2 children **DISCIPLINE** POLITICAL SCIENCE **EDUCATION** New School for Soc Res PhD 67. **CAREER** Sr Spec in Separation of Power, Conpressional Res Service, the Library of Congress, 70; Asst Prof Queens College NY, 67-70. **HONORS AND AWARDS** Louis Brownlow Book Award, National Academy of Public Admin (twice for Pres Spending Power in 75 and Constitutional Dialogues in 88. **MEMBERSHIPS** Ameican Political Sci Assoc, Natl Academy of Public Admin, Amer Soc of Pulbic Admin. **RESEARCH** Constitutional law, presidency, Congress, war powers, budget policy. **SELECTED PUBLICATIONS** Amer Constitutional Law, 3rd ed, Caoline Academic Press, 99; The Polotics of Shared Power, 4th ed, TX A&M Univ Press, 98; Constitutional Conflicts between Congress and the President 4th ed Univ Press of KS, 87; Political Dynamics of Constitutional Law 3rd ed Weed Publishers, 96; Presidential War Power, Univ Press of KS, 95. **CONTACT ADDRESS** Library of Congress, Washington, DC, 20540.

FISHER, MARVIN
PERSONAL Born 11/19/1927, Detroit, MI, m, 1956, 3 children **DISCIPLINE** AMERICAN STUDIES **EDUCATION** Wayne Univ, AB, 50, AM, 52; Univ Minn, PhD, 58. **CAREER** Instr English, Gen Motors Inst, 52-53; instr, Univ Minn, 53-58; from asst prof to assoc prof, 58-66, PROF ENGLISH, ARIZ STATE UNIV, 66-, Huntington Libr res fel, 60; Fulbright lectr, Greece, 61-63, Norway, 66-67; vis prof, Univ Calif, Davis, 69-70; chmn, Ariz State Univ, 77-. **MEMBERSHIPS** MLA; Am Studies Asn; NCTE; Melville Soc Am; AAUP. **RESEARCH** American Renaissance; 19th century technology and its impact on the American imagination; Herman Melville. **SELECTED PUBLICATIONS** Auth, Landry, Tom, An Autobiography, J West, Vol 32, 93; Melville White Jacket and the War Within, Centennial Rev, Vol 37, 93; White Noise, Appalachian J, Vol 23, 95; Virtual Liberty, Index on Censorship, Vol 24, 95; Melville--A Biography, Int Fiction Rev, Vol 24, 97; Critical Essays on Melville, Herman Benito Cereno, Stud Short Fiction, Vol 31, 94; Melville and Turner, Spheres of Love and Fright,Int Fiction Rev, Vol 20, 93; A Little Knowledge is a Useful Thing--Freedom of Information Acts Campaign in England, Index Censorship, Vol 25, 96; The Civil War World of Melville, Herman, Int Fiction Rev, Vol 22, 95; The Sepoys and the Company--Tradition and Transition in Northern India, 1770-1830, Indian Econ Soc Hist Rev, Vol 33, 96; A River Sutra, W Lit Today, Vol 68, 94; Narayan, R. K.--Critical Perspectives, W Lit Today, Vol 69, 95; From Ashes to Glory, J West, Vol 32, 93; Our Famous Guest, Mark Twain in Vienna, Int Fiction Rev, Vol 20, 93; White Noise, Appalachian J, Vol 23, 95. **CONTACT ADDRESS** Dept of English, Arizona State Univ, Tempe, Tempe, AZ, 85281.

FISHER, RAYMOND HENRY
PERSONAL Born 10/21/1907, Los Angeles, CA **DISCIPLINE** RUSSIAN HISTORY **EDUCATION** Univ Calif, AB, 29, AM, 32, PhD, 37. **CAREER** Assoc prof hist, Humboldt State Col, 37-44; country specialist on Russia, US Dept State, 44-46; from asst prof to assoc prof, 46-69, prof, 69-75, EMER PROF HIST, UNIV CALIF, LOS ANGELES, 75-. **HONORS AND AWARDS** Adams Prize, AHA, 44. **MEMBERSHIPS** Am Asn Advan Slavic Studies; Soc Hist Discoveries. **RESEARCH** Russian eastward expansion; Siberia; Russian exploration in the North Pacific. **SELECTED PUBLICATIONS** Auth, The History of Siberia--From Russian Conquest to Revolution, Russ Hist Histoire Russe, Vol 18, 91; Otter Skins, Boston Ships, and China Goods--The Maritime for Trade of The Northwest Coast, 1785-1841, Pac Hist Rev, Vol 62, 93. **CONTACT ADDRESS** Dept of Hist, Univ of Calif, Los Angeles, CA, 90024.

FISHER, ROBERT BRUCE
PERSONAL Born 04/23/1947, Newark, NJ **DISCIPLINE** HISTORY, URBAN STUDIES **EDUCATION** Rutgers Univ, BA, 68; NY Univ, MA, 70, PhD (US hist), 74. **CAREER** Instr hist and polit sci, Grahm Jr Col, 73-76; vis asst prof hist, Union Col, 77-78; ASST PROF HIST, UNIV HOUSTON, DOWNTOWN COL, 78-. **MEMBERSHIPS** AHA; Orgn Am Hists. **RESEARCH** History of urban social change; community organization; United States in the 20th century. **SELECTED PUBLICATIONS** Auth, Ad Hoc Justice Documented--The Paper Daguerreotypes of Fardon, George, Robinson, J West, Vol 33, 94. **CONTACT ADDRESS** Univ Houston Downtown Col, One Main St, Houston, TX, 77002.

FISHER, ROBIN
PERSONAL Born 02/24/1946, Palmerston N., New Zealand **DISCIPLINE** HISTORY **EDUCATION** Massey Univ, BA, 67; Univ Auckland, MA, 69; Univ BC, PhD, 74. **CAREER** Jr lectr hist, Massey Univ, 70; asst prof to prof hist, Simon Fraser Univ, 74-93; co-ed, Can Hist Rev, 84-87; founding ch hist, 93-96, acting dean arts sci, 94-96, dean arts, 96-97, DEAN OF ARTS, SOCIAL AND HEALTH SCIENCES, UNIV NORTHERN BRITISH COLUMBIA, 97-. **HONORS AND AWARDS** John A. Macdonald Prize, Can Hist Asn, 77; Dafoe Book Prize, 92. **SELECTED PUBLICATIONS** Auth, Contact and Conflict: Indian-European Relations in British Columbia 1774-1890, 77; auth, Duff Pattullo of British Columbia, 91; auth, Vancouver's Voyage: Charting the Northwest Coast 1791-1795, 93; co-ed, Captain James Cook and His Times, 79; co-ed, An Account of a Voyage to the North West Coast of America in 1785 and 1786 by Alexander Walker, 82; co-ed, Maps and Metaphors: The Pacific World of George Vancouver, 93. **CONTACT ADDRESS** Univ of No British Columbia, 3333 University Way, Prince George, BC, V2N 4Z9.

FISHMAN, DAVID E.
PERSONAL NY **DISCIPLINE** JEWISH HISTORY **EDUCATION** Yeshiva Univ, BA; Harvard Univ, MA, PhD. **CAREER** Instr, Brandeis Univ; instr, Russ State Univ, Moscow; fel, Hebrew Univ Inst Adv Studies; assoc prof and chr, Dept Jewish Hist, Jewish Theol Sem Am; sr resh assoc, YIVO Inst Jewish Res. **HONORS AND AWARDS** Dir Project Judaica, JTS and YIVO with the Russ State Univ for the Hum; ed, Yivo-Bletter. **SELECTED PUBLICATIONS** Auth, Russia's First Modern Jews, NY Univ Press; Embers Plucked from the Fire: The Rescue of Jewish Cultural Treasures in Vilna,YIVO; numerous articles on the history and culture of East European Jewry. **CONTACT ADDRESS** Jewish Theol Sem of America, 3080 Broadway, New York, NY, 10027. **EMAIL** dafishman@jtsa.edu

FISHMAN, STERLING
PERSONAL Born 04/04/1932, m, 1958 **DISCIPLINE** MODERN EUROPEAN HISTORY **EDUCATION** Wash Univ, BA, 52; Univ Wis, MS, 54, PhD, 60. **CAREER** Asst prof hist, Harpur Col, State Univ NY, 60-61 and Douglas Col, Rutgers Univ, 61-63; asst prof, 63-66, ASSOC PROF HIST GER EDUC, UNIV WIS-MADISON, 67-, Ger govt fel, 58-59; Rutgers Univ Res Coun grant, 63; lectr past and present family, Nat Humanities Ser, 73. **MEMBERSHIPS** AHA; Hist Educ Soc. **RESEARCH** European cultural history; history of European education; comparative history of childhood. **SELECTED PUBLICATIONS** Auth, Laval, Pierre, J Mod Hist, Vol 67, 95; The Republic in Danger--General Ganelin, Maurice and the Politics of French Defense, J Mod Hist, Vol 67, 95; Outwitting the Gestapo, J Mod Hist, Vol 67, 95; The Knight Monks of Vichy France, J Mod Hist, Vol 67, 95; In Search of the Maquis--Rural Resistance in Southern France, J Mod Hist, Vol 67, 95; The Politics of French Business, 1936-1945, J Interdisciplinary Hist, Vol 24, 93; Community in the Expressivist Classroom, College English, Vol 57, 95; Is Expressivism Dead, Coll Eng, Vol 55, 93. **CONTACT ADDRESS** Dept of Educ Policy Studies, Univ of Wis, 455 North Park St, Madison, WI, 53706-1483.

FISHWICK, DUNCAN
PERSONAL Born 05/12/1929, Adlington, England **DISCIPLINE** CLASSICS **EDUCATION** Manchester Univ, BA, 50; Oxford Univ, BA, 53, MA, 56. **CAREER** Lectr, McGill Univ, 56-57; asst prof, Univ Toronto, 57-64; assoc prof, St Francis Xavier Univ, 74-71; assoc prof to prof classics, 71-86, univ prof, 86-94, ch classics, 87-92, UNIV PROF EMER, UNIV ALBERTA, 94-. **HONORS AND AWARDS** Univ Alta Res Prize, 85; McCalla Res Prof, 85-86. **SELECTED PUBLICATIONS** Auth, Studies in Roman Imperial History, 76; auth, The Imperial Cult in the Latin West, vol I, 87, vol II, 91/92; coauth, The Foundations of the West, 64. **CONTACT ADDRESS** Hum Ctr, Univ of Alberta, Edmonton, AB, T6G 2F6.

FISHWICK, MARSHALL W.
DISCIPLINE AMERICAN STUDIES, POPULAR CULTURE **EDUCATION** Univ VA, BA, 44; Univ WI, MA, 46; Yale Univ, PhD, 50; Krakow Univ, Poland, D Phil (hon), 67; Dhaka Univ, Bangladesh, D Litt (hon), 83. **CAREER** Instr, Yale Univ, 49; Prof Am Studies, Dir Honors prog, Washington & Lee Univ, 50-62; vis prof, Univ MN, summer 57; dir, Wemyss Found, consult, Winterthur Museum, 62-64; Distinguished vis prof, Univ WY, summer 63; Prof Humanities, chmn, art dept, chmn, Am studies, Lincoln Univ, 64-70; prof Mass Commun, Temple Univ, 70-76; vis prof, Yale Univ, 84; prof of Humanities in Center for Interdisciplinary Studies and Commun Studies, VA Tech, 76-. **HONORS AND AWARDS** Eight Fulbright grants, 59-85; Sterling fel, Yale Univ, 48-50; Rockefeller Found NY, 51; Glenn grant, Washington & Lee Univ, 55; Indian Ed Found, 64; Yale Alumni grant, 68; Bangladesh Cultural Center, 85; Trumbull Fellows, Yale Univ, 92-96. **MEMBERSHIPS** Nat Ed Asn; Am Studies Asn; Am Hist Asn; Org Am Hist; Modern Lang Asn; AAUP; VA Hist Soc; Southern Hist Asn; British Am Studies Asn; European Studies Asn; Am Studies Res Centre (India); Guild of Scholars; Centro Italiano di Studi Americani, Conseils aux Etudiants d'Anglais, Inst fur Jugendkunde; Fulbright Alumni Asn; Japanese-Am Studies Asn; Soc of Architectural Hist; Popular Culture Asn; Salzburg Adv Fac. **SELECTED PUBLICATIONS** Auth, Heroes and Superheroes, Smithsonian Press, 90; Symbolism, Bowling Green State Univ Popular Press, 90; Revitalizing the Humanities, Popular Press, 92; Popular Religion in America, Hayworth Press, 93; Go and Catch a Falling Star, American Heritage, 95; Preview 2001+, Bowling Green State Univ Press, 95; An American Mosaic, A New Text for a New Age, American Heritage, 97; numerous other publications. **CONTACT ADDRESS** Virginia Tech, 152 Lane Hall, Blacksburg, VA, 24061-0227. **EMAIL** mfishwic@vt.edu

FISS, KAREN A.
DISCIPLINE EUROPEAN CULTURE AND POLITICS BETWEEN THE WORLD WARS **EDUCATION** Yale Univ, PhD, 95. **CAREER** Hist, Washington Univ. **SELECTED PUBLICATIONS** Univ, Discourses: Conversations in Postmodern Art and Cult, M.I.T. Prof and the New Mus, 90; The German Pavilion at the 1937 Paris Exposition Internationale, in Art and Power: Europe under the Dictators, 1930-45, The South Bank Center London, 95. **CONTACT ADDRESS** Washington Univ, 1 Brookings Dr, St. Louis, MO, 63130. **EMAIL** kafiss@artsci.wustl.edu

FITCH, J.G.
DISCIPLINE GREEK; ROMAN DRAMA **EDUCATION** Cornell Univ, BA, 63, Cert Edu, 66, MA, 67, PhD, 74. **CAREER** Prof, 73-; ch. **HONORS AND AWARDS** Pres, Class Assn of Vancouver Island, 82-83; coun mem, Class Assn of Can, 84-86; prog ch, Class Assn of Can, 90. **MEMBERSHIPS** Mem, Amer Philol Assn; Soc for Lit and Sci. **RESEARCH** Senecan tragedy; didactic poetry. **SELECTED PUBLICATIONS** Auth, Seneca's Hercules Furens, Cornell UP, 87; Seneca's Anapaests, Scholars Press, 88; Sense-Pauses and Relative Dating in Seneca, Sophocles and Shakespeare, Amer Jour of Philol 102, 81; coauth, Theory and Context of the Didactic Poem, Florilegium 5, 83. **CONTACT ADDRESS** Dept of Greek and Roman Studies, Victoria Univ, PO Box 1700 STN CSC, Victoria, BC, V8W 2Y2. **EMAIL** fitch@uvvm.uvic.ca

FITE, GILBERT COURTLAND
PERSONAL Born 05/14/1918, Santa Fe, OH, m, 1941, 2 children **DISCIPLINE** HISTORY **EDUCATION** Univ SDak, AB and Am, 41; Univ Mo, PhD, 45. **CAREER** Prof, Wessington Springs Col, 41-42; from asst to prof to prof hist, Univ Okla, 45-58, chmn dept, 55-58, res prof, 58-71; pres, Eastern Ill Univ, 71-76; acting head hist dept, 77-78, RICHARD B RUSSELL PROF HIST, UNIV GA, ATENS, 76-, Ford fel, 54-55; vis prof, Jadavpur Univ, India, 62-63; Guggenheim fel, 64-65; consult, US Off Educ, 65-68; dir, Am Studies Res Ctr, Hyderabad, India, 69-70; Int coun, Phi Alpha Theta, 78-80 (pres, 81-). **HONORS AND AWARDS** DLitt, Seattle Pac Col, 62; DLitt, Univ SDak, 75. **MEMBERSHIPS** AHA; Orgn Am Hists; Agr Hist Soc (pres, 60); Southern Hist Asn (vpres, 73, pres, 74); Econ Hist Asn. **RESEARCH** Farm movements; farm leaders; general recent agricultural history. **SELECTED PUBLICATIONS** Auth, Colleagues Russell, Richard, B. and his Apprentice, Johnnson, J Am Hist, Vol 81, 95 Bale O Cotton--The Mechanical Art of Cotton Ginning, Ark Hist Quart, Vol 52, 93; Interview with Fite, Gilbert, C., Hist, Vol 56, 93; American Agriculture--A Brief History, J Southern Hist, Vol 61, 95. **CONTACT ADDRESS** Dept of Hist, Univ of Ga, Athens, GA, 30602.

FITZGERALD, E.P.
DISCIPLINE HISTORY **EDUCATION** Seton Hall Univ, BA; Univ de Geneve; Yale Univ, MA, PhD. **CAREER** Ch; assoc prof. **HONORS AND AWARDS** Adv, Mention francaise. **RESEARCH** International economic relations and their links to international politics. **SELECTED PUBLICATIONS** Auth, "Economic Constraints on the Continuation of Colonial Rule in French Colonial Africa: The Problem of Recurrent Costs," Proc Fr Colonial Hist Soc, 89; "The Iraq Oil Company, Standard Oil of California and the contest for eastern Arabia, 1930-32," Intl Hist Rev, 91; "Compagnie Francaise des Petroles and the Defense of the Red Line Regime in middle Eastern Oil, 1933-36," Bus and Econ Hist, 91; "Business diplomacy: Walter Teagle, jersey Standard, and the Anglo-French Pipeline Conflict in the Middle East," Bus Hist Rev, 93; "France's Middle Eastern Ambitions, the Sykes-Picot Negotiations, and the Oil Fields of Mosul, 1915-18," Jour Mod Hist, 94; "The Power of the Weak and the Weakness of the Strong: Explaining Corporate Behavior in Middle Eastern Oil, 1946-48," Bus and Econ Hist, 95. **CONTACT ADDRESS** Dept of Hist, Carleton Univ, 1125 Colonel By Dr, Ottawa, ON, K1S 5B6.

FITZPATRICK, ELLEN
DISCIPLINE MODERN AMERICA, WOMEN'S HISTORY, INTELLECTUAL HISTORY **EDUCATION** Brandeis Univ, PhD. **CAREER** Assoc prof, Univ NH, 97-. **HONORS AND AWARDS** Charles Warren Ctr fel, Harvard Univ; Andrew Mellon fac fel in the Hum, Harvard Univ; Spencer Found grant; NEH grant. **RESEARCH** American historians and the memory of modern history. **SELECTED PUBLICATIONS** Auth, Endless Crusade: Women Social Scientists and Progressive Reform; Muckraking: Three Landmark Articles; ed, Century of Struggle by Eleanor Flexner; coed, America in Modern Times. **CONTACT ADDRESS** Univ NH, Durham, NH, 03824. **EMAIL** admissions@unh.edu

FITZPATRICK, MARTIN
DISCIPLINE HISTORY **CAREER** Sr lectr History and Welsh History, Univ Wales, Aberystwyth; vis fel, Ctr Cross-Cult Res, Australian Natl Univ, 98. **RESEARCH** Enlightenment studies. **SELECTED PUBLICATIONS** Ed, Enlightenment and Dissent, pending; Enlightenment Ideas of Conscience, In: Religious Conscience, the State and Law, SUNY, 97; Enlightenment in Britain, and Toleration, In: The Oxford Companion to the Age of Revolutions and Romanticism, Oxford Univ, 98; coauth, The Death of Cook and Other Writings, Cassell, 99. **CONTACT ADDRESS** Dept of Education, Australian National Univ. **EMAIL** Martin.Fitzpatrick@anu.edu.au

FITZSIMMONS, MICHAEL P.
DISCIPLINE HISTORY **EDUCATION** Belmont Abbey Col, BA, 71; Univ NC, Chapel Hill, MA, 76, PhD, 81. **CAREER** Mellon instr, Rice Univ, 82-85; asst prof to PROF, AUBURN UNIV, MONTGOMERY, 85-. **CONTACT ADDRESS** Dept of History, Auburn Univ, Montgomery, PO Box 244023, Montgomery, AL, 36124-4023. **EMAIL** mpfitzsimmons@edla.aum.edu

FLACK, J..KIRKPATRICK
PERSONAL Born 02/11/1937, Brooklyn, NY, m, 1960, 3 children **DISCIPLINE** AMERICAN HISTORY **EDUCATION** Albion Col, BA, 59; Wayne State Univ, MA, 63, PhD(hist), 68. **CAREER** Instr hist, Wayne State Univ, 65-66; from lectr to asst prof, 67-74, ASSOC PROF HIST, UNIV MD, COLLEGE PARK, 74-, Sr Fulbright-Hays lectr, Annamalai Univ & M S Univ, Baroda, India, 74-75; ed, Rec Columbia Hist Soc, 80-. **MEMBERSHIPS** AHA; Orgn Am Historians **RESEARCH** Social history of 19th century America; American urban history; history of Washington, DC; historic preservation. **SELECTED PUBLICATIONS** Auth, The Press in Detroit, 1880-1900, Mich Hist, 66; Desideratum in Washington: The Intellectual Community in the Capital City, 1870-1900, Schenkman, 75; Scientific Societies in Gilded Age Washington, Rec Columbia Hist Soc, 75. **CONTACT ADDRESS** Dept of Hist, Univ of Md, College Park, MD, 20742-0001. **EMAIL** jf14@umail.umd.edu

FLACKS, RICHARD
PERSONAL Born 04/26/1938, Brooklyn, NY, m, 1959, 2 children **DISCIPLINE** SOCIAL PSYCHOLOGY **EDUCATION** Brooklyn Col, BA 58; Univ Michigan, PhD 64. **CAREER** Univ Chicago, asst prof 64-69; Univ Cal SB, prof, 69-, ch, 75-80. **HONORS AND AWARDS** Dist Tchg Awd. **MEMBERSHIPS** ASA; SSSI; SSPP; SPSSI. **RESEARCH** Social movements; Political Consciousness. **SELECTED PUBLICATIONS** Auth, Cultural Politics and Social Movements, co-ed, Temple Univ Press, 95; auth, Beyond the Barricades: The Sixties Generation Grows up, coauth, Temple Univ Press, 89; Reviving Democratic Activism: Thoughts about strategy in a dark time, in: David Trend, ed, Radical Democracy: Identity Citizenship and the State, Routledge, 96; auth, Who Supports the Troops? Vietnam and the Gulf War and the Making of Collective Memory, coauth, Social Problems, 95; auth, The Party's Over-so what's to be done? Social Res, 93. **CONTACT ADDRESS** Dept of Sociology, Univ of California, Santa Barbara, Santa Barbara, CA, 93106. **EMAIL** flacks@alishaw.ucsb.edu

FLADER, SUSAN L.
PERSONAL Born 04/29/1941, Sheboygan, WI **DISCIPLINE** HISTORY **EDUCATION** Univ Wisc, BA, 63; Stanford Univ, MA, 65, PhD, 71. **CAREER** Instr, asst prof, 70-73, 77-78, Univ Wisc; vis lectr, 86, 91, 96, Lanzhou, Qingdao, Nankai, Inner Mongolia, Wuhan, Sichuan, et al Univ, People's Rep of China; Fulbright Sr Lectr, 87-8, Univ Turku, Finland; vis scholar, 95, Univ W Cape S Africa; , asst prof, 73-75, assoc prof, 75-81, prof, 81- Univ Missouri-Columbia. **CONTACT ADDRESS** Dept of History, Univ of Missouri, Columbia, MO, 65211. **EMAIL** histsf@showme.missouri.edu

FLAMMER, PHILIP MEYNARD
PERSONAL Born 06/20/1928, St. Johns, AZ, m, 1954, 4 children **DISCIPLINE** MILITARY HISTORY, UNITED STATES DIPLOMATIC HISTORY **EDUCATION** Utah State Univ, BS, 53; George Washington Univ, MA, 58; Yale Univ, PhD(mil hist), 63. **CAREER** Instr US hist, US Air Force Acad, 58-60, asst prof mil hist, 60-61, from assoc prof to prof, 63-71; assoc prof mil & diplomatic hist, 73-78, PROF MIL & DIPLOMATIC HIST, BRIGHAM YOUNG UNIV, 78- **RESEARCH** The military critic; the struggle for air supremacy over Continental Europe, 1942-1945. **SELECTED PUBLICATIONS** Auth, Weather and the invasion, Mil Rev, 6/63; Image of the aces: A writer's bonanza, Air Univ Rev, 1-2/66; Airpower and 20th Century Warfare, Vol I, Air Force Acad, 67; The attractions of totalitarianism, Air Univ Rev, 5-6/72; The military critic, Proc US Naval Inst, 3/73; Communist propaganda in South Vietnam, Brigham Young Univ Studies, winter 73; Conflicting loyalties and the American military ethic, Behav Scientist, 5-6/76. **CONTACT ADDRESS** Dept of Hist, Brigham Young Univ, Provo, UT, 84602.

FLANAGAN, MAUREEN ANNE
PERSONAL Born 02/20/1948, Chicago, IL **DISCIPLINE** AMERICAN HISTORY **EDUCATION** Loyola Univ, Chicago, PhD (hist), 81. **CAREER** LECTR HIST, LOYOLA UNIV, CHICAGO, 80-. **MEMBERSHIPS** Orgn Am Hists; AHA. **RESEARCH** Urban history; political culture of Chicago. **SELECTED PUBLICATIONS** Auth, Daley, Richard, J--Politics, Race, and the Governing of Chicago, Am Hist Rev, Vol 102, 97; Property Rules--Political Economy in Chicago, 1833-1872, Rev Am Hist, Vol 21, 93; The City Profitable, The City Livable--Environmental Policy, Gender, and Power in Chicago in the 1910s, J Urban Hist, Vol 22, 96; Women in the City, Women of the City--Where Do Women Fit in Urban History, J Urban Hist, Vol 23, 97. **CONTACT ADDRESS** Dept of Hist, Loyola Univ, Chicago, IL, 60626.

FLAYHART III, WILLIAM H.
PERSONAL Born 07/12/1944, Williamsport, PA, m, 1977, 3 children **DISCIPLINE** HISTORY **EDUCATION** Lycoming Col, BA, 66; Univ Va, MA, 68, PhD, 71. **CAREER** Asst Prof, 70-72, Assoc Prof, 72-74, Prof Hist, 74-, Del State Univ; Ch, Dept of Hist, Polit Sci, & Philos, Del State Univ, 93-99. **HONORS AND AWARDS** Vis Prof of Maritime Hist, Univ Lieden, 94-95; Fellow, Int Napoleonic Soc, 97. **MEMBERSHIPS** AHA; SHA; US Naval Inst; NAOHS; CNRO; IMHA. **RESEARCH** Maritime & Naval history; Napoleonic history; British history. **SELECTED PUBLICATIONS** Auth, Counterpoint to Trafalgar: The Anglo-Russian Invasion of Naples, 1805-1806, Univ SC Press, 92; auth, British Rivalries in Sicily and Naples, 1803-1806, Consortium on Revolutionary Europe 1750-1850, Proceedings 1994, Fla State Univ, 95; auth, Oceanic Historiography: The American Dimension (1974-1994), Maritime History at the Crossroads, 249-276, Int Maritime Hist Asn, 95; auth, The Rise of the Compagnie Generale Transatlantique (French Line), Consortium on Revolutionary Europe, La State Univ, 97; auth, The American Line (1871-1902): Stars and Stripes in the Atlantic, WWNorton & Co, Inc, in press. **CONTACT ADDRESS** Dept of Hist & Polit Sci, Delaware State Univ, Dover, DE, 19901. **EMAIL** wflayhar@dsc.edu

FLEENER, CHARLES JOSEPH
PERSONAL Born 11/22/1938, New Orleans, LA, m, 1967, 2 children **DISCIPLINE** LATIN AMERICAN HISTORY **EDUCATION** Georgetown Univ, BSFS, 60; Univ Fla, MA, 63, PhD, 69. **CAREER** From instr to asst prof, 66-76, Assoc Prof Latin Am Hist, St Louis Univ, 76-, Chmn Dept, 76-84, Dean, St Louis Univ/Spain, 92; Vis prof, Columbus Int Col, Spain, 73. **MEMBERSHIPS** Midwest Coun Latin Am Studies (pres, 69-70); AHA. **RESEARCH** Colonial Latin American history, 18th century; expulsions of the Jesuits from Spain and Spanish America. **SELECTED PUBLICATIONS** Coauth, The Guide to Latin American Paperback Literature, Univ Fla, 66; co-ed, Religious and Cultural Factors in Latin America, St Louis Univ, 71. **CONTACT ADDRESS** Dept of Hist, St Louis Univ, 221 N Grand Blvd, Saint Louis, MO, 63103-2097. **EMAIL** fleener@slu.edu

FLEER, JACK DAVID
PERSONAL Born 09/21/1937, Washington, MO, m, 1963, 3 children **DISCIPLINE** POLITICAL SCIENCE **EDUCATION** Okla Baptist Univ, AB, 59; Flor St Univ, MS, 61; Univ N Carolina, Chapel Hill, PhD, 65. **CAREER** Res asst, 59-60, inst for govern res, FL St Univ; res asst, 60-61, inst for res in soc science, part-time inst, dept of political science, 61-64, res asst, institute of govern, sum 62 & sum 63, Univ NC; asst prof, 64-69, chmn dept of politics, 69-77, assoc prof, 69-79, prof, 79-, chmn dept of politics, 85-97, Wake Forest Univ. **MEMBERSHIPS** Amer Political Science Asn; Southern Political Science Asn. **RESEARCH** North Carolina govern & politics; southern politics. **SELECTED PUBLICATIONS** Auth, Interest Groups in North Carolina, NC Focus 2nd ed, NC Center for Public Policy Res, 97; auth, North Carolina Government and Politics, Univ Nebraska Press, 94; auth, North Carolina: Interest Groups in a State in Transition, Interest Group Politics in the Southern States, Univ AL Press, 92. **CONTACT ADDRESS** Wake Forest Univ, Reynolds Station, PO Box 7568, Winston-Salem, NC, 27109. **EMAIL** fleerj@wfu.edu

FLEISCHER, MANFRED PAUL
PERSONAL Born 06/26/1928, Nieder Peilau-Schloessel, Germany, m, 1962, 3 children **DISCIPLINE** EARLY MODERN EUROPE, HISTORY OF IDEAS AND RELIGION **EDUCATION** Wagner Col, BA, 55; Philadelphia Lutheran Theol Sem, MDiv, 59; Univ Pa, MA, 61; Univ Erlangen, PhD (hist ideas and relig), 65. **CAREER** Lectr philos, Wagner Col, 55-56; pastor, Lutheran Church, NY, 59-61; lectr philos and relig, Wagner Col, 61; assoc, 63, from acting instr to assoc prof, 64-77, PROF HIST, UNIV CALIF, DAVIS, 77-, Fulbright res scholar, Univ Strabourg, 67-68. **MEMBERSHIPS** AHA; Am Soc Reformation Res; Soc Hist Ideas, Ger; Am Soc Church Hist. **RESEARCH** Interrelationships between humanism, Reformation, and counter-Reformation in central Europe. **SELECTED PUBLICATIONS** Auth, The Cath Roots of the Protestant Gospel Encounter Between the Middle Ages and the Reformation, Church Hist, Vol 65, 96; The Cath Roots of the Protestant Gospel--Encounter Between the Middle Ages and the Reformation, Church Hist, Vol 65, 96; Screech, M. A--Some Renaissance Studies, Church Hist, Vol 64, 95. **CONTACT ADDRESS** Dept of Hist, Univ of Calif, Davis, CA, 95616.

FLEMING, JAMES RODGER
PERSONAL Born 05/28/1949, Windber, PA, m, 2 children **DISCIPLINE** ATMOSPHERIC SCIENCE, ASTRONOMY **EDUCATION** Princeton Univ, PhD, Hist Sci, 88, MA, Hist Sci, 84; Colorado State, MS, Atmospheric Sci, 73; Penn State Univ, BS, Astron, 71. **CAREER** Colby Col, Assoc Prof Dir, STS Prog, 88-; Ch Interdisc Stud Div, 97-; Am Meteor Soc Hist Consult, 87-88, 94-; Penn State Univ, Vis Prof Global Change, 94; Mass Inst Tech, Vis Schol, STS prog, 92-94; Smithsonian Inst, fel, Papers of Joseph Henry, 85-87; Princeton Univ, fel, Preceptor, Dept Hist, 82-85; Priv Consult Meteor, Miami NY, 74-82; Univ Wash, Res Meteor, Dept Atmosph Sci, 73-74; Nat Cen for Atmosph Resear, Research Meteorologist, 73. **HONORS AND AWARDS** Who's Who in the East, Marquis, 94-98; Dictionary Of Intl Biog, Cambridge, 95; Contemporary Auth, Gale Resea, 96. **MEMBERSHIPS** Am Asn Advan Sci; Am Geophysical Union; Am Meteo Soc; British Soc for Hist of Sci; Hist of Sci Soc; Nat Asn Sci, Technol Soc; Soc for Hist of Tech. **RESEARCH** Hist of meteor, climatology, geophysics; Military relations of Sci; Archives, bibliography. **SELECTED PUBLICATIONS** Historical Perspectives on Climate Change, NY Oxford, Oxford Univ Press, 98; Meteorology in America, 1800-1870, Baltimore, John Hopkins Univ Press, 90; Guide to Historical Resources in the Atmospheric Science, Boulder, National Center for Atmospheric Research, 89; Historical essays on Meteorology, 1919-1995, ed, Boston Am Meteor Soc, 96; Science, Technology and the Environment: Multidisciplinary Perspectives, ed, Akron, Univ Akron Press, 94. **CONTACT ADDRESS** Colby Col, Science, Tech & Society Prog, Waterville, ME, 04901-8858. **EMAIL** jrfleming@colby.edu

FLEMING, JOHN EMORY
PERSONAL Born 08/03/1944, Morganton, NC, m **DISCIPLINE** AFRICAN-AMERICAN STUDIES **EDUCATION** Berea Coll, BA 1966; Univ of KY, 1966-67; Howard U, MA, PhD 1970-74. **CAREER** KY Civil Rights Commn, educ specialist 1966-67; Peace Corps, visual aids special 1967-69; USCR Commn, program officer 1970-71; Inst for the Study of Educ Policy, sr fellow 1974-80; Natl Afro-American Museum, dir 1980-98; Natl Underground Railroad Freedom Ctr, dir, 1998-. **HONORS AND AWARDS** Carter G Woodson Award, Berea College; Martin Luther King Award; OH Library Association Humanities Award. **MEMBERSHIPS** Mem NAACP 1974-87; bd Assoc Study of Afro-Amer Life and History 1978-93; bd Journal of Negro History 1982-96; vice pres bd Art for Comm Expression 1984-87; panel Columbus Foundation 1986-87; v pres Ohio Museums Assoc 1989-90; board member, American Assn of Museums, 1990-95; board member, Museum Trustee Assn, 1989-95; president & board member, African-American Museums Assn, 1991-96; White House Conference on Travel and Tourism, 1995; Ohio Becentennial Commission, 1996-2003. **SELECTED PUBLICATIONS** "The Lenghtening Shadow of Slavery," Howard Univ Press 1976; "The Case for Affirmative Action for Blacks in Higher Education," Howard Univ Press 1978. **CONTACT ADDRESS** National Underground Railroad, 312 Elm St, Cincinnati, OH, 45202.

FLEMING, PATRICIA L.
PERSONAL Born 12/27/1939, Hamilton, ON, Canada **DISCIPLINE** HISTORY **EDUCATION** McMaster Univ, BA, 60; Univ Toronto, BLS, 64, MLS, 70; Univ London, MA, 77, PhD, 80. **CAREER** Staff, Metro Toronto Libr, 64-69; tchg asst to assoc prof, 70-90, PROF, FAC INFORMATION STUD, UNIV TORONTO, 90-; adv bd, Nat Libr Can, 83-86. **HONORS AND AWARDS** Tremaine Medal, 92. **MEMBERSHIPS** Bibliog Soc Can; Am Antiquarian Soc; Can Inst Hist Microrepro (bd mem, vice pres 89-92, pres 92-94), Bibliog Soc Can (coun 82-85, pres 86-89); Am Printing Hist Asn (trustee, 94-). **SELECTED PUBLICATIONS** Auth, Upper Canadian Imprints 1801-1841: A Bibliography, 88; auth, Atlantic Canadian Imprints 1801-1820: A Bibliography, 91. **CONTACT ADDRESS** Fac Info Stud, Univ Toronto, Toronto, ON, M5S 3G6. **EMAIL** fleming@fis.utoronto.ca

FLEMING, RAE B.
PERSONAL Born 05/17/1944, Lindsay, ON, Canada **DISCIPLINE** HISTORY **EDUCATION** Univ Toronto, BA, 66; Univ Sask, MA, 82, PhD, 88. **CAREER** Tchr, lectr, prof, 67-; vis fel, Ctr Can Stud, Univ Edinburgh, 91; lectr, Univ Winipeg; lectr, Univ Guelph; lectr, Ryerson Polytechnic Univ; res assoc, Leslie Frist Ctr, Trent Univ. **HONORS AND AWARDS** Thomas B. Symons Award, Trent Univ; Fred Landon Award, Ont Hist Soc.

MEMBERSHIPS Can Hist Soc. **SELECTED PUBLICATIONS** Auth, Eldon Connections, 75; auth, The Railway King of Canada, 91; ed, Boswell's Children, 92; ed, The Lochaber Immigrants, 94; contribur, Canadian Encyclopedia, 85, 88; contribur, Dictionary of Canadian Biography, 94. **CONTACT ADDRESS** RR 6, Woodville, ON, K0M 2T0.

FLETCHER, JUDITH
DISCIPLINE GREEK DRAMA **EDUCATION** Western, BA, MA; Bryn Mawr, PhD. **CAREER** Asst Prof **SELECTED PUBLICATIONS** Auth, Aeschylus' Cassandra: The Woman Who Knew Too Much; Vision and Representation in Aeschylus' Agamemnon. **CONTACT ADDRESS** Dept of Classics, Wilfrid Laurier Univ, 75 University Ave W, Waterloo, ON, N2L 3C5. **EMAIL** jfletche@mach1.wlu.ca

FLETCHER, MARVIN EDWARD
PERSONAL Born 12/21/1941, San Francisco, CA, m, 1965, 2 children **DISCIPLINE** UNITED STATES HISTORY **EDUCATION** Univ Calif, Berkeley, BA, 63; Univ Wis-Madison, MA, 65, PhD, 68. **CAREER** Asst prof, 68-73, assoc prof hist, Ohio Univ, 73-89; prof hist, Ohio Univ, 89. **MEMBERSHIPS** Orgn Am Historians; Am Jewish Hist Soc; Soc of Am Military Hist. **RESEARCH** Black American history; American military history. **SELECTED PUBLICATIONS** Auth, The Black Volunteer in Reconstruction, 1865-66, 68; auth, The Black Volunteer in the Spanish American War, 73, Mil Affairs; art, The Black Soldier Athlete, Can J Hist Sport & Phys Educ, 73; auth, The Black Soldier and Officer in the United States Army, 1891-1917, Univ Mo, 74; auth, The United States Army in Peacetime, Mil Affairs/Aerospace Historian, 75; auth, The Black Bicycle Corps, Ariz & the West, summer 75; America's First Black General, U Press of Kansas, 89. **CONTACT ADDRESS** Athens, OH, 45701-2979. **EMAIL** mfletcher1@ohiou.edu

FLINT, ALLEN DENIS
PERSONAL Born 11/15/1929, Park River, ND, m, 1953, 5 children **DISCIPLINE** ENGLISH, AMERICAN STUDIES **EDUCATION** Univ Minn, BA, 55, MA, 56, PhD(Am studies), 65. **CAREER** Col Counsel & freshman adv, Col Lib Arts, Univ Minn, 56-58, scholastic comt rep, 58-59, sr scholastic comt rep, 59-62, instr & counsel, 62-64, asst dir, corres studies dept, 64-65, actg dir, 65-66; from asst prof to assoc prof English, Western Ill Univ, 66-70; chmn dept, 71-75, PROF ENGLISH, UNIV MAINE, FARMINGTON, 70-, Fulbright lectr, Romania, CIES, 75-76. **MEMBERSHIPS** MLA; Am Studies Asn. **RESEARCH** American renaissance; Black literature; contemporary literature. **SELECTED PUBLICATIONS** Auth, Hawthorne and the slavery crisis, New Eng Quart, 68; Essentially a daydream: Hawthorne's Blithedale, Hawthorne J, 72; The saving grace of marriage in Hawthorne's fiction, Emerson Soc Quart, 73. **CONTACT ADDRESS** Dept of English, Univ of Maine, Farmington, ME, 04938.

FLINT, JOHN E.
PERSONAL Born 05/17/1930, Montreal, PQ, Canada **DISCIPLINE** HISTORY **EDUCATION** St John's Col, Cambridge, BA, 52, MA, 54; Royal Holloway Col & Sch Orient African Stud Univ London, PhD, 57. **CAREER** Asst lectr to reader, Univ London, King's Col, 54-67; prof, 67-92, ch hist, 68-71, 74-75, dir ctr African stud, 78-83, PROF EMER, DALHOUSIE UNIV, 92-; vis prof, Univ Calif Santa Barbara, 60-61; vis prof, head hist, Univ Nigeria Nsukka, 63-64. **HONORS AND AWARDS** Fulbright fel, 60-61. **MEMBERSHIPS** Can Hist Asn (coun 68-69); Can Asn African Stud (vice pres 69-70, coun mem 77-79, 82-83); Nigerian Hist Soc (coun mem 64-65); African Stud Asn UK. **RESEARCH** History of Africa, Nigeria. **SELECTED PUBLICATIONS** Auth, Sir George Goldie and the Making of Nigeria, 60; auth, Nigeria and Ghana, 66; auth, Cecil Rhodes, 74; ed, West Africa Studies (Mary Kingsley), 64; ed, Travels in West Africa (Mary Kingsley), 65; ed, Cambridge History of Africa, vol V, 77; co-ed, Perspectives of Empire: Essays in Honour of Gerald Sandford Graham, 73; contribur, Oxford History of East Africa, vols I-II, 63, 65. **CONTACT ADDRESS** Dept of History, Dalhousie Univ, Halifax, NS, B3H 3J5.

FLORES, CAROL A.
PERSONAL Lockport, NY, m, 1968 **DISCIPLINE** ARCHITECTURE, HISTORY, THEORY & CRITICISM **EDUCATION** Univ NY Albany, BA, 66; Ga Inst of Tech, MS, 90; Ga Inst of Tech, PhD, archit, 96. **CAREER** Teacher, LaSalle Sch for Boys, 66-71; asst to pres, Environment/One Corp, 71; svc adv, N Eng Telephone, 72-76; chief svc adv, Southern Bell, 76-77; mgr, Southern Bell, 78-79; district mgr, Southern Bell, 80-82; operations mgr, Bell South Svc, 83-85; owner and commercial and residential designer, Design Options, 86-90; grad teaching asst, Col of Archit, Ga Inst of Tech, 89; doctoral fel, Col of Archit, Ga Inst of Tech, 90-94; asst prof, Col of Archit and Planning, Ball State Univ, 96-. **HONORS AND AWARDS** Outstanding rating, Mgt Assessment Prog, Southern Bell, 78; Outstanding Mgt Candidate, Southern Bell, 80; Individual Incentive award, BellSouth Svc, 84; Fel, Colonial Williamsburg Found, Antiques forum, 93; Ga Tech Alumni Asn Student Leadership travel award for Rome study, 93; Scholar, Nineteenth Century Studies Prog in London, Victorian Soc, 94; GTA teaching excellence award, col of archit, Ga Inst of Tech, 94; CETL/AMOCO Found GTA teaching excellence award, 94; pres fel, col of archit, Ga Inst of Tech, 90-94; doctoral fel, col of archit, Ga Inst of Tech, 91-94; Best Article Award, Southeast Chap, Soc of Archit Hist, 95; Outstanding Student in Archit, Ga Inst of Tech, dec, 96; Doctoral prog achievement award, Ga Inst of Tech, may, 97. **MEMBERSHIPS** Soc of Archit Hist; Southeast Chap, Soc of Archit Hist; Vernacular Archit Forum; Soc for Amer City and Regional Planning Hist; Asn of Coll Sch of Archit; Nineteenth-Century Studies Asn; Victorian Soc; Soc for Emblem Studies; Decorative Arts Soc; Intl Soc for Amer City and Regional Planning Hist; Wallpaper Hist Soc. **RESEARCH** 19th-Century British architecture, theory, and decorative arts; Architecture, theory and decorative arts of Owen Jones 1809-1874; Public housing; Symbolism in architecture. **SELECTED PUBLICATIONS** Auth, Owen Jones, Architect, Ga Inst of Tech, 96; contr, The Grammar of Ornament, Professional Artists' Edition, Pasadena, Direct Imagination Inc, 96; auth, US public housing in the 1930s: the first projects in Atlanta, Georgia, Planning Perspectives, 9, 405-430, 94. **CONTACT ADDRESS** College of Architecture and Planning, Ball State Univ, Muncie, IN, 47306-0305. **EMAIL** cflores@wp.bsu.edu

FLORES, DAN
PERSONAL Born 10/19/1948, Vivian, LA, s **DISCIPLINE** HISTORY **EDUCATION** Texas A&M Univ, PhD, 78. **CAREER** Prof, 78-92, Texas Tech Univ; AB Hammond Prof, 92-, Univ Montana. **RESEARCH** Environ hist of the Amer West. **CONTACT ADDRESS** Dept of History, Univ of Montana, Missoula, MT, 59812. **EMAIL** dflores@selway.umt.edu

FLORESCU, RADU R.
PERSONAL Born 10/23/1925, Bucharest, Romania, m, 1951, 4 children **DISCIPLINE** MODERN HISTORY **EDUCATION** Oxford Univ, BA, 47, MA, 50, BLitt, 51; Ind Univ, PhD(Rumanian hist), 59. **CAREER** From instr to asst prof, 53-63, assoc prof hist, Boston Col, 63-; dir East Europ Res Ctr, 80-, Am Philos Soc grant, 61-62; fel, St Antony Col, Oxford Univ, 61-62. **MEMBERSHIPS** AHA; Am Romanian Acad, Mediaeval Acad Am; Soc Romanian Studies; Am Asn Southeastern Europe. **RESEARCH** Rumanian and East European history. **SELECTED PUBLICATIONS** Auth, The origin and development of science in Rumania, Ann Sci, 3/60; Stratford canning and the Wallachian revolution of 1848, J Mod Hist, 9/63; Struggle Against Russia in the Rumanian Principalities, 1821-54, Castaldi, Rome, 63; coauth, In Search of Dracula, NY Graphic Soc, 72; Dracula: A Biography of Vlad the Impaler 1431-1476, Hawthorn, 73; The Dracula debate, E Europ Quart, 74; In Search of Frankenstein, NY Graphic & Warner Books, 75; Dracula Prince of Many Faces, 88, Little Brown, 89, all Dracula books co-auth with Raymond T, McNally, The Essential Dracula, Mayflower Books, 80; 100 Years of American-Romanian Relations, Nagard, 81; co-ed, Romanian between East and West: Profesor C C Giurescu, Columbia Univ East European Monographs. **CONTACT ADDRESS** Boston Col, 140 Commonwealth Ave, Chestnut Hill, MA, 02167-3800. **EMAIL** florescu@BC.edu

FLORI, MONICA ROY
PERSONAL Born 09/17/1944, Montevideo, Uruguay, m, 1968 **DISCIPLINE** LATIN AMERICAN & SPANISH LITERATURE **EDUCATION** Inst Uruguayo de Estudios Prepatorios, 63; Univ Repub Uruguay, Lic Philos, 70; Univ Hawaii, MA, 71; Univ Ore, PhD(Romance lang & lit), 79. **CAREER** Instr Span & Fr, Portland Community Col, 71-74; lectr Span & Fr, 77-79, Prof Lang & Lit, Lewis & Clark Col, 79-. **MEMBERSHIPS** Am Asn Teachers Span; Pac Northwest Foreign Lang Coun; Pac States Lat Am Studies Asn; Southwestern States Latin Am Studies Asn; MLA. **RESEARCH** Contemporary Latin American fiction; Latin American women writers; fiction of the River Plate area. **SELECTED PUBLICATIONS** Auth, Simbolismo existencial en la narrative de Juan Carlos Onetti, Vol I, 80 & Las ventanas en Paseo de Jose Donoso, Vol II, 81, Selecta; Las imagenes sensoriales en El pozo y El astillero de Juan Carlos Onetti, Explicacion de Textos Literarios, Vol X, 81-82; The Hispanic community as resource for a practical Spanish program, Foreign Lang Ann, spring 82; Streams of Silver: Six Contemporary Women Writers from Argentina, Lewisburg, Bucknell University Press, 95, 97; De almibares, perfumes y sedas: La recuperacion historica-biografica en Perfumes de Cartago de Teresa Porzekanski, forthcoming in Alba de America, 98. **CONTACT ADDRESS** Foreign Lang Dept, Lewis & Clark Col, 0615 SW Palatine Hill Rd, Portland, OR, 97219-7879. **EMAIL** flori@lclark.edu

FLORIAN, ROBERT BRUCE
PERSONAL Born 01/17/1930, Hartford, CT, m, 1951, 3 children **DISCIPLINE** ENGLISH HISTORY, MODERN EUROPEAN HISTORY, WEST VIRGINIA HISTORY **EDUCATION** Adrian Col, BA, 51: Garrett Theol Sem, MDiv, 56; WVa Univ, MA, 63, PhD(hist), 73. **CAREER** Instr Relig, Wesley Jr Col, 56-58; assoc prof, 58-75, fac chmn, 80-82, prof Hist, Salem Col, 75-, chmn dept Lib Studies, 74-90, pastor, WVa United Methodist Churches, Haywood, 61-62, Jarvisville, 71-73, Greenwood, 76-78 & Wallace, 79-; mem, WVa State Antiq Comn, 68-69; treas comm on Archives and History, WV conf, United Methodist Church, 84-88, 96. **HONORS AND AWARDS** Citation as Outstanding Instructor by Wva State Legis, 89. **MEMBERSHIPS** AAUP; AHA. **RESEARCH** Tudor England; history of United Methodist Church in West Virginia; Sen Jennings Randolph, 02-98. **SELECTED PUBLICATIONS** Auth, Condensation in Bootstraps, Salem Col Mag, Fall 73; ed, Bicentennial Historical Directory of West Virginia United Methodist Churches, WVa United Methodist, 5/76 & Suppl Article, 10/76; Sir Joh Cheke, Tudor Tutor, 73; Melting Times: A History of West Virginia United Methodism, 84-89. **CONTACT ADDRESS** Dept of Humantities and Soc Sciences, Salem-Teikyo Univ, PO Box 500, Salem, WV, 26426-0500. **EMAIL** Florian@Salem, WVNET.EDU

FLORY, MARLEEN BOUDREAU
PERSONAL Born 01/02/1944, CT, m, 1970 **DISCIPLINE** CLASSICS **EDUCATION** Mount Holyoke Coll, BA, 65; Yale Univ, PhD, 75. **CAREER** Inst, Asst Acad Dean, 70-73, Asst Prof, 70-77, Classics, Mount Holyoke Coll, Classics; Res Fel, 74-75, Sr Assoc Member, 82-83 and 91-92, Amer School of Classical Stud, Athens; Asst Prof, Assoc Prof to Prof, Classic, 78-, Gustavus Alodolophus Coll, Asst Prof, 77-78, Salem Coll, Classics; Andrew W. Mellon Fellow, 85-86, Amer Acad in Rome. **HONORS AND AWARDS** Phi Beta Kappa; Fellow of the Amer Acad. **MEMBERSHIPS** Chair, Classical Association of the Midwest and South; Member of Ed Bd; Consult Evaluator; Executive Bd. **RESEARCH** Roman Society History. **SELECTED PUBLICATIONS** Auth, Octavian's Felicitas, Rheinisches Museum fur Philology, 107, pp 89-112, 94; Deification of Roman Women, Ancient History Bulletin, 95; The Meaning of the Name Augusta in the Julio-Claudian Period, Amer J of Ancient Hist, 97; The Integration of Women in the Roman Triumph, forthcoming in Historia, 98; Review, The Late Roman Army, by P Southern & KR Dixon, in: Religious Studies Review, 98, Atia and Julia and late Republic Political propaganda, CAMWS, 98. **CONTACT ADDRESS** Dept of Classics, Gustavus Adolphus Col, 800 W College Ave, St. Peter, MN, 56082-1498. **EMAIL** mflory@gustavus.edu

FLORY, STEWART GILMAN
PERSONAL Born 10/28/1941, New York, NY, m, 1970 **DISCIPLINE** CLASSICAL LANGUAGES & LITERATURES **EDUCATION** Yale Univ, BA, 64, MA, 67, MPhil, 68, PhD(classics), 69. **CAREER** Asst prof classics, Amherst Col, 69-77; Chmn Dept Classics, Gustavus Adolphus Col, 79-, Am Sch Class Studies fel, Athens, 74-75 & sr assoc, 82-83; Nat Endowment for Humanities fel, Rome, summer, 80 & foreign col teachers, 82-83. **MEMBERSHIPS** Am Philol Asn; Archaeol Inst Am. **RESEARCH** Herodotus; Homer; Plato. **SELECTED PUBLICATIONS** Auth, The Personality of Herodotus, Arion, 69; Laughter, tears and wisdom in Herodotus, Am J Philol, 78; Medea's right hand, Tapa, 78; Who read Herodotus' histories, Am J Philol, Vol 101. **CONTACT ADDRESS** 800 W College Ave, Saint Peter, MN, 56082-1498. **EMAIL** sflory@gac.edu

FLOYD, EDWIN DOUGLAS
PERSONAL Born 05/19/1938, Prescott, AZ, m, 1967, 4 children **DISCIPLINE** CLASSICS **EDUCATION** Yale Univ, BA, 58; Princeton Univ, MA, 60, PhD (classics), 65. **CAREER** Instr ancient lang, Col William and Mary, 62-66; asst prof, 66-72, ASSOC PROF CLASSICS, UNIV PITTSBURGH, 72-. **MEMBERSHIPS** Am Philol Asn; Archaeol Inst Am; Ling Soc Am; Am Oriental Soc. **RESEARCH** Greek poetry; Greek historical linguistics; Sanskrit poetry. **SELECTED PUBLICATIONS** Auth, Homeric Epios Friendly and Vedic Api Friend, Glotta Zeitschrift Griechische Lateinische Sprache, Vol 71, 93; Bacchylides 18.31 and Indo European Poetics, J Indo Europ Stud, Vol 20, 92; Homer Iliad, Book 1, Line 191, Explicator, Vol 53, 95. **CONTACT ADDRESS** Dept of Classics, Univ of Pittsburgh, 207 Hillman Libr, Pittsburgh, PA, 15260-0001.

FLOYD, SAMUEL ALEXANDER
PERSONAL Born 02/01/1937, Tallahassee, FL, m, 1956, 3 children **DISCIPLINE** MUSIC EDUCATION **EDUCATION** Florida A&M Univ, BS, 57; Southern Ill Univ, MME, 65, PhD, 69. **CAREER** Instr, Fla A&M Univ, 62-64; instr/assoc prof, Music, South Ill Univ, Carbondale, 65-78; dir, Inst Res Black Am Music, Fisk Univ, 78-83; DIR, CENTER BLACK MUSIC RES, COLUMBIA COLL, 83-. **MEMBERSHIPS** Coll Music Soc; A, Musicol Soc; Sonneck Soc Am Music **RESEARCH** Music in Black Diaspora. **SELECTED PUBLICATIONS** "Eileen JacksonSouthern: Quiet Revolutionary," New Perspectives on Music: Essays in Honor of Eileen Southern, Harmonie Park Press, 92; "Troping the Blues: From Spirituals to the Concert Hall," Black Music Res Jour, 93; The Power of Black Music, Oxford Univ Press, 95. **CONTACT ADDRESS** Center Black Music Res, Columbia Col, Illinois, 600 S Mich Ave, Chicago, IL, 60605. **EMAIL** sfloyd@popmail.colum.edu

FLUSCHE, DELLA M.
PERSONAL Born 03/02/1936, Muenster, TX **DISCIPLINE** HISTORY **EDUCATION** North Tex State Univ, BA, 56; Marquette Univ, MA, 61; Loyola Univ, Chicago, PhD(hist), 69. **CAREER** Assoc prof, 68-79, prof Hist & Philos, Eastern Mich Univ, 79-; asst prof, 68-73; assoc prof 73-78; prof 78-98; retired 98. **MEMBERSHIPS** Conf Latin Am Hist. **RESEARCH** Colonial Spanish America. **SELECTED PUBLICATIONS** Auth, City councilmen and the Church in seventeenth century Chile, Rec Am Cath Hist Soc Philadelphia, 9/70; The Cabildo and

public health in seventeenth century Santiago Chile, Americas, 10/72; Dowry and Inheritance in Colonial Spanish America: Peninsular Law and Chilean Practice, co-authored with Eugene H Korth, The Americas: A Quarterly Review of Inter-American Cultural History, 87; Marriage and the Family in the Chilean Civil Code of 1855, Locus: Regional and Local History of the Americas, spring, 96. **CONTACT ADDRESS** Dept of History, Eastern Michigan Univ, 701 Pray Harrold, Ypsilanti, MI, 48197-2201. **EMAIL** HIS-Flusche@online.emich.edu

FLYNN, GEORGE QUITMAN

PERSONAL Born 02/12/1937, New Orleans, LA, m, 1960, 3 children **DISCIPLINE** RECENT AMERICAN HISTORY **EDUCATION** Loyola Univ, La, BS, 60; La State Univ, MA, 62, PhD(Hist), 66. **CAREER** Asst prof Hist, Seattle Univ, 66-69; vis assoc prof, Ind Univ, Bloomington, 69-71; assoc prof, Univ Miami, 71-73; assoc prof, 73-75, prof Hist, Tex Tech Univ, 75-. **MEMBERSHIPS** Orgn Am Historians. **RESEARCH** The New Deal and Franklin Delanor Roosevelt; home front World War II; General Lewis B Hershey of selective service system. **SELECTED PUBLICATIONS** Auth, American Catholics and the Roosevelt Presidency, 1932-1936, Univ Ky, 68; Franklin Roosevelt and the Vatican, Cath Hist Rev, 7/72; History and the social sciences, Hist Teacher, 5/74; Roosevelt and Romanism: Catholics and American Diplomacy, 1937-1945, Greenwood, 76; The Mess in Washington: Manpower Mobilization in World War II, Greenwood, 79; Lewis B Hershey, Mr Selective Service, North Carolina, 85; The Draft, 1940-1973, UP of Kansas, 93; Conscription and Equity in Western Democracies, 1940-1975, Journal of Contemporary History, Jan, 98. **CONTACT ADDRESS** Dept of History, Texas Tech Univ, Lubbock, TX, 79409-0001. **EMAIL** ffadq@ttacs.ttu.edu

FLYNN, JAMES THOMAS

PERSONAL Born 04/11/1932, Norwood, MA, m, 1956, 3 children **DISCIPLINE** MODERN EUROPEAN HISTORY **EDUCATION** Boston Col, AB, 54, AM, 55; Clark Univ, PhD (hist), 64. **CAREER** From instr to assoc prof, 60-72, chmn dept, 68-70, PROF HIST, COL OF THE HOLY CROSS, 72-, Assoc, Russ Res Ctr, Harvard Univ, 70-. **MEMBERSHIPS** AHA; Am Cath Hist Asn; Am Asn Advan Slavic Studies. **RESEARCH** Russian higher education; Russian bureaucracy. **SELECTED PUBLICATIONS** Auth, Protestantism and Politics in Eastern Europe and Russia,The Communist and Postcommunist Eras, Slavonic East Europ Rev, Vol 73, 95; A History of the Russian Church, Vol 2, Slavonic East Europ Rev, Vol 71, 93; Alexander I, Russ Rev, Vol 54, 95; Students, Professors, and the State in Czarist Russia, Russ Rev, Vol 52, 93; Missio Moscovitica--The Role of the Jesuits in the Westernization of Russia, 1582-1689, Cath Hist Rev, Vol 83, 97; The American Cath Historical Association Spring Meeting, Cath Hist Rev, Vol 80, 94. **CONTACT ADDRESS** Dept of Hist, Col of the Holy Cross, 1 College St, Worcester, MA, 01610-2322.

FLYNT, WAYNE

PERSONAL Born 10/04/1940, Pontotoc, MS, m, 1961, 2 children **DISCIPLINE** HISTORY **EDUCATION** Howard Col (now Samford Univ), AB, 61; Florida State Univ, MS, 62, PhD, 65. **CAREER** Prof Hist, Samford Univ, 65-77; Head Hist Dept, Auburn Univ, 77-85; Hollifield Prof of So Hist, Auburn Univ, 82-90; Distinguished Prof, Auburn Univ, 90-. **HONORS AND AWARDS** Woodrow Wilson; NDEA; Ford Fellowships; Lillian Smith Award, Non fic, 90; James Sulzby Prize, 91,94; Alabamian of the Year, 92; Humanitarian of the Year, Arthr Soc, 94; Samford Univ Alumnus of the Year, 85. **MEMBERSHIPS** Southern Historical Asn; Organization Am Historians. **RESEARCH** Southern, religious history, history of poverty. **SELECTED PUBLICATIONS** Alabama Baptists:Southern Baptists in the Heart of Dixie, Tuscaloosa, Univ Alabama Press, 98; Taking Christianity to China: Alabama Missionaries in the Middle Kingdom, 1850-1950, with co auth, Gerald W Berkly, Tuscaloosa, Univ Alabama Press, 97; Alabama: The Hist of a Deep South State, co auth, Leah Rawls Atkins, William W Rogers, David Ward, Tuscaloosa, Univ Ala Press, 94; Poor But Proud; Alabamas Poor Whites, Tuscaloosa, Univ Ala Press, 89; Mine Mill and Microchip, Woodland Hills, Cal, Windsor Pub, 87. **CONTACT ADDRESS** 1224 Penny Lane, Auburn, AL, 36830.

FOGARTY, ROBERT STEPHEN

PERSONAL Born 08/30/1938, Brooklyn, NY, 2 children **DISCIPLINE** HISTORY **EDUCATION** Fordham Univ, BS, 60; Univ Denver, MA, 62, PhD, 68. **CAREER** Instr Am studies, Mich State Univ, 63-67; assoc prof, 68-80, chair humanities, 79-80, PROF HIST, ANTIOCH COL, 80-; Mich Hist Comn grant, 71-72; consult, Nat Endowment Humanities, 73, Utopian films in Am, 77-; Am Philos Asn grant, 76; ed, Antioch Rev, 77-; Coord Coun Lit Mag Ed fel, 81. **HONORS AND AWARDS** Vis fel, All Souls, Oxford, 87; NYU Humanities Inst, 89; Lloyd Lews Fel Newberry Libr, 94. **MEMBERSHIPS** Orgn Am Historians; Am Studies Asn. **RESEARCH** Reform movements; literary history; communal history. **SELECTED PUBLICATIONS** Auth, A nice piece of change, Antioch Rev, 69; ed, American Utopianism, AHM Publ, 72; ed, American Utopian Adventure (10 vols), Porcupine, 74; contribr, Wirtschaft und gesselschaft im industriezeitalter, Union Verlag Stuttgart, 74; auth, American communes: 1865-1914, Am Studies, 75; Dictionary of Communal History, Greenwood; The Righteous Remnant: The House of David, Kent State Press, 81; All Things New, Univ Chicago Press, 90; Special Love/Special Sex, Syracuse Univ Press, 94. **CONTACT ADDRESS** Dept of Hist, Antioch Col, 795 Livermore St, Yellow Springs, OH, 45387-1607.

FOGEL, JERISE

PERSONAL Born 11/30/1964 **DISCIPLINE** CLASSICS **EDUCATION** Smith Col, AB, 85; Columbia Univ, MA, 87, MPhil, 90, PhD, 94. **CAREER** Vis asst prof, Smith Col, 90; asst prof, Univ Il Urbana-Champaign, 94-97; asst prof, Gettysburg Col, Pa, 97-98; asst prof, Mich St Univ, 98- . **HONORS AND AWARDS** Mellon Fel, 86-91 **MEMBERSHIPS** Amer Philol Assoc; Archaeol Inst of Amer; AAUW; AAUP; Int Soc for Hist of Rhetoric; Lesbian/Gay/Bisexual Classical Caucus. **RESEARCH** Greek & Roman rhetoric; oratory; political theory. **SELECTED PUBLICATIONS** Auth, Order for Payment to a Banker, Business Letter, Columbia Papyri, 97; Clientela System, Papian-Poppacan Law(Lex Papia-Poppaea, Pax romana, Roman Republic, of The Historical Encyclopedia of world Slavery, 97; Formalized speech in twentieth-century Madagascar and the Late Republic, in Retorica, Politica e Ideologia: Desde la Antiguedad hasta nuestros dias, Salamanca, Spain, 98; Cicero, On Friendship, translation, Copley Publ Co, forthcoming. **CONTACT ADDRESS** Dept of Romance & Classical Lang, Michigan State Univ, East Lansing, MI, 48824. **EMAIL** fogelj@pilot.msu.edu

FOGELSON, ROBERT M.

PERSONAL Born 05/19/1937, New York, NY **DISCIPLINE** URBAN STUDIES, HISTORY **EDUCATION** Columbia Univ, AB, 58; Harvard Univ, AM, 59, PhD, 64. **CAREER** Asst prof hist, Columbia Univ, 64-68; assoc prof, 68-76, prof urban studies & hist, MA Inst Technol, 76, Consult, Pres Comn Law Endorcement & Admin Justice 66; Soc Sci Res Coun fac res grant, 66-67 & legal & govt processes fel, 70-71; consult, Rand Corp, 67-68; mem rev comt, Ctr Metrop & Regional Ment Health Studies, Nat Inst Ment Health, 67-68; consult, Nat Adv Comn Civil Disorders, 68-69 & Urban Inst, 70; Guggenheim fel, 73-74. **RESEARCH** Am urban hist. **SELECTED PUBLICATIONS** Auth, The Fragmented Metropolis: Los Angeles, 1850-1930, Harvard Univ, 67; Los Angeles, 1850-1930, Harvard Univ, 67; White on Black: A Critique of the McCone Commission Report on the Los Angeles Riots, 9/67 & From Resentment to Confrontation: The Police, the Negroes, and the Outbreak of the 1960's riots, 6/68, Polit Sci Quart; coauth, Who Riots: A Study of Participation in the 1967 Riots, US Govt Printing Off, 68; auth, Violence and Grievances: Reflections on the 1960's Riots, J Social Issues, 70; Violence as Protest: A Study of Riots and Ghettos, Doubleday, 71; Big City Police, Harvard Univ, 77; The Morass: An Essay on the Public Employee Pension Problem, Social History and Social Policy, Acad Press, 81; America's Armories: Architecture, Society, and Public Order, Harvard univ press, 89. **CONTACT ADDRESS** Dept of Urban Studies, 77 Massachusetts Ave, Cambridge, MA, 02139-4307.

FOGLEMAN, AARON S.

DISCIPLINE HISTORY **EDUCATION** Okla State Univ, BA; Albert-Ludwigs-Univ, Freiburg, Ger, MA; Univ Mich, PhD. **CAREER** Assoc prof & grad coordr Hist dept, Univ South Al. **RESEARCH** Early america, immigration, religion. **SELECTED PUBLICATIONS** Auth, Hopeful Journeys: German Immigration, Settlement, and Political Culture in Colonial America, 1717-1775, Philadelphia: Univ Pa Press, 96; The Transformation of Immigration into the US during the Era of the American Revolution, J Amer Hist, 98; Moravian Immigration and Settlement in British North America, 1734-1775, Transactions of the Moravian Hist Soc, 29, 96; Immigration, German Immigration, and Eighteenth Century America, in Emigration and Settlement Patterns of German Communities in North America, Indianapolis: Max Kade Ger Amer Ctr, 95 & Women on the Trail in Colonial America: A Travel Journal of German Moravians Migrating from Pennsylvania to North Carolina in 1766, Pa Hist 61, 94. **CONTACT ADDRESS** Dept of History, Univ South Alabama, 344 Humanities, Mobile, AL, 36688-0002. **EMAIL** afoglema@jaguar1.usouthal.edu

FOLDA, JAROSLAV

PERSONAL Born 07/25/1940, Baltimore, MD, m, 1964, 2 children **DISCIPLINE** HISTORY OF ART **EDUCATION** Princeton Univ, AB, 62; Johns Hopkins Univ, PhD, 68. **CAREER** From instr to prof, 68-96, chemn, 83-87, N Ferebee Taylor prof, 96-, Univ NC. **HONORS AND AWARDS** Fulbright Grant, 66-67, Paris France; Younger Humanist Fel, 74-75, Fel, 81-82, Nat Endowment Hum; John Simmon Guggenheim Fel, 88-89; Fel, 95, Univ NC; vis scholar, 95, J. Paul Getty Museum. **MEMBERSHIPS** Medieval Acad Am; Soc francaise d'archeologie; Am Soc Oriental Res; Col Art Asn Am; US Nat Committee Byzantine Stud; Soc Stud Crusades and Latin East. **RESEARCH** Medieval art; iconography; manuscript illumination; art of the crusaders. **SELECTED PUBLICATIONS** Auth, Crusader Manuscript Illumination at Saint-Jean d'Acre: 1275-1291, 76; auth, The Nazareth Capitals and the Crusader Shrine of the Annunciation, 86; auth, The Art of the Crusaders in the Holy Land, 1098-1187, 95; auth, art, Paris, Bibl. Nat., MS lat. 5334 and the Origins of the Hospitaller Master, 97; auth, art, The South Transept Facade of the Church of the Holy Sepulchre in Jerusalem: As Aspect of Rebuilding Zion, 98. **CONTACT ADDRESS** Univ N. Carolina, Chapel Hill, 715 Gimghoul Rd, Chapel Hill, NC, 27514. **EMAIL** jfolda@email.unc.edu

FOLDA III, JAROSLAV T.

PERSONAL Born 07/25/1940, Baltimore, MD, m, 1964, 2 children **DISCIPLINE** ART HISTORY **EDUCATION** Princeton Univ, AB, 62; Johns Hopkins Univ, PhD, 68. **CAREER** Instr, Dept of Art, 68, Asst Prof, 68-72, Assoc Prof, 72-78, Prof, 78-96, Ch Dept of Art, 83-87, N. Ferebee Taylor Prof of Hist of Art, 96-, Univ NC. **HONORS AND AWARDS** Tanner Award for Undergrad Tchng, UNC, 94; Post-baccalaureate Tchng Award, UNC, 98; Younger Humanist Fellow, NEH, 74-75; Fellow for Ind Study & Res, NEH, 81-82; Guggenheim Memorial Fellow, 88-89; Fellow, Ins for the Arts & Hum, UNC, 95; Vis Schol, J Paul Getty Mus, 95; Fellow for Univ Tchrs, NEH, 98-99. **MEMBERSHIPS** Am Soc of Oriental Res; Brit Sch of Archaeol in Jerusalem; Byzantine Stud Conf; Col Art Asn of Am; Medieval Acad of Am; Societe francaise d'archeologie; Soc for the Stud of the Crusades and the Latin E; US Nat Cmte for Byzantine Stud. **RESEARCH** History of Medieval art. **SELECTED PUBLICATIONS** Auth, The Art of the Crusaders in the Holy Land, 1098-1187, Cambridge Univ Press, 95; auth, The Kahn and Mellon Madonnas: Icon or Altarpiece?, Byzantine East, Latin West: Art-Historical Studies in Honor of Kurt Weitzman, Princeton Univ Press, 501-510, 95; auth, The Crusader Period and the Church of St Anne at Sephoris, Sepphoris & Galilee, NC Mus of Art, 100-107, 96; auth, Paris, Bibl. Nat, MS lat 5334 and the Origins of the Hospitaller Master, Montjoie: Studies in Crusade History in Honor of Hans Eberhard Mayer, Variorium, 177-187, 97; auth, The South Transept Facade of the Church of the Holy Sepulchre in Jerusalem: As Aspect of rebuilding Zion, The Crusades and Their Sources: Studies Presented to Bernard Hamilton, Ashgate, 197-218, 98. **CONTACT ADDRESS** Dept of Art, Univ N. Carolina at Chapel Hill, 111 Hanes Art Ctr, Chapel Hill, NC, 27599-3405. **EMAIL** jfolda@email.unc.edu

FOLEY, MARY BRIANT

PERSONAL Born 09/07/1921, Kansasville, WI **DISCIPLINE** AMERICAN HISTORY **EDUCATION** Mt Mary Col, BA, 50; DePaul Univ, MA, 62; Loyola Univ, Ill, PhD, 68. **CAREER** From instr to assoc prof, 66-77, prof hist, Mt Mary Col, 77-, chmn dept Hist & Polit Sci, 77-95; pres, Sch Sisters of Notre Dame, Mequon Prov, 71-75. **MEMBERSHIPS** AHA; Orgn Am Historians. **RESEARCH** United States history, Revolutionary period. **CONTACT ADDRESS** Dept of Hist, Mount Mary Col, 2900 N Menomonee Riv, Milwaukee, WI, 53222-4597. **EMAIL** foleym@mtmary.edu

FOLEY, NEIL

DISCIPLINE AMERICAN CULTURE **EDUCATION** Univ Va, BA; Georgetown Univ, MA, Univ Mich, MA, PhD, 90. **CAREER** Instr, Geo Washington Univ, 75-77; instr, Univ Md, 78-84; res asst, Univ Mich, 87-90; Martin Luther King, Jr/Cesar Chavez/Rosa Parks fel, Univ Mich, 90-91; asst prof, 91-96, assoc dir, Ctr Mexican Am Stud, 96-97, ASSOC PROF, HIST, 97-, UNIV TEXAS, AUSTIN; consult dir, Ctr Mexican Am Studies, 97-98, Univ Tex, Arlington. **CONTACT ADDRESS** Dept of History, Univ of Texas, Austin, TX, 78712-1163. **EMAIL** nfoley@mail.utexas.edu

FOLEY, WILLIAM EDWARD

PERSONAL Born 09/20/1938, Kansas City, MO, m, 1967, 2 children **DISCIPLINE** UNITED STATES HISTORY **EDUCATION** Cent Mo State Univ, BS, 60, MA, 63; Univ Mo, PhD (hist), 67. **CAREER** Asst instr hist, Univ Mo, 63-66; from asst prof to assoc prof, 66-73, PROF HIST, CENT MO STATE UNIV, 73-. **HONORS AND AWARDS** Award of Merit, Am Asn State and Local Hist, 74. **RESEARCH** Missouri territorial history; early national period in United States history; history of the American West. **SELECTED PUBLICATIONS** Auth, Fremont, John Charles--Character as Destiny, Pac Northwest Quart, Vol 84, 93. **CONTACT ADDRESS** Dept of Hist, Central Missouri State Univ, Warrensburg, MO, 64093-8888.

FOLLICK, EDWIN D.

PERSONAL Born 02/04/1935, Glendale, CA, m, 1986 **DISCIPLINE** SOCIOLOGY, RELIGION **EDUCATION** Calif State Univ Los Angeles, BA, 56, MA, 61; Pepperdine Univ, MA, 57, MPA, 77; St Andrews Theol Col, PhD, 58, DTheol, 58; Univ S Calif, MS, 63, MEd, 64, AdvMEd, 69; Blackstone Law, LLB, 66, JD, 67; Cleveland Chiropractic Col, Los Angeles, DC, 72; Academia Theatina, PhD, 78; Antioch Univ, Los Angeles, MA, 90. **CAREER** Instr, Libr Admin, Los Angeles City Sch, 57-68; law libr, Glendale Univ Col of Law, 68-69; col librn, 69-74, dir of educ & admis, 74-84, prof of jurisprudence, 75-, dean student aff, 76-92, dean of educ, 89-, Cleveland Chiropractic Col Los Angeles Campus; assoc prof, Newport Univ, 82; extern prof theology, St Andrews Theol Col, London, 61. **HONORS AND AWARDS** Undergraduate honors in educ & svc & leadership; three sabbatical leaves which included grants to visit the Soviet Union & China twice. **MEMBERSHIPS** ALA; NEA; Amer Assoc Law Librns; Amer Chiropractic Assoc; Int Chiropractors

Assoc; Int Platform Assoc; Phi Delta Kappa, Sigma Chi Psi; Delta Tau Alpha. **RESEARCH** Sociological & religious implications of health. **SELECTED PUBLICATIONS** Auth, The Law and Chiropractic: Administrative Discretion-A Concluding Summary, Part 7, Chiropractic Education: A Management Analysis of Professional Study for the 1990s, Part 1-4, Digest of Chiropractic Economics, 80-92. **CONTACT ADDRESS** 6435 Jumilla Ave, Woodland Hills, CA, 91367.

FOLMAR, JOHN KENT
PERSONAL Foley, AL **DISCIPLINE** UNITED STATES HISTORY **EDUCATION** Stanford Univ, AB, 55; Birmingham-Southern Col, MA, 61; Univ Ala, PhD (hist), 68. **CAREER** Teacher pub sch, Ala, 59-61; instr US hist, Univ Mil Sch, Ala, 61-63; instr, Univ Ala, 65-66; asst prof, Morehead State Univ, 66-69; chmn hist sect, Dept Soc Sci, 71-76, chmn, Dept Hist, 76-78, chmn, Dept Hist and Urban Affairs, 78-79, PROF HIST, CALIFORNIA STATE COL, PA, 69-, DIR, PROJ ADULT COL EDUC, 80-. **HONORS AND AWARDS** Commonwealth distinguished fac award, Asn Pa State Col and Univ Fac, 78. **MEMBERSHIPS** Southern Hist Asn; Orgn Am Hists. **RESEARCH** Civil War and Reconstruction, quantification; local and family history; Southern history. **SELECTED PUBLICATIONS** Auth, Common Labor--Workers and the Digging of North American Canals, 1780-1860, J Southern Hist, Vol 61, 95; The Sinking of the Uss Cairo, Civil War Hist, Vol 42, 96. **CONTACT ADDRESS** Dept of Hist and Urban Affairs, California Univ of Pennsylvania, 250 University Ave, California, PA, 15419-1394.

FOLSOM, LOWELL EDWIN
PERSONAL Born 09/30/1947, Pittsburgh, PA, m, 1969, 1 child **DISCIPLINE** ENGLISH, AMERICAN STUDIES **EDUCATION** Ohio Wesleyan Univ, BA, 69; Univ Rochester, MA, 72, PhD(English), 76. **CAREER** Instr humanities, Eastman Sch Music, 74-75; vis asst prof English, State Univ NY, Geneseo, 75-76; asst prof, 76-81, assoc prof , 81-87, prof English & Am Studies, 87-, ed, Walt Whitman Qtly Rev, 83-, co-dir, Walt Whitman Hypertext Archive, 97-. **HONORS AND AWARDS** Director, NEH Summer Seminar, 84; Collaborative Research Award, NEH, 91-94; Univ Rochester Distinguished Scholar Medal, 95; Iowa Regents Award for Faculty Excellence, 96; Fullbright Senior Professorship, Germany, 96; F. Wendell Miller Distinguished Professorship, 97-. **MEMBERSHIPS** MLA; Midwest MLA; Am Lit Asn; Whitman Studies Asn. **RESEARCH** American poetry and culture; Walt Whitman; contemporary American literature. **SELECTED PUBLICATIONS** Ed, Walt Whitman: The Measure of His Song, Holy Cow! Press, 81, second ed, 98; Choice Best Academic Book, 82; Regions of Memory: Uncollected Prose of W.S. Merwin, Univ of Il Press, 87; W.S. Merwin: Essays on the Poetry, Univ of Il Press, 87; Walt Whitman: The Centennial Essays, Univ of Iowa Press, 94; Walt Whitman and the World, Univ of Iowa Press, 95; Major Authors: Walt Whitman, CD-ROM, Primary Source Media, 97.Auth, Walt Whitman's Native Representations, Cambridge UP, 94; Choice Best Academic Book, 95. **CONTACT ADDRESS** Dept of English, Univ of Iowa, 308 English Phil Bld, Iowa City, IA, 52242-1492. **EMAIL** ed-folsom@uiowa.edu

FOLTZ, RICHARD
PERSONAL Born 04/19/1961, Columbus, OH, m, 1994, 1 child **DISCIPLINE** HISTORY AND MIDDLE EASTERN STUDIES **EDUCATION** Univ Utah, BA, 87, MA, 88; Harvard Univ, PhD, 96. **CAREER** Visiting Asst Prof, Brown Univ, 96-97; Asst Prof, Gettysburg Coll, 97-98; Visiting Asst Prof, Columbia Univ, 98-99 **MEMBERSHIPS** Amer. Hist. Assoc; Amer Acad Religion; Iranian Sudies Assoc; Assoc Asian Studies **RESEARCH** Cultural history of central and south Asia; history of religion; religion and ecology **SELECTED PUBLICATIONS** Conversations with Emperor Jahangir, Mazda Publishers, Costa Mesa, 98; Mughal India and Central Asia, Oxford Univ Press, Karachi, 98; Religions of the Silk Route, St. Martins Press, NY, 99. **CONTACT ADDRESS** Dept of Religion, Columbia Univ, 613 Kent Hall, New York, NY, 10027. **EMAIL** rcf23@columbia.edu

FONER, ERIC
PERSONAL Born 02/07/1943, New York, NY, m, 1980, 1 child **DISCIPLINE** AMERICAN HISTORY **EDUCATION** Columbia Univ, BA, 63, PhD, 69; Oxford Univ, BA, 65. **CAREER** From instr to assoc prof hist, Columbia Univ, 69-73; prof hist, City Col New York, 73-82; prof hist, Columbia Univ, 82-, Vis prof, Princeton Univ, 76-77; vis prof, Univ SC, 78; vis prof, Univ Calif, Berkeley, 79; Pitt prof Am hist and insts, Cambridge Univ, 80-81; dir, Nat Endowment for the Humanities Summer Sem, 80 & 82; Harmsworth Prof Am Hist, Oxford Univ, 93-94. **HONORS AND AWARDS** Los Angeles Times Book Award, 89; Bancroft Prize, 89; Owsley Prize, 89; Parkman Prize, 89; Great Teacher Award, Columbia Univ, 91; Schol of the Year, NY Coun for the Humanities, 95. **MEMBERSHIPS** Am Hist Asn; Southern Hist Asn; Orgn Am Historians (pres, 93-94). **RESEARCH** Civil War period; history of American radicalism; black history. **SELECTED PUBLICATIONS** Auth, Free Soil, Free Labor, Free Men: The Ideology of the Republican Party Before the Civil War, Oxford Univ, 70; ed, America's Black Past, Harper, 70; Nat Turner, Prentice-Hall, 71; auth, Tom Paine and Revolutionary America, 76 & Politics and Ideology in the Age of the Civil War, 81, Oxford Univ; Nothing But Freedom, 83; Reconstruction: America's Unfinished Revolution, 88; Freedom's Lawmakers, 93; The Story of American Freedom, 98. **CONTACT ADDRESS** Columbia Univ, Box 16, Fayerweather, New York, NY, 10027-6900. **EMAIL** ef17@columbia.edu

FONER, ERIC
DISCIPLINE UNITED STATES HISTORY **EDUCATION** Columbia Univ, BA, 63, PhD, 69. **CAREER** DeWitt Clinton prof. **SELECTED PUBLICATIONS** Auth, Politics and Ideology in the Age of the Civil War, 80; Nothing But Freedom: Emancipation and Its Legacy, 83; Reconstruction: America's Unfinished Revolution 1863-1877, 88; Freedom's Lawmakers: A Directory of Black Officeholders During Reconstruction, 93. **CONTACT ADDRESS** Dept of History, Columbia Col, New York, 2960 Broadway, New York, NY, 10027-6902.

FONTANA, BERNARD LEE
PERSONAL Born 01/07/1931, Oakland, CA, m, 1954, 3 children **DISCIPLINE** AMERICAN INDIAN AND SPANISH COLONIAL HISTORY **EDUCATION** Univ Calif, Berkeley, AB, 53; Univ Ariz, PhD (anthrop), 60. **CAREER** Field hist, Univ Ariz Libr, 59-61, ETHNOLOGIST, ARIZ STATE MUS and LECTR ANTHROP, UNIV ARIZ, 62-, FIELD HIST LIBR, 78-, Consult, Papago Indian Tribe, 62-64; mem, Western Regional Adv Comt, Nat Park Serv, 74-78; bd mem, Southwest Parks and Monuments Asn, 79-. **HONORS AND AWARDS** Border Regional Libr Asn Book Award, 79 and 81. **MEMBERSHIPS** Am Soc Ethnohist (pres, 65); Soc Hist Archaeol (pres, 70); Am Ethnol Soc; Soc Post-Medieval Archaeol; Southwestern Mission Res Ctr (pres, 67-). **RESEARCH** Southwestern American Indian ethnology; southwestern colonial history and historical archaeology; contemporary American Indian studies. **SELECTED PUBLICATIONS** Auth, Kelemen, Pal 1894-1993, Hisp Am Hist Rev, Vol 73, 93; Reminiscences, J Southwest, Vol 38, 96; Sharing the Desert--The Tohono Oodham in History, Ethnohistory, Vol 43, 96; Archaeology of the Ak Chin Indian Community West Side Farms Project, Public Hist, Vol 15, 93; Arizona--A History, Ethnohistory, Vol 43, 96; Plants Without Water Ezell, Paul 1974 Manuscript Relating to Arizona and the Sonoran Desert, J Southwest, Vol 36, 94. **CONTACT ADDRESS** Libr, Univ of Arizona, Tucson, AZ, 85721.

FONTIJN, CLAIRE
PERSONAL Born 03/23/1960, Montreal, PQ, Canada **DISCIPLINE** MUSIC, FRENCH, BAROQUE FLUTE, MUSICOLOGY **EDUCATION** Oberlin Col, BA, 82; Royal Conserv of the Hague, cert, 85; Duke Univ, MA, 89, PhD 94. **CAREER** Asst Prof Music, Dir Collegium Musicum, 94-, Wellesley Col. **HONORS AND AWARDS** Prize winner, Case Western Res Univ Baroque Mus Comp, 89; Gladys Krieble Delmas Grant, Venice, 94; Woodrow Wilson Nat Fellow Found Women's Stud Award, 92. **MEMBERSHIPS** Am Musicol Soc; Soc 17th Cent Mus; Int Assoc of Women in Mus; Heinrich Schuetz Soc. **RESEARCH** Baroque Music; Baroque Flute; Women in Music; Women in Baroque Music. **SELECTED PUBLICATIONS** Bembo, Antonia, entry in The Norton/Grove Dict of Women Composers, London, Macmillan, 94; Quantz's 'unegal': implications for the performance of 18th-century music, Early Mus, Feb 95, 55-62; In Honour of the Duchess of Burgundy: Antonia Bembo's Compositions for Marie-Adelaide of Savoy, Cahiers de l'IRHMES, 3, 95, 45-89; Antonia Bembo, in Women Composers: Music Through the Ages, New York, G.K. Hall, 96, 201-16. **CONTACT ADDRESS** Wellesley Col, 106 Central St., Dept. of M, Wellesley, MA, 02481. **EMAIL** cfontijn@wellesley.edu

FOOS, PAUL W.
DISCIPLINE HISTORY **EDUCATION** Univ Mass, BA, 91; Yale Univ, PhD, 97. **CAREER** Author **MEMBERSHIPS** Am Antiquarian Soc **RESEARCH** Mexican Wars, 1835-1853 **CONTACT ADDRESS** 107 Foster St, New Haven, CT, 06511. **EMAIL** paul.foos@yale.edu

FORAGE, PAUL C.
DISCIPLINE HISTORY **EDUCATION** Univ Toronto, PhD. **CAREER** Asst prof. **RESEARCH** Imperial China; Asian frontier history; history of science and technology; military history. **SELECTED PUBLICATIONS** Auth, pubs in Asian history journals. **CONTACT ADDRESS** History Dept, Florida Atlantic Univ, 777 Glades Rd, Boca Raton, FL, 33431. **EMAIL** pforage@fau.edu

FORBES, GERALDINE MAY
PERSONAL Born 01/07/1943, Edmonton, AB, Canada **DISCIPLINE** ASIAN HISTORY **EDUCATION** Univ Alta, BEd, 65; Univ Ill, AM, 68, PhD(hist), 72. **CAREER** Teacher hist, Kings County High Sch, 64-66; asst prof, 71-76, assoc prof Hist, SUNY Oswego, 76-81; prof hist, 81-98; Distinguished Teaching Prof, 98; Dir Women's Studies, SUNY Oswego, 85-. **HONORS AND AWARDS** Rabindra Puraskar (Rabindranath Prize), 79. **MEMBERSHIPS** Asian Studies Asn; National Women's Studies Asn. **RESEARCH** Colonial and Postcolonial Indian History, Gender and Women's Roles. **SELECTED PUBLICATIONS** Auth, Positivism in Bengal: A Case Study in the Transmission and Assimilation of an Ideology (Book selected for the Rabindra Puraskar, awarded by the gov of West Bengal in 1979), Calcutta, Minerva, 75; ed, A Pattern of Life: the Memoirs of an Indian Woman, by Shudha Mazumdar, New Delhi, Manohar, 77; ed and intro, Shudha Mazumdar, Memoirs of an Indian Woman (revised ed of A Pattern of Life), NY, M.E. Sharpe, 89; ed and intro, Manmohini Zutshi Sahgal, An Indian Freedom Fighter Recalls Her Life, NY, M.E. Sharpe, 94; auth, Women in Modern India, New Cambridge History of India series, Cambridge Univ Press, 96; An Historian's Perspective: Indian Women and the Freedom Movement, RCWS Gender Series, S.N.D.T. Women's Univ, Bombay, 97. **CONTACT ADDRESS** Dept of Hist, State Univ of NY Oswego, 431 Mahar, Oswego, NY, 13126-3599. **EMAIL** forbes@oswego.edu

FORBES, JOHN DOUGLAS
PERSONAL Born 04/09/1910, San Francisco, CA, m, 1980, 3 children **DISCIPLINE** ECONOMIC AND ARCHITECTURAL HISTORY **EDUCATION** Univ CA, AB, 31; Stanford Univ, AM, 32; Harvard Univ, AM & PhD(hist), 37. **CAREER** Curator paintings, San Francisco World's Fair, 38-40; chmn dept fine arts, Univ Kansas City, 40-42; mem fac hist, Bennington Col, 43-46; from assoc prof to prof hist & fine arts, Wabash Col, 46-54; prof, 54-80, EMER PROF BUS HIST, GRAD SCH BUS ADMIN, UNIV VA, 80-, Assoc ed, Am Enterprise Asn, 45-46; adv ed, Encycl Britannica, 56-58; mem adv bd, Hist Am Bldg Survey, US Dept Interior, 73-79. **HONORS AND AWARDS** Officier, Ordre des Palmes Academiques (France); Cavaliere, Ordine al Merito (Italy); Phi Beta Kappa. **MEMBERSHIPS** AHA; Soc Archit Hist (secy, 52, vpres, 60-61, pres, 62-63); hon mem Am Inst Archit; AAUP; Col Art Asn Am. **RESEARCH** Economic, political and architectural history. **SELECTED PUBLICATIONS** Auth, Victorian Architect, Ind Univ, 53; Israel Thorndike, Beverly, Mass Hist Soc, 53; Murder in Full View, Caravelle Bks, 68; Death Warmed Over, Pageant, 71; Stettinius, Sr, Portrait of a Morgan Partner, Univ Va, 74; J P Morgon, Jr, 1864-1944, Univ Va, 81; Death Among the Artists, Book Guild, 93. **CONTACT ADDRESS** Box 3607, Charlottesville, VA, 22903.

FORD, ANDREW
PERSONAL New York, NY, m, 2 children **DISCIPLINE** CLASSICS **EDUCATION** Cornell Univ, BA, 74; Yale Univ, PhD, 81. **CAREER** Instr, Smith Col, 80-85; fel, Cornell Univ, 85-87; asst/assoc prof, Princeton Univ, 87-. **HONORS AND AWARDS** NEH fel. **MEMBERSHIPS** Am Philol Asn. **RESEARCH** Classics. **CONTACT ADDRESS** 75 Dryads Green, Northampton, MA, 01060. **EMAIL** aford@princeton.edu

FORD, FRANKLIN LEWIS
PERSONAL Born 12/26/1920, Waukegan, IL, m, 1944, 2 children **DISCIPLINE** HISTORY **EDUCATION** Univ Minn, AB, 42; Harvard Univ, AM, 48, PhD, 50; Suffolk Univ, LHD, 72. **CAREER** Mem fac, Bennington Col, 49-52; from asst prof to prof, 53-68, dean fac arts and sci, 62-70, MCLEAN PROF ANCIENT and MOD HIST, HARVARD UNIV, 68-, Fulbright fel, France, 52-53; Guggenheim fel, Ger, 55-56; fel, Ctr Advan Studies Behav Sci, 61-62; trustee, Bennington Col, 62-72; fel, Inst Advan Studies, 74. **MEMBERSHIPS** Am Philos Soc. **RESEARCH** Modern Germany; early modern Europe; history of political assassination. **SELECTED PUBLICATIONS** Auth, Communities and Conflict in Modern Colmar 1575-1730, Central Europ Hist, Vol 29, 96. **CONTACT ADDRESS** Widener Libr Harvard Univ, Cambridge, MA, 02138.

FORD, PETER ANTHONY
PERSONAL Born 07/11/1934, Providence, RI, m, 1991, 3 children **DISCIPLINE** MEDIEVAL HISTORY **EDUCATION** Providence Col, BA, 56; Univ Notre Dame, MA, 58, MMedieval Stud, 59, DMedieval Stud, 64. **CAREER** From instr to asst prof hist, Tex A&M Univ, 60-65; assoc prof, 65-72, chmn dept, 71-73, actg dean humanities, 78-79, prof history, Merrimack Col 72-, Fulbright scholar, Paris, 59-60. **HONORS AND AWARDS** Tex A&M Univ Arts Sci Coun Award Outstanding Tchr, 63; Edward G Roddy Award Outstanding Teaching, Merrimack Col, 86. **RESEARCH** History of medieval universities; medieval intellectual history; American industrial history. **SELECTED PUBLICATIONS** Auth, The Medieval Account Books of the Parisian College of Dainville, Manuscripta, 11/65; John de Martigny, Principal and Benefactor of the College of Burgundy, In: Studium Generale: Studies Offered to A L Gabriel, Medieval Inst, Univ Notre Dame, 67; An American in Paris: Charles S Storrow and the 1830 Revolution, Proc Mass Hist Soc, 92; Charles S Storrow, Civil Engineer: A Case Study of European Training and Technological Transfer in the Antebellum Period, Technol and Cult, 93. **CONTACT ADDRESS** Dept of History, Merrimack Col, 315 Turnpike St, North Andover, MA, 01845-5800.

FORDE, GERHARD OLAF
PERSONAL Born 09/10/1927, Starbuck, MN, 3 children **DISCIPLINE** CHURCH HISTORY, SYSTEMATIC THEOLOGY **EDUCATION** Luther Col, BA, 50; Luther Theol Sem, BTh, 55; Harvard Divinity Sch, ThD, 67; Oxford Univ, MA, 68. **CAREER** Instr relig, St Olaf Col, 55-56; lectr church hist, Lu-

ther Theol Sem, 59-61; asst prof relig, Luther Col, 61-63; assoc prof church hist, 64-71, Prof Syst Theol, Luther Theol Sem, 71-, Lutheran World Fed lectr, Mansfield Col, Oxford Univ, 68-70; Frederick A Schiotz fel, 72-73. **MEMBERSHIPS** Am Acad Relig. **RESEARCH** Theology of Martin Luther; 19th century theology. **SELECTED PUBLICATIONS** Auth, The Law-Gospel Debate, 69, Where God Meets Man, 72 & coauth, Free To Be, 75, Augsburg; Justification By Faith: A Matter of Death & Life, 82; Theology is for Proclamation, 90; On Being a Theologian of the Cross, 97. **CONTACT ADDRESS** Luther Sem, 2481 Como Ave, St. Paul, MN, 55108-1445. **EMAIL** gfonde@luthersem.edu

FORDERHASE, RUDOLPH EUGENE
PERSONAL Born 01/13/1934, Boonville, MO, m, 1963, 3 children **DISCIPLINE** MIDDLE PERIOD AMERICAN HISTORY **EDUCATION** Univ Mo, AB, 55, MA, 59, PhD, 68. **CAREER** Instr hist, Trenton Jr Col, 59-61 & Univ Mo, St Louis, 64-66; from asst prof to assoc prof, 66-73, prof hist, Eastern Ky Univ, 73-. **MEMBERSHIPS** Orgn Am Historians; Am Studies Asn; Southern Hist Asn. **RESEARCH** Jacksonian democracy; Civil War and Reconstruction. **CONTACT ADDRESS** Dept of History, Eastern Kentucky Univ, 521 Lancaster Ave, Richmond, KY, 40475-3102.

FORDHAM, MONROE
PERSONAL Born 10/11/1939, Parrott, GA, m, 1961, 3 children **DISCIPLINE** HISTORY **EDUCATION** Emporia Kans State Univ, BS, 62, MA, 66; State Univ NY, Buffalo, PhD (hist), 73. **CAREER** Soc studies teacher hist and current issues, Wichita Kans Pub Schs, 62-69; coord Afro-Am studies, Wichita State Univ, 69-70; asst prof, 70-78, ASSOC PROF HIST, STATE UNIV NY COL, BUFFALO, 78-, State Univ NY res fel, 75; ed, Afro-Am in NY Life and Hist: Interdisciplinary J, 76-. **MEMBERSHIPS** Asn Study Afro-Am Life and Hist; African Heritage Studies Asn. **RESEARCH** Afro-American history; Afro-Americans in New York State. **SELECTED PUBLICATIONS** Auth, Between 2 Worlds--African American Identity and American Culture, Public Hist, Vol 17, 95. **CONTACT ADDRESS** Dept of Hist, State Univ NY Col, Buffalo, 1300 Elmwood Ave, Buffalo, NY, 14222-1095.

FOREMAN, GEORGE
DISCIPLINE HUMANITIES AND MUSIC HISTORY **EDUCATION** Univ NMex, BA and MA; Univ Kan, PhD. **CAREER** Dir Bowlus Fine Arts Ctr, Iola Kan, 75; fac, Centre Col, 83-; manage dir, Jane Morton Norton Ctr Arts, present; assoc prof, Hum, present. **HONORS AND AWARDS** Bruce Montgomery Leadership award, 96., Formed and directs the Advocate Brass Band, fdr, Gt Am Brass Band Festival, 90, Danville. **RESEARCH** C. L. Barnhouse; American band history. **SELECTED PUBLICATIONS** Auth, pubs and articles on music history. **CONTACT ADDRESS** Centre Col, 600 W Walnut St, Danville, KY, 40422. **EMAIL** foreman@centre.edu

FORGIE, GEORGE BARNARD
PERSONAL Born 05/31/1941, Philadelphia, PA **DISCIPLINE** AMERICAN HISTORY **EDUCATION** Amherst Col, BA, 63; Stanford Univ, LLB & MA, 67, PhD(Hist), 72. **CAREER** Lectr Am Hist, Princeton Univ, 69-72, asst prof, 72-74; asst prof, 74-80, assoc prof Am Hist, Univ Tex, Austin, 80-. **HONORS AND AWARDS** Allan Nevins Prize, Soc Am Historians, 73. **RESEARCH** American history, 1820-1880. **SELECTED PUBLICATIONS** Auth, Patricide in the House Divided: A Psychological Interpretation of Lincoln and His Age, Norton, 79. **CONTACT ADDRESS** Dept of History, Univ of Texas, Austin, TX, 78712-1163. **EMAIL** forgie@mail.utexas.edu

FORMAN, MARY
PERSONAL Born 09/07/1947, Boise, ID **DISCIPLINE** MEDIEVAL STUDIES **EDUCATION** Idaho St Univ, BS, 70; St. John's Univ, Minn, MA, 82, MA, 88; Univ Toronto, Ctr for Medieval Stud, PhD, 95. **CAREER** Adj fac, Grad Sch of Theol, 90, Saint John's Univ; scholar in res, 96-, Benedictine Spirituality Ctr, Sacred Heart Monastery; adj fac, 97-, theol dept, Univ of Mary. **MEMBERSHIPS** Am Benedictine Acad; Fed of St Gertrude; St Benedict Ctr, Madison, Wis; AAR; ABA; NAPS; Am Pharmaceutical Asn. **RESEARCH** Early monasticism; medieval monastic women; hist of healing and med; early church hist; hist of Christian spirituality; Christian mysticism. **SELECTED PUBLICATIONS** Auth, Scripture and the Rule of Benedict as Sources of Benedictine Spirituality, Am Benedictine Rev, 39, 88; auth, Three Songs About St. Scholastica by Aldhelm and Paul the Deacon, transl, Vox Benedictina, 7, 90; auth, Syncletica: A Spirituality of Experience, Vox Benedictina, 10, 93; auth, Sapere--Tasting the Wisdom of the Monastic Tradition: The Biblical and Patristic Roots of Discerning, Benedictines, 49:1, 96; Ed & Transl, co-auth, Latin Cenobitic Rules of the West: 400-700, Am Benedictine Rev, 48:1, 97; auth, Gertrud of Helfta's Herald of Divine Love: Revelations Through Lectio Divina, Magistra 3.2, 97; auth, Desert Ammas: Midwives of Wisdom, Vetus Doctrina: Stud in Early Christianity in Honor of Fredric W. Schlatter, SJ, Peter Lang Pub, forthcoming; auth, Purity of Heart in the Life and Words of Amma Syncletica, Purity of Heart in Early Ascetical Literature: Essays in Honor of Juana Raasch OSB, Lit Press, 98. **CONTACT ADDRESS** Sacred Heart Monastery, PO Box 364, Richarton, ND, 58652-0364. **EMAIL** maryforman@hotmail.com

FORMAN, MICHAEL LAWRENCE
PERSONAL Born 06/30/1940, Kansas City, MO, m, 1963, 4 children **DISCIPLINE** LIMGUISTICS, ANTHROPOLOGY **EDUCATION** John Carroll Univ, AB, 61; Cornell Univ, PhD, 72. **CAREER** Asst researcher, Pac & Asian Ling Inst, 68-69, acting asst prof, 69-72, asst prof, 72-73, chmn Southeast Asian studies, 77-80, Assoc Prof Ling, Univ Hawaii, Manoa, 73-, Second Language Acquisition faculty; assoc ed, Oceanic Ling; co-ed, The Carrier Pidgeon, 93-96; contribr, Biography: An Interdisciplinary Quart. **HONORS AND AWARDS** Nat Endowment for Humanities study fel, 74-75; Soc Sci Res Inst, 80-82, 93-95; Excellence in Teaching Award, Univ Hawaii Board of Regents, 84, Univ Hawaii Col Lang, Ling, & Lit, 84; Robert W. Clapton Award for Distinguished Community Service, 86. **MEMBERSHIPS** Am Anthrop Asn; Ling Soc Am; Ling Soc Philippines. **RESEARCH** Child language acquisition; pidginization and creolization; Philippine descriptive linguistics. **SELECTED PUBLICATIONS** Auth Kapampangan Grammar Notes, 71 & Kapampangan Dictionary, 71, Univ Hawaii; coauth, Riddles: Expressive models of interrogation, Ethnology, Vol X , Nov 4 & In: Directions in Sociolinguistic Holt, 72; ed, World Englishes 2000, Univ Hawaii Press, 97. **CONTACT ADDRESS** Dept of Ling, Univ of Hawaii Manoa, 1890 E West Rd, Honolulu, HI, 96822-2318. **EMAIL** forman@hawaii.edu

FORMAN, P.
PERSONAL Born 03/22/1937, Philadelphia, PA, d **DISCIPLINE** HISTORY OF SCIENCE **EDUCATION** Reed Col, BA 55-59; Northwestern Univ, grad stud, 59-60; Univ Caifl Berkeley, MA 62, PhD 67. **CAREER** Univ Rochester, asst prof, 67-72; Univ Calif Berk, vis fel, 72-73; Smithsonian Inst NMAH, mod phys curator, 72-; Princeton Univ, vis prof, 87; NY Univ, vis schl, 88-90; Hist Stud Physical Bio Sci, assoc editor, 80-. **HONORS AND AWARDS** APS Fel; AAAS Fel. **MEMBERSHIPS** AHA; HSS; SHT; SSSS; AAAS; APS. **RESEARCH** History of Physics and its social relations in the 20th century; historiography of science. **SELECTED PUBLICATIONS** Auth, Molecular Beam Measurements of nuclear moments before magnetic resonance: II Rabbi and deflecting magnets to 1938, Annals of Science, 98; Recent Science: Late modern and Post modern, in: Thomas Soderqvist, ed, The historiography of contemporary science and technology, London and Chur, Harwood Acad Pub, 97; Into quantum electronics: the maser as gadget of Cold War America, P. Forman, JM Sanchezon, eds, National Military establishments and the advancement of science and technology: studies in 20th century history, Dordrecht, Kluwer Acad Pub, 96; Swords into Ploughshares: breaking new ground with radar hardware and technique in physical research after World War II, Rev of Modern Physics, 95. **CONTACT ADDRESS** MRC-631, Smithsonian Institute, Washington, DC, 20560. **EMAIL** formanp@nmah.si.edu

FORMAN CRANE, ELAINE
DISCIPLINE AMERICAN CONSTITUTIONAL HISTORY **EDUCATION** Univ NY, PhD. **CAREER** Prof, Fordham Univ. **RESEARCH** Domestic violence in Early Am. **SELECTED PUBLICATIONS** Auth, Dependent People: Revolutionary Era, Fordham UP, 85; ed, The Diary of Elizabeth Drinker, 3 volumes, Northeastern UP, 91; I Have Suffer'd Much Today: The Social Dynamics of Pain in Early America, Through a Glass Darkly: Reflections on Personal Identity in Early America, Univ NC Press. **CONTACT ADDRESS** Dept of Hist, Fordham Univ, 113 W 60th St, New York, NY, 10023.

FORMISANO, RONALD P.
DISCIPLINE HISTORY **EDUCATION** Brown Univ, BA, 60; Univ Wis, MA, 62; Wayne State Univ, PhD, 66. **CAREER** Assoc prof, hist, Clark; current, PROF, HIST, UNIV FLA. **HONORS AND AWARDS** Fulbright, Pol Sci, Univ Bologna, 94. **MEMBERSHIPS** Am Antiquarian Soc **RESEARCH** US politics; political culture; social movements. **SELECTED PUBLICATIONS** Auth, The Transformation of Political Culture: Massachusetts Parties, 1790s-1840s, Oxford Univ Press, 83; co-ed, Boston 1700-1980: The Evolution of Urban Politics, Greenwood Press, 84; auth, The Birth of Mass Political Parties, Michigan, 1827-1861, Princeton Univ Press; auth, Toward a Reorientation of 'Jacksonian Politics,': A Review of the Literature, 1959-1974, Jour Am Hist 63, 76; auth, Boston Against Busing: Race, Class, and Ethnicity in the 1960s and 1970s, Univ NC PRess, 91; auth, The Great Lobster War, Univ Mass Press, 97. **CONTACT ADDRESS** Dept of Hist, Univ of Fla, Gainesville, FL, 32601.

FORMWALT, LEE W.
PERSONAL Born 12/19/1949, Springfield, MA, m, 1972, 3 children **DISCIPLINE** HISTORY **EDUCATION** Catholic Univ Am, BA 71; Univ Mass, MA 72; Catholic Univ Am, PhD, 77. **CAREER** Albany State Col, asst prof hist, 77-82, assoc prof 82-88, prof hist 88-, dean grad school, 97-. **HONORS AND AWARDS** NEH; Res of the year; Hist teacher of the year. **MEMBERSHIPS** AHA; SHA; Org Am Histns; Georgia Asn Histns. **RESEARCH** Southern hist; Georgia Hist; African Am Hist. **SELECTED PUBLICATIONS** African American Persistence and Mobility in Postemancipation Southwest Georgia, Georgia Hist Quartly, forthcoming 98; Documenting the Origins of African American Politics in Southwest Georgia, J SW GA Hist, 93; several publications. **CONTACT ADDRESS** The Graduate School, Albany State Univ, Albany, GA, 31705. **EMAIL** lformwal@asurams.edu

FORNARA, CHARLES WILLIAM
PERSONAL Born 11/19/1935, New York, NY **DISCIPLINE** CLASSICS **EDUCATION** Columbia Col, AB 56; Univ Chicago, AM, 58; Univ Calif, Los Angeles, PhD, 61. **CAREER** Instr classics, Ohio State Univ, 61-63; from asst prof to prof, 63-77, Prof Class and Hist, Brown Univ, 77-. **MEMBERSHIPS** Am Philol Asn; Am Hist Asn; Am Asn Ancient Hists; Soc Promotion of Hellenic Studies. **RESEARCH** Greek history; epigraphy and historiography; late antiquity. **SELECTED PUBLICATIONS** Auth, Diodorus Siculus and the 1st Century, Classic Philol, Vol 87, 92; Studies in Ammianus Marcellinus .2. Ammianus Knowledge and Use of Greek and Latin Literature, Hist Zeitschrift Alte Geschichte, Vol 41, 92; Studies in Ammianus Marcellinus .2. Ammianus Knowledge and Use of Greek And Latin Literature, Historia Zeitschrift Alte Geschichte, Vol 41, 92. **CONTACT ADDRESS** Dept of Classics, Brown Univ, 1 Prospect St, Providence, RI, 02912-9127.

FORREST, LARRY W.
PERSONAL Born 05/10/1957, Washington, DC, s **DISCIPLINE** ART HISTORY **EDUCATION** Univ of Louisville, BA, 80, MA, 83; Ind Univ, PhD, 91. **CAREER** PROF OF ART HIST, SAVANNAH COL OF ART AND DESIGN, 90-. **HONORS AND AWARDS** Gennadeion Fel, Am School of Classical Studies of Athens, 86-87. **MEMBERSHIPS** CAA; AIA; Dunbarton Oaks. **RESEARCH** Byzantine architecture; Greek archaeology. **CONTACT ADDRESS** Savannah Col of Art and Design, 212 W Taylor St, PO Box 3146, Savannah, GA, 31402-3146. **EMAIL** lforrest@scad.edu

FORREST-CARTER, AUDREY FAYE
PERSONAL Born 04/01/1956, Greenwood, South Carolina, m, 1983 **DISCIPLINE** EDUCATION **EDUCATION** Bennett Coll, BA 1978; NC A&T State Univ, MA 1979; Miami Univ, PhD 1990. **CAREER** A&T State Univ, teaching asst 1978-79; Winston-Salem State Univ, instructor 1979-84, asst prof 1990-91; Miami Univ, doctoral assoc 1984-88; North Carolina A&T State University, assistant professor of English, 1992-96; Courtesy Kids, owner, currently. **HONORS AND AWARDS** Publ poem Worn Out 1982; DAP Awd Miami Univ 1984-88; Faculty Develop Grant Winston-Salem State Univ 1984-88; Silver Poet Awd World of Poetry 1986; Board of Governor's Grant, Univ of North Carolina at Chapel Hill, 1988-89, 1989-90. **MEMBERSHIPS** Mem NCTE, 1992-; CLA, 1994-; Communities-in-Schools, partner, 1994-; grad comm English dept Miami Univ 1984-85; mem rsch team computers & composition Miami Univ 1985; General Greene Elementary, PTA, bd mem.

FORSCHER WEISS, SUSAN
DISCIPLINE MUSIC HISTORY **EDUCATION** Goucher Col, BA; Smith Col, MA; Univ MD, PhD. **CAREER** Prof, John Hopkins Univ. **HONORS AND AWARDS** Epsilon Musicol Res Awd. **MEMBERSHIPS** Am Musicol Soc. **SELECTED PUBLICATIONS** Auth, pubs for Am and International Musicological Societies. **CONTACT ADDRESS** Dept of Musicology, Johns Hopkins Univ, 1 E Mt Vernon Pl, Baltimore, MD, 21202-2397.

FORSE, JAMES HARRY
PERSONAL Born 01/26/1940, Binghamton, NY, m, 1961, 3 children **DISCIPLINE** MEDIEVAL HISTORY **EDUCATION** State Univ NY, Albany, BA, 62; Univ Ill, MA, 63, PhD (hist), 67. **CAREER** Asst prof, 66-76, ASSOC PROF HIST, BOWLING GREEN STATE UNIV, 76-. **MEMBERSHIPS** Cath Hist Asn; Mediaeval Acad Am. **SELECTED PUBLICATIONS** Auth, The Complete Works of Rather of Verona, Cath Hist Rev, Vol 81, 95; An Echo of Henry IV, Part 2, In a Work by James I, Anq Quart J Short Articles Notes Rev, Vol 8, 95. **CONTACT ADDRESS** Dept of Hist, Bowling Green State Univ, 1001 E Wooster St, Bowling Green, OH, 43403-0001.

FORSLUND, CATHERINE
PERSONAL Born 10/17/1955, Evanston, IL, m, 1984 **DISCIPLINE** HISTORY **EDUCATION** WA Univ, MA, 93, PhD, 97; Univ of IL, BA, 77 **CAREER** Asst Prof, 97-, Col Misericordia; Adj Faculty, 93-96; St Louis Univ **HONORS AND AWARDS** Mellon Travel/Diss Fel, 94-95; Moody Res Grant, 94 **MEMBERSHIPS** Am Hist Asn; Orgn of Am Hist **RESEARCH** Am diplom hist **SELECTED PUBLICATIONS** Auth, Woman of Two Worlds: Anna Chennault and Informal Diplomacy in US-Asian Relations, 1950-1990, WA Univ, Ann Arbor, MI: Univ Microfilms, 97 **CONTACT ADDRESS** Dept of History, Col Misericordia, Dallas, PA, 18612-1098. **EMAIL** cforslun@miseri.edu

FORSTER, MARC R.
DISCIPLINE HISTORY **EDUCATION** Swarthmore Col, BA; Harvard Univ, MA, PhD. **CAREER** Assoc prof; Conn Col, 90-; past vis prof, Ecole des Hautes Etudes en Sci Sociales, Paris; taught, For Lang Across Curric. **HONORS AND AWARDS** Conn Col Meredith prize, 93; Alexander von Humboldt Stiftung grant; Fulbright-Hays grant; Nat Endowment for the Humanities fel, 94; bk prize, Cent Europ Conf Gp of the AHA, 94. **RESEARCH** Early modern European history; German history; religion and society in early modern Germany. **SELECTED PUBLICATIONS** Auth, The Counter Revolution in the Villages. **CONTACT ADDRESS** Dept of History, Connecticut Col, 270 Mohegan Ave, Box 5497, New London, CT, 06320. **EMAIL** mrfor@conncoll.edu

FORSTER, ROBERT
PERSONAL Born 06/07/1926, New York, NY, m, 1955 **DISCIPLINE** HISTORY **EDUCATION** Swarthmore Col, BA, 49; Harvard Univ, MA, 51; Johns Hopkins Univ, PhD (hist), 56. **CAREER** From asst prof to assoc prof hist, Univ Nebr, 58-62; assoc prof mod Europ hist, Dartmouth Col, 62-65; assoc prof, 65-66, PROF MOD EUROP HIST, JOHNS HOPKINS UNIV, 66-, Gustav Bissing res fel, France, 57-58; Soc Sci Res Coun res grant, France, 62 and 64; John Simon Guggenheim res fel, France, 69-70; fel, Inst Advan Study, Princeton, 75-76; US deleg, Int Cong Hist Sci, 75-80; fel, Ctr Advan Study Behav Sci, Stanford, 79-80. **HONORS AND AWARDS** Citoyen d'Honneur, Commune of Vieillevigne, France, 78. **MEMBERSHIPS** AHA; Fr Hist Soc; Fr Col Hist. **RESEARCH** European social history; analyses of social groups in France and in the 18th century, revolutions in 18th century; slavery in French Caribbean. **SELECTED PUBLICATIONS** Auth, 2 Dreams of Commerce--Business and Institution in Lilli 1780-1860 - French, J Interdisciplinary Hist, Vol 24, 93; Being a Patriot in the Tropics, Guadeloupe, Colonization and Revolution 1789-1794, J Caribbean Hist, Vol 25, 91; Revolutionary France--1770-1880, J Interdisciplinary Hist, Vol 25, 94; The Farmers of Ile De France--Ascension of the Tenant Farmers 15th-18th Centuries, J Interdisciplinary Hist, Vol 26, 96; The Fruits of Revolution--Property Rights, Litigation, and French Agriculture, 1700-1860, Am Hist Rev, Vol 98, 93; The Making of Haiti, The Saint Domingue Revolution from Below, J Caribbean Hist, Vol 27, 93; Blood and Belief--Family Survival and Confessional Identity Among the Provincial Huguenot Nobility, Am Hist Rev, Vol 100, 95; A Filleting Knife for Michael, Meanjin, Vol 55, 96; At the Time of the Sugar Islands, History of a Sugar Plantation in Saint Domingue During the 18th Century, J Caribbean History, Vol 25, 91; Recovery Unit Flap 2021, Meanjin, Vol 55, 96; An Historical Geography of France, J Interdisciplinary Hist, Vol 26, 96; From Renaissance Monarchy to Absolute Monarchy, J Mod Hist, Vol 68, 96; History of the French Colonization, Vol 1, The 1st Colonial Empire from its Origins to the Restauration, J Caribbean Hist, Vol 27, 93; ed, Sugar and Slaves, Family and Race, Batterman, 96; ed, European, Non-European Societies, 1450- 1800, Ahgate Pub, 97. **CONTACT ADDRESS** Dept of Hist, Johns Hopkins Univ, Baltimore, MD, 21218.

FORSTER-HAHN, FRANCOISE
DISCIPLINE NINETEENTH AND TWENTIETH-CENTURY ART HISTORY **EDUCATION** Univ Bonn, PhD. **HONORS AND AWARDS** Fel, Alexander von Humboldt Found. **SELECTED PUBLICATIONS** Ed, Imagining Modern German Culture 1889-1910, Nat Gallery of Art, Wash DC, 96. **CONTACT ADDRESS** Dept of Art Hist, Univ Calif, 1156 Hinderaker Hall, Riverside, CA, 92521-0209.

FORSYTH, PHYLLIS
PERSONAL Brookline, MA **DISCIPLINE** CLASSICAL STUDIES/HISTORY/FINE ART **EDUCATION** Mount Holyoke Col, BA, 66; Univ Toronto, MA, 67, PhD, 72. **CAREER** Tchr Fel, Univ Toronto, 67-69: PROF, UNIV WATERLOO 69-, founding ch, dept class studs, 79-88, acting ch 94-. **HONORS AND AWARDS** Distinguished Tchr Awd. **MEMBERSHIPS** Ont Class Asn; Can Fedn Hum; Archeol Inst Am; Can Mediter Inst. **RESEARCH** Latin literature; Aegean Bronze Age; effect of natural disasters on the ancient world. **SELECTED PUBLICATIONS** Auth, Atlantis: The Making of Myth, 80; ed, Labyrinth: A Classical Magazine for Secondary Schs, 73-84, 88-94. **CONTACT ADDRESS** Dept of Classical Studies, Univ Waterloo, 200 University Ave W, Waterloo, ON, N2L 3G1. **EMAIL** forsyth@watarts.uwaterloo.ca

FORTE, ALLEN
PERSONAL Born 12/23/1926, Portland, OR, m, 1950 **DISCIPLINE** THEORY OF MUSIC **EDUCATION** Columbia Univ, BS, 50, MA, 52. **CAREER** Instr music, Columbia Teachers Col, 54-59; instr music theory, Mannes Col Music, 57-59; from instr to assoc prof, Yale Univ, 59-67; prof music, Mass Inst Technol, 67-68; PROF MUSIC, YALE UNIV, 68-, DIR GRAD STUDIES MUSIC, 70-, Ed, J Music Theory, 60-67; Am Coun Learned Soc fel, 65-66; mem proj comt, Contemporary Music Proj, 65-68; mem comt info technol, Am Coun Learned Soc, 69-. **HONORS AND AWARDS** MA, Yale Univ, 68. **MEMBERSHIPS** Col Music Soc; Am Musicol Soc. **RESEARCH** Structure of tonal music; 18th and 19th century music theory; contemporary music and music theory. **SELECTED PUBLICATIONS** Auth, An Octatonic Essay by Webern, Op.9 No.1 of the Six Bagatelles for String Quartet, Mus Theory Spectrum, Vol 16, 94; Mani, the Buddha of Light--A Chinese Manichaean Catechism, Asian Folklore Stud, Vol 51, 92; An Ancient Chinese Monastery Excavated in Kirgiziya Vol 38, Pg 43, Yr 1994, Central Asiatic J, Vol 38, 94; Communications, Mus Theory Spectrum, Vol 15, 93, Concepts of Linearity in Schoenberg Atonal Music--A Study of the Opus 15 Song Cycle, J Mus Theory, Vol 36, 92; Kuwabara Misleading Thesis on Bukhara and the Family Name An, J Am Oriental Soc, Vol 116, 96; An Ancient Chinese Monastery Excavated in Kirgiziya, Central Asiatic J, Vol 38, 94; Secrets of Melody--Line and Design in the Songs of Porter, Cole, Mus Quart, Vol 77, 93. **CONTACT ADDRESS** Dept of Music, Yale Univ, P O Box 208310, New Haven, CT, 06520-8310.

FORTENBAUGH, WILLIAM WALL
PERSONAL Born 07/10/1936, Philadelphia, PA, m, 1959, 3 children **DISCIPLINE** CLASSICS **EDUCATION** Princeton Univ, BA, 58; Oxford Univ, BA, 61; Univ PA, PhD(classics), 64. **CAREER** From instr to asst prof, 64-68, assoc prof, 68-80, prof I, classics, 79-91, prof II, Rutgers Univ, 91-; Ctr Hellenic Studies jr fel, 67-68; Am Coun Learned Soc study fel & hon res fel, Univ Col, London, 72-73; vis prof, Univ WA, spring 87; res fel, Netherlands Inst for advanced study, 90-91; res fel, Alexander von Humboldt-Stiftung, 91-92; Study fel, Bogliasco Found, 99. **HONORS AND AWARDS** Phi Beta Kappa, 58; NEH, summer stipend, 67, project grants, 80-83, 84-85, 88. **MEMBERSHIPS** Am Philol Asn; Soc for Ancient Greek Philos (pres, 76-77, prog comm, 82-98). **RESEARCH** Ancient philosophy. **SELECTED PUBLICATIONS** Auth, Nicomachean Ethics 1096 b26-29, Phronesis, 66; Recent Scholarship on Aristotle's Psychology, Class World, 67; Aristotle on Emotion, Duckworth, London, NY: Barnes & Noble, 74; Quellen zur Ethik Theophrasts, Amsterdam: B R Gruener Verlag, 84; Theophrastus of Eresus: Sources for His Life, Writings, Thought & Influence, 2 vols, ed and trans with P Hughby, R Sharples, & D Gutas, Leiden: E J Brill, 92, reprinted with corrections, 93. **CONTACT ADDRESS** Dept Classics, Rutgers Univ, PO Box 270, New Brunswick, NJ, 08903-0270. **EMAIL** fortenb@rci.rutgers.edu

FORTIER, TED
PERSONAL Born 08/01/1953, Spokane, WA, s **DISCIPLINE** ANTHROPOLOGY **EDUCATION** Washington State Univ, PhD, 95. **CAREER** Res, Dept Natural Resources, 95-97; asst prof, Seattle Univ, 97- . **HONORS AND AWARDS** Mellon fel, 98. **MEMBERSHIPS** Am Acad Relig; Am Anthrop Asn; Soc for Cultural Anthrop. **RESEARCH** Indians of North America; epistemology; culture change; religion. **SELECTED PUBLICATIONS** Auth, Blue Print for Parish Social Ministry, Spokane Diocese, 96; auth, Searching for the Past, Companions, 96; auth, James Schneiders, Coeur d'Alene Council Fires, 97; coauth, Cultural Memory: The Presence of a People, Orbis, 99. **CONTACT ADDRESS** 900 Broadway, Seatle, WA, 98122. **EMAIL** tedf@seattle.edu

FORTIN, MICHEL
PERSONAL Born 03/23/1950, Baie-Comeau, PQ, Canada, 3 children **DISCIPLINE** ARCHAEOLOGY **EDUCATION** Univ of London (England), PhD, 81. **CAREER** Prof adjoint, 81-86; Prof Agrege, 86-91; Prof litulaire, 91-, Univ Laval. **MEMBERSHIPS** Amer Inst of Archaelogy; Amer Schools of Oriental Research **RESEARCH** Near Eastern Archaeology **SELECTED PUBLICATIONS** Auth, Geomorphology Tell'Atij, Northern Syria', Geoarchaelogy, 94; Canadian Excavations at Tell Gudeda (Syria) 92-93, Bulletin of the Canadian Society for Mesopotamian Studies, 94; Canadian Excavations at Tell Atij (Syria) 92-93, Bulletin for the Canadian Society for Meopotamian Studies, 94; On the Fringe of Urbanization in Northern Mesopotamia (3000-2500 B.C.), Debating Complexity, Proceedings of the 26th Annual Chacmool Conference, 96; New Horizons in Ancient Syria, A view from Atij, New Eastern Archaelogy, 98. **CONTACT ADDRESS** Dept of History, Universite Laval, Sainte-Foy, PQ, G1K 7P4. **EMAIL** michel.fortin@hst.ulaval.ca

FORTUNE, GWENDOLINE Y.
PERSONAL Houston, Texas, d **DISCIPLINE** ETHNIC STUDIES **EDUCATION** JC Smith Univ, BS 1948; SC State Coll, MS 1951; Roosevelt Univ, MPh 1972; Nova Univ, EdD 1979. **CAREER** Chicago Public Schools, teacher 1954-66; Dist 68 Skokie IL, team coord 1964-70; Oakton Comm Coll, prof ethnic studies coord 1970-84; Consultant "Discovery", dir 1984-. **HONORS AND AWARDS** Intl Black Writers Conference First Place Non-Fiction 1986; non-fiction second place, International Black Writers Conference 1987; poetry reading, Chicago Cultural Center 1988; poem "Tom Cats" Korone, 1988; other poems published in InnerQuest & Prairie St Companion; Honorable Mention, Poetry, 2 poems: Womanspace, Korone, 1989; Outstanding teaching effectiveness, Oakton Community College, 1981-82. **MEMBERSHIPS** Exec bd IL Council for Black Studies 1980-83; exec comm IL Consultation on Ethnicity in Educ 1980-84; manuscript chair, Off-Campus Writers' Workshop, 1990-. **SELECTED PUBLICATIONS** 2 articles, Black Family Magazine 1986.

FOSS, BRIAN
DISCIPLINE CANADIAN ART HISTORY **EDUCATION** Concordia Univ, MA; Univ London, PhD. **CAREER** Dept Art Hist, Concordia Univ **HONORS AND AWARDS** Curator, co-curator, The imagery of urban site, 98; Young Montreal artists, 93; Military views and maps of Lower Canada, 92; The socio-political implications of the work of portraitist Robert Harris (1849-1919), 92; The visual representation of rural Quebec in the 19th and 20th centuries, 91. **RESEARCH** 19th and 20th-century Canadian art, 20th-century British art and patronage. **SELECTED PUBLICATIONS** Pub(s), articles and essays, especially on the intersections between war art, individual identity and national identity in Can and in Britain. **CONTACT ADDRESS** Dept Art Hist, Concordia Univ, Montreal, 1455 de Maisonneuve W, Montreal, PQ, H3G 1M8. **EMAIL** bffoss@alcor.concordia.ca

FOSS, CLIVE
PERSONAL Born 08/30/1939, London, England **DISCIPLINE** BYZANTINE HISTORY, ARCHEOLOGY **EDUCATION** Harvard Univ, AB, 61, AM, 65, PhD (hist and class archaeol), 73. **CAREER** Lectr, 67-78, PROF ANCIENT HIST and CLASSICS, UNIV MASS, BOSTON, 79-, Mem, Am Sch Class Studies, Athens, 61-62; asst prof hist, Boston Col, 68-69; mem, Sardis Excavation, 69-75 and 79-82; vis fel, Dumbarton Oaks Res Ctr, 73-74; assoc, Ephesus Excavations, 73-74; maitre de conf, Univ Lyon II, 77-79; vis prof, Univ SAfrica, 81. **MEMBERSHIPS** Am Inst Archaeol; British Inst Archaeol; Royal Numis Soc; Am Numis Soc. **RESEARCH** Late antique and Byzantine history and archaeology; historical geography; ancient numismatics. **SELECTED PUBLICATIONS** Auth, Dead Cities of the Syrian Hill Country, Archaeol, Vol 49, 96; Aphrodisias in Late Antiquity, J Roman Stud, Vol 82, 92; Anatolia, Land, Men and Gods in Asia Minor, Vol 1, The Celts and the Impact of Roman Rule, Vol 2, The Rise of the Church, J Roman Studies, Vol 85, 95; Female Innocence as Other in the Portrait of a Lady and What Maisie Knew--Reassessing the Feminist Recuperation of James, Henry, Essays in Lit, Vol 22, 95; Rome and India--The Ancient Sea Trade, Am Neptune, Vol 53, 93; Aphrodisias in Late Antiquity, J Roman Stud, Vol 82, 92; Say it With Flowers, Hist Today, Vol 46, 96; Anatolia, Land, Men and Gods in Asia Minor, Vol 1, The Celts and the Impact of Roman Rule, Vol 2, The Rise of the Church, J Roman Stud, Vol 85, 95. **CONTACT ADDRESS** Dept Hist, Univ Mass, 100 Morrissey Blvd, Boston, MA, 02125-3300.

FOSS, D. PEDAR W.
DISCIPLINE CLASSICAL ART AND ARCHAEOLOGY **EDUCATION** Gustavus Adolphus Col, BA, 88; Univ Mich, MA, 91, PhD, 94. **CAREER** Tutor, Gustavus Adolphus Col, 87-88; Tchg Asst, Univ Mich, 92; Vis Asst Prof, Univ Mich, 95; Lecturer, Univ Mich, 95-96; Vis Asst Prof, Univ Cincinnati, 96-97; Adj Asst Prof, Univ Cincinnati, 97- . **HONORS AND AWARDS** Rackham One-Term Dissertation Grant; Rackham Dissertation/Thesis Grant; Mellon Dissertation Grant; Jacob K. Javits Fel; Alworth & Tozer Foundation Sch. **MEMBERSHIPS** Electronic Publ Comt; Archaeol Inst Am; Eta Sigma Phi. **SELECTED PUBLICATIONS** Coauth, A newly-discovered cryptoporticus and bath at Carthage, J of Roman Archaelogy, 93; coauth, The Rieti Surbey 1988-1001, Part II: Land-use patterns and gazetteer, Papers of the British School at Rome, 95; auth, Watchful Lares: Roman household organization and the rituals of cooking and dining, Domestic Space in the Ancient Mediterranean, 97; auth, Digitizing the ancient world: demograhics, resources, and future opportunities, Archaeological News, 97; auth, Cooking and cuisine, DIning rooms, The social ritual of dining, Oplontis, Boscoreale, and Boscotrecase, all in The Cambridge Guide to Classical Civilization, 98. **CONTACT ADDRESS** Dept of Classics, Univ Cincinnati, PO Box 0226, Cincinnati, OH, 45210-0226.

FOSTER, ANNE L.
DISCIPLINE HISTORY **EDUCATION** Am Univ, BA, 87; Cornell Univ, MA, 91; Cornell Univ, PhD, 95. **CAREER** Asst prof, 97-, St Anselm Col. **RESEARCH** Multiple layers of rel--strategic, economic, polit, and cult--between the US and Asia, particularly Southeast Asia; polit, economic, and cult rel(s) among Am(s), Europ(s), and Southeast Asians in 20th century colonial Southeast Asia; comp look at attempts by the Europ colonial governments and the US to control the use of opium in Southeast Asia from the middle of the th to the middle of the 20th century. **SELECTED PUBLICATIONS** Auth, Secret Police Cooperation and the Coming of the Cold War, Jour American-East Asian Relations, 95; French, Dutch, British and U.S. Reactions to the Nghe-Tinh Rebellions of 30-31 in Imperial Policy and Colonial Revolt, Nordic Inst Asian Studies, 95. **CONTACT ADDRESS** St Anselm Col, 100 Saint Anselm Dr, Manchester, NH, 03102-1310. **EMAIL** afoster@anselm.edu

FOSTER, BENJAMIN READ
PERSONAL Born 11/15/1945, Bryn Mawr, PA, m, 1975, 2 children **DISCIPLINE** ASSYRIOLOGY **EDUCATION** Princeton Univ, BA, 68; Yale Univ, MA, MPhil, 74, PhD, 75. **CAREER** Instr Arabic, 73-75, asst prof Assyriol, 75-81, Assoc Prof Assyriol, Yale Univ, 81-86, prof, 86-; chmn dept Near East lang, 89-98. **HONORS AND AWARDS** Amer Res Inst in Turkey fel, 77, 79; Mellan Fel; NEH Translation Grant, 83-84. **MEMBERSHIPS** Am Orient Soc. **RESEARCH** Soc and economic hist of early Mesopotamia; Akkadian lit. **SELECTED PUBLICATIONS** Umma in the Sargonic Period, Memoirs of Conn Acad of Arts & Sci, No 20, 82; Administration and Use of Institutional Land in Sargonic Sumer, Copenhagen Studies in Assyriology, No 9, 82; coauth, Sargonic Tablets from Telloh in the Istanbul Archeological Museum, Babylonian Sect, Univ Mus, Philadelphia, 82; auth, Before the Muses An Anthology of Akkadian Literature, 93; auth, From Distant Days Myths Tales and Poetry of Ancient Mesopotaria, 95; auth, Un Araboen el Neuro Mindo 1668-1683, 89, (Argentina). **CONTACT ADDRESS** Sterling Mem Libr, Rm 318, Yale Univ, PO Box 208236, New Haven, CT, 06520-8236. **EMAIL** benjamin.foster@yale.edu

FOSTER, DOUGLAS A.
PERSONAL Born 08/30/1952, Sheffield, AL, m, 1979, 2 children **DISCIPLINE** RELIGIOUS HISTORY **EDUCATION** David Lipscomb Univ, BA, 74; Harding Grad Sch of Religion, 76; Scarritt Col, MA, 80; Vanderbilt Univ, PhD, 86. **CAREER** Assoc Min, Jackson Park Church of Christ, 74-83; Arch, Gospel Adv Co, 88-91; Retention, Inst, Asst Prof, David Lipscomb Univ, 85-91; Asst Prof, Assoc Prof, Abilene Christian Univ, 91-94. **HONORS AND AWARDS** Outstanding Tchr Awd, College of Bibl Stud, ACU 94; Outstanding Tchr Awd, DLU, 89; Mayhew Fel Vanderbilt Univ, 83-83. **MEMBERSHIPS** Amer Soc of Church History, Amer Acad of Religion, Conf on Faith and History, disciples of Christ Hist Soc, Rel Res Assn, Soc for the Scientific Stud of Rel, Southern Baptist Hist Soc, Southwest Archivists, TN Archivists. **SELECTED PUBLICATIONS** Holding Back the Tide: T.B. Larimore and the Disciples of Christ and Churches of Christ, Discipliana, 93; Will the Cycle Be Unbroken: Churches of Christ Face the Twenty-First Century, ACU, 94; The Many Faces of Christian Unity: Disciples Ecumenism and Schism, 1875-1900, Nashville Disciples for Christ Hist Soc, 95; Millennial Harbinger, Pop Rel Mag of the USA, 95; Rethinking the History of Churches of Christ: Responses to Richard Hughes, Rest Quart, 96; Reflections on the Writing of Will the Cycle Be Unbroken: Churches of Christ Face the Twenty-First Century, Discipliana, 97. **CONTACT ADDRESS** Abilene Christian Univ, ACU 29429, Abilene, TX, 79699-9429. **EMAIL** foster@bible.acu.edu

FOSTER, E.C.
PERSONAL Born 01/04/1939, Canton, Mississippi, m **DISCIPLINE** HISTORY **EDUCATION** Jackson State Univ, BS 1964; Carnegie-Mellon Univ, MA 1967, DA 1970. **CAREER** Natchez Public School, teacher 1964-65; Brushton Inner City Project, community organizer 1965-66; Pittsburgh Public Schools, teacher 1967-68; Jackson MS City Council, pres 1985-94; Jackson State Univ, prof of history 1969-. **HONORS AND AWARDS** Jackson State Univ Alumni Service Awd 1985; Man of the Year Awd Omega Psi Phi 1985; NAEFO Presidential Citation Awd 1986; Dr Martin Luther King Service Awd JSU/SGA 1986. **MEMBERSHIPS** Pres Faculty Senate (JSU) 1974-79; bd mem Farish St YMCA 1976-79; assoc editor Journal of Negro History 1978-; pres Assn of Soc & Behav Scientists 1982; legislative comm chmn Local PTA 1984; city councilman Jackson MS 1985-; member, Chamber of Commerce, 1986-; member, Vicksburg/Jackson Trade Zone Commission, 1987-; MS Municipal Assn, bd of dirs, 1994-; Natl League of Cities Leadership Training Council, vice chair, 1994. **CONTACT ADDRESS** Jackson State Univ, Jackson, MS, 39217.

FOSTER, KAREN POLINGER
PERSONAL Born 10/07/1950, New York, NY, m, 1975, 2 children **DISCIPLINE** ARCHAEOLOGY **EDUCATION** Mt Holyoke Col, AB, 71; Yale Univ, MA, MPhil, 74, PhD, 76. **CAREER** VIS SCHOLAR, YALE, WESLYAN, Am Philos Soc fel, 77 & 81; Ludwig Vogelstein Found grant, 77; Am Coun Learned Soc fel, 78. **MEMBERSHIPS** Archaeol Inst Am; Am Res Ctr Egypt; Col Art Asn. **RESEARCH** Art and archaeology of the Bronze Age Aegean and ancient Near East. **SELECTED PUBLICATIONS** Auth, Aegean Faience of the Bronze Age, Yale Univ, 79; Murioan Ceranne Relief, Studies in Medit Archeol, 82. **CONTACT ADDRESS** PO Box 208236, New Haven, CT, 06520-8236. **EMAIL** karen.foster@yale.edu

FOSTER, MARK STEWART
PERSONAL Born 05/02/1939, Evanston, IL **DISCIPLINE** AMERICAN HISTORY **EDUCATION** Brown Univ, AB, 61; Univ Southern Calif, MA, 68, PhD (hist), 71. **CAREER** Vis asst prof hist, Univ Mo, St Louis, 71-72; asst prof, 72-76, assoc prof, 76-81, PROF HIST, UNIV COLO, DENVER, 81-, Fac fel, Univ Colo, 77-78; grant, Ford Motor Co Fund, 77-78; Eleanor Roosevelt Inst grant, 79. **MEMBERSHIPS** AHA; Orgn Am Hists; Am Soc Baseball Researchers. **RESEARCH** Technology and urban growth; biography; baseball. **SELECTED PUBLICATIONS** Auth, The end of American Exceptionalism--Frontier Anxiety from the Old West to the New Deal, Rev Am Hist, Vol 22, 94; The Motel in America, NMex Hist Rev, Vol 72, 97; Rocky Mountain West--Colorado, Wyoming, and Montana, 1859-1915, Am Hist Rev, Vol 98, 93; Higgins, Andrew, Jackson and the Boats that Won World War II, Am Hist Rev, Vol 100, 95; The American West in the 20th Century--A Bibliography, J West, Vol 35, 96; American Cities and Towns--Historical Perspectives, J Am Hist, Vol 81, 94; The Lost Dream--Businessmen and City Planning on the Pacific Coast 1890-1920, J West, Vol 34, 95; 722 Miles - The Building of the Subways and how they Transformed New-York, Am Hist Rev, Vol 100, 95; Urban Disorder and the Shape of Disbelief--The Great Chicago Fire, The Haymarket Bomb and the Modern Town of Pullman, Mich Hist Rev, Vol 21, 95. **CONTACT ADDRESS** Univ of Colo, 1100 14th St, Denver, CO, 80202.

FOSTER, STEPHEN
PERSONAL Born 03/08/1942, New York, NY, m, 1971, 1 child **DISCIPLINE** EARLY AMERICAN HISTORY **EDUCATION** Univ Pa, BA, 61; Yale Univ, MA, 64, PhD (hist), 66. **CAREER** Asst prof to assoc prof, Northern Ill Univ, 66-93, pres res prot, 93-97, distinguished res prof, 97-; NEH, 68-69 & 79-80; Guggenheim Mem Found fel, 71-72; vis ed, William & Mary Quart, 77-78; Newberry Library - NEH Fel, 86-87. **HONORS AND AWARDS** Theron R Field Prize, Yale Univ, 66; Annual Award Best Article, William & Mary Quart, 74. **MEMBERSHIPS** AHA; Conf Brit Studies. **RESEARCH** American colonial History; Jacobean-Caroline England. **SELECTED PUBLICATIONS** Auth, The Presbyterian Independents Exorcised: A Ghost Story for Historians, Past & Present, 69; Their Solitary Way, The Puritan Social Ethic in the First Century of Settlement in New England, Yale Univ, 71; coauth, The Puritans' Greatest Success: A Study of Social Cohesion in Massachusetts, J Am Hist, 73; Moving to the New World: The Pattern of Early Massachusetts Immigration, 73; Notes From the Caroline Under-Ground, Alexander Leighton, The Puritan Triumvirate and the Laudian Reaction to Nonconformity, Conf Brit Studies & Archon Bks, 78; auth, The Long Argument: English Puritanism and the Shaping of New England Culture, 1570-1700, Inst of Early am Hist and Cult, and Univ of N Ca Press, 91; The Historiography of British North America in the Seventeenth and Eighteenth Centuries, Oxford History of the British Empire, 5:4, 99. **CONTACT ADDRESS** Dept of Hist, No Illinois Univ, 1425 W Lincoln Hwy, De Kalb, IL, 60115-2825. **EMAIL** sfoster@niu.edu

FOSTER, TEREE E.
PERSONAL Born 09/24/1947 **DISCIPLINE** ENGLISH LITERATURE AND HISTORY **EDUCATION** BA, Univ Ill Chicago Cir, 68; JD, Loyola Univ Chicago Sch of Law, 76. **CAREER** Admis off, Univ Ill Chicago Cir, nov 72-sep 73; co-dir, Dept of Defense, sep 69-sep 72; summer law intern, Off of the State Appelate Defender for the Fourth Jud Dist; jun 74-aug 74; law clerk, Philip H. Corboy and Assoc, sep 74-sep 76; instr, Loyola Univ Chic Sch of Law, sep 76-jan 77; jud law clerk, US Ct of Appeals for the Seventh Circuit, sep 76-aug 77; of coun, Hastie & Kirschner, feb 84-sep 90; vis prof, Oh State Univ Col of Law, 87-88, Univ Fla Col of Law, 88-89, Univ Denver Col of Law, 92-93; asst prof, aug 77-jul 80, assoc prof, jul 80-may 83, prof, may 83-, assoc dean, sep 90-aug 92, Univ Okla Col of Law; dean and prof of law, WV Univ Col of Law, 93-97; dean and prof of law, DePaul Univ Col of Law, jul 97-. **HONORS AND AWARDS** Phi Kappa Phi, 97; 1998 Distinguished Women in Law Award, WV Univ Col of Law Women's Law Caucus, Feb 27, 1998; Who's Who in Amer, 97-; Who's Who in Amer Law, 96-; Intl Who's Who in Prof, 96-. **MEMBERSHIPS** State of Ill Bar; State of Okla Bar; Northern Dist of Ill Bar; Western Dist of Okla Bar; US Ct of Appeals for the Seventh Circuit; US Ct of Appeals for the Tenth Circuit; Amer Law Inst; Soc of Amer Law Tchrs; Asn of Amer Law Sch; Scribes; Okla Bar Asn; WV Bar Asn; Ill Bar Asn; Amer Jud Soc. **SELECTED PUBLICATIONS** Contr, Law and Literature: An Annotated Bibliography of Law-related works, ed Elizabeth Villiers Gemmette, 98; auth, I Want to Live! Federal Judicial Values in Death Penalty Cases: Preservation of Rights or Punctuality of Execution?, A Symposium on Film and the Law, 21, Okla City, U.L. Rev, 63-87, 97; with Mayer-Schonberger, A Regulatory Web: Free Speech and the Global Information Infrastructure, ed Brian Kahin & Charles Nesson, MIT Press, 96; with Mayer-Schonberger, More Speech, Less Noise: Amplifying Contect-Based Speech Regulations Through Binding International Law, 43, BC Intl & Comp Law Rev, 59-135, 95; with Fallon, West Virginia's Pioneer Women Lawyers, 97, WV Law Rev, 702-23, 95; with M. D. Pfefferbaum, Child Witnesses in Okla, 88, Jour Okla State Med Asn, 479-86, 95; Beyond Victim Impact Evidence: A Modest Proposal Reprise, 45, Hastings Law Jour, 1305-27, 94. **CONTACT ADDRESS** 851 W. Roscoe, Chicago, IL, 60657. **EMAIL** tfoster@wppost.depaul.edu

FOTTLER, MYRON D.
PERSONAL Born 09/05/1939, Boston, MA, m, 1972 **DISCIPLINE** BUSINESS **EDUCATION** Northeastern Univ, BS, 62; Boston Univ, MBA, 63; Columbia Univ, PhD, 70. **CAREER** Asst Prof, State Univ NY-Buffalo, 70-75; Assoc Prof, Univ Iowa, 75-76; Assoc Prof to Prof, Univ Ala, 76-83; Prof and Dir PhD Prog in Admin - Health Services, Univ Ala-Birmingham, 83-; ed of book series, Adventures in Health Care Management, JAI Press. **HONORS AND AWARDS** Edgar Hayhow Award for Best Paper in Hospital and Health Services Administration. **MEMBERSHIPS** Acad Mgt; Southern Mgt Asn. **RESEARCH** Health care management. **SELECTED PUBLICATIONS** Co-ed, Strategic Management of Human Resources in Health Services Organizations, Delmar Publ, 2nd ed, 94; coauth, Medical Groups Face the Uncertain Future: Challenges, Opportunities, and Strategies, Ctr for Res in Ambulatory Care Admin, 95; Applications in Human Resources Management, SWestern Publ Co, 3rd ed, 96; co-ed, Essentials of Human Resources Management in Health Services Organizations, Delmar Publ, 98; coauth, Strategic Leadership for Medical Groups: Navigating Your Strategic Web, Jossey-Bass, 98; author of numerous other publications and journal articles. **CONTACT ADDRESS** Dept Health Service Admin, Sch of Health Related Professions, Univ Ala - Birmingham, Birmingham, AL, 35294. **EMAIL** mfottler@fms.uab.edu

FOUCHE, RAYVON
DISCIPLINE HISTORY **EDUCATION** Univ Illinois, Urgana-Champaign, BA, 91; Cornell Univ, MA, 94, PhD, 97. **CAREER** Post-doctoral fel, African-Am Stud, Washington Univ, 96-98; asst prof hist and Af-Am Stud, Purdue Univ, 98- . **RESEARCH** African-American studies; science and technology studies; popular culture. **CONTACT ADDRESS** Dept of History, Purdue Univ, 1358 University Hall, West Lafayette, IN, 47904-1358. **EMAIL** fouche@purdue.edu

FOUQUET, PATRICIA ROOT
PERSONAL Born 06/16/1930, Brooklyn, NY, m, 1978, 2 children **DISCIPLINE** MODERN EUROPEAN HISTORY **EDUCATION** Barnard Col, BA, 53; Univ Calif, San Diego, PhD(hist), 72. **CAREER** Lectr hist, San Diego State Univ, 70; instr, Univ Calif, San Diego Extension, 72-73; lectr, Calif State Univ, Long Beach, 73-76; asst prof, Univ Nebr, Lincoln, 77-78; Asst Prof, 78-84, Assoc Prof Hist, Fayetteville State Univ, 84-98, retired, 98-; Assoc hist, Univ Calif, San Diego, 72-73; tour dir, Am Student Travel Asn, 76-78. **HONORS AND AWARDS** Fulbright Summer Seminar, 84, 86, 89, 94; John C. Moore Prize for Excellence in Teaching Humanities, 90; Col Arts & Sci Teacher of the Year, 92; Dept Geog, Hist, and Pol Sci Teacher of the Year, 97. **MEMBERSHIPS** AHA; Western Soc French Hist; West Coast Asn Women Historians (vpres, 73-75, pres, 75-76). **RESEARCH** The nature of prejudice in fascist movements; discrimination against women in the elite sciences. **SELECTED PUBLICATIONS** Coauth (with Joanna V Scott), The 1934 riots and the emergence of French fascism: The case of Jacques Doriot, 76 & auth, Fascism of the left or renegade Marxism?, The Case of Jacques Doriot, 78, Proc of the Western Soc for French Hist. **CONTACT ADDRESS** 624 8th St, Del Mar, CA, 92014. **EMAIL** prootfouq@aol.com

FOWLER, WILLIAM MORGAN
PERSONAL Born 07/25/1944, Clearwater, FL, m, 1968, 2 children **DISCIPLINE** AMERICAN HISTORY **EDUCATION** Northeastern Univ, BA, 67; Univ of Notre Dame, MA, 69, PhD, 71. **CAREER** Asst prof to prof, Northeastern Univ, 71-97; CO-ED, THE NEW ENGLAND QUARTERLY, 81-; DIR, MASS HIST SOC, 98-; **HONORS AND AWARDS** Distinguished Service Award, USS Constitution Museum; Outstanding alumnus, Northeastern Univ. **MEMBERSHIPS** Mass Hist Soc; Colonial Soc of Mass; United States Naval Inst; Pilgrim Soc; New England Hist Gen Soc; honorary member, Boston Marine Soc. **RESEARCH** American naval history; American colonial and rev; history of Boston and New England. **SELECTED PUBLICATIONS** Auth, William Ellery: A Rhode Island Politic and Lord of Admiralty, Scarecrow, 72; auth, Rebels Under Sail: The American Navy in the Revolution, Charles Scribner's Sons, 76; auth, The Baron of Beacon Hill: A Biography of John Hancock, Houghton Mifflin, 80; auth, Jack Tars and Commodores: The American Navy 1783-1815, Houghton Mifflin, 84; auth, Under Two Flags: The American Navy in the Civil War, Norton, 90; auth, Silas Talbot: Captain of Old Ironsides, Mystic Seaport, 95; auth, Samuel Adams Radical Puritan, Longman, 97; coauth, America and the Sea: A Maritime History, Mystic Seaport, 98. **CONTACT ADDRESS** Massachuettts Historical Society, 1154 Boylston St, Boston, MA, 02215. **EMAIL** wfowler@masshist.org

FOX, FRANK
PERSONAL Born 12/20/1923, Lodz, Poland, m, 1946, 2 children **DISCIPLINE** MODERN HISTORY **EDUCATION** Temple Univ, BS, 51; Univ Pa, MA, 52; Univ Del, PhD (hist), 66. **CAREER** Asst, Univ Del, 61-62; asst prof hist, Temple Univ, 63-67; assoc prof, 67-70, PROF HIST, WEST CHESTER STATE COL, 70-. **MEMBERSHIPS** AHA; Am Asn Advan Slavic Studies; Soc Hist Studies, France. **SELECTED PUBLICATIONS** Auth, A Descriptive Study of Emergency Admissions to Farview State Hospital, Bull Am Acad Psych Law, Vol 24, 96. **CONTACT ADDRESS** 51 Merbrook Lane, Merion Station, PA, 19066.

FOX, FRANK WAYNE
PERSONAL Born 10/07/1940, Salt Lake City, UT, m, 1969, 2 children **DISCIPLINE** AMERICAN SOCIAL HISTORY **EDUCATION** Stanford Univ, PhD, 1973. **CAREER** Prof, Brigham Young Univ, 71-. **HONORS AND AWARDS** Disting. Tchg, 84, 85; Prof of the Year, 83, 97, 98; Alcuin Award; Karl B. Maeser Award. **MEMBERSHIPS** OAH; Am Studies Asn. **RESEARCH** Popular Culture; California; U.S. Constitution. **SELECTED PUBLICATIONS** Auth, Madison Avenue Goes To War: The Strange Wartime Career of American Advertising, 73; J. Reulark: The Public Years, 80; America: A Study in Heritage, 86; California and the Lost Continents: An Inquiry Into the California Garden, 99. **CONTACT ADDRESS** Dept of History, Brigham Young Univ, Provo, UT, 84602.

FOX, MICHAEL
PERSONAL Born 12/12/1940, Detroit, MI, m, 1961, 2 children **DISCIPLINE** BIBLE STUDIES; ANCIENT NEAR EASTERN STUDIES **EDUCATION** Univ Mich, BA, 62; MA, 63; Hebrew Union Col, Rabbinical ordination, 68; Hebrew Univ Jerusalem, PhD, 72. **CAREER** Lectr, Haifa Univ, 71-74; lectr, Hebrew Univ Jerusalem, 75-77; asst prof to prof, Univ Wis-Madison, 77- . **MEMBERSHIPS** Soc for Bibl Lit; Nat Asoc of Profs of Hebrew. **RESEARCH** Biblical literature; ancient Egyptian literature. **SELECTED PUBLICATIONS** Auth, Ideas of Wisdom in Proverbs 1-9, JBL, 97; auth, Words for Folly, ZAH, 97; auth, What the Book of Proverbs is About, VTSup, 97; auth, Qohelet's Catalogue of Times, JNSL, 98; auth, Tearing Down and Building Up: A Rereading of Ecclesi-

astes, forthcoming. **CONTACT ADDRESS** Univ of Wisconsin-Madison, 1220 Linden Dr., Rm. 1346, Madison, WI, 53706. **EMAIL** mfox@lss.wisc.edu

FOX, STEPHEN C.
PERSONAL Born 11/28/1938 **DISCIPLINE** MODERN HISTORY **EDUCATION** DePauw Univ, BA, 60; Univ Cincinnati, MA, 66, PhD, 73. **CAREER** Lectr hist, Univ Cincinnati, 68-69; asst prof, 69-73, assoc prof, 73-77, PROF HIST, HUMBOLDT STATE UNIV, 77-; Am-Italian Hist Asn, advisory board; Oral Hist Asn, editorial board; Una Storia Segreta: When Italian Americans were Enemy Aliens-Traveling Display; Bella Vista: An Unseen View of World War II (video) Internment of Italian seamen at Ft. Missoula, Mt; POW: Italian Prisoners in America (video in progress). **HONORS AND AWARDS** For General John DeWitt and the Proposed Internment of German and Italian Aliens during World War II, Louis Knott Koontz memorial award for most deserving article, 89, presented by the Board of Editors, Pacific Historical Rev; for The Unknown Internment, Gustavus Myers Center for the Study of Human Rights in the United States, Outstanding Book on the subject of human rights in the United States, 91; before Columbus Foundation, Am Book Award, 92. **MEMBERSHIPS** Oral Hist Asn. **RESEARCH** Jacksonian period; World War II. **SELECTED PUBLICATIONS** Auth, Politicians, Issues, and Voter Preference in Jacksonian Ohio: a Critique of an Interpretation, OH Hist, summer 77; The Bank Wars, the Idea of Party, and the Division of the Electorate in Jacksonian Ohio, OH Hist, summer 79; General John DeWitt and the Proposed Internment of German and Italian Aliens during World War II, Pacific Hist Rev 57, Nov 88; The Group Bases of Ohio Political Behavior, 1803-1848, NY: Garland Pub, Inc, 89; The Unknown Internment: An Oral History of the Relocation of Italian Americans during World War II, Boston: Twayne Pubs, 90; The Relocation of Italian Americans during World War II, in Struggle and Success: An Anthology of the Italian Immigrant Experience in California, ed by Paola A. Sensi-Isolani and Phyllis Cancilla Martinelli, NY: Center for Migration Studies, 92; The Deportation of Latin American Germans, 1941-1947: Fresh Legs for Mr. Monroe's Doctrine, Yearbook of German-American Studies 32, 97; Blunderbuss or Rifle? The Impact of World Wat II on Postwar Internal Security Policy (in preparation); Many are the Crimes: A Biography of German American Internment in World War II: History and Memory (completed manuscript); and numerous book reviews. **CONTACT ADDRESS** Dept of Hist, Humboldt State Univ, Arcata, CA, 95521-8299. **EMAIL** stfox@humboldt1.com

FOX-GENOVESE, ELIZABETH
DISCIPLINE HISTORY **EDUCATION** Bryn Mawr Col, AB, 63; Harvard Univ, MA, 66, PhD, 74. **CAREER** Eleonore Raoul Prof Hum. **RESEARCH** Comparative women's history; the antebellum South; cultural, literary, and intellectual history. **SELECTED PUBLICATIONS** Auth, The Origins of Physiocracy; Feminism without Illusions: A Critique of Individualism; Within the Plantation Household; Black and White Women of Old South; The Autobiography of P.S. Du Pont de Nemours; coauth, Fruits of Merchant Capital; "Feminism is Not the Story of My Life:" How Today's Feminist Elite Has Lost Touch with the Real Concerns of Women. **CONTACT ADDRESS** Dept History, Emory Univ, 221 Bowden Hall, 561 Kilgo Cir, Atlanta, GA, 30322-1950. **EMAIL** efoxgen@emory.edu

FRAGER, RUTH
DISCIPLINE HISTORY **EDUCATION** Rochester Univ, BA; York Univ, MA, PhD. **MEMBERSHIPS** Ontario Hist Soc. **RESEARCH** Canadian women's history and women's studies; Canadian hist of immigrants. **SELECTED PUBLICATIONS** Auth, Sweatshop Strife: Class, Ethnicity and Gender in the Jewish Labour Movement of Toronto, 1900-1939. **CONTACT ADDRESS** History Dept, McMaster Univ, 1280 Main St W, Hamilton, ON, L8S 4L9.

FRAKES, GEORGE EDWARD
PERSONAL Born 05/12/1932, Los Angeles, CA, m, 1954, 3 children **DISCIPLINE** AMERICAN HISTORY **EDUCATION** Stanford Univ, AB, 54, MA, 58; Univ Calif, Santa Barbara, PhD (Am hist), 66. **CAREER** Teacher, High Sch, Calif, 58-62; from instr to assoc prof, 62-71, chmn soc sci div, 73-77, PROF HIST, SANTA BARBARA CITY COL, 71-, Lectr, Air Force Reserve Off Training Corps, Univ Southern Calif, 58-59; lectr, exten, Univ Calif, 65-66; supvr studies teachers, Univ Calif, Santa Barbara, 65-66. **MEMBERSHIPS** AHA. **RESEARCH** American colonial history; environmental history; California history. **SELECTED PUBLICATIONS** Auth, Science and the Founding Fathers--Science in the Political Thought of Jefferson, Thomas, Franklin, Benjamin, Adams, John, and Madison, James, Hist, Vol 58, 96. **CONTACT ADDRESS** Dept of Hist, Santa Barbara City Col, Santa Barbara, CA, 93109.

FRAKES, JEROLD C.
PERSONAL Born 11/02/1953, Peoria, IL, s, 2 children **DISCIPLINE** COMPARATIVE LITERATURE, LATIN, GREEK **EDUCATION** Univ of MN, PhD, 82 **CAREER** Asst Prof, 82-87, USC; Guest Prof, 87-, Mittellatein Univ; Prof, 88-93, USC; Prof, 93-97, Prof, 97-, USC **HONORS AND AWARDS** Fulbright, 79 **RESEARCH** Yiddish **SELECTED PUBLICATIONS** Auth, The Fate of Fortune in the Early Middle Ages: The Boethian Tradition, Leiden: E.J. Brill, 87; Brides and Doom: Gender, Property and Power in Medieval German Women's Epic, Philadelphia: Univ of Pennsylvania Press, 94 **CONTACT ADDRESS** Univ of So California, Los Angeles, CA, 90089. **EMAIL** frakes@usc.edu

FRANCE, JEAN R.
PERSONAL Born 08/21/1923, Cleveland, OH, w, 1948, 3 children **DISCIPLINE** ART HISTORY **EDUCATION** Oberlin Col, BA, 46, MA, 48. **CAREER** Archit historian, adj assoc prof, 74-, Univ Rochester. **MEMBERSHIPS** Soc of Architectural Historians; Landmark Soc, Western NY; NY St Preservation League; Natl Trust for Historic Preservation. **RESEARCH** Architects Claude Bragdon, Harvey Ellis, Louis Kahn, Frank Lloyd Wright; Amer arts & crafts movement; local architecture, Rochester region. **SELECTED PUBLICATIONS** Auth, Of Town and the River, A Rochester Guide; auth, Harvey Ellis, Artist, Architect; auth, Made in Rochester (exhib catalogue). **CONTACT ADDRESS** 25 Hardwood Hill Rd,, Pittsford, NY, 14534. **EMAIL** frnc@db6.cc.rochester.edu

FRANCIS, EDITH V.
PERSONAL New York, NY, m **DISCIPLINE** EDUCATION **EDUCATION** Hunter Coll, BA, MA, childhood educ, MS, guidance; NYU, EdD, admin. **CAREER** Ed Dept Media Cntr-Audio Visual Proj Ph I Student Tchr Imp, adj prof 1959-61; Student Tchg, instr suprv 1962-63; Elem Schl, tchr 1963-66; Student Tchg Prog, critic tchr 1963-66; Jr/Sr HS, suprv 1967-68; Campus Schs, asst dir 1968-69; Hunter Coll Elem Sch, princ 1968-69; NY City Bd of Ed, consult 1969-70; Except Gifted Chldrn Proj at PS, coord 1970-71; Princeton Reg Schs, princ 1970-76, act spt of schs 1976-77; Hunter Coll Dept of Curr & Tchg; adj prof 1971-72; US Dept of HEW, consult 1973-; ED TESTING SERV, TECH ASST CONSULT 1975-; Ewing Twnshp Pub Schs, supt of schs 1977-87; Columbia Univ, Teachers College, professor, practitioner/scholar, 1987-91; Irvington Public Schools, superintendent of schools, 1991-92; EAST ORANGE PUBLIC SCHOOLS, DIRECTOR, COMMUNITY AND ADULT EDUCATION, 1992-. **HONORS AND AWARDS** Honorary degrees: PhD, Humanity of Art, Amer Bible Univ, 1969, PhD, Arts Phil World Univ, 1973; Intl Women's Achvmnt Awd, Global News Synd, 1970; Woman of the Year, Zeta of the Year, 1971; NAACP Awd, 1978; Outstanding Woman Award, 1980; Life Membership Award, 1982; Honor Awds: NJ Dept of Ed, Rider Coll, Ewing Cmmty & NJ State Fed Colored Womens Club, 1979; Prof Dev Awd Mercer Cty CC 1980; Awd Trenton St Coll 1980; One of Most Infuential Black Amer, Commendation by Hamilton Twp Mayor, Mansfield M Finney Achvmnt Awd, Ed Awd Gamma Rho Sigma 1981-1984; Black Media Inc citation 1982; Natl Black Monitor Hall of Fame Awd 1982; Alpha Kappa Alpha Awd for dedicated service 1982; Friends of United Negro Coll Fund Awd for Outstanding Ldrshp & Commitment to Furthering Higher Education, 1982; Natl Cncl of Women, The US Inc Woman of Conscience Awd, 1982; speaking engagements include: Rider Coll, Mercer Cty Com Col, Trenton St Coll, Leadership Conf, Cleveland OH; Distinguised African-American Woman's Award, 1995; Leadership America Completion Award, 1998; East Orange Superintendent's Award for Excellence, 1998. **MEMBERSHIPS** Pres Princeton Reg Admin Association 1974-75; chairperson of ed comm Princeton Bicentennial Comm 1974-77; board of directors Public Library 1976-77; Witherspoon Devel Corp 1976-82; legislative comm NJ & Amer Assn of Sch Admin 1977-; board of directors YWCA Trenton NJ, 1977-89; intl pres Grand Basileus of Zeta Phi Beta 1980-86; bd of examiners NJ Ed Dept, 1980-86; board member & trustee Natl Assault on Illiteracy 1982-86; board of directors Helene Fuld Hosp 1982-86; governors task force Trenton NJ 1982-86; board of directors Natl Merit Scholarship Corp 1982-87; Natl Assn of Suprv & Curriculum Devel, Natl Council of Admin Women in Ed, NJ Council of Admin Women in Ed, CUNY Black Professors & Admin Women in Ed, American Association of Sch Admin, American Association of University Professors, Zeta Phi Beta Board of Directors, Schoolmasters of NJ, NJ Association of School Admin, NJ Ed Association, NJ Council of Ed, Phi Beta Kappa; The Links, Inc, 1986-, pres, Central NJ chap, 1997-. **SELECTED PUBLICATIONS** Publications: "Booker T Washington, Temporizer & Compromiser," "Educating Gifted Children," "Gifted Children As We See Them."

FRANCIS, ROBERT D.
PERSONAL Born 09/02/1944, Fenwick, ON, Canada **DISCIPLINE** HISTORY **EDUCATION** York Univ, BA, 67, PhD, 76; Univ Toronto, MA, 68. **CAREER** Instr, York Univ, 74-75; vis lectr, Univ BC, 75-76; asst to assoc prof, 76-88, PROF, UNIV CALGARY, 88-; vis prof, Univ Tsukuba (Japan), 91-93. **HONORS AND AWARDS** Master Tchr Award, Univ Calgary, 82; J.W. Dafoe Book Prize, 86; Award Merit, Asn Can Stud, 89. **MEMBERSHIPS** Can Hist Asn; Alta Hist Asn; Asn Can Stud; Japanese Asn Can Stud. **SELECTED PUBLICATIONS** Auth, Frank H. Underhill, 86; auth, Images of the West, 89; coauth, Origins: Canadian History Before Confederation, 88, 3rd ed 96; coauth, Destinies: Canadian History Since Confederation, 88, 3rd ed 96; co-ed, The Dirty Thirties in Prairie Canada, 80; co-ed, Readings in Canadian History, 2 vols, 82, 5th ed 98; co-ed, The Prairie West, 85, 2nd ed 92; co-ed, The Regions and Peoples of Canada: A Historical Approach (in Japanese), 93. **CONTACT ADDRESS** Univ of Calgary, 2500 University Dr, Calgary, AB, T2N 1N4.

FRANCIS, SAMUEL TODD
PERSONAL Born 04/29/1947, Chattanooga, TN **DISCIPLINE** BRITISH AND WORLD HISTORY **EDUCATION** Johns Hopkins Univ, BA, 69; Univ NC, MA, 71, PhD (hist), 79. **CAREER** Policy analyst--Foreign Affairs, Heritage Found 77-81; LEGIS ASST NAT SECURITY, US SENATE STAFF, 81-, Washington ed, The Southern Partisan, 80-. **RESEARCH** Contemporary political and social conflicts; role of elites and counterelites in world history; sociobiology and political theory. **SELECTED PUBLICATIONS** Authy, Exploring Dance as Concept--Contributions from Cognitive Science, Dance Rsch J, Vol 28, 96. **CONTACT ADDRESS** Apt A1202 2801 Park Ctr, Alexandria, VA, 22302.

FRANK, DAVID
PERSONAL Born 07/30/1949 **DISCIPLINE** CANADIAN HISTORY **EDUCATION** Univ Toronto, BA, 72; Dalhousie Univ, PhD (hist), 79. **CAREER** Mem fac, Col Cape Breton, 78-80; MEM FAC, UNIV NB, 80-, Ed, Acadiensis: J Hist Atlantic Region, 81-. **MEMBERSHIPS** Can Hist Asn. **RESEARCH** History of Atlantic Canada; Canadian social and labour history; international working class history. **SELECTED PUBLICATIONS** Auth, The Makings of the Medieval Hebrew Book--Studies In Paleography and Codicology, J Jewish Stud, Vol 46, 95; Race Relations and the Seattle Labor Movement, 1915-1929,Pac Northwest Quart, Vol 86, 95; Collected Works of Daube, David, Vol 1--Talmudic Law, J Jewish Stud, Vol 46, 95; Jewish Education and Society in The High Middle Ages, J Jewish Stud, Vol 44, 93; Guide to Hebrew Manuscript Collections, J Jewish Stud, Vol 46, 95; 10 Hours Labor Religion, Reform, and Gender in Early New England, J Interdisciplinary Hist, Vol 25, 95; Hebrew Manuscripts of East and West--Towards a Comparative Codicology, J Jewish Stud, Vol 46, 95; Bernstein, Iving Lean Years, Labor Hist, Vol 37, 96; Hebrew Studies--Papers Presented at a Colloquium on Resources for Hebraica in Europe, J Jewish Stud, Vol 46, 95; Bibliotheca Rosenthaliana Treasures of Jewish Booklore, Marking The 200th Anniversary of the Birth of Rosenthal, Leeser, 1794-1994, J Jewish Stud, Vol 46, 95; Fundamentalism and Gender--1875 to the Present, J Rel, Vol 75, 95; Roaring Days--Rosslands Mines and the History of British Columbia, Can Hist Rev, Vol 78, 97; The Jewish Religion--A Companion, J Jewish Stud, Vol 48, 97; The Oxford Dictionary of the Jewish Religion, J Jewish Stud, Vol 48, 97; Minhah Le Nahum--Biblical and other Studies Presented to Sarna, Nahum, M in Honor of his 70th Birthday, J Jewish Studies, Vol 45, 94; The State of Jewish Studies, J Jewish Stud, Vol 44, 93; Karaite Separatism in 19th Century Russia--Lutski, Joseph, Solomon Epistle of Israels Deliverance, J Jewish Stud, Vol 45, 94. GEN Can **CONTACT ADDRESS** Dept of Hist, Univ of NB, Fredericton, NB, E3B 5A3.

FRANK, MORTIMER HENRY
PERSONAL Born 01/14/1933, New York, NY, m, 1961, 1 child **DISCIPLINE** ENGLISH, MUSICOLOGY **EDUCATION** New York Univ, AB, 54, MA, 58, PhD (English), 68. **CAREER** Instr English, New York Univ, 62-65; from instr to assoc prof, 65-74, PROF ENGLISH, BRONX COMMUNITY COL, 74-, Fac res fel, State Univ NY, 73 and 74; producer, Rare Recordings, broadcast by WFUY, 75-; music ed, 17th Century News, 78- and Class Record, Chron Higher Educ, 78-80; cur, Toscanini Collection, Wave Hill, 81-. **MEMBERSHIPS** MLA; Northeast Mod Lang Asn. **RESEARCH** Am Lit; 17th century poetry; relationship between poetry and music. **SELECTED PUBLICATIONS** Auth, The Maestro Myth, Opera News, Vol 57, 93. **CONTACT ADDRESS** Dept of English, Bronx Comm Col, CUNY, 181st St and University Ave, Bronx, NY, 10453.

FRANK, SAM HAGER
PERSONAL Born 07/23/1932, King City, MO, m, 1955, 1 child **DISCIPLINE** MODERN HISTORY **EDUCATION** Fla State Univ, BA, 53, MA, 57; Univ Fla, PhD, 61. **CAREER** Hist consult, Res Studies Inst, Air Univ, 57-58; prof hist and head dept soc sci, Tift Col, 61-65; assoc prof hist, Augusta Col, 66-67; from assoc prof hist and asst dean faculties to prof hist and assoc dean faculties, Jacksonville Univ, 67-72, dean, Col Arts and Sci, 72-78; chancellor, La State Univ, Alexandria, 79-81; PRES, WAGNER COL, 81-, Vis Fulbright prof, Bhagalpur Univ, India, 65-66 and Osmania Univ, India, 66. **MEMBERSHIPS** Am Conf Acad Deans; AHA; Orgn Am Hists; Southern Hist Asn; Am Acad Polit and Soc Sci. **RESEARCH** Military, Far Eastern and United States history. **SELECTED PUBLICATIONS** Auth, Doomed at the Start--American Pursuit Pilots in the Philippines, 1941-1942, J Am Hist, Vol 80, 93; Spaatz, Carl, A. and ahe Air War in Europe, J Amn Hist, Vol 82, 95. **CONTACT ADDRESS** Off of Pres, Wagner Col, Staten Island, NY, 10301.

FRANKEL, NORALEE
DISCIPLINE HISTORY **EDUCATION** George Washington Univ, PhD, 83. **CAREER** Asst dir, Women, Minorities and Teaching, Am Hist Asn. **MEMBERSHIPS** Am Hist Asn. **RESEARCH** Women historians, minority historians. **SELECT-**

ED PUBLICATIONS auth, Break Those Chains at Last: African Americans, 1860-1880, Oxford Univ, 96; co-ed, Gender, Class, Race, and Reform in the Progressive Era, Univ Ky, 91. **CONTACT ADDRESS** American Historical Assn.

FRANKFORTER, ALBERTUS DANIEL

PERSONAL Born 05/17/1939, Waynesboro, PA, m, 1972 **DISCIPLINE** MEDIEVAL ECCLESIASTICAL HISTORY **EDUCATION** Franklin and Marshall Col, Artium Baccalaeurie, 61; Drew Univ, MDiv, 65; Pa State Univ, MA, 69, PhD (medieval hist), 71. **CAREER** Actg chaplain, Williams Col, 63-64; asst prof, 70-80, ASSOC PROF ANCIENT and MEDIEVAL HIST, BEHREND COL, PA STATE UNIV, 80-. **MEMBERSHIPS** Mediaeval Acad Am; Am Soc Church Hist; AHA. **RESEARCH** Medieval English Episcopal registers; medieval female authors. **SELECTED PUBLICATIONS** Auth, A Rural Society After the Black Death--Essex 1350-1525, Church Hist, Vol 64, 95; Between Church and State--The Lives of 4 French Prelates in the Late Middle Ages, Church History, Vol 64, 95; England, Rome and the Papacy, 1417-1464--The Study of a Relationship, Church Hist, Vol 64, 95; Women, Sainthood and Power--The So Called Biographies of Latin Female Saints from the 4th Century to the 7th Century, Church Hist, Vol 64, 95; Between Church And State--The Lives of 4 French Prelates in the Late Middle Ages, Church Hist, Vol 64, 95; Gilbert of Sempringham and the Gilbertine Order, C. 1130-1300, Church History, Vol 66, 97; Unity and Variety--A History of the Church in Devon and Cornwall, Church Hist, Vol 63, 94; Unity and Variety--A History of the Church in Devon and Cornwall, Church Hist, Vol 63, 94; England, Rome and the Papacy, 1417-1464--The Study of a Relationship, Church Hist, Vol 64, 95; The Collegiate Church of Wimborne Minster, Church Hist, Vol 66, 97; Knowledge, Power, and the Struggle for Representation, Coll Eng, Vol 57, 95; The Collegiate Church of Wimborne Minster, Church Hist, Vol 66, 97; Crossfire , Ling Fr, Vol 5, 95; Women, Sainthood and Power--The So Called Biographies of Latin Female Saints from the 4th Century to the 7th Century, Church Hist, Vol 64, 95; Gilbert of Sempringham and the Gilbertine Order, C. 1130-1300, Church Hist, Vol 66, 97. **CONTACT ADDRESS** Dept of Hist, Pennsylvania State Univ, Erie, Station Rd, Erie, PA, 16510.

FRANKLIN, ALLAN DAVID

PERSONAL Born 08/01/1938, Brooklyn, NY, m, 1974 **DISCIPLINE** HISTORY & PHILOSOPHY OF SCIENCE **EDUCATION** Columbia Col, AB, 59; Cornell Univ, PhD(physics), 65. **CAREER** Res assoc physics, Princeton Univ, 65-66, instr, 66-67; asst prof, 67-73, asoc prof physics, Univ Co, 73-82, prof, 82-. **HONORS AND AWARDS** Ch elect, Forum on History of Physics, Am Phys Soc; Exec Bd, Phil of Sci Asn.; Centennial speaker, Am Physical Soc. **MEMBERSHIPS** Fellow of Am Physical Soc; Hist Sci Soc; Phil of Sci Asn. **RESEARCH** The role of experiment in physics. **SELECTED PUBLICATIONS** Auth, The Principle of Inertia in the Middle Ages, CO Assoc Univ, 76; The Discovery and Nondiscovery of Partly Nonconservation, Studies in Hist & Philos of Sci, 10/79; The Neglect of Experiment, Cambridge Univ Press, 1986; Experiment, Right or Wrong, Cambridge Univ Press, 1990; The Rise and Fall of the Fifth Force, Am Institute of Physics, 1993; The Appearance and Disappearance of the 17-keV Neutrino, Rev. Modern Physics, 1995. **CONTACT ADDRESS** Dept of Physics & Astrophysics, Univ Colo, Box 390, Boulder, CO, 80309-0390. **EMAIL** Allan.Franklin@Colorado.edu

FRANKLIN, JAMES L., JR.

PERSONAL Born 07/19/1947, Dayton, OH, s **DISCIPLINE** CLASSICS **EDUCATION** Denison Univ, BA, 69; Queen's Univ, Ontario, MA, 70; Duke Univ, PhD, 75; A.W. Mellon prof in charge, Intercol Ctr Class Stud, Rome, 94-95. **CAREER** Asst prof, Barnard Col, Columbia Univ, 75-76; asst prof, Wellesley Col, 76-77; vis asst prof, Univ Mich, 77-80; asst prof to PROF, IND UNIV, 81-. **HONORS AND AWARDS** Amoco Fdn Award Dist Teach, Ind Univ, 87; NEH fel, 80-81; ACLS grant, 78; Am Acad Rome fel, 73-75; Phi Beta Kappa, 69., Dir, Vergilian Soc Prog, cumae, 87, 89, 90, 93. **MEMBERSHIPS** Am Philol Asn; Am Soc Gr, Lat Epigraphy; Archaeol Inst Am; Asn In d'Epigraphie Gr, Lat; Asn Int Amici di Pompei; Class Asn Middle West, South. **RESEARCH** Pompeian studies; Roman archaeol; Lat lit **SELECTED PUBLICATIONS** Auth, Pompeis Difficile Est: Studies in the Politics of Imperial Pompeii, Univ Mich Press, 99; auth, Pompeii: The Casa del Marinaio and Its History, Monografie della Soprintendenza Archeol di Pompei 3, 90; auth. Cn Alleius Nigidius Maius and the Amphitheatre: Munera and a Distinguished Career at Ancient Pompeii, Historia 46, 97; auth, Aulus Vettius Caprasius Felix of Ancient Pompeii, in Qui Miscuit Utile cum Dulci, Bolchazy-Carducci, 98; auth, Vergil at Pompeii: A Teacher's Aid, class J 92, 96-97. **CONTACT ADDRESS** Dept Class Stud, Indiana Univ, Bloomington, Bloomington, IN, 47405. **EMAIL** franklin@indiana.edu

FRANKLIN, PHYLLIS

PERSONAL New York, NY **DISCIPLINE** AMERICAN REALISM **EDUCATION** Vassar Col, AB, 54; Univ Miami, MA, 65, PhD (English), 69. **CAREER** Teaching asst English, Univ Miami, 65, asst prof, 69-76, assoc prof, 76-81; DIR ENGLISH PROGS and ASN DEPT ENGLISH, MOD LANG ASN, 81-, Nat Endowment for Humanities summer stipend. **HONORS AND AWARDS** Florence Howe Award for feminist criticism, Women's Caucus Mod Lang, 74. **MEMBERSHIPS** MLA; Women's Caucus Mod Lang (vpres, 76-78); Women's Studies Asn. **RESEARCH** American literary realism, Robert Herrick; women's studies; history of English studies in American higher education. **SELECTED PUBLICATIONS** Auth, A History of Western Musical Aesthetics, Mus Times, Vol 134, 93; Schumann Manfred, Mus Times, Vol 135, 94; Blake Violin Concerto, Mus Times, Vol 134, 93; Undertones of Insurrection--Music, Politics and the Social Sphere in the Modern German Narrative, Mus Times, Vol 135, 94; A Mass for the Masses--Proceedings o te Mahler Eight Symposium, Amsterdam 1988, Mus Letters, Vol 75, 94; Schreker, Franz, 1878-1934--A Cultural Biography, Opera, Vol 44, 93; A History of Music Aesthetics, Mus Times, Vol 134, 93; Contemplating Music--Source Readings in the Aesthetics of Music, Vol 3, Essence, Mus Times, Vol 134, 93; Mendelssohn Die Hochzeit des Camacho, Mus Times, Vol 135, 94; Hoffmann, Eta Undine, Mus Times, Vol 135, 94; Mahler Sixth Symphony--A Study in Musical Semiotics, Mus Letters, Vol 78, 97; Musicology and Difference--Gender and Sexuality in Music Scholarship, Mus Letters, Vol 76, 95; Mahler--A Musical Physiognomy, Mus Times, Vol 134, 93; The Music of Pfitzner, Hans, Mus Letters, Vol 74, 93; Report of the Executive Director, PMLA Publications of the Mod Lan Assoc Am, Vol 110, 95; Fragment or Completion--Proceedings of the Mahler Tenth Symposium, Utrecht, 1986, Mus Letters, Vol 75, 94; Schmidt, Franz 1874-1939--A Discussion of his Style with Special Reference to the 4 Symphonies and Das Buch Mit Sieben Siegeln, Mus Letters, Vol 74, 93; Adorno Aesthetics of Music, Mus Times, Vol 135, 94; Strauss, Richard and his World, Mus Times, Vol 134, 93; Report of the Executive Director, PMLA Pubs Mod Lan Assoc Am, Vol 112, 97; Strauss, Richard--New Perspectives on the Composer and his Work, Mus Times, Vol 134, 93; Report of the Executive Director, PMLA Pubs Mod Lan Asso Am, Vol 111, 96; Light in Battle with Darkness, Mus Letters, Vol 74, 93; Ullmann Piano Concerto, Variations Op.5, Second Symphony, Mus Times, Vol 134, 93; Mason Playing Away, Mus Times, Vol 135, 94; Schumann Genoveva, Mus Times, Vol 135, 94; Strauss Also Sprach Zarathustra, Mus Times, Vol 134, 93. **CONTACT ADDRESS** Modern Language Association, 62 Fifth Av, New York, NY, 10011.

FRANKS, KENNY ARTHUR

PERSONAL Born 07/19/1945, Okemah, OK, m, 1996, 3 children **DISCIPLINE** HISTORY **EDUCATION** OK State Univ, PhD, hist 73, MA hist 71; Univ Cen OK, BA hist 69. **CAREER** OK State Univ, Grad tch asst, instr, adjunt asst prof; Univ Cen OK, lectr; Redlands Comm Col, adj instr; OK State Univ, adj facul, res asst, Res and Ed asst to the dir of Will Rogers Project; OK Historical Society and Heritage Society, Editor of the Chronicles of OK, The OK Series, The OK Trackmaker Series, The OK Heritage Magazine, The OK Horizon Series, The OK Heritage County Hist series, The OK Statesman Series, Dir of Publ for OK Historical Society and Dir of Educ and Publ of the OK Heritage Assn; Bk Rev Ed, Rural OK News, 91; Consultant and Legal Consultant; Auth; Ed; Coordr; Writer; etc. **HONORS AND AWARDS** Dean's Honor Roll; Phi Alpha Theta; Pres Hon Roll, Phi Alpha Theta; Awd of Merit from Amer Assn ST Local Hist; Mrs Simon Baruch Univ Awd for Best Book; Jefferson Davis Medal; Distinguished Service Awd, OK Petro Coun; Petro Herit Awd; Mem Okemah Hall Of Fame., Consultant for numerous projects, to list a few, Oil Boom Blues: TV documentary, Cherokee Culture Series of Oral Roberts Univ, Big War Little War: Cen for The Amer Indian, KirkPatrick Cen, USA Postal Ser Commemorative Stamp Series. **MEMBERSHIPS** OHA; OHS. **RESEARCH** Energy, industry, Native Am, Am west. **SELECTED PUBLICATIONS** Oklahoma: Its Land and People, with Paul Lambert, Helena MT, Amer and World Geog Pub, 94; A History of Washington County Oklahoma, with Paul F Lambert, OK City, Oklahoma Herit Assn, 98; Pawnee Pride: A History of Pawnee Country, OK CTY, OK Herit Assn, 94; Glen D Johnston Sr" The Road to Washington, OK Cty, OK Herit Assn, 96; Where the Black Gold Rolls and Flows, OK Today, 97; many, many, more bks, chapters and articles. **CONTACT ADDRESS** Oklahoma Heritage Association, 201 Northwest 14th St, Oklahoma City, OK, 73103. **EMAIL** oha@telepath.com

FRANTZ, JOHN B.

PERSONAL Born 01/10/1932, New Haven, CT, m, 1963, 1 child **DISCIPLINE** AMERICAN HISTORY **EDUCATION** Franklin & Marshall Col, AB, 54; Univ Pa, AM, 56, PhD, 61. **CAREER** From instr to asst prof, 61-66, assoc prof Am hist, PA State Univ, 66-, Adj instr hist, Franklin & Marshall Col, 59-61; Am Philos Soc res grant, 65; Yale Univ Divinity Sch res fel, 67; bus secy, Pa Hist Asn, 65-68, exec coun, 69-77, 98-, pres, 84-86; hist coun, United Church Christ, 75-80. **MEMBERSHIPS** Orgn Am Historians; Am Soc Church Hist, Pa Hist Asn. **RESEARCH** Early Am relig hist; Colonial and Revolutionary Am; PA Ger(s). **SELECTED PUBLICATIONS** Auth, John C Guldin: Pennsylvania German revivalist, Pa Mag Hist & Biog, 4/63; The return to tradition: an analysis of the new measures movement in the German Reformed Church, Pa Hist, 6/64; Revivalism: a thesis concerning its effect on Protestant denominations, Theol & Life, summer 65; ed, Bacon's Rebellion: Prologue to the Revolution?, Heath, 69; auth, The awakening of religion among the German settlers in the middle colonies, William & Mary Quart, 4/76; Religion in Pennsylvania during the Revolution, Pa Heritage, 6/76; Pennsylvania, In: Encyclopedia Americana, Grolier, 76; Religious Freedom: Key to Diversity, Pennsylvania Heritage, 81; Co-ed, Pennsylvania Religions Leaders, 86; Early German Methodist in America, Yearbook of German-American Studies, 91; Franklin and the Pennsylvania Germans, Pa Hist, 98; Co-ed, Beyond Philadelphia: The American Revolution in the Pennsylvania Hinterland, 98. **CONTACT ADDRESS** Dept of Hist, 108 Weaver Bldg, University Park, PA, 16802-5500. **EMAIL** jbf2@psu.edu

FRANTZ, MARY ALISON

PERSONAL Born 09/27/1903, Duluth, MN **DISCIPLINE** ARCHAEOLOGY **EDUCATION** Smith Col, AB, 24; Columbia Univ, PhD, 37. **CAREER** Teacher, Arden Sch, NJ, 25-27; reader Index Christian Art, Princeton Univ, 27-29; MEM STAFF, AGORA EXCAVATIONS, ATHENS, 33-40, 49-, Analyst, Off Strategic Serv, Washington, DC, 42-45; cult attache, Am Embassy, Athens, 46-49; assoc ed, Allied mission to observ Greek elections, 46; vis mem, Inst Advan Study, Princeton, NJ, 76-77. **MEMBERSHIPS** Archaeol Inst Am; Mediaeval Acad Am; Am Philos Soc. **RESEARCH** Byzantine archaeology and literature; early Christian history and architecture; Athens in late antiquity. **SELECTED PUBLICATIONS** Auth, Annual Review of Federal Securities Regulation, Business Lawyer, Vol 51, 96. **CONTACT ADDRESS** 27 Haslet Ave, Princeton, NJ, 08540.

FRANZ, GEORGE W.

PERSONAL m, 2 children **DISCIPLINE** AMERICAN HISTORY **EDUCATION** Muhlenberg Col, AB, 64; Rutgers Univ, MA, 65, PhD(Am hist), 74. **CAREER** Instr, 68-73, asst prof hist, Pa State Univ, 74-, assoc ed, Papers Martin Van Buren, 75-76, proj dir & ed, 76-, dir of Academic Affairs, Penn State Delaware County, 97-. **HONORS AND AWARDS** Outstanding Teacher, Penn State Delaware County, 89; george W. Atherton Award for Excellence in Undergraduate Teaching, Penn State Univ, 90; Outstanding Faculty Advisor, Col of the Liberal Arts, Penn State Iniv, 93; McKay-Donkin Award, Penn State Univ, 94. **MEMBERSHIPS** Orgn Am Historians. **RESEARCH** Colonial and revolutionary Pennsylvania history. **SELECTED PUBLICATIONS** Project dir and ed, The Papers of Martin Van Buren (55 reels of microfilm), Cchadwyck-Healy, 88; Martin Van Buren, Research Guide to American Historical Biography, Beachem, 88; Paxton: A Study of community Structure and Mobility in the Colonial Pennsylvania Backcountry, Garland, 89. **CONTACT ADDRESS** Director of Academic Affairs, Pennsylvania State Univ, 25 Yearsley Mill Rd, Media, PA, 19063-5522. **EMAIL** gwf1@psu.edu

FRASER, JULIUS THOMAS

PERSONAL Born 05/07/1923, Budapest, Hungary, m, 1973, 3 children **DISCIPLINE** STUDY OF TIME, HISTORY OF IDEAS **EDUCATION** Cooper Union, Bee, 51; Univ Hanover, PhD(philos), 70. **CAREER** Jr engineer, MacKay Radio & Telegraph, 51-53; design engineer, Westinghouse Electric Corp, 53-55; sr res scientist, Gen Precision Lab, Inc, 55-71; FOUNDER , INT SOC STUDY TIME, 66-; Adj Assoc Prof Hist Sci, Fordham Univ, 71-, Res asst physics, Mich State Univ, 62-66; vis lectr humanities & sci, Mass Inst Technol, 66-67, guest, 67-69; vis lectr study time, My Holyoke Col, 67-69; vis prof time & intellectual hist, Univ MD. **SELECTED PUBLICATIONS** Auth, Of Time, Passion, and Knowledge: Reflections on the Strategy of Existence, first ed, NY: Braziller, 75; Time as Conflict: a Scientific and Humanistic Study, Basel and Boston: Birkhauser, 78; The Genesis and Evolution of Time: a Critique of Interpretation in Physics, Amherst: Univ MA Press, Brighton, Sussex: The Harvester Press, 82, Tokyo: Kodansha Scientific Ltd, 84; Time, the Familiar Stranger, Amherst: Univ MA Press, 87, Redmond, WA: Tempest Books (paperback), 88, Stuart, FL: Triformation Braille Service, 89; Die Zeit: Vetraut und Fremd, trans of Time, the Familiar Stranger, Basel: Birkhauser Verlag, 88, 2nd ed (paperback), Munchen: Deutscher Taschenbuch Verlag, 91; Il Tempo: una Presenza Sconosciuta, trans of Time, the Familiar Stranger, Milano: Feltrinelli, 91; Genesis y Evolucion del Tiempo, trans of The Genesis and Evolution of Time, Irunea/Pamplona: Pamiela, 95; Time, Conflict, and Human Values, Urbana and Chicago: Univ IL Press, 99; numerous articles, books edited, book reviews, and other publications primarily concerning the study of time. **CONTACT ADDRESS** PO Box 815, Westport, CT, 16880.

FRASER, SARAH

DISCIPLINE ASIAN ART **EDUCATION** Univ Calf, Berkeley, PhD. **CAREER** Prof, Northwestern Univ **MEMBERSHIPS** Turfan-Silk Road archeological team. **RESEARCH** Early Chinese painting, art of central Asia. **SELECTED PUBLICATIONS** Auth, Regimes of Production: The Use of Pounces in Temple Construction, Orientations, 96. **CONTACT ADDRESS** Dept of Art History, Northwestern Univ, 1801 Hinman, Evanston, IL, 60208.

FRASIER, MARY MACK

PERSONAL Born 05/17/1938, Orangeburg, SC, m **DISCIPLINE** EDUCATION **EDUCATION** SC State Coll, BS 1958; SC State Coll, MEd 1971; Univ of CT, PhD 1974. **CAREER**

Univ of GA, Department of Education, professor, psychology, National Research Center on the Gifted and Talented, associate director, 1974-; SC State Coll, dir special serv for disadvantaged students in insts of higher educ 1971-72; Wilkinson High School, Orangeburg SC, instructor Choral Music 1958-71. **MEMBERSHIPS** President, GA Federation-Council for Exceptional Children, 1977-78; exec bd, Nat Assn for Gifted Children 1977-81; National Association for Gifted Children, president, 1983-91; bd of govs, The Assn for the Gifted 1978-80; Pi Lambda Theta, 1973; Delta Sigma Theta Sorority Athens Alumnae Chap, 1974-; Phi Delta Kappa, 1979-; Kappa Delta Pi, 1990. **SELECTED PUBLICATIONS** Articles pub in "The Gifted Child Quarterly, Journal for the Education of the Gifted Exceptional Children"; chap in book "New Voices in Counseling the Gifted" Kendall-Hunt 1979. **CONTACT ADDRESS** 325 Aberhold, Athens, GA, 30602.

FRASSETTO, MICHAEL
DISCIPLINE HISTORY **EDUCATION** LaSalle Univ, BA, 83; MI State Univ, MA, 85; DE Univ, PhD, 93. **CAREER** Asst prof, 90-95; assoc prof, 95-, Jewish Theol Sem Am. **HONORS AND AWARDS** NEH summer sem, Bryn Mawr Col, 93; LaGrange Col summer res grant, 92; Fulbright-Hayes Res Fel, GDR, 1989-1990; Univ Del Grad Res Fel, 88. **RESEARCH** World civilization to 1648 and 1648 to present; ancient Rome; Middle Ages and Renaissance and Reformation. **SELECTED PUBLICATIONS** Auth, The Art of Forgery: The Sermons of Ademar of Chabannes and the Cult of St. Martial of Limoges, Comitatus, 95; Violence, Knightly Piety and the Peace of God in Aquitaine. **CONTACT ADDRESS** Dept of Hist, LaGrange Col, Broad St, PO Box 601, LaGrange, GA, 30240.

FRATIANNI, MICHELE
PERSONAL Born 03/07/1941, Firenze, Italy, m, 3 children **DISCIPLINE** ECONOMICS/MONETARY ECONOMICS **EDUCATION** Ohio State Univ, BA, 67; Ohio State Univ, MA, 67; Ohio State Univ, PhD, 71 **CAREER** W. George Pinnell prof Bus Econ, Indiana Univ, 98-; chair, Bus Econ, Indiana Univ, 97-; visiting prof econ. Latholieke Universiteit te Leuven, Belgium 73-; Allis-Chalmers Distinguished prof Intl Econ, Marquette Univ, 95; Bundesbank prof Intl Monetary Econ, Free Univ, Berlin, 95; prof Bus Econ, Indiana Univ, 79-93 **HONORS AND AWARDS** AMOCO Fel, 93-98; IGIER Visiting Fel, 94; Brit Acad Visiting Prof, 94; Univ Calif, Center for German & European Studies Grant, 91-92; Mont Pelerin Soc, 92-; St. Vincent Prize Econ, 92- **MEMBERSHIPS** Amer Econ Assoc; Intl Trade Finance Assoc **RESEARCH** Monetary Theory and Policy; International Monetary Economics; Political Economy **SELECTED PUBLICATIONS** Auth, "Maxi versus Mini EMU: The Political Economy of Stage III," Columbia Jrnl Europ Law, 98; auth, "Bank Deposit Insurance: The Italian Case," Rev Econ Conditions in Italy, 96; coauth, "Central Banking as a Political Principal-Agent Problem," Econ Inquiry, 97 **CONTACT ADDRESS** Business Economics & Public Policy, Indiana Univ, Bloomington, Kelley School of Business, Rm. 451, Bloomington, IN, 47405. **EMAIL** fratiann@indiana.edu

FRAZER, HEATHER
DISCIPLINE HISTORY **EDUCATION** Duke Univ, PhD. **CAREER** Prof. **HONORS AND AWARDS** Tchg Incentive Prog Awd; Univ Distinguished Tchg Awd. **RESEARCH** India and British Empire; women's history. **SELECTED PUBLICATIONS** Auth, All Quiet on the Hollywood Front: Actor Lew Ayres as Conscientious Objector, 97; Curzon and His Indian Legacy: Consumate Imperialist and Preserver of Ancient Monuments, 95; co-auth, We Have Just Begun Not to Fight, 96. **CONTACT ADDRESS** History Dept, Florida Atlantic Univ, 777 Glades Rd, Boca Raton, FL, 33431. **EMAIL** rinaldi@acc.fau.edu

FRAZER, WILLIAM JOHNSON
PERSONAL Born 10/15/1924, Greenville, AL, d, 1 child **DISCIPLINE** ECONOMICS **EDUCATION** Huntingdon Col, BA, 50; Columbia Univ, MA, Econ, 53; Harvard, Fac Fel, math, 59-60; Univ Pa, Fac Fel, statist, 64-65; Columbia Univ, PhD, 68. **CAREER** Tchg fel, Econ, univ Tex, 51; student asst, Wage Stabilization Bd, 52; instr, Econ, Pratt Inst, 53-54; instr, Econ, Rensselaer Polytechnic Inst, 54-56; asst prof, Univ Fla, 57-65; assoc prof, Univ Fla, 64-68; prof, Univ Fla, 68-95; prof, London Sch Econ, 94; prof, FSUs London Center, 89-90, 92; sr. Econ, Fed Reserve Bank Chi, 66-67; vis assoc prof, Univ Ky, 67-68; econ, PROF, UNIV FLA, 95-. **MEMBERSHIPS** South Econ Asn **RESEARCH** Central banking, Financial markets, Business conditions, Global economy **SELECTED PUBLICATIONS** The Central Banks: Analysis, and International and European Dimensions, Praeger Publ, 94; The Legacy of Keynes and Friedman: Economic Analysis, Money, and Ideology, Praeger Publ, 94; coauth, The Florida Land Boom: Speculation, Money and the Banks, Quorum Bks, 95; The Friedman System: An Economic Analysis of Time Series, Praeger Publ, 97. **CONTACT ADDRESS** Dept Econ, Univ Fla, PO Box 117140, Gainesville, FL, 32611-7140.

FRAZIER, ALISON
DISCIPLINE HISTORY **EDUCATION** Columbia Univ, PhD, 97. **CAREER** Vis asst prof, Dartmouth, 96-99; ASST PROF HIST, UNIV TX, AUSTIN, 99-. **HONORS AND AWARDS** Am Academy Rome, Mellon Awd, 97-98; Newcombe fel, 94-95; Delmas fel, 91; Phi Beta Kappa, 85. **MEMBERSHIPS** AHA, AAR; Am Philol Asn. **RESEARCH** Religious history, Italian Renaissance, biography. **CONTACT ADDRESS** Dept of History, Univ of Texas, Austin, Austin, TX, 78712-1163. **EMAIL** akfrazier@mail.utexas.edu

FREDERICK, RICHARD G.
PERSONAL Born 07/16/1947, Ft. Wayne, IN, m, 1970 **DISCIPLINE** HISTORY **EDUCATION** Ind Univ, Bloomington, AB, 69; St Mary's Univ, San Antonio, MA, 71; Pa State Univ, PhD(hist), 79. **CAREER** Asst Prof to Prof Hist, Univ Pittsburgh, Bradford, 79-. **HONORS AND AWARDS** NEH Res grant **MEMBERSHIPS** Orgn Am Historians. **RESEARCH** United States from 1900-1930: political, social and cultural. **SELECTED PUBLICATIONS** Auth, Warner G. Harding: A Bibliography, Greenwood Press, 92; Coauth, Dictionary of Theoretical Concepts in Biology, Scarecrow Press, 81 **CONTACT ADDRESS** Social Sci Div Univ Pittsburgh, 300 Campus Dr, Bradford, PA, 16701. **EMAIL** rgf1@pitt.edu

FREDERICK, WILLIAM HAYWARD
PERSONAL Born 09/02/1941, Boston, MA, m, 1964, 2 children **DISCIPLINE** HISTORY OF SOUTHEAST ASIA **EDUCATION** Yale Univ BA, 63; Univ Hawaii, PhD (hist), 78. **CAREER** Instr, 73-78, asst prof 78-88; assoc prof, Ohio Univ, 88-, Dir, Int Student Serv, Ohio Univ, 73-78; ed, Southeast Asia Series, Ctr Int Studies Publ, 78-; founder and ed, Antara Kita Bull, Indonesian Studies Comt, 73-76; ed, Southeast Asia Transl Publ Group, Asn Asian Studies, 79-; exec dir, Indonesian Studies Summer Inst, 81-83; vis sr res, Australian Nat Univ, Nordic Inst of Asian Stu and Int Inst for Asian Stu. **MEMBERSHIPS** Asn Asian Studies; Koninklijk Inst voor Taal-, Land- en Volkenkunde. **RESEARCH** Modern Indonesian history; Southeast Asian social change since 1750; literature, the popular arts, and society in contemporary Southeast Asia. **SELECTED PUBLICATIONS** Cotransl, ed, Reflections on Rebellion: Stories from the Indonesian Upheavals of 1948 and 1965, Ohio Univ, 83; auth, Hidden Change in Colonial Urban Society in Indonesia, J of SE Asian Studies XIV, 83; auth, Visions and Heat: The Making of the Indonesian Revolution, Ohio Univ, 89; auth, Southeast Asia, Great Hisotrians of the Modern Age. An International Dictionary, 89,91; auth, Pandangan dan gejolak. Masyarakat kota dan lahirnya Revolusi Indonesia (Suyabaya 1926-1946), Gramedia, 90; auth, Southeast Asia. History, Encyc Britannica, 92; ed, auth, Indonesia. A Country Study, Lib of Cong, 93; auth, The Man Who Knew Too Much. Ch.O. Van der Plas and Postwar Indonesia, Imperial Plolicy and Southeast Asian Nationalism, NIAS-Curzon, 95; auth, The Appearance of Revolution: Cloth, Uniforms, and the 'Pemuda Style' in East Java, 1945-1949, Outward Appearances: Dressing the State and Society in Contemporary Indonesia, KITLV, 97; auth, Brothers of a Kind" Perspectives on Comparing the Indonesian and Vietnamese Revolutions, The Heartbeat of the Indonesian Revolution, Garmedia, 97; auth, Between Intent and Circumstance. Causative Factors in the British Intermezzo on Java (1945-1946): A 'Local History' Perspective, De Leeuw en de Banteng, Instituut Voor Nederlandse Geschiedenis, 97; auth, Dreams of Freedom, Movements of Despair: Armijn Pane and the Imahining of Modern Indonesian Culture, Imagining Indonesia. Cultural Politics and Political Culture, Ohio Univ, 97. **CONTACT ADDRESS** Dept Hist, Ohio Univ, Athens, OH, 45701-2979. **EMAIL** frederic@ohiou.edu

FREDRICK, DAVID
DISCIPLINE ROMAN SOCIAL HISTORY **EDUCATION** Univ Kans, BA, 82, MA, 84; Univ Southern Calif, PhD, 92. **CAREER** English and Lit, Univ Ark. **SELECTED PUBLICATIONS** Areas: violence in Roman elegy, theories of the gaze in rock performance, and Roman wall painting. **CONTACT ADDRESS** Univ Ark, Fayetteville, AR, 72701.

FREDRICKSMEYER, ERNST A.
PERSONAL Born 01/14/1930, Bismarck, ND, m, 1957, 3 children **DISCIPLINE** CLASSICS **EDUCATION** Lakeland Col, BA, 52; Univ Wis, MA, 53, PhD, 58. **CAREER** Instr, Cornell Col, 58-59; instr, Dartmouth Col, 59-60; instr, Bryn Mawr Col, 60-61; asst prof, Univ Wash, 61-66; assoc prof, Univ Colo, 66-71; vis prof, Univ Ore, 71; vis prof, Univ Wis, 78-79; prof, Univ Colo, 71-98. **HONORS AND AWARDS** Tchg Excellence Award, Univ Colo, 87. **MEMBERSHIPS** Am Philos Asn; Class Asn Middle W & S; Am Archeol Inst; Nat Asn Scholars. **RESEARCH** Golden Age Latin poetry; fourth century Greek history. **CONTACT ADDRESS** Dept of Classics, CB 348, Boulder, CO, 80309-0248.

FREDRICKSON, GEORGE M.
DISCIPLINE AMERICAN HISTORY **EDUCATION** Harvard Univ, AB, 56, PhD, 64. **CAREER** Prof, Harvard Univ, Northwestern Univ; prof, Stanford Univ, 84-. **HONORS AND AWARDS** Fulbright Scholar, Univ of Oslo, 56-57; Guggenheim Fel; NEH Sen Fels; Ctr for Advan Study in the Behavioral Scis and the Hums Fel, Stanford Univ; Ford Found Fel, Harvard Univ; Harmsworth vis prof, Oxford; Fulbright lectr, Moscow Univ; Anisfield Wolf Award in Race Relations Co-winner; Pulitzer Prize Finalist; Ralph Waldo Emerson Prize, Phi Beta Kappa; Merle Curti Award, Org of Am Hists. **MEMBERSHIPS** Org of Am Hists; AHA; Southern Hist Asn; Am Antiquarian Soc; Am Acad of Arts and Scis. **RESEARCH** History of race relations in the U.S.; comperative history of race relationss in the U.S. and South Africa; nineteenth century American history; American intellectual history. **SELECTED PUBLICATIONS** Auth, The Inner Civil War: Northern Intellectuals and the Crisis of the Union, 65; The Black Image in the White Mind: The Debate on Afro-American Character and Destiny, 71; White Supremacy: A Comparative Study in American and South African History, 81; The Arrogance of Race: Historical Perspectives on Slavery, Racism, and Social Inequality, 87; Black Liberation: A Comparative History of Black Ideologies in the United States and South Africa, 95; The Comparative Imagination: On the History of Racism, Nationalism, and Social Movement, 97. **CONTACT ADDRESS** Dept of History, Stanford Univ, Stanford, CA, 94305.

FREDRIKSEN, P.
PERSONAL Born 01/06/1951, RI, d, 3 children **DISCIPLINE** RELIGION & HISTORY **EDUCATION** Wellesley, BA, 73; Oxford, Dipl Theol, 74; Princeton, PhD, 79. **CAREER** Asst prof, History Dept, Univ Calif Berkeley, 81-86; assoc prof, Religious Studies, Univ Pitts, 86-89; aurelio prof, scripture, Boston Univ, 90-. **HONORS AND AWARDS** Lady Davis vis prof Jerusalem, 94; NEH Univ res grant, 92-93. **MEMBERSHIPS** Amer Acad Relig; Soc Bibl Lit; Nat Asn Patristic Studies **RESEARCH** Historical Jews; Jews & Gentiles in antiquity; Augustine. **SELECTED PUBLICATIONS** Auth, Augustine on History, the Chrush, and the Flesh, St Augustine the Bishop, Garland Publ, 94; From Jesus to Christ The Contribution of the Apostle Paul,Jews and Christians Speak to Jesus, 94; Torah Observance and Christianity: The Perspective of Roman Antiquity, Mod Theol, 95; What You See is What You Get: Context and Content in Current Research on the Historical Jesus, Theol Today, 95; Did Jesus Oppose the Purity Laws?, Bibl Rev, 95; Excaecati Occulta Iustitia Dei: Augustine on Jews and Judaism, Jour Early Christian Studies, 95; Jerusalem in Christian Thought, The City of the Great King: Jerusalem from David to the Present, Harvard Univ Press, 96; coauth, The Two Souls and the Divided Will, Self, Soul and Body in Religious Experience, E J Brill, 98. **CONTACT ADDRESS** Dept of Relig, Boston Univ, Boston, MA, 02215. **EMAIL** augfred@bu.edu

FREE, KATHERINE B.
DISCIPLINE THEATRE HISTORY **EDUCATION** Marymount Col, BA; Univ Calif, Los Angeles, MA, PhD. **CAREER** Prof; consult & actress, theatre LA. **MEMBERSHIPS** Amer Soc Theatre Res, ASTR; Int Fedn for the Theatre Res, IFTR; Amer Edu Theatre Assoc, ATHE. **RESEARCH** Ancient Greek theatre & the folk theatre of India. **SELECTED PUBLICATIONS** Articles in, Theatre Res Int, Theatre J, & UCLA J of Dance Ethnol. **CONTACT ADDRESS** Dept of Theatre, Loyola Marymount Univ, 7900 Loyola Blvd, Los Angeles, CA, 90045.

FREED, JOANN
DISCIPLINE HISTORY OF ARCHAEOLOGY AT CARTHAGE **EDUCATION** Alberta, PhD. **CAREER** Assoc Prof **SELECTED PUBLICATIONS** Auth, Deep Water Archaeology: A Late-Roman Ship from Carthage and an Ancient Trade Route near Skerki Bank off Northwest Sicily, 94; The Late Series of tunisian Cylindrical Amphoras at Carthage, 95; Early Roman Amphorae in the Collection of the Museum of Carthage, 96. **CONTACT ADDRESS** Dept of Classics, Wilfrid Laurier Univ, 75 University Ave W, Waterloo, ON, N2L 3C5. **EMAIL** jfreed@mach1.wlu.ca

FREED, JOHN BECKMANN
PERSONAL Born 02/06/1944, New York, NY **DISCIPLINE** MEDIEVAL HISTORY **EDUCATION** Cornell Univ, AB, 65; Princeton Univ, PhD, 69. **CAREER** Asst prof, 69-75, ASSOC PROF HIST, ILL STATE UNIV, 75-, Shelby Cullom Davis fel, Princeton Univ, 72. **MEMBERSHIPS** AHA; Mediaeval Acad Am; Am Cath Hist Asn. **RESEARCH** Medieval religious history; medieval German social history. **SELECTED PUBLICATIONS** Auth, The Early Germans, Hist, Vol 55,93; Records of the Collegiate Foundation of St Castulus in Moosburg, Cath Hist Rev, Vol 81, 95; Beguines in the Lake Constance Area, Cath Hist Rev, Vol 81, 95; Communications and Power in Medieval Europe, Vol 2--The Gregorian Revolution and Beyond, Speculum J Medieval Stud, Vol 71, 96; The German Episcopacy and the Implementation of the Decrees of the 4th Lateran Council, Ad 1216-1245--Watchmen on the Tower, Cath Hist Rev, Vol 82, 96; Land and Lordship--Structures of Governance in Medieval Austria, Speculum J Medieval Stud, Vol 69, 94; Peasants in the Middle Ages, Cent Europ Hist, Vol 26, 93; Land and Lordship--Structures of Governance in Medieval Austria--Brunner, O, Speculum J Medieval Stud, Vol 69, 94; The Franciscans in Medieval Luneburg, Cath Hist Rev, Vol 83, 97; Germany in the Early Middle Ages C.800-1056, Cent Europ Hist, Vol 25, 92; Elenchus Fontium Historiae Urbanae, Vol 3, Pt 1--Source Documents on the Early History of the Austrian State up to Ad-1277, Speculum J Medieval Stud, Vol 69, 94; Medieval German Social History--Generalizations and Particularism, Cent Europ Hist, Vol 25, 92; The Cistercian Nunnery in Wald, Cath Hist Rev, Vol 79, 93; Chronicle of the Bishops of Wurzburg 742-1495, Vol 1, From the Beginning until Rugger 1125,

Cent Europ Hist, Vol 26, 93; Elenchus Fontium Historiae Urbanae, Vol 3, Pt 1--Source Documents on the Early History of the Austrian State up to Ad 1277, Speculum J Medieval Stud, Vol 69, 94; Mendicant Orders in Mecklenburg--Contribution to the History of the Franciscans, The Nuns of the Order of Saint Clare, the Dominicans and the Augustinian Hermits in the Middle Ages - German - Ulpts,I/, Cath Hist Rev, Vol 83, 97; Itinerant Kingship and Royal Monasteries in Early Medieval Germany, C.936-1075, Cent Europ Hist, Vol 27, 94; The Letters of Hildegard of Bingen, Vol 1, Cent Europ Hist, Vol 28, 95; The Great Moravian Empire--Reality or Fiction--A New Interpretation of Sources on ihe History of 9th Century Middle Danube Region, Cent Europ Hist, Vol 30, 97; The Tradition of the Polling Foundation, Cath Hist Rev, Vol 80, 94; Fundatio and Memoria--Founders and Cloister Organizers in Images 1100-1350, Cath Hist Rev, Vol 80, 94; Registers of Documents of the Bishops of Passau, Vol 1, Cath Hist Rev, Vol 80, 94; Communications and Power in Medieval Europe, Vol 1--The Carolingian and Ottonian Centuries, Speculum J Medieval Stud, Vol 71, 96; The Making of Europe--Conquest, Colonization and Cultural Change, 950-1350, Cent Europ Hist, Vol 28, 95; Communications and Power in Medieval Europe, Vol 2--The Gregorian Revolution and Beyond, Speculum J Medieval Stud, Vol 71, 96; Schottenkloster--Irish Benedictines in Germany During the High iddle Ages, Cath Hist Rev, Vol 82, 96. **CONTACT ADDRESS** Dept of Hist, Illinois State Univ, Normal, IL, 61761.

FREEDMAN, ROBERT OWEN
PERSONAL Born 04/18/1941, Philadelphia, PA, m, 1965, 2 children **DISCIPLINE** DIPLOMATIC HISTORY; INTERNAL RELATIONS **EDUCATION** Univ Penn, BA 62; Columbia Univ, MA 65; Russian Inst Cert, 65, PhD, 69. **CAREER** Baltimore Hebrew College, pres 97-, acting pres, dean grad sch, 75-97; Marquette Univ, assoc prof, asst prof, 67-75; US Military Acad, 67-70; Univ MD Baltimore, adj prof, 80-92; Geo Washington Univ, adj prof, 84-86; Natnl Sec Agncy, 88-90; Dept State Ser Inst, lectr, 88-90. **HONORS AND AWARDS** U of Penn full schshp, honors grad, Soc Sci honor, Political Sci honor, 2 German Prizes. **MEMBERSHIPS** AIS; APSA; AAASS; MEI; MESA; ISA; JSA. **SELECTED PUBLICATIONS** Auth, The Middle East and the Peace Process, con't ed, Gainesville, Univ Press Florida, 98; Israel Under Rabin, con't ed, Boulder CO, Westview Press, 95; The Middle East After the Iraqi Invasion of Kuwait, co-ed, Gainesville, Univ Press of FL, 93; Moscow and the Middle East: Soviet Policy Since the Invasion of Afghanistan, Cambridge Eng, CUP, 91. **CONTACT ADDRESS** Office of President, Baltimore Hebrew Univ, 5800 Park Heights Ave, Baltimore, MD, 21215. **EMAIL** Freedman@bhu.edu

FREEHLING, WILLIAM W.
PERSONAL Born 12/26/1935, Chicago, IL, m, 1971, 4 children **DISCIPLINE** AMERICAN CULTURAL HISTORY **EDUCATION** Harvard Univ, AB, 58; Univ Calif-Berkeley, MA, 59; Berkeley, PhD, 63. **CAREER** Tchg fel, Berkeley, 59-60 & 62-63; instr Univ S Carolina, 61-62; instr, Harvard Univ, 63-64; asst prof to prof, Univ Mich, 64-72; prof, Johns Hopkins Univ, 72-91; Thomas B. Lockwood Prof Am Hist, SUNY, Buffalo, 91-94; OTIS A. SINGLETARY CHR IN HUM, UNIV KENTUCKY, 94- . **HONORS AND AWARDS** Woodrow Wilson fel, Guggenheim fel, 69-70, nHF fel, 68; Horace Rockham fel, 70-71; Owsley Prize; Bancroft Prize, Nevins Prize; Univ Mich Russel Prize. **MEMBERSHIPS** Am Hist Soc; S Hist Asn; Orgn Am Hist; Am Antiq Soc; Soc Am Hist; Soc Hist of Early Repub; The Hist Soc. **RESEARCH** History of American furniture; History of the Civil War era. **SELECTED PUBLICATIONS** Auth, The Reintegration of American History: Slavery and the Civil War, NY, 94; The Road to Disunion, Disunionists at Bay, 1776-1854, NY, 90; ed, Secession Debated: Georgia's Showdown in 1860, NY, 93; rev, David Gollaher, Ddorothea Dix, Lexington Herald-Leader, 96. **CONTACT ADDRESS** Singletary Chair in the Humanities, Univ of Kentucky, 1715 Patterson Office Tower, Lexington, KY, 40506-0027. **EMAIL** wwfree0@pop.uky.edu

FREEMAN, WILLIAM M.
PERSONAL Born 01/08/1926, Nashville, NC, m **DISCIPLINE** EDUCATION **EDUCATION** DE State Coll, BS 1949; Shaw Univ, BD 1958, MDiv 1970; NC Central Univ, MS 1960; Luther Rice Sem, DMin 1977; UNC, Century Univ, EdD, 1997. **CAREER** Lillington NC, asst vocational agr teacher; Fuquay-Varnia HS, guidance counselor; Fuquay Varnia Elementary School, principal; Fuquay Springs Consolidated HS, principal 1973-75; Wake Co Public Schools NC, dir fed program; Wake Co School Raleigh NC, asst supt 1975-77; Nash Co Sch Nashville NC, asst supt for personnel 1977-83; Congressman Ike Andrews 4th Congressional Dist, staff asst; The Fuquay-Varina Independent NC, columnist "The Other Side of Fuquay"; North Carolina General Assembly, House of Representatives Dist 62; AME Zion Church, staff writer for Sunday school publ bd, dist supt presiding elder 1981-. **HONORS AND AWARDS** Outstanding Serv & Achievement Award in Educ & Govt in 6th Dist Omega Psi Phi; Human Rellations Award Wake Co & NCAE Dist 11; Outstanding Dedication Wake Co; NCAE First Newsletter Editor "The Teachers Pet" 1973; 1st place among Newsletters in the state published by local NCAE Units in 1976; Outstanding Contributor to Fuquay-Varina HS & Comm; School Advisory Council Bd Dir Wake Co Opportunities Inc 1975; Citizen of Yr Fuquay-Varina 1973; Omega Man of Yr 1975-76; Honored as one of top ten grads from Delaware State Coll decade of 1940-49 honored in 1983; inducted into Delaware State Athletic Hall of Fame for Football, Boxing and Wrestling 1985. **MEMBERSHIPS** Mem Phi Delta Kappa; Fuquay-Varina Town Commr 1st Black 1973; Mayor Pro Tem 1st Black 1979-; bd dir Chamber of Commerce; NEA; NC Assn of Educators; mem Omega Psi Phi; Mason; Elk.

FREEZE, GREGORY L.
PERSONAL Born 05/09/1945, Dayton, OH, m, 1994 **DISCIPLINE** HISTORY **EDUCATION** DePauw Univ, BA, 67; Columbia Univ, MA, 68, PhD, 72. **CAREER** From asst, then assoc to full prof, Brandeis Univ, 72- ; res assoc, Davis Ctr for Russian Stud, Harvard Univ, 72- . **HONORS AND AWARDS** Fulbright Fac Res Fel; IREX Fel; Guggenheim Fel; ACLS grant; NEH Summer Sem for Col Tchrs, 88-89; NEH Res Fel, 89-90; NEH Dir of Summer Sem for Col Prof, 92-93, 93-94; principal invesitgator, Nat Coun for Soviet and E Europ Stud, 92-94, 95-97; Mazer grant, 98. **MEMBERSHIPS** Am Asn for the Advanc of Slavic Stud. **RESEARCH** Modern Russian history. **SELECTED PUBLICATIONS** Chief ed, Research Guide to the Central Party Archives, Moscow: Izd-vo Transakta, 93; chief ed, Special Files for I.V. Stalin from the NKVD, Blagovest, 94; chief ed, Russian Archive Series, v.4, Blagovest, 94; chief ed, Russian Archive Series, v.2, Iadatel'stvo Blagovest, 94; co-ed, Russian Archive Series, v.3, pt. 1, Izd-vo Blagovest, 94; chief ed, The Special Files for N.S. Khrushchev from the NKVD, Blagovest, 95; chief ed, The Special Files for V. Molotov from the NKVD, Blagovest, 95; chief ed, The Special Files for L.P. Beria from the NKVD, Blagovest, 96; ed, Russia, A History, Oxford, 97; ed, Pariahs, Partners, Predators: German-Soviet Relations, 1922-1941, Columbia Univ, 97. **CONTACT ADDRESS** Dept of History, Brandeis Univ, Waltham, MA, 02254. **EMAIL** freeze@binah.cc.brandeis.edu

FREIERT, WILLIAM K.
PERSONAL Born 04/26/1941, Baltimore, MD, m, 1970, 1 child **DISCIPLINE** CLASSICS **EDUCATION** St. Louis Univ, AB, 65, MA 66; Univ Minn, PhD, 72. **CAREER** Prof, Gustavus Adolphus Col, 72-; exchange prof, Kansai Gaidai Univ, 92. **HONORS AND AWARDS** Fulbright lectr. **MEMBERSHIPS** Am Philol Asn; Am Class League; Class Asn of Middle West and South; Int Soc for the Class Tradition. **RESEARCH** Classical studies. **SELECTED PUBLICATIONS** Auth, Paul T. Granlund: Spirit of Bronze, Shape of Freedom, 91; "Classical Myth in Post-War American Fiction" in The Class Tradition and the Am, 99; "Platonism in Saul Bellow's 'More Die of Heartbreak'" in J of Inquiry and Res, 93; "Bellow's 'Golden Ass': Greco-Roman Antecedents in 'More Die of Heartbreak'" in Saul Bellow J, 92. **CONTACT ADDRESS** 721 N Washington, St. Peter, MN, 56082-1847. **EMAIL** wfreiert@gac.edu

FREIS, CATHERINE R.
DISCIPLINE GREEK AND LATIN LANGUAGES AND LITERATURES **EDUCATION** Univ Calif, PhD. **CAREER** Dept ch & dir, Core Curric. **HONORS AND AWARDS** Amer Philol Asn awd & Millsaps Cole Distinguished prof awd. **SELECTED PUBLICATIONS** Publ on, drama and language pedagogy. **CONTACT ADDRESS** Dept of Classics, Millsaps Col, 1701 N State St, Jackson, MS, 39210. **EMAIL** freiscr@okra.millsaps.edu

FREIS, RICHARD
DISCIPLINE GREEK AND LATIN LANGUAGES AND LITERATURES **EDUCATION** Univ Calif, PhD. **CAREER** Dept Classics, Millsaps Col **HONORS AND AWARDS** Amer Philol Asn awd & Millsaps Col Distinguished prof awd. **RESEARCH** Greek philosophy; religious studies and comparative literature. **SELECTED PUBLICATIONS** Publ on, class and mod lit & publ poet. **CONTACT ADDRESS** Dept of Classics, Millsaps Col, 1701 N State St, Jackson, MS, 39210. **EMAIL** freissr@okra.millsaps.edu

FRENCH, GOLDWIN S.
PERSONAL Born 01/24/1923, Dresden, ON, Canada **DISCIPLINE** HISTORY **EDUCATION** Univ Toronto, BA, 44, MA, 47, PhD, 58. **CAREER** Lectr to prof hist, McMaster Univ, 47-72, dept ch, 64-70; pres & vice chancellor, 73-87, PROF EMER, VICTORIA UNIV. **HONORS AND AWARDS** Can Coun jr res fel. **MEMBERSHIPS** Can Hist Asn; Am Hist Asn; CIIA; Soc Fr Hist Stud; Can Methodist Hist Soc. **SELECTED PUBLICATIONS** Auth, Parsons and Politics, 62; ed & contrib, Encyclopedia of World Methodism, 74; ed, The Churches and the Canadian Experience, 63; ed, The Shield of Achilles, 68; ed, Can Stud Hist Govt; ed-in-chief, Ont Hist Ser, 71-93. **CONTACT ADDRESS** Victoria Univ, 73 Queen's Park Cr, Toronto, ON, M5S 1K7.

FREY, MARSHA LEE
PERSONAL Born 02/21/1947, Toledo, OH **DISCIPLINE** EARLY MODERN EUROPEAN AND DIPLOMATIC HISTORY **EDUCATION** Ohio State Univ, BA & BS in Ed, 67, MA, 68, PhD, 71. **CAREER** Lectr hist, Ohio State Univ, 71-72; vis asst prof, Univ Ore, 72-73; ASST PROF HIST, KANS STATE UNIV, 73-, Nat Endowment for Humanities grant, 77-78; Am Coun Learned Soc grant, 81; US Off Educ, 82. **MEMBERSHIPS** AHA; Soc Fr Hist Studies; Conf Brit Studies; Western Soc Sci Asn; Western Asn Ger Hist. **RESEARCH** Austria during the War of the Spanish Succession; European diplomatic history; British diplomatic service under Queen Anne. **SELECTED PUBLICATIONS** Coauth, The foreign policy of Frederick I, King in Prussia, 1703-1711: A fatal vacillation, East Europ Quart, spring 75; Frederick I and his Court, 1703-1710, Rev de l'Univ d'Ottawa, 10-12/75; auth, A Boot of Contention: Franco-Austrian Conflict Over Italy, Ann Meeting Western Soc Fr Hist, 76; coauth, The Anglo-Prussian Treaty of 1704, Annales Can Hist, 12/76; The latter years of Leopold I and his Court, Historian, summer 78; co-ed, Observation from the Hague & Ultrecht, Ohio State Univ Libr, 78; co-translr, The Gods are Athirst, Norwood, 78; coauth, Women in the West European Tradition, 82; auth, The History of Diplomats Immunity, 98; auth, Treaties of the War of the Spanish Succession, 95; auth, Societies in Upheaval, 87; Women in Western European History, 82, 84, 86; auth, Frederick I, 84; auth, A Question of Empire, 83. **CONTACT ADDRESS** Dept of History, Kansas State Univ, 208 Eisenhower Hall, Manhattan, KS, 66506-1000.

FREY, SLYVIA RAE
PERSONAL Born 05/03/1935, Eunice, LA **DISCIPLINE** AMERICAN AND BRITISH HISTORY **EDUCATION** Col Sacred Heart, BA, 56; La State Univ, MA, 65; Tulane Univ PhD (hist), 69. **CAREER** Teacher social studies, St Landry Parish Sch, 56-63 and Orleans Parish Sch, 63-66; instr, 69-72, asst prof, 72-81, ASSOC PROF US HIST, TULANE UNIV, 81-. **HONORS AND AWARDS** Moncado Prize, Am Mil Inst, 79. **RESEARCH** Colonial and revolutionary American history. **SELECTED PUBLICATIONS** Auth, Southern Women-Black and White in the Old South, J Southern Hist, Vol 59, 93; Uncommon Ground--Archaeology and Early African America, 1650-1800, Am Hist Rev, Vol 98, 93; Sweet Chariot--Slave Family and Household Structure in 19th Century Louisiana, Southwestern Hist Quart, Vol 97, 94 Rethinking the American Revolution, William Mary Quart, Vol 53, 96; Africans in Colonial Louisiana--Development of Afro- Culture in the 18th CenturyAm Hist Rev, Vol 98, 93. **CONTACT ADDRESS** Dept Hist, Tulane Univ, 6823 St Charles Ave, New Orleans, LA, 70118-5698.

FRIED, RICHARD M.
PERSONAL Born 04/14/1941, Milwaukee, WI, m, 1964, 2 children **DISCIPLINE** RECENT UNITED STATED HISTORY **EDUCATION** Amherst Col, BA, 63; Columbia Univ, MA, 65, PhD (hist), 72. **CAREER** Instr hist, Bowling Green State Univ, 67-70; vis assoc prof, Indiana Univ Pa, 70-71; asst prof, Fairmont State Col, 71-72; asst prof, 72-77, asst dept chmn, 75-77, dir grad studies, 79-81, ASSOC PROF HIST, UNIV ILL, CHICAGO CIRCLE, 77-. **MEMBERSHIPS** AHA; Orgn Am Hists. **RESEARCH** Recent American political history; McCarthy era. **SELECTED PUBLICATIONS** Auth, Un American Activities--The Trials of Remington, William, Rev Am Hist, Vol 24, 96; Not Without Honor--The History of American Anti-communism, Rev Am Hist, Vol 24, 96; Eisenhower and the Anticommunist Crusade, Am Hist Rev, Vol 98, 93; Search for the American Right Wing--An Analysis of the Social Science Record, 1955-1987, Am Hist Rev, Vol 98, 93; The Amerasia Spy Case--Prelude to Mccarthyism, Am Hist Rev, Vol 102, 97. **CONTACT ADDRESS** Dept of Hist, Univ of Ill Chicago Circle, Chicago, IL, 60680.

FRIEDEL, ROBERT D.
DISCIPLINE HISTORY **EDUCATION** Brown Univ, Ba, 71; London MSC, 72; Johns Hopkins Univ, PhD, 77. **CAREER** Assoc prof, PROF, HIST, UNIV MARYLAND **MEMBERSHIPS** Am Antiquarian Soc **RESEARCH** Changes in household materials, 1800-87. **SELECTED PUBLICATIONS** Auth, Edison's Electric Light: A Biography of an Invention, Rutgers Univ Press, 86; auth, "Crazy About Rubber," Am Heritage of Invention & Tech 5, Winter 90; auth, Zipper: An Exploration in Novelty, WW Norton & Co, 94. **CONTACT ADDRESS** Dept Hist, Univ of Maryland, College Park, MD, 20742. **EMAIL** rf27@umail.umd.edu

FRIEDLANDER, WALTER J.
PERSONAL Born 06/06/1919, Los Angeles, CA, m, 1976, 3 children **DISCIPLINE** MEDICAL ETHICS AND HISTORY **EDUCATION** Univ Calif, Berkeley, AB, 41; Univ Calif, San Francisco, MD, 45. **CAREER** Asst prof med, Sch Med, Stanford Univ, 54-56; asst prof neurol, Col Med, Boston Univ, 56-61; from assoc to prof neurol, Albany Med Col, 61-66; dir, Ctr Humanities and Med, 75-80, PROF NEUROL, COL MED, UNIV NEBR, 66-, Prof and Chmn Dept Med Humanities, 80-, Regional humanist, Nebr Comt for Humanities, 76-; consult, Nat Libr Med, 79-. **MEMBERSHIPS** Fel Am Col Physicians; Acad Aphasia. **RESEARCH** Medical history; applied medical ethics; medical sociology. **SELECTED PUBLICATIONS** Auth, The Evolution of Informed Consent in American Medicine, Perspectives Biol Med, Vol 38, 95. **CONTACT ADDRESS** Col of Med, Univ of Nebr, Omaha, NE, 68105.

FRIEDMAN, EDWARD
PERSONAL Born 12/12/1937, m, 1969, 2 children **DISCIPLINE** POLITICAL SCIENCE, EAST ASIA **EDUCATION** Brandeis Univ, BA (Political Sci), 59; Harvard Univ, MA (East Asia), 61, PhD (Political Sci), 68. **CAREER** To prof, Dept of Political Science, Univ WI, 67-; res fel, Univ MI, spring 68; teaching, Harvard Univ, summers 68, 69, 71; res fel, MUCIA, Hong Kong, 70; res fel, Center for Advanced Study, Univ IL, 71; fac, NYU, SUNY-Purchase, CUNY-Brooklyn, 71-72; SSRC, res grant, 73; consult, China Trade Services, fall 80; staff, US House of Representatives, Committee on Foreign Affairs, Jan 81-July 83; advisor, United Nations Develoment prog, Aug 83; lect, USAI: Australia, South Korea, Hong Kong, Burma, France, summer 84; Wang Found Res fel, 85; Guggenheim fel, 86-87; seminar, China and the Pacific Rim, Univ CA, La Jolla, summer 87; NEH fac seminar leader, summer 90; US AID, Albania, summer 92; US Dept of the Defense, consult, 93-94; US Naval Postgraduate School, Monterey, summer week, 93; US Naval Postgraduate School, summer sem, 94. **SELECTED PUBLICATIONS** Auth, Chinese Village, Socialist State China, Yale Univ Press, 91(winner of the Asn for Asian Studies Prize for Best Book on Modern China); What Do Peasants Really Want? An Exploration of Theoretical Categories and Action Consequences, Economic Development and Cultural Change, 41-1, Oct 92; New Nationalist Identities in Post-Leninist Transformations, monograph, Chinese Univ of Hong Kong Press, 92; Ethnic Identity and the De-Nationalization and Democratization of Leninist States, in M Crawford Young, ed, The Rising Tide of Cultural Pluralism, Univ WI press, 93; Anti-Imperialism in Chinese Foreign Policy, in San Kim, ed, China and the World, Westview, forthcoming; The Politics of Democratization, ed, Westview, forthcoming; Korea's Changing Identity, co-ed, under consideration; Why Excuse Oppression, Massacre or Holocaust? Bul of Concerned Asian Scholars, 24-2, April-June 98; Is Democracy A Human Universal?, Ethics and International Affairs, forthcoming; China Misperceived, Bul of Concerned Asian Scholars, forthcoming; numerous other books, book chapters, and articles. **CONTACT ADDRESS** Dept of Political Science, Univ of Wisconsin, Madison, Madison, WI, 53706. **EMAIL** friedman@polisci.wisc.edu

FRIEDMAN, ELLEN G.
PERSONAL Born 03/08/1939, New York, NY, 1 child **DISCIPLINE** EARLY MODERN EUROPE, SPANISH HISTORY **EDUCATION** NY Univ, BA, 67; City Univ New York, PhD (hist), 75. **CAREER** Asst prof hist, Univ Ky, 75-78; ASST PROF HIST, BOSTON COL, 78-, Res grant, Joint Span-US Comt Educ and Cult Affairs, 78-79. **MEMBERSHIPS** Soc Span and Port Hist Studies (secy, 80-82); AHA; N Am Catalan Soc. **RESEARCH** Early modern Spanish social history; history of public health. **SELECTED PUBLICATIONS** Auth, From Plagiarism to Appropriation, PMLA Publications Mod Lan AssocAm, Vol 108, 93; Where are the Missing Contents--Post Modernism, Gender, and the Canon PMLA Publications Mod Lan Assoc Am, Vol 108, 93; Christine and Contemporary Fiction, Mod Fiction Stud, Vol 42, 96. **CONTACT ADDRESS** Dept of Hist, Boston Col, 140 Commonwealth Ave, Chestnut Hill, MA, 02167-3800.

FRIEDMAN, JEAN E.
DISCIPLINE HISTORY **EDUCATION** Moravian, BA, 63; Lehigh, MA, 67, PhD, 76. **CAREER** ASSOC PROF, HIST, UNIV GEOR **MEMBERSHIPS** Am Antiquarian Soc **CONTACT ADDRESS** 124 White St., Watkinsville, GA, 30677.

FRIEDMAN, JEROME
PERSONAL Born 02/05/1943, New York, NY **DISCIPLINE** RENAISSANCE AND REFORMATION, MODERN HISTORY **EDUCATION** Hebrew Univ Jerusalem, BA, 67; Univ Wis-Madison, MA, 68, PhD (hist), 71. **CAREER** Asst prof, 70-76, ASSOC PROF HIST, KENT STATE UNIV, 76-, DIR JEWISH STUDIES, 77-, Lectr, Hillel Found Free Univ Kent State Univ, 73; mem, Ohio Renaissance-Reformation Forum; Nat Endowment for Humanities fel, 78. **MEMBERSHIPS** Am Soc Reformation Res; Sixteenth Century Studies Conf. **RESEARCH** Antitrinitarianism; Jewish-Christian dialogue; Reformation studies, Reformation radicalism. **SELECTED PUBLICATIONS** Auth, Dangerous Familiars--Presentations of Domestic Crime in England, 1550-1700, Am Hist Rev, Vol 100, 95; Essential Papers on Jewish Culture in Renaissance and Baroque Italy, 16th Century J, Vol 24, 93. **CONTACT ADDRESS** Dept of Hist, Kent State Univ, PO Box 5190, Kent, OH, 44242-0001.

FRIEDMAN, LAWRENCE JACOB
PERSONAL Born 10/08/1940, Cleveland, OH, m, 1966, 1 child **DISCIPLINE** AMERICAN HISTORY **EDUCATION** Univ Calif, Riverside, BA, 62, Los Angeles, MA, 65, PhD (hist), 67. **CAREER** Acting instr hist, Univ Calif, Los Angeles, 67; asst prof, Ind Univ, Ft Wayne, 67-68; asst prof, Ariz State Univ, 68-71; assoc prof, 71-77, PROF HIST and AM STUDIES, BOWLING GREEN STATE UNIV, 77-, Ind Univ fac res grant, 68; Nat Endowment for Humanities Younger Humanist fel, 71-72; res grant, Am Coun Learned Soc, 76; Nat Endowment for Humanities fel, 79-80. **MEMBERSHIPS** Orgn Am Hists; Am Studies Asn; Group Use Psychol in Hist. **RESEARCH** American social and intellectual history; psycho history; American race relations. **SELECTED PUBLICATIONS** Auth, Inventing the Feeble Mind--A History of Retardation in the United States, Am Hist Rev, Vol 100, 95; Freud, Jung, and Hall the King Maker--The Historic Expedition to America 1909, J American Hist, Vol 81, 94; Boats Against te Current--American Culture Between Revolution and Modernity, 1820-1860, Revi Am Hist, Vol 22, 94. **CONTACT ADDRESS** Dept of Hist, Bowling Green State Univ, Bowling Green, OH, 43403.

FRIEDMAN, MURRAY
DISCIPLINE AMERICAN JEWISH HISTORY, AMERICAN SOCIAL AND POLITICAL HISTORY **EDUCATION** Georgetown Univ, PhD. **CAREER** Prof, dir, Myer and Rosaline Feinstein Ctr Am Jewish Hist, Temple Univ; lectr, US Infor Agency, African and India, 74; vice-ch, US Civil Rights Comn, DC, 86-89. **MEMBERSHIPS** Mid Atlantic States dir, Am Jewish Comt. **RESEARCH** Am Jews in an age of conservatism. **SELECTED PUBLICATIONS** Auth, Overcoming Middle Class Rage, The Westminster Press, 71; Jewish Life in Philadelphia, 1830-1940, ISHI Publ, 83; The Utopian Dilemma: American Judaism in Public Policy, Ethics and Pub Policy Ctr, 85; Philadelphia Jewish Life: 1940 to 1985, Seth Press, 86; When Philadelphia Was the Capital of Jewish America, Assoc UP, 93; What Went Wrong: The Creation and Collapse of the Black-Jewish Alliance, the Free Press, 95. **CONTACT ADDRESS** Temple Univ, Philadelphia, PA, 19122.

FRIEDMAN, SAUL S
PERSONAL Born 03/08/1937, Uniontown, PA, m, 1964, 3 children **DISCIPLINE** MIDDLE EAST AND JEWISH HISTORY **EDUCATION** Kent State Univ, BA, 59; Ohio State Univ, MA, 62, PhD (hist), 69. **CAREER** Instr hist, Otterbein Col, 66-68 and Ohio Dominican Col, 68-69; asst prof, 69-74, assoc prof, 74-80, PROF HIST, YOUNGSTOWN STATE UNIV, 80-, Mem bd, Anti-Defamation League, Ohio-Ky Region, 72-; vis prof Jewish studies, Kent State Univ, 74; Univ Res Prof, Youngstown State, 76. **MEMBERSHIPS** NEA. **RESEARCH** Holocaust; Zionism and Arab nationalism; Jews in Arab lands. **SELECTED PUBLICATIONS** Auth, Statements of Principles, Business Lawyer, Vol 51, 96; Beyond Gynocriticism and Gynesis, The Geographics of Identity and the Future of Feminist Criticism, Tulsa Stud Womens Lit, Vol 15, 96; Statements of Principles, Business Lawyer, Vol 51, 96; Elational Epistemology and the Question of Anglo American Feminist Criticism, Tulsa Stud Womens Lit, Vol 12, 93; Identity Politics, Syncretism, Cathism, and Anishinabe Religion in Erdrich, Louise Tracks, Rel Li, Vol 26, 94; Woolf, Virginia Pedagogical Scenes of Reading, The Voyage Out, The Common Reader and her Common Readers, Mod Fiction Stud, Vol 38, 92; Identity Politics, Syncretism, Cathism, and Anishinabe Religion in Erdrich, Louise Tracks , Rel Lit, Vol 26, 94; All Rivers Run to the Sea, Cithara Essays in the Judeo Christian Tradition, Vol 35, 96. **CONTACT ADDRESS** Dept of Hist, Youngstown State Univ, One University Plz, Youngstown, OH, 44555-0002.

FRIEND, THEODORE W.
PERSONAL Born 08/27/1931, Wilkinsburg, PA, m, 1960, 3 children **DISCIPLINE** MODERN HISTORY **EDUCATION** Williams Col, BA, 53; Yale Univ, MA, 54, PhD, 58. **CAREER** Asst Instr Hist, Yale Univ, 55-57; from asst prof to prof, State Univ NY, Buffalo, 59-73, fac adv to pres, 68-69, exec asst to pres, 69-70; PRES, SWARTHMORE COL, 73-90, Am Philos Soc grant-in-aid, Philippines & Japan, 58; Rockefeller Found fel int rels, 61-62; Nat Defense Foreign Lang Act fel, Indonesia, 66-67; Guggenheim Found fel, Indonesia, Philippines & Japan, 67-68; nat consult, Nat Endowment for Humanities, 74- **HONORS AND AWARDS** Bancroft Award Am Hist, Diplomacy & Foreign Rels, 66., LLD, Williams Col, 78. **MEMBERSHIPS** AHA; Asn Asian Studies; Soc Historians of Am Foreign Rels. **RESEARCH** History of American foreign relations; Southeast Asian history; Japanese imperialism. **SELECTED PUBLICATIONS** Auth, Between Two Empires: The Ordeal of the Philippines, 1929-1946, Yale Univ, 65; ed, The Philippine Polity: A Japanese View, Yale Southeast Asia Publ, 68. **CONTACT ADDRESS** Swarthmore Col, Swarthmore, PA, 19081.

FRIER, BRUCE WOODWARD
PERSONAL Born 08/31/1943, Chicago, IL **DISCIPLINE** CLASSICAL STUDIES, HISTORY OF LAW **EDUCATION** Trinity Col, Conn, BA, 64; Princeton Univ, PhD, 70. **CAREER** Lectr Latin, Bryn Mawr Col, 68-69; Prof Class Studies, Univ Mich, 69-, Prof Law, Univ Mich, 81-. **HONORS AND AWARDS** Goodwin Award of Merit, 83; Guggenheim Fel, 84-85. **MEMBERSHIPS** Am Philol Asn. **RESEARCH** Roman legal history; Roman social and economic history; ancient demography. **SELECTED PUBLICATIONS** Auth, Libr Annales Pontificum Maximorum: The Origins of the Annalistic Tradition, Am Acad Rome, 79; Landlords and Tenants in Imperial Rome, Princeton Univ, 80; The Rise of the Roman Jurists, Princeton Univ, 85; Casebook on the Roman Law of Delicts, Schol Press, 89; The Demography of Roman Egypt, Cambridge Univ, 94. **CONTACT ADDRESS** Dept of Class Studies, Univ of Mich, 625 S State St, Ann Arbor, MI, 48109-1003. **EMAIL** bwfrier@umich.edu

FRIERSON, CATHY A.
DISCIPLINE RUSSIA AND THE SOVIET UNION, INTELLECTUAL HISTORY, WESTERN CIVILIZATION **EDUCATION** Harvard Univ, PhD. **CAREER** Assoc prof, Univ NH, 91-. **HONORS AND AWARDS** NEH summer stipend, 92; Hist Stud fel, Inst for Adv Stud, 93-95. **RESEARCH** Rural Russia; law and society in Russia. **SELECTED PUBLICATIONS** Auth, Peasant Icons: Representations of Rural People in Late Nineteenth Century Russia, 93; ed and transl, Aleksandr Nikolaevich Engelgardt: Letters from the Country, 1872-1887, 93. **CONTACT ADDRESS** Univ NH, Durham, NH, 03824. **EMAIL** cathyf@christa.unh.edu

FRIES, RUSSELL INSLEE
PERSONAL Born 05/15/1941, Glen Ridge, NJ, m, 1970 **DISCIPLINE** ECONOMIC HISTORY, HISTORY OF TECHNOLOGY **EDUCATION** Yale Univ, BA, 63; Johns Hopkins Univ, MA, 67, PhD (econ hist), 72. **CAREER** Asst prof hist, Southern Methodist Univ, 70-73; asst prof, 73-78, ASSOC PROF HIST, UNIV MAINE, ORONO, 78-, Proj hist, Hist Am Eng Rec, Nat Parks Serv, Dept Interior, 73; dir, Great Falls Hist Dist, 75-76. **HONORS AND AWARDS** Abbott Payson Usher Prize, Soc Hist Technol, 76. **MEMBERSHIPS** AHA; Soc Hist Technol; Soc Indust Archaeol; Hist Sci Soc; Econ Hist Asn. **RESEARCH** Nineteenth Century industrial development and technology; maritime navigation and technology; hydroelectric development. **SELECTED PUBLICATIONS** Auth, The Jours of Gorgas, Josiah, 1857-1878, Technology and Culture, Vol 37, 96; The Jours of Gorgas, Josiah, 1857-1878, Tech Cult, Vol 37, 96. **CONTACT ADDRESS** Dept of Hist, Univ of Maine, Orono, ME, 04473.

FRIGUGLIETTI, JAMES
PERSONAL Born 07/23/1936, Cleveland, OH **DISCIPLINE** MODERN FRENCH HISTORY **EDUCATION** Western Reserve Univ, BA, 58; Harvard Univ, PhD (hist), 66. **CAREER** Asst prof hist, Univ Rochester, 66-69 and Case Western Reserve Univ, 69-76; asst prof, 76-78, ASSOC PROF HIST, EASTERN MONT COL, 78-, Nat Endowment for Humanities fel, 77. **HONORS AND AWARDS** Res Merit Award, Eastern Mont Col, 77; Distinguished Teacher Award, Eastern Mont Col, 79. **MEMBERSHIPS** AHA; Soc Fr Hist Studies; Soc Fr Etude XVIIIe Siecle; Am Soc 18th Century Studies. **RESEARCH** French Revolution; European historiography; French pacifism. **SELECTED PUBLICATIONS** Auth, Gargan, Edward, T. 1922-95, Fr Hist Stud, Vol 19, 95; Reform and Revolution in France--Politics of Transition, 1774-1791, Hist, Vol 59, 97; Art and the French Commune--Imagining Paris After War and Revolution - Boime, A, Hist, Vol 58, 96; Mousnier, Roland 1907-93, Fr Hist Stud, Vol 18, 93. **CONTACT ADDRESS** Dept of Hist, Eastern Montana Col, Billings, MT, 59101.

FRINTA, MOJMIR SVATOPLUK
PERSONAL Born 07/28/1922, Prague, Czechoslovakia, m, 1948, 3 children **DISCIPLINE** HISTORY OF ART, MEDIEVAL ART **EDUCATION** Karlova Univ, Prague, AB, 47; Univ Mich, MA, 53, PhD(art hist), 60. **CAREER** From asst prof to assoc prof, 63-69, prof Hist of Art, 69-93, emeritus, 93-, SUNY Albany; Am Philos Soc grants, 64 & 65; Am Coun Learned Soc grant, 68; S H Kress grant, 70; Nat Endowment for Humanities grant, 77; consult, Soc Sci & Humanities Res Coun Can. **MEMBERSHIPS** Col Art Asn Am; Soc Am Archaeol; Int Inst Conserv Hist & Artistic Works; Int Ctr Medieval Art. **RESEARCH** Fourteenth century painting and sculpture; 15th century Netherlandish painting; medieval art technology. **SELECTED PUBLICATIONS** Auth, The master of the Gerona Martyrology and Bohemian Illumination, 64 & An investigation of the punched decoration of medieval ... panel paintings, 65, Art Bull; The Genius of Robert Campin, Mouton, The Hague, 66; The authorship of the Merode Altarpiece, Art Quart, 68; A Seemingly Florentine yet not really Florentine altar-piece, Burlington Mag, 75; The puzzling raised decorations in the paintings of Magister Theodoric, Simiolus, 76; Deletions from the Oeuvre of Pietro Lorenzetti and related works, Mitteilungen des Kunsthistorischen Insts in Florenz, 76; The quest for a restorer's shop of beguiling invention: Restorations and forgeries in Italian panel painting, Art Bull, 3/78; auth, Punched Decoration on Late Medieval Panel and Miniature Painting, part I: Catalogue, Maxdorf, 98. **CONTACT ADDRESS** Dept of Art, SUNY, Albany, Albany, NY, 12222. **EMAIL** frinta@juno.com

FRISCHER, BERNARD
DISCIPLINE CLASSICAL STUDIES **EDUCATION** Wesleyan Univ, BA, 71; Univ Heidelberg, PhD, 75; FAAR, 76. **CAREER** Asst prof, 76-80; assoc prof, 80-91; ch, 84-88; dir, UCLA Hum Comp Facility, 87-88; dir, Univ Calif Edu Abroad Prog, Italy, 88-90; dir, Univ Calif Edu Abroad Prog, UCLA Campus Off, 92-98; PROF, CLASSICS, UCLA, 91-; vis prof, Univ Bologna, 93; vis prof, Univ Pa, 94; resident class stud, Amer Acad Rome, 96; sec, Acad Sen Univ Calif, 94-96; dir, UCLA Rome Reborn proj, 96; dor.UCLA Cult Virtual Reality lab, 98; dept repr, Legis Assembly, 93-. **HONORS AND AWARDS** Woodrow Wilson fel, 71; jr fel, Mich Soc Fel(S), 71-74; Rome Prize fel, 74-76; ACLS fel, 81-82, 96-97; Paul Mellon sr fel, Ctr Adv Stud in the Visual Arts, Nat Gallery, Wash DC, 96-98., Ch, Cmte to Rev the Summer Sch Roman Topography and Archaeol, Amer Acad Rome, 83; ch, Software

Cmte, Amer Philol Assn, 88. **MEMBERSHIPS** Mem, Amer Philol Assoc, 71-; Archaeol Inst Am, 76-; Adv Cmte, Amer Acad Rome, 76-; ed bd, Class Antiquity, 81-87; adv cmte, proj Perseus, 87-93; Classics Selection Cmte, Fullbright Exchange Commission, 84-88. **SELECTED PUBLICATIONS** Auth, "Horace and the End of Renaissance Humanism in Italy: Quarrels, Religious Correctness, Nationalism and Academic Protectionism," Arethusa 28, 95; "La Villa dei Papiri: Modello per la Villa Sabina di Orazio?," Cronache Ercolanesi 25, 95; "Horazens Sabinum: Dichtung und Wahrheit," Romische Lebenskunst, 96; "Rezeptionsgeschichte and Interpretation: The Quarrel of Antonio Riccoboni and Nicolo Cologno about the Structure of Horace's Ars Poetica," Zeitgenosse Horaz, Der Dichter und seine Leser seit zwei Jahrtausenden, 96; co-auth, Sentence Length and Word-type at Sentence Beginning and End: Reliable Authorship Discriminators for Latin Prose, New Stud on the Authorship of the Hist Augusta, Res Hum Comp 5, Oxford Univ Press, 96; How To Do Things With Words/Stop: Two Studies on the Historia Augusta and Cicero's Orations, Papers from the Seventh Intl Colloquium on Latin Lings, Jerusalem, Innsbrucker Beitrage zur Sprachwissenschaft 96. **CONTACT ADDRESS** Dept of Classics, Univ Calif, 405 Hilgard Ave., Los Angeles, CA, 90095-1417. **EMAIL** frischer49@aol.com

FRITZ, HARRY WILLIAM
PERSONAL Born 09/28/1937, Salisbury, MD, m, 1966, 2 children **DISCIPLINE** EARLY AMERICAN HISTORY **EDUCATION** Dartmouth Col, AB, 60; Mont State Univ, MA, 62; Wash Univ, PhD (hist), 71. **CAREER** Instr hist, Univ Col, Wash Univ, 63-66; from instr to assoc prof, 67-80, PROF HIST, UNIV MONT, 80-. **MEMBERSHIPS** AHA; Orgn Am Hists; Western Soc Sci Asn; Soc Hists Early Am Republic; Southern Hist Asn. **RESEARCH** United States, 1789-1840; political parties; Montana. **SELECTED PUBLICATIONS** Auth, Undaunted Courage--Lewis, Meriwether, Jefferson, Thomas and the Opening of the American, Montana Mag W Hist, Vol 47, 97 American Political Cultures, Hist, Vol 57, 95; Seeking Western Waters--The Lewis and Clark Trail from the Rockies to the Pacific, J Am Hist, Vol 84, 97; An Elusive Victory--The Battle of the Big Hole, Montana Mag W Hist, Vol 44, 94; Roeder, Richard, B., 1930-95--In Commemoration, Montana Mag W Hist, Vol 46, 96. **CONTACT ADDRESS** Dept of Hist, Univ of Mont, Missoula, MT, 59812-0001.

FRITZ, HENRY EUGENE
PERSONAL Born 06/20/1927, Garrison, KS, m, 1950, 3 children **DISCIPLINE** AMERICAN HISTORY **EDUCATION** Bradley Univ, BS, 50, MA, 52; Univ Minn, PhD, 57. **CAREER** Instr Am hist, Univ Wis, Milwaukee, 56-58; from asst prof to assoc prof, 58-68, PROF HIST, ST OLAF COL, 68-, CHMN DEPT, 69-, Fac fel, Newberry Libr Sem in Humanities, Assoc Cols, Midwest, 68-69. **MEMBERSHIPS** AHA; Orgn Am Hists; Western Hist Asn. **RESEARCH** American Indian policies and administration; development of American nationalism, 1800-1850; frontier and territorial expansion of the United States. **SELECTED PUBLICATIONS** Auth, The Fox Wars--The Mesquakie Challenge to New, Hist, Vol 57, 95; They Called it Prairie Light--The Story of Chilocco Indian School, J Am Hist, Vol 82, 95; American Indian Treaties--The History of a Political Anomaly, Pac Northwest Quart, Vol 87, 96; An American Dilemma--Administration of the Indian Estate Under the Dawesm Act and Amendments, J Southwest, Vol 37, 95. **CONTACT ADDRESS** Dept of Hist, St Olaf Col, Northfield, MN, 55057.

FRITZ, ROBERT B.
PERSONAL Born 07/13/1929, Bridgeport, CT **DISCIPLINE** ART **EDUCATION** Syracuse Univ, BA, 51; Columbia Univ, MA, 52, PhD, 63. **CAREER** Prof Fine Arts, 61-92, Fitchburg State College. **RESEARCH** American Architecture. **CONTACT ADDRESS** 30 Clover Lea Place, Stratford, CT, 06615.

FRITZ, STEPHEN G.
DISCIPLINE HISTORY **EDUCATION** Univ Ill, BA, 71, MA, 73, PhD, 80; Goethe Inst, Zertifikat II, 77-78; Univ Heidelberg, Immatirkulation, 77-78. **CAREER** Tchg asst, 74-77, res asst, 78-79, vis instr, 80, Univ Ill; instr, Richland Col, 78; mgmt staff, Ill Res Ctr, 79-80; vis asst prof, Southern Ill Univ, 80-83; codir, 86-94, from asst prof to assoc prof to prof, 84-, East Tenn State Univ. **HONORS AND AWARDS** List of Excellent Teachers, Univ Ill, 76-77; Res Fel, German Acad Exchange Service, 77-78; List of Excellent Teachers, 80-83, Queen Award, 83, Southern Ill Univ; Summer Res Grant, 85, 91, ETSU Res and Development Committee; Col of Arts and Sciences Res Award, 96; Distinguished Univ Fac Res Award, 96., Distinction on PhD Exam. **MEMBERSHIPS** German Stud Asn; Conference Group Central European Hist; Soc German-Am Stud; European Hist Section, Southern Hist Asn; Fulbright Alumni Asn; Phi Alpha Theta; Delta Phi Alpha; Omicron Delta Kappa. **SELECTED PUBLICATIONS** Auth, art, Benito Mussolini and Kaiser Wilhelm II, 91; auth, art, Frankfurt, 92; auth, Frontsoldaten: The German Soldier in World War II, 95; auth, Hitler's Frontsoldaten: Der erzahlte Krieg, 98; auth, art, We are trying to change the face of the world. Ideology and Motivation in the Wehrmacht on the Eastern Front: The View Fom Below, 98. **CONTACT ADDRESS** Dept of History, East Tennessee State Univ, Box 70672, Johnson City, TN, 37614-0672. **EMAIL** fritzs@etsu.edu

FRITZSCHE, PETER
PERSONAL Born 07/03/1959, Chicago, IL, m, 1988, 2 children **DISCIPLINE** HISTORY **EDUCATION** Univ Cal Berk, PhD 86. **CAREER** Univ IL, asst prof, assoc prof, prof, 87 to 94-. **HONORS AND AWARDS** Humboldt Res Fel. **RESEARCH** Modernity; memory; German history. **SELECTED PUBLICATIONS** Auth, Germans into Nazis, Harvard Univ Press, 98; Reading Berlin 1900, Harvard Univ Press, 96; Imagining the Twentieth Century, coed, Univ of IL Press, 97; a Nation of Flyers: German aviation and Popular Imagination, Harvard Univ Press, 92. **CONTACT ADDRESS** Dept of History, Univ of Illinois, 810 S Wright St, Urbana, IL, 61801. **EMAIL** pfritzsc@uiuc.edu

FRIZZELL, ROBERT
PERSONAL Born 06/26/1947, Marshall, MO, m, 1974, 1 child **DISCIPLINE** HISTORY **EDUCATION** Univ Mo, AB, 69; Univ Ill, MA, 73, MSLS, 75. **CAREER** Librn, Wesleyan Univ, 75-89; dir, Hendrix Col, 89-. **HONORS AND AWARDS** Auth Award, 77, State Hist Society Mo. **MEMBERSHIPS** Society for German-Am Studies; Immigration Hist Society; State Hist Society Mo; Ill State Hist Society. **RESEARCH** Immigration history; German immigration to U.S.; Midwestern history. **SELECTED PUBLICATIONS** Auth, German Freethinkers in Bloomington: Sampling a Forgotten Culture, 88; auth, Reticent Germans: The East Frisians of Illinois, 92; auth, The New Bailey Library, 94; auth, Managing Through a Major Building Project: Three Academic Library Leaders Comment, 94; auth, The Low German Settlements of Western Missouri: Examples of Ethnic Cocoons, 98. **CONTACT ADDRESS** Bailey Library, Hendrix Col, 1600 Washington Ave, Conway, AR, 72032. **EMAIL** frizzell@hendrix.edu

FROIDE, AMY
PERSONAL Born 06/22/1967, San Diego, CA, m, 1996 **DISCIPLINE** EARLY MOD BRIT HIST, EUROPEAN WOMEN'S HIST **EDUCATION** Univ San Diego, MAT 90, BA 88; Duke Univ, PhD, 96, MA 93; **CAREER** Vis asst prof, Miami Univ Ohio, 96-98; asst prof, Univ Tenn Chattanooga, 98-. **HONORS AND AWARDS** 98-99 Rockefeller Found Fel Women's Hist; 98 Folger Shakespeare Libr Fel. **MEMBERSHIPS** AHA; NACBS; CCWH; WAWH. **RESEARCH** Women in Pre-Mod Europe; Singlewomen; Soc Hist of premod Brit. **SELECTED PUBLICATIONS** Singlewomen in the European Past, ed, Judith M Bennett & Amy M Froide, Univ Penn, 98; Old Maids: The Lifecycle of Single Women in Early Modern England, ed, Lynn Botelho & Pat Thane; Old Women in Britain, 1500 to the Present, Longman, 99. **CONTACT ADDRESS** Dept of History, Univ of Tennessee, Chattanooga, 615 McCallie Ave, Chattanooga, TN, 37403-2598. **EMAIL** Amy-Froide@utc.edu

FROST, FRANK J.
PERSONAL Born 12/03/1929, Washington, DC, 2 children **DISCIPLINE** ANCIENT HISTORY **EDUCATION** Univ Calif, Santa Barbara, AB, 55, Los Angeles, MA, 59, PhD, 61. **CAREER** Lectr hist and classics, Univ Calif, Riverside, 59-62; asst prof ancient hist, Hunter Col, 62-64; asst prof classics, Univ Calif, Riverside, 64-65; asst prof, 65-67, assoc prof, 68-80, PROF HIST, UNIV CALIF, SANTA BARBARA, 80-, County supvr, 73-77; assoc ed, Am J Ancient Hist, 76-. **MEMBERSHIPS** Soc Promotion Hellenic Studies; Brit Class Asn; Am Philol Asn; Archaeol Inst Am. **RESEARCH** Marine archaeology; Greek historiography, especially Plutarch; Athenian politics in the fifth century, BC. **SELECTED PUBLICATIONS** Auth, Voyages of the Imagination, Archaeol, Vol 46, 93. **CONTACT ADDRESS** 2687 Puesta del Sol, Santa Barbara, CA, 93105.

FROST, GINGER S.
PERSONAL Born 08/19/1962, Sherman, TX **DISCIPLINE** HISTORY **EDUCATION** TX Woman's Univ, BA (Magna Cum Laude), 83; LA State Univ, MA, 86; Rice Univ, PhD, 91. **CAREER** Asst prof, Hist, Wesleyan Col, 91-93; Dept assoc, Northwestern Univ, 93-94; asst prof, Hist, Judson Col, 94-96; ASST PROF, HIST, SAMFORD UNIV, 96-, DIR, HONORS PROG, 98-. **HONORS AND AWARDS** North Am Conf on British Studies Dissertation Year fel, 89-90; Clifford Lefton Lawrence Award in British Hist, Rice Univ, 91; John W. Gardner Award for the Best Dissertation in Humanities and Social Sciences, Rice Univ, 91; Faculty Development grant, Samford Univ, 98., Alumni Federation Graduate fel, LA State Univ, 84-87; Rice Presidential Recognition Award, Rice Univ, 87-88; Lodieska Stockbridge Vaughan Fel, Rice Univ, 89-90; History Dept fel, Rice Univ, 87-91; member: Pi Gamma Mu, Mortar Board, Phi Kappa Phi, Alpha Chi, Phi Alpha Theta, and Alpha Lambda Delta Honor Societies. **MEMBERSHIPS** Am Hist Asn; Southern Hist Asn (European Hist section); Southern Conference of British Studies (exec comm, 97-2000); Southern Asn of Women's Historians; North Am Conference on British Studies; Victorians Inst; Nineteenth Century Studies Asn. **RESEARCH** Modern Britain; family hist; women's hist. **SELECTED PUBLICATIONS** Auth, Through the Medium of the Passions: Cohabitation Contracts in England, 1750-1850, Proceedings of the 23rd Annual Consortium on Revolutionary Europe, 94; I Shall Not Sit Down and Crie: Feminism, Class and Breach of Promise Plaintiffs in England, 1850-1900, Gender and History 6, Aug 94; Promises Broken: Courtship, Class, and Gender in Victorian England, Univ Press VA, Nov 95; Bigamy and Cohabitation in Victorian England, J of Family Hist, 22, July 97; A Shock to Marriage? The Clitheroe Case and the Victorians, in Disorder in the Court, George Robb and Nancy Erber, eds, NY Univ Press, 99. **CONTACT ADDRESS** Dept of Hist, Samford Univ, Birmingham, AL, 35229. **EMAIL** gsfrost@samford.edu

FROST, JAMES ARTHUR
PERSONAL Born 05/15/1918, Manchester, England, m, 1942, 2 children **DISCIPLINE** AMERICAN HISTORY **EDUCATION** Columbia Col, AB, 40; Columbia Univ, AM, 41, PhD, 49. **CAREER** Instr hist, Nutley High Sch, NJ, 46-47; instr, State Univ NY Col Oneonta, 47-50, asst to pres, 50-52, dean, 52-64; assoc provost acad planning, State Univ NY, 64-65, vchancellor univ cols, 65-72; Exec Secy Bd Trustees, Conn State Col, 72-, Exec Dir, 76-, Pres 83-85, PROF EMER, 85- , CONN STATE UNIV, Smith-Mundt prof Am hist, Univ Ceylon, 59-60; mem comn higher educ, Mid States Asn Cols & Sec Schs, 67-73; mem, Comt Res & Develop, Col Entrance Eval Bd, 73-76. **MEMBERSHIPS** AHA. **RESEARCH** American frontier; history of New York state; administration of higher education. **SELECTED PUBLICATIONS** Auth, Life on the Upper Susquehanna, 1783-1860, Columbia Univ, 51; coauth, A History of New York State, Cornell Univ Press, 2nd ed, 67; New York: The Empire State, Prentice-Hall, 5th ed, 80; A History of the United States: The Evolution of a Free People, Follett, 2nd ed, 69; The Establishment of the Connecticut State University, 1965-85, 91; The Country Club of Farmington, Conn, 1892-1995, 96. **CONTACT ADDRESS** 17 Neal Dr, Simsbury, CT, 06070.

FROST, JERRY WILLIAM
PERSONAL Born 03/17/1940, Muncie, IN, m, 1963, 1 child **DISCIPLINE** AMERICAN & CHURCH HISTORY **EDUCATION** DePauw Univ, BA, 62; Univ WI, MA, 65, PhD, 68. **CAREER** Asst prof Am hist, Vassar Col, 67-73; assoc prof & dir relig, Friends Hist Libr, 73-79, prof, 79, Jenkins prof Quaker hist & res, Swarthmore Col, 80-, Fel, John Carter Brown Libr, 70; USIP Fel, 85, Philadelphia Inst for Early Am Studies Fel, 80, Lang Fel, 81, 97; ed, Pa Mag Hist & Biog, 81-86. **HONORS AND AWARDS** Brit Friends Hist Asn, pres, 98. **MEMBERSHIPS** Friends Hist Soc; Am Soc Church Hist. **RESEARCH** Quakers; Am family; peace research. **SELECTED PUBLICATIONS** Auth, Quaker Family in Colonial America, St Martins, 73; Connecticut Education in the Revolutionary Era, Pequot, 74; Origins of the Quaker crusade against slavery: A review of recent literature, spring 78, Quaker Hist; ed, The Keithian Controversy in Early Pennsylvania, 80 & Quaker Origins of Antislavery, 81, Norwood; Years of crisis and separation: Philadelphia yearly meeting, 1790-1860, In: Friends in the Delaware Valley, 81; Seeking the Light, Essays in Quaker History, Pendle Hill, 87; co-auth, The Quakers, Greenwood, 88; auth, A Perfect Freedom: Religious Liberty in Pennsylvania, Cambridge, 90; Our deeds carry our message: The early history of the American Friends Service Committee, Quaker Hist, 92; co-auth, Christianity: a Social and Cultural History, Prentice Hall, 98. **CONTACT ADDRESS** Friends Hist Libr, Swarthmore Col, 500 College Ave, Swarthmore, PA, 19081-1306.

FROST, OLIVIA PLEASANTS
PERSONAL Asbury Park, NJ, w **DISCIPLINE** EDUCATION **EDUCATION** Hunter Coll, BA; Columbia Univ, MA 1951; NY Univ, Dept of Human Relations, Sch of Educ, PhD 1972. **CAREER** Haryou-Contributor to Youth in the Ghetto, rsch assoc 1963-66; NY Urban League, rsch dir 1965-66; Haryou-ACT, rsch assoc 1969-70; New York City Youth Bd Comm Council of NY, rsch assoc; Columbia Univ, MARC Demonstration Proj on Adolescent Minority Females, rsch consultant 1971-75; CUNY, assoc prof 1972-77; Central SEEK, dir prog devel. **HONORS AND AWARDS** Warburg Fellowship, Dept of Human Relations, Sch of Educ, NYU, 1968; grant for doctoral dissertation, Dept of Labor, Washington DC; founder, Assn of Black Women in Higher Educ. **MEMBERSHIPS** Mem Natl Assn Social Workers, Afro-Amer Historical & Genealogical Soc Inc; dir comm study Harlem A Neglected Investment Oppor; mem NAACP, NY Urban League; trustee Schomburg Corp; trustee, Schomburg Corp., chairman, Genealogy Committee with the Schomburg Center for Research in Black Culture, The New York Public Library.

FROST, PETER K.
PERSONAL Born 08/26/1936, Boston, MA, m, 1965, 1 child **DISCIPLINE** HISTORY **EDUCATION** Harvard Univ, BA, 58, MA, 62, PhD, 66. **CAREER** Asst to dean admis & scholar, Harvard Univ, 58-60; from instr to asst prof, 64-72, assoc dean admin, 69-72, dir assoc Kyoto prog, 72-73, assoc prof, 72-80, prof hist, Williams Col, 80-. **MEMBERSHIPS** Assn Asian Studies. **CONTACT ADDRESS** Dept of History, Williams Col, 880 Main St, Williamstown, MA, 01267-2600. **EMAIL** pfrost@williams.edu

FROST, RICHARD HINDMAN
PERSONAL Born 06/15/1930, Brooklyn, NY, m, 1963, 2 children **DISCIPLINE** UNITED STATES HISTORY **EDUCATION** Swarthmore Col, AB, 51; Univ Calif, Berkeley, MA, 54, PhD (hist), 60. **CAREER** Asst prof hist, Univ Winnipeg, 60-

64; lectr, San Francisco State Col, 64-65; vis asst prof, Univ NMex, 65-66; assoc prof, 66-72, PROF HIST, COLGATE UNIV, 72-, CHMN DEPT, 73-, Fel Ctr Hist Am Indian, Newberry Libr, 79-80. **MEMBERSHIPS** Orgn Am Hists; Am Soc Ethnohist. **RESEARCH** Twentieth century United States history; American civil liberties history; American Indian history. **SELECTED PUBLICATIONS** Auth, Pueblo Nations--8 Centuries of Pueblo Indian History, J Am Hist, Vol 80, 93. **CONTACT ADDRESS** Dept of Hist, Colgate Univ, Hamilton, NY, 13346.

FROW, JOHN
DISCIPLINE CULTURAL STUDIES **EDUCATION** PhD. **CAREER** Prof English, Univ Queensland; dep dir, Australian Key Ctr Cult and Media Policy. **RESEARCH** Literary theory. **SELECTED PUBLICATIONS** Auth, Cultural Studies and Cultural Value, pending.

FRY, CHRISTINE L.
PERSONAL Born 04/24/1943, m, 1967 **DISCIPLINE** ANTHROPOLOGY **EDUCATION** Wagner Col, NY, BA, 65; Univ Ariz, MA, 69, PhD, 73. **CAREER** Prof, anthropology, 84-, Loyola Univ Chicago. **HONORS AND AWARDS** Kalish Award for Innovative Publication, 94. **MEMBERSHIPS** Amer Anthropological Asn; Asn for Anthropology & Gerontology; Gerontological Soc of Amer. **RESEARCH** Aging; older people in communities **SELECTED PUBLICATIONS** Coauth, The Aging Experience: Diversity and Commonality Across Cultures, Sage Pub, 94; art, Kin and Kindred: the First and Last Source of Support, Adult Intergenerational Rel: Effects of Societal Change, Springer Pub, 94; art, Kinship and Individuation, Adult Intergenerational Relations: Effects of Societal Change, Springer Pub, 94; art, Age and the Life Course, Aging Experience: Diversity and commonality Across Cultures, Sage Pub, 94; art, Age, Aging and Culture, Handbook of Aging and the Social Sciences, 4th ed, Academic Press, 95; art, Cross-Cultural Perspectives on Aging, Gerontology: Perspectives & Issues 2nd ed, Springer, 97; art, Culture and the Meaning of a Good Old Age, Cultural Contexts of Aging, 2nd ed, Greenwood Press, 97; art, Anthropological theories of age, Handbook of Theories of Aging, Springer Pub, 98. **CONTACT ADDRESS** Dept of Sociology and Anthropology, Loyola Univ, Chicago, Chicago, IL, 60626. **EMAIL** Cfry@luc.edu

FRY, JOSEPH A.
DISCIPLINE HISTORY **EDUCATION** Univ Va, PhD, 74. **CAREER** Prof, Univ Nev Las Vegas. **SELECTED PUBLICATIONS** Auth, John Tyler Morgan and the Search for Southern Autonomy, Knoxville, 92; Henry S. Sanford: Diplomacy and Business in Nineteenth-Century America, Reno, 82. **CONTACT ADDRESS** History Dept, Univ Nev Las Vegas, 4505 Md Pky, Las Vegas, NV, 89154.

FRYD, VIVIEN G.
PERSONAL Born 05/14/1952, Brooklyn, NY, m, 1983, 1 child **DISCIPLINE** ART HISTORY **EDUCATION** Ohio St Univ, BA, 70, MA 74; Univ Wisc, PhD, 84. **CAREER** Asst to Assoc Dean, Univ Wisc, Col Arts & Scui, 81-84; Vis Asst Prof, Ariz St, 84-85; Asst Prof, 85-92, Assoc Prof, 92-, Vanderbilt Univ. **HONORS AND AWARDS** Am Coun of Learned Soc Grant-in-Aid, 89; Smithsonian Short-term Vis Grant, 87; Capital Hist Soc Fellow, 87. **MEMBERSHIPS** Col Art Asn; Am Stud Asn. **RESEARCH** American art, public art, sculpture, Georgia O'Keefe, Edward Hopper, art in the US Capital. **SELECTED PUBLICATIONS** Auth, Art and Empire: The Politics of Ethnicity in the US Capitol, 1815-1860, Yale Univ Press, 92; auth, The Politics of Public Art: Art in the United States Capitol, The J of Art Mgt, Law & Soc, 23, 327-340, 94; auth, Rereading the Indian in Benjamin West's Death of General Wolfe, Am Art, 9, 73-85, 95; auth, Two US Capitol Statues: Horatio Greenough's Rescue and Luigi Persico's Discovery of America, Critical Issues in Am Art, Harper Collins, 93-108, 97; auth, Luigi Persico, Am Nat Bio, Oxford Univ Press, in press. **CONTACT ADDRESS** Dept of Fine Arts, Vanderbilt Univ, Nashville, TN, 37235. **EMAIL** vivien.g.fryd@vanderbilt.edu

FRYER, JUDITH
PERSONAL Born 08/05/1939, Minneapolis, MN, 2 children **DISCIPLINE** AM LIT AND HISTORY **EDUCATION** Univ Minn, PhD (Am studies), 73. **CAREER** Instr women's studies, Am studies and Am lit, Univ Minn, 68-73; asst prof, 74-78, ASSOC PROF AM STUDIES, MIAMI UNIV, OXFORD, OHIO, 78-, DIR AM STUDIES PROG, 74-, Instr Am lit, Macalester Col, St Paul, 72; guest prof Am studies, Univ T¤bingen, West Ger, 76-77; res grants, Miami Univ, summers, 75, 79 and 82, Nat Endowment for the Humanities, summers 76 and 78, 79-80; Fulbright grant, 76; fel, Bunting Inst, Harvard Univ, 79-80. **MEMBERSHIPS** Am Studies Asn; Nat Trust for Hist Preservation; Hist Keyboard Soc. **RESEARCH** Women's studies; early music. **SELECTED PUBLICATIONS** Auth, Review of Developments in State Securities Regulation, Business Lawyer, Vol 49, 93. **CONTACT ADDRESS** American Studies Prog, Miami Univ, Oxford, OH, 45056.

FRYKENBERG, ROBERT E.
PERSONAL Born 06/08/1930, Ootacamund, India, m, 1952, 3 children **DISCIPLINE** SOUTH ASIAN HISTORY **EDUCATION** Bethel Col & Sem, BA, 51, BD, 55; Univ MN, MA, 53; Univ London, PhD, 61. **CAREER** Instr polit sci & hist, Oakland City Col, 57-58; Ford Found res & Carnegie teaching fels & vis asst prof Indian hist, Univ Chicago, 61-62; asst prof SAsian hist, 62-67, assoc prof hist & Indian studies, 67-71, chmn, Dept SAsian Studies, 70-73, dir, Ctr SAsian Studies, 70-74, Prof hist & S Asian studies, Univ WI-Madison, 71-97, Emeritus prof, 97. **HONORS AND AWARDS** Am Coun Learned Soc res grant, SIndia, 62-63; partic, SAsian Microform Proj, 62-; tchr, Peace Corps, 64; Fulbright-Hays fel Indian hist, 65-66; Am Coun Learned Soc-Soc Sci Res Coun grant-in-aid, Asia, 67; Guggenheim fel, 68-69; dir, Summer Prog SAsian Studies, 70-71; hon fel, Am Inst Indian Studies, 65-, trustee, 70-, chmn nominating comt, 73-74; consult, NDEA Title VI Ctr & Fel Progs, US Dept Health, Educ & Welfare, 71 & 73; Nat Endowment for Humanities sr fel & fel, Inst Res in Humanities, Univ WI-Madison, 75; ACLS-SSRC grant for res on SAsia, 77-78; travel fel, Am Inst Indian Studies, 78, 81, 84, 87, 90; Univ WI-Madison research grants, 68, 73-74, 75, 77-78, 79, 81, 82, 86, 88-90 (Vilas assoc), 97; NEH/UW-Madison summer semin dir, 86; IFACS Board, 79-87, 91; AM Phl Soc grant, 83; Woodrow Wilson Center Vis Sch, 86, Fell, 91-92; Rockfell Scholar in Res (Bellagio), 88; Pew (dir, Res Adv Grant: India), 94-97, 98-00; Pew Ev Sch Prog, senior fel, 97-98; Radhakrishnan Memorial Lecturer, vis fel, 98. **MEMBERSHIPS** Asn Asian Studies; fel Royal Asiatic Soc; AHA; fel Royal Hist Soc; India Inst Asian Studies; life member, India Intl Center. **RESEARCH** Hist; politics; relig India ad south Asia; cult and soc conflict in India; land and peasant in S Asia; fund movements ; hist of Christianity within Muslim-Hindu Env. **SELECTED PUBLICATIONS** Auth, India: Today's World in Focus, Ginn, 68 & 73; Elite formation in nineteenth century South India, First Conf Tamil Cult & Hist, Univ Malaysia, 68; auth, Land Control and Social Structure in Indian History, Univ Wis, 69; ed & auth, The partition of India a quarter century after, Am Hist Rev, 3/72; seven chap Asia Sect, In: European History in World Perspective, Heath 74; ed & auth, India's Imperial Tradition: Essays on the Logic of Political Systems, Indo-British Rev, Madras, 75; auth, The last emergency of the Raj, In: India Gandhi's India, West View, 76; ed & auth two chaps in: Land Tenure and Peasant in South Asia, Univ Wis Land Tenure Ctr & Orient Longman, Delhi, 77; co ed, Studies of South India: An Anthology, New Era, Madras, 86; auth ed, Delhi Through the Ages: Essays in History, Culture, and Society, Oxford univ press, 86, revised, 93; Accounting for Fundamentalisims, univ Chicago, 94; auth, History and Belief: The Foundations of Historical Understanding, Eerdmans, 96; auth, Oxford istory of Christianity in Indian World, in progress. **CONTACT ADDRESS** Dept of Hist, Univ of Wisconsin, 455 North Park St, Madison, WI, 53706-1483. **EMAIL** frykenberg@macc.wisc.edu

FRYKMAN, GEORGE AXEL
PERSONAL Born 04/30/1917, South San Francisco, CA, m, 1942, 3 children **DISCIPLINE** HISTORY **EDUCATION** San Jose State Col, AB, 40; Stanford Univ, AM, 47, PhD (hist), 55. **CAREER** Teacher high sch, Calif, 41-42; actg instr hist, Stanford Univ, 49-50; instr, 50-51, asst librn and lectr, 51-53, from instr to asst prof, 53-61, asst to dean, Grad Sch, 61-64, assoc prof, 61-66, PROF HIST, WASH STATE UNIV, 66-, State educ adv, Washington Encycl Americana, 59-64. **MEMBERSHIPS** AHA; Orgn Am Hists. **RESEARCH** Pacific Northwest; historiography; American intellectual history. **SELECTED PUBLICATIONS** Auth, The Triumph of Tradition--The Emergence of Whitman College, 1859-1924, Montana Mag We Hist, Vol 44, 94. **CONTACT ADDRESS** Dept of Hist, Wash State Univ, Pullman, WA, 99164.

FU, POSHEK
DISCIPLINE HISTORY **EDUCATION** Stanford Univ, PhD, 89. **CAREER** Assoc prof, Univ Ill Urbana Champaign. **RESEARCH** Modern Chinese cultural and intellectual history; popular culture and cultural criticism; cinema studies; comparative literature. **SELECTED PUBLICATIONS** Auth, Passivity, Resistance, and Collaboration: Intellectual Choices in Occupied Shanghai, 1957-1945, Stanford, 93; Patriotism or Profit: Hong Kong Cinema during the Second World War, Urban Council, 95; The Ambiguity of Entertainment: Chinese Cinema in Occupied Shanghai, 1941-1945, Cinema J, 97; co-auth, Struggle to Entertain: The Political Ambivalence of Shanghai Film Industry under Japanese Occupation, Urban Council, 94. **CONTACT ADDRESS** History Dept, Univ Ill Urbana Champaign, 52 E Gregory Dr, Champaign, IL, 61820. **EMAIL** p-fu1@uiuc.edu

FUKUYAMA, FRANCIS
PERSONAL Born 10/27/1952, Chicago, IL, m, 1986, 3 children **DISCIPLINE** CLASSICS **EDUCATION** Cornell Univ, BA, 74. **CAREER** Social sci, Rand Corp, 80-81, 83-89, 90-95; State Dept policy planning, 81-82, 89; George Mason Univ Inst of Public Policy, 95- . **HONORS AND AWARDS** Hon doctorate, Conn Col; Permio Capri; Los Angeles Times Critics Award. **MEMBERSHIPS** Am Polit Sci Asn. **RESEARCH** Democracy, economic culture; social capital. **SELECTED PUBLICATIONS** Co-ed, The Soviet Union and the Third World: The Last Three Decades, Cornell, 87; auth, The End of History and the Last Man, Free Press, 92; auth, Trust: The Social Virtues and the Creation of Prosperity, Free Press, 95; auth, The Primacy of Culture, J of Democracy, 95; auth, Confucianism and Democracy, J of Democracy, 95; auth, Immigration, in Alexander, ed, The New Promise of American Life, Hudson Inst, 95; auth, Virtue and Prosperity, Natl Interest, 95; auth, On the Possibility of Writing a Universal History, in Melzer, ed, History and the Idea of Progress, Cornell, 95; auth, Social Capital and the Global Economy, For Aff, 95; auth, Trust Still Counts in a Virtual World, Forbes ASAP, 96; auth, The Illusion of Exceptionalism, J of Democracy, 97; auth, Is It All In the Genes? Commentary, 97; auth, Asian Values and the Asian Crisis, Commentary, 98; auth, Falling Tide: Global Trends and US Civil Society, Harvard Int Rev, 97-98; auth, Women and the Evolution of World Politics, For Aff, 98. **CONTACT ADDRESS** Esther Newberg International Creative Mgt, 40 West 57th St, New York, NY, 10019. **EMAIL** ffukuyam@gmu.edu

FULLER, JUSTIN
PERSONAL Born 07/26/1926, Birmingham, AL, m, 1960, 1 child **DISCIPLINE** AMERICAN HISTORY **EDUCATION** Ga Sch Technol, BS, 48; Emory Univ, MA, 58; Univ NC, PhD (hist), 66. **CAREER** Asst prof hist, Ala Col, 62-63; instr econ hist, Univ Ga, 63-65; from asst prof to assoc prof, 65-76, PROF HIST, UNIV MONTEVALLO, 76-. **MEMBERSHIPS** Southern Hist Asn. **RESEARCH** American business history; history of southern iron and steel industry. **SELECTED PUBLICATIONS** Auth, Les Vieilles Dames Indignes De Havergo Hill, Europe Revue Litteraire Mensuelle, Vol 71, 93; On Formal Verse and Free Verse, Poetry Wales, Vol 28, 93; First Day, Poetry Rev, Vol 85, 95. **CONTACT ADDRESS** 133 Tecumseh Rd, Montevallo, AL, 35115.

FULLER, SARAH
PERSONAL Born 04/23/1939, Bangor, ME, m **DISCIPLINE** MUSIC **EDUCATION** Radcliffe Col, BA, 61; Univ Calif, Berkeley, MA, 63, PhD, 69. **CAREER** From asst to full prof, SUNY Stony Brook, 69- . **HONORS AND AWARDS** Magna cum laude, 61; Alfred Einstein Prize, Am Musicological Soc, 72; Pres Award for Excellence in Tchg, 84. **MEMBERSHIPS** Am Musicological Soc; Col Music Soc; Soc for Music Theory. **RESEARCH** History of Western music; medieval music, history and theory; history of European music theory. **SELECTED PUBLICATIONS** Auth, Tendencies and Resolutions: The Directed Progression in Ars Nova Music, J of Music Theory, 92; auth, Defending the Dodecachordon: Ideological Currents in Glarean's Modal Theory, J of the Am Musicological Soc, 96; auth, Exploring Tonal Structure in French Polyphonic Song of the Fourteenth-Century, in Judd, ed, Tonal Structures in Early Music, Garland, 98. **CONTACT ADDRESS** Dept of Music, SUNY, Stony Brook, Stony Brook, NY, 11794-5475. **EMAIL** sfuller@ccmail.sunysb.edu

FULLINWIDER, S. PENDLETON
PERSONAL Born 10/17/1933, Washington, DC, m, 1964, 1 child **DISCIPLINE** AMERICAN HISTORY **EDUCATION** US Naval Acad, BS, 55; Univ Wis, Madison, MS, 61, PhD (hist), 66. **CAREER** Instr Am hist, Stephens Col, 64-67; asst prof, 68-71, ASSOC PROF HIST, ARIZ STATE UNIV, 71-, Rockefeller Found fel, 75-76. **RESEARCH** American psychiatry. **SELECTED PUBLICATIONS** Auth, The Natural and the Normative--Theories of Spatial PerceptionfFrom Kant to Helmholtz, Stud Hist Philos Science, Vol 24, 93. **CONTACT ADDRESS** Dept of Hist, Arizona State Univ, Tempe, Tempe, AZ, 85281.

FULLMER, JUNE ZIMMERMAN
PERSONAL Born 12/16/1920, IL, m, 1953 **DISCIPLINE** HISTORY OF SCIENCE **EDUCATION** Ill Inst Technol, BSAS, 43, MSChem, 45; Bryn Mawr Col, PhD (phys biochem), 48. **CAREER** Instr chem, Hood Col, 45-46; asst prof, Chatham Col, 50-53; assoc prof and head dept, Newcomb Col, Tulane Univ, 55-64; assoc prof hist, 66-70, PROF HIST, OHIO STATE UNIV, 70-, Am Asn Univ Women fel, 48-49; Am Coun Learned Soc fel, 60-61; Guggenheim Found fel, 63-64. **MEMBERSHIPS** Hist of Sci Soc; Midwest Junto for Hist of Sci (pres, 75-76); Sigma Xi; AAAS; Am Asn Univ Women. **RESEARCH** History of science, especially 19th and 20th century physical sciences; women in science; chemical kinetics. **SELECTED PUBLICATIONS** Auth, Chemical Sciences in the Modern World, Tech Cult, Vol 36, 95; Oppenheimer, Jane, Marion, 19 September 1911 19 March 96, Isis, Vol 88, 97;Stevenson, Robert, Louis, Smithsonian, Vol 26, 95. **CONTACT ADDRESS** 781 Latham Ct, Columbus, OH, 43214.

FUNCHION, MICHAEL FRANCIS
PERSONAL Born 10/04/1943, New York, NY, m, 1976, 2 children **DISCIPLINE** HISTORY **EDUCATION** Iona Col, BA, 66; Loyola Univ Chicago, MA, 68, PhD (hist), 73. **CAREER** Teaching asst, Loyola Univ Chicago, 67-70, lectr, 72; asst prof, 73-77, ASSOC PROF HIST, SDAK STATE UNIV, 77-. **MEMBERSHIPS** AHA; Am Comt for Irish Studies; Orgn Am Hists; Immigration Hist Soc. **RESEARCH** Irish in America; United States immigration; Irish History. **SELECTED PUBLICATIONS** Auth, The Boston Irish--A Political History, J Am Hist, Vol 82, 96. **CONTACT ADDRESS** Dept of Hist, SDak State Univ, Brookings, SD, 57007-0001.

FUNIGIELLO, PHILIP J.
PERSONAL Born 06/28/1939, New York, NY, 1 child **DISCIPLINE** AMERICAN HISTORY **EDUCATION** Hunter Col, AB, 61; Univ Calif, Berkeley, MA, 62; NY Univ, PhD, 66. **CAREER** From asst prof to assoc prof, 66-78, prof hist 78-, Col William & Mary; Fulbright lectr US hist, Univ Genoa, Italy, 77, Fulbright Comn, 77. **MEMBERSHIPS** AHA; Orgn Am Historians. **RESEARCH** History of natl health insurance; politics and public policy 1890-present. **SELECTED PUBLICATIONS** Art, Kilowattis for Defense: the New Deal and The Coming of The Second World War, J Am Hist, 69; auth, City Planning in World War II: the Experience of the National Resources Planning Board, Soc Sci Quart, 72; auth, The Bonneville Power Administration and the New Deal, Prologue: J Nat Arch, 73; auth, The Challenge to Urban Liberalism: Federal City Relations During World War II, Univ Tenn, 78; auth, American-Soviet Trade in the Cold War, Univ NC Press, 88; auth, Florence Lathrop Page: A Biography, Univ Va Press, 93. **CONTACT ADDRESS** Dept of History, Col of William and Mary, Williamsburg, VA, 23185.

FUNK, ARTHUR LAYTON
PERSONAL Born 05/10/1914, Brooklyn, NY, m, 1944, 2 children **DISCIPLINE** HISTORY **EDUCATION** Dartmouth Col, AB, 36; Univ Chicago, PhD, 40. **CAREER** Instr hist, St Petersburg Jr Col, 40-42; asst prof, Drake Univ, 46; assoc prof humanities, Univ Fla, 46-56; cult affairs officer, US Info Agency, 56-62; chmn dept hist, 73-78, PROF HIST, UNIV FLA, 62-, GRAD FAC HIST, 68-, Guggenheim fel, 54-55; mem, Joint Comt Hists and Archivists, 76-79, chmn, 77-79; mem, Dept Army Historical Adv Comt, 81-. **MEMBERSHIPS** AHA, Soc Hist Studies, France; Am Comt Hist 2nd World War (secy, 71-75); Soc Hist Am Foreign Rels; Int Comt Hist 2nd World War (vpres, 75-). **RESEARCH** Political history of World War II; history of France; Europe in the 20th century. **SELECTED PUBLICATIONS** Auth, In Search of the Maquis--Rural Resistance in Southern France, 1942-1944, J Mil Hist, Vol 57, 93; Secret Flotillas--Clandestine Sea Lines to France and French North Africa, 1940-1944, J Mil Hist, Vol 61, 97. **CONTACT ADDRESS** Dept of Hist, Univ of Fla, Gainesville, FL, 32611.

FUNKENSTEIN, AMOS
PERSONAL Born 03/09/1937, Tel Aviv, Israel, m, 1958, 2 children **DISCIPLINE** HISTORY **EDUCATION** Free Univ, Berlin, DPhil(hist, philos), 65. **CAREER** Asst prof medieval hist, Free Univ, Berlin, 65-67; assoc prof, 67-72, PROF JEWISH HIST and MEDIEVAL INTELLECTUAL HIST, UNIV CALIF, LOS ANGELES, 72-. **MEMBERSHIPS** Am Hist Asn; Hist Soc Israel; Mediaeval Acad Am. **RESEARCH** Medieval and early modern Jewish history; medieval and early modern European intellectual history; history of science. **SELECTED PUBLICATIONS** Auth, The Polytheism of James, William, J Hist Ideas, Vol 55, 94; Contemporary Philosophy--A New Survey, Vol 6, Philosophy and Science in the Middle Ages, Pt 1 And Pt 2, Isis, Vol 84, 93; The Aristotelian Scholastic Theory of Movement--Studies on the Commentary on the Physics of Aristotle by Albert of Saxony, Speculum J Medieval Stud, Vol 68, 93. **CONTACT ADDRESS** Dept Hist, Univ Calif, Los Angeles, CA, 90024.

FUQUA, CHARLES
PERSONAL Born 10/05/1935, Paris, France, m, 1961, 3 children **DISCIPLINE** CLASSICS **EDUCATION** Princeton Univ, BA, 57; Cornell Univ, MA, 62, PhD(classics), 64. **CAREER** From instr to asst prof classics, Dartmouth Col, 64-66; chmn dept, 66-78, assoc prof, 66-72, Garfield Prof Ancient Lang, Williams Col, 72-, Mem adv coun, Am Acad Rome, 66- & exec comt, 71-74. **HONORS AND AWARDS** Phi Beta Kappa, 57; Phi Kappa Phi, 64. **MEMBERSHIPS** Am Philol Asn; Class Asn New Eng; Classical Asn Mass; Vergilian Soc. **RESEARCH** Greek epic & drama; Latin lyric poetry. **SELECTED PUBLICATIONS** Auth, Possible implications of the ostracism of Hyperbolus, Trans Am Philol Asn, 65; Horace, Carmina 1.23-25, 1/68 & Aeschylus: Agamemnon 1446-47, 7/72, Class Philol; Studies in the use of myth in Sophocles' Philoctetes and the Orestes of Euripides, 76, The World of myth in Euripides Orestes, 78 & Heroism, Heracles, and the Trachiniae, 80, Traditio; Tyrtaeus and the cult of heroes, Greek, Roman & Byzantine Studies, 81; Hector, Sychaeus, and Deiphobus: Three mutilated figures in Aeneid, Class Philol, 1-6/82; auth, Proper Bevavior in the Odyssey, Ill Classical Stud, 46-58/91; auth, Moral Clusters in the Odyssey, Scholia, 56-68/93. **CONTACT ADDRESS** Dept of Classics, Williams Col, 880 Main St, Williamstown, MA, 01267-2600. **EMAIL** cfuqua@williams.edu

FUQUA, CHARLES J.
DISCIPLINE CLASSICS **EDUCATION** Princeton Univ, AB, 57; Cornell Univ, MA, 62; PhD, 64. **CAREER** Classics Dept, Williams Col **RESEARCH** Homer; Latin lyric; Vergil. **SELECTED PUBLICATIONS** Publ on, Homer, Greek lyric poetry, the Greek tragedians, Horace, Vergil. **CONTACT ADDRESS** Classics Dept, Williams Col, Stetson Hall B25, Williamstown, MA, 01267. **EMAIL** cfuqua@williams.edu

FURDELL, ELLZABETH LANE
PERSONAL Born 04/13/1944, Harrisburg, PA, m, 1968 **DISCIPLINE** ENGLISH HISTORY, POLITICAL SCIENCE **EDUCATION** Univ Wash, BA, 66; Kent State Univ, MA, 68, PhD (hist), 73. **CAREER** Asst prof, 71-74, ASSOC PROF HIST, COL GREAT FALLS, 74-, Contribr, Hist Abstr, 73-78. **MEMBERSHIPS** AHA; Am Polit Sci Asn; Sixteenth Century Study Conf; Rocky Mountain Soc Sci Asn. **RESEARCH** London history; 16th century historiography; urban politics. **SELECTED PUBLICATIONS** Auth, Philanthropy and the Hospitals of London--The Kings Fund, 1897-90, Hist, Vol 55, 93; Hunters and Poachers --A Cultural and Social History of Unlawful Hunting in England, 1485-1640, 16th Century J, Vol 25, 94; Glorianas Face--Women, Public and Private, in the English Renaissance, 16th Century J, Vol 24, 93; Psychiatry for the Rich, A History of Ticehurst Private Asylum, 1792-1917, Albion, Vol 25, 93; The Death of Marlowe, Christopher, 16th Century J, Vol 27, 96; Witnessing Insanity--Madness and Mad Doctors in the English Court, J Mod Hist, Vol 68, 96. **CONTACT ADDRESS** Dept of Soc Sci, Col of Great Falls, Great Falls, MT, 59405.

FURLONG, PATRICK JOSEPH
PERSONAL Born 02/07/1940, Lexington, KY, m, 1965, 2 children **DISCIPLINE** EARLY AMERICAN AND INDIAN HISTORY **EDUCATION** Univ Ky, AB, 61; Northwestern Univ, MA, 62; PhD (hist), 66. **CAREER** Asst prof hist, Ariz State Univ, 65-67; asst prof, 67-71, assoc prof, 71-81, honors coordr, 75-78, PROF HIST, IND UNIV, SOUTH BEND, 81-. **HONORS AND AWARDS** LHD, Manchester Col, 80. **MEMBERSHIPS** Am Soc Church Hist; Orgn Am Hists; AHA; Am Soc Reformation Res; Brethern J Asn. **RESEARCH** Congress; Indiana; American Revolution. **SELECTED PUBLICATIONS** Auth, Development for Exploitation--German Colonial Policies in Main- Land Tanzania, 1884-1914, Hist, Vol 59, 96; The Protestant Experience in Gary, Indiana, 1906-1975--At Home in the City, J Church State, Vol 35, 93; Hope and Despair-English Speaking Intellectuals and South African Politics 1896-1976, Int J African Hist Stud, Vol 27, 94; Posey, Thomas--Son of the American Revolution, J Am Hist, Vol 81, 95; The Fall of the Packard Moto Car Company, J Am Hist, Vol 83, 96. **CONTACT ADDRESS** Dept of Hist, Indiana Univ, South Bend, South Bend, IN, 46615.

FURLOUGH, ELLEN
DISCIPLINE HISTORY **EDUCATION** Lander Col, BA, 75; Univ SC, MA, 78; Brown Univ, PhD, 87. **CAREER** Prof, 96-; asst prof, 86-92; assoc prof, 92- Kenyon Coll. **RESEARCH** Consummerism, contemporary social history. **SELECTED PUBLICATIONS** Coauth, bibliogr, The Sex of Things: Essays on Gender and Consumption, Univ Calif Press, 96; Packaging Pleasures: Club Mediterran and Consumer Culture in France, 1950-1968, Fr Hist Studies, 93, repro, Soc Hist W Civilization, 3rd ed, St Martin's, 95; co-auth, Composing a Landscape: Coastal Mass Tourism and Regional Development in the Languedoc, 1960s-1980s, Intl Jour Maritime Hist, 97. **CONTACT ADDRESS** Dept of Hist, Kenyon Col, Gambier, OH, 43022. **EMAIL** Furlough@Kenyon.edu

FURMAN, NECAH STEWART
PERSONAL Born 01/29/1940, Del Rio, TX, m, 1962, 3 children **DISCIPLINE** HISTORY, AMERICAN STUDIES **EDUCATION** Univ Tex, El Paso, BA, 63; Univ Tex, Arlington, MA, 72; Univ NMex, PhD (Am studies), 75. **CAREER** Lectr US hist, Univ NMex, 76-77; chmn dept hist, Sandia Prep Sch, 76-77; VIS ASST PROF US HIST, UNIV TEX, EL PASO, 77-, Proj dir, New Mexico Humanities Coun grant on Cult Conflict in Borderlands, 76-77; Huntington fel, Southwestern Writers, Huntington Libr and Art Gallery, 77; Nat Endowment Humanities fel Mex and Borderlands Hist, 78. **MEMBERSHIPS** Western Hist Asn; AHA. **RESEARCH** Indian and borderlands history. **SELECTED PUBLICATIONS** Auth, Bighorse, The Warrior, J West, Vol 32, 93; A Visit from Father and other Tales of the Mojave, Nex Hist Rev, Vol 68, 93. **CONTACT ADDRESS** 7421 El Morro Rd N E, Albuquerque, NM, 87109.

FURNISS, ELIZABETH
DISCIPLINE CULTURAL HISTORY **EDUCATION** Univ British Columbia, PhD, 97. **CAREER** Res fel, Ctr for Cross-Cult Res, Australian Natl Univ, 97-99. **RESEARCH** Aboriginal/settler relations in Australia and Canada. **CONTACT ADDRESS** Dept of Education, Australian National Univ. **EMAIL** Elizabeth.Furniss@anu.edu.au

FURTH, CHARLOTTE
DISCIPLINE HISTORY **EDUCATION** Stanford Univ, PhD, 65. **CAREER** Prof, Univ Southern Calif. **RESEARCH** Modern China; Political Thought; Medicine; Social and Cultural, Women. **SELECTED PUBLICATIONS** Auth, A Flourishing Yin: Gender in China's Medical History, 960-1670, Ucal Press, 97; Ting Wen-Chiang: Science and China's New Culture, Harvard, 70; ed and contribur, The Limits of Change: Essays on Conservative Alternatives in Republican China, Harvard, 76. **CONTACT ADDRESS** Dept of History, Univ Southern Calif, University Park Campus, Los Angeles, CA, 90089. **EMAIL** furth@usc.edu

FUSSNER, FRANK SMITH
PERSONAL Born 09/21/1920, Cincinnati, OH, m, 1943, 2 children **DISCIPLINE** HISTORY **EDUCATION** Harvard Univ, BS, 42, PhD (hist), 51. **CAREER** Instr hist and humanities, 50-52, from asst prof to prof, 53-74, EMER PROF HIST, REED COL, 74-, Am Philos Soc grant, 54; Fulbright vis prof, Univ Col Swansea, Wales, 64-65; vis prof, Haverford Col, 68-69. **MEMBERSHIPS** AHA. **SELECTED PUBLICATIONS** Auth, Forms of Nationhood--The Elizabethan Writing of England, Am Hist Rev, Vol 98, 93. **CONTACT ADDRESS** Circle S Ranch, Star Rte, Spray, OR, 97874.

FUTRELL, ROBERT FRANK
PERSONAL Born 12/15/1917, Waterford, MS, m, 1944 **DISCIPLINE** MODERN HISTORY **EDUCATION** Univ Miss, BA, 38, MA, 39; Vanderbilt Univ, PhD, 50. **CAREER** Asst hist, Univ Miss, 38-39; spec consult, US War Dept, 46; Hist, Army Air Force and US Air Force Hist Off, 46-49; assoc prof mil hist, Res Studies Inst, Air Univ, 50-51, prof, Aerospace Studies Inst, 51-71, prof mil hist and sr Hist, Hist Res Ctr, 71-74, EMER PROF MIL HIST, AIR UNIV, 74-, Prof lectr int affairs, George Washington Univ Ctr, 63-68; consult, US Air Force Proj Corona Harvest eval air opers SE Asia, 66-73. **MEMBERSHIPS** Southern Hist Asn; Am Mil Inst; Air Force Hist Found. **RESEARCH** United States military history; airpower history; East Asian history. **SELECTED PUBLICATIONS** Auth, Aerial Interdiction--Air Power and the Land Battle in 3 American Wars, J Am Hist, Vol 83, 93, 97; Camp and Custer--Transcribing the Custer Myth, J Am Hist, Vol 83, 96. **CONTACT ADDRESS** 1871 Hill Hedge Dr, Montgomery, AL, 36106.

G

GABACCIA, DONNA
DISCIPLINE MODERN U.S. SOCIAL HISTORY, WOMEN'S HISTORY, URBAN HISTORY **EDUCATION** Univ MI, PhD, 79. **CAREER** Charles H Stone Prof Hist, Univ NC, Charlotte. **RESEARCH** Migration to the US; the Italian diaspora. **SELECTED PUBLICATIONS** Auth, We Are What We Eat: Ethnic Food and the Making of Americans, Harvard UP, 96. **CONTACT ADDRESS** Univ N. Carolina, Charlotte, Charlotte, NC, 28223-0001.

GABEL, CREIGHTON
PERSONAL Born 04/05/1931, Muskegon, MI, m, 1952, 3 children **DISCIPLINE** ARCHAEOLOGY, ANTHROPOLOGY **EDUCATION** Univ Mich, AB, 53, AM, 54; Univ Edinburgh, PhD(prehist archaeol), 57. **CAREER** From instr to asst prof anthrop, Northwestern Univ, 56-63; assoc prof, 63-69, PROF ANTHROP, BOSTON UNIV, 69-, NSF grants, Northern Rhodisia, 60-61 and Kenya, 66-67; res assoc, African Studies Ctr, 63-; chmn anthrop, Boston Univ, 70-72 and 76-; Sr Fulbright Hays award, Liberia, 73. **MEMBERSHIPS** Soc Am Archaeol; S African Archaeol Soc; Soc Africanist Archaeologists Am. **RESEARCH** Prehistoric archaeology Old World, especially Africa; hunter-gatherers and early agricultural societies. **SELECTED PUBLICATIONS** Auth, Olduvai-Gorge, Vol 4, Pt 1-9, the Skulls, Endocasts and Teeth of Homo-Habilis, Int J African Hist Stud, Vol 0026, 93; Olduvai Gorge, Vol 5, Excavations In Bed-III, Bed-IV, and the Masek Beds 1968-1971, Int J African Hist Stud, Vol 0029, 96; The Peopling of Africa--A Geographic Interpretation, Int J African Hist Stud, Vol 0029, 97. **CONTACT ADDRESS** African Studies Ctr, Boston Univ, 10 Lenox St, Brookline, MA, 02146.

GABEL, JACK
PERSONAL Born 04/19/1930, New York, NY, m, 1974, 1 child **DISCIPLINE** AMERICAN HISTORY **EDUCATION** City Col New York, BA, 53, MA, 56; NY Univ, PhD, 67. **CAREER** From asst prof to assoc prof, 61-74, PROF HIST, LONG ISLAND UNIV, 74-, Asst dean, Col Arts & Sci, Long Island Univ, 80- **HONORS AND AWARDS** David Newton Awd for Excel in Teaching, 92. **MEMBERSHIPS** AHA; Orgn Am Historians. **RESEARCH** Twentieth century United States history; United States diplomatic and American urban history. **CONTACT ADDRESS** Dept of History, Long Island Univ, Brooklyn, 1 University Plz, Brooklyn, NY, 11201-5372.

GADDIS, JOHN LEWIS
PERSONAL Born 04/02/1941, Cotulla, TX, m, 1965, 2 children **DISCIPLINE** UNITED STATES HISTORY **EDUCATION** Univ Tex, Austin, BA, 63, MA, 65, PhD(hist), 68. **CAREER** Asst prof, Ind Univ Southeast, 68-69; from asst prof to assoc prof, 69-76, PROF HIST, OHIO UNIV, 76-, Vis prof strategy, US Naval War Col, 75-77; Bicentennial prof Am hist, Univ Helsinki, 80-81. **HONORS AND AWARDS** Bancroft Prize, 72; Nat Hist Soc Prize Best 1st Bk of Hist, 72; Bernath Prize, Soc Hist Am Foreign Rels, 72. **MEMBERSHIPS** AHA; Orgn Am Historians; Soc Hist Am Foreign Rels. **RESEARCH** Origins of the Cold War; Soviet-American relations; US national security policy. **SELECTED PUBLICATIONS** Auth, The Tragedy of Cold-War History, Diplomatic Hist, Vol 0017, 93; The Devil We Knew--Americans and the Cold-War, Am Hist Rev, Vol 0100, 95. **CONTACT ADDRESS** Dept Hist, Ohio Univ, Athens, OH, 45701.

GAGARIN, MICHAEL
PERSONAL Born 01/04/1942, New York City, NY **DISCIPLINE** CLASSICS **EDUCATION** Stanford Univ, BA, 63; Harvard Univ, MA, 65; Yale Univ, PhD(classics), 68. **CAREER** From instr to asst prof classics, Yale Univ, 68-73; asst prof, 73-80, ASSOC PROF CLASSICS, UNIV TEX, AUSTIN, 80-, Jr fel, Ctr Hellenic Studies, Washington DC, 72-73; vis asst prof classics, Univ Calif, Berkeley, 76-77; Am Coun Learned Soc fel, 80-81. **MEMBERSHIPS** Am Philol Asn; Am Inst Archaeol; Soc Ancient Greek Philos. **RESEARCH** Greek literature; Greek law; Greek philosophy. **SELECTED PUBLICATIONS** Auth, The Poetry of Justice--Hesiod and the Origins of Greek Law, Ramus-Critical Stud in Greek and Roman Lit, Vol 0021, 92; Flow-Backwards-Sacred-Rivers--Tradition and Change in the Classics, Class J, Vol 0087, 92; Plato Penal Code--Tradition, Controversy, and Reform in Greek Penology, Class Rev, Vol 0043, 93; The Shape of Athenian Law, Hist, Vol 0057, 95; Tyranny and Political-Culture in Ancient-Greece, Am Hist Rev, Vol 0100, 95; The First Law of the Gortyn Code Revisited, Greek Roman and Byzantine Stud, Vol 0036, 95; The Justice of the Greeks, Class Philol, Vol 0091, 96; Smith, Gertrude, Elizabeth (1894-85), Class World, Vol 0090, 96; The Torture of Slaves in Athenian Law, Class Philol, Vol 0091, 96; Sardonic Smile--Nonverbal Behavior in Homeric Epic, Hist, Vol 0059, 96; On the Not-Being of Gorgias On Not-Being' (ONB), Philos Rhet, Vol 0030, 97. **CONTACT ADDRESS** Classics Dept, Univ of Tex, Austin, TX, 78712.

GAGLIANO, JOSEPH ANTHONY
PERSONAL Born 04/15/1930, Milwaukee, WI, m, 1961 **DISCIPLINE** LATIN AMERICAN HISTORY **EDUCATION** Marquette Univ, BS, 54, MA, 56; Georgetown Univ, PhD(Latin Am hist), 60. **CAREER** Instr hist, Aquinas Col, 59-62; from asst prof to assoc prof, 62-74, asst dean, 76-78, PROF HIST, LOYOLA UNIV CHICAGO, 74-, ASSOC DEAN GRAD SCH, 78-, Am Coun Learned Soc travel grant to 37th Int Cong Americanists, Buenos Aires and Mar del Plata, 66; Mellon grant, Mex, 79. **MEMBERSHIPS** AHA; Am Cath Hist Asn; Conf Latin Am Hist; Latin Am Studies Asn. **RESEARCH** The Andean republics. **SELECTED PUBLICATIONS** Auth, Religion in the Andes--Vision and Imagination in Early Colonial Peru, Cath Hist Rev, Vol 0079, 93; The Coca Boom and Rural Social-Change in Bolivia, Americas, Vol 0051, 94; Bolivia and Coca--A Study in Dependency, Americas, Vol 0051, 95; History of the Archdiocese of Bogota--Its Evangelist Itinerary, 1564-1993, Cath Hist Rev, Vol 0082, 96; Drug Lessons and Education-Programs in Developing-Countries, Hisp Am Hist Rev, Vol 0076, 96; The Cross and the Serpent--Religious Repression and Resurgence in Colonial Peru, Cath Hist Rev, Vol 0083, 97; The Andean Cocaine Industry, Americas, Vol 0053, 97. **CONTACT ADDRESS** Dept Hist, Loyola Univ, 6525 N Sheridan Rd, Chicago, IL, 60626-5385.

GAGLIARDI, FRANK M.
DISCIPLINE CLASSICAL LANGUAGES **EDUCATION** Carleton Col, BA, 72; Univ Mich, PhD, 76. **CAREER** Prof & dir, Oakley Ctr for the Humanities & Soc Sci. **RESEARCH** Greek Tragedy; archaic Greek literature and culture, especially Homer and lyric poetry; critical theory, especially gender studies and anthropological approaches to Greek culture; Roman comedy. **SELECTED PUBLICATIONS** Publ on, Horace Odes 1.5; Sophocles' Philoctetes. **CONTACT ADDRESS** Classics Dept, Williams Col, Stetson Hall, Williamstown, MA, 01267. **EMAIL** mhoppin@williams.edu

GAGLIARDO, JOHN G.
PERSONAL Born 08/13/1933, Chicago, IL **DISCIPLINE** GERMAN & EARLY MODERN EUROPEAN HISTORY **EDUCATION** Univ Kans, AB, 54, MA, 57; Yale Univ, MA, 58, PhD(hist), 62. **CAREER** Asst instr Western civilization, Univ Kans, 55-57 & 59-60; from instr to asst prof hist, Amherst Col, 60-65; from asst prof to assoc prof, Univ Ill, Chicago, 65-68; assoc prof, 68-70, prof hist, Boston Univ, 70- **HONORS AND AWARDS** Metcalf Cup & Prize for Excellence in Teaching, Boston Univ, 84. **MEMBERSHIPS** AHA; Conf Group Cent Europ Hist; New Eng Hist Asn (pres, 74-75); German Studies Asn. **RESEARCH** European absolutism; German constitutional history; German agrarian history. **SELECTED PUBLICATIONS** Auth, Archives in East Germany, Am Archivist, 7/57; Germans and Agriculture in Colonial Pennsylvania, Pa Mag Hist & Biog, 4/59; Enlightened Despotism, Crowell, 67; Moralism, Rural Ideology and the German Peasant in the Late 18th Century, Agr Hist, 4/68; From Pariah to Patriot: The Changing Image of the German Peasant, 1770-1840, Univ Ky, 69; Reich and Nation: The Holy Roman Empire as Idea and Reality, 1763-1806, Ind Univ, 80; Germany Under the Old Regime 1600-1790, Longman, 91; translator, Otto Busch, Military System and Social Life in Old Regime Prussia, 1713-1807, Humanities Press, 97. **CONTACT ADDRESS** Dept of History, Boston Univ, 226 Bay State Rd, Boston, MA, 02215-1403.

GAICHAS, LAWRENCE EDWARD
PERSONAL Born 03/30/1942, Chicago, IL, m, 1967, 2 children **DISCIPLINE** CLASSICS **EDUCATION** Xavier Univ, Ohio, AB, 64; Ohio State Univ, MA, 68, PhD(classics), 72. **CAREER** Teaching asst classics, Ohio State Univ, 66-68; instr classics and English, Kalamazoo Col, 70-72; instr Columbus Pub Schs, 72-73; asst prof, 73-77, ASSOC PROF CLASSICS, DUQUESNE UNIV, 77-, CHMN DEPT, 78- Concurrent Pos: Circulation mgr, Class World, 78-. **MEMBERSHIPS** Am Philol Asn. **RESEARCH** Graeco-Roman historiography; Graeco-Roman epic; etymology. **SELECTED PUBLICATIONS** Auth, Latin Skills 1 and Latin Skills 2 for the IBM-PC and the PS/2, Version 1.0, Class World, Vol 0089, 1996. **CONTACT ADDRESS** Dept of Classics, Duquesne Univ, Pittsburgh, PA, 15259.

GAISSER, JULIA HAIG
PERSONAL Born 01/12/1941, Cripple Creek, CO, m, 1964, 1 child **DISCIPLINE** CLASSICAL PHILOLOGY **EDUCATION** Brown Univ, AB, 62; Harvard Univ, AM, 66; Edinburgh Univ, PhD, 66. **CAREER** Asst prof classics, Newton Col, 66-69, Swarthmore Col, 70-72 & Brooklyn Col, 73-75; Assoc Prof, 75-84, Prof Latin, Bryn Mawr Col, 84-. **HONORS AND AWARDS** NEH Sr Fel, 85-86, 93-94; ACLS Fel, 89-90; MBE, 90; Res, Bellagio Study & Conf Ctr, Bellagio, Italy, 94; Vis Schol, Phi Beta Kappa, 96-97. **MEMBERSHIPS** Class Asn Atlantic States; Am Philol Asn; Renaissance Soc. **RESEARCH** Greek epic; Latin poetry; classical tradition. **SELECTED PUBLICATIONS** Auth, A structural analysis of the digressions in the Iliad and the Odyssey, Harvard Studies Class Philol, 68; Adaptation of traditional material in the Glaucus-Diomedes episode, Trans Am Philol Soc, 69; Structure and tone in Tibullus 1 6, Am J Philol, 71; Tibullus 1 7: A tribute to Messalla, Class Philol, 71; Noun-epithet combinations in the Homeric hymn to Demeter, Trans Am Philol Soc, 74; coauth, Partons in antiquity, Am J Physics, 77; auth, Mythological Exempla in Propertius 1 2 and, Am J Philol, 77; Tibullus 2 3 and Vergil's Tenth Eclogue, Trans Am Philol, 77; Catullus and his Renaissance Readers, Oxford, 93. **CONTACT ADDRESS** Dept of Latin, Bryn Mawr Col, 101 N Merion Ave, Bryn Mawr, PA, 19010-2899. **EMAIL** jgaisser@brynmawr.edu

GALAMBOS, LOUIS PAUL
PERSONAL Born 04/04/1931, Fostoria, OH, m, 1956, 3 children **DISCIPLINE** ECONOMIC & BUSINESS HISTORY **EDUCATION** Ind Univ, BA, 55; Yale Univ, MA, 57, PhD, 60. **CAREER** Asst prof Hist, Rice Univ, 60-66 assoc prof Hist, 66-70; prof Hist, Livingston Col Rutgers Univ, 70-71; prof Hist, Johns Hopkins Univ, 71-, vis asst prof, Johns Hopkins Univ, 65-66; ed, Papers of Dwight D Eisenhower, 71-; coed, J Econ Hist, 76-78; Nat Endowment for Humanities sr fel, 78-79; Woodrow Wilson Center fel, 85-86. **HONORS AND AWARDS** Pres, Economic Hist Assn; pres, business hist conf, 91-92. **MEMBERSHIPS** AHA; Econ Hist Asn; Bus Hist Asn; Am Econ Asn; Orgn Am Historians. **RESEARCH** American economic history; business history. **SELECTED PUBLICATIONS** Auth, Business History and the Theory of the Growth of the Firm, Explorations in Entrepreneurial Hist, Fall 66; Competition and Cooperation: The Emergence of a National Trade Association, Johns Hopkins Univ, 66; American Business History, Serv Ctr Teachers Hist, 67; coauth, the Changing Economic Order, Harcourt, 68; auth, The Emerging Organizational Synthesis in Modern American History, Bus Hist Rev, Autumn 70; The Public Image of Big Business In America, 1880-1940, John Hopkins Univ, 75; ed, The Papers of Dwight David Eisenhower, Johns Hopkins Univ, Vol VI-IX, 78; co-ed, Studies in Economic History and Policy: The United States in the Twentieth Century, Cambridge Univ Press, 81; The Triumph of Oligopoly, in American Economic Development, Stanford Univ, 93; coauth, The Transformation of the Pharmaceutical Industry in the Twentieth Century, Science in the Twentieth Century, Harwood, 97. **CONTACT ADDRESS** Dept of History, Johns Hopkins Univ, 3400 N Charles St, Baltimore, MD, 21218-2680. **EMAIL** galambos@jhunix.hcf.jhu.edu

GALAVARIS, GEORGE
PERSONAL Born 00/00/1926, Greece, Greece **DISCIPLINE** HISTORY OF ART **EDUCATION** Univ Athens, MA, 51; Princeton Univ, MFA, 57, PhD(art, archaeol), 58. **CAREER** Vis fel Byzantine art, Dumbarton Oaks, Harvard Univ, 52-59; from asst prof to assoc prof, 59-65, PROF HIST OF ART, McGILL UNIV, 65-, Vis prof hist of art, Univ Wis-Madison, 67-68; Can Coun leave award, 70-71, leave fel, 77-78; vis fel, Dept Art and Archaeol, Princeton Univ, 77. **MEMBERSHIPS** Int Asn Byzantine Studies; Mediaeval Acad Am; Am Numis Asn; Ger Soc Thomas von Kempen. **RESEARCH** History of early Christian and Byzantine art; liturgy; East Christian civilization. **SELECTED PUBLICATIONS** Auth, Theodore-Hagiopetrites--A Late Byzantine Scribe and Illuminator, Speculum-J Medieval Stud, Vol 0069, 94. **CONTACT ADDRESS** Dept of Art Hist, McGill Univ, 853 Sherbrooke St W, Montreal, PQ, H3A 2T6.

GALINSKY, KARL
PERSONAL Born 02/07/1942, Strassburg, m, 1986, 2 children **DISCIPLINE** CLASSICS **EDUCATION** Bowdoin, AB, 63; Princeton, PhD, 66. **CAREER** Instr, Princeton, 65-66; asst prof, 66-68; assoc prof, 68-72; dept chair, 74-90; Univ Tex Austin, Prof, 72-; Cailouz Centennial prof, 84-. **HONORS AND AWARDS** Fellowhips at NEH, ACLS, Guggenheim, Humbuldt; Tchg Excellence at Univ Tex, Am Philol Asn. **MEMBERSHIPS** Am Philos Asn; Archaeol Inst of Am; Mommsen Gesellschaft. **RESEARCH** Roman Civilization, Augustan Age. **SELECTED PUBLICATIONS** Auth, Aeneas, Sicily, and Rome, 69; The Herakles Theme, 72; Perspectives of Roman Poetry, 74; Ovid's Metamorphoses, 75; Classical and Modern Interactions, 92; The Interpretation of Roman Poetry, 92; Augustan Culture, 96. **CONTACT ADDRESS** Dept of Classics, Univ of Tex, Austin, TX, 78712-1181. **EMAIL** galinsky@utxvms.cc.utexas.edu

GALISHOFF, STUART
PERSONAL Born 04/18/1940, New York, NY **DISCIPLINE** URBAN HISTORY **EDUCATION** NY Univ, BA, 60, MA, 66, PhD(hist), 69. **CAREER** Asst prof, 68-76, ASSOC PROF HIST, GA STATE UNIV, 76-. **HONORS AND AWARDS** William Adee Whitehead Award, 70. **MEMBERSHIPS** Am Asn Med Hist; AHA; Orgn Am Historians. **RESEARCH** History of public health. **SELECTED PUBLICATIONS** Auth, Dirt and Disease--Polio Before Fdr, J Southern Hist, Vol 0060, 94; Yellow-Fever and Public-Health in the New South, J Urban Hist, Vol 0022, 96; Yellow-Fever and the South, J Urban Hist, Vol 0022, 96; Plague of Strangers--Social-Groups and the Origins of City Services in Cincinnati, J Urban Hist, Vol 0022, 96; Washing the Great Unwashed--Public Baths in Urban America, 1840-20, J Urban Hist, Vol 0022, 96; Living in the Shadow of Death--Tuberculosis and the Social Experience of Illness in American History, J Interdisciplinary Hist, Vol 0026, 96. **CONTACT ADDRESS** Dept of Hist, Georgia State Univ, 33 Gilmer St SE, Atlanta, GA, 30303-3080.

GALLACHER, PATRICK
DISCIPLINE MEDIEVAL STUDIES **EDUCATION** Univ Ill, PhD, 66. **CAREER** Instr, Univ NMex, 66-. **SELECTED PUBLICATIONS** Coed, Hermeneutics and Medieval Culture, 89. **CONTACT ADDRESS** Univ NMex, Albuquerque, NM, 87131.

GALLAGHER, GARY W.
PERSONAL Born 10/08/1950, Los Angeles, CA, m, 1986, 1 child **DISCIPLINE** HISTORY **EDUCATION** Adams State Col, BA, 72; Univ TX Austin, MA, PhD, 77, 82. **CAREER** Archivist, LBJ lib Austin TX, 77-86; vis lectr, Univ TX, Austin, 86; Asst, prof, assoc prof, Penn State, 86-91, hd dept, 91-95, prof, 91-98; Univ VA, prof hist, 98-. **HONORS AND AWARDS** Lincoln Prize, 98; George W Littlefield Lectr, 95-96; Citation, Soc Am Hist, 96; Frank L Klement Lectr, 95; Distg in Hum Awd, Penn State, 95; Richard Barksdale Harwell Awd, 91; Nevins Freeman Awd, 91; Douglas Southall Freman Awd, 90; Founders Awd, 89-90; Mellon Fellow, VA hist soc, 88, 89; Univ fel, Univ TX, Austin, 74, 75, 76, 77. **MEMBERSHIPS** Organ Am Historians; Southern Hist Asn. **RESEARCH** Am civil war; southern hist; military hist. **SELECTED PUBLICATIONS** Lee and His Generals in War and Memory, LA State Univ Press, 98; The Confederate War, Harvard Univ Press, 97; Lee The Soldier, Univ NE Press 96; Jubal A Early, the Lost Cause, and Civil War History: A Persistent Legacy, Marquette Univ Press, 95; many articles and essays. **CONTACT ADDRESS** Corcoran Dept Hist, Univ Virginia, 227 Randall Hall, Charlottesville, VA, 22903-3284. **EMAIL** gallagher@virgina.edu

GALLAGHER, MARY A.Y.
PERSONAL Born 12/09/1939, Hartford, MN, m, 1968, 1 child **DISCIPLINE** HISTORY **EDUCATION** Univ Notre Dame, MA, 67; Queen's Coll, CUNY, PhD, 78. **CAREER** Papers of Robert Morris, asst to assoc ed, 71-86, coeditor, 87-, adjunct prof, 97, Queens Coll, CUNY; adjunct prof, Brooklyn Coll, CUNY, 92-95. **MEMBERSHIPS** Assn Documentary Editors; Omobundo Inst Early Amer History and Culture. **SELECTED PUBLICATIONS** Coed, The Papers of Robert Morris, 1781-1784, vol. VIII, 95; auth, "Charting a New Course for the China Trade: The Late 18th-Century Model," The American Neptune, summer 97; auth, "Reinterpreting the 'very trifiling mutiny' at Philadelphia in 1783," Pennsylvania Magazine of History and Biography, Jan/Apr 95. **CONTACT ADDRESS** 763 E 39th St, Brooklyn, NY, 11210. **EMAIL** catqc@cunyvm.cuny.edu

GALLATIN, HARLIE KAY
PERSONAL Born 12/15/1933, Meadville, MO, m, 1954, 3 children **DISCIPLINE** ANCIENT & MEDIEVAL HISTORY **EDUCATION** William Jewell Col, BA, 55; Cent Baptist Theol Sem, BD, 59; Cent Mo State Univ, MA, 61; Univ Ill, Urbana, PhD(hist), 72. **CAREER** Instr hist & polit sci, 61-65, assoc prof, 67-73, chmn, Interdisciplinary Fac Mid Eastern Studies, 71-80, prof hist, Southwest Baptist Univ, 73-, chmn dept hist & polit sci, 70-, dir spec studies, 76-93. **HONORS AND AWARDS** Parkway Distinguished Prof, 97. **MEMBERSHIPS** AHA; Am Soc Church Hist; Conf Faith & Hist; Assoc of Ancient Hist. **RESEARCH** Relations and interactions between governments and popular religious movements in Hellenistic and Roman times; incidents and results of the use of religious ideology as political propaganda in ancient, medieval, and early modern settings in eastern and western Europe; the development of ancient and medieval Christianity in relation to its cultural context. **SELECTED PUBLICATIONS** Contribr, Eerdmans' Handbook to the History of Christianity, Eerdmans, 77; contribr, A Lion Handbook, The History of Christianity, Lion Publishing, 77, 90; contribr, Evangelical Dictionary of Theology, Baker Book House, 84,94. **CONTACT ADDRESS** Dept of Hist & Political Science, Southwest Baptist Univ, 1600 Univ Ave, Bolivar, MO, 65613-2597. **EMAIL** hgallati@sbuniv.edu

GALLICCHIO, MARC S.
DISCIPLINE HISTORY **EDUCATION** Temple Univ, BA, 75; Pa State Univ, MA, 77; Temple Univ, PhD, 86. **CAREER** Assoc prof. **HONORS AND AWARDS** Bernath Article Prize, Soc of Hist(s) of Amer For Rel(s) Stuart. **RESEARCH** US foreign relations; US military history; US and East Asia. **SELECTED PUBLICATIONS** Auth, The Cold War Begins in Asia: American East Asian Policy and the Fall of the Japanese Empire, 88; The Other China Hands: US Army Officers and America's Failure in China, 1941-1950, J of Amer E Asian Relations, 95; The Kuriles Controversy: US Diplomacy and Strategy in the Soviet-Japan Border Dispute, 1941-1956, Pac Hist Rev, 91; After Nagasaki: George Marshall's Plan for Tactical Nuclear Weapons in Japan, Prologue, 91. **CONTACT ADDRESS** Dept of History, Villanova Univ, 800 Lancaster Ave., Villanova, PA, 19085-1692. **EMAIL** mgallicc@email.vill.edu

GALLUCCI, JOHN
DISCIPLINE RENAISSANCE AND CLASSICAL FRENCH LITERATURE **EDUCATION** BS License es lettres, BS, Strasbourg, 79; Maitrise Avignon, 83; Yale Univ, MA, 82, PhD, 88. **CAREER** Instr, Yale Univ; Actg ch, Comm Acad Advising, 97; ch, Working Comm on FLAC, 92-96; assoc prof-. **HONORS AND AWARDS** Picker fel; fel, Am Coun Learned Soc., Co-organizer, weekend colloquium on for lang tchg, 93. **SELECTED PUBLICATIONS** Auth, Entre copie et autographe: le texte des Pensees de Pascal, Travaux de Litterature; Pascal, Henry Adams and American Modernity, De la morale a l'economie politique; Politique et ecriture: la 'disposition' pascalienne comme principe de liberte, Justice et force: politiques au temps de Pascal; Poetic Pascal, or the Pensees as an Infinite Text, Dalhousie Fr Studies; Pascal and Kenneth Burke: An Argument for a 'Logological' Reading of the Pensees, Fr Seventeenth-Century Lit; Faith and Language: Allegories of Interpretation in Pascal, Fr Forum; Pascal poeta-theologus, Fr Seventeenth-Century Lit; rev(s), The Fr Rev, Papers on Fr Seventeenth-Century Lit; transl, Yale Fr Studies. **CONTACT ADDRESS** Dept of Philos and Relig, Colgate Univ, 13 Oak Drive, Hamilton, NY, 13346. **EMAIL** jgallucci@center.colgate.edu

GALUSH, WILLIAM J.
DISCIPLINE HISTORY **EDUCATION** Minn Univ, PhD. **CAREER** Ed, Mid-Am. **RESEARCH** Ethnic and religious history. **SELECTED PUBLICATIONS** Auth, Purity and Power: Chicago Polonia Feminists, 1880-1914, Polish Am Stud 47, 90. **CONTACT ADDRESS** Fine Arts Dept, Loyola Univ, Chicago, 6525 N. Sheridan Rd., Chicago, IL, 60626. **EMAIL** wgalush@orion.it.luc.edu

GALVARIS, GEORGE
PERSONAL Born 10/17/1926, Greece **DISCIPLINE** ART HISTORY **EDUCATION** Athens, MA, 51; Princeton Univ, MFA, 57, PhD, 58. **CAREER** Vis fel, Dumbarton Oaks, Harvard Univ, 57-59; asst prof, 59, prof art hist, 65, UNIV PROF EMER, McGILL UNIV; vis fel, Princeton Univ, 77; Inst Stud Icon Art, Holland, 78-81; vis prof, Univ Crete, 87, 94-96. **HONORS AND AWARDS** Fel, Royal Soc Can; Acad Athens Award. **MEMBERSHIPS** Founder & first pres, Can Nat Comt Byzantine Stud; corresp mem, Acad Athens; fel, Greek Christian Archaeol Soc; Medieval Acad Am; Am Numismatic Soc; Soc Nubian Stud. **SELECTED PUBLICATIONS** Auth, The Illustrations of the Liturgical Homilies of Gregory Nazianzenus, 69; auth, Bread and the Liturgy, 70; auth, Icons from the Elvehjem Centre, 73; auth, The Illustrations of the Prefaces in Byzantine Gospels, 79; auth, The Icon in the Life of the Church, 81; auth, Zografiki Vizantinon Cheirographon, 95; coauth, The Monastery of St. Catherine at Sinai, The Illuminated Manuscripts, vol 1, 90; coauth, Treasures at Sinai, 90. **CONTACT ADDRESS** 853 Sherbrooke St W, Montreal, PQ, H3A 2T6.

GAMAL, ADEL SULAIMAN
PERSONAL Born 03/14/1937, Cairo, Egypt, m, 1963, 2 children **DISCIPLINE** CLASSICAL ARABIC LITERATURE, ARABIC LANGUAGE **EDUCATION** Cairo Univ, BA, 59, MA, 64, PhD, 70. **CAREER** Instr Arabic lang & lit, Am Univ in Cairo, 62-70; asst prof, Univ Calif, Berkeley, 71-73 & Am Univ in Cairo, 73-75; assoc prof, Univ Ariz, 75-76 & Am Univ in Cairo, 76-78; assoc prof Arabic lang & lit, 78-80, prof, 80-, Univ Ariz. **HONORS AND AWARDS** First prize, Arabic Lang Acad, 94. **MEMBERSHIPS** MidE Studies Asn Nam; Am Asn Teachers Arabic. **RESEARCH** Classical Arabic literature; Arabic language; classical Arabic manuscripts. **SELECTED PUBLICATIONS** Transl, Who's Afraid of Virginia Woolf, In: Majallat al-Masrah, J Theater Art, 3/65; auth, Arabic poetry and the phenomenon of multiple usage of certain verses, 5/66 & The fortitude (Hamasa) books in classical Arabic literature, 3/68, Al-Majalla; The collected Poetry of Al-Ahwas Al-Ansary, Ministry Cult, Cairo, 70; The dissemination of Arabic language in Egypt after the Arab conquest, Majallat ath-Thaqafa, 3/74; Diwan Hatim al-Ta-i, Cairo, Egypt, 75; The basis of selections in the Hamasa Collection, J Arabic Lit, Scotland, 11/76; The conception of nobility in Early Arabic literature, Journal of American Asn Arabic Teachers; auth, al-Muntakhab, 2 vol, 94. **CONTACT ADDRESS** Dept of Oriental Studies, Univ of Arizona, Franklin Rm 403A, Tucson, AZ, 85721-0001. **EMAIL** gamal@u.arizona.edu

GAMBONI, DARIO
DISCIPLINE EUROPEAN ART OF THE 19TH CENTURY **EDUCATION** Univ Lausanne, BA, MA, PhD, 89. **CAREER** Curator, Museums of Fine Arts: Lausanne, Lucerne, Berne and Lugano. **HONORS AND AWARDS** Ailsa Mellon Bruce Sen fel Ctr Adv Study Visual Arts. **MEMBERSHIPS** Institut Universitaire de France; Nat Gallery Art; Revue de l'Art. **SELECTED PUBLICATIONS** Auth, La geographie artistique, Disentis: Desertina, 87, German and Italian translations; La plume et le pinceau. Odilon Redon et la litterature, Paris: Editions de Minuit, 89; The Destruction of Art: Iconoclasm and Vandalism since the French Revolution, New Haven and London: Yale U P, 97, German translation; and Odilon Redon: Das Fass Amontillado, Frankfurt-am-Main: Fischer, 98. **CONTACT ADDRESS** Case Western Reserve Univ, 10900 Euclid Ave, Cleveland, OH, 44106. **EMAIL** dlg11@po.cwru.edu

GANN, LEWIS H.
PERSONAL Born 01/28/1924, Mainz, Germany, m, 1950, 2 children **DISCIPLINE** MODERN HISTORY **EDUCATION** Oxford Univ, BA, 50, MA, 50, MA, 54, MLitt, 55, DPhil(hist), 64. **CAREER** Historian, Rhodes-Livingstone Inst, North Rhodesia, 50-52; asst lectr social and econ studies, Univ Manchester, 52-54; archivist and ed, Nat Archives Rhodesia and Nyasaland, 54-63; sr mem staff, 64-66, SR FEL, HOOVER INST, STANFORD UNIV, 66-, DEP CUR, AFRICANA COLLECTION, 65-, Co-dir, Colonialism in Africa Proj, Cambridge Univ Press, 67; asst ed, Bd of Yearbook Int Communist Affairs, 67-; sr res assoc, St Antony's Col, Oxford Univ; Rehm Found, Earhart Found, Nat Endowment for Humanities grants. **HONORS AND AWARDS** Domus Scholar, Ballid Col, Oxford Univ; L H Gaun, 82. **MEMBERSHIPS** AHA; Conf Brit Studies; African Studies Asn; African Studies Asn, UK; fel Royal Hist Soc. **RESEARCH** European colonialism in Africa; military history; general problems of imperialism. **SELECTED PUBLICATIONS** Auth, Hitler Commanders, Int Hist Rev, Vol 0015, 93; Our Age--English Intellectuals Between the World-Wars--a Group Portrait, Int Hist Rev, Vol 0015, 93; Stalin Generals, Int Hist Rev, Vol 0016, 94; Apartheid Reluctant Uncle--the United-States and Southern Africa in the Early Cold-War, Int Hist Rev, Vol 0016, 94; German-Question, Jewish-Question--Revolutionary Anti-Semitism from Kant to Wagner, Ger Stud Rev, Vol 0017, 94; Tears of Rain--Ethnicity and History in Central-Western Zambia, J Interdisciplinary Hist, Vol 0024, 94; Making War and Waging Peace--Foreign Intervention in Africa, Int Hist Rev, Vol 0017, 95; Weserubung--the German Attack On Denmark and Norway in April 1940, Ger Stud Rev, Vol 0018, 95; The German-Empire, Great-Britain, and the Transvaal, 1896-1902--the Beginnings of German British Estrangement, Int Hist Rev, Vol 0017, 95; Creating a Peoples Army, Without Any Fuss--Studies on the Beginnings of a Secret Rearmament in the Soviet-Zone-of-Occupation German-Democratic-Republic 1947-1952, Ger Stud Rev, Vol 0018, 95; Suicidal Alliance--German-Russian Military Relations 1920-1941, Ger Stud Rev, Vol 0018, 95; Genealogies of Conflict--Class, Identity, and State in Palestine/Israel and South-Africa, Int Hist Rev, Vol 0018, 96; Rich Relations--the American Occupation of Britain, 1942-1945, Int Hist Rev, Vol 0018, 96. **CONTACT ADDRESS** Hoover Inst, Stanford Univ, Stanford, CA, 94305.

GANS, HERBERT J.
PERSONAL Cologne, Germany **DISCIPLINE** SOCIOLOGY **EDUCATION** Univ Chicago, 47, MA, Soc & Soc Sci, 50; Univ Pa, PhD, Plan & Soc. **CAREER** Plan, publ & priv agencies, 50-53; lectr, Dept City Plan, Univ Pa, 53-64; assoc/adj prof, Teachers Coll, 64-69; prof, Soc & Plan, Urban Stud & Plan, MIT, 69-71; prof, Sociol, Columbia Univ, 71-85; ROBERT S LYND PROF, COLUMBIA UNIV, 85-. **RESEARCH** Urban & community studies; Urban poverty & antipoverty plan; Social plan, Social politics; Ethnicity. **SELECTED PUBLICATIONS** The War Against the Poor: The Underclass and Antipoverty Policy, Basic Books, 95. **CONTACT ADDRESS** Dept Sociol, Columbia Univ, 404 Fayerweather Hall, New York, NY, 10027.

GANSON, BARBARA
DISCIPLINE HISTORY **EDUCATION** Univ Tex, PhD. **CAREER** Asst prof. **RESEARCH** Latin America history; Paraguay history; ethnohistory. **SELECTED PUBLICATIONS** Auth, The Evuevi of Paraguay: Adaptive Strategies and Responses to Colonialism 1528-1811, 89; Contacto intercultural: Un estudio des los payaguaes del Paraguay 1528-1870, 89. **CONTACT ADDRESS** History Dept, Florida Atlantic Univ, 777 Glades Rd, Boca Raton, FL, 33431. **EMAIL** rinaldi@acc.fau.edu

GANTT, WALTER N.
PERSONAL Born 05/29/1921, Baltimore, MD, s **DISCIPLINE** EDUCATION **EDUCATION** Coppin State Coll, BS 1942; NY Univ, MA 1949; Univ MD, EdD 1968. **CAREER** Baltimore MD, prin & tchr 1942-68; Univ of MD, assoc prof 1968-78; Comm Coll of Baltimore, personnel admin 1978-85; Peace Corps Honduras 1985-87. **HONORS AND AWARDS** Circulus Scholarum Coppin State Coll; Serv Awd Phi Delta Kappa Univ MD 1975; inductee Maryland Senior Citizens Hall of Fame, 1997. **MEMBERSHIPS** Coord Urban Tchr Educ Ctr 1969-70; asst to the chmn Dept Early Childhood Elem Educ 1971-74; mem Proj Aware; Cit Black History Exhibits; Phi Delta Kappa; chmn Career & Occupational Devel Com; mem Assn Supervision & Curriculum Devel; AAUP; NCSS.

GANZ, ALBERT HARDING
PERSONAL Born 12/12/1938, New York, NY, m, 1970, 2 children **DISCIPLINE** GERMAN & MILITARY HISTORY **EDUCATION** Wittenberg Univ, AB, 61; Columbia Univ, MA, 63; Lt 4th Armored Div, Germany, 64-66; Ohio State Univ, PhD(Ger hist), 72. **CAREER** Instr, Ohio State Univ at Newark, 71-72, asst prof 72-77, assoc prof Europ Hist, 77-. **MEMBERSHIPS** OAH, Ohio Acad of Hist; Soc Mil Hist; Ohio Arms Control Seminar (Mershon). **RESEARCH** Modern German history; Imperial German Navy; armored warfare; military history, national security. **SELECTED PUBLICATIONS** Auth, Abu Ageila-Two Battles, Armor, Part I, 5-6/74, Part II, 7-8/74; co-auth, The German Navy in the Far East and Pacific, In: Kennedy and Moses, Germany in the Pacific and Far East, 1870-1914, Univ Queensland, 77; auth, Colonial Policy and the Imperial German Navy, Militaergeschichtliche Mitteilungen, 1/77; Albion-The Baltic Islands Operation, 4/78, The German Expedition to Finland, 1918, 4/80, Military Affairs; auth, The Holy Roman Empire, ed Zophy, Greenwood Press, 80; auth, Breakthrough to Bastogne, Armor, 11-12/81; Return to Singling, Armor XCIV No 5: 32-39, Sept-Oct 85; Patton's Relief of General Wood, Journal of mil hist 53,3: 257-273, July 89; The 11th Panzers in the Defense, 1944, Armor CIII No 2: 26-27, Mar-Apr 94 (trans into German as Die 11. Panzer-Division an der Westfront 1944; Questionable Objective: The Brittany Ports, 1944, Journal of mil Hist, 59, 1: 77-95, Jan 95; Articles (7) in Spencer C. Tucker, ed, The European Powers in thr First World War, NY & London: Garland Pub, 96. **CONTACT ADDRESS** Dept of Hist, Ohio State Univ, 1179 University Dr, Newark, OH, 43055-1797.

GANZ, DAVID
PERSONAL Born 05/25/1952, Welwyn, England **DISCIPLINE** CLASSICAL AND MEDIEVAL LATIN **EDUCATION** Univ Oxford, BA, 73, DPhil, 80. **CAREER** Res asst hist, Univ St Andrews, Scotland, 79-80; vis asst prof, 80-82, Asst PROF CLASSICS, UNIV NC, CHAPEL HILL, 82-, Ed, Handlist of Alcuin Manuscripts, 79-. **RESEARCH** Latin palaeography; Carotingian Renaissance; Tironian notes. **SELECTED PUBLICATIONS** Auth, Through a Glass Darkly--Aldhelm Riddles in the British-Library-Ms-Royal-12-XXIII, Speculum-a J Medieval Stud, Vol 0068, 93; French, Italian, and Spanish Penitentials From the 8th-Century to the 11th-Century, Vol 1--Paenitentialia-Minora From France and Italy (8th-Century-11th-Century), Speculum-a J Medieval Stud, Vol 0071; Faith, Art and Politics at Saint-Riquier--the Symbolic Vision of Angilbert, Cath Hist Rev, Vol 0083, 97. **CONTACT ADDRESS** Dept of Classics, Univ NC, Chapel Hill, NC, 27514.

GANZ, MARGERY ANN
PERSONAL Born 07/04/1947, Trenton, NJ **DISCIPLINE** RENAISSANCE & MEDIEVAL HISTORY **EDUCATION** Univ Rochester, BA, 69; Syracuse Univ, MA, 71, PhD(Renaissance Hist), 79. **CAREER** Adj instr hist, Onondaga Community Col, 74-79; asst prof, Univ Tenn, Chattanooga, 79-80; asst prof hist, Spelman Col, 81-, Instr hist, Col Cortland, State Univ NY, 71-72 & Le Moyne Col, 76-79; chmn, dept of History, 97; prof History, 98, dir of study abroad, 88; Spelman College. **HONORS AND AWARDS** Harvard Univ Villa I Tatti, fel, 85; NAFSA Lily Von KempererAward, 95; AMOCO Award Outstanding Fac Feaching, 91; UNCF Mellon fel, 88-89. **MEMBERSHIPS** Renaissance Soc Am; Soc Ital Hist Studies; Am Hist Asn. **RESEARCH** Conspiracies against the Medici, 1450-1494; family history in Renaissance Florence; Buon Vivere Civile in the Renaissance. **SELECTED PUBLICATIONS** Auth, Donato Acciaiudi and the Medici: A strategy for survival in Quattrocento Florence, Rinascimento, 82; A Florentine Friendship: Donato Acciaindli & Vespasiano da Bisticci, Renaissance Quarterly 43, 90; Paying the Price for Political Failure: Florentine Women in the Aftermath of 1466, Rinascimento, 34, 94. **CONTACT ADDRESS** Dept of History, Spelman Col, 350 Spelman Lane, Box 1447, Atlanta, GA, 30314-4398. **EMAIL** mganz@spelman.edu

GARA, LARRY
PERSONAL Born 05/16/1922, San Antonio, TX, m, 1946, 2 children **DISCIPLINE** AMERICAN HISTORY **EDUCATION** William Penn Col, BA, 47; Pa State Univ, MA, 48; Univ Wis, PhD, 53. **CAREER** Instr hist & govt, Bluffton Col, 48-49; lectr hist, Mexico City Col, 53-54; from instr to asst prof, Eureka Col, 54-57; prof, Grove City Col, 57-62, chmn, Dept Hist & Polit Sci, 58-62; Assoc Prof, 62-66, Prof Hist & Govt, 71-92, Prof Emeritus, Wilmington Col, Ohio, 92-, Chmn Dept Hist, 71-92. **HONORS AND AWARDS** T. Wistar Brown fel, Haverford Col, 68-69; War Resisters League Annual Peace Award, 84; Distinguished Fac Award, Wilmington Col, 96; Distinguished Service Award, Ohio Acad Hist, 97. **MEMBERSHIPS** Orgn Am Hist; Southern Hist Asn; Ohio Acad Hist; Peace Hist Soc. **RESEARCH** Antislavery and other 19th century reform movements; the American peace movement; the Franklin Pierce Administration. **SELECTED PUBLICATIONS** Auth, Westernized Yankee: The Story of Cyrus Wood-

man, State Hist Soc Wis, 56; The Baby Dodd Story, Contemporary Press, 59, repr, LSU Press, 92; Liberty Line: The Legend of the Underground Railroad, Univ Ky, 61, repr, 96; A Short History of Wisconsin, State Hist Soc Wis, 62; Who was an Abolitionist?, In: The Antislavery Vanguard, Princeton Univ, 65; The Narrative of William Wells Brown, Addison-Wesley, 68; William Still and the Underground Railroad, In: The Making of Black America, Atheneum, 68; Horace Mann: Antislavery Congressman, Historian, 11/69; War Resistance in Historical Perspective Pendle Hill, 70; Propaganda Uses of the Underground Railroad, In: American Vistas 1607-1877, Oxford Univ, 71; Slavery and the Slave Power: a Crucial Distinction, In: The Abolitionists, 73; The Myth of the Underground Railroad, In: Annual Editions: Readings in American History, Dushkin, 81, Vol 1; The Presidency of Franklin Pierce, Univ Press Kans, 91; coauth, A Few Small Candles: War Resisters of World War II Tell Their Stories, Kent State Univ Press (in press for 99). **CONTACT ADDRESS** 251 Ludovic St, Wilmington, OH, 45177-2499. **EMAIL** larry_gara@wilmington.edu

GARBER, MARILYN
PERSONAL Brooklyn, NY, 2 children **DISCIPLINE** HISTORY, LAW **EDUCATION** Univ Calif, Los Angeles, BA, 57, MA, 60, PhD(hist), 67; Southwestern Univ, JD, 77. **CAREER** Prof hist, Calif State Univ, Dominguez Hills, 80-. **MEMBERSHIPS** Calif State Bar. **RESEARCH** Utopia; legal history; labor law; negotiation; conflict resolution **SELECTED PUBLICATIONS** Natural Law Liberalism, 67. **CONTACT ADDRESS** Dept Hist, California State Univ, Dominguez Hills, 1000 E Victoria, Carson, CA, 90747-0005. **EMAIL** mgarber@dhlx20.csudh.edu

GARCIA, AURELIO A.
PERSONAL Born 06/06/1958, Arecibo, Puerto Rico, m, 1995, 1 child **DISCIPLINE** HISTORY OF CHRISTIAN DOCTRINE, REFORMATION STUDIES **EDUCATION** Temple Univ, BA, 79; Princeton Theol Sem, MDiv, 83, PhD, 89. **CAREER** Instr Church Hist, 88-92, adj facC, 92-, Evangelical Sem of PR; Ordained Min Presby Church USA; Pastor, Huto Rey Presby Church. **MEMBERSHIPS** AAR; Calvin Stud Soc. **RESEARCH** Historiography; Reformation studies; Heinrich Bollinger. **SELECTED PUBLICATIONS** Auth Eusebius Theophany: A Christian Neoplatonist Response, The Patristic and Bizantine Rev, 87; The Theology of History and Apologetic Historiography in Heinrich Bullinger, Mellen Res Univ Press, 92. **CONTACT ADDRESS** Entre Rios 137 Plaza Serena, Trujillo Alto, PR, 00976.

GARCIA, JUAN RAMON
PERSONAL Born 07/27/1947, Sebastian, TX, m, 3 children **DISCIPLINE** MEXICAN AMERICAN & AMERICAN HISTORY **EDUCATION** DePaul Univ, BA, 71, MA, 79; Univ Notre Dame, MA, 74, PhD, 77. **CAREER** Asst prof hist, Univ Mich-Flint, 75-78; prog dev bilingual educ, E Mich Univ, 78-79; assoc prof hist, Univ Mich-Flint, 79-81; Assoc prof hist, 81-, Dir Univ Teaching Ctr, 90-94, Assoc Dean, Col Social & Behavorial Sci, 94-98, Prof Hist, 97, Univ AZ; Dir Chicano studies, Univ Mich-Flint, 75-78 & 79-81; consult, Nat Inst Educ, 77-81, Nat Educ Asn, 78-81 & Nat Teacher Corps, 75-80; VP Acad Aff, Col St Mary, Omaha, NE, 98. **MEMBERSHIPS** Nat Asn Chicano Studies; W Soc Sci Asn. **RESEARCH** Mexican immigration history; Mexicans and Mexican Americans in the Midwest 1900-1941; United States History 1918-45. **SELECTED PUBLICATIONS** Auth, A History of the People of Mexican Descent in Chicago Heights, Illinois, 1900-1975, PSC Press, 76; A history of Chicanos in Chicago Heights, Illinois, Aztlan, 78; A History of the Mexican American People: A Teacher's Guide, Univ Notre Dame, 79; The people of Mexican descent in Michigan: A historical overview, Blacks and Chicanos in Urban Michigan, Mich Hist Div, 79; Operation Wetback: The Mass Deportation of Mexican Undocumented Workers, 1954, Greenwood, 81; Midwest Mexicanos in the 1920's: Issues, questions & directions, Social Sci Quart, 82; Perspectives in Mexican American Studies, Volumes 1-6, 1989-1998; Mexicans In The Midwest, 1900-1932, Univ AZ, 98. **CONTACT ADDRESS** VP Acad Aff, Col of Saint Mary, 1901 S 72nd St, Omaha, NE, 68124. **EMAIL** Jgarcia@csm.edu

GARCIA, MATT
DISCIPLINE HISTORY **EDUCATION** Claremont Graduate Sch, PhD, 96. **CAREER** Asst prof, Univ Ill Urbana Champaign. **RESEARCH** Chicano/Latino history; history of American West; popular culture and cultural criticism. **SELECTED PUBLICATIONS** Auth, Just put on that Padua Hills 'smile': The Padua Hills Theatre and The Mexican Players, 1931-1974, Calif Hist, 95; Adjusting the Focus: Padua Hills Theatre and Latino History, 96; Chicana/o history in a changing discipline, Humboldt J Social Relations, 96. **CONTACT ADDRESS** History Dept, Univ Ill Urbana Champaign, 52 E Gregory Dr, Champaign, IL, 61820. **EMAIL** garcia2@uiuc.edu

GARCIA, WILLIAM BURRES
PERSONAL Born 07/16/1940, Dallas, Texas **DISCIPLINE** MUSIC EDUCATION **EDUCATION** Prairie View A&M Univ, music courses 1958-61; N TX State Univ, BMus 1962, MMus Ed 1965; Univ of IA, PhD 1973; Howard Univ, NEH Fellow 1973-74; Carnegie-Mellon Univ, College Mgmt Prog 1984. **CAREER** Philander Smith Coll, instructor of music 1963-64; Langston Univ, asst prof of music 1965-69; Miles Coll, assoc prof of music 1974-77; Talladega Coll, acting academic vice pres 1982-83, prof of music 1977-, chmn of music dept 1977-, chmn of humanities div 1981-85; Selma Univ, acad dean 1986-. **HONORS AND AWARDS** Doctoral Fellowship Grants S Fellowships Fund Inc 1969-73; Ford Found Fellowship Grant for Dissertations in Ethnic Studies 1971-72; Outstanding Educators of Amer 1975; lecture, "John Wesley Work, Choral Composer" Ethnic Music Workshop Coll of Fine Arts 1974; lecture "John Wesley Work, Black Amer Composer" Afro-Amer Music Workshop Ctr for African & Afro-Amer Studies Atlanta Univ 1975; paper, "African Elements in Afro-Amer Music" Anniston Museum of Natl History AL 1982. **MEMBERSHIPS** Mem Phi Mu Alpha Sinfonia 1965; bd Div of Higher Educ Disciples of Christ 1978-81; bd Talladega Arts Council 1981-; life mem Amer Choral Dirs Assn; mem Amer Choral Found; mem Amer Musicological Soc; mem Coll Music Soc; mem Intl Heinrich Schutz Soc; mem Natl Assn of Teachers of Singing; mem Thomas Music Study Club of Natl Assn of Negro Musicians. **SELECTED PUBLICATIONS** "Church Music by Black Composers, A Bibliography of Choral Works" Black Perspective in Music 1974. **CONTACT ADDRESS** Academic Dean, Selma Univ, 1501 Lapsley St, Selma, AL, 36701.

GARDELLA, ROBERT PAUL
PERSONAL Born 02/16/1943, Newark, NJ, m, 1970, 1 child **DISCIPLINE** HISTORY OF MODERN CHINA **EDUCATION** Rice Univ, BA, 65; Univ Wash, MA, 68, PhD(hist), 76. **CAREER** Instr hist, Loyola Univ, La, 73-74; asst prof humanities, US Merchant Marine Acad, 77-. **HONORS AND AWARDS** Chiang Ching-Kuo Res Grant, 96-98. **MEMBERSHIPS** Asn Asian Studies; Soc Ch'ing Studies. **RESEARCH** Social and economic history of Ch'ing and modern China; regional history of southeast China; Chinese business hist. **SELECTED PUBLICATIONS** Auth, Harvesting Mountains: Fujian and the China Tea Trade 1757-1937, Univ Calif Press, 94; Squaring Accounts: Commercial Bookkeeping Methods and Capitalist Rationalism in Late Qing and Republican China, J Asian Studies, 92; From Treaty Ports to Provincial Status, Taiwan: A New History, ME Sharpe, 98; co-ed, Chinese Business History: Interpretive Trends and Priorities for the Future, ME Sharpe, 98. **CONTACT ADDRESS** Dept of Humanities, US Merchant Marine Acad, 300 Steamboat Rd, Kings Point, NY, 11024-1699. **EMAIL** Robert-Gardella@usmma.edu

GARDINIER, DAVID E.
PERSONAL Born 10/13/1932, Syracuse, NY, m, 1966, 3 children **DISCIPLINE** HISTORY OF AFRICA **EDUCATION** State Univ NY Albany, AB, 53; Yale Univ, MAT, 54, PhD(hist), 60. **CAREER** Instr hist, Univ Del, 59-60; from instr to asst prof, Bowling Green State Univ, 60-65; res assoc, Ctr Int Studies, Ohio Univ, 65-66; assoc prof, 66-69, chmn dept, 69-75, PROF HIST, MARQUETTE UNIV, 69-, African sect ed, Am Hist Rev, 64-76. **MEMBERSHIPS** AHA; African Studies Asn; Fr Colonial Hist Soc (vpres, 76-78, pres, 78-80). **RESEARCH** History of French-speaking Africa; equatorial Africa; colonialism. **SELECTED PUBLICATIONS** Auth, The Peace-Corps in Cameroon, Am Hist Rev, Vol 0098, 93. **CONTACT ADDRESS** Dept of Hist, Marquette Univ, Milwaukee, WI, 53233.

GARDNER, BETTYE J.
PERSONAL Vicksburg, MS, s **DISCIPLINE** HISTORY **EDUCATION** Howard Univ, BA 1962, MA 1964; George Washington Univ, PhD 1974. **CAREER** Howard Univ, instructor 1964-69; Social Sys Intervention Inc, sr rsch assoc 1969; Washington DC Bd of Educ, consultant 1969; Black History Calvert Ct MD, consultant; Washington Technical Inst, asst prof 1969-71; Coppin State Coll, dean of arts & sciences 1981-87, prof of history 1982-, chairperson dept of history 1988-90. **HONORS AND AWARDS** Moton Fellowship, Moton Institute, 1978-79; Danforth Assn, Danforth Foundation, 1980-86; Fellowship, Smithsonian, summer 1988. **MEMBERSHIPS** Mem NAACP, Org of Amer Historians, Assoc of Black Women Historians, Assoc for the Study of Afro-Amer Life & History; mem Natl Educ Assn; NCNW, 1980; editorial bd Journal of Negro History; exec counc Asso for the Study of Afro-Amer Life & Hist; vp, Association for Afro-American Life and History, 1993-95, natl pres, 1995-97; publ numerous articles, Educ Licensure Commission, Washington DC, chairperson; Bethune House Federal Commission. **CONTACT ADDRESS** History Dept, Coppin State Col, 2500 W North Ave, Baltimore, MD, 21216.

GAREN, SALLY
PERSONAL Born 10/11/1947, Oak Ridge, TN, m, 1978, 2 children **DISCIPLINE** MEDIEVAL ART HISTORY **EDUCATION** Smith Col, BA, 68; Art Inst of Chicago, MFA, 70; Univ Chicago, MFA, 75, PhD, 85. **CAREER** Lect, DePaul Univ, 77-82; Appreciation of Art Hist teacher, The Madeira School, 90-98. **HONORS AND AWARDS** Smith Col, Alpha Award in the Arts; Univ of Chicago: Cochrane Woods Travel Grant. **MEMBERSHIPS** Soc of Architectural Historians; the Textile Museum; The Pre-Columbian Soc of Washington, DC. **RESEARCH** Visigothic Period Spanish architecture and sculpture. **SELECTED PUBLICATIONS** Auth, book review of Jerrilyn Dodds, Architecture and Ideology in Early Medieval Spain, in JSAH, March 92; Santa Maria de Melque and Church Construction under Muslim Rule, J of the Soc of Architectural Historians, Sept 92. **CONTACT ADDRESS** 1625 Evers Dr, McLean, VA, 22101-5010. **EMAIL** sgaren@aol.com

GARFINKLE, CHARLENE G.
PERSONAL Born 09/01/1955, Inglewood, CA, m, 1977, 1 child **DISCIPLINE** HISTORY OF ART AND ARCHITECTURE; 19TH CENTURY ART AND ARCHITECTURE OF UNITE **EDUCATION** Calif State Univ, BA, 77; Univ Calif Santa Barbara, MA, 86; Univ Calif Santa Barbara PhD, 96 **CAREER** Assoc lctr, Univ Calif Santa Barbara, 90-92; lctr, Univ Calif Santa Barbara, 90-97; instr, Santa Barbara City Col, current **HONORS AND AWARDS** Regents' Fel, 91, 93; Art Affiliates, Art Hist Grad Fel, 92; Newberry Libr Residence Fel, 91; Gen Affiliates, Grad Dissertation Fel, 91; Murray Roman Art Hist Fel, 89-91; **MEMBERSHIPS** Amer Cult Assoc; Amer Studies Assoc; Assoc Historians Amer Art; Assoc Independent Historians Art; Col Art Assoc; Interdisciplinary Nineteenth-Century Studies; Nat Coalition Independent Scholars; Native Amer Art Studies Assoc; Soc Archit Hist **RESEARCH** Nineteenth Century American Art; History of American Women Artists; Nineteenth Century Expositions in the United States; Imagery of Nineteenth-Century American Women **SELECTED PUBLICATIONS** Auth, "Becoming Visible: The 'Coming Woman" Stained Glass of the Woman's Building, World's Columbian Exposition," Stained Glass, forthcoming; contribr, "Anne Whitney" and "Alice Rideout," Amer Ntl Biog, Oxford Univ, 99; **CONTACT ADDRESS** 1030 Kellogg Place, Santa Barbara, CA, 93111. **EMAIL** arthistgar@aol.com

GARGAN, EDWARD T.
PERSONAL Born 02/25/1922, New York, NY, m, 1949, 2 children **DISCIPLINE** MODERN EUROPEAN HISTORY **EDUCATION** Brooklyn Col, BA, 45; Cath Univ Am, MA, 47, PhD, 55. **CAREER** Instr colonial Am hist, Boston Col, 49-52; dir, Sheil Sch Social Studies, 52-53; from asst prof to prof mod Europ hist, Loyola Univ, Ill, 53-63; prof, Wesleyan Univ, 63-66; PROF HIST, UNIV WIS-MADISON, 66-, Am Coun Learned Soc travel grant, Salzburg, Austria, 61; Guggenheim fel, Paris, France, 66-67; Nat Sci Found grant, 70-72; assoc ed, Contemp Fr Civilization, 75-. **HONORS AND AWARDS** Chevalier de Palmes Academiques, France, 63., MA, Wesleyan Univ, 64. **MEMBERSHIPS** AHA; Am Cath Hist Asn (pres, 70-71); Soc Fr Hist Studies (pres, 74-75); Soc Mod Hist, France. **RESEARCH** History of European thought since 1600; France since the French Revolution; historiography of modern Europe since 1600. **SELECTED PUBLICATIONS** Auth, Religion, Society and Politics in France Since 1789, Cath Hist Rev, Vol 0079, 93; Religious History--World-History, Open History--Festschrift for Gadaille, Jacques, Cath Hist Rev, Vol 0079, 93; Expositions--Literature and Architecture in 19th-Century France, Am Hist Rev, Vol 0099, 94; The Jesuit Myth--Conspiracy theory and Politics in 19th-Century France, Am Hist Rev, Vol 0100, 95. **CONTACT ADDRESS** 722 Miami Pass, Madison, WI, 53711.

GARIBALDI, ANTOINE MICHAEL
PERSONAL Born 09/26/1950, New Orleans, LA, s **DISCIPLINE** EDUCATION **EDUCATION** Howard Univ, BA (magna cum laude) 1973; Univ of Minnesota, PhD 1976. **CAREER** Holy Comforter-St Cyprian DC, elem teacher 1972-73; Univ of Minnesota Coll of Educ, rsch asst 1973-75; St Paul Urban League St Acad, principal 1975-77; Natl Inst of Educ, rsch admin 1977-82; Xavier Univ of Louisiana, Dept of Educ, chmn, prof of educ, 1982-89, dean, 1989-91, College of Arts and Sciences, vice pres for academic affairs, 1991-96; HOWARD UNIV, PROVOST AND CHIEF ACADEMIC OFFICER, 1996-. **MEMBERSHIPS** Amer Psychological Assn (Fellow); Amer Educ Rsch Assn; Assn of Black Psychologists; Phi Delta Kappa; Alpha Phi Alpha; Phi Kappa Phi; pres Univ of Minnesota Black Studies Psychological Assn 1974-75; US Army Sci Bd 1979-83; lecturer Howard Univ School of Educ 1981; assoc editor Amer Educ Rsch Journal 1982-84; consultant US Dept of Educ 1983-85; New Orleans Library Bd 1984-93, chairman, 1991-93; Journal of Negro Education, board of directors; co-chmn, Mayor's Foundation for Educ, 1987-90; co-chmn, educ comm, Urban League of Greater New Orleans, 1984-90; American Library Association; Alpha Kappa Mu, Psi Chi; Center for Education of African-American Males, board of directors, 1991-92; Metropolitan Area Committee, board of directors, 1992-96, education fund board, 1991-96. **SELECTED PUBLICATIONS** Author, works include: The Decline of Teacher Production in Louisiana 1976-83; Attitudes Toward the Profession, 1986; Southern Education Foundation monograph, 1986; Educating Black Male Youth: A Moral and Civic Imperative, 1988; editor: Black Colleges and Universities: Challenges for the Future, 1984; "Teacher Recruitment and Retention: With a Special Focus on Minority Teachers", National Education Association, 1989; co-editor: The Education of African-Americans; more than 70 chapters and articles in professional journals and books. **CONTACT ADDRESS** Off of the Provost, 2400 Sixth Street NW, Rm 405, Washington, DC, 20059.

GARLAND, MARTHA
PERSONAL Born 07/18/1942, Salem, IL, m, 1985, 2 children **DISCIPLINE** HISTORY **EDUCATION** Tulane Univ, BA, 64; Cornell Univ, MA, 66; Ohio State, PhD, 75. **CAREER** Asst

Prof, 82-88, assoc prof, 88- , assoc dean, Col of Human, 93-96, actg dean, Arts and Sci, 96-97, VProvost, Undergrad Stud, 97- , Ohio State. **HONORS AND AWARDS** Phi Beta Kappa; Woodrow Wilson Fellow; Phi Kappa Phi; Commencement Speaker, Ohio State, Wint 94. **MEMBERSHIPS** Am Hist Asn; N Am Conf on British Studies; Social Hist Soc UK; Am Asn Higher Ed; Am Asn Col Univ. **RESEARCH** British social and cultural history, 19th and 20th centuries. **SELECTED PUBLICATIONS** Cambridge Before Darwin, CUP, 80. **CONTACT ADDRESS** Ohio State Univ, 190 N Oval Mall, Columbus, OH, 43210. **EMAIL** garland.1@osu.edu

GARLICK, PETER C.
PERSONAL Born 03/07/1923, Sheffield, England, m, 1960, 2 children **DISCIPLINE** ECONOMICS **EDUCATION** Univ Sheffield, UK, BA 49, Diplo edu 50, MA 51; Univ London PhD 62. **CAREER** State Univ NY, New Paltz, prof and ch, econ, current position. **CONTACT ADDRESS** Dept of Economics, State Univ NY, New Paltz, NY, 12561.

GARNER, ROBERTA
PERSONAL m, 2 children **DISCIPLINE** SOCIOLOGY **EDUCATION** Univ of Chicago, AB, 62, AM, 63, PhD, 66. **CAREER** Asst prof, Queens Col, 66-67; asst prof, Barnard Col, 67-69; lectr, Univ of Chicago, 69-71; PROF, DEPAUL UNIV, 71-. **HONORS AND AWARDS** IREX fel, 88; Woodrow Wilson, 63; Phi Beta Kappa, 62. **MEMBERSHIPS** Am Soc Asn. **RESEARCH** Social theory, political sociology; social change; sociology of education; collective behavior. **SELECTED PUBLICATIONS** Auth, Contemporary Movements and Ideologies, McGraw-Hill, 96; coauth, Social Movement Theory and Research: An Annotated Bibliographical Guide, Magill Bibliog, The Scarecrow Press, & Salem Press, 97. **CONTACT ADDRESS** Dept of Sociology, DePaul Univ, 2320 N Kenmore, Chicago, IL, 60614. **EMAIL** rgarner@wppost.depaul.edu

GARRARD, MARY
DISCIPLINE ART HISTORY **CAREER** Prof, Am Univ. **RESEARCH** Italian Renaissance and feminist studies. **SELECTED PUBLICATIONS** Auth, Artemisia Gentileschi; Coauth, The Power of Feminist Art: The American Movement of the 1970's; Feminism and Art History: Questioning the Litany. **CONTACT ADDRESS** American Univ, 4400 Massachusetts Ave, Washington, DC, 20016.

GARRETT, ALINE M.
PERSONAL Born 08/28/1944, Martinville, LA **DISCIPLINE** EDUCATION **EDUCATION** Univ SW LA, BA 1966; Oberlin OH, AM 1968; Univ MA, PhD 1971. **CAREER** Univ of Southwestern LA Lafayette, assoc prof Psychology 1971; Univ of MA Amherst, grad res asst; Summer School Faculty USL, teacher 1970 & 1969; Psychometrist Lafayette Parish Schools, summer 1967; Project Head Start, Lafayette LA, teacher 1966. **HONORS AND AWARDS** Faculty advisor Nat Honor Soc; outstanding black citizen award So Consumers Educ Found Field of Educ 1975; research grant to do family res HEW Office Child Devel 1974-75; SEPA Visting Women Program 1974-. **MEMBERSHIPS** Mem Am Psychol Assn; mem Nat Assn Black Psychol; mem Soc for Research in Child Devel; mem Psi Chi; mem SE Psychol Assn; mem LA Psychol Assn; mem bd dir Nat Council Black Child Devel; mem com on Acad Affairs & Standards 1972; mem Faculty Senate 1973-; mem Grad Faculty 1971-; mem Equal Employment Opportunity Com 1972; mem council on tchr educ coll educ USL 1974-; mem adv bd SGA-USL Child Care Cntr; mem adv bd Cath Soc Serv 1973; mem Health Adv Bd of Tri-Parish Progress Inc 1974; candidate St Martin Parish Sch Bd 1974; mem Agency Parent Council of SMILE Inc USL Rep 1974; mem byappointment Mayor Willis Soc & Economic Com St Martinville 1974; mem bd dir Lafayette Chap Epilepsy Found; mem Alpha Lambda Delta. **CONTACT ADDRESS** Psychology Dept, PO Box 3131 US, Lafayette, LA, 70501.

GARRETT, CLARKE W.
PERSONAL Born 02/26/1935, Evanston, IL, m, 1957, 3 children **DISCIPLINE** MODERN EUROPEAN HISTORY **EDUCATION** Carleton Col, BA, 56, Univ Wis, MS, 57, PhD(hist), 61. **CAREER** Asst prof hist, Wake Forest Col, 61-65; from asst prof to assoc prof, 65-73, prof, 73-81, Dana prof hist, 81-97, PROF EMER, 97-, DICKINSON COL; Nat Endowment for Humanities grant, 70; Huntington Libr fel, 78; Am Philos Soc grant, 81, ACLS Fel 84-85; NEH Fel 91-92. **MEMBERSHIPS** Western Soc French Hist **RESEARCH** European social and intellectual history, 1660-1800; history of popular religion. **SELECTED PUBLICATIONS** Contrib, The Family, Communes and Utopian Societies, Harper, 72; auth, Respectable Folly: Millenarianism and the French Revolution, Johns Hopkins Univ, 74; The spiritual odyssey of Jacob Duche, Proc Am Philos Soc, 75; co-auth, The Wolf and the Lamb: Popular Culture in France, Anma Libri, 77; auth, Women and witches: patterns of analysis, J Women Cult & Soc, 78; auth, "The Myth of the Counterrevolution in 1789" in French Hist Studies, 94; co-auth, Joseph Priestly in America, Carlisle, 94; auth, The Origins of the Shakers, Johns Hopkins Univ, 98. **CONTACT ADDRESS** 249 Stuart Rd, Carlisle, PA, 17013. **EMAIL** garrettc@dickinso.edu

GARRISON, DANIEL
DISCIPLINE CLASSICS **EDUCATION** Harvard Univ, BA, 59; UNC Chapel Hill, MA, 63; UC Berkeley, PhD, 68. **CAREER** Prof, Northwestern Univ, 66-; master, Willard Residential Col; sec, Col Arts and Sci(s) Fac; ch, Undergrad Acad Conduct Comt. **RESEARCH** Vesalius and ancient medical science. **SELECTED PUBLICATIONS** Auth, Mild Frenzy: A Reading of the Hellenistic Love Epigram, Steiner, 78; The Language of Virgil: An Introduction to the Poetry of the Aeneid, Lang, 84, 93; Who's Who in Wodehouse, IPL, 89; The Student's Catullus, Okla, 95; Horace Epodes and Odes, Okla, 91; ed, Lang Class Studies. **CONTACT ADDRESS** Dept of Classics, Northwestern Univ, 1801 Hinman, Kresge 13, Evanston, IL, 60208. **EMAIL** d-garrison@nwu.edu

GARRISON, DAVID H.
PERSONAL Born 12/24/1937, Hamilton, NY, m, 1992, 1 child **DISCIPLINE** CLASSICS **EDUCATION** Harvard Univ, BA 59; Univ NC Chapel Hill, MA 63; Univ Cal Berk, PhD 68. **CAREER** Northwestern Univ, prof 66-. **MEMBERSHIPS** APA; Classical Assoc Middle W & S; Soc Ancient Medicine; AAHM **RESEARCH** Lyric poetry; Medical history **SELECTED PUBLICATIONS** Auth, Sexual Culture in Ancient Greece, Univ Oklahoma Press, forthcoming; Horace Epodes and Odes, A New Annotated Latin edition, Univ OK Press, 91, rev, Class Wld 92, Greece and Rome, 92, Classical Outlook, 93; Andreas Vesalius on the Teeth: An Annotated translation from De humani corporis fabrica, coauth, Clinical Anatomy, 95; Andreas Vesalius on the Larynx and Hyoid Bone, coauth, Medical History, 93; The Locus Inamoenus: Another Part of the Forest, Arion II, 92; **CONTACT ADDRESS** Dept of Classics, Northwestern Univ, Evanston, IL, 60208. **EMAIL** d.garrison@nwu.edu

GARRISON, LORA DEE
PERSONAL Born 10/18/1934, Cleburne, TX, 2 children **DISCIPLINE** AMERICAN INTELLECTUAL & SOCIAL HISTORY **EDUCATION** Fullerton State Col, BA, 68; Univ Calif, Irvine, MA, 69, PhD, 73. **CAREER** Asst prof, 72-80, ASSOC PROF AM HIST, LIVINGSTON COL, RUTGERS UNIV, 80-. **RESEARCH** American intellectual history; women's history. **SELECTED PUBLICATIONS** Auth, Apostles of Culture: The Public Librarian and American Society, 1876-1920, Macmillan, 79; Mary Heaton Vorse, Temple Univ Press, 89. **CONTACT ADDRESS** Dept of Hist, Rutgers Univ, P O Box 5059, New Brunswick, NJ, 08903-5059.

GARRISON, MARK
DISCIPLINE ART AND ARCHAEOLOGY OF ANCIENT WESTERN ASIA **EDUCATION** Univ OK, BA; Univ Ottawa, MA; Univ MI, PhD. **CAREER** Field dir, Tunisia, 90-92; Bilkent Uni excavations at Hacimusalar, Turkey, 95-; assoc prof, 89-. **RESEARCH** Archaeol of Roman North Africa. **SELECTED PUBLICATIONS** Co-auth, Seal Impressions on the Persepolis Fortification Tablets. Fascicule I: Images of Heroic Encounter; Persepolis Seal Studies. An Introduction with Provisional Concordances of Seal Numbers and Associated Documents on Fortification Tablets 1-2087. **CONTACT ADDRESS** Dept of Class, Trinity Univ, 715 Stadium Dr, San Antonio, TX, 78212.

GARRISON, ROMAN
PERSONAL Born 05/09/1953, Cincinnati, OH, m, 1976, 2 children **DISCIPLINE** EARLY CHRISTIANITY **EDUCATION** Westminster Col, BA, 75; Pittsburgh Theological Seminary, MA, 77; Oxford Univ, MliH, 79; Univ of Toronto, PhD, 89. **CAREER** Instr, asst prof, minister. **MEMBERSHIPS** SBL. **RESEARCH** Early Christianity. **SELECTED PUBLICATIONS** Auth, Redemptive Almsgiving in Early Christianity, Sheffield Acad Press; auth, The Graeco-Roman Context of Early Christian Literature, Sheffield Acad Press. **CONTACT ADDRESS** 225 Beechwood Rd., New Wilmington, PA, 16142.

GARROUTTE, EVA
PERSONAL Born 12/29/1962, Johnson City, NY, s **DISCIPLINE** SOCIOLOGY **EDUCATION** Princeton Univ, PhD, 93 **CAREER** Asst Prof, 92-98, Univ of Tulsa; Prof, 98-pres, Boston Col **HONORS AND AWARDS** Ford Found Fel **MEMBERSHIPS** Am Soc Assoc; Am Acad of relig **RESEARCH** Cultural Analysis; Sociology of Religion; Sociology of Science; Race & Ethnicity **SELECTED PUBLICATIONS** Auth, "When Scientists Saw Ghosts and Why They Stopped," Vocabularies of Public Life, 92; Auth, "American Indian Education and the Ideology of Western Science," Proceedings, 92 **CONTACT ADDRESS** Dept of Sociol, Boston Col, Chestnut Hill, MA, 02478. **EMAIL** eva.garroutte@bc.edu

GARTHOFF, RAYMOND L.
PERSONAL Born 03/26/1929, Cairo, Egypt, m, 1950, 1 child **DISCIPLINE** INTERNATIONAL RELATIONS **EDUCATION** Princeton Univ, AB, 48; Yale Univ, MA, 49, PhD, 51. **CAREER** Res mem Soviet affairs, Rand Corp, 50-57; adv, Off Nat Estimates, Cent Intelligence Agency, 57-61; spec asst Soviet bloc polit-mil affairs, US Dept State, 61-68, counsel polit-mil affairs, US Mission to NATO, 68-70, dep dir, Bur Polit-Mil Affairs, 70-73, mem sr sem, 73-74, sr for serv inspector, 74-77; US ambassador to Bulgaria, 77-79; SR FEL, BROOKINGS INST, 80-, Prof lectr, Inst Sino-Soviet Studies, George Washington Univ, 62-64; lectr, Johns Hopkins Univ Sch Advan Int Studies, DC, 64-67. **HONORS AND AWARDS** Arthur S Flemming Award, 65; Superior Honor Award & Medal, US Dept State, 65, Distinguished Honor Award & Gold Medal, 73. **MEMBERSHIPS** Coun Foreign Rels; Am Asn Advan Slavic Studies; Int Inst Strategic Studies; US Strategic Inst; Am Comt East-West Accord. **RESEARCH** Modern Russian history; diplomatic history and international relations; Soviet politics, foreign policy and military affairs. **SELECTED PUBLICATIONS** Auth, The Carter Years--Toward a New Global Order, Am Hist Rev, Vol 0098, 93; The Sputnik Challenge, Am Hist Rev, Vol 0099, 94; Engaging the Enemy--Organization Theory and Soviet Military Innovation, 55-91, Russ Rev, Vol 0053, 94; A Multipolar Peace--Great-Power Politics in the 21st-Century, Slavic Rev, Vol 0054, 95; Leadership-Style and Soviet-Foreign-Policy--Stalin, Khrushchev, Brezhnev, Gorbachev, Russ Rev, Vol 0054, 95; The Cuban Missile Crisis, Am Hist Rev, Vol 0102, 97; Some Observations on Using Soviet Archives, Diplomatic Hist, Vol 0021, 97. **CONTACT ADDRESS** 2128 Bancroft Pl NW, Washington, DC, 20008.

GARTHWAITE, GENE RALPH
PERSONAL Born 07/15/1933, Mt. Hope, WI, m, 3 children **DISCIPLINE** HISTORY OF IRAN & NEAR EAST **EDUCATION** St Olaf Col, BA, 55; Univ Calif, Los Angeles, PhD(hist), 69. **CAREER** Asst prof, 68-75, fac fel, 70-71, assoc prof hist, 75-83, prof hist, Dartmouth Col, 83-, Soc Sci Res Coun grant, 70-71; Am Philos Soc grants, 71-73; Am Coun Learned Soc grant, 78; Nat Endowment Humanities transl grant, 79-80; Jane & Raphael Berstein prof, 98-. **HONORS AND AWARDS** NEH Grant, 79-80, 89, 90, & 92. **MEMBERSHIPS** Am Oriental Soc; Soc Iranian Studies; MidE Studies Asn; Am Inst Iranian Studies. **RESEARCH** Eighteenth, nineteenth and twentieth century history of Iran; social history of Iran. **SELECTED PUBLICATIONS** Auth, Khan, Encyl of the Modern Islamic World, Oxford Univ Press, 95; Mirza Malkum Khan, Encycl of the Modern Islamic World, Oxford Univ Press, 95; Iran: Annotated Biliographic Guide, Guide to His Lit, Oxford Univ Press, 95; Reimagined Internal Frontiers: Tribes and Nationalism-Bakhtiyari and Kurds, Russia's Muslim Frontiers: New Directions in Cross-Cultural Analysis, Indiana Univ Press, 93; Popular Islamic Perceptions of Paradise Gained, Images of Paradise in Islamic Art, Univ of Texas Press, 91; Tribes, Encycl of Asian Hist IV, 88; Qajar Dynasty, Encycl of Asisian Hist III, 88. **CONTACT ADDRESS** Dept of History, Dartmouth Col, 6107 Reed Hall, Hanover, NH, 03755-3506. **EMAIL** gene.r.garthwaite@dartmouth.edu

GARTNER, LLOYD PHILIP
PERSONAL Born 06/03/1927, New York, NY, m, 1961, 2 children **DISCIPLINE** HISTORY **EDUCATION** Brooklyn Col, BA, 48; Univ Pa, MA, 49; Columbia Univ, PhD, 57. **CAREER** Lectr Hebrew and contemporary civilization, Queens Col, NY, 53-57; asst prof Semitic langs, Wayne State Univ, 57-58; from instr to asst prof hist, Jewish Theol Sem, 58-67; assoc prof, City Col New York, 67-73; PROF MOD JEWISH HIST, TEL-AVIV UNIV, 73-, Res fel, Doc Hist Jews in US proj, 54-55; res assoc, Am Jewish Hist Ctr, Jewish Theol Sem, 58-73; ed, Am Div, Encycl Judaica, 67-71; vis prof, Hebrew Univ Jerusalem, 70-72 and Jewish Theol Sem, 76-77; vis lectr hist, Yale Univ, 76-77; sr adv, Open Univ of Israel, 77-79. **MEMBERSHIPS** Am Jewish Hist Soc; fel Am Acad Jewish Res; Hist Soc Israel; Asn Jewish Studies; Asn Am Studies (pres, 77-80). **RESEARCH** Jewish economic, social and intellectual history; history of modern migrations. **SELECTED PUBLICATIONS** Auth, A Recent Look at Anglo-Jewish History--a Review-Essay, Am Jewish Hist, Vol 0080, 91; The Jewish People in America, Vol 1, A Time for Planting--the 1st Migration, 1654-1820, J Am Hist, Vol 0080, 94; The Jewish People in America, Vol 2, A Time for Gathering--the 2nd Migration, 1820-1880, J Am Hist, Vol 0080, 94; The Jewish People in America, Vol 3, A Time for Building--the 3rd Migration, 1880-1920, J Am Hist, Vol 0080, 94; The Jewish People in America, Vol 4, A Time for Searching--Entering the Mainstream, 1920-1945, J Am Hist, Vol 0080, 94; The Jewish People in America, Vol 5, A Time for Healing--American Jewry Since World-War-2, J Am Hist, Vol 0080, 94. **CONTACT ADDRESS** Dept of Jewish Hist Tel-Aviv, Univ Ramat-Aviv, Tel Aviv, ., Il-69978.

GARTON, CHARLES
PERSONAL Born 08/13/1926, Yorkshire, England, m, 1960, 2 children **DISCIPLINE** CLASSICS **EDUCATION** Cambridge Univ, BA, 49, MA, 53. **CAREER** Asst lectr classics, Univ Hull, 51-53; lectr, Univ Newcastle upon Tyne, 53-65; assoc prof, 65-72, actg chmn dept, 73-74, PROF CLASSICS, STATE UNIV NY BUFFALO, 72-, Ed, Arethusa, 68-71, assoc ed, 74-. **MEMBERSHIPS** Class Asn England & Wales. **RESEARCH** Classical and comparative literature; theatre; educational history. **SELECTED PUBLICATIONS** Auth, Fe-Fi-Fo-Fum, in Etymology from 'Jack and the Beanstalk' Fairy-Tale, ANQ-A Quart J Short Articles Notes and Rev, Vol 0006, 93; Magnis-Concede Revisited, in Lucretius, 'De Rerum Natura' 3, 961-2, Class World, Vol 0086, 93; Slipping the Surly Bonds, in the Concept of Soaring Upwards to Make Contact With God, ANQ-A Quart J Short Articles Notes and Rev, Vol 0007, 94. **CONTACT ADDRESS** Dept of Classics, State Univ New York, Buffalo, NY, 14260.

GARVIN, JAMES L.
PERSONAL Born 02/24/1943, Melrose, MA, m, 1969 DISCIPLINE ARCHITECTURAL HISTORY EDUCATION Wentworth Inst, MA 63; Univ New Hampshire, BA 67; Univ Delaware, MA 69; Boston Univ, PhD 83. CAREER Strawbery Banke Museum NH, cur 63-74; Portsmouth Athenaeum NH, curator 71-74; New Hamp Hist Soc, cur 76-87; NH State Hist Preservation Off, State Archit Hist, 87-. HONORS AND AWARDS Winterthur Fel; Spec Univ Fel BU; NewComen Soc NA Hon Mem; Dist Alum Awd WIT; Pres Cit AIA; Dunfey Awd Excel Hum. MEMBERSHIPS SAH; APT; SIA; SPNEA; NSNA; Committee for New Eng Bibliography. RESEARCH Amererican architecture and other material culture; History of tools and technologies; New England history. SELECTED PUBLICATIONS Auth, Early White Mountain Tavern, The Grand Resort Hotels and Tourism in the White Mountains, Hist New Hampshire, 95; auth, Small Scale Brickmaking in New Hampshire, The Jour of the Soc Indust Archaeology, 94; auth, Portsmouth and Piscataqua: Social History and Material Culture, Hist New Hampshire, 71; auth, St. John's Church in Portsmouth: An Architectural Study, Hist New Hampshire, 73; auth, Historic Portsmouth: Early Photographs from the Collection of Strawbery Banke, Somersworth NH, NH Pub Co 74, 2nd ed, with rev by Susan Grigg NH, Peter E Randall for Strawbery Banke Museum, 95; auth, Ebenezer Clifford, Architect and Inventor, Old-Time New Eng, 75; Mail-Order House Plans and American Victorian Architecture, Winterthur Portfolio, 81; auth, The Old New Hampshire State House, Hist NH, 91. CONTACT ADDRESS New Hampshire Historic Preservation Office, 470 North Pembroke Rd, Pembroke, NH, 03275.

GASKELL, IVAN
PERSONAL Born 02/26/1955, Somerset, England, m, 1981, 1 child DISCIPLINE HISTORY OF ART EDUCATION Oxford Univ, England, MA; London Univ, England, MA; Cambridge Univ, England, PhD. CAREER Res fel & Acad Curatorial Asst, Warburg Inst, London Univ, 80-83; fel of Wolfson Col, Cambridge Univ, 83-91; Margaret S. Winthrop Cur, Fogg Art Museum, Harvard Univ Art Museums, 91- . HONORS AND AWARDS Vis scholar, Clark Art Inst, Williamstown, 98. MEMBERSHIPS Col Art Asn. RESEARCH 17th century Dutch art; 17th century European sculpture; 20th century photographic & time-based art; Philos of art; Museology. SELECTED PUBLICATIONS Auth, The Thyssen-Bornemisza Collection: Dutch and Flemish Painting, 90; coed, The Language of Art History, 91; Landscape, Natural Beauty and the Arts, 93; Explanation and Value in the Arts, 98; Vermeer Studies, 98; Nietzsche, Philosophy and the Arts, 98. CONTACT ADDRESS Fogg Art Museum, Harvard Univ, 32 Quincy St., Cambridge, MA, 02138. EMAIL gaskell@fas.harvard.edu

GASKIN, LEROY
PERSONAL Born 06/05/1924, Norfolk, VA, m, 1953 DISCIPLINE ART HISTORY EDUCATION Hampton Inst Hampton VA, BS magna cum laude 1950; Columbia Univ NY, MA 1955, tchrs clge prof diploma 1961; PA State Univ Univ Park PA, Doctor Educ 1972. CAREER Prince George's Cty Pub Schl MD, art instr 1950-67, supr tchr for students of area clges & univ 1954-74; Letcher's Art Ctr Wash DC, comm art instr 1956-59; Prince George's Cty Pub Schl, helping tchr of sec art 1967-70, supr of art K-12 1976-98; lecturer and practicing artist, 1950-. HONORS AND AWARDS Museum & Art Tchr Research Prog Natl Gallery of Art & GW Univ 1966; Art Educ Citation Eastern Arts Assc Kutztown PA 1962; Citation Outstanding Contribution Art Educ Smith-Mason Gallery of Art Wash DC 1971; Community Art Award Assc Preservation & Presentation of Art Inc Wash DC 1977; Natl Art Educ Assc Outstanding Contribution to Art Educ Award State MD Atlanta GA 1980; Natl Art Educ Assc Div of Supr & Admin Outstanding Art Educ Award Eastern Region, Dallas, TX, 1985; Prince George's County Arts Council's Artist Grant, 1992; Outstanding Services in the field of Art Education, Maryland Art Education Assn, 1998. MEMBERSHIPS Spec consult educ Natl Collection of Fine Arts Smithsonian Inst Wash DC 1970-71; eval for summer inst in Art History for hs art tchrs Univ of MD Clge Park MD 1973; eval for Museum & Community Conf for MD Art Educ Assc Baltimore Museum MD 1970; vice pres The Assc for the Preservation and Presentation of the Arts Inc Wash DC 1968-70; pres of DC Art Assc Wash DC 1976-78; pres of MD Art Educ Assc North Englewood MD 1982-84; deacon, Vermont Ave Baptist Church 1959-97.

GASMAN, DANIEL E.
PERSONAL Born 11/18/1933, New York, NY DISCIPLINE MODERN EUROPEAN & INTELLECTUAL HISTORY EDUCATION Brooklyn Col, BA, 55; Univ Chicago, PhD, 69. CAREER Instr hist, State Univ NY, Stony Brook, 60-66; from instr to asst prof, Yeshiva Univ, 66-70; asst prof, 70-72, assoc prof, 72-80; prof hist, John Jay Col & Grad Ctr, City Univ NY, 80-; Directeur D'etudes Ehess, Paris, 6/87; Res grant, City Univ NY, 72-73. MEMBERSHIPS HSS. RESEARCH Ger and Europ intellectual hist. SELECTED PUBLICATIONS Auth, The Scientific Origins of National Socialism, Macdonald, London, 71; Introd to Alfred Fried, Handbuch der Friedensbewegung, Garland, 72; Habeckel's Monism and the Birth of Fascist Ideology, Peter Lang, 98. CONTACT ADDRESS Dept of Hist, John Jay Col of Criminal Justice, CUNY, 445 W 59th St, New York, NY, 10019-1104. EMAIL dgasman@faculty.jjay.cuny.edu

GASSTER, MICHAEL
PERSONAL Born 07/12/1930, New York, NY DISCIPLINE MODERN HISTORY EDUCATION City Col New York, BS, 51; Columbia Univ, MA, 53; Univ Wash, PhD, 62. CAREER Instr hist, Princeton Univ, 61-63; from asst prof to assoc prof, George Washington Univ, 63-66; assoc prof mod Chinese hist and chmn mod Chinese hist proj, Univ Wash, 66-70; ASSOC PROF HIST, LIVINGSTON COL, RUTGERS UNIV, NEW BRUNSWICK, 70-, Inter-Univ fel field training in Chinese, 57-58; Ford Found foreign area training fel, 58-61; mem joint comt contemporary China and comt exchange with Asian Insts, Soc Sci Res Coun-Am Coun Learned Soc, 69-70. HONORS AND AWARDS Einstein Prize Am Diplomacy, Columbia Univ, 53. MEMBERSHIPS Asn Asian Studies; AHA; Soc Ch'ing Studies. RESEARCH Twentieth century Chinese thought and politics; comparative study of revolutions and modernization. SELECTED PUBLICATIONS Auth, The Cambridge History of China, Vol 15, The-Peoples-Republic, Pt 2--Revolutions within the Chinese-Revolution, 1966-1982, Historian, Vol 0055, 93; Popular Protest and Political-Culture in Modern China--Learning from 1989, Am Hist Rev, Vol 0098, 93. CONTACT ADDRESS Dept of Hist, Rutgers Univ, PO Box 5059, New Brunswick, NJ, 08903-5059.

GASTON, PAUL M.
PERSONAL Born 01/31/1928, Fairhope, AK, m, 1952, 3 children DISCIPLINE AMERICAN HISTORY EDUCATION Swathmore Col, BA, 52; Univ NC, MA, 55, PhD, 61. CAREER From instr to assoc prof, 57-71, prof Hist, 71-97, prof emer, Univ VA, 97; Am Coun Learned Soc fel, 61-62, 76-77; vis lectr, Johns Hopkins Univ, 63-64; NEH Summer fel, 83; Rockefeller Humanities fel, 83; vis prof, Univ Cape Town, 86; pres, Southern Regional Coun, 84-88; South African Human Sciences Res Coun, Overseas Res Scholar, 96. HONORS AND AWARDS Lillian Smith Award, 70; Bethune-Roosevelt Award, 78; Lamar lectr, 81; Outstanding Faculty Award, State Coun of Higher Ed in Va, 94; Paul M. Gaston Internship, Southern Regional Coun-Univ of VA, 97. MEMBERSHIPS Southern Hist Asn; Orgn Am Historians; Southern Regional Coun. RESEARCH History of the South; race relations; comparative South-South Africa; utopian communities. SELECTED PUBLICATIONS Auth, The New South Creed, Knopf, 70; Women of Fair Hope, Georgia, 84; Man and Mission, Black Belt, 93; A Southerner in South Africa, Southern Changes, 86. CONTACT ADDRESS 810 Rugby Rd, Charlottesville, VA, 22903. EMAIL pmg@virginia.edu

GATES, JOHN MORGAN
PERSONAL Born 11/06/1937, San Jose, CA, m, 1961, 2 children DISCIPLINE AMERICAN & MILITARY HISTORY EDUCATION Stanford Univ, AB, 59, MA, 60; Duke Univ, PhD, 67. CAREER Asst prof, 67-72, assoc prof, 72-78, prof hist, Col Wooster, 78- HONORS AND AWARDS Harold L Peterson Award, Eastern Nat Park & Monument Asn, 80. MEMBERSHIPS AHA; Orgn Am Hist; Am Mil Inst. SELECTED PUBLICATIONS Auth, Schoolbooks and Krags: The United States Army in the Philippines, 1898-1902, Greenwood, 73; The alleged isolation of US Army officers in the late 19th Century, Parameters, Vol X, 80; The U.S. Army and Irregular Warfare, 98. CONTACT ADDRESS Dept of Hist, Col of Wooster, 1189 Beall Ave, Wooster, OH, 44691-2363. EMAIL jgates@acs.wooster.edu

GATEWOOD, ALGIE C.
PERSONAL Born 12/17/1951, Wadesboro, NC, m, 1973 DISCIPLINE EDUCATION EDUCATION Livingstone Coll, BA Social Science/History 1970-74; Appalachian State Univ, MA Higher Educ/Coll Admin 1976-77; UNC-Charlotte, Certificate in Guidance & Counseling 1982; North Carolina State University, EdD; 1988-94; Winthrop Univ, School Administration Licensing. CAREER Anson Comm Coll, dir of human resources devel, 1974-81; dir of inst research, 1980-81, acting dean of students, 1981-82, dean of students, 1982-97; UNIV OF NC, GEN ADMIN, 1997-. HONORS AND AWARDS Bd mem emeritus, Anson Regional Medical Services, 1997; bd mem of the year, Anson Regional Medical Services, 1996; nominated John B. Grenzebach Award, CASE, 1996; Martin Luther King Jr. Education Award from Association of Univ. Women of Anson. Honored by establishment of the Dr. A.C. Gatewood Scholarship, Alpha Pi Chi Sorority & Women Action Club. MEMBERSHIPS Phi Beta Sigma Fraternity; trustee Ebenezer Baptist Church; 1980-; NC Foundation for Advanced Health Programs, vp; Anson Regional Medical Services, bd mem emeritus; past mem, Anson County Bd of Education; NC Contract Prgms for Denistry, Medicine, and Optometry, comm mem; NC Allied Health Council; NC Trustees Assn, past mem SELECTED PUBLICATIONS "A Model for Assessing the Fund-Raising Effectiveness of Comm Coll Non-profit Foundations in NC"; "A Comparative Analysis & Evaluation of Comm Coll non-profit Foundations in NC," "The Student Recruitment and Retention Manual. CONTACT ADDRESS General Administration, Univ of No Carolina, UNC Research Triangle Park Bldg, Research Triangle Park, NC, 27709.

GATEWOOD, WILLARD BADGETTE
PERSONAL Born 02/23/1931, Pelham, NC, m, 1958, 2 children DISCIPLINE RECENT UNITED STATES HISTORY

EDUCATION Duke Univ, AB, 53, MA, PhD(hist), 57. CAREER Asst prof hist, ETenn State Univ, 57-58 and ECarolina Univ, 58-60; assoc prof, NC Wesleyan Col, 60-64 and Univ Ga, 64-70; ALUMNI DISTINGUISHED PROF HIST, UNIV ARK, FAYETTEVILLE, 70-, Am Acad Arts and Sci grant, 61-62; Am Philos Soc grant, 62-63; Michael res award, Univ Ga, 67. MEMBERSHIPS AHA; Asn Studies Afro-Am Life & Hist, Orgn Am Hist; Southern Hist Asn. RESEARCH Theodore Roosevelt; the 1920's, United States. SELECTED PUBLICATIONS Auth, The Presidency of Roosevelt,Theodore, Rev in Am Hist, Vol 0020, 92; The Promise of the New South--Life After Reconstruction, Ark Hist Quart, Vol 0052, 93; Free Men in an Age of Servitude, 3 Generations of a Black-Family, Miss Quart, Vol 0047, 94; Logan, Rayford,W. and the Dilemma of the African-American Intellectual, J Am Hist, Vol 0081, 94; The Fruits of Integration--Black Middle-Class Ideology and Culture, 1960-1990, Am Hist Rev, Vol 0100, 95; Gods Own Scientists--Creationists in a Secular World, Isis, Vol 0086, 95; Grimke,Archibald--Portrait of a Black Independent, African Am Rev, Vol 0029, 95; The Evolution Controversy in America, Isis, Vol 0086, 95; Cothran,Tilman,C.--2nd-Generation Sociologist, Ark Hist Quart, Vol 0055, 96; Shadow and Light--an Autobiography, African Am Rev, Vol 0031, 97. CONTACT ADDRESS Dept of Hist, Univ of Ark, Fayetteville, AR, 72701-1202.

GAUNT, KYRA D.
DISCIPLINE MUSIC EDUCATION Univ NY, MM; Univ Mich, PhD. CAREER Dept Music, Va Univ RESEARCH Hip-hop; black girls' musical play; hermeneutics of performance and ethnography; sexuality and the body in African American musicking; musical socialization and play; new world performance and African diasporan consciousness; classical music and African Americans. SELECTED PUBLICATIONS Auth, The Musical Games African-American Girls Play: Understanding Gender and the Black Vernacular in Popular Culture, Univ Pittsburgh, 97; African-American Women Between Hopscotch and Hip-Hop, Sage, 95; The Veneration of James Brown & George Clinton in Hip-Hop Music: Is It Live or it Re-Memory?, 95. CONTACT ADDRESS Dept of Music, Virginia Univ, Charlottesville, VA, 22903. EMAIL kg6j@virginia.edu

GAUNT, PHILIP
DISCIPLINE INTERNATIONAL MARKETING, PUBLIC RELATIONS, MEDIA CONSULTING EDUCATION Ind Univ, PhD. CAREER Vis prof, assoc dir, W Europ Ctr; prof, dir, Elliott Sch Commun; Interdisciplinary Commun Res Inst. HONORS AND AWARDS Accredited, Public Rel Soc of Am. SELECTED PUBLICATIONS Publ, 9 bk(s) in Linguistics and Mass Communication in both English and French. CONTACT ADDRESS Dept of Commun, Wichita State Univ, 1845 Fairmont, Wichita, KS, 67260-0062. EMAIL gaunt@elliott.es.twsu.edu

GAUSTAD, EDWIN SCOTT
PERSONAL Born 11/14/1923, m, 1946, 3 children DISCIPLINE AMERICAN RELIGIOUS HISTORY EDUCATION Baylor Univ, AB, 47; Brown Univ, AM, 48, PhD, 51. CAREER Instr relig, Brown Univ, 51-52; Am Coun Learned Soc scholar, 52-53; dean and prof relig and philos, Shorter Col, Ga, 53-57; assoc prof humanities, Univ Redlands, 57-65; assoc prof hist, 65-67, PROF HIST, UNIV CALIF, RIVERSIDE, 67-, Am Coun Learned Soc grant-in-aid, 63-64 and 72-73. MEMBERSHIPS Am Soc Church Hist (pres, 78); Am Studies Asn; Am Acad Relig; AHA; Orgn Am Historians. SELECTED PUBLICATIONS Auth, Williams, Roger and Puritan Radicalism in the English Separatist Tradition, Church Hist, Vol 0061, 92; A History of Christianity in the United-States and Canada, Cath Hist Rev, Vol 0079, 93; The Churching of America, 1776-1990--Winners and Losers in Our Religious Economy, J Relig, Vol 0073, 93; Quakers and Baptists in Colonial Massachusetts, J Interdisciplinary Hist, Vol 0024, 93; Jeffersonian Legacies, J Southern Hist, Vol 0060, 94; American Congregations, Vol 1--Portraits of 12 Religious Communities, Church His, Vol 0064, 95; American Congregations, Vol 2--New Perspectives in the Study of Congregations, Church Hist, Vol 0064, 95; Barbarians and Memory, J Church and State, Vol 0037, 95; When in the Course, William and Mary Quart, Vol 0052, 95; The Shaker Experience in America--A History of the United-Society-of-Believers, J Ecclesiastical Hist, Vol 0047, 96; The Separation of Church and State Defended--Selected-Writings of Wood, James, E, J Church and State, Vol 0038, 96; Modern American Religion, Vol 3--Under God, Indivisible, 1941-1960, Cath Hist Rev, Vol 0083, 97; A Time for Planting--the First Migration, 1654-1820, J Am Ethnic Hist, Vol 0016, 97; Reviving the Ancient Faith--the Story of Churches-of-Christ in America, Cath Hist Rev, Vol 0083, 97. CONTACT ADDRESS Dept of Hist, Univ of Calif, Riverside, CA, 92521.

GAUVREAU, J. MICHAEL
DISCIPLINE HISTORY EDUCATION Laurentian Univ, BA; Univ Toronto, MA, PhD. RESEARCH Social, intellectual, and religious Canadian hist; development of the social sciences in English Canada; cultural hist of the evangelical impulse from 1780 to 1870. SELECTED PUBLICATIONS Auth, The Evangelical Century: College and Creed in English

Canada from the Great Revival to the Great Depression, 91. **CONTACT ADDRESS** History Dept, McMaster Univ, 1280 Main St W, Hamilton, ON, L8S 4L9.

GAVINS, RAYMOND
PERSONAL Born 10/24/1942, Atlanta, GA, m, 1964, 2 children **DISCIPLINE** AMERICAN AND AFRO-AMERICAN HISTORY **EDUCATION** Va Union Univ, AB, 64; Univ Va, MA, 67, PhD(hist), 70. **CAREER** Asst prof, 70-76, ASSOC PROF HIST, DUKE UNIV, 76-, Instr hist and govt, Henrico County Pub Schs, Va, 65-66; minorities studies consult, Durham, NC pub schs, 71; Younger Humanist fel, Nat Endowment Humanities, 74-75. **MEMBERSHIPS** Southern Hist Asn; Orgn Am Hist; Asn Studies Afro-Am Life & Hist. **RESEARCH** Southern Black leadership, 1915-1954; 20th century Southern race relations; Southern Black intellectual history. **SELECTED PUBLICATIONS** Auth, Black, White and Southern--Race-Relations and Southern Culture, 1940 to the Present, Miss Quart, Vol 0045, 92; Woodson, Carter, G.--A Life in Black-History, Va Mag of Hist and Biogr, Vol 0102, 94; Grimke, Archibald--Portrait of a Black Independent, J Southern Hist, Vol 0061, 95. **CONTACT ADDRESS** Dept of Hist, Duke Univ, Durham, NC, 27706.

GAWALT, GERARD WILFRED
PERSONAL Born 02/10/1943, Boston, MA, m, 1966, 3 children **DISCIPLINE** HISTORY **EDUCATION** Northeastern Univ, AB, 65; Clark Univ, MA, 68, PhD(Am hist), 69. **CAREER** HIST SPECIALIST AM HIST, LIBR CONG, WASHINGTON, DC, 69-, Adj prof Am Hist, George Mason Univ, 72 and legal hist, Cath Univ Am, 78; Am Coun Learned Soc fel, 80-81. **MEMBERSHIPS** Am Soc Legal Hist; Orgn Am Historians. **RESEARCH** Development of the professions in the nineteenth century; justice in the American Revolutionary Era; Continental Congress. **SELECTED PUBLICATIONS** Auth, Kings Inns and the Kingdom of Ireland--the Irish Inn of Court 1541-1800, Am J Legal Hist, Vol 0037, 93; Strict Truth--the Narrative of Burwell, William, Armistead, Va Mag of Hist and Biogr, Vol 0101, 93; Monroe, James, Presidential Planter, Va Mag of Hist and Biogr, Vol 0101, 93; Law and Liberty in Early New-England, Criminal-Justice and Due-Process, 1620-1692, William and Mary Quart, Vol 0051, 94; Reason Over Precedents--Origins of American Legal Thought, Am J Legal Hist, Vol 0039, 95. **CONTACT ADDRESS** Libr of Cong, Washington, DC, 20540.

GAYLES-FELTON, ANNE RICHARDSON
PERSONAL Born 06/04/1923, Marshallville, Georgia, w **DISCIPLINE** EDUCATION **EDUCATION** Fort Valley State Coll, BS 1943; Columbia Univ, MA 1949, Prof Diploma, 1953; IN Univ, EdD 1961. **CAREER** Stillman Coll, dir student teaching 1952-54; Albany State Coll, 1954-57; FL A&M Univ, dir student teaching 1957-62, head dept of secondary educ 1962-82, prof of secondary educ 1982-; Fort Valley State Coll, instructor, social sciences, 1949-52; Rust Coll Associate Prof of Social Sciences; Arkansas Baptist Coll Head Dept of Sociology 1950-51; Georgia Public Schools, teacher, 10 years. **HONORS AND AWARDS** Florida A&M University, Teacher of the Year, 1989, College of Education, Teacher of the Year, 1991; Fort Valley State College, Alumni Hall of Fame, Inductee, 1984, Division of Social Science, Distinguished Alumni Award; "A Consortium of Doctors: Women of Color in the Struggle," Banquet Honoree, 1991; FAMU Teacher Incentive Award; Assn of Teacher Educators, Distinguished Teacher Educator, 1990; saluted "Living Legend," Florida A & M Univ, 1997. **MEMBERSHIPS** 1st vice pres Assn of Social & Behavioral Serv 1961-62; exec comm Soc of Prof Educ 1969-70; served on committees Amer Assn in Teacher Educ Coll 1970-80; comm on master teacher Assn of Teacher Educators 1982-85; Delta Sigma Theta; Pi Lambda Theta; Phi Delta Kappa; Kappa Delta Pi; Alpha Kappa Mu; Pi Gamma Mu; Natl Republican Party Presidential Task Force; State of Florida Governors Commemorative Celebration Comm on Dr Martin Luther King, Jr; Governor's Bd of Independent Coll & Univ, State of Florida; Governor's Comm on Quality Educ; Urban League; Republican Party of Florida; United States/China Joint Conference on Education, Beijing, China, invited participant, 1992; United States Military Academy Appointments Board, appointed, several times, by Senator Hawkins (Florida); Citizen Ambassador Program, People to People International, invited participant, 1992. **SELECTED PUBLICATIONS** Author: two books; three monograph; co-author of one book and two monographs; 63 articles; 5 research studies; 5 bibliographies; dissertation; editor, writer, reader for first book devoted soley to Multicultural Education; Delivered paper at the 43rd World Assembly of the Intl Council on Education for Teaching in Amman Jordan; chmn of the Lamson Richardson Scholarship Foundation, founded in 1886. **CONTACT ADDRESS** Professor of Secondary Education, Florida A&M Univ, Tallahassee, FL, 32307.

GAZELL, JAMES A.
PERSONAL Born 03/17/1942, Chicago, IL, m, 1970 **DISCIPLINE** GOVERNMENT **EDUCATION** Roosevelt Univ, BA, 63, MA, 66; Southern Ill Univ at Carbondale, PhD, 68. **CAREER** Asst Prof, 68-72, assoc prof, 72-75, prof, School of Public Admin & Urban Studies, San Diego State Univ, 75-. **HONORS AND AWARDS** Meritorious performance & professional promise award, San Diego State Univ, 88 & 89. **MEMBERSHIPS** Am Soc for Public Admin; Nat Center State Courts. **RESEARCH** Organization theory; judicial administration; research methods. **SELECTED PUBLICATIONS** Auth of five books and 57 articles in professional journals. **CONTACT ADDRESS** School of Public Admin and Urban Studies, San Diego State Univ, San Diego, CA, 92115-4505. **EMAIL** jgazell@mail.sdsu.edu

GEAGAN, DANIEL J.
DISCIPLINE HISTORY **EDUCATION** Boston Univ, BA; Johns Hopkins Univ, PhD. **RESEARCH** Ancient history. **SELECTED PUBLICATIONS** Auth, Roman Athens: Some Aspects of Life and Culture I. 86 B.C. - A.D. 267, 79; auth, Imperial Visits to Athens: the Epigraphical Evidence, 82. **CONTACT ADDRESS** History Dept, McMaster Univ, 1280 Main St W, Hamilton, ON, L8S 4L9.

GEALT, ADELHEID MEDICUS
PERSONAL Born 05/29/1946, Munich, Germany, m, 1969 **DISCIPLINE** HISTORY OF ART **EDUCATION** Ohio State Univ, BA, 68; Indiana Univ, MA, 73; Indiana Univ, PhD, 79 **CAREER** Registrar, Indiana Univ Art Museum, 72-76; adjunct assoc prof, Indiana Univ, 85-89; assoc scholar, Indiana Univ, 86; assoc prof, Henry Radford Hope School Fine Arts, 89-; curator Western Art, Indiana Univ Art Museum, 76-87; Interim/Acting Dir, Indiana Univ Art Museum, 87-89; Dir, Indiana Univ Art Museum, 89- **HONORS AND AWARDS** Ntl Endowment Humanities, 85; Amer Philos Soc Grant, 85; Ntl Endowment Arts, 83; Indiana Univ Res Development Grant, 86,89; Ntl Endowment Art Planning Grant, 82 **MEMBERSHIPS** Commissioner, Indiana Arts Comm, 97; Ntl Endowment Art, Museum Panelist, 91; Assoc Art Museum Directors, 90-; Brauer Museum Art, Valparaiso Univ; Institution Museum Libr Services, 96-98 **RESEARCH** European Art of 17th and 18th Century **SELECTED PUBLICATIONS** Auth, "Disegni di Giuseppe Bernardino Bison nelle collezione nordamericane," Giuseppe Bernardino Bison, pittore e disgegnatore, Cvici Musei, 97; coauth, Domenico Tiepolo: Master Draftsman, IU Press, 96; coauth, Giandomenico Tiepolo, Disegni dal mondo, Electra, 96 **CONTACT ADDRESS** Art Mus, Indiana Univ, Bloomington, East 7th St., Bloomington, IN, 47405.

GEARY, EDWARD ACORD
PERSONAL Born 12/10/1937, Price, UT, m, 1961, 6 children **DISCIPLINE** ENGLISH & AMERICAN LITERATURE & WESTERN REGIONAL STUDIES **EDUCATION** Brigham Young Univ, BA, 60, MA, 63; Stanford Univ, PhD, 71. **CAREER** Instr humanities, Col Eastern Utah, 63-64; asst prof, 68-75, assoc prof, 75-81, PROF ENGLISH, BRIGHAM YOUNG UNIV, 81-, DIR, CHARLES REDD CTR FOR WESTERN STUDIES, 97-. **HONORS AND AWARDS** Rosenblatt Award, UT State Hist Soc, 85; Cert of Commendation, Am Asn for State and Local Hist, 94; Humanities Prize, Utah Academy of Sciences, Arts, and Letters, 94; P.A. Christensen Lectureship, 95. **MEMBERSHIPS** MLA. **RESEARCH** Western Am literature and hist, natural hist. **SELECTED PUBLICATIONS** Auth, An Ashy Halo: Woman as Symbol in Heart of Darkness, Studies Short Fiction, 76; The Need Beyond Reason and Other Essays, Brigham Young Univ, 76; Woman regionalists of Mormon country, Kate Chopin Newsletter, 76; Mormondom's lost generation: the novelists of the 1940s, Brigham Young Univ Studies, 77; The Europeans: a Centennial Essay, Henry James Rev, 82; Community Dramatics in Early Castle Valley, UT Hist Quart, 85; Women Regionalists of Mormon country, Regionalism and the Female Imagination, Hum Sci Press, 85; Goodbye to Poplarhaven, Univ UT, 85; T S Eliot and the fin de siecle, Rocky Mt Rev, 86; Undecidability in Joyce's The Sisters, Studies Short Fiction, 89; A visitable past: Virginia Sorensen's Sanpete, UT Hist Quart, 90; The proper edge of the sky: the high plateau country of UT, Univ UT, 92; History of Emery County, UT State Hist Soc, 96. **CONTACT ADDRESS** Charles Redd Ctr for Western Studies, Brigham Young Univ, Provo, UT, 84602. **EMAIL** edward_geary@byu.edu

GEBHARD, DAVID
PERSONAL Born 07/21/1927, Cannon Falls, MN, m, 1954, 2 children **DISCIPLINE** ARCHITECTURAL HISTORY **EDUCATION** Univ Minn, BA, 49, MA, 51, PhD(art hist), 58. **CAREER** Asst prof art hist, Univ NMex, 53-55; dir, Roswell Mus and Art Ctr, NMex, 55-59; Fulbright prof art hist, Istanbul Tech Univ, 59-61; dir, Art Mus and asst prof, 61-64, assoc prof, 64-68, PROF ARCHIT HIST, UNIV CALIF, SANTA BARBARA, 68-, CUR, ARCHIT DRAWING COLLECTION, 80-, Nat Park Serv grant, 58-59; NSF grant, 64-; Ford Found Near East Studies grant, 65-66; vis prof archit, Sch Environ Design, Univ Calif, Berkeley, 70, 72, 74 and 77; mem, Nat Archit Accrediting Bd, 81- **MEMBERSHIPS** Soc Archit Historians (2nd vpres, 76-78, 1st vpres, 78-80, pres, 80-82); hon mem Am Inst Archit. **RESEARCH** Ottoman Turkish vernacular house, 1500-1900; moderne in the United States, 1925-1942; history of drive-in architecture in the United States. **SELECTED PUBLICATIONS** Auth, The California Garden and the Landscape-Architects Who Shaped It, Calif Hist, Vol 0075, 96; California Gardens--Creating a New Eden, Calif Hist, Vol 0075, 96; The Gardens of California--4 Centuries of Design from Mission to Modern, Calif Hist, Vol 0075, 96; Buildings and Builders in Hispanic California, 1769-1850, Calif Hist, Vol 0075, 96. **CONTACT ADDRESS** 895 E Mountain Dr, Santa Barbara, CA, 93108.

GEBHARD, ELIZABETH REPLOGLE
PERSONAL Born 03/25/1935, Oak Park, IL, m, 1957, 2 children **DISCIPLINE** CLASSICAL ARCHEOLOGY **EDUCATION** Wellesley Col, BA, 57; Univ Chicago, MA, 59, PhD(classics), 63. **CAREER** Vis lectr Classics, Roosevelt Univ, 63-67; asst prof, 69-72, chmn dept, 77-79, ASSOC PROF CLASSICS, UNIV ILL, CHICAGO CIRCLE, 72-, Primary investr, Theater at Stobi, Stobi Excavations, 70-75; CUR and DIR, ISTHMIAN RES PROJ, ISTHMIA MUS, GREECE, 76-; chmn archaeological studies comt, Univ Ill, Chicago, 78-80. **MEMBERSHIPS** Archaeol Inst Am; Am Sch Class Studies at Athens; Am Philol Asn; Asn Field Archaeol; Am Sch Oriental Res. **RESEARCH** Field archaeology; architecture and history of Greek and Roman theatre; materials analysis and techniques of production of artifacts. **SELECTED PUBLICATIONS** Auth, Votives in the Archaic Temple of Poseidon at Isthmia, American J Archaeol, Vol 0098, 94; Seek the Welfare of the City--Christians as Benefactors and Citizens, J Relig, Vol 0076, 96. **CONTACT ADDRESS** Dept of Classics, Univ of Ill, at Chicago Circle, Chicago, IL, 60680.

GEDALECIA, DAVID
DISCIPLINE HISTORY **EDUCATION** Queens Col, AB, 65; Harvard Univ, MA, 67, PhD, 71. **CAREER** Prof. **RESEARCH** Chinese intellectuals in the Mongol Era. **SELECTED PUBLICATIONS** Auth, China Under the Mongols, Princeton UP, 81; Yuan Thought: Chinese Thought and Religion Under the Mongols, Columbia UP, 82; In the Service of the Khan, Wiesbaden, 95; pub, Jour Amer Oriental Soc. **CONTACT ADDRESS** Dept of Hist, Col of Wooster, Wooster, OH, 44691.

GEEHR, RICHARD STOCKWELL
PERSONAL Born 05/06/1938, New Brunswick, NJ, m, 1961 **DISCIPLINE** AUSTRIAN SOCIAL & INTELLECTUAL HISTORY **EDUCATION** Middlebury Col, BA, 60; Columbia Univ, MA, 65; Univ Mass, Amherst, PhD, 73. **CAREER** Instr Ger & hist, Windham Col, 66-67; instr Western civilization, Keene State Col, 67; instr hist, Mark Hopkins Col, 67-68; instr Ger Greenfield Community Col, 67-68; teaching asst, Univ Mass, Amherst, 68-73; instr hist, Lake Mich Col, 73-74 & St Mary's Col, Md, 75-76; asst prof hist, Bentley Col, 77-. **HONORS AND AWARDS** Nat Endowment Humanities Younger Humanist res award, 74; Fulbright res grants, 69, 74, 76, 85, 86; Marion & Jasper Whiting Found grant, 80; Charles P McNear Jr Found grant, 82. **MEMBERSHIPS** AHA; Die Int Robert-Musil Gesellschaft; Historians Film Comt. **RESEARCH** Modern Austrian cultural and intellectual history; film and history. **SELECTED PUBLICATIONS** Auth, Adam Muller-Guttenbrunn and the Aryan Theater of Vienna: 1898-1903, The Approach of Cultural Fascism, Verlag Alfred Kummerle Goppingen, 73; auth, The Aryan theater of Vienna: The Career of Adam Muller-Guttenbrunn, Wiener Libr Bull, UK, 75; ed, Soviet History and Film, Ginn & Co, 80; I Decide Who is a Jew!, The Papers of Dr Karl Lueger, Univ Press Am, 82; auth, Karl Lueger: Mayor of Fin de Siecle Vienna, Wayne State, 90; auth, Letters from the Doomed, University Press of America, 91. **CONTACT ADDRESS** Dept of History, Bentley Col, Beaver & Foster Sts, Waltham, MA, 02155.

GEERKEN, JOHN HENRY
PERSONAL Born 10/11/1938, Colon, Panama, m, 1960, 4 children **DISCIPLINE** EUROPEAN HISTORY **EDUCATION** George Washington Univ, BA, 60; Yale Univ, MA, 61, PhD(hist), 67. **CAREER** From actg instr to instr hist, Yale Univ, 65-68; asst prof, 68-74, assoc prof, 74-82, PROF HIST, SCRIPPS COL, 82-, Consult and res assoc, Machiavelli Proj, Ctr Medieval and Renaissance Studies, Univ Calif, Los Angeles, 75-. **MEMBERSHIPS** AHA; Renaissance Soc Am; Am Soc Legal Hist; Soc Ital Hist Studies. **RESEARCH** History and philosophy of law; Italian Renaissance. **SELECTED PUBLICATIONS** Auth, Guicciardini, Francesco, Jurist--Honorarial Records, Am Hist Rev, Vol 0098, 93. **CONTACT ADDRESS** 1030 Columbia Ave, Claremont, CA, 91711-3948.

GEERTZ, CLIFFORD
PERSONAL Born 08/23/1926, San Francisco, CA, m, 1987, 2 children **DISCIPLINE** ANTHROPOLOGY **EDUCATION** Antioch Col, AB 50; Harvard Univ, PhD 56. **CAREER** Univ Chicago, asst prof to prof, anthrop 60-70; Oxford Univ, Eastman prof 78-79; Princeton Univ, prof of soc sci 70-; Harold F Linder, Prof Soc Sci, Inst for Adv Stud 82. **HONORS AND AWARDS** Hon Doctorates from Harvard, Northern, Chicago, Brandeis, Yale, Princeton, Cambridge, Georgetown Universities and from the following Colleges, Bates, Knox, Swarthmore, Williams, and New Sch for Soc Res; Soc Sci Prize, Amer Acad Arts Sci; NBCC Prize; Fukuoka Asian Cultural Prize. **MEMBERSHIPS** Fell, AAAS, APS, NAS; Corresponding Fell, Brit Acad; Hon Fell, Royal Anthro Inst GB and IRE; AAA; Assn for Asian Stud; MESA. **RESEARCH** Econ develop, soc hist, sociology of relig, organization of traditional marketplaces, peasant agriculture. **SELECTED PUBLICATIONS** After the Fact, 95; Works and Lives, 88; Local Knowledge, 83; The Interpretation of Cultures, 73; Islam Observed, 68. **CONTACT ADDRESS** Sch of Soc Sci, Inst for Advanced Studies, Princeton, NJ, 08540. **EMAIL** geertz@ias.edu

GEGGUS, D.
PERSONAL Born 11/19/1949, Romford, England, m, 1994, 1 child DISCIPLINE HISTORY EDUCATION Oxford Univ, BA, 71; London MA, York PhD, 79. CAREER Prof 82-, Univ Florida; res fel 80-82, Southampton Univ; jr res fel, 76-80, Oxford Univ. HONORS AND AWARDS Guggenheim Fel; Woodrow Wilson Fel; NEH Fel. MEMBERSHIPS SNH; ACH. RESEARCH Caribbean History; Slavery. SELECTED PUBLICATIONS Auth, Slavery War and Revolution, Oxford, 82; coauth, A Turbulent Time, Bloomington, 97; auth, French Revolution Research Collection, Whitney, 93. CONTACT ADDRESS Dept History, Univ Fla, Box 117320, Gainesville, FL, 32611. EMAIL dgeggus@history.ufl.edu

GEIB, GEORGE WINTHROP
PERSONAL Born 10/31/1939, Buffalo, NY, m, 1973, 2 children DISCIPLINE AMERICAN HISTORY EDUCATION Purdue Univ, Lafayette, BA, 61; Univ Wis-Madison, MA, 63, PhD, 69. CAREER From instr to asst prof, 65-72, assoc prof, 73-78, PROF HIST, BUTLER UNIV, 79-, Actg Dean, Liberal Arts, 87-89. HONORS AND AWARDS Phi Alpha Theta; Phi Kappa Phi; Best Book Award, Ind Religious Hist Asn, 90; Sagomore of the Wabash, 97. MEMBERSHIPS OAH; SHEAR; Ind Hist Soc; Soc Mil Hist. RESEARCH Early national American history; urban history; military history; midwest regional. SELECTED PUBLICATIONS Auth, The William F Charters South Seas Collection: An Introduction, Irwin Libr, 70, rev ed, 94; coauth, Indiana's Citizen Soldiers, Ind Armory Bd, 80; auth, Indianapolis Hoosier's Circle City, Continental Heritage Press, 81; Lives Touched By Faith, 87; Indianapolis First, 90; contrib ed, Encyclopedia of Indianapolis, 94. CONTACT ADDRESS Dept of Hist, Butler Univ, 4600 Sunset Ave, Indianapolis, IN, 46208-3443.

GEIGER, MARY VIRGINIA
PERSONAL Born 02/02/1915, Irvington, NJ DISCIPLINE PHILOSOPHY, HISTORY EDUCATION Col Notre Dame, Md, AB, 37; Cath Univ Am, MA, 41, PhD(hist, philos), 43. CAREER Instr hist, 38-56, PROF PHILOS, Col Notre Dame, MD, 56-. HONORS AND AWARDS DHL, Col Notre Dame, Md, 76. MEMBERSHIPS Am Cath Philos Asn; Am Hist Asn. SELECTED PUBLICATIONS Auth, Daniel Carroll II, One Man and His Descendants, 1730-1978, 78; Daniel Carroll, Signer of the Constitution, Cath Univ Am, 43; Genealogy of Charles Carroll of Carrollton, 98; articles in: Catholic Encyclopedia, McGraw, 67; Encyclopedia of American Catholic History, Glazier Shelley Book, Liturgical Press, 97. CONTACT ADDRESS Dept of Philosophy, Col of Notre Dame of Maryland, 4701 N Charles St, Baltimore, MD, 21210-2404. EMAIL VGEIGER@NDM.EDU

GEIGER, REED G.
PERSONAL Born 08/14/1932, Cleveland, OH, m, 1962, 2 children DISCIPLINE MODERN EUROPEAN ECONOMIC HISTORY EDUCATION Col Wooster, BA, 54; Univ Minn, MA, 57, PhD(hist), 64. CAREER Instr, 61-64, asst prof, 64-75, ASSOC PROF HIST, UNIV DEL, 75-. MEMBERSHIPS AHA; Econ Hist Asn. RESEARCH Early industrial revolution in Europe; European radicalism, especially in the 19th century. SELECTED PUBLICATIONS Auth, The Role of Transportation in the Industrial-Revolution--A Comparison of England and France, J Interdisciplinary Hist, Vol 0023, 93. CONTACT ADDRESS Dept of Hist, Univ Del, Newark, DE, 19711.

GEISON, GERALD LYNN
PERSONAL Born 03/26/1943, Savanna, IL, 2 children DISCIPLINE HISTORY OF SCIENCE AND MEDICINE EDUCATION Beloit Col, BA, 65; Yale Univ, MA, 67, PhD(hist of sci & med), 70. CAREER Res fel hist med, Univ Minn, 69-70; asst prof, 70-76, assoc dean col, 77-79, ASSOC PROF HIST, PRINCETON UNIV, 76-, DIR, PROG HIST SCI, 80-, Fel, Inst Hist Med, Med Sch, Johns Hopkins Univ, 72-73; Jonathan Dickinson Bicentennial preceptor, Princeton Univ, 74-77; Nat Endowment for Humanities fel, 75-76; NSF grant, 77-81. MEMBERSHIPS Hist Sci Soc; Am Asn Hist Med. RESEARCH Historical relationship between medical theory and medical practice; life and work of Louis Pasteur; history of physiology in the 19th century. SELECTED PUBLICATIONS Auth, Research Schools and New Directions in the Historiography of Science, Osiris, Vol 0008, 93; The Experimental Life Sciences in the 20th-Century, Osiris, Vol 0010, 95; Lords of the Fly--Drosophila Generics and the Experimental Life, Isis, Vol 0087, 96; Pasteur and the Culture Wars, in Response to Perutz, Max--An Exchange, NY Rev of Bks, Vol 0043, 96. CONTACT ADDRESS Dept of Hist, Princeton Univ, Dickinson Hall, Princeton, NJ, 08544.

GEISSLER, SUZANNE BURR
PERSONAL Born 11/12/1950, Somerville, NJ DISCIPLINE AMERICAN AND CHURCH HISTORY EDUCATION Syracuse Univ, BA, 71, PhD(hist), 76; Rutgers Univ, MA, 72; Drew Univ, MTS, 79. CAREER Instr, State Univ NY Col Cortland, 75-77; lectr, Drew Univ, 77-79; LECTR HIST, UPSALA COL, 79-, Vis lectr, Theol Sch, Drew Univ, 81. MEMBERSHIPS Am Soc Church Hist; Am Studies Asn; AHA; Orgn Am Historians. RESEARCH Early American religious history. SELECTED PUBLICATIONS Auth, A Sense of Deity--The Republican Spirituality of Rush, Benjamin, J Am Hist, Vol 0079, 93. CONTACT ADDRESS 4 Midwood Dr, Florham Park, NJ, 07932.

GELB, JOYCE
PERSONAL Born 06/01/1940, New York, NY, m, 1966, 2 children DISCIPLINE POLITICAL SCIENCE EDUCATION City Col NY, Ba, 62; Univ Chicago, MA, 63; NY Univ, PhD, 69. CAREER Vis prof, Yale Univ, polit sci, 97-98; mem, doctoral fac, Dept Polit Sci, CUNY, 80- ; vis prof, Barnard Col, Smith Col, Conn Col, 78-81; prof, Dept Polit Sci, CCNY, 85-. HONORS AND AWARDS Rockefeller vis scholar, 85; Fulbright grant, 88-89; NY Times Found grant, 90-91; vis scholar, Australia Nat Univ, 93; Ford Found grant, 96. MEMBERSHIPS Am Polit Sci Asn. RESEARCH Women and politics; comparative public policy. SELECTED PUBLICATIONS Co-ed, Women of Japan and Korea: Continuity or Change, Temple Univ, 94; auth, Women and Public Policies, rev ed, Univ Va, 96; auth, Women and Reproductive Choice: Politics and Policy in Japan, in Githens, ed, Abortion: Rhetoric and Reality: Public Policy in Cross Cultural Perspective, Routledge, 96; auth, Feminist Politics in a Hostile Environment: Obstaces and Opportunities, in McAdam, ed, Do Movements Matter? Univ Minn, 97; auth, The Equal Opportunity Law in Japan: A Decade of Change for Japanese Women, Yale Asian/Pacific Rev, forthcoming; coauth, Political Women in Japan: A Case Study of the Seikatsusha Movement, Social Sci J of Japan, 98; coauth, Feminist Organizational Success: The State of US Women's Movement Organizations in the 1990s, in Women and Politics, 99. CONTACT ADDRESS Center for Study of Women and Society, Graduate Sch and Univ Ctr, CUNY, 33 W 42nd St, New York, NY, 10036. EMAIL jgelb@email.gc.cuny.edu

GELBER, STEVEN MICHAEL
PERSONAL Born 02/21/1943, New York, NY, m, 1965, 2 children DISCIPLINE AMERICAN SOCIAL & CULTURAL HISTORY EDUCATION Cornell Univ, BS, 65; Univ WI-Madison, MS, 67, PhD, 72. CAREER Prof hist, Univ Santa Clara, 69. MEMBERSHIPS Orgn Am Hist; AHA. RESEARCH Am business thought; cult hist. SELECTED PUBLICATIONS Auth, Business Ideology and Black Employment, Addison-Wesley, 73; Black Men and Businessmen, Kennikat, 74; co-auth, New Deal Art: California, de Saisset Mus, 76; auth, California's new deal murals, Calif Hist, 79; Culture of the work place and the rise of baseball, J Social Hist, 82; Their hands are all out playing: business and amateur baseball, 185-1917, Jour Sports Hist, spring 84; The eye of the beholder: Images of California by Dorothea Lange and Russell Lee, Calif Hist, fall 85; Sequoia seminar: Th origins of religious sectarianism, Calif Hist, spring 90; Co-auth (with Martin Cook), Saving the Earth: The history of a middle-class millenarian movement, Univ Calif Press, 90; A job you can't lose: Work and hobbies in the Great Depression, J Social Hist, summer 91; Free market metaphor: The historical dyanics of stamp collecting, Comparative Studies in Society and Hist, 10/92; Do-it-yourself: Constructing, repairing and maintaining domestic masculinity, Am Quart, 3/97; Hobbies: Productive learning and the culture of work in America, Columbia Univ Press, 99. CONTACT ADDRESS Dept of Hist, Santa Clara Univ, 500 El Camino Real, Santa Clara, CA, 95053-0285. EMAIL sgelber@scu.edu

GELFAND, LAWRENCE E.
PERSONAL Born 06/20/1926, Cleveland, OH, m, 1953, 3 children DISCIPLINE AMERICAN HISTORY EDUCATION Western Reserve Univ, BA, 49, MA, 59; Univ Wash, PhD, 58. CAREER Asst prof hist, Univ Hawaii, 56-58, Univ Wash, 58-59 and Univ Wyo, 59-62; from asst prof to assoc prof, 62-66, PROF HIST, UNIV IOWA, 66-, Rockefeller Found fel, 64-65; vis prof hist, Univ Wash, 74. MEMBERSHIPS AHA; Orgn Am Hist; Soc Historians Am Foreign Rels (pres, 82); Soc Am Archivists; Acad Polit Sci. RESEARCH History of American foreign relations; First World War and the Paris peace conference. SELECTED PUBLICATIONS Auth, Wilsonian Statecraft--Theory and Practice of Liberal Internationalism During World-War-I, Diplomatic Hist, Vol 0018, 94; Trial by Friendship--Anglo-American Relations, 1917-1918, Rev in Am Hist, Vol 0022, 94; British and American Commercial Relations with Soviet Russia, 1918-1924, Rev in Am Hist, Vol 0022, 94; The Presidency of Wilson, Woodrow, Diplomatic Hist, Vol 0018, 94; The Deliberations of the Council of 4 March 24 June 28, 1919--Notes of the Official Interpreter--to the Delivery to the German Delegation of the Preliminaries of Peace, Diplomatic Hist, Vol 0018, 94; Wilson, Woodrow--A Biography, Diplomatic Hist, Vol 0018, 94; Wilson, Woodrow--A Life for World-Peace, Diplomatic Hist, Vol 0018, 94; Hemispheric Regionalism to Global Universalism--The Changing Face of United-States National Interests, Mid-Am- Hist Rev, Vol 0076, 94; America Secret War Against Bolshevism--US Intervention in the Russian Civil-War, 1917-1920, J Am Hist, Vol 0083, 96. CONTACT ADDRESS Dept of Hist, Univ of Iowa, Iowa City, IA, 52242.

GELLOTT, LAURA S.
DISCIPLINE HISTORY EDUCATION Marquette Univ, BA, 74, MA, 76; Univ WI, PhD, 82. CAREER Assoc prof, Univ of WI, Parkside. HONORS AND AWARDS DAAD fel, 85 & 87; UW-Parkside Tchg Excellence Awd, 86. RESEARCH 20th century Austria; Women; Church-state issues. SELECTED PUBLICATIONS Publ in, Austrian Hist Yearbk, J Contemp Hist, Catholic Hist Rev; contrib to, Liberalism and Catholicism. CONTACT ADDRESS Dept of Hist, Univ of Wisconsin, Parkside, 900 Wood Rd, Molinaro 1, PO Box 2000, Kenosha, WI, 53141-2000. EMAIL laura.gellott@uwp.edu

GELLRICH, MICHELLE
DISCIPLINE GREEK LITERATURE AND PHILOSOPHY, LITERARY THEORY, DRAMA EDUCATION Univ Calif, Berkeley, PhD, 82. CAREER Assoc prof, La State Univ. HONORS AND AWARDS Lily Found tchg grant, 84; ACLS fel, 86; LSU summer fac res stipend, 92; Alpha Lambda Delta, 96. RESEARCH Greek literature and philosophy; classical rhetoric. SELECTED PUBLICATIONS Auth, Tragedy and Theory: The Problem of Conflict Since Aristotle, 88; Aristotle's Poetics and the Problem of Tragic Conflict, Ramus, 94; Aristotle's Rhetoric: Theory, Truth, and Metarhetoric, Cabinet of the Muses, 90; Socratic Magic: Enchantment, Irony, and Persuasion in Some Dialogues of Plato, in Class World, 94. CONTACT ADDRESS Dept of Eng, Louisiana State Univ, 223E Allen Hall, Baton Rouge, LA, 70803.

GENOVESE, EDGAR NICHOLAS
PERSONAL Born 09/18/1942, Baltimore, MD, m, 1969, 2 children DISCIPLINE CLASSICS EDUCATION Xavier Univ, Ohio, AB, 64; Ohio State Univ, PhD(classics), 70. CAREER From asst prof to assoc prof, 70-76, Prof Classics, San Diego State Univ, 76-, Chmn Dept Class & Humanities, 77-. HONORS AND AWARDS Phi Beta Kappa; Phi Kappa Phi. MEMBERSHIPS Amer Philol Assoc; Amer Assoc Univ Profs. RESEARCH Greek and Latin poetry; mythology. SELECTED PUBLICATIONS Auth, Propertius' tardus Amor, Class J, 1/73; Cicero and Sallust: Catiline's ruina, Class World, 74; Symbolism in the Passer poems, Maia, 74; Deaths in the Aeneid, Pac Coast Philol, 75; Case of the poor preposition, Class Outlook, 76; Serpent Leitmotif in the Metamorphoses, Latomus, 83; The Burnett Lectures: A Quarter Century, 93; Mythology: Texts and Contexts, 98. CONTACT ADDRESS Dept Class & Humanities, San Diego State Univ, 5500 Campanile Dr, San Diego, CA, 92182-8143. EMAIL genovese@mail.sdsu.edu

GENOVESE, EUGENE D.
PERSONAL Born 05/19/1930, Brooklyn, NY DISCIPLINE MODERN HISTORY EDUCATION Brooklyn Col, BA, 53; Columbia Univ, MA, 55, PhD(hist), 59. CAREER From instr to asst prof hist and econ, Polytech Inst Brooklyn, 58-63; from asst prof to assoc prof hist, Rutgers Univ, 63-67; prof, Sir George Williams Univ, 68-69; chmn dept, 69-76, PROF HIST, UNIV ROCHESTER, 69-, Soc Sci Res Coun fel, 68-69; fel, Ctr Advan Studies Behav Sci, Stanford, Calif, 72-73. MEMBERSHIPS Southern Hist Asn; Agr Hist Asn; fel Am Acad Arts & Sci; Orgn Am Historians (pres, 77-78). RESEARCH Southern and Afro-American history. SELECTED PUBLICATIONS Auth, The Papers of King, Martin, Luther, Vol 2, Rediscovering Precious Values, July 1951 November 1955, Rev in Am Hist, Vol 0023, 95; The Work of Reconstruction--From Slave to Wage Labor in South-Carolina, 1860-1870, J Soc Hist, Vol 0029, 95. CONTACT ADDRESS Dept of Hist, Univ of Rochester, Rochester, NY, 14627.

GENTLES, IAN
PERSONAL Born 10/25/1941, Kingston, Jamaica DISCIPLINE HISTORY EDUCATION Univ Toronto, BA, 63, MA, 65; Univ London, PhD, 69. CAREER Asst to assoc prof, 69-93, dean students, 70-75, assoc prin acad affairs, 85-87, PROF HIST, GLENDON COL, YORK UNIV, 93-; dept ch, 93-; vis scholar, Corpus Christi Col, 82-83; vis fel, Clare Hall, Cambridge, 93. MEMBERSHIPS Fel, Royal Hist Soc, 78-; ch, London House Asn Can, 84-87. SELECTED PUBLICATIONS Auth, The New Model Army in England, Ireland and Scotland 1645-1653, 92; coauth, Public Policy, Private Voices: The Euthanasia Debate, 92; ed, Care of the Dying and Bereaved, 82; ed, A Time to Choose Life, 90; ed, Euthanasia and Assisted Suicide: the Current Debate, 95. CONTACT ADDRESS Glendon Col, York Univ, 2275 Bayview Ave, Toronto, ON, M4N 3M6.

GENTRY, ATRON A.
PERSONAL El Centro, CA DISCIPLINE EDUCATION EDUCATION Pasadena City Clge, AA 1958; CA State Polytechnic Clge, 1959; CA State Univ at Los Angeles, BA 1966; Univ of MA, EdD 1970. CAREER Apple Creek State Inst OH, asst supr 1975-76; Cleveland State Hosp OH, supr 1976-78; Hull Clge of Higher Educ Hull England, visiting prof 1981; Univ of MA, prof of educ; Visiting Professor in Beijing Tchrs Coll 1986. HONORS AND AWARDS Citizen of the Year Omega Psi Frat 1967; Urban Srv Award Ofc of Econ Apport US Govt 1966; Urban Educ The Hope Factor Philadelphia Sounder 1972; The Politics of Urban Educ for the 80's Natl Assn of Sec Schl Principals 1980; Dedication & Service, Boston Secondary School Project 1987; The Dr. Carter G. Woodson Memorial Uplift Award Tau Iota Chapter, Omega Psi Fraternity 1988; Crispus Attucks Award, National Committee for Commemoration of America's Revolutionary War Black Patriot, 1991.

MEMBERSHIPS Assc dean Schl of Educ Univ of MA 1971-72, 1972-75, dir of the Center for Urban Educ 1968-71; staff mem 1984 Olympic Games L A Olympic Org Comm 1984; Kentucky Colonel 1974; mem Phi Delta Kappa 1971; Dir of Boston Scndry Schls Project, a collaborative prgm between Univ of Mass at Amherst & Boston Secondary Schls. **SELECTED PUBLICATIONS** Author, Learning to Survive: Black Youth Look for Education and Hope; Co-editor, Equity and Excellence in Education. **CONTACT ADDRESS** Educ Dept, Univ of Massachusetts, Amherst, MA, 01002.

GENTRY, JUDITH ANNE FENNER
PERSONAL Born 05/28/1942, Baltimore, MD, m, 1969, 1 child **DISCIPLINE** UNITED STATES CIVIL WAR & ECONOMIC HISTORY **EDUCATION** Univ Md, College Park, BA, 64; Rice Univ, PhD(hist), 69. **CAREER** Asst prof, 69-74, assoc prof hist, Univ Southwestern La, 74-85, prof and dir grad prog hist, 85-. **HONORS AND AWARDS** Mary Hayes Ewing Publ Prize, Rice Univ, 71; Nat Endowment for Humanities res grants, 78 & 79; Fellow, Newberry Library Summer Institute in Quantitative History, 80; Univ of Southwestern La Foundation Outstanding Teacher Award, 94; Fellow, La Historical Asn, 95. **MEMBERSHIPS** AHA; Orgn Am Historians; Southern Hist Asn; AAUP; Southern Asn Women Historians (vpres, 77-78, pres, 78-79); Louisiana Historical Asn, vice-pres, 90-91, pres, 91-92. **RESEARCH** United States Civil War finances. **SELECTED PUBLICATIONS** Auth, A Confederate Success in Europe: The Erlanger Loan, J Southern Hist, 5/70; The Louisiana State Lottery, In: Encyclopedia of Southern History, 79; ed, Eliminating Sex Bias in Vocational Education, Univ Southwestern La Printshop, 80; co-auth with James Dorman, Higher Education and Historical Literacy in Louisiana: An Analsis and Modest Proposal, La Hist, fall 83; An Historical Study of Women in the Southern Historical Association, 1934-1985, J Southern Hist, 5/86; A Private Fortune and the Democratic Process, La History, 87; 7 entries in Directory of Louisiana Biography, 88; Alexander Mouton, Governor of Louisiana and Pierre Dobigny, Arnaud Beavrais, and Jacques Dupre in Joseph G. Dawson The Louisiana Governors from Iberville to Edwards, 90; White Gold: The Confederate Government and Cotton in Louisiana, La Hist, 92; What if the Constitution as Written Had Provided for Equal Rights for Women and Men? in Herb Levine, What if the American Political System Were Different?, 92; The Erlanger Loan, in Encyclopedia of the Confederacy, 93; John A. Stevenson: Confederate Adventurer, La Hist, 94; George Eustis, Jr, in American National Biography, forthcoming; Introduction to Vol 9 of the Jefferson Davis Papers, January- September 1863, 97. **CONTACT ADDRESS** Dept of Hist, Univ of Southwestern La, 200 Hebrard Blvd, Lafayette, LA, 70504-2531. **EMAIL** JFGentry@ucs.usl.edu

GEORGE, CHARLES HILLES
PERSONAL Born 05/22/1922, Kansas City, MO, m, 1951, 1 child **DISCIPLINE** HISTORY **EDUCATION** Princeton Univ, PhD(hist), 50. **CAREER** Instr hist, Stanford Univ, 50-51 and Pomona Col, 51-52; asst prof, Colo Col, 52-53, Univ Rochester, 54-55 and Univ Wash, 56-57; from asst prof to assoc prof, Univ Pittsburgh, 57-61; PROF HIST, NORTHERN ILL UNIV, 61-, Soc Sci Res Coun fel, 55-56. **MEMBERSHIPS** Conf Brit Studies; Am Soc Reformation Res; Hist Asn England. **RESEARCH** Intellectual history of early modern Europe; English history; history of English bourgeoisie. **SELECTED PUBLICATIONS** Auth, The Secularization of Early-Modern England, From Religious Culture to Religious Faith, Albion, Vol 0025, 93; Communications: A Reply to Sommerville, C. John, Albion, Vol 0026, 94; Puritanism and Historical Controversy, Albion, Vol 0029, 97. **CONTACT ADDRESS** Dept of Hist, No Illinois Univ, De Kalb, IL, 60115.

GEORGE, EDWARD V.
PERSONAL Born 12/10/1937, Buffalo, NY, m, 1968 **DISCIPLINE** CLASSICAL LANGUAGES **EDUCATION** Niagara Univ, BA, 59; Canisius Col, MS, 62; Univ Wis, MA, 62, PhD(Classics), 66. **CAREER** Asst prof classics, Univ Tex, Austin, 66-71; assoc prof, 71-78, PROF CLASSICS, TEX TECH UNIV, 78-. **MEMBERSHIPS** Am Philol Asn; Class Asn Midwest & South; Class Asn Southwestern US; Vergilian Soc Am; Am Class League (vpres, 80-82). **RESEARCH** Augustan Latin and Hellenistic Greek poetry; teaching classical humanities; Renaissance Latin Lit. **SELECTED PUBLICATIONS** Auth, Stoics and Neostoics--Rubens and the Circle of Lipsius, Class World, Vol 0087, 94; The Antiquarians and the Myth of Antiquity--the Origins of Rome in Renaissance Thought, Class World, Vol 0090, 96; Andreas and the Ambiguity of Courtly Love, 16th Century J, Vol 0027, 96; Valerius-Maximus and the Rhetoric of the New Nobility, Class World, Vol 0089, 96. **CONTACT ADDRESS** 2007 28th St, Lubbock, TX, 79411.

GEORGE, LUVENIA A.
PERSONAL Born 02/26/1934, Chicago, Illinois, m, 1953 **DISCIPLINE** ETHNOMUSICOLOGY **EDUCATION** Howard University, BMEd, 1952; University of Maryland College Park, MEd, 1969; University of Maryland Baltimore County, PhD, 1995. **CAREER** District of Columbia Public Schools, music teacher, 1954-92; Smithsonian Institution, research scholar, 1993-94, coordinator DE youth proj, 1994-. **HONORS AND AWARDS** African-American Museum, Hall of Fame Inductee, 1997. **MEMBERSHIPS** Sargent Presbyterian Church, organist, 1960-, elder, 1991-; District of Columbia Music Education Association, pres, 1970-72; District of Columbia Choral Directors Association, pres, 1978-80. **SELECTED PUBLICATIONS** Author: "Teaching the Music of Six Different Cultures," 2nd ed, 1987; Lucie Campbell in "We'll Understand It Better Bye & Bye," 1992; Duke Ellington: "Composer Beyond Category," 1993; "The Source of African-American Music," 1991. **CONTACT ADDRESS** CProgram in African-American Culture, Smithsonian Institute, 14th & Constitution Ave, NW, Washington, VT, 20560. **EMAIL** llgeorge@webtv.net

GEORGE, PETER J.
DISCIPLINE HISTORY **EDUCATION** Univ Toronto, BA, MA, PhD; Univ Ottawa, DU. **HONORS AND AWARDS** Pres, McMaster Univ. **RESEARCH** Canadian economic hist. **SELECTED PUBLICATIONS** Auth, Ontario's Mining Industry 1870-1940; auth, Progress Without Planning: The Economic Development of Ontario 1870-1940, 87; co-auth, The Courts and the Development of Trade in Upper Canada, Bus Hist Rev, 86. **CONTACT ADDRESS** History Dept, McMaster Univ, 1280 Main St W, Hamilton, ON, L8S 4L9.

GEPHART, RONALD MICHAEL
PERSONAL Born 09/29/1939, Dayton, OH, m, 1961, 2 children **DISCIPLINE** AMERICAN HISTORY **EDUCATION** Univ Nebr, BA, 63, MA, 65; Northwestern Univ, PhD(Am hist), 80. **CAREER** Lectr colonial and revolutionary Am, Northwestern Am, 68-69; sr bibliogr, 69-75, specialist Am hist, 75-81, ASST ED, LETT DELEG CONGRESS 1774-1789, LIBR CONG, 81-, Co-chmn, Libr Cong Task Force, subcomt bibliog role, Libr Cong, 75-76; consult, Ctr Hist Population Studies, Univ Utah, 77-79. **MEMBERSHIPS** AHA; Orgn Am Historians; Southern Hist Asn; Inst Early Am Hist & Cult; Soc Hist Fed Govt. **RESEARCH** Historical bibliography; documentary editing; American colonial and revolutionary history. **SELECTED PUBLICATIONS** Auth, Who Wrote the 'North American' Essays, William and Mary Quart, Vol 0054, 97. **CONTACT ADDRESS** Hist Publ Off Manuscript Div Libr of Cong, Washington, DC, 20540.

GERATY, LAWRENCE THOMAS
PERSONAL Born 04/21/1940, St. Helena, CA, m, 1962, 2 children **DISCIPLINE** NEAR EASTERN ARCHEOLOGY, OLD TESTAMENT **EDUCATION** Pac Union Col, AB, 62; Andrews Univ, AM, 63, BD, 65; Harvard Univ, PhD(Near Eastern lang & lit), 72. **CAREER** Asst prof, 72-76, assoc prof, 76-80, PROF ARCHAEOL and HIST ANTIQ, ANDREWS UNIV, 80-, Ed, Andrews Univ Monographs, 72-; res grants, Ctr for Field Res, 76 and Nat Endowment for Humanities, 77; trustee, Am Ctr Orient Res, Amman, Jordon, 76-; cur, Andrews Univ Archaeol Mus, 76-; assoc ed, Andrews Univ Sem Studies, 77-. **MEMBERSHIPS** Am Schs Orient Res; Soc Bibl Lit; Am Inst Archaeol; Nat Asn Prof Hebrew; Asn Adventist Forums (pres, 72-73). **RESEARCH** Palestinian archaeology; semitic inscriptions; Old Testament exegesis. **SELECTED PUBLICATIONS** Auth, A Tribute to Horn, Siegfried, H.--March-17, 1908 November-28, 1993--In-Memoriam, Biblical Archaeol, Vol 0057, 94. **CONTACT ADDRESS** Theol Sem, Andrews Univ, Berrien Springs, MI, 49104.

GERBER, DAVID A.
PERSONAL Born 09/28/1944, Chicago, IL, m, 1975 **DISCIPLINE** HISTORY **EDUCATION** Northwestern Univ, BA, 66; Princeton Univ, PhD(hist), 71. **CAREER** Instr hist, Princeton Univ, 70-71; asst prof, 71-77, ASSOC PROF HIST, STATE UNIV NY, BUFFALO, 77-, Davis Ctr Hist Studies, Princeton Univ fel hist, 73. **MEMBERSHIPS** AHA; Orgn Am Historians; Immigration Hist Soc. **RESEARCH** Origins and development of American ethnic pluralism; American immigration history; American Black-white relations. **SELECTED PUBLICATIONS** Auth, News from the Land of Freedom--German Immigrants Write Home, J Am Ethnic Hist, Vol 0012, 93; Heroes and Misfits: Film and War--The Troubled Social Reintegration of Disabled Veterans in the 'Best Years of Our Lives,' Am Quart, Vol 0046, 94; Race, Ethnicity, and Urbanization--Selected Essays, J Southern Hist, Vol 0061, 95; In Search of Schmid, Al; World-War-II--War Hero, Blinded Veteran, Everyman, J Am Stud, Vol 0029, 95; Special Sorrows--the Diasporic Imagination of Irish, Polish, and Jewish Immigrants in the United-States, Am Hist Rev, Vol 0101, 96; The Immigrant Letter Between Positivism and Populism--The Uses of Immigrant Personal Correspondence in 20th-Century American Scholarship, J Am Ethnic Hist, Vol 0016, 97. **CONTACT ADDRESS** Dept of Hist, State Univ NY, Buffalo Amherst, NY, 14261.

GERBER, DOUGLAS E.
PERSONAL Born 09/14/1933, North Bay, ON, Canada, m, 1986, 1 child **DISCIPLINE** CLASSICS **EDUCATION** Univ Western Ontario, BA, 55, MA, 56; Univ Toronto, PhD, 59. **CAREER** Lectr, Univ Toronto, 58-59; lectr, 59-60, asst prof, 60-64, assoc prof, 64-69, prof, 69- , dept ch, 69-97, Univ Western Ontario. **HONORS AND AWARDS** William Sherwood Fox Ch of Classics, 77- ; Pres, Class Asn Canada, 88-90; ed, Transactions Amer Philol Asn, 74-82. **MEMBERSHIPS** Amer Philol Asn; Class Asn, Great Brit; Class Asn Canada; Class Asn Middle West and South. **RESEARCH** Greek Lyric Poetry. **SELECTED PUBLICATIONS** Auth, A Bibliography of Pindar, 1513-1966, Monograph 28 of the Amer Philol Asn, Cleveland, 69; Euterpe, An Anthology of Early Greek Lyric, Elegiac and Iambic Poetry, Hakkert, Amsterdam, 70; Emendations in Pindar, 1513-1972, Hakkert, Amsterdam, 76; Pindar's Olympian One: a Commentary, U of Toronto P, 82; Lexicon in Bacchylidem, Olms, Hildesheim, 84; ed, Greek Poetry and Philosophy, Studies in Honour of Leonard Woodbury, Scholars Press, Chico, 84; Ed, A Companion to the Greek Lyric Poets, Brill, Leiden, 97. **CONTACT ADDRESS** Dept of Classics, Western Ontario Univ, London, ON, N6A 3K7. **EMAIL** degerber@julian.uwo.ca

GERBER, JANE SATLOW
PERSONAL Born 06/17/1938, New York, NY, m, 1964, 3 children **DISCIPLINE** JEWISH AND MIDDLE EASTERN HISTORY **EDUCATION** Wellesley Col, BA, 59; Radcliffe Col, MA, 62; Columbia Univ, PhD(Jewish & Mid E hist), 72. **CAREER** Instr Jewish hist, Stern Col, Yeshiva Univ, 71-72; asst prof, Lehman Col, 72-77; asst prof, 77-81, ASSOC PROF HIST, GRAD CTR, CITY UNIV NEW YORK, 81-, Bk rev ed, Jewish Social Studies J, 68-; mem off-campus fac, Sephardic Inst, Yeshiva Univ, 73-; Fac Res Found grant, City Univ New York, 74 and 75; ed, Shoah: Rev of Holocaust Studies and Commemorations, 78- **MEMBERSHIPS** Am Acad Jewish Res; Am Jewish Hist Soc; Am Asn Jewish Studies (pres); Israel Hist Soc. **RESEARCH** Jewish history in Muslim lands; Jews in Morocco; Sephardic history. **SELECTED PUBLICATIONS** Auth, Sephardi Entrepreneurs in Eretz-Israel--The Amzalak Family, 1816-1918, Jewish Quart Rev, Vol 0084, 94. **CONTACT ADDRESS** Graduate Sch and Univ Ctr, CUNY, 33 W 42nd St, New York, NY, 10018.

GERBERDING, RICHARD A.
PERSONAL Born 09/08/1945, Punxsutawney, PA, s **DISCIPLINE** HISTORY **EDUCATION** Univ Minn, BA, 67; Univ Manitoba, MA, 77; Oxford Univ, PhD, 83. **CAREER** PROF HIST, UNIV ALA, HUNTSVILLE **HONORS AND AWARDS** Am Philol Soc Award Exc Teach Class, 96. **MEMBERSHIPS** Medieval Acad Am **RESEARCH** Frankish hist **SELECTED PUBLICATIONS** Auth, The Rise of the Carolingians and the Liber Historiae Francorum, Clarendon Press, 87; co-auth, Late Merovingian France, Manchester Univ Press, 97. **CONTACT ADDRESS** Dept of History, Univ of Alabama, Huntsville, Huntsville, AL, 35899. **EMAIL** gerberdingr@email.uah.edu

GERLACH, DON R.
PERSONAL Born 06/09/1932, Harvard, NE **DISCIPLINE** AMERICAN HISTORY **EDUCATION** Univ Nebr, BSEd, 54, MA, 56, PhD, 61. **CAREER** Asst hist, Univ Nebr, 57-58, instr, 61-62; instr, Far East Div, Univ Md, 58-59; from asst prof to assoc prof, 62-72, PROF HIST, UNIV AKRON, 72-, Historiographer, Anglican Cath Church; Fulbright scholar, 56-57. **MEMBERSHIPS** AHA; Orgn Am Hist; fel Royal Hist Soc. **RESEARCH** Early America until 1800, especially the revolutionary era. **SELECTED PUBLICATIONS** Auth, The King of the Alley--Duer, William Politician, Entrepreneur, and Speculator, 1768-1799, J Am Hist, Vol 0081, 94. **CONTACT ADDRESS** Dept of Hist, Univ of Akron, Akron, OH, 44325.

GERLACH, LARRY REUBEN
PERSONAL Born 11/09/1941, Lincoln, NE, 1 child **DISCIPLINE** AMERICAN HISTORY **EDUCATION** Univ Nebr, Lincoln, BS, 63, MA, 65; Rutgers Univ, New Brunswick, PhD, 68. **CAREER** Asst prof to assoc prof, 68-76, prof hist, Univ Utah, 77-; vis asst prof hist, Col William & Mary, 70-71; vis bk rev ed, William & Mary Quart, 70-71; fel, NJ Hist Soc, 77; assoc dean, Col Humanities, Univ Utah, 82-. **HONORS AND AWARDS** William A Whitehead Award, NJ Hist Soc, 73; Award of Merit, Am Assn State & Local Hist, 77; Distinguished Achievement Award, NJ Hist Comn, 80; Distinguished Teaching Award, Univ Utah, 81. **MEMBERSHIPS** AHA; Org Am Hist; Am Assn State & Local Hist; Western Hist Assn; North Am Soc Study Sport Hist. **RESEARCH** Colonial America; the American Revolution; sports history. **SELECTED PUBLICATIONS** Ed, The American Revolution: New York as a Case Study, Wadsworth, 72; ed, New Jersey in the American Revolution, NJ Hist Comn, 75; auth, Prologue to Independence: New Jersey in the Coming of the American Revolution, Rutgers Univ, 76; auth, Connecticut Congressman: Samuel Huntington, 1731-1796, Am Revolution Bicentennial Comn Conn, 77; auth, The Men in Blue: Conversations with Umpires, Viking, 80; auth, Blazing Crosses in Zion: The Klu Klux Klan in Utah, Utah State Univ, 82. **CONTACT ADDRESS** Dept of History, Univ of Utah, 217 Carlson Hall, Salt Lake City, UT, 84112-3124. **EMAIL** larry.gerlack@m.cc.utah.edu

GERRISH, BRIAN ALBERT
PERSONAL Born 08/14/1931, London, England, m, 1955, 2 children **DISCIPLINE** RELIGION, HISTORY **EDUCATION** Cambridge Univ, BA, 52, MA, 56; Westminster Col, Eng, cert, 55; Union Theol Sem, STM, 56; Columbia Univ, PhD(philos relig), 58. **CAREER** From instr to assoc prof church hist, McCormick Theol Sem, 58-65; assoc prof hist theol, 65-68, prof hist theol and Reformation hist, 68-72, PROF HIST THEOL,

DIVINITY SCH, UNIV CHICAGO, 72-, Am Asn Theol Schs fac fel, 6i-62; John Simon Guggenheim Mem Found fel, 70-72; CO-ED, J RELIG, 72-; Nat Endowment for Humanities fel, 80-81. **MEMBERSHIPS** Am Acad Relig; Am Soc Reformation Res; Am Soc Church Hist (pres, 79). **RESEARCH** Continental Protestant thought in the 16th and 19th centuries. **SELECTED PUBLICATIONS** Auth, Natural Religion and the Nature of Religion--The Legacy of Deism, J Relig, Vol 0073, 93; Religion and the Religions in the English Enlightenment, J Relig, Vol 0073, 93; Atheism from the Reformation to the Enlightenment, J Relig, Vol 0074, 94. **CONTACT ADDRESS** Univ Chicago, 18541 Klimm Ave, Homewood, IL, 60430.

GERSHENSON, DANIEL ENOCH
PERSONAL Born 03/27/1935, New York, NY, m, 1963, 4 children **DISCIPLINE** GREEK & LATIN **EDUCATION** Columbia Univ, AB, 55, PhD, 61; Jewish Theol Sem Am, BHL, 56. **CAREER** From instr to asst prof Greek & Latin, Columbia Univ, 59-68; actg assoc prof classics, UCLA, 68-69; SR Lectr Class Studies, Tel-Aviv Univ, 69, Nat Sci Found grant, 62. **MEMBERSHIPS** Am Philol Asn. **RESEARCH** Greek mythology. **SELECTED PUBLICATIONS** Auth, The Sic Swans and Arlemis, Mankind Q, 92; auth, Kai Su tekuon: Caesar's Last Words. Shakespeare Q, 92; auth, Greek Proverbs in the Ethics of the Fathers, Grazer Beitrage, 93; auth, Understanding Pushkansa, Acta Orientalia, 94; auth, Hesychias Gennon or Rather Gennon? Rev des Etudes Juiro, 94; auth, A Greek Myth in Jeremiah, Zeitschrift fur die alttestamentliche Wissenschaft, 96; auth, Yiddish Davenen and the Ashkenazic Rite, Yiddish, 96. **CONTACT ADDRESS** Dept of Class Studies, Tel-Aviv Univ, Tel-Aviv, .. **EMAIL** gershens@post.tan.ac.il

GERSON, KATHLEEN
PERSONAL Born 08/06/1947, Montgomery, AL, m, 1981, 1 child **DISCIPLINE** SOCIOLOGY **EDUCATION** Stanford Univ, BA, 69; Univ CA at Berkeley, MA, 74, PhD, 81. **CAREER** Asst prof, 80-87, New York Univ; visiting scholar, Russel Sage Found, 87-88, assoc prof, 88-94, dir of undergraduate studies in sociology, 90-96, prof, 95-present, New York Univ. **HONORS AND AWARDS** NYU Presidential Fel, 85; finalist C. Wright Mills and William J. Goode Book Awards, 86; SWS Feminist Lecturer on Women and Social Change (awarded annually by the Sociologists for Women in Society to a senior scholar who has made a major contribution, 98; research grant, The Alfred P. Sloan Found. **MEMBERSHIPS** Amer Sociol Assn; Easter Sociol Soc; Council on Contemporary Families; Council of Research Advisors, Ctr for Families; Ford Found Project on the Integration of Work, Family, and Community; Sloan Found Research Network on Work Redesign and Work/Family, 95-96; Soc for the Study of Social Problems; Sociologist for Women in Society. **RESEARCH** Gender; the family; families and work; gender and the moral order; Amer Families in transition; the life course and human development; social and individual change processes; qualitative research methods. **SELECTED PUBLICATIONS** Auth, No Man's Land: Men's Changing Commitments to Family and Work, 93; Hard Choices: How Women Decide About Work, Career, and Motherhood, 85; The Social Construction of Fatherhood, in Parenting: Contemporary Issues and Challenges, 97; An Institutional Perspective on Generative Fathering: Creating Social Supports for Parenting Equality, in Generative Fathering: Beyond Deficit Perspectives, 97; Do Americans Feel Overworked? Comparing Actual and Ideal Working Time, in Work and Family: Research Informing Policy, 98; Gender and the Future of the Family: Implications for the Post-Industrial Workplace, pp. 11-21, in Challenges for Work and Family in the 21st Century, 98; Who are the Overworked Americans? Review of Social Economics (Special Issue on The Overworked American Debate, 98. **CONTACT ADDRESS** New York Univ, 269 Mercer St, 4th Fl, New York, NY, 10003. **EMAIL** gerson@soc.mail.nyu.edu

GERSTEIN, LINDA GROVES
PERSONAL Born 04/03/1943, Gouverneur, NY, m, 1964, 2 children **DISCIPLINE** AFRICAN HISTORY **EDUCATION** State Univ NY Col Geneseo, BS, 65; Syracuse Univ, PhD, 72. **CAREER** Asst prof, 67-80, chmn dept, 72-74, prof hist, Westfield State Col, 80-, Consult, NY State Prison Syst, 72; dir, Raymond Patterson Archives, 74-; res grant, Am Philos Soc, 79. **MEMBERSHIPS** AHAG African Studies Asn; Liberian Studies Asn. **RESEARCH** Slavery; slave trade; Liberia. **SELECTED PUBLICATIONS** Auth, Fernando Po and the Anti-Sierra Leonean Campaign: 1826-1834, Int J African Hist Studies, Vol 6, No 2; coauth, Curtin's Atlantic Slave Trade: An Analysis from Two Perspectives, Hist J Western Mass, Vol II, No 1; Immigrants to Liberia, 1843-1754, Inst Liberian Studies, 80; Simon Greenleaf and the Liberian Constitution of 1847, J Liberian Studies, 82. **CONTACT ADDRESS** Dept of Hist, Westfield State Col, 577 Western Ave, Westfield, MA, 01085-2501. **EMAIL** lgerstei@haverford.edu

GERSTEL, SHARON E.J.
DISCIPLINE ART HISTORY **EDUCATION** AB Bryn Mawr Col; MA, PhD NY Univ. **CAREER** Prof, Univ MD. **HONORS AND AWARDS** Samuel H Kress fel; two Dumbarton Oaks fel(s), two Robert Lehman fel(s); grant, NEH; postdoc fel, J Paul Getty. **MEMBERSHIPS** Mem, Prog Comm Intl Ctr for Medieval; Christian Archaeol Assn , Greece. **RESEARCH** Relationship between liturgical and extra-liturgical ceremony and monumental painting of medieval Byzantium. **SELECTED PUBLICATIONS** Auth, Beholding the Sacred Mysteries: Programs of the Byzantine Sanctuary. **CONTACT ADDRESS** Dept of Art Hist, Univ MD, 4229 Art-Sociology Building, College Park, MD, 20742-1335. **EMAIL** sg113@umail.umd.edu

GERTEIS, LOUIS
DISCIPLINE HISTORY **EDUCATION** Antioch Col, BA, 65; Univ Wis, MA, 66; PhD, 69. **CAREER** Prof **RESEARCH** Nineteenth century United States; slavery and emancipation; Civil War and reconstruction; democracy and race. **SELECTED PUBLICATIONS** Auth, From Contraband to Freedman: Federal Policy Toward Southern Blacks, 1861-1865, Greenwood, 73; Salmon P. Chase, Radicalism, and the Politics of Emancipation, 1861-1864, J Am Hist, 73; Slavery and Hart Times: Morality and Utility in American Antislavery Reform, Civil War Hist, 83; Morality and Utility in American Antislavery Reform, Univ NC, 87; Blackface Minstrelsy and the Construction of Race in Nineteenth Century America, Kent, 97. **CONTACT ADDRESS** History Dept, Univ of Missouri, St. Louis, 484 Lucas Hall, St. Louis, MO, 63121. **EMAIL** sisgert@umslvma.umsl.edu

GERVERS, MICHAEL
PERSONAL Born 01/19/1942, Flaunden, England, m, 1967 **DISCIPLINE** MEDIEVAL SOCIAL AND ECONOMIC HISTORY **EDUCATION** Princeton Univ, BA, 64; Univ Poitiers, France, MA, 65; Univ Toronto, PhD(Medieval studies), 72. **CAREER** Asst prof Medieval hist, NY Univ, 72-75; asst prof Medieval art hist, Univ Toronto, 76, asst prof Medieval hist, Erindale Col, 76-77, ASST PROF MEDIEVAL HIST AND ART HIST, SCARBOROUGH COL, UNIV TORONTO, 77-, Res assoc hist, Can Coun Killam Fel, 74-75. **MEMBERSHIPS** Medieval Acad Am; Col Art Asn; Essex Archaeol Soc; Societe Archeologique et Hist Charente; Arms & Armour Soc. **RESEARCH** Social and economic development of the Order of St John of Jerusalem in England; Medieval rock-cut churches of the Mediterranean world; historical ethnography. **SELECTED PUBLICATIONS** Auth, The Military Orders--from the 12th to the Early 14th Centuries, Cath Hist Rev, Vol 0079, 93; The Hospitallers of Rhodes and Their Mediterranean World, Cath Hist Rev, Vol 0080, 94; Templars, Hospitallers, and the Teutonic-Knights--Images of the Military Orders, AD 1128-1291, Speculum-J Medieval Stud, Vol 0070, 95; The Knights of Malta, Int Hist Rev, Vol 0018, 96; The New Knighthood--A History of the Order-of-the-Temple, Speculum-J Medieval Stud, Vol 0071, 96; Military Orders and Crusades, Cath Hist Rev, Vol 0082, 96; Felt and Tent-Carts in the 'Secret History of the Mongols,' J Royal Asiatic Soc, Vol 0007, 97. **CONTACT ADDRESS** Univ Toronto, 46 Chicora, Toronto, ON, M5R 1T6.

GESELL, GERALDINE C.
DISCIPLINE CLASSICAL STUDIES **EDUCATION** Vassar Col, BA, 53; Univ Okla, MA, 55; Univ NC, PhD, 72. **CAREER** Asst prof, 72-79; assoc prof, 79-85; prof, 85-. **MEMBERSHIPS** Advis Counc Am Acad Rome; Archaeol Inst Am; Class Asn Mid W and S; Tennessee Class Asn. **SELECTED PUBLICATIONS** Auth, Town, Palace, and House Cult in Minoan Crete, 85; pubs on Minoan relig and ritual artifacts, preliminary reports of the Kavousi Excavations and pottery technol. **CONTACT ADDRESS** Dept of Classics, Knoxville, TN, 37996. **EMAIL** ggesell@utk.edu

GETTLEMAN, MARVIN EDWARD
PERSONAL Born 09/12/1933, New York, NY, m, 1981, 4 children **DISCIPLINE** MODERN UNITED STATES HISTORY **EDUCATION** City Col New York, BA, 57; Johns Hopkins Univ, MA, 59, PhD(hist), 72. **CAREER** Lectr polit sci & hist, City Col New York, 59-62; lectr US econ hist, 62-63, from instr to asst prof, 63-68, assoc prof, 68-79, prof hist, 79-95, PROF EMER, POLYTECH INST BROOKLYN, 95- ; Consult, proj impact technol change on privacy in US, Asn Bar City New York, 64; Louis M Rabinowitz Found res grant, 68; Nat Endowment for Humanities fel, 73-74; Nat Hist Publ & Records Comn grant, 77-78; mem, Brooklyn Rediscovery Proj, 78-79. **MEMBERSHIPS** AHA; Orgn Am Historians. **RESEARCH** United States foreign policy in Asia; history of higher education; the American Communist Party in the popular front era. **SELECTED PUBLICATIONS** Auth, John Glenn: Hero and America, New Left Rev, 7/8/62; Vietnam: History, Documents, Opinions, Fawcett, US, 65, 2nd ed, Penguin, England, 66 & 3rd ed, New Am Libr/Signet, US, 70; The Dorr Rebellion: A Study in American Radicalism, 1833-1849, Random, 73, 2nd ed, Krieger, 80; Philanthropy and Social Control in Late 19th Century America, Societas, summer 75; An Elusive Presence: The Discovery of John H Finley, Nelson-Hall, 78; auth, An Elusive Presence: John Finley & His America, Nelson-Hall, 79; co-ed, El Salvador: Central America in the New Cold War, Grove, 80; auth, The Johns Hopkins Seminary of History and Politics, 1877-1912, 5 v, Garland, 88-90. **CONTACT ADDRESS** 771 West End Ave, New York, NY, 10025.

GETTY, J. ARCH
PERSONAL Born 11/30/1950, Shreveport, LA, m, 1972, 1 child **DISCIPLINE** RUSSIAN HISTORY **EDUCATION** Univ Pa, AB, 72; Boston Col, MA, 73, PhD(hist), 79. **CAREER** Lectr hist, Boston Col, 77-80; ASST PROF RUSS HIST, UNIV CALIF, RIVERSIDE, 80-, Managing ed, Russ Hist, 78-; sr fel, Russ Inst, Columbia Univ, 81. **MEMBERSHIPS** Am Asn Advan Slavic Studies. **RESEARCH** History of Soviet Communist Party; Russian Revolution; Stalin. **SELECTED PUBLICATIONS** Auth, Stalin--Breaker of Nations, Slavic Rev, Vol 0052, 93; Victims of the Soviet Penal-System in the Prewar Years--A 1st Approach on the Basis of Archival Evidence, Am Hist Rev, Vol 0098, 93; Stalinism--Its Nature and Aftermath--Essays in Honor of Lewin, Moshe, Russ Rev, Vol 0052, 93; Commercialization of Scholarship: Archival Research in the Former Soviet-Union--Do We Need a Code of Behavior, Slavic Rev, Vol 0052, 93; Britain Confronts the Stalin Revolution--Anglo-Soviet Relations and the Metro-Vickers Crisis, Russ Rev, Vol 0055, 96; Bortnevskii, Viktor, G., 1954-1996, Slavic Rev, Vol 0055, 96; Molotov and Soviet Government--Sovnarkom, 1930-41, Slavic Rev, Vol 0056, 97. **CONTACT ADDRESS** Dept of Hist, Univ of Calif, Riverside, CA, 92507.

GEYER, M.
PERSONAL Born 10/30/1947, Germany, m, 1991 **DISCIPLINE** HISTORY **EDUCATION** Albert Ludwigs Univ, PhD summa cum laud, 76, staatsexmem 72. **CAREER** Leipzig Univ, Leibniz Prof, 95-96; John F Kennedy Inst Berlin, vis prof, 93-94; Univ Chicago, prof, 86-; Univ Michigan Ann Arbor, asst prof, assoc prof, 77-86; Univ Bochum Lehrstuh, guest prof, 84. **HONORS AND AWARDS** Woodrow Wilson Fel; St Anthony's Col Sr Res Fel; Stud des Deutschen Volkes Schshp; Grad Schshp Freiburg; APS Tvl Gnt; Ruth M Sinclair Awd; Dist Ser Awd U of M; Max-Planck-Inst Fel; Cen Euro Hist Con Group Article Prize. **MEMBERSHIPS** AHA; AHF; AM; CGCEH; CES; GSA; IISS; SCS; WHA; Karl Lamprecht Gesellschaft; Verein fur Geschicte der Weltsysteme. **RESEARCH** German and European History; History of Modern War and Violence; History of Globalization/World History. **SELECTED PUBLICATIONS** Auth, Germany or: The Twentieth Century as History, S Atlantic Quart, 97; Historians at the Beginning and End of the Twentieth Century, Comparative, 96; Global Violence and Nationalizing wars in Eurasia and the Americas: The Geopolitics of War in the Mid-Nineteenth Century, Comp Stud in Soc and Hist, 96; The Politics of Memory in Contemporary Germany, in: Joan Copjec, ed, Radical Evil, London, NY, Verso, 96; Restorative Elites, German Society and the Nazi Pursuit of War, in: Fascist Italy and Nazi Germany: Comparison and Contrast, ed Richard Bessel, Cambridge, NY, Cambridge Univ Press, 96; Why Culture history? What Future? Which Germany? In: New German critique, 95; Great Men and Postmodern Raptures: Overcoming the Belatedness of German Historiography, coauth, in: German Studies Rev, 95. **CONTACT ADDRESS** Dept of History, Univ of Chicago, Chicago, IL, 60637. **EMAIL** mgeyer@midway.uchicago.edu

GHAZZAL, ZOUHAIR
DISCIPLINE HISTORY **EDUCATION** Sorbonne, PhD. **CAREER** Hist, Loyola Univ. **RESEARCH** Islamic and Middle Eastern societies; the history of ideas. **SELECTED PUBLICATIONS** Auth, Lecture d'un waqf maronite du mont Liban au XIXe siecle, in Le waqf dans l'espace islamique, outil de pouvoir socio-politique, Damascus: Institut Francais de Damas, 94; The Transfer of Property to Women: Judicial Decision-Making in a Maronite Estate in Nineteenth Century Mount Lebanon, Islamic Law and Soc, 2:1, 95. **CONTACT ADDRESS** Fine Arts Dept, Loyola Univ, Chicago, 6525 N. Sheridan Rd., Chicago, IL, 60626. **EMAIL** zghazzal@midway.uchicago.edu

GHILARDUCCI, TERESA
PERSONAL Born 07/22/1957, Roseville, CA, m, 1986, 1 child **DISCIPLINE** ECONOMICS **EDUCATION** Univ of Calif at Berkeley, BA, 78; PhD, 84. **CAREER** Res Asst, Inst of Industrial Relations, Univ of Calif at Berkeley, 79-83; ASST PROF, 84-91, ASSOC PROF, DEPT OF ECONOMICS, 91-, UNIV OF NOTRE DAME; Asst dir of Employee Benefits, Am Fed of Labor, Congress of Industrial Orgs, 94-95. **HONORS AND AWARDS** In residence fel, Mary Ingraham Bunting Inst, Radcliffe Col, 87-88. **MEMBERSHIPS** Am Economics Asn. **RESEARCH** Pensions; social security; labor markets. **SELECTED PUBLICATIONS** Auth, Labor's Capital: The Economics and Politics of Private Pensions, MIT Press, 92; coauth, Pension Practices of Innovative Firms, Pensions, Savings, and Capital Markets, U.S. Gov Printing Office, 96; auth, Pensions in an International Perspective, Rev of Radical Political Economies, 95; auth, The U.S. Social Security Debate and Integenerational Equity, The Role of the State in Pension Provisions: Provider and Regulator, Kluwer Pub, 98; auth, The Progressivity of the Social Security System: A Case Against Means Testing, Topics on Intergenerational Justice, Dushkin Press, 96; auth, Many Faces of American Multiemployer Pension Funds, Supplementary Pensions: Actors, Issues and the Future, Greenwood Press, 95; coauth, Scale Economies in Union Pension Plan Administration: 1981-1993, Industrial Relations Rev, 99; coauth, Labor's Paradoxical Role and the Evolution of Corporate Governance, J of Law and Soc, 97; coauth, Portable Pension Plans for Casual Labor Markets: Lessons from the Operating Engineers Central Pension Fund, Greenwood Press, 95. **CONTACT ADDRESS** Dept of Economics, Univ of Notre Dame, Nortre Dame, IN, 46556. **EMAIL** Ghilarducci.1@nd.edu

GHIRARDO, DIANE
DISCIPLINE ARCHITECTURAL HISTORY AND THEORY **EDUCATION** San Jose State Univ, BA, 73; Stanford Univ, MA, 76, PhD, 82. **CAREER** Prof, USC, 95-; vis prof, Rice Univ, 95; assoc prof, USC, 88-95; asst prof, USC, 84-88; vis prof, SCI-ARC, 86, 87 & 89; asst prof, TX A&M Univ, 83-84; lectr & tchg asst, Stanford Univ, 80-83. **HONORS AND AWARDS** Phi Kappa Phi Fac Recognition Awd, 97; Graham Found Awd, 96; fel, Am Acad, Rome, 87-88; Woodrow Wilson Post Doctoral fel, 87-88, declined; Univ Scholar, USC, 86; Fulbright fel, 76-77. **MEMBERSHIPS** ACSA; Col Art Asn; Soc Arch Hist. **SELECTED PUBLICATIONS** Auth, Architecture After Modernism, Thames & Hudson, 96; Mark Mack, Wasmuth Verlag, 94, monogr; Out of Site: A Social Criticism of Architecture, Bay Press, 91; Building New Communities: New Deal America & Fascist Italy, Princeton, UP, 89; The Case for Letting Malibu Burn, Mortal City, 95; Eisenman's Bogus Avant-Garde, Progressive Arch, 94; Peter Eisenman: Il camouflage dell'avanguardia, Casabella 613, 94; Citta Fascista: Surveillance and Spectacle, J Mod Hist, 94. **CONTACT ADDRESS** School of Archit, Univ of Southern California, University Park Campus, Los Angeles, CA, 90089. **EMAIL** admitusc@usc.edu

GHOSH, RATNA
DISCIPLINE EDUCATION **EDUCATION** Univ Calcutta, BA, 60; Univ Calgary, MA, 73, PhD, 76. **CAREER** Vis prof, Univ Calgary, 76-77; vis prof, OISE, 77; asst prof, 77-81, assoc prof, 81-88, PROF, McGILL UNIV 88-. **HONORS AND AWARDS** Killam predoctoral schol, Univ Calgary, 74; Dame Merit, Order Saint John Jersualem, Knights Malta, 93; Woman Distinction, YWCA, 96. **MEMBERSHIPS** Shastri Indo-Can Inst; Can Human Rights Found; Nat Adv Comt Develop Educ Soc; Comparative & Int Educ Soc. **SELECTED PUBLICATIONS** Auth, Multicultural Policy and Social Integration: South Asian Canadian Women in Indian J Gender Studs, 94; auth, Overview on Women & Development in Women's Studs Encyclopedia, 96; auth, Redefining Multicultural Education, 96. **CONTACT ADDRESS** Dept of Education, McGill Univ, Montreal, PQ, H3A 1Y2. **EMAIL** in3g@musich.mcgill.ca

GIACUMAKIS, GEORGE
PERSONAL Born 07/06/1937, New Castle, PA, m, 1960, 4 children **DISCIPLINE** MEDITERRANEAN STUDIES **EDUCATION** Shelton Col, BA, 59; Brandeis Univ, MA, 61, PhD, 63. **CAREER** Prof, Calif State, Fullerton, 63-78; exec dir, Inst of Holy Land Stud, Jerusalem, 78-84; dir, Mission Viejo Campus, Calif State Univ, Fullerton, 85-98. **HONORS AND AWARDS** Summa cum laude, 59; Who's Who, 90. **MEMBERSHIPS** Am Sci Affil; Bibl Arch Soc; Inst Bibl Res; Middle East Inst; Soc Bibl Lit. **RESEARCH** Middle East studies; Dead Sea Scrolls. **SELECTED PUBLICATIONS** Auth, "Middle East: Cradle of Conflict," video, Bridgestone, 91; "Saladin," World Book Encyclopedia, 93; ed, Bible. International Sandard Version, Davidson, 98. **CONTACT ADDRESS** California State Univ, Fullerton, 28000 Marguerite Pkwy, Mission Viejo, CA, 92692. **EMAIL** ggiacumakis@fullerton.edu

GIBBS, DAVID N.
PERSONAL Born 06/01/1958, New Brunswick, NJ, m, 1994 **DISCIPLINE** POLITICAL SCIENCE **EDUCATION** George Washington Univ, BA, 79; Georgetown Univ, MA, 83; MIT, PhD, 89. **CAREER** MacArthur Postdoctoral Fel, Univ of Wis, Madison, 89-90; ASST PROF OF POLITICAL SCI, 90-96, ASSOC PROF OF POLITICAL SCI, UNIV OF ARIZ, 96-. **HONORS AND AWARDS** Udall Res Fel, Udall Center for Studies in Public Policy, 98. **MEMBERSHIPS** Center for Middle East Studies, Univ of Ariz; Int Studies Asn. **RESEARCH** International relations; U.S. foreign policy; African politics, Middle Eastern politics. **SELECTED PUBLICATIONS** Auth, The Political Economy of Third World Intervention: Mines, Money, and U.S. Policy in the Congo Crisis, Univ of Chicago Press, 91; auth, Is There Room for the Real World in the Postmodernist Universe?, in Squaring the Circle: Int Studies and Ideological Faultlines of the Am Acad, forthcoming-99; auth, The Military-Industrial Complex, Sectoral Conflict, and the Study of U.S. Foreign Policy, in Business and the State in Int Relations, Westview, 96; auth, International Commercial Rivalries and the Zairian Copper Ntionalization of 1967, Review of African Political Economy, 97; auth, Secrecy and International Relations, Journal of Peace Res, 95; auth, Political Parties and Int Relations: The United States and the Decolonization of Subsaharan Africa, Int Hist Review, Univ of Toronto Press, 95; auth, Taking the State Back Out: Reflections on a Tautology, Contention, Ind Univ Press, 94. **CONTACT ADDRESS** Dept of Political Sci, Univ of Ariz, 315 Social Sciences, Tucson, AZ, 85721. **EMAIL** dgibbs@arizona.edu

GIBERT, JOHN C.
DISCIPLINE CLASSICAL HISTORY **EDUCATION** Yale, BA, 82; Harvard, PhD, 91. **CAREER** Asst Prof, 90-92, St Olaf Coll; Asst Prof, 92-, Univ of Colorado, Boulder. **MEMBERSHIPS** Amer Philos Assoc; Class Assoc of the Middle West and South. **RESEARCH** Greek Drama. **SELECTED PUBLICATIONS** Auth, Euripides Hippolytus Plays: Which Came First?, Classical Quarterly 47, pp 80-92, 97; Euripides Hercules 1351 and the Hero's Encounter with Death,, Classical Philology 92, pp 247-58, 97; Change of Mind in Greek Tragedy(Hypomnemata 108), Gottingen, 95; Review of Theseus, Tragedy and the Athenian Empire, by S. Mills, Bryn Mawr Classical Review, 98; Review of Collecting Fragments/Fragmente sammeln, ed, G Most, BMCR, 98; Review of Aristophanes' Birds, ed, N.Dunbar, BMCR 7, 96. **CONTACT ADDRESS** Dept Classics, Univ of Colorado, Boulder, CO, 80309-0348. **EMAIL** John.Gibert@colorado.edu

GIBSON, ANN
DISCIPLINE TWENTIETH-CENTURY AMERICAN AND CONTEMPORARY ART **EDUCATION** Columbia, PhD. **CAREER** Prof, ch. **SELECTED PUBLICATIONS** Auth, Issues in Abstract Expressionism: The Artist-Run Periodicals, UMI, 90; Abstract Expressionism: Other Politics, Yale Univ Press, 97; co-auth, Norman Lewis: The Black Paintings, 98. **CONTACT ADDRESS** Dept of Art Hist, Univ Delaware, 162 Ctr Mall, Newark, DE, 19716. **EMAIL** Ann.Gibson@mvs.udel.edu

GIBSON, WALTER S.
PERSONAL Born 03/31/1932, Columbus, OH, m, 1972 **DISCIPLINE** ART HISTORY **EDUCATION** Ohio State Univ, BFA, 57, MA, 60; Harvard Univ, PhD, 69. **CAREER** Asst prof, 66-71; assoc prof, 71-78, act chair dept art, 70- 71, chair, 71-79, Andrew W. Mellow prof hum, 78-97, PROF EMER, 97-, CASE WESTERN RESERVE UNIV; Murphy Lectr, Univ Kans, Nelson- Atkins Mus ARt, 88; Clark vis prof, Williams Col, 89, 92. **HONORS AND AWARDS** Fulbright Scholarship, Rijksuniversiteit, Utrecht, 60-61; Guggenheim fel, 78-79; Fulbright res grant, Belgium, 84; fel, Netherlands Inst Adv Stud, 95-96. **RESEARCH** Dutch, Flemish painting **SELECTED PUBLICATIONS** Auth, Peter Bruegel the Elder: Two Studies, Franklin D. Murphy LEcture XI, Univ Kans, 91; auth, Hieronymus Bosch, Thames and Hudson, 73, Praeger, 73, reprint, 88, Ger ed, 74, Dutch ed, 74, Jap ed, 89, Span ed (El Bosco), 93, Fr ed (Jerome Bosch), 95, Finnish ed, Czeck ed, Hungarian ed, Rus ed, forthcoming. **CONTACT ADDRESS** RR2., No. 461H, Pownal, VT, 05261-9767. **EMAIL** wsgibson@together.net

GIEBELHAUS, AUGUST WILLIAM
PERSONAL Born 06/01/1943, Rahway, NJ, m, 1967, 2 children **DISCIPLINE** AMERICAN AND ECONOMIC HISTORY **EDUCATION** Rutgers Univ, BA, 64, MA, 70; Univ Del, PhD(hist), 77. **CAREER** Teacher hist, Union County Regional High Sch Dist, Springfield, NJ, 64-71; Hagley fel econ hist, Eleutherian Mills Hagley Found, 71-74 and 75-76; lectr, Univ Birmingham, UK, 74-75; asst prof hist, 76-80, ASSOC PROF HIST, GA INST TECHNOL, 80-, Adj instr, Univ Col, Rutgers Univ, 69-71; asst ed, Technol and Cult, 77-78, assoc ed, 79-81; assoc, Hist Assoc Inc, Washington, DC, 80-. **MEMBERSHIPS** AHA; Econ Hist Asn; Nat Coun Pub hist; Orgn Am Historians; Soc Hist Technol. **RESEARCH** History of American business; energy history; petroleum industry. **SELECTED PUBLICATIONS** Auth, Nordic Energy-Systems--Historical Perspectives and Current Issues, Technol and Cult, Vol 0037, 96; Georgia-Tech Years, Technol and Cult, Vol 0037, 96; Kranzberg,Melvin (22 November 1917-6 December 1995)--Obituary, Soc Stud of Sci, Vol 0026, 96. **CONTACT ADDRESS** Sch of Soc Sci Ga Inst of Technol, 225 North Ave N W, Atlanta, GA, 30332-0002.

GIFFIN, FREDERICK CHARLES
PERSONAL Born 09/10/1938, Pittsburgh, PA, m, 1959, 2 children **DISCIPLINE** RUSSIAN HISTORY **EDUCATION** Denison Univ, BA, 60; Emory Univ, MA, 61, PhD(hist), 65. **CAREER** Vis instr hist, Agnes Scott Col, 63-64; from instr to asst prof, Southern Methodist Univ, 64-67; from asst prof to assoc prof, 67-74, asst dean, Grad Col, 70-72, PROF HIST, ARIZ STATE UNIV, 74-, CHMN DEPT, 82-86. **HONORS AND AWARDS** Grad Coun of Humanities fel, Southern Methodist Univ, 66-67; Outstanding Educr Am Award, 73 **RESEARCH** Russian factory legislation; Soviet-American relations. **SELECTED PUBLICATIONS** Auth, The formative years of the Russian factory inspectorate, 1882-1885, Slavic Rev, 12/66; The prohibition of night work for women and young persons: The Russian Factory Law of June 3, 1885, Can Slavic Studies, summer 68; co-ed, Against the Grain, New Am Libr, 71; auth, I I Yanzhul: Russia's first district factory inspector, Slavonic & East Europ Rev, 1/71; ed, Woman as revolutionary, New Am Libr, 73; auth, Six Who Protested, Kennikat, 77; ed, The Tongue of Angels, Susquehanna Univ Press, 88; auth, James Putnam Goodrich and Soviet Russia, Mid-Am, 10/89; An American Railroad Man East of the Urals, 1918-1922, The Hist, Summer 98. **CONTACT ADDRESS** Dept of History, Arizona State Univ, Tempe, PO Box 872501, Tempe, AZ, 85287-2501. **EMAIL** mfgiff@asu.edu

GIFFIN, WILLIAM WAYNE
PERSONAL Born 04/06/1938, Bellaire, OH, w, 2 children **DISCIPLINE** AMERICAN HISTORY **EDUCATION** Col Wooster, BA, 60; Ohio State Univ, BSEd, 62, MA, 63, PhD(hist), 68. **CAREER** Prof Ethnic Hist, Ind State Univ, 68- **MEMBERSHIPS** Orgn Am Hist; Ind Asn Hist. **RESEARCH** African-American history; immigration. **SELECTED PUBLICATIONS** Auth, Black insurgency in the Republican Party of Ohio, 1920-1932, Ohio Hist, 73; The Mercy Hospital controversy among Cleveland's Afro-American, J Negro Hist, 76; Mobilization of Black militiamen in World War I: Ohio's Ninth Battalion, The Historian, 78; The Political Realignment of Black Voters in Indianapolis, 1924, Ind Mag Hist, 6/83; coauth, Centennial History of the Indiana General Assembly: Three Review Essays, Ind Mag Hist, 12/88; auth, Irish, In: Peopling Indiana: The Ethnic Experience, Ind Hist Soc, 96. **CONTACT ADDRESS** Dept of Hist, Indiana State Univ, 210 N 7th St, Terre Haute, IN, 47809-0002. **EMAIL** HIGIFFN@Ruby.indstate.edu

GIFFORD, BERNARD R.
PERSONAL Born 05/18/1943, Brooklyn, NY, m **DISCIPLINE** **EDUCATION** Long Island Univ, BS 1965; Univ of Rochester Med Sch, MS 1968; Univ of Rochester Med Sch, PhD 1972. **CAREER** Univ of California at Berkeley, prof, currently; Academic Systems Corp, chmn, currently; Russell Sage Found, resident scholar, beginning 1977; New York City Public School System, deputy chancellor & chief of business affairs office 1973-77; New York City Rand Inst, pres 1972-73. **HONORS AND AWARDS** Phi Beta Kappa. **MEMBERSHIPS** Adv Com, John F Kennedy Inst of Politics, Harvard Univ; bd of visitors, City Coll of NY; bd of trustees, NY Univ; acad adv com, US Naval Academy; consultant, CA Supreme Court, 1978-79; consultant, Asst Sec for Com Planning & Devt, Dept of Housing & Urban Devt, 1979; consultant, Natl Acad of Public Admin, 1979-80; consultant, Natl Inst of Educ; bd of dirs, NY Urban Coalition; bd of trustees, German Marshall Fund of US; editorial bd, Urban Affairs Quarterly; bd of edit advs NY Affairs; editorial bd, NY Educ Quarterly; editorial bd, policy Analysis; appointed adj prof, public admin, Columbia Univ, 1975-77; appointed adj lecturer, Public Policy, John F Kennedy School of Govt, Harvard Univ, 1977-78; appointed adjunct & visiting prof, Dept of Urban Studies &Planning, Hunter Coll, City Univ oY, MA Inst of Tech; US Atomic Energy Comm, Fellow in Nuclear Science, 1965-71. **SELECTED PUBLICATIONS** Co-author, "Revenue Sharing & the Planning Process" 1974; author, "The Urbanization of Poverty: A Preliminary Investigation of Shifts in the Distribution of the Poverty Population by Race Residence & Family Structure," 1980; numerous other publications. **CONTACT ADDRESS** Dept Educ, Univ of California, Berkeley, Tolman Hall, Berkeley, CA, 94720.

GIGLIO, JAMES NICHOLAS
PERSONAL Born 03/28/1939, Akron, OH, m, 1965, 2 children **DISCIPLINE** AMERICAN HISTORY **EDUCATION** Kent State Univ, BA, 61, MA, 64; Ohio State Univ, PhD(Am hist), 68. **CAREER** From asst prof to assoc prof, 68-78, PROF AM HIST, SOUTHWEST MO STATE UNIV, 78-. **MEMBERSHIPS** Orgn Am Hist; AAUP. **RESEARCH** Twentieth century United States political history. **SELECTED PUBLICATIONS** Auth, Nixon--Ruin and Recovery, 1973-1990, Historian, Vol 0055, 93; Guide to Historical Materials in the Gerald-R-Ford-Library, J Am Hist, Vol 0079, 93; The Missiles of October--The Declassified Story of Kennedy, John, F and the Cuban Missile Crisis, Am Hist Rev, Vol 0098, 93; Hoover, Herbert--A Bibliography of His Times and Presidency, J Am Hist, Vol 0079, 93; Eisenhower, Dwight, D.--A Bibliography of His Times and Presidency, J Am Hist, Vol 0079, 93; JFK--Reckless Youth, J Am Hist, Vol 0080, 93; Truman, Harry, S--A Life, J Am Hist, Vol 0082, 95; President Kennedy--Profile of Power, Historian, Vol 0058, 95; The Kennedy Persuasion--The Politics of Style Since JFK, Am Hist Rev, Vol 0101, 96; Them Damned Pictures--Explorations in American Political Cartoon Art, Am Hist Rev, Vol 0102, 97. **CONTACT ADDRESS** Dept of Hist, Southwest Mo State Univ, Springfield, MO, 65802.

GILB, CORINNE LATHROP
PERSONAL Born 02/19/1925, Lethbridge, AB, Canada, m, 1945, 2 children **DISCIPLINE** URBAN AND COMPARATIVE HISTORY **EDUCATION** Univ Wash, BA, 46; Univ Calif, Berkeley, MA, 51; Radcliffe Col, PhD(Am civilization), 57. **CAREER** Researcher, Calif State Bar, 49-51; asst hist, Univ Calif, Berkeley, 50-52, head oral hist proj, 53-57; lectr hist, Mills Col, 57-61; prof humanities, San Francisco State Col, 64-67; PROF HIST, WAYNE STATE UNIV, 68-, CO-DIR URBAN STUDIES AND SPEC ADV LAW/HIST PROG, 76-, Res polit scientist labor mgt, Inst Indust Rels, 56-59 and Ctr Studies Law and Soc, 60-66; Soc Sci Res Coun grant, 58; Guggenheim fel, 67; spec consult, Interim Comt Revenue and Taxation, Calif Assembly, 63-64; dir, Planning Dept Detroit, 79. **MEMBERSHIPS** AHA; Orgn Am Historians; Int Soc Comp Study of Civilizations; Soc Am Legal Historians; Soc Sci Hist Asn. **RESEARCH** Comparative world cities; legal history; comparative United States and European history. **SELECTED PUBLICATIONS** Auth, Notebook of a 60s Lawyer--An Unrepentant Memoir and Selected-Writings, Mich Hist Rev, Vol 0018, 92, Layered Violence--The Detroit Rioters of 1943, J Am Ethnic Hist, Vol 0013, 94. **CONTACT ADDRESS** Dept of Hist, Wayne State Univ, Detroit, MI, 48202.

GILBERT, ARLAN KEMMERER
PERSONAL Born 06/29/1933, Emmaus, PA, m, 1959, 3 children **DISCIPLINE** UNITED STATES HISTORY **EDUCATION** Susquehanna Univ, BA, 55; Univ Del, MA, 57. **CAREER** Asst prof, 60-64, chmn dept, 64-70, assoc prof, 64-88, prof us hist, Hillsdale Col, 88-98, WILLIAM AND BERNIECE

GREWCOCK PROF AM HIST, 95-98, PROF EMER, 98-; Teaching asst hist, Univ Wis, 57-59; dir, Model UN assembly for high schs of Mich & Northern Ohio, 60-70. **RESEARCH** American economic history from the colonial period to the Civil War; United States constitutional history; sectionalism and the American Civil War. **SELECTED PUBLICATIONS** Auth, Oliver Evans Memoir on the Origin of Steam Boats and Steam Wagons, Del Hist, 56; auth, Gunpowder Production in post-Revolutionary Maryland, Md Hist Mag, 57; auth, Historic Hillsdale Col, 91; auth, The Permanent Things, 98. **CONTACT ADDRESS** 33 E College St, Hillsdale, MI, 49242-1298.

GILBERT, BENTLEY BRINKERHOFF
PERSONAL Born 04/05/1924, Mansfield, OH, m, 1968, 4 children **DISCIPLINE** HISTORY **EDUCATION** Miami Univ, BA, 49; Univ Cincinnati, MA, 50; Univ Wis, PhD(hist), 54. **CAREER** Instr hist, Univ Cincinnati, 54-55; from asst prof to assoc prof, Colo Col, 55-67; assoc prof, 67-69, PROF HIST, UNIV ILL, CHICAGO CIRCLE, 69-, Nat Inst Health res grant, 62-; consult, Hist Life Sci Studies Group, Nat Inst Health, 72-76; Royal Hist Soc fel, 73; John Simon Guggenheim Found fel, 73-74; exec secy, Conf Brit Studies, 74-78; ed, J Brit Studies, 78. **MEMBERSHIPS** AHA; Conf Brit Studies. **RESEARCH** Twentieth century British social and institutional history; life of David Lloyd George. **SELECTED PUBLICATIONS** Auth, T.J., A Life of Jones, Thomas, Albion, Vol 0025, 1993; Boothby, Robert--A Portrait of Churchill Ally, Historian, Vol 0055, 93; The Peoples Peace--British History, 1945-1989, J Mod Hist, Vol 0065, 93; Parliament and Politics in the Age of Baldwin and Macdonald--The Headlam Diaries, 1923-1935, Albion, Vol 0025, 93; Aspects of Aristocracy, Grandeur and Decline in Modern Britain, Albion, Vol 0026, 94; London Burning--Life, Death and Art in World-War-2, Historian, Vol 0057, 95; The Strategy of the Lloyd-George Coalition, 1916-1918, Albion, Vol 0028, 96; Attlee, Clement, Historian, Vol 0059, 97. **CONTACT ADDRESS** Dept of Hist, Univ of Ill Chicago Circle, Chicago, IL, 60680.

GILBERT, JAMES BURKHART
PERSONAL Born 05/23/1939, Chicago, IL, m, 1964, 2 children **DISCIPLINE** AMERICAN & INTELLECTUAL HISTORY **EDUCATION** Carleton Col, BA, 61; Univ Wis-Madison, MA, 63, PhD(Am hist), 66. **CAREER** From asst prof to assoc prof hist, Univ Md, College Park, 66-71; vis prof social studies, Teachers Col, Columbia Univ, 68-69; vis lectr social hist, Univ Warwick, 71-72; Prof Hist, Univ Md, College Park, 72-; consult, Nat Pub Radio, 77-78. **HONORS AND AWARDS** Nat Endowment for Humanities younger scholar, 68-69; Fulbright Teaching Fel to Sydney Univ, Australia, 87; Walt Whitman Prof, the Netherlands, 91; Distinguished Prof, Uppsala Univ, Sweden, 98. **MEMBERSHIPS** AHA; O.A.H. **RESEARCH** American cultural history; progressive era; 20th century. **SELECTED PUBLICATIONS** Auth, Writers and Partisans, Wiley, 68 (republished, Columbia Univ Press, 92); Designing the Industrial State, Quadrangle, 72; Work Without Salvation, Johns Hopkins Univ Press, 78; coauth, Pursuit of Liberty, Random House, 83 (republished, Wadsworth, 89; Harper/Collins, 95); auth, A Cycle of Outrage, Oxford, 86; Perfect Cities, Chicago, 91; co-ed, Mythmaking Frame of Mind, Wadsworth, 93; auth, Redeeming Culture, Chicago, 97. **CONTACT ADDRESS** Dept of Hist, Univ of Md, College Park, MD, 20742-0001. **EMAIL** jg19@umail.umd.edu

GILBERT, JAMES L.
PERSONAL Born 02/02/1970, Marietta, GA, m, 1996 **DISCIPLINE** PSYCHOLOGY **EDUCATION** Univ W Al, BS, 76, MS, 96 **CAREER** Vis prof, Univ W Al **HONORS AND AWARDS** EMS Instr of the Year, 97; Prof of the Year, 98. **MEMBERSHIPS** Int Critical Incident Stress Found; Int Assoc of Police Counselors/Chaplains; Amer Psychol Assoc. **RESEARCH** Critical incident stress etiology & treatment **CONTACT ADDRESS** Univ W Al, Station 22, Livingston, AL, 35470. **EMAIL** jlg@uwamail.westal.edu

GILBERT, ROBERT EMILE
PERSONAL Born 10/20/1939, New York, NY **DISCIPLINE** POLITICAL SCIENCE **EDUCATION** Fordham Univ, BA (political science), 61, MA (political science), 63; Univ MA, Amherst, PhD (political science), 67. **CAREER** Instr, Boston Col, 65-67, asst prof, 67-73; assoc prof, 73-82, prof of Political Science, Northeastern Univ, 82-. **HONORS AND AWARDS** Phi Kappa Phi;Excellence in Teaching Award, 84; Kennedy Found grantee, 95. **MEMBERSHIPS** Int Soc of Political Psychology; Am Political Science Asn; Center for Study of Presidency. **RESEARCH** Am politics (presidency, mass media). **SELECTED PUBLICATIONS** Auth, Travails of the Chief: Killer Stress Plagues the White House, The Sciences, Feb 93; JFK and Addison's, MD, Noiv 93; The Political Effects of Presidential Illness: The Case of Lyndon B Johnson, Political Psychology, Dec 95; The Physical and Psychological Ailments of Lyndon B Johnson: The Years of Ascent, Presidential Studies Quart, summer 96; Presidential Disability: The Case of John F Kennedy, in Papers on Presidential Disability and the Twenty-Fifth Amendment, Kenneth W Thompson, ed, Univ Press of Am, 96; John F Kennedy: Moral leadership in Civil Rights, in Leadership for the Public Service: Power and Policy in Action, Richard A Loverd, ed, Simon & Schuster, 96; Presidential Disability in Law and Politics: Lessons from 1992, Miller Center J, spring 98; The Mortal Presidency: Illness and Anguish in the White House, 2nd edn, Fordham Univ Press, 98. **CONTACT ADDRESS** Dept of Political Science, Northeastern Univ, Boston, MA, 02115. **EMAIL** rgilbert@lynx.neu.edu

GILDEMEISTER, GLEN A.
PERSONAL Born 05/08/1945, Racine, WI, m, 1968, 2 children **DISCIPLINE** HISTORY **EDUCATION** Univ Wis, BS, 68; Northern Ill Univ, MA, 72, PhD(hist), 77. **CAREER** Co-dir labor hist, Ohio Hist Soc, 75-77; DIR HIST, NORTHERN ILL REGIONAL HIST CTR, 77- **MEMBERSHIPS** Soc Am Archivists; Midwest Archives Conf; Orgn Am Historians. **RESEARCH** Labor history; prison history; regional history. **SELECTED PUBLICATIONS** Auth, Preliminary guide to sources in Ohio labor history, 76 & Labor archives manual, 78, Ohio Hist Soc; The founding of the American Federation of Labor, Labor Hist, 78. **CONTACT ADDRESS** Libr, No Illinois Regional Historical Ctr, 1425 W Lincoln Hwy, De Kalb, IL, 60115-2825.

GILDERHUS, MARK THEODORE
PERSONAL Born 11/15/1941, Rochester, MN, m, 1967 **DISCIPLINE** AMERICAN HISTORY **EDUCATION** Gustavus Adolphus Col, BA, 63; Univ Nebr, MA, 65, PhD(Am hist), 68. **CAREER** Asst prof, 68-73, assoc prof, 73-78, PROF HIST, COLO STATE UNIV, 78-, CHMN, DEPT HIST, 80- **MEMBERSHIPS** AHA; Orgn Am Hist; Conf Latin Am Hist; Soc Hist Am Foreign Rels. **RESEARCH** United States foreign relations, particularly with Latin America; recent United States; United States military history. **SELECTED PUBLICATIONS** Auth, Shoulder to Shoulder, the American-Federation-of-Labor, the United-States, and the Mexican-Revolution, 1910-1924, Hisp Am Hist Rev, Vol 0073, 93; To End All Wars--Wilson,Woodrow and the Quest for a New-World Order, J Am Hist, Vol 0080, 1994; The Premise and the Promise--Free-Trade in the America, Hisp Am Hist Rev, Vol 0074, 94; The Organization-of-American-States, Hisp Am Hist Rev, Vol 0075, 95; FDR Good Neighbor Policy--60 Years of Generally Gentle Chaos, Hisp Am Hist Rev, Vol 0076, 96; Silencing the Past, Power and the Production of History, Americas, Vol 0053, 96; Founding-Father: Society-for-Historians-of-American-Foreign-Relations--Bemis, Samuel, Flagg and the Study of US Latin-American Relations--Presidential-Address, Diplomatic Hist, Vol 0021, 97; Oil, Banks, and Politics--The United-States and Postrevolutionary Mexico, 1917-1924, Americas, Vol 0053, 97. **CONTACT ADDRESS** Dept of Hist, Colorado State Univ, Fort Collins, CO, 80523-0001.

GILDRIC, RICHARD P.
PERSONAL Born 04/18/1945, Norfolk, VA, m, 1966, 2 children **DISCIPLINE** HISTORY & PHILOSOPHY **EDUCATION** Eckerd Col, BA, 66; Univ Va, MA, 68, PhD, 71. **CAREER** Prof, Austin Peay State Univ, 70-. **HONORS AND AWARDS** Kenneth S. Lafaurette Prize. **MEMBERSHIPS** OIEAHC; OAH; AHA; AAUP **RESEARCH** Colonial America; early modern Britian. **SELECTED PUBLICATIONS** Auth, The Profane, The Civil & the Godly: The Reformation of Manners in Orthodox New England 1679-1749, 94. **CONTACT ADDRESS** Dept of History & Philosophy, Austin Peay State Univ, Clarksville, TN, 37044. **EMAIL** gildrier@apsu01.apsu.edu

GILES, GEOFFREY JOHN
PERSONAL Born 08/08/1947, Bournemouth, England **DISCIPLINE** MODERN EUROPEAN HISTORY **EDUCATION** Univ London, BA Hons, 69; Univ Cambridge, cert educ, 70, PhD(hist), 75. **CAREER** Fel, Yale Univ, Yale Higher Educ Res Group, 75-76, res assoc, 76-78 and lectr hist, Yale Col, 76; vis asst prof, 78-79, ASST PROF HIST, UNIV FLA, 79-, Vis fel, Silliman Col, Yale Univ, 76 and res affil, Yale Higher Educ Res Group, 78-80. **MEMBERSHIPS** AHA; Cambridge Hist Soc; Deut Ges fur Hochschulkunde; Soc Hist Soc; Western Asn Ger Studies. **RESEARCH** Modern Germany; history of European higher education. **SELECTED PUBLICATIONS** Auth, The Gestapo and German Society--Enforcing Racial Policy, 1933-1945, J Mod Hist, Vol 0065, 93; Crisis, Radical Change, New Beginning--A Critical and Self-Critical Documentation of GDR Historiography, 1989-1990, Ger Stud Rev, Vol 0017, 94; From Scholar to Public Official, Career Paths and Social-Status of Heidelberg Professors 1914-1933, Am Hist Rev, Vol 0099, 94; Professors and Politics--Political Thinking and Activities of Heidelberg Professors 1914-1935, Am Hist Rev, Vol 0099, 94; The Power of Drunkenness--Cultural and Social-History of Alcohol in Germany, Am Hist Rev, Vol 0101, 96; The Racial State--Germany, 1933-1945, Ger Stud Rev, Vol 0019, 96; Reforming Sex--The German Movement for Birth-Control and Abortion Reform, 1920-1950, Ger Stud Rev, Vol 0020, 97. **CONTACT ADDRESS** Dept of Hist, Univ of Fla, P O Box 117320, Gainesville, FL, 32611-7320.

GILFOYLE, TIMOTHY J.
DISCIPLINE HISTORY **EDUCATION** Columbia Univ, BA, 79, PhD, 87. **CAREER** Assoc prof; assoc ed, J Urban Hist; ed bd(s), The Encycl NY City, Yale Univ Press, 95, Mid-Am, & Stud in Sport and Leisure, Syracuse UP; John Simon Guggenheim Memorial Foun fel, 98-99; sr fel, Mus Am Hist & Smithsonian Inst, 97; NEH-Lloyd Lewis fel, Newberry Libr Chicago, 93-94. **HONORS AND AWARDS** Allan Nevins Prize, Soc Am Hist; Best Manuscript Prize, NY State Hist Asn. **MEMBERSHIPS** Bd dir(s), Chicago Metro Hist Edu Center. **RESEARCH** Late nineteenth-century American city. **SELECTED PUBLICATIONS** Auth, City of Eros: New York City, Prostitution, and the Commercialization of Sex, 1790-1920, NY: W.W. Norton, 92; White Cities, Linguistic Turns, and Disneylands: New Paradigms in Urban History; articles in, Am Quart, Prospects, NY Hist, Miss Rev, & Chicago Hist. **CONTACT ADDRESS** Fine Arts Dept, Loyola Univ, Chicago, 6525 N. Sheridan Rd. 6525 North Sheridan Rd., Chicago, IL, 6062660626. **EMAIL** tgilfoy@orion.it.luc.edu

GILGEN, ALBERT R.
PERSONAL Born 09/19/1930, Akron, OH, m, 1954, 3 children **DISCIPLINE** PSYCHOLOGY **EDUCATION** Princeton Univ, BA, 52; Kent State, MA, 63; Mich State, PhD, 65. **CAREER** Beloit Col, asst, assoc prof, 65-73; Univ Northern Iowa, prof dept hd, Psych, 73-93, prof, 93-. **HONORS AND AWARDS** Fulbright Hays Exch Lectr, Galway Ireland; Distg Schol, Univ N Iowa. **MEMBERSHIPS** APA; APS. **RESEARCH** Hist of Psychol **SELECTED PUBLICATIONS** Soviet and American Psychology during World War II, with C K Carol, VA Koltsova, Y N Olenik, Westport CT Greenwood Press, 97; Post Soviet Perspectives on Russian Psychology, with V A Koltsova, Y N Olenik, C K Gilgen, Westport Ct Greenwood Press, 96; Chaos Theory in Psychology, with F D Abraham, eds, Westport CT Greenwood Press, 95. **CONTACT ADDRESS** Dept Psychology, Univ Northern Iowa, Cedar Falls, IA, 50613. **EMAIL** albert.gilgen@uni.edu

GILINSKY, JOSHUA
PERSONAL Born 10/21/1959, New York, NY **DISCIPLINE** MUSIC THEORY **EDUCATION** Harvard Univ, BA, 81; Manhattan Sch Mus, 90. **CAREER** Asst Ed Dir, Opera Co Boston, 82; Tchg Fel Boston Univ, 84; Compos, Theory and Ear Training Fac, Manhattan Sch Mus Prep Div, 87-98. **HONORS AND AWARDS** Saul Braverman Award for Outstanding Achievement in Mus Theory, Columbia Univ; Pres Fellow. **MEMBERSHIPS** Soc for Mus Theory; Am Musicol Soc. **RESEARCH** Methodological Construction; Orchestration **SELECTED PUBLICATIONS** Unity and Opposition in the Orchestration of Tchaikovsky's Romeo and Juliet Overture, 90. **CONTACT ADDRESS** Columbia Univ, 609 Dodge Hall, New York, NY, 10027. **EMAIL** jeg13@columbia.edu

GILJE, PAUL ARN
PERSONAL Brooklyn, NY, m, 1973, 1 child **DISCIPLINE** AMERICAN HISTORY **EDUCATION** City Univ New York, BA, 74; Brown Univ, AM, 75, PhD(hist), 80. **CAREER** ASST PROF HIST, UNIV OKLA, 80-. **MEMBERSHIPS** Orgn Am Historians; Am Hist Soc; Soc Historians Early Repub; Inst Early Am Hist & Cult. **RESEARCH** Early America; social history; popular culture. **SELECTED PUBLICATIONS** Auth, Before the Melting Pot--Society and Culture in Colonial New-York-City, 1664-1730, Am Hist Rev, Vol 0097, 92; Perry of London--A Family on the Seaborne Frontier, 1615-1753, Rev in Am Hist, Vol 0021, 93; Did Pocahontas Save Smith, John, Miss Quart, Vol 0047, 94; The American-Dream of Smith, John, Miss Quart, Vol 0047, 94; Sweep-O-Sweep-O, African-American Chimney Sweeps and Citizenship in the New Nation, William and Mary Quart, Vol 0051, 94; The Orange Riots--Irish Political Violence in New-York-City, 1870 and 1871, J Am Hist, Vol 0081, 95; On the Waterfront--Maritime Workers in New-York-City in the Early Republic, 1800-1850, NY Hist, Vol 0077, 96; Yankee Sailors in British Jails--Prisoners of War At Forton and Mill, 1773-1783, Am Neptune, Vol 0056, 96; The Transforming Hand of Revolution--Reconsidering the American-Revolution as a Social-Movement, Pa Mag of Hist and Biogr, Vol 0121, 97; The Conundrum of Class--Political Discourse on the Social-Order, Labor Hist, Vol 0038, 97; Clinton, De, Witt and the Rise of the Peoples Men, William and Mary Quart, Vol 0054, 97. **CONTACT ADDRESS** Dept of Hist, Univ of Okla, 455 W Lindsey St, Norman, OK, 73019-2000.

GILL, GERALD ROBERT
PERSONAL Born 11/18/1948, New Rochelle, NY, d **DISCIPLINE** HISTORY **EDUCATION** Lafayette Coll, AB 1966-70; Howard Univ, MA 1974, PhD 1985. **CAREER** City School Dist, New Rochelle NY, social studies teacher 1970-72; Inst for the Study of Educ Policy, research asst 1976-78, research fellow 1978-79; TUFTS UNIV, DEPARTMENT OF HISTORY, ASSOC PROF, 1980-. **HONORS AND AWARDS** Massachusetts College Professor of the Year, 1995. **MEMBERSHIPS** Consult NAACP 1979; consult Ohio Hist Society 1980-85; Office of American Historians; American Hist Assn; Southern Hist Assn; Assn for the Study of Afro-American Life and History; Natl Assn for the Advancement of Colored People. **SELECTED PUBLICATIONS** Co-author: The Case for Affirmative Action for Blacks in Higher Ed 1978; author Meanness Mania 1980; author: The Rightward Drift in Amer in the State of Black America Natl Urban League 1981; co-editor: Eyes On the Prize Civil Rights Reader, 1991. **CONTACT ADDRESS** Dept of History, Tufts Univ, Medford, MS, 02155.

GILL, MARY LOUISE
PERSONAL Born 07/31/1950, Alton, IL, m, 1995 **DISCIPLINE** ANCIENT PHILOSOPHY/CLASSICS **EDUCATION** Barnard Coll, BA, 72; Columbia Univ, MA, 74; Cambridge Univ, PhD 81. **CAREER** Asst prof, Univ Pittsburgh, 81-88; assoc prof, 88-94; prof, 94-. **HONORS AND AWARDS** Chancellor's Distinguished Res Award, Univ of Pittsburgh, 90; Ethel Wattis Kimbal Felhips, Stanford Humanities center, 85-86. **MEMBERSHIPS** Am Philol Asn; Am Philos Asn. **RESEARCH** Ancient Philosophy. **SELECTED PUBLICATIONS** Auth, Aristotle on Substance: The Paradox of Unity, 89; co-translator, Plato: Parmenides, 96; co-ed, self-Motion, From Aristotle to Newton, 94; Unity, Identity, and Explanation in Aristotle's Metaphysics, 94. **CONTACT ADDRESS** Classics Dept, Univ of Pittsburgh, Pittsburgh, PA, 15280. **EMAIL** mlgill@fas.harvard.edu

GILLESPIE, ANGUS K.
PERSONAL Born 04/25/1942, Bryn Mawr, PA, m, 1986, 2 children **DISCIPLINE** AMERICAN CIVILIZATION **EDUCATION** Yale Univ, BA, 64; Univ Pa, PhD, 75. **CAREER** Faculty of Arts & Sci, Rutgers, 73-75; Asst Prof, 75-81; Assoc Prof, 81-. **HONORS AND AWARDS** NJ Hist Commission Award of recognition, 80; Fulbright Award to Philippines, 85-86; travel grants, Partners of the Am, 93; Pres Award for Dist Public Service, Ruitgers Univ, 91; travel grant to Rep of Trinidad & Tobago, US Info Agency, 97; US Speaker & Specialist Grant ot Philippines, US Info Agncy, 98; Douglass Medal, Douglass Col, 98., Pub, New Jersey Folklife: A Statewide Journal; Dir, NJ Folk Festival, 75-. **MEMBERSHIPS** Am Folklore Soc; Am Stud Assoc; Am Asn of Univ Prof; Mid Atl Folklore Soc (vp 80-81, pres, 84-85); Pa Folklore Soc (acting pres 79-80); NJ Folklore Soc (exec committee, 80-85). **RESEARCH** Folklore; regionalism; transportation; engineeering. **SELECTED PUBLICATIONS** Auth, The Jersey Devil is in the Details, NJ Outdoors, 20:4, 93; auth, Stamp Out These Heroes, Rutgers Mag, 76:4, 96; contributor, American Folklore: An Encyclopedia, Garland Publishing, 96; co-auth, Rooted in American Soil: Plants in Symbol and Story, in press. **CONTACT ADDRESS** Dept of Am Stud, Rutgers Univ, 131 George St, New Brunswick, NJ, 08901-1414. **EMAIL** angusgi@rci.rutgers.edu

GILLETT, MARGARET
PERSONAL Wingham, Australia **DISCIPLINE** EDUCATION **EDUCATION** Univ Sydney, BA, 50, Dip Educ, 51; New South Wales Tchr Cert, 52; Russell Sage, Troy, NY, MA, 58; Columbia Univ, EdD, 61. **CAREER** Tchr, Eng & Hist, 51-53, educ off, 54-57, Australia; asst prof, educ, Dalhousie Univ, 61-62; assoc prof, educ, 64-67, ch, dept hist & philos educ, 66-68, prof, 67-82, Macdonald Prof Educ, 82-94, PROF EMER, MCGILL UNIV, 95-. **HONORS AND AWARDS** 75th Anniversary Medal, contrib feminism & higher educ Women, Russell Sage NY, 91; Women Distinction, YWCA, 94; LLD, Univ Sask, 88. **MEMBERSHIPS** Comp Int Educ Soc Can; Am Educ Studs Asn; Can Hist Educ Asn; Can Res Inst Advan Women; Can Women's Studs Asn. **SELECTED PUBLICATIONS** Auth, A History of Education: Thought and Practice, 66; auth, We Walked Very Warily: A History of Women at McGill, 81; auth, Dear Grace: A Romance of History, 86; coauth, A Fair Shake Revisited, 96. **CONTACT ADDRESS** Dept of Educ Studies, McGill Univ, Montreal, PQ, H3A 1Y2. **EMAIL** ingi@musich.mcgill.ca

GILLETTE, WILLIAM
PERSONAL Born 03/02/1933, Bridgeport, CT, m, 1971, 2 children **DISCIPLINE** AMERICAN POLITICAL HISTORY **EDUCATION** Georgetown Univ, BSFS, 55; Columbia Univ, MA, 56; Princeton Univ, MA, 61, PhD(hist), 63. **CAREER** Instr hist, Ohio State Univ, 62-65; actg asst prof, Univ Conn, 65-66; asst prof, Brooklyn Col, 66-67; assoc prof, 67-81, PROF HIST, RUTGERS UNIV, 81-, City Univ New York res grant, 67; Am Philos Soc Penrose Fund grants, 67, 69 and 70; Rutgers Univ Res Coun grants, 68-78, 82; Soc Sci Res Coun fac fel, 70-71; Fulbright prof, Univ Salzburg, 82-83. **HONORS AND AWARDS** Landry Award, 79; Chastain Award, 80. **MEMBERSHIPS** Orgn Am Hist; Southern Hist Asn; AHA; Western Hist Asn; AAUP. **RESEARCH** Reconstruction political history; Civil War; American western history. **SELECTED PUBLICATIONS** Auth, Untitled, J Am Hist, Vol 0083, 96. **CONTACT ADDRESS** Dept of Hist, Rutgers Univ, New Brunswick, NJ, 08903.

GILLIAM, BRYAN
PERSONAL Born 04/23/1953, Lexington, KY, m, 2 children **DISCIPLINE** MUSICOLOGY **EDUCATION** Univ Cincinnati, Bmus, 75; Harvard, AM, 78, PhD, 84. **CAREER** Assoc Prof, Dir Graduate Studies, Dept Music, Duke Univ. **HONORS AND AWARDS** NEH; DAAD Mellon Teaching Award. **MEMBERSHIPS** Am Musicol Soc; Int Richard-Strauss Soc. **RESEARCH** German opera (19th and 20th century); Richard Strauss; Kurt Weill; Anton Bruckner; Hollywood film music. **SELECTED PUBLICATIONS** Various publ: Musical Quarterly, JAMS, 19th-Century Music, and others; Author; Richard Strauss's Elektra, Oxford, 91, 96; Richard Strauss and His World, Princeton, 92; Richard Strauss: New Perspectives, Duke, 92; Music and Performance during the Weimar Republic, Cambridge, 94; The Life of Richard Strauss, Cambridge, 99. **CONTACT ADDRESS** Dept of Music, Duke Univ, 73 Biddle Music Bldg, Durham, NC, 27708. **EMAIL** bgilliam@acpub.duke.edu

GILLIARD, FRANK DANIEL
PERSONAL Born 02/13/1937, Jacksonville, FL **DISCIPLINE** ANCIENT HISTORY **EDUCATION** Univ Fla, BA, 57; Univ Calif, Berkeley, MA, 61, PhD(ancient hist), 66. **CAREER** From asst prof to assoc prof, 66-76, PROF ANCIENT HIST, CALIF STATE UNIV, HAYWARD, 76-, CHMN, DEPT HIST, 80-, Vis asst prof, Hunter Col, 68-69; Am Coun Learned Soc grant, 73. **MEMBERSHIPS** AHA. **RESEARCH** Late Roman Empire. **SELECTED PUBLICATIONS** Auth, More Silent Reading in Antiquity: Reflections on the Earliest Evidence For Non-Vocalized Communal Christian Reading Practice--Non-Omne-Verbum-Sonabat, J Biblical Lit, Vol 0112, 93; Paul and the Killing of the Prophets in 1-Thessalonians-II,15, Novum Testamentum, Vol 0036, 94; Eusebius, Christianity, and Judaism, J Early Christian Stud, Vol 0002, 94. **CONTACT ADDRESS** Dept of Hist, California State Univ, Hayward, 25800 Carlos Bee Bvd, Hayward, CA, 94542-3001.

GILLILAND-SWETLAND, ANNE J.
PERSONAL Born 04/30/1959, Derry, Northern Ireland, m, 1990, 2 children **DISCIPLINE** ARCHIVAL SCIENCE **EDUCATION** Trinity Col, Univ Dublin, MA, 82; Univ Ill, Urbana-Champaign, cert of advan stud in libr and infor sci, MS, 85; Univ Mich, PhD, 95. **CAREER** Archivist, Univ Cincinnati, 85-90; assoc archivist, Univ Mich, 91-92; adj lectr, Sch Libr Infor Sci, Univ Mich, 92-95; dir, Source LINK, Univ Mich Hist Ctr for Health Sci, 93-95; asst prof, Univ Calif, Los Angeles, Libr Infor Sci, 95- . **HONORS AND AWARDS** CFW Coker Award, 98; Norton Award, Midwest Arch Conf, 97; Mellon Found fel, 90, 95, 96; **MEMBERSHIPS** Midwest Arch Conf; Soc of Am Archivists; Asn Lib and Infor Sci Educators; Soc Calif Archivists. **SELECTED PUBLICATIONS** Auth, From Education to Application and Back: Archival Literature and an Electronic Records Curriculum, Am Archivist, 93; coauth, Uses of Electronic Communications to Document an Academic Community: A Research Report; Archivaria, 94; auth, Computer-based Communications and Archives: Documentary Opportunities Not to Be Missed, Archival Issues, 95; auth, Health Sciences Documentation and Networked Hypermedia: An Integrative Approach, Archivaria, 95; auth, Social Science Data Archives in the New World? Proceedings of For the Record Symposium, Royal Irish Academy and National Archives, 96; auth, Policy and Politics: A Case Study in the Management of Electronic Communications at the University of Michigan, Society of American Archivists, 96; auth, Defining Metadada, in, Introduction to Metadada: Pathways to Digital Information, Getty Information Institute, 98; auth, An Exploration of K-12 User Needs for Digital Primary Source Materials, Am Archivist, 98. **CONTACT ADDRESS** Graduate School of Education and Information Studi, Univ of California, Los Angeles, CA, 90095-1520. **EMAIL** swetland@ucla.edu

GILLINGHAM, BRYAN R.
PERSONAL Born 04/12/1944, Vancouver, BC, Canada **DISCIPLINE** MUSIC/HISTORY **EDUCATION** Univ BC, BA, 66, BMus, 68; Toronto Conserv, ARCT, 69; King's Col (UK), MMus, 71; Univ Wash, PhD, 76. **CAREER** Instr, Herdman Col & Memorial Univ, 70-72; lectr, Mt Allison Univ, 72-73; lectr, Univ Alta, 75-76; guest lectr, Univ Ottawa, 77-79; asst prof, 76-80, assoc ch, 80-84, ch, 84-91, PROF MUSIC, CARLETON UNIV, 86-; DIR, INST MEDIAEVAL MUSIC, 85-. **HONORS AND AWARDS** Scholarly Achievement Awards, Carleton Univ, 84, 88; Res Achievement Award, 91. **SELECTED PUBLICATIONS** Auth, The Polyphonic Sequences in Codex Wolfenbuttel, 82; auth, Saint-Martial Mehrstimmigkeit, 84; auth, Medieval Polyphonic Sequences, 85; auth, Modal Rhythm, 86; auth, Medieval Latin Song: An Anthology, 93; auth, Indices to the Notre-Dame Facsimiles, 94; auth, A Critical Study of Secular Medieval Latin Song, 95; co-ed, Beyond the Moon, 90. **CONTACT ADDRESS** Dept of Music, Carleton Univ, 1125 Colonel By Dr, Ottawa, ON, K1S 5B6.

GILLIS, DANIEL J.
PERSONAL Born 09/25/1935, New Bedford, MA **DISCIPLINE** CLASSICS **EDUCATION** Harvard, AB, 57; Cornell Univ, MA, 59, PhD(classics), 63. **CAREER** Instr classics, Brown Univ, 59-60; asst prof, Univ Tex, 64-65 & Swathmore Col, 65-66; from ast prof to assoc prof, 66-76, Prof Classics, Haverford Col, 76-, Ger govt fel, Univ Munich, 63-64; Ford Found humanities res grant, 73. **MEMBERSHIPS** Am Philol Asn. **RESEARCH** Latin poetry; Roman history; Greek politics. **SELECTED PUBLICATIONS** Auth, Furtwangler Recalled, DeGraff, 66; Furtwangler and America, Manyland Bks, 70; Vita, Westworks, 79; Collaboration with the Persians, Steiner, 79; Measure of a Man, Iona Fdn, 82; Eros and Death in the Aeneid, Bretschneider, 82. **CONTACT ADDRESS** Dept of Classics, Haverford Col, 370 Lancaster Ave, Haverford, PA, 19041-1392.

GILLIS, JOHN R.
PERSONAL Born 01/13/1939, Plainfield, NJ, m, 1960, 2 children **DISCIPLINE** EUROPEAN HISTORY **EDUCATION** Amherst Col, BA, 60; Stanford Univ, PhD, 65. **CAREER** Instr, Stanford Univ, 64-65; asst prof, Princeton Univ, 66-71; assoc prof, 71-76, prof hist, Rurtgers Univ, 76, Vis fel hist, St Antony's Col, 69-70; vis prof, Princeton Univ, 82. **HONORS AND AWARDS** NEH Seminar fel, 79-80; Fellow Center for Advan Sutdy in Behavioral Sciences, 93-94. **MEMBERSHIPS** AHA; Am Asn Univ Prof. **RESEARCH** Europ soc hist, 1750-present; hist of family and marriage; Global hist. **SELECTED PUBLICATIONS** auth, The Prussian Bureaucracy in Crisis, Stanford Press, 71; Youth and History, Acad Press, 74; contribr, Crises of Political Development in Europe and the United States, Princeton, 78; For Better, For Worse: British Marriages, 1600-present, Oxford Press, 85; Commemovaticms: The Politics of National Identity, 94; A World of Their Own Making: Myth, Rotual, and the Quest for Family Values, Baric Books, 96. **CONTACT ADDRESS** Hist Dept, Rutgers Univ, PO Box 5059, New Brunswick, NJ, 08903-5059. **EMAIL** 110762.667@compuserve.com

GILLMOR, ALAN
DISCIPLINE FRENCH MUSIC **EDUCATION** Univ Mich, MA, BM; Univ Toronto, PhD. **CAREER** Prof. **HONORS AND AWARDS** Distinguished tchg award, 82; Univ tchg award, 92; 3M tchg fel, 96. **RESEARCH** Life and works of the eccentric composer Erik Satie. **SELECTED PUBLICATIONS** Auth, Erik Satie, Macmillan, 88; paperback ed, W.W. Norton, 92. **CONTACT ADDRESS** Carleton Univ, 1125 Colonel By Dr, Ottawa, ON, K1S 5B6.

GILLMOR, CHARLES STEWART
PERSONAL Born 11/06/1938, Kansas City, MO, m, 1964, 2 children **DISCIPLINE** HISTORY OF SCIENCE **EDUCATION** Stanford Univ, BSEE, 62; Princeton Univ, MA, 66, PhD(hist of sci), 68. **CAREER** Ionospheric physicist GS-12, US Nat Bur Standards, 60-62; instr hist of sci, 67-68, asst prof, 68-72, assoc prof, 73-79, PROF HIST AND SCI, WESLEYAN UNIV, 79-, Res grants, Am Coun Learned Soc, 71, Soc Sci Res Coun, 71-72 and NSF, 72-74; AAASNSF Chautauqua short course lectr, 73-74; NSF grants, 75-76 and 76-78; Fulbright-Hays Sr Res fel, Dept Physics, Cambridge Univ, England, 76. **MEMBERSHIPS** AAAS; Hist Sci Soc; Soc Hist Technol; Am Geophys Union; Am Phys Soc. **RESEARCH** History of physics and engineering, 18th century to present; quantitative measures of science growth; quantitative methods in historical research. **SELECTED PUBLICATIONS** Auth, A History of Antarctic Science, Isis, Vol 0085, 94; No Ordinary Journey--Rae, John, Arctic Explorer, 1813-1893, Isis, Vol 0085, 94. **CONTACT ADDRESS** Dept of Hist, Wesleyan Univ, Middletown, CT, 06457.

GILMORE, AL TONY
PERSONAL Born 06/29/1946, Spartanburg, South Carolina, m **DISCIPLINE** HISTORY **EDUCATION** NC Central Univ, BA 1968, MA 1969; Univ of Toledo, PhD 1972. **CAREER** Howard Univ, prof of history; Univ of MD, prof of history; Natl Afro-Amer Museum Project, consultant director; ASALH, researcher; Natl Educ Assoc, sr policy analyst, currently. **MEMBERSHIPS** Bd dirs Assoc for the Study of Afro Amer Life & History 1977-88; consultant dir Natl Afro-American Museum Project Columbus OH 1979-82; mem Organization of Amer Historians, Amer Historical Assoc; Association for Study of African-American Life & History; pres, The Forum for the Study of Educ Excellence; board of directors, Quality Education for Minorities Project; National Council on Educating Black Children; consultant, California Commission on the Status of African-American Males. **SELECTED PUBLICATIONS** Author of several books "The Natl Impact of Jack Johnson" 1975, "Revisiting the Slave Community" 1979; book reviews and articles have appeared in Washington Post, New York Times, New Republic, American Scholar and others; lectured at over 40 colleges and univs including Harvard, Brown, UCLA, Morehouse and others; editor, African-American Males: The Struggle for Equality. **CONTACT ADDRESS** Sr Policy Analyst, National Education Association, 1201 16th St, NW, Washington, VT, 20036.

GILMORE-LEHNE, WILLIAM JAMES
PERSONAL Born 05/02/1945, Lawrence, MA, 2 children **DISCIPLINE** AMERICAN HISTORY **EDUCATION** Merrimack Col, BA, 66; Univ Va, PhD(US hist), 71. **CAREER** Actg asst prof hist, Univ Va, 71; asst prof, 71-77, assoc prof hist, Stockton State Col, 77-, Co-ed, Psychohistory Rev, 72-81; mem exec coun, Hist Group for Use Psychol in Hist, 73-; Ohio State Univ, fel, 74-75; NJ Hist Comn res grant, 74, 81; Nat Endowment for Humanities res fel, Am Antiq Soc, 79-80, 90-91. **HONORS AND AWARDS** Senior Fulbright fel, 86-87; Weston A Cate, Jr res fel, Vt Hist Soc, 93-94; Global Humanities for the 21st Century Knowledge Soc; RSC Distinguished fac fel, 96. **MEMBERSHIPS** AHA; Orgn Am Historians; Soc Hist Early Am Repub; Group Use Psychol Hist; Soc Study Early Nat Period. **RESEARCH** United States history 1783-1865; psychohistory; American painting to 1900. **SELECTED PUBLICATIONS** Auth, Comments on Donald Capps' interpretations of Orestes Brownson, J Sci Study Relig, 69; Media resources available for teaching psychohistory, 75, The methodology of psychohistory: An annotated bibliography, 76, The individual and the group in psychohistory: Rogin's Jackson, 77, Psychohi-

storical studies: American civilization, 77-78 & Alternatives to psychoanalytical psychohistory, 1979-1981, Psychohist Rev; Psychohistory: An Annotated Bibliography and Essays on the State of the Field, Garland, 82; Literacy in rural New England, Proc Am Antiq Soc, 82; auth, Elementary Literacy on the Eve of the Industrial Revolution: Trends in Rural New England, 1760-1830, Univ Virginia, 82; auth, Truants and Scholars: Daily Attendance in the District School: A Rural New England Case, 1828-29, Vermont Hist, 85; auth, Peddlers and the Dissemination of Printed Material in Northern New England, 1780-1840, Communication, 88; auth, Reading Becomes a Necessity of Life: Material & Cultural Life in Rural New England, 1780-1835, Tennessee, 89; auth, Communications and Migration: Three Classics of Vermont History Revisited: Ludlum, Stilwell & Wilson, Vermont Hist, 91; auth, Literacy, 1585-1990, in, Encyclopedia of American Social History, 93. **CONTACT ADDRESS** Dept of History, Richard Stockton Col, Pomona, NJ, 08240. **EMAIL** gilmorew@pollux.stockton.edu

GIMBUTAS, MARIJA
PERSONAL Born 01/23/1921, Vilnius, Lithuania, m, 1941, 3 children **DISCIPLINE** ARCHAEOLOGY, ANTHROPOLOGY **EDUCATION** Univ Vilnius, MA, 42; Univ Tubingen, PhD, 46. **CAREER** Res scholar old world archaeol, Peabody Mus, Harvard Univ, 50-63, res fel archaeol of E Europe, 55-63; PROF EUROP ARCHAEOL, UNIV CALIF, LOS ANGELES, 63-, CUR OLD WORLD ARCHAEOL, 66-, Fel, Ctr Advan Studies Behav Sci, 61-62; fel, Neth Inst Advan Studies, 73-74. **RESEARCH** Old World archaeology, especially East Baltic area, Russia and Balkans; primitive art; folklore. **SELECTED PUBLICATIONS** Auth, The Indo-Europeanization of Europe, the Intrusion of Steppe Pastoralists from South Russia and the Transformation of Old Europe, Word-J Int Ling Asn, Vol 0044, 93; Prehistoric Anatolia--The Neolithic Transformation and the Early Chalcolithic Period, J Indo-Europ Stud, Vol 0021, 93. **CONTACT ADDRESS** Univ Calif, Los Angeles, 21434 W Entrada Rd, Topanga, CA, 90290.

GIMELLI, LOUIS B.
PERSONAL Born 10/08/1925, Oswego, NY, m, 1951, 2 children **DISCIPLINE** HISTORY, POLITICAL THEORY **EDUCATION** State Univ NY Oswego, BS, 51; NY Univ, MA, 54, PhD(hist), 64. **CAREER** Teacher elem and high schs, NY, 51-66; from assoc prof to prof hist, 66-76, PROF HIST AND PHILOS, EASTERN MICH UNIV, 76-. **MEMBERSHIPS** AHA. **RESEARCH** Jacksonian era, especially New York state politics. **SELECTED PUBLICATIONS** Auth, History of the Cattlemen of Texas, J the W, Vol 0032, 93; The Lance and the Shield--The Life and Times of Sitting-Bull, J the W, Vol 0034, 95; Charreria-Mexicana--An Equestrian Folk Tradition, J the W, Vol 0035, 96; Billy-the-Kid--His Life and Legend, J the W, Vol 0035, 96; Digging Up Butch and Sundance, J the W, Vol 0035, 96. **CONTACT ADDRESS** Dept of Hist and Philos, Eastern Michigan Univ, Ypsilanti, MI, 48197.

GINGERY, GAIL ALVAH
PERSONAL Born 02/02/1928, Princeton, IL, m, 1954, 2 children **DISCIPLINE** VOCAL MUSIC **EDUCATION** Bob Jones Univ, BA, 51, MA, 53; Boston Univ, DMA, 65. **CAREER** Chairman, Div of Music, 56-81, Head, Dept of Voice, Bob Jones Univ, 76-98; regional governor, SE Region of Nat Asn of Teachers of Singing, 67-71; Minister of Music in several churches, incl 25 years at Faith Free Presbyterian Church, Greenville, SC. **HONORS AND AWARDS** Tenor soloist in numerous oratorio performances; tenor roles in Barber of Seville, Magic Flute, Don Pasquale, and in portions of La Traviata and La Boheme. **MEMBERSHIPS** Nat Asn of Teachers of Singing. **RESEARCH** 17th Century Italian Cantata: Dissertation: Solo Cantatas of Alessandro Stradella in MS. 13 E of Fitzwilliam Museum, Cambridge. **CONTACT ADDRESS** 12 Sennet Dr., Greenville, SC, 29609-5111. **EMAIL** ggingery@bju.edu

GINTIS, HERBERT
PERSONAL Born 02/11/1940, Philadelphia, PA, m, 1961, 1 child **DISCIPLINE** ECONOMICS **EDUCATION** Harvard Univ, PhD, 64. **CAREER** Asst prof, Harvard Univ, 75; PROF, UNIV OF MASS, 76-. **MEMBERSHIPS** Am Math Asn; Am Economic Asn. **RESEARCH** Behavioral theory; crime theory. **SELECTED PUBLICATIONS** Coauth, The Moral Economy of Community: Structured Populations and the Evolution of Prosocial Norms, Evolution & Human Behavior, 98; coauth, Wealth Inequality, Credit Constraints, and Economic Performance, Handbook of Income Distribution, 98; coauth, Power and Wealth in a Capitalist Economy, Keizai Seminar, 98; coauth, Escalating Differences and Elusive Skills: Cognitive Abilities and the Explanation of Inequality, Race, Poverty, Inequality, and Domestic Policy, Yale Univ Press, 98; coauth, How Communities Govern: The Structural Basis of Prosocial Norms, Economics, Values, and Organizations, Cambridge Univ Press, 98; coauth, The Use and Abuse of Power in Competitive Exchange, The Politics of Exchange and the Economics of Power, Routledge, 98; coauth, Schooling, Skills, and Earnings: A Principal-Agent Approach, Meritocracy and Economic Inequality, Princeton Univ Press, 98; coauth, Efficient Redistribution: New Rules for Markets, States, and Communities, Politics and Soc, 96; coauth, Recasting Egalitarianism: New Rules for markets, States, and Communities, Verso, 97. **CONTACT ADDRESS** 15 Forbes Ave., Northampton, MA, 01060. **EMAIL** gintls@econs.umass.edu

GIRARDOT, NORMAN J.
PERSONAL Born 04/19/1943, 2 children **DISCIPLINE** HISTORY OF RELIGIONS **EDUCATION** Col Holy Cross, BS, 65; Univ Chicago, MA, 72, PhD, 74. **CAREER** Ed asst, Hist Relig J, 68-70; asst prof Theol, Notre Dame Univ, 72-79; vis asst prof, Oberlin Col, 79-80; assoc prof & chmn, Relig Studies Dept, Lehigh Univ, 80-; prof, 89; Nat Endowment for Humanities fel, 83, 93-95; Chiang Ching-kuo fel, 93-95; Pacific Cult Found fel, 93-95; exec comt, Soc Study Chinese Relig, 75-78; reader Univ Chicago Press, Univ Notre Dame Press, Scholars Press & Greenwood Press. **HONORS AND AWARDS** Phi Beta Kappa . **MEMBERSHIPS** Am Soc for the Study of Religion; Am Acad Relig; Asn Asian Scholars; Soc Study Chinese Relig. **RESEARCH** Taoism; Chinese religion and myth; Western study of Asian religion; Visionary folkart; polular religion. **SELECTED PUBLICATIONS** Auth, The problem of creation mythology in the study of Chinese religion, Vol 15, 76 & co-ed, Current perspectives in the study of Chinese religions, Vol 17, 78, Hist Relig; auth, Returning to the Beginning and the arts of Mr Huntun in the Chuang Tzu, J Chinese Philos, Vol 5, 78; Chaotic order and benevolent disorder in the Chuang Tau, Philos East & West, Vol 28, 78; Taoism, In: Encycl of Bioethics, 78; co-ed, China and Christianity, Notre Dame Univ Press, 79; Imagination and Meaning: The Scholarly and Literary Worlds of Mircea Eliade, Seabury Press, 82; auth, Myth and Meaning in Early Taoism, Univ Calif Press, 82, rb, 89; trans, I Robinet's Tavist Meditation, SUNY, 93. **CONTACT ADDRESS** Relig Studies Dept, Lehigh Univ, 9 W Packer Ave, #5, Bethlehem, PA, 18015-3082. **EMAIL** nvgo@lehigh.edu

GISOLFI, DIANA
DISCIPLINE ART HISTORY **EDUCATION** Radcliffe (Harvard), BA; Univ Chicago, MA, PhD. **CAREER** Ch; prof. **HONORS AND AWARDS** Grant, Delmas Found, 96., Illusr, Classic Ground. **SELECTED PUBLICATIONS** Illus,Yale Univ Art Gallery Bulletin; Artibus et Historiae, Arte Veneta, Art Bulletin, Dictionary of Art, Renaissance Quart, Burlington Mag; co-auth, The Rule, the Bible, and the Council: The Library of the Benedictine Abbey at Praglia, CAA Monograph series. **CONTACT ADDRESS** Dept of Art Hist, Pratt Inst, 200 Willoughby Ave, Brooklyn, NY, 11205.

GISPEN, KEES
DISCIPLINE GERMAN AND EUROPEAN HISTORY **EDUCATION** Univ CA, Berkeley, PhD, 81. **CAREER** Assoc prof, Univ MS, 83-; ed bd, Cent Europ Hist; exec secy and treas, Conf Gp for Cent Europ Hist, 97-. **RESEARCH** The changes in intellectual property rights of inventors, scientists and engineers in Germany between 1890 and 1960. **SELECTED PUBLICATIONS** Auth, New Profession, Old Order: Engineers and German Society, 1815-1914, Cambridge UP, 89. **CONTACT ADDRESS** Univ MS, Oxford, MS, 38677. **EMAIL** hsgispen@olemiss.edu

GITTLEN, BARRY M
PERSONAL Norfolk, VA **DISCIPLINE** NEAR EAST ARCHEOLOGY **EDUCATION** Wayne State Univ, PhB, 65; Univ Pa, PhD(Near East archeol), 77. **CAREER** Asst prof, 72-78, ASSOC PROF ANCIENT NEAR EAST STUDIES, BALTIMORE HEBREW COL, 78-, Am Schs Orient Res fel archeol, 69-70; staff archaeologist, Ben Gurion Univ Excavation Tell esh-Shari'a, Israel, 74-75; field archaeologist joint exped to Cent Negev Highlands, 78-80 and Tell Miqne Exped, 82; vis prof, Towson State Univ. **MEMBERSHIPS** Am Orient Soc; Am Schs Orient Res; Archaeol Inst Am; Asn Jewish Studies; Israel Explor Soc. **RESEARCH** Trade in the Ancient Near East; Cypro-Palestinian relationships in the Bronze Age; the archaeology of Ancient Israel. **SELECTED PUBLICATIONS** Auth, At the Time the Canaanites Were in the Land--Daily Life in Canaan in the Middle-Bronze-Age, Vol 2, 2000-1500-BC, Biblical Archaeol, Vol 0056, 93; The Sociology of Pottery in Ancient Palestine, Biblical Archaeol, Vol 0058, 95. **CONTACT ADDRESS** Baltimore Hebrew Univ, 5800 Park Heights Av, Baltimore, MD, 21215-3932.

GIVENS, STUART R.
PERSONAL Born 04/01/1924, Honolulu, HI, m, 1947, 3 children **DISCIPLINE** MODERN HISTORY **EDUCATION** George Washington Univ, BA, 48; Stanford Univ, MA, 49, PhD(hist), 56. **CAREER** Coordr student activities & instr, 52-56, from asst prof to assoc prof, 56-65, chmn dept, 65-69, prof hist, Bowling Green State Univ, 65-, Univ Historian, 78-, Ed, Ohio Acad of Hist Newslett, 74-. **MEMBERSHIPS** AHA; Nat Educ Asn; Mid-West Brit Studies Asn; Asn Can Studies US; Can Hist Asn. **RESEARCH** Britain and the Commonwealth; Canada. **CONTACT ADDRESS** Dept of History, Bowling Green State Univ, 1001 E Wooster St, Bowling Green, OH, 43403-0001.

GLAAB, CHARLES NELSON
PERSONAL Born 12/19/1927, Williston, ND, m, 1949, 2 children **DISCIPLINE** AMERICAN HISTORY **EDUCATION** Univ NDak, PhB, 51, MA, 52; Univ Mo, PhD (Am hist), 58. **CAREER** Res assoc hist Kansas City proj, Univ Chicago, 56-58; asst prof hist, Kans State Univ, 58-60; from assoc prof to prof, Univ Wis-Milwaukee, 60-68, PROF HIST, UNIV TOLEDO, 68-, Am Asn State & Local Hist res grant, 61; Hist Kansas City Res Proj fel, 62; ed, Urban Hist, Group Newsletter, 61-68; co-ed Northwest Ohio Quart, 95-. **HONORS AND AWARDS** Phi Beta Kappa **MEMBERSHIPS** Orgn Am Historians; Am Hist Asn; Urban Hist Asn. **RESEARCH** Intellectual history; urban history; social history. **SELECTED PUBLICATIONS** Auth, Failure of North Dakota progressivism, Mid-America, 10/57; Visions of metropolis: William Gilpin and theories of city growth in the American West, Wis Mag Hist, autumn, 61; Kansas City and the Railroads, State Hist Soc Wis, 62, 2nd ed, Univ Press of Kans, 93; The American City, Dorsey, 63; Jesup W Soctt and a West of cities, Ohio Hist, summer 64; contrib, The historian and the American city: a bibliographic survey, In: The Study of Urbanization, Wiley, 65; coauth, A History of Urban America, Macmillan, 67, 76, 83 & Factories in the Valley, State Hist Soc Wis, 69; Toledo: Gateway to the Great Lakes, Continental Heritage, 83. **CONTACT ADDRESS** 2801 W Bancroft St, Toledo, OH, 43606-3390. **EMAIL** cglaab@pop3.utoledo.com

GLAD, PAUL WILBUR
PERSONAL Born 08/15/1926, Salt Lake City, UT, m, 1948, 4 children **DISCIPLINE** HISTORY **EDUCATION** Purdue Univ, BS, 47; Ind Univ, MA, 49, PhD(hist), 57. **CAREER** Asst prof hist, Hastings Col, 50-55; assoc prof, Coe Col, 55-64 and Univ Md, 64-66; prof, Univ Wis-Madison, 66-77; MERRICK PROF HIST, UNIV OKLA, 77-, Fulbright prof Am hist, Marburg, Ger, 61-62; Guggenheim Mem fel, 62-63; Am Philos Soc fel, 67; vis prof, Univ Okla, 71-72; fel, Nat Humanities Inst, Univ Chicago, 77-78. **MEMBERSHIPS** AHA; Orgn Am Historians. **RESEARCH** Recent American history; United States political and social history; Western history. **SELECTED PUBLICATIONS** Auth, Boileau, Gerald, J. and the Progressive-Farmer-Labor Alliance--Politics of the New-Deal, J Am Hist, Vol 0082, 95. **CONTACT ADDRESS** Dept of Hist, Univ of Okla, Norman, OK, 73019.

GLAHE, FRED RUFUS
PERSONAL Born 06/30/1934, Chicago, IL, m, 1961, 1 child **DISCIPLINE** ECONOMICS **EDUCATION** BS, aero eng, 57, MS, econ, 63, PhD, econ, Purdue Univ, 64. **CAREER** Engineer, Allsion Division, General Motors, 57-61; economist, Buttelle Memorial Inst, Columbus, Ohio, 64-65; PROF OF ECONOMICS, UNIV OF COLO, 65-. **MEMBERSHIPS** The Mount Pelerin Soc. **RESEARCH** Macroeconomics; Money; History of Economic Thought; Technology. **SELECTED PUBLICATIONS** Auth, Adam Smith and the Wealth of Nations: A Concordance, 95; auth, The Drama: The Hayek Keynes Debate Over the Business Cycle, 99; coauth, Praxeology and the Development of Human Capital, Cultural Dynamics, 97. **CONTACT ADDRESS** Dept of Economics, Univ of Colorado, Campus Box 256, Boulder, CO, 80309. **EMAIL** fred.glahe@colorado.edu

GLASCO, ANITA L.
PERSONAL Born 10/24/1942, Kansas City, KS **DISCIPLINE** EDUCATION **EDUCATION** U Univ So CA, AB 1964; Harvard Univ Law Sch, JD 1967. **CAREER** Univ of Chicago Law Sch, master of comparative law 1970; Southwestern Univ Sch of Law, prof of law 1975-; SW, Asso prof of law 1972-75; Smith & Glascod partner 1971-72; Lewis & Clark Coll, visting prof of law 1975; Univ of Wash, visting prof of law 1974; Univ of TN knoxville, vis prof of law 1980. **HONORS AND AWARDS** Outst Young Woman of Am honoree 1971. **MEMBERSHIPS** Mem CA State Bar Assn 1968-; mem Black Women Lawyers Assn; mem CA Assn of Black Lawyers; chpn Elect of Minority Groups Sect of Assn of Am Law Schs1977; chmn Minority Groups Sect of Assn of Law Schs 1978; fellow Inst French Lang & Civil Univ of Geneva 1968; fellow Inst of French Lang & Civil Univ ofPau 1969; fellow Inst French Lang & Civil Univ of Paris 1969; comparative law fellow Univ of Aix-Marseilles 1969-74. **CONTACT ADDRESS** Sch of Law, SW Univ, 675 S Westmoreland, Los Angeles, CA, 90005.

GLASCO, LAURENCE A.
PERSONAL Born 07/01/1940, Xenia, OH, m, 1969 **DISCIPLINE** AFRO-AMERICAN HISTORY **EDUCATION** Antioch Col, BA, 62; State Univ NY Buffalo, MA, 65, PhD(hist), 73. **CAREER** Instr, 69-73, asst prof, 73-76, ASSOC PROF HIST, UNIV PITTSBURGH, 76-. **MEMBERSHIPS** AHA; Orgn Am Historians; Asn Study of Afro-Am Life & Hist. **RESEARCH** Black middle class; ethnic mobility; family history. **SELECTED PUBLICATIONS** Auth, Making Ethnic Choices--California Punjabi Mexican-Americans, Am Hist Rev, Vol 0098, 93; Cultivation and Culture--Labor and the Shaping of Slave Life in the America, Historian, Vol 0056, 94. **CONTACT ADDRESS** Hist Dept, Univ of Pittsburgh, 3p38 Forbes Quad, Pittsburgh, PA, 15260-0001.

GLASER, DANIEL
PERSONAL Born 12/23/1918, New York, NY, m, 1946, 1 child **DISCIPLINE** SOCIOLOGY **EDUCATION** Univ Chicago, AB, 39, AM, 47, PhD, 54. **CAREER** US Army, 42-46;

US Mil Govt Ger Prison Branch, 46-49; Sociol-actuary, Ill Parole & Pardon Bd, 49-54; asst prof to prof & ch, Sociol Dept, Univ Ill-Urbana, 54-68; Rutgers Univ on 3/4 leave to NY State Narcotic Addiction Control Comn, Res Comnr, 68-69; prof sociol, 70-89, EMER, 89- , UNIV S Cal; SR RES ASSOC, SOC SCI RES INST, 78- ; vis assoc prof, UCLA, 61; vis prof Ariz State Univ, 63-64; distinguished Emer award, U S Cal, 95. **HONORS AND AWARDS** Annual Award John Howard Asn, 65; E H Sutherland Award, 76; August Vollmer Award, 90; Richard A McGee Award, 87; distinguished sociol pract award, 95. **MEMBERSHIPS** Ill Acad Criminol; Am Sociol Asn; Am Soc Criminol; Am Justice Inst; Pac Sociol Asn. **RESEARCH** To expand practical knowledge that canalleviate mankind's problems, seek not just precision, but the grounding of facts in abstract explanatory principles. **SELECTED PUBLICATIONS** Ed, Handbook of Criminology, 74; auth Crime in Our Changing Society, 78; Encyclo Crime and Justice, 83; Evaluation Research and Decision Guidance, 88; Preparing Convicts for Law-Abiding Lifes: The Pioneering Penology of Richard A McGee, 95. **CONTACT ADDRESS** 901 S Ogden Dr., Los Angeles, CA, 90036-4411.

GLASRUD, BRUCE A.
DISCIPLINE HISTORY **EDUCATION** Luther Col, BA; Eastern NMex Univ, MA; Tex Tech Univ, PhD. **CAREER** Prof. **MEMBERSHIPS** Western Soc Sci Asn. **SELECTED PUBLICATIONS** Auth, African Americans in the West: A Bibliography of Secondary Sources, 98; William Henry Dean, Jr., 94; Martha Ostenso, Garland, 94. **CONTACT ADDRESS** Sul Ros State Univ, 1866 Southern Lane, Decatur, GA, 30033-4097. **EMAIL** bglasrud@sulross.edu

GLASS, DOROTHY
DISCIPLINE ART HISTORY **EDUCATION** Johns Hopkins Univ, PhD. **CAREER** Fac, SUNY Buffalo. **HONORS AND AWARDS** Jane and Morgan Whitney Fellow, Metropolitan Museum of Art; Rome Prize, Am Acad Rome; Chancellor's Awd Excellence Tchg, SUNY Buffalo.. Exec Comm, Int Ctr Medieval Art; Coun, Medieval Acad Am. **RESEARCH** Middle Ages; late Medieval Italy; the methodology of art hist. **SELECTED PUBLICATIONS** Auth, Crusade and Pilgrimage: Romanesque Portals in Western Tuscany, 97; Romanesque Sculpture in Campania: Patrons, Programs, and Style, Penn State P, 91; Italian Romanesque Sculpture: An Annotated Bibliography, GK Hall, 83. **CONTACT ADDRESS** Dept Art, SUNY Buffalo, 202 Center for the Arts, Buffalo, NY, 14260-6010.

GLASSBERG, DAVID
DISCIPLINE HISTORY **EDUCATION** Johns Hopkins Univ, PhD, 82. **CAREER** Assoc prof, Univ MA Amherst. **RESEARCH** Public hist; environmental hist. **SELECTED PUBLICATIONS** Auth, American Historical Pageantry: The Uses of Tradition in the Early Twentieth Century, 90. **CONTACT ADDRESS** Dept of Hist, Univ Massachusetts Amherst, Mass Ave, Amherst, MA, 01003.

GLASSNER, MARTIN IRA
PERSONAL Born 07/07/1932, Plainfield, NJ, m, 3 children **DISCIPLINE** POLITICAL SCIENCE, GEOGRAPHY **EDUCATION** BA, Syracuse Univ, 53; MA Goeg and Ploi Sci Calif State Univ, Fullerton, 64; PhD Intl Rel Claremont Grad School, 68. **CAREER** Inst in Poli Mount San Antonio Col Walnut Cal 66; Asst Prof Poli Sci, Univ Puget Sound, Tacoma Washington, 67-68; Asst Prof to Prof Geog, Souther Conn State Univ, 68-93, Org and first Coordr Marine Studies Prog, 77-78; Coordr Marine Dtudies Prog, 81-92; Chm Dept of Goeg, 82-94; bd dir, Conn State Univ Res Found, 86-89; Acting Chm Dept of Geog, 94; Prof Geog Southern Conn State Univ, 93-95; Univ Prof Emeritus, 95-. **HONORS AND AWARDS** Am Men and Women of Sci; Dictionary of Intl Biog; Comm Leaders and Noteworthy Am; Intl Auth and Writer's Who's Who; Natl Dir of Latin Am; Men of Acheivement; Who's Who in Am Edu. **MEMBERSHIPS** Intl Studies Assoc; Assoc Am Geog; Am Soc of Intl Law; Am Branch Intl Law Assoc; Conf of Latin Am Geographers; Acad Council on th UN System. **SELECTED PUBLICATIONS** First Asian-Pacific Regional Conference, Intl Law Assoc(TAIWAN): The Changing Geopolitical Orientation of Land-locked Central Asia, 95; Bibliography on Land Locked States, 4th Revised and Enlarged Ed, Dordrecht: Nijhoff, 95; Political Geography, 2nd ed NY: John Wiley and Sons, 96; The United Nations At Work(ed) Westport, Conn: Praeger, 98; Navigating Diffcult Waters, in Ocean Yearbook 13, 94; New Books on Marine Affairs, in Ocean and Coastal Management, 97; The Polar Regions; A Ploitical Geography by Sanjay Chaturvedi, in Choice, 97; Rediscovering Geography by the National Research Council in Choic, 98. **CONTACT ADDRESS** 742 Paradise Ave, Hamden, CT, 0651.

GLATFELTER, RALPH EDWARD
PERSONAL Born 11/21/1939, Wenatchee, WA, m, 1966 **DISCIPLINE** HISTORY **EDUCATION** Whitman Col, BA, 63; Ind Univ, Bloomington, MA, 68, PhD(hist), 75. **CAREER** Exec dir alumni affairs, Whitman Col Alumni Asn, 63-65; instr, 70-75, asst prof, 75-79, ASSOC PROF HIST, UTAH STATE UNIV, 79-. **MEMBERSHIPS** Am Asn Advan Slavic Studies; Asian Studies Asn; Western Soc Sci Asn. **RESEARCH** Nineteenth century Russian diplomatic history; Siberian history. **SELECTED PUBLICATIONS** Auth, Historical Sources on the Exploration of Siberia During the Period of Capitalism--An Anthology, Jahrbucher Fur Geschichte Osteuropas, Vol 0041, 93; Otter Skins, Boston Ships and China Goods--The Maritime Fur Trade of the Northwest Coast, 1785-1841, Western Hist Quart, Vol 0025, 94. **CONTACT ADDRESS** Dept of Hist, Utah State Univ, 710 University Blvd, Logan, UT, 84322-0710.

GLATZER ROSENTHAL, BERNICE
DISCIPLINE RUSSIAN HISTORY **EDUCATION** Univ CA-Berkeley, PhD. **CAREER** Prof, Fordham Univ. **RESEARCH** Comp intellectual hist and Russ relig philos. **SELECTED PUBLICATIONS** Ed, Nietzsche in Russia, Princeton UP, 86; Nietzsche and Soviet Culture: Ally and Adversary, Cambridge UP, 94; The Occult in Russian and Soviet Culture, Cornell UP, 97; co-auth, Revolution of Spirit: Crisis of Value in Russia, 1890-1924, Fordham UP, 90; auth, The Nature and Function of Sophia in Sergei Bulgakov's Pre-Revolutionary Thought, Russian Religious Thought, Univ Wis Press, 96. **CONTACT ADDRESS** Dept of Hist, Fordham Univ, 113 W 60th St, New York, NY, 10023.

GLAZIER, IRA ALBERT
PERSONAL Born 08/12/1925, New York, NY, m, 1953, 1 child **DISCIPLINE** ECONOMIC HISTORY **EDUCATION** NY Univ, BA, 48; Univ Chicago, MA, 51; Harvard Univ, PhD(hist & econ), 63. **CAREER** Instr econ hist, Ill Inst Technol, 50-51 and Ctr Int Affairs, Harvard Univ, 58-59; lectr hist, Northwestern Univ, 59-60; from instr to asst prof, Mass Inst Technol, 61-66; assoc prof, Boston Col, 66-67; PROF ECON HIST, TEMPLE UNIV, 69-, Old Dominion grant, 64; fac assoc, Columbia Univ, 70-; Fulbright-Hays res scholar, Bocconi Univ, Milan, 71; ed, Journal Europ Econ Hist, 72-; NATO Professorship, Univ Naples, NAtlantic Treaty Orgn, 78-79; Rockefeller grant, 80. **HONORS AND AWARDS** Widener Trust Award, 81. **MEMBERSHIPS** AHA; Am Econ Asn; Royal Econ Soc; Econ Hist Soc; Econ Hist Asn. **RESEARCH** Foreign trade and industrialization; economic development of modern Europe; Soviet-Italian economic relations. **SELECTED PUBLICATIONS** Auth, The National-Integration of Italian Return Migration, 1870-1929, Am Hist Rev, Vol 0098, 93; Crossings--The Great Transatlantic Migrations, 1870-1914, Am Hist Rev, Vol 0099, 94. **CONTACT ADDRESS** Balch Ctr Immigrat Res, Temple Univ, Philadelphia, PA, 19122.

GLAZIER, STEPHEN D.
PERSONAL Born 06/10/1949, New London, CT, m, 1975, 1 child **DISCIPLINE** ANTHROPOLOGY, SOCIOLOGY, THEOLOGY **EDUCATION** Eastern Col, AB, 71; Princeton Univ Sem, MDiv, 74; Univ Conn, PhD, 81. **CAREER** Lectr, Univ Conn, Storrs, 79-81; vis asst prof, Trinity Col, 81-82; vis asst prof, Conn Col, 82-83; asst prof, Wayland Baptist Univ, 83-86; assoc prof, Westmont Col, 86-88; assoc prof, ch, Univ Nebr, Kearney, 88-91; assoc prof, grad fac fel, Univ Nebr, 91-94; prof, grad fac fel, Univ Nebr, 94- . **HONORS AND AWARDS** Sec, Soc Sci Stud Rel, 98- ; VP, Anthrop Rel Sec, Amer Anthrop Assn, 98-99; Prog ed, AnthropRel Sec, 97th Ann Mtg, Am Anthrop Asn, Philadelphia; Delegate, Consciousness stud sum Inst, Univ Ariz and Fetzer Inst, Flagstaff, AZ, 97; tchg fellow, Amer Acad Rel/Lilly Found Wksps, 97-98; Prof Development Leave, vis res fel, Yale Univ Div Sch/Inst Sacred Mus, fall 96; vis scholar, Rackham Grad Sch, Inst Human, Univ Mich, 96; fel, NEH Summer Inst Col Tchrs, 96; fellow, NEH Summer Sem Col Tchrs, 95; Recipient, Pratt-Heins Awd, Univ Nebr at Kearney, 93; fel, NEH Summer Inst, 93; fel, NEH Summer Sem Col Tchrs, 92; fel, NEH Summer Inst Col Tchrs, 91; mem, Exec Coun, Soc Sci stud Rel, 91-93; Participant, UNESCO Conf, Port of Spain, Trinidad, 90; fel, NEH Summer Sem Col Tchrs, Yale Univ, 89; summer fel, Transatlantic Encounters prog, Herman Dunlop Smith Ctr Hist Cartography, Newberry Lib, Chicago, 87; fel, NEH Summer Inst Afro-Amer Rel Hist, Princeton Univ, 86; Mellon Wksp Rel Revivalism, Rice Univ, 86-87; fel, NEH Summer Sem Col Tchrs, Univ Colo, 85. **MEMBERSHIPS** Amers Anthrop Asn; Royal Anthrop Inst; Amer Acad Rel; Soc Anthrop Rel; Soc Sci Stud Rel; Assn Sociol Rel; Intl Assn Caribbean Archaelolgist; Soc des Am de Paris; Amer Folklore Soc; Caribbean Stud Assn; Soc Anthrop Consciousness. **RESEARCH** Anthropology; Religion; Race and Ethnicity; Ethnohistory; Caribbean and Latin America. **SELECTED PUBLICATIONS** Ed, Perspectives on Pentecostalism: Case Studies from the Caribbean and Latin America, Washington, DC, Univ Press Amer, 80; Marchin' the Pilgrims Home: Leadership and Decision-Making in an Afro-Caribbean Faith, Westport, CT, Greenwood, 83; ed, Caribbean Ethnicity Revisited, NY and London, Gordon and Breach, 85; Syncretism and Separation: Ritual Change in an Afro-Caribbean Faith, Jour Am Folklore, 98, 387, 49-62, 85; Mourning in the Afro-Baptist Tradition: A Comparative Study of Religion in the American South and Trinidad, Southern Quart, 23, 3, 85, 141-156; Religion and Social Justice: Caribbean Perspectives, Phylon, 46, 2, 85, 283-299; Caribbean Religions: Pre-Columbian, The Encyclopedia of Religion, 3, M. Eliade, gen ed, NY, Free Press, Macmillan, 87, 81-90; Marchin' the Pilgrims Home: A Study of the Spiritual Baptists of Trinidad, Salem, WI, Sheffield Publ, 91; A Comparative Study of Caribbean Pilgimages: Haiti and Trinidad, Sacred Journeys: The Anthropology of Pilgrimage, A. Morinis, Ed, Westport, CT, Greenwood, 92, 135-147; Slavery and Social Death by O. Patterson; and The Content of Our Character, by S. Steele, in Masterpieces in African-American Literature, F.N. Magill, ed, NY, HarperCollins, 92; Responding to the Anthropologist: When the Spiritual Baptists of Trinidad Read What I Write About Them, in When They Read What We Write: The Politics of Ethnography, C.B. Brettell, ed, NY, Bergin and Garvey, 93, 37-48; Guest editor's introduction: Special issue: Spiritual Baptists, Shango, and other African-Derived Religions in the Caribbean Quart, 39, S.D. Glazier, ed, v-viii, 1-11, 93; New Religions Among Afro-Americans (Caribbean and South America), and New Religions: Afro-Suriname, HarperCollins Dictionary of Religion, J.Z. Smith, gen ed, San Francisco, HarperCollins, 95; New Religious Movements in the Caribbean: Identity and Resistance, Born Out of Resistance: Caribbean Cultural Creativity as a Response to European Expansion, Wim Hoogbergen, ed, Utrecht: Univ Utrecht/ISOR Pres, 95, 253-262; Latin American Perspectives on Religion and Politics, Latin Am Res Rev, 30, 1, 247-255; Changes in the Spiritual Baptist Religion, 1976-1990, Ay BoBo:Afro-Caribbean Cults: Identity and Resistance, Teil 1, Kulte, M. Kremser, Ed, Wien, Institut fur Volkerkunde der Universitat Wien, 96, 107-114; Five entries, American Folklore: An Encyclopedia, J. Brunvand, gen ed, NY, Garland, 96; Authenticity in Afro-Caribbean Religions: Contested Constructs, Contested Rites, Religion and the Social Order, L.F. Carter and D. Bromley, ed, Greenwich, CT, JAI Press, 96, 207-225; New World African Ritual: Genuine and Spurious, Jour Sci Stud Rel, 35, 4, 421-432; ed, Anthropology of Religion: A Handbook, Westport, CT, Greenwood, 97; assoc ed, Forward, Migrants, Regional Cultures, and Latin American Cities, Soc for Latin Amer Anthrop Publ Series 13, Wash DE, Amer Anthrop Assn, 97; Embedded Truths: Creativity and Context in Spiritual Baptist Music, Latin Am Mus Rev, 18, 1, 44-56; ed, Anthropology and Contemporary Religions, Westport CT, Greenwood, 98; Anthropology and Theology: The Legacies of a Link, in Explorations in Anthropology and Theology, Lanham, MD, Univ Press Am, 98; The Noise of Astonishment: Spiritual Baptist Music in Context, Religion, Diaspora and Cultural Identity: A Reader in the Anglophone Caribbean, ed, J.W. Pulis, NY and London, Gordon and Breach, 98, 277-294; Contested Rites of the Aftican Diaspora, in New Trends and Developments in African Religions, P.B. Clarke, ed, London, Greenwood; Anthropology of Religion, and nineteen shorter entries, in The Encyclopedia of Religion and Society, W.H. Swatos, Jr, ed, Walnut Creek, CA, AltaMira Press, Sage, 98; William Wallace Fenn, John Mifflin Brown, and Benjamin W. Arnett, in American National Biography, J.A. Garraty, Ed, NY, Oxford UP, 99. **CONTACT ADDRESS** Dept of Sociology and Anthropology, Nebraska Univ, Kearney, NE, 68849. **EMAIL** glaziers@platte.unk.edu

GLEASON, ABBOTT
DISCIPLINE HISTORY **EDUCATION** Harvard Col, BA, 61; Brown Univ, MA, 63; Harvard Univ, PhD, 69. **CAREER** Teaching Fel, Harvard Univ, 64-68; Asst Prof to Prof, 68-93, Barnaby Conrad and Mary Critchfield Keeney Prof Hist, Brown Univ, 93-; Assoc, Russ Res Ctr, Harvard Univ, 68-79, 82-; Secy, Kennan Inst Advanced Russ Studies, Woodrow Wilson Int Ctr Schol, 80-82. **SELECTED PUBLICATIONS** Auth, The Delegitimation of Government, The Providence J, 12/26/95; Russian Totalitarianism...Again?, Ger Polit and Soc, 96; Russia's View of NATO's Growth, Providence J, 4/1/97; Teaching Totalitarianism, Perspectives, 4/97; Refighting the Last War, Providence J, 4/16/98; The Ideological Structures of Russian Culture, Cambridge Companion to Russian Culture, Cambridge Univ Press (forthcoming); Franco Venturi's Il populismo russo in the English-speaking world, Einaudi Found, forthcoming in a commemorative volume; The Russian Decembrists, The Encyclopedia of Political Revolutions, Congressional Quart Press (forthcoming). **CONTACT ADDRESS** History Dept, Brown Univ, Providence, RI, 02912.

GLEASON, ELISABETH GREGORICH
PERSONAL Born 07/08/1933, Belgrade, Yugoslavia, m, 1954 **DISCIPLINE** EARLY MODERN HISTORY **EDUCATION** Univ Ill, Urbana, BA, 54; Ohio State Univ, MA, 56; Univ Calif, Berkeley, PhD(hist), 63. **CAREER** Instr hist, Univ Calif, Berkeley, 62-63; from asst prof to assoc prof, San Francisco State Col, 63-69; chmn dept, 75-80, PROF HIST, UNIV SAN FRANCISCO, 69-, Soc Relig Higher Educ fel, 66-67; vis prof, Stanford, 76 and Univ Calif, Berkeley, 79; Nat Endowment for Humanities fel, 80; Gladys K Delmas Found fel, 80. **MEMBERSHIPS** AHA; Am Soc Reformation Res; Renaissance Soc Am; Am Soc Church Hist; Soc for Ital Hist Study. **RESEARCH** Reformation history; 16th century Italian history; Venice. **SELECTED PUBLICATIONS** Auth, The Roman Inquisition in Italy in Modern Times--Archives, Methodological Problems and New Research, 16th Century J, Vol 0024, 93; Bruno, Giordano and the Embassy Affair, J Mod Hist, Vol 0065, 93; Trent 1475--Stories of a Ritual Murder Trial, Cath Hist Rev, Vol 0079, 93; The Roman Inquisition and the Counterreformation--Studies on Morone, Giovanni and His Trial for Heresy, 16th Century J, Vol 0025, 94; Cervini, Marcello and Ecclesiastical Government in Tridentine Italy, Church Hist, Vol 0063, 94; Venice Hidden Enemies--Italian Heretics in a Renaissance City, 16th Century J, Vol 0025, 94; Civic Politics in the Rome of Urban VIII, Historian, Vol 0056, 94; Ignatius-of-Loyola--The Psychology of a Saint, Renaissance Quart, Vol 0047, 94; Resolution Adopted at the Annual-Meeting, Cath Hist

Rev, Vol 0081, 95; The Prosecution of Heresy--Collected Studies on the Inquisition in Early-Modern Italy, Church Hist, Vol 0064, 95; Prophetic Rome in the High-Renaissance Period, 16th Century J, Vol 0026, 95; The Birth of the Despot--Venice and the Sublime Porte, Am Hist Rev, Vol 0100, 95; Who Was the 1st Counterreformation Pope, Cath Hist Rev, Vol 0081, 95; The Trial of Davidico, Lorenzo (1555-1560) by the Roman Inquisition--Critical Edition, J Mod Hist, Vol 0067, 95; Creative Women in Medieval and Early-Modern Italy--A Religious and Artistic Renaissance, Cath Hist Rev, Vol 0082, 96; Pius-V, J Ecclesiastical Hist, Vol 0047, 96; The Lateran in 1600--Christian Concord in Counterreformation Rome, Church Hist, Vol 0066, 97. **CONTACT ADDRESS** Dept of Hist, Univ of San Francisco, San Francisco, CA, 94132.

GLEASON, MAUDE
DISCIPLINE CLASSICS **EDUCATION** BA, 75; Oxford Univ, MA, 77; Univ CA Berkeley, PhD, 90. **CAREER** Lctr, Stanford Univ. **RESEARCH** Relig and soc in Late Antiquity and the High Empire; rhetoric; gender. **SELECTED PUBLICATIONS** Auth, Festive Satire: Julian's Misopogon and the New Year at Antioch, JRS, 86; The Semiotics of Gender: Physiognomy and Self-Fashioning in Before Sexuality, 90; Making Men: Sophists and Self-Presentation in the Roman Empire, 95. **CONTACT ADDRESS** Stanford Univ, Bldg 20, Main Quad, Stanford, CA, 94305.

GLEISSNER, STEPHEN
PERSONAL Born 06/27/1962, Wichita, KS, s **DISCIPLINE** ART HISTORY **EDUCATION** Northwestern Univ, PhD, 95. **CAREER** Independent art appraiser and historian **MEMBERSHIPS** Coll Art Assoc; Soc of Architectural Historians, Appraisers Assoc of Amer **RESEARCH** British 17th century art; arts and crafts architecture; decorative arts **SELECTED PUBLICATIONS** Auth, Journal of the History of Collections, Reassembling a Royal Art Collection for the Restored King of Great Britain, 94; Auth, Kings and Connoisseurs: Collecting Art in Seventeenth Century Europe, Review of Jonathan Brown, 97; Auth, Literature and History, Paper Bullets: Print and Kingship Under Charles II, Summer 97; **CONTACT ADDRESS** 115 S. Rutan, Wichita, KS, 67218.

GLEN, ROBERT ALLAN
PERSONAL Born 11/05/1946, Sioux Falls, SD **DISCIPLINE** BRITISH AND EUROPEAN HISTORY **EDUCATION** Univ Wash, BA, 68; Univ Calif, Berkeley, MA, 69, PhD, 78. **CAREER** Instr hist, Univ Wis, Parkside, 75-77 & Univ Vt, 77-78; asst prof, 79-82, assoc prof 82-87, prof Hist, Univ New Haven, 87-; chair, Hist, Univ New Haven 83-87; 94-96; **MEMBERSHIPS** AHA; Hist Asn London; Econ Hist Soc; Social Hist Soc. **RESEARCH** British labor during the industrial revolution; history of English and Caribbean methodism; British urban history. **SELECTED PUBLICATIONS** Auth, The Milnes of Stockport and the export of English technology, Cheshire Hist, 79; The Manchester grammar school in the early nineteenth century, Trans Lancashire & Cheshire Antiquarian Soc, 79; Benjamin Franklin and a case of machine smuggling in the 1780's, Bus Hist, 81; auth, Urban Workers in the Early Industrial Revolution, 84; auth, Man or Beast? English Methodists as Animals in the 18th Centure Satinic Pronts, Conneticut Review, 93; auth, Anatomy of a Religious Revival: The Stockport Methodists in the 1790s, Manchester Region Hist Review, 96. **CONTACT ADDRESS** Dept of History, Univ of New Haven, 300 Orange Ave, West Haven, CT, 06516-1999. **EMAIL** bobglen@charger.newhaven.edu

GLEN, THOMAS L.
DISCIPLINE ART HISTORY **EDUCATION** Princeton Univ, MA, PhD. **CAREER** Assoc prof. **RESEARCH** 17th cent painting and sculpture; Rubens; van Dyck; Poussin; Velazquez. **CONTACT ADDRESS** Dept of Art History, McGill Univ, 845 Sherbrooke St, Montreal, PQ, H3A 2T5.

GLENN, CECIL E.
PERSONAL Born 12/18/1938, Nashville, TN, m **DISCIPLINE** EDUCATION **EDUCATION** BA; MA; PhD 1975. **CAREER** Univ of CO, prof Social Science, head Ethnic Studies; Chicago Dept of Educ, Public Health Serv Civil Rights Envolvement, 10 yrs; teahcer 15 yrs; Higher Educ, area urban sociologist 5 yrs; Mental Health Inc, serv in mental health field chmn 5 yrs. **HONORS AND AWARDS** Recip awds Nat Alliance of Business 1975; Mt Plains Comm Coll Ldshp 1974; Partners corrective progs 1974. **MEMBERSHIPS** Chmn Malcolm X Mental Inc; mem NAACP. **CONTACT ADDRESS** 1100 14 St, Denver, CO, 80202.

GLENN, GEORGE
DISCIPLINE THEATRE HISTORY **EDUCATION** Univ IL, PhD. **CAREER** Prof, ch, grad prog, dept Theater, dir, Iowa Regents London prog, Univ Northern IA, 91/92. **MEMBERSHIPS** Pres, Mid-Am Theatre Conf. **SELECTED PUBLICATIONS** Publ in a variety of areas from nautical drama to the use of firearms on stage. **CONTACT ADDRESS** Univ Northern IA, Cedar Falls, IA, 50614. **EMAIL** susan.chilcott@uni.edu

GLENN, JUSTIN MATTHEWS
PERSONAL Born 04/10/1945, Little Rock, AR, m, 1971, 2 children **DISCIPLINE** GREEK & LATIN LITERATURE **EDUCATION** Stanford Univ, BA, 67; Princeton Univ, MA, 69, PhD(classics), 70. **CAREER** Asst prof Classics, Univ Ga, 70-72; asst prof, 72-76, from assoc prof to prof Classics, Fla State Univ, 76-82; vice pres Classical Assoc of Fla, 85-87. **HONORS AND AWARDS** Teacher of the Year, Classical Assoc of Fla, 92. **MEMBERSHIPS** Class Asn Mid W & S. **RESEARCH** Classical mythology; psychoanalytic criticism; Greek and Latin poetry. **SELECTED PUBLICATIONS** Auth, Mezentius and Polyphemus, Am J Philol, 71; The Polyphemus folktale, Trans Am Philol Asn, 71; Psychoanalytic writings on Greek and Latin authors, Class World, 72; Virgil's Polyphemus, Greece & Rome, 72; Psychoananlytic writings on classical mythology and religion, Classical World, 76-77. **CONTACT ADDRESS** Dept of Classics, Florida State Univ, 205 Dodd Hall, Tallahassee, FL, 32306-1510. **EMAIL** jglenn@mailer.fsu.edu

GLENNY, SHARON
DISCIPLINE MUSIC HISTORY **EDUCATION** Western Conserv London, AMus; McMaster Univ, BMus; Ma; SUNY Buffalo, PhD. **CAREER** Adj lctr, 96, SUNY Binghamton. **RESEARCH** Music hist and theory; music criticism; Morton Feldman. **SELECTED PUBLICATIONS** Auth, Cyclic Form in Debussy's Nocturnes, Cahiers Debussy, 96. **CONTACT ADDRESS** Dept Music, SUNY Binghamton, PO Box 6000, Binghamton, NY, 13902-6000.

GLICK, THOMAS F.
PERSONAL Born 01/28/1939, Cleveland, OH, m, 1963, 2 children **DISCIPLINE** MEDIEVAL HISTORY **EDUCATION** Harvard Univ, BA, 60, PhD, 68; Columbia Univ, MA, 63. **CAREER** From asst prof to assoc prof hist, Univ Tex, Austin, 68-72; assoc prof, 72-79, prof hist, Boston Univ, 79-, Dir, Inst Medieval Hist, 98-. **HONORS AND AWARDS** Guggenheim Fel, 87-88; NSF Fel, 89-90; NEH Fel, 93-94. **MEMBERSHIPS** Hist Sci Soc; Soc Hist Technol. **RESEARCH** Medieval science and technology in Spain and the Islamic world. **SELECTED PUBLICATIONS** Auth, Islamic and Christian Spain in the Early Middle Ages, Princeton Univ Press, 79; From Muslim Fortress to Christian Castle, Manchester Univ Press, 95. **CONTACT ADDRESS** Dept of Hist, Boston Univ, 226 Bay State Rd, Boston, MA, 02215-1403. **EMAIL** tglick@bu.edu

GLOSECKI, STEPHEN O.
DISCIPLINE ANGLO-SAXON ART AND CULTURE **EDUCATION** CA State Univ, PhD, 80. **CAREER** Dept Eng, Univ Ala **SELECTED PUBLICATIONS** Auth, Shamanism and Old English Poetry, Garland Press; Movable Beasts: The Manifold Implications of Early Germanic Animal Imagery, Garland Press. **CONTACT ADDRESS** Univ AL, 1400 University Blvd, Birmingham, AL, 35294-1150.

GLOWACKI, KEVIN T.
DISCIPLINE CLASSICAL STUDIES **EDUCATION** Loyola Univ, BA, 83, MA, 85; Bryn Mawr Col, MA, 87, PhD, 91. **CAREER** Asst prof. **RESEARCH** Greek art and archaeology; Greek sculpture; topography & monuments of Athens; Aegean Bronze & Iron Ages; mythological representation in art. **SELECTED PUBLICATIONS** Auth, A New Fragment of the Erechtheion Frieze, Hesperia, 95; The Acropolis of Athens before 566 B.C, Univ Pa, 97. **CONTACT ADDRESS** Dept of Classical Studies, Indiana Univ, Bloomington, 300 N Jordan Ave, Bloomington, IN, 47405.

GLUCK, CAROL
DISCIPLINE MODERN JAPANESE INTELLECTUAL HISTORY **EDUCATION** Wellesley Col, BA, 62; Columbia Univ, PhD, 77. **CAREER** George Sansom prof. **SELECTED PUBLICATIONS** Auth, Japan's Modern Myths: Ideology in the Late Meiji Period, 85; Showa: the Japan of Hirohito, 92; Asia in Western and World History, 96. **CONTACT ADDRESS** Dept of Hist, Columbia Col, New York, 2960 Broadway, New York, NY, 10027-6902.

GLUECKERT, LEO
DISCIPLINE HISTORY **EDUCATION** Loyola Univ Chicago, PhD, 89. **CAREER** Hist, Loyola Univ. **RESEARCH** Modern European history. **SELECTED PUBLICATIONS** Auth, Between Two Amnesties: Former Polit Prisoners and Exiles in the Roman Revolution of 1848; Papal States: Before 1849, in Encycl of 1848 Revolution; Papal States: Exiles and Polit Prisoners, in Encycl of 1848 Revolution; Origins of Carmel in Kansas, Sword, 90; The World of Therese: France, Church and State in the Late 19th century, in Carmelite Stud, 90; rev, Saveno Fabriani, Catholic Hist Rev, 95. **CONTACT ADDRESS** Fine Arts Dept, Loyola Univ, Chicago, 6525 N. Sheridan Rd., Chicago, IL, 60626. **EMAIL** lglueck@wpo.it.luc.edu

GMELCH, GEORGE
PERSONAL Born 12/28/1945, New York, NY, m, 1969, 1 child **DISCIPLINE** ANTHROPOLOGY **EDUCATION** Stanford, BA, 68; UCSB, PhD, 75. **CAREER** McSU Univ, Asst Prof, 73-75; SUNY, Albany, Asst Prof, 75-80; Union Coll, Prof, 80-present. **MEMBERSHIPS** Amer Anthro Assoc **RESEARCH** Cultural Anthro; Caribbean; Ireland Sport; Urban Anthro; Oral Hist. **SELECTED PUBLICATIONS** In The Ballpark, 98; The Parish Behind God's Back, 97; The Irish Tinker's, 87; Urban Life 93. **CONTACT ADDRESS** Dept of Anthro, Union Coll, Schenectady, NY, 12308. **EMAIL** gmelchg@union.edu

GMELCH, SHARON BOHN
PERSONAL Born 06/02/1947, Balboa, Panama, m, 1968, 1 child **DISCIPLINE** CULTURAL ANTHROPOLOGY **EDUCATION** Univ Calif, Santa Barbara, BA, 69, MA, 71, PhD, 75. **CAREER** PROF, ANTHROP, UNION COLL. **MEMBERSHIPS** Am Anthrop Asn **RESEARCH** Ethnicity; Cultural change; Gender; Visual anthropology; Biography **SELECTED PUBLICATIONS** Tinkers and Travellers: Ireland's Nomads, Mc-Gill Univ Press, 76; edr, Irish Life and Traditions, Syracuse univ Press, 86; Nan: The Life of an Irish Travelling Woman, Waveland Press, 91; The Parish Behind God's Back: The Changing Culture of Rural Barbados, Univ Mich Press, 97; Gender on Campus: Issues for College Women, Rutgers Univ Press, 98. **CONTACT ADDRESS** Dept Anthrop, Union Col, Schenectady, NY, 12308. **EMAIL** gmelchs@union.edu

GOBEL, DAVID W.
PERSONAL Born 06/11/1958, Sierra Madre, CA, m, 1988, 2 children **DISCIPLINE** HISTORY OF ARCHITECTURE **EDUCATION** Princeton Univ, PhD 91; Univ VI, M arch, 88; Princeton Univ, MA 86; Texas Tech Univ, BArch 81. **CAREER** Savannah Col of Art and Design, prof 96-; Univ Oregon, adj asst prof 94-96; Portland State Univ, adj asst prof 93-94; Clackamas Comm Col, inst 93; Portland Comm Col, inst 92-93; Maryhurst Col, inst 91-93; Pacific NW Col, inst 92; Oregon Sch Arch, asst prof 90-91; Princeton Univ, asst inst, res asst, 86-88. **HONORS AND AWARDS** William G. Bowen Fel; Fulbright-Hays Fel; Stanley J. Seeger Fel; Princeton Univ Fels; Omicron Delta Kappa; Tau Sigma Delta. **MEMBERSHIPS** SAH; CAA; SSAH; ASHAHS. **RESEARCH** Renaissance and baroque arch and urbanism; hist of arch and theory. **SELECTED PUBLICATIONS** Auth, The Demise of the City Gate, The U of Penn Archi Jour, 98; Rev of Catherine Wilkinson-Zerner, Juan de Herrera: Architect to Philip of Spain, in: Jour of the Soc of Archi Historians, 95; Assoc ed, The Princeton Journal: Thematic Studies in Architecture, Princeton Arch Press, 89; Gates of Glory, Coll of Charles, 97; The Plan of St. Gall and the Representation of Architecture, Portland St U, 94. **CONTACT ADDRESS** Dept of Architectural History, Savannah Col, PO Box 3146, Savannah, GA, 31402-3146. **EMAIL** dgobel@scad.edu

GOCKING, ROGER S.
PERSONAL Born 10/09/1943, Trinidad and Tobago, s **DISCIPLINE** HISTORY **EDUCATION** Fairfield Univ, BA, 68; Stanford Univ, MA, 72; Stanford Univ, PhD, 81 **CAREER** Instr, Mercy Col, 81-85; asst prof, Mercy Col, 85-91; Fulbright prof, National Univ Lesotho, 91-92; assoc prof, Mercy Col, 92- **HONORS AND AWARDS** Stanford Univ Fel; Fulbright Teaching Award; Research Grant Stanford Univ **MEMBERSHIPS** Amer Alpine Club; New York African Studies Assoc; African Studies Assoc; New England Regional Conf **SELECTED PUBLICATIONS** Auth, Facing Two Ways: Ghana's Coastal Communities Under Colonial Rule, Univ Press Amer; auth, "Colonial Rule and the 'Legal Factor' in Ghana and Lesotho," Africa, 97; auth, "Ghana's Public Tribunals: An Experiment in Revolutionary Justice," African Affairs, 96 **CONTACT ADDRESS** 8 Davids Ln, Ossining, NY, 10562-5940. **EMAIL** Gocking@ibm.net

GODBEER, R.
DISCIPLINE HISTORY **EDUCATION** Oxford Univ, BA, 84; Brandeis Univ, PhD, 89 **CAREER** Instr hist, U.C. Riverside, 89- **RESEARCH** Early America - cultural and religious; gender and sexuality **CONTACT ADDRESS** Univ Calif Riverside, Riverside, CA, 92521.

GODBOLD, E. STANLY
PERSONAL Born 03/15/1942, SC, m, 1 child **DISCIPLINE** HISTORY **EDUCATION** Duke Univ, BA, 63; Southern Methodist Univ, BD, 66; Duke Univ, MA, 68, PhD, 70. **CAREER** Asst prof, hist, Univ Tenn, 69-70; assoc prof, Valdosta State Univ, 70-77; PROF, HIST, MISS STATE UNIV, 77-. **HONORS AND AWARDS** Thomas Wolfe Literary Awd, 91; MSU Alumni Awd, Graduate Teaching, 94; Hum Fac Awd, 95. **MEMBERSHIPS** South Hist Asn. **RESEARCH** South History **SELECTED PUBLICATIONS** Auth, Ellen Glasgow and the Woman Within, LSU Press, 72; auth, Christopher Gadsden and the American Revolution, Univ Tenn Press, 82; auth, Confederate Colonel and the Cherokee Chief: The Life of William Holland Thomas, Univ Tenn Press, 91. **CONTACT ADDRESS** Mississippi State Univ, PO Drawer H, Starkville, MS, 39762. **EMAIL** esg@ra.msstate.edu

GODFREY, AARON W.
PERSONAL Born 01/10/1929, New York, NY, m, 1981, 7 children **DISCIPLINE** CLASSICS **EDUCATION** Fordham Univ, BA, 58; Hunter Col, MA, 60. **CAREER** Asst Latin-Am

rels, Grace Nat Bank, 52-60; instr lang, Newton Col Sacred Heart, 60-61, asst prof hist and class lang, 61-65; dir spec proj, 65-74, Dir Upware Bound Proj, State Univ NY Stony Brook, 66-, LECTR CLASSICS, 67-, Consult, State Educ Dept NY, 67-73; SECY-TREAS, NAT COORD COUN EDUC OPPORTUNITY, 70-, ed, Review; consult, ESEA Title I, New York Schs, 70-72. **MEMBERSHIPS** AHA; Medieval Acad Am; Liturgical Arts Soc; Class Asn Atlantic States; Asn Equality & Excellence Educ (secy, 77-). **RESEARCH** Ancient and medieval history; compensatory education; classical and medieval Latin. **SELECTED PUBLICATIONS** Auth, Catalogus-Translationum-Et-Commentariorum, Vol 7, Medieval and Renaissance Latin Translations and Commentaries, Class World, Vol 0087, 94; Theodoric in Italy, Class World, Vol 0088, 95; Suetonius 'De Grammaticis Et Rhetoribus,' Class World, Vol 0090, 97. **CONTACT ADDRESS** State Univ NY, Stony Brook, Stony Brook, NY, 11794.

GODFREY, MARY F.
DISCIPLINE MEDIEVAL SERMON LITERATURE, MEDIEVAL DRAMA, PSYCHOANALYTIC CRITICISM **EDUCATION** Princeton, PhD. **CAREER** Asst prof, Fordham Univ. **RESEARCH** Post-conquest literary cult in Engl. **SELECTED PUBLICATIONS** Auth, Beowulf and Judith: Thematizing Decapitation in Old English Poetry, Tex Stud Lit and Lang 35, 93; Sir Gawain and the Green Knight: The Severed Head and the Body Politic, Assays: Critical Approaches to Medieval and Renaissance Texts 8, 95. **CONTACT ADDRESS** Dept of Eng Lang and Lit, Fordham Univ, 113 W 60th St, New York, NY, 10023.

GODFREY, WILLIAM GERALD
PERSONAL Born 06/10/1941, Stratford, ON, Canada, m, 1967, 3 children **DISCIPLINE** NORTH AMERICAN AND CANADIAN HISTORY **EDUCATION** Univ Waterloo, BA, 63, MA, 66; Queen's Univ, PhD(hist), 74. **CAREER** Lectr hist, Notre Dame Univ Nelson, 65-67, asst prof, 67-68; asst prof, 70-77, ASSOC PROF HIST, MT ALLISON UNIV, 77-, HEAD DEPT, 80-, Dean men, Notre Dame Univ Nelson, 66-67. **MEMBERSHIPS** AHA; Can Hist Asn. **RESEARCH** Comparative colonial societies; 18th century trans-Atlantic world. **SELECTED PUBLICATIONS** Auth, 19th-Century Cape-Breton--A Historical Geography, J Can Stud-Rev D Etudes Canadiennes, Vol 0028, 93; Trouble in the Woods, Forest Policy and Social-Conflict in Nova-Scotia and New-Brunswick, J Can Stud-Rev D Etudes Canadiennes, Vol 0028, 93; Away, Maritimers in Massachusetts, Ontario and Alberta--An Oral-History of Leaving Home, J Can Stud-Rev D Etudes Canadiennes, Vol 0028, 93; Grenfell-of-Labrador--A Biography, J Can Stud-Rev D Etudes Canadiennes, Vol 0028, 93; The Atlantic Provinces in Confederation, J Can Stud-Rev D Etudes Canadiennes, Vol 0028, 93; Making Adjustments, Change and Continuity in Planter Nova-Scotia, 1759-1800, J Can Stud-Rev D Etudes Canadiennes, Vol 0028, 93; Literature and Society in the Canada, 1817-1850, Histoire Sociale-Soc Hist, Vol 0028, 95; Rawlyk, George Remembered, Acadiensis, Vol 0025, 96. **CONTACT ADDRESS** Hist Dept, Mount Allison Univ, Sackville, NB, E0A 3C0.

GODWIN, JOSCELYN
PERSONAL Born 01/16/1945, Kelmscott, United Kingdom, m, 1979, 1 child **DISCIPLINE** MUSICOLOGY **EDUCATION** Magdalene Coll, BA, Musicol, 65, MusB, 66; Cornell Univ, PhD, 69. **CAREER** Instr, Music, Cleveland State Univ, 69-71; PROF, COLGATE UNIV, MUSIC, 71-. **MEMBERSHIPS** Am Musicol Soc **SELECTED PUBLICATIONS** Robert Fludd; Athanasius Kircher; Mystery Religions in the Ancient World; Harmonies of Heaven and Earth; Music and the Occult; The Mystery of the Seven Vowels; Arktos, the Polar Myth; The Theosophical Enlightenment; coauth, JFH von Dalberg. **CONTACT ADDRESS** Dept Music, Colgate Univ, Hamilton, NY, 13346.

GOEDICKE, HANS
PERSONAL Born 08/07/1926, Vienna, Austria **DISCIPLINE** EGYPTOLOGY **EDUCATION** Univ Vienna, PhD, 49. **CAREER** Res Assoc Egyptol, Brown Univ, 52-56; lectr, 60-62, from asst prof to assoc prof, 62-68, prof, 68-79, CHMN NEAR EASTERN STUDIES, JONHS HOPKINS UNIV, 79-, Howard fel, 56-57; tech asst, Unesco-Centre doc l'ancienne Egypte, Cairo, 57-58; asst, Univ Gottingen, 58-60; Am Philos Soc grant, 66; John Simon Guggenheim Mem fel, 66-67; mem, Am Res Ctr Egypt; dir archaeol exped, Giza, Egypt, 72 and 74 and Tell el Rataba, 77, 78 and 81; corresp mem, Ger Archaeol Inst, 74. **MEMBERSHIPS** Egypt Explor Soc, London. **RESEARCH** Egyptian historical and administrative inscriptions. **SELECTED PUBLICATIONS** Auth, Thoughts About the Papyrus-Westcar, Zeitschrift fur Agyptische Sprache und Altertumskunde, Vol 0120, 93; The Story of Sinuhe, J Near Eastern Stud, Vol 0052, 93; The God Sopdu, J Near Eastern Stud, Vol 0053, 94; Religion in Ancient-Egypt--Gods, Myths, and Personal Practice, J Near Eastern Stud, Vol 0054, 95; The Thutmosis-I Inscription Near Tomas, J Near Eastern Stud, Vol 0055, 96. **CONTACT ADDRESS** Dept of Near Eastern Studies, Johns Hopkins Univ, 3400 N Charles St, Baltimore, MD, 21218.

GOEL, MADAN LAL
PERSONAL Born 06/20/1935, India, m, 1 child **DISCIPLINE** POLITICAL SCIENCE **EDUCATION** The Panjab Univ, BA, 56; Univ of Oregon, MA, 59; State Univ of New York, Buffalo, PhD, 69. **CAREER** Res and teaching asst, State Univ of New York, Buffalo, 63-66; instr to asst prof, Niagra Univ, 66-69; ASST PROF, 69-72, ASSOC PROF 72-78, PROF, UNIV OF WEST FL, PENSACOLA, 68-, dir of int studies, 84-. **HONORS AND AWARDS** Booth Fel in Public Service, Univ of Ore, 58; Grad Fel, State Univ of New York, 63-66; Nat Sci Found Award, Univ of Colo, 70; Distinguished Res and Creative Activities Award, Univ of West Fla, 79; Summer Col Fac Award, Nat Endowment of the Humanities, 90; Distinguished Teaching Award, Univ W Fla, 96; Distinguished Res Award, Univ W Fla, 97; Teaching Incentive Prog Award, Univ W Fla, 97; Professional Excellence Prog Award, Univ W Fla, 97; Fulbright Scholar, 98. **MEMBERSHIPS** Am Political Sci Asn. **RESEARCH** Political participation; comparative politics. **SELECTED PUBLICATIONS** Auth, Political Science Research: A Methods Handbook, Iowa State Univ Press, 88; auth, Political Science Research: A Methods Workbook, Iowa State Univ Press, 88; coauth, Social and Political Science Research Methods, Ajanta Int Pub, 97; auth, International Dimensions of Education at the University of West Florida, Pensacola and the World Project, Univ of West Fla, 78; auth, Foreign Flight Students in the Pensacola Area, Pensacola and the World Project, Univ of West Fla, 79; auth, Pensacola International Directory, Univ of West Fla, 79. **CONTACT ADDRESS** Dept of Govt, Univ of West Florida, Pensacola, FL, 32514. **EMAIL** lgoel@uwf.edu

GOERTZEN, CHRIS
DISCIPLINE MUSIC **EDUCATION** Univ IL, PhD. **CAREER** Prof ethnomusicol, Earlham Col. **RESEARCH** Music of Latin Am; music of Africa; music of Asia. **SELECTED PUBLICATIONS** Auth, Fiddling for Norway: Revival and Identity, Univ Chicago, 97; publ(s) on musics in oral tradition in America. **CONTACT ADDRESS** Music Dept, Earlham Col, Richmond, IN, 47374-4095. **EMAIL** liffeyt@earlham.edu

GOETZMANN, WILLIAM HARRY
PERSONAL Born 07/20/1930, Washington, DC, m, 1953, 3 children **DISCIPLINE** AMERICAN STUDIES **EDUCATION** Yale Univ, BA, 52, PhD(Am studies), 57. **CAREER** Asst instr hist, Yale Univ, 55-57, from instr to assoc prof hist and Am studies, 57-64; from assoc prof to prof, 64-67, dir, Am studies prog, 65-81, STILES PROF AM STUDIES, UNIV TEX, 67-, Am Philos Soc grants, 59-60 and 63-64; Susan B Morse fel, 59-60; Soc Sci Res Coun fel, 62-63; Fulbright vis sr lectr, Cambridge Univ, 67-68; chief hist consult, US Nat Atlas Proj, 62-; Guggenheim fel award, 77-78; fel, Ctr Advan Studies in Behav Sci, 80-81. **HONORS AND AWARDS** Pulitzer Prize, 67; Francis Parkman Prize, Orgn Am Historians, 67; Golden Plate Award, Am Acad Achievement, 68., LLD, St Edwards Univ, 67. **MEMBERSHIPS** Am Studies Asn (pres, 75-76); Western Hist Asn; Soc Am Historians. **RESEARCH** American cultural history; history of the American West; history of science in America. **SELECTED PUBLICATIONS** Auth, Royce, Josiah--From Grass Valley to Harvard, Pacific Northwest Quart, Vol 0084, 93; The Journals of the Lewis-and-Clark-Expedition March 23 June 9, 1806, Vol 7, NMex Hist Rev, Vol 0068, 93; From Maps to Metaphors--The Pacific World of Vancouver, George, Western Hist Quart, Vol 0025, 94; The Journals of the Lewis and Clark Expedition--June 10 to September 26, 1806, Vol 8, NMex Hist Rev, Vol 0069, 94; The Oxford History of the American-West, Southwestern Hist Quart, Vol 0098, 94; Essays on the Changing Images of the Southwes, Southwestern Hist Quart, Vol 0099, 95; Phillips, Bert, Geer and the Taos Art Colony, Pacific Hist Rev, Vol 0064, 95; The Empire of the Eye--Landscape Representation and American Cultural Politics, 1825-1875, Rev in Am Hist, Vol 0023, 95; Daddy-O--Iguana Heads and Texas Tales, Southwestern Hist Quart, Vol 0099, 96; Wild River, Timeless Canyons--Mollhausen,Balduin Watercolors of the Colorado, Southwestern Hist Quart, Vol 0100, 96; Remington,Frederic and Turn-of-the-Century America, J Am Hist, Vol 0083, 96; Drawing the Borderline--Artist-Explorers of the US-Mexico Boundary Survey, Pacific Hist Rev, Vol 0066, 97; Moran, Thomas, the Wests Grandest Painter--A Review-Essay of Morand, Anne 'Thomas Moran, the Field Sketches, 1856-1923' (1996), NMex Hist Rev, Vol 0072, 97; Re-imagining the Modern American-West--A Century of Fiction, History and Art, Western Hist Quart, Vol 0028, 97; Ritual Ground--Bents Old Fort, World Formation, and the Annexation of the Southwest, Southwestern Hist Quart, Vol 0101, 97; A New Significance--Re-envisioning the History of the American-West, J Interdisciplinary Hist, Vol 0028, 98. **CONTACT ADDRESS** Am Studies Prog, Univ of Tex, 0 Univ of Texas, Austin, TX, 78712-1026.

GOFF, BARBARA E.
PERSONAL Born 01/23/1958, London, England, m, 1989, 1 child **DISCIPLINE** CLASSICS **EDUCATION** Berkeley, PhD, 85. **CAREER** Jr Res fel, Kings Col Cambridge, 86-90; Asst prof, 91-98, Assoc Prpf, Univ Texas-Austin, 98- . **MEMBERSHIPS** APA **RESEARCH** Greek tradegy; women in antiquity. **SELECTED PUBLICATIONS** Auth, Euripedes Ion, 88; The Tent, PCPS, 88; The shields of the Phoenissae, GRBS, 88; The Noose of Words: readings of desire, violence and language in Euripide's Hippolytos, Cambridge Univ Press, 90; The sign of the fall: the scars of Orestes and Odysseus, CA, 91; rev Synnove des Bouvrie, Women in Greek Tragedy, AJP, 92; rev, Ruth Padel, In and Out of the Mide, CPhil, 94; auth, Aithra at Eleusis, Helios, 95; The Women of Thebes, CJ, 95; The Figure of Antiquity in the Memoirs of Mme Roland: the classical, the revolutionary, and the feminine, CML, 96. **CONTACT ADDRESS** Classics Dept, Univ Texas Austin, Waggener Hall 123, Austin, TX, 78712-1181.

GOFF, JOHN S.
PERSONAL Born 06/20/1931, Los Angeles, CA, m, 1967, 2 children **DISCIPLINE** UNITED STATES HISTORY **EDUCATION** Univ Southern Calif, AB, 53, AM, 55, PhD(hist), 60; Ariz State Univ, JD, 74. **CAREER** Teaching asst Am civilization, Univ Southern Calif, 55-57; instr hist and polit sci, WTex State Univ, 57-60; chmn educ, philos and soc sci, 62-69, INSTR HIST AND POLIT SCI, PHOENIX COL, 60-, Consult and examr, NCent Accrediting Asn, 70-; consult, Nat Endowment for Humanities, 73- **RESEARCH** Constitutional and legal history; Arizona history. **SELECTED PUBLICATIONS** Auth, From Local Courts to National Tribunals--The Federal District Courts of Florida, 1821-1990, Am Hist Rev, Vol 0098, 93. **CONTACT ADDRESS** Phoenix Col, 1202 W Thomas, Phoenix, AZ, 85013.

GOFF, RICHARD D.
DISCIPLINE HISTORY **EDUCATION** Duke Univ, PhD. **CAREER** Prof and undergrad adv, Eastern Michigan Univ. **RESEARCH** US early national period, US old south. **SELECTED PUBLICATIONS** Coauth, The Twentieth Century, A Brief Global history; World History. **CONTACT ADDRESS** Dept of History and Philosophy, Eastern Michigan Univ, 701 Pray-Harrold, Ypsilanti, MI, 48197.

GOFFART, WALTER A.
PERSONAL Born 02/22/1934, Berlin, Germany **DISCIPLINE** MEDIEVAL HISTORY **EDUCATION** Harvard Univ, AB, 55, AM, 56, PhD, 61. **CAREER** Lectr to assoc prof, 60-71, PROF MEDIEVAL HISTORY, UNIV TORONTO, 71-; vis asst prof, Univ Calif Berkeley, 65-66; vis fel, Inst Advan Stud, Princeton, 67-68; vis fel, Dumbarton Oaks Ctr Byzantine Stud, 73-74. **HONORS AND AWARDS** Connaught sr fel, 83; Can Coun leave fel, 67-68; Coun Learned Soc fel, 73-74; Guggenheim fel, 79-80; SSHRCC leave fel, 85-86, res grant, 90-92; Haskins Medal, Medieval Acad Am, 91; fel, Royal Soc Can, 96. **MEMBERSHIPS** Int Soc Anglo-Saxonists; Hagiography Soc; Can Soc Medievalists; Medieval Acad Am; Royal Hist Soc. **RESEARCH** Late Roman and early medieval history. **SELECTED PUBLICATIONS** Auth, Le Mans Forgeries, 66; auth, Caput and Colonate, 74; auth, Barbarians and Romans A.D. 418-584, 80; auth, The Narrators of Barbarian History (A.D. 550-800), 88; auth, Rome's Fall and After, 89; co-transl, The Origin of the Idea of Crusade, 78; ed bd, Speculum. **CONTACT ADDRESS** Dept of History, Univ of Toronto, Toronto, ON, M5S 3G3.

GOFFEN, RONA
DISCIPLINE ART HISTORY **EDUCATION** Columbia Univ, PhD. **CAREER** Prof, Rutgers Univ. **HONORS AND AWARDS** Asso ed, Renaissance Quart. **RESEARCH** Italian Medieval and Renaissance Art; contextual hist of Italian painting and sculpture from ca. 1250-1600, emphasizing Florence and Venice, and dealing with sacred and polit imagery of the Madonna; the definition of gender in rel to soc realities; "new critical" methologies regarding (self-) imagery and narrative. **SELECTED PUBLICATIONS** Auth, Titian's Women; New Haven and London, 97; Titian's Venus of Urbino; NY and Cambridge, 96; Giovanni Bellini, New Haven and London, 89, Ital ed, Milan, 90, second printing, 94; Piety and Patronage in Renaissance Venice: Bellini, Titian, and the Franciscans; New Haven and London, 86, paperback ed New Haven and London, 90, Ital ed, Venice, 91; Spirituality in Conflict: Saint Francis and Giotto's Bardi Chapel, Univ Park and London, 89. **CONTACT ADDRESS** Dept of Art Hist, Rutgers Univ/Rutgers Col, Hamilton St., New Brunswick, NJ, 08903. **EMAIL** goffen@rci.rutgers.edu

GOHEEN, R.B.
DISCIPLINE HISTORY **EDUCATION** Univ Toronto, BA, 61;, Yale Univ, MA, 62, PhD, 67. **CAREER** Assoc prof. **RESEARCH** The relevance of social philosophic conceptions of consciousness, responsibility and power to historical analyses of political practice. **SELECTED PUBLICATIONS** Auth, "Peasant Politics? Village Community and the Crown in Fifteenth Century England," Amer Hist Rev 96, 91. **CONTACT ADDRESS** Dept of Hist, Carleton Univ, 1125 Colonel By Dr, Ottawa, ON, K1S 5B6.

GOINS, RICHARD ANTHONY
PERSONAL Born 03/01/1950, New Orleans, Louisiana, m, 1990 **DISCIPLINE** HISTORY **EDUCATION** Yale Univ, BA (cum laude), History, 1972; Stanford Univ & Law School, JD, 1975. **CAREER** New Orleans Legal Assist Corp, mgr & staff attorney, 1975-77; deputy dir, 1977-78; exec dir, 1978-81; Hon Adrian G Duplantier, law clerk, 1982; Loyola Univ School of

Law, asst prof, 1981-84; Adams & Reese, asst attorney, 1984-87; attorney, partner, 1987-. **HONORS AND AWARDS** Stanford Univ, School of Law, Reginald Heber Smith Fellowship, 1975. **MEMBERSHIPS** Thomas More Inn of Court, barrister, 1988-; Loyola Univ Law School, adjunct prof, 1984-; Fed bar Assn, bd of dirs local chapter, 1992-; Merit Selection Panel for the Selection & Appointment of US Magistrate, 1992-96; Amer Bar Assn Conference of Minority Partners in Majority/Corporate Law Firm, 1990-; California State Bar, 1977-; Louisiana State Bar Assn, 1975-. **SELECTED PUBLICATIONS** Leadership Louisiana 1992 Participant; Practical Issues in Class Action Litigation, The Practical Litigator, Vol 6,# 1, Jan 1995, Author; Seminar Presenter, LA Public Retirement Seminar, Baton Rouge, LA 1989, 1990, topic: "Fiduciary Responsibilities of Trustees of Pension Plans;" Seminar Presenter, Recent Dev Seminar, Tulane Univ, New Orleans, LA, 1994, topic: "Recent Dev in Labor & Employment Law." **CONTACT ADDRESS** Adams & Reese, 4500 One Shell Sq, New Orleans, LA, 70139.

GOINS, SCOTT

PERSONAL Born 05/02/1961, Cleveland, TN, s **DISCIPLINE** CLASSICS **EDUCATION** Univ Tenn, BA, 83; Fla State Univ, MA, 85, PhD, 88. **CAREER** Vis asst Prof, Classics, Univ of South, 88-89; asst prof, 89-95, assoc prof & asst dept head dept of languages, 95-, Mcneese State Univ, 89-; ed, McNeese Rev. **MEMBERSHIPS** Amer Philol Asn; Class Asn Midwst & S; La Class Asn; Class Asn Can. **RESEARCH** Virgil; Boethius; Fable; Greek drama. **SELECTED PUBLICATIONS** Auth, Penelope and Melantho: A Question of Jealousy in Odyssey 19?, Class Bull, 87;Horace, sermo 1.5.61, Latomus, 87; The Influence of Old Comedy on the Vita Aesopi, Class World, 89; Euripides Fr 863 Nauck, Rheinisches Museum fur Philologie, 89; The Heroism of Odysseus in Euripides, Cyclops Eos, 91; Birds and Erotic Fantasies in Catullus and Goethe, Goethe Yearbook, 92; Two Aspects of Virgils Use of Labor in the Aeneid, Class Jour, 93; Pain and Authority in the Aeneid and Henry V, Class and Modern Lit, 95; The Date of Aeschylus Perseus Tetralogy, Rheinisches Museum fur Philol, 97; The Poetics in the Mythology Syllabus: Nothing to do with Dionysus, Class Bull, 97. **CONTACT ADDRESS** Dept of Languages, McNeese State Univ, Box 93465, Lake Charles, LA, 70609-2655. **EMAIL** sgoins@mcneese.edu

GOIST, PARK DIXON

PERSONAL Born 09/07/1936, Seattle, WA, m, 1987, 1 child **DISCIPLINE** AMERICAN STUDIES, THEATRE **EDUCATION** Univ WA, BA, 58; Univ Rochester, PhD, 67. **CAREER** Instr hist, Colgate Univ, 63 & Kent State Univ, 63-64; from instr to asst prof, 66-71, assoc prof Am studies, Case Western Reserve Univ, 71, Nat Am Studies Fac, 77. **MEMBERSHIPS** Am Studies Asn; Gt Lakes Am Studies Asn. **RESEARCH** Am intellectual hist; Am urban and community studies; Am drama. **SELECTED PUBLICATIONS** Co-ed, The Urban Vision: Selected Interpretations of the Modern American Dity, Dorsey, 70; auth, City and community: the urban theory of Robert Park, Am Quart, spring 71; Seeing things whole: a consideration of Lewis Mumford, 11/72 & Patrick Geddes and the city, 1/74, J Am Inst Planners: Town, City and Community, 1890-1920's, Am Studies, spring 73; Community and self in the Midwest town: Dell's Moon-Calf, Mid America II, 75; From Main Street to State Street: Town, City and Community in America, Kennikat, 77; Oregon Trail Diary, Reserve, 4/81. **CONTACT ADDRESS** Dep Theatre Arts, Case Western Reserve Univ, 10900 Euclid Ave, Cleveland, OH, 44106-4901.

GOKHALE, BALKRISHNA GOVIND

PERSONAL Born 09/04/1919, Dwarka, India, m, 1943, 2 children **DISCIPLINE** HISTORY OF INDIA **EDUCATION** Univ Bombay, BA, 39, MA, 41, PhD, 46. **CAREER** Asst prof Indian hist & Pali-Buddhism, St Xavier's Col, Bombay, 42-54; vis lectr Indian hist, Bowdoin Col, 54-55; assoc prof Indian & Southeast Asian hist, Oberlin Col, 55-56; chmn dept hist, Sidhart Col, India, 56-59; vis lectr Indian hist, Univ Wash, 59-60; prof hist & dir Asian Studies Prog, 60-90, prof emeritus, Wake Forest Univ; Lectr & res guide hist & Pali, Univ Bombay, 48-59. **MEMBERSHIPS** Am Orient Soc; Asn Asian Studies; AHA; fel Royal Asiatic Soc. **RESEARCH** History and civilization of India; Buddhism; Indian culture. **SELECTED PUBLICATIONS** Auth, Indian Thought Through the Ages, 60 & Samudragupta, 62, Asia; Asoka Maurya, Twayne, 66; Buddhism in Maharashtra, Popular Prakashan, 76; Surat in the XVIIth Century, Curzon, 78; Bharatavarsha, Sterling, 82; auth, Poona in the Eighteenth Century, Oxford, 88; auth, The Fiery Quill, Bowker, 98. **CONTACT ADDRESS** 1881 Faculty Dr, Winston-Salem, NC, 27106.

GOLAHNY, AMY

PERSONAL Detroit, MI **DISCIPLINE** ART HISTORY **EDUCATION** Brandeis Univ, BA, 73; Williams Col-Clark Art Inst, MA, 75; Columbia Univ, Mphil, 77, PhD, 84. **CAREER** Curatorial asst, Philadelphia Museum Art, 78; asst prof, Chatham Col, 83-85; assoc prof, Lycoming Col, 85-. **MEMBERSHIPS** Am Asn Netherlandic Stud; Historians of Netherlandish Art. **RESEARCH** Rembrandt; Renaissance European art. **SELECTED PUBLICATIONS** Auth, Rubens Hero and Leander and its Poetic Progeny, 90; auth, Literature, Poetry, and the Visual Arts in the 17th Century, 96; auth, Pieter Lastman in the Literature: From Immortality to Oblivion, 96; auth, Rembrandts Approach to Italian Art: Three Variations, 99; auth, Lastmans Dido Sacrificing to Juno Identified, 99. **CONTACT ADDRESS** Art Dept, Lycoming Col, 700 College Pl, Williamsport, PA, 17701. **EMAIL** golahny@lycoming.edu

GOLANY, GIDEON S.

DISCIPLINE URBAN DESIGN **EDUCATION** Hebrew University, Jerusalem, BA, 56, MA, 62; Inst for Soc Stud, The Hague, The Netherlands, DipCP, 65; Technion-Israel Inst of Tech, Haifa, Israel, MSc, 66; Hebrew Univ, Jerusalem, PhD, 66. **CAREER** Lecturer, Technion-Israel Inst of tech, 63-67; Lecturer, Cornell Univ, 67-68; Asn Prof, Va Polytechnic Inst & State Univ, 68-70; Ch of Grad Prog in Archit, Pa State Univ, 68-70; Sr Member Grad Sch Fac, 70-; Prof of Urban & Reg Planning, 70-87; Coord, China Progs, 84-89; Dir, PhD Prog, 86-89; Res Prof of Urban Des/Planning, 87-91; Distinguished Prof Urban Design, 91-; Aff Prof, Istanbul Tech Univ, Mid-E Tech Univ, Turkey, 96-. **HONORS AND AWARDS** Fulbright Res Award for Japan, 90-91; Nat Endowment for the Arts Grant, 94; Creative Accomplishment & Res Grant, Pa State Univ, 94-95; Fulbright Res Award for Turkey, 95-96; Finalist, Int Ach Award, Pa State Univ, 96, 97., Member, Acad Counc, Babylonian Jewry Heritage Cent, Israel. **MEMBERSHIPS** Am Planning Asn; Asn of Engineers & Archit in Israel; Am Underground Space Asn; Int New-Towns Asn; Int Ctr for Arid & Semi-Arid Land Stud; Asn for Arid Land Stud. **RESEARCH** Urban design/planning; planning for developing society; new-town planning & design; urban design in arid zone; geo-space urban design. **SELECTED PUBLICATIONS** Auth, Ethics and Urban Design: Culture, Form and Environment, John Wiley & Sons, 95; auth, Babylonian Jewelry: Culture, Home and Neighboorhood: Historical Appraisal, in review by press, 95; co-auth, Geo-Space Urban Design, John Wiley & Sons; 96; Japan Urban Environment, Elsevier Sci Ltd & Pergamon Press, 98; numerous multi-lingual publishings and book chapters. **CONTACT ADDRESS** Dept of Archit, Pennsylvania State Univ, 210 Engineering Unit C, University Park, PA, 16802. **EMAIL** gxg3@email.psu.edu

GOLAS, PETER JOHN

PERSONAL Born 04/24/1937, Paterson, NJ, m, 1967, 2 children **DISCIPLINE** HISTORY **EDUCATION** Fordham Univ, AB, 58; Stanford Univ, MA, 64; Harvard Univ, PhD(hist & Far Eastern lang), 72. **CAREER** Asst prof, 73-76, assoc prof Hist, Univ Denver, 76-96, prof History, 96-. **HONORS AND AWARDS** Distinguished Scholar, Univ of Denver. **MEMBERSHIPS** Asn Asian Studies. **RESEARCH** Socio-economic history of Sung China; history of technology in China. **SELECTED PUBLICATIONS** Co-ed, Change in Sung China; Innovation or Renovation?, Heath, 59; coauth, On Contradiction in the Light of Mao Tse-tung's Essay on Dialectical Materialism, China Quart, 7-9/64; auth, Early Ch'ing Guilds, In: The City in Late Imperial China, Stanford Univ, 77; Rural China in the Song, J Asian Studies, 2/80; Science and Civilization in China, Vol 5, Pt 13, Mining, 98. **CONTACT ADDRESS** Dept of Hist, Univ of Denver, 2199 S University, Denver, CO, 80210-4711. **EMAIL** pgolas@du.edu

GOLB, NORMAN

PERSONAL Born 01/15/1928, Chicago, IL, m, 1949, 3 children **DISCIPLINE** JEWISH HISTORY, HEBREW AND JUDEO-ARABIC STUDIES **EDUCATION** Roosevelt Col, BA, 48; Johns Hopkins Univ, PhD, 54. **CAREER** Warburg res fel Judaeo-Arabic studies, Hebrew Univ, Jerusalem, 55-57; vis lectr Semitic lang, Univ Wis, 57-58; from instr to asst prof Mediaeval Jewish studies, Hebrew Union Col, 58-63; from asst prof to prof Hebrew and Judeo-Arabiic Studies, Univ Chicago, 63-88, Rosenberger Prof Jewish Hist and Civilization, 88-. **HONORS AND AWARDS** Adler res fel, Dropsie Col, 54-55; Am Philos Soc grants-in-aid, 59, 63 & 67; Am Coun Learned Soc grants-in-aid, 63 & 65; Guggenheim Mem Found fels, 64-65 & 66-67; voting mem, Orient Inst, 64-; vis fel, Clare Hall, Cambridge Univ, 70; Nat Endowment for Humanities grant, 70-72; Grand Medal of Honor of the City of Rouen, 85; Docteur Honoris Causa (Histoire), Univ of Rouen, 87; Medal of Haute Normandie, 87. **MEMBERSHIPS** Fel Am Acad Jewish Res; life mem, Clare Hall, Cambridge Univ, 80-; Soc de l'Histoire de France, 87-; Founder and vice-pres, Soc for Judeo-Arabic Studies, 84-. **RESEARCH** Jewish History, Hebrew and Judeo-Arabic Studies. **SELECTED PUBLICATIONS** Auth, A Judaeo-Arabic Court Document of Syracuse, AD 1020, J Near Eastern Studies, 73; The Problem of Origin and Identification of the Dead Sea Scrolls, Proc Am Philos Soc, 80; Nature et destination du monument hebraique decouvert a Rouen, Proc Am Acad Jewish Res, 81; coauth (with Omeljan Pritsak), Khazarian Hebrew Documents of the Tenth Century, Cornell Univ Press, 82, trans to Russ, 97; auth, Les Juifs de Rouen au Moyen Age, Presses Univ de Rouen, 85; Who Wrote the Dead Sea Scrolls?, Scribner, 95, translated in Ger, Dutch, Port, Fr, Japanese; The Jews of Medieval Normandy, Cambridge Univ Press, 98; ed, Judeo-Arabic Studies, Harwood Acad Press, 97. **CONTACT ADDRESS** Univ of Chicago, 1155 E 58th St, Chicago, IL, 60637-1540. **EMAIL** n.golb@uchicago.edu

GOLD, ANN G.

PERSONAL Born 12/08/1946, Chicago, IL, m, 1981, 3 children **DISCIPLINE** ANTHROPOLOGY **EDUCATION** Univ Chicago, BA, 75, MA, 78, PhD, 84. **CAREER** Vis asst, adj asst, acting asst, Mellon fel, South Asian Studies, Cornell Univ, 85-93; asst prof, 93-96, prof, Syracuse Univ, relig, 96-. **HONORS AND AWARDS** Fulbright Res scholar, 92-93; Spencer Found major grant, 96-97; NEH fel for univ teachers, 97-98. **MEMBERSHIPS** AAA; AAR; AAS. **RESEARCH** South Asia; Religion; Environment; Oral traditions; Gender. **SELECTED PUBLICATIONS** Co-auth, Listen to the Heron's Words: Reimagining Gender and Kinship in North India, Univ Calif Press, 94; auth, A Carnival of Parting: The Tales of King Bharthari and King Gopi Chand As Sung and Told by Madhu Natisar Nath of Ghatiyali, Rajasthan, India, Univ Calif Press, 92; auth, Fruitful Journeys: The Ways of Rajasthani Pilgrims, Univ Calif Pres, 88; article, Outspoken women: Representations of Female Voices in a Rajasthani Folklore Community, Oral Traditions, 98; auth, Wild Pigs and Kings: Remembered Landscapes in Rajasthan, Amer Anthrop, 97; auth, Khyal: Changed Yearnings in Rajasthani Women's Songs, Manushi, 96; auth, The Jungli Rani and Other Troubled Wives in Rajasthani Oral Traditions, From the Margins of Hindu Marriage, Oxford Univ Press, 95; auth, Mother Ten's Stories, Relig of India in Practice, Princeton Univ Press, 95; auth, Magical Landscapes and Moral Orders: New Readings in Religion and Ecology, Relig Studies Rev, 95; auth, Of Gods, Trees and Boundaries: Divine Conservation in Rajasthan, Folk, Faith and Feudalism, Rawat Publ, 95; auth, Gender, Violence and Power: Rajasthani Stories of Shakti, Women as Subjects: South Asian Histories, Univ Press of Va, 94; auth, Yatra, Jatra, and Pressing Down Pebbles: Pilgrimage within and beyond Rajasthan, The Idea of Rajasth, Manohar Publ, 94; auth, Drawing Pictures in the Dust: Rajasthani Children's Landscapes, Childhood, 94. **CONTACT ADDRESS** Dept. of Religion, 501 Hall of Languages, Syracuse, NY, 13244-1170. **EMAIL** aggold@syr.edu

GOLD, BARBARA K.

PERSONAL Born 03/23/1945, Brooklyn, NY, m, 1986, 1 child **DISCIPLINE** CLASSICS **EDUCATION** Univ Michigan, BA, 66; Univ N Carolina, Chapel Hill, MA, 68, PhD, 75. **CAREER** Lectr, actg asst prof, Univ Calif, Irvine, 71-75; asst prof, Univ Richmond, 76-77; asst prof, Univ Va, 77-78; asst prof classics and comp lit, Univ Texas, 78-86; assoc prof classics, women's stud, Santa Clara Univ, 86-89; assoc prof to prof, 89- , Leonard C Ferguson Prof of Class, 94-97, Prof of Classics and Assoc Dean, 97- , Hamilton Col. **HONORS AND AWARDS** NDEA Fel, 67-68; Mellon Fel, 79; Univ Res Inst sum fel, 79, 81; Univ Res Inst res grant, 79-83, 80, 84; Thomas Terry Award, 88-89; NEH summer stipend, 92. **MEMBERSHIPS** Am Class League; Am Philol Asn; Archaeol Inst Am; Calif Class Asn; Class Asn of the Atlantic States; Class Asn of the Empire State; Class Asn of the Middle West and South; Philol Asn of the Pacific Coast. **RESEARCH** Greek and Roman literature; Roman elegy, lyric and satire; Pindar; Greek tragedy; Plato; comparative literature; women in antiquity. **SELECTED PUBLICATIONS** Ed, Literary and Artistic Patronage in Ancient Rome, Univ Texas, 82; auth, Literary Patronage in Greece and Rome, Univ North Carolina, 87; co-ed, Sex and Gender in Medieval and Renaissance Texts: The Latin Tradition, SUNY, 97; co-ed, Vile Bodies: Roman Satire and Corporeal Discourse, special issue Arethusa, 98. **CONTACT ADDRESS** Dept of Classics, Hamilton Col, Clinton, NY, 13323. **EMAIL** bgold@hamilton.edu

GOLD, CAROL

DISCIPLINE MODERN SCANDINAVIA **EDUCATION** Univ WI, PhD, 75. **CAREER** Univ Alaska **SELECTED PUBLICATIONS** Auth, Educating Middle Class Daughters, Museum Tusculanum Press & the Royal Library, 96. **CONTACT ADDRESS** Univ AK Fairbanks, PO Box 757480, Fairbanks, AK, 99775-7480. **EMAIL** ffcg@aurora.alaska.edu

GOLD, PENNY SCHINE

PERSONAL Born 12/09/1947, Bridgeport, CT, m, 1973 **DISCIPLINE** MEDIEVAL HISTORY **EDUCATION** Univ Chicago, BA, 69; Stanford Univ, MA, 70, PhD(medieval studies), 77. **CAREER** Instr, Univ Cincinnati, 75-76; instr, 76-77, ASST PROF HIST, KNOX COL, 77-, Monticello Col Found fel for Women, Newberry Libr, 79; mem teaching staff, Nat Summer Inst in Women's Studies, 81; vis asst prof, Univ Iowa, summer, 82. **MEMBERSHIPS** AHA; Mediaeval Acad Am; Coord Comt Women Hist Profession; Women Historians Midwest, Nat Womens's Studies Asn. **RESEARCH** Women in the Middle Ages; 12th century France. **SELECTED PUBLICATIONS** Auth, Men Helping Women, A Monastic Case-Study, Sociol of Relig, Vol 0054, 93; The Language of Sex--5 Voices from Northern France around 1200, J Interdisciplinary Hist, Vol 0027, 96. **CONTACT ADDRESS** Dept of Hist, Knox Col, 2 E South St, Galesburg, IL, 61401-4938.

GOLD, ROBERT LEONARD

PERSONAL Born 09/25/1932, Ossining, NY, m, 1962 **DISCIPLINE** LATIN AMERICAN HISTORY **EDUCATION** Columbia Univ, BS, 57; Bowling Green State Univ, MA, 58; Univ Iowa, PhD(Latin Am hist), 64. **CAREER** Asst prof Latin Am hist, Univ S Fla, 63-65; from asst prof to assoc prof, 65-74,

PROF LATIN AM HIST, SOUTHERN ILL UNIV, CARBONDALE, 74-, Assoc ed, Red River Valley Hist Rev, 74-. **MEMBERSHIPS** AHA; Conf Latin Am Hist; AHA. **RESEARCH** Colonial Mexico and the Spanish colonial borderlands; inter-American affairs in the 19th century. **SELECTED PUBLICATIONS** Auth, Florida Indians and the Invasion from Europe, Am Hist Rev, Vol 0102, 97. **CONTACT ADDRESS** Dept of Hist, Southern Ill Univ, Carbondale, IL, 62901.

GOLDBERG, BARRY
DISCIPLINE LATE 19TH AND 20TH CENTURY SOCIAL HISTORY **EDUCATION** Columbia Univ, PhD. **CAREER** Assoc prof; assoc ch, undergrad stud, Fordham Univ. **RESEARCH** Ideological vision of immigration historians. **SELECTED PUBLICATIONS** Auth, Wage Slaves and White Niggers, Garland Press anthology, Critical Race Theory, 97; rev, Let Them Eat Multiculturalism, We Are All Multiculturalists Now, New Politics, 97; **CONTACT ADDRESS** Dept of Hist, Fordham Univ, 113 W 60th St, New York, NY, 10023.

GOLDBERG, ROBERT A.
PERSONAL Born 02/16/1949, New York, NY, s, 2 children **DISCIPLINE** HISTORY **EDUCATION** Ariz State Univ, BA, 71; Univ Wisc-Madison, MA, 72; PhD, 77. **CAREER** Prof, Univ Utah, 70-. **MEMBERSHIPS** Org of Am Hist; W Hist Asn. **RESEARCH** 20th century America; American West. **SELECTED PUBLICATIONS** Auth, Barry Goldwater, Yale Univ Press, 95; co-ed, American Views: Documents in American History, Simon & Schuster, 98; auth, Enemies Within: The Idea of Conspiracy in Modern America, Yale Univ Press, under contract. **CONTACT ADDRESS** Dept of Hist, Univ Utah, 312 Carlson Hall, Salt Lake City, UT, 84112. **EMAIL** bob.goldberg@m.cc.utah.edu

GOLDBERG, SANDER M.
DISCIPLINE CLASSICS **EDUCATION** Univ Rochester, 66-70, BA, 70; Univ Tex, 70-71; Ind Univ, MA, 74, PhD, 77; Univ Col London, 76-77. **CAREER** Vis asst prof, Ind Univ, 77-78; vis lectr, Univ Calif-Berkeley, 80-81; asst prof, Univ Colo, 81-85; asst prof, 85-87; assoc prof, 87-91; PROF, UCLA, 91-. **HONORS AND AWARDS** Phi Beta Kappa, 70; Woodrow Wilson fel, 70; NDEA Title IV fel, Univ Tex, 70-71; Ind Univ grad sch fel, 72-73, 76-77; Wheeler fel, Amer Sch Class Stud, Athens, 76; Fulbright-Hays scholar, 76-77; A.W. Mellon post-doc fel, Stanford Univ, 78-80; NEH fel, 84-85; President's res fel, Univ Calif, 89-90., Ed, Transactions of the Amer Philol Assn, 91-95; ed bd, The Class Jour, 82-83; Helios, 84-90; Bryn Mawr Class Rev, 96-; Comparative Drama, 96-; referee: Amer Jour Philol; Class Antiquity; Class Jour; Class Philol; Comparative Drama; Phoenix; Transactions of the Amer Philol Assn; evaluator, Princeton Univ Press; Johns Hopkins Univ Press; Univ Calif Press; Univ Okla Press; Univ Tex Press; Univ Mich Press. **SELECTED PUBLICATIONS** Auth, The Making of Menander's Comedy, Univ Calif Press, 80; Understanding Terence, Princeton Univ Press, 86; Epic in Republican Rome, Oxford Univ Press, 95; "Improvisation, Plot, and Plautus' Curculio," Plautus und die Tradition des Stegreifspiels, Tubingen, 95. **CONTACT ADDRESS** Dept of Classics, Univ Calif, PO Box 951436, Los Angeles, CA, 90095-1436.

GOLDBERGER, LEO
PERSONAL Born 06/28/1930, Vukovar, Yugoslavia, m, 1970, 1 child **DISCIPLINE** PSYCHOLOGY **EDUCATION** McGill Univ, BA, 51; NYU, PhD, 58. **CAREER** Res Psychologist, NY Hospital-Cornell Medical Center, 53-54; ASST PROF TO PROF, DIR OF RES CENTER OF MENTAL HEALTH, DEPT OF PSYCHOL, NYU, 56-. **HONORS AND AWARDS** NIMH Res Career Development Award, 63-68; Knight's Cross, Queen of Denmark, 93. **RESEARCH** Psychoanalysis; stress & coping; Holocaust rescuers. **SELECTED PUBLICATIONS** Auth, Handbook of Stress, Free Press, 93; auth, The Rescue of the Danish Jews, NYU Press, 87; auth, Psychoanalysis & Contemporary Thought, Quart, 77-. **CONTACT ADDRESS** Dept of Psychology, New York Univ, 6 Washington Pl., New York, NY, 10003. **EMAIL** leo.goldberger@nyu.edu

GOLDEN, LEON
PERSONAL Born 12/25/1930, Teasley City, NJ **DISCIPLINE** CLASSICS **EDUCATION** Univ Chicago, BA, 50, MA, 53, PhD, 58. **CAREER** Instr to asst prof, Col of William & Mary, 58-65; assoc prof to prof, Fl St Univ, 65- . **HONORS AND AWARDS** Phi Beta Kappa **MEMBERSHIPS** Amer Philol Assoc; Classical Assoc of Midwest & South; Amer Comparative Lit Assoc. **RESEARCH** Greek tragedy; Homer; classical literary criticism. **SELECTED PUBLICATIONS** Auth bibliogr, In Praise of Prometheus: Humanism and Rationalism in Aeschylean Thought, Chapel Hill, 66; The Clarification Theory of Catharsis, Hermes, 76; Comic Pleasure, Hermes, 87; Aristotle on Tragic and Comic Mimesis; 92; coauth bibliogr, Horace for Students of Literature: the Ars Poetica and its Tradition, 95. **CONTACT ADDRESS** Dept of Classics, Florida State Univ, Tallahassee, FL, 32306. **EMAIL** lgolden@mnler.fsu.edu

GOLDEN, MARK
PERSONAL Born 06/08/1948, Winnipeg, MB, Canada, m, 1985, 2 children **DISCIPLINE** CLASSICS **EDUCATION** Univ Col, Toronto, BA, 70; Univ Toronto, PhD, 81. **CAREER** Lectr, asst prof, Univ British Columbia, 80-82; asst prof, prof, Univ Winnipeg, 82- . **HONORS AND AWARDS** Fel, Nat Hum Ctr. **MEMBERSHIPS** Class Asn of Can; APA; Asn of Ancient Hist; Soc for Socialist Stud. **RESEARCH** History of childhood; ancient family history; Greek sport. **SELECTED PUBLICATIONS** Co-ed, Inventing Ancient Culture: Historicism, Periodization and the Ancient World, Routledge, 97; auth, Sport and Society in Ancient Greece, Cambridge, 98. **CONTACT ADDRESS** Dept of Classics, Univ of Winnipeg, Winnipeg, MB, R3B 2E9. **EMAIL** mgolden@io.uwinnipeg.ca

GOLDEN, RICHARD MARTIN
PERSONAL Born 06/14/1947, New York, NY, m, 1969, 2 children **DISCIPLINE** EARLY MODERN EUROPEAN HISTORY **EDUCATION** Vanderbilt Univ, BA, 69; Johns Hopkins Univ, MA, 72, PhD(hist), 75. **CAREER** Instr, 74-75, asst prof, 75-80, ASSOC PROF HIST, CLEMSON UNIV, 80-, Fel, Ctr Renaissance Studies, Newberry Libr, 82. **MEMBERSHIPS** AHA; Soc Fr Hist Studies. **RESEARCH** Early modern France; European witchcraft. **SELECTED PUBLICATIONS** Auth, The Duel--Its Rise and Fall in Early-Modern France, J Mod Hist, Vol 0065, 93; Becoming a French Aristocrat--The Education of the Court Nobility, 1580-1715, J Mod Hist, Vol 0065, 93; The Huguenots and French Opinion, 1685-1787--The Enlightenment Debate on Toleration, Am Hist Rev, Vol 0098, 93; Territories of Grace--Cultural-Change in the 17th-Century Diocese of Grenoble, Am Hist Rev, Vol 0098, 93. **CONTACT ADDRESS** Dept of Hist, Clemson Univ, Clemson, SC, 29631.

GOLDFIELD, DAVID
DISCIPLINE THE AMERICAN SOUTH HISTORY **EDUCATION** Univ MD, PhD, 70. **CAREER** Robert Lee Bailey Prof Hist, Univ NC, Charlotte. **RESEARCH** The Am South; the urban South. **SELECTED PUBLICATIONS** Auth, America's Changing Perceptions of Race, 1946-1996, in Cristina Giorcelli and Rob Kroes, eds, Living With America, 1946-1996, VU UP, Amsterdam, 97; Race, Region, and Cities: Interpreting the Urban South, LSU Press; coauth, The American Journey: A History of the United States, Prentice Hall. **CONTACT ADDRESS** Univ N. Carolina, Charlotte, Charlotte, NC, 28223-0001.

GOLDFIELD, MICHAEL
PERSONAL Brooklyn, NY **DISCIPLINE** POLITICAL SCIENCE **EDUCATION** Williams Col, BA, 65; Univ of Chicago, MA, phil, 67, MA, pol science, 78, PhD, 84. **CAREER** Stat prog, 78-79, Natl Opinion Res Center; syst anal/prog, 79-80, Univ Chicago Comp Ctr; prog & fac manage, 80-84, Hines Veterans Admin Hosp; fac fel, 87-88 Soc for Humanities, asst prof, 84-92, Cornell Univ; sr res assoc, 89-93, ctr for labor-manage pol stud, CUNY; asoc prof, CULMA & pol science, adj prof, Africana Stud, 92-98, prof, CULMA & pol science, adj prof, Africana Stud, 98-, Wayne St Univ. **HONORS AND AWARDS** NDEA fel, pol science, Univ Chicago, 68-69; Outstanding Perf Award, Hines Vet Admin Hosp, 81; NBER/Sloan Found Grant, 84-87; Cornell Jr Fac Sum Res Fel, 85; Cornell/IBM proj EZRA Grant 85-88; DAAD sum res grant, 86; Humanities Fac Res Grant, Cornell Univ, 86-87; Fac Fel, Soc for Humanities, Cornell Univ, 87-88; Jonathan R. Meigs Res Grants, 84-92; Amer Coun of Learned Soc Res Grant, 91-92; NSF Supercomputer Grant, 87-94; German Marshall Fund US Grant, 96; Wayne St Humanities Ctr Fel Grant, 96; Prog in Mediating Theory & Dispute Resolution Grant, 97; CULMA Fac Res Grant, 97. **MEMBERSHIPS** APSA; IRRA; MWPSA; HAIMC. **SELECTED PUBLICATIONS** Auth, The Decline of Organized Labor in the United States, Univ Chicago, 87; art, Race and the CIO, Intl Labor & Working Class History, 45, 93; art, The Failure of Operation Dixie: A Critical Turning Point in American Political Development, Race, Class, & Comm in So Labor History, Univ Alabama Press, 94; art, Race and the CIO Revisited - Reply to Critics, Intl Labor & Working Class History, 94; art, Was There a Golden Age of the CIO: Race, Solidarity, and Union Growth During the 1930s and 1940s, Trade Union Pol: Amer Union & Amer Unions and Econ Change, 1960s-1990s, Humanities Press, 95; art, The Limits of Rational Choice Theory, Natl Pol Science Rev & Rational Choice Marxism, 96; auth, The Color of Politics: Race and the Mainsprings of American Politics, New Press, 97; art, Race and the Reuther Legacy, Against the Current, 97; art, Race and US Labor, Monthly Review, 97; art, Assessing Union Leaderships, Against the Current, 97; art, US Unions, Racial Discrimination, and the Post-World War II Social Contract, Along Ethnic Lines: Multicultural Solidarity in the Labor Movement, Lars Maischak, 97; art, Lipset's Union Democracy After 40 Years, Extensions, 98. **CONTACT ADDRESS** Coll of Urban Labor and Metro Affairs, Wayne St Univ, 3247 Faculty/Admin Bldg, Detroit, MI, 48202.

GOLDIN, CLAUDIA
PERSONAL New York, NY **DISCIPLINE** ECONOMICS **CAREER** Harvard Univ Prof econo; Prog Dir, Del of the Am Econ; Res Assoc, Nat Bur of Econ Res. **HONORS AND AWARDS** Hon doc hum letters, Univ NE, 94; fel, Am Acad Arts Sci, 92-; fel, Econ Soc, 91-; Vis sch, Russell Sage Found, 97-98;Galbraith Teach Awd, 95; Irving Kravis Teach Awd, 89; Guggenheim fel, 87-88; Mem, Inst Adv Stud, 82-83; numerous grants. **MEMBERSHIPS** EHA; AEA **SELECTED PUBLICATIONS** Defining the Moment: The Great Depression and the American Economy in the Twentieth Century, ed by M Bordo, C Goldin, E White, Chicago, Univ Chicago, 98; The Regulated Economy: A Historical Approach to Political Economy, ed by C Goldin, G Libecap, Chicago, Univ Chicago Press, 94; Labor Markets in the Twentieth Century, in: S Engerman R Gallman, The Cambr Econ Hist of US, Cambridge Univ Press, forthcoming, many numerous articles and papers. **CONTACT ADDRESS** Dept Economics, Harvard Univ, Cambridge, MA, 02138. **EMAIL** goldin@kuznets.harvard.edu

GOLDIN, MILTON
PERSONAL Born 01/08/1927, Cleveland, OH, m, 1950, 2 children **DISCIPLINE** MUSICOLOGY; PSYCHOLOGY **EDUCATION** New York Univ, BA, 53, MA, 55. **CAREER** Admin dir, Amer Choral Found, 55-61; assoc dir devel, Brookdale Hosp Ctr 63-66; fund raising campaign dir, Wash Sq. Col and Grad Sch, Arts and Sci, NYU, 66-67; VP Oram Assoc, Inc, 67-72, Exec VP, 72-75; fund raising counts, 75-78; Pres The Milton Goldin Co, 78-; mgr Amor Artis Chorale and Orch, 61-78; author of The Music Merchants, 1969, Why They Give, 76; contributing ed, periodicals, 96-. **HONORS AND AWARDS** ASCAP Deems Taylor award, 70; Phi Beta Kappa; Psi Chi; Mu Sigma **MEMBERSHIPS** National Coalition of Independent Scholars (NCIS) **RESEARCH** German economy 1917-1952; american philanthropy; environmental history. **SELECTED PUBLICATIONS** PS, Goldhagen and the Holocaust, Jan 97; The Earth Times, The New York-New Jersey Follies, Mar 97; The Genocide Forum, Allianz's First Trial, Sept 97; History Today, Financing the SS, June 98; Gannett Newspapers, Tourism Isn't Going to Make Up for GM Loss, June 98. **CONTACT ADDRESS** 266 Crest Dr, Tarrytown, NY, 10591-4328. **EMAIL** MiltonG525@aol.com

GOLDMAN, AARON L.
PERSONAL Born 05/10/1938, Chicago, IL, m, 1965, 1 child **DISCIPLINE** MODERN EUROPEAN & DIPLOMATIC HISTORY **EDUCATION** City Col New York, BA, 59; IN Univ, MA, 63, cert Russ area studies, 64, PhD(hist), 67. **CAREER** Instr hist, Univ Col, Univ MD, 63-64; assoc prof, 67-80, prof hist, San Jose State Univ, 80-, coordr Jewish Studies Prog, 80-84; Univ fel, San Jose State Univ, 74-75, fac grant, Off Sponsored Res & Proj Serv, 71,73 & 77-78. **MEMBERSHIPS** Conf Brit Studies; AHA; Am Asn Jewish Studies. **RESEARCH** Modern European diplomatic history; British foreign policy 1930's; modern European Jewish history. **SELECTED PUBLICATIONS** Auth, The Link and the Anglo-German Review, SAtlantic Quart, summer 72; Claud Cockburn, The Week and the Cliveden Set, Jour Quart, winter 72; Defense Regulation 18B: Emergency Internment of Aliens and Political Dissenters in Great Britain during World War Two, J Brit Studies, spring 73; Sir Robert Vansittart's Search for Italian Cooperation against Hitler, 1933-36, J Contemp Hist, 7/74; Stephen King-Hall and the German Newsletter Controversy of 1939, Can J Hist, 8/75; Germans and Nazis: The Controversy over Vansittartism in Britain during the Second World War, J Contemp Hist, 1/79; Two Views of Germany: Nevise Henderson vs Vansittmas and the Foreign Office, Brit J Int Studies, 80; The Resurgence of Anti-Semitism in Britain during World War II, Jewish Social Studies, winter 84; Press Freedom in Britain During World War II, Journalism Hist, winter 97. **CONTACT ADDRESS** Dept Hist, San Jose State Univ, 1 Washington Sq, San Jose, CA, 95192-0117.

GOLDMAN, BERNARD
PERSONAL Born 05/30/1922, Toronto, ON, Canada, m, 1944, 1 child **DISCIPLINE** ANCIENT NEAR EASTERN ART **EDUCATION** Wayne State Univ, AB, 46, AM, 47; Univ Mich, PhD(hist art), 59. **CAREER** PROF HIST OF ART, WAYNE STATE UNIV, 60-, Am Coun Learned Soc fel, 68; dir press, Wayne State Univ, 74-; distinguished vis prof, Hope Col, 81-82. **MEMBERSHIPS** Archaeol Inst Am. **RESEARCH** Ancient Iranian art; ancient Judaic art. **SELECTED PUBLICATIONS** Auth, Nabataean/Syro-Roman Lunate Earrings, Israel Exploration J, Vol 0046, 96. **CONTACT ADDRESS** Wayne State Univ, Detroit, MI, 48202.

GOLDMAN, JEAN
DISCIPLINE ART HISTORY **EDUCATION** Univ Chicago, PhD, 78. **CAREER** Instr, Univ PA; vis lectr, 89. **HONORS AND AWARDS** Kress fel., Cur, Inst Contemp Art, Boston, 65-67; dir, Rennaissance Soc, 76-78 **SELECTED PUBLICATIONS** Ed, Centennial Essays, Art Inst Chicago; auth, Portraits, Art Inst Chicago; Masterpieces, Art Inst Chicago; pub(s), articles on old master drawings. **CONTACT ADDRESS** Dept of Art Hist, Sch of the Art Inst of Chicago, 37 S Wabash Ave, Chicago, IL, 60603.

GOLDMAN, SHELDON
PERSONAL Born 09/18/1939, Bronx, NY, m, 1963, 3 children **DISCIPLINE** POLITICAL SCIENCE **EDUCATION** Harvard Univ, PhD, 65. **CAREER** Prof, political science, 74-, Univ Massachusetts **HONORS AND AWARDS** Phi Beta Kappa; Pi Sigma Alpha Outstanding Tchr Award; Col Outstanding Tchng Award. **MEMBERSHIPS** Amer Political Science Asn; Law and Soc Asn; Northeastern Political Science Asn; Amer Judica-

ture Soc. **RESEARCH** Federal judicial selection; constitutional law; law and politics. **SELECTED PUBLICATIONS** Auth, Picking Federal Judges Lower Court Selection from Roosevelt through Reagan, Yale Univ Press, 97; auth, Federal Judicial Recruitment, Amer Courts A Critical Assessment, CQ Press, 91; art, The Bush Imprint on the Judiciary Carrying on a Tradition, Judicature 74, 91; art, Bushs Judicial Legacy the Final Imprint, Judicature 76, 93; coauth, Clintons NonTraditional Judges, Judicature 78, 94; art, Judicial Selection Under Clinton A Midterm Examination, Judicature 78, 95; coAuth, Clintons First Term Judiciary Many Bridges to Cross, Judicature 80, 97; Coauth, Congress and the Courts A Case of Casting, Great Theater The Amer Congress in Action, Cambridge Univ Press, 98. **CONTACT ADDRESS** Dept of Political Sci, Univ of Massachusetts, Amherst, MA, 01002. **EMAIL** sheldon.goldman@polsci.umass.edu

GOLDMAN, STEVEN
DISCIPLINE HISTORICAL DEVELOPMENT AND THE SOCIAL RELATIONS OF MODERN SCIENCE AND TECHN **EDUCATION** PhD; Boston Univ. **CAREER** Prof, Lehigh Univ **RESEARCH** Medieval and Renaissance roots of modern science; the tansition from 19th to 20th century physics **SELECTED PUBLICATIONS** ed, Science, Technology and Social Progress **CONTACT ADDRESS** Lehigh Univ, Bethlehem, PA, 18015.

GOLDSCHMIDT, ARTHUR E., JR.
PERSONAL Born 03/17/1938, Washington, DC, m, 1961, 2 children **DISCIPLINE** HISTORY **EDUCATION** Colby Col, AB, 59; Harvard Univ, AM, 61; Harvard Univ, PhD, 68. **CAREER** Asst prof to assoc prof to prof, Pa St Univ, 65- **HONORS AND AWARDS** Class of 33 Award for Outstanding Contributions to the Human, 72; Liberal Arts Advising Award, 76; Honorable Mention in First Profess of the Year Contest, 81, AMOCO Teaching Award, 81; Amer Res Center in Egypt Fel, 69, 98; Fulbright Fel, 81., Delta Phi Alpha; Omicron Delta Kappa; Phi Alpha Theta; Phi Beta Kappa; Harvard Grad School of Arts & Sci Fel, 59-60; Nat Defense Foreign Lang Fel, 60-65; Fulbright Travel Grant, 62-63. **MEMBERSHIPS** Amer Hist Soc; Amer Res Center in Egypt; Middle East Stud Assoc; World Hist Assoc. **RESEARCH** Nineteenth-twentieth century Egypt **SELECTED PUBLICATIONS** Auth, Modern Egypt: The Formation of a Nation-State, 88; The Memoirs and Diaries of Muhammad Farid, an Egyptian Nationalist Leader, 92; The Butrus Ghali Family, J of Amer Res Center in Egypt, 93; A Historical Dictionary of Egypt, Scarecrow Press, 94; Van Dyck, Cornelius, Amer Nat Biog, 99. **CONTACT ADDRESS** 108 Weaver Bldg, University Park, PA, 16801-5500. **EMAIL** axg2@psu.edu

GOLDSTEIN, CARL
PERSONAL Born 06/24/1938, New York, NY, m, 2 children **DISCIPLINE** ART HISTORY **EDUCATION** Columbia Univ, PhD, 66. **CAREER** Visiting instr, Wheaton Col, 66; asst prof, Brown Univ, 66-71; ASSOC PROF, 71-80, PROF, 80-, UNIV OF NC. **HONORS AND AWARDS** S.H. Kress Fel, 65; Howard Found Fel, 70-71; Am Philos Soc Summer Grants, 77 & 82. **MEMBERSHIPS** Col Art Asn. **RESEARCH** Renaissance and Baroque art history. **SELECTED PUBLICATIONS** Auth, Visual Fact Over Verbal Fiction. A Study of the Carracci and the Criticism, Theory, and Practice of Painting in Renaissance and Baroque Italy, Cambridge Univ Press, 88; auth, Teaching Art. Academies and Schools from Vasari to Albers, Cambridge Univ Press, 96; auth, The Platonic Beginnings of the Academy of Painting and Sculpture in Paris, Academies of Art, Between Renaissance and Romanticism. Leids Kunsthistorisch Jaarboek, 89; auth, A New Role for the Antique in Academies, Antikenrezeption im Hochbarock, 89; auth, L'academie de Poussin, Nicolas Poussin 1594-1665, Musee du Louvre, 94; auth, Le musee imaginaire de l'acdemie au XVIIe et XVIIIe siecles, Les Musees en Europe a la veille de l'ouverture du Louvre, 95; auth, La fortune: Poussin et les academies au XIXe siecle, Colloque Poussin, 96; auth, Writing History, Viewing Art: The Question of the Humanist's Eye, Text and Image in the Renaissance: Antiquity Transumed, Cambridge Univ Press, forthcoming; auth, The Image of the Artist Reviews, Word and Image, 93. **CONTACT ADDRESS** Art Dept, Univ of N. Carolina at Greensboro, Greensboro, NC, 27412.

GOLDSTEIN, DARRA
DISCIPLINE RUSSIAN **EDUCATION** Vassar Col, AB, 73; Stanford Univ, PhD, 83. **CAREER** Prof, Williams Col, 83-. **HONORS AND AWARDS** Res grants, Int Res & Exchanges Bd, Amer Coun of Learned Soc(s), Kennan Inst, Mellon Found; Julia Child Awd, 93; Sophie Coe Subsidiary Prize, 97. **RESEARCH** Russian poetry; modernism; Russian Avant-Garde Art; Russian cultural studies; culinary history. **SELECTED PUBLICATIONS** Auth, A Taste of Russia, HarperCollins, 83, 93; Art for the Masses, Williams College Museum of Art, 85; Russian Houses, Stewart, Tabori & Chang, 91; The Georgian Feast: The Vibrant Culture and Savory Food of the Republic of Georgia, Harper Collins, 93; Nikolai Zabolotsky: Play for Mortal Stakes, Cambridge UP, 93; coauth, Graphic Design in the Mechanical Age, Yale Univ Press, 98. **CONTACT ADDRESS** Center for Foreign Languages, Literatures and Cult, Williams Col, Williamstown, MA, 01267. **EMAIL** Darra.Goldstein@williams.edu

GOLDSTEIN, JONATHAN
DISCIPLINE HISTORY **EDUCATION** Univ Pa, PhD, 73. **CAREER** Prof. **SELECTED PUBLICATIONS** Auth, pubs on East Asian international relations, and Jewish Diaspora in China. **CONTACT ADDRESS** History Dept, State Univ of West Georgia, Carrollton, GA, 30118.

GOLDSTEIN, JOSHUA S.
DISCIPLINE INTERNATIONAL MILITARY AND ECONOMIC RELATIONS **EDUCATION** Stanford Univ, BA; Mass Inst Technol, MA, PhD. **CAREER** Prof, Am Univ. **RESEARCH** International relations theory **SELECTED PUBLICATIONS** Auth, International Relations, 3rd ed; Harper Collins, 96. **CONTACT ADDRESS** American Univ, 4400 Massachusetts Ave, Washington, DC, 20016.

GOLDSTEIN, LAURENCE ALAN
PERSONAL Born 01/05/1943, Los Angeles, CA, m, 1968, 2 children **DISCIPLINE** 20TH CENTURY **EDUCATION** Univ Calif, Los Angeles, BA, 65; Brown Univ, PhD, 70. **CAREER** From Asst Prof to Assoc Prof, 70-84, prof English, Univ of Mich Ann Arbor, 84-; Ed, Mich Quart Rev, 78-. **RESEARCH** Romantic poetry; film history; contemporary poetry. **SELECTED PUBLICATIONS** Auth, Familiarity and contempt: An essay on the star-presence in film, Centennial Rev, summer 73; Audubon and R P Warren, Contemp Poetry, winter 73; Ruins and Empire: The Evolution of a Theme in Augustan and Romantic Literature, Univ Pittsburgh, 77; Wordsworth and Snyder, Centennial Rev, winter 77; Kitty Hawk and the Question of American Destiny, Iowa Rev, winter 78; The Automobile and American Culture, Mich Quart Rev, fall 80 & winter 81; Lindbergh in 1927: The Response of Poets to the Poem of Fact, Prospects V, Burt Franklyn, 80; The Flying Machine and Modern Literature, Ind Univ Press, 87; The American Poet at the Movies: A Critical History, Univ Mich Press, 94; The Fiction of Arthur Miller, Mich Quart Rev, Fall 98. **CONTACT ADDRESS** Dept of English, Univ of Mich, 505 S State St, Ann Arbor, MI, 48109-1045. **EMAIL** lgoldste@umich.edu

GOLDTHWAITE, RICHARD A.
PERSONAL Born 06/06/1933, Marion, IN **DISCIPLINE** RENAISSANCE HISTORY **EDUCATION** Oberlin Col, BA, 55; Columbia Univ, MA, 57, PhD(hist), 65. **CAREER** From instr to asst prof hist, Kent State Univ, 62-68; asst prof, 68-73, PROF HIST, JOHNS HOPKINS UNIV, 73-, Assoc prof, Kent State Univ, 71-72. **MEMBERSHIPS** AHA; Renaissance Soc Am; Soc Ital Hist Studies. **RESEARCH** Italian Renaissance social and economic history; history of Florence; history of art patronage. **SELECTED PUBLICATIONS** Auth, The Soderini and the Medici--Power and Patronage in 15th-Century Florence, J Interdisciplinary Hist, Vol 0024, 93; Morelli, Lorenzo, Ufficiale-Del-Monte, 1484-1484--Private Interests and Public Offices of a Florentine Silk Merchant at the Time of Medici, Lorenzo, De, Archivio Storico Italiano, Vol 0154, 96. **CONTACT ADDRESS** Dept of Hist, Johns Hopkins Univ, 3400 N Charles St, Baltimore, MD, 21218-2680.

GOLDY, CHARLOTTE NEWMAN
PERSONAL Born 06/14/1949, New York, NY, m, 1988, 1 child **DISCIPLINE** MEDIEVAL HISTORY **EDUCATION** SUNY, BA, 71; MA, 73; PhD, 78 **CAREER** Instr hist, Jr Col Albany, 79-84; asst prof hist, 84-89, assoc prof, 89, dept chmn, Miami Univ, 95; **HONORS AND AWARDS** Phi Beta Kappa **MEMBERSHIPS** Soc Medieval Feminist Studies; Medieval Acad Am; Haskins Soc **RESEARCH** England in the High Middle Ages, especially Jewish and Christian family history. **SELECTED PUBLICATIONS** Auth, The Anglo-Norman Nobility in the Reign of Henry I: The Second Generation, 88. **CONTACT ADDRESS** Dept of History, Miami Univ, Oxford, OH, 45056. **EMAIL** goldycn@muohio.edu

GOLINSKI, JAN
PERSONAL Born 04/09/1957, London, England **DISCIPLINE** HISTORY OF SCIENCE **EDUCATION** Univ Cambridge, BA, 79; Univ Cambridge, MA, 83; Univ Leeds, PhD, 84 **CAREER** Jnr Res Fel, Churchill Col, 86-90; asst prof, Univ NH, 90-94; assoc prof, Univ NH, 94- **HONORS AND AWARDS** Fel, Dibner Inst, MIT, 94; Outstanding Fac Award, Univ NH, 98 **MEMBERSHIPS** Hist Sci Soc; Brit Soc Hist Sci; Amer Hist Assoc **RESEARCH** History of Chemistry & Meteorology; Science in British Society (17th-19th Century); Enlightenment; Historiography **SELECTED PUBLICATIONS** Co-ed, Science as Public Culture: Chemistry and Enlightenment in Britain, 1760-1820, Cambridge, 92; auth, Making Natural Knowledge: Constructivism and the History of Science, Cambridge, 98; co-ed, The Sciences in Enlightened Europe, Univ Chicago, forthcoming **CONTACT ADDRESS** History Dept, Univ NH, Durham, NH, 03824-3586. **EMAIL** jan.golinski@unh.edu

GOLLAHER, DAVID L.
PERSONAL Born 09/10/1949, Glendale, CA, m, 1982, 2 children **DISCIPLINE** HISTORY OF AMERICAN CIVILIZATION, HISTORY OF SCIENCE AND MEDICINE **EDUCATION** Univ Calif Santa Barbara, BA; Harvard Divinity School, MTS; Harvard Univ, PhD. **CAREER** Tchg fel History and Literature, Harvard Univ, 75-80; VP, Scripps Clinic and Res Found, 84-91; Grad School Pub Health, San Diego State Univ, 91-92; PRES CEO, CALIF HEALTHCARE INST, 93-; fel Natl Endowment for Hum, 93; Houghton Libr 50th Anniv Fel, 94. **HONORS AND AWARDS** Avery O Craven Prize, 96. **RESEARCH** History of Medicine. **SELECTED PUBLICATIONS** Voice for the Mad: The Life of Dorothea Dix, Free Press, 95. **CONTACT ADDRESS** California Health Care Inst, 1020 Prospect St, Ste 310, La Jolla, CA, 92037. **EMAIL** gollaher@chi.org

GOLOMBEK, LISA
PERSONAL Born 11/27/1939, Huntington, NY **DISCIPLINE** ISLAMIC ART & ARCHITECTURE **EDUCATION** Barnard Col, BA, 62; Univ Mich, MA, 63, PhD, 68. **CAREER** Asst prof, 68-72, assoc prof, 72-89, PROF MIDDLE EAST & ISLAMIC STUD, UNIV TORONTO, 89-; asst cur, 68-73, assoc cur, 73-80, CURATOR, NEAR EASTERN & ASIAN CIVILIZATIONS DEPT, ROYAL ONTARIO MUSEUM, 80-. **HONORS AND AWARDS** Fel, Royal Soc Can. **SELECTED PUBLICATIONS** Auth, The Timurid Shrine at Gazur Gah, 69; coauth, The Timurid Architecture of Iran and Turan, 2 vols, 88; coauth, Tamerlane's Tableware, 96; co-ed, Timurid Art and Culture, 92. **CONTACT ADDRESS** Near Eastern & Asian Civilizations Dept, Royal Ont Mus, 100 Queens Park, Toronto, ON, M5S 2C6.

GOMEZ-MORIANA, ANTONIO
PERSONAL Born 09/13/1936, Malaga, Spain **DISCIPLINE** INTERDISCPLINARY STUDIES **EDUCATION** Univ Pontificia de Salamanca, Lic, 58, PhD, 62; Ludwig-Maximilians Univ (Munich, Ger), MA, 64, PhD, 65. **CAREER** Tchr, Sanlucar de Barrameda (Spain), 58-59; lectr, Spanisches Kulturinstitut (Munich, Ger), 62-65; Ruhr-Univ (Bochum, Ger), 65-71; prof, 71-74, ch Span, Univ Ottawa, 73-74, ; dir, dept d'etudes anciennes et mod, 74-78, prof, 74-96, prog de litt comp, 87-89, dir-fond, dep de litt comp, Univ Montreal, 89-90; ch Span & Latin Am stud, 92-94, PROF INTERDISCIPLINARY STUD, SIMON FRASER UNIV, 97-. **MEMBERSHIPS** Royal Soc Can; Acad Hum & Soc Sci; Inst Int Sociocritique; Asn Can Hispanistas; Can Semiotic Asn. **SELECTED PUBLICATIONS** Auth, uber den Sinn von 'Congoja' bei Unamuno, 65; auth, Derecha de resistencia y tiranicido, Estudio de una tematica en las 'comedias' de Lope de Vega, 68; auth, Die sprach- und literarhistorische Entwicklung des Spanischen, 73; auth, La subversion du discours rituel, 85; auth, Discourse Analysis as Sociocriticism, 93; coauth, Lecture ideologieue du Lazarillo de Tormes, 84. **CONTACT ADDRESS** Simon Fraser Univ, Burnaby, BC, V5A 1S6.

GONZALES, JOHN EDMOND
PERSONAL Born 09/17/1924, New Orleans, LA **DISCIPLINE** HISTORY **EDUCATION** La State Univ, BS, 43, MA, 45; Univ NC, PhD, 57. **CAREER** From asst prof to prof hist, 45-69, WILLIAM D MC CAIN PROF, UNIV SOUTHERN MISS, 69-, DISTINGUISHED UNIV PROF HIST, 73-, Ed, J Miss Hist, 63-; mem bd dirs, Univ Press Miss, 70-. **MEMBERSHIPS** Southern Hist Asn. **RESEARCH** Southern history, especially Mississippi; American intellectual and social history. **SELECTED PUBLICATIONS** Auth, Portraits of Conflict--A Photographic History of Mississippi in the Civil-War, J Southern Hist, Vol 0060, 94. **CONTACT ADDRESS** Univ So Miss, Hattiesburg, MS, 39406.

GONZALES, MANUEL G.
PERSONAL Born 01/08/1943, Fresno, CA, m, 1969, 2 children **DISCIPLINE** HISTORY **EDUCATION** Univ CA, Santa Barb, BA 65, MA 67, PhD 72. **CAREER** Diablo Valley Col, instr hist 71; Univ CA, Berkeley, vis prof 93. **HONORS AND AWARDS** 5 NEH Fells; NDEA; TIT; FELL. **MEMBERSHIPS** CHS; SIHS; WHA; Nat Assn Chicana. **RESEARCH** Chicana Hist, modern Italian Hist **SELECTED PUBLICATIONS** Andrea Costa and the Rise of Socialism in the Romagna, Univ Press Of Amer, 80; The Hispanic Elite of the Southwest, TX Western Press, 89; Mexicanos: A History of Mexicans in the United States, IN Univ Press, 99. **CONTACT ADDRESS** Dept of Soc Sci(s), Diablo Valley Col, 321 Golf Club Rd, Pleasant Hill, CA, 94523. **EMAIL** magonzal@dvc.edu

GONZALEZ, CATHERINE GUNSALUS
PERSONAL Born 05/20/1934, Albany, NY, m, 1973 **DISCIPLINE** HISTORICAL AND SYSTEMATIC THEOLOGY **EDUCATION** Beaver Col, BA, 56; Boston Univ, STB, 60, PhD(syst theol, hist doctrine), 65. **CAREER** From asst prof to assoc prof Bible and relig, WVa Wesleyan Col, 65-70, dir student relig life, 65-70; assoc prof hist theol, Louisville Presby Theol Sem, 70-73; assoc prof church hist, 74-78, PROF CHURCH HIST, COLUMBIA THEOL SEM, 78-, Mem comt on status of women, Gen Assembly, United Presby Church, 67-70, comt on baptism, 70-72; mem, Faith and Order Comn, Nat Coun Churches, 73-. **MEMBERSHIPS** Presby Hist Soc. **RESEARCH** Liturgical theology; women and theology; comparative systematic theology. **SELECTED PUBLICATIONS** Auth, Between Text and Sermon--Isaiah 43, 8-15, Interpretation-J Bible and Theol, Vol 0048, 94. **CONTACT ADDRESS** Dept of Church Hist, Columbia Theol Sem, PO Box 520, Decatur, GA, 30031-0520.

GONZALEZ, DEENA J.
PERSONAL Born 08/25/1952, Hatch, NM **DISCIPLINE** HISTORY **EDUCATION** NM State Univ, BA, 74; Univ CA, Berkeley, MA, 76, PhD, 85. **CAREER** ASSOC PROF OF HIST AND CHICANO STUDIES, POMONA COL, 83-; vis assoc prof: Hist, Univ NM, 91-92, Chicano Studies, UCSB, 92, Chicano Studies, UCLA, 96-97. **HONORS AND AWARDS** Nat Res Council/Ford Found fel, 87-88; Inst of Am Cultures fel, UCLA, 96-97. **MEMBERSHIPS** Am Hist Asn; Nat Asn of Chicano/a Studies; Org of Am Historians. **RESEARCH** Chicana hist; frontier, 19th century US hist; gay/lesbian hist. **SELECTED PUBLICATIONS** Auth, Series, co-ed with Antonia Castaneda, Chicano Identity Matters Series, Univ TX Press, 96-; La Tules of Santa Fe, forthcoming in Zaragonza Vargas, ed, Major Issues in Chicano History, Houghton-Mifflin, 98; The Unmarried Women of Santa Fe, forthcoming in Zaragoza Vargas, Major Issues in Chicano History, Houghton-Mifflin, 98; The Travail of War: Women and Children in the Years After the US-Mexican War, Sept 98, printed at http://www.pbs.org/kera/usmexican war; On the Lives of Women and Children in the Aftermath of the US-Mexican War, forthcoming in John Bloom, ed, The Treaty of Guadalupe-Hidalgo: Its Impact in New Mexico, 99; Chicana Studies: Paths and Detentions, commissioned by the Julian Samora Inst, MI State Univ, East Lansing, Inst Pubs, 99; Not Honey or Money: Chicana Body Politics, in Debra King, ed, The Body Politic, forthcoming, IN Univ Press, 99; Families and Different Cultural Traditions, commissioned by the AHA, pamphlet series, forthcoming in Antonio Rios-Bustamante, Nell Painter, eds, Teaching Diversity: People of Color and Women of Color, Temple Univ Press, 99; numerous other publications. **CONTACT ADDRESS** Hist Dept, Pomona Col, Claremont, CA, 91711. **EMAIL** dgonzalez@pomona.edu

GONZALEZ, EVELYN
DISCIPLINE HISTORY **EDUCATION** City Col NY, BA, 75; Columbia Univ NY, MA, 77, Mphil, 79, PhD, 93. **CAREER** Asst prof, William Paterson Univ 95-; adj lectr, Stevens Inst Technol, LaGuardia Community Col, Manhattan Col, Baruch Col & LaGuardia Community Col, 80-81; tchg asst, Columbia Univ, 77. **HONORS AND AWARDS** Ford Found fel, 75-80; Phi Beta Kappa, 75; Cromwell Medal, City Col NY, 75, Zimmerman Schol Awd Phi Alpha Theta, 75-76; Phi Alpha Theta Hist Hon Soc, 74. **SELECTED PUBLICATIONS** Auth, Seeds of Decay: The South Bronx Long Before the Sixties, J Urban Hist, 97; The Urban Decay Process: Housing, Crime, and Race in the South Bronx, City Sem, Columbia Univ, 98; Image, Poverty, and Decay: The South Bronx in the 1940s, Sch Mgt & Urban Policy of the New Sch for Soc Res, NY City, 96; Seeds of Decay: The South Bronx Before the Sixties, 26th Annual Meeting of the Urban Aff Asn, NY City, 96; Seven entries on the South Bronx: Mott Haven, Melrose, Morrisania, Claremont, Hunts Point, Crotona Park East, and Fort Apache, The Encycl NY City, New Haven, 95; The Development and Role of New York City's Community Boards, Urban Aff Roundtable of the Special Libr(s) Asn, 80th Annual Conf, NY City, 89; The Development of the Bronx and the Grand Concourse, Bronx Museum of the Arts' sem, 87. **CONTACT ADDRESS** Dept of History, William Paterson Col, 300 Pompton Rd., Atrium 267, Wayne, NJ, 07470. **EMAIL** gonzalez@wilpaterson.edu

GONZALEZ, JUSTO LUIS
PERSONAL Born 08/09/1937, Havana, Cuba, m, 1973, 1 child **DISCIPLINE** HISTORICAL THEOLOGY **EDUCATION** Union Theol Sem, Cuba, STB, 57; Yale Univ, STM, 58, MA, 60, PhD, 61. **CAREER** Prof, 61-68, dean, 68-69, Evangel Sem PR; assoc prof world Christianity, 69-77, Candler Sch Theol, Emory Univ; res & writing, 77-78; Ed, Apuntes; Journal Hispanic Theol, 79-; res fels hist theol, Yale Univ, 68 & 69; consult theol educ, Protestant Episcopal Church, 71-72 & 73-74; mem, Comn Faith & Order, Nat Coun Churches, 73-81; dir, 87-, Hispanic Sum Prog; exec dir, 96-, Hispanic Theol Initiative. **HONORS AND AWARDS** Hon degree, Divinas Letras, Seminario Evangelico de Puerto Rico, 94; Virgilio Elizondo Award; Acad of Cath Hispanic Theologians in US, 91; Gold Medallion Bk Award, Evangelical Christian Publ Assn, 93; Orlando Costas Award, Latino Pastoral Action Ctr, 98. **RESEARCH** Patristics; liberation theology; contemporary Latin American theology. **SELECTED PUBLICATIONS** Auth, Mana: Christian Theology from a Hispanic Perspective, 90; auth, Faith and Wealth, Harper, 90; auth, Out of Every Tribe and Nation: Christian Theology at the Ethnic Roundtable, Abingdon, 92; auth, Santa Biblia: The Bible Through Hispanic Eyes, Abingdon, 96. **CONTACT ADDRESS** PO Box 520, Decatur, GA, 30031. **EMAIL** jgonz02@emory.edu

GONZALEZ DE LEON, FERNANDO JAVIER
DISCIPLINE HISTORY **EDUCATION** Rutgers Col, BA, 81; Univ Virginia, MA, 84; Johns Hopkins Univ, MA, 85, PhD, 91. **CAREER** Vis asst prof, 90-91, SUNY Purchase; vis asst prof, 91-92, Bard Col; asst to assoc prof, 92-, Springfield Col. **RESEARCH** Early modern Europe, early mod Spain, mil hist. **CONTACT ADDRESS** PO Box 145, Hadley, MA, 01035. **EMAIL** fgonzalez@spfldcol.edu

GOOD, DAVID F.
DISCIPLINE HISTORY **EDUCATION** Wesleyan Univ, BA, 65; Univ Chicago, MBA, 67; Univ Pa, PhD, 72. **CAREER** Prof, Temple Univ, 74-90; Univ Minn Twin Cities, 90-. **RESEARCH** European economic history; economic development of Central and Eatern Europe since 1750. **SELECTED PUBLICATIONS** Auth, The Economic Rise of the Habsburg Empire, 1750-1914, Univ Calif, 84; ed, Economic Transformations in East and Central Europe, 94; co-ed, Nationalism and Empire: The Habsburg Empire and the Soviet Union, 92; Austrian Women in the Nineteenth and Twentieth Centuries, 96. **CONTACT ADDRESS** History Dept, Univ of Minnesota, Twin Cities, 614 Social Sciences Tower, 267 19th Ave. S, Minneapolis, MN, 55455. **EMAIL** goodx001@tc.umn.edu

GOOD, IRENE LEE
PERSONAL Born 04/24/1958, Orinda, CA, 2 children **DISCIPLINE** ARCHAEOLOGY **EDUCATION** Boston Univ, BA, 85, MA, 86; Univ Penn, PhD cand, 99. **CAREER** Tchg asst, Boston Univ, 83-86; tchg asst, 88-89, guest lectr, 89, historic preservation, Univ Penn; guest lectr, 93-96, textiles; instr, Archaeology, Univ Penn, 96; guest lectr, Smithsonian Inst, 97. **HONORS AND AWARDS** Travel grant, West Indies, 84; Grad asst, Boston Univ, 84-85, 85-86; tchg asst, 88-89, res asst, 89-92, 96-98, Univ Penn; Univ Res Found Grant, 91-93; fel, Univ Penn, 91-93; dis fel, 93-94; Am Inst iranian Stud Dis Fel, 94; Cotsen Found Res Fel, 97. **MEMBERSHIPS** Am Anthrop Asn, NY Acad of Sci; AAAS. **RESEARCH** Bronze Age; Central Asia; technological innovation and social change; fiber use and weaving/textile technology; long distance exchange/interaction. **SELECTED PUBLICATIONS** Coauth, Quseir al-Aadim, Egypt and the Potential of Archaeological Pollen Analysis in the Near East, in J of Field Archaeol, 95; auth, On the Question of Silk in Pre-Han Eurasia, in Antiquity, 95; auth, Notes on a Textile Fragment from Hami, Xinjiang with Comments on the Significance of Twill, in J of Indo-European Stud, 95; auth, Bronze Age Textiles from the Tarim Basin: The Cherchen Evidence, in Bronze Age and Early Iron Age Peoples of Eastern Central Asia, Univ Penn Museum, 97; auth, Hard Evidence from Fuzzy Data: A Closer Look at Invisible Imports, in Fleeting Identities: Perishable Material Culture in Archaeological Research, Southern Ill, 98. **CONTACT ADDRESS** Dept of Anthropology, Univ of Pennsylvania Museum, 33rd & Spruce Sts, Philadelphia, PA, 19104. **EMAIL** igood@mail.sas.upenn.edu

GOODFRIEND, JOYCE DIANE
PERSONAL Born 10/29/1940, New York, NY **DISCIPLINE** AMERICAN HISTORY **EDUCATION** Brown Univ, BA, 61; Univ Calif, Los Angeles, MA, 68, PhD(hist), 75. **CAREER** Vis asst prof, 72-76, ASST PROF HIST, UNIV DENVER, 76-, DIR AM STUDIES, 81-, Hist consult coun women's hist, Colo Women's Conf Int Women's Decade, 76-77; lectr, Denver Lilly Prog Continuing Educ for Col Teachers, 80. **MEMBERSHIPS** AHA; Orgn Am Historians; Immigration Hist Soc. **RESEARCH** American colonial history; history of women in America; history of ethnic groups in America. **SELECTED PUBLICATIONS** Auth, Traders and Gentlefolk--The Livingstons of New-York, 1675-1790, Am Hist Rev, Vol 0098, 93; A Dutch Family in the Middle Colonies, 1660-1800, William and Mary Quart, Vol 0050, 93; Inheritance and Family-Life in Colonial New-York City, J Am Hist, Vol 0080, 93; Privilege and Prerogative--New-York Provincial Elite, 1710-1776, Am Hist Rev, Vol 0101, 96. **CONTACT ADDRESS** Dept of Hist, Univ of Denver Univ Park, Denver, CO, 80208.

GOODMAN, GRANT KOHN
PERSONAL Born 10/18/1924, Cleveland, OH **DISCIPLINE** JAPANESE HISTORY **EDUCATION** Princeton Univ, BA, 48; Univ Mich, MA, 49, PhD(hist), 55. **CAREER** Actg asst prof hist, Univ Wash, 55-56; instr Far Eastern hist, Univ Del, 56-58; asst prof, State Univ NY Col Fredonia, 58-62; PROF HIST, UNIV KANS, 62-, Fulbright lectr, Univ Philippines, 59-60; NDEA fac fel, Japan and Philippines, 64-65; preceptor, Int Honors Prog, 66-67; vis prof EAsian Hist, Sophia Univ, Japan, 70-71 and 80; vis prof Japan hist, Univ Col, Dublin, Ireland, 75; fel, Neth Inst Advan Study in Humanities and Soc Sci, 76-77; res grantee, Sumitomo Fund-Rockefeller Found, 76-78; Mid-Am State Univs Asn honor lectr, 81-82; mem, Am Adv Comt Japan Found, 81-. **MEMBERSHIPS** AHA; Asn Asian Studies; Asia Soc; Conf Asian Hist (pres, 71-72 & 76-); Midwest Conf Asian Affairs (vpres, 73-74, pres, 74-75). **RESEARCH** Japanese Pan-Asianism; Tokugawa intellectual history; modern Philippine history. **SELECTED PUBLICATIONS** Auth, Winners in Peace--Macarthur, Yoshida, and Postwar Japan, Monumenta Nipponica, Vol 0047, 92; Smith Goes to Tokyo--Japanese Cinema under the American Occupation, 1945-1952, J Am Hist, Vol 0081, 94; The Pacific Basin Since 1945--A History of the Asian, Australasian and the American Rim States and the Pacific Islands, Int Hist Rev, Vol 0017, 95; Illusions of Influence--The Political-Economy of United-States Philippines Relations, 1942-1960, Int Hist Rev, Vol 0017, 95. **CONTACT ADDRESS** Univ Kans, 934 Pamela Lane, Lawrence, KS, 66045.

GOODMAN, LOUIS
DISCIPLINE INSTITUTIONS OF POWER AFFECTING THIRD WORLD DEVELOPMENT **EDUCATION** Darmouth Col, BA; Northwestern Univ, MA, PhD. **CAREER** Prof, Am Univ; Dean Sch Int Service, 86-. **HONORS AND AWARDS** Dir, Latin Am Prog, Woodrow Wilson Int Ctr Scholars; Dir, Latin Am & Caribbean Prog,Soc Sci Res Coun. **RESEARCH** Impact of transnational corporations on National development. **SELECTED PUBLICATIONS** Auth, Small Nations, Giant Firms: Capital Allocation Decisions in Transnational Corporations, Holmes and Mier, 87; The Military and Democracy in Latin America, D.C. Heath-Lexington, 90; Lessons from the Venezuelan Experienc, Johns Hopkins, 95. **CONTACT ADDRESS** American Univ, 4400 Massachusetts Ave, Washington, DC, 20016.

GOODMAN, PAUL
PERSONAL Born 03/01/1934, Brooklyn, NY **DISCIPLINE** HISTORY **EDUCATION** Cornell Univ, BS, 55; Harvard Univ, MA, 57, PhD, 61. **CAREER** Res assoc bus hist, Harvard Univ, 61-62; instr hist, Brooklyn Col, 62-65; from asst prof to assoc prof, 65-70, PROF HIST, UNIV CALIF, DAVIS, 70-, Soc Sci Res Coun grant-in-aid, 62-63; Am Philos Soc grant-in-aid, 64. **MEMBERSHIPS** AHA; Orgn Am Historians. **RESEARCH** Early American history to 1815; political history. **SELECTED PUBLICATIONS** Auth, The Emergence of Homestead Exemption in the United-States--Accommodation and Resistance to the Market Revolution, 1840-1880, J Am Hist, Vol 0080, 93; Passionate Sage--The Character and Legacy of Adams, John, Rev in Am Hist, Vol 0022, 94; Portia--The World of Adams, Abigail, Rev in Am Hist, Vol 0022, 94; Adams, John--A Life, Rev in Am Hist, Vol 0022, 94; Sumner, Charles and the Conscience of the North, J Am Hist, Vol 0082, 95; American Politics in the Early Republic--The New Nation in Crisis, Am Hist Rev, Vol 0100, 95; The American Presidency--An Intellectual History, William and Mary Quart, Vol 0052, 95. **CONTACT ADDRESS** Dept of Hist, Univ of Calif, Davis, CA, 95616.

GOODRICH, THOMAS DAY
PERSONAL Born 00/00/1927, New York, NY **DISCIPLINE** HISTORY, OTTOMAN STUDIES **EDUCATION** Univ Calif, Santa Barbara, BA, 52; Columbia Univ, MA, 53, PhD, 68. **CAREER** PROF HIST, INDIANA UNIV PA, 67-. **MEMBERSHIPS** Am Otological Soc; Mid East Studies Asn; Tolkien Soc Am; AHA; Hist of Discoveries. **RESEARCH** Ottoman history; 16th century. **SELECTED PUBLICATIONS** Auth, Goodrich, Luther, Carrington (1894-1986)--A Bibliography, J Am Orient Soc, Vol 0113, 93. **CONTACT ADDRESS** Dept of Hist, Indiana Univ of Pennsylvania, Indiana, PA, 15701.

GOODSTEIN, ANITA SHAFER
PERSONAL Born 09/12/1929, Brooklyn, NY, m, 1953, 2 children **DISCIPLINE** AMERICAN HISTORY **EDUCATION** Holyoke Col, BA, 51; Cornell Univ, PhD(hist), 58. **CAREER** From instr to assoc prof, 63-77, PROF HIST, UNIV OF THE SOUTH, 77-, Soc Sci Res Coun fac res grant, 67-68; res fel, Nat Endowment Humanities, 79-80. **MEMBERSHIPS** AHA; Orgn Am Historians; Southern Hist Asn. **RESEARCH** Urban frontier; business history. **SELECTED PUBLICATIONS** Auth, Lea, Luke of Tennessee, J Am Hist, Vol 0081, 94. **CONTACT ADDRESS** Dept of Hist, Univ of the South, Sewanee, TN, 37375.

GOODSTEIN, JUDITH RONNIE
PERSONAL Born 07/08/1939, Brooklyn, NY, m, 1960, 2 children **DISCIPLINE** HISTORY OF SCIENCE **EDUCATION** Brooklyn Col, BA, 60; Univ Wash, PhD(hist), 69. **CAREER** Univ archivist, 68-, fac assoc, Calif Inst Technol, 82-, registrar, 89-. **MEMBERSHIPS** Hist Sci Soc. **RESEARCH** Italian science since 1860; 20th century science. **SELECTED PUBLICATIONS** Auth, Sir Humphry Davy: Chemical Theory and the Nature of Matter, Univ Wash, 69; Richard Chace Tolman, In: Dict of American Biography, Suppl 4, Scribner's, 74; Levi-Civita, Einstein and Relativity in Italy, Atti Rend Acc Naz Lincei, 75; ed, The Robert Andrews Millikan Collection at the California Institute of Technology, Guide to a Microfilm Edition, Archives, Calif Inst Technol, 77; Sci & Caltech in the Turbulent Thirties, Calif Hist, 81; co-ed, The Theodore von K rm n Collection at the California Institute of Technology, Guide to the Original Collection and a Microfiche Edition, Archives, 81; coauth, Caltech's Throop Hall, Castle Press, 81; auth, The Rise and Fall of Vito Volterra's World, J Hist of Ideas, 45, 84; Millikan's School: A History of the California Institute of Technology, W. W. Norton, 91; coauth, Feynman's Last Lecture: The Motion of Planets Around the Sun, W. W. Norton, 96. **CONTACT ADDRESS** California Inst of Tech, 1201 E California, Pasadena, CA, 91125-0002. **EMAIL** jrg@cco.caltech.edu

GOODWIN, G.F.
DISCIPLINE HISTORY **EDUCATION** Univ Va, BA, 65; Princeton Univ, PhD, 78. **CAREER** Assoc prof. **RESEARCH** The Democratic Party in the 1920s, J. B. Matthews. **SELECTED PUBLICATIONS** Rev, "Power and Prominence in Washington, D.C.," Can Rev Amer Stud, Vol 16, 85. **CONTACT ADDRESS** Dept of Hist, Carleton Univ, 1125 Colonel By Dr, Ottawa, ON, K1S 5B6. **EMAIL** history@carleton.ca

GOODWIN, JOANNE
DISCIPLINE HISTORY **EDUCATION** Univ Mich, PhD, 91. **CAREER** Assoc prof, Univ Nev Las Vegas. **RESEARCH** American women history; social history. **SELECTED PUBLICATIONS** Auth, Gender and the Politics of Welfare Reform, Univ Chicago, 97. **CONTACT ADDRESS** History Dept, Univ Nev Las Vegas, 4505 Md Pky, Las Vegas, NV, 89154.

GOOSMAN, STUART
DISCIPLINE ETHNOMUSICOLOGY **EDUCATION** Univ WA, PhD. **CAREER** Asst prof; affil fac, Univ Ctr for African & African-Am Stud. **RESEARCH** African Diapora; jazz and popular music; politics and music. **SELECTED PUBLICATIONS** Publ on topics that range from, black group vocal harmony to George Clinton, rap & hip-hop, Juan Luis Guerra & Louis Moreua Gottschalk. **CONTACT ADDRESS** School of Music, Univ of Texas at Austin, 2613 Wichita St, Austin, TX, 78705.

GOOTENBERG, PAUL
PERSONAL Born 10/01/1954, Washington, DC, m, 1996 **DISCIPLINE** HISTORY **EDUCATION** The Col, Univ Chicago, BA, 78; Univ Oxford, St. Anthony's Col, Mphil, 81; Univ Chicago, PhD, 85. **CAREER** Vis asst prof hist, Univ Ill at Chicago, 85-86; mem, Sch of Soc Sci, Inst for Advan Study, 86-87; asst prof Latin Am His, Brandeis Univ, 87-90; vis scholar, Comt on Latin Am and Iberian Studies, Harvard Univ, 90; prof hist, State Univ NY at Stony Brook, 90-present; vis prof, comt hist studies, The New Sch for Social Research, 95; vis scholar, Russel Sage found, 96. **HONORS AND AWARDS** Rhodes Scholar, Oxford Univ; Searle Grad Fel, Univ Chicago; Int Doctoral Res Fel, Soc Sci Res Coun; Fulbright-Hays Diss Res Abroad Award; Soc Sci Res Coun, Postdoctoral Award; res fel for recent recipients of the PhD, Am Coun of Learned Soc; Best Article in Latin Am Studies Award, NECLAS; John M. Olin Fac Fel Hist; Joseph T. Crescenti Best Article Prize, NECLAS; H.G. Davis Best Article Prize; Honorable Mention, NECLAS Best Article Award; John Simon Guggenheim Mem Fel; Res Prize, Lindesmith Ctr/Open Soc Inst; Advan Res Award, Soc Sci Res Coun. **MEMBERSHIPS** CLAH-Am His Asn; Latin Am Studies Asn. **RESEARCH** Latin American history 1400-1990; economic history and development; Andean history; Mexican history; colonial Latin America; historical polititical economics of Latin America; European expansion; Latin American-United States relations 1823-1973; drugs in history. **SELECTED PUBLICATIONS** Auth, The Social Origins of Protectionism and Free Trade in Nineteenth-Century Lima, Jour of Latin Am Studies, 14/2, 82; auth, Beleaguered Liberals: The Failed First Generation of Free Traders in Nineteenth-Century Lima, Guiding the Invisible Hand: Liberalism and the State in Latin American History, Praeger Publ, 88; auth, Tejidos Y Harinas, Corazones Y Mentes: El imperialismo norteamericano del libre comericio en el Peru, 1825-1840, Instituto de Estudios Peruanos, 89; auth, Between Silver and Guano: Commercial Policy and the State in Postindependence Peru, Princeton Univ Press, 89; auth, Carneros y Chuno: Price Levels in Nineteenth-Century Peru, Hispanic American Historical Review, 70/1, 90; auth, North-South: Trae Policy, Regionalism, and Caudillismo in Post-Independence Peru, Jour of Latin Am Studies, 23/2, 91; auth, Population and Ethnicity in Early Republican Peru: Some Revisions, Latin Am Res Review, 26/3, 91; auth, Imagining Development: Economic Ideas in Peru's Fictitious Prosperity of Guano' 1825-1840, Univ Calif Press, 93; aitj. Guano Industry, in Encyclopedia of Latin Am Hist & Culture, 95; auth Caudillismo, Encyclopedia of Soc Hist, 95; auth, Order(s) and Progress in Developmental Discourse: A Case of Nineteenth-Century Peru, Jorn of Hist Sociology, 8/2, 95; auth, Not So Liberal: Protecionist Peru, Latin America and the World Economy: Dependence and Beyond, 96; auth, On Salamanders, Pyramids, and Mexico's 'Growth-without-Change': Anachronistic Reflections on a Case of Bourbon New Spain, Colonial Latin Am Review, 5/1, 96; auth, Paying for Caudillos: The Politics of Emergency Finance in Peru, 1820-45, Liberals, Politics & Power: State Formation in 19th-Century Latin America, Univ Ga Press, 96; auth, Order(s) and Progress in Developmental Discourse: A Case of Nineteenth-Century Peru, in Institute for Latin Am Studies London, 98. **CONTACT ADDRESS** Dept of History, SUNY, Stony Brook, Stony Brook, NY, 11794-4848. **EMAIL** pgootenberg@ccmail.sunysb.edu

GORANSON, STEPHEN
PERSONAL Born 11/05/1950, Surrey, England **DISCIPLINE** RELIGION AND HISTORY **EDUCATION** Brandeis Univ, BA, 72; Duke Univ, PhD, 90. **CAREER** Wake Forest Univ; Univ NC Wilmington; NC State Univ; vis asst prof, Duke Univ, 98-. **SELECTED PUBLICATIONS** Auth, Essene Polemic in the Apocalypse of John, Legal Texts, Legal Issues, Proceedings of the Second Meeting of International Organization for Qumran Studies, Cambridge 1995: Published in Honour of Joseph M. Baumgarten, Cambridge, England, STJD, 23, Leiden, E. J. Brill, 97; auth, The Text of Revelation 22:14, New Testament Studies, 97; auth, 7 vs. 8--The Battle Over the Holy Day at Dura-Europos, Bible Rev, 96; auth, Inkwell, Ostracon with Maria Graffitis, Sepphoris in Galilee: Crosscurrents of Culture, NC Mus of Art, 96; auth, The Exclusion of Ephraim in Rev. 7:4-8 and Essene Polemic Against Pharisees, Dead Sea Discoveries, 95; auth, Posidonius, Strabo, and Marcus Vipsanius Agrippa as Sources on Essenes, Jour of Jewish Studies, 94; auth, Sectarianism, Geography, and the Copper Scroll, Jour of Jewish Studies, 92; auth, Nazarenes and Ebionites, Anchor Bible Dict, 92; auth, Essenes: Etymology from 'asah, Revue de Qumran, 84. **CONTACT ADDRESS** 706 Louise Cir., #30-J, Durham, NC, 27705. **EMAIL** goranson@duke.edu

GORDON, AARON Z.
PERSONAL Born 10/11/1929, Port Gibson, MS, d **DISCIPLINE** EDUCATION **EDUCATION** Univ Mi, BS 1952; Wayne State U, MA 1956; Univ Mi, PhD 1974. **CAREER** Ft Monmouth, Assoc Officers Signal Course 1952; Communications Center Qualification Course, 1952; Teletype Operators School, asst officer in charge; Message Center Clk School, officer in charge; SW Signal School Training Center, Camp San Luis Obispo CA; 3rd Infantry Div AFFE Korea, communication center officer, asst cryptographic officer 1953-54; Br Officers Advance Signal Officers Course, 1963; Command & Gen Staff Coll Ft Levenworth; ICAF, 1974; Air War Coll Maxwell Air Force Base; personnel Officer 1965; S1 5064 USAR Garr, 1967-69; 5032 USAR School, branch officer advanced course instructor 1969-71, dir 1971-73. **HONORS AND AWARDS** Bronze Star Decoration; co-holder worlds record Outdoor Distance Medley Relay; co-holder world's record Indoor Distance Medley Relay; co-holder am record Indoor Two Mile & Relay 1951. **MEMBERSHIPS** Mem Hlth & Curriculum Wrkshp Detroit Pub Schs 1963; co-author Guide to Implementation of Unit of Smiking & Hlth 1963; asst dist ldr E Dist & Dist Ldr 1961-63; com chmn Hlth & Phys Ed Tchrs Inst Day E Dist 1964; sch dist rep Last Two Millage Campaigns Educ TV Tchr Channel 56 Detroit Pub Schs 1964; mem Detroit Orgn Sch Admnstrs & Suprs; Phi Delta Kappa; pgm chmn Detroit Sch Mem's Clu Metro; Detroit Sco Black Educ Admn; Natl All Black Ed; MI Assc Elem Sch Admn Region 1; com mem Midwest Dist AAHPR Conv Detroit 1964; mem Pgmd Educ Soc Detroit 1965; speaker Blue Star Mothers Detroit1963; Carter CME Ch Detroit; bd dir mem Troop 775 BSA 1964; participating guest Focus Negro Life & History Six Wk Work Shop 1967; coordntr Annual Spelling Bee 1967; participant MaximizingBenefits from Testing Workp Test Admn 1968; participant Ed Admn Workshop 1970-73; dir Professional Skills Dev Workshop Metro Detroit Soc Black Ed Admn Ann Arbor 1973; spkr Hampton Sch Detroit 1973; spkr Joyce Sch Grad 1973. **CONTACT ADDRESS** 15000 Trojan, Detroit, MI, 48235.

GORDON, ALLAN M.
PERSONAL Born 08/31/1933, Seminole, OK, m **DISCIPLINE** ART HISTORY **EDUCATION** BA 1955; MA 1962; PhD 1969. **CAREER** CSUS CA, prof art 1969-; OH U, tchg flw 1966-69; Prairie View Clg, asst prof 1964-66. **HONORS AND AWARDS** Award for distinguished publications in Art Criticism Fisk Univ 1974-75; fellow Natl Endowment for the Humanities 1979; Distinguished Alumni Natl Conf of Blacks in Higher Educ 1989. **MEMBERSHIPS** Mem Natl Conf of Artists; Clg Art Assc of Am Inc; mem Alpha Phi Alpha Frat; mem NAACP; bd dirs Crocker Art Gallery Assc Sacramento 1970-74; bd dirs Amistad II Exhib Recip; Awards Comm Chair, Sacramento Metropolitan Arts Commn; College Art Association of America. **SELECTED PUBLICATIONS** Echoes of Our Past: The Narrative Artistry of Palmer C Hayden 1988. **CONTACT ADDRESS** Art Dept, California State Univ, Sacramento, Sacramento, CA, 95819.

GORDON, AMY GLASSNER
PERSONAL Born 02/12/1942, Brooklyn, NY, m, 1964, 2 children **DISCIPLINE** HISTORY **EDUCATION** Conn Col, BA, 63; Univ Chicago, MA, 64, PhD(hist), 74. **CAREER** Lectr hist, City Col New York, 67-68; instr, 68-69, asst prof, 70-72 & 75-78, assoc prof to prof hist, Denison Univ, 78-; Dean of Col, Denison Univ, 87-92. **HONORS AND AWARDS** Newberry Library Research Fellowship, NEH Summer Seminar Grant, Research Grants from Denison Univ and Denison Univ Research Found. **MEMBERSHIPS** Soc Hist Discoveries. **RESEARCH** Sixteenth century French Protestant colonization; Protestant theology and the Amerindians in the 16th century; family in early modern Europe. **SELECTED PUBLICATIONS** Auth, Confronting Cultures: The Effect of the Discoveries on 16th Century French Thought, 76; Mapping La Popeliniere's Thought: Some Geographical Dimensions, Terrae Incognitae, 77; History and Anthropology, J Mod Hist, 78; coauth, History, Values, and Simulation, Simulation in Higher Educ, 79; The First Protestant Missionary Effort: Why Did It Fail?, Int Bulletin of Missionary Research, 84; Autres Temps, Autres Moeurs: French Attitudes to Cultures Revealed by the Discoveries, In: Asia and the West Exchanges, The Age of Exploration, 86. **CONTACT ADDRESS** Dept of Hist, Denison Univ, 1 Denison University, Granville, OH, 43023-1359. **EMAIL** gordona@cc.denison.edu

GORDON, BERTRAM M
PERSONAL Born 04/19/1943, Brooklyn, NY, m, 1965, 2 children **DISCIPLINE** MODERN EUROPEAN HISTORY **EDUCATION** Brooklyn Col, BA, 63; Rutgers Univ, MA, 64, Ph-D(hist), 69. **CAREER** Lectr hist, Brooklyn Col, 67-69; asst prof, 69-76, assoc prof, 76-81, PROF HIST, MILLS COL, 81-, Res grant, Am Philos Soc, 74; vis assoc prof, Calif State Univ, Dominguez Hills, 78-79. **HONORS AND AWARDS** Cert Merit, Western Soc French Hist, 75. **MEMBERSHIPS** AHA; Soc Fr Hist Studies; Western Soc Fr Hist (pres, 74-75). **RESEARCH** Fascism and collaboration in wartime France, 1940-1944; Fascism and youth; food in history. **SELECTED PUBLICATIONS** Auth, The Morphology of the Collaborator, The French Case, J Europ Stud, Vol 0023, 93; The Formation of Degaulle Political-Philosophy--Legacies of the Belle-Epoque, Hist Reflections-Reflexions Historiques, Vol 0019, 93; Tastes of Paradise--A Social-History of Spices, Stimulants, and Intoxicants, Am Hist Rev, Vol 0098, 93; The Repression of the Collaborators, 1942-1952--A Memory of the Past, J Mil Hist, Vol 0058, 94; Collaboration in France During the World-War-2--Deat, Marcel and the Rassemblement-Populaire, Am Hist Rev, Vol 0099, 94; The Vichy-Syndrome Problem in History, Fr Hist Stud, Vol 0019, 95; Good Frenchmen--The French-Police and the German-Occupation-Forces in Occupied-France 1940-1914, Am Hist Rev, Vol 0100, 95; Acquired Taste--The French Origins of Modern Cooking, Am Hist Rev, Vol 0101, 96; Untitled--Reply, Am Hist Rev, Vol 0102, 97; World-War-II, Guide of National Archives in France 1939-1945, J Mil Hist, Vol 0061, 97. **CONTACT ADDRESS** Mills Col, 5000 MacArthur Blvd, PO Box 9962, Oakland, CA, 94613-1000. **EMAIL** bmgordon@mills.edu

GORDON, DANIEL
DISCIPLINE HISTORY **EDUCATION** Univ Chicago, PhD, 90. **CAREER** Assoc prof, Univ MA Amherst. **SELECTED PUBLICATIONS** Auth, The Idea of Sociability in Pre-Revolutionary France, 94. **CONTACT ADDRESS** Dept of Hist, Univ Massachusetts Amherst, Mass Ave, Amherst, MA, 01003.

GORDON, JACOB U.
PERSONAL Born 10/25/1939, Nigeria, m, 1960, 4 children **DISCIPLINE** HISTORY **EDUCATION** Bethune-Cookman College, Daytona Beach, Florida, BA, 62, Howard Univ, Wash,, DC, MA, 64, Michigan State Univ, East Lansing, MI, 67. **CAREER** Assoc Prof and Chm, Dept of Hist and Political Sci, Albany State Univ, Albany, GA, 67-70,Asst Prof and Chm, Dept of African Studies, Univ of KS,70-80,Assoc Prof and Research Fellow, Dept of African and African-American Studies, Univ of KS,80-98,Executive Director, Center for the Multicultural Leadership-Life Span Studies,Univ of KS, 80-98. **HONORS AND AWARDS** Teacher of the year, Rust College,64,Hanline Unive Fellow, 65,Phi Alpha Theta,National Honor Society in Hist,64,The Univ of KS,25 yr pin,Who's Who in the Midwest,79,Men of Achievement-8th edition,81,Wichita School District Service Award,Giftedness Amon African Americans,93,Wally and Marie Steeples Faculty Awasrd for Outstanding Service, Univ of KS,98, KS African American Commission Award for Outstanding Leadership, 98. **MEMBERSHIPS** The Association for the study of Afro-American Life and Hist. **RESEARCH** Black Leadership in America; African Leadership in the 20th century; Substance Abuse Issues in American Society; Public Policy Issues. **SELECTED PUBLICATIONS** Gordon, Jacob U., in progress,Black Leadership for Social Change,Newbury Park,CA,Sage Publications,450pp Gordon,Jacob U., A Systems Change Approach to Substance Abuse Prevention,Lewiston,NY,The Edwon Mellen Press, a94pp,97,Gordon, Jacob U.,and Jackson, Elmer C., in press, A Hist of the National Bar Assoc, New York, NY,Vantage Press,250pp, Gordon, Jacob U.,Supplemental Readings for Training in Multicultural Substance Abuse Continuum of Care for the 21st Century, co-authored with Dr. Edith Freeman and Janine Lee. Topeka, KS,Mainstream, Inc.,290pp, Gordon, Jacob U., and Majors. Richard,The African American Male:His Present Status and His Future, Chicago, Nelson-Hall,372pp, 94, Gordon, Jacob U.,Managing Multiculturalism in Substance Abuse Services, Newbury Park, CA, Sage Publications,262pp, 94, Gordon, Jacob U., Marratives of African Americans in Kansas, Beyond the Exodust Movement, Lewiston, NY, The Edwin Mellen Press, 412pp, 93. **CONTACT ADDRESS** Univ of Kansas, 1028 Dole Human Development Center, Lawrence, KS, 66045. **EMAIL** lbLdr@dole.Lsl.ukans.edu

GORDON, LEONARD ABRAHAM
PERSONAL Born 01/17/1938, New York, NY, m, 1 child **DISCIPLINE** MODERN INDIAN HISTORY, HISTORY OF IMPERIALISM **EDUCATION** Amherst Col, BA, 59; Harvard Univ, MA, 61, PhD, 69. **CAREER** Asst prof hist, Columbis Univ, 67-73; assoc prof, 73-78, prof, New Sch Lib Arts, Brooklyn Col, 78-; Fulbright-Hays sr res fel, India, 71-72; vis assoc prof hist, Columbia Univ, 73-74; sr res assoc, Southern Asian Inst, Columbia Univ, 74-; dir and vpres, Taraknath Das Found, 86-. **HONORS AND AWARDS** Watjmull Prize, AHA, 74. **MEMBERSHIPS** AHA; Asn Asian Studies. **RESEARCH** History of 20th century India; comparative partitions. **SELECTED PUBLICATIONS** Auth, Brothers Against the Raj: A Biography of Indian nationalists Sarat and Subhas Chandra Bose, columbia, 90; co-ed, India Briefing 1992, Westview, 92; auth, Subhas Chandra Bose: la Violence Liberatrice, Calcutta 1905-1971, Editions Autrement, 97; auth, Asias in Enlightenment and Early British Imperial Thought, Asia in Western and World History: A Guide for Teaching, Sharpe, 97; auth, Studying the History of South Asians in America, Indian Archives, 97; auth, Wealth Equals Freedom? The Rockefeller and Ford Foundations in India, The Annals, 97. **CONTACT ADDRESS** 276 Riverside Dr, New York, NY, 10025. **EMAIL** lrgoc@cunyvm.cuny.edu

GORDON, LEONARD H.D.
PERSONAL Born 08/08/1928, New York, NY, m, 1951, 2 children **DISCIPLINE** MODERN CHINESE HISTORY **EDUCATION** Ind Univ, AB, 50, MA, 53; Univ Mich, PhD(hist EAsia), 61. **CAREER** Far Eastern diplomatic historian, US Dept State, 61-63; asst prof EAsian hist, Univ Wis, 63-67, res asst prof hist, Grad Sch, 63; ASSOC PROF CHINESE HIST, PURDUE UNIV, WEST LAFAYETTE, 67-, Ed China sect, Newsletter, Asn Asian Studies, 66-68, ed, 68-71; mem preliminary screening comt, Foreign Area Fel Prog Asia, Joint Comt Soc Sci Res Coun and Am Coun Learned Soc, 71-72, mem nat screening comt, 72-73, 73-74. **MEMBERSHIPS** Asn Asian Studies; Soc Hist Am Foreign Rels. **RESEARCH** History of modern China; diplomatic history of China, 19th and 20th centuries; history of United States-China relations. **SELECTED PUBLICATIONS** Auth, Washington Taiwan Dilemma, 1949-1950--From Abandonment to Salvation, Pacific Hist Rev, Vol 0064, 95. **CONTACT ADDRESS** Dept of Hist, Purdue Univ, West Lafayette, IN, 47907.

GORDON, LINDA
PERSONAL Born 01/19/1940, Chicago, IL **DISCIPLINE** HISTORY **EDUCATION** Swarthmore Coll, BA, Magna cum laude, 61; Yale Univ, MA, 63, PhD, With Distinction, 70. **CAREER** Asst, assoc and full prof, Univ of MA/Boston, 68-84; visiting prof, spring 84, Univ of Amsterdam; prof, 84-, Florence Kelley Prof, 90, Vilas Distinguished Research Prof, 93, Univer of Wisconsin, Madison . **HONORS AND AWARDS** Univ of MA Outstanding Achievement Award, 82-83; Guggenheim Fel 83-84; Inst for Research on Poverty, research awards, 89-90, 90-91, 91-92; Joan Kelley Prize of the /aha, 88; Florence Kelley Professorship, 90; Vilas Research Professorship, 93; Berkshire Prize, 94; Honorary doctorage, SUNY-Binghamton, 97; Kittrell Memorial Lecture, Cornell, 97; Russel Sage Found, 97-98; Eleanor Roosevelt Lecture, Vassar Coll, 98. **SELECTED PUBLICATIONS** Auth, Heroes of Their Own Lives: The Politics and History of Family Violence, 88; Pitied but not Entitled: Single Mothers and the Origins of Welfare, 94, paperback; Teenage Pregnancy and Out-of-Wedlock Birth, Morality and Health, 97; Family Resilience and Family Violence, Promoting Resiliency in Families and Children at Risk, 97; US Women's History, The New American History, 97; Reflections on the Concept of Patriarchy, Radical History Review, spring 98; How Welfare Became a Dirty Word, Journal of International and Comparative Social Welfare, 98. **CONTACT ADDRESS** Univ Wisconsin, Madison, WI, 53706. **EMAIL** Lgordon@facstaff.wisc.edu

GORDON, LYNN DOROTHY
PERSONAL Born 11/25/1946, New York, NY, m, 1981, 2 children **DISCIPLINE** AMERICAN HISTORY, WOMEN'S STUDIES **EDUCATION** Columbia Univ, AB, 68; Univ Chicago, MA, 74, PhD, 80. **CAREER** Teacher social studies, Sweet Home Jr High Sch, 69-73; assoc master of arts prog, Univ Chicago, 74-77; instr educ, Bowdoin Col, 77-78; instr hist, Northern Ill Univ, 79-80; lectr, Princeton Univ, 80-82; from asst prof to assoc prof Educ & Hist, 82-98; Assoc Dean Warner Grad Sch Educ, Univ Rochester, 89-91. **HONORS AND AWARDS** Loewenstein-Wiener Fel Am Jewish Arch, 84; Spencer Found Fel, 91-92; Flora Stone Mather Vis Prof, Case W Reserve Univ, 96. **MEMBERSHIPS** Orgn Am Historians; Nat Women's Studies Asn; Hist Educ Soc (Pres 93); Women Historians Midwest; Berkshire Conf Women Hist. **RESEARCH** History of education and higher education; women's hist; ethnicity and immigration; 20th Century Am Hist. **SELECTED PUBLICATIONS** Auth, Coeducation on two campuses: Berkeley and Chicago 1890-1912, Woman's Being, Woman's Place, 79; Women and the anti-child labor movement in Illinois, Compassion and Responsibility, Univ Chicago, 80; Gender & Higher Education in the Progressive Era, Yale Univ, 90; Why Dorothy Thompson Lost Her Job, Hist Educ Quart, Fall, 94; Race, Class and the Bonds of Womanhood at Spelman Seminary, 1881-1923, Hist Higher Educ Annual, 89. **CONTACT ADDRESS** Dept History, Univ Rochester, Rochester, NY, 14627. **EMAIL** lngo@troi.cc.rochester.edu

GORDON, MARY MCDOUGALL
PERSONAL Toowoomba, Australia **DISCIPLINE** UNITED STATES HISTORY **EDUCATION** Univ Sydney, BA, 50; Radcliffe Col, MA, 52; Univ Pittsburgh, PhD(hist), 74. **CAREER** Asst prof, Carnegie-Mellon Univ, 74-75; asst prof, 75-79, ASSOC PROF US HIST, UNIV SANTA CLARA, 79-, DIR WOMEN'S STUDIES PROG, 80-, Table leader advan placement, Am Hist and Educ Testing Serv; Andrew Mellon fel, Am Asn Univ Women, 69. **MEMBERSHIPS** AHA; Orgn Am Historians; Nat Women's Studies Asn; fel Am Asn Univ Women. **RESEARCH** Nineteenth century social and intellectual history; history of education. **SELECTED PUBLICATIONS** Auth, Missouri 49er--The Journal of Hunter, William, W. on the Southern Gold Trail, Pacific Hist Rev, Vol 0062, 93. **CONTACT ADDRESS** Dept of Hist, Univ of Santa Clara, Santa Clara, CA, 95053.

GORDON, MICHAEL DANISH
PERSONAL Born 01/04/1943, Chicago, IL, m, 1964, 2 children **DISCIPLINE** EUROPEAN HISTORY **EDUCATION** Univ Chicago, BA, 64, MA, 65, PhD(hist), 72. **CAREER** Asst prof, 68-72, assoc prof, 72-80, PROF HIST, DENISON UNIV, 80-, CHMN DEPT, 77-, Yale Univ fel hist, 74. **MEMBERSHIPS** AHA; Soc Span and Port Hist Studies; Am Soc for Legal Hist; Selden Soc. **RESEARCH** European legal history; 16th and 17th century Spanish history; Renaissance political thought. **SELECTED PUBLICATIONS** Auth, An Historical Introduction to Private Law, Am Hist Rev, Vol 0098, 93; The Counterreformation Prince--Anti-Machiavellianism or Catholic Statecraft in Early-Modern Europe, Cath Hist Rev, Vol 0080, 94; Rights of Discovery, Columbus, Christopher Final Appeal to Fernando, Hisp Am Hist Rev, Vol 0075, 95. **CONTACT ADDRESS** Dept of Hist, Denison Univ, 1 Denison University, Granville, OH, 43023-1359.

GORDON, MILTON A.
PERSONAL Born 05/25/1935, Chicago, IL, m **DISCIPLINE** EDUCATION **EDUCATION** Xavier Univ New Orleans, BS 1957; Univ of Detroit, AM 1960; IL Inst of Tech, PhD 1968. **CAREER** Univ of Chicago Math Lab Applied Science, EDUCATION; Chicago Public School System, EDUCATION; Loyola Univ of Chicago, EDUCATION; IL Inst of Tech, EDUCATION; Univ of Detroit, EDUCATION; Chicago State Univ, prof of math 1978-; Coll of Arts & Science, dean 1978-. **HONORS AND AWARDS** Honorary registrar of West Point Mil Acad 1973; **MEMBERSHIPS** Dir Afro-Amer Studies Prog Loyola Math Assoc of Amer, Chicago Math Club, African Assoc of Black Studies, Sigma Xi, Assoc of Social & Behavioral Sci; mem City of Evanston Youth Commiss; chmn Archdiocese of Chicago School Bd 1977-79; bd dir Dem Party of Evanston; mem State of IL Data Comm, Phi Delta Kappa, Amer Conf of Acad Deans, Counc of Coll & Arts & Sci NSF 1964, IL Inst of Tech, Afro-Amer Studies KY State Coll 1971; Rice Univ 1972, Univ of WI 1972, Amer Men & Women of Sci 1972. **SELECTED PUBLICATIONS** Auth, "Enrollment Analysis of Black Students in Inst of Higher Ed from 1940-72"; "Correlation Between HS Performance & ACT & SAT Test Scores by Race & Sex". **CONTACT ADDRESS** Dean, Coll Arts & Science, 6525 N Sheridan Rd, Chicago, IL, 60626.

GORDON-SEIFERT, CATHERINE
PERSONAL Born 01/13/1954, Columbus, OH, m, 1986, 2 children **DISCIPLINE** HISTORY OF MUSIC **EDUCATION** Univ of MI, PhD, 94, MM, 83; IN Univ, MM, 80; Bowling Green St Univ, BM, 76 **CAREER** Facul, 96-98, Boston Conserv of Music; Asst Prof, 98-, Providence Col **HONORS AND AWARDS** Disting Svc Awd for Graduating Sr, Alpha Lambda Delta **MEMBERSHIPS** Am Musicol Asn; Sonneck Soc **RESEARCH** Opera **CONTACT ADDRESS** Dept of Music, Providence Col, Providence, RI, 02918. **EMAIL** cgordon@providence.edu

GOREN, ARTHUR
DISCIPLINE UNITED STATES HISTORY **EDUCATION** Hebrew Univ, BA, 57; Columbia Univ, PhD, 66. **CAREER** Knapp prof. **RESEARCH** American Jewish history. **SELECTED PUBLICATIONS** Auth, New York Jews and the Quest for Community: The Kehillah Experiment 1908-1922, 70, Dissenter in Zion: From the Writings of Judah L. Magnes, 82. **CONTACT ADDRESS** Dept of History, Columbia Col, New York, 2960 Broadway, New York, NY, 10027-6902.

GORHAM, DEBORAH
PERSONAL New York, NY **DISCIPLINE** HISTORY **EDUCATION** McGill Univ, BA, 59; Univ Wisconsin, MA, 63; Univ Ottawa, PhD, 82. **CAREER** Asst prof, 69-78, assoc prof, 78-88, PROF HISTORY, CARLETON UNIV, 88-, dir, Pauline Jewett Inst Women's Studs 94-. **HONORS AND AWARDS** Carleton Univ Scholarly Achievement Award, 82, 86; Arts Fac Bd Tchr Award, 87; 3M Can Inc, 87. **MEMBERSHIPS** Can Comt Women's Hist; Can Hist Asn; Can Friends Peace Now; Temple Israel. **SELECTED PUBLICATIONS** Auth, The Victorian Girl and the Feminist Ideal, 82; auth, The Friendships of Women: Friendship, Feminism and Achievement in Vera Brittain's Life and Work in the Interwar Decades in J Women's Hist, 92; auth, Vera Brittain: A Feminist Life, 96; co-ed, Caring and Curing: Historical Perspectives on Women and Healing in Canada, 94. **CONTACT ADDRESS** Dept of History, Carleton Univ, 1125 Colonel By Dr, Ottawa, ON, K1S 5B6. **EMAIL** dgorham@ccs.carleton.ca

GORING, WILLIAM S.
PERSONAL Born 02/01/1943, NY, m **DISCIPLINE** EDUCATION **EDUCATION** Univ Columbia, BA 1959; Univ San Francisco, JD 1963. **CAREER** Mutual of NY Secur; Minority Educ Devel Univ of San Francisco, dir; Special Opportunity Scholarship Programs Univ of CA Berkeley, exec dir; E Bay Home Care Serv Inc, part owner 1975; Trio Educ Disadvantage Health Educ & Welfare, task force chmn. **CONTACT ADDRESS** 1511 Linden, Oakland, CA, 94607.

GORMAN, CARMA
DISCIPLINE ART HISTORY **EDUCATION** Carleton Col, BA, 91; Univ CA, Berkeley, MA, 94, PhD, 98. **CAREER** Asst prof, School of Art & Design, Southern IL Univ, Carbondale IL, 98-. **HONORS AND AWARDS** Mellon Dissertation-Year Fel, UCB Regents Intern-fellowship, 92-95; Henry Luce/ACLS fel in Am Art, 96-97; Winterthur Res Fel, 96; Robert Wark fel, Huntington Library, 97. **MEMBERSHIPS** Am Studies Asn; Soc of Architectural Historians; Col Art Asn; Vernacular Architecture Forum. **RESEARCH** Am art, architecture, and design. **SELECTED PUBLICATIONS** Auth, Fitting Rooms: The Dress Designs of Frank Lloyd Wright, Winterthur Porfolio 30:4, winter 95. **CONTACT ADDRESS** School of Art & Design, Southern Illinois Univ, Carbondale, IL, 62901-4301. **EMAIL** cgorman@siu.edu

GORMAN, MICHAEL J.
PERSONAL Born 11/03/1955, MD, m, 1976, 3 children **DISCIPLINE** NEW TESTAMENT, EARLY CHURCH HISTORY AND THEOLOGICAL ETHICS **EDUCATION** BA, Gordon Col, 77; M Div, Princeton Theol Sem, 82; PhD, 89. **CAREER** Tchg fel, 81-85, instr, 86, Princeton Theol Sem; adjunct facul, 91-93, assoc dean, 93, assoc prof, 93-98, acting dean, 94-95, dean, 95-, prof, 98-, Ecumenical Inst of Theol, St Mary's Sem & Univ Baltimore. **MEMBERSHIPS** Soc of Bibl Lit. **RESEARCH** NT/early Christian ethics; Paul; Abortion; Non-violence. **SELECTED PUBLICATIONS** Auth, Texts and Contexts, 89, 97; Abortion and the Early Church, 82. **CONTACT ADDRESS** Ecumenical Institute of Theology, St. Mary's Sem & Univ, 5400 Roland Av., Baltimore, MD, 21210. **EMAIL** migorman@aol.com

GORMAN, VANESSA
DISCIPLINE ANCIENT GREECE AND ROME HISTORY **EDUCATION** Univ Pa, PhD, 93. **CAREER** Asst prof, Univ Nebr, Lincoln. **RESEARCH** Archaic and Classical Greek history. **SELECTED PUBLICATIONS** Published articles on Ancient city planning and Latin epic. **CONTACT ADDRESS** Univ Nebr, Lincoln, 619 Oldfat, Lincoln, NE, 68588-0417. **EMAIL** vgorman@unlinfo.unl.edu

GORN, ELLIOTT J.
PERSONAL Born 05/03/1951, Los Angeles, CA, 1 child **DISCIPLINE** HISTORY **EDUCATION** Berkeley, BA, 73; Yale Univ, PhD, 83. **CAREER** Univ Alabama; Miami Univ, Ohio; assoc prof, Am Social and Cultural Hist, Purdue Univ. **HONORS AND AWARDS** Guggenheim fel; Newberry Lib fel; Stanford Hum Ctr fel. **RESEARCH** American social and cultural history. **SELECTED PUBLICATIONS** Auth, The Manly Art: Bare-Knuckle Prize Fighting in America, Cornell, 86; coauth, A Brief History of American Sports, Hill & Wang, 93; co-ed, the Encyclopedia of American Social History, 3 v, Scribners, 93; auth, Mother Jones, in Kaye, ed, The American Radical, Routledge, 94; ed, Muhammad Ali: The People's Champ, Illinois, 96; ed, The McGuffey Readers: Selections from the 1879 Edition, Bedford, 98. **CONTACT ADDRESS** Dept of History, Purdue Univ, West Lafayette, IN, 47907.

GORRELL, DONALD KENNETH
PERSONAL Born 01/24/1928, Cleveland, OH, m, 1951, 3 children **DISCIPLINE** CHURCH HISTORY **EDUCATION** Miami Univ, BA, 49; Western Reserve Univ, MA, 51, PhD, 60; Yale Univ, BD, 55. **CAREER** Minister to students, Ohio State Univ, 55-60; asst prof, 60-68, PROF CHURCH HIST, UNITED THEOL SEM, OHIO, 68-, Am Asn Theol Sch fac fel, 65-66; secy, Gen Comn Arch and Hist, United Methodist Church, 68-72, 76-80 and 80-84 fel, Case-Study Inst, Mass, 72. **MEMBERSHIPS** AHA; Am Soc Church Hist; Orgn Am Historians; World Methodist Hist Soc. **RESEARCH** Social Gospel in the Progressive Era, 1900-1920; American church history in the twentieth century; United Methodist Church history. **SELECTED PUBLICATIONS** Auth, Ambivalent Churchmen and Evangelical Churchwomen--The Religion of the Episcopal Elite in North-Carolina, 1800-1860, J Am Hist, Vol 0081, 94. **CONTACT ADDRESS** United Theol Seminary, 1810 Harvard Blvd, Dayton, OH, 45406.

GORSE, GEORGE L.
PERSONAL Born 01/06/1949, Ithaca, NY, m, 1978 **DISCIPLINE** ART HISTORY **EDUCATION** Brown Univ, PhD 80, MA 73; John Hopkins Univ, BA 71. **CAREER** Pomona Col, prof, Viola Horton Prof, 93-, assoc prof, asst prof, 80-93; Univ Pennsylvania, inst 79-80. **HONORS AND AWARDS** NEH; ACLS fel; Inst Adv Stud Princeton; Villa I Tatti, Florence **MEMBERSHIPS** CAA; SAH; RSA; SCSC. **RESEARCH** Genoese medieval; renaissance and baroque studies; hist of cities and gdns, villas and palaces. **SELECTED PUBLICATIONS** Auth, A Classical Stage for the Nobility: the Strada Nuova in Sixteenth-Century Genoa, Art Bull, 97. **CONTACT ADDRESS** Dept of Art and Art History, Pomona Col, 333 N College Way, Claremont, CA, 91711. **EMAIL** ggorse@pomona.edu

GORSKI, PHILIP
PERSONAL Born 07/19/1963, Livermore, LA, m, 1989, 2 children **DISCIPLINE** SOCIOLOGY **EDUCATION** Deep Springs College, AA, 83; Harvard College, BA, 86; Univ Cal Berkeley, PhD, 96. **CAREER** Asst Prof, 96-, Univ Wisconsin Madison. **HONORS AND AWARDS** IRH UW-M; Adv Stud Cen UM; SSRC Berlin Prog; SSRC West Europe. **MEMBERSHIPS** ASA; SSHA; AHA. **RESEARCH** Comparative Historical Sociology; Sociology of Religion; Early Modern European History. **SELECTED PUBLICATIONS** Auth, Historicizing

the Secularization Debate: Church State and Society in Late Medieval and Early Modern Europe, 1300-1700, Amer Soc Rev, forthcoming; auth, The Protestant Ethic and the Spirit of Bureaucracy, Amer Soc Rev, 95; auth, Calvinism Confessionalism and State-Formation in Early Modern Europein: George Steinmetz ed, State/Culture, Ithaca NY, Cornell U Press, 98; Calvinism and Democracy: Populism Pacification and Resistance in the Dutch Republic 1555-1787, in: Carl Lankowski ed, Breakup Breakdown Breakthrough: Germany's Tortuous Path to Modernity, NY Berghahn, forthcoming; coauth, The German Left: Red Green and Beyond, NY, Oxford U Press, 93. **CONTACT ADDRESS** Dept of Sociology, Univ Wis Madison, Madison, WI, 55760. **EMAIL** pgorski@ssc.wisc.edu

GORSUCH, EDWIN N.
PERSONAL Born 08/28/1939, Wauseon, OH **DISCIPLINE** MEDIEVAL HISTORY **EDUCATION** Bowling Green State Univ, BS, 62, MA, 64; Ohio State Univ, PhD(hist), 67. **CAREER** Asst prof, 67-71, ASSOC PROF HIST, GA STATE UNIV, 71-. **MEMBERSHIPS** AHA. **RESEARCH** Medieval intellectual and economic history. **SELECTED PUBLICATIONS** Auth, Christians and Pagans in Roman Britain, Albion, Vol 0024, 92. **CONTACT ADDRESS** Dept of Hist, Georgia State Univ, 33 Gilmer St SE, Atlanta, GA, 30303-3080.

GOSS, THERESA CARTER
PERSONAL Born 08/22/1932, Latham, AL, m **DISCIPLINE** EDUCATION **EDUCATION** AL State Univ Montg, BS; NC Central Univ Durham, MLS; Nova Univ Ft Lauderdale, EdD. **CAREER** Jackson State Univ, librarian 1954-55; FL A&M Univ, librarian 1956; Pinellas HS, librarian 1956-66; St Petersburg Jr Coll, librarian 1966-81; MM Bennett Library SPSC, dir 1981-. **HONORS AND AWARDS** Girl Scout Leadership Awd 1959; PCPTa Awd for Outstanding Serv 1960; Religious Comm Serv Awd 1961; SOUL Awd for Outstanding Serv 1971; Library Bd Mem Awd City of Clearwater 1976; Alpha Kappa Alpha Awd Outstanding Accomplishments 1979; "Model Library Serv for the Hearing Handicapped" Major Applied Rsch Project Ft Lauderdale Nova Univ 1978, various other publications; Kappa Alpha Psi Awd; Links Awd for Outstanding Serv in Library Science; pres Clearwater Adult Adv Comm. **MEMBERSHIPS** Mem League of Women Voters 1957-; mem Amer Assn of Univ Women 1958-; mem NAACP 1964-; mem Amer Assn of Univ Prof 1979-; mem Women's Adv Com Eckerd Coll 1979-; mem FL Library Assn, Amer Library Assn, Southeast Library Assn, FL Assn of Comm Coll, Phi Delta Kappa, Amer Assn of Univ Women; mem Alpha Kappa Alpha Sor, Links Inc, Silhouettes of Kappa Alpha Psi; Clearwater Airport Authority; Pinellas Co Arts Council. **CONTACT ADDRESS** MM Bennett Library, 6605 5th Ave N, St Petersburg, FL, 33710.

GOSSELIN, EDWARD ALBERIC
PERSONAL Born 02/12/1943, Rutland, VT, m, 1970, 2 children **DISCIPLINE** RENAISSANCE-REFORMATION HISTORY, HISTORY OF SCIENCE **EDUCATION** Yale Univ, BA, 65; Columbia Univ, MA, 66, PhD(hist), 73. **CAREER** Asst prof, 69-74, assoc prof, 74-79, PROF HIST, CALIF STATE UNIV, LONG BEACH, 79-, Assoc, Danforth Found, 73-; dir, Ctr Medieval and Renaissance Studies, 80-83. **MEMBERSHIPS** AHA; Renaissance Soc Am; Am Soc Reformation Res; Medieval Acad Am. **RESEARCH** Sixteenth century intellectual history; medieval, Renaissance and Reformation commentaries on the Psalms; Hermetism and 16th and 17th century science. **SELECTED PUBLICATIONS** Auth, Crautwald and Erasmus--A Study in Humanism and Radical Reform in 16th-Century Silesia, 16th Century J, Vol 0024, 93; The 3rd Force in 17th-Century Thought, 16th Century J, Vol 0024, 93; The Philosophy of Bruno, Giordano--1600-1750, Isis, Vol 0085, 94; The Cult of Remembrance and the Black-Death--6 Renaissance Cities in Central-Italy, 16th Century J, Vol 0025, 94; Complete Works, Vol 1, Isis, Vol 0087, 96; Complete Works, Vol 6, Cabale du Cheval Pegaseen, Isis, Vol 0087, 96; A Dominican Head in Layman Garb--A Correction to the Scientific Iconography of Bruno, Giordano, 16th Century J, Vol 0027, 96; Lefevre-detaples, Jacques (1450-Questionable-1536)--Papers from the November 1992 Colloquium, 16th Century J, Vol 0028, 97. **CONTACT ADDRESS** Dept of Hist, California State Univ, Long Beach, 1250 N Bellflower, Long Beach, CA, 90840-0001.

GOSSETT, PHILIP
PERSONAL Born 09/27/1941, New York, NY, m, 1963, 2 children **DISCIPLINE** MUSICOLOGY **EDUCATION** Amherst Col, BA, 63; Princeton Univ, MFA, 65, PhD, 70. **CAREER** Asst instr, Princeton Univ, 64-65; From asst prof to assoc prof, 68-77, prof music, Univ Chicago, 77-84, Robert W. Reneker Distinguished Service Prof, Univ Chicago, 84-; Chmn, Dept Music, Univ Chicago, 78-84 & 89, Dean, Div hum, Univ Chicago, 89-; Guggenheim fel, 71-72; Nat Endowment for Hum sr scholar, 82-83; coordinating ed, The Works of Giuseppe Verdi; vis assoc prof, Columbia Univ, 75; Meadows Distinguished Vis Prof, Southern Methodist Univ, Fall 80; Professore Associato, Facolta di Musicologia, Universita degli Studi, Parma, Spring 83; Vis prof, Institut de Musicologie, Universite de Paris, France, Spring 88; Five-college vis prof, Amherst, Mount Holyoke, Smith; March 89; Gauss Seminars, Princeton Univ, Feb 91; Professore Associato, Istituto di Musicologia, Universita degli Studi, Roma, Fall 94; Ed board, Jour of Am Musicol Soc, 72-78; Ed board, Critical Inquiry, 74-; Ed board, Nineteenth-Century Music, 76-; Ed board, Cambridge Opera Jour, 87-; Ed board, Performance Practice Rev, 87-98. **HONORS AND AWARDS** Einstein Award, Am Musicol Soc, 69; Quantrell Award, excellence in undergraduate tchg, Univ Chicago, 74; Medaglia d'Oro, prima classe, Italian govt, serv to Italian cult, educ, and arts, 85; Deems Taylor, ASCAP, 86; Hon mem, Accademia Filarmonica di Bolobna, 92; Ryerson Lectr, Univ Chicago, 93; Grand Ufficiale dell'Ordine al Merito, Repub of Italy, 97; Order of Rio Branca, Repub of Brazil, 98; Cavaliere di Gran Cruce, Repub of Italy, 98. **MEMBERSHIPS** Am Musicol Soc (coun, 72-74, 83-85, board dir, 74-76; mem prog comt and local arrangements, chmn for the Annual Meeting of the Soc, Chicago, 73; chmn, Campaign Comt for AMS 50, 84-86; vpres, 86-88; pres, 94-96); Chicago Symphony Orchestra, trustee, 91-; Court Theatre, board dir, 94-; Chicago Comt of the Chicago Coun on For Rel, 95-; Int Musicol Soc (Am rep in the Prog Comt for the Copenhagen Cong, 72); Am Inst of Verdi Studies (board of dir); Societa Italiana di Musicologia; Soc for Textual Scholarship (pres, 93-95); Am Acad of Arts and Sci (special nominating comt, 92-94; board of studies, 95). **RESEARCH** Nineteenth century Italian opera; music theory; Beethoven. **SELECTED PUBLICATIONS** Auth, Techniques of Unificaiton in Early Cyclic Masses and Mass Pairs, JAMS, 66; Gli autografi rossiniani al Museo Teatrale alla Scala di Milano, Bollettino del Centro Rossiniano di Studi, 67; Le fonti autografe delle opere teatrali di Rossini, Nuova Rivista Musicale Italiana, 68; A Provisional Catalogue of the Works of Gioachino Rossini, In: Luigi Rognoni, Gioacchino Rossini, Edizioni RAI Radiotelevisione Italiana, 68, rev ed, Einaudi, Turin, 77; Rossini and Authenticity, The Musical Times, 68; Rossini in Naples: Some Major Works Recovered, Musical Quart, 68, in Italian, Bollettino del Centro Rossiniano di Studi, 71; A facsimile edition of the autograph score of La Cenerentola by Rossini, with an introduction, series Bibliotheca Musica Bononiensis, Arnaldo Forni, 69; Performing Editions: A Middle Ground, Opera Jour, 70; Rossini's Operas and their Printed Librettos, In: Report of the Tenth Congress of the IMS Ljubljana 1967, Ljubljana, 70; Gioachino Rossini and the conventions of Composition, Acta Musicologica, 70; The Operas of Rossini: Problems of Textual Criticism in Nineteenth-Century Opera, 2 vol, Princeton Univ, 70; Tancredi's Candeur virginale, The Musical Times, 71; Treatise on Harmony by Jean-Philippe Rameau, trans, intro and notes, Dover Publ, 71; La gazza ladra: Notes towards a Critical Edition, Bolletino del Centro Rossiniano di Studi, Anno, 72; Beethoven's Sixth Symphony: Sketches for the First Movement, JAMS, 74; Criteri per l'edizione critica di tutte le opere di Gioachino Rossini (with Bruno cagli and Alberto Zedda), Bolletino del Centro Rossiniano di Studi, 74; The Mensural System and the Choralis Constantinus, In: Studies in Renaissance and Baroque Music in Honor of Arthur Mendal, Barenreiter Verlag, 74; Verdi, Ghislanzoni and Aida: The Uses of Convention, critical Inquiry, 74; Editorial Norms for The Works of Giuseppe Verdi, Univ Chicago Press, 76-77; The Tragic Finale of Tancredi, Fondazione Rossini, Pesaro, 77; Early Romantic Opera (Philip Gossett and Charles Rosen, ed), Garland Publ, 78-83; The Overtures of Rossini, 19th Century Music, 79; L'edizione critica delle opere di Verdi, In: Per un progetto Verdi, 80; Rossini e i suoi Peches de Vieillesse, Nuova Rivista Musicale Italiana, 80; Le Sinfonie di Rossini, Fondazione Rossini, Pesaro, 81; Frank Walker, The Man Verdi, Chicago, 82; The Four Versions of Marzelline's Aria: Beethoven as a Composer of Opera, Beethoven-Jahrbuch, 83; Gioachino Rossini, In: The New Grove: Masters of Italian Opera, London, 83; Critical Edition of Verdi's Macbeth, In: A Macbeth Sourcebook, W W Norton, 84; Facsimile of the 1857 Ricordi Catalogo (in ordine numerico) delle opere pubblicate (Agostino Zecca-Laterza, ed), Rome, 84, preface reprinted, Notes, 9/85; Tancredie by Gioachino Rossini, Opera Omnia di Gioachino Rossini, vol 10, Fondazione Rossini, Pesaro, 84; Italian Opera 1810-1840 (Philip Gossett, ed), 25 vol, Garland Publ, 84-92; Anna Bolena and the Maturity of Gaetano Donizetti, Oxford Univ Press, 85; L'edizione critica dell'opera lirica: lo specifico musicale, In: Per la tutela del lavoro musicologico, Milan, 86; Preface to Cent ans de mise en scene lyrique en France (by H. Robert Cohen and Marie-Odile Gigou), New York, 86; Music at the Theatre-Italien, In: Music in Paris in the Eighteen-Thirties, New York, 87; La fine dell'eta borbonica: 1838-1860, In: Il Teatro di San Carolo, Naples, 87; La composizione di Ernani, In: Ernani: ieri e oggi, Atti del convegno internazionale di studi, Modena, Teatro San Carlo, 12/84, Verdi X, 87, Engl trans, The Composition of Ernani, In: Analyzing Opera: Verdi and Wagner, Berkeley, 89; The Works of Giuseppe Verdi, In: Nuove prospettive nella ricerca verdiana, Parma/Milano, 87; Rossini's Ritornelli: A Composer and His Orchestral Soloists, In: Musiques-Signes-Images: Liber amicorum Francois Lesure, Geneva, 88; Omaggio a (liberazione da) Rossini, In: Messa per Rossini: La Storia, Il Teso, La Musica, Quaderni dell-Istituto di Studi Verdiani, 88; Carl Dahlhaus and the Ideal Type, 19th Century Music, 89; Becoming a Citizen: The Chorus in Risorgimento Opera, Cambridge Opera Jour, 90; Censorship and Self-Censorship: Problems in Editing the Operas of Giuseppe Verdi, In: Essays in Musicology: A Tribute to Alvin Johnson, Am Musicol Soc, 90; Audience Education, address, Chicago Symphony Orchestra Centennial Symposium, 6/92, The Aspen Inst Quart, 92; History and Works that Have No History: Reviving Rossini's Neapolitan Operas, In: Disciplining Music: Musicology and Its Canons (Katherine Bergeron and Philip V Bohlman, ed), Chicago, 92; I manoscritti musicali di Rossini, In: Rossini 1792-1992: Mostra Storico-Documentaria, Perugia, 92; Performers and Scholars, address, Am Acad Arts and Science, 11/91, Bull Am Acad of Arts and Sci, Boston, 92; The Rossini Thematic Catalog: When Does Bibliographical Access become Bibliographical Excess, In: Foundations in Music Bibliogrpahy, Part II, Music Reference Serv Quat, 93; New Sources for Stiffelio: A Preliminary Report, Cambridge Opera Jour, 93, reprinted Verdi's Middle Period, Chicago, 97; Translations and Adaptations of Operatic Texts, In: Palimpsest, Ann Arbor, 93; Facsimile edition of the autography manuscript of Il Barbiere di Siviglia, with an introduction, Accademia di Santa Cecilia, Rome, 93; L'ocasione fa il ladro by Gioachino Rossini, Opera Omnia di Gioachino Rossini, vol 8, series (Patricia Brauner, Giovanni Carli-Ballola, and Philip Gossett, ed), Fondazione Rossini, Pesaro, 94; Ermione by Gioachino Rossini, Opera Omnia di Gioachino Rossini, vol 27, series (Patricia Brauner and Philip Gossett, ed), Fondazione Rossini, Pesaro, 95; A New Romanza for Attila, In: Studi Verdiani, 95; Presidential Address: Knowing the Score: Italian Opera as Work and Play, In: Text: Transactions of the Society for Textual Scholarship, Ann Arbor, 95; The Repertory of the Teatro Carolino, In: Culture Musicali, 97; Auth, articles in: Enciclopedia di Musica Ricordi-Rizzoli, Grove's Dictionsary, and Penguin Opera Guide (with Patricia Brauner); Facsimile edition of the autograph manuscript of Don Pasquale with an introduction, Accademia di Santa Cecilia, Rome, 98; Performing Italian Opera, Univ Chicago Press; Thematic Catablogue of the Works of Rossini, Fondazione Rossini, Pesaro. **CONTACT ADDRESS** Dept of Music, Univ of Chicago, 1010 E 59th St, Chicago, IL, 60637-1512. **EMAIL** phgs@midway.uchicago.edu

GOSSMAN, NORBERT JOSEPH
PERSONAL Born 02/21/1924, Ridgeway, IA, m, 1949, 4 children **DISCIPLINE** HISTORY **EDUCATION** Univ Iowa, BA, 47, MA, 48, PhD(hist), 52. **CAREER** Instr hist, Coe Col, 52-53 and Whitman Col, 53-54; asst prof, Wis State Col, Eau Claire, 54-55; from asst prof to assoc prof, 55-69, PROF HIST, UNIV DETROIT, 69-, CHMN DEPT, 77-, Res grant, Univ Detroit, 56 and 58; Soc Sci Res Coun grant, 57-58, Nat Endowment Humanities, 76. **MEMBERSHIPS** AHA; Conf Brit Studies; AAUP. **RESEARCH** English history, especially the 19th century Victorian period. **SELECTED PUBLICATIONS** Auth, The Encyclopedia of the British Press, 1422-1992, Albion, Vol 0025, 93; Popular Radicalism in 19th-Century Britain, Albion, Vol 0028, 96. **CONTACT ADDRESS** 12654 Beaverland, Detroit, MI, 48223.

GOTTHELF, ALLAN
DISCIPLINE ANCIENT GREEK PHILOSOPHY **EDUCATION** Columbia Univ, PhD, 75. **CAREER** Philos, Col NJ. **HONORS AND AWARDS** Vis tchr, Oxford Univ, Tokyo Metropolitan Univ, Georgetown Univ, Swarthmore Col. **SELECTED PUBLICATIONS** Auth, Philosophical Issues in Aristotle's Biology, Cambridge Univ Press 87; Aristotle on Nature and Living Things, Bristol Classical Press 85. **CONTACT ADDRESS** Col of New Jersey, PO Box 7718, Ewing, NJ, 08628-0718.

GOTTLIEB, BEATRICE
PERSONAL Born 06/06/1925, New York, NY, s **DISCIPLINE** HISTORY **EDUCATION** Cornell Univ, BA, 45, MA, 48; Columbia Univ, MA, 68, PhD, 74. **CAREER** Asst prof, Smith Col, 76-77. **MEMBERSHIPS** AHA; Coordinating Council of Women in Hist; Columbia U. Seminars, Soc for the Study of Women in the Renaissance. **RESEARCH** Western Europe 1400-1800, espec family, household, servants. **SELECTED PUBLICATIONS** Auth, The Meaning of Clandestine Marriage, Family and Sexuality in French History, eds Wheaton and Hareven, 80; The Problem of Feminism in the 15th Century, Women of the Medieval World, eds Kirshner and Wemple, 85; The Family in the Western World from the Black Death to the Industrial Age, 93; transl, The Problem of Unbelief in the 16th Century; the Religion of Rabelais, Lucien Febvre, 82. **CONTACT ADDRESS** 501 W. 123 St. Apt. 10 H, New York, NY.

GOTTLIEB, CARLA
PERSONAL Born 07/16/1912, Cernauti, Austria **DISCIPLINE** HISTORY OF ART, ARCHEOLOGY **EDUCATION** Carolina Univ, Cernauti, Licenta, 34; Columbia Univ, PhD(art), 51. **CAREER** Asst hist of art, Bryn Mawr Col, 54-56; prof, New Sch Social Res, NY, 56-60; assoc prof art & chair dept, Ripon Col, 60-62; assoc prof hist of art, Univ IL, Urbana, 62-64, cataloguer, Francois L Schwarz Collection, NY & Paris, 65-70; CURATOR, SAMUEL J LEFRAK COLLECTION, 67-77., mem fac, sem in mod art, Sarah Lawrence Col, 58-59; sr researcher, Albright-Knox Art Gallery, Buffalo, NY, 71; vis prof, Carleton Univ, 72. **HONORS AND AWARDS** Travel and Research Grants: Univ Grant Carolina Univ, Cernauti 33; Univ Grant Columbia Univ NY, 52; Am Phil Soc, 53, 54; de Rothchild Found, 54; Am Asn Univ Women, 57-58; Univ IL, 63, 64; Colloquia: Am Council Learned Soc Participant Athens Greece, 60; UNAM participant Xalapa, Mexico, 77. **MEMBERSHIPS** AAUP; Auth Guild; Auth League Am; Yad Vashem, Jerusalem, Israel; Dorot Inc, NY, Programs for the Elderly; Oxford Medicare Advantage; Hamilton Senior Center, Project Find; Dem Congress Campaign Comm. **RESEARCH** Modern Art; aes-

thetics; iconology. **SELECTED PUBLICATIONS** Auth, Death and modern art, In: The Meaning of Death, McGraw, 59, 65; contrib, Harmony and discord in the visual arts, In: Acts IV International Congress of Aesthetics, Athens, 1960, Menas D Myrtides, Athens, 62; auth, Respiciens per fenestras: The symbolism of the Merode altarpiece, Oud Holland, 70; En ipse stat post parietem nostrum: The symbolism of the Ghent Annunciation, Bull des Musees Royal des Beaux-Arts de Belgique, 70; Beyond Modern Art, Dutton, 74; Fanny Sanin, Profile, 77; From the Window of God to the Vanity of Man, Abaris, 78; Self-Portraiture: From Ancient Egypt to World War II, Dutton, 82; The Window as a Symbol in Western Painting: From Divinity to Doubt, Boian, 82; The Window in the Soap Bubble as Illustration of Psalm 26, Wallraf-Richartz-Jahrbuch vol 43, 82; The Bewitched Mirror Coloquio/Artes vol 71, 2d ser 28, 86; The Window as a Symbol in Western Painting: From Divinity to Doubt (in progress); Self-Portraiture: From Ancient Egypt to WWII (in progress); The Window in Painting: A Study of Its Morphology as a Basis for Motif Classification (in progress); Speech, God's Punishment for Man's Sin (in progress). **CONTACT ADDRESS** 246 W End Ave Apt 10B, New York, NY, 10023.

GOTTSCHALK, PETER
DISCIPLINE HISTORY OF RELIGION **EDUCATION** Col of the Holy Cross, BA, 85; Univ Wis, MA, 89; Univ Chicago, PhD, 97. **CAREER** Asst prof, Southwestern Univ, 97- . **MEMBERSHIPS** AAR; AAS **RESEARCH** Narrative, identity, Hinuism, and Islam in South Asia; Time and space in religion. **CONTACT ADDRESS** Dept of Religions, Southwestern Univ, Box 6318, Georgetown, TX, 78756. **EMAIL** gottschp@southwestern.edu

GOUGH, JERRY B.
DISCIPLINE EARLY BRITAIN HISTORY **EDUCATION** Cornell Univ, PhD, 71. **CAREER** Assoc prof, Washington State Univ. **RESEARCH** Chemistry and wine technology in the 18th century. **SELECTED PUBLICATIONS** Ed, The Plutonium Story: The Journals of Professor Glenn T. Seaborg 1939-1946, Battelle Press, 94. **CONTACT ADDRESS** Dept of History, Washington State Univ, 301 Wilson Hall, PO Box 644030, Pullman, WA, 99164-4030. **EMAIL** gough@wsu.edu

GOUINLOCK, JAMES
DISCIPLINE PHILOSOPHICAL ANTHROPOLOGY **EDUCATION** Columbia Univ, PhD, 69. **CAREER** Philos, Emory Univ. **SELECTED PUBLICATIONS** Auth, John Dewey's Philosophy of Value; Excellence in Public Discourse; and Rediscovering the Moral Life: Philosophy and Human Practice; Ed, The Moral Writings of John Dewey; Coed, Ethics in the History of Western Philosophy. **CONTACT ADDRESS** Emory Univ, Atlanta, GA, 30322-1950.

GOULD, ELIGA H.
DISCIPLINE COLONIAL AND REVOLUTIONARY AMERICA, MODERN BRITAIN, HISTORY OF THE BRITISH **EDUCATION** Johns Hopkins Univ, PhD. **CAREER** Asst prof, Univ NH, 93-. **HONORS AND AWARDS** Charles Warren fel, Harvard Univ, 97-98; NEH; Fulbright-Hays; Huntington Libr fel; Clark Libr fel; Jamestown Prize of the Omohundro Inst of Early Am Hist and Cult. **RESEARCH** Civilizing nature. **SELECTED PUBLICATIONS** Auth, To Strengthen the King's Hands: Militia Reform, Dynastic Legitimacy and Ideas of National Unity in England, 1745-60, Hist J, 91; American Independence and the Cosmopolitan Foundations of Britain's First Counterrevolution, Past and Present, no 154, 97. **CONTACT ADDRESS** Univ NH, Durham, NH, 03824. **EMAIL** ehg@christa.unh.edu

GOULD, LEWIS LUDLOW
PERSONAL Born 09/21/1939, New York, NY, m, 1970 **DISCIPLINE** AMERICAN POLITICAL HISTORY **EDUCATION** Brown Univ, AB, 61; Yale Univ, MA, 62, PhD(hist), 66. **CAREER** From instr to asst prof Hist, Yale Univ, 65-67; from asst prof to assoc prof, 67-76, prof Hist, Univ Tex, Austin, 76-, chmn dept, 80-, Eugene C Barker Centennial prof, American History, Univ Tex, Austin, 88-93; Fel, Nat Endowment for Humanities, 74. **HONORS AND AWARDS** Carr P Collins Prize, Tex Inst Letters, 74. **MEMBERSHIPS** AHA; Orgn Am Historians; Southern Hist Asn. **RESEARCH** American political history, 1880-1920. **SELECTED PUBLICATIONS** Auth, Wyoming: A Political History, 1868-1896, Yale Univ, 68; co-ed, The Black Experience in America: Selected Essays, 70 & auth, Progressives and Prohibitionists Texas Democrats in the Wilson Era, 73, Univ Tex; ed, The Progressive Era, Syracuse Univ, 74; co-auth, Photojournalist: The Career of Jimmy Har, Univ Tex, 77; auth, Reform and Regulation: American Politics, 1900-1916, Wiley, 78; The presidency of William McKinley, Kansas, 80; The Life and Times of Frances Goff, 97. **CONTACT ADDRESS** Dept of History, Univ of Texas, Austin, TX, 78712-1026.

GOUMA-PETERSON, THALIA
DISCIPLINE ANCIENT AND MEDIEVAL ART **EDUCATION** Mills Col; BA, 54, MA, 57; Univ Wis, PhD, 64. **CAREER** Prof. **SELECTED PUBLICATIONS** Ed, auth, monograph on Flack, Harry N Abrams, 92; ed, Bibliography on Women in Byzantium; extensive pubs on Byzantine icons and wall paintings. **CONTACT ADDRESS** Dept of Art, Col of Wooster, Wooster, OH, 44691.

GOUVERNEUR, GRAY HENRY
DISCIPLINE COMPARATIVE RELIGION, ART HISTORY **EDUCATION** Sarah Lawrence, BA, 65; Univ Mich, MA, 80; doctoral work, Univ Kent, Canterbury. **CAREER** Teach, Fordham Univ, Dalton Sch, 66-68; teach, Azhar Acad, Cairo Am Col, 70-78; lect, Cambridge Univ, 88; instr, Bellarmine Col, 91-92; instr, Center Col, 93; DIR, FOUNDER PUB HOUSES: ISLAMIC TEXTS SOC, QUINTA ESSENTIA, FOUNSVITAE, 80-. **CONTACT ADDRESS** 49 Mockingbird Valley Dr, Louisville, KY, 40207. **EMAIL** grayh101@aol.com

GOWANS, ALAN
PERSONAL Born 11/30/1923, Toronto, ON, Canada, m, 1948, 4 children **DISCIPLINE** HISTORY OF ART **EDUCATION** Univ Toronto, BA, 45, MA, 46; Princeton Univ, MFA, 48, PhD, 50. **CAREER** Instr hist art, Rutgers Univ, 48-49, asst prof, 50-53; asst prof, Middlebury Col, 53-54; dir, Fleming Mus, Vt, 54-56; from assoc prof to prof hist art, Univ Del, 56-66, chmn dept, 56-66; prof hist in art & chmn dept, Univ Victoria, BC, 66-81; FEL, CTR FOR ADV STUDY, NAT GALLERY OF ART, WASHINGTON, DC, 81-, Vis prof art hist, Harvard Univ, 72-73; Univ Uppsala, 77-78 & George Washington Univ, 81-83. **MEMBERSHIPS** Soc Archit Hist (secy, 59-63, vpres, 69-71, pres, 71-74). **RESEARCH** Social function of arts, especially popular arts; cross-cultural studies of world civilization; American and Canadian architectural history. **SELECTED PUBLICATIONS** Auth The Comfortable House: Surburban Architecture in North American 1890-1930, MIT Press, 86; Sainte-Croix d'Orleans: A Major Monument too long neglected, Gazette des Beaux-Arts (Paris), 88; Pradigmatic Social Function in Anglican Church Architecture of the Fifteen Colonies, Studies in Art History , Johns Hopkins & Nat Gallery of Art, 89; Styles and Types of North American Architecture: Social Function and Cultural Expression, Harper Collins, 92; Fruitful Fields: Churches of the Aamerican Mission to Hawaii1820-1863, Honolulu: State Historic Preservation Office, 93. **CONTACT ADDRESS** 524-2020 F St NW, Washington, DC, 20006.

GOWER, CALVIN WILLIAM
PERSONAL Born 11/14/1926, Delta, CO, m, 1962, 1 child **DISCIPLINE** AMERICAN HISTORY **EDUCATION** Western State Col, BA, 49; Univ SDak, MA, 50 Univ Kans, PhD(Western Am hist),59. **CAREER** From asst prof to assoc prof, 57-66; chmn dept, 62-70, PROF AM HIST, ST CLOUD STATE UNIV, 66-. **MEMBERSHIPS** AHA; Orgn Am Historians; Western Hist Asn. **RESEARCH** Kansas territory and the Pikes Peak gold rush; the Civilian Conservation Corps, 1933-1942; forest conservation in Minnesota. **SELECTED PUBLICATIONS** Auth, Circles of Tradition--Fine-Arts in Minnesota, J the W, Vol 0032, 93. **CONTACT ADDRESS** Dept of Hist, St Cloud State Univ, St Cloud, MN, 56301.

GRABER, DORIS A.
PERSONAL Born 11/11/1923, St. Louis, MO, m, 1941, 5 children **DISCIPLINE** POLITICAL SCIENCE **EDUCATION** Wash Univ, AB, 41, MA, 42; Columbia Univ, 47. **CAREER** Feat writer, St Louis Count Observer, 39-41; civ dir, US Army Ednl Record Prog, Camp Maxey, 43-45; edr, Commerce Clearing House, 45-56; lectr, Polit Sci, Univ Chicago, 50-51; res assoc, Center for Stud Am For & Mil Pol, 52-71; lectr, Polit Sci, North Park Coll, 52, assoc prof, Univ Ill, 64-69; PROF, POLIT SCI, UNIV ILL, 70-. **MEMBERSHIPS** Int Polit Sci Asn; Int Commn Asn; Asn Educ Journalism; Acad Polit Sci; Am Acad Polit & Soc Sci; Int Soc Polit Psychol **SELECTED PUBLICATIONS** co-edr, The Politics of News: The News of Politics, 97; edr, Political Psychology, 97. **CONTACT ADDRESS** Dept Polit Sci, Univ Ill at Chicago Circle, Chicago, IL, 60680.

GRABOWSKA, JAMES A.
DISCIPLINE MEDIEVAL STUDIES **EDUCATION** Northern State Univ, BS, 82; Univ OK, MA, 91; Univ MN; PhD, 96. **CAREER** Hist, Col St. Benedict. **HONORS AND AWARDS** Phi Kappa Phi, 90; M.J. Meixner Scholarship, 92; Herbert Garvin Scholarship, 93; Fulbright-Hays Scholarship, 94; Herbert Garvin and Bambenek Scholarship, 95; Dissertation Fel, 95. **MEMBERSHIPS** MLA, SCMLA. **SELECTED PUBLICATIONS** Auth, A Multimedia Critical Reader's Guide to Cervantes' Don Quixote, Pending, 97. **CONTACT ADDRESS** Col of Saint Benedict, St. Joseph, MN, 56374-2099. **EMAIL** jgrabowska@csbsju.edu

GRAD, BONNIE L.
PERSONAL Born 06/01/1949, New York, NY, m, 1980, 2 children **DISCIPLINE** ART HISTORY **EDUCATION** Cornell Univ, BA, 71; Univ Va, PhD, 77. **CAREER** Art instr, Cincinnati Art Mus, 67, 68; teaching asst, Univ Va, 73-74; collections asst, Graphic Arts Collection, Princeton Univ, 76-77; asst prof, 77-83, assoc prof, Clark Univ, 83-. **HONORS AND AWARDS** Fulbright-Hayes grant, 74-75; NEH grants, 80-83; Mellon and Higgins grants, Clark Univ, 84-95; Richard A. Florsheim Art Fund grant, 93-94; Seymour N. Logan Facul fel, Clark Univ, 92-94; vis scholar, Pollock-Krasner House and Studies Ctr, 94, 97. **MEMBERSHIPS** Col Art Asn; New England Fulbright Asn. **RESEARCH** Nineteenth and twentieth century art; Landscape painting; Georgia O'Keeffe. **SELECTED PUBLICATIONS** Auth, Georgia O'Keeffe, The Archives of Amer Art Jour, 98; auth, Robert Richenburg: Abstract Expressionist, 94; auth, Stuart Davis, Artibus et Historiae, 91; co-auth, Visions of City and Country: Prints and Photographs of Nineteenth Century France, 82; auth, Milton Avery, 81; auth, Charles Francois Daubigny, The Print Collector's Newsletter, 79. **CONTACT ADDRESS** 21 Willard Rd., Weston, MA, 02493. **EMAIL** bonniegrad@aol.com

GRAEBNER, ALAN
PERSONAL Born 08/06/1938, Pittsburgh, PA, m, 1958 **DISCIPLINE** AMERICAN HISTORY **EDUCATION** Valparaiso Univ, BA, 59; Columbia Univ, MA, 61, PhD(hist), 65. **CAREER** Asst prof, Concordia Col, Morrhead, Minn, 64-69; ASSOC PROF HIST, COL ST CATHERINE, 69-. **RESEARCH** Women and the family in American history; health professions. **SELECTED PUBLICATIONS** Auth, Watchdog of Loyalty--The Minnesota Commission-of-Public-Safety during World-War-I, J the W, Vol 0033, 94; Life at 4-Corners--Religion, Gender, and Education in a German-Lutheran Community, 1868-1945, J Interdisciplinary Hist, Vol 0025, 95. **CONTACT ADDRESS** Dept of Hist, Col of St. Catherine, 2004 Randolph Ave, Saint Paul, MN, 55105-1789.

GRAF, DANIEL WILLIAM
PERSONAL Born 09/20/1940, La Crosse, WI, m, 1967, 2 children **DISCIPLINE** MODERN EUROPEAN HISTORY **EDUCATION** Univ Wis-La Crosse, BS, 65; Univ Nebr, Lincoln, MA, 67, PhD(hist), 72. **CAREER** Asst hist Univ Nebr-Lincoln, 65-67, assoc, 68-69; asst prof, 70-80, PROF HIST, VA WESLEYAN COL, 80-. **MEMBERSHIPS** AHA; Am Asn Advan Slavic Studies. **RESEARCH** Twentieth century Russian society and institutions; reign of Nicholas II and the revolutions of 1917. **SELECTED PUBLICATIONS** Auth, Bayonets Before Bullets--The Imperial Russian Army, 1861-1914, J Mil Hist, Vol 0057, 93; Notes of a Red-Guard, Russ Hist-Histoire Russe, Vol 0021, 94; Russian Hussar--A Story of the Imperial Cavalry, 1911-1920, J Mil Hist, Vol 0058, 94; Vetluga Memoir--A Turkish Prisoner of War in Russia, 1916-1918, J Mil Hist, Vol 0060, 96; Government, Industry and Rearmament in Russia, 1900-1914--The Last Argument of Czarism, J Mil Hist, Vol 0061, 97. **CONTACT ADDRESS** Dept of Hist, Va Wesleyan Col, 1584 Wesleyan Dr, Norfolk, VA, 23502-5599.

GRAF, DAVID FRANK
PERSONAL Born 12/03/1939, Detroit, MI, m, 1963, 2 children **DISCIPLINE** ANCIENT HISTORY (NEAR EAST, GREECE, ROME) **EDUCATION** Harding Coll, BA, 65; McCormick Theological Seminary, BD (with honors), 70; Univ Mich, Near Eastern Languages, MA, 75, History, PhD, 79. **CAREER** Assoc ed, Biblical Archeol, Amer Schools Oriental Research, 80-82; visiting lecturer, Univ Mich, Dept Near Eastern Studies, 82-83, adjunct lecturer, Program on Studies in Religion, 84-86; adjunct asst prof, Montana State Univ, Dept History & Philos, 83-84; asst prof, 86-90, assoc prof, 90-95, prof, 95-, Univ Miami, Dept History. **HONORS AND AWARDS** Senior Fellow, Dumbarton Oaks, 93; summer res grant, NEH, 94; Amer Schools of Oriental Research Archeol Grant, 95; Phi Beta Delta Honor Soc for Intl Scholars, 97; life-time member, chap pres, 97-98, Phi Kappa Phi Honor Soc. **MEMBERSHIPS** Amer Inst Archeol; Amer Schools Oriental Research; Assn Ancient Historians; ARAM: Syro-Mesopotamian Soc. **RESEARCH** Greco-Roman Near East history, especially Roman Arabia; Roman roads; inscriptions. **SELECTED PUBLICATIONS** Co-auth, "The Roman East from the Chinese Perspective," Palmyra and the Silk Road: Les Annales Archeologiques Arabes Syriennes, vol. 42, 96; auth, "The Via Militarias in Arabia," Dumbarton Oaks Papers, vol 51, 97; "Camels, Roads, and Wheels in Late Antiquity," Donum Amicitiae, 97; "The Via Militaris and Limes Arabicus," Roman Frontier Studies 1995, 97; Rome and Its Arabian Frontier from the Nabataeans to the Saracens, 97. **CONTACT ADDRESS** Dept of History, Univ of Miami, PO Box 248107, Coral Gables, FL, 33124-4662. **EMAIL** Dgraf@umiami.ir.miami.edu

GRAFF, HARVEY J.
DISCIPLINE HISTORY **EDUCATION** Nwestern Univ, BA, 70; Univ Toronto, MA, 71, PhD, 75. **CAREER** PROF, HIST & HUM, UNIV TEXAS AT SAN ANTONIO **MEMBERSHIPS** AM Antiquarian Soc **SELECTED PUBLICATIONS** Auth, Conflicting Paths: Growing Up in America, Harvard Univ Press, 95; auth, Literacy, Libraries, Lives: New Cultural and Social Histories, Lib and Cult 26, 91; auth, Remaking Growing Up: Nineteenth Century America, in Histoire sociale - Social History 24, 91; auth, The Literacy Myth, Academic Press, 79 & Transaction, 91; ed, Literacy and Social Development in the West, Cambridge Univ Press, 81; auth, The Legacies of Literacy, Ind Univ Press, 87 & 91; ed, Growing Up in America: Historical Experiences, Wayne State Univ Press, 87; auth, The Labyrinths of Literacy, Falmer, 87, auth, Dallas: The Book. **CONTACT ADDRESS** Div of Behav & Cult Sci, Univ of Texas at San Antonio, 6900 N Loop 1604 W, San Antonio, TX, 78249-0652. **EMAIL** hgraff@utsa.edu

GRAFTON, ANTHONY T.
PERSONAL Born 05/21/1950, New Haven, CT, m, 1972, 2 children **DISCIPLINE** HISTORY **EDUCATION** Chicago, BA, 71, MA, 72, PhD, 75. **CAREER** Instr, Cornell Univ, 74-75; Asst prof, prof, Princeton Univ, 75-85; Mellen prof, 88-93; Dodge Prof, 93- ; Princeton Univ. **HONORS AND AWARDS** LA Times Book Award, 93; Behrmann Award Hum, 96; Brit Acad. **MEMBERSHIPS** Renaissance Soc Am **RESEARCH** Renaissance intellectual history. **SELECTED PUBLICATIONS** Auth, Joseph Scaligen, (1983-93); Commerce with the Classics, 97; The Footnote, 97. **CONTACT ADDRESS** History Dept, Princeton Univ, 129 Dickinson Hall, Princeton, NJ, 08544-1017. **EMAIL** grafton@princeton.edu

GRAHAM, A. JOHN
PERSONAL Born 03/09/1930, Lowestoft, England, m, 1963, 2 children **DISCIPLINE** CLASSICS **EDUCATION** Cambridge Univ, BA, 52, MA, 56, PhD, 57. **CAREER** Asst Lectr, Univ London, 55-57; Asst Lectr to Sr Lectr, Univ Manchester, 57-77; Prof Classical Studies, 77-95, Prof Emeritus, Univ Pa, 95-. **HONORS AND AWARDS** Cromer Greek Prize, British Acad, 56; Hare Prize, Univ Cambridge, 60; NEH Fel, 81-82. **MEMBERSHIPS** Soc Hellenic Studies; British Sch at Athens; Cambridge Philol Soc. **RESEARCH** Greek history; Greek colonization; Greek prose authors; ancient beekeeping. **SELECTED PUBLICATIONS** Auth, Colony and Mother City in Ancient Greece, 2nd ed, 83; Abdera and Teos, J Hellenic Studies 112, 92; Thucydides 7.13.2 and the Crews of Athenian Triremes, Transactions Am Philol Asn 122, 92; A Dedication from the Chersonese at Olympia, Nomodeiktes. Greek Studies in of Martin Ostwald, 93; The Odyssey, History and Women, The Distaff Side, 95; Themistocles' Speech before Salamis: the Interpretation of Herodotus 8.83.1, Classical Quart 46, 96. **CONTACT ADDRESS** Classical Studies Dept, Univ of Pennsylvania, Logan Hall, Philadelphia, PA, 19104-6304.

GRAHAM, GAEL N.
DISCIPLINE MODERN AMERICAN HISTORY **EDUCATION** Univ MI, PhD. **CAREER** Hist Dept, Western Carolina Univ **SELECTED PUBLICATIONS** Auth, Gender, Culture, and Christianity: American Protestant Mission Schools in China, 1880-1930, 95. **CONTACT ADDRESS** Western Carolina Univ, Cullowhee, NC, 28723.

GRAHAM, HUGH DAVIS
PERSONAL Born 09/02/1936, Little Rock, AR, m, 1966 **DISCIPLINE** AMERICAN HISTORY **EDUCATION** Yale Univ, BA, 58; Stanford Univ, MA, 61, PhD(Am hist), 64. **CAREER** Instr US hist, Foothill Col, 63-64; from asst prof to assoc prof, San Jose State Col, 64-67; regional dir training & pub affairs, Peace Corps, 65-66; vis asst prof US hist, Stanford Univ, 67; assoc prof, Johns Hopkins Univ, 67-71; dean soc sci, 71-77, Prof hist, Univ MD Baltimore County, 72-91, Co-dir hist & comp task force, Nat Comn Causes & Prev Violence, 68-69; Guggenheim Found fel, 70-71; Holland M. McTyeire Prof Hist, Vanderbilt Univ 91-; Ch hist dept, Vanderbilt Univ, 94-96. **HONORS AND AWARDS** Chastain Award, Southern Polit Sci Asn, 76; Moody Fel, 80; Fel, Woodrow Wilson Ctr, 85-86; Sen fel, Natl Endowment for the Hum, 89-90; Jury nominee, Pulitzer Prize in Hist, 91; G. Welsey Johnson Prize, 93. **MEMBERSHIPS** Southern Hist Asn; AHA; Am Pol Sci Asn. **RESEARCH** Am polit hist; civil rights; educ policy. **SELECTED PUBLICATIONS** Auth, Crisis in Print, Vanderbilt Univ, 67; Since 1954: Desegregation, Harper, 72; The Uncertain Triumph: Federal Education Policy in the Kennedy and Johnson Years, Univ of NC, 84; The Civil Rights Era: Origins and Development of National Policy, 1960-1972, Oxford Univ Press, 90; Civil Rights and the Presidency, Oxford Univ Press, 92; coauth, Southern Politics and the Second Reconstruction, Johns Hopkins Univ, 75; The Rise of American Research Universities, John Hopkins Univ, 97; ed, Huey Long, Prentice-Hall, 70; Violence, Johns Hopkins Univ, 71; American Politics and Government, Harper, 75; Civil Rights in the United States, PSU Press, 94; co-ed, Violence in America, US Govt Printing Off, 69; Southern Elections, La State Univ, 78; Violence in America, Sage, rev ed, 79; The Carter Presidency: Policy Choices in the Post-New Deal Era, Univ of KS, 98. **CONTACT ADDRESS** Dept of History, Vanderbilt Univ, Nashville, TN, 37235. **EMAIL** hugh.graham@vanderbilt.edu

GRAHAM, HUGH G.
DISCIPLINE HISTORY **EDUCATION** Yale Univ, BA, 58; Stanford, MA, 61, PhD, 65. **CAREER** Prof, Univ Md, 72-91; PROF, POL SCI, 92-, HOLLAND N. MCTYEIRE PROF HIST, 91-, CHAIR, HIST, 94-96, VANDERBILT UNIV. **CONTACT ADDRESS** Dept of History, Vanderbilt Univ, Nachville, TN, 37235. **EMAIL** hugh.graham@vanderbilt.edu

GRAHAM, JOHN THOMAS
PERSONAL Born 03/28/1928, Brookfield, MO, m, 1968, 1 child **DISCIPLINE** MODERN EUROPEAN HISTORY **EDUCATION** Rockhurst Col, BA, 52; St Louis Univ, PhD, 57. **CAREER** From instr to asst prof Europ hist, St Ambrose Col, 57-62; asst prof, Gonzaga Univ, 62-66; asst prof, 66-74, assoc prof, 74-93, PROF, MOD EUROP HIST, UNIV MO-KANSAS CITY, 96-. **MEMBERSHIPS** Soc Sci Hist Asn; AHA; AAUP. **RESEARCH** Nineteenth and twentieth century Europe; history of crisis thought; intellectual history. **SELECTED PUBLICATIONS** Auth, Donoso Cortes: Utopian Romanticism and Political Realism, Univ Mo, 74; A Pragmatist Philosophy of Life: Orteya y Gasset, 94; Theory of History in Orteya y Gasset: The Dawn of Historical Reason, 97. **CONTACT ADDRESS** Dept of Hist, Univ of Mo, 203 Cockefair Hall, 1525 Rockh, Kansas City, MO, 64110-2499.

GRAHAM, LOREN RAYMOND
PERSONAL Born 06/29/1933, Hymera, IN, m, 1955, 1 child **DISCIPLINE** RUSSIAN HISTORY, HISTORY OF SCIENCE **EDUCATION** Purdue Univ, BS, 55; Columbia Univ, MA, 60, PhD, 64; Purdue Univ, DHL, 86. **CAREER** Res engr, Dow Chem Co, 55; lectr hist, Ind Univ, 63-64, asst prof hist, 64-65, asst prof hist of sci, 65-66; from asst prof to assoc prof hist, Columbia Univ, 66-72, prof, 72-80; PROF HIST, MASS INSTECH, 80-; PROF HIST, HARVARD 86-; Am Philos Soc grant, 64; vis asst prof pub law & govt & sr fel, Russ Inst, Columbia Univ, 65-66; Fulbright-Hays grant, 66; mem, Inst Advan Studies, 69-70; Guggenheim fel, 69-70; res fel hist of sci, Harvard Univ, 72-73; consult, NSF, 75-76, NEH, 76-; mem panel on eval sci exhanges, Nat Acad Sci, 75-77; Rockefeller Found Humanities fel 76-77; res fel, Prog Sci & Int Affairs, Harvard Univ, 76-77; adv ed, Isis, 76-. **HONORS AND AWARDS** Saxton Prize, Hist Sci Soc, 96. **MEMBERSHIPS** AHA; Hist Sci Soc, Am Asn Advan Slavic Studies (treas, 67-68); AAAS; Soc Hist Technol; Am Acad Arts & Sci; Am Philos Soc; Russ Acad Natural Scie, foreign mem; Russ Acad Humanitarian Sci, foreign mem. **RESEARCH** History of science; Russian history. **SELECTED PUBLICATIONS** Auth, A Soviet Marxist View of Structural Chemistry: The Theory of Resonance Controversy, Isis, 3/64; Quantum mech and dialectical materialism, Slavic Rev, 9/66; Cybernetics, in Science and Ideology in Soviet Society, Atherton, 67; The Soviet Academy of Sciences and the Communist Party, 1927-1932, Princeton Univ, 67; Science and Philosophy in the Soviet Union, Knopf, 72; ed, Review of US-USSR Interacademy Exchanges and Relations, Nat Acad Sci, 77; auth, Eugenics in Weimar Germany and Soviet Russia in the Twenties, Am Hist Rev, 12/77; Concerns about science and attempts to regulate scientific inquiry, Daedalas, spring 78; Between Science and Values, Columbia Univ, 81; Functions and Uses of Disciplinary History, Dovdeucht, 84; Red Star: The First Bolshevik Science Utopia, Ind Univ, 84; Science, Philosophy, and Human Behavior in the Soviet Union, Columbia Univ, 87; Science and the Soviet Social Order, Harvard Univ, 90; Science in Russia and the Soviet Union: A Short History, Cambridge Univ, 93; The Ghost of the Executed Engineer, Harvard Univ, 93; A Face in the Rock, Island Press, 95; What Have We Learned about Science and Technology from the Russian Experience?, Stanford Univ, 98 **CONTACT ADDRESS** Dept of Hist, Massachusetts Inst of Tech, 77 Massachusetts Ave, Cambridge, MA, 02139-4307. **EMAIL** lrg@mit.edu

GRAHAM, PATRICIA ALBJERG
PERSONAL Born 02/09/1935, Lafayette, IN, m, 1955, 1 child **DISCIPLINE** AMERICAN HISTORY **EDUCATION** Purdue Univ, BS, 55, MS, 57; Columbia Univ, PhD(hist educ), 64. **CAREER** Teacher, High Sch, Va, 55-58; chmn dept hist, St Hilda's and St Hugh's Sch, NY, 58-60; lectr hist educ, Ind Univ, 64-65, asst prof, 65-66; dir educ prog and asst prof educ, Barnard Col, Columbia Univ, 65-68, assoc prof hist educ, 68-72, prof educ and dir educ prog, 72-74, from assoc prof to prof hist educ, Teachers Col, 68-74; prof educ, Harvard Univ, 74-79; dir, Nat Inst Educ, Dept Health, Educ and Welfare, 77-79; prof educ, 74-79, CHARLES WARREN PROF HIST EDUC, HARVARD UNIV, 79-, DEAN GRAD SCH EDUC, 82-, John Simon Guggenheim Found fel and Radcliffe Inst fel, 72-73; dean, Radcliffe Inst and vpres, Radcliffe Col, 74-77; Woodrow Wilson Ctr fel, 82. **MEMBERSHIPS** AHA; Hist Educ Soc. **RESEARCH** History of education. **SELECTED PUBLICATIONS** Auth, Battleships and Schools, Daedalus, Vol 0124, 95. **CONTACT ADDRESS** Hist of Educ, Harvard Univ, Cambridge, MA, 02138.

GRAHAM, RICHARD
PERSONAL Born 11/01/1934, Anapolis, Brazil, m, 3 children **DISCIPLINE** LATIN AMERICAN HISTORY **EDUCATION** Col Wooster, BA, 56; Univ TX, MA, 57, PhD, 61. **CAREER** Asst prof hist, Cornell Univ, 61-68; assoc prof, Univ UT, 68-70; assoc prof, 70-73, prof, 73-86, F. H. NALLE PROF HIST, UNIV TEX, AUSTIN, 86-; Ed asst, Hisp Am Hist Rev, 58, assoc ed, 71-74, ed, 75; series ed, Library of Latin Am, Oxford Univ Press, 94-; Am Philos Soc grant, 62 & 71; Rockefeller Found Int Rels fel, 64-65; Soc Sci Res Coun fac grant, 64-65, 66 & 80-81; Guggenheim Found fel, 72-73; Nat Endowment for Humanities res grant, 72-73, 98-99; Fulbright fel, 74 & 80-81, 91-92. **HONORS AND AWARDS** Bolton Prize, Conf Latin Am Hist, 69; Foreign Corr member, Brazilian Inst Hist and Geog; Teaching Excellence Awards, Univ TX, 96, 97. **MEMBERSHIPS** AHA; Conf Latin Am Hist; Latin Am Studies Asn. **RESEARCH** Brazilian hist; independence in Latin Am hist; hist of slavery; hist of liberalism in Latin Am. **SELECTED PUBLICATIONS** Auth, Causes for the Abolition of Negro Slavery in Brazil, Hisp Am Hist Rev, 66; Britain and the Onset of Modernization in Brazil, 1850-1914, Cambridge Univ, 68; Landowners and the Overthrow of the Empire, Luso-Brazilian Rev, 70; Independence in Latin America, Knopf, 72, 2nd ed, McGrawHill, 94; co-ed, Approaches to Latin American History, Univ Tex, 74; auth, Slave Families on a Rural Estate in Colonial Brazil, J Social Hist, 76; Escravidao, Reforma e Imperialismo, Perspectiva, 79; Slavery and Economic Development: Brazil and the US South, Comparative Studies in Society and History, 81; Brazil from the Middle of the Nineteenth Century to the Paraguayan War, in Leslie Bethell, ed, Cambridge History of Latin America, vol 3, Cambridge Univ, 85; Patronage and Politics in Nineteenth-Century Brazil, Stanford Univ, 90; ed, Idea of Race in Latin america, Univ TX, 90; Dilemas for Democracy in Brazil, in L. Graham and R. Wilson, eds, The Political Economy of Brazil, Univ TX, 90; ed, Brazil and the World System, Univ TX, 91; Mecanismos de integracion en el Brasil del siglo XIX, in A. Annino et al, eds, De los imperios a las naciones: Iberoamerica, IberCaja (Spain), 94; Formando un gobierno central: las elecciones en el Brasil monarquico, in A. Annino, ed, Historia de las elecciones en Iberoamerica, siglo XIX, Fondo de Cultura Economica (Argentina), 95; Ciundadania y jerarquia en el Brasil esclavista, in H. Sabato, ed, La ciudadania politica en America Latina en perspectiva historica, Fondo de Cultura Economica (Mexico), 98; African Brazilians and the State in Slavery Times, in Michael Hanchard, Racial Politics in Contemporary Brazil, NC Univ, 98; ed, Machado de Assis: Contemporary Reflections, Univ TX, 99. **CONTACT ADDRESS** Dept of Hist, Univ of Texas, Univ of TX, Austin, TX, 78712-1063.

GRAHAM, RICHARD
PERSONAL Born 11/01/1934, Brazil, m, 1978, 3 children **DISCIPLINE** HISTORY **EDUCATION** Col Wooster, BA, 56; Univ Texas, Austin, MA, 57, PhD, 61. **CAREER** Asst prof, 61-68, Cornell Univ; Assoc prof, 68-70, Univ Utah; assoc prof, 70-73, prof, 73-86, F H Nalle Prof of History, 86-, Univ Texas, Austin. **RESEARCH** Independence of Latin Am; Brazilian hist, slavery & race; intl econ rels; econ liberalism in Brazil. **CONTACT ADDRESS** Dept of History, Univ of Texas, Austin, TX, 78731-1163.

GRAHAM, W. FRED
PERSONAL Born 10/31/1930, Columbus, OH, m, 1953, 4 children **DISCIPLINE** RELIGION, HISTORY **EDUCATION** Tarkio Col, BA, 52; Pittsburgh Theol Sem, BD, 55; Louisville Presby Sem, ThM, 58; Univ Iowa, PhD(relig), 65. **CAREER** From instr to asst prof relig, 63-65, from asst prof to assoc prof dept relig studies, 66-73, PROF RELIG, MICH STATE UNIV, 73-. **MEMBERSHIPS** Am Soc Church Hist; Calvin Studies Soc; Am Acad Relig; Soc 16th Century Studies. **RESEARCH** Reformation, particularly 16th century Geneva and Calvin; relationship between religion and social, economic and political life and thought; science and religion. **SELECTED PUBLICATIONS** Auth, An Uncounseled King--Charles-I and the Scottish Troubles, 1637-1641, Church Hist, Vol 0062, 93; Calvin, John Preaching, Church Hist, Vol 0063, 94; Where Shall Wisdom Be Found--Calvin Exegesis of Job from Medieval and Modern Perspectives, 16th Century J, Vol 0026, 95; Calvinism in Europe, 1540-1610--A Collection of Documents, Church Hist, Vol 0064, 95; Ecclesia-Reformata--Studies on the Reformation, Vol 2, 16th Century J, Vol 0026, 95; Humanism and Reform--The Church in Europe, England and Scotland, 1400-1643, Church Hist, Vol 0064, 95; Calvin, John Concept of the Law, Church Hist, Vol 0064, 95; Sin and the Calvinists--Morals Control and the Consistory in the Reformed Tradition, Cath Hist Rev, Vol 0082, 96; Politics, Religion, and Diplomacy in Early-Modern Europe--Essays in Honor of Jensen, de, Lamar, Church Hist, Vol 0065, 96; The Uses of Reform--Godly Discipline and Popular Behavior in Scotland and Beyond, 1560-1610, 16th Century J, Vol 0028, 97. **CONTACT ADDRESS** Dept of Relig Studies, Michigan State Univ, East Lansing, MI, 48823.

GRAHAM, WILLIAM C.
PERSONAL Born 04/16/1950, Duluth, MN **DISCIPLINE** HISTORICAL THEOLOGY **EDUCATION** Fordham Univ, PhD, 93. **CAREER** Assoc prof, Caldwell Col, NJ; dir, Caldwell Pastoral Ministry Inst. **HONORS AND AWARDS** Asst ed, Listening; columnist for Natl Cath Reporter. **MEMBERSHIPS** Am Acad Relig; Asn of Grad Prog in Ministry; New Jersey Consortium for Grad Prog in Theol; N Am Acad of Relig. **SELECTED PUBLICATIONS** Co-ed, Common Good, Uncommon Questions: A Primer in Moral Theology, Liturgical, 95; auth, Half Finished Heaven: The Social Gospel in American Literature, Univ Pr Am, 95; ed, More Urgent Than Usual: The Final Homilies of Mark Hollenhorst, Liturgical, 95; auth, Is There A Case Against St. Therese As Doctor of the Church? Sisters Today, 95; auth, Sadness of the City, in Legalized Gambling, Greenhaven, 98; auth, Up In Smoke: Preparation for Ash Wednesday, Mod Liturgy, 97/98; auth, Television, Resistance and Orthodoxy, Natl Cath Reporter, 98; auth, The Preacher and the Abortion Opponent, Celebration, 98. **CONTACT ADDRESS** 326 W 14th St, New York, NY, 10014. **EMAIL** wcgnycpl@aol.com

GRAHAM YATES, GAYLE
PERSONAL m, 2 children **DISCIPLINE** INTERDISCIPLINARY AMERICAN STUDIES **EDUCATION** Univ Minn, PhD, 73. **CAREER** Prof, ch, Women's Stud, Univ Minn, Twin Cities; vis instr, Univ Munich & Univ Amsterdam. **SELECTED PUBLICATIONS** Auth, What Women Want: The Ideas of the

Movement, Harvard, 75; Mississippi Mind: A Personal Cultural History of an American State, Tenn, 90; ed, Harriet Martineau on Women, Rutgers, 85. **CONTACT ADDRESS** Univ Minn, Twin Cities, Minneapolis, MN, 55455. **EMAIL** graha001@maroon.tc.umn.edu

GRANATSTEIN, JACK L.
PERSONAL Born 05/21/1939, Toronto, ON, Canada **DISCIPLINE** HISTORY **EDUCATION** Royal Mil Col Kingston, BA, 61; Univ Toronto, MA, 62; Duke Univ, PhD, 66; Memorial Univ, DLitt, 93; Univ Calgary, LLD, 94. **CAREER** Hist, Directorate Hist, Nat Defence HQ, 64-66; prof history, 66-95, dir, Grad Hist Prog, 84-87; DISTINGUISHED RES PROF HISTORY EMER, YORK UNIV, 95-. **HONORS AND AWARDS** Killam Res Fel, 82-84, 91-93; Tyrrell Medal Can Hist 92; JW Dafoe Prize, 93; Univ BC Medal Can Biog, 93; Vimy Award, Conf Def Asns Inst, 96; Off, Order Can, 97. **MEMBERSHIPS** Fel, Royal Soc Can; Can Inst Int Affairs; Orgn Stud Nat Hist Can. **SELECTED PUBLICATIONS** Auth, The Politics of Survival, 67; Peacekeeping: International Challenge and Canadian Response, 68; Marlborough Marathon, 71; co-ed, The Generals: The Canadian Army's Senior Commanders in the Second World War, 93; Empire to Umpire: Canadian Foreign Policy to the 1990s, 94; Victory 1945, 95; The Good Fight, 95; Yankee Go Home? Canadians and Anti-Americanism, 96; The Canadian 100: The Hundred Most Influential Canadians of the 20th Century, 97; Petrified Campus: Canada's Universities in Crisis, 97. **CONTACT ADDRESS** 53 Marlborough Ave, Toronto, ON, M5R 1X5.

GRANT, EDWARD
PERSONAL Born 04/06/1926, Canton, OH, m, 1951, 2 children **DISCIPLINE** HISTORY OF SCIENCE **EDUCATION** City Col New York, BSS, 51; Univ Wis, MA, 53, PhD(hist of sci), 57. **CAREER** Instr Europ hist and hist of sci, Univ Maine, 57-58; instr hist of sci, Harvard Univ, 58-59; from asst prof to assoc prof, 59-64, chmn, Dept Hist and Philos Sci, 73-79, PROF HIST OF SCI AND MEDIEVAL HIST, IND UNIV, BLOOMINGTON, 64-, NSF res grants, 59-74; Am Coun Learned Soc grant, 61-62; vis asst prof, Univ Wis, 62; Guggenheim fel, 65-66; vis mem, Inst Advan Studies, 65-66; chmn US nat comt, Int Union Hist and Philos Sci, 68-69; mem adv bd, Speculum, J Mediaeval Acad Am, 72-75; Am Coun Learned Soc fel, 75-76. **MEMBERSHIPS** Int Acad Hist Sci; Hist Sci Soc; fel Mediaeval Acad Am; AAUP. **RESEARCH** Ancient and medieval science; medieval cosmology; Medieval and Renaissance Aristotelianism. **SELECTED PUBLICATIONS** Auth, The Aristotelians of Renaissance Italy--A Philosophical Exposition, Isis, Vol 0084, 93; Atomic Theory in the Latin Middle-Ages, Isis, Vol 0087, 96; History, Prophecy, and the Stars--The Christian Astrology of Dailly, Pierre, 1350-1420, Am Hist Rev, Vol 0101, 96; When Did Modern Science Begin, Am Scholar, Vol 0066, 97; Bradwardine, Thomas--A View of Time and a Vision of Eternity in 14th-Century Thought, Speculum-J Medieval Stud, Vol 0072, 97. **CONTACT ADDRESS** Dept of Hist and Philos of Sci, Indiana Univ, Bloomington, 130 Goodbody Hall, Bloomington, IN, 47401.

GRANT, GLEN
PERSONAL Born 02/23/1947, Los Angeles, CA **DISCIPLINE** AMERICAN STUDIES **EDUCATION** Univ Calif, Los Angeles, BA, 68; Univ Hawaii, M.Ed, 74, PhD, 82. **CAREER** Tchg asst, 72-82, instr, 92-, acad chemn, 98-, Hawaii tokai Int Col; educ specialist, Kapiolani Commun Col, 84-91. **HONORS AND AWARDS** Excellence Tchg Award, 79, Univ Hawaii; Living Treasure Hawaii's Multiculturalism, 96, City and County of Honolulu. **RESEARCH** Hawaii's multiculturalism; ethnic studies. **SELECTED PUBLICATIONS** Coauth, Kodomo No Tame Ni (For the Sake of the Children) The Japanese American Experience in Hawaii, 78; coauth, art, Race Relations in the Hawaiian Schools: The Haole Newcomer, 78; auth, art, Living Proof: Is Hawaii the Answer?, 93; auth, art, Hawaiians and Volcanoes, 96; coauth, An Unlikely Revolutionary: The Memoirs of Matsuo Takabuki, 98. **CONTACT ADDRESS** Hawaii Tokai Intl Col, 2241 Kapiolani Blvd, Honolulu, HI, 96826. **EMAIL** ggrant@tokai.edu

GRANT, H. ROGER
PERSONAL Born 11/28/1943, Ottumwa, IA, m, 1966, 1 child **DISCIPLINE** HISTORY **EDUCATION** Simpson Col, BA, 66; Univ Mo, MA, 67, PhD, 70. **CAREER** From asst prof to assoc prof to prof, 70-96, Univ Akron; prof, chemn, Clemson Univ, 96-. **HONORS AND AWARDS** Woodrow Wilson Fel, 66; Woodrow Wilson Dissertation Fel, 68-69; Railroad Hist Book Award; Railway and Locomotive Hist Society, 85. **MEMBERSHIPS** OAH; SHA; Lexington Group in Transportation Hist. **RESEARCH** Transportation history **SELECTED PUBLICATIONS** Auth, Erie Lackawanna: Death of an American Railroad, 1938-1992, 94; auth, Ohio's Railway Age in Postcards, 96; auth, The North Western: A History of the Chicago and North Western Railway System, 96; auth, Ohio in Historic Postcards: Self Portrait of a State, 97; auth, Railroads in the Heartland: Steam and Traction in the Golden Age of Postcards, 97. **CONTACT ADDRESS** 123 Hickory Ridge Rd, Central, SC, 29603-9461. **EMAIL** ggrant@clemson.edu

GRANT, JOHN NEILSON
PERSONAL Born 05/03/1940, Edinburgh, Scotland, m, 1962, 3 children **DISCIPLINE** CLASSICS **EDUCATION** Univ Edinburgh, MA, 62; Cambridge Univ, BA, 64; Univ of St Andrews, PhD(Latin), 70. **CAREER** Lectr classics, Univ Man, 65-67; asst prof, 67-72, assoc prof, 72-80, PROF CLASSICS, UNIV TORONTO, 80-, CHMN, 82-, Can Coun fel, 77-78. **MEMBERSHIPS** Class Asn Can; Am Philol Asn. **RESEARCH** Roman comedy; transmission of texts; republican Latin literature. **SELECTED PUBLICATIONS** Auth, 2 Syntactic Errors in Transcription, Seneca, 'Thyestes 33' and Lucan, 'BC 2.279,' Class Quart, Vol 0044, 94; Taide in 'Inferno 18' and Terence 'Eunuchus 937,' Quaderni D Italianistica, Vol 0015, 94. **CONTACT ADDRESS** Dept Class, Univ Toronto, Toronto, ON, M5S 1A1.

GRANT, SHELAGH D.
PERSONAL Born 06/28/1938, Montreal, PQ, Canada **DISCIPLINE** HISTORY/CANADIAN STUDIES **EDUCATION** Univ Western Ont, Hosp Sick Children, RN, 60; Trent Univ, BA, 81, MA, 83. **CAREER** Tutor/lectr, 82-88, ADJ FAC, HISTORY & CANADIAN STUD, TRENT UNIV, 88-; adv bd, The Northern Rev, 89-; ed adv bd, Arctic, 92-. **MEMBERSHIPS** Can Hist Asn; Am Hist Asn; Asn Can Stud; Can Inst Int Affairs; UN Asn Can; Brit Asn Can Stud; Champlain Soc. **SELECTED PUBLICATIONS** Auth, Sovereignty or Security? Government Policy in the Canadian North 1936-1950, 88; co-ed & contribur, Federalism in Canada and Australia, 89. **CONTACT ADDRESS** Can Stud, Trent Univ, Peterborough, ON, K9J 7B8.

GRANTHAM, DEWEY WESLEY
PERSONAL Born 03/16/1921, Manassas, GA, m, 1942, 3 children **DISCIPLINE** HISTORY **EDUCATION** Univ Ga, AB, 42; Univ NC, MA, 47, PhD, 49. **CAREER** Asst prof hist, NTex State Col, 49-50 and Woman's Col Univ NC, 50-52; from asst prof to prof, 52-77, HOLLAND N MCTYEIRE PROF HIST, VANDERBILT UNIV, 77-, Fund Advan Educ fac fel, 55-56; chmn regional selection comt, Woodrow Wilson Nat Fel Prog, 57-59; Soc Sci Res Coun fac fel, 59, mem, Comt Fac Res Grants, 66-67; Guggenheim Mem Found fel, 60; mem advan placement exam comt Am hist, Col Entrance Exam Bd, 66-67; fel, Henry E Huntington Libr and Art Gallery, 68-69; mem, Regional Archives Adv Coun, Fed Arch and Records Ctr, 70-77; gen ed, Twentieth-Century America Series, Univ Tenn, 76-; Fulbright-Hays lectr, Univ Aix-en-Provence, 78-79; fel, Nat Humanities Ctr, 82-83. **HONORS AND AWARDS** Sydnor Award, Southern Hist Asn, 59. **MEMBERSHIPS** AHA; Am Studies Asn; Orgn Am Historians; Southern Hist Asn, (pres, 67); Am Coun Learned Soc. **RESEARCH** Twentieth century American history; recent Southern history; modern Afro-American history. **SELECTED PUBLICATIONS** Auth, The Papers of Wilson, Woodrow, Vol 65, February 28 July 31, 1920, J Am Hist, Vol 0080, 93; The Papers of Wilson, Woodrow, Vol 66 August 2 December 23, 1920, J Am Hist, Vol 0080, 93; The Papers of Wilson, Woodrow, Vol 67, December 24, 1920-April 7, 1922, J Am Hist, Vol 0080, 93; The Kingfish and His Realm--The Life and Times of Long, Huey, P., J Am Hist, Vol 0080, 94; The Papers of Wilson,Woodrow, Vol 68, April 8, 1922 February 6, 1924, J Am Hist, Vol 0081, 95; The Paper of Wilson, Woodrow, Vol 69, 1918-1924, Contents and Index, Volumes 53-68, J Am Hist, Vol 0081, 95. **CONTACT ADDRESS** Dept of Hist, Vanderbilt Univ, Nashville, TN, 37235.

GRATZ, DELBERT L.
PERSONAL Born 03/05/1920, Allen Co, OH, m, 1943, 4 children **DISCIPLINE** CHURCH HISTORY **EDUCATION** Bluffton Col, AB, 42; Ohio State Univ, MA, 45; Univ Bern, DPhil-(hist), 50; Univ Mich, Ann Arbor, AMLS, 52. **CAREER** LIBRN, MENNONITE HIST LIBR AND COL LIBR AND PROF HIST, BLUFFTON COL 50-, Scholar, Nordrhein-Westfalen Ministry of Educ, Bonn, Ger, 64; fel, Pro Helvetia, Zurich, Switz, 64-65; Ger Acad Exchange Serv fel, Bad Godesberg, 64-65; res scholar, Baptist Theol Sem, Zurich, 64-65 and 71-72; Fulbright travel grant, 71-72. **MEMBERSHIPS** Church Hist Soc; Am Soc Reformation Res; Swiss Am Hist Soc; Mennonite Hist Soc. **RESEARCH** Anabaptist and Mennonite research; genealogical research. **SELECTED PUBLICATIONS** Auth, Helvetia-Sacra--Section 8, Vol 1, The History and Life of the Congregations in Switzerland, 16th-18th-Century, Church Hist, Vol 0065, 96. **CONTACT ADDRESS** Mennonite Hist Libr, Bluffton Col, Bluffton, OH, 45817.

GRAUBARD, STEPHEN RICHARDS
PERSONAL Born 12/05/1924, New York, NY **DISCIPLINE** HISTORY **EDUCATION** George Washington Univ, AB, 45; Harvard Univ, AM, 46, PhD(hist), 52. **CAREER** From instr to asst prof hist and gen educ, Harvard Univ, 52-55, lectr hist, 60-63; PROF HIST, BROWN UNIV, 64-, DIR STUDIES, ASSEMBLY UNIV GOALS AND GOVERNANCE, 69-, Harvard Found grant, 56; managing ed, Daedalus, 60-61, ed, 61-; mem adv comt, Giovanni Agnelli Found, Italy, 70- **HONORS AND AWARDS** DHuL, Providence Col, 71. **MEMBERSHIPS** AHA; Coun Foreign Rels; Am Acad Arts and Sci. **RESEARCH** British labor history; history of the First World War; modern French social and intellectual history. **SELECTED PUBLICATIONS** Auth, Labor at War, France and Britain, 1914-1918, Albion, Vol 0024, 92; Reconstructing Nations and States, Daedalus, Vol 0122, 93; Preface to the Issue China in Transformation, Daedalus, Vol 0122, 93; America Childhood--Preface, Daedalus, Vol 0122, 93; The American Research University--Preface, Daedalus, Vol 0122, 93; Germany in Transition--Preface, Daedalus, Vol 0123, 94; Europe Through a Glass Darkly--Preface, Daedalus, Vol 0123, 94; Pollitt, Harry, Albion, Vol 0026, 94; After Communism--What--Preface, Daedalus, Vol 0123, 94; What Future for the State, Daedalus, Vol 0124, 95; An American Dilemma Revisited--Preface, Daedalus, Vol 0124, 95; We Need to Know More, Daedalus, Vol 0124, 95; The British Communist-Party and the Trade-Unions, 1933-45, Albion, Vol 0028, 96; Social Suffering--Preface, Daedalus, Vol 0125, 96; American Academic Culture in Transformation--50 Years, 4 Disciplines--Preface, Daedalus, Vol 0126, 97. **CONTACT ADDRESS** Dept of Hist, Brown Univ, Providence, RI, 02912.

GRAVELLE, JANE GIBSON
PERSONAL Born 05/22/1947, Sandersville, GA, w, 1969, 1 child **DISCIPLINE** ECONOMICS **EDUCATION** Univ GA, BA, 68, MA, 69; George Washington univ, PhD, 81. **CAREER** Vis Economist, Labor Dept, 77; vis prof, Boston Univ, 88; vis Economist, Treasury Dept, 89-90; Research asst, 69-72; sr specialist in Economic Policy, Economist/Analyst, Congressional Research Service, 72-. **HONORS AND AWARDS** Outstanding Doctoral Dissertation in Public Finance, Nat Tax Asn. **MEMBERSHIPS** Am Economic Asn; Nat Tax Asn. **RESEARCH** Tax policy. **SELECTED PUBLICATIONS** Auth, Effects of the 1981 Depreciation Revisions on the Taxation of Income from Business Capital, Nat Tax J 35, March 82; The Incidence and Efficiency Costs of Corporate Taxation when Corporate and Noncorporate Firms Produce the Same Goods, with Laurence J Kotlikoff, J of Political Economy 97, Aug 89; Differential Taxation of Capital Income: Another Look at thre Tax Reform Act of 1986, Nat Tax J 42, Dec 89; Do Individual Retirement Accounts Increase Savings?, J of Economic Perspectives 5, spring 91; Income, Consumption, and Wage Taxation in a Life-Cycle Model: Separating Efficiency From Redistribution, Am Economic Rev, 81, Sept 91; Equity Effects of the Tax Reform Act of 1986, J of Economic Perspectives 6, winter 92; What Can Private Investment Incentives Accomplish? The Case of the Investment Tax Credit, Nat Tax J 46, Sept 93; Corporate Tax Incidence and Efficiency When Corporate and Noncorporate Goods are Close Substitutes, with Laurence J Kotlikoff, Economic Inquiry 31, Oct 93; Corporate Taxation and the Efficiency Gains of the 1986 Tax Reform Act, with Laurence Kotlikoff, Economic Theory, vol 6, 95; Dynamic tax Models: Why They Do the Things They Do, with Eric Engen and Kent Smetters, Nat Tax J, 42, Sept 97; numerous other articles. **CONTACT ADDRESS** Library of Congress, 101 Independence Ave SE, Washington, DC, 20540-7430. **EMAIL** jgravelle@crs.loc.gov

GRAVELLE, SARAH S.
DISCIPLINE ANCIENT, MEDIEVAL, RENAISSANCE HISTORY **EDUCATION** Sarah Lawrence Col, AB; Univ Mich, PhD. **CAREER** Ch; assoc prof, 81. **HONORS AND AWARDS** Fel(s), Danforth Found; Renaissance Soc Am., Dir, Lib Arts Summer Stud, Volterra, Italy. **RESEARCH** History of Italy in the Renaissance and early modern France. **SELECTED PUBLICATIONS** Auth, articles on Renaissance humanism and philology. **CONTACT ADDRESS** Dept of Hist, Univ Detroit Mercy, 4001 W McNichols Rd, PO BOX 19900, Detroit, MI, 48219-0900. **EMAIL** GRAVELSS@udmercy.edu

GRAVES, MICHAEL W.
PERSONAL Born 10/27/1952, Belleville, IL **DISCIPLINE** ANTHROPOLOGY **EDUCATION** Univ Wash, BA, 71; Univ Ariz, PhD, 81. **CAREER** Asst prof of anthropology, 81-85, dir, Micronesian Res Center, 85-86, Univ Guam; asst prof of anthropology, 86-89, assoc prof of anthropology, 89-95, full prof, 95-, special asst to sr vp and exec vice chancellor, 96- Univ Hawaii at Manoa . **HONORS AND AWARDS** Men of Achievement, biographee, 93-98. **MEMBERSHIPS** Soc for Amer Archaeol; Indo Pacific Assn; Archaeol Inst of Am; Amer Anthropological Assn. **RESEARCH** Archael of Oceania and Asia; archaeol method and theory. **SELECTED PUBLICATIONS** Coauth, "Seriation as a Method of Chronologically Ordering Architectural Design Traits: An Example from Oceania," Archaeology in Oceania, v 31, 96; coauth, "Dryland Agricultural Expansion and Intensification in Kohala, Hawai'i Island," Antiquity, v 70, 96; coauth, "Integration of Global Positioning Systems in Archaeological Field Research: A Case Study from North Kohala, Hawai'i Island," SAA Bulletin, v 16, 98; auth, "The Study of Prehistoric Puebloan Pottery Designs: The Intellectual Tradition of Southwestern Archaeol," The Journal of Archaeol Method and Theory, v 4, 1998; coauth, "The Tongan Maritime Expansion: A Case Study in the Evolutionary Ecology of Social Complexity," Asian Perspectives, v 37, 98. **CONTACT ADDRESS** Office of Senior Vice Pres and Exec Vice Chancellor, Univ of Hawaii, 2444 Doc St, Honolulu, HI, 96822. **EMAIL** mgraves@hawaii.edu

GRAVES, PAMELA
DISCIPLINE HISTORY **EDUCATION** Univ Pitt, PhD. **CAREER** Asst prof, Eastern Michigan Univ. **RESEARCH** Mod-

ern Europe, Europe, labor, history of women. **SELECTED PUBLICATIONS** Auth, Labor Women, Women in British Working Class Politics, 1918-1939. **CONTACT ADDRESS** Dept of History and Philosophy, Eastern Michigan Univ, 701 Pray-Harrold, Ypsilanti, MI, 48197.

GRAVES, ROBERT
DISCIPLINE MUSIC **EDUCATION** Northwestern Univ, PhD. **CAREER** Assoc prof, Univ IL Urbana Champaign . **RESEARCH** Theatre hist; Renaissance theatre; mod theatre. **SELECTED PUBLICATIONS** Auth, publ on Elizabethan staging. **CONTACT ADDRESS** Dept of Music, Univ Illinois Urbana Champaign, E Gregory Drive, PO Box 52, Champaign, IL, 61820.

GRAY, HANNA HOLBORN
PERSONAL Born 10/25/1930, Heidelberg, Germany, m, 1954 **DISCIPLINE** RENAISSANCE & REFORMATION HISTORY **EDUCATION** Bryn Mawr Col, AB, 50; Harvard Univ, PhD, 57. **CAREER** Instr hist, Bryn Mawr Col, 53-54; from instr to asst prof, Harvard Univ, 57-60; from asst prof to assoc prof, Univ Chicago, 61-72; dean arts & sci & prof hist, Northwestern Univ, 72-74; provost & prof hist, Yale Univ, 74-78, actg pres, 77-78; Prof Hist, 78-93, Harry Pratt Judson Distinguished Service Prof Hist, Univ Chicago, 93-, Pres 78-93, Pres Emer 93-; vis lectr, Harvard Univ, 63-64 & Northwestern Univ, 65 & 66; Ctr Advan Studies Behav Sci fel, 66-67; co-ed J Mod Hist, 66-70; vis assoc prof hist, Univ Calif, Berkeley, 70-71; trustee, Yale Univ, 71-74; dir bd dirs, Am Coun Learned Socs, 71-76; mem NEH, 72-77; trustee, Inst Advan Studies, 72-78, Carnegie Found Advan Teaching, 72-75 & Mayo Found, 74-, Bryn Mawr Col, 77-, Ctr Advan Studies Behav Sci, 77-, Mellon Found, 80- & Brookings Inst, 81-; fel, Harvard Univ Corp; Chair, Howard Hughes Med Inst; Chair, Andrew W. Mellon Found; Bd of Regents, Smithsonian Inst; bd mem, Marlboro Sch of Music; mem bd dir, J.P. Morgan & Co, the Cummins Engine Co, and Ameritech; mem, Secretary's Energy Advisory Bd, U.S. Dept Energy. **HONORS AND AWARDS** Newberry Libr fel, 60-61; Phi Beta Kappa; Radcliffe Graduate Medal, 76; Medal of Liberty Award, 86; Presidential Medal of Freedom, 91; Charles Frankel Prize, NEH, 93; Jefferson Medal, Am Philos Soc, 93; Quantrell Award for Excellence in Undergraduate Teaching, Univ Chicago, 96; M. Carey Thomas Award, Bryn Mawr Col, 97; numerous other awards., Sixty honors & awards from US & foreign univs & cols, 71-81. **MEMBERSHIPS** Renaissance Soc Am; fel Am Acad Arts & Sci; Am Philos Soc; Nat Acad Educ; Coun on For Relations of NY; honorary degrees from several colleges and universities, including Oxford, Yale, Brown, Columbia, Princeton, Duke, and Harvard. **RESEARCH** Renaissance intellectual history; historiography; Europe in the Renaissance and Reformation. **SELECTED PUBLICATIONS** Auth, Renaissance humanism: The pursuit of eloquence, in J Hist Ideas, 63; Valla's Encomium of St Thomas Aquinas and the Humanist Conception of Christian Antiquity, Studies Hist & Lit, Newberry Libr, 65; Machiavelli: The art of politics and the paradox of power, in The Responsibility of Power, Doubleday, 68. **CONTACT ADDRESS** Univ of Chicago, 1126 E 59th St., Chicago, IL, 60637-1539. **EMAIL** m-veghte@uchicago.edu

GRAY, LAURA
DISCIPLINE MUSIC **EDUCATION** Univ Western Ontario, BM, 87; Univ British Columbia, MA, 89; Yale Univ, PhD, 97. **CAREER** Asst prof **RESEARCH** 19th and 20th century music, theory and aesthetics. **SELECTED PUBLICATIONS** Auth, pub(s) on Sibelius, and music in the 20th century. **CONTACT ADDRESS** Dept of Music, Conrad Grebel Col, 200 Westmount Rd, Waterloo, ON, N2L 3G6.

GRAY, RALPH D.
PERSONAL Born 10/13/1933, Otwell, IN, m, 1956, 3 children **DISCIPLINE** UNITED STATES HISTORY **EDUCATION** Hanover Col, BA, 55; Univ Del, MA, 58; Univ Ill PhD(hist), 62. **CAREER** Teaching asst, Univ Ill, 60-61; instr, Ohio State Univ, 61-64; from asst prof to assoc prof, Ind Univ Kokomo, 64-68; assoc prof, 68-72, PROF HIST, IND UNIV-PURDUE UNIV, INDIANAPOLIS, 72-, Consult, Stellite Div, Cabot Corp, 71; ed, J Early Repub, 81-. **HONORS AND AWARDS** Thomas McKean Mem Cup Award, Antique Automobile Club Am, 79. **MEMBERSHIPS** Orgn Am Historians; Bus Hist Conf; Lexington Group; Soc Historians of Early Am Republic. **RESEARCH** Indiana history; 19th and 20th century transportation history; 19th and 20 century United States political and economic history. **SELECTED PUBLICATIONS** Auth, Structures in the Stream--Water, Science, and the Rise of the US-Army-Corps-of-Engineers, J Am Hist, Vol 0082, 95; We the People--Voices and Images of the New Nation, Publ Historian, Vol 0017, 95; Common Labor--Workers and the Digging of North-American Canals, 1780-1860, Am Hist Rev, Vol 0102, 97. **CONTACT ADDRESS** Dept of Hist, Indiana Univ-Purdue Univ, Indianapolis, 925 W Michigan St, Indianapolis, IN, 46202.

GRAYBAR, LLOYD JOSEPH
PERSONAL Born 11/29/1937, Bellows Falls, VT **DISCIPLINE** AMERICAN HISTORY **EDUCATION** Middlebury Col, AB, 60; Columbia Univ, MA, 61, PhD, 66. **CAREER** From asst prof to assoc prof, 66-76, PROF HIST, EASTERN KY UNIV, 76-; Vis lectr, Univ NDak, 67; Am Philos Soc grant, 70; Earhart Found grant, 81. **MEMBERSHIPS** Orgn Am Historians; Immigration Hist Group; Am Mil Inst, Comt Hist 2nd World War. **RESEARCH** American social and urban history, 1877-1920; American nuclear testing, 1946-1950; Admiral Ernest J King and the United States Navy, 1900-1945. **SELECTED PUBLICATIONS** Auth, The whiskey war at Paddy's Run, Ohio Hist, winter 66; Albert Shaw's search for the ideal city, Historian, 5/72; Albert Shaw and the founding of the Review of Reviews: An Intellectual Biography, Univ Press Ky, 74; Admiral King's toughest battle, Naval War Col Rev, 2/79; American Pacific strategy after Pearl Harbor: The relief of Wake Island, Prologue, fall 80; The 1946 Atomic Bomb Tests, J Am Hist, 3/86; Ernest J King: Commander of the Two-Ocean Navy, in Quarterdeck & Bridge, Naval Inst Press, 97. **CONTACT ADDRESS** Dept of Hist, Eastern Kentucky Univ, 521 Lancaster Ave, Richmond, KY, 40475-3102.

GRAYBILL, MARIBETH
DISCIPLINE ART HISTORY **EDUCATION** Col Wooster, BA, 71; Univ MI, MA, 75, PhD, 83. **CAREER** Assoc prof art hist; chr Asian studies. **RESEARCH** Japan painting and prints, espec in rel to vernacular narrative traditions. **SELECTED PUBLICATIONS** Auth, Nobuzane and Gotoba In in International Symposium on the Conservation and Restoration of Cultural Property: Periods of Transition in East Asian Art, Tokyo Nat Res Inst Cult Properties, 88; Buson as Heir to Saigy(tm) and Nobuzane: A Study in Self-Fashioning, Kobijutsu, 89; Painting as Family Business: Portraits by Nobuzane and and his Descendants, Bijutsu Kenky, 94. **CONTACT ADDRESS** Swarthmore Col, Swarthmore, PA, 19081-1397. **EMAIL** mgraybi1@swarthmore.edu

GREAVES, RICHARD L.
PERSONAL Born 09/11/1938, Glendale, CA, m, 1959, 2 children **DISCIPLINE** HISTORY **EDUCATION** Bethel Col, BA, 60; Berkeley Baptist Div School, MA, 62; Univ London, PhD, 64. **CAREER** Assoc prof, Fl Mem Col, 64-65; asst prof, William Woods Col, 65-66; asst prof, E Washington St Col, 66-69; assoc prof, Mich St Univ, 69-72; Robert O. Lawton Distinguished Prof, Fl St Univ, 72- . **HONORS AND AWARDS** Outler Prize, Amer Soc of Church Hist; Love Prize, N Amer Conf on British Stud; Fel, Rockefeller Found, Mellon Found, Amer Coun of Learned Soc, Nat Endow for the Humanities, Amer Philos Soc., Robert O. Lawton Distinguished Prof of Hist, Fl St Univ; pres, Amer Soc of Church Hist; pres, Int John Bunyan Soc. **MEMBERSHIPS** Amer Hist Assoc, N Amer Conf on British Stud; Amer Soc of Church Hist. **RESEARCH** Early modern Britain **SELECTED PUBLICATIONS** Auth, Secrets of the Kingdom: British Radicals from the Popish Plot to the Revolution of 1688-1689, Stanford Univ Press, 92; John Bunyan and English Nonconformity, Hambledon Press, 92; God's Other Children: Protestant Nonconformists and the Emergence of Denominational Churches in Ireland, 1660-1700. Stanford Univ Press, 97; Dublin's Merchant-Quaker: Anthony Sharp and the Community of Friends, 1643-1707, Stanford Univ Press, 98; coauth, Instructor's Manual, HarperCollins, 92, 97. **CONTACT ADDRESS** 910 Shadowlawn Dr, Tauahasee, FL, 32312-2446. **EMAIL** rgreaves@mailer.fsu.edu

GREAVES, ROSE LOUISE
PERSONAL Born 02/12/1925, Kansas City, KS, m, 1955 **DISCIPLINE** MODERN DIPLOMATIC & MIDDLE EASTERN HISTORY **EDUCATION** Univ Kans, BA, 46, MA, 47, PhD(hist), 52; Univ London, PhD(hist), 54. **CAREER** From asst instr to instr hist, Univ Kans, 47-51; asst lectr, Univ London, 54-56, res fel, Bedford Col, 56-57; res fel, Europ Ctr, Carnegie Found, 57-67; historian, Brit Petro Co, Ltd, London, 59-67; sr res fel & teaching asst hist & Islamic studies, Univ Toronto, 68; assoc prof hist, 69-73, PROF HIST, UNIV KANS, 73-, Sr assoc mem Mid E hist, St Antony's Col, Oxford Univ, 73 & 74, Hilary & Trinity Terms; vis scholar, Wolfson Col, Cambridge Univ, 81; vis prof, U.S. Army, For Area Officers Course, Fort Bragg, NC, 84-87. **HONORS AND AWARDS** Fulbright Scholar, Eng, 52-54; Res Fel, Carnegie Found, Europ Ctr, 57-59; Am Philos Soc grant, 74; Fel, Am Asn for Univ Women, 75-76; multiple research grants, Univ Kans; Commander's Award for Public Service, Special Warfare Center and School, Fort Bragg, NC, 87; Elected Kans Univ Women's Hal lof Fame, 91; Laurel Leaf Cluster, Commander's Award for Public Service, USMA, West Point, 93. **MEMBERSHIPS** Fel Royal Hist Soc; Royal Soc Asian Affairs. **RESEARCH** Diplomatic relations of the great powers 19th and early 20th centuries; Middle East, especailly Persia, Afghanistan and India; oil. **SELECTED PUBLICATIONS** Auth, Persia and the Defence of India, 1884-1892, The Athlone Press, 59; British Policy in Persia, 1892-1903, 65, & Some Aspects of the Anglo-Russian Convention and its Working in Persia, 1907-1914, 68, Bull Sch Orient & African Studies; National Perceptions and Cultural Identities. The Hidden Infrastructure of the Petroleum Confrontation, A Report from the Center for Mediterranean Studies, Am Universities Field Staff; Profiles of the Third World, River City Publ, 86; The Cambridge History of Iran: Vol 7, From Nadir Shah to the Islamic Republic, Cambridge Univ Press, 91; Durand, Henry Mortimer, Encyclopaedia Iranica, 96; auth of a number of journal articles and book contributions. **CONTACT ADDRESS** Dept of Hist, Univ of Kans, Lawrence, KS, 66045-0001.

GREEN, CAROL HURD
PERSONAL Born 12/25/1935, Cambridge, MA, m, 1967, 2 children **DISCIPLINE** AMERICAN STUDIES **EDUCATION** Regis Col, BA, 57; Georgetown Univ, MA, 60; George Washington Univ, PhD(Am studies), 71. **CAREER** Instr English, Col Notre Dame, MD, 59-63; asst prof, Merrimack Col, 63-64; instr, Boston Col, 64-70; asst prof Am studies, Newton Col, 73-75; co-ed, Notable Am Women, Radcliffe Col, 76-80; assoc dean, col arts & sci, Boston Col, 81-. **HONORS AND AWARDS** Sr Fulbright Scholar, Palacky Univ, Czech Rep, 96-97. **MEMBERSHIPS** Am Studies Asn; Nat Women's Studies Asn. **RESEARCH** Literature and politics; American political trials; women's history. **SELECTED PUBLICATIONS** Auth, The Writer is a Spy: The Poetry of Ann Sexton and Maxine Kumin, Boston Rev of Arts, 73; co-ed, Journeys: Autobiographical Writings by Women, G K Hall, 79; Notable American Women: The Modern Period, Harvard Univ Press, 80; co-ed, American Women Writers: Supplement (Continuum), 94; coauth, American Women in the 1960's: Changing the Future, Twayne, 93; auth, The Suffering Body in M Garber and R Walkowitz, eds, Secret Agents, Routledge, 95. **CONTACT ADDRESS** Col of Arts & Scis, Boston Col, 140 Commonwealth Ave, Chestnut Hill, MA, 02167-3800. **EMAIL** green@bc.edu

GREEN, DOUGLASS MARSHALL
PERSONAL Born 07/22/1926, Rangoon, Burma, m, 1952, 3 children **DISCIPLINE** HISTORY OF MUSIC, MUSIC THEORY **EDUCATION** Univ Redlands, BMus, 49, MMus, 51; Boston Univ, PhD(compos musicol), 58. **CAREER** Sensei music and English, Nanko Gakuen, Sendai, Japan, 51-54; from asst to assoc prof music, St Joseph Col, Conn, 58-66; from asst to assoc prof, Univ Calif, Santa Barbara, 66-70; from assoc prof to prof, Eastman Sch of Music, Univ Rochester, 70-77; PROF MUSIC, UNIV TEX, AUSTIN, 77-. **HONORS AND AWARDS** Am Soc Composers, Arrangers & Publ Deems Taylor award, 78. **MEMBERSHIPS** Am Musicol Soc; Soc Music Theory; Col Music Soc. **RESEARCH** Italian instrumental music of the 18th century; early 20th century music; musical analysis. **SELECTED PUBLICATIONS** Auth, The Berg Companion, J the Arnold Schoenberg Inst, Vol 0014, 91; The Music of Debussy, Claude, Mus Theory Spectrum, Vol 0014, 92; Komar, Arthur (1934-1994)--In-Memoriam, Col Mus Symp, Vol 0033, 94; A History of the Concerto, Notes, Vol 0052, 95; Images--The Piano Music of Debussy, Claude, Notes, Vol 0053, 97. **CONTACT ADDRESS** Dept of Music, Univ Tex, 0 Univ of Texas, Austin, TX, 78712-1026.

GREEN, ELNA C.
DISCIPLINE U.S. HISTORY **EDUCATION** Wake Forest Univ, BA, 82; Wake Forest Univ, MA, 84; Tulane Univ, PhD, 92 **CAREER** Visiting asst prof, Tulane Univ, 92-93; asst prof, Sweet Briar Col, 93-98; assoc prof, Florida State Univ, 98- **HONORS AND AWARDS** Sweet Briar Grant-in-Aid of Res, 93, 96, 97; Amer Council Learned Soc Res Fel, 95; Mellon Res Fel, Virginia Historical Soc, 92; Patricia Harris Dissertation Fel, Tulane Univ, 90-92; **MEMBERSHIPS** Amer Historical Assoc; Orgn Amer Historians; Southern Hist Assoc; Southern Assoc Women Historians; Soc Welfare History Group **SELECTED PUBLICATIONS** Auth, Southern Strategies: Southern Women and the Woman Suffrage Question, Univ North Carolina, 97; auth, "New Women," "True Daughters," and "Mad Women," Atlanta Hist, 96-97; auth, "Ideals of Government, of Home, and of Women': The Ideology of Southern Antisuffragism," Hidden Histories of Women in the New South, Univ Missouri, 94 **CONTACT ADDRESS** 1532 Grape St, Tallahassee, FL, 32303. **EMAIL** egreen@mailer.fsu.edu

GREEN, GEORGE D.
DISCIPLINE HISTORY **EDUCATION** Stanford Univ, PhD, 68. **CAREER** Assoc prof **RESEARCH** Political economy of twentieth-century America. **SELECTED PUBLICATIONS** Auth, Finance and Economic Development in the Old South: Louisiana Banking, 1804-1861, Stanford, 72. **CONTACT ADDRESS** History Dept, Univ of Minnesota, Twin Cities, 614 Social Sciences Tower, 267 19th Ave. S, Minneapolis, MN, 55455. **EMAIL** green007@tc.umn.edu

GREEN, GEORGE N.
PERSONAL Born 04/27/1939, Rockdale, TX, m, 1972, 1 child **DISCIPLINE** LABOR HISTORY, HISTORY OF SOUTHWEST **EDUCATION** Univ Tex, Austin, BA, 61; Fla State Univ, MA, 62, PhD(hist), 66. **CAREER** Instr, Fla State Univ, 64-65 and Tex Woman's Univ, 65-66; from instr to asst prof, 66-72, ASSOC PROF HIST, UNIV TEX, ARLINGTON, 72-, Younger Humanist res fel, Nat Endowment for Humanities, 70-71; coordr, AFL-CIO Fed Prison Prog, 73-74; grant, Tex Comt for Humanities, 77-78. **RESEARCH** Twentieth century political history of the United States. **SELECTED PUBLICATIONS** Auth, Wanderings in the Southwest in 1855, J the W, Vol 0032, 93. **CONTACT ADDRESS** Dept of Hist, Univ of Tex, Arlington, TX, 76019.

GREEN, HARVEY
PERSONAL Born 09/15/1946, Buffalo, NY, m, 1980 **DISCIPLINE** HISTORY **EDUCATION** Univ Rochester, BA, 68; Rutgers Univ, MA, 70, PhD, 76. **CAREER** Chief hist, Strong Mus Rochester NY, 76-82; asst dir, 82-89, Prof of History,

Northeastern Univ, 89-. **HONORS AND AWARDS** Rutgers Univ fel, 75; Fulbright prof hist, Univ Turku, Finland, 95; Bicentennial Prof Am Studies, Univ Helsinki, 99-2000. **MEMBERSHIPS** Am Studies Asn; Nat Coun Public Hist; Am Asn State & Local Orgn Am Hist; Am Hist Asn. **RESEARCH** US Cultural history, 1800-1950; Public history; American material culture; US literary history. **SELECTED PUBLICATIONS** Auth, Light of the Home: An Intimate View of the Lives of Women in Victorian America, Pantheon, 83; Fit for America: Health, Fitness, Sport, and American Society, 1830-1940, Pantheon, 86 & Johns Hopkins Univ Press, 88; The Uncertainty of Everyday Life, 1915-45, Harper, 92. **CONTACT ADDRESS** History Dept, Northeastern Univ, Boston, MA, 02115. **EMAIL** hgreen@lynx.neu.edu

GREEN, JESSE DAWES
PERSONAL Born 02/09/1928, Chippewa Falls, WI, m, 1950, 3 children **DISCIPLINE** AMERICAN STUDIES, HISTORY OF ANTHROPOLOGY **EDUCATION** Reed Col, BA, 51; Univ Calif, Berkeley, MA, 57; Northwestern Univ, PhD(English), 72. **CAREER** Asst prof compos and lit, Univ Cincinnati, 64-68; PROF ENGLISH, CHICAGO STATE UNIV, 68-, Summer grant, National Endowment for Humanities, 76 and 81; fel, National Endowment for Humanities, 82-83. **RESEARCH** History of consciousness; literature and anthropology. **SELECTED PUBLICATIONS** Auth, A Zuni Artist Looks at Cushing, Frank, Hamilton, Cartoons by Hughte, Phil, Am Indian Cult and Res J, Vol 0019, 95. **CONTACT ADDRESS** Chicago State Univ, Chicago, IL, 60628.

GREEN, LEAMON L., JR.
PERSONAL Born 06/28/1959, AL, m, 1996, 1 child **DISCIPLINE** ART **EDUCATION** Cleveland Inst Art; BFA, 82; Temple Univ, MFA, 85. **CAREER** Asst prof, Tx S Univ; 96- **HONORS AND AWARDS** Cosby Fel, 94; Creative Artist Prog Grant, 95; Project Artist, 98. **CONTACT ADDRESS** 1319 W 22nd St, Houston, TX, 77008.

GREEN, MICHAEL KNIGHT
PERSONAL Born 12/26/1935, Spokane, WA, m, 1961, 2 children **DISCIPLINE** AMERICAN HISTORY **EDUCATION** Eastern Wash Univ, BA, 60; Univ Idaho, MA, 62, PhD(hist), 68. **CAREER** Asst prof Am hist, Pac Univ, 64-67; from Asst Prof to Assoc Prof, 67-80, Prof Eastern Wash Univ, 80-. **MEMBERSHIPS** Orgn Am Historians; Western Hist Asn. **RESEARCH** New Deal and post New Deal western history. **CONTACT ADDRESS** Dept of Hist, Eastern Washington Univ, M/S 27, Cheney, WA, 99004-2496.

GREEN, NANCY LASCOE
PERSONAL Born 11/06/1951, Chicago, IL **DISCIPLINE** FRENCH SOCIAL HISTORY **EDUCATION** Univ Wis-Madison, BA, 72; Univ Chicago, MA, 73; Ecole des Hautes Etudes en Sci, Paris, DEA, 78; Univ Chicago, PhD(hist), 80. **CAREER** Teaching and res fel western civilization, Stanford Univ, 80; CHARGEE DE CONF MIGRATION STUDIES, ECOLE DES HAUTES ETUDES EN SCI, PARIS, 80-, Vis asst prof French hist, Stanford Univ Tours, 81-. **RESEARCH** Economic development and labor migration; garment industries in Paris and New York. **SELECTED PUBLICATIONS** Auth, Women, Family, and Utopia--Communal Experiments of the Shakers, the Oneida Community, and the Mormons, Annales-Economies Societes Civilisations, Vol 0048, 93; History of Women in the United-States, Annales-Economies Societes Civilisations, Vol 0048, 93; Art and Industry--The Language of Modernization in the Production of Fashion, Fr Hist Stud, Vol 0018, 94; The Comparative Method and Poststructural Structuralism--New Perspectives for Migration Studies, J Am Ethnic Hist, Vol 0013, 94; Sweatshop Strife--Ethnicity, and Gender in the Jewish Labor-Movement of Toronto, 1900-1939, Histoire Sociale-Soc Hist, Vol 0029, 96; Moving Europeans--Migration in Western-Europe since 1650, Annales-Histoire Sciences Sociales, Vol 0051, 96; Women and Immigrants in the Sweatshop--Categories of Labor Segmentation Revisited, Comp Stud in Soc and Hist, Vol 0038, 96; En-Route to America--The Odyssey of Emigrants in 19th-Century France, Annales-Histoire Sciences Sociales, Vol 0051, 96. **CONTACT ADDRESS** Ecole des Hautes Etudes Sciences Sociales, 54 Blvd Raspail, Paris, ., F-75370.

GREEN, THOMAS ANDREW
PERSONAL Born 03/18/1940, New York, NY, m, 1968 **DISCIPLINE** ANGLO-AMERICAN LEGAL HISTORY **EDUCATION** Columbia Univ, AB, 61; Harvard Univ, PhD(hist), 70, JD, 72. **CAREER** Asst prof hist, Bard Col, 67-69; asst prof law, 72-75, assoc prof, 75-77, PROF LAW, LAW SCH, UNIV MICH, 77-, PROF HIST, HIST DEPT, 80-. **HONORS AND AWARDS** NEH fel, Fel, Guggenheim fel **MEMBERSHIPS** AHA; Medieval Acad Am; Am Soc Legal Hist; Royal Hist Soc; Conf Critical Legal Studies. **RESEARCH** History of criminal law; history of legal and social theory; history of law in America, 1870-present. **SELECTED PUBLICATIONS** Auth, Verdict According to Conscience: Perspectives on the English Criminal Trial Jury, 1200-1800; co-ed, On the Laws and Customs of England: Essays in Honor if Samuel E. Thorn, 81; co-ed, Twelve Good Men and True: The Criminal Jury in England, 1200-1800, Princeton, 88; auth, Freedom and Criminal Responsibility in the Age of Pound: An Essay on Criminal Justice, Mich Law Rev, vol 93; 95. **CONTACT ADDRESS** Law Sch, Univ of Michigan, 625 S State St, Ann Arbor, MI, 48109-1215. **EMAIL** tagreen@umich.edu

GREEN, WILLIAM EDWARD
PERSONAL Born 05/17/1930, Pittsburgh, PA, m, 1950 **DISCIPLINE** EDUCATION **EDUCATION** Univ of Pgh, BS 1953, MEd 1958, EdD 1969. **CAREER** Herron Hill Jr HS, teacher 1955-60; Westinghouse HS, couns 1960-65, vice prin 1965-68, exec asst to supt 1968-69, asst supt 1969-75; Pittsburgh Public Sch, asst supt middle schs 1976-81, asst supt pupil serv 1981-85 retired; W PA Conf United Methodist Church, dir of ethnic minority concerns 1985-93; (retired) Pittsburgh Pist Lay Leader, UM Church, 1990-96. **MEMBERSHIPS** Prince Hall Mason (Boaz 65) 1959-; Phi Eta Sigma 1949-53; dissertation Sch Coll Orientation Prog 1969; bd dir Need 1969-87; Univ of Pgh Alumni Council 1974-77 1979-; chmn PACE 1974-80; PA State Adv Council on Voc Educ 1974-78; State ESEA Title IV Adv Council 1975-78; mem Alpha Phi Alpha; exec dir Pgh Upward Bound Prog; Omicron Delta Kappa; Phi Delta Kappa; lecturer Carnegie Mellon Univ; treas Warren United Methodist Church 1980-94; chmn Ethnic Minority Local Church Coord Comm Western PA Conf United Methodist Church 1980-84; delegate 1984, 1988, and 1994; United Methodist General/ Jurisdictional Conf; 1988; bd of dirs Need, 1969-90; Pace Board, 1984-90.

GREENBAUM, FRED
PERSONAL Born 11/06/1930, Brooklyn, NY, m, 1954, 2 children **DISCIPLINE** AMERICAN HISTORY **EDUCATION** Brooklyn Col, BA, 52; Univ Wis, MA, 53; Columbia Univ, PhD, 62. **CAREER** Lectr hist, Brooklyn Col, 58-59 & Queens Col, 60-61; from instr to assoc prof, 61-70, prof hist, Queensborough Community Col, 70-, lectr, Cooper Union, 61; mem, Prof Staff Cong. **MEMBERSHIPS** AHA; Orgn Am Historians. **RESEARCH** American progressive movement; the New Deal; labor history. **SELECTED PUBLICATIONS** Auth, John Dewey views Karl Marx, Soc Sci, 67; Progressivism: A Complex Phenomenon, New Politics, 68; The Progressive World of Gabirel Kolko, Social Studies, 69; co-ed, Readings in Western Civilization, Early Modern Period, McCutchan, 70; Fighting Progressive, A Biography of Edward P Costigan, Pub Affairs Press, 71; auth, Hiram Johnson and the New Deal, Pac Historian, 74; Robert Marion LaFollette, Twayne, 75; The Foreign Policy of Progressive Irreconcilables, In: Toward a New View of America, Burt Franklin, 77; Empire and Autonomy: The American and Netherland Revolutions, International Social Science Review, 89; Teddy Roosevelt Creates a Draft in 1912, in Theodore Roosevelt, Many Sided American, Heart of the Lakes Pub, 92; Ambivalent Friends, Progressive Era Politicians and Organized Labor, Labors Heritage, 94; American Nation, Whittier pub, 95. **CONTACT ADDRESS** Queensborough Comm Col, CUNY, 22205 56th Ave, Flushing, NY, 11364-1432.

GREENBAUM, LOUIS SIMPSON
PERSONAL Born 02/14/1930, Chicago, IL **DISCIPLINE** HISTORY **EDUCATION** Univ Wis, BA, 50, MA, 51; Harvard Univ, PhD, 55. **CAREER** From instr to assoc prof, 55-69, PROF HIST, UNIV MASS, AMHERST, 69-, Am Philos Soc fel, 63-64; NIH spec fel, 68-69, grant, 72-73; consult hist pop studies, Sch Pub Health, Harvard Univ, 68-72; mem, White House Conf Food, Nutrit and Health, 69. **MEMBERSHIPS** AHA; Soc Fr Hist Studies; Am Soc Church Hist; Am Asn Hist Med; Am Soc 18th Century Studies. **RESEARCH** Church history; 18th century Europe; history of medicine and public health in 18th century France. **SELECTED PUBLICATIONS** Auth, Jefferson, Thomas, the Paris Hospitals, and the University-of-Virginia, 18th-Century Stud, Vol 0026, 93; The End of an Elite--The French Bishops and the Coming of the Revolution, 1786-1790, Cath Hist Rev, Vol 0080, 94. **CONTACT ADDRESS** PO Box 625, North Amherst, MA, 01059.

GREENBERG, CHERYL LYNN
PERSONAL Born 08/13/1958, MA, m, 1990, 2 children **DISCIPLINE** HISTORY **EDUCATION** Princeton Univ, AB (summa cum laude), 80; Columbia Univ, MA, 81, MPhil, 83, PhD, 88. **CAREER** Visiting assoc prof, Dept of Afro-Am Studies, Harvard Univ, 96-97; ASST PROF OF HIST, 86-92, ASSOC PROF OF HIST, 92-, DIR, 98-, AM STUDIES PROG, TRINITY COL. **HONORS AND AWARDS** Carlton C. Qualey Memorial Article Award, Immigration Hist Soc, 97; Working Group on Black-Jewish Relations, 94-97, fel, W.E.B Du Bois Inst for Afro-Am Res, Harvard Univ, 96-97; Fac Res Grant, Trinity Col, 88, 92, & 97; fel, Charles Warren Center for Studies in Am Hist, Harvard Univ, 93-94; res grant, Franklin and Eleanor Roosevelt Inst, 93-94; fel, Am Coun of Learned Socs, 90-91; second prize, Professional Category for paper presented at the Twentieth Annual Dakota Hist Conf, 88; St Anthony Hall Found Summer Res Grant, 87; Danforth Fel, 80-86; Fel, Grad School of Arts and Scis, 80-81,Honorary President's Fel, Columbia Univ, 83-84; Phi Beta Kappa, 80. **RESEARCH** African American history; twentieth century American history; race and ethnicity. **SELECTED PUBLICATIONS** Ed, A Circle of Trust: Remembering SNCC, Rutgers Univ Press, 98; auth, Harold Cruse on Blacks and Jews, The Black Intellectual in Crisis, Routledge Press, 99; auth, The Southern Jewish Community and the Struggle for Civil Rights, African Americans and Jews in the Twentieth Century, Univ of Mo Press, 98; auth, Pluralism and Discontents, Insider/Outsider: Am Jews and Multiculturalism, Univ of Calif Press, 98; auth, Negotiating Coalition: Black and Jewish Civil Rights Agencies In The Twentieth Century, Struggles in the Promised Land: Towards a Hist of Black-Jewish Relations in the United States, Oxford Univ Press, 97; auth, Black and Jewish Responses to Japanese Internment, J of Am Ethic Hist, 95; auth, Ambivalent Allies: Black and Jewish Organizations after WWII, Black Resistance Movements in the U.S. and Africa, 95; auth, God and Man in Harlem, J of Urban Hist, 95. **CONTACT ADDRESS** Dept of History, Trinity Col, Hartford, CT, 06106. **EMAIL** cheryl.greenberg@mail.trincoll.edu

GREENBERG, KENNETH
PERSONAL Born 11/02/1947, Brooklyn, NY, m, 1969, 3 children **DISCIPLINE** HISTORY **EDUCATION** Cornell Univ, BA, 68; Columbia Univ, MA, 70; Univ Wis, PhD, 76. **CAREER** Asst prof Hist, Alfred Univ, 75-77; prof Hist, Suffolk Univ, 78- ; Ch, Hist Dept, 89-present, Suffolk Univ. **HONORS AND AWARDS** Fel, Charles Warren Ctr, Hist Dept, 88; NEH fel, 88; fel in Law and Hist, Harvard Law Sch, 90-91; fel, assoc, W.E.B. DuBois Inst, Harvard Univ; NEH Summer Sem Anthrop and Hist, Northwestern Univ, 80; Va Found Human, Spring 98; Activity dir, fac develop, Title III Grant Suffolk Univ, 82-86; Amer Assn Col Quill grant, 86. **MEMBERSHIPS** Amer Hist Assn; Org Amer Historians; S Hist Assn; Amer Stud Assn. **RESEARCH** United States History; South; Slavery. **CONTACT ADDRESS** Chair, Dept of History, Suffolk Univ, B Ashburton Pl, Boston, MA, 02108. **EMAIL** kgreenbe@acad.suffolk.edu

GREENBERG, NATHAN ABRAHAM
PERSONAL Born 08/23/1928, Boston, MA, m, 1952, 3 children **DISCIPLINE** CLASSICAL PHILOLOGY **EDUCATION** Hebrew Teachers Col, Boston, BJEd, 48; Harvard Univ, AB, 50, AM, 52, PhD, 55. **CAREER** From instr to assoc prof, 56-69, assoc dean humanities, 67-68, chmn dept, 70-76, PROF CLASSICS, OBERLIN COL, 69-, Fulbright scholar, Italy, 55-56; Rockefeller Found study grant, 62-63; Am Coun Learned Soc study grant, 68; Fulbright sr res fel, Belgium, 69-70; vis fel, Wolfson Col, Oxford Univ, 76-77; Am Coun Learned Soc res fel, 76-77. **MEMBERSHIPS** AAUP; Am Philol Asn; Archaeol Inst Am; Vergilian Soc. **RESEARCH** Ancient poetics; political philosophy; computer use in literary study. **SELECTED PUBLICATIONS** Auth, The Attitude of Agamemnon: Homer, 'Iliad', Book-1, Class World, Vol 0086, 93. **CONTACT ADDRESS** Dept of Classics, Oberlin Col, King Bldg, Oberlin, OH, 44074.

GREENBERGER, ALLEN JAY
PERSONAL Born 03/18/1937, Chicago, IL **DISCIPLINE** BRITISH IMPERIAL HISTORY **EDUCATION** Univ Mich, BA, 58, MA, 60, PhD(hist), 66. **CAREER** Instr, Smith Col, 65-66; from asst prof to assoc prof, 66-75, PROF HIST, PITZER COL, 75-. **MEMBERSHIPS** Asn Asian Studies; Conf Brit Studies Res. **RESEARCH** Social and intellectual history of the British empire; social history of the British in India. **SELECTED PUBLICATIONS** Auth, Acts of Supremacy, The British-Empire and the Stage, 1790-1930, Albion, Vol 0024, 92; European Women and the 2nd British-Empire, Int Hist Rev, Vol 0015, 93. **CONTACT ADDRESS** Pitzer Col, 1050 N Mills Ave, Claremont, CA, 91711-6101.

GREENE, GORDON K.
PERSONAL Born 12/27/1927, Cardston, AB, Canada **DISCIPLINE** MUSIC HISTORY **EDUCATION** Univ Alta, AMus, 52, BA, 54, BEd, 55, MA, 61; Ind Univ, PhD, 71. **CAREER** Lectr, Univ Alta, 55-63; fac mem, music hist dept, Univ Western Ont, 66-78; prof 78-93, dean music 79-89, PROF EMER MUSIC HISTORY, WILFRID LAURIER UNIV; vis prof, Univ Toronto, 93-96. **MEMBERSHIPS** Can Univ Music Soc; Am Musicol Soc; Int Musicol Soc. **RESEARCH** Medieval music. **SELECTED PUBLICATIONS** Auth, Polyphonic Music of the Fourteenth Century, 5 vols, 80-87; contribur, Grove's Dictionary of Music and Musicians; contribur, Dictionary of the Middle Ages. **CONTACT ADDRESS** Dept of Music History, Wilfrid Laurier Univ, Waterloo, ON, N2L 3C5.

GREENE, JACK P.
PERSONAL Born 08/12/1931, Lafayette, IN, m, 1990, 2 children **DISCIPLINE** HISTORY **EDUCATION** NC Univ, AB, 51; Ind Univ, MA, 52; Duke Univ, PhD, 56. **CAREER** Instr, 56-59, Mich St Univ; asst, assoc prof, 59-65, Western Reserve; assoc prof, 65-66, Mich St Univ; Andrew W. Mellon Prof, 66-, John Hopkins Univ; dist prof, 90-92, Univ Calif, Irvine. **HONORS AND AWARDS** Fulbright, UK, 53-54; Guggenheim, 64-65; Inst for Advan Stud, 70-71, 85-86; Woodrow Wilson Intl Ctr, 74-75; Harmsworth Prof, Oxford, 75-76; Fulbright, Israel, 79; Ctr for Advan Stud Behavioral Sci, 79-80; Churchill Col Cambridge, 86; Fulbright, France, 86-87; Natl Hum Ctr, 87-88; Phi Beta Kappa LlD, Indiana, 77; Freeman Prof, Richmond, 96; Sweet Prof, Mich St, 97; Royal Hist Soc, 77. **MEMBERSHIPS** AHA; Org of Amer Hist; So Hist Assn. **RESEARCH** Early modern colonial British Amer. **SELECTED PUBLICATIONS** Auth, The Quest for Power: the Lower Houses of As-

sembly in the Southern Royal Colonies, 1689-1776, Norton & Co, 72; coauth, Colonial British America: Essays in the New History of the Early Modern Era, Johns Hopkins Univ Press, 84; auth, Encyclopedia of American Political History, Scribner's Sons, 84; auth, The Diary of Colonel Landon Carter of Sabine Hall 1752-1778, Va Univ Press, Va Hist Soc, 88; auth, Pursuits of Happiness: The Social Development of the Early Modern British Colonies and the Formation of American Culture, Univ NC Press, 88; auth, Peripheries and Center: Constitutional Development in the Extended Polities of the British Empire and the United States 1607-1789, Norton & Co, 90; coauth, The Blackwell Encyclopedia of the American Revolution, Oxford Basil Blackwell, 91; auth, Imperatives, Behaviors and Identities: Essays in Early American Cultural History, Univ Press Va, 92; auth, The Intellectual Construction of America: Exceptionalism and Identity from 1492-1800, Univ NC Press, 93; auth, Negotiated Authorities: Essays in colonial Political and Constitutional History, Univ Press Va, 94; auth, Explaining the American Revolution: Issues, Interpretations, and Actors, Univ Press Va, 95; auth, Interpreting Early America: Historiographical Essays, Univ Press Va, 96. **CONTACT ADDRESS** History Dept, Johns Hopkins Univ, 3400 N Charles St, Baltimore, MD, 21218.

GREENE, JEROME ALLEN
PERSONAL Born 03/23/1942, Watertown, NY, m, 1975 **DISCIPLINE** AMERICAN INDIAN AND AMERICAN MILITARY HISTORY **EDUCATION** Black Hills State Col, BS, 68; Univ SDak, MA, 69. **CAREER** Instr Am Indian hist, Haskell Indian Jr Col, 71-73; HISTORIAN, HIST PRESERV DIV NAT PARK SERV, 73-. **MEMBERSHIPS** Western Hist Asn; Coun Am Military Past; Col Mil Historians; Order Indian Wars; Nat Trust Historic Preservation. **RESEARCH** Indian Wars, 1865-1900; government-Indian relations; US Army uniforms and equipment, 1850-1902. **SELECTED PUBLICATIONS** Auth, The Custer Reader, NMex Hist Rev, Vol 0068, 93; Hokahey--A Good Day to Die--The Indian Casualties of the Custer Fight, Western Hist Quart, Vol 0026, 95; A Good Year to Die--The Story of the Great-Sioux-War, Southwestern Hist Quart, Vol 0100, 96; Custer--The Controversial Life of Custer, George, Armstrong, J Am Hist, Vol 0084, 97; Touched by Fire--The Life Death, and Mythic Afterlife of Custer, George, Armstrong, J Am Hist, Vol 0084, 97. **CONTACT ADDRESS** Denver Serv Ctr, National Park Services, 755 Parfet, Denver, CO, 80225.

GREENE, JOHN C.
PERSONAL Born 03/05/1917, Indianapolis, IN, w, 1945, 3 children **DISCIPLINE** HISTORY **EDUCATION** Univ SD, BA, 38; Harvard Univ, MA, 39, PhD, 52. **CAREER** Prof, Emeritus, 87, Univ Connecticut; Prof, 63-67, Univ Kansas; vis Prof, 62-63, Univ Cal Berkeley; Assoc Prof, Prof, 56-62, Iowa State Univ; Asst Prof, 52-56, Univ Wisc; Instr, 48-52, Univ Chicago. **HONORS AND AWARDS** Harvard Soc of Fellows; Guggenheim Fel; Vis Schl Corpus Christi College. **MEMBERSHIPS** HSS; OAH; AAUP; ISHPSSS. **RESEARCH** History of Evolutionary Thought in the Western World; Early American Science; Historical Relations of Science and Religion. **SELECTED PUBLICATIONS** Auth, Debating Darwin, Regina Books, 99, forthcoming; coauth, The Science of Minerals in the Age of Jefferson, in: Transaction in the American Philo Soc, 78; auth, American Science in the Age of Jefferson, Iowa State U Press, 84; Science Ideology and World View, Essays in the History of Evolutionary Ideas, U of Cal Press, 81. **CONTACT ADDRESS** 10 Thompson Rd, Storrs, CT, 06268.

GREENE, NATHANAEL
PERSONAL Born 04/04/1935, Providence, RI, m, 1959, 4 children **DISCIPLINE** MODERN EUROPEAN HISTORY **EDUCATION** Brown Univ, AB, 57; Harvard Univ, AM, 58, PhD(hist), 64. **CAREER** Teaching fel gen educ, Harvard Univ, 60-63; from instr to assoc prof, 63-74, chmn dept, 73-77, prof hist, 74- , vpres acad affairs, 77-90, Wesleyan Univ; Wesleyan Univ fel, 65; Am Coun Learned Soc fel, 68-69; Guggenheim Mem Found fel, 71-72. **MEMBERSHIPS** AHA; Soc Fr Hist Studies; Soc Span & Port Hist Studies. **RESEARCH** Modern French history; modern Spanish history; French provincial politics, 1918-1940. **SELECTED PUBLICATIONS** Auth, Crisis and Decline: French Socialism in the Popular Front Era, Cornell Univ, 68; Fascism: An Anthology, 68 & From Versailles to Vichy: The Third French Republic, 1919-1940, 70, Crowell; ed, European Socialism Since World War I, Quadrangle, 71; auth, National and Local: Rural Politics, 1932-1936, Fr Hist Studies, spring 76. **CONTACT ADDRESS** History Dept, Wesleyan Univ, Middletown, CT, 06457. **EMAIL** ngreene@wesleyan.edu

GREENE, SANDRA E.
DISCIPLINE HISTORY **EDUCATION** Northwestern Univ, PhD, 81. **CAREER** Assoc prof. **SELECTED PUBLICATIONS** Auth, From Whence They Came: A Note on the Influence of West African Ethnic and Gender Relations on the Organizational Character of the 1733 St. John Slave Rebellion, 94; Gender, Ethnicity and Social Change on the Upper Slave Coast: A History of the Anlo-Ewe, 96; Religion, History and the Supreme Gods of Africa: A Contribution to the Debate, Jour Relig Africa, 96; Sacred Terrain: Religion, Politics and Place in the History of Anloga, Int Jour African Hist Studies, 97. **CONTACT ADDRESS** Dept of History, Cornell Univ, Ithaca, NY, 14853-2801. **EMAIL** seg6@cornell.edu

GREENE, THOMAS R.
PERSONAL Born 10/17/1933, New York, NY, m, 1958, 2 children **DISCIPLINE** MEDIEVAL HISTORY, ENGLISH **EDUCATION** St Francis Col, NY, BA, 58; NY Univ, MA, 61, PhD(medieval hist), 67. **CAREER** Asst prof II Hist, Newark State Col, 63-64; instr, 64-66, ASST PROF II HIST, VILLANOVA UNIV, 66-. **MEMBERSHIPS** AHA. **RESEARCH** Twelfth century church history. **SELECTED PUBLICATIONS** Auth, Oriordan, Michael la 'Recente Insurrezione in Irlanda', 1916, Eire-Ireland, Vol 0028, 93; Starkey, Thomas and the Commonweal--Humanist Politics and Religion in the Reign of Henry-VIII, Church Hist, Vol 0063, 94; Starkey, Thomas and the Commonweal--Humanist Politics and Religion in the Reign of Henry-VIII, Church Hist, Vol 0063, 94; A Question of Character--A Life of Kennedy, John, F., Cath Hist Rev, Vol 0082, 96. **CONTACT ADDRESS** Dept of Hist, Villanova Univ, Villanova, PA, 19385.

GREENE, VICTOR ROBERT
PERSONAL Born 11/15/1933, Newark, NJ, m, 1957, 2 children **DISCIPLINE** AMERICAN HISTORY & STUDIES **EDUCATION** Harvard Univ, AB, 55; Univ Rochester, MA, 60; Univ Pa, PhD, 63. **CAREER** From asst prof to assoc prof hist, Kans State Univ, 63-71; assoc prof hist, 71-77, coordr ethnic studies, 76-78, prof hist, Univ Wis-Milwaukee, 77-, vis prof hist, Cleveland State Univ, 68-69; Warwick Univ, 90-; NE Normal Univ (China), 98-; Am Coun Learned Socs grant-in-aid, 70; Int Res & Exchanges Bd grant, 70-; fel, Nat Humanities Inst, 75-76; demonstration grant, Nat Endowment for Humanities, 77-78; Fulbright Award, Ger, 80-81. **HONORS AND AWARDS** Haiman Award, Polish Am Hist Asn, 81; NEH Senior Fel, 87-88. **MEMBERSHIPS** AHA; Orgn Am Historians; Immigration and Ethnic Hist Soc; Am St Asn. **RESEARCH** American ethnic and labor history; popular culture. **SELECTED PUBLICATIONS** Auth, Origins of Slavic American Self-Consciousness, Church Hist, winter 66; The Slavic Community on Strike, Univ Notre Dame, 68; Slavic American Nationalism, In: American Contributions to 7th Congress of Slavists, Mouton, 73; For God and Country: Polish and Lithuanian Ethnic Consciousness, Soc Press, 75; Becoming American, In: Ethnic Frontier, Erdmans, 77; The Poles, In: Harvard Encycl of American Ethnic Groups, 80; Ethnic Groups and State Universities, In: American Education and the European Immigrant, 82; auth, Immigrant Leaders, Johns Hopkins Univ, 85; A Passion for Polka, Univ Calif, 92; Friendly Entertainers, In: Prospects, 95; A Holistic View of American Ethnic History, In: Polish American Studies, 98. **CONTACT ADDRESS** Dept of Hist, Univ of Wis, PO Box 413, Milwaukee, WI, 53201-0413. **EMAIL** vicgre@uwm.edu

GREENEWALT, CRAWFORD HALLOCK
PERSONAL Born 06/03/1937, Wilmington, DE **DISCIPLINE** CLASSICAL ARCHAEOLOGY **EDUCATION** Harvard Univ, BA, 59; Univ Penn, PhD, 66. **CAREER** Asst Prof, Assoc Prof, Prof, 66 to 78-, Univ Cal Berkeley. **MEMBERSHIPS** APS; GAI; AAI. **RESEARCH** Interconnections between Greece and Anatolia Ancient Lydia, Sardis. **SELECTED PUBLICATIONS** Coauth, The Sardis Campaigns of 1994 and 1995, Amer J Archaeol, 98; auth, Croesus of Sardis and the Lydian Kingdom of Anatolia, in: Civilizations of the Ancient Near East, ed, JM Sasson, NY, Scribner's, 95; Sardis in the Age of Xenophon, in: Dans les des dix-mille, ed, P Briant, Toulouse, Toulouse Univ, 95; George Maxim Anossov Hanfmann, November 1911-13, March 1986, APS, 86. **CONTACT ADDRESS** Dept of Classics, Univ Calif Berkeley, Dwinelle Hall 7303, Berkeley, CA, 94720.

GREENFIELD, GERALD M.
DISCIPLINE LATIN AMERICAN HISTORY, BRAZIL AND MEXICO, LATIN-US RELATIONS, AMERICAN HIS **EDUCATION** SUNY at Buffalo, BA, 67; Brooklyn Col, MA, 69; IN Univ, Bloomington, PhD, 75. **CAREER** Prof & ch, Univ of WI, Parkside. **HONORS AND AWARDS** UW-Parkside, Outstanding Ser Awd, 96; UW-Parkside Outstanding Tchg Awd, 96; Am Philos Soc, 94 & 85. **RESEARCH** Brazilian hist. **SELECTED PUBLICATIONS** Ed,Latin American Urbanization: Historical Profiles of Major Cities, Greenwood Press, 94; co-ed, Latin American Labor Organizations, Greenwood Press, 87; coauth, Western Hemisphere, Silver Burdett & Ginn, 92; The Great Drought and Elite Discourse in Imperial Brazil, Hisp Amer Hist Rev, 92. **CONTACT ADDRESS** Dept of Hist, Univ of Wisconsin, Parkside, 900 Wood Rd, Molinaro 1, PO Box 2000, Kenosha, WI, 53141-2000. **EMAIL** gerald.greenfield@uwp.edu

GREENHILL, PAULINE
PERSONAL Born 03/23/1955, Peterborough, ON, Canada **DISCIPLINE** ANTHROPOLOGY/WOMEN'S STUDIES **EDUCATION** Trent Univ, BA, 76; Memorial Univ Nfld, MA, 81; Univ Texas Austin, PhD, 85. **CAREER** Asst prof, 86-90, assoc prof, Can stud, Univ Waterloo, 90-91; women's stud, 91-96, PROF ANTHROPOLOGY & WOMEN'S STUD, UNIV WINNIPEG, 96-; assoc ed, Canadian Folklore canadien, 96-. **HONORS AND AWARDS** SSHRCC grants; Erica & Arnold Rogers Award Excellence Res Schol; Chicago Folklore Prize, 89; Can Ethnic Stud res grant. **MEMBERSHIPS** Can Women's Stud Asn. **SELECTED PUBLICATIONS** Auth, So We Can Remember: Showing Family Photographs, 81; auth, Lots of Stories: Maritime Narratives from the Creighton Collection, 85; auth, True Poetry: Traditional and Popular Verse in Ontario, 89; auth, Ethnicity in the Mainstream, 94; co-ed, Undisciplined Women: Tradition and Culture in Canada, 97. **CONTACT ADDRESS** Women's Stud, Univ Winnipeg, Winnipeg, MB, R3B 2E9. **EMAIL** pauline.greenhill@uwinnipeg.ca

GREENHOUSE, WENDY
DISCIPLINE HISTORY OF ART **EDUCATION** Yale Univ, BA, 77; Simmons, MLS, 81; Yale Univ, PhD,89. **CAREER** IND ART HIST **MEMBERSHIPS** Am Antiquarian Soc **SELECTED PUBLICATIONS** Auth, "Benjamin West and Edward III: A Neoclassical Painter and Medieval History," Art Hist 8, 85; auth, "The American Portrayal Tudor and Stuart History, 1835-65," PhD diss, 89; coauth, The Art of Archibald J. Motley, Jr., Chicago Hist Soc, 91; auth, "The Landing of the Fathers: Representing the National Past, 1770-1860" in Picturing History: American Painting 1770-1930, Rizzoli, 93; coauth, Herman Menzel: A Rediscovered Regionalist, Chicago Hist Soc, 93; auth, "Imperilled Ideals: British Historical Heroines in Antebellum American History Painting" in Redefining American History Painting, Cambridge Univ Press, 95; "Daniel Huntington and the Ideal of Christian Art," Winterthur Portfolio 31, no 2/3, 96. **CONTACT ADDRESS** 303 N Cuyler Ave, Oak Park, IL, 60302-2302. **EMAIL** mtrenary@uic.edu

GREENLEAF, RICHARD E.
PERSONAL Born 05/06/1930, Hot Springs, AR **DISCIPLINE** LATIN AMERICAN HISTORY **EDUCATION** Univ NMex, BA, 53, MA, 54, PhD(hist), 57. **CAREER** Asst prof hist and int rels, Univ Am, 57-60, assoc prof int rels and chmn dept, 60-62, from asst to assoc dean, Grad Sch, 57-62, prof hist and int rels, acad vpres and grad dean, 62-69; PROF HIST, TULANE UNIV, 69-, DIR, CTR LATIN AM STUDIES, 70-, Univ Am fel, Spain, 62. **MEMBERSHIPS** AHA. **RESEARCH** Social and intellectual history of colonial Latin American and the Hispanic Southwest; modern Mexico. **SELECTED PUBLICATIONS** Auth, Life Between Judaism and Christianity in New-Spain, 1580-1606, Hispanic Am Hist Rev, Vol 0074, 94; A Violent Evangelism--The Political and Religious Conquest of the America, Am Hist Rev, Vol 0099, 94; Persistence of Native Values, the Inquisition and the Indians of Colonial Mexico, Americas, Vol 0050, 94. **CONTACT ADDRESS** Ctr for Latin Am Studies, Tulane Univ, 6823 St Charles Ave, New Orleans, LA, 70118-5698.

GREENLEE, JAMES G.C.
PERSONAL Born 07/04/1945, Hamilton, ON, Canada **DISCIPLINE** HISTORY **EDUCATION** McMaster Univ, BA, 68, MA, 69, PhD, 75. **CAREER** Asst prof, McMaster Univ, 73-77; asst prof to assoc prof, 77-89, PROF HISTORY, GRENFELL COL, MEMORIAL UNIV NFLD, 89-. **MEMBERSHIPS** Hum Asn Can; Asn Atlantic Hist. **SELECTED PUBLICATIONS** Auth, Education and Imperial Unity, 88; auth, Sir Robert Falconer: A Biography, 88. **CONTACT ADDRESS** Grenfell Col, Memorial Univ of Newfoundland, Corner Brook, NS, A2H 6P9.

GREENOUGH, SARAH
DISCIPLINE ART HISTORY **EDUCATION** Univ Penn, BA 73; Univ N Mexico, MA 76, PhD 83. **CAREER** National Gallery of Art, curator of photo, 90-, res curator dept graphic arts 86-89, guest scholar 84-86, guest curator 79-84; Univ New Mexico, tchg assoc, inst, 77-80; Metro museum of Art, res 76-77; Univ New Mexico, grad asst 74-76. **HONORS AND AWARDS** IAAC Best Photog Ex Awd; 2 Book of the Year Awds Marine Photo Wkshp; Focal Press Awd; Awd Dist Content and Design; ICP Photo Book of the Year; Art Critics Awd; Centennial Awd; Silver Medal for Alfred Stieglitz: Photos and Writings; Popejoy Awd; Samuel H. Kress Awd; Ntl Bk Awd; Beaumont Newhall fel; Samuel H Kress Fell; UNM Grad Fel. **MEMBERSHIPS** CAA; NEH Panel; WCP; Smithsonian Inst Adv Panel. **SELECTED PUBLICATIONS** Auth, Harry Callahan, Washington DC, Nat Gallery Art and Bullfinch Press, 96; Robert Frank: Moving Out, ed, coauth, Washington DC, Nat Gallery Art and Bullfinch Press, 94; Stieglitz in the Darkroom, Washington DC, Nat Gallery Art, 92. **CONTACT ADDRESS** Dept of Photographs, National Art Gallery, Washington, DC, 20565.

GREENSHIELDS, MALCOLM
DISCIPLINE HISTORY **EDUCATION** Univ Saskatchewan, BA, 78; Sussex Univ, DPhil. **RESEARCH** European and French history; social history; criminality; religion and popular culture. **SELECTED PUBLICATIONS** Auth, An Economy of Violence in Early Modern France, Penn State, 95. **CONTACT ADDRESS** Dept of History, Lethbridge Univ, 4401 University Dr W, Lethbridge, AB, T1K 3M4. **EMAIL** greenshields@hg.uleth.ca

GREENSPAN, EZRA
PERSONAL Born 02/02/1952, Perth Amboy, NJ, m, 1978, 3 children **DISCIPLINE** AMERICAN STUDIES **EDUCATION** Union Col, BA, 74; Brown Univ, MA, 75; Brown Univ, PhD, 81. **CAREER** Postdoctoral fel, Tel Aviv Univ, 81-82; jr lectr, 83-88; instr, Middlesex County Col, 88-89; asst prof, Univ SC, 90-93; assoc prof, 94- . **HONORS AND AWARDS** Phi Beta Kappa; NEH fel, 93. **MEMBERSHIPS** MLA; South Atlantic MLA; Am Studies Asoc; Soc for the Hist of Authorship, Reading, and Publishing. **RESEARCH** History of authorship and publishing in the U.S.; nineteenth-century U.S. literary history; modern Jewish literary history. **SELECTED PUBLICATIONS** Auth, The Schlemiel Comes to America, 83; auth, Walt Whitman and the American Reader, 90; ed, Cambridge Companion to Walt Whitman, 95; George Palmer Putnam: Representative American Publisher, forthcoming. **CONTACT ADDRESS** English Dept., Univ of South Carolina, Columbia, SC, 29208. **EMAIL** ezra.greenspan@sc.edu

GREENWALD, MAURINE WEINER
PERSONAL Born 05/24/1944, Chicago, IL, m, 1 child **DISCIPLINE** AMERICAN SOCIAL HISTORY **EDUCATION** Univ IL, Urbana, BA, 66; Brown Univ, PhD, 77. **CAREER** Instr hist, RI Col, 71-72; instr, 72-77, asst prof, 77-78, assoc prof hist, Univ Pittsburgh, 78. **HONORS AND AWARDS** Nat Defense Educ Act Title IV fel, Brown Univ, 67-71; Face Arts & Sci Res grant, 77, 82-89, 95-96, 98; Russell Sage Found grant, 93-94; Pittsburgh Center for Social Hist, 93-94; Chancellor's Distinguished Tchg Award, 94; Henry Murray Center Res Expenses grant, 97. **MEMBERSHIPS** Orgn Am Historians; Coord Comt Women in Hist Profession; Golden Key Honor Soc, hon mem, 96. **RESEARCH** Hist of women, work and family in the US during the 19th and 20th centuries. **SELECTED PUBLICATIONS** Auth, Women's History in America, In: American Women and American Studies, Am Studies Asn, 71; Women Workers and World War I: The American Railroad Industry, A Case Study, Jour Am Hist, Dec 75; Women, War and Work: The Impact of World War I on Women Workers in the United States, Greenwood Press, 80, paperback ed, Cornell Univ Press, 90; Women at Work Through the Eyes of Elizabeth Beardsley Butler and Lewis Wickes Hine (intro essay to reprint of Women and the Trades, 1909), Univ Pittsburgh Press, 84; Assessing the Past, Looking to the Future: A Report by the OAH committee on the Status of Women, Org of Am Hist Newsletter, 86; Working-class Feminism and the Family Wage Ideal: The Seattle Debate on Married Women's Right to Work, 1914-1920, Jour Am Hist, June 89; Women and Class in Pittsburgh, 1850-1920, In: City at the Point: Essays on the Social History of Pittsburgh (Samuel P Hayes, ed), Univ Pittsburgh Press, 89; Organized Labor and Women in Modern America, In: Women's Studies Encyclopedia, vol 3 (Helen Tierney, ed), Greenwood Press, 91; Women and Working-Class History in Pennsylvania, Pa Hist, winter 96; Visualizing Pittsburgh in the 1900s: Photographs and Sketches in the Service of Social Reform, In: Pittsburgh Surveyed: Social Science and Social Reform in the Early Twentieth Century, Univ Pittsburgh Press, 96 (co-ed with Margo Anderson); Elizabeth Beardsley Butler, In: American National Biography (John A Garraty, ed), Oxford Univ Press, 99. **CONTACT ADDRESS** Hist Dept, Univ Pittsburgh, 3p01 Forbes Quad, Pittsburgh, PA, 15260-0001. **EMAIL** greenwalt@pitt.edu

GREENWOOD, THERESA M. WINFREY
PERSONAL Born 12/28/1936, Cairo, IL, m **DISCIPLINE** EDUCATION **EDUCATION** Millikin Univ, BA music educ 1959; Ball State Univ, EdM 1963, EdD 1976. **CAREER** E Chicago Pub Schools, music teacher 1959-61; Muncie Pub Schools, teacher 1962-68; Ball State Univ, acad counselor 1971-72; Ball State Univ Burris Lab School, asst prof educ 1979-, teacher of gifted/talented program 1986-. **HONORS AND AWARDS** Soc Studies Grant 1982; Commendation IN Gov Orr 1982; NAACP Award 1980; IN All-Amer Family Awd Family Weekly Mag, Eastern Airlines 1972; fellowship Natl Fellowship Funds Emory Univ 1973-76; BSU Minority Achievement Award, minority Student Development, 1989, currently developing "Tap the Gap," a progam for at-risk students; developing innovative elementary parent partnership; Team program "Connections" for Christa McAuliffe Fellowship; Ford Fellowship 1975- 76 for doctorate; Eli Lilly Foundation, 1989; Teacher of the Year, runner-up, Indiana Dept of Educ, 1982-83; Disney Presents The American Teacher Telecast, 1994; Geraldine R Dodge Grant to design and host "A Celebration of Teaching Conf for Minorities," 1994; Indiana Teacher of the Year Finalist, 1994; Video Report Card,developed and innovated for Christa McAuliffe Fellowship; AAUW Round Table Panelist Natl Gender Study "Gender Bias in the Classroom," 1991; "Women of the Rainbow," Indianapolis Minority Chamber of Commerce, 1992; Served on the Search Committee for Superintendent of University Schools, 1994; Unsung Heros Award, 1998; Fulbright Memorial Scholar to Japan, 1998; "Wood, Paint and a Good Idea: Young Entrepreneurs," The Technology Teacher, 1998; "Traveling Teddy Bears Teach More Than Geography," Teddy Bear Review, 1999, Ball Univ, Jewish Studies Fellowship, 1998. **MEMBERSHIPS** Past pres Sigma Alpha Iota 1958; music adjudicator NISBOVA 1961-; bd of dir United Way, ARC, Huffer Day Care, WIPB-TV 1969-75; mem Kappa Delta Pi 1972-73; mem & state sec Natl League Amer Pen Women 1973-78; testified White House Conf on Families 1980; mem Eastern IN Community Choir; ed bd White River State Park 1983; judge Social Study History Days; adv bd Social Studies Council Natl Publ 1982; recipient Ind & MI Electric Co Mini-Grant 1987; Kodak (Newsletter Pub 1985 & Prie Time Newsletter Pub) 1986; editorial bd Natl Soc Studies Journal; speaker HS Young Writers Conf 1986; media volunteer Pan-American Games 1987. **SELECTED PUBLICATIONS** Feature Story, Ball State University Research Publication Bene Facta; published, Psalms of a Black Mother, Warner Press ,1970, Gospel Graffiti, M Evans, NY, 1978, weekly newspaper column, Muncie Eve Press Poems, "Black Like It Is/Was," 1974, "Break Thru (Upper Room Anthology)," 1972, "Crazy to be Alive in Such a Strange World," 1977; bibliographic, Ladies Home Journal, 1976, Essence Mag, 1975, Church Herald, 1972; article, "Cross-Cultural Educ for Elementary School," The Social Studies Teacher, 1983; published poems in the Saturday Even ing Post, 1974; students gained extensive publicity for "DearWorld" letters to Pres Reagan & Gen Sec Mikhail Gorbachev during Washington Summit (exhibited 10 months at World's Largest Children Museum), 1988; writing, "Open Letter to Miss Crawford, Diary of a Black Girl Growing Up in America," Madison County Magazine, March 1991; Published: Technology Horizons Education Journal, "Let's Pop Some Corn and Watch Your Report Card;" Principal Magazine (NAESP), 1995; Inerviewed for Indianapolis Star and Ball State Information Bureau for national wire services for views on "The Status of Minorities in Teaching" and "Black Creativity and Education;" Created and Produced Educational television show, "What's In The Attic?"; Presented at state and national Gifted Conferences, Indianapolis and Salt Lake City, Utah (Young Entrepreneurs Project); Panel for local PBS telecast, "Parents, The Early Years," 1992; Developed a theoretical, Multiple Intelligence Model based on African Proverbs. **CONTACT ADDRESS** Burris Lab School, Ball State Univ, 2000 Univ, Muncie, IN, 47306.

GREER, ALLAN R.
PERSONAL Born 06/04/1950, New Westminster, BC, Canada **DISCIPLINE** HISTORY **EDUCATION** Univ BC, BA, 72; Carleton Univ, MA, 75; York Univ, PhD, 80. **CAREER** Asst prof, Univ Maine, 80-83; asst to assoc prof, 83-94, PROF HISTORY, UNIV TORONTO, 94-. **HONORS AND AWARDS** John A. Macdonald Award, Can Hist Asn, 85; Alan Sharlin Prize, Soc Sci Hist Asn, 85; Priz Lionel-Groulx, Inst hist Am francaise; John Porter Award, Cam Soc Anthrop Asn. **MEMBERSHIPS** Can Hist Asn; Inst hist Am francaise; Inst Early Am Hist Cultur. **SELECTED PUBLICATIONS** Auth, Peasant, Lord and Merchant: Rural Society in Three Quebec Parishes 1740-1840, 85; auth, The Patriots and the People: The Rebellion of 1837 in Rural Lower Canada, 93. **CONTACT ADDRESS** Univ Col, Univ of Toronto, Toronto, ON, M5S 3H7.

GREGG, EDWARD
PERSONAL Born 04/08/1945, Ashland, KS **DISCIPLINE** HISTORY **EDUCATION** Univ Kans, BA, 67; Univ London, MA, 68, PhD(hist), 72. **CAREER** Asst prof, 72-77, ASSOC PROF HIST, UNIV SC, 77-, Clark Libr, Univ Calif Los Angeles fel hist, 73; Inst Advan Study, Univ Edinburgh fel hist, 78; vis scholar hist, London Sch Econ, 78-79; vis prof, Univ Kans, 79-80. **MEMBERSHIPS** Fel Royal Hist Soc. **RESEARCH** Reign of Queen Anne; Jacobite Movement; reign of Louis XIV. **SELECTED PUBLICATIONS** Auth, Culloden and the '45, 18th-Century Stud, Vol 0026, 93; New Light on the Authorship of the 'Life of James II': Monarchial Memoirs and Biographies and James-II, Eng Hist Rev, Vol 0108, 93; Godolphin, Sidney, Servant of the State, Eng Hist Rev, Vol 0111, 96; The Jacobites--Britain and Europe, 1688-1788, Eng Hist Rev, Vol 0111, 96; The Augustan Court--Anne, Queen and the Decline of Court Culture, Eng Hist Rev, Vol 0111, 96. **CONTACT ADDRESS** Dept of Hist, Univ SC, Columbia, SC, 29208.

GREGG, ROBERT
DISCIPLINE INTERNATIONAL ORGANIZATION **EDUCATION** Colgate Univ, AB; Cornell Univ, PhD. **CAREER** Prof, Am Univ. **RESEARCH** International organizations and the United Nations. **SELECTED PUBLICATIONS** Auth, About Face? The United States and the United Nations, L. Rienner Publs, 93; International Relations on Film, Lynne Rienner, 97. **CONTACT ADDRESS** American Univ, 4400 Massachusetts Ave, Washington, DC, 20016.

GREGG, ROBERT C.
DISCIPLINE CLASSICS **EDUCATION** BA, 60; MDiv, 63; Univ PA, PhD, 74. **CAREER** Prof relig studies/class and dean Memorial Church. **RESEARCH** Early Christianity , institutions, thought, ritual; ; Jews, Pagans, and Christians in Late Antiquity; asceticism in the late Roman and Early Christian periods; Gnostic forms of Christianity. **SELECTED PUBLICATIONS** Auth, Jews, Pagans, and Christians in the Ancient Golan Heights, 96; coauth, Early Arianism, 81; ed, Arianism: Historical and Theological Assessments, 85. **CONTACT ADDRESS** Stanford Univ, Bldg 20, Main Quad, Stanford, CA, 94305.

GREGO, RICHARD
PERSONAL Born 04/03/1963, New York, NY, m, 1987 **DISCIPLINE** HISTORY **EDUCATION** SUNY, BA, 85; Col of St. Rose, MA; SUNY, DA, 97 **CAREER** Adj Inst, 91-pres, Indian Rvr Com Col **MEMBERSHIPS** Am Philos Assoc **RESEARCH** Existentialism, History of Ideas; Comparative Philosophy of Religion **CONTACT ADDRESS** PO Box 3104, Ft. Pierce, FL, 34948.

GREGORY, FREDERICK
PERSONAL Born 12/03/1942, Honesdale, PA, m, 1967, 2 children **DISCIPLINE** HISTORY OF SCIENCE **EDUCATION** Wheaton Col, BS, 65; Gordon-Conwell Theol Sem, BD, 68; Univ Wis, MA, 70; Harvard Univ, PhD(hist sci), 73. **CAREER** Asst prof math and hist sci, Eisenhower Col, 73-78; ASST PROF HIST SCI, UNIV FLA, 78-. **MEMBERSHIPS** Hist Sci Soc; Sigma Xi. **RESEARCH** German science in modern era; science and religion; 19th century science. **SELECTED PUBLICATIONS** Auth, The Creationists--The Evolution of Scientific Creationism, Historian, Vol 0056, 93; Mayer, Robert and the Conservation of Energy, Isis, Vol 0085, 94; Pozzetta, George--Obituary, J Southern Hist, Vol 0061, 95; What I Experienced--From Recorded Recollections, Isis, Vol 0087, 96; The Flight from Science and Reason, Isis, Vol 0088, 97. **CONTACT ADDRESS** Dept of Hist, Univ Florida, 4131 Turlington Hall, Gainesville, FL, 32611.

GREGORY, JUSTINA WINSTON
PERSONAL Born 09/24/1946, Brattleboro, VT, m, 1969, 2 children **DISCIPLINE** CLASSICS **EDUCATION** Smith Col, BA, 67; Harvard Univ, MA, 72, PhD(classics), 74. **CAREER** Asst prof classics, Yale Univ, 74-75; asst prof, Prof Classics, Smith Col, 75-91-, Am Coun Learned Socs fel, 76. **MEMBERSHIPS** Am Philol Asn; Women's Cl Caucus; Class Asn New England. **RESEARCH** Greek tragedy. **SELECTED PUBLICATIONS** Co-translr, Aesop's Fables, Gambit, 75; auth, Euripides' Heracles, Yale Class Studies, 77; Euripides, Alcestis, Hermes, Vol 107, 79; Euripides and the Instruction of the Athenians, Univ Michigan Preaa, 91, second revised ed (paper), 97: Inter...and Geneology in Hecuba, American Journal of Philosophy, 116, 389-97, 95; The Encounter at the Crossroads in Sophocles, Oedipios Tyrnnus, Journal of Hellenic Studies, 115, 141-6, 95; other articles and reviews. **CONTACT ADDRESS** Dept of Classics, Smith Col, 98 Green St, Northampton, MA, 01063-0001. **EMAIL** jgregory@sophia.smith.edu

GREGORY, ROBERT G.
PERSONAL Born 05/16/1924, Denver, CO, m, 1955, 2 children **DISCIPLINE** HISTORY **EDUCATION** Univ Calif, Los Angeles, BA, 48, MA, 50, PhD, 56. **CAREER** Civilian historian, 15th Air Force, March AFB, 57; from asst prof to assoc prof hist, Wake Forest Col, 57-66; assoc prof, 66-71, PROF HIST, SYRACUSE UNIV, 71-; Prof Emeritis, Fac training fel, Am inst Indian Studies, 62-63; humanities fel, cooperative prog humanities, Duke Univ, 64-65; Nat Sci Found award, 68-69, grant, 70-75; chmn, Asn African Studies Prog, 74-77. **MEMBERSHIPS** AHA; African Studies Asn; Asian Studies Asn. **RESEARCH** South Asians in Britain. **SELECTED PUBLICATIONS** Auth, Sidney Webb and East Africa: Labour's Experiment With Native Paramountcy, Univ Calif, 62; Churchill's administration of East Africa: A period of Indian disillusionment, 1906-1922, J Indian Hist, 8/66; coauth, A Guide to the Kenya National Archives, Prog Eastern African Studies, 69; auth, Africana archives and innovative teaching, Africana Libr J, spring 71; India and East Africa: A History of Race Relations Within the British Empire, 1890-1939, Clarendon, 72; auth, H S L Polak and the Indians Overseas Association, Vivekananda Kendra Patrika, spring 73; Co-operation and collaboration in colonial East Africa: The Asians' political role, 1890-1964, African Affairs, 4/81; Literary development in East Africa: The Asian contribution, 1955-1975, Res African Lit, winter 81; The Rise and Fall of Bhizanthropy in East Africa: The Asian Contribution, Transactions, 92; Quest for Equality: Asian Politics in East Africa, 1900-67, Orient Longman, 93; South Asians In East Africa: An Economic and Social History, 1890-1980, Westview, 93. **CONTACT ADDRESS** Dept of Hist, Syracuse Univ, 750 E Adams St, Syracuse, NY, 13210-2399.

GREGORY KOHLSTEDT, SALLY
DISCIPLINE HISTORY **EDUCATION** Univ Ill, PhD, 72. **CAREER** Prof **HONORS AND AWARDS** Pres, Hist Sci Soc. **RESEARCH** American culture participation patterns and institutional development. **SELECTED PUBLICATIONS** Auth, The Formation of the American Scientific Community: The American Association For the Advancement of Science, 1848-1860, 76; co-ed, Historical Writing On American Science, 85; International Science and National Scientific Identity: Australia, Britain, and the United States, 91. **CONTACT ADDRESS** History Dept, Univ of Minnesota, Twin Cities, 64 Classroom Office Bldg, 1994 Buford Ave, Minneapolis, MN, 55455. **EMAIL** kohls001@tc.umn.edu

GRELE, RONALD J.
DISCIPLINE UNITED STATES HISTORY **EDUCATION** Univ Conn, BA, 59; Rutgers Univ, PhD, 78. **CAREER** Prof. **RESEARCH** Historical methods; social history. **SELECTED PUBLICATIONS** Auth, Envelopes of Sound: The Art of Oral

History, 85; A Student Generation in Revolt, 88; co-auth, The Urbanization of New Jersey, 64; ed, Multi-culturalism and Subjectivity in Oral History: An International Anthology, 92. **CONTACT ADDRESS** Dept of History, Columbia Col, New York, 2960 Broadway, New York, NY, 10027-6902.

GRENDLER, PAUL F.
DISCIPLINE HISTORY **EDUCATION** Oberlin Col, BA, 59; Univ Wis, Madison, MA, 61, PhD, 64. **CAREER** Instr, Univ Pittsburgh, 63-64; lectr, 64-65, asst prof, 65- 69, assoc prof, 69-73, prof, 73-98, PORF EMER, 98-, UNIV TORONTO; vis prof, Univ NC, Chapel Hill, 91. **CONTACT ADDRESS** 110 Fern Ln, Chapel Hill, NC, 27514-4206. **EMAIL** pgrendler@compuserve.com

GRENIER, JUDSON A.
PERSONAL Born 03/06/1930, Indianapolis, IN, m, 1954, 4 children **DISCIPLINE** UNITED STATES HISTORY **EDUCATION** Univ Minn, AB, 51; Univ Calif, Berkeley, MA, 51; Univ Calif, Los Angeles, PhD(hist), 65. **CAREER** News analyst, US Inform Agency, US Dept State, 52; instr jour, El Camino Col, 56-60, asst prof hist, 60-65; vis lectr, Univ Calif, Los Angeles, 65-66; from asst prof to assoc prof, 66-72, coordr, interdisciplinary studies, 67-68 and 70-72, chmn urban studies interdept prog, 68-72, chmn dept hist, 68-70, PROF HIST, CALIF STATE UNIV, DOMINGUEZ HILLS, 72-, Reporter, Los Angeles Mirror News, 57; exec secy, Jour Asn Jr Col, 58-60; mem bd dirs, Los Angeles Welfare PLanning Coun, 67-70; Carnegie Found grant, 72-73; mem hist team, Los Angeles Bicentennial Comt, 73-76, Los Angeles 200, 78-81; scribe, Hist Guild Southern Calif, 73-76; senator, Acad Sen Calif State Univ and Col, 73-82, secy, 76-78, vchair, 79-80, mem exec comt, 76-80, mem, Comn Extended Educ, 77-80; assoc Los Angeles, County Mus, 75-; dir and vchair, Hist Soc Southern Calif, 79-82. **HONORS AND AWARDS** Distinguished Prof Award, Calif State Univ, Dominguez Hills, 74. **MEMBERSHIPS** AHA; Asn Educ in Jour; Orgn Am Historians. **RESEARCH** The progressive era, 1898-1919; mass culture and the mass media; California and the West. **SELECTED PUBLICATIONS** Auth, Fleeting Moments--Nature and Culture in American History, Calif Hist, Vol 0071, 92; Los-Angeles and the Great-Depression, Pacific Hist Rev, Vol 0062, 93; Frontier Faiths--Church, Temple, and Synagogue in Los-Angeles, 1846-1888, Pacific Hist Rev, Vol 0062, 93; Haynes, John, Randolph, California Progressive, Pacific Hist Rev, Vol 0063, 94; Yankees in Paradise--The Pacific Basin Frontier, Calif Hist, Vol 0074, 95. **CONTACT ADDRESS** Dept of Hist, California State Univ, Dominguez Hills, Carson, CA, 90747.

GRENNEN, JOSEPH EDWARD
PERSONAL Born 09/03/1926, New York, NY, m, 1950, 6 children **DISCIPLINE** ENGLISH LITERATURE, MEDIEVAL SCIENCE **EDUCATION** Col Holy Cross, BS, 47; Fordham Univ, MA, 54, PhD, 60. **CAREER** Instr, High Sch, NY, 47-50; educ adv, Troop Info and Educ Div, US Army, Ger, 50-55; from asst prof to assoc prof, 56-76, chmn dept, 65-71, PROF ENGLISH, FORDHAM UNIV, 76-, Ed, Thought, 78-80. **MEMBERSHIPS** Mediaeval Acad Am; MLA; AAUP. **RESEARCH** Middle English literature; modern criticism; history of science. **SELECTED PUBLICATIONS** Auth, The Making of Works, Jones, David and the Medieval Drama, Renascence-Essays on Values in Lit, Vol 0045, 93. **CONTACT ADDRESS** Dept of English, Fordham Univ, New York, NY, 10458.

GRESSLEY, GENE M.
PERSONAL Born 06/20/1931, Frankfort, IN, m, 1952, 2 children **DISCIPLINE** HISTORY **EDUCATION** Ind Univ, MA, 56; Univ Ore, PhD(hist), 64. **CAREER** Asst state historian, Colo State Hist Soc, 52-54; res grant, 63, DIR WESTERN HIST RES CTR, UNIV WYO, 60-, RES PROF AM STUDIES, UNIV, 64-, Nat Endowment for Humanities fel, 66-67. **HONORS AND AWARDS** Edwards Award, Agr Hist Soc, 59; Pelzer Award C, Orgn Am Historians, 73. **MEMBERSHIPS** Orgn Am Historians; Agr Hist Soc; Bus Hist Soc; Pac Coast Br AHA. **RESEARCH** American economic history; historiography; 20th century American history. **SELECTED PUBLICATIONS** Auth, Horter, Henry, M.--Rocky-Mountain Empire Builder, Pacific Hist Rev, Vol 0062, 93; The Great Thirst--Californians and Water, 1770s-1990s, Pacific Hist Rev, Vol 0062, 93; The Depression and the Urban West-Coast, 1929-1933--Los-Angeles, San-Francisco, Seattle, and Portland, Montana-Mag of Western Hist, Vol 0043, 93; An Alpha and Omega of 20th-Century Mining History--A Review-Essay, NMex Hist Rev, Vol 0069, 94; Under an Open Sky--Rethinking America Western Past, Montana-Mag of Western Hist, Vol 0044, 94; Sutter, John and a Wider West, Ore Hist Quart, Vol 0096, 95; Colony and Empire--The Capitalist Transformation of the American-West, NMex Hist Rev, Vol 0071, 96; North-American Cattle-Ranching Frontiers--Origins, Diffusion, and Differentiation, Pacific Northwest Quart, Vol 0087, 96; Remaking the Agrarian Dream--New-Deal Rural Settlement in the Mountain West, NMex Hist Rev, Vol 0072, 97. **CONTACT ADDRESS** Univ of Wyo, Laramie, WY, 82071.

GREW, RAYMOND
PERSONAL Born 10/28/1930, San Jose, CA, m, 1952, 3 children **DISCIPLINE** MODERN EUROPEAN HISTORY **EDUCATION** Harvard Univ, AB, 51, AM, 52, PhD, 57. **CAREER** Tutor and teaching fel, Harvard Univ, 55-57; instr hist, Brandies Univ, 57-58; from instr to asst prof, Princeton Univ, 58-64, Rollins preceptor, 61-64; assoc prof, 64-68, dir, Ctr Western Europ Studies, 69-71 and 75-78, PROF HIST, UNIV MICH, ANN ARBOR, 68-, Fulbright fel, Italy, 54-55; Am Philos Soc grant, 62-63; Guggenheim fel, 68; chmn, Coun Europ Studies, 70-71, mem exec comt, 71-74 and 81-84; co-chair, Counc European Studies, 70, 84-87; ed, Comp Studies in Soc and Hist, 74-; dir d'etudes, Ecoles des Hautes Etudes en Sciences Sociales, 76; ed, Comp Study Soc and Hist, 73-; dir, Univ Mich, Florence 73-75 and 81, 84, 96, 98. **HONORS AND AWARDS** First Annual Prize, Soc Ital Hist Studies, 57; Chester Higby Prize, AHA, 62; Unita d'Italia Prize, Ital Govt, 63; Davud Oubjbew Oruze, Soc Fr Hist Stud, 93. **MEMBERSHIPS** AHA; Soc Fr Hist Studies (vpres, 66); Soc Ital Hist Studies; Soc Sci Hist Asn. **SELECTED PUBLICATIONS** Auth, A Sterner Plan for Italian Unity, Princeton Univ, 63; coauth, The Western Experience, Knopf, 74-98; auth, Catholicism in Italy, in Modern Italy, NY Univ, 74; ed, Crises of Political Development in Europe and the United States, Princeton Univ, 78; auth, School, State and Society: Growth of Elementary Schooling in France, Univ Mich, 91; auth, Picturing the People, J Interdisciplinary Hist, 86; auth, On the Prospects of Global History, in Conceptualizing Global History, 93; auth, Seeking the Cultural Context of Fundamentalisms, in Religion, Ethnicity, and Self-Identity, 97; auth, The Paradoxes of Italy's Nineteenth Century Political Cutlure, in Revolutions and Freedom, 96. **CONTACT ADDRESS** Dept of Hist, Univ of Mich, Ann Arbor, MI, 48109-1003. **EMAIL** rgrew@umich.edu

GREWAL, JOYTI
PERSONAL Born 09/21/1962, Patna, India, s **DISCIPLINE** HISTORY **EDUCATION** Delhi Univ, India, BA, 83, MA, 85; Univ Stony Brook NY, PhD, 91. **CAREER** Asst prof, 91-97, assoc prof, 97-, Luther Col. **CONTACT ADDRESS** Dept of History, Luther Col, Decorah, IA, 52101. **EMAIL** grewaljy@luther.edu

GRIBBIN, WILLIAM JAMES
PERSONAL Born 10/02/1943, Washington, DC, 4 children **DISCIPLINE** AMERICAN HISTORY **EDUCATION** Cath Univ Am, BA, 65, MA, 66, PhD(hist), 68. **CAREER** From instr to asst prof Am hist, Va Union Univ, 68-71; asst prof, DC Teachers Col, 72; specialist minority educ, Off Econ Opportunity, 73; legis asst, US Sen James L Buckley, 75-77; sr policy analyst, US Senate Republican Policy Comt, 77-81; dep dir, Off Legis Affairs, White House, 81-82, dep dir, Senate Republican Policy Comt, 82-89; asst to VPres for Legislative Affairs, 89-93; ed-in-chief Republican platforms, 84, 88, 92, 96; Sr Policy Analyst, House Republican Policy Committee, 93-95; COUNSELLOR TO THE U.S. SENATE MAJORITY LEADER, 96-. **RESEARCH** American social and intellectual history; history of religion in the United States. **SELECTED PUBLICATIONS** Auth, Republicanism and Religion in the Early National Period, Historian, 11/72; The Churches Militant: The War of 1812 and American Religion, Yale Univ, 73; Anti-Masonry, Religious Radicalism and the Paranoid Style of the 1820's, Hist Teacher, 2/74; A Greater Than Lafayette is Here: Dissenting Views of the Last American Visit, SAtlantic Quart, summer 74; Republicanism, Reform, and the Sense of Sin in Ante Bellum America, Cithara, 12/74; A Matter of Faith: North America's Religion and South America's Independence, Americas, 4/75; ed, Emblem of Freedom: The American Family in the 1980's, 81 & The Wealth of Families, 82, Am Family Inst; auth, The Family in the Modern World, 82; auth, The Family and the Flat Tax, 84. **CONTACT ADDRESS** Office of the Majority Leader, The Capitol, Room S-230, Washington, DC, 20510.

GRIEB, KENNETH J.
PERSONAL Born 04/03/1939, Buffalo, NY **DISCIPLINE** LATIN AMERICAN HISTORY, AMERICAN DIPLOMATIC HISTORY **EDUCATION** Univ Buffalo, BA, 60, MA, 62; Ind Univ, PhD(hist), 66. **CAREER** Resident lectr hist, Ind Univ South Bend, 65-66; asst prof hist, 66-70, assoc prof hist and int studies, 70-74, coordr Latin Am studies, 68-77, PROF HIST AND INT STUDIES, UNIV WIS-OSHKOSH, 74-, COORDR INT STUDIES, 77-, Ed Newsletter, Midwest Asn Latin Am Studies, 72-77; dir, Interdisciplinary Ctr, 78-. **MEMBERSHIPS** AHA; Conf Latin Am Hist; Latin Am Studies Asn; Soc Hist Am Foreign Rels; Midwest Asn Latin Am Studies (secy, protem, 71, pres, 72-73). **RESEARCH** United States relations with Latin America; Mexico since independence; the Caribbean and Central America in the 20th century. **SELECTED PUBLICATIONS** Auth, Doheney, Edward, L. Petroleum, Power, and Politics in the United-States and Mexico, Pacific Hist Rev, Vol 0062, 93; Historical Dictionary of Costa-Rica, Americas, Vol 0049, 93; Political and Agrarian Development in Guatemala, Hisp Am Hist Rev, Vol 0073, 93; Washington, Somoza, the Sandinistas, State and Regime in United-States-Policy Toward Nicaragua, 1969-1981, Americas, Vol 0052, 95; Origins of Liberal Dictatorship in Central-America, Guatemala, 1865-1873, Hisp Am Hist Rev, Vol 0075, 95; Rural Guatemala--1760-1940, Historian, Vol 0058, 96; The Banana Men--American Mercenaries and Entrepreneurs in Central-America, 1880-1930, Hisp Am Hist Rev, Vol 0077, 97; Oil, Banks and Politics--The United-States and Postrevolutionary Mexico, 1917-1924, Pacific Hist Rev, Vol 0066, 97. **CONTACT ADDRESS** Dept of Hist, Univ of Wis, Oshkosh, WI, 54901.

GRIEDER, TERENCE
PERSONAL Born 09/02/1931, m, 1972, 4 children **DISCIPLINE** ART HISTORY **EDUCATION** Univ Colo, BA, 53; Univ Wisc Madison, MS, 56; Univ Penn, MA, 60, PhD, 61. **CAREER** David Bruton Jr Centennial Prof Art Hist, Univ TexAS Austin, 61- . **MEMBERSHIPS** Col Art Asn; Soc Am Archaeol; Inst Adean Studies **RESEARCH** South American archaeology and art history; Pre-Columbian art; Creative work in painting. **SELECTED PUBLICATIONS** Auth, Signs of an Ideology of Authority, Ancient Images, Ancient Thought: The Archaeology of Ideology, Univ Calgary, 92; Art in the Andes, Discovery: Research and Scholarship at the University of Texas at Austin, 92; A Global View of Central America, Reintrepreting Prehistory of Central America, Univ Press Colo, 93; Informe sobre estudios arquelogicos en Challuabamba, 95; Artist and Audience, Brown & Benchmark, 96; On Two Types of Andean Tombs.Arqueologica Peruana 2, Deutsch-Peruanishce Archaologische Gesellschaft, 97. **CONTACT ADDRESS** Art Dept, Univ Texas Austin, Fine Arts Bldg 2.110, Austin, TX, 78712. **EMAIL** tgrieder@mail.utexas.edu

GRIER, JAMES
DISCIPLINE MUSIC **EDUCATION** Univ Toronto, PhD, 85. **CAREER** Assoc prof **HONORS AND AWARDS** Ed, De Musicae Cult. **RESEARCH** Medieval music; music and liturgy in Aquitaine 900-1200; textual criticism and editing music; popular music post-World War II. **SELECTED PUBLICATIONS** Auth, The Stemma of the Aquitanian Versaria, Jour Am Musicol Soc, 88; Lachmann, Bedier and the Bipartite Stemma: Towards a Responsible Application of the Common-Error method, 88; Some Codicological Observations on the Aquitanian Versaria, Musica Disciplina, 90; Scribal Practices in Aquitanian Versaria of the Twelfth Century: Towards a Typology of Error and Variant, Jour Am Musicol Soc, 92; A New Voice in the Monastery: tropes and Versus from the Eleventh and Twelfth Century Aquitaine, Speculun, 94; Musical Sources and Stemmatic Filiation: A Toll for Editing Music, Jour Am Musicol Soc, 95; Roger de Chabannes (d. 1025), Cantor of St. Martial, Limoges, Early Music Hist, 95; The Critical Editing of Music: History, Method, and Practice, Cambridge, 96; Scripto interrupta: Ademar de Charbannes and the Production of Paris, 97. **CONTACT ADDRESS** Dept of Music, Western Ontario Univ, London, ON, N6A 5B8. **EMAIL** jgrier@julian.uwo.ca

GRIEVES, FOREST L.
PERSONAL Born 09/19/1938, Beatty, NV, m, 1963, 2 children **DISCIPLINE** POLITICAL SCIENCE **EDUCATION** Stanford, BA, 60; Univ Nev, MA, 64, PhD, 67. **CAREER** Tchr, US Army, Europe, 60-62; Tchng Asst, Univ Ariz, 64-67; Asst Prof, W Ill Univ, 67-69; Asst Prof (69) to Assoc Prof (72) to Prof (76), Dept Polit Sci, Univ Mont; Guest Prof, Universitat des Saarlandes, 78-79, 81 2E **HONORS AND AWARDS** Grant, Univ Ariz, 65; Grant, Univ Mont, 70, 72, 74, 87, 92; Grant, Am Philo Soc, 72; Grant, NEH, 73; Grant, Ger Acad Exchange Service, 78, 87; Fulbright Hayes Sr Lectureship, 78-79; Grant, Alexander von Humboldt Foundation, 79, 81. **MEMBERSHIPS** Ger Stud Asn. **RESEARCH** International relations; comparative government; American government. **SELECTED PUBLICATIONS** Auth, Supranationalism and International Adjudication, Univ Ill Press, 69; auth, Conflict and Order: An Introduction to International Relations, Houghton Mifflin, 77; ed, Transnationalism in World Politics and Business, Pergamon Press, 79; co-auth, International Environmental Protection at the Regional Level, International Dimensions of the Environmental Crisis, Westview Press, 82; auth, entries in The African American Encyclopedia, Supplement, Marshall Cavendish Corp, 96. **CONTACT ADDRESS** Dept Polit Sci, Univ Mont, Missoula, MT, 59812. **EMAIL** fgrieves@selway.umt.edu

GRIFFEL, L. MICHAEL
DISCIPLINE MUSIC HISTORY AND LITERATURE **EDUCATION** Columbia Univ, PhD. **CAREER** Dep ch, mus dept & co-ch, Thomas Hunter Hon Prog. **SELECTED PUBLICATIONS** Publ on the symphonies in The Cambridge Companion to Schubert. **CONTACT ADDRESS** Dept of Music, Hunter Col, CUNY, 695 Park Ave, New York, NY, 10021.

GRIFFIN, BETTY SUE
PERSONAL Born 03/05/1943, Danville, Kentucky, d **DISCIPLINE** EDUCATION **EDUCATION** Fisk Univ, BS 1965; OR State Univ, MEd 1976, EdD 1985. **CAREER** Overbrook HS Philadelphia, teacher 1968-70; Model Cities Portland OR, placement dir 1970-72; OR State Univ, dir, field prog 1972-, prof educ psych, dir tchr training prog; KY Dept of Education, dir beginning teacher internship prog 1986-89; Exec Advisor, KY Dept of Education. **HONORS AND AWARDS** Bd mem OR Governors Commiss 1978; Danford Fellow OR State Univ; mem Faculty Networking Stanford Univ 1980; OR Governors Commn on Black Affairs 1985; Governors Scholars Selection Committee 1986; National Forum for Black Public Admin: Eli Fellow. **MEMBERSHIPS** Mem Outstanding Young Women of Ame 1977; ed consult Portland Public Schools 1978-; mem KY Col Assoc 1979, Delta Sigma Theta, Soroptomist; Scholarship committee YMCA Black Achievers; Phi Kappa Phi; Eastern Star. **CONTACT ADDRESS** Office of Instruction, Kentucky Dept of Education, 500 Merd Capital Plaza Tower #1728, Frankfort, KY, 40601.

GRIFFIN, PAUL R.
PERSONAL Born 02/27/1944, Bridgeport, OH, m, 1970, 2 children **DISCIPLINE** RELIGIOUS HISTORY **EDUCATION** Emory Univ, PhD, 83. **CAREER** Asst prof, assoc prof, acad dean, prof, Payne Theol Sem, 79-88; asst prof, assoc prof, chemn, dept of relig, dir African and African American Stud, Wright State Univ, 88- . **HONORS AND AWARDS** Founder, dir, of Black Relig Conf, Wright State Univ, 95; Parity 2000 Award in recognition of acad achievement and commun serv, 97. **MEMBERSHIPS** Am Acad Relig; Am Soc of Church Hist; Am Hist Assoc; Soc for Stud of Black Relig. **RESEARCH** American racism; African American religious history. **SELECTED PUBLICATIONS** Auth, The Struggles for A Black Theology of Education: The Pioneering Efforts of Post Civil War Clergy, Interdenominational Theol Center, 93; auth, Absalom Jones: A Dissenting Voice, Va Sem Jour, 95; auth, Theological Ideas Gone Awry: The Shaping of American Racism, in Turner, ed, Dissent and Empowerment: Essays in Honor of Gayraud S. Wilmore, Westminster, 99; auth, Seeds of Racism in the Soul of America, Pilgrim, 99. **CONTACT ADDRESS** Dept of Religion, Wright State Univ, Dayton, OH, 45435. **EMAIL** PGriffin@desire.wright.edu

GRIFFIN, WILLIAM DENIS
PERSONAL Born 01/19/1936, New York, NY, m, 1960, 2 children **DISCIPLINE** MODERN EUROPEAN HISTORY **EDUCATION** Fordham Univ, AB, 57, MA, 59, PhD, 62. **CAREER** Lectr, Queens Col, NY, 62-65; from instr to asst prof, 65-71, ASSOC PROF MOD EUROP HIST, ST JOHN'S UNIV NY, 71-, Nat Endowment for Humanities res fel, 67-68; assoc ed, Studies in Burke and His Time, 70-75; chmn, Sem Irish Studies, Columbia Univ, 77-79; assoc ed, Dict of Irish Biog, 79-. **MEMBERSHIPS** AHA; Conf Brit Studies; Am Comt Irish Studies; Am Irish Hist Soc (secy-gen, 73-74); Am Soc 18th Century Studies. **RESEARCH** Anglo-Irish political and social history in the 18th and 19th centuries; the Irish overseas; revolutionary era in Europe and America. **SELECTED PUBLICATIONS** Auth, Oconnell, Daniel, Political Pioneer, Cath Hist Rev, Vol 0079, 93. **CONTACT ADDRESS** Dept of Hist, St John's Univ, 8150 Utopia Pky, Jamaica, NY, 11439-0002.

GRIFFIN CARTER, MARVA
DISCIPLINE MUSIC HISTORY AND LITERATURE **EDUCATION** Boston Conserv, Bachelor of Music; New Eng Conserv, Master of Music; Boston Univ, MA; Univ Ill, Urbana, PhD. **CAREER** Asst prof, Ga State Univ. **RESEARCH** The music of the black church. **SELECTED PUBLICATIONS** Areas of publication have included the music of the black church, Hall Johnson and the Negro Spiritual, and the life and music of Will Marion Cook - a pioneer composer of black musical comedies and a conductor of "syncopated" orchestras; she has also published biographical profiles in Notable Black American Women, Black Women in the United States and The Encyclopedia of African-American Culture and History. **CONTACT ADDRESS** Georgia State Univ, Atlanta, GA, 30303.

GRIFFITH, EZRA
PERSONAL Born 02/18/1942, m **DISCIPLINE** AFRICAN-AMERICAN STUDIES **EDUCATION** Harvard Univ BA 1963; Univ of Strasbourg, MD 1973. **CAREER** French Polyclinic Health Center, intern 1973-74; Albert Einstein Coll, chief res psych 1974-77; YALE UNIV SCHOOL OF MEDICINE, asst prof 1977, assoc prof 1982-91, PROFESSOR OF PSYCHIATRY & AFRICAN AND AFRICAN AMERICAN STUDIES 1991-; Connecticut Mental Health Center, assoc dir 1986-89, director 1989-96; DEPT OF PSYCHIATRY, DEPUTY CHAIRMAN, 1996-. **HONORS AND AWARDS** Fellow, American Psychiatric Assn; mem & editorial bd, Hospital and Community Psychiatry; editor-in-chief, Yale Psychiatric Quarterly; Associate Editor, Diversity & Mental Health. **MEMBERSHIPS** Mem Black Psychs of Amer; Amer Psychiatric Assn; Amer Academy Psychiatry and Law; FALK Fellowship; traveling fellow Solomon Fuller Inst 1976; fellow WK Kellogg Found 1980; president, American Academy Psychiatry & Law, 1996-97. **CONTACT ADDRESS** Sch of Med, Yale Univ, 25 Park St, New Haven, CT, 06519.

GRIFFITH, SALLY F.
DISCIPLINE HISTORY **EDUCATION** Radcliffe, AB, 74; Johns Hopkins, MA, 81, PhD, 85. **CAREER** Assoc prof, hist, Villanova Univ; current, IND SCH. **MEMBERSHIPS** Am Antiquarian Soc **SELECTED PUBLICATIONS** Auth, Home Town News: William Allen White and the Emporia Gazette, Oxford Univ Press, 89; ed, The Autobiography of William Allen White, Univ Press Kansas, 90; auth, Order, Discipline, and a Few Cannon: Benjamin Franklin, The Association, and the Rhetoric of Boosterism, Penn Mag of Hist and Bio 116, April 92; auth, A Total Dissolution of the Bonds of Society: Community Wealth and Regeneration in Mathew Carey's Short Account of the Malignant Fever, in A Melancholy Scene of Devastation, Phila Coll of Phys and Library Co of Phila, 97. **CONTACT ADDRESS** 532 Strathmore Rd, Havertown, PA, 19083. **EMAIL** sgriffit@philly.infi.net

GRIFFITHS, NAOMI ELIZABETH SAUNDAUS
PERSONAL Born 04/20/1934, Hove, United Kingdom **DISCIPLINE** MODERN HISTORY **EDUCATION** Univ London, BA, 56, PhD(hist), 69; Univ NB, MA, 57. **CAREER** Lectr hist, 61-64, asst prof, 64-69, assoc dean, 75-79, ASSOC PROF HIST, CARLETON UNIV, 69-, DEAN, 79-, Pres, Acad Staff Asn, Carleton Univ, 71-72, bd of governors, 81-; ed, Can Asn Univ Teachers Monogr Ser, 72-. **MEMBERSHIPS** Can Hist Asn; AHA; Hist Asn, Eng. **RESEARCH** Acadian history; 17th century history; women's history. **SELECTED PUBLICATIONS** Auth, Cajun Country, J Southern Hist, Vol 0059, 93; A Land of Discord Always--Acadia from Its Beginning to the Expulsion of Its People 1604-1755, Am Hist Rev, Vol 0102, 97. **CONTACT ADDRESS** Dept of Hist, Carleton Univ, 1125 Colonel By Dr, Ottawa, ON, K1S 5B6.

GRILL, JOHNPETER HORST
PERSONAL Born 09/24/1943, Munich, Germany, m, 1961, 2 children **DISCIPLINE** MODERN EUROPEAN HISTORY **EDUCATION** Univ Va, BA, 66, MA, 67; Univ Mich, Ann Arbor, PhD, 75. **CAREER** Lectr hist, Univ Mich, 74-75; from Asst Prof to Assoc Prof, 76-92, prof hist, Miss State Univ, 92-. **MEMBERSHIPS** AHA; Cath Hist Asn; Ger Studies Asn. **RESEARCH** Weimar and Nazi Germany; politics and society in Baden; European agriculture; Himmler's SS; racism; American South and Nazi Germany. **SELECTED PUBLICATIONS** Auth, The Nazi Movement in Baden, 1920-1945, Univ NC Press, 83; Josef Stalin, In: Great Leaders/Great Tyrants: Opposing Views of People who have Influenced History, Greenwood Press, 95; Genocide, In: Survey of Social Science: Government and Politics Series, Salem Press, 95; Eugenics, In: The Twentieth Century: Great Events, Supplement, Salem Press, 96; German Officials Seize Plutonium, In: The Twentieth Century: Great Events, Supplement, Salem Press, 96; Racism, In: Encyclopedia of Contemporary Social Issues, Marshall Cavendish, 97; Goebbels, Joseph, In: The Encyclopedia of Propaganda, M.E. Sharpe, 98; author of numerous other articles. **CONTACT ADDRESS** Dept of Hist, Mississippi State Univ, PO Box H, Ms State Univ, MS, 39762-5508. **EMAIL** jhg1@ra.msstate.edu

GRILLO, LAURA
PERSONAL Born 08/22/1956, New York, NY, m, 1998 **DISCIPLINE** HISTORY OF RELIGIONS **EDUCATION** Brown Univ, Ab, 78; Union Theol Sem NY, MDiv, 86; Univ Chicago, PhD, 95. **CAREER** Asst prof, Millsaps Coll, 95-97; Sr Fel, Inst for Advanced Study of Rel, Univ Chicago, 97-98; Vis Asst Prof, Coll Wooster, 98-99. **HONORS AND AWARDS** Charles M Ross Trust grants 80-84, 89-90; Joseph M Kitagawa Scholar, Award in Hist of Rel, 87-88; Jr Fel, Inst for Advanced Study of Rel, 92-93; am Acad of Rel grant, 96; west African Res Asn grant, 97; Nat Endowment for Humanities grant, 97; Inst for Advanced Study of Rel, Univ Chicago Sr Fel, 97-98. **MEMBERSHIPS** Am Acad of Rel; African Studies Asn; West African Res Asn; Int Asn of Hist of Rel; am Asn Univ Prof. **RESEARCH** Method and theory of the Study of Religions; African Religions; Anthropology; Comparative Ethics; Philosophy of religion. **SELECTED PUBLICATIONS** Auth, African Traditional Religions, Encarta Encycl, 97; Divination in Contemporary Urban West Africa, Rel Study News, 98; The Body in African Religions, Purification, The Circle and African Religions, Encycl of Women and World Rel, forthcoming; Dogon: religionsgeschichtlich, Rel in Geschichte und Gegenwart, forthcoming. **CONTACT ADDRESS** 1046 Mindy Ln, #3, Wooster, OH, 44691. **EMAIL** lgrillo@acs.wooster.edu

GRIM, JOHN A.
PERSONAL Born 10/07/1946, ND, m, 1978 **DISCIPLINE** HISTORY OF RELIGION **EDUCATION** St. John's Univ, BA, 68; Fordham Univ, MA, 75, PhD, 79. **CAREER** Adj lectr, Col of Mt St Vincent, 76-79; adj lectr, St Francis Col, 79; adj lectr, Col of New Rochelle, 79-80; vis prof, Fordham Univ, 79-80; vis prof, Maryknoll Grad Sch of Theol, 80-81; assoc prof, Elizabeth Seton Col, 77-87; Hum Div, Sarah Lawrence Col, 86-89; assoc prof, 89-98, PROF, CHAIR RELIG DEPT, BUCKNELL UNIV, 98-; COORD, FORUM ON RELIG AND ECOLOGY, 89-. **HONORS AND AWARDS** V.Kann-Rasmussen Awd, 98; Aga Khan Trust for Culture Grant, 98; Sacharuna Found Grant, 97; Laurance Rockefeller Found Grant, 97; Sr Fel, Center for the Study of World Religions, Harvard Univ, Spring 97. **SELECTED PUBLICATIONS** Auth, The Shaman: Patterns of Siberian and Ojibway Healing, Civilization of the Am Indian Series, Univ of Okla Press, 83, 87; Native North and South American Mystical Traditions, An Anthology of Mysticism, Univ of Calif Press, forthcoming; An Awful Feeling of Loneliness: Native North American Mystical Traditions, Doors of Understanding: Conversations on Global Spirituality in Honor of Ewert Cousins, Franciscan Press, 97; A Comparative Study in Native American Philanthropy, Philanthropy and Culture: A Comparative Perspective, Indiana Univ Press, 97; Rituals Among Native Americans, Handbook in Anthrop of Relig, Greenwood Press, 97; co-ed, Worldviews and Ecology: Religion, Philosophy, and the Environment, Bucknell Univ Press, 93, Orbis Press, 94. **CONTACT ADDRESS** Dept of Relig, Bucknell Univ, Lewisburg, PA, 17837. **EMAIL** grim@bucknell.edu

GRIMSTED, DAVID ALLEN
PERSONAL Born 06/09/1935, Cumberland, WI, m, 1960, 3 children **DISCIPLINE** AMERICAN CULTURAL HISTORY **EDUCATION** Harvard Univ, AB, 57; Univ Calif, Berkeley, MA, 58, PhD, 63. **CAREER** Actg instr, Am hist, Univ Calif, Berkeley, 62-63; asst prof, Bucknell Univ, 63-67; fel, Charles Warren Ctr, Harvard Univ, 67-68; ASSOC PROF AM HIST, UNIV MD, COLLEGE PARK, 68-, Nat Endowment for Humanities fel, 67-68. **MEMBERSHIPS** Am Studies Asn; Orgn Am Historians; AHA. **RESEARCH** Nineteenth century American cultural history; Jacksonian America. **SELECTED PUBLICATIONS** Auth, Booth, Julius, Brutus--Theatrical Prometheus, J Southern Hist, Vol 0060, 94; The Long Affair--Jefferson,Thomas and the French-Revolution, 1785-1800, William and Mary Quart, Vol 0054, 97. **CONTACT ADDRESS** Dept of Hist, Univ of Md, College Park, MD, 20742-0001.

GRIMSTED, PATRICIA KENNEDY
PERSONAL Born 10/31/1935, Elkins, WV, d, 3 children **DISCIPLINE** RUSSIAN & MODERN EUROPEAN HISTORY & ARCHIVES. **EDUCATION** Univ Calif, Berkeley, AB, 57, MA, 59, PhD, 64. **CAREER** Lectr hist, Bucknell Univ, 65-67; fel, Radcliffe Inst, 67-69; assoc prof hist, Am Univ, 70-72; RES ASSOC, UKRAINIAN RES INST & RUSS RES CTR, HARVARD UNIV, 74-, Am Philos Soc grant, 65; assoc, Russ Res Ctr, Harvard Univ, 67-68; sr fel, Russ Inst, Columbia Univ, 68-69, res assoc, 69-74; lectr, Univ Col, Univ Md, 68-70; Am Coun Learned Soc res grant, 69; Int Res & Exchanges Bd res grant, 70; Nat Endowment for Humanities res grant, 71-74; Am Coun Learned Soc-Acad Sci USSR sr exchange scholar, 72-73, 76 & 78; vis res prof, Warsaw Univ, 77, 78, 79 & 81-82; res grant, Ford Found, 78-81. **HONORS AND AWARDS** Leland Prize, Soc Am Archivists, 73. **MEMBERSHIPS** AHA; Am Asn Advan Slavic Studies; Soc Am Archivists; Am Asn Baltic Studies; Int Coun on Arch. **RESEARCH** Soviet-area archival affairs; modern European diplomacy. **SELECTED PUBLICATIONS** Auth, Archives and Manuscript Repositories in the USSR: Moscow and Leningrad, Supplement 1: Bibliographical Addenda, 76 & Archives and Manuscript Collections in the USSR: Finding Aids on Microfiche: Moscow and Leningrad, 76, Int Doc Co; Archives and Manuscript Repositories in the USSR: Estonia, Latvia, Lithuania and Belorussia, Princeton Univ Press, 81; Archives and Manuscript Collections in the USSR: Finding Aids on Microfiche: Estonia, Latvia, Lithuania and Belorussia, Int Doc Co, 81; Archives and Manuscript Repositories in the USSR: The Ukraine and Moldavia, Princeton Univ Press (in press); co-ed (with Irena Sukowska-Kurasiowa) & contribr, The Lithuanian Metrica in Moscow and Warsaw: An Annotated Reedition of the 1887 Ptaszycki Inventory, Orient Res Partners (in press); Recent publications regarding archives and collections in the Soviet Union: A Selected Survey, Slavic Rev (in press); Lenin's legacy to Soviet archival theory and practice, Am Archivist (in press); A Handbook for Archival Research in the USSR, Kennan Inst Advan Russian Stud & Int Res & Exch Bd, 89; The Fate of Ukrainian Cultural Treasures during the Second World War: Plundered Archives, Libraaries, and Museums, Kyiv: Arkheohrafichna komisiia AN URSR, 91; Displaced Archives on the Eastern Front: Restitution Problems from World Ward II and its Aftermath, Int Inst Soc Hist, 95; coauth Arkhivy Rossii: Moskva-Sankt-Petersburg: Spravochnik-obozrenie i bibliograficheskii ukazatel, Moscow, 97; Archives of Russian Five Years After-: Purveyours of Sensations, Int Inst Soc Hist, 97. **CONTACT ADDRESS** Ukrainian Res Inst Harvard Univ, 1583 Massachusetts Ave, Cambridge, MA, 02138. **EMAIL** grimsted @fas.harvard.edu Moscow: abb@glasnet.ru

GRINDE, DONALD ANDREW
PERSONAL Born 08/23/1946, Savannah, GA, m, 1997, 3 children **DISCIPLINE** HISTORY **EDUCATION** Georgia Southern Univ, BA, 66; Univ Delaware, MA, 68; Univ Delaware, PhD, 74 **CAREER** Prof & dir, ALALA/Ethnic Studies, Univ Vermont, 95; George Washington Carver Distinguished prof, Iowa State Univ, 95; prof, Californai Polytechnic State Univ, 91-95; Rupert Costo prof, Univ California Riverside, 89-91; prof, Calif Polytechnic State Univ, 88-89; prof, Gettysburg Col, 87-88 **HONORS AND AWARDS** Rockefeller fel, 94-95; Summer Res Grant, Rockefeller Archives, 90; Rupert Costo Professor Amer Indian Hist, 89-91; Eugene Crawford Mem Fel, 87-88; **MEMBERSHIPS** Amer Assoc Museums; Amer Hist Assoc; Amer Indian Hist Soc; Bus Hist Conf; New York State Amer Studies Assoc; Ontario Archaeol Soc; Southern Hist Assoc; **RESEARCH** American Indian History; U.S. People's of Color **SELECTED PUBLICATIONS** Coauth, Debating Democracy: Native American Legacy of Freedom, Clearlight, 98; coauth, Encyclopedia of Native American Biography, Da Capo, 98; coauth, Apocalypse de Chiokoyhikov, Chef des Iroquois, Laval Univ, 97; coauth, The Ecocide of Native America, Clear Light, 98 **CONTACT ADDRESS** Univ Vermont, Burlington, VT, 05405. **EMAIL** dgrinde@zoo.uvm.edu

GRITSCH, ERIC W.
PERSONAL Born 04/19/1931, Neuhaus, Austria, m, 1955 **DISCIPLINE** RELIGION, HISTORY **EDUCATION** Yale Univ, STM, 55, MA, 58, PhD(relig), 60; Univ Vienna, BD, 56. **CAREER** Instr Bible, Wellesley Col, 59-61; PROF CHURCH HIST, LUTHERAN THEOL SEM, GETTYSBURG, 61-, DIR INST LUTHER STUDIES, 70-, Asn Am Theol Schs fel, Univ Heidelberg, 67-68; rep scholar, Lutheran-Roman Cath Dialog in USA, 72-. **MEMBERSHIPS** Am Soc Church Hist; Am Soc

Reformation Res; AAUP. **RESEARCH** German Reformation to 1900; European history of theology; Thomas Muenzer and Martin Luther. **SELECTED PUBLICATIONS** Auth, The Radical Reformation, 3rd ed, Cath Hist Rev, Vol 0080, 94; Revelation and Revolution--Basic Writings of Muntzer, Thomas, Cath Hist Rev, Vol 0080, 94; The Term Argernis in the Reformation--Concept-Historical Approach to the Biblically Legitimized Political-System of Ethics, Cath Hist Rev, Vol 0083, 97. **CONTACT ADDRESS** Dept of Church History, Gettysburg Col, Gettysburg, PA, 17325.

GROB, GERALD N.
PERSONAL Born 04/25/1931, New York, NY, m, 1954, 3 children **DISCIPLINE** AMERICAN HISTORY **EDUCATION** City Col New York, BSS, 51; Columbia Univ, AM, 52; Northwestern Univ, PhD, 58. **CAREER** From instr to prof Am hist and chmn dept hist, Clark Univ, 57-69; PROF HIST, RUTGERS UNIV, NEW BRUNSWICK, 69-, CHMN DEPT, 81-, NIMH and Nat Libr Med res grants, 60-65 and 67-82; Nat Endowment Humanities sr fel, 72-73; Guggenheim fel, 80-81. **MEMBERSHIPS** AHA; Orgn Am Hist; Am Asn Hist Med. **RESEARCH** American social history; history of American psychiatry and medicine; history and the social and behavioral sciences. **SELECTED PUBLICATIONS** Auth, The Last Great Necessity--Cemeteries in American History, Historian, Vol 0055, 93; Living in The Shadow of Death--Tuberculosis and the Social Experience of Illness in American History, Isis, Vol 0085, 94; The Most Solitary of Afflictions--Madness and Society in Britain, 1700-1900, J Soc Hist, Vol 0027, 94; Doctors and the Law--Medical Jurisprudence in 19th-Century America, J Interdisciplinary Hist, Vol 0025, 95. **CONTACT ADDRESS** Rutgers State Univ, New Brunswick, NJ, 08903.

GROFMAN, BERNARD N.
PERSONAL Born 12/02/1944, Houston, TX **DISCIPLINE** POLITICAL SCIENCE/SOCIAL PSYCHOLOGY **EDUCATION** Univ Chicago, BS, mathematics, 66, MA, political sci, 68, PhD, political sci, 72. **CAREER** Instructor, political sci, 70-71, adjunct asst prof, applied mathematics, 75, asst prof, 71-76, SUNY at Stony Brook; visiting lecturer, political sci, Univ Mannheim (Germany), 73; visiting asst prof, School of Social Scis, visiting asst prof, 75-76; Univ Calif, assoc prof of political sci, 76-80; guest scholar, Brookings Institution, Governmental Studies Program, 84; visiting prof, Univ Wash, Seattle, Dept of Political Sci, 85; fellow, Center for Advanced Study in the Behaviorial Sciences, 85-86; visiting prof, Univ Mich, 89; scholar-in-residence, Inst for Legal Studies, Kansai Univ, Japan, 90; prof of political sci and social psychol, Univ Calif, Irvine, 80-. **HONORS AND AWARDS** Pi Sigma Alpha Award, Best Paper, Annual Meeting of the Midwest Political Science Assn, 79; co-chair, American Political Science Assn, Conf Group on Representation and Electoral Systems, 82-85; Carl B. Allendoerfer Award (corecipient), for mathematical writing for undergraduates, Mathematical Assn of Am, 85; chair, Amer Political Science Assn, Section on Representation and Electoral Systems, 91-93; designation by the Gustavus Myers Center for the Study of Human Rights in North Amer of Controversies in Minority Voting (book) as one of the outstanding books on intolerance published in North America in 1992; Richard Fenno Prize co-recipient, for the best book published in 1994 in the field of legislative studies (Quiet Revolution in the South) , Legislative Studies Section of the Amer Political Science Assn, 95; Lauds and Laurels Award for Professional Achievement, UCI Alumni Assn, 95; Award for Teaching Innovation in the School of Social Sciences, UCI Dean for Undergraduate Education, 96. **MEMBERSHIPS** Chair, American Political Science Assn, Section on Representation and Electoral Systems, 91-93; Inst for Math and Behavioral Sci, 90-. **RESEARCH** Mathematical models of group and individual decision making with a focus on electoral behavior and voter choice and issues connected with representation and redistricting; individual and group information processing and decision heuristics; political propaganda, particularly political cartooning and satire; law and social science, particularly in the domain of civil rights; use of computers as a teaching aid. **SELECTED PUBLICATIONS** Ed, Political Gerrymandering and the Courts, 90; co-editor, Controversies in Minority Voting: The Voting Rights Act in Perspective, 92; ed, Information, Participation and Choice: An Economic Theory of Democracy in Perspective, 93; co-editor, Quiet Revolution in the South: The Voting Rights Act, 1965-1990, 94; ed, Legislative Term Limits: Public Choice Perspectives, 96; ed, Race and Redistricting, 98. **CONTACT ADDRESS** Dept of Politics & Society, Univ of California, Irvine, 3151 Social Science Plaza, Irvine, CA, 92697-5100. **EMAIL** bgrofman@uci.edu

GRONBJERG, KIRSTEN ANDERSON
PERSONAL Born 03/08/1936, Denmark, m, 1970 **DISCIPLINE** SOCIOLOGY **EDUCATION** Pitzer Col, Claremont, CA, BA (Sociol), 68; Univ Chicago, MA (Sociol), 70, PhD (Sociol), 74. **CAREER** Res asst, Pitzer Col, 68; lab asst, Univ Chicago, 68-69; lect in Sociol, Hofstra Univ, 71-73; lect in Sociol, 73-74, asst prof, SUNY at Stony Brook, 74-76; vis prof, School of Social Service Administration, Univ Chicago, 87-88; asst prof of Sociol, 76-78, assoc prof of Sociol, 78-86, prof of Sociol, 86-96, chair, Dept of Sociol and Anthropol, 96, Loyola Univ of Chicago; adjunct prof, in Univ Center on Philanthropy, 97-, School of Public and Environmental Affairs, IN Univ: assoc dean for Academic Affairs, 97-, prof, 97-. **HONORS AND AWARDS** Numerous grants and fellowships from the following sources: Woods Fund, Chicago, Field Found, Chicago, Chicago Community Found, Lyloa Univ, Aspen Inst, prog on non-profit orgs at Yale Univ, Joyce Found, Am Coun of Learned Soc, Ford Res grants, Univ Chicago, SUNY, Albion small fund, Chapin Hall Center for Children, and others, 65-97; Honorable mention, Staley-Robeson-Ryan-St Lawrence Prize, 94; Chmn's Award, United Way of Chicago, 95; Distinguished Service Award, past-pres, ARNOVA, 95; ARNOVA Award for Distinguished Book in Nonprofit and Voluntary Action Res, 95; Architect, Advocate, Advisor Tribute, United Way/Crusade of Mercy, 96. **MEMBERSHIPS** Asn for Res on Nonprofit Orgs and Voluntary Action; Joint Task Force of the Nat Asn for Schools of Public Affairs and the Nonprofit Academic Centers Coun; Am Sociol Asn; ASA Section on Community and Urban Sociol; Midwest Sociol Soc; Soc for the Study of Social Problems; Int Sociol Asn; ISA Res Comm on Poverty, Social Welfare and Social Policy; IL Sociol Asn; Am Soc for Public Admin: Asn for Public Policy Analysis and Management; Population Asn of Am; Am Political Science Asn. **RESEARCH** Charity and nonprofit orgs; orgs and org change; public and private welfare systems; comparative social policies. **SELECTED PUBLICATIONS** Auth, Understanding Nonprofit Funding: Managing Revenues in Social Service and Community Development Organizations, Jossey-Bass Inc Pubs, 93; The NTEE: Human Service and Regional Applications, Nat Center for Charitable Statistics, Voluntas 5, 94; Structure and Adequacy of Human Service Facilities: Challenges for Nonprofit Managers, with Ami Nagle, Nonprofit Management and Leadership, 5, 94; Child Welfare Contracting: Market Forces and Leverage, with Ted Chen and Matthew Stagner, Soc Sci Rev, 69, 95; State and Local Funding for Nonprofit Organizations, in Dilemas of Fiscal Reform: Paying for State and Local Government, ed by Lawrence B Joseph, Center for Urban Res and Policy Studies at the Univ Chicago, 96; the United Way System at the Crossroads: Community Planning and Allocation, with Lori Harmon, Aida Olkkonen, and Asif Raza, Nonprofit and Voluntary Sector Quart 25, 96; Transaction Costs in Social Contracting: Lessons from the USA, The Contract Culture in Public Service: Studies from Britain, Europe, and the USA, ed by Perri and Jeremy Kandall, Arena/Ashgate Pub, 97; Varieties of Nonprofit Funding Sources: Trends and Dimensions, in Financing the Nonprofit Sector, ed by Alan Abramson, forthcoming; numerous other publications. **CONTACT ADDRESS** Office of the Dean, Scho of Public and Env Affairs, Indiana Univ, Bloomington, 10th and Fee Ln, Bloomington, IN, 47405. **EMAIL** kgronbj@indiana.edu

GROPMAN, ALAN LOUIS
PERSONAL Born 02/04/1938, Medford, MA, m, 1960, 3 children **DISCIPLINE** MILITARY HISTORY, BLACK HISTORY **EDUCATION** Boston Univ, AB, 59; Tufts Univ, MA, 70, PhD(hist), 75. **CAREER** Asst prof, US Air Force Acad, 70-74; instr, Univ Md, 76; instr hist, Air War Col, 77-78; INSTR HIST, NAT WAR COL, 81-. **RESEARCH** Black military history; aviation history, World War II. **SELECTED PUBLICATIONS** Auth, Flying Blind--The Politics of the United-States Strategic Bomber Program, J Am Hist, Vol 0080, 93; Crosswinds--The Air Forces Setup in Vietnam, J Am Hist, Vol 0081, 94 ;Untitled, J Am Hist, Vol 0082, 95. **CONTACT ADDRESS** 6015 Kerrwood St, Burke, VA, 22015.

GROSS, DAVID
PERSONAL Born 11/05/1940, Kankakee, IL, m, 1965, 2 children **DISCIPLINE** HISTORY **EDUCATION** St Ambrose Coll, BA, 62; Univ Wis-Mad, MA, 64, PhD, 69. **CAREER** Instr, Univ Wis, 68-69; asst prof, Univ Colo, 69-73; assoc prof, Univ Colo, 73-81; PROF, HIST, UNIV COLO, 81-. **MEMBERSHIPS** Am Hist Asn **RESEARCH** Modern European Intellectual History **SELECTED PUBLICATIONS** "Remembering and Forgetting in the Modern City," Social Epis, 90; The Past in Ruins: Tradition and the Critique of Modernity, Univ Mass Press, 92. **CONTACT ADDRESS** Dept hist, Univ Colo Boulder, Box 234, Boulder, CO, 80309-0234.

GROSS, HANNS
PERSONAL Born 06/20/1928, Stockerau, Austria, m, 1991 **DISCIPLINE** EARLY MODERN EUROPEAN HISTORY **EDUCATION** Univ London, BA, 50; Univ Chicago, AM, 63, PhD(Hist), 66. **CAREER** Asst prof Hist, Southern Ill Univ, 66-67; from asst prof to assoc prof, 67-78, prof Hist, Loyola Univ Chicago, 78-. **MEMBERSHIPS** AHA; Conf Faith & Hist; Am Soc Legal Hist; Am Soc Eighteenth Century Studies; Soc Ital Hist Studies. **RESEARCH** Central European history from 13th to 18th centuries, especially legal, constitutional, administrative and social history; history of the city of Rome in the 18th century; the European city in the preindustrial age; A cultural and intellectual hist of the relationship between Halle Pietism and the early germ enlightenment. **SELECTED PUBLICATIONS** Auth, Empire and Sovereignty: A History of the Public Law Literature in the Holy Roman Empire, 1599-1804, Univ Chicago, 73; Lupold of Bebenburg, National Monarchy and Representative Government in Germany, II Pensiero Politico, 74; The Holy Roman Empire in modern times: Constitutional reality and legal theory, In: The Old Reich: Essays on German Political Institutions, 1495-1806, Etudes presentees a la commission internationale pour l'histoire des assemblees d'etats, 75; Pope Clement XIII In Frank Coppa, ed, Notable Popes A Biocritical Sourcebook, Greenwood Press, forthcoming. **CONTACT ADDRESS** Dept of History Loyola, Univ of Chicago, 6525 N Sheridan Rd, Chicago, IL, 60626-5385. **EMAIL** hgross@wpo.it.luc.ed

GROSS, RITA M.
PERSONAL Born 07/06/1943, Rhinelander, WI **DISCIPLINE** HISTORY OF RELIGIONS **EDUCATION** Univ Wis-Milwaukee, BA, 65; Univ Chicago, MA, 68, PhD(hist relig), 75. **CAREER** Instr theol, Loyola Univ, Chicago, 70-71; instr Indian rel, New Col, Fla, 71-73; instr, 73-75, asst prof, 75-80, ASSOC PROF EASTERN RELIG, UNIV WIS-EAU CLAIRE, 80-, Mem, rev bd relig, Anima; An Experiental J, 73- and Nat Endowment Humanities, 77-. **MEMBERSHIPS** Soc Values Higher Educ; Am Acad Relig; Women's Caucus Am Acad Relig. **RESEARCH** Hindu Theism, especially the Hindu Goddesses; Hindu inconography and mythology. **SELECTED PUBLICATIONS** Auth, Why Me--Methodological-Autobiographical Reflections of a Wisconsin Farm Girl Who Became a Buddhist Theologian when She Grew Up, J Feminist Stud in Relig, Vol 0013, 97; Toward a Buddhist Environmental Ethic: Religious Responses to Problems of Population, Consumption, and Degradation of the Global Environment, J Am Acad of Relig, Vol 0065, 97. **CONTACT ADDRESS** Dept of Philos and Relig Studies, Univ of Wis, Eau Claire, WI, 54701.

GROSS, ROBERT A.
DISCIPLINE HISTORY & AMERICAN STUDIES **EDUCATION** Univ Penn, BA, 66; Columbia Univ, MA, 68, PhD, 76. **CAREER** Assoc prof, Am stud & hist, Amherst; current, MURDEN PROF, AM STUD & HIST & DIR, AM STUD, COLL OF WILL & MARY; CHAIR, AAS PROG FOR THE HIST THE BOOK IN AM CULT. **MEMBERSHIPS** Am Antiquarian Soc **SELECTED PUBLICATIONS** Auth, Printing, Politics and the People, Worcester, 89; auth, Reading Culture, Reading Books, Procs. of the AAS 106, 96; auth, The Minutemen and Their World, 76; auth, Books and Libraries in Thoreau's Concord, Procs of AAS 97, 87; ed, In Debt to Shays: The Bicentennial of an Agrarian Rebellion, 93; auth, The Authority of the Word: Print and Social Change in America, 1607-1880, paper, AAS, 84. **CONTACT ADDRESS** Am Stud Prog, Col of William and Mary, PO Box 8795, Williamsburg, VA, 23187-8795. **EMAIL** ragros@facstaff.wm.edu

GROSS STEIN, JANICE
DISCIPLINE POLITICAL SCIENCE **EDUCATION** McGill Univ, BA, 64, PhD, 69; Yale Univ, MA, 65. **CAREER** Prof. **SELECTED PUBLICATIONS** Auth, Getting to the Table: Processes of International Prenegotiation; Choosing to Cooperate: How States Avoid Loss; We All Lost the Cold War. **CONTACT ADDRESS** Fac of Law, Univ Toronto, 78 Queen's Park, Toronto, ON.

GROSS-DIAZ, THERESA
DISCIPLINE HISTORY **EDUCATION** Northwestern Univ, PhD. **CAREER** Hist, Loyola Univ. **RESEARCH** Medieval England. **SELECTED PUBLICATIONS** Auth, Book manuscript, From Iectio divina to the lecture room: The Psalms Commentary of Gilbert of Poitiers, Brill Publishers, 95. **CONTACT ADDRESS** Fine Arts Dept, Loyola Univ, Chicago, 6525 N. Sheridan Rd., Chicago, IL, 60626. **EMAIL** tgrossdi@orion.it.luc.edu

GROTH, ALEXANDER J.
PERSONAL Born 03/07/1932, Warsaw, Poland, m, 1961, 2 children **DISCIPLINE** POLITICAL SCIENCE **EDUCATION** CUNY, BA, 54, MA, 55; Columbia Univ, PhD, 60. **CAREER** Instr of Political Sci, CCNY, 60-61; asst prof of Political Sci, Harpur Col, 61-62; Asst Prof to Prof of Political Sce, 62-93, Prof Emeritus, Univ Calif Davis, 93-. **HONORS AND AWARDS** Phi Beta Kappa. **MEMBERSHIPS** APSA; Western Political Sci Asn; Policy Studies Org; Western Slavic Studies Asn; Heritage Found. **RESEARCH** Comparative Politics. **SELECTED PUBLICATIONS** Auth, Comparative Politics: A Distributive Approach, Macmillan, 71; Major Ideologies: An Interpretative Survey of Democracy, Socialism and Nationalism, John Wiley, 71, Robert Krieger, 83; People's Poland: Governmaent and Politics, Chandler, 72; Lincoln: Authoritarian Savior, Univ Press of Am, 96; Democracies Against Hitler, forthcoming; ed, Revolution and Politial Change, Dartmouth Pub Co, 96; co-ed & contribur, Public Policy Across Nations: Social Welfare in Industrial Settings, JAI Press, 85. **CONTACT ADDRESS** Dept of Political Sci, Univ of Calif at Davis, Davis, CA, 95616.

GROTH, PAUL
PERSONAL Born 04/25/1949, Mayville, ND **DISCIPLINE** HUMAN GEOGRAPHY **EDUCATION** Univ Cal Berk PhD 83. **CAREER** Univ Cal Berk, Dept Arch, 83-. **HONORS AND AWARDS** Smithsonian Fel; J. B. Jackson Book Prize; Abbott Lowell Cummings prize **MEMBERSHIPS** OAH; SAH; AAG **RESEARCH** Cultural Lands Hist; Urban Hist; Indian Reserv; 19 and 20th Cent; Housing. **SELECTED PUBLICATIONS** Auth, Living Downtown: The History of Residential Hotels in the US, UNW CA Press, 94; Understanding Ordinary Land-

scapes, with Todd Bessi, eds, New Haven, Yale Univ Press, 97. **CONTACT ADDRESS** Dept of Architecture, Univ of California, Berkeley, Berkeley, CA, 94720-1800. **EMAIL** pgroth@uclink4.berkeley.edu

GROTHAUS, LARRY HENRY
PERSONAL Born 01/05/1930, Ft. Wayne, IN, m, 1954, 4 children **DISCIPLINE** UNITED STATES & AFRO-AMERICAN HISTORY **EDUCATION** Concordia Teachers Col, Ill, BSEd, 54; Univ Mo-Columbia, MA, 59, PhD(Hist), 70. **CAREER** Assoc prof Soc Sci, St Paul's Col, 54-68; asst acad dean, 73-77; dean Arts and Sci, 89-94; prof Hist, Concordia Univ, Nebr, 68-98. **MEMBERSHIPS** Orgn Am Historians; Southern Hist Assn. **SELECTED PUBLICATIONS** Auth, Kansas City Blacks, Harry Truman and the Pendergast machine, Mo Hist Rev, 10/74. **CONTACT ADDRESS** Dept of History, Concordia Col, Nebraska, 800 N Columbia Ave, Seward, NE, 68434-1556. **EMAIL** lgrochaus@seward.ccsn.edu

GROTON, ANNE H.
PERSONAL Born 04/08/1954, Oak Park, IL **DISCIPLINE** CLASSICAL STUDIES **EDUCATION** Wellesley Coll, AB, 76; Univ of Michigan, MA. 77, PhD 82. **CAREER** Asst Prof, Assoc Prof to Prof, 81-, St Olaf Coll. **HONORS AND AWARDS** Award for Excellence in the Tchg of Class, Amer Philos Assoc. **MEMBERSHIPS** Amer Philos Assoc; Class Assoc Middle West and South; Class Assoc of Minnesota; Amer Soc Papyrologists; Vergilian Soc. **RESEARCH** Ancient Greek and Roman Drama, especially comedy. **SELECTED PUBLICATIONS** Auth, From Alpha to Omega: A Beginning Course in Classical Greek, Focus Publishing, 95. **CONTACT ADDRESS** Dept Classics, St Olaf Coll, 1520 St Olaf Ave, Northfield, MN, 55057-1098. **EMAIL** groton@stolaf.edu

GROVES, NICHOLAS
PERSONAL Born 11/05/1945, Hyannis, MA, 2 children **DISCIPLINE** MEDIEVAL HISTORY **EDUCATION** Duke Univ, AB, 67; Univ Chicago, MA, 68, PhD, 83. **CAREER** De Andreis Seminary, 80-83; Assoc prof, St Thomas Seminary, 83-87; part-time, 87-91, Loyola Univ. **MEMBERSHIPS** Amer Acad of Relig; Soc for Buddhist Christian Studies. **RESEARCH** Medieval monastic hist; historical theology; Buddhist-Christian Studies. **CONTACT ADDRESS** 6455 N Sheridan Rd, #704, Chicago, IL, 60626.

GRUBB, FARLEY
PERSONAL Born 09/14/1954, Kennewick, WA, m, 1992 **DISCIPLINE** ECONOMICS **EDUCATION** Univ Washington, BA, 77; Univ Chicago, MA, 81, PhD, 84. **CAREER** Asst Prof, Assoc Prof, Prof, 83-93-, Univ Delaware. **MEMBERSHIPS** AEA; EHA; Cliometrics Soc. **RESEARCH** Economic History; Colonial Amer; Contract Labor. **SELECTED PUBLICATIONS** Auth, Lilliputians and Brobdingnagians Stature in British Colonial America: Evidence from Servants, Convicts and Apprentices, Research in Economic Hist, forthcoming; Withering Heights: Did Indentured Servants Shrink from Their Encounter with Malthus?, Econ Hist Rev, forthcoming; Labor Markets and Opportunity: Indentured Servitude in Early America, A Rejoinder to Salinger, Labor Hist, 98; Penal Slavery, in: Seymour Drescher, Stanley Engerman, eds, A Historical Guide to World Slavery, NY Oxford Univ Press, 98; The End of European Immigrant Servitude in the United States: An economic Analysis of Market Collapse 1772-1835, J Econ Hist, 94; German Immigrant Service Contracts Registered at the Port of Philadelphia 1817-1831, Baltimore, Genealogical Pub Co Inc, 94; The Liverpool Emigrant Servant Trade and the Transition to Slave Labor in the Chesapeake 1697-1707: Market Adjustments to War, coed, Explorations in Econ Hist, 94; The Disappearance of Organized Markets for European Immigrant Servants in the United States: Five Popular Explanations Reexamined, Social Science Hist, 94. **CONTACT ADDRESS** Economic Dept, Univ Delaware, Newark, DE, 19716. **EMAIL** grubb@be.udel.edu

GRUBB, JAMES S.
DISCIPLINE HISTORY **EDUCATION** Univ Chicago, PhD. **CAREER** Prof, Univ MD Baltimore County. **RESEARCH** Renaissance and Reformation hist. **SELECTED PUBLICATIONS** Auth, Firstborn of Venice: Vicenza in the Early Renaissance; State and Provincial Families in the Renaissance: Private and Public Life in the Veneto. **CONTACT ADDRESS** Dept of Hist, Univ MD Baltimore County, Hilltop Circle, PO Box 1000, Baltimore, MD, 21250. **EMAIL** connect@umbc.edu

GRUBBS, DONALD HUGHES
PERSONAL Born 12/14/1936, Miami, FL, m, 1979, 3 children **DISCIPLINE** UNITED STATES HISTORY **EDUCATION** Univ FL, BA, 58, MA, 59, PhD, 63. **CAREER** Instr soc sci, Dade County Jr Col, 61-62; assoc prof hist, 63-73, PROF HIST, UNIV OF THE PAC, 73- **RESEARCH** Agricultural, labor and New Deal history. **SELECTED PUBLICATIONS** Auth, Gardner Jackson, STFU and New Deal, Agr Hist, 4/68; Cry from the Cotton: The Southern Tenant Farmers Union and the New Deal, Univ NC, 71; Prelude to Chavez: NFLU in Calif, Labor Hist, fall 75; coauth, Racism: From Irrational to Functional, Rev Black Polit Econ, fall 75; Migrant Workers, in Encyclopedia of Southern Culture, pp 1401-1403, 89; Southern Tenant Farmers' Union, in Encyclopedia of Southern Culture, p 1427, 89. **CONTACT ADDRESS** Dept of Hist, Univ of the Pac, 3601 Pacific Ave, Stockton, CA, 95211-0197.

GRUBER, CARLOS S.
DISCIPLINE HISTORY **EDUCATION** Brandeis Univ, BA, 55;Columbia Univ, MA, 59; PhD, 68. **CAREER** Prof, William Paterson Col, 82-, assoc prof, 77-82 & dept ch, 87-93; asst prof, Rutgers Univ, 72-75; asst prof, Stern Col for Women, Yeshiva Univ, 68-71. **HONORS AND AWARDS** NJ Hist Soc grant, 92; NJ Coun for the Humanities grant, 92; Japan Found grant, 91; Fulbright-Hays fel, Group Study Abroad, Japan, 90; Nat Sci Found, Summer Scholar's Awd, 86, 85 & 82; res grant, 82, 78-80; Nat Endowment for the Humanities, Col Tchr(s) fel, 85-86, Summer Stipend, 78, Younger Humanist fel, 71-72; Charles Thomson Prize, 82. **MEMBERSHIPS** AHA: ch, Local Arrangements Comt, 90 Annual Meeting; US Dept of State, Adv Comt on Hist Diplomatic Doc, rep AHA, 83-86; Berkshire Conf of Women Hist(s): Bd of Trustees, 81-85; ch, Bk Awd Comt, 79-81; Columbia Univ Sem on Amer Civilization: co-chr, 88-91; Orgn Amer Hist(s): Comt on the Status of Women in the Hist Prof, 86-89, ch, 88-89 Membership Comt NJ, 87-89. **SELECTED PUBLICATIONS** Auth, The Overhead System in Government-Sponsored Academic Science: Origins and Early Development, Hist Stud in the Phys and Biol Sci, 95; Jane Addams--Frauen werden Friedenmachen, Der Friedens Nobelpreis von 1901 bis heute, vol IV, Ed Pacis, Munich, 89; rev(s), The Best War Ever, Mil Hist Rev, 95; An Actor in Recent History, James B. Conant: Harvard to Hiroshima and the Making of the Atomic Bomb, Sci, 94; The Cold War and American Science: The Military-Industrial-Academic Complex at MIT and Stanford, Hist Educ Quart, XXX, 94; The Manhattan Story Retold, The Making of the Atomic Bomb, Sci, 87; Academic Freedom Under Pressure, No Ivory Tower: McCarthyism and the Universities, Sci, 87. **CONTACT ADDRESS** Dept of History, William Paterson Col, 300 Pompton Rd., Wayne, NJ, 07470. **EMAIL** gruber@frontier.wilpaterson.edu

GRUBER, HELMUT
PERSONAL Born 07/20/1928, Austria **DISCIPLINE** MODERN EUROPEAN HISTORY **EDUCATION** City Col New York, BSS, 50; Columbia Univ, MA, 51, PhD(hist), 62. **CAREER** From instr to assoc prof hist, 56-75, head dept soc sci, 62-72, PROF HIST, POLYTECH INST NEW YORK, 65-, Consult soc sci div, Univ Sask, 68; vis prof, NY Univ, 74-75 and Maison des sci de l'homme, Paris, 80; chmn univ sem hist working class, Columbia Univ, 75-. **MEMBERSHIPS** AHA; Int Tagung Historiker Arbeiterbewegung (executive mem, 81-84). **RESEARCH** Nineteenth and twentieth century intellectual history of Europe; history of modern Germany; history of international socialism and communism. **SELECTED PUBLICATIONS** Auth, Be Strong and Courageous--40 Years of Jewish Youth in Austria--The Haschomer-Hazair-Movement, Zeitgeschichte, Vol 0022, 95. **CONTACT ADDRESS** Dept of Soc Sci, Polytech Inst of New York, 6 Metro Tech Ctr, Brooklyn, NY, 11201.

GRUBER, IRA DEMPSEY
PERSONAL Born 01/06/1934, Philadelphia, PA, m, 1958, 3 children **DISCIPLINE** ANGLO-AMERICAN HISTORY **EDUCATION** Duke Univ, AB, 55, AM, 59, PhD, 61. **CAREER** Instr hist, Duke Univ, 61-62; fel, Inst Early Am Hist and Cult, 62-65; asst prof, Occidental Col, 65-66; from asst prof to assoc prof, 66-74, PROF HIST, RICE UNIV, 74-, Am Philos Soc res grant, 63 and 74; master, Hanszen Col, Rice Univ, 68-73; Nat Endowment for Humanities summer stipend, 75; John F Morrison prof, US Army Command and Gen Staff Col, 79-80. **HONORS AND AWARDS** George R Brown Award for Super Teaching, Rice Univ, 74. **MEMBERSHIPS** Southern Hist Asn; Assocs Inst Early Am Hist & Cult; Am Mil Inst. **RESEARCH** American Revolution; art of war, Alexander to Napoleon. **SELECTED PUBLICATIONS** Auth, A Quest for Glory--Howe, Robert and the American-Revolution, J Southern Hist, Vol 0059, 93; The Civil-War in the American-West, Hist J, Vol 0036, 93; The Civil-War Memoirs of Seymour, William, J.--Reminiscences of a Louisiana Tiger, Hist J, Vol 0036, 93; Prison Life Among the Rebels--Recollections of a Union Chaplain, Hist J, Vol 0036, 93; The American-Revolution, 1775-1783--An Encyclopedia, Vol 1, a-L, Vol 2, M-Z, J Mil Hist, Vol 0057, 93; An American Profession of Arms--The Army Officer Corps, 1784-1861, Civil War Hist, Vol 0040, 94; Federal Union, Modern World--The Law of Nations in an Age of Revolutions, 1776-1814, Am Hist Rev, Vol 0100, 95; Guide to the Feinstone, Sol Collection of the David Library of the American-Revolution, J Mil Hist, Vol 0060, 96; The War of American Independence, 1775-1783, J Mil Hist, Vol 0060, 96. **CONTACT ADDRESS** Dept of Hist, Rice Univ, Houston, TX, 77251.

GRUDER, VIVIAN REBECCA
PERSONAL Born 01/07/1937, New York, NY, 1 child **DISCIPLINE** MODERN HISTORY **EDUCATION** Barnard Col, AB, 57; Harvard Univ, PhD Hist, 66. **CAREER** Teaching fel gen educ, Harvard Univ, 60-61 & 62-63; instr Hist, Douglass Col, Rutgers Univ, 63-64; lectr, Hunter Col, 64-65, instr, 65-67; asst prof, 67-69, assoc prof Hist, Queens Col, NY, 69-, Am Coun Learned Soc fel, 73-74. **HONORS AND AWARDS** PSC-CUNY Fullbright Travel Grant, 83-84; Res Grant, 83-84, 90-91, 92-96. **MEMBERSHIPS** AHA; Soc Fr Hist Studies; Int Soc Studies 18th Century; Am Soc 18th Century Studies; Int Comn Hist Rep & Parliamentary Insts. **RESEARCH** Eighteenth century French history; the Assembly of Notables, 1787 and 1788. **SELECTED PUBLICATIONS** Auth, The Royal Provincial Intendants: A Governing Elite in Eighteenth Century France, Cornell Univ, 68. **CONTACT ADDRESS** Dept of History, Queens Col, CUNY, 6530 Kissena Blvd, Flushing, NY, 11367-1597. **EMAIL** Gruder@QC.VAXA.ACC.QC.EDU

GRUEN, ERICH S.
PERSONAL Born 05/07/1935, Vienna, Austria, m, 1959, 3 children **DISCIPLINE** ANCIENT HISTORY **EDUCATION** Columbia Univ, BA, 57; Oxford Univ, MA, 60; Harvard Univ, PhD(Hist), 64. **CAREER** Instr Hist, Harvard Univ, 64-66; from asst prof to assoc prof, 66-72, prof Hist, Univ Calif, Berkeley, 72-, consult, Educ Develop Corp, 65-72; Nat Humanities fac fel, 68-70; Guggenheim fel, 69-70; 89-90; mem, Inst Advan Studies, Princeton, 73-74; vis fel, Merton Col, Oxford, 78; vis Distinguished Humanist, Univ Colo, 81; vis prof Princeton, 87-88; NEH fel 84-96; fel First Advan Studies Jerusalem, 96. **HONORS AND AWARDS** Disting Teaching Award, U Calif, 87; Fel Am Academy of Arts & Sciences, 86-. **MEMBERSHIPS** AHA; Am Philol Asn. **RESEARCH** Roman history, Hellenistic history. **SELECTED PUBLICATIONS** Auth, The Last Generation of the Roman Republic, Univ Calif, 74; The origins of the Achaean War, J Hellenic Studies, 76; The Hellenistic World and the Coming of Rome, Univ Calif, 84; Studies in Green Culture & Roman Policy, Brill, 90; Culture & National Identity in Republican Rome, Cornell Univ, 92; Heritage & Hellenism, Univ Calif, 98. **CONTACT ADDRESS** Dept of History, Univ of California, Berkeley, 3229 Dwinelle Hall, Berkeley, CA, 94720-2551.

GRUNDY, KENNETH WILLIAM
PERSONAL Born 08/06/1936, Philadelphia, PA, m, 1960, 3 children **DISCIPLINE** POLITICAL SCIENCE **EDUCATION** Ursinus Col, BA, 58; Penn State, MA, 61, PhD, 63. **CAREER** Asst prof, San Fernando Valley State Col, 63-66; Assoc prof, 66-73, prof, 73-88, M A HANNA PROF OF POLITICAL SCIENCE, CASE W RESERVE UNIV, 66-. **MEMBERSHIPS** Int Studies Asn; African Studies Ans; Int Consortium Armed Forces & Soc. **RESEARCH** International Relations; Comparative Politics, Africa. **SELECTED PUBLICATIONS** auth Guerrilla Struggle in Africa, 72; Confirmation & Accommodation in Southern Africa, 73; Soldiers without Politics, 83; The Militarization of South African Politics, 86 & 88, South Africa, 91. **CONTACT ADDRESS** Case Western Reserve Univ, Mather House 223, Cleveland, OH, 44106-7109. **EMAIL** kwg@po.cwru.edu

GRUPENHOFF, RICHARD
DISCIPLINE FILM PRODUCTION, FILM HISTORY, SCREENWRITING, AND AFRICAN AMERICAN FILM HIS **EDUCATION** Xavier Univ BA; Purdue Univ, MA; Ohio State Univ, PhD. **CAREER** Instr, 75-, ch, dept Radio-TV-Film, Rowan Col of NJ. **SELECTED PUBLICATIONS** Auth, The Black Valentino: The Stage and Screen Career of Lorenzo Tucker. **CONTACT ADDRESS** Rowan Col of NJ, Glassboro, NJ, 08028-1701. **EMAIL** grupenhoff@rowan.edu

GRUSIN, RICHARD A.
DISCIPLINE AMERICAN CULTURAL HISTORY **EDUCATION** Univ Calif, Berkeley, PhD, 83. **CAREER** Ch, Sch of Lit, Commun & Cult, Ga Inst of Technol. **RESEARCH** Cultural origins of the national parks. **SELECTED PUBLICATIONS** Auth, Transcendentalist Hermeneutics: Institutional Authority and the Higher Criticism of the Bible; What Is an Electronic Author?, Configurations, 94; Representing Yellowstone: Photography, Loss, and Fidelity to Nature, Configurations, 95. **CONTACT ADDRESS** Sch of Lit, Commun & Cult, Georgia Inst of Tech, Skiles Cla, Atlanta, GA, 30332. **EMAIL** richard.grusin@lcc.gatech.edu

GRZYMSKI, KRZYSZTOF A.
PERSONAL Born 05/19/1951, Kalisz, Poland **DISCIPLINE** ARCHAEOLOGY/HISTORY **EDUCATION** Lodz Univ, 70-71; Warsaw Univ, MA, 76; Univ Calgary, PhD, 81. **CAREER** Archaeol consult, PIW Publs, Warsaw, 76-77; res & tchg asst, 77-81, res fel, Univ Calgary, 82-84; ASSOC PROF, NEAR & MIDDLE EASTERN CIVILIZATIONS, UNIV TORONTO, 84-; SR CURATOR, EGYPTIAN SECT, ROYAL ONTARIO MUSEUM, 84-; asst dir, 82-84, dir, Dongola Reach Surv, 84-86; dir, ROM Exped Nubia, 86-. **SELECTED PUBLICATIONS** Auth, Archaeological Renaissance in Upper Nubia, 87; coauth, Ancient Egypt and Nubia, 94. **CONTACT ADDRESS** Egyptian Sect, Royal Ontario Museum, 100 Queen's Park, Toronto, ON, M5S 2C6.

GUARNERI, CARL J.
PERSONAL Born 07/15/1950, Yonkers, NY, m, 1974, 2 children **DISCIPLINE** HISTORY **EDUCATION** Univ Penn, BA, 72; Univ Michigan, MA, 74; Johns Hopkins Univ, PhD, 79. **CAREER** Instr, hist and cultural stud, Bates Col, 77-78; from asst prof to assoc prof, 79-93, prof, 93- , hist, Saint Mary's Col,

Calif. **HONORS AND AWARDS** Phi Beta Kappa, 71; ACLS fel, 81-82; res fel, Charles Warren Ctr, Harvard Univ, 81-82; NEH summer stipend, 85; annual book award, Soc for Hist of the Early Am Republic, 92; Irvine Found curric grant, 93; dir, NEH Summer Seminars, 95, 98; USIA lectr, Brazil, 97. **MEMBERSHIPS** AHA; Org of Am Hist; Am Studies Asn; Soc for Hist of the Early Am Republic. **RESEARCH** Antebellum United States and the Civil War; United States intellectual and cultural history; comparative history. **SELECTED PUBLICATIONS** Auth, U.S. Intellectual and Cultural History, 1815-1877, AHA Guide to Historical Literature, Oxford, 95; auth, Utopias, in, Fox, ed, A Companion to American Thought, Blackwell, 95; auth, C. Vann Woodward and the Comparative Approach to American History, Rev in Am Hist, 95; auth, Reconstructing the Antebellum Communitarian Movement: Oneida and Fourierism, J of the Early Republic, 96; auth, Out of Its Shell: Internationalizing the Teaching of American History, AHA Perspectives, 97; ed, America Compared: American History in International Perspective, Houghton Mifflin, 97; auth, Brook Farm, Fourierism, and the Nationalist Dilemma in American Utopianism, in Capper, ed, Transient and Permanent: Transcendentalism in Its Contexts, Univ Mass, 99. **CONTACT ADDRESS** Dept of History, Saint Mary's Col of California, Moraga, CA, 94575. **EMAIL** cguarner@stmarys-ca.edu

GUBERTI-BASSETT, SARAH
DISCIPLINE ART HISTORY **EDUCATION** Smith Col, BA, 76; Univ Chicago, MA, 80; Bryn Mawr Col, PhD, 85. **CAREER** Asst prof, Wayne State Univ, 97-. **HONORS AND AWARDS** Whiting fel in the humanities, 84-58; Dumbarton Oaks fel, 89-90. **MEMBERSHIPS** Archaeol Inst of Amer; Byzantine Studies Conf; Col Art Asn; Intl Ctr for Medieval Art, Nat Comt for Byzantine Studies, Medieval Soc of Amer. **RESEARCH** Late antique & early Christian art & architecture. **SELECTED PUBLICATIONS** Auth, Historiae Custos: Sculpture & Tradition in the Baths of Zeuxippos, Amer Jour of Archaeol, 96; auth, Antiquities in the Hippodrome at Constantinople, Dumbarton Oaks Papers, 91. **CONTACT ADDRESS** Dept. of Art & Art History, Wayne State Univ, 150 Arts Bldg., Detroit, MI, 48202.

GUDDING, GABRIEL
PERSONAL Born 06/16/1966, MN, 1 child **DISCIPLINE** AMERICAN STUDIES/CREATIVE WRITING (POETRY) **EDUCATION** Evergreen Coll, BA, 94; Purdue Univ, MA, 97. **CAREER** Grad stud, Purdue Univ, 95-97; Grad stud, Cornell Univ, 98-. **HONORS AND AWARDS** The Nation "Discovery" Award, 98. **MEMBERSHIPS** Poetry Society of America **RESEARCH** American poetry; history of science **SELECTED PUBLICATIONS** The Phenotype/Genotype Distinction and The Disappearance of the Body, Journal of the History of Ideas, John Hopkins Univ Press, July 96; The Wallace Stevens Jour, I See Your Hammer in the Horologe of Time and I Raise You a Westclock, Spring 97; The Iowa Review, One Petition Lofted into the Ginkgos, Fall 97; The Nation, The Parenthesis Inserts Itself into the Transcripts of The Committee on Un-American Activities, May 18, 1998; River Styx, The Bosun, August 1998; The Beloit Poetry Journal, The Footnote Reconnoiters the Piedmont. **CONTACT ADDRESS** Cornell Univ, 250 Goldwin Smith, Ithaca, NY, 14850. **EMAIL** gwg6@cornell.edu

GUENTNER, FRANCES J.
PERSONAL Born 03/10/1917, LaCrosse, WI **DISCIPLINE** MUSICOLOGY, CLASSICAL LANGUAGES **EDUCATION** St Louis Univ, AB, 39, MA, 42, Wash Univ, MA, 63. **CAREER** From instr to asst prof class lang, 49-64, assoc prof music, 64-70, chmn dept, 69-75; prof music, St Louis Univ, 70-, actg chmn dept, 80-, bk rev ed, Nat Asn Pastoral Musicians, 77- **MEMBERSHIPS** Church Music Asn Am; Nat Asn Pastoral Musicians. **RESEARCH** Baroque music; music theory; synthesizer. **SELECTED PUBLICATIONS** Auth, A nineteenth-century chant revival, Sacred Music, summer 65; Alcestis in ancient drama and early opera, Class Bull, 11/66; Dulces exuviae in sixteenth century Music, Class J, 10-11/72; Medieval Treatise on Cistercian Chant, Am Inst Music, 74; Reassessing a recital heritage, Col Music Symp, fall 77. **CONTACT ADDRESS** Jesuit Hall, St. Louis Univ, 3601 Lindell Blvd, Saint Louis, MO, 63108-3393.

GUICE, JOHN DAVID WYNNE
PERSONAL Born 03/24/1931, Biloxi, MS, m, 1958, 2 children **DISCIPLINE** UNITED STATES COLONIAL HISTORY **EDUCATION** Yale Univ, BA, 52; Univ Tex, El Paso, MA, 53; Univ Colo, Phd(hist), 69. **CAREER** Assoc hist, Univ Colo, Denver Ctr, 67-69; from asst prof to assoc prof, 69-78, PROF HIST, UNIV SOUTHERN MISS, 78-, DIR AM STUDIES PROG, 77-, Part-time instr hist Univ Tex, El Paso, 62-66. **HONORS AND AWARDS** Leroy R Hafen Award, Colo Hist Soc, 77. **MEMBERSHIPS** Western Hist Asn; Orgn Am Historians. **RESEARCH** United States territorial history; old Southwest; frontier legal institutions. **SELECTED PUBLICATIONS** Auth, Before Tennessee--The Southwest Territory, 1790-1796--A Narrative History of the Territory of the United-States South of the River Ohio, J Southern Hist, Vol 0059, 93; North-American Cattle-Ranching Frontiers--Origins, Diffusion, and Differentiation, J Southern Hist, Vol 0061, 95; Territorial Ambition--Land and Society in Arkansas, 1800-1840, J Interdisciplinary Hist, Vol 0026, 95; Old-West, New-West--Quo-Vadis, Pacific Northwest Quart, Vol 0087, 96; A Way Through the Wilderness--The Natchez-Trace and the Civilization of the Southern Frontier, J Southern Hist, Vol 0062, 96; Spanish Expeditions into Texas, 1689-1768, Western Hist Quart, Vol 0027, 96; Politics in the Postwar American-West, Montana-Mag of Western Hist, Vol 0047, 97. **CONTACT ADDRESS** Dept of Hist, Univ of Southern Miss, Hattiesburg, MS, 39401.

GUIDORIZZI, RICHARD PETER
PERSONAL Born 09/26/1937, Brooklyn, NY, m, 1964, 4 children **DISCIPLINE** EARLY NATIONAL HISTORY OF UNITED STATES **EDUCATION** St John's Univ, NY, BA, 59, MA, 61, PhD, 68. **CAREER** From instr to asst prof, 62-68, chmn, Dept Hist & Polit Sci, 72-76, prof hist, Iona Col, 72-. **MEMBERSHIPS** Am Cath Hist Soc; AHA; AAUP; Am Assn State & Local Hist. **RESEARCH** United States diplomatic history; American political parites; immigrant history, oral history project. **CONTACT ADDRESS** Dept of Hist & Polit Sci, Iona Col, 715 North Ave, New Rochelle, NY, 10801-1890.

GUILMAIN, JACQUES
DISCIPLINE ART HISTORY **EDUCATION** Univ NY, BS (biology), 48; Columbia Univ (art history), MA, 52, PhD (art history), 58. **CAREER** Asst, 63-65, assoc, 65-72, chair, dept art, 70-77, prof art, 72-98, PROF EMER, 98-, SUNY, STONY BROOK; vis prof, Columbia Univ, 68, 72; instr, Queens Col, CUNY, 60-63; vis asst prof, Univ Calif, 59-60; vis asst prof, Stanford Univ, 58-59. **CONTACT ADDRESS** Art Dept, SUNY, Stony Brook, Stony Brook, NY, 11794-5400.

GUINAN, MICHAEL DAMON
PERSONAL Born 02/16/1939, Cincinnati, OH **DISCIPLINE** SEMITICS, SYRIAC PATRISTICS **EDUCATION** San Luis Rey Col, BA, 61; Old Mission Theol Sem, STB, 65; Cath Univ Am, STL, 67, MA, 70, PhD(Semitics), 72. **CAREER** Prof Bibl Theol & Semitic Lang, Franciscan Sch Theol, Grad Theol Union, 72-. **MEMBERSHIPS** Cath Theol Soc Am; Cath Bibl Asn; Soc Bibl Lit; Soc for Study of Christian Spirituality. **RESEARCH** Old Testament; Syriac patristic theology. **SELECTED PUBLICATIONS** Auth, The Making of Many Images: Scripture Film and Religious Education, Multimedia Int, 73; Convenant in the Old Testament, Franciscan Herald, 75; Where are the dead?, Purgatory and immedicate retribution in James of Sarug, Proc Syriac Symp of 1972; Jacob of Sarug, In: New Cath Encycl, Vol XVI; The Creation Story of Genesis: Does It Really Establish Evolution?; Angels: Their Meaning for Today; The Menila and the Millenium; Christian Spirituality: Many Styles, One Spirit-Catholic Update, 94, 95, 97, 98. **CONTACT ADDRESS** Franciscan Sch of Theol, 1712 Euclid Ave, Berkeley, CA, 94709-1294. **EMAIL** mdguinan@aol.com

GUINN, PAUL
PERSONAL Born 10/30/1928, The Hague, Netherlands, m, 1971 **DISCIPLINE** MODERN HISTORY **EDUCATION** Swarthmore Col, BA, 50; Harvard Univ, MA, 51, PhD, 62. **CAREER** Analyst nat defense, Legis Ref Serv, Libr Cong, 55-56; instr hist, Simmons Col, 57-58; Univ Md Overseas Prog, UK, 59-60; exec ed, Int Studies Div, Inst Defense Anal, 61-67; ASSOC PROF HIST, STATE UNIV NY BUFFALO, 67-, Instr mil hist, Air Univ, 53-54; instr hist, Univ Baltimore, 55-56; assoc prof and lectr hist and polit sci, George Washington Univ, 65-66; vis assoc prof, Grad Sch Pub and Int Affairs, Univ Pittsburgh, 66; adj assoc prof hist, NY Univ, 66-67; Carnegie Endowment Int Peace vis res scholar, 66-67; Nat Endowment for Humanities sr fel, 71-72. **HONORS AND AWARDS** George Louis Beer Prize, AHA, 65. **MEMBERSHIPS** AHA; Conf Brit Studies; Am Mil Inst. **RESEARCH** Modern Europe; national security policy; international relations. **SELECTED PUBLICATIONS** Auth, British Politics and Foreign-Policy in the Age of Appeasement, 1935-39, Albion, Vol 0025, 93. **CONTACT ADDRESS** Dept of Hist, State Univ NY, Buffalo, NY, 14261.

GULLACE, NICOLETTA F.
DISCIPLINE MODERN BRITAIN, EUROPEAN SOCIAL HISTORY, WOMEN'S HISTORY **EDUCATION** Univ Calif, Berkeley, PhD. **CAREER** Asst prof, Univ NH, 95-. **HONORS AND AWARDS** Fulbright-Hays fel, UK; Mellon dissertation fel; Charlotte Newcombe fel; Olin postdoctoral fel in Mil and Strategic Hist. **RESEARCH** Gender, masculinity, popular culture, and political ideology; the cultural construction of warfare. **SELECTED PUBLICATIONS** Auth, White Feathers and Wounded Men: Female Patriotism and the Memory of the Great War, J of Brit Stud; Women and the Ideology of War: Recruitment, Propaganda, and the Mobilization of Public Opinion in Britain, 1914-1918, Univ Calif, Berkeley; Sexual Violence and Family Honor: British Propaganda and International Law during the First World War, Am Hist Rev, 97. **CONTACT ADDRESS** Univ NH, Durham, NH, 03824. **EMAIL** nfg@hopper.unh.edu

GULLICKSON, GAY LINDA
PERSONAL Born 07/04/1943, Portland, OR **DISCIPLINE** WOMEN'S HISTORY, MODERN EUROPEAN HISTORY **EDUCATION** Pomona Col, BA, 65; Yale Univ, BD, 68, STM, 70; Univ NC, Chapel Hill, PhD(hist), 78. **CAREER** Teacher relig, Day Prospect Hill Sch, 69-72; asst prof hist, Skidmore Col, 78-81; Andrew Mellon fel, Univ Pittsburgh, 81-82; ASST PROF HIST, UNIV MD, 82-, Teaching assoc, Danforth Found, 80-. **MEMBERSHIPS** AHA; Social Sci Hist Asn. **RESEARCH** The French textile industry; rural industrialization; sexual divisions of labor and women's work. **SELECTED PUBLICATIONS** Auth, Property, Production, and Family in Neckarhausen, 1700-1870, Soc Hist, Vol 0018, 93; The Land and the Loom--Peasants and Profit in Northern France, 1680-1800, J Econ Hist, Vol 0054, 94; Industry and Politics in Rural France--Peasants of the Isere, 1870-1914, Am Hist Rev, Vol 0100, 95; Art and the French Commune--Imagining Paris after War and Revolution, Am Hist Rev, Vol 0101, 96; The Flour War--Gender, Class, and Community in Late Ancien-Regime French Society, J Interdisciplinary Hist, Vol 0027, 96; European Women and Preindustrial Craft, J Interdisciplinary Hist, Vol 0028, 97. **CONTACT ADDRESS** Univ Md, College Pk, MD, 20742.

GUMPERZ, JOHN J.
DISCIPLINE LINGUISTICS, ANTHROPOLOGY **EDUCATION** Univ Cincinnati, BA, 47; Univ Mich, PhD(Ger ling), 54. **CAREER** Instr ling, Cornell Univ, 52-54; from instr to assoc prof S Asian lang and ling, 56-67, PROF ANTHROP, UNIV CALIF, BERKELEY, 67-, Ford Found fel ling, India, 54-56; mem comt socioling, Soc Sci Res Coun, 66-73; Trainers of Teachers of Teachers comt, Berkeley sch bd, 69-71. **MEMBERSHIPS** Ling Soc Am; Am Anthrop Asn; Ling Soc India; AAAS. **RESEARCH** Sociolinguistics; linguistics and cognitive anthropology; applied linguistics. **SELECTED PUBLICATIONS** Auth, Treacherous Words--Gender and Power in Academic Assessment, Folia Linguistica, Vol 0030, 96. **CONTACT ADDRESS** Dept of Anthrop, Univ of Calif, 232 Kroeber Hall, Berkeley, CA, 94720.

GUNDERSHEIMER, W.L.
PERSONAL Born 04/07/1937, Frankfurt, Germany, m, 1963, 2 children **DISCIPLINE** HISTORY **EDUCATION** Amherst Univ, BA, 59; Harvard Univ, MA, 60, PhD, 63. **CAREER** Jr Fel, Soc Fels, Harvard Univ, 62-66; Asst Prof to Prof Hist, Univ Pa, 66-84, Dir, Ctr Ital Studies, 80-83, Dept Chair, 76-78; Dir, Folger Shakespeare Libr, 84-. **HONORS AND AWARDS** Order of the Star of Italian Solidarity, Am Philos Soc; Honorary doctorates from Amherst, Williams, Muhlensky, & Davidson Cols; Capitol Hill Community Achievement Award; recipient of numerous fellowships and grants. **MEMBERSHIPS** Medieval Acad; Renaissance Soc Am; Am Hist Asn. **RESEARCH** 15th & 16th century Italian cultural and intellectual history. **SELECTED PUBLICATIONS** Auth, The Italian Renaissance, Prentice-Hall, 65, repr, Univ Toronto Press, 94; Life and Works of Louis LeRoy, Droz, 66; French Humanism, 1470-1600, Macmillan, 69, Harper & Row, 70; Art and Life at the Court of Ercole 1 d'Este: The 'De triumphis religionis' of Giovanni Sabadino degli Arienti, Droz, 72; Ferrara: The Style of a Renaissance Despotism, Princeton Univ Press, 73; Ferrara estense: Lo stile del potere, Modena, Edizioni Panini, 88; author of numerous articles and reviews. **CONTACT ADDRESS** Folger Shakespeare Libr, 201 E. Capitol St. SE, Washington, DC, 20003. **EMAIL** gundersheimer@folger.edu

GUNLICKS, ARTHUR B.
PERSONAL Born 07/07/1936, North Platte, NE, m, 1962, 2 children **DISCIPLINE** COMPARATIVE POLITICS **EDUCATION** Univ of Denver, BA, 58; Univ of Freiburg, Germany, 58-59; Univ of Gottingen, Germany, 64-65; Georgetown Univ, PhD, 67. **CAREER** PROF OF POLITICAL SCI, UNIV OF RICHMOND. **HONORS AND AWARDS** Two Fulbright Res Grants; One Fulbright Travel Grant; Two German Acad Exchange Summer Grants. **MEMBERSHIPS** APSA; So Political Sci Asn; German Studies Asn; European Studies Asn; European Community Studies Asn; Confr Group on German Politics; AAUP. **RESEARCH** Western European politics; German politics; German federalism. **SELECTED PUBLICATIONS** Ed, Campaign & Party Finance in North America & Western Europe, Westview Press, 93; auth, Local Government in the German Federal System, Duke Univ Press, 86; auth, Local Government Reform & Reorganization: An International Perspective, 81. **CONTACT ADDRESS** Dept of Political Science, Univ of Richmond, Richmond, VA, 23173. **EMAIL** agunlick@richmond.edu

GUNTHER, GERALD
PERSONAL Born 05/26/1927, Germany, m, 1949, 2 children **DISCIPLINE** AMERICAN CONSTITUTIONAL LAW AND HISTORY **EDUCATION** Brooklyn Col, AB, 49; Columbia Univ, MA, 50; Harvard Univ, LLB, 53. **CAREER** Law clerk, Judge Learned Hand, 53-54 and Chief Justice Earl Warren, 54-55; from assoc prof to prof law, Sch Law, Columbia Univ, 56-62; prof, 62-72, WILLIAM NELSON CROMWELL PROF LAW, SCH LAW, STANFORD UNIV, 72-, Res dir, Inter-Law Sch Comn Const Simplification, 57-58; Guggenheim fel, 62-63; Fulbright lectr, Ghana, 69; fel, Ctr Advan Studies Behav Sci, 69-70, vis prof const law, Harvard Law Sch, 72-73; Nat Endowment for Humanities fel, 80-81. **HONORS AND AWARDS** Distinguished Alumnus Award, Brooklyn Col, 61. **MEMBER-**

SHIPS Fel Am Acad Arts & Sci; Am Philos Soc; AHA; Am Law Inst; Orgn Am Historians. **RESEARCH** Judicial biography. **SELECTED PUBLICATIONS** Auth, Learned Hand--Outstanding Copyright Judge--The 24th Annual Donald-C-Brace-Lecture, J Copyright Soc of USA, Vol 0041, 94; Objectivity and Hagiography in Judicial Biography--Transcript, NY Univ Law Rev, Vol 0070, 95; Contracted Biographies and Other Obstacles to Truth, NY Univ Law Rev, Vol 0070, 95; Members of the Warren-Court in Judicial Biography--Transcript, NY Univ Law Rev, Vol 0070, 95; Judge Hand, Learned: Examining the Life of an American Jurist--The Choices and Satisfactions of a Biographer, Proc of Am Philos Soc, Vol 0140, 96. **CONTACT ADDRESS** Sch of Law, Stanford Univ, Stanford, CA, 94305.

GUNZERATH, DAVID
DISCIPLINE MEDIA HISTORY **EDUCATION** La Salle Col, PABS, 81; Temple Univ, IAMA, 84, Univ Iowa, Phd, 97. **CAREER** Hist, Old Dominion Univ. **HONORS AND AWARDS** Donald and Geraldine Hedberg Foundation Fel Award. **MEMBERSHIPS** Broadcast Educ Asn; NATPE Educ Div; Popular Cult Asn; Speech Comm Asn. **RESEARCH** Media Industries and Institutions; Media Law and Policy; Television Programming; Marketing and Management; New Technologies; TV Criticism. **SELECTED PUBLICATIONS** Auth, Encyclopedia of Television, Fitzroy Dearborn, 97. **CONTACT ADDRESS** Old Dominion Univ, 4100 Powhatan Ave, Norfolk, VA, 23058. **EMAIL** DGunzera@odu.edu

GUPTA, BRIJEN KISHORE
PERSONAL Born 09/17/1929, Ferozpur, India, m, 1957, 3 children **DISCIPLINE** HISTORY, SOUTH ASIAN STUDIES **EDUCATION** Dayanand Col, India, BA, 52; Yale Univ, MA, 54; Univ Chicago, PhD, 58. **CAREER** Lectr hist & govt, 58-60, Southern Ill Univ; lectr Asian studies, 60-63, Victoria Univ, NZ; asst prof hist, 63-67, assoc prof, 67-69, Brooklyn Col; prof, 69-76, Univ Rochester; prof, 70-76, State Univ NY Col Brockport; sr fel & dir, res & develop, coun int & pub affairs, 76-; vis fel, 61-62, Inst Advan Studies, Australian Nat Univ; Carnegie Soc Sci Res Fund grant, NZ, 61-62; Am Philos Soc grant, 66-67; vis prof, Columbia Univ, 68-69; Swedenberg Found res grant, 71-72; Tarak Nath Das-Ram Mahun Roy lectr, Yale Univ, 75; NEH lectr, Univ Wis-Madison, 76; consult, UN Ctr Transnational Corps, 80-82. **MEMBERSHIPS** AHA; Assn Asian Studies; Indo-Brit Hist Soc. Overbrook fel, Yale Univ, 53-54; Found World Govt fel, 54-55; Univ & Asia Found fel, Univ Chicago,55-58; Rapporteur, Strategy for Peace Conf, Stanley Found, 77; NSF res grant, 78-80; Assn Asian Studies grant, 80-81 **RESEARCH** Indian science policy; comparative intellectual history; urban studies. **SELECTED PUBLICATIONS** Auth, Sirajuddaullah and the East India Company, 1756-57, E J Brill, 62 & 66; coauth, Indian and American Labor Legislations and Practices: A Comparative Analysis, Asia Publ House, 66; auth, India in English Fiction, 1800-1970, Scarecrow-Grolier, 73; art, The Working Class in Modern India, New Polit, 11/73; art, The Ethical System in Sankara and Swedenborg, Indian J Theol, 12/73; coauth, Learning About India: An Annotated Guide for the Nonspecialists, Univ NY Albany, 77; Small Business Development in the Inner City Area of Rochester, 2 vols, NY Coun on Int & Pub Affairs, 78; art, The Political Economy of North-South Relations: Studies in the Transfer of US Science and Technology, Nat Tech Info Serv, 81; auth, India, Amer Bibliographical Center and Clio Press, 84. **CONTACT ADDRESS** 226 Idlewood Rd, Rochester, NY, 14618.

GURVAL, ROBERT ALAN
PERSONAL Born 08/02/1958, Kingston, PA **DISCIPLINE** CLASSICS **EDUCATION** Brown Univ, BA, 80; Univ Calif Santa Barbara, MA, 82; Univ Calif Berkeley, PhD, 88. **CAREER** Lectr, 88-89; asst prof, Univ Ore, 89-90; asst prof, 90-96; ASSOC PROF, UCLA, 96-. **HONORS AND AWARDS** Fel, Am Acad at Rome, 96-97., Academic sen, 92-96; academic sen, gen edu fac adv comm, 94-95; acad sen, Legis Assembly repr, 91-92, 92-93; post-baccalaureate adv, 97-; undergrad adv, 91-92, 92-93, 95-96;, ch, co-ch, Undergrad Aff Comm, 91-92, 92-93, 95-96. **MEMBERSHIPS** APA; Am Numis Soc. **RESEARCH** Roman history; Latin literature; Roman coinage. **SELECTED PUBLICATIONS** Auth, Actium and Augustus, Mich, 96. **CONTACT ADDRESS** Dept of Classics, Univ Calif Los Angeles, Dodd 100, Los Angeles, CA, 90095-1417. **EMAIL** gurval@humnet.ucla.edu

GUSHEE, LAWRENCE
DISCIPLINE MUSIC **EDUCATION** Yale Univ, PhD. **CAREER** Prof emer, 77-, Univ IL Urgana Champaign. **RESEARCH** Medieval music in Europ libr(s); early hist of jazz and related musics. **SELECTED PUBLICATIONS** Auth, Nineteenth-century Origins of Jazz, Black Music Res, 94. **CONTACT ADDRESS** Dept of Music, Univ Illinois Urbana Champaign, E Gregory Dr, PO Box 52, Champaign, IL, 61820. **EMAIL** lgushee@uiuc.edu

GUSTAFSON, DAVID
PERSONAL Born 01/25/1942, Cokate, MN, m, 1964, 2 children **DISCIPLINE** CHURCH HISTORY **EDUCATION** Hamline Univ, BA, 64; M. Div Lutheran School of Theol, 68; Luther Seminary, Th Y, 73; Union Inst, PhD, 90. **CAREER** Lutheran Pastor, 68-98, Univ of St Thomas, St Paul, MN, 98-. **HONORS AND AWARDS** Concordia Hist Inst Book Award, 94. **MEMBERSHIPS** ASCH, LHC, AAR, Sixteenth Century Soc. **RESEARCH** American Religious History. **SELECTED PUBLICATIONS** Auth, The Church: Community of the Crucified or Community that Crucifies?, Lutheran Forum, 97; The ELCA and Ecumenism: Past, Present, and Future, Pieper Lectures in St Louis MO, 97; The ELCA: Its Past, Present, and Future, Logic, Eastertide, 96; A Quiet Week in the ELCA, Forum Letter, 95; Reflections on Bishop Chilstrom's Visit, Lutheran Forum, 95; Suggestions for a New Bishop, Lutheran Forum., 95; Review, A Speaking Life: The Legacy of John Keble, ed, Charles R. Henry, Church Hist, 97. **CONTACT ADDRESS** 5220 Oakley St., Duluth, MN, 55804. **EMAIL** DAGusto@aol.com

GUSTAFSON, MILTON ODELL
PERSONAL Born 11/20/1939, Minneapolis, MN, m, 1962, 2 children **DISCIPLINE** AMERICAN HISTORY **EDUCATION** Gustavus Adolphus Col, BA, 61; Univ Nebr, MA, 63, PhD, 66. **CAREER** Asst prof hist and int rels, Univ of the Americas, 66-67; diplomatic rec specialist, 67-71, CHIEF DIPLOMATIC BR, NAT ARCH, 71-, Lectr, Am Univ, 68; lectr, Univ Md, 69-73. **MEMBERSHIPS** Orgn Am Historians; AHA; Soc Hist Am Foreign Rels; Soc Am Archivists. **RESEARCH** United States diplomatic history. **SELECTED PUBLICATIONS** Auth, Seward Bargain--The Alaska Purchase from Russia, Prologue-Quart of Nat Arch, Vol 0026, 94. **CONTACT ADDRESS** 2706 Shawn Ct, Ft Washington, MD, 20744.

GUTCHEN, ROBERT M.
PERSONAL Born 01/25/1932, Antwerp, Belgium, m, 1955, 3 children **DISCIPLINE** MODERN HISTORY **EDUCATION** Columbia Univ, BS, 55, MA, 57, PhD(hist), 66. **CAREER** Lectr hist, Long Island Univ, 58-61, from instr to asst prof, 61-64; instr English hist, 64-65, from asst prof to assoc prof, 65-76, actg chmn dept, 66-67, asst dean col arts and sci, 66-68, chmn, Dept Hist, 68-71, PROF HIST, UNIV RI, 76-, CHAIRPERSON DEPT, 77-, Am Coun Educ fel, acad admin internship prog, Ind Univ, 67-68. **MEMBERSHIPS** AHA; Conf Brit Studies; AAUP. **RESEARCH** Nineteenth century British administrative history; English poor laws. **SELECTED PUBLICATIONS** Auth, The Victorian Post-Office--The Growth of a Bureaucracy, Am Hist Rev, Vol 0098, 93. **CONTACT ADDRESS** Dept of Hist, Univ of RI, Kingston, RI, 02881.

GUTEK, GERALD LEE
PERSONAL Born 07/10/1935, Streator, IL, m, 1965, 2 children **DISCIPLINE** HISTORY OF EDUCATION **EDUCATION** Univ Ill, Urbana, BA, 57, MA, 59, PhD(educ), 64. **CAREER** From instr to asst prof educ, 63-68, assoc prof found of educ, 68-72, chmn dept found of educ, 69-72, PROF HIST AND FOUND OF EDUC, LOYOLA UNIV CHICAGO, 72-, Am Philos Soc res grant, 68; partic, Foreign Policy Asn Proj Modernization in India, 69. **MEMBERSHIPS** Hist Educ Soc; Philos Educ Soc; Nat Coun Social Studies; Orgn Am Historians. **RESEARCH** History of the Pestalozzian Movement in the United States; educational theory. **SELECTED PUBLICATIONS** Auth, Social-Studies in Schools--A History of the Early Years, Am Hist Rev, Vol 0098, 93; Constitutional Literacy--A Core Curriculum for a Multicultural Nation, Am Hist Rev, Vol 0100, 95. **CONTACT ADDRESS** Found of Educ, Loyola Univ, Chicago, IL, 60611.

GUTIERREZ, RAMON A.
PERSONAL Born 04/19/1951, Albuquerque, NM **DISCIPLINE** LATIN AMERICAN HISTORY **EDUCATION** Univ New Mex, BA, 73; Univ Wisc Mad, MA, 75, PhD, 80. **CAREER** Assoc Chancellor, 96-, 82 to present, Univ California San Diego; 80-82, Pomona College; 74-80, Univ Wisc; 77-78, Inst Ntl de Antroplogia NM; 73-74, U Ntl del Altiplano Peru; 73, Cornell Univ; 72-73, UNM Andean Study Cen, Ecuador; 69-72, Univ New Mexico; 66-69, ST Pius HS NM; Consultant for numerous Institutions, Publications and TV Media; Grant Referee for numerous Foundations, Institutes and Councils; Journal Referee for numerous Reviews and Journals; Manuscript Referee for numerous Press Publications; Prize Referee on numerous committees and associations. **HONORS AND AWARDS** Ray A Billington Awd; Howard Francis Cline Prize; Caroline Bancroft Hist Prize; Herbert E Bolton Prize; Quincentennary of Discovery Prize; Alan Sharlin Prize; John Hope Franklin Awd; Bryce Wood Book Awd; Frederick Jackson Turner Prize; Jane A Rawley Prize; Herbert Herring Prize; AHAP-CB Best Book of the Year; AHACLAH Conference Prize; John D and Catherine MacArthur Foun Genius Prize; Herbert Herring Prize; Reginald Fisher Prize; Getty Cen HAH Sr Schl; Cushwa Cen SAC Fel; Rockefeller postdoc Fel; 2 CASBS Stanford Fel; 2 NEH Fel; Mellon Foun Fel; Haynes Foun Fel; Mex Mins Foreign Rel Fel; Danforth Grad Fel; Fulbright-Hayes Fel; NDEA Foreign Lang Fel; UNM Andean Stud Cen Schshp; Phi Beta Kappa Ntl Vis Prof; Paul Anthony Brick Lectr, U MO; UCSD Chanc Assoc Endowed Ch; PNM Ch Vis Prof U of NM; Stella Jo Morrisett Mem Lect U of OK; Ena H Thompson Dist Lectr, P College., NEH Ntl Council Mem, 94-2000; Dept of Interior, Ntl Pk Ser Adv Bd Mem, 95-99. **MEMBERSHIPS** ASA; OAH; UCHIAC; SHC; CCH; AAC; LSA; NMAH. **SELECTED PUBLICATIONS** Auth, American Society at the End of the Millennium, New Religious Movements, Columbia, U of Missouri Press, under review; Cuando Jesus Ilego las madres del maiz se fueron: Matrimonio sexualidad y poder en Nuevo Mexico, 1500-1846, Mexico, Fondo de la Cultrua Economica, 93; coed, Contested Eden: California Before the Goldrush, Berk, U of Cal Press, 98; ed, Mexican Home Alters, Albuquerque, U NM Press, 97; coauth, The Drama, of Diversity and Democracy: Higher Education and American Commitments, Wash DC, Assoc Amer Colleges and Univ's, 95; coauth, Liberal Learning and the Arts of Connection for the New Academy, Wash DC, Assoc of Amer College Univ, 95; coed, Encyclopedia of the North American Colonies, NY, Charles Scribner's and Sons, 93; auth, Charles Fletcher Lummis and the Orientalization of New Mexico, in: Hispanic Expressive Culture in New Mexico, ed, Francisco Lomeli, Albuquerque, U of NM Press, forthcoming; auth, Chicano History: Paradigm Shifts and Shifting Boundaries, in: Toward a New Paradigm for Chicano History, ed Refugio Rochin, Flint, Mich State U Press, forthcoming; auth, Hispanic Diaspora and Chicano Identity in the USA, in: Diversity of Knowledge and Unity of Science: The Case of Immigration and Diaspora's, ed VT Mudimbe, in press; auth, Crucifixion Slavery and Death: The Hermanos Penitentes of the Southwest, in: Over the Edge: Mapping Western Experiences, ed, Valerie Matsumoto, Blake Allmendinger, Berk, U of Cal Press, forthcoming; auth, Honor and Shame in the Barrio Streets: A Modern Code of Ethic, Cahiers Charles V, Paris, 97; The Hermanos Penitentes Their Alters Their History, Spirit Mag, 97; Introduction to Elsie Clews Parsons Pueblo Indian Religion, Lincoln, U of NE Press, 96; Historical and Social Science Research on Mexican Americans, in: Handbook of Research on Multicultural Education, ed, JA Banks, C McGee, NY, Macmillan Pub, 95. **CONTACT ADDRESS** Chancellor's Complex, Univ Calif San Diego, 9500 Gilman Dr, La Jolla, CA, 92093-0005. **EMAIL** rgutierrez@ucsd.edu

GUTMANN, AMY
PERSONAL Born 11/19/1949, New York, NY, m, 1 child **DISCIPLINE** POLITICAL SCIENCE **EDUCATION** Harvard Univ, BA, 71; London Sch of Econ, MSc, 72; Harvard Univ, PhD, 76. **CAREER** Prof, politics, Laurance S. Rockefeller Univ; Univ Ctr for Human Values, Princeton Univ. **HONORS AND AWARDS** Ralph Bunche Award, Am Polit Sci Asn; North Am Soc of Soc Philos award for best book; Tanner lect, Stanford Univ. **MEMBERSHIPS** APSA; APA. **RESEARCH** Moral and political philosophy; education; race, religion, gender and politics; ethics and public policy; ethics and the professions; democratic theory and practice; multiculturalism. **SELECTED PUBLICATIONS** Coauth, Color Conscious: The Political Morality of Race, Princeton Univ Pr, 96; coauth, Democracy and Disagreement, Harvard Univ Pr, 96; ed, A Matter of Interpretation: Federal Courts and the Law, Princeton Univ Pr, 97; ed, Work and Welfare, Princeton Univ Pr, 98; ed, Freedom of Association, Princeton Univ Pr, 98; ed, The Lives of Animals, Princeton Univ Pr, 99. **CONTACT ADDRESS** Univ Center for Human Values, Princeton Univ, 304 Louis Marx Hall, Princeton, NJ, 08540. **EMAIL** agutmann@princeton.edu

GUTMANN, JOSEPH
PERSONAL Born 08/17/1923, Wurzburg, Germany, m, 1953, 2 children **DISCIPLINE** ART HISTORY, ARCHEOLOGY **EDUCATION** Temple Univ, BS, 49; NY Univ, MA, 52; Hebrew Union Col, Ohio, PhD(medieval Jewish hist & art), 60. **CAREER** Assoc prof Jewish art hist, Hebrew Union Col, Ohio, 60-69; PROF MEDIEVAL CHRISTIAN ART, WAYNE STATE UNIV, 69-, Adj prof, Grad Sch, Univ Cincinnati, 61-66; mem adv bd, Wayne State Univ Press, 70-; Mem Found Jewish Cult grant, 71-72; fac grant-in-aid, Wayne State Univ, 71 and 73; consult, Spertus Mus Judaica, Ill, 71- and Choice Asn Col and Res Libr, 73; mem adv bd, Int Survey of Jewish Monuments of CAASAH, 77-. **MEMBERSHIPS** Art Asn Am; Cent Conf Am Rabbis; Soc Bibl Lit. **RESEARCH** Early Christian and byzantine art; medieval illuminated manuscripts; biblical archaeology. **SELECTED PUBLICATIONS** Auth, Inculturation and Christian Art--An Indian Perspective, J Ecumenical Stud, Vol 0029, 92; Jewish Historiography and Iconography in Early and Medieval Christianity, J Ecumenical Stud, Vol 0030, 93; Loeb, Mortiz, 'Abraham Urjella or the Struggle over Principle': A Reprint of a 19th-Century Story of a Jewish Immigrant in America, Am Jewish Hist, Vol 0083, 95. **CONTACT ADDRESS** Dept of Art/Art Hist, Wayne State Univ, Detroit, MI, 48202.

GUTMANN, MYRON P.
PERSONAL Born 11/04/1949, Chicago, IL, m, 1970 **DISCIPLINE** HISTORY, DEMOGRAPHY **EDUCATION** Columbia Univ, BA, 71; Princeton Univ, PhD(hist), 76. **CAREER** Res assoc demog, Univ Pa, 75-76; ASST PROF HIST, UNIV TEX, AUSTIN, 76-. **MEMBERSHIPS** AHA; Soc Sci Hist Asn; Pop Asn Am; Asn Hist Family. **RESEARCH** Economic and demographic history of early modern Europe; methodology of historic demography. **SELECTED PUBLICATIONS** Auth, Marriage and Migration on the Frontier, Marital Patterns in Texas, 1850-1910, Hist Mexicana, Vol 0042, 92; Land, Climate, and Settlement on the Texas Frontier, Southwestern Hist Quart, Vol 0099, 95; Small-Town Communities in The Counties of Dalhem and Limburg 16th-18th Centuries--Origins, Structures, Evolution, Am Hist Rev, Vol 0101, 96; The Social-

Context of Child-Mortality in the American Southwest, J Interdisciplinary Hist, Vol 0026, 96; The Shape of Texas--Maps as Metaphors, Southwestern Hist Quart, Vol 0100, 97; A School for the Social-Science--From Section-6 to the Ecole-Des-Hautes-Etudes-En-Sciences-Sociales, J Interdisciplinary Hist, Vol 0028, 98. **CONTACT ADDRESS** Dept of Hist, Univ of Texas, Austin, TX, 78712.

GUTOWSKI, CAROLYN
PERSONAL Pittsburgh, PA **DISCIPLINE** HUMAN SERVICES **EDUCATION** LaRoche Coll, BA, 69; Duquesne Univ, MAT, 73; Walden Univ, PhD, 89. **CAREER** Adj prof, Mary-Mount Univ, 61-; teacher, Pittsburgh parochial schs, 61-; founder, dir, Bonaventure Soc Svcs Ctr, 76-80; prof coord, Ctr App Res and the Apostolate, 87-88; prog coord Nat Inst for the Family, 80-87; EXEC DIR, ADVISORY NEIGHBORHOOD COMN 3-C, 92-. **MEMBERSHIPS** Am Acad Rel; Am Soc Aging; Environ Alliance Senior Involvement; N Am Coalittion Rel & Ecology (NACRE). **RESEARCH** Grandparenting; spirituality and aging. **SELECTED PUBLICATIONS** Auth, Grandparents are Forever, Paulist Press, 94; auth, The Regenerative Role of Grandparents, AARP/Cornell Univ, 91; auth, Grandparents are Forever, Catholic Woman, Sept 94. **CONTACT ADDRESS** 8101 Connecticut Ave, N410, Chevy Chase, MD, 20815.

GUTTMANN, ALLEN
DISCIPLINE AMERICAN STUDIES **EDUCATION** Univ MN, PhD, 61. **CAREER** Prof, Amherst Col, 59; coed, Olympika. **SELECTED PUBLICATIONS** Auth, The Wound in the Heart: America and the Spanish Civil War, 62; From Ritual to Record: The Nature of Modern Sports, 78; Games and Empires, 94; The Erotic in Sports, 96. **CONTACT ADDRESS** Amherst Col, Amherst, MA, 01002-5000.

GUTZWILLER, KATHRYN
PERSONAL Born 09/25/1948, Hinton, WV, m, 1971, 1 child **DISCIPLINE** CLASSICS **EDUCATION** Marshall Univ, BA, 70; Bryn Mawr Col, MA, 71; Univ Wis, Madison, PhD, 77. **CAREER** Vis lect, Univ Mass, Amherst, 77-78; asst prof, Univ Cincinnati, 78-85, asst to assoc prof, Case WEstern Univ, 86-89; assoc to Prof, Univ Cincinnati, 89-. **HONORS AND AWARDS** Gildersleeve Award **MEMBERSHIPS** Am Phil Asn; Class Asn of Middle West & South **RESEARCH** Greek poetry, ; women in intiquity; genre theory. **SELECTED PUBLICATIONS** Auth, Poetic Garlands: Hellenistic Epigrams in Context, Univ Calif Press, 98; auth, Theocritus' Pastoral Analogies, Univ Wis Press, 91; auth, Studies in the Hellenistic Epyllion, , 81. **CONTACT ADDRESS** Dept Classics, Univ of Cincinnati, Cincinnati, OH, 45221-0226. **EMAIL** kathryn.gutzwiller@uc.edu

GUY, DONNA JAY
PERSONAL Cambridge, MA **DISCIPLINE** HISTORY **EDUCATION** Brandeis Univ, BA, 67; Ind Univ, AM, 69, PhD(hist), 73. **CAREER** Instr hist, 72-73, asst prof, 73-80, ASSOC PROF HIST, UNIV ARIZ, 80-, Bk rev ed, Hispanic Am Hist Rev, 75-80; Foreign Area fel, 70-72; Midwest Consortium for Int Activ fel, 70-71; Fulbright Hays res grant, 78; Fulbright Hays sr lectr, Great Britain, 82-83. **MEMBERSHIPS** AHA; Latin Am Studies Asn; Conf Latin Am Hist. **RESEARCH** Argentine economic history; entrepreneurial history, womens history. **SELECTED PUBLICATIONS** Auth, Between Civilization and Barbarism--Women, Nation, and Literary Culture in Modern Argentina, Hispamerica-Rev de Lit, Vol 0022, 93; Oro-Blanco--Cotton, Technology, and Family Labor in 19th-Century Argentina, Americas, Vol 0049, 93; The Hour of Eugenics, Race, Gender, and Nation in Latin-America, Americas, Vol 0050, 93; Gay and Lesbian Themes in Latin-American Writing, Hisp Am Hist Rev, Vol 0073, 93; Future-Directions in Latin-American Gender History: Paper Presented to the Conference on Latin-American History, Jan 1994, Americas, Vol 0051, 94; Woman and Crisis, Responses to the World Recession, Hisp Am Hist Rev, Vol 0075, 95; Revolutionizing Motherhood--The Mothers of The Plaza-De-Mayo, Am Hist Rev, Vol 0100, 95; Researching Women in Latin-America and The Caribbean, Americas, Vol 0051, 95; Unequal Burden, Economic Crises, Persistent Poverty, and Womens Work, Hisp Am Hist Rev, Vol 0075, 95; Where Cultures Meet, Frontiers in Latin-American History, Americas, Vol 0051, 95; Latin-American Male Homosexualities, Hisp Am Hist Rev, Vol 0077, 97; How Latin-America Fell Behind--Essays on the Economic Histories of Brazil and Mexico, 1800-1914, J Interdisciplinary Hist, Vol 0028, 98. **CONTACT ADDRESS** Dept of Hist Soc Sci, Univ of Ariz, 1 University of Az, Tucson, AZ, 85721-0001.

GUY, FRED
DISCIPLINE ANCIENT PHILOSOPHY **EDUCATION** Auburn Univ, BA, Univ Ga, MA, PhD. **CAREER** Assoc Prof, Univ Baltimore, 77-; Chairman, dept hist & philos, Univ Baltimore, 77-92; Codir, Hoffberger Ctr Professional Ethics, 91-94; Dir, Hoffberger Ctr Professional Ethics, 91-94. **MEMBERSHIPS** Asn Practical & Professional Ethics; Am Asn Philos Tchrs; Am Philos Asn; Asn Advancement Community Col Tchrs; Soc Values Inquiry; Soc Business Ethics. **SELECTED PUBLICATIONS** Auth, The Role of Praxis Today, Jour Value Inquiry, 91; auth, Ethics in the Workplace: Top to Bottom, Chesapeake Human Resource Asn, 97; auth, Personal, Professional, and Business Ethics, Woods Memorial Presbyterian Church, 97; auth, An Ethical Life in Today's World, Suburban Club Baltimore County, 97. **CONTACT ADDRESS** Univ Baltimore, 1420 N. Charles Street, Baltimore, MD, 21201.

GUY, MARY E.
PERSONAL Born 12/02/1947, Carlinville, IL, d **DISCIPLINE** POLITICAL SCIENCE **EDUCATION** Jacksonville Univ, 69; Univ Fla, Master Rehab Counseling, 70; Univ SC, MA, 76, PhD, 81. **CAREER** Psychologist, SC Dept Mental Health, 73-82; Prof, Univ Ala - Birmingham, 82-97; Pres, Am Soc Public Admin, 97-98; Jerry Collins Prof Public Admin, Fla State Univ, 97-. **HONORS AND AWARDS** Distinguished Res Award, Am Soc Public Admin, 91; Dimock Award, Am Soc Public Admin, 94; Fac Mentor Award, Am Polit Sci Asn, 96. **MEMBERSHIPS** Am Soc Public Admin; Am Polit Sci Asn; Acad Management. **RESEARCH** Public management; American government; gender & workplace issues. **SELECTED PUBLICATIONS** Auth, Professionals in Organizations, 85; From Organizational Decline to Organizational Renewal, 89; Ethical Decision Making in Everyday Work Situations, 90; Women and Men of the States, 92. **CONTACT ADDRESS** Askew Sch Public Admin & Policy, Florida State Univ, Tallahassee, FL, 32306-2250.

GUZMAN, GREGORY G.
PERSONAL Born 12/25/1939, Stevens Point, WI, m, 1964, 3 children **DISCIPLINE** ANCIENT & MEDIEVAL EUROPEAN HISTORY **EDUCATION** Wis State Univ, Stevens Point, BS, 63; Univ Pittsburgh, MA, 64; Univ Cincinnati, PhD(hist), 68. **CAREER** From asst prof to full prof, 67-77, prof hist, Bradley Univ, 77-, NDEA Fulbright-Hays grant, Southeast Asia, 70; fel, Intercult Studies Prog, East-West Ctr, 72. **HONORS AND AWARDS** Award for Professional Excellence, Bradley Univ, 77. **MEMBERSHIPS** Midwest Medieval Conf; Medieval Acad Am. **RESEARCH** Thirteenth century papal missions to the Mongols; Simon of Saint-Quentin; Vincent of Beauvais and his encyclopedia; Speculum Historiale. **SELECTED PUBLICATIONS** Auth, The Cambron Manuscript of the Speculum Historiale, Manuscripta, XIII: 95-104; Simon of Saint-Quentin and the Dominican Mission to the Mongol Baiju: A Reappraisal, Speculum, LXVI: 232-249; Simon of Saint-Quentin as Historian of the Mongols and Seljuk Turks, Medievalia et Humanistica, new ser, 3:155-178; coauth, Origins of Tomorrow (2 vols), Holbrook, 73; auth, The Encyclopedist Vincent of Beauvais and his Mongol Extracts from John of Plano Carpini and Simon of Saint-Quentin, Speculum, XLIX: 287-307; A Growing Tabulation of Vincent of Beauvaus' Speculum Historiale Manuscripts, Scriptorium, XXIX: 122-125; ed, Vincent of Beauvais Newsletter, 76-; Were the Barbarians a Negative or Positive Factor in Ancient & Medieval History, in The Historian, L, 558-72, 88; Vincent of Beauvais' Epistola actoris ad regem Ludoricum: A Critical Analysis and a Critical Editiom, in Vincent Beauvais: Intentious et Receptious d'une oevre encyclopedique au Moyen Age, ed by M. Paulmia-Foucart, S. O. Lusignam, & A. Nadeau, Paris & Montreal, 1990, pp 57-85; Report of Mongol Cannabilism in the Thirteenth-Century Latin Source: Oriental Fact or Western Fiction?, in Discovering New Worlds: Essays on Medieval Exploration and Immigration, ed by Scott D. Westrem, NY, 91, pp 31-68; The Testimony of Medieval Dominicain Concerning Vincent Beauvain, in Latin et Compilator: Vincent de Beauvain, frere precheur un intellectuel et son milieu au XIIIe riecle, ed by S. Lusignam & M. Paulmier-Foucart, Royarmt, 96, pp 303-326; European Clerical Envoys to the Mongols: reports of Western Merchants in Eastern Europe and Central Asia, 1231-1255, in Journal of Medieval Hist, XXII, 53-69, 96, Assoc ed, Medieval Travel, Trade, & Exploration: An Encyclopedia (525-1492), Garland Press, NY, forthcoming 98. **CONTACT ADDRESS** Dept of Hist, Bradley Univ, 1501 W Bradley Ave, Peoria, IL, 61625-0002. **EMAIL** ggg@bradley.bradley.edu

GWYN, ALEXANDRA
PERSONAL Born 05/17/1935, St. John's, NF, Canada **DISCIPLINE** HISTORY **EDUCATION** Dalhousie Univ, BA, 55; DLitt(hon), Memorial Univ Nfld, 91. **CAREER** Infor off, Nat Gallery Can, 57-61; freelance journalist & auth, 61-; Ottawa ed, Saturday Night Mag, 75-80. **HONORS AND AWARDS** Found Arts & Lett awards, 77, 78, 94; Nat Mag Awards, 79, 85; Gov Gen Award Non-fiction, 84; Nfld & Labrador Arts Coun Hall Honour, 96. **MEMBERSHIPS** Dir, PEN Can, 93-. **SELECTED PUBLICATIONS** Auth, The Private Capital: Ambition and Love in the Age of Macdonald and Laurier, 84; auth, Tapestry of War: A Private View of Canadians in the Great War, 92. **CONTACT ADDRESS** 300 Carlton St, Toronto, ON, M5A 2L5.

GWYN, JULIAN
PERSONAL Born 03/30/1937, Birmingham, England, m, 1961, 5 children **DISCIPLINE** MODERN HISTORY **EDUCATION** Loyola Col Montreal, BA, 56; McGill Univ, MA, 58; Oxford Univ, BLitt, 61, DPhil(hist), 71. **CAREER** Lectr, 61-63, from asst prof to assoc prof, 63-78, PROF HIST, UNIV OTTAWA, 78-, Sessional lectr, Carleton Univ, 71-72; Can Coun fel, 71-73 and 75-77; asst ed, Hist Sociale-Social Hist, 72-. **MEMBERSHIPS** Soc Nautical Res. **RESEARCH** Eighteenth century British and Irish history; American colonial and economic history; British naval history. **SELECTED PUBLICATIONS** Auth, Wealth Distribution in Nova-Scotia During the Confederation Era, 1851 and 1871, Can Hist Rev, Vol 0073, 92; Maritime Capital--The Shipping Industry in Atlantic Canada, 1820-1914, Histoire Sociale-Soc Hist, Vol 0026, 93; Cole, Robert World--Agriculture and Society in Early Maryland, Histoire Sociale-Soc Hist, Vol 0027, 94; The Insatiable Earl--A Life of Montagu, John, 4th Earl of Sandwich, 1718-1792, Am Hist Rev, Vol 0100, 95; Surgeons, Smallpox and the Poor--A History of Medicine and Social Conditions in Nova-Scotia, 1749-1799, Histoire Sociale-Soc Hist, Vol 0028, 95; While the Women Only Wept--Loyalist Refugee Women in Eastern Ontario, Histoire Sociale-Soc Hist, Vol 0029, 96; Warpaths--Invasions of North-America, Int Hist Rev, Vol 0018, 96; Anatomy of a Naval Disaster--The 1746 French Naval Expedition to North-America, William and Mary Quart, Vol 0054, 97. **CONTACT ADDRESS** Dept of Hist, Univ of Ottawa, Ottawa, ON, K1N 6N5.

GYTHIEL, ANTHONY P.
DISCIPLINE WESTERN CIVILIZATION I, THE MIDDLE AGES, THE RENAISSANCE, THE REFORMATION. **EDUCATION** Univ Detroit, PhD, 71. **CAREER** Dept Hist, Wichita State Univ **HONORS AND AWARDS** Regents award for excellence in tchg; Wichita State Univ, 76; Emory Lindquist excellence in hon(s), 93; John Barrier distinguished tchg award; summer grants, (6) NEH; internal grants (7), Wichita State Univ. **RESEARCH** Trinitarian experience and vision in biblical and patristic tradition. **SELECTED PUBLICATIONS** Transl, seven bk(s) that deal with the theology of the early Christian East. **CONTACT ADDRESS** Dept of Hist, Wichita State Univ, 1845 Fairmont, Wichita, KS, 67260-0062.

GYUG, RICHARD F.
DISCIPLINE MEDIEVAL LITURGY, RELIGION AND SOCIETY **EDUCATION** Univ Toronto, PhD. **CAREER** Dir, grad stud; assoc prof, Fordham Univ. **RESEARCH** Studying the liturgical manuscripts of the Beneventan region. **SELECTED PUBLICATIONS** Auth, Missale ragusinum: The Missal of Dubrovnik, 90; The Diocese of Barcelona during the Black Death: The Register 'Notule communium' 15, 94; The Pontificals of Monte Cassino, L'Eta dell'abate Desiderio, 92. **CONTACT ADDRESS** Dept of Hist, Fordham Univ, 113 W 60th St, New York, NY, 10023.

H

HAAR, JAMES
PERSONAL Born 07/04/1929, St. Louis, MO **DISCIPLINE** HISTORY OF MUSIC **EDUCATION** Harvard Univ, BA, 50, PhD(music), 61; Univ NC, MA, 54. **CAREER** From instr to asst prof music, Harvard Univ, 60-67; assoc prof, Univ Pa, 67-69; prof, NY Univ, 69-78; W R KENAN JR PROF MUSIC, UNIV NC, 78-, Villa I Tatti fel music, 65; Am Coun Learned Soc fel, 73. **MEMBERSHIPS** Am Musicol Soc (vpres, 72-74, pres, 76-78); Renaissance Soc Am. **RESEARCH** Italian Madrigal; history of theory; humanism and music. **SELECTED PUBLICATIONS** Ed, Cimello, Giovanthomaso as Madrigalist, Studi Musicali, Vol 0022, 93; Italian Music Incunabula--Printers and Type, Romance Philol, Vol 0048, 94; Classicism and Mannerism in 16th-Century Music, Int Rev of Aesthet and Sociol of Mus, Vol 0025, 94; A Correspondence of Renaissance Musicians, Renaissance 0048, 95; Palestrina as Historicist--The 2 L'homme Arme' Masses, J Royal Mus Asn, Vol 0121, 96; The Squarcialupi Codex--Manuscript-Mediceo-Palatino-87, Biblioteca-Laurenziana in Florence, A Facsimile Ed Quart, Vol 0047, 94; Musical Humanism and Its Legacy--Essays in Honor of Palisca, Claude, V., Notes, Vol 0050, 94; The Birth of Opera, Early Mus, Vol 0022, 94; The Court-Musicians in Florence during the Principate of the Medici, with a Reconstruction of the Artistic Establishment, Renaissance Quart, Vol, J Am Musicol Soc, Vol 0049, 96; Mourning into Joy--Music, Raphael, and Cecilia, Saint, Renaissance Quart, Vol 0050, 97; The Rise of European Music, 1380-1500, Renaissance Quart, Vol 0050, 97. **CONTACT ADDRESS** Dept of Music, Univ of NC, Chapel Hill, NC, 27514.

HAARBAUER, DON WARD
PERSONAL Born 09/17/1940, Charleroi, PA, m, 1964, 2 children **DISCIPLINE** THEATRE HISTORY **EDUCATION** Univ Ala, Tuscaloosa, BS, 62, MA, 65; Univ Wis, Madison PhD(theatre), 73. **CAREER** Asst prof speech & theatre, 68-73, asst dean sch humanities, 73-75, asst prof theatre, 73-77, chmn performing arts, 73-81, assoc prof, 77-80, prof theatre, Univ Ala, Birmingham, 80-, assoc dean sch arts & humanities, 81-, dir, Horn in the West, Boone, NC, 67-71. **MEMBERSHIPS** Southeastern Theatre Conf (admin vpres, 77-79, vpres, 79-80, pres, 80-81). **RESEARCH** Pre-twentieth century English theatre. **SELECTED PUBLICATIONS** Auth, The Birmingham theatres of Frank O'Brien, Southern Theatre, summer 77. **CONTACT ADDRESS** Univ of Alabama, 301 Humanities Bldg, Birmingham, AL, 35294-1260. **EMAIL** whaar@uab.edu

HAAS, ARTHUR G.
DISCIPLINE HISTORY **EDUCATION** Univ Chicago, PhD. **CAREER** Prof. **SELECTED PUBLICATIONS** Auth, Metternich, Reorganization and Nationality 1813-1818, Univ Tennessee. **CONTACT ADDRESS** Dept of History, Knoxville, TN, 37996.

HAAS, PETER J.
PERSONAL Born 11/29/1947, Detroit, MI, m, 1971, 3 children **DISCIPLINE** HISTORY OF RELIGIONS AND JUDAISM **EDUCATION** Univ Mich, BA, 70; Hebrew Union Col, MAHL, 74; Brown Univ, PhD, 80. **CAREER** Asst prof, Vanderbilt Univ, 80-88; assoc prof, Vanderbilt Univ, 88-. **HONORS AND AWARDS** Fel, sci and soc, Robert Penn Warren Ctr, Vanderbilt Univ, 94; Lilly endow teaching fel, 95; Templeton Sci Relig course award, 97. **MEMBERSHIPS** AAR; SBL; Asn of Jewish Studies; Western Jewish Studies Asn; Central Conf of Amer Rabbis Jewish Law Asn. **RESEARCH** Jewish ethics; Rhetoric of Jewish ethics; Science and religion. **SELECTED PUBLICATIONS** Auth, Responsa: Literary History of a Rabbinic Genre, Atlanta, Scholar Press, Semeia Studies, 96; ed, Recovering the Role of Women: Power and Authority in Rabbinic Jewish Society, Atlanta, Scholar Press, 92; article, The sacred and the Mundane: The Message of Leviticus, The Christ Century, 114, 27, 877-882, 8 oct, 97; rev essay, A Time to Kill and a Time to Heal, Jews, Medicine and Medical Society, Menorah Rev, 38, 3-4, fall, 96; rev essay, Who Do You Say I Am?, A Rabbi Talks with Jesus, Menorah Rev, 37, 1-2, spring/summer, 96; article, The Emergence of Rabbinic Legal Rhetoric: The Sheelot Uteshuvot Genre, Jewish Law Asn Studies, VIII, Atlanta, Scholar Press, 55-63, 96; article, What We Know Today that We Didn't Know Fifty Years Ago: Fifty Years of Holocaust Scholarship, CCAR Jour, 1-15, fall, 95; article, Nineteenth Century Science and the Formation of Nazi Policy, The United Theol Sem Jour of Theol, XCIX, 6-30, 95; article, How to Develop the Moral Personality: Immanuel Etke's Rabbi Israel Salanter and the Musar Movement: Seeking the Torah of Truth, Menorah Rev, 35, 6-7, fall, 95; article, The Quest for Hebrew Bible Ethics: A Jewish Response, Ethics and Politics in the Hebrew Bible, Semeia, 66, 151-159, 95. **CONTACT ADDRESS** Religious Studies Dept., Vanderbilt Univ, Box 1556, Nashville, TN, 37235. **EMAIL** peter.j.haas@vanderbilt.edu

HABEL, DOROTHY
DISCIPLINE ART **EDUCATION** Univ Mich, PhD, 77. **CAREER** Assoc prof. **HONORS AND AWARDS** Alumni Outstanding Tchg Awd, 85. **SELECTED PUBLICATIONS** Auth, Architects and Clods: The Emergence of Planning in the Context of Palace Architecture in Seventeenth-Century Rome, Pa State Univ, 93; The Projected Palazzo Chigi al Corso and S. Maria in Via Lata: The Palace-Church Component of Alexander VIIs Program for the Corso, 91; Alexander VII and The Private Builder, Jour Soc Archit Hist, 90. **CONTACT ADDRESS** Dept of Art, Knoxville, TN, 37996.

HABER, CAROLE
DISCIPLINE AMERICAN HISTORY, MEDICAL, SOCIAL, AND FAMILY HISTORY, VICTORIAN CULTURE **EDUCATION** Univ PA, PhD, 79. **CAREER** Prof, ch, dept Hist, Univ NC, Charlotte; exec bd, Behav and Soc Sci Sect, Gerontological Soc Am. **MEMBERSHIPS** Gerontological Soc Am. **RESEARCH** Old age; insanity; death. **SELECTED PUBLICATIONS** Auth, Witches, Widows, Wives and Workers: The Historiography of Elderly Women in America, in Jean M. Coyle, ed, Handbook on Women and Aging, Greenwood Press. **CONTACT ADDRESS** Charlotte, NC, 28223-0001.

HABER, SAMUEL
PERSONAL Born 05/05/1928, New York, NY, m, 1949, 3 children **DISCIPLINE** UNITED STATES HISTORY **EDUCATION** Univ Calif, AB, 52, MA, 53, PhD, 61. **CAREER** Asst prof US Hist, Univ Del, 61-65; asst prof, 65-67, from assoc prof to prof US History, Univ Calif, Berkeley, 67-95; prof grad school, 95-. **RESEARCH** American intellectual history. **SELECTED PUBLICATIONS** Auth, Efficiency and Uplift, Univ Chicago, 64; contribr, The professions and higher education, an historical analysis, In: Higher Education and the Labor Market, 73; The Quest for Authority and Honor in the American Professions, 1750-1900, Univ Chicago, 91. **CONTACT ADDRESS** Dept of History, Univ of California, Berekely, 2321 Dwinelle Hall, Berkeley, CA, 94720-2551. **EMAIL** zanvil@socratesberkeley.edu

HACKENBURG, MICHAEL
DISCIPLINE HISTORY **EDUCATION** Wichita St Univ, BA, 69; Univ Calif, Berkeley, MLS, 73, PhD, 83. **CAREER** Asst prof, librnshp, Univ Chicago; current, PARTNER, BOLERIUM BOOKS, SAN FRANCISCO. **MEMBERSHIPS** Am Antiquarian Soc **RESEARCH** Subscription publishing; Underground Railroad; Robert Sears of NY. **SELECTED PUBLICATIONS** Auth, Hawking Subscription Books in 1870: A Salesman's Prospectus from Western Pennsylvania, PBSA 78, 84; ed & auth, The Subscription Publishing Network in Nineteenth- Century America, in Getting the Books Out: Papers of the Chicago Conference on the Book in the 19th-Century America, Lib Congress, 87. **CONTACT ADDRESS** Bolerium Books, 2141 Mission, Ste 300, San Francisco, CA, 94110.

HACKETT, DAVID ANDREW
PERSONAL Born 01/29/1940, Rensselaer, IN, m, 1974, 3 children **DISCIPLINE** EUROPEAN HISTORY **EDUCATION** Earlham Col, BA, 62; Univ Wis, MA, 65, PhD(hist), 71. **CAREER** Asst prof hist, Kans State Col, Pittsburg, 68-71; asst prof hist, 71-, chemn, Univ Tex, El Paso, 96- **HONORS AND AWARDS** Chancellor's Award for Outstanding Teaching; Fulbright, Univ Munich, 67-68; Fulbright, Ger, 80 & 93; DAAD Fellowship, 84. **MEMBERSHIPS** AHA; Western Ger Studies Asn. **RESEARCH** Germany-Weimar & Nazi period; electoral behavior; Holocaust. **SELECTED PUBLICATIONS** Ed & transl, The Buchenwald Report, Westview Press, 95; ed, Der Buchenwald Report, C.H. Beck, 96; Buchenwald: Symbol and Metaphor for the Changing Political Culture of East Germany, Stud in GDR Culture and Soc, Univ Press Am, 96. **CONTACT ADDRESS** Dept of History, Univ Texas, El Paso, 500 W University Ave, El Paso, TX, 79968-0532. **EMAIL** dhackett@utep.edu

HACKETT, DAVID H.
DISCIPLINE AMERICAN RELIGIOUS HISTORY, SOCIOLOGY OF RELIGION **EDUCATION** Emory Univ, PhD, 86. **CAREER** Assoc prof. **RESEARCH** Gender and American culture, American catholicism. **SELECTED PUBLICATIONS** Auth, Religion and American Culture: A Reader, Routledge, 95; Gender and Religion in American Culture, 1870-1930, Rel and Amer Cult, 95; The Silent Dialogue: Zen Letters to a Trappist Monk, Continuum, 96. **CONTACT ADDRESS** Dept of Rel, Univ Fla, 226 Tigert Hall, Gainesville, FL, 32611. **EMAIL** dhackett@religion.ufl.edu

HACKMANN, WILLIAM KENT
PERSONAL Born 08/12/1937, Denver, CO, m, 1960, 2 children **DISCIPLINE** ENGLISH AND MODERN EUROPEAN HISTORY **EDUCATION** Yale Univ, BA, 59; Univ Mich, MA, 62, PhD(hist), 69. **CAREER** Teaching fel hist, Univ Mich, 62-65; instr, Muskingum Col, 65-67, col archivist, 66-67; from asst prof to assoc prof hist, 67-77, PROF HIST, UNIV IDAHO, 77-, Bus mgr, Albion, 69-73. **MEMBERSHIPS** Conf Brit Studies; AHA; Selden Soc Brit Mus Soc; Am Soc Eighteenth-Century Studies. **RESEARCH** British amphibious operations on the French coast in the eighteenth century. **SELECTED PUBLICATIONS** Auth, British Politics and Society from Walpole to Pitt, 1742-1789, Albion, Vol 0025, 93; Pitt, William, Earl of Chatham 1708-1778--A Bibliography, Albion, Vol 0026, 94; Bate, R. B. of the Poultry, 1782-1847--The Life and Times of a Scientific Instrument Maker, Isis, Vol 0086, 95. **CONTACT ADDRESS** Dept of Hist, Univ Idaho, Moscow, ID, 83843.

HADDAD, GLADYS
PERSONAL Born 09/12/1930, Cleveland, OH, s **DISCIPLINE** AMERICAN STUDIES **EDUCATION** Allegheny Col, BA, 52; Case Western Reserve Univ, MA, 61; Lake Erie Col, BFA, 74; Case Western Reserve Univ, PhD, 80. **CAREER** Prof, dean, exec asst to pres, Lake Erie Col, 63-89; prof, dir Studies Symposia, Case Western Reserve Univ, 91-. **HONORS AND AWARDS** Biographical entries in Who's Who in the Midwest, 79-,Who's Who of Am Women, 79-, Two Thousand Notable Am Women, 93-,Who's Who in Am Educ, 95-,Who's Who in the World, 95-; Grad Alumni Res Grant, Case Western Reserve Univ, 79; Nat Forum: Am Coun on Educ Nat Idnetification Progr for the Advancement of Women in Higher Educ, 81; Rockefeller Res Grant, 83; Am Asn for State and Local Hist Cert of Commendation Award for Western Reserve Studies Symposium/ Western Reserve Studies: A J of Regional Hist and Cult, 88; Am Asn for State and Local Hist Grant-in Aid for Anthology of Western Reserve Lit, 88; Northern Ohio Live Achievement Award, 91; Nat Endowment for the Hums, Vassar Col, 93; Flora Stone Mather Alumnae Asn Grant, 94; Nat Television Broadcasting Silver Telly Highest Award for Documentary Video Samuel Mather: Vision, Leadership, Generosity, 95; Case Western Reserve Univ Fel, 96; Ohio Hums Coun Grant for film script, 96. **MEMBERSHIPS** Am Studies Asn; Great Lakes Am Studies Asn; Ohio Hist Soc. **RESEARCH** Regional Studies: History, literature, and art; Women's Studies: biography. **SELECTED PUBLICATIONS** Auth, Early Western Reserve Impressions: The Surveyor, The Artist, The Land Speculator, in Mapping the Land: Western Reserve Scapes and Shapes, Western Reserve Studies Symposium, 92; Interpreters of the Western Reserve: William Sommer, Henry Keller, Frank Wilcox, in Cleveland As a Center of Regional Am Art, Cleveland Artist Found, 93; A Brief History of Cleveland's Fortnightly Musical Club, in Centennial Program Book, 94; Samuel Mather: Vision, Leadership, Generosity, a Video Documentary, Dedication-Samuel Mather Pavilion, Univ Hospitals, 94; Samuel and Flora Stone Mather: Partners in Philanthropy, a Video Documentary, Western Reserve Studies Symposium, 95; Laukhoff's Book Store: Cleveland's Literary and Artistic Landmark, in Cleveland's Artistic Heritage, Cleveland's Artists Found, 96; Laukhoff's Book Store of Cleveland: An Epilogue, Northern Ohio Bibliophilic Soc, 97; Flora Stone Mather: A Legacy of Stewardship, aVideo Documentary, Col of Arts and Scis, Case Western Reserve Univ, 97; rev, Converting the West: A Biography of Narcissa Whitman, The Western Hist Soc Quart, XXIII, 92. **CONTACT ADDRESS** Dept of American Studies, Case Western Reserve Univ, Cleveland, OH, 44106. **EMAIL** qmh3@po.cwru.edu

HADDAD, MAHMOUD
DISCIPLINE MODERN MIDDLE EASTERN HISTORY **EDUCATION** Amer Univ Beirut, BA, 70; Columbia Univ, PhD, 89. **CAREER** Assoc prof. **RESEARCH** Modern Islamic nationalism. **SELECTED PUBLICATIONS** Auth, The Rise of Arab Nationalism Reconsidered, Intl Jour Middle Eastern Stud, 94. **CONTACT ADDRESS** Dept of Hist, Columbia Col, New York, 2960 Broadway, New York, NY, 10027-6902.

HADDAD, ROBERT MITCHELL
PERSONAL Born 10/10/1930, New York, NY, m, 1964, 4 children **DISCIPLINE** ISLAMIC HISTORY **EDUCATION** Univ Pittsburgh, BS, 52; Univ Mich, MA, 54; Harvard Univ, PhD(hist, Mid Eastern studies), 65. **CAREER** Lectr nonwestern studies, Amherst, Smith, Mt Holyoke Cols & Univ Mass, 60-63; lectr hist, 63-65, asst prof, 65-68, assoc prof hist & relig, 68-73, prof hist & relig, 73- 82; Sophia Smith Prof hist & prof relig, 82-93, SOPHIA SMITH PROF HIST & PROF RELIG EMER, 93- , SMITH COL; pres, Am Univ Beirut, 93-96. **HONORS AND AWARDS** Soc Sci Res Coun grant, 66-67 **MEMBERSHIPS** AHA; Mid E Studies Asn N Am; AAUP. **RESEARCH** Syrian Christianity in the Muslim era; Greater Syria in the Ottoman period. **SELECTED PUBLICATIONS** Syrian Christians in Muslim Society: An Interpretation, Princeton Univ, 70; auth;The Conversion of Eastern Christians to the Unia, in Gervers, ed, Conversion and Continuity: Indigenous Christian Communities in Islamic Lands, Eighth to Eighteenth Centuries, Pontifical Inst of Mediaeval Stud in Toronto, 90; auth, Constantinople over Antioch, 1516-1724: Patriarchal Politics in the Ottoman Era, in, J of Ecclesiastical Hist, 90; auth, A Response of Rev David M. Petras' The Ecumenical Status of the Eastern Catholic Churches, Greek Orthodox Theol Rev, 92. **CONTACT ADDRESS** Dept of History, Smith Col, Northampton, MA, 01060.

HADDEN, SALLY E.
PERSONAL m, 1994 **DISCIPLINE** HISTORY **EDUCATION** Univ NC, BA, 84; Harvard Univ, MA, 85, PhD, 93; Harvard Law Sch, JD, 89. **CAREER** Asst prof, 93-95, Univ Toledo; asst prof, 95-, Fl St Univ. **HONORS AND AWARDS** Mark DeWolfe Howe Fund res grant, 90, 91; Charles Warren Center for Amer His res grant, 90, 91; Va Hist Soc Res Fel, 91; Josephine de Karman Found Dissertation Fel, 92-93; res assoc, Univ Toledo, 93-94; Kate B & Hall J Peterson Fel, 94; Archie K Davis Fel, 97; W B H Dowse Fel, 98., Phi Beta Kappa **MEMBERSHIPS** AHA; ASLH; OAH; SHA. **RESEARCH** Legal & constitutional hist; colonial Amer; the South. **SELECTED PUBLICATIONS** Auth, James Madison, in Statesmen Who Changed the World, Greenwood Press, 93; auth, The War of 1812, Events that Shaped Nineteenth-Century American, Greenwood Press, 97; art, Redefining the Boundaries of Public History: Mystic Seaport Goes Online and On Board with Amistad, OAH Newsletter, 98; auth, Thomas Ruffin and State v. Mann: A Reconsideration, Race and Criminal Justice in the American South, 1800-1900, Univ Ga Press, 99; art, Colonial and Revolutionary Era Slave Patrols in Virginia, Lethal Imagination: Violence and Brutality in American History, NY Univ Press, 99. **CONTACT ADDRESS** Dept of History, Florida State Univ, Tallahassee, FL, 32306-2200. **EMAIL** shadden@mailer.fsu.edu

HAFTER, DARYL MASLOW
PERSONAL Born 01/17/1935, Elizabeth, NJ, m, 1957, 2 children **DISCIPLINE** MODERN EUROPEAN HISTORY **EDUCATION** Smith, Col, BA, 56; Yale Univ, MA, 58, PhD(Fr hist), 64 **CAREER** Lectr, 68-69, asst prof, 69-76, assoc prof, 76-81, PROF HIST & PHILOS, EASTERN MICH UNIV, 81-; Res grant, Am Philos Soc, 75; consult, Nat Endowment for Humanities, 77-. **MEMBERSHIPS** Soc Hist Technol; Women Historians Midwest; AHA; Fr Hist Asn **RESEARCH** French eighteenth century; women's history; history of technology. **SELECTED PUBLICATIONS** Auth, Philippe de Lasalle: From Mise-en-carte to Industrial Design, Winterthur Portfolio XII; ed, European Women and Preindustrial Craft, Ind Univ Press, 95; Female masters in the Ribbonmaking Guild of Eighteenth Century Rouen, French Hist Studies, winter 97. **CONTACT ADDRESS** Dept of Hist, Eastern Michigan Univ, 701 Pray Harrold, Ypsilanti, MI, 48197-2201. **EMAIL** his_hafter@online.emich.edu

HAGAN, KENNETH JAMES
PERSONAL Born 02/20/1936, Oakland, CA, m, 1964, 3 children **DISCIPLINE** AMERICAN DIPLOMATIC AND NAVAL HISTORY **EDUCATION** Univ Calif, Berkeley, AB, 58, MA, 64; Claremont Grad Sch, PhD(hist), 70. **CAREER** Instr hist, Claremont Men's Col, 68-69; asst prof, Kans State Univ, 69-73; asst prof, 73-77, ASSOC PROF HIST, US NAVAL ACAD, 77-. **MEMBERSHIPS** AHA; Orgn Am Historians; Soc Historians Am Foreign Rels; Am Mil Inst; NAm Soc Oceanic Hist. **RESEARCH** US Naval and diplomatic history; American foreign relations and naval history; Soviet-American naval strategy. **SELECTED PUBLICATIONS** Auth, How Navies Fight--The United-States-Navy and Its Allies, Int Hist Rev, Vol 0017, 95; 100 Years of Sea Power--The United-States-Navy, 1890-1990, Int Hist Rev, Vol 0017, 95. **CONTACT ADDRESS** Dept of Hist, US Naval Acad, Annapolis, MD, 21402.

HAGAN, WILLIAM THOMAS
PERSONAL Born 12/19/1918, Huntington, WV, m, 1943, 4 children **DISCIPLINE** AMERICAN HISTORY **EDUCATION** Marshall Univ, BA, 41; Univ Wis, PhD, 50. **CAREER** From asst prof to prof hist, NTex State Univ, 50-65; prof, 65-75, distinguished prof hist, State Univ NY Col, Fredonia, 75-88; prof History, Univ Okla, 89-95; Adv comt, Newberry Libr Ctr Indian Hist, 72-86; bd eds, Western Hist Quart, 73-78; ed consult, Ariz & West, 78-84. **HONORS AND AWARDS** W Hist Asn Prize, 89 **MEMBERSHIPS** Orgn Am Historians; Am Hist Asn; Am Soc Ethnohistory (pres, 63); Western His Asn. **SELECTED PUBLICATIONS** Auth, The Sac and Fox Indians, Univ Okla, 58 & 80; American Indians, Univ Chicago, 61 & 79 & 93; The Indian in American History, Am Hist Asn, 63 & rev ed, 71; Indian Police and Judges, 71 & United States-Comanche Relations, Yale Univ, 76; The Indian Rights Association, Univ Arizona, 85; Quanah Parker, Comanche Chief, Univ Okla, 93; Theodore Roosevelt and Six Friends of the Indian, Univ Okla, 97. **CONTACT ADDRESS** 2542 Cypress Ave, Norman, OK, 73072. **EMAIL** Whagan5281@AOL.com

HAGAN, WILLIE JAMES
PERSONAL Born 12/17/1950, Montgomery, AL, m, 1979 **DISCIPLINE** EDUCATION **EDUCATION** Mitchell College, New London, CT, AS, 1971; University of Connecticut, Storrs, CT, BA, 1973, MA, 1975, PhD, currently. **CAREER** Dept of Higher Education, Hartford, CT, assistant director of legislative services; UNIVERSITY OF CONNECTICUT, STORRS, CT, director of government relations, 1986-90, acting vice president, 1990, ASSOCIATE VICE PRES, 1990-. **MEMBERSHIPS** Member, Government Relations and Communications Officers, 1982-87. **CONTACT ADDRESS** External Affairs, Univ of Connecticut, U-166, Storrs, CT, 06268.

HAGEDORN, NANCY L.
DISCIPLINE HISTORY **EDUCATION** Univ Cincinnati, BA; Will & Mary Coll, PhD, 95. **CAREER** ASST PROF, HIST, ST JOHN'S **HONORS AND AWARDS** Hon Mention Award in Kerr Hist Prize Comp of NY Hist Asn, 96. **MEMBERSHIPS** Am Antiquarian Soc **SELECTED PUBLICATIONS** Auth, Faithful, Knowing, and Prudent: Andrew Montour as Interpreter and Cultural Broker, 1740-1772, in Between Indian and White Worlds: The Cultural Broker, Univ Okla Press, 94; auth, A Friend to Go Between Them: Interpreters Among the Iroquois, 1664-1775, Will & Mary Coll, 95; auth, A Friend to Go Between Them: The Interpreter as Cultural Broker during Anglo-Iroquois Councils, 1740-70, Ethnohistory 35, 88; coauth, Tools: Working Wood in Eighteenth Century America, Colonial Williamsburg Found, 93; auth, Broker of Understanding: Interpreters as Agents of Cultural Exchange in Colonial New York, NY Hist, Oct 95. **CONTACT ADDRESS** Hist Dept, St John's, 8000 Utopia Pkwy, Jamaica, NY, 11439. **EMAIL** nlhagedorn@prodigy.net

HAGEN, WILLIAM WALTER
PERSONAL Born 10/24/1942, Butte, MT, m, 1961, 2 children **DISCIPLINE** MODERN EUROPEAN HISTORY **EDUCATION** Harvard Univ, BA, 65; Univ Chicago, MA, 67, PhD(hist), 71. **CAREER** Asst prof, 70-77, ASSOC PROF HIST, UNIV CALIF, DAVIS, 77-. **MEMBERSHIPS** AHA; Am Asn Advan Slavic Studies; Western Slavic Asn. **RESEARCH** Polish-German-Jewish nationality conflict in Prussian Poland 1772-1918; nineteenth century German social history; social and political history of Poland and Hapsburgh Empire. **SELECTED PUBLICATIONS** Auth, Seigneurial Strongholds and Force of Local Nobility--Authoritarian Penetration of Rural Regions between the Elbe and Aller 1300-1700, J Mod Hist, Vol 0064, 92; Internal Peripheries in European-History, J Econ Hist, Vol 0053, 93; Peasants in the Middle-Ages, J Econ Hist, Vol 0054, 94; Citizenship and Nationhood in France and Germany, J Mod Hist, Vol 0067, 95; Before the Final-Solution--Toward a Comparative-Analysis of Political Anti-Semitism in Interwar Germany and Poland, J Mod Hist, Vol 0068, 96; Hunger Crises in Prussia During the First Half of the 19th-Century, J Soc Hist, Vol 0029, 96; Biographies, Families, Households--Farmers and Cottagers in the Parish of Belm near Osnabruck During the Proto-Industrial Era, Cent Europ Hist, Vol 0029, 96; The Sanctity of Rural Life--Nobility, Protestantism, and Nazism in Weimar Germany, Cent Europ Hist, Vol 0029, 96; Inventing Eastern-Europe--The Map of Civilization on the Mind of the Enlightenment, J Mod Hist, Vol 0069, 97. **CONTACT ADDRESS** Dept of Hist, Univ of Calif, Davis, CA, 95616-5200.

HAGER, HELLMUT
DISCIPLINE ITALIAN AND GERMAN BAROQUE AND ROCOCO ARCHITECTURE **EDUCATION** Bonn University, Dr Phil. **CAREER** Prof, Pa State Univ, 71-, Hd dept Art Hist, 72-96. **HONORS AND AWARDS** Fel, Instit Arts and Humanistic Stuc; Evan Pugh Professor. **RESEARCH** Italian architects Carlo Fontana, Filippo Juvarra, and the school of Bernini. **SELECTED PUBLICATIONS** Coauth, Loyola: Historia y Arquitectura; Carlo Fontana: The Drawings at Windsor Castle, London; Filippo Juvarra e il concorso di modelli del 1715 bandito da Clemente XI per la nuova sacrestia di S. Pietro. **CONTACT ADDRESS** Pennsylvania State Univ, 201 Shields Bldg, University Park, PA, 16802. **EMAIL** axc6@psu.edu

HAGGIS, DONALD
DISCIPLINE CLASSICAL ARCHAEOLOGY **EDUCATION** Wayne State Univ, AB, 82, MA, 85; Univ MN, PhD, 92. **CAREER** Asst prof, Univ NC, Chapel Hill; assoc mem, Am Schl Class Stud, Athens, 89-92, Schl Archaeol, Athens, 90-91. **RESEARCH** Archaeol of bronze age Crete; early iron age Greece; early state soc. **SELECTED PUBLICATIONS** Auth, East Crete in the Middle Minoan Period: A Pre-State Society, Am J of Archaeol 98, 94; An Early Minoan I Pottery Assemblage from East Crete, Am J of Archaeol 99, 95; Archaeological Survey at Kavousi, East Crete: Preliminary Report, Hesperia 65, 96; The Port of Tholos in Eastern Crete and the Role of a Roman Horreum along the Egyptian 'Corn Route,' Oxford J of Archaeol 15, 96; Excavations at Kalo Khorio, East Crete, Am J of Archaeol 100, 96; coauth, Aspects of Vernacular Architecture in Postpalatial and Early Iron Age Crete, Am J of Archaeol 98, 94. **CONTACT ADDRESS** Univ N. Carolina, Chapel Hill, Chapel Hill, NC, 27599. **EMAIL** dchaggis@email.unc.edu

HAHM, DAVID EDGAR
PERSONAL Born 09/30/1938, Milwaukee, WI, m, 1964, 4 children **DISCIPLINE** CLASSICAL LANGUAGES, ANCIENT PHILOSOPHY, INTELLECTUAL HISTORY **EDUCATION** Northwestern Col, Wis, BA, 60; Univ Wis-Madison, MA, 62, PhD(classics), 66. **CAREER** Asst prof class lang, Univ Mo-Columbia, 66-69; from asst prof to assoc prof class, 69-78, PROF CLASSICS, OHIO STATE UNIV, 78-, Fel, Ctr Hellenic Studies, Wash, DC, 68-69. **MEMBERSHIPS** Am Philol Asn; Am Philos Asn; Hist Sci Soc; Class Asn Midwest & South. **SELECTED PUBLICATIONS** Auth, The Nature of Man in Early Stoic Philosophy, Phoenix-J Class Asn of Can, Vol 0045, 91; The Chain of Change--A Study of Aristotles Physics, Pt 7, Isis, Vol 0084, 93. **CONTACT ADDRESS** Dept of Greek & Latin, Ohio State Univ, 230 N Oval Mall, Columbus, OH, 43210-1335. **EMAIL** hahm.1@osu.edu

HAHN, FRANCIS V. HICKSON
DISCIPLINE CLASSICS **EDUCATION** Univ NC, Chapel Hill, PhD, 86. **CAREER** ASSOC PROF, UNIV CALIF, SANTA BARBARA. **RESEARCH** Religion of the Roman Republic. **SELECTED PUBLICATIONS** Auth, Roman Prayer Language: Livy and the Aeneid of Vergil, Teubner, 93; "Patruus: Paragon or Pervert? The Case of a Literary Split Personality," Syllecta Classica 4, 93; "Augustus Triumphator: Manipulation of the Triumphal Theme in the Political Program of Augustus," Latomus, 91; "Roman Religion," The Dictionary of Religion, Harper-Collins and Amer Acad of Rel, 95. **CONTACT ADDRESS** Dept of Classics, Univ Calif, Santa Barbara, CA, 93106-7150. **EMAIL** fhahn@humanitas.ucsb.edu

HAHN, HARLAN
PERSONAL Born 07/09/1939, Osage, IA **DISCIPLINE** POLITICAL SCIENCE **EDUCATION** BA, magna cum laude, St Olaf Col, 60; PhD, Harvard Univ, 64; MS, Calif State Univ, 82. **CAREER** Asst Prof Res, Assoc, Univ MI, 64-67; Assoc Prof, Prof Univ CA 67-72; Prof, Ministry of S CA, 72-98. **HONORS AND AWARDS** Who's Who; Alexander Hamilton; Woodrow Wilson, Robert A Taft, Ed Robets, NIHR Fellowships. **MEMBERSHIPS** Soc of Disability Studies. **RESEARCH** Disability Studies; Discrimination. **SELECTED PUBLICATIONS** Urban-Rural Conflicr: The Polotics of Change, Sage Publ, 71; Health Politics and Policy; Antidiscrimination Laws and Social Research: The Minority Group Perspective; Behavioral Sciences and the Law Vol 14, 96; The Apperance of Physical Differences: A New Agenda for Political Research, Journal of Health and Human Rsources Admin Vol17, 95; Feminist Perspectives, Disability, Sexuality and Law: New Issues and Agendas, Southern California Review of Law and Women's Studies Vol 4 No 1, 94; Civil Rights in Robert P Martinelli and Arthur E Dell Orto eds Encylopedia of Rehabilitation, MacMillan(in press); Embodied Differences: Achieving a Positive Identity, In Motion Vol 6, 96. **CONTACT ADDRESS** Dept Political Sci, Univ S California, Los Angeles, CA, 90089-0044.

HAHN, ROGER
PERSONAL Born 01/05/1932, Paris, France, m, 1955, 2 children **DISCIPLINE** HISTORY OF SCIENCE **EDUCATION** Harvard Univ, BA, 53, MAT, 54; Ecole Pratique des Hautes Etudes, Paris, dipl, 55; Cornell Univ, PhD, 62. **CAREER** Instr hist, Univ Del, 60-61; from instr to assoc prof, 61-74, PROF HIST, UNIV CALIF, BERKELEY, 74-, SPEC ASST TO DIR SCI AFFAIRS, BANCROFT LIBR, 71-, Fulbright scholar, 54-55; NSF fels, 59-60 & 64-65; adv ed, Isis, 71-76, Hist Sci, 72-, Soc Studies Sci, 74- & Eighteenth Century Studies, 76-; Am Coun Learned Soc fel, 73-74. **HONORS AND AWARDS** Bk-of-the-Year Award, Pac Coast Br, AHA, 72; Chevalier Palmes Academiques, 77. **MEMBERSHIPS** AHA; Hist Sci Soc; Soc Fr Hist Studies, fel AAAS; corresp mem Int Acad Hist Sci **RESEARCH** Eighteenth century science; history of scientific institutions; French history. **SELECTED PUBLICATIONS** Auth, L'Hydrodynamique au 18e siecle, Palais Decouverte, Paris, 65; Laplace as a Newtonian Scientist, W A Clark Libr, 67; The Anatomy of a Scientific Institution: The Paris Academy of Sciences, 1666-1803, Univ Calif, 71; Scientific research as an occupation in 18th century France, Minerva, 75; New directions in the social history of science, Physis, 75; L'autobiographie de Lacepede retrouvee, Dix-huitieme Siecle, 75; Laplace and the Mechanistic Universe, God and Nature, 86; The Meaning of the Mechanistic Age, The Boundaries of Humanity, 91; The Ideological and Institutional Difficulties of a Jesuit Scientist in Paris, R J Boscovich, 93. **CONTACT ADDRESS** Dept of Hist, Univ of Calif, 3229 Dwinelle Hall, Berkeley, CA, 94720-2550. **EMAIL** rhahn@socrates.berkeley.edu

HAHN, THOMAS
DISCIPLINE SPONSORSHIP, PRODUCTION, AND INTERPRETATION OF TEXTS AND IMAGES FROM THE EA **EDUCATION** UCLA, PhD. **CAREER** Assoc prof; taught at, UCLA; assoc, Susan B. Anthony Inst for Women's Stud. **HONORS AND AWARDS** NEH prog grant, 89-95; NEH & ACLS fel., Collab proj, Chaucer Bibliog & TEAMS Middle Eng Texts ser. **RESEARCH** Emerging Europ identities, including women, Indians, Jews, heretics, outlaws, virtuous pagans, popular chivalric heroes, and other monstrous types. **SELECTED PUBLICATIONS** Auth, articles on, writing in Britain in the 12th and 13th centuries, Cambridge Hist of Middle Eng Lit, the paradox of popular chivalric romance, the hist of the lang, medieval manuscripts, Latin writing, Chaucer, Dante, medieval drama, romances of Alexander of Macedon, medieval and Renaissance cult and intellectual hist, post-modern readers & medieval texts; ed, Reconceiving Chaucer: Literary Theory and Historical Interpretati on; Sir Gawain: Eleven Romances and Tales; The Letter of Alexander, gen ed, The Chaucer Bibliog. **CONTACT ADDRESS** Dept of Eng, Univ of Rochester, 601 Elmwood Ave, Ste. 656, Rochester, NY, 14642. **EMAIL** thhn@db1.cc.rochester.edu

HAHNER, JUNE EDITH
PERSONAL Born 07/08/1940, New York, NY **DISCIPLINE** LATIN AMERICAN HISTORY **EDUCATION** Earlham Col, AB, 61; Cornell Univ, MA, 63, PhD, 66. **CAREER** Foreign Area Fel Prog fel, Brazil & Cornell Univ, 64-66; asst prof Latin Am hist, Tex Technol Col, 66-68; asst prof, 68-72, assoc prof, 72-80, PROF LATIN AM HIST, STATE UNIV NY ALBANY, 80-; NEH fel, 71 & 82-83; Rockefeller Found fel, 86-87; Fulbright fel, 80; coord, Comn Women in Hist, 1998-2000; mem, ed bd, The American, 74-92 and Latin Am Res News, 94-96. **HONORS AND AWARDS** NECLAS Book Prize, 87. **MEMBERSHIPS** Latin Am Studies Asn; Conf Latin Am Hist; AHA; Int Conf Group Mod Portugal. **RESEARCH** Urban change and politics in Brazilian empire and republic; women in Latin America; Brazilian armed forces in Brazil. **SELECTED PUBLICATIONS** Auth, Civilian Military Relations in Brazil, 1889-1898, Univ SC, 69; The Brazilian Armed Forces and the overthrow of the monarchy: Another perspective, Americas, 10/69; A molestia do Imperador e as interpretacoes da queda do Imperio, Rev Inst Hist Geog Brasileiro, 10-12/71; Floriano Peixoto: Brazil's iron marshal: A reevaluation, Americas, 6/74; ed, Women in Latin American History: Their Lives and Views, Univ Calif, Los Angeles, 76, rev ed, 80; auth, Jacobinos vs Galegos: Urban radicals vs Portuguese immigrants in Rio de Janeiro in the 1890's, J Inter Am Studies & World Affairs, 5/76; Women and work in Brazil, 1850-1920, in Essays Concerning the Socioeconomic History of Brazil and Portuguese India, Univ Fla, 77; ed, A Mulher No Brasil, Editora Civilisacao Brasileira, 78; The Nineteenth-Century feminist press and women's rights in Brazil, in latin American Women, A Historical Perspective, Greenwood, 78; auth, Feminism, women's rights, and the suffrage movement in Brazil, 1850-1932, Latin Am Res Rev, 80; auth, A Mulher Brasileira e Suas Lutas Sociais e Politicas, 1850-1937, Brasiliense, 81; Women's place in politics and economics in Brazil since 1964, Luso-Brazilian Rev, 82; Researching the history of Latin American women: Past and future directions, Inter-Am Rev of Bibliog, 83; Recent research on women in Brazil, Latin Am Res Rev, 85; Poverty and Politics. The Urban Poor in Brazil, 1870-1920, Univ NM, 86; Women's work in Brazil. Recent researach and publications, Inter-Am Rev of Bibliog, 88; La historiografia de la mujer. Problemas y perspectivas, in Seminario de Estudios sobre la Mujer, Min de Cultura de CR, 89; Emancipating the Female Sex. The Struggle for Women's Rights in Brazil, 1850-1940, Duke, 90; Educacao e ideologia: Profissionais liberais na America latina do seculo XIX, Estudos Feminista, 94; Recent tendencies in the historiography of women in Latin America, Noticia Bibliografica e Historica, 96; Educacao e ideologia. Profissionais pioneiras na Amerca Latina do Seculo SIX, in Educacao na America Latina, EDUSP, 96; Women in Brazil, rev ed, Latin Am Inst, Univ NM, 98; ed, Women through Women's Eyes. Latin American Women in Nineteenth-Century Travel Accounts. **CONTACT ADDRESS** Dept of Hist, State Univ NY, 1400 Washington Ave, Albany, NY, 12222-1000. **EMAIL** hahner@csc.albany.edu

HAIKEN, ELIZABETH
DISCIPLINE HISTORY **EDUCATION** Univ Ca, PhD. **CAREER** Asst prof. **RESEARCH** U.S. history; history of medicine. **SELECTED PUBLICATIONS** Auth, Venus Envy: A History of Cosmetic Surgery, Johns Hopkins Univ. **CONTACT ADDRESS** Dept of History, Knoxville, TN, 37996.

HAIMOWITZ, NATALIE READER
PERSONAL Born 05/27/1923, Brooklyn, NY, m, 1948, 3 children **DISCIPLINE** PSYCHOLOGY **EDUCATION** Univ Chi-

cago, PhD, Human Devel, 48; Ohio St Univ, MA, Clinical Psychol, 45; Brooklyn Col, BA, Psychol, 44. **CAREER** Res Asst, Comm Human Devel, Univ Chicago, 45-46; Fac, Dept Psychol, Brooklyn Col, 47-48; Instr, Univ Chicago, 53-58; Clinical Priv Pract, 55-; Chief Psychol, Woman's Childs Hosp, 55-59; Psychol, Milwaukee Psych Ser, 60-64; Co-Dir, Haimowoods Inst, 72-; Faculty, Univ WI, Parkside, Dept Psychol, Behavioral Sci Div, 78-79; Clinical Pvt Practice, current. **SELECTED PUBLICATIONS** Human Development, co auth, Dr Morris Haimowitz, pub, Thomas Y Crowell, 60, rev, 66, 73; Suffering is Optional, co auth, Dr Morris Haimowitz, pub, Haimowoods Press, 76; Success in Psychotherapy, W Wolff, J A Precker, chap 3, Personality Changes in Client-Cen Therapy, pub, Grune and Stratton, 52; Encyclopedia of Psychology, chaps on Deprivation & Middle Age, NY, John Wiley and Sons, 87. **CONTACT ADDRESS** 1101 Forest Av, Evanston, IL. **EMAIL** GREENSUP@EARTHLINK.NET

HAINES, GERALD KENNETH
PERSONAL Born 05/19/1943, Detroit, MI, m, 1969 **DISCIPLINE** UNITED STATES DIPLOMATIC HISTORY **EDUCATION** Wayne State Univ, BA, 65, MA, 67; Univ Wis, Madison, PhD(diplomatic hist), 73. **CAREER** Teacher social studies, Detroit Pub Schs, 65-67; instr Am hist, Wayne County Community Col, 73-74; ARCHIVIST AM HIST, NAT ARCH, 74-81; vis assoc prof, Univ Tex, San Antonio, 81-82. **MEMBERSHIPS** Orgn Am Historians; AHA; Soc Historians Am Foreign Rels; Soc Am Archivists; Soc Hist Fed Govt. **RESEARCH** US-Latin American relations; US-Asian relations. **SELECTED PUBLICATIONS** Auth, Unequal Giants--Diplomatic Relations between the United-States and Brazil, 1889-1930, Diplomatic Hist, Vol 0017, 93; Goillot, Virginia, Hall--Career Intelligence Officer, Prologue-Quart of the Nat Arch, Vol 0026, 94; The Rich Neighbor Policy--Rockefeller and Kaiser in Brazil, Diplomatic Hist, Vol 0019, 95. **CONTACT ADDRESS** 202 N Highland, Arlington, VA, 22201.

HAIR, JOHN
PERSONAL Born 10/08/1941, Gulf Port, Mississippi, m, 1988 **DISCIPLINE** EDUCATION **EDUCATION** Wayne State Univ, BS Ed 1969, MS Ed 1971; GA State Univ, EdS 1978; Western MI Univ, EdD 1986. **CAREER** Detroit Public Schools, band dir 1969-71; Grand Rapids OIC, exec dir 1973-77; Grand Rapids Job Corps, mgr of educ 1981-82; Davenport Coll, faculty 1982-, dir of minority affairs 1983-88, dean of minority affairs, 1988-90; vice president for student affairs, 1990-; vice pres, cabinet member, 1992-. **HONORS AND AWARDS** Grad Rsch Asst GA State Univ 1976-77; Band Leader 13 piece band Amway Grand Hotel 1982-85; "GIANTS" Phyllis Scott Activist Award 1988; "HEROES" Hispanic Community Service (non-Hispanic) Award of Merit 1988; chair personnel and Junior College Conn Grand Rapids Public School Board 1988-90. **MEMBERSHIPS** Mem Phi Delta Kappa 1980-, MI Academy of Sci Arts & Letters 1983-; higher educ comm mem NABSE 1984-; mem IL Comm Black Concern in Higher Educ 1985-; secondary/higher educ comm AAHE 1986-; adv bd mem Grand Rapids Cable TV 1986-; mem industrial adv council Grand Rapids OIC; mem Grand Rapids Urban League; mem exec adv comm Sara Allen Family Neighborhood Ctr; bd mem, Grand Rapids Public School 1987-90; vice president, Black Educational Excellence Program, 1990-; Sigma Pi Phi, 1992-. **CONTACT ADDRESS** Vice President for Student Affairs, Davenport Col of Business, Grand Rapids, 415 E Fulton, Grand Rapids, MI, 49503.

HALAL, WILLIAM E.
PERSONAL Born 06/29/1933, Lebanon, m, 1972, 2 children **DISCIPLINE** BUSINESS & ECONOMICS **EDUCATION** Purdue Univ BSc; Univ CA Berkeley, MBA, PhD. **CAREER** George Washington Univ, prof mgmt 79; Am Univ, assoc prof mgmt 71-79. **HONORS AND AWARDS** Awarded Mitchell Prize; George Washington Honor Medal Freedoms Found, Smithsonian Awd, Speaker; Conference Maker; Consultant. **MEMBERSHIPS** Academy of Management World Future Soc. **RESEARCH** Engineering Technol; The New Management. **SELECTED PUBLICATIONS** Creating the New Organization, book/cd rom in progress, pub Jossey-Bass; 21st Century Economics, in progress, pub St Martin's Press; The New Management: Democracy and Enterprise Are Transforming Organizations, San Fran, Berrett-Koehler, 96; Encyclopedia of the Future, Ed Bd, MacMillan, 96; Organization for the Year 2000: The New Portable MBA, Wiley, 95;Creating Internal Markets, Enterprise, 94; The IT Generation, Eng Horizons, 93; numerous pub, articles. **CONTACT ADDRESS** Dept of Management Serv, George Washington Univ, Washington, DC, 20052. **EMAIL** halal@gwu.edu

HALBERSLEBEN, KAREN I.
DISCIPLINE HISTORY **EDUCATION** SUNY Buffalo, BA, 79; MA, 83; PhD, 87. **CAREER** Assoc prof, SUNY Oswego. **HONORS AND AWARDS** NEH Summer Fellow, 90. **RESEARCH** Mod Brit hist; Europ women's hist. **SELECTED PUBLICATIONS** Auth, Women's Participation in the Brit Antislavery Movement 1824-1865, Mellen, 93; Elizabeth Pease: One Woman's Vision of Peace, Justice and Human Rights, Quaker Hist, 95; Epilogue to Play "Seneca Falls, 1848: All Men and Women are Created Equal," Willson, 84. **CONTACT ADDRESS** Dept Hist, SUNY Oswego, 433 Mahar Hall, Oswego, NY, 13126. **EMAIL** halbers@oswego.edu

HALE, CHARLES ADAMS
PERSONAL Born 06/05/1930, Minneapolis, MN, m, 1952, 4 children **DISCIPLINE** LATIN AMERICAN HISTORY **EDUCATION** Amherst Col, BA, 51; Univ Minn, MA, 52; Univ Strasbourg, dipl, 53; Columbia Univ, PhD(Latin Am hist), 57. **CAREER** Instr soc sci, Univ NC, 56-57; asst prof hist, Lehigh Univ, 57-63 and Amherst Col, 63-66; from asst prof to assoc prof, 66-70, chmn dept, 77-80, PROF HIST, UNIV IOWA, 70-, Soc Sci Res Coun and Am Coun Learned Soc Latin-Am study grant, 62-63, 65-66 and 76-77; Nat Endowment for Humanities fel, 69-70; Guggenheim Found fel, 73-74; adv ed, Hisp Am Hist Rev, 77. **HONORS AND AWARDS** Robertson Prize, Conf Latin Am Hist, 66, Conf Prize, 74. **MEMBERSHIPS** Conf Latin Am Hist; AHA; Latin Am Studies Asn. **RESEARCH** Mexico; Latin American social and political thought. **SELECTED PUBLICATIONS** Auth, Imaginary Citizens--Memorial to the Trials and Tribulations of Virtue and Apology for Triumphant Vice in the Mexican-Republic, Touching on Public Morality, Hisp Am Hist Rev, Vol 0074, 94; Revolution in the Countryside--Rural Conflict and Agrarian-Reform in Guatemala, 1944-1954, Am Hist Rev, Vol 0100, 95; Tannenbaum, Frank and the Mexican-Revolution, Hisp Am Hist Rev, Vol 0075, 95; The Political Myths of the Mexican Nation--Liberalism and Revolution, Hist Mexicana, Vol 0046, 97. **CONTACT ADDRESS** 250 Black Springs Circle, Iowa City, IA, 52240.

HALE, JANICE ELLEN
PERSONAL Born 04/30/1948, Ft. Wayne, IN, 1984 **DISCIPLINE** EDUCATION **EDUCATION** Spelman Coll, BA 1970; Interdenominational Theol Center, MRE 1972; GA State Univ, PhD 1974. **CAREER** Early Childhood Educ Clark Coll, asso prof; Dept of Psychol Yale Univ, rsrch asso; Afro-Am Studies Prog, lecturer 1980-81; Cleveland State Univ, assoc prof; Wayne State University, professor, currently. **HONORS AND AWARDS** Publications "Christian Educ for Black Liberation" in For You Who Teach in th Black Church 1973; "The Woman's Role The Strength of Blk Families" in 1st World, An Intl Jrnl of Black Thought 1977; "De-Mythicizing the Educ of Black Children" 1st World, An Intl Journal of Black Thought 1977; numerous other publications; recipient of grant Spencer Found; numerous presentations on Research for the following institutions and associations: Black Child Devel Inst, Natl Council for Black Child Devel, Natl Assn for the Educ of Young Children, NC Assn for the Educ of Young Children, Univ of SC, SC State Coll, Spelman Coll, Morehouse Coll, GA State Univ, Univ of the West Indies, NY Univ, Head Start Prog of Omaha NE, CO Springs, CO Public Schools; author of Black Children, Their Roots, Culture and Learning Styles, John Hopkins Univ Press, revised edition 1986; 50 Future Leaders, Ebony Magazine, 1978; Distinguished Alumna, College of Educ, Georgia State Univ 1982; nominated for Pulitzer Prize, 1995. **MEMBERSHIPS** Founder, Visions for Children, African-Amer Early Childhood Educ Rsch Demonstration Prog; governing bd mem, Natl Assn for the Educ of Young Children, 1988-92. **SELECTED PUBLICATIONS** Author, Unbank the Fire: Visions for the Education of African-American Children, Johns Hopkins University Press, fall 1994. **CONTACT ADDRESS** Early Childhood Educ, Wayne State Univ, 213 Educ Bldg, Detroit, MI, 48202.

HALES, PETER BACON
PERSONAL Born 12/13/1950, Pasadena, CA, 2 children **DISCIPLINE** AMERICAN HISTORY **EDUCATION** Haverford Col, BA, 72; Univ of Tx at Austin, MA, PhD, 80. **CAREER** Lectr, Calif State Univ, 80; ASST PROF TO PROF, UNIV OF ILL AT CHICAGO. **HONORS AND AWARDS** Amoco Teaching Award, 84; Univ of Ill Teaching Award, 90; Focus/Infinity Artist's Grant, 87-88; Nat Endowment for the Humanities Fel, 87; Herbert Hoover Prize, 98; Ill Arts Coun Grant, 83. **MEMBERSHIPS** Am Studies Asn. **RESEARCH** American cultural landscape; history of photography. **SELECTED PUBLICATIONS** Coauth, The Perfect City: Photographs and Meditations, Johns Hopkins Univ Press, 94; auth, Atomic Spaces: Living on the Manhattan Project, Univ of Ill Press, 97; auth, Topographies of Power: The Forced Spaces of the Manhattan Project, Mapping Am Culture, Univ of Iowa Press, 92; auth, Life Presents the Atomic Bomb, Looking at Life, Smithsonian Inst Press, 99; auth, Surveying the Field: Artists Make Art History, Artjournal, 95; auth, Discipline/Survey, Artjournal, 95; auth, The Mass Aesthetic of Holocaust: American Media Construct the Atomic Bomb, Yearbook of the Japanese Asn for Am Studies, 96. **CONTACT ADDRESS** Art Hist Dept, M/C 201, Univ of Ill at Chicago, 935 W. Harrison St., Chicago, IL, 60607. **EMAIL** pbhale@uic.edu

HALEY, EVAN W.
PERSONAL Born 08/02/1954, Tacoma, WA, m, 1987, 1 child **DISCIPLINE** HISTORY **EDUCATION** Dartmouth Col, AB, 77; Columbia Univ, PhD, 86. **CAREER** Vis Asst Prof, 87-89, Univ of Oregon; Vis Asst Prof, 90-, Franklin & Marshall Col; Asst Prof, 90-96, Assoc Prof, 96-, McMaster Univ. **HONORS AND AWARDS** Fulbright-Hays Scholar, Spain, 84-85. **MEMBERSHIPS** Amer Philological Asn; Archeol Inst of Amer; Assoc of Ancient Hist **RESEARCH** Roman Social Economic and Political History; Pioneers of the Roman Empire. **SELECTED PUBLICATIONS** Migration and Economy in Roman Imperial Spain, Univ of Barcelona Press, 91; A Palace of Maximianus Herculius at Corduba?!, Zeitschrift fur Papyrologie und Epigraphik, 94; Rural Settlement in the Conventus Astigitanus, (Baetica) Under the Flarians, Pheonix, 96. **CONTACT ADDRESS** McMaster Univ, Dept of Classics, Hamilton, ON, L8S 4M2. **EMAIL** haley@mcmaster.ca

HALL, DAVID D.
DISCIPLINE HISTORY **EDUCATION** Harvard Univ, BA, 58; Yale Univ, PhD, 64. **CAREER** Prof, hist, Univ Boston; current, PROF AM REL HIST, HARVARD DIVINITY SCH. **HONORS AND AWARDS** Co-winner, Merle Curti Prize, 91 **MEMBERSHIPS** Am Antiquarian Soc **SELECTED PUBLICATIONS** Auth, A World of Wonders: The Mentality of the Supernatural in Seventeenth Century New England, in Seventeenth Century New England, Boston, 84; auth, Worlds of Wonder, Days of Judgment: Popular Religious Belief in Early New England, Knopf, 89; auth, The Faithful Shepherd: A History of the New England Ministry in the Seventeenth Century, Chapel Hill, 72; auth, Puritanism in Seventeenth Century Massachusetts, 68; co-ed, Saints and Revolutionaries: Essays on Early American History, 83; auth, Witch-hunting in New England, 1638-1692: A Documentary History, Boston, 90; auth, The Uses of Literacy in New England, 1600-1850, in Printing and Society in Early America, AAS, 83. **CONTACT ADDRESS** Harvard Divinity Sch, Harvard Univ, Cambridge, MA, 02138.

HALL, FREDERICK A.
PERSONAL Born 07/02/1944, Niagara-on-the-Lake, ON, Canada **DISCIPLINE** HISTORY OF MUSIC **EDUCATION** McGill Univ, BMus, 69; Univ Toronto, MA, 70; PhD 78. **CAREER** ASSOC PROF SCHOOL OF ART, DRAMA AND MUSIC, MCMASTER UNIV, 72-, chmn, 80-86, assoc dean, Hum, 88-96, acting dean, Hum, 96-97. **SELECTED PUBLICATIONS** Ed, Songs I to English Texts, 85; Songs IV to English Texts, 93; co-ed, Musical Canada: Words and Music Honouring Helmut Kallmann, 88; The Romantic Tradition, 92; contribur, Encyclopedia of Music in Canada; The Canadian Encyclopedia; Dictionary of Canadian Biography, vols XIII & XIV; Studies in Eighteenth Century Culture; Canadian Music: Issues of Hegemony and Identity. **CONTACT ADDRESS** Sch of Art, Drama & Music, McMaster Univ, 1280 Main St W, Hamilton, ON, L8S 4M2.

HALL, GENE E.
PERSONAL Born 06/19/1941, Rutland, VT, m, 1965, 2 children **DISCIPLINE** SCIENCE EDUCATION **EDUCATION** Catleton State Col, BS, 64; Syracuse Univ, MS, 65; PhD, 68. **CAREER** Prof, Proj and Ctr Dir, R&D Ctr for Teacher Educ, Univ Tex-Austin, 68-86; prof, Univ Fla, 86-88; dean, Univ Northern Col, 88-93; prof, 88- . **MEMBERSHIPS** Am Educ Res Asoc. **RESEARCH** Change proven in organizations; leadership during change; implementation evaluation; teacher education r&d and policy. **SELECTED PUBLICATIONS** Auth with S.M. Hord, Change in Schools: Facilitating the Process, 87; auth, The Local Education Change Process and Policy Implementation, J Res Sci Teaching, 92; auth with W.H. Shieh, Supervision and Organizational Development, Handbook of Research on Supervision, 98; auth with J. Johnson, V. Dupuis, D. Musial, and D. Gollnick, Introduction to the Foundations of American Education, 99. **CONTACT ADDRESS** Educational Leadership and Policy Studies, Univ of Northern Colorado, 412 McKee Hall, Greeley, CO, 80639. **EMAIL** gehall@bentley.unco.edu

HALL, GWENDOLYN MIDLO
PERSONAL Born 06/27/1929, New Orleans, LA, m, 1956, 3 children **DISCIPLINE** CARIBBEAN AND LATIN AMERICAN HISTORY **EDUCATION** Univ Am, BA, 62, MA, 63; Univ Mich, PhD(hist), 70. **CAREER** Instr hist, Elizabeth City State Col, 65; lectr Afro-Am studies, Univ Mich, 69; res asst, Mich Hist Collections, 70; asst prof, 71-73, ASSOC PROF HIST, RUTGERS UNIV, 73-. **MEMBERSHIPS** Asn Caribbean Historians. **RESEARCH** Comparative slavery; race relations. **SELECTED PUBLICATIONS** Auth, Africa and Africans in the Making of the Atlantic World, 1400-1680, J Am Hist, Vol 0080, 93; Cultivation and Culture--Labor and the Shaping of Slave Life in the America, J Southern Hist, Vol 0060, 94; American Slavery--1619-1877, Am Hist Rev, Vol 0100, 95; African-Americans at Mars-Bluff, South-Carolina, Southern Cult, Vol 0001, 95; Our Rightful Share--The Afro-Cuban Struggle for Equality, 1886-1912, Am Hist Rev, Vol 0101, 96; Maroon Heritage--Archaeological, Ethnographic, and Historical Perspectives, Hisp Am Hist Rev, Vol 0076, 96; Slave Cultures and the Cultures of Slavery, Am Hist Rev, Vol 0102, 97; Slavery, the Civil-Law and the Supreme-Court of Louisiana, African Am Rev, Vol 0031, 97. **CONTACT ADDRESS** Hist Dept, Rutgers Univ, P O Box 5059, New Brunswick, NJ, 08903-5059.

HALL, JACQUELYN DOWD
PERSONAL Born 01/14/1943, Pauls Valley, OK **DISCIPLINE** AMERICAN HISTORY **EDUCATION** Rhodes Col, BA, 65; Columbia Univ, MA, 67, PhD, 74. **CAREER** Instr Am hist, Columbia Univ, summer, 71; instr, 73-74, asst prof, 74-79, assoc prof hist, 79-88, Julia Cherry Spruill Prof of Hist, 89-,Univ NC, Chapel Hill; dir, Southern Oral History Prog, 73-. **HONORS AND AWARDS** Lillian Smith Award, Southern

Regional Coun, 79; Francis B Simkins Award, Southern Hist Asn, 79-80; Merle Curti Social History Award, 86-87; Albert J. Beveridge Award; Philip Taft Labor History Prize; Lyndhurst Prize, 89; UNC distinguished teaching award, 97. **MEMBERSHIPS** Orgn Am Historians; Oral Hist Asn; Southern Hist Asn; Am Stud Asn; S Asn of Women Hist; Am Hist Asn; Soc of Am Hist; Univ NC Press Bd Gov; Ctr for the Study of the Am South, exec bd. **RESEARCH** Women in United States history; labor history; history of the United States south. **SELECTED PUBLICATIONS** Auth, Class, A Companion to American Thought, Kloppenberg, 95; contribur, What We See and Can't See in the Past: A Round Table, J of Am Hist, 97; auth, O Delight Smith: A Labor Organizer's Odyssey, Forgotten Heroes from America's Past: Inspiring Portraits from Our Leading Historians, Free Press, 98; auth, Open Secrets: Memory, Imagination, and the Refashioning of Southern Identity, Am Q, 98; auth, You Must Remember This: Autobiography as Social Critique, J of Am Hist, 98. **CONTACT ADDRESS** History Dept, Univ of NC, Chapel Hill, NC, 27514. **EMAIL** jhall@email.unc.edu

HALL, JONATHAN M.
DISCIPLINE CLASSICS **EDUCATION** Univ Oxford, BA, 88, MA, 91; Univ Cambridge, PhD, 93. **CAREER** Tchg fel, Marlboro Col, 88-89; Undergrad Supvr, Univ Cambridge, 89-96; Lectr, British Sch at Athens Summer Sch, 92-93; Res Fel, Downing Col, 93-96; Aff lectr, Univ Cambridge, 95-96; Asst prof, Univ Chicago, 96-. **SELECTED PUBLICATIONS** Auth, Ethnic identity in Greek antiquity, Cambridge, 97. **CONTACT ADDRESS** Dept of Classics, Univ Chicago, 1010 E 50th St, Chicago, IL, 60637. **EMAIL** jhall@midway.uchicago.edu

HALL, MICHAEL G.
PERSONAL Born 01/08/1926, Princeton, NJ, m, 1972, 4 children **DISCIPLINE** HISTORY **EDUCATION** Princeton Univ, BA (magna cum laude), 49; Johns Hopkins Univ, PhD, 56. **CAREER** ASST PROF, 59-64, ASSOC PROF, 64-70, PROF, 70-, CHEMN, DEPT OF HIST, UNIV OF TEX, 76-80; sr fulbright lectr, Pakistan, 94-95; advisory coun, Omohundro Inst of Early Am Hist and Culture, 90-92. **HONORS AND AWARDS** C.O. Joline Prize, Princeton Univ; book of the year Awd, Confr on Christianity & Lit, 88. **MEMBERSHIPS** Am Antiquarian Soc; Mass Hist Soc; Colonial Soc of Mass. **RESEARCH** Early America; Native America; world history. **SELECTED PUBLICATIONS** Auth, Edward Randolph and the American Colonies 1676-1703, Chapel Hill, 60; The Last American Puritan: The Life of Increase Mather, Weslayn Univ Press, 88; ed, The Autobiography of Increase Mather, Am Antiquarian Society, 62; co-ed, The Glorious Revolution in America, Chapel Hill, 63; Science and Society in the United States, 66. **CONTACT ADDRESS** Dept of Hist, Univ of Texas, Austin, TX, 78712. **EMAIL** mghall@mail.utexas.edu

HALL, PETER G.
DISCIPLINE GEOGRAPHY **EDUCATION** Univ of Cambridge, BA, 53, MA, 57, PhD, 59. **CAREER** Asst Lecturer, Lecturer, Birkbeck Col, London, 57-65; Reader, London Sch of Econ, 66-67; Prof, Univ Reading, 68-88, Emeritus, 88; Prof, Univ Calif, Berkeley, 80-92, Emeritus, 92; Prof, Univ Col London, 92. **HONORS AND AWARDS** FBA; MAE; 6 honorary degrees; Knighthood, 98. **MEMBERSHIPS** Hon MRTPI; APA. **RESEARCH** Urban planning; transportation planning; urban history. **SELECTED PUBLICATIONS** Co-auth, The Rise of the Gunbelt, 91; co-auth, Technopoles of the World, 94; co-auth, Sociable Cities, 98; auth, Cities in Civilization, 98. **CONTACT ADDRESS** Bartlett Sch of Planning, Univ Col London, 22 Gordon St, WCI H OQB, London, .. **EMAIL** p.hall@ucl.ac.uk

HALL, TIMOTHY D.
PERSONAL Born 01/25/1955, Kansas City, KS, m, 1979, 2 children **DISCIPLINE** HISTORY **EDUCATION** Dallas Theolog Sem, ThM, 84; Univ Chicago, MA, 86; Northwestern Univ, PhD, 91. **CAREER** Res asst prof, Northwestern Univ, 91-92; vis asst prof, Colgate Univ, 92-93; assoc prof, Central Mich Univ, 93-. **HONORS AND AWARDS** Charlotte W. Newcombe Doctoral Dissertation Fel. **MEMBERSHIPS** Am Hist Asn; Orgn of Am Hist. **RESEARCH** Early American cultural and religious history. **SELECTED PUBLICATIONS** Auth, Contested Boundaries: Itinerancy and the Reshaping of the Colonial American Religious World, 94; auth, art, Structuring Provencial Imagination: The Rhetoric and Experience of Social Change in Eighteenth-Century New England, 98. **CONTACT ADDRESS** Dept of History, Central Michigan Univ, Mt. Pleasant, MI, 48859. **EMAIL** tim.d.hall@cmich.edu

HALL, TOM
PERSONAL Born 02/13/1955, Teaneck, NJ, m, 1986, 1 child **DISCIPLINE** MUSIC **EDUCATION** Univ Maryland, DMA, 96. **CAREER** Music Dir, Baltimore Choral Arts Soc, 82-; Dir Choral Activities, Goucher Col, 83-; Chorus Master, Baltimore Opera Company, 83-93; Music Dir, Concord Chorus, 79-82. **MEMBERSHIPS** Chorus Am; Am Choral Dir Asn; Am Symphony Orchestra League; Am Handel Soc; Am Musicol Soc. **RESEARCH** Handel; Bach; Haydn; Mozart. **SELECTED PUBLICATIONS** Voice Magazine; Hist Performance Magazine; Baltimore Sun; Choral Journal. **CONTACT ADDRESS** Baltimore Choral Arts Soc, 1316 Park Ave, Baltimore, MD, 21217. **EMAIL** thall1@erols.com

HALL, VAN BECK
PERSONAL Born 09/03/1934, Charleston, WV, m, 2 children **DISCIPLINE** AMERICAN HISTORY **EDUCATION** Oberlin Col, AB, 56; Univ Wis, MS, 61, PhD(hist), 64. **CAREER** Asst prof, 64-71, ASSOC PROF HIST, UNIV PITTSBURGH, 71- , dept chm, 91-92. **MEMBERSHIPS** AHA; Orgn Am Historians. **RESEARCH** Political economy of Virginia, 1790-1830; politics in the United States, 1790-1830. **SELECTED PUBLICATIONS** Auth, Politics Without Parties: Massachusetts 1780-1791, Univ Pittsburgh, 72; A Fond Farewell to Henry Adams in Human Dimensions of Nation Building, Hist Soc Wis, 76; auth, Appalachian Politics, in Mitchell, ed, Appalachian Frontiers, Tennessee, 90. **CONTACT ADDRESS** 5854 Douglas St, Pittsburgh, PA, 15217.

HALLENBECK, JAN TRAVER
PERSONAL Born 04/13/1940, New York, NY, m, 1963, 2 children **DISCIPLINE** MEDIEVAL HISTORY **EDUCATION** Kenyon Col, BA, 61; NY Univ, MA, 62, PhD(hist), 66. **CAREER** Lectr contemporary civilization, Queen's Col, NY, 62-63; asst hist, NY Univ, 63-65; asst prof, Ind Univ, Fort Wayne, 66-69; from asst prof to assoc prof, 69-77, chmn dept, 74-78, PROF HIST, OHIO WESLEYAN UNIV, 77-. **MEMBERSHIPS** AHA; Medieval Acad Am; Am Cath Hist Asn. **RESEARCH** Eighth century Roman and Papal history; history of the Lombard Monarchy; early medieval Papal, Frankish, Lombard and Byzantine relations. **SELECTED PUBLICATIONS** Auth, The Lives of the 8th-Century Popes (Liber-Pontificalis)--The Ancient Biographies of 9 Popes from AD-715 to AD-817, Cath Hist Rev, Vol 0079, 93; Before the Normans--Southern Italy in the 9th and 10th Centuries, Cath Hist Rev, Vol 0079, 93; Miasmas and Disease--Public-Health and the Environment in the Preindustrial Age, Am Hist Rev, Vol 0099, 94; Ambrose-of-Milan and the End of the Nicene-Arian Conflicts, Historian, Vol 0058, 96. **CONTACT ADDRESS** Dept of Hist, Ohio Wesleyan Univ, 61 S Sandusky St, Delaware, OH, 43015-2398.

HALLER, ARCHIBALD O.
PERSONAL Born 01/15/1926, San Diego, CA, m, 1989, 5 children **DISCIPLINE** SOCIOLOGY **EDUCATION** Hamline Univ, BA, 50; Univ Minn, MA, 51; Univ Wisc, PhD, 54. **CAREER** Prof Emeritus Sociology, Univ Wisc, 94-; Distinguished vis prof Rural Sociology, Ohio St Univ, 82-83; prof Sociology, Univ Wisc, 65-94; assoc prof to prof Sociology, Mich St Univ, 56-65; res assoc Sociology, Univ Wisc, 54-56. **HONORS AND AWARDS** Order of Merit, Grand Officer, Govt Brazil, 81; Fulbright Fel to Brazil, 62, 74, 79, 83, 87, 88, 89; Distinguished Rural Sociologist, Rural Sociologist Soc, 90. **MEMBERSHIPS** Amer Sociological Assoc Fel 59-; Industrial Relations Res Assoc, 76-; Intl Industrial Relations Assoc, 76-; Intl Rural Sociological Assoc; Intl Sociological Assoc for Rural Sociology; Latin Amer Res Assoc; Midwest Sociological Soc; NY Acad of Sci; Rural Sociological Soc; Sigma Xi; Soc for Intl Development; Sociological Res Assoc **RESEARCH** Societal Stratification Structures; Social Status Allocation Processes; Socioeconomic Development. **SELECTED PUBLICATIONS** Concepts and Indicators of Development: An Empirical Analysis, Jour of Developing Societies, 98; The Socioeconomic Development Levels of the People of Amazonian Brazil-1970 and 1980, Jour Developing Areas, 96; Social Structure and Behavior: Essays in Honor of William Hamilton Seward, Academic Pr, 82. **CONTACT ADDRESS** Dept of Rural Sociology, 350 Agriculture Hall, Madison, WI, 53706. **EMAIL** haller@ssc.wisc.edu

HALLER, MARK HUGHLIN
PERSONAL Born 12/22/1928, Washington, DC, s **DISCIPLINE** HISTORY, CRIMINAL JUSTICE **EDUCATION** Wesleyan Univ, BA, 51; Univ of MD, MA, 54; Univ of Wis, PhD, 59. **CAREER** Instr & asst prof of Hist, Univ of Chicago, 59-68; ASSOC PROF & PROF OF HIST & CRIMINAL JUSTICE, 68-, TEMPLE UNIV. **MEMBERSHIPS** Am Hist Assoc, Org of Am Historians; Am Soc of Criminology; Law & Soc Asn. **RESEARCH** History of American urban crime; the structure of organized crime. **SELECTED PUBLICATIONS** Auth, Historical Roots of Police Behavior: Chicago 1890-1925, Law & Soc Rev, 76; auth, Bootleggers as Businessmen: From City Slums to City Builders, Law, Alcohol, and Order: Perspectives on Nat Prohibiton, 85; auth, Loansharking in American Cities: Historical Analysis of a Marginal Enterprise, Am J of Legal Hist, Illegal Enterprise: A Theoretical and Historical Interpretation, Criminology, 90; auth, Policy Gambling, Entertainment, and the Emergence of Black Politics: Chicago from 1900 to 1940, J of Soc Hist, 91; auth, Life under Bruno: The Economics of an Organized Crime Family, Pa Crime Comn, 91; auth, The Bruno Family of Philadelphia: Organized Crime as a Regulatory Agency, Handbook of Organized Crime in the United States, 94. **CONTACT ADDRESS** Dept of History, Temple Univ, Philadelphia, PA, 19122. **EMAIL** hallerm@vm.temple.edu

HALLETT, JUDITH P.
PERSONAL Born 04/04/1944, Chicago, IL, m, 1966, 2 children **DISCIPLINE** CLASSICAL PHILOLOGY **EDUCATION** Wellesley Univ, BA, 66; Harvard Univ, MA, 67, PhD, 71. **CAREER** Lectr and Vis Asst Prof, Clark Univ, 72-74; Asst Prof, Boston Univ, 74-82; Asst Prof Mellon Found, Brandeis Univ, 82-83; Assoc Prof, 83-93, Prof, Univ Md, 93-, Dept Chair, 96-. **HONORS AND AWARDS** Blegen Vis Schol, Vassar Col, 80; NEH Fel Col Teachers, 86-87; Distinguished Scholar-Teacher, Univ Md, 92-93. **MEMBERSHIPS** Am Philol Asn; Classical Asn Atlantic States; Phi Beta Kappa; Am Asn Univ Prof; Women's Classical Caucus. **RESEARCH** Latin language and literature; Roman culture; women, sexuality, and the family in classical antiquity; the classical tradition. **SELECTED PUBLICATIONS** Auth, Fathers and Daughters in Roman Society: Women and the Elite Family, Princeton Univ Press, 84; Feminist Theory, Historical Periods, Literary Canons and the Study of Greco-Roman Antiquity, Feminist Theory and the Classics, 93; Martial's Sulpicia and Propertius, Women in Classical Antiquity: Essays in Honor of Joy K. King, Oak Park, 93; ed and contribr, Six ¤North Americanl Women Classicists, special issue of Classical World, Nov/Dec 96-Jan/Feb 97; co-ed and contribr, The Personal Voice in Classical Scholarship, Routledge, 96; Roman Sexualities, Princeton, 97; author of numerous articles and other publications. **CONTACT ADDRESS** Classics Dept, Univ of Maryland, College Park, MD, 20742. **EMAIL** jh10@umail.umd.edu

HALLION, RICHARD PAUL
PERSONAL Born 05/17/1948, Washington, DC **DISCIPLINE** HISTORY OF TECHNOLOGY AND AVIATION **EDUCATION** Univ Md, BA, 70, PhD(Am hist), 75. **CAREER** Mus cur, Nat Air and Space Mus, Smithsonian Inst, 74-80; assoc prof gen admin, Univ Col, Univ Md, 80-82; HISTORIAN HIST AVIATION, AIR FORCE FLIGHT TEST CTR, EDWARDS AFB, 82-, Adj assoc prof hist, Univ Md, 75-82, lectr, Dept Aerospace Eng, 76-82; vis fel, Silliman Col, Yale Univ, 77; mus consult, Toshihiko Sakow Assoc Inc, 79-; consult and auth, Time-Life Bks, 79-82. **HONORS AND AWARDS** Am Inst Aeronaut and Astronaut, Hist Manuscript Award, 76 and Young Engineer and Scientist Award, 79; Robert H Goddard Award, Nat Space Club, 80. **MEMBERSHIPS** Am Inst Aeronaut and Astronaut; Soc Hist Tech; US Naval Inst; Air Force Hist Found; Aviation and Space Writers Asn. **RESEARCH** History of aviation, especially aerodynamics and flight testing; military history, especially 20th century development of military technology; United States social and cultural history since 1945. **SELECTED PUBLICATIONS** Auth, NASA Engineers and the Age of Apollo, Pub Historian, Vol 0016, 94; Untitled, J Am Hist, Vol 0082, 95; Race to the Moon--America Duel with the Soviets, J Am Hist, Vol 0081, 95. **CONTACT ADDRESS** Off Af Historian, USAF, Bolling AFB, Washington, DC, 20330.

HALPENN, PAUL G.
PERSONAL Born 01/27/1937, New York, NY **DISCIPLINE** HISTORY **EDUCATION** Univ Va, BA, 58, Harvard Univ, AM, 61, PhD, 66. **CAREER** Vis prof, Naval War Col, 86-87; instr to asst prof to assoc prof to prof, Fl St Univ, 66- . **HONORS AND AWARDS** Phi Beta Kappa, Phi Eta Sigma; Woodrow Wilson Fel, 58; Fel, Royal Hist Soc, 93. **MEMBERSHIPS** Navy Records Soc; Amer Hist Soc. **RESEARCH** Naval hist; late nineteenth & twentieth century. **SELECTED PUBLICATIONS** Ed, The Keyes Papers, George Allen & Unwin, 79-81; The Royal Navy in the Mediterranean, 1915-1918, Temple Smith, 87; auth, The Naval War in the Mediterranean, 1914-1918, Naval Inst Press, 87; A Naval History of World War I, UCL Press, 94; Anton Haus: Osterreich-Ungarns Grossadmiral, Verlag Styria, 98. **CONTACT ADDRESS** Dept of History, Florida State Univ, Tallahassee, FL, 32306. **EMAIL** phalpenn@mailer.fsu.edu

HALPERIN, DAVID M.
PERSONAL Born 04/02/1952, Chicago, IL **DISCIPLINE** CLASSICAL & COMPARATIVE LITERATURE, QUEER THEORY **EDUCATION** Oberlin Col, BA, 73; Stanford Univ, MA, 77, PhD(classics & humanities), 80. **CAREER** Teaching asst classics, Oberlin Col, 71-73; teaching fel classics & humanities, Stanford Univ, 74-76; actg instr classics, Intercol Ctr Class Studies, Rome, 77-78; Prof Lit, Dept Humanities, Mass Inst Technol, 79-96, Assoc dir archaeol, Sch Class Studies, Am Acad, Rome, 77-78; teaching asst humanities, Stanford Univ, 78; sr lectr, sociol, Univ New South Wales, Sydney, 96- . **MEMBERSHIPS** Am Acad Rome; Am Philol Asn; Women's Class Caucus; Petronian Soc; Joseph Conrad Soc Am. **RESEARCH** Bucolic and pastoral poetry; Russian literature; platonic love. **SELECTED PUBLICATIONS** Auth, The role of the lie in The First Circle, In: Aleksandr Solzhenitsyn: Critical Essays and Documentary Materials, 2nd ed, Collier Bks, 75; Lord Jim and the pear tree caper, Am Notes & Queries, Vol 14, No 8, 76; Man's fate in the Aeneid, Va Quart Rev, Vol 53, No 1, 77; Solzhenitsyn, Epicurus and the ethics of Stalinism, Critical Inquiry, Vol 7, 80/81; Continuities in Solzhenitsyn's ethical thought, In: Solzhenitsyn in Exile, 82; Before Pastoral: Theocritus and the Ancient Tradition of Bucohe Poetry, Yale Univ Press, 83; auth, One Hundred Years of Homosexuality, Routledge, 90; ed, Before Sexuality, Princeton, 90; ed, The Lesbian and Gay Studies Reader, Routledge, 93; ed, GLQ: A Journal of Lesbian and Gay Studies, 93- ; auth, Saint Foucault, Oxford, 95. **CONTACT ADDRESS** School of Sociology, Univ of New South Wales, Sydney, ., 2052. **EMAIL** d.halperin@unsw.edu.au

HALPERN, PAUL G.
PERSONAL Born 01/27/1937, New York, NY **DISCIPLINE** MODERN EUROPEAN HISTORY **EDUCATION** Univ Va, BA, 58; Harvard Univ, AM, 61, PhD, 66. **CAREER** From instr to assoc prof, 65-74, prof hist Fla State Univ, 74- **HONORS AND AWARDS** Fel, Royal Hist Soc, 93. **MEMBERSHIPS** AHA; Co Mil Historians; Navy Rec Soc, Eng; The Naval Ref, Eng. **RESEARCH** Modern France; diplomatic and naval history. **SELECTED PUBLICATIONS** Auth, The Anglo-French-Italian naval convention of 1915, Hist J, 3/70; The Mediterranean Naval Situation, 1908-1914, Harvard Univ, 71; ed, The Keyes papers, 1914-1918, Vol I, 72, Vol II: 1919-1938, 78, Vol III: 1939-1945, 81, Navy Rec Soc; auth, The Naval War in the Mediterranean, 1914-1918, Allen & Unwin, 87; ed, The Toyal Navy in the Mediterranean, 1915-1918, Navy Rec Soc, 87; auth, A Naval History of World War I, Naval Inst Press, 94; auth, Admiral Haus, Verlag Styria, 98. **CONTACT ADDRESS** Dept of History, Florida State Univ, 600 W College Ave, Tallahassee, FL, 32306-1096. **EMAIL** phalpern@mailer.fsu.edu

HALPORN, JAMES WERNER
PERSONAL Born 01/04/1929, New York, NY, m, 1951, 2 children **DISCIPLINE** GREEK, LATIN **EDUCATION** Columbia Univ, AB, 49, MA, 50; Cornell Univ, PhD(Greek, Latin), 53. **CAREER** Instr Greek & Latin, Columbia Col, 54-58; vis lectr classics, Carleton Univ, 58-59; vis asst prof, Univ Mo, 59-60; asst prof, 60-64, assoc prof, 64-68, Prof Class Studies & Comp Lit, Ind Univ, Bloomington, 68-, Fulbright fel, Univ Vienna, 53-54; rep adv coun, Am Acad Rome, 62-, mem class jury Rome Prize fels, 70-71; Am Coun Learned Soc/Int Bus Mach Corp fel, 66-67; chmn region IX, Woodrow Wilson Nat Fel Found, 69-; vis prof classics & comp lit, Univ Calif, Berkeley, 71-72; mem comt on placement, Am Philol Asn, 80-83; vis scholar classics, Harvard Univ, 81-82 **MEMBERSHIPS** Am Philol Asn; NAm Patristic Soc; Class Asn Gt Brit; Soc Promotion Roman Studies; Soc Promotion Hellenic Studies. **RESEARCH** Late Latin literature; Latin palaeography; Greek and Latin metrics. **SELECTED PUBLICATIONS** Auth, Pause and Effect--An Introduction to the History of Punctuation on the West, J Medieval Studies, Vol 0069, 94; Early Printed Editions of Cassiodorus 'De Anima', Traditio-Studies Ancient Medieval Hist Thought Relig, Vol 0051, 96; Liutprand-Of-Cremona and the Freising-Codex, Munich-Clm-6388, J Medieval Studies, Vol 0070, 95. **CONTACT ADDRESS** 702 Ballantine Rd, Bloomington, IN, 47401.

HALTMAN, KENNETH
DISCIPLINE ART HISTORY **EDUCATION** Wesleyan, BA, 80; Yale Univ, MA, 85, PhD, 92. **CAREER** ASST PROF, ART HIST & AM STUD, MICH STATE UNIV **MEMBERSHIPS** Am Antiquarian Soc **SELECTED PUBLICATIONS** Auth, "Private Impressions and Public Views: The Long Expedition Sketchbooks of Titian Ramsay Peale, 1819-1820," Yale Univ Art Gallery Bull, 89; auth, "Between Science and Art: Titian Ramsay Peale's Long Expedition Sketches, Newly Discovered at the State Historical Society of Iowa," Palimpsest: Jour of Iowa State Hist Soc 74, 93; auth, "Titian Ramsay Peale: Specimen Portraiture, or Natural History as Family History," in The Peale Family: Creation of a Legacy, 1770-1870, Abbeville Press with Natl Port Gall, 96; auth, "The Poetics of Geologic Reverie: Figures of Source and Origin" in Samuel Seymour's Landscapes of the Rocky Mountains, Huntington Library Q, Fall 97; auth, entries in Reader's Encyclopedia of the American West, Yale Univ Press; auth, Earth and Reveries of Will, Gaston Bachelard, Jose Corti, 97; auth, Figures in A Western Landscape: Expeditionary Art and Science in the Early Republic, Princeton Univ Press. **CONTACT ADDRESS** Michigan State Univ, 113 Kresge Art Ctr, East Lansing, MI, 48824-1119. **EMAIL** haltman@pilot.msu.edu

HALTON, THOMAS
PERSONAL Born 02/06/1925, Cavan, Ireland **DISCIPLINE** GREEK, LATIN **EDUCATION** Maynooth Col, Ireland, BA, 46, STB, 49; Univ Col, Dublin, MA, 58; Cath Univ Am, PhD, 63. **CAREER** Assoc prof, 60-75, Prof Greek & Latin, Cath Univ AM, 75- **MEMBERSHIPS** Early Christian Greek **SELECTED PUBLICATIONS** Auth, The Martyrdom of Pionios-French, Cath Hist Rev, Vol 0081, 95; John-Chrysostom, The Homilies on the Statues--An Introduction, Cath Hist Rev, Vol 0080, 94. **CONTACT ADDRESS** Dept of Greek & Latin Cath, Catholic Univ of America, 620 Michigan Ave N E, Washington, DC, 20064-0002.

HALTTUNEN, KAREN
DISCIPLINE HISTORY **EDUCATION** Brown Univ, BA, 73; Yale Univ, PhD, 79. **CAREER** Assoc prof, hist & Am cult, Northwestern Univ; current, PROF HIST, UNIV CALIF DAVIS. **MEMBERSHIPS** Am Antiquarian Soc **SELECTED PUBLICATIONS** Auth, "Domestic Differences: Competing Narratives of Womanhood in the Murder Trial of Lucretia Chapman," in The Culture of Sentiment: Race, Gender, and Sentimentality in 19th Century America, Oxford Univ Press, 92; auth, "Early American Narratives: The Birth of Horror", in The Power of Culture: Critical Essays in American History, Univ Chicago Press, 93; auth, Murder Most Foul! The Killer and the American Gothic Imagination, Harvard Univ Press, 98; auth, Confidence Men and Painted Women: A Study of Middle-Class Culture in America, 1830-1870, 83; auth, "Gothic Imagination and Social Reform: The Haunted Houses of Lyman Beecher, Henry Ward Beecher, and Harriet Beecher Stowe," in New Essays on Uncle Tom's Cabin, 86; auth, "The Domestic Drama of Louisa May Alcott," Feminist Studies 10, 84. **CONTACT ADDRESS** Dept of Hist, Univ of Calif, Davis, CA, 95616.

HAM, DEBRA NEWMAN
PERSONAL Born 08/27/1948, York, PA, m, 1989, 2 children **DISCIPLINE** AFRICAN HISTORY **EDUCATION** Howard Univ, BA, 70, PhD, 84; Boston Univ, MA, 71. **CAREER** African-Am hist spec, National Archives, 72-86; ms div African Am hist spec, Libr Cong, 86-95; PROF HIST, MORGAN STATE UNIV, 95-. **HONORS AND AWARDS** Soc Am Arch Coker prize, 85; Univ Va Chesapeake fel, 98. **MEMBERSHIPS** Asn Stud Afro-Am Life, Hist; Afro-Am Hist, Genealogical Soc; Mid-Atlantic Reg Arch Conf. **RESEARCH** African-Am women; African diaspora. **SELECTED PUBLICATIONS** Auth, Black History: A Guide to Civilian Records in the National Archives, National Archives, 84; auth, We Shall Overcome, Someday: Collections Relating to the Civil Rights Movement in the Manuscript Division of the Library of Congress, Libr Congr Info Bull, Feb 90; ed, The African-American Mosaic: A Libary of Congress Resource Guide for the Study of Black History and Culture, Libr Cong, 93; auth, The Role of African American Women in the Founding of Liberia, in Global Dimensions of the African Diaspora, 2d ed, Howard Univ Press, 93; ed, The African American Odyssey, Libr Cong, 98. **CONTACT ADDRESS** Dept Hist, Morgan State Univ, Cold Spring Ln & Hillen Rd, Baltimore, MD, 21251. **EMAIL** dham@moac.morgan.edu

HAM, F. GERALD
PERSONAL Born 04/13/1930, Toms River, NJ, m, 1953, 4 children **DISCIPLINE** AMERICAN HISTORY **EDUCATION** Wheaton Col, Ill, AB, 52; Univ Ky, MA, 55, PhD(hist), 62. **CAREER** Assoc curator arch, WVa Univ Libr, 58-64; STATE ARCHIVIST, STATE HIST SOC, WIS, 64-, Lectr Am hist, WVa Univ, 62-63, asst prof, 63-64; lectr, Univ Wis Libr Sch, 67- **MEMBERSHIPS** Fel Soc Am Archivists (exec secy, 68-72, vpres, 72-73, pres, 73-74). **RESEARCH** American social and religious history; American archival institutions and practices; 19th century communitarian experiments. **SELECTED PUBLICATIONS** Auth, Is the Past Still Prologue--History And Archival Education, Am Archivist, Vol 0056, 93. **CONTACT ADDRESS** 3527 Tallyho Ln, Madison, WI, 53705.

HAMALAINEN, PEKKA KALEVI
PERSONAL Born 12/28/1938, Finland, m, 1965, 4 children **DISCIPLINE** EUROPEAN HISTORY **EDUCATION** IN Univ, AB, 61, PhD, 66. **CAREER** Actg asst prof hist, Univ CA, Santa Barbara, 65-66, asst prof, 66-70; assoc prof, 70-76, PROF HIST, UNIV WI-MADISON, 76-, CHMN WESTERN EUROP AREA STUDIES PROG, 77-, fac res grants, Univ CA, Santa Barbara, 66-69; Ford Found grant, 67-68; fac res grants, Univ WI-Madison, 71-; Am Philos Soc res grant, 73-74; mem, Nat Screening Comt, Fulbright-Hays Prog, 74-75; Am Coun Learned Socs fel, 76-77, res grant, 78; cons Dept of State, DC, 91-; Chair, Grad Educ Comm, Univ Wis, 96-97. **HONORS AND AWARDS** Vilas Associate, 96. **MEMBERSHIPS** AHA; Soc Advan Scand Studies. **RESEARCH** North European hist, twentieth century European hist; Finnish hist. **SELECTED PUBLICATIONS** Auth, Kielitaistelu Suomessa, 1917-1939, Werner Soderstrom Osakeyhtio, 68; Nationnalitetskampen och sprakstriden i Finland, 1917-1939, Holger Schildts Forlag, 69; In Time of Storm: Revolution, Civil War and the Ethnolinguistic Issue in Finland, State Univ NY, 78; Luokka ja Kieli vallankumouksen suomessa, Suomen Hist Seura, 78; Uniting Germany: Actions and Reactions, 94. **CONTACT ADDRESS** Dept of Hist, Univ Wisconsin, 455 North Park St, Madison, WI, 53706-1483.

HAMBLY, GAVIN RICHARD GRENVILLE
PERSONAL Born 07/04/1934, Sevenoaks, England, 2 children **DISCIPLINE** INDIAN HISTORY **EDUCATION** Cambridge Univ, BA, 58, MA & PhD(hist), 62. **CAREER** Lectr, Brit Coun, Tehran, Iran, 61-63, dir studies, Ankara, Turkey, 64-66, asst rep, New Delhi, India, 66-68; from asst prof to assoc prof hist of India, Yale Univ, 68-75; PROF HIST, UNIV TEX, DALLAS, 75-, DEAN SCH ARTS & HUMANITIES, 77-, Smuts Mem Fund Commonwealth Study res grant, Cambridge Univ, 63-64; res grants, Soc Sci Res Coun, 70 & Nat Endowment for Humanities, 71 & fel, 76-77. **MEMBERSHIPS** Asn Asian Studies; Mideast Studies Asn; Royal Cent Asian Soc; Brit Inst Persian Studies; Asn Brit Orient. **RESEARCH** Mughal and British rule in India; Iranian civilization and its spread in India and Central Asia; Indian and Iranian urban history. **SELECTED PUBLICATIONS** Auth, Nur Jahan--Empress Of Mughal India, Am Hist Rev, Vol 0099, 94. **CONTACT ADDRESS** Sch of Arts & Humanities JO 45, Univ of Tex at Dallas, Box 688, Richardson, TX, 75080.

HAMBRICK, CHARLES HILTON
PERSONAL Born 05/14/1931, Atlanta, GA, m, 1955, 3 children **DISCIPLINE** HISTORY OF RELIGIONS, JAPANESE STUDIES **EDUCATION** Vanderbilt Univ, BA, 52; Drew Univ, BD, 59; Univ Chicago, MA, 67, PhD(hist of relig), 71. **CAREER** From instr to asst prof, 69-75, Assoc Prof Hist Of Relig, Vanderbilt Univ, 75- **MEMBERSHIPS** Am Acad Relig; Asn Asian Studies. **RESEARCH** Japanese religion; religion and Eastern cultures; methods in the study of religion. **SELECTED PUBLICATIONS** Auth, Religion and Society in Modern Japan--Selected-Readings, Monumenta Nipponica, Vol 0049, 94. **CONTACT ADDRESS** Dept of Relig Studies, Vanderbilt Univ, Sta B, Box 64, Nashville, TN, 37235.

HAMBY, ALONZO LEE
PERSONAL Born 01/13/1940, Humansville, MO, m, 1967 **DISCIPLINE** HISTORY **EDUCATION** Southeast Mo State Col, BA, 60; Columbia Univ, MA, 61; Univ Mo, PhD(hist), 65. **CAREER** From Asst prof to Prof, 65-96, DISTINGUISHED PROF HIST, OHIO UNIV, 96-, Fac Senate, 80-83, Univ Compensation Comt, 80-82, Univ Grad Coun, 93-96, Col Arts and Sci Staffing Advisory Comt, 83-84, 87-89, Dir Grad Studies, Dept Hist, 78-80, 87-88, 95-, Chmn, Dept Hist, 80-83; mem, Ohio Hist Records Preserv Adv Bd, 78-. **HONORS AND AWARDS** Woodrow Wilson Fel, 60-61; Nat Defense Educ Act Fel, 62-64; Univ Mo Wilson Fel, 64-65; Harry S. Truman Libr Inst grants, 64, 66, 67, 69; Am Philos Soc grant, 67; Ohio Univ Res Coun grants, 67, 76, 83; Ohio Univ Baker Fund awards, 69, 86; Nat Endowment for Humanities fel, 72-73; Evans fel, Harry S Truman Libr Inst, 73-74; David D Lloyd Prize, Harry S. Truman Inst, 74; First Book Award, Phi Alpha Theta, 74; Publ Award, Ohio Acad Hist, 74; Phi Beta Kappa, Lambda of Ohio, honorary membership, 77; SE Mo State Univ Outstanding History Alumnus, 85; NEH Summer Fel, 85; Harry S. Truman Library Inst Sr Fel, 86-87; Col of Liberal Arts Alumni Merit Award, 90; Fel, Woodrow Wilson Int Ctr for Schol, 91-92; Herbert Hoover Book Award, 96; Harry S. Truman Book Award, 96; Ohio Acad of Distinguished Serv Award, 98. **MEMBERSHIPS** AHA; Orgn Am Historians,; Southern Hist Asn; Soc Historians Am Foreign Rels. **RESEARCH** United States history, 1607-present; Twentieth-century America; American Historiography; contemporary history. **SELECTED PUBLICATIONS** Ed, The New Deal, Analysis and Interpretation, Weybright & Talley, 69, 2nd ed, Longman, 80; auth, The Liberals, Truman and FDR as symbol and myth, J Am Hist, 3/70; The vital center, the Fair Deal, and the quest for a liberal political economy, Am Hist Rev, 6/72; Beyond the New Deal: Harry S Truman and American Liberalism, Columbia Univ, 73; ed and contribr, Harry S. Truman and The Fair Deal, Heath, 74; auth, The clash of perspectives..., In: The Truman Period as a Research Field, 2nd ed, Univ Mo, 74; The Imperial Years: The United States Since 1939, Weybright & Talley, 76; co-ed & contribr, Historian, Archivists, and Access to The Papers of Recent Public Figures, Orgn Am Historians, 78; auth, Liberalism and Its Challengers: F.D.R. to Reagan, Oxford Univ Press, 85, 2nd ed, 92; Man of the People: A Life of Harry S. Truman, Oxford Univ Press, 95; numerous articles and book reviews published or forthcoming in scholarly journals or magazines and essay collections, and pieces for encyclopedias and other reference works. **CONTACT ADDRESS** Dept of History, Ohio Univ, Athens, OH, 45701-2979. **EMAIL** hambya@oak.cats.ohiou.edu

HAMDANI, ABBAS HUSAYN
PERSONAL Born 08/11/1926, Surat, India, m, 1961, 2 children **DISCIPLINE** MIDDLE EASTERN HISTORY, ISLAMIC CIVILIZATION **EDUCATION** Univ Bombay, BA, 45, LLB, 47; Univ London, PhD, 50. **CAREER** Prof Islamic hist, SM & Islamia Cols, Univ Karachi, 51-62; prof Arabic studies, Am Univ Cairo, 62-69; vis lectr hist, Univ Wis-Madison, 69-70, PROF HIST, UNIV WIS-MILWAUKEE, 70-; Chmn, Comt Mid Eastern and NAfrican Studies, Univ Wis-Milwaukee, 72-. **HONORS AND AWARDS** NEH res fel, Am Res Ctr Egypt, 74-75, 78-79, 88-89; Fulbright Fel, India, 92, Egypt, 96-97. **MEMBERSHIPS** Fel Mid E Studies Asn NAm; Am Orient Soc; Am Inst Res in Yemen. **RESEARCH** Fatimid movement and caliphate; South Arabian history; medieval Islamic social history. **SELECTED PUBLICATIONS** Auth, Islamic Fundamentalism, Mediterranean Quart, Fall 93; Islam and Politics: Egypt, Algeria and Tunisia, The Digest of Middle Eastern Studies, Summer 94; A Time-Table for Palestinian-Israeli Peace, The Digest of Middle Eastern Studies, Winter 94; An Overview of the Current Status of the Muslim countries of the Former Soviet Union, Islamic Studies, Vol 33, 94; A Critique of Casanova's Dating of the Rasa' il lkhwan al Safa', In: Essays in Medieval Isma' ili History and Thought, Cambridge Univ Press, 95; author of numerous other articles. **CONTACT ADDRESS** Dept of Hist, Col Lett & Sci, Univ of Wis-Milwaukee, PO Box 413, Milwaukee, WI, 53201-0413.

HAMELIN, MARCEL
PERSONAL Born 09/18/1937, Saint-Narcisse, PQ, Canada, m, 1962, 3 children **DISCIPLINE** HISTORY **EDUCATION** Univ Laval, LL, 61, DL, 72. **CAREER** Prof hist, 66-, dept ch, 68-70, vice dean grad stud, 72-74, dean arts, 74-90, RECTOR & VICE CHANCELLOR, UNIV OTTAWA, 90-. **MEMBERSHIPS** Asn canadienne-francaise pour l'avancement des sciences; Can Hist Asn; Royal Soc Can; vice pres, Inter-Am Orgn Higher Educ; dir, Canada-US Fulbright Prog. **SELECTED PUBLICATIONS** Auth, Les premieres annees du parlementarisme quebecois: 1867-1878, 75; coauth, Les moeurs electorales dans le Quebec, de 1791 a nos jours, 62; coauth, Apercu de la

politique canadienne au XIXe siecle, 65; coauth, Confederation 1867, 66; coauth, Les elections provinciales dans le Quebec, 69; ed, Les memoires de l'honorable Raoul Dandurand, 67; ed, Les debats de l'Assemblee legislative de la province de Quebec 1867-1870, vol I-IV, 74; ed, Les debats de l'Assemblee legislative de la province de Quebec 1871-1875, vol V-VIII, 76; ed, Les debats de l'Assemblee legislative de la province de Quebec 1875-1878, vol IX-XI, 77. **CONTACT ADDRESS** Univ of Ottawa, 550 Cumberland, Ottawa, ON, K1N 6N5.

HAMEROW, THEODORE STEPHEN
PERSONAL Born 08/24/1920, Warsaw, Poland, m, 1954, 2 children **DISCIPLINE** MODERN HISTORY **EDUCATION** City Col New York, BA, 42; Columbia Univ, MA, 47; Yale Univ, PhD, 51. **CAREER** Instr hist, Wellesley Col, 50-51 & overseas prog, Univ Md, 51-52; from instr to assoc prof, Univ Ill, 52-58; assoc prof, 58-61, chmn dept, 73-76, PROF HIST, UNIV WIS-MADISON, 61-, Consult ed, Dorsey Press, 61-70; Fulbright scholar & Soc Sci Res Coun fel, 62-63. **MEMBERSHIPS** AHA; Conf Group Cent Europ Hist (secy-treas, 59-61, pres, 76). **RESEARCH** Modern European history; modern Germany; the 19th century. **SELECTED PUBLICATIONS** Auth, Frankfurt-Am-Main--History of the City in 9 Parts, J Modern Hist, Vol 0066, 94; History of Thuringia 1866-1914, J Modern Hist, Vol 0066, 94; In the Beginning--The Advent of the Modern-Age--Europe in the 1840s, Am Hist Rev, Vol 0100, 95; The Transformation of European Politics, 1763-1848, Hist, Vol 0057, 95; Hitler and Stalin--Parallel Lives, J Modern Hist, Vol 0067, 95. **CONTACT ADDRESS** Univ of Wisconsin, Madison, 466 S Segoe Rd, Madison, WI, 53711.

HAMILTON, CAROL
DISCIPLINE MODERNIST AND POSTMODERNIST CULTURAL POLITICS **EDUCATION** Univ Calif, PhD. **CAREER** Pol Sci, Carnegie Mellon Univ. **MEMBERSHIPS** Area: anarchism and modernism. **CONTACT ADDRESS** Carnegie Mellon Univ, 5000 Forbes Ave, Pittsburgh, PA, 15213.

HAMILTON, EDWIN
PERSONAL Born 07/24/1936, Tuskegee, Alabama, m, 1960 **DISCIPLINE** EDUCATION **EDUCATION** Tuskegee Univ, BS 1960, MEd 1963; The Ohio State Univ, PhD 1973. **CAREER** Macon County Schools, dir 1965-70; Ohio State Univ, rsch asst 1971-73; FL International Univ, prof 1973-74; Howard Univ, prof 1974-. **HONORS AND AWARDS** Fulbright Scholar (Nigeria) CIES/USIA 1982-83; Writer's Recognition Univ of DC 1984; Certificate of Appreciation Phi Delta Gamma Johns Hopkins Univ 1986; Certificate of Awd Phi Delta Kappa Howard Univ 1987-89; Distinguished Alumni Citation NAFEO/Tuskegee Univ, 1988; President's Award Howard Univ, PDK, 1989; designed study-travel to China Tour, 1989. **MEMBERSHIPS** Mem AAACE/ASTD 1975-87; presidential assoc Tuskegee Univ 1980-; mem Intl Assoc CAEO/ICA 1984-87; rsch rep Phi Delta Kappa Howard Univ 1986-87; adjunct prof Univ of DC 1986; educ leader Professional Seminar Consultants's (Russia) 1986; adjunct prof OH State Univ 1987; pres, Howard Univ PDK, 1989-89; elections judge, P G Bd of Elections, Uppermarlboro, MD, 1986-87; chief elections judge, 1988-95. **CONTACT ADDRESS** Professor of Education, Howard Univ, Washington, VT, 20059.

HAMILTON, JOHN DANIEL BURGOYNE
PERSONAL Born 10/19/1939, Los Angeles, CA **DISCIPLINE** CLASSICAL LANGUAGES, GREEK MYTHOLOGY & RELIGION **EDUCATION** St Louis Univ, AB, 63; AM, 64; Weston Col, Cambridge, MS, MDiv, 69; Univ MN, PhD, 73. **CAREER** Instr classics, Univ Santa Clara, 65-66; asst prof, 72-76, assoc prof Classics, 77-, GRAD STUDIES ADV, CLASSICS, COL OF THE HOLY CROSS, 89-. **MEMBERSHIPS** Am Philol Asn; Class Asn New England; Class Asn Midwest & South; Soc Promotion Hellenic Studies; Class Asn Gt Brit. **RESEARCH** Greek epic and drama; mythology; Roman satire. **SELECTED PUBLICATIONS** Auth, Justin's Apology 66: A review of scholarship, 72 & The church and the language of mystery, 77, Ephemerides Theol Lovanienses; transl (with B Nagy), L Gernet, The Anthropology of Ancient Greece, Johns Hopkins, 81; Antigone: Kinship, Justice and the Womb, in Myth and the Pelis, Cornell, 91; At Sea with Myth: A Bibliography for Charting a Course, NE Clas J, Dec 89; contrib, articles in The World Book Encyclopedia, 93. **CONTACT ADDRESS** Dept of Classics, Col of the Holy Cross, 1 College St, Worcester, MA, 01610-2395. **EMAIL** jhamilto@holycross.edu

HAMILTON, PAUL L.
PERSONAL Born 04/01/1941, Pueblo, CO, d **DISCIPLINE** EDUCATION **EDUCATION** Univ of Denver, BA 1964, MA 1972; Univ of N CO, EdD 1975. **CAREER** Denver Public Schools, teacher 1964-91, principal, 1991-95; State of Colorado, representative 1969-73; Univ of Denver, instructor, 1971, lecturer & rsch asst 1971-72, prof of history, 1982-96; Univ of Colorado, instructor, 1995-96; Hamilton Education Consultants, pres, currently; Power Learning Systems, district dir, 1995-; R A Renaissance Publications, pres, 1993-. **HONORS AND AWARDS** Denver Assn for Retired Citizens, Educator of the Year, 1991; Univ of Color ado, Black Alumni Award, 1995; Omega Psi Phi Fraternity, Chi Phi Chapter, Citiz en of the Year, 1995. **MEMBERSHIPS** Assn for the Study of Classical African Civilizations; National Alliance of Black School Educators; Univ of Denver National Honor Society; Renaissance Publications, pres. **SELECTED PUBLICATIONS** Author: Teacher's Guide for Afro American History; African People's Contributions to World History: Shattering the Myths, Vol 1.

HAMILTON, RICHARD
PERSONAL Born 12/19/1943, Bryn Mawr, PA, m, 1965, 2 children **DISCIPLINE** GREEK LITERATURE **EDUCATION** Harvard Col, AB, 65; Univ Mich, PhD(class), 71. **CAREER** From Asst Prof to Assoc Prof, 71-88, Prof Greek, Bryn Mawr Col, 88-. **MEMBERSHIPS** Am Philol Asn. **RESEARCH** Greek literature; Greek religion. **SELECTED PUBLICATIONS** Auth, Epinikion: General Form in the Odes of Pindar, Mouton, The Hague, 74; The Architecture of Hesiod's Theogany and Works and Days, Hopkins, 89; Choes and Anthesteria, Mich, 92; Treasure Map, Mich (forthcoming 98). **CONTACT ADDRESS** Dept of Greek, Bryn Mawr Col, 101 N Merion Ave, Bryn Mawr, PA, 19010-2899. **EMAIL** rhamilto@brynmawr.edu

HAMILTON, RICHARD FREDERICK
PERSONAL Born 01/18/1930, Kenmore, NY, m, 1957, 2 children **DISCIPLINE** SOCIOLOGY **EDUCATION** Univ Chicago, AB, 50; Columbia Univ, MA, 53, PhD, 63. **CAREER** Instr, Skidmore Col, 57-59; instr, State Univ NY, Binghamton, 59-64; asst prof, Princeton Univ, 64-66; assoc to full prof, Univ WI, 66-70; prof, McGill Univ, Montreal, Can, 70-86; prof, 86-98, prof Emeritus, OH State Univ, 98-. **HONORS AND AWARDS** Distinguished Scholar award, 93. **RESEARCH** Political sociology; historical sociol. **SELECTED PUBLICATIONS** Auth, Affluence and the French Worker in the Fourth Republic, Princeton Univ Press, 67; Class and Politics in the United States, John Wiley & Sons, 72; Restraining Myths: Critical Studies of US Social Structure and Politics, Sage Pubs, 75; Who Voted for Hitler?, Princeton Univ Press, 82; with James Wright, The State of the Masses, Aldine Press, 86; The Bourgeois Epoch: Marx and Engels on Britain, France, and Germany, Univ NC Press, 91; The Social Misconstruction of Reality: Validation and Verification in the Scholarly Community, Yale Univ Press, 96; and numerous other articles. **CONTACT ADDRESS** Menhon Center, Ohio State Univ, 1501 Neil Ave, Columbus, OH, 43201-2602. **EMAIL** hamilton.1@osu.edu

HAMILTON, VICTOR PAUL
PERSONAL Born 09/26/1941, Toronto, ON, Canada, m, 1965, 4 children **DISCIPLINE** OLD TESTAMENT STUDIES, ANCIENT NEAR EASTERN HISTORY **EDUCATION** Houghton Col, BA, 63; Asbury Theol Sem, BD, 66, ThM, 67; Brandeis Univ, MA, 69, PhD, 71. **CAREER** From asst prof to assoc prof, 71-85, prof Old Testament, Asbury Col, 85-. **MEMBERSHIPS** Soc Bibl Lit; Evangelical Theol Soc. **RESEARCH** Old Testament languages. **SELECTED PUBLICATIONS** Auth, The Shepherd Psalm: Psalm 23, Asbury Seminarian, 72; Handbook on the Pentateuch, Baker, 82; Genesis Chapters 1-17, Eerdmans, 92; Genesis, Chapters 18-50, Eerdmans, 95. **CONTACT ADDRESS** 1 Macklem Dr, Wilmore, KY, 40390-1198. **EMAIL** victor.hamilton@asbury.edu

HAMILTON, VIRGINIA V.
PERSONAL Kansas City, MO **DISCIPLINE** UNITED STATES HISTORY **EDUCATION** Birmingham-Southern Col, AB, 41, MA, 61; Univ Ala, PhD(hist), 68. **CAREER** Asst prof hist, Univ Montevallo, 51-55; asst to pres, Birmingham-Southern Col, 55-65; lectr, 65-69, from asst prof to assoc prof, 69-75, PROF HIST, UNIV ALA, BIRMINGHAM, 75-, CHAIRPERSON DEPT, 75- **HONORS AND AWARDS** Award of Merit, Am Asn State & Local Hist, 73. **MEMBERSHIPS** Southern Hist Asn; Soc Am Historians; AHA; Orgn Am Historians; Am Asn State & Local Hist. **RESEARCH** Southern politics since 1900. **SELECTED PUBLICATIONS** Auth, Unheard Voices--The 1st Historians of Southern Women, J S Hist, Vol 0060, 94. **CONTACT ADDRESS** Dept of Hist, Univ Col Univ of Ala, Birmingham, AL, 35294.

HAMLIN, CHRISTOPHER S.
DISCIPLINE HISTORY **EDUCATION** Antioch Col, BA, 74; Univ Wis, MA, 77, PhD, 82. **CAREER** Assoc fel, Joan B. Kroc Inst for Intl Peace Stu, prof. **RESEARCH** History of technology; history of medicine. **SELECTED PUBLICATIONS** Auth, What Becomes of Pollution? Adversary Science and the Controversy on the Self-Purification of Rivers in Britain, 1850-1900, 87; A Science of Impurity: Water Analysis in Nineteenth-Century Britain, 90; Concepts of Predisposing Causes in the Early Nineteenth Century Public Health Movement, 92; Reflexivity in Technology Studies: Toward a Technology of Technology (and Science)?, 92; Between Knowledge and Action: Themes in the History of Environmental Chemistry, 93; Environmental Sensibility in Edinburgh, 1839-1840: the 'Fetid Irrigation' Controversy, 94; Public Health and Social Justice in the Age of Chadwick: Britain 1800-1854, 98; co-auth, Deep Disagreement in U.S. Agriculture: Making Sense of Policy Conflict, 93. **CONTACT ADDRESS** History and Philosophy of Science Dept, Univ of Notre Dame, Notre Dame, IN, 46556. **EMAIL** Christopher.S.Hamlin.1@nd.edu

HAMM, MICHAEL FRANKLIN
PERSONAL Born 08/29/1943, Ithaca, NY, m, 2 children **DISCIPLINE** RUSSIAN HISTORY, EAST & EUROPE, MODERN EUROPEAN HISTORY **EDUCATION** Macalester Col, BA, 65; Ind Univ, Bloomington, AM, 67, PhD, 71. **CAREER** Asst prof, 70-76, assoc prof, 76-86, Prof hist Centre Col KY, 86-, Ewing T Boles Prof Hist, 93-, ch, Div Soc Sci, 91-95, ch, Hist Prog, 84-89, 95-; Am Philos Soc fel, Helsinki, 73; res fel, Int Res & Exchanges Bd, IREX, 76-77; Nat Endowment for Hum grant, 78 & 81. **HONORS AND AWARDS** IREX & Fulbright grants, USSR, 86; Phi Beta Kappa, 89; Antonovych Found Prize, Most Outstanding Work on Ukraine, 95. **MEMBERSHIPS** Am Asn Slavic Studies; AAUP. **RESEARCH** Russ urban and soc hist. **SELECTED PUBLICATIONS** Auth, Liberalism and the Jewish question; the progressive bloc, Russ Rev, 4/72; Liberal politics in wartime Russia: an analysis of the progressive bloc, Slavic Rev, 74; ed, The City in Russian History, Univ Ky, 76; coauth, The breakdown or urban modernization: a prelude to the revolutions of 1917, In: City in Russ Hist; auth, The modern Russian city: an historiographical analysis, J Urban Hist, 77; Riga's municipal election of 1913: A study in Baltic urban politics, Russ Rev, 4/80; Khar'Kov's progressive Duma, 1910-1914: A study in Russian municipal reform, Slav Rev, spring 81; The City in Late Imperial Russia, Ind Univ Press, 86; Kiev: A Portrait, 1800-1917, Princeton Univ Press, 93; Teaching in Almaty, kazakstan: Autumn 1995, ISRE Newsletter on Russian & Eurasian Educ, spring 96; Kishinev: The Character and Development of a Tsarist Frontier Town, Nationalist Papers, 3/98, ed, Moldova - The Forgotten Republic, Nationalistc Papers, 3/98. **CONTACT ADDRESS** Centre Col, 600 W Walnut St, Danville, KY, 40422-1394.

HAMM, THOMAS D.
PERSONAL Born 06/08/1957, New Castle, IN, m, 1984 **DISCIPLINE** HISTORY **EDUCATION** Butler Univ, BA, 79; Ind Univ, MA, 81, PhD, 85. **CAREER** Vis asst prof, Ind Univ-Purdue Univ, 85-87; ARCH, ASSOC PROF HIST, EARLHAM COL, 87-. **HONORS AND AWARDS** An Soc Church Hist Brewer Prize, 87. **MEMBERSHIPS** AHA; OAH; SHEAR; SAA; AAUP; Am Soc Church Hist. **RESEARCH** Am rel hist; antebellum reform; Quakerism. **SELECTED PUBLICATIONS** Auth, George Fox and the Politics of Late Nineteenth-Century Quaker Historiography, in New Light on George Fox, 1624-1691: A Collection of Essays, Sessions, 94; auth, Hicksite Quakers and the Antebellum Nonresistance Movement, Church Hist 63, Dec 94; auth, Quakers and African Americans, in Encyclopedia of African American Culture and History, Macmillan, 89; auth, Gurneyites and Hicksites, 1871-1917, in Quaker Crosscurrents: Three Hundred Years of Friends in the New York Yearly Meetings, Syracuse Univ Press, 95; auth, God's Government Begun: The Society for Universal Inquiry and Reform, Earlham College: A History, 1847- 1997, Ind Univ Press, 97. **CONTACT ADDRESS** Lilly Libr, Earlham Col, Richmond, IN, 47374. **EMAIL** tomh@earlham.edu

HAMMOND, JAMES MATTHEW
PERSONAL Born 07/10/1930, Keanansville, North Carolina, m **DISCIPLINE** PSYCHOLOGY **EDUCATION** Oakwood Coll, BA 1953; SC State Coll, MSc 1960; Catholic Univ of Amer, MA 1975; Friendship Coll, DDiv 1963; S IL Univ, PhD 1973. **CAREER** Atkins HS, guidance counselor 1960-61; Sci Dept Bekwai Teachers Coll, chair 1961-68; Seventh Day Adventist Church of Sierra Leone, pres 1968-70; SDA Church of North Ghana, exec dir 1972-74; Metro Family Life Council, mem 1979; Pan African Develop Coop, bd mem 1981; MD Psychological Assoc, mem 1982-; Columbia Union Coll, chair/prof of psychology. **HONORS AND AWARDS** UNESCO Fellow United Nations Organs 1972; Phi Delta Kappa mem SIU Chap 1972. **MEMBERSHIPS** Mem Metro Family Life Council 1979; bd mem Pan African Develop Coop 1981; mem MD Psychological Assoc 1982; chaplain (maj) Civil Air Patrol 1983. **CONTACT ADDRESS** Chair/Prof of Psychology, Columbia Union Col, 7600 Flower Ave, Takoma Park, MD, 20912.

HAMMOND, MASON
PERSONAL Born 02/14/1903, Boston, MA, m, 1935, 3 children **DISCIPLINE** ROMAN HISTORY, LATIN LITERATURE **EDUCATION** Harvard Univ, AB, 25; Oxford Univ, BA, 27, BLitt, 30. **CAREER** From instr to Pope prof, 28-73, Emer Pope Prof, Latin Lang & Lit, Harvard Univ, 73-, From instr to prof, Radcliffe Col, 28-42; prof in charge class studies, Am Acad Rome, 37-39 & 55-57, vis prof, 51-52 & 63; actg dir, Villa I Tatti, Harvard Ctr Renaissance Studies, Florence, Italy, 72 & 73; vis prof classics, Univ Wis-Madison, 74; emer trustee, Am Acad Rome & St Mark's Sch; trustee, Isabella Stewart Gardner Mus, Boston. **HONORS AND AWARDS** LHD, St Bonaventure Univ, 78. **MEMBERSHIPS** Am Philol Asn; Archaeol Inst Am; Am Acad Arts & Sci; hon mem Ger Archaeol Inst. **RESEARCH** Roman history; Latin literature. **SELECTED PUBLICATIONS** Auth, The Politics Of Immorality in Ancient-Rome, Classical World, Vol 0088, 95; Restless Youth in Ancient-Rome, Classical World, Vol 0088, 95; The Edges of the Earth in Ancient-Thought, Classical World, Vol 0086, 93; Space, Geography, and Politics in the Early Roman-Empire, Classical World, Vol 0086, 92. **CONTACT ADDRESS** Harvard Univ, Widener Libr H, Cambridge, MA, 02138.

HAMMOND, PAUL Y.
DISCIPLINE POLITICAL SCIENCE **EDUCATION** Univ Utah, BA, 49; Harvard Univ, MA, 51, PhD, 53. **CAREER** Instr, Govt, Harvard Univ, 53-55; lectr, Publ Law & Govt, Columbia Univ, 56-57; fell, Naval Hist, US Naval Acad, 55-56; asst prof, Polit Sci, Yale Univ, 57-62; res assoc/Rockefeller fell, Wash Ctr For Policy Res, Johns Hopkins Univ, 62-64; sr scientist, Rand Corp, 64-76; PROF, UNIV PITTSBURGH, 76-. **RESEARCH** US foreign & security policy; Presidency & foreign relations; Information systems for public organizations; Regional foreign policy; NATO & Asia; Policy formation & policy implementation with respect to foreign relations **SELECTED PUBLICATIONS** "Central Organization in the Transition from Bush to Clinton," Am Defense Annual 1994, Lexington Books, 94; "Towards a Workable European Architecture: Political-Military Problems in the New Europe," The International System after the Collapse of the East-West Order, Martinus Nijhoff, 94; "Security and Morality in a Contingent World," Moral Perspectives on US Security Policy: View from the LDS Community, David M Kennedy Center for International Studies, 95; "Doing Without America?", The Evolving Pacific Power Structure , Inst of Southeast Asian Studies, 97; "On Taking Peacekeeping Seriously," To Sheath the Sword: Civil-MilitaryRElations in the Quest for Democracy, Greenwood Press, 97. **CONTACT ADDRESS** Grad Sch Public & Int Affairs, Univ Pitts, 3N23 Forbes Quadrangle, Pittsburgh, PA, 15260. **EMAIL** PYH@pitt.edu

HAMPTON, BARBARA L.
DISCIPLINE ETHNOMUSICOLOGY **EDUCATION** Columbia Univ, PhD. **CAREER** Prof & dir, Grad Prog in Ethnomusicol. **MEMBERSHIPS** Served on, nat exec bd, Soc for Ethnomusicol. **SELECTED PUBLICATIONS** Contribur, Garland Encycl World Mus; JVC Anthology Mus and Dance in the Americas & Int Encycl of Dance; ed, Through African-Centered Prisms and Mus and Gender. **CONTACT ADDRESS** Dept of Music, Hunter Col, CUNY, 695 Park Ave, New York, NY, 10021.

HAMPTON, GRACE
PERSONAL Born 10/23/1937, Courtland, AL **DISCIPLINE** EDUCATION **EDUCATION** Art Inst Chicago, BAE 1961; IL State U, MS 1968; AZ State U, PhD Dec 1976. **CAREER** IL State Univ, prof Art Educ; Northern IL Univ; School Art Inst Chicago; CA State Univ Sacramento; Univ of OR. **MEMBERSHIPS** Mem Nat Art Educ Assn; Nat Conf of Black Artist; Art-ist-in-residence Hayden House Phoenix; presented papes local & natl conferences; del Festac 1977. **CONTACT ADDRESS** Art Dept, California State Univ, Sacramento, Sacramento, CA, 95819.

HAMPTON, ROBERT L.
PERSONAL Born 11/18/1947, Michigan City, IN, m **DISCIPLINE** SOCIOLOGY **EDUCATION** Princeton Univ, AB 1970; Univ of Michigan, MA 1971, PhD 1977. **CAREER** Connecticut Coll, asst prof 1974-83; Harvard Med School, lectr of ped 1981-93; Connecticut Coll, assc prof 1983-89, prof 1989-94, dean, 1987-94; professor of Family Studies, professor of Sociology, 1994-; Acad Affairs, assoc provost, dean for undergraduate studies, currently. **HONORS AND AWARDS** Danforth Assc Danforth Found 1979; NIMH Post Doc Flwshp 1980; NRC Flwshp Natl Rsrch Cncl 1981; Rockfeller Flwshp Rockefeller Found 1983. **MEMBERSHIPS** Consultant Urban Inst 1975; consultant Women in Crisis 1979-82; consultants Childrens Hospital Boston 1982; mem exec com Peguot Comm Found 1983-86; chr Oprtns Dev Corp 1977-78; pres of bd Child & Family Agency 1987-90; New London County Child Sexual Abuse Task Force; United Way of Southeastern Connecticut, 1992-95; Prince Georges County Superintendent of Schools, advisory comm; Inst for Women's Policy Research, advisory comm. **CONTACT ADDRESS** Univ of Maryland, College Park, MD, 20742-5031.

HAMRE, JAMES S.
PERSONAL Born 10/28/1931, Montevideo, MN, m, 1957, 2 children **DISCIPLINE** RELIGION IN AMERICAN HISTORY **EDUCATION** Augsburg Col, BA, 53; Luther Theol Sem, Minn, BTh, 57; Univ Chicago, MA, 59; Univ Iowa, PhD(-Relig), 67. **CAREER** Prof Religion & Philosophy, Waldorf Col, Iowa, 78-94; Emeritus prof, 94-; visiting lec, Luther Theo Sem, MN, Spring 76, Augsburg Col, MN, Spring 81, District College, Volda, Norway, Spring 95. **HONORS AND AWARDS** Endowment for Humanities, 74, 87; Regents Outstanding Fac Award, Waldorf Col, 84; Holmen Fac Achievement Award, Waldorf Col, 92. **MEMBERSHIPS** Norwegian-American Historical Association. **RESEARCH** Life and thought of Georg Sverdrup; Norwegian immigrant experience; American religious history. **SELECTED PUBLICATIONS** Auth, Georg Sverdrup concerning Luther's principles in America, Concordia Hist Inst Quart, 70; Georg Sverdrup's concept of theological education in the context of a free church, Lutheran Quart, 70; A Thanksgiving Day Address by Georg Sverdrup, Norweg-Am Studies, 70; The Augsburg Triumvirate and the Kvartal-Skrift, Luther Theol Sem Rev, 72; Georg Sverdrup and the Augsburg Plan of Education, Norweg-Am Studies, 74; John O Evjen: Teacher, theologian, biographer, 74 & Georg Sverdrup's Errand into the Wilderness: Building the Free and Living Congregation, 80, Concordia Hist Inst Quart; Norwegian immigrants respond to the common school: A case study of American values and the Lutheran Tradition, Church Hist, 81; The Creationist-Evolutionist Debate and the Public Schools, Journal of Church and State, 91. **CONTACT ADDRESS** Dept of Religion & Philosophy, Waldorf Col, 106 S 6th St, Forest City, IA, 50436-1713. **EMAIL** hamrej@Waldorf.edu

HAMSCHER, ALBERT NELSON
PERSONAL Born 08/19/1946, Philadelphia, PA **DISCIPLINE** EARLY MODERN & FRENCH HISTORY **EDUCATION** Pa State Univ, BA, 68; Emory Univ, MA, 70, PhD, 73. **CAREER** From Asst Prof to Assoc Prof, 72-86, prof hist, Kans State Univ, 86-. **HONORS AND AWARDS** Nat Endowment for Humanities fel, 76, 80-81, 87, 88-89; Am Philos Soc res grant, 77; mem, Inst for Advanced Study, 88-89. **MEMBERSHIPS** Soc Fr Hist Studies. **RESEARCH** Seventeenth century France; administrative history; history of law. **SELECTED PUBLICATIONS** Auth, The Parlement of Paris After the Fronde, 1653-1673, Univ Pittsburgh, 76; The Conseil Priv and the Parlements in the Age of Louis XIV: A Study in French Absolutism, Am Philos Soc, 87; author of numerous articles. **CONTACT ADDRESS** Dept of Hist, Kansas State Univ, 208 Eisenhower Hall, Manhattan, KS, 66506-1000. **EMAIL** aham@ksu.edu

HANAK, WALTER KARL
PERSONAL Trenton, NJ, m, 1959, 4 children **DISCIPLINE** BYZANTINE & MEDIAEVAL SLAVIC HISTORY **EDUCATION** Univ Tex Austin, BA, 57; Ind Univ, Bloomington, MA, 65, PhD(hist), 73. **CAREER** Instr hist, Univ Tex Austin, 59-60, asst archivist, 60-63; teaching asst hist, Ind Univ, Bloomington, 67; instr, Univ Va, 67-70; from asst prof to assoc prof, 70-78, PROF HIST, SHEPHERD COL, 78-, Ed, Byzantine Studies/ Etudes Byzantines, 72-; mem, US Nat Comt Byzantine Studies. **MEMBERSHIPS** Mediaeval Acad Am; Medieval Acad Am; Asn Int des Etudes Byzantines. **RESEARCH** History of the Byzantine Empire, 700-1000; history of the Kievan Russia, 860-1240; history of the Great Moravian Empire and Bohemia/ Moravia to 1200. **SELECTED PUBLICATIONS** Auth, The Origins of Christianity in Bohemia--Sources and Commentary, J Medieval Studies, Vol 0068, 93; Genghis-Khan--His Life And Legacy, J Medieval Studies, Vol 0070, 95; A Bibliography of Byzantine Studies German, English, French, Italian, Byzantinoslavica, Vol 0053, 92; The Origins of Christianity In Bohemia--Sources And Commentary, J Medieval Studies, Vol 0068, 93; Genghis-Khan--His Life And Legacy, Speculum, Vol 0070, 95. **CONTACT ADDRESS** Dept of Hist, Shepherd Col, Pox Box 3210, Shepherdstown, WV, 25443-3210.

HANAWALT, BARBARA A.
PERSONAL Born 03/04/1941 **DISCIPLINE** HISTORY **EDUCATION** Douglass Col, BA, 63; Univ Mich, MA, 64, PhD, 70. **CAREER** Instr, San Fernando Valley State Col, 70-72; vis asst prof, Univ So Calif, 72; vis asst prof, Univ Oregon, 72-73; asst prof, 74-78, assoc prof, 78-84, prof, 84-87, dir, Criminal Justice Consortium, 85-87, Indiana Univ; prof, 87-98, dir Center for Medieval Stud, 91-97, Univ Minn; King George III Prof British Hist, 99- , Ohio State Univ. **HONORS AND AWARDS** Phi Beta Kappa; Woodrow Wilson fel, 63-64, dissertation fel, 66-68; AAUW fel, 68-69; ACLS fel, 75-76; Am Philos Soc grant, 71, 78; NEH sr res fel, 79-80; NEH fel and mem, School for Hist Stud, Inst for Advanced Stud, Princeton, NJ, 82-83; Fulbright travel grant, 88-89; Guggenheim fel, 88-89; fel, Wissenschaftskolleg zu Berlin, 90-91; fel, Royal Hist Soc, 94- ; Scholar-of-the-College, Univ Minn, 95-98; NEH res fel, 97-98; fel, Natl Hum Ctr, 97-98. **MEMBERSHIPS** Am Hist Asn; Royal Hist Soc; British Stud Asn; Medieval Acad of Am; Social Sci Hist Asn; Past and Present Soc. **RESEARCH** Medieval history including history of crime, children, family and women, peasants, urban history, law. **SELECTED PUBLICATIONS** Auth, Growing Up in Medieval London: The Experience of Childhood in History, Oxford, 93; auth, Of Good and Ill Repute: Gender and Social Control in Medieval England, Oxford, 98; coauth, The Western Experience, McGraw Hill, 7th ed, 98; auth, An Illustrated History of the Middle Ages, Oxford, 99. **CONTACT ADDRESS** Dept of History, Ohio State Univ, 230 West 17th St, Columbus, OH, 43210. **EMAIL** hanawalt.4@osu.edu

HANCHETT, TOM
PERSONAL Born 01/16/1956, Chicago, IL, m, 1 child **DISCIPLINE** URBAN HISTORY; HISTORIC PRESERVATION **EDUCATION** Cornell Univ, BA, 78; Univ Chicago, MA, 86; Univ North Carolina, PhD, 93 **CAREER** Asst prof, Youngstown State Univ, 95-98; asst prof, Cornell Univ, 98- **HONORS AND AWARDS** Catherine Bauer Wurster Prize, 95-97; Mellon Postdoctoral Teaching Fel, 94-95; Best Dissertation Urban Hist, 93; Best Dissertation Southern Studies, 92-93; First Place Hist Book Award, 87 **MEMBERSHIPS** Soc Amer City & Regional Planning Hist; Soc Archit Historians; Nat Trust Historic Preservation; Urban Hist Assoc; Orgn Amer Historians **RESEARCH** Forces shaping the built environment in the US during 19th and 20th Centuries **SELECTED PUBLICATIONS** Auth, SORTING OUT THE NEW SOUTH CITY: Race, Class and Urban Development in Charlotte, 1875-1975, UNC, 98; auth, "US Tax Policy and the Shopping Center Boom of the 1950s and 1960s," Amer Historical Rev, 96; auth, "Roots of the 'Renaissance:' Federal Incentives to Urban Planning, 1941-1948," PLANNING THE TWENTIETH CENTURY AMERICAN CITY, Johns Hopkins, 96 **CONTACT ADDRESS** Dept City & Reg Planning, Cornell Univ, Ithaca, NY, 14853-6701. **EMAIL** twh3@cornell.edu

HANCHETT, WILLIAM
PERSONAL Born 05/25/1922, Evanston, IL, m, 1945, 2 children **DISCIPLINE** UNITED STATES HISTORY **EDUCATION** Southern Methodist Univ, BA, 48; Univ Calif, MA, 49, PhD, 52. **CAREER** Asst prof US hist, Univ Colo, 54-55 & Colo State Univ, 55-56; PROF US HIST, SAN DIEGO STATE UNIV, 56- **RESEARCH** Lincoln; Lincoln's assassination; Civil War and Reconstruction. **SELECTED PUBLICATIONS** Auth, The Inner World of Lincoln, Abraham--Burlingame, J Am Hist, Vol 0083, 96; Lincoln--Donald, J Am Hist, Vol 0083, 96. **CONTACT ADDRESS** Dept of Hist, San Diego State Univ, San Diego, CA, 92115.

HANCOCK, VIRGINIA
PERSONAL Born 02/13/1941, Phoenix, AZ **DISCIPLINE** MUSIC **EDUCATION** Reed Col, BA (chem), 62; Harvard Univ, AM (chem), 63; Univ Oregon, DMA (music hist), 77. **CAREER** Reed Col, prof (music), 91-. **MEMBERSHIPS** Am Musicol Soc, Am Brahms Soc **RESEARCH** Vocal music of Johannes Brahms **SELECTED PUBLICATIONS** Brahms: Volkslied/Kunstlied, in The Nineteenth-Century German Lied, ed Rufus Hallmark, Schirmer Books, 96; Brahms and Early Music: Evidence from His Library and His Choral Compositions, in Brahms Studies: Analytical and Hist Perspectives, ed George S. Bozarth, Oxford Univ Press, 90; Brahms's links with German Renaissance music: A discussion of selected choral works, in Brahms 2: Biographical, Documentary and Analytical Studies, ed Michael Musgrave, Cambridge Univ Press, 87; Brahms's performances of early choral music, 19th Century Music VIII/2, 84; Brahms's Choral Compositions and His Library of Early Music, UMI Res Press, 83; The growth of Brahms's interest in early choral music, and its effect on his own choral compositions, in Brahms: Biographical, Documentary and Analytical Studies, ed Robert Pascall, Cambridge Univ Press, 83; Sources of Brahms's manuscript copies of early music in the Archiv of the Gesellschaft der Musikfreunde in Wien, Fontes Artis Musicae 24, 77. **CONTACT ADDRESS** Music Dept, Reed Col, 3203 SE Woodstock Blvd, Portland, OR, 97202. **EMAIL** virginia.hancock@reed.edu

HAND, SAMUEL B.
PERSONAL Born 08/20/1931, New York, NY, m, 1957, 3 children **DISCIPLINE** UNITED STATES HISTORY **EDUCATION** NY Univ, BA, 52; Syracuse Univ, PhD(hist), 60. **CAREER** Asst prof hist, Slippery Rock State Col, 60-61; from instr to assoc prof, 61-70, chmn dept, 74-76, PROF HIST, UNIV VT, 70-, Ed, Oral Hist Rev, 73-79. **HONORS AND AWARDS** Stephen Greene Award, Stephen Greene Press, 76. **MEMBERSHIPS** AHA; Orgn Am Historians; Oral Hist Asn. **RESEARCH** Recent political history; Vermont history; oral history. **SELECTED PUBLICATIONS** Auth, The Vermont State Constitution--A Reference Guide, J Am Hist, Vol 0080, 94. **CONTACT ADDRESS** Dept of Hist, Univ of Vt, Burlington, VT, 05401.

HANDLIN, OSCAR
PERSONAL Born 09/29/1915, Brooklyn, NY, m, 1937, 3 children **DISCIPLINE** AMERICAN HISTORY **EDUCATION** Brooklyn Col, AB, 34; Harvard Univ, AM, 35, PhD, 40. **CAREER** From instr to prof, 39-72, CARL H PFORZHEIMER UNIV PROF HIST, HARVARD UNIV, 72-, Vchmn, US Bd Foreign Scholar, 62-65, chmn, 65-66; dir, Charles Warren Ctr Study Am Hist, 65-72; dir, Harvard Univ Libr, 79- **HONORS AND AWARDS** Pulitzer Prize, 52; Dunning Prize, AHA, 41., LittD, Brooklyn Col, 72, Oakland Univ, 68; LLD, Colby Col, 62, Univ Cincinnati, 81; LHD, Hebrew Union Col, 67, Northern Mich Univ, 69, Seton Hall Univ, 72 & Boston Col, 75, Univ Lowell, 80. **MEMBERSHIPS** AHA; Nat Acad Educ; Nat Educ Asn; Am Acad Arts & Sci; Am Jewish Hist Soc (vpres, 73-). **RESEARCH** Social and economic history; commonwealth. **SELECTED PUBLICATIONS** Auth, The Bill-Of-Rights in its Context, Am Scholar, Vol 0062, 93; Being Jewish--The Endless Quest, Am Scholar, Vol 0066, 97; A Career at Harvard, Am Scholar, Vol 0065, 96; The 'Unmarked Way', Am Scholar, Vol 0065, 96. **CONTACT ADDRESS** Harvard Univ, 210 Robinson Hall, Cambridge, MA, 02138.

HANDSMAN, RUSSELL G.
DISCIPLINE HISTORY **EDUCATION** Franklin & Marshall, BA, 70; Am Univ, PhD, 76. **CAREER** IND SCH **MEMBERSHIPS** Am Antiquarian Soc **RESEARCH** John Milton Earle, Mass Indians **CONTACT ADDRESS** 5 Periwinkle St, Saunderstown, RI, 02874-2711.

HANE, MIKISO
PERSONAL Born 01/16/1922, Hollister, CA, m, 1948, 2 children **DISCIPLINE** ASIAN HISTORY **EDUCATION** Yale Univ, BA, 52, MA, 53, PhD, 57. **CAREER** Instr Japanese, Yale Univ, 49-53; Fulbright res grant, Japan, 57-58; asst prof hist,

Univ Toledo, 59-61; from asst prof to prof, 61-75, SZOLD DISTINGUISHED SERV PROF HIST, KNOX COL, 75-, Fulbright grant, Univ Mysore, India, 63; Japan Found res fel, 73; Nat Endowment Humanities res grant, 79-80. **MEMBERSHIPS** AHA; Asn Asian Studies. **RESEARCH** Modern Japanese history. **SELECTED PUBLICATIONS** Auth, Roosevelt, Theodore and Korea--The US Response to the Japanese Policy to Make Korea its Protectorate, J Am Hist, Vol 0082, 96. **CONTACT ADDRESS** Dept of Hist, Knox Col, Galesburg, IL, 61401.

HANEY, RICHARD CARLTON
PERSONAL Born 11/01/1940, Stoughton, WI **DISCIPLINE** TWENTIETH CENTURY UNITED STATES HISTORY **EDUCATION** Univ Wis-Whitewater, BEd, 63; Univ Wis-Madison, MS, 64, PhD(Am hist), 70; post-PhD(Traditional Hist Program), USMA West Point, 89. **CAREER** Teacher hist, Monroe High Sch, Wis, 64-66; prof hist, Univ Wis-Whitewater, 66-, Publ ed on six-vol hist of Wis proj, Wis State Hist Soc, 70; coordr student internship prog, Old World Wis Outdoor Ethnic Mus, Univ Wis-Whitewater, 76-80. **HONORS AND AWARDS** Disabled Student Serv Teaching Award, 87; Teaching Excellence Award, Wis Asn for Promotion of Hist, 91. **MEMBERSHIPS** AHA; Orgn Am Historians. **RESEARCH** State, local and regional history; political history; ethnic immigrant history. **SELECTED PUBLICATIONS** Auth, A case study of the midwestern Ku Klux Klan of the 1920's: Whitewater, Wis, 10/69 & JFK's Catholic vote in the 1960 Wisconsin presidential primary: A reassessment, 10/70, Paper Wis Asn Teachers Col Hist; The rise of Wisconsin's New Democrats: A Political Realignment in the Mid-Twentieth Century, Wis Mag Hist, winter 74-75; A Concise History of the Modern Republican Party of Wisconsin: 1925-1975, Kramer & Republican Party Wis, 76; Wallace in Wisconsin: The Presidential Primary of 1964, Wis Mag Hist, summer 78; ed, Between the Wars: America 1919-1941, Houghton-Mifflin, 79; auth, From Black Earth to Liverpool: Transatlantic Observations by George W Bate, Wis Mag Hist, autumn 81; William Jennings Bryan: Orator was a force in American life for three decades, Cameo Speech Quart, autumn 81; auth, Campus Cornerstones at UW-Whitewater: Biographical Sketches of People for Whom Buildings and Facilities are Names, 97. **CONTACT ADDRESS** Dept of Hist, Univ of Wis, 800 W Main, Whitewater, WI, 53190-1790.

HANFT, SHELDON
PERSONAL Born 08/06/1939, Brooklyn, NY, m, 1960, 3 children **DISCIPLINE** MODERN & TUDOR-STUART BRITISH HISTORY **EDUCATION** City Col New York, BA, 61; NY Univ, MA, 64, PhD(hist), 69. **CAREER** Teacher social studies, Eli Whitney Voc High Sch, Brooklyn, 61-69, asst chemn dept 65-69; prof hist, Appalachian State Univ, 69-, ed consult, Can Rev Studies Nationalism, 73-76; bus mgr, Albion, 73-80; secy-treas, Carolinas Symposium on Brit Studies, 75-97; Nat Endowment for Humanities res fel, 76. **HONORS AND AWARDS** S HANFT CSBS Annual Travel Award. **MEMBERSHIPS** Conf Brit Studies; Southern Conf Brit Studies; Anglo-Am Assocs; AHA. **SELECTED PUBLICATIONS** Auth, A Variation on the Term Paper: The Slice of Life, Hist Teacher, 11/71; The Scottish Monarchy Captures the English Throne, Scottish Tradition, fall 72; The Image of Women in Foxe's Book of Martyrs, Am Hist Asn Proc, 2/78. **CONTACT ADDRESS** Dept of History, Appalachian State Univ, 238 Whitener Hall, Boone, NC, 28608-0001. **EMAIL** hanfts@appstate.edu

HANKIN, ALAN LEE
DISCIPLINE ENVIRONMENTAL SCIENCE RESEARCH **EDUCATION** Boston Univ, BA; SUNY, PhD. **CAREER** Emerson Col. **HONORS AND AWARDS** Ch, Secy's Advy Gp Environmental Educ. **SELECTED PUBLICATIONS** Coauth, Barrier Beaches, Salt Marshes and Tidal Flats; An Inventory of Massachusetts Coastal Resources; Commonwealth's Benchmarks on the Way to Environmental Literacy. **CONTACT ADDRESS** Emerson Col, 100 Beacon Street, Boston, MA, 02116-1596.

HANKINS, THOMAS LEROY
PERSONAL Born 09/09/1933, Lawrence, KS, m, 1960, 2 children **DISCIPLINE** HISTORY OF SCIENCE **EDUCATION** Yale Univ, BS, 56; Harvard Univ, MAT, 58; Cornell Univ, PhD(hist), 64. **CAREER** Instr physics, Phillips Acad, 56-60; asst prof, 64-69, assoc prof, 69-75, PROF HIST, UNIV WASH, 75-**HONORS AND AWARDS** Zeitlin-Verbrugge Prize, Hist Sci Soc, 80. **MEMBERSHIPS** Hist Sci Soc; AHA; Am Soc Eighteenth Century Studies. **RESEARCH** History of mechanics; the French enlightenment; scientific biography. **SELECTED PUBLICATIONS** Auth, Dalembert, Jean, Le Rond Philosopher, ISIS, Vol 0086, 95; The Ocular Harpsichord Of Castel, Louis, Bertrand or The Instrument That Wasn't, Osiris, Vol 0009, 94. **CONTACT ADDRESS** DP-20 Dept of Hist, Univ of Wash, Seattle, WA, 98195.

HANLEY, SARAH
PERSONAL NY **DISCIPLINE** HISTORY **EDUCATION** Univ Pittsburgh, BA, 67; Univ IA, MA, 70, PhD, 75. **CAREER** Instr, 69-70, vis asst prof, 75-76, Coe Col; asst, 77, assoc prof, 82, asst chair and dir, 84-85, prof, 87, fac dean, 87-90, Univ IA. **HONORS AND AWARDS** Fel, 90-91, Nat Hum Ctr; Seminar Fel, 93, Univ Bielefeld; Fel, 93-94, John Simon Guggenheim Memorial Found; Fel, 97, Camargo Found; Fel, 98, Huntington Libry; Mary Parker Follett Award, 98, Am Political Science Asn. **MEMBERSHIPS** Soc French Hist Studies; Am Hist Asn; Soc French Hist Studies; Western Soc French Hist; Social Science Hist; Am Soc Legal Hist. **RESEARCH** Early modern France, 1500-1800, political culture, society, law, and litigation critical theory and interpretation. **SELECTED PUBLICATIONS** Auth, The Lit de Justice of the Kings of France: Constitutional Ideology in Legend, Ritual, and Discourse, Princeton Univ Press, 83; Le Lit de Justice des Rois de France: L'Ideologie Constitutionnelle dans la Legende, le Rituel, et le Discours, Aubier, 91; auth, "Mapping Rulership in the French Body Politic: Political Identity, Public Law, and The King's One Body," Hist Reflections, 97; "Social Sites of Political Practice in France: Lawsuits, Civil Rights, and the Separation of Powers in Domestic and State Government, 1500-1800," Am Hist Rev, 97; "The Politics of Identity and Monarchic Governance in France: The Debate over Female Exclusion," Women Writers and the Early Modern British Political Tradition, Hilda L. Smith, ed, 98. **CONTACT ADDRESS** Dept of History, Univ of Iowa, Iowa City, IA, 52242. **EMAIL** sarah-hanley@uiowa.edu

HANNA, MARTHA
DISCIPLINE HISTORY **EDUCATION** Georgetown Univ, PhD, 89. **CAREER** Instr, 88, asst prof, 89-96, assoc prof, Univ Colo, 96-. **SELECTED PUBLICATIONS** Auth, The Mobilization of Intellect: French Scholars and Writers during the Great War, Harvard, 96; Metaphors of Malaise and Misogyny in the Rhetoric of the Action francaise, Hist Reflections, 94; The Catholic Construction of the Great War, W Soc French Hist, 94; Metaphors of Malaise and Misogyny in the Rhetoric of the Action francaise, Hist Reflections, 94; Natalism, Homosexuality, and the Controversy over Corydon, Oxford, 96. **CONTACT ADDRESS** History Dept, Univ of Colorado, Boulder, Boulder, CO, 80309. **EMAIL** hanna@spot.colorado.edu

HANNAN, BARBARA
DISCIPLINE PHILOSOPHY OF MIND, PHILOSOPHY OF SCIENCE, EARLY ANALYTIC PHILOSOPHY, WITTG **EDUCATION** Randolph-Macon Woman's Col, BA, 79; Univ Ariz, JD, 82, PhD, 89. **CAREER** Assoc prof, Univ NMex. **SELECTED PUBLICATIONS** Auth, Subjectivity and Reduction, Westview, 94; contribur, Love Analyzed, Westview, 96. **CONTACT ADDRESS** Univ NMex, Albuquerque, NM, 87131.

HANSEN, BOB
DISCIPLINE THEATRE HISTORY, DRAMATIC LITERATURE **EDUCATION** Univ MN, BA; FL State Univ, MA; Univ MN, PhD. **CAREER** Instr, ch, dept Theatre, mng dir, Huron Playhouse, Bowling Green State Univ; instr, 86-, hd, dept, Broadcasting/Cinema and Theatre, Univ NC, Greensboro. **MEMBERSHIPS** NC Theatre Asn; USITT-Ohio; Am Theatre Asn; Southeastern Theatre Conf; Nat Asn Sch Theatre. **SELECTED PUBLICATIONS** Auth, Scenic and Costume Design for the Ballets Russes, UMI Res Press. **CONTACT ADDRESS** Univ N. Carolina, Greensboro, Greensboro, NC, 27412-5001. **EMAIL** rchansen@dewey.uncg.edu

HANSEN, DEBRA GOLD
PERSONAL Born 09/16/1953, Orange, CA, m, 1977 **DISCIPLINE** HISTORY **EDUCATION** Calif State Univ Fullerton, BA, 75; MA, 79; MA Libr and Information Sci, 83; Univ Calif Irvine, PhD, 88. **CAREER** Ed, Oral Hist Program, Calif State Univ Fullerton, 75-79; freelance indexer for acad presses, 80-93; hist bibliogr, ref librn, Honnold Libr, Claremont Coll Calif, 84-89; asst coordr biblogr instructions, Pomona Coll Claremont Calif, 88-89; archivist, Anaheim Public Libr Calif, 89-90; instr, Calif State Univ Fullerton, 90; aasst prof, San Jose Univ calif, 89-95; assoc dir, School of Libr and Infor Sci, San Jose Univ Calif, 95-. **HONORS AND AWARDS** Grad with Honors, Calif State Univ Fullerton, 75; Joint recipient of Robert G Athearn Award Western Hist Asn, 92; Contemporary Authors; Who's Who in the West, 96-97. **RESEARCH** Nineteenth Century American Social History; Women's History; Family and Ethnic History. **SELECTED PUBLICATIONS** Auth, The Boston Female Anti-Slavery Society and the Limits of Gender Politics, The Abolitionist Sisterhood: Antislavery and Women's Political Culture, 94; coauth, Interactive Video and Female Learning: Imlications for a Feminized Profession, Feminist Collections, 96. **CONTACT ADDRESS** San Jose State University - University Library, California State Univ, Fullerton, Box 4150, Fullerton, CA, 92834-4150. **EMAIL** Dhansen@wahoo.sjsu.edu

HANSEN, JULIE
DISCIPLINE ARCHAEOLOGY **EDUCATION** Univ MN, MA, 75, PhD, 80. **CAREER** Asst prof, 85-93, assoc prof, 93-, chmn, dept of archaeol, 95-, Boston Univ. **HONORS AND AWARDS** NEH Univ Tchrs Fel; NMERTP Fel to Acor, Amman; Fulbright Fel. **MEMBERSHIPS** Archaeol Inst of Am; Am Schools of Oriental Res; Soc of Am Archaeol; Soc of Ethnobiology; Soc of Economic Botany. **RESEARCH** East Mediterranean prehistory; palaeoethnobotany. **SELECTED PUBLICATIONS** Auth, The Palaeoethnobotany of Franchthi Cave, IN Univ Press, 91; auth, L'Agricultura del Neolitic Antic a L'Egeu, Cota Zero, 93; auth, Beyond the Site: Palaeoethnobotany in Regional Perspective, Beyond the Site: Reg Stud in the Aegean Area, Univ Press Am, 94; auth, Preliminary Report on the Plant Remains (1986, 1988-1991), Fouilled Recentes a Khirokitia (Chypre) 1988-91, Ed Recherche sur les civilisations, ADPF, 94; auth, Ethnobotany, and Paleobotany, Oxford Encycl of Archaeol in the Near East, 96. **CONTACT ADDRESS** Dept of Archaeology, Boston Univ, 675 Commonwealth Ave, Boston, MA, 02215. **EMAIL** jmh@bu.edu

HANSEN, KLAUS JUERGEN
PERSONAL Born 11/29/1931, Kiel, Germany, m, 1959, 4 children **DISCIPLINE** AMERICAN HISTORY **EDUCATION** Brigham Young Univ, BA, 57, MA, 59; Wayne State Univ, PhD, 63. **CAREER** Instr hist, Eastern Mich Univ, 63 & Ohio State Univ, 63-65; asst prof, Utah State Univ, 65-68; assoc prof, 68-78, PROF HIST, QUEEN'S UNIV, ONT, 78-, Consult, Am Heritage Dictionary, Houghton Mifflin, 69; Queen's res awards, 69-70 & 72-73; vis fel, Yale Univ, 74-75; Can Coun fel, 74-75. **HONORS AND AWARDS** Award of Merit, Am Asn State & Local Hist, 68; Book Award, Mormon Hist Asn, 68. **MEMBERSHIPS** AHA; Orgn Am Historians; Am Studies Asn; Am Soc Church Hist; Can Asn Am Studies. **RESEARCH** American cultural history; American race relations; American religion. **SELECTED PUBLICATIONS** Auth, The 'Journals of Addison Pratt, Being a Narrative of Yankee Whaling in the 1820s, A Mormon Mission to the Society Islands, and of Early California and Utah in the 1840s And 1850s', Church Hist, Vol 0064, 95; The Angel and the Beehive--The Mormon Struggle with Assimilation, J Church State, Vol 0037, 95; Mormon Odyssey--The Story of Udall, Ida, Hunt, Plural Wife, Church Hist, Vol 0064, 95; Growing-Up in Hitler Germany, Queens Quarterly, Vol 0103, 96; The Journals of Mclellin, 1831-1836, Church Hist, Vol 0064, 95; The Mormon Hierarchy--Origins of Power, Church Hist, Vol 0065, 96; An Intimate Chronicle--The Journals of Clayton, Church Hist, Vol 0066, 97; An Intimate Chronicle--The Journals Of Clayton, William, Church Hist, Vol 0066, 97; Science, Religion, and Mormon Cosmology, Church Hist, Vol 0064, 95; Mormon Americana--A Guide to Sources and Collections in the United-States, Church Hist, Vol 0066, 97. **CONTACT ADDRESS** Dept of Hist, Queen's Univ, Kingston, ON, R7L 3N6.

HANSEN, PETER H.
PERSONAL Born 10/31/1961, New Haven, CT, m, 1988, 2 children **DISCIPLINE** HISTORY **EDUCATION** Carleton Col, BA, 84; Harvard Univ, MA, 86, PhD, 91. **CAREER** Tchng fel, 86-88, Harvard Univ; vis mem, 88-90, Inst for Hist Res, Univ London; adj asst prof, 91-92, Lehman Col, CUNY; vis fel, 95-96, Clare Hall, Cambridge Univ; vis fel, 98, Australian Nat Univ, Hum Res Centre; asst prof, 92-98, dir of int stud, 95-, assoc prof, 98-, Worchester Polytechnic Inst. **HONORS AND AWARDS** Phi Beta Kappa, 84; NYC Urban fel, 84-85; Krupp Found Fel in European Stud, 88-89; Bowdoin Grad Diss Prize, Harvard Univ, 91; Nat Endowment for the Hum, travel to collections grant, 93; Royal Geographical Soc, Inst of British Geographers, Young Res Award, 96; Nat Endowment for the Hum, fel for Col Tchrs, 95-96. **MEMBERSHIPS** Am Hist Asn; North Am Conference on British Studies; North East Conference on British Studies; World Hist Asn; Soc for Cinema Studies; Royal Hist Soc, fel; Royal Geographical Soc, Inst British Geographers, fel; Clare Hall, Cambridge, life member. **SELECTED PUBLICATIONS** Auth, Albert Smith, the Alpine Club, and the Invention of Mountaineering in Mid-Victorian Britain, J of Brit Stud 34, 95; auth, Mountaineering, in Twentieth-Century Britain: an Encycl, Garland, 95; auth, International Education and Sustainable Development: An American Experience in Bangkok, Venice, and Guayaquil, The Environmentalist 15, 95; auth, Vertical Boundaries, National Identities: Victorian Mountaineering on the Frontiers of Europe and the Empire, 1868-1914, J of Imperial and Commonwealth Hist, 24, 96; auth, The Dancing Lamas of Everest: Cimema, Orientalism, and Anglo-Tibetan Relations in the 1920's, Am Hist Rev, 1010, 96; Der tibetische Horizont, Tibet im Kino des Fruhen 20, Jahrhunderts, in Mythos Tibet: Wahrnehmungen, Projektionen, Phantasien, ed Thierry Dodin and Heinz Rather, DuMont, 97; auth, Debate: Tenzing's Two Wrist-Watches: the Conquest of Everest and Late Imperial Culture in Britain, 1921-1953: Comment, Past and Present, 157, 97; auth, Partners: Guides and Sherpas in the Alps and Himalayas, 1850s-1950s, Voyages and Visions: Towards a Cultural History of Travel, 98; contrib, New Dictionary of National Biography, Oxford Univ Press. **CONTACT ADDRESS** Dept of Humanities and Arts, Worcester Polytech Inst, 100 Institute Rd, Worcester, MA, 01609-2280. **EMAIL** phansen@wpi.edu

HANSEN, WELLS S.
PERSONAL Born 12/08/1964, Southport Island, ME, s **DISCIPLINE** CLASSICAL LANGUAGE AND LITERATURE **EDUCATION** Boston Col, BA, 87; Univ Chicago, MA,88. **CAREER** Tchr, Mount Alvernia Acad, 87; lectr, Univ Chicago, 98-92; tchr, Princeton Day Sch, 93; tchr, Milton Acad, 93-. **HONORS AND AWARDS** Weiner Classics Medal, 87; Shorey Fel and Bobrinsky Fel, 90, 92; Klingenstein Sum Fel, 94; Fulbright Grant, 98; McKinlay Fel, 98. **MEMBERSHIPS** Am Philol Asn; Class Asn Mass; Pearl River Gibonian Soc.

RESEARCH Latin literature, pedagogy of classical languages in secondary schools. **SELECTED PUBLICATIONS** "Catullus 75 and the Poetics of Separation," New Engl Classic J, 98. **CONTACT ADDRESS** Ware Hall, Suite 516, Milton, MA, 02186. **EMAIL** wells_hansen@milton.edu

HANSEN, WILLIAM F.
PERSONAL Born 06/22/1941, Fresno, CA, m, 1994, 1 child **DISCIPLINE** CLASSICAL STUDIES, FOLKLORE **EDUCATION** Univ Calif, Berkeley, BA, 65, PhD, 70. **CAREER** From asst prof to assoc prof, Class Stud & Fel of the Folklore Inst, 70-85, prof, 85-92, prof Class Stud & Folklore, 92- , assoc dean fac, 86-92, chemn, Class Stud, 97- co-dir Program in Mythology Stud, 98- , Indiana Univ, Bloomington. **HONORS AND AWARDS** Phi Beta Kappa, 65; NEH Younger Hum Fel, 72-73; Am Coun Learned Soc fel, 77-78, 92. **MEMBERSHIPS** Am Philol Asn; Class Asn of the Middle West and South; Am Folklore Soc; Calif Folklore Soc; Hoosier Folklore Soc; Int Soc for Folk-Narrative Res; Int Soc for Contemp Legend Res. **RESEARCH** Mythology; folklore; early Greek epic; early fiction. **SELECTED PUBLICATIONS** Auth, The Theft of the Thunderweapon: A Greek Myth in Its International Context, Classica et Mediaevalia, 95; auth, Abraham and the Grateful Dead Man, in Bendix, ed, Folklore Interpreted: Essays in Honor of Alan Dundes, Garland, 95; auth, The Protagonist on the Pyre: Herodotean Legend and Modern Folktale, Fabula, 96; auth, Phlegon of Tralles' Book of Marvels, Univ Exeter, 96; auth, Homer and the Folktale, in Morris, ed, A New Companion to Homer, Brill, 97; auth, Idealization as a Process in Ancient Greek Story-Formation, Symbolae Osloenses, 97; auth, Mythology and Folktale Typology: Chronicle of a Failed Scholarly Revolution, J of Folklore Res, 97; ed, Anthology of Ancient Greek Popular Literature, Indiana, 98. **CONTACT ADDRESS** Classical Studies Dept, Indiana Univ, Bloomington, 1020 E Kirkwood Ave, Bloomington, IN, 47405-7103. **EMAIL** hansen@indiana.edu

HANSON, CARL AARON
PERSONAL Born 11/02/1946, Washington, DC, m, 1969 **DISCIPLINE** PORTUGUESE & ECONOMIC HISTORY **EDUCATION** Univ Denver, BA, 68, MA, 69; Univ NMex, PhD(hist), 78. **CAREER** Asst prof hist, Grad Ctr, Univ NMex, Santa Fe, 79; VIS SCHOLAR HIST, UNIV NMEX, ALBUQUERQUE, 80- **MEMBERSHIPS** Soc Span & Port Hist Studies; Int Conf Group Mod Port; AHA; Conf Latin Am Hist. **RESEARCH** Early modern Portugal; European economic history; history of science, cosmology. **SELECTED PUBLICATIONS** Auth, Pombal--Paradox of the Enlightenment, Am Hist Rev, Vol 0101, 96. **CONTACT ADDRESS** Univ New Mexico, 701 Ridgecrest SE, Albuquerque, NM, 87108.

HANSON, CHARLES PARKER
DISCIPLINE HISTORY **EDUCATION** Harvard Univ, AB, 82; Univ Calif at Berkeley, MA, 89, PhD, 93. **CAREER** ASST PROF, HIST, DOANE COLL **MEMBERSHIPS** Am Antiquarian Soc **SELECTED PUBLICATIONS** Auth, A Necessary Virtue: The Reconfiguration of Religious Differences in Revolutionary New England, Univ Press of Va. **CONTACT ADDRESS** Dept of Hist, Doane Col, 1014 Boswell Ave, Crete, NE, 68333. **EMAIL** chanson@doane.edu

HANSON, ERIC O.
PERSONAL Born 03/05/1942, San Francisco, CA, m, 1972, 2 children **DISCIPLINE** POLITICAL SCIENCE **EDUCATION** Stanford, PhD, 76. **CAREER** Donahoe Prof of Polit Sci, 92-. **RESEARCH** Religion & politics; Asian politics. **SELECTED PUBLICATIONS** Auth, Catholic Politics in China and Korea, Orliss, 80; auth, The Catholic Church in World Politics, Princeton, 87. **CONTACT ADDRESS** Dept of Polit Sci, Santa Clara Univ, Santa Clara, CA, 95053.

HANSON, JOHN
DISCIPLINE MUSIC HISTORY **EDUCATION** Eastman Schl Music, BM; MA; PhD. **CAREER** Fac, Univ KS, Carroll Col, Eastman Sch Music; assoc prof, 77. **HONORS AND AWARDS** Founder/Pres, Music Theory Soc NY State. **MEMBERSHIPS** Music Theory Soc NY State. **SELECTED PUBLICATIONS** Auth, articles in Theory and Practice, Cole Music Symposium, and Jour Music Theory Pedag; Music Fundamentals Workbook. **CONTACT ADDRESS** Dept Music, SUNY Binghamton, PO Box 6000, Binghamton, NY, 13902-6000.

HANYAN, CRAIG
DISCIPLINE HISTORY **EDUCATION** Yale Univ, BA; Harvard Univ, AM, PhD. **CAREER** Prof. **HONORS AND AWARDS** Presidential Released Time award, 96. **RESEARCH** New York politics and society in the early national period. **SELECTED PUBLICATIONS** Auth, King George, Queen Caroline and the Albany Regency, NY Hist; De Witt Clinton and the Rise of the People's Men, McGill-Queen's UP, 96. **CONTACT ADDRESS** Dept of Hist, Brock Univ, 500 Glenridge Ave, St Catharines, ON, L2S 3A1.

HAO, YEN-PING
DISCIPLINE HISTORY **EDUCATION** Harvard Univ, PhD. **CAREER** Lindsay Young prof. **SELECTED PUBLICATIONS** Auth, The Comprador in Nineteenth Century China: Bridge Between East and West, Harvard; Commercial Revolution in Nineteenth-Century China: The Rise of Sino-Western Mercantile Capitalism, Univ Ca Pr. **CONTACT ADDRESS** Dept of History, Knoxville, TN, 37996.

HARBISON, CRAIG
DISCIPLINE ART HISTORY **EDUCATION** Princeton Univ, PhD, 72. **CAREER** Prof, 74-. **RESEARCH** Study of social origins and functions of sixteenth-century Flemish still-life painting; history of the iconographic method; sixteenth-century northern artists in Italy; sexuality and gender issues in northern Renaissance art. **SELECTED PUBLICATIONS** Auth, Sexuality and Social Standing in Jan van Eyck's Arnolfini Double Portrait, Renaissance Quarterly, 90; The Play of Realism, London (rev), Reaktion Bk, 91; Meaning in Venetian Renaissance art: the issues of artistic ingenuity and oral tradition, Art Hist, 92; Miracles Happen: Image and Experience in Jan van Eyck's Madonna in a Church, Princeton, 93; The Sexuality of Christ in the Early Sixteenth Century in Germany, Princeton, 94; The Mirror of the Artist: Northern Renaissance Art in its Historical Context, Abrams, 95. **CONTACT ADDRESS** Art History Dept, Univ of Massachusetts, Amherst, 325 Bartlett Hall, Amherst, MA, 01003. **EMAIL** craighar@arthist.umass.edu

HARBOTTLE, GARMAN
PERSONAL Born 09/25/1923, Dayton, OH, m, 1949, 1 child **DISCIPLINE** CHEMISTRY **EDUCATION** Cal Inst Tech, BS, 44; Columbia Univ, PhD, 49. **CAREER** Assoc Chemist, Chemist, Chemist ten, Sr Chemist, 49 to 68-, Prof Emeritus, 98-, Brookhaven Nat Lab; postdoc Fel, 51-52, Cambridge Univ, AEC; vis scientist, 59, Amer Univ Beirut; Lectr, 60, US Atomic Eng Comm Mexico; Dir div res/lab, 65-67, Intl Atomic Energy Agcy, Austria; vis exch scientist, 71, Hungary, 73, US Acad Sci MAE Romania; Adj Prof anthro sci, 83-92, SUNY Stony Brook. **HONORS AND AWARDS** Guggenheim Fel; George Hevesy Medal co-recip; Univ IL Miller Lectr, ; Bowdoin College Root Lectr, ; SAA Roald Fryzell Medal; ANS Glen Seaborg Medal; World Who's Who in Science; Amer Men and Women of Science; Who's Who in Amer and Sci and Technology. **MEMBERSHIPS** SAS Pres. **SELECTED PUBLICATIONS** Assoc Editor, J Radioanalytical Chemistry, 76-; Assoc editor, Archaeometry, 84-94; Editorial Bd, J Mediterranean Archaeology, 88-92; Bd Consul Editors, Studies in Archaeological and Museum Studies, 90-. **CONTACT ADDRESS** Dept of Chemistry, Brookhaven National Lab, Upton, NY, 11973. **EMAIL** garman@bnl.gov

HARBUTT, FRASER J.
DISCIPLINE HISTORY **EDUCATION** Univ Otago, BA, 60, LLB, 60; Univ Auckland, LLM, 67; Univ Calif Berkeley, PhD, 76. **CAREER** Assoc prof **HONORS AND AWARDS** Stuart L. Bernath Mem Bk Prize, Soc Hist Am For Rel, 86. **RESEARCH** International history; United States diplomatic and political history; US-Soviet relations. **SELECTED PUBLICATIONS** Auth, The Iron Curtain: Churchill, America and the Origins of the Cold War. **CONTACT ADDRESS** Dept History, Emory Univ, 221 Bowden Hall, 561 Kilgo Cir, Atlanta, GA, 30322-1950. **EMAIL** fharbut@emory.edu

HARCAVE, SIDNEY SAMUEL
PERSONAL Born 09/12/1916, Washington, DC, m, 1947 **DISCIPLINE** HISTORY **EDUCATION** City Col New York, BS, 37; Univ Chicago, PhD(hist), 43. **CAREER** Foreign affairs analyst, Foreign Broadcast Intelligence Serv, 42-44; res analyst, Off Strategic Serv, 44-45 & US Dept State, 45-46; instr hist, Univ Wyo, 46-47; asst prof, Champlain Col, State Univ NY, 47-50 & 51-53; from asst prof to assoc prof, 53-57, chmn dept, 56-59 & 60-65, div soc sci, 56-59, dir Russ & East Europ Prog, 70-73, prof, 57-81, EMER PROF HIST, STATE UNIV NY, BINGHAMTON, 81-, Hon fel, Yale Univ, 46; Soc Sci Res Coun fel, 46, grant-in-aid, 57; res assoc, Russ Res Ctr, Harvard Univ, 50-51; consult, Ford Found, 56-59; Inter-Univ Comt Travel Grants travel grant, 57 & mem final selection comt, Soviet exchange prog, 62; vis prof, Univ Mich, 62. **MEMBERSHIPS** AHA **RESEARCH** Russian and modern European history. **SELECTED PUBLICATIONS** Auth, Russia: A History, Lippincott, 1st ed, 52, 4th ed, 59, 6th ed, 68; Structure and Functioning of the Lower Party Organs of the Soviet Union, US Air Force 54; The Revolution of 1848, Russ Rev, 7/55; coauth, The Transformation of Russian Society, Harvard Univ, 60; ed, Readings in Russian History, Crowell, 62; auth, Years of the Golden Cockerel, Macmillan, 68; The Russian Revolution of 1905, Collier, 70; auth, The Hessen Redaction of the Witte Memoirs, Jahrbucher fur Geschichte Osteuropas 36, 88; trans, ed, The Memoirs of Count Witte, M. E. Sharpe, 90. **CONTACT ADDRESS** 20 Fuller Hollow Rd, Binghamton, NY, 13903.

HARDEMAN, CAROLE HALL
PERSONAL Muskogee, OK **DISCIPLINE** EDUCATION **EDUCATION** Fisk Univ, BA Music; Univ of OK, MA 1975, PhD Ed Admin 1979; Harvard Univ, MLE Program, 1988. **CAREER** Univ of OK, Coll of Educ & Human Relations, adj prof 1980-85; Southwest Center for Human Relations Studies, exec dir 1982-85; Adroit Publ Inc, pres; LeMoyne-Owen College, vice president for academic affairs, 1990-92, vp for research and development 1992-97; LANGSTON UNIVERSITY, ASSOCIATE DEAN OF GRADUATE STUDIES, 1997-. **HONORS AND AWARDS** Regents Doct Fellow OK State Regents for Higher Ed 1975-79; Outstanding Faculty/Staff Univ of OK 1984; Commiss by Natl Ctr for Ed Stat US Dept of Ed Rsch & Stat Div to write paper addressing policy issues & admin needs of Amer ed syst through the year 2001; Spec Consult for Sci Projects Harvard Univ; Roscoe Dungee Awd for Excellence in Print Journalism OK Black Media Assoc 1984; editor, NABSE; Journal, NABSE Research Roundtable Monographs, editor; Tennessee Higher Education Commission Community Svc Awd, 1997. **MEMBERSHIPS** Exec bd Natl Alliance/Black School Ed 1996-; founder OK Alliance for Black School Educators 1984; mem Links Inc, Jack & Jill Inc, NABSE, Urban League, NAACP, NAMPW, AASA, ASCD, AERA, Alpha Kappa Alpha, YWCA, Assoc of Women in Math; keynote speaker, Univ of DE, Univ of Pittsburgh, Univ of OK, State Dept of Ed-PA, DC Public Schools, Chicago IL, New Orleans Chap One, Las Vegas; Natl Task Force on Multicultural Ed; member, Memphis Arts Council Committee of 100; bd of dir, Planned Parenthood; bd of dirs, Southern Region of Planned Parenthood, exec bd, 1994-; Memphis in May, Memphis Literacy Council. **CONTACT ADDRESS** Graduate Studies, Langston Univ, 4001 Lincoln Blvd, Oklahoma City, OK, 73105.

HARDING, VINCENT
PERSONAL Born 07/25/1931, New York, NY, m **DISCIPLINE** HISTORY **EDUCATION** City Coll NY, BA 1952; Columbia, MS 1953; Univ of Chgo, MA 1956; PhD 1965. **CAREER** Seventh Day Adventist Church Chicago, sply pastor 1955-57; Woodlawn Mennoite Church Chicago, lay assoc pastor 1957-61; Mennonite Central Com Atlanta, southern rep 1961-64; Spelman Coll Atlanta, asst prof History, dept chmn History Social Sciences 1965-69; Martin Luther King Jr Center, dir 1968-70; Institute of Black World, Atlanta, GA, dir 1969-74; Blackside, Inc, Boston, MA, academic adviser to "Eyes on the Prize" documentary, 1985-90; Iliff School of Theology, professor, 1981-. **HONORS AND AWARDS** Kent fellow Soc Rel in Hghr Edn; Honorary Doctorate, Lincoln University, Swarthmore Coll, 1987; Member, Howard Thurman Trust, 1990; Humanist of the Year, Colorado Council of the Humanities, 1991. **SELECTED PUBLICATIONS** Must walls divide, 1965; There Is a River, 1981; Hope and History, 1990; contrib ed, mem, ed bd, Concern Christianity & Crisis Christian Country; also poems, short stories, articles, sermons to professional pubs. **CONTACT ADDRESS** Relig, Social Change, Iliff Sch of Theol, 2201 S University Blvd, Denver, CO, 80210.

HARDY, B. CARMON
PERSONAL Born 12/24/1934, Vernal, UT, m, 1954, 5 children **DISCIPLINE** HISTORY **EDUCATION** Wash State Univ, BA, 57; Brigham Young Univ, MA, 59; Wayne State Univ, PhD, 63. **CAREER** Asst prof, Brigham Young Univ, 61-66; ASST PROF TO FULL PROF, 66-98, PROF EMERITUS, CALIF STATE UNIV, 98-. **RESEARCH** American Constitutional history; American intellectual history; history of religion. **SELECTED PUBLICATIONS** Auth, Solemn Covenant: Mormonism's Polygamous Passage, Univ of Ill Press, 92; The Sonora, Sinaloa and Chihuahua Railroad, Jahrbuch Fur Geschichte Von Staat, Mirtshcaft Und Gesellschaft Lateinamericas, 75; The Schoolboy God: A Mormon American Model, J of Religious Hist, 76; The Third Amendment, The Bill of Rights: A Lively Heritage, Va State Libr and Archives, 87; Early Mormon Polygamy in Mexico and Canada: A Legal and Historiographical Review, Univ of Alberta Press, 90. **CONTACT ADDRESS** History Dept, California State Univ, Fullerton, Fullerton, CA, 92634.

HARE, JOHN
PERSONAL m, 2 children **DISCIPLINE** CLASSICAL PHILOSOPHY **EDUCATION** Princeton Univ, PhD, 75 **CAREER** Staff Assoc, House Foreign Affairs Comm, Washington DC, 82-83; Amer Philos Assn Congressional fel, 81-82; vis fel, Hum, Medical Col Penn, 78-81; vis asst prof, Univ Mich, 75; Instr, 74, asst prof, 75-81, assoc prof, 81-87, prof 85, Lehigh Univ; prof, Calvin Col, 89. **HONORS AND AWARDS** Inst Adv Christian Stud (IFACS) Bk prize, 97; Pew Evangelical fel, 91-92; Jr Lindback awd for disting tchg, 81; Elected Hon Mem Phi Beta Kappa, 79. **MEMBERSHIPS** APA; APA Congressional fel selection comm, 83-89; Mem NY Aristotle Group, 75-81; Prog Comm APA Central Div, 96-97. **SELECTED PUBLICATIONS** Auth, The Apology as an Inverted Parody of Rhetoric, Arethusa, 14.2, Fall, 81, 205-216; Ethics and International Affairs, London, MacMillan, 82; Plato's Euthyphro, Bryn Mawr, 81, 2nd ed, 85; The Unfinished Business of the Peace Process in the Middle East, Report of Congressional Study Mission to Europe and the Middle East, Nov 82, House Foreign Affairs Comm, 97th Congress, 2nd Session; The Hospice Movement and the Acceptance of Death, Hospice USA, ed Austin H. Kutscher, New York, Columbia UP, 83, 9-17; Threats and Intentions, Evangelical Perspective on the Catholic Bishops' Pastoral Letter, ed Dean Curry, Grand Rapids, Eerdmans, 84, 139-157; Philosophy in the Legislative Process, Intl Jour Applied Ethics, 2, 2, Fall 84, 81-88; Credibility and Bluff, in Nuclear Weapons and the Future of Humanity, Totowa, Rowman and

Allanheld, 86, 191-199; Nuclear Deterrence as Bluff, in Political Realism and International Morality: Ethics in the Nuclear Age, Boulder, Westview Press, 87, 144-152; Aristotelian Justice and the Pull to Consensus, in Intl Jour Applied Ethics, 3,3, Spring 89, 37-49; Commentary on Timothy J. Brennan, Academic Disciplines and Representative Advocacy, Bus and Prof Ethics Jour, 6, 1, 88, 56-62; Il Movemento Hospice e L'accettazione della Morte, Progressi Clinici: Medicina, 3, 3, 88, 137-140; Eleutheriotes in Aristotle's Ethics, in Ancient Philos, Spring, 88, 19-32; The Moral Argument for the Existence of God, and The Claims of Religious Experience, in Evidence for Faith, Richardson, Probe, 90, 231-252, and 253-273; Jackie Kennedy and the Seven Dwarfs, in Dialogue, April/May, 91, 23, 6, 20-31; The Atonement: How Does Christ Bridge the Gap, in The Banner, April 13, 92, 4-6; Government, Ethics in, in Encycl of Ethics, 92, 412-416, rev 97; Puffing up the Capacity, Jour Philos Res, XIX, 94, 75-88; Commercial Contracts and the Moral Contract, in Christian Scholar's Rev, XXIII, 3, 94, 259-266; The Invitation, poem, Dialogue, March/April 95, 8; The Atonement, Perspectives, May 95, 16-18; The History of Christian Ethics, in New Dictionary of Christian Ethics and Pastoral Theology, ed David Kingon, InterVarsity Press, 95, 33-42; The Unhappiest Man, in Kierkegaard's Either/Or, International Kierkegaard Commentary, Mercer Press, 95, 91-108; Kantian Ethics, International Politics and the Enlargement of the Foedus Pacificum, in Sovereignty at the Crossroads, Rowman, 96, 71-92; The Moral Gap, Oxford, Clarendon Press, 96; Atonement, Justification, and Santification, in A Companion to the Philosophy of Religion, Blackwell, 97, 549-555; Augustine, Kant and the Moral Gap, The augustinian Tradition, ed Gareth Matthews, U of California P, 97, 220-230; Why Bertrand Russell was not a Christian, Bk (s) and Cult, May/June, 98, 26-28. **CONTACT ADDRESS** Univ of Notre Dame, Flanner 1112, Notre Dame, IN, 46556. **EMAIL** hare.2@nd.edu

HARE, JOHN ELLIS
PERSONAL Born 04/30/1933, Toronto, ON, Canada, m, 1954, 7 children **DISCIPLINE** SOCIAL HISTORY & LITERATURE OF FRENCH CANADA **EDUCATION** Laval Univ, BPhilos, 55, MA, 56 & 62, PhD(ling), 70. **CAREER** Instr educ & English, LavalUniv, 59-66; asst prof, 66-71, assoc prof, 71-80, PROF CAN STUDIES, UNIV OTTAWA, 80- **HONORS AND AWARDS** Marie Tremaine Medal, Can Bibliog Soc, 73. **RESEARCH** Social and cultural history of French Canada. **SELECTED PUBLICATIONS** Auth, Literary-Life in Quebec, Vol 1, 1764-1805, The French Of New British Subjects, Rev Hist Am French, Vol 0046, 93. **CONTACT ADDRESS** Dept of Can Studies, Univ of Ottawa, Ottawa, ON, K1N 6N5.

HARGREAVES, MARY WILMA MASSEY
PERSONAL Born 03/01/1914, Erie, PA, m, 1940 **DISCIPLINE** HISTORY **EDUCATION** Bucknell Univ, AB, 35; Radcliffe Col, MA, 36, PhD, 51. **CAREER** Res asst, Baker Libr, Bus Sch, Harvard Univ, 37-39; from asst prof to assoc prof, 64-73, res-ed/co-ed, proj dir, 73-79, Henry Clay Papers, 52-79, asst prof, 64-69, assoc prof, 69-73, prof, 73-84, PROF EMER, 84- , UNIV KY, 73-, Assoc ed, Henry Clay Papers, 52-73; Brookings Inst fel, 39-40; Phi Beta Kappa; Phi Alpha Theta; Sigma Tau Delta; Hallam prof, 75-77; Saloutos fel, 95. **HONORS AND AWARDS** Saloutos Awaard, 94 **MEMBERSHIPS** Agr Hist Soc (pres, 75-76); Orgn Am Historians; AHA: Southern Hist Asn; Econ Hist Asn; SHEAR; KHS. **RESEARCH** Agricultural history of the Northern Great Plains; dryland agriculture; land utilization. **SELECTED PUBLICATIONS** Auth, Dry Farming Alias Scientific Farming, 48; Dry Farming in the Northern Great Plains, Harvard Univ, 57; Presidency of John Quincy Adams, Kansas, 85; Dry Farming in the Northern Great Plains, Readjustment Years, 1920-1990, Kansas, 93; assoc ed, Papers of Henry Clay, Univ Ky, Vols I, II & III, 59, 61 & 63, 72, 73, 81; co-ed, Vols IV, V & VI, 72, 73 & 81; auth, The Durum Wheat Controversy, 7/68, Women in the agricultural settlement of the Northern Plains, 1/76, Land-use planning in response to drought: Experience of the thirties, 10/76 & Dry-farming movement in retrospect, 1/77, Agr Hist; Rural Education in the Northern Plains Frontier, Jour of West, 79. **CONTACT ADDRESS** 237 Cassidy Ave, Lexington, KY, 40502-2303.

HARING, LEE
PERSONAL Born 06/30/1930, New York, NY **DISCIPLINE** FOLKLORE **EDUCATION** Haverford Col, AB, 51; Columbia Univ, AM, 52, PhD, 61. **CAREER** Asst prof Eng, Guilford Col, 53-56; lectr, 57-61, from instr to asst prof, 61-72, assoc prof, 72-80, prof eng, Brooklyn Col, 80-, Lectr speech, Greensboro Col, 55-56; lectr Eng, City Col NY, 56; admin secy, African Prof, Friends World Inst, 67-69. **MEMBERSHIPS** Am Folklore Soc; Soc Ethnomusicol; Int Folk Music Coun. **RESEARCH** African folk narrative; Am folklore and folk narrative. **SELECTED PUBLICATIONS** Ed, Treasure chest of American folk song, 61 & Folk banjo styles, 62, Elektra Rec; auth, The Gypsy Laddie Hargail Music, 62; ed, Folk Songs for Guitar, Novello, 64; A college course in the ballad, NY Folklore Quart, 67; Performing for the interviewer, Southern Folklore Quart, 72; East African oral narrative, Res African Lit, fall 72. **CONTACT ADDRESS** Dept of Eng, Brooklyn Col, CUNY, 2901 Bedford Ave, Brooklyn, NY, 11210-2813.

HARLAN, LOUIS R.
PERSONAL Born 07/13/1922, Clay Co, MS, m, 1947, 2 children **DISCIPLINE** AMERICAN HISTORY **EDUCATION** Emory Univ, BA, 43; Vanderbilt Univ, MA, 48; Johns Hopkins Univ, PhD, 55. **CAREER** From asst prof to assoc prof hist, ETex State Col, 50-59; from assoc prof to prof, Univ Cincinnati, 59-66; vis prof, 66-67, PROF HIST, UNIV MD, COLLEGE PARK, 67-, Am Coun Learned Soc fel, 63-64; Guggenheim fel, 75; Walter Lynwood Fleming lectr southern hist, La State Univ, 77; Ctr for Advan Study in Behav Sci fel, 80-81. **HONORS AND AWARDS** Bancroft Prize, Am Coun Learned Soc, 73. **MEMBERSHIPS** AHA; Orgn Am Historians; Southern Hist Asn; Asn Study Afro-Am Life & Hist; fel Soc Am Hist. **RESEARCH** Recent United States history; Afro-American history; Southern history since 1865. **SELECTED PUBLICATIONS** Auth, Logan, Rayford, and the Dilemma of the African-American Intellectual, Am Hist Rev, Vol 0100, 95. **CONTACT ADDRESS** Dept of Hist, Univ of Md, College Park, MD, 20742.

HARLESTON, ROBERT ALONZO
PERSONAL Born 01/28/1936, Hempstead, NY, m **DISCIPLINE** CRIMINAL JUSTICE **EDUCATION** Howard University, Washington, DC, BA, 1958; Michigan State University, East Lansing, MI, MS, 1965; Georgetown Law Center, Washington, DC, JD, 1984. **CAREER** CRIMINAL JUSTICE PROGRAM, UNIVERSITY OF MARYLAND, EASTERN SHORE, DIRECTOR, currently. **HONORS AND AWARDS** Maryland Classified Employees Association, Martin Luther King Jr Award, 1996. **MEMBERSHIPS** Govenors Education Coordinating Committee on Correctional Institutions, 1997-; bd of dirs, Eastern Shore Red Cross, 1990-93; bd of dirs, Delmarva Boy Scouts, 1990-93; member, Rotary Club, 1990-93; member, Black Advisory Committee to the Episcopal Bishop, 1990-; sire archon, Gamma Theta Boule, Sigma Pi Phi, 1996; member, Omega Psi Phi, 1953-; Interview Committee, Habitat for Humanity, 1995-. **CONTACT ADDRESS** Criminal Justice Program, Univ of Maryland Eastern Shore, Princess Anne, MD, 21853.

HARLEY, MARIA ANNA
PERSONAL Born 12/30/1957, Warsaw, Poland, m, 3 children **DISCIPLINE** MUSICOLOGY **EDUCATION** J Elsner State High Sch of Music, Warsaw, 79; Summer Courses for Young Composers 83-86; Ctr Acanthes Summer Course in New Music, 87; Univ Warsaw, MA Musicology, 86; F Chopin Acad of Music, MA, sound engineering, 87; McGill Univ, PhD, musicology, 94. **CAREER** Transl & libr, Int Soc Contemporary Music, Warsaw, 84-86; grad asst, McGill Univ, 88-90; instr, McGill Univ, 91-94; SSHRC postdoctoral res fel, McGill Univ, 94-96; ASST PROF, SCH OF MUSIC, UNIV SO CAL, 96-; ED, POLISH MUSIC J, 1998-; GEN ED, POLISH MUSIC HISTORY SERIES, 98-. **HONORS AND AWARDS** M Kopernik St High Sch Gold Medal for Best Grad, 76; Rector's Awards for Outstanding Students, 76-79; Wilk Prize for Res in Polish Music, 95. **MEMBERSHIPS** Amer Musicology Soc; Canadian Univ Music Soc; Int Alliance for Women in Music; Int Musicological Soc; Int Soc for Contemporary Music; Mu Phi Epsilon; Sonneck Soc for Amer Mus; Polish Inst of Arts & Sciences in Amer; Polish Inst of Arts & Sciences in Canada; World Forum for Acoustic Ecology. **RESEARCH** 20th-century music; Music and/as culture. **SELECTED PUBLICATIONS** auth, Technika komedii w 'Falstafie' Verdiego, Muzyka, 91; auth, Stowik I tajemnice nocy: o realizmie I symbolice spiewu slowika w muzyce, Polish Musicological Quart, 92; auth, From Point to Sphere: Spatial Organization of Sound in Contemporary Music (after 1950), Canadian Univ Music Rev, 94; auth, Birds in Concert: North-American Birdsong in Bartok's Piano Concerto No. 3, Tempo, Ju 94; auth, Musique, espace, et spatialisation: Entretien de Iannis Xenakis ave Maria Harley, Circuit, 94; auth, Spatial Sound Movement in the Instrumental Music of Iannis Xenakis, Interface, Aug 94; auth, 'To Be God with God': Catholic Composers and the Mystical Experience, Contemporary Music Rev, 95; auth, O (bez)uzytecznosci analizy dla potrzeb wykonawstwa muzyki dwudziestowiecznej (Xenakis, Bartok, Strawinski), Monochord, 95; auth, Notes on Music Ecology as a New Research Paradigm, Acoustic Ecology J, 95; auth, Natura Naturans, Natura Naturata and Bartok's Nature Music Idiom, Studia Musicologica Acad Sci Hungaricae, 95; auth, Notes on Polish Women Composers, Bulletin of the Polish Inst of Arts & Sci in Canada and the Polish Libr, 96; auth, Ritual und Klanglandschaft Zur Musik von R Murray Schafer, MusikTexte, 97; coauth, Triumphs of Modernity: Xenakis's Kraanerg at the National Arts Centre, Musicworks, 97; auth, Natura naturans, natura naturata a idiom 'muzyki natury' Bartoka, Polish Musicological Quart, 97; auth, An American in Space: Henry Brants' 'Spatial Music,' Amer Music, spring 97; auth, Polski sonoryzm I jego europejski kontekst, Dysonanse, 97; auth, Bacewicz, Picasso and the Making of Desire, J of Musicological Res, 97; auth, Into the City, Onto the Lake: Sit-Specific Music of Henry Brant and R Murray Schafer, Contemporary Mus Rev, 97; auth, Polish School as Sonorism and Its European Context, Crosscurrents and Counterpointes: Offerings in Honor of Bengt Hambraeus at 70, 98; auth, Maria Szymanowska's Vocal Music, Women Compsers, vol 4, 98; auth, Music of Sound and Light: Xenakis's Polytopes, Leonardo, 98; auth, About Life and Music: A Semi-Serious Conversation with Henryk Mikolaj Gorecki, Musical Quart, 98; auth, Gorecki and the Paradigm of the 'Maternal', Musical Quart, 98; auth, Music as Text, Musical Movement and Spatio-temporal Features of the Musical Work, Proceedings of the Int Kongress der Gesellschft fur Musikforschung 'Musik als Text,' 98; auth, At Home with Phenomenology: Roman Ingarden's Work of Music Revisited, Int J of Musicology, 98; auth, Technika ruchu dzwicku w muzyce instrumentalnej Xenakisa, Muzyka, 98; auth, Iannis Xenakis, Polish Musicological Quart, 98; auth, A Mystic in the Cathedral: Music, Image and Symbol in Andriessen's Hadewijch, Amer J of Semiotics, 98; auth, Canadian Identity, Deep Ecology and R Murray Schafer's The Princess of the Stars, Soundscape Yearbook, 98; auth, Sacred/Secular Constructs of National Identity: A Convoluted History Polish Anthems, Critical Musicology J, 98; ed, After Chopin: Essays on Polish Music, Friends of Polish Music at USC, 98; auth, Dans La Nuit: The Themes of Night and Death in Lutoslawski's Oeuvre, Lutoslawski Studies, Oxford Univ, 99; auth, Bogurodzica Reborn: A Medieval Anthem in Contemporary Polish Music, The Yearning for the Middle Ages, 99; ed, trans, auth, Gorecki: An Autumn Portrait, 99 **CONTACT ADDRESS** Dept of Music, History & Lit, Univ So California, Los Angeles, CA, 91214-0851. **EMAIL** maharley@usc.edu

HARMON, DANIEL P.
PERSONAL Born 05/03/1938, Chicago, IL **DISCIPLINE** CLASSICS **EDUCATION** Northwestern Univ, MA, 65, PhD, 68. **CAREER** Asst prof, 67-75, assoc prof, 75-89, prof, 84- , chemn, Dept of Classics, 76-91, co-dir, 92- , Univ Washington Rome Ctr. **MEMBERSHIPS** APA; Archaeol Inst of Am; AAUP; Societe des Etudes Latines. **RESEARCH** Greek and Roman religion; Roman archaeology; classical linguistics. **SELECTED PUBLICATIONS** Auth, The Poet's Initiation and the Sacerdotal Imagery of Propertius 3.1-5, Stud in Latin Lit and Roman Hist, Coll Latomus, 79; auth, Religion in the Latin Elegists, in Haase, ed, Augstieg und Niedergang der Romischen Welt: Geschichte und Kultur Roms im Spiegel der Neuren Forschung, Walter de Gruyter, 85; auth, The Religious Significance of Games in the Roman Age, in Raschke, ed, The Archaeology of the Olympics, Univ Wisconsin, 87; auth, contribur, World Book Encyclopedia, 93; auth, Feriae, Der Neue Pauly, v.4, J.B. Metzger Verlag, forthcoming. **CONTACT ADDRESS** Dept of Classics, Univ of Washington, PO Box 353110, Seattle, WA, 98195. **EMAIL** dph@u.washington.edu

HARMOND, RICHARD PETER
PERSONAL Bronx, NY **DISCIPLINE** UNITED STATES HISTORY, HISTORY OF TECHNOLOGY **EDUCATION** Fordham Univ, BA, 51; Columbia Univ, MA, 54, PhD(hist), 66. **CAREER** Assoc prof hist, St John's Univ, NY, 57-. **MEMBERSHIPS** Orgn Am Historians; Soc Hist Technol. **RESEARCH** Social history; local history. **SELECTED PUBLICATIONS** Auth, The Recollections of Nathaniel S. Prime, J Long Island Hist, 81; Technology in the Twentieth Century, Kendall Hunt, 83; Counting Board, Altar and Vista: The Bradys and Inisfada, New York Irish, 87; Robert Roosevelt and the Early Conservation Movement, Theodore Roosevelt Assoc Journal XIV, 88; JP Morgan, St James Guide to Bio, St James Press, 91; Robert Cushman Murphy: Environmental Issues on Long Island, Long Island Hist J, Vol. VIII, 95; co-ed, A Biographical Dictionary of North American Environmentalists and Naturalists, Greenwood Press, 97. **CONTACT ADDRESS** Dept of History, St. John's Univ, 8000 Utopia Pky, Jamaica, NY, 11439-0002.

HARNETTY, P.
PERSONAL Born 06/06/1927, Brighton, England, m, 1956, 1 child **DISCIPLINE** MODERN INDIAN HISTORY **EDUCATION** Univ BC, BA, 53; Harvard Univ, AM, 54, PhD(hist), 58. **CAREER** From instr hist to assoc prof, 58-71, head, Dept Asian Studies, 75-81, PROF HIST & ASIAN STUDIES, UNIV BC, 71-, Can Coun sr fel, 64-65 & 71-72; Nuffield Found fel, 64-65; assoc ed, Pac Affairs, 66-69 & 78-; pres, Shastri Indo-Can Inst, 70-71; Soc Sci & Humanities Res Coun of Can sr fel, 80-81. **MEMBERSHIPS** Asn Asian Studies; Econ Hist Asn; Can Soc Asian Studies; Hist Asn. **RESEARCH** India, modern, social and economic history. **SELECTED PUBLICATIONS** Auth, Land and Caste in South-India--Agricultural Labor in the Madras Presidency During the 19th-Century, J Economic Hist, Vol 0053, 93; The British Raj in India, Am Hist Rev, Vol 0102, 97. **CONTACT ADDRESS** Univ BC, 3026 W 34th, Vancouver, BC, V6N 2K1.

HARP, STEPHEN
PERSONAL Born 05/06/1964, LaGrange, m, 1989, 2 children **DISCIPLINE** EUROPEAN HISTORY **EDUCATION** Manchester Col, BA, 86; Ind Univ, MA (Hist), 88, MA (French), 88 PHD, 93. **CAREER** Asst prof hist, Univ Akron, 93-98, assoc prof hist, 98-. **HONORS AND AWARDS** Spencer Found fel, 97, 94; DAAD fel, 88, 90-91. **MEMBERSHIPS** AHA; Hist of Education Soc; Phi Alpha Theta; Soc sci Hist Asn; Soc for French Hist Studies; Western Soc for French Hist **RESEARCH** Education; Nat Identity; Tourism; World War I; Current Project: "Pushing Pneus: A Cult Hist of Michelin, 1900-1940. **SELECTED PUBLICATIONS** Learning to Be Loyal: Primary Schooling as Nation Building in Alsace and Lorraine, 1850-1940, Northern Ill Univ Press, 98. **CONTACT ADDRESS** Univ of Akron, Olin 201, Akron, OH, 44235-1902. **EMAIL** sharp@uakron.edu

HARPER, KATHERINE
DISCIPLINE ART HISTORY **EDUCATION** UCLA, PhD, 77. **CAREER** Prof. **RESEARCH** Art History of Zen Buddhism, Islamic Art and the Arts of Prehistory from Europe to Ancient India **SELECTED PUBLICATIONS** published widely on the subject of Ancient Goddesses including a book entitled, "The Iconography of the Saptamatrikas: Seven Hindu Goddesses of Spiritual Transformation, " (Lewiston, New York: The Edwin Mellen Press, 1989) **CONTACT ADDRESS** Dept of Art and Art History, Loyola Marymount Univ, 7900 Loyola Blvd, Los Angeles, CA, 90045. **EMAIL** kharper@lmumail.lmu.edu

HARRIGAN, PATRICK JOSEPH
PERSONAL Born 07/26/1941, Detroit, MI, m, 1966, 1 child **DISCIPLINE** MODERN HISTORY **EDUCATION** Univ Detroit, AB, 63; Univ Mich, AM, 64, PhD(hist), 70. **CAREER** Lectr hist, Univ Mich, 68-69; asst prof, 69-75, assoc prof, 75-82, PROF HIST, UNIV WATERLOO, 82-, Res fel, Shelby Cullom Davis Ctr Hist Studies, Princeton Univ, 71-72. **MEMBERSHIPS** Fr Hist Soc; Can Asn Univ Teachers. **RESEARCH** French social history; education in 19th century France. **SELECTED PUBLICATIONS** Auth, Women Teachers and Popular Education in 19th-Century France--Social Values and Corporate Identity at the Normal School Institution, Am Hist Rev, Vol 0102, 97; French Society in the 19th-Century--Tradition, Transition, Transformation, Social Hist, Vol 0027, 96. **CONTACT ADDRESS** Dept of Hist, Univ of Waterloo, Waterloo, ON, N2L 3G1.

HARRINGTON, ANN M.
DISCIPLINE HISTORY **EDUCATION** Claremont, PhD, 77. **CAREER** Hist, Loyola Univ. **RESEARCH** 19th-20th century Japanese history. **SELECTED PUBLICATIONS** Auth, Japan's Hidden Christians, Chicago: Loyola UP, 93; Women and Higher Education in the Japanese Empire, J Asian Hist, 87; Meiji Imperialism: Not Based on Preordained Design in Japan Examined: Perspectives on Modern Japanese History, Honolulu: Univ Hawaii Press, 83. **CONTACT ADDRESS** Fine Arts Dept, Loyola Univ, Chicago, 6525 N. Sheridan Rd., Chicago, IL, 60626. **EMAIL** aharri1@orion.it.luc.edu

HARRINGTON, DANIEL JOSEPH
PERSONAL Born 07/19/1940, Arlington, MA **DISCIPLINE** BIBLICAL STUDIES, JEWISH HISTORY **EDUCATION** Boston Col, BA, 64, MA, 65; Harvard Univ, PhD(Oriental lang), 70; Weston Sch Theol, BD, 71. **CAREER** PROF NEW TESTAMENT, WESTON JESUIT SCH THEOL, 72-; Vis lectr Old Testament, Harvard Divinity Sch, 72-; ed, New Testament Abstracts, 72-; pastoral assoc, St Agnes Church, Mass, 72-; coordr, New Testament Colloquium, Boston, 77-; trustee, Holy Cross Col, Mass, 78- **MEMBERSHIPS** Cath Bibl Asn of Am, pres 85-86; Soc Bibl Lit; Soc New Testament Studies. **SELECTED PUBLICATIONS** Auth, The Gospel According to Matthew, Collegeville: Liturgical, 83; The Gospel According to Mark, NY: Sadlier, 83; The Gospel According to Luke, NY: Sadlier, 83; Pentecost 2, Series B, Philadelphia: Fortress, 85; The New Testament: A Bibliography, Wilmington: Glazier, 85; Targum Jonathan of the Former Prophets, Wilmington: Glazier, 87; The Maccabean Revolt: Anatomy of a Biblical Revolution, Wilmington: Glazier, 88; John's Thought and Theology: An Introduction, Wilmington: Glazier, 90; The Gospel of Matthew, Collegeville: Liturgical, 91; Paul on the Mystery of Israel, Collegeville: Liturgical, 92; How to Read the Gospels, Hyde Park, NY: New City Press, 96; Wisdom Texts from Oumran, London: Routledge, 96; Paul's Prison Letters, Hyde Park, NY: New City Press, 97; Romans. The Good News According to Paul, Hyde Park, NY: New City Press, 98; and author of many other articles in directories, encyclopedias, scholarly journals, and other publications. **CONTACT ADDRESS** Bibl Studies Dept, Weston Jesuit Sch of Theol, 3 Phillips Place, Cambridge, MA, 02138-3495.

HARRINGTON, JESSE DREW
PERSONAL Born 11/21/1933, Tallahassee, AL **DISCIPLINE** ANCIENT & AMERICAN HISTORY **EDUCATION** Samford Univ, BA, 57; Univ Ky, MA, 63, PhD(hist), 70. **CAREER** Instr, Georgetown Col, 65-68; PROF HIST, WESTERN KY UNIV, 68- **MEMBERSHIPS** Asn Ancient Historians; Am Philol Asn; AHA. **RESEARCH** Comparative study of slavery in the ancient world and the antebellum South; early Roman Empire; Greek history and historiography. **SELECTED PUBLICATIONS** Auth, The Greeks in History, Classical World, Vol 0087, 94; Work, Identity, and Legal Status at Rome--A Study of the Occupational Inscriptions, Classical World, Vol 0087, 94; International Law in Archaic Rome--War and Religion, Classical World, Vol 0088, 95. **CONTACT ADDRESS** Dept of Hist, Western Kentucky Univ, Bowling Green, KY, 42101.

HARRINGTON, KEVIN
PERSONAL Born 07/14/1944, Rochester, NY, m, 1968 **DISCIPLINE** HISTORY OF ARCHITECTURE **EDUCATION** Colgate Univ, BA 67; Cornell Univ, MA 74, PhD 81. **CAREER** IL Inst Technology, inst, asst prof, assoc prof, prof, 78 to 98-. **HONORS AND AWARDS** Graham Foun Fel; 4 NEH Gnts. **MEMBERSHIPS** SAH; CAA; VAF; ACSA; NTHP; CAC. **RESEARCH** Chicago architecture and urbanism; Mies Van der Rohe. **SELECTED PUBLICATIONS** Auth, Chicago's Famous Buildings, co-ed, 4th ed, Chicago IL, Univ Chicago Press, 93; forthcoming, Mies Vander Rohe's design of the IIT Campus, 5th edition, and an electronic version of Chicago's famous buildings. **CONTACT ADDRESS** Dept of Humanities, Illinois Inst of Tech, 3717 N Janssen Ave, Chicago, IL, 60613. **EMAIL** kevinhar@charlie.iit.edu

HARRIS, ANN SUTHERLAND
PERSONAL Born 11/04/1937, Cambridge, England, m, 1965, 1 child **DISCIPLINE** ART HISTORY **EDUCATION** Univ London, Courtauld Inst, BA, 61; PhD, 65. **CAREER** Asst lectr, Art Dept, Univ of Leeds, 64-65; asst lectr, Barnard & Columbia Col; asst prof, Dept of Art & Archeol, 66-71, adjunct prof, Columbia Univ, 80; vis lectr, Dept of Art Hist, Yale Univ, 72-73; asst prof, Art Dept, Hunter Col, CUNY, 71-73; asst prof, Art Dept, SUNY at Albany, 73-77; vis assoc prof, Inst of Fine Arts, NYU, 74; Arthur Kittredge Watson Chair for Acad Affairs, Metropolitan Museum of Art, 77-81; part-time member of liberal arts fac, Juilliard School, 78-83; Amon Carter Distinguished vis prof of Art Hist, Univ Tx at Arlington, 82; Mellon prof of Art Hist, Univ Pittsburgh, 84; adjunct prof, Art Dept, Carnegie-Mellon Univ, 89; Eleanor Tufts Distinguished vis prof, Southern Methodist Univ, 93; **HONORS AND AWARDS** Guggenheim Found Fel, 70-71; Ford Found Fac Fel, 75-76; Andrew W. Mellon Fel, Metropolitan Museum of Art, 77; Mademoiselle Magazine Woman of the Year, 77; NEA Museum Professional Fel, 81; Honorary Doctor of Arts, Eastern Mich Univ, 81; Pittsburgh YWCA Woman of the Year in the Arts, 86; Sr Res Fel, Nat Endowment for the Humanities, 81-82; guest scholar, J. Paul Getty Museum, 88; Honorary Doctor of Humanities, Atlanta Col of Art, 90. **SELECTED PUBLICATIONS** Coauth, The Collections of the Detroit Institute of Arts: Italian, French and English Drawings and Watercolors, Hudson Hills Press, 92; auth, Cool Waves and Hot Blocks: The Art of Edna Andrade, Pa Acad of the Fine Arts, 93; The Katalan Collection of Italian Drawings, 95-96; Nicolas Poussin dessinateur, Nicolas Poussin 1594-1665, Galeries nationales du Grand Palais, 94-95; Ludovico, Agostino, Annibale: ...l'abbiam fatta tutti noi, Academia Clementina, Atti e memorie, Nuova Serie, 94; Domenichino's Caccia di Diana: Art and Politics in Seicento Rome, Shope Talk, Studies in Art Hist for Seymour Slive, Harvard Univ, 95; Le mariage mystique de Sainte Catherine: attribution, commanditaire, iconographie, Nicolas Poussin (1594-1665), Actes du colloque...Octobre, 1994, 96; Artemisia Gentileschi: The Literate Illiterate or Learning from Example, Docere, Delectare, Movere: Affetti e Rettorica nel Linguaggio Artistico nel Primo Barocco Romano, Rome and the Biblioteca Hertziana, 97; Guido Reni's First Thoughts, Master Drawings Vol 36, 98. **CONTACT ADDRESS** Univ Pittsburgh, Frick Fine Arts Bldg, Pittsburgh, PA, 15260.

HARRIS, CHARLES DAVID
PERSONAL Born 01/06/1939, Minneapolis, MN, d, 3 children **DISCIPLINE** MUSICOLOGY **EDUCATION** Northwestern Univ, BMus, 60, MMus, 61; Univ MI, PhD, 67. **CAREER** Asst prof, 65-71, assoc prof, 71-77, prof music, Drake Univ, 77, Fulbright res grant, Austrian-Am Educ Comn, Vienna, 71-72. **HONORS AND AWARDS** Ellis and Nelli Levitt Prof of Music Hist and Harpsichord, 89-; NEH grants, 89, 92 **MEMBERSHIPS** Am Musicol Soc. **RESEARCH** Baroque music hist and performance practice. **SELECTED PUBLICATIONS** Critical ed, A-R Editions, and The Broude Trust (Art of the Keyboard Series). **CONTACT ADDRESS** Fine Arts Center, Drake Univ, 2507 University Ave, Des Moines, IA, 50311-4505. **EMAIL** david.harris@drake.edu

HARRIS, EDWARD E.
PERSONAL Born 02/27/1933, Topeka, KS **DISCIPLINE** EDUCATION **EDUCATION** Lincoln U, AB 1954; Univ IA, AM 1958, PhD 1963; WI U, post grad 1972. **CAREER** IN Univ, Purdue Univ Indianapolis, assoc prof sociology 1968-; CA State Coll, asst prof 1965-68; Prairie View A&M Coll, TX, assoc prof 1963-64. **MEMBERSHIPS** Mem Am & No Central Sociological Assns ed bd Coll Student Journal 1971-. **SELECTED PUBLICATIONS** Contrib articles to professional jrnls. **CONTACT ADDRESS** Indiana Univ-Purdue Univ, Indianapolis, Indianapolis, IN, 46208.

HARRIS, J. WILLIAM
DISCIPLINE HISTORY **EDUCATION** Johns Hopkins Univ, PhD. **CAREER** Assoc prof, 85-, ch, dept Hist, Univ NH. **HONORS AND AWARDS** Nat Hum Ctr fel; Charles Warren Ctr fel, Harvard Univ; Fulbright lectr, Ital, 97. **RESEARCH** Comparative social history of three Southern regions in the era of segregation. **SELECTED PUBLICATIONS** Auth, Plain Folk and Gentry in a Slave Society, 85; ed, Society and Culture in the Slave South, 92. **CONTACT ADDRESS** Univ NH, Durham, NH, 03824. **EMAIL** jwharris@christa.unh.edu

HARRIS, JAMES F.
PERSONAL Born 09/29/1940, Cleveland, OH, m, 1963, 2 children **DISCIPLINE** MODERN EUROPEAN & GERMAN HISTORY **EDUCATION** Loyola Univ, Ill, BA, 62; Univ Wis, MS, 64, PhD(hist), 68. **CAREER** Instr hist, Univ Wis, 66-67; lectr, 67-68, ASST PROF HIST, UNIV MD, COLLEGE PARK, 68- **MEMBERSHIPS** AHA **RESEARCH** German liberalism; the second empire in Germany, 1848-1914. **SELECTED PUBLICATIONS** Auth, Rethinking the Categories of the German Revolution of 1848--The Emergence of Popular Conservatism in Bavaria, Central Europ Hist, Vol 0025, 92; The European Revolutions, 1848-1851, Central Europ Hist, Vol 0027, 94; Imperial Germany, 1871-1914--Economy, Society, Culture and Politics, J Military Hist, Vol 0060, 96; The Village in Court--Arson, Infanticide, and Poaching in the Court Records of Upper Bavaria, 1848-1910, Central Europ Hist, Vol 0029, 96; Frederick III--Germany Liberal Emperor, J Modern Hist, Vol 0069, 97; The Transformation of European Politics, 1763-1848, Central Europ Hist, Vol 0030, 97. **CONTACT ADDRESS** Dept of Hist, Univ of Md, College Park, MD, 20740.

HARRIS, JANICE HUBBARD
PERSONAL Born 03/30/1943, Los Angeles, CA, m, 1966, 2 children **DISCIPLINE** BRITISH FICTION; WOMEN'S STUDIES; POST COLONIAL STUDIES **EDUCATION** Stanford Univ, AB, 65; Brown Univ, PhD, 73. **CAREER** Instr English, Tougaloo Col, 69-73; asst prof English, 75-81, Assoc prof English, 81-88, Assoc Dean Arts Sci. 83-84; Dir Univ Honors Prog, 82-86, prof English, 88-, dir Women's Studies, 95-,Univ Wyo, 80-, Danforth Teaching fel, 81. **MEMBERSHIPS** MLA; Nat Women's Studies Asn; Women's Caucus Mod Lang. **RESEARCH** Modern British fiction; women's studies; Post-Colonial Literatures. **SELECTED PUBLICATIONS** Auth, D H Lawrence and Kate Millett, Mass Rev, summer 74; Our mute, inglorious mothers, Midwest Quart, 4/75; Insight and experiment in D H Lawrence's early short fiction, Philol Quart, summer 76; Sexual antagonism in D H Lawrence's early leadership fiction, Mod Lang Studies, spring 77; The moulting of the plumed serpent, Mod Lang Quart, 3/79; Bushes, bears and the beast in the jungle, Studies in Short Fiction, spring 81; Gayl Jones' Corregidora, Frontiers, Vol 3; Feminist Representations of Wives and Work: An Almost Irreconcilable' Edwardian Debate, Women's Stud, 93; Challenging the Script of the Heterosexual Couple: Three Marriage Novels by May Sinclair, Papers on Lang & Lit, 93; Wifely Speech and Silence: Three Marriage Novels by H G Wells, Stud in Novel, 94; Edwardian Stories of Divorce, Rutgers Univ, 96. **CONTACT ADDRESS** Dept English, Univ Wyo, PO Box 3353, Laramie, WY, 82071-3353. **EMAIL** JHARRIS@vwyo.edu

HARRIS, JOSEPH E.
PERSONAL Born 07/02/1929, Rocky Mount, NC, m, 1958, 2 children **DISCIPLINE** AFRICAN HISTORY **EDUCATION** Howard Univ, BA, 52, MA, 56; Northwestern Univ, PhD(hist), 65. **CAREER** Prof hist, 75- , distinguished prof, 92- , Howard Univ. **HONORS AND AWARDS** Rockefeller Found fel, 72-74; Woodrow Wilson Ind Ctr for Scholars fel, 81-82; fel Nat Hum Ctr, 85; vis fel Ctr for Hum and Soc Sci, Williams Col, 89; res award, Black Management Forum, 92; James Kwegir Aggrey Medal awarded by Phelps-Stokes Fund, 94; Outstanding Author award, Howard Univ, 95; Troyer Steele Anderson Prize awarded by Am Hist Asn, 95; Howard Univ Scholar-in-Residence, Cape Town, 97. **MEMBERSHIPS** UNESCO, Int Sci Comt for the Slave Route Project to Promote Intercultural Cooperation; Nat Mus of African Art, Smithsonian Inst; West African Res Asn; World Found for the Preservation of Goree, Senegal; Goree Hist Trust Soc; Hist Asn of Kenya; Coun of For Rel; Asn for the Study of Afro-American Life and Hist; Int African Stud Asn. **RESEARCH** African history; the African diaspora. **SELECTED PUBLICATIONS** Rev, Eurasia and Africa: The Growth of Civilization to AD 200, Rand McNally, 91; rev, Africa in 1815 and the Partition of Africa, Rand McNally, 92; auth, Scope of the Dispersion to 1873, and, Return Movements and Outreach Activities to 1945, African Diaspora Map Series, Rand McNally, 90, 92; auth, Africans and Their History, New American Library, rev eds, 87, 98; ed and contrib, Global Dimensions of the African Diaspora, Howard Univ, rev ed, 93; auth, African-American Reactions to War in Ethiopia, 1936-1941, Louisiana, 94. **CONTACT ADDRESS** Dept of History, Howard Univ, 2400 6th St NW, Washington, DC, 20059-0002.

HARRIS, JOSEPH JOHN, III
PERSONAL Born 10/10/1946, Altoona, PA, m, 1988 **DISCIPLINE** EDUCATION **EDUCATION** Highland Park College, AS, 1967; Wayne State University, BS, 1969; University of Michigan at Ann Arbor, MS, 1971, PhD, 1972. **CAREER** Detroit Public Schools, teacher, assistant principal, 1968-73; Highland Park Public School, consulting project director, 1973; Pennsylvania State Univ, assistant professor, 1973-76; Indiana University, associate professor, 1976-83, professor, chair, center director, 1983-87; Cleveland State University, professor, dean, 1987-90; UNIVERSITY OF KENTUCKY, PROFESSOR, DEAN, 1990-. **MEMBERSHIPS** Editorial board, CSU Magazine, 1989-; board of trustees, Greater Cleveland Literacy Coalition, 1988-; advisory board, National Sorority of Phi Delta Kappa, 1988-; board of trustees, National Public Radio Affiliate-WCPNW, 1988-; board of directors, Marotta Montessori School/Cleveland, 1987-90; National Organization on Legal Problems in Education, board of directors, 1988-91; Lexington Arts and Cultural Center, board of directors; Holmes Group Ed Schools, E Lansing, board of directors. **SELECTED PUBLICATIONS** Author: "Education, Society & the Brown Decision," Journal of Black Studies, 1982; "The Outlaw Generation," Educational Horizons, 1982; "Identifying Diamond in the

Rough," The Gifted Child Today, 1990; "Public School-Univ Collaboration," Community Education Journal, 1989; "The Resurrection of Play in Gifted...," Journal for the Education of the Gifted, 1990; "The Elusive Definition of Creativity," The Journal of Creative Behavior, 1992; "Dissonance in the Education Ecology," Metropolitan Universities, 1991; "The American Achievement Ideology and Achievement Differentials Among Preadolescent Gifted and Nongifted African-American Males and Females," Journal of Negro Education, 1992. **CONTACT ADDRESS** Col of Education, Univ of Kentucky, 103 Dickey Hall, Lexington, KY, 40506-0017.

HARRIS, LAURILYN J.

DISCIPLINE THEATRE HISTORY AND DRAMATURGY **EDUCATION** Ind Univ, BA; Univ Iowa, MA, PhD. **CAREER** Prof & dir Grad Stud, Washington State Univ.. **SELECTED PUBLICATIONS** Publ in, Theatre Res Int; Theatre Hist Stud; J Creative Behavior; Theatre J; Notable Women in the Amer Theatre; Theatre Annual; Theatre Southwest; Amer Theatre Companies; Stud in Amer Drama; Nineteenth Century Theatre Res; Confronting Tenn Williams' Streetcar Named Desire. **CONTACT ADDRESS** Dept of Music and Theater, Washington State Univ, Pullman, WA, 99164-5300.

HARRIS, LESLIE M.

DISCIPLINE HISTORY **EDUCATION** Columbia Univ, BA, 88; Stanford Univ, MA, 89, PhD, 95. **CAREER** Asst prof **RESEARCH** Pre-Civil War African-American; American labor and social history. **SELECTED PUBLICATIONS** Auth, Creating the African-American Working Class in New York City, 1626-1863. **CONTACT ADDRESS** Dept History, Emory Univ, 221 Bowden Hall, 561 Kilgo Cir, Atlanta, GA, 30322-1950. **EMAIL** lharr04@emory.edu

HARRIS, MICHAEL D.

PERSONAL Cleveland, OH, m, 2 children **DISCIPLINE** ART **EDUCATION** Bowling Green St Univ, BS, 71; Howard Univ, MFA, 79; Yale Univ, MA, 89, MPhil, 91, PhD, 96. **CAREER** Teacher, 71-73, Cleveland Pub Sch; artist-in-res, 77, Dougherty Co Public Sch; artist-in-res, gallery dir, 80-81, Neighborhood Arts Center, Atlanta; adj prof, 80-82, Atlanta Jr Col; adj prof, 84-85, Ga St Univ; tech svc ed, 88-90, Yale Univ; adj prof, 92, Wellesley Col; asst prof, 81-93, Morehouse Col; asst prof, 93-95, Ga St Univ Atlanta; asst prof, 95-, Univ NC Chapel Hill. **HONORS AND AWARDS** Artist Initiated Grant, 81, 83; Coors Found Grant, 84; Bronze Jubilee Award, 85; Mayor's Fel, Atlanta, 87; Charles Dana Faculty Improvement Fel, 88-89; Foreign Lang Area Stud Fel, 89; Patricia Roberts Harris Fel, 89-92; Foreign Res Grant, 91-92; Nat Endow for the Humanities Faculty Grand Study Fel, 92; Andrew W Mellon Pre-Dissertation Fel, 93; art work purchased for Hartsfield Int Airport, 95. **MEMBERSHIPS** ACASA; CAA. **RESEARCH** Contemporary African art; African Amer art. **SELECTED PUBLICATIONS** Auth, Beyond Aesthetics: Visual Activism in Ile-Ife, the Yoruba Artist: New Theoretical Perspective on African Arts, Smithsonian Inst Press, 94; auth, Hand Me Downs: Innovation Within a Tradition, Afro-Amer Cultural Center, 95; auth, Crosscurrents: Ile-Ife, Washington, DC and the TransAfrican Artist, African Arts, 97; art, The Past is Prologue but is Parody and Pastiche Progress?: A Conversation, Int Rev of African Amer Art, 97; auth, Memories and Memorabilia, Art and Identity: Is Aunt Jemima Really a Black Woman, Third Text, 98. **CONTACT ADDRESS** Dept of Art, Univ NC, Box 3405, Chapel Hill, NC, 27599-3405. **EMAIL** mharris1@email.unc.edu

HARRIS, MICHAEL H.

DISCIPLINE HISTORY **EDUCATION** Univ of N Dakota, BA, 63; Univ Ill, MSLS, 64; Univ Ind, PhD, 71. **CAREER** Asst prof, lib sci, Univ Kentucky; current, DIR, THE HIGH DAKOTA GROUP. **MEMBERSHIPS** Am Antiquarian Soc **SELECTED PUBLICATIONS** Auth, "Books Stocked by Six Indiana General Stores, 1800-1850," Jour of Lib Hist 9, 74; auth, "Subscription Book Sales on the Frontier," Am Book Collector 26, 76; auth, "Books! Books! Books! The Estate Auction as a Source of Books in Frontier Southern Indiana, 1800-1850," Proof 5, 77; coauth, Justin Winsor: Scholar-Librarian, 80; auth, "Spiritual Cakes upon the Waters: The Church as a Disseminator of the Printed Word on the Ohio Valley Frontier to 1850," in Getting the Books Out, Lib Congress, 87; auth, The Age of Jewett: Charles Coffin Jewett and American Librarianship, 1841-1868, Libraries Unlimited, 75. **CONTACT ADDRESS** The High Dakota Group, PO Box 2248, Ormond Beach, FL.

HARRIS, MICHAEL WESLEY

PERSONAL Born 11/09/1945, Indianapolis, IN, d **DISCIPLINE** HISTORY, AFRICAN-AMERICAN STUDIES **EDUCATION** Ball State University, Muncie, IN, 1963-66; Andrews University, Berrien Springs, MI, BA, 1967; Bowling Green State University, Bowling Green, OH, MM, 1968; Harvard University, Cambridge, MA, PhD, 1982. **CAREER** Oakwood College, Huntsville, AL, instructor of music/German, 1968-71; University of Tenn-Knoxville, Knoxville, TN, asst prof of religious studies, 1982-87; Temple University, Philadelphia, PA, visiting asst prof of religious studies, 1987-88; Wesleyan University, Middletown, CT, associate professor of history, 1988-91; UNIVERSITY OF IOWA, PROFESSOR, HISTORY AND AFRICAN-AMERICAN WORLD STUDIES, currently. **HONORS AND AWARDS** Rockefeller Humanities Fellowship, Rockefeller Foundation, 1985-86; Research Fellowship, Smithsonian Institution, 1979-80; National Fellowships Fund Dissertation Fellowship, 1976-77; Board of Editors, History and Theory, 1990-92. **MEMBERSHIPS** Member, board of directors and co-chair of program committee, National Council of Black Studies, 1988-90; council member, American Society of Church History, 1990-93; member, American Historical Association, 1978-; member, American Studies Association, 1987-. **SELECTED PUBLICATIONS** Author: The Rise of Gospel Blues: The Music of Thomas A Dorsey in the Urban Church, Oxford University Press, 1992. **CONTACT ADDRESS** History & African-American World Studies, Univ of Iowa, 205 Schaeffer Hall, Iowa City, IA, 52242.

HARRIS, P.M.G.

DISCIPLINE AMERICAN COLONIAL HISTORY **EDUCATION** Columbia Univ, PhD. **CAREER** Assoc prof, Temple Univ. **HONORS AND AWARDS** Res grant, Nat Inst for Ment Hea, Nat Sci Found, Am Coun of Learned Soc, NEH. **RESEARCH** The evolution of the Am colonies. **SELECTED PUBLICATIONS** Auth, Of Two Minds, Falsely Sundered: Faith and Reason, Duality and Complexity, 'Art' and Science in Perry Miller and in Puritan New England, Am Quart, 82; The Demographic Development of Colonial Philadelphia in Some Comparative Perspective, in Susan Klepp, ed, The Demographic History of the Philadelphia Region, 1600-1860, 89; Economic Growth in Demographic Perspective: The Example of the Chesapeake, 1607-1775, in John J. McClusker, et al, eds, Lois Green Carr: The Chesapeake and Beyond -- A Celebration, Md Dept of Housing and Commun Develop, May 92; Inflation and Deflation in Early America 1634-1860: Patterns of Change in the British-American Economy, Soc Sci Hist, Vol 20, No 4, 96. **CONTACT ADDRESS** Temple Univ, Philadelphia, PA, 19122.

HARRIS, PAUL W.

PERSONAL Born 04/11/1954, Rochester, NY, m, 1984, 2 children **DISCIPLINE** HISTORY **EDUCATION** Univ NY Binghamton, BA, 76; Univ Mich, MA, 89, PhD, 86. **CAREER** Fulbright lectr, Universitat Oldenburg, Germany, 84-85; prof, Moorhead St Univ, 86- . **HONORS AND AWARDS** Phi Beta Kappa, 76; Charlotte Newcomb Fel; Woodrow Wilson Nat Fel Found, 82-83. **MEMBERSHIPS** Org of Amer Hist **RESEARCH** Hist of Amer Protestant foreign missions; polit & soc thought 1650-1850. **SELECTED PUBLICATIONS** Auth, A Checkered Life: Yung Wing's American Education, Amer J of Chinese Stud, 94; Cultural Imperialism and American Protestant Missions: Collaboration and Dependency in Mid-Nineteenth-Century Chine, Pac Hist Rev, 91, 95; David Brainerd and the Indians: Cultural Interaction and Protestant Missionary Ideology, Amer Presbyterians, 94; Nothing but Christ: Rufus Anderson and the Ideology of Protestant Foreign Missions, Oxford Univ Press, forthcoming. **CONTACT ADDRESS** Moorhead State Univ, Moorhead, MN, 56563. **EMAIL** harrispa@mhdl.moorhead.msus.edu

HARRIS, ROBERT ALLEN

PERSONAL Born 01/09/1938, Detroit, MI, m, 1963 **DISCIPLINE** MUSICOLOGY **EDUCATION** Wayne State Univ, BS 1960, MA 1962; Michigan State Univ, PhD 1971. **CAREER** Detroit Public Schools, teacher 1960-64; Wayne State Univ, asst prof 1964-70; MI State Univ, assoc prof, prof 1970-77; NORTHWESTERN UNIV, MUSIC DEPARTMENT, PROFESSOR, 1977-. **HONORS AND AWARDS** Distinguished Alumni Award Wayne State Univ 1983. **MEMBERSHIPS** Dir of music Trinity Church of the North Shore 1978-. **SELECTED PUBLICATIONS** Publ, Composer Boosey & Hawkes, Carl Fisher Inc, Mark Foster Publ, Heritage Music Press, Oxford Univ Press. **CONTACT ADDRESS** Sch of Music, Northwestern Univ, 711 Elgin Rd, Evanston, IL, 60208.

HARRIS, ROBERT DALTON

PERSONAL Born 12/24/1921, Jamieson, OR **DISCIPLINE** EUROPEAN HISTORY **EDUCATION** Whitman Col, BA, 51; Univ Calif, Berkeley, MA, 53, PhD(hist), 59. **CAREER** Teaching asst, Univ Calif, Berkeley, 56-58, assoc soc sci, 58-59; from instr to assoc prof, 59-74, PROF HIST, UNIV IDAHO, 74-. **MEMBERSHIPS** AHA; Soc Fr Hist Studies. **RESEARCH** France in the 18th century and revolutionary era. **SELECTED PUBLICATIONS** Auth, French Politics, 1774-1789--From the Accession of Louis-XVI to the Fall of the Bastille, Am Hist Rev, Vol 0101, 96; France and America in the Revolutionary Era--The Life of Dechaumont, Jacques, Donatien, Leray, 1725-1803, Am Hist Rev, Vol 0102, 97. **CONTACT ADDRESS** Dept of Hist, Univ of Idaho, Moscow, ID, 83843.

HARRIS, ROBERT L., JR.

PERSONAL Born 04/23/1943, Chicago, Illinois, m, 1964 **DISCIPLINE** HISTORY **EDUCATION** Roosevelt University, Chicago, IL, BA, 1966, MA, 1968; Northwestern University, Evanston, IL, PhD, 1974. **CAREER** St Rita Elementary Sch, Chicago, IL, 6th grade teacher, 1965-68; Miles College, Birmingham, AL, instructor, 1968-69; Univ of Illinois, Urbana, IL, asst prof, 1972-75; Cornell University, Ithaca, NY, director, 1986-91, assistant to associate professor, beginning 1975, associate professor, currently, special assistant to the provost, 1994. **HONORS AND AWARDS** Teaching Afro-Amer History, American Historical Assn, 1992; Black Studies in the United States, The Ford Foundation, 1990; Rockefeller Humanities Fellow, SUNY at Buffalo, 1991-92; WEB DuBois Fellow, Harvard Univ, 1983-84; Ford Foundation Fellow, 1983-84; National Endowment for the Humanities Fellow, 1974-75. **MEMBERSHIPS** President, Assn for the Study of Afro-Amer Life & Hist, 1991-92; chair/membership comm, American Historical Assn, 1989-94; chair/program comm, American Historical Assn, 1995; member/bd of directors, New York Council for the Humanitites, 1983-87; member/editorial bd, Journal of Negro History, 1978-96; member/editorial bd, Western Journal of Black Studies, 1990-; National Advisory Board, The Society for History Education, 1996-; General Editor, Twayne African American Histroy Series, 1990-. **CONTACT ADDRESS** Africana Studies & Research Center, Cornell Univ, 310 Triphammer Rd, Ithaca, NY, 14850.

HARRIS, STEPHEN JOHN

PERSONAL Born 03/31/1948, Toronto, ON, Canada, m, 1980 **DISCIPLINE** MILITARY & CANADIAN HISTORY **EDUCATION** McMaster Univ, BA, 69, MA, 70; Duke Univ, PhD(hist), 79. **CAREER** Instr, Exten Sch, Can Forces Col, 70-74; HISTORIAN, DIRECTORATE OF HIST, DEPT OF NAT DEFENCE, ONT, 79- **MEMBERSHIPS** Can Hist Soc. **RESEARCH** Officer professional development in the Canadian Armed Forces; military planning in Canada post World War I; the air war, 1939-1945. **SELECTED PUBLICATIONS** Auth, Dieppe Revisited, A Documentary Investigation, Int Hist Rev, Vol 0018, 96. **CONTACT ADDRESS** Directorate of Hist, Nat Defence Hq, Ottawa, ON, K1A 0K2.

HARRIS, VICTORIA

DISCIPLINE MUSIC **EDUCATION** Eastman Sch Mus, Rochester, BA, 61; Ohio State Univ, Columbus, MA, 63; Univ Iowa, MA, 68, PhD, 80. **CAREER** Dept Music, Mt Union Col **MEMBERSHIPS** Alliance Commun Concerts, bd dir; Amer Guild Organists, Akron; Mem-at-large, Canton; Amer Musicol Soc; Amer Mus Scholar Asn; Col Mus Soc; Hymn Soc Am; MENC-OMEA; Mus Teachers Nat Asn; Nat Guild of Piano Teachers: Nat Conf on Piano Pedagogy; Organ Hist Soc; Riemenschneider Bach Inst & Sigma Alpha Iota. **SELECTED PUBLICATIONS** Ed, First Lady of the Organ: Diane Bish, 95; rev, 85 Univ Kans Church Mus Inshtute, The Diapason, 86; concert rev, The Alliance Rev, 88-. **CONTACT ADDRESS** Dept of Music, Mount Union Col, 1972 Clark Ave, Alliance, OH, 44601. **EMAIL** harrisvb@muc.edu

HARRIS, WALTER, JR.

PERSONAL Born 01/27/1947, Suttles, AL, m, 1976 **DISCIPLINE** EDUCATION **EDUCATION** Knoxville College, Knoxville, TN, BS, 1968; Michigan State University, East Lansing, MI, MM, 1969, PhD, 1979; Harvard University, Cambridge, MA, diploma, 1990. **CAREER** Knoxville College, Knoxville, TN, dir, choral activities, chair, music dept, dir, division arts and humanities; ARIZONA STATE UNIVERSITY, TEMPE, AZ, coord, undergraduate studies, music, asst dean, College of Fine Arts, acting dean, College of Fine Arts, associate dean, College of Fine Arts, interim asst vice pres academic affairs, VICE PROVOST, currently. **HONORS AND AWARDS** Luce Fellow, Luce Foundation, 1977; NEH Fellow, 1974; Pi Kappa Lamda Honorary Fraternity, Michigan State University, 1968. **MEMBERSHIPS** President, Arizona Alliance for Arts Education, 1991-93; member, board of trustees, Phoenix Boys Choir, 1990-; member, board of directors, Phoenix Symphony Orchestra, 1990-; member, International Council of Fine Arts Deans, 1985-; regional chairperson, American Choral Directors Assn, 1987-. **CONTACT ADDRESS** Academic Affairs, Arizona State Univ, Tempe, Off of the Sr VP & Provost, Adm 211, Tempe, AZ, 85287-2803.

HARRIS, WILLA BING

PERSONAL Born 03/12/1945, Allendale, South Carolina, m, 1972 **DISCIPLINE** EDUCATION **EDUCATION** Bennett Coll, BA 1966; Bloomsburg State Coll, MEd 1968; Univ of IL, EdD 1975. **CAREER** White Haven State School & Hospital, classroom teacher, 1967-69; Albany State Coll, instructor, 1969; SC State Coll Orangeburg, asst prof & suprv of graduate practicum students, 1969-70; Univ of Illinois at Urbana-Champaign, Upward Bound, head counselor, 1971, asst to major advisor, 1971-73; Barber-Scotia Coll, asst prof of educ & psychology 1975-76; Alabama State Univ, Montgomery, coord, Central AL Regional Educ In-Serv Center, coord 1985-88, dir, Rural & Minority Special Educ Personnel Preparation, 1988, assoc prof & coord for special educ, 1976-, dir of emotional conflict, teacher preparation program, 1990-98. **HONORS AND AWARDS** USOE Fellow Univ of IL 1970-73; Ford Found Fellow Univ of IL 1972-73; Ed of Year AL Assoc Retarded Citizens 1982; Outstanding Educ, Montgomery County Assn for Retarded Citizens, 1982; Volunteer Services Award, Montgomery County Assn for Retarded Citizens, 1985; Distinguished Alumni Award, C V Bing High School, Allendale, SC, 1988. **MEMBERSHIPS** Consult Head Start 1977-80, 1984-85; lay delegate annual conf AL-West FL Conf United Meth Church 1980-90; bd of dir United Meth Children's Home Selma AL 1984-94, 1996; ASU Credit Union 1984-87, Nellie Burge

Comm Ctr 1985-91; mem Amer Assoc on Mental Deficiency-Mental Retardation, AAUP, AL Consortium of Univ Dirs Spec Ed, Black Child Devel Inst, Council for Excep Children, Council for Children with Behavior Disorders, Div for Children with Commun Disorders, Div for Mental Retardation, Teacher Ed Div, IL Admin of Spec Ed, Kappa Delta Pi, Natl Assoc for Ed of Young Children, Natl Assoc for Retarded Citizens, Montgomery Cty Assoc for Retarded Citizens, Phi Delta Kappa, ASU Grad Faculty, AL State Univ Woman's Club, Montgomery Newcomers Club, Tot'n'Teens, Peter Crump Elem School-PTA State & Natl Chapt,tropolitan United Methodist Church, Adult II Sunday School Class, Committee Chmn Fund Raising Choir Robes, Organizer of United Meth Youth Fellow, Admin Bd; jurisdictional coordinator, Black Methodists for Southeastern Jurisdiction Church Renewal, 1989-; board member/finance chair, National Black Methodists for Church Renewal, 1989-; president/board of directors, United Methodist Children's Home, 1990-94. **CONTACT ADDRESS** Prof of Spec Educ, Alabama State Univ, Box 288, Montgomery, AL, 36101-0271.

HARRIS, WILLIAM C.
PERSONAL Born 02/07/1933, Mt Pleasant, AL, m, 1960, 3 children **DISCIPLINE** UNITED STATES HISTORY **EDUCATION** Univ Ala, AB, 54, MA, 59, PhD(hist), 65. **CAREER** From asst prof to assoc prof hist, Millsaps Col, 63-68; assoc prof, 69-76, PROF HIST, NC STATE UNIV, 76-, Nat Endowment for Humanities younger scholar's fel, 68-69. **MEMBERSHIPS** Southern Hist Asn; Orgn Am Historians. **RESEARCH** History of southern reconstruction; the middle period in United States history; biography of William Woods Holden of North Carolina. **SELECTED PUBLICATIONS** Auth, Conservative Unionists and the Presidential-Election of 1864, Civil War Hist, Vol 0038, 92; Lincoln Loyalists--Union Soldiers From the Confederacy, Southwestern Hist Quarterly, Vol 0097, 93; Multiparty Politics in Mississippi, 1877-1902, Am Hist Rev, Vol 0102, 97; Political Culture in the 19th Century South Mississippi, 1830-1900, Civil War Hist, Vol 0042, 96. **CONTACT ADDRESS** Dept of Hist, No Carolina State Univ, Raleigh, NC, 27650.

HARRIS, WILLIAM MCKINLEY, SR.
PERSONAL Born 10/29/1941, Richmond, VA, m **DISCIPLINE** EDUCATION **EDUCATION** Howard U, BS Physics 1964; Univ Washington, MUP Urban Plng 1972, PhD Urban Plng 1974. **CAREER** Cntr for Urban Studies Western Washington State Clg, dir 1973-74; Black Studies Dept Portland St U, chrmn 1974-76; Off Afro Am Afrs, dean 1976-81; Univ of Virginia, prof of city planning, 1987-; planning consultant, 1987-. **HONORS AND AWARDS** Danforth Assc Danforth Found VA 1980; outstanding serv Comm Dev Soc VA 1984; Citizen Ambassador Program, delegation leader to China, 1992, 1994; Monticello Community Action Agency, Teacher of the Year, 1990; Portland, Oregon Citizen of the Year, 1975. **MEMBERSHIPS** Charlottesville Planning Commission, 1981-; Charlottesville Bd of Zoning Appeals, 1991-; TJ United Way, bd of dirs, 1990-; American Inst of Certified Planners, 1978-; American Planning Assn, 1976-; NAACP, 1964-; People to People's Citizen Ambassador Program, 1993-; Development Training Inst, bd mem, 1988-. **SELECTED PUBLICATIONS** Author of: "Environmental Racism: A Challenge to Community Development," Journal of Black Studies, 1995; "African American Economic Development in Baltimore," The Urban Design and Planning Magazine, 1993; "Technology Education for Planners: A Century for African and People of African Descent," African Technology Forum, 1992; "Professional Education of African Americans: A Challenge to Ethical Teaching," Business and Professional Ethics Journal, 1990; Black Community Development, 1976; Charlottesville Little League Basketball, coach, championships, 1982, 1988, 1992. **CONTACT ADDRESS** Dept Urban & Regional Planning, Jackson State Univ, 3825 Ridgewood Rd, Box 23, Jackson, MS, 39211.

HARRIS, WILLIAM VERNON
PERSONAL Born 09/13/1938, Nottingham, England **DISCIPLINE** ANCIENT HISTORY **EDUCATION** Oxford Univ, BA, 61, MA, 64, PhD, 68. **CAREER** Lectr ancient hist, Queen's Univ Belfast, 64-65; from instr to assoc prof, 65-76, prof hist Columbia Univ, 76-95; Shepherd prof hist 95; Am Coun Learned Soc fel, 70-71; Herodotus fel & mem, Inst Advan Study, NJ, 70-71 & 78; foreign mem, Inst Etruscan & Ital Studies, Florence, Italy, 73; vis fel, Corpus Christi Col, Oxford, 75; Nat Endowment for Humanities fel, 78; res, Am Acad Rome, 78; dir, Nat Endowment for Humanities summer sem Col Teachers, 79 & 81; vis fel, All Souls Col, Oxford, 83. **MEMBERSHIPS** AHA Am Philol Asn; Archaeol Inst Am; Asn Ancient Historians. **RESEARCH** Cultural & social history of Greece & Rome. **SELECTED PUBLICATIONS** Auth, Rome in Etruria and Umbria, Oxford Univ, 71; ed, Columbia Studies in the Classical Tradition (ser), Brill, Leiden, 76-; auth, War and Imperialism in Republican Rome, Oxford Univ, 79; Towards a Study of the Roman Slave Trade, Memoirs of the American Academy in Rome, 80; Roman terracotta lamps: The organization of an industry, J Roman Studies, 80; The Imperial Rescript from Vardagate, Athenaeum, 81; The theoretical possibility of extensive infanticide in the Graeco-Roman world, Class Quart, 82; contribr, Cambridge Ancient History, Vol VIII, 2nd ed. **CONTACT ADDRESS** Dept Hist, Columbia Univ, 2960 Broadway, New York, NY, 10027-6900. **EMAIL** wvh1@columbia.edu

HARRIS-CLINE, DIANE
DISCIPLINE CLASSICAL ARCHAEOLOGY **EDUCATION** Stanford Univ, BA, 83; Princeton Univ, MA, 86; PhD, 91. **CAREER** Vis instr, Portland State Univ, 90-91; Asst prof, Calif State Univ, 91-94; Assoc prof, Calif State Univ, 94-96; Vis Assoc prof, Univ Cincinnati, 94-95; Asst prof, Univ Cincinnati, 95-. **HONORS AND AWARDS** NEH grant, 92, 94; Samuel H. Kress Found, 96-97; Regional Symposia Grant, 97; Vis Sch, Stanford Univ, 97-98; Spears & Berry Funds Travel Grants, 85; Seeger Fel, 86; Spears Travel Grant, 86; Hencken Prize Travel Grant, 89; Princeton Univ Fel, 83-87; Doreen C. Spitzer Fel, 88-89; Eugene Vanderpool Fel, 89-90. **RESEARCH** Greek art and archeology; ancient history; Greek epigraphy; mythology. **SELECTED PUBLICATIONS** Auth, The Inventory Lists of the Parthenon Treasures, Univ Microfilms Int, 91; auth, The Treasures of the Parthenon and the Erechtheion, Oxford Monographs on Classical Archaeology, Oxford Univ Press, 95. **CONTACT ADDRESS** Dept of Classics, Univ Cincinnati, PO Box 0226, Cincinnati, OH, 45210-0226. **EMAIL** diane.harris@uc.edu

HARRIS-WARRICK, REBECCA
DISCIPLINE MUSIC **EDUCATION** Brandeis Univ, BA, 71; Stanford Univ, DMA, 78. **CAREER** Assoc prof **HONORS AND AWARDS** Nat Endowment for the Humanities res fel, 85-86; Mellon Found grant, 89; NEH Summer fel, 91; Honorable Mention, De la Torre Bueno Prize, Dance Perspectives Found, 95. **MEMBERSHIPS** Coun mem, Amer Musicol Soc, 95-98; bd dir, Soc Dance Hist Scholars, 93-99; Soc for 17th-Century Music. **RESEARCH** French Baroque music and dance; J.-B. Lully; opera in France (17th-19th century); music editing. **SELECTED PUBLICATIONS** Auth, Magnificence in Motion: Stage Musicians in Lully's Ballets and Operas, Cambridge Opera J 6/3, 94; Interpreting Pendulum Markings for French Baroque Dances, Hist Performance 6/1, 93; Critical ed of G. Donizetti's opera, La Favorite, Milan: Casa Ricordi, 97; coauth, Musical Theatre at the Court of Louis XIV: Le Mariage de la Grosse Cathos, Cambridge: Cambridge UP, 94. **CONTACT ADDRESS** Dept of Music, Cornell Univ, 104 Lincoln Hall, Ithaca, NY, 14853. **EMAIL** rh14@cornell.edu

HARRISON, ALGEA OTHELLA
PERSONAL Born 02/14/1936, Winona, WV **DISCIPLINE** EDUCATION **EDUCATION** Bluefield State Coll, BS (Magna Cum Laude) Ed 1956; Univ of MI, MA Ed 1959, PhD Psych, Ed 1970. **CAREER** Detroit Public School System, teacher; Inkster School System, Rsch Design, Urban Action Needs Analysis, Wayne County Headstart Program, MI Dept of Educ, consultant 1962-66; Highland Park School System, school diagnostician 1968-69; Oakland Univ, prof currently. **HONORS AND AWARDS** Horace Rackham Predoctoral Fellow 1969-70; US Publ Health Grants, 1965-68; graduated second highest mem of class. **MEMBERSHIPS** Mem Amer Psych Assoc, MI Psych Assoc, Assoc of Black Psych, Soc for Rsch in Child Devel, Assoc of Soc & Behavioral Sci; bd trustees New Detroit Inc, Roeper City & Cty Schools; mem Founders Soc, Your Heritage House A Black Museum, Natl Org for Women, Child Care Coord Council. **CONTACT ADDRESS** Psychology Dept, Oakland Univ, Rochester, MI, 48309.

HARRISON, CAROL
DISCIPLINE MODERN HISTORY **EDUCATION** La State Univ, BA, 90; Oxford Univ, DPhil, 93. **CAREER** Asst prof, hist, Auburn Univ, 93-97; asst prof, hist, Kent State Univ, 97-. **HONORS AND AWARDS** Eccles Res Fellow, Tanner Human Ctr, Univ Utah 96-97; Rhodes Scholar, 90-93. **MEMBERSHIPS** Am Hist Asn, Soc French Hist Stud; West Soc French Hist. **RESEARCH** Modern Europe, France, cultural and gender history. **SELECTED PUBLICATIONS** The Unsociable Frenchman: Associations and Democracy in Historical Perspective, The Tocqueville Rev, 17, 96, 37-56. **CONTACT ADDRESS** Kent State Univ, Bowman Hall, Kent, OH, 44242. **EMAIL** charris1@kent.edu

HARRISON, CYNTHIA
PERSONAL Born 10/29/1946, Brooklyn, NY **DISCIPLINE** HISTORY **EDUCATION** Brooklyn Col, BA, 66; Columbia Univ, MS, 67 PhD, 82. **CAREER** Dep Dir, Amer Hist Assoc, 82-88; chief, Hist Off, Fed Judicial Center, 88-94; assoc prof, George Washington Univ, 95- . **HONORS AND AWARDS** Res Fel, Brookings Inst, 79-80; CETA Dissertation Grant, US Dept of Labor, 78-79; Lyndon Baines Johnson Found Grant, 78; Eleanor Roosevelt Inst Grant, 77; Harry S. Truman Inst Grant, 77; Columbia Univ Readership, 74-75; Columbia Univ Scholar, 66-67; NYS Regents' Scholar, 63-66; Dir Award, Fed Judicial Center, 92. **MEMBERSHIPS** Amer Hist Assoc; Org of Amer Hist; Coord Comm for Women in the Hist Prof/Conf Group in Women's Hist; Amer Soc for Legal Hist. **SELECTED PUBLICATIONS** Auth, On Account of Sex: The Politics of Women's Issues, 1945 to 1968, Univ Calif Berkeley Press, 88, 89; Women, Gender, Values, and Public Policy, in Democracy, Social Values, and Public Policy, Greenwood Press, 98; A Revolution But Half Accomplished, Columbia Univ Press, forthcoming; Constitutional Equality for Women: Losing the Battle or Winning the War?, in Time to Reclaim: American Constitutional History at the Millennium, forthcoming. **CONTACT ADDRESS** 3707 Harrison St NW, Washington, DC, 20015-1815. **EMAIL** harrison@gwu.edu

HARRISON, DAPHNE DUVAL
PERSONAL Born 03/14/1932, Orlando, FL, m **DISCIPLINE** MUSICOLOGY **EDUCATION** Talladega Coll, BMus 1953; Northwestern Univ, MMus 1961; Univ of Miami FL, EdD 1971. **CAREER** Marion & Broward Co FL, music tchr 1953-66; Broward Co FL, TV instr 1966-68; FL Atlantic Univ, asst prof educ 1969-70; Hallandale Middle Sch FL, dean of girls 1970-71; Benedict Coll, asso prof fine arts 1971-72; Univ of MD Baltimore County, assoc prof, chairperson, prof, Africana studies dept 1981-96, Center for the Study of Humanities, director, 1996-. **HONORS AND AWARDS** NEH Fellowship for University Professors, 1992-; NEH African Humanities Fellow UCLA 1979; Moton Ctr for Independent Studies Fellow Philadelphia 1976-77; So Fellowships Univ of Miami 1969-70; Theodore Presser Awd Talladega Coll 1951; Fulbright Fellow 1986; Outstanding Faculty of the Year, Black Student Union, UMBC 1988-89. **MEMBERSHIPS** Proj dir, summer inst African & African Amer History culture & literature, 1984-85; proj dir Racism Intervention Develop Proj UMBC 1975-77; social planner New Town Harbison SC 1971-72; consult FL Sch Desegregation Consult Ctr 1965-70; ch music dir St Andrews Ch Hollywood FL 1960-70; bd mem CTD FL Educators Assn 1965-67; bd mem FL State Tchrs Assn 1963-65; mem Natl Assn of Negro Business & Professional Women, Alpha Kappa Alpha, Assn for the Study of Afro-Amer Life & Hist; Co-chair Black Family Committee of African American Empowerment Project; Commissioner of the Maryland Commission on African-American History & Culture; Sonneck Society; Intl Assn for Study of Popular Music. **SELECTED PUBLICATIONS** Black Pearls: Blues Queens of the 1920's, Rutgers Univ Press 1988; The Classic Blues and Women Singers, Blackwell Press Guide to the Blues 1989. **CONTACT ADDRESS** Ctr Study of Humanities, Univ of Maryland, Baltimore County, 5401 Wilkens Ave, Baltimore, MD, 21228.

HARRISON, DON K., SR.
PERSONAL Born 04/12/1933, Nashville, NC, m **DISCIPLINE** EDUCATION **EDUCATION** North Carolina Central Univ, BA 1953; Wayne State Univ, MA 1958; Univ of Michigan, PhD 1972; Licensed Psychologist. **CAREER** Univ of Michigan Rehabilitation Rsch Inst, assoc prof and dir 1976; Univ of Michigan Rehabilitation Counseling Educ, assoc prof and dir 1975; Guidance and Counseling Program, Univ of Michigan, chmn 1974-77; Guidance and Counseling Program, Univ of Michigan, asst prof 1972-76; Vocational Rehabilitation, Wayne State Univ, adjunct asst prof 1972. **HONORS AND AWARDS** Outstanding Srv Awd MI Prsnl & Guid Assn 1976. **MEMBERSHIPS** Dir PRIME Inc Detroi MI 1970-80; mem Am Psychol Assn; mem Personnel & Guidance Assn Rehab Couns Traineeship Rehab Srv Admin 1975. **CONTACT ADDRESS** Rehabilitation Research, Univ of Michigan, 1360 School of Educ, Ann Arbor, MI, 48109.

HARRISON, GEORGE MALLORY
PERSONAL Born 07/29/1951, Milwaukee, WI, m, 1988, 1 child **DISCIPLINE** ARCHAEOLOGY **EDUCATION** John Hopkins, PhD, 85. **CAREER** Assoc Prof, Chair of Classics, 85-, Xavier Univ, Cincinnati. **MEMBERSHIPS** AIA, Poe Society. **RESEARCH** Archaeology of Roman Empire in the East; Plutarch Seneca. **SELECTED PUBLICATIONS** Auth, Romans and Crete, 94; ed, Oxford Moralia Papers(Plutarch), 95; Seneca in Production, 99. **CONTACT ADDRESS** 3788 Ault Park Ave, Cincinnati, OH, 45208-1704. **EMAIL** Harrison@xavier.xu.edu

HARRISON, LOWELL HAYES
PERSONAL Born 10/23/1922, Russell Springs, KY, m, 1948 **DISCIPLINE** HISTORY **EDUCATION** Western Ky State Col, AB, 46; NY Univ, MA, 47, PhD, 51. **CAREER** Instr hist, NY Univ, 47-50, asst dir foreign student ctr, 50-51; assoc prof, W Tex State Col, 52-57, prof & head dept, 57-67, chmn div soc sci, 61-67; res prof history, W Ky Univ, 67-88, Fulbright fel, London Sch Econ, 51-52; Southern Fel fac res grant, 59; co-ed, Panhandle-Plains Hist Rev, 59-68. **HONORS AND AWARDS** Fac Excellence Award, WTex State Univ, 65; Fac Award, Minnie Stevens Piper Found, 66; Fac Res Award, Western Ky Univ, 71; Filson Club Hist Soc; Kentucky Hist Soc. **MEMBERSHIPS** Nat Hist Soc; Orgn Am Historians; Southern Hist Asn; Soc Historians Early Am Republic. **RESEARCH** Southern history; United States history, 1789-1865; Kentucky history. **SELECTED PUBLICATIONS** Auth, John Breckinridge, Jeffersonian Republican Filson Club Hist Soc, 69; The Civil War in Kentucky, 75, George Rogers Clark and the War in the West, 76, co-ed, A Kentucky Sampler, 77 & Antislavery Movement in Kentucky, 78, Univ Press Ky; Kentucky's Governors, 85; Western Kentuck University, 87; Kentuckys Road to Statehood, 92; coauth A New History of Kentucky, 99. **CONTACT ADDRESS** 704 Logan Ave, Bowling Green, KY, 42101.

HARRISON, TIMOTHY P.
PERSONAL Born 08/13/1965, Ft. Wayne, IN, m, 1989, 2 children **DISCIPLINE** ARCHAEOLOGY **EDUCATION** Wheaton Col, BA, 87; Univ Chicago, MA, 91, PhD, 95. **CAREER** Lectr, Oriental Inst, 93-94, lectr, The College, 94-95, res assoc, 95-97, Univ of Chicago; asst prof, 97-, Univ of Toronto. **HONORS AND AWARDS** White-Levy Found Pub Award, 97-98, Sr Post-Doct Res Fel, NMERTA Program, 96-97, Stuart Taye

Tchng Award, The College, Univ of Chicago, 94. **MEMBERSHIPS** Amer Anthropological Asn; Amer Schools of Oriental Res; Archaeological Inst of Amer. **RESEARCH** Near Eastern Archaeology; emergence of early civilizations; urbanism; ethnicity; exchange networks; ceramic analysis; spatial analysis; archaeological method/theory. **SELECTED PUBLICATIONS** Art, The Early Umayyad Settlement at Tabariyah A Case of Yet Another Misr, Jour of New Eastern Stud, 92; art, Economics with an Entrepreneurial Spirit Early Bronze Trade with Late Predynastic Egypt, Biblical Archaeologist, 93; art, Madaba Region Early Bronze Age Survey, Amer Jour of Archaeology, 94; art, A Sixth-Seventh Century Ceramic Assemblage from Madaba Jordan, Annual of the Dept of Antiquities of Jordan (ADAJ), 94; art, The Surface Survey, pp 18-23 in Madaba Cultural Heritage, Amer Center of Oriental Res, 96; art, The History of Madaba, pp 1-17 in Madaba Cultural Heritage, Amer Center of Oriental Res, 96; art, Tell Madaba Excavations 1996, Liber Annuus, 96; art, Field D The Lower Southern Terrace pp 99-175, Madaba Plains Project III The 1989 Season at Tell el-'Umeiri and Vicinity, Andrews Univ Press, 97; art, Investigations of Urban Life in Madaba Jordan, Biblical Archaeologist, 97; coauth, Tell Madaba, Amer Jour of Archaeology, 97; art, Intrasite Spatial Analysis and the Settlement History of Madaba, Stud in the History and Archaeology of Jordan, 97; art, Shifting Patterns of Settlement in the Highlands of Central Jordan During the Early Bronze Age, Bull of the Amer Schools of Oriental Res, 97; art, Retrieving the Past Essays on Archaeological Research and Methodology in Honor of Gus W van Beek, Biblical Archaeologist, 97. **CONTACT ADDRESS** Dept of Near and Middle Eastern Civ, 4 Bancroft Ave, Toronto, ON, M5S 1C1. **EMAIL** tim.harrison@utoronto.ca

HART, DARRYL GLENN

DISCIPLINE CHURCH HISTORY, THEOLOGICAL BIBLIOGRAPHY **EDUCATION** Temple Univ, BA, 79; Westminster Theol Sem, MAR, 81; Harvard Univ, MTS, 83; Johns Hopkins Univ, MA, 85, PhD, 88. **CAREER** Tchg asst, Johns Hopkins Univ, 85-88; post-dr fel, lectr, Divinity Sch, Duke Univ, 88-89; dir, Inst Stud of Amer Evangelicals, Wheaton Cole, 89-93; assoc prof, Westminster Theol Sem, 93-. **HONORS AND AWARDS** Co-ed, Dictionary of the Presbyterian and Reformed Tradition in America, 91-; bk rev ed, Fides et Historia 92-96; ed, Westminster Theol Jour, 96-; **SELECTED PUBLICATIONS** Auth, J. Gresham Machen and the Crisis of Conservative Protestantism in Modern America; The Troubled Soul of the Academy: American Learning and the Problem of Religious Studies, Rel and Amer Cult, 92; The Legacy of J. Gresham Machen and the Identity of the Orthodox Presbyterian Church, Westminster Theol Jour 53, 92. **CONTACT ADDRESS** Westmininster Theol Sem, PO Box 27009, Philadelphia, PA, 19118.

HART, JEFFREY ALLEN

PERSONAL Born 12/29/1947, New Kensington, PA, m, 1968, 1 child **DISCIPLINE** POLITICAL SCIENCE **EDUCATION** Swarthmore Col, BA, 69; Univ CA, Berkeley, PhD, 75. **CAREER** Asst prof, 73-80, Princeton Univ; assoc prof, 81-87, prof,87-, Ind Univ. **HONORS AND AWARDS** NDEA Title IV Fel, 69-72; Interuniversity Consortium for World Order Studies, 73l; Paul Henri Spaak Fel in US-European Relations, 82-83; John D. and Catherine T. MacArthur Found, Postdoctoral Fel, Univ CA, Berkeley, 89; Alfred P. Sloan Found, 96-98. **MEMBERSHIPS** Am Polit Sci Asn; Int Stud Asn. **RESEARCH** Int political economy; int competitiveness; high technology industries. **SELECTED PUBLICATIONS** Auth, Rival Capitalists: International Competitiveness in the United States, Japan, and Europe, Cornell Univ Press, 93; auth, Consumer Electronics, in Bjorn Wellenius, Electronics Industry Devel, World Bank, 93; auth, Ernst B. Haus and Kenneth Waltz, Amer Polit Sci: A Dict, Greenwood Press, 93; auth, Policies Toward Advanced Display in the Clinton Administration, Advanced Flat Panel Displays Engg, Proceed of SPIE The Int Soc for Optical Engg, 94; auth, A Comparative Analysis of the Sources of America's Relative Economic Decline, Understanding American Economic Decline, Cambridge Univ Press, 94; auth, Maquiladorization as a Global Process, Foreign Direct Investment in a Changing Political Economy, Macmillan, 95; auth, Aerospace, Encycl of US Foreign Relations, vol 1, Oxford Univ Press, 97; auth, The Politics of International Economic Relations, 5th ed, St. Martin's Press, 97; co-ed, Globalization and Governance; co-ed, Coping With Globalization, 2 vols; auth, Digital Divergence: The Politics of High Definition Television. **CONTACT ADDRESS** Dept of Political Science, Indiana Univ, Bloomington, Bloomington, IN, 47405. **EMAIL** hartj@indiana.edu

HART, JOHN MASON

PERSONAL Born 02/14/1935, Los Angeles, CA, m, 1957, 2 children **DISCIPLINE** HISTORY **EDUCATION** UCLA, PhD, 70. **CAREER** Asst Prof, Univ North Dakota, 69-73; Assoc Prof, 73-78, Prof, 78-, Univ Houston **HONORS AND AWARDS** SSRC/ACLS Post Doctoral Research, 75; Visiting research Fel, UCSD, 88; NEH Senior Univ Research Fel, 91; Shelby Cullom Davis Fel, Princeton, 91; Conference Prize, 75; Herring Prize, 81; Johnson Prize, 88. **MEMBERSHIPS** Amer Historical Assoc. **RESEARCH** Mexico **SELECTED PUBLICATIONS** Auth, Revolutionary Mexico: The Coming and Process of the Mexican Revolution, 10th Anniv Ed, 98; Auth, Border Crossings: Mexican and Mexican American Workers, 98; auth, Empire and Revolution: The Americanism in Mexico since the Civil War, forthcoming. **CONTACT ADDRESS** Dept of History, Univ of Houston, Houston, TX, 77204-3785. **EMAIL** jhart@uh.edu

HART, STEPHEN

PERSONAL Born 02/14/1946, Chicago, IL, m, 1977 **DISCIPLINE** SOCIOLOGY **EDUCATION** Univ Calif, PhD, 79; Univ Calif, MA, 68; Harvard Col, AB, 67 **CAREER** Frontier Science & Tech Res Found Analysis, 98-; Center Theolog Inquiry, 97; Center Study Amer Relig Princeton Univ, 97; Ntl Endowment Humanities Fel, 96; adjunct asst prof, State Univ New York-Buffalo, 93-; freelance contract res, 90- **RESEARCH** Religion; Culture; Politics; Social Movements **SELECTED PUBLICATIONS** The Culture of Political Action: Public Discourse in Grassroots Organizations, Univ Chicago Pr, 99; What Does the Lord Require? How American Christians Think about Economic Justice, Oxford Pr, 96; "The Cultural Dimension of Social Movements: A Theoretical Reassessment and Literature Rev," Sociology of Relig, 96 **CONTACT ADDRESS** Dept Sociology, SUNY Buffalo, Buffalo, NY, 14260-4140. **EMAIL** sahart@buffalo.edu

HARTGROVE, JOSEPH DANE

PERSONAL Born 02/12/1947, Winston-Salem, NC, m, 1978 **DISCIPLINE** RUSSIAN HISTORY, AMERICAN DIPLOMATIC HISTORY **EDUCATION** Duke Univ, AB, 69; Univ NC, Chapel Hill, PhD(hist), 75. **CAREER** ARCHIVIST, DIPLOMATIC BR, NAT ARCHIVES, 76- **MEMBERSHIPS** AHA; Am Asn Advan Slavic Studies; Soc Historians Am Foreign Rels. **RESEARCH** Russian-American relations; the Russian Revolution and Civil War; Russian military and naval history. **SELECTED PUBLICATIONS** Auth, Indeitsy Tlinkity V Period Russkoi Ameriki, 1741-1867 The Tlingit Indians in the Period of Russian America, 1741-1867, J Am Hist, Vol 0081, 94; History of US Foreign-Policy and Diplomacy, 1775-1877, J Am Hist, Vol 0082, 95. **CONTACT ADDRESS** Diplomatic Br Nat Archives Eighth & Pennsylvania A, Washington, DC, 20408.

HARTIGAN, KARELISA V.

PERSONAL Born 03/05/1943, Stillwater, OK, m, 1992, 5 children **DISCIPLINE** CLASSICS **EDUCATION** Col of Wooster, BA, 65; Univ Chicago, AM, 66, PhD, 70. **CAREER** Asst prof, St Olaf Col, 69-73; asst prof, 73-76, assoc prof, 76-90, PROF, UNIV FL, 90-. **HONORS AND AWARDS** Various undergraduate awards, including Phi Beta Kappa; Woodrow Wilson fel, 65; Ford Found MA fel, 66; Univ Chicago fel, 66-68; Woodrow Wilson Dissertation fel, 68-69; numerous teaching awards, Univ FL; Amer Philos Assoc Nat Teaching Award; Distinguished Alumni Prof, Univ FL; Classical Assoc of Middle West and South Ovatio Award. **MEMBERSHIPS** Classical Assoc of Middle West and South, pres 92-93; Amer Philol Assoc; Modern Greek Studies Assoc. **RESEARCH** Greek drama; mythology; ancient cities; comparative lit. **SELECTED PUBLICATIONS** Auth, The Poets and the Cities, Anton Hain, 79; Ambiguity and Self Deception, Apollo & Artemis Plays of Euripides, Peter Lang, 91; Greek Drama on the American Stage, Greenwood, 95; Muse on Madison Avenue, Greenwood, 99; Myths Behind Our Words, Forbes, 98; over 2 dozen articles on Greek drama, comparative lit, and myth in film; also slide sets with commentary: 4, with Pictures of Record. **CONTACT ADDRESS** Dept of Classics Dauer 3-C, Univ FL, Box 117435, Gainesville, FL, 32611. **EMAIL** kvhrtgn@classics.ufl.edu

HARTMAN, MARY SUSAN

PERSONAL Born 06/25/1941, Minneapolis, MN, m, 1966 **DISCIPLINE** HISTORY **EDUCATION** Swarthmore Col, BA, 63; Columbia Univ, MA, 64, PhD, 70. **CAREER** Instr, hist, 68-69, asst prof, 69-75, assoc prof, 75-82, acting dean, 81-82, dean, 82-94, prof, history, 82-, dir, Inst for Women's Leadership, 94-, Douglas Col, Rutgers Univ. **HONORS AND AWARDS** Magna Cum Laude; Phi Beta Kappa, 63; Woodrow Wilson Fel, 63-64; Columbia Univ grant, 64-65; Fulbright Fel to France, 65-66; NEH, sum grant, 72; Rutgers Univ Fac Leave Grant, 74, 77, 85; Hannah G. Solomon Award; NJ Chapter of the Natl Coun of Jewish Women, 93; Girl Scout Award, Delaware-Rarian Girl Scout Council Women of Distinction Award, 93; Women of the Year, Hispanic Women's Task Force of NJ, 93; Woman of Achievement, Middlesex County Comm on the Status of Women, 93; NJ Women of the Year, NJ Woman Magazine, 93; NJ Woman of Achievement, 96. **MEMBERSHIPS** Amer Hist Asn; Berkshire Conf of Women Historians; Amer Asn of Univ Women; NJ Coalition for Women's Education; Women's Col Coalition; Chmn, Public Leadership Ed. Network. **RESEARCH** French & English social and political history; women's history. **SELECTED PUBLICATIONS** Auth, Victorian Murderesses: A True History of Thirteen Respectable French English Women Accused of Unspeakable Crimes, Jeremy Robson, 85; art, The Hall-Mills Murder Case: The Most Fascinating Unsolved Homicide in America, Jour Rutgers Univ Libraries, 84; art, Mills Students Provide Eloquent Testimony to the Value of Women's Colleges, Point of View ed, Chronicle of Higher Ed, 90; art, Leadership: The Agenda for Women, NJ Bell Jour, Vol 14, 91; art, The Sacrilege Law of 1825 in France: A Study in Anticlericalism and Mythmaking, Jour of Modern History, Vol LXLIV, 92; Auth, Talking Leadership: conversations With Powerful Women, Rutgers Univ Press, 99. **CONTACT ADDRESS** Inst for Women's Leadership, Rutgers, The St Univ of NJ, 162 Ryders Lane, New Brunswick, NJ, 08901-8555. **EMAIL** msh@rci.rutgers.edu

HARVEY, PAUL

DISCIPLINE MODERN AMERICAN HISTORY **EDUCATION** Okla Baptist Univ, BA, 83; Univ Calif, Barkely, PhD, 92. **CAREER** Lectr, Univ Calif, Berkeley, 92; vis prof, Colo Col, 91, 93; asst prof, 96-; fac ch, 97. **HONORS AND AWARDS** Postdoc tchg fel, Valparaiso Univ, 93-94, 94-95; postdoc fel, Yale Univ, 95-96. **MEMBERSHIPS** Mem, Amer Hist Assn; S Hist Assn; Amer Acad Rel; Amer Soc Church Hist; Org Amer Hist. **SELECTED PUBLICATIONS** Auth, Redeeming the South: Religious Cultures and Racial Identities Among Southern Baptists, 1865-25, Univ NC, 97; Sweet Homes, Sacred Blues, Religious Orders: The Search for the Meaning of Southern Religious History, Rel Stud Rev, 97;The Ideal of Professionalism and the Southern Baptist Ministry, 1870-20, Rel and Amer Cult, 95; Sweet Home Alabama: Southern Popular Culture and the American Search for Community, Southern Cult, 95; Yankee Faith and Southern Redemption: Southern Baptist Ministers and the Public World, 1850-1890, Rel and the Amer Civil War, Oxford Univ Press, 98; The Holy Spirit Come to Us and Denied the Negro Taking a Second Place: Richard H. Boyd and Black Religious Activism in Nashville, Tennessee, 1895-20, Tenn Hist Quart, 96; Easily Centered: the Reformed Tradition and American Religious History, Amer Hist, 95; The Politicization of White and Black Southern Baptist Missionaries, Amer Baptist Quart, 94; Southern Baptist Missionaries and the Expansion of Evangelical Protestantism, CrossRoads: A Jour of S Stud, 94; The Importance of Being Elvis: Fame, Religion and the Color Line in 50s America, Cresset, 95; rev, Southern Baptists and the Social Gospel: White Religious Progressivism in the South, 1895-20, Fides et Hist, 95. **CONTACT ADDRESS** Dept of Hist, Univ Colo, PO Box 7150, Colorado Springs, CO, 80933-7150. **EMAIL** pharvey@mail.uccs.edu

HARWOOD, ROBIN

DISCIPLINE PHILOSOPHY OF MIND, PHILOSOPHY OF RELIGION, ANCIENT AND MEDIEVAL PHILOSOPHY **EDUCATION** Reading, Eng, PhD, 95. **CAREER** Lectr, Ga State Univ. **SELECTED PUBLICATIONS** Auth, The Survival of the Self. **CONTACT ADDRESS** Georgia State Univ, Atlanta, GA, 30303. **EMAIL** phlrrh@panther.gsu.edu

HASKELL, GUY H.

PERSONAL Born 03/08/1956, New York, NY, m, 1988, 2 children **DISCIPLINE** FOLKLORE ANTHROPOLOGY **EDUCATION** IN Univ, PhD, 85; MA, 79; State Univ of NY, Stony Brook, BA, 76. **CAREER** Visiting Asst Prof, Dept Middle Eastern Studies, Emory Univ, 94-; Dir Judaic and Near Eastern Studies, Oberlin Coll, 88-94; Asst Prof, Judaic and Near Eastern Studies, Oberlin Coll, 88-94; Lecurer, Jidaic and Near Eastern Studies; Dir, Judaic and Near Easter Studies Program House, Oberlin Coll, 85-88; Assoc Inst, Dept of Near Eastern Langs and Cultures, IN Univ, 82-85; Interim Dir B'nai B'rith Hillel Found, IN Univ, 81-82; Assoc Inst, Folklore Dept, IN Univ, 79-80; Assoc Inst, Dept of Near Eastern Langs and Cultures, IN Univ, 78-79. **HONORS AND AWARDS** Phi Beta Kappa, Emory Univ Recognition for Excellent Teaching, 98; H.H. Powers Travel Grant, Bugaria and Israel, 92; Lilly Endowment Curricc Devel Frant for Minority Concerns, 91; Mellon Freshman-Sophomore Colloquium Devel Grant, 90; Grant in Aid Oberlin Coll Acculturation and Ethnicity in Israel-The Second Generation of Jews form Bulgaria, Tel Aviv, 86; Grant in Aid, IN Univ, 84; Dissertation Writing Grant, IN Univ, 83; Title VI Foreign Lang Fellowshop Arabic, 77; Hon BA, State Univ of NY,Stony Brook. **MEMBERSHIPS** Chair Comm for the Anthro of Jews and Judaism; Amer Anthro Assoc; Exec Board Gen Anthro Div; Chair Jewish Folklore and Ethnology Section, Amer Folklore Soc Section, Cord Folklore and Anthro Assoc for Jewish Studies; Assoc for Israel Studies; Israel Anthro Assoc; Bulgarian Studies Assoc; Natl Assoc of Pfor of Hebrew; Midwest Jewish Studies Assoc; Assoc for the Social Sci Study of Jewry; World Congress of Jewish Studies. **RESEARCH** Immigration; Ethnicity; Israeli Soc Sci; Jews of Bulgaria. **SELECTED PUBLICATIONS** From Sofia to Jaffa: The Jews of Bulgaria and Israel; Jewish Floklore and Anthro Series; ed, with a preface by Raphael Patai, Detroit Wayne State Univ Press, 94; Steven Sowman Choice 32, pp5729, 95; Jean Carasso Letter Sepharad, 95; pp8-10, Carol Silverman Jewish Folklore and Ethnology Review 17, 95; Walter Weiker Contemporary Jewry 16, 95; Committee for the Anthropology of Jews and Judaism: Background, Anthro of Rel Section, ed, Andrew Buckser Anthropology Newsletter Vol 39 No 4, 98; The Dossolution of Sephardic Cultrue in Bulgaria in Yeddish and Norman Stillman eds, From Iberia to Diaspora: Studies in Sephardic History and Culture, Leiden: Brill Forthcoming ,98; The hws of Bulgaria and the Final Solution, Jewish Folklore and Ethnology Review Vol 20 No 1, 98; Committee for the Anthropology of Jews and Judaism, Anthropology Newsletter Vol 38 No 5, 97; Publication Board General Anthropology Beneral Anthro Div Amer Anthro Assoc, Ed Board Jewish Folklore and Anthro Series, Wayne State Univ Press, (Dan Ben-Amos,ed in Chief), Joelle Bahloul, The Arcjitecture of Memory in Religious Studies Review, forthcoming. **CONTACT ADDRESS** Dept of Middle Eastern Studies, Emory Univ, Callaway S317, Atlanta, GA, 30022. **EMAIL** ghaskel@emory.edu

HASKELL, THOMAS LANGDON
PERSONAL Born 05/26/1939, Washington, DC, m, 1966, 2 children **DISCIPLINE** AMERICAN SOCIAL & INTELLECTUAL HISTORY **EDUCATION** Princeton Univ, BA, 61; Stanford Univ, PhD(hist), 73. **CAREER** From instr to asst prof, 70-77, ASSOC PROF US HIST, RICE UNIV, 77-, Fel, Nat Humanities Inst, Yale Univ, 75-76; vis mem, Inst Advan Study, Princeton Univ, 78-79; fel, Rockefeller Found, 78-79. **MEMBERSHIPS** AHA; Orgn Am Historians. **RESEARCH** History of social thought in the 19th and 20th centuries; intellectual consequences of modernization; attitudes toward criminal responsibility. **SELECTED PUBLICATIONS** Auth, Intellect and Public-Life--Essays on the Social-History of Academic Intellectuals in the United-States, J Social Hist, Vol 0027, 94; The Definition of a Profession--The Authority of Metaphor in the History of Intelligence-Testing, 1890-1930, J Am Hist, Vol 0081, 94; Death of the Guilds--Professions, States, and the Advance of Capitalism, 1930 to the Present, New York Rev Bk, Vol 0044, 97. **CONTACT ADDRESS** Dept of Hist, Rice Univ, Houston, TX, 77251.

HASSING, ARNE
PERSONAL Born 04/02/1943, Umtali, Rhodesia, m, 1966, 2 children **DISCIPLINE** RELIGION, HISTORY **EDUCATION** Boston Univ, BA, 64; Garrett-Evangel Theol Sem, MDiv, 68; Northwestern Univ, PhD(relig), 74. **CAREER** Asst Prof Humanities, Northern Ariz Univ, 73 **HONORS AND AWARDS** Jesse Lee Prize, Gen Comn Arch & Hist, United Methodist Church, 77. **MEMBERSHIPS** Am Soc Church Hist; Am Acad Relig; Soc Advan Scand Study; World Methodist Hist Soc. **RESEARCH** History of religion in Scandinavia; religion and modern culture; history of Christianity in the American Southwest. **SELECTED PUBLICATIONS** Auth, The Hedstroms and the Bethel Ship Saga--Methodist Influence on Swedish Religious Life, Am Hist Rev, Vol 0099, 94; Rome and the Counterreformation in Scandinavia, Vol 3, Jesuit Educational Strategy, 1553-1622, Vol 4, The Age Of Gustavus Aldolphus, and Queen Christina of Sweden, 1622-1656, Am Hist Rev, Vol 0098, 93. **CONTACT ADDRESS** Dept of Humanities, No Arizona Univ, Box 6031, Flagstaff, AZ, 86011-0001.

HASSING, RICHARD F.
DISCIPLINE HISTORY AND PHILOSOPHY OF SCIENCE **EDUCATION** Cornell Univ, PhD. **CAREER** Philos, Catholic Univ Am. **RESEARCH** Atistotle; hist of physics & philos of nature. **SELECTED PUBLICATIONS** Auth, The Use and Non-Use of Physics in Spinoza's Ethics; The Southwestern Jour Philos 11, 80; Wholes, Parts, and Laws of Motion; Nature and System 6, 84; Thomas Aquinas on Physics VII;1 and the Aristotelian Science of the Physical Continuum, Catholic Univ Press, 91; Animals versus the Laws of Inertia; Rev Metaphysics 46, 92, Introduction, and Modern Natural Science and the Intelligibility of Human Experience, Catholic Univ Press, 97; The Exemplary Career of Newton's Mathematics, The St John's Rev 44, 97. **CONTACT ADDRESS** Catholic Univ of America, 620 Michigan Ave Northeast, Washington, DC, 20064. **EMAIL** hassing@cua.edu

HASSRICK, PETER H.
PERSONAL Born 04/27/1941, Philadelphia, PA, m, 1963, 2 children **DISCIPLINE** ART HISTORY, HISTORY **EDUCATION** Univ CO, Boulder, BA (Hist, minor Classics), 63; Univ Denver, MA (Art Hist), 69. **CAREER** Instr, TX Christian Univ, Fort Worth, 74-75; Curator of Collections, Amon Carter Museum, Fort Worth, TX, 69-75; Curator, Buffalo Bill Hist Center, Whitney Gallery of Western Art, Cody, WY, 76-96; Dir, Buffalo Bill Hist Center, Cody, WY, 76-96; Dir, The Georgia O'Keefe Museum, Santa Fe, NM, 96-97; DIR, CHARLES M. RUSSELL CENTER FOR THE STUDY OF ART OF THE AMERICAN WEST AND CHARLES MARION RUSSELL ENDOWED CHAIR, ART HIST AT THE UNIV OK, NORMAN, 98-. **HONORS AND AWARDS** Leadership Award, Yellowstone Nat Park, 89; WY Governor's Art Award, 89; Who's Who in America, 95-., MA Thesis: Artists Employed on the United States Government Expeditions to the Trans-Mississippi West Before 1850. **RESEARCH** Am 19th-20th century art. **SELECTED PUBLICATIONS** Auth, Frederic Remington: Paintings, Drawings, and Sculpture in the Amon Carter Museum and the Sid W. Richardson Foundation Collections, Harry Abrams, Inc., 73; chief coord and ed, Amon Carter Museum of Western Art, Catalogue of the Collection 1972, Amon Carter Museum, 73; The American West Goes East, Am Art Rev, 75; The Artists, Buffalo Bill and the Wild West, The Brooklyn Museum, 81; Intro, Alfred Jacob Miller: Artist on the Oregon Trail, Amon Carter Museum, 82; The Rocky Mountains: A Vision for Artists in the Nineteenth Century, with Patricia Trenton, Univ OK Press, 83; Intro, American Frontier Life: Early Western Paintings and Prints, Abbeville Press, 87; coauth with Michael Shapiro and others, Frederic Remington: The Masterworks, Harry N. Abrams, 88; Charles Russell, Harry N. Abrams, 89; Western Art Museums: A Question of Style or Content, Montana, summer 92; with Melissa Webster, Frederic Remington: A Catalogue Raisonne in 2 vols with CD-ROM, Buffalo Bill Hist Center, 96; Frederic Remington's Studio: A Reflection, Antiques, Nov 94; Georgia O'Keefe's West, Antiques, Nov 97; ed and auth with others, The Georgia O'Keefe Museum, Harry N. Abrams, Inc., 97. **CONTACT ADDRESS** 520 Parrington Oval, Room 202, Norman, OK, 73019. **EMAIL** hassrick@ou.edu

HATA, DONALD TERUO
PERSONAL Los Angeles, CA, m, 1966 **DISCIPLINE** HISTORY **EDUCATION** Univ So Calif, BA, 62, MA, 64, PhD, 70. **CAREER** Vis instr his, Occidental Coll, 67-68; adj inst, LA Cty probation dept staff training, 72-75; asst prof hist, 70-73, assoc prof, 73-74, PROF, HIST, 74-. **HONORS AND AWARDS** Lyle Gibson Distinguished Teaching Award, Calif State Univ, Dominguez Hills, 77; Award of Merit, Calif Hist Soc, 80; Board of Trustees systemwide outstanding prof award, Calif State Univ, 90; Outstanding prof award, Asn Students, Inc, Calif State Univ, Dominguez Hills, 98. **MEMBERSHIPS** Amer hist asn; org of Amer historians, Asn for Asian Studies; Calif Hist Soc; Hist Soc of So Calif; LA Conservancy; Asian Amer Studies Asn **RESEARCH** Hist of Asian Calif; hist of multicultural, race, ethnicity and gender relations in Los Angeles; unexplored dimensions of the evacuation and incarceration of persons of Japanese ancestry in United States during WWII. **SELECTED PUBLICATIONS** Coauth, Asian-Pacific Angelinos: Model Minorities and Indipensable Scapegoats, in: 20th Century Los Angeles: Power, Promotion, and Social Conflict, Regina Books, 2nd ed, 91; coauth, Thinking Historically in the classroom, American Hist Asn perspectives, 95; coauth, Japanese Americans and World War II, Exclusion, Internment and Redress, 2nd ed, Harlan Davidson, 95. **CONTACT ADDRESS** Dept of Hist, California State Univ, Dominguez Hills, 1000 E. Victoria St, Carson, CA, 90747. **EMAIL** DHATA@DHVX20.CSUDH.EDU

HATA, NADINA ISHITANI
PERSONAL Born 03/15/1941, Honolulu, HI, m, 1966 **DISCIPLINE** HISTORY, FAR EASTERN STUDIES **EDUCATION** Univ Hawaii, BA, 63; Univ Mich, Ann Arbor, MA 65. **CAREER** Asst prof hist, Calif State Univ, Long Beach, 67-68; lectr, Calif State Univ, Dominguez Hills, 69-70; PROF HIST, EL CAMINO COL, 70-; Acting VP-instruction, El Camino Col, 92-93; VP-ACA AFFAIRS, EL CAMINO COL, 93-. **HONORS AND AWARDS** Award of Merit, Calif Hist Soc, 80; Selection Committee, 89 Carl What Award, Hist Soc of So Calif; Nancy Roelker Mentorship Award Committee, Amer Hist Asn, 92-96; Distinguished Woman Award, 97. **MEMBERSHIPS** Amer Hist Asn; Org of Amer Historians; Asn for Asian Studies; Calif Hist Soc; Hist Soc of So Calif, LA Conservancy; Community Coll Humanities Asn; Asian Amer Studies Asn **RESEARCH** History of Asian and Pacific Americans in LA, Calif and the west coast; historic preservation in Calif; hist of multicultural, race, ethnicity and gender relations in LA. **SELECTED PUBLICATIONS** Coauth, Asian-Pacific Angelinos: Model Minorities and Indispensable Scapegoats, in: 20th Centruty Los Angeles: Power, Promotion and Social Conflict, Regina Books 2nd ed, 91; The Historic Preservation Movement in California, 1940-1976, California State Dept of parks and Rec, 92; coath, Thinking Historically in the Classroom, Amer Hist Asn, Perspective, 95; coath, Japanese Americans and World War II, Exclusion, Internment, and Redress, 2nd ed, Harlan Davidson, 95. **CONTACT ADDRESS** El Camino Col, 16007 Crenshaw Boulevard, Torrance, CA, 90506. **EMAIL** Nhata@elcamino.cc.ca.us

HATAB, LAWRENCE J.
DISCIPLINE 19TH- AND 20TH-CENTURY CONTINENTAL PHILOSOPHY **EDUCATION** Fordham Univ, PhD, 76. **CAREER** Chair, Philos dept. **RESEARCH** Ancient philos, and social and political philos. **SELECTED PUBLICATIONS** Auth, Nietzsche and Eternal Recurrence ;Myth and Philos ;A Nietzschean Defense of Democracy: An Experiment in Postmodern Politics **CONTACT ADDRESS** Old Dominion Univ, 4100 Powhatan Ave, Norfolk, VA, 23058. **EMAIL** LHatab@odu.edu

HATCH, GEORGE
DISCIPLINE EARLY CHINA **EDUCATION** Yale Univ, BA, 59; Univ Wash, PhD, 72. **CAREER** Instr to assoc prof, Wash Univ, 68-. **SELECTED PUBLICATIONS** Transl, Yonezawa Yoshiho and Kawakita Michiaki, Arts China, Iii: Paintings In Chinese Museums, New Collection, Kodansha Int, 70; Contribr, Sung Bibliographies, Ostasiatische Studien, 76; A Sung Bibliography, Chinese Univ Profess, 78; Su Hsun's Profagmatic Statecraft, Ordering The World: Approfoaches To State And Society In Sung Dynasty China. **CONTACT ADDRESS** Washington Univ, 1 Brookings Dr, St. Louis, MO, 63130.

HATCH, MARTIN
DISCIPLINE MUSIC **EDUCATION** Cornell Univ, PhD. **CAREER** Assoc prof **HONORS AND AWARDS** Grant for study in Southeast Asia: Asian Cult Coun, NY, 87/88. **MEMBERSHIPS** Bd, treas, Soc Asian Music; Soc Ethnomusicol. **RESEARCH** Song in Southeast Asia; socio-cultural construction of music genres. **SELECTED PUBLICATIONS** Ed, Asian Music, jour, 85-96; Khmer Shadow Theater, 95. **CONTACT ADDRESS** Dept of Music, Cornell Univ, 104 Lincoln Hall, Ithaca, NY, 14853. **EMAIL** mfh2@cornell.edu

HATCH, NATHAN O.
DISCIPLINE HISTORY **EDUCATION** Wheaton Coll, BA, 68; Univ Wash, MA, 72, PhD, 74. **CAREER** Asst prof, PROF HIST, AND PROVOST UNIV NOTRE DAME **MEMBERSHIPS** Am Antiquarian Soc **SELECTED PUBLICATIONS** Auth, "The Christian Movement and the Demand for a Theology of the People," Jour of Am Hist, 80; co-ed, The Bible in America, 82; co-ed, Jonathan Edwards and the American Experience, Oxford, 88; ed, The Professions in American History, Univ Notre Dame, 88; The Democratization of American Christianity, Yale Univ Press, 89. **CONTACT ADDRESS** Univ of Notre Dame, 240 Hayes Healy, Notre Dame, IN, 46556.

HATCH, ROBERT A.
DISCIPLINE SCIENTIFIC HISTORY **EDUCATION** Univ Wis, BS, 70, MA, 72, PhD, 78. **CAREER** Asst prof, hist of sci, Univ Fla, 78-83; assoc prof 83-; Co-ed, hist of sci sect, The Eighteenth Century: A Current Bibliography, Am Soc Eighteenth Century Studies, 81-82. **HONORS AND AWARDS** Finalist Univ Teacher of the Yr, 96; CLAS Teacher of the Yr, 96; Mahon Teaching Awd, 96; TIP Teaching Awd, 93, 96. **MEMBERSHIPS** Hist Sci Soc; Soc Fr Hist Studies; Midwest Junto for Hist Sci; Southern Asn Hist Sci & Technol; Southern Hist Asn; British Soc Hist Sci. **RESEARCH** Seventeenth-century science; French science; correspondence networks in the Scientific Revolution. **SELECTED PUBLICATIONS** Auth, The Collection Boulliau, (BN, FF 13019-13059): An Inventory, Am Philos Soc, 82. **CONTACT ADDRESS** Dept of History, Univ of Florida, PO Box 117320, Gainesville, FL, 32611-7320. **EMAIL** ufhatch@nersp.nerdc.ufl.edu

HATFIELD, DOUGLAS WILFORD
PERSONAL Born 05/22/1939, Baton Rouge, LA, m, 1966, 1 child **DISCIPLINE** MODERN EUROPEAN HISTORY **EDUCATION** Baylor Univ, BA, 60; Univ Ky, MA, 61, PhD(hist), 69. **CAREER** Instr, Univ Tenn, Knoxville, 64 & Rhodes Col, 65-66; asst prof, Baylor Univ, 66-67; asst prof, 67-70, assoc prof, 70-79, prof hist, 80-, dir, interdisciplinary humanitites, 85-, JJ McComb prof hist, 89-, Rhodes Col, vis lectr, Memphis Acad Arts, 68-74; mem, Inst Hist Res, Univ London, 73; vis fel, Princeton Theol Sem, 80, 83. **HONORS AND AWARDS** Sears Interdisciplinary Teaching Award; Diehl Soc Fac Service Award, 94. **MEMBERSHIPS** Phi Beta Kappa; Phi Alpha Theta. **SELECTED PUBLICATIONS** Auth, Kulturkampf: The Relationship of Church and State and the Failure of German Political Reform, J Church & State, Vol 23, No 3; German Protestantism and the Kulturkampf, Red River Valley Hist J, Vol 5, No 4; Reform in the Prussian Evangelical Church and the Concept of the Londesherr, J Church & State, Vol 24, 3; Coauth, Celebrating the Humanities: A Half-Century of the Search Course at Rhodes College, Vanderbilt Press, 96. **CONTACT ADDRESS** Dept of History, Southwestern at Memphis, 2000 N Parkway, Memphis, TN, 38112-1690. **EMAIL** hatfield@rhodes.edu

HATHAWAY, JANE
DISCIPLINE HISTORY **EDUCATION** Univ Tex, BA, 82, MA, 86; Princeton Univ, PhD, 92. **CAREER** From asst prof to assoc prof, 92-, Ohio State Univ. **HONORS AND AWARDS** Turkey Fel, Am Res Inst, 88-89, 90, 93, 97; Fulbright Fel, 88-89; Whiting Fel, 91-92; SSRC postdoctoral Fel, 93-94; **MEMBERSHIPS** Middle East Stud Asn; Am Hist Asn; Turkish Stud Asn; Am Oriental Soc; World Hist Asn. **RESEARCH** Ottoman empire; Ottoman eunuchs. **SELECTED PUBLICATIONS** Auth, art, The Grand Vizier and the False Messiah: The Sabbatie Sevi Controversy and Ottoman Reform in Egypt, 97; Auth, art, Eunuchs, Ghulams, Janissaries, Slavery in the Ottoman Empire, 98; auth, art, Egypt in the Seventeenth Century, 98; auth, art, Mamluk Households' and Mamluk Factions' in Ottoman Egypt: A Reconsideration, 98; auth, art, Cerkes Mehmed Bey: Rebel, Traitor, Hero?, 98. **CONTACT ADDRESS** Dept of History, Ohio State Univ, 230 W 17th Ave, Columbus, OH, 43210.

HATHEWAY, JAY
PERSONAL Born 08/20/1949, Los Angeles, CA, s **DISCIPLINE** MODERN EUROPEAN HISTORY **EDUCATION** Claremont McKenna Col, BA, 71; Monterey Inst Int Studies, MA, 79; Univ Wis - Madison, PhD, 92. **CAREER** Asst Prof Hist, Edgewood Col, 97-, Dept Chair, 97-99. **MEMBERSHIPS** Am Hist Asn; Soc Hist Gilded Age & Progressive Era. **RESEARCH** Gilded Age ideological consensus; SS ideology; Gilded Age theories of homosexuality. **SELECTED PUBLICATIONS** Auth, The Pre-1920 Origins of the Nazi Party, J Contemp Hist, 94; Gay Liberation Front, The Encyclopedia of Contemporary Social Issues, Salem Press, 96; Anti-Modernism and the Contract with America, Ways of Co-Existing: Urban, Suburban, and Global Communities, Kendall/Hunt Publ Co, 97; Edgewood Col Dept Hist Web Site, 12/97; In Perfect Formation: SS Ideology and the SS-Junkerschule-Tulz, Schiffer Publ Ltd, Fall 98. **CONTACT ADDRESS** Edgewood Col, 855 Woodrow St., Madison, WI, 53711. **EMAIL** hatheway@edgewood.edu

HATHEWAY, JOSEPH G.
DISCIPLINE MODERN EUROPEAN HISTORY **EDUCATION** Claremont McKenna Col, BA, 71; Diploma, Cert Achievement, Defense Lang Inst, Presidio Monterey, Federal

Republic Germany, 72, 73; Monterey Inst Int Stud, MA, 79; Univ Wis, Madison, PhD, 92. **CAREER** Tchg asst, 82-84, reader, 83-, Univ Wis, Madison; adj prof, Cardinal Stritch Col, 87-93; adj prof, Lakeland Col, 95; instr, lectr, asst prof, 91-, Edgewood Col, Madison. **HONORS AND AWARDS** Chicago Resource Ctr Grant, 84; Ameritech Award, 94; **MEMBERSHIPS** Soc Hist Gilded Age and Progressive Era; Soc German-American Stud; Max Kade Inst; Council European Stud; Gay & Lesbian Caucus Am Hist Asn; Am Hist Asn. **SELECTED PUBLICATIONS** Auth, art, The Pre-1920 Origins of the Nazi Party, 94; auth, art, The Puritan Covenant Revisited: Anti-Modernism and the Contract with America, 95; auth, art, Gay Liberation Front, 96; auth, art, Anti-Modernism and the Contract With America, 97; auth, In Perfect Formation: SS Ideology and the SS-Junkerschule-Tolz, 98. **CONTACT ADDRESS** 217 W Washington St, Stoughton, WI, 53589. **EMAIL** hatheway@edgewood.edu

HATTAWAY, HERMAN MORELL
PERSONAL Born 12/26/1938, New Orleans, LA, m, 1961 **DISCIPLINE** UNITED STATES & MILITARY HISTORY **EDUCATION** La State Univ, Baton Rouge, BA, 61, MA, 63, PhD(hist), 69. **CAREER** Asst prof, 69-73, assoc prof, 73-81, prof Hist, Univ MO, Kansas City, 81-, vis asst prof hist, La State Univ, Baton Rouge, 72, prof Religion Studies, Univ MO, Kansas City, 96-. **HONORS AND AWARDS** Jefferson Davis award, 76, 86. **MEMBERSHIPS** AHA; Southern Hist Asn. **RESEARCH** Civil War Reconstruction; generalship; Jefferson Davis new south: United Confederate veterans. **SELECTED PUBLICATIONS** Auth, Some Aspects of Tudor Military History, Brit Army Quart & Defence J, 4/69; Clio's Southern Soldiers: the United Confederate Veterans and History, La Hist, summer 71; General Stephen D Lee, Univ Miss, 76; coauth, How the North Won: A Military Analysis of the Civil War, Univ Ill, 82; Shades of Blue and Gray, Univ Mo Press, 97. **CONTACT ADDRESS** Dept of Hist, Univ of Mo, 5100 Rockhill Rd, Kansas City, MO, 64110-2499.

HATZENBUEHLER, RONALD LEE
PERSONAL Born 06/09/1945, Dallas, TX, m, 1970 **DISCIPLINE** HISTORY **EDUCATION** Southwestern at Memphis, BA, 67; Kent State Univ, MA, 69, PhD(hist), 72. **CAREER** From asst prof to chmn dept, 72-77, ASSOC PROF HIST, IDAHO STATE UNIV, 77- **MEMBERSHIPS** Orgn Am Historians; Inst Early Am Hist & Cult; Soc Historians Am Foreign Relations; Southern Hist Soc; Soc Sci Hist Asn. **RESEARCH** United States early National Period; United States diplomacy; quantitative methods. **SELECTED PUBLICATIONS** Auth, Principle and Interest-- Thomas Jefferson and the Problem of Debt, Virginia Magazine of History and Biography, Vol 0104, 96; Western Rivermen, 1763-1861--Ohio and Mississippi Boatmen and the Myth of the Alligator Horse, NMex Hist Rev, Vol 0068, 93. **CONTACT ADDRESS** Dept of Hist, Idaho State Univ, Pocatello, ID, 83209.

HAUBEN, PAUL J.
PERSONAL Born 07/02/1932, Brooklyn, NY **DISCIPLINE** EARLY MODERN EUROPEAN HISTORY **EDUCATION** Brooklyn Col, BA, 58; Princeton Univ, PhD(hist), 63. **CAREER** Instr hist, Lafayette Col, 60-63; vis lectr, Univ Calif, Davis, 63-64; asst prof, Portland State Col, 64-65 & Mich State Univ, 65-69; assoc prof, 69-74, PROF HIST, UNIV OF THE PAC, 74-, ASSOC DEAN, COL PAC, 80-, Am Philos Soc grants-in-aid, 64-66. **RESEARCH** Early modern Spain; reformation; aspects of 18th century Spain. **SELECTED PUBLICATIONS** Auth, The End of Days--A Story Of Tolerance, Tyranny, and the Expulsion of the Jews From Spain, J Church State, Vol 0039, 97. **CONTACT ADDRESS** Dean's Office, Univ of the Pacific, Stockton, CA, 95211.

HAUCK, PAUL A.
PERSONAL Born 09/15/1924, Germany, m, 1953, 3 children **DISCIPLINE** PSYCHOLOGY **EDUCATION** Drew univ, BA 48; Univ UT, MA 51, PhD 53. **CAREER** Rock Island IL, Clinical Psychologist, 68-; Peoria Mental Health Clinic, Chief Psychol. **HONORS AND AWARDS** Dist Psychol Awd; Fell of APA; Outstanding Educ of Am., Frequent visitor on radio and television. **MEMBERSHIPS** UMVPA; APA **SELECTED PUBLICATIONS** The Rational Management of children, Libra Press; the following from Westminster Press, Reason in Pastoral Counseling, Over Coming Frustration and Anger, Overcoming Depression, Overcoming worry and Fear, Brief Counseling with RET, Overcoming Jealousy and Possessiveness, How to get the Most Out of Life, Overcoming the rating game, The Three Faces of Love, Marriage is a Loving Business, How to stand Up for Yourself, How to Cope with People Who Drive You Crazy. **CONTACT ADDRESS** Safety Building, suite 302, Rock Island, IL, 61201.

HAUPTMAN, LAURENCE MARC
PERSONAL Born 05/18/1945, New York, NY, m, 1970 **DISCIPLINE** UNITED STATES HISTORY **EDUCATION** NY Univ, BA, 66, MA, 68, PhD(Am hist), 71. **CAREER** Lectr, 71-72, asst prof, 71-75, ASSOC PROF US HIST, STATE UNIV NY COL NEW PALTZ, 75- **MEMBERSHIPS** AHA; Orgn Am Historians; Western Hist Asn; Am Soc Ethnohist. **RESEARCH** American Indian-white relations; the frontier in American history; American diplomatic history. **SELECTED PUBLICATIONS** Auth, Cultivating a Landscape of Peace--Iroquios European Encounters in 17th Century America, J Interdisciplinary Hist, Vol 0026, 95; On Our Own Ground--The Complete Writings of William Apess, A Pequot, J Am Hist, Vol 0080, 93; The White Earth Tragedy--Ethnicity and Dispossession at a Minnesota Anishinaabe Reservation, 1889-1920, J Am Hist, Vol 0082, 95; Historic Contact--Indian People and Colonists in Todays Northeastern United-States in the 16th Through 18th Centuries, J Am Hist, Vol 0083, 96; The Taos Indians and the Battle for Blue Lake, Hispanic Am Hist Rev, vol 0076, 96; American-Indian Children at School, 1850-1930, Historian, Vol 0056, 94; The States Men, The Salvation Seekers and the Seneca--The Supplemental-Treaty-Of-Buffalo-Creek, 1842, NY Hist, Vol 0078, 97; Retained by the People--A History of American-Indians and the Bill-Of-Rights, Am Hist Rev, Vol 0100, 95. **CONTACT ADDRESS** Dept of Hist, State Univ Col, 75 S Manheim Blvd, New Paltz, NY, 12561-2400.

HAUSE, STEVEN C.
PERSONAL Born 09/15/1942, Fort Wayne, IN, m, 1992 **DISCIPLINE** MODERN EUROPEAN HISTORY **EDUCATION** Northwestern Univ, BS, 64; WA Univ, AM, 66, PhD, 69 . **CAREER** Asst prof, 69-80, assoc prof hist, Univ MO, St Louis, 80-87, Res assoc int studies, Univ MO, St Louis, 70-72 & 82-85, Fellow, 86-, Prof, 87. **HONORS AND AWARDS** Phi Alpha Theta Best First Bk, 85; MO Conference on Hist, Distinguished Bk Award, 85 and 88; UM-St Louis Chancellor Award for Excellence in Tchg, 96. **MEMBERSHIPS** AHA; Soc French Hist Studies; Western Soc French Hist; Soc Hist; Soc Hist Mod; Southern Hist Asn. **RESEARCH** Polit and soc hist of the French Third Republic; women's rights in mod France. **SELECTED PUBLICATIONS** The Evolution of Social History, French Hist Studies, 96; Anti-Protestant Rhetoric in the Early Third Republic, French Hist Studies, 89; More Minerva Than Mars: The French Womans Rights Campaign and the First World War, IN Margaret Higonnet et al, Behind the Lines Gender and Discourse in the Two World Wars, Yak UP, 86; Western Civilization, with William Maltby, Wadsworth, 98; Feminisms of the Belle Epoque, with Jennifer Waelti-Walters, Neb UP, 95; Hubertine Auckrt: The French Suffagette, Yak UP, 87; Women's Suffrage and Social Politics in the French Third Republic, Princeton UP, with Anne R Kenney, 84; The development of the Catholic women's suffrage movement in France, Cath Hist Rev, 81; The limits of suffragist behavior: Legalism & militancy in France, Am Hist Rev, 81. **CONTACT ADDRESS** Dept Hist, Univ MO, 8001 Natural Bridge, Saint Louis, MO, 63121-4499. **EMAIL** schause@umslvma.umsl.edu

HAUSER, WILLIAM BARRY
PERSONAL Born 05/02/1939, Washington, DC, m, 1973, 3 children **DISCIPLINE** JAPANESE, ASIAN AMERICAN, & ASIAN HISTORY **EDUCATION** Univ Chicago, SB, 60; Yale Univ, MA, 62, PhD(hist), 69. **CAREER** Lectr hist, Univ Mich, Ann Arbor, 67-69, asst prof, 70-74; asst prof, 74-77, assoc prof, 77-83, PROF HIST, UNIV ROCHESTER, 83-, CHMN DEPT, 79-85, Nat Endowment for Humanities younger humanist fel, 71-72; Japan Found fel, 76; Mellon Found Fac fel, Univ Rochester, 77; Nat Endowment Humanities fel, 82-83. **MEMBERSHIPS** Asn Asian Studies. **RESEARCH** Economic and social change in Tokugawa Japan; Japanese local history; Asian women's history; Asian Am hist, lit. **SELECTED PUBLICATIONS** Auth, Kinsei Osaka ni okeru shogyo kiko no henshitsu katei--Osaka wata tonya no baai, Shakai Keizai Shigaku, 70; Economic Institutional Change in Tokugawa Japan--Osaka and Kinai Cotton Trade, Cambridge Univ, 74; The diffusion of cotton processing and trade in the Kinai region in Tokugawa, Japan, J Asian Studies, Vol XXXIII, 74; The Early Development of Osaka and Rule by Status, Miyamoto Mataji sensei koki kinen ronbunshu, Kindai Keizai no rekishiteki kiban, 77; Osaka: A commercial city in Tokugawa Japan, Urbanism Past & Present (transl, Sasaki Gin'ya, Sengoku Daimyo Rule and Commerce), 78; Japan Before Tokugawa: Political Consolidation and Economic Growth, 1500-1650, Princeton Univ, 81; Burghers, In: Japan Handbuch, Wiesbaden: Frank Steiner Verlag, 81; auth, Woman and War: The Japanese Film Image, in Recreating Japanese Women, 1600-1945, Univ Calif, 91; auth, Why so Few? Female Household Heads in Early Modern Osaka, J Fam Hist, II, 4, 86; auth, Fires on the Plain: The Human Costs of the Pacific War, in Reforming Japanese Cinema, Univ Tnchana, 92; auth, Tokugawa Japan, in Asian in Western and World History, ME Sharpe, 97. **CONTACT ADDRESS** Dept of Hist, Univ of Rochester, 500 Joseph C Wilson, Rochester, NY, 14627-9000.

HAVEMAN, ROBERT H.
PERSONAL Born 07/22/1936, Grand Rapids, MI, m, 1983, 3 children **DISCIPLINE** ECONOMICS, PUBLIC FINANCE **EDUCATION** Calvin Col, AB, 58; Vanderbilt Univ, PhD, econo, 63. **CAREER** John Bascom Prof, Dept Econo La Follette Inst Pub Aff; Res Assoc, Inst Res on Poverty, Univ WI-Madison; Inst to Prof, Econ, Grinnel Col, 62-70; Brookings Res Prof, 65-66; Sr Econ, Jt Econ Comm, 68-69; Fel, Neth Inst for Advn Study Soc Ser, Human, Wassenaar, The Neth, 75-76, 96-97; Tinbergen Prof, Erasus Univ, Neth, 84-85; Chair, Dept Econ, Univ WI-Madison, 93-; Board of Editors, Am Econ Rev, 91-95, J Econ Lit, 83-87, Public Fin, 83-, Evaluation Quart, 76-80, co ed, Am Econ Rev, 85-91. **MEMBERSHIPS** Pres, Intl Inst of Pub Fin, 97-; Pres, Midwest Econ Asn,92-93; Mem, Bd Dir, Resources for the Future, 90-; Pres, Midwest Econ Asn, 92-93. **SELECTED PUBLICATIONS** Poverty Policy and Poverty Research: The Great Society and Social Sciences, Univ Wisconsin Press, 87; Starting Even: An Equal Opportunity Program for the Nation's New Poverty, NY, Simon and Schuster, 88; Earnings Inequality" The Influence of Changing Opportunities and Choices, Washington, DC, Urban Inst Press, 94; Succeeding Generations: On the Effects of Investments in Children, with B Wolfe, NY, Russell Sage Found, 94; The Work Alternative, ed and auth with D Nightingale, Washington DC, Urban Inst Press, 94. **CONTACT ADDRESS** Dept Economics, Univ Wisconsin, 3412 Social Science Bldg, Madison, WI, 53706. **EMAIL** haveman@lafollette.wisc.edu

HAVRAN, MARTIN JOSEPH
PERSONAL Born 11/12/1929, Windsor, ON, Canada, m, 1958, 1 child **DISCIPLINE** HISTORY **EDUCATION** Univ Detroit, PhB, 51; Wayne State Univ, MA, 53; Western Reserve Univ, PhD(hist), 57. **CAREER** Res assoc Can hist, Essex County Hist Asn, Windsor, Ont, 52-53; instr to assoc prof English hist, Kent State Univ, 57-68; assoc prof, 68-72, chemn dept hist, 74-79, dir, Self-Study Prog, 84-86, prof English hist, Univ Va, 72-, Consult, Scott, Foresman & Co Publ, 64-70; vis assoc prof, Northwestern Univ, 67-68; mem bd overseers, Case Western Reserve Univ, 76-79. **HONORS AND AWARDS** Whittaker Hist Prize, Wayne State Univ, 53; Alumni Distinguished Prof Award, 86; Raven Soc Distinguished Fac Award, 87; Distinguished Teacher Award, 64, 66, 92; Omicron Delta Fac Award for Teaching, 97; Arthur Stodser Distinguished Fac Award, 97. **MEMBERSHIPS** AHA; North Am Conf Brit Studies (pres, 79-81); Am Cath Hist Asn (pres, 82); Asn Can Studies in US; fel Royal Hist Soc. **RESEARCH** Tudor and Stuart England; the English Reformation; history of Canada. **SELECTED PUBLICATIONS** Auth, Catholics in Caroline England, Stanford Univ & Oxford Univ, 62; co-ed, Readings in English History, Scribner, 67; coauth, England: Prehistory to the Present, Doubleday & Praeger, 68; Caroline Courtier: The Life of Lord Cottington, Macmillan, London & Univ SC, 73. **CONTACT ADDRESS** Corcoran Dept of Hist, Univ of Virginia, 205 Randall Hall, Charlottesville, VA, 22903-3244. **EMAIL** mjh6f@virginia.edu

HAW, JAMES A.
DISCIPLINE HISTORY **EDUCATION** Univ Va, PhD, 72. **CAREER** Prof. **RESEARCH** American Colonial history; American Revolution. **SELECTED PUBLICATIONS** Coauth, Stormy Patriot: the Life of Samuel Chase, 80. **CONTACT ADDRESS** Dept of History, Indiana Univ-Purdue Univ, Fort Wayne, 2101 Coliseum Blvd, Fort Wayne, IN, 46805. **EMAIL** haw@smtplink.ipfw.edu

HAWES, JOSEPH
PERSONAL Born 05/09/1938, Fort Davis, TX, m, 1989, 2 children **DISCIPLINE** HISTORY **EDUCATION** Rice Univ, AB, 60; Okla State Univ, MA, 62; Univ Tex, PhD, 69. **CAREER** Asst Prof, Ind Univ Southeast, 69-71; asst prof, Kans State Univ, 71-73; assoc prof to prof, dept hd, Kans State Univ 73-84; prof, Univ Memphis, 84-present. **HONORS AND AWARDS** Phi Alpha Theta and Phi Kappa Phi; Outstanding Academic Book, Choice Mag, 93; Outstanding Fac Member, Univ Col, 95-96. **MEMBERSHIPS** AHA; Orgn Am Historians; Southern Hist Asn; Hist Educ Society; Am Studies Asn; Am Asn of Univ Prof. **RESEARCH** History of childhood in the United States. **SELECTED PUBLICATIONS** Auth, Children in Urban Society, Oxford Univ Press, 71; ed, Law and Order in American History, Kennikat Press, 73; co-ed, American Childhood, Greenwood Press, 85; co-ed, American Families, Greenwood Press, 85; co-ed, Growing Up in America, Univ Ill Press, 85; auth, The Children's Rights Movement, Twayne Publ, 91; co-ed, Children in Historical and Comparative Perspective, Greenwood Press, 91; auth, Children Between the Wars, Twayne Publ, 97. **CONTACT ADDRESS** Univ of Memphis, Campus Box 526120, Memphis, TN, 38152-6120. **EMAIL** jhawes@memphis.edu

HAWKINS, DORISULA WOOTEN
PERSONAL Born 11/15/1941, Mt. Pleasant, TX, m **DISCIPLINE** EDUCATION **EDUCATION** Jarvis Christian Coll, BS 1962; East TX State Univ, attended 1965; Prairie View A&M Univ, MS 1967; TX A&M Univ, attended 1970; Univ of Houston, EdD 1975. **CAREER** Jarvis Coll, sec & asst public relations dir 1962-63; Roxton School Dist, instructor business 1963-66; Prairie View A&M Univ, assoc prof, 1966-96, head general business dept 1976-88; Jarvis christian Coll, dev officer, 1996-97, prof business administration, 1997-. **HONORS AND AWARDS** Dist Business Tchr of the Yr TBEA 1981; Disting Alumnus Jarvis Coll 1982; nominee State Tchr of Yr TBEA 1982; Disting Alumni Citation (NAFEO) 1986. **MEMBERSHIPS** Adv bd Milady Publishing Co; exec bd mem TX Assn of Black Personnel in Higher Educ 1978-83; bd mem TX Bus Educ (TBEA) Assn 1978-83; pres Alpha Kappa Alpha 1982-85; chmn TX Business Thcr Educ Cncl 1985-87; mem Natl Bus Educ Assoc; mem Jarvis Christian Coll Bd of Trustees, 1986-88; pres Natl Alumni Assoc 1986-88. **SELECTED PUBLICATIONS** "Can Your Office Administration be Justified" TX Business Educator 1979. **CONTACT ADDRESS** Jarvis Christian Col, PO Box Drawer G, Hawkins, TX, 75765-0893.

HAWKINS, HUGH DODGE
PERSONAL Born 09/03/1929, Topeka, KS **DISCIPLINE** AMERICAN HISTORY **EDUCATION** DePauw Univ, AB, 50; Johns Hopkins Univ, PhD(hist), 54. **CAREER** Instr hist, Univ NC, 56-67; instr Am studies, 57-59, from asst prof to assoc prof hist & Am studies, 59-69, prof, 69-75, ANSON D MORSE PROF HIST & AM STUDIES, AMHERST COL, 75-; Fulbright lectr, Goettingen, WGer, 73-74; vis assoc, Ctr Studies in Higher Educ, Univ Calif, Berkeley, 78-79 & 82-83; Fulbright Lectr, Hamsburg, Ger, 93-94. **HONORS AND AWARDS** Moses Coit Tyler Prize, AHA, 59; Guggenheim fel, 61-62; Nat Endowment Humanities fel, 82-83. **MEMBERSHIPS** AHA; Orgn Am Historians; Hist Educ Soc; Mass Hist Soc. **RESEARCH** Social and intellectual history; race in American history. **SELECTED PUBLICATIONS** Auth, Pioneer: A History of the Johns Hopkins University, 1874-1889, Cornell Univ, 60; The Emerging University and Industrial America, 70 & The Abolitionists: Means, Ends and Motivations, 2nd ed, 72, Heath; auth, Between Harvard and America: The Educational Leadership of Charles W Eliot, Oxford Univ, 72; ed, Booker T Washington and His Critics: Black Leadership in Crisis, 2nd ed, Heath, 74; coauth, Education at Amherst Reconsidered: The Liberal Studies Program, Amherst Col Press, 78; auth, Transatlantic discipleship: Two American biologists and their German mentor, Isis, Vol LXXI, 80; University Identity: The Teaching and Research Functions, In: The Organization of Knowledge in Modern America, 1860-1920, Johns Hopkins Univ, 79; Edward Jones, marginal man, In: Black Apostles at Home and Abroad, G.K. Hall, 82; Banding Together: The Rise of National Associations in American Higher Education, 1887-1950, Johns Hopkins Univ, 92; The University, In: Encyclopedia of the United States in the Twentieth Century, Vol IV, Scribner's, 96. **CONTACT ADDRESS** Dept of Am Studies, Amherst Col, Amherst, MA, 01002-5000. **EMAIL** hhawkins@amherst.edu

HAWKINS, MERRILL M.
PERSONAL Born 12/04/1963, Vicksburg, MS, m, 1988, 1 child **DISCIPLINE** HISTORY; THEOLOGY **EDUCATION** BA, History; PhD **CAREER** Grad Asst, Baylor Univ, 90-95; Asst Prof, Carson-Newman Col, 95-. **HONORS AND AWARDS** Outstanding Graduate Student, Baylor Univ, 93; Faculty Research Award, Carson-Newman Col, 98. **MEMBERSHIPS** Amer Soc of Church History; Amer Acad of Religion; Southern Historical Assoc. **RESEARCH** American religious history; religion in the American South; religion and social activism **SELECTED PUBLICATIONS** Coauth, Texas Baptist Educational Institutions, Texas Baptist History, 90; Auth, Private Schools, Public Funds, Report from the Capital, 90; Roger Williams on Separation, Report from the Capital, 92; The Ecumenical and Social Leadership of G. Bromley Oxnam, Methodist History, 95; Attitudes toward the White House, Baptist History and Heritage 32, 97; Will Campbell: Radical Prophet of the South, 97; J.B.Tidwell, The Handbook of Texas, forthcoming. **CONTACT ADDRESS** Carson-Newman Col, CNC Box 71919, Jefferson City, TN, 37760. **EMAIL** hawkins@cncacc.cn.edu

HAWKINS, RALPH K.
PERSONAL Born 06/24/1969, Yuma, AZ, m, 1990, 1 child **DISCIPLINE** BIBLICAL LANGUAGES **EDUCATION** David Lipscomb Univ, BA, 90, MA, 95; Univ of the South, DMin, 98. **HONORS AND AWARDS** Endow for Bibl Res, 97. **MEMBERSHIPS** Am Schools of Orient Res; Cath Bib Asn; Soc of Bibl Lit. **RESEARCH** Archaeology; Historiography of ancient Israel. **SELECTED PUBLICATIONS** Auth, A Heritage in Crisis. **CONTACT ADDRESS** 275 North Carolina Ave, Sewanee, TN, 37355. **EMAIL** Hawkirk9@sewanee.edu

HAWLEY, ELLIS WAYNE
PERSONAL Born 06/02/1929, Cambridge, KS, m, 1953, 3 children **DISCIPLINE** HISTORY **EDUCATION** Univ Wichita, BA, 50; Univ Kans, MA, 51; Univ Wis, PhD(hist), 59. **CAREER** Instr hist, NTex State Univ, 57-58, from asst prof to prof, 58-68; prof, Ohio State Univ, 68-69; PROF HIST, UNIV IOWA, 69-, Hist consult, Pub Paper of Hoover Presidency Proj, Off Fed Reg, 73-78. **MEMBERSHIPS** AHA; Orgn Am Historizns; AAUP. **RESEARCH** Recent United States history. **SELECTED PUBLICATIONS** Auth, The Presidency of Woodrow Wilson, J Southern Hist, Vol 0059, 93; America Welfare-State--From Roosevelt to Reagan, Labor Hist, Vol 0034, 93; Giannini and the Bank-Of-America, Historian, Vol 0059, 96; Wilsonian Idealism in America, Am Hist Rev, Vol 0101, 96. **CONTACT ADDRESS** Dept of Hist, Univ of Iowa, Iowa City, IA, 52242.

HAWTHORNE, GERALD F.
PERSONAL Born 08/16/1925, Los Angeles, CA, m, 1955, 3 children **DISCIPLINE** CLASSICAL GREEK, NEW TESTAMENT **EDUCATION** Wheaton Col, Ill, BA, 51, MA, 54; Univ Chicago, PhD, 69. **CAREER** From instr to assoc prof, 53-73, Prof Class Greek & New Testament Exegesis, Wheaton Col, Ill, 73- **MEMBERSHIPS** Am Acad Relig; Soc Bibl Lit; Evangel Theol Soc; Studiorum Novi Testamenti Soc; Inst Bibl Res (treas, 73-). **RESEARCH** Early Christian literature and church history; New Testament studies. **SELECTED PUBLICATIONS** Auth, Chained in Christ--The Experience and Rhetoric of Paul Imprisonments, J Biblical Lit, Vol 0116, 97. **CONTACT ADDRESS** Wheaton Col, Wheaton, IL, 60187.

HAY, CARLA HUMPHREY
PERSONAL Born 11/12/1942, Louisville, KY, m, 1966 **DISCIPLINE** ENGLISH & MODERN EUROPEAN HISTORY **EDUCATION** Spalding Col, BA, 64; Univ Ky, PhD(hist), 72. **CAREER** Lectr hist, Cardinal Stritch Col, 67-68, instr, 68-70; instr, 70-73, asst prof, 73-79, ASSOC PROF HIST, MARQUETTE UNIV, 79-, Lectr hist, Cardinal Stritch Col, 70-73; Am Philos Soc fel, 75; Nat Endowment for Humanities fel, summer, 76. **MEMBERSHIPS** AHA; Conf Brit Studies; Hist Asn, Eng; Soc 18th-Century Studies. **RESEARCH** Eighteenth century English intellectual history; 18th century English radicals, James Burgh, Catharine Macaulay and John Sawbridge; women in 18th century England. **SELECTED PUBLICATIONS** Auth, Catharine Macaulay and the American Revolution, Historian, Vol 0056, 94. **CONTACT ADDRESS** Dept of Hist, Marquette Univ, Milwaukee, WI, 53233.

HAY, FRED J.
PERSONAL Born 10/03/1953, Toccoa, GA, m, 1983, 1 child **DISCIPLINE** ANTHROPOLOGY; LIBRARY SCIENCE **EDUCATION** Rhodes Col, BA, 75; Univ Va, MA, 81; Fl St Univ, MLIS, 87; Univ Fl, PhD, 85. **CAREER** Asst prof, St Cloud St Univ, 85-86; librn, asst prof, Ks St Univ, 88-89; librn, Harvard Univ, 89-94; prof, librn, Appalachian St Univ, 94- . **HONORS AND AWARDS** Douglas W. Bryant Fel, 92-93; Brenda McCullum Mem Prize, Amer Folklore Soc, 97. **MEMBERSHIPS** Amer Anthrop Assoc; Appalachian Stud Assoc; Amer Libr Assoc; Assoc of Col & Res Libr; Assoc of Black Anthrop; Progressive Librn Guild. **RESEARCH** Appalachia, African-American cultures; Black music; soc sci bibliogr & documentation, southern US, Caribbean. **SELECTED PUBLICATIONS** Auth, Tozzer Library: How to Access the World's Largest Anthropology Bibliography, Cult Anthrop Methods Newsletter, 92; OCLC: An Essential Tool for Anthropological Documentation, Cult Anthrop Methods Newsletter, 93; The Significance of Caribbeanist Anthropology: A Bibliographic History, Ref Svc Rev, 95; coed, Documenting Cultural Diversity in the Resurgent American South: Collectors, Collecting and Collections; Assoc of Col & Res Libr; ed, auth, When Night Falls: Kric! Krac!, Libr Unlimited, 98. **CONTACT ADDRESS** W. L. Evry Appalachian Col, Appalachian State Univ, Belk Library, Boone, NC, 28608. **EMAIL** hayfj@appstate.edu

HAY, MELBA PORTER
PERSONAL Born 03/16/1949, Somerset, KY, m, 1977 **DISCIPLINE** AMERICAN HISTORY **EDUCATION** Univ Ky, BA, 71, MA, 73, PhD, 80. **CAREER** Instr Am Hist, 74-78, Asn Ed Papers of Henry Clay, Univ Ky, 80-87; ed & dir, Papers of Henry Clay, 87-91; DIVISION MANAGER OF RESEARCH AND PUBLICATIONS, KENTUCKY HISTORICAL SOCIETY, 91- . **MEMBERSHIPS** Southern Hist Asn; Kentucky Hist Soc; Kentucky Coun Arch. **RESEARCH** United States political history; women's history; Southern history. **SELECTED PUBLICATIONS** Auth, Madeline McDowell Breckinridge: Her Role in the Kentucky Women Suffrage Movement, 1908-1920, 10/74 & ed, The memoirs of Charles Henry Daily, 4/78, Regist Ky Hist Soc; contribr, James D Dole, Suppl VI, Frederick Hale, Supple VII & Owen Brewster, Suppl VII, Dict Am Biog, Scribners; The Election of 1824, Running for President, NY, 94; Suffragist Triumphant: Madeline McDowell Breckinridge and the Nineteenth Amendment, The Register, 95; Letitia Tyler and Julia Gardiner Tyler, American First Ladies: Their Lives and Their Legacies, Lewis Gould, 96; Compromiser or Conspirator? Henry Clay and the Graves-Cilley Duel, A Mythic Land Apart: Reassessing Southerners and Their History, Westport, CT, 97. **CONTACT ADDRESS** 126 Buckwood Dr, Richmond, KY, 40475. **EMAIL** melba.hay@mail.state.ky.us

HAY, ROBERT PETTUS
PERSONAL Born 10/23/1941, Eagleville, TN, m, 1966 **DISCIPLINE** AMERICAN HISTORY **EDUCATION** Mid Tenn State Univ, BS, 62; Univ Ky, PhD(Am hist), 67. **CAREER** Lectr hist, Univ Ky, 66-67; asst prof, 67-71, asst chmn dept, 75, chmn dept & dir grad study, 75-79, ASSOC PROF HIST, MARQUETTE UNIV, 71-, Res grant, Marquette Univ, 68; Nat Endowment for Humanities fel, 69-70; assoc hist ed, USA Today, 80- **MEMBERSHIPS** Southern Hist Asn; Orgn Am Historians; AAUP; Soc Historians of the Early Am Republic. **RESEARCH** American intellectual history; American nationalism; Jeffersonian and Jacksonian democracy. **SELECTED PUBLICATIONS** Auth, Henry Clay--Statesman for the Union, Historian, Vol 0055. **CONTACT ADDRESS** Dept of Hist, Marquette Univ, Milwaukee, WI, 53233.

HAYCOCK, RONALD G.
PERSONAL Born 06/30/1942, Ingersoll, ON, Canada **DISCIPLINE** MILITARY HISTORY **EDUCATION** Wilfrid Laurier Univ, BA, 68; Univ Waterloo, MA, 69; Univ Western Ont, PhD, 76. **CAREER** Lectr, Waterloo Lutheran Univ, 69-71; instr, Wilfrid Laurier Univ & Univ Western Ont, 72-75; lectr to assoc prof, 75-87, PROF, ROYAL MILITARY COL CANADA, 87-, head hist dept, 90-93. **HONORS AND AWARDS** Moncado Prize Mil Hist, Am Soc Mil Hist, 79. **MEMBERSHIPS** Soc Mil Hist; past pres Can Mil Hist Gp, Can Hist Asn, 83-92; ed bd, Ont Hist, 82-; ed bd, War and Society, 83-. **SELECTED PUBLICATIONS** Auth, Image of the Indian, 72; auth, Sam Hughes, 86; auth, Clio and Mars in Canada, 95; ed, Regular Armies and Insurgency, 79; co-ed, Men, Machines and War, 88; co-ed, The Cold War and Defense, 90; co-ed, Canada's Defense, 93. **CONTACT ADDRESS** Royal Mil Col, Kingston, ON, K7K 5L0.

HAYDEN, ALBERT A.
PERSONAL Born 09/18/1923, Cape Girardeau, MO, m, 1954, 2 children **DISCIPLINE** BRITISH HISTORY **EDUCATION** Univ Ill, BA, 50, Bucknell Univ, MA, 52; Univ Wis, PhD, 59. **CAREER** From instr to assoc prof, 59-70, PROF HIST, WITTENBERG UNIV, 70-, Managing ed, Study Brit Hist & Cult. **MEMBERSHIPS** AHA; NAm Conf British Studies; Midwest Conf British Studies. **RESEARCH** British imperial history; 19th century Britain. **SELECTED PUBLICATIONS** Auth, Lord Curzon--The Last of the British Moghuls, Historian, Vol 0057, 94; Gladstone Imperialism in Egypt--Techniques of Domination/, Historian, Vol 0059, 96; Capitalism, Culture, and Decline in Britain 1750-1990, Historian, Vol 0056, 94; Joseph Chamberlain--Entrepreneur in Politics, Historian, Vol 0058, 95. **CONTACT ADDRESS** 1329 Eastgate Rd, Springfield, OH, 45503.

HAYDEN, JAMES MICHAEL
PERSONAL Born 06/04/1934, Akron, OH, m, 1961, 3 children **DISCIPLINE** MODERN EUROPEAN HISTORY **EDUCATION** John Carroll Univ, MA, 58; Loyola Univ, Ill, PhD, 63. **CAREER** From instr to asst prof hist, Univ Detroit, 61-66; from asst prof to assoc prof, 66-74, PROF HIST, UNIV SASK, 74-, Ed, Can J Hist, 70-73. **MEMBERSHIPS** Soc Fr Hist Studies; Can Hist Asn; Western Soc Fr Hist. **RESEARCH** Early modern European history, especially social, institutional and religious; France, late 16th-early 17th centuries. **SELECTED PUBLICATIONS** Auth, Iron and Blood--Civil-Wars in 16th-Century France, Manuscripta, Vol 0036, 92; The Clergy of Early-17th-Century France--Self-Perception and Society Perception, French Hist Studies, Vol 0018, 93; Good News From Fraunce--French Anti-League Propaganda in Late Elizabethan England, Sixteenth Century J, Vol 0028, 97. **CONTACT ADDRESS** Dept of Hist, Univ of Sask, Saskatoon, SK, S7N 0W0.

HAYES, ANNAMARIE GILLESPIE
PERSONAL Born 09/06/1931, Flint, MI, m **DISCIPLINE** EDUCATION **EDUCATION** MI St, BA, MA, MS, PhD. **CAREER** Pontiac Public Schools, Inkster Public Schools, public school teacher; MI-OH Regional Lab, teacher trainer; MI State Univ, educ specialist; Univ WI Madison, rsch assoc; Coll of Educ Wayne State Univ, presently assoc prof. **HONORS AND AWARDS** Woman of yr awd MI State Univ 1971; USAF Europe awd 1972; fellow resrch Williams Coll. **MEMBERSHIPS** Nat Assn Negro Bus & Professional Women; Nat Assn Black Fin Aid Adminstr; Nat All Black Educ; Am Educ Resrch Assn; Assn Study Negro Life & Hist; bd dir Intl Afro-Am Museum; Shrine Black Madonna Detroit; Councilwoman Erma Henderson Women's Concerns Conf.

HAYES, CHARLES LEONARD
PERSONAL Born 12/16/1921, Baton Rouge, LA, m **DISCIPLINE** EDUCATION **EDUCATION** Leland Coll, AB 1947; Loyola U, EdM 1949; Univ No CO, EdD 1958. **CAREER** Chicago, teacher 1948-49; NC A&T State Univ, instr 1949-52, asst prof 1952-56, prof 1958-61, chmn 1961-66; George Washington Univ, ace fellow 1966-67; US Office of Educ HEW, chief 1967-69; Albany State Coll, pres 1969-80; NC A&T State Univ, chmn beginning 1980, adjunct faculty, currently. **MEMBERSHIPS** Am Assn of Univ Profs; Assn of Higher Edn; NEA; Phi Delta Kappa; Am Personnel & Guidance Assn; Am Coll Personnel Assn; Assn of Counselor Educators & Suprs; NC Psychol Assn; Kappa Delta Pi; bd dir Albany Urban League; Albany USO Council; exec bd Chehaw Council Boy Scouts of Am; Nat Conf of Christian& Jews; YMCA; Citizens Adb Com; mem Drug Action Council, Volunteers to the Courts. **CONTACT ADDRESS** No Carolina A&T State Univ, 1601 E Market St, Greensboro, NC, 27411.

HAYES, FLOYD WINDOM, III
PERSONAL Born 11/03/1942, Gary, IN, m **DISCIPLINE** HISTORY **EDUCATION** Univ of Paris, Cert d'Etudes 1964; NC Central Univ, BA (Cum Laude) 1967; Univ of CA Los Angeles, MA (w/Distinction) 1969; Univ of MD, PhD 1985. **CAREER** Univ of CA Los Angeles, instruction specialist 1969-70; Princeton Univ, lecturer dept of pol exec sec Afro-Amer studies 1970-71; Swarthmore Coll, vstg lecturer dept of history 1971; Univ of MD, asst coord Afro-Amer studies 1971-73, instructor 1971-77; Cornell Univ, instructor Africana studies 1977-78; Close Up Found, prog instructor 1979-80; Howard Univ, res asst, res fellow inst for the study of ed policy 1980-81, 1981-85; US Equal Employment Oppor Com, special asst to chmn 1985-86; San Diego State Univ, asst prof Africana studies 1986-. **HONORS AND AWARDS** Outstanding Young Men of Amer 1977; Phi Delta Kappa Professional Educ Frat Howard Univ Chap 1982. **MEMBERSHIPS** Consultant Union Township Sch System 1971, Comm Educ Exchange Prog Columbia Univ 1972, MD State Dept of Educ 1973-75; mem Early Childhood Educ Subcomm FICE US Dept of Educ 1986. **SELECTED PUBLICATIONS** "The Future, A Guide to Information Sources," World Future Soc 1977; "The African Presence in

America Before Columbus," Black World July 1973; "Structures of Dominance and the Political Economy of Black Higher Education," Institute for the Study of Educational Policy Howard Univ 1981; "The Political Economy, Reaganomics, and Blacks," The Western Journal of Black Studies 1982; "Politics and Education in America's Multicultural Society," Journal of Ethnic Studies 1989; "Governmental Retreat and the Politics of African American Self-Reliant Development," Journal of Black Studies 1990. **CONTACT ADDRESS** San Diego State Univ, Dept of Africana Studies, San Diego, CA, 92182.

HAYES, JACK I., JR.
PERSONAL Born 08/13/1944, Danville, VA, m, 1966, 2 children **DISCIPLINE** HISTORY **EDUCATION** Hampden Sydney Col, BA, 66; Va Polytechnic Inst, MA, 68; Univ SC, PhD, 72; Averett Col, BS, 87. **CAREER** Dir, Univ SC, 72-74; from asst prof to assoc prof to prof to W.C. Daniel prof, 72-, Averett Col; adj prof, Va Polytechnic Inst, 77-79; Archival Consult, Dibrell Brothers Inc, 90-91. **HONORS AND AWARDS** Who's Who in the South and Southwest; Outstand Young Man in Am; Westmoreland Davis Memorial Found Fel; Lewis P. Jones Res Fel. **RESEARCH** Twentieth-Century United States **SELECTED PUBLICATIONS** Auth, A History of Averett College, 84; auth, Dan Daniel and the Persistence of Conservatism in Virginia, 97; auth, art, John Taylor Averett, 98. **CONTACT ADDRESS** 245 Linden Dr, Danville, VA, 24541. **EMAIL** jhayes@averett.edu

HAYES, JEFFREY R.
DISCIPLINE ART HISTORY **EDUCATION** Wake Forest Univ, BA, 67; Johns Hopkins Univ, MLA, 82; Univ Md, PhD. **CAREER** Instr, Trinity Col, 76-77; instr, Univ Md, 77-80; lectr, Smithsonian Inst, 81; asst prof, 82-88; assoc prof, 88-96; assoc prof, 88-96; prof, 96-. **RESEARCH** American painting and sculpture; folk and nonacademic art. **SELECTED PUBLICATIONS** Auth, Oscar Bluemner, Cambridge, 91; Foreword, 96; Use to Beauty: The Artful Decoy, 96; Oscar Julius (FLORIANUS) Bluemner, 95; Carl Mckenzie: Life and Art of a Southern Highlander, 94; Artworks by Carl McKenzie in the Exhibition, 94; Oscar Bluemner 1867-1938, Providence, Rhode Island, 1923, 94. **CONTACT ADDRESS** Dept of Art History, Univ of Wisconsin, Milwaukee, PO Box 413, Milwaukee, WI, 53201. **EMAIL** jhayes@csd.uwm.edu

HAYES, LEOLA G.
PERSONAL Rocky Mount, NC, m **DISCIPLINE** EDUCATION **EDUCATION** BS; MA; MS prof diploma; PhD 1973. **CAREER** William Paterson Coll of NJ, chmn Special Educ Dept, currently; Fair Lawn NJ, supervisor, spl educ 1957-64; Fair Lawn NJ, teacher of handicapped children; Blind Chicago, consultant 1954-57; Blind NY Inst for Blind, teacher 1953-54. **HONORS AND AWARDS** Recipient: Human Relations Award, Natl Bus & Professional Women; Nat Comm Ldrs Award; Hannah G Solomon Award; Ernest Melly Award. **MEMBERSHIPS** CEC; Vocational Rehab Soc; AAMD; NJEA; Drug Abuse Prog 1973-; Young People Counseling Session, Alpha Kappa Alpha Sorority. **CONTACT ADDRESS** Spec Educ, William Paterson Col, 300 Pompton Rd, Wayne, NJ, 07470.

HAYES, ROBERT MAYO
PERSONAL Born 12/03/1926, Los Angeles, CA, m, 1952, 1 child **DISCIPLINE** MATHEMATICS **EDUCATION** Univ Calif-Los Angeles, BA, 47, MA, 49, PhD, 52. **CAREER** Systems analyst, Nat bur Standards, 49-52, Hughes Aircraft, 52-54, Nat Cash Register, 54-55, Magnavox Res Labs, 55-59; pres, Advanced Infor Systems, 59-64; prof, Libr & Info Sci, UCLA, 64-91; PROF EMER, LIBR & INFOR SCI, UCLA, 91-. **MEMBERSHIPS** Am Soc Info Sci; Infor Sci & Automat Div, Am Libr Asn, Am Asn Advancement Sci **SELECTED PUBLICATIONS** Strategic Management for Academic Libraries, Greenwood Press, 93; Strategic Management for Public Libraries, Greenwodd Press, 96. **CONTACT ADDRESS** Sch Libr Sci, Univ Calif, Los Angeles, CA, 90024. **EMAIL** rhayes@ucla.edu

HAYES, ZACHARY JEROME
PERSONAL Born 09/21/1932, Chicago, IL **DISCIPLINE** HISTORY OF CHRISTIAN THEOLOGY **EDUCATION** Quincy Col, BA, 56; Univ Bonn, Ger, ThD, 64. **CAREER** Lectr syst theol, St Joseph Sem, Ill, 64-68; assoc prof, 68-74, Prof Hist Of Theol, Cath Theol Union, Chicago, 74. **HONORS AND AWARDS** Res grant, Asn of Theol Schs, 77, res scholar, 78, Scholar-in-Residence, 84, 91; J.C. Murray Award, CTSA, 85; LittD, Quincy Univ, 85., LittD, St Bonaventure Univ, 74. **MEMBERSHIPS** Cath Theol Soc Am; Soc for Sci Study Relig. **RESEARCH** Mediaeval philos and theol; contemp theological developments, particularly in Christology. **SELECTED PUBLICATIONS** Auth, The General Doctrine of Creation in the Thirteenth Century, Schoningh, 64; transl, The Theology of History in St Bonaventure, Franciscan Herald, 71; What Manner of Man? Sermons on Christ by St Bonaventure, Franciscan Herald, 64; The meaning of Convenientia in the metaphysics of St Bonaventure, Franciscan Studies, 74; Incarnation and creation in the theology of St Bonaventure, In: Studies Honoring Ignatius Brady, Franciscan Inst, 76; Christology and metaphysics, J of Relig, 78; Disputed Questions on the Trinity, Franciscan Inst, 79; The Hidden Center, Paulist, 81; Visions of a Future, Glazier, 89; Disputed Questions on the Knowledge of Christ, Franciscan Inst, 92; Reduction of the Arts to Theology, Franciscan Inst, 96; A Window to the Divine, Franciscan Press, 96. **CONTACT ADDRESS** Catholic Theol Union at Chicago, 5401 S Cornell Ave, Chicago, IL, 60615-6200. **EMAIL** zach@ctu.edu

HAYIM YERUSHALMI, YOSEF
DISCIPLINE MEDIEVAL AND MODERN JEWISH HISTORY **EDUCATION** Yeshiva Univ, BA, 53; Columbia Univ, PhD, 66. **CAREER** Instr, Harvard Univ; prof-. **SELECTED PUBLICATIONS** Spanish Court to Italian Ghetto, 71; Haggadah and History, 75; The Lisbon Massacre of 1506, 76; Zakhor: Jewish History and Jewish Memory, 82; A Jewish Classic in the Portuguese Language, 89; Freud's Moses, 91; Ein Feld in Anathoth, 93; Diener von Koenigen und nicht Diener von Dienern, 95. **CONTACT ADDRESS** Dept of Hist, Columbia Col, New York, 2960 Broadway, New York, NY, 10027-6902.

HAYNER, LINDA K.
PERSONAL Born 09/11/1946, Jackson, MI, s **DISCIPLINE** HISTORY **EDUCATION** Western Mich Univ, BA, 68, MA, 70; Vanderbilt Univ, PhD, 82. **CAREER** PROF, BOB JONES UNIV, 71-; CHAIR, HIST DEPT, 92- **HONORS AND AWARDS** Bob Jones Univ Alumni Asn Hon Life Member, Univ fel, WMU, 68-69; teach fel, hist dept, Vanderbilt, 74-75; Ethel MacWilson Scholarship, 75. **MEMBERSHIPS** SC Hist Asn; SC Comn Hum Scholars Forum; SE Renaissance Conf. **RESEARCH** Tudor-Stuart **SELECTED PUBLICATIONS** Auth, "Biblical Christianity: Its Relationship to the Humanities," SCCH Proceedings, 83; "The Responsibilities of the Parishes of England for the Poor, 1640-1660," SCHA Journal, 83; The Foundling, 97. **CONTACT ADDRESS** 211 Batesview #127, Greenville, SC, 29607. **EMAIL** lhayner@bju.edu

HAYNES, EDWARD S.
DISCIPLINE MODERN SOUTH ASIAN AND MIDDLE EASTERN HISTORY AND CIVILIZATION **EDUCATION** Duke Univ, BA, MA, MPhil, PhD. **CAREER** Tchng Asst and Course Coord South Asian Civilization, Duke Univ, 75 Vis Instr, Kansas State Univ75-76; Vis Scholar South Asian Studies, Skidmore Col, 76-77; Adj Asst prof, State Univ NY, 77-78; Asst Prof, Univ of Northern Iowa, 78-80; Occasional Tchng, Dept History, Duke Univ, 84-87; Asst Prof (87-92) & Assoc Prof (92), Winthrop Col/Univ, 87-. **HONORS AND AWARDS** NDEA Title VI Grad Fel in Hindi-Urdu; 72; Am Inst Indian Studies Summer Hindi fel; 1973 Shell Companies Foundation Res fel; 73-74; Am Inst Indian Studies; supplementary Res grant; 73-74; NEH Summer Seminar Fel; 80; Am Inst Indian Studies Senior Res Fel; 80-81, 85-/86; Winthrop Col/ Univ Res Coun grants; 88, 90, 94, 95, 98; Fulbright-Hays Gp Seminar Fel, 88; Winthrop Col Pres Citation Meritorious Service, 89; Joseph J. Malone Fac Felships in Arab and Islamic Studies; 92, 93; Listed in Who's Who in the South and Southwest; 24th and 25th editions; Spec Award Nat Coun U.S.-Arab Rel. **RESEARCH** Modern Southern Asian and Middle Eastern history and civilization. **SELECTED PUBLICATIONS** Co-ed, Guide to Buddhist Religion, G. K. Hall, 81; Guide to Islam, G. K. Hall, 83; Guide to Chinese Religion, G. K. Hall, 85 **CONTACT ADDRESS** Winthrop Univ, 346 Bancroft hall, Rock Hill, SC, 29733-0001. **EMAIL** haynese@winthrop.edu

HAYNES, HOLLY
PERSONAL Born 11/02/1965, TX **DISCIPLINE** CLASSICS **EDUCATION** Univ Washington, PhD 96. **CAREER** NY Univ, asst prof 95 to 98-. **MEMBERSHIPS** APA **RESEARCH** Critical Theory; Historiography **CONTACT ADDRESS** Dept of Classics, New York Univ, 25 Waverly Pl, 7th Fl, NYC, NY, 10003. **EMAIL** hh13@is5.nyu.edu

HAYNES, JAMES H.
PERSONAL Born 11/27/1953, Pensacola, FL, s **DISCIPLINE** EDUCATOR **EDUCATION** Pensacola Jr Coll, AA 1973; Morebouse Coll, BA 1975; Georgia State Univ, MEd 1977; Univ of IA, PhD 1979. **CAREER** Atlanta Public Sch System, teacher 1975-77; Philadelphia Training Center, asst dir 1979-80; FL A&M Univ, dir of planning 1980-83; MORGAN STATE UNIV, dir of inst research 1983-84, vice pres of planning 1984, TITLE III COORD, 1988-. **HONORS AND AWARDS** Honorary membership in Promethean Kappa Tau, Phi Delta Kappa, Phi Alpha Theta; Governor's Citation for services to youth in Baltimore community; Mayor's Citation for services to youth in Baltimore city. **MEMBERSHIPS** Woodrow Wilson Nat'l Fellowship Foundation, 1980; Title III Prog Bowie State Coll, counsultant 1984-; Assoliation of Minority Hlth Profession Sch, consultant 1982; supervisor of admin for NTE, GMAT 1984-; Alpha Phi Alpha, Baltimore Morehouse Alummi Club, sec; NAACP; Morehouse Coll Nat'l Alumni Assoc; board of directors, Baltimore Employment Network. **CONTACT ADDRESS** Morgan State Univ, Cold Spring Ln & Hillen Rd, Baltimore, MD, 21239.

HAYNES, JOHN E.
PERSONAL Born 11/22/1944, Plant City, FL, m, 1971, 3 children **DISCIPLINE** HISTORY **EDUCATION** Fla State Univ, BA, 66; Univ Minn, MA, 68, PhD, 78. **CAREER** 20th century polit hist, manuscript div, Libr of Congress, 87-. **HONORS AND AWARDS** Magna cum laude with honors, hist, Fla State Univ, 66. **MEMBERSHIPS** Phi Beta Kappa; Phi Alpha Theta; The Hist Soc. **RESEARCH** Communism; Anti-communism; Liberalism; Labor. **SELECTED PUBLICATIONS** Ed, Calvin Coolidge and the Coolidge Era: Essays on the History of the 1920s, Libr of Congress and Univ Press of New England, 98; coauth, with Harvey Klehr and Kyrill Anderson, The Soviet World of American Communism, Yale Univ Press, 98; auth, Red Scare or Red Menace? American Communism and Anti-communism in the Cold War Era, Ivan Dee, 96; coauth, with Harvey Klehr and Fridrikh Firsov, The Secret World of American Communism, Yale Univ Press, 95; coauth, with Harvey Klehr, The American Communist Movement: Storming Heaven Itself, Twayne Publ, 92; auth, Communism and Anti-communism in the United States: An Annotated Guide to Historical Writings, Garland Publ, 87; Dubious Alliance: The Making of Minnesota's DFL Party, Univ Minn Press, 84. **CONTACT ADDRESS** Manuscript Div, Library of Congress, Washington, DC, 20540-4689. **EMAIL** jhay@loc.gov

HAYNES, KEITH A.
PERSONAL Born 07/09/1951, Beloit, WI, m, 1977, 1 child **DISCIPLINE** HISTORY **EDUCATION** Northern Ill Univ, PhD, 81. **CAREER** Vis asst prof, hist, Univ Vermont, 84-85; assoc prof hist, 85-90, chemn Dept of Hist and Polit Sci, 90-98, College of Saint Rose. **MEMBERSHIPS** Conf of Latin Am Hist; Latin Am Stud Asn. **RESEARCH** Latin America; Mexico; United States foreign policy. **SELECTED PUBLICATIONS** Auth, Imperialism, Ultraimperialism, and Postimperialism: International Relations and the Periodization of Corporate Capitalism, Radical Hist Rev, 93; contribur, Beede, ed, The War of 1898 and U.S. Interventions, 1898-1934: An Encyclopedia, Garland, 94; auth, The Mexican Revolution as a Province of Postimperialism, in, Becker, ed, Postimperialism in World Politics, Praeger, forthcoming. **CONTACT ADDRESS** The Col of Saint Rose, 432 Western Ave, Albany, NY, 12203. **EMAIL** haynesk@rosnet.strose.edu

HAYNES, LEONARD L., III
PERSONAL Born 01/26/1947, Boston, MA, m, 1968 **DISCIPLINE** EDUCATION **EDUCATION** Southern University, Baton Rouge, LA, BA, 1968; Carnegie-Mellon Univ, Pittsburgh, PA, MA, 1969; Ohio State University, Columbus, OH, PhD, 1975. **CAREER** Institute for Services to Education, Washington, DC, dir, desegregation unit, 1976-79; National Assn State/Land Grant College, Washington, DC, director, public black colleges, 1979-82; Southern University System, Baton Rouge, LA, executive vice president, 1982-85, professor of history, 1985-88; Louisiana Depart of Education, Baton Rouge, LA, assistant superintendent, 1988-89; US Department of Education, Washington, DC, assistant secretary, 1989-91; adjunct faculty, The Brookings Institute, 1991-92; UNITED STATES INFORMATION AGENCY, DIR OF ACADEMIC PROGRAMS, 1992-; senior consultant & national education goals panel, 1993; Univ of MD, visiting scholar, 1994; THE AMERICAN UNIVERSITY, SENIOR ASSISTANT TO THE PRESIDENT, 1994-. **HONORS AND AWARDS** Honorary Doctor of Laws, Ohio State Univ, 1990; Honorary Doctor of Humane Letters, Tougaloo College, 1990; Honorary Doctor of Laws, University of St Thomas, 1990; Honorary Doctor of Laws, Alabama A&M Univ, 1990; Honorary Doctor of Laws, Stockton State College, 1991; Honorary Doctor of Public Administration, Bridgewater College, 1992. **MEMBERSHIPS** Omega Psi Phi Fraternity, 1968-; Jack & Jill Inc, 1988.

HAYS, JO N.
DISCIPLINE HISTORY **EDUCATION** Univ Chicago, PhD, 70. **CAREER** Hist, Loyola Univ. **RESEARCH** History of science and Med, especially British. **SELECTED PUBLICATIONS** Auth, The Burdens of Disease: Epidemics and Human Response in Western History, Rutgers UP, 98; essay rev on med in, Fr & Indust Revolutions, Perspectives in Biol & Med 33, 90; res articles in, Anns of Sci, Brit J for Hist of Sci; Metropolis and province; Pa Mag of Hist; Perspectives in Biol & Med. **CONTACT ADDRESS** Fine Arts Dept, Loyola Univ, Chicago, 6525 N. Sheridan Rd., Chicago, IL, 60626. **EMAIL** jhays@wpo.it.luc.edu

HAYS, ROSALIND CONKLIN
PERSONAL Born 12/01/1940, Chicago, IL, m, 1966 **DISCIPLINE** MEDIEVAL & ENGLISH HISTORY **EDUCATION** Univ Chicago, BA, 60, MA, 61, PhD(hist), 64. **CAREER** Instr hist, Wells Col, 64-66; asst prof, 66-68, ASSOC PROF HIST, HIST, ROSARY COL, 68- **MEMBERSHIPS** AHA; AAUP; Medieval Acad. **RESEARCH** Medieval English social history of the 13th through the 15th centuries; Tudor social history; the Crusades. **SELECTED PUBLICATIONS** Auth, The Widening Gate--Bristol and the Atlantic Economy, 1450-1700, Ethnohist, Vol 0040, 93. **CONTACT ADDRESS** Dept Hist, Rosary Col, 7900 W Division, River Forest, IL, 60305-1099.

HAYS, SAMUEL PFRIMMER
PERSONAL Born 04/05/1921, Coydon, IN, m, 1948, 4 children **DISCIPLINE** HISTORY **EDUCATION** Swarthmore Col, BA, 48; Harvard Univ, MA, 49, PhD, 53. **CAREER** Instr hist, Univ Ill, 52-53; from asst prof to assoc prof, State Univ

Iowa, 53-60; prof & chmn dept, 60-73, DISTINGUISHED SERV PROF HIST, UNIV PITTSBURGH, 73-, Mem bd dirs, Harry S Truman Libr Inst, 57-70; mem, Soc Sci Res Coun, 66-72; chmn comt, Am Soc Polit, Woodrow Wilson Int Ctr Scholars, 80- ; Fulbright lectr Aus, 70; Harmsworth Prof Am Hist, Oxforc Univ, 83-84; Lectr Acad Sinica, Taiwan, 87; fel Forest Hist Soc, 80. **HONORS AND AWARDS** Penn Distinguished Hum Award, 91; Hist Makers Award, Hist Soc W. Penn, 93; Career Achievement Award, Am Soc Environ Hist, 97. **MEMBERSHIPS** Orgn Am Historians; Social Sci Hist Asn; Am Asn Environ Hist. **RESEARCH** Social analysis of American politics; urbanization; the politics of environmental conservation. **SELECTED PUBLICATIONS** Auth, The Response to Industrialism, Univ Chicago, 57; Conservation and the Gospel of Efficiency, Harvard Univ, 58; American Political History as Social Analysis, Univ Tenn, 80; Politics and Society: Beyond the Political Party, In: The Evolution of American Electoral Systems, Greenwood Press, 81; The Structure of Environmental Politics Since World War II, J Social Hist, summer 81; Political Choice in Regulatory Administration, In: Regulation in Perspective: Historical Essays, Harvard Univ Press, 81; ed City at the Point, Univ Pitt Press, 85; coauth Beauty, Health and Permanence: Environmental Politics in the United States, 1955-1985, Cambridge Univ Press, 87; Response to Industrialism, 95; Explorations in Environmental History, Univ Pitts Press, 98. **CONTACT ADDRESS** Dept of Hist, Univ of Pittsburgh, Forbes Quadrangle, Pittsburgh, PA, 15260. **EMAIL** sph1+@pitt.edu

HAYS, WILLARD MURRELL
PERSONAL Born 07/26/1928, Lewisburg, TN, m, 1964, 2 children **DISCIPLINE** AMERICAN HISTORY **EDUCATION** Va Mil Inst, BA, 51; Univ Tenn, MA, 58, PhD(hist), 71. **CAREER** Teaching asst, Univ Tenn, 57-58, instr eve sch, 58-59; instr hist, West Tex State Col, 59-61; from asst prof to assoc prof, 61-75, PROF HIST, VA MIL INST, 75- **MEMBERSHIPS** AHA; Orgn Am Historians. **RESEARCH** American revolution; 19th century United States history; American thought. **SELECTED PUBLICATIONS** Auth, Struggle for a Continent--The Wars of Early America, J Military Hist, Vol 0057, 93. **CONTACT ADDRESS** Dept Hist, Va Military Inst, Lexington, VA, 24450.

HAYWOOD, C. ROBERT
PERSONAL Born 08/27/1921, Fowler, KS, m, 1942, 3 children **DISCIPLINE** UNITED STATES HISTORY **EDUCATION** Univ Kans, AB, 47, MA, 48; Univ NC, PhD, 56. **CAREER** From instr US hist to dean, Southwestern Col, 48-66; dean, Col Arts & Sci, Millikin Univ, 66-69; prof hist, vpres acad affairs & dean, 69-81, VPRES & PROVOST, WASHBURN UNIV, 81- **MEMBERSHIPS** Orgn Am Historians; Southern Hist Soc; Am Conf Acad Deans. **SELECTED PUBLICATIONS** Auth, The Old West, J West, Vol 0032, 93; Unplighted Troths--Causes For Divorce in a Frontier Town Toward the End of the 19th-Century, Great Plains Quarterly, Vol 0013, 93; Brushwork Diary--Watercolors of Early Nevada, J West, Vol 0033, 94. **CONTACT ADDRESS** Acad Affairs, Washburn Univ, Topeka, KS, 66621.

HAYWOOD, RICHARD MOWBRAY
PERSONAL Born 04/28/1933, Baltimore, MD, m, 1965, 2 children **DISCIPLINE** RUSSIAN & EAST EUROPEAN HISTORY **EDUCATION** NY Univ, BA, 54; Oxford Univ, MA, 60; Columbia Univ, PhD(Russ hist), 66. **CAREER** From asst prof to assoc prof Russ hist, Eastern Mich Univ, 65-69; ASSOC PROF RUSS & E EUROP HIST, PURDUE UNIV, WEST LAFAYETTE, 69-, Nat Endowment for Humanities younger scholar fel, 69. **HONORS AND AWARDS** Nat Endow Humanities younger scholar fel, 69; Fulbright-Hays fac res abroad prog, 83; IREX sr scholar fel, 83; IREX short term res scholar, 90. **MEMBERSHIPS** Am Asn Advan Slavic Studies **RESEARCH** Nineteenth century Russia; Russian transportation **SELECTED PUBLICATIONS** Auth, The Beginnings of Railway Development in Russia in the Reign of Nicholas I, 1835-1842, Duke Univ, 69; The Question of Standard Gauge for Russian Railways, 1836-1860, 3/69 & The Ruler Legend: Tsar Nicholas I and the Route of the St Petersburg-Moscow Railway, 1842-1843, 12/78, Slavic Rev; The Winter Palace in St Petersburg: Destruction by Fire and Reconstruction, December 1837-March 1839, Jahrbucher fur Geschichte Osteuropas, No 2, 79; The Development of Steamboats on the Volga River and its Tributaries, 1817-1856, Res in Econ Hist, Vol 6, 81; Russia Enters the Railway Age, 1842-1855, East European Monographs, Columbia Univ, 98. **CONTACT ADDRESS** Dept of Hist, Purdue Univ, West Lafayette, IN, 47907-1968.

HEAD, LAURA DEAN
PERSONAL Born 11/03/1948, Los Angeles, California, s **DISCIPLINE** AFRICAN-AMERICAN STUDIES **EDUCATION** San Francisco State Coll, BA 1971; Univ of MI, MA 1974, PhD 1978. **CAREER** Univ of CA Riverside, 1973-76; Urban Inst for Human Develop, project dir 1978-80; Far West Lab for Educ Rsch & Develop, project dir 1980-81; San Francisco State Univ, prof black studies 1978-. **HONORS AND AWARDS** Minority Fellowship Prog Amer Psych Assn 1976-77; Meritorious Promise Award San Francisco State Univ 1984. **MEMBERSHIPS** Chair of bd Marin City Multi-Serv Inst 1978-; chair Black Child Develop Inst 1978-81; Comm on School Crime CA State Dept of Educ 1981; bd of dir Oakland Men's Project 1988-; Committee to Organize the 20th Anniversary Commemoration of the 1968 San Francisco State University Student Strike 1988. **CONTACT ADDRESS** Professor of Black Studies, San Francisco State Univ, 1600 Holloway Ave, San Francisco, CA, 94132.

HEAD, THOMAS F.
DISCIPLINE MEDIEVAL FRANCE **EDUCATION** Harvard Univ, BA, MA, 78, PhD, 85. **CAREER** Asst prof, Sch Theol Claremont, 85-89; Asst prof, Pomona Col, 89-90; Assoc prof, Yale Univ, 90-94; Asst prof, Washington Unive, 94-. **SELECTED PUBLICATIONS** Auth, Monks And Their Enemies: A Comparative Approfoach Speculum, 91; The Peace God: Social Violence And Religious Response In France Around The Year One Thousand, Cornell Univ, 92; Soldiers Christ: Saints And Saints' Lives From Late Antiquity And The Early Middle Ages, Pa State Univ, 94; Contribr, Dictionary The Middle Ages, 82-89; Lexicon Des Mittelalters, 80-; An Encyclopedia Continental Women Writers, 91; The Orlanais, 950-1130; Hagiographies, 94; Medieval France: An Encyclopedia, 95, Harper's Dictionary Religion, 96; Encyclopedia Medieval Women, 96. **CONTACT ADDRESS** Washington Univ, 1 Brookings Dr, St. Louis, MO, 63130.

HEADLEY, JOHN M.
PERSONAL Born 10/23/1929, New York, NY **DISCIPLINE** EARLY MODERN EUROPEAN HISTORY **EDUCATION** Princeton Univ, BA, 51; Yale Univ, PhD, 60. **CAREER** Instr hist, Univ Mass, 59-61; res assoc, St Thomas More Proj, Yale Univ, 61-62; instr hist, Univ BC, 62-64; from instr to assoc prof, 64-70, PROF HIST, UNIV NC, CHAPEL HILL, 70-, Chmn, Southeastern Inst Medieval & Renaissance Studies, 67; Guggenheim fel, 74. **MEMBERSHIPS** Am Soc Reformation Res (vpres, 78-80); Renaissance Soc Am; AHA. **RESEARCH** Historiography and church history in the Reformation Period; intellectual history. **SELECTED PUBLICATIONS** Auth, The 16th-Century Venetian Celebration of the Earths Total Habitability--The Issue of the Fully Habitable World for Renaissance Europe, J World Hist, Vol 0008, 97; Spain Struggle for Europe, 1598-1668, Sixteenth Century J, Vol 0027, 96; Nuptial Arithmetic-- Marsilio Ficino 'Commentary on the Fatal Number in Book-VIII of Platos Republic', Renaissance Quarterly, Vol 0049, 96; The Burden of European Imperialisms, 1500-1800, Int Hist Rev, Vol 0018, 96; Spain Asian Presence, 1565-1590--Structures and Aspirations, Hisp Am Hist Rev, Vol 0075, 95; Isabel The Queen--Life and Times, Sixteenth Century J, Vol 0026, 95. **CONTACT ADDRESS** Dept of Hist, Univ of NC, Chapel Hill, NC, 27514.

HEADRICK, ANNABETH
DISCIPLINE ART HISTORY **EDUCATION** Colo Col, BA, 85; MA Univ Tex Austin, MA, 91; PhD 96. **CAREER** Achaeol lab asst, Espey, Houston and Assoc, 93; lab dir, camp mgr, K'axob archaeol project, 92; Valley archaeol proj, 95; lab dir, Belize, 95; asst instr, tchg asst, Univ Tex, 90-93; vis instr, Colo Col, 94-95; vis asst prof, Baylor Univ, 95-96; asst prof, Western State Col, 96-. **MEMBERSHIPS** Col Art Assn; Soc Am Archaeol; Am Anthropol Assn. **SELECTED PUBLICATIONS** Co-founder, ed, contrib auth, Free Food For Thought, Univ Tex Art; co-auth, The Teotihuacan Trinity: Mythological Justification of Power, Narratives of Power: Monumental Architecture in Mesoamerica; Iconographic Expression in the Agrarian Context, The Genesis of Ancestor Veneration; Maya Help You? When Mesoamerica Beckons, Artists and Scientists Answer the Call, The Edge, 93. **CONTACT ADDRESS** Dept of Art Hist, Western State Col, Gunnison, CO, 81231.

HEADRICK, DANIEL RICHARD
PERSONAL Born 08/02/1941, Bay Shore, NY, m, 1992, 3 children **DISCIPLINE** EUROPEAN HISTORY **EDUCATION** Swarthmore Col, BA, 62; Johns Hopkins Sch Advan Int Studies, MA, 64; Princeton Univ, MA & PhD(hist), 71. **CAREER** From instr to asst prof hist, Tuskegee Inst, 68-75, dir freshman study prog, 73-75; assoc prof soc sci, Roosevelt Univ, 75-, fel, Shelby Cullom Davis Ctr Hist Study, 72. **MEMBERSHIPS** AHA; Soc Hist Technol. **RESEARCH** Modern Spain; industrial revolution; 19th and 20th century European imperialism. **SELECTED PUBLICATIONS** Auth, Spain and the Revolutions of 1848, Europ Studies Rev, 4/76; The Tools of Imperialism: Technology and the Expansion of the European Colonial Empires in the Nineteenth Century, J Mod Hist, Vol 51, No 2; Canovas del Castillo y el Conde-Duque de Olivares, Historia-16, 2/80; The Tools of Empire: Technology and European Imperialism in the Nineteenth Century, Oxford Univ Press, 81; Ejercito y Politica en Espana, 1866-1898, Ed Tecnos, 81; The Tentacles of Progress: Technology Transfer in the Age of Imperialism, 1850-1940, Oxford Univ Press, 88; The Invisible Weapon: Telecommunications and International Politics, 1851-1945, Oxford Univ Press, 91; The Earth and its Peoples: A Global History, Houghton Mifflin, 97. **CONTACT ADDRESS** Roosevelt Univ, 430 S Michigan Ave, Chicago, IL, 60605-1394. **EMAIL** dheadric@roosevelt.edu

HEALEY, ROBERT MATHIEU
PERSONAL Born 06/01/1921, New York, NY, m, 1953, 1 child **DISCIPLINE** CHURCH, HISTORY **EDUCATION** Princeton Univ, BA, 42; Yale Univ, MFA, 47, BD, 55, MA, 56, PhD(relig), 59. **CAREER** Instr English, Mercersburg Acad, 42-44 & Rensselaer Polytech Inst, 48-52; assoc prof commun, 56-63, from assoc prof to prof Am church hist, 63-74, chnin div hist & theol, 68-70, interim acad dean, 70-71, Prof Church Hist, Theol Sem, Univ Dubuque, 74-, Mem comt relig & pub educ, Nat Coun Churches, 58-62; consult, Nat Studies Conf Church & State, Ohio, 64; theologian in residence, Am Church in Paris, 65-66; mem bd dirs, Asn Theol Fac Iowa, 67-71 & 76-80; consult Gen Coun, United Presby Church USA, 71-72; resident scholar, Ecumenical Inst Advan Theol Studies, Israel, 73-74; pres, Asn Fac & Theol Educ Prof Theol Sem, Univ Dubuque, 73-77; vis prof, Univ Edinburgh, 80-81; Asn Theol Schs in US & Can basic res grant, 80-81. **MEMBERSHIPS** Am Soc Church Hist; Am Acad Relig; Presby Hist Soc. **RESEARCH** Relationships of church, state and education in the United States and in France; Andrew Melville (1545-1622), and Scottish reformation; Judaism in American religious history. **SELECTED PUBLICATIONS** Auth, The Mainstream Protestant Decline--The Presbyterian Pattern, Church Hist, Vol 0064, 95; The Organizational Revolution--Presbyterian and American Denominationalism, Church Hist, Vol 0064, 95; The Language of Liberty 1660-1832--Political Discourse and Social Dynamics in the Anglo-American World, Church Hist, Vol 0066, 97; John Duns-Scotus, Doctor of the Church, J Ecumenical Studies, Vol 0030, 93; Waiting For Deborah-- John Knox, And 4 Ruling Queens, Sixteenth Century J, Vol 0025, 94. **CONTACT ADDRESS** Dept of Hist & Theol Theol Sem, Univ of Dubuque, Dubuque, IA, 52001.

HEATH, DWIGHT BRALEY
PERSONAL Born 11/19/1930, Hartford, CT, m, 1 child **DISCIPLINE** SOCIAL/CULTURAL ANTHROPOLOGY **EDUCATION** Harvard Univ, AB (magna cum laude), 52; Yale Univ, PhD (anthropology), 59. **CAREER** Prof of Anthropology, Brown Univ, 59-; various years, part-time vis prof of anthropology at: Univ WI, Universidad de Costa Rica; frequent consultant to govt and international organizations around the world. **HONORS AND AWARDS** Frequent res grants: Nat Science Found; Nat Inst on Alchohol Abuse & Alchoholism; Wenner-Gren Found; Fulbright; Soc Sci res Coun; et al. **MEMBERSHIPS** Cross-cultural and historical perspectives on alcohol & drugs; social hist; political socialization; ethnography. **SELECTED PUBLICATIONS** Author of several books on Pilgrims at Plymouth; Latin American cultures & societies; alcohol in sociocultural perspective; historical dictionary of Bolivia; International Handbook on Alcohol and Culture, Greenwood, 95; The World of Drink, Taylor & Francis, 99. **CONTACT ADDRESS** Dept of Anthropology, Brown Univ, Providence, RI, 02912. **EMAIL** katherine_grimaldi@brown.edu

HEATH, JIM FRANK
PERSONAL Born 04/09/1931, Clarendon, TX, m, 1975, 2 children **DISCIPLINE** MODERN UNITED STATES HISTORY **EDUCATION** Univ NMex, BBA, 53, MA, 55; Stanford Univ, PhD(hist), 67. **CAREER** From asst prof to assoc prof, 67-74, dean undergrad studies, 77-81, PROF HIST, PORTLAND STATE UNIV, 74-, Am Coun Learned Soc grant-in-aid, 73-74; Danforth teaching assoc, 70. **MEMBERSHIPS** Orgn Am Historians; Am Comt Hist 2nd World War. **RESEARCH** The Kennedy and Johnson administration; United States domestic history during World War II. **SELECTED PUBLICATIONS** Auth, Shifting The Burden--The Struggle Over Growth and Corporate-Taxation, J Am Hist, Vol 0081, 94. **CONTACT ADDRESS** Dept of Hist, Portland State Univ, Portland, OR, 97207.

HEATH, KINGSTON W.
DISCIPLINE ARCHITECTURAL HISTORY **EDUCATION** Brown Univ, PhD. **CAREER** Assoc prof, Univ NC, Charlotte. **SELECTED PUBLICATIONS** Auth, False-Front Architecture on Montana's Urban Frontier, in Perspectives in Vernacular Architecture, III ,eds, Thomas Carter and Bernard L. Herman, 89; Crossing the Vemacular Threshold: The Transformation of the American HouseTrailer from a Standardized Consumer Product to a Vehicle for Regional Exploration, The Harvard Archit Rev, 10, 93; Timber Frame, III, Balloon Frame, in the Dictionary of Art, MacMillan Publ Ltd, 93. **CONTACT ADDRESS** Univ N. Carolina, Charlotte, Charlotte, NC, 28223-0001. **EMAIL** kwheath@email.uncc.edu

HEATH, ROBIN L.
PERSONAL Born 10/07/1946, Prince Rupert, BC, Canada, s **DISCIPLINE** ANTHROPOLOGY **EDUCATION** Univ Ky, PhD, 98. **MEMBERSHIPS** Am Anthrop Asn; Am Public Health Asn; Asn Anthrop and Gerontology. **RESEARCH** Brain and behavior; humor. **SELECTED PUBLICATIONS** Coauth, Lay Concepts of Stroke in Kentucky, What Works? Synthesizing Effective Biomedical and Psychosocial Strategies for Healthy Families in the 21st Century, Ind Univ, 94; Prosodic Characteristics of Speech Pre and Post Right Hemisphere Stroke, Brain and Lang 51, 95; Cognitive Model of Stroke, Indian J Gerontology, 96; Farm Youth and Horse-Related Injuries:

A Case for Safety Helmets, J Agromedicine 5, 98; The Interpersonal Management of Crying Among Survivors of Stroke, Sociological Spectrum 18, 98. **CONTACT ADDRESS** Anthrop Dept, Univ Kentucky, Lafferty Hall, Lexington, KY, 40536. **EMAIL** rlheat00@ukcc.uky.edu

HECK, MARLENE
DISCIPLINE ART HISTORY **EDUCATION** Univ Tex Austin, BA; Univ VA, MAH; Univ PA, MA, PhD. **CAREER** Sr letr. **RESEARCH** Archit hist, soc hist, material cult studies, Islamic art & archit. **SELECTED PUBLICATIONS** Auth, Building Status: Virginia's Winged Pavilion Dwellings, in Shaping Communities: Perspectives in Vernacular Architecture VI, Univ TN P, 97; var other articles. **CONTACT ADDRESS** Dartmouth Col, 3529 N Main St, Ste. 207, Hanover, NH, 03755. **EMAIL** marlene.heck@dartmouth.edu

HECK, THOMAS F.
PERSONAL Born 07/10/1943, Washington, DC, m, 1968, 2 children **DISCIPLINE** MUSICOLOGY **EDUCATION** Univ Notre Dame, BA, 65; Yale Univ, PhD, 70; Univ Southern Calif, MLS, 77. **CAREER** Head, Music/Dance Lib, Ohio State Univ, 78- ; asst prof, Mus Hist and Libr, Wis Conserv Mus, 77-78; Vis asst prof Mus Hist, Chapman Col, 75-76; vis asst prof mus, John Carroll Univ, 74-75; asst prof Mus Hist, Case Western Res Univ, 71-74. **HONORS AND AWARDS** Netherlands Inst Adv Stud Human and Soc Sci Fellow, 94-95; USIA Fac Exchange Fellow to the Univ Genoa, June 90; Fulbright Fellow, Italy, 85-86; Fulbright Fellow, Austria, 68-69. **MEMBERSHIPS** Am Musicol Soc; Mus Libr Asn; Inter Asn Mus Libr; Am Soc Theatre Res; Int Fed Theatre Res; Guitar Found Am. **RESEARCH** Music & Theatre History; Iconography; Commedia dell'arte; European cultural history in general; the history of the guitar. **SELECTED PUBLICATIONS** Mauro Giuliani: virtuoso guitarist and composer, Columbus, Editions Orphee, 95; The 'music information explosion' and its implications for college teachers and students, Missoula, Col Mus Soc, 92; Commedia dell'arte: a guide to the primary and secondary literature, NY, Garland, 88, xiv; The illustration of music periodicals, c.1880-1914: a question of halftones and 'whole'-tones, Fontes artis musicae 44, Dec 97, 307-330; The uses of music in Commedia performance, Theatre Symposium: A Jour Southeastern Theatre Conf, 1, 93, 7-12; The operatic Christopher Columbus: three hundred years of musical mythology, Annali d'italianistica, 10, 92, 236-278. **CONTACT ADDRESS** Ohio State Univ, 1813 N High St, Columbus, OH, 43210-3929. **EMAIL** heck.3@osu.edu

HEDREEN, GUY
PERSONAL Born 12/12/1958, Dallas, TX, m, 1985, 2 children **DISCIPLINE** CLASSICAL ARCHAEOLOGY **EDUCATION** Bryn Mawr Col, PhD 88, MA 83; Pomona Col, BA cum laude 81. **CAREER** Williams Col, ch, assoc prof, asst prof, act dir, 90 to 98-; Middlebury College, asst prof, 89-90; Franklin and Marshall Col, vis asst 88-89; Bryn Mawr Col, tchg asst, 83-84. **HONORS AND AWARDS** NEH Sr Fel; NHC Fel; NEH Doc Fel; Humboldt Stiftung Fel; Whiting Fel; BMC Fel; Kress Fel; Samuel and Lucy Chew Fel; Asstshp BMC. **MEMBERSHIPS** ASCS at Athens; AIA; CAA. **SELECTED PUBLICATIONS** Auth, Landscape Narrative and the Trojan War in Greek Art, under consideration, Univ Michigan Press; auth, Sliens in Attic Black-figure Vase-painting: Myth and Performance, Univ Michigan Press, 92; auth, Image Text and Story in the Recovery of Helen, Classical Antiquity, 96; auth, Narrative art, I.3. Greece and Rome, in: The Dictionary of Art, ed Jane Turner, NY, 96; auth, Sir Lawrence Alma-Tadema's Women of Amphissa, The Jour of the Walters art Gallery, 96; Silens Nymphs and Maenads, Jour of Hellenic Studies, 94; The Fall of Troy in Early Greek Poetry and Art, Michael J. Anderson, Bryn Mawr Classical Rev, forthcoming; auth, Dionysian Imagery in Fifth-Century Athens, Thomas H Carpenter, Oxford 97, Bryn Mawr Classical Rev, 98; auth, Polygnotos and Vase Painting in Classical Athens, Susan Matheson, Madison 95, Bryn Mawr Classical Rev, 97. **CONTACT ADDRESS** Dept of Art, Williams Col, Williamstown, MA, 01267.

HEDRICK JR., CHARLES W.
PERSONAL 2 children **DISCIPLINE** GREEK AND ROMAN HISTORY **EDUCATION** Univ Penn, PhD, 84. **CAREER** Instr, Buffalo Univ, NY; PROF, UNIV CALIF, SANTA CRUZ. **SELECTED PUBLICATIONS** Ed, The Decrees of the Demotionidai, 90; co-edr, The Birth of Democracy: an Exhibition, 93; Demokratia, 96. **CONTACT ADDRESS** Dept of Hist, Univ Calif, 1156 High St, Santa Cruz, CA, 95064.

HEFFERNAN, CHARLES
DISCIPLINE MUSIC **EDUCATION** Univ Mich, BM, MM, PhD. **CAREER** Assoc prof. **HONORS AND AWARDS** Dir, Bach Soc Amherst. **SELECTED PUBLICATIONS** Auth, Choral Music: Technique and Artistry, 83; pubs on music education, vocal music, choral conducting, and aesthetics. **CONTACT ADDRESS** Music and Dance Dept, Univ of Massachusetts, Amherst, 720 Massachusetts Ave, Amherst, MA, 01003.

HEFFRON, PAUL THAYER
PERSONAL Born 11/05/1920, Newton, MA, m, 1963 **DISCIPLINE** POLITICAL SCIENCE; AMERICAN HISTORY **EDUCATION** Boston Col, AB, 42, MA, 47; Fordham Univ, PhD, 51. **CAREER** Assoc prof Am govt, Boston Col, 50-66; Historian, Libr of Cong, 66-. **MEMBERSHIPS** AHA; Am Polit Sci Asn; Am Soc for Legal Hist; Orgn Am Historians; Supreme Court Hist Soc. **RESEARCH** American constitutional law; American presidency: twentieth century political history. **SELECTED PUBLICATIONS** Auth, Theodore Roosevelt and the appointment of Mr Justice Moody, Vanderbilt Law Rev, 3/65; Secretary Moody and naval administrative reform, Am Neptune, 1/69; William Moody: Profile of a Public Man, Supreme Court Hist Soc Yearbk, 80. **CONTACT ADDRESS** Manuscript Div Libr of Cong, Washington, DC, 20540.

HEFLIN, JOHN F.
PERSONAL Born 04/07/1941, Sweetwater, TX, m **DISCIPLINE** EDUCATION **EDUCATION** NM Highlands Univ, BA 1963; Stanford Univ, MA 1972, PhD 1977. **CAREER** Portland State Univ, asst prof educ admin 1976-; OR Dept D, EEO program coord 1974-76; Stanford Univ, asst to dean 1971-74; Merced Union High School, Merced, CA, teacher/coach 1965-70; US Dept Interior Denver, CO, cartographer 1964-65. **HONORS AND AWARDS** NW Association of Black Elected Officials; Foundation Leadrship Development Program fellow 1970-71. **MEMBERSHIPS** Portland Urban League; OR Assembly for Black Affairs; OR Alliance of Black School Educators; CA Teachers Assn; OR Educators Assn; NEA; Natl Cnl Social Studies; Policy Student Orgn; Phi Delta Kapp; bd dir Mid-Peninsula Task Force Integrated Ed; Am Ed Research Assn; ed dir NAACP; Natl Alliance of Black School Educators; ntl chmn Rsrch Focus on Black Ed (Am Ed Research Assn); commissioner Portland Metro Human Realtions Committee; Assn for Supervision & Curriculm Dev. **CONTACT ADDRESS** Portland State Univ, PO Box 751, Portland, OR, 97207.

HEIBRON, JOHN L.
PERSONAL Born 03/17/1934, San Francisco, CA, m, 1995 **DISCIPLINE** PHYSICS; HISTORY **EDUCATION** Univ of Cal-Berkeley, BA, 55, MA, 58, PhD, 64. **CAREER** Asst Prof, Univ of PA, 64-67; Asst prof, Assoc prof, prof, 67-94, Vice Chancellor, 90-94, Prof Emer, 94-, Univ Cal-Berkeley; Sr Research Fel, Museum of the History of Science, Worcester Col, Oxford, 96-. **HONORS AND AWARDS** Laurea in Phil, Univ of Bologna; Berkeley Citation; George Sarton Medal. **MEMBERSHIPS** Royal Swedish Acad of Sci; Amer Phil Soc; Amer Acad of Arts and Sciences; Academic internationale d'histoire des sciences; History of Science Soc; British Soc for the History of Science. **RESEARCH** History of the Physical Sciences **SELECTED PUBLICATIONS** coed, The Quantifying Spirit in the 18th Century, 90; auth, Weighing Imponderables and other Quantitative Science around 1800, 93; Geometry Civilized: History, Culture and Technique, 98; The Sun in the Church: Cathedrals as Big Science Facilities, 99; coauth, Science and Technology in the 20th Century, forthcoming; Ernest Rutherford, forthcoming. **CONTACT ADDRESS** April House, Shilton, OX18 4AB. **EMAIL** jlheilbron@ohst7.berkeley.edu

HEIDEN, BRUCE A.
PERSONAL Born 09/04/1951, Brooklyn, NY, d, 2 children **DISCIPLINE** CLASSICAL PHILOLOGY **EDUCATION** Columbia, BA, 72; Cornell, PhD, 84. **CAREER** Asst prof, 84-80, assoc prof, 90-, Ohio State Univ, 84-. **MEMBERSHIPS** Amer Philol Asn; Brit Class Asn; Class Asn of Midwst & S **RESEARCH** Homer; Greek drama; Cognitive science. **SELECTED PUBLICATIONS** Rev, Journal of Hellenic Studies, 93; auth, Sic te servato: An Interpretation of Propertius 1.21, Class Philol, 95; The Three Movements of the Iliad, Greek, Roman, and Byzantine Studies, 96; The Ordeals of Homeric Song, Arethusa, 97; The Simile of the Fugitive Homicide: Analogy, Foiling and Allusion, Am Jour Philol, 98; The Placement of Book-Divisions in the Iliad, Jour Hellenic Studies, 98. **CONTACT ADDRESS** Dept of Greek & Latin, Ohio State Univ, Columbus, OH, 43210. **EMAIL** heiden.1@osu.edu

HEILBRON, JOHN L.
PERSONAL Born 03/17/1934, San Francisco, CA, m, 1959 **DISCIPLINE** HISTORY OF SCIENCE **EDUCATION** Univ Calif, Berkeley, AB, 55, MA, 58, PhD(hist), 64. **CAREER** Asst dir, Sources Hist Quantum Physics, 61-64; asst prof hist & philos sci, Univ Pa, 64-67; from asst prof to assoc prof, 67-73, PROF HIST, UNIV CALIF, BERKELEY, 73-, DIR, OFF FOR HIST OF SCI & TECHNOL, 73-, Ed, Historical Studies in the Physical Sciences, 79- **MEMBERSHIPS** Hist Sci Soc; Brit Soc Hist Sci. **RESEARCH** History of physical science and its institutions since the Renaissnce. **SELECTED PUBLICATIONS** Auth, Science for a Polite Society--Gender, Culture, and the Demonstration of Enlightenment, Annals Sci, Vol 0053, 96; Geometry-French--Durer,, Annals Sci, Vol 0053, 96; A Social-History of Truth--Civility and Science in 17th-Century England, Annals Sci, Vol 0052, 95; The Affair of the Countess Gorlitz, Am Philos Soc, Vol 0138, 94. **CONTACT ADDRESS** Dept of Hist, Univ of Calif, Berkeley, CA, 94720.

HEILMAN, SAMUEL C.
PERSONAL Born 05/26/1946, Karlsruhe, Germany, m, 1969, 4 children **DISCIPLINE** SOCIOLOGY, ANTHROPOLOGY **EDUCATION** Brandeis Univ, BA, 68; New Sch for Soc Res, MA, 70; Univ Pa, PhD(sociology), 73. **CAREER** Instr, St. Joseph's Univ, 72-73; instr, Univ Pa, 72-73; from asst prof to assoc prof, 73-82, prof, sociology, 82-, Harold Proshansky Chair in Jewish Studies, 93-, grad chair, Dept Sociology, 76-78, chair dept, 79-80, dir, Jewish Studies Prog, 80-86, dir, Ctr for Jewish Studies, 80-87, Queens Col, City Univ New York; vis prof, Max Weinreich Ctr for Advanced Jewish Studies, YIVO Inst Jewish Res, 76; vis prof, Hebrew Univ Jerusalem, 79, 88; vis prof, Tel Aviv Univ, 84; Vis Fulbright Prof, Universities of New South Wales, Sydney, and Melbourne, 86; Fel, Inst for Advanced Study, Jerusalem, 91-92. **HONORS AND AWARDS** Grad Fac Fel, New Sch for Social Res, 68-70; Teaching Fel in Soc Psychol, Univ Pa, 70-71; Dissertation Fel, Univ Pa Ctr for Urban Ethnography, 72-73; Distinguished Fac Award, CUNY, 85, 87, 94; The Present Tense Mag Lit Award for best book of the year in the religious thought category, for The Gate Behind the Wall, 84; Nat Jewish Book Award, for A Walker in Jerusalem, 86; recipient of numerous grants. **SELECTED PUBLICATIONS** Auth, Synagogue Life: A Study in Symbolic Interaction, Univ Chicago Press, 76; auth, The People of the Book: Drama, Fellowship and Religion, Univ Chicago Press, 83; auth, The Gate Behind the Wall, Summit Books/Simon & Schuster, 85; coauth, A Walker in Jerusalem, Summit Books/Simon & Schuster, 86, 2nd ed, J.P.S, 95; coauth, Cosmopolitans and Parochials: Modern Orthodox Jews in America, Univ Chicago Press, 89; auth, Defenders of the Faith: Inside Ultra-Orthodox Jewry, Schocken, 92; auth, Portrait of Jewish Americans: The Last Half of the Twentieth Century, Univ Wash Press, 95. **CONTACT ADDRESS** Dept Sociology, Queens Col, CUNY, 6530 Kissena Blvd, Flushing, NY, 11367.

HEIMAN, LAWRENCE FREDERICK
PERSONAL Born 08/24/1917, Decatur, IN **DISCIPLINE** CHURCH MUSIC **EDUCATION** Cath Univ Am, MA, 49; Pontifical Inst Sacred Music, Rome, LCG, 58, MCG, 59, DS Mus, 70. **CAREER** Prof Emeritus Music & Dir Emeritus Rensselaer Prog Church Music & Liturgy, St Joseph's Col, IN, 44. **HONORS AND AWARDS** Papal Gold Medal res work in Gregorian Chant, 70; Nat Merit Award, Nat Cath Music Educr Asn, 72; President's Fel, St Joseph's Col; Doctor of Letters, honoris causa, St. Joseph's Col, 96. **MEMBERSHIPS** Int Asn Studies Gregorian Chant; Int Consociatio Sacred Music; N Am Acad Liturgy; Nat Asn Pastoral Musicians. **SELECTED PUBLICATIONS** Auth, The Rhythmic Value of the Final Descending Note After a Puncture in Neums of Codex 239 of the Library of Laon, Etudes Gregoriennes, 72. **CONTACT ADDRESS** St Joseph's Col, PO Box 81J, Rensselaer, IN, 47978-0929. **EMAIL** lheiman@saintjoe.edu

HEIMERT, ALAN
PERSONAL Born 11/10/1928, Oak Park, IL, m, 1962, 2 children **DISCIPLINE** AMERICAN CIVILIZATION **EDUCATION** Harvard Univ, AB, 49, PhD, 60; Columbia Univ, MA, 50. **CAREER** Instr hist lit & Eng, 59-60, from asst prof to assoc prof, 61-69, chmn dept Eng, 72-76, Powell M Cabot prof Am lit, Harvard Univ, 70, Master Eliot House, 68-, Mem Inst Advan Studies, Princeton Univ, 60-61. **MEMBERSHIPS** Am Studies Asn; mod lang asn; Am antiq soc. **RESEARCH** Colonial lit and hist; 19th century intellectual hist. **SELECTED PUBLICATIONS** Auth, Puritanism, the wilderness, and the frontier, New Ent Quart, 53; Moby Dick and American political symbolism, Am Quart, 63; coauth, A Nation So Conceived, Scribner, 63; auth, Perry Miller: an appreciation, Harvard Rev, 64; Religion and the American Mind: From the Great Awakening to the Revolution, Harvard Univ, 66; co-ed, The Great Awakening, Bobbs, 67; co auth, The Puritans in America, harvard, 85. **CONTACT ADDRESS** Harvard Univ, Barker 129, 12 Quincy st, Cambridge, MA, 02138-3800. **EMAIL** aheimert@fas.harvard.edu

HEINEMANN, RONALD
PERSONAL Born 07/24/1939, Flushing, NY, m, 1962, 2 children **DISCIPLINE** HISTORY **EDUCATION** Dartmouth College, BA, 61; Univ Virginia, MA, 67, PhD, 68. **CAREER** Squires Prof Hist, 68-, Hamden-Sydney College. **HONORS AND AWARDS** Phi Beta Kappa; Cabell and Fuqua Awds for Excell in Teaching; Mettauer and Wilson Awds for Excell in Research. **MEMBERSHIPS** OAH; SHA; VHS; AAUP. **RESEARCH** 20th Century US and Virginia History. **SELECTED PUBLICATIONS** Auth, Depression and New Deal in Virginia; The Enduring Dominion, 83; Harry Byrd of Virginia, 96. **CONTACT ADDRESS** Box 122, Hampden-Sydney, VA, 23943. **EMAIL** ronaldh@tiger.hsc.edu

HEINZ, VIRA I.
DISCIPLINE MODERN WESTERN CIVILIZATION **EDUCATION** Conception Sem Col, 81-85; Divinity Sch Univ Chicago, MA, 87, PhD, 93. **CAREER** Lang fel, Amer Inst Indian Stud, Calcutta, 89-90; assoc prof. **MEMBERSHIPS** Mem, Amer Hist Assn; Org Amer Historians; Soc Historians Amer For Rel; Univ Calif Hist Assoc; NATO Assoc Lyman L Lemnitzer Ctr NATO Stud; Ger Hist Inst; Ohio Acad Hist; Assn Asian StudInc; Amer Inst Contemp Ger Stud. **RESEARCH**

Nineteenth-century Bengali texts. **SELECTED PUBLICATIONS** Auth, Kali's Child: The Mystical and the Erotic in the Life and Teachings of Ramakrishna, Univ Chicago Press, 95. **CONTACT ADDRESS** Rel, Hist, Philos, Classics Dept, Westminster Col, New Wilmington, PA, 16172-0001.

HEISS, MARY ANN
PERSONAL Born 01/25/1961, Cleveland, OH, m, 1997 **DISCIPLINE** HISTORY **EDUCATION** Miami Univ, BA, 83, MA, 84; Ohio State Univ, PhD, 91. **CAREER** Asst prof, 92-98, assoc prof, 98- , Kent State Univ. **MEMBERSHIPS** Am Hist Asn; Org Am Historians; Soc Historians Am Foreign Rel. **RESEARCH** US foreign relations. **SELECTED PUBLICATIONS** Empire and Nationhood: The United States, Great Britain, and Iranian Oil, 1950-1954, NY, Columbia Univ Press, 97; Coed, NATO in the Post-Cold War Era: Does It Have a Future, NY, St Martin's Press, 95. **CONTACT ADDRESS** Dept of History, Kent State Univ, PO Box 5190, Kent, OH, 44242-0001. **EMAIL** mheiss@kent.edu

HEISSER, DAVID C. R.
PERSONAL Born 10/22/1942, Charleston, SC **DISCIPLINE** HISTORY, LIBRARY SCIENCE **EDUCATION** Col of Charleston, BS, 64; Univ NC, Chapel Hill, MA, 67, PhD, 72; Columbia Univ, MS, 75. **CAREER** Assoc prof, Head of Reference, Tufts Univ Library, 78-89; assoc prof & Government Documents Librarian, Univ Miami, 89-92; asst prof & Walterboro Librarian, Univ SC, Salkehatchie, 92-95; ASST PROF & REFERENCE/DOCUMENTS LIBRARIAN, THE CITADEL, 95-. **HONORS AND AWARDS** Fulbright fel; Woodrow Wilson fel; res grant, Cushwa Center for the Study of American Catholicism. **MEMBERSHIPS** Am Library Asn; Special Libraries Asn; SC Library Asn; SC Hist Soc; Am Cath Hist Asn. **RESEARCH** Government information; hist of SC; emblematica & symbolism. **SELECTED PUBLICATIONS** Auth, Marketing US Government Depository Libraries, Government Pubs Rev 13, 86; with Peter Hernon, GPO Regional Depositories, The Reference Librarian 32, 91; South Carolina's Mace and Its Heritage, House of Representatives of SC, 91; The State Seal of South Carolina: A Short History, SC Dept of Archives and Hist, 92; Warrior Queen of Ocean: The Story of Charleston and Its Seal, SC Hist Mag 93, 92; Jean Mayer: A Bibliography, 1948-1993, Tufts Univ Library, 98; Bishop Lynch's Civil War Pamphlet on Slavery, Cath Hist Rev 84, 98; Federal Depository Program at the Crossraods: The Library Administrator's Perspective, Government Information Quart 16, 99. **CONTACT ADDRESS** Daniel Library, The Citadel, Charleston, SC, 29409. **EMAIL** David.Heisser@Citadel.edu

HEITZMANN, WILLIAM RAY
PERSONAL Born 02/12/1948, Hoboken, NJ, d, 2 children **DISCIPLINE** EDUCATION **EDUCATION** Villanova Univ, BS; Univ Chicago, MAT. **CAREER** Dir, grad Tchr Educ Prog & prof, author, writer, Villanova Univ. **HONORS AND AWARDS** Listed, Who's Who in Am, Who's Who in Am Educ; MSCSS Gold Medal, 89; Outstanding Alumnus Award, 88; Outstanding Serv Award, Nat Coun for Soc Stud, 80; writer in residence, Ragdale Found, Ill; mem, Adv Coun, Int Biog Ctr; bd mem, Res Bd Adv, Am Biog Inst; proposal eval, Nat Sea Grant Col Prog, NOAA, NEH. **MEMBERSHIPS** Oceanic Soc; US Naval Inst; No Am Soc of Oceanic Hist; Commun Col Social Sci Asn; Naval Hist Asn; Kappa Delta Pi; Phi Delta Kappa; Delta Tau Kappa; Nat Coun for Soc Stud; Int Oceanographic Soc; Nat Asn Basketball Coaches; Penn Asn for Curriculum Dev and Supervision; Del Valley Read Asn; Cousteau Soc; Mystic Seaport Soc; Phila Writers' Org. **SELECTED PUBLICATIONS** Coauth, Sources of Cartoons, Insight, 95; auth, Historical Cartoons: Opportunities to Motivate and Educate, Insight, 95; auth, The Power of Political Cartoons in a Presidential Year, Hist Matters, 96; auth, The Power of Political Cartoons in the Classroom: Opportunities to Motivate and Educate, Nat Soc Sci Perspectives J, 97; auth, The Course Profile: Instructional and Marketing Dynamite, Trends and Issues, 97; auth, Targeted Homework: Opportunities to Motivate and Educate, Today's Cath Tchr, 97; auth, Writing for Publication in Marine and Maritime Education, J of Marine Educ, 98; auth, The Professor as Evaluator: The Promise of Criterion Referenced Measurement, Soc Stud J, 98; auth, A St Patrick's Day Tragedy, Cath NY,; auth, Ten Steps to Classroom Success, MSCSS 1998 Yearbook. **CONTACT ADDRESS** Dept of Education and Human Services, Villanova Univ, Villanova, PA, 19085.

HELD, BEVERLY ORLOVE
DISCIPLINE HISTORY **EDUCATION** Univ of Penn, BA, 72; MA, 74, PhD, 87. **CAREER** LECT, HIST, SAN FRANCISCO STATE UNIV **MEMBERSHIPS** Am Antiquarian Soc **CONTACT ADDRESS** 1340 Lombard St. No. 304, San Francisco, CA, 94109.

HELD, DIRK
PERSONAL Born 03/24/1939, New York, NY, m, 1962, 2 children **DISCIPLINE** CLASSICS **EDUCATION** Brown **CAREER** Instr Classics and Inst for Lib Arts, Emory Univ, 68-71; asst prof to prof of Classics, Conn Col, 71-; Univ fel philos, Univ Penn, 66-67; NEH fel for Interrelations Sci and Hum, 74-75. **MEMBERSHIPS** Am Philol Asn; Soc Ancient Greek Philos; Int Soc Classical Tradition. **RESEARCH** Greek philosophy; Classical tradition 18th-19th Century. **SELECTED PUBLICATIONS** Auth Why Individuals didn't exist in classical Antiquity, N Eng Classical Newsl & Jour, 91; Megalopsychia in Nicomachean Ethics IV, Ancient Philos, 93; Bernard Williams Shame and Necessity, Int Jour Philos Stud, 95; Shaping Eurocentrism: The Uses of Greek Antiquity, Greeks and Barbarians: Essays on the Interactions between Greeks and Non-Greeks in Antiquity and the Consequences of Eurocentrism, CDL Press, 97; Plato and Aristotle on Memory, Knowledge and the Self, Memory, History and Critique, European Identity at the Millenium, Proceedings of the Fifth Conference of the International Society for the Study of European Ideas, Utrecht, 98. **CONTACT ADDRESS** Classics Dept, Connecticut Col, 270 Mohegan Ave, New London, CT, 06320. **EMAIL** dthel@conncoll.edu

HELD, JOSEPH
PERSONAL Born 10/14/1930, Budapest, Hungary, m, 1954, 2 children **DISCIPLINE** MODERN EUROPEAN HISTORY **EDUCATION** Rutgers Univ, AB, 62, MA, 63, PhD, 68. **CAREER** Asst mod Europ hist, Rutgers Univ, 62-65; instr, Newark Col Eng, 66; asst prof Hungarian & E Europ studies, 66-68, asst prof hist & Hungarian studies, 68-70, dir, E Europ Soviet Studies, 76, ASSOC PROF HIST & HUNGARIAN STUDIES, UNIV COL, RUTGERS UNIV, NEW BRUNSWICK, 70-, CHMN DEPT, 74-, Int Res & Exchanges Bd, Soc Sci Res Coun fel, 71-72. **MEMBERSHIPS** AHA; Am Asn Advan Slavic Studies. **RESEARCH** Social, political and economic history; Hungarian society in the early 15th century. **SELECTED PUBLICATIONS** Auth, Jadwiga-Of-Anjou and the Rise of East-Central-Europe, English Hist Rev, Vol 0110, 95; The Rural Society of Hungary in the Interwar Period, English Hist Rev, Vol 0109, 94; Hungarian Economy and Society During World-War-II, Int Hist Rev, Vol 0016, 94. **CONTACT ADDRESS** Dept of Hist, Univ Col Rutgers Univ, 84 College Ave, New Brunswick, NJ, 08903.

HELFANT, IAN M.
DISCIPLINE RUSSIAN **EDUCATION** Harvard Univ, BS, 86, MA, 92, PhD, 96. **CAREER** Vis asst prof, Williams Col,97-98. **HONORS AND AWARDS** Mellon fel, 89-91, 94-95; USIA/ACTR Res Scholar in Petersburg, 94; FLAS fel, 90-91, 92-93; Harvard Frederick Sheldon Traveling fel in Eastern Europe, 86-87. **RESEARCH** 19th-century Russian literature; cultural and gender studies; Autobiographical genres; reader response and risk theory. **SELECTED PUBLICATIONS** Auth, Sculpting a Persona: The Path from Pushkin's Caucasian journal to Puteshestvie v Arzrum, Russ Rev, 97. **CONTACT ADDRESS** Center for Foreign Languages, Literatures and Cult, Williams Col, Williamstown, MA, 01267. **EMAIL** Ian.M.Helfant@williams.edu

HELGUERA, J. LEON
PERSONAL Born 10/29/1926, New York, NY, m, 1950, 3 children **DISCIPLINE** LATIN AMERICAN HISTORY **EDUCATION** Univ of Americas, Mex, BA, 48; Univ NC, MA, 51, PhD(Latin Am hist & polit sci), 58. **CAREER** Actg instr hist, Univ Tenn, 55; actg asst prof, Lynchburg Col, 56 & Univ NC, Ft Bragg, 56; actg instr, NC State Col, 57, instr, 57-59, from asst prof to assoc prof, 59-63; assoc prof, 63 & 68, PROF LATIN AM HIST, VANDERBILT UNIV, 68-, US res rep, John Boulton Found Caracas, Venezuela, 58-; US consult, Simon Bolivar Biog Proj Venezuelan Govt & Bolivarian Soc of Venzuela, 63; vis sr fel, St Antony's Col, Oxford Univ, 72-73. **HONORS AND AWARDS** Order of Andres Bello, Venezuelan Govt, 71. **MEMBERSHIPS** Conf Latin Am Hist; Southeastern Conf Latin Am Studies; Southern Hist Asn; corresp mem Centro de Estudios Montaneses, Santander; Gran Colombianist Comt. **RESEARCH** Colombian and Venezuelan history, the national period since 1830; foreigners in the independence movement of Northern South America, 1810-1830; social-economic history of Southwestern Colombia in the 19th century. **SELECTED PUBLICATIONS** Auth, Bello and Bolivar--Poetry and Politics in the Spanish-American Revolution, Am Hist Rev, Vol 0099, 94; Posada and Mexican Engraving from the Famed Engraver of Popular Themes Up to Contemporary-Artists, Studies Latin Am Popular Cult, Vol 0012, 93. **CONTACT ADDRESS** Vanderbilt Univ, Sta B, Box 1606, Nashville, TN, 37235.

HELLER, HENRY
PERSONAL Born 07/17/1938, New York, NY, 2 children **DISCIPLINE** FRENCH RENAISSANCE HISTORY **EDUCATION** Univ Mich, BA, 59; Cornell Univ, PhD(hist), 69. **CAREER** Lectr, 63-66, asst prof, 66-69, assoc prof, 69-79, PROF HIST, UNIV MANITOBA, 79-, Can Coun fels & grants, 71, 72 & 78-79. **MEMBERSHIPS** Can Cath Hist Soc (vpres, 69); Can Hist Asn; AHA; Renaissance Soc Am; Am Soc Reformation Res. **RESEARCH** French Renaissance and Reformation; early modern Europe. **SELECTED PUBLICATIONS** Auth, Copernican Ideas in 16th-Century France--Philosophy, Astronomy, Renaissance Reformation, Vol 0020, 96; Atoms, Pneuma and Tranquillity--Epicurean and Stoic Themes in European Thought, Renaissance Reformation, Vol 0018, 94; Bodin on Slavery and Primitive Accumulation, Sixteenth C J, Vol 0025, 94; The Economics of Power--The Private Finances of the House of Foix-Navarre-Albret During the Religious-Wars, Sixteenth C J, Vol 0025, 94; The Kings Army--Warfare, Soldiers and Society During the Wars-Of-Religion in France, 1562-1576, J Military Hist, Vol 0061, 97; The Paris Studium--Robert-Of-Sorbonne and His Legacy--Selected Studies, Sixteenth C J, Vol 0024, 93; Putting History Back into the Religious-Wars, a Reply to Mack Holt, French Hist Studies, Vol 0019, 96. **CONTACT ADDRESS** Dept of Hist, Univ of Manitoba, Winnipeg, MB, R3T 2N2.

HELLIE, RICHARD
PERSONAL Born 05/08/1937, Waterloo, IA, m, 1998, 1 child **DISCIPLINE** RUSSIAN HISTORY **EDUCATION** Univ Chicago, AB, 58, AM, 60, PhD, 65. **CAREER** Asst prof Russ hist, Rutgers Univ, 65-66; asst prof, 66-71, assoc prof, 71-80, prof Russ hist, Univ of Chicago, 80-, Guggenheim fel, 73-74; Nat Endowment for Humanities fel, 78-79 & 82-83. **HONORS AND AWARDS** Herbert Baxter Adams Prize, AHA, 72. **MEMBERSHIPS** Am Soc Legal Hist; Hist Early Mod Europe; Am Asn Slavic Studies. **RESEARCH** Early modern Russian social, institutional, economic, and legal history. **SELECTED PUBLICATIONS** Auth, Muscovite Society, 67 & Enserfment and Military Change in Muscovy, 71, Univ Chicago; Ivan the Terrible reconsidered, in Ivan the Terrible, Acad Int, 74; The Petrine Army, Can-Am Slavic Studies, summer 74; The structure of modern Russian history: Toward a dynamic model, 1/77 & The stratification of Muscovite society: The townsmen, 78, Russ Hist; Muscovy, in Mod Encycl Russian and Soviet Hist, 81; Slavery in Russia, 1450-1725, Univ Chicago Press, 82; Late Medieval and Early Modern Russian Civilization and Modern Neuroscience, in UCLA Slavic Studies 3, 97; The Economy and Material Culture of Russia 1600-1725, Univ Chicago Press, 98. **CONTACT ADDRESS** Dept of Hist, Univ of Chicago, 1126 E 59th St, Chicago, IL, 60637-1587. **EMAIL** hell@midway.uchicago.edu

HELLY, DOROTHY O.
PERSONAL Born 02/02/1931, Torrington, CT, m, 1956, 1 child **DISCIPLINE** MODERN BRITISH HISTORY **EDUCATION** Smith Col, AB, 52; Radcliffe Col, AM, 53, PhD, 61. **CAREER** Ed, Col Dept, Ginn & Co, Boston, 57-59; sr ed, Col Dept, Holt, Rinehart & Winston, Inc, NY, 61-63; instr, 63-69, asst prof, 69-80, assoc prof, 80-87, prof hist, 87-, assoc dean, Sch Gen Studies, 77-84, Hunter Col; mem, Berkshire Conf Women Historians, 69-, co-chemn prog comm, 84-87. **HONORS AND AWARDS** CUNY fac res grant, 68; Ford Found grant, 92-94; Hunter Col Pres Fac Incentive and Tchg grant, 96-97; AAUW awards, 97; res assoc, Queen Elizabeth House, oxford Univ, 98; mem, steering comt, seminar, Women Writing Women's Lives, 98-. **MEMBERSHIPS** AHA; fel Royal Geog Soc; Northeast Conf Victorian Studies; Inst Res Hist; Mid-Atlantic Conf Brit Studies. **RESEARCH** Women and society in Victorian England; British attitudes toward tropical Africa since 1860; Reverend Horace Waller, 1833-1896, a study in British humanitarianism and empire; biography of Flora Shaw, Lady Lugard (1852-1929). **SELECTED PUBLICATIONS** Ed, Family History, Haworth, 85; auth, Livingstone's Legacy: Horace Waller and Victorian Mythmaking, Ohio, 87; co-ed, Gendered Domains: Rethinking Public and Private in Women's History, Cornell, 92; coauth, Women's Realities, Women's Choices: An Introduction to Women's Studies, Oxford, 95; coauth, Journalism as Active Politics; Flora Shaw, The Times, and South Africa, The South African War, Manchester, 98. **CONTACT ADDRESS** Hunter Col, CUNY, 695 Park Ave, New York, NY, 10021-5085. **EMAIL** dhelly@shiva.hunter.cuny.edu

HELM, JAMES JOEL
PERSONAL Born 12/17/1937, Chicago, IL, m, 1960, 2 children **DISCIPLINE** CLASSICAL STUDIES **EDUCATION** Elmhurst Col, BA, 59; Union Theol Sem, MDiv, 63; Univ Mich, Ann Arbor, MA, 65, PhD(class studies), 68. **CAREER** Instr class studies, Univ Mich, Ann Arbor, 66-68; asst prof, 68-74, chmn dept, 76-82, Assoc Prof Classics, Oberlin Col, 74-, Vis assoc prof classics, Scripps Col, 78-79. **MEMBERSHIPS** Am Philol Asn; Archaeol Inst Am; Class Asn Mid West & South. **RESEARCH** Greek paleography; computer applications in classical studies; poetry of Catullus. **SELECTED PUBLICATIONS** Auth, Koros--From Satisfaction to Greed, Classical World, Vol 0087, 93. **CONTACT ADDRESS** Dept of Classics, Oberlin Col, 135 W Lorain St, Oberlin, OH, 44074-1076.

HELMER, STEPHEN
PERSONAL Born 08/31/1944, Cleveland, OH, m **DISCIPLINE** ART HISTORY; ARCHITECTURE AND CITY DESIGN **EDUCATION** Principia Col, BA, 66; Cornell Univ, PhD, 80. **CAREER** Asst Prof Art Hist, Principia Col, 96-. **MEMBERSHIPS** Soc Archit Hist. **RESEARCH** History of city design; history of architecture. **SELECTED PUBLICATIONS** Auth, Gammage Auditorium and the Baghdad Opera Project: Two Late Designs by Frank Lloyd Wright, The Frank Wright Newsletter, vol 3, 80; Hitler's Berlin: A New Look at the Plan of Nazi Masterbuilder, Albert Speer, Archetype, Fall 80; Totaliarianism and the Modern Planning Tradition: Nazi Berlin Revisited, Planning Hist Bull, no 2, 82; Hitler's Berlin: The Speer Plans for Reshaping the Central City, UMI Res Press, 85. **CONTACT ADDRESS** Principia Col, Elsah, IL, 62028. **EMAIL** SHD@PRIN.EDU

HELMHOLZ, R.H.
PERSONAL Born 07/01/1940, Pasadena, CA **DISCIPLINE** HISTORY, LAW **EDUCATION** Princeton Univ, AB, 61; Harvard Univ, LLB, 65; Univ Calif, Berkeley, MA, 66, PhD(hist), 70; Trinity Col, Dublin, LLD(h.c.), 92. **CAREER** Asst Prof Hist to Prof Law and Hist, Washington Univ, St. Louis, 70-81; Prof Law, 81-84, Ruth Wyatt Rosenson Prof Law, Univ Chicago, 84-; co-ed, Comparative Studies in Continental and Anglo-Am Legal Hist, 97-; assoc ed, New Dictionary of Nat Biography, 98-. **HONORS AND AWARDS** Fulbright Schol, Univ Kent, 68-69; Royal Hist Soc, Fel, 78-; Guggenheim Fel, 86-87; Cambridge Univ, Maitland Lectr and Vis Fel Commoner, Trinity Col, 86-87; Am Acad of Arts and Sci, Fel, 91-; Alexander von Humboldt Found, Res Prize, 92-93; Medieval Acad of Am, Fel, 97-; All Souls Col, Oxford, vis fel, Michaelmas term, 98. **MEMBERSHIPS** Selden Soc; Am Soc Legal Hist; Royal Hist Soc. **RESEARCH** Legal history. **SELECTED PUBLICATIONS** Auth, Canonical Defamation, Vol 15, Am J Legal Hist, 72; Marriage Litigation in Medieval England, Cambridge Univ, 74; Assumpsit and fidei laesio, Law Quart Rev, Vol 91, 75; Writs of prohibition and ecclesiastical sanctions, Minn Law Rev, 76; Support Orders, Church Courts and the Rule of Filius Nullius, Va Law Rev, Vol 63, 77; Early Enforcement of Uses, Columbia Law Rev, Vol 79, 79; Canon Law and English Common Law, London, 83; Select Cases on Defamation to 1600, Seldon Soc, Vol 101, 85; Canon Law and the Law of England, London, 87; Roman Canon Law in Reformation England, Cambridge, 90; coauth, Notaries Public in England since the Reformation, London, 91; ed and contribur, Canon Law in Protestant Lands, Berlin, 92; auth, The Spirit of Classical Canon Law, Athens, Ga, 96; coauth, The Privilege against Self-Incrimination: its Origins and Development, Chicago, 97. **CONTACT ADDRESS** Law Sch, Univ of Chicago, 1111 E 60th St., Chicago, IL, 60637-2702. **EMAIL** dick_helmholz@law.uchicago.edu

HELMREICH, ERNST CHRISTIAN
PERSONAL Born 08/26/1902, Crescent City, IL, m, 1932, 2 children **DISCIPLINE** HISTORY **EDUCATION** Univ Ill, AB, 24, AM, 25; Harvard Univ, PhD, 32. **CAREER** Instr hist & govt, Purdue Univ, 24-26; asst hist, Radcliffe Col, 27-29 & 30-31; from instr to prof hist & govt, 31-59, Thomas Brackett Reed prof, 59-72, EMER THOMAS BRACKETT REED PROF HIST & POLIT SCI, BOWDOIN COL, 72-, Prof, Fletcher Sch Law & Diplomacy, 43-44. **MEMBERSHIPS** AHA **RESEARCH** Modern European and diplomatic history; Church and state in Germany. **SELECTED PUBLICATIONS** Auth, Twisted Cross--The German Christian Movement in the Third-Reich, Cath Hist Rev, Vol 0083, 97. **CONTACT ADDRESS** Bowdoin Col, 6 Boody St, Brunswick, ME, 04011.

HELMREICH, JONATHAN ERNST
PERSONAL Born 12/21/1936, Brunswick, ME, 3 children **DISCIPLINE** MODERN EUROPEAN HISTORY **EDUCATION** Amherst Col, AB,58; Princeton Univ, MA, 60, PhD(hist), 61. **CAREER** Asst instr, Princeton Univ, 61; US Int Educ Exchange scholar, Free Univ Brussels, 61-62; from asst prof to assoc prof, 62-72, dean instr, 66-81, sec of fac, 91-93, prof hist, 72-88, prof emeritus, 88-, col historian, Allegheny Col, 98-. **HONORS AND AWARDS** BA degree magna cum laude; Phi Beta Kappa; Raymond P Shafer Award for Distinguished Community Service. **MEMBERSHIPS** AHA; Phi Beta Kappa; Phi Alpha Theta; Rotary Int; Meadville Lit Union. **RESEARCH** Nineteenth and 20th century European diplomacy; modern Belgium. **SELECTED PUBLICATIONS** Auth, Is There an Honors Inflation?, Col & Univ, 77; A Prayer for the Spirit of Acceptance, Hist Mag Protestant Episcopal Church, 12/77; From Paris to Cannes: Belgium's Fight for Priority Reparation Payments, Studia Diplomatica, 12/80; The Serbs: A Warning from a Past Contributer, Contemp Rev, 93; US Foreign Policy and the Belgian Congo in the 1950s, Historian, winter 96; Historic Ties, Allegheny 17, fall/winter 97; Installation of a King, Allegheny, spring 98; Brand Whitlock, The United States in the First World War: An Encycl, Garland, 95; co-ed, The Civil War Diaries of Seth Waid III, Crawford County Hist Soc, 93; The Lake as it Was: An Informal History and Memoir of Conneaut Lake, Crawford County Hist Soc, 94; Place Names of Crawford County, Crawford County Hist Soc, 96, 98; ed, Pioneer Life in Crawford County, Pennsylvania, Crawford County Hist Soc, 96; Motering to Conneaut Lake: A Memoir by Bronson B. Luty, Pittsburgh History, spring 97. **CONTACT ADDRESS** Dept of History, Allegheny Col, 520 N Main St, Meadville, PA, 16335-3902. **EMAIL** jhemrei@alleg.edu

HELMREICH, PAUL CHRISTIAN
PERSONAL Born 07/13/1933, Brunswick, ME, m, 1956, 3 children **DISCIPLINE** HISTORY **EDUCATION** Amherst Col, BA, 55; Harvard Univ, MA, 57, PhD(hist), 64. **CAREER** From instr to assoc prof, 57-74, chm dept, 68-75, prof hist, 74-99, PROF EMER, 99- WHEATON COL, MASS; lectr current events, Katherine Gibbs Sch, 65-78; vis assoc prof Rhode Island Col, 69; vis prof, Brown Univ, 70; consult, Hist Prog, Roger Williams Col, 71 and Bentley Col, 90; trustee's adv comt humanities, Southeastern Mass Univ, 79-82. **HONORS AND AWARDS** NEH summer stipend fel, 67; prentice Prof, 82-85. **MEMBERSHIPS** AHA; New Eng Hist Asn; AAUP. **RESEARCH** Diplomatic history of Europe 1918-1939; New England higher education for women; 19th and 20th centuries. **SELECTED PUBLICATIONS** Auth, From Paris to Sevres: The Partition of the Ottoman Empire at the Peace Conference of 1919-1920, Ohio State, 74; auth, The Diary of Charles G Lee in the Andersonville and Florence Prison Camps, 1864, Conn Hist Soc Bull, 76; auth, Italy and the Anglo-French Repudiation of the 1917 St Jean de Maurienne Agreement, J Mod Hist, 77; auth, Wheaton College, 1834-1912: The Seminary years, Wheaton, 85; auth, Switzerland, Americana Annual, Grolier, 68-99; auth, Lucy Larcom at Wheaton, New England Q, 91. **CONTACT ADDRESS** Dept of History, Wheaton Col, Norton, MA, 02766.

HELMS, JOHN DOUGLAS
PERSONAL Born 06/29/1945, Union County, NC **DISCIPLINE** AMERICAN HISTORY **EDUCATION** Univ NC, Chapel Hill, AB, 67; Fla State Univ, MA, 70, PhD(hist), 77. **CAREER** Archivist, Nat Arch & Rec Serv, 73-81; HISTORIAN, SOIL CONSERV SERV, 81-, Smithsonian Inst fel, 78-79. **MEMBERSHIPS** Agr Hist Soc; Orgn Am Historians; Southern Hist Asn; Forest Hist Soc; Soil Conserv Soc Am. **RESEARCH** Agricultural history; conservation history; Southern United States. **SELECTED PUBLICATIONS** Auth, Outstanding in His Field--Perspectives on American Agriculture in Honor of Wayne Rasmussen, Public Historian, Vol 0018, 96; National Soil Conservation Policies--A Historical Case-Study of the Driftless Area, Agricultural Hist, Vol 0070, 96. **CONTACT ADDRESS** Soil Conserv Serv, PO Box 2890, Washington, DC, 20013.

HELZLE, MARTIN
PERSONAL Born 08/17/1961, Stuttgart, Germany, m, 1987, 3 children **DISCIPLINE** CLASSICS **EDUCATION** Univ of Leeds, BA, 83; Univ of Cambridge, PhD, 88. **CAREER** Univ of Bristol, 80-87; Univ Wales, 87-88; Cleveland State Univ, 89, part time, John Carroll Univ; asst prof, 89-95, assoc prof, 96-present, Case Western Reserve Univ. **HONORS AND AWARDS** Jopson research fel; RIG from State of Ohio; Humboldt Fel. **MEMBERSHIPS** APA; CAMWS; OCC; Mommsengesellschaft. **RESEARCH** Latin Poetry **SELECTED PUBLICATIONS** P Ouidii Nasonis Epistualarum ex Ponto liber IV: A commentary on Poems 1-7 and 16, 89; Die Charakterisierung Scipios in Silius Italicus' Classica et Mediaevalia, 95; Der Stil ist der Mensch, Redner und Reden im romischen Epos, 96. **CONTACT ADDRESS** Dept of Classics, Case Western Reserve Univ, 10900 Euclid Ave, Cleveland, OH, 44106-7111. **EMAIL** mxh13@po.cwru.edu

HEMPHILL, C. DALLETT
DISCIPLINE HISTORY AND AMERICAN STUDIES **EDUCATION** Brandeis Univ, PhD. **CAREER** Prof, Ursinus Col. **HONORS AND AWARDS** NEH grant. **RESEARCH** American history before the Civil War. **SELECTED PUBLICATIONS** Published several articles on early modern American culture. **CONTACT ADDRESS** Ursinus Col, Collegeville, PA, 19426-1000.

HENCH, JOHN BIXLER
PERSONAL Born 02/21/1943, Colorado Springs, CO, m, 1966, 2 children **DISCIPLINE** AMERICAN HISTORY **EDUCATION** Lafayette Col, AB, 65; Clark Univ, AM, 68, PhD, 79. **CAREER** Asst prof hist, Mankato State Col, 70-73; ed publ, 73-77, res & publ officer, 77-81, asst dir res & publ, 81-84, Am Antiquarian Soc; assoc dir res & publ, 84-89, dir res & publ, 89-96, vice pres & public progs, 96- ed, 73-96, Proc Am Antiquarian Soc & Early Am Imprints Ser; proj dir, NAm Imprints Prog, 79-89; affil prof hist, 92-, Clark Univ. **MEMBERSHIPS** Am Printing Hist Assn; AHA; Orgn Am Historians; Assn Bibliog Hist. **RESEARCH** American printing and publishing history; United States early national period; American Revolution. **SELECTED PUBLICATIONS** Ed, Three Hundred Years of the American Newspaper, Am Antiquarian Soc, 91; co-ed, Under It's Generous Dome: The Collections and Programs of the American Antiquarian Society, Am Antiquarian Soc, 92; ed, Serendipity and Synergy: Collection Development, Access, and Research Opportunities at the American Antiquarian Society in the McCorison Era, Am Antiquarian Soc, 93; auth, Toward a History of the Book in America, Publ Research Quart, 94. **CONTACT ADDRESS** Am Antiquarian Soc, 185 Salisbury St, Worcester, MA, 01609. **EMAIL** jbh@mwa.org

HENDEL, KURT KARL
DISCIPLINE REFORMATION HISTORY **EDUCATION** Concordia Sr Col; Concordia Sem; Ohio State Univ, PhD. **CAREER** Dir, MA prog; ch, Division II; assoc prof-. **HONORS AND AWARDS** Fulbright scholar, Univ Gottingen. **RESEARCH** Sixteenth-century reformer, Johannes Bugenhagen. **SELECTED PUBLICATIONS** Auth, various articles on Reformation and general church history; The Doctrine of the Ministry: The Reformation Heritage, Currents in Theology and Mission. **CONTACT ADDRESS** Dept of Reformation History, Lutheran Sch of Theol, 1100 E 55th St, Chicago, IL, 60615. **EMAIL** khendel@lstc.edu

HENDERSON, ALEXA BENSON
PERSONAL Born 01/08/1944, Elberton, GA, m, 1967 **DISCIPLINE** AMERICAN HISTORY **EDUCATION** Fort Valley State Col, BS, 65; Atlanta Univ, MA, 66; Ga State Univ, PhD(hist), 75. **CAREER** Instr soc sci, Savannah State Col, 66-67; assoc prof, 67-79, PROF HIST, CLARK COL, 79-, Partic soc sci, Inst Ser Educ, 67-74; adj prof, Atlanta Univ, 78-81; consult historian, Nat Park Serv; fel, Col Teachers, Nat Endowment Humanities, 82-83. **MEMBERSHIPS** Asn Study Afro-Am Life Hist; Southern Hist Asn; Asn Gen & Liberal Studies. **RESEARCH** Afro-American history; business history; urban history. **SELECTED PUBLICATIONS** Auth, Richard Wright and the National-Negro-Bankers-Association--Early Organizing Efforts Among Black Bankers, 1924-1942, Penn Magazine Hist Biography, Vol 0117, 93. **CONTACT ADDRESS** Clark Atlanta Univ, 204 Chestnut St SW, Atlanta, GA, 30314.

HENDERSON, GEORGE
PERSONAL Born 06/18/1932, Hurtsboro, AL, m **DISCIPLINE** EDUCATION **EDUCATION** Wayne State U, BA 1957, MA 1959, PhD 1965. **CAREER** Church Youth Svc, soc caseworker 1957-59; Detroit Housing Commn, soc economist 1960-61; Detroit Urban League, com serv dir 1961-63; Detroit Mayors Youth Commn, pgm dir 1963-64; Detroit Pub Sch, asst supt 1965-67; Univ of OK, prof of human relations, currently. **HONORS AND AWARDS** Citation for Achievements in Human Relations, Oklahoma State Senate, 1978; Distinguished Community Serv Award, Urban League of Oklahoma City, 1981; Citation for Affirmative Action Activities in Higher Educ, Oklahoma House of Representatives, 1984; David Ross Boyd Distinguished Prof, Univ of Oklahoma, 1985; Civilian Commendation, Tinker AFB, Oklahoma, 1986; Outstanding Faculty Award, Univ of Oklahoma Black People's Union, 1987; Outstanding Contributions, Osan Air Base, Korea, 1987; Trail Blazer Award, Oklahoma Alliance for Affirmative Action, 1988; Outstanding Teacher, Univ of Oklahoma Black Alumni Assn, 1988; Human Rights Award, Oklahoma Human Rights Commission, 1989; Oklahoma Black Public Administrators Excellence Award, 1990; Martin Luther King Jr Award, Univ of Oklahoma College of Health Black Student Assn, 1990; Regent's Distinguished Professor, University of Oklahoma, 1989; Distinguished Service Award, University of Oklahoma, 1992; American Association for Higher Education, Black Caucus Award for Educational Service, 1992; Cultural Diversity in the Workplace, 1994; Social Work Interventions, 1994; Migrant, Immigrants & Slaves, 1995; Human Relations Issues in Management, 1996. **MEMBERSHIPS** Disting visiting prof USAF Acad 1980-81; consult US Dept of Def, US Dept of Justice, US Commn on Civil Rights, Social Sec Admin, Am Red Cross; mem Kappa Alpha Psi Frat; mem Am Sociological Assn; mem Assn of Black Sociologist; mem Assn for Supr & Curriculum Devel. **SELECTED PUBLICATIONS** "Understanding Indigenous and Foreign Cultures", 1989; "Values in Health Care,", 1991; "Police Human Rel" 1981; "Transcultural Hlth Care" 1981; "Physician-Patient Communication" 1981; "The State of Black OK" 1983; "The Human Rights of Profsnl Helpers" 1983; "Psychosocial Aspects of Disability" 1984; "Mending Broken Children" 1984; "College Survival for Student Athletes," 1985; "Intl Business & Cultures" 1987; "Our Souls to Keep," 1998; **CONTACT ADDRESS** Col of Liberal Studies, Univ of Oklahoma, 1700 Asp Ave, Ste 226, Norman, OK, 73072.

HENDERSON, H. JAMES
DISCIPLINE HISTORY **EDUCATION** Boston, AB, 50; Columbia Univ, MA, 57, PhD, 62. **CAREER** RETIRED PROF, HIST, OKLAHOMA STATE UNIV **MEMBERSHIPS** Am Antiquarian Soc **SELECTED PUBLICATIONS** Auth, Party Politics in the Continental Congress, 74; auth, "The Continental Congress and the Nationalization of American Politics," in Liberation in the Americas, San Diego, 79; auth, "Taxation and Political Culture: Massachusetts and Virginia, 1760-1800," Will & Mary Quart, Vol xlvii, 90. **CONTACT ADDRESS** 163 Spring St, Marshfield, MA, 02050.

HENDERSON, JEFFREY
PERSONAL Born 06/21/1946, Montclair, NJ, m, 1996 **DISCIPLINE** CLASSICS **EDUCATION** Kenyon Col, BA, 68; Harvard Univ, MA, 70, PhD, 72. **CAREER** Asst prof, 72-78, Yale Univ; assoc prof, 78-82, Univ Mich; prof, 82-91, USC; prof, chmn, 91-, Boston Univ. **HONORS AND AWARDS** LHD, Kenyon Col, 94; Guggenheim fel, 97-98. **MEMBERSHIPS** APA; Asn of Literary Scholars & Critics. **RESEARCH** Greek lit, esp. drama; textual criticism. **SELECTED PUBLICATIONS** Auth, The Maculate Muse: Obscene Language in Attic Comedy, Yale Univ Press, 75, Oxford Univ Press, 90; auth, Aristophanes: Essays in Interpretation, contr ed, Yale Classical Studies XXVI, Cambridge Univ Press, 80; ed with intro and commentary, Aristophanes Lysistrara, Clarendon Press, 87, 90; ed and transl, Aristophanes, Loeb Class Lib, Harvard Univ Press, 98. **CONTACT ADDRESS** Dept of Classical Studies, Boston Univ, 745 Commonwealth Ave, Boston, MA, 02215. **EMAIL** jhenders@bu.edu

HENDERSON, JOHN B.
DISCIPLINE RELIGIONS OF CHINA AND JAPAN **EDUCATION** Univ Calif, Berkeley, PhD, 77. **CAREER** Prof Hist and Relig Stud, La State Univ. **SELECTED PUBLICATIONS** Auth, Scripture, Canon, and Commentary: A Comparison of Confucian and Western Exegesis, Princeton, 91. **CONTACT ADDRESS** Dept of Philos and Relig Stud, Louisiana State Univ, 106 Coates Hall, Baton Rouge, LA, 70803.

HENDERSON, LINDA
DISCIPLINE 20TH-CENTURY ART **EDUCATION** Yale Univ, PhD, 75. **CAREER** Prof; Univ TX at Austin, 78-; curator, Mod Art, Mus of Fine Arts, Houston, 74-77; Guggenheim fe, 88-89. **HONORS AND AWARDS** Vasari awd, Dallas Mus Art; Col Fine Arts Tchg Excellence awd, 81; Who's Who in Am Art. **RESEARCH** Interdisciplinary study of modernism; rel of mod art to fields such as geometry; sci and technol; mystical and occult philos. **SELECTED PUBLICATIONS** Auth, The Fourth Dimension and Non-Euclidian Geometry in Modern Art, Princeton, 83; Duchamp in Context: Science and Technology in the 'Large Glass' and Related Works, Princeton Press, 97. **CONTACT ADDRESS** Dept of Art and Art Hist, Univ of Texas at Austin, 2613 Wichita St, FAB 2.122, Austin, TX, 78705.

HENDON, DAVID WARREN
PERSONAL Born 09/11/1947, Atlanta, GA **DISCIPLINE** HISTORY **EDUCATION** Vanderbilt Univ, BA, 69; Emory Univ, MA, 74, PhD(hist), 76. **CAREER** ASST PROF HIST, BAYLOR UNIV, 77-, Managing ed, Cent European Hist, 76-77, assoc ed, 78-; exchange prof, Seinan Gakuin Univ, Japan, 80-81. **MEMBERSHIPS** AHA; Conf Group Cent European Hist; Western Asn Ger Studies. **RESEARCH** Agrarian politics; political Catholicism. **SELECTED PUBLICATIONS** Auth, Notes on Church-State Affairs, J Church State, Vol 0038, 96. **CONTACT ADDRESS** Dept of Hist, Baylor Univ, Waco, TX, 76703.

HENDRICK, IRVING GUILFORD
PERSONAL Born 08/30/1936, Los Angeles, CA, m, 1996, 3 children **DISCIPLINE** HISTORY OF EDUCATION **EDUCATION** Whittier Col, AB, 58, MA, 60; Univ Calif, Los Angeles, EdD, 64. **CAREER** Teacher, jr high sch, Calif, 59-62; asst prof educ, Flint Col, Univ Mich, 64-65; from asst prof to assoc prof, 65-74, prof educ, 74-, assoc dean, sch educ, 75-, Univ Calif, Riverside; Ex officio mem, Calif Comn Teacher Prep & Licensing, 77-. **MEMBERSHIPS** Hist Educ Soc; Am Educ Res Assn; Nat Soc for Study Educ. **RESEARCH** History of education in the United States; history of minority group education in the United States; history of teacher education and certification requirements. **SELECTED PUBLICATIONS** Auth, The Development of a School Integration Plan in Riverside, California, Riverside Sch Study, 68; auth, The Education of Non-Whites in Clifornia, 1849-1970, R & E Res Assocs, 75; art, Federal Policy Affecting the Education of Indians in California, Hist Educ Quart, summer 76; auth, California Education, Boyd & Fraser, 80. **CONTACT ADDRESS** Sch of Educ, Univ of California, Riverside, 900 University Ave, Riverside, CA, 92521-0001. **EMAIL** irving.hendrick@ucr.edu

HENDRICKS, JAMES EDWIN
PERSONAL Born 10/19/1935, Pickens Co, SC, m, 1958, 3 children **DISCIPLINE** AMERICAN HISTORY **EDUCATION** Furman Univ, BA, 57; Univ Va, MA, 59, PhD, 61. **CAREER** From asst prof to assoc prof, 61075, PROF HIST, WAKE FOREST UNIV, 75-, Mem, NC Am Revolution Bicentennial Comn, 67-; restoration consult, Harriton Asn, Pa, 68-; R J Reynolds res leave, 72; dir hist preserv prog, Wake Forest Univ, 73-; mem, Nat Trust Hist Preserv & US Nat Comt Int Coun Monuments & Sites. **MEMBERSHIPS** AAUP **RESEARCH** Historic preservation; local history; revolutionary and early national United States history. **SELECTED PUBLICATIONS** Auth, Papers of William Thornton, 1781-1802, J Southern Hist, Vol 0063, 97; The Governors Palace in Williamsburg--A Cultural-Study, J Southern Hist, Vol 0059, 93; Abner Cook--Master Builder on the Texas Frontier, J Southern Hist, Vol 0061, 95; Nancy Lancaster--Her Life, Her World, Her Art, J Southern Hist, Vol 0063, 97. **CONTACT ADDRESS** Dept of Hist, Wake Forest Univ, P O Box 7806, Winston Salem, NC, 27109-7806.

HENGGELER, PAUL R.
PERSONAL Born 02/02/1955, Wantah, NY, m, 1997, 2 children **DISCIPLINE** AMERICAN HISTORY **EDUCATION** State Univ of NY, Cort, BA hist 77; Bowling Green State Univ, MA hist 85, PhD hist 89. **CAREER** 80-83, tchr, Western OH Yth Cen; 89-91, asst prof, Bowling Green State Univ; 92-96, asst prof, Univ TX; 96, assoc prof, hist Univ TX-Pan Amer, TX. **MEMBERSHIPS** AHA; OAH; Cen for the Study of the Pres; HS. **RESEARCH** Mod US presidency, 1960's political cult, Cesas Chavez. **SELECTED PUBLICATIONS** After The Harvest: Rise and Fall of Cesar Chavez, forthcoming; The Kennedy Persuasion: The Politics of Style Since JFK, Chi, Ivan R Dee, 95; In His Steps: Lyndon Johnson and the Kennedy Mystique, Chi, Ivn R Dee, 91; several reviews. **CONTACT ADDRESS** Univ of Texas, Pan American, 1702 West Smith, Edinburg, TX, 78539. **EMAIL** henggeler@panam.edu

HENIG, GERALD S.
PERSONAL Born 10/09/1942, New York, NY, m, 1972, 2 children **DISCIPLINE** HISTORY **EDUCATION** Brooklyn Col, BA, 64; Univ Wis, MA, 65; City Univ NY, PhD (hist), 71. **CAREER** Res asst, CUNY, 65-68; lectr hist, Hunter Col, 68-69; asst prof, 70-75, assoc prof hist, 75-79, prof hist 79-, Calif State Univ, Hayward, 75- **HONORS AND AWARDS** Arthur Rosenberg Award in Hist, 64; Outstanding Prof Award, Ca State Univ, 83; Pi Kappa Delta Award for Best Lectr, Ca State Univ, 79, 83, 85, 90. **MEMBERSHIPS** AHA; Orgn Am Historians. **RESEARCH** US political and social history, 1850-1876; Maryland political and social history, 1850-1865; California Jewish history. **SELECTED PUBLICATIONS** Auth, Henry Winter Davis, The Encycl of the United States Congress, Macmillan, 94; To Dwell Together in Freedom: The Jews in America, 87; The Jacksonian Attitude Toward Abolitionism in the 1830s, Tenn Hist Quart, spring 69; ed, Give My Love to All: The Civil War Letters of George S Rollins, Civil War Times Illus, 11/72; auth, Henry Winter Davis and the Speakership Contest of 1859-1860, Md Hist Mag, spring 73; Henry Winter Davis: Antebellum and Civil War Congressman From Maryland, Twayne, 73; A Neglected Cause of the Sioux Uprising, Minn Hist, fall 76; ed, A Marylander's Impressions of Europe During the Summer of 1854, Md Hist Mag, summer 77; Soldiering is One Hard Way of Serving the Lord: The Civil War Letters of Martin D Hamilton, Ind Mil Hist J, 10/77. **CONTACT ADDRESS** Dept of History, California State Univ, Hayward, 25800 Carlos Bee Bvd, Hayward, CA, 94542-3001. **EMAIL** ghenig@csuhayward.edu

HENNING, RANDALL
DISCIPLINE POLITICS AND INSTITUTIONS OF ECONOMIC POLICY MAKING **EDUCATION** Stanford Univ, BA; Tufts Univ, PhD. **CAREER** Prof, Am Univ. **RESEARCH** International and comparative political economy;International economic organizations; European integration; Exchange rate policy making, and macroeconomic conflict and cooperation. **SELECTED PUBLICATIONS** Auth, Currencies and Politics in the United States, Germany and Japan, Inst Int Econ, 94; coauth Global Economic Leadership and the Group of Seven, Inst Int Econ, 96. **CONTACT ADDRESS** American Univ, 4400 Massachusetts Ave, Washington, DC, 20016.

HENRETTA, JAMES A.
DISCIPLINE HISTORY **EDUCATION** Swarthmore, BA, 62; Harvard Univ, MA, 63, PhD, 68. **CAREER** Prof, hist, Boston; current, BURKE PROF OF HIST, UNIV OF MARYLAND. **MEMBERSHIPS** Am Antiquarian Soc **SELECTED PUBLICATIONS** Auth, The Rise and Decline of Democratic Republicanism: Political Rights in New York and the Several States, Albany Law Review, 89; auth, The Slow Triumph of Liberal Individualism: Law and Politics in New York 1780-1850, in American Chameleon: Individualism in US History, 91; auth, The Nineteenth-Century Revolution in Civil Liberties: From Rights in Property to Property in Rights, This Constitution, Fall 91; auth, Rethinking the State Constitutional Tradition, Rutgers Law Journal 22, Fall 91; auth, The First Contract with American, Wilson Q 20, Winter 96; auth, The Strange Birth of Liberal America, New York Hist 77, Apr 96; Charles Evans Hughes and the Strange Death of Liberal America, Studies in Am Political Devel, Spring 98; coauth, America's History, 87, 92,96; auth, The Origins of American Capitalism, 91; coauth, The Transformation of Early American History, 91; coauth, Evolution and Revolution: American Society, 1600-1820, D. C. Heath & Co., 87. **CONTACT ADDRESS** Dept of Hist, Univ of Maryland, College Park, MD, 20742-7315. **EMAIL** jh35@umail.umd.edu

HENRY, ERIC PUTNAM
PERSONAL Born 03/15/1943, Greensboro, NC, m, 1976, 2 children **DISCIPLINE** CHINESE LITERATURE & HISTORY **EDUCATION** Amherst Col, BA, 72; Yale Univ, Mph, 76, PhD, 79. **CAREER** Vis asst prof Chinese lang & lit, Dartmouth Col, 80-82; LECTR CHINESE LANG, UNIV NC, 82- . **MEMBERSHIPS** Asn Asian Studies; Warring States Project. **RESEARCH** Chinese drama and fiction; Chinese legendary history; Chinese social history. **SELECTED PUBLICATIONS** Auth, Chinese Amusement: The Lively Plays of Li Yu, Shoe String Press, 80. **CONTACT ADDRESS** Asian Studies Curric, Univ N. Carolina, Campus Box 3267, Chapel Hill, NC, 27514. **EMAIL** henryhme@bellsouth.net

HENRY, MILDRED M. DALTON
PERSONAL Tamo, Arkansas **DISCIPLINE** EDUCATION **EDUCATION** AM&N College Pine Bluff, BS Music Ed 1971; Southern IL Univ Edwardsville, MS counselor ed 1976; Southern IL Univ Carbondale, PhD counselor ed 1983. **CAREER** AM&N Coll, sec bus office 1949-51; St Paul Public Library, library asst 1956-58; AM&N Coll, lib asst/secty 1968-71; Pine Bluff School Dist, music teacher 1971-75; Southern IL Univ Edwardsville, library asst 1975; Watson Chapel School Dist, counselor 1976-77; Univ of AR at Pine Bluff, counselor 1978-80; Southern IL Univ at Carbondale, grad asst 1981; Carbondale Elem Sch Dist, teacher 1981-83; CA State Univ San Bernardino, asst prof 1983-. **HONORS AND AWARDS** Leadership Awards Atlanta Univ & UCLA 1978 & 1979; Citizen of Day Radio Station KOTN Pine Bluff 1980; Dean's Fellowship Southern IL Univ Carbondale 1980-81; Outstanding Scholastic Achievement Black Affairs Council SIUC 1981. **MEMBERSHIPS** Adv bd Creative Educators Inc Riverside 1983-; city commissioner Fontanta CA 1984-; exec bd Rialto/Fontana NAACP 1984-; pres Provisional Educ Services Inc 1984-; Amer Assn of Univ Profs; Natl Educ Assn; CA Faculty Assn; CA Teachers Assn; CA Assn of Counseling Develop; Assn of Teacher Educators; CA Black Faculty and Staff Assn; CA State Employees Assn, Inland Empire Peace Officers Assn; NAACP; Natl Council of Negro Women; steering comm San Bernardino Area Black Chamber of Commerce; San Bernardino Private Industry Council. **SELECTED PUBLICATIONS** Auth, "Setting Up a Responsive Guidance Program in a Middle School" The Guidance Clinic 1979. **CONTACT ADDRESS** California State Univ, San Bernardino, 5500 University Pkwy, San Bernardino, CA, 92407.

HENRY, SAMUEL DUDLEY
PERSONAL Born 10/09/1947, Washington, District of Columbia, m, 1988 **DISCIPLINE** EDUCATION **EDUCATION** DC Teachers Coll, BS 1969; Columbia Univ, MA 1974, EdD 1978. **CAREER** Binghamton, eng/soc studies teacher 1971-73; HMLI Columbia Univ Teachers Coll, rsch assoc 1975-77; Sch of Ed Univ MA Amherst, asst prof 1977-78; Race Desegregation Ctr for NY, NJ, VI & PR, dir 1978-81; San Jose State Univ, dir of Equal Opportunity & Affirmative Action; CSU Northridge, Northridge CA, School of Education, assoc dean (acting) 1988-; San Jose State Univ, San Jose CA, School of Social Sciences, assoc dean 1987-88, assistant vice pres for Student Affairs, 1989-92; Portland State University, executive director, Portland Educational Network, 1992-94; Urban Fellow and Associate Professor of Education, beginning 1994-; Depaun Univ, chair of ed dept, 1998-99. **HONORS AND AWARDS** Outstanding Serv Awd Disabled Students SJSU 1982-83; Commendation Curr Study Comm East Side Union HS Dist 1984; AA in Higher Educ/2nd Annual Conf on Desegregation in Postsecondary 1984. **MEMBERSHIPS** Exec bd Greenfield Secondary Sch Comm 1977-79; sponsor Harlem Ebonetts Girls Track Team 1980-81; exec bd Santa Clara Valley Urban League 1982-83; exec bd CAAAO,CA Assoc of Affirmative Action Off 1983-84; mem Prog Comm No CA Fair Employ Roundtable 1983-85; mem ASCD Assoc of Supr of Curr Ser 1984-85; mem bd of dirs Campus Christian Ministry 1984-85; San Jose Roundtable, chair-drug prevention task force. **CONTACT ADDRESS** Urban Fellow & Associate Professor of Education, PO Box 751, Portland, OR, 97207-0751.

HENRY TSAI, SHIN SHAN
DISCIPLINE HISTORY **EDUCATION** Univ Oregon, PhD. **CAREER** Prof. **SELECTED PUBLICATIONS** Auth, The Chinese Experience in America, Univ Ind, 86; The Eunuchs in the Ming Dynasty, SUNY, 96. **CONTACT ADDRESS** History Dept, Univ of Arkansas, Fayetteville, 505 Old Main, Fayetteville, AR, 72701. **EMAIL** htsai@comp.uark.edu

HENWOOD, JAMES N.J.
PERSONAL Born 04/17/1932, Upper Darby, PA **DISCIPLINE** AMERICAN & MODERN EUROPEAN HISTORY **EDUCATION** West Chester State Col, BSEd, 54; Univ PA, AM, 58, PhD, 75. **CAREER** Tchr, high sch, PA, 58-66; assoc prof, 66-75, prof hist, East Stroudsburg Univ, 75; bk rev ed, Railroad Hist, and National Railway Bulletin. **MEMBERSHIPS** Orgn Am Historians; AHA; Nat Railway Hist Soc; Steamship Hist Soc Am; Railway & Locomotive Hist Soc. **RESEARCH** Twentieth century Am hist; railroad and maritime hist. **SELECTED PUBLICATIONS** Auth, Team teaching, Pa Sch J, 3/68; A Short Haul to the Bay, Greene, 69; A Cruise on the USS Sabine, Am Neptune, 4/69; Experiment in relief: The CWA in Pennsylvania, Pa Hist, 1/72; coauth, Monroe County, An Area in Transition, Pa Heritage, 10/84; Laurel Line: An Anthracite Region Railway, Interurban Press, 86; auth, Country Carrier of the Poconos: The Delaware Valley Railroad, Railroad Hist 174; contribr, Railroads in the Age of Regulation, 1900-1980; contribr, American National Biography, Oxford, 98. **CONTACT ADDRESS** Dept of Hist, East Stroudsburg Univ of Pennsylvania, 200 Prospect St, East Stroudsburg, PA, 18301-2999.

HERBENICK, RAYMOND M.
DISCIPLINE CLASSICAL PHILOSOPHY, LOGIC **EDUCATION** Georgetown Univ, Phd, 68. **CAREER** Dept Philos, Univ Dayton **RESEARCH** Applied ethics, history of Slavic philosophy. **SELECTED PUBLICATIONS** Auth, Remarks on Abortion, Abandonment, and Adoption Opportunities, Philosophy and Public Affairs, Princeton Univ Press, 75; Basic Logic: A Systems Approach to the Structures and Principles of Logical Reasoning, Ginn, 85; Carpatho-Rusyn American Index: A Computerized Bibliography Vols1-11 (78-88), Carpatho-Rusyn Res Ctr, 91; Augustine's Moral Thermometer of Human Goodness, Univ Dayton Rev, 94. **CONTACT ADDRESS** Dept of Philos, Univ Dayton, 300 Col Park, Dayton, OH, 75062. **EMAIL** herbenic@checkov.hm.udayton.edu

HERBER, CHARLES JOSEPH
PERSONAL Born 07/04/1930, Allentown, PA, m, 1957 **DISCIPLINE** MODERN EUROPEAN HISTORY **EDUCATION** Dickinson Col, AB, 52; Univ Calif, Berkeley, MA, 57, PhD(hist), 65. **CAREER** Asst prof, 60-65, chmn dept, 71-73, assoc prof Europ hist, 65- , chemn dept, 83-84, George Washington Univ. **HONORS AND AWARDS** Woodrow Wilson fel, 55-56. **MEMBERSHIPS** AHA; Conf Group Cent Europ Hist; AAUP; Ger Stud Asn. **RESEARCH** Politics of peace in time of war, 1916-1918; German history in the modern era; the age of Austrian Baroque. **SELECTED PUBLICATIONS** Auth, Economic and social aspects of Austrian Baroque architecture,

Eighteenth-Century Life, 6/77; auth, Eugenio Pacelli's Mission to germany and the Papal Peace Proposals of 1917, Cath Hist Rev, 79; co-auth, Conflict and Stability: Modern Europe, 1870-1970, Lexington, MA, 83; auth, Secular Implications of Religious Building Construction, in, Sangallensia in Washington, New York, 93; auth, Regulation or Disequilibration: Intervention in Economic and Social Matters in Late Eighteenth-Century German Lands, in, Consortium on Revolutionary Europe, 1750-1850: Selected papers, 1995, Tallahassee, 95. **CONTACT ADDRESS** Dept of History, George Washington Univ, 2035 H St NW, Washington, DC, 20052-0001. **EMAIL** cherber@gwu.edu

HERBERT, EUGENIA WARREN
PERSONAL Born 09/08/1929, Summit, NJ, m, 1953, 3 children **DISCIPLINE** HISTORY **EDUCATION** Wellesley Col, BA, 51; Yale Univ, MA, 53, PhD(hist), 57. **CAREER** Asst prof, 78-80, assoc, 80-85, E. Nevius Rodman prof hist, 85-97, E. NEVIUS RODMAN PROF HIST EMER, MOUNT HOLYOKE COL, 97-, Stevens traveling fel hist, Wellesley Col, 68-69; book rev ed, African Studies Review, 97-. **HONORS AND AWARDS** Winship Book Award, Boston Globe, 76. **MEMBERSHIPS** African Studies Asn; Hist Metal Soc; Royal Geog Soc. **RESEARCH** History of copper in Africa; historical roles of women in Africa. **SELECTED PUBLICATIONS** Auth, Alcune istituzioni commerciali anseatiche del medioevo, Rivista di Storia del Diritto Italiano, 55; coauth, Artists and anarchism: unpublished letters of Pissarro, Signac and others, Burlington Mag, 60; auth, The Artist and Social Reform, Yale Univ, 61; Aspects of the use of copper in pre-colonial West Africa, J African Hist, 73; Portuguese adaptation to trade patterns, Guinea to Angola, 1443-1640, African Studies Rev, 74; Smallpox inoculation in Africa, J African Hist, 75; coauth, The Private Franklin, W W Norton, 75; contribr, Timbuktu: a case study of the role of legend in history, West African Culture Dynamics, Mouton, 78; auth, Red Gold of AFrica: Copper in Precolonial History and Culture, Univ Wis Press, 84; auth, Iron, Gender and Power: Rituals of Transformation in African Socieites, Indiana Univ Press, 93; co- ed, Social Approaches to an Industrial Past: The Archaeology and Anthropology of Mining, Routledge, 98. **CONTACT ADDRESS** Dept of Hist, Mount Holyoke Col, South Hadley, MA, 01075. **EMAIL** eherbert@mtholyoke.edu

HERBERT, LUFT
DISCIPLINE MODERN EUROPEAN HISTORY **EDUCATION** Pepperdine Univ, BA, 65, MA, 66; Univ S CA, PhD, 76. **CAREER** Prof, Pepperdine Univ, 67-; asst, Ger, 67-74; assoc, 75-82; full prof, 82-; exec VP, Pepperdine Univ, 81-83; dean, Europ Prog Pepperdine Univ, 83-93. **HONORS AND AWARDS** Outstanding Young Men of Am, 87, 96; scholar(s) for the dream, 95; Phi Alpha Theta Hist hon. **MEMBERSHIPS** Mem, Am Hist Assn; Ger Studies Assn; Soc Who's Who in die World, 95, 96; Who's Who in the West, 92; Who's Who in CA, 97. **RESEARCH** Africa in late nineteenth century. **SELECTED PUBLICATIONS** Rev(s), Norman M. Naimark, The Russians in Germany, The History of the Soviet Occupation 45-49, Harvard UP, 95; Eugene Davidson, The Unmaking of Adolf Hitler, 97; Hamerow, Theodore S, On the Road to the Wolfs Lair, German Resistance to Hitler, The Belknap Press Harvard UP, 97; Micham Jr, Samuel W, Why Hitler? The Genesis of the Nazi Reich Preaeger, Ger Studies Assn Jour, 98 **CONTACT ADDRESS** Pepperdine Univ, 24255 Pacific Coast Hwy, Malibu, CA, 90263. **EMAIL** hluft@pepperdine.edu

HERBERT, SANDRA
PERSONAL Born 04/10/1942, Chicago, IL, m, 1966, 2 children **DISCIPLINE** INTERDISCIPLINARY STUDIES **EDUCATION** Wittenberg Univ, BA, 63; Brandeis Univ, MA, 65, PhD, 68. **CAREER** Asst prof, 73-78, assoc prof, 78-86, prof, 86-, Univ Maryland; vis asst prof, 76, vis assoc prof, 84, Princeton Univ. **CONTACT ADDRESS** Dept of History, Univ of Maryland, Baltimore County, 1000 Hilltop Circle, Baltimore, MD, 21250. **EMAIL** herbert@umbc.edu

HERBERT, SANDRA SWANSON
PERSONAL Born 04/10/1942, Chicago, IL, m, 1966, 2 children **DISCIPLINE** SCIENCE/HISTORY **EDUCATION** Wittenberg Univ, BA, 63; Brandeis Univ, MA, 65. PhD, 68. **CAREER** Vis cur, Hist Sci, Smithsonian Inst, 67-68; postdoctoral fel, Smithsonian Inst, 70-71; asst prof, Hist, Univ Md, 73-78; vis asst prof, Hist/Philos Sci, Princeton Univ, 76; vis assoc prof, Hist Sci, Princeton Univ, 84; PROF, HIST, UNIV MD, 86-; sr postdoctoral fel, Smithsonian Inst, 89-90. **MEMBERSHIPS** Hist Sci Soc; Am Hist Asn; Am Asn Univ Prof **SELECTED PUBLICATIONS** edr, The Red Notebook of Charles Darwin, Cornell Univ Press, 80; co-edr, Charles Darwin's Notebooks, 1836-1844: Geology, Transmutation of Species, Metaphysical Enquiries, Cornell Univ Press, 87. **CONTACT ADDRESS** Univ Md, Baltimore, MD, 21228.

HERLAN, RONALD WALLACE
PERSONAL Born 03/19/1942, Buffalo, NY, m, 1966, 2 children **DISCIPLINE** EARLY MODERN EUROPEAN & ENGLISH HISTORY, WORLD & LOCAL HISTORY **EDUCATION** Houghton Col, BA, 64; State Univ NY, Buffalo, MA, 67, PhD(hist), 73. **CAREER** Asst prof, 70-80, assoc prof hist, State Univ NY Col Brockport, 79-, State Univ NY Res Found grant-in-aid, 74 & 77 & fac res fel, 76-77; Willmott Found Grant, 87. **MEMBERSHIPS** Conf Brit Studies; Past & Present Soc; Hist Film Comt; London Rec Soc. **RESEARCH** Tudor-Stuart England; English poor relief; historical demography; local hist. **SELECTED PUBLICATIONS** Auth, Social articulation and the configuration of parochial poverty in London on the eve of the restoration, 4/76, Poor relief in the London parish of Antholin's budge row, 1638-1664, 4/77 & Poor relief in the London Parish of Dunstan in the west during the English revolution, 10/77, Guildhall Studies London Hist; Relief of the poor in Bristol from late Elizabethan times until the Restoration Era, Proc Am Philos Soc, Vol 126, 82; Local History materials in Drake Memorial Library, SUNY Col Brockport: An annotated bibliography with index of names and places, 1988; Hillside Cemetery. 125 Years, 92. **CONTACT ADDRESS** Dept of History, SUNY, Brockport, 350 New Campus Dr, Brockport, NY, 14420-2956. **EMAIL** rherlan@po.brockport.edu

HERMAN, BERNARD L.
DISCIPLINE ART HISTORY **EDUCATION** Col William and Mary, BA, 73; Univ Pa, PhD, 78. **CAREER** Lectr, Amer stud prog, 77-80; res assoc, 81-85; asst dir, Ctr Hist Arch and Engg, 84-85; asst prof, dept hist, 81-89; asst prof, Col Urban Aff and Pub Policy, 85-89; sr policy sci, 85-93; assoc prof, dept hist, 89-98; prof, dept hist, 98-; assoc prof, Col Urban Aff and Pub Policy, 89-98; prof, Col Urban Aff and Pub Policy, 98-; assoc dir, Ctr Hist Arch and Engg, 85-; assoc prof, 93-98; prof, 98-. **HONORS AND AWARDS** Abbott Lowell Cummings award, Vernacular Arch Forum, 87, 93; excellence in tchg, Univ Del, 92; Fred Kniffen prize, Pioneer Amer Soc, 92; Univ Del gen res grant, 95; summer res fel, NEH, 95; res fel, NEH, 96-97., Ch, Evaluation Comm, Univ Delaware Seaford Hist Soc, 92-93; bk rev recognition, NY Times. **MEMBERSHIPS** Mem, Vernacular Arch Forum; Soc Hist Archaeol. **RESEARCH** Folklore and folklife. **SELECTED PUBLICATIONS** Coauth, A Land and Life Remembered: Americo-Liberian Folk Architecture, Univ Ga Press, 88; Everyday Architecture of the Mid-Atlantic: Looking at Buildings and Landscapes, Johns Hopkins Univ Press, 97; auth, Architecture and Rural Life in Central Delaware: 1700-00, Tenn Univ Press, 87; The Stolen House, Va Univ Press, 92; ed, Historical Archaeology and the Study of American Culture, Tenn Univ Press, 96; rev(s), North Carolina Architecture by Catherine Bishir, Jour Soc Arch Hist, 94; Back of the Big House by John Vlach, SC Hist Mag, 94; The Old Village and the Great House: An Archaeological and Historical Example of Drax Hall Plantation, St. Anne's Bay, Jamaica by Douglas V. Armstrong, Jour Amer Folklore, 95; Housing Culture: Traditional Architecture in an English Landscape by Matthew Johnson, Amer Anthrop, 95. **CONTACT ADDRESS** Dept of Art Hist, Univ Delaware, 162 Ctr Mall, Newark, DE, 19716.

HERMAN, GERALD HARVEY
PERSONAL Born 09/13/1944, Brooklyn, NY, m, 1965, 2 children **DISCIPLINE** CONTEMPORARY HISTORY **EDUCATION** Hunter Col, BA, 65; Northeastern Univ, MA, 67. **CAREER** Instr, 65-71, asst prof hist, Northeastern Univ, 71, Spec Asst to the Provost, 78-88, Spec Asst to the Univ Counsel, 88, Actg Chmn Dept Hist, 98-99; hist consult, WGBH-Boston, 76-; fac develop officer, Northeastern Univ, 77. **HONORS AND AWARDS** Mellon Found grant, 73-74; OH State Award for Excellence in Educational, Informational, and Public Affairs Broadcasting, 80; Northeastern Univ Excellence in Tchg Award, 83; "Reaching for New Standards: Partnerships Take the Lead" Award, Am Asn Higher Educ, 92. **MEMBERSHIPS** AHA; Hist Sci Soc; Film Comt. **RESEARCH** Contemp philos of hist; tchg of hist; Romanticism; media in hist. **SELECTED PUBLICATIONS** Ed, World War I: The Destroying Fathers Confirmed, Northeastern Univ, 72; auth, Making multimedia lectures for classroom use: A case history, Film & Hist, 12/72; coauth, To Know Thyself, Northeastern Univ, 73; A mediated instructional model to assure student competence in the history of Western civilization, Int J Instrnl Media, 76-77; auth, An integration of teacher and technology in a western civilization program, Soc Hist Educ Network News Exchange, fall 77; For God and Country: Khartoum as an Object Lesson for Global Policemen, Film & Hist, 79; coauth, Wien 1910, Film & Hist, 83; Media and History, In: The Craft of Public History, 83; World History on the Screen, 90, repr, 95; co-prodr, Public History Today, 90; auth, The Pivotal Conflict, 92; coauth, U.S. History on the Screen, 94; auth, The Great War Revisioned, In: Hollywood's World War I, 97. **CONTACT ADDRESS** Dept of Hist, Northeastern Univ, 360 Huntington Ave, Boston, MA, 02115-5000. **EMAIL** GHerman@lynx.neu.edu

HERMAN, PHYLLIS
PERSONAL Born 03/20/1946, Los Angeles, CA, m, 1973, 1 child **DISCIPLINE** HISTORY **EDUCATION** UCLA, PhD, 79. **CAREER** Calif State Univ Northridge, lectr, asst prof, 75-. **HONORS AND AWARDS** Calif State Univ, Gold Key Society Award. **MEMBERSHIPS** AAR, AAUW, SCICSA. **RESEARCH** Hinduism; women and religion. **SELECTED PUBLICATIONS** Auth, Relocating Ramarajya, Int Jour Hindu Studies, 98. **CONTACT ADDRESS** Dept of Religious Studies, California State Univ, Northridge, 18111 Nordhoff St, Northridge, CA, 90024. **EMAIL** prk45739@csuni.csun.edu

HERMANN, RICHARD
DISCIPLINE MUSIC **EDUCATION** Yale Univ, PhD. **CAREER** Assoc prof, Univ N Mex. **HONORS AND AWARDS** Ed, Winds Quarterly. **SELECTED PUBLICATIONS** Auth, Music Theory Online, Theory and Practice, Sonus, J Musicol Res; ed, Concert Music, Rock, and Jazz since 1945: Essays and Analytical Studies Rochester, Ken Dorn, 95. **CONTACT ADDRESS** Music Dept, Univ NMex, 1805 Roma NE, Albuquerque, NM, 87131. **EMAIL** paaffair@unm.edu

HERR, RICHARD
PERSONAL Born 04/07/1922, Guanajuato, Mexico, m, 1968, 4 children **DISCIPLINE** HISTORY **EDUCATION** Harvard Col, AB, 43; Univ Chicago, PhD, 54. **CAREER** Instr to asst prof, Yale Univ 52-29; asst to assoc to prof PROF EMER, UNIV CALIF, BERKELEY, 55-. **HONORS AND AWARDS** Bronze medal, Col de France, Paris, 85; Clare Hall, Cambridge, Eng, vis life member, 85-, Chancellor's fel, Univ Calif, Berkeley, 87-90; Comendador, Order of Isabel La Catolica, Spain, 88; Fel, Am Acad Arts & Sci, 90; Am Hist Asn Gershoy Prize for Rural Change and Royal Finances in Spain, 90; The Berkeley Citation, Univ Calif-Berkeley, 91, Am Philos Soc. **MEMBERSHIPS** Inst for Hist Stud; Soc for Spanish and Portuguese Hist Stud; Asn de Hist Demografica; Asn de Hist Economica. **RESEARCH** History of modern Spain, history of agriculture, modern history of group identities. **SELECTED PUBLICATIONS** Ed & contr, Themes in the Rural History of the Western World, Iowa State Univ Press, 93; ed & contr, The New Portugal: Democracy and Europe, Univ Calif, Intl and Area Stud, 93; auth, "The Constitution of 1812 and the Spanish Road to Parliamentary Monarchy," in Revolution and the Meanings of Freedom in the Nineteenth Century, Stanford Univ Press, 96; "El principio de la virtud y la critica politica: los origenes de la Monarquia constitucional en Francia y Espana," in Sociedad Espanola de Estudios del Siglo XVIII, El Mundo hispancio en el siglo de las luces, 96. **CONTACT ADDRESS** 1541 Hawthorne Terr, Berkeley, CA, 94708-1805. **EMAIL** rherr@socrates.berkeley.edu

HERREN, MICHAEL W.
PERSONAL Born 12/15/1940, Santa Ana, CA **DISCIPLINE** HUMANITIES/CLASSICS **EDUCATION** Claremont Men's Col, BA, 62; Pontif Inst Medieval Stud, MSL, 67; Univ Toronto, PhD, 69. **CAREER** High sch tchr, Calif, 62-64; asst to assoc prof, 69-78, PROF HUMANITIES AND CLASSICS, YORK UNIV, 78-, ch hum, 82-85; grad fac medieval stud, Univ Toronto, 90-. **HONORS AND AWARDS** Assoc fel, Clare Hall, Cambridge Univ, 74; SSHRCC leave fel, 80-81, 87-88; Alexander von Humboldt res fel, Munich, 81-82; Atkinson Col res fel, 86-87; sr res fel, class, King's Col London, 87-88; DAAD fel, 92; Killam res fel, 95-97. **MEMBERSHIPS** Medieval Acad Am; Medieval Latin Asn Am; Soc Promotion Eriugenian Stud; Soc Hiberno-Latin Stud. **SELECTED PUBLICATIONS** Auth, Hisperica Famina I: The A-Text, 74, II: Related Poems, 87; auth, Aldhelm: The Prose Works, 79; auth, Johannis Scotti Eriugenae Carmina, 93; ed, Insular Latin Studies, 82; ed, The Sacred Nectar of the Greeks, 88; ed, J Medieval Latin, 91-; comp, Latin Letters in Early Christian Ireland, 96. **CONTACT ADDRESS** York Univ, 4700 Keele St, North York, ON, M3J 1P3.

HERRERA, ROBERT ANTHONY
PERSONAL Born 10/31/1933, Spring Lake, NJ, m **DISCIPLINE** MEDIEVAL PHILOSOPHY, PHILOSOPHY OF RELIGION **EDUCATION** Col St Thomas, BA, 53; New Sch Soc Res, MA, 65, PhD, 75. **CAREER** Vis asst prof philos, Rutgers Univ, 70-71; assoc prof, 73-79, Prof Philos, Seton Hall Univ, 79-97, Prof Emeritus, 98-; Adj fac, New Sch Soc Res, 68-73, Baruch Col, 70-72 & Immaculate Conception Sem, 70-71; consult, Judeao-Christian Inst, Seton, 76- & Christendom Col, 77. **HONORS AND AWARDS** Seton Hall Univ res grant, 77, 78, 79, 82, 84; Canagie summer grant, 70; NS Hum grant, 82; Wilbur Found grant, 95; Earhart Found grant, 98. **MEMBERSHIPS** Am Philos Asn; Am Cath Philos Asn. **RESEARCH** Early medieval thought (emphasis on Anselm); the Augustinian tradition; 19th-20th century Span polit thought (emphasis on Donoso Cortes). **SELECTED PUBLICATIONS** Auth, John of the Cross: Introductory studies, Rev Espiritualidad, Madrid, 68; contribr, God in Contemporary Thought Nauwelaerts, Louvain, 77; auth, Anselm's Proslogion, Univ Press, 78; contribr, J Hist Philos, Mod Schoolman, Angus Triniana, Philos Today & Analecta Anselmiana; Lamps of Fire, St Bedes Pub, 79; Donoso Contes: Cassandrs of the Age; Eerdmans, 95; ed, Mystics of the Book, Peter Lang, 93; Saints Scholars and Sovereigns, Peter Lang, 94. **CONTACT ADDRESS** Dept of Philos, Seton Hall Univ, 400 S Orange Ave, South Orange, NJ, 07079-2697.

HERRING, GEORGE C.
PERSONAL Born 05/23/1936, Blacksburg, VA, m, 1995, 2 children **DISCIPLINE** HISTORY **EDUCATION** Roanoke Col, BA, 57; Univ Va, MA, 62, PhD, 65. **CAREER** Prof, 65-69, Ohio Univ; alumni prof, chair, distinguished prof, 69-, Univ Ky; vis prof, 91, Univ Otago, Dunedin, New Zealand; vis prof, 93-94, US Milit Acad. **HONORS AND AWARDS** NEH FEL, 76-77; Fulbright Award, 91; Guggenheim Fel, 97-98; Moncado Award for Excellence in Milit Hist, 81; **MEMBERSHIPS** Soc

for Hist of Amer Foreign Rel; Amer Hist Assoc. **RESEARCH** U S Foreign relations; Vietnam War. **SELECTED PUBLICATIONS** Auth, America's Longest War: The United States and Vietnam, 1950-1975, McGraw-Hill, 96; auth, The Secret Diplomacy of the Vietnam War: The Negotiating Volumes of the Pentagon Papers, Univ Tx Press, 83; auth, LBJ and Vietnam: A Different Kind of War, Univ Tx press, 94. **CONTACT ADDRESS** History Dept, Univ Ky, Lexington, KY, 40506-0027. **EMAIL** gherrin@pop.uky.edu

HERSEY, GEORGE LEONARD
PERSONAL Born 08/30/1927, Cambridge, MA, m, 1953, 2 children **DISCIPLINE** HISTORY OF ART **EDUCATION** Harvard Univ, BA, 51; Yale Univ, MFA, 54, MA, 61, PhD(hist of art), 64. **CAREER** From instr to asst prof art, Bucknell Univ, 54-59, actg chmn dept, 58-59; from instr to prof hist of art, Yale Univ, 63-; dir grad studies, 68-71; dir spec prog humanities, Yale Col, 75-76; mem adv board Conn Preservation Trust, 77-79; mem Conn State Commn Capitol Restoration, 77-79; lectr, Princeton Univ, Columbia Univ, others; mem adv board: J of Pre-Raphaelite and Aesthetic Studies; art exhibition co-orgnr, The Taste of Angels: Neapolitan Paintings in North America, 1650-1750, Yale Univ Art Gallery and other museums, 87-88. **HONORS AND AWARDS** Recipient Monticello Prize, 61; Fulbright scholar, Italy, 62; Am Philos Soc fel, Italy, 62; Morse fel, Yale Univ, 66-67; Schepp fel, Florence, Italy, 72. **MEMBERSHIPS** Renaissance Soc Am; Col Art Asn; Soc Archit Historians, dir, 71-73; Victorian Soc (US and Gr Brit), dir chapt; Dunky Club. **RESEARCH** Italian Renaissance art; Victorian art. **SELECTED PUBLICATIONS** Auth, J C Loudon and Architectural Associationism, Archit Rev, 68; The Arch of Alfonso in Naples and its Pisanellesque Design, Master Drawings, 69; Alfonso II and the Artistic Renewal of Naples, 1485-1495, Yale Univ, 69; Associationism and Sensibility in Eighteenth-Century Architecture, 18th Century Studies, spring 71; High Victorian Gothic: A Study in Associationism, Johns Hopkins Univ, 72; The Aragonese Arch at Naples, 1443-1475, Yale Univ, 73; auth, Poggioreale: Notes on a Reconstruction, and an Early Replication, Architectura, 73; Pythagorean Palaces: Architecture and Magic in the Renaissance, Cornell Univ, 76; Architecture, Poetry, and Number in the Royal Palace at Caserta, 83; co-ed, Architectura, 71-; ed, Yale Publs in History of Art, 74-. **CONTACT ADDRESS** Dept Hist of Art, Yale Univ, New Haven, CT, 06520-0000. **EMAIL** glherse@pantheon.yale.edu

HERSHKOWITZ, LEO
PERSONAL Born 11/21/1924, New York, NY, m, 1953, 2 children **DISCIPLINE** HISTORY **EDUCATION** Hunter Col, BA, 50; Columbia Univ, MA, 54; NY Univ, PhD(hist), 60. **CAREER** From instr to assoc prof, 60-70, prof Hist, Queens Col, NY, 70-. **MEMBERSHIPS** AHA; Am Jewish Hist Soc. **RESEARCH** New York City history. **SELECTED PUBLICATIONS** Auth, Native American Democratic Association in New York City, 1/62 & Loco Foco party of New York, 7/62, NY Hist Soc Quart; Troublesome Turk: An Illustration of Judicial Process in New Amsterdam, NY Hist, 10/65; ed, Wills of Early New York Jews, 67 & co-ed, Letters of the Franks Family, 68, Am Jewish Hist Soc; auth, Tweed's New York: Another Look, Doubleday, 76. **CONTACT ADDRESS** Dept of Hist, Queens Col, CUNY, 6530 Kissena Blvd, Flushing, NY, 11367-1597.

HERVEY, NORMA J.
PERSONAL Born 10/28/1935, Akron, OH, m, 1955, 6 children **DISCIPLINE** HISTORY **EDUCATION** Univ Akron, BA, 56; SUNY, Geneseo, MLS, 72; St Bonaventure Univ, MA, 80; Univ Minn, PhD, 91. **CAREER** Instr, asst prof, 70-80, Bonaventure Univ; assoc prof, 80-81, Univ Arkansas; assoc prof, 81-88, Gustavus Adolphus Col; vis prof, 94-95, Palackeho Univ, Czech Rep; prof, 88-, Luther Col. **RESEARCH** Ethnicity, human rights, peace stud, comm stud; soc & econ hist. **CONTACT ADDRESS** Luther Col, 700 College Drive, Decorah, IA, 52101. **EMAIL** herveynj@luther.edu

HERZMAN, RONALD BERNARD
PERSONAL Born 11/17/1943, Brooklyn, NY, m, 1970, 2 children **DISCIPLINE** ENGLISH LITERATURE, MEDIEVAL STUDIES **EDUCATION** Manhattan Col, BA, 65; Univ Del, MA, 67, PhD(English), 69. **CAREER** Instr English, Univ Del, 68-69; asst prof, 69-79, ASSOC PROF ENGLISH, STATE UNIV NY, GENESEO, 79-, Fel in residence English, Univ Chicago, 78-79. **MEMBERSHIPS** Dante Soc Am. **RESEARCH** Dante; Chaucer; interdisciplinary medieval studies. **SELECTED PUBLICATIONS** Auth, Squaring the Circle--Exploring the Artistry of Dante in His 'Divine Commedia'--'Paradiso', and the Poetics of Geometry, Traditio-Studies Ancient Medieval Hist Thought Relig, Vol 0049, 94. **CONTACT ADDRESS** Dept of English, State Univ of NY, 1 College Cir, Geneseo, NY, 14454-1401.

HERZSTEIN, ROBERT EDWIN
PERSONAL Born 09/26/1940, New York, NY, s **DISCIPLINE** HISTORY **EDUCATION** NY Univ, BA, 61, PhD, 64. **CAREER** Asst prof, M.I.T., 66-72; from assoc prof to prof, Univ of SC, 78- ; Carolina distinguished prof, 90- . **HONORS AND AWARDS** Distinguished scholarship by an alumnus, NY Univ; Russell Award in the Humanities and Soc Scis, Univ of SC. **MEMBERSHIPS** German Studies Asns; Soc for Hists of Am Foreign Relations; Southern Hist Asn. **RESEARCH** Germany, espec World War II and Holocaust; Recent U.S. history; Media and politics in Germany and the U.S. **SELECTED PUBLICATIONS** Auth, Adolf Hitler and the German Trauma: An Interpretation of the Nazi Phenomenon 1913-1945, 74; Western Civilization, 75; The War that Hitler Won: Goebbels and the Nazi Media Campaign, 78; The Nazis, Time-Life World War II series, 80; When Nazi Dreams Come True: The Third Reich's Internal Struggle Over the Future of Europe after a German Victory, 82; Waldheim: The Missing Years, 88; Roosevelt and Hitler: Prelude to War, 89; Henry R. Luce: A Political History of the Man Who Created the American Century, 94, Marketing America's Cold War in Asia: Henry R. Luce, Time Inc., and the Politics of Intervention, forthcoming; ed, The Holy Roman Empire, 66; Adolf Hitler and the Third Reich, 71; coed, The Evolution of Western Society, 3 vols, 74-78; contribur, Image as Artifact: The Historical Analysis of Film and Television, 90; Historians and Archivists: Essays in Modern German History and Archival Policy, 91; George C. Marshall's China Mediation Mission, December 1945-January 1947. **CONTACT ADDRESS** Dept of History, South Carolina Univ, Columbia, SC, 29208. **EMAIL** Herzstein@Garnet.CLA.sc.edu

HESLA, DAVID H.
PERSONAL Born 10/14/1929, Stevens Point, WI, m, 1956, 2 children **DISCIPLINE** LITERATURE; HISTORY OF IDEAS **EDUCATION** St Olaf Col, BA, 51; Univ Chicago, AM, 56, PhD, 64. **CAREER** Instr English, St Olaf Col, 55-56; from instr to asst prof, Cornell Col, 61-65; instr lit & theol, 65-70, assoc prof humanities, Emory Univ, 70-, consult, Miles Col, 71-72. **HONORS AND AWARDS** Fulbright lectr, US Educ Found, Finland, 72-73. **MEMBERSHIPS** Am Acad Relig. **RESEARCH** Religious dimensions of literature; modern British and American literature; literary criticism and theory. **SELECTED PUBLICATIONS** Auth, Theological ambiguity in the Catholic novels, In: Graham Greene, Univ KY, 63; The two roles of Norman Mailer, Adversity & Grace, 68; The Shape of Chaos: An Interpretation of the Art of Samuel Beckett, Univ Minn, 71. **CONTACT ADDRESS** Emory Univ, 1364 Clifton Rd NE, Atlanta, GA, 30322-0001. **EMAIL** iladhh@emory.edu

HESS, GARY R.
PERSONAL Born 03/23/1937, Pittsburgh, PA, m, 1966, 1 child **DISCIPLINE** AMERICAN HISTORY **EDUCATION** Univ Pittsburgh, AB, 59; Univ Va, MA, 62, PhD(Hist), 65. **CAREER** From instr to assoc prof, 64-72, prof Hist, Bowling Green State Univ, 72-, chmn dept, 73-81, 85-93-; act dean, Col Arts & Sciences, 81-82; disting research prof, 88-; Nat Endowment for Humanities res fel, 78-79. **HONORS AND AWARDS** Pres, Soc for Historians of Am Foreign Relations, 91; Olscamp Research Award, Bowling Green State Univ, 88; John M Burns Vis Prof, Univ of Hawaii, 93. **MEMBERSHIPS** AHA; Soc Hist Am Foreign Rels; Orgn Am Historians. **RESEARCH** United States foreign policy in South and Southeast Asia; United States diplomacy in World War II; United States foreign policy in early Cold War. **SELECTED PUBLICATIONS** Auth, Sam Higginbottom of Allahabad: Pioneer of Point Four to India, Univ Va, 67; American agricultural missionaries and efforts at economic improvement in India, Agr Hist, 1/68; The Hindu in America: Immigration and naturalization policy and India, 1917-1946, Pac Hist Rev, 2/69; American Encounters India, 1941-1947, Johns Hopkins Univ, 71; Franklin Roosevelt and Indochina, J Am Hist, 9/72; ed, America and Russia: From Cold War Confrontation to Coexistence, Crowell, 73; auth, The Iranian Crisis of 1945-46 and the Cold War, Polit Sci Quart, 4/74; United States policy and the origins of the French-Viet Minh War, 1945-46, Peace & Change, Summer-Fall 75; The Unending Debate: Historians & the Vietnam War, Diplomatic History, Spring, 94. **CONTACT ADDRESS** Dept of History, Bowling Green State Univ, 1001 E Wooster St, Bowling Green, OH, 43403-0001. **EMAIL** ghess@bgnet.bgsu.edu

HESS, WILLIAM HUIE
PERSONAL Born 12/24/1933, Arkadelphia, AR, m, 1954, 2 children **DISCIPLINE** CLASSICS **EDUCATION** Univ TX, BA, 55, MA, 59; Princeton Univ, MA, 62, PhD, 63. **CAREER** Spec instr class, 59-60, from instr to asst prof classics, Univ TX, 62-68; assoc prof, 68-78, Prof Lang & Chmn Dept, Univ UT, 78-83, Prof Emer, 98. **MEMBERSHIPS** Camus **RESEARCH** Greek comedy; ancient relig; hist of ideas. **CONTACT ADDRESS** 1860 Laurelwood Cir, Salt Lake City, UT, 84121-1220.

HESTER, KARLTON EDWARD
DISCIPLINE MUSIC **EDUCATION** Univ Tex at El Paso, BM; San Francisco State Univ, MM; City Univ NY, PhD. **CAREER** Asst prof and Herbert Gussman dir Jazz Stud. **HONORS AND AWARDS** Mellon Postdoct fel, Cornell Univ, 91-92; Nat Endowment for the Arts, composition, 85, 89. **MEMBERSHIPS** Musicians Local 802; ASCAP. **RESEARCH** Contemporary composition; African American music innovators; world music. **SELECTED PUBLICATIONS** Auth, Afrocentric Innovations Some Call 'Jazz' Vols I and II, Fairleigh Dickenson UP, 98; The Melodious and Polyrhythmic Developments in John Coltrane's Spontaneous Compositions within a Racist Society, Edwin Mellen Press, 97; Video review of Tryin' to Get Home: A History of African American Song by Kerrigan Black, for Notes, quart jour Music Libr Asn, 95. **CONTACT ADDRESS** Dept of Music, Cornell Univ, 104 Lincoln Hall, Ithaca, NY, 14853. **EMAIL** keh6@cornell.edu

HETHERINGTON, NORRISS SWIGART
PERSONAL Born 01/30/1942, Berkeley, CA, m, 1966, 2 children **DISCIPLINE** HISTORY OF SCIENCE **EDUCATION** Univ of Calif, Berkeley, BA, 63, MA (astronomy), 65, MA (hist), 67; Indiana Univ, PhD, 70. **CAREER** Res aid, Univ of Calif Forest Products Laboratory, 59; res asst, Univ of Calif Space Sci Laboratory, 63-66; res asst, Lick Observatory, 64; instr, San Mateo Col, 67; instr, Agnes Scott Col, 67-68; asst prof, Atkinson Col, York Univ, 70-72; asst prof, 72-76, chm, Program in History and Philos of Sci, 73-74, staff, Western Civilization Senior Honors, 75-76, Univ Kansas; visiting fel, Henry E. Huntington Libr, 73; asst prof, Razi Univ, 76-77; visiting scholar, hist and philos of sci, Cambridge Univ, 77-78; visiting assoc prof, Univ of Ok, 81; RES ASSOC, OFFICE FOR THE HIST OF SCI AND TECH, UNIV OF CALIF, 78-; DIR, INST FOR THE HIST OF ASTRONOMY, 88-. **HONORS AND AWARDS** Robert H. Goddard Hist Essay Award, 74. **MEMBERSHIPS** Berkeley Sci Historians; Hist Comn, Int Astronomical Union; Inst for the Hist of Astronomy; ed advisory board, Cosmos and Culture; ed advisor, The Oxford Companion to the History of Science and Its Uses. **RESEARCH** History of cosmology; U.S. science, technology, & society. **SELECTED PUBLICATIONS** Auth, Hubble's Cosmology: A Guided Study of Selected Texts, Pachart Pub House, 96; auth, Converting an Hypothesis into a Research Program: T.C. Chamberlin, his Planetesimal Hypothesis, and its Effect on Research at the Mount Wilson Observatory, The Earth, the Heavens, and the Carnegie Inst of Washington: Historical Perspectives after Ninety Years, History of Geophysics, 93; auth, Isaac Newton and Adam Smith: Intellectual Links between Natural Science and Economics, Action and Reaction: Proceedings of a Symposium to Commemorate the Tercentenary of Newton's Principia, 93; auth, Plato and Eudoxus: Instrumentalists, Realists, or Prisoners of Themata?, Studies in Hist and Philos of Sci, 96; auth, Early Greek Cosmology: A Historiographical Review, Culture and Cosmos, 97; ed & contribur, Encyclopedia of Cosmology: Historical, Philosophical, and Scientific Foundations of Modern Cosmology, Garland Pub, 93; auth, Cosmology: Historical, Literary, Philosophical, Religious, and Scientific Perspectives, Garland Pub, 93. **CONTACT ADDRESS** Office for History of Science and Technology, Univ of Calif, 543 Stephens Hall, Berkeley, CA, 94720. **EMAIL** norriss@ohst7.berkeley.edu

HETTINGER, MADONNA
DISCIPLINE HISTORY **EDUCATION** St Francis Univ, AB, 77; Ind Univ, MA, 79, PhD, 86. **CAREER** Assoc prof. **RESEARCH** Women's writing and women's performance in the Renaissance. **SELECTED PUBLICATIONS** Auth, Defining the Servant, The Work of Work, Cruithne Press, 94. **CONTACT ADDRESS** Dept of Hist, Col of Wooster, Wooster, OH, 44691.

HEUCHEMER, DANE
DISCIPLINE MUSIC **EDUCATION** Univ Northern Colo, BM, 88; Ithaca Col, MM, 90; Univ Cincinnati, DPhil, 97. **CAREER** Asst prof mus, 97- ,vis inst mus, 95-97, Kenyon Col. **HONORS AND AWARDS** Presser Scholar, 94. **MEMBERSHIPS** AMS; Hist Brass Soc; Col Band Dir Nat Asn. **RESEARCH** Renaissance Music, particularly in Germany and Italy; Performance Practice. **SELECTED PUBLICATIONS** Italian Musicians in Dresden in the Second Half of the Sixteenth Century, with an Emphasis on the Lives and Works of Antonio Scandello and Giovanni Battista Pinello di Ghirardi, Univ Cincinnati, 97. **CONTACT ADDRESS** Music Dept, Kenyon Col, Gambier, OH, 43022. **EMAIL** heuchemerd@kenyon.edu

HEWLETT, RICHARD GREENING
PERSONAL Born 02/12/1923, Toledo, OH, m, 1946 **DISCIPLINE** HISTORY OF TECHNOLOGY **EDUCATION** Univ Chicago, MA, 48, PhD, 52. **CAREER** Intel specialist, 51-52, US Air Force, Wash DC; prog analyst, 52-57, chief hist, 57-75, US Atomic Energy Comn, Wash, DC; chief hist, US Energy Res & Develop Admin, 75-77; chief hist, US Dept Energy, 77-80; sr vice pres, sr hist, 80-, chmn, 90-98, History Assoc, Inc, Rockville MD; Regents Lect, Uiv Calif, 82; historiographer, Wash Natl Cathedral & Episcopal Diocese of Wash, 78-. **HONORS AND AWARDS** David D Lloyd Prize, Truman Libr Inst, 70; Dist Serv Award, US Atomic Energy Comn, 73; Richard W. Leopold Prize, orgn Am Hist, 90; Henry Adams Prize, Soc Hist in Fed Govt, 90; Franklin D Roosevelt Award, Soc Hist in Fed Govt, 93. **MEMBERSHIPS** AHA; Orgn Am Historians; Soc Hist Technol; Am Nuclear Soc Hist Sci Soc; Soc Hist in Fed Govt; Natl Coun on Public Hist; Hist Soc Episcopal Church. **RESEARCH** History of science and technology; history of the Episcopal Church. **SELECTED PUBLICATIONS** Coauth, The New World, 1939-1946, Vol I, 62 & Atomic shield, 1947-1952, Vol II, Atomic Energy Commission History, Pa State Univ, 69; auth, Nuclear Navy, 1939-1962, Univ Chicago, 74; auth, Atoms for Peace and War, 1953-1962, vol III, Univ Calif, 89; auth, Jessie Ball DuPont, Univ Fla, 92. **CONTACT ADDRESS** 7909 Deepwell Dr, Bethesda, MD, 20034. **EMAIL** rghewlett@compuserve.com

HEWSEN, ROBERT
DISCIPLINE RUSSIAN AND BYZANTINE HISTORY **EDUCATION** Univ Md, BA; Georgetown Univ, PhD, 67. **CAREER** Instr, Rowan Col of NJ. **HONORS AND AWARDS** Cofounder, Soc for the Stud of Caucasia. **MEMBERSHIPS** Pres, Soc for the Stud of Caucasia. **RESEARCH** History of the Caucasis. **SELECTED PUBLICATIONS** Published several books and numerous articles on the history of the Caucasus, especially Armenia. **CONTACT ADDRESS** Rowan Col of NJ, Glassboro, NJ, 08028-1701.

HEYCK, THOMAS WILLIAM
PERSONAL Born 09/17/1938, Beaumont, TX, m, 1964, 2 children **DISCIPLINE** HISTORY **EDUCATION** Rice Inst, BA, 60; Rice Univ, MA, 62; Univ Tex, Austin, PhD(hist), 69. **CAREER** Asst prof, 68-73, ASSOC PROF HIST, NORTHWESTERN UNIV, 73-, ASSOC DEAN, 80-, Am Coun Learned Socs fel Brit hist, 74-75. **MEMBERSHIPS** AHA; Midwest Conf Brit Studies; Midwest Victorian Studies Asn. **RESEARCH** Modern British history; intellectual history; history of Ireland. **SELECTED PUBLICATIONS** Auth, The Decline of Christianity in 20th-Century Britain, Albion, Vol 0028, 96; Englishness and the Study of Politics--The Social and Political-Thought of Ernest Barker, Am Hist Rev, Vol 0101, 96; A Moralist in and out of Parliament-- John Stuart Mill, at Westminster, 1865-1868, Am Hist Rev, Vol 0098, 93. **CONTACT ADDRESS** Dept of Hist, Northwestern Univ, Evanston, IL, 60201.

HEYRMAN, CHRISTINE L.
DISCIPLINE HISTORY **EDUCATION** Macalester, BA, 71; Yale Univ, PhD, 76. **CAREER** Asst prof, hist, Univ Calif Irvine; current, PROF, HIST, UNIV DELAWARE **MEMBERSHIPS** Am Antiquarian Soc **SELECTED PUBLICATIONS** Auth, A Model of Christian Charity: The Rich and the Poor in Colonial New England, 1630-1730, 77; auth, "Spectres of Subversion, Societies of Friends: Dissent and the Devil in Provincial Essex County, Massachusetts," in Saints and Revolutionaries: Essays in Early American History, Nortin, 83; auth, Commerce and Culture: The Maritime Communities of Colonial Massachusetts, 1690-1750, Norton, 84; coauth, Nation of Nations: A Narrative History of the American Republic, McGraw-Hill, 90, 94; auth, Southern Cross: The Beginnings of the Bible Belt, Knopf, 97. **CONTACT ADDRESS** Dept of Hist, Univ of Delaware, Newark, DE, 19716. **EMAIL** christine.heyrman@mvs.udel.edu

HICKEY, DAMON
PERSONAL Born 10/30/1942, Houston, TX, m, 1967, 1 child **DISCIPLINE** HISTORY **EDUCATION** Rice Univ, BA, 65; Princeton Theol Sem, MDiv, 68; Univ NC-Chapel Hill, MSLS, 75; Univ NC-Greensboro, MA, 82; Univ SC-Columbia, PhD, 89. **CAREER** Assoc Libr Dir, 75-91, Curator, Friends Hist Collect, 82-91, Guilford Col; Dir Libr, Col Wooster, 91-. **MEMBERSHIPS** Org Am Hist; South Hist Asn; NC Hist Soc; NC Friends Hist Soc; Friends Hist Asn; Am Soc Church Hist; Am Libr Asn, Acad Libr Asn Ohio. **RESEARCH** American religious history, southern history, history of late 19th-century United States. **SELECTED PUBLICATIONS** Sojourners No More: The Quakers in the New South, 1865-1930, Greensboro, NC, Friends Hist Soc, 67. **CONTACT ADDRESS** The Col of Wooster, Libraries, Wooster, OH, 44691. **EMAIL** dhickey@acs.wooster.edu

HICKEY, DONALD ROBERT
PERSONAL Born 03/03/1944, Berwyn, IL **DISCIPLINE** HISTORY **EDUCATION** Univ Ill, Urbana, BA, 66, MA, 68, PhD(hist), 72. **CAREER** Vis lectr hist, Univ Ill, Urbana, 72-73; vis asst prof, Univ Colo, 73-75; lectr, Univ Calif, Santa Barbara, 76-77; vis asst prof hist, Tex Tech Univ, 78; from asst prof to prof hist, Wayne State Col, 78- **MEMBERSHIPS** Soc Historians Early Am Repub; Society for Military History. **RESEARCH** American Early National, Jacksonian and Colonial history. **SELECTED PUBLICATIONS** Auth, The War of 1812: A ShortHistory, U of Illinois Press, 95. **CONTACT ADDRESS** Div of Soc Sci, Wayne State Col, 1111 Main St, Wayne, NE, 68787-1172. **EMAIL** dhickey@wscgate.wsc.edu

HICKEY, MICHAEL C.
PERSONAL Born 07/22/1960, Itasca, IL, m **DISCIPLINE** HISTORY **EDUCATION** Northern IL Univ, BA, 81, MA, 83, PhD, 93. **CAREER** Asst Prof, Assoc Prof, 92 to 96-, Bloomsburg Univ; Instr, 90-92, Univ Minn; Instr, 85,90, N IL Univ. **HONORS AND AWARDS** U IL REEC Res Lab Assoc 85, 98; 4 BU Res Gnts; Kennan Inst Adv Stud; NEH; Hayter Endow Res Gnt; NIU Grad Diss Fel; Fulbright-Hays Fel; NIU Haynes outstanding Stud Awd; NIU Hist Res Prize; NIU Hist Fel. **MEMBERSHIPS** AHA; AAASS; MASA; SSA; DE Valley Sem Russ Hist; CO U Sem Slavic Hist and Cult; Wildman Stud Grp Hist Russ Labor. **RESEARCH** 19th and 20th Century Russia. **SELECTED PUBLICATIONS** Auth, Urban Zemliachestva and Rural Revolution: Petrograd and the Smolensk Countryside in 19171, The Sov and Post Sov Rev, 98; auth, Gorod Smolensk v 1917 godu: Revoliusiia kak politicheskii protsess problemy I istochniki, in: E V Kodin ed, Stalinizm v Rossiiskoi provintsii sbornik statei, Smolensk, Smolensk Pedagogical Univ, 99; Russian Migrant Laborers in Helsinki on the Eve of World War one: A Res Note, J Baltic Stud, 96; Revolution on the Jewish Street: Smolensk 1917, J Social Hist, 98; Peasant Autonomy Soviet Power and Land Distribution in Smolensk Province, November 1917-May 1918, Revolution Russ, 96; Local Govt and State Authority in the Provinces: Smolensk Feb-Jun 1917, Slavic Rev, 97; Discourses of Public Identity and Liberalism in the February Revolution: Smolensk 1917, The Russian Rev, 96. **CONTACT ADDRESS** Dept of History, Bloomsburg Univ of Pennsylvania, 400 East Second St, Bloomsburg, PA, 17815. **EMAIL** Hickey@planetx.bloomu.edu

HICKS, DAVID L.
PERSONAL Born 08/12/1927, Kansas City, MO, m, 1947, 1 child **DISCIPLINE** EARLY MODERN EUROPEAN HISTORY **EDUCATION** Columbia Univ, AB, 49, AM, 50, PhD(hist), 59. **CAREER** Historian, US Air Force, 54-60; instr hist, Columbia Col, 60-62; asst prof, 62-65, ASSOC PROF HIST, NY UNIV, 65- **RESEARCH** Siena; Italian political and social hostory in the late Middle Ages and Renaissance. **SELECTED PUBLICATIONS** Auth, Sienese society in the Renaissance, Comp Study Soc & Hist, 7/60; The education of a prince: Lodovic il Moro and the rise of Pandolfo Petrucci, Study in Renaissance, 61; coauth, European History in a World Perspective, Heath, 64, rev ed, 75; auth, The Sienese state in the Renaissance, In: From Renaissance to Counter-Reformation, Random, 65; auth, sources of wealth in Renaissance Siena: business men and land owners, Bulletino senese di storia patria, 93/86; auth, from democracy to oligarchy: the transformation of the Siene government in the Renaissance Duquesne History Forum, 89; auth, the Sienese oligarchy and the rise of Pandolfo Petrucci, La Toscana al tempo di Lorenzo di Medici, 96. **CONTACT ADDRESS** Dept of Hist, New York Univ, 53 Washington Sq S, New York, NY, 10011. **EMAIL** david.hicks@nyu.edu

HICKS, L. EDWARD
PERSONAL Born 06/05/1946, Dyersburg, TN, m, 1968, 2 children **DISCIPLINE** HISTORY **EDUCATION** Claremont McKenna Col, BA 68; Claremont Grad Univ, MA 71; Grad Study: Ed, Admin, Calif State Univ and Claremont Grad Univ 71-76, relig, Harding Grad Sch Relig, 82-85; Univ Memphis, PhD 90. **CAREER** Faulkner Univ, asst prof, assoc prof, ch hum fine arts, ch soc behav sci, fac rep pres cab bd dir's, 91-97; Christian Bros Univ, instr 90-91; Univ Memphis, teach asst 85-87; BD Hicks Ent Inc, vpres, pres, 76-91; Fullerton Jr Col, adj instr 70-76; Buena Park HS, tchr, coach, asst Dept hd, hd varsity bb coach, var fb off coord, 70-76; Fullerton Union HS, tchr, coach, 68-70; Claremont McKenna Col, grad tchg asst, 68-69. **HONORS AND AWARDS** Phi Alpha Theta; Outstanding Grad Stud; AUSCS Res Awd; Belle McWilliams Endow Res Gnt; Who's Who Amg Amer Univ Profs; NAIA All Amer CMC. **MEMBERSHIPS** AAUP; ASCH; AHA; AAH; BAS; CFH; NEAS; OAH; SCS; SHA. **SELECTED PUBLICATIONS** Auth, Sometimes in the Wrong But Never in Doubt: George S. Benson and the Education of the New Religious Right, Knoxville, The U of Tenn Press, 95; Donald C. Swift, Religion and The American Experience, 1765-1997, Armonk NY, ME SHarpe Inc, 97, rev, Hist Rev of New Books, 98; auth, George Stuart Benson, Dict of Arkansas Biography, Fort Smith, AR Univ Press, 98; auth, Martin E Marty, Modern Amer Religion, vol 3 Under God Indivisible 1941-1960, Chicago, U of Chicago Press, 96, rev, Hist Rev of New Books, 97; auth, Diana Hochstedt Butler, Standing Against the Whirlwind: Evangelical Episcopalians in Nineteenth Century America, NY Oxford U Press, 95, rev, Hist Rev New Bks, 96; auth, Randy J. Sparks, On Jordan's Stormy Banks: Evangelicalism in Mississippi, 1773-1876, Athens GA, U of GA Press, 94, rev, Hist of New Bks Rev, 95. **CONTACT ADDRESS** Dept of Social and Behavioral Sciences, Faulkner Univ, 5345 Atlanta Hwy, Montgomery, AL, 36109-3398.

HIGASHI, SUMIKO
DISCIPLINE HISTORY **EDUCATION** Univ Ca, BA, PhD. **CAREER** Prof. **RESEARCH** American film history; American cultural history; Film criticism. **SELECTED PUBLICATIONS** Auth, Cecil B. DeMille and American Culture: The Silent Era, Univ Ca, 94; Postmodernism versus Illusionist Narrative as History: Walker and Mississippi Burning, Princeton Univ, 95; Night of the Living Dead: A Horror Film about the Horrors of the Vietnam Era, Rutgers, 90; Melodrama, Realism, and Race: World War II News Reels and Propaganda Film, Cinema Jour, 98; Rethinking Film as American History, 98. **CONTACT ADDRESS** Dept of History, State Univ NY Col Brockport, Brockport, NY, 14420. **EMAIL** shigashi@acspr1.acs.brockport.edu

HIGBEE, MARK
DISCIPLINE HISTORY **EDUCATION** Columbia Univ, PhD. **CAREER** Asst prof, Eastern Michigan Univ. **RESEARCH** US, African-American. **SELECTED PUBLICATIONS** Publ in, J Negro Hist; Ind mag Hist. **CONTACT ADDRESS** Dept of History and Philosophy, Eastern Michigan Univ, 701 Pray-Harrold, Ypsilanti, MI, 48197. **EMAIL** his_higbee@online.emich.edu

HIGGINBOTHAM, R. DON
PERSONAL Born 05/22/1931, Fresno, CA, 3 children **DISCIPLINE** UNITED STATES HISTORY **EDUCATION** Wash Univ, AB & MA, 54; Duke Univ, PhD, 58. **CAREER** Instr hist, Duke Univ, 57-58; asst prof, Col William & Mary, 58-59 & Longwood Col, 59-60; from asst prof to assoc prof, La State Univ, 60-67; assoc prof, 67-70, prof Hist, DOWD PROF, 88-; UNIV NC, CHAPEL HILL, 70-, CHMN DEPT, 80-, Nat Hist Publ Comn grant, 67-68; VIS PROF HISTORY, US MIL ACAD, 75-76 & 98-99. **HONORS AND AWARDS** NY Revolution Roundtable Award for best bk on Am Revolution, 71; R D W Connor Award for best article on phase of NC Hist, 72; Outstanding Civilian Serv Medal, US Army, 76; Pres Hist Asn, 91-92; Pres Soc Hist of the Early Republic, 94-95. **MEMBERSHIPS** AHA; Southern Hist Asn; Orgn Am Historians. **RESEARCH** Colonial and Revolutionary America; early national period to 1815. **SELECTED PUBLICATIONS** Auth, Daniel Morgan: Revolutionary Rifleman, Univ NC, 61; American historians and the military history of the American revolution, Am Hist Rev, 64; The War of American Independence, Macmillan, 71; James Iredell's efforts to preserve the first British Empire, NC Hist Rev, 72; coauth, Atlas of the American Revolution, Rand McNally, 74; contribr, Military leadership in the eighteenth century, In: Leadership in the American Revolution, Libr Cong, 74; ed, The Papers of James Iredell (2 vols), Arch & Hist, 76; Reconsiderations on the Revolutionary War, Greenwood, 78; George Washington and the American Military Tradition, Univ Ga Press, 85; War and Society in Revolutionary America, Univ S Carolina Press, 88; The Martial Spirit in the Antebellum South, Jour S Hist, 92; of Revolution, Jour Early Repub, 94; The Federalized Militia Debate: A Neglected Aspect of Seonc Admendment Scholarship, Wm & Mary Quart, 98. **CONTACT ADDRESS** Dept of Hist, Univ of N. Carolina, Chapel Hill, NC, 27599-3195. **EMAIL** higginbo@email.unc.edu

HIGGINS, HANNAH
DISCIPLINE ART HISTORY **EDUCATION** Univ Chicago, PhD. **CAREER** Assoc prof. **SELECTED PUBLICATIONS** Auth, pubs in New Art Examiner. **CONTACT ADDRESS** Art Hist Dept, Univ Illinois Chicago, S Halsted St, PO Box 705, Chicago, IL, 60607.

HIGGINS, WILLIAM E.
PERSONAL Born 01/18/1945, Newark, NJ **DISCIPLINE** CLASSICS **EDUCATION** Georgetown Univ, BA, 66; Harvard Univ, PhD, 71; New York Univ, MBA, 81. **CAREER** Asst prof, Brandeis Univ, 71-79. **HONORS AND AWARDS** Phi Beta Kappa, Jr Fel, Ctr for Hellenic Stud, Washington, DC, 77-78. **MEMBERSHIPS** Am Philol Asn. **RESEARCH** Greek literature; ancient history. **SELECTED PUBLICATIONS** Auth, Aspects of Alexander's Imperial Administration, Athenaeum, 80; Deciphering Time in the Herakles of Euripides, Quaderni Urbinati, 84; rev of Osborne, Demos, AHR, 86; rev of Hirsch, The Friendship of the Barbarians, AHR, 87; rev of Garner, Law and Society in Classical Athens, AHR, 89. **CONTACT ADDRESS** 489 Summit Ave, Maplewood, NJ, 07040. **EMAIL** william.higgins@prudential.com

HIGGINSON, JOHN
DISCIPLINE HISTORY **EDUCATION** Univ MI, PhD, 79. **CAREER** Prof, Univ MA Amherst. **RESEARCH** Hist of South Africa; comp labor hist. **SELECTED PUBLICATIONS** Auth, A Working Class in the Making: The Union Miniere du Haut-Katanga and the African Mineworkers 1907-1949, Univ Wis, 89; Liberating the Captives: Watchtower as an Avatar of Colonial Revolt in Southern Africa and Katanga Province, Belgian Congo, 1907-1941, Jour Soc Hist. **CONTACT ADDRESS** Dept of Hist, Univ Massachusetts Amherst, Mass Ave, Amherst, MA, 01003.

HIGGS, CATHERINE
DISCIPLINE HISTORY **EDUCATION** Yale Univ, PhD. **CAREER** Assoc prof. **RESEARCH** African history. **SELECTED PUBLICATIONS** Auth, The Ghost of Equality: The Public Lives of D.D.T. Jabavu of South Africa 1885-1959 Ohio Univ, 97. **CONTACT ADDRESS** Dept of History, Knoxville, TN, 37996.

HIGHAM, JOHN
PERSONAL Born 10/26/1920, Jamaica, NY, m, 1948, 4 children **DISCIPLINE** HISTORY **EDUCATION** Johns Hopkins Univ, AB, 41; Univ Wis, AM, 42, PhD(hist), 49. **CAREER** Asst ed, Am Mercury, 45-46; from instr to asst prof hist, Univ Calif, Los Angeles, 48-54; from assoc prof to prof, Rutgers Univ, 54-60; prof, Univ Mich, Ann Arbor, 60-68, Tyler univ prof, 68-71 & 72-73, chmn prog Am cult, 69-71; prof, 71-80, Vincent prof hist, 73-89, PROF EMERITUS, 89-, JOHNS HOPKINS UNIV; Fund Advan Educ fel, 55-56; vis assoc prof, Columbia Univ, 58-59; vis fel, Coun Humanities, Princeton Univ, 60-61; fel, Ctr Advan Studies Behav Sci, 65-66; Commonwealth Fund lectr Am hist, Univ Col, London, 68; sr fel, Mich Soc Fels, 70-73; vis scholar, Phi Beta Kappa, 72-73; mem, Inst Advan Studies, 73-74; consult ed, Comp Studies Soc & Hist, 74-; Ecole des Hautes Etudes en Sciences Sociales, Paris, directeur d'etudes, 81-82. **HONORS AND AWARDS** Dunning Prize, AHA, 56. **MEMBERSHIPS** Orgn Am Historians (vpres, 72-73, pres, 73-74); hon mem New Soc Letts, Sweden; Am Antiq Soc; AHA; Immigration Hist Soc (pres, 79-82). **RESEARCH** American immigration and ethnic history; American cultural and intellectual history since 1830. **SELECTED PUB-**

LICATIONS Auth, Strangers in the Land, Rutgers Univ, 55; coauth & ed, Reconstruction of American History, Hutchinson & Co, 62; coauth, History: Humanistic Scholarship in America, Prentice-Hall, 65; auth, From Boundlessness to Consolidation: The Transformation of American Culture, 1848-1860, Clements Libr, 69; Writing American History, Ind Univ, 70; Send These to Me: Jews and Other Immigrants in Urban America, Atheneum, 75; ed, Ethnic Leadership in America, Johns Hopkins Univ, 78; ed, Civil Rights and Social Wrongs: Black-White Relations Since World War II, Pa State Univ Press, 97. **CONTACT ADDRESS** Dept of Hist, Johns Hopkins Univ, 3400 N Charles St, Baltimore, MD, 21218. **EMAIL** jhigham@jhu.edu

HIGHAM, ROBIN
PERSONAL Born 06/20/1925, London, England, m, 1950, 4 children **DISCIPLINE** HISTORY **EDUCATION** Harvard Univ, AB, 50, PhD, 57; Claremont Grad Sch, MA, 53. **CAREER** Instr Eng & hist, 50-52, Webb Sch, Calif; instr hist, 54-57, Univ Mass; asst prof, 57-63, Univ NC; assoc prof, 63-66, prof mod Brit & mil hist, 66-98, Kans St Univ; Soc Sci Res Coun Natl Security Policy res fel, 60-61; historian, 60-66 & 75-79, Brit Overseas Airways Corp; adv ed, 67-, Technol & Cult; ed, 68-88, Mil Affairs; adv, 70-88, Aerospace Historian; grad fac lectr, 71, Kans St Univ; mil adv, 70-75, Univ Ky Press; ed, 76-85, Bd Int Comn on Mil Hist; ed, J of the West, 77-. **MEMBERSHIPS** Am Aviation Hist Soc; Soc Hist Technol; Am Mil Inst; Orgn Am Historians. **RESEARCH** Modern British; military and technological history. **SELECTED PUBLICATIONS** Auth, Air Power: A Concise History, Macdonald's, London, 72 & St Martin's, NY, 73; ed, Civil Wars in the Twentieth Century, 72-98 Intervention or Abstention: The Dilemma of US Foreign Policy, Univ Ky, 74; co-ed, A Guide to the Sources of US Military History, Archon Bks, 75; co-ed, Flying Combat Aircraft of the USAAF-USAF, 75 & Flying Combat Aircraft II, Iowa State Univ, 78; auth, Soviet Aviation and Air Power, Westview, 78; auth, BOAC, 1939-1974, The Inside Story, 79; auth, The Bases of Air Geology: Building Airfields for the RAF 1915-1945, Airlife, 98; co-ed, Russian Aviation & Air Power, Cass, 98. **CONTACT ADDRESS** President, Sunflower Univ, Box 1009, Manhattan, KS, 66506-1000.

HIGONNET, PATRICE
DISCIPLINE HISTORY **EDUCATION** Harvard Univ, BA, 58; Oxford Univ, BA, 60; Harvard Univ, PhD, 65. **CAREER** Prof, fr hist, Harvard Univ. **SELECTED PUBLICATIONS** Auth, Goodnen Beyond Virtue, Harvard Univ Press, 98. **CONTACT ADDRESS** Harvard Univ, Cambridge, MA, 02138.

HILDERBRAND, ROBERT CLINTON
PERSONAL Born 08/24/1947, Marshalltown, IA, m, 1986, 1 child **DISCIPLINE** UNITED STATES HISTORY, AMERICAN FOREIGN RELATIONS **EDUCATION** Univ Iowa, BA, 69, MA, 74, PhD(hist), 77. **CAREER** Asst prof hist, Univ SDak, 77-78; asst prof, Univ NC, 78-79; asst prof, Univ Mo, 79-80; asst prof, 80-87, PROF HIST, UNIV SDAK, 87-. **HONORS AND AWARDS** Univ Teacher of the Year Award, 84, 92. **MEMBERSHIPS** AHA; Soc Historians Am Foreign Rels; Phi Beta Kappa. **RESEARCH** Management of United States public opinion in foreign affairs; creation of United Nations; World War II. **SELECTED PUBLICATIONS** Auth, Power and the People: Executive Management of Public Opinion in Foreign Affairs, 1897-1921, Univ NC Press, 81; The Press Conference of Woodrow Wilson, 85; Dumberton Oaks: The Origins of the United Nations and the Search for Postwar Security, Univ NC Press, 90. **CONTACT ADDRESS** Dept of Hist, Univ SDak, 414 E Clark St., Vermillion, SD, 57069-2390. **EMAIL** rhilderb@usd.edu

HILDRETH, GLADYS JOHNSON
PERSONAL Born 10/15/1933, Columbia, MS, m **DISCIPLINE** EDUCATION **EDUCATION** So Univ Baton Rouge LA, BS 1953; Univ of WI Madison, MS 1955; MI State Univ East Lansing, PhD 1973. **CAREER** So Univ, assoc prof 1960-68; LA State Univ School of Human Ecology, prof family studies 1974-90; Texas Woman's Univ, Denton, TX, professor, 1990-. **HONORS AND AWARDS** Grad School Fellowship MI State Univ Human Ecology 1970; Thelma Porter Fellowship MI State Univ Human Ecology 1970; Recipient of the LA Home Econ Assn Disting District & State Serv Awd 1986; Nominated for Amer Council on Educ Fellow; Distinguished Faculty Fellowship Award, Louisiana State University; Distinguished Service Award, Southeast Council on Family Relations; Natl Council of Family Rel, Marie Peters Ethnic Minority Award. **MEMBERSHIPS** Chmn jr div adv council LA State Univ 1979-80; state chmn aging serv LA Home Econ Assn 1978-80; consult Natl Assn for Ed of Young Children 1974-; Ctr for the Family Amer Home Econ Assn 1977-79; Delta Sigma Theta 1970-; mem Phi Upsilon Omicron So Univ Home Econ, Omicron Nu MI State Univ Human Ecology; National Council on Family Relations; Sect, TCFR; Texas Consortium On Geriatric Education. **CONTACT ADDRESS** Family Sciences, Texas Woman's Univ, Denton, TX, 76205.

HILES, TIMOTHY
DISCIPLINE ART **EDUCATION** Pa State Univ, PhD, 92. **CAREER** Assoc prof. **HONORS AND AWARDS** Creative Ach Awd, 90. **SELECTED PUBLICATIONS** Auth, Keith Haring, 94; Hector Guimards Paris Mtro Stations, 93; ed, Impressionism; Post-Impressionism; Symbolism, Art Nouveau. **CONTACT ADDRESS** Dept of Art, Knoxville, TN, 37996.

HILL, BENNETT DAVID
PERSONAL Born 09/27/1934, Baltimore, MD, s **DISCIPLINE** HISTORY **EDUCATION** Princeton Univ, AB 1956; Harvard Univ, AM 1958; Princeton Univ, PhD 1963. **CAREER** University of Western Ontario, London CN, assistant professor, 1962-64; University of Illinois, Urbana, assistant and associate professor, 1964-78, dept of history, professor, 1975-81, chm, 1978-81; Benedictine Monk of St Anselm's Abbey, Washington District of Columbia, 1980-; University of Maryland, visiting professor, 1984-87; Roman Catholic priest ordained, 1985; Georgetown University visiting professor, 1987-. **HONORS AND AWARDS** Flw Amer Cncl of Learned Soc 1970-71. **MEMBERSHIPS** Consltnt Natl Endowmnt for the Humanities 1978, Woodrow Wilson Natl Fdtn 1982; bd of dir American Benedictine Review; Princeton Club of Washington. **SELECTED PUBLICATIONS** Author, English Cistercian Monasteries and Their Patrons in the Twelfth Century, 1970; Church and State in the Middle Ages, 1970; co-author, A History of Western Society, 1979, 6th edition, 1990, 6th edition, 1998; A History of World Societies, 4th edition, 1991, 5th edition, 1999. **CONTACT ADDRESS** History Dept, Georgetown Univ, 604 ICC Bldg, Washington, DC, 20057.

HILL, CHRISTOPHER V.
PERSONAL Born 04/14/1953, Salt Lake City, UT, m, 1979, 2 children **DISCIPLINE** HISTORY **EDUCATION** Univ Ut, BA, 80; Univ Va, MA, 82, PhD, 87. **CAREER** Assoc prof, Lock Haven Univ Pa, 90-93; assoc prof to chair, Col Univ, Colorado Springs, 93-. **HONORS AND AWARDS** First Aldo Leopold Award, Amer Soc for Environ Hist, 93. **MEMBERSHIPS** Assoc Asian Stud; Amer Soc Environ Hist. **RESEARCH** Colonial India; global environ hist. **SELECTED PUBLICATIONS** Auth, River of Sorrow: Environment and Agrarian control in Riparian North India, 1770-1994, Assoc Asian Stud Monograph, 97; art, Ideology and Public Works: Managing the Mahanadi River in Colonial North India, Capitalism, Nature, Socialism, 95; art, Philosophy and Reality in Riparian South India: British Famine Policy and Migration in Colonial North India, Modern Asian Stud, 91; art, Water and Power: Riparian Legislation and Agrarian Control in Colonial Bengal, Environmental History Review, 90. **CONTACT ADDRESS** Dept of History, Univ of Col, Colorado Springs, CO, 80918-3733. **EMAIL** chill@mail.uccs.edu

HILL, EUGENE DAVID
PERSONAL Born 02/25/1949, New York, NY **DISCIPLINE** RENAISSANCE LITERATURE, INTELLECTUAL HISTORY. **EDUCATION** Columbia Univ, BA, 70; Princeton Univ, PhD(English), 80. **CAREER** Instr, 78-80, asst prof Eng, Mt Holyoke Col, 80-86; from assoc prof to prof Eng, 86-94. **MEMBERSHIPS** Renaissance Soc Am. **RESEARCH** John Milton, John Donne, Thomas Kyd. **SELECTED PUBLICATIONS** Auth, The trinitarian allegory of the moral play of Wisdom, Mod Philol, 75; The place of the future, Sci Fiction Studies, 82; Parody and History in Arden of Feversham, Huntington Library Quarterly, 93. **CONTACT ADDRESS** Dept of English, Mount Holyoke Col, 50 College St, South Hadley, MA, 01075-6421.

HILL, JOHN
DISCIPLINE ASIAN HISTORY **EDUCATION** Okla Baptist Col, BA, Duke Univ, MA, PhD. **CAREER** Assoc prof. **RESEARCH** Evolution of Indian nationalism, Muslim politicization, British famine and agricultural policy. **SELECTED PUBLICATIONS** Ed, The Congress and Indian Nationalism: Historical Perspectives, Curzon Press, 91. **CONTACT ADDRESS** Dept of Hist, Concordia Univ, Montreal, 1455 de Maisonneuve W, Montreal, PQ, H3G 1M8.

HILL, JOHN WALTER
DISCIPLINE MUSIC **EDUCATION** Univ Chicago, BA; Harvard Univ, MA, PhD. **CAREER** Prof, 78-, Univ IL Urbana Champaign. **MEMBERSHIPS** Am Musicol Soc. **RESEARCH** Music of the Baroque and Class periods. **SELECTED PUBLICATIONS** Auth, The Life and Works of Francesco Maria Veracini; Vivaldi's Ottone in Villa. **CONTACT ADDRESS** Dept of Music, Univ Illinois Urbana Champaign, E Gregory Dr, PO Box 52, Champaign, IL, 61820. **EMAIL** jwhill@uiuc.edu

HILL, JONATHAN D.
PERSONAL Born 02/21/1954, Charlotte, NC, d, 1 child **DISCIPLINE** ANTHROPOLOGY **EDUCATION** Univ Chicago, BA, 76; Indiana Univ, PhD, 83. **CAREER** Vis asst prof, Dept of Anthropology, 83-86, Univ of Georgia; asst prof, 86-90, assoc prof, 90-96, Dept of Anthropology, SIUC; vis assoc prof, 93-94, Dept of Anthropology, UCLA; prof, Dept of Anthropology, 96-, SIUC. **HONORS AND AWARDS** NDEA Title VI Fellowship in Portuguese and Latin Amer Studies, Indiana Univ, 77-78; Fulbright-Hays Training Grant, Doctoral Dissertation Abroad Program to Venezuela, 80-81; Fulbright-Hays Fac Res Abroad Grant to Venezuela, 84-85; Smithsonian Postdoctoral Fellowship, 87-88; Cultural Survival Grant for fieldwork in Columbia, 89; Office of Res and Development S IL Univ for fieldwork and archival res in Venezuela, 93. **MEMBERSHIPS** Amer Anthrop Asn; Amer Ethnological Soc; Amer Soc for Ethnohistory; Cult Survival Scholars Network; Latin Amer Stud Asn; NY Acad of Sciences; Soc for Cultural Anthrop; Soc for Ethnomusicology; Soc for Linguistic Anthrop. **RESEARCH** Ethnology, ecology and history of Lowland South America; ethnomusicology; performance studies; symbolic and semiotic anthropology; nationalism and ethnicity; critical studies of culture; power and history. **SELECTED PUBLICATIONS** Ed, Anthropological Discourses and the Expression of Personhood in South American Inter-Ethnic Relations, S Amer Indian Stud, Bennington Col, 93; auth, Keepers of the Sacred Chants The Poetics of Ritual Power in an Amazonian Soc, Univ of Arizona Press, 93; ed, History Power and Identity Ethnogenesis in the Americas 1492-1992, Univ of Iowa Press, 96; art, Introduction Ethnogenesis in the Americas 1492-1992, History Power and Identity Ethnogenesis in the Americas After 1492, Univ of Iowa Press, 96; art, Northern Arawakan Ethnogenesis and Historical Transformations, History Power and Identity Ethnogenesis in the Americas After 1492, Univ of Iowa Press, 96; art, South America Tropical Forests, Encyclopedia of Cultural Anthropology, Henry Holt Co, 96. **CONTACT ADDRESS** Dept of Anthropology, Southern Ill Univ, Mail Code 4502, Carbondale, IL, 62901-4502. **EMAIL** jhill@siu.edu

HILL, LAMAR MOTT
PERSONAL Born 02/23/1938, New York, NY, m, 1960, 2 children **DISCIPLINE** HISTORY **EDUCATION** Kenyon Col, AB, 60; Western Reserve Univ, MA, 65; Univ London, PhD(hist), 68. **CAREER** Asst prof hist, 68-73, asst vice chancellor acad affairs, 76-77, ASSOC PROF HIST, UNIV CALIF, IRVINE, 73-, Inst Hist Res, London, res fel hist, 68; Nat Endowment Humanities fel hist, 73-74; consult, Gen Educ Proficiency, Educ Testing Serv, 76-77. **MEMBERSHIPS** AHA; Historians Early Mod Europe; Conf Brit Studies; Selden Soc; fel Royal Hist Soc. **RESEARCH** Tudor-Stuart English history; social structure of Tudor-Stuart politics; English law and administration. **SELECTED PUBLICATIONS** Auth, Court, Country, and Culture--Essays on Early-Modern British History in Honor of Perez Zagorin, Albion, Vol 0025, 93; The Plumpton Correspondence, Albion, Vol 0025, 93; The Administration of the County Palatine of Chester 1442-1485, Am Hist Rev, Vol 0097, 92; The Marian Experience-Of-Defeat--The Fate of Roman-Catholics in Reformation England--The Case of John Bourne, Sixteenth Century J, Vol 0025, 94. **CONTACT ADDRESS** Dept of Hist, Univ of Calif, Irvine, CA, 92717.

HILL, ORDELLE GERHARD
PERSONAL Born 09/04/1935, Brookings, SD, m, 1961 **DISCIPLINE** MEDIEVAL ENGLISH **EDUCATION** Augustana Col, BA, 57; Auburn Univ, MA, 59; Univ Ill, PhD(14th century English), 65. **CAREER** Instr English, Luther Col, 60-61; asst prof, Merrimack Col, 65-66; assoc prof, 66-68, PROF ENGLISH, EASTERN KY UNIV, 68- **MEMBERSHIPS** SAtlantic MLA; MLA. **RESEARCH** Medieval English literature. **SELECTED PUBLICATIONS** Auth, A Conduct Book For Richard II, Philol Quarterly, Vol 0073, 94. **CONTACT ADDRESS** Dept of English, Eastern Kentucky Univ, 521 Lancaster Ave, Richmond, KY, 40475-3102.

HILL, PATRICIA
DISCIPLINE NINETEENTH-CENTURY U.S. CULTURAL HISTORY **EDUCATION** Col Wooster, BA; Harvard Univ, MTS; Harvard Univ, PhD. **CAREER** Wesleyan Univ. **SELECTED PUBLICATIONS** Auth, The World Their Household: The American Woman's Foreign Mission Movement And Cultural Transformation, 1870-1920. **CONTACT ADDRESS** Wesleyan Univ, Middletown, CT, 06459. **EMAIL** phill@wesleyan.edu

HILL, PAUL GORDON
PERSONAL Born 03/15/1933, Gary, IN, m, 1989 **DISCIPLINE** EDUCATION **EDUCATION** IN State Univ, PhD 1973; Kent State Univ, Adv cert 1965; TN A&I State Univ, MA 1965; IN State Univ, BA 1955. **CAREER** Chicago Publ School, instr 1955-61, couns 1961-67, coord of guid in career devel prog 1967-68; IN State Univ, doctoral fellow 1968-70; Govs State Univ, dir stud serv & prof of human learning & devel 1970-73, disting univ prof of human learning & devel 1973-1989, retired, 1990. **HONORS AND AWARDS** Blue Key Natl Scholastic Hon Soc; Pi Gamma Mu Hon Soc; Hulman 4.0 Average Scholarship Cert IN Univ; Kappa Delta Pi Hon Soc. **MEMBERSHIPS** Workshop IL Coll Personnel Assoc 1972; conflict resolution team Rich Twp Schl dist 1972-73; co-dir Non-Whites in NASPA 1975-76; mem Natl Assoc of St Personnel Admin 1974-77, Amer Personnel & Guid Assoc 1973-77, World Future Soc 1975, IL Assoc for Non-White Concern 1974-75, Amer Assoc for Higher Ed 1974-75; rsch task force handicapped Bur for Ed of Handicapped & Ed Testing Serv 1975; bd of dir Gavin Meml Found 1974-76; dir Proj Aquarius 1977-97; career devel workshop Amer Personnel & Guid Assoc Conf 1975; mem Amer Assn for Counseling and Devel. **SELECTED PUBLICATIONS** Author, "TAS/The Allegory of a Slave."

HILL, PETER PROAL
PERSONAL Born 10/04/1926, Concord, MA, m, 1953, 1 child **DISCIPLINE** AMERICAN DIPLOMATIC & EARLY NATIONAL HISTORY **EDUCATION** Tufts Univ, AB, 48; Boston Univ, MA, 54; George Washington Univ, PhD(hist), 66. **CAREER** From instr to assoc prof, 60-74, PROF HIST, GEORGE WASHINGTON UNIV, 74- **MEMBERSHIPS** AHA; Soc Fr Hist Study; Soc Historians Am Foreign Rels. **RESEARCH** Federalist era diplomacy; Franco-American relations. **SELECTED PUBLICATIONS** Auth, America and France--2 Revolutions, J Am Hist, Vol 0081, 94. **CONTACT ADDRESS** Dept of Hist, George Washington Univ, Washington, DC, 20052.

HILLGARTH, JOCELYN NIGEL
PERSONAL Born 09/22/1929, London, England, m, 1966 **DISCIPLINE** MEDIEVAL HISTORY **EDUCATION** Cambridge Univ, BA, 50, MA, 54, PhD(hist), 57. **CAREER** Sr res fel hist, Warburg Inst, London, 59-62; mem, Inst Advan Studies, 63-64; vis lectr, Univ Tex, Austin, 64-65; lectr, Harvard Univ, 65-66, asst prof, 66-70; from assoc prof to prof, Boston Col, 70-77; PROF HIST, PONTIFICAL INST MEDIAEVAL STUDIES, TORONTO, 77-, Guggenheim fel, 67-68; Am Coun Learned Soc fel, 76-77; Lady Davis vis prof, Hebrew Univ, Jerusalem, fall 80. **MEMBERSHIPS** Mediaeval Acad Am; Soc Span & Port Hist Studies. **RESEARCH** Medieval Spain; medieval intellectual and church history. **SELECTED PUBLICATIONS** Auth, Ramon-Lull, Opera-Latina, Speculum, Vol 0069, 94; Conversos, Inquisition and the Expulsion of the Jews From Spain, Cath Hist Rev, Vol 0083, 97; Christian Life and Culture in Spain from the 7th-Century to the 10th-Century, Speculum, J Medieval Studies, Vol 0069, 94; The Evangelical Rhetoric of Ramon Llull--Lay Learning and Piety in the Christian West Around 1300, Cath Hist Rev, Vol 0083, 97; The Origins of the Christian Balearics from Their Development Through the Arab-Muslim Conquest, Speculum, Vol 0069, 94; The Martyrs of Cordoba--Community and Family Conflict in an Age of Mass Conversion, Am Hist Rev, Vol 0101, 96; Ramon-Llull New Rhetoric--Text and Translation of Llull 'Rethorica Nova', Speculum, Vol 0071, 96; The Learned King--The Reign of Alfonso-X-Of-Castile, Cath Hist Rev, Vol 0080, 94. **CONTACT ADDRESS** Pontifical Inst of Mediaeval Studies, 59 Queens' Park CR E, Toronto, ON, M5s 2C4.

HILLMER, GEORGE NORMAN
PERSONAL Born 11/24/1942, Niagara Falls, ON, Canada **DISCIPLINE** HISTORY **EDUCATION** Univ Toronto, BA, 66; MA 67; Cambridge Univ, PhD, 74. **CAREER** Lectr to adj prof, 72-89, PROF HISTORY, CARLETON UNIV, 90-; hist, Directorate Hist Dept Nat Defence, 72-90; vis prof, Leeds Univ (Eng), 78-79. **HONORS AND AWARDS** Commonwealth Scholar, 68-70; IODE, Univ London, Mackenzie King & Can Counc Fels, 70-72; Queen's Silver Jubilee Medal, 77; Carleton Excellence Tchg Award, 94; Marston LaFrance Fel, 95; Prime Minister's Publ Award, Japan, 97. **MEMBERSHIPS** Can Hist Asn **SELECTED PUBLICATIONS** Auth, Negotiating Freer Trade: The United Kingdom, the United States, Canada, and the Trade Agreements of 1938, 89; For Better or For Worse: Canada and the United States to the 1990s, 91; Empire to Umpire: Canada and the World to the 1990s, 94; ed, Int J, 97-. **CONTACT ADDRESS** Dept of History, Carleton Univ, 1125 Colonel By Dr, Ottawa, ON, K1S 5B6. **EMAIL** nhillmer@ccs.carleton.ca

HILSON, ARTHUR LEE
PERSONAL Born 04/06/1936, Cincinnati, OH, m, 1982 **DISCIPLINE** AMERICAN STUDIES **EDUCATION** Wheaton College, Springfield Christian Bible Seminary, Wheaton, IL, bachelor of theology; Andover Newton Theological Seminary, Newton Center, MA, MDiv; University of Massachusetts, Amherst, MA, MEd, 1974, EdD, 1979. **CAREER** Human Resources Development Center, Newport, RI, human relations consultant, 1973; University of Massachusetts at Amherst, MA, administrative assistant to dean of graduate affairs, School of Education, 1973-75, department head, Veterans Assistance and Couseling Services, 1976-78, department head, University Placement Services, 1978-87, executive director, Public Safety, 1987-92; UNIVERSITY OF NH, FACULTY, AMERICAN STUDIES FOR STUDENT AFFAIRS, 1993-; NEW HOPE BAPTIST CHURCH, PASTOR, 1991-. **HONORS AND AWARDS** Developed and faciliated over 100 workshops on human/race relations and multicultural communications; Kellogg Fellow, Kellogg Foundation, 1973-74. **MEMBERSHIPS** Member, Phi Delta Kappa; member, American Personnel Officers Assn; member, Eastern College Personnel Officers Assn; member, College Placement Council; member, NAACP; bd member, American Veterans Committee; chairman, Natl Assn of Minority Veterans Program Administrators; bd member, Natl Assn of Veterans Program Administrators; bd member, interim director, Veterans Outreach Center of Greenfield, MA; member, Intl Assn of Campus Law Enforcement Administrators; member, Intl Assn of Chiefs of Police; chairman, United Christian Foundation; charter president, Amherst NAACP; member, bd of dirs, Western Massachusetts Girl Scouts; member, bd of dirs, United Way of Hampshire County; School Bd, elected mem. **CONTACT ADDRESS** New Hope Baptist Church, 263 Peverly Hill Rd, Portsmouth, NH, 03801.

HILTON, KATHLEEN C.
DISCIPLINE SOCIAL HISTORY **EDUCATION** Seattle Univ, BEd, cum laude, 69; Carnegie Mellon Univ, MA, 82, PhD, 87. **CAREER** Assoc prof, coordr, Soc Stud educ prog, Univ NC, Pembroke. **RESEARCH** Progressive Era adolescent socialization patterns; women's hist. **SELECTED PUBLICATIONS** Auth, Domesticity, in Encycl of Soc Hist, Garland Press. 94; Both in the Field, Each With a Plow: Race Gender, and Women's Work in the Rural South, 1907-1929, in Hidden Histories of Women in the New South, Unvi Mo Press, 94. **CONTACT ADDRESS** Univ N. Carolina, Pembroke, Pembroke, NC, 28372-1510. **EMAIL** kch@papa.uncp.edu

HILTS, VICTOR L.
PERSONAL Born 11/01/1937, Great Falls, MT, m, 1965 **DISCIPLINE** HISTORY OF SCIENCE & SOCIAL SCIENCE **EDUCATION** Harvard Univ, AB, 59, PhD, 67. **CAREER** Asst prof, 65-71, chmn dept, 77-81, 87-90 & 91-94, assoc prof, 71-85, PROF HIST SCI, UNIV WIS-MADISON, 85-. **MEMBERSHIPS** Hist Sci Soc; AAAS; Midwest J Hist Sci. **SELECTED PUBLICATIONS** Auth, Statistics and social science, in Foundations of Method, Ind Univ, 73; Guide to Francis Galton's English Men of Science, Am Philos Soc, 75; Allis exterendum: Or, origins of the statistical society of London, Isis, 78; Statist and Statistician, Arno Press, 81; Obeying the laws of hereditary descent: Phrenological views on inheritance and eugenics, J Hist Behav Sci, 82; Enlightenment view, in Transformation and Tradition in the Sciences, Cambridge Univ Press, 84; Towards the social organism: Herbert Spencer and William B Carpenter on the analogical method, in The Natural Sciences and the Social Sciences, Kluwer Acad Press, 94. **CONTACT ADDRESS** Dept of Hist of Sci, Univ of Wis, 1180 Observatory Dr, Madison, WI, 53706-1393.

HILTY, JAMES
DISCIPLINE TWENTIETH CENTURY UNITED STATES POLITICAL HISTORY **EDUCATION** Univ MO, Columbia, PhD. **CAREER** Assoc prof, Temple Univ. **RESEARCH** Biog of Robert F. Kennedy. **SELECTED PUBLICATIONS** Auth, John F. Kennedy: An Idealist without Illusions, Forum Ser in Hist, 76; Senatorial Papers and the 'New' Political History, in Senators' Papers, ed, Richard A. Baker, 79; Harry S. Truman and the New Deal, The Truman Encycl, ed, Richard S. Kirkendall, 89; John F. Kennedy and Robert F. Kennedy, in Leaders of the World, Ann Commire, ed, 93; coauth, Prologue: The Senate Voting Record of Harry S Truman, J of Interdisciplinary Hist, 73. **CONTACT ADDRESS** Temple Univ, Philadelphia, PA, 19122.

HIMMELBERG, ROBERT F.
DISCIPLINE AMERICAN ECONOMIC HISTORY **EDUCATION** Penn State Univ, PhD. **CAREER** Prof; dean, Grad Sch Arts and Sci. **RESEARCH** Study of the Democratic party in Congress during the Republican Era. **SELECTED PUBLICATIONS** Co-auth, The Great Depression and American Capitalism, D C Heath, 68; Herbert Hoover and the Crisis of American Capitalism, Cambridge, Schenckman, 74; auth, Does Antitrust Matter? A Comparative History of Antitrust Policy and The Evolving Corporation in Britain and the United States, Rev(s) Amer Hist 21, 93; The Origins of the National Recovery Administration: Business, Government and the Trade Association Issue, 1921-1933, Fordham UP, 76, revised, 93; Business and Government in America Since 1870, 94; co-ed, Historians and Race: Autobiography and the Writing of History , 96. **CONTACT ADDRESS** Dept of Hist, Fordham Univ, 113 W 60th St, New York, NY, 10023.

HIMMELFARB, GERTRUDE
PERSONAL Born 08/08/1922, New York, NY, m, 1942, 2 children **DISCIPLINE** MODERN HISTORY **EDUCATION** Brooklyn Col, BA, 42; Univ Chicago, MA, 44, PhD, 50. **CAREER** Prof hist, 65-78, exec officer, 74-79, distinguished prof, Grad Sch & Univ Ctr, 78-87, prof emeritus, 87- , City Univ NY; Res & writing, 52-; fels, Am Asn Univ Women, 51-52, Am Philos Soc, 53-54, Guggenheim Found, 55-56 & 57-58 & Rockefeller Found, 62-63 & 63-64; Nat Endowment for Humanities sr fel, 68-69; Am Coun Learned Socs fel, 72-73; mem, Presidential Adv Comt Econ Role of Women, 72-; vis comt, Univ Chicago, 72-79; mem bd overseers, Hoover Inst, Stanford Univ, 73-79; mem adv coun, Acad Jewish Studies, Univ Haifa, 74; mem bd trustees, Nat Humanities Ctr, 76-88; Woodrow Wilson Int Ctr fel, 76-77; Rockefeller Found Humanities fel, 80-81; mem bd dir, Int Coun on Future of the Univ, 80-83. **HONORS AND AWARDS** Jefferson Lecture, NEH, 91; Templeton Found Award for Outstanding Book, 97., LittD, Smith Col, 77, Jewish Theol Sem & Lafayette Col, 78; LHD, Rhode Island Col, 76. **MEMBERSHIPS** Fel Am Acad Arts & Sci; Soc Am Historians; fel Royal Hist Soc; British Acad; Am Philos Soc. **RESEARCH** Nineteenth century English history; modern intellectual history; social history. **SELECTED PUBLICATIONS** Auth, Lord Acton: A Study in Conscience and Politics, Univ Chicago, 52; Darwin and the Darwinian Revolution, Doubleday, 59; ed, T S Malthus, On Population, Mod Libr, 60; J S Mill, Essays on Politics and Culture, Doubleday, 62; auth, Victorian Minds, Knopf, 68; contribr, The Victorian City, Routledge & Kegan Paul, 73; auth, On Liberty and Liberalism, Knopf, 74; ed, On Liberty, Penquin, 74; auth, The Idea of Poverty, Knopf, 84; auth, Marriage and Morals Among the Victorians, Knopf, 86; auth, The New History and the Old, Harvard, 87; auth, Poverty and Compassion, Knopf, 92; auth, On Looking Into the Abyss, Knopf, 94; auth, The De-Moralization of Society, Knopf, 95; ed, Alexis de Tocqueville, Memoir on Pauperism, Ivan Dee, 97. **CONTACT ADDRESS** Dept of History, Graduate Sch and Univ Ctr, CUNY, New York, NY, 10036.

HINCKLEY, TED C.
PERSONAL Born 10/04/1925, New York, NY, m, 1948, 2 children **DISCIPLINE** HISTORY **EDUCATION** Claremont Men's Col, BA, 50; Northwest Mo State Col, BS, 51; Univ Kansas City, MA, 53; Ind Univ, PhD(hist), 61. **CAREER** Instr hist, Barstow Sch, 51-53; instr & asst to pres, Claremont Men's Col, 53-55; headmaster, St Katharine's Sch, 55-57; assoc prof US hist, 63-67, PROF HIST, SAN JOSE STATE UNIV, 67-, Am Philos Soc grants, 62 & 66; Danforth assoc, 62; lectr, Nat Endowment for Humanities, 67 & 76; Am Asn State & Local Hist grant, 69; Huntington Libr grant, 71; dir, Sourisseau Acad Calif State & Local Hist, 71-73. **HONORS AND AWARDS** Distinguished Teaching Award, Calif State Cols, 67, Outstanding Professor Award, 81. **MEMBERSHIPS** AHA; Orgn Am Historians; Presby Hist Soc: Western Hist Asn. **RESEARCH** Pacific Basin, 1500-1941; Alaska, 1867-1897; 19th century United States. **SELECTED PUBLICATIONS** Auth, Glimpses of Societal Change Among 19th-Century Tlingit Women--Alaskan Native-American Indians, J West, Vol 0032, 93. **CONTACT ADDRESS** Dept of Hist, San Jose State Univ, San Jose, CA, 95192.

HINDMAN, E. JAMES
PERSONAL Lubbock, TX, m, 2 children **DISCIPLINE** HISTORY OF THE UNITED STATES **EDUCATION** TX Tech Univ, BA, 66, MA, 68, PhD, 72. **CAREER** Instr, Lamar Univ, 70; asst prof, 72-, ch, dept Hist, Sul Ross State Univ; dean, Col of Liberal Arts and Sci, dir, Honors Mentoring Prog, Eastern NMex Univ, 86; assoc vice pres for Acad Aff, 88, prof, Univ Northern Colo; provost and vice pres for Acad Aff, Mid Tenn State Univ; prof, Pres, Angelo State Univ, 94-; bd trustees, UP Colo, 89-91. **MEMBERSHIPS** Bd dir, TX Asn for Advan of Hist; San Angelo Chamber of Com; Rotary Club. **SELECTED PUBLICATIONS** Publ a variety of scholarly articles on hist and educ. **CONTACT ADDRESS** Angelo State Univ, San Angelo, TX, 76909. **EMAIL** President@angelo.edu

HINDMAN, SANDRA L.
DISCIPLINE MEDIEVAL MANUSCRIPTS, EARLY PRINTED BOOK **EDUCATION** Cornell Univ, PhD. **CAREER** Prof, Ch Art History dpt, Northwestern Univ. **RESEARCH** Gothic art, women in medieval art and society. **SELECTED PUBLICATIONS** Auth, Sealed in Parchment: Rereadings of Knighthood in the Illuminated Manuscripts of Chretien de Troyes, Univ Chicago Press, 94; Christine de Pizan's "Epistre Othea": Painting and Politics at the Court of Charles VI; ed, Printing the Written Word: The Social History of Books, c.1450-1520. **CONTACT ADDRESS** Dept of Art History, Northwestern Univ, 1801 Hinman, Evanston, IL, 60208.

HINE, WILLIAM CASSIDY
PERSONAL Born 10/16/1943, Dodge City, KS **DISCIPLINE** UNITED STATES HISTORY **EDUCATION** Bowling Green State Univ, BS, 65; Univ Wyo, MA, 67; Kent State Univ, PhD, 79. **CAREER** From Instr to Assoc Prof, 67-83, prof hist, SC State Univ, 83-; Vis prof, Idaho State Univ, 80. **MEMBERSHIPS** Orgn Am Historians; Southern Hist Asn; Asn Study Afro-Am Life Hist. **RESEARCH** United States reconstruction; United States African-American; black higher education. **SELECTED PUBLICATIONS** Contribr, Dr Benjamin A Boseman Jr: Charleston's black physician-politician, in Southern Black Leaders During Reconstruction, Univ Ill Press, 6/82; auth, Black politicians in reconstruction Charleston, J of Southern Hist, 11/83; South Carolina State College, Agr Hist, Spring 91; South Carolina's Challenge to Civil Rights, Agr and Human Values, Winter 92; Civil Rights and Campus Wrongs, SC Magazine of Hist, 10/96; Thomas E. Miller and the Early Years of South Carolina State University, Carologue, Winter 96; encyclopedia articles in Black Women in America: An Historical Encyclopedia, Encyclopedia of the Confederacy, and American National Biography (forthcoming 99) **CONTACT ADDRESS** S. Carolina State Univ, 300 College St NE, Box 7207, Orangeburg, SC, 29117-0001. **EMAIL** WHINE@scsu.edu

HINES, JAMES ROBERT
PERSONAL Born 10/27/1937, Springfield, IL, d, 1 child **DISCIPLINE** MUSICOLOGY **EDUCATION** Old Dominion Univ, BA, 65; Va Commonwealth Univ, MM, 69; Univ NC, PhD(musicol), 74 **CAREER** Fac, Tidewater Community Col, 74-75; dir music, 75-92, PROF FINE & PERFORMING ARTS, CHRISTOPHER NEWPORT UNIV, 92-; Dir, Norfolk Camerata, 74-; music critic, Norfolk Virginian-Pilot, 74-77. **HONORS AND AWARDS** Outstanding Faculty **MEMBERSHIPS** Am Musicological Soc; Sonneck Soc Am Music **RESEARCH** Nineteenth century American music, folk music of Guyana. **SELECTED PUBLICATIONS** Ed, A performance practices bibliography, third supplement, Current Musicology, 73. **CONTACT ADDRESS** Christopher Newport Univ, 1 University Pl, Newport News, VA, 23606. **EMAIL** jhines@cnu.edu

HINES, THOMAS S.
DISCIPLINE HISTORY **EDUCATION** Univ Mississippi, BA, 58, MA, 60; Univ Wis, Madison, PhD, 71. **CAREER** Prof Hist & Arch, UCLA, 68-; vis prof, Sch of Arch & Am Stud Prog, Univ Texas, 74-75; Fulbright prof, Am Stud, Univ Exeter, Eng, 84-84. **HONORS AND AWARDS** John H. Dunning Prize, Am Hist Asn, 76; NEH Fel, 78-79; Fulbright Fel, 84-85; Guggenheim Fel, 87-88; Am Acad Arts, Scis, 94; Getty Scholar, 96-97. **SELECTED PUBLICATIONS** Auth, "The Search for Frank Lloyd Wright: History, Biography, Autobiography," Jour Soc Arch Hist, 95;auth, William Faulkner and the Tangible Past: The Architecture of Yoknapatawpha, Univ Calif Press, 96; auth, "The Blessing and the Curse: The Achievement of Lloyd Wright," in The Architecture of Lloyd Wright," Thames and Hudson, 98; **CONTACT ADDRESS** Dept of History, Univ California, Los Angeles, 405 Hilgard Ave, Los Angeles, CA, 90024.

HINSLEY, CURTIS M.
DISCIPLINE HISTORY **EDUCATION** Princeton Univ, BA, 67; Univ Wis Madison, MA, 71, PhD, 76. **CAREER** Assoc prof, hist, Colgate Univ; current, PROF HIST, N ARIZ. **MEMBERSHIPS** Am Antiquarian Soc **SELECTED PUBLICATIONS** Auth, Savages and Scientists: The Smithsonian Institution and the Development of American Anthropology, 1846-1910, Smithsonian Inst Press, 81; auth, Zunis and Brahmins: Cultural Ambivalence in the Gilded Age, in History of Anthropology 6: Romantic Motives: Essays on Anthropological Sensibility, 169-207; auth, Revising and Revisioning the History of Archaeology: Reflections on Region and Context, in Tracing Archaeology's Past: The Historiography of Archaeology, So Ill Univ Press, 89; auth, Collecting Cultures and Cultures of Collecting: The Lure of the American Southwest, 1880-1915, in Museum Anthropology 16, 92; auth, In Search of the New World Classical, in Collecting the Pre-Columbian Past, Dumbarton Oaks, 93. **CONTACT ADDRESS** Dept of Hist, No Arizona Univ, Flagstaff, AZ, 86011-6023.

HINSON, E. GLENN
PERSONAL Born 07/27/1931, St. Louis, MO, m, 1956, 2 children **DISCIPLINE** CHURCH HISTORY **EDUCATION** Washington Univ; BA 54; Southern Baptist Theological Seminary; BD, ThD, 57,62; Oxford Univ; D Phil 74. **CAREER** Southern Baptist Theological Sem; prof, 62-92, prof of spirituality, John Loftis Prof of church hist, 92-99; Wake Forest Univ; prof 82-84. **HONORS AND AWARDS** Johannes Quasten Medal; Cuthbert Allen Awd; 2 ATS Fell; Prof of the Year SBTS. **MEMBERSHIPS** ASCH; AAR; IPS; EIS; NAPS; NABPR; ITMS. **RESEARCH** Early Christianity and Spirituality. **SELECTED PUBLICATIONS** Auth, Love At the Heart of Things: A Biography of Douglas V. Steer, Pendle Hill Pub, 98; The Early Church, Abingdon, 96; The Church Triumphant: A History of Christianity up to 1300, Mercer Univ, 95; A Serious Call to a Contemplative Lifestyles, rev, ed, Smith & Helwys 93. **CONTACT ADDRESS** Dept of Church History, S Baptist Theological Sem, 3400 Brook Rd, Richmond, VA, 23227.

HIRSCH, ARNOLD RICHARD
PERSONAL Born 03/09/1949, Chicago, IL, m, 1971, 2 children **DISCIPLINE** AMERICAN & URBAN HISTORY **EDUCATION** Univ Ill, Chicago Circle, BA, 70, MA, 72, PhD(US hist), 78. **CAREER** Asst prof US hist, Univ Ill, Chicago Circle, 78; ASST PROF US & URBAN HIST, UNIV NEW ORLEANS, 79-, Vis lectr Urban hist, Univ Mich, 79. **MEMBERSHIPS** AHA; Orgn Am Historians. **RESEARCH** Urban politics and policy; race relations; immigration and ethnicity. **SELECTED PUBLICATIONS** Auth, Property Rules--Political-Economy in Chicago, 1833-1872, Am J Legal Hist, Vol 0037, 93; Black Neighbors--Race and the Limits of Reform in the American Settlement-House-Movement, 1890-1945, Rev Am Hist, Vol 0022, 94; Building a New Boston--Politics and Urban-Renewal, 1950-1970, Am Hist Rev, Vol 0099, 94; Black Dixie--Afro-Texan History and Culture in Houston, Southwestern Hist Quarterly, Vol 0097, 94; Black San-Francisco--The Struggle for Racial Equality in the West, 1900-1954, J Am Hist, Vol 0081, 94; On the Edge--A History of Poor Black-Children and Their American Dreams, Am Hist Rev, Vol 0100, 95; Waterfront Workers in New-Orleans--Race, Class and Politics, 1863-1923, J Urban Hist, Vol 0021, 95; Massive Resistance in the Urban North--Trumbull-Park, Chicago, 1953-1966, J Am Hist, Vol 0082, 95; Creoles of Color of the Gulf South, J Southern Hist, Vol 0063, 97; The Separate City--Black-Communities in the Urban South, 1940-1968, Am Hist Rev, Vol 0102, 97. **CONTACT ADDRESS** Dept Hist, Univ New Orleans, 2000 Lakeshore Dr, New Orleans, LA, 70148-0001.

HIRSCH, HERBERT
PERSONAL Born 04/29/1941, New York, NY, m, 1998, 4 children **DISCIPLINE** POLITICAL SCIENCE **EDUCATION** Concord Col, BA, 63; Villanova Univ, MA, 65; Univ KY, PhD, 68. **CAREER** Asst prof, Univ TX, Austin, 68-73, assoc prof, 73-80; prof and chair, 81-90, dir, Int studies, 90-91, prof of Political Science, VA Commonwealth Univ, 91-. **HONORS AND AWARDS** Distinguished lect, VA Commonwealth Univ, 89. **MEMBERSHIPS** Int Coun for the Inst of the Holocaust & Genocide; Gouldnet Holocaust Symposium, Oxfordshire, England; Int Network on Holocaust & Genocide, Sydney, Australia; Inst on Holocaust & Genocide, Jerusalem. **RESEARCH** Politics of war; violence and genocide. **SELECTED PUBLICATIONS** Auth, Poverty and Politicization: Political Socialization in an American Sub-Culture, The Free Press, 71; Comparative Legislative Systems: A Reader in Theory and Research, with M Donald Hancock, The Free Press, 71; Violence as Politics: A Series of Original Essays, with David C Perry, Harper & Row, 73; Learning to Be Militant: Ethnic Identity and the Development of Political Militance in a Chicago Community, with Armando Gutierrez, R & E Res Assocs, 77; The Right of the People: An Introduction to American Politics, Univ Press of Am, 80; Persistant Prejudice: Prespectives in Anti-Semitism, with Jack Spiro, George Mason Univ Press, 88; Genocide and the Politics of Memory: Studying Death to Preserve Life, Univ NC Press, April 95; articles in The Am Political Science Rev, Western Political Quart; Social Science Quart, Aztlan, Int J of Group Tensions, Ed Forum, Armenian Rev, Australian J of Jewish Studies. **CONTACT ADDRESS** Dept of Political Science, Virginia Commonwealth Univ, 923 Franklin St, Richmond, VA, 23284. **EMAIL** HHirsch@prodigy.com

HIRSCH, SUSAN E.
DISCIPLINE HISTORY **EDUCATION** Univ Mich, PhD, 74. **CAREER** Hist, Loyola Univ. **RESEARCH** Labor; work; soc structure. **SELECTED PUBLICATIONS** Auth, Roots of the American Working Class: The Industrialization of Crafts in Newark, 1800-1860, Philadelphia: Univ Pa Press, 78; coauth, A City Comes of Age: Chicago in the 1890s, Chicago Hist Soc, 90; co-ed, The War in American Culture: Society and Consciousness during World War II, Univ Chicago Press, 96. **CONTACT ADDRESS** Fine Arts Dept, Loyola Univ, Chicago, 6525 N. Sheridan Rd., Chicago, IL, 60626. **EMAIL** shirsch@orion.it.luc.edu

HIRSCH, WERNER Z.
DISCIPLINE ECONOMICS **EDUCATION** Univ Cal Berkeley, PhD, 49. **CAREER** Prof, Univ Cal Los Angeles. **MEMBERSHIPS** Am Econ Asoc. **RESEARCH** Law and economics. **CONTACT ADDRESS** 11601 Bellagio Rd., Los Angeles, CA, 90049. **EMAIL** whirsch@ucla.edu

HIRSCHMANN, DAVID
DISCIPLINE RURAL DEVELOPMENT **EDUCATION** Univ Witwatersrand, Johannesburg, BA, LLB, MA, PhD. **CAREER** Prof, Am Univ. **RESEARCH** Development management; Decentralization; Women and development, Democracy. **SELECTED PUBLICATIONS** Auth, Women Farmers in Malawi, UCLA, 84; Changing Attitudes of Black South Africans toward the United States, E. Mellen Press, 89. **CONTACT ADDRESS** American Univ, 4400 Massachusetts Ave, Washington, DC, 20016.

HIRSH, RICHARD FREDERIC
PERSONAL New York, NY **DISCIPLINE** HISTORY OF SCIENCE & TECHNOLOGY **EDUCATION** Middlebury Col, BA, 74; Univ Wis-Madison, MA, 76, PhD(hist sci), 79, MS, 80. **CAREER** Asst prof hist sci, Univ Md, 79; fel, Lilly Found, Univ Fla, 79-80; ASST PROF HIST, VA POLYTECH INST & STATE UNIV, 80-, Consult, Am Inst Physics, 80-81. **HONORS AND AWARDS** Henry Schuman Prize, Hist Sci Soc, 76; Hist Manuscript Award, Am Inst Aeronaut & Astronaut, 80. **MEMBERSHIPS** Hist Sci Soc; Soc Hist Technol; Am Asn Physics Teachers; AAAS. **RESEARCH** History of astronomy; history of electric power industry; science, technology and public policy. **SELECTED PUBLICATIONS** Auth, Momentum Shifts in the American Electric Utility System--Catastrophic Change, or No Change At All, Tech Cult, Vol 0037, 96; Wolf Creek Station--Kansas Gas and Electric Company in the Nuclear Era, Tech Cult, Vol 0037, 96; Electrifying Eden--Portland-General-Electric, 1889-1965, J West, Vol 0032, 93. **CONTACT ADDRESS** Dept of Hist, Va Polytech Inst & State Univ, Blacksburg, VA, 24061.

HIRST, DEREK M.
DISCIPLINE EARLY-MODERN BRITAIN **EDUCATION** Cambridge Univ, BA, 69; PhD, 74. **CAREER** Hist, Washington Univ. **HONORS AND AWARDS** Nat Endowment Hum sr fel, Folger Library, 79; Guggenheim fel, 81-82; Vis sr res fel, Gonville & Caius College, 81-82., Fel, Royal Hist Socy, Trinity Hall; Dir Studies History, 74-75; Asst prof to prof, Washington Univ, 75-; Clark Lect, Univ Calif, 83; Codir, Folger Inst seminar,91. **SELECTED PUBLICATIONS** Auth, The Lord Profotector, Oliver Cromwell And The English Revolution, Longmans, 90; The Political Context Literature In The 1650s, The Seventeenth-Century, 90; Liberty, Revolution And Beyond, Parliament And Liberty From The Reign Elizabeth To The Civil War, Stanford Univ Profess, 91; The Failure Godly Rule In The English Republic, Past And Profesent, 91; Coauth, High At Nunappleton, 1651: Andrew Marvell And Lord Fairfax's Occasions, Histl Jour, 93; The Rupturing The Cromwellian Alliance English Historical Rev, 93; 'The English Republic And The Meaning Britain,' Jour Mod Hist, 94; 'Milton And The Drama Justice,' The Theatrical City,Cambridge Univ Profess, 95; 'British Isles 1450-1800', Aha Guide To Histl Lit, Oxford, 95. **CONTACT ADDRESS** Washington Univ, 1 Brookings Dr, St. Louis, MO, 63130.

HIRT, PAUL W.
DISCIPLINE HISTORY, AMERICAN WEST **EDUCATION** Univ Ariz, PhD, 91. **CAREER** Asst prof, Washington State Univ. **HONORS AND AWARDS** Rockefeller Found fel, Univ Kansas, 93. **SELECTED PUBLICATIONS** Auth, A Conspiracy of Optimism: Management of the National Forests Since World War II, Univ Nebr Press, 94 & Timber Dreams: Fifty Years of National Forest Planning, Inner Voice, 94. **CONTACT ADDRESS** Dept of History, Washington State Univ, 301 Wilson Hall, PO Box 644030, Pullman, WA, 99164-4030. **EMAIL** forrest@wsunix.wsu.edu

HISE, GREG
DISCIPLINE HISTORY OF ARCHITECTURE, ARCHITECTURE **EDUCATION** Univ CA, Berkeley, AB (Architecture, with honors), 80-84, PhD (Hist of Arch), 87-92. **CAREER** Asst prof, School of Urban Planning and Development, Univ Southern CA, 92-98, assoc prof, School of Policy, Planning, and Development, 98-; vis assoc, Div of Humanities and Social Sciences, Cal Tech, 97-98. **HONORS AND AWARDS** John Reps Prize, Soc of Am City & Regional Planning Hist, 93; Spiro Kostof Book Prize for Architecture and Urbanism, Soc of Architectural Historians, for Magnetic Los Angeles, 98. **SELECTED PUBLICATIONS** Auth, Home Building and Industrial Decentralization in Los Angeles: The Roots of the Postwar Urban Region, J of Urban Hist, Feb 93; Building the World of Tomorrow: Regional Visions, Modern Community Housing and America's Postwar Urban Expansion, Center: A J for Architecture in Am, 93; The Airplane and the Garden City: Regional Transformations during World War II, in Donald Albrecht, ed, World War II and the American Dream: How Wartime Building Changed a Nation, MIT Press with the Nat Building Museum, 95; From Roadside Camps to Garden Homes: Housing and Community Planning for California's Migrant Workforce, 1935-41, in Elizabeth Cromley and Carter L Huggins, eds, Gender, Race, and Shelter: Perspectives in Vernacular Architecture V, Univ TN Press, 95; Building Design as Social Art: The Public Architecture of William Wurster, 1935-1950, in Marc Treib, ed, An Everyday Modernism: The Houses of Willaim Wurster, UC Press with SFMOMA, 95; ed, Rethinking Los Angeles, with Michael J Dear and H Eric Schockman, Sage Pub, 96; Magnetic Los Angeles: Planning the Twentieth-Century Metropolis, Johns Hopkins Univ Press, 97. **CONTACT ADDRESS** School of Policy, Planning, and Development, Univ of Southern California, Von Kleinsmid Center 351, Los Angeles, CA, 90089-0626.

HITCHENS, MARILYNN JO
PERSONAL Born 12/14/1938, w, 1974, 2 children **DISCIPLINE** HISTORY **EDUCATION** Miami Univ, BA, 60; Univ Colo, MA, 75, PhD, 79. **CAREER** Research/Writer, US Congress, 68-70; Teacher Russ & Hist, Jefferson County Schools, 70-95; Instr World & Russ Hist, Univ Colo, 94-98; International Legal Res, Holme Roberts & Owen LLP, 95-. **HONORS AND AWARDS** Phi Beta Kappa **MEMBERSHIPS** Am Hist Asn; World Hist Asn. **RESEARCH** World history. **SELECTED PUBLICATIONS** Auth, Germany, Russia and the Balkans: Prelude to the Nazi-Soviet Non-Aggression Pact; SATII World History; Aspen World History Handbooks I & II; Discovering World History; Discovering Nation States; Essays in World History; Readings in World History. **CONTACT ADDRESS** 720 Josephine, Denver, CO, 80206. **EMAIL** Hitchem@hro.com

HITCHINS, KEITH
PERSONAL Born 04/02/1931, Schenectady, NY **DISCIPLINE** MODERN HISTORY **EDUCATION** Union Col, NY, AB, 52; Harvard Univ, AM, 53, PhD(Hist), 64. **CAREER** Instr Hist, Wake Forest Univ, 58-60 & 62-64, asst prof, 64-65; asst prof, Rice Univ, 66-67; assoc prof, 67-69, prof Hist, Univ Ill, Urbana Champaign, 69-, Am Coun Learned Soc grant, 65-66, res fel, Hungary & Rumania, 69-70; mem, Nat Screening Comt Fulbright-Hays Awards for Poland, Rumania & Yugoslavia, 66-68; mem East Europ adv comt, Coun Int Exchange of Scholars, 70-79; mem East Europ screening comt, Int Res & Exchange Bd, 72-75, res fel for Hungary, 73; The Romanians, 1774-1866, Oxford, 96; Mit si realitate in istoriografia romaneasca, Enciclopedica, 97. **HONORS AND AWARDS** Honorary Member, Romanian Academy, 91; Doctor honoris causa, U of Cluj, 91, Univ Sibiu, 93. **RESEARCH** Southeastern Europe; Habsburg monarchy; the Caucasus. **SELECTED PUBLICATIONS** Auth, The Rumanian National Movement in Transylvania, 1780-1849, Harvard Univ, 69; ed, Rumanian Studies, E J Brill, Leyden Vol I, 70, Vol II, 71-72, Vol III, 73-75, Vol IV, 76-79; coauth, Corespondenta lui Ioan Ratiu cu George Baritiu, 70, auth, Studii privind istoria moderna a Transilvaniei, 70 & Cultura si nationalitate in Transilvania, 72, Dacia; The Nationality Problem in Austria-Hungary, 74 & ed, Studies in East European Social History, Vol 1,77, Vol II, 81, E J Brill, Leyden; auth, Orthodoxy and Nationality: Andreiu Saguna and the Rumanians of Transylvania, 1846-1873, Harvard Univ, 77; Hungarica, 1961-1974, Historische Zeitschrift, Sonderheft 9. **CONTACT ADDRESS** Dept of History, Univ of Illinois, Urbana-Champaign, 810 S Wright St, Urbana, IL, 61801-3611.

HIXSON, WALTER LAWRENCE
PERSONAL Born 10/18/1955, Louisville, KY, m, 2 children **DISCIPLINE** HISTORY **EDUCATION** Univ Ky, BA, 78; W Ky Univ, MA, 81; Univ Co, PhD, 86. **CAREER** Vis asst prof, NW Univ, 87-89; PROF, 89-, CHR, 98-, UNIV AKRON, 89-. **HONORS AND AWARDS** Bernath Prize, Soc Hist of Am For Rel, 89. **MEMBERSHIPS** Soc Hist Am For Rel; Orgn Am Hist. **RESEARCH** United States foreign relations; Cold War. **SELECTED PUBLICATIONS** auth Parting the Curtain: Propaganda, Culture, and the Cold War, 1945-1961, St Martin's Press, 96; Charles A. Lindbergh, Lone Eagle, Harper-Collins, 96. **CONTACT ADDRESS** Univ Akron, 201 Olin Hall, Akron, OH, 44325-1902. **EMAIL** walter4@uakron.edu

HOARD, R.J.
PERSONAL Born 04/03/1956, Chicago Heights, IL, m, 1984, 3 children **DISCIPLINE** ANTHROPOLOGY **EDUCATION** Univ NE, Lincoln, BA (anthropol), 82; Univ OR, MA (Anthropol), 85; Univ MO, Columbia, PhD (Anthropol), 92. **CAREER** Grad teaching asst, field school inst, Dept of Anthropol, Univ OR, 84-85; grad instr, grad teaching asst, Dept of Anthropol, Univ MO, Columbia, 86-91; Instr, Dept of Social and Behavioral Sciences, 98. **HONORS AND AWARDS** Grant-in-aid, Soc of the Sigma Xi, 89. **MEMBERSHIPS** Soc for Am Archaeology; Plains Anthropol Soc; MO Archaeol Soc; Human Behavior and Evolution Soc. **RESEARCH** Archaeology, primarily early agricultural societies; geographic emphasis: North Am (midwest); res foci: ceramic technology, materials science, archaeometry, Late Woodland. **SELECTED PUBLICATIONS** Auth, Technical Dimension of Woodland-Period Cooking Vessels From Missouri, dissertation, Univ Microfilm, Ann Arbor, MI, 92; with S R Holen, M D Glascock, H Neff, and J M Elam, Neutron Activation Analysis of Stone from the Chadron Formation and a Clovis Site on the Great Plains, J of Archaeol Sci, 92; with J R Bozell, S R Holen, M D Glascock, H Neff, and J M Elam, Source Determination of White River Group Silicates From Two Archaeological Sites in the Great Plains, Am Antiquity, 93; with M J O'Brien, T D Holland, and G L Fox, Materials Science and Midwestern Pottery: Generating Data for a Selectionist Framework, J of Archaeol Method and Theory, 94; with S R Holen, M D Glascock, H Neff, Additional Comments on Neutron Activation Analysis of Stone From the Great Plains: Reply to Church, J of Archaeol Sci, 95; with M J O'Brien, M Ghazavy Khorasgany, and V S Gopalaratnam, A Materials Science Approach to Understanding Limestone-Tempered Pottery From the Midwest, J of Archaeol Sci, 95; with M J O'Brien, Ceramic Vessels, in Burkemper: A Study of Middle and Late Woodland Subsistence and Ceramic Technology in the Central Mississippi River Valley, IL State Musueum Reports of Investigations, no 52, 96; with T M Prawl, the Origins and Evolution of Rock Feces in Missouri, Material Culture, 98; Archaeological Investigations at Richterkessing Mound, 23SC501, St Charles County, Missouri, The MO Archaeol, forthcoming. **CONTACT ADDRESS** Preliminary Studies-Cultural Resources, Missouri Dept of Transportation, PO Box 270, Jefferson City, MO, 65102. **EMAIL** hoardr@mail.modot.stste.mo.us

HOBBS, WAYNE
DISCIPLINE MUSIC HISTORY AND LITERATURE **EDUCATION** FL State Univ, BME; New Orleans Baptist Theol Sem, MCM; Tulane Univ, PhD. **CAREER** Hd, dept Mus, Western KY Univ; ch, dept Mus, Univ New Orleans; prof Mus, dir, Sch Mus, TX Tech Univ, 87-94. **RESEARCH** The early baroque; Am music. **SELECTED PUBLICATIONS** Publ articles in the fields of music administration, musicology, interdisciplinary arts, music theory, and choral music. **CONTACT ADDRESS** Texas Tech Univ, Lubbock, TX, 79409-5015. **EMAIL** a5sjm@ttuvm1.ttu.edu

HOBERMAN, LOUISA SCHELL
PERSONAL Born 06/01/1942, Boston, MA, m, 1968 **DISCIPLINE** LATIN AMERICAN & URBAN HISTORY **EDUCATION** Radcliffe Col, BA, 63; Columbia Univ, MA, 66, PhD(hist), 72. **CAREER** Instr hist, Univ Calif Exten, Berkeley, 70; asst prof, Pomona Col, 72-76; asst prof hist, Wesleyan Univ, 76-80; RES & WRITING, 80-, Vis scholar, Inst Latin Am Studies, Univ Texas, Austin, 79-80; Mary I Bunting Inst Radcliffe Col fel, 77-78. **MEMBERSHIPS** Conf Latin Am Hist; AHA; Latin Am Studies Asn; Women's Coalition Latin Americanists; Nat Coun on Pub Hist. **RESEARCH** Business history **SELECTED PUBLICATIONS** Auth, Social Assistance and Bureaucratic Politics--The Montepios of Colonial Mexico, 1767-1821, J Interdisciplinary Hist, Vol 0024, 94; Gazeta-De-Mexico January-July-1785, Hisp Am Hist Rev, Vol 0075, 95; Science and Technology in America Urbanization, Hisp Am Hist Rev, Vol 0077, 97. **CONTACT ADDRESS** 2637 West 49th St, Austin, TX, 78731.

HOBGOOD-OSTER, LAURA
PERSONAL Born 09/18/1964, Indiana, m, 1995 **DISCIPLINE** HISTORICAL THEOLOGY **EDUCATION** St Louis Univ, PhD, 97; Vanderbilt Univ, Mdiv, 89; James Madison Univ, BA, 85. **CAREER** Asst Prof of Rel, 98-, Southwestern Univ; Lectr/Instr of Rel Studies, 97-98, Cal State Univ. **HONORS AND AWARDS** Pres Fellow, 94-97, St Louis Univ; Faculty Merit Scholar, 88-89, Vanderbilt Univ. **MEMBERSHIPS** AAR **RESEARCH** Christianity in America, Theology of Nature, Gnostic Christianity, Women and Religion. **SELECTED PUBLICATIONS** Auth, As Heaven and Earth Combine: Perceptions of Nature in American Shakerism, Esoteric Studies, 98; She Glanceth From Earth to Heaven: The Phenomenon of Love Mysticism Among Women in Antebellum Virginia and Maryland, Univ Press of the South, 98; Mary Magdalene, Gnostic Revealer, Koinonia Journal, Princeton Seminary Graduate Forum 96; Sexuality-One of God's Gifts, A Year in the Life, St Louis, Chalice Books, 93; Building Self Esteem, Christian Children's Fellowship Manual, Chalice Books, 92; ed, The Sabbath Journal of Judith Lomax, Scholar Press, Texts and Translations Series, forthcoming; **CONTACT ADDRESS** Southwestern Univ, 1001 E University, Georgetown, TX, 78626. **EMAIL** hoboster@southwestern.edu

HOBSBAWM, ERIC
DISCIPLINE HISTORY **EDUCATION** Cambridge Univ, PhD, 51. **CAREER** Prof Pol and Soc Emeritus and sr lctr grad fac. **RESEARCH** Comp polit, soc, and economic hist. **SELECTED PUBLICATIONS** Auth, Nations and Nationalism Since 1780, 90; Echoes of the Marseillaise, 90; The Age of Empire 1875-1914, 89; The Age of Capital 1848-1875, 75; Industry and Empire, 68; The Age of Revolution 1789-1848, 62. **CONTACT ADDRESS** Eugene Lang Col, New Sch for Social Research, 66 West 12th St, New York, NY, 10011.

HOBSON, CHARLES FREDERIC
PERSONAL Born 03/27/1943, Mobile, AL, m, 1969, 2 children **DISCIPLINE** UNITED STATES HISTORY **EDUCATION** Brown Univ, BA, 65; Emory Univ, MA, 66, PhD(hist), 71. **CAREER** Instr hist, Ga State Univ, 70-72; asst ed, Papers of James Madison, Univ Va, 72-73, assoc ed, 73-77, co-ed, 77-79; ED, PAPERS OF JOHN MARSHALL, INST EARLY AM HIST & CULTURE, WILLIAMSBURG, 79-, Colonial Williamsburg res grant, 72; lectr, Col William & Mary, 79- **HONORS AND AWARDS** Hamer Award, Soc Am Archivists, 76. **MEMBERSHIPS** Southern Hist Asn; Am Soc Legal Hist; Asn Doc Ed; Soc Historians Early Am Repub. **RESEARCH** Revolution and early national period; 18th century Virginia. **SELECTED PUBLICATIONS** Auth, Law--Interpretation, Ideology, and Interest--Contributions in Legal Studies, No-77 (rev), Am J Legal Hist, Vol 0039, 95. **CONTACT ADDRESS** Papers of John Marshall, Box 220, Williamsburg, VA, 23187.

HOBSON, WAYNE K.
PERSONAL Born 07/01/1941, Moscow, ID, m, 1966, 2 children **DISCIPLINE** AMERICAN STUDIES, HISTORY **EDUCATION** Univ Ore, BA, 65; Reed Col, MAT, 66; Stanford Univ, MA, 69, PhD(hist), 77. **CAREER** Asst prof, 73-78, ASSOC PROF AM STUDIES, CALIF STATE UNIV, FULLERTON, 78- **MEMBERSHIPS** Am Studies Asn; AHA; Orgn Am Historians. **RESEARCH** American social and cultural history; late 19th and early 20th centuries; cultural history of image and reality of crime and violence in America. **SELECTED PUBLICATIONS** Auth, New-Deal Justice--The Life of Stanley Reed of Kentucky, Am Hist Rev, Vol 0101, 96; The Quest for Authority and Honor in the American Professions, 1750-1900, Am Studies Int, Vol 0031, 93. **CONTACT ADDRESS** Dept of Am Studies, California State Univ, Fullerton, Fullerton, CA, 92634.

HOCHMAN, JIRI
PERSONAL Born 03/06/1926, Prague, Czechoslovakia, m, 1963, 2 children **DISCIPLINE** HISTORY **EDUCATION** Ohio State Univ, PhD, 80. **CAREER** Vis Prof, 74-77, from Assoc Prof to Prof, 83-95, Prof Emeritus Hist, Ohio State Univ, 95-. **HONORS AND AWARDS** Czechoslovakia Press Prize, 64; Am Pen Club, 84. **MEMBERSHIPS** Czechoslovakia Hist Conf. **RESEARCH** European history. **SELECTED PUBLICATIONS** Auth, The Soviet Union and the Failure of Collective Security, 1934-1938, Cornell Univ Press, 84; coauth, Hope Dies Last, An Autobiography of Alexander Dubcek, Kodansha Amerrica, 93; auth, Historical Dictionary of the Czech State, Scarecrow Press, 98. **CONTACT ADDRESS** 103 Putter Dr., Palm Coast, FL, 32164. **EMAIL** jirhoch@pcfl.net

HOCHSTADT, STEVE
DISCIPLINE EUROPEAN HISTORY **EDUCATION** Brown Univ, BA, 71, PhD, 83. **CAREER** PROF HIST, CHAIR HIST DEPT, BATES COL, 79-. **CONTACT ADDRESS** History Dept, Bates Col, Lewiston, ME, 04240. **EMAIL** schochsta@bates.edu

HOCKLEY, ALLEN
DISCIPLINE ART HISTORY **EDUCATION** Univ Victoria, BA; Univ British Columbia, MA; Univ Toronto, PhD. **CAREER** Asst prof, Dartmouth Col. **HONORS AND AWARDS** Ed, E Asia Forum, 90-92). **RESEARCH** Japanese prints, early photography in Asia, Buddhist art. **SELECTED PUBLICATIONS** Auth, Harunobu and the Megane-e Tradition, Ukiyo-e guijutsu, 89l; Harunobu's Relationship with Hiraga Gennai, Andon, 89. **CONTACT ADDRESS** Dartmouth Col, 3529 N Main St, Ste. 207, Hanover, NH, 03755. **EMAIL** allen.hockley@dartmouth.edu

HOCKS, ELAINE
DISCIPLINE HUMANITIES COURSE **EDUCATION** Mo Univ, PhD, 91. **CAREER** Adj prof; dir, Learning Center's Writing Lab & coordr, Stretch Engl 20; **MEMBERSHIPS** Elected pres, Alpha chap of Phi Beta Kappa, 96-97, still on bd. **RESEARCH** Post-critical theorists and their relationship between Samuel Taylor Coleridge and Michael Polanyi. **CONTACT ADDRESS** Dept of English, Univ of Missouri-Columbia, 309 University Hall, Columbia, MO, 65211.

HODDESON, LILLIAN
DISCIPLINE HISTORY **EDUCATION** Columbia Univ, PhD, 66. **CAREER** Assoc prof, Univ Ill Urbana Champaign **RESEARCH** History of twentieth century science and technology; oral history. **SELECTED PUBLICATIONS** Auth, Mission Change in the Large Laboratory: the Los Alamos Implosion Program, 1943-1945, Stanford, 92; Critical Assembly: a History of Los Alamos During the Oppenheimer Years, 1943-1945, Cambridge, 93; co-auth, The Mirage of the World Accelerator for World Peace and the Origins of the SSC, Hist Studies Physical and Biological Sci, 93. **CONTACT ADDRESS** History Dept, Univ Ill Urbana Champaign, 52 E Gregory Dr, Champaign, IL, 61820. **EMAIL** hoddeson@uiuc.edu

HODGE, ROBERT WHITE
PERSONAL Born 10/03/1939, Grand Rapids, MI **DISCIPLINE** UNITED STATES HISTORY **EDUCATION** Cent Mich Univ, BS, 61, MA, 63; Mich State Univ, PhD(US foreign rels), 68. **CAREER** From instr to asst prof, 66-72, assoc prof, 72-79, PROF HIST, BELOIT COL, 79-, Vis prof, Univ Nottingham, 73. **MEMBERSHIPS** AHA; Orgn Am Historians. **RESEARCH** United States diplomatic history in the twentieth century. **SELECTED PUBLICATIONS** Auth, Cobb Would Have Caught It--The Golden-Age of Baseball in Detroit, Michigan Hist Rev, Vol 0018, 92. **CONTACT ADDRESS** Dept of Hist, Beloit Col, 700 College St, Beloit, WI, 53511-5595.

HODGES, JAMES A.
DISCIPLINE HISTORY **EDUCATION** N Ala Univ, BS, 55; Vanderbilt Univ, MA, 59, PhD, 63. **CAREER** Michael O Fisher prof. **RESEARCH** Study on textile unionism in the modern South. **SELECTED PUBLICATIONS** Auth, articles in Tenn Histl Quart; auth, Encycl S Hist; auth, New Deal Labor Policy and the Southern Cotton Textile Industry, 1933-1941, Univ Tenn Press, 86. **CONTACT ADDRESS** Dept of Hist, Col of Wooster, Wooster, OH, 44691.

HODGINS, BRUCE W
PERSONAL Born 01/29/1931, Kitchener, ON, Canada, m, 1958, 2 children **DISCIPLINE** CANADIAN & COMMONWEALTH HISTORY **EDUCATION** Univ Western Ont, BA, 53; Queen's Univ, Ont, MA, 55; Duke Univ, PhD(hist), 65. **CAREER** Chmn dept hist, Prince of Wales Col, 55-58; 61-62; lectr, Univ Western Ont, 62-64, asst prof, 64-65; from asst prof to assoc prof, 65-72, PROF HIST, TRENT UNIV, 72-, CHMN, DEPT HIST, 80-, Spec adv federalism, Govt P E I, 57-58, prov archivist, 61-62; mem, Nat Exec Coun, UN Asn in Can, 61-62 & 65-, vchmn, Nat Admin Comt, 66-67, chmn, 67-68, Nat Policy Coun, 68-; vis fel hist, Australian Nat Univ, 70. **HONORS AND AWARDS** Can Centennial Medal, 67; Ont Hist Cruikshank Award, 68. **MEMBERSHIPS** Can Hist Asn; Asn for Cancer Studies. **RESEARCH** Canadian politics, 1841-1873 and 1956 to the present; French Canadian society; Canadian North. **SELECTED PUBLICATIONS** Auth, Protected Places, a History of Ontario Provincial-Parks System, Can Hist Rev, Vol 0076, 95; Rebirth, Political, Economic, and Social-Development in 1st Nations, Can Hist Rev, Vol 0076, 95. **CONTACT ADDRESS** Dept of Hist, Trent Univ, Peterborough, ON, K9J 7B8.

HOEVELER, J. DAVID
PERSONAL Born 07/31/1943, Bridgeport, CT, m, 1972, 2 children **DISCIPLINE** HISTORY **EDUCATION** Lehigh Univ, BA, 65; Univ Ill-Urbana Champaign, PhD, 71. **CAREER** Asst prof, Univ Wis, 71-77; assoc prof, Univ Wis, 77-82; PROF, UNIV WIS, 82-. **MEMBERSHIPS** Org Am Hist; Am Soc for 18th Cent Stud **RESEARCH** American thought & culture. **SELECTED PUBLICATIONS** Watch on the Right: Conservative Intellectuals in the Reagan Era, Univ Wis Press, 92; The Postmodernist Turn: American Thought and Culture in the 1970s, Twayne Publ, 96. **CONTACT ADDRESS** Dept History, Univ Wis, PO Box 413, Milwaukee, WI, 53201. **EMAIL** jdh2@csd.uwm.edu

HOEY, LAWRENCE R.
DISCIPLINE ART HISTORY **EDUCATION** Univ Rochester, BA, 73; Univ Chicago, MA, 74, PhD, 81. **CAREER** Asst prof, 81-88; assoc prof, 88-. **MEMBERSHIPS** Soc Antiquaries London; British Archaeol Asn; Soc Archit Hist; Int Center Medieval Art; AVISTA. **SELECTED PUBLICATIONS** Auth, A Problem in Romanesque Aesthetics: The Articulation of Groin and Early Rib Vaults in the Larger Churches of England and Normandy, 96; Style, Patronage, and Artistic Creativity in Kent Parish Church Architecture in the Early English Period, 96; The 13th-Century Choir and Transepts of Rievaulx Abbey, 95; Stone Vaults in English Parish Churches in the Early Gothic and

Decorated Periods, 94; Pier Design in Early Gothic Architecture in East-Central Scotland c.1170-1250, 94. **CONTACT ADDRESS** Dept of Art History, Univ of Wisconsin, Milwaukee, PO Box 413, Milwaukee, WI, 53201. **EMAIL** 1hoey@csd.uwm.edu

HOFF, JOAN
PERSONAL Born 06/27/1939, Butte, MT **DISCIPLINE** U.S. HISTORY **EDUCATION** Univ MT, BA 57; Cornell Univ, MA, 60; Univ Calif, PhD, 69. **CAREER** Prof Calif State Univ, 73-76; Sr Prof Ariz State Univ, 76-81; Kathe Tappe Vernon Vis prof, Dartmouth, 80; vis prof, Univ Va, 81; prof, Ind Univ, 81-97; co-ed/co-founder, The Journal of Women's History 88-96; pres and CEO, Ctr for Study of the Presidency, 95-96; ed, Pres Stu Qrt, 95-97; dir, Contemp Hist Inst, prof, Ohio Univ 97-98. **HONORS AND AWARDS** Fel, Soc of Am Historians; Sr Lectr Fulbright Prog, IU-Bloomington; Distinguished Fac Res Lectr; USIS Fac Lectr Warsaw Univ; Mary Ball Washington Ch, Univ Col, Dublin; Hon Doctorate, MT State Univ. **MEMBERSHIPS** OAH, SNAFR, Peace Hist Soc. **RESEARCH** Modern Presidency; U.S. 20th century for policy and politics; U.S. women's history. **SELECTED PUBLICATIONS** Auth, Law, Gender, and Injustice: A Legal History of U.S. Women from the American Revolution to the Present, NY Univ Press 91; auth, Nixon Reconsidered, Basic Books, 94; co-ed, Voices of Irish Women: Past and Present, Ind Univ Press 95; co-ed, The Nixon Presidency, NY Ctr for the Study of the Presidency, 95. **CONTACT ADDRESS** Contemporary History Inst, Ohio Univ, Brown House, Athens, OH, 45701. **EMAIL** hoffj@oak.cats.ohiou.edu

HOFFECKER, CAROL E.
PERSONAL Born 12/29/1938, Wilmington, DE **DISCIPLINE** AMERICAN HISTORY **CAREER** Asst prof hist, Sweet Briar Col, 63-66; coordr Hagley Fel Prog, Hagley Mus, Univ Del, 70-73; asst prof, 70-75, assoc prof, 75-81, prof hist, 82-, Univ Del. **HONORS AND AWARDS** Francis Alison Prof; Richards Prof; Medal of Distinction, Univ Del; Del Women's Hall of Fame. **MEMBERSHIPS** Orgn Am Historians; AHA. **RESEARCH** History of Delaware; urban history. **SELECTED PUBLICATIONS** Auth, U.S. District Court for Delaware, 92; auth, Beneath Thy Guiding Hand: A History of Women at the University of Delaware, 94. **CONTACT ADDRESS** Dept of History, Univ of Del, Newark, DE, 19711. **EMAIL** Carol.Hoffecker@mvs.udel.edu

HOFFECKER, J.F.
PERSONAL Born 12/16/1952, London, England, m, 1985, 2 children **DISCIPLINE** ARCHAEOLOGY **EDUCATION** Univ Chicago, anthropology 86; Yale Univ, archaeology 75. **CAREER** Argonne National Laboratory, environ scientist, 84-98; Univ of Colorado, Inst of Arctic and Alpine Research, 98-. **HONORS AND AWARDS** Dist Performance Awd ANL. **MEMBERSHIPS** SAA **RESEARCH** Stone age archaeology of Russia; early prehistory of Alaska. **SELECTED PUBLICATIONS** Auth, Neanderthal Ecology in the northwestern Caucasus: Faunal remains from the Borisovskoe Gorge sites, coauth, in: Quaternary Paleozoology in the Northern Hemisphere, eds J.J. Saunders B.W. Styles G. Baryshnikov, IL State Museum Scientific Papers, 98; Un site Micoquien Est-European du Caucases du Nord, resultsats preliminaires de l'etude de la grotte Mezmaiskaya, les fouilles des annees 1987-1993, coauth, L'Anthropologie, Paris, 98; The Archaeology of the European Neanderthals: East and west, The Rev of Archaeology, 97; The Last Neanderthals, London, Weidenfeld and Nicolson, 97; Introduction to the Archaeology of Beringia, in: American Beginnings, ed FH West, Chicago, UCP, 96; Zooarchaeology and palaeoecology of Mezmaiskaya Cave, Northwestern Caucasus, coauth, Jour of Arch Sci, 96; Mousterian hunters of the NW Caucasus: Preliminary results of recent investigations, coauth, Jour of Field Arch, 94. **CONTACT ADDRESS** Dept of Environmental Assessment, Argonne National Laboratory, 7876 South Niagara Way, Englewood, CO, 80112. **EMAIL** JFHoffeck@aol.com

HOFFECKER, W. ANDREW
DISCIPLINE CHURCH HISTORY **EDUCATION** Dickinson Col, BA; Gordon-Conwell, MDiv; Brown Univ, PhD. **CAREER** Prof, Grove City Col; prof. **HONORS AND AWARDS** Captain, US Army. **SELECTED PUBLICATIONS** Auth, Piety and the Princeton Theologians; ed, Building a Christian World View. **CONTACT ADDRESS** Dept of Church History, Reformed Theol Sem, 5422 Clinton Blvd, Jackson, MS, 39209-3099.

HOFFER, PETER CHARLES
PERSONAL Born 08/03/1944, Brooklyn, NY, m, 1970, 1 child **DISCIPLINE** AMERICAN HISTORY **EDUCATION** Univ Rochester, AB, 65; Harvard Univ, MA, 66, PhD(hist), 70. **CAREER** Asst prof hist, Ohio State Univ, 70-77; vis asst prof hist, Univ Notre Dame, 77-78; asst prof, 78-82, assoc prof hist, Univ GA, 82-86, prof, 86, research prof, 93-, Grants, Nat Endowment for Humanities, 75, 90, Am Philos Soc, 77, Colonial Williamsburg Found, 78, Project '87, 79 & Am Bar Found, 80. **HONORS AND AWARDS** Golieb Fellow, N.Y.O. Law School, 92, 95, 96; Lyans Visiting Prof, Brooklyn Col, 93-94. **MEMBERSHIPS** AHA; Orgn Am Historians; Inst Early Am Hist & Cult; Am Soc Legal Hist. **RESEARCH** Early American legal and constitutional history. **SELECTED PUBLICATIONS** Coauth, Murdering Mothers, Infanticide in England and New England, 1558-1803, NY Univ Press, 81; Criminal Proceedings in Colonial Virginia, the Richmond County, Virginia, Record, 1711-1754, Am Legal Rec Ser, Am Hist Asn, Vol 10, 82; coauth, Impeachment in America, 1635-1805, Yale Univ Press, 84; auth, Revolution and Regeneration, Univ of GA Press, 81; auth, The Law's Conscience, Univ of NC Press, 90; auth, Law and People in Colonial America, John Hopkins Univ Press, 1st ed, 92, 2nd ed, 98; auth, The Devil's Disciples: M...of the Salem Witchcraft Trials, John Hopkins Univ Press, 96; auth, The Salem Witchcraft Trials: A Legal History, Univ Press of Kansas, 97; co-auth, Reading and Writing in American History, Houghton-Miffin, 2nd ed, 98.. **CONTACT ADDRESS** Dept of Hist, Univ of Ga, LeConte Hall, Athens, GA, 30602-0001. **EMAIL** vchoffer@arches.uga.edu

HOFFMAN, ANNE
DISCIPLINE MODERN EUROPEAN FICTION, JEWISH LITERARY HISTORY **EDUCATION** Columbia Univ, PhD. **CAREER** Prof, Fordham Univ. **RESEARCH** Lit and psychoanalysis, feminist theory, contemp critical theory. **SELECTED PUBLICATIONS** Auth, A Book That Was Lost and Other Stories, Schocken Bk(s), 95. **CONTACT ADDRESS** Dept of Eng Lang and Lit, Fordham Univ, 113 W 60th St, New York, NY, 10023.

HOFFMAN, DANIEL
PERSONAL Born 01/07/1957, Hamilton, OH, m, 1987 **DISCIPLINE** ANCIENT AND CHURCH HISTORY **EDUCATION** Miami Univ, PhD, BS Ed; Trinity Evangelical Divinity School, MA; Moody Bible Inst, BA. **CAREER** Asst Prof of Hist, 94-, Lee Univ of Cleveland; Tchr, Dept Chr, 86-94, Soc Stud, Charlotte Christian School. **HONORS AND AWARDS** John Stephenson Fellowships; Who's Who in Amer Tchr; Lee Univ Faculty Res Grants. **MEMBERSHIPS** NAPS, ASOR, The Conf on Faith and Hist. **RESEARCH** Gnosticism; Women in the Early Church; Karak Region of Jordan during the Roman Era. **SELECTED PUBLICATIONS** Auth, The Status of Women and Gnosticism in Irenaeus and Tertullian, Studies in Women and Religion 36, Lewiston NY, Edwin Mellen, 95; Bathe, Jewish and Prisons in: A Dictionary of Biblical Manners and Customs, eds, RK Harrison, M Wilson, S Carroll & E Yamauchi, Grand Rapids, Zondervan, forthcoming; Walter Bauer, Suetonius, in: Encyclopedia of Historians and Historical Writing, ed, K Boyd, London, Fitzroy Dearborn, 97; Phoenix, The Anchor Bible Dictionary, ed, DN Freedman, NY, Doubleday, 92. **CONTACT ADDRESS** Dept of Behavioral and Social Science, Lee Univ, Box 3450, Cleveland, TN, 37320-3450. **EMAIL** dhoffman@leeuniversity.edu

HOFFMAN, DONALD STONE
PERSONAL Born 12/10/1936, Albany, NY, m, 1963, 2 children **DISCIPLINE** MODERN GERMAN HISTORY **EDUCATION** Syracuse Univ, AB, 58; Univ Del, PhD(hist), 69. **CAREER** Lectr hist, Univ Western Ont, 65-69, asst prof, 69-71; assoc prof, 71-77, PROF HIST, EDINBORO Univ PA, 71-, COORDR ACAD RES, 73-, Mem publ comt, Can Coun, 68-71; Can Coun res award, 69. **MEMBERSHIPS** AHA; Conf Group Cent Europ Hist. **RESEARCH** Germany in the 19th century; railway history; economic history of Europe. **SELECTED PUBLICATIONS** Auth, Science and the American Dream, In: The American Fabric, Edinboro, 73; The Real Cost of Industrial Progress, In: Regional Public Affairs, 10/75; ConRail and America's National Needs, In: Regional Public Affairs, 4/75; The Preservation of America, In: The American Fabric, Dubuque, Iowa, 76; Obstacles to Modern Nationalism: Myth and Nineteenth Century German Particularism, Sind J Hist & Polit Sci, winter 77; Some Perspectives on Architecture, The Edinboro Rev, 12/77; The Arts and Politics of College Administration, Analytical Review of Kenneth E Eble, The Art of Admin, 78 & The Edinboro Rev, 12/78; German Railways in the 1850's: Did They Aid Unification?, Sind J Hist & Polit Sci, winter 80. **CONTACT ADDRESS** Dept of Hist, Edinboro Univ of Pennsylvania, Edinboro, PA, 16444. **EMAIL** dhoffman@edinboro.edu

HOFFMAN, PAUL
DISCIPLINE HISTORY OF EARLY MODERN PHILOSOPHY **EDUCATION** UCLA, PhD. **CAREER** ASSOC PROF, UNIV CALIF, RIVERSIDE. **RESEARCH** Moral psychology; Philosophy of mind. **SELECTED PUBLICATIONS** Coauth, "Alternative Possibilities: A Reply to Lamb," Jour Philos 91, 94; "Responses to Chappell and Watson," Philos Stud 77, 95; "Strength and Freedom of Will: Descartes and Albritton," Philos Stud 77, 95; "The Being of Leibnizian Phenomena," Studia Leibnitiana 28, 96; "Descartes on Misrepresentation," Jour Hist of Philos 34, 96. **CONTACT ADDRESS** Dept of Philos, Univ Calif, 1156 Hinderaker Hall, Riverside, CA, 92521-0209. **EMAIL** phoffman@ucrac1.ucr.edu

HOFFMAN, PETER C.W.
PERSONAL Born 08/13/1930, Dresden, Germany **DISCIPLINE** HISTORY **EDUCATION** Univ Stuttgart; Univ Tubingen; Univ Zĩrich; Northwestern Univ; Univ Munich, PhD, 61. **CAREER** PROF HISTORY, McGILL UNIV, 70-, William Kingsford Prof, 88-. **HONORS AND AWARDS** Mem, Royal Soc Can. **MEMBERSHIPS** Ger Stud Asn; Deutsche Schillergesellschaft; Bibliothekgesellschaft; Can Comt Hist Second World War; Wĩrttembergischer Geschichts- und Altertumsverein. **SELECTED PUBLICATIONS** Auth, Widerstand, Staatsreich, Attentat, 69, 4th rev ed, 85; auth, Die Sicherheit des Diktators, 75; auth, The History of the German Resistance 1933-1945, 77, 3rd rev ed, 96; auth, Hitler's Personal Security, 79; auth, Widerstand gegen Hitler: Probleme des Umsturzes, 79, 4th rev ed, 94; auth, La resistance allemande contre Hitler, 84; auth, German Resistance to Hitler, 88; auth, Claus Schenk Graf von Stauffenberg und seine Bruder, 92; auth, Stauffenberg: A Family History 1905-1944, 95. **CONTACT ADDRESS** Dept of History, McGill Univ, 855 Sherbrooke St W, Montreal, PQ, H3A 2T7.

HOFFMAN, PIOTR
DISCIPLINE HISTORY OF PHILOSOPHY AND CONTINENTAL PHILOSOPHY **EDUCATION** Univ Paris, Sorbonne, PhD, 70. **CAREER** Prof, Univ Nev, Reno. **RESEARCH** Ontological implications of the political philosophies of Hobbes, Locke, and Rousseau. **SELECTED PUBLICATIONS** Auth, The Anatomy of Idealism, Kluwer/Martinus Nijhoff, 82; The Human Self and the Life and Death Struggle, Univ Fla, 83; Doubt, Time, and Violence, Univ Chicago, 86; Violence in Modern Philosophy, Univ Chicago, 89; The Quest for Power: Hobbes, Descartes and the Emergence of Modernity, Hum Press, 96. **CONTACT ADDRESS** Univ Nev, Reno, Reno, NV, 89557. **EMAIL** unrug@unr.edu

HOFFMAN, RONALD
PERSONAL Born 02/10/1941, Baltimore, MD, m, 1965, 2 children **DISCIPLINE** HISTORY **EDUCATION** George Peabody Coll, BA, 64; Univ Wash, MA, 65; PhD, 69. **CAREER** Asst prof, Univ Md, 69-73; assoc prof, 74-92; prof, 92-95; prof, Coll of William and Mary, 93-; dir, Omohundro Inst of Early Am Hist and Culture, 93-; ed, Charles Carroll of Carrollton Papers. **HONORS AND AWARDS** Nat Endowment for Humanities Grant, 78; Nat Hist Publ and Records Comn Grant, 80-; E Harold Hugo Memorial Book Prize; Va Found for the Humanities Grant. **MEMBERSHIPS** Am Hist Asn; Org of Am Hist; Soc for the Hist of the Early Repub. **RESEARCH** Irish History; American History. **SELECTED PUBLICATIONS** Auth, A Spirit of Dissension: Economics, Politics, and the Revolution in Maryland, 73; numerou s publications on American and Irish history, 69-; coauth, The Pursuit of Liberty: A History of the American People, 83. **CONTACT ADDRESS** Omohundro Inst of Early American History and Culture, Box 8781, Williamsburg, VA, 23187-8781. **EMAIL** ieahc1@facstaff.wm.edu

HOFFMAN, STEVEN J.
DISCIPLINE HISTORY **EDUCATION** Carnegie Mellon Univ, PhD. **CAREER** Hist, SE Missouri St Univ. **RESEARCH** Exploring the role of race and class on the city building process. **SELECTED PUBLICATIONS** Auth, Toronto's American Tragedy 1900-1950 (rev), Johns Hopkins Univ, 96; The Separate City: Black Communities in the Urban South 1940-1968, Univ Ky, 95; The Saga of Pittsburgh's Liberty Tubes: Geographical Partisanship on the Urban Fringe,Pittsburgh Hist, 92; 'A Plan of Quality:' The Development of Mt. Lebanon, A 1920s Automobile Suburb, Jour Urban Hist, 92. **CONTACT ADDRESS** Hist Dept, SE MO State Univ, 1 University Plz, Cape Girardeau, MO, 63701. **EMAIL** shoffman@semovm.semo.edu

HOFFMANN, DONALD
PERSONAL Born 06/24/1933, Springfield, IL, m, 1958, 5 children **DISCIPLINE** ART HISTORY **EDUCATION** Univ Chicago **CAREER** Reporter to art and archit critic, The Kansas City Star, 56-90; police reporter, The Illinois State Register, 54-56; office, City News Bureau of Chicago, 54. **HONORS AND AWARDS** NEA fel, 74; NEH grant, 70; asst ed, J of the Soc of Archit Historians, 70-71. **MEMBERSHIPS** Soc Archit Historians; Art Inst of Chicago (Life). **RESEARCH** Architecture; photography. **SELECTED PUBLICATIONS** Auth, Frank Lloyd Wright's Dana House, 96; Understanding Frank Lloyd Wright's Archit, 95; Frank Lloyd Wright's Fallingwater, 2nd rev ed, 94; Frank Lloyd Wright's Hollyhock House, 93. **CONTACT ADDRESS** 6441 Holmes St., Kansas City, MO, 64131.

HOFFMANN, STANLEY
PERSONAL Born 11/27/1928, Vienna, Austria **DISCIPLINE** GOVERNMENT; POLITICS. **EDUCATION** Institut d'Etudes Politiques, diplome, Paris, 45-48; Institut des Hautes Etudes Internationales, Paris, diplome, 48-50; Law Sch, Univ of Paris, licence 48, doctorate, 53; Harvard Univ, Dept of Govt, MA, 52. **CAREER** Instr, 55-57, Asst prof, 57-59, assoc prof, 59-62, 60-68 chmn, Committee on Degrees in Social Studies, prof, 63-present, Harvard; visiting prof, 75-76, Institut d'Etudes Politiques, visiting prof, chair of Amer civilization, ecole des Hautes Edtudes en Sciences Sociales, 83-84; president, Intl Inst of Political Psychology, 84-85; Paul and Catherine Buttenwieser University Professorship, 97. **HONORS AND AWARDS** Carnegie Endow for Intl Peace, Intl Org Prize, 55; John Simon Guggenheim Mem Found Grant, 65; Rockefeller Found aand Amer Council of Lrnd Societies Grants, 69-70; Chevalier, French Legion of Honor, 76; Prix Adolphe Bentinck,

82; Officier, French Legion of Honor; Commander's Cross of the Order of Merit of the Federal Republic of Germany; Balzan Prize in Intl Relations. **MEMBERSHIPS** Amer Acxad of Arts and Sci; Amer Political Sci Assn; Amer Soc of Intl Law; Council on Foreign Relations; French-American Found; French Historical Studies; Assn Francaise de Sci Politique; Intl Soc of Political Psychology **SELECTED PUBLICATIONS** Auth, After the Cold War, 93; The European Sisyphus:Essays on Europe, 1964-1994, 95; The Ethics and Problems of Humanitarian Intervention, 97; **CONTACT ADDRESS** Harvard Univ, Cambridge, MA, 02138.

HOGAN, HEATHER
PERSONAL Born 09/20/1949, Mineola, NY, m, 1975, 1 child **DISCIPLINE** RUSSIAN HISTORY **EDUCATION** BA, Northwestern Univ, 71; Univ of MI, MA, 76, PhD, 81. **CAREER** Prof, 86-present, Oberlin Col. **HONORS AND AWARDS** NDFL,IREX,NEH, Culpepper. **MEMBERSHIPS** AHA, AWSS **RESEARCH** Imperial, Soviet, post-Soviet hist. **SELECTED PUBLICATIONS** Forging Revolution: Metalworkers, Managers and the State in St. Petersburg, 1890-1914, IN Univ Press, 93. **CONTACT ADDRESS** Dept of Hist, Oberlin Col, Rice Hall 307, Oberlin, OH, 44074. **EMAIL** fhogan@oberlin.edu

HOGAN, LAWRENCE DANIEL
PERSONAL Born 06/01/1944, Stamford, CT, m, 1968, 3 children **DISCIPLINE** HISTORY **EDUCATION** Fairfield Univ, BA; Univ Conn, MA; Indiana Univ, PhD. **CAREER** Consul/curator, 98, Middlesex County Hist Museum. **HONORS AND AWARDS** New Jersey Historical Comm, Award of Recog, outstanding svc. **MEMBERSHIPS** Garden St Immigration History Consortium. **RESEARCH** History of Black Baseball in New Jersey. **SELECTED PUBLICATIONS** Auth, A Black National News Service: The Associated Negro Press and Claude Barnett, 1919-1945; auth, Afro-American History as Immigration History: the Anguillians of Perth Amboy, Give Me Your Tired, Your Poor...? Voluntary Black Migration to The United States, 86. **CONTACT ADDRESS** Union County Col, Cranford, NJ, 07016. **EMAIL** hogan@hawk.ucc.edu

HOGAN, MICHAEL J.
PERSONAL Born 10/01/1943, Waterloo, IA, m, 1967, 4 children **DISCIPLINE** HISTORY **EDUCATION** Univ N Iowa, BA, 65; Univ Iowa, MA, 67, PhD, 74. **CAREER** Asst prof to assoc prof to prof, 77-86, Miami Univ, Ohio; prof, chair, 86-, Oh St Univ. **HONORS AND AWARDS** Bernath Lecture Prize for Excellence in Scholar & Teaching, 84; Oh Acad Book Award, 88; Quincy Wright Book Prize, 88; Stuart L Bernath Book Prize, 88; George Louis Beer Book Prize, 88; Louis Martin Sears Distinguished Professorship, 90; Univ Distinguished Scholar Award, 90; Distinguished Alumni Award, 92. **MEMBERSHIPS** Org of Amer Hist; Soc for Hist of Amer Foreign Rel; Amer Hist Assoc. **RESEARCH** Modern Amer hist; Amer foreign rel; nat security stud. **SELECTED PUBLICATIONS** Auth, The End of the Cold War: Its Meaning and Implications, Cambridge Univ Press, 92; auth, America in the World: The Historiography of American Foreign Relations Since 1941, Cambridge Univ Press, 95; auth, Hiroshima in History and Memory, Cambridge Univ Press, 96; auth, The American Century, Cambridge Univ Press, 99. **CONTACT ADDRESS** Dept of History, Ohio State Univ, 106 Dulles Hall, 230 W 17th Ave, Columbus, OH, 43210-1367.

HOGAN, PATRICIA
DISCIPLINE HISTORY **EDUCATION** St Francis Xavier Univ, BA, 64; Univ Toronto, Pontif Inst Medieval Studs, LMS, 67, PhD, 71. **CAREER** Asst prof, 70-75, assoc prof, 75-94, PROF, ST FRANCIS XAVIER UNIV, 95-. **HONORS AND AWARDS** Pontif Inst Medieval Studs Fel, 65-67; Ont Grad Fel, 67-69; Can Coun Doctoral Fel, 69-70. **SELECTED PUBLICATIONS** Auth, Medieval Villainy: A Study in the Meaning of Crime and Social Control in a Medieval Village, in Studs in Medieval and Renaissance Hist, 87; auth, Clays, Culturae and The Cultivator's Wisdom-Management Efficiency at Fourteenth-Century Wistow, in Brit Agricultural Hist Rev, 88; auth, The Slight to Honor-Slander and Wrongful Prosecution in Five English Medieval Villages, in Studs in Medieval and Renaissance History, 91. **CONTACT ADDRESS** Dept of History, St. Francis Xavier Univ, Antigonish, NS, B2G 2W5. **EMAIL** phogan@stfx.ca

HOGE, DEAN R.
PERSONAL Born 05/27/1937, New Knoxville, OH, m, 1965, 2 children **DISCIPLINE** SOCIOLOGY **EDUCATION** OH State Univ, Barch 60; Harvard Divinity School, BD 64; Harvard Univ, PhD 70. **CAREER** Princeton Theological Seminary, asst prof 69-74; Cath Univ of Am, assoc and ord prof 74. **HONORS AND AWARDS** Distg Bk Awd for Vanishing Boundaries, co auth. **MEMBERSHIPS** ASA; ASR; SSSR; RRA. **RESEARCH** Am churches; relig trends. **SELECTED PUBLICATIONS** Money Matters: Personal Giving in American Churches, with Dean R Hoge, Charles Zech, Patrick McNamara, Michael Donahue, Louisville, Westminster John Knox Press, 96; Laity, American and Catholic: Transforming the Church, with William V D'Antonio, James D Davidson, Dean R Hoge, Ruth A Wallace, Kansas City MO, Sheed and Ward, 96; Changes in Satisfaction and Institutional Attitudes of Catholic Priests, 1970-1993, with Dean R Hoge, Joseph J Shields, Douglas L Griffin, Sociology of Religion, 95; numerous articles and bks. **CONTACT ADDRESS** Dept of Sociology, Catholic Univ of America, Washington, DC, 20064. **EMAIL** hoge@cua.edu

HOGLUND, ARTHUR WILLIAM
PERSONAL Born 09/04/1926, Baltimore, MD **DISCIPLINE** AMERICAN HISTORY **EDUCATION** Cornell Univ, BA, 49; Univ Wis, MA, 50, PhD, 57. **CAREER** Asst prof Am hist, Muskingum Col, 57-61; from asst prof to assoc prof, 61-68, PROF AM HIST, UNIV CONN, 68-, Trustee, The Balch Inst Ethnic Studies, 75- **MEMBERSHIPS** AHA; Orgn Am Historians; Am Studies Asn; Agr Hist Soc; Immigration Hist Soc. **RESEARCH** Immigrants in America; New York agriculture; American social and intellectual history. **SELECTED PUBLICATIONS** Auth, A Century of European Migrations, 1830-1930, Rev Am Hist, Vol 0022, 94; To Make America--European Emigration in the Early-Modern Period, Rev Am Hist, Vol 0022, 94; The Course of Industrial Decline--The Boott-Cotton-Mills of Lowell, Massachusetts, 1835-1955, Historian, Vol 0056, 94. **CONTACT ADDRESS** Dept of Hist, Univ of Conn, Storrs, CT, 06268.

HOHLFELDER, ROBERT L.
PERSONAL Born 09/21/1938, Brooklyn, NY **DISCIPLINE** HISTORY **EDUCATION** Bowdoin Col, BA, 60; Univ Ind, MA, 62; PhD, 66. **CAREER** Asst prof, 69-73, assoc prof, 73-78, dept ch, 89-91, prof, Univ Colo, 78-. **SELECTED PUBLICATIONS** Auth, Ancient Paphos Beneath the Sea: A Survey of the Submerged Structures, Univ Cyprus, 95; ICOMOS Goes to Sea, 95; Evidence for a Lighthouse at Nea Paphos?, Univ Cyprus, 95. **CONTACT ADDRESS** History Dept, Univ of Colorado, Boulder, Boulder, CO, 80309. **EMAIL** Hohlfeld@spot.Colorado.edu

HOIDAL, ODDVAR KARSTEN
PERSONAL Born 07/26/1938, Alesund, Norway, m, 1966, 1 child **DISCIPLINE** HISTORY **EDUCATION** San Diego State Col, BA, 61; Univ Southern CA, PhD, 70. **CAREER** Asst prof, 67-71, assoc prof, 71-80, PROF HIST, SAN DIEGO STATE UNIV, 80-; Res scholar hist, Fulbright-Hayes, 71-72. **MEMBERSHIPS** Soc Advan Scandinavian Studies; Norwegian Hist Asn; Am Hist Asn. **RESEARCH** Modern Norwegian history; Scandinavian history; modern European history. **SELECTED PUBLICATIONS** Auth, Vidkun Quisling's Decline as a Political Figure in Prewar Norway, J Mod Hist, 9/71; Quisling's Position at the Norwegian Legation in Moscow, June 1927-December 1929, Historisk Tidsskrift, 74; Hjort, Quisling, and Nasjonal Samling's Disintegration, fall 75 & Okonomisk Verneplikt and Nordiske Folkereisning: Two Predecessors of Nasjonal Samling, fall 77, Scand Studies; The unwelcomed exile: Leon Trotsky's failure to receive asylum in Norway, 1929, Scand Studies, winter 80; Norsemen and the North American forests, J Forest Hist, 10/80; Quisling and the Agrarian Party in the spring of 1933, Historisk Tidsskrift, 78; Quisling: A Study in Treason, Oslo: The Norwegian Univ Press, 89; Betrayal and Rescue: The Fate of the Jews in Scandinavia during World War II, in Michalczyk, John J., ed, Resistors, Rescuers and Refugees: Historical and Ethical Issues, Kansas City: Sheed & Ward, 97. **CONTACT ADDRESS** Dept of Hist, San Diego State Univ, 5500 Campanile Dr, San Diego, CA, 92182-0002. **EMAIL** hoidal@mail.sdsu.edu

HOLBERT, RAYMOND
PERSONAL Born 02/24/1945, Berkeley, CA, m, 1984, 3 children **DISCIPLINE** ART HISTORY **EDUCATION** Univ Calif, BA, 70, MA, 72, MFA, 74. **CAREER** Instr, chemn, City Col San Francisco. **MEMBERSHIPS** Col Art Asn; Org African Art Stud. **RESEARCH** International imagery in art history. **CONTACT ADDRESS** 50 Phelan St, San Francisco, CA, 94112. **EMAIL** rholbert@ccsf.cc.ca.us

HOLBO, PAUL S.
PERSONAL Born 07/10/1929, Wildrose, ND, m, 1962, 2 children **DISCIPLINE** AMERICAN HISTORY **EDUCATION** Yale Univ, BA, 51; Univ Chicago, MA, 55, PhD, 61. **CAREER** From instr to prof Am & Latin Am hist, 59-75, actg dean, Col Lib Arts, 73-74, assoc dean, 70-73, PROF HIST, UNIV ORE, 75-, Lectr, Univ Chicago, 56-58; examr, Col Entrance Exam Bd, 65-71, chmn test develop Am hist, 81-; chief reader, adv placement, Am Hist Educ Testing Serv, Princeton, NJ, 68-71; found & interim ed, J Diplomatic Hist, 76. **HONORS AND AWARDS** Binkley-Stephenson Award, Orgn Am Historians, 69. **MEMBERSHIPS** AHA; Orgn Am Historians; Soc Historians Am Foreign Rels. **RESEARCH** American diplomatic and political history; historiography of American foreign relations; United States foreign relations in the Gilded Age. **SELECTED PUBLICATIONS** Auth, Edward Doheny, Petroleum, Power, and Politics in the United-States and Mexico, Pacific NW Quarterly, Vol 0084, 93. **CONTACT ADDRESS** Dept of Hist, Univ of Ore, Eugene, OR, 97403.

HOLCOMBE, LEE
PERSONAL Spartanburg, SC **DISCIPLINE** HISTORY **EDUCATION** Mt Holyoke Col, BA, 49; Columbia Univ, MA, 50, PhD(hist), 62. **CAREER** Instr hist & govt, Queens Col, NC, 50-51, Westlake Sch, Calif, 51-52 & Quinnipiac Col, Conn, 61-62; lectr hist, Univ Conn, Groton, 67-73; asst prof hist, Univ Conn, Storrs, 73-74; ASSOC PROF HIST, UNIV SC, SPARTANBURG, 75- **MEMBERSHIPS** AHA; Conf Brit Studies; Southern Asn Women Historians. **RESEARCH** Nineteenth century British history; women's history. **SELECTED PUBLICATIONS** Auth, Lady Inspectors, the Campaign for a Better Workplace, 1893-1921, Albion, Vol 0024, 92. **CONTACT ADDRESS** Dept of Hist, Univ SC, Spartanburg, SC, 29303.

HOLIFIELD, E. BROOKS
PERSONAL Born 01/05/1942, Little Rock, AR, m, 1963, 2 children **DISCIPLINE** AMERICAN RELIGIOUS HISTORY **EDUCATION** Hendrix Col, BA, 63; Yale Div Sch, BD, 66; Yale Univ, PhD, 70. **CAREER** Asst prof, 70-75, assoc prof, 75-80, prof, 80-84, C H Candler prof, 84-, Emory Univ. **HONORS AND AWARDS** Woodrow Wilson fel, 63; Danforth fel, 63; Yale Sterling fel, 69; NEH fel, 76, 83, 91; Lilly and PEW fel, 98. **MEMBERSHIPS** Am Soc of Church Hist; Am Acad of Relig; Am Hist Asn; Orgn of Am Hist. **RESEARCH** Religious thought in America. **SELECTED PUBLICATIONS** Auth, The Covenant Sealed, 74; auth, The Gentlemen Theologians, 78; auth, History of Pastoral Care in America, 83; auth, Health and Medicine in the Methodist Tradition, 86; auth, Era of Persuasion: American Thought and Culture, 1521-1680, 89. **CONTACT ADDRESS** Bishops Hall, Emory Univ, Atlanta, GA, 30322. **EMAIL** eholifi@emory.edu

HOLLAND, ANTONIO F.
PERSONAL Born 12/05/1943, Petersburg, VA, m, 1975, 2 children **DISCIPLINE** HISTORY **EDUCATION** Northeastern Univ, BA, 67, MA, 69; Univ Mo, Columbia, PhD, 84. **CAREER** Inst, asst prof, assoc prof, PROF HISTORY, SOC SCIS, HEAD DEPT SOC & BEH SCIS, 86-, LINCOLN UNIV, 70-; military svc, 68-70; lt col, Mo Army Nat Guard, 78-. **HONORS AND AWARDS** Lawrence Prize, Boston Public Schs, Lewis Athenton fel, Hist dept, Univ Mos, 83,84; Martin Luther King Jr Award, Ctr Mo, 99; Nat Teach fel; Phelps-Stokes Fund Fel to West Africa; NEH rev. **MEMBERSHIPS** Asn Stud Afro-Am Life, Hist; So Hist Asn; Mo Hist Soc; Mo Folklore Soc; Mo Nat Guard Asn. **RESEARCH** African-Am hist; Mo hist. **SELECTED PUBLICATIONS** Co-auth, Missouri's Black Heritage, Univ Mo Press, 93; auth, Education over Politics: Nathan B Young at Florida A & M College, 1901-1923, Ag Hist, 65:2. **CONTACT ADDRESS** 306 W El Cortez Dr, Columbia, MO, 65203.

HOLLAND, JAMES C.
PERSONAL Born 11/03/1935, Baltimore, MD, m, 1968 **DISCIPLINE** HISTORY **EDUCATION** Univ of Maryland, BA, 59, MA, 65; Catholic Univ of America, PhD, 68. **CAREER** From asst prof to assoc prof, Albertus Magnus Col, New Haven, CT; from assoc prof to prof, Shepherd Col, Shepherdstown, WV. **MEMBERSHIPS** Am Cath. Hist Asn **RESEARCH** Victorian England; History of Ideas; Old South and the American Civil War. **SELECTED PUBLICATIONS** Auth, A Capital in Search of a Nation, 86; The Legacy of an Education, 97; coauth, Lord Acton: The Decisive Decade, 1864-1874, 70; The Correspondence of Lord Acton and Richard Simpson, 3 vols, 71-75; The Correspondence of Lord Acton and Mr. Gladstone, forthcoming. **CONTACT ADDRESS** Dept of History, Sheperd Col, Sheperdstown, WV, 25443.

HOLLEY, LINDA TARTE
PERSONAL Born 10/06/1940, Darlington, SC, m, 1962, 2 children **DISCIPLINE** MEDIEVAL ENGLISH **EDUCATION** Winthrop Col, AB, 62; Tulane Univ, MA, 70, PhD(English), 76. **CAREER** ASST PROF PROF ENGLISH, NC STATE UNIV, 76-, Folger fel, 81. **MEMBERSHIPS** MLA; SAtlantic Mod Lang Asn; Southeastern Medieval Asn. **RESEARCH** Chaucer; Middle English. **SELECTED PUBLICATIONS** Auth, Seeing the Gawain-Poet--Description and the Act of Perception, J English Germanic Philol, Vol 0093, 94. **CONTACT ADDRESS** Dept of English, No Carolina State Univ, Raleigh, NC, 27607.

HOLLI, MELVIN
PERSONAL Born 02/22/1933, Ishpeming, MI, m, 1961, 2 children **DISCIPLINE** HISTORY **EDUCATION** Suomi Col, assoc in arts, 52-54; Northern Mich Univ, BA, 54-57; Univ Mich, MA, 57-66, PhD. **CAREER** Cur, Univ Mich, 63-65; from asst prof to assoc prof to prof, 65-, Univ Ill, Chicago. **HONORS AND AWARDS** Hist Book Award, 81, 84, Soc Midland Authors; Ill State Hist Soc Award, 88., Nat Woodrow Wilson Fel, 57-58; NEH Fel, 69-70; Fulbright Prof, 78, 89. **MEMBERSHIPS** Organization Am Historians; Immigration Hist Soc; Urban Hist Asn. **RESEARCH** US Urban ethnic and political history. **SELECTED PUBLICATIONS** Auth, Restoration: Chicago Elects Another Daley, 91; auth, The Mayors: The Chicago Political Tradition, 95; auth, Ethnic Chicago: A Multicultural Portrait, 95; auth, art, Emil E Hurja: Michigan's Presidential Pollster, 95; auth, art, American Mayors: The Best and The Worse Since 1960, 97. **CONTACT ADDRESS** 1311 Ashland Ave, River Forest, IL, 60305. **EMAIL** mholl.@uic.edu

HOLLIDAY, VIVIAN LOYREA
PERSONAL Born 02/25/1935, Manning, SC **DISCIPLINE** CLASSICS, ANCIENT HISTORY **EDUCATION** Winthrop Col, AB, 57; Univ Mo, MA, 59; Univ NC, PhD(classics), 61. **CAREER** Instr classics, 61-63, from asst prof to assoc prof, 63-69, Aylesworth Prof Classics, Col Wooster, 69-, Dean Fac, 77-85, mem managing comt, Am Sch Class Studies, Athens, 67. **MEMBERSHIPS** Am Philol Asn; Am Inst Archaeol. **RESEARCH** Republican Rome; comparative literature; modern Greek literature. **SELECTED PUBLICATIONS** Auth, Pompey in Cicero's Letters and Lucan's Civil War, Mouton, The Hauge, 69; Kazantzakis, Odyssey, Neo-Hellenika, Vol III, 78; Job Satisfaction for the Faculty, Academic Job Satisfaction: Varieties and Values, 80; Classical and Modern Narratives of Leadership, (pub 1999). **CONTACT ADDRESS** Dept of Classics, Col of Wooster, 1189 Beall Ave, Wooster, OH, 44691-2363. **EMAIL** IN%vholliday@acs.wooster.edu

HOLLINGER, D.A.
PERSONAL Born 04/25/1941, Chicago, IL, m, 1967, 2 children **DISCIPLINE** HISTORY **EDUCATION** LaVerne Col, BA 63; Univ Cal Berk, PhD 70. **CAREER** SUNY Buffalo, asst prof, assoc prof, 69-77; Univ Michigan, prof, 77-92; Univ Cal Berk, prof, 92-. **HONORS AND AWARDS** Guggenheim Fel; AAAS 97 **MEMBERSHIPS** AHA; OAH; HSS **RESEARCH** US intellectual history. **SELECTED PUBLICATIONS** Auth, Science Jews and Secular Culture, 96; Post-ethnic America, 95; In the American Province, 85; Morris R Cohen and the Scientific Ideal, 75. **CONTACT ADDRESS** Dept of History, Univ of California, Berkeley, Berkeley, CA, 94720.

HOLLINGSWORTH, JOSEPH ROGERS
PERSONAL Born 07/26/1932, Anniston, AL, m, 1957 **DISCIPLINE** HISTORY **EDUCATION** Emory Univ, BA, 54; Univ Chicago, PhD, 60. **CAREER** Instr soc sci, Univ Chicago, 57-59; asst prof hist, Univ Ill, Urbana, 60-64; assoc prof, 64-69, partic mem, Law Sch, 66-70, PROF HIST, UNIV WISMADISON, 69-, CHAIRPERSON PROG COMP WORLD HIST, 77-, Andrew Mellon fel, 62-63; Am Coun Learned Soc fel, 66-67; Nat Endowment for Humanities grant, 67-68; Rockefeller Fund vis prof hist, Univ Ibadan, 69-71; fel, Prog Law Sci & Med, Yale Univ & German Marshall Found, 75-76; staff mem, Inst Res Poverty, Univ Wis, 75-; fel, Woodrow Wilson Int Ctr Scholars, 77; Commonwealth Fund fel, 77; fel, Am Scand Found, 81. **MEMBERSHIPS** AHA; Orgn Am Historians; Am Sociol Asn; Am Polit Sci Asn. **RESEARCH** Comparative historical politics; American social history; comparative public policy. **SELECTED PUBLICATIONS** Auth, Cages of Reason--The Rise of the Rational State in France, Japan, The United-States, and Great-Britain, J Am Hist, Vol 0082, 95. **CONTACT ADDRESS** Dept of Hist, Univ Wis, Madison, WI, 53705.

HOLLIS, DANIEL W.
PERSONAL Born 11/02/1942, Talladega, AL, m, 1966, 2 children **DISCIPLINE** HISTORY **EDUCATION** Univ GA, AB 64; Auburn Univ, MA 68; Vanderbilt Univ, PhD 72. **CAREER** Jacksonville State Univ, asst prof 71, assoc prof 72, prof 82. **HONORS AND AWARDS** Fac Schl Lectr, Jackson St Univ. **MEMBERSHIPS** Conf British Stud; Phi Alpha Theta. **RESEARCH** 16th-18th century England; Euro Intellect; Media Hist. **SELECTED PUBLICATIONS** Niccolo Machiavelli in: J E Finding & F W Thackeray, eds, Statesman Who Changed the World, Greenwood Press, 93; The ABC-CLIO World History Companion to Utopian Movements, ABC CLIO Press, 98; The ABC CLIO Companion to the Media in America, ABC CLIO Press, 95;The Great Reform Bill in: J E Findling and F W Thackeray, eds, Events That Changed the World, Greenwood Press, 96. **CONTACT ADDRESS** Dept History, Jacksonville State Univ, Jacksonville, AL, 36265-1602. **EMAIL** dhollis@jsuss.jsu.edu

HOLLISTER, C. WARREN
PERSONAL Born 11/02/1930, Los Angeles, CA, m, 1952, 3 children **DISCIPLINE** MEDIEVAL HISTORY **EDUCATION** Harvard Univ, AB, 51; Univ Calif, Los Angeles, MA, 57, PhD, 58. **CAREER** Teaching asst, Univ Calif, Los Angeles, 55-57, from instr to asst prof hist, Santa Barbara, 58-62; vis asst prof, Stanford Univ, 62-63; assoc prof, 63-64, PROF HIST, UNIV CALIF, SANTA BARBARA, 64-, Grants-in-aid, Soc Sci Res Coun, 61 & Am Coun Learned Soc, 62 & 63; vis res fel, Merton Col, Oxford, 65-66; Guggenheim fel, 65-66; Fulbright Res fel, UK, 65-66 & travel grant to Italy, 67; Nat Endowment for Humanities res grant, 75-78; fel, Australian Nat Univ, Canberra, 78. **HONORS AND AWARDS** Triennial Bk Prize, Conf Brit Studies, 60-62; E Harris Harbison Award for Distinguished Teaching, Danforth Found, 66; Walter D Love Mem Prize, Conf Brit Studies, 81. **MEMBERSHIPS** Conf Brit Studies; fel Royal Hist Soc; AHA; fel Mediaeval Acad Am. **RESEARCH** Normandy and England, 1066-1154; The reign of Henry I of England. **SELECTED PUBLICATIONS** Auth, Lincolnshire Domesday, Vol 1, Folios And Maps, Vol 2, Introduction and Translations, Vol 3, Domesday-Book Studies, Albion, Vol 0025, 93; Conquest and Colonization--The Normans in Britain, 1066-1100, Int Hist Rev, Vol 0018, 96; Law and Government in Medieval England and Normandy--Essays in Honor of James Holt, J Ecclesiastical Hist, Vol 0047, 96. **CONTACT ADDRESS** Dept of Hist, Univ of Calif, Santa Barbara, CA, 93106.

HOLLOWAY, ROBERT ROSS
PERSONAL Born 08/15/1934, Newton, MA, m, 1960, 2 children **DISCIPLINE** CLASSICAL ARCHAEOLOGY **EDUCATION** Amherst Col, AB, 56; Univ Pa, AM, 57; Princeton Univ, MA & PhD, 60. **CAREER** Staff mem, archaeol exped Sicily, Princeton Univ, 58-62; vis asst prof class archaeol, 62-63; asst prof archaeol, Univ NC, Chapel Hill, 63-64; from asst prof to assoc prof class archaeol, 64-69, prof Meditr Archaeol, Brown Univ, 69-, Am Acad Rome fel, 60; Am Philos Soc grant, 61; Am Coun Learned Soc fel, 69-70; archaeologist in residence, Am Acad, Rome, 69-70; Nat Endowment for Humanities grant, 72 & 79, fel, 77; consult cur ancient art, Mus Art, RI Sch Design, 72-; pres, Int Ctr Numis Study, Naples, 81-; vpres, Whitlesey Found, New York, 73-; dir archaeol exped, Mediter, 64-; dir, Ctr Old World Archaeol & Art, 78-. **HONORS AND AWARDS** MA, Brown Univ, 67; HLD Amherst Col, 76; Docteur hc Univ Louvain, Belgium, 97; Gold Medal, Archaeol Inst Am, 95., MA, Brown Univ, 67; HLD, Amherst Col, 76. **MEMBERSHIPS** Ger Archaeol Inst; Royal Numismatic Soc; Royal Belgian Numismatic Soc; Italian Inst Prehist and Protohist; Nat Inst Etruscan and Italic Stud. **RESEARCH** Ancient Greek numismatics; ancient art; archaeology of Italy and Sicily. **SELECTED PUBLICATIONS** Auth, The Thirteen Months Coinage of Hieronymos of Syracuse, De Gruyter, Berlin, 68; Satrianum, 68 & A View of Greek Art, 73, Brown Univ; Buccino, De Luca, Rome, 73; Styles and influences in the late archaic and early classical sculpture of Magna Graecia and Sicily, Cath Univ Louvain, 76; Art and Coinage in Magna Graecia, Edizioni Arte e Monota, 78; Italy and the Aegean, Archaeologia Transatlantica, 81; Morgantina Studies II, the Coins, Princeton, 88; La Muculufa, Providence and Louvain, 90; Ustica I, Archaeologia Transatlantica 14, Providence and Louvain, 95. **CONTACT ADDRESS** Ctr for Old World Archaeol, Brown Univ, Box 1837, Providence, RI, 02912-9127.

HOLLOWAY, THOMAS HALSEY
PERSONAL Born 06/24/1944, Enterprise, Ore, m, 1963, 2 children **DISCIPLINE** LATIN AMERICAN HISTORY **EDUCATION** Univ Calif, Santa Barbara, BA, 68; Univ Wis-Madison, MA, 69, PhD(Latin Am hist), 74. **CAREER** Asst prof, 74-80, assoc prof, 80-91, prof, Cornell Univ, 91-, Dir, Latin Am Studies Prog, Cornell Univ, 82-87 **MEMBERSHIPS** Conf Latin Am Hist; Latin Am Studies Asn. **RESEARCH** History of Brazil. **SELECTED PUBLICATIONS** Auth, The Brazilian Coffee Valorization of 1906, State Hist Soc Wis, 75; Immigrants on the Land: Coffee and Society in Sao Paulo, 1886-1934, Univ NC Press, 80; auth, Policing Rio De Janerio: Repression and Resistance in a 19th Century City, Stanford Univ, 93. **CONTACT ADDRESS** Dept of Hist, Cornell Univ, Mcgraw Hall, Ithaca, NY, 14853-0001.

HOLLY, MICHAEL ANN
DISCIPLINE ART HISTORY/VISUAL AND CULTURAL STUDIES **EDUCATION** Cornell Univ, PhD, 81. **CAREER** Ch & prof, Univ of Rochester. **HONORS AND AWARDS** Getty Summer Inst on Visual and Cult Stud, 98; Ailsa Bruce Mellon sr fel, Ctr for Advanced Study in the Visual Arts, Nat Gallery of Art, DC, 96-97; Guggenheim fel, 91-92; ACLS grant, 89 & NEH Summer Inst grants (dir), 87, 89. **RESEARCH** Art historiography and criticism; intellectual hist of the hist of art; ancient, medieval and renaissance art. **SELECTED PUBLICATIONS** Auth, Past Looking: Historical Imagination and the Rhetoric of the Image, Ithaca, Cornell UP, 96; Iconography and Iconology, Milan: Jaca Publ, 92 & Panofsky and the Foundations of Art History, Ithaca, Cornell UP, 84; ed, The Subjects of Art History: Historical Objects in Contemporary Perspectives, NY: Cambridge UP, 98; Visual Culture: Images and Interpretation, Hanover, UP New Eng for Wesleyan UP, 94 & Visual Theory: Painting and Interpretation, NY, Harper & Row, 90. **CONTACT ADDRESS** Dept of Art and Art Hist, Univ of Rochester, 601 Elmwood Ave, Ste. 656, 424 Morey , Rochester, NY, 14642. **EMAIL** holy@db1.cc.rochester.edu

HOLMBERG, I.E.
DISCIPLINE GREEK LITERATURE **EDUCATION** Univ Vermont, BA, 80; Yale Univ, PhD, 90. **CAREER** Asst prof, 91. **RESEARCH** Homer and early Greek poetry; critical theory. **SELECTED PUBLICATIONS** Auth, The Sign of Metis, Arethusa, 97; The Odyssey and Female Subjectivity, Helios, 95; Euripides' Helen: Most Noble and Most Chaste, AJP 116, 95. **CONTACT ADDRESS** Dept of Greek and Roman Studies, Victoria Univ, PO Box 1700 STN CSC, Victoria, BC, V8W 2Y2. **EMAIL** ingrid@uvic.ca

HOLMES, BARBARA J.
PERSONAL Born 06/26/1934, Chicago, IL, m **DISCIPLINE** EDUCATION **EDUCATION** Talladega Coll, attended 1951-53; Univ CO, BA 1973, MA 1974, PhD 1978. **CAREER** Natl Assessment of Educ Progress, writer 1977-83; State Educ Policy Seminary Prog co-sponsored by Educ Commn of the States & the Inst for Educ Leadership, natl coord; Former Director of Policy Studies, ECS; other educ prof organs, presentations; Consultant on Recruitment & Retention of Minority Teachers. Expertise in Teacher Education, Work Force Literacy, currently. **HONORS AND AWARDS** Phi Beta Kappa Hon Soc 1974; Acad Fellowships Whitney M Young 1973-74. **MEMBERSHIPS** Mem Delta Sigma Theta Public Serv Sor; mem bd of dirs Whitney M Young Jr Memorial Foundation 1974-84; fellow Educ Policy Fellowship Prog 1982-83. **SELECTED PUBLICATIONS** Published over 20 articles and reports.

HOLMES, BLAIR R.
PERSONAL Born 06/29/1942, Driggs, ID, m, 1965, 6 children **DISCIPLINE** HISTORY **EDUCATION** Brigham Young Univ, BA, 66; Univ of Colo, MA, 68, PhD, 72. **CAREER** ASST PROF TO ASSOC PROF, BRIGHAM YOUNG UNIV, 71-99. **RESEARCH** Social history; Austrian empire. **SELECTED PUBLICATIONS** Auth, When Truth Was Treason: German Youth Against Hitler, Univ of Ill Press, 95. **CONTACT ADDRESS** Brigham Young Univ, 406 KMB, Provo, UT, 84602. **EMAIL** Blair_Holmes@byu.edu

HOLMES, LARRY E.
DISCIPLINE HISTORY **EDUCATION** McPherson Col, BA; Eastern NMex Univ, MA; Univ Kans, PhD. **CAREER** Prof, Univ South Al.. **SELECTED PUBLICATIONS** Auth, The Kremlin and the Schoolhouse: Reforming Education in Soviet Russia, 1917-1931, Ind UP, 91. **CONTACT ADDRESS** Dept of History, Univ South Alabama, 344 Humanities, Mobile, AL, 36688-0002. **EMAIL** lholmes@jaguar1.usouthal.edu

HOLMES, ROBERT A.
PERSONAL Born 07/13/1943, Shepherdstown, WV, 3 children **DISCIPLINE** POLITCAL SCIENCE; PUBLIC LAW AND GOVERNMENT **EDUCATION** Shepherd Coll, BS, 64; Columbia Univ, MA, 66, PhD, 69. **CAREER** Coordinator, 68, Harvard-Yale-Columbia Intensive Summer Study Program; Assoc prof, 69-70; Southern Univ; Dir, 70-71, Search for Elevation, Education and Knowledge; prof, 71-75, 76-, Atlanta Univ; dir, 89-, Southern Ctr for Studies in Public Policy, Clark Atlanta Univ. **HONORS AND AWARDS** Georgia Environmental Council Legislator of the Year; Shepher Coll Alumni of the Year; Sickle Cell Found of Georgia Torchbearer Award; Concerned Black Clergy Father of the Year. **MEMBERSHIPS** Natl Conf of Black Political Scientists **RESEARCH** Environmental policy; African Amer politics; Urban politics **SELECTED PUBLICATIONS** Coed and auth, Appropriations/Budget, Governmental Affairs and Other Issues, Georgia Legislative Review 1997, 97; auth, Vital Issues In Election '97: Improving Management and Reducing Racial Disparity, Election Issues '97, 97; Reapportionment Strategies in the 1990s, Race and redistricting in the 1990s, 97; Affirmative Action Under Siege, Endarch, Fall 97; co auth, The Great Debate: White Support and Black Opposition to the Confederate Battle Flag, Old Times They're not Forgotten Confederate Symbols in the South, 97. **CONTACT ADDRESS** Dept of Political Sci, Atlanta Univ, 223 Chesnut St. SW, Atlanta, GA, 30314. **EMAIL** bholmes@cau.edu

HOLMES, STEVEN J.
PERSONAL Born 10/21/1960, San Francisco, CA, s **DISCIPLINE** AMERICAN CIVILIZATION **EDUCATION** Harvard Univ, PhD, 96; Harvard Div Sch, MTS, 87; Univ of Notre Dame, MA, 83 **CAREER** Lect, 96-pres, Harvard Univ **RESEARCH** Environmental Biography & Autobiography; History of American Attitudes toward Nature; Disability Studies **SELECTED PUBLICATIONS** Auth, The Young John Muir: An Environmental Biography, University of Wisconsin Press, 99 **CONTACT ADDRESS** 170 Walter St #1, Roslindale, MA, 02131.

HOLMES, WILLIAM F.
PERSONAL Born 10/31/1937, Greenwood, MS, m, 1965, 2 children **DISCIPLINE** HISTORY **EDUCATION** Univ Notre Dame, BA, 59; Univ Del, MA, 61; Rice Univ, PhD(hist), 64. **CAREER** Asst prof hist, Univ Tex, Arlington, 64-67; assoc prof, 68-79, PROF HIST, UNIV GA, 79-. **HONORS AND AWARDS** Nat Endowment for Humanities fel, 67-68 & 77-79; Am Philos Soc fel, 68. **MEMBERSHIPS** Orgn Am Historians; Southern Hist Asn (secy-treas, 86-) **RESEARCH** History of the American South. **SELECTED PUBLICATIONS** Auth, The White Chief: James Kimble Vardaman, La State Univ, 70; Whitecapping: Agrarian violence in Mississippi, Mid-Am, 4/73; The demise of the Colored Farmers' Alliance, J Southern Hist, 75; A History of Georgia, Univ Ga, 77; Moonshining and Collective Violence: Georgia, 1889-1895, J Am Hist, 80; Labor Agents and the Georgia Exodus, 1899-1900, S Atlantic Quart, 80; Populism: In Search of Context, Agr Hist, Fall 90; Charivari: Race, Honor, and Post Office Politics, Sharon, Georgia, 1890, Ga Hist Quart, Winter 96. **CONTACT ADDRESS** Dept of History, Univ of Georgia, Athens, GA, 30602-0001. **EMAIL** wfholmes@arches.uga.edu

HOLOKA, JAMES P.
PERSONAL Born 01/19/1947, Rochester, NY, m, 1968, 3 children **DISCIPLINE** ANCIENT HISTORY **EDUCATION** Univ Rochester, BA, 69; SUNY-Binghamton, MA, 72; Univ Mich, PhD, 74. **CAREER** Teaching asst/fel, 69-72; lectr, Eastern Mich Univ, 74-76; from asst prof to prof, Eastern Mich Univ, 76-. **HONORS AND AWARDS** Rackham Prize Fel, Univ Mich, 73-74; NEH Summer Stipend, 76; Distinguish Fac Award for Excellence in Teaching and Commitment to Students, 80; Scholarly Recognition Award, 91. **MEMBERSHIPS**

Am Philol Asn; Class Asn of the Mid West and South; Cen Intl d'Etudes Homeriques. **RESEARCH** Greek and Roman epic, lyric, and satire; Ancient history; Women in antiquity; Comparative literature and literary theory. **SELECTED PUBLICATIONS** Co-auth, A Survey of Western Civilization, 97; Lives and Times: A World History Reader, 95; World History, 91; auth, "Homeric Originality: A Survey," 78; "Homer Studies 1971-1977," 79; "Looking Darkely: Reflections on Status and Decorum in Homer," 83; "Homer Studies 1978-1983 Pt. 1," 90; "Homer Studies 1978-1983 Pt. 2," 90; "Homer, Oral Poetry Theory and Comparative Literature: Major Trends and Controversies in Twentieth-Century Criticism," 91; "Nonverbal Communication in the Classics: Research Opportunities," 92. **CONTACT ADDRESS** 7685 Paint Creek Dr, Ypsilanti, MI, 48197. **EMAIL** fla_holoka@online.emich.edu

HOLSEY, LILLA G.
PERSONAL Born 08/26/1941, San Mateo, FL **DISCIPLINE** EDUCATION **EDUCATION** Hampton Institute, BS 1963; FL State University, MS 1971, PhD 1974. **CAREER** East Carolina Univ, assoc prof home economics 1974-; FL State Univ, graduate rsch asst 1971, 1973; Gainesville High School, home economics teacher 1970-72; Lincoln High School, 1964-70. **HONORS AND AWARDS** Ford Foundation felllowship 1973-74; Danforth associate 1977; charter mem Putnam Co Educ Hall of Fame Palatha FL. **MEMBERSHIPS** Natl & Amer Home Econ Assns; Amer & Vocational Assn; NC Consumer Assn; Bethel AME Church; bd trustees Alpha Kappa Alpha; Kappa Delta Pi & Omicron Nu Honor Society; Phi Kappa Delta. **CONTACT ADDRESS** East Carolina Univ, 1000 E Fifth St, Greenville, NC, 27858.

HOLSINGER, M. PAUL
PERSONAL Born 01/31/1938, Philadelphia, PA, m, 1958, 4 children **DISCIPLINE** AMERICAN & CANADIAN HISTORY **EDUCATION** Duke Univ, AB, 59; Univ Denver, MA, 60, PhD(hist), 64. **CAREER** From instr to asst prof hist, Ore State Univ, 62-67; asst prof Am thought & lang, Mich State Univ, 67-69; assoc prof, 69-76, PROF HIST, ILL STATE UNIV, 76-, Eppley prof hist, Culver Mil Acad, Ind, 65-66. **HONORS AND AWARDS** Louis Knott Koontz Prize, Pac Hist Quart, 69. **MEMBERSHIPS** Southern Hist Asn; Asn Can Studies US. **RESEARCH** American legal and constitutional history; Canadian studies; environmental history. **SELECTED PUBLICATIONS** Auth, Iwo Jima--Monuments, Memories, and the American Hero, J Am Cult, Vol 0016, 93. **CONTACT ADDRESS** Dept of Hist, Illinois State Univ, Normal, IL, 61761.

HOLSTI, OLE R.
PERSONAL Born 08/07/1933, Geneva, Switzerland, m, 1953, 2 children **DISCIPLINE** POLITICAL SCIENCE **EDUCATION** Stanford Univ, BA, 54; Wesleyan Univ, MAT, 56; Stanford Univ, PhD, 62. **CAREER** Instr and asst prof, polit sci, Stanford Univ, 62-65; res coordr and assoc dir, Studies in Int Conflict and Integration, Stanford Univ, 62-67; assoc prof and prof, polit sci, Univ British Columbia, 67-74; George V. Allen Prof, Dept Polit Sci, Duke Univ, 74- ; chemn dept, 78-83; Dir Undergrad Studies, 92- . **HONORS AND AWARDS** Own D. Young Fel, GE Found, 60-61; Canada Coun Res Grant, 69; fel, Ctr for Adv Study in Behavioral Sci, 72-73; Ford Found Fac Res Fel, 72-73; NSF Res Grant, 75-77, 79-81; Guggenheim Fel, 81-82; Best Published Paper Award, Int Studies Q, 79-81; NSF Res Grant, 83-85, 88-90; Nevitt Sanford Award, Int Soc of Polit Psychol, 88; Pew Fac Fel, Harvard Univ, 90; NSF Res Grant, 92-94, 96-98; Alumni Distinguished Undergrad Tchg Award, 95. **SELECTED PUBLICATIONS** Coauth, Enemies in Politics, Rand McNally, 67; auth, Content Analysis for The Social Sciences and Humanities, Addison-Wesley, 69; auth, Crisis, Escalation, War, McGill-Queen's, 72; auth, Unity and Disintegration in International Alliances: Comparative Studies, Wiley, 73; co-ed, Change in the International System, Westview, 80; coauth, American Leadership in World Affairs: Vietnam and The Breakdown of Consensus, Allen & Unwin, 84; auth, Public Opinion and American Foreign Policy, Michigan, 96; co-ed, Encyclopedia of U.S. Foreign Relations, Oxford, 96. **CONTACT ADDRESS** Dept of Political Science, Duke Univ, Durham, NC, 27706.

HOLT, MICHAEL FITZGIBBON
PERSONAL Born 07/08/1940, Pittsburgh, PA, m, 1967, 3 children **DISCIPLINE** AMERICAN HISTORY **EDUCATION** Princeton Univ, AB, 62; Johns Hopkins Univ, PhD(hist), 67. **CAREER** Actg instr hist, Yale Univ, 65-67, from asst prof to assoc prof, 67-73, assoc prof, 74-80, PROF HIST, UNIV VA, 80-, Vis assoc prof, Stanford Univ, 73-74; Nat Endowment for Humanities sr fel, 76-77. **MEMBERSHIPS** Orgn Am Historians; AHA; SHA **RESEARCH** United States political history 1840-1860. **SELECTED PUBLICATIONS** Auth, Nativism and Slavery--The Northern Know Nothings and the Politics of the 1850s, Am Hist Rev, Vol 0098, 93; auth, Political Parties and American Political Development from the Age of Jackson to the Age of Lincoln, LSU, 92. **CONTACT ADDRESS** Dept of Hist, Univ of Va, 1 Randall Hall, Charlottesville, VA, 22903-3244. **EMAIL** mfh6p@virginia.edu

HOLT, PHILIP
DISCIPLINE ANCIENT GREECE AND ROME **EDUCATION** Stanford Univ, PhD, 76. **CAREER** Assoc prof; Univ WY, 87-. **RESEARCH** Greek myth and drama; Greek and Roman epic poetry. **SELECTED PUBLICATIONS** Publ in, scholarly jour in NAm & Europe. **CONTACT ADDRESS** Dept of Mod and Class Lang(s), Univ WY, PO Box 3964, Laramie, WY, 82071-3964. **EMAIL** PHOLT@UWYO.EDU

HOLTMAN, ROBERT BARNEY
PERSONAL Born 08/26/1914, Kenosha, WI, m, 1952, 2 children **DISCIPLINE** MODERN EUROPEAN HISTORY **EDUCATION** Univ Wis, BS & AM, 35, PhD, 41. **CAREER** Instr, Western Wash Col Educ, 41-42; from asst prof to assoc prof, 46-61, assoc dean grad sch, 70-74, PROF HIST, LA STATE UNIV, BATON ROUGE, 61-, Am Philos Soc res grant, 67; mem bd consult, Hist Teachers Asn, 67-71. **MEMBERSHIPS** AHA; Southern Hist Asn; Soc Fr Hist Studies (vpres, 66-67, treas, 74); Soc Mod Hist, France. **RESEARCH** Nineteenth and 20th century France; Napoleonic and Hitlerian wartime propaganda. **SELECTED PUBLICATIONS** Auth, Napoleon Integration of Europe, J Modern Hist, Vol 0066, 94; Legitimism and the Reconstruction of French Society, 1852-1883, J Modern Hist, Vol 0067, 95; Bonapartism and Revolutionary Tradition in France--The Federes of 1815, Am Hist Rev, Vol 0097, 92. **CONTACT ADDRESS** Dept of Hist, Louisiana State Univ, Baton Rouge, LA, 70803.

HOLZ, ROBERT K.
PERSONAL Born 11/03/1930, Kankakee, IL, m, 1951, 2 children **DISCIPLINE** GEOGRAPHY **EDUCATION** Southern Illinois Univ, BA 59, MA 60; Mich State Univ, PhD 63. **CAREER** Mich State Univ, instr 61-62; Univ Texas, Austin, asst prof 62-67, assoc prof 67-72, prof 72-. **HONORS AND AWARDS** Eric W Zimmerman Regent Prof; NASA Grp Achmt Awd; Asn Geog Remote Sensing, Grp Medal. **MEMBERSHIPS** AAG; Am Soc Photogrammetry. **RESEARCH** Cartography; remote sensing of the Environment. **CONTACT ADDRESS** Dept Geography, Univ Texas, Austin, TX, 78712.

HOMAN, GERLOF DOUWE
PERSONAL Born 08/28/1929, Appingedam, Netherlands, m, 1953, 3 children **DISCIPLINE** MODERN EUROPEAN HISTORY **EDUCATION** Bethel Col, Kans, BA, 54; Univ Kans, MA, 56, PhD, 58. **CAREER** Assoc prof hist, Cent State Col, Okla, 58-63; vis assoc prof, Univ Okla, 63-64; assoc prof, Kans State Col Pittsburg, 64-68; assoc prof, 68-72, PROF HIST, ILL STATE UNIV, 72-, CHMN DEPT, 76- **MEMBERSHIPS** AHA; Soc Fr Hist Studies. **RESEARCH** The French Revolution and Napoleon; the Netherlands in French Revolution and Napoleon Era; Netherlands-American relations and the Indonesian revolution. **SELECTED PUBLICATIONS** Auth, The Netherlands and the Rise of Modern Imperialism--Colonies and Foreign-Policy, 1870-1902, Am Hist Rev, Vol 0098, 93. **CONTACT ADDRESS** Dept of Hist, Illinois State Univ, Normal, IL, 61761.

HOMEL, MICHAEL W.
DISCIPLINE HISTORY **EDUCATION** Grinnell Col, BA; Univ Chicago, MA, PhD. **CAREER** Prof, Eastern Michigan Univ. **RESEARCH** US 20th-Century, US urban. **SELECTED PUBLICATIONS** Auth, Down From Equality: Black Chicagoans and the Public Schools, 1920-1941; Southern Cities, Southern Schools; The Politics of Public Education in Black Chicago, 1910-1941, J Negro Educ 65, 76; Race and Schools in Nineteenth-Century Chicago, Integrated Educ 12, 74; The Lilydale School Campaign of 1936: Direct Action in the Verbal Protest Era, J Negro Hist 59, 74; contribur, Biographical Dictionary of American Mayors, 1820-1980. **CONTACT ADDRESS** Dept of History and Philosophy, Eastern Michigan Univ, 701 Pray-Harrold, Ypsilanti, MI, 48197. **EMAIL** his_homel@online.emich.edu

HOMER, FRANCIS XAVIER JAMES
PERSONAL Born 07/30/1941, Scranton, PA **DISCIPLINE** MODERN EUROPEAN & BRITISH HISTORY **EDUCATION** Univ Scranton, AB, 54; Univ Va, MA, 66, PhD(hist), 71. **CAREER** From instr to assoc prof, 68-84, prof hist, Univ Scranton, 84-. **MEMBERSHIPS** AHA; AAUP; Soc Historians Am Foreign Rels; Northeast Asn of Pre-Law Advisors, Membership Dir, 89-; Pre-Law Advisor Nat Council, Newsletter Co-ed, 91-; Board of Trustees, Scranton Preparatory School, 94-. **RESEARCH** Twentieth century British diplomacy; Nazi Germany. **SELECTED PUBLICATIONS** Co-ed, Germany and Europe in the Era of the Two World Wars, Univ Press Va, 86. **CONTACT ADDRESS** Dept of History, Univ of Scranton, Scranton, PA, 18510-4674. **EMAIL** homerf1@uofs.edu

HOMER, WILLIAM I.
DISCIPLINE ART HISTORY **EDUCATION** Princeton Univ, BA, 51; Harvard Univ, MA, 54; PhD, 61. **CAREER** Asst dir, Art Museum, Princeton Univ, 56-57; cur, Princeton Univ, 56-57; cur, Mus Amer Art, 55, 56, 58; asst prof, Princeton Univ, 61-64; lectr, 59-61; instr, 55-59; assoc prof, Cornell Univ, 64-66,; ch, 88-93; act ch, 86-87; ch, 66-81; prof, 66-84; prof, 84-. **HONORS AND AWARDS** Jr fel, Princeton Univ, 62-63; fel, Amer Coun Learned Soc, 64-65; John Simon Guggenheim Memorial fel, 72-73; NEH fel, 80-81; Univ Del Francis Alison Fac award, 80; distinguished fac lectureship, 81; fel, 85-86; Delaware Hum Forum, res fel, 88-89. **MEMBERSHIPS** Mem, Col Art Assn Am; Pictorial Photogr Am; Photog Soc Philadelphia. **SELECTED PUBLICATIONS** Auth, Seurat and the Science of Painting, MIT Press, 64, repr ed, 85; Robert Henri and His Circle, Cornell Univ Press, 69, second ed, 88; Alfred Stieglitz and the American Avant-Garde, Little, Brown, 77; Alfred Stieglitz and the Photo-Secession, Little, Brown, 83; Thomas Eakins: His Life and Art, Abbeville Press, 92; Preface, Randall C. Griffin, Thomas Anshutz: Artist and Teacher, Wa Univ Press, 94; Robert Henri as a Portrait Painter, Valerie Leeds, My People: The Portraits of Robert Henri, Orlando Museum of Art, 94, 95; The Watercolors of Abraham Walkowitz, Abraham Walkowitz (1878-65): Watercolors from 05 through 20 and Other Works on Paper, Zabriskie Gallery, 94, 95; Unheralded Genius: Karl Struss, Photographer, New York to Hollywood: The Photography of Karl Struss, Amon Carter Mus and Albuquerque, Nmex Univ Press, 95; Karl Struss, Photographer: Unheralded Genius, Amer Art Rev, 95; Charles Demuth: Flowers, 150 Years of Philadelphia Still-Life Painting, The Schwarz Gallery, 97; Collaborative Efforts: Genesis and Fulfillment, The Gist of Drawing, Delaware Art Museum, 97; Whitman, Eakins, and The Naked Truth, Walt Whitman Quart Rev, 97; Visual Culture: A New Paradigm, Amer Art, 98. **CONTACT ADDRESS** Dept of Art Hist, Univ Delaware, 162 Ctr Mall, Newark, DE, 19716.

HOMZE, EDWARD L.
PERSONAL Born 10/13/1930, Canton, OH, m, 1959, 2 children **DISCIPLINE** MODERN & GERMAN HISTORY **EDUCATION** Bowling Green State Univ, BA, 52, MA, 53; Pa State Univ, PhD(Europ hist), 63. **CAREER** Asst prof Europ hist, Kans State Teachers Col, 61-65; assoc prof, 65-71, prof Europ Hist, Univ Nebr, Lincoln, 71-, Nat Found Arts & Humanities fel, 68. **MEMBERSHIPS** AHA. **RESEARCH** Twentieth century Europe; modern Germany. **SELECTED PUBLICATIONS** Auth, Foreign Labor in Nazi Germany, Princeton Univ, 67; coauth, Germany: The Divided Nation, 70 & Willy Brandt, 74, Nelson; auth, Arming the Luftwaffe, Univ Nebr, 76. **CONTACT ADDRESS** History Dept, Univ Nebr, PO Box 880327, Lincoln, NE, 68588-0327. **EMAIL** ehomze@unl.edu

HONDROS, JOHN L.
DISCIPLINE HISTORY **EDUCATION** Univ NC, AB, 59; Vanderbilt Univ, MA, 63, PhD, 69. **CAREER** Prof. **RESEARCH** Origins of the Cold War. **SELECTED PUBLICATIONS** Auth, Greece in the 1940s: A Nation in Crisis, New Eng UP; Occupation and Resistance: The Greek Agony, 1941-1944, Pella Pub Co, 83. **CONTACT ADDRESS** Dept of Hist, Col of Wooster, Wooster, OH, 44691.

HONEYCUTT, DWIGHT A.
PERSONAL m, 3 children **DISCIPLINE** CHURCH HISTORY **EDUCATION** Mercer Univ, BA; Midwestern Baptist Sem, BD; Intl Baptist Theol Sem, Switzerland, ThM; New Orleans Baptist Theol Sem, ThD. **CAREER** Instr, ch, Acad Comm, Intl Baptist Theol Sem, Cali, Colombia, 77; vis prof, New Orleans Baptist Theol Sem; Midwestern Baptist Theol Sem, 87-88; prof, 88; William A. Carleton prof, Golden Gate Baptist Theol Sem, 92-. **HONORS AND AWARDS** Assoc secy, missionary personnel, S Baptist For Mission Bd, 72. **SELECTED PUBLICATIONS** Pub(s), Theol Educator; Bolotin Teologico de ABITHA; El Heraldo; Dialogo Teologica; Jour Church and State; SBC Quart Rev. **CONTACT ADDRESS** Golden Gate Baptist Theol Sem, 201 Sem Dr, Mill Valley, CA, 94941-3197. **EMAIL** DwightHoneycutt@ggbts.edu

HOOD, DAVID CROCKETT
PERSONAL Born 04/21/1937, Tulsa, OK, m, 1961, 2 children **DISCIPLINE** ANCIENT HISTORY **EDUCATION** Univ Calif, Santa Barbara, BA, 61; Univ Southern Calif, PhD(Hist), 67. **CAREER** Asst prof Hist, Wichita State Univ, 65-66; from asst prof to assoc prof, 66-75, prof hist, Calif State Univ, Long Beach, 75-. **HONORS AND AWARDS** So Calif Classical Assoc; chmn, Academic Senate, 9a5-98; chmn, Friends of Ancient Hist in So Calif, 82. **MEMBERSHIPS** Soc Prom Hellenic Studies; Am Philol Asn; Soc Prom Roman Studies. **RESEARCH** Roman historiography. **SELECTED PUBLICATIONS** Ed, The Rise of Rome: How to Explain It?, Heath, 70. **CONTACT ADDRESS** Dept of History, California State Univ, Long Beach, 1250 N Bellflower, Long Beach, CA, 90840-1601. **EMAIL** dhood@csulb.edu

HOOD, MANTLE
DISCIPLINE ETHNOMUSICOLOGY **EDUCATION** Univ Calif, MA, BA; Univ Amsterdam, PhD. **CAREER** Prof emer, UCLA; vis prof; adj prof-. **HONORS AND AWARDS** Sr fel, NEH; Fulbright fel; Ford Found fel., Former pres, Soc ethnomusicology. **MEMBERSHIPS** Soc for Ethnomusicology. **RESEARCH** Indonesian music. **SELECTED PUBLICATIONS** Publ, twenty books and book chapters as well as over sixty articles in scholarly journals and encyclopedias. **CONTACT ADDRESS** Dept of Mus, W Va Univ, PO Box 6009, Morgantown, WV, 26506-6009.

HOOGENBOOM, ARI
PERSONAL Born 11/28/1927, Richmond Hill, NY, m, 1949, 3 children **DISCIPLINE** AMERICAN HISTORY **EDUCATION** Atlantic Union Col, AB, 49; Columbia Univ, AM, 51, PhD, 58. **CAREER** Lectr Am hist, Columbia Univ, 55-56; from instr to asst prof hist, TX Western Col, 56-58; from instr to asst prof, PA State Univ, 58-62, from assoc prof to prof Am hist, 62-68; chmn dept, 68-74, prof hist, Brooklyn Col, City Univ NY, 68-98, Emeritus 98-, Am Philos Soc grants-in-aid, 59, 60; Guggenheim fel, 65-66. **HONORS AND AWARDS** Fulbright Award, Ger, 91-92. **MEMBERSHIPS** AHA; Orgn Am Historians. **RESEARCH** Post Civil War Am hist; Am bureaucratic hist; the Am Civil War. **SELECTED PUBLICATIONS** Auth, The Pendleton Act and the Civil Service, American Hist Rev, 59; Outlawing the Spoils: A History of the Civil Service Reform Movement, 1865-1883, Univ IL, 61; Thomas A Jenckes and Civil Service reform, Miss Valley Hist Rev, 3/61; Gustavus Fox and the relief of Fort Sumter, Civil War Hist, 12/63; coauth, The Enterprising Colonials: Society on the Eve of the Revolution, Argonaut, Inc, 65; co-ed, The Gilded Age, 67 & An Interdisciplinary Approach to American History (2 vols), 73, Prentice-Hall; coauth, A History of Pennsylvania, McGraw, 73, 2nd ed, PA State Univ Press, 80; A History of the ICC: From Panacea to Palliative, Norton, 76; The Presidency of Rutherford B. Hayes, Univ Press of KS, 88; Rutherford B. Hayes: Warrior and President, Univ Press of KS, 95. **CONTACT ADDRESS** Dept of Hist, Brooklyn Col, CUNY, 2901 Bedford Ave, Brooklyn, NY, 11210-2813.

HOOGLAND VERKERK, DOROTHY
DISCIPLINE ART HISTORY **EDUCATION** Rutgers Univ, PhD. **CAREER** Asst prof, Univ NC, Chapel Hill. **RESEARCH** Late antique, Celtic, early medieval art and cult. **SELECTED PUBLICATIONS** Auth, Exodus and Easter Vigil in the Ashburnham Pentateuch, Art Bull 77, 95. **CONTACT ADDRESS** Univ N. Carolina, Chapel Hill, Chapel Hill, NC, 27599. **EMAIL** dverkerk@email.unc.edu

HOOLEY, DANIEL M.
DISCIPLINE LATIN AND GREEK LITERATURE **EDUCATION** Minn Univ, MA, PhD, Class, PhD, Engl. **CAREER** Assoc prof; Univ Mo, 92-; actv, Honors Col Humanities sequence; taught at, Allegheny Col, Carleton Col & Princeton Univ. **RESEARCH** Satire; later Latin; Classical tradition; translation studies. **SELECTED PUBLICATIONS** Auth, The Classics in Paraphrase: Ezra Pound and Modern Translators of Latin Poetry & The Knotted Thong: Structures of Imitation in Persius. **CONTACT ADDRESS** Dept of Classical Studies, Univ of Missouri-Columbia, 309 University Hall, Columbia, MO, 65211. **EMAIL** clstuddh@showme.missouri.edu

HOOPER, PAUL FRANKLIN
PERSONAL Born 07/31/1938, Walla Walla, WA, m, 1960, 1 child **DISCIPLINE** AMERICAN STUDIES **EDUCATION** Eastern Wash Univ, BA, 61; Univ Hawaii, MA, 65, PhD, 72. **CAREER** Prof, ch, Dept stud, 72 to present, Univ Hawaii; exec Asst mng Dir, 85-86, City and County of Honolulu; Fulbright Sr Lectr, 83-84, Beijing For Stud Univ; ch clerk, 81, St Sen Comm Trans; exec sec, 76-77, Univ HI Intl Rel Counc. **HONORS AND AWARDS** Numerous Res and Pub Gnts Most Recently from Shibusawa Foundation. **MEMBERSHIPS** AAUP; ASA; HCFR. **RESEARCH** Asian-Pacific-American Relations; Hawaii History and Politics; Inst of Pacific Relations. **SELECTED PUBLICATIONS** Auth, From friend to Foe: Pre-WWII Japanese-American Relations Within The Inst Of Pacific Relations, in: Economic Development in East Asia: The Intl Context, ed, Aiko Ikeo, London, Routledge, 97; Forward, Linguistic Americanization of Japanese-Americans in Hawaii, Nobuhiro Adachi, Osaka, Osaka Kyoiku Tosho, 96; Remembering the Inst of Pacific Relations: The Memoirs of Wm L Holland, Tokyo, Ryukei Shyosha, 95. **CONTACT ADDRESS** Dept of American Studies, Univ Hawaii, Honolulu, HI, 96822. **EMAIL** hooper@hawaii.edu

HOOPER, WILLIAM LOYD
PERSONAL m, 2 children **DISCIPLINE** MUSIC **EDUCATION** Southwest Bapt Col, cert, Bolivar, Mo, 51; William Jewell Col, BA, Philos, 53, Liberty, Mo; Univ Iowa, MA, music, 56; PhD, music, 66, minor in higher educ, George Peabody Col, Vanderbilt Univ, Nashville, Tenn; music composition study with, Philip Bezanson, 55-56, Univ Iowa, Philip Slates, 60-61, Peabody Col, Vanderbilt Univ, Humphrey Searle, 69-70, Royal Col of Music, London, England; training in psychotherapy, Westminster Pastoral Found, 82-83, London, England. **CAREER** Music tchr, K-12, Essex Pub Sch, Essex, Iowa, 53-55; music tchr, 9-12, Atalissa Pub Sch, Atalissa, Iowa, 55-56; pastor, Denver Bapt Church, Denver, Mo, 53-55; prof of music, Southwest Bapt Col, Bolivar, Mo, 56-60; minister of music and educ, First Bapt Church, Old Hickory, Tenn, 60-62; prof of music, New Orleans Bapt Sem, New Orleans, La, 62-74; acting dean, Sch of Church Music, New Orleans Bapt Sem, 64-65, dean, 65-74; head of music dept, Newstead Wood Sch for Girls, London Borough of Bromley England, 74-79; assoc pastor and minister of music, Emmanuel Bapt Church, Gravesend, Kent, England, 74-79; sr pastor, 79-83; chief examiner in music, Southeast Reg Examining Bd, Tunbridge Wells, Kent, England, 75-80; dean, prof of music, Sch of Fine Arts, Southwest Bapt Univ, 83-89; dir of assessment, dir of intl studies, prof of music, Southwest Bapt Univ, 89-98. **HONORS AND AWARDS** David Duce Award in Philos, William Jewell Col, 53; Outstanding Young Men of Amer, 63; Citation for Achievement, William Jewell Col, 67; First Place winner, Delius Compos Competition, 73; First place winner, New Times Compos Competition, 74. **SELECTED PUBLICATIONS** Auth, Fundamentals of Music, Conv Press, 86; Ministry and Musicians, Broadman Press, 83; Music Fundamentals, Conv Press, 67; Church Music in Transition, Broadman Press, 63; compos, Jubilee, Cantata, Carl Fischer Co, Litany of Praise, Cantata, Carl Fischer Co, And He Shall Come, Cantata, Broadman Press, Sing Joyfully, choral collection, Broadman Press; incidental music for prof of Anouihl's Becket, Le Petit Theatre du Vieux Carre, New Orleans, La. **CONTACT ADDRESS** 116 W. Auburn St., Bolivar, MO, 65613.

HOOPES, JAMES
DISCIPLINE HISTORY **EDUCATION** Bowling Green Univ, BA, 65; Univ Wis, MA, 69; Johns Hopkins, MA, 71, PhD, 73. **CAREER** PROF, HIST, BABSON COLL **MEMBERSHIPS** Am Antiquarian Soc **SELECTED PUBLICATIONS** Auth, Van Wyck Books: In Search of American Culture, 77; Oral History: An Introduction for Students, 79; auth, Consciousness in New England, Johns Hopkins, 89; auth, Peirce on Signs: Writings on Semiotics by Charles Sanders Peirce, Univ of NC Press, 91; auth, Two Myths of Pragmatic Liberalism: The Philosophical Errors of Twentieth-Century American Political Theory, Cornell. **CONTACT ADDRESS** Hist & Soc Div, Babson Col, Wellesley, MA, 02157. **EMAIL** hoopes@cc01.babson.edu

HOOVER, DWIGHT W
PERSONAL Born 09/15/1926, Oskaloosa, IA, m, 1954, 3 children **DISCIPLINE** AMERICAN INTELLECTUAL HISTORY **EDUCATION** William Penn Col, BA, 48; Haverford Col, MA, 49; State Univ Iowa, PhD, 53. **CAREER** Prof, chmn dept & head div soc sci, Bethune-Cookman Col, 53-55 & 58; asst prof gen studies, Kans State Univ, 58-59; from asst prof to assoc prof soc sci, 59-67, PROF HIST, BALL STATE UNIV, 67-, Consult urban hist, Nat Endowment for Humanities, 71-72 & pub progs, 76-77; prof hist sociol, Univ Va, 77-78. **MEMBERSHIPS** AHA; Orgn Am Historians; Am Studies Asn; AAUP. **RESEARCH** Intellectual origins of racism; recent historiography; urban history, particularly of Muncie, Indiana. **SELECTED PUBLICATIONS** Auth, Venice West--The Beat Generation in Southern California, J West, Vol 0032, 93. **CONTACT ADDRESS** Dept of Hist, Ball State Univ, Muncie, IN, 47306.

HOOVER, HERBERT THEODORE
PERSONAL Born 03/09/1930, Millville, MN, m, 1957, 2 children **DISCIPLINE** AMERICAN FRONTIER & INDIAN HISTORY **EDUCATION** NMex State Univ, BA, 60, MA, 61; Univ Okla, PhD, 66. **CAREER** Asst prof hist, ETex State Univ, 65-66; assoc prof, 67-74, grad adv, 71-76, prof hist, Univ S Dak, Vermillion, 74-, mem SDak Comt on Humanities, NEH, 75-78; fel, Newberry Libr, Chicago, 77; dir, SDak Oral Hist Ctr, 77-78; adv panelist, Res Div, NEH, 77-78; NEH res award, 78-81. **HONORS AND AWARDS** Western America Award, Augustana Ctr for Western Studies, 84; Chair, Rhodes Schol S Dakota State Selection Comt, 91-98. **MEMBERSHIPS** Western Hist Asn; Orgn Am Historians. **RESEARCH** American frontier; American Indian history; oral history. **SELECTED PUBLICATIONS** Coauth, To Be An Indian, Holt, 71; The Practice of Oral History, Microfilming Corp of Am, 75; auth, The Chitimacha People, Indian Tribal Series, 75; Yankton Sioux tribal claims against the United States, 1917-1975, in Western Hist Quart, 76; The Sioux: A Critical Bibliography, Ind Univ Press, 79; Bibliography of the Sioux, Scarecrow Press, 80; The Yankton Sioux, Chelsea House Publ, 88; South Dakota Leaders, Univ Publ Assoc, 89; Yanktonai Sioux Images: The Watercolors of John Saul, Augustana Col Ctr for Western Studies, 93; South Dakota History: An Annotated Bibliography, Greenwood Press, 93; The Sioux and Other Native American Cultures of the Dakotas: An Annotated Bibliography, Greenwood Press, 93; "South Dakota" entries in Encycl Am 76-, Wordmark Encycl 81, Encycl Brittanica 90, Dict Am Hist 96, Encarta Encycl 96; author of numerous other journal articles and book chapters. **CONTACT ADDRESS** Dept of Hist, Univ of South Dak, 414 E Clark St., Vermillion, SD, 57069-2390.

HOOVER, WILLIAM DAVIS
PERSONAL Born 04/25/1941, Columbus, OH, m, 1964, 3 children **DISCIPLINE** JAPANESE HISTORY **EDUCATION** Muskingum Col, BA, 63; Univ Mich, Ann Arbor, MA, 65, PhD, 73. **CAREER** From Instr to Assoc Prof, 68-85, prof hist, Univ Toledo, 85, Chmn Dept, 79-94. **HONORS AND AWARDS** Japan Found Res Fel, Tokyo, 95-96. **MEMBERSHIPS** Asn Asian Studies; AHA; SHAFR. **RESEARCH** Meiji Japan; Pacificism in Japan hist; soc, cult and intellectual exchange with Japan; US-Japanese rels. **CONTACT ADDRESS** 2801 W Bancroft St, Toledo, OH, 43606-3390. **EMAIL** whoover@pop3.utoledo.edu

HOPKINS, DIANNE MCAFEE
PERSONAL Born 12/30/1944, Houston, Texas, m, 1982 **DISCIPLINE** EDUCATION **EDUCATION** Fisk University, Nashville, TN, BA, 1966; Atlanta University, Atlanta, GA, MSLS, 1967; Western Michigan University, Kalamazoo, MI, EdS, 1973; University of Wisconsin-Madison, Madison, WI, PhD, 1981. **CAREER** Houston Independent School District, Houston, TX, librarian, 1967-71; Dept of Education, Michigan, Lansing, MI, school librarian consultant, 1972-73; West Bloomfield Schools, West Bloomfield, MI, high school librarian, 1973-74; University of Michigan, Ann Arbor, MI, school librarian consultant, 1974-77; Wisconsin Dept of Public Instr, Madison, dir, school librarians, 1977-87; University of Wisconsin-Madison, professor, 1987-92, associate prof, 1992-. **HONORS AND AWARDS** Recipient, US Dept of Education Grant, 1989; Beta Phi Mu International Library Fraternity, 1967; Phi Delta Kappa, 1980; Exceptional Performance Award, Wisconsin Dept of Public Instr, 1982; Winner, ALISE Research Award, 1992; Winner, Distinguished Service Award, American Association of School Librarians; Co-principal Investigator, Natl Library Power Evaluation, Dewitt Wallace-Readers Digest Fund, 1994-. **MEMBERSHIPS** Executive committee, educators of school library media specialists, 1988-91, member, editorial board, school library media quarterly, 1988-91, chair, AASL White House conference, 1986-92, American Assn of School Librarians; member, ALA presidents White House conference task force, American Library Assn, 1990-92; chair, local arrangement committee ALISE national conference, Assn of Library and Information Science Education, 1990-91; ALA Intellectual Freedom Comm, 1991-; AASL Vision Comm for New Natl Guidelines, 1995-. **CONTACT ADDRESS** Univ of Wisconsin-Madison, 600 N Park St, 4251 Helen C White Hall, Madison, WI, 53706.

HOPKINS, FRED
PERSONAL Born 11/19/1935, Staten Island, NY, m, 1961, 2 children **DISCIPLINE** HISTORY **EDUCATION** Gettysburg Coll, BA, 56; Univ of Md, MEd, 64, PhD, 69. **CAREER** Anne Arundel County Public High Sch, 59-70; Assoc prof, Univ Baltimore, 70-71; Adj Fac, Univ Baltimore, 71-92; Prof, Univ Baltimore, 93-. **HONORS AND AWARDS** Phi Beta Kappa. **MEMBERSHIPS** Inst of Nautical Archaeol; Md Hist Soc; North Am Soc of Oceanic Hist. **SELECTED PUBLICATIONS** Auth, Tom Boyle, Master Privateer, Tidewater Press, 76; Coauth, War on the Patuxent, 1814, Calvert Marine Museum Press, 81. **CONTACT ADDRESS** Univ Baltimore, 1420 N. Charles Street, Baltimore, MD, 21201.

HOPKINS, JOHN ORVILLE
PERSONAL Born 01/27/1930, Missoula, MT **DISCIPLINE** EDUCATION **EDUCATION** Gonzaga U, BA 1956, MA 1957; Columbia U, MPhil, PhD 1976; Columbia Univ Rsrch Prof, prep kndergrad educ 1977-78. **CAREER** State Univ of NY, prof 1976-77; MARC Public Educ Assn, educ dir 1970-74; Bd of Educ Baltimore, asst supt 1968-69; Fed Civil Rights Officer for Educ 1965-67; Amer Philos Assn, parish priest, teacher 1962-64. **HONORS AND AWARDS** Columbia Univ Pub Speaking Awds Univ MT, Seattle U, Gonzaga U, Elks, Rotary Club. **MEMBERSHIPS** Am Assn of Sch Adminstrs; NAACP; Assn fcor Study of Black Religion; Minority Parents Assn; African Studies Assn; corporate bds MD Day Care Council; dir S African Rsrch Progm. **CONTACT ADDRESS** 420 W 118th St 1318, New York, NY, 10027.

HOPKINS, RICHARD JOSEPH
PERSONAL Born 10/25/1939, Deposit, NY, m, 1961, 2 children **DISCIPLINE** AMERICAN URBAN & SOCIAL HISTORY **EDUCATION** Univ Rochester, BA, 61; Emory Univ, MA, 65, PhD(hist), 72. **CAREER** Instr hist, Univ Wis, Milwaukee, 68-69; instr, 69-72, ASST PROF HIST, OHIO STATE UNIV, 72- **MEMBERSHIPS** AHA; Orgn Am Historians; Southern Hist Asn **RESEARCH** American urbanization, especially occupational and residential mobility. **SELECTED PUBLICATIONS** Auth, The Pursuit of Public Power--Political-Culture in Ohio, 1787-1861, Historian, Vol 0058, 95. **CONTACT ADDRESS** Dept of Hist, Ohio State Univ, 230 W 17th Ave, Columbus, OH, 43210.

HOPKINS, THOMAS J.
PERSONAL Born 07/28/1930, Champaign, IL, m, 1956, 4 children **DISCIPLINE** HISTORY OF RELIGIONS **EDUCATION** Col William & Mary & Mass Inst Technol, BS, 53; Yale Univ, BS, 58, MA, 59, PhD, 62. **CAREER** From instr to assoc prof, 61-72, Prof Relig, 72-96, EMER PROF RELIG SCI, 96-, FRANKLIN & MARSHALL COL, 61- ; Dir India Studies prog, Cent Pa Consortium, 71-75; chmn group Indian philos & relig, Coun Intercult Studies & Prog, 72-77; chr AAR Asian Relig/Hist Relig Sect, 75-80; co-chr AAR Comp Stud Relig Section, 80-87. **MEMBERSHIPS** Asn Asian Studies; Am Orient Soc; Am Acad Relig; Am Soc Study Relig. **RESEARCH** Indian history; phenomenology of religion. **SELECTED PUBLICATIONS** Auth, The social teaching of the Bhagavata Purana, In: Krishna: Myths, Rites and Attitudes, East-West, 66; The Hindu Religious Tradition, Dickenson, 71; Contribr, Six Pillars: Introduction to the Major Works of Sri Avrobindo, Conchocheague Assoc, 74; contrib Hare Krishna, Hare Krishna, Grove Press, 83; Krishna Consciousness in the West, Bucknell Univ Press, 89; Death and Afterlife: Perspectives of World Religions, Greenwood Press, 92. **CONTACT ADDRESS** 323 N West End Ave, Lancaster, PA, 17603.

HOPKINS, VASHTI EDYTHE JOHNSON
PERSONAL Born 08/22/1924, Virginia, m **DISCIPLINE** EDUCATION **EDUCATION** Virginia Seminary & Coll, BS 1963; St Paul's Coll, BS Elem Educ 1967; Univ of Virginia, MEd 1969; Southwestern Univ, PhD Educ 1984. **CAREER** Amherst City Public Schools, teacher 1963-67; Lynchburg Public Schools, teacher 1967-74; Sandusky Middle School, teacher 1974-82; Virginia Seminary & Coll, prof of English, 1991-97. **HONORS AND AWARDS** Achievement Award Order of Eastern Star Chapter 40 1984; Outstanding Achievement Grand Chapter of Virginia OESPHA 1984; Golden Poet Award, World of Poetry 1989-96; **MEMBERSHIPS** Dep organizer Order of Eastern Star PHA 1967-91; Eastern Theological Center; mem Zeta Chap Zeta Phi Beta Sor; life mem NEA, VEA, LEA, Univ of Virginia Alumni Assoc, Century Club St Paul's Coll; mem Daughter of Isis, Golden Circle Past LL Ruler; past pres Episcopal Church Women, pres Amity Soc, Bridgette Soc; mem Natl Sor of Phi Delta Kappa Inc Alpha Tau Chapter Lynchburg Virginia Chapter; Phi Delta Kappa Fraternity, past vice pres of membership; past pres, Lynchburg Retired Teachers, 1989-90; pres, District F Retired Teachers, 1990-92. **SELECTED PUBLICATIONS** poems published in 1989, 1992; Golden Treasury of Great Poems.

HORD, FREDERICK LEE
PERSONAL Born 11/07/1941, Kokomo, IN, d, 3 children **DISCIPLINE** BLACK STUDIES: LITERATURE/HISTORY **EDUCATION** Ind State Univ, BS, 63, MS, 65; Union Grad School, PhD, 87. **CAREER** Asst prof English, Wabash Col, 72-76; lectr, Howard Univ, 84-87; Dir Ctr Black Cult & Res, W Va Univ, 87-88; DIR BLACK STUDIES & FULL PROF, KNOX COL, 88- **HONORS AND AWARDS** ACM grant for Blacks-Jews Relationships; Ed bd, Jour of Black Stud; First Poets Series Award. **MEMBERSHIPS** Nat Asn Black Cult Ctrs; Nat Coun Black Studies; ILL Comm Black Concerns Higher Educ. **RESEARCH** African American literature; black philosophy; black psychology; history of black intellectuals; black culture centers. **SELECTED PUBLICATIONS** Auth, After Hours; Reconstructing Memory; coed, Life Sentences; I Am Because We Are: Readings in Black Philosophy. **CONTACT ADDRESS** Knox Col, 2 E South St, Galesburg, IL, 61401. **EMAIL** fhord@knox.knox.edu

HORGAN, PAUL
PERSONAL Born 08/01/1903, Buffalo, NY **DISCIPLINE** MODERN HISTORY **CAREER** Librn, NMex Mil Inst, 26-42, asst to pres, 47-49; adj prof English, 67-71, dir, 62-67, AUTH IN RESIDENCE, WESLEYAN UNIV, 67-, EMER PROF ENGLISH, 71-, Guggenheim fels, 46, 50, 59; lectr, Grad Sch Lett, Univ Iowa, 46; mem bd mgr & exec comt, Sch Am Res, 63-; mem Nat Coun on Humanities, 66-72; hon fel, Saybrook Col, Yale, 66-, lectr English, 70; scholar in residence, Aspen Inst Humanistic Studies, 68, 71 & 73. **HONORS AND AWARDS** Harper Prize, 33; Pulitzer Prize in Hist, 55 & 77; Bancroft Prize hist, 55; Campion Award, 57., LittD, Wesleyan Univ, 56, Southern Methodist Univ, 57, Univ Notre Dame, 58, Boston Col, 59, NMex State Univ, 61, Col Holy Cross, 63, Univ NMex, 63, Lincoln Col, Ill, 68, St Bonaventure Univ, 70, Loyola Col, Md, 70 & LaSalle Col, 71; LHD, Canisius Col, 60, Georgetown Univ, 62, Fairfield Univ, 64, D'Youville Col, 65, Pace Col, 67, Cath Univ Am, 73 & Yale, 77. **MEMBERSHIPS** AHA; Cath Hist Asn (vpres, 57, pres, 58); Nat Inst Arts & Lett; Soc Am Historians; life fel Am Acad Arts & Sci. **RESEARCH** Southwest United States history; United States biography; English literature criticism. **SELECTED PUBLICATIONS** Auth, Edmund Wilson at Wesleyan, Am Poetry Rev, Vol 0022, 93; Vachel Lindsay and the 'Book Of The Dead'--The Poet and New-Poetry, Am Scholar, Vol 0062, 93. **CONTACT ADDRESS** Wesleyan Univ, Middletown, CT, 06457.

HORN, MARTIN
DISCIPLINE HISTORY **EDUCATION** Univ Western Ontario, BA; McMaster Univ, MA; Univ Toronto, PhD. **RESEARCH** Economics; power. **SELECTED PUBLICATIONS** Art, International Hist Rev; art, Guerres Mondiales et Conflits Contemporains. **CONTACT ADDRESS** History Dept, McMaster Univ, 1280 Main St W, Hamilton, ON, L8S 4L9.

HORN, VERNON
DISCIPLINE HISTORY **EDUCATION** Univ Md, MA, PhD cand. **CAREER** Commun assoc, Am Hist Asn. **MEMBERSHIPS** Am Hist Asn. **CONTACT ADDRESS** American Historical Assn.

HORNSBY, ALTON
PERSONAL Born 09/03/1940, Atlanta, GA, m, 1965, 2 children **DISCIPLINE** HISTORY **EDUCATION** Morehouse Col, BA, 61; Univ Texas, MA, 62, PhD, 69. **CAREER** Instr, hist, 62-65,Tuskegee Inst; asst prof, actng chmn, dept hist, 68-71, assoc prof, chmn, dept hist, 71-74, prof, 74-, Fuller E. Callaway Prof of History, 89-, Morehouse Col. **HONORS AND AWARDS** Woodrow Wilson Fel, 61-62; S Ed Found Fel, 66-68; Univ Fel, Univ Texas, 69; S Fel Fund Fel, 78-79; United Negro Col Fund Hum Fel, Sum, 81; NEH Fel for Col Tchrs, 81-82; Amer Coun of Learned Soc Grant-in-aid, Sum, 82; United Negro Col Fund Dist Scholar, 82-83; Morehouse Col Fac Res Grant, 71-73; Alpha Phi Alpha Tchr of the Year, Morehouse Col, 71-72; Danforth Found Assoc, 78-81; Rockefeller Hum Fel, 77-78; Phi Alpha Theta; Phi Beta Kappa; WEB Du Bois Award, 89; Fuller E Callaway Prof of Hist, 89. **MEMBERSHIPS** Assn for Stud for Afro-Amer Life & Hist; Assn of Soc & Behav Sci; Georgia Assn of Hist; Atlanta Hist Soc; Org of Amer Hist; Assn of St and Local Hist; Natl Coun for Black Stud; St Comm on Life & Hist of Black Georgians; So Conf on Afro-Amer Stud; So Hist Assn. **SELECTED PUBLICATIONS** Ed & intro, In The Cage: Eyewitness Accounts of the Freed Negro in Southern Society 1877-1929, Chicago, 71; auth, The Black Almanac, Woodbury, 77; auth, The Negro in Revolutionary Georgia, Atlanta, 72; auth, The City Too Busy to Hate: Atlanta Businessmen and Desegregation, in So Businessmen & Desegregation, Baton Rouge, 82; auth, Georgia, The Black Press in the South, Westport, 83; auth, The Black Revolution, Black History, and Professor Franklin, The Atlanta Univ Ctr Sampler, 72; auth, Black History in a Vacuum, The Black Collegian, 72; art, The Freedman's Bureau Schools in Texas, S Hist Quart, 73; art, The Colored University Issue in Texas Politics: Prelude to Sweatt vs. Painter, J Negro Hist, 76; art, The Negro in Atlanta Politics, 1961-1973, Atlanta Hist J, 77. **CONTACT ADDRESS** Dept of History, Morehouse Col, 223 Chestnut SW, Atlanta, GA, 30314.

HORNSBY, ROGER ALLEN
PERSONAL Born 08/08/1926, Nye, WI, m, 1960 **DISCIPLINE** CLASSICS **EDUCATION** Western Reserve Univ, BA, 49; Princeton Univ, MA, 51, PhD(classics), 52. **CAREER** Instr Latin & Greek, 54-58, from asst prof to assoc prof classics, 58-67, chmn dept, 66-81, Prof Classics, Univ Iowa, 67-, Coun Learned Soc fel, 70-71; consult, Nat Endowment for Humanities, 71-72; ed, Text Book Series APA, 75-81, Am Acad Rome resident, 83. **HONORS AND AWARDS** Ovatio, Classic Asn Midwest & South, 80. **MEMBERSHIPS** Am Philol Asn; Classic Asn Midwest & South (pres, 68-69); Archaeol Inst Am; Am Numis Soc; Mediaeval Acad Am. **RESEARCH** Latin poetry; stoicism; Greek poetry. **SELECTED PUBLICATIONS** Auth, A Students Latin Grammar, Classical World, Vol 0087, 94; A New Topographical Dictionary of Ancient-Rome, Classical Bul, Vol 0069, 93. **CONTACT ADDRESS** Dept Classics, Univ Iowa, Iowa City, IA, 52242.

HORNSTEIN, SHELLEY
DISCIPLINE ART HISTORY **EDUCATION** Univ des Sciences Humaines de Strasbourg, LL, 76, Diplome des Etudes Approfondies, DEA, 76, ML, 78, PhD, 81. **CAREER** Lectr, 82, instr, 83-84, Laval Univ; coordr, visual arts, 87-89, ch, fine arts, 88-90, ASSOC PROF ATKINSON COL, YORK UNIV, 88-, assoc dean, 90-92, CH, FINE ARTS 95-. **MEMBERSHIPS** Art Gallery York Univ; Ctr Feminist Res, York Univ. **SELECTED PUBLICATIONS** Auth, Interstices of Romance, in C Mag vol 9, 86; auth, Architecture on the Edge, in J Archit Planning Res, 89; auth, The Architecture of the First Montreal Teaching Hospitals of the 19th Century, in J Art Hist, vol X111 & X1V, 91; co-ed, Capital Culture: A Reader on Modernist Legacies, State Institutions and the Values of Art. **CONTACT ADDRESS** Dept of Fine Arts, York Univ, North York, ON, M3J 1P3. **EMAIL** shelley@yorku.ca

HOROWITZ, DANIEL
PERSONAL Born 03/23/1938, New Haven, CT, m, 1963, 2 children **DISCIPLINE** AMERICAN STUDIES; HISTORY **EDUCATION** Yale Col, BA, 60; Pembroke Col, 60-61; Harvard Univ, 61-67. **CAREER** Asst prof to prof, Scripps Col, 73-88; prof and Dir Am Studies Prog, Smith Col, 89- . **HONORS AND AWARDS** NEH fel, 73; Nat Human Ctr fel, 84-85; NEH fel for Col Teachers, 95; Hon Vis Fel, Schlesinger Libr, Radcliffe Col, 96-98; Constance Rourke Prize, Am Studeis Assoc, 97. **MEMBERSHIPS** ASA; AHA; OAH. **RESEARCH** History of consumer culture; social criticism. **SELECTED PUBLICATIONS** Auth, The Morality of Spending: Attitudes Toward the Consumer Society in America, 1875-1940; auth, Vance Packard and American Social Criticism, 94; Betty Friedan and the Making of the Feminine Mystique: The American Left, The Cold War, Modern Feminism, 98. **CONTACT ADDRESS** American Studies Program, Smith Col, Northampton, MA, 01063. **EMAIL** dhorowit@sophia.smith.edu

HOROWITZ, DAVID A.
PERSONAL Born 08/17/1941, Bronx, NY, m, 1996 **DISCIPLINE** HISTORY **EDUCATION** Antioch Col, BA, 64; Univ of Minn, PhD, 71. **CAREER** INSTR TO PROF OF HISTORY, PORTLAND STATE UNIV, 68-. **MEMBERSHIPS** Org of Am Historians. **RESEARCH** 20th century U.S. cultural and political history. **SELECTED PUBLICATIONS** Ed & annotator, Inside the Klavern: The Secret History of a 1920 Klu Klux Klan, Southern Ill Univ Press, forthcoming in 99; coauth, On the Edge: The U.S. in the 20th Century, West/Wadsworth, 98; auth, The Normality of Extremism: The Ku Klux Klan Revisited, Soc, 98; auth, Beyond Left and Right: Insurgency and the Establishment, Univ of Ill Press, 97; auth, An Alliance of Convenience: Independent Exhibitors and Purity Crusaders Battle Hollywood 1920-1940, Historian, 97; auth, Senator Borah's Crusade to Save Small Business from the New Deal, Historian, 93; auth, The Cross of Culture: La Grande, Oregon in the 1920s, Ore Hist Quart, 93. **CONTACT ADDRESS** Dept of Hist, Portland State Univ, Portland, OR, 97207.

HOROWITZ, MARYANNE CLINE
PERSONAL Born 06/29/1945, Boston, MA, m, 1968, 3 children **DISCIPLINE** RENAISSANCE HISTORY **EDUCATION** Brown Univ, AB, 65; Harvard Univ, MAT, 66; Univ Wis-Madison, MA, 68, PhD, 70. **CAREER** Instr govt, 70-71, res assoc, 71-73, Cornell Univ; asst prof polit, Ithaca Col, 72-73; asst prof, 73-80, assoc prof, 80-88, PROF HIST, OCCIDENTAL COL, 88-, chair, women's studies, 77-79, 82-85, chair, hist dept, 88-91; assoc, Center for Medieval & Renaissance Studies, Univ Calif Los Angeles, 88-; vis fac, Divinity Sch, Harvard Univ, 79-80, hist, UCLA, 92; reader, Huntington Libr, Warburg Inst, Getty Center. **HONORS AND AWARDS** Mellon Found 79, 98; Ford fel, 90, 91; NEH Summer, 71, 86, 90; ACLS Travel, 84; Haynes, 74, 77. **MEMBERSHIPS** AHA; APSA; Renaissance Soc Am (exec bd, 86-98); Sixteenth Century Studies Conf (counc 77-80); WAWH. **RESEARCH** Moral, educational, and political ideas and images. **SELECTED PUBLICATIONS** Auth, The Image of God in Man - Is Woman Included?, J Hist Biol, 76; Marie de Gournay, Ed of the Essaies of Michel de Montaigne, Sixteenth Century J, 86; Renaissance Rereadings: Intertext and Context, 88; Drogue medicinale ou vieux conte, in Montaigne et l'histoire, 89; Politics of Gender in Early Modern Europe, 89; Race, Gender and Rank: Early Modern Ideas of Humanity, 91; Playing with Gender: A Renaissance Pursuit, 91; Race, Class, and Gender in Nineteenth-Century Culture, 91; Bodin and Judaism, Il pensiero politico, 97; Seeds of Virtue and Knowledge, Princeton, 98. **CONTACT ADDRESS** Dept of Hist, Occidental Col, 1600 Campus Rd, Los Angeles, CA, 90041-3314. **EMAIL** horowitz@oxy.edu

HOROWITZ, MICHAEL M.
DISCIPLINE ANTHROPOLOGY **EDUCATION** Columbia Univ, PhD, 59; MA, 59; Berlin Coll, BA, Hon, 55. **CAREER** Prof, Anthro, Binghamton Univ, 61-; Dir Inst, Devel Anthro, 76-. **HONORS AND AWARDS** Keynote Speaker Proposal 21, Tokyo, 96; Distinguished Lecturer, Pakistan Soc of Devl Ecib, 95; Elizabeth Colson Lecturer, Oxford Univ, 91; Fulbright Sr Res Scholar, Bergen Univ, 66-67; Phi Beta Kappa; Sigma XI; Woodrow Wilson fellow; Soc Sci Res Council Fellow; Columbia Univ Fellow. **MEMBERSHIPS** Amer Anthro Assoc; Soc for Applied Anthro; Amer Fed of Teacher (AFL-CIO) Intl Comm on the Anthro of Food; Amer Civil Liberties Union; African Studies Assoc. **RESEARCH** Soc and Env Sustainable Eco Devel; Human Rights; The Soc of Pastoralisml; The Soc of Riparian Peoples; African Sowest Asia South Asia SE Asia. **SELECTED PUBLICATIONS** Environment and Society in the Lower Mekong Basin: A Landscaping Review of the Literature, Pamela McElwee and Michael M Horowitz Binghamton NY Inst for Devel Anthro for Oxfam America 98; Ethenicity and Socioeconomic Vulnerability in Pakistan, Forour Jowkar, Michael M Hororwitz et al, Binghamton NY Inst for Devel Anthro, 95; Les Barrages de la Controverse; M Salem-Murdock,M Niasse J Magistro, M Horowitz et al; Paris: L'Harmattan, 94; Large Dams and Small People Producer director writer, senior anthropological advisor; An Inst for Devel Anthro Production, 93; Awarded screenings at Rencontre Median Mord-Sud, Geneva March 93; WSKG Public Television, 94; Enviornmental Film Festival in the Nation's Capital, 96; Soc of Wetland Sci, 96; On Not Offending the Borrower:(Self?)-Ghettoization fo Soc Sci at the World Band Devel Anthro 14(1-2):1-12, 96; The Sustainability of Anthro and Devel, Keynote Address to Proposal 21, Tokyo, 96; Devel Anthro (forthcoming); The Green Revolution, In The Dicitionary of Anthropology, Thomas J Barfield, ed, Oxford Blackwell Publishers, 97; Devel-Induced Food Insecurity in the Middle Senegal Valley, Michael M Horowitz and Muneera-Salem Murdock, GeoJournal 30(2) 179-184, 93. **CONTACT ADDRESS** Dept of Anthro, State Univ of NY, Binghamton, NY, 13902-6000. **EMAIL** mhorowi@binghamton.edu

HORSMAN, REGINALD
PERSONAL Born 10/24/1931, Leeds, England, m, 1955, 3 children **DISCIPLINE** HISTORY **EDUCATION** Univ Birmingham (England), BA, 52, MA, 55; Ind Univ, PhD, 58. **CAREER** From instr to prof, 58-73, Distinguished Prof Hist, Univ Wis-Milwaukee, 73. **HONORS AND AWARDS** Guggenheim Fel, 65; Kiekhofer Award for Excellence in Teaching, Univ Wis, 61; Univ Wis Alumni Award for Teaching Excellence, 95. **MEMBERSHIPS** Org Am Hist; Soc Am Hist; Soc Hist Early Am Republic (pres 87-88); State Hist Soc Wis. **RESEARCH** 19th century American history; race and expansion; War of 1812; American Indian policy; medical history. **SELECTED PUBLICATIONS** Auth, The Causes of the War of 1812, Univ Pa Press, 62; auth, Expansion and American Indian Policy, 1783-1812, Mich State Univ Press, 67, paperback ed, Okla State Univ Press, 93; auth, The War of 1812, Alfred Knopf, Inc/ Eyre & Spottiswood, Ltd, 69, 72; auth, The Frontier in the Formative Years, 1783-1815, Holt, Rhinehart, and Winston, Inc, 70; auth, Race and Manifest Destiny: The Origins of American Racial Anglo-Saxonism, Harvard Univ Press, 81; auth, The Diplomacy of the New Republic, 1776-1815, Harlan Davidson, Inc, 85; auth, Frontier Doctor: William Beaumont, America's First Great Medical Scientist, Univ Mo Press, 96. **CONTACT ADDRESS** Dept Hist, Univ Wis-Milwaukee, PO Box 413, Milwaukee, WI, 53201. **EMAIL** horsman@csd.uwm.edu

HORST, IRVIN BUCKWALTER
PERSONAL Born 05/31/1915, Lancaster, PA, m, 1944, 4 children **DISCIPLINE** HISTORY, RELIGION **EDUCATION** Goshen Col, BA, 49; Univ Pa, MA, 51; Univ Amsterdam, Ph-D(theol), 66. **CAREER** Dir relief in Neth, Mennonite Cent Comt, 46-48; assoc prof hist, Eastern Mennonite Col, 55-66, prof church hist, 66-67; PROF MENNONITE HIST, UNIV AMSTERDAM, 67-, Secy, Teylers Godgeleerd Genootschap & consult ed, Mennonite Quart Rev, 68-; secy commissie tot uitgave van Documenta Anabaptistica, Neerlandica, 68-; ed, Doopsgezinde Bijdragen, 77- **MEMBERSHIPS** Am Soc Church Hist; Bibliog Soc, England; Renaissance Soc Am. **RESEARCH** Dutch and English Reformation history; Anabaptists; bibliography. **SELECTED PUBLICATIONS** Auth, Between Known Men and Visible Saints--A Study in 16th-Century English Dissent, Church Hist, Vol 0065, 96. **CONTACT ADDRESS** Univ van Amsterdam Herengracht, 514-516 1017 CC, Amsterdam, ..

HORSTMAN, ALLEN
PERSONAL Born 08/01/1943, Seymour, IN, 2 children **DISCIPLINE** HISTORY, LAW **EDUCATION** Purdue Univ, BS, 65; Harvard Law Sch, LLB, 68; Univ Calif, Berkeley, PhD, 77. **CAREER** Prof hist, Albion Col, 77-. **MEMBERSHIPS** AHA; Am Bar Asn; Conf Brit Studies. **RESEARCH** English legal history; American legal history. **CONTACT ADDRESS** Dept of History, Albion Col, 611 E Porter St, Albion, MI, 49224-1831. **EMAIL** ahorstman@albion.edu

HORTON, LOREN NELSON
PERSONAL Born 03/16/1933, Hopeville, IA, m, 1957 **DISCIPLINE** UNITED STATES HISTORY **EDUCATION** Univ Northern Iowa, BA, 55, MA, 60, PhD, 78. **CAREER** Teacher hist, Toledo Pub Schs, 55-57, Cedar Falls Community Schs, 60-62, Shimer Col, 63, St Katharine's Sch, 63-68 & Palmer Jr Col, 65-73; hist specialist, 73-79, ASSOC DIR, STATE HIST SOC, IOWA, 79-, Chmn soc sci div, Independent Schs Asn Cent States, 67-68; mem, Nat Trust Hist Preserv, 70- **HONORS AND AWARDS** Outstanding Educr, NEA, 72. **MEMBERSHIPS** Am Asn State & Local Hist; Am Asn Mus; Asn Preserv Technol. **RESEARCH** Town planning and architecture in the Mississippi River towns of Iowa; Urbanization process on the American frontier; territorial and state census records, genealogical source material. **SELECTED PUBLICATIONS** Auth, The Worlds Columbian Exposition, J West, Vol 0033, 94; Nebraska Moments--Glimpses of Nebraska Past, J West, Vol 0034, 95. **CONTACT ADDRESS** 3367 Hanover Ct, Iowa City, IA, 52240.

HORWARD, DONALD D.
PERSONAL Born 01/09/1933, Pittsburgh, PA, m, 1958 **DISCIPLINE** MODERN HISTORY **EDUCATION** Waynesburg Col, BA, 55; Ohio Univ, MA, 56; Univ Minn, PhD, 62. **CAREER** Asst, Ohio Univ, 55-56; asst, Univ Minn, 56-58, fac adv & coun, 58-61; from instr to assoc prof, 61-70, chmn dept, 72-75, Prof Hist, Fla St Univ, 70-, Mem, Defesa Nacional, Port, 65-; Am rep, Comt Honor, Soc Chateau Imperial Pont-de-Briques, 66-68; Calouste Gulbenkian Found award, Port, 67 & 72, fel, 76; mem bd dirs, Consortium Revolutionary Europe, 1750-1850, 71-; Am Coun Learned Socs travel grant, 76; Dir, Inst on Napoleon and the French Revolution, 90; Ben Weider Eminent Scholar Chair in Napleonic History, Fl St Univ, 98. **HONORS AND AWARDS** Standard Oil Ind Award, 67; Calouste Gulbenkian Fnd Awd, 78, 80, 82, 84, 86, 87, 89; French Min of Culture; Edwin P. Conquest Chair in Human, Va Milit Inst, 84; Chair of Milit Hist, US Milit Acad, 86-87; Chair of Milit Aff, US Marine War Col, 93, 95, 96, 97, 98; Chair of Milit Stu, US Marine Sch of Advan Warfighting, 94; Excel in Teach, 93, 95, 98; Distinguished Teach Prof, 90; Chavalier, Palmes Academiques; Officier, Palmes Academiques, 91; Grand Off, Ordem da Infante Dom Henrique, 92; Outstand Civil Svc Medal, US Army; Medal of Merit, Ohio Univ; Mancado Prize, Soc of Mil Hist, 89. **MEMBERSHIPS** AHA; Soc Fr Hist Studies; Soc Mod Hist France; Soc Army Hist Res; Inst Napoleon; Portuguese Acad Hist; British Hist Soc Portugal; Soc Litteraire et Historique de la Brie; Int Napoleonic Soc, Napoleonic All; Soc Mil Hist **RESEARCH** Napoleon; the Peninsular Wars; French Revolution. **SELECTED PUBLICATIONS** Auth, The Battle of Busaaco: Massena vs Wellington, Fla St Univ, 65, 2nd ed, 67; L'Opinion Americaine et Waterloo, Rev de l'Inst Napoleon, 72; The archives de Massena, Fr Hist Studies, 72; Massena et Napoleon: L'abandon de Portugal, Rev Hist de l'armees, 73; The French Campaign in Portugal, 1810-1811, an Account by Jean Jacques Pelet, Univ Minn & Oxford Univ, 73; The French Revolution and Napoleon Collection at Florida State University: A Bibliographical Guide, Fla State Univ Friends Libr, 73; consortium on Revolutionary Europe Proceedings 1974, 74 ed, Univ Fla, 78; auth, Naploeon and Iberia: The Twin Sieges of Ciudad Rodrigo and Almeida, 1819, Univ of Fl, 84, Greenhill, 94; coauth, Napoleon and America, New Orleans, La, State Museum, 89; auth, Napoleonic Military History: A Bibliography, Garland, 86; coauth, Warfare in the Western World, D.C. Heath, 96; ed, Proceedings, Consortium on Revolutionary Europe, 94, 95, 96, 97, 98. **CONTACT ADDRESS** Dept of History, Florida State Univ, 429 Bellamy Hall, Tallahassee, FL, 32306. **EMAIL** dhorward@mailer.fsu.edu

HORWITZ, HENRY GLUCK
PERSONAL Born 08/02/1938, New York, NY, m, 1963, 3 children **DISCIPLINE** EARLY MODERN ENGLISH HISTORY **EDUCATION** Haverford Col, BA, 59; Oxford Univ, DPhil(English hist), 63. **CAREER** From asst prof to assoc prof, 63-70, prof hist, Univ Iowa, 70-, Nat Endowment for Humanities younger scholar award, 69; Guggenheim fel, 78. **RESEARCH** Later seventeenth and eighteenth century English political and legal history. **SELECTED PUBLICATIONS** Auth, Revolution Politicks: The Career of Daniel Finch, 2nd Earl of Nottingham, Cambridge Univ, 68; ed, The Parliamentary Diary of Narcissus Luttrell, Clarendon, 72; auth, Parliament, Policy and Politics in the Reign of William III, Manchester Univ, 77; Chancery Equity Records and Proceedings 1600-1800, HMSO, 95. **CONTACT ADDRESS** Dept of Hist, Univ of Iowa, 280 Schaeffer Hall, Iowa City, IA, 52242-1409.

HOSOI, Y. TIM
DISCIPLINE HISTORY OF NON-WESTERN RELIGIOUS IDEAS **EDUCATION** Univ Chicago, PhD. **CAREER** Philos, Oregon St Univ. **HONORS AND AWARDS** Dir, Prog Ethics, Sci, Environment. **MEMBERSHIPS** Cascade-W Japan Am Soc. **RESEARCH** Japanese Religions. **SELECTED PUBLICATIONS** Contribur The Oxford Companion to World Religions. **CONTACT ADDRESS** Dept Philos, Oregon State Univ, Corvallis, OR, 97331-4501. **EMAIL** thosoi@orst.edu

HOSTETLER, THEODORE J.
PERSONAL Born 02/07/1951, Canton, OH, m, 1975, 3 children **DISCIPLINE** LIBRARY SCIENCE/HISTORY **EDUCATION** Univ of IA, MA, 74; Bluffton Col, BA, 73 **CAREER** Libr Dir, 93-, Randolph-Macon Woman's Col; Head Access Svcs, 89-93, Univ of CA; Head Access Svcs, 79-89, Syracuse Univ; Head Circulation, 78-79 Univ of S FL **HONORS AND AWARDS** ALA, Univ of CA Achievement Awd, 92 **MEMBERSHIPS** VLA; ALA **RESEARCH** Reference; Undergraduate educ exp **SELECTED PUBLICATIONS** Auth, Introduction, 95; Coauth, Issue of Library Trends **CONTACT ADDRESS** Lipscomb Libr, Randolph-Macon Woman's Col, Lynchburg, VA, 24503. **EMAIL** thostetler@rmwc.edu

HOUGHTON, EDWARD FRANCIS
PERSONAL Born 10/07/1938, New Brunswick, NJ, m, 1964, 3 children **DISCIPLINE** MUSICOLOGY **EDUCATION** Rutgers Univ, BA, 62; Univ Nev, MA, 63; Univ Calif, Berkeley, PhD(Music), 71. **CAREER** Asst prof Music, Rutgers Univ, 67-70; asst prof, 70-73, from assoc prof to prof Music, 81-; dean Arts Div, 92; Univ Calif, Santa Cruz, 73-, dir, Univ Calif Educ Abroad Prog, Italy, 76-78. **HONORS AND AWARDS** NEH Fell, 80-81, 87. **MEMBERSHIPS** Academia Tartiniana; Am Musicol Soc; Renaissance Soc Am. **RESEARCH** Music of the 15th century. **SELECTED PUBLICATIONS** Auth, Rhythm and meter in 15th century polyphony, J Music Theory, Spring 74; A new motet by Johannas Regis, Tijdschrift, 83. **CONTACT ADDRESS** Div of the Arts, Univ of California, Santa Cruz, 1156 High St, Santa Cruz, CA, 95064-0001.

HOULD, CLAUDETTE
PERSONAL Born 00/00/1942, Montreal, PQ, Canada **DISCIPLINE** ART HISTORY **EDUCATION** Univ Montreal, BA, 65, LL, 69, MA, 71; Ecole des Hautes Etudes en Sciences sociales (Paris), PhD, 90. **CAREER** Tchr, 60-71; cur, Montreal Mus Fine Arts, 75-76; PROF ART HISTORY, UNIV QUEBEC MONTREAL, 76-, dir dept, 79-81, 83-89. **HONORS AND AWARDS** Prix d'excellence, Asn Musees can, 89; Medaille argent du Bicentenaire de la Revolution francaise, 89; Prix Publication, Asn Musees Que, 90. **MEMBERSHIPS** Soc d'histoire de l'art francais; Am Soc Eighteenth Century Stud; Conseil int des musee; Asn d'art des universites can. **SELECTED PUBLICATIONS** Auth, Repertoire des livres d'artistes au Quebec 1900-1982, 82; auth, Repertoire des livres d'artistes au Quebec 1981-90, 93; ed, Iconographie et image de la Revolution francaise, 90; co-ed, Code d'ethique de l'estampe originale, 82. **CONTACT ADDRESS** Art History Dept, Univ Quebec, Montreal, Montreal, PQ.

HOUSER, CAROLINE
DISCIPLINE ART HISTORY **EDUCATION** Mills Col, BA; Harvard Univ, MA, PhD. **CAREER** Dir, Archaeol Prog. **RESEARCH** Golden Greek and Graeco-Roman statues. **SELECTED PUBLICATIONS** Auth, a catalogue Dionysos & His Circle to accompany an exhibition she curated at Harvard Univ; bk on, a monument in the Athenian Agora; 2 bk(s) on, the large bronze sculptures of ancient Greece. **CONTACT ADDRESS** Dept of Art, Smith Col, Hillyer Hall 318, Northampton, MA, 01063. **EMAIL** chouser@sophia.smith.edu

HOUSTON, GEORGE W.
PERSONAL Born 11/15/1941, New York, NY, m, 1962, 2 children **DISCIPLINE** CLASSICS **EDUCATION** Haverford Coll, BA, 63; Univ of NC, PhD, 71. **CAREER** Instr to Prof and Chr, 69-, Dept of Classics, Univ of NC, Chapel Hill; Vis Prof, 82, Inst di Filologia, Univ of Bologna, Italy. **HONORS AND AWARDS** Rome Prize, Amer Acad; Fulbright Fellowship. **MEMBERSHIPS** APA, Soc for the Promotion of Roman Stud, Amer Soc of Greek and Latin Epigraphy. **RESEARCH** Latin Literature and Roman History; Latin Epigraphy; Ancient Technology. **SELECTED PUBLICATIONS** Auth, Vespasian's Adelction of Men in Senatum, American Journal of Philology, 77; Tiberius on Capri, Greece and Rome, 85; State of the Art, Current Work in the Technology of Ancient Rome, Classical Journal, 92; What Uses Might Roman Farmers Have Made of the Loans They Received in the Alimenta Program?, Rivista Storica dell'Anthichita, 93; Fasti Broughtoniani, The Professional Activities and Published Works of Thomas Robert Shannon Broughton, in Jerry Linderski, ed, Imperium Sine Fine, T. Rovert S, Broughton and the Roman Republic, Stuttgart, Franz Steiner, 96. **CONTACT ADDRESS** 704 Tinkerbell Rd, Chapel Hill, NC, 27514. **EMAIL** gwhousto@email.unc.edu

HOVANEC, EVELYN ANN
PERSONAL Born 12/23/1937, Uniontown, PA **DISCIPLINE** ENGLISH, FOLKLORE, HISTORY AND LORE OF COAL MINERS **EDUCATION** Duquesne Univ, BEd, 62, MA, 66; Univ Pittsburgh, PhD, 73. **CAREER** Teacher social studies & English, Pittsburgh pub jr high schs, 62-66; ASSOC prof English, PA State Univ, Fayette, 66-88, dir Acad Aff, PA State, McKeesport 85-92. **HONORS AND AWARDS** PSF Awd for Pub Svc, 94; PSM Awd for Svc, 89; PSF Awd for Teach Excel, 97; PSF Min Stu Org Fac Awd, 98. **MEMBERSHIPS** Nat Coun Teachers English; Col English Asn; MLA. **RESEARCH** Mining literature and lore; mythology; Henry James. **SELECTED PUBLICATIONS** Auth, 3 poems, Earth & You, 72; coauth, Making the humanities human, WVa Rev Educ Res, fall 73; auth, Horses of the Sun (2 poems), In: Cathedral Poets II, Boxwood, 76; coauth, Patch/Work Voices: The Culture & Lore of a Mining People, Harry Hoffman, 77; auth, Coal culture & communities, Pa Oral Hist Newslett, 77; The Sea (poem), In: Strawberry Saxifrage, Nat Soc Publ Poets, 77; coauth, Making the Humanities Human, West VA Review of Educ Res 1, 46-47, 73; auth, A Mythological Approach to Tomorrow, Assoc of Teach Educ Review 3, 78; auth, Reader's Guide to Coal Mining Fiction and Selected Prose Narratives, Bul of Biblio, 41-57, Sept, 86; auth, Marie Belloc Lowndes, An Encyclopedia of British Women Writers, Garland, 297-298, 88. **CONTACT ADDRESS** Pennsylvania State Univ, PO Box 519, Uniontown, PA, 15401-0519. **EMAIL** eah2@psu.edu

HOVENDICK, KELLY B.
PERSONAL Born 12/18/1970, Hanover, PA, m, 1996, 1 child **DISCIPLINE** HISTORY; ANTHROPOLOGY; LIBRARY SCIENCE **EDUCATION** E NM Univ, BS, 94; Univ Az, MA, 99. **MEMBERSHIPS** Amer Libr Assoc **RESEARCH** Gender & libr sci; technophobia. **CONTACT ADDRESS** 804 E 7th St, Tucson, AZ, 85719. **EMAIL** kbhovend@u.arizona.edu

HOVEY, KENNETH
DISCIPLINE FINE ARTS AND HUMANITIES **EDUCATION** Cornell Univ, BA; Grade Theol Union, Berkeley, MA; Univ VA, MA, PhD. **CAREER** Assoc prof; taught at, Univ Cincinnati, Univ NC at Greensboro & NC Wesleyan Col. **HONORS AND AWARDS** NEH fel; UTSA's President's Distinguished Achievement Awd for Tchg Excellence, 93; 2 fac fel, UNC & UTSA. **RESEARCH** Renaissance lit; Milton and 17th-century poetry; 17th-century philos and sci; early Am lit and cult, espec Poe; Bible as lit. **SELECTED PUBLICATIONS** Auth, Poe's Materialist Metaphysics of Man, in A Companion to Poe Stud, Greenwood Press, 96; publ on, Poe, Longfellow, Bradford, Bacon & Herbert; in, Am Quart, Am Transcendental Quart, Early Am Lit, PMLA, Renaissance Quart & Stud in Philol. **CONTACT ADDRESS** Col of Fine Arts and Hum, Univ Texas at San Antonio, 6900 N Loop 1604 W, San Antonio, TX, 78249. **EMAIL** khovey@lonestar.utsa.edu

HOWARD, ANGELA
DISCIPLINE FAR EASTERN ART **EDUCATION** NY Univ, PhD. **CAREER** Assoc prof, Rutgers, The State Univ NJ, Univ Col-Camden. **RESEARCH** Buddhist art of southwest China; Central Asian Buddhist art. **SELECTED PUBLICATIONS** Auth, The Imagery of the Cosmological Buddha, E.J.Brill, Leiden, 86; Tang Buddhist Sculpture of Sichuan: Unknown and Forgotten, The Mus of Far Eastern Antiq, Stockholm 60, 88; In Support of a New Chronology for the Kizil Mural Paintings, in Arch of Asian Art 44, 91; Buddhist Cave Sculpture of the Northern Qi Dynasty: Shaping a New Style, Formulating New Iconographies, in Arch of Asian Art 49, 96; Buddhist Monuments of Yunnan: Eclectic Art of a Frontier Kingdom, in Arts of the Song and Yuan, Hearn, M. and Smith, J. eds, The Metropolitan Mus of Art, NY, 96; The Dharani Pillar of Kunming, Tunnan. A Legacy of Esoteric Buddhism and Burial Rites of the Bai People in the Kingdom of Dali (937-1253), in Artibus Asiae 57, 1/2, 97. **CONTACT ADDRESS** Dept of Art Hist, Rutgers, The State Univ NJ, Univ Col-Camden, Voorhees Hall, 71 Hamilton St, New Brunswick, NJ, 08903.

HOWARD, JOHN ROBERT
PERSONAL Born 01/24/1933, Boston, MA, m **DISCIPLINE** SOCIOLOGY **EDUCATION** Brandeis Univ, BA 1955; NY Univ, MA 1961; Stanford Univ, PhD 1965; J Du Pace Univ 1985. **CAREER** Univ of OR, asst prof 1965-68; Rutgers Univ, assoc prof 1969-71; State Univ of NY, dean & prof 1971-80, State Univ of NY, prof of sociology 1971-; atty in private prac-

tice 1986-. **HONORS AND AWARDS** Publ Lifestyles in the Black, WW Norton 1969; The Cutting Edge, J B Lippincott Publ 1974; Urban Black Politics, Annals of the Am Acad 1978; various articles. **MEMBERSHIPS** Bd mem United Way of Westchester 1976-78; bd of advs Inst for Urban Design 1978-; vice pres Soc for the Study of Social Problems 1978-79; bd mem Street Theater Inc 1978-80; bd Friends of the Nueberger Museum 1982-85. **CONTACT ADDRESS** Sociology Dept, SUNY, Lincoln Ave, Purchase, NY, 10577.

HOWARD, THOMAS A.
PERSONAL Born 11/20/1967, Tuscaloosa, AL, m, 1994, 1 child **DISCIPLINE** HISTORY **EDUCATION** Univ Alabama, BA, 90; Univ of VA, 96, PhD. **CAREER** Lilly fel and lect, Hist and Humanities, Valparaiso Univ, 97-. **HONORS AND AWARDS** DAAD grant, 94-95; AAR grant, 97. **MEMBERSHIPS** AHA, AAR, German Studies Asn. **RESEARCH** Modern Germany; European intellectual hist. **SELECTED PUBLICATIONS** Auth, Religion and Rise of Historicism, Cambirdge, UP, forthcoming. **CONTACT ADDRESS** Lily Fellows Program, Valparaiso Univ, Valparaiso, IN, 46383. **EMAIL** tal.howard@valpo.edu

HOWARD, THOMAS CARLTON
PERSONAL Born 07/27/1938, Miami, FL, m, 1962, 2 children **DISCIPLINE** ENGLISH & AFRICAN HISTORY **EDUCATION** Washington & Lee Univ, AB, 60; Fla State Univ, MA, 62, PhD(hist), 65. **CAREER** Asst prof, 66-77, ASSOC PROF HIST, VA POLYTECH INST & STATE UNIV, 77-, Dir, NDEA Inst Advan Studies Hist, 67-68; vis prof African hist, Univ Wis-Madison, 69-70; Nat Endowment for Humanities fel, 72-73; Am Philos Soc fel, 72-73. **MEMBERSHIPS** AHA; Southern Asn Africanists; African Studies Asn; Royal African Soc; Southeastern Regional Sem African Studies. **RESEARCH** African history; English history; imperial history. **SELECTED PUBLICATIONS** Auth, Imperialism, the State and the 3rd-World, Albion, Vol 0026, 94; British Imperialism, Crisis and Deconstruction, 1914-1990, Albion, Vol 0026, 94. **CONTACT ADDRESS** Dept of Hist, Va Polytech Inst & State Univ, Blacksburg, VA, 24061.

HOWARTH, THOMAS
PERSONAL Born 05/01/1914, Wesham, England **DISCIPLINE** ARCHITECTURE/HISTORY **EDUCATION** Univ Glasgow, PhD, 49. **CAREER** Lectr, Glasgow Sch Archit & Glasgow Sch Art, 39-46; lectr to sr lectr, Univ Manchester, 46-58; dir, sch archit, 58-67, dean, 67-74, PROF EMER ARCHITECTURE, UNIV TORONTO, 82-; campus planner, Glendon Col & adv to bd, York Univ, 60-87; campus planner, Laurentian Univ, 61-87. **HONORS AND AWARDS** Annual Bk Award, Soc Archit Hist (US); Alice Davis Hitchcock Medal, 53; Rockefeller res scholar, 55-56; Killam sr res scholar, 78. **MEMBERSHIPS** Can Soc Decorative Arts; Royal Ont Mus; Charles Rennie Makintosh Soc Glasgow. **SELECTED PUBLICATIONS** Auth, Charles Rennie Mackintosh and the Modern Movement, 52, 77, 90; auth, RAIC College of Fellows, 62, 77; auth, Two Cultures Two Cities, 76; contribur, A History of Architecture on the Comparative Method, 61; contribur, Chambers Encyclopedia; contribur, Encyclopedia Britannica; contribur, Macmillan's Encyclopedia of Architecture. **CONTACT ADDRESS** 131 Bloor St W, #1001, Toronto, ON, M5S 1R1.

HOWE, JOHN MCDONALD
PERSONAL Born 03/13/1947, Alameda, CA, m, 1974, 3 children **DISCIPLINE** MEDIEVAL HISTORY **EDUCATION** Univ San Francisco, BA, 69; Univ Calif, Los Angeles, MA, 71, CPhil, 73, PhD, 79. **CAREER** Res asst, Ctr Medieval & Renaissance Studies, Univ Calif, Los Angeles, 71-72 & 76-77; teaching fel hist, Univ Calif, Los Angeles, 73-75; teacher social studies, Harvard School, spring 80; vis asst prof relig studies, Ariz State Univ, spring, 81; asst prof, 81-88, assoc prof, 88-98, PROF HIST, TEX TECH UNIV, 98-. **HONORS AND AWARDS** TTU fac award, Creative Excellence Teaching, 88; TTU Pres Excellence Teaching, 95; TTU fac sen pres, 96-97. **MEMBERSHIPS** Medieval Acad Am AHA; Archeol Inst Am; Am Cath Hist Asn. **RESEARCH** Medieval hagiography; medieval mysticism; medieval technology. **SELECTED PUBLICATIONS** Auth, The Nobility's Reform of the Medieval Church, Am Hist Rev, 88; Church Reform and Social Change in Eleventh-Century Italy, 97. **CONTACT ADDRESS** Dept Hist, Tex Tech Univ, Lubbock, TX, 79409-1013. **EMAIL** john.howe@ttu.edu

HOWE, JOHN R.
DISCIPLINE HISTORY **EDUCATION** Yale Univ, PhD, 62. **CAREER** Prof **RESEARCH** American political history. **SELECTED PUBLICATIONS** Auth, The Changing Political Thought of John Adams, the Role of Ideology in the American Revolution, From the Revolution to Jackson. **CONTACT ADDRESS** History Dept, Univ of Minnesota, Twin Cities, 614 Social Sciences Tower, 267 19th Ave. S, Minneapolis, MN, 55455. **EMAIL** howex002@tc.umn.edu

HOWE, SONDRA WIELAND
PERSONAL Born 04/30/1938, Bridgeport, CT, m, 1961, 3 children **DISCIPLINE** MUSIC **EDUCATION** Wellesley Col, AB, 60; Radcliffe Col, AMT, 61; Univ Minn, MA, 85, PhD, 88. **CAREER** Independent Scholar **MEMBERSHIPS** ISME; MENC; MTNA; AMS; Sonneck Soc Am Mus; AGO. **RESEARCH** History of Music Education; Women composers. **SELECTED PUBLICATIONS** Luther Whiting Mason: International Music Educator, Warren, Mich, Harmonie Park Press, 97; Pauline Duchambge, Loisa Puget, Dora Pejacevic, Jane Vieu, Women Composers: Music Through the Ages, G.K. Hall, 96-99; **CONTACT ADDRESS** 135 Chevy Chase Dr, Wayzata, MN, 55391. **EMAIL** howex009@tc.umn.edu

HOWELL, ALLEN C.
PERSONAL Born 03/18/1962, Portland, OR, m, 1997, 3 children **DISCIPLINE** MUSIC **EDUCATION** Whitman Col, BA, 84; Portland St Univ, MAT, 85; Univ Or, DMA, 93. **CAREER** Asst prof, Columbus St Univ, 94-96; dir, First Unit Methodist Church, Erie, Pa, 96- ;asst prof, Edinboro Univ Pa Edinboro, 96- . **HONORS AND AWARDS** Pi Kappa Lambda, Univ Or; Virginia Johnson Whitfield Mem Scholar, Univ Or; Rose M. Gross Scholar, Univ Or, 89; Presser Found Prize, Outstanding Musical Ability, Whitman Col, 84; David Campbell Award, Outstanding Sr Recital, Whitman Col, 84; Sarah Johnson Mem Scholar, Outstanding Personal & Scholar Cal, Whitman Col, 80. **MEMBERSHIPS** Pi Kappa Lambda, Amer Choral Dir Assoc; Music Educ Nat Conf; Pa Music Educ Assoc; Orff Schulwerk Assoc; Col Music Soc. **RESEARCH** Choral methods; general music methods; conducting & rehearsal pedagogy; curriculum develop; res methods, tech in music educ **SELECTED PUBLICATIONS** Auth, Effect of Repeated Testing on Knowledge Acquisition of Secondary Choral Students, res paper symp & poster presentation, 92; Planning for Rehearsals: The Instructional Planning Thoughts and Practices of a Few Exemplary Public School Music Ensemble Teachers, res poster presentation, 93; Planning for Rehearsals: The Instructional Planning Thoughts and Practices of Selected High School and Middle School Band and Choral Directors, 96; copresenter, Assessing the Student Teaching Experience, 98. **CONTACT ADDRESS** Dept of Music, Edinboro Univ of Pennsylvania, Edinboro, PA, 16444. **EMAIL** Dr_Howell@hotmail.com

HOWELL, MARTHA
DISCIPLINE SOCIAL HISTORY OF NORTHERN EUROPE **EDUCATION** Georgetown Univ, BS, 66; Columbia Univ, PhD, 79. **CAREER** Ch dept; prof. **RESEARCH** Urban society, economy, culture and gender. **SELECTED PUBLICATIONS** Auth, Women, Production, and Patriarchy in Late Medieval Cities, 86. **CONTACT ADDRESS** Dept of Hist, Columbia Col, New York, 2960 Broadway, New York, NY, 10027-6902.

HOWELL, RICHARD WESLEY
PERSONAL Born 09/06/1926, Berkeley, CA, m, 1948, 4 children **DISCIPLINE** ANTHROPOLOGY, LINGUISTICS **EDUCATION** Univ Calif, Berkeley, AB, 49, PhD,(anthrop), 67; Univ Hawaii, MA, 51. **CAREER** Asst prof anthrop, Richmond Col, NY, 67-69; assoc prof sociol, Univ Sask, 69-70; Assoc Prof Anthrop, Univ Hawaii At Hilo, 70-, Vis assoc prof E Asian Lang, Univ Hawaii, Manoa, 75-76; vis assoc prof ling, Int Christian Univ, Tokyo, 76-77. **MEMBERSHIPS** Am Anthrop Asn; Southern Anthrop Asn. **RESEARCH** Japanese ethnology; sociolinguistics; social conflict. **SELECTED PUBLICATIONS** Auth, Following the Brush--An American Encounter with Classical Japanese Culture, J Asian Hist, Vol 0029, 95. **CONTACT ADDRESS** Dept of Anthrop, Univ Hawaii at Hilo, Hilo, HI, 96720.

HOWELL, SARAH MCCANLESS
PERSONAL Born 08/09/1930, Morristown, TN, m, 1954, 1 child **DISCIPLINE** UNITED STATES SOCIAL & INTELLECTUAL HISTORY **EDUCATION** Vanderbilt Univ, BA, 52, MAT, 54, MA, 67, PhD, 70. **CAREER** Asst prof, 70-74, fac res grant, 72, assoc prof, 74-, PROF HIST, MID TENN STATE UNIV, 74-96, Prof Emerita, 96. **MEMBERSHIPS** Orgn Am Historians; Am Studies Asn. **RESEARCH** Social and intellectual changes of late 19th century United States; nineteenth century American utopias; intellectual conflicts of the 1920's. **SELECTED PUBLICATIONS** Auth, The editorials of Arthur S Colyar, Nashville prophet of the New South, Tenn Hist Quart, fall 68; Jesse Wills and the Conflicts of the 1920s, Tenn Hist Quart, spring 88; James I. Vance: Transformations in Religion and Society, 1922-32, Tenn Hist Quart, spring 90; articles on Vance, black leader Charles S. Johnson, and film director Delbert Mann in forth coming Tennessee Encyclopedia. **CONTACT ADDRESS** Dept of Hist, 700 Crescent Rd, Nashville, TN, 37205-1918. **EMAIL** SallyMH@aol.com

HOXIE, FREDERICK E.
DISCIPLINE HISTORY **EDUCATION** Brandeis Univ, PhD, 77. **CAREER** Prof, Univ Ill Urbana Champaign **HONORS AND AWARDS** Pres, Am Soc Ethnohist. **RESEARCH** American Indian communities in the twentieth century. **SELECTED PUBLICATIONS** Auth, A Final Promise: The Campaign to Assimilate the Indians, 1880-1920, 84; Parading Through History: The Making of the Crow Nation in America, 1805-1935, 95; ed, Encyclopedia of North American Indians, 96. **CONTACT ADDRESS** History Dept, Univ Ill Urbana Champaign, 52 E Gregory Dr, Champaign, IL, 61820. **EMAIL** hoxie@uiuc.edu

HOXIE, RALPH GORDON
PERSONAL Born 03/18/1919, Waterloo, IA, m, 1953 **DISCIPLINE** HISTORY POLITICAL SCIENCE **EDUCATION** Univ Northern Iowa, BA, 40; Univ Wis, MA, 41; Columbia Univ, PhD, 50. **CAREER** Asst to provost, Columbia Univ, 48-49; asst prof hist, ed studies, Soc Sci Found & asst to chancellor, Univ Denver, 50-53; proj assoc, Bicentennial, Columbia Univ, 53-54; dean col lib arts & sci, Long Island Univ, 54-55, dean, C W Post Col, 55-60, provost, 60-62, pres col, 62-68; pres dep, Mitchel Col, 55-60, vpres univ, 62, chancellor, 64-68; FOUNDER,PRES,CHM EMERY, CTR FOR STUDY OF PRESIDENCY, 69-97: Vis lectr numerous univs & cols; consult col training & develop progs & educ policies; adv mil educ progs, US Air Force, Brig Gen, ret; mem adv coun, Robert A Taft Inst Govt; dir, Greater NY Coun Foreign Studies; secy, Comn Govt Rev Nassau County; co-chmn, Nassau-Suffolk Conf Christians & Jews; pub mem, US State Dept Selection Bd, 69. **HONORS AND AWARDS** Legion of Merit Distinguished Serv Medal, City New York; Gold Medal, Paderewski Found; Korean Cult Medal; Gold Medal, Univ Northern Iowa, 65; LLD, Chungang Univ, Korea, 65; LittD, Youville Col, 66; LHD, Gannon Univ, 88; Wesley Col, 89; Univ N Iowa, 90; Shepherd Col, 92; Teiko Post Univ, 94; Long Island Univ, 95; Fitchburg State Col, 97; Alumni Achievement Award, Columbia Univ, 97., LLD, Chungang Univ, Korea, 65; LittD, D'Youville Col, 66. **MEMBERSHIPS** Am Soc Pub Admin; AHA; Acad Polit Sci; Am Polit Sci Asn. **RESEARCH** History of education; American presidency; American foreign policy. **SELECTED PUBLICATIONS** Auth, Presidential Studies Quart, 71-; The Presidency of the 1970's, 73; contrib, The Coattailless Landslide, Tex Western, 74; Power and the Presidency, Scribner's, 76; auth, Command Decision and the Presidency, Reader's Digest, 77; coauth, Organizing and Staffing the Presidency, 80; Presidency and Information Policy, 81; contribr, Encycl Britannica World Book Encycl, Greenwood Encycl of American Institutions. **CONTACT ADDRESS** Ctr Study of Presidency, 208 E 75th St, New York, NY, 10021. **EMAIL** thecsp@aol.com

HOYT-O'CONNOR, PAUL E.
PERSONAL Born 04/01/1960, Brooklyn, NY, m, 1987, 1 child **DISCIPLINE** PHILOSOPHY; HISTORY **EDUCATION** Fordham Univ, BA, 92; Boston Col, PhD, 92. **CAREER** Asst prof, 94- , Spalding Univ. **MEMBERSHIPS** APA; Amer Catholic Philos Assn; Kentucky Philos Assn **RESEARCH** Social and political philos; Ethical theory. **SELECTED PUBLICATIONS** Auth, Lonegan and Bellah: Social Science in Public Philosophy, American Catholic Philosophy Quarterly, 95; auth, Progress Without End, International Philosophical Quarterly, 98. **CONTACT ADDRESS** Spalding Univ, 851 S 4th St, Louisville, KY, 40203. **EMAIL** spalding@humanities.net

HOZESKI, BRUCE WILLIAM
PERSONAL Born 02/28/1941, Grand Rapids, MI, m, 1967, 1 child **DISCIPLINE** ENGLISH LITERATURE, HISTORY OF LANGUAGE, MEDIEVAL BRITISH LITERATURE **EDUCATION** Aquinas Col, BA, 64; Mich State Univ, MA, 66, PhD(medieval English lit), 69. **CAREER** Grad asst English, Mich State Univ, 64-69; instr, Lansing Community Col, 68-69; PROF ENGLISH, BALL STATE UNIV, 69-, Chair, University Senate, 96-, Dir Grad Programs in English, 98-01; Exec Secy and Treas of Lambda Iota Tau, The Nat Honor Soc for Lit, 90-; founder and president, Int Soc of Hildegard von Bingen Studies, 84-89, lifetime mem of exec coun; mem Bd of Dir, Christian Ministries of Delaware County, 97-03. **MEMBERSHIPS** AAUP; MLA; Midwest Mod Lang Asn; NCTE; Medieval Acad Am. **RESEARCH** Medieval English literature; medieval drama; Hildegard of Bingen. **SELECTED PUBLICATIONS** Auth, Hildegard of Bingen's Ordo Virtutum: The earliest discovered liturgical morality play, Am Benedictine Rev, 75; A mathematical error in Jonathan Swift's A Modest Proposal, Am Notes & Queries, 76; The parallel patterns in Hrotsvitha of Gandersheim, a tenth century German playwright, and in Hildegard of Bingen, a twentieth century German playwright, Annuale Mediaevale, 78; The parallel patterns in Prudentia's Psychomachia and Hildegarde of Bingen's Ordo Virtutum, 14th Century, English Mystics Newslett, 82; Hildegard of Bingen's Scivias, 86; Hildegard von Bingen's Mystical Visions, 95; Hildegard of Bingen: The Book of the Rewards of Life: Liber Vitae Meritorum, 97; regular contribr to An Annotated Chaucer Bibliography - Studies in the Age of Chaucer, 91-present. **CONTACT ADDRESS** Dept of English, Ball State Univ, 2000 W University, Muncie, IN, 47306-0460. **EMAIL** 00bwhozeski@bsuuc.edu

HRABOWSKI, FREEMAN ALPHONSA, III
PERSONAL Born 08/13/1950, Birmingham, AL, m **DISCIPLINE** EDUCATION **EDUCATION** Hampton Inst, BA 1970; Univ of IL, MA 1971, PhD 1975. **CAREER** Univ of IL at Urbana-Champaign, math instr 1972-73, admin intern 1973-74, asst dean 1974-76; AL A&M Univ Normal, assoc dean 1976-77; Coppin State Coll Baltimore, dean arts & scis div 1977-81, vice pres academic affairs 1981-87; Univ of MD, Baltimore County, vice provost, 1987-90, executive vice president, 1990-92, interim pres, 1992-93; Univ of Maryland, Catonville, pres, 1993-. **HONORS AND AWARDS** Scholarship for Study Abroad Amer Univ Cairo Egypt 1968-69; Phi Delta Kappa, Univ of IL at Urbana-Champaign 1971; Outstanding Alumni Awd, Hampton Univ, Baltimore Chapter; Outstanding Commu-

nity Service Award, Tuskegee Univ. **MEMBERSHIPS** Alpha Phi Alpha; Hampton Inst, sr class pres, 1969-70; bd of trustees, Baltimore City Life Museums; Florence Crittenton Services Inc, advisory council; Peabody Institute, Johns Hopkins Univ; evaluator, Middle States Assn of Coll and Schools; Baltimore Equitable Society; Unity of MD Medical Systems; bd mem: Amer Coun on Educ, Baltimore Gas & Electric Co, Baltimore Comm Foundation, Ctr Stage, Greater Baltimore Comm, Joint Ctr for Political & Economic Development, McCormick & Co, Mercantile Safe Deposit & Trust Co, Merrick & France Foundation, Suburban Maryland High-Technology Coun. **SELECTED PUBLICATIONS** Co-author, Beating the Odds, 1998. **CONTACT ADDRESS** Univ of Maryland, Baltimore County, 1000 Hilltop Circle, Baltimore, MD, 21250.

HSU, CHO-YUN
PERSONAL Born 07/10/1930, Amoy, China, m, 1969, 1 child **DISCIPLINE** CHINESE HISTORY **EDUCATION** Nat Taiwan Univ, BA, 53, MA, 56; Univ Chicago, PhD, 62. **CAREER** Assoc prof hist, Nat Taiwan Univ, 62-65, prof & chmn dept, 65-70; prof hist & sociol, Univ Pittsburgh, 70-, distinguished serv prof, 79-, asst res fel hist, Inst Hist & Philol, Acad Sinica, 56-62, assoc res fel, 62-67, res fel, 67-; Fulbright fel, Off Educ, Dept Health, Educ & Welfare, 77-78. **MEMBERSHIPS** AHA; Asn Asian Studies; Chinese Hist Soc; Bd Dir Chiang Ching-Kuo Found, 89-; China Times Found, 87-. **RESEARCH** Peasant life and rural economy; 19th century China; comparative social history. **SELECTED PUBLICATIONS** Auth, Ancient China in trasition, Stanford Univ, 65; auth, The farming technique in Chou China, 72, Bull Inst Hist & Philol; I-lan in the 19th century, Bull Inst Ethnol, 73; co-ed, History of ancient China series, Acad Sinica, 73-; auth, Urbanization and commercial development in the Chou period, Bull Inst Hist & Philol, 78; The founding of Eastern Chou, Bull Acad Sinica, 78; Han Agriculture, Univ Wash, 80; Western Chou Civilization, Yale Univ, 88. **CONTACT ADDRESS** Dept Hist, Univ Pittsburgh, 3M38 Forbes Quad, Pittsburgh, PA, 15260-0001. **EMAIL** cyhsu@pitt.edu

HUACO, GEORGE A.
PERSONAL Born 12/21/1927, Oakland, CA, m, 1978, 2 children **DISCIPLINE** SOCIOLOGY **EDUCATION** Univ Calif-Berkeley, BA, 54; Univ Calif-LA, MA, 59, Univ Calif-Berkeley, PhD(sociology), 63. **CAREER** Asst prof, Yale Univ, 63-69; assoc prof, SUNY-Buffalo, 69-71; prof soc, Univ NMex, 71-. **MEMBERSHIPS** Nat Asn Scholars; Foundation Shamanic Studies. **RESEARCH** Contemporary theory; Marx; neo-Darwinism. **SELECTED PUBLICATIONS** Auth, The Sociology of Film Art, Basic Books, 65; auth, The Sociological Model, in The Sociology of Art and Literature, Praeger, 70; auth, Toward a Sociology of Western Philosophy, in Knowledge and Society: Studies in the Sociology of Culture, JAI Press Vol 5, 84; author of several journal articles. **CONTACT ADDRESS** Dept Sociology, Univ New Mexico, SSCI-1072, Albuquerque, NM, 87131-0000. **EMAIL** georgeh@unm.edu

HUANG, RAY
PERSONAL Born 06/25/1918, Changsha, China, m, 1966, 3 children **DISCIPLINE** CHINESE HISTORY **EDUCATION** Univ Mich, BA, 54, MA, 57, PhD(hist), 64. **CAREER** Asst prof hist, Southern Ill Univ, 64-66; vis assoc prof, Columbia Univ, 66-67; assoc prof, State Univ NY, 67-71, prof, 71-80. Am Coun Learned Soc fel, 66 & 72; Harvard Univ res fel, 70-71; Nat Sci Found grant, 73; Guggenheim fel, 75. **MEMBERSHIPS** PEN **RESEARCH** Social-economic history of China; Ming Dynasty in China; History of science in China. **SELECTED PUBLICATIONS** Auth, Kai-Shek Chiang and His Diary as a Historical Source--Proposals for the Revision of Modern Chinese History, Chinese Studies Hist, Vol 0029, 96. **CONTACT ADDRESS** Dept of Hist, State Univ NY, New Paltz, NY, 12561.

HUBBARD, NANCY
DISCIPLINE ARCHITECTURE **EDUCATION** Univ Ill, BA, 68; Northwestern Univ, PhD, 84. **CAREER** Lectr, Univ Chicago, 77-84; instr, Northeastern Ill Univ, 86-87; asst prof, 88-93; assoc prof, 93-. **HONORS AND AWARDS** Phalin/Field Enterprises Prize Res, 77. **MEMBERSHIPS** AIA; Soc Archit Hist; Col Asn; Asn Preservation Tech. **RESEARCH** Criticism; historic preservation; professional practice and legal issues in architecture. **SELECTED PUBLICATIONS** Auth, Dollars for Design: A Case Study of Design Review in a Facade Rebate Program, Univ Cinn, 92; Landscape in Civil War Cemeteries, 92. **CONTACT ADDRESS** Sch of Architecture and Urban Planning, Univ of Wisconsin, Milwaukee, PO Box 413, Milwaukee, WI, 53201. **EMAIL** nanhub@uwm.edu

HUBBARD, THOMAS K.
PERSONAL Born 07/19/1956, Oklahoma City, OK, s **DISCIPLINE** CLASSICS **EDUCATION** Santa Clara Univ, BA, 75; Univ of Cal Berkley, MA, 77; Yale Univ, PhD, 80. **CAREER** Bard Col, vis asst prof, 80-81; Skidmore Col, asst prof, 82-84; Univ Minn, vis asst prof 84-85; Cornell Univ., asst prof, 86-88; Univ Texas Austin, vis lectr, asst prof, assoc prof, prof, 85-86, 88-. **HONORS AND AWARDS** NEH Fel, NEH Fel, Alexander von Humboldt Fel. **MEMBERSHIPS** APA, CAC, CAMWS **RESEARCH** Greek lyric and drama; Latin lyric and elegy; gay and lesbian stud. **SELECTED PUBLICATIONS** Auth, The Pindaric Mind: A Study of Logical Structure in Early Greek Poetry, 85; The Mask of Comedy: Aristophanes and the Intertextual Parabasis, 91; The Pipes of Pan: Intertextuality and Literary Filiation in the Pastoral Tradition from Theocritus to Milton, 98. **CONTACT ADDRESS** Dept of Classics, Texas Univ, Austin, TX, 78712-1181. **EMAIL** tkh@mail.utexas.edu

HUBBARD, WILLIAM H.
DISCIPLINE HISTORY **EDUCATION** Columbia Univ, PhD. **CAREER** Prof. **RESEARCH** Social and economic history of German-speaking Europe in the nineteenth century. **SELECTED PUBLICATIONS** Auth, Familiengeschichte, Munich, 83; Auf dem Weg zur Grossstadt, Graz 1857-1914, Vienna, 84; Sozial- und Wirtschaftsgeschichte Europas im 20 Jahrhundert, Munich, 86; editions in English, 89; Spanish, 92; Japanese, 92; ed, Making a Historical Culture: Norwegian Historiography, Oslo, 95. **CONTACT ADDRESS** Dept of Hist, Concordia Univ, Montreal, 1455 de Maisonneuve W, Montreal, PQ, H3G 1M8.

HUBBELL, JOHN THOMAS
PERSONAL Born 11/23/1934, Okay, OK, m, 1958, 2 children **DISCIPLINE** UNITED STATES HISTORY **EDUCATION** Northeastern State Col, BA, 59; Univ Okla, MA, 61; Univ Ill, PhD(hist), 69. **CAREER** Ed, Civil War Hist, Univ Iowa, 65-68; asst prof, 68-74, assoc prof hist, Kent State Univ, 74-, Ed, Civil War Hist, Kent State Univ, 68-; prof Hist, Kent State Univ, 81-; dir, Kent State Univ Press, 85-. **HONORS AND AWARDS** Distinguished Teaching Award, 80. **MEMBERSHIPS** Southern Hist Asn **RESEARCH** Civil War and Reconstruction. **SELECTED PUBLICATIONS** Auth, Three Georgia Unionists and the Compromise of 1850, Ga Hist Quart, 9/67; The desegregation of the University of Oklahoma, 1946-1950, J Negro Hist, 10/72; The Douglas Democrats and the Election of 1860, Mid-Am, 4/73; ed, Battles Lost and Won; Essays from Civil War History, Greenwood, 75; co-ed, Biographical Dictionary of the Union: Northern Leaders of the Civil War, Greenwood Press, 95. **CONTACT ADDRESS** Kent State Univ, PO Box 5190, Kent, OH, 44242-0001.

HUBER, DONALD L.
DISCIPLINE CHURCH HISTORY **EDUCATION** Capital Univ, BA, 62; Evangel Lutheran Theol Sem, BD, 66; Duke Univ, PhD, 71; Univ Mich, MALS, 73. **CAREER** Instr, ELTS, 69-72; librarian, ELTS, 73-78; librarian, 78-91; sec fac, 78-80; act dean Acad Aff, 84-85; guest lectr, Luther Sem, Adelaide, Australia, 86-87; prof, Trinity Lutheran Sem, 88-; archiv, Trinity Lutheran Sem, 91-. **SELECTED PUBLICATIONS** Auth, Luther A. Gottwald, John H. Tietjen, Dictionary of Heresy Trials in Amer Christianity, Greenwood, 97; Teddy, Rah! Theodore Roosevelt and German-Americanism, Timeline, Ohio Hist Soc, 96; Red, White, and Black: The Wyandot Mission at Upper Sandusky, Timeline XIII, 96; The Rise and Fall of Lane Seminary: An Antislavery Episode, 95. **CONTACT ADDRESS** Hist, Theol, Soc Dept, Trinity Lutheran Sem, 2199 E Main St, Columbus, OH, 43209-2334. **EMAIL** dhuber@trinity.capital.edu

HUDDLE, T.S.
PERSONAL Born 01/20/1955, Bath, ME, m, 1998 **DISCIPLINE** HISTORY **EDUCATION** Univ Ill Urbana Champaign, BS, 77, AM, 83, MD, 85, PhD, 88. **CAREER** Internal med residency, Univ Wisc Madison, 86-89; fel, general internal med, Univ Penn, 89-91; asst prof, med, Univ Ala Birmingham, 91-98. **MEMBERSHIPS** Amer Asn Hist of Med; Hist Sci Soc; Amer Col Physicians. **RESEARCH** History of American medical education. **SELECTED PUBLICATIONS** Competition and Reform at the Medical Department of the University of Pennsylvania 1847-1877, Jour of the Hist of Med and Allied Sci, 51, 251-92, Jul, 96; rev, Medical Lives and Scientific Medicine at Michigan, 1891-1969, Univ Mich Press, Jour of General Internal Med, 11, 65-66, 96; Osler's Clinical Clerkship: Origins and Interpretations, Jour of the Hist of Med and Allied Sci, 49, 483-503, 94; rev, A History of Education in Public Health, Health that Mocks the Doctor's Rules, NY, Oxford Univ Press, Jour of General Internal Med, 9, 240, 94; rev, Beyond Flexner: Medical Education in the Twentieth Century, Jour of General Internal Med, 8, 287-88, 93; auth, Basic Science and the Undergraduate Medical Curriculum, Perspectives in Bio and Med, 36, 550-64, Summer, 93; auth, Looking Backward: The 1871 Reforms at Harvard Medical School Reconsidered, Bull of the Hist of Med, 65, 340-365, 91; rev, The Caring Physician: The Life of Dr. Francis W. Peabody, Boston, Harvard Univ Press, Jour of General Internal Med, 8, 287-88, 92; rev, In Sickness and in Wealth: American Hospitals in the Twentieth Century, NY, Basic Books, Jour of General Internal Med, 6, 271, 91; essay rev, Educating Competent and Humane Physicians, Ind Univ Press, Jour of General Internal Med, 7, 129-130, 91; auth, Science, Practice and the Reform of American Medical Education, Univ Ill, 88. **CONTACT ADDRESS** 700 19th St. South, 11-P, Birmingham, AL, 35233. **EMAIL** thuddle@uas.edu

HUDSON, BARTON
DISCIPLINE MUSIC HISTORY & LITERATURE **EDUCATION** Midwestern Univ, BA; Ind Univ, MA, PhD. **CAREER** Ed, Early Keyboard Jour; contrib ed, New Josquin Ed; prof-. **HONORS AND AWARDS** Fulbright scholar, Ger; Fulbright res fel, 92-93; maj Text/Editions grant, outstanding tchr and Benedum distinguished scholar, W Va Univ., Mus ed, Opera Omnia of Antoine Brumel and Thomas Crecquillon. **SELECTED PUBLICATIONS** Publ, articles in the Jour of Amer Musicol Soc, The Mus Quart, The New Grove Dictionary of Mus. **CONTACT ADDRESS** Dept of Mus, W Va Univ, PO Box 6009, Morgantown, WV, 26506-6009. **EMAIL** bhudson@wvu.edu

HUDSON, CHARLES M.
PERSONAL Born 12/24/1932, Monterey, KY, m, 1968, 2 children **DISCIPLINE** ANTHROPOLOGY **EDUCATION** Univ Kentucky, AB, 59; Univ N Carolina, PhD, 65. **CAREER** Asst prof, 64-68, assoc prof, 68-77, prof, 77-93, Franklin Prof, 93-, Univ Georgia, 64- . **HONORS AND AWARDS** GA Gov Award in Hum, 88; James Mooney Award, 91; Rembert W Patrick Award, 94. **MEMBERSHIPS** Am Anthrop Asn; Am Soc Ethnohistory. **RESEARCH** Culture and history of the native people of the Southeastern US. **SELECTED PUBLICATIONS** Coauth, Knights of Spain, Warriors of the Sun: Hernando de Soto and the South's Ancient Chiefdoms, Univ Georgia Press, 97; Hernando do Soto and the Indians of Florida, Univ Press Fla, 93; coed, The Forgotten Centuries: Indians and Europeans in the American South, Univ Georgia Press, 94. **CONTACT ADDRESS** Anthropology Dept, Univ Georgia, Athens, GA, 30602. **EMAIL** chudson@arches,uga.edu

HUDSON, G. ELIZABETH
PERSONAL Born 12/31/1961, Walnut Creek, CA, m, 1991, 1 child **DISCIPLINE** MUSICOLOGY **EDUCATION** Smith Col, BA, 86; Cornell Univ, MA, 90, PhD, 93. **CAREER** Asst prof, 91-98, assoc prof, Univ Va, 98- . **HONORS AND AWARDS** NEH Fellow, 95-96; AMS 50 Fellow, 91. **MEMBERSHIPS** AMS **RESEARCH** 19th and 20th century performance practice, analysis, and criticism; 19th century Italian opera; Feminist operatic criticism. **SELECTED PUBLICATIONS** Introduzione storica, in Donizetti's Maria Stuarda, ed. Anders Wiklund, Milan, Ricordi, 91. Gilda seduced: A tale untold, Cambridge Opera Jour, 4/3, 92; Les vpres siciliennes, Simon Boccanegra, Un ballo in maschera, La forza del destino, Macbeth, Don Carlos, Aida, Othello, and Falstaff, in Dict des oeuvres de l'art vocal, ed. Marc Honegger and Paul Prevost, Paris, Bordas, 92; Telling Tales: Verdi, Jago, and the Undoing of Otello, Royal Gala prog book, Royal Opera House, Covent Garden, 92. Entry on "Puccini" and each of his operas, in The Viking Opera Guide, London: Viking and Penguin, 93; Masking Music: A Reconsideration of Light and Shade in Un ballo in maschera, in Verdi's Middle Period: Source Studies, Analysis and Performance Practice (1849-59), ed Martin Chusid, Univ Chicago Press, 97; Ed, Critical Edition of Giuseppe Verdi's Il corsaro, Univ Chicago Press, 98. **CONTACT ADDRESS** Univ of Virginia, 112 Old Cabell Hall, Charlottesville, VA, 22903. **EMAIL** eh6v@virginia.edu

HUDSON, GEORGE C., JR.
DISCIPLINE RENAISSANCE STUDIES **EDUCATION** Duke Univ, AB, 59, MA, 61; Univ MN, PhD, 74. **CAREER** Instr, Univ Louisville; prof, 69-. **RESEARCH** 17th century Brit poetry, post-16th century Japanese poetry. **SELECTED PUBLICATIONS** Auth, Expository Writing: Study and Practice; co-ed, Six Dark Questions, 66; articles, Kyoto Eng Cent News and Museum Travel. **CONTACT ADDRESS** Dept of Eng, Colgate Univ, 13 Oak Drive, Hamilton, NY, 13346.

HUDSON, HERMAN C.
PERSONAL Born 02/16/1923, m **DISCIPLINE** AFRICAN-AMERICAN STUDIES **EDUCATION** Univ MI, BA1945; Univ MI, MA 1946; Univ MI, PhD 1961. **CAREER** IN U, prof 1978; Afro-Am Affairs, dean, minority achievers program, currently; Dept of AfroAm Studies IN U, chmn 1970-72; Dept of Applied Linguistics IN U, chmn 1969-70; IN U, asso prof 1968-69; Univ MI, ind reading 1967-68; TC Columbia Univ English Prgm in Afghanistan, asst prof, dir 1961-67; VA State Coll, consult 1960; NC Coll, asst prof 1959-60; Univ Puerto Rico, asst prof 1957-59; Univ MI, tchng fellow 1953-57; FL A&M U, instr 1946-51. **HONORS AND AWARDS** Publs; "The Black Studies Prgm Strategy & Structure" 1971; "From Paragraph to Theme" 1972; "From Paragraph to Essay" 1975; "How To Make It In Coll" 1977; "The Black Composer Speaks" 1978. **CONTACT ADDRESS** Minority Achievers Program, Indiana Univ, Bloomington, Memorial Hall West 003A, Bloomington, IN, 47405.

HUDSON, JAMES BLAINE, III
PERSONAL Born 09/08/1949, Louisville, KY, m **DISCIPLINE** EDUCATION **EDUCATION** Univ of Louisville, BS 1974, MEd 1975; Univ of Kentucky, EdD 1981. **CAREER** School of Educ Univ of Louisville, admin coord 1974-75; West Louisville Educ Program Univ of Louisville, admin coord 1975-77, asst dir 1977-80, dir 1980-82; Univ of Louisville, assoc dir; Univ of Louisville Preparatory Division, associate director, 1982-92; assistant professor, Pan-African Studies, University of Louisville, 1992-. **HONORS AND AWARDS** Nat'l Merit Schlr 1967; Haggin Fellowshp Univ of K 1977-78; Black Faculty/Staff Mem of the yr Univ of L 1982. **MEMBERSHIPS** Mem APGA, KPGA, ACPA 1976-; MENSA 1984-. **CONTACT ADDRESS** Pan-African Studies, Univ of Louisville, Louisville, KY, 40208.

HUDSON, LEONNE
PERSONAL Born 07/23/1954, Andrews, SC, m, 1991, 1 child **DISCIPLINE** HISTORY **EDUCATION** Voorhees Col, BA, 76; Kent State Univ, MA, 78, PhD, 80. **CAREER** Asst prof, Kent State Univ, 91-. **HONORS AND AWARDS** Phi Alpha Theta; Omicron Delta Kappa; Alpha Kappa Mu; Alpha Chi; Prof of Excellence Award, Kent State Univ, 95; Prof of Distinction Award, Kent State Univ, 96. **MEMBERSHIPS** Southern Hist Asn; Org of Am Hists; Ohio Acad of Hist; Soc of Civil War Hists **RESEARCH** Civil War; Military. **SELECTED PUBLICATIONS** Auth, A Confederate Victory at Grahamville: Fighting at Honey Mill, in South Carolina Hist Mag, 93; Gustavus W. Smith and the Battle of Seven Pines, in Confederate Veteran Mag, 93; Valor at Wilson's Wharf, in Civil War Times Illustrated, 98; Robert E. Lee, in Leaders of the Civil War, 98; The Odyssey of a Southerner: The Life andTimes of Gustavus Woodson Smith, 98; Foreword, in Dogs of War and Stories of Other Beasts in the Civil War, 98. **CONTACT ADDRESS** Dept of History, Kent State Univ, PO Box 5190, Kent, OH, 44242-0001.

HUDSON, LEONNE
PERSONAL Andrews, SC **DISCIPLINE** 19TH CENTURY UNITED STATES **EDUCATION** Voorhees Coll, BA, 76; Kent State Univ, MA, 78, PhD, 90. **CAREER** ASST PROF, KENT STATE UNIV, 91-. **HONORS AND AWARDS** Phi Alpha Theta; Omicron Delta Kappa; Alpha Kappa Mu. **MEMBERSHIPS** Southern Historical Asn; Org Am Historians, Ohio Acad Hist; Soc Civil War Historians. **RESEARCH** Civil war, military. **SELECTED PUBLICATIONS** Auth, The Odyssey of a Southerner: The LIfe and Times of Gustavus Woodson Smith, Mercer Univ Press, 98; A Confederate Victory at Grahamville: Fighting ata Honey Mill, SC Hist Mag, 93; Gustavus W. Smith and the Battle of Seven Pines, Confederate Veteran Mag, 93; Valor at Wilson's Wharf, Civil War Times Illustrated, 98; Robert E Lee, in Leaders of the Civil War, Greenwood Press, 98. **CONTACT ADDRESS** Dept Hist, Kent State Univ, PO Box 5190, Kent, OH, 44242-0001.

HUDSON, LEONNE M.
PERSONAL Born 07/23/1954, Andrews, SC, m, 1991, 1 child **DISCIPLINE** HISTORY **EDUCATION** Voorhees Col, BA, 76; Kent St Univ, MA, 78, PhD, 90. **CAREER** Dir, proj Upward Bound, 79-81, Williamsburg Tech Col; asst prof, 91-, Kent St Univ. **RESEARCH** Civil War, Old South, African Amer **CONTACT ADDRESS** Dept of History, Kent St Univ, PO Box 5190, Kent, OH, 44242-0001. **EMAIL** 1hudson@kent.edu

HUDSON, ROBERT
DISCIPLINE HISTORY AND PHILOSOPHY OF SCIENCE AND EPISTEMOLOGY **EDUCATION** W Ontario Univ, PhD. **CAREER** Dept Philos, Concordia Univ **RESEARCH** Contemporary experimental microbiology. **SELECTED PUBLICATIONS** Pub(s), in Synthese; Stud in Hist and Philos of Sci. **CONTACT ADDRESS** Dept of Philos, Concordia Univ, Montreal, 1455 de Maisonneuve W, Montreal, PQ, H3G 1M8. **EMAIL** hudsonr@alcor.concordia.ca

HUDSON, ROBERT VERNON
PERSONAL Born 08/29/1932, Indianapolis, IN, 2 children **DISCIPLINE** HISTORY OF MASS COMMUNICATION **EDUCATION** Ind Univ, Bloomington, BS, 54; Univ Ore, MS, 66; Univ Minn, Minneapolis, PhD(mass commun), 70. **CAREER** City ed, News-Sentinel, Rochester, Ind, 54; staff corresp, United Press, Indianapolis, 54-56; reporter, Chicago Daily News, 56-57 & Fairchild Publ, Chicago, 57-58; serv exec, Pub Rels Bd, Chicago, 58-59; publ asst, Traffic Inst & Transp Ctr, Northwestern Univ, 60-61, news bur mgr, 61-63, info serv dir, 63; asst dir, News Bur, Ariz State Univ, 63-65; asst prof, 68-73, asst chmn, Sch Joun, 72-74, actg asst dean, Col Commun Arts, 74, assoc prof to prof Jour, Mich State Univ, 73-98, prof emeritus, 98-; freelance writer, 49-; staff writer, Traffic Dig & Rev, 60-61; TV prod-writer-anchorman, Phoenix, Ariz, 64-65; prof jour & head dept, Calif Polytech State Univ, San Luis Opispo, 75-76. **MEMBERSHIPS** Jack London Soc; Am Lit Asn. **RESEARCH** Biography; mass media history; The First Amendment; Jack London. **SELECTED PUBLICATIONS** Coauth, Johnson's Information Strategy for Vietnam: An Evaluation, autumn 68, auth, Will Irwin's Pioneering Criticism of the Press, summer 70 & FoI Crusade in Perspective: Three Victories for the Press, spring 73, Jour Quart; Will Irwin's Crusade for the League of Nations, Jour Hist, autumn 75; The English roots of Benjamin Franklin's jour, Jour Hist, autumn 76; Non-indigenous Influences on Benjamin Franklin's Jour, In: Newsletters to Newspapers: Eighteenth-Century Jour, WVa Univ, 77; The Writing Game: A Biography of Will Irwin, Iowa State Univ Press, 82; auth, Mass MediaL A Chronological Encyclopedia of Television, Radio, Motion Pictures, Magazines, Newspapers, and Books in the United States, Garland Publ, 87. **CONTACT ADDRESS** Michigan State Univ, 305 Comm Arts & Scie, East Lansing, MI, 4882 1212.

HUEL, RAY
DISCIPLINE HISTORY **EDUCATION** Univ Regina, BA; MA; Alberta Univ, PhD. **RESEARCH** Canadian and French Canadian history. **SELECTED PUBLICATIONS** Auth, pubs on moutaineering in the Canadian Rockies, French minorities in western Canada, anti Catholicism and Francophobia in Saskatchewan and the Metis and Oblate missionaries in western Canada. **CONTACT ADDRESS** Dept of History, Lethbridge Univ, 4401 University Dr W, Lethbridge, AB, T1K 3M4. **EMAIL** huel@hg.uleth.ca

HUESTON, ROBERT FRANCIS
PERSONAL Born 08/25/1941, Darby, PA **DISCIPLINE** UNITED STATES HISTORY **EDUCATION** Col of the Holy Cross, AB, 63, Univ Notre Dame, MA, 65, PhD, 72. **CAREER** From instr to asst prof, 68-76, assoc prof hist, Univ Scranton, 76. **MEMBERSHIPS** Am Cath Hist Soc; Hist Soc PA; The Hist Soc. **RESEARCH** Hist of Am immigration; Am Cath Hist. **SELECTED PUBLICATIONS** Auth, Noah Webster's linguistic nationalism, Bull Hist Teacher's Club, Notre Dame Univ, 12/65-1/66; The Catholic Press and Nativism, 1840-1860, ser on Irish Americans, Arno, 76. **CONTACT ADDRESS** Dept of Hist, Univ of Scranton, Scranton, PA, 18510-0000.

HUFF, CAROLYN BARBARA
PERSONAL Born 04/30/1943, Maryville, TN **DISCIPLINE** UNITED STATES HISTORY, BLACK STUDIES **EDUCATION** Maryville Col, BA, 65; Univ NC, Chapel Hill, MA, 66, PhD(hist), 69. **CAREER** Asst prof, 69-75, assoc prof, 75-80, prof hist, Lenoir Rhyne Col, 80-, chmn dept, 72-, Danforth Found fel, Atlanta Univ, 71-72. **HONORS AND AWARDS** Bost Distinguished Professor Award. **MEMBERSHIPS** Orgn Am Historians. **RESEARCH** Nineteenth century United States social history; the abolitionist crusade; African history, the apartheid system in South Africa. **SELECTED PUBLICATIONS** Auth, The Black Experience in Catawba County, various reviews. **CONTACT ADDRESS** Dept of Hist, Lenoir-Rhyne Col, 743 6th St N E, Hickory, NC, 28601-3976. **EMAIL** huff_c@LRC.edu

HUFF, PETER A.
PERSONAL Born 11/01/1958, Atlanta, GA, m, 1994, 1 child **DISCIPLINE** HISTORICAL THEOLOGY **EDUCATION** Mercer Univ, BA, 80; Southern Baptist Theol Seminary, MDiv, 84; St Louis Univ, PhD, 94. **CAREER** Asst Prof, Univ Puget Sound, 94-95; Asst Prof Theol, St. Anselm Col, 95-. **HONORS AND AWARDS** Phi Beta Kappa. **MEMBERSHIPS** Am Acad Relig; Am Soc Church Hist; Col Theol Soc. **RESEARCH** Religion in American culture; religion and literature; catholic studies. **SELECTED PUBLICATIONS** Coauth, Knowledge and Belief in America: Enlightenment Traditions and Modern Religious Thought, Cambridge Univ Press, 95; auth, With the Body of This World: Allen Tate's Quarrel with Modern Gnosticism, Fides et Hist, 95; New Apologists in America's Conservative Catholic Subculture, Horizons, 96; Allen Tate and the Catholic Revival: Trace of the Fugitive Gods, Isaac Hecker Studies in Religion and American Culture, Paulist Press, 96; John Locke and the Prophecy of Quaker Women, Quaker Hist, 97. **CONTACT ADDRESS** Theology Dept, St. Anselm Col, 100 Saint Anselm Dr., Manchester, NH, 03102. **EMAIL** pehuff@anselm.edu

HUFF, TOBY E.
PERSONAL Born 04/24/1942, Portland, ME, m, 1989, 2 children **DISCIPLINE** SOCIOLOGY **EDUCATION** NE Univ, AB, 65, MA, 67; New Sch for Soc Res, PhD, 71. **CAREER** Asst to full Prof, 71, 81, Univ Mass, Dartmouth; Founder & Dir, Ctr for Policy Analysis, Univ Mass, 84-86; Chancellor Prof, 9/98. **HONORS AND AWARDS** Postdoc Fellow at Univ Calif Berkeley, 76-77; Inst for Adv Stud, Princeton, 78-79. **MEMBERSHIPS** Am Sociol Asn; Hist of Sci Soc; Mid E Stud Asn; Int Soc for Comp Stud of Civilization. **RESEARCH** Comparative historical sociology; science in the Muslim world; women in the Islamic world; comp sociology of law. **SELECTED PUBLICATIONS** Ed, On the Road to Modernity: Conscience, Science and Civilizations, Rowman & Littlefield, 81; auth, Max Weber and the Methodology of the Social Sciences, Transaction Books, 84; auth, The Rise of Early Modern Science: Islam, China, and the West, Cambridge Univ Press, 93, 95; auth, Science and the Public Sphere: Comparative Institutional Developments in Islam and the West, Soc Epistem, A J of Knowledge, Cult, and Soc Policy, 11:1, 25-27, 97; co-ed, Max Weber and Islam, Interpretations and Critiques, Transaction Books, 98. **CONTACT ADDRESS** Dept Sociol & Anthrop, Univ Mass at Dartmouth, 285 Old Westport Rd, N Dartmouth, MA, 02747-2350. **EMAIL** thuff@umassd.edu

HUFFMAN, CARL A.
PERSONAL Born 12/27/1951, Denver, CO, m, 1986, 3 children **DISCIPLINE** CLASSICS **EDUCATION** Univ Colo, BA, 74, MA, 76; Univ Tex, PhD, 81. **CAREER** From asst prof to assoc prof to prof, DePauw Univ, 81-. **HONORS AND AWARDS** John Simon Guggenheim Found Fel, 95-96; Howard Found Res Fel, 89-90; NEH Fel Independent Study & Res, 83-84; Bye Fel, Robinson Col, Cambridge Univ, 83-84. **MEMBERSHIPS** Am Philos Asn; Soc Ancient Greek Philos. **RESEARCH** Ancient philosophy. **SELECTED PUBLICATIONS** Auth, Philolaus of Croton: Pythagorean and Presocratic, 93; auth, The Pythagorean Tradition, Cambridge Companion to Early Greek Philos, 99; auth, Die Pythagoreer, Philosophen der Antike I, 96; auth, Pythagorisme, Le Savior Grec, 96; auth, Philolaus' Cosmogony, Ionian Philos, 89; auth, The Role of Number in Philolaus' Philosophy, Phronesis, 88; auth, The Authenticity of Archytas Fragment 1, Class Quart, 85. **CONTACT ADDRESS** Dept of Classics, DePauw Univ, 400 S Locust, Greencastle, IN, 46135. **EMAIL** cahuff@depauw.edu

HUFFMAN, JAMES LAMAR
PERSONAL Born 10/17/1941, Plymouth, IN, m, 1964, 2 children **DISCIPLINE** MODERN JAPANESE HISTORY **EDUCATION** Ind Wesleyan Univ, Ind, AB, 63; Northwestern Univ, Evanston, MSJ, 64; Univ Mich, Ann Arbor, MA, 67, PhD, 72. **CAREER** Reporter, Minneapolis Tribune, 64-66; asst prof hist, Univ Nebr, Lincoln 72-75; asst prof, Marion Col, Ind 75-77; from Asst Prof to Assoc Prof, 77-87, prof hist, Wittenberg Univ, 87-; sr translr-ed consult, Japan Interpreter, 74-75; Am Advisory Comt, Japan Found, 95-. **HONORS AND AWARDS** Fulbright-Hays res grant; Fulbright-Hayes res grant, Tokyo, 83-84; Japan Found res grant, Tokyo, 94-95. **MEMBERSHIPS** Asn Asian Studies; Midwest Japan Sem (chmn, 78-81). **RESEARCH** The press and modernization in 19th century Japan; comparative press history; Edward H House and early American images of Japan. **SELECTED PUBLICATIONS** Auth, Modern History, transl, in Introductory Bibliography for Japanese Studies, Japan Found, 75; Meiji roots and contemporary practice of Japanese Press, Japan Interpreter, spring 77; Modernization of Japan (TV script) for: Japan: The Living Tradition, Univ Mid-Am, 78; Politics of the Meiji Press: Life of Fukuchi Genichiro, Univ Hawaii, 80; Nationalism in Japan, in Nationalism in East Asia: Annotated Bibliography, Garland, 81; Creating a Public: People and Press in Meiji Japan, Univ Hawaii, 97; ed, Modern Japan: An Encyclopedia of History, Culture, and Nationalism, Garland, 98. **CONTACT ADDRESS** Dept of Hist, Wittenberg Univ, PO Box 720, Springfield, OH, 45501-0720. **EMAIL** jhuffman@wittenberg.edu

HUFFMAN, JAMES RICHARD
PERSONAL Born 05/08/1944, Liberal, KS, m, 1965, 2 children **DISCIPLINE** ENGLISH, AMERICAN STUDIES **EDUCATION** Harvard Col, BA, 66; MI State Univ, MA, 67; PhD, 70. **CAREER** Asst prof Eng & Am lit, 70-75, assoc prof Eng, 75-85, prof eng, State Univ NY Col, Fredonia, 85, Dir Am Studies, 74-, Assoc prof, UER Des Pays Anglophones, Univ Paris III, Sorbonne Nouvelle, Paris, 76-77. **MEMBERSHIPS** Am Cult Asn; Popular Cult Asn. **RESEARCH** Am lit; popular cult; psychology and cult. **SELECTED PUBLICATIONS** Auth, Jesus Christ Superstar: Popular art and unpopular criticism, J Popular Culture, fall 72; The cuckoo clocks in Kesey's Nest, Mod Lang Studies, spring 77; A psychological redefinition of Styron's Confessions of Nat Turner, Literary Rev, winter 81; A psychological critique of American culture, Am J Psychoanalysis, 82; Murray Krieger and the impasse in contextualist poetics, In: Murray Krieger and Contemporary Critical Theory (Bruce Henriksen, ed), Columbia Univ, 86; Coauth (with Julie L Hoffman), Sexism and cultural lag: The rise of the jailbait song, 1955-1985, J Popular Culture, fall 87; Young Man Johnson, The Am J of Psychoanalysis, 9/89; A Norreyan approach to American literature, In: Dionysius in Literature: Essays on Literary Madness (Branimis M Rieger, ed), Bowling Green Univ Popular Press, 94. **CONTACT ADDRESS** Dept of Eng, State Univ of NY Col, Suny at Fredonia, Fredonia, NY, 14063-1143. **EMAIL** huffman@ait.fredonia.edu

HUGHES, ANDREW
PERSONAL Born 08/03/1937, London, England **DISCIPLINE** MUSIC/HISTORY **EDUCATION** Merchant Taylor's Sch, 50-55; Worcester Col (Oxford), 57-64. **CAREER** Lectr, Queen's Univ (Belfast), 62-64; asst prof, Univ Ill, 64-67; assoc prof, Univ N Carolina, 67-69; PROF, UNIV TORONTO, 69-. **HONORS AND AWARDS** Henry Hadow scholar, Oxford, 55; John Lowell Osgood Mem Prize, Oxford, 58; Guggenheim fel, 73-74; fel, Trinity Col, Univ Toronto, 80; Killam res fel, 93-95. **MEMBERSHIPS** Am Musicol Soc; Medieval Acad Am. **SELECTED PUBLICATIONS** Auth, Manuscript Accidentals: Ficta in Focus, 72; auth, A Bibliography of Medieval Music, 74, 2nd ed, 80; auth, Medieval Manuscripts for Mass and Office, 81, 86; auth, Style and Symbol: Medieval Music 800-1453, 89; auth, Late Medieval Liturgical Offices: Resources for Electronic Research: Texts, 94; auth, Late Medieval Liturgical Offices: Resources for Electronic Research: Sources and Chants, 96; ed, Fifteenth Century Liturgical Music, 68; co-ed, The Old Hall Manuscript, 69, 73. **CONTACT ADDRESS** Ctr Medieval Stud, Univ of Toronto, Toronto, ON, M5S 1A1.

HUGHES, CARL D.
PERSONAL Indianapolis, IN, m **DISCIPLINE** EDUCATION **EDUCATION** WV State Coll Inst, BS 1942; Wharton Sch of Finance Univ of PA, MA 1943; Christian Theol Sem, BD 1957; Christian Theol Sem, MA 1958; Centrl Bapt Theol Semin of IN, DD 1975; Christian Theol Sem, MDiv 1972; IN Univ Sch of Law Wayne State Univ & Univ of Detroit, Post Grad Studies. **CAREER** Mt Zion Bapt Ch Indianapolis, ministers asst 1952; Second Bapt Ch Lafayette 1952-56; St John Missionary Bapt Ch 1956-60; Christian Educ Met Bapt Ch Detroit, dir 1960-61; Bethel Bapt Ch East Detroit, pastor 1961; Hughes Enterprise Inc, vice pres treas; Detroit Christian Training Cntr, former dean; Bus Educ Detroit Pub Sch, former tchr; Ch Bldr

& Bus Educ Detroit Pub Sch, dept hd; Calvary Dist Assn Detroit, former instr; Wolverine State Conv SS & BTU Cong MI, former instr; Nat Bapt SS & BTU Congress, former instr; Central Bible Sem, former instr. **HONORS AND AWARDS** Received First John L Webb Award Nat Bapt Conv 1948; **MEMBERSHIPS** Membership com YMCA; membership Com NAACP; former mem Grand Bd Dir Kappa Alpha Psi Nat Coll Frat; Mason; budget com Nat Negro Bus League; treas StEmma Military Acad Parent Assn of Detroit; chmn bd of trustees Todd-Phillips Children Home of the Wolverine State Missionary Bapt Conv Inc; chmn of Finance Pastors' Div of the Nat Bapt Congress of Christian Edn. **SELECTED PUBLICATIONS** Auth, The Church Orgnzd For A Meaning Ministry; Financing the Local Church Property. **CONTACT ADDRESS** Bethel Baptist Church East, 5715-33 Holcomb, Detroit, MI, 48213.

HUGHES, JOHNSON DONALD
PERSONAL Born 06/05/1932, Santa Monica, CA, m, 1964, 2 children **DISCIPLINE** ANCIENT HISTORY, ENVIRONMENTAL HISTORY **EDUCATION** Univ Calif, Los Angeles, AB, 54; Boston Univ, STB, 57, PhD(hist), 60. **CAREER** Asst prof hist, Calif Western Univ, 61-66 & Pierce Col, Greece, 66-67; from asst prof to assoc prof, 67-77, dir Class Athens & Rome humanities progs, 71-77, PROF HIST, UNIV DENVER, 77-, Danforth assoc, 65-; bd mem, Environmental Ethics, 81- **MEMBERSHIPS** AHA; Am Soc Environ Hist **RESEARCH** Ancient history, particularly environmental history of the Mediterranean. **SELECTED PUBLICATIONS** Auth, Water Management in Ancient-Greek Cities, Am Hist Rev, Vol 0099, 94; On Rims and Ridges--The Los-Alamos Area Since 1880, NMex Hist Rev, Vol 0069, 94; The Mountains of the Mediterranean World--An Environmental History, Am Hist Rev, Vol 0099, 94; The Sacred Groves of South-India--Ecology, Traditional Communities and Religious Change, Social Compass, Vol 0044, 97; Green Imperialism--Colonial Expansion, Tropical Island Edens and the Origins of Environmentalism, 1600-1860, J World Hist, Vol 0007, 96. **CONTACT ADDRESS** Dept of Hist, Univ of Denver, Denver, CO, 80208.

HUGHES, JUDITH MARKHAM
PERSONAL Born 02/20/1941, New York, NY, m, 1964, 1 child **DISCIPLINE** HISTORY **EDUCATION** Swarthmore Col, BA, 62; Harvard Univ, MA, 63, PhD(hist), 70; Clinical Assoc, San Diego Pschoanalytic Inst, 91-. **CAREER** Asst prof soc studies, Harvard Univ, 70-75; assoc prof hist, 75-84, prof hist, Univ Calif, San Diego, 84-. **HONORS AND AWARDS** Phi Beta kappa; Woodrow Wilson Fel, 62-63; Nat Endowment of the Humanities Fel, 74. **RESEARCH** History of psychoanalysis. **SELECTED PUBLICATIONS** Auth, To the Maginot Line: The Politics of French Military Preparation in the 1920's, Harvard Univ, 71; Emotion and High Politics: Personal Relations at the Summit in Late Nineteenth-Century Britain and Germany, Univ Calif Press, 83; Reshaping the Psychoanalytic Domain: The Work of Melanie Klein, W R D Fourbaurn and D W Winnicott, Univ Calif Press, 89; From Freud's Consulting Room: The Unconscious in a Scientific Age, Harvard Univ Press, 94; Fruedian Analysts/Feminist Issues, Yale Univ Press (in press). **CONTACT ADDRESS** Dept of History, Univ of California, San Diego, 9500 Gilman Dr, La Jolla, CA, 92093-5003. **EMAIL** jhughes@ucsd.edu

HUGHES, KEVIN L.
PERSONAL Born 11/12/1969, Baltimore, MD, m, 1995, 1 child **DISCIPLINE** HISTORY OF CHRISTIANITY **EDUCATION** Univ Chicago, PhD, 97. **CAREER** Arthur J Ennis postdoc fel hum, 97-, Villanova Univ. **HONORS AND AWARDS** Phi Beta Kappa, 90; Pres Scholar, Villanova Univ, 87-91; Dist Stud Award (Relig Studies), Villanova Univ, 91; summa cum laude, Villanova Univ, 91; Valedictorian, Villanova Univ, 91; Century Fel, Univ Chicago, 91-95; jr fel, Inst for Advanced Stud of Relig, 95-96. **MEMBERSHIPS** Am Soc of Church Hist; AAR; Soc of Bibl Lit. **RESEARCH** Theology, religion, and culture of the Middle Ages; history of biblical exegesis; apocalypticism. **SELECTED PUBLICATIONS** Auth, A Theology of Antichrist? Peter Lombard's Commentary on 2 Thessalonians in its Medieval Exegetical Context, Proceed of Am Soc of Church Hist, Theol Res Exchange Network, 97; rev, Carthusian Spirituality: The Writings of Hugh of Balma and Guigo de Ponte, Church Hist, forthcoming; auth, Adso and His Sources: Notes on Antichrist and the Exegetical Tradition at the Millenium, The Apocalyptic Year 1000: Religious Expectation and Social Change in Western Europe, 968-1033, Oxford Univ Press, forthcoming; auth, Augustine and Antichrist: Strategies of Synthesis in Early Medieval Exegesis, in History, Apocalypse, and the Secular Imagination, An Interdisciplinary Symposium on Augustine's City of God, forthcoming; coauth, Second Thessalonians: Two Early Medieval Apocalyptic Commentaries, TEAMS Medieval Comm Series, forthcoming. **CONTACT ADDRESS** Core Humanities, Villanova Univ, 800 Lancaster Ave, Villanova, PA, 19085. **EMAIL** khughes@email.villanova.edu

HUGHES, THOMAS PARKE
PERSONAL Born 09/13/1923, Richmond, VA, m, 1948, 3 children **DISCIPLINE** HISTORY OF TECHNOLOGY & SCIENCE **EDUCATION** Univ Va, BME, 47, MA, 50, PhD(hist), 53. **CAREER** Instr eng English, Univ Va, 52-54; asst prof mod Europ hist, Sweet Briar Col, 54-56; from asst prof to assoc prof, Wash & Lee Univ, 56-63; assoc prof hist, Mass Inst Technol, 63-66; vis assoc prof, Johns Hopkins Univ, 66-69; prof hist technol, Inst Technol, Southern Methodist Univ, 69-73; chmn dept hist & sociol sci, 77-81, PROF HIST OF TECHNOL, UNIV PA, 73-, Fulbright res grant, Ger, 58-59; adv ed, Technol & Cult, Soc Hist Technol, 60-; vis prof hist tech, Univ Wis, 63; vis scholar, Univ Ctr Va, 66; fel, Ctr Recent Am Hist, Johns Hopkins Univ, 66-68; Am Coun Learned Soc fel, Smithsonian Inst, 68; Nat Sci Found grant, 73-74; mem hist adv comt, Atomic Energy Comn, 73-77 & NASA, 73-79; mem, US Comt, Int Union for Hist & Philos of Sci, 74-, chmn, 75-77; Rockefeller Found humanities grant, 76; chmn hist adv comn comt, NASA, 77-79; coun mem, Hist Sci Soc, 77-; fel, Forschung Inst, Univ Bielefeld, 79. **HONORS AND AWARDS** Tex Inst Lett Bk Award, 72; Dexter Prize, Soc Hist Technol, 72. **MEMBERSHIPS** Hist Sci Soc; Soc Hist Technol (pres, 77-80). **RESEARCH** History of technology and science in the modern West; biography of inventors, engineers and entrepreneurs; history of invention and discovery. **SELECTED PUBLICATIONS** Auth, Stanley Cyril Smith, 1903-1992--Memorial, Tech Cult, Vol 0034, 93. **CONTACT ADDRESS** Dept of Hist & Sociol of Sci, Univ of Pa, Philadelphia, PA, 19174.

HUHTA, JAMES KENNETH
PERSONAL Born 08/27/1937, Ashtabula, Ohio, m, 1958, 2 children **DISCIPLINE** HISTORY, HISTORIC PRESERVATION **EDUCATION** Baldwin-Wallace Col, BA, 59; Univ NC, Chapel Hill, MA, 63, PhD(Am colonial & revolutionary hist), 65. **CAREER** Res asst hist, Univ NC, Chapel Hill, 60-62 & 63-65; asst ed, NC Colonial Rec Proj, 62-63; from asst prof to assoc prof, 65-73, asst vpres acad affairs, 76-79, PROF HIST & DIR HIST PRESERV PROG, MIDDLE TENN STATE UNIV, 73-, Instr hist, NC State Univ, 63-65; bd trustees, Comt Preserv Services, 77-79; reviewer, Nat Heritage Trust Task Force, US Dept Interior, 77-78; nat bd mem, Preserv Action, 77-82, chmn nominating comt, 81, vpres southern region, 81-82; chmn, Nat Coun Preserv Educ, 78-81; dir, Mid-South Humanities Proj, Nat Endowment Humanities, 78-83; reviewer & panelist consult, Nat Endowment Humanities, 78-; mem bd adv, Ctr Study Southern Hist & Culture, Univ Mississippi, 79-, Boston/ Newton Local Hist Collaborative, 80-, Hiram Regional Studies Proj, 81- & Nat Trust Hist Preserv, 81-; chmn, Comt Historic Preserv, 81 & Comt Public Hist, 82; comt archit conserv, Nat Conserv Adv Coun, Smithsonian Inst, 81- **MEMBERSHIPS** Orgn Am Historians; Soc Hist Archaeol; Asn Preserv Technol; Am Asn State & Local Hist; Soc Archit Historians. **RESEARCH** Historic preservation textbook; grant support alternatives for historic preservation; use of community cultural heritage resources for the teaching of history. **SELECTED PUBLICATIONS** Auth, Instructor's Manual for Teaching American History (2 vols), Ronald, 68; coed, The Regulators in North Carolina, 1759-1776: A Documentary History, NC State Dept Arch & Hist, 71; auth, Tennessee and the American Revolution Bicentennial, Tenn Hist Quart, 72; co-ed, Preservation: Toward an Ethnic for the 1980's, Preserv Press of the Nat Trust Hist Preserv, 80; contribr, Historic Preservation in Small Towns: A Manual of Practice, Am Asn State & Local Hist, 80. **CONTACT ADDRESS** Dept of Hist, Middle Tennessee State Univ, Murfreesboro, TN, 37132-0001. **EMAIL** jhuta@frank.mtsu.edu

HULL, HENRY LANE
PERSONAL Born 10/05/1942, Washington, DC **DISCIPLINE** RUSSIAN HISTORY, MODERN EUROPEAN HISTORY **EDUCATION** Georgetown Univ, BA, 64, MA, 69, PhD(Russ hist), 70. **CAREER** Intern hist, Smithsonian Inst, 65; lectr hist, Georgetown Univ, 67-70; Relm Found fel, 70-71; asst prof, 71-77, chmn Int Studies Comt, 75-76, ASSOC PROF HIST, UNIV ALA, HUNTSVILLE, 77-, CHMN INT STUDIES COMT, 81-, Mem acad adv coun, Charles Edison Mem Youth Fund, 72-; mem, Nat Captive Nations Comt, 79- **MEMBERSHIPS** Am Asn Advan Slavic Studies; Am Cath Hist Asn; Consortium on Revolutionary Europe; Southern Conf Slavic Studies. **RESEARCH** Soviet diplomacy of the 1920's and 1930's; Russian religious history; papal history. **SELECTED PUBLICATIONS** Auth, Michel Dherbigny and Russia--A Pre-Ecumenical Approach to Christian Unity, Cath Hist Rev, Vol 0079, 93; Eastern Christianity and Politics in the 20th-Century, Cath Hist Rev, Vol 0079, 93. **CONTACT ADDRESS** Dept of Hist, Univ of Ala, Huntsville, AL, 35807.

HULL, KENNETH
DISCIPLINE MUSIC **EDUCATION** Univ Waterloo, BA, 76; Univ Western Ontario, BM, 77; MM, 80; Princeton, PhD, 89. **CAREER** Assoc prof **MEMBERSHIPS** Can Liturgical Soc. **SELECTED PUBLICATIONS** Auth, pub(s) on music of Brahms, musical allusion and twentieth century hymnody. **CONTACT ADDRESS** Dept of Music, Conrad Grebel Col, 200 Westmount Rd, Waterloo, ON, N2L 3G6. **EMAIL** krhull@uwaterloo.ca

HULL, N.E.H.
PERSONAL Born 08/27/1949, New York, NY, m, 1970, 2 children **DISCIPLINE** LAW, HISTORY **EDUCATION** Ohio State, Univ, BA, 74; Columbia Univ, PhD, 81; Univ of Georgia, JD, 85. **CAREER** Assoc prof, 87-93, prof, 93-97, distinguish prof of law and hist, 97-present, Rutgers Univ. **HONORS AND AWARDS** Scribes Book Award for 1998; Erwin Surrency Prize of Amer Soc for Legal Hist, 99. **MEMBERSHIPS** ABA, New Jersey Bar Assn; AHA; ASLA; OAH **RESEARCH** Amer Legal and Jurisprudential Hist **SELECTED PUBLICATIONS** Auth, Vital Schools of Jurisprudence: Roscoe Pound, Wesley Newcomb Hohfeld, and the Promotion of an Academic Jurisprudential Agenda, 1910-1919, Journal of Legal Education, 95; The Romantic Realist: Art, Literature and the Enduring Legacy of Karl Llewellyn's Jurisprudence, 40 American Journal of Legal History, 96; Roscoe Pound & Karl Llewellyn: Searching for an American Jurisprudence, 97; Back to the Future of the Institute: William Draper Lewis's Vision of the ALI's Mission During Its First Twenty-Five Years and The Implications for the Institute's Seventy-Fifth Anniversary, 98. **CONTACT ADDRESS** Sch Law-Camden, Rutger Univ, 217 N. Fifth St., Camden, NJ, 08102-1203. **EMAIL** nehhul@crab.rutgers.edu

HULL, RICHARD W.
PERSONAL Born 08/29/1940, Hackensack, NJ, 2 children **DISCIPLINE** AFRICAN HISTORY **EDUCATION** Rutgers Univ, BA, 62; Columbia Univ, MA, 64, prof cert African studies, 65, PhD, 68. **CAREER** ASSOC PROF TO PROF, AFRICAN HIST, NY UNIV, 68-; Pres, African Consults, Inc. **MEMBERSHIPS** African Studies Asn. **RESEARCH** Race relations in Southern Africa; architecture in pre-colonial Africa. **SELECTED PUBLICATIONS** Auth, Munyakare: African Civilization before the Batuuree, Wiley, 72; African Cities and Towns before the European Conquest, Norton, 77; American Enterprise in South Africa, NYU Press, 90. **CONTACT ADDRESS** Dept of Hist, New York Univ, 53 Wash Sq S, New York, NY, 10012. **EMAIL** rwh1@is.nyu.edu

HULSE, JAMES W.
PERSONAL Born 06/04/1930, Pioche, NV, m, 1962, 2 children **DISCIPLINE** MODERN EUROPEAN HISTORY **EDUCATION** Univ Nev, BA, 52, MA, 58; Stanford Univ, PhD, 62. **CAREER** Asst prof Hist, Cent Wash State Col, 61-62; from asst prof to assoc prof, 62-70, prof Hist, Univ Nev, Reno, 70-97; prof Emeritus, 97-; Danforth Assoc, 81-. **HONORS AND AWARDS** Grace A Griffen chemn hist, 92-98; Disting Fac Award, 96. **MEMBERSHIPS** AHA; Am Asn Advan Slavic Studies. **RESEARCH** European socialism; modern Communism and Russia; intellectual history. **SELECTED PUBLICATIONS** Auth, The Forming of the Communist International, Stanford Univ, 64; The Nevada Adventure: A History, Univ Nev, 65, 5th ed, 81; Revolutionists in London, Oxford Univ, 70; The University of Nevada: A Centennial History, Univ Nev, 74; The Reputations of Socrates: The Afterlife of a Gadfly, Peter Lang, 95; The Silver State: Nevada's Heritage Reinterpreted, Univ Nev, 91, 98. **CONTACT ADDRESS** Dept of History, Univ of Nevada, Reno, NV, 89557-0001. **EMAIL** Jhulse@unr.edu

HULTS, LINDA
DISCIPLINE RENAISSANCE AND BAROQUE ART **EDUCATION** Ind Univ, BA, 71; Univ NC, PhD, 78. **CAREER** Assoc prof. **SELECTED PUBLICATIONS** Auth, The Print in the Western World: An Introductory History, Univ Wis Press, 96. **CONTACT ADDRESS** Dept of Art, Col of Wooster, Wooster, OH, 44691.

HUME, RICHARD L.
PERSONAL Born 11/09/1939, Prescott, AZ, m, 1961 **DISCIPLINE** JEFFERSONIAN JACKSONIAN AMERICA, THE CIVIL WAR, RECONSTRUCTION **EDUCATION** Univ Wash, PhD, 69. **CAREER** Prof, Washington State Univ. **MEMBERSHIPS** Southern Hist Asn; Orgn Am Historians. **SELECTED PUBLICATIONS** Co-ed, God Made Man, Man Made the Slave: The Autobiography of George Teamoh, Mercer UP, 90; publ in, J Amer Hist; J Southern Hist & Virginia Mag Hist and Biog. **CONTACT ADDRESS** Dept of History, Washington State Univ, 301 Wilson Hall, PO Box 644030, Pullman, WA, 99164-4030. **EMAIL** rhume@wsu.edu

HUMPHREYS, LEONARD A.
DISCIPLINE HISTORY **EDUCATION** Stanford Univ, MA, 60, PhD, 75. **CAREER** Prof emer, Univ Pacific. **SELECTED PUBLICATIONS** Auth, The Way of the Heavenly Sword: The Japanese Army in the 1920s, Stanford. **CONTACT ADDRESS** Hist Dept, Univ Pacific, Pacific Ave, PO Box 3601, Stockton, CA, 95211.

HUMPHREYS, MARGARET
PERSONAL Born 12/06/1955, New Orleans, LA, d **DISCIPLINE** HISTORY **EDUCATION** Univ Notre Dame, BA, 76; Harvard Univ, MA, 77, PhD, 83; Harvard Medical School, MD, 87. **CAREER** Lect, instr, Harvard Univ, 87-93; staff physician, Harvard Comm Health Plan, 90-93; ASST PROF, HIST & ASST PROF, MEDICINE, DUKE UNIV, 93-. **HONORS AND AWARDS** Phi Beta Kappa, 76; Sigma Xi, 79. **MEMBERSHIPS** Am Asn Hist Med; Soc for Gen Internal Med; Am Hist Asn; Hist for Sci Soc. **RESEARCH** Hist med; US public health. **SELECTED PUBLICATIONS** Auth, "Kicking a Dying Dog: DDT and the Demise of Malaria in the American

South, 1942-1952," Isis 87, 96; "Yellow Fever Since 1793: History and Historiography," in A Melancholy Scene of Devastation: The Public Response to the 1793 Philadelphia Yellow Fever Epidemic, 97; essays on "Chlorosis," "Dengue," "Malaria," "Tuberculosis," "Typhoid Fever," and "Yellow Fever," in Plague, Pox and Pestilence in History, 97; "Water Won't Run Uphill:The New Deal and Malaria Control in the American South, 1933-1940," Parassitologia 40, 98; biographies of "James Lawrence Cabell," "Jerome Cochran," Henry Rose Carter," "John Maynard Woodworth," and "Stanford Emerson Chaille," in American National Biography, 99. **CONTACT ADDRESS** Dept of History, Duke Univ, Box 90719, Durham, NC, 27708.

HUNDERT, EDWARD J.
PERSONAL Born 05/28/1940, New York, NY, m, 1967, 1 child **DISCIPLINE** MODERN & INTELLECTUAL HISTORY **EDUCATION** City Col New York, BA, 61; NY Univ, MA, 63; Univ Rochester, PhD(hist), 69. **CAREER** Asst hist, Univ Rochester, 63-65; asst prof, Univ Calgary, 66-68; asst prof, 68-71, ASSOC PROF HIST, UNIV BC, 71-, Can Coun res grants, 69-71, fel, 72-73 & leave fel, 78-79. **MEMBERSHIPS** AHA; Past & Present Soc, England; Am Philos Asn; Soc Study Hist Philos; Conf for Study of Polit Thought. **RESEARCH** Development of the work ethic; psychoanalysis and history; relationship of the social sciences and history. **SELECTED PUBLICATIONS** Auth, The Politics of Skepticism in the Ancients, Montaigne, Hume, and Kant, Am Hist Rev, Vol 0099, 94; Bernard Mandeville and the Enlightenments Maxims of Modernity, J Hist Ideas, Vol 0056, 95; Stalin and My Father--A Childhood Memoir, Queens Quarterly, Vol 0104, 97; Defining the Common Good--Empire, Religion and Philosophy in 18th-Century Britain, J Modern Hist, Vol 0068, 96. **CONTACT ADDRESS** Dept of Hist, Univ of BC, Vancouver, BC, V6T 1W5.

HUNDLEY, NORRIS CECIL
PERSONAL Born 10/26/1935, Houston, TX, m, 2 children **DISCIPLINE** HISTORY **EDUCATION** Mt. San Antonio Col, AA, 56; Whittier Col, AB, 58; UCLA, PhD, 63. **CAREER** Instr, Univ of Houston, 63-64; ASST PROF OF AM HIST, 64-69, ASSOC PROF, 69-73, PROF, 73-, UCLA; chemn, exec comt, Inst of Am Cultures, 76-93; chemn, Univ prog on Mex, 81-94; acting dir, 89-90, dir, 90-94, Latin Am Center; mem, exec comt, Univ of Calif Consortium on Mex and the U.S., 81-86; mem, adv comt, Calif water atlas project, Calif Office Planning and Res, 77-79. **HONORS AND AWARDS** Award of Merit, Calf Hist Soc, 79; Am Philos Soc grantee, 64 & 71; Ford Found Grantee, 68-69; Univ of Calif Water Resources grantee, 72; NEH Grantee, 83-89; Hewlett Found Grantee, 86-89; Univ of Calif Regenis Fac Fel in Humanities, 75; Guggenheim Fel, 78-79; Hist Soc of Southern Calif Fel, 96-. **MEMBERSHIPS** Am Hist Asn, Western Hist Asn, Orgn Am Hist. **SELECTED PUBLICATIONS** Auth, Dividing the Waters: A Century of Controversy Between the United States and Mexico, 66; auth, Water and the West: The Colorado River Compact and the Politics of Water in the American West, 75; auth, The Great Thirst: Californians and Water, 1770s-1990s, 92; coauth, The California Water Atlas, 79; California: History of a Remarkable State, 82; ed, The American Indian, 74; ed, The Chicano, 75; ed, The Asian American, 76; co-ed, The American West: Frontier and Region, 69; co-ed, Golden State series, 78-; managing ed, Pacific History Review, 68-97. **CONTACT ADDRESS** Dept of History, Univ of Calif, Los Angeles, CA, 90095.

HUNGERFORD, CONSTANCE CAIN
DISCIPLINE ART HISTORY **EDUCATION** Wellesley Col, BA; Univ CA Berkeley, MA; PhD. **CAREER** Prof, Swarthmore Col. **RESEARCH** 19th century French painting. **SELECTED PUBLICATIONS** Auth, Charles Marville..., The Origins of a Photographic Sensibility, 85; numerous articles and essays on Jean-Louis-Ernest Meissonier (1815-1891), and contributions to the catalog for "Ernest Meissonier--Retrospective," an exhibition curated for the Musee des Beaux-Arts. **CONTACT ADDRESS** Swarthmore Col, Swarthmore, PA, 19081-1397. **EMAIL** chunger1@swarthmore.edu

HUNT, BRUCE J.
PERSONAL Born 06/23/1956, Walla Walla, WA, m, 1992, 2 children **DISCIPLINE** HISTORY; PHYSICS; HISTORY OF SCIENCE **EDUCATION** Univ Wash, BA & BS, 79; Johns Hopkins Univ, PhD, 84. **CAREER** Postdoctoral fel, Smithsonian Inst, 84-85; asst prof History, 85-92, ASSOC PROF HISTORY 92-, UNIV TEXAS AT AUSTIN, 85-; vis fel, Cambridge Univ, 89-90. **MEMBERSHIPS** Hist Sci Soc; Soc Hist Technol; Lone Star Hist Sci. **RESEARCH** History of physics; Electrical science; Technology **SELECTED PUBLICATIONS** auth The Ohm is Where the Art Is: British Telegraph Engineers and the Development of Electrical Standard, Osiris, 94; The Maxwellians, Cornell Univ Press, 94; "Scientists, Engineers and Wildman Whitehouse: Measurement and Credibility in Early Cable Telegraphy," Brit Jour Hist Sci, 96; Doing Science in a Global Empire: Cable Telegraphy and Victorian Physics, Victorian Sci in Context, Univ Chicago Press, 97; Insulation for an Empire: Gutta-Percha and the Development of Electrical Measurement in Victorian Britian, Semaphores to Short Waves, Royal Soc Arts, 98. **CONTACT ADDRESS** Dept of History, Univ of Texas at Austin, Austin, TX, 78712. **EMAIL** bjhunt@matl.utexas,edu

HUNT, JAMES
PERSONAL m **DISCIPLINE** AMERICAN HISTORY, HISTORICAL, POLITICAL AND INTERNATIONAL STUDIES **EDUCATION** Univ Wash, BA, MA, PhD, 73. **CAREER** Tchg, Univ Wash; Core prog; Cent Amer Stud/Serv prog; US and World survey classes; prof-. **HONORS AND AWARDS** Burlington Northern award; tchg excellence, grants, FIPSE, NEH. Wash Comm for Hum. **RESEARCH** Latin American Colonial History. **SELECTED PUBLICATIONS** Publ, articles on the faith journeys of Frederick Douglass and Jane Addams. **CONTACT ADDRESS** Dept of Hist, Whitworth Col, 300 West Hawthorne Rd, Spokane, WA, 99251. **EMAIL** junt@whitworth.edu

HUNT, JOHN M., JR.
PERSONAL Born 09/21/1943, Bryn Mawr, PA, s **DISCIPLINE** CLASSICS **EDUCATION** Lafayette Col, AB, 65; Cornell Univ, Post-grad fel, 65-66; Bryn Mawr Col, MA, 68, PhD, 70 **CAREER** Inst, Lafayette Col, 70; Asst Prof, 70-76, Villanova Univ; Visit Assoc Prof, 78-80, Univ of CA, Santa Barbara; Assoc Prof, 84-90, Prof, 91-, Villanova Univ **HONORS AND AWARDS** Who's Who in Am Educ **MEMBERSHIPS** Soc of Mayflower Descendants in PA; Sons of the Revolution; PA Soc **RESEARCH** Latin lit; textual criticism **CONTACT ADDRESS** Wayne, PA, 19087-2423.

HUNT, MICHAEL H.
PERSONAL Born 12/19/1942, Pearsall, TX, m **DISCIPLINE** HISTORY **EDUCATION** Georgetown Univ, BSFS, 68; Yale Univ, MA, 67, PhD, 71. **CAREER** Teaching asst, 67-68, instr, 71-72, asst prof, Yale Univ, 72-78; assoc prof, Colgate Univ, 78-80; assoc prof, 80-83, prof, 83-94, Everett H. Emerson Prof, Univ NC, Chapel Hill, 94-. **HONORS AND AWARDS** Phi Beta Kappa, 65; Fel, 79-80, grant, NEH, 85; res award, Nat Prog for Advanced Study and Res in China, 89; Stuart L. Bernath Memorial Book Award, 84; Fel, Woodrow Wilson Int Center for Scholars, Smithsonian Inst, 90-91; vis scholar grant, Fairbank Center for East Asian Studies, Harvard Univ, 91; Woodrow Wilson grad fel, 65-66; NDEA title IV, 66-69; Fulbright-Hays, 69-70. **MEMBERSHIPS** Am Hist Asn; Asn for Asian Studies; Soc for Hist of Am Foreign Relations; Org of Am Hist. **RESEARCH** The history of U.S. relations; cold war Asia; the Vietnam war; the world since 1945. **SELECTED PUBLICATIONS** Auth, Lyndon Johnson's War: America's Cold War Crusade in Vietnam 1945-1968, Hill and Wang, 96 & 97; Crisis in U.S. Foreign Policy: An International History Reader, Yale Univ Press, 96; The Genesis of Chinese Communist Foreign Plicy, Columbia Univ Press, 96 & 98; Studying the Vietnam War: Between and Implacable Force and an Immovable Object, New England J of Hist, 98; Traditions of American Diplomacy: From Colony to Great Power, Am Foreign Relations Reconsidered 1890-1993, Routledge, 94; Beijing and the Korean Crisis, June 1950-June 1951, Political Sci Quart, 92; The Long Crisis in U.S. Diplomatic History: Coming to Closure, Diplomatic Hist, 92; co-ed, Toward a History of Chinese Communist Foreign Relations 1920s-1960s: Personalities and Interpretive Approaches, Woodrow Wilson Center Asia Prog, 95; **CONTACT ADDRESS** History Dept, Univ of N. Carolina at Chapel Hill, Chapel Hill, NC, 27599-3195.

HUNT, PATRICK
DISCIPLINE CLASSICS **EDUCATION** BA, 77; Dallas Theol Sem, MA, 82; Univ London, PhD, 91. **CAREER** Lctr, Stanford Univ. **RESEARCH** Archaeol and papyrology. **SELECTED PUBLICATIONS** Auth, Holy Moountian, Sacred Stone, Precolumbian Art Res Inst, 94; Maya and Olmec Stone Contests: Basalt and Limestone Weathering Contrasts, Precolumbian Art Res Inst, 94; Sensory Images in the Song of Solomon, 95. **CONTACT ADDRESS** Stanford Univ, Bldg 20, Main Quad, Stanford, CA, 94305.

HUNT, RICHARD ALLEN
PERSONAL Jersey City, NJ **DISCIPLINE** HISTORY **EDUCATION** Rutgers Univ, BA, 64; Univ Pa, MA, 65, PhD(hist), 73. **CAREER** Historian, US Mil Assistance Command, Vietnam, 70-71; HISTORIAN, US ARMY CTR MIL HIST, 71-, Univ Pa teaching fel, 65-67. **MEMBERSHIPS** AHA; French Hist Studies; Soc Historians Am Foreign Rels; US Comn Military Hist. **RESEARCH** Vietnam war; American foreign policy; France. **SELECTED PUBLICATIONS** Auth, Winning Hearts and Minds--British Governments, the Media and Colonial Counterinsurgency, 1944-1960, J Military Hist, Vol 0061, 97; Remembering World-War-II--The Role of Oral-History, Public Historian, Vol 0016, 94. **CONTACT ADDRESS** US Army Ctr Mil Hist, Pulaski Bldg, Washington, DC, 20314.

HUNT, RICHARD M.
PERSONAL Born 10/16/1926, Pittsburgh, PA, m, 1955, 3 children **DISCIPLINE** HISTORY SOCIAL SCIENCE **EDUCATION** Yale Univ, BA, 49; Columbia Univ, MA, 51; Harvard Univ, PhD, 60. **CAREER** SR LECTR SOCIAL STUDIES & DIR MELLON FAC FELS, HARVARD UNIV, 75-, Pres, Am Coun on Ger, New York. **MEMBERSHIPS** AHA **RESEARCH** Nazi German history; 20th century European intellectual history; contemporary sociological theory. **SELECTED PUBLICATIONS** Auth, Surviving the Swastika--Scientific-Research in Nazi Germany, J Interdisciplinary Hist, Vol 0026, 95; The Logic of Evil--The Social Origins of the Nazi Party, 1925-1933, J Interdisciplinary Hist, Vol 0028, 97. **CONTACT ADDRESS** Harvard Univ, 10 Coolidge Hill Rd, Cambridge, MA, 02138.

HUNT, WILLIAM RAYMOND
PERSONAL Born 08/01/1929, Seattle, WA, m, 1963, 2 children **DISCIPLINE** EARLY MODERN HISTORY **EDUCATION** Seattle Univ, BSS, 51; Univ Wash, LLB, 58, MA, 66, PhD(hist), 67. **CAREER** From asst prof to assoc prof, 67-74, PROF HIST, UNIV ALASKA, FAIRBANKS, 74-, HEAD DEPT, 71- **RESEARCH** Travel and exploration; crime and roguery; Arctic. **SELECTED PUBLICATIONS** Auth, Going to Meet a Man--Denver Last Legal Public Execution, 27 July 1886, Pacific NW Quarterly, Vol 0084, 93. **CONTACT ADDRESS** Dept of Hist, Univ of Alaska, Fairbanks, AK, 99701.

HUNTER, GARY
PERSONAL Born 09/23/1946, Coatesville, PA, m, 1969, 3 children **DISCIPLINE** HISTORY **EDUCATION** Lincoln Univ, BA, 69; Atlanta Univ, MA, 70; Univ Mich, PhD, 77. **CAREER** Inst, Fisk Univ, 70-71; vis prof, Univ Calabar, 81-83; Rowan Univ, 74-. **HONORS AND AWARDS** NAACP Citizenship Award; New Jersey Black Educators Award for Teaching. **MEMBERSHIPS** Am Hist Asn; African Hist Asn. **RESEARCH** African American and African history. **SELECTED PUBLICATIONS** Auth, Neighborhoods of Color: African American Communities of South Jersey, 90. **CONTACT ADDRESS** Dept of History, Rowan Univ, Glassboro, NJ, 08028. **EMAIL** hunter@rowan.edu

HUNTER, JOHN
DISCIPLINE RENAISSANCE ART HISTORY **EDUCATION** Wayne State Univ, BPh, 65, MA, 71; Univ Mich, MA, 77, PhD, 83. **CAREER** Edu cur, Detroit Inst Arts; assoc prof, ch; instr, 82-. **RESEARCH** Study of portraits of renaissance cardinals. **SELECTED PUBLICATIONS** Auth, monograph of the sixteenth-century Roman painter Girolamo Siciolante da Sermoneta (Girolamo Siciolante: Pittore da Sermoneta, Rome, 96; publ, articles on renaissance topics, The Art Bulletin, Romisches Jarhbuch fur Kunstgeschichte, Master Drawings, Storia dell'Arte. **CONTACT ADDRESS** Dept of Art, Cleveland State Univ, 83 E 24th St, Cleveland, OH, 44115.

HUNTER, LESLIE GENE
DISCIPLINE HISTORY **EDUCATION** Univ Ariz, BA, 64, MA, 66, PhD, 71. **CAREER** Asst prof, 69-74, assoc prof, 74-81, prof, 81-98, REGENTS PROF, 98-, TEX A&M UNIV, KINGSVILLE; Chair dept hist, Tex A&M Univ, Kingsville, 86-90, 91-96. **CONTACT ADDRESS** Dept of History, Texas A&M Univ, Kingsville, MSC 166, Kingsville, TX, 78363. **EMAIL** kflgh00@tamuk.edu

HUNTER, PHYLLIS A.
DISCIPLINE HISTORY, AMERICAN STUDIES **EDUCATION** Harvard Univ, BA, 65; So Flor, MA, 90; Will & Mary, PhD, 96. **CAREER** ASST PROF, HIST, NC AT GREENSBORO **MEMBERSHIPS** Am Antiquarian Soc **SELECTED PUBLICATIONS** Auth, Ship of Wealth: Massachusetts Merchants, Foreign Goods, and the Transformation of Anglo-America, 1670-1760; reviews in Va Mag Hist and Biog and Gender and Hist. **CONTACT ADDRESS** Hist Dept, Univ of N Carol at Greensboro, 219 McIver, Greensboro, NC, 27412-5001. **EMAIL** pwhunter@fagan.uncg.edu

HUNTING, MARY ANNE
PERSONAL Born 07/26/1957, Grand Rapids, MI, s **DISCIPLINE** HISTORY OF DECORATIVE ARTS **EDUCATION** BA, Vanderbilt Univ, MDA, Parsons School of Design. **CAREER** Asst ed, The Magazine Antiques, 90-94; freelance writer, antiques, 94-98. **MEMBERSHIPS** Show Catalogue. **RESEARCH** 19th century interiors and decorative arts. **CONTACT ADDRESS** 186 Riverside Dr., Apt. 16C, New York, NY, 10024. **EMAIL** mhunt6994@aol.com

HUPCHICK, DENNIS P.
PERSONAL Born 09/03/1948, Monongahela, PA, m, 1976, 2 children **DISCIPLINE** HISTORY **EDUCATION** Univ Pittsburgh, Ba, 70, MA, 72, PhD, 83. **CAREER** ASSOC PROF, HIST, WILKES UNIV, 90-. **HONORS AND AWARDS** Fulbright res scholar Bulgaria, 89; Wilkes Univ Fac Lect award, 94; Int Res, Exch Bd Res Exch Scholar, Bulgaria, 76-77; NDFL-VI Lang gel, Univ Pittsburgh, 77-78, 75-76, 74-75., Dir, Wilkes Univ E European, Rus Stud Prog **MEMBERSHIPS** Bulgarian Studies Asn; Am Asn Adv Slavic Stud. **RESEARCH** Hist Bulgaria, Balkans, Ottoman Emp, Byzantine Emp, East Europe. **SELECTED PUBLICATIONS** Co-auth, A Concise Historical Atlas of Eastern Europe, St. Martin's Press, 96; auth, Conflict and Chaos in Eastern Europe, St. Martin's Press, 95; auth, Culture and History in Eastern Europe, St. Martin's Press, 94; co-ed, Bulgaria, Past & Present: Transitions & Turning Points, vol 9 of Balkanistica, 96; auth, Seventeenth-Century Cultural Contacts Between Bulgarians and Romanians, Romanian Civilization 5, no 3, winter 96-97; auth, A Statistical Overview of Seventeenth-Century Bulgarian Orthodox Society and

Culture, Bulgaria, Past & PResent: Transitions & Turning Points, in Balkanistica 9, 96. **CONTACT ADDRESS** History Dept, Wilkes Univ, Wilkes-Barre, PA, 18766. **EMAIL** dhupchi@wilkes1.wilkes.edu

HUPPERT, GEORGE
PERSONAL Born 02/21/1934, Tesin, Czechoslovakia, m, 1956, 5 children **DISCIPLINE** HISTORY **EDUCATION** Univ Calif Berkeley, PhD, 62. **CAREER** Prof, 65-, Univ Il Chicago. **HONORS AND AWARDS** Guggenheim Fel; NEH Fel, ACLS Fel; Bronze Medal, Col de France. **MEMBERSHIPS** Hist Soc; Soc for French Hist Stud. **RESEARCH** Renaissance France **SELECTED PUBLICATIONS** Auth, The Idea of Perfect History: Historical Erudition and Historical Philosophy in Renaissance France, Univ Il Press, 70; auth, Les Bourgeois Gentilshommes: An Essay on the Definition of Elitesin Renaissance France, Univ Chicago Press, 77; auth, Public Schools in Renaissance France, Univ Il Press, 84; auth, After the Black Death: A Social History of Early Modern Europe, Ind Univ Press, 98; auth, Il Mulino, Bologna, Italy, 90; auth, The Style of Paris: Renaissance Origins of the French Enlightenment, Ind Univ Press, 99. **CONTACT ADDRESS** 832 Seventeenth St, Wilmette, IL, 60091. **EMAIL** huppert@uic.edu

HURLEY, ALFRED FRANCIS
PERSONAL Born 10/16/1928, Brooklyn, NY, m, 1953, 5 children **DISCIPLINE** MODERN HISTORY **EDUCATION** St John's Univ, NY, BA, 50; Princeton Univ, MA, 58, PhD, 61. **CAREER** US Air Force, 52-80, from instr to asst prof, 58-62, res assoc, 62-63, actg head dept, 66-67, prof hist, US Air Force Acad, 66-80, head dept, 67-80, chmn humanities div, 77-80; vpres admin affairs, 80-82, PROF HIST, NTEX STATE UNIV, 81-, PRES, 82-; CHANCELLOR, TEX COL OSTEOPATHIC MED, 82-, Guggenheim fel, 71-72; dir, Am Comt Hist 2nd World War, 73-; trustee, Am Mil Inst, 73-; dir, US Comn Mil Hist, 75-; fel, Eisenhower Inst Hist res, Smithsonian Inst, 76-77; trustee, Air Force Hist Fedn, 80- **MEMBERSHIPS** AHA; Orgn Am Historians **RESEARCH** Modern military and diplomatic history. **SELECTED PUBLICATIONS** Auth, Carl Spaatz, and the Air War in Europe, Am Hist Rev, Vol 0100, 95. **CONTACT ADDRESS** 828 Skylark, Denton, TX, 76201.

HURLEY, ANDREW J.
PERSONAL Born 06/19/1961, New York, NY **DISCIPLINE** HISTORY **EDUCATION** Johns Hopkins Univ, BA, MA, 83; Northwestern Univ, PhD, 88. **CAREER** Asst prof, Rhodes Col, 88-91; assoc prof, Univ Mo St. Louis, 91-99. **SELECTED PUBLICATIONS** Auth, Creating Ecological Wastelands: Oil Pollution in New York City, 1870-1900, J of Urban Hist, 94; Environmental Inequalities: Class, Race, and Industrial Pollution in Gary, Indiana, 1945-1980, Univ of NC Press, 95; Fiasco at Wagner Electric: Environmental Justice and Urban Geography, Environmental Hist, 97; From Hash House to Family Restaurant: The Transformation of the Diner and Post-War II Consumer Culture, J of Amer Hist, 97; ed, Common Fields: An Environmental History of St. Louis, Mo Hist Soc Press, 97. **CONTACT ADDRESS** Dept of History, Univ of Mo St. Louis, St. Louis, MO, 63121. **EMAIL** sahurle@umslvma.emsl.edu

HURLEY, DAVID
DISCIPLINE MUSIC HISTORY AND OBOE **EDUCATION** Univ Mich, BA, 80; Univ Chicago, MA, PhD, 90, 91. **CAREER** Asst prof, 96- **RESEARCH** Seventeenth- and eighteenth-century music, G. Fl handel. **SELECTED PUBLICATIONS** Publ, articles and rev(s), The Jour of Musicol Res, The Mus Quart. **CONTACT ADDRESS** Dept of Mus, Pittsburg State Univ, 1701 S Broadway St, Pittsburg, KS, 66762. **EMAIL** dhurley@pittstate.edu

HURLEY, FORREST JACK
PERSONAL Born 08/28/1940, Ft. Worth, TX, m, 1961, 3 children **DISCIPLINE** AMERICAN SOCIAL HISTORY, HISTORY OF PHOTOGRAPHY **EDUCATION** Austin Col, BA, 62; Tulane Univ, MA, 66, PhD(hist), 71. **CAREER** Instr, 66-71, asst prof, 71-76, assoc prof, 76-81, PROF HIST, MEMPHIS STATE UNIV, 81-; Humanist in residence, Int Mus Photog George Eastman House, Rochester, 74-75; vis prof, Austin Col, summer, 80. **HONORS AND AWARDS** Young Humanist Award, Nat Endowment for the Humanities, 72, BiCentennial Award, 74-75; Lyndhurst Prize, 90, for distinguished and original writing on photography and culture. **MEMBERSHIPS** Southern Hist Asn; Soc Hist Technol. **RESEARCH** History of photography as a social force in American culture; southern regional social and cultural history; history of technology. **SELECTED PUBLICATIONS** Auth, Portrait of a Decade, LA State Univ Press, 72; Russell Lee: Photographer, Morgan & Morgan, 78; ed, Industry and the Photographic Image, Dover, 80; coauth, Tennessee Traditional Singers, Univ TN Press, 80; co-ed, Southern Eye: Southern Mind--A Photographic Inquiry, Memphis Acad of the Arts, 81; Marion Post Wolcott: A Photographic Journey, Univ NM Press, 89. **CONTACT ADDRESS** Hist Dept, Memphis State Univ, 3706 Alumni St, Memphis, TN, 38152-0001. **EMAIL** jhurley@cc.memphis.edu

HURLEY, JAMES
DISCIPLINE MARRIAGE; FAMILY THERAPY **EDUCATION** Harvard Univ, BA; Cambridge Univ, PhD; Florida State Univ, PhD. **CAREER** Dept ch; prof. **HONORS AND AWARDS** Gold Medallion awd as the Evangel Bk Yr, Man and Woman in Bibl Perspective., Clinical supervisor, Amer Assn for Marriage and Family Therapy. **MEMBERSHIPS** Bd mem, Miss Assn for Marriage and Family Therapy; Pastoral Counseling Inst. **RESEARCH** New Testament, theology, and counseling. **SELECTED PUBLICATIONS** Auth, Man and Woman in Biblical Perspective. **CONTACT ADDRESS** Dept of Marriage and Family Therapy, Reformed Theol Sem, 5422 Clinton Blvd, Jackson, MS, 39209-3099.

HUSTON, JAMES ALVIN
PERSONAL Born 03/24/1918, Fairmount, IN, m, 1946, 2 children **DISCIPLINE** HISTORY **EDUCATION** Ind Univ, Ab, 39, AM, 40; NY Univ, PhD, 47. **CAREER** From instr to prof hist, Purdue Univ, 46-72; PROF HIST & INT RELS & DEAN, LYNCHBURG COL, 72-, King prof maritime hist, US Naval War Col, 59-60; NATO fel, 63-64; prof foreign affairs, Nat War Col, 66-67, dir Europ studies, 71-72. **MEMBERSHIPS** AHA; Am Mil Inst; Inst Strategic Studies, Eng; London Inst World Affairs. **RESEARCH** National security policy; United States military history; political geography. **SELECTED PUBLICATIONS** Auth, A Dam and Bloody Ground--The Hurtgen Forest and the Roer River Dams, 1944-1945, J Am Hist, Vol 0083, 96. **CONTACT ADDRESS** Lynchburg Col, Lynchburg, VA, 24501.

HUSTON, RICHARD P.
DISCIPLINE HISTORY **EDUCATION** Greenville Col, BA, 78; Asbury Sem, MDiv, 86; Univ Calif, Los Angeles, Phd, 93. **CAREER** Assoc prof, Aldersgate Col, 92-94; DEPT CHAIR, HIST, GREENVILLE COL, 94-. **CONTACT ADDRESS** 315 E College Ave, Greenville, IL, 62246. **EMAIL** rhuston@greenville.edu

HUTCHESON, JOHN AMBROSE, JR.
PERSONAL Born 07/18/1944, Winston - Salem, NC, m, 1967, 2 children **DISCIPLINE** HISTORY **EDUCATION** Univ N Carolina, Chapel Hill, AB, 66, MA, 68, PhD, 73. **CAREER** Instr, 73-74, Univ N Carolina; asst prof, 74-90, assoc prof, 90-97, prof, 97-, chmn, div of Soc Sci, 97-, Dalton St Col. **RESEARCH** 19th & 20th century Britain; conservative party, naval & maritime hist. **CONTACT ADDRESS** Div of Soc Sci, Dalton Col, Dalton, GA, 30720. **EMAIL** jhutcheson@ca_pet.dalton.peachnet.edu

HUTCHESON, THOM
DISCIPLINE MUSIC **EDUCATION** Univ Tex-El Paso, BA; Northwestern Univ, MA; Fla State Univ, PhD. **CAREER** Dept Muis, Middle Tenn State Univ **HONORS AND AWARDS** Composer-of-the-Yr, Tenn Mus Teachers Asn. **MEMBERSHIPS** Past dir, Amer Soc Univ Composers. **SELECTED PUBLICATIONS** Auth, Synvironment, Atlanta Int Film Festival; The Tightrope Walker March, for Concert Band; Macarena, for Jazz Ensemble & Multiphonix, for Percussion Ensemble. **CONTACT ADDRESS** Dept of Music, Middle Tennessee State Univ, 1301 E Main St, Murfreesboro, TN, 37132-0001. **EMAIL** lthutch@frank.mtsu.edu

HUTCHINSON, GEORGE
PERSONAL Born 12/19/1938, Albuquerque, NM, m **DISCIPLINE** EDUCATION **EDUCATION** California State Univ Los Angeles, BS 1969, MS 1971; United States International Univ, PhD 1977; National University, San Diego, California, Post Doctoral Law 1988. **CAREER** CALIFORNIA STATE UNIV, ASSOC DEAN EDUC SUPPORT SERV 1986-; SAN DIEGO STATE UNIV, asst prof dept of recreation 1973-79, asst dean 1974-77 assoc dean 1978-81 college of professional studies and fine arts, ASSOC PROF DEPT OF RECREATION 1979-, DIR STUDENT OUTREACH SERV DIR 1981-. **HONORS AND AWARDS** Honorary Mem US Navy ROTC Selection Bd Chief of Naval Opers Washington DC 1979-82; Distinguished Alumna San Diego Comm Leadership Develop 1980; Honorary Member Phi Kappa Phi San Diego State Univ 1980-86; Letter of Commendation, Mayor, City of San Diego, 1989; Proclamation, Board of Supervisors, 1990; Resolution, Assemblyman Chacon 75th District, 1990; San Diego Urban League, Letter of Commendation, 1991; National Black Child Dev Inc, Certificate of Appreciation, 1992; San Diego Housing Commission, Proclamation, 1992. **MEMBERSHIPS** Mem Advisory Council for Minority Officer Recruiting US Navy 1977-; mem at large Industry Educ Council Greater San Diego 1980-; mem Phi Kappa Phi; mem bd dirs Amer Cancer Society 1984-; mem Athletic Adv Comm 1985-; mem Senate Comm Minority; mem CA Academic Partnership Program 1985-; mem Naval Reserve Officers Assn, Navy League of the US; member, San Diego Chapter, Urban League; member, State Bar of California, 1988-; president, Boy Scouts of America Explorers Division, 1988-. **SELECTED PUBLICATIONS** Publications including "Trends Affecting Black Recreators in the Professional Society," California Parks and Recreation Society Magazine 1981; Role of Higher Educ in Educational Reform of Adolescents 1988; Meeting the Challenge of Technology 1988. **CONTACT ADDRESS** Student Outreach Serv, San Diego State Univ, San Diego, CA, 92182-0777.

HUTCHISON, JANE CAMPBELL
PERSONAL Born 07/20/1932, Washington, DC **DISCIPLINE** ART HISTORY **EDUCATION** Western Md Col, BA, 54; Oberlin Col, MA, 58; Univ Wis, PhD, 64. **CAREER** From instr to assoc prof, 63-75, chmn dept, 77-80, PROF ART HIST, UNIV WIS-MADISON, 75-; Consult, NEH, 71-. **HONORS AND AWARDS** Elected Print Counc Am, 94; Trustee Alumni Award, Western Md Col; Major grant, DAAD, ACLS, Fulbright. **MEMBERSHIPS** Col Art Asn Am; Mediaeval Acad Am; Mid-Am Col Art (secy, 69-70); AAUP; Midwest Art Hist Soc (treas, 81-83); Hist Netherlandish Art (treas, 94-); Am Asc Netherlandis Studies. **RESEARCH** Fifteenth century German graphics; fifteenth century Flemish, Dutch and German portraiture; seventeenth century Flemish and Dutch low-genre p ainting. **SELECTED PUBLICATIONS** Auth, The housebook master and the folly of the wise man, Art Bull, 3/66; The Housebook Master, Collectors Ed, Van Nostrand, 72; 17th Century Dutch and Flemish Paintings from Private Collections, exhib catalogue, E lvehjem Art Ctr, 75; The housebook master and the Mainz Marienleben, Prin t Rev: A Tribute to Wolfgang Stechow, 2/76; Der vielgefeierte Durer, in Deutsche Feiern, Athenaion, Wiesbaden, 77; Early German Artists: Master E S-Schongauer, The Illustrated Bartsch 8, 80; Early German Artists: Wenze l von Qlmutz-Monogrammists, The Illustrated Bartsch 9, 81; Albrecht Durer : A Biography, Princeton Univ Press, 90; Albrecht Durer: Eine Biographie, Campus Verlag, 94. **CONTACT ADDRESS** Elvehjem Art Ctr, Univ of Wis, 800 University Ave, Madison, WI, 53706-1479. **EMAIL** jchutchi@facstaff.wisc.edu

HUTCHISON, WILLIAM ROBERT
PERSONAL Born 05/21/1930, San Francisco, CA, m, 1952, 4 children **DISCIPLINE** AMERICAN HISTORY **EDUCATION** Hamilton Col, BA, 51; Oxford Univ, Fulbright Scholar, BA, 53, MA, 57; Yale Univ, PhD(hist), 56. **CAREER** Instr hist, Hunter Col, 56-58; assoc prof Am studies, Am Univ, 58-64, prof hist & Am studies, 64-68; Charles Warren prof Hist Relig in Am, Harvard Univ, 68-, Master Winthrop House, 74-79; Guggenheim fel, 60-61; ed consult, UNESCO, 62-69; Am Philos Soc grant, 65; vis assoc prof hist, Univ Wis, 63-64; res fel, Charles Warren Ctr, Harvard Univ, 66-67; mem Am studies adv comt, Am Coun Learned Soc, 68-71; Fulbright sr res grant, Free Univ, Berlin, 76; Asn Theol Schs grants, 79; Fulbright distinguished lectr Am hist, India, 81, Indonesia, 93; Fulbright Regional Reasearch grant, W Europe, 87; Olaus Petri Lecturer, Uppsala Univ, Sweden, 96. **HONORS AND AWARDS** Egleston Prize, Yale Univ, 56; Brewer Prize, Am Soc Church Hist, 57, Nat'l Rel Book Award, 76., MA, Harvard Univ, 68. **MEMBERSHIPS** AHA; Am Studies Asn; Am Soc Church Hist (pres, 81); Orgn Am Historians; Unitarian Hist Soc; Am Acad Relig. **RESEARCH** American intellectual history; American religious history; comparative cultural history. **SELECTED PUBLICATIONS** Auth, Transcendentalist Ministers: Church Reform in the New England Renaissance, Yale Univ, 59; Liberal Protestantism and the End of Innocence, Am Quart, summer 63; ed, American Protestant Thought: The Liberal Era, Harper, 68; contribr, UNESCO History of the Scientific and Cultural Development of Mankind, Laffont, Paris, Vol V, 69; auth, Cultural Strain and Protestant Liberalism, Am Hist Rev, 71; The Americanness of the Social Gospel: an Inquiry in Comparative History, Church Hist, 9/75; The Modernist Impulse in American Protestantism, Harvard Univ, 76; Errand to the World: American Protestant Thought and Foreign Missions, Univ of Chicago, 87; ed, Between the Times: The Travail of the Protestant Establishment in America, 1900-1960, Cambridge Univ, 89; co-ed with H. Lehman, Many are Chosen: Divine Election and Western Nationalism, Fortress, 94. **CONTACT ADDRESS** Divinity Sch, Harvard Univ, 45 Francis Ave, Cambridge, MA, 02138-1994. **EMAIL** whutchis@fas.harvard.edu

HUTTENBACH, HENRY R.
PERSONAL Born 10/15/1930, Worms, Germany, 5 children **DISCIPLINE** HISTORY **EDUCATION** Gonzaga Univ, BA, 51; Univ WA, PhD(hist), 61. **CAREER** Instr hist, Univ Seattle, 56-59; asst prof, E TX State Univ, 60-61; asst prof, LA State Univ, 61-66; from asst prof to assoc prof, 66-78, prof hist, City Col New York, 78-; US State Dept Cult Exchange Scholar, Moscow State Univ, 64-65 & 75. **MEMBERSHIPS** AHA; Am Asn Advan Slavic Studies; Asn Jewish Studies; Asn for the Study of Nationalities. **RESEARCH** 15th and 16th century Russian history; contemporary German Jewish history; genocide. **SELECTED PUBLICATIONS** Contribr, Russian Expansionism, Rutgers Univ Press, 72; The Emigration Book of Worms, Koblenz, 74; The Destruction of the Jewish Community of Worms, 1933-1945, New York, 81. **CONTACT ADDRESS** Dept Hist, City Col, CUNY, 160 Convent Ave, New York, NY, 10031-9198.

HUTTON, JOHN
DISCIPLINE NINETEENTH-CENTURY EUROPEAN AND AMERICAN ART **EDUCATION** Northwestern Univ, PhD. **CAREER** Assoc prof, Truman State Univ. **SELECTED PUBLICATIONS** Pub(s), relationship of art and soc. **CONTACT ADDRESS** Dept of Art Hist, Trinity Univ, 715 Stadium Dr, San Antonio, TX, 78212. **EMAIL** jhutton@trinity.edu

HUTTON, PATRICK H.
PERSONAL Born 03/16/1938, Trenton, NJ, m, 1991, 5 children **DISCIPLINE** MODERN EUROPEAN HISTORY **EDUCATION** Princeton Univ, AB, 60; Univ Wis, MA, 64, PhD, 69. **CAREER** From Instr to Assoc Prof, 68-82, Prof Hist, Univ Vt, 82-, Chair, Dept Hist, 92-. **HONORS AND AWARDS** Kent fel, 65-68; Am Coun Learned Socs grant-in-aid, 74-75; UVM bicentennial fel, 88; Sr Fulbright research fel, France, 95-96. **MEMBERSHIPS** Soc Values Higher Educ; Soc Fr Hist Studies; Am Hist Asn; Fulbright Asn. **RESEARCH** French history; European intellectual history; historiography. **SELECTED PUBLICATIONS** Auth, The Cult of the Revolutionary Tradition, Univ Calif Press, 81; History as an Art of Memory, Univ Press New Eng, 93; ed, Historical Dictionary of the Third French Republic, 1870-1940, Greenwood Press, 86; co-ed, Technologies of the Self: A Seminar with Michael Foucault, Univ Mass Press, 88; ed, Vico for Historians, special issue of Historical Reflections XXII/3, 96. **CONTACT ADDRESS** Dept Hist, Univ Vt, Burlington, VT, 05405-0164. **EMAIL** phutton@polyglot.uvm.edu

HUTTON, WILLIAM E.
PERSONAL Born 07/26/1961, Bellefonte, PA, m, 1991 **DISCIPLINE** CLASSICS **EDUCATION** Penn State Univ, BA, 82; Univ Tex Austin, MA, 85; PhD, 95. **CAREER** Vis asst prof, Univ Wis Madison, 91-92; instr, Univ Calgary, 92-96; vis asst prof, Truman State Univ, 96-97; vis asst prof, Coll of William and Mary, 97-. **HONORS AND AWARDS** Phi Beta Kappa; Phi Alpha Theta; Phi Kappa Phi; James R Wheeler Fel; Jacob Hirsch Fel; Eugene Vaderpool Fel, Am School of Classical Studies in Athens. **MEMBERSHIPS** Am Philol Asn; Archaeol Inst of Am; Classical Asn of the Middle W and S; Classical Asn of Va. **RESEARCH** Greek Prose; Greek History; Greek Historiography; Greek topography. **SELECTED PUBLICATIONS** Auth, The Meaning of ge-te-o in Linear B, Minos, 90-91. **CONTACT ADDRESS** Dept of Classical Studies, Col of William and Mary, Box 8795, Williamsburg, VA, 23187-8795. **EMAIL** wehutt@facsraff.wm.edu

HUZAR, ELEANOR GOLTZ
PERSONAL Born 06/15/1922, St. Paul, MN, m, 1950 **DISCIPLINE** ANCIENT HISTORY **EDUCATION** Univ Minn, BA, 43; Cornell Univ, MA, 45, PhD(hist), 49. **CAREER** Instr hist, Stanford Univ, 48-50; from instr to asst prof classics, Univ Ill, 51-55; assoc prof hist, Southeastern Mo State Col, 55-59; assoc prof classics, Carleton Col, 59-60; from asst prof to assoc prof, 60-70, PROF HIST, MICH STATE UNIV, 70-, CHMN PROG CLASS STUDIES, 64- **MEMBERSHIPS** AHA; Am Philol Asn; Class Asn Mid W & S; Asn Ancient Historians; Archaeol Inst of Am. **RESEARCH** Relations between the Roman Republic and Egypt; the Fall of the Roman Republic; Greek athletics. **SELECTED PUBLICATIONS** Auth, Philhellenism and Imperialism--Ideological Aspects of the Roman Conquest of the Hellenistic World from the 2nd Macedonian War to the War Against Mithridates, Am Hist Rev, Vol 0097, 92. **CONTACT ADDRESS** Dept of Hist, Michigan State Univ, East Lansing, MI, 48824.

HYATT, IRWIN T., JR.
DISCIPLINE HISTORY **EDUCATION** Emory Univ, BA, 57, MA, 58; Harvard Univ, PhD, 69. **CAREER** Assoc prof **RESEARCH** East Asian history, especially modern Chinese history and Sino-American relations. **SELECTED PUBLICATIONS** Auth, Ordered Lives Confess. **CONTACT ADDRESS** Dept History, Emory Univ, 1380 Oxford Rd NE, Atlanta, GA, 30322-1950.

HYDE JR., JAMES F.
DISCIPLINE MODERN LITERARY CRITICISM, MEDIEVAL, BAROQUE AND CLASSICAL GERMAN LITERATUR **EDUCATION** Princeton Univ, AB; IN Univ, AM, PhD. **CAREER** Prof, ch, dept Ger, dir, Bonn prog, Ripon Col. **HONORS AND AWARDS** NEH grants. **SELECTED PUBLICATIONS** Publ widely on medieval, baroque and class Ger lit, baroque novel, Goethe and Schiller. **CONTACT ADDRESS** Ripon Col, Ripon, WI. **EMAIL** HydeJ@mac.ripon.edu

HYER, PAUL V.
PERSONAL Born 06/02/1926, Ogden, UT, m, 1948, 8 children **DISCIPLINE** ASIAN HISTORY, CULTURE **EDUCATION** Brigham Young Univ, BA, 51; Univ Calif, Berkeley, MA, 53, PhD, 60. **CAREER** Asst prof to prof, 58-66, Coordr, Asian Studies Prog, 61-67, Prof hist & Asian Studies, Brigham Young Univ, 66-; res, Toyo Bunko on Mongolia & China border lands, 63-64, Academia Sinica, 66-67; vis prof, Chengchi Univ, 71-72; ed, Mongolia Soc Bull, 69-; vis prof, Inner Mongolia Univ, 81. **HONORS AND AWARDS** Maeser Award for Excellence in Res. **MEMBERSHIPS** Asn of Asian Studies; Mongolia Soc; Int Altaistic Conf. **RESEARCH** Modern Mongolian & Tibetan history; Japanese expansion. **SELECTED PUBLICATIONS** Ed, Papers of the CIC Far Eastern Language Institute, Univ of Mich, 63; The Cultural Revolution in Inner Mongolia, China Quart, 68; articles in: Encycl Americana, 70; Hu Shih: The Diplomacy of Gentle Persuasions, The Diplomats in Crisis, Am Bibliog Ctr, 74; The Mongolian Nation Within the People's Republic of China, Case Studies on Human Rights and Fundamental Freedoms, The Hague, 75; The Chin-tan-tao Movement: A Chinese Revolt in Mongolia, Altaica, Helsinki, 77; Mongolian Stereotypes and Images, J Mongolian Studies, 78; Mongolia's Culture and Society, Praeger's Westview, 79. **CONTACT ADDRESS** Kennedy Center for Int Studies, Brigham Young Univ, HRCB, Provo, UT, 84602-0002. **EMAIL** pnkhyer@aol.com

HYERS, M. CONRAD
PERSONAL Born 07/31/1933, Philadelphia, PA, m, 1955, 3 children **DISCIPLINE** COMPARATIVE MYTHOLOGY & HISTORY OF RELIGIONS **EDUCATION** Carson-Newman Col, BA, 54; Eastern Theol Sem, BD, 58; Princeton Theol Sem, ThM, 59, PhD(phenomenol relig), 65. **CAREER** From instr to assoc prof hist relig, Beloit Col, 65-77; assoc prof, 77-81, PROF HIST RELIG, GUSTAVUS ADOLPHUS COL, 81-97, PROF EMER 97-. **HONORS AND AWARDS** Humanities develop grant, 69; Assoc Col Midwest non-Western studies fel, East-West Ctr, 70; Nat Found Humanities fel, 70-71; Fund Studies Great Relig fel, 71; Nat Found Humanities res fel, 75-76. **MEMBERSHIPS** Am Acad Relig **RESEARCH** A phenomenological study of the mythological motifs of Paradise Lost, fall and degeneration; a phenomenological study of the nature and function of comedy and humor in relation to the sacred; interfaith relations. **SELECTED PUBLICATIONS** Auth, Holy Laughter: Essays on Religion in the Comic Perspective, Seabury, 69; The Dialectic of the Sacred and the Comic, Cross Currents, winter 69; The Ancient Ch'an Master as Clown Figure and Comic Midwife, Philos East & West, winter, 69-70; The Comic Perspective in Zen Literature and Art, Eastern Buddhist, 72; Zen and the Comic Spirit, Rider, London, 73; The Chickadees: A Contemporary Zen Fable, Westminster, 74; The Comic Vision and the Christian Faith, Pilgrim, 81; The Meaning of Creation: Genesis and Modern Science, John Knox, 84; And God Created Laughter, The Bible as Divine Comedy, John Knox, 86; Once-Born, Twice-Born Zen, The Soto and Rinzai Schools of Japan, Hollowbrook, 89; The Laughing Buddha, Hollowbrook, 90; The Spirituality of Comedy, Comic Heroism in a Tragic World, Transaction Publ, 96. **CONTACT ADDRESS** 2162 Harbor View Drive, Dunedin, FL, 34698.

HYMAN, HAROLD MELVIN
PERSONAL Born 07/24/1924, New York, NY, m, 1946, 3 children **DISCIPLINE** UNITED STATES HISTORY **EDUCATION** Univ Calif, BA, 48; Columbia Univ, MA, 50, PhD, 52. **CAREER** Asst prof hist, Earlham Col, 52-55; vis asst prof, Univ Calif, Los Angeles, 55-56, from assoc prof to prof, 57-63; prof, Univ Ill, 63-68; WILLIAM HOBBY PROF AM HIST, RICE UNIV, 68-, Fund for Repub fel, 56; assoc prof, Ariz State Univ, 56-57; Soc Sci Res Coun res award, 59; Nat Endowment for Humanities sr fel hist & law, 70-71; juror, Pulitzer Prize Selection Jury, 72 & 77; Fulbright sr lectr, Univ Tokyo & Keio Univ, 73; Meyer vis distinguished prof, NY Univ Sch Law, 82-. **HONORS AND AWARDS** Beveridge Award, AHA, 52; Hillman Award, 59. **MEMBERSHIPS** AHA Orgn Am Historians. **RESEARCH** Civil War, legal and constitutional histories; legal history of cities; civil-military relationships. **SELECTED PUBLICATIONS** Auth, One Dies, Get Another--Convict Leasing in the American South, 1866-1928, Labor Hist, Vol 0037, 96. **CONTACT ADDRESS** Dept of Hist, Rice Univ, Houston, TX, 77001.

I

IACOVETTA, FRANCA
PERSONAL Born 09/14/1957, Toronto, ON, Canada **DISCIPLINE** CANADIAN HISTORY **EDUCATION** York Univ, BA, 80, MA, 81, PhD, 88. **CAREER** Postdoctoral fel, Univ Guelph, 88-89; Canada res fel, SSHRCC, 89-90; PROF CANADIAN HISTORY, UNIV TORONTO, 90-. **HONORS AND AWARDS** Hilda Neatby Prize, 86; Univ Toronto Jr Connaught Res fel, 91; Floyd Chalmers Award Ont hist, 92; Toronto Hist Bd Award Merit, 92. **MEMBERSHIPS** Can Hist Asn. **SELECTED PUBLICATIONS** Auth, Such Hardworking People, 92; co-ed, Gender Conflicts, 92; co-ed, Social History of Canada (ser), 92-94; co-ed, Studies in Gender and History (ser), 94-; co-ed, Teaching Women's History, 95; co-ed, Themes in Social History (ser), 96-; chief ed, A Nation of Immigrants: Women, Workers & Communities in Canadian History 1840s-1960s, 97. **CONTACT ADDRESS** Dept of History, Univ Toronto, Toronto, ON, M5S 3G3.

IDE, HARRY
DISCIPLINE ANCIENT, HELLENISTIC, AND MEDIEVAL PHILOSOPHY **EDUCATION** Cornell Univ, PhD, 88. **CAREER** Assoc prof, Univ Nebr, Lincoln. **RESEARCH** Aristotle's views about possibility and necessity. **SELECTED PUBLICATIONS** Auth, Dunamis in Metaphysics 9, Apeiron 35, 92; Aristotle, Metaphysics 6.2-3, and determinism, Ancient Philos 13, 93; Hobbes Contractarian Account of Individual Responsibility for Group Actions, J of Value Inquiry 27, 93. **CONTACT ADDRESS** Univ Nebr, Lincoln, Lincoln, NE, 68588-0417.

IGGERS, GEORG G.
PERSONAL Born 12/07/1926, Hamburg, Germany, m, 1948 **DISCIPLINE** HISTORY OF CULTURE **EDUCATION** Univ Richmond, BA, 44; Univ Chicago, AM, 45, PhD, 51. **CAREER** Instr, Univ Akron, 48-50; assoc prof, Philander Smith Col, 50-57; prof, Dillard Univ, 57-67; assoc prof, Roosevelt Univ, 63-65; prof, 65-77, distinguished prof, 78-, prof emer, 97-, SUNY/BUFFALO, 65-. **HONORS AND AWARDS** Guggenheim, fel; NEH fel; Fulbright fel; A V Humboldt res. **MEMBERSHIPS** Ctr Interdisciplinary Res; Ctr Res Contemp Hist; Woodrow Wilson Ctr; Acad Sci GDR; AHA; Int Comn Hist & Theory Historiography. **RESEARCH** Historiography; European intellectual history. **SELECTED PUBLICATIONS** Auth, Geschichtswissenschaft im 20. Jahrhundert. Ein kritischer Uberblick im internationalen Vergleich, Vanderhoeck & Ruprecht, 93; coed, Die Geschichtswissenschaft der DDR als Forschungsproblem, Hist Z, 98. **CONTACT ADDRESS** Dept of History, SUNY/Buffalo, 592 Park Hall, Buffalo, NY, 14260-4130. **EMAIL** iggers@acsu.buffalo.edu

ILARDI, VINCENT
PERSONAL Born 05/15/1925, Newark, NJ, m, 1 child **DISCIPLINE** RENAISSANCE HISTORY **EDUCATION** Rutgers Univ, AB, 52; Harvard Univ, AM, 53, PhD, 58. **CAREER** Instr hist, Carnegie Inst Technol, 56-57; instr, 57-59, from asst prof to assoc prof, 60-69 prof hist, Univ Mass, Amherst, 69-95; VIS PROF HIST, YALE UNIV, 90-99. **HONORS AND AWARDS** Fulbright res scholar, Italy, 59-60; Am Philos Soc res grant, 60-63; Rockefeller Found res grant, 61-63, int res grant, 63-64; chm, Fulbright Nat Screening Comt for Greece & Italy, 63-64; Guggenheim fel, 70-71; Nat Endowment for Humanities res grant, 76-85. **MEMBERSHIPS** Renaissance Soc Am; Am Soc Reformation Res; Mediaeval Acad Am. **RESEARCH** Renaissance political and diplomatic history; origins of modern diplomatic institutions and of modern nationalism. **SELECTED PUBLICATIONS** Auth, France and Milan: The Uneasy "Alliance, 1452-1466, in Gli Sforza a Milano e in Lombardia e i Loro Rapporti con gli State Italiani ed Europei, 1450-1535, 82; auth, The Banker-Statesman and the Condottiere-Prince: Cosimo de' Medici and Francesco Sforza, 1450-1464, In; Florence and Milan: Comparisons and Relations, 89; auth, Crosses and Carets: Renaissance Patronage and Coded Letters of Recommendation, Am Hist Rev, 87; auth, Renaissance Florence: The Optical Capital of the World, J of Europ Econ Hist, 93; auth, The First Permanent Embassy Outside Italy: The Milanese Embassy at the French Court, 1464-1483, in Politics, Religion and Diplomacy in Early Modern Europe, 94; auth, Towards the Tragedia d'Italia: Ferrante and Galeazzo Maria Sforza, Friendly Enemies and Hostile Allies, and, The Ilardi Microfilm Collection of Renaissance Diplomatic Documents, ca1450-ca1500, Index, In, Abulafia, ed, The French Descent Into Renaissance Italy, 1494-95, 95, and Studies in Italian Renaissance Diplomatic History, London, 86. **CONTACT ADDRESS** 238 N Main St, Sunderland, MA, 01375.

ILLICK, JOSEPH E.
PERSONAL Born 11/15/1934, Bethlehem, PA, m, 1956, 3 children **DISCIPLINE** COLONIAL AMERICAN HISTORY, PSYCHOHISTORY **EDUCATION** Princeton Univ, BSE, 56; Univ Pa, MA, 58, PhD, 63. **CAREER** Asst instr civil eng, Univ Pa, 56-58, asst instr hist, 58-61; instr, Kalamazoo Col, 61-62; instr, Lafayette Col, 62-63; from asst prof to assoc prof, 63-71, prof hist, San Francisco State Univ, 71-, Bk ed, The Am West, 66-70; prof, San Francisco Psychoanal Inst, 74-75 & 78-79. **MEMBERSHIPS** AHA **RESEARCH** Colonial Pennsylvania; American biography; psychohistory. **SELECTED PUBLICATIONS** Auth, William Penn the Politician, Cornell Univ, 65; The Pennsylvania grant: a re-evaluation, Pa Mag Hist & Biog, 62; ed, America and England, 1558-1776, Appleton, 70; auth, Bibliographic essay, In: Anglo-American Political Relations, 1675-1775, Rutgers Univ, 70; Robert Proud, In: The Colonial Legacy, 71 & Anglo-American Child Rearing in Seventeenth Century, In: History of Childhood, 74, Harper; Colonial Pennsylvania: A History, Scribner, 76; At Liberty, Univ of Tenn, 89. **CONTACT ADDRESS** Dept of Hist, San Francisco State Univ, 1600 Holloway Ave, San Francisco, CA, 94132-1740. **EMAIL** illick@sfsu.edu

IMHOLT, ROBERT JOSEPH
PERSONAL Born 05/22/1946, Cincinnati, OH, m, 1973, 3 children **DISCIPLINE** HISTORY **EDUCATION** Washington & Lee Univ, BA, 67; Univ Ky, MA, 69, PhD, 74. **CAREER** From instr to assoc prof, 71-81, prof hist & chemn dept, 82-, Albertus Magnus Col. Ed, NEHA News, newsletter New Eng Hist Asn, 77-83. **MEMBERSHIPS** Orgn Am Historians; Southern Hist Asn; New Eng Hist Asn. **RESEARCH** Timothy Dwight; early American Republic. **CONTACT ADDRESS** Dept of History, Albertus Magnus Col, 700 Prospect St, New Haven, CT, 06511-1189. **EMAIL** imholt@albertus.edu

INGALLS, ROBERT PAUL
PERSONAL Born 05/19/1941, New York, NY, m, 1967, 2 children **DISCIPLINE** HISTORY **EDUCATION** Purdue Univ, BA, 63; Columbia Univ, MA, 65, PhD(hist), 73. **CAREER** Asst cur, Herbert Lehman Papers, Columbia Univ, 67-68 & 72-74; asst prof, 74-78, ASSOC PROF HIST, UNIV SOUTH FLA, 78-, CHMN, HIST DEPT, 79-, Adj asst prof hist,

Hunter Col, City Univ NY, 67-74; consult, Impeachment Inquiry Staff of House Comt Judiciary, 74. **MEMBERSHIPS** Orgn Am Historians; Southern Hist Asn **RESEARCH** American labor history during the 1930's; anti-labor vigilantism in the South. **SELECTED PUBLICATIONS** Auth, No Crooked Death--Coatesville, Pennsylvania, and the Lynching of Walker, Zachariah, Pa Mag Hist and Biography, Vol 0117, 93; Stories of Scottsboro, Amer Hist Rev, Vol 0100, 95; Untitled--Reply, Amer Hist Rev, Vol 0101, 96; Twice the Work of Free Labor--The Political-Economy of Convict Labor in the New South, J Southern Hist, Vol 0063, 97. **CONTACT ADDRESS** Dept of Hist, Univ S Fla, 4202 Fowler Ave, Tampa, FL, 33620-9951.

INGHAM, JOHN NORMAN
PERSONAL Born 03/15/1939, Green Bay, WI, m, 1961, 3 children **DISCIPLINE** AMERICAN URBAN & SOCIAL HISTORY **EDUCATION** Univ Wis-Milwaukee, BA, 63; Univ Pittsburgh, MA, 64, PhD(hist), 73. **CAREER** Lectr hist, Carnegie-Mellon Univ, 67-68; instr, Univ Bridgeport, 68-70; from asst prof to assoc prof, State Univ NY Col Brockport, 70-77, coordr, Annual Conf Social & Polit Hist, 71-77; ASSOC PROF HIST, UNIV TORONTO, 77-. **HONORS AND AWARDS** Wallace K Ferguson Prize, Can Hist Asn, 80. **MEMBERSHIPS** Orgn Am Historians; Urban Hist Group **RESEARCH** American urban upper classes; urban history; social history. **SELECTED PUBLICATIONS** Auth, Mill and Mine--the Cf-and-I in the 20th-Century, Can Rev Amer Stud, Vol 0023, 93; Making America Corporate, 1870-1920, Can Rev Amer Stud, Vol 0024, 94; Harrisburg Industrializes--The Coming of Factories to an American Community, Technol and Culture, Vol 0035, 94; Harrisburg Industrializes--The Coming of Factories to an American Community, Technol and Culture, Vol 0035, 94; Sloss Furnaces and the Rise of the Birmingham District--An Industrial Epic, J Amer Hist, Vol 0082, 95; Platt Brothers and Company--Small Business in American Manufacturing, Amer Hist Rev, Vol 0100, 95. **CONTACT ADDRESS** Dept of Hist, Univ of Toronto, Toronto M5S 1A1, Toronto, ON, M5S 1A1.

INGLE, HAROLD NORMAN
PERSONAL Born 09/20/1938, m, 1969 **DISCIPLINE** EUROPEAN & RUSSIAN HISTORY **EDUCATION** Johns Hopkins Univ, BA, 64, MA, 65; Univ Calif, Davis, PhD(hist), 72. **CAREER** Lectr Europ hist, Univ New S Wales, 70-73; RES & WRITING, 73- **MEMBERSHIPS** Am Hist Asn; Am Asn Advan Slavic Studies; Acad Polit Sci; Orgn Am Hist; AAAS. **RESEARCH** International history. **SELECTED PUBLICATIONS** Auth, Late Soviet Culture--From Perestroika to Novostroika, Can Slavonic Papers-Revue Canadienne des Slavistes, Vol 0035, 94. **CONTACT ADDRESS** 780 D St #C, Arcata, CA, 95521.

INGLE, HOMER LARRY
PERSONAL Born 10/09/1936, Greensboro, NC, m, 1958, 2 children **DISCIPLINE** RECENT UNITED STATES HISTORY **EDUCATION** Wake Forest Col, BA, 58; Am Univ, MA, 61; Univ Wis, PhD(hist), 67 **CAREER** Asst prof hist, Wilmington Col, 61-63; asst prof, Presby Col, 64-67; asst prof, 67-69, assoc prof, 69-84, prof hist, 84-97, PROF EMER, UNIV TENN, CHATTANOOGA, 97-; Danforth fel Black studies, Yale Univ, 69-70; Fulbright fel hist, Univ Cape Coast, 73-74. **HONORS AND AWARDS** Pres, Friends Hist Soc (London), 97. **MEMBERSHIPS** Orgn Am Historians **RESEARCH** Populism; Nixon; Quakerism. **SELECTED PUBLICATIONS** Coauth, American History: A Brief View, Little, 78; Quakers in Conflict: The Hicksite Reformation, Univ Tenn Press, Knoxville, 86, 2nd ed, Pendle Hill Publ, 98; First among Friends: George Fox and the Creation of Quakerism, Oxford Univ Press, 94. **CONTACT ADDRESS** 1106 Collins Circle, Chattanooga, TN, 37411. **EMAIL** larry-ingle@utc.edu

INGLIS, JOHN
DISCIPLINE MEDIEVAL PHILOSOPHY **EDUCATION** Univ Ky, PhD, 93. **CAREER** Dept Philos, Univ Dayton **RESEARCH** Relation between philosophy and theology. **SELECTED PUBLICATIONS** Auth, Philosophical Anatomy and the Historiography of Medieval Philosophy, Brit Jour Hist Philos, 97. **CONTACT ADDRESS** Dept of Philos, Univ Dayton, 300 Col Park, Dayton, OH, 75062. **EMAIL** inglis@checkov.hm.udayton.edu

INGRAM, EARL GLYNN
DISCIPLINE HISTORY **EDUCATION** La Polytech Univ, BA, 62; Auburn Univ, MA, 63; Univ GA, PhD, 73. **CAREER** Asst prof hist, 66-73, assoc prof hist, 73-, La Tech Univ. **MEMBERSHIPS** Autrey House Mus Comt, 91-; Autrey House Restoration Comt, 85-92; N La Hist Asn, 79-80. **RESEARCH** Europ hist; Brit hist. **SELECTED PUBLICATIONS** Auth, Huey P. Long: A Synopsis, With a Selected Bibliography of Works on Huey P. Long and His Era, McGinty, 94; Dictionary of Louisiana Biography, La Hist Asoc, 88; North Louisiana: An Historical Overview, Ruston, 84. **CONTACT ADDRESS** Dept of Hist, Louisiana Tech Univ, PO Box 3178, Ruston, LA, 71272.

INGRAM, NORMAN
DISCIPLINE HISTORY OF MODERN FRANCE **EDUCATION** Univ Alberta, BA; Univ Toronto, MA; Univ Edinburgh, PhD. **CAREER** Assoc prof. **HONORS AND AWARDS** Killam Post-Doc fel; Can res fel, Univ Alberta, 88-92. **SELECTED PUBLICATIONS** Auth, The Politics of Dissent: Pacifism in France, 1919-1939, Clarendon Press, 91. **CONTACT ADDRESS** Dept of Hist, Concordia Univ, Montreal, 1455 de Maisonneuve W, Montreal, PQ, H3G 1M8. **EMAIL** ingram@vax2.concordia.ca

INGRAO, CHARLES WILLIAM
PERSONAL Born 03/15/1948, New York, NY, m, 1971, 2 children **DISCIPLINE** EUROPEAN HISTORY **EDUCATION** Wesleyan Univ, BA, 69; Brown Univ, MA, 71, PhD(hist), 74. **CAREER** Asst prof, 76-82, assoc prof Hist, Purdue Univ, 82-87, prof 87-, Alexander von Humboldt Found fel, Institut fur Europaische Geschichte, Mainz, 80-82. **MEMBERSHIPS** Soc Austrian Habsburg History. **RESEARCH** Eighteenth century central Europe. **SELECTED PUBLICATIONS** Auth, In Quest and Crisis: Emperor Joseph I and the Habsburg Monarchy, Purdue Univ, 79; Guerilla Warfare in Early Modern Europe: The Kuruc War, In: War and Society in East Central Europe, Vol I, Brooklyn Col Studies, 79; The Pragmatic Sanction and the Theresian Succession: A Reevaluation, Etudes Danubiennes, Vol 9, 93; Empress Wilhelmine Amalia and the Pragmatic Sanction, Mitteilungen des Osterreichischen Staatsarchivs, 81; Kaiser Josef I, Styria Verlag, rev ed, 82; Austrian Strategy and Geopolitics in the Eighteenth Century, In: War and Society in East Central Europe, Vol II, Brooklyn Col Studies, 82; Barbarous Strangers: Hesse-Cassel and the American Revolution, Am Hist Rev, Vol 87, 82; The Hessian Mercenary State, Cambridge Univ, 87; The Habsburg Monarchy 1618-1815, Cambridge Univ, 94; The Problem of Enlightened Absolutism and the German States, J of Modern History, Vol 58, 86. **CONTACT ADDRESS** Dept of Hist, Purdue Univ, West Lafayette, IN, 47907-1358. **EMAIL** cingrao@purdue.edu

IRELAND, ROBERT M.
PERSONAL Born 08/16/1937, Lincoln, NE, m, 1959, 3 children **DISCIPLINE** HISTORY **EDUCATION** Stanford Univ, JD, 62; Univ Nebr, BA, 59; PhD, 67. **CAREER** Asst Prof, 67-71, Assoc Prof, 71-77, Prof, 77-, Univ Ky. **HONORS AND AWARDS** Distinguished Tchr, Col of Arts & Sci, Univ Ky, 96-. **MEMBERSHIPS** Org of Am Hist; Am Soc for Legal Hist. **RESEARCH** 19th century American legal history; Constitutional history of Kentucky. **SELECTED PUBLICATIONS** Auth, The Problem of Concealed Weapons in Nineteenth Century Kentucky, Register of the Ky Hist Soc, 91, 370-385, 93; auth, Privately Funded Prosecution of Crime in the Nineteenth Century United States, Am J of Legal Hist, 39, 43-58, 95; auth, The Hargis-Green Affair and the Politics of the Elective Judiciary in Nineteenth Century Kentucky, Filson Club Quart, 69, 366-389, 10/95; auth, The Politics of the Elective Judiciary during the Period of Kentucky's Third Constitution (1850-1891), Register of the Ky Hist Soc, 93, 387-421, 95; auth, The Suicide of Judge Richard Reid: Politics and Honor Run Amok, Filson Club Quart, 71, 123-145, 4/97; auth, The Kentucky State Constitution: A Reference Guide, Greenwood Press, in press. **CONTACT ADDRESS** Dept of Hist, Univ Ky, 1733 Patterson Off Twr, Lexington, KY, 40506-0279. **EMAIL** rmirel00@pop.uky.edu

IRISH, SHARON
PERSONAL Born 11/12/1952, Seattle, WA, m, 1982, 2 children **DISCIPLINE** ART HISTORY **EDUCATION** Univ of NM, BA, 76; Northwestern Univ, MA, 82, PhD, 85. **CAREER** Grad coll scholar, 86-, Univ of IL, Urbana. **MEMBERSHIPS** CAA, SAH, SHT. **RESEARCH** American architecture & public sculpture, history of civil engineering. **SELECTED PUBLICATIONS** Auth, Cass Gilbert Architect, Modern Traditionalist, NY, Monacelli Press, 99; Cass Gilbert in Practice 1884-1934, in: Cass Gilbert Ten Projects, NY, NY Hist Soc, 99; Memorial, Carl W Condit 1914-1997, in: Technology and Culture, 97; What Might a Polluted Creek Teach Us about Architecture? in: Design for the Environment/Proceedings of the 1995 ACSA West Central Regional Conference, 95; Physical Spaces and Public Life, in: Nordic J of Arch Research, 94; West Hails East, Cass Gilbert in Montana, in: Minnesota Hist, 93. **CONTACT ADDRESS** 608 West Iowa St, Urbana, IL, 61801-4036. **EMAIL** s-irishl@uiuc.edu

IRSCHICK, EUGENE FREDERICK
PERSONAL Born 08/15/1934, Kodaikanal, m, 1963 **DISCIPLINE** HISTORY, ANTHROPOLOGY **EDUCATION** Gettysburg Col, AB, 55; Univ Pa, AM, 59; Univ Chicago, PhD(hist), 64. **CAREER** Instr Indian civilization & Carnegie Corp teaching internship, Univ Chicago, 60-61; asst prof hist, 63-69, assoc prof, 69-78, PROF HIST, UNIV CALIF BERKELEY, 78-, Am Inst Indian Studies grant, 67-68 & 79; Fulbright res fel, India, 71-72 & 80. **HONORS AND AWARDS** Walmull Prize, 69. **MEMBERSHIPS** Asn Asian Studies; Am Hist Asn. **RESEARCH** South Asian history; social change; peasant culture and economy. **SELECTED PUBLICATIONS** Auth, The Nation and its Fragments--Colonial and Postcolonial Histories, Int Hist Rev, Vol 0017, 95; Gandhi,Mahatma--Nonviolent Power in Action, J Interdisciplinary Hist, Vol 0026, 95; Caste, Nationalism and Communism in South-India, Malabar, 1900-1948, J Interdisciplinary Hist, Vol 0027, 96; Hindu Nationalists in India--The Rise of the Bahratiya-Janata Party, J Church and State, Vol 0038, 96; The Origins of Industrial Capitalism in India--Business Strategies and the Working Classes in Bombay, 1900-1940, J Interdisciplinary Hist, Vol 0027, 97. **CONTACT ADDRESS** Univ Calif Berkeley, 1523 Walnut St, Berkeley, CA, 94720.

IRVINE, B.J.
DISCIPLINE ART HISTORY **EDUCATION** Univ Ind, PhD. **CAREER** Adj assoc prof. **SELECTED PUBLICATIONS** Auth, pubs on women in academic librarianship. **CONTACT ADDRESS** Dept of History and Art, Indiana Univ, Bloomington, 300 N Jordan Ave, Bloomington, IN, 47405. **EMAIL** irvine@indiana.edu

IRWIN, ELEANOR
PERSONAL Toronto, ON, Canada **DISCIPLINE** CLASSICS **EDUCATION** Univ Toronto, BA, 59, MA, 60, PhD, 67. **CAREER** Asst prof, 68-73, ASSOC PROF, SCARBOROUGH COL, UNIV TORONTO, 73-, assoc ch, 80-82, 94-, vice prin & assoc dean, 89-93. **HONORS AND AWARDS** D.R. Campbell Award Outstanding Contrib Scarborough Col, 84. **MEMBERSHIPS** Class Asn Can; Can Soc Patristic Studs; Int Soc Class Tradition. **SELECTED PUBLICATIONS** Auth, Colour Terms in Greek Poetry, 74; auth, Evadne, Iamos and Violets in Pindar's Sixth Olympian in Hermes, 96. **CONTACT ADDRESS** Scarborough Col, Univ Toronto, Toronto, ON, M1C 1A4. **EMAIL** irwin@macpost.scar.utoronto.ca

IRWIN, JOHN THOMAS
PERSONAL Born 04/24/1940, Houston, TX **DISCIPLINE** AMERICAN LITERATURE, HISTORY OF IDEAS **EDUCATION** Univ St Thomas, BA, 62; Rice Univ, MA & PhD, 70. **CAREER** Supvr pub affairs libr, Ling-Temco-Vought, NASA Manned Spacecraft Ctr, 66-67; asst prof Eng, Johns Hopkins Univ, 70-74; Ed, Ga Rev, Univ GA, 74-77; Prof Lit & English, 77-84, Decker Prof in the Humanities, The Writing Seminars, Johns Hopkins Univ, 84-, Chmn Dept, 77-96; ed, Johns Hopkins Fiction and Poetry Series, 79. **HONORS AND AWARDS** Danforth fel, Rice Univ, 70; Guggenheim fel, 91; Christian Gauss Prize, Phi Beta Kappa, 94; Scaglione Prize in Comparative Lit, MLA, 94. **MEMBERSHIPS** MLA. **RESEARCH** Mod Am poetry; 19th century Am novel; 20th century Am novel. **SELECTED PUBLICATIONS** Coauth, The structure of Cleanness: Parable as effective sign, Medieval Studies, 73; auth, Doubling and Incest/Repetition and Revenge, Johns Hopkins Univ, 75; The Heisenberg Variations, Univ Ga, 76; American Hieroglyphics, Yale Univ Press, 80; The Mystery to a Solution, Johns Hopkins Press, 94; Just Let Me Say This About That, Overlook Press, 98. **CONTACT ADDRESS** The Writing Seminars Johns Hopkins Univ, 3400 N Charles St, Baltimore, MD, 21218-2680.

IRWIN, JOYCE LOUISE
PERSONAL Born 11/04/1944, Joplin, MO, m, 1980 **DISCIPLINE** REFORMATION & POST-REFORMATION THOUGHT, HISTORY OF CHRISTIANITY **EDUCATION** Wash Univ, AB, 66; Yale Univ, MA, 68, MPhil, 69, PhD(relig studies), 72. **CAREER** Asst prof hist, Univ Ga, 70-77; ASST PROF PHILOS & RELIG, COLGATE UNIV, 77-82. **MEMBERSHIPS** Am Soc Reformation Res; Am Acad Relig; Am Soc Church Hist. **RESEARCH** Theology and music; women in religion. **SELECTED PUBLICATIONS** Auth, Crautwald and Erasmus--A Study in Humanism and Radical Reform in 16th-Century Silesia, Renaissance Quart, Vol 0047, 94; The Radical Reformation, Renaissance Quart, Vol 0047, 94. **CONTACT ADDRESS** Colgate Univ, 8 West Kendrick, Hamilton, NY, 13346.

ISAAC, EPHRAIM
PERSONAL Born 05/29/1936, Nedjio, Ethiopia, m **DISCIPLINE** HISTORY, PHILOLOGY **EDUCATION** Concordia Coll, BA 1958; Harvard Univ Div School, BD 1963; Harvard Univ, PhD 1969. **CAREER** Harvard Univ, instr 1968-69, lecturer 1969-71, assoc prof 1971-77; Hebrew Univ, visiting prof 1977-79; Inst for Advanced Study Princeton, fellow 1979-80; Princeton Theol Sem/Hunter Coll, visiting prof 1980-81; Bard Coll, visiting prof 1981-83; Lehigh Univ, visiting prof of religion Princeton Univ, visiting prof, 1983-85; Institute of Semitic Studies, dir 1985. **HONORS AND AWARDS** Second Prize Ethiopian HS Matric Award 1954; Ethiopian Natl Prize for literacy (Humanity) 1967; Outstanding Educators of Amer 1972; Fellow Endowment for the Humanities 1979; NEH Rsch Grant 1976-77; Harvard Univ Faculty Fund Rsch Grants; Concordia Coll Scholarships 1956-58; Univ Coll of Addis Ababa Fellowship 1954-56. **MEMBERSHIPS** Dir general Natl Literacy Campaign of Ethiopia 1966-72; bd mem Amer Assn for Ethiopian Jews 1973-; pres Ethiopian Student Assn in North Amer 1959-62; vice chmn Ethiopian Famine Relief Comm 1984-; bd mem African Studies Heritage Assoc 1969-73; chmn Comm for Ethiopian Literacy 1963-68; treas Harvard Graduate Student Assoc 1962-65; chorale dir Harvard Graduate Chorale 1962-64. **SELECTED PUBLICATIONS** Ethiopic Book of Enoch, Doubleday, 1983; A History of Religions in Africa, Oxford. **CONTACT ADDRESS** Inst of Semitic Studies, 9 Grover Ave, Princeton, NJ, 08540-3601.

ISAAC, GORDON L.
DISCIPLINE ADVENT CHRISTIAN STUDIES, CHURCH HISTORY **EDUCATION** Seattle Pacific Univ, BA; Western Evangel Theol Sem, MDiv; Luther Theol Sem, MTh; Marquette Univ, PhD. **CAREER** Berkshire asst prof, Gordon-Conwell Theol Sem, 97-. **HONORS AND AWARDS** Dir, Ctr Advent Christian Stud. **MEMBERSHIPS** Mem, Sixteenth Century Soc; Amer Soc Church Hist. **RESEARCH** Theology of Martin Luther, history of exegesis, Trinitarian theology, the Early Church Fathers. **SELECTED PUBLICATIONS** Assoc ed, Luther Digest. **CONTACT ADDRESS** Gordon-Conwell Theol Sem, 130 Essex St, South Hamilton, MA, 01982.

ISAAC, LARRY
PERSONAL Born 06/12/1949, Cleveland, OH, m, 1969, 2 children **DISCIPLINE** SOCIOLOGY **EDUCATION** Indiana Univ, PhD. 79. **CAREER** Prof, Fla State Univ, 78-. **HONORS AND AWARDS** Nat Inst of Mental Health Fel, 75-77; Moore Award, ASA, 80; ASA/NSF Award, 90; NSF Dissertation Endowment Award; Vice Pres of Southern Sociol Soc. **MEMBERSHIPS** Am Sociol Asn; Soc for the Study of Social Problems; Southern Sociol Soc. **RESEARCH** Social Movements; Labor; Comparative-Historical Methods; Social Change; Political Sociology. **SELECTED PUBLICATIONS** Auth, Transforming Localities: Reflections on Time, Causality, and Narrative in Contemporary Historical Sociology, Hist Methods, 97; Class Conflict, Encycl of Violence, Peace, and Conflict, 98; coauth, Introduction to Time-Series Analysis; Quality of Quantity in Comparative-Historical Analysis: temporally Changing Wage Labor Regimes in the United States and Sweden, in The Comparative Political Economy of the Welfare State: New Methodologies and Approaches, 94; Analyzing Historical Contingency With Formal Methods: The Case of the 'Relief Explosion' and 1968, in Sociol Methods and Res, 94; Regimes of Power and the Power of Analytic Regimes: Explaining US Military Procurement Keynesianism as Historical Process, Hist Methods, 97; Degradation of Labor, cultures of Co-Operation: Braverman's 'Labor', Lordstown, and the Social Factory, in Rethinking the Labor Process: The Braverman Legacy and Beyond, 98; Temporally Recursive Regression and Social Historical Inquiry: An Example of Cross-Movement Militancy Spillover, in Int Rev of Soc Hist, 98. **CONTACT ADDRESS** Dept of Sociology, Florida State Univ, Tallahassee, FL, 32306. **EMAIL** lisaac@garnet.acns.fsu.edu

ISAACMAN, ALLEN
DISCIPLINE HISTORY **EDUCATION** City Coll, New York, BA; Univ Wis, MA, PhD. **CAREER** Chemn, Am Council of Learned Societies/Soc Sci Res Council Joint Africa Comm, 80-88; dir, MacArthur Prog on Peace and Intl Coop, 88-; prof, 65-. **HONORS AND AWARDS** Melville Herkovits Awd, 73. **RESEARCH** Pre-Colonial southern and central Africa. **SELECTED PUBLICATIONS** Auth, Mozambique: The Africanization of a European Institution: The Zambesi Prazos, 1750-1902, 73; The Tradition of Resistance in Mozambique: A Luta Continua and Mozambique: From Colonialism To Revolution, 1900-1982; Cotton Is the Mother of Poverty: Peasants, Work, and Struggle in Colonial Mozambique; co-ed, Cotton, Colonialism and Social History in Colonial Africa. **CONTACT ADDRESS** History Dept, Univ of Minnesota, Twin Cities, 614 Social Sciences Tower, 267 19th Ave. S, Minneapolis, MN, 55455. **EMAIL** isaac001@tc.umn.edu

ISEMINGER, GORDON LLEWELLYN
PERSONAL Born 02/22/1933, DeSmet, SD, m, 1958, 3 children **DISCIPLINE** MODERN EUROPEAN HISTORY **EDUCATION** Augustana Col, SDak, BA, 59; Univ SDak, MA, 60; Univ Okla, PhD(Europ hist), 65. **CAREER** From asst prof to assoc prof hist, 62-73, PROF HIST, UNIV N DAK, 73-. **HONORS AND AWARDS** Standard Oil Ind Outstanding Teacher Award, Univ NDak, 68. **MEMBERSHIPS** AHA **RESEARCH** Late nineteenth century British diplomatic history; nineteenth-century British social history; immigration history. **SELECTED PUBLICATIONS** Auth, Family, Church, and Market--A Mennonite Community in the Old and the New Worlds, 1850-1930, J Amer Hist, Vol 0081, 94; North Dakota Cornhusking Contests, 1939-1941, Agr Hist, Vol 0071, 97; North Dakota Cornhusking Contests, 1939-1941, Agr Hist, Vol 0071, 97. **CONTACT ADDRESS** Dept of Hist, Univ of NDak, Grand Forks, ND, 58201.

ISENBERG, NANCY G.
DISCIPLINE HISTORY, AMERICAN STUDIES **EDUCATION** Rutgers, BA, 78; Univ Wis, MA, 83, PhD, 90. **CAREER** ASST PROF, HIST, UNIV N IOWA **MEMBERSHIPS** Am Antiquarian Soc **SELECTED PUBLICATIONS** Auth, "Eleanor Roosevelt: Joseph Lash's Eternal Mother," Bio 10, 87. **CONTACT ADDRESS** Dept of Hist, Univ of N Iowa, 319 Seerley Hall, Cedar Falls, IA, 50614-0701.

ISENBERG, SHELDON ROBERT
PERSONAL Born 10/21/1941, Fall River, MA **DISCIPLINE** HISTORY OF JUDAISM & EARLY CHRISTIANITY **EDUCATION** Columbia Univ, AB, 62; Harvard Univ, MA, 65, PhD (relig), 69. **CAREER** Asst prof relig, Duke Univ, 68-69 & Princeton Univ, 69-73; asst prof relig, 73-76, ASSOC PROF RELIG, CTR JEWISH STUDIES, UNIV FLA, 76-, Assoc Dir Ctr, 73-, Soc Relig Higher Educ cross-disciplinary fel, 72-73. **MEMBERSHIPS** Asn Jewish Studies; Soc Values Higher Educ; Am Acad Relig; Soc Bibl Lit. **RESEARCH** Judaism in Greco-Roman Palestine; Biblical text criticism; historical method from social psychological and social anthropoligical perspectives. **SELECTED PUBLICATIONS** Auth, The Lamp of God--A Jewish Book of Light, J Amer Acad Rel, Vol 0060, 92; Education for Shalom--Religion Textbooks and the Enhancement of the Catholic and Jewish Relationship, J Ecumenical Stud, Vol 0034, 97. **CONTACT ADDRESS** Ctr for Jewish Studies, Univ of Fla, Gainesville, FL, 32611.

ISETT, CHRISTOPHER
DISCIPLINE HISTORY **EDUCATION** Univ Mich, BA, 85, MA, 90; Univ Calif Los Angeles, PhD, 98. **CAREER** Asst prof **RESEARCH** Asian history. **SELECTED PUBLICATIONS** Auth, Sugar Manufacture and the Agrarian Economy of Nineteenth-Century Taiwan, Modern China, 94. **CONTACT ADDRESS** History Dept, Univ of Minnesota, Twin Cities, 614 Social Sciences Tower, 267 19th Ave. S, Minneapolis, MN, 55455. **EMAIL** isett003@tc.umn.edu

ISHERWOOD, ROBERT M.
PERSONAL Born 04/18/1935, Waynesburg, PA, m, 1959, 2 children **DISCIPLINE** EARLY MODERN EUROPEAN HISTORY **EDUCATION** Allegheny Col, BA, 57; Univ Chicago, MA, 59, PhD(hist), 64. **CAREER** Asst prof hist, Univ NH, 64-67; asst prof, 67-71, ASSOC PROF HIST, VANDERBILT UNIV, 71-. **MEMBERSHIPS** AHA; Soc Hist Studies, France; Am Soc 18th Century Studies; Soc Fr Etude XVIIIe Siecle. **RESEARCH** Politics and culture in the reign of Louis XIV; music and ideas in the French Enlightenment; popular entertainment in 18th century Paris. **SELECTED PUBLICATIONS** Auth, Music and the French Enlightenment--Reconstruction of a Dialog, 1750-1764, Amer Hist Rev, Vol 0099, 94. **CONTACT ADDRESS** Dept of Hist, Vanderbilt Univ, Nashville, TN, 37240.

ISRAEL, FRED L.
PERSONAL Born 02/08/1934, New York, NY **DISCIPLINE** AMERICAN HISTORY **EDUCATION** City Col New York, BS, 55; Columbia Univ, MA, 56, PhD, 59. **CAREER** From instr to assoc prof, 56-74, prof hist, City Col NY, 74. **MEMBERSHIPS** AHA; Orgn Am Historians **RESEARCH** Contemp Am hist. **SELECTED PUBLICATIONS** Auth, Nevada's Key Pittman, 63 & War Diary of Breckinridge Long, 65, Univ Nebr; ed, State of the Union Messages of the Presidents, 1789-1966, 66 & Major Peace Treaties of Modern History, 1648-1967, 67, Chelsea House; co-ed, History of American Presidential Elections, McGraw, 71. **CONTACT ADDRESS** Dept of Hist, City Col, CUNY, 160 Convent Ave, New York, NY, 10031-9198.

ISRAEL, MILTON
PERSONAL Born 07/27/1936, Hartford, CT **DISCIPLINE** HISTORY **EDUCATION** Trinity Col (Hartford), BA, 58; Univ Mich, MA, 59, PhD, 65. **CAREER** Lectr 64, assoc prof, 72, assoc ch dept, 72-74, vice provost, 74-79, dir, ctr South Asian stud, 81-91, PROF HISTORY, UNIV TORONTO, 90-. **HONORS AND AWARDS** Fulbright fel, India, 63-64; Int Stud fel (Univ Toronto), India, 70-71; Shastri Inst fel, 80-81. **MEMBERSHIPS** Multicultur Hist Soc Ont; Shastri-Indo Can Inst; Asn Asian Stud; Can Ethnic Stud Adv Comt; Heritage Can. **SELECTED PUBLICATIONS** Auth, Communications and Power, Propaganda and the Press in the Indian Nationalist Struggle 1920-1947, 94; auth, In the Further Soil: A Social History of Indo-Canadians in Ontario, 94; ed, Pax Britannica, 68; ed, Islamic Society and Culture: Essays in Honor of Professor Aziz Ahmad, 83; ed, National Unity: The South Asian Experience, 83; ed, Nehru and the Twentieth Century, 91; co-ed, Religion and Society in Maharashtra, 87; co-ed, City, Countryside and Society in Maharashtra, 88; co-ed, Sikh History and Religion in the Twentieth Century, 88. **CONTACT ADDRESS** Univ of Toronto, Stanley Smith Hall, #2045, Toronto, ON, M5S 3G3.

ISSEL, WILLIAM HENRY
PERSONAL Born 04/27/1940, San Francisco, CA, 4 children **DISCIPLINE** AMERICAN POLITICS, SOCIETY, CULTURE **EDUCATION** San Francisco State Col, BA, 63, MA, 64; Univ Pa, AM, 66, PhD(Am civilization), 69. **CAREER** Prog assoc & ed, Inst Serv Educ, Rutgers Univ, 67-68; from instr to assoc prof hist, 68-76, prof hist & urban studies, San Francisco State Univ, 76-, coordr Am studies, 77-78, sr lectr, Fulbright-Hays grant, Am Studies Resources Ctr, Polytech Cent London, 78-79. **HONORS AND AWARDS** Phi Beta Kappa Alumni Member, 90; Univ Merit Award, 94, 96. **MEMBERSHIPS** AHA; Orgn Am Historians; Urban Hist Asn. **RESEARCH** Business, Labor, Religion, and Urban Politics and Policy. **SELECTED PUBLICATIONS** Auth, Teachers and Educational Reform during the Progressive Era, Hist Educ Quart, summer 67; Modernization to Philadelphia School Reform, 1882-1905, Pa Mag Hist & Biog, 7/70; History, Social Science and Ideology, Hist Teacher, 11/75; School Reform Ideology in Industrial Pennsylvania, 1880-1910, J Social Hist, summer 79; coauth, San Francisco: Presidio, Port and Pacific Metropolis, Boyd & Fraser, 81; Class and Ethnic Conflict in San Francisco Political History, Labor Hist, summer 77; The Politcs of Public School Reform in Pennsylvania, 1880-1911, Pa Mag Hist & Biog, 1/78; auth, Social Change in the U.S., 1945-1983, 85; co auth, San Francisco, 1865-1932: Politics, Power, and Urban Development, Univ of Ca, 86; Business and Urban Policy in San Francisco and Los Angelos, 1890-1932, Pacific Historical Review, Nov 88; Business Power and Political Culture in San Francisco, 1900-1940, Journal of Urban History, Nov 89; Liberalism and Urban Policy in San Francisco from the 30's to the 60's, Western Historical Quart, Nov 91. **CONTACT ADDRESS** Dept of Hist, San Francisco State Univ, 1600 Holloway Ave, San Francisco, CA, 94132-1740. **EMAIL** BI@sfu.edu

ISSER, NATALIE K.
PERSONAL Born 07/12/1927, Philadelphia, PA, m, 1947, 4 children **DISCIPLINE** MODERN EUROPEAN HISTORY **EDUCATION** Univ PA, BA, 47, MA, 48, PhD(hist), 62. **CAREER** Asst prof, 63-75, Assoc prof Hist, PA State Univ, Ogontz Campus, 75-85; Prof Hist, PA State Univ, Abington Col, 85-95, Emer prof Hist, PA State Univ, Abington Col, 95-. **MEMBERSHIPS** AHA; Soc Fr Hist Studies. **RESEARCH** Public opinion during the Second Empire, France; anti-semitism during the Second Empire. **SELECTED PUBLICATIONS** Auth, The Second Empire and the Press, Nijhoff, 74; Antisemitism During the Second French Empire, 90; coauth, AmSchools and Melting Pot, 86. **CONTACT ADDRESS** Dept of History, Pennsylvania State Univ, Abington, PA, 19001. **EMAIL** Nxi1@psu.edu

IUDIN-NELSON, LAURIE
DISCIPLINE RUSSIAN **EDUCATION** St. Olaf Col, BA; Univ Minn, MA; Univ Wis-Madison, PhD. **CAREER** Asst prof; dir, Luther Col Balalaika Ensemble; resident dir, Univ Wis-Moscow State Univ Exch Prog; vis Dana fel, Dartmouth Col, 93;employed in, Concordia Lang Vlg, 84-; dean, Russ Vlg, 89-. **RESEARCH** Utilizing music in L2 pedagogy, integration of this methodology into the Russian language. **SELECTED PUBLICATIONS** Auth, An Anthology of Russian Song, Concordia Lang Villages. **CONTACT ADDRESS** Dept of Modern Languages, Luther Col, 700 College Dr, Decorah, IA, 52101. **EMAIL** iudinnel@luther.edu

IVERS, LOUISE H.
PERSONAL Born 05/30/1943, New Haven, CT **DISCIPLINE** ART **EDUCATION** Boston Univ, BFA, 64; Univ Nmex, MA, 67; PhD, 75. **CAREER** Chair Art Dept, 86-91and 96-98; asst, assoc, prof, Calif State Univ Dominguez Hills, 71-. **HONORS AND AWARDS** Univ Fel, Univ Nmex, 66-68, 69-70; Jr Consultantship in Am Studies, Univ Nmex, 68; Del Amo Found Fel, Los Angeles Calif, 77; Outstanding Contributor of Merit, Southwest Heritage, Vol 8, Montezuma Hotel, 80; Affirmative Action Fac Develop Award for Res, Calif State Univ Dominguez Hills, 84; Univ Found Award, 84; Honorable Mention, Long Beach Art Asn Open Juried Photographic Exhibition, 88; Sunbird Grant, Getty Center for Educ in Arts and Calif State Univ, 89; Women's Archi League grant for publication of Cecil Schilling catlogue, 94. **RESEARCH** American and Colonial Latin American Architecture. **SELECTED PUBLICATIONS** Auth, Cecil Schilling, Jazz Age Architect, 94; Cecil Schilling, Long Beach Architect, Southern Calif Quart, 97. **CONTACT ADDRESS** Art Dept, California State Univ, Dominguez Hills, Carson, CA, 90747. **EMAIL** livers@dhux20.csudh.edu

IVES, EDWARD DAWSON
PERSONAL Born 09/04/1925, White Plains, NY, m, 1951, 3 children **DISCIPLINE** FOLKLORE; ORAL HISTORY **EDUCATION** Hamilton Col, AB, 48; Columbia Univ, MA, 50; Ind Univ, PhD, 62. **CAREER** Instr English, Ill Col, 50-53; lectr English, City Col New York, 53-54; from instr to assoc prof English, 55-67, assoc prof, 67-70, PROF FOLKLORE, UNIV MAINE, ORONO, 70-, Coe res fund grant & Guggenheim fel, 65-66; lectr, NY State Hist Asn; Sem Am Cult, Cooperstown, NY, 67; assoc ed, J Am Folklore, 68-73; dir, Northeast Arch of Folklore & Oral Hist, 72-; folk arts panelist, Nat Endowment Arts, 77-80; ed, Northeast Folklore; LLD Univ Prince Edward Is, 86; Litt D, Mem Univ Nfld, 96. **HONORS AND AWARDS** Marius Barbeau Medal, Can Fol Stud Asn, 91. **MEMBERSHIPS** Am Folklore Soc; Can Folk Studies Asn; Can Folk Music Coun; Northeast Folklore Soc; Oral Hist Asn. **RESEARCH** All aspects of the folklore of the Northeast; the authorship of folksongs; oral history. **SELECTED PUBLICATIONS** Auth, Twenty-one folksongs from Prince Edward Island, Northeast Folklore, 63; Larry Gorman: The Man Who Made the Songs, Ind Univ, 64; coauth, Folksongs and Their Makers, Bowling Green Univ, 70; auth, Lawrence Doyle: Farmer poet of Prince Edward Island, Maine Studies, 71; Argyle boom, Northeast Folklore, 76; Joe Scott: The Woodsman Songmaker, Univ Ill, 78; The tape-recorded interview, 80; George Magoon and the Down East Game War, Univ Ill, 85; Folksongs of New Brunswick, Goose Lane, 89; The Bonn of Earl of Murray: The Man, The Murder, The Ballard, Univ Ill, 97. **CONTACT ADDRESS** Univ of Maine, South Stevens Hall, Orono, ME, 04473. **EMAIL** sandy_ives@vnut.maine.edu

IZENBERG, GERALD NATHAN
PERSONAL Born 06/30/1939, Toronto, ON, Canada, m, 1963, 2 children **DISCIPLINE** HISTORY **EDUCATION** Univ To-

ronto, BA, 61; Harvard Univ, AM, 62, PhD, 69. **CAREER** Asst prof hist of ideas, Brandeis Univ, 68-75; assoc prof hist, WA Univ, 76-, Nat Endowment for Hum res fel, Boston Univ, 75-76; prof, WV, 91. **MEMBERSHIPS** AHA **RESEARCH** Mod Europ intellectual hist; methodology; psychohist. **SELECTED PUBLICATIONS** Auth, Psychohistory and intellectual history, History & Theory, 75; The Existentialist Critique of Freud: The Crisis of Autonomy, Princeton Univ, 76; Die Aristokratisierung der b?rgerlichen Kultur im 19 Jahrhundert In: Legitimationskrisen des deutschen Adels 1200-1900, 79; Seduced and Abandoned: The Rise and Fall of Freuds Seduction Theory, The Cambridge Campanion to Freud, Cambridge, 92; Impossible Individuality: Romanticism, Revolution and The Origins f Modern Selfhood 1787-1802, Princeton, 92. **CONTACT ADDRESS** Dept of Hist, Washington Univ, 1 Brookings Dr, Saint Louis, MO, 63130-4899.

J

JABLON, HOWARD
PERSONAL Born 12/21/1939, Brooklyn, NY, m, 1961, 2 children **DISCIPLINE** UNITED STATES DIPLOMATIC & RECENT HISTORY **EDUCATION** Hofstra Col, BA, 61; Rutgers Univ, MA, 62, PhD, 67. **CAREER** From asst prof to assoc prof, 66-75, prof hist, Purdue Univ, 75. **HONORS AND AWARDS** Phi Alpha Theta; Hofstra Honors; NEH Summer Fel - Symposium, Yale Univ, 74; Resident Humanist Series, Univ Wis extension, 75; Humanist-in-Residence, Ind Libr Asn, 79; Fel, Berlin Seminar, AHA & West Berlin Govt, 82. **MEMBERSHIPS** AHA; Orgn Am Historians; Soc Study Am Foreign Fels; Soc Hist Am For Rels; Conf Peace Res Hist. **RESEARCH** US New Deal diplomatic and twentieth century hist. **SELECTED PUBLICATIONS** Auth, FDR and Spanish Civil War, Social Studies, 2/65; State Department and collective security, 1933-34, Historian, 2/71; Cordell Hull, His Associates and Relations with Japan 1933-1936, Mid-Am, 7/74; Crossroads of Decision, Univ Press Ky, 83; General David M. Shoup: Warrior & War Protestor, J Mil Hist, 96; Diaries of Michael & Patterson Lewark, Oregon-Calif Trails Asn, Fall 98. **CONTACT ADDRESS** Dept of Hist, Purdue Univ, 1402 S U S Hwy 421, Westville, IN, 46391-9542. **EMAIL** hjablon@purduenc.edu

JACKLIN, THOMAS M.
DISCIPLINE MODERN AMERICA **EDUCATION** Allegheny Col, BA; Northern Ariz Univ, MA; Johns Hopkins Univ, PhD. **CAREER** Vis fel, Univ Baltimore, 79-80; Asst prof, Univ Baltimore, 80-; Dir, Interdisciplinary Studies Prog, Univ Baltimore, 83-91; Dir, Hist prog, Univ Baltimore, 91-94, 96-97; Dir, Public hist, Univ Baltimore, 95-96. **MEMBERSHIPS** Org Am Hist; Nat Coun Public Hist; Baltimore Hist Res Gp; Frederick Jackson Turner Soc; Lexington Gp Transportation Hist; Railway & Locomotive Hist Soc; B&O Hist Soc; Nat Railway Hist Soc; Soc Industrial Archeology. **SELECTED PUBLICATIONS** Auth, The Civic Awakening: Social Christianity and the Usable Past, Mid-Am, LXIV, 82; auth, History in the Roundhouse, Md Hum, 95; auth, Railroading and American Life in the Nineteenth Century, America's Great Road, 96. **CONTACT ADDRESS** Univ Baltimore, 1420 N. Charles Street, Baltimore, MD, 21201.

JACKS, PHILIP
PERSONAL Born 06/10/1954, St. Louis, MO, m, 1990, 2 children **DISCIPLINE** HISTORY OF ART **EDUCATION** Univ Chic, PhD, 81; Cornell Univ, BA, 76; Univ Ill, M.Arch, 81. **CAREER** Asst prof, Yale Univ, 88-92; assoc prof, Yale Univ, 93-96; vis assoc prof, Univ Mich, 96-97; asst prof Fine Arts & Art History, George Washington Univ, 97. **HONORS AND AWARDS** Univ Facilitating Fund Fel George Washington Univ, 98; Getty Grant Prog, 96; FW Hilles Awards, 92, 95; Ntl Endowment Humanities, 93/94; Gladys Krieble Delmas Found Fel, 87, 96; Morse Jr Fac Fel, Yale Univ, 90-91; Samuel H Kress Instn Fel, 81-83; Fulbright-Hays Fel to Italy, 81-82 **MEMBERSHIPS** Spiro Kostof Award Committee, 97-99; Soc Archit Historians. **SELECTED PUBLICATIONS** Coauth, The Spinelli. Merchants, Bankers, and Patrons of Renaissance Florence, Penn St Pr, forthcoming; Vasari's Florence: Artists and Literati at the Medicean Court, Cambridge Univ Pr, 98; Vasari's Florence: Artists and Literati at the Medicean Court, Yale Univ Art Gallery, 94; The Antiquarian and the Myth of Antiquity: The Origins of Rome in Renaissance Thought, Cambridge Univ Pr, 93. **CONTACT ADDRESS** Dept of Fine Arts & Art History, George Washington Univ, 801 22nd St, Washington, DC, 20052.

JACKSON, AGNES MORELAND
PERSONAL Born 12/02/1930, Pine Bluff, AR, m **DISCIPLINE** EDUCATION **EDUCATION** Univ Redlands, BA, cum laude, 1952; Univ of WA, MA, 1953; Columbia Univ, PhD, 1960. **CAREER** Spelman College, instructor 1953-55; College of Basic Studies, Liberal Arts, Boston Univ, instructor, asst prof 1959-63; CA State Univ LA, asst & assoc prof 1963-69; Pitzer College, The Intercollegiate Dept of Black Studies, English prof 1969-. **HONORS AND AWARDS** United Church of Christ Danforth Grad Fellowship 1952-59; So Fellowships Fund Award 1955; Society for Values in Higher Ed Cross-Disciplinary Post-Doctoral Fellowship; Distinguished Service Award Univ of the Redlands Alumni Assn 1973. **MEMBERSHIPS** Society for Values in Higher Educ Central Committee 1971-74; bd of dirs 1985-88, Modern Lang Assn; AAUP; Amer Assn of Univ Women; Danforth Assn Prog 1971-; adv counc & panels/symposia at various English & other professional society meetings; bd of trustees 1981-85, 1985-89, pres 1983-84 Pomona Unified School District; nominating committee 1981-84, 1987-90 bd of dir 1984-86, 1988 Spanish Trails Girl Scout Council; Phi Beta Kappa Univ of Redlands 1982-. **CONTACT ADDRESS** English Dept, Pitzer Col, Claremont, CA, 91711.

JACKSON, ANDREW
PERSONAL Born 02/02/1945, Montgomery, Alabama, m **DISCIPLINE** PSYCHOLOGY **EDUCATION** Yale Univ, Study Prog 1966; Univ of Nairobi Kenya, Ed 1969-70; Univ of CA, MA Ed, Psych 1970, MA 1972, PhD Soc 1974. **CAREER** Desegregation Inst Emergency School Aid Act, consult 1977; Fisk Univ, adj prof 1978-; US Dept of Labor, hbc faculty fellow 1980; Natl Assoc for Equal Oppty in Higher Ed, consult 1981; TN State Univ, prof of soc 1973-. **HONORS AND AWARDS** Delegate Crisis of Black Family Summit NAACP 1984. **MEMBERSHIPS** Pres Assoc of Social & Behavioral Scientists Inc 1983-84; mem Ed Bd Jrnl of Soc & Behavioral Sci 1984-; chairperson, bd of dir Sankofa Dance Theatre1984-; mem Amer Soc Assoc, Amer Acad of Political & Soc Sci, Southern Soc Assoc, Amer Assoc of Univ Prof, Kappa Alpha Psi, Islamic Ctr Inc; life mem Assn of Social and Behavioral Scientists Inc. **SELECTED PUBLICATIONS** Article "Illuminating the Path to Community Self-Reliance" Journal of Soc & Behavioral Sci 1984; Textbook Sci of Soc, 1985; article "Apartheid, the Great Debate and Martin Luther King Jr" The AME Church Review Jan-March 1985. **CONTACT ADDRESS** Professor of Sociology, Tennessee State Univ, 3500 John A Merritt Blvd, Nashville, TN, 37203.

JACKSON, CARL THOMAS
PERSONAL Born 03/24/1934, Santa Rita, NM, m, 1955, 3 children **DISCIPLINE** UNITED STATES INTELLECTUAL & SOCIAL HISTORY **EDUCATION** Univ NMex, BA, 56; Univ Calif, Los Angeles, PhD(hist), 64. **CAREER** From instr to assoc prof, 62-73, prof US Hist, Univ Tx, El Paso, 73-, Dean of Lib Arts, 89-96. **HONORS AND AWARDS** Ralph Henry Gabriel Prize in American Studies, 79; Teaching Excellence Award, Amoco Found, 81. **MEMBERSHIPS** Orgn Am Historians; Am Hist Asn; World Hist Asn; Amer Acad of Relig. **RESEARCH** Influence of Asian thought upon American culture; Asian religions in the United States; meeting of East and West. **SELECTED PUBLICATIONS** Auth, The Meeting of East and West: The Case of Paul Carus, J Hist Ideas, 1-3/68; The Orient in Post-Bellum American Thought: Three Pioneer Popularizers, Am Quart, spring 70; Oriental Ideas in American Thought, In: Dict of the History of Ideas, Vol III, Scribner's, 73; The New Thought Movement and the 19th Century Discovery of Oriental Philosophy, J Popular Cult, winter 75; The Oriental Religions and American Thought, Nineteenth Century Explorations, Greenwood Press, 81; The Orient in American transcendentalism: The Later Phase, South Asian Rev, 7/81; Theodore Parker and the Orient, Amer Transend Q., fall 81; Zen, Mysticism, and Counter-culture: The Pilgramage of Alan Watts, Indian J of Amer Stud, Jan 84; The Influence of Asia upon Amer Thought: A Bibliographical Essay, Amer Stud Internts, Apr. 84; D.T.Suzuki in America, Zen Stud, Jul 87; The Counterculture looks East: Beat Writers and Asian religion, Amer Stud, Spring 89; Vedanta for the West: The Ramakrishna Movement in the United States, Indiana Univ Press, 94. **CONTACT ADDRESS** Dept of Hist, Univ of Tex, 500 W University Ave, El Paso, TX, 79968-0532. **EMAIL** cjackson@utep.edu

JACKSON, CARLTON LUTHER
PERSONAL Born 01/15/1933, Blount Co, AL, m, 1954, 4 children **DISCIPLINE** UNITED STATES HISTORY **EDUCATION** Birmingham-Southern Col, BA, 58, MA, 59; Univ GA, PhD, 63; Oxford Univ, cert, 66. **CAREER** Tchr, Birmingham Univ Sch, AL, 57-59; asst prof hist, AL Col, 59-60; tchg asst, Univ GA, 60-61; from Asst Prof to Assoc Prof, 61-67, Prof Hist, 67-96, Univ Distinguished Prof, Western KY Univ, 96-; Fulbright vis lectr, Bangalore Univ & lectr, 16 univs & cols, India, 71-72 & Univ Islamabad, 74-75; US Info Agency lectr, Greece, Iran & India, 72; vis prof, Pahlavi Univ, 78 & Univ Graz, 81; lectr, US Int Commun Agency tour in Ger, 80. **HONORS AND AWARDS** Fulbright Lectr, Univ Dhaka, Bangladesh, 85; Fulbright Centennial Chair Am Studies, Univ Helsinki, Finland, 89-90; Fulbright Selection Comt, Scandinavia, 91-94, Dipl (Am studies), John F Kennedy Univ, 76. **MEMBERSHIPS** Am Culture Asn. **RESEARCH** Presidential powers, vetoes; biog; Am studies. **SELECTED PUBLICATIONS** Auth, Presidential Vetoes, 1792-1945, Univ GA, 67; Bronson Alcott's Temple, PHP-Int, Japan, 4/71; Pulitzer Prize winning novels as social history, J Hist Studies, Univ Mysore, 3/72; Come drink the brew and sing a fine song (short story), Southern Humanities Rev, 6/72; coauth, US History Textbook (8th and 9th grades), Laidlaw, 74; auth, Zane Grey, Twayne, 73; Apostle of Nonconformity: A Life of J I Rodale, Pyramid, 74; The Great Lili, Strawberry Hill, 78; The Dreadful Month, Popular Press; Hounds of the Road, Popular Press; Picking up the Tab: The Life and Movies of Martin Rhitt, Popular Press; ed, Befriending, The American Samaritans, Popular Press; A Social History of the Scottish-Irish, Madison Bks; Forgotten Tragedy: The Sinking of HMT Rohna, Naval Inst Press. **CONTACT ADDRESS** Dept of Hist, Western Kentucky Univ, 1 Big Red Way St, Bowling Green, KY, 42101-3576. **EMAIL** carlton.jackson@wku.edu

JACKSON, CHARLES O.
PERSONAL Born 08/22/1935, Orlando, FL, m, 1954, 2 children **DISCIPLINE** AMERICAN SOCIAL & INTELLECTUAL HISTORY **EDUCATION** Oglethorpe Univ, AB, 60; Emory Univ, MA, 62, PhD(Am hist), 67. **CAREER** Instr hist, Reinhardt Col, 60-61; instr, Ga Col Milledgeville, 62-65, asst prof, 66-69; assoc prof, 69-75, asst dean col lib arts, 72-77, PROF HIST, UNIV TENN, KNOXVILLE, 75-, ASSOC DEAN COL LIB ARTS, 77- **MEMBERSHIPS** Southern Hist Asn; AHA; Am Asn Hist Med; Am Studies Asn. **RESEARCH** History of medicine in America; 20th century American cultural currents. **SELECTED PUBLICATIONS** Auth, Deadly Dust--Silicosis and the Politics of Occupational Disease in 20th entury America, Amer Hist Rev, Vol 0097, 92. **CONTACT ADDRESS** Dept of Hist, Univ of Tenn, Knoxville, TN, 37996.

JACKSON, DONALD DEAN
PERSONAL Born 06/10/1919, Glenwood, IA, m, 1943, 2 children **DISCIPLINE** AMERICAN HISTORY **EDUCATION** Iowa State Univ, BS, 42; State Univ Iowa, MA, 47, PhD(commun), 48. **CAREER** Ed, Univ Ill Press, 48-66, assoc dir, 66-68; PROF HIST & ED PAPERS GEORGE WASHINGTON, UNIV VA, 68-76, Mem, Secy Navy's Comt Naval Hist, 71-79. **HONORS AND AWARDS** Am Asn State & Local Hist Award of Merit, 67; Western Hist Asn Award of Merit, 79. **MEMBERSHIPS** AHA; Orgn Am Historians; Western Hist Asn; Asn Doc Hist. **RESEARCH** Trans-Mississippi history; United States exploration; Washington and his times. **SELECTED PUBLICATIONS** Auth, Hot on the Cold Trail Left By Frobisher,Martin, Smithsonian, Vol 0023, 93; Mama-Poc, Smithsonian, Vol 0023, 93; the Aye-Aye and I, Smithsonian, Vol 0024, 93; One Mans Soaring, Stately Pleasure Dome for the People, Smithsonian, Vol 0023, 93; Just Plain Bob Was the Best Friend Wilderness Ever Had + Marshall,Bob %1901-1939, American Champion of Wilderness Preservation, Smithsonian, Vol 0025, 94; Broadsides From the Other Orders--A Book of Bugs, Smithsonian, Vol 0024, 94; The Diet Biz--Fat Profits out of Thin Air--The Art of Wishful Shrinking Has Made a Lot of People Rich, Smithsonian, Vol 0025, 94; Remember the 1st Rule of Selling--Dont Drop the Money on the Ground, Smithsonian, Vol 0024, 94; Burns, Ken Puts His Special Spin on the Old Ball Game, Smithsonian, Vol 0025, 94; Sapelos People, Smithsonian, Vol 0025, 94; Tales of a Shamans Apprentice, Smithsonian, Vol 0025, 94; They Were Poor, Hungry, and They Built toLast, Smithsonian, Vol 0025, 94; A Naturalist in Florida, Smithsonian, Vol 0025, 95; The Last Panda, Smithsonian, Vol 0026, 95; Daring Deeds, Bold Dreams, in a Lang Removed From Time, Smithsonian, Vol 0026, 95; Chimpanzee Travels, Smithsonian, Vol 0026, 95; Believe it or Not, Rip Was Almost as Odd as His Items, Smithsonian, Vol 0025, 95; Scenes From the Life of a City, Smithsonian, Vol 0026, 95; I Lost a Baby, and When I Got Him Back he Was a Toddler, Smithsonian, Vol 0026, 95; As Long as Life, Smithsonian, Vol 0025, 95; Doctors on Horseback, Smithsonian, Vol 0025, 95; People Say, You Poor Thing, and Im Thinking, I Have 4 Healthy Kids + The Joys and Worries of Supertwins, Smithsonian, Vol 0027, 96; An Adirondack Passage, Smithsonian, Vol 0026, 96; When Dad Makes Tennis a Family Game, Love Means More Than 0, Smithsonian, Vol 0027, 96; Red, Hot and Blue--The Smithsonian Celebrates American Musicals, Smithsonian, Vol 0027, 96; Eyewitness toAmerica, Smithsonian, Vol 0028, 97; a Stout Ships Heartbreaking Ordeal By Ice + Icebound 2 Months After Setting Out for the Pole, the Jeannette and her Crew Began a Long Fight for Survival, Smithsonian, Vol 0027, 97; Illumination in the Flatwoods, Smithsonian, Vol 0027, 97; Barrymore, John--A Profile in Just about Everything, Smithsonian, Vol 0028, 97. **CONTACT ADDRESS** 3920 Old Stage Rd, Colorado Springs, CO, 80906.

JACKSON, JACQUELINE DOUGAN
PERSONAL Born 05/03/1928, Beloit, WI, 4 children **DISCIPLINE** LITERATURE, CLASSICS **EDUCATION** Beloit Col, BA, 50, Univ Mich, Ann Arbor, MA, 51. **CAREER** Lectr lit, Kent State Univ, 66-68; ASSOC PROF LIT, SANGAMON STATE UNIV, 70-, Consult, Rockford Teacher Develop Ctr, Ill, 68-70; radio lectr, Univ Wis, WHA Sch of the Air, 69- **HONORS AND AWARDS** Dorothy Canfield Fisher Award, 67., DLitt, MacMurray Col, 76; DHL, Beloit LCol, 77. **MEMBERSHIPS** MLA **RESEARCH** Creativity in children and adults; children's literature, current and historical; fantasy. **SELECTED PUBLICATIONS** Auth, the Taste of Spruce Gum, 66, Missing Melinda, 67, Chicken Ten Thousand, 68 & auth & illusr, the Ghost Boat, 69, Little; auth, Spring Song, Kent State Univ, 69; The Orchestra Mice, Reilly & Lee, 70; coauth, The Endless Pavement, Seabury, 73; auth, Turn Not Pale, Beloved Snail, Little, 74. **CONTACT ADDRESS** Dept of English, Sangamon State Univ, Springfield, IL, 62708.

JACKSON, JOE C.
PERSONAL Born 04/24/1911, Gene Autrey, OK, 1 child **DISCIPLINE** HISTORY, GOVERNMENT **EDUCATION** Univ

Okla, BSEd, 34, EdM, 40, EdD(hist, govt), 50. **CAREER** Instr speech, hist & govt, Sulphur High Sch, 34-37; vprin, Bristow High Sch, 37-40; dean, Bristow Jr Col, 40-44; prin, Bristow Jr High Sch, 44-48; assoc prof hist & govt, 48-51, dean col, 51-59, prof hist & polit sci, 51-76, EMER PROF HIST & POLIT SCI, CENT STATE UNIV, 76-, VPRES ACAD AFFAIRS, 69-. **MEMBERSHIPS** NEA **RESEARCH** History of the Southwest. **SELECTED PUBLICATIONS** Auth, Born to Wander--Autobiography of Ball, John, Oregon Hist Quart, Vol 0096, 95. **CONTACT ADDRESS** Academic Affairs, Central State Univ, Oklahoma, Edmond, OK, 73034.

JACKSON, KENNELL A., JR.
PERSONAL Born 03/19/1941, Farmville, VA **DISCIPLINE** HISTORY **EDUCATION** Hampton Inst VA, BA; King's Coll Cambridge Univ England; UCLA, PhD. **CAREER** Stanford Univ Dept of History, asst prof 1969-78, assoc prof, 1979-; **HONORS AND AWARDS** Woodrow Wilson Scholar 1962; John Hay Whitney Scholar Univ Ghana 1963; Fulbright Scholar, Cambridge Univ, 1964-65; Foreign Areas Fellow, Kenya, 1965-68; Lloyd W Dinkelspiel Serv Undergrad Educ, Stanford Univ, 1972; Fellow, Society for the Humanities, Cornell Univ, 1997-98; Univ Fellow, Stanford Univ; Allan V Cox Award, Fostering Undergrad Research; chair, African-American Studies, 1980-89. **SELECTED PUBLICATIONS** Publications: "America is Me: The Most Asked and Least Understood Questions About Black American History," Harper Collins. **CONTACT ADDRESS** Dept History, Stanford Univ, Palo Alto, CA, 94305.

JACKSON, KENNETH T.
DISCIPLINE UNITED STATES HISTORY **EDUCATION** Univ Memphis, BA, 61; Univ Chicago, PhD, 66. **CAREER** Jacques Barzun prof. **SELECTED PUBLICATIONS** Auth, The Ku Klux Klan in the City 1915-1930, 67; Cities in American History, 72; Crabgrass Frontier: The Suburbanization of the United States, 85; co-auth, Silent Cities: The Evolution of the American Cemetery, 90; ed, The Encyclopedia of New York City, 95. **CONTACT ADDRESS** Dept of History, Columbia Col, New York, 2960 Broadway, New York, NY, 10027-6902.

JACKSON, KENT PHILLIPS
PERSONAL Born 08/09/1949, Salt Lake City, UT, m, 1975, 5 children **DISCIPLINE** ANCIENT NEAR EASTERN LANGUAGES **EDUCATION** Brigham Young Univ, BA, 74; Univ Mich, MA, 76, PhD(Near Eastern studies), 80. **CAREER** Teaching asst world hist, Brigham Young Univ, 74-75; ed, Am Schs Orient Res, 76-80; ASST PROF ANCIENT SCRIPTURE, BRIGHAM YOUNG UNIV, 80-, Teaching asst world relig, Univ Mich, 78; Old Testament area dir, Brigham Young Univ, 82- **MEMBERSHIPS** Mormon Scripture Soc; Soc Bibl Lit; Am Schs Orient Res. **RESEARCH** Canaanite inscriptions; West Semitic personal names; Biblical history. **SELECTED PUBLICATIONS** Auth, Revolutionaries in the First-Century + Zealots, Rebellion, and the 1st Jewish Revolt Against the Roman-Empire, Brigham Young Univ Stud, Vol 0036, 97. **CONTACT ADDRESS** Dept of Anicent Scriptures, Brigham Young Univ, Joseph Smith Bldg, Provo, UT, 84602-0002.

JACKSON, PHILIP TAYLOR
PERSONAL Born 08/18/1937, Crawfordsville, IN, m, 1965, 1 child **DISCIPLINE** MUSICOLOGY **EDUCATION** Univ Richmond, Va, BA, 63; Univ NC, Chapel Hill, MA, 65, PhD(music), 68. **CAREER** Asst prof music, Occidental Col, 67-69; asst prof music hist, Conserv Music, Oberlin Col, 69-77; ASSOC PROF MUSICOL, BAYLOR UNIV, 77-80. Nat Endowment Humanities fel music, 67-69. **MEMBERSHIPS** Am Musicol Soc; Music Libr Asn; Int Musicol Soc; Col Music Soc; Renaissance Soc Am. **RESEARCH** Renaissance polyphonic Mass; Jachet of Mantua (16th century French composer active in Italy); Italian madrigal. **SELECTED PUBLICATIONS** Auth, Goostly Psalmes and Spirituall Songes--English and Dutch Metrical Psalms from Coverdale to Utenhove, 1535-1566, 16th Century J, Vol 0024, 93. **CONTACT ADDRESS** Ball State Univ, 1420 E Jackson, Muncie, IN, 47306.

JACKSON, RICHARD A.
PERSONAL Born 05/09/1937, Minneapolis, MN, m, 2 children **DISCIPLINE** HISTORY **EDUCATION** North Park Col, 55-57; Free Univ of Berlin, 58-59; Univ of Minn, BA, 60, MA, 63; PhD, 67. **CAREER** Instr, Creighton Univ, 64; INSTR, 65-67, ASST PROF, 67-70, ASSOC PROF, 70-94, PROF, UNIV OF HOUSTON, 94-; exchange prof, 79-80, vis prof, Univ of Strasborg, 80-83. **HONORS AND AWARDS** Grant, Am Philos Soc, 69 & 74; Fel, 70-71, grant, 75, Am Coun of Learned Soc; travel grant, Count for Int Exchange of Scholars, 75; summer stipend, 85, grant, NEH, 94-95. **MEMBERSHIPS** Medieval Acad of Am; Soc de l'Histoire de France; MAJESTAS. **RESEARCH** Ceremonial coronation; kingship; France 1300-1600. **SELECTED PUBLICATIONS** Auth, Vive le Roi!, Univ of NC, 84; Manuscripts, Texts, and Enigmas of Medieval French Coronation Ordines, Viator, 92; Who Wrote Hincmar's Ordines, Viator, 94; Ordines Coronationis Franciae, Univ of Pa, 95; Le pouvoir monarchique dans la ceremonie du sacre et couronnement des rois de France, Representation, pouvoir et royaute, 95; Robert L. Benson, Majestas 5, 97; joint ed, European Monarchy, Franz Steiner Verlag, 84; Majestas 1-5, 93-97. **CONTACT ADDRESS** Dept of Hist, Univ of Houston, Houston, TX, 77204-3785. **EMAIL** rjackson@uh.edu

JACKSON, W. SHERMAN
PERSONAL Born 05/21/1939, Crowley, LA, m **DISCIPLINE** HISTORY **EDUCATION** So Univ, AB 1962; NC Central Univ, MA 1962-63; OH State Univ, PhD 1969. **CAREER** Alcorn Coll Lorman MS, instr 1963-64; Central State Univ, instr 1966-68; Univ of Lagos Nigeria, sr fulbright lecturer 1972-73; Amer Constitutionalism Miami Univ, prof 1969-. **MEMBERSHIPS** History ed NIP Mag 1969-71; assoc ed NIP Mag 1971-75; ed consult Pentagon Ed Testing Svc; pres, founder Assoc for Acad Advancement 1969-; pres Oxford NAACP 1979-; consult NEH. **CONTACT ADDRESS** Miami Univ, 241 Irvin, Oxford, OH, 45056.

JACKSON, WILLIAM TURRENTINE
PERSONAL Born 04/05/1915, Ruston, LA **DISCIPLINE** AMERICAN HISTORY **EDUCATION** Tex Western Col, AB, 35; Univ Tex, AM, 36, PhD, 40. **CAREER** Instr hist, Univ Calif, Los Angeles, 40-41; from instr to assoc prof, Iowa State Col, 41-42, 43-47; asst prof, Univ Chicago, 47-49; from asst prof to assoc prof, 50-56, chmn dept, 59-60, PROF HIST, UNIV CALIF, DAVIS, 56-, Vis prof Am hist, Univ Glasgow, Scotland, 49-50; res grants, Rockefeller Found, Fulbright award, Huntington Libr, Am Hist Res Ctr, Am Philos Soc & Soc Sci Res Coun; Am Asn State & Local Hist award, 56; Guggenheim fel, 57-58; consult, Governor's Calif Hist Comn, 64-66; Fulton Found lectr, Univ Nev, 64; Guggenheim fel, 65; hist consult, Wells Fargo Bank, 65-82; Nat Sci Found grant, 68-73; Inst Humanities award, 71-72; Huntington Libr res fel, 72; Am Coun Learned Soc grant-in-aid, 72; Calif Coun for Humanities, 75-80; Walter Prescott Webb lectr, Univ Tex, 76; mem coord bd, Calif Water Resources Ctr, 77-81; distinguished Am specialist lectr for western Europe, Dept State, 78; consult, US Army Corp Engrs, Tetra Tech, Inc & Teknekron, Inc; Am Historical Asn rep, Nat Arch, 81- **MEMBERSHIPS** AHA; Orgn Am Historians; Western Hist Asn (pres, 76-77). **RESEARCH** The West in American history, especially trans-Mississippi western frontier influences; European contribution to economic development of the West; environmental history. **SELECTED PUBLICATIONS** Auth, Texas Crossings--The Lone Star State and the American Far West, 1836-1986, Southwestern Hist Quart, Vol 0096, 93; Trails, Toward a New Western History, Western Hist Quart, Vol 0024, 93; Surveying the Canadian Pacific--Memoir of a Railroad Pioneer, Western Hist Quart, Vol 0024, 93; The Great Thirst--Californians and Water, 1770s-1990s, Montana-Mag Western Hist, Vol 0044, 94; Turning on Water With a Shovel--The Career of Mead,Elwood, Montana-Mag Western Hist, Vol 0044, 94; The Lost Frontier--Water Diversion in the Growth and Destruction of Owens Valley Agriculture, Pacific Hist Rev, Vol 0064, 95. **CONTACT ADDRESS** Dept of Hist, Univ of Calif, Davis, CA, 95616-5200.

JACOBS, DONALD MARTIN
PERSONAL Born 05/17/1937, Cambridge, MA, m, 1967, 1 child **DISCIPLINE** UNITED STATES & AFRICAN-AMERICAN HISTORY **EDUCATION** Brown Univ, BA, 59; Boston Univ, MA, 62, PhD(hist), 68. **CAREER** Asst prof hist, Bridgewater State Col, 66-69; assoc prof, 72-78, PROF HIST, NORTHEASTERN UNIV, 78-; Lectr Afro-Am hist, Boston Univ, 70-71. **MEMBERSHIPS** AHA; Orgn Am Hist; Asn Study Afro-Am Life & Hist; New England Hist Asn. **RESEARCH** Nineteenth century pre-Civil War Black history; antebellum reform in America; Civil War and Reconstruction. **SELECTED PUBLICATIONS** Ed, Afro-American History: A Bibliography, Northeastern Univ, 70; auth, The 19th Century Struggle over Segregated Education in the Boston Schools, J Negro Educ, winter 70; David Walker: Boston Race Leader, 1825-1830, Essex Inst Hist Collections, 1/71; William Lloyd Garrison's Liberator and Boston's Blacks, New Eng Quart, 6/71; coauth, America's Testing Time: 1848-1877, Allyn & Bacon, 73; ed, Antebellum Black Newspapers, Greenwood, 76; ed, Index to the American Slave, Greenwood, 81; ed, Courage and Conscience: Black and White Abolitionists in Boston, Bloomington, IN: Univ IN Press, 93. **CONTACT ADDRESS** Dept of Hist, Northeastern Univ, 360 Huntington Ave, Boston, MA, 02115-5000.

JACOBS, LYNN F.
DISCIPLINE NORTHERN RENAISSANCE **EDUCATION** Princeton Univ, BA; NY Univ, MA, PhD. **CAREER** Univ Ark **SELECTED PUBLICATIONS** Auth, The Marketing and Standardization of South Netherlandish Carved Altarpieces: Limits on the Role of the Patron,Art Bull, 89, The Inverted "T"-Shape in Early Netherlandish Altarpieces: Studies in the Relationship Between Painting and Sculpture, Zeitschrift fur Kunstgeschichte, 91; The Master of Getty Ms. 10 and 15th Century Manuscript Illumination in Lyon, J. Paul Getty Mus Jour, 93; The Commissioning of Early Netherlandish Carved Altarpieces: Some Documentary Evidence, Princeton, 94; . **CONTACT ADDRESS** Univ Ark, Fayetteville, AR, 72701.

JACOBS, RUTH HARRIET
PERSONAL Born 11/15/1924, Boston, MA, d, 2 children **DISCIPLINE** SOCIOLOGY **EDUCATION** Boston Univ, BS, 61; Brandeis Univ, PhD, 69. **CAREER** Prof, Boston Univ, 69-82; chemn Sociol Dept, Clark Univ, 82-87; sr lectr, Regis Col, 87-; res, Wellesley Col Ctr for Res on Woman, 87- ; adj prof, School of Human Serv, Manchester, NH, 87- . **HONORS AND AWARDS** NSF; Nat Inst of Mental Health; US Dept of Educ; Southport Found Athena Award. **MEMBERSHIPS** Am Soc on Aging; Nat Coun on Aging. **RESEARCH** Social gerontology; women and agine. **SELECTED PUBLICATIONS** Auth, Older Women: Surviving and Thriving, Familia Int, 89; auth, Women Who Touched My Life: A Memoir, Knowledge Ideas and Trends, 96; auth, Be an Outrageous Older Woman, Harper Collins, 97; auth, Button, Button, Who Has the Button? Knowledge Ideas and Trends, 97. **CONTACT ADDRESS** Center for Research on Women, Wellesley Col, Wellesley, MA, 02482.

JACOBS, SYLVIA MARIE
PERSONAL Born 10/27/1946, Mansfield, Ohio, m, 1980 **DISCIPLINE** HISTORY **EDUCATION** Wayne State Univ, Detroit MI, BS, 1969, MBA 1972; Howard Univ, Washington DC, PhD, 1975. **CAREER** McKerrow Elementary School, Detroit MI, teacher, 1969-72; Federal City Coll, Washington DC, visiting lecturer, 1973; Univ of AR, Pine Bluff AR, asst prof, 1975-76; North Carolina Central Univ, Durham NC, assoc prof, 1976-82, professor 1982-92, dept chair, 1992-; Univ of North Carolina, Chapel Hill, visiting prof, 1982; Univ of Florida, Gainesville, NEH seminar leader, 1988. **HONORS AND AWARDS** Letitia Brown Memorial Publication Prize, Assn of Black Women Historians, 1984, 1992; Fellowship for Coll Teachers, Natl Endowment for the Humanities, 1984-85; Distinguished Achievement Award, Howard Univ Alumni Club, 1985; Fellowship for Minority-Group Scholars, Rockefeller Foundation, 1987-88. **MEMBERSHIPS** Mem, Delta Sigma Theta, 1968-; executive council, mem, Assn for the Study of Afro-Amer Life and History, 1995-98; co-convener, Southeastern Regional Seminar in African Studies, 1983-87; natl dir, Assn of Black Women Historians, 1984-88, co-publications dir, 1995-97; mem, Natl Council of Negro Women Inc, 1985-; mem, Southern Poverty Law Center, 1985-; mem, Committee on the Status of Minority Historians and Minority History, Organization of Amer Historians, 1987-90; mem, Organization of American Historians; mem, NAACP 1987-; mem, Amer Historical Assn; mem, African Studies Assn, 1976-. **SELECTED PUBLICATIONS** Editor, works include: Black Americans and the Missionary Movement in Africa, 1982; 36 articles, 1975-93; 8 book reviews, 1975-88; author: The African Nexus: Black American Perspectives on the European Partitioning of Africa, 1981. **CONTACT ADDRESS** Department of History, North Carolina Central Univ, Durham, NC, 27707.

JACOBS, TRAVIS B.
DISCIPLINE 20TH CENTURY AMERICA; HISTORY OF AMERICAN FOREIGN RELATIONS; AMERICAN HIST **EDUCATION** Princeton Univ, AB; Columbia Univ, MA, PhD. **CAREER** Prof, 65-; Fletcher D. Proctor prof Amer Hist, 92. **SELECTED PUBLICATIONS** Auth, America and the Winter War, 39-40; Navigating the Rapids, 18-71. **CONTACT ADDRESS** Dept of History, Middlebury Col, Middlebury, VT, 05753. **EMAIL** tjacobs@panther.middlebury.edu

JACOBSEN, NILS
DISCIPLINE HISTORY **EDUCATION** Univ Calif Berkeley, PhD, 82. **CAREER** Assoc prof, Univ Ill Urbana Champaign. **RESEARCH** Latin American history; politics and society in nineteenth century Peru. **SELECTED PUBLICATIONS** Auth, Mirages of Transition: The Peruvian Altiplano, 1780-1930, Univ Calif, 93. **CONTACT ADDRESS** History Dept, Univ Ill Urbana Champaign, 52 E Gregory Dr, Champaign, IL, 61820. **EMAIL** njacobse@uiuc.edu

JACOBSEN, THORKILD
PERSONAL Born 06/07/1904, Copenhagen, Denmark, m, 1966, 4 children **DISCIPLINE** ASSYRIOLOGY **EDUCATION** Univ Copenhagen, MA, 27, Dr Phil(Assyriol), 39; Univ Chicago, PhD(Syriac), 29. **CAREER** Field Assyriologist, Orient Inst, Univ Chicago, 29-37, res assoc Assyriol, 37-42, from asst prof to prof soc insts, 42-62, chmn dept Near Eastern lang & lit & dir Orient Inst, 46-48, dean div humanities, 48-51; PROF ASSYRIOL, HARVARD UNIV, 63-74. Haskell lectr, Oberlin Col, 52; Am Coun Learned Soc lectr hist relig, 66-67; Guggenheim fel, 68-69. **HONORS AND AWARDS** MA, Harvard Univ, 63. **MEMBERSHIPS** Am Philos Soc; Am Acad Arts & Sci; corresp mem Royal Danish Acad Arts & Sci, Brit Acad; Am Soc Studies Relig. **RESEARCH** Ancient Mesopotamian languages; archaeology; civilization. **SELECTED PUBLICATIONS** Auth, The Historian and the Sumerian Gods, J Amer Oriental SOC, Vol 0114, 94. **CONTACT ADDRESS** E Washington Rd, Bradford, NH, 03221.

JACOBSON, HOWARD
PERSONAL Born 08/21/1940, Bronx, NY, m, 1965, 4 children **DISCIPLINE** CLASSICAL LITERATURE **EDUCATION** Columbia Col, NY, BA, 62; Univ Chicago, AM, 63; Columbia Univ, PhD, 67. **CAREER** Instr Greek & Latin, Columbia Univ, 66-68; from Asst Prof to Assoc Prof, 68-80, Prof Classics, Univ Ill, Urbana, 80-; Lady Davis Vis Prof, Hebrew Univ, Jerusalem, Winter 83. **HONORS AND AWARDS** C.J. Goodwin Award of Merit, 85. **MEMBERSHIPS** Am Philol Asn. **RESEARCH** Latin literature; Hellenistic Judaism; comparative literature. **CONTACT ADDRESS** Dept of Classics, Univ of Ill, 707 S Mathews Ave, Urbana, IL, 61801-3625.

JACOBSON, PAUL A.
PERSONAL Born 09/01/1957, Evanston, IL, s **DISCIPLINE** MUSIC **EDUCATION** Blackburn Col, BA, 79; Yale Univ Inst Sacred Mus, MM & MAR, 83; Grad Theol Union Berkeley, PhD, 96. **CAREER** Tchg asst, Blackburn Col, 77-79; tchg asst, Yale Divinity School, 81-83; interim choral conductor 85-86, donor campaign, 89-91, inst music, 84-91, Col St Catherine; interim choral conductor, St Paul Sem School Divinity, 98; adj fac, 92-95, asst to pres, 96-97, acting vp develop & publ rel, 97-, Jesuit School Theol Berkley. **HONORS AND AWARDS** George Marshall Fel, 79; Edwin Stanley Seder Scholar, 83; Alpha Chi **MEMBERSHIPS** N Amer Acad Liturgy; Soc Liturgica; Am Guild Organists; Asn Anglican Musicians; Col Mus Soc; Organ Hist Soc. **RESEARCH** Early Medieval (Carolingian) liturgy; Liturgy & music. **SELECTED PUBLICATIONS** Auth, The Benedictiones episcopales: A Case Study in the Gallicanization of the Roman Liturgy, 96; Sicut Samuhel unxit David: Early Carolingian Royal Anointings Reconsidered, Essays in Medieval Liturgy, Garland, 97; contrib Worship Music: A Concise Dictionary, Liturgical Press; auth, So That None Would Be Lost: Jacques de Vitry's Vita Mariae Oigniacensis, Int Medieval Cong, 97; Reform and Function: An Introduction to Visual Theology, San Anselmo Organ Festival, 97; rev, Ave verum Corpus: Music & the Eucharist, CTSA, 97. **CONTACT ADDRESS** 623 Hayes St, San Francisco, CA, 94102. **EMAIL** jacobson@jstb.edu

JACOBY, SANFORD M.
PERSONAL Born 05/13/1953, New York, NY, m, 1984, 2 children **DISCIPLINE** ECONOMICS **EDUCATION** Univ Penna, AB, 74; Univ Calif - Berkeley, PhD, 81. **CAREER** Prof, 80-, UCLA. **RESEARCH** US Labor, economic & bus hist. **CONTACT ADDRESS** Univ of California, Los Angeles, Los Angeles, CA, 90095-1481. **EMAIL** sjacoby@agsm.ucla.edu

JACOWAY, ELIZABETH
PERSONAL Born 06/16/1944, Little Rock, AR **DISCIPLINE** AMERICAN HISTORY **EDUCATION** Univ Ark, BA, 66; Univ NC, MA, 68, PhD(hist), 74. **CAREER** Asst prof behav studies, Univ Fla, 72-75; asst prof hist, 75-78, ASSOC PROF HIST, UNIV ARK, 78-, Nat Endowment Humanties fel hist, 76; Am Philos Soc grant-in-aid, 77. **MEMBERSHIPS** Southern Hist Asn; Oral Hist Asn. **RESEARCH** New South; race relations; civil rights. **SELECTED PUBLICATIONS** Auth, Down From the Pedestal--Gender and Regional Culture in a Lady-Like Assault on the Southern Way of Life, Ark Hist Quart, Vol 0056, 97. **CONTACT ADDRESS** Dept of Hist, Univ of Ark, Little Rock, AR, 72204.

JAENEN, CORNELIUS JOHN
PERSONAL Born 02/21/1927, Cannington Manor, SK, Canada, m, 1949, 9 children **DISCIPLINE** HISTORY **EDUCATION** Univ Man, BA, 47, MA, 50, BEd, 58; Univ Bordeaux, dipl, 48; Univ Ottawa, PhD, 63. **CAREER** Hist master, St John's-Ravenscourt, Winnipeg, 48-52; lectr hist, Haile Sellassie Inst, Ethiopia, 52-55; asst prof, Mem Univ, 58-59; from asst to assoc prof, Univ Winnipeg, 59-67; chmn dept, 70-72, PROF HIST, UNIV OTTAWA, 67-, Consult, Fortress Louisbourg Nat Hist Park, 68-72; mem Can comn, UNESCO, 70-72; consult, Fed Dept Secy State, Ottawa, 71- & Fed Dept Indian Affairs, 80- **HONORS AND AWARDS** Ronsard Medal, 47; Gold Medal Educ, 58; Ste Marie Prize in Can Hist, Ont Ministry Cult, 74; Book Prize, Fr Colonial Hist Soc, 76., LLD, Univ Winnipeg, 81. **MEMBERSHIPS** Can Hist Asn Soc Fr Hist Studies (vpres, 71-72); Soc Hist Am Fr; Can Ethnic Studies Asn (pres, 71-73); Fr Colonial Hist Soc. **RESEARCH** New France; French Amerindian relations; ethnic groups. **SELECTED PUBLICATIONS** Auth, Problems of Assimilation in New France, Fr Hist Studies, 66; Amerindian Views of French Culture, Can Hist Rev, 74; Ethiopia before the Congo, Inst Int Coop, Ottawa, 74; Friend and Foe: Aspects of French-Amerindian Contact, McClelland & Stewart, Toronto & Columbia Univ, 76; The Role of the Church in New France, McGraw-Hill-Ryerson, Toronto, 76; Glimpses of the France-Manitoban Community, Univ Winnipeg, 76; Conceptual Frameworks for French Views of America, Fr Col Studies, 78; Mutilated Multiculturalism, Canadian Education in the 1980's Calgary, 81. **CONTACT ADDRESS** Dept of Hist, Univ of Ottawa, Ottawa, ON, K1N 6N5.

JAFFA, HARRY VICTOR
PERSONAL Born 10/07/1918, New York, NY, m, 1942, 3 children **DISCIPLINE** POLITICAL SCIENCE **EDUCATION** Yale Univ, BA, 39; New Sch Social Res, PhD(polit sci), 51. **CAREER** Mem fac, Queens Col, NY, 45-48, City Col New York, 48-49, Univ Chicago, 49-51 & Ohio State Univ, 51-64; prof, 64-71, Henry Salvatori Res Prof Polit Philos, Claremont Men's Col & Claremont Grad Sch, 71-, Ford fac fel, 52-53; Rockefeller fel, 56-57 & 59-60; Guggenheim fel, 61-62; Relm Found fel, 64-65. **MEMBERSHIPS** Winston S Churchill Asn (pres, 69). **RESEARCH** Political philosophy; American government. **SELECTED PUBLICATIONS** Auth, The Return of Sutherland,George--Restoring a Jurisprudence of Natural Rights, Univ Chicago Law Rev, Vol 0063, 96. **CONTACT ADDRESS** Dept of Polit Sci, Claremont Men's Col, Claremont, CA, 91711.

JAFFE, DAVID P.
DISCIPLINE HISTORY **EDUCATION** Harvard Univ, BA, 76; MA, 80, PhD, 82. **CAREER** Teach fell, Harvard Univ, 81-82; asst prof, PROF, HIST, CITY COLL NY, 88-. **MEMBERSHIPS** Am Antiquarian Soc **SELECTED PUBLICATIONS** Auth, "'One of the Rural Sort': Portrait-Makers in Rural America, 1760-1860," in Rural America: 1780-1900, Essays in Soc Hist, Chapel Hill, 86; auth, "The Village Enlightenment in the Rural North," Wm & Mary Quart 47, 90;auth, "Peddlers of Progress and the Transformation of the Rural North, 1760-1860," Jour of Am Hist 78, 91; auth, "The Age of Democratic Portraiture: Artisan-entrepreneurs and the Rise of Consumer Goods," in Meet Your Neighbors: New England Portraits, Painters, & Society, 1790-1850, 92. **CONTACT ADDRESS** Dept of Hist, City Col, CUNY, 138th and Convent Ave, New York, NY, 10031. **EMAIL** dpjhist@mail.humanities.ccny.cuny.edu

JAFFE, LORNA S.
DISCIPLINE HISTORY **EDUCATION** Tulane, BA, 63; Yale Univ, MA, 65, PhD, 82. **CAREER** Tchg Fellow, Yale Univ, 66-68; Instr, 68-71, Acad Advisor, 71-72, Temple Univ; Historian, US Army Materiel Command, 84-85; Hist, SE Asia Branch, Hist Div, US Army Ctr of Mil Hist, 85-87; Hist, Joint Staff Hist Div, 87-93; Deputy Chief, Joint Staff Hist Branch, Joint Hist Office, 93-. **HONORS AND AWARDS** Phi Beta Kappa; Woodrow Wilson Fellow. **MEMBERSHIPS** Soc for Hist of Am Foreign Relations; Soc for Hist in the Fed Govt; US Commission on Mil Hist; Dept of Defense Sr Professional Women's Asn. **RESEARCH** 20th century European and US diplomatic history; contemporary national security policy; Joint Staff. **SELECTED PUBLICATIONS** Auth, The Decision to Disarm Germany: British Policy towards Postwar German Disarmament, 1914-1919, Allen & Unwin, 85; auth, Abolishing War? Military Disarmament at the Paris Peace Conference, 1919, Arms Limitation and Disarmament, Praeger, 92; auth, The Development of the Base Force, 1989-1992, Joint Hist Office, 93; co-auth, The Chairmanship of the Joint Chiefs of Staff, Joint Hist Office, 95. **CONTACT ADDRESS** Joint History Office, Office of the Ch of the Joint Chiefs of Staff, Washington, DC, 20318-9999.

JAHER, FREDERIC COPLE
PERSONAL Born 03/17/1934, Beverly, MA **DISCIPLINE** AMERICAN CIVILIZATION **EDUCATION** City Col New York, BA, 55; Harvard Univ, MA, 57, PhD, 61. **CAREER** Instr hist, City Col New York, 61-64; asst prof, Long Island Univ, 64-65; asst prof, Univ Chicago, 65-68; assoc prof, 68-78, PROF HIST, UNIV ILL, URBANA, 78-, Am Philos Soc grant, 67; Am Philos Soc res fel, Ctr Advan Studies, Univ Ill, 71-72. **HONORS AND AWARDS** The Newcomen Award in Business History, Am Newcomen Soc, 76. **MEMBERSHIPS** AHA; Orgn Am Historians; Am Studies Asn **RESEARCH** American social and intellectual history. **SELECTED PUBLICATIONS** Auth, Doubters and Dissenters, Free Press, 64; Businessman and gentleman: Nathan and Thomas Gold Appleton, an exploration in intergenerational history, Explor Entrepreneurial Hist, fall 66; coauth & ed, America in the Age of Industrialism, Free Press, 68; Nineteenth century elites in Boston and New York, J Social Hist, fall 72; coauth & ed, The Rich, the Welborn and the Powerful, Univ Ill, 72; coauth, The Chicago business elite: 1830-1930, a collective profile, Bus Hist Rev, autumn 76; The Urban Establishment, Univ Ill Press, 82; auth, A Scapegoat in the New Wilderness, Harvard Univ Press, 94. **CONTACT ADDRESS** Dept of History, Univ of Illinois, Urbana-Champaign, 810 S Wright St, Urbana, IL, 61801-3611. **EMAIL** f-jaher@uiuc.edu

JAIMES-GUERRERO, MARIANA
PERSONAL Born 09/10/1946, Mesa, AZ, s, 2 children **DISCIPLINE** AMERICAN HISTORY; SECONDARY EDUCATION; HIGHER EDUCATION AND PUBLIC POLICY **EDUCATION** AZ State Univ, BA, 71, MA, 78, EdD, 90. **CAREER** Vis prof, Cornell Univ, Soc for the Humanities, 91-92; vis prof, School of Judaic Studies, AZ State Univ, 94-95; ASSOC PROF, WOMEN'S DEPT, HUMANITIES COL AT SAN FRANCISCO STATE UNIV, 95-. **HONORS AND AWARDS** Humanities fel, Australian Nat Univ, 96; Humanities fel, Cornell Univ, Soc for the Humanities, 91-92. **MEMBERSHIPS** Amer Academy Relig; World Philos Congress; Native Amer Methodist Assoc. **RESEARCH** Indigenous perspectives and experiences; Native women and cancer control res; impact of peoples, cultures, and ecology. **SELECTED PUBLICATIONS** Auth, The State of Native America, SEP, 92; numerous articles in academic journals; several works in progress; brd, Aboriginal Voices; reviewer brd, Journal of American Indian Education, CIE at ASU, Tempe, AZ. **CONTACT ADDRESS** College of Humanities, San Francisco State Univ, 1600 Holloway Ave., Room 363, San Francisco, CA, 94132. **EMAIL** guerrero@athena.sfsu.edu

JAKLE, JOHN ALLAIS
PERSONAL Born 05/16/1939, Terre Haute, IN, m, 1957, 2 children **DISCIPLINE** HISTORICAL & SOCIAL GEOGRAPHY **EDUCATION** Western Mich Univ, BBA, 61; Southern Ill Univ, MA, 63; Ind Univ, PhD(geog), 67. **CAREER** Asst prof, Univ Maine, 65-66; instr, Western Mich Univ, 66-67; asst prof, 67-70, ASSOC PROF GEOG, UNIV ILL, URBANA, 70-. **MEMBERSHIPS** Pioneer Am Soc; Asn Am Geog; AHA **RESEARCH** History of American built environment; vernacular architecture. **SELECTED PUBLICATIONS** Auth, Beautiful Machine--Rivers and the Republican Plan, 1755-1825, J Amer Hist, Vol 0080, 93; The Mountainous West--Explorations in Historical Geography, Pacific Northwest Quart, Vol 0088, 97. **CONTACT ADDRESS** Dept of Geog, Univ of Ill, 607 S Mathews Ave, Urbana, IL, 61801-3601.

JALAL, AYESHA
DISCIPLINE SOUTH ASIAN HISTORY **EDUCATION** Wellesley Univ, BA, 78; Cambridge Univ, PhD, 83. **CAREER** Assoc prof. **SELECTED PUBLICATIONS** Auth, The Sole Spokesman: Jinnah, the Muslim League, and the Demand for Pakistan, 85; The State of Martial Rule: the Origins of Pakistan's Political Economy of Defense, 90; Democracy and Authoritarianism in South Asia: a Comparative and Historical Perspective, 95. **CONTACT ADDRESS** Dept of History, Columbia Col, New York, 2960 Broadway, New York, NY, 10027-6902.

JAMES, BETTY HARRIS
PERSONAL Born 06/21/1932, Gadsden, Alabama, w **DISCIPLINE** EDUCATION **EDUCATION** Univ of Pittsburgh, BS Educ, MEd (Magna Cum Laude) 1971, PhD 1974; Marshall Univ, MA 1976. **CAREER** WV State Coll, prof of educ 1974-84, special asst to pres 1981-84; Livingstone Coll, assoc vice pres academic affairs 1984-86; Appalachia Educ Lab, dir regional liaison ctr 1986-. **HONORS AND AWARDS** Danforth Assoc 1976; Faculty Meritorious Serv WV State Coll 1977; Meritorious Serv Livingstone Coll Student Govt 1985. **MEMBERSHIPS** Pres Charleston Branch NAACP 1979-81; mem Comm Council Job Corps 1979-; consultant WV Human Rights Commn 1980-; mem Phi Lambda Theta Hon Soc, Kappa Delta Phi. **CONTACT ADDRESS** Appalachia Educational Laboratory, 1031 Quarrier St, Atlas Bldg, Charleston, WV, 25301.

JAMES, DAVID PHILLIP
PERSONAL Born 09/02/1940, Greenville, NC, m **DISCIPLINE** EDUCATION **EDUCATION** Elizabeth City State Univ, NC, BS, 1962; Georgetown Univ, Washington, DC, MA, 1971; Nova Univ, Fort Lauderdale, FL, EdD 1978. **CAREER** Pitt Co NC, teacher/coach, 1962-63; Clarke Co VA, social sci teacher/coach, 1963-67; Washington, DC Public Schools, Social Science teacher/coach, 1967-71; Prince George's Community Coll, educ admin, 1971-, dean of educational development and extension centers & special programs, currently. **HONORS AND AWARDS** Outstanding Teacher of the Year, Washington, DC Public Schools, 1971; Phi Alpha Theta Intl Award, History, Georgetown Univ, 1971; 1st Black Assoc Dean, Prince George's Community Coll, 1979; Honored Graduate, Elizabeth City State Coll, NC, 1962; Honored as the Outstanding Admin, Prince George Community Coll, 1988; Honorable Mention Recipient, Maryland Assn for Higher Educ as Outstanding Educator, 1989; Named Project Dir of the Black & Minority Student Retention Programs, Prince George's Community Coll, 1988. **MEMBERSHIPS** Part-time consultant, self-employed, 1978-; Student Retention; mem, Natl Council Community Serv & Continued Educ, 1973-; mem, Adult Educ Assn, 1978-; mem, Amer Assn for Higher Educ, 1982. **SELECTED PUBLICATIONS** Auth, "Black Issues in Higher Education," 1988, "Increasing the Retention Rates of Black & Minority Students Through Mentoring & Tutorial Services at Prince George's Community College," 1989. **CONTACT ADDRESS** Dean, Prince George's Community Col, 301 Largo Rd, Largo, MD, 20772.

JAMES, ELRIDGE M.
PERSONAL Born 03/23/1942, Eunice, LA, m **DISCIPLINE** EDUCATION **EDUCATION** Grambling State U, BS 1966; Wayne State U, MEd 1969; MI State U, PhD 1973. **CAREER** NE LA Univ, mem grad faculty, asst prof sec & coun educ 1975-76; Quachia Parish Bd of Educ, asst prof & clinical prof 1974-; Grambling State Univ, assoc prof 1973-74; MI State Univ, graduate asst 1972; Great Lakes Steel Corp, indus instructor 1969-70; Ecorse HS, teacher 1968-70; CJ Miller Elementary School; Great Lakes Steel Corp, dir educ 1968-70; Ford Motor Co, supvr 1966-68. **HONORS AND AWARDS** Dean's list of outstanding grads MI State U. **MEMBERSHIPS** LA Indsl Arts Assn; Am Vocat Assn; LA Assn Pub Sch Adult Edn; So Assn for Counselor Educ & Supervision; LA State Reading Council; Assn Supr & Curriculum Devel; mem Phi Delta Kappa; Scottish Rite Mason King Solomon's Lodge; Omega Psi Phi. **SELECTED PUBLICATIONS** Wrote several articles & books for Grambling Coll. **CONTACT ADDRESS** Sec Coun Educ, Northeast Louisiana Univ, Monroe, LA, 71202.

JAMES, FELIX
PERSONAL Born 11/17/1937, Hurtsboro, Alabama, m, 1985 **DISCIPLINE** HISTORY **EDUCATION** Fort Valley State Coll, Fort Valley, GA, BS, 1962; Howard Univ, Washington, DC, MA, 1967; Ohio State Univ, Columbus, PhD, 1972; New Orleans Baptist Theological Seminary, New Orleans, Masters of Arts in Christian Education, 1991. **CAREER** Columbia Public Schools, Columbia, SC, instructor of social studies, 1962-64; Howard Univ, Washington, DC, reserve book librarian, 1965-67; Tuskegee Inst, Tuskegee, AL, instructor of history, 1967-

70; Southern IL Univ, Carbondale, asst prof of history, 1972-74; Southern Univ in New Orleans, chairman of history dept, 1974-75, prof of history, 1979-; Salvation Baptist Church, pastor and moderator; Mt Zion Miss Bapt, assoc, currently. **MEMBERSHIPS** Assn for the Study of Afro-Amer Life and History, state direc, 1973-, co-chair of program comm, 1979-80, member of exec bd; member, New Orleans Martin Luther King Steering Comm, 1977-; member, faculty coun, Southern Univ in New Orleans, 1980-85; vice-chair of arrangement comm, ASBS Annual Meeting in New Orleans, 1983; member of exec bd, Louisiana Historical Assn, 1984-86; member of advisory bd, Annual City-Wide Black Heritage Celebration, 1985-; commr, New Orleans Bicentennial Comm, 1987-91; consultant, Ethnic Minorities Cultural Center, Univ of N Iowa, 1988; senior warden, DeGruy Lodge, Prince Hall Free and Accepted Masons, 1989; member, bd of direcs, S Christian Leadership Conf, 1983-; worshipful master, DeGruy Lodge No 7, Prince Hall Free & Accepted Masons, 1991-; Illustrious Comman of Kadosh, Eureka Consistory, No 7-Masons. **SELECTED PUBLICATIONS** Author of The American Addition: History of a Black Community, Univ Press of Amer, 1978; contributor to Dict of Amer Negro Biography, 1982, Dict of Louisiana Biography, 1986, Black Leadership in the 20th Century, 1989, Edn of the Black Adult in the US, 1989, and Twentieth Century Black Leaders, 1989. **CONTACT ADDRESS** Dept of History, Southern Univ in New Orleans, 6400 Press Dr, New Orleans, LA, 70126.

JAMES, FRANK
DISCIPLINE CHURCH HISTORY **EDUCATION** Oxford Univ, PhD. **CAREER** Instr, Ctr for Medieval and Renaissance Stud, affil Keble Col, Oxford Univ; assoc prof-. **HONORS AND AWARDS** Transl, ch, Ed Comm of the Peter Martyr Lib. **SELECTED PUBLICATIONS** Auth, Peter Martyr Vermigli: Praedestinatio Dei in the Thought of an Italian Reformer; ed/transl, Selected Works of Peter Martyr Vermigli: Theological Treatises; co-ed, Via Augustini: Augustine in the Later Middle Ages, Renaissance and Reformation; gen ed, Peter Martyr Lib; sr ed, Library of Classical Protestant Theology Texts on CD-ROM; consult ed, The Blackwell Encycl of Medieval, Renaissance and Reformation Christian Thought. **CONTACT ADDRESS** Dept of Church History, Reformed Theol Sem, 1015 Maitland Ctr Commons, Maitland, FL, 32751.

JAMES, HAROLD
PERSONAL Born 01/19/1956, Bedford, United Kingdom, m, 1991, 2 children **DISCIPLINE** HISTORY **EDUCATION** Cambridge Univ, BA, 78, PhD, 81. **CAREER** Peterhouse, Cambridge, lectr, 78-86; Princeton Univ, prof hist, 86-. **HONORS AND AWARDS** Fin Times Global Bus Book of the Year Awd, 96. **MEMBERSHIPS** AHA; Econo Hist Asn. **RESEARCH** Econo Hist; Hist of Germany **SELECTED PUBLICATIONS** The German Slump, Politics and Economics, 1924-1936, OUP, 86; A German Identity, Weidenfeld, Nicolson, 89; International Monetary Cooperation Since Bretton Woods, OUP and Intl Monetary Fund, 96; The Deutsche Bank, 1870-1995, Co auth C H Beck, 95. **CONTACT ADDRESS** Dept History, Princeton Univ, Princeton, NJ, 08544. **EMAIL** Ljames@princeton.edu

JAMES, WINSTON
DISCIPLINE UNITED STATES HISTORY **EDUCATION** Leeds Univ, BA, 78; London Sch Econ, PhD, 93. **CAREER** Asst prof. **RESEARCH** Caribbean and African-American history. **SELECTED PUBLICATIONS** Auth, Holding Aloft the Banner of Ethiopia: Caribbean Radicalism in America 1900 to 1932, 97; co-auth, Inside Babylon: The Caribbean Diaspora in Britain, 93. **CONTACT ADDRESS** Dept of History, Columbia Col, New York, 2960 Broadway, New York, NY, 10027-6902.

JAMES, WOODROW C.
PERSONAL Born 01/03/1936, Biloxi, MS, m, 1989 **DISCIPLINE** MUSIC **EDUCATION** La St Univ, BA, 58; Univ Ms, MM, 60; Mich St Univ, PhD, 66. **CAREER** Grad asst, 58-60, Univ Miss; grad asst, 61-64, Mich St Univ; asst prof, 64-65, Florence St Col; asst prof, 65-68, McNeese St Col; prof, 68-71, Univ Ok; prof, 72-73, Calif St Univ, Northridge; prof, 73-74, Calif St Univ, Pomona; prof, 74-90, Los Angeles City Col; vis prof, 98, E Los Angeles Col; vis prof, 99, Glendale Commun Col; prof, 90-, Los Angeles Valley Col. **HONORS AND AWARDS** First Place Composition Award, 66, 67; Nat Endow for the Humanities fel, 78; Vocational Music Grant, 89; Jazz Educator of the Year, 93., First Place composition Award, 61. **MEMBERSHIPS** Amer Soc of Composers, Authors & Publ; Amer Federation of Musicians; Amer Federation of Teachers; Unit Prof of Calif; Music Assoc; Amer Soc of Music Arrangers & Composers. **RESEARCH** Music in England in the 18th cent; hist of jazz. **SELECTED PUBLICATIONS** Auth, Elegy for Trumpet and Band, Ludwig Music, 62; auth, The Use of the Harmonic Tritone in Twentieth-Century Music, Univ Mich, 65; auth, Brass Quartet (three movements), Mixomodian Music, 76; auth, Computer Assisted Instruction in the Fundamentals of Music, Los Angeles Commun Col, 88; auth, Professional Music in Los Angeles, 93, Los Angeles Commun Col, 94. **CONTACT ADDRESS** 18135 Hatton St, Reseda, CA, 91335.

JAMESON, ELIZABETH
DISCIPLINE WESTERN AMERICA, U.S. SOCIAL, WOMEN'S HISTORY **EDUCATION** Univ Mich, PhD. **CAREER** Assoc prof, Univ NMex. **RESEARCH** Women's and gender history; labor history. **SELECTED PUBLICATIONS** Auth, Building Colorado: The United Brotherhood of Carpenters and Joiners in the Centennial State, 84; coed, The Women's West, 87. **CONTACT ADDRESS** Univ NMex, Albuquerque, NM, 87131.

JAMESON, JOHN R.
PERSONAL Born 05/30/1945, Annapolis, MD, m, 1968, 2 children **DISCIPLINE** US HISTORY **EDUCATION** Austin Col, BA, 67; Tex A&M Univ at Commerce, MA, 70; Univ Toledo, PhD, 74. **CAREER** Asst prof, Washington State Univ, 79-84; assoc prof, Washington State Univ, 84-88; assoc prof, Kent State Univ, 88-97; prof and chair, Kent State Univ, 97-. **RESEARCH** U.S. 20th century; environmental; public. **SELECTED PUBLICATIONS** Auth, "The Quest for a National Park in Texas", in West Texas Historical Asn Yearbook, vol. 50, 74; auth, Big Bend National Park: The Formative Years, Western Press, 80; auth, "The National park System in the United States: An Overview with a Survey of Selected Government Documents and Archival Materials", in Government Publications Review, vol. 7A, 80; auth, "Walter Prescott Webb, Public Historian", in Public Historian, vol. 7, 85; auth, "From Dude Ranches to Haciendas: Master Planning at Big Bend National Park, Texas", in Forest and Conservation History, vol. 38, 94; auth, The Story of Big Bend National Park, Univ Texas Press, 96. **CONTACT ADDRESS** Department of History, Kent State Univ, PO Box 5190, Kent, OH, 44242-0001. **EMAIL** jjameson@kent.edu

JAMESON, MICHAEL H.
DISCIPLINE CLASSICS **EDUCATION** BA, 42; Univ Chicago, PhD, 49. **CAREER** Edward Clark Crossett Prof Emeritus Hum Studies and prof emeritus class/hist. **RESEARCH** Greek hist; relig; epigraphy; archaeol. **SELECTED PUBLICATIONS** Auth, Sophocles, The Women of Trachis in Complete Greek Tragedies, 57; A Decree of Themistokles from Troizen, Hesperia, 60; Agriculture and Slavery in Classical Athens, CJ, 77-8; Sacrifice Before Battle in Hoplites, 91; coauth, A Greek Countryside: The Southern Argolid from Prehistory to Present Day, 92. **CONTACT ADDRESS** Stanford Univ, Bldg 20, Main Quad, Stanford, CA, 94305.

JAN, GEORGE POKUNG
PERSONAL Born 01/06/1925, China, m, 1946, 3 children **DISCIPLINE** POLITICAL SCIENCE **CAREER** Vis prof, Political Science, Beijing Univ, 88; asst, assoc prof, and prof, Univ SD, 61-68; prof, Political Science, 68-93; prof Emeritus, Univ Toledo, 93-. **HONORS AND AWARDS** Phi Beta Kappa; Pi Sigma Alpha; Pi Gamma Mu; Phi Kappa Phi; Phi Beta Delta; Honorary res fel, Res Inst of Contemporary China, Beijing Univ, 88-. **MEMBERSHIPS** Am Political Science Asn; Asn for Asian Studies; Am Assoc for Chinese Studies. **RESEARCH** Government, politics and international relations in the Asian-Pacific region, with special interest in China. **SELECTED PUBLICATIONS** Auth, Government of Communist China; International Politics of Asia; the Chinese Commune Experiment; How to Do Business With China; and numerous articles published in professional journals. **CONTACT ADDRESS** 3041 Valleyview Dr, Toledo, OH, 43615. **EMAIL** AITJE@aol.com

JANKOWSKI, JAMES PAUL
PERSONAL Born 07/17/1937, Buffalo, NY, m, 1965, 2 children **DISCIPLINE** MODERN AND MIDDLE EAST HISTORY **EDUCATION** Univ Buffalo, BA, 59; Univ Mich, MA, 63, PhD(hist), 67. **CAREER** From instr to assoc prof, 66-78, PROF HIST, UNIV COLO, BOULDER, 78- . **HONORS AND AWARDS** Nat Endowment for Humanities grant, summer, 69; res fel, Am Res Ctr in Cairo Egypt, 74-75; res fel, Inst for Advan Studies, Hebrew Univ Jerusalem, 82. **MEMBERSHIPS** AHA; fel Mid East Studies Asn NAm **RESEARCH** Twentieth century Egypt; modern Arab history. **SELECTED PUBLICATIONS** Coauth, The Middle East: A Social Geography, Duckworth, England & Aldine-Atherton, 70; auth, The Egyptian Blue Shirts and the Egyptian Wafd, 1935-1938, Mid East Studies, 1/70; Egypt's Young Rebels: Young Egypt, 1933-1952, Hoover Inst, 75; Egyptian Responses to the Palestine Problem in the Interwar Period, Int J Mid East Studies, 80; Nationalism in Twentieth Century Egypt, Middle East Rev, 79; The Government of Egypt and the Palestine Question, 1936-1939, Mid East Studies, 10/81; coauth, Redefining the Egyptian Nation, 1930-1945, Cambridge Univ, 95; coauth, Egypt, Islam, and the Arabs: The Search for Egyptian Nationhood, 1900-1930, Oxford Univ, 86; coed, Rethinking Nationalism in the Arab Middle East, Columbia Univ, 97. **CONTACT ADDRESS** Dept of History, Univ of Colorado, Box 234, Boulder, CO, 80309-0234. **EMAIL** james.jankowski@colorado.edu

JANOWSKY, OSCAR I.
PERSONAL Born 01/15/1900, Russia, m, 1922, 3 children **DISCIPLINE** MODERN HISTORY **EDUCATION** City Col New York, BSS, 21; Columbia Univ, AM, 22, PhD, 33. **CAREER** From asst prof to prof, 35-66, dir, Grad Studies, 51-57, EMER PROF HIST, CITY COL NEW YORK, 66-, Consult, League of Nations High Comnr for Refugees, 35; dir, Surv of Nat Jewish Welfare Bd, 46-47; chmn, Comn Study Jewish Educ in US, 52-57; Jacob Ziskind vis prof hist, Brandeis Univ, 66-67. **HONORS AND AWARDS** DHL, Jewish Theol Sem, 66 & Hebrew Union Col, 67. **RESEARCH** National minorities; human rights; imperialism. **SELECTED PUBLICATIONS** Auth, Forgotten Worlds--An Unfinished Memoir--Rethinking the American Jewish Experience, Amer Jewish Arch, Vol 0046, 94. **CONTACT ADDRESS** 247-C Mayflower Way, Jamesburg, NJ, 08831.

JANSEN, MARIUS BERTHUS
PERSONAL Born 04/11/1922, Netherlands, m, 1 child **DISCIPLINE** HISTORY **EDUCATION** Princeton Univ, AB, 43; Harvard Univ, MA, 48, PhD(hist), 50. **CAREER** From asst prof to prof Japanese hist, Univ WA, 50-59; dir E Asian studies prog, 61-68, chmn E Asian studies, 68-72, Prof hist, Princeton Univ, 59-, Ford fel, Japan, 55-56; exec assoc, Int House, Japan, 60-61; Nat Endowment for Hum fel, 71; Fulbright fel, 72. **HONORS AND AWARDS** DLitt, Middlesbury Col, 76. **MEMBERSHIPS** Asn Asian Studies (pres, 76-77); AHA; Coun For Rels. **RESEARCH** Mod Japanese hist, espec Meiji Restoration and Sino-Japanese rels). **SELECTED PUBLICATIONS** Auth, The Japanese and Sun Yat-sen; Sakamoto Ryoma and the Meiji Restoration, 61, coauth, Changing Japanese Attitudes Toward Modernization, 65 & Studies in the Institutional History of Early Modern Japan, 68, Princeton Univ; Japan and China From War to Peace, 1894-1972, Rand McNally, 75; auth, Japan and Its World: Two Centuries of Change, Princeton, 81, auth, China in the Tokugawa World, Harvard Press, 92; ed, Cambridge History of Japan, 89-99. **CONTACT ADDRESS** Dept of Asian Studies, Princeton Univ, 211 Jones Hall, Princeton, NJ, 08540.

JANSEN, VIRGINIA
PERSONAL m **DISCIPLINE** ART HISTORY AND ARCHITECTURAL HISTORY **EDUCATION** Smith Col, AB, 64; Univ Calif Berkeley, MA, 67; Univ Calif Berkeley, PhD, 75. **CAREER** Tchg asst, Franzosisches Gymnasium, Berlin, Ger, 64-65; assoc cur, Montreal Mus of Fine Arts, Montreal, Que, 67-68; instr, div of fine arts, Foothill Col, Los Altos Hills, Calif, 72-73; vis lectr, dept of design, Univ of Calif, Davis, fall, 72; lectr, dept of fine arts, Univ Santa Clara, Santa Clara, Calif, 73-75; asst prof, 75-83, assoc prof, 83-93, prof, art hist, Univ of Calif, Santa Cruz. **HONORS AND AWARDS** Graham Found for Advan Studies in the Fine Arts, 93; Favorite Prof Award, Student Alum Asn, Univ Calif Santa Cruz, 93; Univ Calif Pres Res Fel in the Humanities, 89; Amer Coun of Learned Soc, grant-in-aid, 86; NEH Summer Inst: The Tech of Hist Archit, dir Robert Mark, Princeton Univ, 86; Elliott Prize, Medieval Acad of Amer, Superposed Wall Passages and the Triforium Elevation of St. Weburg's, Chester, 81; Amer Philos Soc, res grant from Penrose Fund, 81; Nat Endowment for the Humanities, summer stipend, 79; Facul Res grants, Univ Calif Santa Cruz; instr improvement grants, 76-78, 80, 91, 94-96; dean's descretionary award, 92-93; Regents' Jr Facul Fel, Univ Calif Santa Cruz, 78, 80-81; Humanities Fel Summer Stipend, Univ Calif Santa Cruz, 76; Mabelle McLeod Lewis Memorial Fund Grant, 70-71; Univ Calif Regents' Intern Fel for PhD studies, Univ Calif Berkeley, 68-72; NDEA Fel, Title IV, Univ Calif Berkeley, 66-67. **MEMBERSHIPS** Soc of Archit Hist; The Medieval Acad of Amer; Col Art Asn; The Brit Archaeol Asn; Soc Francaise d'Archeol; The Intl Ctr of Medieval Art; Asn Villard de Honnecourt for the Interdisciplinary Study of Medieval Tech, Sci and Art; Medieval Asn of the Pacific. **RESEARCH** Medieval architecture, both ecclesiastical and secular, particularly Gothic, in cultural context; Urbanism in the Middle Ages. **SELECTED PUBLICATIONS** Auth, Salisbury Cathedral and the Episcopal Style in the Early Thirteenth Century, Medieval Art and Archit at Salisbury, Brit Archaeol Asn Conf Transactions XVII, ed Thomas Cocke and Laurence Keen, 32-39, 96; Medieval Service Architecture: Undercrofts, Medieveal Archit and its Intellectual Context: Studies in Honour of Peter Kidson, ed Eric Fernie and Paul Crossley, London, The Hambledon Press, 73-79, 90; Dying Mouldings, Vertical Springer Blocks and Hollow Chamfers in Thirteenth Century Architecture, Jour of the Brit Archaeol Asn, CXXXV, 35-54, 82; Superposed Wall Passages and the Triforium Elevation of St. Werburg's, Chester, Jour of the Soc of Archit Hist, XXXVIII, 223-243, 79; Lambeth Palace Chapel, the Temple Choir, and Southern English Gothic Architecture of c. 1215-1240, Eng in the Thirteenth Cent, proceed of the 1984 Harlaxton Symposium, ed W. M. Ormrod, Grantham, Lincolnshire, Eng, 95-99, 85; The Design and Building Sequence of the Eastern Arm of Exeter Cathedral, c 1270-1310: A Qualified Study, Medieval Art and Archit at Exeter Cathedral, Brit Archaeol Asn Conf Transactions XI ed Francis Kelly, 35-56, 91; Architectural Remains of King John's Abbey, Beaulieu, Hampshire, Studies in Cistercian Art and Archit, II, ed Meredith Lillich, 76-114, 84. **CONTACT ADDRESS** Cowell College, Univ of California, Santa Cruz, CA, 95064. **EMAIL** goth@cats.ucsc.edu

JANSON, ANTHONY F.
DISCIPLINE ART HISTORY **EDUCATION** Columbia Univ, BA; NY Univ, MA; Harvard Univ, PhD. **CAREER** Instr, SUNY, Buffalo; instr, Col Charleston; cur, Indianapolis Mus of Art, John and Mable Ringling Mus of Art, Sarasota, NC Mus

of Art; vis prof, 94-, ch, dept Art and Theater, Univ NC, Wilmington, 96-98. **RESEARCH** American l9th-century painting. **SELECTED PUBLICATIONS** Author of numerous articles on a wide range of art, from the Renaissance to the present day. **CONTACT ADDRESS** Univ N. Carolina, Wilmington, Wilmington, NC, 28403-3297. **EMAIL** jansona@uncwil.edu

JANSON, CAROL
DISCIPLINE ART HISTORY **EDUCATION** Univ Minn, BA, BFA, 76; MA, 80; PhD, 82. **CAREER** Dept Art, Western Wash Univ **MEMBERSHIPS** Mem, Hist Netherlandish Art; Sixteenth Century Soc; Col Age Assn. **SELECTED PUBLICATIONS** Auth, Artists' Confraternities and Craftsmen's Guild, Dutch History in Art, Gouda as an Artistic Center, Dutch Art from 1475 to 1990: An Encyclopedia, Garland Press, 96; Pieter Bruegel, Encycl Reformation, Oxford Univ Press, 95; Public Places, Private Lives: The Reformed Church as Historical Monument; The Public and Private--Dutch Culture of the Golden Age, Univ Delaware Press, 98. **CONTACT ADDRESS** Dept of Art, Western Washington Univ, 516 High St., Bellingham, WA, 98225. **EMAIL** janson@henson.cc.wwu.edu

JANSON-LA PALME, BAYLY
PERSONAL Born 07/31/1943, Baltimore, MD, m, 1997 **DISCIPLINE** HISTORY **EDUCATION** Randolf-Macon Woman's Col, AB, 65; Univ Maryland, PhD, 79 **CAREER** Curator Manuscripts, Maryland Historical Soc, 67-69; prof, Catonsville Comm Col, 69-95 **MEMBERSHIPS** Maryland Historical Soc; Res Soc for Amer Periodicals **RESEARCH** 18th and 19th century Maryland History **SELECTED PUBLICATIONS** Auth, "William Wilkins Glenn," Encyclopedia of American Biography, Oxford, 96; auth "Tax Assessor's Portrait of a County," History Trails, 96; auth, "Rakes, Nippers, and Tongs, Oystermen in Antebellum St. Mary's County," Maryland Hist Mag, 93 **CONTACT ADDRESS** 7 Byford Ct, Chestertown, MD, 21620.

JARRELL, RICHARD A.
PERSONAL Born 08/29/1946, Connersville, IN **DISCIPLINE** HISTORY OF SCIENCE **EDUCATION** Indiana Univ, AB, 67; Univ Toronto, MA, 69, PhD, 72. **CAREER** PROF HISTORY, YORK UNIV, 70-; vis lectr, Univ Toronto, 76-78; founding ed, Scientia Canadensis, 76-88; co-founder, Can Sci & Technol Hist Asn, 80; Atkinson Col Res Fel, 84-85. **MEMBERSHIPS** Hist Sci Soc; Can Hist Asn; Royal Astron Soc Can; Can Soc Hist & Phil Sci. **SELECTED PUBLICATIONS** Auth, Science, Technology and Canadian History, 80; Critical Issues in the History of Canadian Science, Technology & Medicine, 83; The Cold Light of Dawn, 88; Science, Technology and Medicine in Canada's Past, 91; Building Canadian Science, 92; Dominions Apart, 95. **CONTACT ADDRESS** Dept of History, York Univ, 4700 Keele St, North York, ON, M3J 1P3.

JARVIE, IAN CHARLES
PERSONAL Born 07/08/1937, South Shields, England, m, 1962, 2 children **DISCIPLINE** PHILOSOPHY, ANTHROPOLOGY **EDUCATION** Univ London, BS, 58, PhD(philos), 61. **CAREER** Lectr philos, Univ Hong Kong, 62-66; chmn dept, 76-79, PROF PHILOS, YORK UNIV, 67-. **MEMBERSHIPS** Royal Anthrop Inst; Brit Soc Philos Sci; Soc Cinema Studies. **RESEARCH** Philosophy of the social sciences; anthropological theory; movies. **SELECTED PUBLICATIONS** Auth, Shared Pleasures--A History of Movie Presentation in the United States, Hist J Film Radio and Television, Vol 0014, 94. **CONTACT ADDRESS** Dept of Philos, York Univ, Downsview, ON, M3P 1P3.

JARVIS, CHARLES AUSTIN
PERSONAL Born 12/21/1941, Easton, MD, m, 1966, 2 children **DISCIPLINE** UNITED STATES HISTORY **EDUCATION** DePauw Univ, BA, 63; Univ MoColumbia, MA, 64, PhD(hist), 70. **CAREER** Asst prof, 69-73, ASSOC PROF HIST, DICKINSON COL, 73-, Nat Endowment for Humanities fel, Univ Mich, 75-76; dir, Dickinson Ctr Europ Studies, Bologna, Italy, 78-80. **MEMBERSHIPS** AHA; Orgn Am Historians; Southern Hist Asn **RESEARCH** United States history, 19th century; United States diplomatic history; Afro-American history. **SELECTED PUBLICATIONS** Auth, Jefferson, Thomas, Passionate Pilgrim--The Presidency, the Founding of the University, and the Private Battle, Pennsylvania Magazine of History and Biography, Vol 0117, 93; The Political-Philosophy of Jefferson, Thomas, Pa Mag Hist and Biography, Vol 0117, 93; Matthew 11-16-30, Interpretation-J Bible and Theology, Vol 0050, 96. **CONTACT ADDRESS** Dept of Hist, Dickinson Col, 1 Dickinson College, Carlisle, PA, 17013-2897.

JARVIS, JOSEPH ANTHONY
PERSONAL Born 04/05/1939, Queens, NY, m, 1966, 2 children **DISCIPLINE** AMERICAN HISTORY **EDUCATION** St John's Univ, NY, BA, 60; Columbia Univ, MA, 61; NY Univ, PhD, 70. **CAREER** Instr hist, St John's Univ, NY, 61-65; asst prof, State Univ NY Col Potsdam, 65-67; assoc prof, E Stroudsburg State Col, 67-, Kellogg fel pub affairs leadership prog, Pa State Univ, 73-75. **MEMBERSHIPS** AHA; AAUP **RESEARCH** New York City politics, 1880-1890; urban American history. **CONTACT ADDRESS** Dept of Hist, East Stroudsburg Univ of Pennsylvania, 200 Prospect St, East Stroudsburg, PA, 18301-2999. **EMAIL** JJarvis@esu.edu

JARVIS, MICHAEL J.
PERSONAL Born 07/21/1968, East Stroudsburg, PA, m, 1995, 1 child **DISCIPLINE** HISTORY **EDUCATION** Rutgers Univ, BA, 89; Col William and Mary, MA, 93, PhD, 98. **CAREER** Tchg asst, 92-94, 98, lectr, 94, 98, Col William and Mary; asst prof, Long Island Univ, 98-. **HONORS AND AWARDS** Henry Rutgers Scholar, 88-89, Rutgers Univ; Albert O. Vietor Fel, 96, John Carter Brown Library. **MEMBERSHIPS** Am Hist Asn **RESEARCH** Colonial Bermuda; the atlantic world; maritime history in age of sail. **SELECTED PUBLICATIONS** Auth, art, The Henry Tucker House: 280 Years of Bermudian Social History, 94; auth, art, The Fastest Vessels in the World: The Origin and Evolution of the Bemuda Sloop, 95; auth, art, The Long, Hot Summer of 1863, 96; auth, art, The Vingboons Chart of the James River, circa 1617, 97; auth, art, Bemuda's Architectural Heritage: Saint George's, 98. **CONTACT ADDRESS** Dept of History, Col of William and Mary, PO Box 8795, Williamsburg, VA, 23187-8795.

JASHEMSKI, WILHELMINA F.
PERSONAL Born 07/10/1910, Yory, NE, m, 1945 **DISCIPLINE** ANCIENT HISTORY **EDUCATION** York Col, AB, 31; Univ Nebr, AM, 33; Univ Chicago, PhD, 42. **CAREER** Teacher, Walthill High Sch, 34-35; mem fac Latin, Greek & hist, Ind Cent Col, 35-37, 38-40; mem fac hist, Lindenwood Col Women, 42-45; from asst prof to assoc prof, 46-65, prof, 65-80, fel, Dumbarton Oaks, 80-81, distinguished scholar-teacher, 82, EMER PROF GREEK & ROMAN HIST, UNIV MD, COLLEGE PARK, 80-, SR FEL & PROJ DIR, UNIV MD, DUMBARTON OAKS, 81-, Biomed sci support grant, 67-68; Nat Endowment for Humanities sr fel, 68-69 & res grants, 72-78. **HONORS AND AWARDS** Tatiana Warscher Award for Archaeol Res, Am Acad Rome, 68; Bradford Williams Award, Am Soc Landscape Architects, 77., Dr humanities, Univ Nebr, 80. **MEMBERSHIPS** Soc Prom Roman Studies; Archaeol Inst Am; Am Philol Asn; Int Asn Classical Archaeol. **RESEARCH** Roman provinces; ancient gardens of pompeii and the Roman Empire. **SELECTED PUBLICATIONS** Auth, Excavations in the Gardens in the House of Bacchus and Ariadne and in the East Temple at Thuburbo-Majus, Amer Jf Archaeol, Vol 0098, 94; Roman Gardens in Tunisia--Preliminary Excavations in the House of Bacchus and Ariadne and in the East Temple at Thuburbo Maius, Amer J Archaeol, Vol 0099, 95. **CONTACT ADDRESS** Univ Maryland, 415 Pershing Dr Silver, College Pk, MD, 20742.

JAY, MARTIN EVAN
PERSONAL Born 05/04/1944, New York, NY, m, 1974, 2 children **DISCIPLINE** MODERN EUROPEAN INTELLECTUAL HISTORY **EDUCATION** Union Col, NY, BA, 65; Harvard Univ, PhD(hist), 71. **CAREER** Asst prof, 71-75, assoc prof, 75-80, prof Hist, 80-97, SIDNEY HELLMAN EHRMAN PROF, UNIV CA, BERKELEY, 97-; Sr assoc mem, St Antony's Col, 74-75; Col internationale de philosophie, 84-85;Sr assoc member, Clare Hall, Cambridge, 89; Sr fel, Stanford Humanities Center, 97-98; Guggenheim Found fel, 74-75; Nat Endowment for Humanities fel, 79-80; sr ed, Theory and Society, 80-; Rockefeller Found fel, 84-85; ACLS fel, 89-90; Univ CA Presidential fel in the Humanities, 93-94; regular columnist, Salmagundi, 87-. **HONORS AND AWARDS** Herbert Baxter Adams Prize, AHA, 73; Am Academy of Arts and Sciences, 96. **MEMBERSHIPS** AHA; Soc for Exile Studies. **RESEARCH** Twentieth century European intellectual history; history of Marxist theory; history of German exiles to Am; visual culture. **SELECTED PUBLICATIONS** Auth, The Dialectial Imagination: A History of the Frankfurt School and the Institute of Social Research, 1923-1950, Little, Brown, 73, 2nd ed, Univ CA Press, 96; Marxism and Totality, Univ CA Press, 84; Adorno, Harvard, 84; Permanent Exiles, Columbia Univ Press, 85; Finde-siecle Socialism, Routledge, 89; Force Fields, Routledge, 93; Downcast Eyes, Univ CA Press, 93; Cultural Semantics, Univ MA Press, 98; Ed: An Unmastered past, Univ CA Press, 87; The Weimar Republic Sourcebook, Univ CA Press, 94; Vision in Context, Routledge, 97. **CONTACT ADDRESS** Dept of Hist, Univ of California, 3229 Dwinelle Hall, Berkeley, CA, 94720-2551. **EMAIL** martjay@socrates.berkeley.edu

JEFFERS, JACK
PERSONAL Born 12/10/1928, m **DISCIPLINE** MUSIC HISTORY **EDUCATION** Northeastern Univ, BS 1951; New York Univ Sch of Law, JD 1982. **CAREER** STATE UNIV OF NY, PROF EMERITUS OF MUSIC. **MEMBERSHIPS** Chmn 7 Arts Chap CORE 1964-66.

JEFFERSON, ALPHINE W.
DISCIPLINE HISTORY **EDUCATION** Univ Chicago, AB, 73; Duke Univ, MA, 75, PhD, 79. **CAREER** Assoc prof. **RESEARCH** Blacks and Jews in Chicago. **SELECTED PUBLICATIONS** Auth, Contemporary Diaspora and the Future, Africana Stud; auth, articles in African-American history. **CONTACT ADDRESS** Dept of Hist, Col of Wooster, Wooster, OH, 44691.

JEFFERSON, CARTER
PERSONAL Born 07/12/1927, Dallas, TX, m, 1955, 1 child **DISCIPLINE** HISTORY **EDUCATION** George Washington Univ, BA, 49; Southern Methodist Univ, MA, 55; Univ Chicago, PhD, 59. **CAREER** Instr hist, Wayne State Univ, 58-59 & Univ Mich, 59-62; from asst prof to assoc prof, Rutgers Univ, 62-69; PROF HIST, UNIV MASS, BOSTON, 69-80. **MEMBERSHIPS** AHA; Soc Fr Hist Studies; Soc Mod Hist France; Hist Educ Soc. **RESEARCH** European political and social history. **SELECTED PUBLICATIONS** Auth, Incentive Problems in Canada Land Markets--Emphasis on Ontario, J Agr & Env Ethics, Vol 0009, 96. **CONTACT ADDRESS** 6 Cazenove St, Boston, MA, 02116.

JEFFERSON, JOSEPH L.
PERSONAL Born 11/08/1940, Pensacola, FL, m **DISCIPLINE** EDUCATION **EDUCATION** TX Southern Univ, BA, 1968, MA, 1971; OH State Univ, PhD, 1974. **CAREER** Vocational Guidance Houston, counselor 1971; TX Southern Univ, admin asst to dean coll of arts & sciences dir inst; TX Southern Univ, assoc dir Office of Inst Research, prof College of Educ. **HONORS AND AWARDS** Recip Grad Fellow TX So Univ 1970-71; Acad Year Inst Study Grant 1972-73 OH State U. **MEMBERSHIPS** Mem Am Educ & Research Assn; Phi Delta Kappa; Assn for Inst Research; Am Counseling Assn; TX Counseling Assn; Kappa Alpha Psi Frat; Houston Jr Chamber of Commerce; Houston Lion's Club. **CONTACT ADDRESS** 3100 Cleburne, Houston, TX, 77004.

JEFFERY, PETER
PERSONAL Born 10/19/1953, New York, NY, m, 1983, 2 children **DISCIPLINE** MUSIC HISTORY **EDUCATION** City Univ NY, BA, 75; Princeton Univ, MFA, 77, PhD, 80. **CAREER** Hill Monastic Manuscript Libr, 80-82; asst prof, Univ Delaware, 84-87; assoc prof, 87- 93; PROF, PRINCETON UNIV, 93-. **MEMBERSHIPS** SBC, Medieval Acad Am; Am Musicol Soc. **RESEARCH** Medieval Christian chant **SELECTED PUBLICATIONS** Auth, "A Proposal for a "Palaeographical Manual of the Byzantine Musical Notations'," in Palaeobyzantine Notations: A Reconstruction of the Source Material, A.A. Bredius Found, 95; auth, "Rome and Jerusalem: From Oral Tradition to Written Repertory in Two Ancient Liturgical Centers," in Essays on Medieval Music in Honor of David Hughes 207-47, 95. ed, Paths and Bridges: The Study of Liturgical Chant, East and West, Princeton Univ Press; co-auth, Ethiopian Christian Liturgical Chant: An Anthology, 93-97; **CONTACT ADDRESS** Music Dept, Princeton Univ, Princeton, NJ, 08544. **EMAIL** jeffery@princeton.edu

JEFFREY, DAVID LYLE
PERSONAL Born 06/28/1941, Ottawa, ON, Canada **DISCIPLINE** ENGLISH LITERATURE, ART HISTORY **EDUCATION** Wheaton Col, Ill, BA, 65; Princeton Univ, MA, 67, PhD(English), 68. **CAREER** Asst prof, Univ Victoria, BC, 68-69 & Univ Rochester, 69-72; assoc prof English & chmn dept, Univ Victoria, BC, 73-78; chmn dept, 78-81, PROF ENGLISH, UNIV OTTAWA, 78-, Gen ed, Dict Biblical Tradition in English Lit, 77-; Can Coun leave fel, 77-78; adj prof, Regent Col, 78-, **HONORS AND AWARDS** Bk of Year Award, Conf Christianity & Lit, 75; Solomon Katz Distinguished Lectr in Humanities, Univ Wash, 77. **MEMBERSHIPS** MLA; Conf Christianity & Lit; Mediaeval Acad Am; Asn Can Univ Teachers English; Am Acad Relig & Soc Biblical Lit. **RESEARCH** Medieval, modern and biblical literature. **SELECTED PUBLICATIONS** Auth, A History of the Bible as Literature, Vol 1, From Antiquity to1700, Vol 2, From 1700 tothe Present Day, J Rel, Vol 0075, 95. **CONTACT ADDRESS** Dept of English, Univ of Ottawa, Ottawa, ON, K1N 6N5.

JEFFREY, JULIE ROY
PERSONAL Born 03/20/1941, Boston, MA, m, 1963, 2 children **DISCIPLINE** AMERICAN HISTORY **EDUCATION** Radcliffe Col, FA, 62; Rice Univ, PhD, 72. **CAREER** Asst prof, 72-80, assoc prof, 80-84, PROF AM HIST, GOUCHER COL, 84-; DIR, HISTORIC PRESERVATION, 76-84, Comnr, Comn Historic & Archit Preservation Baltimore City, 77-86 & Nat Historic Recs & Publ Comn, 79-84; Newberry Libr fel, 79. **HONORS AND AWARDS** Elizabeth Connolly Todd Prof 89-94; Am Counc Educ fel 87-88; Fulbright sr lectr, 92; Sudler Award, 92; NEH Award 95-96. **MEMBERSHIPS** Orgn Am Historians; Am Hist Asn; Coordinating Comt Women Hist Profession; Soc Hist Early Republic. **RESEARCH** American reform; American women in the nineteenth century; architecture and social roles. **SELECTED PUBLICATIONS** Coauth, An experiment in combat simulation: The battle of Cambrai, J Interdisciplinary Hist, winter 72; auth, The southern alliance and women: Another look at equal rights to all, special privileges to none, Feminist Studies, fall 75; coauth, Historical preservation projects, Newberry Papers in Family & Community Hist, 1/78; auth, Education for Children of the Poor: A Study of the Origins and Implementation of the Elementary andSecondary Education Act of 1975, Ohio State Univ, winter 78; auth, Beautiful walls for Baltimore, in Baltimore Museum of Fine Arts Catalogue, Baltimore Museum, spring 78; Buildings in and out of the classroom, Teaching Hist, spring 79; Frontier Women: Women in the Trans Mississippi West, 1840-1880, Hill & Wang, spring 79; The other half of the calling: Methodist clergy wives on the trans-Mississipi frontier, in Women in the Methodist Tradition, Abingdon Press, fall 81; co-auth, The American People: A History of a Nation and a Society, Longman, 4th ed, 87; The Making of a Missionary: Narcissa Whitman and Her

Vocation, Idaho Yesterdays, summer 87; There Is Some Splendid Scenery: Women's Responses to the Great Plains Landscape, Great Plains Quart, spring 88; Narcissa Whitman: The Significanceof a Missionary's Life, Mont Mag of Western Hist, spring 91; Empty Harvest at Waiilatpu: The Mission Life of Narcissa Whitman, Columbia Mag of Northwest Hist, fall 92; Converting the West: A Biography of Narcissa Whitman, Univ Okla, 92, 94; The Great Silent Army of Abolitionism: Ordinary Women in the Abolitionist Movement, Univ NC, 98; The Heathen Are Far Different from What You Imagine: Narcissa Whitman's Conflict between Imagination and Reality, in Terra Pacifica: People and Place in the Northwestern States and Canada, Wash State Univ Press, 98. **CONTACT ADDRESS** Dept of Hist, Goucher Col, 1021 Dulaney Vlly Rd, Baltimore, MD, 21204-2780. **EMAIL** riezler@aol.com

JEFFREY, KIRK
PERSONAL Born 09/05/1944, Washington, DC, m, 1965, 2 children **DISCIPLINE** AMERICAN HISTORY **EDUCATION** Harvard Univ, BA, 66; Stanford Univ, MA, 67, PhD(hist), 72. **CAREER** From instr to asst prof, 70-77, ASSOC PROF HIST, CARLETON COL, 77-, Am Coun Learned Soc grant-in-aid, 73; fac fel, Newberry Libr Sem Humanities, 73-74. **MEMBERSHIPS** Orgn Am Hist; Am Studies Asn **RESEARCH** Nineteenth century American cultural history; history of the family; history of women. **SELECTED PUBLICATIONS** Auth, Pacing the Heart--Growth and Redefinition of a Medical Technology, 1952-1975, Technol and Culture, Vol 0036, 95. **CONTACT ADDRESS** Dept of Hist, Carleton Col, Northfield, MN, 55057.

JEFFREY, THOMAS EDWARD
PERSONAL Born 09/05/1947, Chelsea, MA **DISCIPLINE** HISTORY **EDUCATION** Cath Univ Am, AB, 69, MA, 70, MSLS, 73, PhD(hist), 76. **CAREER** Microfiche ed hist, Papers Benjamin Henry Latrobe, Md Hist Soc, Baltimore, 74-77; ASSOC ED, THOMAS A EDISON PAPERS, RUTGERS UNIV, 79-, Consult hist ed, Nat Hist Publ & Records Comn, 77. **MEMBERSHIPS** Southern Hist Asn; Orgn Am Historians; Asn Doc Ed. **RESEARCH** Antebellum US politics; North Carolina history. **SELECTED PUBLICATIONS** Auth, The Papers of Reid, David,Settle, Vol 1--1829-1852, J Southern Hist, Vol 0061, 95. **CONTACT ADDRESS** Thomas Edison Papers, Rutgers Univ, P O Box 5059, New Brunswick, NJ, 08903-5059.

JEFFRIES, JOHN W.
DISCIPLINE HISTORY **EDUCATION** Yale Univ, PhD. **CAREER** Prof, Univ MD Baltimore County. **RESEARCH** Twentieth century Am; Am polit and policy hist. **SELECTED PUBLICATIONS** Auth, Testing the Roosevelt Coalition and Wartime America: The World War II Homefront; publ(s) on polit(s) and policy of the Franklin D. Roosevelt era; World War II American homefront. **CONTACT ADDRESS** Dept of Hist, Univ MD Baltimore County, Hilltop Circle, PO Box 1000, Baltimore, MD, 21250. **EMAIL** jeffries@research.umbc.edu

JEFFRIES, LEONARD
DISCIPLINE AFRICAN-AMERICAN STUDIES **EDUCATION** PhD. **CAREER** New York State Commission on Education, Task Force on Deficiency Correction in Curriculum Regarding People of Color, former consultant, former member; City College of New York, Dept of African American Studies, chairman, until 1992, professor, currently. **SELECTED PUBLICATIONS** Task Force's final report entitled, "A Cirriculum of Inclusion". **CONTACT ADDRESS** Department of African-American Studies, City Col, CUNY, 138th & Covant St, Rm 4150, New York, NY, 10031.

JEFFRIES, ROSALIND R.
PERSONAL Born 06/24/1936, New York, NY, m, 1965 **DISCIPLINE** ART HISTORY **EDUCATION** Hunter Coll, BA 1963; Columbia Univ, MA, 1968; Yale Univ, PhD, 1990. **CAREER** Bishop's Bible College Church of God in Christ, New York, NY, assistant professor, 1991; Jersey City State College, Jersey City, assistant professor, currently; School of Visual Arts, New York, NY, senior teaching faculty, currently; City Univ NY, art hist, artist, prof 1972-; San Jose St Univ, asst prof 1969-72; Brooklyn Museum, lectr 1969; Group Seminars, Africa, co-ldr 1966-72; US Govt USIS, Abidjan, & Ivory Cst, W Africa, dir exhib 1965-66. **HONORS AND AWARDS** Listed, Black Artists On Art; Afro-am Artist; Arts Achievement Award, President of Senegal, 1986. **MEMBERSHIPS** Lectr, univs, colls & comm cntrs-num one-woman art shows; cat writer, Museums; mem, Coll Arts Assn; CA St Art Historians; Nat Conf Artists; board of directors, Kem-Were Science Consortium, 1986-; director of art & culture, Association for the Study of African Classical Civilizations, 1986-; member, Blacklight Fellowship, Black Presence in the Bible, 1991-. **SELECTED PUBLICATIONS** Negro in Music & Art 1969; African Arts Mag, UCLA 1974; Enstooled as Queen Mother, Ashantehene Traditional Government of Ghana, 1988. **CONTACT ADDRESS** City Col, CUNY, 138 St & Convent Ave, New York, NY, 10031.

JEGEDE, DELE
PERSONAL Born 04/19/1945, Nigeria, m, 1975, 4 children **DISCIPLINE** ART HISTORY **EDUCATION** Ahmadu Bello Univ, Zaria, Nigeria, BA, 73; Ind Univ Bloomington, MA, 81, PhD, 83. **CAREER** Assoc prof, Ind St Univ Terre Haute **HONORS AND AWARDS** Fulbright Scholar-in-residence, Spelman Col, 87-88; ACASA Traveling Award, Art & Archaeology in Africa Program, 92; Ind St Univ res grant, 95; Smithsonian Sr Post-doctoral res grant, 95 **MEMBERSHIPS** African Stud Assoc; Arts Coun of African Stud Assoc; Col Art Assoc; Midwest Art Hist Soc. **SELECTED PUBLICATIONS** Auth, Recent Offerings in Contemporary African Art, rev essay, Res in African Lit, 94; Contemporary Art in Post-Colonial Africa, in An Inside Story: African Art of Our Time, Setagaya Art Museum, 95; The Essential Emokpae, in Seven Stories About Modern Art in Africa, Whitechapel, 95; New Currents, Ancient Rivers Contemporary African Artists in a Generation of Change, in African Arts, 96; On Scholars and Magicians: A Review of Contemporary Art of Africa, in Issues in Contemporary Art, 98. **CONTACT ADDRESS** Dept of Art, Indiana State Univ, Terre Haute, IN, 47809. **EMAIL** arjeged@ruby.indstate.edu

JELAVICH, BARBARA
PERSONAL Born 04/12/1923, Belleville, IL, m, 1944, 2 children **DISCIPLINE** HISTORY **EDUCATION** Univ Calif, AB, 43, AM, 44, PhD, 48. **CAREER** From asst prof to assoc prof, 62-64, PROF HIST, IND UNIV, BLOOMINGTON, 67-, Am Asn Univ Women Palmer fel & Harnach grant, Deutscher Akademikerinnenbund, 60-61; Rockefeller Found fel, 63-64; Nat Endowment for Humanities grant & Am Coun Learned Soc res grant, 69-70, 76-77; Off Educ Am Coun Learned Soc fel, 77-79. **RESEARCH** European and Russian diplomatic history; Balkan history. **SELECTED PUBLICATIONS** Auth, Destruction of Russia as a Major Power--British Military Goals in the Crimean War, Amer Hist Rev, Vol 0099, 94. **CONTACT ADDRESS** Dept of Hist, Indiana Univ, Bloomington, Bloomington, IN, 47401.

JELKS, EDWARD BAKER
PERSONAL Born 09/10/1922, Macon, GA, m, 1944, 1 child **DISCIPLINE** ARCHAEOLOGY, HISTORICAL ARCHAEOLOGY **EDUCATION** Univ Tex, BA, 48, MA, 51, PhD(anthrop), 65. **CAREER** Archaeologist, Smithsonian Inst, 50-53; archaeologist, Nat Park Serv, 63-56, supvry archaeologist, 56-58; dir, Tex Archaeol Salvage Proj, Univ Tex, 58-65, lectr anthrop, 63-65; assoc prof, Southern Methodist Univ, 65-68; PROF ANTHROP & DIR MIDWESTERN ARCHEOL RES CTR, ILL STATE UNIV, 68-, Dir, Signal Hill, Nfld Proj, Can Govt, 65-67; dir excavations, Ft Lancaster, San Saba, Ft Leaton & Washington-on-the-Brazos, Tex Hist Sites Prog, State Tex, 65-69; fel, Smithsonian Inst, 68; collabr improv soc sci teaching, US Off Educ, 70-72; dir, Archaeol Surv Mackinaw River & Cent Ill River Valleys, Ill Hist Sites Prog & Const Island Proj, US Mil Acad, 71-72. **MEMBERSHIPS** Fel AAAS; fel Am Anthrop Asn; Soc Am Archaeol; Soc Hist Archaeol (pres, 68); Soc Prof Archeologists (pres, 76). **RESEARCH** North American archaeology; historical archaeology. **SELECTED PUBLICATIONS** Auth, The Founding Meeting of the Society-For-Historical-Archaeology, 67, Hist Arch, Vol 0027, 93; Jc Harrington Medal in Historical Archaeology--Gilmore, Kathleen, Kirk 95, Hist Arch, Vol 0029, 95. **CONTACT ADDRESS** 605 N School St, Normal, IL, 61790.

JENKINS, A. LAWRENCE
PERSONAL Born 08/02/1959, Spain, m **DISCIPLINE** ART HISTORY **EDUCATION** Harvard Univ, BA, 81; Inst of Fine Arts, MA, 85, PhD, 95. **CAREER** Asst prof, Univ New Orleans, Dept of Fine Arts, 94-. **HONORS AND AWARDS** NEH fel, 97-98. **MEMBERSHIPS** CAA; SAH; Renaissance Soc of Am. **RESEARCH** Italian Renaissance architecture; fifteenth century; Sienese art of the Renaissance. **SELECTED PUBLICATIONS** Co-ed, Pratum Romanum: Richard Krautheimer zum 100 Geburstag, Ludwig Reichert Verlag, 97; rev, Massimo Bulgarelli, All'ombra Delle Volte: Architettura del Quattrocento a Firenze e Venezia, Jour of Soc of Archit Hist, 97; auth, Pius II and His Loggia in Siena, in, Pratum Romanum: Richard Krautheimer zum 100 Geburstag, Ludwig Reichert Verlag, 97; auth, Caterina Piccolomini and the Palazzo delle Papesse in Siena, in Wilkins, ed, Beyond Isabella: Secular Women Patrons of Art in Renaissance Italy, Thomas Jefferson, 99. **CONTACT ADDRESS** Dept of Fine Arts, Univ of New Orleans, New Orleans, LA, 70148. **EMAIL** aljfa@uno.edu

JENKINS, FRED W.
PERSONAL Born 04/13/1957, Cincinnati, OH, m, 1992 **DISCIPLINE** CLASSICAL PHILOLOGY **EDUCATION** Univ Cincinnati, BA, 79; Univ Ill Urbana-Champaign, AM, 81, PhD, 85, MS, libr & info sci, 86. **CAREER** Catalog spec and asst prof, 87-96, coord & head collection mgt and assoc prof, 96-, Univ Dayton Libr. **HONORS AND AWARDS** Phi Beta Kapp, 78; Acad Libr Asn of Oh Res grant, 93, 97; Choice Outstanding Acad Book, 96; Oh Libr Found Res award, 97. **MEMBERSHIPS** Amer Soc of Papyrologists; Amer Libr Asn. **RESEARCH** Later Latin literature; Papyrology; History & bibliography of classical studies. **SELECTED PUBLICATIONS** Co-auth, Reorganizing Collection Development and Acquisitions in a Medium-sized Academic Library, Libr Acquisitions: Practice and Theory, 22.3, 287-293, fall, 98; auth, Classical Studies, Mag for Libr, 9th ed, 356-362, 97; co-auth, Internet Resources for Classical Studies, Col & Res Libr News, 58.4, 255-259, apr, 97; auth, A Ptolemaic Account, Bull of the Amer Soc of Papyrologists, 33, 21-23, 96; auth, Classical Studies: A Guide to the Reference Literature, Libr Unlimited, 96; auth, A Coptic Account from the Michigan Collection, Archiv fur Papyrusforschung, 41.2, 191-193, 95; auth, A Fourth-Century Receipt from the Michigan Collection, Bull of the Amer Soc of Papyrologists, 31.3-4, 137-139, 94. **CONTACT ADDRESS** Univ of Dayton, 105F Roesch Library, Dayton, OH, 45469-1360. **EMAIL** jenkins@data.lib.udayton.edu

JENKINS, JENNIFER L.
DISCIPLINE MODERN EUROPE **EDUCATION** Stanford Univ, BA, 88; Univ Mich, MA, 91, PhD, 96. **CAREER** Hist, Washington Univ. **HONORS AND AWARDS** Krupp Found Intern Profog fel, Stanford Univ, 87; Regents Fel, Univ Mich, 89-92; Mellon Candidacy Fel, Univ Michigan, 92; Germanistic Socy Am Dissertation Grant, 92-93; Rackham Profedoctoral Fel, Univ Michigan, 94-95; Dissertation Res Grant, Nat Endowment Hum, 95-96. **SELECTED PUBLICATIONS** Coauth, The Kaiserreich in the 1990s: New Research, New Agendas, New Directions German History, 91; Die Kulturreformbewegung um 1900 am Beispiel Hamburgs Materialien Jugendliteratur Und Medien heft 30, 93; Collaborative paper, Postmordernism and Television: Speaking Twin Peaks, Full Secrets: Critical Approfoaches To Twin Peaks, Wayne State Univ Profess, 94. **CONTACT ADDRESS** Washington Univ, 1 Brookings Dr, St. Louis, MO, 63130.

JENNINGS, ROBERT RAY
PERSONAL Born 11/15/1950, Atlanta, Georgia **DISCIPLINE** SOCIOLOGY **EDUCATION** Univ of Ghana Legon West Africa, Charles Merrill Scholar 1971; Morehouse Coll, BA, Sociology, 1972; Atlanta Univ, MA, Educ Psych, 1974; GA State Univ Sch of Educ, Certificate in Gifted Educ 1975; Univ of GA, Certificate in Adult Basic Educ, 1978; Atlanta Univ, Educ Specialist in Interrelated Learning, 1979; Doctorate, Admin, 1982. **CAREER** Atlanta Univ, asst to dir of public relations, 1973; Atlanta Public Sch, Hoffman reading coord 1973-76; Literacy Action Inc Atlanta, reading consultant 1974-75; Reading Learning Ctr Inc East Point, dir 1975-79; Atlanta Public Schs, tchr of the gifted 1976-79; Atlanta Univ, consultant dean's grant proj 1979-80; Atlanta Area Tech Sch, part-time prof 1979-84; Equal Employ Comm US Govt, equal oppor specialist 1979-82; Morris Brown Coll Atlanta, assoc prof 1982-84; US Equal Employment Oppor Commn, Atlanta Dist, official commn rep office of dir 1982-84, Washington, employee devel specialist 1984-85; asst vice pres, devel & placement, Atlanta Univ, 1985-88; Norfolk State Univ, vice pres of development, 1988-91; Albany State University, vp for institutional advancement, 1991-97; North Carolina Agricultural and Technical State University, vice chancellor for Development and University Relations and CEO for the Foundation, 1997-. **HONORS AND AWARDS** Outstanding Achievement Award, Economic Opportunity Atlanta 1972; Outstanding Serv Awd Atlanta Inquirer Newspaper 1972; Director's Award Frederick Douglass Tutorial Inst Morehouse Coll 1972; Outstanding Serv Award Student Natl Educ Assn, 1972; Awd of Excellence Student Mississippi Teacher's Assn, 1972; WSB TV & Radio Fellow 1975; Teacher of the Year Home Park School Atlanta 1976; Award of Excellence Wm Finch Sch PTA, 1976; Appreciation Award for Outstanding Leadership SM Inman Sch PTA 1976; Outstanding Chapter Mem of the Yr Atlanta Univ 1979; Best of Service Award Frank Lebby Stanton Sch Atlanta 1979; Alumnus of the Yr Atlanta Univ 1980; Special Serv Award, Council for Exceptional Children, Atlanta, 1981; Special Serv Award, Natl Bd of Dirs, Atlanta Univ Alumni, 1981; Phi Delta KappaPrssional Fraternity in Educ, 1982; cited by Atlanta Journal & Constitution Newspaper as one of Atlanta's Most Outstanding Volunteers, 1982; Outstanding Serv Award, United Way of Metro Atlanta, 1984; First Recipient Leadership Award in Educ, Delta Sigma Theta Sor, 1986; Outstanding Atlantan, 1986. **MEMBERSHIPS** Pres, Atlanta Univ Natl Alumni Assn, 1979-81; mem, bd of dirs, Exodus Right-to-Read Program Adult Literacy Prog, 1980; bd of advisors, Volunteer Atlanta, 1980-84; parlimentarian Council for Exceptional Children Atlanta Area Chap 1980-81; bd of dirs, Parents Anonymous of GA, 1981-84; bd of trustees, Atlanta Univ 1981-85; founder and editor-in-chief Alumni Update of Leadership Atlanta 1982-; Self-Study Evaluation Comm, Morris Brown Coll, 1983-84; bd of dirs, Planned Parenthood, 1983-87; exec bd, Leadership Atlanta 1986-87; vice pres, Council for Advancement of Public Black Colleges & Universities, 1989-; NAACP Education Legal Advisory Board, chairman, 1987-; Leadership Albany, 1992-93; Southwest Georgia Comprehensive Health Institute, board of directors, 1992-; Community Relations Council and Turner Job Corp, Inc, Albany GA, mem board of directors, 1996-98; American Lung Assn, Albany Chap, mem board of directors, 1994-; West End Church of Christ, mem, 1988-; American Assn for Higher Educ, 1988-; American Biographical Inst, honorary mem, bd of advisors, 1987-; Council for the Advancement & Support of Education, 1984-; Phi Delta Kappa, 1982-. **CONTACT ADDRESS** North Carolina A&T State Univ, Greensboro, NC, 27411.

JENSEN, BILLIE B
PERSONAL Born 08/18/1933, Boulder, CO, m, 1955 **DISCIPLINE** AMERICAN HISTORY **EDUCATION** Univ Colo,

BA, 55, MA, 59, PhD, 62. **CAREER** Lectr hist, Denver Exten Ctr, Univ Colo, 60-61; from instr to assoc prof, 62-71, PROF HIST, SAN JOSE STATE UNIV, 71-, Assoc ed, San Jose Studies, 75-. **MEMBERSHIPS** Am Studies Asn; AHA; Orgn Am Historians; Western Hist Asn. **RESEARCH** American diplomatic history; American social and intellectual history; history of women in the United States. **SELECTED PUBLICATIONS** Auth, in the Weird and Woolly West--Anti-Suffrage Women, Gender Issues, and Woman Suffrage in the West, J West, Vol 0032, 93; Girl on a Pony, Nmex Hist Rev, Vol 0070, 95. **CONTACT ADDRESS** Dept of Hist, San Jose State Univ, 1 Washington Sq, San Jose, CA, 95192-0001.

JENSEN, DE LAMAR
PERSONAL Born 04/22/1925, Roseworth, ID, m, 1951, 5 children **DISCIPLINE** MODERN EUROPEAN HISTORY **EDUCATION** Brigham Young Univ, AB, 52; Columbia Univ, AM, 53, PhD, 57. **CAREER** Teacher, high sch, Idaho, 47-48; instr of Western civilization, NY Univ, 54-57; from instr to assoc prof, 57-66, chmn dept, 67-72, PROF HIST, BRIGHAM YOUNG UNIV, 66-, RES FUND GRANT, 59-, Fac res fel, Brigham Young Univ, 63; Rockefeller Found res grant early mod diplomacy in Europe, 64-65; newsletter ed, Historians Early Mod Europe, 65-; Nat Endowment for Humanities res grant, 70-71; consult ed, Forums in hist ser, Forum Press, 72-; ed exec, Biog Dictionary Early Mod Europ, 73- **MEMBERSHIPS** AHA; Renaissance Soc Am; Am Soc Reformation Res; Hist Asn, Eng. **RESEARCH** Early modern diplomatic history; Renaissance and Reformation; European thought. **SELECTED PUBLICATIONS** Auth, Isabel the Queen--Life and Times, Amer Hist Rev, Vol 0099, 94. **CONTACT ADDRESS** Dept of Hist, Brigham Young Univ, Provo, UT, 84602.

JENSEN, JOAN MARIA
PERSONAL Born 12/09/1934, St. Paul, MN **DISCIPLINE** UNITED STATES HISTORY **EDUCATION** Univ Calif, Los Angeles, BA, 57, MA, 59, PhD(hist), 62. **CAREER** Teaching asst, Univ Calif, Los Angeles, 59-61; from asst prof to assoc prof hist, US Int Univ, 62-71; asst prof, 76-78, assoc prof, 78-82, PROF HIST, NMEX STATE UNIV, 82-, Vis asst prof hist, Ariz State Univ, 74-75; vis lectr hist, Univ Calif, Los Angeles, 75-76; mem ex bd, Southwest Labor Studies, 78-79. **MEMBERSHIPS** Orgn Am Historians; AHA; Coord Comt Women in Hist Professions. **RESEARCH** United States intelligence and internal security in the 20th century; women in American labor history; Asian immigration. **SELECTED PUBLICATIONS** Auth, Western Womens History Revisited + Afterword, Pacific Hist Rev, Vol 0061, 92; The Death of Rosa--Sexuality in Rural America, Agr Hist, Vol 0067, 93. **CONTACT ADDRESS** Dept of Hist, New Mexico State Univ, Las Cruces, NM, 88003.

JENSEN, TIM
PERSONAL Edmore, MI, m, 2 children **DISCIPLINE** RELIGIONS OF ASIA **EDUCATION** Dana Col, BA, 66;Univ Chicago, MA, 70, PhD, 76. **CAREER** Instr, Mary Washington Col, 72-78; instr, Sturt Col of Advan Educ, Adelaide, S Australia, 78-82; instr, Univ Nebr, Omaha. **HONORS AND AWARDS** Off of Educ grant, 73. **RESEARCH** Christianity. **SELECTED PUBLICATIONS** Published in the areas of Hinduism and Guddhism; published an article on Danish immigration to the U.S. and Canada. **CONTACT ADDRESS** Univ Nebr, Omaha, Omaha, NE, 68182.

JENSON, CAROL ELIZABETH
PERSONAL Born 11/27/1939, Albert Lea, MN, m, 1976 **DISCIPLINE** AMERICAN CONSTITUTIONAL HISTORY **EDUCATION** St Olaf Col, BA, 61; Brown Univ, MA, 63; Univ Minn, Minneapolis, PhD(hist), 68. **CAREER** Instr Hist, Gogebic Community Col, 63; instr, Dakota State Col, 63-64; ref librn, Chicago Hist Soc, 64; asst prof hist, 68-72, assoc prof, 72-79, PROF HIST, UNIV WIS-LA CROSSE, 79-, Nat Endowment for Humanities fel, 77-78. **HONORS AND AWARDS** Solon J Buck Award, Minn Hist Soc Writing Award, 73. **MEMBERSHIPS** Orgn Am Historians; Am Civil Liberties Union; AHA; Am Soc Legal Hist; Women Historians Midwest. **RESEARCH** American civil liberties in the twentieth century; women's history; women and the law. **SELECTED PUBLICATIONS** Auth, Promise to the Land--Essays On Rural Women, J West, Vol 0032, 93. **CONTACT ADDRESS** Dept of Hist, Univ of Wis, La Crosse, WI, 54601.

JERVIS, ROBERT
DISCIPLINE INTERNATIONAL AFFAIRS **EDUCATION** Oberlin Coll, BA, 62; Univ Calif-Berkeley, PhD, 68. **CAREER** Asst prof, harvard Univ, 68-74; prof, UCLA, Polit Sci, 74-80; PROF, COLUMBIA UNIV, INT AFFAIRS. **SELECTED PUBLICATIONS** The Meaning of Nuclear Revolution, Cornell Univ Press, 89; System Effects: Complexity in Political and Social Life, Princeton Univ Press, 97. **CONTACT ADDRESS** Dept Polit Sci, Columbia Univ, New York, NY, 10027.

JETT, STEPHEN C.
PERSONAL Born 10/12/1938, Cleveland, OH, m, 1995, 1 child **DISCIPLINE** GEOLOGY; GEOGRAPHY **EDUCATION** Princeton Univ, AB, 60; Johns Hopkins Univ, PhD, 64 **CAREER** Prof Textiles, Univ Calif Davis, 96-; prof Geography, Univ Calif Davis, 79-; assoc prof Geography, Univ Calif Davis, 72-79; asst prof Geography, Univ Calif Davis, 64-72 **HONORS AND AWARDS** Navajo Wildlands Top 50 Bks of Yr, 97 **MEMBERSHIPS** Amer Assoc Advancement Science; Assoc Amer Geographers; Amer Geographical Soc; Soc Amer Archaeology. Explorers Club **RESEARCH** Historical Geography; Historical Culture; Pre-Columbian Transoceanic Influences; Material Culture; Sacred Places; Placenames **SELECTED PUBLICATIONS** "Dyestuffs and Possible Early Southwestern Asian/South American Contacts," Across before Columbus? Evidence for Transoceanic Contact with the Americas prior to 1492, NEARA Publications, 98; "Resist-Dyeing as a Possible Ancient Transoceanic Transfer," Mormons, Scripture, and the Ancient World: Studies in Honor of John L. Sorenson, 98; "Place-Naming, Environment, and Perception among the Canyon de Chelly Navajo of Arizona," The Professional Geographer, 97 **CONTACT ADDRESS** Div of Textiles and Clothing, Univ Calif, 1 Shields, Davis, CA, 95616.

JEWSBURY, GEORGE FREDERICK
PERSONAL Born 11/26/1941, Colchester, IL, m, 1964, 3 children **DISCIPLINE** RUSSIAN & EAST EUROPEAN HISTORY **EDUCATION** Mankato State Col, BA, 62; Univ Wash, MA, 65, PhD(hist), 70; Univ Bucharest, dipl Romanian studies, 68. **CAREER** From instr to asst prof, 67-76, ASSOC PROF HIST, OKLA STATE UNIV, 76-, Fulbright teaching fel, Univ Nancy, 71-72. **MEMBERSHIPS** Am Asn Advan Slavic Studies; Fulbright Alumni Asn; Am Asn southeastern Europ Studies. **RESEARCH** Russian activities in the Danubian principalities; Russia in the nineteenth century; French Emigres in Russia. **SELECTED PUBLICATIONS** Auth, Nicholas-I and the Russian Intervention in Hungary, Russ Hist, Vol 0020, 93; Russia Balkan Entanglements 1806-1914, Russ Hist, Vol 0020, 93; Revolution and Genocide--On the Origins of the Armenian Genocide and the Holocaust, Historian, Vol 0055, 93; Alexander-I, Int Hist Rev, Vol 0017, 95; Conflict and Chaos in Eastern-Europe, Amer Hist Rev, Vol 0101, 96; Culture and History in Eastern-Europe, Amer Hist Rev, Vol 0101, 96. **CONTACT ADDRESS** Dept of Hist, Oklahoma State Univ, Stillwater, OK, 74078.

JICK, LEON ALLEN
PERSONAL Born 10/04/1924, St. Louis, MO, m, 1959, 4 children **DISCIPLINE** IMMIGRATION HISTORY, MODERN JEWISH HISTORY **EDUCATION** Washington Univ, BA, 47; Hebrew Union Col, MA, 54; Columbia Univ, PhD(Am immigration hist), 73. **CAREER** Asst prof, 66-69, dean col, 69-71, dir contemp Jewry, Inst for Jewish Life, 71-73, assoc prof, 69-80, SCHNEIDER ASSOC PROF AM JEWISH STUDIES, BRANDEIS UNIV, 80-, Trustee, Boston Hebrew Col, 72-76. **MEMBERSHIPS** Asn for Jewish Studies (pres, 70-72); Am Jewish Hist Soc; Inst for Contemp Jewry, Jerusalem; Acad Jewish Studies; Boston Hebrew Col. **RESEARCH** American Jewish history. **SELECTED PUBLICATIONS** Auth, Wise, Isaac, Meyer--Shaping American Judaism, Amer Jewish Arch, Vol 0046, 94; Comments on the Washington Hebrew Congregation Article--Response, Amer Jewish Hist, Vol 0084, 96. **CONTACT ADDRESS** Lown Ctr, Brandeis Univ, 415 South St, Waltham, MA, 02154.

JIMENEZ-RAMIREZ, TALIA
PERSONAL Born 02/25/1972, Mexico City, Mexico **DISCIPLINE** MUSIC, MUSICOLOGY **EDUCATION** Ithaca Col, BA, 93; NYUniv, MA, 98. **CAREER** Admin Asst and Prof, Technol Inst Monterrey, Mexico City, 93-96. **HONORS AND AWARDS** Fullbright Travel Scholar, 89; Ithaca Col Scholar, 89-93; Truman Scholar 91, 93; Emerson Scholar, 92-93; Dana Intern, 90, 92; McCracken Scholar 96-98; Dean's Scholar, 96-98; DAAD Ger Stud Scholar, 97; NYU Summer Paper Travel Scholar, 98. **MEMBERSHIPS** Oracle Soc; Phi Kappa Phi. **RESEARCH** Perception and emotion in music; Contemporary music and systems theory; Mexican concert music in the twentieth century. **CONTACT ADDRESS** New York Univ, 24 Waverly Pl, 2nd Fl, New York, NY, 10003. **EMAIL** tj201@is5.nyu.edu

JODZIEWICZ, THOMAS W.
PERSONAL Born 03/07/1944, Alburquerque, NM, m, 1967, 2 children **DISCIPLINE** HISTORY **EDUCATION** Providence Col, AB; Tufts Univ, MA; Col William and Mary, PhD. **CAREER** Dept ch; prof, Dallas Univ. **RESEARCH** Early American history, particularly New England and American Catholic. **SELECTED PUBLICATIONS** Auth, A Curious Soaking Rain to Night Thanks Be to God: Gershom Bulkeley's 1710 Diary, Conn Hist Soc, Bul LVI, 91, 93; An Unexpected Coda for the Early American Captivity Narrative: A Letter from a Romish Priest, Cath Hist Rev LXXXI, 95. **CONTACT ADDRESS** Dept of History, Univ of Dallas, 1845 E Northgate Dr, Braniff 244, Irving, TX, 75062. **EMAIL** tjodz@acad.udallas.edu

JOHANNES, JOHN R.
PERSONAL Born 12/15/1943, Milwaukee, WI, m, 1967, 3 children **DISCIPLINE** POLITICAL SCIENCE **EDUCATION** Marquette Univ, BS, Math & Polit Sci, 66; Harvard Univ, GOVT, AM, 68, PhD, 70. **CAREER** Instr, Marquette Univ, 70; vis asst prof, Harvard Univ, 72; asst prof, Marquette Univ, 70-75; assoc prof, Marquette Univ, 75-84; ch, Marquette Univ, 80-88; prof, Marquette Univ, Polit Sci, 84-95; dean, Marquette Univ, Coll Arts & Sci, 88-93; VPRES, VILLANOVA UNIV, ACAD AFFAIRS & PROF POLIT SCI, 95-. **HONORS AND AWARDS** Lynde and Harry Bradley Found Res Grant, 94 **MEMBERSHIPS** Am Polit Sci Asn; Midwest Polit Sci Asn; South Polit Sci Asn; West Polit Sci Asn; Wisconsin Polit Sci Asn; Asn Am Coll & Univ; Am Asn High Educ **SELECTED PUBLICATIONS** "Casework in the House," The House at Work, Glencoe Books, 93; "Constituency Service and Congressional Elections," Encyclopedia American Political Parties and Elections, Garland Press, 91. **CONTACT ADDRESS** Off Acad Affairs, Villanova Univ, 800 Lancaster Ave, Villanova, PA, 19085. **EMAIL** jjohanne@email.vill.edu

JOHANNSEN, ROBERT W.
PERSONAL Born 08/22/1925, Portland, OR, m, 1949, 2 children **DISCIPLINE** HISTORY **EDUCATION** Univ Wash, PhD, 53. **CAREER** Prof, Univ Ill Urbana Champaign. **RESEARCH** Cultural history of early nineteenth century America. **SELECTED PUBLICATIONS** Auth, To the Halls of the Montezumas: The Mexican War in the American Imagination, Oxford, 85; Lincoln, the South, and Slavery: The Political Dimension, La State Univ, 91. **CONTACT ADDRESS** History Dept, Univ Ill Urbana Champaign, 52 E Gregory Dr, Champaign, IL, 61820.

JOHANSEN, BRUCE ELLIOTT
PERSONAL Born 01/30/1950, San Diego, CA **DISCIPLINE** AMERICAN HISTORY, CROSS-CULTURAL COMMUNICATIONS **EDUCATION** Univ Wash, BA, 72, PhD(comm), 79; Univ Minn, MA, 75. **CAREER** Staff writer, Seattle Times, 70-76; teaching assoc newswriting, Univ Wash, 76-79; grant coord, El Centro de la Raza, 80-81; asst to full prof Commun, Robert T. Reilly Diamond Prof, Univ Nebr, Omaha, 82-, co-ord Native American Studies, Univ of Nebr at Omaha, 98-, consult, El Centro de la Raza, 76-, Seattle Times, 77, Ford Found, 77 & Nat Endowment for Humanities, 81-. **HONORS AND AWARDS** Univ of Omaha's Award for Outstanding Research or Creative Activity, 97.RG **RESEARCH** American Revolutionary history; American Indian history and contemporary issues; Chicano history and contemporary issues. **SELECTED PUBLICATIONS** Auth, The Reservation Offensive, In: Essential Sociology, Scott, Foresman & Co, 79; coauth (with Roberto Maestas), Wasi'chu: The Continuing Indian Wars, Monthly Rev Press, 79, Span transl, Fondo Cultura y Economica, Mexico City, 62 & Arabic transl, Hindi, Beruit; auth, Black Hills uranium rush, In: America's Energy: Reports from the Nation on 100 Years of Struggles for the Democratic Control of Our Resources, Pantheon, 81; The Forgotten Founders: Benjamin Franklin, the Iroquois and the Rationale for American Revolution, Gambit, 82; coauth (with Roberto Maestas), El Pueblo: The Gallegos Family's American Journey, 1503-1980, Monthly Rev Press, 82; Exemplar of Liberty: Native America and the Evolution of Democracy, with Dr. Donald A. Grinde, Jr., Los Angelos: American Indian Study Center, UCLA, 91; Life and Death in Mohawk Country, Golden, Co: North American Press/ Fulcrum Pubs, 93; Eccocide of Native America: Ecology, Economics, and the Environment, with Donald A. Grinde, Jr., Santa Fe, NM: Clear Light Pubs, 95; Native American Political Systems and the Evolution of Democracy: An Annotated Bibliography, Westport, Conn: Greenwood Press, 96; So Far From Home: Manila's Santo Tomas Internment Camp, 1942-1945, Omaha: NE: PBI Press (self-published), 96; The Encyclopedia of Native American Biography, with Donald A. Grinde, Jr., New York: Henry Holt, 97; Debating Democracy: The Iroquois Legacy of Freedom, Santa Fe: Clear Light Pubs, 98; The Encyclopedia of Native American Legal Tradition, Westport, Conn: Greenwood Press, 98; The Encyclopedia of Native American Economic History, Westport, Conn: Greenwood Press, est 99; The Haudeosaunee (Iroquois) Encyclopedia, Westport, Conn: Greenwood Press, est 2000; Native American Political Systems and the Evolution of Democracy; An Annotated Bibliography, Vol II, Westport, Conn: Greenwood Press, est 2000; The Shapers of the Great Debates: Native Americans, Land, Spirit, and Power, Wesrport, Conn: Greenwood Press, est 2000. **CONTACT ADDRESS** Dept of Commun, Univ Nebr, 6001 Dodge St, Omaha, NE, 68182-0002. **EMAIL** johansen@cwis.unomaha.edu

JOHANSON, HERBERT A.
DISCIPLINE CONST LAW, AND LEGAL HISTORY **EDUCATION** Columbia Univ, AB, 55, MA, 61, PhD, 65; NY Law Sch, LLB, 60. **CAREER** Ernest F. Hollings prof Const Law, Univ of SC. **SELECTED PUBLICATIONS** Auth, casebk on Amer legal and const hist & textbk on the hist of criminal justice. **CONTACT ADDRESS** School of Law, Univ of S. Carolina, Law Center, Columbia, SC, 29208. **EMAIL** Hjohnson@law.law.sc.edu

JOHN, JAMES J.
PERSONAL Born 07/25/1928, Long Prairie, MN, m, 1952, 6 children **DISCIPLINE** MEDIEVAL HISTORY, LATIN PALEOGRAPHY **EDUCATION** Univ Notre Dame, BA, 48, MA, 50, MMS, 51, DMS(mediaeval studies), 59. **CAREER** Asst paleography, Inst Advan Studies, 51-61, res assoc, 62-64; PROF

PALEOGRAPHY & MEDIEVAL HIST, CORNELL UNIV, 65-, Vis lectr, Princeton Univ, 59, Bryn Mawr Col & Fordham Univ, 61-62; consult, Free Libr Philadelphia, 60-65; fel, Inst Res Humanities, Univ Wis, 64-65; Am Philos Soc grant, 69-70; Am Coun Learned Soc grant, 69-70, fel, 72-73; mem, Inst Advan Studies, 69-70 & 72-73; Nat Endowment for Humanities grant, 72-73; vis prof, State Univ NY Binghamton, 74. **MEMBERSHIPS** Am Cath Hist Asn; Mediaeval Acad Am **RESEARCH** Medieval intellectual history; Latin paleography. **SELECTED PUBLICATIONS** Auth, The Cartulary of Flavigny, 717-1113, Speculum-J Medieval Stud, Vol 0068, 93; The Ex-Libris in 'Codices Latini Antiquiores' + Provenance and Ownership Claims in Early-Medieval Latin Literary Manuscripts, Scriptorium, Vol 0050, 96; The Ex-Libris in 'Codices Latini Antiquiores' + Provenance and Ownership Claims in Early-Medieval Latin Literary Manuscripts, Scriptorium, Vol 0050, 96. **CONTACT ADDRESS** Dept of Hist, Cornell Univ, Mcgraw Hall, Ithaca, NY, 14853-0001.

JOHN, RICHARD R.
DISCIPLINE HISTORY **EDUCATION** Harvard Univ, BA, 81; MA, 83, PhD, 89. **CAREER** Inst, hist & lit, Harvard Univ; asst prof, ASSOC PROF, HIST, UNIV ILL AT CHICAGO. **HONORS AND AWARDS** Allan Nevins Prize, Herman E Kroos Prize. **MEMBERSHIPS** Am Antiquarian Soc **SELECTED PUBLICATIONS** Auth, "Taking Sabbatarianism Seriously: The Postal System, the Sabbath, and the Transformation of American Political Culture," Jour of the Early Repub, 90;"Communications and Information Processing," in Encycl of Soc Hist, 93; auth, "American Historians and the Concept of the Communications Revolution," in Information Acumen: The Understanding and Use of Knowledge in Modern Business, Routledge, 94; auth, Spreading the News: The American Postal System from Franklin to Morse, Harvard Univ Press, 95; auth, "Leonard D. White and the Invention of American Administrative History," Rev in Am Hist 24, 96; auth, "Champions, Critics, and Skeptics: Alfred D. Chandler's The Visible Hand, Organizational Innovation, and the Stages of American Economic Development," Bus Hist Rev, 97; auth, "Hilland Hall's 'Report on Incendiary Publications': A Forgotten Nineteenth-Century Defense of the Constitutional Guarantee of the Freedom of the Press,." Am Jour of Legal Hist; auth, "Eben Norton Horsford, the Northmen, and the Founding of Massachusetts," Cambridge Hist Soc Procs. **CONTACT ADDRESS** Dept of Hist, Univ of Ill at Chicago, 601 S Morgan St, Chicago, IL, 60607-7049. **EMAIL** rjohn@uic.edu

JOHNSON, ARTHUR L.
PERSONAL Born 11/15/1933, Natick, MA, m, 1960, 2 children **DISCIPLINE** AMERICAN & CANADIAN HISTORY **EDUCATION** Kenyon Col, BA, 55; Univ Maine, MA, 66, PhD(Am hist), 71. **CAREER** Instr hist, Univ Maine, 67-68; asst prof, 68-73, assoc prof, State Univ NY Col Potsdam, 73-. **MEMBERSHIPS** Org Am Historians; Can Hist Asn; Asn Can Studies US; Steamship Hist Soc Am; Railway and Locomotive Hist Soc. **RESEARCH** East Coast steamship lines; United States and Canada. **SELECTED PUBLICATIONS** Auth, Historic Night Line Revived, Steamboat Bill, spring 72; The International Line: A History of the Boston-Saint John Steamship Service, Am Neptune, 4/73; Steam Navigation Between Boston and the Maritimes, Abstrs for Colloquium on Maritime Provinces Hist, 72; From Eastern State to Evangeline, Am Neptune, 7/74; No Firebell in the Night, Steamboat Bill, fall 74; The Transportation Revolution on Lake Ontario, Ont Hist, 12/75; The Boston-Halifax Steamship Lines, Am Neptune, 10/77; The Montreal Secondary: Origins and History, Railroad Hist, Spring 98. **CONTACT ADDRESS** Dept of Hist, State Univ, 44 Pierrepont Ave., Potsdam, NY, 13676-2299. **EMAIL** johnsoal@potsdam.edu

JOHNSON, BOBBY HAROLD
PERSONAL Born 11/09/1935, Overton, TX, m, 1959, 2 children **DISCIPLINE** AMERICAN & JOURNALISM HISTORY **EDUCATION** Abilene Christian Col, BA, 58; Univ Okla, MA, 62, PhD(hist), 67. **CAREER** From asst prof to assoc prof, 66-77, PROF HIST, STEPHEN F AUSTIN STATE UNIV, 77-, Dir, Off Univ Info, Stephen F Austin State Univ, 79-82. **MEMBERSHIPS** Orgn Am Historans; Western Hist Asn **RESEARCH** American West, especially Oklahoma territory; history of American journalism; history of aviation. **SELECTED PUBLICATIONS** Auth, The Cartwrights of San-Augustine--3 Generations of Agricultural Entrepreneurs in 19th-Century Texas, Southwestern Hist Quart, Vol 0098, 95. **CONTACT ADDRESS** Dept of Hist, Stephen F Austin State Univ, Box 3013, Nacogdoches, TX, 75962.

JOHNSON, CALVERT
DISCIPLINE MUSIC **EDUCATION** Kalamazoo Co, BA, 71; Northwestern Univ, MM, 72, DM, 76. **CAREER** Dir music, 1st Un Methodist Church, 75-77; assoc prof, Northeastern Okla State Univ, 77-86; PROF MUSIC, AGNES SCOTT COL, 86-. **CONTACT ADDRESS** Agnes Scott Col, 141 E College Ave, Decatur, GA, 30030. **EMAIL** cjohnson@agnesscott.edu

JOHNSON, CHARLES W.
DISCIPLINE HISTORY **EDUCATION** Univ Mich, PhD. **CAREER** Assoc prof. **SELECTED PUBLICATIONS** Coauth, City Behind a Fence: A History of Oak Ridge, Tennessee. **CONTACT ADDRESS** Dept of History, Knoxville, TN, 37996.

JOHNSON, CHRISTOPHER HOWARD
PERSONAL Born 11/22/1937, Washington, IN, m, 1960, 2 children **DISCIPLINE** MODERN EUROPEAN SOCIAL HISTORY **EDUCATION** Wabash Col, BA, 60; Univ Wis-Madison, MA, 62, PhD(Hist), 68. **CAREER** Instr Hist, Univ Wis Ctr-Wausau, 65-66; from instr to asst prof, 66-75, assoc prof, 75-79, prof Hist, Wayne State Univ, 79-, Leverhulme vis fel, Univ E Anglia, UK, 70-71; Nat Endowment for Humanities younger humanist fel, 74-75; Guggenheim fel, 81-82. **HONORS AND AWARDS** Fac Recognition Award, Bd Govs, Wayne State Univ, 76, 89, 96; Prof of the Year, Wayne State Univ, 97; Acad of Scholars, Wayne State, 98. **MEMBERSHIPS** AHA; Soc Fr Hist Studies. **RESEARCH** Eighteenth/Nineteenth century French social and cultural history; working class US history. **SELECTED PUBLICATIONS** Auth, Etienne Cabet and the problem of class antagonism, Int Rev Social Hist, 66; Communism and the working class before Marx: The Icarian experience, Am Hist Rev, 71; Utopian Communism in France: Cabet and the Icarians, 1839-1851, Cornell Univ, 74; The Revolution of 1830 in French economic history, In: 1830 in France, New Viewpoints, 75; Economic change and artisan discontent: the Tailors' history, 1800-1848, In: Revolution and Reaction: 1848 and the Second French Republic, Croom Helm, 75; Patterns of proletarianization: Parisian tailors and Lodeve woolen workers, In: Consciousness and Class Experience in Nineteenth Century Europe, Holmes and Meier, 79; Capitalism and the State: Capital Accumulation and Proletarianization in the Languedocian Woolens Industry, In the Workplace before the Factory, Cornell, 93; The Life and Death of Industrial Languedoc, 1700-1920: The Politics of Deindustrialization, Oxford U Press, 95. **CONTACT ADDRESS** Dept of History, Wayne State Univ, 838 Mackenzie, Detroit, MI, 48202-3919. **EMAIL** c.h.Johnson@Wayne.edu

JOHNSON, CURTIS
DISCIPLINE 19TH CENTURY AMERICAN SOCIAL AND RELIGIOUS HISTORY **EDUCATION** Univ Minn, PhD, 85. **CAREER** Dept Hist, Mt. St. Mary's Col **SELECTED PUBLICATIONS** Auth, Redeeming America: Evangelicals and the Road to Civil War. **CONTACT ADDRESS** Dept of History, Mount Saint Mary's Col, 16300 Old Emmitsburg Rd, Emmitsburg, MD, 21727-7799. **EMAIL** johnson@msmary.edu

JOHNSON, DAVID ALAN
PERSONAL Born 03/16/1950, Altadena, CA, m, 1981, 2 children **DISCIPLINE** AMERICAN HISTORY & STUDIES **EDUCATION** Univ Calif, Irvine, BA, 72; Univ Pa, MA, 73, PhD, 77. **CAREER** Lectr Am civilization, Univ Pa, 76-77, hist, San Diego State Univ, 77-78, & Univ Calif, Los Angeles, 78-79; asst prof, 79-82, assoc prof, 82-92, PROF HIST, PORTLAND STATE UNIV, 92-, fac asst to Univ pres, 92-93, chair, hist dept, 93-96; Planning analyst, Univ Pa, 76-77; consult, Acad & Financial Planning, Univ Southern Calif, 79; dir, Grad Prog Pub Hist, Portland State Univ, 79-82; managing ed, Pacific Hist Rev, 96-. **HONORS AND AWARDS** Haynes Found res fel, Huntington Libr, 94; Burlington Northern Teach Award, Portland State Univ, 92; Pacific Coast Br, Am Hist Asc Book Award, 92. **MEMBERSHIPS** Orgn Am Historians; Am Studies Asn; Soc Sci Hist Asn; AAUP. **RESEARCH** American social and intellectual history; American West; history of violence in American. **SELECTED PUBLICATIONS** Ed, American Culture and the American Frontier & auth, Vigilance and the law: The moral authority of popular justice in the far West, in American Culture and the American Frontier, Am Quart (spec issue), winter 81; Founding the Far West: California, Oregon, Nevada, 1840-1890, Univ Calif Press, 92. **CONTACT ADDRESS** Portland Historical Review, Portland State Univ, 487 Cramer Hall, Portland, OR, 97207-0751. **EMAIL** johnsonda@pdx.edu

JOHNSON, DAVID RALPH
PERSONAL Born 12/20/1942, Rockford, IL, m, 1973, 1 child **DISCIPLINE** HISTORY **EDUCATION** Univ of Ill, BA, 65; Univ of Chicago, MA, 66; Univ of Chicago, PhD, 72. **CAREER** Inst, 70-72, asst prof, 72-75, Univ of New Orleans; ASST PROF, 75-79, ASSOC PROF, 79-85, PROF, 85-, ASSOC VICE PRES FOR FAC AFFAIRS, 97-, UNIV OF TEX AT SAN ANTONIO; ED, BOOKS IN THE HISTORY OF CRIME AND CRIMINAL JUSTICE SERIES, 96-. **HONORS AND AWARDS** Univ Fac Res Grant, 82; Travel to Collections Grant, Nat Endowment for the Humanities, 85 & 88; NEH summer Seminar for Coll Teachers, Columbia Univ, 87; President's Distinguished Achievement Award for Teaching Excellence, 94; President's Distinguished Achievement Award for Excellence in Univ Service, 95. **MEMBERSHIPS** Urban Hist Asn; Amer Hist Asn. **RESEARCH** Urban History; Crime & Criminal Justice. **SELECTED PUBLICATIONS** Auth, Police and Fire Protection, Encyc of Am Soc Hist, Charles Scribner's Sons, 93; auth, Homegrown Gangsters: Urban Crime in the Twentieth Century West, Journal of the West, 95; auth, Gambling, in The Encyc of New York City, Yale Univ Press, 95; auth, Illegal Tender: Counterfeiting and the Secret Service 1863-1899, Smithsonian Inst Press, 95. **CONTACT ADDRESS** Division of Behavioral and Cultural Scis, Univ of Tex, San Antonio, TX, 78285. **EMAIL** djohnson@utsa.edu

JOHNSON, DONALD DALTON
PERSONAL Born 01/10/1917, Hartford, CT, m, 1945, 3 children **DISCIPLINE** HISTORY **EDUCATION** Univ Calif, Los Angeles, AB, 38; Univ Southern Calif, MA, 41, PhD(hist), 46. **CAREER** Lectr hist & int rels, Univ Southern Calif, 44-46; asst prof hist, State Col Wash, 46-49; from asst prof to assoc prof, 49-58, chmn dept, 60-64, prof, 58-80, EMER PROF HIST, UNIV HAWAII, 80-, Fulbright lectr, New SWales Univ & Univ Queensland, Australia, 56; prof lectr, George Washington Univ, 62-63 & Univ Md, 63; consult, City & County of Honolulu, 68-, State of Hawaii, 71-; vis scholar hist, Ctr SPac Studies, Univ Calif, Santa Cruz, 76. **MEMBERSHIPS** AHA; Asn Asian Studies **RESEARCH** History of the Pacific area; United States diplomatic history; local history, Hawaii. **SELECTED PUBLICATIONS** Auth, The United States in the Pacific: a Syllabus, 57 & US in the Pacific: Special Interests and Public Policy, 64, Univ Hawaii. **CONTACT ADDRESS** Dept of Hist, Univ of Hawaii, Honolulu, HI, 96822.

JOHNSON, DONALD ELLIS
PERSONAL Born 04/07/1918, Plaistow, NH, m, 1942, 3 children **DISCIPLINE** HISTORY, INTERNATIONAL RELATIONS **EDUCATION** Mass State Col Fitchburg, BSEd, 40; Clark Univ, AM, 41, PhD(hist & int rels), 53. **CAREER** From instr to assoc prof, 46-66, head dept hist, 68-74, PROF HIST, WORCESTER POLYTECH INST, 66-, HEAD DEPT HUMANITIES, 74-, Vis lectr US dipl hist, Col Holy Cross, 68; abstractor, Hist Abstr. **MEMBERSHIPS** AHA; AAUP **RESEARCH** Local United States Colonial history; Worcester in the war for independence. **SELECTED PUBLICATIONS** Coauth, Pioneer Class, LaVigne, 66. **CONTACT ADDRESS** 16 Lowell Ave, Holden, MA, 01520.

JOHNSON, EMILY
DISCIPLINE RUSSIAN **EDUCATION** UCLA, BA, 87; Columbia Univ, MA, 90, MPhil, 93. **CAREER** Vis asst prof, Williams Col, 98-99. **HONORS AND AWARDS** ACTR res fel, 96-97; Meier's fel, 97-98. **RESEARCH** Russian language and culture; 19th and 20th century Russian literature; travel literature; contemporary Russian films. **SELECTED PUBLICATIONS** Auth, NP Antsiferov and the Origin of the Literary Excursion, AATSEEL Conf, 97; Morbid Dread: Vampires in Bolshevik Propaganda from the 1920s, Northeast Reg Conf, 95. **CONTACT ADDRESS** Center for Foreign Languages, Literatures and Cult, Williams Col, Williamstown, MA, 01267. **EMAIL** Emily.Johnson@williams.edu

JOHNSON, EVANS COMBS
PERSONAL Born 11/14/1922, Langdale, AL **DISCIPLINE** HISTORY **EDUCATION** Univ Ala, AB, 43, MA, 47; Univ NC, PhD, 53. **CAREER** Asst prof hist & polit sci, Huntingdon Col; asst prof, 53-61, PROF HIST & POLIT SCI, STETSON UNIV, 61-, CHMN DEPT HIST, 71-, Southern Fels Fund grant, 55; chmn dept hist & polit sci, Armstrong State Col, 69-70. **MEMBERSHIPS** Southern Hist Asn **RESEARCH** Recent American history. **SELECTED PUBLICATIONS** Auth, Adventures of a Contrarian, Daedalus, Vol 0125, 96. **CONTACT ADDRESS** 722 N Arlington Ave, DeLand, FL, 32720.

JOHNSON, HAROLD BENJAMIN
PERSONAL Born 11/17/1931, Hastings, NE, s **DISCIPLINE** HISTORY **EDUCATION** Cambridge Univ, BA, 53, MA, 60; Univ of Chicago, PhD, 63. **CAREER** Instr, 61-63, Univ of Chicago; Asst Prof, 69-72, Assoc Prof, 72-81, Scholar in Res, 81-, Univ of Virginia. **HONORS AND AWARDS** SSRC Fel 64-65, 68-69; Ford Found Fel, 65-66. **MEMBERSHIPS** Amer Hist Assoc; Soc for the History of Discoveries; Yale Library Assoc; Friends of the Univ of Arizona Library; Amer Friends of the Univ of Arizona **RESEARCH** Medieval, Early Modern Portugal; Colonial Brazil. **SELECTED PUBLICATIONS** Portrait of a Portuguese Parish Santa Maria de Alvarenga in 1719, Lisboa, 83; The Settlement of Brazil 1500-1580, Cambridge Hist of Latin Amer, 84; CoAuth, O Imperio Luso-Brasileiro 1500-1620, Lisbon, 92; Distribuicao de Rendimentos numa Aldeia Medieval Portuguesa, Ler Historia, 97. **CONTACT ADDRESS** PO Box 89669, Tucson, AZ, 85752. **EMAIL** mvesgate@aol.com

JOHNSON, HERBERT ALAN
PERSONAL Born 01/10/1934, Jersey City, NJ, m, 1983, 2 children **DISCIPLINE** AMERICAN LEGAL & CONSTITUTIONAL HISTORY **EDUCATION** Columbia Univ, AB, 55, MA, 61, PhD(hist), 65; NY Law Sch, LLB, 60. **CAREER** Res asst John Jay Papers, Columbia Univ, 61-63; lectr hist, Hunter Col, 64-65, asst prof, 65-67; assoc ed, Papers of John Marshall, Inst Early Am Hist & Cult, 67-70, co-ed, 70-71, ed, 71-77; prof Hist & Law, Univ SC, 77-90, HOLLINGS PROF OF CONSTITUTIONAL LAW, 91-; Lectr hist, City Col New York, 62-63 & Col William & Mary, 67-77; Am Philos Soc grant-in-aid, 71; mem res & publ adv comt, Heritage 76 Comt, Am Revolution Bicentennial Comn, 73-75; Am Coun Learned Soc fel, 74-75; Lucy Hampton Bostick vis res prof, Univ SC, 76& 77; advan sr res fel, US Army Military Hist Inst, 81; Liberty Fund fel, Inst for Humane Studies, 81, 85; vis scholar, Centre for Comparative Constitutional Studies, Univ Melbourne, 92; vis res scholar, Univ Toronto, 95; vis prof, Univ Birmingham, UK, 98. **HONORS AND AWARDS** Paul S Kerr Hist Prize, NY State Hist

Asn, 70. **MEMBERSHIPS** Osgoode Soc; AHA; Am Soc Legal Hist (vpres, 72-73, pres, 74-75); Selden Soc; Stair Soc; Jean Bodin Soc. **RESEARCH** American legal history; American constitutional history. **SELECTED PUBLICATIONS** Auth, The Law Merchant and Negotiable Instruments in Colonial New York, 1664-1730, Loyola Univ, 63; John Jay, 1745-1829, NY State Educ Dept, 70; ed, The Papers of John Marshall, Vol I, 74, Vol II, 77, Univ NC; coauth, Historical Courthouses of New York, Columbia Univ, 77; Imported Eighteenth-Century Law Treatises in American Law Libraries 1700-1799, Knoxville: Univ of TN Press, 78; South Carolina Legal History, Spartanburg: The Reprint Co, 80; co-auth with George L. Haskins, Foundations of Power--John Marshall, 1801-1815, vol 2, History of the Supreme Court of the United States, Paul A. Freund, ed, New York: Macmillan Co, 81; Essays on New York Colonial Legal History, Westport: Greenwood Press, 81; History of Criminal Justice, Cincinnati: Anderson Pub Co, 88, 2nd ed, with Nancy Travis Wolfe, Anderson Pub Co, 95; John Jay: Colonial Lawyer, New York: Garland Pub Co, 89; American Legal and Constitutional History: Cases and Materials, San Francisco: Austin and Winfield, 94; The Chief Justiceship of John Marshall, 1801-35, Columbia: Univ SC Press, 97, paperback ed, 98; author of numerous book chapters, law review articles, essays, book reviews, and other publications. **CONTACT ADDRESS** School of Law, Univ of S. Carolina, Columbia, SC, 29208. **EMAIL** HJOHNSON@LAW.SC.EDU

JOHNSON, IVORY
PERSONAL Born 06/11/1938, Oakland, MS, m **DISCIPLINE** EDUCATION **EDUCATION** Harris Tchrs Coll St Louis, AA 1960; BA 1962; St Louis U, MEd 1969; PhD 1974. **CAREER** Ferguson-Florissant Reorganized School Dist, Title I prog dir; Berkeley School Dist St Louis Co, elem sch prin 1969-; St Louis Univ, instructor 1973-; St Louis Bd of Educ, teacher 1962-69; Urban Rural Teacher Renewal Inst St Louis Public School System, consultant 1974. **HONORS AND AWARDS** J Jerome Peters Professionalism Award Kappa Alpha Psi 1975. **MEMBERSHIPS** Mem MO State Tchrs Assn; St Louis Suburban Principals Assn; MO Assn Elem Sch Prins; White House Conf Edn; Nat Assn Elem Sch Prins; Urban League; YMCA; MO PTA; bd dirs Metroplex; Kappa Alpha Psi NDEA Fellowship 1968.

JOHNSON, JACOB EDWARDS, III
PERSONAL Born 02/21/1922, Charleston, WV, w, 1944 **DISCIPLINE** CRIMINAL JUSTICE **EDUCATION** West Virginia State College, Institute, ES, 1928; North Carolina Central University, 1940; Kentucky State University, 1940-43; University of Wisconsin Law School, 1949; Howard University Law School, LLB, 1950, JD, 1968; National University Law School, 1952; George Washington University, 1956. **CAREER** US Department of Justice, federal legal liaison, retired; District of Columbia Department of Justice, Corrections, and Parole Board, 35 years; PROFESSOR OF LAW AND CRIMINAL JUSTICE, currently. **HONORS AND AWARDS** Kappa Alpha Psi, 50 Year Award, 1991; IBPO Elks, Past grand Exalted Ruler, with Honors, 1984. **MEMBERSHIPS** IBPO Elks, past grand exalted ruler(w/honors), legal liaison officer, 1984-91, W Grand Federal Census, officer, 1989-92, Elks Veterans, national service officer, 1984-91, Civil Liberties Department, Elks grand commissioner, 1992; life member, commander, 1983-84, American Legion Post 5, Washington, DC, 1983-84; life member, vice commander, 1989-91, Veterans of Foreign Wars Post 7456, Fairmount, MD, 1983-91; life member, service officer, 1983-91, Disabled American Veterans Post 7, Camp Springs, MD; life member, NAACP; life member, National Bar Association; numerous others. **CONTACT ADDRESS** Col, Lodge #85, 1846 3rd St NW, Washington, DC, 20001.

JOHNSON, JAMES M.
PERSONAL Born 06/28/1947, Montezuma, GA, m, 1969, 2 children **DISCIPLINE** HISTORY **EDUCATION** USMA, BS, 69; Duke Univ, MA, 77; PhD, 80; US Naval War Col, MA, Natl Security & Strategic Scholar, 95. **CAREER** Off, field artillery, 69-99, Colonel, 91, US Army; instr, asst prof, 77-80, assoc prof, 87-94, prof, 94-99, USMA. **RESEARCH** Colonial and Amer revolutionary hist; hist of the US Army. **CONTACT ADDRESS** 214 Wilson Rd, West Point, NY, 10996. **EMAIL** kj4213@trotter.usma.edu

JOHNSON, JAMES PEARCE
PERSONAL Born 08/20/1937, Birmingham, AL, m, 1959, 2 children **DISCIPLINE** AMERICAN HISTORY **EDUCATION** Duke Univ, AB, 59; Columbia Univ, MA, 62, PhD(hist), 68. **CAREER** From instr to assoc prof, 66-80, chmn dept, 72-78, PROF HIST, BROOKLYN COL, 80-; Danforth fellow, 61-67; Mem, Bd Educ, Westfield, NJ, 72-75; assoc, Danforth Found, 77; consult var NJ & Brooklyn pub high Schs, 77-. **HONORS AND AWARDS** Louis Pelzer Award, Orgn Am Historians, 66. **RESEARCH** Psychohistory; twentieth century American politics. **SELECTED PUBLICATIONS** Auth, Drafting the NRA Code of Fair Competition for the Bituminous Coal Industry, J Am Hist, 12/66; The Fuel Crisis, Largely Forgotten, of 1918, Smithsonian, 12/76; Westfield: From Settlement to Suburb, Westfield Bicentennial Comt, 77; The Wilsonians as War Managers, Prologue: J Nat Archives, winter 77-78; How Mother Got Her Day, Am Heritage, 4/79; Nixon's Use of Metaphor: The Real Nixon Tapes, Psychoanalytic Rev, summer 79; The Assassination in Dallas: A Search for Meaning, Psychoanalytic Rev, summer 79; The Politics of Soft Coal: From the First World War to the New Deal, Univ IL Press, 79; New Jersey: History of Ingenuity and Industry, Windsor Pubs, 87; with Timothy B. Benford, Righteous Carnage: The John E. List Murders, Scribner, 91. **CONTACT ADDRESS** 716 Clark St, Westfield, NJ, 07090.

JOHNSON, JOHN W.
DISCIPLINE HISTORY **EDUCATION** St. Olaf Col, BA, 68; MA, 70, PhD, 74, Univ Minnesota **CAREER** Clemson Univ, 76-88; Prof, 88-, Univ Northern Iowa **CONTACT ADDRESS** Dept of History, Univ of No Iowa, Cedar Falls, IA, 50614-0701. **EMAIL** john.johnson@uni.edu

JOHNSON, JOHNNY B.
PERSONAL Born 02/17/1920, Rison, Arkansas, m **DISCIPLINE** EDUCATION **EDUCATION** Agricultural Mechanical & Normal Coll, BS 1948; MI State Univ, MS 1948, MA 1955; Univ of AR, EdD 1963. **CAREER** AM&N Coll, dean of men 1949-61; Univ of AR-Pine Bluff, prof 1963-73, interim chancellor 1973-74, vice chancellor academic affairs 1974-76, prof acting chancellor vice chancellor 1976-86, provost/vice chancellor. **HONORS AND AWARDS** Fellowship Southern Educ Foundation 1962; listed Outstanding Educators of Amer 1975; Outstanding Civilian Service Awd Army ROTC 1974. **MEMBERSHIPS** Mem AR Educ Assoc, Natl Educ Assoc, Amer Assoc of Higher Educ 1949-86; mem Kiwanis Intl 1975-86.

JOHNSON, JUDITH R.
DISCIPLINE TWENTIETH CENTURY UNITED STATES, AND LATIN AMERICAN HISTORY **EDUCATION** BS, MA, PhD. **CAREER** Asst prof **RESEARCH** Oral history projects; reform movements with emphasis on the New Deal, and Civil Rights.. **SELECTED PUBLICATIONS** Auth, The Penitentiaries in Arizona, Nevada, New Mexico, and Utah From 1900 to 1980, 97; John Weinzirl: A Personal Search for the Conquest of Tuberculosis; Kansas in the Grippe, The Spanish Influenza Epidemic of 1918. **CONTACT ADDRESS** Dept of Hist, Wichita State Univ, 1845 Fairmont, Wichita, KS, 67260-0062. **EMAIL** jjohnson@wsuhub.uc.twsu.edu

JOHNSON, LEROY
DISCIPLINE EDUCATION **CAREER** MILES COLLEGE, BIRMINGHAM, AL, PRES/CHANCELLOR, currently. **CONTACT ADDRESS** Miles Col, Birmingham, AL, 35208.

JOHNSON, LEROY RONALD
PERSONAL Born 01/25/1944, Smithville, Georgia, d **DISCIPLINE** HISTORY **EDUCATION** Univ of Caen France, Licence-es Lettres Ancient & Medieval History 1966-69; The Sorbonne Univ of Paris, Maitrise-es Lettres Medieval History 1971; Univ of MI, PhD African History 1981. **CAREER** Inst St Jean-Eudes France, dir & teacher 1969-70; Inst St Joseph Paris, dir & teacher 1970-72; MI State Univ, instructor 1973-77; Univ of FL, asst prof history 1977-78; Bryn Mawr Coll, lecturer African Hist; Towson State University, asst prof of history; Moorhead State University, assoc prof, dept of humanities, currently. **HONORS AND AWARDS** French govt scholarship Caen, Paris France 1967-68, 1971-72; Natl Defense Foreign Lang Fellowship MI State Univ 1972-73; Rackham Fellowship Univ of MI 1973-75. **MEMBERSHIPS** Reg officer French Fed of Basketball Coaches 1964-72; hon mem African Students Assoc France 1966-72, West Indian Students Assoc France 1966-72; lecturer Ctr for Afro-Amer & African Studies Univ of MI 1978-79; sr lecturer history Univ of Lagos Nigeria 1982-83; lecturer history Bryn Mawr Coll 1983-86. **CONTACT ADDRESS** Humanities & Multicultural Studies Dept, Moorhead State Univ, Moorhead, MN, 56560.

JOHNSON, M. GLEN
PERSONAL Born 11/18/1936, Pikeville, KY, m, 1963, 2 children **DISCIPLINE** POLITICAL SCIENCE **EDUCATION** Georgetown College (KY), BA, 58; Univ of NC, Chapel Hill, MA, 61, PhD, 66. **CAREER** Inst of Political Sci, Univ of Ky, 63-64; instr, 64-66, ASST PROF, 66-72, ASSOC PROF, 72-77, PROF OF POLITICAL SCI, 77-, ACTING PRES, 97-98, VASSAR COLL; dir, Am Studies Res Centre, Hyderabad, India, 90-93. **HONORS AND AWARDS** Fulbright Prof, Poena Univ, India, 77-78; Fulbright Prof & Dir, Am Studies Res Centre, Hyderabad, India, 90-93. **MEMBERSHIPS** Amer Political Sci Asn; Int Studies Asn; Asn for Asian Studies. **RESEARCH** U.S. Foreign Policy; International Human Rights; South Asia. **SELECTED PUBLICATIONS** Coauth, The Universal Declaration of Human Rights: 45th Anniversary, 1948-1993, UNESCO, 94 & 98; auth, Structures, Order and Interests: Coping with the End of the Westphalian Era, in Ganging Global Political/Ideological Context and Afro-Asia: Strategies for Development, South Asian Pubs Pvt. Ltd., 96; auth, Some Reflections on Federalism in India and the United States, in Democracy and Federalism, Andhra Pradesh Judicial Acad, 95. **CONTACT ADDRESS** Dept of Political Sci, Vassar Col, 124 Raymond Ave, Poughkeepsie, NY, 12604-0376. **EMAIL** johnsong@vassar.edu

JOHNSON, OWEN V.
PERSONAL Born 02/22/1946, Madison, WI, m, 1969, 2 children **DISCIPLINE** EAST EUROPEAN MEDIA AND HISTORY, HISTORY OF JOURNALISM **EDUCATION** Washington State Univ, BA, 68; Univ Mich, MA, 70, cert Russ & East Europ studies & PhD(hist), 78. **CAREER** Lect East Europ hist, Univ Mich, 78-79; asst prof journalism, Southern Ill Univ, Carbondale, 79-80; Asst Prof, 80-87, Assoc Prof Journalism, Ind Univ, 87-, Adjunct Prof Hist, 97-, Dir, Russ & East Europ Inst, 91-95; Producer, ed & reporter, WUOM, Ann Arbor & WVGR, Grand Rapids, 69-77. **HONORS AND AWARDS** Am Philos Soc grant, 79; Int Res & Exchanges Bd res grant, Czech, 82; ACLS Conf grant, 83; Head, Hist Div, Asn Educ in Journalism, 85-86; Stanley Pech Award, Czechoslovak Hist Conf, 87-88; Nat Coun Soviet & East Europe Res Grant, 88-90. **MEMBERSHIPS** AHA; Am Asn Advan Slavic Studies; Asn Educ Jour and Mass Commun; Czechoslovak Hist Conf; OAH; Slovak Studies Asn (pres 88-90). **RESEARCH** The theory and practice of journalism in the Central and Eastern Europe. **SELECTED PUBLICATIONS** Auth, Slovakia 1918-1938: Education and the Making of a Nation, Columbia Univ Press/East Europ Monographs, 85; Whose Voice?: Freedom of Speech and the Media in Central Europe, In: Creating a Free Press in Eastern Europe, Univ Ga, 93; coauth, Mass Media and the Velvet Revolution, In: Media and Revolution: Comparative Perspectives, Univ Press Ky, 95; Professional Roles of Russian and U.S. Journalists: A Comparative Study, Journalism & Mass Commun Quart, Autumn 96; auth, The Media and Democracy in Eastern Europe, In: Communicating Democracy, Lynne Rienner, 98; contribr, Journalism and the Education of Journalists in the New East/Central Europe, Hampden Press (in press); author of numerous other articles. **CONTACT ADDRESS** Sch of Journalism, Indiana Univ, Bloomington, 1 Indiana University, Bloomington, IN, 47405. **EMAIL** johnsono@indiana.edu

JOHNSON, PAUL B.
PERSONAL Born 06/07/1921, Paw Paw, MO, m, 1947 **DISCIPLINE** MODERN AMERICAN & BRITISH HISTORY **EDUCATION** Univ Chicago, AB, 42, PhD(hist), 54. **CAREER** Instr hist, Denison Univ, 47-49; lectr Europ hist, Univ Chicago, 49-52; from asst prof to assoc prof, 52-62, PROF AM HIST, ROOSEVELT UNIV, 62-, Sr Fulbright lectr, Univ Edinburgh, 66-67; lectr Brit hist, Univ Ill, Chicago Circle, 74. **MEMBERSHIPS** Midwest Conf Brit Studies (secy, 70-). **RESEARCH** British housing, planning and reform, 1900-1949. **SELECTED PUBLICATIONS** Auth, Citizens Participation in Urban Renewal, Hull-House, 60; Land Fit for Heroes, Univ Chicago, 68; War, reform and hope: British Labour's perceptions, in: Im Gegenstrom, Peter Hammer, 77. **CONTACT ADDRESS** Dept of Hist, Roosevelt Univ, 600 S Michigan Ave, Chicago, IL, 60605-1901.

JOHNSON, PAUL E.
DISCIPLINE HISTORY **EDUCATION** Univ Calif Berkeley, BA, 65; UCLA, MA, 68, PhD, 75. **CAREER** Guest lect, hist, Princeton; current, PROF, HIST, UNIV UTAH **MEMBERSHIPS** Am Antiquarian Soc **SELECTED PUBLICATIONS** Auth, A Shopkeeper's Millenium: Society and Revivals in Rochester, New York, 1815- 1837, Hill & Wang, 78; auth, "The Modernization of Mayo Greenleaf Patch: Land, Family, and Marginality in New England, 1766-1818," New Eng Quart 55, 82; auth, "Drinking, Temperance, and the Construction of Identity in Nineteenth-Century America," Soc Sci Info 25, 86; auth, "Art and the Language of Progress in Early Industrial Paterson: Sam Patch at Clinton Bridge, Am Quart, Dec 88; auth, "Democracy, Patriarchy, and American Revivals, 1780-1830," Jour of Soc Hist 24, 91; auth, "The Market Revolution," in Encyclopedia of Am Soc Hist, Charles Scribner's Sons, 93; African-American Christianity: Essays in History, Univ Calif Press, 94; coauth, The Kingdom of Matthias: A Story of Sex and Salvation in Nineteeth-Century America, Oxford Univ Press, 94. **CONTACT ADDRESS** Dept of Hist, Univ of Utah, Salt Lake City, UT, 84112.

JOHNSON, PENELOPE DELAFIELD
PERSONAL Born 03/02/1938, New York, NY, m, 1957, 2 children **DISCIPLINE** MEDIEVAL HISTORY, WOMEN'S HISTORY **EDUCATION** Yale Univ, BA, 73, MPhil, 76, PhD, 79. **CAREER** Teaching asst history, Yale Univ, 74-75, lectr, 77; asst prof hist, NY UNIV, 79-. **HONORS AND AWARDS** Phi Beta Kappa, Summa Cum Laude, Yale Univ, 73; ACLS Fel, 81; NEH Summer Fel, 81; ACLS Fel 85-86; Rockefeller Fel 85-86; NYU Research Challenge Grant, 89; Great Teacher Award, NYU, 92. **MEMBERSHIPS** AHA; Medieval Acad Am; Soc Archeol Sci et Lit du Vendomois; New England Hist Asn. **RESEARCH** Medieval religious women; medieval monasticism; medieval mysticism. **SELECTED PUBLICATIONS** Auth, Virtus: Transition from classical Latin to the De civitate Dei, Augustinian Studies, 75; La Legende de fondation de la Trinite, Vendome, Bull Soc Archeol Sci et Lit du Vendomois, 78; Pious legends & historical realities: The foundation myths of la Trinite, Bonport & Holyrood, Rev Benedictine, 81; Prayer, Patronage & Power: The Abbey of la Trinite, Vendome, 1032-1187, NY Univ, 81; Equal in Monastic Profession: Religious Women in Medieval France, Chicago Univ, 91; Priere, Patronage et pouvoir: l'abbaye de la Trinite de Vendome (1032-1187), Cherche-Lune, 97. **CONTACT ADDRESS** Dept Hist, New York Univ, 53 Washington Sq South, New York, NY, 10012-4556. **EMAIL** penny.johnson@nyu.edu

JOHNSON, PHIL BRIAN
DISCIPLINE LATIN AMERICAN HISTORY **EDUCATION** Univ Minn, BA 63; Tulane Univ, MA, 66, PhD(hist), 71. **CAREER** Assoc prof, 68-80, PROF HIST, SAN FRANCISCO STATE UNIV, 80-, Dir Latin Am Studies, Monterey Inst Foreign Studies, 68-71; Dept of Health, Educ, Welfare res grant, 75; contribr ed, New Scholar, 75- **MEMBERSHIPS** Pac Coast Coun Latin Am Studies; Latin Am Studies Asn; AHA; Southern Hist Asn. **RESEARCH** Ruy Barbosa; waste disposal in Latin America; teaching innovation in Latin American area studies. **SELECTED PUBLICATIONS** Auth, Stevenson, Robert, Louis, Smithsonian, Vol 0026, 95. **CONTACT ADDRESS** Dept of Hist, San Francisco State Univ, San Francisco, CA, 94132.

JOHNSON, RICHARD RIGBY
PERSONAL Born 07/06/1942, Tunbridge Wells, England **DISCIPLINE** AMERICAN HISTORY **EDUCATION** Oxford Univ, BA, 64; Univ Calif, Berkeley, MA, 65, PhD(hist), 72. **CAREER** Instr hist, Univ Calif, Berkeley, 68-69 & 71-72; asst prof, 72-80, ASSOC PROF HIST, UNIV WASH, 80-, William andrews Clark Libr fel, 76. **HONORS AND AWARDS** Rotary Found fel, 64-65; William andrews Clark Libr fel, 76. **MEMBERSHIPS** AHA; Orgn Am Historians. **RESEARCH** Colonial America; Anglo-American political relations. **SELECTED PUBLICATIONS** Auth, Imperatives, Behaviors, and Identities, Rev(S) in Amer Hist, Vol 0021, 93; The Radicalism of the American Revolution, J Interdisciplinary Hist, Vol 0024, 94; Warpaths--Invasions of North America, William and Mary Quart, Vol 0053, 96. **CONTACT ADDRESS** Dept of Hist, Univ of Wash, Seattle, WA, 98195.

JOHNSON, RICHARD RONALD
PERSONAL Born 09/24/1937, Santa Rita, NM **DISCIPLINE** ANCIENT HISTORY **EDUCATION** Univ Calif, Los Angeles, BA, 60, PhD(hist), 68. **CAREER** From instr to asst prof, 66-70, ASSOC PROF HIST, UNIV HOUSTON, 70-. **MEMBERSHIPS** Am Soc Papyrologists; Hellenic Soc; Soc Promotion Roman Studies; Medieval Acad Am. **RESEARCH** Classical palaeography; Roman Empire; Early Byzantine history. **SELECTED PUBLICATIONS** Auth, Ancient and Medieval accounts of the Invention of Parchment, Calif Studies Class Antiq, 70; Bicolor Membrana, Class Quart, 73. **CONTACT ADDRESS** Dept of Hist, Univ Houston, Houston, TX, 77004.

JOHNSON, ROBERT C.
PERSONAL Born 08/27/1945, Richmond, VA **DISCIPLINE** EDUCATION **EDUCATION** Lincoln Univ, BA 1967; Institut D'Etudes Francaises France 1967; MAT 1969; MA 1974; Washington Univ, PhD 1976; Washington Univ, BS 1984. **CAREER** Lincoln Univ Foreign Lang Lab, student dir 1964-67; Washington Univ, lectr 1969-71; Educ Cntr of E St Louis, dir 1969-72; Fontbonne Coll, lectr 1971; Inst Black Studies St Louis, dir educ 1971; Washington Univ, asst prof 1971-84; Grambling State Univ, assoc prof 1984-. **HONORS AND AWARDS** Numerous publ appearances/addresses/publications in field; 1st Intl Black Merit Acad Award 1973; World Future Soc; Amer Assn for the Advancement of Sci; Eval Network; African Heritage Studies Assn; Outstanding Young Men in Amer 1974, 1977; Men of Achievement 1977; Comm Ldrs & Noteworthy Amer 1977; numerous scholarships/fellowships/grants. **MEMBERSHIPS** Numerous consultantships in field; mem Amer Assn for Higher Educ 1973-, Amer Assn Univ Profs 1971-, Assn for the Study of Afro-Am Life & Hist 1970-, Educators to Africa Assn 1972-, Natl & Reg Assn African-Am Educators 1969-72, Phi Delta Kappa 1969-; bd dirs Trainers Tchr Trainers Prog 1969-71; spl serv Washington Univ 1970-71; Inst Black Studies 1970-; Educ Center of E St Louis 1972-; mem So IL Univ Citizens Adv Com 1970-72; Comp Educ Comm 1970; E St Louis Model Cities Planning Com 1969-71; Afro-Am Studies Curriculum Adv Com 1972; St Louis Com on Africa 1970-; UN Assn 1973-. **CONTACT ADDRESS** Dept of Educ, The Master's Col, PO Box 91322, Newhall, CA, 91322.

JOHNSON, ROBERT E.
PERSONAL Born 08/07/1943, New York, NY **DISCIPLINE** RUSSIAN & EAST EUROPEAN STUD **EDUCATION** Antioch Col, BA, 65; Cornell Univ, PhD, 75. **CAREER** Fac mem hist, Erindale Col, 71-, mem grad fac, 79-, DIR, CTR RUSSIAN & EAST EUROPEAN STUD, UNIV TORONTO, 89-; vis scholar, Russian Inst Hist, 83, 91; proj dir, Archives of the Stalin Era, 94-. **SELECTED PUBLICATIONS** Auth, Peasant and Proletarian, 79; auth, Contadini e Proletari, 93; coauth, The Seam Allowance, 82. **CONTACT ADDRESS** Robarts Libr, Univ of Toronto, 130 St. George St, Toronto, ON, M5S 1A5.

JOHNSON, ROGER A.
DISCIPLINE HISTORY; THEOLOGY **EDUCATION** Northwestern Univ, BA, 52; Yale Divinity Sch, BD, 55; Harvard Divinity Sch, ThD, 66. **CAREER** Elisabeth Luce Moore Prof of Christian Studies, Wellesley Col, 59-. **CONTACT ADDRESS** 7 Appleby Rd., Wellesley, MA, 02181. **EMAIL** rjohnson@mediaone.net

JOHNSON, ROGER N.
PERSONAL Born 04/22/1939, Dayton, OH, m, 1968, 2 children **DISCIPLINE** PSYCHOLOGY **EDUCATION** Swarthmore Col, BA, 61; Univ Conn, MA, 62, PhD, 66. **CAREER** Univ Mass, 65; Amherst Coll, 65-68; Tufts Univ, 68-71; Rampao Col, 71- ; Univ Jyvaskyla, 79; New Sch for Soc Res, 80-82; Richmond Coll, 88. **HONORS AND AWARDS** Who's Who in Am; Who's Who in the East; am Men and Women of Sci; Who's Who in Writers, Editors & Poets; Who's Who of Int Auth and Writers; Int Dir of Distinguished Leadership; Int Dict of Contemporary Achievement; Dir of Am Scholars. **MEMBERSHIPS** APA; Int Soc for Research on Aggression; Eastern Psych Asn; Int Soc for Political Psychology. **SELECTED PUBLICATIONS** Auth, Aggression in Man and Animals, Missouri, 96; Bad News Revisited, Peace and Conflict, 96. **CONTACT ADDRESS** Ramapo Col, New Jersey, Mahwah, NJ, 07430. **EMAIL** rjohnson@ramapo.edu

JOHNSON, RONALD C.
PERSONAL Born 07/18/1927, Duluth, MN, w, 1954, 3 children **DISCIPLINE** PSYCHOLOGY **EDUCATION** Univ Minn, BA, psychology, 49, PhD, child development; Denver Univ, MA, sociol, 50. **CAREER** Instr, Univ Minn, 56-57; asst to assoc prof, San Jose State Coll, 57-62; assoc prof, 62-65, prof, 70-93, prof emeritus, 93-, Univ Hawaii; assoc prof, Univ Colorado, 65-70; dir, Behavioral Biology Lab, 72-93. **HONORS AND AWARDS** Distinguished Sci Contribution Award, Hawaii Psychol Assn, 95; Dobzhansky Award, Behavior Genetics Assn, 97. **MEMBERSHIPS** Amer Assn Advancement Sci; Amer Psychol Soc; Behavior Genetics Assn; Soc Study Social Biol. **RESEARCH** Human viability; behavior genetics; ethology; psychometrics. **SELECTED PUBLICATIONS** Coauth, "Intergroup Similarities in Judgments of Psychiatric Symptom Severity," Cultural Diversity and Mental Health, vol 3, no 1, 97; coauth, "Kinship and the Quest for Wealth and Power in the Punjab, 1839-1845," Evolution and Human Behavior, 97; coauth, "Active Phenotypic Assortment in Mate Selection," Social Biology, vol 44, 97; coauth, "Depressive Symptomatology among Filipino-American Adolescents," Cultural Diversity and Mental Health, vol 4, no 1, 98; coauth, "Prediction of Major Depression and Dsythymia from CES-D Scores among Ethnic Minority Adolescents," Journ Amer Acad Child and Adolescent Psychiatry, vol 37, no 5, 98. **CONTACT ADDRESS** 23 Kalaka Pl, Kailua, HI, 96734.

JOHNSON, RONALD MABERRY
PERSONAL Born 10/15/1936, Kansas City, MO, m, 1965, 3 children **DISCIPLINE** AMERICAN SOCIAL & CULTURAL HISTORY **EDUCATION** Col Emporia, BA, 61; Univ Kans, MA, 65; Univ Ill, Urbana, PhD(Am social & intellectual hist), 70. **CAREER** Asst prof Afro-Am hist, Cleveland State Univ, 69-72; asst prof urban & Afro-Am hist, 72-76, assoc prof Am Hist, Georgetown Univ, 76-86, prof Am Hist, Georgetown, 86-, dir Am Studies, 79-85, 89-. **MEMBERSHIPS** ASA; AHA; Orgn Am Historians. **RESEARCH** Social and cultural history; history of race relations; educational history. **SELECTED PUBLICATIONS** Auth, Schooling the Savage: Andrew S Draper and Indian Education, Phylon, 3/74; coauth, Forgotten Pages: Black Literary Magazines in the 1920s, J Am Studies, 12/74; auth, Politics and Pedagogy: The 1892 Cleveland School Reform, Ohio Hist, autumn 75; Captain of Education: Andrew S Draper, 1848-1913, Societas, summer 76; Black History and White Students: Broadening Cultural Horizons, Negro Educ Rev, 1/77; coauth, Away from Acommodation: Radical Editors and Protest Journalism, J Negro Hist, 10/77; Propaganda and Aesthetics: Literary Politics of Afro-American Magazines in the Twentieth Century, Univ Mass Press, 79, rev ed, 92. **CONTACT ADDRESS** Dept of Hist, Georgetown Univ, 1421 37th St N W, Washington, DC, 20057-0001. **EMAIL** johnson2@gusun.georgetown.edu

JOHNSON, RONALD WILLIAM
PERSONAL Born 07/29/1937, Rockford, IL, 1 child **DISCIPLINE** HISTORY OF ART, PSYCHOLOGY **EDUCATION** San Diego State Univ, MA, 63; Univ Calif, Berkeley, MA, 65, PhD(art hist), 71. **CAREER** Asst prof art hist, Univ Iowa, 70-73; prof art hist, Humboldt State Univ, 74-. **MEMBERSHIPS** Col Art Asn Am. **RESEARCH** Late 19th and early 20th century art history. **SELECTED PUBLICATIONS** Auth, Picasso's Old Guitarist and the Symbolist Sensibility, Artforum XIII, 12/74; Dante Rossetti's Beata Beatrix and the New Life, Art Bull, 12/75; Poetic Pathways to Dada: Marcel Duchamp and Jules Laforgue, 5/76, Picasso's Parisian Family and the Saltimbanques, 1/77, Vincent van Gogh and the Vernacular: His Southern Accent, 6/78, Arts Mag; Picasso's Demoiselles d'Avignon and the Theatre of the Absurd, 10/80 & Whistler's Musical Modes: Symbolist Symphonies, 4/81, Arts Mag. **CONTACT ADDRESS** 1 Harps St, Arcata, CA, 95521-8299.

JOHNSON, TIMOTHY
DISCIPLINE MUSIC THEORY **EDUCATION** Univ Mass, BM; Univ Conn, MM; State Univ NY, PhD. **CAREER** Asst prof. **MEMBERSHIPS** Col Music Soc; Soc Music Theory. **SELECTED PUBLICATIONS** Auth, pubs on Charles Ives, John Adams, minimalism, 17th-century theory, and technology. **CONTACT ADDRESS** Dept of Music History, Theory and Composition, Ithaca Col, 100 Job Hall, Ithaca, NY, 14850. **EMAIL** tjohnson@ithaca.edu

JOHNSON, W. RALPH
DISCIPLINE CLASSICS **EDUCATION** Univ Calif, BA, 61, MA, 63, PhD, 66. **CAREER** Asst to Assoc Prof, UC Berkeley, 66-74; Assoc Prof to Prof, Cornell, 74-81; Prof, Univ Chicago, 81-. **HONORS AND AWARDS** Distinguished Tchg Award; Christian Gauss Award; Martin Lectures; Townsend Lectures. **SELECTED PUBLICATIONS** Auth, Luxuriance and Economy: Cicero and the Alien Style, Ucal Press,71; auth, Darkness Visible: A Study of Vergil's Aeneid, Univ Calif Press,76; auth, The Idea of Lyric, Univ Calif Press, 82; auth, Momentary Monsters: Lucan and his Heroes, Cornell, 87; auth, Horace and the Dialectic of Freedom, Cornell Univ Press, 93. **CONTACT ADDRESS** Univ Chicago, 1010 E 59th St, Chicago, IL, 60637.

JOHNSON, WALKER C.
PERSONAL Born 07/24/1935, Stevens Point, WI, m, 1958, 3 children **DISCIPLINE** ARCHITECTURE/HISTORY **EDUCATION** Univ Wisc, BS, hist, 58; Univ of Illinois, BArch, 66. **CAREER** Adj prof, Univ VA, 87-88. **HONORS AND AWARDS** Fel, AIA. **MEMBERSHIPS** AIA; SAH; APT. **RESEARCH** Architectural history; building pathology & restoration. **SELECTED PUBLICATIONS** Auth, Twentieth Century Building Materials, Terrazzo, Natl Park Svc, McGraw-Hill, 95. **CONTACT ADDRESS** Johnson-Lasky Architects, 22 West Monroe St, Ste 1601, Chicago, IL, 60603. **EMAIL** jlarch@ibm.net

JOHNSON, WENDY DASLER
DISCIPLINE HISTORY AND THEORY OF RHETORIC **EDUCATION** Univ Oregon, PhD. **CAREER** Asst prof, Washington State Univ. **RESEARCH** Gender studies, sentimentalism, poetics, critical theory, popular culture including Pee Wee Herman. **SELECTED PUBLICATIONS** Publ on, 19th-century poets Julia Ward Howe and Lydia Huntley Sigourney; pedagogy & connections between writing and antebellum women's lives. **CONTACT ADDRESS** Dept of English, Washington State Univ, 1 SE Stadium Way, PO Box 645020, Pullman, WA, 99164-5020. **EMAIL** johnsonw@vancouver.wsu.edu

JOHNSON, WILLIAM M.
PERSONAL Born 10/24/1939, Columbia, MO **DISCIPLINE** ART HISTORY **EDUCATION** Univ Missouri, BA, 60, MA, 62; Princeton Univ, MFA, 64, PhD, 65. **CAREER** Lectr to assoc prof, 65-76, PROF FINE ART, UNIV TORONTO, 77-. **HONORS AND AWARDS** Fulbright fel, 60-61; Guggenheim fel, 78-79; Prix Bernier Acad Beaux-Arts, Inst France, 82. **MEMBERSHIPS** Am Soc Eighteenth Stud; Renaissance Soc Am; Soc hist de l'art francais. **SELECTED PUBLICATIONS** Auth, French Lithography: The Restoration Salons 1817-1824, 77; auth, French Royal Academy of Painting and Sculpture: Engraved Reception Pieces 1673-1789, 82; auth, Art History: Its Use and Abuse, 88; auth, Hugues-Adrien Joly: Lettres a Karl-Heinrich von Heinecken 1772-1789, 88; coauth, Estienne Jodelle, Le Recueil des Inscriptions 1558, 72; coauth, The Paris Entries of Charles IX and Elisabeth of Austria 1571, 74; coauth, The Royal Tour of Charles IX and Catherine de Medici 1564-1566, 79; ed, Ontario Association of Art Galleries Art Gallery Handbook, 82. **CONTACT ADDRESS** Dept of Fine Art, Univ of Toronto, 100 St. George St, Toronto, ON, M5S 1A1.

JOHNSON-ODIM, CHERYL
DISCIPLINE HISTORY **EDUCATION** Northwestern Univ, PhD, 78. **CAREER** Hist, Loyola Univ. **MEMBERSHIPS** Ed bd(s), Hist Encycl Chicago Women, J Women's His, Nat Women's Stud Asn J. **RESEARCH** Women's history; African; African American history. **SELECTED PUBLICATIONS** Auth, monograph For Women and the Nation: Funmilayo Ransome-Kuti of Nigeria, Univ Ill Press, 97; Lady Oyinkan Abayomi, Nigerian Women in Historical Perspective, Nigeria: Sankore Press, 92; Common Themes, Different Contexts: Third World Women and Feminism, Ind UP, 91; co-ed, Expanding the Boundaries of Women's History, Ind UP, 92; guest ed on special issue of Nat Women's Stud Asn J on, Global Perspectives on Gender, 96. **CONTACT ADDRESS** Fine Arts Dept, Loyola Univ, Chicago, 6525 N. Sheridan Rd., Chicago, IL, 60626. **EMAIL** cjohns1@wpo.it.luc.edu

JOHNSTON, CAROLYN
DISCIPLINE HISTORY **EDUCATION** Univ Ca, PhD. **CAREER** Prof. **RESEARCH** American intellectual history; history of radical and working class movements; history of women in America. **SELECTED PUBLICATIONS** Auth, Jack London: An American Radical, 84; Sexual Power: Feminism and the Family, 92. **CONTACT ADDRESS** Dept of History, Eckerd Col, 54th Ave S, PO Box 4200, St Petersburg, FL, 33711.

JOHNSTON, CHARLES MURRAY
PERSONAL Born 04/01/1926, Hamilton, ON, Canada, m, 1953, 4 children **DISCIPLINE** MODERN HISTORY **EDUCATION** McMaster Univ, BA, 49; Univ Pa, MA, 50, PhD(hist), 54. **CAREER** From lectr to assoc prof, 53-66, PROF HIST, McMASTER UNIV, 66-, Can Coun res grants, 60, 61 & 63, res fel for overseas studies, 63-64, 75-76, 82-83; consult, Ont Centennial Ctr Sci & Technol, 64-65; mem, Archaeol & Hist Sites Bd, Ont, 65-70; mem, Soc Sci Res Coun Can, 67-71;

Ont Prov Govt res grant for biog of E C Drury, 72. **MEMBERSHIPS** Can Hist Asn; Can Asn Am Studies. **RESEARCH** British imperial, Canadian and Ontario history. **SELECTED PUBLICATIONS** Auth, The Chiefs, Warriors and Cadets of Academe--Recent Writings on Canadian Higher-Education, Acadiensis, Vol 0022, 92; Mcquesten, Thomas, Baker, Public-Works, Politics, and Imagination, Can Hist Rev, Vol 0074, 93; The British Abroad--The Grand Tour in the 18th-Century, Historian, Vol 0056, 94; Matters of Mind-- Univ in Ontario, 1791-1951, Dalhousie Rev, Vol 0075, 95. **CONTACT ADDRESS** Dept of History, McMaster Univ, 1280 Main St W, Hamilton, ON, L8S 4M4.

JOHNSTON, PATRICIA ANN
PERSONAL Chicago, IL **DISCIPLINE** CLASSICAL LANGUAGES **EDUCATION** Univ Calif, Los Angeles, AB, 67; Univ Calif, Berkeley, MA, 72, PhD(classics), 75. **CAREER** Asst prof, 75-82, ASSOC PROF CLASSICS, BRANDEIS UNIV, 82-, Vis asst prof, Univ Southern Calif, 78-79. **MEMBERSHIPS** Am Philol Asn; Class Asn New England; Vergilian Soc. **RESEARCH** Latin language and literature; Greek language and literature. **SELECTED PUBLICATIONS** Auth, Love and Laserspicium in Catullus 7, Classical Philol, Vol 0088, 93; The Roman Theater and its Audience, Classical Philol, Vol 0088, 93. **CONTACT ADDRESS** Dept Class & Oriental Studies, Brandeis Univ, Waltham, MA, 02254.

JOHNSTON, ROBERT H.
DISCIPLINE HISTORY **EDUCATION** Univ Toronto, BA; Yale Univ, MA, PhD. **HONORS AND AWARDS** Humanities Bk Prize, 90. **RESEARCH** Russian exile migrant communities. **SELECTED PUBLICATIONS** Auth, New Mecca, New Babylon, Paris and the Russian Exiles 1920-1945, 88; auth, Soviet Foreign Policy 1918-1945, 91. **CONTACT ADDRESS** History Dept, McMaster Univ, 1280 Main St W, Hamilton, ON, L8S 4L9.

JOHNSTON, WILLIAM
DISCIPLINE SOCIAL AND CULTURAL CHANGE **EDUCATION** Elmira Col, BA, Harvard Univ, MA, PhD. **CAREER** Wesleyan Univ. **SELECTED PUBLICATIONS** Auth, The Modern Epidemic: A History Of Tuberculosis In Japan. **CONTACT ADDRESS** Wesleyan Univ, Middletown, CT, 06459. **EMAIL** wjohnston@wesleyan.edus

JOHNSTON, WILLIAM M.
DISCIPLINE HISTORY **EDUCATION** Harvard Univ, PhD, 65. **CAREER** Prof, Univ MA Amherst. **HONORS AND AWARDS** Austrian Hist Prize, 69. **RESEARCH** Mod Europe; intellectual hist of relig(s). **SELECTED PUBLICATIONS** Auth, In Search of Italy: Foreign Writers in Northern Italy, 87; Celebrations, 91; Recent Reference Books in Religion, 96. **CONTACT ADDRESS** Dept of Hist, Univ Massachusetts Amherst, Mass Ave, Amherst, MA, 01003.

JOINER, BURNETT
PERSONAL Born 11/10/1941, Raymond, MS, m **DISCIPLINE** AFRICAN-AMERICAN STUDIES **EDUCATION** Utica Jr Coll, AA 1962; Alcorn State Univ, BS 1964; Bradley Univ, MA 1968; Univ of SC, PhD 1975. **CAREER** Oliver School Clarksdale, MS, principal 1968-71; York School Dist #1, asst supt of schls 1971-73; SC Coll Orangeburg, SC, asst prof 1974-75; Atlanta Univ Atlanta, GA, exec dir/assoc prof 1975-80; Grambling State Univ, exec academic dean and prof, 1984-91; LEMOTNE-OWENS COLLEGE, PRES, 1991-. **MEMBERSHIPS** Mem Ouachita Valley Boy Scouts 1982-; charter mem Grambling Lion's Club 1983-; consultant US Dept Educ 1983-85; commr LA Learning Adv Commn 1984-85; commr LA Internship Commn 1984-85; mem Natl Inst of Education Study Group on Teacher Edn; chaired special comm in Coll of Educ Univ of SC on student advisement; past mem Curriculum Comm Sch of Educ at SC State Coll; mem Ruston-Lincoln C of C; vice chairperson Comm on Social Concerns Lewis Temple Church; conducted numerous workshops and seminars for more than 50 schools, agencies and community groups; mem of the bd of dir Teacher Ed Council for State Coll and Univ, American Assoc of Coll for Teacher Ed; mem of the Governor's Internship Commission and Learning Adv Commission. **SELECTED PUBLICATIONS** Publications, "The Teacher Corps Policy Board; Three Perspectives on Role and Function" 1979; "A Documentation Primer; Some Perspectives from the Field" 1979; "New Perspectives on Black Education History" Book Review for the Journal of Negro History in progress; "Identifying Needs and Prioritizing Goals Through Collaboration" 1978; "Education That Is Multicultural; A Process of Curriculum Development" 1979; "The Design, Implementation and Evaluation of a Pre-Service Prototype Competency-Based Teacher Education Model" 1975; "Maximizing Opportunities for Professional Improvement" 1983; Improving Teacher Education: A Conscious Choice, co-author. **CONTACT ADDRESS** LeMoyne-Owen Col, 807 Walker Ave, Memphis, TN, 38126.

JOINER, DOROTHY
DISCIPLINE ART **EDUCATION** Emory Univ, PhD. **CAREER** Prof. **SELECTED PUBLICATIONS** Auth, Hieronymus Bosch's Temptation of Saint Anthony and the Hieros Gamos, Duke, 85; A New Methodology for Bosch, Emory Univ, 89; Figurative Art and Portaiture, Macon, 88. **CONTACT ADDRESS** Art Dept, State Univ of West Georgia, Carrollton, GA, 30118.

JONAITIS, ALDONA
PERSONAL Born 01/27/1948, New York, NY, s **DISCIPLINE** ART HISTORY **EDUCATION** SUNY, BA, 69; Columbia Univ, MA, 73, PhD, 77. **CAREER** Lecturer, Asst Prof, Assoc Prof, Prof, SUNY Stony Brook, 73-89; Ch, Dept Art, SUNY, 81-84; Assoc Provost, SUNY, 84-86; V Provost for Undergrad Stud, SUNY, 86-89; VP for Public Progs, Am Mus of Nat Hist, 89-93; Adjunct Prof of Art Hist & Archaeol, Columbia univ, 90-93; Prof Anthrop, Univ Alaska, Fairbanks, 93-; Dir, Univ of Alaska Mus, 93-. **MEMBERSHIPS** Otsego Inst for Native Am Art, Founding Bd member, 96-; Native Am Art Stud Asn (founding member, pres 93-95). **RESEARCH** NW Coast Indian Art. **SELECTED PUBLICATIONS** Auth, Traders of Tradition: The History of Haida Art, Robert Davidson: Eagle of the Dawn, 1st ed, The Vancouver Art Gallery, 3-23, 93; co-auth, Power, History and Authenticity: The Mowachaht Whaler's Washing Shrine, Eloquent Obsessions: Writing Cultural Criticism, Duke Univ Press, 157-84, 94; auth, Introduction, Eagle Transforming: The Art of Robert Davidson, Univ Washington Press, 1-11, 94; ed, A Wealth of Thought: Franz Boas on Native American Art, Univ Wash Press, 3-37, 306-337, 95; auth, The Beauty and the Magic of His Horse, Heritage, 4-15, spring/summer 97; ed, Looking North: Art from the University of Alaska Museum, Univ Wash Press/.Univ Alaska Mus, 13-43, 98; The Yuquot Whalers' Shrine: A Study of Representation, Univ Wash Press, in press. **CONTACT ADDRESS** Univ Alaska Mus, 907 Yukon Dr, Fairbanks, AK, 99775. **EMAIL** ffaj@uaf.edu

JONAS, MANFRED
PERSONAL Born 04/09/1927, Mannheim, Germany, m, 1952, 4 children **DISCIPLINE** AMERICAN HISTORY **EDUCATION** City Col New York, BS, 49; Harvard Univ, AM, 50, PhD, 59. **CAREER** Mil Intel analyst, US Dept Defense, 51-54; asst prof Am hist, Free Univ Berlin, 59-62; assoc prof hist, Widener Col, 62-63; from asst prof to assoc prof, 63-67, dir grad prog Am studies, 64-74, chmn div soc sci, 71-74, chmn dept, 70-81, prof hist, 67-80, WASHINGTON IRVING PROF HIST & MOD LIT, UNION COL, NY, 80-, Lectr, Exten Div, Univ Md, 54; consult, Choice: bks Collibr, 64-; dir, NDEA Insts Advan Study Hist, 66-68; consult, US Off Educ, 67; mem, NY State Col Proficiency Exam Comt Am Hist, 70-; sr Fulbright-Hays lectr US hist, Univ Saarland, 73; res fel, Charles Warren Ctr Studies Am Hist, Harvard Univ, 77-78. **MEMBERSHIPS** AHA; Orgn Am Historians; Ger Soc Am Studies; Soc Historians Am Foreign Rels. **RESEARCH** Ideas and politics in twentieth century America; isolationism; United States foreign relations. **SELECTED PUBLICATIONS** Auth, Foreign Relations of the United States, 1955-1957, Vol 26, Cent and Southeastern Europe, J Amer Hist, Vol 0080, 93; Prussia and National Socialism, a Conference Held in Potsdam, November 5-7, 1992, Zeitschrift Fur--Geschichtswissenschaft, Vol 0041, 93; Kennedy and Johnson Policy Toward Germany --Different Approaches Within the American Government, Amer Hist Rev, Vol 0098, 93; A Preponderance of Power-National Security, the Truman Administration and the Cold War, Historian, Vol 0055, 93; America Germany--Mccloy, John, J. and the Federal Republic of Germany, Diplomatic Hist, Vol 0017, 93; Foreign Relations of the United States, 1955-1957, Vol 24, Soviet Union--Eastern Mediterranean, J Amer Hist, Vol 0080, 93; Confrontation and Cooperation--Germany and the United-States in the Era of World War I, 1900-1924, Central Europ Hist, Vol 0027, 94; The Occupied Ally--The American Germany Policy, 1949-1955, J Amer Hist, Vol 0081, 94; When the Old Left Was Young--Student Radicals and America 1st Mass Student Movement, 1929-1941, Historian, Vol 0056, 94; American Intelligence Warfare Against Germany--Subversion, Propaganda, and Political Planning By the Office of Strategic Services During World War 2, J Amer Hist, Vol 0082, 95; The Greatest of Friends--Roosevelt, Franklin, D. and Churchill, Winston, 1941-1945, J Amer Hist, Vol 0083, 96; Hard Bargain--How Fdr Twisted Churchills Arm, Evaded the Law, and Changed the Role of the American Presidency, Amer Histl Rev, Vol 0101, 96. **CONTACT ADDRESS** Dept of Hist, Union Col, Schenectady, NY, 12308.

JONES, AMELIA
PERSONAL Born 07/14/1961, Durham, NC, m, 1987, 1 child **DISCIPLINE** ART HISTORY **EDUCATION** Harvard Univ, BA, 83; Univ PA, MA, 87; UCLA, PhD, 91. **CAREER** Instr, UCLA, 89; instr, Art Ctr Col of Design, 90-91; assoc prof, Univ CA, Riverside, 91-; instr, USC, 92; exec ed, Los Angeles Ctr Photog Studies, 95-98. **HONORS AND AWARDS** Elizabeth Agassiz Scholarship, Harvard Univ; Deans Fel, 86-87, Univ PA; Dickson Fel, 89-91, UCLA; Affirmative Action Career Development Award, 93, Distinguished Humanist Achievement Award, 93-94, Univ CA, Riverside; Postdoctoral Fel, 94-95, Am Coun Learned Soc; Group Fel, 95, Graham Found; Best Exhibition Catalogue, third place, 95-96, Int Asn Art Critics. **MEMBERSHIPS** Col Art Asn; Educ Publications Committee; Ctr For Photographic Studies; Asn Art Historians. **RESEARCH** Contemporary art and theory; 20th century European and Am art; feminist art theory; history and theory of photog. **SELECTED PUBLICATIONS** Auth, "Clothes Make the Man: The Male Artist as a Performative Function," Oxford Art Jour, 95; ed, coauth, Sexual Politics: Judy Chicago's Dinner Party in Feminist Art History,Univ CA Press, 96; auth, "Margaret Morgan/Mr. Clean," Art + Text, 97; auth, "'Presence' in absentia: Experiencing Performance as Documentation," Art Jour, 98; coed, coauth, "In Between," Framework, 98. **CONTACT ADDRESS** Dept of Art History, Univ of California, Riverside, 339 S Orange Dr, Los Angeles, CA, 90036-3008. **EMAIL** jonessher@aol.com

JONES, ANN R.
PERSONAL Born 07/05/1921, New Castle, Pennsylvania, m **DISCIPLINE** EDUCATION **EDUCATION** Livingstone Coll, BA 1944; Univ of Pittsburgh, MSW 1964, PhD 1978. **CAREER** Irene Kaufmann Ctr, prog dir 1952-60; Anna Heldman Ctr, prog dir 1960-64; Action Housing, dir of training 1964-66; Community Action, dir of training 1966-70; Univ of Pittsburgh, prof emeritus until 1998, interim dir of affirmative action, 1989-91. **HONORS AND AWARDS** Post-Gazette Disting Woman 1969; Black Studies Univ of Pittsburgh Black Studies 1980; Disting Alumni Univ of Pittsburgh 1985; Task Force Recognition Cty Commissioners 1986; Three Rivers Adoption Council, Person of the Year, 1997; Foster Parents Support Award, 1996. **MEMBERSHIPS** Provost adv comm Womens Concerns; dir Soc Work Field Educ; nom comm Natl Council Soc Work; site visitor Natl Council Social Educ Work; mem adv comm Allegheny Children Youth Svcs; pres Hazelwood Neighborhood Council; mem bd dir Three Rivers Adoption Council.

JONES, BARNEY LEE
PERSONAL Born 06/11/1920, Raleigh, NC, m, 1944, 5 children **DISCIPLINE** AMERICAN CHURCH HISTORY, BIBLICAL LITERATURE **EDUCATION** Duke Univ, BA, 41, PhD(Am Christiani y), 58; Yale Univ, BD, 44. **CAREER** Instr Bible, Duke Univ, 48-50, chaplain, 53-56, asst dean, Trinity Col, 56-64, assoc prof relig, 64-72, PROF RELIG, 72-80. **MEMBERSHIPS** Soc Relig Higher Educ; Am Soc Church Hist. **RESEARCH** Colonial American church history, particularly New England area; Charles Chauncy, 1707-1782. **SELECTED PUBLICATIONS** Auth, John Caldwell, critic of the Great Awakening in New England, in: A Miscellany of American Christianity, Duke Univ, 63. **CONTACT ADDRESS** 2622 Pickett Rd, Durham, NC, 27705.

JONES, BEVERLY WASHINGTON
PERSONAL Born 12/13/1947, Durham, NC, m, 1970, 3 children **DISCIPLINE** AMERICAN & AFRO-AMERICAN HISTORY **EDUCATION** NC, Cent Univ, BA, 70, MA, 71; Univ NC Chapel Hill, PhD(Am hist), 80. **CAREER** Teacher US hist, Guy B Phillips Jr High Sch, 71-72; instr hist, 72-76, asst prof, 76-80, prof hist, NC Cent Univ, 80-; Consult, Nat Endowment Humanities, 75-76, reviewer, 77-78; vis assoc, Univ NC Chapel Hill, 80-. **MEMBERSHIPS** Orgn Black Women Historians; Asn Study Afro-Am Life & Hist; Orgn Am Historians. **RESEARCH** Black women's history; labor history, especially labor concerns of tobacco workers and domestics; psycho history, motivational concepts of Black leaders. **SELECTED PUBLICATIONS** Auth, Mary Church Terrell and the National Association of Colored Women, 1896-1901, J Negro Hist (in press); Mary Church Terrell: A new woman, Negro Hist Bull (in press); Before Montgomery and Greensboro: The desegregation movement in the District of Columbia, Phylon (in press). **CONTACT ADDRESS** 1801 Fayetteville St, Durham, NC, 27707-3129. **EMAIL** Bjones@wpo.nccu.edu

JONES, BYRD LUTHER
PERSONAL Born 10/06/1938, Huron, NY, m, 1962, 2 children **DISCIPLINE** MODERN AMERICAN HISTORY, URBAN EDUCATION **EDUCATION** Williams Col, BA, 60; Yale Univ, PhD(Am studies), 66. **CAREER** From instr to asst prof hist, Calif Inst Technol, 63-69; dir, ctr Urban Educ, 71-73, chair, Div Instructional Leadership, 77-79, acad coordr, Teacher Corps, 79-82, PROF EDUC, UNIV MASS, AMHERST, 72-, Soc Sci Res Coun fel econ, Stanford Univ, 68-69; mem, Mass Task Force Equity Educ; instr paraprof, Brooklyn, NY, 69. **RESEARCH** American economic thought; recent United States history; staff development in schools. **SELECTED PUBLICATIONS** Auth, In the Kingdom of Grass, Great Plains Quart, Vol 0015, 95. **CONTACT ADDRESS** 11 Overlook Dr, Amherst, MA, 01002.

JONES, CHRISTOPHER P.
PERSONAL Born 08/21/1940, Chislehurst, England **DISCIPLINE** CLASSICS, ANCIENT HISTORY **EDUCATION** Oxon (Oxford), BA, 61, MA, 67; Harvard, PhD, 65. **CAREER** Lect, 65-66, Univ Toronto; asst prof, 66-68, assoc prof, 68-75, prof, 65-92, prof of class & hist, 92-97, George Martin Lane Prof of Classics & Hist, 97-, Harvard Univ. **HONORS AND AWARDS** Fel, Royal Soc of Canada; Corresp mem, Ger Archaeol Inst, 92; fel, Am Numismatic Soc, 93; The Am Philos Soc, 96; fel, Am Acad of Arts & Sci, 98. **MEMBERSHIPS** APA; Bd of Sr Fellows, Byzantine Stud, Dumbarton Oaks Res Lib & Collection, Harvard Univ; Class Asn of Canada; Inst for Advanced Stud, Princeton, Sch of Hist Stud; Soc for the Promotion of Hellenic Stud; Soc for Promotion of Roman Stud. **RE-**

SEARCH Greek lit of the Roman period; Hellenistic and Roman hist; Greek epigraphy. **SELECTED PUBLICATIONS** Auth, Philostratus: Life of Apollonius of Tyana, Penguin Books, 71; auth, Plutarch and Rome, Oxford Univ Press, 71, 72; auth, The Roman World of Dio Chrysostom, Harvard Univ Press, 78; auth, Culture and Society in Lucian, Harvard Univ Press, 86; auth, Louis Robert, Le Martyre de Pionios, pretre de Smyrne, mis au point et complete par G. W. Bowerstock et C. P. Jones, Dumbarton Oaks Res Lib & Collection, Wash, 94; auth, Kinship Diplomacy in Classical Antiquity, Harvard Univ Press, forthcoming 99. **CONTACT ADDRESS** Dept of Classics, Harvard Univ, 319 Boylston Hall, Cambridge, MA, 02138. **EMAIL** cjones@fas.harvard.edu

JONES, EDWARD LOUIS
PERSONAL Born 01/15/1922, Georgetown, TX, m, 1964 **DISCIPLINE** HISTORY **EDUCATION** Univ of WA, BA (2) 1952, BA 1955; Univ of Gonzaga, JD 1967. **CAREER** Hollywood Players Theatre, prod, dir 1956-58; Roycroft Leg Theatre, prod, dir 1958-59; WA State Dept of Publ Asst, soc worker 1958; Seattle Water Dept, cost acctg clerk 1960-61; State of WA, atty gen office 1963-66; Seattle Oppty Indust Ctr, suprv 1966-68; Univ of WA, asst dean a&s 1968-, lecturer. **HONORS AND AWARDS** Moot Court Contest, First Place, 1953. **MEMBERSHIPS** Consult State Attny Gen Adv Comm on Crime, State Supr of Counseling; vice pres WA Comm on Consumer Interests, Natl Council on Crime & Delinquency; bd mem Natl Acad Adv & Assn; ed NACADA Jrnl; mem Natl Assn of Student Personnel Admin, The Amer Acad of Pol & Soc Sci, The Smithsonian Assn; historical advisor, Anheuser Busch. **SELECTED PUBLICATIONS** Author: Profiles in African Heritage, Black Zeus, 1972; Tutankhamon, King of Upper & Lower Egypt, 1978; Orator's Workbook, 1982; The Black Diaspora: Colonization of Colored People, 1989; co-author, Money Exchange Flashcards, Currency Converters, 1976; From Rulers of the World to Slavery, 1990; President Zachary Taylor and Senator Hamlin: Union or Death, 1991; Why Colored Americans Need an Abraham Lincoln in 1992; Forty Acres & a Mule: The Rape of Colored Americans, 1995. **CONTACT ADDRESS** Ethnic Cultural Ctr, HH-05, Univ of Washington, 3931 Brooklyn Ave, NE, Seattle, WA, 98195.

JONES, ELWOOD HUGH
PERSONAL Born 05/06/1941, SK, Canada, m, 1964, 2 children **DISCIPLINE** HISTORY **EDUCATION** Univ Sask, BA, 62; Univ Western Ont, MA, 64; Queen's Univ, Ont, PhD(hist), 71. **CAREER** Archivist, Pub Arch Can, 64-67; lectr hist, 69-70, asst prof, 70-75, assoc prof, 75-81, PROF HIST, TRENT UNIV, 81-, Dir, Can Hist Asn, 70-73, dir, Nat Archival Appraisal Bd, 71-. **MEMBERSHIPS** Can Hist Asn; Orgn Am Historians; Inst Early Am Hist & Cult; Inst Fr-Am Hist; Can Church Hist Soc (pres, 78-). **RESEARCH** Canada; political and religious development, nineteenth century; urban history. **SELECTED PUBLICATIONS** Co-ed, A letter on the Reform Party, 1860: Sandfield Macdonald and the London Free Press, Ont Hist, 65; Union List of Manuscripts in Canadian Repositories, Queen's Printer, 68; auth, Ephemeral compromise: the Great Reform Convention revisited, J Can Studies, 68; contribr, Illustrated Historical Atlas of Peterborough County 1825-1875, Hunter Rose, 75; St John's Peterborough, the Sesquicentennial History of an Anglican Parish 1826-1976, Peterborough St John's Church, 76; auth, Localism and Federalism in Upper Canada to 1865, in: Early Canadian and Australian Federalism, Waterloo, 78; coauth, Toronto Waterworks 1840-1877: Continuity and change in 19th century Toronto politics, Can Hist Rev, 79; auth, The Church in the Backwoods: Anglican missionaries in the Peterborough area, J Can Church Hist Soc, 81. **CONTACT ADDRESS** Trent Univ, Peterborough, ON, K9J 7B8.

JONES, HOUSTON GWYNNE
PERSONAL Born 01/07/1924, Caswell Co, NC **DISCIPLINE** UNITED STATES HISTORY **EDUCATION** Appalachian State Teachers Col, BS, 49; Peabody Col, MA, 50; Duke Univ, PhD(hist), 65. **CAREER** Prof hist & polit sci, Oak Ridge Mil Inst, 50-53; prof & chmn dept, WGa Col, 55-56; state archivist, NC Div Arch & Hist, 56-68, dir, 68-72, state historian & dir, 72-74; Cur, NC Collection, DAVIS RESEARCH HISTORIAN, 94- ; Univ NC Libr, Chapel Hill, 74-93; Adj prof hist, NC State Univ, 66-73; arch consult, State Calif, 66, State Fla, 67 & State Va, 68; chmn, America's Four Hundredth Anniversary Comt, 77-80; adj prof hist, Univ NC, 79-90; comnr, Nat Hist Publ & Rec Comn, 79-83; ed, NC Hist Rev, 68-74 & NCarolinian Soc Imprints, 78- . **HONORS AND AWARDS** Leland Prize, Soc Am Archivists, 67 & 81; Award of Merit, Am Asn State & Local Hist, 68; Crittenden Mem Award, NC Lit & Hist Asn, 77; Award of Distinction, AASLH, 89. **MEMBERSHIPS** Fel Soc Am Archivists (treas, 61-67, pres, 68-69); AHA; Orgn Am Historians; Am Asn State & Local Hist (secy, 78-); Nat Trust Hist Preserv. **RESEARCH** History of North Carolina; archival administration in the United States; Arctic history and Inuit culture. **SELECTED PUBLICATIONS** Auth, Bedford Brown: State Rights Unionist, 55; Guide to State and Provincial Archival Agencies, 1961, Soc Am Archivists, 61; For History's Sake, Univ NC, 66; The Records of a Nation, Atheneum, 69; Archival training in American universities, 4/68 & The Pink Elephant Revisited, 10/80, Am Archivist; Local Government Records, Am Asn State & Local Hist, 80; N Carolina Illustrated, Univ NC Press, 84; N. Carolina Hist: A Bibliography, Greenwood, 95. **CONTACT ADDRESS** Library, Univ N. Carolina, Campus Box 3930, Chapel Hill, NC, 27514-8890. **EMAIL** hgjones@email.unc.edu

JONES, HOWARD
PERSONAL Born 10/21/1940, Lebanon, TN, m, 1962, 2 children **DISCIPLINE** AMERICAN FOREIGN POLICY **EDUCATION** Ind Univ, BS, Educ, 63, MA, Hist, 65, PhD, Hist, 73. **CAREER** Vis asst prof, univ Nebr, 72-74; RES PROF & CHR, HIST, UNIV ALA, 74-. **MEMBERSHIPS** South Hist Asn; Soc Historians Am For Relations; Org Am Historians; Am Hist Asn; Phi Alpha Theta **RESEARCH** American foreign policy; Civil War; Vietnam War; Cold War; pre-Civil War. **SELECTED PUBLICATIONS** Prologue to Manifest Destiny: Anglo-American Relations in the 1840s, 97; Quest for Security: A History of US Foreign Relations, 96; Abraham Lincoln and a New Birth fo Freedom: The Union and Slavery in the Diplomacy of the Civil War. **CONTACT ADDRESS** Dept Hist, Univ Ala, University, AL, 35486. **EMAIL** Hjones@TenHoor.as.ua.edu

JONES, JACQUELINE
DISCIPLINE HISTORY **EDUCATION** Univ Del, BA, 70; Univ Wis, MA, 72, PhD, 76. **CAREER** TRUMAN PROF, AM CIVILIZATION, BRANDEIS UNIV **MEMBERSHIPS** Am Antiquarian Soc **SELECTED PUBLICATIONS** Auth, Soldiers of Light and Love: Northern Teachers and Georgia Blacks, 1865-73, 80; auth, Labor of Love, Labor of Sorrow; Black Women, Work and the Family: From Slavery to the Present, Basic, 85; auth, American Work: Black and White Labor Since 1600, Norton, 85; auth, The Dispossessed: America's Underclasses form the Civil War to the Present, Basic, 92. **CONTACT ADDRESS** Dept of Hist, Brandeis Univ, Waltham, MA, 02254.

JONES, JAMES HOWARD
PERSONAL Born 03/22/1943, Bauxite, AR, m, 1965, 3 children **DISCIPLINE** AMERICAN HISTORY **EDUCATION** Henderson State Teachers Col, BA, 64; East Tex State Univ, MA, 66; Ind Univ, PhD(hist), 73. **CAREER** Teacher Am hist, Carlisle Pub High Sch, 64-65; instr, Henderson State Teachers Col, 66-68; prog officer, Nat Endowment Humanities, 73-81; ASSOC PROF AM HIST, UNIV HOUSTON, 81-, Sr res scholar, Kennedy Inst Ethics, Georgetown Univ, 75; consult ed, Free Press, 82- **HONORS AND AWARDS** Best Bks 81 Award, NY Times Bk Rev, 81. **MEMBERSHIPS** AHA; Orgn Am Historians; Southern Hist Asn. **RESEARCH** United States history since 1900; social history of medicine. **SELECTED PUBLICATIONS** Auth, Sentinel for Health--A History of the Centers for Disease Control, J Amer Hist, Vol 0081, 94; The Psychiatric Persuasion--Knowledge, Gender, and Power in Modern America, J Amer Hist, Vol 0082, 95; Fundamental Developments of the Social Sciences--Rockefeller Philanthropy and the United States Social Science Research Council, Amer Hist Rev, Vol 0100, 95. **CONTACT ADDRESS** Dept of Hist, Univ of Houston, Houston, TX, 77004.

JONES, KATHERINE ELIZABETH BUTLER
PERSONAL Born 03/19/1936, New York, NY, m **DISCIPLINE** AFRICAN-AMERICAN STUDIES **EDUCATION** Mt Holyoke Coll, BA 1957; Simmons Coll, MS 1967; Harvard Univ, EdD 1980. **CAREER** Boston Public Schools, teacher 1958-59; Newton Public Schools, coord for ed prog 1966-76; Simmons Coll, instr 1967-69; School Systems Public & Independent MA, consult 1968-; Wheelock Coll, instr 1976; Cambridge Public Schools, supvr staff & prog 1977-81; self-employed as EDUC CONSULTANT, currently. **HONORS AND AWARDS** Ed Excellence Scholarship to Student Black Citizens of Newton 1976; Serv to METCO City of Newton 1976; Contrib to Integrated Ed METCO Boston Staff 1976; Serv Above Self Newton Chamber of Commerce 1974; Doctoral Dissertation School Consolidation in Newton 1980; Citizens Who Make a Difference Contrib to Mental Health MA Assoc of Mental Health 1982; Tribute to 350 years of Black Presence in Massachusetts Honoree, Museum of Afro-American History 1988; Nominating Committee for Alumnae Trustees Mt Holyoke College, 1990-92; Schomberg Scholar in Black Culture New York Public Library, 1991-92; Award Black Alumnae Conference, Mt Holyoke College, 1994; Faculty Boston Univ, Afro-American Studies Program, 1993-95; Newton Citizen Recognition of Distinction, 1994; New England Pen Writers, Discovery Author Non-Fiction, 1996; Family History Exhibitor Museum of our National Heritage, Lexington, MA, 1995. **MEMBERSHIPS** Bd dir METCO 1966-73; bd trustees Mt Holyoke Coll 1973-78; 1st black mem Newton School Comm 1978-85; minority affairs comm Natl Assoc of IN Schools 1984-89; bd Boston Childrens Serv 1985-; bd Family Serv Assn 1986-, vice chairperson 1989-91; Massachusetts Coalition for the Homeless 1989-99. **SELECTED PUBLICATIONS** Published Garnets, Diamonds and Other Black Jewels, American Visions, 1998; "They Called It Timbukto," Orion Magazine.

JONES, KENNETH PAUL
PERSONAL Born 03/15/1937, Brooklyn, NY, 3 children **DISCIPLINE** HISTORY **EDUCATION** Univ MO, Kansas City, BA, 59; Columbia Univ, MIA, 61; Univ WI, Madison, PhD, 70. **CAREER** Instr hist, Mansfield State Univ; 61-65, teaching asst, Univ Wis, Madison, 65-66, instr, Rock County Ctr, 66-69; assoc prof, 70-80, PROF HIST, 80-,ASSOC VICE CHANCELLOR FOR ACADEMIC AFFAIRS AND DEAN OF GRADUATE STUDIES, 97-, UNIV TENN, MARTIN; Guest prof, Johannes Gutenberg Univ, Mainz, 74-75; screening comt grad study USA, Deutscher Akademischer Austauschdienst, 74-75; Fulbright jr lectr, Coun Int Exchange Persons, 74-75; Deutscher Akademischer Austauschdienst travel study grant, summer 78. **HONORS AND AWARDS** Wilson Scholarship (UMKC), 55-59; Columbia Univ Fel, 59-61; Ford Found Dissertation Completion Grant, 68-69; US Dept of State Scholar-Diplomat Seminar, March 71; UTM Fac Res grants, 72, 78, 84, 87; Fulbright Lecturer, Mainz Univ, GER, 74-75; German Academic Exchange Service, Research Grant, summer 78; NEH Summer Seminar, Yale Univ, 74; NEH Travel to Collections Grant, 84; Who's Who in Am Ed, 92-; Dict of Int Biography, 93-, Member, Nat Steering Comm, POD Network in Higher Ed, 83-86; TN Conf of Grad Schools, pres, 93-94, vice pres, 92-93; TN Asn of Inst Res: pres, 95-96; vice pres, 94-95. **MEMBERSHIPS** AHA Conf Group Cent Europ Hist; Soc Historians Am Foreign Rels; AAHE; AAUP; POD Network in Higher Ed; Phi Kappa Phi; Phi Alpha Theta; Am Hist Asn; AHA Comm on Hist in the Classroom; Soc for Hist Ed. **RESEARCH** The diplomacy of the Ruhr Crisis, 1923-1924; German-American relations, 1919-1933. **SELECTED PUBLICATIONS** Auth, Discord and Collaboration: Choosing an Agent General for Reparations, Diplomatic Hist, spring 77; Stresemann, the Ruhr Crisis, and Rhenish Separatism: A Case Study of Westpolitik, Europ Studies Rev, 7/77; US Diplomats in Europe, 1919-1941, Santa Barbara: ABC-Clio Press, 81, rev paperback ed, 83; book revs in the Am Hist Rev, Choice, History, and The Hist Teacher; book-length manuscript on The Diplomacy of the Ruhr Crisis: Germany and the West, 1922-24, in prep. **CONTACT ADDRESS** Admin Bldg, Rm 312, Univ of Tenn, 554 University St, Martin, TN, 38238-5001. **EMAIL** kpjones@utm.edu

JONES, LAIRD
DISCIPLINE WORLD HISTORY, AFRICAN HISTORY **EDUCATION** Carleton Col, BA, 82; MSU, MA, 85, PhD, 92. **CAREER** Grad tchg asst, MSU, 83-87, 89-91; asst prof Hist, Lock Haven Univ Pa, 91-. **HONORS AND AWARDS** Nat rsrc lang fel, MSU, 83-87; net rsrc summer lang fel, Kenya, 85; res stipend, MSU, 87; Hinman fel , MSU, 87-88; Fulbright-Hayes doctoral dissertation abroad fel, Tanzania, 87-88; doctoral writing fel, MSU, 91; fac develop grant, LHU, 92; alternative workload leave, LHU, 1998. **MEMBERSHIPS** African Stud Asn; Can African Stud Asn; NY African Stud Asn; Phi Beta Delta-Honor Soc for Int Scholars; Tanzania Stud Asn; World Hist Asn. **RESEARCH** German trading house branch activities in early colonial East Africa. **SELECTED PUBLICATIONS** Auth, Commercial Politics and the Overstocking Crisis in Mwanza Province, 1927-35, African Econ Hist, 95; Rev of Cotton, Colonialism, and Social History in Sub-Saharan Africa, eds Allan Issacman and Richard Roberts, in H-AFRICA, 96. **CONTACT ADDRESS** Lock Haven Univ, Pennsylvania, Lock Haven, PA, 17745. **EMAIL** ljones@eagle.lhup.edu

JONES, LARRY EUGENE
PERSONAL Born 02/16/1940, El Dorado, KS **DISCIPLINE** MODERN EUROPEAN & GERMAN HISTORY **EDUCATION** Univ Kans, BA, 61, MA, 63; Univ Wis, PhD(hist), 70. **CAREER** Asst prof, 68-73, assoc prof, 74-79, PROF HIST, CANISIUS COL, 80-, Res fel, Alexander von Humboldt-Stiftung, Univ Bochum, W Ger, 75-77. **MEMBERSHIPS** AHA **RESEARCH** German history, 1918-1945; history of Marxism. **SELECTED PUBLICATIONS** Auth, The dying middle, Weimer Germany and the fragmentation of bourgeois politics, Cent Europ Hist, 73; Streemann and the crisis of German liberalism, Europ Studies Rev, 74; Between the fronts: The German National Union of Commercial Employees from 1928 to 1933, J Mod Hist, 76; Sammlung oder Zersplitterung? Die Bestrebungen zur Bildung einer neuen Mittelpartei in der Endphase der Weimarer Republik 1930-1933, Vierteljahrshefte fur Zeitgeschichte, 77; Inflation, revaluation, and the crisis of middle-class politics, A study in the dissolution of the German party system 1923-28, Cent Europ Hist, 79; Adam Stegerwald und die Krise des deutschen Parteiensystems: Ein Beitrag zur Deutung des Essener Programms vom November 1920, Vierteljahrshefte fur Zeitgeschichte, 79; The Dissolution of the Bourgeois Party System in the Weimar Republic, in: Social Change and Political Development in Weimar Germany, London, 81. **CONTACT ADDRESS** Dept of Hist, Canisius Col, 2001 Main St, Buffalo, NY, 14208-1098.

JONES, LOUIS CLARK
PERSONAL Born 06/28/1908, Albany, NY, m, 1932, 3 children **DISCIPLINE** HISTORY, LITERATURE **EDUCATION** Hamilton Col, BA, 30; Columbia Univ, MA, 31, PhD(Eng lit), 42. **CAREER** From instr to assoc prof English & Am lit, NY State Col Teachers, Albany, 34-46; dir, 46-72, EMER DIR, NY STATE HIST ASN & FARMERS MUS, 72-; PROF AM FOLK ART, COOPERSTOWN GRAD PROG, STATE UNIV NY COL ONEONTA, 73-, Guggenheim fel, 46; mem, NY Coun on Hist Sites, 54-58, NY Coun on Hist Sites, 60-72 & NY State Hist Trust, 66-72; dir, Coopertown Grad Prog, State Univ NY col Oneonta, 64-72; Nat Endowment for Humanities res grant, 72-73. **HONORS AND AWARDS** Award of Distinction, Am Asn State & Local Hist, 70; Katherine Coffee Prize, 81., LHD, Ham-

ilton Col, 62. **MEMBERSHIPS** Am Asn Mus (vpres, 52-68); Am Asn State & Loal Hist (vpres, 50-57); fel Am Folklore Soc. **RESEARCH** Eighteenth century social history; New York state folklore; folklore of the supernatural; American folk art. **SELECTED PUBLICATIONS** Auth, Clubs of the Georgian Rakes, Columbia Univ, 42; Spooks of the Valley, Houghton, 48; Things that Bump in the Night, Hill & Wang, 59; ed, Growing up in the Cooper Country, Syracuse Univ, 65; Murder at Clearry Hill, 82; Three Eyes on the Past, Syracuse Univ Press, 82. **CONTACT ADDRESS** 11 Main St, Box 351, Cooperstown, NY, 13326.

JONES, MICHAEL OWEN
PERSONAL Born 10/11/1942, Wichita, KS, m, 1964, 1 child **DISCIPLINE** AMERICAN FOLKLORE, FOLK ART & TECHNOLOGY **EDUCATION** Univ Kans, BA, 64; Ind Univ, MA, 66, PhD(folklore and Am studies), 70. **CAREER** Actg asst prof, 68-70, asst prof, 70-75, assoc prof, 75-81, PROF FOLKLORISTICS & HIST, UNIV CALIF, LOS ANGELES, 81-, Consult & reviewer, Nat Endowment for Humanities, 79- **MEMBERSHIPS** Am Folklore Soc; Am Studies Asn; Popular Cult Asn; Soc Anthrop of Work. **RESEARCH** Organizational folklore; folk art and aesthetics; folk belief and custom. **SELECTED PUBLICATIONS** Auth, 'Spirits in the Woods, the Chainsaw Art of Skip Armstrong', J Amer Folklore, Vol 0107, 94; 'Traditions in Clay C.J. and Cleater Meaders', J Amer Folklore, Vol 0107, 94; The 1995 Archer Taylor Memorial Lecture, Why Make Folk Art, Western Folklore, Vol 0054, 95. **CONTACT ADDRESS** Folklore & Mythol Ctr, Univ of Calif, 1037 Grad Sch Mgt, Los Angeles, CA, 90024.

JONES, NICHOLAS FRANCIS
PERSONAL Born 08/22/1946, Lynwood, CA, m, 1971, 2 children **DISCIPLINE** ANCIENT HISTORY, CLASSICAL PHILOLOGY **EDUCATION** Univ Southern Calif, BA, 68; Univ Calif, Berkeley, MA, 72, PhD(classics), 75. **CAREER** Instr, 75-76, asst prof 76-81, assoc, 82-97, PROF CLASSICS, UNIV PITTSBURGH, 97-, Am Coun Learned Soc res fel hist, 78-79. **MEMBERSHIPS** Am Philol Asn; Archaeol Inst Am; Asn Ancient Historians. **RESEARCH** Greek and Roman hist; classical philol. **SELECTED PUBLICATIONS** Auth, Public Organization in Ancient Greece, Am Philos Soc, 87; auth, Ancient Greece: State and Society, Prentice Hall, 97; auth, The Associations of Classical Athens. The Response to Democracy, Oxford Univ Press, 99. **CONTACT ADDRESS** Dept of Classics, Univ Pittsburgh, 1518 CL, Pittsburgh, PA, 15260-0001. **EMAIL** NFJ2+@Pitt.edu

JONES, NORMAN L.
PERSONAL Born 04/27/1951, Twin Falls, ID, m, 1994 **DISCIPLINE** HISTORY **EDUCATION** Idaho State Univ, BA, 72; Univ Colo, MA, 74; Cambridge Univ, PhD, 78. **CAREER** Prof & Ch, Dept Hist, Utah State Univ. **HONORS AND AWARDS** Whitefield Prize for the Best Book in Stud in Hist Series, 82; Vis Fellow, Institut d'Histoire de la Reformation, Univ de Geneve, SWI, 85; NZL V Chancellors' Casual Vis, 8/94; Fowler Hamilton Vis Res Fellow, Christ Church, Oxford Univ, 98. **RESEARCH** 16th cent Britain; Parliamentary history; Reformation Europe. **SELECTED PUBLICATIONS** Auth, Faith by Statute: Parliament and the Settlement of Religion, 1559, Royal Hist Soc, 82; co-ed, Interest Groups and Legislation in Elizabethan Parliaments: Essays Presented to Sir Geoffrey Elton, Parliamentary Hist, 8:2, 89; auth, God and the Moneylenders, Usury and Law in Early Modern England, Basil Blackwell, 89; co-ed, The Parliaments of Elizabethan England, Basil Blackwell, 90; auth, The Birth of the Elizabethan Age, England in the 1560s, Blackwell Pubs, 93, 95; auth, Living the Reformation, Religion and Social Change in Early Modern England, Blackwell Pubs, forthcoming. **CONTACT ADDRESS** Dept Hist, Utah State Univ, Logan, UT, 84322-0710. **EMAIL** njones@wpo.hass.usu.edu

JONES, PAUL HENRY
PERSONAL Born 06/28/1949, Richmond, VA, m, 1976, 2 children **DISCIPLINE** HISTORICAL THEOLOGY **EDUCATION** Yale Univ, BA, 72; Brite Div Sch, Tex Christian Univ, MDiv, 78; Vanderbilt Univ, MA, 84, PhD, 88. **CAREER** Dean of the Chapel, assoc prof, prog dir Rel, Transylvania Univ, 85-; tchg asst, Vanderbilt Univ, 81-83. **HONORS AND AWARDS** Alpha Omicron Pi Awd for tchg excellence, 98, Transylvania Univ; Bingham Awd excellence tchg, 97, Transylvania Univ; T.A. Abbott Awd fac excellence, Div higher educ, Christian Church, 97; John H. Smith fel, Vanderbilt Univ; Theta Phi Hon Soc, Fac Bk Awd (s) in New Testament, Hebrew Bible, Rel ed, and Christian Board of Publ Awd (s) for scholastic excellence at Brite Div Sch. **SELECTED PUBLICATIONS** Auth, An Eidetics of the Eucharist, Mid-stream: An Ecumenical Jour, Jan 91; Worship as Identity Formation, Lexington Theol Quart, April 91; Tarry at the Cross: A Christian Response to the Holocaust, Perspectives, March 92; The Meaning of the Eucharist: Its Origins in the New Testament Texts, Encounter, Spring 93; Christ's Eucharistic Presence: A History of the Doctrine, NY, Peter Lang Publ, 94; Making a Differnce is Imperative, The Disciple, Aug 94; We Are How We Worship: Corporate Worship as a Matrix for Christian Identity Formation, Worship, July 95; Worship and Christian Identity, The Disciple, Dec 96; Disciples at Worship: From Ancient Order to Thankful Praise, in Christian Faith Seeking Historical Understanding, Macon, GA, Mercer UP, 97; coauth, 500 Illustrations: Stories from Life for Preaching and Teaching, Nashville, Abingdon Press, 98. **CONTACT ADDRESS** Dept of Religion, Transylvania Univ, 352 Melbourne Way, Lexington, KY, 40502. **EMAIL** pjones@mail.transy.edu

JONES, PETER D'A
PERSONAL Born 06/09/1931, Hull, England **DISCIPLINE** ECONOMIC HISTORY **EDUCATION** Univ Manchester, Eng, BA, 52, MA, 53; London Sch Econ, PhD, 63. **CAREER** Asst lectr Am hist & insts, Dept Am Studies, Univ Manchester, 57-58; vis asst prof econ & hist, Tulane Univ, 59-60; from asst prof to prof hist, Smith Col, 60-68; PROF HIST, UNIV ILL, CHICAGO CIRCLE, 68-; AM SPECIALIST, US DEPT STATE, 76-, Danforth teaching fel, 63; ed in hist & soc sci, Pegasus, New York, 66-68; mem hist comt, Grad Rec Exam, Educ Testing Serv, Princeton Univ, NJ, 66-70; vis prof US hist, Univ Hawaii, 72, 76; vis prof Am hist, Univ Warsaw, 73-74; mem Am studies comt, Am Coun Learned Soc, 73-; vis prof, Univ Dusseldorf, 74-75. **MEMBERSHIPS** AHA; Econ Hist Asn; Econ Hist Soc; Am Econ Asn; Conf Brit Studies. **RESEARCH** United States social and economic history; comparative history; foreign affairs. **SELECTED PUBLICATIONS** Auth, Economic History of the US since 1783, Routeledge, 56, coauth, The Christian Socialist Revival, 1877-1914: Religion, Class, and Social Conscience in Late-Victorian England, Princeton Univ, 68; The Robber Barons Revisited, Heath, 68; auth, Since Columbus: Pluralism and Poverty in the History of the Americas, Heinemann, London, 75; The USA: A History of its People and Society (2 vols), Dorsey, 76; co-ed, The Ethnic Frontier: Group Survival in Chicago and the Midwest, Eerdmans, 77; Ethnic Chicago, Eerdmans, 81; Biographical Dict of American Mayors, Greenwood Press, 82. **CONTACT ADDRESS** Dept of Hist, Univ of Illinois, Chicago, Chicago, IL, 60680.

JONES, PHILLIP ERSKINE
PERSONAL Born 10/26/1940, Chicago, IL, m **DISCIPLINE** EDUCATION **EDUCATION** Univ of IL, BS 1963; Univ of IA, MA 1967, PhD 1975. **CAREER** Chicago Youth Ctrs, group work counselor 1963-64; Flint Comm Schs, secondary tchr phys ed 1967-68; Univ of IA, dir special support serv 1970-75, asstvice pres & dir affirmative action asst prof of counselor educ 1975-78, assoc dean of student serv & asst prof of counselor educ 1978-83, dean of student serv & asst prof of counselor educ 1983-89, associate vice president of academic affairs & dean of students, 1989-97, vice pres for student services and dean of students, 1997-. **HONORS AND AWARDS** Rep US Ethnic Professional Exchange Prog to W Germany; Sister Cities Intl; Carl Duisberg-Gesellschaft; and Instut fur Auslandsbeziehungen; proceedings of the 1972 ACT Invitational Conf Iowa City. **MEMBERSHIPS** Mem IA City Human Relations Comm 1972-74; chair IA City Human Relations Comm 1974-75; human relations training sessions IA City Fire Dept 1985; field reader for spec serv prog US Office of Educ 1980-87; human relations workshop Dept of Correction Serv Session 1981; reentry workshop for tchrs IA City Sch Dist; consul redevelopment of training prog for Educators in USOE; field reader for grad & professional oppor progs US Office of Educ 1978; consul HUD. **SELECTED PUBLICATIONS** Special Educ & Socioeconomic Retardation, J for Spec ducators, Vol 19 No 4 1983; "Student Decision Making, When and How"; College/Career Choice, Right Student Right Time Right Place. **CONTACT ADDRESS** Vice President for Student Services, Univ of Iowa, Rm 114 Jessup Hall, Iowa City, IA, 52242.

JONES, REGINALD L.
PERSONAL Born 01/21/1931, Clearwater, FL, m **DISCIPLINE** EDUCATION **EDUCATION** Morehouse Coll, AB 1952; Wayne State Univ, MA 1954; OH State Univ, PhD 1959. **CAREER** Miami Univ, asst prof 1959-63; Fisk Univ, assoc prof 1963-64; UCLA, asst prof 1964-66; OH State Univ, prof vice chmn dept of psychol 1966-69; Univ of CA Riverside, chmn & prof dept of educ 1969-72; Haile Selassie Univ Addis Adaba Ethiopia, prof & dir testing ctr 1972-74; Univ of CA Berkeley, prof 1973-75; Univ of CA Berkeley, chmn dept of afro-amer studies prof of educ 1975-78, 1985-87, faculty, asst to the vice chancellor, 1982-84, 1987-90; Hampton Univ, Dept of Psychology, chair and distinguished prof, 1991-94; Hampton Univ Center for Minority Special Education, dir, 1991-96. **HONORS AND AWARDS** Scholarship Award, Assn of Black Psychologists, 1979, 1986; J E Wallace Wallin Award, Council for Exceptional Children, 1983; Education Award, American Assn on Mental Retardation, 1988; Citation for Distinguished Achievement, OH State Univ, 1983; Berkeley Citation, Univ of CA, Berkeley, 1991. **MEMBERSHIPS** Natl chmn Assn of Black Psychol 1971-72; fellow Amer Psychol Assn; mem Council for Exceptional Children; guest ed Journal of Black Psychology; assoc ed Amer Journal of Mental Deficiency; editor Mental Retardation 1979-83; 100 Black Men of the Virginia Peninsula; Alpha Alpha Chapter, Omega Psi Phi.

JONES, ROBERT
DISCIPLINE HISTORY **EDUCATION** Cornell Univ, PhD, 68. **CAREER** Prof, Univ MA Amherst. **SELECTED PUBLICATIONS** Auth, Emancipation of the Russian Nobility 1763-1785, 73; Provincial Development in Russia: Catherine II and Jakob Sievers, 84. **CONTACT ADDRESS** Dept of Hist, Univ Massachusetts Amherst, Mass Ave, Amherst, MA, 01003.

JONES, ROBERT EDWARD
PERSONAL Born 01/11/1942, Wilkes-Barre, PA, m, 1966, 1 child **DISCIPLINE** RUSSIAN HISTORY **EDUCATION** Lafayette Col, BA, 63; Cornell Univ, PhD(hist), 68. **CAREER** Asst prof, 68-73, assoc prof, 73-80, PROF HIST, UNIV MASS, AMHERST, 80-. **MEMBERSHIPS** AHA; Am Asn Advan Slavic Studies. **RESEARCH** Eighteenth century Russia. **SELECTED PUBLICATIONS** Auth, Catherine II and the reform of provincial administration, Can Slavic Studies, fall 70; Urban planning and the development of provincial towns in Russia, 1762-1796, in: The Eighteenth Century in Russia, Clarendon, 73; The Emancipation of the Russian Nobility, 1762-1785, Princeton Univ, 73; Jacob Sievers, Enlightened Reform, and the development of a Third Estate in Russia, Russ Rev, 10/77. **CONTACT ADDRESS** Dept of Hist, Univ of Mass, Amherst, MA, 01002.

JONES, ROBERT FRANCIS
PERSONAL Born 03/10/1935, Philadelphia, PA, m, 1959, 5 children **DISCIPLINE** AMERICAN HISTORY **EDUCATION** La Salle Col, BA, 56; Univ Notre Dame, MA 58, PhD, 67. **CAREER** Teacher, high sch, Pa, 60-61; instr hist, Sch Bus, 61-65, asst prof, Fordham Col, 65-76, assoc prof, 76-93, prof hist, Fordham Col and Grad Sch, Fordham Univ, Am Philos Soc grants, 69-71 & 80-81. **MEMBERSHIPS** Orgn Am Historians; Inst Early Am Hist & Cult. **RESEARCH** Federal period in United States history, political and commercial. **SELECTED PUBLICATIONS** Auth, Naval Thought of Benjamin Stoddert, First Secretary of the Navy, 1798-1801, Am Neptune, 1/64; ed, The Formation of the Constitution, Holt, 71; auth, William Duer and the Business of Government in the Era of the American Revolution, William & Mary Quart, 7/75; contribr, Power and the Presidency, Scribner, 76; auth, George Washington: A Biography, Twayne, 79; George Washington and the Politics of the Presidency, Presidential Studies Quart, 1/80; auth, Economic Opportunism and the Constitution in New York: the Example of William Due, New York History, 87; auth, The King of the Alley: The Career of William Duer, Politician, Entrepreneur, and Speculator, 1768-1799, Memories of American Philosophical Society, 92; ed, Astorian Adventure: The Journal of Alfred Seton, 1811-1815, Fordham, 93, **CONTACT ADDRESS** Dept of History, Fordham Univ, 441 E Fordham Rd, Bronx, NY, 10458-5191. **EMAIL** rjones@murray.fordham.edu

JONES, ROBERT LESLIE
PERSONAL Born 04/04/1906, Cobden, ON, Canada, m, 1939, 2 children **DISCIPLINE** AGRICULTURAL HISTORY **EDUCATION** Queen's Univ, Can, BA, 27, MA, 28; Harvard Univ, AM, 32, PhD, 38. **CAREER** From instr to asst prof hist, 38-45, prof & head dept, 45-72, andrew U Thomas prof, 66-72, EMER PROF HIST, MARIETTA COL, 72-. **MEMBERSHIPS** AHA; Orgn Am Historians; Can Hist Asn; Agr Hist Soc. **RESEARCH** History of agriculture in Ontario, 1613-1880; history of agriculture in Quebec; flatboating on the Ohio River. **SELECTED PUBLICATIONS** Contribr, The Old Northwest: Studies in Regional History, 1787-1910, Univ Nebr, 69; auth, History of Agriculture in Ohio 1750-1865, Ohio Hist Soc, 78. **CONTACT ADDRESS** Marietta Col, Marietta, OH, 45750.

JONES, WARD
DISCIPLINE CLASSICAL STUDIES **EDUCATION** Univ Richmond, BA, 52; Univ NC at Chapel Hill, MA, 57, PhD, 59. **CAREER** Instr, Ohio State Univ, 59-61; assoc prof, 61-67; prof, 67- & Chancellor prof, 68-, Col William and Mary; vis assoc prof, Tufts Univ in Naples, Italy, 65-66 & Univ NC, 66. **HONORS AND AWARDS** Ovatio awd, Class Asn Mid W and S, New Orleans, 88; Listed in Whols Who in Am, 85-; VP, 65-66 & pres, 66-67, Class Asn Va; sec-treas, 66-68 & pres, 80-82, Class Asn Mid W and S, Southern Sect; exec comt, Class Asn Mid W and S, 79-82; mng ed, Class J, 70-80; nominating comt, Class Asn Mid W and S; dir, 70-, VP, 78-80 & pres, 80-, Mediter Soc Am; VP, 86-88 & Marshal, 90-92, Alpha Chap of Phi Beta Kappa & pres, Alpha Delta Gamma, Hon Medieval and Renaissance Fraternity, 94-95; fel Inst Advanced Study in Arts and Humanities, Univ Minn, 67 - $300,00; fel Southeastern Inst Medieval and Renaissance Stud, Duke Univ & Univ NC, 66 - $600,00; 67 -600,00; 68 - $600.00 & 69-70 - $14,000,00; fac res assignments, William and Mary, 78 & 92-93. **RESEARCH** Vergil; Legend of the Sack of Troy; early history of the College of William and Mary. **SELECTED PUBLICATIONS** Auth, A New Latin Quitrent Poem of the College of William & Mary, Va Mag Hist and Biog, vol 96, 88; The So-Called Silvestris Commentary on the Aeneid and Two Other Interpretations, Speculum, 89 & A Latin Munusculum among the Papers of Francis Nicholson, Bodleian Libr Record, 93; coauth, The Commentary on the First Six Books of the Aeneid of Vergil Commonly Attributed to Bernardus Silvestris, Univ Nebr Press, 77 & An Aeneid Commentary of Mixed Type: the Glosses in MSS Harley 4946 and Ambrosianus Glll inf, The Pontifical Inst Mediaeval Stud, Toronto, 96; co-ed, Solomon Henning's Chronicle of Courland and Livonia, Baltic Stud Ctr, Madison, 92; rev, Schreiber and Maresca, Commentary on the First Six Books of Vergilis Aeneid by Bernardus Silvestris, in Vergilius,

80. **CONTACT ADDRESS** Dept of Classical Studies, Col of William and Mary, Morton Hall, Williamsburg, VA, 23187-8795. **EMAIL** jwjone@facstaff.wm.edu

JONES, WILBUR DEVEREUX
PERSONAL Born 09/28/1916, Youngstown, OH, m, 1943, 2 children **DISCIPLINE** HISTORY **EDUCATION** Youngstown Col, AB, 40; Western Reserve Univ, AM, 47, PhD(hist), 49. **CAREER** Instr hist, Western Reserve Univ, 47-49; from instr to assoc prof, 49-61, PROF HIST, UNIV GA, 62-. **RESEARCH** Nineteenth century British history; Anglo-American relations; ancient history. **SELECTED PUBLICATIONS** Auth, Make Believe Ballroom + Roadhouse Musicians of the 1930s, A Personal Account, Amer Heritage, Vol 0045, 94. **CONTACT ADDRESS** 420 S Milledge Ave, Athens, GA, 30601.

JONES, WILLIAM J.
PERSONAL Born 07/04/1932, London, England **DISCIPLINE** HISTORY **EDUCATION** Univ Col, London, BA, 54, PhD, 58, DLitt(hon), 84. **CAREER** Hist Parliament Trust, Westminster, 57-61; fac mem to prof, 61-91, chmn hist, 75-77, PROF EMER HISTORY, UNIV ALBERTA, 92-; vis prof, Univ Calif Davis, 65-66; vis assoc prof, Univ Calif Berkeley, 67. **HONORS AND AWARDS** Guggenheim fel, 68; fel, Royal Hist Soc, 73; fel, Royal Soc Can, 82. **MEMBERSHIPS** Econ Hist Soc; Selden Soc; Past Present Soc; N Am Conf Brit Stud; Hist Asn; Am Soc Legal Hist. **SELECTED PUBLICATIONS** Auth, The Elizabethan Court of Chancery, 67; auth, Politics and the Bench, 71; auth, The Foundations of English Bankruptcy, 79; contribur, History of Parliament 1559-1601, 3 vols, 82-83. **CONTACT ADDRESS** Dept of History, Univ of Alberta, Edmonton, AB, T6G 2H4.

JONES, WILLIAM JOHN
PERSONAL Born 07/04/1932, London, England, m, 1958, 3 children **DISCIPLINE** EARLY MODERN HISTORY **EDUCATION** Univ London, BA, 54, PhD(hist), 58. **CAREER** From asst prof to assoc prof, 61-69, chmn dept hist, 75-77, PROF HIST, UNIV ALTA, 69-, Am Coun Learned Soc grant, 63; vis assoc prof, Univ Calif, Davis, 65-66; Am Bar Found grant, 66; Guggenheim fel, 68-69; Can Coun grants, 70 & 75, leave fel, 72; mem adv bd, Legal Hist Prog, Am Bar Found, 71; McCalla res prof, Univ Alta, 81-82; Soc Sci & Humanities Res Coun Can leave fel, 79 & grant, 81-82. **MEMBERSHIPS** Fel Royal Hist Soc; Selden Soc; Past & Present Soc, Eng; Econ Hist Soc; Am Soc Legal Hist. **RESEARCH** Early modern British legal, parliamentary, political and administrative history. **SELECTED PUBLICATIONS** Auth, Starkey, Thomas and the Commonwealth--Humanist Politics and Religion in the Reign of Henry Viii, Renaissance and Reformation, Vol 0017, 93; Glossary of Concepts and Index for Ulrich Von Zatzikhoven 'Lanzelet', Medium Aevum, Vol 0063, 94. **CONTACT ADDRESS** Dept of Hist, Univ of Alta, Edmonton, AB, T6G 2E1.

JORAVSKY, DAVID
PERSONAL Born 09/09/1925, m, 1949, 2 children **DISCIPLINE** MODERN HISTORY **EDUCATION** Univ Pa, BA, 47; Columbia Univ, MA, 49, Russ Inst, cert, 49, PhD, 58. **CAREER** Instr hist, Cornell Univ, 53, Marietta Col, 53-54 & Univ Conn, 54-58; from asst prof to assoc prof, Brown Univ, 58-66; PROF HIST, NORTHWESTERN UNIV, EVANSTON, 66-, CHMN DEPT, 80-, Res grants-in-aid, Am Acad Arts & Sci & Am Philos Soc, Brown Univ, 58-61; NSF & Am Coun Learned Soc, Russ Res Ctr, Harvard Univ, 61-72; mem screening comt, Foreign Area Fel Prog, 62-63; NSF & Am Coun Learned Soc res grants, 69-70 & 73-74; fel, Woodrow Wilson Ctr, Smithsonian Inst, 77-78. **HONORS AND AWARDS** Pfizer Prize, Hist Sci Soc, 71. **MEMBERSHIPS** AHA; Hist Sci Soc; Am Asn Advan Slavic Studies. **RESEARCH** Russian intellectual history; history of science; history of communism. **SELECTED PUBLICATIONS** Auth, Communism in Historical Perspective, Amer Hist Rev, Vol 0099, 94; History and Literature in Contemporary Russia, Slavic Rev, Vol 0056, 97. **CONTACT ADDRESS** Dept of History, Northwestern Univ, Evanston, IL, 60201.

JORDAN, ABBIE H.
PERSONAL Wilcox County, GA, m **DISCIPLINE** EDUCATION **EDUCATION** Albany State Coll, BS 1949; Atlanta Univ, MA 1953; Univ of GA, PhD, 1979. **CAREER** Tuskegee Inst, instr; Atlanta Univ Complex, instr of reading; Jr HS Ben Hill Cty, principal; Veterans School, principal, instr; GA-SC Read Conf, org & dir; Savannah Morning News, ed-op columnist; Savannah State Coll Reading Inst, founder; US Office of Education (EPDA). **HONORS AND AWARDS** Outstanding Teacher of the Year 1973; featured in Essence Mag 1976; Novelet "Ms Lily" 1977; authored numerous articles; featured in Atlanta Constitution Journal, June 1988; Jet, Sept 28, 1992, Oct 5, 1992. **MEMBERSHIPS** Consultant in reading for the Southeastern Area of the US; mem adv comm IRA Resol Comm 1974-; exec sec/treasurer Savannah Hospital Authority 1975-; mem adv comm GA Hist Found 1974-80, Telfair Art Acad 1975-80, Basic Ed & Reading 1977-78; mem, exec bd NAACP 1977-83; coord/founder of the Society of Doctors Inc 1986-; founder/director, The Consortium of Doctors, Ltd, 1989. **CONTACT ADDRESS** The Consortium of Doctors Ltd, PO Box 20402, University System, Savannah, GA, 31404.

JORDAN, BORIMIR
PERSONAL Born 11/05/1933, Sofia, Bulgaria, m, 1961, 3 children **DISCIPLINE** CLASSICS **EDUCATION** Univ Calif, Berkeley, PhD, 68. **CAREER** Asst prof, Univ So Calif, 67-68; asst prof, assoc prof, prof, Univ Calif, Santa Barbara, 68- . **MEMBERSHIPS** APA. **RESEARCH** Ancient Greek history; Greek historical writers; Greek religion. **SELECTED PUBLICATIONS** Auth, The Athenian Navy, Berkeley, 75; Servants of the gods, Gottingen, 79. **CONTACT ADDRESS** Dept of Classics, Univ of California, Santa Barbara, Santa Barbara, CA, 93106. **EMAIL** bjordan@humanitas.ucsb.edu

JORDAN, DAVID P.
PERSONAL Born 01/05/1939, Detroit, MI, m, 1973 **DISCIPLINE** MODERN EUROPEAN HISTORY **EDUCATION** Univ Mich, BA, 61; Yale Univ, MA, 62, PhD(hist), 66. **CAREER** Asst prof hist, Brooklyn Col, 66-68; asst prof, 68-71, assoc prof, 71-79, PROF HIST, UNIV ILL, CHICAGO CIRCLE, 79-. **RESEARCH** European intellectual history of the seventeenth and eighteenth centuries; historiography; French revolution. **SELECTED PUBLICATIONS** Auth, Gibbon's Age of Constantine and the fall of Rome, Hist & Theory, 70; LeNain de Tillemont: Gibbon's surefooted mule, Church Hist, 70; Gibbon and his Roman Empire, Univ Ill, 71; Edward Gibbon: The historian of the Roman Empire, Daedalus, summer 76; Robespierre, J Mod Hist, 77; The King's Trial, Univ Calif Press, 79. **CONTACT ADDRESS** Dept of Hist, Univ of Ill at Chicago Circle, Box 4348, Chicago, IL, 60680.

JORDAN, DONALD A.
PERSONAL Born 06/06/1936, Chicago, IL, m, 1963, 3 children **DISCIPLINE** MODERN ASIAN HISTORY **EDUCATION** Allegheny Col, BA, 58; Univ Pittsburgh, MA, 63; Univ Wis, PhD(E Asian hist), 67. **CAREER** Asst prof, 67-74, dir summer inst China, 72-75, dir, Southeast Asia Studies Ctr, 77-81, ASSOC PROF E ASIAN HIST, OHIO UNIV, 74-, Nat Endowment for Humanities fel, 82. **MEMBERSHIPS** Asn Asian Studies; Nat Educ Asn; Mid-west China Sem; Tri-state China Sem. **RESEARCH** Republican China; Sino-Japanese relations. **SELECTED PUBLICATIONS** Auth, The Diplomacy of Imperial Retreat--Britain South China Policy, 1924-1931, Amer Hist Rev, Vol 0098, 93; The Kwangsi Way in Kuomintang China, 1931-1939, Amer Hist Rev, Vol 0100, 95. **CONTACT ADDRESS** Dept of Hist, Ohio Univ, Athens, OH, 45701-2979.

JORDAN, EDDIE JACK, SR.
PERSONAL Born 07/29/1927, Wichita Falls, TX, w **DISCIPLINE** EDUCATION **EDUCATION** Langston Univ, BA 1948; IA Univ, MA 1949; State Univ of IA, MFA 1956; IN Univ, MS 1973, DEd 1975. **CAREER** Claflin Univ, chmn dept of art 1950-Army; Allen Univ, chmn dept of art 1954-56; Langston Univ, chmn dept of art 1956-61; Southern Univ at NO, chmn dept of art 1961-. **HONORS AND AWARDS** Rec'd 44 awds in local regional & natl competition; Sculpture Awd Rhode Island Natl, Philbrook Museum in OK, Walker ARt Ctr MN, Gibbs Art Museum SC, Carnegie Inst Pgh; 2 sculptures as a first of Blacks purchased for IN Museum 1974; Delta Phi Delta Natl Hon Art Frat. **MEMBERSHIPS** Natl co chmn Comm for Devel of Art in Negro Colls 1962-; pres, adm bd Bethany United Ch 1968-80; mem comm Phi Delta Kappa Inc 1980-81; pres bd of dirs Natl Conf of Artists 1983-; sec treas New Orleans Ctr of Creative Arts 1983-; life mem NAACP; life mem Alpha Phi Frat Inc; life mem, National Conference of Artists. **CONTACT ADDRESS** Art Dept, Southern Univ of New Orleans, 6400 Press Dr, New Orleans, LA, 70126.

JORDAN, ERVIN L.
PERSONAL Born 00/00/1954, Norfolk, VA, m, 1985 **DISCIPLINE** HISTORY **EDUCATION** Norfolk State Col, BA cum laude 73; Old Dominion Univ, MA 79. **CAREER** Univ Virginia, asst prof, assoc curator, assoc prof, cur, 81 to 96-; Piedmont Virginia Comm Col, adj fac, 93-. **HONORS AND AWARDS** Sergeant Kirkland Awd; Cert of Hon Civil War Rnd Table; Outstanding Alumnus; VFH; Floyd W Crawford Awd; H. H. Clay Humane Awd; Who's Who in the South; Who's Who in the World; Phi Kappa Phi, Member of the Advisory Comm on African-Amer Interpretation at Monticello; appointed to the Bd Of Trustees of the VA Museum of Natural Hist and the State Historical Advisory Bd; has been the subject of numerous television, radio and newspaper interviews; and commentator on Nat Pub radio, All Things Considered, program. **MEMBERSHIPS** SHA; NAAAS; ASAALH; SAA; MARAC. **RESEARCH** Civil war hist; afro/amer history; southern history; amer hist. **SELECTED PUBLICATIONS** Auth, Black Confederates and Afro-Yankees in Civil War Virginia. A Nation Divided: New Studies in Civil War History, ed, James I. Robertson Jr, Charlottesville and London, U press of VA, 95; Jamestown Virginia, 1607-1907: An Overview, Jamestown Virtual Website, 98; Battlefield and Home Front: African Americans and the Civil war, 1860-1865, in: The African American Odyssey: An Exhibition at the Library of Congress, ed, Debra Newman Ham, Washington, Library of Congress, 98; Slave Laws in Virginia, by Philip J. Schwarz, Athens and London, U of GA press, rev in: the Jour of Amer Hist, 97; Hearts at Home: Southern Women in the Civil War, coauth, Charlottesville, U of VA Print and Press, 97; George Washington: A Hero for American Students?, coauth, The Social Studies, 97. **CONTACT ADDRESS** Dept of History, Piedmont Virginia Comm Col, 811 Harris Rd, Charlottesville, VA, 22902.

JORDAN, JIM
DISCIPLINE ART HISTORY **EDUCATION** Univ IA, BA, MFA; Inst Fine Arts NY Univ, PhD. **CAREER** Prof, Dartmouth Col. **RESEARCH** Art of the first half of the 20th century, espec abstract art. **SELECTED PUBLICATIONS** Auth, Paul Klee and Cubism, Princeton UP, 84; Graphic Legacy of Paul Klee (exh cat), 83; var other articles; coauth, The Paintings of Arshile Gorky, NY UP, 82. **CONTACT ADDRESS** Dartmouth Col, 3529 N Main St, Ste. 207, Hanover, NH, 03755. **EMAIL** jim.jordan@dartmouth.edu

JORDAN, ROBERT WELSH
PERSONAL Born 12/20/1936, Miami Beach, FL, m, 1962, 1 child **DISCIPLINE** PHILOSOPHY, PHILOSOPHY OF HISTORY **EDUCATION** Univ Houston, BS, 57; New Sch Social Res, MA, 70. **CAREER** Asst prof, 70-82, ASSOC PROF PHILOS, CO STATE UNIV, 82-. **MEMBERSHIPS** Husserl Circle; Soc Phenomenol & Existential Philos; Am Soc Value Inquiry. **RESEARCH** Twentieth century Continental philosophy; German philosophy since Kant; philosophy of history and social science. **SELECTED PUBLICATIONS** Auth, Vico and Husserl: History and Historical Science, In: Giambattista Vico's Science of Humanity, John's Hopkins Univ Press, 76; Vico and the Phenomenology of the Moral Sphere, Social Res, Vol 43, 76; Das transzendentale Ich als Seiendes in der Welt, Perspecktiven Philos, Vol 5, 79; Das Gesetz, die Anklage und Klc Prozess: Franz Kafka und Franz Brentano, Jahrbuch deutschen Schillerges, Vol 24, 80; auth, intro to & transl of Husserl's Inaugeral Lecture at Freiburg im Breisgau (1917): Pure Phenomenology, its Method and its Field of Investigation, In: Husserl: The Shorter Works, Univ Notre Dame Press, 80; Extended Critical Review of Edmind Husserl's Vorlesungen uper Ethik and Wertlehre, 1908-1914, ed by Ullrich Melle (Husserliana, vol 28), Dordrecht, Boston, London: Kluwer Academic Pubs, 88, in Husserl Studies 8, 92; Phenomenalism, Idealism, and Gurwisch's Account of the Sensory Noema, in To Work at the Foundations, J. C. Evans and R. W. Stufflebeam, eds, Kluwer Academic Pubs, 97; The Part Played by Value in the Modification of Open into Attractive possibilities, Ch 5 oh Phenomenology of Values and Valuing, J. G. Hart and Lester Embree, eds, Kluwer Academic Pubs, 97; Hartmann, Nicolai, in Encyclopedia of Phenomenology, Lester Embree, gen ed, Kluwer Academic Pubs, 97; Value Theory in Encyclopedia of Phenomenology, Lester Embree, gen ed, Kluwer Academic Pubs, 97. **CONTACT ADDRESS** Dept of Philos, Colorado State Univ, Fort Collins, CO, 80523-0001. **EMAIL** rjordan@vines.colostate.edu

JORDAN, WILLIAM CHESTER
PERSONAL Chicago, IL, m, 4 children **DISCIPLINE** MEDIEVAL HISTORY **EDUCATION** Ripon Col, AB, 69; Princeton Univ, PhD(hist), 73. **CAREER** Instr, 73-74, lectr, 74-75, asst prof, 75-81, from assoc prof to prof Hist, Princeton Univ, 81-86; dir Shelby Cullom Davis Ctr for Historical Studies, 94-; vis lectr, Univ PA, 81-82; vis assoc prof Swarthmore Col, 85. **HONORS AND AWARDS** Mellon Found humanities fel, 85-76; Rockefeller Found humanities fel, 82-83; Annenburg Res Inst fel, 89-90; Behrman Senior Fel, Princeton Univ, 90-94. **MEMBERSHIPS** Medieval Acad Am, Am Hist Assn. **RESEARCH** Medieval law and administration; Jewish-Christian relations; serfdom; famile; credit. **SELECTED PUBLICATIONS** Auth, On Bracton and Deus Ultor, Law Quart Rev, 72; co-ed, Order and Innovation in the Middle Ages, Princeton Univ Press, 76; auth, The lamb triumphant and the municipal seals of Western Languedoc, Rev belge de numismatique et de sigillographie, 77; Jews on top: Women and the availability of consumption loans in northern France, J Jewish Studies, 78; Louis IX and the Challenge of the Crusade, Princeton Univ Press, 79; Stephaton: The origin of the name, Class Folia, 79; The Aristotelevy vrata: Problems in reconstructing an ideology, Jahrbocher for Geschichte Osteuropas, 80; Approaches to the court scene in the bond story: Equity and mercy or reason and nature, Shakespeare Quart, 82; Women and Credit in Pre-Industrial and Developing Societies, Univ Pa Press, 93; The Great Famine: Northern Europe in the Early Fourteenth Century, Princeton Univ Press, 96. **CONTACT ADDRESS** Dept of History, Princeton Univ, Dickinson Hall, Princeton, NJ, 08544-1098. **EMAIL** wchester@princeton.edu

JOUKOWSKY, MARTHA SHARP
PERSONAL Born 09/02/1936, Cambridge, MA, m, 1956, 3 children **DISCIPLINE** NEAR EASTERN ARCHAEOLOGY **EDUCATION** Amer Univ Beirut, Lebanon, MA, 72; Univ Paris Sorbonne, PhD, 82. **CAREER** Prof, Brown Univ, 97-; assoc prof, Brown Univ, 88-97; asst prof, Brown Univ, 87-88. **MEMBERSHIPS** Archaeol Inst Amer; Amer Schools of Oriental Res; Amer Center Oriental Res. **RESEARCH** Near Eastern Archaeology **SELECTED PUBLICATIONS** Early Turkey: An Introduction to the Archaeology of Anatolia from Prehistory through the Lydian Period, Kendall-Hunt, 96; The Great Temple at Petra," Amer Jour Archaeol, 98; Re-Discovering Elephants at Petra! Ancient Egyptian and Mediterranean Studies: In Memory of William A. Ward, Brown Univ, 98. **CONTACT ADDRESS** Dept of Archaeology, Brown Univ, Box 1921, Providence, RI, 02912. **EMAIL** martha_joukowsky@brown.edu

JOY, MARK S.
PERSONAL Born 03/10/1954, Maryville, MO, m, 1975, 3 children **DISCIPLINE** AMERICAN HISTORY **EDUCATION** Central Christian Col, BA, 76; E NM Univ, MA, 83; Ks St Univ, MA, 85, PhD, 92. **CAREER** Vis prof, 88-89, Washburn Univ; asst prof to assoc prof, 91-, Jamestown Col. **HONORS AND AWARDS** Best paper W Hist, 84; Phi Alpha Theta **MEMBERSHIPS** Conf on Faith & Hist; Amer Soc of Church Hist; Org Amer Hist. **RESEARCH** Relig in Amer, espec primitivists & restorationist groups **SELECTED PUBLICATIONS** Auth, Caleb May: Kansas Territorial Pioneer and Politician, Prairie Scout, 85; art, Missions to Native Americans, Protestant, Dictionary of Christianity in American, Inter-Varsity Press, 90; art, Riggs, Stephen Return, The Blackwell Dictionary of Evangelical Biography, 1760-1830, Basil Blackwell Ltd, 95. **CONTACT ADDRESS** 6045 College Ln, Jamestown, ND, 58405. **EMAIL** joy@acc.jc.edu

JOYCE, DAVIS D.
PERSONAL Born 06/19/1940, Greenwood, AR, m, 1975, 5 children **DISCIPLINE** HISTORY **EDUCATION** Eastern NM Univ, BS, 61; NM State Univ, MA, 63; Univ OK, PhD, 68. **CAREER** Asst to assoc prof, Hist, Univ Tulsa, 66-83; vis prof, American studies, Univ Keele (England), 81; Soros Prof Am studies, Kossuth Univ (Hungary), 94-96; assoc prof Hist, East Central Univ, 87-. **HONORS AND AWARDS** Nat Endowment for the Humanities grants, 71, 76, 80, 83, 88, 90, 92; McCasland Award for Excellence in Teaching OK Hist, OK Heritage Asn, 97. **MEMBERSHIPS** OK Hist Soc; OK Asn of Prof Hist; Am Asn of Univ Profs. **RESEARCH** Am historiography; OK hist. **SELECTED PUBLICATIONS** Auth, A History of the United States by Edward Channing, ed, Univ Press Am, 93; An Oklahoma I Had Never Seen Before: Alternative Views of Oklahoma History, ed, Univ OK Press, 94; United States History: A Brief Introduction for Hungarian Students, with Tibor Glant, Kossuth Univ Press, 96. **CONTACT ADDRESS** Dept of History, East Central Univ, Ada, OK, 74820. **EMAIL** djoyce@mailclerk.ecok.edu

JOYCE, JANE W.
DISCIPLINE CLASSICS **EDUCATION** Bryn Mawr Col, BA; Univ Tex Austin, MA and PhD. **CAREER** Fac, 78-; prof. **HONORS AND AWARDS** Disting Prof Hum, Centre Col. **RESEARCH** Latin language and literature, ancient epic and lyric poetry, Greco-Roman drama, classical mythology and creative writing. **SELECTED PUBLICATIONS** Auth, Beyond the Blue Mountains; The Quilt Poems, Mill Springs Press, 84/86, Gnomon, 91; transl, Lucan's Pharsalia, Cornell Univ Press, 93. **CONTACT ADDRESS** Centre Col, 600 W Walnut St, Danville, KY, 40422. **EMAIL** joycej@centre.edu

JOYCE, ROSEMARY A.
PERSONAL Born 04/07/1956, Lackawanna, NY, m, 1984 **DISCIPLINE** ANTHROPOLOGY/ARCHAEOLOGY **EDUCATION** Cornell Univ, AB, 78; Univ Ill, Urbana-Champaign, PhD, 85. **CAREER** Asst curator, 85-94, asst dir, 86-89, Peabody Museum, Harvard Univ; asst prof, 89-91, assoc prof, 91-94, anthrop, Harvard Univ; dir, Phoebe Hearst Museum of Anthropology, 94-, assoc prof, anthrop, Univ Calif Berkeley, 94. **HONORS AND AWARDS** Resident fellowships: Bunting Inst, Radcliffe Coll, Harvard Univ, 92-93; Stanford Univ Center Study Behavioral Scis, 98 (deferred); Univ Calif Humanities Research Inst, spring 99; research grants: Getty Grant Program; Wenner-Fren Found Anthrop Research; Heinz Charitable Fund; Nat Sci Foundation; Nat Endowment for the Humanities; Fulbright-Hays Prog. **MEMBERSHIPS** Soc Amer Archeol; Amer Anthrop Assn; Coun Museum Anthrop; Amer Assn Museums. **RESEARCH** Archaeology of Central America and Mesoamerica; the archaeology of gender; ceramic analysis; Maya writing; the anthropology of representation and identity; museum anthropology. **SELECTED PUBLICATIONS** Coauth, Encounters with the Americas: The Latin American Gallery of the Peabody Museum, 95; auth, "The Construction of Gender in Classic Maya Monuments," in Gender in Archaeology: Essays in Research and Practice, 96; co-ed, Women in Prehistory: North American and Mesoamerica, 97; co-ed, Social Patterns in Pre-Classic Mesoamerica, 98; auth, "Performing the Body in Prehispanic Central America," RES: Anthropology and Aesthetics, spring 98. **CONTACT ADDRESS** Phoebe Hearst Museum of Anthropology, Univ of California, Berkeley, Kroeber Hall, #3720, Berkeley, CA, 94720-3712. **EMAIL** joyce@montu.berkeley.edu

JOYCE STONE, ANDREA
DISCIPLINE ART HISTORY **EDUCATION** Univ Fla, BA, 74; Univ Tex, MA, 77, PhD, 83. **CAREER** Asst prof, 84-91; assoc prof, 91-. **SELECTED PUBLICATIONS** Auth, Images from the Underworld: Naj Tunich and the Tradition of Maya Cave Painting, Univ Tex, 95; The Petroglyphs in the Guianas and Adjacent Areas of Brazil and Venezuela (rev), 89; A Dream of Maya (rev), Univ NMex, 89; The Mesoamerican Ballgame (rev), Univ NMex, 89; Arte rupestre colonial y republicano de Bolivia y paises vecinos, Latin Am Indian Lit, 89. **CONTACT ADDRESS** Dept of Art History, Univ of Wisconsin, Milwaukee, PO Box 413, Milwaukee, WI, 53201. **EMAIL** stone@csd.uwm.edu

JUDD, JACOB
PERSONAL Born 07/16/1929, New York, NY, m, 1951, 2 children **DISCIPLINE** AMERICAN HISTORY **EDUCATION** NY Univ, BA, 50, MA, 53, PhD, 59. **CAREER** Instr hist & polit sci, Sch Com, NY Univ, 55-56; res assoc Am hist, Sleepy Hollow Restorations, 56-63; from asst prof to assoc prof, 63-78, PROF AM HIST, LEHMAN COL, 78-, Lectr, Sch Gen Studies, Hunter Col, 58-59, 62-63, Grad Div, 62; George N Shuster grant, 67-68; res coord, Sleepy Hollow Restorations, 69-; assoc, Columbia Univ Sem Early Am Hist, 70-; Nat Endowment for Humanities res grant, 75-76; GRAD FAC, GRAD CTR, CITY UNIV NEW YORK, 79-. **MEMBERSHIPS** Am Asn State & Local Hist; Am Studies Asn; AHA; Orgn Am Historians. **RESEARCH** American Colonial history; development of urbanism; the Hudson Valley in American history. **SELECTED PUBLICATIONS** Auth, The Bronx in the Frontier Era--From the Beginning to 1696, J Amer Hist, Vol 0082, 95. **CONTACT ADDRESS** Dept of Hist, Lehman Col, CUNY, Bronx, NY, 10468.

JUDGE, EDWARD H.
PERSONAL Born 06/07/1945, Detroit, MI, m, 1970, 4 children **DISCIPLINE** RUSSIAN AND SOVIET HISTORY **EDUCATION** Univ of Detroit, BA, 67; Univ Mich, MA, 69, PhD, 75. **CAREER** Asst prof hist, SUNY Plattsburgh, 77-78; asst to prof of hist, LeMoyne Col, 78- . **HONORS AND AWARDS** IREX USSR Young Scholar Exchange, 76-77; NEH res and travel grant, 86, 90, 93; NEH summer sem grant, 86; LeMoyne Scholar of the year, 84; J.T. Georg endowed professorship, 97-2000. **MEMBERSHIPS** Am Asn for Advanc of Slavic Stud; Central NY Russian Hist. **RESEARCH** History of late Imperial Russia; history of the Cold War. **SELECTED PUBLICATIONS** Auth, Plehve: Repression and Reform in Imperial Russia, 1902-1904, Syracuse Univ, 83; auth, Easter in Kishinev: Anatomy of a Pogrom, NY Univ, 92; coauth, Modernization and Revolution: Dilemmas of Progress in Late Imperial Russia, East European Monographs, 92; coauth, A Hard and Bitter Peace: A Global History of the Cold War, Prentice-Hall, 96; coauth, The Cold War: A History Through Documents, Prentice-Hall, 99. **CONTACT ADDRESS** Dept of History, LeMoyne Col, 1419 Salt Springs Rd, Syracuse, NY, 13214. **EMAIL** judge@maple.lemoyne.edu

JUHNKE, JAMES CARLTON
PERSONAL Born 05/14/1938, Newton, KS, m, 1963, 2 children **DISCIPLINE** AMERICAN HISTORY **EDUCATION** Bethel Col, Kans, AB, 60; Ind Univ, MA, 64, PhD, 68. **CAREER** Asst prof, 66-71, assoc prof, 73-77, prof hist, Bethel Col, Kans, 77-, Dir, Mennonite Libr & Arch, 73-75; co-ed, Mennonite Life, 75-80. **MEMBERSHIPS** AHA; Asn Am Historians; Conf Faith & Hist. **RESEARCH** American Mennonite history; conscientious objection in World War I; modern Christian missions. **SELECTED PUBLICATIONS** Co-ed, Voices Against War, Bethel Col, 73; auth, The Victories of Nonresistance, Fides et Hist, fall, 74; A People of Two Kingdoms, Faith and Life, 75; Mob Violence and Kansas Mennonites in 1918, Kans Hist Quart, autumn 77; A People of Mission, A History of General Conference Mennonite Overseas Missions, Faith and Life Press, 79; General Conference Mennonite Missions to the American Indians in the Late Nineteenth Century, Menn Quart Rev, 4/80; The Response of Christians to Conscription in United States History, in Mennonites and Conscientious Objection, Mennonite Central Comt, 80; Gustav H Enss, Mennonite Alien, Mennonite Life, 12/81; Dialogue With a Heritage: Cornelius H. Wedel and the Beginnings of Bethel College, Bethel Col, 87; Vision, Doctrine, War: The Mennonite Experience in America 1890-1930, Herald Press, 89; co-ed, Nonviolent America: History Through the Eyes of Peace, Bethel Col, 93; Creative Crusader: Edmund G. Kaufman and Mennonite Community, Bethel Col, 94. **CONTACT ADDRESS** Dept of Hist, Bethel Col, 300 E 27th St, North Newton, KS, 67117-8061. **EMAIL** jjuhnke@bethelks.edu

JUMONVILLE, NEIL TALBOT
PERSONAL Born 10/07/1952, Portland, OR, m, 1998 **DISCIPLINE** HISTORY **EDUCATION** Reed Col, BA, 77; Columbia Univ, MA, 79; Harvard Univ, AM, 83, PhD, 87. **CAREER** Teaching fel, resident tutor, lectr, 82-90, Harvard Univ; asst prof to assoc prof to prof, 90-, Fl St Univ. **HONORS AND AWARDS** Reed Col Faculty commendation for Acad Excellence, 75, 76; Phi Beta Kappa, 77; Univ Teaching Award, Fl St Univ, 94. **MEMBERSHIPS** Amer Hist Assoc; Org of Amer Hist; Signet Soc. **RESEARCH** US intellectual & cultural hist; Amer historiography; Amer stud, twentieth century US. **SELECTED PUBLICATIONS** Auth, Critical Crossing: the New York Intellectuals in Postwar America, Univ Calif Press, 91; art, The New York Intellectuals' Defense of the Intellect, Queen's Quart, 90; auth, The Origin of Henry Steele Commager's Activist Ideas, His Teacher, 96; auth, Henry Steele Commager: Midcentury Liberalism and the History of the Present, Univ NC Press, 99. **CONTACT ADDRESS** Dept of History, Florida State Univ, Tallahassee, FL, 32306-2200. **EMAIL** njumonvi@mailer.fsu.edu

JURICEK, JOHN T.
PERSONAL Born 05/17/1938, Chicago, IL, 2 children **DISCIPLINE** HISTORY **EDUCATION** Univ Chicago, BA, 59, MA, 62, PhD, 70. **CAREER** Assoc prof **RESEARCH** American colonial history; the Indian in American history. **SELECTED PUBLICATIONS** Ed, Early American Indian Documents: Treaties and Laws, 1607-1789. **CONTACT ADDRESS** Dept History, Emory Univ, 221 Bowden Hall, 561 Kilgo Cir, Atlanta, GA, 30322-1950. **EMAIL** jjurice@emory.edu

JUSCZYK, P.W.
PERSONAL Born 01/31/1948, RI, m, 1971, 2 children **DISCIPLINE** PSYCHOLOGY **EDUCATION** Brown Univ, BS, 70; Univ Penn, MA, 71; Univ Penn, PhD, 75 **CAREER** Asst to assoc prof, Dalhousie Univ, 75-80; assoc to prof, Univ Oregon, 80-90; prof, SUNY, 90-96; Johns Hopkins Univ, 96- **HONORS AND AWARDS** Sloane Fel, Univ Penn, 84; Fulbright Schola, Cath Univ; NIMH Senior Scientist Award, 97-2002 **MEMBERSHIPS** Sigma Xi; Soc Res Child Develop; Acoustical Soc Amer; Amer Psychol Soc; Cognitive Sci Soc; Psychonomic Soc **RESEARCH** Psycholinguistics; Speech Perception; Infant Language Acquisition; Cognitive Development **SELECTED PUBLICATIONS** coauth, "18 month olds' sensitivity to relationships between morphemes: Interactions among relationships, frequency and processing," Proceedings of the 22nd Annual Boston University Conference on Language Development, Vol. 2, 98; coauth, "Talker-specificity and persistence of infants' word representations," Proceedings of the 22nd Annual Boston University Conference on Language Development, Vol. 1, 98; coauth, "American infant discrimination of Dutch and French word lists," Proceedings of the 21st Annual Boston University Conference on Language Development, Vol. 2, 97 **CONTACT ADDRESS** Dept Psychol, Johns Hopkins Univ, Ames Hall, Baltimore, MD, 21218. **EMAIL** jusczyk@jhu.edu

K

KACZYNSKI, BERNICE M.
DISCIPLINE HISTORY **EDUCATION** Univ Pittsburgh, BA; Yale Univ, MA, PhD. **HONORS AND AWARDS** Assoc ed, Jour Medieval Latin. **RESEARCH** Intellectual hist of late Antiquity and the early Middle Ages. **SELECTED PUBLICATIONS** Auth, Greek in the Carolingian Age: The St. Gall Manuscripts, 88. **CONTACT ADDRESS** History Dept, McMaster Univ, 1280 Main St W, Hamilton, ON, L8S 4L9.

KAEGI, WALTER EMIL
PERSONAL Born 11/08/1937, New Albany, IN, m, 1969, 2 children **DISCIPLINE** HISTORY **EDUCATION** Haverford Coll, BA, 59; Harvard Univ, MA, 60, PhD, 65. **CAREER** Teach fel, 61-63, Harvard; Asst Prof, 65-69, Assoc Prof, 69-74, Prof, 74-, vote mem Oriental Instr, 97-, Univ of Chicago. **HONORS AND AWARDS** Harv Fel, Dum Oaks/Harv Fel, IRH Fel, ACLS Fel, SHS Fel, IAS Fel, NEH Fel, Guggenheim Fel, NHC Fel, 2 Fulbright Fel, SSRC Mid East Fel. **MEMBERSHIPS** Mid-east Medievalists, SAHS, USNCBS, MAA. **RESEARCH** Byzantine & Islamic history, seventh century & early Islamic conquests, Byzantino-Arabica history. **SELECTED PUBLICATIONS** Auth, Byzantium and the Decline of Rome, Princeton, Princeton Univ Press, 68; Byzantine Military Unrest 471-843, An Interpretation, Amsterdam & Las Palmas, AM Hakkert, 81; Byzantium and the Early Islamic Conquests, Cambridge Eng, Cambridge Univ Press, 92; Byzantine Logistics, Problems and Perspectives, in: The Feeding of Mars, ed J A Lynn, Boulder, Westview Press, 93; The Capability of the Byzantium Army for Military Operations in Italy, in: Teodorico e i Goti, ed, A Carile, Ravenna Longo Editore, 95. **CONTACT ADDRESS** Dept of History, Univ of Chicago, 1126 E 59th St, Chicago, IL, 60637-1539. **EMAIL** kwal@midway.uchicago.edu

KAEUPER, RICHARD WILLIAM
PERSONAL Born 06/20/1941, Richmond, IN, m, 1965 **DISCIPLINE** MEDIEVAL HISTORY **EDUCATION** Capital Univ, BA, 63; Princeton Univ, MA, 65, PhD, 67. **CAREER** Lectr hist, Kenyon Col, 67-68; asst prof, IL State Univ, 68-69; asst prof, 69-73, assoc prof hist, Univ Rochester, 73, chmn dept, 77, Am Philos Soc grant, 71; res grant, Guggenheim Found, 78; R T French vis prof, Worcester Col Oxford, 79-80. **HONORS AND AWARDS** H.F. Gugeneim grt, 89-91. **MEMBERSHIPS** AHA; Mediaeval Acad Am; fel Royal Hist Soc. **RESEARCH** Medieval Eng institutions. **SELECTED PUBLICATIONS** Auth, Bankers to the Crown: The Riccardi of Lucca and Edward I, Princeton Univ, 73; The Role of Italian Financiers in the Conquest of Wales, Welsh Hist Rev, 73; The Frescobaldi of Florence and the English Crown, Studies Medieval & Renaissance Hist, 73; Royal Finance and the Crisis of 1297, In: Order and Innovation in the Middle Ages, Princeton Univ, 76; Law and Order in Fourteenth Century England, Speculum, 79, An Historians Reading of the Tale of Gamelyn, 83; War Justice Public Order, Clarendon Press, Oxford, 88; Chivalry and the Problem of Violence, Clarendon Press, Oxford, (in press); Co auth, The Book of Chivalry of Geoffroide Charny, Univ PA Press, 96. **CONTACT ADDRESS** Dept of Hist, Univ Rochester, 500 Joseph C Wilson, Rochester, NY, 14627-9000. **EMAIL** rkpr@uhurs.cc.rochester.edu

KAFKER, FRANK ARTHUR
PERSONAL Born 12/18/1931, New York, NY, m, 1953, 2 children **DISCIPLINE** MODERN EUROPEAN HISTORY **EDUCATION** Columbia Col, BA, 53; Columbia Univ, MA, 54, PhD(hist), 61. **CAREER** From instr to assoc prof hist, Corning Community Col, 58-62; from asst prof to assoc prof, 62-72, PROF HIST, UNIV CINCINNATI, 72-, Charles P Taft grant, Univ Cincinnati, 72-73 & 78; Am Philos Soc grant, 78. **MEMBERSHIPS** AHA Soc Fr Hist Studies; Am Soc 18th Century Studies; Soc Fr Etude XVIIIe Siecle. **RESEARCH** France during the Old Regime and the Revolution; the history of encyclopedias, especially Diderot's Encyclopedia and the French encyclopedists; European intellectual history. **SELECTED PUBLICATIONS** Auth, Publishing and Sedition--Universe of 18th-Century Underground Literature, Amer Hist Rev, Vol 0097, 92; Diderot--A Critical Biography, Amer Hist Rev, Vol 0099, 94. **CONTACT ADDRESS** Dept of Hist, Univ of Cincinnati, P O Box 210373, Cincinnati, OH, 45221-0373.

KAGAN, RICHARD C.
PERSONAL Born 06/24/1938, Los Angeles, CA, m, 1962, 2 children **DISCIPLINE** FAR EASTERN HISTORY **EDUCATION** Univ Calif, Berkeley, BA, 60, MA, 63; Univ Pa, PhD(hist), 69. **CAREER** Instr hist, Boston State Col, 69-71; res assoc, Ctr Chinese Studies, Univ Mich, Ann Arbor, 71-72; asst prof hist, Grinnell Col, 72-73; asst prof, 63-73, ASSOC PROF HIST, HAMLINE UNIV, 73-. **MEMBERSHIPS** AHA; Asn Asian Studies. **RESEARCH** Communist Revolution; Shamanism in China; political and economic development of Taiwan. **SELECTED PUBLICATIONS** Auth, Following Ho Chi Minh--Memoirs of a North Vietnamese Colonel, Historian, Vol 0059, 97. **CONTACT ADDRESS** Dept of Hist, Hamline Univ, 1536 Hewitt Ave, Saint Paul, MN, 55104-1284.

KAGAN, RICHARD LAUREN
PERSONAL Born 09/18/1943, Newark, NJ **DISCIPLINE** EARLY MODERN HISTORY **EDUCATION** Columbia Univ, AB, 65; Cambridge Univ, PhD, 68. **CAREER** Asst prof hist, Ind Univ, Bloomington, 68-72; asst prof, 72-74, assoc prof, 74-79, prof hist, Johns Hopkins Univ, 79-, fel, Shelby Cullom Davis Ctr Hist Studies, NJ, 69-70; US Dept Health, Educ & Welfare Comt Basic Res Educ res grant, 71-72; Herodotus fel, Inst Advan Study, Princeton, 76-77; US-Span Joint Comt res grant, 80. **HONORS AND AWARDS** John Simon Guggenheim Fel, 82; Quincentenary Fel, US-Spanish Joint Comm, 91-92; Sr Research Fel, The Getty Trust, 93-95; Collab Proj Grant, NEH, 94-97; Knight Comdr, Order of Isabel the Catholic. **MEMBERSHIPS** AHA; Soc Span & Port Hist Studies; Ctr for Advan Study in Visual Arts, Wash, DC. **RESEARCH** Early modern Spain; history of European education; history of law. **SELECTED PUBLICATIONS** Auth, Universities in Castile, 1500-1700, Past & Present, 70; Students and Society in Early Modern Spain, Johns Hopkins Univ, 74; Universities in Castile, 1500-1810, Universities in Society: Studies in the History of Higher Education, Princeton Univ, 74; Law students and legal careers in eighteenth-century France, Past & Present, 75; Lawsuits and Litigants in Castile, 1500-1700, Univ NC, 81; The Toledo of El Greco, El Greco et Toledo, 82; Spanish Cities of the Golden Age, 89; Lucrecia's Dreams: Politics & Prophecy in Sixteenth Century Spain, 90; Spain, Europe and the Atlantic World, Cambridge Univ, 95; Prescott's Paradigm: American Historical Scholarship and the Decline of Spain, Am Hist Rev, April 96. **CONTACT ADDRESS** Dept Hist, Johns Hopkins Univ, 3400 N Charles St, Baltimore, MD, 21218-2680. **EMAIL** Kagan@jhu.edu

KAGAN, ROBERT A.
PERSONAL Born 06/13/1938, Newark, NJ, m, 1967, 1 child **DISCIPLINE** POLITICAL SCIENCE **EDUCATION** Harvard, BA, 59; Columbia, LLB, 62; Yale Univ, PhD, 74. **CAREER** Prof of Poli Sci, 74-, Prof of Law, 88-, Dir, Center for the Study of Law & Society, 93-, Univ of Cal, Berkeley. **HONORS AND AWARDS** AAAS Member **MEMBERSHIPS** APA, L&SA **RESEARCH** Sociolegal studies, government regulation of business, comparative legal institutions. **SELECTED PUBLICATIONS** Auth, Regulatory Justice, Implementing a Wage-Price Freeze, Russell Sage Foundation, 78; Patterns of Port Development, Government Intermodal Transportation and Innovation in the United States, China and Hong Kong, 90; Adversarial Legalism and American Government, J of Public Policy Analysis and Management, 91; Regulatory Enforcement, in: Handbook of Administrative Law and Regulation, eds, D Rosenbloom & R D Schwartz, Marcel Dekker, 94; Should Europe Worry About Adversarial Legalism? Oxford J Legal Studies, 97; Adversarial Legalism, An International Perspective, in: Comparative Disadvantages? Social Regulations and the Global Economy, ed, Pietro Nivola, Washington DC, Brookings Instr, 97. **CONTACT ADDRESS** Center for the Study of Law and Society, Univ of Calif Berkeley, Berkeley, CA, 94720-2150. **EMAIL** rak@uclink4.berkeley.edu

KAGAN, SUSAN
PERSONAL Born 12/27/1929, New York, NY, m, 1955, 2 children **DISCIPLINE** MUSICOLOGY **EDUCATION** Columbia Univ, BS, 51; Hunter Col CUNY, MA, 75; CUNY Grad School, PhD, 83. **CAREER** Pianist, St Louis Symphony Orchestra, 58-62 & Pitt Symphony Orchestra, 62-63; adj lectr, Bronx Comm Col, CUNY, 72-77; adj lectr, vis asst prof, substitute asst prof, PROF, HUNTER COL, CUNY; Am Asn Univ Women Diss Fel, 77; Rosa Riegelman Heintz Scholar, Hunter Col, 70. **MEMBERSHIPS** Am Musicol Soc; Local 802 Am Fedn Musicians; Int Franz Schubert Inst; Am Schubert Inst; Am Beethoven Soc; Berlioz Soc. **RESEARCH** 19th and 20th Century music. **SELECTED PUBLICATIONS** Ed Archduke Rudolph: Forty Variations on a Theme by Beethoven; Sonata in F for Violin and piano, 92; Archduke Rudolph: Variations in F for Violin and Piano, 95; Half and Half: Anthology of Workes for Piano Four Hands, 98; discography Archduke Rudolph: Sonata in F Minor for Violin and Piano & Variations in F for Violin and Piano, Koch Int Classics, 92; Archduke Rudolph: Sonata in A for Clarinet and Piano: Trio in Eb for Clarinet, Cello, and Piano, Koch Int Classics, 95; W A Mozart: Piano Concertos K 413, 414, 449; Vox Classics, 95; W A Mozart: Piano Concertos K 246, 271 & Rondo in A, K 386, Koch Discover Int, 96; Edvard Grieg: Complete Sonatas for Violin and Piano, Koch Int Classics, 97. **CONTACT ADDRESS** Music Dept, Hunter Col, CUNY, 695 Park Ave, New York, NY, 10021. **EMAIL** Susankagan@AOL.com

KAHAN, ALAN S.
PERSONAL Born 07/24/1959 **DISCIPLINE** HISTORY **EDUCATION** Princeton Univ, BA, 80; Univ Chicago, PhD, 87. **CAREER** Mellon asst prof, Rice Univ, 88-92; asst prof, hist, Fla Intl Univ, 92-94; assoc prof, hist, Fla Intl Univ, 95-. **HONORS AND AWARDS** NEH Transl Grant, 95-96. **RESEARCH** European liberalism; Tocqueville; Burckhardt; J.S. Mill. **SELECTED PUBLICATIONS** Auth, Alexis de Tocqueville, The Old Regime and the Revolution, a new transl, The Univ of Chicago Press, vol 1, 98; Aristocratic Liberalism: The Social and Political Thought of Jacob Burckhardt, John Stuart Mill and Alexis de Tocqueville, Oxford Univ Press, 92; articles, Defining Opportunism: The Political Writings of Eugene Spuller, Hist of Polit Thought, winter, 94; Liberalism and Realpolitik in Prussia, 1830-52: The Case of David Hansemann, German Hist, oct, 91; Guizot et le modele anglais, in Francois Guizot et la culture politique de son temps, Paris, Gallimard, 91; The Victory of German Liberalism?, Rudolf Haym, Liberalism and Bismarck, Cent Europ Hist, mar, 90; Tocqueville's Two Revolutions, Jour of the Hist of Ideas, oct, 85. **CONTACT ADDRESS** History Dept, Florida Intl Univ, Miami, FL, 33199. **EMAIL** kahana@fiv.edu

KAHN, B. WINSTON
PERSONAL Born 10/23/1932, Hsin-shih, m, 1970, 3 children **DISCIPLINE** MODERN JAPANESE HISTORY **EDUCATION** Nat Taiwan Univ, BA, 55; Univ Minn, Minneapolis, MA, 59; Univ Pa, PhD(int rels), 69. **CAREER** Asst prof, 66-78, ASSOC PROF HIST, ARIZ STATE UNIV, 78-, Asst ed, Asian Forum, 71-73; Fulbright res grant, Japan, 79-80. **MEMBERSHIPS** AHA; Asn Asian Studies. **RESEARCH** Japanese expansion; modern Japanese intellectual history; United States-Japanese relations. **SELECTED PUBLICATIONS** Contribr, Taiwan's Future?, Union Res Inst, 74; auth, Hani Goro: A radical democrat's critique of Japanese society, Japan Interpreter, fall 76; The diplomacy of Matsuoka Yosuke, 1940-1941, Asian Forum, spring-summer 79; contribr, China and Japan: A Search for Balance since World War I, ABC-Clio, 78. **CONTACT ADDRESS** Dept of Hist, Arizona State Univ, Tempe, Tempe, AZ, 85281.

KAHN, CHARLES H.
PERSONAL Born 05/29/1928, New Iberia, LA, m, 1951, 2 children **DISCIPLINE** HISTORY OF PHILOSOPHY **EDUCATION** Univ Chicago, BA, 46, MA, 49; Columbia Univ, PhD, 58. **CAREER** From instr to assoc prof Greek & Latin, Columbia Univ, 57-65; assoc prof, 65-68, chmn dept, 75-78, PROF PHILOS, UNIV PA, 68-, Univ Chicago exchange fel to Univ Paris, 49-50; Cutting traveling fel, Columbia Univ, 55-56; Am Coun Learned Soc res fel, 63-64; co-ed, Arch Geschichte Philos, 65-; mem managing comt, Am Sch Class Studies in Athens, 70-, vis prof, 74-75; Nat Endowment for Humanities fel, 74-75. **MEMBERSHIPS** Am Philos Asn; Soc Ancient Greek Philosophers (pres, 76-78). **RESEARCH** Greek philosophy, especially Presocratics, Plato and Aristotle; political philosophy. **SELECTED PUBLICATIONS** Auth, The Chronology of Plato Dialogs, Classical J, Vol 0088, 92; Proleptic Composition in the 'Republic', or Why Book-1 Was Never a Separate Dialogue + Plato, Classical Quart, Vol 0043, 93. **CONTACT ADDRESS** Dept of Philos/CN, Univ of Pa, 34th and Spruce St, Philadelphia, PA, 19104.

KAHN, DAVID
PERSONAL Born 02/07/1930, New York, NY, d, 2 children **DISCIPLINE** MODERN HISTORY **EDUCATION** Bucknell Univ, AB, 51; Oxford Univ, PhD, 74. **CAREER** Assoc Ed, Newsday, 79-; Assoc Prof, Journalism, 75-79. **RESEARCH** Hist of Intelligence; Hist of Cryptology. **SELECTED PUBLICATIONS** Auth, Seizing the Enigma, The Race to Crack the German U-Boat Codes, 1939-1943, Houghton Mifflin, 91; Kahn on Codes: Secrets of the New Cryptology, Macmillan, 84; Woodrow Wilson on Intelligence, Intelligence and National Security, 94; U S Unveils WWII Decode Secrets, Newsday, 96; British Knew of Holocaust in 41, Newsday, 96; Seizing the Enigma, Book on tape, 10 Cassettes, Audio Books, 96; Let Feds Overhear Cellular-Phone Talk, Newsday, 97; How to Share a Secret, Newsday, 97; Francis Harry Hinsley 79, British Historian, Newsday, 98. **CONTACT ADDRESS** Great Neck, NY, 11023. **EMAIL** DAVEK120@aol.com

KAHN, JONATHAN
PERSONAL Born 08/06/1958, Cambridge, MA **DISCIPLINE** HISTORY **EDUCATION** Yale Univ, BA, 80; Boalt Hall Sch of Law, JD, 88; Cornell Univ, PhD, 92. **CAREER** Asst Prof, Bard Col, 92-98 **HONORS AND AWARDS** Mellon Fel; Order of the Caif; Sage Fel; Yee Fel **MEMBERSHIPS** AHA; APSA; OAH; SHGAGE; ASLH **RESEARCH** U.S political culture; legal studies **CONTACT ADDRESS** Bard Col, 13 Hollis St, Cambridge, MA, 02140. **EMAIL** kahn@bard.edu

KAIMOWITZ, JEFFREY H.
PERSONAL Born 11/03/1942, New York, NY, m, 1987, 1 child **DISCIPLINE** CLASSICS **EDUCATION** Johns Hopkins, AB, 64; Univ of Cincinnati, PhD, 70; Columbia Univ, MS, 76 **CAREER** Asst Prof, 69-73, Miami Univ, OH; Libr Trainee, 73-77, NY Pub Lib; Curator, 77-, Watkinson Lib, Trinity Col, Hartford **HONORS AND AWARDS** Phi Beta Kappa, 64; Woodrow Wilson Fel, 64-65; Fulbright Fel, 66-67 **MEMBERSHIPS** Am Lib Asc; Grolier Club **RESEARCH** Translating Latin poetry; Printing hist **CONTACT ADDRESS** Watkinson Lib, Trinity Col, Hartford, CT, 06106. **EMAIL** jeffrey.kaimowitz@trincoll.edu

KAIN, JOHN FORREST
PERSONAL Born 11/09/1935, Fort Wayne, IN, m, 1957, 2 children **DISCIPLINE** ECONOMICS **EDUCATION** Bowling Green State Univ, AB (Honors in Economics and Political Science), 57; Univ CA, Berkeley, MA, PhD, 61. **CAREER** Grad res asst, 57-61, lect, Business Admin & Economics, Univ CA, Berkeley, 59-61; assoc prof, economics, US Air Force Academy, 62-64; asst prof economics, Harvard Univ, 65-67, prof, 68-90, dir, prog in Regional and Urban Economics, 67-78; Henry Lee prof of Economics and prof of Afro-American Studies, Harvard Univ, 91-97, chmn, dept of economics, 88-91, Emeritus, 97-; The Cecil and Ida Green chair for the Study of Science and Society, prof of Economics and prof of Political Economy, dir, Cecil and Ida Green Center for the Study of Science and Society, Univ TX, Dallas, 97-; vis res assoc, London School of Economics, 64; vis res scholar, dept economics, Univ TX, Arlington, 87-88; vis fel, Korean Devel Inst, 91; vis prof, School of Social Sciences, Univ TX, Dallas, 91-92, 96-97; non-resident fel, WEB DuBois inst for Afro-American res, Harvard Univ, 97-. **HONORS AND AWARDS** Scholarship, Bowling Green State Univ, 54-57; fel, Real Estate Res prog, Univ CA, Berkeley, 59-61; Harvard Univ, AM (honorary), 68; Taussig Res Prof, Dept of Economics, 87-88. **MEMBERSHIPS** Am Economics Asn, 61-; Am Real Estate and Urban Economics Asn, 80-; Asn for Public Policy Analysis and Management, 98-. **RESEARCH** Urban economics; transportation; determinants of student achievement and performance of schools and teachers. **SELECTED PUBLICATIONS** Auth, with William C Apgar Jr, Housing and Neighborhood Dynamics: A Simulation Study, Harvard Univ Press, 85; A Defense of Demand Subsidies--The Cost-Effective Way of Assisting Low Income Households, in Joseph Pechman and Michael S McPherson, eds, Fulfilling America's Promise, Cornell Univ Press, 92; The Use of Strawmen in the Economic Evaluation of Transport Investments, Am Economic Rec, May 92; The Spatial Mismatch Hypothesis: Three Decades Later, Housing Policy Debate, vol 3, issue 2, 92; The Impacts of Congestion Pricing on Transit and Carpool Demand and Supply, in Committee for the Study of Urban Transportation Congestion Pricing, Transportation Res Bd, Nat Res Coun, Curbing Gridlock: Peak-Period Fees to Relieve Traffic Congestion: Vol 2, Commissioned papers, Washington, DC, Nat Academy Press, 94; with Kraig Singleton, Equality of Educational Opportunity Revisited, New England Economic Rev, May/June 96; with Jeffrey Zax, Moving to the Suburbs: Do Relocating Companies Leave Their Black Employees Behind?, J of Labor Economics, July 96; Cost-Effective Alternatives to Atlanta's Costly Rapid Transit System, of Transport Economics and Policy, vol XXI, no 1, Jan 97; The Case for Bus Rapid Transit, Nieman Reports, winter 97; numerous other publications. **CONTACT ADDRESS** Dir, The Cecil and Ida Green Center for the Study of Science and Society, Univ of Texas, Dallas, PO Box 830688, Richardson, TX, 75083-0688. **EMAIL** jkain@utdallas.edu

KAISER, DANIEL HUGH
PERSONAL Born 07/20/1945, Philadelphia, PA, m, 1968, 2 children **DISCIPLINE** RUSSIAN & FAMILY HISTORY **EDUCATION** Wheaton Col, Ill, AB, 67; Univ Chicago, AM, 70, PhD(Russ hist), 77. **CAREER** Instr hist, King's Col, NY, 68-71; asst prof, Trinity Col, Ill, 71-73; vis asst prof, Russ hist, Univ Chicago, 77-78; asst prof hist, Univ Chicago, 77-78; asst prof hist, Grinnell Iowa Coll, 79-84; assoc prof, 84-86; prof hist, 86-; Joseph F Rosenfield prof social studies, 84-; chemn dept hist, 89-90, 96-98; Lectr & tour dir, Smithsonian Inst tours to USSR, 76-. **HONORS AND AWARDS** Mem adv bd Soviet Studies in History, 79-85; editl bd Slavic Rev, 96; Fel Nat Endowment Humanities, 79, 92-93, John Simon Guggenheim Meml Found, 86; Fulbright-Hays Fac Research Abroad Found, 86. **MEMBERSHIPS** AHA; Am Assn Advan Slavic Studies;

Early Slavic Studies Assn, vp, 95-97; Slavonic and East European Medieval Studies Group, UK; Study Group on 18th Century Russia, UK; 18th Century Russian Studies Assn. **RESEARCH** Russian and comparative law; Russian and comparative family history; Historical climatology. **SELECTED PUBLICATIONS** Trans ed, The Laws of Rus Tenth to Fifteenth Centuries, Charles Schlacks Jr, Publisher, 92; co-ed, with Gary Marker, Reinterpreting Russian History 860-1860s, 94; The Growth of the Law in Medieval Russia, Princeton Univ Press, 80; Muscovite Law, 1300-1500, Dict Middle Ages (in press). **CONTACT ADDRESS** Dept of History, Grinnell Col, PO Box B, Grinnell, IA, 50112-0805. **EMAIL** kaiser@ac.grin.edu

KAISER, THOMAS ERNEST
PERSONAL Born 06/10/1947, New York, NY, m, 1975, 1 child **DISCIPLINE** HISTORY **EDUCATION** Univ Mich, BA, 68; Harvard Univ, PhD, 76. **CAREER** Asst prof, 76-80, assoc prof, 80-94, prof hist, 94-, Univ Ark, Little Rock; Univ Ark, Little Rock fac res grant, 77; Am Coun Learned Soc grant-in-aid, 78. **HONORS AND AWARDS** Article Award, Southeastern Am Soc 18th-Century Studies, 81. **MEMBERSHIPS** Am Soc 18th Century Studies; Soc French Hist Studies. **RESEARCH** Eighteenth-century French political and cultural history. **SELECTED PUBLICATIONS** Auth, Property, Sovereignth, the Declaration of the Rights of Man, and the Tradition of French Jurisprudence, The French Idea of Freedom: The Old Regime and the Declaration of Rights of 1789, Stanford, 94; auth, Madame de Pompadour and the Theaters of Power, French Hist Stud, 96; auth, The Drama of Charles Edward Stuart, Jacobite Propaganda, and French Political Protest, 1745-1750, Eighteenth-Century Stud, 97; auth, Louis le Bien-Aime and the Rhetoric of the Royal Body, From the Royal to the Republican Body: Incorporating the political in Seventeenth and Eighteenth Century France, California, 98; auth, Enlightenment, Public Opinion and Politics in the Work of Robert Darnton, The Darnton Debate: Books and Revolution in the Eighteenth Century, Oxford, 98; art, The Evil Empire: Constructing Turkish Despotism in Eighteenth-Century French Political culture, J of Modern Hist, 99. **CONTACT ADDRESS** Dept of History, Univ of Ark, 2801 S University Ave, Little Rock, AR, 72204-1000. **EMAIL** tekaiser@uar.edu

KAISER, WALTER C., JR.
PERSONAL Born 04/11/1933, Folcroft, PA, m, 1957, 4 children **DISCIPLINE** BIBLICAL ARCHAEOLOGY **EDUCATION** Wheaton Col, AB, 55, BD, 58; Brandeis Univ, MA, 62, PhD, 73. **CAREER** Instr, 58-60, asst prof of Bible, 60-64, actg dir of archaeol & Near Eastern stud, 65-55, Wheaton Col; asst prof, 66-70, assoc prof, 70-75, chmn dept of OT, 75-79, sr vice pres, acad dean, 80-92, sr vice pres of Distance Learning, 92-93, Trinity Evangel Divin Schl; Coleman M Mockler Dist Prof of OT, 93-96; pres, 97-, Gordon Conwell Theol Sem. **HONORS AND AWARDS** Danforth Tchr Stud grant. **MEMBERSHIPS** Evangel Theol Soc; Inst of Bibl Res; Near Eastern Archaeol Soc; Soc of Bibl Lit. **RESEARCH** Old Testament Theol; Israel, history and archaeology; ethics. **SELECTED PUBLICATIONS** Auth, The Journey Isn't Over: The Pilgrim Psalms (120-134) for Life's Challenges and Joys, Baker 93; coauth, An Introduction to Biblical Hermeneutics: The Search for Meaning, Zondervan, 94; auth, The Book of Leviticus: Introduction, Commentary and Reflections, New Interpreter's Bible, Abingdon, 94; auth, Proverbs: Wisdom for Everyday Life, Zondervan, 95; auth, Psalms: Heart to Heart with God, Zondervan, 95; auth, The Messiah in the Old Testament, Zondervan, 95; auth, Hard Sayings of the Bible, InterVarsity, 96; auth, A History of Israel, Broadman & Holman, 98; auth, The Christian and the "Old" Testament, US Ctr for World Mission, 98; auth, An Urgent Call For Revival and Renewal in Our Times: Sixteen Revivals in the Old and New Testament with a Study Guide, Broadman & Holman, 99; auth, Are the Old testament Documents Reliable?, InterVarsity, 99. **CONTACT ADDRESS** Gordon-Conwell Theol Sem, 130 Essex St, South Hamilton, MA, 01982. **EMAIL** wckaiser@gcts.edu

KALAS, ROBERT
DISCIPLINE WESTERN CIVILIZATION **EDUCATION** NY Univ, PhD **CAREER** Dept Hist, Mt. St. Mary's Col **RESEARCH** Roles of widows within noble families during 16th and 17th century France. **SELECTED PUBLICATIONS** Publ on, structure of the nobility in 16th and 17th century France **CONTACT ADDRESS** Dept of History, Mount Saint Mary's Col, 16300 Old Emmitsburg Rd, Emmitsburg, MD, 21727-7799. **EMAIL** kalas@msmary.edu

KALE, STEVEN D.
DISCIPLINE MODERN EUROPEAN HISTORY **EDUCATION** Univ Wis, Madison, PhD, 87. **CAREER** Assoc prof, Washington State Univ. **MEMBERSHIPS** Mem Gov Coun, Western Soc for Fr Hist. **RESEARCH** History of modern France. **SELECTED PUBLICATIONS** Auth, Legitimism and the Reconstruction of French Society, 1852-1883, La State UP, 92. **CONTACT ADDRESS** Dept of History, Washington State Univ, 301 Wilson Hall, PO Box 644030, Pullman, WA, 99164-4030. **EMAIL** kale@wsu.edu

KALLMANN, HELMUT
PERSONAL Born 08/07/1922, Berlin, Germany **DISCIPLINE** MUSIC HISTORY **EDUCATION** Royal Conserv Mus, 48; Univ Toronto, BMus, 49, LLD, 71. **CAREER** CBC Toronto Mus Libr, 50-70; Chief Mus Div, Nat Libr Can, 70-87 (RETIRED). **HONORS AND AWARDS** Can Mus Coun Medal Outstanding Serv Can Mus life, 77; mem, Order Can, 86. **MEMBERSHIPS** Can Mus Coun (vice pres, 71-76); Can Asn Mus Librs; Int Asn Mus Librs; Bibliog Soc Can; Soc quebecoise de recherche en musique; chmn, Can Mus Heritage Soc, 82-. **SELECTED PUBLICATIONS** Auth, Catalogue of Canadian Composers, rev ed 52; A History of Music in Canada 1534-1914, 60, repr, 69, 87; ed, The Canadian Musical Heritage, vol 8: Music for Orchestra 1, 90; co-ed, Encyclopedia of Music in Canada, 81, 2nd ed, 92; Encyclopedie de la Musique au Canada, 83, 2nd ed, 93. **CONTACT ADDRESS** 38 Foothills Dr, Nepean, ON, K2H 6K3.

KALLMYER, NINA
DISCIPLINE EIGHTEENTH AND NINETEENTH CENTURY EUROPEAN ART **EDUCATION** Princeton, PhD. **CAREER** Prof, assoc ch. **SELECTED PUBLICATIONS** Auth, French Images from the Greek War of Independence: Art and Politics under the Restoration, Yale Univ Press, 89; Eugene Delacroix Prints, Politics and Satire 1814-1822, Yale Univ Press, 92. **CONTACT ADDRESS** Dept of Art Hist, Univ Delaware, 162 Ctr Mall, Newark, DE, 19716. **EMAIL** nina@udel.edu

KALMAN, LAURA
PERSONAL Born 03/19/1955, Los Angeles, CA, m, 1984 **DISCIPLINE** HISTORY **EDUCATION** Pomona Col, BA, 74; UCLA, JD, 77; Yale Univ, PhD, 82. **CAREER** Asst prof, Univ Calif Santa Barbara, 82-85; assoc prof, 85-91; prof, 91-. **HONORS AND AWARDS** Golieb Res Fel, NYU Law School, 81-82; Am Coun of Learned Soc Fel, 84-85; Am Bar Found Fel, 84-85; Visiting Res Fel, Am Bar Found, 86-87; Littleton-Griswold Prize, Am Hist Asoc, 91; Charles Warren Res Fel, 94-95. **MEMBERSHIPS** Am Hist Asoc; Am Soc for Legal Hist; Orgn of Am Hist. **RESEARCH** Recant American legal and political history. **SELECTED PUBLICATIONS** Auth, Legal Realism at Yale, 1927-1960, 86; auth, Abe Fortas: A Biography, 90; auth, The Strange Career of Legal Liberalism, 96. **CONTACT ADDRESS** Dept. of History, Univ of California, Santa Barbara, Santa Barbara, CA, 93106. **EMAIL** kalman@humanitas.ucsb.edu

KALVODA, JOSEF
PERSONAL Born 01/15/1923, Czechoslovakia, m, 1956 **DISCIPLINE** HISTORY, POLITICAL SCIENCE **EDUCATION** Hunter Col, BA, 56; Columbia Univ, MA, 56, PhD, 60. **CAREER** From instr to assoc prof polit sci & hist, St Joseph Col, Conn, 57-61; assoc prof, Col for Women, Univ San Diego, 61-64, prof, 64-77; assoc prof govt, La State Univ, 66-68; PROF POLIT SCI & HIST, ST JOSEPH COL, CONN, 68-. **MEMBERSHIPS** AAUP; Am Asn Advan Slavic Studies; Am Polit Sci Asn. **RESEARCH** East central Europe; international relations; comparative government. **SELECTED PUBLICATIONS** Auth, Tightening the Noose--Secret Documents on Czechoslovakia in 1968, Slavic Rev, Vol 0055, 96. **CONTACT ADDRESS** 9 Greenwood Dr, Avon, CT, 06001.

KAMAU, MOSI
PERSONAL Born 05/05/1955, Chicago, Illinois, s **DISCIPLINE** AFRICAN-AMERICAN STUDIES **EDUCATION** Univ of Minnesota, BFA 1979; Florida State Univ, MFA 1983; Temple Univ, PhD, African-Amer Studies, 1989-. **CAREER** Tutle Contemporary Elem School, pottery instructor, 1977-78 Talbot Supply Co Inc, welder 1979-80; Florida State Univ, asst preparator 1980-81; Williams Foundry, foundryman 1981-82; St Pauls Coll, asst prof of art 1984-89. **HONORS AND AWARDS** Intl Exchange Scholarship from Univ of Minnesota to Univ of Ife Ile, Ife Nigeria 1976-77; Sculpture/$5000 Natl Endowment of the Arts, Visual Arts, Washington DC 1984-85. **MEMBERSHIPS** Natl Council of Black Studies; African American Assn of Ghana; African Heritage Assn. **CONTACT ADDRESS** St Pauls Col, PO Box 901, Lawrenceville, VA, 23868.

KAMHI, MICHELLE MARDER
PERSONAL Born 06/09/1937, New York, NY, m, 1987, 1 child **DISCIPLINE** ART HISTORY **EDUCATION** Bernard Coll, BA, 58; Hunter Coll CUNY, MA, 70. **CAREER** Ed, Columbia Univ Press 66-70; freelance ed and writer, 71-84; assoc ed, ARISTOS, 84-91; Co-ed, ARISTOS, 92-. **HONORS AND AWARDS** Fulbright scholar, Univ Paris, 58-59. **MEMBERSHIPS** Am Philos Asn; Am Soc for Aesthetics; Asn of Literary Scholars and Critics. **RESEARCH** Philosophy of Art. **SELECTED PUBLICATIONS** Auth, Limiting What Students Shell Read: Books and Other Learning Materials in Our Schools, 81; Censorship vs Selection: Choosing Books for School, Am Educ, 82; Today's 'Public Art': Rarely Public, Rarely Art, Aristos, 88; The Misreading of Literature: Context, Would-Be Censors, and Critics, Aristos, 86; coauth, Ayn Rand's Philosophy of Art: A Critical Introduction, 91-92; What Art Is: The Esthetic Theory of Ayn Rand, forthcoming. **CONTACT ADDRESS** Aristos, Radio City Station, PO Box 1105, New York, NY, 10101. **EMAIL** aristos@aristos.org

KAMINSKI, JOHN PAUL
PERSONAL Born 01/16/1945, Bridgeton, NJ, m, 1967, 2 children **DISCIPLINE** AMERICAN HISTORY **EDUCATION** Ill State Univ, BS, 66, MS, 67; Univ Wis-Madison, PhD(US hist), 72. **CAREER** DIR, CTR STUDY AM CONSTITUTION, UNIV WIS-MADISON, 81-, Assoc ed, Doc Hist Ratification Constit & Bill of Rights, 69-80, prin investr & co-ed, 80. **MEMBERSHIPS** Orgn Am Historians; Asn Doc Ed. **RESEARCH** United States Constitution; American Revolution. **SELECTED PUBLICATIONS** Auth, The Constitutional Thought of Jefferson, Thomas, Virginia Mag Hist and Biography, Vol 0104, 96. **CONTACT ADDRESS** Dept of Hist, Univ of Wis, Madison, WI, 53706.

KAMLA, THOMAS A.
DISCIPLINE MEDIEVAL GERMAN LITERATURE, 18TH-20TH CENTURY GERMAN LITERATURE, GERMAN LAN **EDUCATION** St John's Univ, Univ of MN, BA, 61; Univ WI, MA, 69, PhD, 73. **CAREER** Univ Scranton, 78-; Univ NE, 76-78; Carnegie Mellon Univ, 72-76. **RESEARCH** 19th-20th century Ger lit; psychoanalytic criticism; turn of the century; expressionism; exile lit. **SELECTED PUBLICATIONS** Auth, scholarly bk:Confrontation with Exile: Studies in the German Novel; articles,19th and 20th century Ger authors. **CONTACT ADDRESS** Dept of For Lang(s) and Lit(s), Univ of Scranton, Scranton, PA, 18510. **EMAIL** Kamlatl@tiger.uofs.edu

KAMMAN, WILLIAM
PERSONAL Born 03/23/1930, Geneva, IN, m, 1957, 3 children **DISCIPLINE** UNITED STATES DIPLOMATIC HISTORY **EDUCATION** Ind Univ, AB, 52, PhD(hist), 62; Yale Univ, MA, 58. **CAREER** Assoc prof, 62-69, prof hist, N Tx State Univ, 69-, chmn dept, 77-89, 93-94, assoc dean of A&S, 96-97, 98-, interim dean of A&S, 97-98. **MEMBERSHIPS** AHA; Orgn Am Historians; Soc Hist Am Foreign Rels, exec sec-treas, 85-89. **RESEARCH** United States Foreign policy in the 1920's and 1930's. **SELECTED PUBLICATIONS** Auth, A Search for Stability: United States Diplomacy Toward Nicaragua, 1925-1933, Univ Notre Dame, 68; contribr, Makes of American Diplomacy, 74 & Encycl of American Foreign Policy, 78, Scribner's; Encyclopedia World Biography, McGraw Hill, 73; 20th Century Encyl World Biography, Jack Heraty & Assoc, 87, 92; The War of 1898 and U.S. Intervention, 1898-34: An Encyl, Garland, 94. **CONTACT ADDRESS** Dept of Hist, No Texas State Univ, PO Box 310650, Denton, TX, 76203-0650. **EMAIL** Kamman@UNT.EDU

KAMMEN, MICHAEL
DISCIPLINE HISTORY **EDUCATION** PhD. **CAREER** Prof. **HONORS AND AWARDS** Pulitzer Prize, 73; The Francis Parkman Prize, 87; Henry Adams Prize, 87; Nat Bk Awd, Popular Cult Asn, 96., Pres, Org Am Hist, 95-96. **RESEARCH** U.S. cultural history; historical relationship between government and culture in the U.S. **SELECTED PUBLICATIONS** Auth, Mystic Chords of Memory; The Transformation of Tradition in American Culture, 91; Selvages and Biases: The Fabric of History in American Culture, 87; A Machine That Would Go of Itself: The Constitution in American Culture, 86. **CONTACT ADDRESS** Dept of History, Cornell Univ, Ithaca, NY, 14853-2801. **EMAIL** mgk5@cornell.edu

KAMOCHE, JIDLAPH GITAU
PERSONAL Born 12/01/1942, Kabete, Kenya, m **DISCIPLINE** HISTORY **EDUCATION** Amherst Col, BA 1967; Univ of MA, MA 1969; State Univ of NY at Buffalo, PhD 1977. **CAREER** African & Afro-Amer Studies Univ of OK, asst prof of History dir 1977-; State Univ Coll Buffalo, asst prof History 1972-77; African & Afro-Amer, dir; State Univ Coll Buffalo, stud 1970-72. **HONORS AND AWARDS** Recipeint inst of intl Educ Fellowship NY 1968-69; author Afro-am Life & Hist 1977; recipient coll of arts research fellowship Univ of OK 1979-80. **MEMBERSHIPS** Mem Several African & Afro-am Studies Orgns 1970-80; past vice pres Assn of Black Personnel Univ of OK 1978-79. **SELECTED PUBLICATIONS** author articles & book reviews in several scholarly journs 1977-; author "Umoja" 1980. **CONTACT ADDRESS** Department of History, Univ of Oklahoma, 455 W Lindsey, Norman, OK, 73019.

KANDO, THOMAS M.
PERSONAL Born 04/08/1941, Budapest, Hungary, m, 1973, 2 children **DISCIPLINE** SOCIOLOGY **EDUCATION** Univ MN, MA, 67, PhD, 69. **CAREER** Asst prof, Univ CA, Riverside, 72-73; assoc prof, PA State (main campus), 77-79; prof, CA State Univ, Sacremento, 79-. **HONORS AND AWARDS** Fulbright fel, 60-61; fel, Univ Amsterdam, 62-65; fel, Univ MN, 67; Merit Awards, CA State Univ, Sacramento, 85, 97. **MEMBERSHIPS** Am Sociol Asn; Phi Beta Kappa Honor Soc; Am Asn of Univ Profs (pres, local and statewide, 76-78); Int Sociol Asn; Int Committee on Sports Sociol. **RESEARCH** Sociol of marriage and sexuality; social psychology; sociol of leisure; criminology and deviance. **SELECTED PUBLICATIONS** Auth, L A Debate: Police are also Victims, Wall Street J, March 19, 91; Clintonomics, Int J on World Peace, summer 93; Eastern Europe: Prospects for Progress, Int J on World Peace, June 94; Interstellar Travel, Gold River Scene, spring 95; Postmodernism: Old Wine in New Bottles?, Int J on World

Peace, Sept 96; The Family in Global Transition, Int J on World Peace, March 97; The Influence of the Family on the Formation of Selfhood, in Identity and Character: the Main Influence of Family and Society on Personality Development, N Pitrie, ed, PWPA Press, 98; numerous other scholarly articles, book reviews, and newspaper and magazine articles. **CONTACT ADDRESS** Dept of Sociol, California State Univ, Sacramento, Sacramento, CA, 95819. **EMAIL** kandotom@csus.edu

KANE, STANLEY
DISCIPLINE PHILOSOPHY OF RELIGION, HISTORY OF PHILOSOPHY, ENVIRONMENTAL PHILOSOPHY **EDUCATION** Barrington Col, BA; Brown Univ, AM; Harvard Univ, PhD. **CAREER** Prof, Miami Univ **RESEARCH** Philosophy of religion. **SELECTED PUBLICATIONS** Publ on, problems of God and evil; nature of God; nature of religious lang; Anselm's theory of free will; Aquinas' doctrine of the soul and personal identity; 17th century mechanism philos & histl roots of the env crisis. **CONTACT ADDRESS** Dept of Philosophy, Miami Univ, Oxford, OH, 45056. **EMAIL** kanegs@muohio.edu

KANET, ROGER E.
PERSONAL Born 09/01/1936, Cincinnati, OH, m, 1963, 2 children **DISCIPLINE** POLITICAL SCIENCE **EDUCATION** Berchmanskolleg, Pullach-bei-Munchen, Germany, PhB, 60; Xavier Univ, AB, 61; LeHigh Univ, MA, 63; Princeton Univ, AM, 65, PhD, 66. **CAREER** Asst to Assoc Prof, Univ Kans, 67-74; Dir, Undergrad Stud, 69-70; Assoc Ch, Dept Polit Sci, 70-71; Vis Assoc Prof to Assoc Prof to Prof, Univ Ill at UC, 73-97; Hd of Dept of Polit Sci, 84-87; Assoc V Chan, 89-97; Mem, Russian & E European Ctr, 74-97; Prof Emeritus, 97-; Prof, Dean, Sch of Int Stud, Univ Miami, Coral Gables, 97-. **HONORS AND AWARDS** Joint Sr Fellow, Columbia Univ, 72-73; Fellow, Am Counc of Learned Soc, 72-73, 78; IREX Fellow in Hungary & Poland, 76; NATO Fac Fellow, 77; Assoc, Ctr for Adv Stuf, UIUC, 81-82; Awards for Excellence in Udergrad Tchng, 81; Burlington N Fac Ach Award, UIUC, 89. **MEMBERSHIPS** Counc on Foreign Relations; Chicago Comt of Chicago Counc on Foreign Relations; Int Commission of the Nat Asn of State Univ & Land Grant Col, 89-97; Bd of Dir, MidW Univ Cons for Int Activities, 89-97; Asn of Int Educ Admin (exec committee, 95-); Int Polit Sci Asn; Int Comte for Cent & E Eur Stud; Am Polit Sci Asn; Int Stud Asn; Am Asn for the Adv of Slavic Stud. **RESEARCH** Foreign & domestic policies of Russia & other countries of Central & Eastern Europe; democratization in postcommunist states. **SELECTED PUBLICATIONS** Co-ed, Soviet Foreign Policy in Transition, Cambridge Univ Press, 92; Coping with Conflict after the Cold War, Johns Hopkins Univ Press, 96; co-ed, The Foreign Policy of the Russian Federation, St Martin's Press, 97; co-ed, Resolving Regional Conflict, Univ Ill Press, 98; co-ed, The Post-Communist States in the World Community, St Martin's Press, 98. **CONTACT ADDRESS** Sch of Int Stud, Univ Miami, PO Box 248123, Coral Gables, FL, 33124-3010. **EMAIL** rkanet@sis.miami.edu

KANG, SOO Y.
PERSONAL Born 07/24/1964, Seoul, Korea, s **DISCIPLINE** ART HISTORY **EDUCATION** Univ So Calif, BA, 85; Univ Calif, Berkeley, MA, 89; Univ Calif, Santa Barbara, PhD, 94. **CAREER** Lectr, Univ Calif, Santa Barbara, 95; lectr, Santa Barbara City Col, 95; asst prof Art Hist, Chicago State Univ, 95- . **MEMBERSHIPS** Col Art Asn; Lancanian Soc, Chicago. **RESEARCH** Modern art; feminist art, religious art of the Twentieth Century. **SELECTED PUBLICATIONS** Auth, The Political Dimension of Roucault's Art, Cummer Stud, 96; auth, Voicing Post-Modern Women, Una Kim exhibition catalogue, Seoul, 98-99; auth, Roucault in Perspective; Contextual and Theoretical Study of His Art, International Scholars, 99. **CONTACT ADDRESS** 600 N McClung Ct, 3908A, Chicago, IL, 60611. **EMAIL** bisyk@csu.edu

KANG, WI JO
PERSONAL Born 03/10/1930, Chinju, Korea, m, 1961, 4 children **DISCIPLINE** HISTORY OF RELIGIONS, MISSIONS **EDUCATION** Concordia Sem, BA, 57, 1313, 60; Univ Chicago, MA, 62, PhD, 67. **CAREER** Instr hist of relig, Columbia Univ, 64-66; asst prof, Valparaiso Univ, 66-68; assoc prof, Concordia Sem, 68-74 & Christ Sem-Seminex, 74-78; vis prof, Yonsei Univ, Korea, 78-79; Prof of Mission, Wartburg Sem, 80-; Christ and Caesar in Modern Korea: A History of Christianity and Politics, State Univ NY Press, 97. **MEMBERSHIPS** Am Acad Relig; Am Hist Soc; Int Soc Buddhist Studies; Am Soc Missiology; Am Soc Church Hist. **RESEARCH** History of religions in Asia; history of Christian missions in East Asia; world religions and politics. **SELECTED PUBLICATIONS** Auth, Korean Religions Under the Japanese Government (in Japanese), Seibunsha, Tokyo, 76; In Search of Light (in Korean), 76 & Religion and Politics of Korea Under Japanese Rule (in Korean), 77, Christian Lit Soc Korea, Seoul; The secularization of Korean Buddhism, Actes du XXIXe Cong Int des Orient Paris L'Asiatheque, 77; Religious response to Japanese rule, Ctr for Korean Studies, Kalamazoo, Mich, 77; co-ed, Christian Presence in Japan, Seibunsha, Tokyo, 81; auth, Christianity under the government of Chung Hee Park, Missiology: Int Rev, 81; Christianity in China, Currents in Theol & Mission, 82. **CONTACT ADDRESS** Wartburg Theol Sem, 333 Wartburg Place, Dubuque, IA, 52003-5050. **EMAIL** KANGWI.JO@MACLEODUSA

KANIPE, ESTHER SUE
PERSONAL Born 03/22/1945, Rockingham, NC **DISCIPLINE** EUROPEAN & WOMEN'S HISTORY **EDUCATION** Univ NC, Greensboro, BA, 67; Univ Wis, MA, 70, PhD(hist), 76. **CAREER** Instr hist, Grinnell Col, 73-75; asst prof, Lawrence Univ, 75-76; asst prof, 76-82, ASSOC PROF HIST, HAMILTON COL, 82-, Nat Endowment for the Humanities fel hist, Brown Univ, 80-81; consult, Nat Endowment for the Humanities, 81- **MEMBERSHIPS** AHA; Soc French Hist Studies. **RESEARCH** Modern French social history; World War I. **SELECTED PUBLICATIONS** Auth, Women and Medicine in the French Enlightenment--The Debate Over Maladies Des Femmes, J Hist Sexuality, Vol 0004, 94. **CONTACT ADDRESS** Dept of Hist, Hamilton Col, 198 College Hill Rd, Clinton, NY, 13323-1292.

KANTOWICZ, EDWARD ROBERT
PERSONAL Born 06/20/1943, Chicago, IL, m, 1967, 2 children **DISCIPLINE** UNITED STATES HISTORY **EDUCATION** St Mary of the Lake Sem, BA, 65; Univ Chicago, MA, 66, PhD(hist), 72. **CAREER** Asst prof, 69-75, ASSOC PROF HIST, CARLETON UNIV, 75-, Fel, Can Coun, 75-76. **RESEARCH** Immigration to the United States; American Catholic history; American urban history. **SELECTED PUBLICATIONS** Auth, Research Guide toAmerican Historical Biography, J Amer Hist, Vol 0079, 93; Research Guide toAmerican Historical Biography, Vol 4, J Amer Hist, Vol 0079, 93; Research Guide toAmerican Historical Biography, Vol 5, J Amer Hist, Vol 0079, 93; Unmeltable Ethnics--Politics and Culture in American Life, J Amer Ethnic Hist, Vol 0016, 97. **CONTACT ADDRESS** 509-1701 Kilborn, Ottawa, ON, K1H 6M8.

KAO, ARTHUR MU-SEN
DISCIPLINE ART HISTORY **EDUCATION** Nat Taiwan Univ, BA, 67; Univ Chinese Culture, MA, 70; Univ Kans, MA, 74, MPh, 75, PhD, 79. **CAREER** Instr, Chinese Univ Hong Kong, 79-85; assoc prof, Kent State Univ, 85-89; PROF, 89-, DIR, SCH ART, SAN JOSE STATE UNIV. **CONTACT ADDRESS** Sch Art and Design, San Jose State Univ, 1 Washington Sq, San Jose, CA, 95192.

KAPLAN, BENJAMIN J.
DISCIPLINE HISTORY **EDUCATION** Yale Univ, BA, 81; Harvard Univ, MA, 83, PhD, 89. **CAREER** Tutor, tchg fel, Harvard Univ, 84-86, 88; asst prof, Brandeis Univ, 89-96; from asst prof to assoc prof, 96-, Univ IA. **HONORS AND AWARDS** Harold K. Gross Prize, 90; Harold J. Grimm Prize, 95; Rowland Bainton Prize, 96; Philip Schaff Prize, 97; Old Gold Summer Fel, 97, Univ IA; Frederick Solmnsen Fel, 97, Univ WI; Mazer Award, fac res, 94, Brandeis Univ. **SELECTED PUBLICATIONS** Auth, art, Remnants of the Papal Yoke: Apathy and Opposition in the Dutch Reformation, 94; auth, art, Confessionalism and Popular Piety in the Netherlands, 95; auth, Calvinists and Libertines: Confession and Community in Utrecht, 1578-1620, 95; auth, art, Possessed by the Devil? A Very Public Dispute in Utrecht, 96; auth, art, Connfessionalism and Its Limits: Religion in Utrecht, 1600-1650, 97. **CONTACT ADDRESS** Dept of History, Univ of Iowa, 280 Schaeffer Hall, Iowa City, IA, 52242. **EMAIL** benjamin-kaplan@uiowa.edu

KAPLAN, HERBERT HAROLD
PERSONAL Born 06/05/1932, New York, NY **DISCIPLINE** HISTORY **EDUCATION** Brooklyn Col, AB, 54; Columbia Univ, AM, cert prof E Cent Europe, 56, PhD(hist), 60. **CAREER** From instr to assoc prof, 60-70, PROF HIST, IND UNIV, BLOOMINGTON, 70-, Am Coun Learned Soc grant, 61; Inter-Univ Comt Travel Grants grant, Moscow State Univ, 64-66; Ger Acad Exchange Serv vis scholar fel, Ger, 68; Guggenheim Mem Found fel, 70-71; off Ind Univ rep, Anglo-Am Conf Historians, London, 72; Russ & E Europ Inst cross cult fel, Ind Univ, 73-74; consult, Slavic Rev, 74-; Pres Coun Int Prog grant, Ind Univ, 78. **MEMBERSHIPS** AHA; Am Asn Advan Slavic Studies; Am Soc Eighteenth Century Studies. **RESEARCH** Russian commerce with Great Britain during the second half of the 18th century; social and economic management of landed estates in 18th century Russia; history of the Polish-Lithuanian Commonwealth from 1569-1795. **SELECTED PUBLICATIONS** Auth, England and the German Hanse, 1157-1611--A Study of Their Trade and Commercial Diplomacy, Cent Europ Hist, Vol 0025, 92; Teplov, Grigorii--A Statesman at the Court of Catherine the Great, Slavic Rev, Vol 0052, 93; The Hanseatic League and the German East, Slavic Rev, Vol 0053, 94; After the Deluge-Poland Lithuania and the 2nd Northern-War 1655-1660, Slavic Rev, Vol 0053, 94. **CONTACT ADDRESS** Dept of Hist, Indiana Univ, Bloomington, Bloomington, IN, 47401.

KAPLAN, LAWRENCE SAMUEL
PERSONAL Born 10/28/1924, Cambridge, MA, m, 1948, 2 children **DISCIPLINE** HISTORY **EDUCATION** Colby Col, BA, 47; Yale Univ, MA, 48, PhD(hist), 51. **CAREER** Lectr hist, Univ Bridgeport, 50; historian, US Dept Defense, 51-54; from instr to prof, 54-77, UNIV PROF HIST, KENT STATE UNIV, 77-, DIR, CTR NATO STUDIES, 79-, Fulbright lectr Am hist, Univ Bonn, 59-60 & Univ Louvain, 64-65; Am Philos Soc grant, 67 & 69 & vis res scholar US hist, Univ London, 69-70; fel, Woodrow Wilson Int Ctr Scholars, 74; consult, Histori-an Off, Off Secy Defense, 75-80; vis prof, Europ Univ Inst, Florence, Italy, 78; NATO res fel, 80-81. **MEMBERSHIPS** AHA; Orgn Am Historians; Soc Hist Am Foreign Rels (secy-treas, 74-79, pres, 81); Am Studies Asn; Soc Historians Early Am Repub. **RESEARCH** American diplomatic history; American politico-military history. **SELECTED PUBLICATIONS** Auth, Cold Economic Warfare + 2nd Opposing View on a Recent Dissertation By Forland, Egil--The Creation and Prime of Cocom, 1948-1954, Historisk Tidsskrift, Vol 0071, 92; British Foreign Policy in the Age of the American Revolution, J Modern Hist, Vol 0065, 93; Franks, Oliver, Founding Father, J Mil Hist, Vol 0057, 93; The Origins of the Cold-War in Europe--International Perspectives, J Mil Hist, Vol 0059, 95; Nationalist Ferment--Origins of United States Foreign-Policy, Diplomatic Hist, Vol 0021, 97. **CONTACT ADDRESS** Dept of Hist, Kent State Univ, Kent, OH, 44242.

KAPSCH, ROBERT J.
PERSONAL Born 07/25/1942, Elizabeth, NJ, m, 1970 **DISCIPLINE** AMERICAN STUDIES; ENGINEERING & ARCHITECTURE **EDUCATION** Univ Md, PhD, 93; Cath Univ Amer, PhD, 83; George Washington Univ, MA, 78; MS, 74; Rutgers Univ, BS, 64. **CAREER** Special Asst to Dir, Ntl Park Service, 95-; Chief, Historic Amer Buildings Survey/Historic Amer Engineering Record, Ntl Park Service, 80-95; Program Manager, Dept Housing & Urban Develop, 78-80; Amer Polit Sci Assoc Congressional Fel, 77-78. **HONORS AND AWARDS** US Dept Interior Meritorious Service Medal, 93; Ntl Park Service First Vail Partnership Award, 94; Amer Inst Architects Honorary Membership Award, 94. **MEMBERSHIPS** Amer Soc Civil Engineers; Amer Inst Architects; Soc Industrial Archeol; Soc Archit Historians; Washington Historical Soc; US Capitol Historical Soc; Ntl Trust for Historical Preservation. **RESEARCH** Historic Architecture and Engineering of US **SELECTED PUBLICATIONS** Auth, Building the Infrastructure of the New Federal City, 1793-1800, Civil Engineering History, Engineers Make History, Proceedings of the First National Symposium on Civil Engineering History, 96; auth, Blacks and the Construction of the White House, 1793-1800, Amer Vision Mag, 95; auth, A Labor History of the Construction and Reconstruction of the White House, 1793-1817, Univ Maryland, 93. **CONTACT ADDRESS** Dept of National Park Service, Univ of Maryland, 15220 DuFief Dr, N Potomac, MD, 20878. **EMAIL** bobhist@erols.com

KARAMANSKI, THEODORE J.
DISCIPLINE HISTORY **EDUCATION** Loyola, PhD, 80. **CAREER** Act grad prog dir; pres, Nat Coun Publ Hist, 89-90. **RESEARCH** 19th century Frontier history; midwest public history. **SELECTED PUBLICATIONS** Auth, Fur Trade and Exploration, Okla, 83; Rally Round the Flag: Chicago and the Civil War, Nelson Hall, 92; Deep Woods Frontier: a History of Logging in Northern Michigan, Wayne State Press, 89; ed, Ethics and Public History: An Anthology, Krieger, 90. **CONTACT ADDRESS** Fine Arts Dept, Loyola Univ, Chicago, 6525 N. Sheridan Rd., Chicago, IL, 60626. **EMAIL** tkarama@wpo.it.luc.edu

KARAVITES, PETER
PERSONAL Born 04/05/1932, Patras, Greece, m, 1968, 2 children **DISCIPLINE** HISTORY **EDUCATION** Univ Chicago, MA, 59; Loyola Univ, Chicago, PhD, 71. **CAREER** Tchg asst, Loyola Chicago, 65-69; asst prof, Univ N Carolina, Boone, 71-77; Asst prof, Prof, Bridgewater State Col, 78- ; NEH Summer Sem; Schmitt Scholar Loyola, 69-70; grant Inst Advanced Studies, 86. **HONORS AND AWARDS** NEH Summer Sem(s); Schmitt Scholar, Loyola, 69-70; grant, Am Counc Learned Soc, 86 **MEMBERSHIPS** APA; Assoc Ancient Hist; Friendly Ancient Hist; New Eng Colloquium; AHEPA. **RESEARCH** Greek history 5th century; homeric treaties; Patristic writings. **SELECTED PUBLICATIONS** Auth, Gregory Nazianzinos and Byz Hymnography, Jour Hellenic Studies, 93; St Basil and Byzantine Hymnology, The Greek Orthodox Theol Rev, 92; From Clement of Alexandria to Gregory Nazianzinus via Heracleitus, Alpha to Omega: Studies in Honor of George Zsemler on his Sixty-Fifth Birthday, Ares, 93; Melito of Sardes, A Note on His Influence, The Ancient World, 96; Evil-Freedom of the Will & The Road to Perfection in Clement of Alexandria, E J Brill, 98. **CONTACT ADDRESS** 470 Hayward St., Bridgewater, MA, 02324. **EMAIL** PKaravites@bridgew.edu

KARETZKY, STEPHEN
PERSONAL Born 08/29/1946, Brooklyn, NY, m, 1985 **DISCIPLINE** HISTORY **EDUCATION** Queens Col, BA, 67; Columbia Univ, MA, 69, PhD, 78; Calif St Univ, MA, 91. **CAREER** Asst prof, 74-76, Buffalo, 77-78, Geneseo, SUNY; assoc prof, 78-81, Haifa Univ, Israel; ed, 81-82, Shapolsky, Staimatzky Pub NY; assoc prof, 82-85, Calif St Univ, San Jose; sr ed, 86-86, Shapolsky Pub, NY; lib dir & assoc prof, 86-, Felician Col, Lodi NJ. **HONORS AND AWARDS** Who's Who in Amer; Who's Who in the World; 2nd place, Book of the Year, Amer Soc Info Science, 83. **MEMBERSHIPS** Historians;

Amer Soc for Info Science. **RESEARCH** U.S. History **SELECTED PUBLICATIONS** Auth, Reading Research and Librarianship: A History and Analysis, 82; auth, The Cannons of Journalism, 84; auth, The Media's Coverage of the Arab-Israeli Conflict, 89; auth, Not Seeing Red: American Librarianship and the Soviet Union 1917-1960, 98. **CONTACT ADDRESS** Felician Col, 262 S Main St, Lodi, NJ, 07644.

KARGON, ROBERT
PERSONAL Born 10/18/1938, Brooklyn, NY, m, 1962, 2 children **DISCIPLINE** HISTORY OF SCIENCE **EDUCATION** Duke Univ, BS, 59; Yale Univ, MS, 60; Cornell Univ, PhD (hist), 64. **CAREER** Asst prof hist, Univ Ill, 64-65; from asst prof to assoc prof, 65-72, prof, 72-77, WILLIS K SHEPARD PROF HIST OF SCI, JOHNS HOPKINS UNIV, 77-, CHMN DEPT, 72-, Am Philos Soc grant, 71-72; Nat Endowment for Humanities grant, 72-73, fel, 76-77; Nat Sci Found grant, 75-79. **MEMBERSHIPS** Hist of Sci Soc. **RESEARCH** History of physics of the 17th and 19th centuries; social history of science; American science. **SELECTED PUBLICATIONS** Auth, Science and the Founding Fathers--Science in the Political Thought of Jefferson, Franklin, Adams, and Madison, Amer Hist Rev, Vol 0102, 97. **CONTACT ADDRESS** Dept of Hist of Sci, Johns Hopkins Univ, 3400 N Charles St, Baltimore, MD, 21218-2680.

KARKHANIS, SHARAD
PERSONAL Born 03/08/1935, Khopoli, India **DISCIPLINE** POLITICAL SCIENCE, AMERICAN GOVERNMENT **EDUCATION** Bombaby Libr Asn, diploma, 56; Univ of Bombay, BA, 58; Rutgers State Univ, MLS, 62; Brooklyn Col, CUNY, MA, 67; NY Univ, PhD, 78. **CAREER** Librn, U.S. Infor Service Libr, 55-58; Libr Trainee, Leyton Public Libr, 58-59; Librn Trainee, Montclair Public Libr, 59-60; librn, East Orange Pub Libr, 60-63; Prof of Libr & Political Sci, Kingsborough Community Col, CUNY, 64-. **HONORS AND AWARDS** Distinguished Service Award, Asian/Pacific Am Librn Asn, 89; Taraknath Das Award, NY Univ Grad School, 77; Certificate of Appreciation by the Libr Asn of the City Univ of NY, 73. **MEMBERSHIPS** Am Libr Asn, 64-; Asian/Pacific Am Libr Asn, 80-. **RESEARCH** Press and politics of India; Judaism in America. **SELECTED PUBLICATIONS** Auth, Jewish Heritage in America: An Annotated Bibliography, Garland Pub, 88; Indian Politics and the Press, Vikas Pub, 81. **CONTACT ADDRESS** Kingsborough Comm Col, CUNY, 2001 Oriental Blvd, Brooklyn, NY, 11235. **EMAIL** sharadka@worldnet.att.net

KARL, BARRY D.
PERSONAL Born 07/24/1927, Louisville, KY, m, 1957, 2 children **DISCIPLINE** UNITED STATES HISTORY **EDUCATION** Univ Louisville, BA, 49; Univ Chicago, MA, 51; Harvard Univ, PhD(Am civilization), 60. **CAREER** Head tutor hist & lit, Harvard Univ, 60-62; asst prof, 62-63, prof hist, Wash Univ, 63-68; prof hist, Brown Univ, 68-71; PROF AM HIST, UNIV CHICAGO, 71-, Mem, Joint Comt Res Philanthropy, 75-; chmn dept hist, Univ Chicago, 76-; Norman & Edna Freehling Prof Social Sci & Am Hist, 77-. **RESEARCH** Social science and public policy in the twentieth century; public administration. **SELECTED PUBLICATIONS** Auth, Struggles for Justice--Social-Responsibility and the Liberal State, J Southern Hist, Vol 0059, 93; Science Policy and Politics, Rev(s) in Amer Hist, Vol 0023, 95; The Rich Man and the Kingdom--Rockefeller, John, D., Jr, and the Protestant Establishment, J Rel, Vol 0077, 97. **CONTACT ADDRESS** Dept of Hist, Univ Chicago, Chicago, IL, 60637.

KARLSEN, CAROL F.
DISCIPLINE HISTORY **EDUCATION** Univ of Maryland, BA, 70; NY Univ, MA, 72; Yale Univ, PhD, 80. **CAREER** ASSOC PROF, HIST, UNIV MICH **MEMBERSHIPS** Am Antiquarian Soc **RESEARCH** Iroquois Indians, 1750-1900. **SELECTED PUBLICATIONS** Co-ed, The Journal of Esther Edwards Burr, 1754-1757, Yale Univ Press, 84; auth, The Devil in the Shape of a Woman: Witchcraft in Colonial New England, Norton, 87, Vintage, 89; auth, The Salem Witchcraft Outbreak of 1692, Oxford Univ Press, 98. **CONTACT ADDRESS** Divinity Sch, Harvard Univ, 45 Francis Ave, Cambridge, MA, 02139.

KARMAN, JAMES
PERSONAL Born 08/12/1947, Moline, IL, m, 1968 **DISCIPLINE** ART **EDUCATION** Augustana Col, BA, 69; Univ Iowa, MA, 71; Syracuse Univ, PhD, 76. **CAREER** Postdoctoral fel, Syracuse Univ, 76-77; ast prof, 77-84, asoc prof, 84-87, prof coord, 87-, Calif St Univ, Chico. **HONORS AND AWARDS** Res fel, Nat Endowment Hum, 98-99. **MEMBERSHIPS** Robinson Jeffers Tor House Found; Robinson Jeffers Asn; MLA; Col Art Asn; Am Acad Relig; Asn for Documentary Editing; Soc for Textua Scholar. **RESEARCH** Art; religion; literature; twentieth century history and culture; life and work of Robinson Jeffers. **SELECTED PUBLICATIONS** Ed, Critical Essays on Robinson Jeffers, GK Hall, 90; auth, Robinson Jeffers: Poet of California, rev., Story Line, 95; ed, Of Una Jeffers, Story Line, 98. **CONTACT ADDRESS** Dept of English, California State Univ, Chico, Chico, CA, 95929-0830. **EMAIL** Jkarman@oavax.csuchico.edu

KARON, BERTRAM PAUL
PERSONAL Born 04/28/1930, Tantan, MA, m, 3 children **DISCIPLINE** PSYCHOLOGIST **EDUCATION** Harvard Univ, BA 52; Princeton Univ, MA 54, PhD 57. **CAREER** Educational Testing Ser, res fel 52-55; Direct Analysis, intern 52-56; Princeton Univ, fel 56-57; Annandale NJ Reformatory, sr clin psychol 58; Phil Psych Hosp, res psycho 58-59, post doc fel 59-61; Private Prac PA 61-62; MI State Univ, asst prof 62-63, assoc prof 63-68, prof 68-; MI State Psychotherapy Proj Dir 66-81. **HONORS AND AWARDS** Psychoanal Awd; Distg Psychoanal Awd; Raymon D Fowler Awd; MST Lectr Awd; Distg Practitioner; Fellow APA; Fell MPA; Fell Academy of Clinic Psychol. **MEMBERSHIPS** APA; Midwest PA; MI PA; ASA; Soc PR; Mich Soc Clinic Gerontology; MPC; World Fed Mental Health; APP; Intl Symposia Psychotherapy of Schizophrenia. **SELECTED PUBLICATIONS** Video tape, The APA Psychotherapy Videotape Series: Effective Psychoanalytic Therapy of Schizophrenia and Other Severe Disorders, Washington DC, APA, 94; Ch by B P KARON, In Search of Truth, 95, How To Become A Schizophrenic: The Case Against Biological Psychiatry, Everett, WA Appolyer Press; Psychotherapy For Schizophrenia; Dynamic Therapies for Psychiatric Disorders, Axis I NY, Basic Books, 94; The Future of Psychoanalysis; A History of the Division of Psychoanalysis of the Amer Psychol Assn, Hillsdale NJ, Erlbaum; et al; BOOKS; Psykoterapi vid schizofreni: Overstattning av qun zetterstrom, Stockholm, Wahlstrom & Widstrand, 85; Psychotherapy of Schizofrene: The Treatment of Choice, NY, Aronson; et al; ARTICLES; with M A Teiexeira, 95, Guidelines for the Treatment of Depression in Primary Care, and the APA response, Amer Psycho; 95, Becoming a First Rate Psychologist Despite Graduate Education, Prof Psychol: Res and Pract; 95, Provision of Psychotherapy under managed health care: A growing crisis and national nightmare, Prof Psychol: Res and Pract; et al. **CONTACT ADDRESS** Psychology Dept, Michigan State Univ, East Lansing, MI, 48824. **EMAIL** karon@pilot.msu.edu

KARP, STEPHEN A.
PERSONAL Born 08/28/1928, Brooklyn, NY, d, 3 children **DISCIPLINE** PSYCHOLOGY **EDUCATION** Brookly Col, BA 49; New Sch Soc Research, MA 52; NY Univ, PhD 62. **CAREER** George Washington Univ, assoc prof to prof 69; Chief Psychol, Sinai Hosp Balt, Assoc Prof, John Hopkins Univ, 64-69; Univ NY, Dwntn Med Cen, instr 54-64. **MEMBERSHIPS** APA; Soc for Personality Assess; APS. **RESEARCH** Psychological Tests **SELECTED PUBLICATIONS** The Karp Objective Word Association Test KOWAT manual, Brooklandville MD, 98; Apperceptive Personality Tests, consolidated manual: child and adult brief versions, with D E Silber, R W Holmstrom, OH, IDS Pub Corp, 93; Outcomes of Thematic Apperception Test and Apperceptive Personality Test stories, with D E Silber, R W Holmstrom, V Banks, J Karp, Perceptual and Motor Skills, 92; Personality of rape survivors as a group and by relation to survivor to perpetrator, Journal of Clinical Psychology, 95; Personalities of women reporting incestuous abuse during childhood, Perceptual and Motor Skills, 95. **CONTACT ADDRESS** Dept Psychology, George Washington Univ, Washington, DC, 20052. **EMAIL** skarp@gwu.edu

KARPF, JUANITA
PERSONAL Born 10/31/1951, Rochester, NY **DISCIPLINE** MUSICOLOGY **EDUCATION** State Univ Col, Potsdam, NY, BM, 73; Univ Ga, MM, 86, DMA, 92. **CAREER** Asst Prof, Mus and Women's Stud, 95- . **MEMBERSHIPS** Am String Tchr Asn; Am Musicol Soc; Col Mus Soc, Mus Ed Nat Conf; Nat Women's Stud Assoc; Gender Res in Mus Ed; Sonneck Soc Am Mus. **RESEARCH** Feminist theory, women and music, African American history, American music history. **CONTACT ADDRESS** Univ of Georgia, School of Music, 250 River Rd, Athens, GA, 30602-7287. **EMAIL** nkarpf@arches.uga.edu

KARPINSKI, GARY S.
PERSONAL Born 07/20/1957, Philadelphia, PA, m, 1983, 2 children **DISCIPLINE** MUSIC **EDUCATION** Temple Univ, BM, MM; City Univ NY, PhD. **CAREER** Asst prof of Music, Univ of Ore, 87-93; ASSOC PROF OF MUSIC, UNIV OF MASS, 93-. **HONORS AND AWARDS** Ed, J Music Theory Pedagogy; pres, Asn Tech Music Instruction. **MEMBERSHIPS** Soc for Music Theory; Soc for Music Perception and Cognition; Am Musicological Soc. **RESEARCH** Musical Theory; aural skills; perception. **SELECTED PUBLICATIONS** Auth, Structural Functions of the Interval Cycles, Int J of Musicology, 95; Reviews of Recent Textbooks in Theory and Musicianship: Aural Skills, Music Theory Spectrum, 93; A Model for Music Perception and Its Implications in Melodic Dictation, J of Music Theory Pedagogy, 90; Hypercard: A Powerful Tchg Tool, The Computer and Music Educator, 90. **CONTACT ADDRESS** Dept of Music and Dance, Univ of Massachusetts, Amherst, MA, 01003. **EMAIL** garykarp@music.umass.edu

KARS, MARJOLEINE
DISCIPLINE HISTORY **EDUCATION** Duke Univ, PhD. **CAREER** Asst prof, Univ MD Baltimore County. **RESEARCH** Am women's hist; popular cult and relig in the eighteenth century. **SELECTED PUBLICATIONS** Auth, publ(s) on tchg. **CONTACT ADDRESS** Dept of Hist, Univ MD Baltimore County, Hilltop Circle, PO Box 1000, Baltimore, MD, 21250. **EMAIL** kars@umbc7.umbc.edu

KARSTEN, PETER
PERSONAL Born 07/27/1938, New Haven, CT, m, 1965, 3 children **DISCIPLINE** HISTORY **EDUCATION** Yale Univ, BA 60; Univ Wis, PhD 68. **CAREER** Univ Pitts, faculty, 67-; Univ Col Dublin, Washington Prof, 79-80; USN, off, 60-63. **HONORS AND AWARDS** Phi Alpha Theta; Best Bk Awd; Surrency Prize; Fulbright Sr Res Fel; Gastprof Angsburg Univ. **MEMBERSHIPS** ASLH; ASMH; Aus/NZ Law and Hist Forum; Forum on Euro Expansion and Global Interaction; Intr-Univ sem on Armed forces and soc. **RESEARCH** Common Law; Popular Norms in NA the Antipodes Polynesia and S Africa; Military systems. **SELECTED PUBLICATIONS** Auth, Heart Versus Head: Judge-made Law in nineteenth Century America, U of N Carolina Press, 97; auth, The Military and Society, five vol set of essays, Garland Press 98; auth, Cows in the Corn Pigs in the Garden and The Problem of Social Costs: High and Low Legal Cultures and Resolution of Animal Trespass Disputes in the British Diaspora Lands of the 17th, 18th, and 19th Centuries, Law and Society Rev, 98; auth, The Coup d'Etat and Civilian Control of the Military in Competitive Democracies, To Sheathe the sword, ed, John Lovell, Greenwood Press, 97; auth, Supervising the Spoiled Children of Legislation: Judicial judgements of Quasi-Public Corporations of the Nineteenth Century, Amer Jour of Legal Hist, 97; auth, American Culture war and the Military, in: The Oxford Companion to American Military History, ed, John Chambers, Oxford Univ Press, 97. **CONTACT ADDRESS** Dept of History, Univ of Pittsburgh, Pittsburgh, PA, 15260. **EMAIL** pjk2@pitt.edu

KASSON, JOHN FRANKLIN
PERSONAL Born 10/20/1944, Muncie, IN, m, 1968, 3 children **DISCIPLINE** AMERICAN HISTORY **EDUCATION** Harvard Univ, BA, 66; Yale Univ, PhD, 71. **CAREER** Asst prof, 71-76, assoc prof, 76-81, prof hist, 81-, Univ NC, Chapel Hill; NEH fel, 74; Rockefeller Humanities fel, 80-81; Nat Humanities Ctr fel, 80-81; Humanities Inst Fel, Univ Calif, Davis, 87-88; Guggenheim fel, 99. **HONORS AND AWARDS** Soc of Am Historians, 91; Bowman & Gordon Gray Professorship for inspirational tchng, 93-96. **MEMBERSHIPS** Am Studies Assn; AHA; OAH. **RESEARCH** Modes of American cultural expression; technology and American culture; the popular arts. **SELECTED PUBLICATIONS** Auth, Civilizing the Machine: Technology and Republican Values in America, 1776-1900, Grossman/ Viking, 76 & Penguin, 77; auth, Amusing the Million: Coney Island at the Turn of the Century, Hill & Wang, 78; auth, Rudeness and Civility: Manners in Nineteenth-Century Urban America, Hill & Wang, 90. **CONTACT ADDRESS** Dept of Hist, Univ of North Carolina, Chapel Hill, Chapel Hill, NC, 27599. **EMAIL** jfkasson@email.unc.edu

KASSOW, SAMUEL D.
PERSONAL Born 10/03/1946, Stuttgart, Germany **DISCIPLINE** RUSSIAN HISTORY **EDUCATION** Trinity Col, BA, 66; London Sch Econ, MsC, 68; Princeton Univ, PhD(hist), 76. **CAREER** Asst prof, 76-78, ASSOC PROF HIST, TRINITY COL, 78-. **MEMBERSHIPS** Am Asn Advan Slavic Studies; Asn Jewish Studies. **RESEARCH** Modern Russian history; modern European history; East European Jewish history. **SELECTED PUBLICATIONS** Auth, Warsaw Before the 1st World War--Poles and Jews in the 3rd City of the Russian Empire, 1880-1914, Slavic Rev, Vol 0052, 93; Poland Between the Wars - 1918-1939, Slavic Rev, Vol 0052, 93; East European Jews in 2 Worlds--Studies From the Yivo Annual, Slavic Rev, Vol 0053, 94; Gender, Class, and the Professionalization of Russian City Teachers, 1860-1914, Amer Hist Rev, Vol 0101, 96; Jews and Jewish Life in Russia and the Soviet Union, Slavic Rev, Vol 0055, 96. **CONTACT ADDRESS** Dept of Hist, Trinity Col, 300 Summit St, Hartford, CT, 06106-3186.

KASTER, ROBERT A.
PERSONAL Born 02/06/1948, New York, NY, m, 1969, 2 children **DISCIPLINE** LATIN LANGUGE AND LITERATURE. **EDUCATION** Dartmouth Coll, AB, 69; Harvard Univ, MA, 71; PhD, 75. **CAREER** Harvard Univ: Tchg Fel, 72-73; Instr, Colby Col, 73-74; asst prof, 75-82, assoc prof, 82-89, prof, 89-97 Univ Chicago; prof, Princeton Univ; 97- **HONORS AND AWARDS** Nat Endowment Hum Fel, 80-81; John Simon Guggenheim Memorial Found Fel, 91-92; Charles J. Goodwin Award of Merit, 91., Pres, Am Philol Asn, 96; Avalon Found Distinguished Service Prof, 96-97. **MEMBERSHIPS** Am Philol Asn; Asn Ancient Historians; Women's Class Caucus. **RESEARCH** Origins of Rome; Greek: Plato; Euripides; Sophocles. **SELECTED PUBLICATIONS** Auth, Guardians of Language: The Grammarian and Society in Late Antiquity, TheTransformation of the Classical Heritage, /vik 11, Berkeley-Univ Calif Press, 88; Studies on the Text of Suetonius De Grammaticis et Rhetoribus, The American Philological Association: American Classical Studies, Scholars Press, 92; Suetonius: De Grammaticis et Rhetoribus, Clarendon Press, 95. **CONTACT ADDRESS** Princeton Univ, 1 Nassau Hall, Princeton, NJ, 08544. **EMAIL** kaster@princeton.edu

KATADA, SAORI
DISCIPLINE INTERNATIONAL RELATIONS **EDUCATION** Univ NC at Chapel Hill, PhD, 94. **CAREER** Asst prof, Univ Southern Calif. **RESEARCH** International relations of the Pacific Rim including East Asia and Latin America; Japa-

nese foreign policy; Japanese politics. **SELECTED PUBLICATIONS** Auth, Official Flows to China: Recent Trends and Major Characteristics; grants and Debt Forgiveness to SPA Countries: a Descriptive Analysis. **CONTACT ADDRESS** East Asian Studies Center, Univ Southern Calif, University Park Campus, Los Angeles, CA, 90089.

KATER, MICHAEL H.
PERSONAL Born 07/04/1937, Zittau, Germany **DISCIPLINE** HISTORY **EDUCATION** Univ Toronto, BA, 59, MA, 61; Univ Heidelberg, PhD, 66. **CAREER** Lectr, Univ Maryland, 65-66; asst prof to prof, 67-91, DISTINGUISHED RES PROF HISTORY, ATKINSON COL, YORK UNIV, 91-; Jason A. Hannah vis prof hist med, McMaster Univ, 85-86; Jason A. Hannah vis prof hist med, Univ Toronto, 97-98. **HONORS AND AWARDS** Can Coun leave fel, 73-74; Guggenheim fel, 76-77; Killam sr fel, 78-79, 79-80, 93-94, 94-95; SSHRCC leave fel, 82-83; Atkinson res fel, 84-85; York Walter L. Gordon fel, 90-91; Am Hist Asn First Prize, central Europ hist, 72; Konrad Adenauer res award, 90-91; Jason A. Hannah Medal, 91. **SELECTED PUBLICATIONS** Auth, Das 'Ahnenerbe' der SS 1935-1945, 74; auth, Studentenschaft und Rechtsradikalismus in Deutschland 1918-1933, 75; auth, The Nazi Party: A Social Profile of Members and Leaders 1919-1945, 83; auth, Doctors Under Hitler, 89; auth, Different Drummers: Jazz in the Culture of Nazi Germany, 92; auth, The Twisted Muse: Musicians and Their Music in the Third Reich, 3rd ed, 97. **CONTACT ADDRESS** Dept of History, York Univ, 4700 Keele St, North York, ON, M3J 1P3.

KATES, GARY
PERSONAL Born 11/09/1952, Los Angeles, CA, m, 1978, 2 children **DISCIPLINE** HISTORY **EDUCATION** Pitzer Col, BA, 74; Univ Chicago, PhD, 78 **CAREER** Vis asst prof, Pitzer Col, 78-79; from asst prof to assoc prof to prof, 80-, chemn, 95-98, dean, 99-00, Trinity Univ. **MEMBERSHIPS** Am Hist Asn; Society French Hist Stud; Western Society French Hist; Am Society 18th Century Stud. **RESEARCH** 18th Century France **SELECTED PUBLICATIONS** Ed, French Revolution: Recent Debates and New Controversies, 98; auth, article, The Transgendered World of the Chevalier/Chevaliere d'Eon, 95; auth, article, Introduction to Special Issue on Fashion Gender, 96; auth, article, Introduction to Forum: Royal and Aristocratic Family Politics in Eighteenth-Century France and England, 96. **CONTACT ADDRESS** Dept of History, Trinity Univ, San Antonio, TX, 78212-7200. **EMAIL** gkates@trinity.edu

KATSAROS, THOMAS
PERSONAL Born 02/02/1926, New York, NY **DISCIPLINE** HISTORY, AREA STUDIES **EDUCATION** NY Univ, BA, 53, MA, 56, MBA, 58, PhD(area studies), 63. **CAREER** Asst prof soc studies, State Univ NY, 63-65; from asst prof to assoc prof hist, Univ New Haven, 65-70, prof & chmn dept, 70-80, assoc Dean, Business School, Univ New Haven, 84-95, PROF AND CHAIR, HISTORY DEPT, 96-, DIR OF UNIV NEW HAVEN PRESS AND DIR OF BUSINESS RESEARCH, 96-. **MEMBERSHIPS** AHA **RESEARCH** Anglo-Soviet relations during World War II. **SELECTED PUBLICATIONS** Coauth, The Western Mystical Tradition, Col & Univ Press, 69; auth, Early Modern Science and Mysticism, Essays in Arts & Sciences, spring 72; coauth, American Transcendentalism: Its Mystical and Philosophical Origins, Col & Univ Press, 75; A Brief History of the Western World, 78 & Capitalism: A Cooperative Venture, 81, Univ Press Am; auth, The Development of the Welfare State in the Western World, Univ Press Am, 95. **CONTACT ADDRESS** 11 Carriage Dr, North Haven, CT, 06574.

KATZ, IRVING
PERSONAL Born 09/24/1932, New York, NY, 2 children **DISCIPLINE** AMERICAN POLITICAL & JEWISH HISTORY **EDUCATION** City Col NY, BA, 54; NY Univ, MA, 59, PhD(hist), 64. **CAREER** Res assoc bus hist, Harvard Univ, 61-64; asst prof, 64-68, assoc prof, 68-81, PROF HIST, IND UNIV, BLOOMINGTON, 81-, Am Philos Soc res grant, 68. **MEMBERSHIPS** AHA; Orgn Am Historians; Am Jewish Hist Soc. **RESEARCH** American political history; immigration and labor history; investment banking. **SELECTED PUBLICATIONS** Auth, From Philanthropy toActivism--The Political Transformation of American Zionism in the Holocaust Years, 1933-1945, Amer Hist Rev, Vol 0100, 95; Giannini, A.P and the Bank of America, Montana-the Magazine of Western History, Vol 0045, 95; The Man Who Found the Money--Kennedy, John, Stewart and the Financing of the Western Railroads, J Amer Hist, Vol 0084, 97. **CONTACT ADDRESS** Dept of Hist, Indiana Univ, Bloomington, Bloomington, IN, 47401.

KATZ, MARILYN A.
DISCIPLINE CLASSICAL LANGUAGES **EDUCATION** Columbia Univ, BA, 66, Yale Univ, MA, 68, PhD, 75. **CAREER** Trinity Col, Hartford, CT, 66; Lectr Trinity Col, Hartford, CT, 67, 68; Vis Instr, Wesleyan Univ, Middletown, CT, 70-71; Tchng Intern, Brooklyn Col, CUNY, 72-73, P/T Instr; 73-75, F/T Instr; 75, Instr, Sarah Lawrence Col, 75, 76; Vis Instr, Columbia Col, Columbia Univ, 75-77; Asst Prof; 76, 77, Asst Prof, Vis Lectr, Yale Col, Guest Fel, Morse Col, 80, Wesleyan Univ, Asst Prof, 78-83; Assoc Prof, 83-90; Prof 90-. **HONORS AND AWARDS** Yale Univ fel, 68; Mary Cady Tew Profize, 68; Samuel K. Bushnell Fel, 69-70; Elizabeth & A. Varvick Stout Fel, 71-72; Biddle Travel Sch, 73; Mem, Sch Hist, Studies, Inst Adv Study, 77-78; ACLS Fel Recent Ph.D.'s, 78; Nat Endowment Hum, 79, 80, 89, 90-91; Fac fel, Ctr Hum, 82; Elected mem, Am Philol Asn, 84-87, 87-90; Nat Endowment Hum, 87; Chair, Am Philol Asn, 89-90; Guggenheim Found, 93. **MEMBERSHIPS** Am Philological Asn, 67; Women's Classical Caucus, 72; Columbia Univ Seminar on Women and Society, 74; Am Asn Univ Prof, 79; Mod Lang Asn, 79, Columbia Univ Sem Clas Civilization, 83; Gardiner Seminar, 86; Soc Biblical Lit, 86; Yale Univ Judaic Studies Fac Seminar, 86. **SELECTED PUBLICATIONS** Sexuality and the Body in Ancient Greece, Metis. Revue d'anthropologie du monde grec ancient 4.1, 89, 155 - 79; Profoblems Sacrifice in Ancient Cultures, In The Bible in the Light Cuneiform Literature. Scripture in Context III, Edwin Mellen Profess, 90; Patriarchy and Inheritance in Greek and Biblical Antiquity: The Epiclerate and the Levirate. Profoceedings the Xth World Congress Jewish Studies, Magnes Profess, 90; Penelope's Renown: Meaning and Indeterminacy in Homer's Odyssey. Profinceton, New Jersey: Profinceton Univ Profess, 91; Review Suzanne Dixon, The Roman Mother, New England Clas Newsl & Jour 17, 90; Review Robert Garland, The Greek Way Life, The Classical Outlook 69, 91-92; Bouphonia and Goring Ox: Homicide, Animal Sacrifice, and Judicial Profocess, invited contribution to refereed volume, Nomodeiktes: Greek Studies in Honor Martin Ostwald, Univ Mich Profess, 92; Did the Greeks Believe in Their Myths? An Essay on the Constitutive Imagination History and Theory 31, 92; Ox Slaughter and Goring Oxen: Homicide, Animal Sacrifice, and Judicial Profocess, Yale Jour Law & Hum, 92; Politics and Pomegranates, in Essays on the Homeric Hymn to Demeter, Profinceton Univ Profess, 93; Ideology and 'the Status Women' in Ancient Greece, History and Theory Beiheft 31: History and Feminist Theory, 92; Homecoming and Hospitality: Recognition and the Construction Identity in the Odyssey,' in Epic and Epoch, Texas Tech Univ Pess, 94; The Character Tragedy: Women and the Greek Imagination, Arethusa 27.1, 94; Ideology and 'the Status Women' in Ancient Greece, in Feminists Revision History, Rutgers Univ Profess, 93; Ideology and 'the Status Women' in Ancient Greece, in Women in Antiquity: New Assessments, Routledge, 95. **CONTACT ADDRESS** Wesleyan Univ, Middletown, CT, 06459. **EMAIL** mkatz@wesleyan.edu

KATZ, MICHAEL B.
PERSONAL Born 04/13/1939, Wilmington, DE **DISCIPLINE** AMERICAN SOCIAL HISTORY **EDUCATION** Harvard Univ, BA, 61, MAT, 62, EdD, 66. **CAREER** Res asst hist educ, Harvard Univ Grad Sch Educ, 64-65, instr & res assoc, 65-66; from asst prof to prof hist educ, Univ Toronto & Ont Inst Studies in Educ, 66-74; prof hist & educ, York Univ, 74-78; PROF EDUC & HIST, UNIV PA, 78-, Vis mem, Inst Advan Studies, 73-74; Guggenheim fel, 77-78. **HONORS AND AWARDS** Albert C Corey Award, Am & Canadian Hist Asns, 78. **MEMBERSHIPS** Orgn Am Historians; Hist Educ Soc (pres, 75-76); Can Hist Asn; Am Hist Soc; Soc Sci Hist Asn. **RESEARCH** Nineteenth century social history; history of social structure; history of the family. **SELECTED PUBLICATIONS** Auth, The Family and Medical Leave Act of 1993, Labor Law J, Vol 0044, 93; The Transformation of Charity in Postrevolutionary New-England, Amer Hist Rev, Vol 0098, 93; The Good Society, Amer Hist Rev, Vol 0098, 93; Working People of Holyoke--Class and Ethnicity in a Massachusetts Mill Town, 1850-1960, Labor Hist, Vol 0034, 93; A Very Social Time--Crafting Community in Antebellum New England, New Eng Quart-Hist Rev New Eng Life and Letters, Vol 0067, 94; A Very Social Time--Crafting Community in Antebellum New England, New Eng Quart- Hist Rev New Eng Life and Letters, Vol 0067, 94; Migrants, Emigrants, and Immigrants--A Social History of Migration, J Interdisciplinary Hist, Vol 0025, 95; Brutal Need--Lawyers and the Welfare Rights Movement, 1960-1973, J Amer Hist, Vol 0081, 95; Politics and Welfare in Birmingham, 1900-1975, Amer Hist Rev, Vol 0101, 96. **CONTACT ADDRESS** Grad Sch of Educ, Univ Penn, 3401 Walnut St, Philadelphia, PA, 19104-6228.

KATZ, PHYLLIS
PERSONAL Born 05/23/1936, New Haven, CT **DISCIPLINE** CLASSICS **EDUCATION** Wellesley Col, BA, 58; Univ Calif, Los Angeles, MA, 63; Columbia Univ, phD, 69. **CAREER** Lectr, Mount St Mary's Col, 62-63; Lectr, Barnard Col, 65- 66; asst prof, 69, instr, 68-69, Univ Ill; instr, CUNY, City College NY, 71-72; vis asst prof, Col New Rochelle, 74; lectr, 76, vis asst prof, 74-75; SUNY, Purchase; teach, 77-83, Miss Porter's Sch; lectr, fac mem, Class Asn New Eng, Summer Inst, summers 87-97; vis lectr, Univ Mass, 93; vis lectr, Wesleyan Univ, Grad Lib Stud Prog, 92; vis scholar, vis lectr, sen lectr, DARTMOUTH COL, 90-. **CONTACT ADDRESS** Dept of Classics, Dartmouth Col, HB 6086, Reed Hall, PO Box 1048, Norwich, VT, 05055-1048.

KATZ, STANLEY NIDER
PERSONAL Born 04/23/1934, Chicago, IL, m, 1960 **DISCIPLINE** AMERICAN LEGAL HISTORY **EDUCATION** Harvard Univ, AB, 55, MA, 59, PhD(Am colonial hist), 61. **CAREER** From instr to asst prof hist, Harvard Univ, 61-65, Allston Burr sr tutor, Leverett House, 63-65; from asst prof to assoc prof hist, Univ Wis-Madison, 65-70; prof legal hist, Law Sch, Univ Chicago, 70-78; prof, Princeton Univ, 78-82; PROF HIST, WOODROW WILSON SCHOOL, 82-, Res fel, Charles Warren Ctr, Harvard Univ, 66-67, fel law and hist, Law Sch, 69-70; Am Bar Asn fel legal hist, 66-67; Am Coun Learned Soc fel, 69-70; MEM COMT ON OLIVER WENDEL HOLMES, 77-; Vis Meme, Inst Advan Study, 81-82. **HONORS AND AWARDS** LLD, Stockton State Col, 81. **MEMBERSHIPS** AHA Orgn Am Historians; Am Soc Legal Hist (pres, 78-80); Am Studies Asn; Selden Soc. **RESEARCH** Anglo-Am legal history; Am colonial history. **SELECTED PUBLICATIONS** A Peoples Charter--The Pursuit Of Rights in Am, Am Hist Rev, Vol 97, 92; Official Hist--The Holmes Devise Hist Of The Supreme-Court, Proceedings Of The Am Philos Soc, Vol 141, 97; Freed,Doris,Jonas--In-Memoriam, Family Law Quart, Vol 27, 93; The Child's Attorney--A Guide to Representing Children in Custody, Adoption, and Protection Cases, Family Law Quart, Vol 27; Giving--Charity and Philanthropy in Hist, J Interdisciplinary Hist, Vol 26, 95. **CONTACT ADDRESS** Dept of Hist, Princeton Univ, Princeton, NJ, 08540.

KATZMAN, DAVID MANNERS
PERSONAL Born 10/25/1941, New York, NY, m, 1965, 2 children **DISCIPLINE** AMERICAN HISTORY **EDUCATION** Queens Col, NY, BA, 63; Univ Mich, Ann Arbor, PhD (hist), 69. **CAREER** From asst prof to assoc prof, 69-78, prof, 78-90, PROF AND CHAIR AM STUDIES, UNIV KANS, 90-, assoc dean, col lib arts & scis & dir honors prog, 80-87, Inst Southern Hist sr res fel, Johns Hopkins Univ, 71-72; Nat Endowment for Humanities Afro-Am studies fel, 72-73; res fel ethnic studies, Harvard Univ, 72-73; Ford Found fel, 75-76; vis prof mod hist, Univ Col Dublin, Ireland, 76-77; assoc ed, Am Studies, 77-; Guggenheim fel, 79-80, vis prof eco hist, Univ Birmingham, Eng, 84-85, vis prof Amer Stud, Univ Tokushima, Japan, 94, vis prof hist & Amer Studies, Hong Kong Univ, 95, NEH fel, 94-95; ed, American Studies, 98-. **HONORS AND AWARDS** Certificate of Commendation, Am Asn State & Local Hist, 74; Philip Taft Labor History Prize, 79; Byron Caldwell Smith Award, Humanistic Scholarship, 80. **MEMBERSHIPS** AHA; Orgn Am Historians; Am Jewish Hist Soc; Immigrant Hist Soc; Am Studies Asn. **RESEARCH** Ethnic groups; Afro-American history; American working class. **SELECTED PUBLICATIONS** Auth, Ann Arbor: Depression City, Mich Hist, 12/66; Black Slavery in Michigan, Midcontinent Am Studies J, fall 70; contribr, Perspectives in Geography II: Geography of the Ghetto, Northern Ill Univ, 72; auth, Before the Ghetto: Black Detroit in the Nineteenth Century, Univ Ill, 73; coauth, Three Generations in 20th Century America, Dorsey, 77, rev ed, 82; auth, Seven Days a Week: Women and Domestic in Industrializing America, Oxford Univ, 78 & Univ Ill, 81; coauth, A People & A Nation, Houghton Mifflin, 82, 86, 90, 94, 98; co-ed, Plain Folk: The Life Stories of Undistinguished Americans, Univ Ill, 82; co-ed, Technical Knowledge in American Culture, Univ Ala, 96; contr, La storia americana e le scienze sociali, Inst della Enciclopedia Italiana, 96. **CONTACT ADDRESS** Dept of Hist, Univ of Kans, Lawrence, KS, 66045-0001. **EMAIL** dkatzman@ukans.edu

KATZNELSON, IRA
DISCIPLINE UNITED STATES HISTORY **EDUCATION** Columbia Univ, BA, 66; Cambridge Univ, PhD, 69. **CAREER** Ruggles prof. **RESEARCH** Comparative politics; political theory. **SELECTED PUBLICATIONS** Auth, Black Men, White Cities, 73; City Trenches: Urban Politics and the Patterning of Class in the United States, 81; Liberalism's Crooked Circle: Letters to Adam Michnik, 96; co-auth, Schooling for All, 85; co-ed, Working Class Formation: Nineteenth-century Patterns in Western Europe and the United States, 88; Paths of Emancipation, 95. **CONTACT ADDRESS** Dept of History, Columbia Col, New York, 2960 Broadway, New York, NY, 10027-6902.

KAUFFMAN, GEORGE B.
PERSONAL Born 09/04/1930, Philadelphia, PA, m, 1952, 2 children **DISCIPLINE** HISTORY OF SCIENCE **EDUCATION** Univ Pa, BA, 51; Univ Fla, PhD(chem), 56. **CAREER** Instr, Univ Tex, 55-56; asst prof, 56-61, assoc prof, 61-66, PROF CHEM, CALIF STATE UNIV, FRESNO, 66-, Res mem, Oak Ridge Nat Lab, 55; res chemist, Humble Oil and Refining Co, 56 and Gen Elec Co, 57 and 59; Exec comt, Am Chem Soc, 70-73, guest lectr, Coop Lect Tours, 71; Guggenheim fel, 72; CONTRIB ED, J COL SCI TEACHING, 73-& HEXAGON, 80-; ed, Hist Chem Series, Am Chem Soc, 75-81; vis scholar, Univ Calif, Berkeley, 76 and 77 and Univ Puget Sound, 78; consult, Educ Testing Serv and Am Col Testing Prog; contrib scholar, Isis Critical Bibliog Hist Sci. **HONORS AND AWARDS** Outstanding Prof, Calif State Univ and Col Syst, 73; Col Chem Teacher Award, Mfg Chemists Asn, 76; Lev Aleksandrovich Chugaev Mem Dipl and Bronze Medal, Acad Sci USSR, 76; Dexter Award, Am Chem Soc, 78. **MEMBERSHIPS** AAAS; Am Chem Soc; Hist Sci Soc; Soc Hist Alchemy and Chem; Strindberg Soc. **RESEARCH** Hist of chemistry; translation of chemical classics; biographies of famous chemists. **SELECTED PUBLICATIONS** The Atomic-Energy Commission Under Nixon--Adjusting To Troubled Times, Isis, Vol 85, 94; Haber,Fritz--Chemist, Nobel Laureate, German, Jew, Annals Sci, Vol 52, 95. **CONTACT ADDRESS** Dept of Chem, California State Univ, Fresno, Fresno, CA, 93740.

KAUFMAN, BURTON
PERSONAL Born 11/26/1940, Boston, MA, m, 1966 **DISCIPLINE** AMERICAN HISTORY **EDUCATION** Brandeis Univ, BA, 62; Rice Univ, MA, 64; PhD(hist), 66. **CAREER** From asst prof Am hist to assoc prof hist, La State Univ, New Orleans, 66-73; assoc prof, 73-77, PROF HIST, KANS STATE UNIV, 77- **MEMBERSHIPS** Orgn Am Historians; Newcomen Soc; Soc Hist Am Foreign Rel. **RESEARCH** Am foreign policy. **SELECTED PUBLICATIONS** Report Of The Working Group On Conflicts-Of-Interest, Fordham Law Rev, Vol 64, 96. **CONTACT ADDRESS** Dept of Hist, Kansas State Univ, Manhattan, KS, 66506.

KAUFMAN, DEBORAH RENEE
PERSONAL Born 04/02/1941, Cleveland, OH, m, 1963, 2 children **DISCIPLINE** SOCIOLOGY **EDUCATION** Univ of Michigan, BA, 63, MA, 66; Cornell Univ, PhD, 75. **CAREER** Prof of Sociol, Northeastern Univ, 66- . **HONORS AND AWARDS** Matthews Distinguished Prof, 94. **MEMBERSHIPS** Am Sociol Asn; Eastern Sociol Soc; Assoc for Jewish Stud. **RESEARCH** Identity politics; feminist studies; work and professions; gender studies; women and religion. **SELECTED PUBLICATIONS** Coauth, Achievement and Women: Challenging the Assumptions, Free Press, 82; auth, Rachel's Daughters: New Orthodox Jewish Women, Rutgers, 91; auth, Rethinking, Reflecting and Rewriting: Teaching Feminist Methodology, J of Radical Educ and Cultural Stud, 96; auth, The Holocaust and Sociological Inquiry: A Feminist Inquiry, Contemp Jewry, 96; auth, Embedded Categories: Identity Among Jewish Young Adults in the United States, Race, Class and Gender, 98. **CONTACT ADDRESS** Holmes Sociology, Rm 515, Northeastern Univ, Boston, MA, 02115. **EMAIL** dkaufman@nuhub.neu.edu

KAUFMAN, GEORGE G.
PERSONAL Born 03/06/1933, Germany, s **DISCIPLINE** ECONOMICS/FINANCE **EDUCATION** Oberman Col, BA, 54; Univ of Mich, MA, 55; Univ of Iowa, PhD, 62. **CAREER** Res Economist, Federal Reserve Bd, Chicago, 59-70; John Rocfres Prof of Finance, Univ of Ore, 70-80; JOHN SMITH PROF OF FINANCE AND ECONOMICS, LOYOLA UNIV, 81-. **MEMBERSHIPS** Western Finance Asn; Midwest Finance Asn; Am Finance Asn; Am Economic Asn. **RESEARCH** Banking; financial regulation; bond management. **SELECTED PUBLICATIONS** Auth, Designing an Efficient, Incentive Compatible, Government-Provided Deposit Insurance for Developing and Transitional Economies, Review of Pacific Basin Financial Markets and Policies, 98; auth, Preventing Banking Crises in the Future: Lessons From Past Mistakes, Independent Review, 97 and Review of Monetary and Financial Studies, 97; auth, The New Depositor Preference Act: Time Inconsistency in Action, Managerial Finance Vol 23, No 11, 97; auth, Comment on Financial Crises, Payment System Problems and Discount Window Lending, Journal of Money, Credit and Banking, 96; coauth, FDICIA After Five Years, Journal of Economic Perspectives, 97; auth, The Appropriate Role of Bank Regulation, Economic Journal, 96; auth, Managing Interest Rate Risk with Duration Gaps to Achieve Multiple Targets, Journal of Financial Engineering, 96; auth, Is the Banking and Payments System Fragile?, Journal of Financial Services Res, 95. **CONTACT ADDRESS** Col of Business Admin, Loyola Univ, Chicago, 820 N. Michigan Ave, Chicago, IL, 60611. **EMAIL** gkaufma@luc.edu

KAUFMAN, MARTIN
PERSONAL Born 12/06/1940, Boston, MA, m, 1968, 3 children **DISCIPLINE** HISTORY OF MEDICINE, AMERICAN SOCIAL HISTORY **EDUCATION** Boston Univ, AB, 62; Univ Pittsburgh, MA, 63; Tulane Univ, PhD(hist), 69. **CAREER** Instr hist, Worcester State Col, 68-69; from asst prof to assoc prof, 69-76, PROF HIST, WESTFIELD STATE COL, 76- . **HONORS AND AWARDS** Ed dir, Hist J Mass, 72-; dir, Inst Mass Studies, 80-98. **MEMBERSHIPS** Am Asn Hist Med; Orgn Am Historians. **RESEARCH** History of American medical education; unorthodox practitioners; women and minorities in medicine. **SELECTED PUBLICATIONS** Auth, The American Antivaccinationists and Their Arguments, Bull Hist Med, 67; Homepathy in America, Johns Hopkins Univ, 71; coauth, Body-Snatching in the Midwest, Mich Hist, 71; co-ed, The Ethnic Contribution to the American Revolution, Westfield Bicentennial Comt, 76; auth, American Medical Education, The Formative Years, Greenwood, 76; The Admission of Women to Nineteenth Century American Medical Societies, Bull Hist Med, 76; The University of Vermont College of Medicine, Univ Vt, 79. **CONTACT ADDRESS** Dept of History, Westfield State Col, 577 Western Ave, Westfield, MA, 01085-2501.

KAUFMAN, STEPHEN ALLAN
PERSONAL Born 09/11/1945, Minneapolis, MN, m, 1972, 2 children **DISCIPLINE** ANCIENT NEAR EASTERN LANGUAGES, OLD TESTAMENT **EDUCATION** Univ Minn, BA, 62; Yale Univ, PhD(Near Eastern lang and lit), 70. **CAREER** Asst prof North-West semitics, Univ Chicago, 71-76; assoc prof, 76-81, PROF BIBLE and COGNATE LIT, HEBREW UNION COL, 81-, Vis sr lectr, Haifa Univ, Israel, 74-76; ED, SOC BIBL LIT, ARAMAIC SERIES, 79- **MEMBERSHIPS** Am Oriental Soc; Soc Bibl Lit. **RESEARCH** Aramaic studies; humanities micro computing. **SELECTED PUBLICATIONS** The Causative Stem in Ugartic and the Causative Form in Semitic--A Morphologic-Semantic Analysis of the S-Stem and Disputed Non-Sibilant Causative Stems in Ugartic, J Am Oriental Soc, Vol 113, 93; Old Aramaic Grammar of Texts from 7th-8th Century BC, J Am Oriental Soc, Vol 115, 95; A Scholars; Dictionary of Jewish Palestinian Aramaic--An Article Rev of Sokoloff, Michael Dictionary, J Am Oriental Soc, Vol 114, 94; The Dead Sea Scrolls on Microfiche--A Comprehensive Facsimile Edition of the Texts from the Judean Desert, Vol 3, Inventory List of Photographs, J Am Oriental Soc, Vol 116, 96; The Function of the Niphal in Biblical Hebrew in Relationship to Other Passive-Reflexive Verbal-Systems and to the Pual and Hophal in Particular--Siebesma,Pa, Cath Bibl Quart, Vol 56, 94; Living Waters--Scandinavian orientalistic Studies Presented to Lokkegaard,Frede on His 75th Birthday, January 27th, 1990, J Am Oriental Soc, Vol 113, 93; The Dead-Sea-Scrolls on Microfiche--A Comprehensive Facsimile Edition of the Texts from the Judean Desert, Vol 2, Companion Volume, J Am Oriental Soc, Vol 116, 96; The Dead-Sea-Scrolls Catalog--Documents, Photographs, and Museum Inventory Numbers, J Am Oriental Soc, Vol 116, 96. **CONTACT ADDRESS** Dept Bible and Cognate Lit, Hebrew Union Col, Cincinnati, OH, 45220.

KAUFMAN, SUZANNE
PERSONAL Born 09/22/1965, New York, NY, s **DISCIPLINE** MODERN EUROPEAN HISTORY **EDUCATION** Wesleyan Univ, BA, 87; Rutgers Univ, MA, 92, PhD, 96. **CAREER** Vis Asst Prof, Miami Univ, 96-97; Asst Prof, Ga State Univ, 97-98; Asst Prof Hist, Loyola Univ - Chicago, 98-. **HONORS AND AWARDS** Chateaubriand Dissertation Res Fel, 92-93; NEH Dissertation Grant, 94-95. **MEMBERSHIPS** Am Acad Relig; Am Hist Asn; Soc Fr Hist Studies. **RESEARCH** Modern European social and cultural history; modern France; history of religion & popular culture; history of women & gender. **SELECTED PUBLICATIONS** Auth, Influence of Christianity on women in France, The Feminist Companion to French Literature, Greenwood Press, 99. **CONTACT ADDRESS** History Dept, Loyola Univ, Chicago, 6525 N Sheridan Rd., Chicago, IL, 60640. **EMAIL** SKaufma@luc.edu

KAUFMANN, FRANK
PERSONAL Born 12/23/1952, New York, NY, m, 1982, 3 children **DISCIPLINE** CHURCH HISTORY **EDUCATION** Vanderbuilt Univ, PhD 85. **CAREER** Pace Univ, adj prof, Univ Theol Sem, adj prof. **HONORS AND AWARDS** Vanderbilt Univ Schshp; F U Berlin Schshp. **MEMBERSHIPS** AAr **RESEARCH** Religion and society; New religions; Inter religious dialogue. **SELECTED PUBLICATIONS** Auth, Religion and the Future of South African Societies, ed, forthcoming; Christianity in the Americas, ed, NY, Paragon Pub, 98; Dialogue and Alliance, assoc ed, Quart Jour; Newsletter of the Inter-religious Federation for World Peace, assoc ed, quart; Today's World, sr ed consul, monthly; The Foundations of Modern Church History, NY, Lang Pub, 89; Religion and Peace in the Middle East, NY, New Era Books, 87. **CONTACT ADDRESS** Inter Religious Federation, Pace Univ, 4 West 43rd St, New York, NY, 10036. **EMAIL** fortl@pipeline.com

KAUFMANN, THOMAS DACOSTA
PERSONAL Born 05/07/1948, New York, NY, d, 1 child **DISCIPLINE** ART HISTORY **EDUCATION** Harvard Univ, PhD, 77. **CAREER** Asst to full prof, Princeton Univ, 77-. **HONORS AND AWARDS** Guggenheim fel. **MEMBERSHIPS** Col Art Asn. **RESEARCH** Art of central Europe; Latin America; Historiography; Art & science; Geography of art. **SELECTED PUBLICATIONS** Auth, Cloister, Court, and City. The Art and Culture of Central Europe, 1450-1800, London, Univ Chicago Press, 95; auth, Empire of Curiosity, Tokyo, Kousakusha, 95; auth, The Mastery of Nature, Aspects of Art, Science and Humanism in the Renaissance, Princeton Univ Press, 93; article, Archduke Albrecht as an Austrian Habsburg and Prince of the Empire, Albrecht and Isabella, Brussels, Sept, 98; rev, Dazwischen. Kulturwissenschaft auf Warburgs Spuren (Saecula Spiritalia 29), Winckelmann and the Notion of Aesthetic Education, The Absolute Artist; The Historiography of a Concept, Past Looking. Historical Imagination and the Rhetoric of the Image, Art Bull, lxxx.no 3, 581-85, Sept, 98; article, Planeten im kaiserlichen Universum. Prag und die kunst an den deutschen Furstenhofen zur Zeit Rudolfs II, Hofkunst der Spatrenaissance. Braunschweig - Wolfenbuttel und das kaiserliche, Prag um 1600, Braunschweig, 9-19, 98; article, The Adoration of the Shepherds, Master Paintings, London-NY, Colnaghi, no 7, 98; article, Lessons of History, The New York Times, A18, 4 May, 98; article, Gothico More Nondum Visa: The Modern Gothic Architecture of Jan Blazej Santini Aichl, Artes atque humaniora. Studia Stanislao Mossakowski sexagenario dicata, Warsaw, 317-331, 98; article, Caprices of Art and Nature: Arcimboldo and the Monstrous, Kunstform Capricccio. Von der Groteske zur Spieltheorie der Moderne, Verlag der Buchhandlung Walther Konig, 33-51, 97; article, Kunst und Alchemie, Moritz der Gelerhrte--ein Renassancefurst in Europa, Lemgo, Minerva, 370-77, 97; article, Architecture and Sculpture, Schubert's Vienna, Yale Univ Press, 143-73, 97. **CONTACT ADDRESS** Dept. of Art and Archaeology, Princeton Univ, McCormick Hall, Princeton, NJ, 08840. **EMAIL** tkaufman@princeton.edu

KAVORK DOHANIAN, DIRAN
DISCIPLINE ART HISTORY **EDUCATION** Harvard Univ, PhD. **CAREER** Prof, Univ of Rochester. **RESEARCH** Hist of the art and cult of ancient Lanka; Buddhism: art and cult; comp studies of the art of east and west; art as relig expression; elite cult: arts of China, arts of Japan; popular art: east/west; connoisseurship and collecting. **SELECTED PUBLICATIONS** Auth, Sinhalese Sculptures in the Pallava Style, Archives of Asian Art, XXXVI, 83; The Mahayana Buddhist Sculpture of Ceylon, NY and London: Garland Pub, 77; The Wata-Da-Ge in Ceylon: the Circular Relic House of Polonnaruva and its Antecedents, Arch Asian Art, XXIII & The Colossal Buddha at Aukana, Arch of the Chinese Art Soc in Am, XIX. **CONTACT ADDRESS** Dept of Art and Art Hist, Univ of Rochester, 601 Elmwood Ave, Ste. 656, 424 Morey , Rochester, NY, 14642. **EMAIL** urhomepage@cc.rochester.edu

KAWASHIMA, YASUHIDE
PERSONAL Born 10/22/1931, Nagasaki, Japan **DISCIPLINE** EARLY AMERICAN AND AMERICAN LEGAL HISTORY **EDUCATION** Keio Univ, Japan, LLB, 54, LLM, 56; Univ Calif, Santa Barbara, BA, 61, MA, 63, PhD(hist), 67. **CAREER** From instr to asst prof, 66-73, assoc prof, 73-80, PROF AM HIST, UNIV TEX, EL PASO, 80-, Colonial Williamsburg Found grant-in-aid, 70; fel, John Carter Brown Libr, Brown Univ, 71; Soc Sci Res Coun res training fel, 71-72; Charles Warren fel, Am legal hist, Harvard Law Sch, 71-72; Am Philos Soc res grant, 73; Huntington Libr fel, 80; Japan Found Professional fel, 81-82. **MEMBERSHIPS** AHA; Orgn Am Historians; Asn Asian Studies; Western Hist Asn; Am Soc Legal Hist. **RESEARCH** Indian-white relations; early Am legal history; history of Amn-Japanese legal relations. **SELECTED PUBLICATIONS** Racial Fault Lines--The Hist Origins of White Supremacy in California, Am Hist Rev, Vol 101, 96; Frontier and Pioneer Settlers--A Study of the Am Westward Movement, J Am Hist, Vol 83, 96; Exemplar of Liberty--Native Am and the Evolution of Democracy, Am Hist Rev, Vol 98, 93; The New-Deal and Am Capitalism--From a ViewpoInt of Popular Movements, J Am Hist, Vol 81, 94; Am Holocaust--The Conquest of the New-World, Western Hist Quart, Vol 25, 94; Essays on English Law and the Am Experience, J Am Hist, Vol 82, 95; Civil-Law in Qing and Republican China, Am J Legal Hist, Vol 40, 96; The New-Deal and Am Democracy--The Political-Process of the Agricultural Policy, J Am Hist, Vol 81, 94; The Fox Wars--The Mesquakie Challenge to New France, Am Hist Rev, Vol 100, 95. **CONTACT ADDRESS** Dept of Hist, Univ of Tex, 500 W University Ave, El Paso, TX, 79968-0001.

KAWIN, BRUCE FREDERICK
PERSONAL Born 11/06/1945, Los Angeles, CA **DISCIPLINE** FILM HISTORY; MODERN LITERATURE **EDUCATION** Columbia Univ, AB, 67; Cornell Univ, MFA, 69, PhD, 70. **CAREER** Asst prof English, Wells Col, 70-73; lectr English & Film, Univ Calif, Riverside, 73-75; assoc prof, 75-80, prof English & Film, Univ Co, Boulder, 80-, Specialist, Ctr for Advan Film Studies, Am Film Inst, 74. **MEMBERSHIPS** MLA; SCS. **RESEARCH** Narrative theory; relations between literature and film. **SELECTED PUBLICATIONS** Auth, Slides (poem), Angelfish, 70; Telling It Again and Again: Repetition in Literature and Film, Cornell Univ, 72, repr Univ Press Co, 89; Faulkner and Film, Ungar, 77; Me Tarzan, you junk, Take One, 78; Mindscreen: Bergman, Godard and First-Person Film, Princeton Univ, 78; ed, To Have and Have Not--The Screenplay, Univ Wis, 80; The Mind of the Novel: Reflexive Fiction and the Ineffable, Princeton Univ, 82; Faulkner's MGM Screenplays, Univ Tenn, 82; How Movies Work, MacMillan, 87, repr Univ Ca Press, 92; co-auth, A short History of the Movies, 5th ed, MacMillan, 92; 6th ed, Allyn & Bacon, 96; 7th ed Allyn & Bacon, 99. **CONTACT ADDRESS** Dept of English, Univ Co, Box 226, Boulder, CO, 80309-0226. **EMAIL** bkawin@aol.com

KAY, GERSIL NEWMARK
PERSONAL Philadelphia, PA, m, 1980 **DISCIPLINE** PHYSICS; BUSINESS ADMINISTRATION **EDUCATION** Univ Pa; Wharton Sch. **CAREER** Adj Prof, Drexel Univ; Pres, Conservation Lighting Int'l; Founder/Chmn, Building Conservation Int'l. **HONORS AND AWARDS** Victorian Society; Pa Hist and Mus Comn; BOMA; Asoc of Gen Contractors; 1st Pres of the United States Hist Preserv Award. **MEMBERSHIPS** AIA; CSI; IAEI; AIC; SAH; SIA; AASHH; AAM. **RESEARCH** Conservation lighting; older building construction techniques. **SELECTED PUBLICATIONS** Mechanical/Electrical Systems for Historic Buildings, 92; Fiber Opitcs in Architectural Lighting, 98. **CONTACT ADDRESS** 1901 Walnut St., Ste. 902, Philadelphia, PA, 19103.

KAY, THOMAS O.
DISCIPLINE HISTORY **EDUCATION** Wheaton Col, AB, 53; Univ Chicago, MA, 54, PhD, 74. **CAREER** ASSOC PROF, 75-, CHAIR HIST, 80, COORD INTERDISC & GEN STUD, 89-, WHEATON COL; **CONTACT ADDRESS** History Dept, Wheaton Col, Wheaton, IL, 60187. **EMAIL** Thomas.O.Kay@wheaton.edu

KAYE, HARVEY JORDAN
PERSONAL Born 10/09/1949, Englewood, NJ, m, 1973, 2 children **DISCIPLINE** HISTORY OF CULTURE **EDUCATION** Rutger Univ, BA, 71; Univ London, MA 73; La St Univ, PhD 76. **CAREER** Inst, hist & sociology, La St Univ, 74, 75; asst prof social sci, St. Cloud St Univ, 77-78; from asst prof to assoc prof, Univ Wisc, 78-86, BEN & JOYCE ROSENBERG PROF OF SOCIAL CHANGE & DEVELOP & DIR, CTR FOR HIST & SOCIAL CHANGE, 1986- . **HONORS AND AWARDS** Honors Res Student in Hist, Rutger Col, 70-71; Fel, La St Univ, 74-75 & 75-76; post-doctoral fel, Lilly Endowment, 78-79; Nat Endowment for the Humanities Fel, 81 & 83; Visiting Fel, Inst for Advanced Res in the Humanities, Univ Birmingham, Engl, 87; Ed & Executor, George Rude Lit Estate, 88-; Endowed Chair, Rosenberg Professorship, 90-; Bd of Dir, Wisc Hist Soc, 81-; Deutscher Memorial Lect, London Sch of Econ, 94; Teaching Award, St. Cloud St Univ, 77-78; Award for Excellence in Scholarship, UWGB Founders Assn, 85; Isaac Deutscher Memorial Prize, 93., Scholarship, Columbia Univ, 77. **MEMBERSHIPS** Amer Historical Assn; Amer Studies Assn; Org of Amer Historians. **RESEARCH** Amer History; politics; ideas; intellectuals; critics and radicals. **SELECTED PUBLICATIONS** Auth, British Marxist Historians: An Introductory Analysis, Polity Press/Blackwell, 84; auth, The Powers of the Past: Reflections on the Crisis and the Promise of History, Simon & Schuster & Univ Minn, 91; auth, The Education of Desire: Marxists and the Writing of History, Routledge, 92; auth, Why Do Ruling Classes Fear History? and Other Questions, St Martin's/Macmillan, 96; auth, Thomas Paine-A Young People's Biography, Oxford Univ, 99; ed History, Classes and Nation-States: Selected Writings of VG Kiernan, Polity Press/ Blackwell, 88; ed Face of the Crowd: Selected Essays of George Rude, Simon & Schuster & Humanities Press, 88; ed, Poets, Politics and the People: Selected Writings of VG Kiernan, Verso, 89; co-ed, EP Thompson: Critical Perspectives, Polity Press & Temple Univ, 90; co-ed, American Radical, Routledge, 94; ed, Imperialism and Its Contradictions: Selected Writings of VG Kiernan, Routledge, 95; ed, Ideology and Popular Protest, Univ NCar, 95; series co-ed, American Radicals, Routledge, 92-98. **CONTACT ADDRESS** Dept of Social Change & Develop, Univ of Wisconsin--Green Bay, Green Bay, WI, 54301. **EMAIL** kayeh@uwgb.edu

KAYE, JOEL
DISCIPLINE MEDIEVAL HISTORY **EDUCATION** Univ Pa, Phd, 91. **CAREER** Asst prof, Bernard Col. **SELECTED PUBLICATIONS** The Impact of Money on the Emergence of Scientific Thought, Jour Medieval Hist, 88; Economy and Nature in the Fourteenth Century: Money, Market Exchange, and the Emergence of Scientific Thought, 97. **CONTACT ADDRESS** Dept of Hist, Columbia Col, New York, 2960 Broadway, New York, NY, 10027-6902.

KAZEMZADEH, FIRUZ
PERSONAL Born 10/27/1924, Moscow, USSR, m, 1959, 3 children **DISCIPLINE** RUSSIAN HISTORY **EDUCATION** Stanford Univ, BA, 46, MA, 47; Harvard Univ, PhD(hist), 51. **CAREER** Res fel, Hoover Inst, 49-50; consult publ, US Dept State, 51-52; head Soviet affairs unit, Info Dept, Radio Free Europe, 52-54; res fel, Russian Res Ctr and Ctr Mid Eastern Studies, Harvard Univ, 54-56, instr hist and lit, 55-56; from instr to assoc prof, 56-67, chmn coun Russ and E Europ Studies, 68-69, dir grad studies hist, 75-76, master Davenport Col, 76-81, PROF HIST, YALE UNIV, 67-, Morse fel, 58-59; Ford fac grant Int studies, 66-67. **MEMBERSHIPS** AHA; Am Asn Advan Slavic Studies; Soc Iranian Studies. **RESEARCH** Russian imperial history; foreign relations; modern Persian history. **SELECTED PUBLICATIONS** Nationalism and Hist--The Politics of Nation Building in Post-Soviet Armenia, Azerbaijan and Georgia, Slavic Rev, Vol 54, 95; The Soviet Socialist Republic of Iran, 1920-1921--Birth Of The Trauma, Am Hist Rev, Vol 102, 97. **CONTACT ADDRESS** Dept of Hist, Yale Univ, New Haven, CT, 06520.

KAZEMZADEH, MASOUD
DISCIPLINE POLITICAL SCIENCE **EDUCATION** Univ Southern California, PhD, 95 **CAREER** Asst Prof, 99-, Utah Valley State Col. **CONTACT ADDRESS** Utah Valley State Col, 800 West 1200 S, Orem, UT, 84058-5999. **EMAIL** kazemzma@uvs.edu

KAZIN, ALFRED
PERSONAL Born 06/05/1915, Brooklyn, NY, m, 1952, 2 children **DISCIPLINE** AMERICAN STUDIES **EDUCATION** City Col New York, BSS, 35; Columbia Univ, MA, 38. **CAREER** Tutor English, City Col New York, 39-42; lectr English and gen lit, New Sch Social Res, 41-42, 48-49, 51, 52-53, 58-63; vis lectr, Harvard Univ, 53; Neilson res prof, Smith Col, 54-55; prof Am Studies, Amherst Col, 55-58; distinguished prof English, State Univ NY, Stony Brook, 63-73; vis prof English, Univ Notre Dame, 78-79. Vis lectr, Ger, Eng, France, Sweden and Norway; vis lectr, Black Mountain Col, 44; Berg prof, NY Univ, 57-58; vis prof, Univ PR, 59; Gauss lectr, Princeton Univ, 62; Gallagher prof, City Col New York, 63; Beckman prof, Univ Calif, Berkeley, 63; DISTINGUISHED PROF ENGLISH LIT, CITY UNIV NY, 73-; Nat Endowment Humantiies, sr fel, 77-78; Ctr for Advancec Study Behavioral Scis, fel, 77-78. **HONORS AND AWARDS** MA, Amherst Col, 56; LittD, Adelphi Univ, 64, Univ New Haven, 76. **MEMBERSHIPS** Am Acad Arts and Sci; Nat Inst Arts and Lett. **RESEARCH** Am literature; English literature; modern European literature. **SELECTED PUBLICATIONS** 1920 Diary, NY Rev Bks, Vol 42, 95; Cold Mountain, NY Rev Bks, Vol 44, 97; Collected Stories--Babel,I, Mcduff,D, NY Rev Bks, Vol 42, 95; The Complete Stories, NY Rev Bks, Vol 44, 97; Talking Horse-Malamud, Bernard on Life and Work, NY Rev Bks, Vol 44, 97; Her Holiness--Stowe,H arriet Beecher and Her Famous Book, 'Uncle Toms Cabin,' NY Rev Bks, Vol 41, 94; Culture of Complaint--The Fraying of America, NY Rev Bks, Vol 40, 93; A Genius of the Spiritual Life--Weil, Simone, NY Rev Bks, Vol 43, 96; Loves Story Told--A Life of Murray, Henry, A, NY Rev Bks, Vol 40, 93; Religion As Culture--Adams, Henry 'Mont-Saint-Michel and Chartres', Transactions of the Am Philosophical Society, Vol 83, 93; The 'Book of Intimate Grammar,', NY Rev Bks, Vol 41, 94; The Polish Invasion--Authors Reply, NY Rev Bks, Vol 42, 95; The 'Actual,' NY Rev Bks, Vol 44, 97. **CONTACT ADDRESS** Dept of English, Univ Notre Dame, Notre Dame, IN, 46556.

KEALEY, EDWARD J.
PERSONAL Born 08/01/1936, New York, NY **DISCIPLINE** MEDIEVAL HISTORY **EDUCATION** Manhattan Col, BA, 58; Johns Hopkins Univ, MA and PhD, 62. **CAREER** From asst prof to assoc prof, 62-73, adv grad studies, 64-69, PROF HIST, COL HOLY CROSS, 73-, CHMN HIST DEPT, 80-, Lectr pub speaking and parliamentary law, Labor Rels and Res Ctr, Univ Mass, 69-76; Nat Endowment for Humanities fel, 76; Holy Cross Col fac fel, 72 and 78-79; Am Philos Soc fel, 80. **MEMBERSHIPS** AHA; Am Cath Hist Asn; Conf Brit Hist; Soc Values Higher Educ; Medieval Acad Am. **RESEARCH** Medieval history, England and France in the 12th century; European and Am archaeology; pre-Columbian Am. **SELECTED PUBLICATIONS** The English Hospital, 1070-1570, Albion, Vol 28, 96. **CONTACT ADDRESS** Dept of Hist, Col of the Holy Cross, Worcester, MA, 01610.

KEALEY, GREGORY S.
PERSONAL Born 10/07/1948, Hamilton, ON, Canada **DISCIPLINE** HISTORY **EDUCATION** Univ Toronto, BA, 70; Univ Rochester(Mass) MA, 71, PhD, 77. **CAREER** Asst prof, 74-79, assoc prof hist, Dalhousie Univ, 79-81; assoc prof, 81-83, prof hist, 83-, univ res prof, 92-, DEAN GRAD STUD, MEMORIAL UNIV NFLD, 97-; vis prof, Univ Alta, 84; vis prof, Univ Guelph, 85; Univ Sydney, Univ New Eng, Griffith Univ, 93; scholar res, Laurentian Univ, 96. **HONORS AND AWARDS** Maurice Cody Memorial Prize, Univ Toronto, 70; Sir John A Macdonald Prize, Can Hist Asn, 80; AB Corey Prize, Can & Amer Hist Asns, 84; Pres Award Outstanding Res, Memorial Univ Nfld, 85. **MEMBERSHIPS** Royal Hist Soc; Can Hist Asn; Can Comt Labour Hist; Asn Can Stud; Can Asn Learned Jour. **SELECTED PUBLICATIONS** Auth, Toronto Workers Respond to Industrial Capitalism, 1867-1892, 80; Workers and Canadian History, 95; co-auth, Dreaming of What Might Be, 82; Labour and Hibernia, 93; ed, Labour/Le Travail, 76-97; McClelland & Stewart Social History Series, 80-96; Oxford Univ Press Social History Series, 96-. **CONTACT ADDRESS** Grad Stud, Memorial Univ of Newfoundland, St. John's, NF, A1C 5S7.

KEALEY, LINDA
PERSONAL Rochester, NY **DISCIPLINE** HISTORY **EDUCATION** Univ Toronto, BA, 69, BLS, 70, MA, 74, PhD, 82. **CAREER** Vis asst prof, 80-81, asst prof, 81-86, ASSOC PROF HISTORY, MEMORIAL UNIV NEWFOUNDLAND 86-, head dept, 94-. **MEMBERSHIPS** Royal Hist Asn; Can Women's Studs Asn; Can Res Inst Advan Women. **SELECTED PUBLICATIONS** Auth, A Not Unreasonable Claim: Women and Reform in Canada, 1880s-1920s, 79; auth, Canadian Socialism and the Women Question 1900-14, in Labour/Le Travail, 84; auth, The Status of Women in the Historical Profession in Canada, 1989 Survey, in Can Hist Rev, 91. **CONTACT ADDRESS** History Dept, Memorial Univ of Newfoundland, St. John's, NF, A1C 5S7. **EMAIL** lkealey@morgan.ucs.mun.ca

KEANEY, JOHN J.
DISCIPLINE CLASSICS **EDUCATION** Boston Coll, AB, 53; Harvard Univ, PhD, 59. **CAREER** Prof, Princeton Univ. **RESEARCH** Greek paeography and lexicography; Greek political theory. **SELECTED PUBLICATIONS** Auth, The Composition of Aristotle's Athenaion Politeia; ed, Harpocration: Lexeis of the Ten Orators; Contributing ed, Theophrastus of Eresus: Sources for his Life, Writings, Thought, and Influence. **CONTACT ADDRESS** Princeton Univ, 1 Nassau Hall, Princeton, NJ, 08544.

KEBEDE, ASHENAFI AMDE
PERSONAL Born 05/07/1938, Addis Ababa, Ethiopia, d, 1964 **DISCIPLINE** AFRICAN-AMERICAN STUDIES **EDUCATION** University of Rochester, BA, 1962; Wesleyan University, MA, 1969, PhD, 1971. **CAREER** US Peace Corps, counselor/teacher, summer 1962; Ethiopian Ministry of Education, director/teacher, 1962-68; Wesleyan University, instructor, 1968-71; Queens College, CUNY, assistant professor, 1971-75; Brandeis University, assistant professor, 1976-80; Florida State University, Center for African-American Culture, professor/ director, 1980-. **HONORS AND AWARDS** Haile Selassie Foundation, Outstanding Young Ethiopian Scholar, 1958; UNESCO, UNESCO Expert to Sudan, 1979; Institute for International Education, Senior Fulbright Scholar to Israel, 1986-87. **MEMBERSHIPS** Ethiopian National Music Committee, president, 1963-71; International Music Council, UNESCO, 1964-69; Society for Ethnomusicology, 1964-90; Florida Arts Council for African-American Affairs, executive director, 1982-90; Ethius, Inc, executive director, 1989-. **SELECTED PUBLICATIONS** Founded Ethiopia's Institute of Music, 1963; first African to conduct the Hungarian State Orchestra in Budapest, 1967; commissioned by UNESCO, wrote the syllabus for Sudan's Institute of Music, Dance and Drama, 1979; numerous books, monograms, articles and compositions in Black Perspectives in Music, Musical Quarterly, Ethnomusicology. **CONTACT ADDRESS** Center for African-American Culture, Florida State Univ, 210 S Woodward Ave, B-105, Tallahassee, FL, 32306.

KEBRIC, ROBERT BARNETT
PERSONAL Born 04/30/1946, Palo Alto, CA, m, 1971 **DISCIPLINE** ANCIENT HISTORY **EDUCATION** Univ Southern Calif, AB, 68; State Univ NY Binghamton, MA, 71, PhD (ancient hist), 72. **CAREER** From instr to asst prof, 73-77, vchmn dept, 77-79, ASSOC PROF HIST, UNIV LOUISVILLE, 77- **MEMBERSHIPS** Asn Ancient Historians. **RESEARCH** Greek history; Roman history; classical culture and literature. **SELECTED PUBLICATIONS** Law, Sexuality, and Society--The Enforcement of Morals in Classical Athens, Am J Legal Hist, Vol 37, 93. **CONTACT ADDRESS** Dept of Hist, Univ of Louisville, Louisville, KY, 40208.

KEDDIE, NIKKI R.
PERSONAL Born 08/30/1930, New York, NY **DISCIPLINE** MIDDLE EAST HISTORY **EDUCATION** Radcliffe Col, BA, 51; Stanford Univ, MA, 51; Univ Calif, PhD(hist), 55. **CAREER** Res historian, Univ Calif, 55-56; instr hist, Univ Ariz, 57; from instr to asst prof, Scripps Col, 57-61; from asst prof to assoc prof, 61-71, PROF HIST, UNIV CALIF, LOS ANGELES, 71-, Soc Sci Res Coun Near and Mid E fel, 59-60, 76; Guggenheim Mem Found Fel, 63-64; vis prof hist, Univ Paris, 3, 76-78; Rockefeller fel, 80-82; Woodrow Wilson fel, 82. **MEMBERSHIPS** Asn Asian Studies; Mid East Inst; Mid East Studies Asn. **RESEARCH** Middle East; intellectual and social history. **SELECTED PUBLICATIONS** The Political Dimensions of Religion, Hist Relig, Vol 36, 97; The Revolt Of Islam, 1700 To 1993--Comparative Considerations and Relations to Imperialism, Comp Studies Soc Hist, Vol 36, 94; Women and the Political-Process in 20th-Century Iran, Am Hist Rev, Vol 102, 97; The Political Dimensions of Religion, Hist Relig, Vol 36, 97. **CONTACT ADDRESS** Dept of Hist, Univ of Calif, Los Angeles, CA, 90024.

KEE, HOWARD CLARK
PERSONAL Born 07/28/1920, Beverly, NJ, m, 1951, 3 children **DISCIPLINE** RELIGION, HISTORY **EDUCATION** Bryan Col, BA, 40; Dallas Theol Sem, ThM, 44; Yale Univ, PhD(relig), 51. **CAREER** Instr relig thought, Univ Pa, 51-53; from asst prof to prof New Testament, Drew Univ, 53-67; Rufus Jones prof hist relig, Bryn Mawr Col, 68-77; prof New Testament, 77-82, WILLIAM GOODWIN AURELIO PROF BIBLICAL STUDIES and DIR GRAD DIV RELIG STUDIES, SCH THEOL, BOSTON UNIV, 82-, Vis prof relig, Princeton Univ, 55-56; mem bd managers and chmn transl comt, Am Bible Soc, 58-; Am Asn Theol Schs fel, Marburg, Ger, 59-60; Guggenheim Found fel archaeol, Jerusalem, 66-67; ed, Soc Bibl Lit Dissertation Ser; BD ADV, YALE UNIV INST SACRED MUSIC, 79- **MEMBERSHIPS** Soc Relig Higher Educ; Soc Bibl Lit; Am Acad Relig; Aaup; Soc New Testament Studies. **RESEARCH** Hist and literature of early Christianity; archaeology of the Hellenistic and early Roman periods; social setting of early Christianity in the Graeco-Roman world. **SELECTED PUBLICATIONS** Theios-Aner and the Markan Miracle Traditions--A Critique of the Theios-Aner Concept As An Interpretative Background of the Miracle-Tradition Used by Mark, Cath Bibl Quart, Vol 54, 92; The Changing Meaning of Synagogue--A Response to Oster, Richard, New Test Studies, Vol 40, 94; Encyclopedia of Early Christianity, J Church State, Vol 35, 93; Jesus in Current Approaches to an Analysis of A Puzzling Designation in the Q-Tradition Q-VII, 18-35--A Glutton and a Drunkard, New Test Studies, Vol 42, 96; The Land Called Holy--Palestine in Christian History and Thought, Am Hist Rev, Vol 99, 94; A Century of Quests for the Culturally Compatible Jesus in an Examination of Recent Scholarship from the So-Called Jesus-Seminar and AN Overview of 20th-Century Research into the Christ Figure, Theology Today, Vol 52, 95; Defining the 1st-Century-Ce Synagogue--Problems and Progress, New Test Studies, Vol 41, 95; Foundational Writings of the Testament of the 12 Patriarchs--An Investigation on the Size, Contents and Characteristics of the Original Writings, Cath Bibl Quart, Vol 55, 93. **CONTACT ADDRESS** Sch of Theol, Boston Univ, Boston, MA, 02215.

KEEFE, SUSAN ANN
PERSONAL Born 05/21/1954, RYE, NY **DISCIPLINE** MEDIEVAL INTELLECTUAL HISTORY **EDUCATION** Univ

Pa, BA, 75; Univ Toronto, MA, 76, PhD(medieval studies), 81. **CAREER** MELLON INSTR HIST, CALIF INST TECHNOL, 81- **MEMBERSHIPS** Medieval Acad Am; Medieval Asn Pac; AHA; Inst Relig Life. **RESEARCH** Carolingian liturgical expositions; manuscript evidence for the teaching and celebration of Christian initiation in the early Middle Ages. **SELECTED PUBLICATIONS** Liturgy and Sacramental Theology in History, Speculum-A J Medieval Studies, Vol 68, 93; Law and Liturgy in the Latin Church, 5th-12th Centuries, Cath Hist Rev, Vol 82, 96; Liturgy and Sacramental Theology in History, Speculum-A J Medieval Studies, Vol 68, 93. **CONTACT ADDRESS** Duke Univ, Durham, NC, 27706.

KEEFE, SUSAN E.
PERSONAL Born 12/01/1947, Spokane, WA, m, 1970, 1 child **DISCIPLINE** CULTURAL ANTHROPOLOGY **EDUCATION** Univ of CA, Santa Barbara, BA, Anthro, 69; MA, Anthro, 71; PhD, Anthro, 74. **CAREER** Asst Res, Anthro Soc Process Inst, Univ CA, Santa Barbara, 74-78; Asst Prof, Dep of Anthro, Appalachian State Univ, 78-82; Assoc Prof, Anthro, 82-87; prof Anthro, 87-; Chp 92-. **HONORS AND AWARDS** Natl Sci Found Graduate Traineeship, UCSB, 71-72; Woodrow Wilson Dissertation Fellowship, UCSB, 72-73; Co-principal Investigator NIMH grant Mental Health Service Utilization by Medican American, UCSB, 74-79; Principal Investigator NSF grant, Ethenicity and Education in Southern Appalachia, Appalachian State Univ, 82-83; Advisory Board member, Appalachian Journal, 82-; Editorial Board member, Hispanic Journal of Behavioral Sciences, 85-; Phi Kappa Phi Hon Soc member, 87-; Outstanding Scholar Award Coll of Arts and Sci, Appalachian State Univ, 97. **MEMBERSHIPS** Amer Anthro Assn; Soc for Applied Anthro; Souther Anthro Soc; Soc of Medical Anthro; Applachian Studies Assn. **RESEARCH** Ethnicity; Soc Org; Medical Anthro; Applied Anthro; Applachia; Mexican Amer. **SELECTED PUBLICATIONS** Keefe, Susan Emley(-ed), Appalachian Mental Health, Lexington KY, Univ of Kentucky Press, 88; Negotiating Ethnicity: The Impact of Anthropological Theory and Practice, Wash DC; American Anthropological Assoc Natl Assoc for the Practice of Anthrop Bulletin #8, 89; Keefe, Susan E. and Amado M. Padilla, Chicano Ethninity Albuquerque NM, Univ of New Mexico Press, 87; Keefe, Susan Emley, Appalachia Americans In Many Americas: Perspective on Racism,Ethnicity, and Cultural Identity, Gregory R. Campbell(ed), Dubuque 10 Kendall/Hunt, 98; The Development of and Undergraduate Applied Anthropology Training Program, In Practicing Anthropology in the South, James M, Tim Wallace(ed), Southern Anthropology Society Proceedings # 30, Athens GA, Univ of GA Press, pp 81-90, 97; Keefe, Susan Emley Urbanism Reconsidered: A Southern Appalachian Perspective City and Society, Annual Review Vol 1, pp 20-34, 94; Southern Appalachia: Analytical Models, Social Services and Native Support Systems American Journal of Community Psychology, 14:479-498, 86; Help-Seeking Behavior Among Foreigh-Born and Native Born Mexican Americans, Social Science and Medicine 16: 1467-1472, 82; Reck, U. Mae, Gregory G. Reck and Susan E. Keefe Implications of Teachers Perceptions of Students in An Appalachian School, Journal of Research and Development in Education: 26(2) 117-121, 93. **CONTACT ADDRESS** Dept Of Anthro, Appalachian State Univ, Boone, NC, 28608. **EMAIL** keefese@appstate.edu

KEEFE, THOMAS KEELIN
PERSONAL Born 12/02/1946, Highland Park, IL, m, 1970, 1 child **DISCIPLINE** MEDIEVAL ENGLAND **EDUCATION** Univ Calif, Santa Barbara, BA, 69, PhD(medieval hist), 78. **CAREER** ASST PROF HIST, APPALACHIAN STATE UNIV, 78- **MEMBERSHIPS** Royal Hist Soc; Pipe Roll Soc; Soc Medieval Archaeol; Conf Brit Studies; Haskins Soc Anglo-Norman and Angevin Hist (vpres, 82-). **SELECTED PUBLICATIONS** Richard-I Coeur-De-Lion--Kingship, Chivalry and War in the 12th-Century, Speculum-A J Medieval Studies, Vol 71, 96; English Castles--A Guide by Counties, Albion, Vol 29, 97; Charters of the Redvers Family and the Earldom of Devon, 1090-1217, Albion, Vol 27, 95. **CONTACT ADDRESS** Dept of Hist, Appalachian State Univ, 1 Appalachian State, Boone, NC, 28608-0001.

KEEFE, THOMAS M.
PERSONAL Born 12/25/1933, Chicago, IL **DISCIPLINE** MODERN GERMANY **EDUCATION** St Mary's Col, Minn, BA, 56; Univ Denver, MA, 57; Loyola Univ, Ill, PhD(hist), 66. **CAREER** Asst prof hist, St Mary's Col, Minn, 63-64; lectr, Sch Bus, Loyola Univ, Ill, 64-65; from instr to asst prof, 65-71; ASSOC PROF HIST, ST JOSEPH'S UNIV, PA, 71- **MEMBERSHIPS** AHA; Am Cath Hist Asn; Conf Group Cent Europ Hist; Hist Asn, Eng; Soc Hist Educ. **RESEARCH** Germany, 19-1939; Am press; nativism. **SELECTED PUBLICATIONS** Germany Rude Awakening--Censorship in the Land of the Brothers Grimm, Historian, Vol 55, 93; Hecker, Isaac--An American-Catholic, Church Hist, Vol 64, 95. **CONTACT ADDRESS** 25 Old Lancaster Rd, Bala-Cynwyd, PA, 19004.

KEELER, MARY FREAR
PERSONAL Born 01/01/1904, State College, PA, m, 1938, 1 child **DISCIPLINE** HISTORY **EDUCATION** Pa State Univ, AB, 24; Yale Univ, MA, 29, PhD(hist), 33. **CAREER** Instr hist, Univ Wyo, 29-31; instr, NJ Col Women, 31-32; from instr to asst prof, Pa State Univ, 33-38; lectr, Vassar Col, 52-53 & Wellesley Col, 53-54; lectr hist, 54-58, prof, 58-71, dean fac, 54-69, EMER DEAN FAC, HOOD COL, 69-; EXEC ED PARLIAMENTARY DEBATES, YALE CTR PARLIAMENTARY HIST, 74-, Am Asn Univ Women fel, 35-36; sr fel, Folger Shakespeare Libr, 71-72; res assoc hist, Yale Univ, 74-76; consult, Yale Ctr Parliamentary Hist, 76-; co-ed, Commons Debates 1628, Yale Univ, 77-83. **HONORS AND AWARDS** AAUW Fel, 35-36; Am Phil Soc grant, 72-73. **MEMBERSHIPS** AHA; Conf Brit Studies; fel Royal Hist Soc; Berkshire Conf Women Historians; Soc Hist Discoveries. **RESEARCH** History of Parliament; English and modern European history; Elizabethan explorations. **SELECTED PUBLICATIONS** Auth, The Long Parliament, 1640-1641, Am Philos Soc, 54; ed, Bibliography of British History, Stuart Period, Clarendon, 2nd ed, 70; Sir Francis Drake's West Indian Voyage, 1585-1586, Hakluyt Soc, 81. **CONTACT ADDRESS** 302 W 12th St, Frederick, MD, 21701.

KEEN, BENJAMIN
PERSONAL Born 04/25/1913, m, 1937, 4 children **DISCIPLINE** LATIN AMERICAN HISTORY **EDUCATION** Muhlenberg Col, AB, 36; Lehigh Univ, MA, 39; Yale Univ, PhD(hist), 41. **CAREER** Instr hist, Yale Univ, 43-45; asst prof, Amherst Col, 45-46; assoc prof, WVa Univ, 46-56; prof hist, Jersey City State Col, 56-59; PROF HIST, NORTHERN ILL UNIV, 59- **MEMBERSHIPS** Conf Latin Am Hist; AHA. **RESEARCH** Pre-Columbian Am; social history of colonial Latin Am; historiography of colonial Latin Am. **SELECTED PUBLICATIONS** Aesthetic Recognition of Ancient Amerindian Art, Ethnohistory, Vol 39, 92; Indian Law, Studies, Vol 1, The Visitas-Generales in Spanish-America 16th-Century to 17th-Century, Vol 2, Sources--Legal Documents--Public-Law--Spanish, Hispanic Am Hist Rev, Vol 73, 93; The Only Way, Cath Hist Rev, Vol 79, 93; Mesoamerican Elites--An Archaeological Assessment, Historian, Vol 57, 95; Portraits from the Age of Exploration--Selections from Thevet, Andre 'Vrais Pourtraits Et Vies Des Hommes Illustres,', Hispan Am Hist Rev, Vol 74, 94; Men of the Ocean, Hispan Am Hist Rev, Vol 73, 93; Cortes--The Great Adventurer and the Fate of Aztec Mexico, Historian, Vol 56, 94; The Armature of Conquest--Spanish Accounts of the Discovery of America, 1492-1589, Ams, Vol 50, 94; Collecting the Pre-Columbian Past, Ethnohistory, Vol 41, 94; The America in the Spanish World Order--The Justification for Conquest in the 17th-Century, Cath Hist Rev, Vol 82, 96; Lascasas in Mexico, History and Unknown Works, Ams, Vol 51, 94; Hanke, Lewis 1905-93, Hispan Am Hist Rev, Vol 73, 93; Las Casas--In Search of the Poor of Christ, Jesus, Am Hist Rev, Vol 100, 95. **CONTACT ADDRESS** Dept of Hist, No Illinois Univ, De Kalb, IL, 60115.

KEEN, J. ERNEST
PERSONAL Born 02/15/1937, Indianapolis, IN, m, 3 children **DISCIPLINE** PSYCHOLOGY **EDUCATION** Harvard Univ, PhD 63. **CAREER** Bucknell Univ, Psychologist/tchr 64. **HONORS AND AWARDS** Linbach Awd for Tchg. **RESEARCH** Psychopharmacology; drugs and society. **SELECTED PUBLICATIONS** Drugs Therapy and Professional Power, Praeger, 98. **CONTACT ADDRESS** Dept of Psychology, Bucknell Univ, Lewisberg, PA, 17837. **EMAIL** keen@bucknell.edu

KEENAN, J.G.
PERSONAL Born 01/19/1944, New York, NY **DISCIPLINE** CLASSICS **EDUCATION** Col of the Holy Cross, AB 65; Yale Univ, MA 66, PhD 68. **CAREER** Univ Cal Berk, asst prof 68-73; Loyola Univ, assoc to full prof 74 to 98-. **HONORS AND AWARDS** NEH **MEMBERSHIPS** ASP; AIP; APA; ARCE; CAMS **RESEARCH** Papyrology, ancient , social, economic and legal history; Byzantine and medieval Egypt. **SELECTED PUBLICATIONS** Auth, Egypt A.D. 425-600, Cambridge Ancient History, forthcoming; Review of Stanley Burstein, Ancient African Kingdoms, and Derek A. Welsby, The Kingdom of Kush, for The Classical Bull, forthcoming; Review of David Tandy, Warriors into Traders: The power of the Market in Early Greece, for Classical Bull, forthcoming; More From the Archive of the Descendents of Eulogius, with Todd Hickey, Analecta Papyrologica, 98; Gilgamesh: An Appreciation, in: Danny P. Jackson, trans, The Epic of Gilgamesh, rev ed, Bolchazy Carducci Pub, Wauconda Il, 97; George Sphrantzes: A Brief Review, The Ancient World, 96; The Aphrodito Murder Mystery: A Return to the Scene of the Crimes, BASP, 95; The Will of Gaius Longinus Castor, BASP, 94. **CONTACT ADDRESS** Dept of Classic Studies, Loyola Univ, 6525 N Sheridan Rd, Chicago, IL, 60626. **EMAIL** jkeenan@orion.it.luc.edu

KEENE, JENNIFER D.
DISCIPLINE HISTORY **EDUCATION** George Wash Univ, BA, 84; Carnegie Mellon Univ, PhD, 91. **CAREER** Asst prof, Redland Univ. **RESEARCH** American Diplomatic History; Civil War and Reconstruction; American Political History; War and Society; African-American History; American Social History. **SELECTED PUBLICATIONS** Auth, Americans in France During the Great War, 94; Intelligence and Morale in the Army of a Democracy: The Genesis of Military Psychology During the First World War, Military Psychol, 94; Between Mutiny and Obedience: The Case of the French Fifth Infantry Division during World War I (rev), J Social Hist, 95. **CONTACT ADDRESS** History Dept, Univ Redlands, 1200 E Colton Ave, Box 3090, Redlands, CA, 92373-0999. **EMAIL** keene@jasper.uor.edu

KEEP, JOHN L.H.
PERSONAL Born 01/21/1926, Orpington, m, 1948 **DISCIPLINE** RUSSIAN HISTORY **EDUCATION** Univ London, BA, 50, PhD(Russ hist), 54. **CAREER** Lectr Russ and reader hist, Univ London, 54-70; PROF HIST, UNIV TORONTO, 70-, Vis assoc prof hist, Univ Wash, 64-65. **MEMBERSHIPS** Can Asn Slavists; Am Asn Advan Slavic Studies. **RESEARCH** Social history of Russian army; Russian revolution. **SELECTED PUBLICATIONS** Without the Right to Think--Historians in the Era of the Great Terror, Jahrbucher fur Geschichte Osteuropas, Vol 43, 95; A Historical Encyclopedia of the Soviet Union 1917/22 to 1991, Jahrbucher fur Geschichte Osteuropas, Vol 42, 94; 2 Legal Investigations Against Ginzburg, Evgeniya--Case-Number, Political Victims of Totalitarianism in Russia, Jahrbucher fur Geschichte Osteuropas, Vol 43, 95. **CONTACT ADDRESS** Dept Hist, Univ Toronto, Toronto, ON, M5S 1A1.

KEGLEY, CHARLES W.
PERSONAL Born 03/05/1944, Evanston, IL, d, 1 child **DISCIPLINE** INTERNATIONAL RELATIONS **EDUCATION** Syracuse Univ, Maxwell School, PhD 71; Am Univ, Sch Intl Ser, BA 66. **CAREER** Univ of SC, prof 70-99, Pearce Prof Intl Rel 84-, Ch 81-85; Rutgers Univ, vis prof 89; Univ TX, vis assoc prof 76; Georgetown univ, asst prof 71-72. **HONORS AND AWARDS** Distg Sch For Pol Analy Awd; Pres ISA; Pew Facul Fell; Dist Alumni Awd. **MEMBERSHIPS** APSA; ISA. **RESEARCH** Intl Rel Theory, comparable for policy, peace res, intl ethics, quantitative methodology. **SELECTED PUBLICATIONS** World Politics: Trend and Transformation, 7th ed, NY, St Martins Press, co auth Eugene R Wittkopf, 99; How Nations Make Peace, NY, Macmillan, co auth, Gregory A Raymond, 99; Controversies in International Relations Theory: Realism and the Neoliberal Challenge, NY, St Martins Press, 95; Controlling Economic Competition In the Pacific Rim, USA Today, 98; Placing Global Ecopolitics in Peace Studies, Peace Review, 97; The U S Use of Military Intervention to Promote Democracy : Evaluating the Recoed, Intl Interactions, co auth Margaret G Hermann, 98. **CONTACT ADDRESS** Dept of Govt and International Studies, Univ of S. Carolina, 401 Gambrell Hall, Columbia, SC, 29208. **EMAIL** kegletc@garnet.cla.sc.edu

KEHL, JAMES ARTHUR
PERSONAL Born 02/16/1922, Pittsburgh, PA, m, 1972, 1 child **DISCIPLINE** HISTORY **EDUCATION** Univ Pittsburgh, BA, 44, MA, 47; Univ Pa, PhD, 54. **CAREER** Lectr hist, 46-47, from instr to assoc prof, 47-65, admin asst dept, 55-58, admin asst to chancellor, 58-60, asst dean soc sci, 60-65, dean col arts & sci, 65-69, prof hist, 65-92, prof emeritus, 92-, Univ Pittsburgh; instr, Carnegie Mellon Univ, 46-47. **HONORS AND AWARDS** Distinguished Alumnus Award, Univ Pittsburgh; Meritorious Service Award, Phi Alpha Theta. **RESEARCH** Pennsylvania history; history of American political parties. **SELECTED PUBLICATIONS** Auth, Ill Feeling in the Era of Good Feeling, Western Pennsylvania Political Battles, 1815-1825, Univ Pittsburgh; art, Defender of the Faith: Orphan Annie and the Conservative Tradition, SAtlantic Quart, 77; art, A Bull Moose Responds to the New Deal, Pa Mag of Hist & Biog, 64; art,The Unmaking of a President, 1889-1892, Pa Hist, 72; art,The Delegate Convention: Agent of the Democratic Process, SAtlantic Quart, 73; art, Albert Gallatin: Man of Moderation, WPa Hist Mag, 78; art, Boss Rule in the Gilded Age: Matt Quay of Pennsylvania, Univ Pittsburgh, 81; art, White House or Animal House, SAtlantic Quart, 80; auth, When Civilians Manned the Ships: Life in the Amphibious Fleet During World War II, Brandylane, 97. **CONTACT ADDRESS** 5057 Brownsville Rd, Pittsburgh, PA, 15236.

KEHOE, DENNIS P.
DISCIPLINE ROMAN IMPERIAL HISTORY, SOCIAL AND ECONOMIC HISTORY LATIN LITERATURE **EDUCATION** Dartmouth Col, AB, 73-77; Oxford Univ, Magdalen Col, BA, 77-79; Univ MI, PhD, 79-82. **CAREER** Prof, Tulane Univ. **RESEARCH** Roman law, papirology. **SELECTED PUBLICATIONS** Auth, The Economics of Agriculture on Roman Imperial Estates in North Africa, HYPOMNEMATA 89, Vandenhoeck und Ruprecht, 88; Management and Investment on Estates in Roman Egypt during the Early Empire, Papyrologische Texte und Abhandlungen 40, Habelt, 92; Legal Institutions and the Bargaining Power of the Tenant in Roman Egypt, Archv fur Papyrusforschung 41, 95; Roman-Law Influence on Louisiana's Landlord-Tenant Law: The Question of Risk in Agriculture, Tulane Law Rev 70, 96; Investment, Profit, and Tenancy: The Jurists and the Roman Agrarian Economy, Univ Mich Press, 97. **CONTACT ADDRESS** Dept Class Stud, Tulane Univ, 6823 St Charles Ave, New Orleans, LA, 70118. **EMAIL** kehoe@mailhost.tcs.tulane.edu

KEIGHTLEY, DAVID NOEL
PERSONAL Born 10/25/1932, London, England, m, 1965, 2 children **DISCIPLINE** CHINESE HISTORY **EDUCATION** Amherst Col, BA, 53; NY Univ, MA, 56; Columbia Univ, PhD(Chinese hist), 69. **CAREER** Asst prof, 69-75, assoc prof, 75-79, PROF HIST, UNIV CALIF, BERKELEY, 79-; ed, Early

China, 75-; vis prof, Peking Univ, spring 81; assoc ed, J Asian Studies, 81-. **HONORS AND AWARDS** Fels, Humanities Res Inst, Univ Calif, Berkeley, 72-73; fel, Am Counc Learned Socs, 75-76; Guggenheim fel, 78-79; MacArthur Fel, 86-91. **MEMBERSHIPS** Asn Asian Studies; Soc Study Early China; Am Orient Soc. **RESEARCH** Ancient Chinese history; oracle bone inscriptions; Shang religion. **SELECTED PUBLICATIONS** Auth, Religion and the rise of urbanism, J Am Orient Soc, 10-12/73; On the misuse of ancient Chinese inscriptions: An astronomical fantasy, Hist Sci, 77; Ping-ti Ho and the origins of Chinese civilization, Harvard J Asiatic Studies, 12/77; Archaeology and history in Chinese society, In: Paleoanthropology in the People's Republic of China, Nat Acad Sci, 77; The religious commitment: Shang theology and the genesis of Chinese political culture, Hist Relig, 2-5/78; Sources of Shang History: The Oracle Bone Inscriptions of Bronze Age China, Calif, 78; Akatsuka Kiyoshi and the study of early China: A study in historical method, Harvard J Asiatic Studies, 6/82; The late Shang state: When, where, and what?, In: Origins of Chinese Civilizations, Calif, 83; Late Shang Divination: The Magico-Religious Legacy, In: Explorations in Early Chinese Cosmology, J of the Am Acad of Relig Studies, 84; Archaeology and Mentality: The Making of China, Representations, Spring 87; Shang Divination and Metaphysics, Philos East and West, 10/88; Clean Hands and Shining Helmets: Heroic Action in Early Chinese and Greek Culture, In: Religion and Authority, Univ Mich Press, 93; A Measure of Man in Early China: In Search of the Neolithic Inch, Chinese Sci 12, 94-95; Art, Ancestors, and the Origins of Writing in China, Representations, Fall 96; The Shang: China's First Historical Dynasty, In: The Cambridge History of Ancient China, Cambridge Univ Press, 99. **CONTACT ADDRESS** Dept of History, Univ of California, Berkeley, 3229 Dwinelle Hall, Berkeley, CA, 94720-1742. **EMAIL** keightle@socrates.berkeley.edu

KEIL, CHARLES M.H.
PERSONAL Born 08/12/1939, Norwalk, CT, m, 1964, 2 children **DISCIPLINE** ANTHROPOLOGY, MUSIC **EDUCATION** Yale Univ, BA; Univ Chicago, MA, 64; PhD, 79. **CAREER** From asst prof to prof, Dept of Am Stud, SUNY Buffalo, 70- ; acting chemn, 78-89, 92, 94-95, Dir Undergrad Stud, 86-89, dir Grad Stud, 70-77, 79-82; vis prof, music, Univ Natal, 93; vis lectr, sociol of music, 82, 83. **HONORS AND AWARDS** Chicago Folklore Prize, co-winner, 80; Chicago Folklore Prize, 95; Woodrow Wilson Fel, 61-62; Ford Found Fel, 62-63; NIMH Fel, 63-64; Foreign Area Fel Prog, 65-67; Rockefeller Found Res Grant, 75; Guggenheim fel, 79-80. **SELECTED PUBLICATIONS** Auth, Urban Blues, Univ Chicago, 66; auth, Tiv Song: The Sociology of Art in a Classless Society, Univ Chicago, 79; coauth, Polka Happiness, Temple Univ, 92; co-ed, My Music, Wesleyan Univ, 93; coauth, Music Grooves: Essays and Dialogues, Univ Chicago, 94. **CONTACT ADDRESS** Dept of American Studies, SUNY Buffalo, Buffalo, NY, 14260. **EMAIL** amsckeil@acsu.buffalo.edu

KEILLOR, ELAINE
DISCIPLINE BAROQUE AND CLASSICAL PERIODS, ETHNOMUSICOLOGY **EDUCATION** Univ Toronto, BA, MA, PhD. **CAREER** Lectr, York Univ, 75-76; instr, Queen's Univ, 76-77; asst prof, 77-82, assoc prof, 82-95, PROF CARLETON UNIV 95-. **HONORS AND AWARDS** Chappell Medal, 58; Merit Award, Fac Arts, Carleton Univ, 81., Principal investigator, The Can Mus Heritage Soc; co-ch, Another Organized Res Unit. **MEMBERSHIPS** Can Musical Heritage; Am Musicol Soc; Int Musicol Soc; Soc Ethnomusicol; Can Univ Music Soc; Can Soc Traditional Music. **RESEARCH** Canadian music. **SELECTED PUBLICATIONS** Auth, monograph John Weinzweig and His Music: The Radical Romantic of Canada, 94; **CONTACT ADDRESS** Dept of Mus, Carleton Univ, 1125 Colonel By Dr, Ottawa, ON, K1S 5B6. **EMAIL** elaine_keillor@carleton.ca

KEITER, ROBERT B.
PERSONAL Born 07/05/1946, Bethesda, MD, m, 1976, 2 children **DISCIPLINE** LAW; HISTORY **EDUCATION** Northwestern Univ, JD 72; Washington Univ, BA 68. **CAREER** Univ Utah Col Law, Wallace Stegner prof, dir, 93-; Wallace Stegner Cen Land Resource Environ, prof, James I. Farr prof, 93-98, Univ Wyoming College of Law, assoc prof, interim dean, prof, Winston S. Howard dist prof, 78-93; Univ Utah, vis prof, 85; Southwestern Univ, assoc prof, 76-78; Idaho Legal Aid, managing att, 75-76; Appalachian Res Def Fund, Reginald Heber Smith Fel, 72-74. **HONORS AND AWARDS** Omicron delta Kappa; Phi Kappa Phi; Sr Fulbright Sch **MEMBERSHIPS** ABA; State Bars of Wyoming, Idaho, West Virginia; RMMLF Trustee. **RESEARCH** Nat Resources Law and Policy; Constitutional Law. **SELECTED PUBLICATIONS** Auth, Reclaiming the Native Home of Hope: Community Ecology and the West, ed, Univ Utah Press, 98; Visions of the Grand Staircase-Escalante: Examining Utah's Newest National Monument, co-ed, Wallace Stegner Cen Utah Museum Natural Hist, 98; The Greater Yellowstone Ecosystem: Redefining America's Wilderness Heritage, coed, Yale Univ Press, 91; Ecosystems and the Law: Toward an Integrated Approach, Ecolo Apps, Preserving Nature in the Provincial Parks: Law Policy and Science in a Dynamic Environment, rev, Denver U L, 97; Ecological Policy and the Courts: Of rights Processes and the Judicial Role, Human Ecolo Rev, 97; Greater Yellowstone's Bison: The Unraveling of an Early American Wildlife Conservation Achievement, Jour of Wildlife Mgmt, 97; Law and Large Carnivore Conservation in the Rocky Mountains of the Us and Canada, coauth, Conservation Biology, 96. **CONTACT ADDRESS** College of Law, Utah Univ, 332 S. 1400 E. Front, Salt Lake City, UT, 84112. **EMAIL** keiterb@law.utah.edu

KELLEHER, PATRICIA
DISCIPLINE HISTORY **EDUCATION** Univ Wis, Madison, PhD. **CAREER** Asst prof, Univ NH, 95-. **HONORS AND AWARDS** Soc Sci Res Coun fel; Nat Sci Found fel; Newberry Libr fel, Chicago. **RESEARCH** Gender dynamics in 18th- and 19th-century Ireland and among Irish immigrants in North America. **SELECTED PUBLICATIONS** Coauth, Women, Social Institutions and Social Change, in Irish Women and Irish Immigration, ed. Patrick O'Sullivan, 95. **CONTACT ADDRESS** Univ NH, Durham, NH, 03824.

KELLER, CLAIR WAYNE
PERSONAL Born 01/??/1932, FARGO, ND, m, 1959, 2 children **DISCIPLINE** COLONIAL HISTORY **EDUCATION** Univ Wash, BA, 57, MA, 62, PhD(hist), 67. **CAREER** Teacher soc studies, Lake Wash High Sch, 57-59 and Sammamish High Sch, 60-66; instr hist, Univ Wash, 66-67; chmn dept soc studies, Interlake High Sch, Wash, 67-69; assoc prof, 69-80, PROF HIST and EDUC, IOWA STATE UNIV, 80- **MEMBERSHIPS** Nat Coun Soc Studies; AHA; Orgn Am Historians; Soc Hist Educ. **RESEARCH** Pennsylvania government, 1701-1740. **SELECTED PUBLICATIONS** Pennsylvania Reconsideration and Passage of the 1st Proposed Amendment on Representation in Constitutional History, Pa Mag Hist Biog, Vol 117, 93. **CONTACT ADDRESS** Dept of Hist, Iowa State Univ, Ames, IA, 50010.

KELLER, KENNETH WAYNE
PERSONAL Born 10/29/1943, St. Louis, MO, m **DISCIPLINE** AMERICAN HISTORY **EDUCATION** Wash Univ, AB, 65; Yale Univ, MPhil, 68, PhD(hist), 71. **CAREER** From instr to asst prof hist, OH Univ, 70-74; asst prof, OH State Univ, 74-81; assoc prof, 81-87, prof, Mary Baldwin Col, 87-. **HONORS AND AWARDS** Phi Beta Kappa. **MEMBERSHIPS** AHA; Orgn Am Historians; Soc Historians Early Am Repub. **RESEARCH** United States early national history; frontier; American colonial history. **SELECTED PUBLICATIONS** Auth, The Philadelphia Pilots' Strike of 1792, Labor Hist, winter 77; Alexander McNair and John B C Lucas: The Background of Early Missouri Politics, Bull Mo Hist Soc, 7/77; contribr, The Reader's Encycl of the American West, 77; The Encycl of Southern History, 79; coauth, Tenancy and Assetholding in Late Eighteenth Century Washington County, Pennsylvania, Western PA Hist Mag, 1/82; coauth, Rural Pennsylvania in 1800: A Portrait from the Septennial Census, PA Hist, 4/82; coauth, New Jersey Wealth-holding and the Republican Congressional Victory of 1800, NJ Hist, 82; auth, Rural Politics and the Collapse of Pennsylvania Federalism, Trans Am Philos Soc, 82; Cultural Conflict and Early Nineteenth Century Pennsylvania Politics, PA Mag of Hist and Biog, Oct 86; From the Rhineland to the Virginia Frontier: Flax Production as a Commercial Enterprise, VA Mag Hist and Biog, July 90; What is Distinctive About the Scotch-Irish?, in Robert Mitchell, ed, Appalachian Frontiers, 91; Origins of Ulster--Scots Emigration to America, 1600-1800: A Survey of Recent Research, Am Presbyterians, summer 92; The Outlook of Rhinelanders on the Virginia Frontier, in Michael Puglisi, ed, Diversity and Accomodation; Merchandising Nature: The H J Weber and Sons Nursery, MO Hist Rev, April 95; Cyrus McCormick, The Inventor as Creator of Controversy, Proceedings of the Asn for Living History Farms and Museums, 97. **CONTACT ADDRESS** Mary Baldwin Col, Staunton, VA, 24401. **EMAIL** kkeller@cit.mbc.edu

KELLER, MORTON
PERSONAL Born 03/01/1929, Brooklyn, NY, m, 1951, 2 children **DISCIPLINE** AMERICAN HISTORY **EDUCATION** Univ Rochester, BA, 50; Harvard Univ, MA, 52, PhD, 56. **CAREER** Instr hist, Univ NC, 56-58; from asst prof to assoc prof hist, Univ Pa, 58-64; prof hist, Brandeis Univ, 64-, Guggenheim fel, 59-60; Soc Sci Res Coun auxiliary res award, 59-60; fel, Harvard Ctr Studies Hist Liberty in Am, 60-61; Nat Sci Found soc sci res grant, 62; Am Philos Soc res award, 62; vis lectr, Harvard Univ, 63-64; res fel, Charles Warren Ctr Studies Am Hist, 67-68; mem US deleg, UNESCO Gen Conf, 68; lib arts fel, Harvard Law Sch, 70-71; sr fel, Nat Endowment for Hum, 74-75; resident scholar, Bellagio Study & Res Ctr, 76; Commonwealth Fund Lectr Am Hist, Univ Col, London, 79; Harmsworth prof Am hist, Oxford Univ, 80-81. **MEMBERSHIPS** Soc Am Historians; Am Acad Arts & Sci. **RESEARCH** Am polit, institutional and legal hist. **SELECTED PUBLICATIONS** Auth, The Life Insurance Enterprise, 1885-1910: A Study in the Limits of Corporate Power, Harvard Univ, 63; Affairs of State: Public Life in Late Nineteenth Century America, Harvard Univ, 77; Regulating a New Economy, Harvard Univ, 90; Regulating a New Society, Harvard Univ, 94. **CONTACT ADDRESS** Dept of Hist, Brandeis Univ, 415 South St, Waltham, MA, 02154-2700. **EMAIL** keller@binah.cc.brandeis.edu

KELLER, ROBERT J.
PERSONAL Born 02/07/1952, Grand Forks, ND, s **DISCIPLINE** SOCIOLOGY **EDUCATION** Graduate Theol Union, PhD, 93. **CAREER** Author **MEMBERSHIPS** AAR; ASR. **RESEARCH** Cath social teaching; sociology-theology of work; the works of M.-D. Chenu, 20th century French Dominican). **CONTACT ADDRESS** 1815 Las Lomas NE, Albuquerque, MN, 87106. **EMAIL** FBJK@juno.com

KELLER, WILLIAM
PERSONAL Born 01/27/1920, Newark, NJ **DISCIPLINE** EUROPEAN HISTORY **EDUCATION** Seton Hall Univ, AB, 43; Cath Univ Am, STL, 47; Fordham Univ, AM, 61. **CAREER** Lectr relig, Seton Hall Univ, 51-56, asst prof social studies, 56-61, dir grad info off, 60-79, assoc prof hist, 61-79. NJ CATH REC COMN, 76- **RESEARCH** Ancient Greece and Rome, early church; Eighteenth century England and Ireland; Renaissance reformation. **SELECTED PUBLICATIONS** Words of Introduction for Debruyn, Gunter, Goethe Jahrbuch, Vol 112, 95; Opening Remarks at the 73rd Annual-Meeting of the Goethe-Gesellschaft in Weimar, June 3-5, 1993, Goethe Jahrbuch, Vol 110, 93; 74th General-Meeting of the Goethe-Gesellschaft Held in Weimar, June 8-10, 1995--Preface, Goethe Jahrbuch, Vol 112, 95; Foreword in Introduction 'Goethe-Jahrbuch' 96, Goethe Jahrbuch, Vol 113, 96; Opening Address of the President of the Goethe-Gesellschaft in 74th General-Meeting Held in Weimar, June 8-10, 1995, Goethe Jahrbuch, Vol 112, 95; Introduction and Welcome for Semprun,Jorge in 74th General-Meeting of the Goethe-Gesellschaft Held in Weimar, June 8-10, 1995, Goethe Jahrbuch, Vol 112, 95; Opening Remarks by the President of the Goethe-Gesellschaft at the Opening Ceremony of the 72nd Annual-Meeting of the Inte-Goethe Gesellschaft in Weimar, May 23-25, 1991, Goethe Jahrbuch, Vol 108, 91; Karelski, Albert, January 31, 1936 to June 24, 1993--In Memoriam, Goethe Jahrbuch, Vol 110, 93. **CONTACT ADDRESS** 104 Clark Glen, Ridge, NJ, 07028.

KELLEY, BROOKS MATHER
PERSONAL Born 08/18/1929, Lake Forest, IL, m, 1980, 3 children **DISCIPLINE** AMERICAN HISTORY **EDUCATION** Yale Univ, BA, 53, Univ Chicago, MA, 56, PhD, 61. **CAREER** From instr to asst prof hist, 61-67, lectr, 68, cur hist manuscripts, libr & univ archivist, 64-66, dir res, Off Univ Develop, 67, res assoc, 68-73, res fel 73-75, res affiliate hist, Yale Univ, 75-; Writer Am hist, 70-, Vis prof hist, Brown Univ, 69-70. **MEMBERSHIPS** AHA, Orgn Am Historians. **RESEARCH** Educ hist; 19th century Am history. **SELECTED PUBLICATIONS** Auth, Simon Cameron and the senatorial nomination of 1867, 10/63 & Fossildom, old fogeyism, and red tape, 1/66, Pa Mag Hist & Biog; Yale, A History, Yale Univ, 74; New Haven Heritage, New Haven Preservation Trust, 74; coauth (with Daniel J Boorstin), A History of the United States, Ginn & Co, 81. **CONTACT ADDRESS** 91 Andrews Rd, Guilford, CT, 06437.

KELLEY, DONALD B.
PERSONAL Born 10/04/1937, Charleston, WV, m, 1961, 3 children **DISCIPLINE** AMERICAN INTELLECTUAL HISTORY **EDUCATION** Wheeling Col, BA, 60; Univ Miss, MA, 62; Tulane Univ, PhD, 65. **CAREER** Asst prof, 65-69, dir honors prog, 67-72, ASSOC PROF HIST, VILLANOVA UNIV, 69-, Vis prof, Univ Kent, 72-73. **MEMBERSHIPS** AHA; AAUP; Southern Hist Asn. **RESEARCH** Am colonial history; Am Quaker history. **SELECTED PUBLICATIONS** The Papers Washington, George, Revolutionary-War Series, Vol 4, April-June 1776, Pa Mag Hist Biog, Vol 118, 94. **CONTACT ADDRESS** Villanova Univ, Villanova, PA, 19085.

KELLEY, DONALD R.
PERSONAL m, 1979, 3 children **DISCIPLINE** EUROPEAN HISTORY **CAREER** James Westfall Thompson Prof Hist, Rutgers, 91- ; exec ed, J of the Hist of Ideas. **HONORS AND AWARDS** Davis Center, Princeton Univ, 87-88; Woodrow Wilson Center, 92-93; Princeton Inst Advanced Stud, 96-97. **MEMBERSHIPS** Am Philos Soc, 95- . **SELECTED PUBLICATIONS** Auth, The Human Measure; Social Thought in the Western Legal Tradition, Harvard, 90; auth, Renaissance Humanism, Twayne, 91; auth, the Writing of History and the Study of Law, Variorum, 97; ed, History and the Disciplines: The Reclassification of Knowledge in Early Modern Europe, Rochester, 97; auth, Faces of History: Historical Inquiry from Herodotus to Herder, Yale, 98. **CONTACT ADDRESS** Dept of History, Rutgers Univ, New Brunswick, NJ, 08901. **EMAIL** dkelley@rei.rutgers.edu

KELLEY, JOHN T.
DISCIPLINE HISTORY **EDUCATION** Amherst, BA, 70; Harvard Univ, MA, 71, PhD, 77, MD, 79. **CAREER** Teach fell, hist, Harvard Univ; current, V.P. & DIR OF MED AFF, STRAT PRDT PLAN & MARKETPLACE, HBO & CO. **MEMBERSHIPS** Am Antiquarian Soc **RESEARCH** Am almanacs **SELECTED PUBLICATIONS** Auth, Practical Astronomy During the Seventeenth Century: A Study of Almanac-Makers in America and England, Garland Press, 91. **CONTACT ADDRESS** 5 Country View Rd, Malvern, PA, 19355. **EMAIL** john.kelly@hboc.com

KELLEY, MARY
DISCIPLINE HISTORY **EDUCATION** Mt Holyoke, BA, 65; New York Univ, MA, 70; Univ Iowa, PhD, 74. **CAREER** Prof, WHEELOCK PROF, HIST, DARTMOUTH COLL **MEMBERSHIPS** Am Antiquarian Soc **SELECTED PUBLICATIONS** Auth, Private Woman, Public Stage: Literacy Domesticity in Nineteenth-Century America, Oxford Univ Press, 84; coauth, The Units of Sisterhood: The Beecher Sisters on Human Rights and Women's Sphere, Univ NC Press, 88; "'Vindicating the Equality of Female Intellect': Women and Authority in the Early Republic," Prospects: An Ann of Am Cult Stud 17, 92; ed, The Power of Her Sympathy: The Autobiography and Journal of Catherine Maria Sedgwick, Northeastern Univ Press, 93; ed, The Portable Margaret Fuller, Viking, 94; auth, "Designing a Past for the Present: Women Writing Women's History in Nineteenth-Century America," Procs of the AAS 105, 95; auth, "Reading Women/Women Reading: The Making of Learned Women in Antebellum America," Jour of Am Hist LXXXIII, Sept 96. **CONTACT ADDRESS** Dept of Hist, Dartmouth Col, Hanover, NH, 03755.

KELLNER, GEORGE
DISCIPLINE AMERICAN IMMIGRATION; URBAN HISTORY; AMERICA, 1815-77 **EDUCATION** Hiram Col, BA; Univ MO, Columbia, MA, PhD. **CAREER** Instr, RI Col. **RESEARCH** Immigration; urban hist; RI hist. **SELECTED PUBLICATIONS** Auth, Providence: A Century of Greatness, 1832-1932, RI Hist; coauth, Rhode Island: The Independent State. **CONTACT ADDRESS** Rhode Island Col, Providence, RI, 02908.

KELLNER, HANS
PERSONAL Born 05/12/1945, Pittsburgh, PA, m, 1980, 3 children **DISCIPLINE** HISTORY **EDUCATION** Harvard Univ, AB, 66; Univ Rochester, PhD, 72. **CAREER** Prof, Mich State Univ, 77-91; prof, Univ Tex-Arlington, 91- . **SELECTED PUBLICATIONS** Co-ed with F.R. Ankersmit, A New Philosophy of History, 95; auth, Language and Historical Representation, The Postmodern History Reader, 97; auth, Never Again is Now, The Postmodern History Reader, 97; Etyczny moment w teorii historii; przedstawiajac doswiadczenie poznania, Historia: o jeden swiat za daleko?, 97; Hans Kellner, Interviews on Philosophy of History, forthcoming. **CONTACT ADDRESS** Dept. of English, Univ of Texas-Arlington, Arlington, TX, 76019-0035. **EMAIL** kellner@uta.edu

KELLOGG, FREDERICK
PERSONAL Born 12/09/1929, Boston, MA, m, 1975, 1 child **DISCIPLINE** EUROPEAN HISTORY **EDUCATION** Stanford Univ, AB, 52; Univ Southern Calif, MA, 58; Ind Univ, PhD, 69. **CAREER** Admin asst, Univ Southern Calif, 57-58; asst, Univ Calif, Berkeley, 59-60; from instr to assoc prof hist, Boise State Univ, 62-67; from instr to asst prof, 67-71, assoc prof hist, Univ Ariz, 71-; United States-Romania Cultural Exchange res scholar, 60-61; vis asst prof, Univ Idaho, 65; Fulbright-Hays sr res scholar, 69-70; res scholar, Am Coun Learned Soc, Soviet Union, 70; Int Res and Exchanges Bd, Romania, 73-74; managing ed, Southeastern Europe, 74-. **HONORS AND AWARDS** Hon Mem, Institutul de istorie Alexandru D. Xenopol, Alexandru D. Xenopol Inst Hist, 91; Cert Recognition, Soc Romanian Stud, 93; Nicolae Orga Prize, Academia Romaana, 97. **MEMBERSHIPS** AHA; Am Asn Advan Slavic Studies; Southeast Europ Studies Assoc; Int Comn on Historiography of the Int Comt Hist Sci. **RESEARCH** East European history; Romanian history. **SELECTED PUBLICATIONS** Auth, Historical research materials in Rumania, J Cent Europ Affairs, 64; Conventia comerciala din 1875: un pas catre independenta, Studii: Rev de Istorie, 72; The historiography of Romanian independence, E Europ Quart, 78; The Structure of Romanian Nationalism, Canadian Review of Studies in Nationalism, 84; Dwa studia z dziejow historiografii rumunskiej XVII i XVII w: Dziela historyczne Mirona Kostyna i Dymitra Kantemira, Studia historyczne, 90; A History of Romanian Historical Writing, 90; The Road to Romanian Independence, 95; o Istorie a istoriografiei romane, 96; The Life and Historical Works of David Prodan, SE Europe, 97; A Quest to Understand Nationalism, SE Europe, 97. **CONTACT ADDRESS** Dept History, Univ AZ, 1 University of AZ, Tucson, AZ, 85721-0027. **EMAIL** kellogg@u.arizona.edu

KELLUM, BARBARA
DISCIPLINE VISUAL CULTURE OF THE ANCIENT ROMAN WORLD **EDUCATION** Univ Southern CA, AB, AM; Univ MI, AM; Harvard Univ, PhD. **CAREER** Art, Smith Col. **HONORS AND AWARDS** Initiated, Dept's crse in Art Hist Methods and Film & Art Hist. **RESEARCH** Aspect of life in ancient Roman and Etruscan times. **SELECTED PUBLICATIONS** Publ on, res interest. **CONTACT ADDRESS** Dept of Art, Smith Col, Hillyer Hall 317, Northampton, MA, 01063. **EMAIL** bkellum@julia.smith.edu

KELLY, ALFRED HERBERT
PERSONAL Born 02/22/1947, Detroit, MI, m, 1977, 1 child **DISCIPLINE** EUROPEAN INTELLECTUAL & GERMAN HISTORY **EDUCATION** Univ Chicago, BA, 69; Univ Wis, MA, 71 & PhD(hist), 75. **CAREER** Vis asst prof hist, Va Commonwealth Univ, 76-77; adj asst prof, Univ Richmond, 77-78; mem fac, Shimer Col, 80-81; from Asst Prof to Prof, 81-93, Edgar B. Graves prof hist, Hamilton Col, 93-. **MEMBERSHIPS** AHA; Ger Studies Asn. **RESEARCH** Cultural impact of Darwinism; German working class culture; philosophy of history; nationalism. **SELECTED PUBLICATIONS** Auth, The Descent of Darwin: The Popularization of Darwinisim in Germany, 1860-1914, Univ NC Press, 81; ed & transl, The German Worker: Working-Class Autobiographies from the Age of Industrialization, Univ Calif Press, 87. **CONTACT ADDRESS** Hist Dept, Hamilton Col, 198 College Hill Rd., Clinton, NY, 13323-1292. **EMAIL** akelly@hamilton.edu

KELLY, CATHIE
DISCIPLINE RENAISSANCE AND BAROQUE ART AND ARCHITECTURE **EDUCATION** Pa State Univ, PHD, 80. **CAREER** Instr, Univ Nev, Las Vegas, 80. **HONORS AND AWARDS** Outstanding Tchr of the Yr Award, Univ Nev, Las Vegas. **RESEARCH** Rome. **SELECTED PUBLICATIONS** Published in architectural history journals, as well as in collected essay volumes. **CONTACT ADDRESS** Univ Nev, Las Vegas, Las Vegas, NV, 89154.

KELLY, DAVID H.
PERSONAL Born 09/23/1929, Philadelphia, PA, 3 children **DISCIPLINE** CLASSICAL LINGUISTICS **EDUCATION** Cath Univ Am, BA, 52; Univ PA, MA, 54, PhD, 58. **CAREER** From asst prof to assoc prof class & ling, La Salle Univ, 61-70, chmn dept for lang, 67-69, dean arts & sci, 69-70; Prof Class, Montclair State Col, 70. **HONORS AND AWARDS** MSU Distinguished Tchr, 98. **MEMBERSHIPS** Am Philol Asn; Class Asn Atlantic States (pres, 77-78). **RESEARCH** Lang tchg methodology; class hum; syntax of Greek and Latin. **SELECTED PUBLICATIONS** Auth, Distinctive feature analysis in Latin phonology, Am J Philol, 67; Transformations in the Latin nominal phrase, Class Philol, 68; Tense in the Latin independent operative, Glotta, 72; Latin the tool subject, Class Outlook, 73; Revolution in classical studies, Class J, 73; Egyptians and Ethiopians: Color, race, and racism, Class Outlook, 91; Case: Grammar and terminology, Class World, 93. **CONTACT ADDRESS** Dept of Class, Montclair State Univ, 1 Normal Ave, Montclair, NJ, 07043-1699. **EMAIL** kellyd@mail.montclair.edu

KELLY, DAVID H.
PERSONAL Born 09/23/1929, Philadelphia, PA, m, 1997, 3 children **DISCIPLINE** CLASSICS **EDUCATION** Catholic Univ of Amer, BA, 52; Univ of Penn, MA, 54; PhD, 58. **CAREER** Asst to Assoc Prof, LaSalle Univ, 61-70; Assoc, Prof, Montclair St Univ, 70-. **HONORS AND AWARDS** Lindback Awd, 66; Dist Tchr Awd Montclair St Univ, 98. **MEMBERSHIPS** APA; Class Asn of the Atlantic States; NJ Class Assoc **RESEARCH** General classics; classical linguistics **SELECTED PUBLICATIONS** Articles and reviews in: The Classical World and the Classical Outlook. **CONTACT ADDRESS** Dept of Classics and General Humanities, Montclair State Univ, Upper Montclair, NJ, 07043. **EMAIL** Kellyd@mail.montclair.edu

KELLY, DAVID H.
PERSONAL Born 11/10/1942, Chicago, IL, m, 1992, 2 children **DISCIPLINE** HISTORY **EDUCATION** Univ Chicago, BA, 65; Ind Univ, MA, 68, PhD, 76. **CAREER** Bibliographic res, Univ Wi, 70-74; hist to adjunct to prof, D'Youville Col, 75-. **MEMBERSHIPS** OAH; AHA. **RESEARCH** Social & institutional history **SELECTED PUBLICATIONS** Coauth, Women's Education in the Third World: An Annotated Bibliography of Published Research, 89; ed, Women's Education: a Selected Bibliography of Published Works, International Handbook of Women's Education, Greenwood Press, 89; auth, Women in Higher Education: A Select International Bibliography, St Univ NY, Buffalo, 90; ed, International Feminist Perspectives on Educational Reform, the Work of Gail Kelly, 96; ed, The Education of Gail Paradise Kelly: A Memoir, International Feminist Perspectives on Educational Reform, Garland, 96. **CONTACT ADDRESS** 131 Greenfield, Buffalo, NY, 14214.

KELLY, THOMAS
DISCIPLINE HISTORY **EDUCATION** Univ Ill, PhD, 64. **CAREER** Prof **RESEARCH** Greek history. **SELECTED PUBLICATIONS** Auth, A History of Argos To 500 B.C., 77. **CONTACT ADDRESS** History Dept, Univ of Minnesota, Twin Cities, 614 Social Sciences Tower, 267 19th Ave. S, Minneapolis, MN, 55455. **EMAIL** kelly004@tc.umn.edu

KELMAN, STEVEN
PERSONAL Born 05/01/1948, New York, NY, m, 1980, 2 children **DISCIPLINE** POLITICAL SCIENCE **EDUCATION** Harvard Col, AB, 70; Harvard Univ, PhD, 78. **CAREER** Asst and assoc prof, 78-86, prof of pub mgt, 86-, Harvard Univ, JFK Sch of Govt. **HONORS AND AWARDS** Nat Achievement Award, Nat Contract Mgt Asn, 97; Distinguished Pub Svc Award, Amer Soc of Pub Admin, Wash chap, 96; Gabriel Almond Award, Outstanding Dissertation in Comparative Polit, Amer Polit Sci Asn, 80; Fulbright scholar, Univ Stockholm, 70-71; Harvard Univ Sheldon Traveling fel, 70-71; Junior Twelve, Phi Beta Kappa, 69; Harvard Nat Scholar, 66-70. **MEMBERSHIPS** Coun for Excellence in Govt; GTSI Inc; Fed Sources Inc; Nat Acad of Pub Admin; Nat Contract Mgt Asn; Jour of Pub Admin Res and Theory; The Amer Prospect; Acad Adv Bd, Volvo Res Found; Intl Adv Grp; Amer Coun on Ger. **RESEARCH** Public management. **SELECTED PUBLICATIONS** Auth, American Democracy and the Public Good, Harcourt Brace, 96; Procurement and Public Management: The Fear of Discretion and the Qualtiy of Public Performance, Amer Enterprise Inst, 90; Making Public Policy: A Hopeful View of American Government, Basic Books, 87; coauth, with Sidney Verba, Elites and the Idea of Equality, Harvard Univ Press, 87; auth, What Price Incentives? Economists and the Environment, Auburn House, 81; Regulating American, Regulating Sweden: A Comparative Study of Occupational Safety and Health Policy, MIT Press, 81; Improving Doctor Performance: A Study in the Use of Information and Organizational Change, Human Sci Press, 79; Behind the Berlin Wall, Houghton Mifflin, 71; Push Comes to Shove, Houghton Mifflin, 70. **CONTACT ADDRESS** JFK School of Government, Harvard Univ, Cambridge, MA, 02138. **EMAIL** steve_kelman@harvard.edu

KEMENY, PAUL CHARLES
PERSONAL Born 12/13/1960, Morristown, NJ, m, 1983, 1 child **DISCIPLINE** AMERICAN RELIGIOUS HISTORY **EDUCATION** Wake Forest, BA, 83; Westminster Sem, MAR, 86, MDiv, 87; Duke Univ, ThM, 88; Princeton Sem, PhD, 95. **CAREER** Vis fel, ctr stud (s) Amer Rel, Princeton Univ, 95-96; asst prof, Rel, Calvin Col, 96- . **HONORS AND AWARDS** Woodrow Wilson awd, 97 **MEMBERSHIPS** AAR; HEQ; AHA; ASOH; Conf Earth Hist. **CONTACT ADDRESS** Dept of Religion and Theology, Calvin Col, 3201 Burton St SE, Grand Rapids, MI, 49546.

KEMP, HENRIETTA J.
DISCIPLINE GERMAN, HISTORY, LIBRARY SCIENCE **EDUCATION** Univ Iowa, BA, 66; Univ Pittsburgh, MLS, 71. **CAREER** LIBR, 81-, SUPERV, FINE ARTS COLLECT, 89-, LUTHER COL. **CONTACT ADDRESS** Library, Luther Col, 700 College Dr, Decorah, IA, 52101. **EMAIL** kempjane@luther.edu

KENEZ, PETER
PERSONAL Born 04/05/1937, Budapest, Hungary, m, 1959 **DISCIPLINE** RUSSIAN HISTORY **EDUCATION** Princeton Univ, BA, 60; Harvard Univ, MA, 62, PhD, 67. **CAREER** From asst prof to assoc prof, 66-75, prof hist, Univ CA, Santa Cruz,75, Int Res & Exchange Bd studies grant in USSR, 69-70; nat fel, Hoover Inst, 73-74. **RESEARCH** Russ revolution and civil war; hist of the Russ Army. **SELECTED PUBLICATIONS** Auth, The volunteer army and Georgia, Slavonic Rev, 70; Civil War in South Russia, 1918, 71 & Coalition politics in the Hungarian Soviet Republic, In: Revolution in Perspective, 72, Univ CA; A profile of the pre-revolutionary officer corps, Calif Slavic Studies, 73; Civil War in South Russia, 1919-1920, Univ CA, 76; The birth of the propaganda state: Soviet methods of mobilization, 1917-29, Cambridge Univ, 85; Co-ed (with Abbott Gleason and Richard Stites), Bolsheviks culture, Ind Univ, 85; Cinema in Soviet society, 1917-1953, Cambridge Univ, 92; Varieties of fear, Am Univ, 95; A history of the Soviet Union from the beginning to the end, Cambridge Univ, 99. **CONTACT ADDRESS** Dept of Hist, Stevenson Col Univ of California, 1156 High St, Santa Cruz, CA, 95064-0001.

KENFIELD, JOHN F., III
DISCIPLINE ART HISTORY **EDUCATION** Princeton Univ, PhD. **CAREER** Assoc prof, Rutgers Univ. **RESEARCH** Greek sculpture with emphasis on the Hellenistic and archaic periods, espec Western Greece or Magna Graecia (Southern Italy and Sicily). **SELECTED PUBLICATIONS** Auth, The Mosaics and Wall Paintings in The Palatial Late Roman Villa at Castle Copse, Great Bedwyn, Wiltshire, Ind UP, 97; An East Greek Master Coroplast at late Archaic Morgantina, Hesperia, 90; A Modelled Terracotta Frieze from Archaic Morgantina: Its East Greek and Central Italic Affinities, Deliciae Fictiles, 93; The Case for a Phokaian Presence at Archaic Morgantina as Evidenced by the Site's Archaic Architectural Terracottas, Varia Anatolica III, 93; High Classical and High Baroque in the Architectural Terracottas of Morgantina, Hesperia Suppl, 94. **CONTACT ADDRESS** Dept of Art Hist, Rutgers Univ/ Rutgers Col, Hamilton St., New Brunswick, NJ, 08903.

KENISTON MCINTOSH, MARJORIE
DISCIPLINE HISTORY **EDUCATION** Radcliffe Col, BA, 62; Harvard Univ, MA, 63; PhD, 66. **CAREER** Asst prof, 89-96, assoc prof, 94-, dir grad stu prog, Univ Colo, 96. **SELECTED PUBLICATIONS** Auth, A Community Transformed: The Manor and Liberty of Havering, 1500-1620, Cambridge, 91; Autonomy and Community: The Royal Manor of Havering, 1200-1500, Cambridge, 86; Finding Language for Misconduct: Jurors in Fifteenth-Century Local Courts, Univ Minn, 96. **CONTACT ADDRESS** History Dept, Univ of Colorado, Boulder, Boulder, CO, 80309. **EMAIL** McIntosh@spot.colorado.edu

KENNEDY, BENJAMIN W.
DISCIPLINE HISTORY **EDUCATION** Univ Ga, PhD, 66. **CAREER** Prof. **RESEARCH** French Revolution; Napoleon; 18th and 19th century Europe; historiography. **SELECTED PUBLICATIONS** Auth, pubs on France history, the age of revolution in the late 18th century, and French impacts on Ireland and Spain in 1789-1799. **CONTACT ADDRESS** History Dept, State Univ of West Georgia, Carrollton, GA, 30118. **EMAIL** bkennedy@westga.edu

KENNEDY, DANE KEITH
PERSONAL Born 05/30/1951, Bonne Terre, MO, m, 1974, 1 child **DISCIPLINE** BRITISH & COMMONWEALTH HISTORY **EDUCATION** Univ Calif, Berkeley, BA, 73, MA, 75, PhD(Brit hist), 81. **CAREER** Prof And Ch Brit Hist, Univ Nebr-Lincoln, 81-. **HONORS AND AWARDS** Fel, Royal Hist Soc; Distinguished Teaching Award, Univ Nebr, 89. **MEMBERSHIPS** Am Hist Asn; Conf Brit Studies; World Hist Asn. **RESEARCH** British colonialism in Africa and India. **SELECTED PUBLICATIONS** Auth, Islands of White: Settler Society & Culture in Kenya and Southern Rhodesia, 1890-1939, Duke Univ Press, 87; The Magic Mountains: Hill Stations and the British Raj, Berkeley: Univ Calif Press, 96, Delhi: Oxford Univ Press, 96; numerous articles in: J of Mod Hist; J of Brit Studies; Int J of African Hist Studies; Albion; South Asia; Clio; J of Imperial and Commonwealth Hist; The Nation; and others. **CONTACT ADDRESS** History Dept, Univ of Nebr, PO Box 880327, Lincoln, NE, 68588-0327. **EMAIL** dkennedy@unlinfo.unl.edu

KENNEDY, GEORGE A.
PERSONAL Born 11/26/1928, Hartford, CT, m, 1955, 1 child **DISCIPLINE** CLASSICS **EDUCATION** Princeton Univ, AB, 50; Harvard Univ, AM, 52, PhD, 54. **CAREER** Kennedy Traveling Fel, 54-55, instr and tutor of English, Hist, & Lit, 55-58, sec of Classics fac, 55-58, board of freshman advisers, 56-58, commencement commt, 58, visiting asst prof, Harvard Univ, 59; asst prof of Greek, 58-59, asst prof of Classics, 59-63, assoc prof of Classics, 63-65, chemn, search commt for a librarian, 62, acad coun, 63-64, Haverford Col; prof of Classics & chemn, Dept of Classics, Univ of Pittsburgh, 65-66; prof of Classics, 66-72, dir, Am Office of L'Annee Philologique, 68-74, Paddison Prof of Classics, 72-95, chemn, Dept of Classics, 66-76, chemn, Dept of Linguistics, 75-76, chemn, Curriculum of Comparative Lit, 89-93, chemn of Univ fac, 85-88, Univ of NC at Chapel Hill. **HONORS AND AWARDS** Fulbright fel, 64-65; Guggenheim fel, 64-65; Charles J. Goodwin Award, Am Philological Asn; Distinguished Scholar Award, Nat Commun Asn; Thomas Jefferson Award, UNC-CH. **MEMBERSHIPS** Am Acad of Arts & Sci; Am Philosophical Soc; Am Philological Asn; Int Soc for the Hist of Retoric. **SELECTED PUBLICATIONS** Auth, The Art of Persusion in Greece, Princeton Univ Press, 63; auth, Quintilian, Twayne Pubs, 69; auth, The Art of Rhetoric in the Roman World, Princeton Univ Press, 72; auth, Greek Rhetoric Under Christian Emperors, Princeton Univ Press, 83; auth, New Testament Interpretation through Rhetorical Criticism, Univ of NC Press, 84; auth, Aristotle, On Rhetoric: A Theory of Civic Discourse, Newly Translated with Introduction, Notes, and Appendices, Oxford Univ Press, 91; auth, A New History of Classical Rhetoric, Princeton Univ Press, 94; auth, Comparative Rhetoric: An Historical and Cross-Cultural Introduction, Oxford Univ Press, 98. **CONTACT ADDRESS** PO Box 271880, Fort Collins, CO, 80527-1880.

KENNEDY, JANET
DISCIPLINE MODERN ART **EDUCATION** Columbia Univ, PhD. **CAREER** Assoc prof. **RESEARCH** Reception of Western European art in late nineteenth; early twentieth century Russia. **SELECTED PUBLICATIONS** Auth, Mir iskustva, 77; Shrovetide Revelry: Alexandre Benois's Contribution to Petrushka; Line of Succession: Three Productions of Tchaikovsky's Sleeping Beauty. **CONTACT ADDRESS** Dept of History and Art, Indiana Univ, Bloomington, 300 N Jordan Ave, Bloomington, IN, 47405. **EMAIL** kennedy@indiana.edu

KENNEDY, JOYCE S.
PERSONAL Born 06/15/1943, St. Louis, MO, d **DISCIPLINE** EDUCATION **EDUCATION** Harris Tchr Coll, AB 1965; St Louis U, MEd 1968; MI State U, PhD 1975. **CAREER** Coll of Arts & Sciences Governors State Univ, occupational educ coordinator, prof 1975-; Meramec Jr Coll, counselor 1971-74; Forest Park Jr Coll, counselor 1969-71; St Louis Job Corps Center for Women, counselor 1968-69; Carver Elementary School, teacher 1966-68. **HONORS AND AWARDS** Cert of Recognition for Outstanding Serv IL Guidance adn Personnel Assn 1977; Distinguished Prof Governors State Univ 1977; Outstanding Young Woman of Am Award 1978. **MEMBERSHIPS** Mem Am Personnel and Guidance assn; mem IL Assn of Non-White Concerns; mem IL Guidance and Personnel Assn; keynote speaker Roseland Community Sch Graduation 1978; facilitator Career Awareness Workshop 1978; speaker Harvey Pub Library 1978; Urban Counseling Fellowship Nat Mental Health Inst MI State Univ 1972-74. **CONTACT ADDRESS** Col of Arts & Sciences, Governors State Univ, University Park, IL, 60466.

KENNEDY, KENNETH ADRIAN RAINE
PERSONAL Born 06/26/1930, Oakland, CA, m, 1969 **DISCIPLINE** ANTHROPOLOGY **EDUCATION** Univ Calif-Berkeley, BA, 53, MA, 54, PhD, 62. **CAREER** PROF, ECOL & SYSTEMATICS, BIOL SCI, CORNELL UNIV, 64-. **MEMBERSHIPS** Am Asn Physical Anthrop; Am Anthropol Asn; AmAsn Advancement Sci; Am Acad Forensic Sci; Anthrop Soc India; Archaeol Inst Am; Asn South Asian Archaeolog West Europ; Indo-Pacific Prehist Asn; Inst Human Origins; Int Asn Human Biol; Nat Center Sci Edu; Northeast Forensic Anthrop Asn; Paleopath Asn **RESEARCH** Biological anthropology; Palaeoecology & palaeodemography; Human paleontology; Forensic anthropology; Palaeopathology. **SELECTED PUBLICATIONS** South Asia: India and Sri Lanka, Anthropol Prehist Inst Royal Sci Naturelles Belgique; Reconstruction of Life from the Skeleton, Wiley/Liss, 89; "The Wrong Urn," Commingling of Cremains in Mortuary Practices, Jour Forensic Sci, 96; "A Canine Tooth from the Siwaliks: First Recorded Discovery of a Fossil Ape," Abstract of 97th Ann Mtg Am Anthrop Asn, 97. **CONTACT ADDRESS** Sect Ecol & Systematics, Cornell Univ, Corson Hall, Ithaca, NY, 14853. **EMAIL** KAK10@cornell.edu

KENNEDY, LAWRENCE W.
PERSONAL Born 08/04/1952, Riverside, CA, m, 1974, 2 children **DISCIPLINE** HISTORY POLITICAL SCIENCE **EDUCATION** Boston Col, BA, polit sci, 75, MA, hist, 78, PhD, hist, 87. **CAREER** St Sebastion's Country Day Sch, 75-76; Boston Col HS, teacher, 76-85; Univ Mass, Northeastern univ, Tufts univ, adjunt faculty, 87-92; Boston Redel Auth, consult histn, 87-92; Boston col, lectr, 87-92; asst prof, 92-98; Univ Scranton, assoc prof, 98-. **HONORS AND AWARDS** Outstanding Fac Mem Awd, 98; Alph Sigma nu, 98; Phi Alpha theta, 93; Who's Who in the East, 96-98; Intl Writ and Auth's Who's Who, 97. **MEMBERSHIPS** Am cath hist asn; NEHA; OAH; Soc of hist of the guilded age and progress era; Urban hist asn. **RESEARCH** Boston; urban; ethnic; religious hist; planning hist and architectural **SELECTED PUBLICATIONS** Boston: A Topographical History, co auth Walter Muir Whitehill, 3d ed, Cambridge MA, Harvard Univ Press, forthcoming; Planning the City upon a Hill: Boston since 1630, Amherst MA, Univ Mass Press, 92; pp bk 94; Boston's First Irish Mayor: Hugh O' Brien, 1885-1889, in: Mass Politics: Selected Hist Essays, Westfield MA, Inst Mass Stud, 98; numerous other articles. **CONTACT ADDRESS** Dept History, Univ Scranton, 800 Linden St, Scranton, PA, 18510. **EMAIL** kennedyL1@uofs.edu

KENNEDY, THOMAS C.
DISCIPLINE HISTORY **EDUCATION** Univ SC, PhD. **CAREER** Prof. **RESEARCH** 19th and 20th Century Britain; imperialism. **SELECTED PUBLICATIONS** Auth, Female Friends and the Pacifist Impulse, Univ Toronto, 96; Comments on Military/Civilian Relations in Britain and Germany, Univ Tex, 90. **CONTACT ADDRESS** History Dept, Univ of Arkansas, Fayetteville, 409 Old Main, Fayetteville, AR, 72701. **EMAIL** tkennedy@comp.uark.edu

KENNEDY, THOMAS L.
DISCIPLINE CHINESE AND EAST ASIAN HISTORY **EDUCATION** Columbia Univ, PhD, 68. **CAREER** Prof, Washington State Univ. **SELECTED PUBLICATIONS** Auth, Testimony of a Confucian Women: The Autobiography of Mrs. Nie Zeng Jifen, 1852-1942, Univ Ga Press, 93; Li Hung-chang and the Kiangnan Arsenal, 1860-1865, Li Hung-chang and China's Early Modernization, 94. **CONTACT ADDRESS** Dept of History, Washington State Univ, 301 Wilson Hall, PO Box 644030, Pullman, WA, 99164-4030. **EMAIL** kennedyt@wsu.edu

KENNEDY, W. BENJAMIN
PERSONAL Born 04/15/1938, Tifton, GA, m, 1959, 3 children **DISCIPLINE** MODERN EUROPEAN HISTORY **EDUCATION** Georgetown Col, AB, 60; Univ NC, MA, 62; Univ Ga, PhD, 66. **CAREER** From instr to assoc prof, 62-76, from actg head dept to head dept, 67-71, prof hist, State Univ of Western Goergia, 76- . **MEMBERSHIPS** AHA; Soc Fr Hist Studies. **RESEARCH** Military history in the French Revolution; 18th century Europe. **SELECTED PUBLICATIONS** Auth, Without any guarantee on our part: The French Directory's Irish policy, In: Proceedings of the Consortium on Revolutionary Europe, Univ Fla, 73; ed, Siege of Savannah in 1779, Beehive, 74; The Irish Jacobins, Studia Hibernica, Dublin, 76; The French are on the sea: Irish, French and British reactions to the abortive bantry expedition in 1796, Proceedings Western Soc Fr Hist, 77; auth, Biographical sketches of William Duckett, William Jackson, Edward John Lewines, Henry Sheares, Matthew Tone, In: Biographical Dictionary of Modern British Radicals, Harvester, 79; Conspiracy tinged with blarney: Wolfe Tone and other Irish emissaries to Revolutionary France, Proceedings of the Consortium on Revolutionary Europe, Univ Ga, 80. **CONTACT ADDRESS** Dept of History, State Univ of Western Georgia, 1601 Maple St, Carrollton, GA, 30117-4116. **EMAIL** bkennedy@westga.edu

KENNETT, DOUGLAS
PERSONAL Born 06/16/1967, Los Angeles, CA **DISCIPLINE** ANTHROPOLOGY **EDUCATION** Univ Calif, Santa Barbara, PhD, 98. **CAREER** Asst prof, anthrop, Calif State Univ, Long Beach. **MEMBERSHIPS** Am Anthrop Asn; Soc for Am Archaeol. **RESEARCH** Anthropological archaeology; evolutionary ecology; isotope geochemistry. **CONTACT ADDRESS** Dept of Anthropology, California State Univ, Long Beach, Long Beach, CA, 90840. **EMAIL** dkennett@csulb.edu

KENNY, KEVIN
PERSONAL Born 07/11/1960, London, England, m, 1992, 1 child **DISCIPLINE** HISTORY **EDUCATION** Univ Edinburgh UK, BA, MA 87; Columbia Univ, MA 89, MPhil 90, PhD 94. **CAREER** CUNY, City Col, adj instr, 93-94; Columbia Univ, vis asst prof, 94; Univ Texas Austin, asst prof, 94-. **HONORS AND AWARDS** Whiting Foun Fel; Albert J Beveridge Res Gnt. **MEMBERSHIPS** AHA; OAH. **RESEARCH** US Labor and Immigration. **SELECTED PUBLICATIONS** Auth, Making Sense of the Molly Maguires, NY, Oxford U Press, 98; The American Irish: A Concise History Since 1700, Addison Wesley Longman, forthcoming; Development of the Working Classes, William L. Barney ed, Blackwell Companion to Nineteenth-Century America, Oxford, Blackwell, forthcoming; Ethnicity and Immigration in: Eric Foner ed, The New American History, rev ed, Temple Univ Press, 97, pamphlet in series, The New American History, AHA; The Molly Maguires in Popular Culture, Jour of Amer Ethnic Hist, 95; The Molly Maguires and the Catholic Church, Labor Hist, 95; The Encyc of the City of New York, 38 entries, Yale Univ Press, 95; The Readers Companion to American History, 9 entries, Houghton Mifflin, 91. **CONTACT ADDRESS** Dept of History, Texas Univ, Austin, TX, 78712. **EMAIL** kenny@mail.utexas.edu

KENSETH, JOY
DISCIPLINE ART HISTORY **EDUCATION** Hiram Col, BA; Harvard Univ, MA, PhD. **CAREER** Prof, Dartmouth Col. **RESEARCH** Sculpture of Bernini; painting of Caravaggio; the art of dying in Roman Baroque sculpture. **SELECTED PUBLICATIONS** Auth, The Age of the Marvelous (exh cat), 91; Bernini's David, excerpts of studies p ubl in Basic Design: Systems, Elements, Application, Prentice Hall, 83; var a rticles. **CONTACT ADDRESS** Dartmouth Col, 3529 N Main St, Ste. 207, Hanover, NH, 03755. **EMAIL** joy.kenseth@dartmouth.edu

KENZER, ROBERT C.
PERSONAL Born 02/11/1955, Chicago, IL, m, 1976, 1 child **DISCIPLINE** HISTORY **EDUCATION** Univ Calif Santa Barbara, BA, 76; Harvard Univ, MA, 77; PhD, 82. **CAREER** Inst, 81-82, Harvard Univ; asst prof to assoc prof, 82-93, Brigham Young Univ; assoc prof, 93-99, Univ Richmond. **HONORS AND AWARDS** Archie K Davis res fel, 88; Donald B Hoffman Award, 88; Albert J Beveridge res grant, 89. **MEMBERSHIPS** Amer Hist Assoc; Org of Amer Hist; S Hist Assoc; Soc of Civil War Hist. **RESEARCH** Nineteenth Century US; Civil War era; Amer S. **SELECTED PUBLICATIONS** Auth, Kinship and Neighborhood in a Southern Community: Orange County, North Carolina, 1849-1881, Univ Tn Press, 87; auth, Enterprising Southerners: Black Economic Success in North Caroline, 1865-1915, Univ Press of Va, 97. **CONTACT ADDRESS** Dept of History, Univ Richmond, Richmond, VA, 23173. **EMAIL** rkenzer@richmond.edu

KEOHANE, NANNERL O.
DISCIPLINE POLITICAL SCIENCE **EDUCATION** Wellesley College, BA, 61; Oxford Univ, BA/MA, 63; Yale Univ, PhD, 67. **CAREER** Prof, Pres, 93-, Duke Univ; Prof, Pres, 81-93, Wellesley College; Asst Prof, Assoc Prof, Chmn, 73-81, Stanford Univ; Lectr, Asst Prof, 67-73, Swarthmore College; vis Lectr, 70-72, Univ Penn. **HONORS AND AWARDS** Phi Beta Kappa; Marshall Schshp; Woodrow Wilson fel; Gores Awd Excell Teach; CASBS Fel; Wilbur Cross Medal; AAAS Fel; APS Fel; OU St Anne's Hon Fel; Ntl Women's Hall of Fame; AAA Golden Plate Awd; Eleven Honorary Degrees. **MEMBERSHIPS** APSA **RESEARCH** Political Philosophy; Feminism; Education. **SELECTED PUBLICATIONS** Auth, Moral Education in the Modern University, Proceedings of the Amer Philo Soc, 98; The Mission of the Research University, in: DAEDALUS, J the Amer Acad of Arts and Sciences, 93; The Role of the President, in: Strategy and Finance of Higher Education, by WF Massy, Joel W Myerson, Peterson's Guides, Princeton NJ, 92; Women and the Transformation of the World, in: Preparing for the 21st Century: Models for Social Change, AAUW Edu Foun Occasional Paper, 89. **CONTACT ADDRESS** 207 Allen Bldg, Box 90001, Durham, NC, 27708-0001. **EMAIL** nkeohane@mail.duke.edu

KERBER, LINDA KAUFMAN
PERSONAL Born 01/23/1940, New York, NY, m, 1960, 2 children **DISCIPLINE** AMERICAN HISTORY **EDUCATION** Barnard Col, AB, 60; NY Univ, MA, 61; Columbia Univ, PhD, 68. **CAREER** Instr hist, Stern Col, Yeshiva Univ, 63-67, asst prof, 68; instr, San Jose State Col, 69-70; vis asst prof, Stanford Univ, 70-71; assoc prof, 71-75, prof hist, Univ IA, 75-, May Brodbeck Prof Lib Arts & Prof Hist, 85; Penrose Fund grant; Am Philos Soc, 71-72; fel, National Endowment for Humanities, 76; mem ann prize comt, Am Quart, 76-78; biog jury, Pulitzer Prize, 77-78; J S Guggenheim Found, Nat Humanities Center, Rockefeller Found Residency, Bellagio. **HONORS AND AWARDS** Phi Beta Kappa Nat Vis Scholar, 98-99

MEMBERSHIPS AHA; Orgn Am Historians; Am Studies Asn, pres 88-89; Am Acad Arts & Sci; Soc Relig Higher Educ; Soc Am Historians; Berkshire Conf Women Hist. **RESEARCH** Early Am hist; women's hist. **SELECTED PUBLICATIONS** Auth, Federalists in Dissent: Imagery and Ideology in Jeffersonian America, Cornell Univ, 70, paperback, 80; Women of the Republic: Intellect and ideology in revolutionary America, Univ NC Press, 80, 2nd paperback, W W Norton, 86, 3rd paperback, UNC Press, 97; co-ed (with Jane Sherron De Hart), Women's America: Refocusing the Past, Oxford Univ Press, 82, 4th ed, 95; co-ed (with Emory Elliott, A Walton Litz and Terence Martin), American Literature: An Anthology, 2 vol, Prentice-Hall, 91; co-ed (with Alice Kessler-Harris and Kathryn Kish Sklar), U S History as Women's History: New Feminist Essays, UNC Press, 95; Toward an Intellectual History of Women: Essays by Linda K Kerber, UNC Press, 97; No Constitutional Right to Be Ladies: Women and the Obligations of Citizenship, Hill and Wang, 9/98. **CONTACT ADDRESS** Dept of Hist, Univ of IA, 280 Schaeffer Hall, Iowa City, IA, 52242-1409. **EMAIL** linda-kerber@uiowa.edu

KERN, GILBERT RICHARD
PERSONAL Born 12/05/1932, Detroit, MI, 6 children **DISCIPLINE** CHURCH & AMERICAN HISTORY **EDUCATION** Findlay Col, AB, 54; Winebrenner Theol Sem, BD, 58; Univ Chicago, MA, 60, PhD, 68. **CAREER** From lectr to prof church hist, Winebrenner Theol Sem, 60-70, pres, 63-70; Prof Relig, 70-75, Prof Hist, 75-98, Professor Emeritus, The Univ of Findlay, 98-; Lectr Hist, Winebrenner Theol Sem, 72-84. **MEMBERSHIPS** Am Soc Church Hist; Am Hist Asn. **RESEARCH** Nineteenth century Am church. **SELECTED PUBLICATIONS** Auth, John Winebrenner: 19th Century Reformer, Cent Publ House 74; Findlay College: The first one hundred years, 82. **CONTACT ADDRESS** Dept Hist, The Univ of Findlay, 1000 N Main St, Findlay, OH, 45840-3695. **EMAIL** kern@lucy.findlay.edu

KERN, ROBERT
DISCIPLINE IBERIAN HISTORY, MODERN EUROPE **EDUCATION** Univ Chicago, PhD. **CAREER** Prof, hd, Europ sec, Univ NMex. **HONORS AND AWARDS** Grant, Harkness Found, NEH, Am Philos Soc. **RESEARCH** Western U.S. labor. **SELECTED PUBLICATIONS** Auth, Caciquismo and the Luso-Hispanic World, 72; Liberals, Reformers, and Caciques in Restoration Spain, 74; Red Years/Black Years: The Political History of Spanish Liberalism, 78; The Labor History of New Mexico, 83; Building New Mexico, 84; The Regions of Spain, 95; coauth, European Women on the Left, 82; Historical Dictionary of Modern Spain, 1700 to Present, 90. **CONTACT ADDRESS** Univ NMex, Albuquerque, NM, 87131.

KERN, STEPHEN
DISCIPLINE HISTORY **EDUCATION** Columbia Univ, PhD, 70 **CAREER** Asst Prof, Northern Illinois Univ, 70-77; Asst Prof and administrator, Northern Illinois Univ Salzburg Program, 71; Assoc Prof, 77-84, Prof, 84-, Northern Illinois Univ. **CONTACT ADDRESS** Dept of History, No Illinois Univ, Dekalb, IL, 60115. **EMAIL** skern@elnet.com

KERR, JOAN
DISCIPLINE CULTURAL HISTORY **CAREER** Prof and convenor, Cultural History, Ctr Cross-Cult Res, Australia Natl Univ. **RESEARCH** Feminist art; Australian art; cultural art. **SELECTED PUBLICATIONS** co-ed, Past Present: Documents on the National Women's Art Exhibition, Art & Australia Books, pending. **CONTACT ADDRESS** Dept of Education, Australian National Univ. **EMAIL** Joan.Kerr@anu.edu.au

KERR, KATHEL AUSTIN
PERSONAL Born 08/29/1938, St. Louis, MO, m, 1967, 3 children **DISCIPLINE** RECENT AMERICAN HISTORY **EDUCATION** Oberlin Col, AB, 59; Univ Iowa, MA, 60; Univ Pittsburgh, PhD, 65. **CAREER** Asst prof, 65-72, assoc prof hist, Ohio State Univ, Columbus, 72-; prof hist, Ohio State Univ, Columbus, 84; Fulbright lectr, Univ Tokyo & Waseda Univ, Japan, 73. **HONORS AND AWARDS** Sr Fulbright Lectr, Univ Tokyo, Waseda Univ, Japan, 73; Sr Fulbright Lectr, Univ Hamburg, Germany, 82-83. **MEMBERSHIPS** Am Hist Asn; Business Hist Conf; Ohio Acad of Hist; Ohio Hist Soc; Alcohol & Temperance Hist Group; Orgn Hist. **RESEARCH** American political and business history. **SELECTED PUBLICATIONS** Auth, Organized for Prohibition: An New History of the Anti-Saloon League, Yale University, 85; auth, Local Businesses: Exploring Their History, American Association State and Local History, 90; auth, BF Goodrich: Traditions and Transformations, Ohio State University, 96. **CONTACT ADDRESS** Dept of History, Ohio State Univ, 230 W 17th Ave, Columbus, OH, 43210-1361. **EMAIL** kerr.6@osu.edu

KERSEY, HARRY A.
DISCIPLINE HISTORY **EDUCATION** Univ Ill, PhD. **CAREER** Prof. **MEMBERSHIPS** Am Philos Soc; Am Asn State Local Hist. **RESEARCH** Southeastern Native American history; Florida history. **SELECTED PUBLICATIONS** Auth, Pelts, Plumes and Hides: White Traders Among the Seminole Indians 1870-1930; An Assumption of Sovereignty: Social and Political transformation Among the Florida Seminoles 1953-1979, 96. **CONTACT ADDRESS** History Dept, Florida Atlantic Univ, 777 Glades Rd, Boca Raton, FL, 33431. **EMAIL** rinaldi@acc.fau.edu

KERTZER, DAVID ISRAEL
PERSONAL Born 02/20/1948, New York, NY, m, 1970, 2 children **DISCIPLINE** ANTHROPOLOGY **EDUCATION** Brown Univ, BA, 69; Brandeis, PhD, 74. **CAREER** William Kenan Prof of Anthropology, Bowdoin Col, 89-92; PAUL DUREE UNIV PROF, PROF OF ANTHROPOLOGY & HIST, BROWN UNIV, 92-. **HONORS AND AWARDS** Guggenheim fel; NEH fel; NSF fel; NIH fel; Center for Advanced Study in the Behavior Scis fel. **MEMBERSHIPS** PEN; Am Anthropological Asn; Soc Sci Hist Asn; Population Asn of Am; Int Union for the Sci Study of Population. **RESEARCH** European social history; politics and symbolism; anthropological population studies. **SELECTED PUBLICATIONS** Auth, Politics and Symbols: auth, The Italian Communist Party and the Fall of Communism, Yale Univ Press, 96; The Kidnapping of Edgardo Mortara, Knopf, 97; auth, Family Strategies and Changing Labour Relations, Economic and Soc Hist in the Neth, 94; auth, Class Formation and Political Mobilization in Turn-of-the-century Milan, Soc Sci Hist, 95; auth, Qualitative and Quantitative Approaches to Historical Demography, Population and Development Rev, 97; co-ed, Aging in the Past: Demography, Society, and Old Age, Univ of Calif Press, 95; coed, Italian Politics, 1996, Il Mulino, 96; coed, Anthropological Demography: Towards a New Synthesis, Univ of Chicago Press, 97; coauth, Growing up as an Abandoned Child in Nineteenth-century Italy, Hist of the Family, 97. **CONTACT ADDRESS** Dept of Anthropology, Brown Univ, Box 1921, Providence, RI, 02912. **EMAIL** David_Kertzer@brown.edu

KESELMAN, THOMAS A.
PERSONAL Born 12/21/1948, Perth, NJ, m, 1973, 3 children **DISCIPLINE** HISTORY **EDUCATION** Univ MI, Ann Arbor, PhD 79. **CAREER** Univ Notre Dame, asst prof 79-84, assoc prof 85-91, prof 92. **HONORS AND AWARDS** John Gilmart Shea Prize; NEH Fell; Guggenheim Fell. **MEMBERSHIPS** AHS; Soc for Fr Hist Stud; WSFH; ACHS; ASCH. **RESEARCH** Mod France; Modern Europe, Religious Hist. **SELECTED PUBLICATIONS** Death and Afterlife in Modern France, Prin, Prin Univ Press, 93; Miracles and Prophecies in Nineteenth Century France, New Brunswick, NJ, Rutgers Univ Press, 83; Belief in History: Innovative Approaches to European and American Religion, Notre Dame, Univ Notre Dame, 91; The Perraud Affair: Clergy, Church, and Sexual Politics in Fin-de-Siecle France, Journal of Modern Hist, 98; Religion as Enduring Theme in French Cultural Conflict, in: Memory, History and Critique: Europea Identity at the Millennium, eds, Frank Brinkhuis and Sascha Talmor, Cambridge, MIT Press, 97. **CONTACT ADDRESS** Dept of Hist, Univ of Notre Dame, Notre Dame, IN, 46656. **EMAIL** thomas.a.kselman.1@nd.edu

KESSLER, HERBERT LEON
PERSONAL Born 07/20/1941, Chicago, IL, m, 1976, 1 child **DISCIPLINE** ART HISTORY **EDUCATION** Univ Chicago, BA, 61; Princeton Univ, MFA, 63, PhD(art hist), 65. **CAREER** From asst prof art & col to prof art & New Testament & early Christian lit, Univ Chicago, 65-76, assoc chmn, Dept Art, 68-69, chmn, 73-76, univ dir of fine arts, 75-76; Prof Hist Art & Chmn Dept, 76-98, Charlotte Bloomberg Prof, Johns Hopkins Univ, 84-, Dean, Krieger Sch of Arts and Sci, 98-; mem, Int Ctr Medieval Studies, 71-; mem bd dirs, 74-76; Richard Krautheimer Guest Prof, Bibliotheca Hertziana, Rome, 96-97. **HONORS AND AWARDS** Nat Endowment for Humanities fel, 67; Herodotus fel, Inst Advan Study, Princeton, 69-70; Guggenheim fel, NY, 72-73; fel, Am Acad Learned Soc, 79-80 & Am Philos Soc, 80; sr fel, Dumbarton Oaks, Wash, 80-86; Fel, Am Acad Rome, 84-85; Fel, Medieval Acad of Am, 91; Fel, Am Acad Arts and Sci, 95-. **MEMBERSHIPS** Col Art Asn Am; Mediaeval Acad Am. **RESEARCH** Carolingian manuscript illumination; early Christian art; medieval art. **SELECTED PUBLICATIONS** Auth, French and Flemish Illuminated Manuscripts from Chicago Collections, Newberry Libr, 69; ed, Studies in Classical and Byzantine Manuscript Illumination, Univ Chicago, 71; auth, The Illustrated Bibles From Tours, Princeton Univ, 77; coauth, The Cotton Genesis, Princeton Univ Press, 86; The Frescoes of the Dura Synagogue and Christian Art, Dumbarton Oaks Studies XXVIII, Dumbarton Oaks, 90; auth, Studies in Pictorial Narrative, Pindar Press, 94; coauth, The Poetry and Paintings in the First Bible of Charles the Bald, Recentiores: Later Latin Texts and Contexts, Univ Mich Press, 97; The Holy Face and the Paradox of Representation, Villa Spelman Studies, vol 6, 98. **CONTACT ADDRESS** Sch Arts and Sci, Johns Hopkins Univ, 3400 N Charles St, Baltimore, MD, 21218-2680. **EMAIL** hlk@jhu.edu

KESSLER, S. ANN
DISCIPLINE CHURCH HISTORY, PASTORAL MINISTRY **EDUCATION** Mt Marty Col, BA, 53;Creighton Univ, Omaha, MA, 57; Univ Notre Dame, PhD, 63. **CAREER** Prof emer, Mt Marty Col; part-time prof, Hist, Geog & Polit Sci; part-time, plan giving coordr, Develop Dept & prof. **MEMBERSHIPS** Benedictine Sisters of Sacred Heart Monastery; Phi Alpha Theta; SDak Hist Soc; Yankton Hist Soc; Hist Women Relig Organ & Amer Benedictine Acad. **SELECTED PUBLICATIONS** Auth, Benedictine Men and Women of Courage: Roots and History. **CONTACT ADDRESS** Dept of Religious Studies, Mount Marty Col, 1105 W 8th St, Yankton, SD, 57078-3724. **EMAIL** akessler@rs6.mtmc.edu

KESSLER-HARRIS, ALICE
PERSONAL Born 06/02/1941, Leicester, England, m, 1982, 3 children **DISCIPLINE** HISTORY **EDUCATION** Goucher Col, AB, 61; Rutgers Univ, MA, 63, PhD, 68. **CAREER** Vis fac, Sarah Lawrence Col, 74-76; Dir, Women's Hist Prog, 75-76; Vis Sr Lecturer, Univ Warwick, 79-80; Vis Prof, SUNY, 85; Asst Prof, Hofstra Univ, 68-74; Assoc Prof, Hofstra Univ, 74-81; Prof Hist, Hofstra Univ, 81-88; Prof Hist, Temple Univ, 88-90; Prof Hist, Rutgers Univ, 90-; Prof II, 94; Dir Women's Stud, 90-95. **HONORS AND AWARDS** NEH Fellow, 76-77, 85-86; Fellow, Rockefeller Found, 88-89; Fellow, Guggenheim Mem Found, 89-90; Res Assoc, Ctr for Stud of Soc Change, 89-90; Vis Fellow, Swed Coll for Adv Stud in the Soc Sci, 91; Doctor of Laws, Honoris causa, Goucher Col, 91; Vis Fellow, Inst for Soc Res, Oslo, 94-95; Dr of Philos, honoris causa, Uppsala Univ, Sweden, 95; Fulbright Award, Aus & N Zealand, 95; Fellow, Swedish Coll for Adv Stud in Soc Sci, 97. **MEMBERSHIPS** Soc Am Hist; Am Hist Asn; Org of Am Hist; Am Stud Asn; Berkshire Conf of Women Hist; Columbia Univ Seminar in Am Civ; Columbia Univ Seminar on Women in Soc; ACLU. **RESEARCH** History, women's studies. **SELECTED PUBLICATIONS** Auth, Treating the Male as Other: Re-Defining the Parameters of Labor History, Labor Hist, 34, 190-204, 93; auth, Gendered Interventions: Exploring the Historical Roots of US Social Policy, The Jap J of Am Stud, 5, 3-22, 93-94; auth, Designing Women and Old Fools: The Construction of the Social Security Amendments of 1939, US History as Womens' History, Univ NC Press, 87-106, 95; auth, The Paradox of Motherhood: Night Work Laws in the United States, Protecting Women, Univ Ill, 95; auth, A Principle of Law but not of Justice: Men, Women, and Income Taxes in the United States, 1913-1948, S Calif, Rev of Law & Women's Stud, 6, 331-360, 97. **CONTACT ADDRESS** 141 E 88th St, NY, NY, 10128. **EMAIL** akh@rci.rutgers.edu

KESSNER, THOMAS
PERSONAL Born 12/20/1946, Germany **DISCIPLINE** HISTORY **EDUCATION** Brooklyn Col, City Univ NY, BA, 67; Columbia Univ, MA, 68, PhD(hist), 75. **CAREER** Assoc prof hist, 71-91, PROF HIST, KINGSBOROUGH COMMUNITY COL & GRAD CTR, CITY UNIV NEW YORK, 91- ; acting exec officer, PhD Prog in Hist, CUNY Graduate School and Univ Ctr. **HONORS AND AWARDS** Phi Beta Kappa; Am Coun Learned Soc fel hist, 76; Nat Endowment for Humanities fel hist, 76-77; City Univ Inst New Hist fel hist, 76; consult ethnic heritage, NY City Bd Educ Community Dist 22, 78-79; assoc dir, Hist & Humanities Prog, City Univ New York Grad Ctr, 81-; consult, Select Pres Comn Refugee & Immigration Policy & Harvard Encycl Am Ethnic Groups; Rockefeller Found res fel; Distinguished Alumnus Medal, Brooklyn Col, 89; CUNY PSC-BHE Res Award, 82-87, 91, 95-97; CUNY Fac Excellence Award, 90-96. **MEMBERSHIPS** Am Jewish Hist Soc; Orgn Am Historians; Immigrant Hist Soc. **RESEARCH** American urban history; American immigrant history; Jewish history. **SELECTED PUBLICATIONS** Auth, Gershom Mendes Seixas: A Jewish Minister, Am Jewish Hist Soc, 6/69; The Golden Door: Italian and Jewish Immigrant Mobility in New York City, 1880-1915, Oxford Univ, 1/77; coauth, Immigrant Women at Work, J Ethnic Hist, 12/77; auth, New York's Immigrants in Prosperity and Depression, In: Ravitch and Goodenow, Educating an Urban People, 81; Repatriation in American History, Report of Select Comn Refugee & Immigration Policy, 81; Today's Immigrants, Their Stories: A New Look at the Newest Americans, Oxford Univ Press, 81; Jobs, Ghettos and the Urban Economy, Am Jewish Hist, 81; auth, Fiorello H. La Guardia and the Making of Modern New York, McGraw Hill, 89; auth, Capital Metropolis: New York's Rise to Dominance, 1869-1898, Simon and Schuster, forthcoming. **CONTACT ADDRESS** Graduate School and University Center, City Univ, 33 West 42 St, New York, NY, 10036-8099.

KETCHAM, RALPH LOUIS
PERSONAL Born 10/28/1927, Berea, OH, m, 1958, 2 children **DISCIPLINE** AMERICAN STUDIES **EDUCATION** Allegheny Col, AB, 49; Colgate Univ, MA, 52; Syracuse Univ, PhD, 56. **CAREER** Res assoc polit sci, Univ Chicago, 56-60, assoc ed, Papers of James Madison, 56-60; from assoc prof to prof Am studies, 63-68, prof Am Studies, Polit Sci & Hist, Syracuse Univ, 68-, Res assoc hist & assoc ed, Papers of Benjamin Franklin, Yale Univ, 61-63, lectr, 62-63; lectr Am civilization, Tokyo Univ, 65; vis prof, Univ Tex, 67-68; vis prof Am hist, Univ Sheffield, 71-72; Fulbright lectr, India, 74; scholar-in-residence, Aspen Inst for Humanistic Studies, 75-76; Fulbright lectr, Netherlands, 87; vis prof, Public Affairs, George Mason Univ, 91; vis prof, Am Hist, Massey Univ, NZ, 98. **HONORS AND AWARDS** Hon DLitt, Allegheny Col, 85; CASE Prof of the Year, 87; Maxwell Prof of Citizenship and Public Aff, 94. **MEMBERSHIPS** Orgn Am Hist; Am Studies Asn. **RESEARCH** American intellectual history and political theory; American revolutionary and early national period. **SELECTED PUBLICATIONS** Auth, Presidents above Party: The First American Presidency, 1789-1829, Univ North Carolina, 84;

auth, Individualism and Public Life: A Modern Dilemma, Blackwell, 87; auth, Framed for Posterity: The Enduring Philosophy of the Constitution, Univ Kansas, 93. **CONTACT ADDRESS** Maxwell Sch, Syracuse Univ, Syracuse, NY, 13244. **EMAIL** rketcham@mailbox.syr.edu

KETCHUM, RICHARD J.
PERSONAL Born 05/06/1941, Lexington, KY, m **DISCIPLINE** ANCIENT PHILOSOPHY **EDUCATION** Beloit Col, BA; Albert Ludwig's Univ, 61-62; Univ Penn, PhD 71. **CAREER** Vanderbilt Univ, inst, asst prof, 68-73; Univ Rochester, vis lect, 72; Univ Cal SB, asst prof, 73-79; FL INTL Univ, vis prof, 79-80; Univ Texas, vis prof, 80-81; Univ Missouri, vis prof, 81-83; Lindenwood Col, asst prof, 83-85; New Mexico State Univ, asst prof, assoc prof, 85 to 91-. **MEMBERSHIPS** APA; SAGP **RESEARCH** Ancient philosophy **SELECTED PUBLICATIONS** Auth, Philosophy is not a Trivial Pursuit, coauth, Champaign, Stipes Pub, 97; Plato: Parmenides, trans by Mary Louise Gill and Paul Ryan, in: Can Philo Rev, IN, Hackett Pub, 96; Companions to Ancient Thought: Language, ed, Steven Everson, Cambridge, Cambridge Univ Press, 94; in: Ancient Philo, 96; On the Impossibility of Epistemology, Philosophical Studies: Ab Intl Jour for the Analytic Tradition, 97;C. S. Pierce on Naturalism, Philosophia Scientiae: Travaux d' Histoire et de Phil des Sciences, Archives Cen d'Etudes et de Recherche Henri Poine, 96. **CONTACT ADDRESS** Dept of Philosophy, New Mexico State Univ, Las Cruces, NM, 88003. **EMAIL** rketchum@nmsu.edu

KETT, JOSEPH FRANCIS
PERSONAL Born 03/11/1938, Brooklyn, NY, m, 1965, 2 children **DISCIPLINE** AMERICAN HISTORY, HISTORY OF EDUCATION **EDUCATION** Holy Cross Col, AB, 59; Harvard Univ, MA, 60, PhD (hist), 64. **CAREER** Instr hist, Harvard Univ, 65-66; from asst prof to assoc prof, 66-76, prof hist, Univ VA, 76-, mem panel on youth, President's Sci Adv Coun, 71-72, chair, hist dept, 85-90. **MEMBERSHIPS** Orgn Am Hist. **RESEARCH** American social and intellectual history; history of education. **SELECTED PUBLICATIONS** Auth, The Formation of the American Medical Profession, Yale Univ, 68; Adolescence and youth in nineteenth century America, J Interdisciplinary Hist, 71; Growing up in rural New England, 1800-1840, in: Anonymous Americans, Prentice-Hall, 72; Rites of Passage: Adolescence in America, 1790 to the Present, Basic Bk, 77; The perils of precocity, in: Turning Points, Univ Chicago Press, 78; The Adolescence of Vocational Education, Stanford Univ Press, 82; The Pursuit of Knowledge Under Difficulties: From Self Improvement to Adult Education in America, 1750-1990, Stanford Univ Press, 94; co-auth, The Enduring Vision: A History of the American People, Houghton Mifflin, 96; Dictionary of Cultural Literacy, 93. **CONTACT ADDRESS** Dept of History, Univ of Virginia, 1 Randall Hall, Charlottesville, VA, 22903-3244. **EMAIL** jfk9v@virginia.edu

KETTNER, JAMES HAROLD
PERSONAL Born 10/04/1944, Greenville, OH **DISCIPLINE** AMERICAN HISTORY **EDUCATION** Harvard Univ, AB, 66, PhD(hist), 73; Univ Sussex, BA, 68. **CAREER** Actg asst prof, 73-74, lectr, 74-77, asst prof to assoc prof, 77-90, PROF HIST, UNIV CALIF, BERKELEY, 90-; Mem, Joint Comt Proj 87, Am Hist Asn/Am Polit Sci Asn, 78-80. **HONORS AND AWARDS** Jamestown Prize, Inst Early Am Hist & Cult, 75. **MEMBERSHIPS** AHA; Orgn Am Historians; Am Soc Legal Hist; Asn Marshall Scholars Alumni. **RESEARCH** American colonial & early national periods; American legal history. **SELECTED PUBLICATIONS** Auth, The development of American citizenship in the Revolutionary Era: the idea of volitional allegiance, Am J Legal Hist, 7/74; Subjects or citizens? A note on British views respecting the legal effects of American independence, Va Law Rev, 6/76; The Development of American Citizenship, 1608-1870, Univ NC, 78; Persons or Property? The Pleasants Slaves in the Virginia Courts, 1792-1799, In: Launching the Extended Republic: The Federalist Era, Univ Va, 96. **CONTACT ADDRESS** Dept of History, Univ of California, Berkeley, 3229 Dwinelle Hall, Berkeley, CA, 94720-2551.

KEUCHEL, EDWARD F.
PERSONAL Born 09/20/1934, Kansas City, KS, m, 1967, 2 children **DISCIPLINE** HISTORY **EDUCATION** Rockhurst Col, BS, 56; Univ KS, MA, 61; Cornell Univ, PhD, 70. **CAREER** Instr, hist, OH State Univ, 65-68; asst prof, 68-74, assoc prof, 74-81, PROF, HISTORY, FL STATE UNIV, 81-. **MEMBERSHIPS** FL Hist Soc; Southern Hist Soc; Oral Hist Asn. **RESEARCH** FL hist; US military hist. **SELECTED PUBLICATIONS** Co-auth, Civil War Marine: A Diary of the Red River Expedition, 1864, 75; co-auth, American Economic History: From Abundance to Constraint, 81; auth, A History of Columbia County Florida, 81; Florida: Enterprise Under the Sun, 90; Family, Community, Business Enterprise: The Millers of Crescent City, Florida, 97. **CONTACT ADDRESS** Dept of Hist, Florida State Univ, Tallahassee, FL, 32306-2200. **EMAIL** ekeuchel@mailer.fsu.edu

KEVERN, JOHN
DISCIPLINE CHURCH HISTORY **EDUCATION** Univ Paris-Sorbonne, Dipl Sup, 74; Univ Ill, BA, 75; Gen Theol Sem, MDiv, 80; Univ Chicago Divinity Sch, PhD, 97. **CA-**

REER Asst prof, Cooke Ch of Hist Theol, Bexley Hall Sem, 92-; dean, Bexley Hall Sem, 96. **SELECTED PUBLICATIONS** Auth, The Future of Anglican Theology, Anglican Theol Rev 75th Anniversary Ed, 94; Form in Tragedy: A Study in the Methodology of Hans Urs von Balthasar, In Communio, 94; The Fullness of Catholic Identity, In The Anglican Cath, 96; The Trinity and the Search for Justice, Anglican Theol Rev, 97. **CONTACT ADDRESS** Hist, Theol, Soc Dept, Trinity Lutheran Sem, 2199 E Main St, Columbus, OH, 43209-2334. **EMAIL** jkevern@trinity.capital.edu

KEVLES, DANIEL JEROME
PERSONAL Born 03/02/1939, Philadelphia, PA, m, 1961, 2 children **DISCIPLINE** MODERN AMERICAN HISTORY; HISTORY OF SCIENCE **EDUCATION** Princeton Univ, BA, 60, PhD(hist), 64. **CAREER** From asst prof to assoc prof, 64-78, exec officer humanities, 78-81, prof hist, Calif Inst Technol, 78-, Nat Sci Found grant, 65, 73-74 & 78-80; Old Dom fel, Calif Inst Technol, 66-67; consult, Ranger Hist Proj, Jet Propulsion Lab, 72-77; Am Coun Learned Soc grant-in-aid, 73; vis res fel, Univ Sussex, 76; fel panel, Nat Sci Found, 78; vis prof, Univ Pa, 79; fel, Charles Warren Ctr, Harvard Univ, 81-82; adv ed, Isis, 81-; Nat Endowment Humanities sr fel, 81-82; Guggenheim fel, 82-83; mem coun, Hist Sci Soc, 80-82. **HONORS AND AWARDS** Nat Hist Soc Prize, 79; Page One Award, 84. **MEMBERSHIPS** Orgn Am Historians AAAS (pres, 83); Am Asn Hist Medicine. **RESEARCH** The social and political history of modern science, especially in the United States; history of physics, genetics and eugenics. **SELECTED PUBLICATIONS** Auth, The Physicists, Knopf, 78; The Code of Codes: Scientific and Social Issues in the Human Genome Project, edited with Leroy Hood, Cambridge: Harvard University Press, 92; paperback, 93; published in Germany, Artemis and Winkler, spring, 94; Japan, Ague Shotu-Sha, 97; The Baltimore Case: A Trial of Politics, Science, and Character; Norton, 98. **CONTACT ADDRESS** Div of Humanities & Soc Sci, California Inst of Tech, 1201 E California, Pasadena, CA, 91125-0002. **EMAIL** kevles@cco.caltech.edu

KEYLOR, WILLIAM ROBERT
PERSONAL Born 08/15/1944, Sacramento, CA, m, 1968 **DISCIPLINE** MODERN EUROPEAN HISTORY **EDUCATION** Stanford Univ, BA, 66; Columbia Univ, MA, 67, cert & PhD, 71. **CAREER** Lectr mod hist, Rutgers Univ, Newark, 68-69; lectr Am studies, Univ Paris, Vincennes, 69-70; instr mod hist, Rutgers Univ, 70-72; asst prof, 72-75, assoc prof, 75-79, PROF MOD HIST, BOSTON UNIV, 80-; Vis assoc prof, Mass Inst Technol, 79-80. **HONORS AND AWARDS** Chevalier de L'Ordre National du Merite (France). **MEMBERSHIPS** Soc Fr Hist Studies; AHA; AAUP. **RESEARCH** Modern French history; European diplomatic history; Franco-American relations since 1919. **SELECTED PUBLICATIONS** Auth, Academy and Community: The Foundation of the French Historical Profession, Harvard Univ, 75; co-ed, From Parnassus: Essays in Honors of Jacques Barzun, 76 & auth, Clio on trial: Charles Peguy as historical critic, in From Parnassus: Essays in Honor of Jacques Barzun, 76, Harper & Row; Jacques Bainville and the Renaissance of Royalist History in Twentieth Century France, La State Univ, 79; Prohibition Diplomacy: An Incident of Franco-American Misunderstanding, French Civilization, spring 81; The Twentieth Century World: An International History, 3rd ed, 96; ed, The Legacy of the Great War: Peacemaking, 1919, 97. **CONTACT ADDRESS** Dept of Hist, Boston Univ, 226 Bay State Rd, Boston, MA, 02215-1403. **EMAIL** wrkeylor@bu.edu

KEYSSAR, ALEXANDER
DISCIPLINE HISTORY **EDUCATION** Harvard Col, BA, 69; Harvard Univ, PhD, 77. **CAREER** Tutor, Harvard Univ, 71-73; instr, Fed State County, Municipal Employees, NY, 74; asst prof, Mass Inst Tech, 76-77; asst prof, Brandeis Univ, 77-85; vis scholar, Russel Sage Fdn, 85-86; asst prof, 86-87, assoc prof, 87-91, Duke Univ; guest dir d'Edtudes, L'Ecole Hautes Etudes Scis Soc, Paris, 91-95; prof, Mass Inst Tech, 91-93; prof, Duke Univ, 92-97; PROF HIST, PUB POLICY, DUKE UNIV, 97. **CONTACT ADDRESS** History Dept, Duke Univ, 223 Carr Bldg, Durham, NC, 27708.

KHODARKOVSKY, MICHAEL
PERSONAL Born 02/12/1955, Kiev, Yugoslavia, m **DISCIPLINE** HISTORY **EDUCATION** Univ Chicago, PhD, 87. **CAREER** Assoc prof, Loyola Univ-Chicago, 91-; NEH, 96; Fulbright-Hays, 83; Woodrow Wilson Ctr, 82-83; NCREER, 97. **RESEARCH** Russian Imperial and Early Modern History. **CONTACT ADDRESS** 726 W Melrose St, Chicago, IL, 60657. **EMAIL** mkhodar@orion.it.luc.edu

KHOURY, PHILIP S.
PERSONAL Born 10/15/1949, Washington, DC, m, 1980 **DISCIPLINE** HISTORY **EDUCATION** Trinity Col, BA, 71; Harvard Univ, PhD, 80. **CAREER** From asst prof to prof and dean, Mass Inst of Technol, 81-. **HONORS AND AWARDS** Pi Gamma Mu, 71; T.J. Watson Fel, 71; Nat Defense Foreign Langs Fels, 71-72, 73-74, 77-78; St Antony's Col Assoc, Univ of Oxford, 74-75, 76-77; Fulbright Scholar, 76-77; Soc Sci Res Coun Post-doctoral Fel, 83-84; Mellon Fel, 84-85; Class of 1922 Career Develop Prof, M.I.T., 84-86; G. Louis Beer Prize,

AHA, 87; Navas Award, M.I.T., 90, 92; Pres, Middle East Studies Asn of North Am, 98. **MEMBERSHIPS** Brit Soc for Middle Eastern Studies; Middle East Inst; Am Asn for the Advancement of Sci; Middle East Studies Asn. **SELECTED PUBLICATIONS** Auth, Urban Notables and Arab Nationalism, 83; Syria and the French Mandate, 87; coed, Tribes and State Formation in the Middle East, 90; Recovering Beirut: Urban Design and Post-war Reconstruction, 93; The Modern Middle East: A Reader, 93. **CONTACT ADDRESS** Dean's Office, Sch of Humanities and Social Science, 77 Mass Inst of Tech, E51-255, Cambridge, MA, 02139. **EMAIL** khoury@mit.edu

KIAH, RUTH JOSEPHINE
PERSONAL Born 04/16/1927, Elkhart, IN, m, 1980 **DISCIPLINE** EDUCATION **EDUCATION** Wayne State University, Detroit, MI, BS, 1948, MEd, 1954, EdD, 1975. **CAREER** Mercy College Reading Methods Course, instr, 1966-67, consultant, 1962-74, facilitator of change needs assessment trainer & problem analysis for school staff, 1974-83; Detroit Public Schools, Office of Adult Cont Educ, coordinator, 1967-72, dept of staff devel & tchr training, tchr corps coordinator, 1972-; teacher, Detroit Public Schools MGT Academy, on camera teacher reading, 1962-67, WTVS 56; administrative asst, 1968-84; Wayne State University, Detroit, MI, executive director of Detroit Center for Professional Growth and Development, 1984-, adjunct associate professor, 1985-. **HONORS AND AWARDS** Award in recognition & of creativity pioneering spirit & serv to youth Womens Fellowship & Youth Ministry Plymouth United Ch of Christ Detroit 1971; Quarterly Publications Professional Development Programs with Thematic Inservice Modules 1984-; A Multi Faceted Approach to Staff Development and Its Relationship to Student Achievement 1975; Distinguished Contribution to Field Reading Instruction, Wayne County Reader Assn, 1988; Distinguished Alumna, Wayne State University, 1988; Outstanding Service Award, Friends International Institute, 1990. **MEMBERSHIPS** Mem Women's Economic Club, 1982; board of directors, membership chairperson, secretary, 1978-91, Friends International Institute; board of directors Michigan Coalition of Staff Development and School Improvement 1987-92; board of directors Effective Instruction Consortium 1987-91; mem Assn of Supervisors and Curriculum, 1980-; mem Phi Delta Kappa, Wayne State University Chapter 1985-; executive board, Michigan Coalition for Staff Development and School Improvement, 1984-; faculty advisory/member, Phi Lambda Theta, 1986-. **SELECTED PUBLICATIONS** Author of several books. **CONTACT ADDRESS** Detroit Ctr for Prof Growth & Devel, Wayne State Univ, 114 College of Education, Detroit, MI, 48202.

KICKLIGHTER, JOSEPH ALLEN
PERSONAL Born 08/14/1945, Macon, GA **DISCIPLINE** HISTORY **EDUCATION** Univ the South, BA 67; Emory Univ, MA, 70, PhD(medieval hist), 73. **CAREER** Instr social studies, Woodward Acad, 73-75; from Asst Prof to Assoc Prof, 75-91, PROF HIST, AUBURN UNIV, 91-. **MEMBERSHIPS** Mediaeval Acad Am; AHA. **RESEARCH** Anglo-French relations in the High and Late Middle Ages; Medieval French royal institutions; the Papacy in the late Middle Ages. **SELECTED PUBLICATIONS** Auth, La Carriere de Beraud de Got, Annales du Midi, 73; An unknown brother of Pope Clement V, Mediaeval Studies, 76; French jurisdictional supremacy in Gascony: One aspect of the ducal government's response, J Medieval Hist, 79; Les monasteres de gascogne et le conflit Franco-Anglais, 1270-1327, Annales du Midi, 79; English Bordeaux in Conflict: the Execution of Pierre Vigier de la Rouselle and its Aftermath, J Medieval Hist, 83; The Parlement of Paris, Dictionary of the Middle Ages, 87; Arnaud Caillau: Maire de Bordeaux et officier d'Edouard II, Annales du Midi, 87; The Nobility of English Gascony: the Case of Jourdain de l'Isle, J Medieval Hist, 87; English Legal Representatives at the Parlement of Paris, 1259-1337, In: Documenting the Past: Essays in Honor of G.P. Cuttino, 89; The Abbey of Sainte-Croix de Bordeaux versus the King of England/Duke of Aquitaine Phillipps Charter 6 in the John Rylands Library, Bulletin of the John Rylands Library, 90; English Gascony, The Parlement of Paris and the Origins of the Hundred Years War, 1330-1337, Sewanee Medieval Studies, 90; Appeal, Negotiation and Conflict: The Evolution of an Anglo-French Legal Relationship during the Hundred Years War, Proceedings of the Western Soc for Fr Hist, 90. **CONTACT ADDRESS** Dept of History, Auburn Univ, Auburn, AL, 36849. **EMAIL** kicklja@mail.auburn.edu

KICZA, JOHN EDWARD
PERSONAL Born 07/29/1947, Northhampton, MA, m, 1980, 2 children **DISCIPLINE** LATIN AMERICAN & SOCIAL HISTORY **EDUCATION** Amherst Col, BA, 69; Univ Mass, MA, 73; Univ Calif, Los Angeles, PhD(hist), 79. **CAREER** Instr hist, Univ Santa Clara, 77-78; asst prof, Loyola Marymount Univ, 79-80; from asst prof to prof, 80-96, Edward R. Meyer Distinguished Professor Hist, Wash State Univ, 96-. **MEMBERSHIPS** AHA; Conf Latin Am Hist; Latin Am Studies Asn; Pac Coast Coun Latin Am Studies. **RESEARCH** Social history of Latin America; race relations in the history of the Americas; colonial Mexico. **SELECTED PUBLICATIONS** Auth, Colonial urban social history: The case of Mexico, Proc Rocky Mt Coun Latin Am Studies, 79; The Pulque Trade of Late Colonial Mexico City, The Americas, 10/80;

Mexican demographic history of the nineteenth century, Statist Abstract Latin Am, 81; Women and business life in late colonial Mexico City, J Univ Autonoma Metropolitana, Azcapotzalco, 81; The great families of Mexico: Elite maintenance and business, Hisp Am Hist Rev, 8/82; Colonial Entrepreneurs: Families and Business in Bourbon Mexico City, Univ NMex Press, 83; auth, The Social and Ethnic Historiography of Colonial Latin America: The Last Twenty Years, William and Mary Quart, 3rd series, July 88; auth, Patterns in Early Spanish Overseas Expansion, William and Mary Quart, 3rd series, April 92; ed, The Indian in Latin American History: Resistence, Resilience, and Acculturation, Schol Resources, 93; auth, The Social and Political Position of Spanish Immigrants in Bourbon America and the Origins of the Independence Movements, Colonial Latin Am Rev, 4:1, 95; auth, The Native Peoples and Civilizations of the Americas Before Contact, Washington DC: Am Hist Asn Essays on Global and Comparitive Hist, 98. **CONTACT ADDRESS** Dept of Hist, Wash State Univ, PO Box 644030, Pullman, WA, 99164-4030. **EMAIL** jekicza@wsu.edu

KIDWELL, CLARA SUE
PERSONAL Born 07/08/1941, Tahlequah, OK **DISCIPLINE** HISTORY OF SCIENCE **EDUCATION** BA, letters, 62; MA, history of science, 63; PhD, history of science, 70. **CAREER** Instr history, Kansas City Art Inst, 68-69; instr social sci, Haskell Jr Coll, 70-72; asst prof Amer Indian Studies, Univ Minnesota, 72-74; assoc to full prof Native Amer Studies, Univ Calif Berkeley, 74-93; asst dir cultural resources, Natl Museum Amer Indian, Smithsonian Inst, 93-95; prof history, dir Native Amer Studies, Univ Oklahoma, 95-. **HONORS AND AWARDS** Rockefeller Found Fel, 75-76; summer res fel, Smithsonian Inst, 84; Newberry Library Summer Res Fel, 84; Humanities Res Inst Fellowship, Univ Calif Irvine, spring 92. **MEMBERSHIPS** Amer Hist Assn; Org Amer Historians; Amer Soc Ethnohistory. **RESEARCH** History of Choctaw Indians; Amer Indian science and technology. **SELECTED PUBLICATIONS** Auth, "Choctaws and Missionaries in Mississippi Before 1830," American Indian Culture and Research Journ, vol XI, no 2, 87; auth, "Systems of Knowledge," in America in 1492, 91; auth, "Indian Women as Cultural Mediators," Ethnohistory, spring 92; auth, "Choctaw Women as Cultural Mediators," Ethnohistory, spring 92; auth, "Choctaw Women and Cultural Persistence in Mississippi," in Negotiators of Change: Historical Perspectives on Native American Women, 95; auth, Choctaws and Missionaries in Mississippi 1818-1918, 95. **CONTACT ADDRESS** 455 W Lindsey, Rm 804, Norman, OK, 73019. **EMAIL** cskidwell@ou.edu

KIECKHEFER, RICHARD
PERSONAL Born 06/01/1946, Minneapolis, MN, m, 1986, 2 children **DISCIPLINE** PHILOSOPHY, HISTORY **EDUCATION** Saint Louis Univ, BA, 68; Univ Tex Austin, MA Philos, 70; PhD Hist, 72. **CAREER** Instr, Univ Tex Austin, 73-74; lectr, 74; asst prof, Philips Univ, 75; asst prof, 75-79; assoc prof, 79-84, Prof, Northwest Univ, 84-. **HONORS AND AWARDS** Tchg citation from Council for Advancement and Support of Education, 82, 83; Nat Endowment for the Humanities Fel, 87-88; Guggenheim Found Fel, 92-93; Fel of Medieval Acad Of Am, 98. **MEMBERSHIPS** Medieval Acad Of Am; Am Soc of Church Hist; An Acad of Rel; Societas Magica. **RESEARCH** Late medieval religious culture-including mystical theology, magic and witchcraft, and church architecture to parish religion. **SELECTED PUBLICATIONS** Auth, The holy and the unholy: sainthood, witchcraft, and magic in late medieval Europe, J of Medieval And Renaissance Studies, 94; The specific rationality of medieval magi, Am Hist Rev, 94; Forbidden Rites: A Necromancer's manual of the fifteenth Century, 98; The office of inquisition and medieval heresy: the transition from personal to institutional jurisdiction, J of Ecclesiastical Hist, 95; Avenging the blood of children: anxiety over child victims and the origins of the European witch trials, the Devil, Heresy and Witchcraft in the Middle Ages: Essays in Honor of Jeffrey B Russel, 98; The Devils' contemplative: the Liber iuratus, the Liber visionum, and Christian appropriation of Jewish occultism, Conjuring Spirits: Texts and Traditions of Medieval Ritual magic, 98. **CONTACT ADDRESS** Dept of Religion, Northwestern Univ, 1940 Sheridan Rd, Evanston, IL, 60208-4050.

KIEFT, DAVID
DISCIPLINE HISTORY **EDUCATION** Univ Calif Berkeley, PhD, 66. **CAREER** Assoc prof **RESEARCH** Diplomatic history; German history. **SELECTED PUBLICATIONS** Auth, Belgium'S Return to Neutrality, 72. **CONTACT ADDRESS** History Dept, Univ of Minnesota, Twin Cities, 614 Social Sciences Tower, 267 19th Ave. S, Minneapolis, MN, 55455. **EMAIL** kieft001@tc.umn.edu

KIESWETTER, JAMES KAY
PERSONAL Born 03/08/1942, Dodge City, KS **DISCIPLINE** FRENCH & MODERN EUROPEAN HISTORY **EDUCATION** Univ Colo, Boulder, BM, 63, MA, 65, PhD(hist), 68. **CAREER** From asst prof to assoc prof, 68-76, prof hist, Eastern Wash Univ, 76-, Nat Endowment for Humanities summer stipend, 69; Am Philos Soc grant, 69. em exam comt, Educ Testing Serv Col Level Exam Prog, 72-. **MEMBERSHIPS** AHA; Soc Fr Hist Studies; Western Soc Fr Hist. **RESEARCH** French Restoration; French Revolution and Napoleon; 19th century European diplomatic history. **SELECTED PUBLICATIONS** Auth, French diplomacy at the congresses of Troppau and Laiback, Can J Hist, 9/69; ed, Documents Illustrative of the Origin, Development and Application of Metternich's Intervention Policy at the Congresses of Troppau and Laiback, Eastern Wash State Col, 70; auth, Metternich and the Bourbon succession 1819-1820, E Europ Quart, 9/72; France and the American Revolution, Historians Bicentennial Newslett, 3/75; Etienne-Denis Pasquier: The Last Chancellor of France, Am Philos Soc, 77; War and American Society 1914-1975, Geront Uses Hist, Fed Admin Aging, 81. Auth, The Imperial Restoration, The Historian, November 82; auth, 109 articles in: Historical Dictionary of France from the 1815 Restoration to the Second Empire, Greenwood Press, 87; auth, articles on Napoleon I, and French Revolutionary-Napoleonic Wars, In: International Military and Defence Encyclopedia, Pergamon-Brassey, 93; auth, articles on French Revolutionary-Napoleonic Wars, and Napoleon I, In: Brassey's Encyclopedia of Military History and Biography, Brassey, 94. **CONTACT ADDRESS** Dept of Hist, Eastern Washington Univ, M/S 27, Cheney, WA, 99004-2496.

KIGER, JOSEPH CHARLES
PERSONAL Born 08/19/1920, Covington, KY, m, 2 children **DISCIPLINE** HISTORY **EDUCATION** Birmingham-Southern Col, AB, 43; Univ Ala, MA, 47; Vanderbilt Univ, PhD, 50. **CAREER** Instr hist, Univ Ala, 50 & Wash Univ, 50-51; dir res, House Select Comt Investigate Found, 52-53; staff assoc, Am Coun Educ, 53-55; asst dir, Southern Fel Fund, 55-58; assoc prof hist, Univ Ala, 58-61; chm dept, 69-74, PROF HIST, UNIV MISS, 61-, Guggenheim fel, 60-61; Rockefeller grant, 61; consult on philanthropists, Dictionary of American Biography, 68-; Am Coun Learned Soc grant, 80. **MEMBERSHIPS** AHA; Org Am Historians; Southern Hist Asn. **RESEARCH** Intellectual and social history; history of philanthropy; history of educational and research institutions. **SELECTED PUBLICATIONS** Auth, Operating Principles of the Larger Foundations, Russell Sage, 54; coauth, Sponsored Research Policy of Colleges and Universities, Am Coun Educ, 54; Am Learned Societies, Pub Affairs, 63; Inovation in Education, In: Foundation Support of Educational Innovation by Learned Societies, Councils and Institutes, Columbia Univ, 64; Disciplines and American Learned Societies, In: Encyclopedia of Education, MacMillan, 71; Frederick P Keppel, In: Dictionary of American Biography, 73 & Learned Societies, In: Dictionary of American History, 76, Scribner's; ed, Research Institutions and Learned Societies, Greenwood, 82. **CONTACT ADDRESS** Dept of History, Univ Miss, University, MS, 38677.

KIKUCHI, AKIRA
DISCIPLINE HISTORY **EDUCATION** Hokkaido Univ, PhD, 65. **CAREER** Prof, PROF EMER, LIB ARTS, OTARU UNIV COM; PROF EMER, HIST, SEISHU UNIV. **MEMBERSHIPS** Am Antiquarian Soc **SELECTED PUBLICATIONS** Auth, The Original Version of Faulkner's "Sanctuary": A Study Through the Manuscript and the Typescript; "Participating Constructions on Hemingway's Works," Current Eng Stud, 67; auth, "Contact Between Two Different Cultures: A Comparative Study Between John Smith's Expeditions and Takeshiro Matsuura's Explorations, Lang Stud 2, Otaru Univ Commerce, 94; auth, "John Smith and Takeshiro Matsuura: A Study From a Comparative Cultural Viewpoint," The Rev of Seishu Univ 1, 94; auth, "The Life of John Smith: With Some Literary Historical Problems Concerning the Pocahontas Episode," Jour of Seisha Univ. 2, 95; auth, "The Formation of Colonial Chesapeake Society: With Inquiries into The Cavalier Myth," Jour of Seisha Univ. 3, 96. **CONTACT ADDRESS** Minami-ku, Sapporo, ., 005.

KILLEN, LINDA
PERSONAL Born 04/02/1945, Washington, DC, s **DISCIPLINE** DIPLOMATIC HISTORY **EDUCATION** Univ N Carolina, PhD 75, MA 71; Univ Wisconsin Madison, BA honors 66. **CAREER** Radford Univ, prof 76-; Univ N Carolina CH, lectr 75-76. **HONORS AND AWARDS** SCHEV Outstanding Tchg Awd nom; Fulbright Res Gnt; Woodrow Wilson Gnt; Radford Foun Gnt; Donald Dedmon Awd for Excell., Photo Exhibition, Flossie Martin Gallery 98, Local Black History **MEMBERSHIPS** SHAFR; VSHT; NRVHS; RHF. **RESEARCH** Diplomatic; Local. **SELECTED PUBLICATIONS** Auth, Variations on New World Order: Eastern Europe as a Factor in Past present and Future US-Soviet/Russian Relations, The Soviet and Post-Soviet Rev, 95; auth, Testing the Peripheries: US Econ Relations with Interwar Yugoslavia, Boulder, E Euro Mono Series, 94; auth, Life At Pepper's Ferry, 1826-1865, taken from ledger accounts, compiled and ed, 97; auth, Radford's Early Black Residents 1880-1925, compiled, 97; auth, Freedmen's Bureau: Reports of Charles S. Schaeffer 1866-1868, ed, 97; These People live in a Pleasant Valley: A History of Slave and Freedmen in Nineteenth Century Pulaski County, Radford, A&S Occasional Pub, 96; auth, The Wharton's Town: New River Depot 1870-1940, A&S Occasional Pub, 94. **CONTACT ADDRESS** Dept of History, Radford Univ, Radford, VA, 24142. **EMAIL** lkillen@runet.edu

KILMER, ANNE DRAFFKORN
PERSONAL Born 06/01/1931, Chicago, IL, d, 1 child **DISCIPLINE** ANCIENT NEAR EASTERN HISTORY & LITERATURE **EDUCATION** State Univ Iowa, BA, 53; Univ Pa, PhD(Assyriol), 59. **CAREER** Res asst assyriol, Orient Inst, Chicago, 57-63; vis lectr, 63-64, from asst prof to assoc prof, 65-72, chmn, Dept Near Eastern Studies, 70-72, 89-91, 97-; dean humanities, Col Lett & Sci, 72-76 & 80-82, chmn, Berkeley Academic Senate, 91-92; prof Near Eastern Studies, Univ Calif, Berkeley, 72-, Guggenheim fel, 61-63; Am Asn Univ Women res fel, 64-65; Humanities Inst res grant & fel, Univ Calif, Berkeley, 67, 69, 70, 76, 79 & 82; Nat Endowment for Humanities res grant studies in Ancient music, Univ Calif, Berekeley, 76-77. **MEMBERSHIPS** Am Schs Orient Res; Am Orient Soc. **RESEARCH** Ancient Mesopotamian music, games and entertainment; Sumero-Akkadian lexical texts; Sumero-Akkadian literature and mythology. **SELECTED PUBLICATIONS** Coauth, Materialien zum Sumerischen Lexikon, Vol VIII/1, 60 & Vol VIII/2, 63, Pontif Bibl Inst; auth, The Mesopotamian Concept of Overpopulation and its Solution as Reflected in the Mythology, Orientalia, 72; Symbolic gestures, J Am Oriental Soc, 74; Akkadian Contracts from Alalakh and Ugarit: Another Interpretation, Rev Assyriologie, 74; coauth, Sounds from Silence: Recent Discoveries in Ancient Near Eastern Music (bk and 12 inch stereo rec), Bit Enki Pulb, 76; Note on overlooked word play in Akkadian Gilgamesh, In: Zikir Shumim, Leiden, 82; Musik, Reallexikon der Assyriologie VIII, pp. 463-482, 95; Fugal Features of Atrahasis: The Birth Theme, Mesopotamian Poetic Language: Sumerian and Akkadian, Proceedings of the Groningen Group for the Study of Mesopotamian Literature, Vol 2, Styx Publications, pp 127-139, 96. **CONTACT ADDRESS** Dept of Near Eastern Studies, Univ of Calif, 250 Barrows Hall, Berkeley, CA, 94720-1941. **EMAIL** adkilmer@uc.link4.berkeley.edu

KILMKO, RONALD
DISCIPLINE MUSIC **EDUCATION** Milton Col, BA; Univ Wis Madison, MA, PhD. **CAREER** Prof. Hartford Univ. **HONORS AND AWARDS** Ed, Int Double Reed Soc. **SELECTED PUBLICATIONS** Auth, Bassoon Performance Practices & Teaching in the United States & Canada, 74; co-auth, Bassoon Performance & Teaching Materials, Techniques & Methods, 93. **CONTACT ADDRESS** Lionel Hampton Sch Music, Univ Idaho, 415 W 6th St, Moscow, ID, 83844.

KILPATRICK, ROSS S.
PERSONAL Born 10/03/1934, Toronto, ON, Canada, m, 1960, 3 children **DISCIPLINE** CLASSICS **EDUCATION** Univ Toronto, BA, 57, MA 64; Yale Univ, MA, 65, PhD, 67. **CAREER** Tchr, East York Collegiate, 57-64; instr, 67-68, asst prof, classics, 68-70, Yale Univ; assoc prof, 70-85, actg head dept, 84, asst to VP, 85, head dept, 85-95, prof, Queen's Univ, 85- . **HONORS AND AWARDS** OVATIO, Classical Assoc of the Middle West and South, 96. **MEMBERSHIPS** Am Philol Asn; Class Asn Can; Class Asn Middle West and South; Int Soc for Class Tradition; Ontario Class Asn; Soc of Fel of Am Acad in Rome; Vergilian Soc Am. **RESEARCH** Latin and Greek literature; classical tradition in Renaissance art and in English and Canadian literature. **SELECTED PUBLICATIONS** Ed, Smethurst, Classics at Queens: A Short History, Queen's Univ, 93; auth, In Praise of Nurses: T.R. Glover, Queen's Q, 94; auth, The Sea Took Pity, Studies, 95; auth, The Stuff of Doors and Dreams, Vergilius, 95; auth, Old Friends and Good Temper: T.R. Glover and Horace, Arethusa, 95; auth, Fortuna Regum: An Anonymous Landscape in the Bader Collection at Queen's, Int J for Class Trad, 97; auth, Yoshio Markino: A London Portfolio, Queen's Q, 97; auth, Yoshio Markino in the West London Hospital, J of Med Biog, 97; auth, A Missed Literary Source for Sir Charles G.D. Roberts' Out of Pompeii, Can Poetry, 97; auth, Giorgione's Tempest and the Flight of Hagar, Artibus et Historiae, 97; auth, Amicus Medicus: Medicine and Epicurean Therapy in Lucretius, Mem of the Am Acad in Rome, 97; ed, Sir Charles G D Roberts' Orion, and Other Poems, Canadian Poetry, forthcoming 98; auth, Education, Culture, and the Classics in Haliburton's Nova Scotia, Stud in Honor of Margaret Thomson, in Cahiers des Etudes Class, forth 98; auth, Nam Unguentum Dabo: Catullus 13 and Servius' Unguent of Phaon, Class Q, 98; auth, Horace, Vergil,and the Jews of Rome, Dionysius, forthcoming 98; auth, T R Glover at Queen's, Class Views, forthcoming 98; auth, Winnie-the-Pooh and the Canadian Connection, Queen's Q, forthcoming 98. **CONTACT ADDRESS** Dept of Classics, Queen's Univ, Kingston, ON, K7L 3N6. **EMAIL** kilpatri@post.queensu.ca

KILPATRICK, THOMAS L.
PERSONAL Born 11/27/1937, Springville, TN, s **DISCIPLINE** HIGHER EDUCATION **EDUCATION** Vanderbilt Univ, PhD, 82 **CAREER** Asst educ librn, 64-75, Ill Librn, 1975-1993; ACCESS SVCS LIBRN, 92-, SOUTHERN ILL UNIV, CARBONDALE. **HONORS AND AWARDS** Ill Asn Col, Res Librs Acad Librn Year, 98; MCB Univ Press Award Exc, 97; SO Ill Univ Libr Aff Outstanding Fac Award. **MEMBERSHIPS** ALA, Ill Lib Asn. **RESEARCH** Ill lit, libr resource sharing; libr computer applications. **SELECTED PUBLICATIONS** Auth, Illinois! Illinois! An Annotated Bibliography of Fiction: A Twenty-Year Supplement, 1976-1996; Ill State Libr, 98; auth, Microcomputers and Libraries: A Bibliographic Sourcebook, 1986-1989, Scarecrow Press, 90;

co-auth, Cutting Out the Middle- Man: Patron-Initiated Interlibrary Loans, Library Trends 46, Oct 98; auth, A Critical Look at the Availability of Gay and Lesbian Periodical Literature in Libraries and Standard Indexing Services, Serials Rev 22, Winter 96; co-auth, Serial Cuts and Interlibrary Loan: Filling in the Gaps, Interlending & Document Supply 24, no 1, 96; auth, Tales of the Windy City, Libr J 120, June 95. **CONTACT ADDRESS** 106 S Mark Ct, Carbondale, IL, 62901. **EMAIL** tkilpatr@lib.siu.edu

KIM, HYUNG KOOK
DISCIPLINE RURAL DEVELOPMENT **EDUCATION** Lewis and Clark Col, BA; Korea Univ, BS; John Hopkins Univ, PhD. **CAREER** Prof, Am Univ. **HONORS AND AWARDS** Dir, Ctr Asian Studies, Am Univ. **RESEARCH** Japan and the United States and Contemporary Korea and East Asia. **SELECTED PUBLICATIONS** Auth, The Division of Korea and the Alliance-Making Process: Internationalization of Internal Conflict and Internalization of International Struggle, Univ Press Am, 95. **CONTACT ADDRESS** American Univ, 4400 Massachusetts Ave, Washington, DC, 20016.

KIM, YOUNG HUM
PERSONAL Born 12/19/1920, Korea, m **DISCIPLINE** HISTORY, POLITICAL SCIENCE **EDUCATION** Schinheung Univ, Korea, BA, 53; Bradley Univ, BS, 55; Univ Southern CA, MA, 56, PhD, 60. **CAREER** Instr, Inchon Commerce Inst, Korea, 48-50; res assoc Soviet studies, Sch Int Rel, 60-61; from asst prof to assoc prof, 61-70, prof hist & polit sci, US Int Univ, CA, 70, Asst dir, Soviet-Asian Studies Ctr, Univ Southern CA. **MEMBERSHIPS** AHA; Am Polit Sci Asn; Asn Asian Studies; Am Acad Polit & Social Sci; Coun For Rel. **RESEARCH** US diplomatic hist. **SELECTED PUBLICATIONS** Auth, East Asia's Turbulent Century, Appleton, 66; Patterns of Competitive Coexistence: USA vs USSR, Putnam, 66; Struggle Against History: US Foreign Policy in an Age of Revolution, Simon & Schuster, 68; The Central Intelligence Agency: Problems of Secrecy in a Democracy, Heath, 68; Twenty Years of Crisis: The Cold War Era, Prentice-Hall, 68; American Frontier Activities in Asia: Nelson-Hall, 81; Ideology vs National Interests, USA Today, 85; Centennial History of American Diplomacy in Asia, Shinku Cultural Press, Korea, 88; Women Liberation Issue in Korea, Jeonju Univ Press, Korea, 88; War of No Return: The Korean War, 2 vol, Kwiin Publ, Korea, 88; U S-Asian Relations in the 20th Century, Edwin Mellen Press, 96. **CONTACT ADDRESS** Dept of Hist & Polit Sci, US Int Univ, 10455 Pomerado Rd, San Diego, CA, 92131-1717. **EMAIL** ykim1@san.rr.com

KIMBALL, JEFFREY PHILIP
PERSONAL Born 12/14/1941, New Orleans, LA, m, 1963, 2 children **DISCIPLINE** UNITED STATES HISTORY **EDUCATION** Univ New Orleans, BA, 63; Queen's Univ, Ont, MA, 64; La State Univ, Baton Rouge, PhD(hist), 69. **CAREER** From instr to asst prof, 68-69, assoc prof hist, Miami Univ, 74-89, prof hist, 90-, vis prof, Univ New Orleans, summer 74; Science Found Title VI grant, 78, sr res fel, Norwegian Nobel Institute, Oslo, Norway, Jan. 10, 95-June 30, 95; Air Force Historical Research Agency Research Grant, 93; The Mershon Center National Security Award, summer, 87. **HONORS AND AWARDS** Moncado Award Best Article, Vol XXXI, Military Affairs; Twenty-sixth Annual Norman Thomas Memorial Lecture, April 29, 97, Ohio State Univ, Marion, Ohio; Norwegian Nobel Institute Senior Fellow, spring 95; Eighth Annual Eleazer Wood Lecturer in Military History, Bowling Green State Univ, 83. **MEMBERSHIPS** Soc Historians Am Foreign Relations; Peace History Soc; International Peace Research Asn. **RESEARCH** War and the military in American history; causes of war and peace; the U.S. -Vietnam War; the Nixon presidency. **SELECTED PUBLICATIONS** Auth, The Battle of Chippawa: Infantry Tactics in the War of 1812, Mil Affairs, winter 67-68; Primitive War, Human Nature, and the Problem of Definition, In: Peace and Change: A Journal of Peace Research, Vol II, spring, 74; contribr, Great Events in History: American Series, Salem, 75; Encyclopedia of Southern Hist, La State Univ Press, 79; The Fog and Friction of Frontier War: The Role of Logistics in American Offensive Failure during the War of 1812, In: The Old Northwest, Vol V, winter 79; The Causes of War and the Teaching of Peace History, Peace and Change: A Journal of Peace Research 9: 69-73, winter 84; The Influence of Ideology on Interpretive Disagreement: A Report on a Survey of Diplomatic, Military, and Peace Historians on the Causes of 20th-Century U.S. Wars, The History Teacher 17: 356-384, May 84; Realism, Diplomatic History, and American Foreign Policy: A Conversation with Norman A. Graebner, The SHAFR Newsletter 18: 11-19, June 87; The Stab-in-the-Back Legend and the Vietnam War, Armed Forces and Society 14: 433-458, spring, 88; Lessons of the Vietnam War: The Myth of the Liberals' Lost, Limited War, Indochina Newsletter, no 55: 1-8, Jan-Feb 89; To Reason Why: The Debate About the Causes of American Involvement in the Vietnam War, contrib ed, NY: McGraw Hill, 90, Philadelphia: Temple Univ, 90; Alternatives to War in History, Org of Am Hists Magazine of History 8: 5-9, spring 94; On Peace Research in History, Org of Am Hists Magazine of History 8: 4, spring 94; How Wars End: The Vietnam War, Peace and Change: A Journal of Peace Research 20: 181-200, April 95; Nixon's Vietnam War, Lawrence: Univ Press of Kansas, 98; three chapters in books or monographs, and other publications. **CONTACT ADDRESS** Dept of Hist, Miami Univ, Upham Hall, Oxford, OH, 45056-1618. **EMAIL** kimbaljp@muohio.edu

KIMBALL, WARREN F.
PERSONAL Born 12/24/1935, Brooklyn, NY, m, 1959, 3 children **DISCIPLINE** AMERICAN DIPLOMATIC HISTORY **EDUCATION** Villanova Univ, BA, 58; Georgetown Univ, MA, 65, PhD(hist), 68. **CAREER** Instr hist, US Naval Acad, 61-65; instr Am hist, Georgetown Univ, 65-66, asst prof, 66-67; asst prof, Univ GA, 67-70; assoc prof, 70-75, prof 75-86, prof II, 86-93, RBT. TREAT PROF OF HIST, RUTGERS UNIV, 93-; Fulbright sr lectr, Univ Madrid, Spain, 75-76, Australia, 90; Pitt Prof, Univ of Cambridge, England, 88-89; State Dept hist adv cmte, chair 92-. **HONORS AND AWARDS** George P Hammond Prize, 64; Rutgers res excellence award, 85; AAP book award, 85; vis fel, Corpus Christi Col, Cambridge, 97; archive by-fel, Churchill Col, Cambridge, 98. **MEMBERSHIPS** AHA; Orgn Am Historians; Soc Hist Am Foreign Rels, pres 93; Int Churchill Soc, academic bd, 93-; WWII Studies Asn, bd of dirs, 77-79, 85-90, 92-. **RESEARCH** Foreign policy of Franklin Roosevelt; 20th century Anglo-Am relns; WWII int relns; Thatcher-Reagan era dipl. **SELECTED PUBLICATIONS** Auth, The Most Unsordid Act: Lend-Lease, 1939-1941, Johns Hopkins Univ, 69; Lend-lease and the Open Door, Polit Sci Quart, 6/71; The Cold War Warmed Over, Am Hist Rev, 10/74; Swords or Ploughshares?: The Morgenthau Plan for Defeated Nazi Germany, Lippincott, 76; ed, Churchill and Roosevelt: The Complete Correspondence, Three Volumes, 1939-1945, Princeton Univ, 84; The Juggler: Franklin Roosevelt as Wartime Statesman, Princeton Univ, 91; ed, America Unbound: World War II and the Making of a Super-Power, St Martins, 92; Roosevelt and the Southwest Pacific: Merely a Facade?, J of Am-East Asian Relations, summer 94; co-ed, Allies at War: The Soviet, American, and British Experience, 1939-44, St Martins, 95; Stalingrad: A Chance for Choices, J of Mil Hist, 1/96; Forged in War: Roosevelt, Churchill, and the Second World War, Wm Morrow, 97; A Victorian Tory: Churchill, the Americans, and Self-Determination, in More Adventures with Britannia, Oxford Univ (in press). **CONTACT ADDRESS** Dept of Hist, Rutgers Univ, 175 University Ave, Newark, NJ, 07102-1814. **EMAIL** wkimball@andromeda.rutgers.edu

KIMES, DON
PERSONAL Born 11/18/1953, Oil City, PA, m, 1978, 3 children **DISCIPLINE** ART **EDUCATION** Westminster Col, BA, 75; Brooklyn Col, MFA, 80. **CAREER** Prog dir, 80-85, NY Stud Sch; artistic dir, 86-, Chautaugua Inst; dir, 98-, Int Inst Art & Archit, Corciano, Italy; prof, chair, 88-, Amer Univ. **HONORS AND AWARDS** US Dept of Interior Award; Eisenhower Found Award, 86; Camerata di Todi, Italy, 94-95; Mellon Grant, 96; Artiste in the Manicomium, 96. **RESEARCH** Painting, drawing, sculpture, printmaking. **SELECTED PUBLICATIONS** Exhibitor, Claudia Carr Gallery, New York City, 99; exhib, Kennedy Museum of Art, Oh Univ, Athens, Oh, 99; exhib, Goya Girl Press, Baltimore, 99; exhib, McClean Project for the Arts, Arlington, Va, 99; exhib, Montpelier Center for the Arts, Laurel, Md, 99; exhib, Univ of Md, College Park, Md, 99. **CONTACT ADDRESS** 902 Gilbert Rd, Rockville, MD, 20851. **EMAIL** dKimes@american.edu

KIMMEL, RICHARD H.
PERSONAL Dayton, OH **DISCIPLINE** ANTHROPOLOGY AND ARCHAEOLOGY **EDUCATION** Univ NC, anthrop, MA, 78. **CAREER** Archaeol, US Army Corps of Engineers. **MEMBERSHIPS** Soc for Hist Archaeol; Southeastern Archaeol Conf. **RESEARCH** Mid-Atlantic and southeast U.S. historical archaeology, ecology and climate. **SELECTED PUBLICATIONS** Papers, Notes on the Cultural Origins and Functions of Sub-Floor Pits, Hist Archaeol, 27, 3, 102-113, 93; Estimating Magnetic Anomaly Sampling Fractions in Underwater Archaeology: Resolving Funding and Date Limitations, Underwater Archaeol Proceedings: Soc for Hist Archaeol Conf, 90-93, 90; Mitigating the Federal Review Process: A Preliminary Formulation of Data Contexts for the Ecological Interpretation of Small Craft, Underwater Archaeol Proceedings: Soc for Hist Archaeol Conf, 64-70, 89; Introduction to the Symposium: Current Research and Management Perspectives on Confederate Maritime Trade, Underwater Archaeol Proceedings: Soc for Hist Archaeol Conf, 19, 85. **CONTACT ADDRESS** US Army Corps Engineers, Environmental Resources Branch, PO Box 1890, Wilmington, NC, 28402-1890.

KINDALL, SUSAN CAROL
PERSONAL Born 02/26/1967, Greenville, SC **DISCIPLINE** MUSIC **EDUCATION** Bob Jones Univ, BM, 88, MM, 90; Univ Ok, DMA, 94. **CAREER** Prof, Bob Jones Univ, 98- **HONORS AND AWARDS** Gail Boyd DeStwolinski Award, 93; OMTA Piano competition, 91., Private study, Alexander technique **MEMBERSHIPS** Music Teachers Assoc; Crescent Music Club. **RESEARCH** Twentieth-century Amer piano music; music tech & its application to piano pedagogy. **SELECTED PUBLICATIONS** Auth, The Twenty-Four Preludes for Solo Piano by Richard Cumming: A Pedagogical and Performance Analysis, UMI, 94. **CONTACT ADDRESS** Bob Jones Univ, PO Box 34444, Greenville, SC, 29614. **EMAIL** kindall@gateway.net

KING, ANTHONY D.
DISCIPLINE ART HISTORY **EDUCATION** Brunel Univ, PhD, 83. **CAREER** Prof, SUNY Binghamton. **RESEARCH** Soc production of building form; urbanism and colonialism; world syst and postcolonial theory; ethnic archit and develop. **SELECTED PUBLICATIONS** Auth, Re-Presenting the City: Ethnicity, Capital and Culture in the 21st Century Metropolis, Macmillan Educ and NY UP, 96; The Bungalow, The Production of a Global Culture, 2d ed, Oxford UP, 95;. Writing Colonial Space, in Comparative Studies Soc Hist, 95; Vernacular, Transnational, Postcolonial, Casabella, 95; The Times and Spaces of Modernity (Or Who Needs Postmodernism?) in Global Modernities, Sage, 95. **CONTACT ADDRESS** SUNY Binghamton, PO Box 6000, Binghamton, NY, 13902-6000. **EMAIL** adking@binghamton.edu

KING, BEN L.
PERSONAL Born 01/31/1967, Bloomington, IN, s **DISCIPLINE** CLASSICS **EDUCATION** Princeton Univ, PhD, 97. **CAREER** Vis asst prof, Univ VA, 96-97; lectr, Univ Cal Riverside, 97-. **MEMBERSHIPS** Amer Philol Asn **RESEARCH** Greek intellectual history; Homer; Greek and Roman historigraphy. **SELECTED PUBLICATIONS** Auth, The Rhetoric of the Victim: Odysseus at the Swineherds Hut, Classical Antiquity, 99. **CONTACT ADDRESS** 600 Central Ave., #30, Riverside, CA, 92507. **EMAIL** BENKING@verac1.ucr.edu

KING, H. ROGER
DISCIPLINE HISTORY **EDUCATION** Vanderbilt Univ, PhD. **CAREER** Prof and grad adv, Eastern Michigan Univ. **RESEARCH** US colonial period, US revolutionary war. **SELECTED PUBLICATIONS** Auth, Cape Cod and Plymouth Colony in the Seventeenth Century. **CONTACT ADDRESS** Dept of History and Philosophy, Eastern Michigan Univ, 701 Pray-Harrold, Ypsilanti, MI, 48197. **EMAIL** his_king@online.emich.edu

KING, JOHN O.
DISCIPLINE HISTORY **EDUCATION** Princeton univ, AB, 65; Univ Wis, PhD, 76. **CAREER** Asst prof, hist, Univ Mich; current, IND SCH. **MEMBERSHIPS** Am Antiquarian Soc **SELECTED PUBLICATIONS** Auth, "Demonic New World and Wilderness Land: The Making of America," Prospects: The Ann of Am Cult Stud 7, 82; auth, The Iron of Melancholy, Wesleyan Univ Press, 83; auth, "On the Effectual Work of the Word: William James and the Practice of Puritan Confession," Texas Stud in Lang & Lit 25, 85. **CONTACT ADDRESS** 419 Second St, Ann Arbor, MI, 48103.

KING, MARGARET LEAH
PERSONAL Born 10/16/1947, New York, NY, m, 1976, 2 children **DISCIPLINE** HISTORY **EDUCATION** Sarah Lawrence Col, BA, 67; Stanford Univ, MA, 68, PhD, 72. **CAREER** Asst prof hist, Calif State Col, Fullerton, 69-70; asst prof, 72-76, Assoc Prof Hist, 72-76, Prof Brooklyn Col & Grad Ctr, CUNY, 87-; Am Coun Learned Soc fel hist, 77-78; Gladys Krieble Delmas Found fel Venetian hist, 77-78. **HONORS AND AWARDS** Woodrow Wilson Fel, 67-68; Danforth Found Fel, 67-72; CUNY, New Fac Res Award, 73; CUNY, Fac Res Award, 73-74; PSC/CUNY Award, 77-78, 80, & 90; Brooklyn Col Favorite Teacher, 93; Tow Award for Distinction in Scholarship, Brooklyn Col 94-95; **MEMBERSHIPS** Renaissance Soc Am; AHA; Soc Values in Higher Educ. **RESEARCH** Venetian history; intellectual history; Renaissance history; Women's history. **SELECTED PUBLICATIONS** Auth, Personal, Domestic and Republican values in the moral philosophy of Giovanni Caldiera, Renaissance Quart, 75; The patriciate and the intellectuals: Power and ideas, Societas, 75; Caldiera and the Barbaros on marriage and the family: Humanist reflections of Venetian realities, J Medieval & Renaissance Studies, 76; Thwarted ambitions: Six learned women of the Italian Renaissance, 76 & The social role of intellectuals: Antonio Gramsci and the Italian Renaissance, 78, Soundings; The religious retreat of Isotta Nogarola: Sexism and its consequences in the fifteenth century, Signs, 78; A study in Venetian humanism: Filippo da Rimini and his symposium de paupertate, Part I, 78, Part II, 79 & Part III, 80, Studi Veneziani; Jacobo Antonio Marcello and the War for the Lombard Plain, in Continuita e discontinuita nella storia politica, economica e religiosa: Studi in onore di Aldo Stella (Vicenza: Neri Pozza) 63-88, 93; Isotta Nogarola, in Italian Women Writers: A Bio-Bibliographical Sourcebook, ed, Rinaldina Russell, Westport, CT:Greenwood 313-23, 94; Iter Kristellerianum: The European Journey 1905-1939, Renaissance Quarterly 47:4 95; The Death of the Child Valerio Marcello, Univ Chicago, 94. **CONTACT ADDRESS** Dept Hist, Brooklyn Col, CUNY, 2900 Bedford Ave, Brooklyn, NY, 11210-2813. **EMAIL** margking@worldnet.att.net

KING, ORA STERLING
PERSONAL Born 10/15/1931, Delta, AL, m **DISCIPLINE** EDUCATION **EDUCATION** Spelman Coll, BA 1954; Atlanta Univ, MA 1969; Univ of Maryland, PhD, 1982. **CAREER** Atlanta Public Schools, teacher/instructional coord 1954-72; Federal City Coll, reading dept chair 1975-78; Univ of the District of Columbia, asst prof of educ 1978-81; COPPIN STATE COLL, prof & dept chair of C&I, 1981-88, dean Division of Education, 1988-90, dean, Division of Education and Graduate

Studies, 1990-91, PROF OF EDUCATION, COORD OF MASTERS OF ARTS IN TEACHING, 1991-. **HONORS AND AWARDS** Mem editorial adv bd Reading World Coll Reading Assn 1982-84; mem US Delegation to the People's Republic of China US China Scientific Exchange 1985; twenty articles published in educational journals 1979-92.received NAFEO Distinguished Alumni Award, 1988; Fulbright Scholarship Recipient, Monrovia, Liberia, 1988. **MEMBERSHIPS** 1st vice pres Natl Alumnae Assn of Spelman Coll 1982-86; mem editorial adv bd Innovative Learning Strategies Intl Reading Assn 1985-86; pres Natl Alumnae Assn of Spelman Coll 1986-88; mem Alpha Kappa Alpha Iota Lambda Chap; president Columbia Chapter NAASC 1990-95. **SELECTED PUBLICATIONS** Published textbook Reading & Study Skills for the Urban College Student, Kendall/Hunt Publ 1984, 1988, 2nd ed. **CONTACT ADDRESS** Education, Coppin State Col, 2500 W North Ave, Baltimore, MD, 21216.

KING, PETER JOHN
DISCIPLINE AMERICAN HISTORY **EDUCATION** Cambridge Univ, BA, 57, MA, 61; Univ Ill, PhD, 61. **CAREER** Prof. **RESEARCH** Eighteenth-century American intellectual history. **SELECTED PUBLICATIONS** Auth, Utilitarian Jurisprudence in America: The Influence of Bentham and Austin on American Legal Thought in the 19th Century, Garland, 86. **CONTACT ADDRESS** Dept of Hist, Carleton Univ, 1125 Colonel By Dr, Ottawa, ON, K1S 5B6. **EMAIL** pking@ccs.carleton.ca

KING, RICHARD D.
DISCIPLINE HISTORY **EDUCATION** Univ Ill, Urbana-Champaign, PhD. **CAREER** Assoc prof, Ursinus Col. **HONORS AND AWARDS** NEH res sem, Russia, 90, 94. **RESEARCH** Russian, Middle Eastern, and East European history. **SELECTED PUBLICATIONS** Auth, Sergei Kirov and the Struggle for Soviet Power in the Terek Region, 1917-1918. **CONTACT ADDRESS** Ursinus Col, Collegeville, PA, 19426-1000.

KING, WALTER JOSEPH
PERSONAL Born 01/10/1943, Leominster, MA, m, 1964, 1 child **DISCIPLINE** HISTORY **EDUCATION** Univ Mich, BA, 67, MA, 69, PhD(hist), 77. **CAREER** Asst prof, Upper Iowa Univ, 76-80; asst prof hist & philos, Northern State Univ, 80-, adj lectr hist, Univ Northern Iowa, 77. **HONORS AND AWARDS** Distinguished South Dakota Regental Professor, 90; Burlington Northern Excellence-in-Research Award, 86; Outstanding Faculty Member, 84. **MEMBERSHIPS** AHA; Social Hist Soc England; Conf on British Studies; NAm Nietzsche Soc. **RESEARCH** Illegal behavior in early modern England; causes of change in history. **SELECTED PUBLICATIONS** Auth, Punishment for Bastardy in Early Seventeenth-Century England, Albion, 9/78; Modern European History, Univ Press, 78; Vagrancy and Local Law Enforcement: Why be a Constable in Stuart Lancashire?, The Historian, 2/80; Leet Jurors and the Search for Law and Order: Galling Persecution or Reasonable Justice?, Social Hist, 11/80; Regulation of Ale Houses in Stuart Lancashire: An Example of Discretionary Administration of the Law, Trans of the Hist Soc of Lancashire and Cheshire, 80; Out-of-Court Settlements in 17th Century England: Can Historians of Crime Trust Quantification?, 81 & Is Crime normal? Attitudes Toward Crime Since About 1500, 82, The Northern Soc Sci Rev; Untapped Resources for Social Historians: Court Leet Records, Journal Of Social History, spring 82; Early Stuart Courts Leet: Still Needful and Useful, Histoire Sociale-Social History, Nov 92; The Holocaust: Questions and Implications for Christianity, Journal of Ethnical Studies, Jan-March 92; How High is Too High? Disposing of Dung in Seventeenth-Century Prescot, Sixteenth-Century Journal, fall 92. **CONTACT ADDRESS** Dept of Hist & Philos, No State Univ, 1200 S Jay St, Aberdeen, SD, 57401-7198. **EMAIL** kingw@wolf.northern.edu

KING-HAMMOND, LESLIE
PERSONAL Born 08/04/1944, Bronx, NY, d **DISCIPLINE** ART HISTORY **EDUCATION** Queens College CUNY, BA 1969; Johns Hopkins Univ, MA 1973, PhD 1975. **CAREER** Performing Arts Workshops of Queens, New York, NY, chair dept of art, 1969-71; HARYOU-ACT, Inc, Harlem, NY, program writer, 1971; MD INSTITUTE, COLLEGE OF ART, LECTURER 1973-, DEAN OF GRAD STUDIES 1976-; Corcoran School of Art, lecturer 1977, visiting faculty 1982; Howard Univ, Dept of African Studies, doctoral supervisor, 1977-81; Civic Design Commission Baltimore City, commissioner 1983-87; Afro-Amer Historical & Cultural Museum, art consultant, 1990-96; PHILIP MORRIS SCHOLARSHIPS FOR ARTISTS OF COLOR, PROJECT DIRECTOR, 1985-. **HONORS AND AWARDS** Horizon Fellowship, 1969-73; Kress Fellowship, John Hopkins Univ, 1974-75; Guest curator, Montage of Dreams Deferred, Baltimore Museum of Art 1979; published Celebrations: Myth & Ritual in Afro-American Art, Studio Museum in Harlem, 1982; Mellon Grant for Faculty Research, MD Institute, College of Art, 1984; guest curator, The Intuitive Eye, MD Art Place 1985; Trustee Award for Excellence in Teaching 1986; co curator, Woman of the Year 1986, Women's Art Caucus, 1986; Mellon Grant for faculty research, 1987; curator, 18 Visions/Divisions, Eubie Blake Cultural Center and Museum, 1988; co curator, Art as a Verb: The Evolving Continuum, 1988; curator, Black Printmakers and the WPA, Lehman Gallery of Art, 1989; coordinated Hale Woodruff Biennial, Studio Museum in Harlem, 1989; Masters, Makers and Inventors, Artscape, 1992; MCAC, 1992; Tom Miller Retrospective, Baltimore Museum of Art & Maryland Art Place, 1995; Hale Woodruff Biennale, Studio Museum in Harlem, 1994; Co-curator, Three Generations of African-American Women Sculptors, African-American Historial and Cultural Museum, Philadelphia, Equitable Gallery, NY, The Smithsonian, 1996-98; Exhibiting Artist, Artist-Scholar: In Search of A Balance, Ctr for African American History & Culture; The Smithsonian, 1997. **MEMBERSHIPS** Panelist, Natl Endowment for the Humanities 1978-80; panelist Natl Endowment for the Arts 1980-82; mem bd Baltimore School for the Arts 1984-; mem, Natl Conf of Artist; College Art Association; mem bd Community Foundation of Greater Baltimore 1984-87; consult MD Arts Council 1985-; mem bd Art Commission, Baltimore City, Office of the Mayor, 1988; bd of drs, CAA, 1991-99, pres, 1996-98; bd, Alvin Ailey Dance Theatre Found of Maryland, 1990-93; bd of overseers, School for the Arts, Baltimore, 1996-99. **CONTACT ADDRESS** Maryland Inst Col of Art, 1300 W Mt Royal Ave, Baltimore, MD, 21217. **EMAIL** lkingha@mica.edu

KINGDON, ROBERT MCCUNE
PERSONAL Born 12/29/1927, Chicago, IL **DISCIPLINE** HISTORY **EDUCATION** Oberlin Col, AB, 49; Columbia Univ, MA, 50, PhD, 55. **CAREER** From instr to asst prof hist, Univ Mass, 52-57; from asst prof to pr of hist, State Univ Iowa, 57-65; PROF HIST, UNIV WIS, MADISON, 65-98, DIR, INST RES HUMANITIES, 75-87; Vis instr, Amherst Col, 53-54; Am Coun Learned Soc fel, 60-61; vis prof, Stanford Univ, 64 & 80; mem, Inst Advan Studies, 65-66; pres bd, Center Reformation Res, 67-; Guggenheim Found fel, 69-70; ed-in-chief, Sixteenth-Century J, 73-97; Folger Shakespeare Libr sr fel, 73-74; mem, Inst Res Humanities, 74-98 **HONORS AND AWARDS** Docteur es lettres, honoris causa, Univ Geneva, 86; Alexander von Humboldt Res Award, Germany, 92-94; Fel, Inst Advan Studies, Hebew Univ, Jerusalem, 98; Recipient of Festschrift, Essays Presented to Robert M. Kingdon, Sixteenth Century Essays and Studies, Sixteenth Century J, 87 **MEMBERSHIPS** Am Soc Reformation Res (secy-treas, 63-69, pres, 70-71); AHA; Am Soc Church Hist (pres, 80); Renaissance Soc Am; Int Fed Renaissance Socs & Insts (secy-treas, 67-89). **RESEARCH** History of the Calvinist Reformation and Catholic Reformation; business history of early printing industry. **SELECTED PUBLICATIONS** Auth, Geneva and the Coming of the Wars of Religion in France, 1555-1563, Librarie E Droz, Geneva, 56; The Plantin Breviaries, Biblio d'Humanisme et Renaissance, 60; coed, Registres de la Compagnie des Pasteurs de Geneve au Temps de Calvin, Librairie Droz, Geneva, 62 & 64; The Execution of Justice in England & A Defense of English Catholics, Cornell Univ, 65; auth, Geneva and the Consolidation of the French Protestant Movement, 1564-1572, Droz, Geneva & Univ Wis, Madison, 67; ed, Du Droit des Magistrats, Droz, 71; Transition and Revolution: Problems and Issues of European Renaissance and Reformation History, Burgess, 74; The Political Thought of Peter Martyr Vermigli, Libr E Droz, Geneva, 80; Church and Society in Reformation Europe, Variorum, London, 85; Myths about St Bartholomew's Day Massacres, 1572-1576, Harvard Univ Press, 88; Adultery and Divorce in Calvin's Geneva, Harvard Univ Press, 95; co-ed, Registres du Consistoire deGeneve au temps de Calvin, vol 1, Librairie Droz, Geneva, 96. **CONTACT ADDRESS** Inst for Res in the Humanities, Univ of Wis, 455 North Park St, Madison, WI, 53706-1483. **EMAIL** rkingdon@facstaff.wisc.edu

KINGHORN, KENNETH CAIN
PERSONAL Born 06/23/1930, Albany, OK, m, 1955, 4 children **DISCIPLINE** CHURCH HISTORY **EDUCATION** Ball State Univ, BS, 52; Asbury Theol Sem, BD, 62; Emory Univ, PhD, 65. **CAREER** From prof church hist to Dean Sch Theol, Asbury Theol Sem, 65-. **MEMBERSHIPS** Am Soc Church Hist. **RESEARCH** Wesley studies; Protestant Reformation; spiritual formation. **SELECTED PUBLICATIONS** Auth, Dynamic Discipleship, Fleming H Revell, 73; Fresh Wind of the Spirit, 75, Gifts of the Spirit, 76 & Christ Can Make You Fully Human, 79, Abingdon; Discovering Your Spiritual Gifts, 81 & A Celebration of Ministry, 82, Francis Asbury Publ Co; The Gospel of Grace, Abingdon, 92. **CONTACT ADDRESS** Dept of Church Hist, Asbury Theol Sem, 204 N Lexington Ave, Wilmore, KY, 40390-1199. **EMAIL** ken_kinghorn@ats.wilmore.ky.us

KINKLEY, JEFFREY CARROLL
PERSONAL Urbana, IL, m, 1981, 1 child **DISCIPLINE** HISTORY **EDUCATION** Univ Chicago, BA, 69; Harvard Univ, MA, 71, PhD, 77. **CAREER** Lectr, Harvard Univ, Hist, 77-79; asst prof, St Johns Univ, 79; assoc prof, 86; instr, Rutgers Univ, 92; PROF, ST JOHNS UNIV, 93-; vis prof, Columbia Univ, Asian Lang & Cult, 97. **MEMBERSHIPS** Asn Asian Stud; Am Hist Asn; Am Asn Chinese Comparative Lit **RESEARCH** History & literature of modern China. **SELECTED PUBLICATIONS** Shen Congwen bixia de Zhongguo Shehui yu Wenhua, East China Normal UP, 94; Shen Congwen. Imperfect Paradise: Stories by Shen Congwen, Univ Hawaii, 95; Chinese Justice, the Fiction: Law and Literature in Modern China, Stanford Univ Press, Escape from the Law: Crime, Law and Literature in Post-Mao China. **CONTACT ADDRESS** Hist Dept, St Johns Univ, Jamaica, NY, 11439. **EMAIL** jkinkley@worldnet.att.net

KINNEAR, MICHAEL S.R.
PERSONAL Born 08/13/1937, Saskatoon, SK, Canada **DISCIPLINE** HISTORY **EDUCATION** Univ Sask, BA, 60; Univ Oregon, MA, 61; Oxford Univ, DPhil, 65. **CAREER** PROF HISTORY, UNIV MANITOBA, 65-. **HONORS AND AWARDS** Can Coun scholar, leave fel; Woodrow Wilson fel; IODE scholar; SSHRC leave fel. **SELECTED PUBLICATIONS** Auth, The British Voter, 68, 81; auth, The Fall of Lloyd George, 73, 74; auth, Gleanings and Memoranda 1893-1968, 75; coauth, A History of the Vote in Canada, 97. **CONTACT ADDRESS** History Dept, Univ of Manitoba, Winnipeg, MB, R3T 2M8.

KINSELLA, DAVID
DISCIPLINE WORLD POLITICS **EDUCATION** Univ Calif, Irvine BA; Yale Univ, MA, Mphil, PhD. **CAREER** Asst prof; Univ Miss; Prof, Am Univ. **HONORS AND AWARDS** Mershon postdoctoral fel, Ohio State Univ. **RESEARCH** World politics, internatioal relations theory, national secirity, arms trade. **SELECTED PUBLICATIONS** Contribur, Am Jour Pol Sci; Intl Studies Quart, Jour Conflict Resolution. **CONTACT ADDRESS** American Univ, 4400 Massachusetts Ave, Washington, DC, 20016.

KINSER, SAMUEL
PERSONAL Born 06/04/1931, Davenport, IA, m, 3 children **DISCIPLINE** MODERN HISTORY **EDUCATION** Carleton Col, BA, 53; Cornell Univ, PhD(hist), 60. **CAREER** Asst prof hist, Wash State Univ, 60-65; assoc prof, 65-70, prof hist, Northern Ill Univ, 70-, Newberry Libr grants-in-aid, 64 & 69; Am Philos Soc grant, 64-65 & 79; Weil Found fel, 64; Am Coun Learned Soc grant-in-aid, 65; Inst Res in Humanities fel, Madison, Wis, 68-69. **HONORS AND AWARDS** Inst for Adv Studs in Humanities Fel, Univ of Edinburgh, 79; Nat Endowment for Humanities Fel, 93-94; Presidential Res Prof, North Ill Univ, 94-98. **RESEARCH** The relation of ideology and style to social and psychological formation in the Renaissance period; the emergence of concepts of historical process, social science and culture; European folk culture. **SELECTED PUBLICATIONS** Auth, Rabelais's Carnival: Text, Context, Metatext, Univ Cal Press, Berkeley, 90; Carnival American Style, Mardi Gras at new Orleans and Mobil, Univ Chicago Press, Chicago, 90; D'Aubigne and the murder of Concini: Complaintes du sang du grand Henry, Studies Philol, 65; The Works of Jacques-Auguste de Thou, Nijhoff, The Hague, 66; The ingratitude of princes: An unedited French poem by Jacques-Auguste de Thou, Biblio Humanisme & Renaissance, 67; ed, Memoirs of Philippe de Commynes, Univ SC, Vols I & II, 69 & 73; auth, Ideas of temporal change and cultural process in France, 1470-1535, In: Renaissance Studies in Honor of Hans Baron, Florence, Italy & De Kalb, Ill, 71; The Language of History, Clio, 74; Saussure's anagrams: Ideological work, Mod Lang Notes 78; Annaliste paradigm?, The geohistorical structuralism of Fernand Braudel, Am Hist Rev, 81. **CONTACT ADDRESS** Dept of History, No Illinois Univ, 1425 W Lincoln Hwy, De Kalb, IL, 60115-2825. **EMAIL** sakinser@aol.com

KINSEY, WINSTON LEE
PERSONAL Born 03/07/1943, Lampasa, TX, m, 1964, 3 children **DISCIPLINE** MODERN EUROPEAN & AFRICAN HISTORY **EDUCATION** Baylor Univ, BA, 64, MA, 65; Tx Tech Univ, PhD, 69. **CAREER** Teacher social studies, Tx City Independent Schs, 65-66; asst prof, 69-74, asst dean, Col Arts & Sci, 71-73, assoc prof hist to full prof, 74-91, Appalachian State Univ, 74-. **MEMBERSHIPS** African Studies Asn; SE Reg Sem N African St; AHA; Agr Hist Soc; Asn Hist NC. **RESEARCH** Recent Ghana; recent Africa; Texas agriculture, Agriculture in Western NC. **SELECTED PUBLICATIONS** Auth, Black Americans and the African Republic of Ghana, Faculty Publications, Appalachian State Univ, 70; The Immigrant in Texas Agriculture During Reconstruction, Agricultural History, 1/79. **CONTACT ADDRESS** Dept Hist, Appalachian State Univ, 1 Appalachian State, Boone, NC, 28608-0001. **EMAIL** KinseyWL@appstate.edu

KINTIGH, KEITH W.
PERSONAL Born 05/19/1951, Kansas City, MO, m, 1988, 1 child **DISCIPLINE** ANTHROPOLOGY **EDUCATION** Stanford Univ, BA, 74, MS, 74; Univ Michigan, PhD, 82. **CAREER** Assoc archeol, Ariz State Mus, Univ Ariz, 80-85; asst, assoc prof, anthrop, Univ Calif, Santa Barbara, 85-87; res assoc, Zuni Archeol Prog, 86- ; assoc and prof, Dept Anthrop, Ariz State Univ, 87- . **HONORS AND AWARDS** Pres recognition Award, Soc for Am Archeol, 91, 95, 97. **MEMBERSHIPS** Am Anthrop Asn; Ariz Archeol and Hist Soc; Ariz Archeol Coun; Sigma Xi; Soc for Am Archeol. **SELECTED PUBLICATIONS** Coauth, Archaeological Settlement Pattern Data from the Chalco, Zochimilco, Ixtapalapa, Texcoco and Zumpango Regions, Mexico, Univ Mich, 83; auth, Settlement, Subsistence, and Society in Late Zuni Prehistory, Univ Ariz, 85; coauth, Demographic Alternatives: Consequences for Current Models of Southwestern Prehistory, in Gumerman, ed, Understanding Complexity in the Prehistoric Southwest, Addison Wesley, 94; coauth, Processes of Aggregation in the Prehistoric Southwest,

in Gumerman, ed, Themes in Southwest Prehistory, Sch of Am Res Press, 94; auth, Chaco, Communal Architecture, and Cibolan Aggregation, in Wills, ed, The Ancient Southwestern Community: Methods and Models for the Study of Prehistoric Social Organizations, New Mexico, 94; auth, Contending with Contemporaneity in Settlemant Pattern Studies, Am Antiquity, 94; auth, A Test of the Relationship between Site Size and Population, Am Antiquity, 96; auth, Post-Chacoan Social Integration at the Hinkson Site, New Mexico, Kiva, 96; coauth, Archaeological Identification of Kin Groups Using Mortuary and Biological Data: An Example from the American Southwest, Am Antiquity, 96; coauth, Ceramic Seriation and Site Reoccupation in Lowland South America, Latin Am Antiquity, 96; coauth, Determining Gender and Kinship at Hawikku: A Reply to Corruccini, Am Antiquity, 98. **CONTACT ADDRESS** Dept of Anthropology, Arizona State Univ, Tempe, Tempe, AZ, 85287-2402. **EMAIL** Kintigh@asu.edu

KIPLE, KENNETH FRANKLIN
PERSONAL Born 01/29/1939, Waterloo, IA, m, 1974, 4 children **DISCIPLINE** LATIN AMERICAN AND AMERICAN HISTORY **EDUCATION** Univ S FL, BA, 65; Univ FL, PhD, 70. **CAREER** Instr soc sci, Univ Fla, 69-70; asst prof, 70-77, assoc prof, 78-80, prof hist, Bowling Green State Univ, 81-94, Joint Soc Sci Res Coun & Am Coun Learned Soc grant, 77-79, distin prof, 94. **HONORS AND AWARDS** Natl inst health, natl lib meds - pub grant 98-99, OH coun for human gra, 92, natl lib med extralmurals prog gra, 91-92, Guggenheim mem found gra, 90-91, natl endow human fell, 88, Earhart found gra, 87, milbank mem fund gra, 86. **MEMBERSHIPS** Conf Latin Am Hist; AHA; Southern Hist Asn, Am Asn Hist Med. **RESEARCH** Slavery in the Am; Spain and Portugal; med hist; Hist food nutrit. **SELECTED PUBLICATIONS** Auth, Slave Nutrition, Disease and Infant Mortality in the Caribbean, J Interdisciplinary Hist, Vol XI, No 2, autumn 80; The African Connection: Slavery, Disease and Racism, Phylon, Vol XLI, fall 80; Another Dimension to the Black Diaspora: Diet, Disease and Racism, Cambridge Univ Press, 81; ed, The Caribbean Slave: A Biologiacal History, Cambridge univ Press, 84; The African Exchange: Toward a Biological History of Black People, Duke Univ Press, 88; The Cambridge World history of Human Disease, Cambridge Univ Press, 93; Plague, Pox, Pestilence: Disease in History, Weidenfeld and Nicolson in London, Barnes and Nobel in NY, 97. **CONTACT ADDRESS** Dept of Hist, Bowling Green State Univ, 1001 E Wooster St, Bowling Green, OH, 43403-0001.

KIPP, RITA
PERSONAL Born 04/04/1948, Wilburton, OK, m, 1969, 3 children **DISCIPLINE** ANTHROPOLOGY **EDUCATION** Univ Pittsburg, PhD, 76 **CAREER** Prof, Keyon Coll, 76-present. **MEMBERSHIPS** Asian Studies Assn; Amer Anthropological Assn. **RESEARCH** Cultural Anthropology; Religion; Ethnicity **SELECTED PUBLICATIONS** Co-ed, Indonesian Religions in Transition, Univ of AZ Press, 87; The Early Years of a Dutch Colonial Mission: The Karo Field, Univ of Mich Press, 90; Dissociated Identities: Ethnicity, Religion, and Class in an Indonesian Society, Univ of Mich Press, 93. **CONTACT ADDRESS** Dept of Anthropology and Sociology, Kenyon Col, Gambier, OH, 43022. **EMAIL** kipp@kenyon.edu

KIRBY, ALEC
PERSONAL Born 07/24/1962, Royal Oak, MI **DISCIPLINE** HISTORY **EDUCATION** Muskingum Col, BA, 84; MA, 86, PhD, 92, George Washington Univ. **CAREER** Lectr in History and Govt, 91-97; Sr. Lectr, Univ Wisconsin-Stout, 97-. **MEMBERSHIPS** Amer Historical Assoc. **RESEARCH** 20th century political history **CONTACT ADDRESS** Box 72, Menomonie, WI, 54751. **EMAIL** kirbya@uwstout.edu

KIRBY, JACK TEMPLE
PERSONAL Born 08/22/1938, Portsmouth, VA, 2 children **DISCIPLINE** AMERICAN HISTORY **EDUCATION** Old Dom Col, BA, 63; Univ Va, MA, 64, PhD, 65. **CAREER** From Asst Prof to Prof, 65-88, W.E. Smith Prof Hist, Miami Univ, 88, 74. **HONORS AND AWARDS** Phi Alpha Theta Book Prize, 88. **MEMBERSHIPS** Am Studies Asn; Southern Hist Asn; Orgn Am Historians; Agr Hist Soc (pres 96); Am Soc Environmental Hist; VA Hist Soc. **RESEARCH** Am South; environment. **SELECTED PUBLICATIONS** Auth, Westmoreland Davis: Virginia Planter, Univ Va, 68; Darkness at the Dawning: Race and Reform in the Progressive South, Lippincott, 72; Media-Made Dixie: The South in the America Imagination, La State Univ, 78; Rural Worlds Lost: The American South 1920-1960, La State Univ, 87; Poquosin: A Study of Rural Landscape and Society, NC, 95; The Countercultural South, Ga, 95. **CONTACT ADDRESS** Dept Hist, Miami Univ, Oxford, OH, 45056-1602.

KIRBY, JOHN T.
PERSONAL Born 05/09/1955, New Haven, CT, 2 children **DISCIPLINE** CLASSICS & COMPARATIVE LITERATURE **EDUCATION** Choate Sch, diploma, 73; Univ NC Chapel Hill, AB, 77; Univ NC Chapel Hill, MA, 81; Univ NC Chapel Hill, PhD, 85. **CAREER** Asst prof, class lang and lit, Smith Col, 85-87; founding chair, prog in class studies, Purdue Univ, 88-94; chair, prog in comparative lit, Purdue Univ, 94-. **HONORS AND AWARDS** Phi Eta Sigma, 74; Phi Beta Kappa, 76; Morehead Scholar, Univ NC, 73-77; Univ Res Asst, Univ NC, 80-81; Classics Teaching fel, Univ NC, 83-84; Software develop grant, ACIS Found of IBM, 85; Robert E. Frane Memorial Scholar, 85; Morris House fel, Smith Col, 86; Facul Teaching Award nominee, Smith Col, 86; Libr Scholars grant prog award, Purdue Univ, 87; Facul teaching award nominee, Smith Col, 87, 88; XL Summer facul grant, Purdue Res Found, 88; Univ Outstanding Undergraduate Teaching Award nominee, Purdue Univ, 88; XL summer facul grant, Purdue Res Found, 90; XL Intl Travel grant, Purdue Res Found, 91; res leave, dept foreign lang and lit, Purdue Univ, spring, 91; NEH fel, Univ Iowa, fall, 91; fel, Ctr for Humanistic Studies, Purdue Univ, spring, 93; Scholar-in-residence, Choate Rosemary Hall, fall, 93; Sch of Liberal Arts Outstanding Teaching award, Purdue Univ, 93; Amer Philol Asn award for Excellence in the Teaching of the Classics, 96; Twentieth Century award for achievement, Intl Bio Ctr, 97., Man of the Year, Am Biog Inst, 96; International Man of the Year, Int Biog Ctr, 96-97; listed in Int Dir of Distinguished Leadership, 7th Ed, 97; listed in Int Who's Who of Intellectuals, 12th Ed, 97. **MEMBERSHIPS** Mod Lang Asn; Amer Comparative Lit Asn; Amer Philol Asn; Calif Class Asn; Class Asn of the Middle West and South; Amer Soc for the Hist of Rhetoric. **RESEARCH** Classical Greek and Latin literature; Classical rhetoric and poetics; Literary theory. **SELECTED PUBLICATIONS** Auth, The Rhetoric of Cicero's Pro Cluentio, 90; ed, The Comparative Reader: A Handlist of Basic Reading in Comparative Literature, 98; jour articles, Amer Jour of Philol, 118, 517-554, 97; Philos and Rhetoric, 30, 190-202, 97; Voices in Italian Amer, 7, 207-211, 96; Ill Class Studies, 20, 77-81, 95; Voices in Italian Amer, 6, 71-76, 95; book chap, Ciceronian Rhetoric: Theory and Practice, 13-31, Roman Eloquence: Rhetoric in Society and Literature, 97; Classical Greek Origins of Western Aesthetic Theory, 29-45, 96; The Great Triangle in Early Greek Rhetoric and Poetics, 3-15, 94; The Neo-Latin Verse of Joseph Tusiani, 180-204, Joseph Tusiani: Poet, Translator, Humanist, 94; auth, Secret of the Muses Retold: Classical Influences on Itlaian Authors of the Twentieth Century, Chicago: University of Chicago Press, in press; ed, Landmark Essays on Ciceronian Rhetoric, Davis CA: Hermagoras Press/Erlbaum, in press. **CONTACT ADDRESS** Dept of For Lang and Lit, Purdue Univ, 1080 Schleman Hall, W. Lafayette, IN, 47907-1354. **EMAIL** corax@purdue.edu

KIRBY, TORRANCE W.
PERSONAL Born 07/04/1955, Red Deer, AB, Canada, m, 1980, 2 children **DISCIPLINE** RENAISSANCE & REFORMATION **EDUCATION** Oxford Univ, DPhil, 88. **CAREER** Commonwealth Schol, Christ Church, Oxford, 80-84; Fel, King's Col, Nova Scotia, 84-89; Tutor, St. John's Col, 89-96; Mem, Princeton Ctr Theol Inquiry, 96-; Prof Church Hist, Mc McGill Univ, 97-. **HONORS AND AWARDS** Univ Medal in Classics, Dalhousie, 77; Killam Fel, Dalhousie, 77-79. **MEMBERSHIPS** Am Acad Relig; Soc Christian Ethics; Sixteenth Century Studies Conf; Atlantic Theol Conf. **RESEARCH** Richard Hooker; Peter Martyr Vermigli; Reformation and Neoplatonism. **SELECTED PUBLICATIONS** Auth, Richard Hooker as an Apologist of the Magisterial Reformation in England, Richard Hooker and the Construction of Christian Community, Medieval and Renaissance Texts and Studies, vol 165, MRTS, 97; Praise as the Soul's Overcoming of Time in the Confessions of St. Augustine, Pro Ecclesia, vol VI, Summer 97; The Theology of Richard Hooker in the Context of the Magisterial Reformation, Princeton Seminary Press, (in press 98); The Neoplatonic Logic of Richard Hooker's Generic Division of Law, Renaissance and Reformation (forthcoming 1999); The Political and Social Thought of Peter Martyr Vermigli, The Peter Martyr Libr, 2nd series (forthcoming). **CONTACT ADDRESS** 3520 University St., Montreal, PQ, H3A 2A7. **EMAIL** tkirby@wilson.lan.mcgill.ca

KIRCH, PATRICK V.
PERSONAL Born 07/07/1950, Honolulu, HI, m **DISCIPLINE** ANTHROPOLOGY **EDUCATION** Pa Univ, BA, 71; Yale, M Philos, 74, PhD, 75. **CAREER** Affiliate Fac, Univ Hawaii, 79-84; archaeol, Bernice P Bishop Museum, 75-84; prof, Univ Washington, (dir, Burke Muiseum), 84-89; prof anthrop, Univ Calif, Berkeley, 89-. **HONORS AND AWARDS** Nat Acad Sci, USA, 90; Am Acad Arts & Sci, 92; Fellow, Am Asn for the Advancement of Sci, 96; Carty Award for the Advan of Sci (NAS), 97; Fellow, Calif Acad of Sci, 97; Fellow, Ctr for Advan Stud in the Behav Sci, 97-98; Am Philos Soc, 98; Staley Prize (Sch Am Res), 98., Curator of Oceanic Archaeol, PA Hearst Museum of Anthrop. **MEMBERSHIPS** AAAS; Am Anthrop Assoc; Soc Am Archaeol; Pac Sci Assoc; Sigma Xi; Asn Field Archaeol; Polynesian Soc; Prehist Soc; New Zealand Archaeol Assoc 2E **RESEARCH** Archaeology. **SELECTED PUBLICATIONS** Co-auth, Anahulu: The Anthropology of History in the Kingdom of Hawaii, 92; auth, Legacy of the Landscape, Hawaii, 96; Historical Ecology in the Pacific Islands, Yale, 97; The Lapita Peoples: Ancestors of the Oceanic World, Blackwell, 97. **CONTACT ADDRESS** Dept of Anthrop, Univ Calif, Berkeley, CA, 94720.

KIRK, WYATT D.
PERSONAL Born 05/10/1935, Elgin, IL, m **DISCIPLINE** EDUCATION **EDUCATION** Western MI U, BA 1963; Western MI U, MA 1969; Western MI U, EdD 1973; Licensed Psycologist 1978; NBCC 1984. **CAREER** NC A&T State Univ Dept of Human Development & Services, chairperson; Benton Harbor HS, tchr 1963-67; Ft Custer Job Corps, counselor 1967-68; Kalamazoo Pub Sch, counselor 1967-68; Western MI U, counselor 1968-70; Kalamazoo Resources Devel Council, assistance to founder, dir 1968-69; Experimental Program toEmploy Ex-Consult & Drug Users Ford Motor Co Dearborn, consult 1969-71; In-Serv Training Program for Tchr Grand Rapids Pub Sch, consult 1970; Western MI U; assoc prof 1970-78; Staff Relations Kalamazoo Planned Parenthood, consult 1972; Basic Treatment Counseling Techniques for Minorities MI Probate Ct, consult 1975; NC A&T St Univ, professor/chairperson. **HONORS AND AWARDS** MI Personnel & Guidance Assn serv awd 1976; Faculty Research Grant for Scholarly & Creative Research 1977; Presidents Citation, the Natl Assn of Nonwhite Concerns in Personnel & Guidance 1977 & 1978; Assn Counselor Educ & Spvsn recognition awd for successful completion of the Accreditation Workshop Training 1979; grants awds Kalamazoo Fdn Doctoral Research, Grand Rapids Fnd, Title IV Desegregation Inst, Intern, Cmty-Based Alternatives, State of NC, Dept of Human Resources, Managerial Schlrshp Centerfor Creative Leadership, Greensboro, NC; several publications published & non-published. **MEMBERSHIPS** Pres elect Amer Assoc for Counseling Dev; Assn Counselor Educ & Sprvsn; MI Personnel & Guidance Assn; MI Coll Personnel Assn; MI and NC Assn for Non-White Concerns; NC Assn Counselor Educ & Supervision; NC Personnel & Guidance Assn; Assn of Black Psychologists; charter mem MI and mem Natl Alliance of Black School Educ; Kappa Alpha Psi Inc; vice pres NAACP; bd mem, treas Churches United Effort; Equal Empl for the Disadvantaged & Minority chrmn; bd of trustees for the Lift Fdn; Inter-Faith Housing Council bd of dir; Greater Kalamazoo Cncl vice chairperson; Kalamazoo Cnty Substance Abuse bd mem; Greater Kalamazoo United Way Allocation & Budget Committeel editorial bd Journal of Multicultural Counseling and Develop; chairperson NC Assoc for Counseling and-Develop; mem AMCD Comm. **CONTACT ADDRESS** No Carolina A&T State Univ, 212 Hodgin Hall, Greensboro, NC, 27411.

KIRK-DUGGAN, CHERYL ANN
PERSONAL Born 07/24/1951, Lake Charles, LA, m, 1983 **DISCIPLINE** THEOLOGY, MUSICOLOGY **EDUCATION** University of Southwestern Louisiana, BA 1973; University of Texas at Austin, MM 1977; Austin Presbyterian Theological Seminary, MDiv 1987; Baylor University, PhD, 1992. **CAREER** Univ of Texas at Austin, music of Black Amers coach accomp 1974-77; Austin Community College, music of Black Amers 1976-77; Prairie View A&M Univ, teacher 1977-78; The Actor's Inst, teacher 1982-83; Williams Inst CME Church, organist, choir dir 1979-83; Self-employed, professional singer, voice teacher, vocal coach 1980-85; Christian Methodist Church, ordained minister, deacons orders 1984, elders orders 1986; Baylor University, Institute of Oral History, graduate asst, 1987-89, Dept of Religion, teaching asst, 1989-90; Meredith College, assistant professor, 1993-96; CENTER FOR WOMEN & RELIGION, DIR, GRADUATE THEOLOGICAL UNION, ASST PROF, 1997-; EDITORIAL BD, CONTAGION: JOURNAL OF VIOLENCE, MIMESIS & CULTURE, 1994-; ASSN FOR BLACK AWARENESS, MEREDITH COLLEGE, ADVISOR, 1994-. **HONORS AND AWARDS** University of Southwestern Louisiana, Magna Cum Laude; University of Texas at Austin, University Fellowship, 1975-77; Fund for Theological Education, Fellowship for Doctoral Studies, 1987-88, 1988-89. **MEMBERSHIPS** Pi Kappa Lambda, 1976-; Omicron Delta Kappa, 1977-; associate pastor, Trinity CME Church, 1985-86; president, Racial Ethnic Faith Comm, Austin Seminary, 1986-87; Golden Key Honor Society, 1990; Colloquim On Violence & Religion; Society of Biblical Literature; American Academy of Religion; Center for Black Music Research; Society of Christian Ethics; American Society for Aesthetics; Sigma Alpha Iota. **SELECTED PUBLICATIONS** Carnegie Hall debut, 1981; featured: "Life, Black Tress, Das Goldene Blatte, Bunte," 1981, 1982; recording: "Third Duke Ellington Sacred Concert," Virgil Thompson's Four Saints in Three Acts, EMI Records, 1981-82; author: Lily Teaching Fellow, 1995, 1996; Collidge Scholar with Assoc for Religion & Intellectual Life, 1996; "African-American Spirituals: Exorcising Evil Through Song," A Troubling in My Soul: Womanist Perspectives on Evil and Suffering, Orbis Press, 1991; "Gender, Violence and Transformation," Curing Violence: The Thought of Rene Girard, Polebridge Press, 1991; African-American Special Days: 15 Complete Worship Services, Abingdon Press, 1996; It's In the Blood: A Trildgy of Poetry Harvested from a Family Tree, River Vision, 1996; Exorcizing Evil: A Womanist Perspective on the Spirituals, Orbis, 1997. **CONTACT ADDRESS** Ctr for Women, Religion, 2400 Ridge Rd, Berkeley, CA, 94709-5298.

KIRKPATRICK, DIANE MARIE
PERSONAL Born 06/28/1933, Grand Rapids, MI **DISCIPLINE** HISTORY OF ART **EDUCATION** Vassar Col, BA, 55; Cranbrook Acad Art, MFA, 57; Univ Mich, Ann Arbor, MA, 65, PhD, 69. **CAREER** Manuscript & layout ed, Fideler Publ Co, Mich, 57-58; serv club dir, US Army Europe, Ger, 58-60; dir children's educ art hist & appreciation, Grand Rapids Art Mus, Mich, 61-63; lectr hist of art, 68-69, instr, 69-70, asst

prof, 72-74, dir, Prog in Film Video Studies, 77-78, assoc prof, PROF, 82- , HIST OF ART, UNIV MICH, ANN ARBOR, 74-, Sr fel, Mich Soc Fels, 73-78; Nat Endowment for grant to spec exhibs, 92. **HONORS AND AWARDS** Thurman Prof Hist of Art, 97; Time-Warner Media Develop Award, 95-99; H R Bloch Fund Spec Award Course Develop, 97-98. **MEMBERSHIPS** Col Art Asn Am. **RESEARCH** Twentieth century Western art; movies; popular culture. **SELECTED PUBLICATIONS** Auth, Eduardo Paolozzi, Studio Vista, 70; The Creation of Art (10 TV progs), Univ Mich TV Ctr, 74-75; An interview with film pioneer Frank Goldman, Cinegram, 77; Sonia Sharidan: Mind and machine, Afterimage, 78; Imaging and the machine, In: Chicago: The City and Its Artists 1945-1978, Univ Mich Mus Art, 78; The Artistic Vision of Jim Pallas, Detroit Inst Arts, 78; Making Waves: Recent Art, Science, and Technology Interactions in Chicago, Evanston Art Ctr, 86; Gardners Art Through the Ages, Harcourt, Brace, Jovanovitch, 90; Time and space in the Work of Laszlo Moholy-Nagy, Hungarian Stud Rev, 89; The Artists of the IG: Backgrounds and Continuities, The Independent Group: Postwar Britain and the Aesthetics of Plenty, MIT Press, 90; La Fotografia e la Nuova Tecnologia, Fotologia, 92; In-Visibility: Art and Disability, Mich Quart Rev, 98. **CONTACT ADDRESS** Dept of Hist of Art, Univ of Mich, 519 S State St, Ann Arbor, MI, 48109-1357. **EMAIL** diank@umich.edu

KIRKWOOD, GORDON MACDONALD
PERSONAL Born 05/07/1916, Toronto, ON, Canada, m, 1940, 2 children **DISCIPLINE** CLASSICAL PHILOLOGY **EDUCATION** Univ Toronto, AB, 38; Cornell Univ, AM, 39; Johns Hopkins Univ, PhD(Greek), 42. **CAREER** Latin master, Lower Can Col, 45-46; from instr to prof, 46-73, chmn dept, 63-72, Frederic J Whiton Prof Classics, Cornell Univ 73-, Ford fel, 53-54; Guggenheim fel, 56-57; Am Coun Learned Soc fel, 62-63; co-ed, Cornell Studies in Class Philol; Nat Endowment for Hum fel, 77. **MEMBERSHIPS** Am Philol Asn; Class Asn Atlantic States; AAUP. **RESEARCH** Greek lit. **SELECTED PUBLICATIONS** Auth, A Study of Sophoclean Drama, Cornell Univ, 58; A Short Guide to Classical Mythology, Holt, 60; Early Greek Monody, 74 & ed, Poetry and Poetics, Studies in Honor of James Hutton, 75, Cornell Univ; Selections from Pindar, Am Philol Asn, 82. **CONTACT ADDRESS** Dept of Classics, Cornell Univ, Ithaca, NY, 14850. **EMAIL** GMK4@Cornell.edu

KIRSHNER, ALAN MICHAEL
PERSONAL Born 02/01/1938, New York, NY, m, 2 children **DISCIPLINE** WESTERN CIVILIZATION, LATIN AMERICAN HISTORY **EDUCATION** Hofstra Univ, BA, 59; City Col New York, MA, 63; NY Univ, PhD(Hist), 70. **CAREER** Asst prof Hist, Univ WFla, 69-71; assoc prof, 71-76, prof Hist, Ohlone Col, 76-. **MEMBERSHIPS** AHA. **RESEARCH** Mexico, 1930-1935; marginal groups in Western civilization; masculinity. **SELECTED PUBLICATIONS** Auth, A Setback for Tomas Garrido Canabal's Desire to Eliminate the Church in Mexico, J Church & State, Autumn 71; Closing Phases of Global Exploration: The Evolution of the Early Works of Halford J Mackinder, Community Col Soc Sci Quart, Spring 72; Tomas Garrido Canabal y el Movimiento de los Camisas Rojas, Sep-Setentas, 76; Teaching the History Survey Course: Looking to the 1980's--The Need to Introduce Popular Culture, Popular Culture Methods, 6/77; Heretical Interpretations of Western Civilization: A Teaching Method, Community Col Soc Sci Asn, Fall 77; Masculinity in an Historical Perspective: Readings and Discussions, Univ Press Am, 77; Masculinity in American Comics, In: Men in Difficult Times, Prentice-Hall, 81; Tomas Garrido Canabal and the Repression of Religion in Tabasco, In: Religion in Latin American Life and Literature, Baylor Univ Press, 81; In the Course Of Human Events: Essays in American Government, Simon & Schuster, 98. **CONTACT ADDRESS** Dept of History, Ohlone Col, 43600 Mission Blvd, Fremont, CA, 94539-5884. **EMAIL** AKirshner@ohlone.cc.ca.us

KIRSHNER, JULIUS
PERSONAL Born 07/12/1939, New York, NY, m, 1965, 1 child **DISCIPLINE** MEDIEVAL & RENAISSANCE HISTORY **EDUCATION** Pace Col, BA, 61; Vatican Paleog & Diplomatic Sch, dipl paleog & diplomatics, 69; Am Acad Rome, dipl, 69; Columbia Univ, PhD, 70. **CAREER** Instr hist, Pace Col, 63-65; Lectr hist, City Col New York, 64-65; asst prof, Bard Col, 65-70; from Asst Prof to Assoc Prof, 70-83, prof hist, Univ of Chicago, 83-. **HONORS AND AWARDS** Herodotus fel, Inst Advan Studies, 72-73; I Tatti fel, 78-79; Nat Endowment Humanities fel, 78-79. **MEMBERSHIPS** Medieval Acad Am; Renaissance Soc Am. **SELECTED PUBLICATIONS** Auth, Papa Eugenio IV e il Monte Comune, Arch Storico Ital, 69; The Moral Theology of Public Finance, Archivum Fratrum Praedicatorum, 70; Civitas Sibi Faciat Civem: Bartolus of Sassoferrato's Doctrine on the Making of a Citizen, Speculum, 73; The Dowry Fund and the Marriage Market in Early Quattrocento Florence, J Mod Hist, 78; Between Nature and Culture: An Opinion of Baldus of Perugia on Venetian Citizenship as Second Nature, J Medieval and Renaissance Studies, 79; co-ed, University of Chicago Readings in Western Civilization, Univ Chicago Press, 9 vols, 86-87; ed, Italy, 1530-1630, Longman, 88; coauth, A Grammar of Signs: Bartolo da Sassoferrato's Tract on Insignia and Coats of Arms, Studies in Comparative Legal Hist, Publ of The Robbins Collection in Relig and Civil Law, Univ Calif, 94; ed and contribr, The Origins of the State in Italy, 1300-1600, Univ Chicago Press, 96. **CONTACT ADDRESS** Dept of Hist, Univ of Chicago, 1126 E 59th St, Chicago, IL, 60637-1539.

KISER, JOY
DISCIPLINE ART HISTORY, LIBRARY AND INFORMATION SERVICES **EDUCATION** Univ Akron, BA, 88; Case Western Reserve Univ, MA, 90; Kent State Univ, MLIS, 94. **CAREER** HEAD LIBR, CLEVELAND MUS NAT HIST; med libr Wooster Community Hosp. **CONTACT ADDRESS** 15307 Clinton Rd, Doylestown, OH, 44260. **EMAIL** jkiser@cmnh.org

KISSLING, PAUL J.
PERSONAL Born 08/03/1957, Toledo, OH, m, 1979, 2 children **DISCIPLINE** BIBLICAL LANGUAGES **EDUCATION** Univ of Sheffield, PhD, 91. **CAREER** Great Lakes Christian Col MI, prof, 91-; Co-editor, Col Press, NIV Old Testament Commentary. **MEMBERSHIPS** SBL, IBR **RESEARCH** Hebrew narrative research **SELECTED PUBLICATIONS** Auth, Reliable Characters in the Primary History, in: JSOTSup, 96. **CONTACT ADDRESS** Dept of Old Testament, Great Lakes Christian Col, 4808 Omar Dr, Lansing, MI, 48917. **EMAIL** pjk@voyager.net

KITAO, T. KAORI
DISCIPLINE ART HISTORY **EDUCATION** Univ CA, BA; MA; Harvard Univ, PhD. **CAREER** Fac, RI Sch Design, 63-66; fac, Swarthmore Col, 66; Chp, 75-81; William R. Kenan, Jr. Prof Art Hist, present. **HONORS AND AWARDS** VP Int Soc Comp Study of Civs, 80-83. **RESEARCH** Renaissance and Baroque art and archit; Am archit; cinema, design, and visual semiotics; material cult as hist of ideas; Bernini's archit. **SELECTED PUBLICATIONS** Auth, Oval and Circle in the Square of St. Peter's; scholarly articles in the Art Bulletin and the Journal of the Society of Architectural Historians; writings also on Japanese gardens **CONTACT ADDRESS** Swarthmore Col, Swarthmore, PA, 19081-1397. **EMAIL** tkitao1@swarthmore. edu

KITCHEL, MARY JEAN
PERSONAL New York, NY **DISCIPLINE** PHILOSOPHY, MEDIEVAL STUDIES **EDUCATION** Rice Univ, BA, 64; Pontif Inst Mediaeval Studies, MSL, 68; Univ Toronto, PhD, 74. **CAREER** Asst prof philos, Univ St Thomas, TX, 68-69; asst prof, Emmanuel Col, MA, 69-74; loan asst, Student Financial Aid, Houston Community Col Syst, 76-77; asst prof, 77-79, assoc dean extended educ, 80-82, Assoc Prof Philos, Univ St Thomas, TX, 79-88, Prof Phil, 88-, Dean Acad Serv, 90-93, Dept Ch Phil, 96-, Asst prof church hist, St Mary's Sem, TX, 68-69; res assoc philos & text ed, Pontif Inst Mediaeval Studies, Toronto, 73-75; Nat Endowment for Hum grant, 79. **HONORS AND AWARDS** Piper Professorship, 90; Sears-Roebuck Found Award, 90 **MEMBERSHIPS** Am Cath Philos Asn. **RESEARCH** Ed and analysis of texts of Walter Burley; philos psychol, philos of hum person; medl ethics. **SELECTED PUBLICATIONS** Auth, The De potentis animae of Walter Burley, 71, Walter Burley's Doctrine of the Soul: Another view, 77 Mediaeval Studies; Walter Burley and radical Aristotelanism, Proc World Cong on Aristotle (in press). **CONTACT ADDRESS** Dept of Philos, Univ of St Thomas, 3800 Montrose, Houston, TX, 77006-4696. **EMAIL** kitchel@stthom.edu

KITCHELL, KENNETH F.
PERSONAL Born 10/24/1947, Brockton, MA, m, 1970, 1 child **DISCIPLINE** CLASSICAL STUDIES **EDUCATION** Coll of Holy Cross, BA, 69; Loyola Univ Chicago, MA, 73; PhD, 76. **CAREER** Loyola Univ, 74; Quigley Preparatory Sem S Chicago, 74-76; Cath High School Baton Rouge, 80-81; Am School of Class Studies Athens Greece, 89; co-dir, Program in Greece Vergilian Soc of Am, 90; instr, 76-78; asst prof, 83-94, assoc prof, 94-97, prof, LA State Univ, 97-; vis prof, Univ Mass, 98-99. **HONORS AND AWARDS** Amoco Found award for Outstanding Undergraduate Techg, 80; Am Philol Asn Award for excellence in Tchg of Classics, 83; LSU Student Govt Asn Fac Award, 91; Robert L Amborski Distinguished Honors Prof Award, 93; Ovatio, Clasical Asn of the Middle W and S, 94; Summer Scholar Centre for Hellenic Studies Wash DC, 97; Lsu Alumni Asn Distinguished Fac Award, 97; Who's Who in the South and Southwest; Who's Who of Emerging Leaders in America; Men of Achievement; Dictionary of International Biography; Who's Who in American Education. **MEMBERSHIPS** Am Philol Asn; Archaeol Inst Am; Am Class League; Asn of Ancient Hist; Class Asn of the Middle west and S; Class Asn of New England, Joint Asn of Class Tchrs; Mass Foreign Lang Asn; Class Asn of Mass; Class Asn of the Pacific Northwest Am Council on the Tchg of Foreign Lang. **RESEARCH** Latin and Greek Pedagogy; Crete. **SELECTED PUBLICATIONS** Entering the Stadiun, Approaches to Ancient Greek Athletics, Class Bull, 98;coauth, A Trilogy on the Herpetology of Linnaeus's Systema Naturae X, Smithsonian Herpetological Service, 94; Albertus Magnus De Animalibus: A Medieval Summa Zoologica, 98. **CONTACT ADDRESS** The Dept of Classics, Univ of Mass, 520 Herter Hall, Amherst, MA, 01003. **EMAIL** kkitchel@classics.umass.edu

KITCHEN, MARTIN
PERSONAL Born 12/21/1936, Nottingham, England **DISCIPLINE** HISTORY **EDUCATION** Univ London, BA, 63, PhD, 66. **CAREER** Fac mem, 66-76, PROF HISTORY, SIMON FRASER UNIV, 76-. **SELECTED PUBLICATIONS** Auth, British Policy Towards the Soviet Union During the Second World War, 86; auth, Europe Between the Wars, 88; auth, The Origins of the Cold War in Comparative Perspective: American, British and Canadian Relations with the Soviet Union 1941-1948, 88; auth, A World in Flames, 90; auth, Empire and After, 94; auth, Nazi Germany at War, 94; auth, The British Empire and the Commonwealth, 96. **CONTACT ADDRESS** Dept of History, Simon Fraser Univ, Burnaby, BC, V5A 1S6.

KITTELSON, JAMES
DISCIPLINE CHURCH HISTORY **EDUCATION** St. Olaf Col, Phi Beta Kappa grad, 63; Stanford Univ, MA, 64, PhD, 69. **CAREER** Instr, Ohio State Univ, 71; vice-ch, Ohio State Univ, 74-77; ch, grad stud, Ohio State Univ, 89-91; vis grad prof, Luther Northwestern Theol Sem, 92; Concordia Univ. 97; prof, 97-; dir, Lutheran Brotherhood Res Prog. **HONORS AND AWARDS** Pres, bd of the Sixteenth Century Stud (s) Conf; exec comm, Coun Amer Soc for Reformation Res; Soc for Reformation Res; bd of dir(s), Ctr for Reformation Res. **SELECTED PUBLICATIONS** Auth, Luther the Reformer: The Story of the Man and His Career, 86; sr ed, Oxford Encycl of the Reformation, 96. **CONTACT ADDRESS** Dept of Church History, Luther Sem, 2481 Como Ave, St. Paul, MN, 55108. **EMAIL** jkittels@luthersem.edu

KITTERMAN, DAVID HAROLD
PERSONAL Born 04/01/1940, Denver, CO, m, 1964, 3 children **DISCIPLINE** MODERN EUROPEAN HISTORY **EDUCATION** Univ Utah, BA, 64, MA, 66; Univ Wash, PhD(Europ hist), 72. **CAREER** Instr hist, Utah State Univ, 69-70; asst prof, 70-78, ASSOC PROF HIST, NORTHERN ARIZ UNIV, 78-. **MEMBERSHIPS** AHA; Western Soc Sci Asn; Asn Ger Studies (pres, 76-78). **RESEARCH** Twentieth century German social, cultural and intellectual history; World War II and World War I history; modern Russian history. **SELECTED PUBLICATIONS** The Justice of the Wehrmacht Legal System in Servant or Opponent of National-Socialism, Cent Europ Hist, Vol 0024, 91. **CONTACT ADDRESS** Dept of Hist, No Arizona Univ, Flagstaff, AZ, 86001.

KIVISTO, PETER
PERSONAL Born 11/17/1948, Ishpeming, MI, m, 1973, 2 children **DISCIPLINE** SOCIOLOGY **EDUCATION** Univ Mich, BA, 70; Yale Univ, MDiv, 73, New School for Social Research, MA, 77, PhD, 82. **CAREER** ASST PROF TO FULL PROF, AUGUSTANA COL, 82-. **HONORS AND AWARDS** Fulbright, NEH Fel, Am Scandinavian Found Grant **MEMBERSHIPS** Am Sociol Asn, Midwest Sociol Soc, Soc for the Study of Social Problems, Immigration Hist Soc, Soc Sci Hist Asn, Asn for Sociol of Relig **RESEARCH** Race/ethnicity, theory, relig. **SELECTED PUBLICATIONS** Assoc ed, The Encyclopedia of Religion and Society, 98, AltaMira Press; auth, Key Ideas in Sociology: Their Origins, Careers, and Contemporary Relevance, 98, Pine Forge Press; ed, Illuminating Social Life, 98, Pine Forge Press; auth, Americans All: Ethnic and Race Relations in Historical, Structural, and Comparative Perspectives, 95, Wadsworth Publishing; co-ed, The Rapture of Politics: The Christian Right as the United States Approaches the Year 2000, 95, Transaction; co-ed, Scandinavian Immigrants and Education in North America, 95, Swedish Am Hist Soc; coauth, For Democracy, 93, Greenwood Press; auth, "Multiculturalism as a Factor in Shaping National Identity in Europe Today," in Dylematy Tozsamosci Europejskich Pod Koniec Drigiego Tysiaclecia, 97, Nicholas Copernicus Univ Press; coauth, "Multicultural America: Approaching the Twenty-First Century," in Race, Ethnicity, and Gender in Global Perspective, 97, Kendall/Hunt; auth, "Stanford M. Lyman's Sociology of Race and Ethnic Relations: Conundrums of Color and Culture," International Journal of Politics, Culture, and Society, 95; auth, "Finns and the Public Schoools, 1930-40," in Scandinavian Immigrants and Education in North America, 95, Swedish-Am Hist Soc; auth, "Does Ethnicity Matter for European Americans? Interpreting Ethnic Identity in the Post-Civil Rights Era," Finnish Am Reporter, 95; auth, "Toward an Antifoundational Yet Relevant Sociology: Can Gottdiener Have It Both Ways?" The Sociol Quarterly, 94; auth, "The Rise or Fall of the Christian Right?: Conflicting Reports from the Frontline," Sociol of Relig, 94; auth, "Robert E. Park's Dialectic of Racial Enlightenment," Int Jour of Politics, Culture, and Soc, 93; auth, "Intermarriage and the Melting Pot in Moline, 1910," in Swedes in America: New Perspectives, 93, The Emigrant Inst; auth, "Interpreting the Finnish American Experience," in Nordics in America: The Future of Their Past, 93, Norwegian-Am Hist Asn; coauth, "Symbolic Ethnicity and American Jews: The Relationship of Ethnic Identity to Behavior and Group Affiliation," Soc Sci Jour, 93; auth, "Religion and New Immigrants," in A Future for Religion?: Trends in Social Analysis, 93, Sage Publ. **CONTACT ADDRESS** Dept of Anthrop, Augustana Col, Rock Island, IL, 61201. **EMAIL** Sokivisto@augustana.edu

KLAASSEN, WALTER
PERSONAL Born 05/27/1926, Laird, SK, Canada, m, 1952, 3 children **DISCIPLINE** HISTORY, THEOLOGY **EDUCATION** McMaster Univ, BA, 54; McMaster Divinity Sch, BD, 57; Oxford Univ, DPhil(hist theol), 60. **CAREER** Assoc prof Bible, Bethel Col, Kans, 60-62, chmn dept Bible and relig, 62-64; assoc prof Bible and relig, 64-70, assoc prof hist, 71-73, PROF HIST, CONRAD GREBEL COL, UNIV WATERLOO, 73-; Can Coun grants, 70-73 and 78-79. **MEMBERSHIPS** Am Soc Church Hist; Can Soc Church Hist; Mennonitischer Geschichtsverein; NAm Comt for Doc Free Church Origins (secy, 71). **RESEARCH** Just war theory; dissent in the 16th century; unilateral peace initiatives in history. **SELECTED PUBLICATIONS** Jesus, A Crucified Pharisee, J Ecumenical Studies, Vol 0029, 92; Homosexuality in the Church in Both Sides of the Debate, J Ecumenical Studies, Vol 0033, 96. **CONTACT ADDRESS** Conrad Grebel Col, Waterloo, ON, N2L 3G6.

KLANG, DANIEL M.
PERSONAL Born 09/12/1934, San Francisco, CA, m, 1967 **DISCIPLINE** MODERN EUROPEAN HISTORY **EDUCATION** Univ Calif, Berkeley, BA, 59; Princeton Univ, PhD(hist), 63. **CAREER** Asst prof, 63-70, ASSOC PROF HIST, UNIV BC, 70-. **MEMBERSHIPS** AHA **RESEARCH** Western Europe, 1600-1918. **SELECTED PUBLICATIONS** Auth, , Political Science and Revolution in Works of Fabbroni,Giovanni 1752-1822, Intellectual and Civil Servant in Lorraine, J Mod Hist, Vol 0064, 92; Culture, Intellectuals and Circulation of Ideas in the 18th Cent, J Modern Hist, Vol 0064, 92; 18th-Century Reform, Vol 5, Italy of the Enlightenment, Pt 2, The Republic of Venice, 1761-1797, Engl Hist Rev, Vol 0109, 94. **CONTACT ADDRESS** Dept of Hist, Univ of BC, Vancouver, BC, V6T 1W5.

KLARE, MICHAEL T.
PERSONAL Born 10/14/1942, New York, NY **DISCIPLINE** INTERNATIONAL PEACE & SECURITY STUDIES **EDUCATION** Columbia Col, BA, 63; Columbia Univ, MA, 68; Union Inst, PhD, 76. **CAREER** Dir, Nat Security Proj, Inst for Policy Stud, Wash, DC, 76-84; Five Col Prof of Peace & World Security Stud, Hampshire Col, 85-. **MEMBERSHIPS** Comm on Int Security Stud; Am Acad of Arts & Sci. **RESEARCH** Military strategy; arms control & disarmament. **SELECTED PUBLICATIONS** Auth, War Without End, Knopf, 72; auth, American Arms Supermarket, Univ Tex Press, 84; co-ed, Low Intensity Warfare, Pantheon, 88; auth, Rogue States and Nuclear Outlaws, Hill & Wang, 95; co-ed, Lethal Commerce, Am Acad of Arts & Sci, 95; co-ed, World Security, 3rd ed, St. Martin's Press, 97. **CONTACT ADDRESS** Peace & World Security Stud, Hampshire Col, Amherst, MA, 01002. **EMAIL** mklare@hampshire.edu

KLAREN, PETER FLINDELL
PERSONAL Born 10/18/1938, Summit, NJ, m, 1963, 1 child **DISCIPLINE** LATIN AMERICAN HISTORY **EDUCATION** Dartmouth Col, AB, 60; Univ Calif, Los Angeles, MA, 64, PhD(hist), 68. **CAREER** Asst prof hist, Wash State Univ, 68-70; adj asst prof, Dartmouth Col, 71-72; asst prof, 72-75; assoc prof, 75-79, prof hist, George Washington Univ, 79-, Soc Sci Res Coun fel, 73-74; fel, Andrew Mellon Found, Aspen Inst Humanistic Studies, 75-76 & Am Philos Soc, 76-77. **HONORS AND AWARDS** Trachtenberg Teaching Prize, GWU, 95. **MEMBERSHIPS** AHA; Latin Am Studies Asn. **RESEARCH** Late 19th and early 20th century social and economic history of Latin America; Peru. **SELECTED PUBLICATIONS** Auth, Las Haciendas Azucareras y los Origines del Apra, Inst Peruvian Studies, Lima, 70 & 2nd ed, 76; Modernization, Dislocation and Aprismo: Origins of the Peruvian Aprista Party, 1870-1932, Univ Tex, 73; contrib, The social and Economic Consequences of Modernization in the Peruvian Sugar Industry, 1860-1940, In: Land and Labour in Latin America: Essays in the Development of Agrarian Capitalism, Cambridge Univ, 77; Orgins of Modern Peru, 1880-1930, In: Vol V, Cambridge History of Latin America, Cambridge Univ Press, 86; contrib, Historical Background, Peru: A Country Study, ed by Rex Hudson, Washington, 93. **CONTACT ADDRESS** Dept of Hist, George Washington Univ, 2035 H St N W, Washington, DC, 20052-0001. **EMAIL** klaren@gwis2.circ.gwu.edu

KLASSEN, PETER JAMES
PERSONAL Born 12/18/1930, AB, Canada, m, 1959, 3 children **DISCIPLINE** EARLY MODERN EUROPEAN HISTORY **EDUCATION** Univ BC, BA, 55; Univ Southern Calif, MA, 68, PhD(hist), 62. **CAREER** Prin, Fraser Lake Sch, BC, Can, 53-54; lectr hist, Univ Southern Calif, 58-60, admin supvr, Dept Gen Studies, 60-62; head dept hist and cur arch, Pac Col, 62-66; from asst prof to assoc prof, 66-69, chmn dept, 69-74, dir conflict resolution prog, 73-75, PROF HIST, CALIF STATE UNIV, FRESNO, 69-; DEAN, SCH SOC SCI, 80-. **MEMBERSHIPS** AHA; Am Soc Church Hist; Am Soc Reformation Res; Renaissance Soc Am. **RESEARCH** The Reformation; western civilization; Mennonite history. **SELECTED PUBLICATIONS** Auth, The Early Reformation in Europe, German Studies Rev, Vol 0016, 93; Enacting the Reformation in Germany in Essays on Institution and Reception, Ger Studies Rev, Vol 0018, 95; Wondrous in His Saints in Counterreformation Propaganda in Bavaria, Ger Studies Rev, Vol 0018, 95. **CONTACT ADDRESS** Dept of Hist, California State Univ, Fresno, Fresno, CA, 93710.

KLAUSNER, CARLA LEVINE
PERSONAL Born 11/09/1936, Kansas City, MO, m, 1963, 3 children **DISCIPLINE** MIDDLE EAST AND MEDIEVAL EUROPEAN HISTORY **EDUCATION** Barnard Col, Columbia Univ, AB, 58; Radcliffe Col, AM, 60; Harvard Univ, PhD (Mid E hist), 63. **CAREER** Teaching asst Islamic insts, Harvard Univ, 61-62; lectr Mid E hist and civilization, 64-65, asst prof, 65-72, assoc prof, 72-80, PROF MID E HIST AND CIVILIZATION AND MEDIEVAL HIST, UNIV MOKANSAS CITY, 80-. **HONORS AND AWARDS** Shelby Storck Award, Univ MoKansas City, 77. **MEMBERSHIPS** AHA; MidE Studies Asn NAm. **RESEARCH** Islamic civilization and modern Middle East history; medieval and contemporary Jewish history; medieval European civilization. **SELECTED PUBLICATIONS** Auth, The Distant Shrine in The Islamic Centuries in Jerusalem, Am Hist Rev, Vol 0099, 94. **CONTACT ADDRESS** Dept of Hist, Univ of Mo, 5100 Rockhill Rd, Kansas City, MO, 64110-2499.

KLEBER, BROOKS EDWARD
PERSONAL Born 04/15/1919, Trenton, NJ, m, 1946 **DISCIPLINE** MILITARY HISTORY **EDUCATION** Dickinson Col, PhB, 40; Univ Pa, MA, 48, PhD, 57. **CAREER** Historian, US Army Chem Corps Hist off, 50-59, asst chief, 59-63; chief historian, US Continental Army Command, 63-73; chief historian, US Army Training and Doctrine Command, 73-80; DEP CHIEF HISTORIAN, US ARMY CTR MIL HIST, 80-. **MEMBERSHIPS** AHA; Am Mil Inst US Comn Mil Hist. **RESEARCH** Colonial American and military history. **SELECTED PUBLICATIONS** Auth, Observance of the 50th Anniversary of D-Day, Pub Hist, Vol 0017, 95. **CONTACT ADDRESS** 440 Summer Dr, Newport News, VA, 23606.

KLEHR, HARVEY
PERSONAL Born 12/25/1945, Newark, NJ, m, 1998, 3 children **DISCIPLINE** POLITICAL SCIENCE **EDUCATION** Franklin and Marshall Col, BA, 67; Univ NC, PhD, 71. **CAREER** Asst prof, assoc prof, prof, Emory Univ, 71-; Samuel Candler Dobbs prof polit, 86-95; Andrew Mellon prof polis and hist, 96-. **HONORS AND AWARDS** Emory Williams tchg award, 83; F&M Alumni medal, 85; scholar/tchr of the year award, 95. **MEMBERSHIPS** Am Polit Sci Asn; Orgn of Am Hist. **RESEARCH** American Communism. **SELECTED PUBLICATIONS** Auth, the Heyday of American Communism: The Depression Decade, Basic, 84; auth, Far Left of Center: The American Radical Left Today, Transaction, 88; coauth, The American Communist Movement: Storming Heaven Itself, Twayne, 92; coauth, The Secret World of American Communism, Yale, 95; coauth, The American Spy Case: Prelude to McCarthyism, Univ North Carolina, 96; coauth, The Soviet World of American Communism, Yale, 98. **CONTACT ADDRESS** Political Science Dept, Emory Univ, Atlanta, GA, 30322. **EMAIL** hklehr@ps.emory.edu

KLEIMOLA, ANN
DISCIPLINE MEDIEVAL RUSSIAN HISTORY **EDUCATION** Univ Mich, PhD, 70. **CAREER** Prof, Univ Nebr, Lincoln. **HONORS AND AWARDS** NEH Inst, 94. **SELECTED PUBLICATIONS** Auth, Justice in Medieval Russia, Am Philos Soc, 75; coed, Culture and Identity in Muscovy, 1359-1584, Moscow, 97. **CONTACT ADDRESS** Univ Nebr, Lincoln, 635 Oldfat, Lincoln, NE, 68588-0417. **EMAIL** akleimol@unlinfo.unl.edu

KLEIN, BERNARD
PERSONAL Born 10/15/1928, Czechoslovakia, m, 1961, 2 children **DISCIPLINE** MODERN & JEWISH HISTORY **EDUCATION** Rabbi, Torah Vodaath Talmudical Sem, 53; Brooklyn Col, BA, magna cum laud, 54; Columbia Univ, MA, 56, PhD, 62. **CAREER** Lectr hist, Brooklyn Col, 58-61 & City Col New York, 64; from instr to assoc prof, 65-69, chmn, Div Behav & Soc Sci, 68-70, chmn, Dept Hist & Polit Sci, 70-71, chmn, Dept Hist & Philos, 72-79, PROF HIST, KINGSBOROUGH COMMUNITY COL, 69-, CHMN DEPT SOC SCI, 79-95, CHMN DEPT HIST, PHILOS & POLIT SCI, 95-; Lectr, Long Island Univ, 60; consult, Nat Curric Res Inst, Am Asn Jewish Educ, 65-67; mem educ coun, Fed Jewish Philanthropists, pres, 67-69; pres, Jewish Fac Asn, City Univ New York, 79-. **HONORS AND AWARDS** Phi Beta Kappa, 54; Fel, Conf Material Claims Jews against Ger, 57-58, 59-60; Fel, Res Found State Univ NY, 71. **MEMBERSHIPS** AHA **RESEARCH** German international policy during the Nazi Period; the right-radical movements in Hungary during the inter-war period; Jewish history and the Nazi Holocaust. **SELECTED PUBLICATIONS** Auth, Rudolf Kasztner and the Hungarian Rescue Effort, in Perspective, Vol I, 59; The Judenrat, Jewish Social Studies, 1/60; New developments in Jewish school curricula, Am Asn Jewish Educ, 65 & in Jewish Education Register and Directory, 65; The decline of a Sephardic community in Transylvania, Studies in Honor of M J Benardete, 65; Hungarian politics and the Jewish question, 4/66 & Anti-Jewish demonstrations in Hungarian universities, 1932-1936: Their role in the struggle for political power between Istvan, Bethlen, and Gyula Gombos, 82, Jewish Soc Studies, 82; Hungarian politics and the Jewish question, in Hostages of Modernization: Studies on Modern Antisemitism, 1870-1933/39, Walter de Gruyer, 93. **CONTACT ADDRESS** Dept Hist, Philos & Polit Sci, Kingsborough Comm Col, CUNY, 2001 Oriental Blvd, Brooklyn, NY, 11235-2333. **EMAIL** bklein@kbcc.cuny.edu

KLEIN, HERBERT S.
DISCIPLINE LATIN AMERICAN HISTORY **EDUCATION** Univ Chicago, BA, 57, PhD, 63. **CAREER** Prof. **SELECTED PUBLICATIONS** Slavery in the Americas, A Comparative History of Cuba and Virginia, 67; Origenes de la Revolucion Nacional Boliviana: La Crisis de la generacion del Chaco, 68, 93; Parties and Political Change in Bolivia, 1880-1952, 69; The Middle Passage: Comparative Studies in the Atlantic Slave Trade, 78; Bolivia: The Evolution of a Multi-Ethnic Society, 82; African Slavery in Latin America and the Caribbean, 86; Haciendas y Ayllus, Rural Society in the Bolivian Andes in the 18th- and 19th-century, 93. **CONTACT ADDRESS** Dept of Hist, Columbia Col, New York, 2960 Broadway, New York, NY, 10027-6902.

KLEIN, IRA N.
PERSONAL Born 12/07/1931, New York, NY, m, 1966, 3 children **DISCIPLINE** MODERN EUROPEAN & ASIAN HISTORY **EDUCATION** Columbia Univ, BS, 56, MA, 60, PhD, 68. **CAREER** Lectr contemporary civilization, Queens Col, NY, 67-68; asst prof mod Europ hist, 68-72, assoc prof mod europ & asian hist, Am Univ, 72-, Nat Endowment for Humanities fel, 72 & 75-76; Ford-Rockefeller fel, Population Policy, 77-78. **HONORS AND AWARDS** Outstanding Tchr Col Arts & Sci Am Univ, 91-92; Distinguished Serv, Nat Gold Key Soc, 93; Outstanding Commun Serv, Stud Life, Am Univ, 94 & 96. **RESEARCH** Modern European diplomacy; British imperialism in Asia; development of modern India. **SELECTED PUBLICATIONS** Auth Imperialism Ecology & Presence Indian Econ Soc ist Rev, 94; Plague & Popular Responses in India, Jour Indian Hist, 98; Materialism, Modernization & Mutiny in India, Mod Asian Study. **CONTACT ADDRESS** Dept Hist, American Univ, 4400 Mass Ave NW, Washington, DC, 20016-8200.

KLEIN, LAWRENCE E.
DISCIPLINE HISTORY **EDUCATION** Johns Hopkins Univ, PhD, 83. **CAREER** Assoc prof, Univ Nev Las Vegas. **SELECTED PUBLICATIONS** Auth, Britain History; Early Modern Europe; Cultural History; Shaftesbury and the Culture of Politeness, Cambridge, 94. **CONTACT ADDRESS** History Dept, Univ Nev Las Vegas, 4505 Md Pky, Las Vegas, NV, 89154.

KLEIN, MARTIN A.
PERSONAL Born 04/09/1934, New York, NY, m, 1963, 2 children **DISCIPLINE** AFRICAN HISTORY **EDUCATION** Northwestern Univ, BA, 55; Univ Chicago, MA, 59, PhD(hist), 64. **CAREER** Instr hist, Univ RI, 61-62; asst prof, Univ Calif, Berkeley, 65-70; assoc prof, 70-79, PROF HIST, UNIV TORONTO, 79-; Mem, Comt Comp Studies New Nations, Univ Chicago, 64-65; vis assoc prof, Louvanium Univ, Kinshasa, 68-69. **MEMBERSHIPS** AHA; African Studies Asn. **SELECTED PUBLICATIONS** Auth, Africa in Endurance and Change South of the Sahara, Int J African Hist Studies, Vol 0026, 93; Birth of Guine in Portuguese and Africans in Senegambia 1841-1936, Jour African Hist, Vol 0034, 93; The Era of Power, Int J African Hist Studies Vol 0028, 95; Pragmatism in the Age of Jihad in The Precolonial State of Bundu, J Interdisciplinary Hist, Vol 0026, 96; Leisure and Society in Colonial Brazzaville, J Interdisciplinary Hist, Vol 0028, 97; Cotton, Colonialism, and Social-History in Sub-Saharan Africa, J African Hist, Vol 0038, 97; Status and Identity in West Africa, J Interdisciplinary Hist, Vol 0027, 97; Migration, Jihad and Muslim Authority, The Future Colonies in Karta, J African Hist, Vol 0038, 97. **CONTACT ADDRESS** Dept of Hist, Univ of Toronto, Toronto, ON, M5S 1A1.

KLEIN, MAURY
DISCIPLINE US SOCIAL, CULTURAL, AND BUSINESS HISTORY BETWEEN 1860 AND 1945 **EDUCATION** Emory Univ, PhD, 65. **CAREER** Dept Hist, Univ RI **HONORS AND AWARDS** URI Res Excellence awd. **RESEARCH** Mod cult. **SELECTED PUBLICATIONS** Publ on, hist of the Civil War; the railroad industry & the late 19th and 20th century. **CONTACT ADDRESS** Dept of Hist, Univ of RI, 8 Ranger Rd, Ste. 1, Kingston, RI, 02881-0807.

KLEIN, MICHAEL EUGENE
PERSONAL Born 07/30/1940, Philadelphia, PA **DISCIPLINE** ART HISTORY **EDUCATION** Rutgers Col, BA, 62; Columbia Univ, MA, 65, PhD, 71. **CAREER** Lectr, Douglass Col, 69-70; asst prof, State Univ NY Col Brockport, 71-73 & Univ SC, 73-77; asst prof, 77-81, assoc prof art hist, Western KY Univ, 81, Vis cur, Hirshhorn Mus & Sculpture Garden, Smithsonian Inst, 75. **MEMBERSHIPS** Col Art Asn Am. **RESEARCH** Twentieth century Am painting; 19th century Eng painting. **SELECTED PUBLICATIONS** Auth, John Covert's Time: Cubism, Duchamp, Einstein--a quasi-scientific fantasy, Art J, summer 74; John Covert and the Arensberg Circle: Symbolism, cubism and protosurrealism, Arts Mag, 5/77; John Covert's studios in 1916 and 1923: Two views into the past, Art J, fall 79. **CONTACT ADDRESS** Dept of Art, Western Kentucky Univ, 1 Big Red Way St, Bowling Green, KY, 42101-3576.

KLEIN, MILTON M.
PERSONAL Born 08/15/1917, New York, NY, m, 1963, 2 children **DISCIPLINE** AMERICAN HISTORY **EDUCATION** City Col New York, BSS, 37, MSEd, 39; Columbia Univ, PhD, 54. **CAREER** Lectr hist, Columbia Univ, 54-58; Chmn dept hist, Long Island Univ, 58-62; Dean col lib arts and sci, 62-66; Dean grad studies, State Univ NY Col Fredonia, 66-69; Prof hist, 69-77, Alumni Distinguished Serv prof, 77-80, LINDSAY YOUNG PROF HIST, UNIV TENN, KNOXVILLE, 80-; Ford Found fel, 55-56; Lilly fel, Clements Libr, Ann Arbor, Mich, 61; Fulbright lectr, Univ Canterbury, NZ, 62; Am Philos Soc res grant, 73; ADV ED, 18TH CENTURY STUDIES, 75-; Walter E Meyer vis prof, NY Univ Sch Law, 76-77. **HONORS AND AWARDS** Kerr Hist Prize, NY State Hist Asn, 74; Articles Prize, Am Soc for 18th-Century Studies, 76. **MEMBERSHIPS** Orgn Am Historians; AAUP; Am Hist Asn; Am Soc Legal Hist (secy, 75-77, vpres, 78-79, pres, 80-); Southeast Am Soc 18th Century Studies. **RESEARCH** American colonial history; New York history; American legal history. **SELECTED PUBLICATIONS** Auth, The Republican Synthesis Revisited and Politics and the American Revolution in Essays in Honor of Billias, George, Proc Am Antiq Soc, Vol 0102, 92; Political Thought and the American Judiciary, Am J Legal Hist, Vol 0038, 94; Budapest and New York in Studies in Metropolitan Transformation, 1870-1930, NY Hist, Vol 0075, 94; The Pleasures of Teaching and Writing History, William Mary Quart, Vol 0052, 95; Mythologizing the United States Constitution, Soundings, Vol 0078, 95; Political Partisanship in the American Middle Colonies, 1700-1776, William Mary Quart, Vol 0053, 96. **CONTACT ADDRESS** Dept of Hist, Univ of Tenn, Knoxville, TN, 37996.

KLEIN, OWEN
DISCIPLINE THEATRE HISTORY; IMPROVISATION **EDUCATION** Villanova, MA; Ind Univ, PhD. **CAREER** Adj assoc prof. **SELECTED PUBLICATIONS** Pub (s), Theatre Hist in Can and 19th century Theatre Res; contrib ed, Oxford Companion to Canadian Drama and Theatre. **CONTACT ADDRESS** Dept of Dramatic Art, Univ of Windsor, 401 Sunset Ave, Windsor, ON, N9B 3P4. **EMAIL** dumala@uwindsor.ca

KLEINBAUER, W. EUGENE
DISCIPLINE EARLY CHRISTIAN, BYZANTINE ART **EDUCATION** Princeton Univ, PhD. **CAREER** Prof. **SELECTED PUBLICATIONS** Auth, Modern Perspectives in Western Art History, 71; Research Guide to the History of Western Art, 83; Early Christian and Byzantine Architecture, 92. **CONTACT ADDRESS** Dept of History and Art, Indiana Univ, Bloomington, 300 N Jordan Ave, Bloomington, IN, 47405. **EMAIL** kleinbau@indiana.edu

KLEINBAUER, W. EUGENE
PERSONAL Born 06/15/1937, Los Angeles, CA, 2 children **DISCIPLINE** MEDIEVAL ART HISTORY, HISTORIOGRAPHY OF ART **EDUCATION** Univ Calif, Berkeley, BA, 59, MA, 62; Princeton Univ, PhD(Hist of Art), 67. **CAREER** Asst prof Hist of Art, Univ Calif, Los Angeles, 65-71, assoc prof, 72; chmn, Dept Fine Arts, 73-76, assoc prof, 73-77, prof Hist of Art, Ind Univ, Bloomington, 77-, Nat Endowment for the Humanities fel, 76-77; Zacks vis prof, Hebrew Univ, Jerusalem, 78; Frederic L Morgan prof, U of Louisville, 96; ed, Int Ctr Medieval Art, Gesta, 80-83. **MEMBERSHIPS** Col Art Asn; Mediaeval Acad Am; Int Ctr Medieval Art; Midwest Art Hist Soc; Archaeol Inst Am. **RESEARCH** Byzantine art; early medieval art. **SELECTED PUBLICATIONS** Auth, Modern Perspectives in Western Art History, Holt, Rinehart & Winston, 71; Origins and functions of aisled Tetraconch churches in Syria and Mesopotamia, Dumbarton Oaks Papers, 27: 89-114; ed, Art of Byzantium and Medieval West: Selected Studies by Ernst Kitzinger, Ind Univ Press, 76; Aedita in Turribus: Superstructure of S Lorenzo, Milan, Gesta, 15: 1-9; Tradition and Innovation in The Design of Zvartnots, Acad Sci Armenian, 81; Ornts in the Mosaic Decoration of the Rotunda at Thessaloniki, Cahiers archeologiques, Vol 30, 82; coauth, Research Guide to the History of Western Art, Am Libr Asn, 82; Early Christian and Byzantine Architecture, 92. **CONTACT ADDRESS** Dept of Art History, Indiana Univ, Bloomington, Bloomington, IN, 47405. **EMAIL** kleinbau@indiana.edu

KLEINBERG, SUSAN JANET
PERSONAL Born 10/20/1947, New York, NY **DISCIPLINE** HISTORY **EDUCATION** Univ Pittsburgh, BA, 68, MA, 70, PhD(hist), 73. **CAREER** Asst prof hist, Univ Calif, San Diego, 72-75; Asst prof interdisciplinary studies, Miami Univ, Ohio, 75-77; Asst prof hist, Univ Tenn, 77-80; BRIT SUB-AQUA CLUB RES FEL SPORTS HIST, 78-. **MEMBERSHIPS** AHA; Orgn Am Historians; Social Sci Hist Asn; Coord Comt Women Hist Prof; British Asn Am Studies. **RESEARCH** Urban history; labor history; history of women. **SELECTED PUBLICATIONS** Auth, From the Corn-Mothers to Starship-Enterprise in Gender in American Studies, J Am Studies, Vol 0028, 94; Population and Resources in Western Intellectual Traditions, Engl Hist Rev, Vol 0109, 94; Second To None in a Documentary History of American Women from the 16th Century to 1865, Vol I, from 1865 to the Present, Vol II J Am Studies, Vol 0030, 96. **CONTACT ADDRESS** Eaton Mill Lodge Mill Lane Enton NR Goldalming Sur.

KLEINERT, SYLVIA
DISCIPLINE ART HISTORY **EDUCATION** PhD **CAREER** Fel, Ctr Cross-Cult Res, Australian Natl Univ. **RESEARCH** Aboriginal art; tourist trade between aborigines and mainstream Australians. **SELECTED PUBLICATIONS** contrib, The Heritage of Namatjira,92; Lying About the Landscape, pending; co-ed, Oxford Companion to Aboriginal Art and Culture, pending. **CONTACT ADDRESS** Dept of Education, Australian National Univ. **EMAIL** Sylvia.Kleinert@anu.edu.au

KLEINFELD, GERALD R
PERSONAL Born 11/08/1936, New York, NY **DISCIPLINE** MODERN EUROPEAN HISTORY **EDUCATION** NY Univ, BA, 56, PhD, 61; Univ Mich, MA, 57. **CAREER** Vis instr hist, Bates Col, 61-62; from asst prof to assoc prof, 62-77, PROF HIST, ARIZ STATE UNIV, 77-; ASST DEAN OFF-CAMPUS INSTR, 77-; Vis asst prof, State Univ NY Col Fredonia, 67-68; ED, GER STUDIES REV, 77-. **MEMBERSHIPS** AHA; Conf Group Cent Europ Hist; Am Comt Hist 2nd World War; Western Asn Ger Studies; Coun Ger Studies Mod Lang Asn. **RESEARCH** Central European history. **SELECTED PUBLICATIONS** Auth, German Errors in False Interpreters and Accomplices of the Sed-Dictatorship in the West, Ger Studies Rev, Vol 0016, 93. **CONTACT ADDRESS** Dept of Hist, Arizona State Univ, Tempe, Tempe, AZ, 85281.

KLEINSASSER, JEROME
PERSONAL Born 03/28/1939, St. Paul, MN, m, 1980, 2 children **DISCIPLINE** MUSICOLOGY **EDUCATION** Univ Minn, PhD, 70. **CAREER** Prof Music, Calif State Univ, 72-. **MEMBERSHIPS** Am Musicol Soc, Col Mus Soc **RESEARCH** Opera **CONTACT ADDRESS** California State Univ, Bakersfield, 9001 Stockdale Hwy, Bakersfield, CA, 93311-1099. **EMAIL** jkleinsasser@academic.csubak.edu

KLEPAK, HAL
DISCIPLINE HISTORY **EDUCATION** McGill Univ, BA; London Univ, MA, PhD. **CAREER** Prof, Royal Milit Col. **MEMBERSHIPS** Canadian Found for the Ams (FOCAI) **RESEARCH** Latin American security issues; Canadian foreign and defense policy; conventional strategy. **SELECTED PUBLICATIONS** Auth, Canada and Latin American Security, 1996; Natural Allies? Canadian and Mexican Views on International Security, 1996. **CONTACT ADDRESS** Royal Military Col Canada, PO Box 17000, Kingston, ON, K7K 7B4. **EMAIL** klepak_h@rmc.ca

KLINE, RONALD R.
PERSONAL Born 04/21/1947, Oswego, KS, m, 1976, 5 children **DISCIPLINE** HISTORY OF SCIENCE & TECHNOLOGY **EDUCATION** Univ Wisc-Madison, PhD, 83. **CAREER** Dir, IEEE Ctr for Hist of Elec Eng, 84-87; Asst Prof, Hist & Tech, 87-93, Assoc Prof, 93-, Cornell Univ. **HONORS AND AWARDS** Soc for Hist of Tech, IEEE Life embers Prize in Elec Hist, 88; Soc of Nat Asn Pubs, Best Editorial or Column, 92; Soc for Tech Commun, 1st Place Award of Distinction for editorial excellence, 97, editing prize-winning paper, 96; Cornell Col of Eng, recognized for exemplary tchng, 96., Assoc Ed for Hist, IEEE Transactions on Educ, 88-94; Ed Bd, IEEE Spectrum, 89-91; Ed, IEEE Tech & Soc Magazine, 95-97; Advisory ed, Isis, 96-98, Tech & Culture, 98-00. **MEMBERSHIPS** IEEE Soc on Soc Implications of Tech, (pres 91-92). **RESEARCH** History of urban technology in rural life; history of engineering; history of information technology. **SELECTED PUBLICATIONS** Auth, Stienmetz: Engineer and Socialist, Johns Hopkins Stud in the Hist of Tech, Johns Hopkins Univ Press, 92; auth, Construing Technology as Applied Science: Public Rhetoric of Scientists and Engineers in the United States, 1880-1945, Isis, 86, 194-221, 95; auth, Ideology and the New Deal Fact Film Power and the Land, Public Understanding of Science, 6, 19-30, 97; auth, Ideology and Social Surveys: Reinterpreting the Effects of Laborsaving Technology on American Farm Women, Tech & Culture, 38, 355-385, 97. **CONTACT ADDRESS** Cornell Univ, 394 Rhodes Hall, Ithaca, NY, 14850. **EMAIL** rrk1@cornell.edu

KLING, BLAIR B.
DISCIPLINE HISTORY **EDUCATION** Univ Pa, PhD, 60. **CAREER** Prof, Univ Ill Urbana Champaign **RESEARCH** Modern South Asian business and entrepreneurial history; industrialization; urban history. **SELECTED PUBLICATIONS** Auth, The Blue Mutiny: The Indigo Disturbances in Bengal 1859-1862, Univ Pa, 66; Partner in Empire: Dwarkanath Tagore and the Age of Enterprise in Eastern India, Univ Calif, 76. **CONTACT ADDRESS** History Dept, Univ Ill Urbana Champaign, 52 E Gregory Dr, Champaign, IL, 61820. **EMAIL** b-kling@uiuc.edu

KLING, DAVID
PERSONAL Born 04/21/1950, Mora, MN, m, 1985, 4 children **DISCIPLINE** HISTORY OF CHRISTIANITY, RELIGION IN AMERICAN LIFE **EDUCATION** Trinity Col, IL, BA, 72; Northern IL Univ, 76; Univ Chicago, PhD, 85. **CAREER** Asst prof hist, Palm Beach Atlantic Col, 82-86; Univ administration, Univ Miami, 86-93; asst prof of relig studies, 93-95, assoc prof, Univ Miami, 95-. **HONORS AND AWARDS** Kenneth Scott Latourette Prize in Religion and Modern Hist (Best Book Manuscript), 92. **MEMBERSHIPS** Am Academy of Relig; Am Soc of Church Hist. **RESEARCH** Revivalism in Am; biblical texts in hist of Christianity. **SELECTED PUBLICATIONS** Auth, A Field of Divine Wonders: The New Divinity and Village Revivals in Northwestern Connecticut, 1792-1822, PA State Univ Press, 93; For Males Only: The Image of the Infidel and the Construction of Gender in the Second Great Awakening in New England, J of Men's Studies 3, May 95; twenty-five entries in The Blackwell Dictionary of Evangelical Biography, 1730-1860, ed Donald M Lewis, 2 vols, Blackwell Pubs, 95; The New Divinity and Williams College, 1793-1836, Religion and American Culture: A Journal of Interpretation 6, summer 96; By the Light of His Example: New Divinity Schools of the Prophets and Theological Education in New England, 1750-1825, in American Theological Education in the Evangelical Tradition, eds D G Hart and R Albert Mohler, Jr, Baker Books, 96; Smyth, Newman, in Dictionary of Heresy Trials in American Christianity, ed George H Shriver, Greenwood Press, 97; New Divinity Schools of the Prophets, 1750-1825: A Case Study in Ministerial Education, History of Ed Quart 37, summer 97. **CONTACT ADDRESS** Dept of Relig Studies, Univ of Miami, PO Box 248264, Miami, FL, 33124. **EMAIL** dkling@miami.edu

KLINGHOFFER, ARTHUR JAY
PERSONAL Born 07/30/1941, New York, NY, m, 1969, 1 child **DISCIPLINE** POLITICS, SOVIET FOREIGN POLICY **EDUCATION** Columbia Univ, PhD, 66 **CAREER** Prof, Rutgers Univ, 70- **HONORS AND AWARDS** Fulbright (2), Nobel **RESEARCH** Russian politics, African politics, politics of oil **SELECTED PUBLICATIONS** The International Dimension of Genocide in Rwanda, 98; Red Apocalypse, 96 **CONTACT ADDRESS** Dept Political Sci, Rutgers Univ, Camden, NJ, 08102. **EMAIL** klinghof@crab.rutgers.edu

KLOTTER, JAMES CHRISTOPHER
PERSONAL Born 01/17/1947, Lexington, KY, m, 1966, 3 children **DISCIPLINE** HISTORY **EDUCATION** Univ Ky, BA, 68, MA, 69, PhD(hist), 75. **CAREER** Res analyst, 73-75; asst ed, 75-78, managing ed, 78-80, GEN ED, THE REGISTER, KY HIST SOC, 80-. **MEMBERSHIPS** Orgn Am Historians; Southern Hist Asn. **RESEARCH** Kentucky history; Appalachian history; history of the family. **SELECTED PUBLICATIONS** Auth, The Pattons in A Personal History of an American Family, J Southern Hist, Vol 0062, 96; How the West was Lost in The Transformation of Kentucky from Boone, Daniel To Clay, Henry, J Am Hist, Vol 0084, 97. **CONTACT ADDRESS** PO Box H, Frankfort, KY, 40602.

KLUNDER, WILLARD C.
PERSONAL Chicago, IL **DISCIPLINE** POLITICAL HISTORY **EDUCATION** St. Olaf Col; Univ Ill, MA, PhD. **CAREER** Vis profships, Ind Univ; Univ Cincinnati; assoc prof, 86-. **HONORS AND AWARDS** Asst ed, Jour Early Republic. **RESEARCH** Antebellum political history. **SELECTED PUBLICATIONS** Ed, transl, The Story of My Life, by Frederick Finnup, Finney County Hist Soc; auth, Lewis Cass and the Politics of Moderation, 1782-1866, Kent State Univ Press, 96. **CONTACT ADDRESS** Dept of Hist, Wichita State Univ, 1845 Fairmont, Wichita, KS, 67260-0062.

KNAFLA, LOUIS A.
PERSONAL Born 07/27/1935, Bakersfield, CA, m, 1965, 1 child **DISCIPLINE** EARLY MODERN HISTORY **EDUCATION** Claremont Mens Col, BA, 57; Univ Calif, Los Angeles, MA, 61, PhD (Tudor-Stuart English), 65. **CAREER** Lectr Brit hist, Calif State Col, Long Beach, 64-65; from asst prof to asoc prof, 65-77, asst chmn to chmn dept, 68-69, PROF HIST, UNIV CALGARY, 77-; Ed, Can Soc Legal Hist, 71-73; Can Coun res grants, 70-71, 73-75 and 79-82, leave fel, 75; chmn, Law Lib Arts Minor, 76-80; Killam resident fel, 77; ASSOC ED, CRIMINAL JUSTICE HIST, 81-. **MEMBERSHIPS** AHA; Renaissance Soc Am; Am Soc Legal Hist; Can Soc Legal Hist (pres, 73-78); fel Royal Hist Soc. **RESEARCH** England in the 16th and 17th centuries; history of English law; history of Canadian law, crime and criminal justice. **SELECTED PUBLICATIONS** Auth, Fundamental Authority in Late Medieval English Law, Hist Polit Thought, Vol 0013, 92. **CONTACT ADDRESS** Dept of Hist, Univ of Calgary, Calgary, AB, T2N 1N4.

KNAPP, ARTHUR BERNARD
PERSONAL Born 09/06/1941, Akron, OH **DISCIPLINE** ARCHAEOLOGY AND ANCIENT HISTORY **EDUCATION** Univ Akron, BA, 67; Univ Calif, Berkeley, MA, 76, PhD(ancient hist and mediter archaeol), 79. **CAREER** Teaching asst archaeol and ancient hist, 73-75, assoc, 75-76, actg instr, 76-79, LECTR ARCHAEOL and ANCIENT HIST, UNIV CALIF, BERKELEY, 79-; Instr, Extension Div, Univ Calif, Berkeley, 76-77. **MEMBERSHIPS** Archaeol Inst Am; Am Orient Soc; Asn Field Archaeol; Soc Am Archaeol; Am Schs Orient Res. **RESEARCH** Trade and interaction in eastern Mediterranean prehistory; island archaeology, especially in the Mediterranean; method and theory in archaeology. **SELECTED PUBLICATIONS** Auth, Gordion Excavation Final Reports, Vol 3, The Bronze-Age J Hellenic Studies, Vol 0112, 92; Thalassocracies in Bronze-Age Eastern Mediterranean Trade in Making And

Breaking A Myth, World Archaeol, Vol 0024, 93; The Prehistory of Cyprus in Problems and Prospects, J World Prehistory, Vol 0008, 94; Provenance Studies and Problem Solving On Bronze-Age Cyprus, American J Archaeol, Vol 0098, 94; Volatile Bodies in Bodies Evidence On Prehistoric Cyprus, American J Archaeol, Vol 0100, 96; Recent Excavations In Israel in A View to the West, Reports on Kabri, J Am Orient Soc, Vol 0117, 97 **CONTACT ADDRESS** Dept of Near East Studies, Univ of Calif, Berkeley, CA, 94720.

KNAPP, ROBERT CARLYLE
PERSONAL Born 02/12/1946, m, 1974, 2 children **DISCIPLINE** ANCIENT HISTORY, CLASSICS **EDUCATION** Cent MI Univ, BA, 68; Univ PA, PhD, 73. **CAREER** Vis asst prof classics, Colby Col, 73; ass 73-74; asst prof, 74-80, Assoc Prof Classics, Numismatics, Univ CA, Berkeley, 80-87; Prof 87. **HONORS AND AWARDS** Am Council of Learned Societies Fellowship, 82-83. **MEMBERSHIPS** Asn Ancient Historians; Am Philol Asn; Archaeological Institute of Am Fellow; Royal Numismatic Society. **RESEARCH** Roman Spain; Roman Cult Studies. **SELECTED PUBLICATIONS** Auth, Aspects of the Roman Experience in Iberia, 206-100 BC, Anejos IX Hisp Antiqua, 77; The date and purpose of the Iberian denarii, Numis Chronicle, 77; The origins of provincial prosopography in the West, Ancient Soc, 78; Cato in Spain, 195-194 BC, In: Studies in Latin Literature and Roman History II, C Deroux, Brussells, 80; La epigrafia y la historia de la Cordoba romana, Annario, de Filologia, 80; Festus 262L and Praefecturae in Italy, Athenaeum, 80; L Axius Naso and Pro legato, Phoenix, 81; Roman Cordoba, Univ Calif press, 83; Latin Inscriptions from Central Spain, Univ Calif, 92; Mapping Ancient Iberia: Progress and Perspectives, intro, ed (and contribution, Ptolemy Mapping Baetica, pp 29-36) Classical Bulletin, special issue, 96. **CONTACT ADDRESS** Dept Class, Univ California, 7303 Dwinelle Hall, Berkeley, CA, 94720-2521. **EMAIL** RCKNAPP@SOCRATES.Berkeley.edu

KNAPP, RONALD G.
PERSONAL Born 08/15/1940, Pittsburgh, PA, m, 1968, 3 children **DISCIPLINE** CULTURAL GEOGRAPHY **EDUCATION** Stetson Univ, BA, 62; Univ of Pittsburgh, PhD, 68. **CAREER** SUNY exchange prof, Nanyang Univ, 71-72; asst prof, 68-71, assoc prof, 71-78, prof, 78-98, Distinguished prof, State Univ of NY, NEW PALTZ, 98-. **HONORS AND AWARDS** Woodrow Wilson Nat Fel, 62-63; ACLS/Mellon Found Postdoctoral Fel for Advanced Training in Chinese Studies, 78; Summer Seminar, 79, Fel, Nat Endowment for the Humanities, 84 & 94; Nat Geographic Soc Comt for Res and Exploration Grant, 87; Nat Geographic Soc Comt for Res and Exploration, 80; Chiang Ching-kuo Found, 96. **MEMBERSHIPS** Asn of Am Geographers; Asn for Asian Studies; Vernacular Archit Forum; Int Asn for the Study of Traditional Environments; NY Conf on Asian Studies. **RESEARCH** The cultural and historical geography of China, especially the frontier settlement and the evolution of cultural landscapes; Chinese vernacular architecture; Chines folk symbols and household ornamentation. **SELECTED PUBLICATIONS** Auth, Chinese Bridges, Oxford Univ Press, 93; China's Living Houses: Folk Ornamentation and popular Culture, Univ of Hawaii Press, 98; Popular Rural Architecture, Handbook of Chinese Popular Culture, Greenwood Pub Group, 94; China's didactic landscapes: the folk tradition and the built environment, History and Culture of Vernacular Architecture, South Cina Univ of Tech, 95; Chinese Villages as Didactic Texts, Landscape, Culture, and Power in Chines Soc, Inst of East Asian Studies, Univ of Calif, 98; The Shaping of Taiwan's Landscapes, Taiwan: A Hist 1600-1994, M.E. Sharpe, 98. **CONTACT ADDRESS** Dept of Geography, State Univ of NY New Paltz, New Paltz, NY, 12561-2499. **EMAIL** knappr@npvm.newpaltz.edu

KNAPP, THOMAS A.
DISCIPLINE HISTORY **EDUCATION** Catholic Univ, PhD. **CAREER** Hist, Loyola Univ. **RESEARCH** Modern European history. **SELECTED PUBLICATIONS** Auth, Joseph Karl Wirth, Badische Biographien 2, 82. **CONTACT ADDRESS** Fine Arts Dept, Loyola Univ, Chicago, 6525 N. Sheridan Rd., Chicago, IL, 60626. **EMAIL** tknapp@wpo.it.luc.edu

KNEPPER, GEORGE W.
PERSONAL Born 01/15/1926, Akron, OH, m, 1949, 2 children **DISCIPLINE** HISTORY **EDUCATION** Univ Akron, BA, 48; Univ Mich, MA, 50, PhD(hist), 54. **CAREER** Asst adv men, 48-49, from instr to assoc prof hist, 54-65, head dept, 59-62, dean Col Lib Arts, 62-72, vpres acad affairs, 72, PROF HIST, UNIV AKRON, 65-; DIR EDUC RES and DEVELOP CTR, 72-. **MEMBERSHIPS** AHA; Orgn Am Historians. **RESEARCH** American Colonial and Revolutionary history; state and local history; history of higher education. **SELECTED PUBLICATIONS** Auth, Hayes, Rutherford,B in Warrior and President, Civil War Hist, Vol 0041, 95. **CONTACT ADDRESS** 1189 Temple Trails, Stow, OH, 44224.

KNIGHT, FRANKLIN W.
PERSONAL Born 01/10/1942, m **DISCIPLINE** HISTORY **EDUCATION** Univ Coll of WI London, BA (honors) 1964; Univ of WI Madison, MA 1965, PhD 1969. **CAREER** SUNY at Stony Brook, asst/assoc prof 1968-73; Johns Hopkins Univ, assoc prof 1973-77, prof 1977-; Leonard & Helen R Stulman Prof of History, 1991-; Latin Amer Studies Program, dir, 1992-95. **HONORS AND AWARDS** Fellow Natl Endowment for Humanities 1976-77; Fellow Center for Adv Study in Behav Sciences 1977-78; Fellow Natl Humanities Center 1986-87. **MEMBERSHIPS** Visit prof Univ of TX at Austin 1980; bd dirs Social Sci Rsch Council 1976-79; consultant NEH 1977-85; comm mem Inter-American Found 1984-86; rsch comm Amer Historical Assn 1984-86; chmn Intl Scholarly Relations Comm Conf of Latin Amer Historians 1983-86; exec comm Assn of Caribbean Hist 1982-85; pres, Latin Amer Studies Assn, 1998-2000. **SELECTED PUBLICATIONS** Auth, "Slave Society in Cuba During 19th Century" 1970; "The Caribbean, Genesis of a Fragmented Nationalism" 1990. **CONTACT ADDRESS** Dept of History, Johns Hopkins Univ, 3400 N Charles St, Baltimore, MD, 21218.

KNIGHT, FRANKLIN WILLIS
PERSONAL Born 01/10/1942, Manchester, Jamaica, m, 1965, 3 children **DISCIPLINE** LATIN AMERICAN HISTORY **EDUCATION** Univ Col West Indies, BA, 64; Univ WI, Madison, MA, 65, PhD, 69. **CAREER** From instr to assoc prof hist, State Univ NY, Stony Brook, 68-73; assoc prof, 73-77, Prof hist, Johns Hopkins Univ, 77-91, Stulman Prof, 91-, Mem joint comt Latin Am studies, Soc Sci Res Coun & Coun Learned Socs, 71-73; Nat Endowment for Hum fel, 77-78; Ctr Advan Study in Behav Sci fel, 77-78. **HONORS AND AWARDS** Hum Award, Black Acad Arts & Lett, 70. **MEMBERSHIPS** AHA; Latin Am Studies Asn (pres, 98-2000); Soc Span & Port Hist Studies. **RESEARCH** Late colonial and early nat Latin Am hist; Am slave sys(s); Caribbean region. **SELECTED PUBLICATIONS** Auth, Slave Society in Cuba During the Nineteenth Century, Univ Wis, 70; A colonial response to the glorious revolution in Spain, In: La Revolucion de 1868..., Americas, 70; Cuba, In: Neither Slave nor Free, Johns Hopkins, 72; Slavery, In: Encycl Americana, 73; African Dimension in Latin American Societies, Macmillan, 74; The Caribbean: The Genesis of a Fragmented Nationalism, Oxford Univ, 90; Atlantic Port Cities, Tenn, 91; Slave Societies in Caribbean, UNESCO, 97. **CONTACT ADDRESS** Dept of Hist, Johns Hopkins Univ, 3400 N Charles St, Baltimore, MD, 21218-2680. **EMAIL** fknight@jhu.edu

KNIGHT, ISABEL FRANCES
PERSONAL Born 11/24/1930, Los Angeles, CA **DISCIPLINE** MODERN EUROPEAN HISTORY **EDUCATION** Univ Calif, Los Angeles, BA, 51, MA, 58; Yale Univ, PhD (hist), 64. **CAREER** Instr hist, Yale Univ, 61-64; lectr, 64-72, ASSOC PROF HIST, PA STATE UNIV, UNIVERSITY PARK, 72-; Am Coun Learned Socs interdisciplinary studies fel, 70-71. **MEMBERSHIPS** AHA; Conf on Utopian Studies. **RESEARCH** Intellectual history of psychoanalysis; social criticism; Utopian thought. **SELECTED PUBLICATIONS** Auth, Crowds, Psychology, and Politics 1871-1899, Am Hist Rev, Vol 0099, 94. **CONTACT ADDRESS** Dept of Hist, Pennsylvania State Univ, University Park, PA, 16802.

KNIPE, DAVID MACLAY
PERSONAL Born 11/25/1932, Johnstown, PA, m, 3 children **DISCIPLINE** HISTORY OF RELIGION, SOUTH ASIAN STUDIES **EDUCATION** Cornell Univ, AB, 55; Union Theol Sem, MA, 58; Univ Chicago, MA, 65, PhD(hist relig), 71. **CAREER** Lectr, 67-69, from instr to asst prof, 69-73, assoc prof, 73-79, PROF SOUTH ASIAN STUDIES, UNIV WIS-MADISON, 79-; Sr res fel, Am Inst Indian Studies, 71-72, and 80. **MEMBERSHIPS** Am Acad Relig; Asn Asian Studies; Am Soc Study Relig. **RESEARCH** Vedic religion; Hinduism Jainism; methodology and religion. **SELECTED PUBLICATIONS** Auth, Asceticism and Healing in Ancient-India in Medicine In The Buddhist Monastery Isis, Vol 0084, 93; Hindu Spirituality in Vedas Through Vedanta, J Am Orient Soc, Vol 0117, 97. **CONTACT ADDRESS** Dept of S Asian Studies, Univ of Wis, 1220 Linden Drive, Madison, WI, 53706-1557.

KNOBEL, DALE THOMAS
PERSONAL Born 09/14/1949, East Cleveland, OH, m, 1971, 2 children **DISCIPLINE** AMERICAN HISTORY **EDUCATION** Yale Univ, BA, 71; Northwestern Univ, PhD(hist), 76. **CAREER** Instr hist and Am cult, Northwestern Univ, 76-77; ASST PROF HIST, TEX AM UNIV, 77-; Info Syst consult, G D Searle and Co, 76-77. **MEMBERSHIPS** Orgn Am Historians; Immigration Hist Soc; Soc Ger-Am Studies. **RESEARCH** American intellectual and cultural history; American immigration and ethnic history; race relations. **SELECTED PUBLICATIONS** Auth, Erin Heirs in Irish Bonds of Community, Am Hist Rev, Vol 0097, 92; The Invention of the White Race, Vol 1, Racial Oppression and Social-Control, Am Hist Rev, Vol 0101, 96. **CONTACT ADDRESS** Dept of Hist, Texas AandM Univ, College Station, TX, 77843.

KNOLL, PAUL W.
DISCIPLINE HISTORY **EDUCATION** Lewis and Clark Col, BA, 60; Univ Colo, MA, 61, PhD, 64. **CAREER** Prof, Purdue Univ, 64-69; Prof, Univ Southern Calif. **HONORS AND AWARDS** Kosciuszko Foundation prize, Prof, Univ Southern Calif, 69-. **RESEARCH** Medieval & Renaissance periods in European history; history & civilization of the western Slavs. **SELECTED PUBLICATIONS** Auth, The Rise of the Polish Monarchy, Piast Poland in East Central Eurpoe, 1320-1370. **CONTACT ADDRESS** Dept of History, Univ Southern Calif, University Park Campus, Los Angeles, CA, 90089. **EMAIL** knoll@usc.edu

KNORR, WILBUR RICHARD
PERSONAL Born 08/29/1945, Brooklyn, NY **DISCIPLINE** HISTORY OF SCIENCE **EDUCATION** Harvard Univ, BA, 66, AM, 68, PhD (hist sci), 73. **CAREER** Asst prof lib arts and sci, Univ Calif, Berkeley, 71-73; NSF and NATO fel, Cambridge Univ, 73-74; asst prof lib arts and sci, Brooklyn Col, 75-78; vis mem, Inst Advan Study, Princeton, NJ, 78-79; ASST PROF HIST SCI, STANFORD UNIV, 79-; Am Coun Learned Soc fel, Inst Advan Study, Princeton, NJ, 78-79; NSF grant, Am Acad Arts and Sci, 79-80. **MEMBERSHIPS** Hist Sci Soc **RESEARCH** History of mathematics and mathematical science, including cosmology: ancient, medieval, including Arabic and early modern; specialization: ancient geometry with its applications and transmission. **SELECTED PUBLICATIONS** Auth, On an Alleged Error in Archimedes Conoids, Prop-1, Historia Mathematica, Vol 0020, 93; Plato in Timee, Critias, Isis, Vol 0084, 93; Arithmetike-Stoicheiosis in on Diophantus and Hero of Alexandria, Historia Mathematica, Vol 0020, 93. **CONTACT ADDRESS** Dept of Philos, Stanford Univ, Stanford, CA, 94305.

KNOTT, ALEXANDER W.
PERSONAL Born 10/14/1938, Chicago, IL, m, 1963, 2 children **DISCIPLINE** HISTORY **EDUCATION** Univ Colo, BA, 61, MA, 63, PhD, 68. **CAREER** From asst prof to assoc prof, 68-, Univ Northern Colo. **MEMBERSHIPS** Society for Hist of Am Foreign Relations; Am Hist Asn; Orgn of Am Hist. **RESEARCH** United States foreign policy. **SELECTED PUBLICATIONS** Auth, World War I Battles, 73; auth, World War I: Causes, 73; coauth, Power, Justice, and Foreign Relations in the Confederation Period: The Marbois-Longchamps Affair, 80; coauth, Essays in Twenthieth Century American Diplomatic History Dedicated to Daniel M. Smith, 82; coauth, The Longchamps Affair (1784-1786) the Law of Nations, and the Shaping of Early American Foreign Policy, 86. **CONTACT ADDRESS** Univ of No Colorado, Greeley, CO, 80639. **EMAIL** awknott@bentley.unco.edu

KNOWLTON, ROBERT JAMES
PERSONAL Born 01/16/1931, Akron, OH, m, 1958, 2 children **DISCIPLINE** LATIN AMERICAN HISTORY **EDUCATION** Miami Univ, BA, 53; Western Reserve Univ, MA, 59; State Univ lowa, PhD(hist), 63. **CAREER** Asst, State Univ lowa, 59-61; from instr to assoc prof, 62-72, PROF HIST, UNIV WIS, STEVENS POINT, 72-; Improvement leave, Univ Wis, 66-67 and 71; ASSOC, LATIN AM CTR, UNIV WIS, MILWAUKEE, 72; MEM POLICY COMT, 74-; chmn policy comt, 77-82. **MEMBERSHIPS** AHA; Latin Am Studies Asn; Conf Latin Am Hist; MidW Asn Latin Am Studies; N Cent Coun Latin Americanist (pres, 68-69). **RESEARCH** Mexican history, 19th century; expropriation of corporate property in 19th century Mexico and Colombia. **SELECTED PUBLICATIONS** Auth, Origins of Instability in Early Republican Mexico, Am Hist Rev, Vol 0098, 93; Federal-Courts and Rural Lands in 19th Century, Mexico in the Semanario Judicial De La Federacion, Historia Mexicana, Vol 0046, 96. **CONTACT ADDRESS** Dept of Hist, Univ of Wis, Stevens Point, WI, 54481.

KNOX, BERNARD MACGREGOR WALKER
PERSONAL Born 11/24/1914, Bradford, England, m, 1 child **DISCIPLINE** CLASSICAL PHILOLOGY **EDUCATION** Cambridge Univ, BA, 36; Yale Univ, PhD, 48, LHD, 83. **CAREER** Instr Classics, Yale Univ, 47-48; asst prof & fel, Branford Col,48-54, from assoc prof to prof, 54-60; Dir, Ctr Hellenic Studies, Washington DC 61-85, Guggenheim fel, 56-57; Sather lectr, Univ Calif, Berkeley, 63; chmn, Soc Preserv Greek Heritage, 77-; Martin lectr, Oberlin Col, 81; West lectr, Stanford Univ, 84; Nellie Wallace lectr, Oxford Univ, 75; Spielvogel-Diamonstein award PEN, 90; Frankel priize, NEH, 90; NEH Jefferson lectr, 92. **HONORS AND AWARDS** Award for Lit, Nat Inst Arts & Lett, 67; George Jean Nathan Award for Dramatic Criticism, Mfrs Hanover Trust, 78., MA, Harvard Univ, 61; LittD, Princeton Univ, 64; DHL, George Washington Univ, 77; Georgetown Univ, LHD, 88; LHD (HON) Univ Mich, 85. **MEMBERSHIPS** Am Philol Soc; Am Archaeol Inst; AAAS; Am Philol Asn (pres 80). **RESEARCH** Greek tragedy; Latin and Greek literature. **SELECTED PUBLICATIONS** Auth, Oedipus at Thcbes, Yale Univ, S7; The Heroic Temper, Univ Calif, 64; Word and action: Essays on the ancient theater, Johns Hopkins Press, 79; asst ed & contribr, Cambridge History of Classical Literature, Vol I (in press); coauth (with Robert Foyles), The Theban plays of Sophocles, Viking Press (in prep); Essays Ancient and Modern, 89; The Oldest Dead White European Males, 93; Backing into the Future, 94 **CONTACT ADDRESS** 13013 Scarlet Oak Dr, Darnestown, MD, 20878-3551.

KOCHANEK, STANLEY ANTHONY
PERSONAL Born 05/10/1934, Bayonne, NJ, w, 1984, 2 children **DISCIPLINE** POLITICAL SCIENCE **EDUCATION** Univ Pennsylvania, PhD, 63; Rutgers Univ, MA, 57; Rutgers Univ, BA, 56 **CAREER** Prof Polit Sci, Pennsylvania State

Univ, 73-; assoc prof Polit Sci, Pennsylvania State Univ, 67-73; assist prof Polit Sci, Pennsylvania State Univ, 63-67 **HONORS AND AWARDS** Research Fel, Amer Inst Pakistan Studies, 96-97; Fulbright South Asia Regional Research Fel, 93-94; Faculty Research Fel, Amer Inst of Bangladesh Studies, 90-91 **MEMBERSHIPS** Amer Polit Sci Assoc; Assoc Asian Studies; Amer Pakistan Research Orgn **RESEARCH** India, Pakistan and Bangladesh **SELECTED PUBLICATIONS** CoauthIndia: Government and Politics in a Developing Nation, Harcourt Brace, 99; Patron Client Politics and Business in Bangladesh, Sage, 93; "Ethnic Conflict and the Politicization of Pakistan Business." Pakistan 1995, Westview, 95 **CONTACT ADDRESS** Dept Polit Sci, Pennsylvania State Univ, N166 Burrowes Bldg, University Park, PA, 16802.

KOCLITSCHEK, THEODORE
PERSONAL Born 05/19/1951, Elizabeth, NJ, d, 1 child **DISCIPLINE** EUROPEAN HISTORY **EDUCATION** Rutgers Univ, AB, 73; Princeton Univ, MA, 75, PhD, 81. **CAREER** Lectr, Princeton Univ, 78-79; asst prof, Univ of Calif at Irvine, 80-87; asst prof, Worcester Polytchenic, 88-89; ASST PROF, 89-91, ASSOC PROF, UNIV OF MO, 91-. **HONORS AND AWARDS** Harper fel, Univ of Chicago, 70-80; Herbert Baxter Adams Prize, 91; Robert Livingston Schuyler Prize, 91; Shelby Cullon Davis Post Doctoral Fel, Princeton Univ, 83. **MEMBERSHIPS** Am Hist Asn; North Am Confr on British Studies. **SELECTED PUBLICATIONS** Auth, Class Formation and Urban Industrial Society: Bradford 1750-1850, Cambridge Univ Press, 90; The Dynamics of Class Formation in Nineteenth Century Bradford, The First Modern Soc: Essays in Honour of Lawrence Stone, Cambridge Univ Press, 89; Marxism and the Historiography of Modern Britain: From Engles, To Thompson, To Deconstruction, and Beyond, hist, Economic Hist and the Future of Marxism: Essays in Honour of Tom Kemp, Porcupine Press, 96; The Gendering of the British Working Class, Gender and History, 97. **CONTACT ADDRESS** Univ of Mo, 101 Reed Hall, Columbia, MO, 65211. **EMAIL** histtk@showme.missouri.edu

KOEGEL, JOHN
DISCIPLINE MUSIC HISTORY **EDUCATION** Calif State Univ, Northridge, BA; Calif State Univ, Los Angeles, MA; CUNY, MA; Cambridge Univ, MA; Claremont Grad Sch, PhD. **CAREER** Asst prof; Univ Mo, 97-. **HONORS AND AWARDS** NEH, Univ Tex-Austin, 96. **RESEARCH** Latin American music; music of Mexico and the Hispanic southwest; Spanish music. **SELECTED PUBLICATIONS** Co-ed, Music in Performance and Soc. **CONTACT ADDRESS** Dept of Music, Univ of Missouri-Columbia, 140 Fine Arts Bldg, Columbia, MO, 65211. **EMAIL** musicjk@showme.missouri.edu

KOELSCH, WILLIAM ALVIN
PERSONAL Born 05/16/1933, Morristown, NJ **DISCIPLINE** AMERICAN HISTORY & GEOGRAPHY **EDUCATION** Bucknell Univ, ScB, 55; Clark Univ, AM, 59; Univ Chicago, PhD(hist), 66. **CAREER** Vis asst prof geog, Clark Univ, 63; from instr to asst prof hist, Fla Presby Col, 63-67; asst prof, 67-69, assoc prof, 69-81, univ archivist, 72-82, prof hist & geog, Clark Univ, 81-98, univ historian, 82-90, comnr, Mass Arch Adv Comn, 74-96; registrar-historiographer, Episcopal Diocese of Mass, 92-98; corresp mem, Int Geog Union Comn, 75-. **HONORS AND AWARDS** Prof Emeritus, 98-. **MEMBERSHIPS** Hist Educ Soc; Am Geog Soc; Orgn Am Historians. **RESEARCH** History of geography and related fields; history of American higher education. **SELECTED PUBLICATIONS** Auth, A Propound Through Special Erudition?: Justin Winsor as Historian of Discovery, Proc Am Antiquarian Soc, 4/83; Coauth, Psychoanalysis Arrives in America, Am Psychologist, 85; contribur, The Episcopal Diocese of Massachusetts, Boston, 84; Aspects of Antiquity in the History of Education, Lax, 92; Geographers: Biobibliographical Studies, 79. **CONTACT ADDRESS** 3310 First Ave, Apt 3C, San Diego, CA, 92103.

KOENEN, LUDWIG
PERSONAL Born 04/05/1931, Cologne, Germany, m, 1955, 4 children **DISCIPLINE** CLASSICAL PHILOLOGY, PAPYROLOGY **EDUCATION** Univ Cologne, Dr(class philol), 57, Drhabil(class philol), 69. **CAREER** From asst prof to assoc prof and from cur to chief cur class philol and papyrology, Univ Cologne, 56-75; PROF PAPYROLOGY, UNIV MICH, ANN ARBOR, 75-; Res study papyri Cairo, Univ Cologne, 62-65; field dir papyri, Photog Arch Egyptian Mus, Cairo Int Asn Papyrologists, 69, 71, 73 and 76; corresp mem, Ger Archaeol Inst, 75. **MEMBERSHIPS** Am Philol Asn; Am Soc Papyrologists (vpres, 78-80, pres, 81-); Int Asn Papyrologists. **RESEARCH** Classical philology; papyrology; patristics. **SELECTED PUBLICATIONS** Auth, Phoenix From the Ashes in the Burnt Archive from Petra, Mich Quart Rev, Vol 0035, 96. **CONTACT ADDRESS** 1312 Culver, Ann Arbor, MI, 48103.

KOENIGSBERG, LISA M.
DISCIPLINE AMERICAN STUDIES **EDUCATION** Johns Hopkins, BA, 79; MA, 79, PhD, 88. **CAREER** PHD CAND IN AM STUD, YALE UNIV **MEMBERSHIPS** Am Antiquarian Soc **SELECTED PUBLICATIONS** "Emblem for an Era: Selected Images of America Victorian Womanhood from the Yale University Community, 1837-1911," Yale exhibition, 82; auth, "Renderings from Worcester's Past: Nineteenth-Century Architectural Drawings at the American Antiquarian Soc," Procs of the AAS 96, 86. **CONTACT ADDRESS** Landmarks Preserv Comm, City of New York, 225 Broadway, New York, NY, 10007.

KOENKER, DIANE P.
DISCIPLINE HISTORY **EDUCATION** Univ Mich, PhD, 76. **CAREER** Prof, Univ Ill Urbana Champaign. **HONORS AND AWARDS** Ed, Slavic Rev. **RESEARCH** Society in Soviet Russia. **SELECTED PUBLICATIONS** Auth, Men Against Women on the Shop Floor in Early Soviet Russia: Gender and Class in the Socialist Workplace, Am Hist Rev, 95; Factory Tales: Narratives of Industrial Relations in the Transition to NEP, Russian Rev, 96; co-auth, Strikes and Revolution in Russia, 1917, Princeton, 89. **CONTACT ADDRESS** History Dept, Univ Ill Urbana Champaign, 52 E Gregory Dr, Champaign, IL, 61820. **EMAIL** dkoenker@uiuc.edu

KOEPKE, ROBERT L.
PERSONAL Born 06/17/1932, Arcadia, IA, m, 1960 **DISCIPLINE** MODERN HISTORY **EDUCATION** Univ Iowa, BA, 59; Stanford Univ, MA, 61, PhD(hist), 67. **CAREER** Instr hist, Stanford Univ, 63-65; instr, 65-67, ASST PROF HIST, SIMON FRASER UNIV, 67-. **MEMBERSHIPS** AHA; Soc Fr Hist Studies. **RESEARCH** Modern French history. **SELECTED PUBLICATIONS** Auth, Cooperation, Not Conflict, Parisian Bureaucracy and the Third-Republic, Ministry-of-Education in Cures and Primary-School, Inspectors in July-Monarchy France, Church Hist. Vol 0064, 95. **CONTACT ADDRESS** 5017 Howe Sound Lane W, Vancouver, BC, V7W 1L3.

KOERPER, PHILLIP ELDON
PERSONAL Born 06/23/1941, Ironton, OH, m, 1964, 2 children **DISCIPLINE** BRITISH HISTORY, EUROPEAN HISTORY **EDUCATION** Fla Southern Col, BA, 67; Univ Ga, MA, 68, PhD (hist), 71. **CAREER** Assoc Prof, 69-83, Prof Brit Europ Hist, Jacksonville State Univ, 83-. **HONORS AND AWARDS** English Speaking Union res grant, 70. **MEMBERSHIPS** Southeastern Conf Latin Am Studies; AHA; Int Churchill Soc. **RESEARCH** British Empire; modern Britain; early modern Europe. **SELECTED PUBLICATIONS** Auth, Cable Imbroglio in the Pacific, Hawaiian J Hist, 75; Ernest Belfort Bax, William Pember Reeves, David James Shakleton & H R L Sheppard, In: Biographical Dictionary of Modern British Radicals, Vol III, 78; Classics in Western Civilization, 2 vols, Ginn & Co, 86-87; author of numerous journal articles/entries. **CONTACT ADDRESS** Dept of Hist Col of Letters & Sci, Jacksonville State Univ, 700 Pelham Rd N, Jacksonville, AL, 36265-1602.

KOERTGE, NORETTA
PERSONAL Born 10/07/1935, Olney, IL **DISCIPLINE** PHILOSOPHY OF SCIENCE, HISTORY OF SCIENCE **EDUCATION** Univ Ill, BS, 55, MS, 56; London Univ, PhD(philos of sci), 69. **CAREER** Instr chem, Elmhurst Col, 60-63; head chem sect, Am Col for Girls, Instanbul, Turkey, 63-64; lectr philos of sci, Ont Inst for Studies Educ, 68-69; asst prof, 70-73, assoc prof, 74-81, PROF HIST and PHILOS OF SCI, IND UNIX, BLOOMINGTON, 81-; AM REP, BRIT SOC FOR PHILOS OF SCI, 76-. **MEMBERSHIPS** Philos Sci Asn. **RESEARCH** Theories of scientific method; historical development of philosophy of science; Poppers philosophy of science. **SELECTED PUBLICATIONS** Auth. The Myth of the Framework, In Defense of Science and Philosophy of Science, Vol 0064, 97. **CONTACT ADDRESS** Indiana Univ, Bloomington, 130 Goodbody Hall, Bloomington, IN, 47401.

KOGINOS, MANNY T.
PERSONAL Born 03/12/1933, New Castle, PA, m, 2 children **DISCIPLINE** AMERICAN DIPLOMATIC HISTORY **EDUCATION** Bowling Green State Univ, BA, 54; Am Univ, MA, 60, PhD, 66. **CAREER** Instr Am hist, Ohio Wesleyan Univ, 64-65; asst prof, Purdue Univ, 65-67; assoc prof Am Hist, State Univ NY Col Buffalo, 67-. **HONORS AND AWARDS** NY State grant-in-aid, 68-69; vis prof Am hist, Didesbury Col, Univ Manchester, England, 71-72; vis prof, Univ Hawaii, Hilo, 81-82; vis prof, Kansai Univ of For Studies, Osaka, Japan, 86. **MEMBERSHIPS** AHA; Orgn Am Historians; Soc Hist Am Foreign Rels; Western Hist Asn. **RESEARCH** American-Far Eastern and American-Japanese relations. **SELECTED PUBLICATIONS** Auth, The Panay Incident: Prelude to War, Purdue Univ, 67. **CONTACT ADDRESS** Dept of Hist, State Univ of New York Col, 1300 Elmwood Ave, Buffalo, NY, 14222-1095.

KOHL, BENJAMIN GIBBS
PERSONAL Born 10/26/1938, Middletown, DE, m, 1961, 2 children **DISCIPLINE** RENAISSANCE HISTORY **EDUCATION** Bowdoin Col, AB, 60; Univ Del, MA, 62; Johns Hopkins Univ, PhD(hist), 68. **CAREER** Instr hist, Johns Hopkins Univ, 65-66; from instr to asst prof, 66-74, assoc prof, 74-81; PROF HIST, VASSAR COL, 81-; ASSOC, COLUMBIA UNIV COLLOQUIUM HIST LEGAL and POLIT THOUGHT, 68-; Rome prize fel post-classical humanistic studies, Am Acad Rome, 70-71. **MEMBERSHIPS** Mediaeval Acad Am; Renaissance Soc Am; Dante Soc Am; Soc Ital Hist Studies; Econ Hist Asn. **RESEARCH** Fourteenth century Italian history; Renaissance intellectual history. **SELECTED PUBLICATIONS** Auth, Mulcaster,Richard 1531-1611 and Educational-Reform in the Renaissance, Renaissance Quart, Vol 0046, 93; Venice, A Documentary History, 1450-1630,J, Editors, Sixteenth Century J, Vol 0024, 93; Women of the Renaissance, Am Hist Rev, Vol 0098, 93; Barbaro, Francesco in Critical Edition of Letters, Vol 1, Renaissance Quart, Vol 0047, 94; From Politics to Reason of State, The Acquisition and Transformation of the Language of Politics, 1250-1600, Am Hist Rev, Vol 0099, 94; Sopra-Le-Acque-Salse, Power and Society in Venice at the End of the Middle-Ages, Sixteenth Century J, Vol 0025, 94; The History of the University of Oxford, Vol 2, Late-Medieval Oxford Vol 0026, 94; Bracciolini, Poggio, De Varietate Fortunae in Italian and Latin, Renaissance Quart, Vol 0048, 95; Petrarch Genius in Pentimento and Prophecy, J Am Acad Relig, Vol 0063, 95; A Moral Art in Grammar, Society, and Culture in Trecento, Florence, Am Hist Rev, Vol 0100, 95; Northern English Books, Owners, and Makers in the Late-Middle-Ages, Vol 0028, 96; Schools, Teachers and Basic Education in the Middle-Ages and the Renaissance in Venice, Am Hist Rev, Vol 0101, 96; The Civilization of Europe in the Renaissance, Vol 0059, 97. **CONTACT ADDRESS** Dept of Hist, Vassar Col, Poughkeepsie, NY, 12601.

KOHLER, ERIC DAVE
PERSONAL Born 10/24/1943, Cincinnati, OH, m, 1968 **DISCIPLINE** MODERN EUROPEAN HISTORY, GERMAN HISTORY **EDUCATION** Brown Univ, AB, 65; Stanford Univ, MA, 67, PhD (hist), 71. **CAREER** Asst prof hist, Calif State Univ, Humbolt, 70-71; asst prof, 71-78, ASSOC PROF HIST, UNIV WYO, 78-. **MEMBERSHIPS** AHA; Conf Group Cent Europ Hist. **RESEARCH** Prussian state in the Weimar Republic; European labor history; national socialism. **SELECTED PUBLICATIONS** Auth, Weimar Prussia, 1925-1933 in the Illusion of Strength, Ger Studies Rev, Vol 0016, 93; The German Bourgeoisie in Essays on the Social-History of the German Middle-Class From the Late 18th-Century to the Early-20th-Century, Ger Studies Rev, Vol 0016, 93; Himmler Auxiliaries, The Volksdeutsche-Mittelstelle and the German National Minorities of Europe, 1933-1945, Ger Studies Rev, Vol 0017, 94; Red Vienna, Experiment in Working-Class Culture, 1919-1934, Ger Studies Rev, Vol 0018, 95; German Social-Democracy and the Rise of Nazism, Ger Studies Rev, Vol 0018, 95; National-Socialist Leadership and Total War, 1941-1945 Ger Studies Rev, Vol 0018, 95; Medicine and Health-Policy in the Nazi Period in German Ger Studies Rev, Vol 0019, 96. **CONTACT ADDRESS** Dept of Hist, Univ of Wyo, P O Box 3198, Laramie, WY, 82071-3198.

KOHLER, SUE A.
PERSONAL Born 11/27/1927, Grand Rapids, MI, w, 1953, 3 children **DISCIPLINE** HISTORY; HISTORY OF ART **EDUCATION** Univ Mich, BA, 49, MA, 50. **CAREER** Asst to cur, Mus of Cranbrook Acad of Art, 51-53; archit hist, US Comn of Fine Arts, 74-. **HONORS AND AWARDS** Phi Beta Kappa; Phi Kappa Phi. **MEMBERSHIPS** Soc of Archit Hist; Nat Trust for Hist Preserv; Victorian Soc in Amer; Class Amer; Nat Building Mus; Hist Soc of Wash DC. **RESEARCH** 19th and 20th century American architecture. **SELECTED PUBLICATIONS** Auth, chapt, The Grand American Avenue, Amer Archit Found, 94; auth, The Commission of Fine Arts: A Brief History, 1910-1995, The Comn of Fine Arts, 95; co-auth, Sixteenth Street Architecture, vol 2, The Comn of Fine Arts, 88; co-auth, Sixteenth Street Architecture, vol 1, The Comn of Fine Arts, 78; co-auth, Massachusetts Avenue Architecture, vol 2, The Comn of Fine Arts, 75. **CONTACT ADDRESS** U.S. Commission of Fine Arts, National Building Museum, Suite 312, 441 F. Str, Washington, DC, 20001. **EMAIL** Sue_Kohler@ios.doi.gov

KOHLS, WINFRED A.
PERSONAL Born 07/07/1929, Yingtak, China, m, 3 children **DISCIPLINE** MODERN EUROPEAN HISTORY **EDUCATION** Augustana Col, SDak, AB, 51; Univ Calif, Berkeley, MA, 59, PhD (hist), 67. **CAREER** Instr hist, Univ Md, Overseas Br, 57-58; from asst prof to assoc prof, 63-72, chmn dept, 73-78, PROF HIST, MORAVIAN COL, 72-; Participant, Soviet-Am Inter-Univ Cult Exchange, 68-69; ADJ PROF HIST, LEHIGH UNIV, 69-; sr res fel, Alexander von Humboldt Found, Ger and vis res prof, Univ Marburg, 72-73; BK REV ED, RUSSIAN HISTHISTOIRE RUSSE, 75-; AM ED, UNITAS FRATRUM, 76-; res fel, Kennan Inst Advan Russ Res, Washington, DC, 78. **HONORS AND AWARDS** Lindback Found Award Distinguished Teaching. **MEMBERSHIPS** AHA; Am Asn Advan Slavic Studies. **RESEARCH** Russian history, 19th century; history of Russian education; German history, post World War I. **SELECTED PUBLICATIONS** Auth,. A Mennonite in Russia in the Diaries of Epp, Russ Hist-Histoire Russe, Vol 0020, 93; Chapters in the History of Foreign Colonization in Russia, The Sarepta Crisis in Its Historical Context, The Herrnhuter-Brudergemeinde, The Moravian Church, Established in the Volga Region in 1765, Russ Hist-Histoire Russe, Vol 0020, 93. **CONTACT ADDRESS** Dept of Hist, Moravian Col, 1200 Main St, Bethlehem, PA, 18018-6650. **EMAIL** mewak@moravian.edu

KOHLSTEDT, SALLY GREGORY
PERSONAL Born 01/30/1943, Ypsilanti, MI, m, 1966, 2 children **DISCIPLINE** HISTORY OF SCIENCE AND TECHNOLOGY **EDUCATION** Valparaiso Univ, BA, 65; Mich State Univ, MA, 66; Univ Il., Urbana, PhD, 72. **CAREER** Simmons Col, Dept of Hist, Syracuse Univ, Dept of Hist, 75-88, acting ch, 80-81; women's studies dir, 80-81; Fulbright vis prof, Univ of Melbourne, spring, 83; visiting prof, Cornell Univ, spring, 89; assoc dean, Inst of Tech, 89-95; vis prof, Amer-Inst, Univ of Munich, spring, 97; prof, Prog in Hist of Sci and Tech; dir, Ctr for Advan Feminist Studies. **HONORS AND AWARDS** Mortar bd; Valparaiso Univ; Nat Sci Found, res funding, summer, 69, 78-79, 93-94, 95; conference funding, 84, 95; Smithsonian Inst Pre-Doctoral Fel, 70-71; Syracuse Univ Facul Res Grant, 76, 82; Amer Philos Soc Res Grant, 77; Amer Antiquarian Soc, Haven Res Fel, oct, 82, mem, 84; Woodrow Wilson Ctr Fel, fall, 86; Smithsonian Inst Sr Fel, spring, 87; Hist of Sci Soc Plenary Lectr, 88; Univ of Minn Facul Res Grant, 90, 97-98; UMN TEL award: Outstanding Computer Aided Course Project, 98. **MEMBERSHIPS** Amer Asn for the Advan of Sci; Amer Hist Asn; Hist of Sci Soc; Intl Congress for the Hist of Sci; Orgn of Amer Hist. **RESEARCH** Science in America; Women, gender and science; Science in public culture, including museums and amateur associations. **SELECTED PUBLICATIONS** Ed, with Helen Longino, Women, Gender and Science: New Directions, Osiris, 12, Chicago, Univ Chicago Press, 97; ed, with Barbara Laslett, Helen Longino and Evelyn Hammonds, Gender and Scientific Authority, Chicago, Univ Chicago Press, 96; ed, The Origins of Natural Science in the United States: The Essays of George Brown Goode, Wash, Smithsonian Inst Press, 91; ed, with R. W. Home, International Science and National Scientific Identity: Australia between Britain and America, Holland, Kluewer Acad Publ, 91; ed, with Margaret Rossiter, Historical Writing on American Science, Osiris, 2nd series, 1, 85; auth, The Formation of the American Scientific Community: The American Association for the Advancement of Science, Urbana, Univ Ill Press, 76. **CONTACT ADDRESS** Univ of Minnesota, 123 Pillsbury Hall, Minneapolis, MN, 55455. **EMAIL** sgk@mailbox.mail.umn.edu

KOHN, RICHARD HENRY
PERSONAL Born 12/29/1940, Chicago, IL, m, 1964, 2 children **DISCIPLINE** MILITARY AND AMERICAN HISTORY **EDUCATION** Harvard Univ, AB, 62; Univ Wis-Madison, MS, 64, PhD(hist), 68. **CAREER** Asst prof hist, City Col New York, 68-71; asst prof, Rutgers Univ, New Brunswick, 71-75, assoc prof, 75-81. Nat Endowment for Humanities bicentennial grant, 70-71; Am Philos Soc res grant, 70-71; Am Coun Learned Soc fel, 77-78; Harold Keith Johnson vis prof military hist, US Army Military Hist Inst, US Army War Col, 80-81. **HONORS AND AWARDS** Binkley-Stephenson Prize, Orgn Am Historians, 73. **MEMBERSHIPS** Am Mil Inst; AHA; Orgn Am Historians; Inter-Univ Sem on Armed Forces and Soc; Air Force Historical Found. **RESEARCH** Military history; civil-military relations; American warfare. **SELECTED PUBLICATIONS** Auth, History and the Culture Wars in the Case of the Smithsonian-Institution Enola-Gay Exhibition, J Am Hist, Vol 0082, 95; Untitled, J Am Hist, Vol 0083, 96; The Practice of Military History in the Us Government in the Department of Defense, J Military History, Vol 0061, 97. **CONTACT ADDRESS** US Air ForceCho Bolling AFB, Bldg 5681 Hg, Washington, DC, 20332.

KOHUT, THOMAS A.
PERSONAL Born 03/11/1950, Chicago, IL, m, 1975, 2 children **DISCIPLINE** HISTORY; PSYCHOANALYSIS **EDUCATION** Oberlin College, BA 72; Univ Minnesota, MA 75, PhD 83; Cincinnati Psychoanalytic Inst, graduate 84. **CAREER** Williams College, asst prof, assoc prof, Sue and Edgar Wachenhein III Prof, 84 to 95-; Univ Cincinnati; asst clin prof 82-84. **MEMBERSHIPS** AHA; GSA. **RESEARCH** Modern European intellectual and cultural history; Modern German history **SELECTED PUBLICATIONS** Auth, The Creation of Wilhelm Busch as a German Cultural Hero, 1902-1908, Enlightenment Culture and Passion: Essays in Honor of Peter Gay, eds, Mark S. Micale Robert Dietle, Stanford, SUP, in press; Wilhelm Busch: Die Erfindung eines literarischen Nationalhelden, 1902-1908, Zeitschrift fur Literaturwissenschaft und Linguistik, in press; Commentary on Robert Jay Lifton's Reflections on Aum Shinrikyo' and on the 25th Anniversary of the Group for the Use of Psychology in History, The Psycho History Rev, 97. **CONTACT ADDRESS** Dept of History, Williams Col, Williamstown, MA, 01267. **EMAIL** Thomas.A.Kohut@williams.edu

KOISTINEN, PAUL ABRAHAM CARL
PERSONAL Born 03/27/1933, Wedena, MN, m, 1961, 2 children **DISCIPLINE** AMERICAN HISTORY **EDUCATION** Univ CA, Berkeley, AB, 56, MA, 59, PhD (hist), 64. **CAREER** From asst prof to assoc prof, 63-73, prof hist, CA State Univ Northridge, 73-, res grants, CA State Univ, Northridge, 65-66, 68-70, 72-73, 76-78 & 79-98; res fel, Charles Warren Ctr Studies Am Hist, Harvard Univ, 7 4-75; Am Coun Learned Soc, 75; NEH, 88; vis scholar, US Military Acad, 79 & US Air Force Acad, 82. **MEMBERSHIPS** AHA; Orgn Am Historians; Am Comt Hist 2nd World War; Conf Peace Res in Hist; Inter-Univ Sem Armed Forces & Soc. **RESEARCH** American political, economic and military history. **SELECTED PUBLICATIONS** Auth, The Industrial-Military Complex in Historical Perspective: World War I, Bus Hist Rev, winter 67; The Industrial-Military Complex in Historical Perspective: the Interwar Years, J Am Hist, 3/70; Mobilizing the World War II Economy: Labor and the Industrialmilitary Alliance, Pac Hist Rev, 11/73; The Hammer and the Sword: Labor, the Military, and Industrial Mobilization, 1920-1945, Arno Press, 79; The Military-Industrial Complex: A Historical Perspective, Praeger, 80; Warfare and Power Relations in America: Mobilizing the World War II Economy, in Home Front and War in the 20th Century, ed James Titus, Air Force Academy, 84; Towards A Warfare State: Militarization in America During the Period of the World Wars, in Militarization of the Western World, ed John Gillis, Rutgers, 89; The Political Economy of Warfare in America, 1865-1914, in Anticipating Total War? The United States and Germany, 1871-1914, ed Stig Forster, Cambridge, 98; assoc ed, American National Biography, 89-98; Beating Plowshares into Swords: The Political Economy of American Warfare, 1606-1865, KS, 97; Planning War, Pursuing Peace: The Political Economy of American Warfare, 1920-1939, KS, 98 -- the above three volumes are part of a 5 vol study of the political economy of warfare in America (vol 4 will cover WWII, vol 5, the Cold War years). **CONTACT ADDRESS** Dept Hist, California State Univ, Northridge, 18111 Nordhoff St, Northridge, CA, 91330-8200.

KOLB, ROBERT
PERSONAL Born 06/17/1941, Fort Dodge, IA, m, 1965 **DISCIPLINE** REFORMATION HISTORY, HISTORY OF THEOLOGY **EDUCATION** Concordia Sr Col, BA, 63; Concordia Sem, BD, 67, STM, 68, MDiv, 72; Univ Wis-Madison, MA, 69, PhD(hist), 73. **CAREER** Exec dir, Found Reformation Res and res fel, 72-77; ASST PROF RELIG and HIST, CONCORDIA COL, 77-; Part-time instr church hist, Concordia Sem, 72-77; ASSOC ED, SIXTEENTH CENTURY J, 73-. **MEMBERSHIPS** Am Soc Reformation Res; Am Soc Church Hist; Sixteenth Century Studies Conf; Am Acad Relig Res. **RESEARCH** Lutheran church history 1550-1600; history of piety or popular Christianity; 16th century martyrology. **SELECTED PUBLICATIONS** Auth, Bodying the Word in Textual Resurrections in the Martyrological Narratives of Foxe, Crespin, Beze And Aubigne Sixteenth Century J, Vol 0024, 93; The Influence of Luther, Martin Galatians Commentary of 1535 on Later 16th Century Lutheran Commentaries on Galatians, Archiv Fur Reformationsgeschichte-Archive For Reformation History, Vol 0084, 93; Problems of Authority in the Reformation Debates Church Hist, Vol 0063, 94; Sermon and Society in Lutheran Orthodoxy in Ulm, 1640-1740, Am Hist Rev, Vol 0099, 94; Andreae,Johann,Valentin Collected Works, Vol 7 in Veri Christianismi Solidaeque Philosophiae Libertas, Sixteenth Century J, Vol 0026, 95; God Gift of Martyrdom in the Early Reformation Understanding of Dying for the Faith, Church Hist, Vol 0064, 95; Whether Secular Government Has the Right to Wield the Sword in Matters of Faith, A Controversy in Nurnberg, 1530, Church History, Vol 0066, 97; Obituaries, Autobiographical Writings and Cosmonexus of Andreae,Johann,Valentin, Sixteenth Century J, Vol 0028, 97. **CONTACT ADDRESS** Concordia Col, Minnesota, Hamline and Marshall Ave St, St Paul, MN, 55104.

KOLKO, GABRIEL
PERSONAL Born 08/17/1932, Paterson, NJ, m, 1955 **DISCIPLINE** AMERICAN HISTORY **EDUCATION** Kent State Univ, BA, 54; Univ Wis, MS, 55; Harvard Univ, PhD (hist), 62. **CAREER** Soc Sci Res Coun fel, 63-64; assoc prof hist, Univ Pa, 64-68; prof hist, State Univ NY, Buffalo, 68-70; PROF HIST, YORK UNIV, 70-; Guggenheim Found fel, 66-67; Inst Policy Studies fel, 67-68; Am Coun Learned Soc fel, 71-72. **MEMBERSHIPS** AHA; Orgn Am Historians. **RESEARCH** American political and economic history since 1876; American diplomatic history in the 20th century. **SELECTED PUBLICATIONS** Auth Vietnam in Winning the War and Losing the Peace, Ponte, Vol 0052, 96. **CONTACT ADDRESS** Dept of Hist, York Univ, Downsview, ON, M3J 1P3.

KOLLANDER, PATRICIA
DISCIPLINE HISTORY **EDUCATION** Brown Univ, PhD. **CAREER** Assoc prof. **HONORS AND AWARDS** Tchg Incentive Prog Awd. **RESEARCH** Modern Germany history; European diplomatic history; Russia history. **SELECTED PUBLICATIONS** Auth, Frederick III: Germany's Liberal Emperor, Greenwood, 95; Politics for the Defence?: Bismarck, Battenberg and the Formation of the Cartel of 1887, 95; Bismarck, Crown Prince Frederick William, and the Hohenzollern Candidacy for the Spanish Throne, 96. **CONTACT ADDRESS** History Dept, Florida Atlantic Univ, 777 Glades Rd, Boca Raton, FL, 33431. **EMAIL** rinaldi@acc.fau.edu

KOLLAR, NATHAN RUDOLPH
PERSONAL Born 07/20/1938, Braddock, PA, m, 1972, 3 children **DISCIPLINE** RELIGIOUS STUDIES, HISTORY **EDUCATION** St Bonaventure Univ, BA, 60; Cath Univ Am, STL, 64, STD, 67; Univ Notre Dame, MA, 68. **CAREER** Instr theol, Whitefriars Hall, 64-67; asst prof, Washington Theol Coalition, 68-71; asst prof relig studies, St Thomas Univ, 71-74; assoc prof, 74-82, PROF RELIG STUDIES, ST JOHN FISHER COL, 82-; CHMN DEPT, 79-; Consult relig educ, Div Adult Educ, US Cath Conf, 71-73; dir relig, Ctr Study Relig N Am, 73-77; dir relig and educ, Resource Ctr Death Educ, 77. **MEMBERSHIPS** Am Acad Relig; Col Theol Soc; Soc Sci Study Relig; Can Soc Study Relig; Forum for Death Educ and Coun. **RESEARCH** North American culture and religion; dying, death and religion; eschatology. **SELECTED PUBLICATIONS** Auth, Death in the Midst of Life in Perspectives on Death From Christianity and Depth-Psychology, Horizons, Vol 0020, 93. **CONTACT ADDRESS** St John Fisher Col, Rochester, NY, 14618.

KOLLMANN, NANCY SHIELDS
PERSONAL Born 09/09/1950, Brockton, MA, m, 1976 **DISCIPLINE** RUSSIAN AND POLISH HISTORY **EDUCATION** Middlebury Col, BA, 72; Harvard Univ, MA 74, PhD(hist), 80. **CAREER** Teaching fel Russ and Europ hist, Harvard Univ, 75-80 and lectr, 80-82; ASST PROF HIST, STANFORD UNIV, 82-; Allston Burr sr tutor, Harvard Univ, 80-82. **MEMBERSHIPS** AHA; Am Asn Advan Slavic Studies. **RESEARCH** Musovite political history, 15th-17th centuries; muscovite social history; Polish-Lithuanian history. **SELECTED PUBLICATIONS** Auth, Reflections on Russia, Slavic Rev, Vol 0052, 93; Sophia, Regent of Russia, 1657-1704, Russian Rev, Vol 0052, 93; Medieval Russia 980-1584, Am Hist Rev, Vol 0102, 97. **CONTACT ADDRESS** Dept of Hist, Stanford Univ, Stanford, CA, 94305-1926.

KOLMER, ELIZABETH
PERSONAL Born 12/11/1931, Waterloo, IL **DISCIPLINE** AMERICAN HISTORY **EDUCATION** St Louis Univ, BS, 61, MA, 62; PhD, 65. **CAREER** From lectr to asst prof, 64-73, coordr Am Studies Prog, 69-81, assoc prof, 73-80, prof hist, 80, prof Am studies, St Louis Univ, 81- **MEMBERSHIPS** Mid America Am Studies Asn. **RESEARCH** Feminist movement; The Shakers; St. Louis history; women in religion. **SELECTED PUBLICATIONS** Auth, Nineteenth century woman's rights movement: Black and white, Negro Hist Bull, 12/72; McGuffey readers: Exponents of American classical liberalism, J Gen Educ, 76; Religious women and the Women's Movement, Am Quart, 78; Nationalism in eighteenth century American schoolbooks, 79 & Domestic economy: The whole duty of woman, 81, Am Studies; The Sisters of St. Mary & The Sick Poor of St. Louis, Soc Justice Rev, 11-12/82; Religious Women in the United States Since 1950, Michael Glazier, Inc, 84; Blessed are the Peacemakers: The Shakers as Pacifists, in Locating the Shakers, Univ Exeter Press, 90; A New Heaven and a New Earth: The Progressive Shakers and Social Reform, Hungarian J English and Am Studies (forthcoming 98). **CONTACT ADDRESS** Dept of Am Studies, St Louis Univ, 221 N Grand Blvd, Saint Louis, MO, 63103-2097. **EMAIL** kolmere@slu.edu

KOME, PENNY J.
PERSONAL Born 11/02/1948, Chicago, IL **DISCIPLINE** WOMEN'S STUDIES **CAREER** RES ASSOC, CAN RES INST FOR THE ADVANCEMENT OF WOMEN. **HONORS AND AWARDS** Robertine Barry Prize, CRIAW, 84. **SELECTED PUBLICATIONS** Auth, Somebody Has To Do It: Whose Work is Housework?, 82; auth, The Taking of Twenty-Eight, 83; auth, Women of Influence: Canadian Women & Politics, 85; auth, Every Voice Counts, 89; auth, Working Wounded: The Politics of Musculoskeletal Injuries, 98; co-ed, Peace: A Dream Unfolding, 86. **CONTACT ADDRESS** 2319 Uxbridge Dr NW, Calgary, AB, T2N 3Z7.

KONIG, DAVID THOMAS
PERSONAL Born 01/22/1947, Baltimore, MD **DISCIPLINE** EARLY AMERICAN AND LEGAL HISTORY **EDUCATION** NY Univ, AB, 68; Harvard Univ, AM, 69, PhD(hist), 73. **CAREER** Asst prof, 73-80, ASSOC PROF HIST, WASHINGTON UNIV, 80-; Dir, Nat Endowment for Humanities summer sem, 80; Fulbright sr lectr, Italy, 81-82. **RESEARCH** American legal development; colonial through Jacksonian America; science and witchcraft. **SELECTED PUBLICATIONS** Auth, A Summary View of the Law of British America, William Mary Quart, Vol 0050, 93; Virginias Historic Courthouses, Va Mag Hist Biog, Vol 0104, 96; Southern Slavery and the Law, 1619-1860, William Mary Quart, Vol 0054, 97. **CONTACT ADDRESS** Dept of Hist, Washington Univ, 1 Brookings Dr, Saint Louis, MO, 63130-4899.

KONISHI, HARUO
PERSONAL Born 12/20/1932, Tokyo, Japan, m, 1984 **DISCIPLINE** GREEK HISTORIOGRAPHY **EDUCATION** Int Christian Univ, BA, 56; Univ Penn, MA, 60; Univ Liverpool, PhD, 66. **CAREER** Asst prof, assoc prof, prof, Univ New Brunswick, 67-98. **MEMBERSHIPS** Class Asn of Canada; Am Philol Asn. **RESEARCH** Grek epic; Greek history; Greek drama. **SELECTED PUBLICATIONS** Auth, Thucydides' Method in the Episodes of Pausanias and Themistocles, Am J of Philol, 70; auth, Thucydides History, Tokyo, 76; auth, The Composition of Thucydides' History, Am J Philol, 80; auth, Thucydides History as a Finished Piece, Liverpool Class Monthly, 87; auth, Agamemnon's Reasons for Yielding, Am J Philol, 89; auth, The Plot of Aeschylus Oresteia: A Literary Commentary, Amsterdam, 91; auth, Did Thucydides Write a History? PEDILAVIUM, 97. **CONTACT ADDRESS** 86 Burnham Ct, Fredericton, NB, E3B 5T7. **EMAIL** konishi@unb.ca

KONSTAN, DAVID
PERSONAL Born 11/01/1940, New York, NY, m, 1994, 2 children **DISCIPLINE** CLASSICS **EDUCATION** Columbia Col, BA, 61; Columbia Univ, MA, 63, PhD, 67. **CAREER** Lectr classics, Hunter Col, 64-65, Brooklyn Col, 65-67; dir Hum prog, 72-74, chr, 75-77, 78-80, asst prof, 67-72, assoc prof, 72-77, Jane A. Seney prof Greek, 77-87, Wesleyan Univ; Dir Grad Stud, 88-89, CHR, 89-90, 92-94, 98-2001, PROF CLASSICS & COMP LIT, 87- , JOHN ROW WORKMAN DISTINGUISHED PROF CLASSICS & HUMANISTIC TRAD, BROWN UNIV; vis prof, Am Univ Cairo, 81-83; vis schol Univ Texas-Austin, 86-90; vis prof, UCLA, 87; Fulbright lectr, 88; vis prof, Univ Sydney, 90-91; vis prof, Univ Natal, 93, Univ La Plata, 97. **MEMBERSHIPS** Am Philol Asn. **RESEARCH** Ancient literature; culture. **SELECTED PUBLICATIONS** Auth, Sexual Summetry: Love in the Anceint Novel and Related Genres, Princeton Univ Press, 94; Greek Comedy and Ideology, Oxford Univ, 95; Friendship in the Classical World, Cambridge Univ Press, 97; Philodemus on Frank Criticism: Introduction, Translation and Notes, Soc Bibl Lit Texts & Transl, 98; The greek Commentaries on Aristotle's Nicomachean Ethics 8 and 9, Cornell Univ Press. **CONTACT ADDRESS** Dept Classics, Brown Univ, Providence, RI, 02912. **EMAIL** dkonstan@brown.edu

KONVITZ, JOSEF WOLF
PERSONAL Born 07/27/1946, New York, NY, m, 1969, 2 children **DISCIPLINE** EUROPEAN URBAN HISTORY **EDUCATION** Cornell Univ, BA, 67; Princeton Univ, MA, 71, PhD(hist), 73. **CAREER** Asst prof, 73-78, ASSOC PROF HIST, MICH STATE UNIV, 78-; Newberry Libr fel, 76; Nat Endowment for Humanities fel, 79-80. **MEMBERSHIPS** AHA; Soc French Hist Studies. **RESEARCH** Urban history; history of cartography; early modern Europe. **SELECTED PUBLICATIONS** Auth, Megalopolis, Introduction, J Urban Hist, Vol 0019, 93; The Widening Gate in Bristol and the Atlantic Economy, 1450-1700, J Urban Hist, Vol 0019, 93; Brides of the Sea in Port Cities of Asia From the 16th-20th Centuries, J Urban Hist, Vol 0019, 93; Atlantic Port Cities in Economy, Culture, and Society in the Atlantic World, 1650-1850, J Urban Hist, Vol 0019, 93; The Crises of Atlantic Port Cities, 1880 To 1920, Comparative Studies in Society and History, Vol 0036, 94; Urban Rivalries in the French-Revolution, J Interdisciplinary Hist, Vol 0025, 94; Small Towns in Early-Modern Europe, J Interdisciplinary Hist, Vol 0027, 97; Maps and Civilization, Cartography in Culture and Society, Technology and Culture, Vol 0038, 97; The Assassination of Paris, J Urban Hist, Vol 0023, 97; Building Paris in Architectural Institutions and the Transformation of the French Capital, 1830-1870, J Urban Hist, Vol 0023, 97. **CONTACT ADDRESS** Dept of Hist, Michigan State Univ, East Lansing, MI, 48824.

KOONZ, CLAUDIA
DISCIPLINE HISTORY **EDUCATION** Univ WI Madison, BA, 62; Columbia Univ, MA, 64; Rutgers Univ, PhD, 69. **CAREER** Prof, Duke Univ. **HONORS AND AWARDS** Nat Bk Awd, 87. **RESEARCH** Twentieth century Europ hist; women's hist; genocide. **SELECTED PUBLICATIONS** Co-ed, Becoming Visible: Women in European History, 87. **CONTACT ADDRESS** Dept of Hist, Duke Univ, Carr Bldg, Durham, NC, 27706. **EMAIL** ckoonz@acpub.duke.edu

KOOT, GERARD M.
PERSONAL Born 11/17/1944, Breezand, Netherlands, m, 1967 **DISCIPLINE** EUROPEAN HISTORY **EDUCATION** Assumption Col, Mass, BA, 67; State Univ NY, Stony Brook, MA, 69, PhD(hist), 72. **CAREER** Asst prof, 72-78, ASSOC PROF HIST, SOUTHEASTERN MASS UNIV, 78-; Kress fel, Harvard Univ, 72. **MEMBERSHIPS** AHA; Conf Brit Studies; Soc Hist Econ Thought. **RESEARCH** History of British economic throught and policy; neo-mercantilist British economic thought and policy; domestic impact of late 19th century British imperialism. **SELECTED PUBLICATIONS** Auth, Political-Economy and Colonial Ireland, in The Propagation and Ideological Function of Economic Discourse in the 19th-Century, Victorian Studies, Vol 0036, 93; The Market for Political-Economy, The Advent of Economics in British University Culture, 1850-1905, Albion, Vol 0026, 94; Industrial-Development and Irish National Identity, 1922-1939, Am Hist Rev, Vol 0099, 94; An Economist Among Mandarins in a Biography of Hall,Robert, 1901-1988, Albion, Vol 0027, 95; British Monetary-Policy, 1945-51, Am Hist Rev, Vol 0100, 95; A Soaring Eagle in Marshall,Alfred, 1842-1924, Albion, Vol 0028, 96; A Woman in History in Power, Eileen, 1889-1940, Albion, Vol 0029, 97; Lse in a History of the London School of Economics and Political Science, 1895-95, Am Hist Rev, Vol 0102, 97. **CONTACT ADDRESS** Dept of Hist, Southeastern Mass Univ, 285 Old Westport Rd, North Dartmouth, MA, 02747-2300.

KOPF, DAVID
PERSONAL Born 03/12/1930, Paterson, NJ, m, 1955, 2 children **DISCIPLINE** MODERN SOUTH ASIAN HISTORY **EDUCATION** NY Univ, BA, 51, MA, 56; Univ Chicago, PhD(hist), 64. **CAREER** Asst prof S Asian Hist, Univ Mo, 64-67; assoc prof, 67-76, PROF S ASIAN HIST, UNIV MINN, MINNEAPOLIS, 73-; S Asian ed, Newsletter of Asn Asian Studies, 65-68, res coun grant, 66; UNIV MINN OFF INT PROG GRANTS, 68- and travel grant to participate Rammohun Roy Bi-Centenary Symp, Jawaharlal Nehru Arch, New Delhi, 72; sr fel, Am Inst Indian Studies, Calcutta, 69-71; TRUSTEE, AM INST INDIAN STUDIES, UNIV PA, 71-; Ford Found vis prof fel, Inst Bangladesh Studies, Rajshahi Univ, Bangladesh, 75; Guggenheim fel, Genesis of Hinduism, Bengal, 79-80. **HONORS AND AWARDS** Watumull Prize, AHA, 69. **MEMBERSHIPS** AHA Asn Asian Studies, Bengal Studies Group. **RESEARCH** Socio-religious modernism and search for modern identity in Bengal under the British focused on history of Brahmo Samaj movement and community; comparative history of Asian civilizations; translation of selected works in contemporary Bangaldeshi literature. **SELECTED PUBLICATIONS** Auth, 3 Deltas in Accumulation and Poverty in Rural Burma, Bengal, and South-India, J Interdisciplinary Hist, Vol 0023, 93; Asia Before Europe in Economy and Civilization of the Indian-Ocean From the Rise of Islam to 1750, Hist, Vol 0055, 93; Ungoverned Imaginings in Mill, James the History of British India and Orientalism, J Am Orient Soc, Vol 0114, 94; Economy, Society and Politics in Bengal in Jalpaiguri, 1869-1947, J Interdisciplinary Hist, Vol 0026, 95; Subaltern Studies .7. Writings on South Asian History and Society, J Interdisciplinary Hist, Vol 0026, 95; Sati, The Blessing and the Curse in the Burning of Wives in India, J Am Orient Soc, Vol 0115, 95; Society and Ideology in Essays inn South Asian History Presented to Professor Ballhatchet, K.A, J Interdisciplinary Hist, Vol 0026, 95; Broken Promises in Popular Protest, Indian Nationalism and the Congress Party in Bihar, 1935-1946, J Interdisciplinary Hist, Vol 0026, 95; Rural India in Land, Power and Society Under British Rule, J Interdisciplinary Hist, Vol 0026, 95; Factories of Death, Japanese Biological Warfare, 1932-1945, and the American Cover-Up, J World Hist, Vol 0007, 96; Subaltern Studies, Vol 8, J Am Orient Soc, Vol 0116, 96; The Unhappy Consciousness in Bankimchandra-Chattopadhyay and the Formation of Nationalist Discourse in India, Am Hist Rev, Vol 0102, 97; Ray,Raja,Rammohan in the Father of Modern India, Am Hist Rev, Vol 0102, 97. **CONTACT ADDRESS** Dept of Hist, Univ of Minn, 267 19th Ave S, Minneapolis, MN, 55455-0499.

KOPFF, EDWARD CHRISTIAN
PERSONAL Born 11/22/1946, Brooklyn, NY **DISCIPLINE** GREEK, LATIN **EDUCATION** Haverford Col, BA, 68; Univ NC, Chapel Hill, PhD(classics), 74. **CAREER** Asst dir classics, Intercol Ctr Class Studies, Rome, Italy 72-73; asst prof, 73-76, Assoc Prof Classics, Univ Colo, Boulder, 76, BK REV ED, CLASS J, 77-; Nat Endowment for the Humanities fel, Am Acad Rome, 78-79; AM ED, QUADERAI DI STORIS, 82-. **MEMBERSHIPS** Am Philol Asn; Asn Ancient Historians; Class Asn Midwest and South. **RESEARCH** Transmission of ancient literature; Greek palaeography; ancient drama. **SELECTED PUBLICATIONS** Auth, Sophocles in Trachiniae in Greek and English, Editor, Am J Philol, Vol 0114, 93; Sophocles in Fabulae in Greek and English, Am J Philol, Vol 0114, 93. **CONTACT ADDRESS** Dept of Classics, Univ of Colo, Box 248, Boulder, CO, 80309-0248.

KOPPES, CLAYTON R
PERSONAL Born 09/24/1945, Lincoln, NE **DISCIPLINE** HISTORY **EDUCATION** Bethel Col, Kans, AB, 67; Emory Univ, Atlanta, MA, 68; Univ Kans, PhD(hist), 74. **CAREER** Coordr curric, Independent Study Ctr, Univ Kans, 70-72; sr res fel hist, Calif Inst Technol, 74-78; ASST PROF HIST, OBERLIN COL, 78-; US Steel Found fel, 68-70. **MEMBERSHIPS** Orgn Am Historians; Am Hist Asn, Forest Hist Soc; Am Asn Soc Environ Hist. **RESEARCH** American political history 20th century; international oil policy. **SELECTED PUBLICATIONS** Auth, Popular Culture and Political-Change in Modern-America, J Am Hist, Vol 0079, 93; Under an Open Sky in Rethinking America Past, Pac Hist Rev, Vol 0062, 93; Columbia Pictures in Portrait of A Studio, Pac Historical Rev, Vol 0062, 93; On The Home Front in the Cold-War, Legacy of the Hanford Nuclear Site, Pac Hist Rev, Vol 0063, 94; Hollywood Overseas Campaign in the North-Atlantic Movie Trade, 1920-1950, Am Hist Rev, Vol 0099, 94; The Sputnik Challenge, Hist, Vol 0056, 94; Hollywood as Mirror in Changing Views of Outsiders and Enemies in American Movies, J Am Hist, Vol 0081, 95 Forcing the Spring in the Transformation of the American Environmental Movement, Pac Hist Rev, Vol 0064, 95; Hard Bodies in Hollywood Masculinity in the Reagan-Era, Revs In American History, Vol 0023, 95; Reagan,Ronald In Hollywood in Movies and Politics, Rev Am Hi, Vol 0023, 95; Crossing-Over the Line in Legislating Morality and the Mann-Act, J Hist Sexuality, Vol 0006, 95; Gay New York, Urban Culture, and the Making of the Gay Male World, Rev Am Hist, Vol 0024, 96; The Missile and Space Race, Pac Hist Rev, Vol 0066, 97. **CONTACT ADDRESS** Dept of Hist, Oberlin Col, OH, 44704.

KORNBERG, JACQUES
PERSONAL Born 08/10/1933, Antwerp, Belgium, m, 1965, 3 children **DISCIPLINE** MODERN INTELLECTUAL HISTORY **EDUCATION** Brandeis Univ, BA, 55; Harvard Univ, PhD(hist), 64. **CAREER** Instr hist, Stanford Univ, 64-67; asst prof intellectual hist mod Europe, 68-71, ASSOC PROF INTELLECTUAL HIST MOD EUROP, UNIV TORONTO, 71-; Can Coun fel, 69-70. **MEMBERSHIPS** AHA **RESEARCH** Nineteenth and 20th century European social thought; theories of Wilhelm Dilthey; modern Jewish History. **SELECTED PUBLICATIONS** Auth, Elusive Prophet in Haam, Ahad and The Origin of Zionism, Am Hist Rev, Vol 0100, 95; Vienna, The 1890s in Jews in the Eyes of Their Defenders The Verein-Zur-Abwehr-Des-Antisemitismus, Cent European Hist, Vol 0028, 95; On Modern Jewish Politics, J Interdisciplinary History, Vol 0026, 96. **CONTACT ADDRESS** Dept of Hist, Univ of Toronto, Toronto, ON, M5S 1A1.

KORNBLITH, GARY J.
DISCIPLINE HISTORY **EDUCATION** Amherst Coll, BA, 73; Princeton Univ, MA, 75, PhD, 83. **CAREER** Asst prof, ASSOC PROF, HIST, OBERLIN COLL **MEMBERSHIPS** Am Antiquarian Soc **RESEARCH** Master mechanics in New Eng, 1780s-1850s. **SELECTED PUBLICATIONS** Auth, "The Rise of the Mechanic Interest and the Campaign to Develop Manufacturing in Salem, 1815-1830," Essex Inst Coll 121, 85; auth, "Self-Made Men: The Development of Middling-Class Consciousness in New England," Mass Rev 26, 85; auth, "Cementing the Mechanic Interest": Origins of the Providence Association of Mechanics and Manufacturers," Jour of the Early Rep 6, 88; auth, "The Artisanal Response to Capitalist Transformation," Jour of the Early Rep 10, 90; coauth, "The Making and Unmaking of an American Ruling Class, " in Beyond the American Revolution: Explorations in the History of American Radicalism, No Ill Univ Press, 93; auth, "Artisan Federalism: New England Mechanics and the Political Economy of the 1790s," in Launching the "Extended Republic": The Federalist Era, UPV, 96; auth, "Becoming Joseph T. Buckingham: The Struggle for Artisanal Independence in Early Nineteenth-Century Boston," in American Artisans: Explorations in Social Identity, Johns Hopkins Univ Press. **CONTACT ADDRESS** Hist Dept, Oberlin Col, Rice Hall, Oberlin, OH, 44074. **EMAIL** gary.kornblith@oberlin.edu

KORNBLUTH, GENEVA
DISCIPLINE ART OF MEDIEVAL WESTERN EUROPE **EDUCATION** Pomona Col, AB; Univ NC, MA, PhD. **CAREER** Prof, Univ MD. **HONORS AND AWARDS** Fel, Ctr Advan Stud in the Visual Arts; visitorship, Sch Hist Stud; Inst Advan Stud, Princeton; support, Millard Meiss Publ Fund, Col Art Assn; J Paul Getty postdoc fel; Dumbarton Oaks summer fel., Adv bd, Intl Ctr of Medieval Art; ch, organization's prog comm. **SELECTED PUBLICATIONS** Auth, Engraved Gems of the Carolingian Empire. **CONTACT ADDRESS** Dept of Art and Archeol, Univ MD, 4229 Art-Sociology Building, College Park, MD, 20742-1335.

KORR, CHARLES P.
DISCIPLINE HISTORY **EDUCATION** Univ Calif, Los Angeles, BA, 61, MA, 65, PhD, 69. **CAREER** Inst, Stanford Univ, 67-70; asst prof, 70-76, assoc prof, 76-86, Univ Mo, St Louis; asst to mayor, City St Louis, 77-81; vis prof, Univ WEstern Cape, S Africa, 93; chair dept hist, 92- 95, dir, ctr hum, 95-97, PROF HIST, UNIV MO, ST LOUIS, 86-. **CONTACT ADDRESS** Dept of History, Univ of Missouri, St. Louis, St. Louis, MO, 63121. **EMAIL** cpkorr@umsl.edu

KORS, ALAN CHARLES
PERSONAL Born 07/18/1943, Jersey City, NJ, m, 1975, 1 child **DISCIPLINE** INTELLECTUAL AND EARLY MODERN HISTORY **EDUCATION** Princeton Univ, BA, 64; Harvard Univ, MA, 65, PhD(hist), 68 **CAREER** Asst Prof, 68-74, ASSOC PROF HIST, UNIV PA, 74-; Am Coun Learned Soc res fel hist, 75-76; bk rev ed, Am Soc 18th Century Studies, 76-78; adv ed, 18th Century Life, Eastern Soc Am Soc 18th Century Studies. **HONORS AND AWARDS** Lindback Found Award, 75. **MEMBERSHIPS** Am Soc 18th Century Studies; AHA; Eastern Soc Am Soc 18th Century Studies. **RESEARCH** French enlightenment; origins and development of materialism in early modern France; philosophy and revolution. **SELECTED PUBLICATIONS** Auth, Monsters and the Problem of Naturalism in French Thought Teratology, Eighteenth-Century Life, Vol 0021, 97.. **CONTACT ADDRESS** Dept of Hist, Univ of Pa, 3401 Walnut St, Philadelphia, PA, 19104-6228.

KORTEPETER, CARL MAX
PERSONAL Born 05/27/1928, Indianapolis, IN, m, 1957, 7 children **DISCIPLINE** HISTORY, NEAR EASTERN LANGUAGES **EDUCATION** Harvard Univ, BA, 50, McGill Univ, MA, 54; Univ London, PhD(hist), 62; Rytgers Univ, M.Sc., 89. **CAREER** Instr sci, Robert Col, Istanbul, 50-53; Prof, Russ hist, U.S. Army, 54-56;lectr Islamic studies, Univ Toronto, 61-64, from asst prof to assoc prof, 64-67; Sr fel, Am Res Inst, Turkey, 66-67, bd mem & secy, 69-71; vis prof, Princeton Univ, 71-72; dir, Princeton Mid E Syst, 76-; Am Res Ctr Egypt sr fel, 78; Assoc prof hist & near eastern lang, NY Univ, 67-96. **MEMBERSHIPS** MidEast Instr; Turkish Studies Asn; Am Res Ctr Egypt; MidEast Studies Asn. **RESEARCH** Turko-Slavic contacts; institutions of the Islamic Ottoman state; the US and Soviet rel(s) in the Middle East. **SELECTED PUBLICATIONS** Auth, Ottoman Imperial Policy and the Economy of the Black Sea Region, J Am Orient Soc, 66; The Islamic-Ottoman Social Structure: The Quest for a Model of Ottoman History, In: Near East Round Table I: Turkish History and Politics, NY Univ, 69; ed, Literature and Society: The Modern Near East, 71 & auth, Ottoman Imperialism during the Reformation: Europe and the Caucasus, 72, NY Univ; auth, The origins and Nature of Turkish power, Fakueltesi Tarih Arastirmalari Dergisi, Ankara Univ,

72, The Ottoman Turks: Nomad Kingdon to Worl Empire, 91; Co-auth, The Human Experience, Columbus, 85; Co-ed, The Transformation of Turkish Culture: The Ataturk Legacy, Princeton, 86; ed, Literature and Society: The Modern Middle East, 73; Oil and Economic Geography, 93. **CONTACT ADDRESS** Kevorkian Ctr Near Eastern Studies, New York Univ, Washington Sq, New York, NY, 10003. **EMAIL** cmaxadk@aol.com

KORTH, PHILIP ALAN
PERSONAL Born 08/06/1936, Fairmont, MN, m, 1963, 3 children **DISCIPLINE** AMERICAN STUDIES **EDUCATION** Univ Minn, BA, 61, MA, 65, PhD(Am studies), 67. **CAREER** Asst prof, 67-70, assoc prof, 70-77, PROF AM THOUGHT and LANG, MICH STATE UNIV, 77-; Proj dir, Rockefeller Found res grant, 72-75. **MEMBERSHIPS** Am Studies Asn; Orgn Am Historians; Nat Educ Asn. **RESEARCH** American cultural history; American labor history; American literature 1865-1940. **SELECTED PUBLICATIONS** Auth, Labor Into Art in the Theme of Work in 19th-Century American, J American Culture, Vol 0016, 93. **CONTACT ADDRESS** Dept of Am Thought and Lang, Michigan State Univ, East Lansing, MI, 48823.

KOSAR, ANTHONY J.
DISCIPLINE MUSIC THEORY **EDUCATION** W Liberty State Col, BM; Southern Ill Univ, MM; Ohio State Univ, PhD. **CAREER** Assoc prof, Westminster, 84-. **HONORS AND AWARDS** Highest hon(s), BM. **MEMBERSHIPS** Mem, Soc Mus Theory; Pi Kappa Lambda and Phi Kappa Phi. **RESEARCH** Theory pedagogy and 19th-century theory. **SELECTED PUBLICATIONS** Publ, articles, The Jour of Mus Theory Pedag. **CONTACT ADDRESS** Dept of Theory and Mus Hist, Westfield State Col, 577 Western Ave., Westfield, MA, 01085.

KOSCHMANN, JULIEN VICTOR
PERSONAL Born 12/30/1942, Fairbanks, AK, m, 1964, 3 children **DISCIPLINE** JAPANESE HISTORY **EDUCATION** Int Christian Univ, Tokyo, BA, 65; Sophia Univ, Tokyo, MA, 71; Univ Chicago, PhD Hist, 80. **CAREER** Transl & assoc ed, Japan Interpreter, 71-76; lectr Social Sci, Univ Chicago, 78-80; asst prof Japanese Hist, Cornell Univ, 80-, instr Asian Studies, Sophia Univ, Tokyo, 75-76. **MEMBERSHIPS** Asn Asian Studies. **RESEARCH** Thought and action in the domain of Mito, late Tokugawa period; post-World War II Japanese intellectual and social history; 20th century intellectual history. **SELECTED PUBLICATIONS** Ed, Authority and the Individual in Japan: Citizen Protest in Historical Perspective, Univ Tokyo Press, Tokyo, 78; auth, The debate on subjectivity in postwar Japan: Foundations of modernism as a political critique, Pac Affairs, Winter 81; co-ed (with Tetsuo Najita), Conflict in Modern Japanese History: The Neglected Tradition, Princeton Univ Press, 82; Revolution and Subjectivity in Postwar Japan, Univ of Chicago Press, 96. **CONTACT ADDRESS** Dept of History, Cornell Univ, Mcgraw Hall, Ithaca, NY, 14853-0001. **EMAIL** jvk1@cornell.edu

KOSHKIN-YOURITZIN, VICTOR
PERSONAL Born 12/20/1942, New York, NY **DISCIPLINE** ART HISTORY **EDUCATION** Williams Col, BA, 64; N Y Univ, MA, 67. **CAREER** Instr, Vanderbilt Univ, Nashville Tn, 68-69; instr, Tulane Univ, 69-72; asst prof to assoc prof to prof, Univ Ok, 72- . **HONORS AND AWARDS** Univ of Al Alumni Assoc Baldwin Award for Excellence , Undergraduate teaching, 87; Univ Ok Stud Assoc Award, outstanding faculty member, 89, 94; Honorable citation, Ok St House of Rep, 93; David Ross Boyd Distinguished Prof in Art Hist, Univ Ok, 97., NEH panel, 84; panelist, Prog on Film. **MEMBERSHIPS** Mabee-Gerrer Museum of Art; Koussevitzky Recordings Soc, Inc; Ogden Museum of South Art. **SELECTED PUBLICATIONS** Auth, Oklahoma Treasures: Paintings, Drawings, and Watercolors for Public and Private Collections, The Ok Art Center, 86; Koussevitzky: Missing in Action, Los Angeles Times, 88; coauth, American Watercolors from The Metropolitan Museum of Art, Amer Federation of Arts, 91; Twentieth-Century Russian Drawings from a Private Collection, Ar Arts Center, 97, auth, Paintings by Glenda Green: A Focus on the Oklahoma Years, Mabee-Gerrer Museum of Art, 1999. **CONTACT ADDRESS** 1721 Oakwood Dr, Norman, OK, 73069. **EMAIL** vky@ou.edu

KOSLOFSKY, CRAIG
DISCIPLINE HISTORY **EDUCATION** Univ Mich, PhD, 94. **CAREER** Asst prof, Univ Ill Urbana Champaign **RESEARCH** Late medieval; early modern German history. **SELECTED PUBLICATIONS** Auth, pubs on late medieval history and early modern German history. **CONTACT ADDRESS** History Dept, Univ Ill Urbana Champaign, 52 E Gregory Dr, Champaign, IL, 61820. **EMAIL** koslof@uiuc.edu

KOSS, DAVID HENRY
PERSONAL Born 11/24/1935, Elgin, IL **DISCIPLINE** CHURCH HISTORY **EDUCATION** NCentral Col, BA, 56; Evangelical Theol Sem, BD, 59; Princeton Theol Sem, ThM, 61; Northwestern Univ, PhD, 72. **CAREER** Clergyman, Methodist Church, Earlville, Ill, 66-71; faculty relig, IL coll, 72-; Scarborough prof of relig, 90. **MEMBERSHIPS** Am Soc Church Hist; AAR. **RESEARCH** Am and Mod Europ church hist. **CONTACT ADDRESS** Dept of Relig, Illinois Col, 1101 W College Ave, Jacksonville, IL, 62650-2299. **EMAIL** koss@hilltop.ic.edu

KOSTELANETZ, RICHARD
PERSONAL Born 05/14/1940, New York, NY **DISCIPLINE** AMERICAN CULTURE **EDUCATION** Brown Univ, AB, 62; Columbia Univ, MA, 66. **CAREER** RES and WRITING, 62-; Guggenheim fel, 67-68; compiler, ASSEMBLING, 70-; CO-PARTNER, ASSEMBLING PRESS, 70-; CONTRIB ED, NY ARTS J, 80-; PUSHCART PRIZE, 77-; prog assoc thematic studies, John Jay Col Criminal Justice, 72-73; Nat Endowment for Arts grant, 76; sr staff, Univ Indiana Writers Conf, 76; vis prof, Am Studies and English, Univ Tex, Austin, 77; co-ed, Precisely: A Critical Jour, 76-; Vogelstein found, 80; grant, Investigative Jour, 80; Coord Coun Lit Mag, ed fel, 81. **RESEARCH** Experimental literature, particularly in North America; arts and artists in America; criticism of avant- garde arts, particularly literature. **SELECTED PUBLICATIONS** Auth, Avant Garde American Radio Art, North Am Rev, Vol 0278, 93; Flood in a Novel in Pictures, Am Book Rev, Vol 0014, 93; The Roaring Silence in Cage, John, A Life, Notes, Vol 0049, 93; Caxon, Caxton, a Predating, A Definition, and a Supposed Derivation, Notes and Queries, Vol 0040, 93; Not Wanting to Say Anything About Cage, John 1912-92, Chicago Rev, Vol 0038, 93; Grrrhhhh, Amn Book Rev, Vol 0014, 93; The Phenomenology of Revelation, Am Book Rev, Vol 0014, 93; Minimal Audio Plays, Western Hum Rev, Vol 0048, 94; It Too Shall Pass, Modern Languages Association Rev, Am Book Rev, Vol 0016, 94; Hysterical Pregnancy , North Am Rev, Vol 0279, 94; The Boulez-Cage Correspondence, Am Book Rev, Vol 0016, 95; Literary Video, Visible Language, Vol 0029, 95; Postmodern American Poetry in a Norton Anthology, Am Book Rev, Vol 0016, 95; Preface to Solos, Duets, Trios, and Choruses Membrane Future, Midwest Quart-A J Contemporary Thought, Vol 0037, 95; A Poetry-Film Storyboard in Transformations, Visible Lang, Vol 0030, 96; Anarchist Voices in an Oral-History of Anarchism in America, Am Book Rev, Vol 0017, 96; Interview With Schwartz, Tony, American Horspielmacher, Perspectives New Mus, Vol 0034, 96; Conservative Subversion, Am Book Rev, Vol 0017, 96; Format And Anxiety, Am Book Rev, Vol 0017, 96; The Year of the Hot Jock and Other Stories, Am Book Rev, Vol 0019, 97; A Star in the Family, Am Book Rev, Vol 0019, 97; Newsreel, Am Book Rev, Vol 0019, 97; Jim Dandy, Am Book Rev, Vol 0019, 97; The File on Stanley Patton Buchta, Am Book Rev, Vol 0019, 97; Roar Lion Roar and Other Stories, Am Book Rev, Vol 0019, 97; The Steagle, Am Book Rev, Vol 0019, 97; The Winner of the Slow Bicycle Race, Am Book Rev, Vol 0018, 97; Willy Remembers, Am Book Rev, Vol 0019, 97; Foreign Devils, Am Book Rev, Vol 0019, 97. **CONTACT ADDRESS** Canal St, PO Box 73, New York, NY, 10013.

KOSTO, ADAM
DISCIPLINE MEDIEVAL HISTORY **EDUCATION** Yale Univ, BA, 89; Harvard Univ PhD, 96. **CAREER** Asst prof. **SELECTED PUBLICATIONS** Rev, Pierre Bonnassie, From Slavery to Feudalism in South-Western Europe, Cambridge, 91; Parergon 26, 96; Paul Freedman, The Origins of Peasant Servitude in Medieval Catalonia, Cambridge, 92, Paragon 26, 96. **CONTACT ADDRESS** Dept of Hist, Columbia Col, New York, 2960 Broadway, New York, NY, 10027-6902.

KOSZTOLNYIK, ZOLTAN JOSEPH DESIDERIUS
PERSONAL Born 12/15/1930, Heves, Hungary, m, 1966, 2 children **DISCIPLINE** MEDIEVAL HISTORY **EDUCATION** St Bonaventure Univ, BA, 59; Fordham Univ, MA, 61; NY Univ, PhD, 68. **CAREER** From instr to asst prof, 67-72, assoc prof, 72-81, PROF HIST, TEX A&M UNIV, 81-. **HONORS AND AWARDS** Univ Fund Organized Res grants, Tex A&M Univ, 70 & 72; Phi Kappa Phi, 79; Distinguished Teaching Award, TAMU/Col Lib Arts, 95. **MEMBERSHIPS** Mediaeval Acad Am; AHA; Am Cath Hist Asn. **RESEARCH** Church and state in Hungary in the reign of the Arpads, 9th century to 1301; intellectual eleventh century Hungary, Gerard of Csanad; intellectual twelfth century Germany, Gerhoch of Reichersberg. **SELECTED PUBLICATIONS** Auth, Eventuelle spanische (Leon-aragonosche) und westliche Wirkingen in der Zusammenstellung der Landtage wahrend Regierugszeit Andreas' III, Aetas, 94; Early Hungarian towns and town life in the record of western chronicles, Specimina nova Universitatis de Iano Pannonio nominate, 95; Hungary in the Thirteenth Century, EEM-Columbia Univ Press, 96; The question of belonging: religious politics over Pannonia at the time of Magyars' arrival in the 890's, Cithara, 98. **CONTACT ADDRESS** Dept of Hist, Tex A&M Univ, College Station, TX, 77843-4236. **EMAIL** z-kosztolnyik@tamu.edu

KOTLER, NEIL G.
PERSONAL Born 04/17/1941, Chicago, IL, m, 1971, 1 child **DISCIPLINE** POLITICAL SCIENCE **EDUCATION** Branders Univ, AB, 62; Univ Wisconsin, MS, 63; Univ Chicago, PhD, 74. **CAREER** Smithsonian Inst, 86-; Georgetown Univ, 81; Legislative Aide US House of Repr, 75-84; Univ TX, Austin, 74-75; Dartmouth Col, 71-74; de Paul univ, 69-71. **HONORS AND AWARDS** Phi Beta Kappa **RESEARCH** Popular Image and Perception Politics; the experiences visitors have in museums. **SELECTED PUBLICATIONS** Museum Strategy and Marketing; Designing Missions; Building Audiences; Generating revenue and Resources, Jossey-Bass Inc, 98. **CONTACT ADDRESS** Office of the Provost, Smithsonian Inst, Washington, DC, 20560. **EMAIL** nkotler@si.edu

KOTLER, PHILIP
PERSONAL Born 05/27/1931, Chicago, IL, m, 1955, 3 children **DISCIPLINE** MARKETING **EDUCATION** Univ Chicago, MA, 53; PhD, MIT, 56; Hon Doctorate, DePaul Univ, 88. **CAREER** Asst then Assoc Prof, Roosevelt Univ, 57-61; Asst Prof to Prof, NW Univ, 62-69; A Montgomery Ward Prof, 69-73; Harold T Martin Prof, 73-88; SC Johnson & Son Dist Prof, 89-. **HONORS AND AWARDS** Graham & Dodd Award Fin Analysts Fedn, 62; MacLaren Advt Res Award, 64; McKinsey Award, 65; Alpha Kappa Psi Found Award, 78; Philip Kotler Award for excellence in Health Care Marketing, 85; Charlse Coolidge Parlin Nat Mktg Award, 89; Marketer of the Yr, 83., Marketing Ed, Holt, Rinehart & Winston, 65-78; Ch, Col Mktg, Inst Mgt Sci. **MEMBERSHIPS** Am Mktg Asn (bd 70-72); Inst Mgt Sci, Mktg Sci Inst (trustee 74-84); Phi Beta Kappa. **RESEARCH** Marketing. **SELECTED PUBLICATIONS** Auth, Marketing Management: Analysis, Planning and Control, 9th ed, 96; auth, Strategic Marketing for Nonprofit Organizations, 5th ed, 96; auth, Principles of Marketing, 7th ed, 96. **CONTACT ADDRESS** 624 Central St, Evanston, IL, 60201-1733.

KOUMOULIDES, JOHN A.
PERSONAL Born 08/23/1938, Athens, Greece **DISCIPLINE** MODERN HISTORY, ANCIENT EUROPEAN HISTORY **EDUCATION** Montclair State Col, BA, 60, MA, 61; Univ Md, PhD, 67. **CAREER** Asst prof ancient hist & 19th century Europ, 63-65, 67-68, Austin Peay State Univ; res studies hist, Cambridge Univ, 65-67; from asst prof to assoc prof ancient hist, 68-75, prof hist 75-, Ball State Univ; res grants, 69-71, 74 & 79; Am Coun Learned Soc travel grants, 69, 71 & 74; vis fel, Fitzwilliam Col, Cambridge Univ, 71-72; Am Philosophical Soc res grants, 73 & 81; Fulbright-Hays sr res scholar, Greece, 77-78; vis tutor, Campion Hall, Oxford, England, 80-81; Fulbright-Hays Sr Res Scholar, Greece, 87-88; vis fel, Wolfson Coll, Oxford, 83-84; dis vis fel, Fitzwilliamcol, Cambridge, 89-90; guest Scholar, Woodrow Wilson Int Cen for Scholars, 82. **HONORS AND AWARDS** Archon Chartophylax of the Ecumenical Patriarchate, Ecumenical Patriarch Dimitrios I, 79; Honorary Mem, The Society for the Promotion of Hellenic Studies, UK, 93; Corresponding Member, The Academy of Athens, 93; Commander of the Order of Phoenix, Greece, 97. **MEMBERSHIPS** AHA; Hist Assn, Eng; Soc Promotion Hellenic Studies; Archaeol Inst Am; Mod Greek Studies Assn; AAUP. **RESEARCH** Ancient history; Neo-Hellenic history; 19th century European history. **SELECTED PUBLICATIONS** Auth, Helenic Perspectives: Essays in the History of Greece, Univ Press Am, 80; auth, The Monastery of Tatarna: History and Treasures, 91; auth, The Good Idea: Democracy in Ancient Greece, 95; auth, Greece: The Legacy, 98. **CONTACT ADDRESS** Dept of History, Ball State Univ, 2000 W University, Muncie, IN, 47306-0002.

KOURVETARIS, YORGOS A.
PERSONAL Born 11/21/1933, Eleochorion, Greece, m, 1998, 3 children **DISCIPLINE** SOCIOLOGY **EDUCATION** Teacher's Col, Tripolis, Greece, Assoc degree, 55; Loyola Univ, BSc, 63; Roosevelt Univ, MA, 65; Northwestern Univ, PhD, 69. **CAREER** Northwestern Univ, Dept fel and Lectr, 67-68; Chicago City Col, asst prof, 67; Northern IL Univ, asst prof, 69-73, assoc prof, 73-78, prof, 78-. **HONORS AND AWARDS** Delta Tau Kappa; Heritage Awd by Greek Am Com; Recog Awd Hellenic Coun on Edu. **MEMBERSHIPS** ASA; Modern Greek Stud Asn; Europ Comm Stud Asn; SE Europ Asn; KRIKOS; **RESEARCH** Ethnicity; Multiculturalism; Ethno Nationalism. **SELECTED PUBLICATIONS** Social Thought, 94; A Book on Poetry, 92; The Impact of European Integration, co ed, 96; Political Sociology: Structure and Process, 96; Studies on Greek Americans, 97; numerous other articles. **CONTACT ADDRESS** Dept Sociology, No Illinois Univ, DeKalb, IL, 60115. **EMAIL** tk0gak1@corn.cso.niu.edu

KOUSSER, JOSEPH MORGAN
PERSONAL Born 10/07/1943, Lewisburg, TN, m, 1968, 2 children **DISCIPLINE** HISTORY **EDUCATION** Princeton Univ, AB, 65; Yale Univ, MPhil, 68, PhD(hist), 71. **CAREER** From instr to asst prof, 69-74, assoc prof hist, 74-79, prof hist & soc Sco, Calif Inst Technol, 80-; Nat Endowment for Humanities res grant, 74-75, consult, 76; Graves Found fel, 76; vis instr, Univ Mich, 80; vis prof, Harvard Univ, 81-82; Nat Endowment for Humanities res grant, 81-83. **MEMBERSHIPS** Orgn Am Historians; Soc Sci Hist Asn; Southern Hist Assoc. **RESEARCH** Quantitative history; Southern United States history; American political history. **SELECTED PUBLICATIONS** Auth, Ecological Regression and the Analysis of Past Politics, J Interdisciplinary Hist, autumn 73; The Shaping of Southern Politics, Yale Univ, 74; The New Political History: A Methodological Critique, Rev Am Hist, 3/76; Separate But Not Equal: The First Supreme Court Case on Racial Discrimination in Education, 80 & Progressivism for Middle-Class Whites Only: The Distribution of Taxation and Expenditures for Edu-

cation in North Carolina, 1800-1910, 80, J Southern Hist; Quantitative Social Scientific History, In: The Past Before Us: Contemporary Historical Writing in the US, Cornell Univ Press, 80; Making Separate Equal: The Integration of Black and White School Funds in Kentucky, J Interdisciplinary Hist, 79; coauth (with Gary W Cox), Turnout and Rural Corruption: New York as a Test Case, Am J Polit Sci, 81; Estimating the Partisan Consequences of Redistricting Plans - Simply, Legislative Studies Q, 96; Ironies of California Redistricting, 1971-2001, In: Governing the Golden State: Politics, Government, and Public Policy in California, U of CA Press, 97; Reapportionment Wars: Party, Race, and Redistricting in California, 1971-92, Agathon Press, 98; Colorblind Injustice: Minority Voting Rights and the Undoing of the Second Reconstruction, U North Carolina, 99. **CONTACT ADDRESS** Div of Humanities & Social Sciences 228-77, California Inst of Tech, 1201 E California, Pasadena, CA, 91125-0002. **EMAIL** kousser@hss.caltech.edu

KOVACS, PAUL DAVID
PERSONAL Born 11/12/1945, Kenosha, WI, m, 1969, 2 children **DISCIPLINE** CLASSICAL LANGUAGE & LITERATURE **EDUCATION** Col Wooster, BA, 67; Harvard Univ, AM, 69, PhD(class philol), 76. **CAREER** Asst prof, 76-82, assoc prof, 82-89, PROF CLASS, UNIV VA, 90-; Jr fel, Ctr for Hellenic Studies, DC, 81-82. **MEMBERSHIPS** Am Philol Asn; Class Asn Middle West & South. **RESEARCH** Greek tragedy; Greek textual criticism. **SELECTED PUBLICATIONS** Auth, Three Passages from the Andromache, Harvard Studies in Class Philol, 77; Andromache 1009-1018, Am J of Philol, 78; Four Passages from Euripidesion, Trans of the Am Philol Asn, 79; Shame, Pleasure and Honor in Phaedra's Great Speech, Am J of Philol, 80; Euripides Hippolytus 100 and the Meaning of the Prologue, Class Philol, 80; The Andromache of Euripides, Scholars Press, 81; Tyrants and Demagogues in Tragic Interpolation, Greek, Roman, and Byzantine Studies, 82; ed and trans, Loeb Classical Library Euripides, 94-. **CONTACT ADDRESS** Dept of Class, Univ of Va, 401 New Cabell Hall, Charlottesville, VA, 22903-3125.

KOVALEFF, THEODORE PHILIP
PERSONAL Born 02/08/1943, New York, NY, m, 2 children **DISCIPLINE** MODERN AMERICAN AND LEGAL HISTORY **EDUCATION** Columbia Univ, BA, 64, MA, 66; NY Univ, PhD, 72. **CAREER** From instr to asst prof hist, St John's Univ, NY, 69-75; lectr hist, 75-77, Barnard Col; dir admis, sch law, 77-80, asst dean, Sch Law, Columbia Univ, 77-92, hist adv, Westinghouse Broadcasting Co, 72-80; moderator & producer, Nighttalk, WOR radio, New York City; adv bd, The Antitrust Bull, 88-; ed bd, Presidential Stud Q, 91-; anal, small banks/ thrifts, national securities, 96-. **HONORS AND AWARDS** NY Univ Founder's Day Award, 73; Borough Pres Certificate of Service, 77; Borough Pres Citation for Service to the Commun, 83; City of NY Certification of Appreciation, 87; Ted Kovaleff Day proclaimed by Borough Pres Ruth Messinger, Jan 18, 1996, in recognition of service to Manhattan. **MEMBERSHIPS** AHA; Orgn Am Historians; AAUP; Bus Hist Conf. **RESEARCH** Diplomatic history; antitrust. **SELECTED PUBLICATIONS** Coauth, Poland and the Coming of World War II, Ohio, 77; auth, Business and Government During the Eisenhower Administration, Ohio, 80; auth, The Antitrust Impulse, Sharpe, 94; ed, J of Reprints for Antitrust Law and Econ, 94; ed, The Antitrust Bull, 94; auth, Interview with Anne Bingaman, The Antitrust Bull, 94. **CONTACT ADDRESS** 454 Riverside Dr, New York, NY, 10027.

KOVALIO, JACOB
DISCIPLINE MODERN JAPANESE DIPLOMATIC AND POLITICAL HISTORY **EDUCATION** Tel-Aviv Univ, BA, 69, Univ Pittsburgh, MA, 72, PhD, 81. **CAREER** Assoc prof. **RESEARCH** Asia-Pacific politics, international relations, and nationalism. **SELECTED PUBLICATIONS** Auth, Gendai Nihonron, Nyumon gendai chiiki kenkyu ¤An Introduction to Area Studiesl, Kyoto, Showado, 92; A.J. Toynbee and Japan, Japan in Focus, APRRC/Captus, 94; "Old and new clash in recent Japanese politics," APRRC Newsletter, 94; Japanese antisemitism in the 1990s, Antisemitism Worldwide 1994, Tel Aviv UP, 95; Japan - a security profile, Security Challenges in Asia, Bandung, 96; ed, Japan in Focus, APRRC/Captus UP, 94. **CONTACT ADDRESS** Dept of Hist, Carleton Univ, 1125 Colonel By Dr, Ottawa, ON, K1S 5B6. **EMAIL** jacob_kovalio@carleton.ca

KOVARIK, EDWARD
DISCIPLINE MUSIC HISTORY **EDUCATION** Northwestern Univ, BM, BME, MM; Harvard, MA, PhD. **CAREER** Assoc prof; dir, Windsor Collegium & mus dir and conductor, Windsor Commun Orchestra; first violin, Coventry Quartet of Windsor. **SELECTED PUBLICATIONS** Auth, pub (s), 15th and 16th century music. **CONTACT ADDRESS** Dept of Music, Univ of Windsor, 401 Sunset Ave, Windsor, ON, N9B 3P4. **EMAIL** kovarik@uwindsor.ca

KOWALESKI, MARYANNE
DISCIPLINE MEDIEVAL ECONOMIC AND SOCIAL HISTORY **EDUCATION** Univ Toronto, PhD. **CAREER** Prof, Fordham Univ. **RESEARCH** Maritime hist. **SELECTED PUBLICATIONS** Auth, Local Markets and Regional Trade in Medieval Exeter, 95; ed, The Local Customs Accounts of the Port of Exeter, 1266-1321, 93; co-ed, Women and Power in the Middle Ages. **CONTACT ADDRESS** Dept of Hist, Fordham Univ, 113 W 60th St, New York, NY, 10023.

KOWALKE, KIM H.
PERSONAL Born 06/25/1948, Monticello, MN, m, 1978, 1 child **DISCIPLINE** MUSICOLOGY **EDUCATION** Macalester Col, BA, 70; Yale Univ, MA, 72; Mphil, 74; PhD, 77. **CAREER** Conductor, 102nd Nat Guard Band, 71-77, Greater New Haven Youth Symphony, 73-75; musical dir, Yale Dramat and Yale Cabaret, 73-74; principal conductor, Col Light Opera Company, Falmouth, Mass, 74, 75, 77, 79; teaching fel, Yale Univ, 74-75; conductor, Collegiate Symphony Orchestra of Occidental Col and Calif Inst of Technol, 77-83; musical dir and conductor, many productions of musical theater, Occidental Col, 77-86; from asst prof to assoc prof, Occidental Col, 77-86; prof, Univ of Rochester, 86- ; conductor, Happy End, Univ of Rochester, Street Scene, Eastman Opera Theatre 91; music dir, A Salute to Stephen Sondheim, Univ of Rochester, 95; conductor, Eastman Opera Theatre: There Once Was A Girl Named Jenny: A Celebration of the Music of Kurt Weill, 95; coproducer and -conductor, Broadway: The George Abbott Way, Eastman Theatre, 97. **HONORS AND AWARDS** Nat Merit Scholar, 66-70; W. Wilson Nat Fel, 70; Yale Univ Fel, 71-75; Martha Baird Rockefeller Fund for Music Grant in Musicology, 75-76; Whiting Prize Dissertation Fel, 76-77; Theron Rockwell Field Prize, 78; Mellon Found Grant, 78; ACLS Res Grant for Recent Recipients of the PhD, 80; The Arnold L. and L. S. Graves Award in the Hums, 84-85; 3-Time Winner of ASCAP's Deems Taylor Award for excellence in writing about music, 86, 90, 97; Irving Lowens Prize, Sonneck Soc for Am Music, 97; George Friedley Award for outstanding book in the performing arts, 97. **MEMBERSHIPS** Phi Beta Kappa; Sonneck Soc for Am Music; Int Brecht Soc; Col Music Soc, Am Musicological Soc; Kurt Weill Found for Music. **RESEARCH** Whitman and Music; Adorno and the aesthetics of modernism; Wagner; post-Wagnerian symphonists; neo-Classicism. **SELECTED PUBLICATIONS** Ed, A New Orpheus: Essays on Kurt Weill, 86; coed, A Stranger Here Myself: Kurt Weill Studien, 93; Street Scene: A Sourcebook, 94; Der Silbersee: A Sourcebook, 95; Aufstieg und Fall der Stadt Mahagonny: A Sourcebook, 95; Lady in the Dark: A Sourcebook, 97; auth, Kurt Weill in Europe, 81; The Threepenny Opera in America, in: Die Dreigroscshenoper, ed. by S. Hinton, 90; Hin und zurueck: Kurt Weill at 90, in The Musical Times, 90; Singing Brecht vs. Brecht Singing: Performance in Theory and Practice, in Cambridge Opera Journal 5/1, 93; Dancing on a Volcano: Berg and Weill, in Stagebill, Dec., 93; Kurt Weill, Modernism, and Popular Culture: Oeffentlicheit als Stil, in Modernism/Modernity 2, 95; Ein Ehemaliger Deutscher: Kurt Weill in Amerika, in Kurt Weill: Berlin-Paris-New York , 95; Mahagonny and Robert W. Service, in Kurt Weill Newsletter 13, 95; Hindemith and Whitman: An American Requiem, in Stagebill, Sept., 95; Response to the 'Bourges Resolution', in The Brecht Yearbook 21, 96; Blitzstein and Bernstein: Remaking The Threepenny Opera, introductory essay for Vol. 1 of the Kurt Weill Edition, a facsimile of the Holograph Partitur of Die Dreigroschenoper, 96; Putting Sondheim in Musical Theater Focus, in The Sondheim Rev 3, 97; Orff and Weill: The Brecht Connection, in Stagebill, 97; For Those We Love: Hindemith, Whitman, and An American Requiem', in Journal of the Am Musicological Soc, 97. **CONTACT ADDRESS** The Col Music Program, Univ of Rochester, 210 Todd, Rochester, NY, 14627. **EMAIL** kkwk@db1.cc.rochester.edu

KRAABEL, ALF THOMAS
PERSONAL Born 11/04/1934, Portland, OR, m, 1956, 3 children **DISCIPLINE** RELIGIOUS STUDIES, CLASSICS **EDUCATION** Luther Col, BA, 56; Univ Iowa, MA, 58; Luther Theol Sem, BD, 61; Harvard Univ, ThD, 68. **CAREER** Asst prof classics and relig studies, 67-70, assoc prof classics and chmn rclig studies, 70-76, PROF CLASSICS and RELIG STUDIES, UNIV MINN, MINNEAPOLIS, 76-; CHMN DEPT and DIR GRAD STUDY, 80-; Assoc dir, Joint expedition to Khirbet Shema, Israel, 69-73; Sabbatical fel, Am Coun Learned Soc, 77-78. **MEMBERSHIPS** Soc Bibl Lit; Am Acad Relig; Am Soc Study Relig; Soc Values Higher Educ. **RESEARCH** Greco-Roman religions; archaeology. **SELECTED PUBLICATIONS** Auth, Jewish Communities in Asia-Minor, Cath Bibl Quart, Vol 0055, 93; Ancient Jewish Epitaphs in An Introductory Survey of a Millennium of Jewish Funerary Epigraphy Cath Bibl Quart, Vol 0055, 93; From Synagogue to Church in Public Services and offices in the Earliest Christian Communities Interpretation-A, J Bible Theol, Vol 0048, 94; Mission and Conversion in Proselytizing in the Religious History of the Roman Empire, J Early Christian Studies, Vol 0004, 96; Early Christian Epitaphs from Anatolia, Cath Bibl Quart, Vol 0058, 96. **CONTACT ADDRESS** Dept of Classics, Univ of Minn, 310A Folwell Hall, Minneapolis, MN, 55455.

KRABBE, JUDITH
DISCIPLINE GREEK AND LATIN AND SANSKRIT LANGUAGES AND LITERATURES **EDUCATION** Cath Univ, PhD. **CAREER** Dept Classics, Millsaps Col **SELECTED PUBLICATIONS** Auth, The Metamorphoses of Apuleius; coauth, An Introduction to Sanskrit. **CONTACT ADDRESS** Dept of Classics, Millsaps Col, 1701 N State St, Jackson, MS, 39210. **EMAIL** krabbjk@orka.millsaps.edu

KRAEHE, ENNO EDWARD
PERSONAL Born 12/09/1921 **DISCIPLINE** HISTORY **EDUCATION** Univ Mo, AB, 43, AM, 44; Univ Minn, PhD, 48. **CAREER** From asst prof to prof hist, Univ Ky, 48-64; prof hist, Univ NC- 64-68; prof, 68-71, Commonwealth prof, 71-77, WILLIAM W CORORAN PROF HIST, UNIV VA, 77-; Fulbright res scholar, Austria, 52-53; specialist, US Dept State, Ger, 53; vis assoc prof, Univ Tex, 55-56; Guggenheim fel, 60-61; Am Coun Learned Soc fel, 69; screening comt, Sr Fulbright-Hays Prog, 70-73; Nat Endowment for Humanities res grant, 73-74; chmn Europ sect, Soc Hist Asn, 75; Nat Endowment for Humanities fel, 80. **MEMBERSHIPS** AHA; Southern Hist Asn; Conf Group Cent Europ Hist. **RESEARCH** Modern European history; Central Europe; diplomatic history. **SELECTED PUBLICATIONS** Auth, The Origins of the Crimean-War, J Mil Hist, Vol 0059, 95. **CONTACT ADDRESS** Dept of Hist, Univ of Va, 216 Randall Hall, Charlottesville, VA, 22903.

KRAFT, JAMES P.
DISCIPLINE AMERICAN HISTORY, LABOR-BUSINESS **EDUCATION** Univ S Calif, PhD, 90. **CAREER** ASSOC PROF, UNIV HAWAII, MANOA, PRESENTLY. **CONTACT ADDRESS** History Dept, Univ of Hawaii, Manoa, 2530 Dole St, Honolulu, HI, 96822.

KRAFT, ROBERT ALAN
PERSONAL Born 03/18/1934, Waterbury, CT, m, 1955, 4 children **DISCIPLINE** HISTORY OF WESTERN RELIGION **EDUCATION** Wheaton Col, IL, BA, 55, MA, 57; Harvard Univ, PhD, 61. **CAREER** Asst lectr New Testament studies, Univ Manchester, 61-63; from asst prof to assoc prof relig thought, 63-76, acting chmn dept, 72-73, 92, Prof Relig Studies, Univ PA, 76-, Chmn Grad Studies, 73-84, 96-, Chmn Dept, 77-84; Vis lectr, Lutheran Theol Sem, Philadelphia, 65-66; ed, Monogr ser, Soc Bibl Lit, 67-72 & Pseudepigrapha ser, 73-78; task force on scholarly publ, Coun Studies Relig, 71-72. **HONORS AND AWARDS** Fels, Guggenheim, 69-70 & Am Coun Learned Soc, 75-76. **MEMBERSHIPS** Soc Bibl Lit; Int Orgn Septuagint & Cognate Studies; NAm Patristic Soc; Studiorum Nov Testamenti Societas; Am Soc Papyrologists. **RESEARCH** Judaism in the Hellenistic era, especially Greek-speaking Judaism; Christianity to the time of Constantine, espec the second century; computers and Ancient lit. **SELECTED PUBLICATIONS** Auth, Was There a Messiah-Joshua Tradition at the Turn of the Era?, RKMESSIA ARTICLE on the IOUDAIOS Electronic Discussion Group, 6/10/92; Philo's Text of Genesis 2.18 (I will make a helper), on the IOUDAIOS Electronic Discussion Group, 6/10/93; The Pseudepigrapha in Christianity, In: Tracing the Threads: Studies in the Vitality of Jewish Pseudepigrapha, SBL Early Judaism and Its Literature 6, Scholars, 94; coauth, Jerome's Translation of Origen's Homily on Jeremiah 2.21-22 (Greek Homily 2; Latin 13), Revue Be/ne/dictine 104, 94; auth, The Use of Computers in New Testament Textual Criticism, In: The Text of the NT in Contemporary Research, Studies and Documents 46, 95; Scripture and Canon in Jewish Apocrypha and Pseudepigrapha, In: Hebrew Bible/Old Testament: The History of its Interpretation, I: From Beginnings to the Middle Ages (Until 1300), 1: Antiquity, Vandenhoeck & Ruprecht, 96; author of numerous other articles. **CONTACT ADDRESS** Relig Studies, Univ of PA, Logan Hall, Philadelphia, PA, 19104-6304. **EMAIL** kraft@ccat.sas.upenn.edu

KRAHMALKOV, CHARLES R.
PERSONAL Born 06/06/1936, New York, NY, m, 1968, 2 children **DISCIPLINE** ANCIENT NEAR EAST HISTORY **EDUCATION** Univ Calif, Berkeley, AB, 57; Harvard Univ, PhD(Hebrew and Northwest Semitic philol), 65. **CAREER** Asst prof Near E lang and lit, Univ Mich, 65-66; asst prof, Univ Calif, Los Angeles, 66-68; asst prof, 68-71, assoc prof, 71-79, PROF NEAR EAST LANG and LIT, UNIV MICH, ANN ARBOR, 80-. **RESEARCH** Early Northwest Semitic philology; Egyptology; Biblical exegesis. **SELECTED PUBLICATIONS** Auth, The Byblian Phoenician Inscription of Bd-Smn in A Critical Note on Byblian Grammar, J Semitic Studies, Vol 0038, 93; Notes on Tripolitanian Neo Punic, J Am Orient Soc, Vol 0114, 94; **CONTACT ADDRESS** 1905 Dunmore, Ann Arbor, MI, 48103.

KRAMER, ARNOLD PAUL
PERSONAL Born 08/15/1941, Chicago, IL, m, 2 children **DISCIPLINE** MODERN EUROPE, GERMAN HISTORY **EDUCATION** Univ Wis-Madison, BS, 63, MS & cert Russ area studies, 65, PhD(mod Ger), 70; Univ Vienna, dipl, 64. **CAREER** Fac preceptor, Parsons Col, 65-68; asst prof mod Europe, Russ & Ger hist, Rockford Col, 70-74; assoc prof, 74-79, PROF MOD GER HIST, TEX A&M UNIV, 79-, Am Coun Learned Soc grant & Am Philos Soc grant, 72; Nat Endowment for Hum grant, 75; prin investr, Ctr for Energy & Mineral Resources, Tex A&M Univ, 76-; vis prof, Rice Univ, 80; Nat Sci Found, 82; vis prof Tubingen Univ, 93-94. **HONORS AND AWARDS** Bk of Yr Award, Jewish Bk Coun Am, 75, Sen Fulbright Fel 92, Tubingen Univ, Germany. **MEMBERSHIPS** Historians Second World War; Soc Hist Am For Rels; Western Asn Ger Studies. **RESEARCH** International brigades in Spanish Civil War; heavy industry in Nazi Ger; Ger Prisoners of War in the US during World War II. **SELECTED PUBLICATIONS** Auth, Germans against Hitler: The Thaelmann Brigade,

J Contemp Hist, 4/69; Russian Counterfeit Dollars: A Case of Early Soviet Espionage, Slavic Rev, 12/71; L'Aide Militarie Tchecoslovaque a Israel, 1948, Rev L'Est, 1/74; The Forgotten Friendship: Israel and the Soviet Bloc, 1947-1953, Univ Ill, 74; German Prisoners of War in the United States, Mil Affairs, 4/76; Fueling the Third Reich, Technol & Cult, 7/78; Technologyb as War Booty, Technol & Cult, 81; Japanese Prisoners of War in America, Pacif Hist rev, 83 German Prisoners of War in America, Stein & Day, 79; PW-Gefangen in America, Motorbuch Verlag, Stuttgart, 82; Enemy Diplomats in WW II, Prologue, 85; German Generals during WW II, J Mil Host, 90; Operation PLUTO, Technol & Cult, 92; Deutsche Zivilinternierte in den USA, 41-46, Vierteljahrshefte fur Zeitgeschichte, 96. **CONTACT ADDRESS** Dept of History, Tex A&M Univ, 1 Texas A&M Univ, College Station, TX, 77843. **EMAIL** apkrammer@aol.com

KRAMER, CARL EDWARD
PERSONAL Born 05/22/1946, New Albany, IN **DISCIPLINE** AMERICAN HISTORY **EDUCATION** Anderson Col, AB, 68; Roosevelt Univ, AM, 70; Univ Louisville, MS, 72; Univ Toledo, PhD(Am hist), 80. **CAREER** Pop analyst, US Bur Census, 70-71; res planner, Louisville and Jefferson County Planning Comn, 71-72; archit historian, Louisville Hist Landmarks and Preserv Dist Comn, 77-79; PRES, KENTUCKIANA HIST SERV, 81-; ADJ LECTR HIST, INST COMMUNITY DEVELOP, UNIV LOUISVILLE, 76- and IND UNIV SOUTHEAST, 78-. **MEMBERSHIPS** AHA; Orgn Am Historians; Community Develop Soc; Am Soc Pub Admin. **RESEARCH** Urbanization and land development; urban imagery; urban politics and planning. **SELECTED PUBLICATIONS** Auth, Koneski, Blaze, 1921-93 in In Memoriam, Slavic E European J, Vol 0038, 94; The Slavonic Languages, Slavic E European J, Vol 0039, 95; The Semantics and Pragmatics of Verbal Categories in Bulgarian, Slavic Rev, Vol 0054, 95; The Slavonic Languages, Slavic E European J, Vol 0039, 95. **CONTACT ADDRESS** 210 Ettles Lane No 112, Clarksville, IN, 47130.

KRAMER, JOHN E.
PERSONAL Born 05/19/1935, Philadelphia, PA, m, 1958, 2 children **DISCIPLINE** SOCIOLOGY **EDUCATION** Dartmouth Col, AB, 56; George Washington Univ, MA, 61; Yale Univ, MA, 63, PhD, 65. **CAREER** Asst prof, Univ of Mo at St Louis, 65-68; assoc prof, 68-69, prof, 69-97, prof emeritus, SUNY Brockport, 97-. **RESEARCH** Sociology of literature; fiction about higher education. **SELECTED PUBLICATIONS** Auth, North American Suburbs, Glendessary, 72; The American College Novel, Garland Pub, 81; College Mystery Novels, Garland Pub, 83; coauth, Strategy and Conflict in Metropolitan Housing, Heinemann, 78. **CONTACT ADDRESS** Dept of Sociology, State Univ of NY Brockport, Brockport, NY, 14420. **EMAIL** Jkramer-Brock@att.net.worldnet

KRAMER, LAWRENCE ELIOT
PERSONAL Born 08/21/1946, Philadelphia, PA, m, 1973, 1 child **DISCIPLINE** MUSICOLOGY **EDUCATION** Univ Pa, AB, 68; Yale Univ, MPhil, 70, PhD, 72. **CAREER** Asst prof English, Univ Pa, 72-78; asst prof, 78-81, assoc prof Eng, Fordham Univ Lincoln Ctr., 81-87, prof Eng and Comp Lit 87-95; prof Eng and Mus 95-. **MEMBERSHIPS** Am Music Soc; Soc for Music Theory; World Music Assoc. **RESEARCH** Romantic poetry; Romantic music; psychoanalytic criticism. **SELECTED PUBLICATIONS** Auth, Music and Poetry, the 19th Century and After, Univ Cal, 84; auth, Music as Cultural Practice, 1800-1900, Univ Cal, 90; auth, Classical Music and Postmodern Knowledge, Univ. Cal, 95; auth, After the Lovedeath: Sexual Violence and the Making of Culture, Univ Cal, 97; auth, Franz Schubert: Sexuality, Subjectivity, and Song, Cambridge Univ, 98. **CONTACT ADDRESS** Dept of English, Fordham Univ, 113 W 60th St, New York, NY, 10023-7484. **EMAIL** leonard@bard.edu

KRANTZ, GROVER S.
PERSONAL Born 11/05/1931, Salt Lake City, UT, m, 1982 **DISCIPLINE** ANTHROPOLOGY **EDUCATION** Univ Minn, PhD, 71. **CAREER** Asst prof to prof, Wash State Univ, 68- . **MEMBERSHIPS** Int Soc Cryptozoology. **RESEARCH** Evolution; races; linguistics; sasquatch. **SELECTED PUBLICATIONS** auth, Big Footprints: A Scientific Inquiry into the Reality of Sasquatch, Boulder Johnson Bks, 92; auth, The Antiquity of Race, Student Bookstore, 94; auth, The Process of Human Evolution, 2nd Ed, Student Bookstore, 95; auth, Only a Dog, Hoflin Publ Co, 98. **CONTACT ADDRESS** Dept Anthrop, Wash State Univ, Pullman, WA, 99164. **EMAIL** grover@mail.wsu.edu

KRANZBERG, MELVIN
PERSONAL Born 11/22/1917, St. Louis, MO, m, 1943, 2 children **DISCIPLINE** HISTORY OF SCIENCE **EDUCATION** Amherst Col, AB, 38; Harvard Univ, AM, 39, PhD, 42. **CAREER** Instr and tutor, Harvard Univ, 46; instr, Stevens Inst Technol, 46-47; asst prof hist, Amherst Col, 47-52; from assoc prof to prof, Case Western Reserve Univ, 52-72; CALLAWAY PROF HIST OF TECHNOL, GA INST TECHNOL, 72-; Assoc economist, off Price Admin, 42-43; consult, Opers Res off, Johns Hopkins Univ, 51-52; ed, Technol and Cult, Soc Hist Technol, 59-; vpres, Int Comt Coopin Hist of Technol, 65-68; chmn hist adv comt, NASA, 66-69; mem panel on technol assessment, Nat Acad Sci, 69-71, mem comt on surv of mat sci and eng, 71-73; mem adv panel, Prog on Sci, Technol and Values, Nat Endowment for Humanities, 75-77; chmn adv panel, Div Policy Res and Anal, NSF, 77-80; chmn comt on sci, eng and public policy, AAAS, 78-80. **HONORS AND AWARDS** Leonardo da Vinci Medal, Soc Hist Technol, 68; Roe Medal, Am Soc Mech Engrs, 80., LHD, Denison Univ, 67; LittD, Neward Col Eng, 68 and Northern Mich Univ, 72; Dr English, Worcester Polytech Inst, 81. **MEMBERSHIPS** AHA; AAAS (vpres, 65-66); Soc Hist Technol (secy, 58-74); Soc Fr Hist Studies (vpres, 58-59); Sigma Xi (pres, 79-80). **RESEARCH** History of technology; innovation and technology transfer; technology assessment. **SELECTED PUBLICATIONS** Auth, Glennan, T.Keith, 1905-95, Memorial, Technol Cult, Vol 0037, 96. **CONTACT ADDRESS** Dept of Soc Sci, Georgia Inst of Tech, Atlanta, GA, 30332.

KRAUS, MATTHEW A.
PERSONAL Born 08/21/1963, Cincinnati, OH, m, 1991, 2 children **DISCIPLINE** CLASSICS **EDUCATION** Harvard-Radcliffe, BA, 85; Hebrew Union Col, Jewish Inst of the Religion, Rabbinic ordination, 91; Univ MI, PhD, 96. **CAREER** ASST PROF CLASSICS AND JEWISH STUDIES, WILLIAMS COL, 96-. **MEMBERSHIPS** AJS; AAR-SBL; APA. **RESEARCH** Jerome; Judaism and the Greco-Roman world; late Antique Latin lit. **CONTACT ADDRESS** Dept of Classics, Williams Col, Stetson Hall, Williamstown, MA, 01267. **EMAIL** mkraus@williams.edu

KRAUSE, CORINNE AZEN
PERSONAL Born 03/03/1927, Pittsburgh, PA, m, 1948, 4 children **DISCIPLINE** HISTORY, SOCIOLOGY **EDUCATION** Univ Mich, BA, 48; Carnegie-Mellon Univ, MA, 66; Univ Pittsburgh, PhD(hist), 70. **CAREER** Teacher, Chatham Col, Carnegie-Mellon Univ and Univ Pittsburg, Greensburg; proj dir, Women, Ethnicity, and Mental Health Oral Hist Study, Am Jewish Comt, 75-78; RES and WRITING, 78-; Proj dir, Roots and Branches, exhibit Pittsburghs Jewish hist. **MEMBERSHIPS** Inst Res Hist; Orgn Am Historians; Am Jewish Hist Soc; AHA; Oral Hist Soc. **RESEARCH** Womens history in United States; United States Jewish history; Latin American history. **SELECTED PUBLICATIONS** Auth, Immigrant Family Patterns in Demography, Fertility, Housing, Kinship, and Urban Life, Vol 11, of American Immigration and Ethnicity, J Am Ethnic Hist, Vol 0013, 94. **CONTACT ADDRESS** 7 Darlington Ct, Pittsburgh, PA, 15217.

KRAUSE, LINDA R.
DISCIPLINE ARCHITECTURE **EDUCATION** Temple Univ, BA; Western Reserve Univ, MA; Yale Univ, PhD. **CAREER** Instr, Yale Univ, 76-77; asst prof, 84-. **MEMBERSHIPS** Col Art Asn; Soc Archit Hist; Midwest Art Hist Soc. **SELECTED PUBLICATIONS** Auth, The Image of the House of Images; Detours On the Roads Not Taken, 90; The New Brutalism: Frampton Reconsidered, 90; Milwaukee: In Praise of the Commonplace, 90. **CONTACT ADDRESS** Sch of Architecture and Urban Planning, Univ of Wisconsin, Milwaukee, PO Box 413, Milwaukee, WI, 53201. **EMAIL** lrkrause@uwm.edu

KRAUT, ALAN M.
PERSONAL Born 10/06/1946, Bronx, NY, m, 1973, 1 child **DISCIPLINE** HISTORY **EDUCATION** Hunter Col, BA, 68; Cornell Univ, MA, 71, PhD, 75. **CAREER** Asst prof, 74-78, ASSOC PROF AM HIST, AM UNIV, 78-. **MEMBERSHIPS** AHA; Orgn Am Historians; Southern Hist Asn; Social Sci Hist Asn; Immigration Hist Soc. **RESEARCH** Nineteenth century United States political and social history; immigration and ethnic history; Civil War and reconstruction. **SELECTED PUBLICATIONS** Auth, The Nation of Nations ... Still and American Immigrants, Proteus, Vol 0011, 94; A Century of European Migrations, 1830-1930, J Am Ethnic Hist, Vol 0013, 94; Dictionary of American Immigration History, J Am Hist, Vol 0081, 95; To See a Promised Land in Americans and the Holy Land in the 19th Century, Am Hist Rev, Vol 0101, 96. **CONTACT ADDRESS** Dept of Hist, American Univ, 4400 Mass Ave NW, Washington, DC, 20016-8200.

KRAUT, BENNY
PERSONAL Born 12/24/1947, Munich, Germany, m, 1972, 3 children **DISCIPLINE** MODERN JEWISH HISTORY, MODERN JUDAISM **EDUCATION** Yeshiva Univ, BA, 68; Brandeis Univ, MA, 70, PhD(Jewish hist), 75. **CAREER** Vis asst prof Judaica, Vassar Col, 75-76; ASSOC PROF JUDAICA, UNIV CINCINNATI, 76-. **MEMBERSHIPS** Orgn Am Historians; Asn Jewish Studies; World Union Jewish Studies. **RESEARCH** Development of American Judaism; religious and theological responses to the Holocaust; Jewish-Christian relations in American history. **SELECTED PUBLICATIONS** Auth, Wise, Isaac, Mayer in Shaping American Judaism, Am Hist Rev, Vol 0099, 94; Alternatives to Assimilation in The Response of Reform Judaism to American Culture, Am Hist Rev, Vol 0101, 96. **CONTACT ADDRESS** Judaic Studies, Univ of Cincinnati, P O Box 210169, Cincinnati, OH, 45221-0169.

KRAYBILL, DONALD B.
DISCIPLINE SOCIOLOGY **EDUCATION** Temple Univ, PhD, 75. **CAREER** Prof, Elizabethtown Col, Pa, 71-96; Provost, Messiah Col, Pa, 96-98. **HONORS AND AWARDS** Best relig book. **RESEARCH** Anabaptist Groups - Amish, Mennonites, Hutterites. **SELECTED PUBLICATIONS** The Riddle of Amish Culture; Amish Enterprise; Menonite Peacemaking; Mennonite Mutual Aid. **CONTACT ADDRESS** Office of the Provost, Messiah Col, Grantham, PA, 17027. **EMAIL** DKraybil@messiah.edu

KREKIC, BARISA
PERSONAL Born 10/14/1928, Dubrovnik, Croatia **DISCIPLINE** MEDIEVAL HISTORY, BYZANTINE HISTORY **EDUCATION** Univ Belgrade, BA, 51; Serbian Acad Arts and Sci, PhD(medieval hist), 54. **CAREER** Asst Byzantine hist, Byzantine Inst, Belgrade, 51-56; from asst prof to prof medieval hist, Univ Novi Sad, 56-70; prof, Ind Univ, Bloomington, 68-69; PROF SOUTHEAST EUROP HIST, UNIV CALIF, LOS ANGELES, 70-; Res teacher, Nat Ctr Sci Res, Paris, 57, 58 and 60; mem, Yugoslav Nat Comt Byzantine Studies, 66-70; US NAT COMT BYZANTINE STUDIES, 71-; prof hist, Dumbarton Oaks Byzantine Ctr, Harvard Univ, 75-76. **MEMBERSHIPS** AHA; Am Asn Advan Slavic Studies. **RESEARCH** Medieval Balkans; Byzantine history; Italian cities. **SELECTED PUBLICATIONS** Auth, A State of Deference in Ragusa Dubrovnik in the Medieval Centuries, J Medieval Studies, Vol 0069, 94; The Serbs in the Middle-Ages, J Medieval Studies, Vol 0070, 95; East-Central Europe in the Middle-Ages, 1000-1500, Am Hist Rev, Vol 0100, 95. **CONTACT ADDRESS** Dept of Hist, Univ of Calif, Los Angeles, CA, 90024.

KREMER, GARY R.
PERSONAL Born 09/03/1948, Jefferson City, MO, m, 1968, 2 children **DISCIPLINE** AMERICAN HISTORY **EDUCATION** Lincoln Univ, BA, 71, MA, 72; American Univ, PhD(hist), 78. **CAREER** ASST PROF HIST, LINCOLN UNIV, 72-; DIR, BLACK HIST SITES PROJ, 78-. **MEMBERSHIPS** Orgn Am Historians; Southern Hist Asn; Inst Study of Early Am Life and Hist. **RESEARCH** History of prisons; black history; social history. **SELECTED PUBLICATIONS** Auth, Climbing Jacob Ladder in The Enduring Legacy of African-American Families, Historian, Vol 0056, 94. **CONTACT ADDRESS** Dept of Soc Sci, Lincoln Univ, Jefferson City, MO, 65101.

KREN, GEORGE M.
PERSONAL Born 06/03/1926, Austria, 1 child **DISCIPLINE** MODERN EUROPEAN HISTORY **EDUCATION** Colby Col, BA, 48; Univ Wis, MA, 49, PhD, 60. **CAREER** Instr hist, Oberlin Col, 58-59; asst prof, Elmira Col, 59-60; from instr to asst prof, Lake Forest Col, 60-65; assoc prof, 65-77, PROF HIST, KANS STATE UNIV, 77-; Contrib ed, J Psychohist, 75-. **RESEARCH** European intellectual and cultural history; 19th and 20th century Germany; historiography and psychohistory. **SELECTED PUBLICATIONS** Co-ed, Varieties of Psychohistory, Springer Publ, 76; auth, Psychohistory in the university, J Psychohist, winter 77; The SS: A Social and Psychohistorical Analysis, In: Int Terrorism in the Contemporary World, Greenwood Press, 78; Psychohistorical Interpretation of National Socialism, German Studies Rev, 5/78; The Jew the Image as Reality, J Psychohist, 78; The Literature of the Holocaust, Choice, 1/79; Psychohistory and the Holocaust, J Psychohist, winter 79; coauth, The Holocaust and the Crisis of Human Behavior, Holmes & Meier, 80. **CONTACT ADDRESS** Dept of History, Kansas State Univ, 208 Eisenhower Hall, Manhattan, KS, 66506-1000. **EMAIL** kreng@ksu.edu

KRENTZ, PETER MARTIN
PERSONAL Born 07/11/1953, St. Louis, MO, m, 1981 **DISCIPLINE** ANCIENT HISTORY **EDUCATION** Yale Univ, BA, 75, MA, 76, PhD, 79. **CAREER** PROF CLASSICS & HIST, DAVIDSON COL, 79-. **MEMBERSHIPS** Asn Ancient Historians; Am Philol Asn; Class Asn Can. **RESEARCH** Greek political and military history; Greek orators; Greek epigraphy. **SELECTED PUBLICATIONS** Auth, The Thirty at Athens, Cornell Univ Press, 82; Xenophon, Hellenika, I-II.3.10, Aris & Phillps, 89; Xenophon, Hellenika, I.3.11-IV.2.8, Aris & Phillips, 95 **CONTACT ADDRESS** Dept Classics, Davidson Col, PO Box 1719, Davidson, NC, 28036-1719. **EMAIL** pekrentz@davidson.edu

KRESS, LEE BRUCE
PERSONAL Born 06/19/1941, Baltimore, MD, m, 1968, 1 child **DISCIPLINE** LATIN AMERICAN & AMERICAN HISTORY **EDUCATION** Johns Hopkins Univ, BA, 63; Columbia Univ, MA & cert Latin Am Studies, 67, PhD(hist), 72. **CAREER** Instr hist & polit, Baltimore Col of Com, 69-71; from instr to asst prof hist, Univ Md, 71-73; from asst prof to assoc prof hist, Rowan Univ, 73-, Res grants, NJ Comt for Humanities, 74 & Glassboro State Col, 77-78 & 79; instr & consult, Pace Prog, Old Dominion Univ, 76-78; adj instr, Camden County Col, 77-. **MEMBERSHIPS** Conf Latin Am Hist; AHA; Latin Am Studies Asn; Inter-Am Coun; Middle Atlantic Conf on Latin Am Studies. **RESEARCH** Latin American history, Argentine and Mexico; American history, diplomatic, military and Western. **SELECTED PUBLICATIONS** Auth, Central-

ism and federalism in Latin America, J Int & Comp Studies, 73; Argentine liberalism and the church, The Americas, 74; Development of Spanish-speaking community in New Jersey, NJ Hist, 77; co-ed, Terrorism in the Contemporary World, Greenwood, 78. **CONTACT ADDRESS** Dept of History, Rowan Univ, 201 Mullica Hill Rd, Glassboro, NJ, 08028-1702. **EMAIL** lbkress@rowan.edu

KREVANS, NITA
DISCIPLINE COMPARATIVE LITERATURE, CLASSICS **EDUCATION** Yale Col, BA, 75; Cambridge Univ, BA, 77; Princeton Univ, PhD; 84. **CAREER** Assoc prof, Univ Minn, Twin Cities. **RESEARCH** Hellenistic and Latin lyric. **SELECTED PUBLICATIONS** Auth, Print and the Tudor Poets, in Reconsidering the Renaissance, ed, M A Di Cesare, Medieval and Renaissance Texts and Studies, 93, Binghamton, 92; Ilia's Dream: Ennius, Virgil, and the Mythology of Seduction, HSCP 95, 93; Fighting against Antimachus: the 'Lyde' and the 'Aetia' Reconsidered, in Hellenistica Groninganа. 1. Callimachus, eds, M A Harder, R F Regtuit, and G C Wakker, Groningen, 93; Medea as Foundation-heroine, in Medea, eds, Clauss and Johnston, Princeton UP, 97. **CONTACT ADDRESS** Dept of Class and Near Eastern Stud, Univ Minn, Twin Cities, Minneapolis, MN, 55455. **EMAIL** Nita.Krevans-1@tc.umn.edu

KREY, GARY DE
PERSONAL m, 1 child **DISCIPLINE** BRITAIN, EARLY MODERN EUROPE **EDUCATION** Princeton, PhD, 78. **CAREER** History, St. Olaf Col. **SELECTED PUBLICATIONS** Area: seventeenth-century London. **CONTACT ADDRESS** St Olaf Col, 1520 St Olaf Ave, Northfield, MN, 55057. **EMAIL** dekrey@stolaf.edu

KREY, PHILIP D.W.
DISCIPLINE EARLY; MEDIEVAL CHURCH HISTORY **EDUCATION** Univ Mass/Boston, BA, 72; Lutheran Theol Sem at Gettysburg, MDiv, 76; Cath Univ Am, MA, 85;; Univ Chicago, PhD, 90. **CAREER** Dean; prof-. **HONORS AND AWARDS** Fulbright fel, Univ Munich, 89., Co-founder, Soc Stud of the Bible in the Middle Ages. **SELECTED PUBLICATIONS** Auth, transl, medieval Franciscan's Revelation Commentary - Nicholas of Lyra; co-ed, Sources of Medieval Christian Thought, Cath UP. **CONTACT ADDRESS** Dept of History and Systematic Theology, Lutheran Theol Sem, 7301 Germantown Ave, Philadelphia, PA, 19119 1794. **EMAIL** Pkrey@ltsp.edu

KRICK, ROBERT KENNETH
PERSONAL m, 1966, 2 children **DISCIPLINE** AMERICAN HISTORY **EDUCATION** Pac Union Col, BA, 65; San Jose State Col, MA, 67. **CAREER** Chief historian, Ft McHenry Nat Monument, 67-69; supt, Ft Necessity Nat Battlefield, 69-72; CHIEF HISTORIAN, FREDERICKSBURG and SPOTSYLVANIA NAT MIL PARK, 72-. **RESEARCH** The Army of Northern Virginia, 1862-1865. **SELECTED PUBLICATIONS** Auth, Hotchkiss,Jedediah in Rebel Mapmaker and Virginia Businessman, J Southern Hist, Vol 0060, 94; Jackson, Stonewall Deadly Calm and Coming to Terms with the Most Compelling and Mysterious of Civil-War Heroes, Am Heritage, Vol 0047, 96. **CONTACT ADDRESS** PO Box 1327, Fredericksburg, VA, 22402.

KRIEGER, LEONARD
PERSONAL Born 08/28/1918, Newark, NJ **DISCIPLINE** MODERN EUROPEAN HISTORY **EDUCATION** Rutgers Univ, AB, 38; Yale Univ, AM, 42, PhD, 49. **CAREER** Polit analyst, US Dept State, 46; asst instr, Yale Univ, 46-47, from instr to prof hist, 48-62; univ prof, Univ Chicago, 62-69; prof, Columbia Univ, 69-72; UNIV PROF HIST, UNIV CHICAGO, 72-; Fel, Ctr Advan Studies Behav Sci, 56-57; mem, Inst Advan Study, 63 and 69-70; ED, CLASSIC EUROPEAN HISTORIANS, UNIV CHICAGO, 67-; vis comt for dept hist, Harvard Univ, 70-73; MEM COUNC, AM ACAD ARTS and SCI, 75-; MEM UNIV COUNC and CHMN VIS COMT FOR GRAD SCH, YALE UNIV, 76-. **HONORS AND AWARDS** Soc Sci Res Counc demobilization awards, 46-48. **MEMBERSHIPS** AHA; Am Acad Arts and Sci; Am Soc Polit and Legal Philos; Int Soc Hist Ideas; Am Philos Soc. **RESEARCH** Intellectual history; philosophy of history. **SELECTED PUBLICATIONS** Auth, Teaching Professional Judgment, Wash Law Rev, Vol 0069, 94. **CONTACT ADDRESS** Dept of Hist, Univ of Chicago, Chicago, IL, 60637.

KRIGGER, MARILYN FRANCIS
PERSONAL Born 03/27/1940, St. Thomas, Virgin Islands of the United States, m **DISCIPLINE** HISTORY **EDUCATION** Spelman Coll Atlanta GA, BA Social Sci 1959; Columbia Univ NY, NY, MA History 1960; Univ of DE, Newark, DE, PhD-History 1983. **CAREER** Charlotte Amalie High Schl St Thomas, soc stud tchr 1960-66; University of the Virgin Islands St Thomas, history prof 1967-. **HONORS AND AWARDS** Grd flw John Hay Whitney Found Flwshp 1959-60; study-travel flw African Am Inst Ed-to-Africa Prog 1972; Natl Endowment for the Humanities, Summer Fellowships, 1976, 1988. **MEMBERSHIPS** Mem Virgin Islds Histl Soc mem Assoc of Caribbean Histn; mem Phi Alpha Theat; consult Virgin Islds Dept of Ed; mem Virgin Islds, Hum Coun; mem VI State Rev Brd for hist; Pres Founder Virgin Island 2000; mem VI Brd of Ed 1974-76; co-chair, VI Status Commission, 1988-93. **CONTACT ADDRESS** History Dept, Univ of the Virgin Islands, St Thomas, 00802.

KRIMSKY, SHELDON
PERSONAL Born 06/26/1941, New York, NY, m, 1970, 2 children **DISCIPLINE** PHILOSOPHY; HISTORY OF SCIENCE **EDUCATION** Brooklyn Col, BS, 63; Purdue Univ, MS, 65; Boston Univ, PhD(philos), 70. **CAREER** Assoc dir urban & environ studies, 75-78, actg dir, 78-80, from Asst Prof to Assoc Prof, 80-90, Prof Dept Urban & Environ Policy, 90-; Res assoc philos & hist sci, Boston Univ, 73-. **HONORS AND AWARDS** NDEA Fel; Distinguished Alumnus, Boston Univ **MEMBERSHIPS** AAAS **RESEARCH** Biotechnology; science and society; bioethics; chemicals and health. **SELECTED PUBLICATIONS** Auth, The Muliple-World Thought Experiment and Absolute Space, Nous, 72; The Use and Misuse of Critical Gedankenexperimente, zeitschrift fur allgemeine Wissenschafts theories Vol IV, No 2; Regulating Recombinant DNA Research in Controversy: Politics of Technical Decisions, Sage, 78; The role of the citizen court in the recombinant DNA debate, Bull Atomic Scientists, 10/78; coauth, Recombinant DNA research: The scope and limits of regulation, The Am J Pub Health, 12/79; auth, Genetic Alchemy: The Social History of the Recombinant DNA Debate, MIT Press, 82; Patents for life forms sui generis: Some new questions for science law and society, Recombinant DNA Tech Bull, 4/81; coauth, Environmental Hazards, Auburn House Publ Co, 88; Social Theories of Risk, Praeger, 92; auth, Biotechnics and Society, Praeger, 92; coauth, Agricultural Biotechnology and the Environment, Univ Ill Press, 96. **CONTACT ADDRESS** Dept of Urban Environ Policy, Tufts Univ, 97 Talbot Ave, Medford, MA, 02155-5555. **EMAIL** skrimsky@emerald.tufts.edu

KRINSKY, CAROL HERSELLE
PERSONAL Born 06/02/1937, New York, NY, m, 1959, 2 children **DISCIPLINE** HISTORY OF ART **EDUCATION** Smith Col, BA, 57; New York Univ, MA, 60, PhD, 65. **CAREER** Instr, 65-77, prof, New York Univ, 78-. **HONORS AND AWARDS** Phi Beta Kappa; ACLS grant; NEA grant; Arnold Buckner Award of NY City Chapter, Am Inst of Architects; Nat Jewish Book Award. **MEMBERSHIPS** Soc of Architectural Hist (pres, 84-86); Col Art Asn; Int Survey of Jewish Monuments; Int Center for Medieval Art; Urban History Asn. **RESEARCH** Architectural history; 15th century Netherlandish painting. **SELECTED PUBLICATIONS** Auth, Vitruvius de Architectura, como, 1511, Munich: Wilhelm Fink Verlag, 59; Rockefeller Center, NY: Oxford Univ Press, 78; Synagogues of Europe, NY: Cambridge, Architectural History Found/MIT Press, 85; Gordon Bunshaft of Skidmore, Owings and Merrill, NY: Cambridge, 88; Contemporary Native American Architecture, NY: Oxford Univ Press, 96; numerous articles, book reviews, book chapters, and introductions to books. **CONTACT ADDRESS** New York Univ, 303 Main, 100 Washington Sq SE, New York, NY, 10003-6688. **EMAIL** chk1@as2.nyu.edu

KRISLOV, JOSEPH
PERSONAL Born 08/14/1927, Cleveland, OH, m, 1956, 1 child **DISCIPLINE** ECONOMICS **EDUCATION** Univ of Wisconsin, PhD, 54. **CAREER** PROF, ECON, UNIV of KY, 64-. **HONORS AND AWARDS** Fulbright Fel, Ireland, India, and Brazil. **MEMBERSHIPS** Nat Acad of Arbitrators. **RESEARCH** Labor organizations; arbitration. **SELECTED PUBLICATIONS** auth, "Entry and Advancement in the Arbitrator Profession," The Profession and Practice of Labor Arbitration in Am, 92; auth, "Disclosure Problems of the Academic Labor Arbitrator," Dispute Resolution J, 97. **CONTACT ADDRESS** Dept of Econ, Univ of Kentucky, Lexington, KY, 40517.

KRISTOF, JANE
PERSONAL Born 05/25/1932, Chicago, IL, m, 1956, 1 child **DISCIPLINE** ART HISTORY **EDUCATION** Columbia Univ, PhD, 72; Univ Chicago, MA, 56, BA, 50. **CAREER** Lectr, Instr, Asst Prof, Assoc Prof, Prof, 73 to 92-, Portland State Univ, Instr, 72-73, Mount Hood Comm College; Lectr, 70-71, Univ Waterloo, ON CA. **MEMBERSHIPS** CAA; RSA; NWRS; CLA; SCS; INCS; AHNCA. **SELECTED PUBLICATIONS** Auth, The Feminization of Piety in Nineteenth Century Art, in: Reshaping Religion: Innovation and Pluralization in the Nineteenth Century, ed, Linda Woodward, forthcoming; Rouault and the Catholic Revival in France, in: Through a Glass Darkly: Essays in the Religious Imagination, ed, John Hawley, Fordham Univ Press, 96; Mary Stevenson Cassatt in Great Lives from History: American Women, Salem Press, 95; Blacksmiths Weavers and Artists: Images of Labor in Nineteenth Century Contexts, 93. **CONTACT ADDRESS** Art Dept, Portland State Univ, Portland, OR, 97207. **EMAIL** kristofj@pdx.edu

KRISTOFCO, JOHN P.
DISCIPLINE EDUCATION **EDUCATION** John Carroll Univ, BA, 70; Cleveland State Univ, MA, 76; Wright State Univ, Eds, 87; Ohio State Univ, PhD, 90. **CAREER** Asst dir, Commun Learning Ctr, Cuyahugo Community Col, 76- 77; fac, 77-86; chair, Educ Svcs Div, 86-91, assoc dean, 91-97, Clark State Community Col; adj assoc prof, grad sch educ, Wright State Univ, 92-97; DEAN, WAYNE COL, 97-. **CONTACT ADDRESS** Wayne Col, 1901 Smucker Rd, Orrville, OH, 44667.

KRODEL, GOTTFRIED G.
PERSONAL Born 07/14/1931, Redwitz, Germany, m, 1956, 1 child **DISCIPLINE** CHURCH HISTORY **EDUCATION** Univ Erlangen, ThD, 55. **CAREER** Instr church hist, Univ Chicago, 56-59; from asst prof to assoc prof relig, Concordia Col, Moorhead, Minn, 59-65; assoc prof hist and church hist, 65-71, PROF HIST and CHURCH HIST, VALPARAISO UNIV, 71-. **MEMBERSHIPS** Am Soc Church Hist; Am Soc Reformation Res; AHA; Renaissance Soc Am; Lutber Ges. **RESEARCH** History of Christian thought; Renaissance and humanism; constitutional history of 16th century Germany. **SELECTED PUBLICATIONS** Auth, A Mystics Passion in The Spirituality of Staupitz, Johannes, Von in His 1520 Lenten Sermons, Church Hist, Vol 0062, 93; Erasmus, Church Hist, Vol 0063, 94; Erasmus, Lee and the Correction of the Vulgate in The Shaking of the Foundations, Church Hist, Vol 0064, 95; The Kings Bedpost in Reformation and Iconography in a Tudor Group-Portrait, Church Hist, Vol 0066, 97. **CONTACT ADDRESS** Dept of Hist, Valparaiso Univ, Valparaiso, IN, 46383.

KROEBER, CLIFTON BROWN
PERSONAL Born 09/07/1921, Berkeley, CA, m, 1944, 4 children **DISCIPLINE** HISTORY **EDUCATION** Univ Calif, AB, 43, MA, 47, PhD, 51. **CAREER** Asst prof hist, Univ Wis, 51-55; from asst prof to assoc prof, 55-64, NORMAN BRIDGE PROF HISP AM HIST, OCCIDENTAL COL, 64-. **MEMBERSHIPS** AHA Latin Am Studies Asn. **RESEARCH** Latin American history. **SELECTED PUBLICATIONS** Auth, Violence, Resistance, and Survival in the America in Native-Americans and the Legacy of Conquest, Pacific Hist Rev, Vol 0064, 95; Theory and History of Revolution, J World Hist, Vol 0007, 96. **CONTACT ADDRESS** Occidental Col, 1600 Campus Rd, Los Angeles, CA, 90041.

KROEGER, KARL D.
DISCIPLINE MUSIC HISTORY **EDUCATION** Univ Louisville, BM, 54; MM, 59; Univ Ill, MS, 61; Brown Univ, PhD, 76. **CAREER** Music Libr, PROF EMER, UNIV COLO **MEMBERSHIPS** Am Antiquarian Soc **RESEARCH** William Billings **SELECTED PUBLICATIONS** Auth, The Complete Works of William Billings, vol 4; auth, The Worcester Collection of Sacred Harmony, Isaiah Thomas as a Music Publisher, Procs of AAS 86, 76; auth, The Complete Works of William Billings, v. 4, Am Musol Soc and Coll Soc Mass, 90; auth, Catalog of the Musical Works of William Billings, Greenwood, 91; auth, The Complete Works of William Billings, vol 1, 80, vol. 3, 86; auth, Pelissier's Columbian Melodies; researches in American Music, vol 13-14, 84; auth, "Collected Works of Daniel Reed" in Music of the United States of America, vol 4, A-R Editions, 95; auth, Music of the New American Nation: Sacred Music 1780-1820, 15 vols, Garland Press, 95. **CONTACT ADDRESS** Univ of Colo, C. B. 301, Boulder, CO, 80309. **EMAIL** karl.kroeger@spot.colorado.edu

KROG, CARL EDWARD
PERSONAL Born 03/02/1936, Cedar Rapids, IA, m, 1962, 3 children **DISCIPLINE** HISTORY **EDUCATION** Univ Chicago, BA, 58, MA, 60; Univ Wis, Madison, PhD(hist), 71. **CAREER** Instr hist and geog, Concordia High Sch, Wis, 59-63; instr hist, Univ-Cent High Sch, Wis, 65-66; from instr to asst prof, 66-75, ASSOC PROF HIST, UNIV WIS CTR, MARINETTE, 75-; Instr hist, Univ Wis, Green Bay, Marinette Campus, 69-72. **MEMBERSHIPS** Orgn Am Historians. **RESEARCH** Great Lakes regional history. **SELECTED PUBLICATIONS** Auth, Great-Lakes Lumber on the Great-Plains in The Laird, Norton Lumber Company In South-Dakota, Mont Mag Western Hist, Vol 0045, 95. **CONTACT ADDRESS** Univ of Wis, Ctr Bay Shore Rd, Marinette, WI, 54143.

KROLL, JOHN HENNIG
PERSONAL Born 02/12/1938, Washington, DC, m, 1969, 3 children **DISCIPLINE** GREEK ARCHEOLOGY, ANCIENT NUMISMATICS **EDUCATION** Oberlin Col, BA, 59; Harvard Univ, MA, 61, PhD(class archaeol), 68. **CAREER** Excavation numismatist, Agora Excavation, Athens, Greece, 70-74; asst prof, 74-78, from assoc prof to prof Classics, Univ Tex, Austin, 78-93. **HONORS AND AWARDS** Nat Endowment for Humanities fel, 81; ACLS Fell, 86. **MEMBERSHIPS** Archaeol Inst Am; Am Numis Soc Am Sch Class Studies Athens; Soc Ancient Historians; Am Philol Asn. **RESEARCH** Greek coinage from the Agora Excavations; Athenian government and monuments. **SELECTED PUBLICATIONS** Auth, Athenian Bronze Allotment Plates, Harvard Univ, 72; Greek Coins: The Athenian Agure, vol 26, 93. **CONTACT ADDRESS** Dept of Classics, Univ of Texas, Austin, TX, 78712-1026. **EMAIL** jKroll@utxvms.cc.utexas.edu

KRONENFELD, DAVID B.
PERSONAL Born 12/21/1941, Miami Beach, FL, m, 1964, 2 children **DISCIPLINE** ANTHROPOLOGY **EDUCATION** Harvard Univ, AB, 63; Stanford Univ, MA, 65, PhD, 69. **CA-**

REER From asst prof to assoc prof,69-76; prof, anthrop, Univ Calif Riverside, 81- ; dept chair, 81-93. **HONORS AND AWARDS** Magna Cum Laude, 63; NSF Fel 64-65, 65-66; NIMH Fel, 66-69; Fel AAAS, 83- . **MEMBERSHIPS** Am Anthrop Asn; Am Ethnol Soc; Ling Soc of Am; AAAS; Royal Anthrop Inst; Soc for Cult Anthrop; Soc for Ling Anthrop; Soc for Psychol Anthrop; Soc for Econ Anthrop. **RESEARCH** Social anthropology; kinship; social organization; ethnicity and stranger communities; linguistic anthropology, semantics; cognitive anthropology, computer and mathematical applications; culture as distributed cognition; Africa. **SELECTED PUBLICATIONS** Coauth, Starlings and Other Critters: Simulating Society, in J of Quantitative Anthrop, 93; auth, Language, Nineteen Eighty-Four, and 1989, in Language in Soc, 94; auth, Componential Analysis, Kinship Terminology, in Encyclopedia of Cultural Anthropology, 96; auth, Plastic Glasses and Church Fathers: Semantic Extension from the Ethnoscience Tradition, Oxford Univ Pr, 96. **CONTACT ADDRESS** Dept of Anthropology, Univ of California, Riverside, CA, 92521-0418. **EMAIL** kfeld@citrus.ucr.edu

KROSS, JESSICA
PERSONAL Born 09/20/1943, New York, NY **DISCIPLINE** HISTORY **EDUCATION** Brandeis Univ, BA, 65; Univ Mich, MA, 69, PhD(hist), 74. **CAREER** Asst prof, Southwest Mo State Univ, 74-75; ASST PROF HIST, UNIV SC, 75-. **MEMBERSHIPS** AHA; Orgn Am Historians; Econ Hist Asn; Social Sci Hist Asn. **RESEARCH** Colonial America; social history; American Revolution. **SELECTED PUBLICATIONS** Auth, New York in the Age of the Constitution, 1775-1800, William Mary Quart, Vol 0050, 93; The Estonian National Character, Sinn Form, Vol 0045, 93; The Rude Hand of Innovation in Religion and Social Order in Albany, New-York 1652-1836, J Urban Hist, Vol 0021, 94; Die Flucht, Sinn Form, Vol 0046, 94; Possessing Albany, 1630-1710 in The Dutch and English Experiences, J Urban Hist, Vol 0021, 94; Before the Melting Pot in Society and Culture in Colonial New York City, 1664-1730, J Urban Hist, Vol 0021, 94; Mohawk Frontier in The Dutch Community of Schenectady, New-York, 1661-1710, J Urban Hist, Vol 0021, 94; Deadly Medicine in Indians and Alcohol in Early America, Pa Mag Hist Biog, Vol 0120, 96; Schattenwurf, Akzente Zeitschrift Lit, Vol 0044, 97. **CONTACT ADDRESS** Dept of Hist, Univ SC, Columbia, SC, 29208.

KRUMAN, MARC WAYNE
PERSONAL Born 12/13/1949, Brooklyn, NY, m, 1977, 1 child **DISCIPLINE** AMERICAN HISTORY **EDUCATION** Cornell Univ, BS, 71; Yale Univ, MA and MPhil, 73, PhD(hist), 78. **CAREER** Instr, 75-78, ASST PROF HIST, WAYNE STATE UNIV, 78-; Andrew W Mellon fac fel, Harvard Univ, 80-81; vis asst prof hist, Harvard Univ, 81. **MEMBERSHIPS** AHA; Orgn Am Historians; Southern Hist Asn. **RESEARCH** American political history; 19th century American history; Southern history. **SELECTED PUBLICATIONS** Auth, The Presidency of Jackson, Andrew, J Am Hist, Vol 0081, 94. **CONTACT ADDRESS** Dept of Hist, Wayne State Univ, 838 Mackenzie, Detroit, MI, 48202-3919.

KRUMHANSL, CAROL L.
PERSONAL Born 09/17/1947, Providence, RI **DISCIPLINE** PSYCHOLOGY **EDUCATION** Wellesley Col, BA, 69; Brown Univ, MA, 73; Stanford Univ, PhD, 78. **CAREER** Asst prof, Rockefeller Univ, 78-79; asst prof, Harvard Univ, 79-80; asst prof, 80-84, assoc prof, 84-90, prof, 90-, Cornell Univ. **HONORS AND AWARDS** APA distinguished sci award, 83; fel, Am Psychol Soc, 93; mem, Soc of Experimental Psychol, 93. **MEMBERSHIPS** Psychonomic Soc; Am Psychol Soc; Soc for Music Perception and Cognition; European Soc for Cognitive Sci of Music; Soc for Res in Psychol of Music and Music Educ; Int Coop in Syst and Comp Musicol. **RESEARCH** Music perception and cognition. **SELECTED PUBLICATIONS** Auth, Cognitive Foundations of Musical Pitch, Oxford, 90; coauth, Infant's Perception of Phrase Structure in Music, Psychol Sci, 90; auth, Music Psychology and Music Theory: Problems and Prospects, Music Theory Spectrum, 95; auth, A Perceptual Analysis of Mozart's Piano Sonata, K.282: Segmentation, Tension and Musical Ideas, Music Perception, 96; coauth, Can Dance Reflect the Structural and Expressive Qualities of Music? A Perceptual Experiment on Balanchine's Choreography of Mozart's Divertimento no. 15, Musicae Scientiae, 97; auth, An Exploratory Study of Musical Emotions and Psychophysiology, Can Jour of Pshchol, 98. **CONTACT ADDRESS** Dept of Psychology, Cornell Univ, Ithaca, NY, 14853. **EMAIL** clk4@cornell.edu

KRUMMEL, DONALD WILLIAM
PERSONAL Born 07/12/1929, Sioux City, IA, m, 1956, 2 children **DISCIPLINE** LIBRARY SCIENCE, MUSIC **EDUCATION** Univ Mich, BA, Music, 51, MA, 53, MA, MLS, 54; PhD, 58. **CAREER** Instr, Music Lit, Univ Mich, 52-56; Library of Congress, 56-61; hd ref dept, Newberry Libr, 62-69; assoc prof/prof, Univ Ill; PROF EMER, UNIV ILL, 70-. **MEMBERSHIPS** Music Libr Asn; Am Libr Asn; Am Antiquarian Soc; Am Musicological Soc; Int Asn Music Librs **RESEARCH** History bibliography and libraries; Music bibliography **SELECTED PUBLICATIONS** The literature of Music Bibliography, Fallen Leaf Press, 92; "The Variety and uses of Music Bibliography," Foundations in music Bibliography, Hayworth, 93; "The Bay Psalm Book Tercentenary, 1698-1998," 1998. **CONTACT ADDRESS** Univ Ill, 501 E Daniel St, Champaign, IL, 61820.

KRUPPA, PATRICIA STALLINGS
PERSONAL Born 10/02/1936, Corpus Christi, TX, m, 1975, 1 child **DISCIPLINE** BRITISH HISTORY **EDUCATION** Univ Houston, BA, 58; Columbia Univ, MA, 59, PhD(Brit hist), 68. **CAREER** Instr hist, Towson State Col, 61-64; instr, 67-80, ASSOC PROF HIST and DIR WOMENS STUDIES, UNIV TEX, AUSTIN, 80-; Asst dean col social and behav sci, Univ Tex, Austin, 71-73. **MEMBERSHIPS** AHA **RESEARCH** Anglo-American history; history of popular religion in the 19th century; womens history. **SELECTED PUBLICATIONS** Auth, Secularism, Art and Freedom, Albion, Vol 0026, 94; Austen,Jane and the Clergy, Am Hist Rev, Vol 0100, 95. **CONTACT ADDRESS** 101 E 31st S St, Austin, TX, 78705.

KRUZE, ULDIS
PERSONAL Born 03/11/1944, Riga, Latvia, m, 1970 **DISCIPLINE** HISTORY **EDUCATION** Yale Univ, BA, 66; Northwestern Univ, MA, 68; Ind Univ, PhD, 76. **CAREER** ASST PROF HIST, UNIV SAN FRANCISCO, 77-; Res scholar, Ctr Chinese Studies, Univ Calif, Berkeley, 76-. **MEMBERSHIPS** Asn Asian Studies; Comt Concerned Asian Scholars. **RESEARCH** Modern Chinese and Japanese history. **SELECTED PUBLICATIONS** Trans, An Economic History of the Major Capitalist Countries (Kang Fau, et al), M E Sharpe, 92. **CONTACT ADDRESS** Dept of Hist, Univ of San Francisco, 2130 Fulton St, San Francisco, CA, 94117-1080. **EMAIL** kruzeu@usfca.edu

KRYSIEK, JAMES
DISCIPLINE HISTORY **EDUCATION** York Univ, MA; Marquette Univ, PhD. **CAREER** Fac, Mt Saint Mary's, 88-. **RESEARCH** Establishment of The University of Toronto and the status of women in twentieth-century Quebec. **SELECTED PUBLICATIONS** Publ on, Anglo-Dutch relations during the 1820s, New Perspectives on the Belgian Rev. **CONTACT ADDRESS** Dept of History, Mount Saint Mary's Col, 16300 Old Emmitsburg Rd, Emmitsburg, MD, 21727-7799. **EMAIL** krysiek@msmary.edu

KUBEY, ROBERT W.
PERSONAL Born 07/20/1952, Berkeley, CA, m, 1981, 2 children **DISCIPLINE** PSYCHOLOGY, BEHAVIORAL SCINCE, HUMAN DEVELOPMENT **EDUCATION** Univ Calif, Santa Cruz, AB, 74; Univ Chicago, MA, 78, PhD, 84. **CAREER** Asst prof, 85-91, ASSOC PROF COMMUN, 91-, DIR, MASTER'S PROG COMMUN INFO STUD, RUTGERS UNIV, 97-. **HONORS AND AWARDS** Res award, Sch Commun, Rutgers Univ, 97-98; merit awards, Rutgers Univ; Rutgers Univ Res Counc grants; investigator, Dept Health and Hum Svcs grant 88-93; res stipend, Fordham Univ, 88- 89; Annenberg Scholar, 93; Ctr Critical Analysis of Contemporary Cult fel, 86-87; fel, Nat Inst Mental Health. **MEMBERSHIPS** Nat Commun Asn; Int Commun Asn; Asn Media Literacy. **RESEARCH** Media analysis, production and soc of culture; media literacy; psychol and polit impact of media. **SELECTED PUBLICATIONS** Co-auth, Television and the Quality of Life: How Viewing Shapes Everyday Experience, Lawrence Erlbaum Assoc, 90; ed, Media Literacy in the Information Age: Current Perspectives, in Information and Behavior, Vol 6, Transaction Publishers, 97; auth, Creating Television: Then and Now, Lawrence Erlbaum Assoc, forthcoming; auth, Obstacles to the Development of Media Education in the United States, J of Commun, 48, 98. **CONTACT ADDRESS** MCIS Prog, Rutgers Univ, 4 Huntington St, New Brunswick, NJ, 08901-1071. **EMAIL** kubey@scils.rutgers.edu

KUBLER, GEORGE
PERSONAL Born 07/26/1912, Los Angeles, CA **DISCIPLINE** HISTORY OF ART **EDUCATION** Yale Univ, AB, 34, AM, 36, PhD, 40. **CAREER** From instr to prof, 38-75, STERLING PROF HIST OF ART, YALE UNIV, 75-; FEL, JONATHAN EDWARDS COL. Ed in chief, Art Bull, 45-47; anthropologist, inst soc anthrop, Smithsonian Inst, Lima, Peru, 48-49; Fulbright res grant, Spain and Portugal, 63-64; sr res fel, Nat Endowment for Humanities, 78-79. **HONORS AND AWARDS** Hitchcock Award, Soc Archit Hist, 63; Premio Figueiredo for bk, Nat Acad Fine Arts, Port, 73., LittD, Tulane Univ, 72. **MEMBERSHIPS** Corresp mem Hisp Soc Am; Am Acad Arts and Sci; corresp mem San Fernando Royal Acad Fine Arts, Spain; Acad Belas Artes, Lisbon, Port. **RESEARCH** Spanish and Portuguese architecture; Latin American art and archaeology. **SELECTED PUBLICATIONS** Auth, Circa 1492 in Art in the Age of Exploration, J Medieval Studies, Vol 0068, 93. **CONTACT ADDRESS** Dept of Hist of Art, Yale Univ, 56 High St, New Haven, CT, 06520.

KUCZYNSKI, MICHAEL
DISCIPLINE MEDIEVAL STUDIES **EDUCATION** St Joseph's Univ, BA, 79; Univ NC, PhD, 87. **CAREER** Instr, 88. **SELECTED PUBLICATIONS** Auth, A Classical Allusion in Gulliver's Travels, The Explicator, 83; A New Manuscript of Nicholas of Lynn's Kalendarium, Oxoniensia, 86; Gower's Metaethics, John Gower: Recent Readings, Kalamazoo: The Medieval Inst, 89; A Fragment of Richard Rolle's Form of Living in MS Bodley 554, Bodleian Lib Record, 94; Prophetic Song: The Psalms as Moral Discourse in Late Medieval England, Univ Pa Press, 95. **CONTACT ADDRESS** Dept of Eng, Tulane Univ, 6823 St Charles Ave, New Orleans, LA, 70118.

KUEHL, JOHN WILLIAM
PERSONAL Born 11/18/1941, Wausau, WI, m, 1966, 2 children **DISCIPLINE** AMERICAN HISTORY **EDUCATION** St Olaf Col, BA, 63; Univ Wis, Madison, MA, 64, PhD(hist), 68. **CAREER** Asst prof, 68-73, ASSOC PROF HIST, OLD DOMINION UNIV, 73-; CHMN DEPT HIST, 81-. **RESEARCH** American early national period; history of American nationalism; history of American thought. **SELECTED PUBLICATIONS** Auth, Redeeming the Republic in Federalists, Taxation and the Origins of the Constitution, Historian, Vol 0057, 94; Justice, Republican Energy, and the Search for Middle Ground in Madison, James and the Assumption of State Debts, Va Mag Hist Biog, Vol 0103, 95. **CONTACT ADDRESS** Dept of Hist, Old Dominion Univ, Norfolk, VA, 23508.

KUEHMANN, KAREN MARIE
PERSONAL Born 12/28/1954, Monravia, CA **DISCIPLINE** MUSIC **EDUCATION** Bob Jones Univ, BS, 76, MA, 78; Az St Univ, EdD, 87. **CAREER** SoundForth Music dir, prof, Bob Jones Univ, 79- **HONORS AND AWARDS** Who's Who in Amer Col & Univ, 76 **MEMBERSHIPS** Music Educ Nat Conf **RESEARCH** Music educ in Christian schools **SELECTED PUBLICATIONS** Auth, Music for Christian Schools, Bob Jones Univ Press; Perspectives in Music for Christian Schools, bob Jones Univ Press; Since I Have Been Redeemed, SoundForth, 99. **CONTACT ADDRESS** Bob Jones Univ, Box 34581, Greenville, SC, 29614. **EMAIL** kkuehman@bju.edu

KUEHN, D.D.
PERSONAL Born 11/25/1952, Bismarck, ND, m, 1990 **DISCIPLINE** ARCHAEOLOGY; GEOARCHAEOLOGY **EDUCATION** Texas A&M Univ, PhD, 95. **CAREER** Assoc dir Ctr for Ecol Archaeol and adj asst prof, anthrop, Texas A&M Univ, 95-98; geoarchaeological consult, 95- ; asst prof, dept of sociol and anthrop, Luther Col, 98- . **HONORS AND AWARDS** Outstanding Student Research Paper Award, Geol Soc Am, 93; dissertation award, 94; Interdisciplinary Research Initiative award, 94-96. **MEMBERSHIPS** Soc of Am Archaeol; Am Anthrop Asn; Soc for African Archaeol; Geol Soc Am; Olains Anthrop Soc. **RESEARCH** Geoarchaeology, stratigraphy, soils, site formation in archaeology; paleoenvironmental reconstruction; hunter-gatherer archaeology; arid landa; U.S. Great Plains, Midwest, Southwest, East Africa, Chile. **SELECTED PUBLICATIONS** Auth, Landforms and Archaeological Site Location in the Little Missouri Badlands: A New Look at Some Well Established Patterns, Geoarchaeology: An Int J, 93; auth, The Aggie Brown Member of the Oahe Formation: A Late Pleistocene/Early Holocene Marker Horizon in Western North Dakota, Current Res in the Pleistocene, 96; auth, A Geoarchaeological Assessment of Bison Kill Site Preservation in the Little Missouri Badlands, Plains Anthrop, 97; auth, Late Quaternary Vegetation and Climate Change in the North American Great Plains: Evidence from Stable Carbon Isotopic Composition of Paleosol Organic Carbon, Isotope Techniques in the Study of Environmental Change, 98; auth, Late Wisconsin-Age Proboscideans from Southern New Mexico, Texas J of Sci, forthcoming; auth, Stratigraphy and Non-Cultural Site Formation at the Shurmai Rockshelter, GnJm1, North-Central Kenya, Geoarchaeology: an Int J, forthcoming. **CONTACT ADDRESS** Dept of Sociology and Anthropology, Luther Col, 700 College Dr, Decorah, IA, 52101. **EMAIL** kuehndav@luther.edu

KUEHN, MANFRED
DISCIPLINE THE HISTORY OF EARLY MODERN PHILOSOPHY **EDUCATION** McGill Univ, PhD. **CAREER** Prof, Purdue Univ. **RESEARCH** 18th century philosophy; Immanuel Kant, Hume, Reid. **SELECTED PUBLICATIONS** Auth, Scottish Common Sense in Germany, 1768-1800. **CONTACT ADDRESS** Dept of Philos, Purdue Univ, 1080 Schleman Hall, West Lafayette, IN, 47907-1080.

KUETHE, ALLAN JAMES
PERSONAL Born 02/01/1940, Waverly, IA, m, 1962, 4 children **DISCIPLINE** LATIN AMERICAN HISTORY **EDUCATION** Univ Iowa, BA, 62; Univ Fla, MA, 63, PhD(Latin Am hist), 67. **CAREER** Asst prof Latin Am hist, 67-72, assoc prof, 72-80, PROF HIST, TEX TECH UNIV, 80-. **MEMBERSHIPS** AHA; Conf Latin Am Hist; InterUniv Sem Armed Forces and Soc. **RESEARCH** Bourbon reforms in eighteenth century New Granada and Cuba. **SELECTED PUBLICATIONS** Auth, United States Expansionism Cuban Annexationism in the 1850s, Hisp Am Hist Rev, Vol 0073, 93; The Expedition of Belalcazar, Sebastian, De To The North Sea and His Arrival in New-Granada, Hisp Am Hist Rev, Vol 0074, 94; Bouligny, Francisco, A Bourbon Soldier in Spanish Louisiana, Hispanic Am Hist Rev, Vol 0075, 95; The Army and Armed Forces in the American Colonial World, Hisp Am Hist Rev, Vol 0076, 96; The American Defense System in 18th Century, Hispanic Am Hist Rev, Vol 0076, 96; Garrison Life in American Cities

During The Enlightenment, Hispanic Am Hist Rev, Vol 0076, 96; Indian Reservations in the New Kingdom of Granada, Hispanic Am Hist Rev, Vol 0076, 96. **CONTACT ADDRESS** Dept of Hist, Tex Tech Univ, Lubbock, TX, 79409-0001.

KUHN, GARY G.
PERSONAL Born 07/22/1937, St. Paul, MN **DISCIPLINE** LATIN AMERICAN HISTORY **EDUCATION** Univ MN, BA, 59, MA, 61, PhD, 65. **CAREER** Assoc Prof Hist to PROF EMERITUS, UNIV WI, LA CROSSE, 65-, teaches part time (fall semester only) since retirement in 96. **MEMBERSHIPS** Conf Latin Am Hist; NCent Coun Latin Americanists; Am Aviation Hist Soc. **RESEARCH** Latin American aeronautical hist; 19th century Central America. **SELECTED PUBLICATIONS** Auth, United States Maritime Influence in Central America, 1863-1865, Am Neptune, Vol XXXII No 4, 72; Liberian Contract Labor in Panama, 1887-1897, Liberian Studies J, 75. **CONTACT ADDRESS** Dept of Hist, Univ Wisconsin, 1725 State St, La Crosse, WI, 54601-3788. **EMAIL** kuhn@mail.uwlax.edu

KUHN, THOMAS SAMUEL
PERSONAL Born 07/18/1922, Cincinnati, OH, m, 1948, 3 children **DISCIPLINE** HISTORY AND PHILOSOPHY OF SCIENCE **EDUCATION** Harvard Univ, BS, 43, MA, 46, PhD(physics), 49. **CAREER** Civilian employee, off Sci Res and Develop, Harvard Univ, 43-45, instr gen educ, 51-52, asst prof gen educ and hist of sci, 52-56; from asst prof to prof hist of sci, Univ Calif, Berkeley, 56-74; prof, Princeton Univ, 64-68, M Taylor Pyne Prof, 69-79; PROF PHILOS and HIST SCI, MASS INST TECHNOL, 79-; Lowell lectr, 51; Guggenheim fel, 54-55; fel, Ctr Advan Studies Behav Sci, 58-59; dir, Sources Hist of Quantum Physics Proj, 61-64; bd dirs, Soc Sci Res Coun, 64-67; assoc ed physics, Dict Sci Biog, 64-; dir prog hist and philos of sci, Princeton Univ, 67-72; mem, Inst Advan Study, 72-79; MEM, ASSEMBLY BEHAV and SOC SCI, 80-. **HONORS AND AWARDS** Howard T Behrman Award, Princeton Univ, 77., LLD, Univ Notre Dame, 73; DHL, Rider Col, 78; Doctorate, Linkoping Univ, Sweden, 80. **MEMBERSHIPS** Nat Acad Sci; Am Philos Soc; Am Acad Arts and Sci; Hist Sci Soc (pres, 68-70); Am Philos Asn. **RESEARCH** Reconstruction of out-of-date scientific ideas; description and abstract analysis of the way languag an ideas change in scientific development. **SELECTED PUBLICATIONS** Auth, The Road Since Structure, Arbor Ciencia Pensamiento Cult, Vol 0148, 94. **CONTACT ADDRESS** Dept of Ling and Philos Mass, Massachusetts Inst of Tech, Cambridge, MA, 02139.

KUISEL, RICHARD F.
PERSONAL Born 10/17/1935, Detroit, MI, m, 1960, 2 children **DISCIPLINE** MODERN EUROPEAN HISTORY **EDUCATION** Univ Mich, AB, 57; Univ Calif, MA, 59, PhD, 63. **CAREER** Instr Western civilization, Stanford Univ, 61-63; asst prof 20th century Europe, Univ Ill, 63-67; asst prof mod Fr hist, Univ Calif, Berkeley, 67-70; assoc prof, 70-80, PROF MOD FR HIST, STATE UNIV NY STONY BROOK, 80-; Am Coun Learned Soc fel, 76-77; Lehrman Inst fel, 76-78; nat selection comt, Soc Sci Res Coun, 76-78. **HONORS AND AWARDS** William Koren Prize, Soc Fr Hist Studies, 70. **MEMBERSHIPS** AHA; Soc Fr Hist Studies; Conf Group Fr Politics; Inst Fr Studies; Cent Int Univ dEtudes Europeennes. **RESEARCH** Modern French history; 20th century European history; economic policy. **SELECTED PUBLICATIONS** Auth, The Politics of French Business, 1936-1945, J Mod Hist, Vol 0066, 94; France and the United States in The Cold Alliance Since World War II, Diplomatic Hist, Vol 0018, 94; American Historians in Search of France in Perceptions and Misperceptions, French Hist Studies, Vol 0019, 95. **CONTACT ADDRESS** Dept of Hist, Univ of NY, Stony Brook, NY, 11790.

KUKLA, REBECCA
DISCIPLINE HISTORY OF MODERN PHILOSOPHY, SOCIAL PHILOSOPHY, GENDER THEORY AND CULTURAL **EDUCATION** Univ Toronto, BA, 90; Univ Pittsburgh, PhD, 95. **CAREER** Asst prof, Univ NMex. **RESEARCH** The writing of Jean-Jacques Rousseau. **SELECTED PUBLICATIONS** Published in The Brit J for Psihol of Sci, Metaphilosophy, J of Speculative Philos, J of Brit Soc for Phenomenol, Poznan Stud, Eidos, and Anal, as well as contributing chapters to volumes on Rousseau, Feminist Theory, and Popular Cult. **CONTACT ADDRESS** Univ NMex, Albuquerque, NM, 87131.

KUKLICK, BRUCE
PERSONAL Born 03/13/1941, Philadelphia, PA, m, 4 children **DISCIPLINE** HISTORY **EDUCATION** Univ Pa, BA, 63, MA, 66, PhD(Am civilization), 68; Bryn Mawr Col, MA, 65. **CAREER** From instr to asst prof philos, Am Studies Prog, Yale Univ, 68-72; Assoc Prof to Prof, 72-96, NICHOLS PROF HIST, UNIV PA, 96-; ed, Am Quart, 74-83; **HONORS AND AWARDS** Am Coun Learned Soc fel, 73; Guggenheim fel, 76-77; fel, Ctr Advan Study Behav Sci, 78-79; Rockefeller Humanities fel, 82; NEH Fel, 93. **MEMBERSHIPS** Orgn Am Historians. **RESEARCH** Diplomatic history; American philosophy; philosophy of history; intellectual history. **SELECTED PUBLICATIONS** Auth, The mind of the historian, Hist & Theory, 69; History as a way of learning, Am Quart, 70; Myth and symbol in American studies, Am Quart, 72; United States and the Division of Germany, Cornell Univ, 72; Josiah Royce, Bobbs, 72; Rise of American Philosophy, Yale Univ, 77; Churchmen and Philosophies, Yale, 85; The Good Ruler, Rutgers, 88; To Everything a Season, Princeton, 91; Puritans in Babylon, Princeton, 96. **CONTACT ADDRESS** Dept of History, Univ of Pennsylvania, 3401 Walnut St, Philadelphia, PA, 19104-6228. **EMAIL** bkuklick@sas.upenn.edu

KULCZYCKI, JOHN J.
PERSONAL Born 04/27/1941, Milwaukee, WI, m, 1971 **DISCIPLINE** HISTORY **EDUCATION** Col of the Holy Cross, BS, 63; Columbia Univ, MA, 66, PhD, 73. **CAREER** Admin Dir & instr, Haile Selassie Univ Exten Ctr, 63-65; asst prof, Brooklyn Col, CUNY, 72-75; lectr, Univ Vermont, 76; sr res fel, Columbia Univ, 75-78; vis assoc prof, NW Univ, 92; asst prof, 78-82, assoc prof, 82-95, PROF, 95- , UNIV ILLINOIS-CHICAGO. **HONORS AND AWARDS** Numerous fellowships, grants, & awards. **MEMBERSHIPS** Am Hist Asn; Am Asn Advan Slavic Stud; Polish Inst Arts & Sci Am. **RESEARCH** Polish national identity and Polish nationalism. **SELECTED PUBLICATIONS** Auth, School Strikes in Prussian Poland, 1901-1907: The Struggle over Bilingual Education, Columbia Univ Press, 81; The Foreign Worker and the German Labor Movement: Xenophobia and Solidarity in the Coal Fields of the Ruhr, 1871-1914, Berg Publ, 94; The Polish Coal Miners' Union and the German Labor Movement in the Ruhr, 1902-1934: National and Social Solidarity, Berg, 97. **CONTACT ADDRESS** 1560 N Sandburg Ter, 3902, Chicago, IL, 60610. **EMAIL** kul@uic.edu

KULIKOWSKI, MARK
DISCIPLINE HISTORY **EDUCATION** SUNY Binghamton, BA; MA; PhD. **CAREER** Assoc prof, SUNY Oswego. **RESEARCH** 20th century Russ Am For Policy. **SELECTED PUBLICATIONS** Auth, articles, bk revs on Russ and East Europe, 79-. **CONTACT ADDRESS** Dept Hist, SUNY Oswego, 427 Mahar Hall, Oswego, NY, 13126.

KUNIHOLM, BRUCE ROBELLET
PERSONAL Born 10/04/1942, Washington, DC, d, 2 children **DISCIPLINE** HISTORY **EDUCATION** Dartmouth Col, BA, 64; Duke Univ, MA, 72, MAPPS & PhD, 76. **CAREER** Instr English, Robert Acad, Robert Col, Turkey, 64-67; lectr policy sci & hist, 75-77, asst prof policy sci & hist & aid undergrad studies, 77-78, 80-84, assoc prof pub policy stud and hist, 84-87, prof, 87-, chemn dept, 89-94, vice provost for acad and int affairs, 96-, Duke Univ; Nat Endowment Humanities Int Affairs fel, Coun Foreign Rel, 78-79; mem policy planning staff, Dept State, 79-80; dir Terry Sanford Inst Pub Policy, 89-94; vis prof Int Rels Koc U, Istanbul, 95-96. **HONORS AND AWARDS** Phi Beta Kappa; Stuart L Bernath Prize, Soc Historians Am Foreign Rel, 81; Decorated Bronze Star with V device; Distinguished Tchg award, Duke Univ, 89; res grant Harry S Truman Libr, 84; Duke Univ Res Coun, 85-86; Ctr Soviet and East European Stud grant, 91; Fulbright fel, Turkey, 86-87; sr fel Nobel Inst, 94. **MEMBERSHIPS** AHA; Orgn Am Historians; Soc Historians Am Foreign Rel; Middle East Inst; Coun Foreign Relations; Middle East Stud Asn; Int Inst Strategis Stud. **RESEARCH** Cold War; Arab-Israeli problem; United States policy in Persian Gulf. **SELECTED PUBLICATIONS** Auth, The Origins of the Cold War in the Near East: Great Power Conflict and Diplomacy in Iran, Turkey, and Greece, Princeton Univ, 80; art, What the Saudis Really Want: A Primer for the Reagan Administration, Orbis, spring 81; auth, The Persian Gulf and United States Policy, 84; auth, The Palestine Problem and United States Policy, 86. **CONTACT ADDRESS** Office Provost, Duke Univ, PO Box 90006, Durham, NC, 27706-0006. **EMAIL** Bruce.Kuniholm@duke.edu

KUNIHOLM, PETER IAN
PERSONAL Born 09/30/1937, Washington, DC, m, 1959, 2 children **DISCIPLINE** CLASSICAL ARCHEOLOGY **EDUCATION** Brown Univ, AB, 58; Vanderbilt Univ, AM, 63; Univ Pa, PhD(class archaeol), 77. **CAREER** Instr English, Worcester Acad, Mass, 60-62; instr, house master, dean and dir athletics, Robert Col, Istanbul, Turkey, 62-68; instr, house master and dir athletics, Verde Valley Sch, Ariz, 68-70; fel, Am Res Inst, Turkey, 73-76, dir class archaeol, 74-76; ASST PROF CLASSICS and CUR CLASS ANTIQ, CORNELL UNIV, 76-; Res fel classics, Cornell Univ, 77-78. **MEMBERSHIPS** Archaeol Inst Am; Am Inst Nautical Archaeol; Am Res Inst Turkey; Am Orient Soc; Brit Inst of Archaeol Ankara. **RESEARCH** Aegean dendrochronology and dendroclimatology; the Greek Dark Ages. **SELECTED PUBLICATIONS** Auth, Dendrochronology, Am J Archeol, Vol 0099, 95; The Absolute Chronology of the Aegean Early Bronze Age, Archeology, Radiocarbon and History, Am J Archeol, Vol 0100, 96. **CONTACT ADDRESS** Dept of Classics, Cornell Univ, 35 Goldwin Smith Hal, Ithaca, NY, 14853-0001.

KUNNIE, JULIAN
DISCIPLINE AFRICAN STUDIES **EDUCATION** United Theol Col, BD, 81; Pacific School of Relig, MA, 84; Grad Theol Union, Univ Calif, Berkeley, ThD, 90. **CAREER** Asst prof, theol, 90-94, chair, Intercultural Stud Program, 91-94, Valparaiso Univ; dir African Stud, asst prof relig, Kalamazoo Col, 94-96; assoc prof and acting dir African American Stud, Univ Arizona, 96- . **HONORS AND AWARDS** Lilly Found grant, 91; Newhall Fel, 87-88, 89-90; eight academic prizes from United Theol Col for academic excellence; Award of Merit, 85; res grants, 90, 94; Kellogg Found grant 94, 96; Hum Res Initiative Grant, 96. **MEMBERSHIPS** Chemn, Indigenous Religious Traditions Sect, Am Acad of Relig; chemn, Ad Hoc Comm on African Study Abroad, Univ Ariz; African Stud Asn; Am Acad Relig/ Soc Bibl Lit; Asn for Study of Afro-American Life and Hist; Ed Advisory Board, Collegiate Press; Nat Coun for Black Stud; Nat Asn of Black Cultural Stud Centers; Southern African Asn for Culture and Develop Stud; Peace and Justice Comn; South African Asn for Literacy and Educ; Int Asn of Black Prof in Int Affairs; UMTAPO Center, S Africa. **RESEARCH** Systematic theology and philosophy; global religions; indigenous religions; ancient and contgemporary African religions; African politics; religions and society; Black religion and society in the United States; Black theologies; Third World liberation theologies; womanist and feminist theologies. **SELECTED PUBLICATIONS** Auth, Doing Social Analysis in Black Theology in Post-Apartheid Society in South Africa, in, Perspectives in Mission and Theology from South Africa: Signs of the Times, Mellen Research University, 93; auth, Models of Black Theology: Issues in Class, Culture, and Gender, Trinity, 94; auth, Black Churches in South Africa and the United States: Similarities and Differences, in, Afro-Christianity at the Grassroots, Brill, 94; auth, The Life, Thought, and Works of Desmond Tutu, in, The New Handbook of Christian Theologians, Abingdon, 96. **CONTACT ADDRESS** African Studies, Univ of Arizona, Martin Luther King Bldg, Room 305, PO Box 210128, Tucson, AZ, 85721-0128. **EMAIL** jkunnie@u.arizona.edu

KUNREUTHER, HOWARD
DISCIPLINE DECISION SCIENCES **EDUCATION** Bates Coll, AB (magna cum laude), economics, 59; MIT, PhD, economics, 65. **CAREER** Fulbright Scholar, Econometric Inst , Netherlands School of Econ, 63-64; econ, Inst Defense Analyses, Econ Political Studies Div, 64-66; asst prof, Univ Chicago, Graduate Sch Bus, 66-72; res adv, Pakistan Inst Development Econ (under Ford Found-Yale Univ Pakistan Project), 70-71; assoc prof, decision sciences, 72-75, chm, Decision Sciences Dept, 77-80, sr fellow, Wharton Financial Institutions Center, currently, co-dir, Wharton Risk Mgt Decision Processes Center, currently, Cecelia Yen Koo Professor Decision Sci Public Policy, currently, Univ Pa; task leader, Risk Group, Intl Inst Applied Analysis, 80-82; prog mgr, Decision Risk and Mgt Sci Program, Natl Sci Found, 88-89. **HONORS AND AWARDS** Fellowships and grants received: "Socioeconomic Impacts of Sitting High Level Radioactive Waste Repository," State of Nevada, 87-; with other faculty, EPA cooperative agreement on "Implementing the Clean Air Act," 93-; with Financial Institutions Center, "Managing Catastrophic Risks," 97-; Natl Sci Found, "role of Insurance and Other Policy Instruments in Managing Catastrophic Risks," 98-. **MEMBERSHIPS** Natl Sci Found Mentoring Program Natural Hazards, 96-98; Building Seismic Safety Comn, Natl Res Coun, 93-; Phi Beta Kappa; Amer Econ Assn;. **RESEARCH** Catastrophic risk management. **SELECTED PUBLICATIONS** Assoc ed, Risk Analysis, 84-; assoc ed, Journ of Risk and Uncertainty, 87-; assoc ed, Journ of Regulatory Econ, 88-; co-editor, "Challenges in Risk Assessment and Management," Annals of Amer Acad Polit Social Sci, May 96; co-auth, "Energy, Environment and the Economy: Asian Perspectives, 96; auth, "Managing Catastrophic Risks Through Insurance and Mitigation," Proceedings of the 5th Alexander Howden Conf on Financial Risk Mgt for Natural Catastrophes, 97; co-auth, Managing Environmental Risk Through Insurance, 97; co-auth, "Utilizing Third Party Inspections for Preventing Major Chemical Accidents," Risk Analysis, Apr 98. **CONTACT ADDRESS** Dept of Operations and Information Management, Univ of Pennsylvania, The Wharton School, Philadelphia, PA, 19104-6366. **EMAIL** kunreuther@wharton.upenn.edu

KUO, LENORE
PERSONAL New York, NY **DISCIPLINE** METAPHYSICS, ETHICS AND THE HISTORY OF PHILOSOPHY **EDUCATION** Univ Wis, Madison, BA, MA, PhD. **CAREER** Assoc prof Philos and Women's Stud, Univ Nebr, Omaha, 85-. **RESEARCH** Social policy analysis. **SELECTED PUBLICATIONS** Published on topics as diverse as surrogate mothering, corruption in bureaucracy and recent U.S. attempts to require women to use Norplant (a form of birth control) as a condition of probation. **CONTACT ADDRESS** Univ Nebr, Omaha, Omaha, NE, 68182.

KUPPERMAN, KAREN ORDAHL
PERSONAL Born 04/23/1939, Devil's Lake, ND, m, 1964 **DISCIPLINE** HISTORY **EDUCATION** Univ Missouri, BA, 61; Harvard Univ, MA, 62; Cambridge Univ, PhD, 78. **CAREER** Mellon Fac Fel, 80-81, Harvard Univ; asst prof - prof, 78-95, Univ Connecticut; prof, hist, NY Univ, 95-. **HONORS AND AWARDS** Binkley-Stephenson Award, 80, Org of Amer Historians; Amer Phil Soc Fel, 81; Res Fel, 84-85, Amer Coun of Learned Soc; Fel, 84-85, Natl Humanities Center; Rockefeller Found Fel, Villa Servelloni, Bellagio, 88; NEH Fel, 89, John Carter Brown Lib; Albert J Beveridge Award, 95, Amer Hist Asn; Times-Mirror Found Dist Fel, 95-96, Huntington Lib.

MEMBERSHIPS Soc Amer Hist; Colonial Soc of MA; Sr Assoc Mem, Oxford Amer Hist Asn; Assoc of the Omohundro Inst of Early Amer History and Culture; Org of Amer Historians, Amer Soc for Ethnohistory, New England Hist Asn. **RESEARCH** Early modern Atlantic world; transplantation of English society to America; American Indian-European relationships in early America **SELECTED PUBLICATIONS** Auth, Providence Island, 1630-1641: The Other Puritan Colony, Cambridge Univ Press, 93; art, The Connecticut River: A magnet for Settlement, CT History, Reshaping Traditions: Native Amer and Europeans in Southern New England, 94; art, Needs and Opportunities: British Expansion, Itinerario, 94; art, Scandinavian Colonists Confront the New World, New Sweden in Amer, Univ DE Press, 95; auth, America in European Consciousness, Univ NC Press for the Inst of the Early Amer Hist and Culture, 95; art, The Founding Years of Virginia and the United States, Virginia Mag of Hist & Biography, 96; art, A Continent Revealed: Assimilation of the Shape and Possibilities of North America's East Coast, North Amer Exploration, Univ NB Press, 96; art, Presentment of Civility: English Response to American Self-Presentation 1580-1640, Wm & Mary Quart, 97. **CONTACT ADDRESS** 53 Washington Square So., New York, NY, 10012-1098. **EMAIL** karen.kupperman@nyu.edu

KURLAND, JORDAN EMIL
PERSONAL Born 07/18/1928, Boston, MA, m, 1947, 4 children **DISCIPLINE** HISTORY **EDUCATION** Boston Univ, AB, 49, AM 50; Columbia Univ, cert, 52. **CAREER** Instr hist, Univ NC, Greensboro, 54-57, asst prof hist and Russ, 57-65; staff assoc, 65-67, assoc secy, 67-69, ASSOC GEN SECY, AM ASN UNIV PROFS, 69-; Instr and admin asst, Russ Inst, Columbia Univ, 55-56; Inter-Univ Comt Travel Grants exchange fel, 59-60; reserve off res and anal, US Info Agency, 60-; asst prof hist, Ind Univ, 62. **MEMBERSHIPS** AHA; Conf Slavic and East Europ Hist; Neth-Am Inst; Am Asn Advan Slavic Studies; Am Asn Teachers Slavic and East Europ Lang. **RESEARCH** Russian history and language; diplomatic history. **SELECTED PUBLICATIONS** Auth, Compromised Campus in the Collaboration of Universities With the Intelligence Community, 1945-1955, Slavic Rev, Vol 0052, 93. **CONTACT ADDRESS** General Secy, American Assn of Universities, Washington, DC, 20036.

KURODA, TADAHISA
DISCIPLINE EARLY AMERICAN HISTORY **EDUCATION** Yale Col, BA; Columbia Univ, MA, PhD. **CAREER** Prof, Skidmore Col. **HONORS AND AWARDS** Winner, essay contest sponsored by, NY State Hist Asn & NY State Bicentennial Comn. **RESEARCH** Early national US hist. **SELECTED PUBLICATIONS** Auth, New York and the First Presidential Election, New York History LXIX, 88; The Origins of the Twelfth Amendment: The Electoral College in the Early Republic, Westport: Greenwood Press, 94; coauth, The United States: Creating the Republic, in Establishing Democracies, Boulder: Westview Press, 96. **CONTACT ADDRESS** Dept of Hist, Skidmore Col, 815 North Broadway, Saratoga Springs, NY, 12866. **EMAIL** tkuroda@skidmore.edu

KURTH, WILLIAM CHARLES
PERSONAL Born 10/23/1932, Waterloo, IA, m, 1958, 3 children **DISCIPLINE** LATIN, GREEK **EDUCATION** Univ Northern Iowa, AB, 53; Univ Tex, MA, 59, Univ NC, PhD, 65. **CAREER** Tchr, 55-56, high Sch, Wis; instr Latin, 57-59, Baylor Univ; from instr to asst prof classics, 62-67, Univ Ill; assoc prof, 67-73, chmn dept, 67-76, prof classics, 73-, Luther Col, Iowa; consult programmed Latin, 67, Macalester Col; NEH fel, Univ Tex, 77-78. **MEMBERSHIPS** Am Philol Assn; Am Class League; Class Assn Mid W & S. **RESEARCH** Aulus Gellius; the minor Latin rhetoricians. **CONTACT ADDRESS** Dept of Classics, Luther Col, 700 College Dr, Decorah, IA, 52101-1045. **EMAIL** kurthwmc@luther.edu

KURTZ, MICHAEL L.
PERSONAL Born 08/26/1941, New Orleans, LA, m, 1966, 1 child **DISCIPLINE** HISTORY **EDUCATION** Tulane Univ, PhD, 71. **CAREER** Prof of Hist & Govt, SE La Univ, 67-; Dean of Grad Sch, SE La Univ, 97-. **HONORS AND AWARDS** L Kemper Williams Prize for Best Manuscript (83) & Best Book (90) in La Hist. **MEMBERSHIPS** La Hist Asn; Southern Hist Asn; Org of Am Hist; Phi Alpha Theta; Author's Guild. **RESEARCH** JFK assassination; recent US history; recent Louisiana history. **SELECTED PUBLICATIONS** Co-auth, Louisiana: A History, 3rd ed, 96; ed, Louisiana Since the Longs, 98; auth, Crime of the Century: The Kennedy Assassination From a Historian's Perspective, 2nd ed, 93; auth, Oliver Stone, JFK, and History, 99. **CONTACT ADDRESS** Dept of Hist & Govt, Southeastern La Univ, SLU 10809, Hammond, LA, 70402. **EMAIL** mkurtz@selu.edu

KUSHNER, DAVID Z.
PERSONAL Born 12/22/1935, Ellenville, NY, m **DISCIPLINE** MUSICOLOGY **EDUCATION** Boston Univ, BM, 57; Col-Conservatory of Music, Univ of Cincinnati, MM, 58; Univ of Mich, PhD, 66. **CAREER** Asst prof of Music, Miss Univ for Women, 64-66; assoc to full prof, Radford Univ, 66-69; Prof & grad prog head, Musicology, Univ Fla, 69-. **HONORS AND AWARDS** Teaching Incentive Prog and Professorial Excellence Prog Awards, Fla Stat Univ; Master Teacher Certificate in Music Hist, Music Teachers Nat Asn; Man of the Year, Am Bio Inst; Int Man of the Year, Int Bio Centre; Musician of the Year, Found for the Promotion of Music. **MEMBERSHIPS** Am Musicological Soc; 19th-Century Studies Asn; Col Music Soc, Soneck Soc for Am Music; Music Teachers Nat Asn; Pi Kappa Lambda. **RESEARCH** Life and music of Ernest Bloch and Jaromir Weinberger; nationalism in 19th- and 20th-century music; music criticism; American music. **SELECTED PUBLICATIONS** Auth, Jaromir Weinberger, Int Dictionary of Opera, St James Press, 93; Bloch's Macbeth, Int Dictionary of Opera, St James Press, 93; Ellen Taaffee Zwilich, Great Lives from Hist: Am Women, Salem Press, 95; Creative Teaching and the Practical Applications of Knowledge, Proceedings of the Eighteenth-Nat Conf on Successful Col Teaching, Valdosta State Col, 95; numerous entries including: Ernest Bloch, John Powell, Marc Blitzstein, Scott Huston, and Jaromir Weinberger, The New Grove Dictionary of Music and Musicians, Macmillan, 99; **CONTACT ADDRESS** Dept of Music, Univ of Fla, Gainesville, FL, 32611. **EMAIL** DZK777@gator.net

KUSHNER, HOWARD I.
DISCIPLINE HISTORY OF MEDICINE **EDUCATION** Rutgers Univ, AB; Cornell Univ, MA, PhD. **CAREER** Prof & dir, MA in Liberal Arts, San Diego State Univ; vis scholar, Univ Calif, San Diego, 94-and 96-97; past Jennifer Allen Simons prof, Simon Fraser University's Harbour Ctr in Vancouver, BC; adj prof, Simon Fraser Univ; res on childhood movements disorders, Brown Univ Med School's Child Neuro-Psychiatric Develop Clinic and at the Neuropsychiatric Clinic at Children's Hospital, Univ BC, 94-; ed adv bd, J Hist NeuroSci; sci consult, Discovery Network's tv ser World of Wonder. **HONORS AND AWARDS** Nat Endowment for the Humanities, Sci, and Technol grant, $108,000, 94-96; San Diego State Univ Alumni Asn awd for Outstanding Fac Contrib to the Univ, 95; Univ Prof Performance awd(s), 96 and 97. **RESEARCH** Historical and clinical aspects of Gilles de la Tourette's syndrome and associated neuropsychiatric disorders. **SELECTED PUBLICATIONS** Auth, American Suicide: A Psychocultural Exploration, Rutgers UP, 91; Chinese Translation San Min Book Co, Ltd., Taipei, Taiwan, 97; The Cursing Brain The Histories of Tourette Syndrome, Harvard UP, 99. **CONTACT ADDRESS** Dept of History, San Diego State Univ, 5500 Campanile Dr, San Diego, CA, 92182.

KUSHNER, HOWARD IRVIN
PERSONAL Born 07/21/1943, Camden, NJ, m, 1965, 1 child **DISCIPLINE** UNITED STATES SOCIAL HISTORY **EDUCATION** Rutgers Univ, New Brunswick, AB, 65; Cornell Univ, MA, 68, PhD(hist), 70. **CAREER** From asst prof to assoc prof hist, State Univ NY Col Fredonia, 70-77; assoc prof hist, Concordia Univ, Montreal, 77-79; PROF HIST, SAN DIEGO STATE UNIV, 79-; Vis asst prof hist, San Francisco State Univ, 73-74; vis assoc prof, Cornell Univ, 76-77. **MEMBERSHIPS** AHA; Orgn Am Historians; Can Asn Am Studies. **RESEARCH** Suicide in United States history; psychoanalytic methodology. **SELECTED PUBLICATIONS** Auth, Suicide, Gender, and the Fear of Modernity in 19th Century Medical and Social Thought, J Soc Hist, Vol 0026, 93; Medical Fictions in the Case of the Cursing Marquise and the Reconstruction of Delatourette, Gilles Syndrome, Bul Hist Med, Vol 0069, 95; Silent Travelers in Germs, Genes, and The Immigrant Menace, J Am Ethnic Hist, Vol 0014, 95; Plague in the Late Medieval Nordic Countries in Epidemiologic Studies, J interdisciplinary Hist, Vol 0025, 95; The Science of Sickness in The Establishment of Psychiatry in Quebec, 1800-1914, J Am Hist, Vol 0081, 95; The Controversy Over the Classification of Gilles De La Tourettes Syndrome, 1800-95, Perspectives Biology Med, Vol 0039, 96; The Romance of American Psychology in Political Culture in the Age of Experts, Am Hist Rev, Vol 0101, 96; The History of Pain, Am Hist Rev, Vol 0102, 97. **CONTACT ADDRESS** Dept of Hist, San Diego State Univ, 5500 Campanile Dr, San Diego, CA, 92182-0002.

KUSHNER, JAMES ALAN
PERSONAL Born 04/14/1945, Philadelphia, PA, m, 1970, 3 children **DISCIPLINE** LAW, CONSTITUIONAL HISTORY **EDUCATION** Univ Miami, BBA, 67; Univ Md, LLB & JD, 68. **CAREER** Adj prof housing law, Univ Mo-Kansas City, 73; vis lectr, Univ Calif, Berkeley, 74-75; assoc prof, 75-78, PROF LAW, SOUTHWESTERN UNIV, CALIF, 78-; Consult, Am Bar Asn, 74-76; vis lectr, Univ Va, 81; vis prof, UCLA, 83 & 93. **MEMBERSHIPS** Am Asn Law Schs. **RESEARCH** Race and Law; urban housing and planning. **SELECTED PUBLICATIONS** Auth, Apartheid in America, Carrollton Press, 80; Urban Transportation Planning, Urban Law & Policy, Vol 4, 81; Housing & Community Development (with Mandelker et al), Michie/Bobbs-Merrill, 81, 2nd ed, 89; The Reagan Urban Policy: Centrifugal Force in the Empire, UCLA J Environ Law & Policy, 82; Non-Owner Rights in Real Property and the Impact on Property Taxes, Urban Law & Policy, 85; Government Discrimination, West, 88; DMS: The Development Monitoring System is the Latest Technique for Subdivision Review and Growth Management, Zoning and Planning Law Report, 88; Unfinished Agenda: The Federal Fair Housing Enforcement Effort, Yale Law & Pol Review, 88; Substantive Equal Protection: The Rehnquist Court and the Fourth Tier of Judicial Review, Mo Law Rev, 88; The Fair Housing Amendments Act of 1988: The Second Generation of Fair Housing, Vanderbilt Law Rev, 89; Subdivision Law and Growth Management, West, 91; Property and Mysticism: The Legality of Exactions as a Condition for Public Development Approval in the Time of the Rehnquist Court, J Land Use & Environ Law, 92; Vested Development Rights, in 1992 Zoning and Planning Law Handbook, 92; A Tale of Three Cities: Land Development and Planning for Growth in Stockholm, Berlin, and Los Angeles, Urban Lawyer, 93; Growth Management and the City, Yale Law & Pol Rev, 94; Fair Housing: Discrimination in Real Estate, Community Development and Revitalization, 2nd ed, West, 95; Growth for the Twenty-First Century: Tales from Bavaria and the Vienna Woods -- Comparative Images of Urban Planning in Munich, Salzburg, Vienna, and the United States, Southern Calif Interdisciplinary Law J, 97; co-auth, Land Use Regulation: Cases and Materials, Aspen Law and Business, forthcoming; co-auth, Housing and Community Development: Cases and Materials, 3rd ed, Carolina Acad Press, forthcoming. **CONTACT ADDRESS** School of Law, Southwestern Univ, 675 S Westmoreland Ave, Los Angeles, CA, 90005-3905. **EMAIL** jkushner@swlaw.edu

KUSMER, KENNETH L.
PERSONAL Born 06/19/1945, Cleveland, OH, d **DISCIPLINE** AMERICAN HISTORY **EDUCATION** Oberlin Col, BA, 68; Kent State Univ, MA, 70; Univ Chicago, MA, 80, PhD, 80. **CAREER** Public sch tchr, Crestwood High Sch, OH, 69; instr hist, Cleveland State Univ, 69-71; from Asst Prof to Assoc Prof, 76-87, prof hist, Temple Univ, 87, Ed, The Temple Univ Historian, 77-; Vis Prof, Univ PA, 84-85; Bancroft Prof, Univ Guttingen, 87-88. **HONORS AND AWARDS** Louis Pelzer Award, Org Am Hist, 73. **MEMBERSHIPS** Org Am Historians; Immigration Hist Soc. **RESEARCH** Am soc hist since 1850; Afro-Am hist; recent Am hist. **SELECTED PUBLICATIONS** Auth, African Americans in the City since World War II: From the Industrial to the Postindustrial Era, J Urban Hist, 5/95; Black Cleveland and the Central-Woodland Community 1865-1930, In: Cleveland: A Metropolitan Reader, Kent State Univ Press, 95; The Homeless Unemployed in Industrializing America, 1865-1930: Perception and Reality, Amerikastudien, 12/95; The Urban Crisis as History, Rev Am Hist, 12/97; Ghettos Real and Imagined, Int J Urban & Regional Res, 12/97; Toward a Comparative History of Racism and Xenophobia in the U.S. and Germany, 1870-1933, In: Bridging the Atlantic: The United States and Germany in the Modern World, Cambridge Univ Press (in press); author of numerous other articles and publications. **CONTACT ADDRESS** Dept of Hist, Temple Univ, 1114 W Berks St, Philadelphia, PA, 19122-6029.

KUSTUS, GEORGE L.
DISCIPLINE CLASSICS **CAREER** Fac, Harvard Univ, 53; prof emer, SUNY Buffalo, present. **RESEARCH** Ancient rhetoric; Class and Medieval lit, drama, educational hist. **SELECTED PUBLICATIONS** Auth, Studies in Byzantine Rhetoric, Thessalonica, 73; publ on rhetoric. **CONTACT ADDRESS** Dept Classics, SUNY Buffalo, 712 Clemens Hall, Buffalo, NY, 14260.

KUTLER, STANLEY I.
PERSONAL Born 08/10/1934, Cleveland, OH, m, 1956, 4 children **DISCIPLINE** AMERICAN HISTORY **EDUCATION** Bowling Green State Univ, BA, 56; Ohio State Univ, PhD, 60. **CAREER** Teaching asst hist, Ohio State Univ, 58-59; vis instr, Ohio Wesleyan Univ, 59; instr, Pa State Univ, 60-62; asst prof, San Diego State Col, 62-64; from asst prof to assoc prof, 64-70, prof hist, 70-80, E Gordon Fox Prof Am Hist & Insts, Univ Wis-Madison, 80-, Am Philos Soc res grant, 61 & 63; Am Coun Learned Soc fel, 67-68; Russell Sage residency law & soc sci, 67-68; Guggenheim fel, 71-72; ed, Rev Am Hist, 73-; Fulbright lectr, Japan, 76-77. **MEMBERSHIPS** Orgn Am Historians; AHA; Am Soc Legal Hist. **RESEARCH** American legal and constitutional history. **SELECTED PUBLICATIONS** Auth, Ex Parte McCardle: Judicial Impotence?, in Am Hist Rev, 4/67; ed, Dred Scott Decision, Houghton, 67; Supreme Court and the Constitution, Norton, 68 & 77; auth, Judicial Power and Reconstruction Politics, Univ Chicago, 68; Privilege and Creative Destruction, Norton, 71 & 78; co-ed, New Perspectives on American Past (2 vols), Little, 71 & 74; auth, Looking for America (2 vols), Norton, 76 & 79; The American Inquisition: Justice and Injustice in the Cold War, Hill & Wang, 82; The Wars of Watergate, Norton, 92; Abuse of Power, The Free Press, 97. **CONTACT ADDRESS** Dept of Hist, Univ of Wis, 455 North Park St, Madison, WI, 53706-1483. **EMAIL** sikutler@facstaff.wisc.edu

KUTOLOWSKI, JOHN FRANCIS
PERSONAL Born 11/18/1931, Lynn, MA, m, 1971, 2 children **DISCIPLINE** MODERN EUROPEAN HISTORY **EDUCATION** Univ Mass, BA, 53; Univ Chicago, PhD, 66. **CAREER** Asst prof hist, Univ Dayton, 62-66; asst prof, 66-70, assoc prof hist, State Univ NY Col, Brockport, 70-. **MEMBERSHIPS** AHA; Polish Inst Arts & Sci Am. **RESEARCH** Victorian England; history of modern war. **SELECTED PUBLICATIONS** Auth, British Economic Interests and the Polish Insurrection of 1861-1864, The Polish Review, XXIX, 84; auth, Victorian Provincial Businessmen and Foreign Affairs: The Case of the Polish Insurrection, 1863-64, Northern History, XXI, 85. **CONTACT ADDRESS** Dept of History, SUNY, Brockport, 350 New Campus Dr, Brockport, NY, 14420-2914.

KUTOLOWSKI, KATHLEEN SMITH
PERSONAL Born 03/05/1942, Batavia, NY, m, 1971, 2 children **DISCIPLINE** AMERICAN HISTORY **EDUCATION** Gettysburg Col, BA, 64; Cornell Univ, MA, 66; Univ Rochester, PhD(hist), 73. **CAREER** Instr, 70-73, asst prof, 73-81, assoc prof hist, State Univ NY Col Brockport, 81-. **HONORS AND AWARDS** Chancellor's Award for Excellence in Teaching, State Univ NY, 77; NEH Fel, 84-85. **MEMBERSHIPS** Orgn Am Historians; Soc Historians Early Am Republic. **RESEARCH** Nineteenth century American social and political history. **SELECTED PUBLICATIONS** Auth, Moore's rural New Yorker: A farm program for the 1850's, Agr Hist, 1/71; Identifying the religious affiliations of nineteenth century local elites, Hist Methods Newslett, 12/75; contribr, Antimasonry and Masonry: The genesis of protest, 1826-1827, Am Quart, summer 77; auth, The Janus face of New York's local parties: Genesee County, 1821-1827, NY Hist, 4/ 78; co-auth, Canvasses and Commission: Politics and the Militia in Western New York, 1803-1845, 1/82; Freemasonry and Community in The Early Republic: The Case for Antimasonic Anxieties, American Quarterly, 82; Antimasonry Reexamined: Social Bases of the Grassroots Party, Journal of American History, 84. **CONTACT ADDRESS** Dept of History, SUNY, Brockport, 350 New Campus Dr, Brockport, NY, 14420-2914. **EMAIL** kkutolow@acspr1.acs.brockport.edu

KUZDALE, ANN E.
PERSONAL Born 01/01/1958, Dunkirk, NY, s **DISCIPLINE** HISTORY AND MEDIEVAL STUDIES **EDUCATION** Boston Col, MA, hist, 80; Harvard Univ, MTS, church hist, 85; Univ Toronto, PhD, medieval studies (hist), 95. **CAREER** Instr, Trent Univ, Peterborough, Ont, 96; asst prof, Chicago State Univ, 96-. **HONORS AND AWARDS** Pontifical Inst of Medieval Studies res assoc, 95-96. **MEMBERSHIPS** AHA; AAR; Cath Hist Asn; North Amer Patristics Soc; Ital Hist Soc; Hagiography Soc. **RESEARCH** Late antiquity; Early middle ages; Hagiography; Papacy. **SELECTED PUBLICATIONS** Book rev, Jour of the Amer Acad of Relig, v 66, 191-194, spring, 98. **CONTACT ADDRESS** History Dept., Chicago State Univ, 9501 S. King Dr., Chicago, IL, 60628-1598. **EMAIL** ae-kuzdale@csu.edu

KUZMIC, PETER
PERSONAL m, 3 children **DISCIPLINE** WORLD MISSIONS, EUROPEAN STUDIES **EDUCATION** S Calif Col, BA; Wheaton Col Grad Sch, MA; Univ Zagreb, MTh, DTh. **CAREER** Dir, Evangel Theol Sem, Osijek, Croatia; ch, Theol Commn of World Evangel Fel, 86; Eva B. and Paul E. Toms Distinguished prof, Gordon-Conwell Theol Sem, 93-. **HONORS AND AWARDS** Hon DD degree award, Asbury Theol Sem, 92., Co-founder, ch, Coun Evangelical Christians of (former) Yu; pres, Protestant Evangel Coun Croatia; founding pres, Agape and New Europe Vision.; founding exec, Coun Evangel Christians of Yu. **MEMBERSHIPS** Mem, Lausanne Comm for World Evangelization. **SELECTED PUBLICATIONS** Pub(s), On The Influence of Slavic Bible Translations Upon Slavic Literature, Language and Culture; auth, The Gospel of John and Biblical Hermeneutic; ed, Izvori. **CONTACT ADDRESS** Gordon-Conwell Theol Sem, 130 Essex St, South Hamilton, MA, 01982.

KUZMINSKI, ADRIAN
PERSONAL Born 02/21/1944, Washington, PA, m, 1966, 2 children **DISCIPLINE** HISTORY, PHILOSOPHY **EDUCATION** Amherst Coll, BA, 66; Univ of Rochester, PhD, 73. **CAREER** Prof of Hist, 71-80, Univ of Hawaii; Res Scholar in Philos, 96-, Hartwick Coll. **HONORS AND AWARDS** Fulbright and Wilson Fellow. **MEMBERSHIPS** APA **RESEARCH** Consciousness, political economy. **SELECTED PUBLICATIONS** The Soul, Peter Lang Pub, NY, 94. **CONTACT ADDRESS** RD #1, Box 68, Fly Creek, NY, 13337. **EMAIL** adrian@clarityconnect.com

KUZNICK, PETER J.
PERSONAL Born 07/25/1948, Brooklyn, NY, d, 1 child **DISCIPLINE** HISTORY **EDUCATION** Rutgers Univ, PhD, 84. **CAREER** Dir, Nuclear Studies Inst, 95-; assoc prof, hist, Amer Univ, 86-. **HONORS AND AWARDS** Woodrow Wilson fel; Smithsonian Postdoctoral fel; NEH summer fel. **MEMBERSHIPS** AHA; DAH. **RESEARCH** U.S. cultural history; Recent American history; Nuclear history; Radicalism; History and film. **SELECTED PUBLICATIONS** Auth, Beyond the Laboratory: Scientists as Political Activists in 1930s America, Univ Chicago Press, 87. **CONTACT ADDRESS** Dept. of History, American Univ, Washington, DC, 20016. **EMAIL** kuznick@american.edu

KUZNIEWSKI, ANTHONY JOSEPH
PERSONAL Born 01/28/1945, Carthage, MO **DISCIPLINE** AMERICAN HISTORY, CHURCH HISTORY **EDUCATION** Marquette Univ, AB, 66; Harvard Univ, AM, 67, PhD(hist), 73; Loyola Univ Chicago, MDiv, 80. **CAREER** Teaching fel hist, Harvard Univ, 68-72; asst prof, Col Holy Cross, 74-76 and Loyola Univ Chicago, 80-81; ASST PROF HIST, COL HOLY CROSS, 81-; Res tutor hist, Kirkland, House Harvard Col, 70-72; Vis lectr, Loyola Univ Chicago, 76-77. **HONORS AND AWARDS** Oscar Halecki Award, Polish Am Hist Asn and Am Hist Asn, 81. **MEMBERSHIPS** Polish Am Hist Asn (pres, 82-83); Am Cath Hist Asn; Orgn Am Historians. **RESEARCH** Polish immigrants in the United States; the religious life of Polish Americans; the interaction of various Catholic immigrant groups in the United States. **SELECTED PUBLICATIONS** Auth, This Confident Church in Catholic Leadership and Life in Chicago, 1940-1965, Am Hist Rev, Vol 0099, 94; Contending with Modernity in Catholic Higher Education in the 20th Century, Am Hist Rev, Vol 0102, 97. **CONTACT ADDRESS** Dept of Hist, Col of the Holy Cross, Worcester, MA, 01610.

KWOK, D.W.Y.
PERSONAL Born 09/03/1932, Shanghai, China, m, 1954, 2 children **DISCIPLINE** CHINESE HISTORY **EDUCATION** Brown Univ, BA, 54; Yale Univ, PHD, 59. **CAREER** Lectr hist & area studies, Inst Far Eastern Lang, Yale Univ, 57-59; from instr to asst prof hist, Knox Col, 59-61; from Asst Prof to Assoc Prof, 61-68, dir Asian studies prog, 69-75, Prof Hist, 68-97, Prof Emeritus, Univ Hawaii, Manoa, 97-; vis prof, Nanyang Univ, 65-67; sr specialist, Inst Advan Proj, East-West Ctr, Univ Hawaii, 68-69; Soc Sci Res Coun fel, 75-76; vis scholar, Hong Kong Univ, 75-76; external examiner hist, Univ Hong Kong, 79-82; vis res prof, Univ Hong Kong, 82-83; Tan Kah Kee Prof, Nanyang Tech Univ, 98. **HONORS AND AWARDS** Honorary Prof, State Commission on Educ, China. **MEMBERSHIPS** Asn Asian Studies; AHA. **RESEARCH** Mod Chinese intellectual hist; early mod Chinese hist; late Ming thought. **SELECTED PUBLICATIONS** Auth, Scientism in Chinese Thought, 1900-1950, Yale Univ, 65; Anarchism and traditionalism, J Inst Chinese Studies, Univ Hong King, 12/71; contrib, Chinas grosse wandlung, C H Beck, 72; Die Sohne des Drachen, List Verlag, Munich, 74; Chinas Handbuch, Bertelsmann, Dusseldorf, 74; Ming Biographical Dictionary, Columbia Univ, 76; Mao Tsetung and Populism, Centre Asian Studies, Univ Hong Kong, 79; coauth, Cosmology, Ontology, and Human Efficacy, Univ Hawaii, 93; ed & transl, Turbulent Decade, Univ Hawaii, 96; auth, The Urbane Imagination, Kendall/Hunt, 97. **CONTACT ADDRESS** Dept of Hist, Univ of HI, 2530 Dole St, Honolulu, HI, 96822-2303. **EMAIL** dkwok@hawaii.edu

KYTE, GEORGE WALLACE
PERSONAL Born 03/01/1918, Berkeley, CA **DISCIPLINE** HISTORY **EDUCATION** Univ Calif, AB, 40, MA, 41, PhD, 43. **CAREER** Assoc res analyst, res br, off Strategic Serv, 43-45; from instr to assoc prof hist, Lehigh Univ, 46-66; assoc prof, 66-68, PROF HIST, NORTHERN ARIZ UNIV, 68-. **MEMBERSHIPS** AHA; Orgn Am Historians; Conf Brit Studies; Conf Early Am Hist. **RESEARCH** Anglo-American colonial history in the 18th century; British Empire history and Anglo-American colonial history; American colonial history, especially the War for American Independence. **SELECTED PUBLICATIONS** Auth, Bouligny,Francisco in A Bourbon Soldier in Spanish Louisiana, Am, Vol 0051, 94. **CONTACT ADDRESS** No Arizona Univ, Box 5718, Flagstaff, AZ, 86011.

KYVIG, DAVID EDWARD
PERSONAL Born 03/08/1944, Ames, IA, m, 1988, 2 children **DISCIPLINE** AMERICAN HISTORY **EDUCATION** Kalamazoo Col, BA, 66; Northwestern Univ, PhD(Am hist), 71 **CAREER** Archivist, Off Presidential Libr, Nat Arch, 70-71; asst prof, 71-79, assoc prof, 79-85, PROF HIST, UNIV AKRON, 85-; Vis asst prof hist, Kalamazoo Col, 72; Am Coun Learned Soc fel, 80-81; Fulbright prof, Univ Tromso, Norway, 87-88 **HONORS AND AWARDS** Pres, Nat Counc Public Hist, 90-91; Bancroft Prize, Columbia Univ, 97; Henry Adams Prize, Soc Hist in Fed Gov, 97; Ohio Acad Hist Book Prize, 97. **MEMBERSHIPS** Orgn Am Historians; Am Hist Asn; Nat Coun Pub Hist; Ohio Humanities Counc; Ohio Bicentennial Comn **RESEARCH** America since 1900; constitutional amendments **SELECTED PUBLICATIONS** Ed, FDR'S America, Forum, 76; coauth, Your Family History: A Handbook for Research and Writing, AHM Publ, 78; auth, Repealing National Prohibition, Univ Chicago Press, 79; coauth, Nearby History: Exploring the Past Around You, Am Asn State & Local Hist, 82; ed, Law, Alcohol, and Order: Perspectives on National Prohibition, Greenwood, 85; ed, New Day/New Deal: A Bibliography of the Great American Depression, 1929-1941, Greenwood, 88; ed, Reagan and the World, Greenwood, 90; auth, Explicit and Authentic Acts: Amending the U S Constitution, 1776-1995, Kansas, 96. **CONTACT ADDRESS** Dept of Hist, Univ of Akron, Akron, OH, 44325-1902. **EMAIL** kyvig@vakron.edu

L

L'ABATE, LUCIANO
PERSONAL Born 09/19/1928, Brindisi, Italy, d, 2 children **DISCIPLINE** PSYCHOLOGY **EDUCATION** Tabor Coll, BA, 50; Wichita State Univ, MA, 53; Duke Univ, PhD, 56. **CAREER** PROF EMER, PSYCHOL, GA STATE UNIV. **MEMBERSHIPS** Am Psychol Asn; Am Asn Marriage & Family Ther **RESEARCH** Computer assisted interventions; Prgrammed distance writing. **SELECTED PUBLICATIONS** Edr, Family Psychopathology: The Relational Roots of Dysfunctional Behavior, Guilford Press, 98; "How Should a Theory of Personality Socialization in the Family Be evaluated? Strategies of Theory Testing," Famiglia, Interdisciplinarita', Ricera: Rivista di Studi Familiari, 98; "Increasing Intimacy in Couples Through Distance Writing and Face-to-Face Approaches," The Intimate Couple, 98; coauth, "The Forgotten Others: The Importance of Prevention With Couples and Families," The Family and Family Therapy in International Perspective, 98. **CONTACT ADDRESS** Dept Psychol, Georgia State Univ, Univ Plaza, Atlanta, GA, 30303. **EMAIL** labate@gsu.edu

L'ALLIER, LOUIS
PERSONAL Born 02/27/1961, PQ, Canada **DISCIPLINE** CLASSICAL STUDIES **EDUCATION** Univ Ottawa, MA, 89; Laval Univ, PhD, 96. **CAREER** Lectr, Laval Univ, 96-. **MEMBERSHIPS** Am Philol Asn; Class Asn of Can; Soc des Etudes Anciennes du Quebec. **RESEARCH** Ancient Greek literature. **SELECTED PUBLICATIONS** Auth, "Le Heros Xenophontique et les Femmes," 98; "Le Domaine de Scillonte; Xenophon et l'Exemple Perse," 98; "Xenophon's Park at Scillua: Some Ancient and Modern Views on Nature," 97. **CONTACT ADDRESS** 24 Benedict St, Hull, PQ, J8Y 5G1. **EMAIL** l.lallier@sympatico.ca

LA FORTE, ROBERT SHERMAN
PERSONAL Born 09/08/1933, Frontenac, KS, m, 1959, 3 children **DISCIPLINE** UNITED STATES HISTORY & BIBLIOGRAPHY **EDUCATION** Kans State Col Pittsburg, BSE & MS, 59; Univ Tex, Austin, MLS, 68; Univ Kans, PhD(hist), 66. **CAREER** From instr to asst prof hist, East Tex State Univ, 64-67; from asst prof to assoc prof, 68-74, prof hist, N Tex State Univ, 77-, dept chair, 89-93, Univ Archivist, 75-85, Higher Educ Act fel, 67-68. **HONORS AND AWARDS** UNT Pres Teaching Award, 92; Shelton Teaching Award, 94; 'Fessor' Graham Award, 95. **MEMBERSHIPS** The Hist Soc. **RESEARCH** Nineteenth and Twentieth century United States; History of Kansas. **SELECTED PUBLICATIONS** Auth, Leaders in Reform, Kansas' Progressive Republicans, Univ Kans, 74; Down the Corridor of Years, A Centennial History of U.N.T., 1890-1990, UNT Press, 89; co-ed, Remembering Pearl Harbor, SR Books, 91; co-ed, Building the Death Railway, SR Books, 93; co-ed, With Only the Will to Live, SR Books, 94. **CONTACT ADDRESS** Dept of Hist, Univ North Tex, PO Box 310650, Denton, TX, 76203-0650. **EMAIL** cb36@jove.unt.edu

LABIANCA, OYSTEIN S.
PERSONAL Born 09/10/1949, Kristiansand, Norway, m, 1972, 3 children **DISCIPLINE** ANTHROPOLOGY **EDUCATION** Andrews Univ, BA, 71; Loma Linda Univ, MA, 76; Brandeis Univ, PhD, 87; Cambridge Univ, Eng, Post-doc fel, 90. **CAREER** Assoc dir, Inst Archaeol, 81-, Andrews Univ; dir, Hinterland proj, 82-, Madaba Plains Proj, Jordan; res prof, dept beh sci, 91-, Andrews Univ. **HONORS AND AWARDS** NEH Res Grant, 79; NEH Fel, 89; NGS Res Grant, 97. **MEMBERSHIPS** Amer Antaro Assn; Soc Amer Archaeol; Amer Schls of Orient Res. **RESEARCH** Ancient and modern food systems **SELECTED PUBLICATIONS** Auth, Sedentarization and Nomadization: Food System Cycles at Hesban and Vicinity in Transjordan, Andrew Univ Press, 90; art, Food Systems Research: An Overview and a Case Study From Madaba Plains, Food & Foodways 4, 91; art, Residential Caves and Rock Shelters, Amer J of Anthrop 96:541, 92; auth, The Fluidity of Tribal Peoples in Central Transjordan: Four Millenia of Sedentarization and Nomadization on the Madaba Plains, Middle East - Unity & Diversity papers from the 2nd Nordic Conf on Middle East Stud, 93. **CONTACT ADDRESS** 4075 Lake Chapin Rd, Berrien Springs, MI, 49103-9654. **EMAIL** labianca@andrews.edu

LABUDDE, KENNETH J.
PERSONAL Born 01/20/1920, Sheboygan, WI **DISCIPLINE** AMERICAN STUDIES **EDUCATION** Univ Wis, BA, 41; BLS, 42; Univ Minn, MA, 48; PhD, 54. **CAREER** Sr libr asst, Milwaukee Public Libr, 42; libr, Sheboygan Press, 44-46; instr, 46-47; lecturer, Univ Minn, 50; prof, Univ Mo-Kansas City, 62-85; dir univ libr, 50-85; prof emeritus, 85- . **HONORS AND AWARDS** Thomas Jefferson Award, Univ Mo, 88. **MEMBERSHIPS** Am Studies Asoc; ALA; Bibliog Soc of Am; Orgn of Am Historians; Soc of Archit Historians. **RESEARCH** Art forms in the history of idea; nineteenth-century American art; Thomas Cole. **CONTACT ADDRESS** 309 Bursh Creek Blvd., #504, Kansas City, MO, 64112.

LABYS, WALTER CARL
PERSONAL Born 07/25/1937, Latrobe, PA, w, 1967, 2 children **DISCIPLINE** ECONOMICS **EDUCATION** Carnegie Mellon Univ, SB, 59; Duquesne Univ, MBA, 62; Harvard Univ, MA, 65; Nottingham Univ, PhD, 68. **CAREER** Visiting prof, Grad Inst of Int Studies, Univ of Geneva, 69-75; res assoc, Nat Bureau of Economic Res, 77-81; visiting scholar, Energy Lab, MIT, 81-82; chemn, Dept of Mineral and Energy Resource Economics, 84-87; res assoc, Minerals Trade Project, Inst for Applied Systems Analysis, 83-84; res fel, Inst for Int Economic Studies, Univ of Stockholm, 83-85; visiting prof, Inst Superieure de Petrochemie et de Synthese Organique Industrielle, Univ d' Aix-Marseille, 87; Gunnar Myrdal Scholar in Residence, United Nations Economic Comn for Europe, 90-91; vis-

iting prof, Centre d;Econometrie pour L'enterprise, Univ de Montpellier and the Res Center on World Commodity Markets, Conservatoire des Arts et Metiers de Paris, 90-91; PROF OF RESOURCE ECONOMICS, ADJUNCT PROF OF ECONOMIS, FAC RES ASSOC-REGIONAL RES INST, & BENEDUM DISTINGUISHED SCHOLAR, WEST VA UNIV; RES ASSOC, GREQAM, & VISITING PROF, FACULTE D'ECONOMIE APPLIQUEE, UNIV D'AIX-MARSEILLE; VISITING PROF, LAMETA, UNIV DE MONTPELLIER; VISITING PROF, APPLIED ECONOMICS DEPT, INST FOR ADVANCED STUDIES; RES FEL, RES GROUP ON INT COMMODITY MARKETS, FACULTE DES SCIS ECONOMIQUES, UNIVERSITE PIERRE-MENDES FRANCE; LECTR, INTER-UNIVERSITY CONSORTIUM FOR POLITICAL AND SOC SCI RES, UNIV OF MICH. **HONORS AND AWARDS** Alumnus of Distinction, St. Vincent Col, 97; Outstanding Res, Col of Agriculture and Forestry, West Va Univ, 97; Master Knight, Order of the Vine, Sacramento Chapter, 94; Claude Worthington Benedum Distinguished Scholar, Wes Va Univ, 90; Gunnar Myrdal Scholar, United Nations Economic Comn for Europe, 90; visiting scholar, MIT, 81-82; honorary member, Societe d'Honneur Francaise, 81. **MEMBERSHIPS** Am Economics Asn; Mineral Economics and Management Soc. **RESEARCH** International commodity market modeling and forecasting; time series analysis; resources, environment, trade, & development; mineral, energy, & agricultural market analyses. **SELECTED PUBLICATIONS** Coauth, Fractional Dynamics in International Commodity Prices, J of Futures Markets, 97; coauth, Long Term Memory In Commodity Futures Prices, Financial Rev, 97; coauth, Spatial Price Equilibrium as the Core to Spatial Commodity Modeling, Regional Sci Papers, 96; coauth, Uncertainty, Carbon Dioxide Concentrations and Fossil Fuel Use, Int J of Environment and Pollution, 96; coauth, CO2 Emissions and Concentration Coefficients Revisited, Int J of Global Energy Issues, 94; coauth, Divergences in Manufacturing Energy Consumption between the North and the South, Energy Policy, 94; coauth, Wavelet Analysis of Commodity Price Behavior, Advances in Computational Economics, Chapman Hall Pub Co, 97; coauth, An Econometric Approach to CO2 Concentration Modeling, Measuring and Accounting Environmental Nuisances and Benefits: Essays in Environmetrics, 97; coauth, Le Chatelier's principle and the allocation sensitivity of spatial commodity models, Recent advances in spatial equilibrium modeling: Methodology and application (essays in honor of Takashama Takayama, 96; coauth, Modeling of the petroleum spot market: A vector autoregressive appraoch, Models for Energy Policy, Routledge Pub Co, 96. **CONTACT ADDRESS** Resource Economics, West Virginia Univ, PO Box 6108, Morgantown, WV, 26506-6108. **EMAIL** wlabys@wvu.edu

LACCETTI, SILVIO R.
PERSONAL Born 01/14/1941, Teaneck, NJ **DISCIPLINE** MODERN EUROPEAN HISTORY, URBAN STUDIES **EDUCATION** Columbia Univ, AB, 62, MA, 63, PhD(Europ hist), 67. **CAREER** From instr to assoc prof, 65-87, PROF HUMANITIES, STEVENS INST TECHNOL, 88-; Spec adv, Hudson County Dist Atty Off, 68-70; educ consult, NJ Regional Drug Abuse Agency, 70; exec dir, N Bergen Drug Prog, Inc, 70-72; planning consult, N Hudson Mayor's Coun, 71-72; prof dir, Citizenship Inst, 74-76; chmn, Hudson Bicentennial Cong, 74-76; gen ed, Pub Policy Series, Commonwealth Books; Danforth Teaching Assoc, 78-; NJ Master Fac prog, 89-91; Stevens Teacher of the Year, 90, 93. **MEMBERSHIPS** AHA; AAUP **RESEARCH** Drug abuse education; municipal studies; international politics; regional econ; embroidery industry, 95-98. **SELECTED PUBLICATIONS** Co-ed, The City in Western Civilization, Vol I, In: Cities in Civilization, Speller, 71; auth, Drug Dilemma, J Forum Contemp Hist, 1/73; Dialogue on Drugs, Exposition, 74; ed, New Jersey Colleges and Vocational Schools, 77, Casebook in New Jersey Studies, 78 & contribr, Major Development Plans for New Jersey, In: Casebook for New Jersey Studies, 78, Wm Wise; NJ Profiles in Public Policy, Commonwealth, 90. **CONTACT ADDRESS** Dept of Humanities Stevens, Stevens Inst of Tech, 1 Castle Point Ter, Hoboken, NJ, 07030-5991.

LACEY, BARBARA E.
DISCIPLINE HISTORY **EDUCATION** Smith Coll, BA, 58; Univ Conn, MA, 71; Clark, PhD, 82. **CAREER** ASSOC PROF, HIST, ST. JOSEPH COLL **MEMBERSHIPS** Am Antiquarian Soc **SELECTED PUBLICATIONS** Auth, "The World Hannah Heaton: Autobiography an 18th Century Connecticut Farm Woman," Wm & Mary Quart 45, 88; auth, "Gender, Piety and Secularization in Connecticut Religion, 1720-1775," Jour of Soc Hist, Summer 91; auth, "Visual Images of Blacks in Early American Imprints," Wm & Mary Quart 53, 96. **CONTACT ADDRESS** Dept of Hist & Pol Sci, St Joseph Coll, 1678 Asylum Ave, W Hartford, CT, 06117.

LACEY, JAMES
PERSONAL Born 10/15/1933, New York, NY, m, 1958, 2 children **DISCIPLINE** AMERICAN STUDIES **EDUCATION** St Peter's Col, AB, 55; Boston Col, MA, 58; NY Univ, PhD(Am civilization), 68. **CAREER** From instr to asst prof English, St Francis Col, NY, 58-68; assoc prof, 68-71, PROF AM LIT AND AM STUDIES, EASTERN CONN STATE COL, 71-, Ger Acad Exchange Serv res grant, Am Inst, Univ Munich, 65-66. **MEMBERSHIPS** MLA; Am Studies Asn; Aaup. **RESEARCH** American literature and history; Henry David Thoreau in German criticism, 1881-1965. **SELECTED PUBLICATIONS** Auth, The 1994 American Studies Conference in Tubingen, Amer Stud Int, Vol 0032, 94; The 1995 American Studies Conference in Hamburg, Amer Stud Int, Vol 0033, 95. **CONTACT ADDRESS** Dept of English, Eastern Connecticut State Univ, 83 Windham St, Willimantic, CT, 06226-2211.

LACHAN, KATHARINE
PERSONAL Ottawa, ON, Canada **DISCIPLINE** CURATOR/PRINTS/DRAWINGS **EDUCATION** Univ Toronto, BA, 68, MA, 71; Univ London, Courtauld Inst, PhD, 82. **CAREER** Cur asst, European dept, ROM, 68-69; cur asst, 69-71, asst cur, 71-76, CURATOR, PRINTS & DRAWINGS, ART GALLERY ONT 76-; fac mem, Art Hist, Univ Toronto, 92-. **HONORS AND AWARDS** J. Paul Getty Trust, Scholar, 87; Award Merit, Ryerson Polytechnic Inst, 91. **MEMBERSHIPS** Can Museum Asn; Master Print and Drawing Soc Ont; Massey Col, Univ Toronto; Print Coun Am; William Soc Can; Opera Atelier; Toronto Hist Board. **SELECTED PUBLICATIONS** Auth, The Etchings of James McNeil Whistler, 84; auth, Whistler's Etchings and the Sources of His Etching Style, 87; coauth, The Earthly Paradise: Arts and Crafts by William Morris and His Circle of Friends from Canadian Collections, 93. **CONTACT ADDRESS** Art Gallery of Ontario, 317 Dundas St W, Toronto, ON.

LADD, DORIS
PERSONAL Born 12/17/1933, Los Angeles, CA, 1 child **DISCIPLINE** HISTORY **EDUCATION** Stanford Univ, AB, 55, MA, 56 & 63, PhD(Hist), 70. **CAREER** Teacher Span & Biol, High Schs, Calif, 56-59; teacher English, USIA Schs, Lucca, Italy, 59, Madrid, 60-63; instr Hist, Col Notre Dame, Belmont, 70; asst prof Hist, Univ Hawaii, Manoa, 70-, asst prof Hist, Univ Tex, Austin, 74-76. **HONORS AND AWARDS** Bolton Prize, Conf Latin Am Hist, AHA, 77. **MEMBERSHIPS** Conf Latin Am Hist; AHA. **RESEARCH** Mexico; social & economic history; women. **SELECTED PUBLICATIONS** Coauth, Simon Bolivar and Spanish American Independence, Anvil, 68; auth, The Mexican Nobility at Independence, Univ Tex, 76; contribr, The Solitude of Self by Elizabeth Cady Stanton, Press Pacifica, 78; The Making of a Strike, 88. **CONTACT ADDRESS** Dept of History, Univ of Hawaii, Manoa, 2530 Dole St, Honolulu, HI, 96822-2303. **EMAIL** dladd@hawaii.edu

LADEWIG, JAMES L.
DISCIPLINE MUSIC HISTORY, MUSICOLOGY, MUSIC APPRECIATION **EDUCATION** Northwestern Univ, BM, 71; Univ CA, Berkeley, MA, 73, PhD, 78. **CAREER** Prof; Univ RI, 85-; taught at, Vassar Col & Wellesley Col; vis scholar, Harvard Univ; past ed, nat Newletter, Am Musicol Soc. **HONORS AND AWARDS** Am Coun Learned Soc & URI Found, grants. **MEMBERSHIPS** Am Musicol Soc; Soc for 17th-century Music & Renaissance Soc Am; past pres, New Eng Chap, Am Musicol Soc. **RESEARCH** Renaissance and Baroque eras; instrumental and keyboard music of Italy. **SELECTED PUBLICATIONS** Publ on, Variation canzona, Frescobaldi, Luzzaschi I Bach; in, J Musicol, Frescobaldi Stud & Studi Musicali; completed ed, 30-vol series Italian Instrumental Music of the 16th and Early 17th Centuries: Previously Unpubl Full Scores of Major Works from the Renaissance and Early Baroque, New York & London: Garland Publ. **CONTACT ADDRESS** Dept of Music, Univ of RI, 8 Ranger Rd, Ste. 1, Kingston, RI, 02881-0807.

LAEL, RICHARD LEE
PERSONAL Born 09/16/1946, NC, m, 1987, 2 children **DISCIPLINE** HISTORY, US DIPLOMATIC HISTORY **EDUCATION** Lenoir-Rhyne Col, BA, 68; Univ NC, Chapel Hill, MA, 72, PhD, 76. **CAREER** Instr, NC State Univ, 75-77, vis asst prof, 77-78; asst prof, 78-84, assoc prof, 84-90, prof, Westminster Col, 91-, chair, Div of Humanities, 98-. **HONORS AND AWARDS** MO Conference of Hist Distinguished Book Award for The Yamashita Precedent, 83. **MEMBERSHIPS** Org Am Historians; Soc for Historians of Am Foreign Relations; Phi Alpha Theta (Hist Honor Soc). **RESEARCH** War crimes; Latin America; local hist. **SELECTED PUBLICATIONS** Auth, The Yamashita Precedent: War Crimes and Command Responsibility, 82; co-auth with Dr Linda Killen, Versailles and After: An Annotated Bibliography of American Foreign Relations, 1919-1933, 83; auth, Arrogant Diplomacy: US Policy Toward Columbia, 1903-1922, 87; The Rating Game in American Politics: An Interdisciplinary Approach, ed Ann McLaurin and William Pederson, 87; The War of 1989 and US Interventions, 1898-1934, ed Benjamin Beede, 94; articles in the following journals: Diplomatic History, 78; Mid-America, 79; Business History Rev, 82. **CONTACT ADDRESS** Dept of History, Westminster Col, 501 Westminster Ave, Fulton, MO, 65251-1299. **EMAIL** Laelr@jaynet.wcmo.edu

LAFEBER, WALTER
PERSONAL Born 08/30/1933, Walkerton, IN, m, 1955, 2 children **DISCIPLINE** AMERICAN HISTORY **EDUCATION** Hanover Col, BA, 55; Stanford Univ, MA, 56; Univ Wis, PhD, 59. **CAREER** Asst prof Am hist, 59-63, from assoc prof to prof, 63-68, chmn dept, 68-69, Noll prof hist, Cornell Univ, 68-, Soc Sci Res Coun grant, 63-64; Am Philos Soc grant, 67-68; mem adv comt, Hist Div, US Dept of State, 71-74; commonwealth lectr, Univ London, 73; Edmundson lectr, Baylor Univ, 80. **HONORS AND AWARDS** Clark Teaching Award, Col Arts & Sci, Cornell Univ, 66; Albert J Beveridge Award, AHA, 62; Bancroft Prize, 98; Hawley Prize, 98, Weiss Presidential teaching Fel, 94-99. **MEMBERSHIPS** AHA; Orgn Am Historians; Soc Historians Foreign Rels. **RESEARCH** American diplomatic history. **SELECTED PUBLICATIONS** Auth, The New Empire: An Interpretation of American Expansion, 1860-1898, Cornell Univ, 63; John Quincy Adams and American Continental Empire, Quadrangle, 65; America, Russia, and the Cold War, 67, rev ed, 72, 81 & The United States and the Cold War: 20 Years of Revolution and Response, 69, Wiley; coauth, Creation of the American Empire, Rand McNally, 73, rev ed, 76; The American Century, Wiley, 75, rev ed, 79.97; auth, The Panama Canal: The Crisis in Historical Perspective, Oxford Univ, 78; The Third Cold War, Baylor Univ, 81; The American Search for Opportunity 1865-1912, 93; The Clash: the United States and Japan Throughout History, 97. **CONTACT ADDRESS** Dept of History, Cornell Univ, Mcgraw Hall, Ithaca, NY, 14853-0001.

LAFLEUR, RICHARD ALLEN
PERSONAL Born 09/22/1945, Newburyport, MA, m, 1967, 3 children **DISCIPLINE** CLASSICAL STUDIES **EDUCATION** Univ Va, BA, 68, MA, 70; Duke Univ, PhD, 73. **CAREER** Asst prof, 72-77, ASSOC PROF CLASSICS, UNIV GA, 77-, Head Dept, 80-, Ed, Class Outlook, 79-; chmn, comt Prom Latin, 79-81, exec comt, 79-83, S sect secy-treas, 78-; Class Asn Midwest & South. **HONORS AND AWARDS** Am Philol Asn Award, Excellence in Teaching Classics, 84; Classical Asn Midwest & South, Ovatio, 85; Am Classical League, pres, 84-86, hon pres for life, 86-; Univ GA, Bronze Medallion, Public Service, 88; For Lang Asn Ga, Teacher of the Year, 88; Ga Governors Award, Humanities, 89. **MEMBERSHIPS** Am Class League; Am Philol Asn; Archaeol Inst Am; Class Asn Mid W & S; Vergilian Soc. **RESEARCH** Juvenal; Roman satire; Latin pedagogy. **SELECTED PUBLICATIONS** Auth, The Teaching of latin in American Schools, Scholars Press, 87; Latin Poetry for the Beginning Student, Longman, 87; Wheelock's Latin, Harper Collins, 95; Love and Transformation: An Ovid Reader, Scott Foresman-Addison Wesley 98; Latin for the 21st Century: From Concept to Classroom, Scott Foresman-Addison Wesley, 98. **CONTACT ADDRESS** Dept Classics, Univ of Ga, Athens, GA, 30602-0001. **EMAIL** rlafleur@parallel.park.uga.edu

LAGEMANN, ELLEN CONDLIFFE
PERSONAL Born 12/20/1945, New York, NY, m, 1969, 1 child **DISCIPLINE** AMERICAN AND WOMEN'S HISTORY **EDUCATION** Smith Col, AB, 67; Columbia Univ, MA, 68, PhD(hist and educ), 78. **CAREER** Asst prof, 78-81, ASSOC PROF HIST AND EDUC, TEACHERS COL, COLUMBIA UNIV, 81-, RES ASSOC, INST PHILOS AND POLITICS EDUC, 78-. **MEMBERSHIPS** Hist Educ Asn; AHA; Orgn Am Historians; Coord Comt Women Hist Professions; Am Educ Res Asn. **RESEARCH** History of American education; history of American philanthropy, 20th century; women's history. **SELECTED PUBLICATIONS** Auth, The Power and Passion of Careythomas, M., Amer Hist Rev, Vol 0101, 96. **CONTACT ADDRESS** Teachers Col Columbia Univ, New York, NY, 10027.

LAGUERRE, MICHAEL SATURNIN
PERSONAL Lascaholoas, Haiti **DISCIPLINE** SOCIAL ANTHROPOLOGY **EDUCATION** Univ Quebec, BA, 71; Roosevelt Univ, MA, 73; Univ Ill Urbana, PhD, 76. **CAREER** PROF ANTHROPOLOGY & AMERICAN STUDIES, UNIV CAL BERKELEY, 78- . **HONORS AND AWARDS** Barbara Weinstock Lectureship, 94-95. **MEMBERSHIPS** Am Pouological Asn; Am Anthrop Asn **RESEARCH** Immigration; Globalization; Multiculturalism; Ethnic Communities in the US; American cities. **SELECTED PUBLICATIONS** Urban Poverty in the Caribbean, St Martin's Press, 90; The Military and Society in Haiti; Univ Tenn Press, 93; The Informal City, St Martin's Press, 94; Diasporic Citizenship, St Martin's Press, 98; Minoritized Space: An Inquiry into the Spatial Order of Tgubgs, Inst of Govt Studies Press, 98. **CONTACT ADDRESS** Dept of Afro-American Studies, Univ Cal, 660 Barrows Hall, Berkeley, CA, 94720. **EMAIL** mlaguerr@ucliak.berkeley.edu

LAIRD, PAUL
PERSONAL Born 10/26/1958, Louisville, KY, m, 1982, 1 child **DISCIPLINE** MUSIC HISTORY **EDUCATION** Ohio State Univ, BM, 80, MA, 82; Univ NC-Chapel Hill, PhD, 86. **CAREER** Asst Prof, 91-94, Assoc Prof, Univ Kans, 97-; Asst Prof, 91-94, Univ Denver; Asst Prof, SUNY-Binghamton, 88-91; Vis Asst Prof, Penn State Univ, 87-88. **HONORS AND AWARDS** Prog for Cultural Coop Between Spain's Ministry of Culture and US Univ Grant; NEH travel grant. **MEMBERSHIPS** Am Musicol Soc; Col Mus Soc; Early Mus Am; Soc Espanola de Musicol; Sonneck Soc Am Mus. **RESEARCH** Spanish and Latin American villancico; music of Leonard Bernstein; Broadway musicals early stringed instruments. **SELECTED PUBLICATIONS** Towards A History of the Spanish Villancico, Warren, MI, Harmonie Park Press, 97. **CONTACT ADDRESS** Univ of Kansas, 907 Christie Ct, Lawrence, KS, 66049-4148. **EMAIL** plaird@falcon.cc.ukans.edu

LAIRD, WALTER ROY
DISCIPLINE MEDIEVAL HISTORY **EDUCATION** Concordia Univ, BA, 76; Univ Toronto, MA, 78, PhD, 83. **CAREER** Assoc prof. **RESEARCH** Medieval and renaissance Aristolelianism, Impact in the Middle Ages and Renaissance. **SELECTED PUBLICATIONS** Auth, Patronage of Mechanics and Theories of Impact in Sixteenth-Century Italy, Patronage and Institutions: Science, Technology, and Medicine at the European Court, 1500-1750, Woodbridge, Suffolk: Boy dell-Brewer, 91; Archimedes Among the Humanists, Isis, 82, 91. **CONTACT ADDRESS** Dept of Hist, Carleton Univ, 1125 Colonel By Dr, Ottawa, ON, K1S 5B6. **EMAIL** roy_laird@carleton.ca

LAITOS, JAN GORDON
PERSONAL Born 05/06/1946, Colorado Springs, CO **DISCIPLINE** LAW, AMERICAN LEGAL HISTORY **EDUCATION** Yale Univ, BA, 68; Law Sch, Univ Colo, JD, 71; Law Sch, Univ Wis, SJD, 74. **CAREER** Law clerk, Colo Supreme Ct, 71-72; atty, Off Legal Coun, US Dept of Justice, 74-76; PROF LAW, LAW SCH, UNIV DENVER, 76-, Sr legal adv, Solar Energy Res Inst, 78-81; consult, Colo State Dept of Natural Resources, 79-80, US Dept of Interior, 79-80 and US Dept of Energy, 80-81. **MEMBERSHIPS** Natural resources law; energy law. **RESEARCH** Auth, Causation and the Unconstitutional Conditions Doctrine--Why the City of Tigards Exaction Was a Taking, Denver Univ Law Rev, Vol 0072, 95; National Parks and the Recreation Resource, Denver Univ Law Rev, Vol 0074, 97. **CONTACT ADDRESS** Law Sch, Univ of Denver, Denver, CO, 80208.

LAKER, JOSEPH ALPHONSE
PERSONAL Born 03/17/1941, Indianapolis, IN **DISCIPLINE** HISTORY, JAPANESE STUDIES **EDUCATION** Marian Col, BA, 63; IN Univ, MA, 67, PhD, 75. **CAREER** Instr hist, St Olaf Col, 67-70; asst prof, 74-80, assoc prof, 80-94, PROF HIST, WHEELING COL, 94-; NEH Summer Seminar, Brown Univ, 79; Fulbright/Hays Summer Seminar, Korea, 87; co-dir, NEH Summer Inst for High Sch Tchr(s), summer 95. **MEMBERSHIPS** Asn Asian Studies; Econ Hist Asn; Bus Hist Asn. **RESEARCH** The develop of the Japan beer industry; mod Japan economic and soc hist; Japan Colonialism. **SELECTED PUBLICATIONS** Encyclopedia of World War II, Cord Publ, 78; Oligopoly at home and expansion abroad: The develop of the Japan beer industry, 1907-1937, Proc Second Int Symp Asian Studies, 80; coauth, Tchr Outreach in Japanese Studies, Educ About Asia, fall 96. **CONTACT ADDRESS** Wheeling Jesuit Col, 316 Washington Ave, Wheeling, WV, 26003-6243. **EMAIL** lakerj@wju.edu

LALONDE, GERALD VINCENT
PERSONAL Born 05/18/1938, Bellingham, WA, m, 1969, 2 children **DISCIPLINE** CLASSICS, ANCIENT HISTORY **EDUCATION** Univ Wash, BA, 62, MA, 64, PhD(classics), 71. **CAREER** Instr classics, Univ Wash, 68-69; from instr to asst prof, 69-74, assoc prof, 74-79, PROF CLASS, GRINNELL COL, 80. **MEMBERSHIPS** Archaeol Inst Am; Am Philol Asn; Brit Class Asn. **RESEARCH** Greek epigraphy, history and archaeology. **SELECTED PUBLICATIONS** Auth, Reading the Past-Ancient Writing From Cuneiform to the Alphabet, Class World, Vol 0087, 94; Ig I-3, 1055 A and B--Zeus on the Hill of the Nymphs, Amer J Archaeol, Vol 0100, 96. **CONTACT ADDRESS** Dept of Classics, Grinnell Col, P O Box 805, Grinnell, IA, 50112-0805.

LAM, TRUONG BUU
PERSONAL Born 03/23/1933, Tan-An, Vietnam, d, 1 child **DISCIPLINE** MODERN HISTORY, SOUTHEAST ASIA **EDUCATION** Cath Univ Louvain, D(hist), 57. **CAREER** Asst prof hist, Univ Saigon & Univ Hue, 57-64; res assoc, E Asian Res Ctr, Harvard Univ, 64-65, Southeast Asia Studies, Yale Univ, 65-66 & Southeast Asia Prog, Cornell Univ, 66-71; assoc prof hist, State Univ NY Stony Brook, 71-72; assoc prof hist, Univ Hawaii, Manoa, 72-, dir, Inst Hist Res, Saigon, 57-64; Soc Sci Res Coun grant, 66-69; adj asst prof, State Univ NY, Stony Brook, 68-71; res fel, Inst Southeast Asian Studies, Singapore, 77-78; dir, SE Asia Res Ctr, Univ Hawaii, 85-86. **RESEARCH** Tributary systems in China and Vietnam; impact of the West on Southeast Asia; Vietnamese nationalism. **SELECTED PUBLICATIONS** Auth, Patterns of Vietnamese Response to Foreign Intervention, 1858-1900, Yale Southeast Asia Studies, 67; Tributary Versus Intervention, a Case-Study in Vietnamese History, 1789-1792, Chinese World Order, 68; A Vietnamese Viewpoint, In: The Pentagon Papers, Vol V, Quadrangle, 71; Japan and the Disruption of the Vietnamese Nationalist Movement, In: Aspects of Vietnamese History, Univ Hawaii, 72; auth, Revolution, ISEAS, Singapore, 84; coauth, An Annotated Bibliography of the VAN-SU-DIA, 85. **CONTACT ADDRESS** Dept of Hist, Univ of Hawaii at Manoa, 2530 Dole St, Honolulu, HI, 96822-2303. **EMAIL** lamb@hawaii.edu

LAMAR, HOWARD ROBERTS
PERSONAL Born 11/18/1923, Tuskegee, AL, m, 1959, 2 children **DISCIPLINE** AMERICAN HISTORY **EDUCATION** Emory Univ, BA, 45; Yale Univ, MA, 45, PhD(Am hist), 51. **CAREER** Instr hist, Univ Mass, 45-46 and Wesleyan Univ, 48-49; from instr to assoc prof, 49-64, chmn dept, 67-70, PROF HIST, YALE UNIV, 64-; DEAN, YALE COL, 79-, Morse fel, 53-54; Am Coun Learned Soc fel, 59-60; Soc Sci Res Coun fel, 60-61. **HONORS AND AWARDS** DHumL, Emory Univ, 75. **MEMBERSHIPS** AHA; Orgn Am Historians; Western Hist Asn (pres, 72). **RESEARCH** American frontier history; family history; comparative history. **SELECTED PUBLICATIONS** Auth, Sutter, John, Augustus, Wilderness Entrepreneur, California Hist, Vol 0073, 94; Coming into the Mainstream at Last--Comparative Approaches to the History of the American West, J West, Vol 0035, 96; The Dust Rose Like Smoke--the Subjugation of the Zulu and the Sioux, Ethnohist, Vol 0044, 97. **CONTACT ADDRESS** Dept of Hist, Studies Yale Univ, 237 Hall of Grad, New Haven, CT, 06520.

LAMARCHE, JEAN
PERSONAL Born 04/29/1945, Manchester, NH, m, 1996 **DISCIPLINE** ARCHITECTURE **EDUCATION** Lawrence Technol Univ, BS, 81; Univ Michigan, ArchD, 95. **CONTACT ADDRESS** 6456 Hamilton Dr, Derby, NY, 14047. **EMAIL** lamarche@ap.buffalo.edu

LAMB, CHARLES M.
PERSONAL Born 03/01/1945, Murfreesboro, TN, s **DISCIPLINE** POLITICAL SCIENCE **EDUCATION** Middle Tenn State Univ, BA, 67; Univ of Ala, MA, 70, PhD, 74. **CAREER** Res sci, George Washington Univ, 73-75; equal opportunity specialist, U.S. Comn on Civil Rights, 75-77; Asst prof of Pol Sci, 77-84, asst prof of Pol Sci, SUNY Buffalo, 84-. **HONORS AND AWARDS** Choice Outstanding Book Award, 83; listed in Who's Who in the East; Who's Who in Emerging Leaders in Am; Who's Who in Am Ed; Contemporary Authors. **MEMBERSHIPS** Am Political Sci Asn. **RESEARCH** Civil rights; civil liberties; constitutional law; constitutional history; judicial behavior. **SELECTED PUBLICATIONS** Auth, Supreme Court Activism and Restraint, 82; Implementation of Civil Rights Policy, 84; Judicial Conflict and Consensus, 86; The Burger Court, 91; Presidential Influence and Fair Housing Policy, forthcoming. **CONTACT ADDRESS** Dept of Political Sci, State Univ of NY Buffalo, 520 Hall Park, Buffalo, NY, 14260.

LAMBERG-KARLOVSKI, CLIFFORD CHARLES
PERSONAL Born 10/02/1937, Prague, Czechoslovakia, m, 1959, 2 children **DISCIPLINE** ANTHROPOLOGY **EDUCATION** Dartmouth Coll, BA, 59; Univ Pa, MA, 64; PhD, 65; Harvard Univ, AM, 70. **CAREER** Asst curator of Old World Archaeology, Peabody Museum, Harvard Univ, 64-69; asst prof, Harvard Univ, 64-69; asst prof, Franklin and Marshall College Lancaster Pa, 64-65; dir, Peabody Museum, Harvard Univ, 77-91; prof, Harvard Univ, 69-91; curator on Near Eastern Archaeol, Peabody Museum, Harvard Univ, 69-; Univ assoc, Columbia Univ NY, 71-; Stephen Phillips prof, 91-. **MEMBERSHIPS** Am Acad of Arts and Sci; Fel of the Soc of Antiquaries of Great Britain and Ireland; Soviet Acad of Sci; Istituto para Medio e Extremo Orient, Italian Acad Rome; AM Anthropol Asn; Am Asn for the Advancement of Sci; Am School of Oriental Res; Am School of Prehistoric Res; Am Inst of Iranian Studies; Archaeol Inst of Am; Sigma Xi Socl Am Inst of Archaeol Pakistan. **SELECTED PUBLICATIONS** Auth, Beyond the Tigris and Euphrates Bronze Age Civilizations, 96; numerous books, monographs and articles, 65-. **CONTACT ADDRESS** Peabody Museum, Harvard Univ, Cambridge, MA, 02138. **EMAIL** karlovski@fas.harvard.edu

LAMBERT, BYRON C.
DISCIPLINE CHRISTIAN DOCTRINE; HISTORY OF CULTURE **EDUCATION** Univ Buffalo, BA, 45, MA, 46; Butler Univ sch Rel, BD, 50; Univ Chicago, PhD, 57. **CAREER** Assoc prof English, Milligan Col, 57-60; dean, assoc prof English, Simpson Col, 60-62; dean, 62-65, campus dean, 65-71, assoc prof Hum, 71-75, assoc dean, Col ed, 71-75, Fairleigh Dickinson Univ; Prof Philos, 75-85, actg dean, Arts and Sci, 82-83, acting Provost, Madison Campus, 81.. **HONORS AND AWARDS** Fairleigh Dickinson Univ, Campus Achieve Awd, 74; Pres James A. Garfield Awd, Emmanuel Sch Rel, Tenn, 98. **MEMBERSHIPS** Amer Philos Asn; Soc Christian Philso; Disciples of Christ Hist Soc. **RESEARCH** C.S. Lewis; Paul Elmer More; Christian theology, sacraments, Holy Spirit.. **SELECTED PUBLICATIONS** Auth, The Essential Paul Elmer More, 72; The Rise of the Anti-Mission Baptist, 80; The Recovery of Reality, 80; The Restoration of the Lord's Supper and the Sacramental Principle, 92; Experience-Different Semantic Worlds, Wasleyan Theol Jour, Spring 95; Shifting Gronтiers and the Invisible Hand, Discipliana, Fall 95; The Middle Way of Frederick Doyle Kershner, 98; The Regrettable Silence of Paul Elmer More, Modern Age, Fall 98; C.S. Lewis and the Moral Law, Stone-Campbell Jour, Fall 98. **CONTACT ADDRESS** 300 North Perry St, Hagerstown, IN, 47346.

LAMBERT, LYNDA J.
PERSONAL Born 08/27/1943, PA, m, 1961, 5 children **DISCIPLINE** FINE ARTS; HUMANITIES **EDUCATION** Slippery Rock Univ Pa, BFA, MA; WV Univ, MFA **CAREER** Instr, Commun Col of Beaver Co, Monaca, Pa, 85-88; instr, Slippery Rock Univ Pa, 90; teaching asst, WV Univ, 89-91; exec dir, Hoyt Inst, New Castle, Pa, 92-96, asst prof, Geneva Col, Beaver Falls, Pa, present. **MEMBERSHIPS** Assoc Artists of Pittsburgh; Assoc for Integrative Stud; Group A; Amer Assoc of Museums; Inst of Museum Svcs; Nat Assoc of Women Artists Inc; Pa Rural Arts Alliance, Women's Caucus for Art; Cal Art Assoc; Handweaver's Guild of Amer. **RESEARCH** Viking glass; African Amer art & lit; African art; ancient art. **SELECTED PUBLICATIONS** Auth, MacLennan, Rosalind, Abstract art exhibition invites interpretation, Butler Eagle, 95; MacLennan, Rosalind, Painter, sculptor complement each other, Butler Eagle, 95; Mabin, Connie, Artists painting Aliquippa portrait as a city of pride, Beaver Valley Times, 95; Marcello, Patricia Cornin, Parade of 25 Successful women for 1996, Successful Women Mag, 96; Wilson, Gladys Blews, Painter chooses unusual medium for her prints, Beaver Valley Times, 96. **CONTACT ADDRESS** 104 River Rd, Ellwood City, PA, 16117. **EMAIL** llambert@geneva.edu; llambert@pathway.net

LAMBERT, RICHARD THOMAS
PERSONAL Born 03/28/1943, Rochester, NY, m, 1978, 3 children **DISCIPLINE** HISTORY OF PHILOSOPHY, LOGIC, ETHICS **EDUCATION** St Bernard's Col, BA, 65; Univ Notre Dame, PhD, 71. **CAREER** Asst prof, 70-80, philos dept chmn, 77-82, assoc prof 80-, prof philos, Carrol Col, Mont, Dir, Summer, 81-82, Dir, Continuing Educ, 81-85, Exchange prof philos, Loras Col, 76-77. **HONORS AND AWARDS** NY State Regents Scholar, 61-65; NDEA Grad Fel, 66-70; Exec Comt, Delta Epsilon Sigma, 90-94, vpres & pres, 94-98. **MEMBERSHIPS** Int Berkeley Soc; Am Cath Philos Asn; Am Philos Asn; Delta Epsilon Sigma. **RESEARCH** Berkeley; Aquinas; Camus. **SELECTED PUBLICATIONS** Auth, Berkeley's use of the relativity argument, Idealistic Studies, 10: 107-121; Albert Camus and the paradoxes of expressing a relativism, Thought, 56: 185-198; A textual study of Aquinas' comparison of the intellect to prime matter, New Scholasticism, Vol 56; Berkeley's commitment to relativism, Berkeley: Critical and Interpretive Essays, Univ Minn Press, 82; Habitual knowledge of the soul in St Thomas Aquinas, Mod Schoolman, 40: 1-19; The literal intent of Berkeley's Dialogues, Philos & Lit, 6: 165-171; Nonintentional experience of oneself in Thomas Aquinas, New Scholasticism, 59: 253-275; Teaching Camus's The Plague in an introductory philosophy course, Approaches to Teaching Camus's The Plague, MLA, 85; transl, Thomas Aquinas, Disputed Question on the Soul's Knowledge of Itself, Clearinghouse for Medieval Philos Transl, 87; Conferring honors in a democratic society, Delta Epsilon Sigma Jour, 33: 59-60; President's report to the membership, Delta Epsilon Sigma Jour, 43: 77-78; Ethics column, Helena Independent Record, 90. **CONTACT ADDRESS** Carroll Col, Montana, 1601 N Benton Ave, Fac Box 49, Helena, MT, 59625-0002. **EMAIL** rlambert@carroll.edu

LAMBERTI, MARJORIE
PERSONAL Born 09/30/1937, New Haven, CT **DISCIPLINE** HISTORY **EDUCATION** Smith Col, BA, 59; Yale Univ, MA, 60, PhD, 66. **CAREER** Prof History, Middlebury Col, 64-, **HONORS AND AWARDS** Nat Endowment Humanities fel, 68-69 & 81-82; fell at the Inst for Adv Stud, Princeston, NJ, 92-93; fel Woodrow Wilson Ctr, Washington, DC, 97-98. **MEMBERSHIPS** AHA. **RESEARCH** German history. **SELECTED PUBLICATIONS** Auth, Lutheran Orthodoxy and the Beginning of Conservative Party Organization in Prussia, Church Hist, 68; The Attempt to Form a Jewish Bloc: Jewish Notables and Politics in Wilhelminian Germany, Cent Europ Hist, 70; The Prussian Government and the Jews--Official Behavior and Policy-Making in the Wilhelminian Era, 72 & The Jewish Struggle for the Legal Equality of Religions in Imperial Germany, Leo Baeck Inst Yearbk, 78; Jewish Activism in Imperial Germany: The Struggle for Civil Equality, Yale Univ Press, 78; Liberals, Socialists and the Defence against Antisemitism in the Wilhelminian Period, 80 & From Coexistence to Conflict: Zionism and the Jewish Community in Germany, 1897-1914, 82, Leo Baeck Inst Yearbk; Elementary School Teachers and the Struggle Against Social Democracy in Wilhelmine Germany, History of Education Quarterly, 92. **CONTACT ADDRESS** Dept of History, Middlebury Col, Middlebury, VT, 05753-6001. **EMAIL** Lamberti@panther.middlebury.edu

LAMBI, I.N.
PERSONAL Born 07/14/1931, Tallinn, Estonia, m, 1955, 5 children **DISCIPLINE** MODERN HISTORY **EDUCATION** Univ Toronto, BA, 52, MA, 55; Univ Minn, PhD(hist), 58. **CAREER** Lectr hist, Univ Toronto, 58-60; instr, Univ Omaha, 60-61; from asst prof to assoc prof, 61-67, head dept, 69-74, PROF HIST, UNIV SASK, 67-, Univ Sask humanities and soc sci res grants, 62-68 and 74-75; ed, Can J Hist, 66-; Can Coun sr fel, 67-68, res grant, 73; Alexander von Humboldt fel, 67-69; mem, Soc Sci Res Coun Can, 69-73; mem, Acad Panel, Soc Sci and Human Res Coun Can, 79-82. **MEMBERSHIPS** Can Hist Asn (vpres, 70-71, pres, 71-72); AHA; Conf Group Cent Europ Hist. **RESEARCH** German diplomacy and defense, 1871-1914; the role of the navy in Germany's defense, 1883-1914. **SELECTED PUBLICATIONS** Auth, Building the Kaiser Navy--the Imperial Navy Office and German Industry in the Vontirpitz Era, 1890-1919, Amer Hist Rev, Vol 0098, 93; Bismarck and Mitteleuropa, Int Hist Rev, Vol 0018, 96. **CONTACT ADDRESS** Univ Saskatchewan, 509 Quance Ave, Saskatoon, SK, S7N OWO.

LAMIRANDE, EMILIEN
PERSONAL Born 05/22/1926, St-Georges de Windsor, Canada **DISCIPLINE** HISTORY OF CHRISTIANITY **EDUCATION** Univ Ottawa, BA, 49, LPh, 50, MA, 51, LTh, 55; Univ Innsbruck, DTh, 60; Union Theol Sem, NY, STM, 65;. **CAREER** Assoc prof theol, Univ Ottawa, 60-65; prof, St Paul Univ, Ont, 65-70, dean fac theol, 67-69; chmn dept, 72-74, PROF RELIG STUDIES, UNIV OTTAWA, 70-. **MEMBERSHIPS** Am Acad Relig; Can Cath Hist Asn; Can Theol Soc (vpres, 67-70); Asn Can d'Estudes Patristiques (vpres, 79-). **RESEARCH** Early Christianity; North African Church; ecclesiology. **SELECTED PUBLICATIONS** Auth, Sulpician Priests in Canada--Major Figures in Their History, Stud in Rel-Sciences Religieuses, Vol 0022, 93; Body of the Church, Body of Christ--Sources for the Ecclesiology of the Communion, Stud in Rel-Sciences Religieuses, Vol 0022, 93; Writings of the Reformation Fathers, Stud in Rel-Sciences Religieuses, Vol 0025, 96; The Aggiornamento and Its Eclipse--Free Thinking in the Church and in the Faithful, Stud in Rel-Sciences Religieuses, Vol 0025, 96. **CONTACT ADDRESS** Dept of Relig Studies, Univ of Ottawa, Ottawa, ON, K1H 8M5.

LAMPLUGH, GEORGE RUSSELL
PERSONAL Born 05/20/1944, Wilmington, DE, m, 1967, 2 children **DISCIPLINE** AMERICAN AND EUROPEAN HISTORY **EDUCATION** Univ Del, BA, 66; Emory Univ, MA, 71, PhD(hist), 73. **CAREER** Teaching asst hist, Emory Univ, 70-71, teaching assoc, 72-73; instr, Ga Inst Technol, spring 73; TEACHER HIST, THE WESTMINSTER SCH, 73-, Vis asst prof, Emory Univ, summer 75. **MEMBERSHIPS** Orgn Am Historians; Soc Historians of the Early Am Repub; Southern Hist Asn. **RESEARCH** Factions and parties in Georgia, 1776-1806; development of political parties in early National United States; southern history. **SELECTED PUBLICATIONS** Auth, Calhoun, John, C--A Biog, Amer Hist Rev, Vol 0100, 1995 **CONTACT ADDRESS** Dept of Hist, The Westminster Sch, Atlanta, GA, 30327.

LANCASTER, JANE FAIRCHILD
PERSONAL Hamilton, MS, m, 2 children **DISCIPLINE** EDUCATION, HISTORY **EDUCATION** MS State Univ, BA Sci, 66; MS Univ for Women, MA, 69; PhD, 86. **CAREER** Amory HS, Amory MS, Teacher, Dept head, 81-86; MS State Univ, fel Teaching Asst, 81-86; Historian, Auth, 86-. **HONORS AND AWARDS** Grad fellowship, MS Univ for Women; Garner Fellowship and Grant, MS State Univ; Listed in Contemporary Authors, Who's Who in the South and Southwest, Outstanding Young Women of Am. **MEMBERSHIPS** Phi Alpha Theta; Southern Hist Asn; Organization Am Historians; Asn Univ Women; Oklahoma Historical Soc; Monroe County Historical Soc. **RESEARCH** Native Am Hist, USA **SELECTED PUBLICATIONS** Historical Dict of the Gilded Age, M E Sharp Inc, (in press); Removal Aftershock: The Seminole's Struggles to Survive in the West, 1836-1866, Univ TN Press, 94; William Tecumseh Sherman's Introduction to War, 1840-1842, Lesson for Action, Florida Historical Quarterly, 93; Non-historical article in Ostomy Quarterly, 92; Tallahassee Jail-In and Nashville Sit-ins, Encyclopedia of African Am Civil Rights from Emancipation to Present, Greenwood Press, 92; Hamilton: Take Your place in History as the First County Seat of Monroe, self pub, 75; Book Reviews, J Am Hist; J Southern Hist; J MS Hist; MS Quarterly; Florida Hist Quarterly. **CONTACT ADDRESS** 40191 Hwy 373, Hamilton, MS, 39746.

LANDAU, ELLEN G.
DISCIPLINE EUROPEAN AND AMERICAN MODERN ART **EDUCATION** Cornell Univ, BA; George Washington Univ, MA, Delaware, PhD, 81. **CAREER** Guest curator, Library Congress traveling exhib. **HONORS AND AWARDS** Fel, Am Coun Learned Societies; Rockefeller Found, National Mus Am Art , Smithsonian Institution, John S. Diekhoff Award., Dept chait, Art Hist. **SELECTED PUBLICATIONS** Auth, Jackson Pollock, Harry N. Abrams, Pub, 89. **CONTACT ADDRESS** Case Western Reserve Univ, 10900 Euclid Ave, Cleveland, OH, 44106. **EMAIL** exl3@po.cwru.edu

LANDAU, SARAH BRADFORD
PERSONAL Born 03/27/1935, Raleigh, NC, m, 1959, 2 children **DISCIPLINE** ART HISTORY **EDUCATION** Univ NC Greensboro, BFA, 57; NY Univ, MA, 59, PhD, 78. **CAREER** Instr, 71-73, 76-78, asst prof, 78-84, assoc prof, 84-96, prof, fine arts, 96-, NY Univ; mem, 87-96, com v chmn, 93-96, NY City Landmarks Preservation Comm. **HONORS AND AWARDS** Am Inst of Archit Intl Archit bk award, 97; Victorian Soc in Am bk award, 97; Lucy G. Moses award for preservation leadership, 97. **MEMBERSHIPS** Col Art Asn; Soc of Archit Hist; Victorian Soc of Am. **RESEARCH** History of Am archit; hist of 19th to early 20th century NYC archit. **SELECTED PUBLICATIONS** Ed, The Grand American Avenue 1850-1920, Pomegranite Artbks & Am Archit Found, 94; coauth, Rise of the New York Skyscraper, 1865-1913, Yale Univ Press, 96; auth, Potter & Robertson 1875-1880, Long Island Country Houses & their Archit, 1860-1940, WW Norton, 97; auth, George B Post, Architect: Picturesque Designer and Determined Realist, Monacelli Press, 98. **CONTACT ADDRESS** Dept of Fine Arts, New York Univ, 100 Washington Sq E, New York, NY, 10003-6688. **EMAIL** sarah.landau@nyu.edu

LANDER, JACK ROBERT
PERSONAL Born 02/15/1921, Hinckley, England **DISCIPLINE** MEDIEVAL ENGLISH HISTORY **EDUCATION** Cambridge Univ, BA, 42, MA, 45, MLitt, 50. **CAREER** From lectr to sr lectr hist, Univ Ghana, 50-63; assoc prof, Dalhousie Univ, 63-65; PROF HIST, UNIV WESTERN ONT, 65-, Leverhulme res fel, 59-60. **MEMBERSHIPS** AHA; Hist Asn, Eng; Royal Hist Soc. **RESEARCH** Italian Renaissance; late medieval and early modern England. **SELECTED PUBLICATIONS** Auth, Lordship, Kingship and Empire--the Idea of Monarchy, 1400-1525, Albion, Vol 0025, 93; Richard of England, Hist Today, Vol 0044, 94; Richard III--a Medieval Kingship, Hist Today, Vol 0044, 94; Gaunt, John--the Exercise of Princely Power in 14th-Century Europe, Amer Hist Rev, Vol 0099, 94; From Personal Duties Towards Personal Rights, Late-Medieval and Early Modern Political Thought, 1300-1600, Albion, Vol 0027, 95; Crown, Government and People in the 15th-Century, Albion, Vol 0029, 97. **CONTACT ADDRESS** Dept of Hist Soc Sci Ctr, Univ of Western Ont, London, ON, N6A 3K7.

LANDON, MICHAEL DE LAVAL
PERSONAL Born 10/08/1935, St. John, NB, Canada, m, 1959, 2 children **DISCIPLINE** MODERN HISTORY **EDUCATION** Oxford Univ, BA, 58, MA, 61; Univ Wis, MA, 62, PhD, 66. **CAREER** From asst prof to assoc prof, 64-72, prof hist, Univ Miss, 72-, Am Philos Soc res grant, 66-67. **MEMBERSHIPS** Fel Royal Hist Soc Gt Brit; Conf Brit Studies; AHA; Am Soc Legal Hist. **RESEARCH** 17th century England; English legal history; sub-Sahara Africa. **SELECTED PUBLICATIONS** Auth, The position of the public schools in postwar Britain, Soc Studies, 10/67; The Bristol Artillery Company and the Tory triumph in Bristol, 1679-1684, Proc Am Philos Soc, 4/70; The Triumph of the Lawyers, Univ Ala, 70; Burke on the law and the legal profession, Enlightenment Essays, winter 70; Fact and fiction in Bacon's Henry VII, Univ Miss, 71; Serjeant Maynard's family, Devon & Cornwall, 75-76; The learned Glynne and Maynard--Two characters dashed out of Samuel Butler's Hudibras, Proc Am Philos Soc, 6/76. **CONTACT ADDRESS** Dept of History, Univ of Mississippi, General Delivery, University, MS, 38677-9999. **EMAIL** hslandon@olemiss.edu

LANDOW, GEORGE PAUL
PERSONAL Born 08/25/1940, White Plains, NY, m, 1966, 2 children **DISCIPLINE** ENGLISH LITERATURE, DIGITAL CULTURE, ART HISTORY **EDUCATION** Brandeis Univ, MA, 62; Princeton Univ, AB, 61, MA, 63, PhD(English), 66; Brown Univ, MA, 72. **CAREER** Instr English, Columbia Univ, 65-68, asst prof, 69-70; vis assoc prof, Univ Chicago, 70-71; assoc prof, 71-78, Prof English & Artist Hist, Brown Univ, 78-; Fel, Soc for Humanities, Cornell Univ, 68-69; Guggenheim Found fels, 73 & 78; consult lit & art, Museum Art, RI Sch Design, 76-79; vis fel, Brasenose Col, Oxford Univ, 77; fac fel, Brown Univ Inst for Res in Information and Scholarship (IRIS), 85-92; NEA, 84-85; NEH Summer Inst, Yale, 88, 91; British Academy vis prof, Univ of Lancaster, vis res fel, Electronics and Computer Science, Univ of Southampton (UK), vis prof Univ of Zimbabwe, 97: IL SU, 98; Distinguished vis prof, Nat Univ of Singapore, 98. **HONORS AND AWARDS** Gustave O Arldt Award, Coun Grad Schs US, 72; .EDUCOM/NCRIPTAL award innovative courseware in the humanities, 90; many awards for websites. **MEMBERSHIPS** ACM; Tennyson Soc; Trollope Soc. **RESEARCH** Hypertext and digital culture; Victorian British poetry and nonfiction; Victorian painting and visual arts; theology and literature. **SELECTED PUBLICATIONS** Auth, Your Good Influence on Me: The Correspondence of John Ruskin and W H Hunt, John Rylands Libr, England, 76; William Holman Hunt and Typological Symbolism, Yale Univ, 79; ed, Approaches to Victorian Autobiography, Ohio Univ, 79; Victorian Types, Victorian Shadows: Biblical Typology and Victorian Literature, Art and Thought, Routledge & Kegan Paul, 80; Images of Crisis: Literary Iconology 1750 to the Present, Routledge & Kegan Paul, 82; Ruskin, Oxford Univ Press, 85; ed with others, Pre-Raphaelite Friendship, UMI, 85; ed, Ladies of Shalott: A Victorian Masterpiece and its Contexts, Brown, 86; Elegant Jeremiahs: The Sage from Carlyle to Mailer, Cornell, 86; ed with P. Delany, Hypermedia and Literary Studies, MIT, 91; Hypertext: The Convergence of Contemporary Critical Theory and Technology, Johns Hopkins, 92; ed with P. delany, Digital Word: Text-Based Computing in the Humanities, MIT, 93; Hyper/Text/Theory, Johns Hopkins, 94; Hypertext 2.0, Johns Hopkins, 97. **CONTACT ADDRESS** Dept of English, Brown Univ, Box 1852, Providence, RI, 02912-9127. **EMAIL** george@landow.com

LANDRUM, LARRY N.
PERSONAL Huntington, IN, 2 children **DISCIPLINE** AMERICAN LITERATURE, POPULAR CULTURE **EDUCATION** Purdue Univ, BA, 65, MA, 67; Bowling Green State Univ, PhD, 73. **CAREER** Instr, Ctr Studies Popular Culture, Bowling Green State Univ, 70-73; from Asst Prof to Assoc Prof, 73-84, prof eng, MI State Univ, 84; Adv ed, J Popular Cult, 67-85; bibliogr, J Popular Film, 72-; bibliogr, Popular Culture Asn, 73-85. **MEMBERSHIPS** Midwest Popular Cult Asn (vpres & treas, 77-78); MLA; Popular Cult Asn. **RESEARCH** Am lit; Am studies; popular cult. **SELECTED PUBLICATIONS** Co-ed, Challenges in American Culture, Bowling Green State Univ, 71; Theories and Methodologies in Popular Culture, 76 & Dimensions of Detective Fiction, 76, Popular Press; auth, American Popular Culture, Gale, 82; co-ed, New Dimensions in Detective Fiction, Greenwood Press, 99; auth, American Mystery and Detective Novels, Greenwood Press, 99. **CONTACT ADDRESS** Dept of Eng, Michigan State Univ, 201 Morrill Hall, East Lansing, MI, 48824-1036. **EMAIL** landrum@pilot.msu.edu

LANDSMAN, NED C.
PERSONAL Born 09/30/1951, New York, NY, m, 1982 **DISCIPLINE** AMERICAN AND SCOTTISH HISTORY **EDUCATION** Columbia Univ, BA, 73; Univ Pa, PhD(hist), 79. **CAREER** ASST PROF HIST, STATE UNIV NY, STONY BROOK, 79-, Assoc ed, Papers of William Penn, 79; Am Coun Learned Soc res fel, 80. **MEMBERSHIPS** Orgn Am Historians. **RESEARCH** Scottish colonization of North America; transatlantic influences in American social development. **SELECTED PUBLICATIONS** Auth, Scottish Emigration to Colonial America, 1607-1785, William and Mary Quart, Vol 0052, 95; Adapting to a New World--English Society in the 17th-Century Chesapeake, Virginia Mag Hist and Biog, Vol 0103, 95. **CONTACT ADDRESS** Dept Hist, State Univ NY, 100 Nicolls Rd, Stony Brook, NY, 11794-0002.

LANE, ALCYEE
DISCIPLINE TWENTIETH-CENTURY AMERICAN LITERATURE **EDUCATION** UCLA, PhD, 96. **CAREER** ASST PROF, ENG, UNIV CALIF, SANTA BARBARA. **RESEARCH** Gay and lesbian lit; queer, feminist, crit race theory; African Am lit and cult. **SELECTED PUBLICATIONS** Auth, "Black Bodies/Gay Bodies: The Politics of Race in the Gay/Military Battle," Callaloo, 95. **CONTACT ADDRESS** Dept of Eng, Univ Calif, Santa Barbara, CA, 93106-7150. **EMAIL** lane@humanitas.ucsb.edu

LANE, BARBARA MILLER
PERSONAL Born 11/01/1934, New York, NY, m, 1956 **DISCIPLINE** EUROPEAN HISTORY **EDUCATION** Univ Chicago, BA, 53; Barnard Col, BA, 56; Radcliffe Col, MA, 57; Harvard Univ, PhD, 62. **CAREER** Tutor hist and lit, Harvard Univ, 60-61; from lectr to assoc prof, 62-75, prof hist, 75-81, ANDREW W MELLON PROF HUMANITIES, 81-, DIR COMT GROWTH and STRUCT CITIES, 73-, Am Coun Learned Soc Fel, 67-68; John Simon Guggenheim Mem Found fel, 77-78; mem bd dir, Int Planning Hist group, Soc Archit Historians, 77-80; mem exec bd, Conf Group Cent Europ Hist, 77-79. **MEMBERSHIPS** AHA; Soc Archit Historians. **RESEARCH** Modern Germany; architectural history; Italian and German urban history. **SELECTED PUBLICATIONS** Auth, Berlin Cabaret, Cent Europ Hist, Vol 0029, 96. **CONTACT ADDRESS** Dept of Hist, Bryn Mawr Col, 101 N Merion Ave, Bryn Mawr, PA, 19010-2899.

LANE, ROGER
PERSONAL Born 01/17/1934, Providence, RI, m, 1974, 3 children **DISCIPLINE** AMERICAN HISTORY **EDUCATION** Yale Univ, BA, 55; Harvard Univ, PhD, 63. **CAREER** From asst prof to assoc prof, 63-76, prof hist, 76-81, Benjamin R. Collins Prof Am Hist, Haverford Col, 81-. **HONORS AND AWARDS** Bancroft Award, 87; Urban Hist Asn Best Book Award, 92. **MEMBERSHIPS** AHA **RESEARCH** History of 19th century police forces; local government and American criminal patterns. **SELECTED PUBLICATIONS** Auth, Policing the City: Boston 1822-1885, Harvard Univ, 67; Violent Death in the City: Suicide, Accident & Murder in 19th Century Philadelphia, Harvard Univ, 79; Roots of Violence in Black Philadelphia, Harvard Univ, 80; William Dorsey's Philadelphia & Ours, CY Revel, 91; Murder in America: A History, Ohio State, 97. **CONTACT ADDRESS** Dept of Hist, Haverford Col, 370 Lancaster Ave, Haverford, PA, 19041-1392. **EMAIL** rlane@haverford.edu

LANG, MABEL LOUISE
PERSONAL Born 11/12/1917, Utica, NY **DISCIPLINE** CLASSICAL PHILOLOGY **EDUCATION** Cornell Univ, AB, 39, Bryn Mawr Col, AM, 40, PhD, 43. **CAREER** From instr to assoc prof class philol, 43-59, actg dean, 58-59 & 60-61, Prof Greek to PROF EMERITUS, Bryn Mawr Col, 59-, Fulbright res grant, Greece, 59-60; chmn comt admis & fels, Am Sch Class Studies, Athens, 67-72, chmn managing comt, 75-80; Blegen Distinguished Vis Res prof, Vassar Col, 76-77; Martin lectr, Oberlin Col, 82. **HONORS AND AWARDS** LittD, Holy Cross Col, 75, Colgate Univ, 78. **MEMBERSHIPS** Archaeol Inst Am; Am Philol Asn; Am Philos Soc. **RESEARCH** Greek history, literature and epigraphy. **SELECTED PUBLICATIONS** Auth, Pylos tablets, 1957-1962, Am J Archaeol, 58-63; The Athenian Citizen, 60 & Weights and Measures of the Athenian Agora, 64, Am Sch Class Studies, Athens; The palace of Nestor, Vol II, in The Frescoes, Princeton Univ, 68; The Athenian Agora, XXI, Graffiti and Dipinti, 76 & Socrates in the Agora, 78, Am Sch Class Studies, Athens; auth, Herodotean Narrative and Discourse, Harvard Univ Press, 84; auth, The Athenian Agora, Ostraca, 90. **CONTACT ADDRESS** Dept of Greek, Bryn Mawr Col, Bryn Mawr, PA, 19010. **EMAIL** mlang@brynmawr.edu

LANGER, ERICK DETLEF
PERSONAL Born 05/22/1955, Richland, WA, m, 1978, 4 children **DISCIPLINE** HISTORY **EDUCATION** Univ Wash, BA, 77; Stanford Univ, MA, 79, PhD, 84. **CAREER** Vis lectr, Ctr Lat Am Stud, Univ Calif, Los Angeles, 84; vis fac, Univ Pittsburgh, 85; vis prof, Univ Catolica Salta, Argentina, 88; asst prof, Carnegie Mellon Univ, 84-90; adj assoc prof, Univ Pittsburgh, 90-98; adj assoc prof, 94-98, assoc prof hist, 90-98, Carnegie Mellon Univ; ASSOC PROF HIST, GEORGETOWN UNIV, 99-. **HONORS AND AWARDS** Fulbright-Hays fel, 81; Inter-Am Fdn fel, 81; Soc Sci Res Counc fel, 81; James Alexander Robertson Mem prize best article, hon men, 85; NEH summer stipend, 85; Albert J. Beveridge res grant, 88; Am Philos Soc res grant, 88; Fulbright res award, 88; Fulbright Lect award, Inst Nac Antropol, 90; Soc Sci Res Counc res grant, 92; Oversears Ministries Stud Ctr res grant, 94; Rocky Mountain Council Lat Am Stud, McGann Prize Best Article, 88. **MEMBERSHIPS** Soc Geo Hist Tarija; Am Soc Ethnohistory; Phi Alpha Theta; Soc Boliviana Hist; Conf Lat Am Hist; Soc Geo Hist Sucre; Lat Am Stud Asn; AHA. **RESEARCH** Lat Am hist, 19th, 20th cent; Andean peasants; econ dev Andes; Lat Am frontier hist; Cath missions Lat Am. **SELECTED PUBLICATIONS** Co-auth, Experiencing World History, NY Univ Press, forthcoming; co-ed, The New Latin American Mission History, Univ Neb Press, 95; auth, Periodo y regiones: Una perspectiva historica, Memoria de JALLA Tucuman 1995, v 2, Univ Nac Tucuman, 97; auth, Foreign Cloth in the Lowland Frontier: Commerce and Consumption of Textiles in Bolivia, 1830-1930, The Allure of the Foreign: The Role of Imports in Post-Colonial Latin America, Univ Mich Press, 97; auth, Indigenas y exploradores en el Gran Chaco: Relaciones indio-blancas en la Bolivia del siglo XIX, Archivo y Biblioteca Nacionales de Bolivia Anuario 1996, Editorial Tupac Katari, 97; auth, The Barriers to Proletarianization: Bolivian Mine Labour, 1826-1918, Peripheral Labour? Studies in the History of Partial Proletarianization, Cambridge Univ Press, 97. **CONTACT ADDRESS** Dept of History, Georgetown Univ, Washington, DC, 22207-3401. **EMAIL** langere@gunet.georgetown.edu

LANGFORD, PAUL
DISCIPLINE HISTORY **EDUCATION** Oxford Univ, BA, 64; MA, PhD, 71. **CAREER** Fell, hist, Oxford Univ; current, PROF, MOD HIST, OXFORD. **MEMBERSHIPS** AM Antiquarian Soc **SELECTED PUBLICATIONS** Auth, British Correspondence in the Colonial Press, 1763-75, in The Press and the American Revolution; ed, The Writings and Speeches of Edmund Burke; A Polite and Commercial People: England, 1727-83, Oxford Univ Press, 89; auth, Public Life and the Propertied Englishman, 1689-1798, Oxford Univ Press, 91. **CONTACT ADDRESS** Lincoln Col, Oxford, ., OX1 3DR.

LANGILL, RICHARD L.
DISCIPLINE US AND WORLD AFFAIRS **EDUCATION** CA State Univ, BA, 65, MA, 67; Am Univ, PhD, 74. **CAREER** Peace Corps Vol, 67-69; Instr, Am Univ, 72-74; Dir, Blackburn Col, 80-86; Chair, Polit Sci Dept, Blackburn Col, 75-86; Dir, Soc sci div, Blackburn Col, 81-86; Vice-Pres, Acad Affairs, Saint Martin's Col , 86-97; prof, Saint Martin's Col, 97-98. **HONORS AND AWARDS** Cote Award , 60; Nat Defense For Lang Fel , 69-72, Am Univ Tchg fel, 72-74; Malone Fel Prog , 92, 98. **MEMBERSHIPS** Am Polit Sci Asn; Int studies Asn; Wash Comt US-Arab Relations; Olympia World Affairs Coun. **SELECTED PUBLICATIONS** Auth, Americans in Southeast Asia, Potomac Rev, 75; Book Review of The Giants: Russia and America by Richard Barnet in Magill's Literacy Annual, Salem Int Publ, 78; Reunification of Vietnam, Great Events From History, Salem Int Publ, 79; The Fall of Saigon, Great Events From History, Salem Int Publ, 79; The Problem of Civic Illiteracy in American Education, Burnian Mag, 83. **CONTACT ADDRESS** Saint Martin's Col, 5300 Pacific Ave, Lacey, WA, 98503-1297.

LANGLEY, HAROLD D.
DISCIPLINE HISTORY **EDUCATION** Catholic Univ, BA, 50; Univ Penn, MA, 51, PhD, 60. **CAREER** Assoc cur, Mus Hist & Tech, Smithsonian Inst; current, CUR NAV HIST EMER, NATL MUS OF AM HIST, SMITHSONIAN INST & ADJ PROF, HIST, CATHOLIC UNIV. **HONORS AND AWARDS** John Lyman Book Award **MEMBERSHIPS** Am Antiquarian Soc **RESEARCH** Peace of Ghent **SELECTED PUBLICATIONS** Ed, To Utah with the Dragoons, 74; co-ed, Roosevelt and Churchill: Their Secret Wartime Correspondence, Saturday Review/EP Dutton, 75; ed, So Proudly We Hail: The History of the United States Flag, 81; auth, "Medical Men of the Old Navy: A Study in the Development of a Profession, 1797- 1833," New Aspects of Naval History, Naval and Aviation Pub, 85; auth, "Robert F. Stockton," in Command Under Sail, Annapolis, 85; auth, Medicine in the Early U.S. Navy, 1794-1842, Johns Hopkins Univ Press, 95; auth, "Robert F. Stockton" in Quarterdeck & Bridge: Two Centuries of American Naval Leaders, Annapolis, 97; auth, A History of Medicine in the Navy, 1797-1860, Johns Hopkins Univ Press. **CONTACT ADDRESS** 2515 N Utah St, Arlington, VA, 22207.

LANGLEY, LESTER DANNY
PERSONAL Born 08/07/1940, Clarksville, TX, m, 1962, 2 children **DISCIPLINE** HISTORY **EDUCATION** WTex State Univ, BA, 61, MA, 62; Univ Kans, PhD(hist), 65. **CAREER** Asst prof hist, Tex A&M Univ, 65-67 & Cent Wash State Col, 67-70; from Assoc Prof to Prof, 70-88, Reearch Prof Hist, Univ Ga, 88-. **MEMBERSHIPS** AHA; Orgn Am Historians; Conf Latin Am Hist; Soc Hist Am Foreign Rel. **RESEARCH** Latin American history; inter-American relations; history of the Americas. **SELECTED PUBLICATIONS** Ed, United States, Cuba, and the Cold War, Heath, 70; co-ed, United States & Latin America, Addison-Wesley, 71; auth, Senator Kennedy on United States Foreign Policy in Latin America, Rev Interam, fall 72; The Diplomatic Historians: Bailey & Bemis, Hist Teacher, fall 72; Cuba, Forum, 73; Struggle for the American Mediterranean: US-European Rivalry in Gulf Caribbean, Ga Univ, 76; The Jacksonians and the Origins of Inter-American Distrust, Inter-Am Affairs, Vol 30; The US, Latin America, and the Panama Canal, Forum, 78; The US and the Caribbean in the 20th Century, Ga Univ, 80, 82, 85, & 89; The Banana Wars, Kentucky, 83; Central America: The Real Stakes, Crown, 85; MexAmerica: Two Countries, One Future, Crown, 88; America and the Americas: The United States in the Western Hemisphere, Univ Ga, 89; Mexico and the United States, Twayne, 91; coauth, The Banana Men, Kentucky, 94; auth, The Americas in the Age of Revolution, 1750-1850, Yale, 96. **CONTACT ADDRESS** Dept of History, Univ of Georgia, Athens, GA, 30602-0001. **EMAIL** llangley@athens.net

LANGMUIR, GAVIN INCE
PERSONAL Born 04/02/1924, Toronto, ON, Canada **DISCIPLINE** HISTORY **EDUCATION** Univ Toronto, BA, 48; Harvard Univ, AM, 49, PhD(hist), 55. **CAREER** Instr hist, Harvard Univ, 55; from asst prof to assoc prof, 55-77, PROF HIST, STANFORD UNIV, 77-. **MEMBERSHIPS** Asn Jewish Studies; Mediaeval Acad Am; AHA; Medieval Asn Pac; Comn Francaise Arch Juives. **RESEARCH** Medieval political, legal and institutional history; formation of anti-Semitism. **SELECTED PUBLICATIONS** Auth, Alienated Minority--the Jews of Medieval Latin Europe, Amer Hist Rev, Vol 0099, 94; The Holocaust in Historical Context, Vol 1, the Holocaust and Mass Death Before the Modern Age, Amer Hist Rev, Vol 0100, 95. **CONTACT ADDRESS** Dept of Hist, Stanford Univ, Stanford, CA, 94305.

LANGSAM, MIRIAM ZELDA
PERSONAL Born 02/09/1939, Brooklyn, NY **DISCIPLINE** AMERICAN INTELLECTUAL AND SOCIAL HISTORY **EDUCATION** Brooklyn Col, BA, 60; Univ Wis, MS, 71, PhD(hist), 67. **CAREER** Resident lectr, 64-67, asst prof, 67-72, assoc prof, 72-81, PROF HIST, IND UNIV, INDIANAPOLIS, 81-, Lilly fel, 75; dir, Honors Prog and prof hist, Ind Univ-Purdue Univ at Indianapolis. **MEMBERSHIPS** AHA; Orgn Am Historians. **RESEARCH** Nineteenth century social history; urban and penal history. **SELECTED PUBLICATIONS** Auth, In the Web of Class--Delinquents and Reformers in Boston, 1810s-1930s, Amer Hist Rev, Vol 0098, 93; Orphanages Reconsidered-Child Care Institutions in Progressive era Baltimore, Amer Hist Rev, Vol 0100, 95. **CONTACT ADDRESS** Indiana Univ-Purdue Univ, Indianapolis, 4125 Ashbourne Ln, Indianapolis, IN, 46202.

LANGSAM, WALTER E.
PERSONAL Born 06/24/1935, Manhattan, NY, d, 1 child **DISCIPLINE** ARCHITECTURE **EDUCATION** Miami Univ, BA, 60; Yale Univ, MA 68; work towards PhD. **CAREER** Prod ed, Prentice-Hall, 60-64; arts ed, Yale Univ Pr, 65-66; asst prof, Art History, Univ Louisville, 70-74; asst dir, Kentucky Heritage Comn, 74-78; hist preserv asst, Lexington-Fayette Co Hist Comn, 78-82; Hist Preserv Off, Kovington KY, 82-85; adj asst prof, architecture, Univ of Cincinnati, 85- . **HONORS AND AWARDS** Ohioana Lib Prize, 98., Founder and pres, Isaiah Rogers/Ohio River Valley Chapter of Soc of Archit Hist. **MEMBERSHIPS** Archit Found Cincinnati; Cincinnati Preservation Asn; Historic Southwest Ohio; Historic Northern Kentucky Found; Ohio River Valley Chapter of Victorian Soc in Am. **RESEARCH** Cincinnati architecture; American art, architecture, interior design history; historic preservation; British architecture. **SELECTED PUBLICATIONS** Auth, Louisville Mansions from the Civil War to World War II, in Mag Antiques, 74; auth, Introduction, in The Kentucky Governor's Mansion, A Restoration, by Seale, Harmony House, 84; co-auth, Historic Architecture of Bourbon County, Kentucky, Ky Heritage Council, 85; auth, Great Houses of the Queen City: 200 Years of Historic and Contemporary Architecture and Interiors in Cincinnati and Northern Kentucky, Museum Ctr at Union Terminal, 97. **CONTACT ADDRESS** 2355 Fairview Ave, Cincinnati, OH, 45219.

LANIER, MARSHALL L.
PERSONAL Born 01/12/1920, Halifax Co, VA, m **DISCIPLINE** EDUCATION **EDUCATION** Tuskegee Univ AL, BSA 1948, MSA 1950; TX A&M, PhD 1971. **CAREER** Marvell Independent Sch Dist, instr of vets 1950-51; County Agr Agent, Texarkana, Ark, 1951-54; Sparkman Training Sch Sparkman AR, prin & teacher 1957-60; E AR Community Coll, dir spec serv 1976-77; Jarvis Christian Coll Hawkins, TX, dir student teaching 1977-85. **HONORS AND AWARDS** Recipient plaque for Outstanding Advisor, Jarvis Christian Coll 1975; Blue & Gold Plaque, Jarvis Christian Coll 1978. **MEMBERSHIPS** Mem Assn of Tchr Educators; mem TX State Tchrs Assn; mem Phi Delta Kappa; mem Assn for Supervision & Curriculum Devel; mem Kappa Delta Pi; mem Omega Psi Phi Frat.

LANIER BRITSCH, R.
PERSONAL Born 11/16/1938, Provo, UT, m, 1961, 6 children **DISCIPLINE** HISTORY **EDUCATION** BYU, BA, 63, MA, 64; Claremont Grad Univ, PhD, 67. **CAREER** From instr to asst prof to assoc prof to prof, 66-, vp, academics, BYU, Hawaii Campus, 86-90; dir, David M. Kennedy Ctr, 91-97. **HONORS AND AWARDS** Nat Defense Foreign Lang Fel, 65-66; Fel, Blaisdell Inst, 66; Fulbright-Hays Summer Sem, 68; BYU Res Grant, 73; LDS Church Historians Grant, 74; Prof Development Leave, 78, 95, 97, 98. **MEMBERSHIPS** Mormon Hist Asn. **RESEARCH** History of the Church of Jesus Christ of Latter-day Saints in Asia and the Pacific; Christian mission history in Asia. **SELECTED PUBLICATIONS** Auth, Unto the Islands of the Sea: A History of the Latter-day Saints in the Pacific, 86; auth, Moramona: The Mormon in Hawaii, 89; auth, From the East: The History of the Latter-day Saints in Asia, 1851-1996, 98; auth, art, Faithful, Good, Virtuous, True: Pioneers in the Philippines, 98; auth, art, Mormon Intruders in Tonga: The Passport Act of 1922, 98. **CONTACT ADDRESS** Dept of History, Brigham Young Univ, Provo, UT, 84602. **EMAIL** rlb23@email.byu.edu

LANKEVICH, GEORGE J.
PERSONAL Born 04/23/1939, New York, NY, m, 1965, 2 children **DISCIPLINE** AMERICAN HISTORY **EDUCATION** Fordham Col, BSS, 59; Columbia Univ, MA, 60, PhD(Am hist), 67. **CAREER** From instr to assoc prof, 64-75, PROF HIST, BRONX COMMUNITY COL, 75-, City Univ New York fac res fel, 68. **MEMBERSHIPS** AAUP; AHA; Orgn Am Historians. **SELECTED PUBLICATIONS** Auth, Foley and Lardner--Attorneys at Law, 1842-1992, J Amer Hist, Vol 0081, 94. **CONTACT ADDRESS** Dept of Hist, Bronx Comm Col, CUNY, Bronx, NY, 10453.

LANKFORD, NELSON DOUGLAS
DISCIPLINE HISTORY **EDUCATION** Univ Richmond, BA, 70; Ind Univ, Bloomington, MA, 72, PhD(hist), 76. **CAREER** Coordr, Ind Univ-Hist New Harmony Inst, 76-77; researcher, Centennial Hist of Ind Gen Assembly, 77-78; ASST ED, AM HIST REV, 78-. **MEMBERSHIPS** AHA **RESEARCH** Victorian social history; British imperial and commonwealth history; US business history. **SELECTED PUBLICATIONS** Auth, of Locks and Picklocks, Va Mag Hist and Biog, Vol 0103, 95. **CONTACT ADDRESS** 914 Atwater, Bloomington, IN, 47405.

LANSEN, OSCAR
DISCIPLINE 20TH CENTURY WORLD, HOLOCAUST **EDUCATION** Katholieke Unversiteit Nijmegen, PhD, 88. **CAREER** Lectr, Univ NC, Charlotte. **RESEARCH** World War II; war and soc. **SELECTED PUBLICATIONS** Auth, Welkom Yankee Bevrijders: Soldiers and Civilians During the Liberation of the Netherlands 1944-1945, in William Shetter, ed, Publ of the Am Asn for Netherlandic Stud, UP of Am; Gerhard Durlacher's Verzameld Werk, USHMM, Holocaust and Genocide Stud, Oxford UP. **CONTACT ADDRESS** Univ N. Carolina, Charlotte, Charlotte, NC, 28223-0001.

LANZILLOTTI, ROBERT F.
PERSONAL Born 06/19/1921, Washington, DC, m, 1945, 2 children **DISCIPLINE** ECONOMICS **EDUCATION** Columbia Univ, US Navy Midshipman Sch, 44; Am Univ, BA, 46, MA, 47; Univ Calif, Berkeley, PhD, 53. **CAREER** Tchng Fellow, Univ Calif Berkeley, 47-49; Asst to Assoc to Prof of Econ, Wash State Univ, 49-61; Res Assoc, Brookings Inst, 56-57, 74-75; Prof & Ch, Mich State Univ, 61-69; Vis Prof, Cornell Univ, 65-82; Dean, Grad Sch Bus, Univ Fla, 69-86; Member, US Price Commission, 71-73; Dean Emeritus & Dir, Pub Policy Res Ctr, Grad Sch of Bus, Univ Fla, 86-. **HONORS AND AWARDS** Phi Beta Kappa; Beta Gamma Sigma; Omicron Delta Kappa; Fla Blue Key; Am Men in Sci; Fellow, Swift & Co, 53; Fellow, US Steel Corp, 54; Fellow, Merrill Ctr for Econ, 56; N Atl Treaty Org Res Fellow, 64; Member, Vis Sci Prog, Am Econ Assoc, 68-71; D. Litt, Tampa Univ (hon), 79; DSc, Fla Inst of Tech (hon), 79. **MEMBERSHIPS** Am Econ Asn; S Econ Asn; Am Bar Asn, Antitrust Section; Fla Council of 100, 73-88,91-; Int Joseph A Schumpter Soc, Bd of Mgmt (pres-elect); Bd of Dir, Univ Fla Foundation Bd, 83-; Am Law & Econ Asn. **RESEARCH** Antitrust economics & industrial organization. **SELECTED PUBLICATIONS** Co-auth, Measuring Damage in Commercial Litigation: Present Value of Lost Opportunities, J of Acctng, Auditing & Finance, Winter/Spring 90; auth, The Great Milk Conspiracies of the 1980s, Rev of Ind Org, vol II, 413-458, 8/96; auth, Coming to Terms With Daubert in Sherman Act Complaints: A Suggested Economic Approach, Neb Law Rev, forthcoming, 98. **CONTACT ADDRESS** Col of Bus Admin, Univ Fla, PO Box 117154, Gainesville, FL, 32611-7154. **EMAIL** lanz@dale.cba.ufl.edu

LAPIDUS, IRA M.
PERSONAL Born 06/09/1937, New York, NY, m, 1983, 1 child **DISCIPLINE** HISTORY **EDUCATION** Harvard Univ,

AB, 58, PhD, 64. **CAREER** Prof, hist, Univ Calif Berkeley, 65-94; chair, Ctr for Middle Eastern Studies, Univ Calif Berkeley, 79-94; pres, Middle East Studies Asn, 83-84. **HONORS AND AWARDS** Mem, Amer Philos Soc; Guggenheim fel; SSRC fel. **MEMBERSHIPS** Middle East Studies Asn; Urban Hist Asn. **RESEARCH** Islam; Middle East history; Urban history. **SELECTED PUBLICATIONS** Article, Islamic Revival and Modernity: The Contemporary Movements and the Historical Paradigms, Jour of the Econ and Soc Hist of the Orient, 38, 444-460, 97; article, Islamism, Encycl Ital, 100-114, 96; article, Death in the Muslim Tradition, Facing Death: Where Culture, Religion and Medicine Meet, Yale Univ Press, 148-159, 96; article, A Sober Survey of the Islamic World, Orbis, 391-404, 96; article, State and Relgion in Islamic Societies, Past and Present, 151, 3-27, 96; article, The Golden Age: The Political Concepts of Islam, The Annals of the American Academy of Political and Social Science, Polit Islam, v 524, 13025, nov, 92; article, An Historian Looks at the Current Crisis, Confrontation in the Gulf, Berkeley, 101-112, 92; article, Islamisches Sketirertum und das Rekonstruktions--und Umgestaltungs potential der Islamischen Kultur, Kulturen der Achsenzeit, Frankfurt am Main, 161-188, 92; article, Sufism and Ottoman Islamic Society, The Dervish Lodge, Berkeley, 15-32, 92. **CONTACT ADDRESS** 2671 Shasta Rd., Berkeley, CA, 94708. **EMAIL** ilapidus@uclink4.berkeley.edu

LAPOMARDA, VINCENT ANTHONY
PERSONAL Born 02/28/1934, Portland, ME **DISCIPLINE** UNITED STATES HISTORY, AMERICAN DIPLOMACY, AMERICAN RELIGIOUS HISTORY, GREA **EDUCATION** Boston Col, AB, 57, MA, 58, STL, 65; Boston Univ, PhD, 68. **CAREER** Teacher English, hist, Latin & relig, Boston Col High Sch, 58-61; asst prof, 69-74, assoc prof hist, Col of the Holy Cross, 74-, Dir, The Jesuits of Holy Cross Col, Inc, 71-87, secy, 72-87, mem educ policy comt, Col of the Holy Cross, 72-74, dir Washington internship prog, 74-75, coordr, Holocaust Collection, Col of the Holy Cross, 79-, dir, Italian Am Collection, Col of the Holy Cross; chmn comt hist memorials, Int Order Alhambra, 81-. **HONORS AND AWARDS** Coe Fel, 59; Phi Alpha Theta, 66; Batchelor Fel, 69, 70; Knight of Holy Sepulchre, 87; Alhambran of the Year, 87; Fac Service Award, Col of the Holy Cross, 95. **MEMBERSHIPS** AHA; Am Cath Hist Asn; Orgn Am Historians; Am Ital Hist Asn. **RESEARCH** Jesuits in history; Italian Americans; The Holocaust. **SELECTED PUBLICATIONS** Auth, The Jesuit Heritage in New England, Worcester, 77; The Knights of Columbus in Massachusetts, Needham, 82, 2nd ed, Norwood, 92; The Jesuits and the Third Reich, Lewiston, 89; The Order of Alhambra, Baltimore, 94; The Boston Mayor Who Became Truman's Secretary of Labor, NY, 95; Charles Nolcini, Worcester, 97; author of numerous journal articles, letters, and reviews. **CONTACT ADDRESS** Col of the Holy Cross, 1 College St, Worcester, MA, 01610-2322. **EMAIL** vlapomar@holycross.edu

LAPORTE, ROBERT, JR.
PERSONAL Born 02/12/1940, Detroit, MI, m, 1962, 2 children **DISCIPLINE** POLITICAL SCIENCE, PUBLIC ADMINISTRATION **EDUCATION** Wayne State Univ, BA, 62, MA, 63; Syracuse Univ, PhD, 67. **CAREER** Asst prof, 66-69, assoc prof, 69-75, prof of public admin, 75-94; prof of public admin & political sci, The Pa State Univ, 94-. **MEMBERSHIPS** Am Political Sci Asn; Am Soc for Public Admin; Asn of Asian Studies. **RESEARCH** Public administrative systems; South Asian studies; development studies; comparative politics and government; political/governmental institutions. **SELECTED PUBLICATIONS** Auth, Pakistan: A Nation Still in the Making, India and Pakistan, Woodrow Wilson Center Press/ Cambridge Univ Press, 98; Another Try at Democracy, Contemporary Problems of Pakistan, Westview Press, 93; Pakistan in 1996: Starting Over Again, Asian Survey, Feb 97; Pakistan in 1995: The Continuing Crises, Asian Survey, Feb, 96; Elements of unity, Dawm, Aug 97; coauth, Liberalization of the Economy Through Privatization, Pakistan in 1997, Westview Press, 98; Public Enterprise Management: Pakistan, Public Enterprise Management: Int Case Studies, Greenwood Press, 93. **CONTACT ADDRESS** Pennsylvania State Univ, Box 314, University Park, PA, 16802. **EMAIL** rql@psu.edu

LAPP, RUDOLPH MATHEW
PERSONAL Born 08/19/1915, Chicago, IL, m, 1943 **DISCIPLINE** AFROAMERICAN HISTORY **EDUCATION** Roosevelt Univ, Chicago, BA, 48; Univ Calif, Berkeley, MA, 52, PhD(Am hist), 56. **CAREER** PROF AM HIST, COL SAN MATEO, 55-, Nat Endowment Humanities fel, 72-73. **MEMBERSHIPS** Southern Hist Asn; Study Negro Life and Hist. **SELECTED PUBLICATIONS** Auth, Parallel Communities-African Americans in California East Bay, 1850-1963, PAC HIST REV, Vol 0064, 95. **CONTACT ADDRESS** Col of San Mateo, 1700 Hillsdale Blvd, San Mateo, CA, 94402.

LAQUEUR, THOMAS WALTER
PERSONAL Born 09/06/1945, Istanbul, Turkey **DISCIPLINE** HISTORY **EDUCATION** Swarthmore Col, BA, 67; Princeton Univ, MA, 69, PhD(hist), 73. **CAREER** Instr social sci, Concord Col, 68-69; asst prof, 73-80, ASSOC PROF HIST, UNIV CALIF, BERKELEY, 80-, Nat Endowment for Humanities fel, 76. **MEMBERSHIPS** AHA **SELECTED PUBLICATIONS** Auth, Womens Bodies in Classical Greek Science, Isis, Vol 0086, 95; Hanging the Head--Portraiture and Social Formation in 18th-Century England, Amer Hist Rev, Vol 0100, 95. **CONTACT ADDRESS** Dept of Hist, Univ Calif, 3229 Dwinelle Hall, Berkeley, CA, 94720-2551.

LARDINOIS, ANDRE P.M.H.
DISCIPLINE ARCHAIC GREEK POETRY, GREEK TRAGEDY, GREEK AND ROMAN MYTHOLOGY **EDUCATION** Free Univ, Neth, BA, 84, MA, 88; Princeton Univ, MA, 91, PhD, 95. **CAREER** Asst prof, Univ Minn, Twin Cities. **RESEARCH** Voices of women in Greek literature and society. **SELECTED PUBLICATIONS** Auth, Lesbian Sappho and Sappho of Lesbos, in J N Bremmer, ed, From Sappho to de Sade: Moments in the History of Sexuality, London-NY, 89; Greek Myths for Athenian Rituals: Religion and Politics in Aeschylus' Eumenidesand Sophocles' Oedipus Coloneus, GRBS 33/4, 92; Subject and Circumstance in Sappho's Poetry, TAPA 124, 94; Wisdom in Context: The Use of Gnomic Statements in Archaic Greek Poetry, PhD Diss, Princeton Univ, 95; Who Sang Sappho's Songs?, in E Greene, ed, Reading Sappho: Contemporary Approaches, Berkeley, 96; Modern Paroemiology and the Use of Gnomai in Homer's Iliad, CP 92, 97; coauth, Tragic Ambiguity: Anthropology, Philosophy and Sophocles' Antigone, Leiden, 87. **CONTACT ADDRESS** Dept of Class & Near Eastern Stud, Univ Minn, Twin Cities, Minneapolis, MN, 55455. **EMAIL** lardi001@tc.umn.edu

LAREW, KARL GARRET
PERSONAL Born 12/09/1936, Ithaca, NY, m, 1972 **DISCIPLINE** MODERN EUROPEAN MILITARY AND INTELLECTUAL HISTORY **EDUCATION** Univ Conn, BA, 59; Yale Univ, MA, 60, PhD(hist), 64. **CAREER** From asst prof to assoc prof, 66-73, PROF HIST, TOWSON STATE UNIV, 73-. **MEMBERSHIPS** AHA; Am Comt Hist 2nd World War; AAUP. **RESEARCH** Nineteenth and 20th century European and American military and diplomatic history; intellectual history of 19th and 20th century Western civilization. **SELECTED PUBLICATIONS** Auth, War Plan Orange--the United States Strategy to Defeat Japan, 1897-1945, Historian, Vol 0057, 94; Planet Women--the Image of Women in Planet Comics, 1940-1953, Historian, Vol 0059, 97. **CONTACT ADDRESS** Dept of Hist, Towson State Univ, Baltimore, MD, 21204.

LARKIN, JACK
PERSONAL Born 06/26/1943, Evergreen Park, IL, m, 1970, 2 children **DISCIPLINE** AMERICAN SOCIAL HISTORY AND MATERIAL CULTURE **EDUCATION** Harvard Col, AB, 65; Brandeis Univ, MA, 68; Museum Management Inst, J. Paul Getty Trust, 95. **CAREER** From coord to asst dir to res hist to chief hist to dir res, 71-, Old Sturbridge Village. **HONORS AND AWARDS** Am Quarterly Award, 82; Finalist & Distinguished Mention, 89; PEN, 89; Mem Am antiquarian Society, 94; President's Award, 96; Kidger Award, 99. **MEMBERSHIPS** Org Am Hist: Asn Am Museums; Am Asn State Local Hist. **RESEARCH** Social history; historical ethnography and material culture of rural New England, 1780-1860; public history and museums. **SELECTED PUBLICATIONS** Auth, art, Rural Life in the North 1620-1980, 93; auth, art, Notes on a Native Daughter: Dolly Smith and New England Culture, 94; auth, art, From Country Mediocrity to Rural Improvement: Transforming the Slovenly Countryside in the Early Republic, 95; con **CONTACT ADDRESS** Director of Research, Collections & Library, Old Sturbridge Village, 1 Old Sturbridge Village Rd, Sturbridge, MA, 01566-1138. **EMAIL** jlarkin@osv.org

LAROCCA, JOHN JOSEPH
PERSONAL Born 06/01/1946, New York, NY **DISCIPLINE** HISTORY **EDUCATION** Fordham Univ, BA, 69; Rutgers Univ, MA, 71, PhD(hist), 77. **CAREER** Asst prof History, 77-81, from assoc prof to prof History, chmn dept, Xavier Univ, 81-87. **HONORS AND AWARDS** Midwest Conf on Brit Studies; Ecclesiastical Hist Soc, Gr Brit; Cath Record Society, Gr Brit. **MEMBERSHIPS** AHA; Cath Rec Soc; Conf Brit Studies. **RESEARCH** Elizabethan and Jacobean Recusancy; reformation. **SELECTED PUBLICATIONS** Auth, Time, death and the next generation: The early Elizabethan Recusancy Policy, 1558-1574, Albion (in press); The Recusant Rolls for London and Middlesex Counties, 1603-1625, The Catholic Record Society, Spring, 1996; Jacobean Recusant Rolls for Middlesex: an Abstract in English, trans and ed Catholic Record Society Publications, Record Series, Vol 76, Hampshire, 97. **CONTACT ADDRESS** Dept of History, Xavier Univ, 3800 Victory Pky, Cincinnati, OH, 45207-1092. **EMAIL** larocca@admin.xu.edu

LAROCHE, ROLAND ARTHUR
PERSONAL Born 03/04/1943, Berlin, NH, m, 1965, 3 children **DISCIPLINE** CLASSICS **EDUCATION** Boston Col, BA, 65; Tufts Univ, MA, 66, PhD(classics), 72. **CAREER** Teacher French, Latin and Greek, Pingree Sch, S Hamilton, Mass, 66-70; asst prof classics, State Univ NY, Potsdam, 70-77; teacher Latin and French, Cheshire Acad, Conn, 77-81; TEACHER LATIN AND GREEK AND CHMN, FOREIGN LANG DEPT, ALBANY ACAD, 81-. **MEMBERSHIPS** Am Class League; Class Asn Atlantic States. **RESEARCH** Greek and Roman numerical practices; Livy; early Roman historiography. **SELECTED PUBLICATIONS** Auth, Popular Symbolic-Mystical Numbers in Antiquity, Latomus, Vol 0054, 95; Number Symbolism, Latomus, Vol 0055, 96. **CONTACT ADDRESS** Albany Acad, Albany, NY, 12210.

LAROUCHE, MICHEL
PERSONAL Born 01/25/1951, PQ, Canada, m, 1973, 1 child **DISCIPLINE** HISTORY OF ART **EDUCATION** Univ Que, Montreal, BA, 73; Univ Montreal, BA, 73, MA, 75, PhD(-French), 80. **CAREER** Prof film, Col Bois-de-Boulogne, 73-75 and Col Andre-Laurendeau, 75-80; PROF FILM, ART HIST DEPT, UNIV MONTREAL, 80-, Prof, art hist dept, Univ Que, Montreal, 75-80. **MEMBERSHIPS** Univ Art Asn of Can; Film Studies Asn of Can. **RESEARCH** The film style of Alexandro Jodorowsky; the experimental film; the animated film. **SELECTED PUBLICATIONS** Auth, Kane,Cheikh,Hamidou L'aventure Ambigue'--From Novel to Screenplay, Etudes Francaises, Vol 0031, 95; Cinema in Red and Black--30 Years of Film-Criticism in Quebec, Univ Toronto Quart, Vol 0065, 95. **CONTACT ADDRESS** Art History Dept, Univ of Montreal, Montreal, PQ, H3C 3J7.

LARSEN, GRACE H.
PERSONAL Born 12/04/1920, Pomona, CA, m, 1943, 2 children **DISCIPLINE** AMERICAN HISTORY **EDUCATION** Univ Calif, Berkeley, AB, 42, MA, 45; Columbia Univ, PhD, 55. **CAREER** Lectr Europ hist, Rutgers Univ, 47-49, US hist, 52-55; from asst specialist to assoc specialist agr econ, Univ Calif, Berkeley, 55-66; assoc prof hist, 66-71, chmn dept hist, 67-70, acad dean, 70-80, PROF HIST, HOLY NAMES COL, CALIF, 71-, Lectr, Bryn Mawr Col, 49-50 and Swarthmore Col, 49-51; Huntington Library grant; Nat Endowment Humanities summer grant. **MEMBERSHIPS** AHA; Agr Hist Soc. **RESEARCH** American colonial history; agricultural history; women on the land. **SELECTED PUBLICATIONS** Auth, The Economics and Structure of the Citrus Industry--Comment on Papers by Moses, H.,Vincent and Tobey, Robert and Wetherell, Charles, Calif Hist, Vol 0074, 95. **CONTACT ADDRESS** Holy Names Col, 3500 Mountain Blvd, Oakland, CA, 94619.

LARSEN, LAWRENCE H.
PERSONAL Born 01/18/1931, Racine, WI, m, 2 children **DISCIPLINE** AMERICAN HISTORY **EDUCATION** Lawrence Col, BS, 53; Univ Wis, MS, 55, PhD, 62. **CAREER** Asst hist, Univ Wis, 55-57, 58-59, instr hist, Exten Ctr, 57-58; asst archivist, State Hist Soc Wis, 59-61; instr hist, Carroll Col, 61-62; asst prof, Wis State Col, Oshkosh, 62-64; asst prof to assoc prof, 64-69, actg chmn dept, 65-66, PROF HIST, UNIV MO-KANSAS CITY, 69-, Instr, Univ Wis, 61, specialist, Exten Div, 62. **MEMBERSHIPS** Orgn Am Historians. **RESEARCH** Eisenhower administration; urban history; administrative history. **SELECTED PUBLICATIONS** Auth, The President Wore Spats, a Biography of Glenn Frank, 65; coauth, Factories in the Valley: Neenah-Menasha, 1870-1915, 69; co-ed, Aspects of American History, 1776-1970 (2 vols), Kendall-Hunt, 70, Urban Crisis in Modern America, Heath, 71 & The Eisenhower Administration, 1953-1961: A Documentary History, Random, 71; auth, The Urban West at the End of the Frontier, Regents Press of Kans, 78; coauth, The Gate City: A History of Omaha, Pruett Publ Co, 82; auth, Wall of Flames, North Dakota St Univ, 84; auth, the Rise of the Urban South, Univ Press of Kent, 85; auth, The Urban South: A History, Univ Press of Kent, 90; coauth, The University of Kansas Medical Center: A Pictoral History, Univ Press of Kans, 92; auth, Federal Justice in Western Missouri: The Judgesm the Cases, the Times, Univ of MO, 94; coauth, The Gate City: A History of Omaha, enlarged ed, Univ of Neb 97; coauth, Pendergast!, Univ of MO, 97. **CONTACT ADDRESS** Dept of History, Univ of Missouri, Kansas City, 5100 Rockhill Rd, Kansas City, MO, 64110-2499.

LARSON, BRUCE LLEWELLYN
PERSONAL Born 01/10/1936, Hawley, MN **DISCIPLINE** AMERICAN HISTORY **EDUCATION** Concordia Col Moorhead, BA, 59; Univ NDak, MA, 61; Univ Kans, PhD(hist), 71. **CAREER** Instr hist, Concordia Col, 62-63; from asst prof to assoc prof, 65-76, PROF HIST, MANKATO STATE UNIV, 76-, Elmer L and Eleanor J Andersen Found fel grant, 72-73; narrator and consult, TV Documentary on Charles a Lindbergh, KTVI, Mo, 77. **MEMBERSHIPS** AHA; Orgn Am Historians; Agr Hist Soc; Swed Pioneer Hist Soc; Am Aviation Hist Soc. **RESEARCH** Midwest and Scandinavian-American politics; Lindbergh history; Minnesota history. **SELECTED PUBLICATIONS** Auth, Norwegian Americans and the Politics of Dissent, 1880-1924, Scand Stud, Vol 0065, 93. **CONTACT ADDRESS** Dept of Hist, Mankato State Univ, Mankato, MN, 56001.

LARSON, CALVIN J.
PERSONAL Born 09/25/1933, Oakland, CA, m, 1959, 2 children **DISCIPLINE** SOCIOLOGY **EDUCATION** Univ Cal Berk, BA 56; San Jose State Univ, MS 60; Univ Oregon, PhD 65. **CAREER** Purdue Univ, asst prof, 65-70; Univ Vermont, assoc prof, 70-71; Univ Mass Boston, 71-. **RESEARCH** Soc Theory; crime and correction; family violence and deviant behavior. **SELECTED PUBLICATIONS** Auth, Crime, Justice

and Society, with Gerald Garrett, Gen Hall Inc, 96; Pure and Applied Sociology Theory: Problems and Issues, Har Brace Jovanovich, 93; Child Abuse, Ready Ref Fam Life, Salem Press, 96; White-collar Crime, Encycl of Soc Issues, Salem Press, 96; Theory and Applied Sociology, Jour of Appl Soc, 95. **CONTACT ADDRESS** Dept of Sociology, Univ of Massachusetts, Boston, MA, 02125. **EMAIL** larsonc@umbsky.cc.umb.edu

LARSON, DORAN
DISCIPLINE FINE ARTS AND HUMANITIES **EDUCATION** Univ CA at Santa Cruz, BA; SUNY at Buffalo, MA, PhD. **CAREER** Asst prof; taught at, SUNY Buffalo, Univ Paris & Univ WI Madison and Richland campuses. **HONORS AND AWARDS** Over 10 grants & awd(s) for tchg excellence, tchg develop & fiction writing. **SELECTED PUBLICATIONS** Auth, 2 novels, Bantam, 85 & Permanent, 97; articles in, Mod Lang Stud, AR Quart, Cinema J; stories in, IA Rev, Boulevard, Va Quart Rev, Other Voices. **CONTACT ADDRESS** Col of Fine Arts and Hum, Univ Texas at San Antonio, 6900 N Loop 1604 W, San Antonio, TX, 78249. **EMAIL** dlarson@lonestar.utsa.edu

LARSON, JOHN LAURITZ
DISCIPLINE HISTORY **EDUCATION** Luther Col, BA, 72; Brown Univ, AM, 76, PhD, 81. **CAREER** Teach asst, Brown Univ, 75-78; dir res and collections, Conner Prairie Pioneer Settlement, 79-83; lectr, Earlham Col, 79- 83; ASSOC PROF HIST, PURDUE HIST, 88-; CO-ED JOURNAL OF EARLY REPUBLIC, 94-. **CONTACT ADDRESS** Dept of History, Purdue Univ, West Lafayette, IN, 47906. **EMAIL** larsonjl@purdue.edu

LARSON, ROBERT H.
PERSONAL Born 03/03/1942, New York, NY, 3 children **DISCIPLINE** MODERN EUROPEAN HISTORY **EDUCATION** The Citadel, BA, 63; Univ Va, MA, 68, PhD, 73. **CAREER** Instr, 69-72, asst prof, 72-79, assoc prof mod Europ hist, 79-88, prof 88-98, Shangraw Prof of Hist, Lycoming Col. **HONORS AND AWARDS** Templer Medal, Soc for Army Hist Res, Eng, 84. **MEMBERSHIPS** AHA **RESEARCH** Military history of 19th- and 20th-century Europe. **SELECTED PUBLICATIONS** Auth, "B.H. Liddell Hart: Apostle of Limited War," Military Affairs, 4/80; auth, The British Army and the Theory of Armored Warfare, 1918-1940, Delaware, 84; coauth, Williamsport: From Frontier Village to Regional Center, Windsor, 84. **CONTACT ADDRESS** History Dept, Lycoming Col, 700 College Pl, Williamsport, PA, 17701-5192. **EMAIL** larson@lycoming.edu

LARSON, ROBERT WALTER
PERSONAL Born 03/20/1927, Denver, CO, 2 children **DISCIPLINE** UNITED STATES HISTORY **EDUCATION** Univ Denver, AB, 50, Am, 53; Univ NMex, PhD(US hist), 61. **CAREER** Instr hist, pub schs, Colo, 50-56, supv teacher, 56-58; assoc prof, 60-68, PROF HIST, UNIV NORTHERN COLO, 68-, Hist consult, Britannica Jr Encycl, 69-; ed consult, NMex Hist Rev, 76- **HONORS AND AWARDS** Distinguished Scholar Award, Univ Northern Colo, 77. **MEMBERSHIPS** AHA; Orgn Am Historians; Western Hist Asn. **RESEARCH** Southwestern history, especially New Mexico; Progressive period during the administrations of Theodore Roosevelt and William Howard Taft; Western populism. **SELECTED PUBLICATIONS** Auth, Donnelly, Ignatius--Portrait of a Politician, J the West, Vol 0032, 93; Founding the Far West--California, Oregon, and Nevada, 1840-1890, Amer Hist Rev, Vol 0098, 93; Populism in the Western United-States, 1890-1900, Montana-Mag Western Hist, Vol 0044, 94; Rocky-Mountain West--Colorado, Wyoming, and Montana, 1859-1915, Nmex Hist Rev, Vol 0069, 94; In the Peoples Interest--a Centennial History of Montanab State University, Pac Hist Rev, Vol 0063, 94; Desert Lawmen--the High Sheriffs of New Mexico and Arizona, 1846-1912, J Amer Hist, Vol 0081, 94; Red Cloud .2. the Reservation Years, Trial and Transition for the Great Lakota Leader, Montana-Mag Western Hist, Vol 0047, 97; Red Cloud + the Great Lakota Leaders Rise to Prominence .1. the Warrior Years, Montana-Mag Western Hist, Vol 0047, 97. **CONTACT ADDRESS** Dept of Hist, Univ of Northern Colo, Greeley, CO, 80639.

LARSON, TAFT ALFRED
PERSONAL Born 01/18/1910, Wakefield, NE **DISCIPLINE** HISTORY **EDUCATION** Univ Colo, AB, 32, AM, 33; Univ Ill, PhD, 37. **CAREER** From instr to prof hist, 36-69, William Robertson Coe Prof Am Studies, 69-75, EMER PROF AM STUDIES, UNIV WYO, 75-; MEM HOUSE REP, WYO STATE LEGIS, 76-, Vis prof, Columbia Univ, 50-51; mem US Nat Comn for UNESCO, 63-66. **MEMBERSHIPS** Western Hist Asn (pres, 70-71). **RESEARCH** Western American history; Wyoming history; history of woman suffrage. **SELECTED PUBLICATIONS** Auth, Rocky Mountain West--Colorado, Wyoming, and Montana, 1859-1915, Montana-Mag Western Hist, Vol 0044, 94. **CONTACT ADDRESS** Univ Wyoming, 810 Clark, Laramie, WY, 82071.

LARUE, LEWIS HENRY
PERSONAL Born 01/30/1938, Bartley, WV, m, 1962, 2 children **DISCIPLINE** AMERICAN CONSTITUTIONAL LAW, JURISPRUDENCE **EDUCATION** Washington & Lee Univ, AB, 59; Harvard Univ, LLB, 62. **CAREER** Trial atty, US Marine Corps Reserve, 62-65 & US Dept Justice, 65-67; asst prof, 67-70, assoc prof, 70-74, PROF LAW, WASHINGTON & LEE UNIV, 74-. **RESEARCH** Literature. **SELECTED PUBLICATIONS** Auth, A Comment on Fried, Summers, and the Value of Life, Cornell Law Rev, Vol 57, 72; A Jury of One's Peers, Washington & Lee Law Rev, Vol 33, 76; Politics and the Constitution, Yale Law J, Vol 86, 77; The Rhetoric of Powell's Bakke, Washington & Lee Law Rev, Vol, 38, 81; A Student's Guide to the Study of Law: An Introduction, Matthew Bender & Co, 87; Political Discourse: A Case Study of the Watergate Affair, Univ of GA Press, 88; Constitutional Law as Fiction: Narrative in the Rhetoric of Authority, PA State Press, 95. **CONTACT ADDRESS** Sch of Law, Washington & Lee Univ, Lexington, VA, 24450-0303. **EMAIL** lhl@wlu.edu

LARZELERE, R.E.
PERSONAL Born 04/03/1945, Greensburg, PA, m, 1972, 2 children **DISCIPLINE** PSYCHOLOGY **EDUCATION** Wabash Col, BA, 67; Georgia Tech, MS, 74; Penn State Univ, PhD, 79. **CAREER** Asst prof, hd Psych Dept; Bryan Col, 77-79; asst prof, Western Con Baptist Sem, 80-82; assoc prof, Rosemead Sch of Psych, Biola Univ, 82-90; dir behavioral health care res, Boys Town, 90-. **HONORS AND AWARDS** NIMH fel, 79-80, 88-89; Who's Who in the Midwest; Omicron Nu; Psi Chi. **MEMBERSHIPS** Am Psychol Asn; Soc for Res in Child Develop; Asn for Advan of Behavior Ther; Nat Coun on Family Relations; Am Prof Soc on the Abuse of Children. **RESEARCH** Stat anal and res methodology; parental discipline; eval and treatment of children in out-of-home placement. **SELECTED PUBLICATIONS** Auth, Response to Oosterhuis: Empirically Justified Uses of Spanking: Toward a Discriminating View of Corporal Punishment, J of Psychol and Theol, 93; auth, Should the Use of Corporal Punishment by Parents be Considered Child Abuse? No., in Debating Children's Lives, 94; coauth, The Effectiveness of Parental Discipline for Toddler Misbehavior at Different Levels of Child Distress, in Family Rel, 94; auth, Discipline, in Encyclopedia of Marriage and the Family, 95; coauth, Predictive Validity of the Suicide Probability Scale Among Adolescents in a Group Home Treatment, in J of Am Acad of Child and Adolescent Psychiat, 96; coauth, The Effects of Discipline Responses in Delaying Toddler Misbehavior Recurrences, Child & Family Behavior Therapy, 96; auth, A Review of the Outcomes of Parental Use of Nonabusive or Customary Physical Punishment, in Pediatrics, 96; coauth, Nonabusive Spanking: Parental Liberty or Child Abuse?, in Children's Legal Rights J, 97; auth, Effective vs. Counterproductive parental Spanking: Toward More Light and Less Heat, in Marriage and Family, 98; coauth, Punishment Enhances Reasoning's Effectiveness as a Disciplinary Response to Toddlers, in J of Marriage and the Family, 98; coauth, Two Emerging Perspectives of Parental Spanking, Archiv of Pediatric & Adolescent Med, 98; coauth, Group Treatment for Sexually Abused Adolescent Females: PTSD-related Mediators of Its Effectiveness, in J of Traumatic Stress, in press. **CONTACT ADDRESS** Youth Care Bldg, Father Flanagan's Boys Home, Boys Town, NE, 68010. **EMAIL** larzelerer@boystown.org

LASKA, VERA
PERSONAL Born 07/21/1928, Kosice, Czechoslovakia, m, 1949, 2 children **DISCIPLINE** UNITED STATES HISTORY, LATIN AMERICAN CIVILIZATION **EDUCATION** Charles Univ, Prague, MA, 45 & 46; Univ Chicago, PhD, 59. **CAREER** Exec secy, War Crime Invest, Prague, 45-46; foreign studies adv admis, Univ Chicago, 54-59; asst prof, 66-72, assoc prof, 72-80, prof hist, Regis Col, MA, 80, Chmn Div soc sci, 68-, Fulbright Comn, Brazil, 61-64; Fulbright Prof, Charles Univ, Prague, Czech Republic, 93; consult, Inst Int Educ, NY, 64-66; mem, Mass Adv Bd for Bicentennial Am Revolution. **HONORS AND AWARDS** Masaryk Scholar, 46; Outstanding Educ of Am, 72; Kidger Award for Excellence in Hist; George Washington Honor Medal, Commun. **MEMBERSHIPS** AHA; Nat Asn Foreign Study Affairs; Latin Am Studies Asn; Czech Soc Arts & Sci Am. **RESEARCH** Cult exchange of persons; US hist & Latin Am civilization. **SELECTED PUBLICATIONS** Auth, One of Us, Nova Doba, Chicago, 46-47; Reference works on the evaluation of foreign education, Nat Asn Foreign Study Adv, 59; Historical Towns of Minas Gerais, Sao Paulo Bull, 63-64; Refugee students in the United States, Ann Czech Soc Arts & Sci Am, 68; Remember the Ladies--Outstanding Women of the American Revolution, Mass Bicentennial Comn, 76; Czechs in America, Oceana, 78; Franklin and Women, 79; Benjamin Franklin, Diplomat, 82; Women in the Resistance and in the Holocaust, Greenwood Press, 83; Nazism, Resistance & Holocaust, Scarecrow Press, 85; Two Loves of Benjamin Franklin, Grafoprint, Prague, 94. **CONTACT ADDRESS** 235 Wellesley St, Weston, MA, 02193-1505. **EMAIL** Verandy@aol.com

LASLETT, JOHN HENRY MARTIN
PERSONAL Born 05/07/1933, Watford, England, m, 1959, 2 children **DISCIPLINE** AMERICAN AND COMPARATIVE SOCIAL HISTORY **EDUCATION** Oxford Univ, BA, 57, DPhil(hist), 62. **CAREER** Asst lectr polit theory and insts, Univ Liverpool, 61-62; assoc prof soc sci, Univ Chicago, 63-64 and Am hist, 64-68; assoc prof, 68-75, PROF HIST, UNIV CALIF, LOS ANGELES, 75-, Willett res award, Univ Chicago, 64; Soc Sci Res Coun res fel, 70-71; Am Coun Learned Soc fac award, 70-71; vis prof hist, Ctr Study Social Hist, Univ Warwick, 73-74; fel, Inst Ind Relations, Univ Calif, Los Angeles, 81-82. **MEMBERSHIPS** AHA **RESEARCH** Comparative Euro-American history; immigrant history; mining history. **SELECTED PUBLICATIONS** Auth, The German American Radical Press--the Shaping of a Left Political Culture, 1850-1940, J Amer Hist, Vol 0080, 93; The Spirit of 1848--German Immigrants, Labor Conflict, and the Coming of the Civil War, J Amer Hist, Vol 0080, 93; Gender, Class, Or Ethno Cultural Struggle + Garment-Workers Union--the Problematic Relationship Between Pesotta, Rose and the Los Angeles Ilgwu, Calif Hist, Vol 0072, 93; Woman From Spillertown--a Memoir of Wieck, Agnes, Burns, Labor Hist, Vol 0034, 93; The Conundrum of Class--Public Discourse on the Social Order in America, J Amer Hist, Vol 0083, 96; American Exceptionalism--a Double Edged Sword, J Soc Hist, Vol 0031, 97. **CONTACT ADDRESS** Dept of Hist, Univ of Calif Los, Los Angeles, CA, 90024.

LASS, WILLIAM EDWARD
PERSONAL Born 11/27/1928, Beresford, SD, m, 1955, 2 children **DISCIPLINE** AMERICAN HISTORY **EDUCATION** Univ SDak, BA, 51, MA, 54; Univ Wis, PhD, 60. **CAREER** Asst prof hist, Southwestern State Col, 57-60; from asst prof to assoc prof, 60-66, chmn dept, 73-80, PROF HIST, MANKATO STATE UNIV, 66-, DIR, SOUTHERN MINN HIST CTR, 69-, Nebr Hist Soc Woods fel Nebr hist, 61-63; Minn Hist Soc pub affairs fel, 71-72. **MEMBERSHIPS** Western Hist Asn; Orgn Am Historians; Am Asn State and Local Hist. **RESEARCH** Frontier transportation; Minnesota history. **SELECTED PUBLICATIONS** Auth, The Iron Horse and the Constitution--the Railroads and the Transformation of the 14th Amendment, J Amer Hist, Vol 0081, 94; Norwegian Yankee--Nelson,Knute and the Failure of American Politics, 1860-1923 , J Amer Hist, Vol 0082, 96; The Man Who Found the Money--Kennedy, John, Stewart and the Financing of the Western Railroads, Western Hist Quart, Vol 0028, 97. **CONTACT ADDRESS** Dept of Hist, Mankato State Univ, Mankato, MN, 56001.

LATEINER, DONALD
PERSONAL Born 06/01/1944, New Rochelle, NY, m, 1 child **DISCIPLINE** CLASSICAL STUDIES, ANCIENT HISTORY **EDUCATION** Univ Chicago, BA, 65; Cornell Univ, MA, 67; Stanford Univ, MA, 70, PhD(classics), 72. **CAREER** Lectr hist, San Francisco State Col, 68-69; acting asst prof classics, Stanford Univ, 71-72; asst prof class studies, Univ PA, 72-79; asst prof, 79-82, Assoc Prof Humanities-Classics, 82-85, prof, 85-92, JOHN WRIGHT PROF GREEK & HUMANITIES, OH WESLEYAN UNIV, 93-. **HONORS AND AWARDS** Am School of Classical Studies @ Athens, Seymour fel, 69-70; Center for Hellenic Studies, Washington, D.C., vis Sr Scholar, 99. **MEMBERSHIPS** Am Philol Asn; Am Asn Ancient Historians; Archaeol Inst Am; Friends Ancient Hist. **RESEARCH** Greek epic; nonverbal behaviors in ancient lit; Greek historiography; Latin elegy; Greek oratory. **SELECTED PUBLICATIONS** Auth, The Speech of Teutiaplus, Greek, Roman & Byzantine Studies, 75; Tissaphernes and the Phoenician fleet, Trans Am Philol Asn, 76; Obscenity in Catullus, Ramus, 77; No Laughing Matter: A Lterary Tactic in Herodotus, Trans Am Philol Asn, 77; An Analysis of Lysias' Defense Speeches, Rivista Storica dell' Antichita, 81; The Historical Method of Herodotus, Tornto, 89; The Failure of the Ionian Revolt, Historia, 82; Mimetic Syntax: Metaphor from World Order, Am J of Philol, 90; Sardonic Smile, Nonverbal Behavior in Homeric Epic, Ann Arbor, 95. **CONTACT ADDRESS** Dept of Humanities-Classics, Ohio Wesleyan Univ, 61 S Sandusky St, Delaware, OH, 43015-2398. **EMAIL** dglatein@cc.owu.edu

LATHAM, MICHAEL E.
DISCIPLINE AMERICAN HISTORY **EDUCATION** UCLA, PhD, **CAREER** Asst prof, Fordham Univ. **RESEARCH** Intellectual hist. **SELECTED PUBLICATIONS** Co-ed, Knowledge and Postmodernism in Historical Perspective, Routledge, 95 **CONTACT ADDRESS** Dept of Hist, Fordham Univ, 113 W 60th St, New York, NY, 10023.

LATNER, RICHARD BARNETT
PERSONAL Born 03/04/1944, New York, NY, m, 1974 **DISCIPLINE** AMERICAN HISTORY **EDUCATION** Swarthmore Col, BA, 65; Univ Wis, MA, 67, PhD(hist), 72. **CAREER** Asst prof hist, Univ Mich, 70-74; assoc ed Mich hist, Mich Hist Div Dept State, Mich, 74-75; asst prof, 75-78, ASSOC PROF HIST, NEWCOMB COL, TULANE UNIV, 78-, DIR AM STUDIES, 80-, Nat Endowment Humanities fel, 79-80. **MEMBERSHIPS** Orgn Am Historians; Southern Hist Asn; Am Studies Asn. **RESEARCH** Jacksonian political history; political issues involving slavery. **SELECTED PUBLICATIONS** Auth, The Papers of Jackson, Andrew, Vol 3, 1814-1815, J Southern Hist, Vol 0059, 93; Liberty and Power--the Politics of Jacksonian America, J Southern Hist, Vol 0059, 93; The Papers of Jackson, Andrew, Vol 4, 1816-1820, J Southern Hist, Vol 0061, 95; Principle and Interest--Jefferson, Thomas and the Problem of Debt, Amer Hist Rev, Vol 0102, 97. **CONTACT ADDRESS** Dept of Hist, Tulane Univ, 6823 St Charles Ave, New Orleans, LA, 70118-5698.

LATOUSEK, ROB
PERSONAL Born 07/10/1956, Evanston, IL **DISCIPLINE** CLASSICS **EDUCATION** Holy Cross Col, BA, 78; Loyola Univ, Chicago, MA, 85. **CAREER** Univ Wisconsin, Madison, proj asst, 86-88, Centaur Systems Ltd, Pres, 84-. **HONORS AND AWARDS** HCC, Bean Scholarship, 74-78, Loyola Univ., Condon Fel, 82-84 **MEMBERSHIPS** APA, ACL, CAMS **RESEARCH** Classical computing **SELECTED PUBLICATIONS** Auth, Software Directory for the Classics, ACL, 93-95, Random Access, Classical Outlook, ACL, 89-, Survey of latin Instructional Software for the Microcomputer, ACL, 85-91, software pub, Tutrix, 88; Latin Vocab Drill, 87; Latin Flash Drill, 85; Centaur Sys Ltd. **CONTACT ADDRESS** Centaur Systems Ltd, 407 North Brearly St, Madison, WI, 53703-1603. **EMAIL** Latousek@centaursystems.com

LATTIMORE, STEVEN
PERSONAL Born 05/25/1938, Bryn Mawr, PA **DISCIPLINE** CLASSICS, CLASSICAL ARCHEOLOGY **EDUCATION** Dartmouth Col, AB, 60; Princeton Univ, MA, 64, PhD(class archaeol), 68. **CAREER** Instr class archaeol, Dartmouth Col, 64; instr Greek, Haverford Col, 65-66; asst prof classics and class archaeol, Intercol Ctr Class Studies, Rome, 66-67; asst prof, 67-74, ASSOC PROF CLASSICS, UNIV CALIF, LOS ANGELES, 74-, Guggenheim Found fel, 75-76. **MEMBERSHIPS** Archaeol Inst Am; Am Philol Asn. **RESEARCH** Classical sculpture; Greek literature; mythology. **SELECTED PUBLICATIONS** Auth, The 'Odyssey' and Ancient Art--an Epic in Word and Image, Class World, Vol 0087, 94; Proc Int Symp on the Olympic Games, 5-9 September 1988, Class World, Vol 0089, 96; The Chariot Racers on the Francois Vase, Amer J Archaeol, Vol 0101, 97. **CONTACT ADDRESS** Dept of Classics, Univ of Calif, Los Angeles, CA, 90024.

LAUBER, JACK M.
PERSONAL Born 10/08/1934, Archbold, OH, m, 1964, 2 children **DISCIPLINE** MODERN HISTORY **EDUCATION** Bowling Green State Univ, BSEd, 59, MA, 60; Univ Iowa, PhD(Russ hist), 67. **CAREER** Instr Russia and western civiliation, Ohio State Univ, 64-67; asst prof, 67-69, assoc prof, 69-77, PROF RUSS HIST, UNIV WIS-EAU CLAIRE, 77-. **MEMBERSHIPS** Conf Slavic and East Europ Hist; Am Asn Advan Slavic Studies; Am Soc 18th Century Studies. **RESEARCH** Russian socioeconomic history of the 18th century; Russian revolutionary history of the 19th century. **SELECTED PUBLICATIONS** Auth, A History of Singapore, Historian, Vol 0056, 93; Paul I of Russia, 1754-1801, Historian, Vol 0056, 93. **CONTACT ADDRESS** Dept of Hist, Univ of Wis, Eau Claire, WI, 54701.

LAUDON, ROBERT TALLANT
PERSONAL Born 12/30/1920, St. Paul, MN **DISCIPLINE** MUSICOLOGY AND MUSIC **EDUCATION** Univ Minn, BA, 47, MA, 50; Univ Ill, PhD, 69. **CAREER** Assoc Prof, Jamestown Col, 52-55; Asst Prof, St Cloud State Col, 55-62; Prof, Univ Minn, 62-86, Prof Emeritus, 86- . **HONORS AND AWARDS** BA magna cum laude, Phi Beta Kappa; Pi Kappa Phi; Pi Kappa Lambda; Phi Mu Alpha Sinfonia. **MEMBERSHIPS** Am Musicol Soc; Minn Mus Tchr Assoc; Nat Mus Tchr Assn; Minn Hist Soc. **RESEARCH** 19th-century symphony; Minn music and musicians. **SELECTED PUBLICATIONS** Symphonic Genres, Current Musicol, 78; Sources of the Wagnerian Synthesis, Munich, 79; Eduard Sobolewski, Frontier Kapellmeister, Mus Quart, 89; Visual Image and Couperin's Harpsichord Music, Alexander L Ringer Festschrift, 91; Debate about Consecutive Fifths, A Context for Brahm's Manuscript, Music and Letters, 92. **CONTACT ADDRESS** 924-18th Ave SE, Minneapolis, MN, 55414. **EMAIL** laudo001@maroon.tc.umn.edu

LAUGHLIN, JOHN C.H.
PERSONAL Born 09/05/1942, Asheboro, NC, m, 1965, 1 child **DISCIPLINE** HEBREW BIBLE STUDIES, NEAR EASTERN ANTHROPOLOGY AND PHILOSOPHY **EDUCATION** Wake Forest Univ, BA, Greek, 67; Southern Bapt Theol Sem, M Div, 71; PhD, 75. **CAREER** Pastor, Col Ave Bapt Church, Bluefield, WV, 75-76; asst prof relig, Hardin-Simmons Univ, Abilene, TX, 76-77; asst prof relig, Palm Beach Atlantic Col, West Palm Beach, Fla, 77-79; prof relig and cha, dept relig, Averett Col, Danville, Va, 79-. **MEMBERSHIPS** Nat Asn Bapt Prof of Relig; Amer Sch of Oriental Res; Soc of Bibl Lit; Bibl Archaeo Soc. **RESEARCH** Archaeology and the Bible; Near Eastern Archaeology; Biblical Studies. **SELECTED PUBLICATIONS** Articles, Mercer Dict of the Bible, 90; Capernaum from Jesus' Time and After, Bibl Archaeol Rev, 54-61, 90, 93; Joshua, Mercer Commentary on the Bible, 95; Israel and the Liberation of Canaan, Joseph A. Callaway's Faces of the Old Testament, Mercer Univ Press, 95; Digging Archaeology, The Bibl Illusr, fall, 97; Samaria the Strong, The Bibl Illusr, fall, 98. **CONTACT ADDRESS** Averett Col, 420 W. Main St., Danville, VA, 24541. **EMAIL** laughlin@averett.edu

LAUMAKIS, STEPHEN J.
DISCIPLINE MEDIEVAL PHILOSOPHY: ST. THOMAS AQUINAS **EDUCATION** St. Charles Sem, BA, 82; Villanova Univ, MA, 84; Univ Notre Dame, PhD, 91. **CAREER** Phil, St. John Vianney Col Sem **MEMBERSHIPS** MN Philos Soc; Am Philos Asn; Am Catholic Philos Asn; Soc Christian Philos. **SELECTED PUBLICATIONS** Auth, Is Christian Science Possible?,Science & Theology, Univ St Thomas, 96; The Role of Chance in the Philosophy of Teilhard De Chardin, Villanova Univ, 84. **CONTACT ADDRESS** St. John Vianney Col Sem, 2115 Summit Ave, St Paul, MN, 55105-1095.

LAUREN, PAUL GORDON
PERSONAL Born 02/17/1946, Seattle, WA, m, 1967, 2 children **DISCIPLINE** HISTORY **EDUCATION** Wash State Univ, BA, 68; Stanford Univ, MA, 69, PhD(Hist & Polit Sci), 73. **CAREER** Asst prof, 74-77, from assoc prof to prof Hist, Univ Mont, 78-82; Regents prof, 91-; Peace fel Hist, Hoover Inst & Stanford Univ, 73-74; vis asst prof Hist, Stanford Univ, 74; vis assoc prof Hist, Stanford Univ, 79 & 82; Rockefeller Found Humanities fel, 80. **HONORS AND AWARDS** Disting Expert, UN, 90; CASE Prof of Year, Montana, 91; Harris Fel, Rotary Int, 94; Sen Fulbright Scholar, 94; Disting Am Scholar, Fulbright, 97. **MEMBERSHIPS** AHA; Int Studies Asn. **RESEARCH** European diplomatic history; national security and peace research; the Cold War. **SELECTED PUBLICATIONS** Auth, Human Rights in History: Diplomacy and Racial Equality, In: Diplomatic History, 78; ed, Diplomatic History: New Approaches, Free Press Macmillan, 79; Crisis Management: History and Theory, In: International History Review, 79; Crisis Management: An Assessment, J Conflict Resolution, 80; Destinies Shared, Westview, 89; Kokka to Jinshuhenken, TBS Britannica, 95; Power and Prejudice, 2nd ed, HarperCollins, 96; Between Pandemonium and Order, In: Am Behavioral Scientist, 96; The Evolution of International Human Rights: Visions Seen, Univ Penn Press, 98. **CONTACT ADDRESS** Dept of History, Univ of Montana, Missoula, MT, 59812-0001.

LAURENT, JANE KATHERINE
PERSONAL Born 08/03/1947, Gainesville, FL, m, 1982, 2 children **DISCIPLINE** RENAISSANCE & EUROPEAN SOCIAL HISTORY **EDUCATION** Univ Ga, BA, 68, MA, 70; Brown Univ, PhD, 76. **CAREER** Adj prof, Univ Fla, 76-79; Asst prof, 79-85, ASSOC PROF HIST, UNIV NC CHARLOTTE, 79-. **MEMBERSHIPS** AHA; Renaissance Soc Am; Southeastern Medieval-Renaissance Asn; Southern Hist Asn. **RESEARCH** Political history of Renaissance city-states; agricultural history: 1300-1600. **SELECTED PUBLICATIONS** Auth, The signory and its supporters: The este of Ferrara, J Medieval Hist, 77; Feudalesimo e la signoria, Arch Storico Ital, 79; The exiles and the signory: The case of Ferrara, J Medieval & Renaissance Studies, 81; Patterns of agrarian control in fourteenth century Ferrara, Peasant Studies, 82. **CONTACT ADDRESS** Hist Dept, Univ of N. Carolina, 9201 University City, Charlotte, NC, 28223-0002. **EMAIL** jklauren@email.uncc.edu

LAURENT, PIERRE HENRI
PERSONAL Born 05/15/1933, Fall River, MA, m, 1958, 4 children **DISCIPLINE** MODERN EUROPEAN DIPLOMATIC AND FRENCH HISTORY **EDUCATION** Colgate Univ, AB, 56; Boston Univ, AM, 60, PhD(hist), 64. **CAREER** Instr polit econ and hist, Boston Univ, 61-64; asst prof hist, Sweet Briar Col, 64-66; vis asst prof, Univ Wis-Madison, 66-67; from asst prof to assoc prof, Tulane Univ, 67-70 assoc prof, 70-75, PROF HIST, TUFTS UNIV, 75-, Fel, Belgium-Am Educ Found, 62; vis prof, Northwestern Univ, 65; NATO res fel humanities, 67; Nat Endowment for Humanities fel, 69; Tufts Univ fac res award, 71; adj prof, Fletcher Sch Law and Diplomacy, 75-; Found Paul-Henri Spaak fel, 77-78; mem col bd adv, Europ Hist Placement Exam, 78-82. **MEMBERSHIPS** AHA; Soc Fr Hist Studies; Am Comt Hist 2nd World War; Inst Rel Int Belgium. **RESEARCH** History of the Lowlands; modern France; comtemporary Europe. **SELECTED PUBLICATIONS** Auth, The European Rescue of the Nation State, Amer Hist Rev, Vol 0098, 93; The Action of the King in Belgium Since 1831--Power and Influence--a Typological Study of Royal Modes of Action, Amer Hist Rev, Vol 0099, 94. **CONTACT ADDRESS** Tufts Univ, Medford, MA, 02155.

LAURIE, BRUCE
PERSONAL Born 03/01/1943, Elizabeth, NJ, m, 1 child **DISCIPLINE** U.S. HISTORY **EDUCATION** Rutgers Univ, BA, 65; Univ Pittsburgh, MA, 67, PhD, 71. **CAREER** From asst prof to prof, Univ of Mass., 71-. **HONORS AND AWARDS** Phi Beta Kappa **MEMBERSHIPS** Orgn of Am Hists; Am Hist Asn; Soc Sci Hist Asn. **RESEARCH** U.S. Labor & Politics. **SELECTED PUBLICATIONS** Auth, Working People of Philadelphia, 1800-1850, 80; Artisans into Workers: Labor in Nineteenth Century America, 89; coauth, Labor Histories, 98. **CONTACT ADDRESS** Dept of History, Amherst, MA, 01003. **EMAIL** Laurie@History.umass.edu

LAURITSEN, FREDERICK MICHAEL
PERSONAL Born 03/10/1938, Montevideo, MN, m, 1968, 2 children **DISCIPLINE** ANCIENT HISTORY **EDUCATION** Univ Minn, Minneapolis, BA, 61, MA, 65, PhD(hist), 73. **CAREER** Librn, Winona State Col, 65-67 & Univ Iowa, 67-69; from asst prof to assoc prof, 69-80; prof hist, Eastern Wash Univ, 80-, Mem, Brit Inst Archaeol Ankara, 68-; numis consult, Cheney Cowles State Mem Mus, Spokane, 74-. **MEMBERSHIPS** Archaeol Inst Am; Am Numis Soc; Am Orient Soc; fel Royal Numis Soc. **RESEARCH** Numismatics; cuneiform studies. **SELECTED PUBLICATIONS** Auth, Rare nineteenth-century Latin American periodicals, Bks Iowa, 11/69. **CONTACT ADDRESS** Dept of Hist, Eastern Washington Univ, M/S 27, Cheney, WA, 99004-2496. **EMAIL** flauritsene@ewu.edu

LAURSEN, JOHN CHRISTIAN
DISCIPLINE POLITICAL THEORY **EDUCATION** Harvard Univ, JD, 77; Johns Hopkins Univ, PhD, 85. **CAREER** Prof polit sci, Univ Calif, Riverside. **SELECTED PUBLICATIONS** Auth, The Politics of Skepticism: in the Ancients, Montaigne, Hume, and Kant, Leiden, 92; ed, New Essays on the Political Thought of the Huguenots of the Refuge, Leiden, 95; co-ed, Difference and Dissent: Theories of Toleration in Medieval and Early Modern Europe, Rowman & Littlefield, 96; co-ed, Beyond the Persecuting Society: Religious Toleration Before the Enlightenment, Univ Pa Press, 98. **CONTACT ADDRESS** Dept Polit Sci, Univ Calif, Riverside, CA, 92521. **EMAIL** Laursen@wizard.ucr.edu

LAUSHEY, DAVID MASON
PERSONAL Born 01/30/1934, Colonial Heights, VA, m, 1958, 3 children **DISCIPLINE** HISTORY OF MODERN INDIA **EDUCATION** Univ Va, BSEd, 61, MA, 63, PhD(hist of India), 69. **CAREER** Asst prof hist, Midwestern Univ, 65-68; asst prof, 68-76, ASSOC PROF HIST, GA STATE UNIV, 76-. **MEMBERSHIPS** Asn Asian Studies. **RESEARCH** Terrorism and Marxism in Bengal. **SELECTED PUBLICATIONS** Auth, The New Cambridge History of India, Vol 3, Pt 4, Ideologies of the Raj, Hist, Vol 0058, 96. **CONTACT ADDRESS** Dept of Hist, Georgia State Univ, Atlanta, GA, 30303.

LAUX, JAMES MICHAEL
PERSONAL Born 11/04/1927, La Crosse, WI, m, 1952, 3 children **DISCIPLINE** HISTORY **EDUCATION** Univ Wis, BS, 50; Univ Conn, MA, 52; Northwestern Univ, PhD, 57. **CAREER** Instr hist, Wis State Col, La Crosse, 55-57; from asst prof to assoc prof, 57-69, PROF HIST, UNIV CINCINNATI, 69-, Vis assoc prof, Northwestern Univ, 66-67; vis prof hist, Ohio State Univ, 69. **MEMBERSHIPS** AHA; Soc Fr Hist Studies; Soc Automotive Historians. **RESEARCH** France since 1789; French economic history; auto and aviation history. **SELECTED PUBLICATIONS** Auth, The Right Wing in France (transl, Remond, La droite en France), Univ Pa, 66; co-ed, French Revolution: Conflicting Interpretations, Random, 68, 76; Rise and fall of Armand Deperdussin, Fr Hist Studies, spring 73; In First Gear, McGill-Queen's, 76; coauth, La Revolution Automobile, Albin Michel, Paris, 77; auth, Gnome et Rhone in 1914-1918, L'Autre Front, Ed Ouvrieres, 77; auth, Economic History of the Third Republic, Third Republic/ Traisieme Rapublique, spring 78; coauth, Steaming through New England with Locomobile, J Transport Hist, 9/79; transl, as the Automobile Revolution, Univ NC Press, 82. **CONTACT ADDRESS** Dept of Hist, Univ of Cincinnati, Cincinnati, OH, 45221.

LAVERY, GERARD B.
PERSONAL Born 02/03/1933, Brooklyn, NY **DISCIPLINE** CLASSICAL LANGUAGES **EDUCATION** Fordham Univ, AB, 55, MA, 56, PhD(classics), 65. **CAREER** Asst prof, 61-72, ASSOC PROF CLASS LANG, COL OF THE HOLY CROSS, 72-, Batchelor Ford fac fel, 69. **MEMBERSHIPS** Am Philol Asn; AAUP. **RESEARCH** Plutarch; Roman history and politics; Lucretius. **SELECTED PUBLICATIONS** Auth, Plutarch 'Lucullus' and the Living Bond of Biog, Class J, Vol 0089, 94; Never Seen in Public--Seneca and the Limits of Cosmopolitanism, Latomus, Vol 0056, 97. **CONTACT ADDRESS** Col of the Holy Cross, Box 89 A, Worcester, MA, 01610.

LAVIN, DAVID E.
PERSONAL Born 09/28/1931, New York, NY, m, 1997, 3 children **DISCIPLINE** SOCIOLOGY OF EDUCATION **EDUCATION** New York Univ, PhD, 66. **CAREER** Res fel in social relations, Harvard U, 60-62; asst to assoc prof, Univ Pa, 62-70; PROF, CITY UNIV GRAD SCH AND LOHMAN COL, 70- . **MEMBERSHIPS** Am Sociol Asoc; Eastern Sociol Asoc; Am Educ Res Asoc. **RESEARCH** Education and Social Inequality **SELECTED PUBLICATIONS** auth, Right vs. Privilege: Open Admissions Experiment at City University of New York, 81; Changing the Odds: Open Admissions and Life Chances of the Disadvantaged, 96. **CONTACT ADDRESS** Graduate Sch and Univ Ctr, CUNY, 33 W 42nd St., New York, NY, 10036. **EMAIL** delbh@cunyum.cuny.edu

LAWALL, GILBERT WESTCOTT
PERSONAL Born 09/22/1936, Detroit, MI, m, 1957, 2 children **DISCIPLINE** CLASSICS **EDUCATION** Oberlin Col, AB, 57; Yale Univ, PhD, 61. **CAREER** Instr classics, Yale Univ, 61-63 & 64-65, jr fel, Ctr Hellenic Studies, 63-64; asst prof classics, Amherst Col, 65-67; from asst prof to assoc prof, 67-72, PROF CLASSICS, UNIV MA, AMHERST, 72-. **HONORS AND AWARDS** Barlow-Beach Award Distinguished Serv, Class Asn New England, 79; Oustanding contrib For Lang Educ, Class Asn Empire State, 79. **MEMBERSHIPS** Am Philol Asn; Class Asn New Eng (vpres, 72-73, secy-treas, 80-87); Vergilian Soc; Archaeol Inst Am; Am Class League (pres,

76-80). **RESEARCH** Hellenistic Greek poetry; Senecan tragedy; Catullus; Horace; Latin pedagogy. **SELECTED PUBLICATIONS** Auth, Theocritus' Coan Pastorals: A Poetry Book, Ctr Hellenic Studies, 67; The green cabinet and the pastoral design: Theocritus, Euripides, and Tibullus, Ramus: Critical Studies Greek & Roman Lit, 75 & In: Ancient Pastoral: Ramus Essays on Greek and Roman Pastoral Poetry, Aureal, Melbourne, 75; Herodas 6 and 7 reconsidered, Class Philol, 76; Teaching the classics in England and America today and some thoughts for the future, Class Outlook, 78; The Phaedra of Seneca: Latin Text and Study Materials, Bolchazy-Carducci Publ, 81; Death and perspective in Seneca's Troades, Class J, No 77, 82; Petronius: Selections from the Satyricon: Introduction, Notes, and Vocabulary by Gilbert Lawall, Bolchazy-Carducci Pubs, 75, large type, MA Dept of Ed, Div Special Ed, Vision Resources Lib, 79, 2nd rev ed, 80, 3rd rev ed, 95; Plautus' Menaechmi: ed with Introduction and Running Vocabularies by Gilbert Lawall and Betty Nye Quinn, Bolchazy-Carducci Pubs, Chicago, 81; Euripides Hippolytus: A Companion and Translation by Gilbert and Sarah Lawall, Bristol Classical Press, 86; ed and coauth, Cicero's Somnium Scipionis: The Dream of Scipio, Sally Davis and Gilbert Lawall, Longman Inc, 88; The Aulularia of Plautus: The Pot of Gold, Gilbert Lawall and Betty Nye Quinn, Longman Inc, 88; ed, The Romans Speak for Themselves: Books I and II, Longman Inc, 89, rev ed, 95; coauth, Maurice Balme and Gilbert Lawall, Athenaze: An Introduction to Ancient Greek, Book I, NY: Oxford Univ Press, 90, Book II, NY: Oxford Univ Press, 91; coauth rev, Fabulae Graecae: A Revised Edition of Richie's Fabulae Faciles, ed by Gilbert Lawall, Stanley Iverson, and Allen Wooley, White Plains, NY: Longman Inc, 91; coauth rev and ed with David Perry, Fabulae Romanae: Stories of Famous Romans, White Plains, NY: Longman Inc, 93; chief rev ed, Ecce Romani: A Latin Reading Program, 2nd ed, Longman Inc, 95. **CONTACT ADDRESS** Dept of Classics, Univ Massachusetts, Amherst, MA, 01003-3905. **EMAIL** glawall@classics.umass.edu

LAWES, CAROLYN J.
DISCIPLINE HISTORY **EDUCATION** Univ Calif at Santa Clara, BA, 80; Univ Calif at Davis, MA, 84; PhD, 92. **CAREER** Assoc instr, hist, Univ Calif at Davis; current, ASST PROF, HIST, OLD DOMINION UNIV. **MEMBERSHIPS** Am Antiquarian Soc **SELECTED PUBLICATIONS** Auth, "Trifling with Holy Time: Women and the Formation of the Calvinist Church of Worcester, Massachusetts," Rel & Am Cult, Winter 98. **CONTACT ADDRESS** Dept of Hist, Old Dominion Univ, Norfolk, VA, 23529-0091.

LAWHEAD, WILLIAM F.
DISCIPLINE HISTORY OF PHILOSOPHY, PHILOSOPHY OF RELIGION **EDUCATION** Wheaton Col, BA; Univ TX, Austin, PhD. **CAREER** Prof, Univ MS, 80-. **RESEARCH** God and time. **SELECTED PUBLICATIONS** Auth, The Voyage of Discovery: A History of Western Philosophy, Wadsworth Publ Co, 96. **CONTACT ADDRESS** Univ MS, Oxford, MS, 38677. **EMAIL** wlawhead@olemiss.edu

LAWSON-PEEBLES, ROBERT
DISCIPLINE ENGLISH, AMERICAN STUDIES **EDUCATION** Sussex, BA, 75; MA, 76; Oxford, DPhil, 83. **CAREER** Lect, SR LECT, ENG & AM STUD, UNIV EXETER **MEMBERSHIPS** Am Antiquarian Soc **SELECTED PUBLICATIONS** Auth, Landscape and Written Expression in Revolutionary America, Cambridge Univ Press, 88; co-ed, Views of American Landscapes, Cambridge Univ Press, 89; auth, "Some Approaches to American Amplitude," Renaissance & Mod Stud 35, 92; auth, "America as Interpreted by Foreign Observers," in Encyclopedia of American Social History, Scribner, 93; auth, "Property, Marriage, Women, and Fenimore Cooper's First Fictions," in James Fenimore Cooper: New Historical and Literary Contexts, Editions Rodopi, 93; co-ed, Modern American Landscapes, in European Contributions to American Studies 26, VU Univ Press, 95; ed, Approaches to the American Musical, Exeter Univ Press, 96. **CONTACT ADDRESS** Sch of Eng & Am Stud, Univ of Exeter, Queen's Bldg, Exeter, ., EX4 4QH. **EMAIL** r.lawson-peebles@exeter.ac.uk

LAWTON, CAROL
PERSONAL Born 03/21/1949, Cumberland, MD, m, 1984 **DISCIPLINE** ART HISTORY **EDUCATION** Vassar Col, BA, 71; Univ Pittsburgh, MA, 72; Princeton Univ, MA, 75, Phd, 84. **CAREER** Instr to asst prof to assoc prof, chair, curator, 80-, Lawrence Univ; vis assoc prof, UC Berkeley, 86; Elizabeth Whitehead vis prof, Amer Sch of Classical Stud, Athens, 99-00. **HONORS AND AWARDS** NDEA Title IV Fel, 71-73; Kress Found Fel, 74; Vanderpool Fel, Amer Sch Athens, 77; Lawrence Univ Young Teacher Award, 82; Amer Philos Soc Grant, 85, 94; J Paul Getty Postdoctoral Fel, 87-88; NEH Sr Fel, 95-96; Solow Found Summer Res Fel, 98; Freshman Stud Teaching Award, 98. **MEMBERSHIPS** Archaeol Inst of Amer; Col Art Assoc. **RESEARCH** Greek sculpture, classical archaeol. **SELECTED PUBLICATIONS** Auth, An Attic Document Relief in the Walters Art Gallery, J of the Walters Art Gallery, 93; auth, Four Document Reliefs from the Athenian Agora, Hesperia, 95; ed, Bearers of Meaning: the Ottilia Buerger collection of Ancient and Byzantine Coins, Lawrence Univ Press, 95; auth, Attic Document Reliefs: Art and Politics in Ancient Athens, Oxford Univ Press, 95; auth, Votive Reliefs and Popular Religion in the Athenian Agora: the Case of Asklepios and Hygieia, Proceedings of the XVth Int Cong of Classical Archaeol, Amsterdam, 98. **CONTACT ADDRESS** Art Dept, Lawrence Univ, Appleton, WI, 54912. **EMAIL** carol.l.lawton@lawrence.edu

LAYTON, EDWIN THOMAS
DISCIPLINE HISTORY **EDUCATION** Univ Calif Los Angeles, PhD. **CAREER** Prof **HONORS AND AWARDS** Dexter Prize, 71., Pres, Soc Hist Tech, 85-86; pres, Am Asn Advancement Sci, 89-91. **RESEARCH** History of the engineering profession in France, England, and America; impact of Newtonian science on technology and invention in America; impact of technology on society and its ethical implications. **SELECTED PUBLICATIONS** Auth, Revolt of the Engineers, Social Responsibility and the American Engineering Profession, John Hopkins, 86; ed, Mirror Image Twins, the Communities of Science and Technology in 19th-Century America, Harper and Row, 73; co-ed, The Dynamics of Science and Technology, Reidel, 78. **CONTACT ADDRESS** History Dept, Univ of Minnesota, Twin Cities, 614 Social Sciences Tower, 267 19th Ave S, Minneapolis, MN, 55455. **EMAIL** layto001@tc.umn.edu

LAZAREVICH, GORDANA
PERSONAL Belgrade, Yugoslavia **DISCIPLINE** MUSIC **EDUCATION** Univ Toronto, Art & Lic dipl, 60; Juilliard Sch Music, BS, 62, MS, 64; Columbia Univ, PhD, 70. **CAREER** Instr, Barnard Col, 69-71; asst prof, 71-74, Columbia Univ; asst prof, 74-76, assoc prof, 76-83, PROF MUSICOLOGY, UNIV VICTORIA, 83-, dean grad stud, 92-97. **MEMBERSHIPS** Mem, SSHRC Adjudicating Ctte Art Hist; Soc 18th Century Studs; Can Asn Univs Schs Music; Can Univ Music Soc; Can Fedn Hum. **SELECTED PUBLICATIONS** Auth, The Musical World of Frances James and Murray Adaskin, 88. **CONTACT ADDRESS** 1557 Orelton Pl, Victoria, BC, V8N 5S7.

LAZZERINI, EDWARD JAMES
PERSONAL Born 09/14/1943, Hartford, CT, m, 1966, 1 child **DISCIPLINE** HISTORY **EDUCATION** Trinity Col, BA, 65; Fordham Univ, MA, 67; Univ Wash, PhD(hist), 73. **CAREER** Asst prof, 73-80, ASSOC PROF HIST, UNIV NEW ORLEANS, 80-. **MEMBERSHIPS** Am Asn Advan Slavic Studies; AHA; Asn Studies Nationalities. **RESEARCH** Late Imperial Russian history; history of the Russian Islamic community. **SELECTED PUBLICATIONS** Auth, Russia Muslim Frontiers--New Directions in Cross Cultural Analysis, Slavic Rev, Vol 0054, 95; Muslim Resistance to the Tsar--Shamil and the Conquest of Chechnia and Daghestan, Russ Rev, Vol 0054, 95. **CONTACT ADDRESS** Dept of Hist, Univ New Orleans Lakefront, New Orleans, LA, 70148.

LE GOFF, T.J.A.
PERSONAL Born 12/12/1942, Vancouver, BC, Canada **DISCIPLINE** HISTORY **EDUCATION** Univ BC, BA, 65; Univ Col London, PhD, 70. **CAREER** Lectr to asst prof, 69-73, ASSOC PROF HISTORY, YORK UNIV, 73-; lectr, Univ Reading (UK), 79-80; vis prof, Univ Laval, 83; vis fel, Balliol Col, Oxford, 83-84; vis prof, Col France, 91. **HONORS AND AWARDS** WK Ferguson Prize, Can Hist Asn, 84; Keith Matthews Prize, Can Nautical Res Soc, 87; fel, Royal Hist Soc, 95. **MEMBERSHIPS** Soc Fr Hist Stud; Soc d'hist moderne et contemporaine; Can Hist Asn. **SELECTED PUBLICATIONS** Auth, Vannes and its Region: A Study of Town and Country in Eighteenth Century France, 81; ed bd, Fr Hist Stud, 81-83; ed bd, Fr Hist, 86-; ed bd, Histoire sociale/Social History, 87-91. **CONTACT ADDRESS** Dept of History, York Univ, 4700 Keele St, North York, ON, M3J 1P3.

LEAB, DANIEL JOSEF
PERSONAL Born 08/29/1936, Berlin, Germany, m, 1964, 3 children **DISCIPLINE** AMERICAN HISTORY **EDUCATION** Columbia Univ, BA, 57, MA, 61, PhD(hist), 69. **CAREER** From instr to asst prof hist, Columbia Univ, 66-74, assoc dean, Columbia Col, 69-71, asst dean fac, univ, 71, spec asst, exec vpres and provost, 73-74; assoc prof, 74-79, PROF HIST, SETON HALL UNIV, 79-, DIR, AM STUDIES, 74-, Consult, Atomic Energy Comn, 72-73; contrib ed, Columbia Jour Rev, 74-78 and Atlas World Press Rev, 74-78; ed, Labor Hist, 74-; Fulbright Sr lectureship, Univ Cologne, Ger, 76; mem exec comt, Univ Sem, 76-; Nat Endowment for Humanities fel, 81. **MEMBERSHIPS** AHA; Orgn Am Historians; Labor Hist; Hist Film Comt; Soc for Cinema Studies (secy-treas, 79-). **RESEARCH** Twentieth century United States social and political history; labor history; media history. **SELECTED PUBLICATIONS** Auth, Symposium on Brody, David, Steelworkers in America--the Nonunion Era, and the Beginnings of the New Labor History, Labor Hist, Vol 0034, 93; Price, Clement, 'Liberators' and Truth in History + War Films and African Americans--a Comment, Hist J Film Radio and Television, Vol 0014, 94; Making Movies Black--the Hollywood Message Movie From World War II to the Civil Rights Era, J Amer Hist, Vol 0081, 94; Preface, Labor Hist, Vol 0035, 94; No Surprises, Please--Movies in the Reagan Decade, Hist J Film Radio and Television, Vol 0015, 95; 'In the Name of the Emperor' + Choy,Christine Documentary--War Guilt and the Medium of Film, Hist J Film Radio and Television, Vol 0015, 95; News-workers--Toward a History of the Rank and File, J Amer Hist, Vol 0083, 96; Forging American Communism--the Life of Foster, William, Z., Historian, Vol 0058, 96; Introduction + American Film and Television Archives, Hist J Film Radio and Television, Vol 0016, 96; The Red Menace and Justice in the Pacific-Northwest + Mccarthyism--the 1946 Trial of the Soviet Naval Lieutenant Redin, Nikolai, Gregorevitch, Pac Northwest Quart, Vol 0087, 96; Populism and the Capra Legacy, Hist J Film Radio and Television, Vol 0016, 96; Hollywood Other Blacklist--Union Struggles in the Studio System, Hist J Film Radio and Television, Vol 0017, 97; The Hidden Foundation--Cinema and the Question of Class, Hist J Film Radio and Television, Vol 0017, 97. **CONTACT ADDRESS** Seton Hall Univ, S Orange, NJ, 07079.

LEACH, ELEANOR W.
DISCIPLINE CLASSICAL STUDIES **EDUCATION** Bryn Mawr Col, BA, 59; Yale Univ, PhD, 63. **CAREER** Prof. **RESEARCH** Latin texts. **SELECTED PUBLICATIONS** Auth, Absence and Desire in Cicero's De Amicitia, CW, 93; Oecus on Ibycus: Investigating the Vocabulary of the Roman House, Oxbow, 97. **CONTACT ADDRESS** Dept of Classical Studies, Indiana Univ, Bloomington, 300 N Jordan Ave, Bloomington, IN, 47405.

LEAF, MURRAY JOHN
PERSONAL Born 06/01/1939, New York, NY, m, 1965 **DISCIPLINE** ANTHROPOLOGY **EDUCATION** Reed Col, BA, 61; Univ Chicago, MA, 63, PhD, 66. **CAREER** Asst prof, Anthropology, Pomona Col, 66-67; asst prof, Anthropology, UCLA, 67-75; assoc prof, 75-81, PROF, ANTHROPOLOGY & POLITICAL ECONOMY, UNIV TX, 81-. **MEMBERSHIPS** Am Anthrop Asn; Asn for Asian Studies; Royal Anthrop Inst of Great Britain & Ireland. **RESEARCH** South Asia: politics, social organization, history, and culture-particularly as they affect development; irrigation sociology; irrigation and development; social organization; pragmatism; development; history of social thought. **SELECTED PUBLICATIONS** Auth, Punjabi, The Encyclo of World Cultures Vol III: South Asia, Macmillan Pub Co, 92; Irrigation and Authority in Rajasthan, Ethnology, 92; Agriculture and Farming Systems, The Encycl of Cultural Anthrop, Henry Holt, 96; Local Control Versus Technocracy: The Bangladesh Flood Response Study, J of Int Affairs, Columbia Univ Press, 97; Pragmatism and Development: the Prospect for Pluralist Transformation in the Third World, Bergen and Garvey, 98. **CONTACT ADDRESS** School of Soc Sci, Univ Texas at Dallas, Richardson, TX, 75080.

LEAHY, DAVID G.
DISCIPLINE CLASSICS **EDUCATION** St. Peter's Col, BA, 59; Fordham Univ, MA, 64. **CAREER** Lectr, Iona Col, 63-64; Assoc Prof, NY Univ, 64-72; Assoc Prof, C.W. Post Col LIU, 72-76; Mgt Consult, 76-89; Adj Assoc Prof, Brooklyn Col CUNY, 85-92; Vis Assoc Prof & Dir Undergrad Relig Studies, NY Univ, 91-98; Distinguished Vis Prof Philos, Loyola Col Md, 98-; Vis Assoc Prof, SUNY - Stony Brook, 95. **HONORS AND AWARDS** Scholarship to St. Peter's Col; Nat Oratorical Contest Col & Univ Scholarships; Scholarship to Fordham Univ; NYU Lindback Found Award for Distinguished Teaching; **MEMBERSHIPS** Am Philos Asn; Soc Advancement Am Philos; Am Acad Relig. **SELECTED PUBLICATIONS** Auth, To Create The Absolute Edge, J Am Acad Relig, 89; The New Beginning: Beyond the Post-Modern Nothingness, J Am Acad Relig, 94; Novitas Mundi: Perception of the History of Being, SUNY Press, repr, 94; Foundation: Matter The Body Itself, SUNY Press, 96; The Golden Bowl Structure, Geodesic Math Links, Geodesic Designs, Inc, 96-98 (http://www.geod.com/main/geomath.htm) **CONTACT ADDRESS** 104 Yorkleigh Rd., Towson, MD, 21204. **EMAIL** dgl@dgleahy.com

LEAHY, MARGARET E.
DISCIPLINE INTERNATIONAL RELATIONS THEORY, INTERNATIONAL POLITICAL ECONOMY, THIRD WORL **EDUCATION** San Francisco State Univ, BA, MA; Univ Southern CA, PhD. **CAREER** Assoc prof, ch, dept Soc Sci and Int Rel, Golden Gate Univ. **MEMBERSHIPS** Exec comt, Int Stud Asn. **SELECTED PUBLICATIONS** Auth, Development Strategies and the Status of Women; The Harassment of Nicaraguanists and Fellow Travelers. **CONTACT ADDRESS** Golden Gate Univ, San Francisco, CA, 94105-2968.

LEAMON, JAMES SHENSTONE
PERSONAL Born 12/09/1930, Melrose, MA **DISCIPLINE** AMERICAN COLONIAL HISTORY **EDUCATION** Bates Col, BA, 55; Brown Univ, PhD, 61. **CAREER** Inst hist, Wartburg Col, 60-61; asst prof, Lebanon Valley Col, 61-64; from asst prof to assoc prof, 64-77, Prof Hist, Bates Col, 77-. **MEMBERSHIPS** Orgn Am Historians; Coun for NE Hist Archaeol; Maine Hist Soc; New Eng Hist Asn; Orgn of Am Hist. **RESEARCH** American Colonial history; American revolution; Maine history; historical archaeology. **SELECTED PUBLICATIONS** Auth, Governor Fletcher's recall, William & Mary Quart, 10/63; The Stamp Act crisis in Maine: the case of Scarborough, Maine Hist Soc Newslett, winter 72; Maine's Swedish Pioneers, Swedish Pioneer Hist Quart, 4/75; co-ed, Maine in the Revolution: a readers guide, Maine Hist Soc Quart, spring 76;

auth, The Search for Security: Maine After Penobscot, Maine Hist Soc Quart, Winter 82; co-ed and auth, Maine in the Early Republic: From Revolution to Statehood, 88; auth, In Shay's Shadow: Separation and Ratification of the Constitution in Maine, In: In Debt to Shays, 93; Revolution Downeast: The War for American Independence in Maine, 93; King William's War (1689-1697), In: Colonial Wars of North America, 1512-1763: An Encyclopedia, 96. **CONTACT ADDRESS** Dept of Hist, Bates Col, Lewiston, ME, 04240-6018. **EMAIL** jleamon@abacus.Bates.edu

LEARS, T.J. JACKSON
PERSONAL Born 07/26/1947, Annapolis, MD, m, 1969, 1 child **DISCIPLINE** AMERICAN HISTORY AND LITERATURE **EDUCATION** Univ Va, BA, 69; Univ NC, Chapel Hill, MA, 73; Yale Univ, PhD(Am studies), 78. **CAREER** Instr Am studies, Yale Univ, 77-79; ASST PROF US HIST, UNIV MO, COLUMBIA, 79-. **MEMBERSHIPS** Am Studies Asn. **RESEARCH** American advertising; literary modernism; cultural impact of modernization. **SELECTED PUBLICATIONS** Auth, Making Fun of Popular Culture, Amer Hist Rev, Vol 0097, 92. **CONTACT ADDRESS** 212 N William St, Columbia, MO, 65201.

LEARY, DAVID E.
DISCIPLINE HISTORY & PHILOSOPHY OF PSYCHOLOGY **EDUCATION** San Luis Rey Col, CA, BA, 68; San Jose State, CA, MA, 71; Univ Chicago, IL, PhD, 77. **CAREER** Vis asst prof of Psychology, Graduate Theol Union, Berkeley, CA, 71-72; instr Psychol, Holy Names Col, Oakland, CA, 72-74; instr psychol, San Francisco State Univ Ext Services and Univ CA Ext Services, 73-74; instr of Psychol, Univ Chicago, 75; asst prof of the History and Philos of Psychol, Univ NH, Durham, 77-81, co-dir, grad prog in the Theory and History of Psychol, 77-89, assoc prof Psychol & Humanities, 81-87; fel, Center for Advanced Study in the Behavioral Sciences, Stanford, CA, 82-83, co-dir, summer inst on the Hist of Social Scientific Inquiry, 86; assoc prof Humanities, Cambridge Univ Summer prog, 84; Chairperson, Dept of Psychol, 86-89, prof of Psychol, Hist, and the Humanities, Univ NH, Durham, 87-89; prof of Psychology, dean of Arts and Sciences, Univ Richmond, VA, 89-. **HONORS AND AWARDS** San Luis Rey College Memorial Fund Scholarship, 63-68; Special Honors, PhD dissertation, 77; Univ NH Merit Award, 78, 82; Asn of Am Pubs Award, 85; Phi Beta Kappa, 87; numerous grants, fellowships, and stipends from the NEH, Univ NH, Nat Sci Found, Mellon Found, and others. **MEMBERSHIPS** Am Asn of Higher Ed; Am Conf of Academic Deans (member of the bd, 93-2000, chair of the bd, 98-99); Am Hist Asn; Am Psychol Asn (Pres, 83-84, Pres, Div of Theoretical and Philos Psychol, 94-95); Am Psychol Soc; Asn of Am Colleges and Universities; Cheiron: Int Soc for the History of the Behavioral and Social Sciences; Forum for the Hist of Human Science; Hist of Science Soc; Soc for the Hist of Science in Am. **RESEARCH** The intellectual, social, and cultural history of psychology, with a special focus on the relations between psychology and the humanities (eg, literature, philosophy, and religion) and the other sciences. **SELECTED PUBLICATIONS** Auth, An Introduction to the Psychology of Guilt, Lansford Co, 75; A Century of Psychology as Science, co-ed with Sigmund Koch, MacGraw-Hill, 85 (recipient of the Asn of Am Pubs Award, 85), 2nd ed reissued with a new postscript, Am Psychol An, 92; Metaphors in the History of Psychology, Cambridge Univ Press, 90, paperback, 94; William James, the Psychologist's Dilema, and the Historiography of Psychology: Cautionary Tales, Hist of Human Sciences, 8, 95; Naming and Knowing: Giving Forms to Things Unknown, Social Res 62, 95; William James and the Art of Human Understanding, in Ludy T Benjamin, Jr, ed, A History of Psychology: Original Sources and Contemporary Research, 2nd ed, McGraw-Hill, 97 (reprinted from 92); Sigmund Koch (1917-1996), co-auth with Frank Kessel and William Bevan, Am Psychologist 53, 98; numerous other publications. **CONTACT ADDRESS** Dean of Arts and Sciences, Univ of Richmond, Richmond, VA, 23173.

LEARY, WILLIAM M.
PERSONAL Born 05/06/1934, Newark, NJ, m, 1977, 4 children **DISCIPLINE** HISTORY **EDUCATION** Wayne State Univ, BA 63; Princeton univ, MA 65, PhD, 66. **CAREER** Princeton Univ, res assoc asst ed for The Papers of Woodrow Wilson, 66-68; San Diego state Univ, asst prof 68-69; Univ Victoria, assoc prof 69-73; Univ Georgia, prof 73-, E Merton Coulter Prof of Hist 95. **HONORS AND AWARDS** Phi Beta Kappa; Woodrow Wilson fell; Stud Intell Awd; Chas A Linbergh chair in Areospace hist. **MEMBERSHIPS** SMH **RESEARCH** Aeronautical Hist, Intelligence Hist. **SELECTED PUBLICATIONS** Under Ice: Waldo Lynd the Development of the Arctic Submarine, 99; Project Coldfeet: Secret Mission to a Soviet Ice Station, 96; Aerial Pioneers: The U S Air Mail Service, 1918-1927, 85; Perilous Missions: Civil Air Transport and CIA Covert Operations in Asia, 84. **CONTACT ADDRESS** Dept of Hist, Univ of Georgia, Athens, GA, 30602. **EMAIL** wleary@arches.uga.edu

LEAVELL, LINDA
DISCIPLINE LATE 19TH THROUGH CONTEMPORARY AMERICAN LITERATURE **EDUCATION** Rice Univ, PhD,

86. **CAREER** Engl, Okla St Univ. **HONORS AND AWARDS** SCMLA book award. **MEMBERSHIPS** Okla Am Asn Univ Profs; SCMLA. **SELECTED PUBLICATIONS** Auth, Marianne Moore and the Visual Arts: Prismatic Color, La State Univ Press, 95. **CONTACT ADDRESS** Oklahoma State Univ, 101 Whitehurst Hall, Stillwater, OK, 74078.

LEAVER, ROBIN A.
PERSONAL Born 05/12/1939, Aldershot, England, m, 1988 **DISCIPLINE** SACRED MUSIC **EDUCATION** Trinity Col, Theol Dip, Bristol, England; Rijksuniversiteit Groningen, Dtheol cum laude **CAREER** Pres, Intl Arbeitsgemeinschaft fur Hymnologie, 85-89; bd dir(s), Charles Wesley Soc, 89-; contrib ed, Jahrbuch fur Liturgik und Hymnologie, 76-; The Hymnology Annual, 89-; lectr, Taverner Choir and Players; Early Mus Ctr; Eng Bach Fest; The Gabrieli Consort; The Bach Choir Bethlehem; The Berkeley Fest; consult, Brit Broadcasting Corporation, Oxford UP; vis prof, Drew Univ, 88-. **HONORS AND AWARDS** Winston Churchill fel, 71; ed, Studies in Liturgical Musicol; co-editor, Drew Liturgical Studies., Listed, Contemp Auth(s), Dictionary of Intl Biog, Who's Who in the World, Latimer House, Oxford, 77-84; Wycliffe Hall, Oxford, 84-85. **MEMBERSHIPS** Hon mem, Riemenschneider Bach Inst, 73; mem, Scholarly Adv Comm Kessler Reformation Coll, Emory University, 95-. **RESEARCH** Theory pedagogy and 19th-century theory. **SELECTED PUBLICATIONS** Auth, Bachs theologische Bibliothek, 83; J S Bach and Scripture, 85; The Theological Character of Music in Worship, 89; Goostly psalmes and spirituall songes: English and Dutch Metrical Psalters from Coverdale to Utenhove 1535-1566, 91; Come to the Feast: The Original and Translated Hymns of Martin H. Franzman, 94; co-auth, Liturgy and Music: Lifetime Learning, 98. **CONTACT ADDRESS** Dept of Theory and Mus Hist, Westfield State Col, 577 Western Ave., Westfield, MA, 01085. **EMAIL** Leaver@enigma.rider.edu

LEAVITT, JUDITH WALZER
PERSONAL Born 07/22/1940, New York, NY, m, 1966, 2 children **DISCIPLINE** AMERICAN MEDICAL HISTORY **EDUCATION** Antioch Col, BA, 63; Univ Chicago, MA, 66, PhD(hist), 75. **CAREER** Instr hist C W Post Col, 68-70; asst prof, 75-80, ASSOC PROF MED HIST AND WOMEN'S STUDIES, UNIV WIS, MADISON, 80-, CHAIRPERSON, HIST MED, 81-. **MEMBERSHIPS** Am Asn Hist Med; Orgn Am Historians; AHA; Am Pub Health Asn. **RESEARCH** US public health history; US urban history, 19th century; US women's health history. **SELECTED PUBLICATIONS** Auth, Typhoid Mary Strikes Back--Bacteriological Theory and Practice in Early 20th-Century Public Health, Isis, Vol 0083, 92; Death in Childbirth--an International Study of Maternal-Care and Maternal Mortality 1800-1950--Loudon,I, Soc Hist Med, Vol 0007, 94; Untitled, Isis, Vol 0086, 95; A Worrying Profession--the Domestic Environment of Medical Practice in Mid 19th Century America, Bull Hist Med, Vol 0069, 95. **CONTACT ADDRESS** Univ Wis, 1300 Univ Ave, Madison, WI, 53706.

LEBEAU, BRYAN
PERSONAL Born 07/23/1947, North Adams, MA, m, 1967, 1 child **DISCIPLINE** HISTORY **EDUCATION** North Adams St Col, BA, 70, MA 71; Penn St Univ, PhD, 82 **CAREER** Assoc Prof, Creighton Univ **HONORS AND AWARDS** Creighton Univ Award for Teaching, 87; Creighton Univ Award for Service, 90; Creighton Univ Award for Collaboration, 95; Creighton Univ Award for Res, 98 **MEMBERSHIPS** Am Hist Assoc; Am Studies Assoc; Org of Amer Historians **RESEARCH** Religious History; Early American Culture **SELECTED PUBLICATIONS** Auth, History of the Salem Witch Trials, Prentice Hall, 98 **CONTACT ADDRESS** Dept of Hist, Creighton Univ, Omaha, NE, 68178. **EMAIL** blbeau@creighton.edu

LEBLANC, ALBERT
PERSONAL Born 09/18/1942, Baton Rouge, LA, m, 1971 **DISCIPLINE** MUSIC EDUCATION **EDUCATION** Univ Illinois, MS 69, PhD 75; Louisiana State Univ, B Mus Ed 65. **CAREER** Michigan state Univ, prof 76-; Cemrel Inc, eval specialist, 73-76; Thibodaux LA, HS band dir, 65-70. **HONORS AND AWARDS** Mus Educ Nat Conf Sr res awd. **MEMBERSHIPS** MENC; SAH. **RESEARCH** Music listening preferences; music performance anxiety. **SELECTED PUBLICATIONS** Auth, Effects of style tempo and performing medium on children's music preference, in: Music edu research: An anthology from the Jour of Research in Music edu, ed, Harry E Price, Reston VA, MENC, 98; Effect of audience on music performance anxiety, coauth, Jour of res in Music Edu, 97; rev of, Experiencing music technology: Software and Hardware, by David Brian Williams, Peter Richard Webster, Music Edu Jour, 97; Building theory in music education: A personal account, Philo of Music Edu Rev, 96; Music style preferences of different age listeners, Jour of Res in Music Edu, 96; rev of, Music matters: A new philosophy of music education, by David J. Elliott, Music Edu Jour, 96; Differing results in research on preferences for music tempo, Perceptual and Motor Skills, 95; A theory of music performance anxiety, Quart Jour of Music teaching and Learning, 94. **CONTACT ADDRESS** School of Music, Michigan State Univ, East Lansing, MI, 48824-1043. **EMAIL** aleblanc@pilot.msu.edu

LEBLANC, PHYLLIS
PERSONAL Moncton, NB, Canada **DISCIPLINE** HISTORY **EDUCATION** Univ Moncton, BA, 76, MA, 78; Univ Ottawa, PhD, 89. **CAREER** Policy Adv & Hist Res, Dept of Indian Affairs & Northern Dev, 84-88; asst prof, hist, Univ Winnipeg, 88-90; assoc prof, 90-95, PROF HISTORY UNIV MONCTON 95-. **HONORS AND AWARDS** Can Coun Special MA Scholar, 76; Scholar in Residence, Ctr Louisiana Studs, Univ Southwestern Louisiana, 95-96. **MEMBERSHIPS** Gorsebrook Inst Atlantic Can Studs; Asn Can Studs; Can Hist Soc. **SELECTED PUBLICATIONS** Auth, The Vatican and the Roman Catholic Church in Atlantic Canada: Policies Regarding Ethnicity and Language 1878-1922, in Papal Diplomacy in the Mod Age, 94; auth, Francophone Minorities: the Fragmentation of the French-Canadian Identity, in Beyond Quebec: Taking Stock of Canada, 95; co-ed, Economie et societe en Acadie 1985-1950, 96. **CONTACT ADDRESS** Dept of History, Univ Moncton, Moncton, NB, E1A 3E9. **EMAIL** leblanpc@bosoleil.umoncton.ca

LEBOVICS, HERMAN
PERSONAL Born 09/06/1935, Nagy Szollosa, Czechoslovakia **DISCIPLINE** MODERN EUROPEAN HISTORY **EDUCATION** Univ Conn, BA, 57; Yale Univ, MA, 58, PhD(hist), 65. **CAREER** Instr Europ hist, Brooklyn Col, 62-65; vis asst prof, Oberlin Col, 65-66; asst prof, 66-69, ASSOC PROF EUROP HIST, STATE UNIV NY, STONY BROOK, 69-. **MEMBERSHIPS** AHA; Conf Group Cent Europ Hist; Soc Fr Hist Studies. **RESEARCH** German social and intellectual history of the late 19th century; French social and intellectual history of the late 19th century; comparative history. **SELECTED PUBLICATIONS** Auth Present Past--Modernity and the Memory Crisis, Amer Hist Rev, Vol 0099, 94; The Past in French History, Amer Hist Rev, Vol 0099, 94. **CONTACT ADDRESS** Dept of Hist, State Univ of NY, 100 Nicolls Rd, Stony Brook, NY, 11794-0002.

LECKIE, SHIRLEY A.
PERSONAL Born 06/15/1937, Claremont, NH, m, 1975, 3 children **DISCIPLINE** AMERICAN HISTORY **EDUCATION** Univ Mo-Kansas City, BA, 67; MA, 69; Univ Toldeo, PhD. **CAREER** Dir of Adult Lib Studies, Univ Toledo, 73-80; asst dean of continuing educ, 80-81; assoc dean of continuing educ, Millsaps Col, 81-82; dir of continuing educ, Univ NC-Asheville, 83-85; asst prof, Univ Central Fla, 85-88; assoc prof, 88-95; prof, 95-. **HONORS AND AWARDS** Evans Bigraphy Award, 93; Julian J. Rothbam Prize, 93. **MEMBERSHIPS** Western Hist Asoc; Southern Hist Asoc; Orgn of Am Hist. **RESEARCH** Women in American history; urban history; Western history; military history. **SELECTED PUBLICATIONS** Co-auth with William H. Leckie, Unlikely Warrors: General Benjamin H. Grierson and His Family, 84; ed, The Colonel's Lady on the Western Frontier: The Correspondence of Alice Kirk Grierson, 89; auth, Custer's Luck Runs Out, Montana, 93; auth, Elizabeth Bacon Custer and the Making of a Myth, 93; auth, Gender as a Force in History and Biography: The Custer Myth through the Prism of Domestic Ideals, North Dakota History, 97. **CONTACT ADDRESS** History Dept., Univ of Central Florida, Orlando, FL, 32816. **EMAIL** sleckie@pegasus.cc.ucf.edu

LEDFORD, KENNETH F.
PERSONAL Born 08/17/1953, Gulfport, MS, m, 1977, 2 children **DISCIPLINE** HISTORY; LAW **EDUCATION** Univ NC, BA, 75, JD, 78; Johns Hopkins Univ, BA, 84, PhD, 89. **CAREER** Adjunct asst prof history, Univ MD, 88-89; vis asst prof history, 89, lectr Paul H. Nitze School Adv Int Studies, 88-91, Johns Hopkins Univ; res fel/ed, German Hist Inst, 89-91; asst prof history & law, 91-97, ASSOC PROF HISTORY & LAW, 97-, CASE WESTERN RESERVE UNIV, 91-; German Marshall Fund US res fel, 98-99; Fulbright fel, 97-98; ed bd Law Hist Rev, 96-; DAAD fel, 85-86; Mellon Found fel, 82-84; John Motley Morehead fel Univ NC, 75-78; Phi Beta Kappa, 74; Phi Eta Sigma, 72. **HONORS AND AWARDS** John Snell Mem Essay Prize S Hist Asn, 83; Seymour W Wurfel Prize Int Law Univ NC, 78. **MEMBERSHIPS** Am Hist Asn' Am Soc Legal Hist; Conf Grp Cent Europ Hist; S Hist Asn; Ger Stud Asn; Law Soc Asn; VA State Bar. **RESEARCH** German social history; German and European legal history; history of Central European professions; history of the German Burgertum; historiography of German. **SELECTED PUBLICATIONS** Conflict within the Legal Professions: Simultaneous Admission and the German Bar 1903-1927, German Professions, 1800-1950, Oxford Univ Press, 90; Lawyers, Liberalism, and Procedure: The German Imperial Justice Laws of 1877-79, Central European History, 93; "German Lawyers and the State in the Weimar Republic," Law and History Review, 95; "Identity, Difference, and Enlightenment Heritage: Comment on The Right to Be Punished," Law and History, 98; Lawyers and the Limits of Liberalism: The German Bar in the Weimar Republic, Lawyers and the Rise of Western Political Liberalism, Clarendon Press, 98; From General Estate to Special Interest: German Lawyers 1878-1933, Cambridge Univ Press, 96. **CONTACT ADDRESS** Dept of History, Case Western Reserve Univ, Cleveland, OH, 44106-7107. **EMAIL** KXL15@po.cwru.edu

LEE, ANTHONY A.
PERSONAL Born 08/05/1947, m, 1979, 3 children **DISCIPLINE** HISTORY **EDUCATION** Univ of Calif, Los Angeles, BA, 68, MA, 74, CPhil 76. **CAREER** Instr, Cypress Col, 92-98; El Camino Col, 96-98; Oxnard Col, 92; Ventura Col, 91; online courses for NetNoir, 94-96. **HONORS AND AWARDS** Grad Advan Prog Fel, UCLA, 72-75., Ford Found, Nat Fels Fund Awards, 74-75, 75-76; NDEA, Title VI, 73-74, 74-75; Rackham Fel, Univ of Mich, Ann Arbor, 68-69; Regents' Sch, UCLA 64-68. **MEMBERSHIPS** Soc for Scholarly Publ. **RESEARCH** Baha'i Studies; African Religions; African American History. **SELECTED PUBLICATIONS** Ed, Studies in Baha'I History, 82; **CONTACT ADDRESS** 826 Dianthus St, Manhattan Beach, CA, 90266. **EMAIL** Member1700@aol.com

LEE, DAVID DALE
PERSONAL Born 08/05/1948, Cincinnati, OH **DISCIPLINE** AMERICAN HISTORY **EDUCATION** Miami Univ, BA, 70; Ohio State Univ, MA, 71, PhD(hist), 75. **CAREER** Asst prof, 75-81, ASSOC PROF HIST, WESTERN KY UNIV, 81-, Nat Endowment for Humanities summer sem, 79, summer grant, 82; Hoover Libr Asn grant, 82. **HONORS AND AWARDS** Fac Excellence Award, Western Ky Univ, 81. **MEMBERSHIPS** Orgn Am Historians; Southern Hist Asn. **RESEARCH** American South in the twentieth century; The United States in the 1920s and 1930s. **SELECTED PUBLICATIONS** Auth, The Paradox of Southern Progressivism, 1880-1930, Amer Hist Rev, Vol 0099, 94. **CONTACT ADDRESS** Dept of Hist, Western Kentucky Univ, 1 Big Red Way St, Bowling Green, KY, 42101-3576.

LEE, DOUGLAS
PERSONAL Born 11/03/1932, Carmel, CA, m, 1961 **DISCIPLINE** MUSIC/MUSICOLOGY **EDUCATION** DePauw Univ, BMus, 54; Univ Mich, MMus, 58 PhD, 68. **CAREER** Asst prof, Mt. Union Col, 59-61; Rackham Fel, Univ Mich, 61-63; Wichita State Univ, prof, chmn, musicol, 64-86; prof, chmn, musicol, Vanderbilt Univ, 86-98. **HONORS AND AWARDS** Rector Scholar, Depauw U, 50-54 Rackham Fel, Univ Mich, 61-63; Res grant, NEH, 79-80; Am Philosophical Soc, 80; res grants Wichita State Univ, Vanderbilt Univ; Kansas Arts Council; Tennessee Arts Commission; Outstanding Educators of Am, 75; Who's Who in Am; Int'l Dir of Music and Musicians; other biographical citations. **MEMBERSHIPS** Am Musicol Soc; Sonneck Soc for Am Music; Mus Teachers Nat Assoc; Am Soc for 18th Century Studies. **RESEARCH** Early classic 19th cent instrumental music; hist keyboard concerto; Am music 19th cent; Am Symphony Orchestra. **SELECTED PUBLICATIONS** A Musician at Court, 98; Christoph Nichelmann and the Free Fantasia, in CPE Bach Studies, 88; ed, 6 kb concertos for The C.P.E.Bach Edition (awaiting publication); articles in Groves Dictionary of Music and Musicians, 80; Groves Dictionary of Am Music, 84; ca 50 articles in Musical Quarterly; Sonneck Soc Bulletin; European Studies J; Studies in Biography. **CONTACT ADDRESS** Vanderbilt Univ, 2400 Blakemore Ave, Nashville, TN, 37212. **EMAIL** Douglas.A.Lee@Vanderbilt.edu

LEE, GEORGE ROBERT
PERSONAL Born 09/17/1933, Dawn, MO, m, 1964, 2 children **DISCIPLINE** HISTORY **EDUCATION** Northeastern State Col, BA, 54; Univ Okla, MA, 59; Johns Hopkins Univ, cert, 70. **CAREER** Teacher social studies, Wichita Pub Schs, 55-56; teacher hist, Oswego Pub Schs, Kans, 56-57 & Sterling Pub Schs, Colo, 57-61; instr, Lamar Jr Col, 61-62; from asst prof to prof hist, 62-98, PROF EMERITUS HIST, CULVER-STOCKTON COL, 98-. **MEMBERSHIPS** State Hist Soc Mo. **RESEARCH** Southern history and slavery. **SELECTED PUBLICATIONS** Auth, Slavery and Emancipation in Lewis County, Mo, Mo Hist Rev, 4/71; The Beaubiens of Chicago, Lee, 73; Carl Johann, Culver-Stockton Col, 75; James Shannon's Search for Happiness, Mo Hist Rev, 10/78; Conf Refugees, Encycl Southern Hist, La State Univ Press, 79; Culverton-Stockton College, the First 130 Years, Culverton-Stockton Col, 84; Decisions that Shaped America, Mark Twain, 93; China and the United States, Mark Twain, 94; World War II, Mark Twain, 95; Holocaust, Mark Twain, 98. **CONTACT ADDRESS** Dept of History, Culver-Stockton Col, 1 College Hill, Canton, MO, 63435-1299.

LEE, GUY MILICON, JR.
PERSONAL Born 05/24/1928, East Chicago, IN, m **DISCIPLINE** EDUCATION **EDUCATION** Roosevelt Univ, BA, 1954; Inidana Univ, MS, 1959; Ball State Univ, EdD, 1969. **CAREER** Gary Comm Schools IN, public school teacher 1956-64, administrator 1964-70; Saginaw Valley State Coll, dir of student teaching 1970-73, assoc dean sch of educ prof 1973-75, admin asst to the pres 1975-78, asst to the pres 1978-82, dean sch of educ 1982-86, prof of educ 1986-95, prof emeritus, 1995-. **HONORS AND AWARDS** High Scholastic Achievement Award IN Univ Bloomington 1953; Doctoral Fellowship Ball State Univ Muncie IN 1968-69; Citizen of the Age of Enlightement Award for Educ Am Found for the Sci of Creative Intelligence 1976; Keyman Award for community Serv United Way of Saginaw Co MI 1979. **MEMBERSHIPS** Mem, Assn Supervison & Curriculum Devel; mem, Natl Org on Legal Problems in Educ; mem, Amer Assn of School Admin; rep, United Way of Saginaw Co; mem, Assn Teach Educ; mem, Amer Asoc Higher Educ; mem, Assn of Super and Curr Devel; bd of dir League of United Latin Amer Citizens, 1982-95; Metro Fayette Kiwanis Club, 1998-.

LEE, HUGH MING
PERSONAL Born 02/10/1945, Honolulu, HI **DISCIPLINE** CLASSICS **EDUCATION** St Mary's Col, Calif, BA, 66; Stanford Univ, MA, 71, PhD(classics), 72. **CAREER** Instr classics, Ind Univ, Bloomington, 71-72, asst prof, 72-78; asst prof, Miami Univ, Ohio, 78-79; ASST PROF CLASSICS, UNIV MD, COLLEGE PARK, 79-, Nat Endowment for Humanities fel, 79-80. **MEMBERSHIPS** Am Philol Asn; Archaeol Inst Am; Vergilian Soc; Classical Asn Atlantic States. **RESEARCH** Pindar; Greek and Roman athletics; Greek Literature. **SELECTED PUBLICATIONS** Auth, Baths and Bathing in Classical Antiquity, Class World, Vol 0087, 94; Stadia and Starting Gates, Archaeol, Vol 0049, 96; Athletics and Mathematics in Ancient Corinth--the Origins of the Greek Stadion, Class World, Vol 0090, 97. **CONTACT ADDRESS** Dept of Classics, Univ of Md, College Park, MD, 20742-0001.

LEE, JEAN B.
DISCIPLINE HISTORY **EDUCATION** Univ Va, PhD, 84. **CAREER** Asst prof, Col of Wm & Mary, 84-86; 89-91; asst prof, Univ Wisc, Madison 87-89; 92-95, assoc prof, 95- , Univ Wisc-Madison. **HONORS AND AWARDS** NEH, Mellon fel; fel Wintenthur Mus & Libr; fel Va Hist Soc; fel David Libr Am Revolution; fel Inst Early Am Hist & Cult. **MEMBERSHIPS** Am Hist Soc; Orgn Am Hist; S Hist Asn; S Asn Women Hist. **RESEARCH** American revolution; early national period; the South to 1835. **SELECTED PUBLICATIONS** Auth, The Problem of Slave Community in the Eighteenth-Century Chesapeake, Wm and Mary Quart, 86; The Price of Nationhood: The American Revolution in Charles County, W W Norton, 94; Experiencing the American Revolution, Taking Off the White Gloves: Annual Addresses of the S Asn Women Hist, Univ Mo Press, 98. **CONTACT ADDRESS** History Dept, Univ Wisconsin Madison, 455 N Park St., Madison, WI, 53706.

LEE, LOYD ERVIN
PERSONAL Born 07/16/1939, Broadway, OH, m, 1963, 2 children **DISCIPLINE** MODERN EUROPEAN HISTORY **EDUCATION** Ohio State Univ, BA, 61; Cornell Univ, PhD, 67. **CAREER** Tchng asst hist, 62-64, Cornell Univ; asst prof, 65-67, Ark Agric, Mech & Norm Col; asst prof, 67-71, assoc prof, 71-81, prof hist, 81-, SUNY, New Paltz. **HONORS AND AWARDS** Phi Beta Kappa, Chancellor's Award for Excel tchng, 93. **MEMBERSHIPS** AHA; Am Comt Hist Second World War. **RESEARCH** European social history; military history, WW II. **SELECTED PUBLICATIONS** Auth, Afro-Eurasian Worlds, 1500-1800, World Hist, The Am Hist Assn Guide to Hist Lit, Oxford Univ Press, 95; auth, The Rise of an Interdependent World, Asia in World Hist & Western Hist: A Guide for Col Tchrs, M E Sharpe, 97; auth, World War II in Europe, Africa, and the Americas, with General Sources, A Handbook of Literature and Research, Greenwood Pub, 97; auth, World War II in Asia and the Pacific and the War's Aftermath, with General Themes, A Handbook of Literature and Research, Greenwood Pub, 98; auth, World War II, Greenwood Pub, 98. **CONTACT ADDRESS** JFT814, 755 Manheim Blvd, New Paltz, NY, 12581. **EMAIL** leel@npvm.newpaltz.edu

LEE, M. OWEN
PERSONAL Born 05/28/1930, Detroit, MI **DISCIPLINE** CLASSICS **EDUCATION** Univ Toronto, BA, 53, MA, 57; St Michael's Col, Univ Toronto, STB, 57; Univ BC, PhD, 60. **CAREER** From lectr to asst prof classics, St Michael's Col, Univ Toronto, 60-68; from assoc prof to prof, Univ St Thomas, Tex, 68-72; assoc prof, Loyola Univ Chicago, 72-75; assoc prof, 75-79, PROF CLASSICS, UNIV TORONTO, 79-. **MEMBERSHIPS** Am Philol Asn. **RESEARCH** Myth of Orpheus; Roman poets; Wagner. **SELECTED PUBLICATIONS** Auth, Correspondence + Amara, Lucine, Opera Quart, Vol 0009, 92; Die 'Aeneis' as the Subject of Opera--Dramaturgical Changes From the Early Baroque to Berlioz, Phoenix-J Class Assoc of Can, Vol 0046, 92; Correspondence + Burroughs, Bruce, Opera Quart, Vol 0009, 93; Wagner 'Schwarzschwanenreich' + Johanning, Raffeiner, Quandt, Bach--Marco Polo 8 223777 8, Opera Quart, Vol 0012, 96; Correspondence + Farkas Rev of Lee 'First Intermissions'--Comment, Opera Quart, Vol 0012, 96; Wagner die 'Meistersinger Von Nurnberg' + Wiener, Thomas, Watson, Keilberth-Eurodisc 69008 2 Rg, Opera Quart, Vol 0012, 96; Wagner 'Tristan Und Isolde' + Jerusalem, Meier, Barenboim--Teldec 94568 2, Opera Quart, Vol 0013, 96; Wagner die 'Meistersinger Von Nurnberg' + Schoffler, Seider, Seefried, Bohm Preiser 90234, Opera Quart, Vol 0012, 96. **CONTACT ADDRESS** St Michael's Col, 81 St Mary St, Toronto, ON, M5S 1A1.

LEE, ROY ALTON
PERSONAL Born 05/24/1931, White City, KS, m, 1963, 2 children **DISCIPLINE** HISTORY **EDUCATION** Kans State Teachers Col, BS, 55, MS, 58; Univ Okla, PhD, 62. **CAREER** Teacher, high sch, Kans, 55-57; asst, Kans State Teachers Col, 57-58 and Univ Okla, 58-61; Harry S Truman Libr Inst res grant, 61; asst prof Am hist, Cent State Col, Okla, 61-66; assoc prof, 66-69, chmn dept, 70-73, PROF US HIST, UNIV SDAK, VERMILLION, 69-. **MEMBERSHIPS** Orgn Am Historians. **RESEARCH** Recent American history; United States constitutional history. **SELECTED PUBLICATIONS** Auth, Kaiser, Henry, J.--Builder in the Modern American West, J West, Vol 0032, 93; Campus Wars--the Peace Movement at American State-Universities in the Vietnam Era, Historian, Vol 0056, 93; United States Labor-Relations, 1945-1989--Accommodation and Conflict, Labor Hist, Vol 0035, 94; Truman in Retirement--a Former President View the Nation and the World, J Amer Hist, Vol 0081, 95; Introduction + Labor in the West, J West, Vol 0035, 96. **CONTACT ADDRESS** Dept of Hist, Univ of SDak, Vermillion, SD, 57069.

LEE, SHERMAN E.
DISCIPLINE ART HISTORY **EDUCATION** Western Reserve Univ, PhD. **CAREER** Adj prof, Univ NC, Chapel Hill. **RESEARCH** Far Eastern art. **SELECTED PUBLICATIONS** Auth, Japanese Decorative Style, Cleveland Mus Art, 61; Chinese Landscape Painting, Cleveland Mus Art, 62; Reflections of Reality in Japanese Art, Cleveland Mus of Art, 83; History Far Eastern Art, Abrams, 62, 73, 82, 84, 94. **CONTACT ADDRESS** Univ N. Carolina, Chapel Hill, Chapel Hill, NC, 27599.

LEE ORR, N.
DISCIPLINE MUSIC HISTORY AND LITERATURE **EDUCATION** Univ NC, Chapel Hill, PhD. **CAREER** Prof, Ga State Univ; ed bd, 19th-Century Stud J; ed bd, Organ Hist Soc Press. **RESEARCH** American church music of the 19th century. **SELECTED PUBLICATIONS** Auth, Church Music Handbook, Abingdon Press, 91; Alfredo Barili and the Rise of Classical Music in Atlanta, Scholars Press-Emory Univ, 96; coed, the stage works of John Hill Hewitt, Garland Press. **CONTACT ADDRESS** Georgia State Univ, Atlanta, GA, 30303.

LEEB, ISIDORE LEONARD
PERSONAL Born 10/11/1934, Philadelphia, PA, m, 1960 **DISCIPLINE** MODERN EUROPEAN HISTORY **EDUCATION** Univ Pa, BA, 55; Columbia Univ, PhD(hist), 70. **CAREER** Lectr contemp civilization, Queens Col, NY, 60-62; lectr hist, Yeshiva Univ, 62-63 and Brooklyn Col, 63-64; from instr to asst prof, 64-69, ASSOC PROF HIST, POLYTECH INST NEW YORK, 69-, HEAD DEPT SOC SCI, 71-, Nat Endowment for Humanities fel, 70-71. **MEMBERSHIPS** Werkgroep 18e EEUW, Neth; Nederlands Hist Genoot; AHA. **RESEARCH** Historiography and political theory in the Dutch Republic; 18th century intellectual history; theory and practice of imperialism. **SELECTED PUBLICATIONS** Auth, Enlightenment and Conservatism in the Dutch-Republic--the Political-Thought of Luzac, Elie 1721-1796, Amer Hist Rev, Vol 0099, 94; Patriots Republicanism-Political Culture in the Netherlands 1766-1787, Amer Hist Rev, Vol 0102, 97. **CONTACT ADDRESS** Polytech Inst of New York, 6 Metro Tech Ctr, Brooklyn, NY, 11201.

LEES, ANDREW
PERSONAL Born 11/15/1940, New York, NY, m, 1965, 2 children **DISCIPLINE** HISTORY **EDUCATION** Amherst Col, BA, 63; Harvard Univ, MA, 64, PhD(hist), 69. **CAREER** Instr hist, Amherst Col, 68-69, asst prof, 69-74; asst prof, 74-76, assoc prof, 76-85, prof hist, Rutgers Univ, Camden, 85-; mem Ger Acad Exchange Serv, 79, 87, 94; fel col teachers, NEH, 81-82; member, Inst for Advanced Study, 95. **MEMBERSHIPS** AHA; Conf Group Cent Europ Hist; Urban Hist Asn. **RESEARCH** Nineteenth and 20th century European intellectual and social history; modern Germany; modern England. **SELECTED PUBLICATIONS** Auth, Revolution and Reflection: Intellectual Change in Germany During the 1850's, Martinus Nijhoff, 74; co-ed, The Urbanization of European Society in the Nineteenth Century, Heath, 76; Critics of Urban Society in Germany, 1854-1914, J Hist Ideas, 79; Historical Perspectives on Cities in Modern Germany, J Urban Hist, 79; The Metropolis and the Intellectual, In: Metropolis, 1890-1940, Mansell, 82; Cities Perceived: Urban Society in European and American Thought, 1820-1940, Columbia Univ Press, 85; Social Reform, Social Policy and Social Welfare in Modern Germany, J Social Hist, 89; Berlin and Modern Urbanity in German Discourse, 1845-1945, J Urban Hist, 91; Das Denken uber die Grobstadt um 1900, Berichte zur Wissenschaftsgeschichte, 92; State and Society, in Imperial Germany, Greenwood, 96. **CONTACT ADDRESS** Dept Hist, Rutgers Univ, 311 N 5th St, Camden, NJ, 08102-1461. **EMAIL** alees@camden.rutgers.edu

LEES, LYNN HOLLEN
PERSONAL Born 10/06/1941, Akron, OH, m, 1965, 2 children **DISCIPLINE** MODERN EUROPEAN HISTORY **EDUCATION** Swarthmore Col, AB, 63; Harvard Univ, AM, 64, PhD(hist), 69. **CAREER** Lectr hist, Mt Holyoke Col, 68-69, asst prof, 69-73; from Asst Prof to Assoc Prof, 74-86, PROF HIST, UNIV PA, 86-. **HONORS AND AWARDS** Howard Found fel, Brown Univ, 72-73; fel, Shelby Cullom Davis Ctr, Princeton Univ, 75-76; Am Coun Learned Soc fel, 78-79; mem W Europ fel screening comt, Soc Sci Res Coun, 76-78; Guggenheim fel, 78-79; John Ben Snow Prize, 82; Ford Grant, Am Coun of Learned Soc, 85-86; NEH Fel, 93; Rotary Found Fel, 95-96. **MEMBERSHIPS** AHA; Soc Sci Hist Asn; World Hist Asn; N

Am Conf on Brit Studies. **RESEARCH** Urban history; 19th century European social history; history of British Empire. **SELECTED PUBLICATIONS** Auth, Patterns of Lower-Class Life: Irish Slum Communites in Nineteenth Century London, In: Nineteenth Century Cities, Yale Univ, 69; The Metropolitan Type: London and Paris compared, In: The Victorian City: Images and Reality, Routledge & Kegan Paul, 73; coauth, The people of June, 1848, In: Annales: Economies, Societes, Civilisation, 74; co-ed, The Urbanization of European Society, Heath, 76; The Irish Countryman Urbanized: A Comparative Perspective on the Famine Migration, J Urban Hist, 77; auth, Exiles of Erin: Irish Migrants in mid-Nineteenth Century London, Cornell Univ & Manchester Univ 78; coauth, The Making of Urban Europe, 1000-1950, Harvard Univ Press, 95; auth, The Solidarities of Strangers: The English Poor Laws and the People, 1900-1948, Cambridge Univ Press, 98. **CONTACT ADDRESS** Dept of History, Univ of Pennsylvania, 3401 Walnut St, Philadelphia, PA, 19104-6228. **EMAIL** lhlees@history.upenn.edu

LEFF, MARK H.
DISCIPLINE HISTORY **EDUCATION** Univ Chicago, PhD, 78. **CAREER** Assoc prof, Univ Ill Urbana Champaign **RESEARCH** Twentieth century United States; public policy. **SELECTED PUBLICATIONS** Auth, The Limits of Symbolic Reform: The New Deal and Taxation, 1933-1939, Cambridge, 84; The Politics of Sacrifice on the American Home Front in World War II, J Am Hist, 91; Revisioning U.S. Political History, Am Hist Rev, 95. **CONTACT ADDRESS** History Dept, Univ Ill Urbana Champaign, 52 E Gregory Dr, Champaign, IL, 61820.

LEFFLER, M.P.
PERSONAL Born 05/31/1945, New York, NY, m, 1968, 2 children **DISCIPLINE** HISTORY **EDUCATION** Cornell Univ, BS, 66; Ohio St Univ, PhD, 72. **CAREER** Asst prof, 72-77, assoc prof, 77-86, Vanderbilt Univ; prof, 86-, chmn, 90-95, hist dept, Edward R. Stettinius Prof, Amer hist, 93-, dean, col & grad schl arts & sci, 97-, Univ Va. **HONORS AND AWARDS** Nobel Fel, 98; Bancroft Prize, 93; Hoover Prize, 93; Ferrell Prize, 93; Bernath Art Prize, 84. **MEMBERSHIPS** AHA; Org of Amer Hist; Soc for Hist of Amer For Rels. **RESEARCH** US foreign relations; cold war; morality & for policy; US economic foreign policy. **SELECTED PUBLICATIONS** Auth, Specter of Communism; auth, A Preponderance of Power: National Security, the Truman Administration, and the Cold War; auth, The Elusive Quest: America's Pursuit of European Stability and French Security, 1919-1933. **CONTACT ADDRESS** Office of the Dean, Univ of Virginia, Charlottesville, VA, 22903. **EMAIL** MPL4j@virginia.edu

LEFKOWITZ, JOEL M.
PERSONAL Born 10/17/1940, New York, NY, m, 1974, 2 children **DISCIPLINE** INDUSTRIAL; ORGANIZATIONAL PSYCHOLOGY **EDUCATION** CWRU, PhD 65. **CAREER** CUNY Baruch Col, asst prof to prof, 65-; Head of PhD prog in I/O Psychology. **HONORS AND AWARDS** ABPP in I/O psychol. **MEMBERSHIPS** APA; APS; NY ACAD of SCI. **RESEARCH** Fair employment practices in industry. **SELECTED PUBLICATIONS** Auth Dimensions of biodata items and their relationships to item validity, coauth, Jour of Occupational and Organizational Psychology, in press; The shelflife of a test validation study: A survey of expert opinion, coauth, Jour of Business and Psychology, 97; auth, Potential sources of criterion bias in supervisor ratings used for test validation, coauth, Jour of Business and Psychology, 95; Sex-related differences in job attitudes and dispositional variables: Now you seem them.... Acad of Mgmt j, 94. **CONTACT ADDRESS** Dept of Psychology, Baruch Col, CUNY, 17 Lexington Ave, PO Box G-1126, New York, NY, 10010. **EMAIL** jmlbb@cunyvm.cuny.edu

LEFKOWITZ, MARY ROSENTHAL
PERSONAL Born 04/30/1935, New York, NY, m, 1982, 2 children **DISCIPLINE** CLASSICS **EDUCATION** Wellesley Col, BA, 57; Radcliffe Col, MA, 59, PhD, 61. **CAREER** Instr Greek, 59-63, from asst prof to assoc prof Greek & Latin, 63-75, chemn dept, 70-72, 75-78, 81-87, 91-94, & 96-, prof Greek & Latin, Wellesley Col, 75-; Andrew W Mellon prof humanities, 79-; fel, Radcliffe Inst, 66-67, 72-73, Am Coun Learned Soc fel, 72-73; mem managing comt, Am Sch Class Studies, Athens, 71-; vis prof, Univ Calif, Berkeley, 78; vis fel, St Hilda's Col, Oxford, 79-80; dir Nat Endowment Summer Seminar, 84-85; Nat Endowment for Humanities fel, 79-80, 91. **HONORS AND AWARDS** Honorary Fel, St. Milda's Col, 94-; LHD, Trinity College, 96. **MEMBERSHIPS** Am Philol Asn; Archaeol Inst Am. **RESEARCH** Greek poetry; classical mythology; ancient biography. **SELECTED PUBLICATIONS** Auth, The Victory Ode, Noyes, 76; Heroines and Hysterics, St Martin's, 81; The Lives of the Greek Poets, 81; co-ed, Women's Life in Greece and Rome, Johns Hopkins, 82, 2nd ed, 92; auth, Women in Greek Myth, John's Hopkins, 86; First-Person Fictions, Oxford, 91; Not Out of Africa, Basic Books, 96; co-ed Black Athena Revisited, North Carolina, 96. **CONTACT ADDRESS** Dept of Classical Studies, Wellesley Col, 106 Central St, Wellesley, MA, 02481-8252. **EMAIL** mlefrowitz@wellesley.edu

LEGAN, MARSHALL SCOTT
PERSONAL Born 02/17/1940, Louisville, MS, m, 1961, 2 children **DISCIPLINE** HISTORY OF THE SOUTH **EDUCATION** Miss State Univ, BS, 61, MA, 62; Univ Miss, PhD(hist), 68. **CAREER** Teacher social studies, Ackerman High Sch, 62-63; asst prof, 68-75, ASSOC PROF HIST, NORTHEAST LA UNIV, 75-, DEPT HEAD HIST and GOVT, 75-, Abstractor, Am Hist and Life, ABC-Clio Press. **MEMBERSHIPS** Southern Hist Asn; Railway and Locomotive Hist Soc. **RESEARCH** Railroad history; medical history. **SELECTED PUBLICATIONS** Auth, Yellow Fever and the South, J Southern Hist, Vol 0060, 94; Stricklin, Thomas, E. -in Memoriam, J Southern Hist, Vol 0062, 96. **CONTACT ADDRESS** Dept of Hist and Govt, Northeast Louisiana Univ, 700 University Ave, Monroe, LA, 71209-9000.

LEGGE, ELIZABETH
DISCIPLINE ART HISTORY **EDUCATION** Univ Toronto, BA, 73; Mt Allison Univ, studio art, 73-74; Cambridge Univ, BA, 76; Courtauld Inst, Univ London, MA, 79, PhD, 86. **CAREER** Lectr, 79-81, asst prof, 85-87, Univ Winnipeg; cur, Winnipeg Art Gallery, 79-81; Univ art cur, 88-, ASST PROF FINE ART, UNIV TORONTO 96-. **HONORS AND AWARDS** Joseph Henderson Memorial Award, Trinity Col, Univ Toronto, 69-73; Rainmaker Prize, Girton Col, Cambridge Univ, 76; Commonwealth Scholar, 81-84. **MEMBERSHIPS** Inst Contempory Culture, ROM. **SELECTED PUBLICATIONS** Auth, Posing Questions: Max Ernst's Oedipus Rex and the Implicit Sphinx, in Arts Mag, 86; auth, Max Ernst: The Psychoanalytic Sources, 89; auth, Thirteen Ways of Looking at a Virgin: Picabia's La Sainte Vierge, in Word and Image, 96. **CONTACT ADDRESS** Dept of Fine Art, University Col, Univ Toronto, Toronto, ON, M5E 1A1.

LEGON, RONALD
DISCIPLINE GREEK HISTORY **EDUCATION** Cornell Univ, PhD, 66. **CAREER** Instr, CUNY, 65-66; Asst prof, CUNY, 66-67; Asst prof, Univ Ill, 67-70; assoc prof, Univ Ill, 70-82; Vis assoc prof, Univ Chicago, 82; Prof, Univ Ill, 82-92; Vis prof, Univ Chicago, 83-94; Prof, Univ Baltimore, 92-. **SELECTED PUBLICATIONS** Auth, The Political History of a Greek City-State to 336 B.C., Cornell Univ Press, 81; auth, Thucydides and the Case for COntemporary History, Essays in Honor of Donald Kagan, 97. **CONTACT ADDRESS** Univ Baltimore, 1420 N. Charles Street, Baltimore, MD, 21201.

LEGUIN, CHARLES A
PERSONAL Born 06/04/1927, Macon, GA, m, 1953 **DISCIPLINE** HISTORY **EDUCATION** Emory Univ, PhD(hist), 56. **CAREER** Instr hist, Syracuse Univ, 49-50; asst prof, Mercer Univ, 52-55; instr, Emory Univ, 55-56; asst prof, Univ Idaho, 56-59; from asst prof to assoc prof, 59-68, PROF HIST, PORTLAND STATE UNIV, 68-, Vis assoc prof, Emory Univ, 62-63. **MEMBERSHIPS** AHA; Soc Fr Hist Studies; Soc Mod Hist, France. **RESEARCH** French revolution. **SELECTED PUBLICATIONS** Auth, Trials of the Earth--the Autobiog of Hamilton, Mary, J Southern Hist, Vol 0060, 94. **CONTACT ADDRESS** Dept of Hist, Portland State Univ, Portland, OR, 97207.

LEHMAN, CYNTHIA L.
PERSONAL Born 11/25/1968, Sunbury, PA, s **DISCIPLINE** AFRICAN AMERICAN STUDIES **EDUCATION** Temple Univ, MA, 95, PhD, 97. **CAREER** Asst prof, Eastern Ill Univ, 97-. **HONORS AND AWARDS** Phi Alpha Theta (Int Hist Honor Soc). **MEMBERSHIPS** AHA; AAUW; NCBS; NCA. **RESEARCH** African-American/Native American history & culture; curriculum revision. **SELECTED PUBLICATIONS** The Social and Political Views of Charles Chestnutt: Reflections on his Major Writings, J of Black Studs, 1/96. **CONTACT ADDRESS** 2003 S 12th St #16, Charleston, IL, 61920. **EMAIL** cfcll1@eiu.edu

LEHMANN, CLAYTON M.
DISCIPLINE HISTORY **EDUCATION** Augustana Col, BA, 78; Univ Md, MA, 80; Univ Chicago, PhD, 86. **CAREER** Adj prof, Mont State Univ, 86-87; from asst to assoc prof, Univ SDak, 88-. **MEMBERSHIPS** AIA; Am Philos Asn; ASOR; AAAH. **RESEARCH** Greek history; Greek and Roman epigraphy; 16th Century Europe. **SELECTED PUBLICATIONS** Auth, Observations on the Latin Dedicatory Inscriptions from Caesarea Maritima, Bibl Archeol Today, 90; auth, Xenoi, Proxenoi, and Early Greek Traders, Helios, 94; auth, The Combined Caesarea Expeditions: The Excavation of Caesarea's Byzantine City Wall, 1989, Annual Am Sch Oriental Res, 94; auth, The City and the Text, Caesarea Maritima: Retrospective After Two Millennia, 96. **CONTACT ADDRESS** Dept of History, Univ of South Dakota, Vermillion, SD, 57069-2390. **EMAIL** clehmann@usd.edu

LEHMBERG, STANFORD E.
DISCIPLINE HISTORY **EDUCATION** Univ Kansas, BA, 53, MA, 54; Cambridge Univ, PhD, 56. **CAREER** Prof, Univ Texas Austin, 56-69; prof, Univ Minn Twin Cities, 69-. **RESEARCH** History of England during Tudor and Stuart periods. **SELECTED PUBLICATIONS** Auth, Writings of English Cathedral Clergy (1600-1700), Anglican Theol Rev, 93; The Peoples of the British Isles, From Prehistoric Times to 1688, 91; The Reformation of Cathedrals: Cathedrals in English Society, 1485-1603, Princeton, 88; Henry VIII and the Cathedrals, Huntington Library Quarterly, 86. **CONTACT ADDRESS** History Dept, Univ of Minnesota, Twin Cities, 614 Social Sciences Tower, 267 19th Ave. S, Minneapolis, MN, 55455. **EMAIL** lehmb001@tc.umn.edu

LEHUU, ISABEL
DISCIPLINE HISTORY **EDUCATION** Paris-Sorbonne, BA, 78; MA, 79; Ecole des Hautes Etudes en Sciences Sociales, Paris, DEA, 83; Cornell, MA, 87, PhD, 92. **CAREER** ASST PROF, HIST, UNIV. DU QUEBEC. **MEMBERSHIPS** AM Antiquarian Soc **SELECTED PUBLICATIONS** Auth, "Sentimental Figures: Reading Goley's Lady's Book in Antebellum America" in The Culture of Sentiment: Race, Gender, and Sentimentality in 19-Century America, Oxford Univ Press, 92; auth, "Une Tradition de Dialogue: L'histoire Culturelle et Intellectuelle," in Chantiers d'Histoire Americaine, Belin, 94; auth, "Ephemeral Myriads of Books": The Work of Popular Reading in America, 1830-1860, Univ NC Press. **CONTACT ADDRESS** Dept d'Histoire, Universite du Quebec a Montreal, succ. Centre-ville, Montreal, PQ, H3C 3PB.

LEIBSOHN, DANA
DISCIPLINE ART HISTORY **EDUCATION** Bryn Mawr, BA; Univ CO, MA; UCLA, PhD. **CAREER** Act, Lat Am Stud Progr, Smith Col & 5 Col Native Am Stud Comt; post-doctoral fel, Getty Ctr. **RESEARCH** Indigenous visual cult after the Span conquest of Mexico, particularly on maps, histories, and modes of writing. **SELECTED PUBLICATIONS** Publ on, maps and indigenous bk(s) from colonial Mexico. **CONTACT ADDRESS** Dept of Art, Smith Col, Hillyer Hall 312, Northampton, MA, 01063. **EMAIL** dleibsoh@julia.smith.edu

LEICHTY, ERLE VERDUN
PERSONAL Born 08/07/1933, Alpena, MI, m, 1963 **DISCIPLINE** ASSYRIOLOGY **EDUCATION** Univ Mich, BA, 55, MA, 57; Univ Chicago, PhD(Assyriol), 60. **CAREER** From res asst to res assoc Assyriol, Orient Inst, Univ Chicago, 60-63; from asst prof to assoc prof ancient hist, Univ Minn, 63-68; assoc prof Assyriol, 68-71, prof Assyriol, Univ Pa, 71-97, Clark Research prof of Assyriol, Univ Pa, 98-, Cur Akkadian Lang & Lit, Univ Mus, 68-95, Guggenheim fel, 64-65; ed, Expedition, 70-73 & J Cuneiform Studies, 72-91; ed, Occasional Publications of the Babylonian Fund, 76-; ed, for the Ancient Near East, The Am Hist Asn's Guide to Historical Literature, Oxford, 95; Curator of Tablet collections, Univ Museum, Univ Pa, 96-. **HONORS AND AWARDS** Fel, Am Numismatic Soc, 56; alternate Fulbright to England, 62-63; Fulbright to England, 63-64 (declined); annual prof of the Baghdad Schools of the American Schools of Oriental Research, 63-64 (declined); fel of the Guggenheim Foundation, 64-65; trustee, Institute of Semitic Studies, Princeton, NJ, 85-90. **MEMBERSHIPS** Am Orient Soc; Archaeol Inst Am; Am Schs Orient Res; Assoc of Current Anthropology; British School of Archaeology in Iraq. **RESEARCH** Ancient Near Eastern history. **SELECTED PUBLICATIONS** Auth, A Bibliography of the Kuyunjik Collection of the British Museum, Trustees Brit Mus, 64; The Omen Series Shumma Izbu, J J Augustin, 69; A Remarkable Forger, 70 & Demons and Population Control, 71, Expedition; Two Late Commentaries, Arch fur Orientforsch, 73; The Fourth Tablet of Erimhaus, Alter Orient und Altes Testament, 75; Literary Notes, Essays on the Ancient Near East in Memory of J. J. Finkelstein, 77; A Collection of Recipes for Dyeing, Alter Orient und Altes Testament-Sonderreihe 203, 79; The Curator's Write: The Summerian Dictionary, Expedition 24, 82; An Inscription of Ashur-etel-ilani, Journal of the American Oriental Soc, 83; Bel-epush and Tammaritu, Anatolian Studies 33, 83; A Legal Text from the Reign of Tiglath-Pileser III, American Oriental Series 67, 87; Omens from Doorknobs, Journal of Cuneiform Studies 39, 87; Catalogue of Babylonian Tablets in the British Museum, vol 6, London, 86, vol 7, London, 87, vol 8, London, 88; Ashurbanipal's Library at Ninevah, Syro-Mesopotamian Studies Bulletin, 88; Making Dictionaries, Humanities 9/3, 88; Guaranteed to Cure, A Scientific Humanist, Studies in Memory of Abraham Sachs, 89; Feet of Clay, Dumu-e2-dub-ba-a, Studies in Honor of Ake W. Sjoberg, 89; Esarhaddon's 'Letter to the Gods," Ah, Assyria..., Studies in Assyrian History and Ancient Near Eastern Historiography presented to Hayim Tadmor, Scripta Hierosolymitana 33, 90; A Tamitu from Nippur, Lingering Over Words, Studies in Ancient Near Eastern Literature in Honor of William L. Moran, 90; Sheep Lungs, The Tablet and Scroll, Near Eastern Studies in Honor of William W.Hallo, 93; Ritual, Sacrifice, and Divination in Mesopotamia, Ritual and Sacrifice in the Ancient Near East, OLA 55, 93; The Origins of Scholarship, Die Rolle der Astronomie in den Kulturen Mesopotamiens, Grazer Morgenlandishe Studies 3, 93; The Distribution of Agricultural Tools in Mesopotamia, Sulma IV, 93; Esarhaddon, King of Assyria, Civilizations of the Ancient Near East, 2, 95; Section 5: Ancient Near East, Guide to Historical Literature, 95; Angurinnu, Weiner Zeitschrift fur die Kunde des Morgenlandes 86, 96; Divination, Magic, and Astrology, Assyria 1995, 97; qabutu, sahu, and me-gati, Oelsner Fs, in press; An Old Babylonian Chronicle, Cagni Mem Vol, in press; The Fifth Tablet of Summa Izbu, CTMMA 2, in press. **CONTACT ADDRESS** Dept Orient Studies, Univ Pa, 255 S 36th St, Philadelphia, PA, 19104-3805.

LEIGHOW, SUSAN
DISCIPLINE HISTORY **CAREER** Asst prof; fac, Shippensburg Univ, 92. **HONORS AND AWARDS** Bloomsburg State Col, BSEd; Kutztown State Col, MA; Univ Pittsburgh, PhD. **RESEARCH** Classroom methodology; women's hist; US hist. **SELECTED PUBLICATIONS** Auth, Nurses' Questions; Womens' Questions. **CONTACT ADDRESS** Dept Hist and Philos, Shippensburg Univ PA, 1871 Old Main Dr., Shippensburg, PA, 17257-2299. **EMAIL** pmgigo@ship.edu

LEIGHTEN, PATRICIA
DISCIPLINE ART HISTORY **EDUCATION** Rutgers Univ, PhD. **CAREER** Prof, Duke Univ. **RESEARCH** Late nineteenth and early twentieth-century art and the hist of photography. **SELECTED PUBLICATIONS** Auth, Re-Ordering the Universe: Picasso and Anarchism, 1897-1914; Anarchism and Audience in Avant-Guerre Paris; co-auth, Cubism and Culture. **CONTACT ADDRESS** Dept of Art and Art Hist, Duke Univ, East Duke Building, Durham, NC, 27706.

LEIMAN, SID ZALMAN
PERSONAL Born 11/03/1941, New York, NY **DISCIPLINE** HISTORY, RELIGION **EDUCATION** Brooklyn Col, BA, 64; Mirrer Yeshivah, BRE, 64; Univ Pa, PhD(Orient studies), 70. **CAREER** Lectr Jewish hist and lit, Yale Univ, 68-70, from asst prof to assoc prof relig studies, 70-78; prof Jewish hist and dean, Vervard Revel Grad Sch, Yeshiva Univ, 78-81; PROF AND CHMN DEPT JUDAIC STUDIES, BROOKLYN COL, 81-, Nat Found Jewish Cult res grant, 67-68; Morse fel, Yale Univ, 71-72; vis scholar Jewish law and ethics, Kennedy Inst Ethics, Georgetown Univ, 77-78; Mem Found Jewish Cult res grant, 81-82. **MEMBERSHIPS** Am Schs Orient Res; Soc Bibl Lit; Am Acad Relig; Asn Jewish Studies; Am Jewish Hist Soc. **RESEARCH** Jewish history; Jewish ethics; Biblical studies. **SELECTED PUBLICATIONS** Auth, Horowitz, Jacob on the Study of Scripture--From the Pages of 'Tradition', Tradition-J Orthodox Jewish Thought, Vol 0027, 92; From the Pages of Tradition--Friedman, David of Karlin--the Ban on Secular Study in Jerusalem, Tradition-J Orthodox Jewish Thought, Vol 0026, 92; Dwarfs on the Shoulders of Giants + the Study of Torah Despite a Theology of Generational Regression, Tradition-J Orthodox Jewish Thought, Vol 0027, 93; Carlebach, Joseph, Wuerzburg and Jerusalem--a Conversation Between Bamberger, Seligmann, Baer and Salant, Shmuel, Tradition-J Orthodox Jewish Thought, Vol 0028, 94; Ha Kohen Kook, Abraham, Isaac--Invocation at the Inauguration of the Hebrew-University--Excerpt From the Pages of Tradition April-1, 1925, Tradition-J Orthodox Jewish Thought, Vol 0029, 94; Rabbi Schwab,Shimon + Respone on the Torah and Derekh-Eretz Movement Concerning Jewish Education--a Letter Regarding the Frankfurt Approach--From the Pages of 'Tradition', Tradition-J Orthodox Jewish Thought, Vol 0031, 97. **CONTACT ADDRESS** Dept of Judaic Studies, Brooklyn Col, CUNY, Brooklyn, NY, 11367.

LEINIEKS, VALDIS
PERSONAL Born 04/15/1932, Liepaja, Latvia **DISCIPLINE** CLASSICS **EDUCATION** Cornell Univ, BA, 55, MA, 56; Princeton Univ, PhD, 62. **CAREER** From instr to asst prof classics, Cornell Col, 59-64; assoc prof, Ohio State Univ, 64-66; assoc prof, 66-71, Prof Classics, Univ Nebr, Lincoln, 71-, Chm Dept, 67-95, Chm Comp Lit Prog, 70-86. **MEMBERSHIPS** Am Philol Asn; Am Classical League; Classical Asn of the Middle West and South. **RESEARCH** Greek and Latin literature and linguistics; linguistic theory. **SELECTED PUBLICATIONS** Auth Morphosyntax of the Homeric Greek Verb, Mouton, 64; The Structure of Latin: An Introductory Text Based on Caesar and Cicero, MSS Educ Publ, 75; Index Nepotianus, Univ Nebr, 76; The plays of Sophokles, Gr¤ner, 82; The City of Dionysos, Teubner, 96. **CONTACT ADDRESS** Dept of Classics, Univ of Nebr, Lincoln, NE, 68588-0337. **EMAIL** rgorman@unlinfo.unl.edu

LEIREN, TERJE IVAN
PERSONAL Born 05/14/1943, Stamneshella, Norway, m, 1967, 2 children **DISCIPLINE** SCANDINAVIAN HISTORY **EDUCATION** Calif State Univ, Los Angeles, BA, 66, MA, 70; North Tex State Univ, PhD(hist), 78. **CAREER** Lectr hist and English, Lindaas Gymnas, Knarvik, Norway, 75-76; res asst and lectr mod Europ hist, Univ Oslo, 76-77; ASST PROF, SCAND HIST, UNIV WASH, 77-, Lectr, Univ Oslo, summers; assoc ed, Scand Studies. **MEMBERSHIPS** Soc Advan Scand Studies; Norweg-Am Hist Asn; AHA; Norweg Hist Asn. **RESEARCH** Norwegian history: 19th and 20th centuries: interwar years (1918-1940); nationalism in Norway and the establishment of modern Norwegian monarchy, 1905; Scandinavian immigration. **SELECTED PUBLICATIONS** Auth, Swedish American Life in Chicago--Cultural and Urban Aspects of an Immigrant People, 1850-1930, Scand Stud, Vol 0065, 93; New Land, New Lives--Scandinavian Immigrants to the Pacific-Northwest, Pac Northwest Quart, Vol 0086, 95; Becoming Norwegian, Ibsen, Sigurd in America 1886-1888 + Son of Playwright Ibsen, Henrik, Scand Stud, Vol 0068, 96; Ethnicity on Parade--Inventing the Norwegian American Through Celebration, Amer Hist Rev, Vol 0101, 96; **CONTACT ADDRESS** Dept of Scand, Univ Wash, Seattle, WA, 98195.

LEITAO, DAVID
PERSONAL Born 06/18/1964, CT **DISCIPLINE** CLASSICS **EDUCATION** Dartmouth, AB, 86; Univ Mich, MA, 90, PhD, 83. **CAREER** Vis asst prof, 93-95, Ohio St Univ; asst prof, 95-, San Francisco St Univ. **RESEARCH** Gender & sexuality; anthropology of ancient world; computers in classics. **SELECTED PUBLICATIONS** Art, Classical Antiquity; art, Mnemosyne; art, Bucknell Review; art, Neve Parly. **CONTACT ADDRESS** 825 Mountain View Dr. #4, Daly City, CA, 94014. **EMAIL** dleitao@sfsu.edu

LEITH, JAMES A.
PERSONAL Born 10/26/1931, Toronto, ON, Canada, m, 1956, 2 children **DISCIPLINE** MODERN EUROPEAN HISTORY **EDUCATION** Univ Toronto, BA, 53, PhD(hist), 60; Duke Univ, MA, 55. **CAREER** Lectr hist, Univ Sask, 58-61; from lectr to assoc prof, 61-68, head dept, 68-73, PROF HIST, QUEEN'S UNIV, ONT, 68-, Can Coun fels, 61, 65, 68, 70, 75, 76 and 77; vis prof, Cornell Univ, 64; R H McLaughlin res prof, 65-66; vis prof, Oxford Univ, 70-71 and Australian Inst Advan Studies, 74-75; French govt fel, 74. **MEMBERSHIPS** Soc Fr Hist Studies; Soc Mod Hist France; AHA; Can Hist Asn; Can Soc 18th Century Studies. **RESEARCH** Eighteenth century French cultural and intellectual history, especially ideas about education and mass indoctrination. **SELECTED PUBLICATIONS** Auth, Worthy Monuments-Art Museums and the Politics of Culture in 19th Century France, Amer Hist Rev, Vol 0097, 92; Ledoux, Claude, Nicolas--Architecture and Social-Reform at the End of the Ancien-Regime, J Mod Hist, Vol 0066, 94; As Befits a Legend--Building a Tomb for Napoleon, 1840-1861, Amer Hist Rev, Vol 0100, 95; The Future of the Past in Canada on the Eve of the 21st Century, J Can Hist Assoc-Revue De La Societe Historique Du Can, Vol 0006, 95; Building Paris--Architectural Institutions and the Transformation of the French Capital, 1830-1870, Histoire Sociale-Soc Hist, Vol 0029, 96; Emulation--Making Artists for Revolutionary France, Amer Hist Rev, Vol 0101, 96; Unruly Women of Paris--Images of the Commune, Amer Hist Rev, Vol 0102, 97. **CONTACT ADDRESS** Dept of Hist, Queen's Univ, Kingston, ON, K7L 3N6.

LEMAHIEU, DAN LLOYD
PERSONAL Born 05/09/1945, West Bend, WI **DISCIPLINE** BRITISH HISTORY **EDUCATION** Lawrence Univ, BA, 67; Harvard Univ, MA, 68, PhD(hist), 73. **CAREER** Vis asst prof hist, Univ Nebr-Lincoln, 73-74; asst prof, 74-80, PROF HIST, LAKE FOREST COL, 80-, Rockefeller Found humanities fel, 78-79. **MEMBERSHIPS** AHA; NAm Conf Brit Studies. **RESEARCH** British culture 1920s and 1930s. **SELECTED PUBLICATIONS** Auth, The British Press and Broadcasting Since 1945, Albion, Vol 0024, 92; A Social History of British Broadcasting, Vol 1, 1922-1939, Serving the Nation, Albion, Vol 0024, 92; Politics and Military Morale, Current Affairs and Citizenship Education in the British Army, 1914-1950, Albion, Vol 0025, 93; Bentham, Byron, and Greece--Constitutionalism, Nationalism, and Early Liberal Political Thought, Amer Hist Rev, Vol 0098, 93; The Origins of Railway Enterprise--the Stockton-and-Darlington Railway, 1821-1863, Historian, Vol 0057, 94; Popular Reading and Publishing in Britain, 1914-1950, Amer Hist Rev, Vol 0099, 94; The History of Bbc Broadcasting in Scotland, 1923-1983, Amer Hist Rev, Vol 0100, 95; The Christian Philosopher, Cath Hist Rev, Vol 0081, 95; Propaganda and the Role of the State in Interwar Britain, Amer Hist Rev, Vol 0101, 96; Narrating the Thirties--a Decade in the Making--1930 to the Present, Albion, Vol 0028, 96; British Writers and the Media, 1930-45, Albion, Vol 0029, 97; The New Statesman--Portrait of a Political Weekly, 1913-1931, Albion, Vol 0029, 97. **CONTACT ADDRESS** Dept of Hist, Lake Forest Col, 555 N Sheridan Rd, Lake Forest, IL, 60045-2399.

LEMAY, HELEN RODNITE
PERSONAL Born 03/05/1941, New York, NY, 1 child **DISCIPLINE** MEDIEVAL INTELLECTUAL HISTORY **EDUCATION** Bryn Mawr Col, AB, 62; Columbia Univ, MA, 65, PhD(medieval hist), 72. **CAREER** Asst medieval hist, Columbia Univ, 64-67; instr hist, 70-71, asst prof, 71-76, ASSOC PROF HIST, STATE UNIV NY STONY BROOK, 76-. **MEMBERSHIPS** Int Soc Neoplatonic Studies; Soc Pour L'Etude de la Philos Medievale; Soc Italian Hist Studies. **RESEARCH** Medieval sexuality in medical and astrological literature; Twelfth-century school of Chartres. **SELECTED PUBLICATIONS** Auth, La 'Novele Cirurgerie', a Compendium of Rhymed Pharmaceutical Recipes, Speculum-J Medieval Stud, Vol 0068, 93; The Meanings of Sex Difference in the Middle Ages--Medicine, Science, and Culture, Speculum-J Medieval Stud, Vol 0069, 94; The Misfortunes of Dinah--the Book of Human Generation--Jewish Gynecological Texts From the Middle-Ages, Speculum-J Medieval Stud, Vol 0069, 94; The Bridling of Desire--Views of Sex in the Later Middle Ages, Speculum-J Medieval Stud, Vol 0069, 94; The History of Obstetrics and Gynecology, Isis, Vol 0086, 95; 'Tractatus De Sterilitate' by Anonymous of Montpellier 14th Century, Originally Attributed to Arnald of Villanova, Raymond De Moleriis, and Jordanus De Turre, Speculum-J Medieval Stud, Vol 0070, 95. **CONTACT ADDRESS** Dept of Hist, State Univ NY, 100 Nicolls Rd, Stony Brook, NY, 11794-0002.

LEMAY, RICHARD
PERSONAL Born 06/30/1916, Montreal, PQ, Canada, m, 1971, 1 child **DISCIPLINE** MEDIEVAL EUROPEAN INTELLECTUAL HISTORY **EDUCATION** Univ Montreal, BA, 36, Lic, 40 and 46; Columbia Univ, PhD (hist), 58. **CAREER** Teacher relig educ, Ecole Normale Jacques Cartier, Montreal, 40-41; foreign corresp UN, Le Devoir Newspaper, 47-49; lectr medieval hist, Columbia Univ, 56-58; asst prof hist, Am Univ Beirut, 58-65; sr researcher medieval hist, Nat Ctr Sci Res, Paris, 65-70; assoc prof hist, 70-75, PROF HIST, CITY COL AND GRAD SCH, CITY UNIV NEW YORK, 75-, Assoc dir, Ecole Pratique des Hautes Etudes, Paris, 63; lectr, Ctr Higher Studies Medieval Civilization, Poitiers, France, 73. **RESEARCH** Arabic background of medieval European science; Arabic and Latin astrology in the Middle Ages; Renaissance philosophy. **SELECTED PUBLICATIONS** Auth, The 'Speculum Astronimiae' and its Enigma--Astrology, Theology and Science in Albertus Magnus and his Contemporaries, Speculum-J Medieval Stud, Vol 0069, 94; Abu Masar, the 'Abbreviation of the Introduction to Astrology' Together With the Translation of Adelard of Bath, Speculum-J Medieval Stud, Vol 0071, 96. **CONTACT ADDRESS** Dept of Hist, City Univ, New York, NY, 10021.

LEMELLE, TILDEN J.
PERSONAL Born 02/06/1929, New Iberia, LA, m **DISCIPLINE** AFRICAN-AMERICAN STUDIES **EDUCATION** Xavier Univ New Orleans, AB 1953, MA 1957; Univ of Denver, PhD 1965. **CAREER** Grambling Coll LA, asst prof 1957-63; Fordham Univ NY, assoc prof 1966-69; Ctr Intl Race Rel Univ Denver, prof, dir 1969-71; Hunter Clge NY, prof & acting dean 1971-, provost, vice pres, currently; Amer Com on Africa, treas 1973-; Univ of the District of Columbia, past pres. **HONORS AND AWARDS** John Hay Whitney Fellow NY 1963-65; The Black Coll Praeger NY 1969; Hon Consul-Senegal Denver CO 1969-71; Race Among Nations Heath-Lexington MA 1971. **MEMBERSHIPS** Trustee Africa Today Assoc Inc 1967-; bd office pres Amer Comm on Africa 1973-; trustee New Rochelle Bd of Educ 1976-;mem Cncl on Foreign Rel 1978-; trustee Social Sci Found 1979-; trustee Africa Fund 1979-; trustee Intl League for Human Rights 1980-; trustee Nurses Educ Fund 1984-; Council For International Exchange of Scholars, Fulbright, 1991-. **SELECTED PUBLICATIONS** Editor/publ Africa Today 1967-; **CONTACT ADDRESS** Univ of District of Columbia, 4200 Connecticut Ave NW, Washington, DC, 20008.

LEMIEUX, GERMAIN
PERSONAL Born 01/05/1914, Cap-Chat, PQ, Canada **DISCIPLINE** HISTORY/FOLKLORE **EDUCATION** Univ Laval, BA, 35, MA, 56, PhD, 61; York Univ, LLD(hon), 77; Univ Ottawa, LittD(hon), 78; Univ Laurentienne, LittD(hon), 84. **CAREER** Prof, Col Sacre-Coeur, Sudbury, 41-44, 49-50, 51-53, 56-59; prof Univ Laurentienne, 61-65; prof, Univ Laval, 66-69; prof dep folklore, Univ Sudbury, 70-80. **HONORS AND AWARDS** Prix Champlain, 73; Medaille Luc-Lacourciere, 80; Prix du Nouvel-Ontario, 83; Carnochan Award, Ont Hist Soc, 83; mem, l'Ordre Can, 84; Medaille Marius-Barbeau, 86; mem, l'Ordre de l'Ontario, 92; commandeur, l'Ordre des Palmes, 96. **SELECTED PUBLICATIONS** Auth, Chansonnier franco-ontarien, 2 vols, 74, 76; auth, Les vieux m'ont conte, 33 vols, completee 91; ed, Les jongleurs du billochet, 72; ed, Le four de glaise, 82; ed, La vie paysanne (1860-1900), 82. **CONTACT ADDRESS** 38 rue Xavier, Sudbury, ON, P3C 2B9.

LEMIEUX, LUCIEN
PERSONAL Born 04/30/1934, St-Remi, PQ, Canada **DISCIPLINE** HISTORY, RELIGION **EDUCATION** St-Jean Col, BA, 54; Univ Montreal, LTh, 58; Gregorian Univ, DHist, 65. **CAREER** Prof hist, St-Jean Col, 65-68; asst prof church hist, Univ Montreal, 67-73, ASSOC PROF, 73-79. Mem, Centre Hist Relig Can, 67-. **HONORS AND AWARDS** Prix Litteraire Du Quebec, 68. **MEMBERSHIPS** Can Soc Theol. **RESEARCH** Religious history of citizens of Quebec, 1760-1840. **SELECTED PUBLICATIONS** Auth, Leger, Paul, Emile--Evolution of his Philosophy, 1950-1967, Revue D Histoire De L Amerique Francaise, Vol 0048, 95; The Seminaire-De-Quebec From 1800 to 1850, Revue D Histoire De L Amerique Francaise, Vol 0049, 96. **CONTACT ADDRESS** Dept of Theol, Univ of Montreal, Montreal, PQ, H3C 3J7.

LEMIRE, BEVERLY
DISCIPLINE HISTORY **EDUCATION** Univ Guelph, BA, 79, MA, 81; Balloil Col, Oxford Univ, DPhil, 85. **CAREER** Instr, Wilfred Laurier Univ, 85; instr, Univ Guelph, 85; asst prof, Univ Lethbridge, 86-87; ASSOC PROF HISTORY UNIV NEW BRUNSWICK 87-. **SELECTED PUBLICATIONS** Auth, Fashion's Favorite: The Cotton Trade and the Consumer in Britain, 1660-1800, 91; auth, Peddling Fashion: Salesmen, Pawnbrokers, Tailors, Thieves and the Secondhand Clothes Trade in England, 1680-1800 in Textile Hist, 91; auth, Dress, Culture and Commerce: The English Clothing Trade before the Factory, 97. **CONTACT ADDRESS** Dept of History, Univ New Brunswick, Fredericton, NB, E3B 5A3. **EMAIL** lmre@unb.ca

LEMKE, WERNER ERICH
PERSONAL Born 01/31/1933, Berlin, Germany, m, 1959, 3 children **DISCIPLINE** OLD TESTAMENT, ANCIENT HISTORY **EDUCATION** Northwestern Univ, BA, 56; NPark Theol Sem, BD, 59; Harvard Univ, ThD(Old Testament), 64. **CAREER** Asst prof Bibl interpretation & lectr ancient hist, NPark Col & Theol Sem, 63-66; assoc prof, 66-69, actg dean, 73-74, Prof Old Testament Interpretation, Colgate Rochester Divinity Sch, 69-, Archaeol fel, Hebrew Union Col, Jerusalem, 69-70; prof, W F Albright Inst Archaeol Res Jerusalem, 72-73; vis prof in relig studies, Univ Rochester, 70, 74, 77. **MEMBERSHIPS** Colloquium Old Testament Res (secy-treas, 69-); Soc Bibl Lit; Am Schs Orient Res. **RESEARCH** Hebrew; Old Testament interpretation; ancient Near Eastern languages, literatures and history. **SELECTED PUBLICATIONS** Auth, The snyoptic problem in the chronicler's history, Harvard Theol Rev, 10/65; Nebuchadrezzar, my servant, Cath Bibl Quart, 1/66; Magnalia Dei: The Mighty Acts of God, Essays on the Bible and Archaeology presented to G Ernest Wright, Doubleday, 76; The way of obedience: I Kings 13 and the structure of the Deuteronomistic history, In: Magnalia Dei, Doubleday, 76; The near and distant God, J Bibl Lit, 12/81; Revelation through history in recent Biblical theology, Interpretation, 1/82. **CONTACT ADDRESS** Colgate Rochester Divinity Sch, 1100 S Goodman St, Rochester, NY, 14620-2530. **EMAIL** wlemke@crds.edu

LEMKE-SANTANGELO, GRETCHEN
DISCIPLINE HISTORY **EDUCATION** BA, 86, MA, 88, San Francisco State Univ; Duke Univ, PhD, 93. **CAREER** Dir of Women's Studies, St. Mary's, 95-97; Asst Prof, 93-97, Assoc Prof, 97-, St. Mary's Col. **CONTACT ADDRESS** Dept of History, St. Mary's Col, Moraga, CA, 94575.

LEMMON, SARAH MCCULLOH
PERSONAL Born 10/24/1914, Davidsonville, MD **DISCIPLINE** HISTORY **EDUCATION** Madison Col, BS, 34; Columbia Univ, AM, 36; Univ NC, PhD, 52; Meredith Col, BA, 91; ord, Episcopal Deacon, 95. **CAREER** Acad supvr, 40-43, Oldfields Sch Girls; assoc prof, 43-47, La Grange Col; from asst prof to assoc prof, 47-63, prof hist, 63-, head dept hist & polit sci, 62-, dean cont educ & spec progs, 77-84, Meredith Col; chmn, 77-81, NC Hist Comn. **MEMBERSHIPS** Southern Hist Assn; Soc Am Historians. **RESEARCH** Eugene Talmadge of Georgia; North Carolina history; Episcopal Church history. **SELECTED PUBLICATIONS** Ed, The Pettigrew Papers vol I 1685-1818, 71, vol 2, 1819-1843, NC State Dept Arch & Hist, 81; co-ed, The Episcopal Church in North Carolina 1701-1959, Episcopal Diocese of NC, 87; auth, Candido Portinari, The Protest Period, Lain American Art, 91. **CONTACT ADDRESS** Box 2001, Southern Pines, NC, 28388-2001.

LEMOINE, FANNIE J.
DISCIPLINE CLASSICAL STUDIES **EDUCATION** Bryn Mawr Univ, PhD, 68. **CAREER** Dept Classics, Wisc Univ **RESEARCH** Latin literature; medieval studies; science fiction. **SELECTED PUBLICATIONS** Auth, Martianus Capella: A Literary Re-Evaluation; pubs on medieval topics and Latin teaching issues. **CONTACT ADDRESS** Dept of Classics, Univ of Wisconsin, Madison, 500 Lincoln Drive, Madison, WI, 53706. **EMAIL** lemoine@macc.wisc.edu

LEMON, ROBERT S., JR.
PERSONAL Born 10/01/1938, Pittsburg, KS, m, 1967, 2 children **DISCIPLINE** ART HISTORY **EDUCATION** Univ Mo at KC, BA; Ohio Univ, MA, PhD. **CAREER** Asst, assoc prof, 73-87, prof, art hist & art dept chmn, 87-, Rollins Col. **RESEARCH** N Amer Indian art, 20th century art. **CONTACT ADDRESS** Rollins Col, PO Box 2684, Winter Park, FL, 32789.

LEMONS, STANLEY J.
DISCIPLINE AMERICAN CULTURAL HISTORY, WOMEN'S HISTORY, GILDED AGE, PROGRESSIVE ERA **EDUCATION** William Jewell Col, AB; Univ Rochester, MA; Univ MO, Columbia, PhD. **CAREER** Instr, RI Col. **RESEARCH** African-Am hist; RI hist relig hist. **SELECTED PUBLICATIONS** Auth, The Woman Citizen: Social Feminism in the 1920's; The First Baptist Church in America; coauth, The Elect: Rhode Island's Women Legislators, 1922-1990; Rhode Island: The Independent State; ed., Aspects of the Black Experience. **CONTACT ADDRESS** Rhode Island Col, Providence, RI, 02908.

LENIOR, TIMOTHY
PERSONAL Born 02/07/1948 **DISCIPLINE** HISTORY **EDUCATION** St Mary's Col, BA, 70; Indiana Univ, PhD, 74. **CAREER** Asst prof, Univ of nore Dame, 74-78; res assoc, Univ Calif Berkley, 78-79; asst prof, 78-83, assoc prof, 83-86, Univ Ariz; assoc prof, Hebrew Univ of Jerusalem, 85-87; Julian Bers Assoc Prof, Univ Penn, 86-87; dir, Center for Hist and Philos of Science, Tech and Med, The Hebrew Univ of Jerusalem, 85-87; assoc prof, 87-93, chair, Program in Hist and Philos of Sci, 90-92, prof, Stanford Univ, 93-. **HONORS AND AWARDS** Indiana Univ Fel, 71; NSF Traineeship, 71-72; NDEA Fel, 73-74; Deutscher Akademischer Austauschdienst Fel, 74-75; NATO PostDoc Fel in Science, 75-76; NSF Res Grant, 78-80; Univ AZ Humanities Counc Grant, 81; Alexander von Humboldt-Stiftung Fel, 82-84; Zeitlin-Ver Brugge Prize, Hist of Science Soc, 82; NSF Res Grant, 82-84; Univ AZ Soc Sciences Res Inst Grant, 85; John Simon Guggenheim Fel, 87-88; Inst Advanced Studies Fel, Berlin, 87-88; John W. Hagerty Dist Lectr, St Mary's Col, 90; Natl Science Found Res Grant, 89-90; Bing Innovative Tchng Grant, Stanford Univ, 94; Provost's Res Fund Award, Stanford Univ, 94; Stanford Humanities Center Fel, 94-95; GastProf, Graduierten Kolleg, Deutsches Museum Munich, 94; Natl Science Found Res Grant, 94; Alfred P. Sloan Found Grant, 97-99; Bing Fel for Excel in Tchng, 98. **MEMBERSHIPS** History of Science Soc; West Coast History of Science Soc, Pres, 89-91; Amer Asn For the Advancement of Science; Soc for the History of Technology; Soc for Social Stud of Science; Gesellschaft fur Wissenschaftsgeschichte. **RESEARCH** Intro of computing into biomedicine, 1960's-1980's, esp, development of computational chemistry and molecular graphics; constructing a multi-media database "siliconbase", for the history of silicon valley; history of the development of nuclear med as a medical specialty from WW II through recognition as a med board specialty. **SELECTED PUBLICATIONS** Auth, The Gottingen School and the Development of transcendental Naturphilosophie in the Romantic Era, Stud in the History of Biology Vol 5, Johns Hopkins Univ Press, 81; auth, Models and Instruments in the Development of Electrophysiology 1945-1912, Hist Stud in the Physical Sciences Vol 17, Univ CA Press, 87; coed, Practice, Context, and the Dialogue between Theory and Experiment, Science in Context Vol 2, 88; auth, The Strategy of Life: Teleology and Mechanics in Nineteenth Century German Biology, Univ Chicago, 89; auth, Politik im Tempel der Wissenschaft: Forschung und Machtausubung im deutschen Kaiserreich, Campus Verlag, 92; auth, Instituting Science: Essays on Discipline and the Culture of Science, Stanford Univ Press, 97; ed, Inscribing Science, Stanford Univ Press, 97. **CONTACT ADDRESS** Dept of History, Stanford Univ, Building 200-033, Stanford, CA, 94305-2024. **EMAIL** Tlenior@leland.stanford.edu

LENK, RICHARD WILLIAM
PERSONAL Born 08/29/1936, Hackensack, NJ **DISCIPLINE** HISTORY **EDUCATION** Fairleigh Dickinson Univ, NJ, BA, 59; NY Univ, PhD(hist), 69. **CAREER** Lectr hist, Long Island Univ, 64-65 & Brooklyn Col, 65-67; asst prof, 69-73, assoc prof, 73-80, prof 80-97, PROF EMERITUS, BERGEN COMMUNITY COL, 98-. **MEMBERSHIPS** Am Hist Soc; Orgn Am Historians; Archaeol Inst Am. **RESEARCH** American history; ancient history; New Jersey history. **CONTACT ADDRESS** Dept of Social Sci, Bergen Comm Col, 400 Paramus Rd, Paramus, NJ, 07652-1595.

LENNOX, JAMES GORDON
PERSONAL Born 01/11/1948, Toronto, ON, Canada, m, 1969, 1 child **DISCIPLINE** ANCIENT PHILOSOPHY, PHILOSOPHY OF BIOLOGY **EDUCATION** York Univ, BA(hons), 71; Univ Toronto, MA, 73, PhD(philos and Greek), 78. **CAREER** ASST PROF HIST AND PHILOS SCI, UNIV PITTSBURGH, 77-, Mem med ethics, Prog Human Values Health Care, 77-. **MEMBERSHIPS** Am Philos Asn; Soc Ancient Greek Philos; Philos Sci Asn; His Sci Soc. **RESEARCH** Ancient Greek metaphysics and science; medical ethics; history and philosophy of biology. **SELECTED PUBLICATIONS** Auth, Darwin Was a Telelogist, Biology and Philos, Vol 0008, 93; Aristotles Physicsa, Isis, Vol 0084, 93; Natural-Selection and the Struggle for Existence, Stud in Hist and Philos of Sci, Vol 0025, 94; Teleology by Another Name--a Reply, Biology and Philos, Vol 0009, 94; The Meaning of Evolution--the Morphological Construction and Ideological Reconstruction of Darwin Theory, Philos Sci, Vol 0061, 94. **CONTACT ADDRESS** Dept of Hist and Philos of Sci, Univ Pittsburgh, 1017 Cathedral/Learn, Pittsburgh, PA, 15260-0001.

LENTNER, HOWARD H.
PERSONAL Born 09/08/1931, Detroit, MI, d, 3 children **DISCIPLINE** POLITICAL SCIENCE **EDUCATION** Miami Univ, BS, 58; Syracuse Univ, MA, 59, PhD, 64. **CAREER** Instr, 62-63, Asst Prof, 63-68, Western Reserve Univ; Assoc Prof, McMaster Univ, 68-72; Assoc Prof, 73-76, Prof Polit Sci, 77-, Bernard M Baruch Col of CUNY. **MEMBERSHIPS** Am Polit Sci Asn; Int Polit Sci Asn; Int Stud Asn; NE Polit Sci Asn; Acad Coun on the UN System. **RESEARCH** International politics; comparative politics; globalization; East Asian politics. **SELECTED PUBLICATIONS** Auth, State Formation in Central Americas: The Struggle for Autonomy, Development, and Democracy, Greenwood Pub Co, 93; auth, International Politics: Theory and Practice, W Publishing Co, 97; auth, Realism and Asian Studies, Asian Stud in Am, 10, 3, 7, 98; auth, Central American Development Strategies: Concepts and Choices, Adv in Developmental Policy Stud, vol 3, JAI Press, forthcoming. **CONTACT ADDRESS** 19 Abeel St, 6H, Yonkers, NY, 10705. **EMAIL** HowardH.Lentner@worldnet.att.net

LENZ, JOHN RICHARD
PERSONAL Born 07/03/1957, New York, NY, m, 1994, 1 child **DISCIPLINE** CLASSICAL STUDIES **EDUCATION** Columbia Univ, PhD, 93. **CAREER** 90-91, Union College; 91-94, Chmn 94-, Drew Univ. **HONORS AND AWARDS** Fulbright Travel Grant, Greece, 88-89. **MEMBERSHIPS** Bertrand Russell Society, Pres; NJ Classical Assoc, VP. **RESEARCH** Bertrand Russell, ancient Greece. **CONTACT ADDRESS** Dept of Classics, Drew Univ, Madison, NJ, 07940. **EMAIL** jlenz@drew.edu

LEONARD, HENRY BEARDSELL
PERSONAL Born 11/08/1938, Boston, MA, m, 1960, 2 children **DISCIPLINE** AMERICAN HISTORY **EDUCATION** Harvard Univ, AB, 60; Univ Calif, Berkeley, MA, 61; Northwestern Univ, PhD, 67. **CAREER** Asst prof, 67-77, ASSOC PROF HIST, KENT STATE UNIV, 77-, chmn, 92-96; prof emer, 96-. **MEMBERSHIPS** AHA; Orgn Am Historians. **RESEARCH** American immigrant history. **SELECTED PUBLICATIONS** Auth, Louis Marshall and Immigration Restriction, 1906-1924, Am Jewish Arch, 4/72; Ethnic Conflict and Episcopal Power: The Diocese of Cleveland, 1847-1870, Cath Hist Rev, 7/76; Ethnic Cleavage and Industrial Conflict: The Cleveland Rolling Mill Company Strikes of 1882 and 1885, Labor Hist, fall 79. **CONTACT ADDRESS** Dept of Hist, Kent State Univ, PO Box 5190, Kent, OH, 44242-0001.

LEONARD, KAREN ISAKSEN
PERSONAL Born 12/04/1939, Madison, WI, w, 1962, 2 children **DISCIPLINE** ANTHROPOLOGY **EDUCATION** Univ of Wis, BA, 62; MA, 64, PhD, 69. **CAREER** Assoc of Center for South and Southeast Asian Studies, 67-68, visiting lectr, Univ of Mich, 68; lectr in hist, Univ of San Diego, 69; lectr in hist, 69, full-time lectr, Univ of Calif at San Diego, 70; ASST PROF, PROG IN COMPARATIVE CULTURE, 72-78, ASSOC PROF, SOCIAL RELATIONS, 78-85, PROF, SOCIAL RELATIONS, 85-87, PROF, 88-, DEPT OF ANTHROPOLOGY, UNIV OF CALIF AT IRVINE; dir of Women's Studies, UCI, 78-79; visiting asst prof in Indian Hist, Univ of Va, 78; asst ed, J of Asian Studies, 78-80; ed comt, 83-87, mem of three-person Policy Subcomt, Univ of Calif Press, 86-87. **HONORS AND AWARDS** Phi Beta Kappa, Mortar Board, 62; Nat Defense Foreign Lang fels, 62-66; Ford Found fel, Univ of Chicago, 63; Res fel, Univ of Chicago, 67; Am Inst of Indian Studies Fac Res Fel, 70-71, 76, & 83; UCI Fac Fel, 73; grant, Innovative Training Funds for Women's Studies, 75; UC Instructional Improvement Grants for Women's Studies Core Corse, 76-77 & 77-78; SSRC Grant, 77; Fulbright Res Fel, Pakistan, 92-93; CAORC Smithsonian Grant, 95-96; Rupee grant from His Exalted Highness the Nizam's Charitable Trust, 95-96. **MEMBERSHIPS** Reviewer for J of Asian Studies, Am Anthropologist, Amerasia J, Int Migration Rev, Am Ethnologist; referee for NSF Anthropology Prog, NEH, Oxford Univ Press, Univ of Calif Press, Univ of Chicago Press; referee for grants, Wenner-Gren Found. **SELECTED PUBLICATIONS** Auth, Social History of an Indian Caste: The Kayasths of Hyderabad, Oxford Univ Press, 78 & Longman, 92; auth, Making Ethnic Choices: California's Punjabi-Mexican-Americans, Temple Univ Press, 92 & 94; auth, The South Asian Americans, Greenwood Press, 97; auth, Finding One's Own Place: Asian Landscapes Re-Visioned in Rural California, Culture, Power, Place: Explorations in Critical Anthropology, Duke Univ Press, 97; auth, Identities in the Diaspora: Surprising Voices, Cultural Compass: Ethnographic Explorations of Asian America, Temple Univ Press, forthcoming; auth, Remembering/Claiming Homelands: California's Punjabi Pioneers, Movement and Memory: The Mastery of Displacement in South Asian Experience 1800-1995, Univ of Iow Press, forthcoming. **CONTACT ADDRESS** Dept of Anthropology, Univ of California, Irvine, CA, 92717. **EMAIL** kbleonar@uci.edu

LEONARD, THOMAS CHARLES
PERSONAL Born 10/17/1944, Detroit, MI, m, 1969, 2 children **DISCIPLINE** AMERICAN HISTORY **EDUCATION** Univ Mich, Ann Arbor, BA, 66; Univ Calif, Berkeley, PhD(hist), 73. **CAREER** Asst prof hist, Columbia Univ, 73-76; asst prof, 76-80, PROF JOUR & ASSOC DEAN, UNIV CALIF, BERKELEY, 80- . **HONORS AND AWARDS** Chm, Columbia Univ Sem Am Civilization, 75-76. **MEMBERSHIPS** AHA; Orgn Am Historians; Asn Educ Jour. **RESEARCH** Role of war in American culture; the expose as a form of journalism and social criticism; propaganda; notoriety. **SELECTED PUBLICATIONS** Auth, Red, White, and the Army Blue: Anger and Empathy in the American West, Am Quart, 5/74; George Creel, Walter Duranty, Hegley Farson, John T Flynn & Robert Wagner, In: Dict Am Biog, Suppls V-VII, Scribner's, 77-81; Above the Battle: War-Making in America from Appomattox to Versailles, Oxford Univ, 78; News for a Revolution: The expose in America, 1768-1773, J Am Hist, 6/80; auth, The Power of the Press: The Birth of American Political Reporting, Oxford, 86; auth, News for All: America's Coming-of-Age with the Press, Oxford, 95. **CONTACT ADDRESS** Sch of Journalism, Univ Calif Berkeley, 121 North Gate Hall, Berkeley, CA, 94720-5860.

LEONARD, THOMAS MICHAEL
PERSONAL Born 11/08/1937, Elizabeth, NJ, m, 1960, 6 children **DISCIPLINE** HISTORY **EDUCATION** Mt St Mary Col, BS, 59; Georgetown Univ, MA, 64; Am Univ, PhD(US diplomatic), 69. **CAREER** Sales expeditor, Weston Instruments, 59-60; sec social studies teacher, Baltimore County Pub Sch, 60-62; from asst prof to assoc prof hist, St Joseph Col, 62-73, chmn dept, 71-73; assoc prof, 73-79, coordr lib studies, 74-79, PROF

HIST, UNIV N FLA, 80-, CHMN DEPT, 80-, Consult hist, State Dept Educ, WVa 70, Md, 72, Fla, 75; prog evaluator, Fla Endlwment Humanities, 75- **MEMBERSHIPS** Soc Historians Am Foreign Rel; Conf Latin Am Hist; AHA. **RESEARCH** United States diplomatic history; World War II and the Cold War; Inter-American relations. **SELECTED PUBLICATIONS** Auth, Patriarch and Folk--the Emergence of Nicaragua 1798-1858, Americas, Vol 0049, 93; Central America and the United States, Overlooked Foreign Policy Objectives, Americas, Vol 0050, 93; The United States and Somoza, 1933-1956--a Revisionist Look, Pac Hist Rev, Vol 0063, 94; Political Parties and Democracy in Central America, Hisp Amer Hist Rev, Vol 0074, 94; Managing Democracy in Central America--a Case Study, United States Election Supervision in Nicaragua, 1927-1933, Americas, Vol 0050, 94; Economic and Financial Aspects of Social-Security in Latin America and the Caribbean--Tendencies, Problems and Alternatives for the Year 2000, Hisp Amer Hist Rev, Vol 0075, 95; Washington, Somoza and the Sandinistas--State and Regime in United States Policy Toward Nicaragua, 1969-1981, Pac Hist Rev, Vol 0064, 95; Central America and the United States--the Clients and the Colossus, J Amer Hist, Vol 0082, 95; The Caribbean World and the United States--Mixing Rum and Coca Cola, J Amer Hist, Vol 0082, 95; Changing Social Security in Latin America--Toward Alleviating the Social Costs of Economic Reform, Hisp Amer Hist Rev, Vol 0075, 95; The Social Security Reform and Pensions in Latin America--Importance and Evaluation of Alternatives to Privatization, Hisp Amer Hist Rev, Vol 0075, 95; The Banana Men--American Mercenaries and Entrepreneurs in Central America, 1880-1930, Amer Hist Rev, Vol 0101, 96; The Social Causes of Environmental Destruction in Latin-America, J Latin Amer Stud, Vol 0028, 96. **CONTACT ADDRESS** Univ N Florida, 8889 Brierwood Rd, Jacksonville, FL, 32216.

LEONARD, VIRGINIA WAUGH

PERSONAL Willimantic, CT **DISCIPLINE** LATIN AMERICAN & AMERICAN HISTORY **EDUCATION** Univ Calif, Berkeley, BA, 63; Hofstra Univ, MA, 67; Univ Fla, Gainesville, PhD(hist), 75. **CAREER** Teacher social studies, Colegio Lincoln, Buenos Aires, 70; instr world hist, NY Inst Technol, 73-75; biblingual teacher social studies, Seward Park High Sch, New York City, 75-77; prof Hist, Western Ill Univ, 77-; Task force on women, Latin Am Studies Asn, 82-83. **HONORS AND AWARDS** Peter Guilday Prize, Am Cath Hist Asn, 79. **MEMBERSHIPS** AHA; Latin Am Studies Asn; Orgn Am Historians; Midwest Asn Latin Am Studies; NCent Coun Latin Americanists. **RESEARCH** Church-state relations in education in Argentina; women's history; U.S. Navy and suppression of slavery. **SELECTED PUBLICATIONS** Auth, Education and the church-state clash in Argentina, Cath Hist Rev, 1/80; Politicians, Pupils, and Priests, Peter Lang Press, 89; Back to the Future: Haiti in 1915 and 1994, Low Intensity Conflict and Law Enforcement, Winter 97. **CONTACT ADDRESS** Dept Hist, Western Illinois Univ, 1 University Cir, Macomb, IL, 61455-1390. **EMAIL** virginia_leonard@ccmail.wiu.edu

LEONTIADES, MILTON

PERSONAL Born 11/25/1932, Athens, Greece, m, 1968, 2 children **DISCIPLINE** BUSINESS **EDUCATION** Indiana Univ, BA, 54, MBA, 57; Am Univ, PhD, 66. **CAREER** Management Consultant, 66-71; Dir, Econ Dev, IU Int, 71-73; Sr Planner, Gen Electric, 73-74; Dean & Prof, Rutgers Univ, 74-. **RESEARCH** Corporate strategy; company diversification & change. **SELECTED PUBLICATIONS** Auth, Strategies for Diversification & Change, Little Brown, 80; Management Policy, Strategy and Plans, Little Brown, 82; Policy, Strategy, and Implementation, Random Hse, 83; Managing the Unmanageable, Addison-Wesley, 86; Mythmanagement, Basil Blackwell, 89. **CONTACT ADDRESS** 14 Tallowood Dr, Voorhees, NJ, 08043.

LEOSHKO, JANICE

DISCIPLINE ART AND ART HISTORY **EDUCATION** OH State Univ, PhD. **CAREER** Asst prof; Univ TX at Austin, 93-; assoc curator art Indian and Southeast Asian, Los Angeles County Museum of Art, 7 yrs. **HONORS AND AWARDS** Co-curating, int loan exhibition, Romance of the Taj Mahal. **MEMBERSHIPS** Past pres, Am Coun Southern Asian Art. **RESEARCH** Ways in which relig imagery developed in South Asia. **SELECTED PUBLICATIONS** Ed & contrib vol, Bodhgaya, the Site of Enlightenment. **CONTACT ADDRESS** Dept of Art and Art Hist, Univ of Texas at Austin, 2613 Wichita St, FAB 1.110, Austin, TX, 78705.

LEPLIN, JARRETT

PERSONAL Born 11/20/1944, Houston, TX **DISCIPLINE** HISTORY AND PHILOSOPHY OF SCIENCE **EDUCATION** Amherst Col, BA, 66; Univ Chicago, MA, 67, PhD(philos), 72. **CAREER** Instr philos, Ill Inst Technol, 67-70 and Univ Md Baltimore County, 70-71; asst prof, 71-76, ASSOC PROF PHILOS, UNIV NC, GREENSBORO, 76-. **MEMBERSHIPS** Am Philos Asn; Hist Sci Asn; AAAS; Brit Soc Hist Sci; Philos Sci Asn. **RESEARCH** Scientific methodology; theory comparison, philosophy of space and time. **SELECTED PUBLICATIONS** Auth, Kitcher, Philip the Advancement of Science--Science Without Legend, Objectivity Without Illusion, Philos of Sci, Vol 0061, 94. **CONTACT ADDRESS** Dept of Philos, Univ of NC, Greensboro, NC, 23412.

LEPORE, JILL

DISCIPLINE HISTORY **EDUCATION** Tufts, BA, 87; Univ Mich, MA, 90; Yale Univ, MA, 92; MPhil, 95; PhD, 95. **CAREER** ASST PROF, HIST, BOSTON UNIV **HONORS AND AWARDS** Ralph Henry Gabriel Prize, ASA, 95. **MEMBERSHIPS** Am Antiquarian Soc **SELECTED PUBLICATIONS** Auth, "Dead Men Tell No Tales: John Sassamon and the Fatal Consequences of Literacy," Am Quart 46, 94; auth, The Name of War: King Philip's War and the Origins of American Identity, Knopf, 98. **CONTACT ADDRESS** Dept of Hist, Boston Univ, 226 Bay State Rd, Boston, MA, 02215. **EMAIL** jlepore@bu.edu

LERNER, B. H.

PERSONAL Born 09/27/1960, Boston, MA, m, 1990, 2 children **DISCIPLINE** HISTORY **EDUCATION** Columbia Univ MD 86; Univ Washington PhD 96. **CAREER** Columbia Univ, asst prof 93-; Presbyterian Hosp, asst att phys 93-; Univ Washington, inst 91-93; Columbia Univ, inst 89-91; Presbyterian Hosp, asst phys 89-91. **HONORS AND AWARDS** Rbt Wood Johnson Foun Sch 97-2001; Richard Shryock Medal; Phi Beta Kappa; Summa Cum Laude; Jos Garrison Parker prize; Arnold P. Gold award **MEMBERSHIPS** AAHM; ASBH; SGIM; SHHV; OAH. **RESEARCH** History of bioethics, tuberculosis, and cancer. **SELECTED PUBLICATIONS** Auth, Contagion and Confinement: Controlling Tuberculosis Along the Skid Road, Baltimore MD, John Hopkins Univ Press, 98; Fighting the war on breast cancer: debates over early detection, 1945 to present, Ann Intern Med, 98; Nonadherence in tuberculosis treatment: predictors and consequences in New York City, coauth, Amer Jour Med, 97; Can stress cause disease? Revisiting the tuberculosis research of Thomas Holmes, 1949-61, Ann Intern Med, 96; Temporarily detained: tuberculosis alcoholics in Seattle, 1949-60, Am Jour Pub Health, 96; Knowing when to say goodbye: Final Exit and Suicide among the elderly, Suicide and Life Threatening Behavior, 95. **CONTACT ADDRESS** Dept of History, Columbia Univ, 630 West 168th Street, Box 11, NYC, NY, 10032. **EMAIL** BHL5@columbia.edu

LERNER, WARREN

PERSONAL Born 07/16/1929, Boston, MA, m, 1959, 3 children **DISCIPLINE** RUSSIAN HISTORY, HISTORY OF SOCIALISM **EDUCATION** Boston Univ, BS, 52; Columbia Univ, cert and MA, 54, PhD, 61. **CAREER** Asst prof hist, Roosevelt Univ, 59-61; from asst prof to assoc prof, 61-72, PROF HIST, DUKE UNIV, 72-, Nat Endowment for Humanities sr fel, 74-75; mem exec coun, Conf Slavic and E Europ Hist, 78-80. **MEMBERSHIPS** Am Asn Advan Slavic Studies. **RESEARCH** History of Russia and east Europe; Soviet history; history of socialism and communism. **SELECTED PUBLICATIONS** Auth, Lenin--a New Biog, Historian, Vol 0059, 97. **CONTACT ADDRESS** Dept of Hist, Duke Univ, Durham, NC, 27706.

LEROY, PERRY EUGENE

PERSONAL Born 03/17/1930, New York, NY **DISCIPLINE** AFRICAN HISTORY **EDUCATION** Univ Conn, BA, 52; Ohio State Univ, MA, 53, PhD, 60. **CAREER** Asst prof Latin Am, Memphis State Univ, 60-61; asst prof Latin Am and mod imperialism, 61-66, assoc prof, 66-68, PROF AFRICAN AND LATIN AM HIST, MOREHEAD STATE UNIV, 68-. **MEMBERSHIPS** AHA; NEA **RESEARCH** Latin America, Africa and colonial America. **SELECTED PUBLICATIONS** Auth, Discipline in the NW Militia During the War of 1812, Ohio Anthony Wayne Bd; Discipline and Humanity, Academe, 59. **CONTACT ADDRESS** Dept of Hist, Morehead State Univ, Morehead, KY, 40351.

LESCH, JOHN EMMETT

PERSONAL Born 11/24/1945, Vallejo, CA, m, 1980, 1 child **DISCIPLINE** HISTORY OF SCIENCE AND MEDICINE **EDUCATION** Univ Mich, AB, 68; Univ London, MSc, 71; Princeton Univ, PhD(hist), 77. **CAREER** ASST PROF HIST, UNIV CALIF, BERKELEY, 77- **MEMBERSHIPS** Hist Sci Soc; West Coast Hist Sci Soc; Am Inst Hist Pharm. **RESEARCH** History of physiology, 19th century; history of chemotherapy, 20th century. **SELECTED PUBLICATIONS** Auth, Krebs, Hans, Vol 1, the Formation of a Scientific Life 1900-1933, Amer Hist Rev, Vol 0100, 95; Krebs,Hans, Vol 2, Architect of Intermediary Metabolism 1933-1937, Amer Hist Rev, Vol 0100, 95; Quantification and the Quest for Medical Certainty, Isis, Vol 0087, 96. **CONTACT ADDRESS** Dept of Hist, Univ of Calif, 3229 Dwinelle Hall, Berkeley, CA, 94720-2551.

LESHER, JAMES

DISCIPLINE GREEK PHILOSOPHY **EDUCATION** Univ VA, BA; Univ Rochester, PhD. **CAREER** Mem, philos dept, 67; prof, dept(s) class and philos, 93; asst to the pres of the Univ. **HONORS AND AWARDS** ACLS Study fel for postdoc res; jr fel, Ctr Hellenic Stud, 81-82. **SELECTED PUBLICATIONS** Auth, Xenophanes of Colophon: Text, Translation, and Commentary, Univ Toronto Press, 92; Early Interest in Knowledge, Cambridge Companion to Early Greek Philos; auth, more than 30 articles on various aspects of ancient Greek philos and lit. **CONTACT ADDRESS** Dept of Class, Univ MD, 4229 Art-Sociology Building, College Park, MD, 20742-1335. **EMAIL** jlesher@arhu.umd.edu

LESHKO, JAROSLAV

DISCIPLINE ART HISTORY **EDUCATION** Columbia Univ, BA, MA, MPhil, PhD. **CAREER** Art, Smith Col. **HONORS AND AWARDS** Curated an exhibition of, Kokoschka's prints, 87-88. **RESEARCH** Vienna ca 1900, specifically the works of the Austrian Expressionist, Oskar Kokoschka. **SELECTED PUBLICATIONS** Auth, a catalogue, Orbis Pictus-the Prints of Oscar Kokoschka; Jacques Hnizdousky, a catalogue of paintings and prints, Ukrainian Mus NY, 95-96. **CONTACT ADDRESS** Dept of Art, Smith Col, Hillyer Hall 313, Northampton, MA, 01063.

LESKO, LEONARD HENRY

PERSONAL Born 08/14/1938, Chicago, IL, m, 1966 **DISCIPLINE** EGYPTOLOGY **EDUCATION** Loyola Univ Chicago, AB, 61, MA, 64; Univ Chicago, PhD(Egyptol), 69. **CAREER** Instr Latin and Greek, Quigley Prep Sem S, Chicago, 61-64; res asst, Orient Inst, Univ Chicago, 64-65; actg instr Egyptology, Univ Calif, Berkeley, 66-67, actg asst prof, 67-69, from asst prof to assoc prof, 69-72, dir, Near Eastern Studies Ctr, 73-75, chmn dept Near Eastern studies, 75-77 and 79-81, prof, 77-82, chmn prog ancient hist and archaeol, 78-79; WILBUR PROF EGYPTOLOGY AND CHMN DEPT, BROWN UNIV, 82-, Nat Endowment for Humanities younger humantist fel, 70-71; collab ed Coffin texts, Orient Inst, Univ Chicago, 71-; Am Coun Learned Soc award, 73-74; Nat Endowment for Humanities proj grant, 75-79. **HONORS AND AWARDS** FIAT Fac fel, Turin, 90; NEH Hum Inst, 94-95; RI Comt Hum Grant, 98. **MEMBERSHIPS** Egypt Explor Soc; Am Orient Soc; Am Res Ctr Egypt; Fondation Egyptol Reine Elisabeth, Brussels; Int Asn Egyptologists. **RESEARCH** Ancient Egyptian religious literature; Egyptian history and language. **SELECTED PUBLICATIONS** Auth, High Tech Projects for Research and Distribution, Zeitschrift fur Agyptische Sprache Und Altertumskunde, Vol 0121, 94; Voyage to Lower and Upper Egypt, Amer J Archaeol, Vol 0098, 94; Black Athena--the Afroasiatic Roots of Classical Civilization .2. the Archaeological and Documentary Evidence, J Interdisciplinary Hist, Vol 0024, 94; Popular Religion in Egypt During the New-Kingdom, J Near Eastern Stud, Vol 0054, 95; A Dictionary of Late Egyptian, 5 vols, Berkeley & Providence, 82- 90; auth, Egyptological Studies in Honor of Richard A Parker, Hanora & London, 86; co-auth, Religion in Ancient Egypt, Ithaca, 91; ed, Pharoah's Workers: The Villagers of Deir al-Madina, Ithaca, 94; co-ed, Exodus: Egyptian Evidence, Winona Lake, 97; ed, Ancient Egyptian and Mediterranean Studies in Memory of William A Wood, Providence, 98. **CONTACT ADDRESS** Dept of Egyptology, Brown Univ, Box 1899, Providence, RI, 02912. **EMAIL** LLosko@Brownvm.Brown.edu

LESSER, GLORIA

PERSONAL Montreal, PQ, Canada **DISCIPLINE** ART HISTORY/DESIGN **EDUCATION** Chicago Sch Interior Design, Dipl, 63; Concordia Univ, BA, 77, MFA, 83. **CAREER** Sch tchr, 56-60; substitute tchr, 60-78; PROF ART HISTORY & INTERIOR DESIGN, CHAMPLAIN REGIONAL COL, 84-. **MEMBERSHIPS** Can Soc Decorative Arts; Interior Designers' Soc Que; Interior Designers Can. **SELECTED PUBLICATIONS** Auth, Ecole du Meuble 1930-50: Interior Design and Decorative Art in Montreal, 89; auth, The Homes and Furnishings of R.B. Angus, Montreal in Living in Style, 93; auth, Sources and Documents: R.B. Angus Collection, Paintings, Watercolours and Drawings, in J Can Art Hist, No 1, 94; auth, Carl Poul Peterson: Master Danish-Canadian Silversmith, in Material Hist Rev, 43, 96. **CONTACT ADDRESS** 4870 Cote des Neiges, E-305, Montreal, PQ, H3V 1H3.

LESSER, JEFFREY

DISCIPLINE HISTORY **EDUCATION** Brown Univ, BA, MA; NY Univ, PhD. **CAREER** Assoc prof, Conn Col, 90-; assoc dir, Res Ctr Int Stud and Liberal Arts. **HONORS AND AWARDS** Best bk prize, New Eng Coun Latin Amer Stud; Natl Endowment for the Hum grant; Fulbright Comn, grant; North-South Ctr grant; Mellon Initiative for Multiculturalism Across the Curric grant; Amer Coun Learned Soc grant. **RESEARCH** Latin American history; Brazilian history; Modern Jewish history; Ethnic history; Immigration history. **SELECTED PUBLICATIONS** Auth, Welcoming the Undesirables: Brazil and the Jewish Question, 94; Jewish Colonization in Rio Grande do Sul, 1904-1925; Neither Slave nor Free, Neither Black nor White: The Chinese in Early Nineteenth Century Brazil, 94; Immigration and Shifting Concepts of National Identity in Brazil during the Vargas-Era, 94. **CONTACT ADDRESS** Dept of History, Connecticut Col, 270 Mohegan Ave, New London, CT, 06320. **EMAIL** jhles@conncoll.edu

LESTER, DAVID

PERSONAL Born 06/01/1942, London, England, m, 1987, 1 child **DISCIPLINE** PSYCHOLOGY **EDUCATION** Brandeis Univ, PhD 68 **CAREER** Wellesley Col, asst prof 67-69; Suicide Prev Cen, Buff, dir res 69-71; Richard Stockton Col, prof 71. **HONORS AND AWARDS** Dublin Awd. **MEMBERSHIPS** Amer Assn of Suicidology. **RESEARCH** Thanatology, Biography. **SELECTED PUBLICATIONS** Suicide in Creative Women, Commack NY, Nova Sci, 93; Judy Garland, in: F N Magill ed, Great Lives from History: Amer Women, Pasadena, Salem 95; Amy Lowell, in: F N Magill ed, Great lives from hist: Amer Women, Pasadena, Salem, 95; The unconscious and suicide in literature, in" A A Leenaars D Lester eds, Suicide and the Unconscious, Northvale NJ, Jason Aronson, 96; An Encyclopedia of Famouds Suicides, Commack NY, Nova Science, 96. **CONTACT ADDRESS** Psychology Program, The Richard Stockton Col of NJ, Pomona, NJ, 08240-0195.

LEVEN, CHARLES LOUIS

PERSONAL Born 05/02/1928, Chicago, IL, m, 1971, 5 children **DISCIPLINE** MATHMATICS, ECONOMICS **EDUCATION** Northwestern Univ, BS 50, MA 56, PhD 57. **CAREER** Consult, Pub Pol Inst Cal, 98-; Consult, Pulmonary Diseases, Wash Univ Sch Med, 96-; Trustee, Univ City MO Pen Funds, 94-; Adv, Reg Econo Analysis Lab, 93-; Dist Vis Teacher, Reg Sci, Univ Reading, UK, 92-; Distg Prof Pub Pol, Univ MO-St Louis, 91-; Prof Econo Emer, Washington Univ, 91-; Prof Econo, Wash Univ, 65-91; Mem Exec Council, Soc Prof Emer, Wash Univ, 95-98; Mem Intl Adv Bd, Handbook Urban Stud, 95-97; Prof In Res, Arch Plan, Tech Univ, 95; Consult, Munic Rotterdam, 94; Consult, Spirit St Louis Airport, 94; Adv, Ukrain Nat Cen for Mkts Entreprshp, 92; Consult, Behavioral Med, Jewish Hosp, 91-95; Consult, Boatmen's Bank, 91-93; Adv, Metro St Louis Sewer Dist, 92; Prof in Res, Univ Lodz Poland, Dept Urban Econo, 91; Consult, Cardio Div, Jewish Hosp, 90-95; Mem, Bd Electors Land Econo, Cambridge Univ, 90-91; Vis Dist Scholr, Pub Pol Res Cent, Univ MO, 90-91; Consult, St Louis Civic Prog, 90, 96-97; Adv, Polish Found Local Democ, 90-91; Adv, Pol Min Plan Const, 89-91; Consult, IL, Office of the Auditor Gen, 87-89; Consult, Stockholm Reg Plan Off, 87; Chmn, Dept Econo, Wash Univ, 75-80; Chmn, Urban Studies, Wash Univ, 70-71, 82-85. **HONORS AND AWARDS** Walter Isard Award Dist Scholar Reg Sci, 95; RIA Res Award, Univ MO-St Louis, 93; Donald Robertson Mem Lect, Univ Glasgow, 91; Dist Fel So Reg Sci Asn, 91; Am Plan Asn, Mo ch, Excellence in Planning, 86; Nat Inst Health Grant, 85; US Dept Housing Urban Devel Grant, 78; Mercantile Bancorp Symp Grant, 76; Nat Sci Foun Res Grant, 68,73; Comm Urban Econo Res Grant, 65, 66; Soc Sci Res Council, Grant-in-aid-of-Res, 60; Alumni Achiev Fund Award, Iowa State Col, 58; Soc Sci Res Council Res Train Fellowshp, 56; BS with Honors Mathematics, Northwestern Univ, 50. **MEMBERSHIPS** AEA; Midwest Econo Asn; So Econo Asn; **RESEARCH** Urban reg economs; health economs; quality of life measurement. **SELECTED PUBLICATIONS** An analytical Framework for regional Development, with J Legler and P Shaprio, MIT press, 70; Spatial Regional and Population Economics: Essays in Honor of Edgar M Hoover, ed with Mark Perlman and Benjamin Chintz, NY London, Gordon and Breach, 72; Neighborhood Change: Lessons in the Dynamics of Urban Decay, with J Little, H Nourse and R Read, NY, Praeger, 76; The Mature Metropolis, Ed, Lexington, DC, Heath, 78; Gaming in the Us: Taxation Revenues and Economic Impact, with D Phares and c Louishomme, in W B Hildreth and J A Richardson, eds, Handbook on Taxation, NY, forthcoming; Casino Gaming in Missouri: The Spending Displacement Effect and Gamings Net Economic Impact, with D Phares, Proceedings of the National Tax Asn, forthcoming; Economic Impact of Casino Gaming in Missouri, with D Phares and C Luishomme, St Louis, Civic Progress, 98. **CONTACT ADDRESS** Washington Univ, 1 Brookings Dr, Campus Box 1208, St Louis, MO, 63130. **EMAIL** leven@wuecon.wustl.edu

LEVENTHAL, FRED MARC

PERSONAL Born 05/17/1938, New York, NY, m, 1967, 1 child **DISCIPLINE** MODERN BRITISH HISTORY **EDUCATION** Harvard Univ, AB, 60, PhD, 68. **CAREER** Instr hist, Harvard Univ, 67-69; from Asst Prof to Assoc Prof, 69-84, PROF HIST, BOSTON UNIV, 84-; Co-Ed, Twentieth Century British History, 95-; res fel, Inst Advan Studies in Humanities, Univ Edinburgh, 74; vis prof, Univ Kent-Canterbury, 78-79; vis prof, Univ Sydney, 86; vis fel, St. Catherine's Col, Oxford Univ, 97; vis prof, Harvard Univ, 99. **HONORS AND AWARDS** Recipient of numerous grants from NEH, American Coun Learned Soc, Am Philos Soc, and others. **MEMBERSHIPS** NAm Conf Brit Studies (pres 97-99); AHA; Fel, Royal Hist Soc. **RESEARCH** 20th century British culture and politics. **SELECTED PUBLICATIONS** Auth, Respectable Radical: George Howell and Victorian Working Class Politics, Harvard Univ, 71; ed, Trade Unionism New and Old, Harvester, 73; auth, H N Brailsford and the New Leader, J Contemp Hist, 1/74; chap, In: Edwardian radicalism: Aspects of British Radicalism, 1900-14, Routledge & Kegan Paul, 74; chap, In: Essays in Labour History 1918-1939, Croom Helm, 77; The Last Dissenter: H.N. Brailsford and His World, Clarendon Press, 85; Arthur Henderson, Manchester Univ Press, 89; ed, Twentieth-Century Britain: An Encyclopedia, Garland Publ, 95; author of several book chapters and journal articles. **CONTACT ADDRESS** Dept of Hist, Boston Univ, 226 Bay State Rd, Boston, MA, 02215-1403. **EMAIL** fleventh@bu.edu

LEVERING, RALPH BROOKS

PERSONAL Born 02/27/1947, Mt. Airy, NC, m, 1967, 2 children **DISCIPLINE** HISTORY **EDUCATION** Univ NC, BA, 67; Princeton Univ, MA, 69, PhD, 72. **CAREER** Asst to assoc prof, 72-81, Western MD Col; assoc prof, 81-86, Earlhan Col,; assoc to full prof, 86-, Davidson Col. **HONORS AND AWARDS** Phi Beta Kappa, 67; NEH fel, 76-77. **MEMBERSHIPS** Soc of Hist of Am Foreign Relations; AHA; Org of Am Hist; Peace Hist Soc. **RESEARCH** US foreign relations since 1939; public opinion and US foreign policy. **SELECTED PUBLICATIONS** Auth, American Opinion and the Russian Alliance, 1945-1972, Univ NC Press, 76; auth, The Public and American Foreign Policy, 1918-1978, William Morrow, for the Foreign Policy Asn, 78; co-auth, The Kennedy Crises: The Press, the Presidency, and Foreign Policy, Univ NC Press, 83; auth, The Cold War: A Post-Cold War History, Harlan Davidson, 94; auth, Citizen Action for Global Change: The Neptune Group and Law of the Sea, Syracuse Univ Press, 99. **CONTACT ADDRESS** History Dept, Davidson Col, PO Box 1719, Davidson, NC, 28036. **EMAIL** ralevering@davidson.edu

LEVERING LEWIS, DAVID

DISCIPLINE AFRICAN-AMERICAN HISTORY **EDUCATION** London Sch of Econ and Polit Sci, PhD, 62. **CAREER** Prof, Martin Luther King, Jr Univ Prof, Rutgers, State Univ NJ, Livingston, 94-. **RESEARCH** African-American history; conceptions of race and racism; the dynamics of European colonialism, especially in Africa. **SELECTED PUBLICATIONS** Auth, W.E.B. Du Bois: Biography of a Race, 1868-1919 Vol I, Henry Holt and Co, 93; The Portable Harlem Renaissance Reader, Viking, 94; The Harlem Renaissance, in Robert O'Meally and Jack Salzman, eds, Encyclopedia of African-American Culture and History, Macmillan, 94; Rev of Carter G. Woodson: A Life in Black History, by Jacqueline Goggin, J of Am Hist, 94; Khartoum, in Past Imperfect: History According to Hollywood, Henry Holt, 95; W.E.B. Du Bois: A Reader, Henry Holt and Co, 95. **CONTACT ADDRESS** Dept of Hist, Rutgers, State Univ NJ, Livingston Col, Van Dyck Hall CAC, Piscataway, NJ, 26745. **EMAIL** lcdean@rci.rutgers.edu

LEVERNIER, JAMES ARTHUR

PERSONAL Born 07/26/1949, Highland Park, IL **DISCIPLINE** ENGLISH, AMERICAN STUDIES **EDUCATION** Marquette Univ, BA, 71; Univ Pa, MA, 73, PhD(English), 75. **CAREER** Asst prof, 76-80, ASSOC PROF ENGLISH, UNIV ARK, LITTLE ROCK, 80-, DIR, AM STUDIES, 78-. **MEMBERSHIPS** MLA; Children's Lit Asn; Am Studies Asn. **RESEARCH** Early American literature; native American studies; folklore. **SELECTED PUBLICATIONS** Auth, Style as Protest in the Poetry of Wheatley, Phillis, Style, Vol 0027, 93; The Collected Works of Wheatley, Phillis, Resources for Amer Lit Study, Vol 0019, 93; Wheatley, Phillis C.1735-1784 + Legacy Profile, Legacy, Vol 0013, 96. **CONTACT ADDRESS** Univ Arkansas, 2801 S University Av, Little Rock, AR, 72204-1000.

LEVESQUE, GEORGE AUGUST

PERSONAL Born 06/08/1936, West Warwick, RI **DISCIPLINE** UNITED STATES & AFRO-AMERICAN HISTORY **EDUCATION** RI Col, BA, 62; Harvard Law Sch, LLB, 65; Brown Univ, AM, 69; State Univ NY Binghamton, PhD(hist), 76. **CAREER** Asst dean men, Univ Ottawa, 64-66; asst prof US hist, State Univ NY Morrisville, 66-71; teaching fel urban hist, State Univ NY Binghamton, 71-72; Nat Endowment for Humanities-Charles Warren fel ethnic studies, Harvard Univ, 72-73; Fulbright scholar Afro-Am hist, Anglo-Am Sect, Univ Montpellier, 73-74; teaching fel, State Univ NY Binghamton, 74-75; asst prof hist, Ill State Univ, 75-77; asst prof Afro-Am studies, Ind State Univ, Terre Haute, 77-78, assoc prof, 78-81; assoc prof Afro-Am studies, 81-94, prof, Afro-Am studies, Univ Ctr, State Univ Ny Albany, 94-, Am Coun Learned Soc grant-inaid, 77; consult, Nat Endowment for Humanities, 78-81; T Wistar Brown fel, Haverford Col, 79-80; sr Fulbright award, Univ Yaounde, CAmoon, 78-79 & John F Kennedy Prof, US Hist, Free Univ Berlin, 82-83. **HONORS AND AWARDS** Littleton-Griswold Res Grant, Am Hist Asn, 91-92; DuBois Inst Res Fel, Harvard univ, 87. **RESEARCH** Afro-American history, 1750-1865; 18th and 19th century American social-urban history; antebellum reform. **SELECTED PUBLICATIONS** Auth, Black Abolitionists in the Age of jackson, J Black Studies, 12/70; Inherent Reformers-Inherited Orthodoxy: Black Baptists in Boston, J Negro History, 9/75; LeRoi Jones' Dutchman: Myth & Allegory, Obsidian, 79; Politicians in Petticoats: Interracial Sex and Leg, Politics in Antebellum Massachusetts, New England J Black Studies, 83; Slavery in the Ideology & Politics of the Revolutionary Generation, Canadian Rev, Am Studies, 87; Slave Names and Naming Practices, Dictionary of Afro-Am Slavery, 88 & 97. **CONTACT ADDRESS** Dept of African-Am Studies, SUNY, Albany, 1400 Washington Ave, Albany, NY, 12222-1000.

LEVI, DARRELL ERVILLE

PERSONAL Born 11/14/1940, San Francisco, CA, m, 1963, 2 children **DISCIPLINE** HISTORY **EDUCATION** Univ Calif, Berkeley, BA, 63; Univ Calif, Davis, MA, 69; Yale Univ, PhD(hist), 74. **CAREER** Asst prof, 74-79, ASSOC PROF HIST, FLA STATE UNIV, 79-, Fla State Univ prof development grant, 78. **MEMBERSHIPS** Conf Latin Am Hist, Latin Am Studies Asn. **RESEARCH** Social history of Brazil; history of Puerto Rico; Latin American nationalism. **SELECTED PUBLICATIONS** Auth, The Social Origins of Democratic Socialism in Jamaica, Americas, Vol 0050, 94; To Hell With Paradise, a History of the Jamaican Tourist Industry, Hisp Amer Hist Rev, Vol 0075, 95; Distant Neighbors in the Caribbean, the Dominican Republic and Jamaica in Comparative Perspective, Hisp Amer Hist Rev, Vol 0075, 95; The Jamaican People, 1880-1902--Race, Class and Social Control, Americas, Vol 0052, 95; Noises in the Blood--Orality, Gender, and the Vulgar Body of Jamaican Popular-Culture, Hisp Amer Hist Rev, Vol 0077, 97. **CONTACT ADDRESS** Dept of Hist, Florida State Univ, 600 W College Ave, Tallahassee, FL, 32306-1096.

LEVIN, DAVID S.

PERSONAL Born 05/30/1933, New York, NY, m, 1959, 2 children **DISCIPLINE** UNITED STATES HISTORY **EDUCATION** Hunter Col, BA, 57; Columbia Univ, MA, 60, PhD(hist), 69. **CAREER** From instr to asst prof hist, Adelphi Univ, 63-69; asst prof hist & asst dean fac, Dowling Col, 69-70; asst prof hist, John Jay Col Criminal Justice, 70-73; prof hist & chemn soc sci, Mercer County Comm Col, 73-; dean Arts, Communication & Engineering Technology, 83-; Chmn East Mid-Atlantic regional selection comt, Danforth Assoc Prog, 72-75; co-dir, Community Col Intern Prog, Princeton Univ, 75-; consult, Mid-Career Fels Prog, NJ Consortium on Community Cols, 77-. **MEMBERSHIPS** AHA; Orgn Am Historians; AAUP. **RESEARCH** Stock market regulation; Great Depression and the New Deal. **CONTACT ADDRESS** Dept of Soc Sci, Mercer County Comm Col, PO Box B, Trenton, NJ, 08690-0182. **EMAIL** levind@mccc.edu

LEVIN, DONALD NORMAN

PERSONAL Born 02/01/1927, Rochester, NY, m, 1949, 2 children **DISCIPLINE** CLASSICS **EDUCATION** Cornell Univ, BA, 49, MA, 52; Harvard Univ, MA, 54, PhD(class), 57. **CAREER** Asst class, Tufts Col, 53-54; Ford Found intern class and humanities, Reed Col, 54-55; from instr to asst prof class, Wash Univ, 56-59; asst prof, Mt Holyoke Col, 59-63; assoc prof, 63-68, PROF CLASS, RICE UNIV, 68-, Wash Univ res grants, 57-59. **MEMBERSHIPS** Am Philol Asn; Archaeol Inst Am; Asn Int Papyrologues; Class Asn Midwest and South; Soc Ancient Greek Philos. **RESEARCH** Greek drama and early Greek philosophy; Hellenistic literature; Latin poetry, especially elegy and lyric. **SELECTED PUBLICATIONS** Auth, 'Aethiopica' 3-4, Greek Dunces, Egyptian Sage + Heliodorus, Athenaeum Studi Periodici Di Letteratura E Storia Dell Antichita, Vol 0080, 92. **CONTACT ADDRESS** Dept of Classics, Rice Univ, Houston, TX, 77251.

LEVIN, EVE

PERSONAL Born 03/28/1954, Chicago, IL **DISCIPLINE** HISTORY **EDUCATION** Mount Holyoke Col, BA, 75; Ind Univ, MA, 76, PhD, 83. **CAREER** Ohio State Univ, asst prof, 83-90, assoc prof ed, 90-. **HONORS AND AWARDS** Phi Beta Kappa, IREX/Fulbright-Hays, 81-82, 90; ACLS post-doctoral fel, 86-87; Heldt Prize for best translation in Slavic Women's Studies, 97. **MEMBERSHIPS** AAASS; Early Slavic Studies Asn; AHA; Medieval Acad Am; Asn Women Slavic Studies. **RESEARCH** Russian and Balkan hist, 900-1750. **CONTACT ADDRESS** Dept of History, Ohio State Univ, 106 Dulles Hall, 230 W 17th Ave, Columbus, OH, 43210. **EMAIL** levin.2@osu.edu

LEVIN, SAUL

PERSONAL Born 07/13/1921, Chicago, IL, m, 1951, 6 children **DISCIPLINE** CLASSICS **EDUCATION** Univ Chicago, AB, 42, PhD(Greek), 49. **CAREER** Instr hist, Univ Chicago, 49-51; from asst prof to assoc prof classics, Wash Univ, 51-61; prof, 61-65, PROF ANCIENT LANG, STATE UNIV NY BINGHAMTON, 65-, Fund Advan Educ fac fel, 53-54. **MEMBERSHIPS** Am Philol Asn; Soc Bibl Lit; Nat Asn Prof Hebrew; Am Orient Soc; Ling Asn Can and US (pres, 80-81). **RESEARCH** Comparison of Semitic and Indo-European languages; classical Greek, especially the Homeric dialect; Hebrew scriptures. **SELECTED PUBLICATIONS** Auth, Overlapping Verbs, Concubare and Concumbere, Class World, Vol 0087, 93; Hezekiah Boil + Suggestions on the Diagnostic Possibilities Presented by Illnesses Contained in Biblical Texts Isaiah-Xxxviii and 2-Kings-Xx, Judaism, Vol 0042, 93; Semitic Studies in Honor of Leslau,Wolf on the Occasion of his 85th Birthday--, Word-J Int Ling Asn, Vol 0045, 94; Jacob Limp + a Psychoanalytical and Clinical Interpretation Assuming a Genital Focus in the Biblical Story of Jacobs-Dream Genesis-Xxxii,25f, Judaism, Vol 0044, 95; 'After the Jahiliyya', Stand Mag, Vol 0037, 96; Let My Right Hand Wither + a Medical Opinion on the Hebrew Word Tishkakh From Psalm-Cxxxvii, Judaism, Vol 0045, 96. **CONTACT ADDRESS** Dept of Classics and Near Eastern Stud, State Univ of NY, Binghamton, NY, 13901.

LEVIN, WILLIAM R.

DISCIPLINE ART HISTORY **EDUCATION** Northwestern Univ, BA; Univ Mich, MA and PhD. **CAREER** Instr, Mankato State Univ; fac, Centre Col, 86-; assoc prof, current. **MEMBERSHIPS** Int Cong Med Studies; SE Col Art Conf; Col Art Asn. **RESEARCH** History and art of Late-Medieval and Early Renaissance philanthropic institutions in Italy; works of art dealing with the concept of charity. **SELECTED PUBLICATIONS** Auth, Images of Love and Death in Late Medieval and Renaissance Art Univ Mich P, 76. **CONTACT ADDRESS** Centre Col, 600 W Walnut St, Danville, KY, 40422. **EMAIL** levin@centre.edu

LEVINE, ALEXANDER
PERSONAL Born 07/21/1966, Minneapolis, MN **DISCIPLINE** EIGHTEENTH CENTURY PHILOSOPHY **EDUCATION** Reed Coll, BA, 88; Univ Calif, C Phil, 91; PhD, 94.

LEVINE, DANIEL
PERSONAL Born 12/31/1934, New York, NY, m, 1954, 2 children **DISCIPLINE** AMERICAN HISTORY **EDUCATION** Antioch Col, BA, 56; Northwestern Univ, MA, 57, PhD, 61. **CAREER** Asst prof hist, Earlham Col, 60-63; from asst prof to assoc prof, 63-72, PROF HIST, BOWDOIN COL, 72-; Fulbright sr lectr hist, Univ Copenhagen & Aarhus, 69-70; Guggenheim fel, Denmark, 72-73; Fulbright sr lectr, Munich, 79-80. **MEMBERSHIPS** AHA; Orgn Am Historians. **RESEARCH** American intellectual history since the Civil War; modern Danish social history; comparative social welfare history. **SELECTED PUBLICATIONS** Auth, Varieties of Reform Thought, State Hist Soc Wis, 64; John Dewey, Randolph Bourne and the legacy of liberalism, Antioch Rev, summer 69; Jane Addams and the Liberal Tradition, State Hist Soc Wis, 71; Den ideologiske baggrnd for Dansk social-lovgivning, 1890-1933, Scandia, Oslo, 73; Conservation & tradition in Danish social welfare legislation, 1890-1933, Comp Studies Soc & Hist, 78; Social Democrats, socialism and social insurance: Germany and Denmark, 1918-1933, Comparative Soc Res, vol 6, 83; Poverty and Society, Rutgers, 88; A single standard of civilization, Ga Hist Quart, spring 97 **CONTACT ADDRESS** Dept of Hist, Bowdoin Col, 9900 College Station, Brunswick, ME, 04011-8499. **EMAIL** dlevine@polar.bowdoin.edu

LEVINE, DANIEL
DISCIPLINE GREEK LITERATURE **EDUCATION** Univ Minn, BA, 75; Univ Cincinnati, PhD, 80. **CAREER** English and Lit, Univ Ark. **HONORS AND AWARDS** Excellence Tchng Classics; Burlington Northern Outstanding Fac-Scholar Tchng Award., Chair, Classical Studies Prog. **SELECTED PUBLICATIONS** Area: Greek epic, lyric, dramatic, and historical texts. **CONTACT ADDRESS** Univ Ark, Fayetteville, AR, 72701.

LEVINE, DANIEL BLANK
PERSONAL Born 09/22/1953, Cincinnati, OH **DISCIPLINE** CLASSICAL LANGUAGE AND LITERATURE **EDUCATION** Univ Minn, BA, 75; Univ Cincinnati, PhD(classics), 80. **CAREER** ASST PROF CLASSICS, UNIV ARK, 80-, Ed, Ark Class Newslett, 80-. **MEMBERSHIPS** Class Asn Mid West and South; Am Philol Asn. **RESEARCH** Epic poetry; archaic Greek history. **SELECTED PUBLICATIONS** Auth, Hubris in Josephus Jewish Antiquities 1-4, Hebrew Union Coll Annual, Vol 0064, 94. **CONTACT ADDRESS** Dept of Foreign Lang, Univ of Ark, Fayetteville, AR, 72701-1202.

LEVINE, DAVID OSCAR
PERSONAL Born 08/16/1955, Middletown, NY, m, 1981, 2 children **DISCIPLINE** HISTORY OF AMERICAN CIVILIZATION **EDUCATION** Univ PA, BA, Magna Cum Laude with Distinction, 76; Harvard Univ, MA, History, 78, PhD, Hist and Am Civilization, 81. **CAREER** Visiting asst prof, dept hist, Univ Calif, Los Angeles, 81-87; exec dir, Touch Am Hist Foundation, 87-. **RESEARCH** Hist Am Edu **SELECTED PUBLICATIONS** The American College and the Culture of Aspiration, Cornell Univ Press, 86. **CONTACT ADDRESS** Touch Am History, 4201 Via Marina, Marina del Rey, CA, 90292. **EMAIL** levzach@earthlink.net

LEVINE, PETER D.
PERSONAL Born 06/23/1944, Brooklyn, NY, m, 1965, 1 child **DISCIPLINE** AMERICAN HISTORY **EDUCATION** Columbia Col, BA, 65; Columbia Univ, MA, 66; Rutgers Univ, PhD, 71. **CAREER** From instr to assoc prof, 69-84, prof Am hist, MI State Univ, 84. **RESEARCH** Hist of sport in Am. **SELECTED PUBLICATIONS** Auth, The Behavior of State Legislative Parties in the Jacksonian Era: New Jersey, 1829-44, J Am Hist, 12/75; Fairleigh Dickinson Univ, J Am Hist, 77; Draft Evasion in the North During the Civil War, 1863-1865, J Am Hist, 3/81; A.G. Spalding & the Rise of Baseball, Oxford Univ Press, 85; Ellis Island to Ebbets Field, Sport & the American Jewish Experience, Oxford Univ Press, 92; coauth, Idols of the Game, A Sporting History of 20th Century America, Turner, 95. **CONTACT ADDRESS** Dept of Hist, Michigan State Univ, 301 Morrill Hall, East Lansing, MI, 48824-1036. **EMAIL** levinep@pilot.msu.edu

LEVINE, ROBERT M.
PERSONAL Born 03/26/1941, New York, NY, 2 children **DISCIPLINE** LATIN AMERICAN HISTORY **EDUCATION** Colgate Univ, AB, 62; Princeton Univ, AM, 64, PhD, 67. **CAREER** From asst prof hist to assoc prof, State Univ NY Stony Brook, 66-78, prof, 78-80; prof hist, Univ Miami, 80-, Dir, Latin Am Studies, Chmn comt, Brazilian studies, Conf Latin Am Hist, Hisp Found, 70-71; chmn sem Latin Am, Columbia Univ, 72-73; sr Fulbright-Hays lectr, Brazil, 73 & 80. **MEMBERSHIPS** AHA; Latin Am Studies Asn; Hisp Am Hist Soc; Conf Latin Am Hist. **RESEARCH** Mod Brazil; mod Latin Am. **SELECTED PUBLICATIONS** Auth, The Vargas Regime, Columbia Univ, 70; Pernambuco and the Brazilian Federation, 1889-1937, Stanford Univ, 74; Vale of Tears, Univ CA, 92; Father of the Poor?, Cambridge Univ, 98; Brazilian Legacies, Sharpe, 98. **CONTACT ADDRESS** Dept of Hist, Univ of Miami, PO Box 248107, Miami, FL, 33124-4662. **EMAIL** rlevine@miami.edu

LEVINE, ROBERT M.
PERSONAL Born 03/26/1941, New York, NY, 2 children **DISCIPLINE** LATIN AMERICAN HISTORY **EDUCATION** Colgate Univ, AB, 62; Princeton Univ, AM, 64, PhD(hist), 67. **CAREER** From asst prof hist to assoc prof, State Univ NY Stony Brook, 66-78, prof, 78-80; PROF HIST, UNIV MIAMI, 80-, dir of Lat Am stu, Chmn comt, Brazilian studies, Conf Latin Am Hist, Hisp Found, 70-71; chmn sem Latin Am, Columbia Univ, 72-73; sr Fulbright-Hays lectr, Brazil, 73 & 80. **MEMBERSHIPS** AHA; Latin Am Studies Asn; Hisp Am Hist Soc; Conf Latin Am Hist. **RESEARCH** Modern Brazil; modern Latin America. **SELECTED PUBLICATIONS** Auth, The Jorges Regime, Columbia Univ, 70; auth, Pernambuco and the Brazilian Federation , 1889-1937, Standford Univ, 74; auth, Vale of Tears, Univ Calif, 92; auth, Father of the Poor?, Cambridge Univ, 98; auth, Brazilian Legacies, Sharpe, 98. **CONTACT ADDRESS** Dept of Hist, Univ of Miami, P O Box 24810, Miami, FL, 33124-4662. **EMAIL** rlevine@miami.edu

LEVINE, SURA
DISCIPLINE ART HISTORY **EDUCATION** Univ MI, BA; Univ Chicago, MA, PhD. **CAREER** Assoc prof, Hampshire Col. **RESEARCH** Soc hist of 19th and 20th century Europ and Am art. **SELECTED PUBLICATIONS** Auth, Politics and the Graphic Art of the Belgian Avant-Garde; Belgian Art Nouveau Sculpture; Print Culture in the Age of the French Revolution; Constantin Meunier: A Life of Labor; Constantin Meunier's Monument au travail. **CONTACT ADDRESS** Hampshire Col, Amherst, MA, 01002.

LEVY, BARRY
DISCIPLINE HISTORY **EDUCATION** Cornell Univ, BA, 68; Univ Penn, PhD, 76. **CAREER** ASSOC PROF, HIST, UNIV MASS AMHERST **MEMBERSHIPS** Am Antiquarian Soc **SELECTED PUBLICATIONS** Auth, Quakers and the American Family: British Settlement in the Deleware Valley, 1650- 1785, Oxford Univ Press, 98. **CONTACT ADDRESS** Dept of Hist, Univ of Mass at Amherst, Herter Hall, Amherst, MA, 01002. **EMAIL** bjl@history.umass.edu

LEVY, BARRY
DISCIPLINE HISTORY **EDUCATION** PA Univ, PhD, 76. **CAREER** Assoc prof, Univ MA Amherst. **SELECTED PUBLICATIONS** Auth, Quakers and the American Family: British Settlement in the Delaware Valley, 88. **CONTACT ADDRESS** Dept of Hist, Univ Massachusetts Amherst, Mass Ave, Amherst, MA, 01003.

LEVY, DAVID BENJAMIN
PERSONAL Born 03/29/1948, New York, NY, m, 1968, 2 children **DISCIPLINE** MUSIC **EDUCATION** Eastman Sch of Music, BM, 69, MA, 71; Univ Rochester, PhD, 80. **CAREER** Prof, Chair, Wake Forest Univ, 76- . **HONORS AND AWARDS** Advisory Bd, Amer Beethoven Soc; Outstanding Acad Book, Choice, 96. **MEMBERSHIPS** Amer Musicological Soc; Amer Beethoven Soc. **RESEARCH** Beethoven stud; Berlioz; Wagner; nineteenth century music. **SELECTED PUBLICATIONS** Auth, Ritter Berlioz' in Germany, Berlioz Stud, Cambridge Univ Press, 92; The Contrabass Recitative in Beethoven's Ninth Symphony Revisited, Hist Performance, 92; To the Ninth, Power, Wake Forest Univ Mag, 95; Beethoven: The Ninth Symphony, Schirmer Books, 95; assoc ed, Historical Performance, 93-95. **CONTACT ADDRESS** Dept of Music, Wake Forest Univ, Box 7345, Winston-Salem, NC, 27109. **EMAIL** levy@wfu.edu

LEVY, DAVID WILLIAM
PERSONAL Born 05/06/1937, Chicago, IL **DISCIPLINE** AMERICAN INTELLECTUAL HISTORY **EDUCATION** Univ Ill, BA, 59; Univ Chicago, MA, 61; Univ Wis, PhD(hist), 67. **CAREER** Instr hist, Ohio State Univ, 64-67; asst prof, 67-71, ASSOC PROF HIST, UNIV OKLA, 71-, Nat Endowment for Humanities grants, 67-69, 71-73; Rockefeller Found grant, 80-81. **MEMBERSHIPS** Orgn Am Historians. **RESEARCH** American intellectual history; political philosophy in the Progressive Era. **SELECTED PUBLICATIONS** Auth, The Challenge of Our Time--Wilson, Woodrow, Croly, Herbert, Bourne, Randolph and the Making of Modern America, J Amer Hist, Vol 0080, 93; The People V Darrow,Clarence--the Bribery Trial of America Greatest Lawyer, J Amer Hist, Vol 0081, 94; Shaping Modern Liberalism--Croly,Herbert and Progressive Thought, Amer Hist Rev, Vol 0099, 94; Working Class War--American Combat Soldiers and Vietnam, J Amer Hist, Vol 0081, 94; Wesleyan University, 1831-1910--Collegiate Enterprise in New England, Rev(s) In Amer Hist, Vol 0023, 95; Parrington, V.L.--Through the Avenue of Art, Rev(s) in Amer Hist, Vol 0023, 95; Bad Times for Good Ol Boys--the Oklahoma County Commissioner Scandal, J West, Vol 0035, 96; Managing Legal Uncertainty--Elite Lawyers in the New Deal, J Amer Hist, Vol 0083, 97. **CONTACT ADDRESS** Dept of Hist, Univ of Okla, Norman, OK, 73019.

LEVY, EUGENE DONALD
PERSONAL Born 12/04/1933, Los Angeles, CA, m, 1960, 2 children **DISCIPLINE** AMERICAN SOCIAL HISTORY **EDUCATION** Univ Calif, Riverside, AB, 56; Yale Univ, MA, 60, PhD, 70. **CAREER** Actg instr hist & Am studies, Yale Univ, 62-65; asst prof, 65-71, assoc prof hist, Carnegie-Mellon Univ, 71-95; NEH jr fac fel, 71-72; Am Coun Learned Soc res grant, 72; Pa Humanities Coun grant, 81. **MEMBERSHIPS** Orgn Am Historians; Am Assn State & Local Hist. **RESEARCH** Afro-American history; ethnic American history; industrial America. **SELECTED PUBLICATIONS** Art, Ragtime and Race Pride, J Popular Cult, winter 68; co-ed, In Search of America, Dryden, 72; auth, James Weldon Johnson: Black Leader, Black Voice, Univ Chicago, 73; art, Is the Jew a White Man? Press Reaction to the Leo Frank Case, Phylon, 6/74; coauth, America's People, Harper & Row, 82; art, High Bridge Low Bridge, Places, Summer, 93; art, The Aesthetics of Power: High Voltage Transmission Systems and the American Landscape, Technology and Cultures, 6/97. **CONTACT ADDRESS** Dept of History, Carnegie Mellon Univ, 5000 Forbes Ave, Pittsburgh, PA, 15213-3890. **EMAIL** elil@andrew.cmu.edu

LEVY, IAN CHRISTOPHER
PERSONAL Born 02/24/1967, New York, NY **DISCIPLINE** HISTORICAL THEOLOGY **EDUCATION** Univ of New Mexico, BA, 89; Vanderbilt, MA, 91; Marquette Univ, PhD, 97. **CAREER** Marquette Univ, tchg asst, 94-96, Nashotah House Episcopal Sem, adj prof, 97; Marquette Univ, adj prof, 97-, Carroll Col, adj prof, 98-. **HONORS AND AWARDS** Phi Beta Kappa, Marquette Univ, Schmitt fell. **MEMBERSHIPS** MAA, MAMW, SBL, ASCH **RESEARCH** Medieval Theol; esp biblical interpretations and sacraments. **SELECTED PUBLICATIONS** Auth, John Wyclif and Augustinian Realism, in: Augustiniana, 98; Biographical Dictionary of Christian Theologians, contributing auth, eds P. Carey, J. Lienhard, Greenwood Pub Co, forthcoming; auth, Was John Wyclif's Theology of the Eucharist Donatistic? in: Scottish Jour of Theol, forthcoming. **CONTACT ADDRESS** Dept of Theology, Marquette Univ, 5400 W Washington Blvd, Milwaukee, WI, 53208. **EMAIL** ian.levy@marquette.edu

LEVY, LEONARD WILLIAMS
PERSONAL Born 04/09/1923, m, 1944, 2 children **DISCIPLINE** HISTORY **EDUCATION** Columbia Univ, BA, 47, MA, 48, PhD(hist), 51. **CAREER** Res asst hist, Columbia Univ, 50-51; instr Am civilization, Brandeis Univ, 51-54, from asst prof to prof hist, 54-70, Earl Warren prof Am consitutional hist, 57-70, chmn dept hist, 67-68, assoc dean fac and dean grad sch, 58-63, dean fac, 63-66, chmn grad prog hist, 66-67, 69-70; William W Clary prof hist, 70-74, ANDREW W MELLON ALL-CLAREMONT PROF HUMANITIES AND HIST, CLAREMONT GRAD SCH, 74- CHMN GRAD FAC HIST, CLAREMONT COLS, 70-, Guggenheim fel, 57-58; sr res fel, Ctr Study Hist Liberty Am, Harvard Univ, 61-62; mem, Nat Comn Law and Social Action, Am Jewish Cong, 62-67; mem, US Bicentennial Comn Am Revolution, 67-68; Am Bar Found fel legal hist, 73-74; Nat Endowment for Humanities sr fel, 74; bicentennial speaker, City St Louis, 76; consult ed, Encycl Britannica; Pulitzer Prize juror and chmn. **HONORS AND AWARDS** Pulitzer Prize in hist, 69; Gaspar Bacon lectr, Boston Univ, 72; Sheldon Elliott lectr, Law Sch, Univ Southern Calif, 72. **MEMBERSHIPS** Am Acad Polit and Soc Sci; Am Soc Legal Hist; Orgn Am Historians; Am Antiq Soc; Inst Early Am Hist and Cult. **RESEARCH** History of the Bill of Rights; American legal and constitutional history; history of religion. **SELECTED PUBLICATIONS** Auth, The Godless Constitution--the Case Against Religious Correctness, Rev(s) in Amer Hist, Vol 0024, 96; Foreign Policy and War Powers--the Presidency and the Framers, Amer Scholar, Vol 0066, 97. **CONTACT ADDRESS** Dept of Humanities and Hist, Claremont Graduate Sch, Claremont, CA, 91711.

LEVY, RICHARD S.
PERSONAL Born 05/10/1940, Chicago, IL, m, 1967 **DISCIPLINE** GERMAN AND EUROPEAN HISTORY **EDUCATION** Univ Chicago, BA, 62; Yale Univ, MA, 64, PhD(hist), 69. **CAREER** Instr-asst hist, Univ Mass, Amherst, 66-70; asst prof, 70-76, ASSOC PROF HIST, UNIV ILL, CHICAGO CIRCLE, 76-. **MEMBERSHIPS** AHA **RESEARCH** German anti-Semitism; the German Empire, 1871-1918. **SELECTED PUBLICATIONS** Auth, Modernity Within Tradition--the Social History of Orthodox Jewry in Imperial Germany, Historian, Vol 0056, 94; Art, Ideology, and Economics in Nazi Germany--the Reich Chambers of Music, Theater, and the Visual Arts, Ger Stud Rev, Vol 0018, 95. **CONTACT ADDRESS** Dept of Hist, Univ of Ill, Chicago Circle, Chicago, IL, 60680.

LEWARNE, CHARLES PIERCE
PERSONAL Born 08/16/1930, Kirkland, WA, m, 1956, 3 children **DISCIPLINE** UNITED STATES HISTORY **EDUCATION** Western Wash State Col, BA and BA in Ed, 55; Univ Calif, Berkeley, MA, 58; Univ Wash, PhD(hist), 69. **CAREER** Teacher hist, Battle Ground Sch Dist, Wash, 55-57; TEACHER HIST, EDMONDS SCH DIST 15, 58-, Part-time instr hist, Everett Community Col, 62-65 and Edmonds Community Col, 67. **MEMBERSHIPS** Orgn Am Historians; Western Hist Asn; NEA; Nat Hist Communal Soc Asn. **RESEARCH** Late 19th

century communitarian movement; PACIFIC Northwest history; radicalism in the PACIFIC Northwest. **SELECTED PUBLICATIONS** Auth, Carstensen, Vernon 1907-1992, Pac Northwest Quart, Vol 0084, 93; Spokane and the Inland Empire--an Interior Pacific-Northwest Anthology, Ore Hist Quart, Vol 0094, 93; Washington Comes of Age--the State in the National Experience, Ore Hist Quart, Vol 0095, 94; The Pacific Northwest--an Interpretive History, Pac Northwest Quart, Vol 0088, 97. **CONTACT ADDRESS** 20829 Hillcrest Pl, Edmonds, WA, 98020.

LEWELLEN, TED CHARLES
PERSONAL Born 06/26/1940, Redding, CA, m, 1985 **DISCIPLINE** CULTURAL ANTHROPOLOGY **EDUCATION** Alaska Methodist Univ, BA, Philos/Comp Relig, 63; NY Univ, MA, Anthrop, 73; Univ Colo, PhD, Cult Anthrop, 77. **CAREER** Vis asst prof, Anthrop, Tex Tech Univ, 77-78; asst prof to prof, Univ Richmond, 78- **HONORS AND AWARDS** Prof of the year, Omicron Delta Kappa, Univ of Richmond, 82; Distinguished Tchr, Mortarboard Leadership Soc, Univ of Richmond, 81. **MEMBERSHIPS** Am Anthrop Asn; World Acad Develop and Coop. **RESEARCH** Postmodernism and science wars in anthropology; anthropology development theory. **SELECTED PUBLICATIONS** Auth,"Holy and Unholy Alliances: The Politics of Catholicism in Revolutionary Nicaragua," Jour Church and State, 89; auth, "Individualism and Heirarchy: A Grid/Group Analysis of American Political Culture," Polar-Polit & Legal Anthrop Rev, 93; "Structures of Terror: A Systems Analysis of Repression in El Salvador," Human Rights and Third World Develop, 85; auth, "The U.S. and State Terrorism in the Third World," Terrible Beyond Endurance: Foreign Policy of State Terrorism, 88; auth, Dependency and Development: An Introduction to the Third World, Bergin and Garvey, 95. **CONTACT ADDRESS** Dept Soc and Anthrop, Univ Richmond, Richmond, VA, 23173. **EMAIL** tlewelle@richmond.edu

LEWENSTEIN, BRUCE V.
PERSONAL Born 09/18/1957, Palo Alto, CA, m, 1983, 3 children **DISCIPLINE** HISTORY **EDUCATION** Univ Chicago, BA 80; Univ Penn, MA 85; PhD 87. **CAREER** Cornell Univ, asst prof, assoc prof, 87-. **CONTACT ADDRESS** Dept of Communication, Cornell Univ, Ithaca, NY, 14853.

LEWIN, LINDA
PERSONAL Born 05/07/1941, Baltimore, MD **DISCIPLINE** LATIN AMERICAN HISTORY **EDUCATION** Univ Calif, Berkeley, AB, 63; Columbia Univ, MA, 68, PhD(hist), 75. **CAREER** From instr to asst prof hist, John Jay Col, City Univ New York, 71-76; asst prof, Princeton Univ, 76-82; ASST PROF HIST, UNIV CALIF, BERKELEY, 82-, Vis res scholar, Boston Col Law Sch, 80-81. **HONORS AND AWARDS** Best article prize Latin Am hist, Conf Latin Am Hist, AHA, 80. **MEMBERSHIPS** Conf Latin Am Hist; Latin Am Studies Asn. **RESEARCH** Brazilian family history and family law; oligarchical politics in Brazil's Old Republic; history of the Brazilian northeast. **SELECTED PUBLICATIONS** Auth, Millenarian Vision, Capitalist Reality--Brazil Contestado Rebellion, 1912-1916, Amer Hist Rev, Vol 0098, 93; Policing Rio De Janeiro--Repression and Resistance in a 19th-Century City, Histoire Sociale-Soc Hist, Vol 0027, 94; The Family in Bahia, Brazil, 1870-1945, Hisp Amer Hist Rev, Vol 0074, 94. **CONTACT ADDRESS** Hist Dept, Univ of Calif, 3229 Dwinelle Hall, Berkeley, CA, 94720-2551.

LEWIS, ANDREW WELLS
PERSONAL Born 09/05/1943, Savannah, GA, m, 1970 **DISCIPLINE** MEDIEVAL AND RENAISSANCE HISTORY **EDUCATION** Dartmouth Col, BA, 66; Univ Chicago, MA, 67; Harvard Univ, PhD(hist), 73. **CAREER** Vis asst prof hist, Univ Md College Park, 73-74; cur medieval collections, Stanford Univ Libr, 74-75; vis lectr hist, Univ Western Ont, 75-76; vis asst prof, Southern Ill Univ, Edwardsville, 76; Mellon fel, St Louis Univ, 77; asst prof, 77-80, ASSOC PROF HIST, SOUTHWEST MO STATE UNIV, 80-, Am Philos Soc grant, 75. **MEMBERSHIPS** Mediaeval Acad Am; AHA. **RESEARCH** Medieval France, 900-1328; medieval social history. **SELECTED PUBLICATIONS** Auth, The Career of Philip the Cleric, Younger Brother of Louis-VII + a Study of Supplemental Information From Contemporaneous 12th-Century Parisian Chronicles--Apropos of an Unpublished Charter, Traditio-Studies in Ancient and Medieval Hist Thought and Res; Forest Rights and the Celebration of May--2 Documents From the French Vexin, 1311-1318, Mediaeval Stud, Vol 0053, 91; 6 Charters of Henry-II and his Family for the Monastery of Dalon, Engl Hist Rev, Vol 0110, 95. **CONTACT ADDRESS** Dept of Hist, SW Mo State Univ, Springfield, MO, 65802.

LEWIS, ARNOLD
PERSONAL Born 01/13/1930, New Castle, PA, m, 1958, 3 children **DISCIPLINE** ART HISTORY **EDUCATION** Univ Wis, PhD 62, MA 54; Allegheny Col, BA 52. **CAREER** Wells Col, instr 62-64; Col of Wooster, asst prof, 64-96, emeritus prof, 96-. **HONORS AND AWARDS** Nat Trust Fel; Fulbright Gnt; SAH Founder's Awd; SAH Western Reserve Bk Awd; SAH Dir; Jacques Barzun Bk Awd. **MEMBERSHIPS** CAA; SAH. **RESEARCH** 19th Century Architecture. **SELECTED PUBLICATIONS** Auth, An Early Encounter With Tomorrow: Europeans Chicago's Loop and the World's Columbian Exposition, Urbana, Univ IL Press, 97; auth, The Disquieting Progress of Chicago, in: Amer Pub Architecture: Euro Roots and Native Expressions: Papers in Art Hist from the Penn State Univ, 88; auth, Imaging the Real, Lee Waisler-Mostra Retrospectiva 1968-1988, Ferrara, Galleria Civica d'Arte Moderna, 88, with Beth Irwin Lewis; American Country House of the Gilded Age, NY, Dover Press, 83; auth, Wooster in 1876, Wooster, College of Wooster, 76. **CONTACT ADDRESS** Col of Wooster, 614 Kieffer St, Wooster, OH, 44691. **EMAIL** alewis@acs.wooster.edu

LEWIS, DAVID LANIER
PERSONAL Born 04/05/1927, Bethalto, IL, m, 1953, 4 children **DISCIPLINE** BUSINESS HISTORY **EDUCATION** Univ Ill, BS, 48; Boston Univ, MS, 55; Univ Mich, MA, 56, PhD(hist), 59. **CAREER** Reporter, Edwardsville Intelligencer, Ill, 48; state ed, Alton Telegraph, 48-50; ed publ, Ford Motor Co, 50-51; press rel rep, Borden Co, 52; supvr, Indust Arts Awards, Ford Motor Co, 52-55; pub rel staff exec, Gen Motors Corp, 59-65; assoc prof, 65-68, PROF BUS HIST, UNIV MICH, 68-, Contrib ed, Model T Times, 71-, V-8 Times, 71-, Horseless Carriage, 72-, Model A News, 72- and Old Car Illustrated, 76-; consult indust properties, Div Hist, Mich Dept State, 73-; assoc ed, Cars and Parts, 73-; feature ed, Bulb Horn, 74-; trustee, Nat Automotive Hist Collection, 75- **HONORS AND AWARDS** Cuqnot Award, Soc Automotive Historians, 77; Duryea Award, Antique Automobile Club Am, 77; Award of Merit, Mich Hist Soc, 77. **MEMBERSHIPS** AHA; Econ Hist Asn; Soc Automotive Historians (dir, 74-, pres, 82-). **RESEARCH** Henry Ford; auto history; entrepreneurial history. **SELECTED PUBLICATIONS** Auth, International public relations, in: Handbook of Public Relations, McGraw, 60; Automobile industry, Collier's Encycl, 67; Automobile industry, Collier's Encycl Year Bk, annually, 68-; The Square Dancing Master, Am Heritage, 72; Milton Snavely Hershey, Dict of Am Biog, 73; The Public Image of Henry Ford, Wayne State Univ, 76; guest ed, Mich Quart Rev, fall 80 and winter 81. **CONTACT ADDRESS** Grad Sch of Bus Admin, Univ of Mich, 435 S State St, Ann Arbor, MI, 48109-1003.

LEWIS, DAVID RICH
PERSONAL Born 04/13/1957, Ogden, UT, m, 1990, 2 children **DISCIPLINE** HISTORY **EDUCATION** Ut St Univ, BS, 79; Univ Toronto, MA, 80; Univ Wi Madison, MA, 83, PhD, 88. **CAREER** Asst prof to assoc prof, Ut St Univ, 88- ; coed, W Hist Quart, 92- . **HONORS AND AWARDS** Bert M. Fireman Prize, W Hist Assoc, 84; Pre-doctoral Fel, D'Arcy McNickle Center for the Hist of the Amer Indian, Newberry Libr, Chicago, Il, 85-86; Honors Prof, Ut St Univ Honors Prog, 96-97; Res of the Year, Col of Humanities, Arts, & Soc Sci, Ut St Univ, 97. **MEMBERSHIPS** W Hist Assoc; Org of Amer Hist; Amer Soc for Ethnohistory; Amer Soc for Environ Hist. **RESEARCH** Native Amer; Amer W; environ Utah **SELECTED PUBLICATIONS** Auth, Major Problems in the History of the American West, Houghton Mifflin, 97; Neither Wolf Nor Dog: American Indians, Environment and Agrarian Change, Oxford Univ Press, 94, 97; Sins of the Fathers (and Mothers): Utah, Past and Present, Mag of the Mountainwest, 99; Great Basin and Rocky Mountain Indians, in American Heritage Encyclopedia of American History, Henry Holt & Co, 98; Native Americans: The Original Westerners, in The Rural West Since World War II, Univ Press Ks, 98. **CONTACT ADDRESS** Dept of History, Ut St Univ, 0710 Old Main Hill, Logan, UT, 94322-0710. **EMAIL** dlewis@hass.usu.edu

LEWIS, DOUGLAS
PERSONAL Born 04/30/1938, Centreville, MS, w, 1969 **DISCIPLINE** HISTORY OF ART; HISTORY OF ARCHITECTURE ITALIAN RENAISSANCE **EDUCATION** Yale Col, BA, 59 & 60; Univ Cambridge, BA, 62, MA, 63; Yale Univ, MA, 63, PhD, 67. **CAREER** Lectr, Bryn Mawr Col, 67-68; curator of sculpture, Nat Gallery Art, 68-; vis prof, Univ Calif Berkeley, 70 & 79; adj prof, Johns Hopkins Univ, 73-77; prof lectr, Georgetown Univ, 80-93; lectr in univ honors, Univ Maryland College PK, 88-. **HONORS AND AWARDS** Mellon fel, Clare Col, 60-62; Chester Dale fel, Amer Acad Rome, 64-65; Rome Prize fel, AAR, 65-66; David E Finley fel, Nat Gallery Art, 65-68; Ailsa Mellon Bruce Cur Sabbatical fel, Nat Gallery Art, 97-87. **MEMBERSHIPS** Col Art Asn; Asn Art Hist; Soc Archit Hist; Nat Trust Hist Preserv; Amer Acad Rome. **RESEARCH** Italian Renaissance; Baroque art & architecture 1300-1800. **SELECTED PUBLICATIONS** contribur & ed, Essays in Art and Architecture in Memory of Carolyn Kolb: Artibus et Historiae, 97; auth, Longhena and His Patrons: The Creation of the Venetian Baroque, 97; The Last Gems: Italian Neoclassical Gem Engravings and Their Impressions, Engraved Gems, Survivals and Revivals, Stud in the Hist Art, 97. **CONTACT ADDRESS** National Gallery of Arts, 4th St at Constitution Ave NW, Washington, DC, 20565-0001. **EMAIL** m.beck@nga.gov

LEWIS, GEORGE H.
PERSONAL Born 10/18/1943, Houlton, ME, m, 1970, 1 child **DISCIPLINE** SOCIOLOGY **EDUCATION** Bowdoin Col, BA, 65; Univ Oregon, MA, 69, PhD, 70. **CAREER** Prof, sociology, Univ of the Pacific. **HONORS AND AWARDS** Distinguished fac awd, 84, distinguished fac res lec, 86, Univ of the Pacific; Eberhart Teacher/Scholar Awd, 90; Fishwick Awd, 91., Bd of gov, Am Cult Asn. **MEMBERSHIPS** Am Cult Asn; Pop Cult Asn; Pacific Sociol Asn. **RESEARCH** Popular culture; popular music; food and culture. **SELECTED PUBLICATIONS** Auth, Side Saddle on the Golden Calf: Social Structure and Popular Culture in America, Goodyear, 72; auth, Storm Blowing From Paradise: Social Protest and Oppositional Idealogy in Popular Hawaiian Music, in Pop Music, 91; auth, All that Glitters: Country Music in America, Popular, 93; auth, Shell Games in Vacationland: Homanus Americanus and the State of Maine, in Usable Pasts: Traditions and Group Expressions in N Am, Utah State Univ Pr, 97. **CONTACT ADDRESS** Sociology Dept, Univ of the Pacific, Stockton, CA, 95211. **EMAIL** glewis@uop.edu

LEWIS, JAMES A.
PERSONAL Born 07/29/1942, Galion, OH, m, 1969, 3 children **DISCIPLINE** HISTORY **EDUCATION** Ohio State Univ, BA, 64; Northern Ill, MA, 68; Duke Univ, PhD, 75. **CAREER** From asst prof to assoc prof to prof, 72-, WCU. **HONORS AND AWARDS** Daniel Creigton Sossomon Endowed Chemn, WCU, 88-92; Spain in Am Quincontennial Prize, Spanish Ministry of Culture, 88. **MEMBERSHIPS** SLAH; SECOLAS; Asn Carribean Hist; SC Hist Soc. **RESEARCH** Colonial Latin America; Spanish Carribean; Am revolution. **SELECTED PUBLICATIONS** Coauth, Guide to Cherokee Documents in Foreign Archives, 83; auth, The Final Campaign of the American Revolution: Rise and Fall of the Spanish Bahamas, 91. **CONTACT ADDRESS** Dept of History, Western Carolina Univ, Cullowhee, SC, 28723. **EMAIL** lewis@wcu.edu

LEWIS, JAMES F.
PERSONAL Born 06/21/1937, m, 1958, 3 children **DISCIPLINE** HISTORY OF RELIGIONS **EDUCATION** Bethel Col, BA, 60; Bethel Theol Sem, BD, 63; Univ Iowa, PhD, 76. **CAREER** Asst prof and dept chair, world relig, Union Bibl Sem, Pune, Maharashtra, India, 77-81; assoc prof and dept chair, world relig, St. Bonifacius, 81-94; assoc prof, world relig, Wheaton Col, 94-. **MEMBERSHIPS** Evang Theol Soc; Asn of Asian Studies; Amer Acad of Relig. **RESEARCH** Religion in Vietnam; Religion in Modern India. **SELECTED PUBLICATIONS** Co-auth, Religious Traditions of the World, Zondervan, 91. **CONTACT ADDRESS** 501 College Av., Wheaton, IL, 60187. **EMAIL** james.f.lewis@wheaton.edu

LEWIS, JAN ELLEN
PERSONAL Born 07/10/1949, St. Louis, MO, m, 1 child **DISCIPLINE** AMERICAN HISTORY & STUDIES **EDUCATION** Bryn Mawr Col, BA, 71; Univ Mich, MA(Am studies), 72, MA(hist), 74, PhD(hist), 77. **CAREER** Asst prof to assoc prof, 77-94, PROF HIST, RUTGERS UNIV, NEWARK, 94-, chair, 87-93, graduate dir, 94-, grad fac, Rutger Univ, New Brunswick, 89-; vis prof hist, Princeton Univ, fall 95. **HONORS AND AWARDS** NEH fel, independent study and res, 85-86; Sr fel, Philadelphia Center Early Am Studies, spring 88; fel, Center Hist Freedom, Wash Univ, spring, 91. **MEMBERSHIPS** Am Hist Asn; Orgn Am Historians; Am Studies Asn; Southern Hist Asn; Soc Historians of Early Am Repub **RESEARCH** American history to 1865; Southern history; history of the family and women. **SELECTED PUBLICATIONS** Auth, Domestic Tranquility and the Management of Emotion among the Gentry of Pre-Revolutionary Virginia, Willliam & Mary Quart, 1/82; The Pursuit of Happiness: Family and Values in Jefferson's Virginia, Camabridge Univ Press, 83, paperbk ed, 85; The Republican Wife: Virtue and Seduction in the Early Republic, William and Mary Quart, 87; co-auth, Sally Has Been Sick: Pregnancy and Family Limitation among Virginia Gentry Women, 1780-1830, Jour Soc Hist, 88; Mother's Love: The Construction of an emotion in Nineteenth-Century America, In: Social History and Issues in Consciousness: Some Interdisciplinary Connections, NY Univ Press, 89; Mother's as Teachers: Reconceptualizing the Role of the Family as Educator, In: Education and the American Family: A Research Synthesis, NY Univ Press, 89; Motherhood and the Construction of the Male Citizen in the United States, 1750-1850, In: Constructions of Self, Rutgers Univ Press, 92; The Blessings of Domestic Society: Thomas Jefferson's Family and the Transformation of American Politics, In: Jeffersonian Legacies, Univ Press Va, 93; Southerners and the Problem of Slavery in Political Discourse, In: Devising Liberty: Preserving and Creating Freedom in the New American Republic, Stanford Univ Press, 95; Of Every Age, Sex & Condition: The Representation of Women in the Constitution, Jour Early Republic, 95; co-auth, American Synecdoche: Thomas Jefferson as Image, Icon, Character, and Self, Am Hist Rev, 2/98; ed & contribr, Those Scenes for which Along My Heart Was Made: Affection and Politics in the Age of Jefferson and Hamilton, In: An Emotional History of the United States, NY Univ Press, 98. **CONTACT ADDRESS** Dept of Hist, Rutgers Univ, 175 University Ave, Newark, NJ, 07102-1897. **EMAIL** janlewis@andromeda.rutgers.edu

LEWIS, JANE E.
PERSONAL Born 04/14/1950, London, England **DISCIPLINE** HISTORY OF MEDICINE **EDUCATION** Reading

Univ, BA, 71; Memorial Univ Nfld, MA, 74; Univ Western Ont, PhD, 79. **CAREER** Lectr to prof, London Sch Econ 79-96; FEL, ALL SOULS COL, OXFORD & DIR, THE WELLCOME UNIT FOR THE HISTORY OF MEDICINE, 96-; Kirsten Hesselgren vis prof, Stockholm, 90; vis prof, Europ Univ Inst, 95. **HONORS AND AWARDS** Mem, Royal Soc Can. **MEMBERSHIPS** Soc Social Hist Med; Brit Soc Asn; Social Policy Asn; Econ Hist Soc; Social Hist Soc. **SELECTED PUBLICATIONS** Auth or coauth, Women and Social Action in Victorian and Edwardian England, 91; auth or coauth, Women in Britain Since 1945, 92; auth or coauth, Whom God Hath Joined, 92; auth or coauth, The Voluntary Sector, the State and Social Work in Britain, 95; auth or coauth, Implementing the new Community Care, 96. **CONTACT ADDRESS** All Soul's Col, Oxford, ., 0X1 4AL.

LEWIS, LIONEL STANLEY
PERSONAL Born 07/29/1933, Ottawa, Canada, m, 1962, 2 children **DISCIPLINE** SOCIOLOGY **EDUCATION** Washington Univ, BA, 57; Cornell Univ, MA, 58; Yale Univ, PhD, 61. **CAREER** Asst prof, sociol, Univ Nev, 61-63; from asst prof to prof, sociol, SUNY Buffalo, 63- ; dir grad stud, 71-72, 94-96; chemn dept, 88-91; adj prof Higher Educ, SUNY Buffalo, 73- . **HONORS AND AWARDS** Phi Beta Kappa; Woodrow Wilson Fel, 57-58; Soc Sci Res Coun Fac Res Grant, 69-70; cited as auth of Outstanding Book on the Subject of Human Rights in 1994, Myers Ctr for Stud of Human Rights. **RESEARCH** Sociology of higher education. **SELECTED PUBLICATIONS** Auth, Scaling the Ivory Tower: Merit and Its Limits in Academic Careers, Johns Hopkins, 75; auth, Cold War on Campus: A Study of the Politics of Organizational Control, Transaction, 88; auth, Marginal Worth: Teaching and the Academic Labor Market, Transaction, 96. **CONTACT ADDRESS** Dept of Sociology, State Univ of NY, Buffalo, 430 Park Hall, Buffalo, NY, 14260. **EMAIL** soclsl@acsu.buffalo.edu

LEWIS, MARTHA HOFFMAN
PERSONAL Born 11/08/1922, Newton, MA, m, 1954, 2 children **DISCIPLINE** CLASSICS **EDUCATION** Univ Calif, Berkeley, AB, 43; Bryn Mawr Col, MA, 49, PhD, 51. **CAREER** Teacher Latin and English, Red Bluff High Sch, Calif, 44-45, Piedmont High Sch, 45-48; Fulbright scholar and fel, Am Acad Rome, 51-53; asst prof classics and educ, Univ Ill, 53-56; asst prof Latin, 63-66, ASSOC PROF LATIN AND ENGLISH, ROCKHURST COL, 66-. **MEMBERSHIPS** Am Philol Asn; Am Asn Ancient Historians. **RESEARCH** Roman history, especially late republic and early empire; modern poetry. **SELECTED PUBLICATIONS** Auth, Steamboats and Ferries on White River--a Heritage Revisited, Ark Hist Quart, Vol 0055, 96. **CONTACT ADDRESS** 716 W 109th Terr, Kansas City, MO, 64114.

LEWIS, MEHARRY HUBBARD
PERSONAL Born 08/02/1936, Nashville, TN, m **DISCIPLINE** EDUCATION **EDUCATION** TN State Univ, BA 1959; TN State Univ, MS 1961; IN Univ, PhD 1971. **CAREER** IN Univ, NDEA fellow 1966-67; Student Activities Office IN Univ, frat affairs adv 1967-69, lecturer 1970, visiting asst prof 1970-72; Macon Cty Bd Ed, coord rsch & eval 1972-73; Natl Alliance of Black School Educators, dir rsch proj 1973-74; School of Educ, prof of educ, asst dean Tuskegee Inst, dir institutional rsch & planning 1974-84; MGMT Inc, pres, dir 1984-; Bullock County Bd of Education, counselor, currently. **HONORS AND AWARDS** Presidents Awd Natl Alliance of Black School Educators 1974. **MEMBERSHIPS** Mem natl Alliance Black School Ed, Kappa Delta Pi, Phi Delta Kappa Intl, Alpha Kappa Mu Natl Honor Soc, Amer Personnel & Guid Assoc, ACES Div & Assoc for Non-White Concerns; general sec, trust Church of the Living God, Pillar & Ground of the Truth Inc; mem youth comm YMCA 1963-66; mem Beta Kappa Chi. **SELECTED PUBLICATIONS** Publisher of several poems & articles. **CONTACT ADDRESS** Bullock County Board of Education, PO Box 5108, Union Springs, AL, 36089.

LEWIS, NATHANIEL
DISCIPLINE AMERICAN LITERATURE AND IMAGES OF THE WEST **EDUCATION** Harvard Univ, PhD. **CAREER** Eng, St. Michaels Col. **SELECTED PUBLICATIONS** Area: cult of the Am West. **CONTACT ADDRESS** St. Michael's Col, Winooski Park, Colchester, VT, 05439. **EMAIL** nlewis@smcvt.edu

LEWIS, PETER
DISCIPLINE COMPARATIVE POLITICS **EDUCATION** Univ Calif, Berkeley, BA; Princeton Univ, MA, PhD. **CAREER** Prof, Am Univ. **RESEARCH** International political economy, and Third World development. **SELECTED PUBLICATIONS** Articles, World Polit, World Develop & Jour Modern African Studies. **CONTACT ADDRESS** American Univ, 4400 Massachusetts Ave, Washington, DC, 20016.

LEWIS, SAMELLA
PERSONAL Born 02/27/1924, New Orleans, LA, m, 1948 **DISCIPLINE** ART HISTORY **EDUCATION** Hampton Inst, BS 1945; OH State Univ, MA 1948, PhD 1951; Postdoctoral studies, Tung Hai Univ, NYU, Univ of Southern CA. **CAREER** Art Hist Scripps Coll, prof; LA Co Museum of Art; Coordinator of Educ, CA State Univ; Univ State of NY; FL A&M Univ; Morgan State Univ; Hampton Inst. **HONORS AND AWARDS** Permanent collections, Baltimore Museum Art, VA museum fine arts, palm springs museum, high Mus Atlanta; Delta Sigma Theta Scholarship, Dillard Univ; Art Scholarship Hampton Inst; Amer Univ Fellowship OH State; Fulbright Fellowship Chinese Studies; NDEA Fellowship; NY Ford Found Grant; Honorary Doctorate, Chapman Coll, 1976; Fellowships, Fulbright Found, Ford Found. **MEMBERSHIPS** Mem, Expansion Arts Panel, NEA 1975-78; pres Contemp Crafts Inc; bd mem Museum African Amer Art; Art Educ Black Art Intl Quarterly Natl Conf of Artists; Coll Art Assn of Amer; Pres, Oxum Intl, 1988-; Dir/founder, Museum of African Amer Art, 1976-80. **SELECTED PUBLICATIONS** Published, Art African Amer, 1978; "Black Artist on Art," volumes I & II, 1969-71; "Art: African Amer", 1978. **CONTACT ADDRESS** The Intl Review of African American Art, 3000 Biscayne Blvd, Ste 505, Miami, FL, 33137.

LEWIS, THEODORE GYLE
PERSONAL Born 12/02/1941, m, 1984, 2 children **DISCIPLINE** COMPUTER SCIENCE **EDUCATION** Ore State Univ, BS, 66; Washington State Univ, MS, 70, PhD, 71. **CAREER** Fac, Univ of Miss-Rolla, 71-73; fac, Univ Southwestern La, 73-76; prof, Ore State Univ, 77-93; Dir of OACIS, 88-91; PROF, NAVAL POSTGRADUATE SCHOOL, 93-. **MEMBERSHIPS** IEEE Computer Soc. **RESEARCH** Software Engineering; Parallel & Distributed Processing. **SELECTED PUBLICATIONS** Auth, The Friction-Free Economy, Harper Collins, 97; auth, Information Appliances: Gadget Netopia?, Computer, 98; auth, Is Microsoft a Natural Monopoly?, Scientific Am, 98; auth, Cares, Phones, and Tamagotchi Tribes, Computer, 97; auth, www.batmobile.car, Scientific Am, 97; auth, VoIP: Killer App for the Internet? IEEE Internet Computing, 97; coauth, Introduction to Parallel & Distributed Computing, Prentice-Hall, 98; auth, Parallax: A Tool for Parallel Program Scheduling, IEEE Parallel & Distributed Tech, 93. **CONTACT ADDRESS** 13260 Corte Lindo, Salinas, CA, 93908. **EMAIL** tedglewis@frictionfree-economy.com

LEWIS, THOMAS T.
PERSONAL Born 10/21/1941, Paris, TX, m, 1968, 2 children **DISCIPLINE** HISTORY **EDUCATION** Okla Christian Univ, BA, 63; Southern Methodist Univ, MA, 65; Univ Okla, PhD, 70. **CAREER** Asst prof, Eastern Ky Univ, 69-71; prof, chemn, Mount Senario Col, 71-. **HONORS AND AWARDS** Tchr of the Year, 90-91, 93-94., Fulbright lectr, 73-74, Univ Metz. **MEMBERSHIPS** Am Hist Asn; Western Society for French Hist. **RESEARCH** History of law; constitutional history. **SELECTED PUBLICATIONS** Auth, Carl Popper's Situational Logic; auth, Authoritarian Attitudes and Personality's; auth, Alternative Psychological Interpretations of Woodrow Wilson. **CONTACT ADDRESS** Mount Senario Col, 1500 College Ave W, Ladysmith, WI, 54848. **EMAIL** tlewis@mscsf.edu

LEWIS, V. BRADLEY
PERSONAL Born 02/20/1965, Wayne, MI **DISCIPLINE** GOVERNMENT, INTERNATIONAL STUDIES **EDUCATION** Univ of Maryland, BA, 87; Univ of Notre Dame, MA, 89, PhD, 97. **CAREER** Asst Prof, 97-, Sch Philos, Catholic Univ of Amer. **HONORS AND AWARDS** H.B. Earhart Dissertation Fellowship, 93-94. **MEMBERSHIPS** Amer Philos Assoc; Soc Ancient Greek Philos; Amer Catholic Philos Assoc; Soc for Greek Polit Thought. **RESEARCH** Classical Political Philosophy, Natural right and natural law. **SELECTED PUBLICATIONS** Auth, Natural Law in Irish Constitutional Jurisprudence, Catholic Social Science Review, 97; The Nocturnal Council and Platonic Political Philosophy, History of Political Thought, 98; Politeia kai Nomoi: On the Coherence of Plato's Political Philosophy, Polity, forthcoming, Jan 99. **CONTACT ADDRESS** School of Philosophy, Catholic Univ of America, Washington, DC, 20064. **EMAIL** lewisb@cua.edu

LEWIS, WALTER DAVID
PERSONAL Born 06/24/1931, Towanda, PA, m, 1954, 3 children **DISCIPLINE** AMERICAN HISTORY **EDUCATION** Pa State Univ, BA, 52, MA, 54; Cornell Univ, PhD(hist), 61. **CAREER** Instr pub speaking, Hamilton Col, 54-57; fel coord, Eleutherian Mills-Hagley Found, 59-65; assoc prof hist, State Univ NY Buffalo, 65-71, prof, 71, dir undergrad sem hist, 65-67, dir honors prog hist, 65-70; HUDSON PROF HIST AND ENGINEERING, AUBURN UNIV, 71-, Instr, Univ Del, 59-61, lectr, 61-65; grants-in-aid, Eleutherian Mills Hist Libr, 70-72; Nat Endowment for Humanities grant, 74; dir, Proj Technol, Human Values and Southern Future, Auburn Univ, 74-78; exec co-producer film, About US: the Changing American South, 75-77; Delta Air Lines Found res grants, 75-78; fel, Nat Humanities Inst, Univ Chicago, 78-79. **MEMBERSHIPS** Soc Hist Technol; Bus Hist Conf; G A Henty Soc England. **RESEARCH** History of technology; American social and intellectual history; business history. **SELECTED PUBLICATIONS** Auth, The Politics of International Aviation, Technol and Culture, Vol 0034, 93; The Emergence of Birmingham as a Case Study of Continuity Between the Antebellum Planter Class and Industrialization in the 'New South', Agr Hist, Vol 0068, 94; A Nation of Steel--the Making of Modern America, 1865-1925, J Amer Hist, Vol 0083, 96; Iron and Steel--Class, Race, and Community in Birmingham, Alabama, 1875-1920, Technol and Culture, Vol 0038, 97. **CONTACT ADDRESS** Dept of Hist, Auburn Univ, Auburn, AL, 36849.

LEYENDECKER, LISTON EDGINGTON
PERSONAL Born 01/19/1931, Laredo, TX, m, 2 children **DISCIPLINE** AMERICAN WESTWARD MOVEMENT **EDUCATION** Univ N Mex, BA, 58; Univ Denver, MA, 61, PhD(Am studies), 66. **CAREER** Instr Am hist, Del Mar Col, 63-64, instr Am Hist & Western Civilization, 64-65; Dep State Historian, State Hist Soc Colo, 65-66; instr & acting chmn Dept Am Hist & Western Civilization, Arapahoe Jr Col, 66-67, instr & chmn Dept Am & Colo Hist, 67-68; from asst prof to assoc prof Am & Colo Hist, 68-78, prof Hist, Colo State Univ, 78-, researcher & consult, Hist Georgetown Loop Mining Area prof, Colo State Univ, 69-, dir, Georgetown Soc, Inc, 78-. **HONORS AND AWARDS** Harris T Guard Award, Colo State Univ, 75. **MEMBERSHIPS** Western Hist Asn; Mining History Assn, Historic Georgetown; Am Asn State & Local Hist. **RESEARCH** Mining in 19th century Colorado; preservation and restoration in Colorado; latter 19th century United States. **SELECTED PUBLICATIONS** Auth, The History of Rufugio County Hospital, Jack Bonner Co, 65; Colorado and the Paris Universal Exposition, 1867, Colo Mag, Winter 69; contribr, The restoration of Black Hawk and Central City: the preliminary pains, panics and problems, In: Western American History in the Seventies, Educ Media & Info Systs, 73; auth, Washington Hall: Gilpin County's Oldest Courthouse (booklet), Colo State Univ Coop Exten Serv, 75; Georgetown: Colorado's Silver Queen, 1859-1876 (booklet), Centennial Publ, 77; Georgetown 1878: One Year in the Life of Colorado's Silver Queen, The Georgetown/Silver Plume National Historic Landmark District Journal, Feb 97; Palace Car Prince: A Biography of George Mortimer Pullman, University Press of Colorado, 98. **CONTACT ADDRESS** Dept of History, Colorado State Univ, Fort Collins, CO, 80523-0001.

LEYERLE, BLAKE
PERSONAL Born 08/16/1960, Boston, MA, s **DISCIPLINE** HISTORY OF CHRISTIANITY **EDUCATION** Duke Univ, PhD 91. **CAREER** Univ Notre Dame, asst prof, assoc prof, 91 to 98-. **MEMBERSHIPS** NAPS; AAR. **RESEARCH** Social Hist of Early Christianity; John Chrysostom; Pilgrimage; Monasticism. **SELECTED PUBLICATIONS** Auth, Meal Customs in the Greco-Roman World, Passover and Easter: The Liturgical Structuring of a Sacred Season, eds, Paul Bradshaw, Lawrence A. Hoffman, Univ Notre dame Press, forthcoming; Appealing to Children, The Jour of Early Christian Studies, 97; auth, Landscape as Cartography in Early Christian Pilgrimage Narratives, Jour of Amer Acad Relig, 96; auth, Clement of Alexandria on the Importance of Table Etiquette, The Jour of Early Christian Studies, 95; auth, John Chrysostom on Almsgiving and the Use of Money, Harv Theol Rev, 94; auth, John Chrysostom on the Gaze, The Jour of Early Christian Studies, 93. **CONTACT ADDRESS** Dept of Theology, Univ of Notre Dame, 327 O'Shaughnessy Hall, Notre Dame, IN, 46556. **EMAIL** Leyerle@nd.edu

LI, CHU-TSING
PERSONAL Born 05/26/1920, Canton, China, m, 2 children **DISCIPLINE** ART HISTORY **EDUCATION** Univ Nanking, BA, 43; State Univ Iowa, MA, 49, PhD(Art hist), 55. **CAREER** Instr and cur prints and slides, Art Dept, State Univ Iowa, 54-55; actg asst prof fine arts, Oberlin Col, 55-56; from instr to prof hist of art, Univ Iowa, 56-66; chmn dept, 72-78, prof, 66-78, JUDITH HARRIS MURPHY DISTINGUISHED PROF HIST OF ART, UNIV KANS, 78-, Ford Found training and res fel Orient art, Harvard Univ and Princeton Univ, 59-60; Am Coun Learned Soc and Soc Sci Res Coun res grants Chinese art, Far East, 63-64; Fulbright-Hays Ctr fac fel, 68-69; vis prof fine arts, Chinese Univ Hong Kong, 72-73; dir, Nat Endowment for Humanities summer sem on Chinese art hist, 75 and 78; res cur orient art, William Rockhill Nelson Gallery Art, 66- **MEMBERSHIPS** Col Art Asn Am; Asn Asian Studies; Midwest Art Hist Soc; Asia Soc. **RESEARCH** History of Yuan Dynasty painting; contemporary Chinese art; history of Kwangtung painting. **SELECTED PUBLICATIONS** Auth, Recent Studies on Zhao Mengfu Painting in China, Artibus Asiae, Vol 0053, 93. **CONTACT ADDRESS** Dept of Art Hist, Univ of Kans, Lawrence, KS, 66045.

LIBBY, JUSTIN HARRIS
PERSONAL Born 12/04/1937, Cincinnati, OH, m, 1965, 2 children **DISCIPLINE** AMERICAN DIPLOMATIC HISTORY **EDUCATION** Univ Cincinnati, BA, 65, MA, 66; Mich State Univ, PhD(Am hist), 71. **CAREER** From instr to asst prof, 69-78, assoc prof to prof Am Hist, Ind Univ, Indianapolis, 78-, Ind Univ study & res grants-in-aid, 74-77, 93, 94, 96; scholar-diplomat sem E Asian affairs, Dept State, 76. **MEMBERSHIPS** AHA; Orgn Am Historians; Asian Hist Soc; Soc Hist Am Foreign Rel; Foreign Policy Asn; Navy League of the United States; Naval Intelligence Professionals; United States Naval Institute. **RESEARCH** American-Japanese diplomatic relations; American diplomatic relations with countries bordering the Pacific; modern Japanese history, especially political re-

lations with the West. **SELECTED PUBLICATIONS** Auth, Senators King and Thomas and the Coming War with Japan, Utah Hist Quart, fall 74; The Irreconcilable Conflict: Key Pittman and Japan During the Interwar Years, Nev Hist Quart, fall 75; Anti-Japanese Sentiment in the Pacific Northwest: Senators Schwellenbach and Congressman Coffee Attempt to Embargo Japan, Mid-Am, 10/76; contribr, Wendell Willkie and the Election of 1940, In: Gentlemen From Indiana, Ind Hist Soc, 77; auth, Congress and American-Japanese Relations, 1931-1941, Pac Historian, fall 78; The Irresolute Years: American Congressional Opinion Towards Japan, 1937-1941, Hong Kong: Asian Monograph Series, 84; A Wedding of Contradictions, Journal of Caribbean Studies, VIII: 197-218, winter 91; The Search for a Negotiated Peace: Japanese Diplomats Attempt to Surrender Japan Prior to the Bombing of Hiroshima and Nagasaki, World Affairs, CLVI: 35-45, summer 93; Hamilton Fish and the Origins of Anglo-American Solidarity, Mid-America, LXXVI: 205-226, fall 94; Essay on The Conditional Surrender of Japan, Naval War College Review, XLVIII: 89-91, winter 95; Rendezvous with Disaster: There Never Was a Chance for Peace in American-Japanese Relations, World Affairs, CLVIII: 137-147, winter 96; Pan Am and the Navy: Pacific Partners, Navy History, forthcoming 98. **CONTACT ADDRESS** Dept of Hist, Indiana Univ-Purdue Univ, Indianapolis, 425 University Blvd, Indianapolis, IN, 46202-5140. **EMAIL** jhlibby@iupui.edu

LIBIN, KATHRYN
DISCIPLINE MUSIC HISTORY AND THEORY **EDUCATION** Oberlin Conserv, BM; NY Univ, PhD. **CAREER** Vis Instr, Vassat Col; recitals, Boston Early Mus Festival, Metropolitan Mus Art, Moravian Mus in Bethlehem, Pa, Vassar Col. **RESEARCH** Music of the late 18th and early 19th centuries; the history and performance practice of early keyboard instruments. **SELECTED PUBLICATIONS** Contribu, Metropolitan Mus Art; notes have appeared in Stagebill for Great Performers, Lincoln Center; auth, liner notes for complete cycles of the Mozart solo keyboard works & sonatas for violin and keyboard. **CONTACT ADDRESS** Classics Dept, Vassar Col, 124 Raymond Ave., Poughkeepsie, NY, 12604.

LIBO, KENNETH HAROLD
PERSONAL Born 12/04/1937, Norwich, CT **DISCIPLINE** JEWISH AMERICAN STUDIES **EDUCATION** Dartmouth Col, BA, 59; Hunter Col, MA, 68; City Univ NY Grad Ctr, PhD(Eng), 74. **CAREER** Asst prof Eng, City Col, City Univ NY, 71-78; ED, Jewish Daily Forward, 78-; Natl Museum of Am Jewish Hist, 86-89; Museum of Jewish Heritage, 89-92. **HONORS AND AWARDS** Nat Bk Award, Am Acad & Inst Arts & Lett, 77. **MEMBERSHIPS** Gomez Foundation **RESEARCH** Jewish immigration; Lower East Side; Am Jewish Hist. **SELECTED PUBLICATIONS** Auth, World of Our Fathers, Harcourt Brace Jovanovich, 76; How We Lived, Richard Marek Publ, 79; We Lived There Too, St. Martin's Press, 84; All in a Life Time, John Loeb Publishers, 96. **CONTACT ADDRESS** 365 W 20th St, New York, NY, 10011. **EMAIL** KENLIBO@aol.com

LICHTENBERG, PHILLIP
PERSONAL Born 10/01/1926, Schenectady, NY, m, 1949, 4 children **DISCIPLINE** PSYCHOLOGY **EDUCATION** Case Western Reserve Univ, BS, 48, MA, 50, PhD, 52. **CAREER** Bryn Mawr Col, Mary Hale Chase Prof Emer, Soc Sci, Soc Wk, Soc research, 96-, Mary Hale Chase Prof Soc Sci, Soc Wk, Soc Research, 90-96, Professor, 68-90, Assoc Prof, 61-68; Co Director, Gestalt Therapy Institute, Phil, 83-; Assoc Soc Psych, Mental Health Research Unit, NY Dept Mental Hygiene, Syracuse, NY, 57-61; Clinical Asst Prof, Psychiatry, Dept of Psychiatry State Univ NY, Upstate Medical Cen, Syracuse, NY, 57-61; Research Psychologist, Inst for Psychosomatic Psychiatric Research and Training, Michael Reese Hosp, Chicago, Ill, 54-57; Research Consultant, Sonia Shankman Orthogenic School, Univ Chicago, 57; Research Asst Psychology Prof, Research Cen Human Relations, NY Univ, 52-54; Research Fellow, Clinical Psychology, Dept Soc Relations, Harvard Univ, 51-52. **HONORS AND AWARDS** Phi Beta Kappa, 48; Mary Hale Chase Professorship, 90. **MEMBERSHIPS** Am Psychol Asn; Penn Psychol Asn; Eastern Psychol Asn; Soc for the Psychol Study of Soc Issues; Am Asn Advancement Science; Am Asn Univ Profs; Am Orthopsychiatric Asn; Intl Soc Pol Psychol; Phil Soc Clinical Psychols; Gestalt Therapy Inst Phil; Soc Advancement Field Theory; Psychols Soc Responsibility; Bertha Capen Reynolds Soc. **RESEARCH** Clinical Contributions to Social Change. **SELECTED PUBLICATIONS** Motivation for Child Psychiatry Treatment, Russell and Russell, 60; Psychoanalysis: Radical and Conservative, Springer, 69; Getting Even: Equalizing Law of Relationship, Univ Press Am, 88; Undoing the Clinch of Oppression, Peter Lang Pub, 90; Encountering Bigotry: Befriending, Projecting Persons in Everyday Life, Jason Aronson, 97. **CONTACT ADDRESS** 25 Lowry's Lane, Bryn Mawr, PA, 19010-1402. **EMAIL** plichtenberg@erols.com

LIDDLE, WILLIAM D.
PERSONAL Born 08/31/1937, Nashville, TN, m, 1958, 2 children **DISCIPLINE** HISTORY **EDUCATION** George Peabody Col, BA, 59; Claremont Grad School, MA, 61, PhD, 70. **CAREER** Vis asst prof, Univ of Tenn, summer 74; INSTR TO PROF, 62-99, DIR OF GRAD STUDIES, DEPT OF HIST, SOUTHWEST TEX STATE UNIV, 95-. **HONORS AND AWARDS** Woodrow Wilson Nat Fel, 59-60; presidential scholar, 81, honors prof of the Year, Southwest Tex State Univ, 97. **MEMBERSHIPS** AAUP; Org of Am Historians; Southern Hist Asn; Soc of Historians of the Eaflly Republic; Am Soc for 18th Century Studies; Asn of the Omohundro; Inst of Early Am Hist and Culture; Tex Fac Asn. **RESEARCH** Eighteenth-Century America; intellectual history of the Eighteenth-Century. **SELECTED PUBLICATIONS** Auth, Virtue and Liberty: An Inquiry into the Role of the Agrarian Mythin the Rhetoric of the American Revolutionary Era, South Atlantic Quart, 78; A Patriot King or None: Lord Bolingbroke and the American Renunciation of George III, J of Am Hist, 79; Edmund S. Morgan, The Dictionary of Literary Bio. **CONTACT ADDRESS** Dept of Hist, Southwest Texas State Univ, San Marcos, TX, 78666. **EMAIL** wl01@academia.swt.edu

LIDOV, JOEL
PERSONAL Born 03/13/1945, Chicago, IL, m **DISCIPLINE** GREEK & LATIN LANGUAGE & LIT **EDUCATION** Columbia Coll, BA, 66; Columbia Univ, MA, 67, PhD, 72. **CAREER** Visiting/acting, asst prof, Univ of CA Berkeyly, 70-73; Visiting asst prof, 73-75, Stanford Univ; asst to assoc prof, the graduate sch, City Univ of NY **HONORS AND AWARDS** Phi Beta Kappa, 65; Earle Prize in classics, 66; woodbridge distinguished fel, 70; gildersleev prize (John Hopkins Univ Press), 93. **MEMBERSHIPS** Amer Philogical Assn **RESEARCH** Classical Greek Lit (especially Archaic, classical poetry) **SELECTED PUBLICATIONS** Auth, Alternating Rhythm in Archaic Greek Poetry, Trans, American Philological Assoc, 89; What am I? What am I not?: Three Recent Pindars, Classical Journal, 93; The Secon Stanza of Sappho, Another Look, American Journal of Philology, 93; Pindar's Hym to Cybele, Meter, Form and Syncretism, Greek, Roman and Byzantine Studies, 96. **CONTACT ADDRESS** Dept of Classical Middle-Eastern & Asian Langs, Queens Col, CUNY, 6530 Kissena Blvd, Flushing, NY, 11367. **EMAIL** joel_lidov@qc.edu

LIDTKE, VERNON LEROY
PERSONAL Born 05/04/1930, Avon, SD, m, 1951 **DISCIPLINE** MODERN EUROPEAN HISTORY **EDUCATION** Univ OR, BA, 52, MA, 55; Univ CA, Berkeley, PhD, 62. **CAREER** Instr, High Sch, OR, 53-55; assoc soc sci, Univ CA, Berkeley, 60-62; from asst prof to assoc prof Europ hist, MI State Univ, 62-68; assoc prof, 68-73, chmn dept hist, 75-79, prof Europ hist, Johns Hopkins Univ, 73-, Nat Endowment for Hum younger scholar fel, 69-70; fel, Davis Ctr Hist Studies, Princeton Univ, 74-75; vis scholar, Humboldt Universitat, Berlin, Ger Democratic Repub, 5-6/86; fel, Wissenschaftskolleg zu Berlin (Inst Advan Study, Berlin), 87-88; fel, Max-Planck-Instut fur Geschichte, Gottingen, summer 96; mem exec coun, Conf Group Ger Polit, 75-80; chmn, Conf Group Central Europ Hist, 86; pres, Friends Ger Hist Inst, 91-94; chair, Mod Europ Sect, Am Hist Assoc, 92. **HONORS AND AWARDS** Award for Excellence in Tchg, Johns Hopkins Univ, 4/97. **MEMBERSHIPS** AHA; Conf Group Cent Europ Hist (secy-treas, 72-74); Conf Group Ger Polit. **RESEARCH** Mod Ger; Europ soc movements; popular cult of Central Europe. **SELECTED PUBLICATIONS** Auth, The Outlawed Party: Social Democracy in Germany, 1878-1890, Princeton Univ, 66; Revisionismus, Sowjetsystem und Demokratische, Ges, 71; contribr, Kultureller Wandel im 19 Jahrhundert, Vandenhoeck & Ruprecht, 73; auth, Naturalism and socialism in Germany, Am Hist Rev, 2/74; contribr, Storio del Marxismo Contemporaneo, Feltrinelli, 74; auth, Songs and politics: An exploratory essay on Arbeiterlieder in the Weimar Republic, Archiv fur Sozialgeschichte, 74; Lieder der deutschen Arbeiterbewegung, 1864-1914, Geschichte und Gesellschaft, 79; Social class and secularization in Imperial Germany: The working classes, In: Yearbook of the Leo Baeck Institute, Vol XXV, 80; Songs and Nazis: Political music and social change in Twentieth-Century Germany, In: Essays on Culture and Society in Modern Germany, Tex A M Press, 82; The Alternative Culture: Socialist Labor in Imperial Germany, Oxford Univ Press, 85; Recent literature on worker's culture in Germany and England, In: Arbeiter und Arbeiterbewegung im Vergleich, Berichte zur internationalen historischen Forschung, Historische Zeitschrift, Oldenbourg Verlag, 86; Twentieth-Century Germany: The cultural, social, and political context of the work of Oskar Schlemmer, In: Oskar Schlemmer, Baltimore Mus Art, 86; Burghers, workers and problems of class relationships 1870 to 1914: German comparative perspective, In: Arbeiter und Burger im 19 Jahrhundert, Varianten ihres Verhaltinisses im europaischen Vergleich, Oldenbourg Verlag, 86; Cahtolics and politics in Nineteenth-Century Germany, Central Europ Hist, 3/86; Museen und die Zeitgenossische Kunst in der Weimarer Republik, In: Sammler, mazene und Mussen, Kunstforderung in Deutschland im 19 un 20 jahrhundert, Bohlau Verlag, 93; The Socialist labor movement, In: Imperial Germany: A Historigraphical Companion, Greenwood Press, 96. **CONTACT ADDRESS** Dept of Hist, Johns Hopkins Univ, 3400 N Charles St, Baltimore, MD, 21218-2680. **EMAIL** lidtke@jhu.edu

LIEBERMAN, STEPHEN JACOB
PERSONAL Born 03/21/1943, Minneapolis, MN **DISCIPLINE** ASSYRIOLOGY, LINGUISTICS **EDUCATION** Univ Minn, BA, 63; Harvard Univ, PhD(Near Eastern lang), 72. **CAREER** From asst prof to assoc prof Near Eastern studies, New York Univ, 71-75; res specialist, Sumerian Dict, Univ Mus, Univ Pa, 76-79; ASSOC PROF ASSYRIOL AND SEMITIC LING, DROPSIE UNIV, 82-, Fel Mesopotamian civilization, Baghdad Ctr Comt, Am Schs Orient Res, 70-71; Nat Endowment for Humanities fel, 75-76; Guggenheim fel, 79-80; Inaugural fel, Found for Mesopotamian Studies, 80- **MEMBERSHIPS** Am Orient Soc; AHA; Archaeol Inst Am; Ling Soc Am; NAm Conf Afro-Asiatic Ling. **RESEARCH** Sumerian and Akkadian languages and cultures; Semitic linguistics; Mesopotamian history. **SELECTED PUBLICATIONS** Auth, Bar Ilan Studies in Assyriology Dedicated to Artzi, Pinhas, J Amer Oriental Soc, Vol 0112, 92. **CONTACT ADDRESS** Dept Assyriol and Semitic Ling, Dropsie Univ, Philadelphia, PA, 19132.

LIEBERSOHN, HARRY
DISCIPLINE HISTORY **EDUCATION** Princeton Univ, PhD, 79. **CAREER** Assoc prof, Univ Ill Urbana Champaign **RESEARCH** European cultural and intellectual history; history of the social sciences. **SELECTED PUBLICATIONS** Auth, Religion and Industrial Society: The Protestant Social Congress in Wilhelmine Germany, Am Philos Soc, 86; Fate and Utopia in German Sociology, 1870-1923, MIT, 88; Discovering Indigenous Nobility: Tocqueville, Chamisso, and Romantic Travel Writing, Am Hist Rev, 94. **CONTACT ADDRESS** History Dept, Univ Ill Urbana Champaign, 52 E Gregory Dr, Champaign, IL, 61820. **EMAIL** hliebers@uiuc.edu

LIEDL, JANICE
DISCIPLINE HISTORY **EDUCATION** Univ Ottawa, BA, MA; Purdue Univ, PhD. **CAREER** Assoc prof. **SELECTED PUBLICATIONS** Art, The Penitent Pilgrim: William Calverley and the Pilgrimage of Grace, Sixteenth Century Jour, 94; auth, Richard Morison, 94; co-ed, Love and Death in the Renaissance, Dovehouse, 91. **CONTACT ADDRESS** Dept of History, Laurentian Univ, 935 Ramsey Lake Rd, Sudbury, ON, P3E 2C6.

LIENHARD, JOSEPH T.
DISCIPLINE HISTORICAL THEOLOGY **EDUCATION** Fordham Univ, BA, MA,; Woodstock Univ, PhL, BD, STM; Habil, Freiburg ThD. **CAREER** Asst ch, grad stud; prof, 90, Fordham Univ. **RESEARCH** Augustine's late works. **SELECTED PUBLICATIONS** Auth, The Bible, the Church, and Authority: The Canon of the Christian Bible, Hist and Theol, Collegeville, 95; transl, Gospel according to Luke, Origen: Homilies on Luke; Fragments on Luke, Wash, 96. **CONTACT ADDRESS** Dept of Relig, Fordham Univ, 113 W 60th St, New York, NY, 10023.

LIGHT, IVAN
PERSONAL Born 11/03/1941, Chicago, IL, m, 1966, 2 children **DISCIPLINE** SOCIOLOGY **EDUCATION** Univ CA, Berkeley, PhD 69. **CAREER** UCLA, Prof sociology, 69. **HONORS AND AWARDS** 4 Times NSF Grantee **MEMBERSHIPS** ISA; ASA **RESEARCH** Immigration, entrepreneurship. **SELECTED PUBLICATIONS** Globalization, Vacancy Chains, or Migration Networks? Immigrant Employment and income in Greater Los Angeles, 1970-190, ed by Don Kalb Marco van der Land, Bart van Steenbergen, Richard Staring and Nico Wilterdink, forthcoming, 99; Ethnic Entrepreneurs in America's Largest Metropolitan Areas, Journal of Urban Affairs, 98; The ethnic economy, NY Academic, forthcoming, with Steven Gold; Just Who Do You Think You Aren't? Society, 97. **CONTACT ADDRESS** Dept of Sociology, Univ of California, Los Angeles, CA, 90095. **EMAIL** light@soc.ucla.edu

LIGHTNER, DAVID LEE
PERSONAL Born 05/13/1942, Bethlehem, PA **DISCIPLINE** AMERICAN HISTORY **EDUCATION** Pa State Univ, BA, 63; Univ Pa, AM, 64; Cornell Univ, PhD(hist), 69. **CAREER** Asst prof hist, Univ Ill, Chicago Circle, 69-70; asst prof, St Olaf Col, 70-74; res asst, Inst Social Hist, City Col, City Univ New York, 74-75; asst prof hist, Univ Conn, 75-77; ASST PROF, UNIV ALTA, 77-. **MEMBERSHIPS** AHA; Orgn Am Historians; Econ Hist Asn; Can Asn Univ Teachers. **RESEARCH** American economic history; labor and business; nineteenth century. **SELECTED PUBLICATIONS** Auth, Lincoln in American Memory, Can Rev Amer Stud, Vol 0025, 95; The Last Best Hope of Earth, Lincoln, Abraham and the Promise of America, Can Rev Amer Stud, Vol 0025, 95; Common Labor, Workers and the Digging of North American Canals, 1780-1860, Can Rev Amer Stud, Vol 0025, 95; The Lincoln Persuasion, Remaking American Liberalism, Can Rev Amer Stud, Vol 0025, 95; Managing Madness + Recent Publications by Gamwell, Lynn, Gollaher, David, and Grob, Gerald, N., Can Rev Amer Stud, Vol 0026, 96. **CONTACT ADDRESS** Dept of Hist, Univ of Alta, Edmonton, AB, T6G 2E1.

LIGHTNER, ROBERT P.
PERSONAL Born 04/04/1931, Cleona, PA, m, 1952, 3 children **DISCIPLINE** THEOLOGY, MODERN HISTORY **EDUCATION** Baptist Bible Col, ThB, 55; Dallas Theol Sem, ThM, 59, ThD, 64; Southern Methodist Univ, MLA, 72. **CA-**

REER Instr Bible & Theol, 59-61, from Asst Prof to Assoc Prof Systematic Theol, Baptist Bible Sem, 63-68, Dept Chmn, 63-66; from Asst Prof to Prof Systematic Theol, 68-98, Adjunct Prof, Dallas Theol Sem, 98-. **HONORS AND AWARDS** Graduated with honors from Dallas Theol Sem., Started churches in NY and AR; Pastor and Interim Pastor in NY, PA, AR, OK, LA, and TX; mission trips to Paraguay, Venezuela, and Peru. **MEMBERSHIPS** Grace Evangelical Soc; Conservative Theol Soc; Pre-Trib Study Group. **RESEARCH** Pre-millennial, A-millennial, and post-millennial theology. **SELECTED PUBLICATIONS** Auth, The Toungues Tied, Speaking in Tongues and Divine Healing; The Death Christ Died: A Case for Unlimited Atonement; Prophecy in the Ring; Truth for the Good Life; James: Apostle of Practical Christianity; The God of the Bible; The Saviour and the Scriptures; Triumph though Tragedy; Neo-Liberalism; Neo-Evangelicalism Today; Church-Union: A Layman's Guide; The God of the Bible and other gods; Last Days Handbook; author of numerous other publications and articles. **CONTACT ADDRESS** 324 Clear Springs Dr, Mesquite, TX, 75150-0000.

LIGO, LARRY L.
DISCIPLINE ART HISTORY **EDUCATION** Muskingum Col, AB; Princeton Sem, BD; Univ NC Chapel Hill, PhD. **CAREER** Prof, Davidson Col. **RESEARCH** 19th-century Europ painting; Edouard Manet; early 20th-century painting and sculpt (1890-1945); the hist of photography; mod archit. **SELECTED PUBLICATIONS** Auth, The Concept of Function in 20th Century Architectural Criticism; articles in Arts Magazine and Gazette des Beaux-Arts. **CONTACT ADDRESS** Dept Art, Davidson Col, 102 N Main St, PO Box 1719, Davidson, NC, 28036. **EMAIL** laligo@davidson.edu

LIGON, DORIS HILLIAN
PERSONAL Born 04/28/1936, Baltimore, MD, m **DISCIPLINE** AFRICAN-AMERICAN HISTORY, ART HISTORY **EDUCATION** Morgan State Univ, BA Sociology (Summa Cum Laude) 1978, MA Art Hist/Museology 1979; Howard Univ, PhD courses African Hist. **CAREER** Natl Museum of African Art Smithsonian Inst, docent (tour guide) 1976-88; Morgan State Univ, art gallery rsch asst 1978-79; HOWARD CTY MD SCHOOL SYST, CONSULTANT AFRICAN ART & CULTURE 1980-; MD MUSEUM OF AFRICAN ART, FOUNDER/EXEC DIR 1980-. **HONORS AND AWARDS** Goldseeker Fellowship for Graduate Studies MSU 1978-79; Phi Alpha Theta (Natl History Hon Soc); Alpha Kappa Mu; Nirmaj K Sinha Award for highest honors in Sociology 1978. **MEMBERSHIPS** Mem Assn Black Women Historians, African-American Museums Assn; charter mem Eubie Blake Cultural Center 1984; charter mem Columbia (MD) Chap Pierians Inc 1983; mem Morgan State Univ Alumni; mem NAACP; mem Urban League; mem Arts Council of the African Studies Assn. **CONTACT ADDRESS** African Art Museum of Maryland, 5430 Vantage Point Rd, Columbia, MD, 21044.

LILLIBRIDGE, GEORGE DONALD
PERSONAL Born 07/20/1921, Mitchell, SD, m, 1943, 4 children **DISCIPLINE** AMERICAN HISTORY **EDUCATION** Univ SDak, AB, 42; Univ Wis, MA, 48, PhD(hist), 51. **CAREER** Instr hist, State Univ NY Teachers Col Albany, 50-52; from asst prof to assoc prof, 52-65, PROF HIST, CALIF STATE UNIV, CHICO, 65-, CHMN DEPT, 73-. **MEMBERSHIPS** AHA; Orgn Am Historians. **RESEARCH** The American impact abroad. **SELECTED PUBLICATIONS** Auth, So Long, Maestro, Amer Scholar, Vol 0066, 97. **CONTACT ADDRESS** Dept of Hist, California State Univ, Chico, Chico, CA, 95929.

LIMBAUGH, RONALD H.
DISCIPLINE HISTORY **EDUCATION** Col ID, BA, 60, MA, 62, PhD, 67. **CAREER** Prof, Univ Pacific. **SELECTED PUBLICATIONS** Auth, John Muir's Stickeen, Univ Alaska; Lessons of Nature, Univ Alaska. **CONTACT ADDRESS** Hist Dept, Univ Pacific, Pacific Ave, PO Box 3601, Stockton, CA, 95211.

LIN, YU-SHENG
PERSONAL Born 08/07/1934, Mukden, China, m, 1966, 2 children **DISCIPLINE** CHINESE INTELLECTUAL HISTORY **EDUCATION** Nat Taiwan Univ, AB, 58; Univ Chicago, PhD, 70. **CAREER** Vis asst prof hist, 66-67, acting asst prof, 67-68, Univ Va; asst prof, Univ Ore, 68-69; Soc Sci Res Coun & Am Coun Learned Soc res fel, EAsian Res Ctr, Harvard Univ, 69-70; asst prof, 70-75, assoc prof, 75-81, prof hist & E Asian lang & lit Univ Wis, Madison, 81-. **MEMBERSHIPS** Life Member, Adademia Sinica, 94-. **RESEARCH** The Chinese Ideas of Political Order from the Neolithic Age to the End of Mao: A comparative approach **SELECTED PUBLICATIONS** Auth, From the Perspective of Civil Society (in Chinese), Taipei: Linking Publishing Co, 98 **CONTACT ADDRESS** Dept of History, Univ of Wisconsin, 455 North Park St, Madison, WI, 53706-1483. **EMAIL** ylin1@facstaff.wisc.edu

LINCOLN, BRUCE
PERSONAL Born 03/05/1948, Philadelphia, PA, m, 1971, 2 children **DISCIPLINE** HISTORY OF RELIGIONS **EDUCATION** Haverford Col, BA, 70; Univ Chicago, MA, 73, PhD, 76. **CAREER** Asst prof Humanities, 76-79, assoc prof, 79-86, prof Comparative Studies in Discourse & Soc, 86-94, Univ Minn; PROF HISTORY OF RELIGIOUS & ASSOC MEMBER DEPT ANTHROP & CLASSICS, CTR FOR MIDDLE EASTERN STUDIES, COMM ANCIENT MEDITERRANEAN WORLD, UNIV CHICAGO, 94-; vis prof, Univ Siena, 84-85, Uppsala Univ, 85, Novosibrisk Univ, 91, Univ Copenhagen, 98; Guggenheim fel, 82-83; Scholar of the Col, Univ Minn, 90-93. **HONORS AND AWARDS** ACLS Book Award, 81. **RESEARCH** Religion & other ideological systems; Discourse and the construction of social borders and hierarchies; Politics of myth, ritual, and cosmatogy. **SELECTED PUBLICATIONS** Priest, Warriors, and Cattle: A Study in the Ecology of Religions, Univ Cal Press, 81; Emergin from the Chrylasis: Studies in Rituals of Women's Initiation, Harvard Univ Press, 81; Myth, Cosmos, and Society: Indo-European Themes of Creation and Destructions, Harvard Univ Press, 86; Discourse and the Construction of Society: Comparative Studies of Myth, Ritual, and Classification, Oxford Univ Press, 89; Death, Warm and Sacrifice: Studies in Ideology and Practice, Univ Chicago Press, 91; Authority: Construction and Corrosion, Univ Chicago Press, 94. **CONTACT ADDRESS** Swift Hall, Univ of Chicago, 1025 E 58th St, Chicago, IL, 60637. **EMAIL** blincoln@midway.uchicago.edu

LINCOLN, HARRY B.
PERSONAL Born 03/06/1922, Fergus Falls, MN, m, 1947, 3 children **DISCIPLINE** MUSIC HISTORY **EDUCATION** Macalester Col, BA, 46; Northwestern Univ, M Mus, 47, PhD(music hist), 51. **CAREER** From instr to assoc prof, 51-63, chmn dept, 73-76, prof music, 63-87, DIST SERV PROF EMER, STATE UNIV NY BINGHAMTON, 87-; US Off Educ grants, 67-69; Nat Endowment for Humanities res grants, 77-78 & 79-80; res grants, ACLS, Am Phil Soc, 92. **MEMBERSHIPS** Col Music Soc (pres, 68-70); Am Musicol Soc; Music Libr Asn; Int Musicol Soc. **RESEARCH** Sixteenth century Italian music; development of computer techniques for thematic indexing. **SELECTED PUBLICATIONS** Auth, I manuscritti Chigiani di Musica organocembalistica, L 'Organo, 67; Some criteria and techniques for developing computerized thematic idices, Elecktronische Datenverarbeitung Musikwissenschaft, 67; The Madrigal Collection L'Amorosa Ero: Brescia, 1588, State Univ NY, 68; Early Seventeenth-Century Keyboard Music in the Vatican Library Chigi Manuscripts, Am Inst Musicol, 68; ed, The Computer and Music, Cornell Univ, 70; auth, Uses of the computer in music composition and research, In: Advances in the Computer, Acad Press, 72; Encoding, decoding and storing melodies for a data base of Renaissance polyphony, Proc Third Int Conf on Very Large Data Bases, Tokyo, 10/77; auth, The Italian Madrigal and Related Repertories, Yale Univ Press, 88; The Latin Motet, Inst Mediaeval Music, 93; co-auth, Study Scores of Historical Styles, Prentice Hall, 86; Dir Music Faculties in American Col and Univ, 4 eds, 67-72. **CONTACT ADDRESS** Dept of Music, SUNY, Binghamton, NY, 13901. **EMAIL** BG0056@bingvmb.cc.binghamton.edu

LINCOLN, WILLIAM BRUCE
PERSONAL Born 09/06/1938, Stafford Springs, CT, m, 1984, 2 children **DISCIPLINE** RUSSIAN HISTORY; MODERN EUROPEAN HISTORY **EDUCATION** Col William & Mary, AB, 60; Univ Chicago, PhD(Russ & mod Europ hist), 66. **CAREER** Asst prof Russ hist, Memphis State Univ, 66-67; from Asst Prof to Distinguished Res Prof Russ Hist, Northern Ill Univ, 67-. **HONORS AND AWARDS** Exchange fel to USSR, Int Res & Exchanges Bd, 70-71, sr exchange fel, 73-74, 78 & 82; Fulbright-Hays fac res awards, Russ & Soviet Studies, 70-71 & Poland, 74; sr res fel, Russ Inst, Columbia Univ, 78; recipient of over 70 research grants, honors and awards from the Int Res and Exchanges Bd, Am Coun of Learned Soc, Soc Sci Res Coun, and others; **MEMBERSHIPS** Am Asn Advan Slavic Studies. **RESEARCH** Russian bureaucracy, Russian reform movements, 1801-1881; Russian society and culture, 1825-1918. **SELECTED PUBLICATIONS** Auth, The Romanovs: Autocrats of All the Russias, 81; In War's Dark Shadow: Russians before the Great War, 83; Passage through Armageddon: The Russians in War and Revolution, 86; Red Victory: A History of the Russian Civil War, 89; The Great Reforms: Autocracy, Bureaucracy, and the Politics of Change in Imperial Russia, 90; The Conquest of a Continent: Siberia and the Russians, 94; Between Heaven and Hell: A History of the Russian Artistic Experience, Viking Penguin, 98; author of over 130 scholarly papers, essays, reviews, and journal articles. **CONTACT ADDRESS** Dept of History, No Illinois Univ, 1425 W Lincoln Hwy, De Kalb, IL, 60115-2825. **EMAIL** brucel@niu.edu

LINDAHL, CARL
PERSONAL Born 12/02/1947, Boston, MA **DISCIPLINE** FOLKLORE, ENGLISH, MEDIEVAL STUDIES **EDUCATION** Harvard Univ, BA, 71; Indiana Univ, Bloomington, MA, 76, PhD, 80. **CAREER** Asst prof, 80-86, assoc prof, 86-97, prof, 97- , English Dept, Univ Houston. **HONORS AND AWARDS** Magna Cum Laude, 71; fel, Am Coun Learned Soc, 83; tchg excellence awd, 93; Alcee Fortier Awd, Am Folklore Soc, 96; fel, Virginia Found for Hum, 97; Lib of Cong Parsons Grant, 98., Founder and ed, World Folktale Library, Garland and Univ Pr Miss; editorial bd, Folklore; dist ed bd, Medieval Folklore. **MEMBERSHIPS** Am Folklore Soc; Folklore Soc, London; Int Soc for Contemp Legend Res; Int Soc for Folk Narrative Res; New Chaucer Soc; Nordic Inst of Folklore, **RESEARCH** Folk narrative; medieval literature; medieval folklore; American folklore. **SELECTED PUBLICATIONS** Auth, Earnest Games: Folkloric Patterns in the Cantebury Tales, Indiana, 87; auth, Jacks: the Name, the Tales, the American Traditions, in Jack in Two Worlds, Univ NC Pr, 94; auth, the Oral Undertones of Late Medieval Romance, in Oral Tradition in the Middle Ages, Medival and Renaissance Texts Series, 95; auth, Bakhtin's Carnival Laughter and The Cajun Country Mardi Gras, in Folklore, 96; auth, the Presence of the Past in the Cajun Country Mardi Gras, in J of Folklore Res, 96; auth, Some Uses of Numbers, in J of Folklore Res, 97; auth, the Oral Aesthetic and the Bicameral Mind, in Gilgamesh: A Reader, Bolchazy-Carducci, 97; auth, the Power of Being Outnumbered, in La Folklore Miscellany, 97; auth, Chaucer and the Shape of Performance, in Critical Essays on Geoffrey Chaucer, GK Hall, 98; auth, Sir Gawain and the Green Knight, Robert Burns's 'Halloween,' and Myth in its Time, in telling Tales, Medieval Narratives and the Folk Tradition, St Martins, 98; ed, Outlaws and Other Medieval Heroes, Southern Folklore, 96; co-ed, Swapping Stories: Folktales from Louisiana, Mississippi, 97; co-auth, Cajun Mardi Gras Masks, Mississippi, 97. **CONTACT ADDRESS** Dept of English, Univ of Houston, Houston, TX, 77204-3012. **EMAIL** clindahl@uh.edu

LINDBERG, DAVID C.
PERSONAL Born 11/15/1935, Minneapolis, MN, m, 1959, 2 children **DISCIPLINE** HISTORY OF SCIENCE **EDUCATION** Wheaton Col, BS, 57; NWestern Univ, MS, 59; Ind Univ, PhD, 65. **CAREER** Asst Prof, Univ Mich, 65-67; Asst Prof to Hilldale Prof, Univ Wis, 67-, Dir, Inst Res Humanities, 87-93. **HONORS AND AWARDS** Guggenheim Fel, 77-78; Fel, Medieval Acad Am; Fel, Am Acad Arts & Sci; Fel, Int Acad Hist Sci; Watson Davis Bk Prize of the Hist Sci Soc, for: "The Beginnings of Western Science..." **MEMBERSHIPS** Hist Sci Soc (pres 94-95); British Soc Hist Sci; Medieval Acad Am; Renaissance Soc Am. **RESEARCH** Medieval and early modern science. **SELECTED PUBLICATIONS** Auth, Theories of Vision from al-Kindi to Kepler, Univ Chicago Press, 76; The Beginnings of Western Science: The European Scientific Tradition in Philosophical, Religious, and Institutional Context, 600 B.C. - A.D. 1450, Univ Chicago Press, 92; Roger Bacon and the Origins of Perspectiva in the Middle Ages: A Critical Edition and English Translation of Bacon's Perspectiva, with Introduction and Notes, Clarendon Press, 96; co-ed, The Cambridge History of Science, 8 vols, Cambridge Univ Press (forthcoming); Science Encounters Christianity: Twelve Case Histories, Univ Chicago Press (forthcoming). **CONTACT ADDRESS** History Dept, Univ Wisconsin, 7143 Social Science, 1180 Observatory Dr., Madison, WI, 53706-1393. **EMAIL** dclindbe@facstaff.wisc.edu

LINDBERG, JOHN
PERSONAL Born 10/22/1955, Merrill, WI, m, 1980, 3 children **DISCIPLINE** MUSICOLOGY **EDUCATION** Univ Fla, BM, 76; Univ Mo-Columbia, MA, 79; Univ Cincinnati, PhD, 89. **CAREER** Assoc prof music, Mankato State; asst prof, music, Univ Northern Iowa. **HONORS AND AWARDS** Fulbright Scholar, Frankfurt-am-Main, 79-80; Fulbright Fel, Nuremberg, 87-88. **MEMBERSHIPS** Col Mus Soc; Am Musicol Soc. **RESEARCH** Music of Germany before 1800, the Basson **SELECTED PUBLICATIONS** The Lied before 1800, in Reader's Guide to Music: History, Theory, and Criticism; Christoph Graupner, Concerti grossi for 2 violins, 96; Christoph Graupner, Concerto grosso for 2 oboes, 98. **CONTACT ADDRESS** Music Dept, Mankato State Univ, PO Box 8400, Mankato, MN, 56001. **EMAIL** john.lindberg@mankato.msus.edu

LINDEMANN, ALBERT S.
PERSONAL Born 05/19/1938, Santa Monica, CA, m, 1963 **DISCIPLINE** MODERN EUROPEAN HISTORY **EDUCATION** Pomona Col, BA, 60; Harvard Univ, MA, 62, PhD(hist), 68. **CAREER** Instr hist Western civilization, Stanford Univ, 65-66; asst prof, 69-73, ASSOC PROF HIST, UNIV CALIF, SANTA BARBARA, 73-. **MEMBERSHIPS** AHA **RESEARCH** History of European socialism. **SELECTED PUBLICATIONS** Auth, On Socialists and the Jewish Question After Marx, Cent Europ Hist, Vol 0025, 92; Jews and the German State--the Political History of a Minority, 1848-1933, Cent Europ Hist, Vol 0026, 93; Marxist Intellectuals and the Working Class Mentality in Germany, 1887-1912, Cent Europ Hist, Vol 0027, 94; The British Labor Party and the German Social Democrats, 1900-1931--a Comparative Study, Cent Europ Hist, Vol 0029, 96. **CONTACT ADDRESS** Dept of Hist, Univ of Calif, 552 University Rd, Santa Barbara, CA, 93106-0001.

LINDENFELD, DAVID FRANK
PERSONAL Born 01/25/1944, Bethlehem, PA **DISCIPLINE** GERMAN HISTORY; EUROPEAN INTELLECTUAL HISTORY; HISTORY OF SOCIAL SCIENCE **EDUCATION** Princeton Univ, AB, 65; Harvard Univ, MAT, 66; Univ Chicago, PhD, 73. **CAREER** Lectr, Univ Chicago, 69; asst prof, Ohio State Univ, 72-74; asst prof, 74-80, assoc prof, 80-97, prof

hist, LA State Univ, 97-. **MEMBERSHIPS** Am Hist Assoc, German Stud Assoc, World Hist Assoc. **RESEARCH** Theory and philosophy of history. **SELECTED PUBLICATIONS** Contribr, Jenseits von Sein und Nichtsein, Akad Druck-und Verlagsanstalt, 72; auth, Oswald Kulpe and the Wurzburg School, J Hist Behav Sci, 78; The Transformation of Positivism, Alexius Meinong and European Thought 1880-1920, Univ Calif, 80; On Systems and Embodiments as Categories for Intel History, Hist & Theory, 88; The Myth of the Older German Historical School of Economics, Cent Europ Hist, 93; The Practical Imagination, The German Sciences of State in the Nineteenth Century, Univ Chicago, 97; The Prevalence of Irrational Thinking in the Third Reich, Cent Europ Hist, 98. **CONTACT ADDRESS** Dept Hist, Louisiana State Univ, Baton Rouge, LA, 70803. **EMAIL** dlinden@whflemming.hist.lsu.edu

LINDER, ROBERT DEAN
PERSONAL Born 10/06/1934, Salina, KS, m, 1957, 4 children **DISCIPLINE** EUROPEAN HISTORY, HISTORY OF CHRISTIANITY **EDUCATION** Emporia State Univ, BS, 56; Cent Baptist Theol Sem, MDiv, MRE, 58, Univ IA, MA, 60, PhD, 63. **CAREER** Instr western civilization, Univ IA, 58-61; asst prof hist, William Jewell Col, 63-65; from asst prof to assoc prof, 65-73, prof KS State Univ, 73-, Sr res fel, The Centre for the Study of Christianity, Macquerie Univ, Sydney, Australia, 95-, Ed, Fides et Historia, Conf Faith & Hist, 68-78; Mayor, Manhattan, KS, 71-72, 78-79; Dir, Relig Studies Prog, KS State Univ, 79-82. **HONORS AND AWARDS** KS State Univ Distinguished Tchg Award, 68; Phi Kappa Phi Outstanding Scholar, 1980; Sr Fac Award for Res Excellence, Inst for Soc & Behav Res, KS State Univ, 97. **MEMBERSHIPS** AHA; Am Soc Church Hist; Am Soc Reformation Res (secy, 71-79); Renaissance Soc Am; Rocky Mountain Soc Sci Asn; Conf Faith & Hist. **RESEARCH** Reformation and Renaissance hist; hist of Christianity; Australian relig hist. **SELECTED PUBLICATIONS** Auth, The Political Ideas of Pierre Viret, Droz, Geneva, 64; co-ed, Protest and Politics: Christianity and Contemporary Politics, Attic, 68; coauth, Calvin and Calvinism: Sources of Democracy?, Heath, 70; ed, God and Caesar: Case Studies in the Relationship between Christianity and the State, Conf Faith & Hist, 71; co-ed, The Cross and the Flag, Creation House, 72; coauth, Politics and Christianity, InterVarsity, 73; co-ed, The Eerdman's Handbook to the History of Christianity, Eerdmans, 77; coauth, Twilight of the Saints: Biblical Christianity and Civil Religion in America, InterVarsity, 78; coauth, Civil Religion and the Presidency, Zonervan, 88; co-ed, The Dictionary of Christianity in America, InterVarsity, 90; co-ed, The History of Christianity, Fortress, 90; co-ed, A Concise Dictionary of Christianity in America, InterVarsity, 95; auth, The People of God and the Great War: Australian Evangelicals in World War I, CSAC, 98. **CONTACT ADDRESS** Dept of Hist, Kansas State Univ, 208 Eisenhower Hall, Manhattan, KS, 66506-1002. **EMAIL** rdl@ksu.edu

LINDERSKI, JERZY
DISCIPLINE CLASSICS **EDUCATION** Univ Cracow, MA, 55, PhD, 60. **CAREER** Prof, Univ NC, Chapel Hill; vis mem, Inst for Advan Stud, Princeton Univ, 77-78. **HONORS AND AWARDS** Ford Found fel, 62-63; Deut Forschungsgemeinschaft fel, Univ Cologne, 70-71; Guggenheim fel, 77-78; NEH fel, 85-86. **RESEARCH** Cicero; Roman law. **SELECTED PUBLICATIONS** Auth, Broughton, Thomas Robert Shannon, in W.W. Briggs, Jr, ed, Biog Dictionary of N Am Classicists, Westport, Ct., 94; Zum Wandel d/l: medulla / melila, Glotta 71 93, 94; Thomas Robert Shannon Broughton, Gnomon 67, 95; A Missing Ponticus, Am J of Ancient Hist 12, 87, 95; Games in Patavium, Ktema 17, 92, 96; Q. Scipio Imperator, in Jerzy Linderski, ed, Imperium Sine Fine: T.R.S. Broughton and the Roman Republic, Hist Einzelschriften 105, 96; Cato Maior in Aetolia, in Robert W. Wallace and Edward M. Harris, eds, Transitions to Empire. Essays in Greco-Roman History 360 -146 B.C. in Honor of Ernst Badian, Norman, OK, 96; Agnes Kirsopp Michels and the Religio, Class J 92.4, 97; Fatalis: A Missing Meretrix, Rheinisches Mus 140, 97; ed, Imperium Sine Fine: T.R.S. Broughton and the Roman Republic, Hist Einzelschriften 105, Steiner Verlag, 96; coauth, T. Robert S. Broughton, In Memoriam, Am Philol ASn Newsl 17.2, 94. **CONTACT ADDRESS** Univ N. Carolina, Chapel Hill, Chapel Hill, NC, 27599.

LINDGREN, C. E.
PERSONAL Born 11/20/1949, Coeburn, VA, s **DISCIPLINE** MEDIEVAL HISTORY, HISTORY OF EDUCATION **EDUCATION** Univ Miss, MEd, 77, EdS, 93; Coll of Preceptors, MPhil, 93; UNISA, DEd, 98. **CAREER** Dir, Delta Hills Educ Asn, 76-80; dir, Educ consultants of Oxford, 81-95; prof, LaSalle Univ, 95-98; chm, Hist & Phil of Educ, Greenwich Univ, 98-. **HONORS AND AWARDS** Robert A. Taft Fel; EDPA Fel; hon fel, World Jnana Sadhak Soc; assoc IIPS, knighthood, Orthodox Order of St. John. **MEMBERSHIPS** Royal Soc Arts; Royal Asiatic Soc; Col of Preceptors; Royal Hist Soc; Am Acad Relig; Medieval Acad of Am; PSA; Hist of Ed Soc. **RESEARCH** Egyptology; medieval history; Qu Gong; metagogics; religion. **CONTACT ADDRESS** 10431 Hwy51, Courtland, MS, 38677. **EMAIL** paschal@panola.com

LINDGREN, JAMES M.
DISCIPLINE UNITED STATES HISTORY **EDUCATION** College of William and Mary, PhD 84. **CAREER** SUNY, asst prof, assoc prof, prof 84 to 94-. **HONORS AND AWARDS** G Wesley Johnson Prize; Phi Beta Kappa; Phi Alpha Theta. **MEMBERSHIPS** ASA; OAH; NCPH. **RESEARCH** Us historic preservation and historic sites; US maritime museums; Amer traditionalism, memory and material change. **SELECTED PUBLICATIONS** Auth, Preserving Historic New England: Preservation Progressivism and the Remaking of Memory, NY, Oxford, OUP, 95; Preserving the Old Dominion: Historic Preservation and Historic Traditionalism, Charlottesville, London, UPV, 93; A New Departure in Historic Patriotic Work: Personalism Professionalism and Conflicting Concepts of Material Culture in the Late Nineteenth and Early Twentieth Centuries, The Pub Historian, 96; That every Mariner May Possess the History of the World: A cabinet for the East India Marine Society of Salem, New Eng Quart, 95; The Rising Grandeur of a Nation and the Decay of its Virtue: Historic Preservation at the Fin de Siecle, in: Fin-de-Siecle: Comparisons and Perspectives, ed, Jugen Kleist and Bruce Butterfield, NY, Peter Lang, 96. **CONTACT ADDRESS** Dept of History, SUNY, Plattsburgh, NY, 12901-2698. **EMAIL** lindgrjm@splava.cc.plattsburgh.edu

LINDGREN, RAYMOND ELMER
PERSONAL Born 02/10/1913, Kansas City, KS, m, 1940, 3 children **DISCIPLINE** HISTORY **EDUCATION** Univ Calif, AB, 35, AM, 40, PhD, 43. **CAREER** Asst prof, Occidental Col, 42-45; assoc prof hist, Vanderbilt Univ, 45-52; vis lectr, Univ Wis, 52-54; from assoc prof to prof, Occidental Col, 54-61, chmn dept, 55-61; prof, 61-80, EMER PROF HIST, CALIF STATE UNIV, LONG BEACH, 80-, Vis lectr, Univ Minn, 49-50; Fulbright res grant, Norway, 50-51; Gustaf V fel, 50-51; prof and resident dir, Calif State Cols, Int Prog, Sweden, 67-69; Rockefeller Found fel, Villa Servelloni Conf Ctr, 73; sub-ed, Scandinavia, Am Hist Rev Knight, Order of the NStar, Sweden. **HONORS AND AWARDS** Gustav Adolf Medal, Uppsala Univ, 80. **MEMBERSHIPS** AHA; Norweg Hist Soc; Danish Hist Soc; Swedish Hist Soc. **RESEARCH** Scandinavian history; 18th century Europe; immigration in the southwest United States. **SELECTED PUBLICATIONS** Auth, Oga Mot Oga, World Lit Today, Vol 0067, 93; Eftertradaren, World Lit Today, Vol 0067, 93; Historien Med Hunden, Ur En Texansk Konkursdomares Dagbocker Och Brev, World Lit Today, Vol 0068, 94; Sju Huvudens Historia, World Lit Today, Vol 0068, 94; Under Tiden, World Lit Today, Vol 0068, 94; Ett Minnepalats, Vertikala Memoarer, World Lit Today, Vol 0069, 95; Angel Bland Skuggor, World Lit Today, Vol 0069, 95. **CONTACT ADDRESS** Dept of Hist, California State Univ, Long Beach, 1250 Bellflower Blvd, Long Beach, CA, 90840.

LINDHEIM, SARA H.
DISCIPLINE CLASSICS **EDUCATION** Brown Univ, PhD, 95. **CAREER** ASST PROF. **RESEARCH** Latin poetry, Sappho, critical and feminist theory. **SELECTED PUBLICATIONS** Auth, Female prophetic figures in Virgil's Aeneid and in Lucan; Cross-dressing and gender identity in Propertius 4.9. **CONTACT ADDRESS** Dept of Classics, Univ Calif, Santa Barbara, CA, 93106-7150. **EMAIL** lindheim@humanitas.ucsb.edu

LINDNER, RUDI PAUL
PERSONAL Born 07/17/1943, Stockton, CA **DISCIPLINE** MEDIEVAL HISTORY **EDUCATION** Harvard Col, AB, 65; Univ Wis-Madison, MA, 67; Univ Calif, Berkeley, PhD(hist), 76. **CAREER** Jr fel hist, Ctr Byzantine Studies, Dumbarton Oaks, 72-74; Instr, Tufts Univ, 74-77; ASST PROF HIST, UNIV MICH, ANN ARBOR, 77-. **RESEARCH** Byzantine, Turkish and Inner Asian history. **SELECTED PUBLICATIONS** Auth, The Rise and Rule of Tamerlane, J Amer Oriental Soc, Vol 0113, 93; The Ottoman Empire, 1300-1481, J Amer Oriental Soc, Vol 0113, 93; The Seljuks of Anatolia--Their History and Culture According to Local Muslim Sources, Bull Sch Oriental and African Stud, Univ London, Vol 0059, 96. **CONTACT ADDRESS** Hist Dept, Univ of Mich, 435 S State St, Ann Arbor, MI, 48109-1003.

LINDO-FUENTES, HECTOR
DISCIPLINE HISTORY **EDUCATION** Univ Chicago, PhD. **CAREER** Prof, Fordham Univ. **HONORS AND AWARDS** Co-dir, interdisciplinary prog, Latin Am Stud Lincoln Ctr campus. **RESEARCH** The evolution of the state in the nineteenth century and the polit economy of educ. **SELECTED PUBLICATIONS** Auth, Weak Foundations: The Economy of El Salvador in the Nineteenth Century, 90; co-auth, Central America 1821-1871: Liberalism Before Reform, 95; Historia de El Salvador, 94. **CONTACT ADDRESS** Dept of Hist, Fordham Univ, 113 W 60th St, New York, NY, 10023.

LINDSAY LEVINE, VICTORIA
DISCIPLINE MUSIC **EDUCATION** San Francisco State Univ, BA, 77; MA, 80; Univ Ill Urbana, PhD, 90. **CAREER** Assoc prof, Columbia Col Columbia. **SELECTED PUBLICATIONS** Auth, pubs on Ethnomusicology, American Indian Musical Cultures, Music of the American Southwest, and Latino Music of the US; co-auth, book on Choctaw Indian Music. **CONTACT ADDRESS** Music Dept, Columbia Col, Columbia, 14 E Cache La Poudre St, Colorado Springs, CO, 80903.

LINDSTROM, DIANA
PERSONAL Born 09/09/1944, Jamestown, NY, 1 child **DISCIPLINE** HISTORY **EDUCATION** Alfred Univ, BA, 66; Univ Del, MA, 69, PhD(hist), 74. **CAREER** Asst prof hist, 71-77, ASSOC PROF HIST AND WOMEN'S STUDIES, UNIV WIS, MADISON, 78-, Am Coun Learned Soc fel hist, 76 and Reg Econ Hist Res, 78-79. **HONORS AND AWARDS** Allan Nevins Prize Econ Hist, Columbia Univ, 74. **MEMBERSHIPS** Econ Hist Asn; Agr Hist Soc; Bus Hist Soc. **RESEARCH** American economic 1815-1860; American domestic trade. **SELECTED PUBLICATIONS** Auth, North American Patterns of Growth and Development--the Continental Context, J Economic History, Vol 0053, 93; The Republic of Labor--Philadelphia Artisans and the Politics of Class, 1720-1830, Pa Mag Hist and Biog, Vol 0118, 94; Fair to Middlin--the Antebellum Cotton Trade of the Apalachicola--Chattahooche River Valley, J Southern Hist, Vol 0060, 94; American Economic Development in Historical Perspective, J Econ Hist, Vol 0055, 95; A Place to Live and Work--the Disston,Henry Saw Works and the Tacony Community of Philadelphia, Amer Hist Rev, Vol 0100, 95; Early American Technology--Making and Doing Things From the Colonial Era in 1850, J Interdisciplinary Hist, Vol 0027, 96; Technological Innovation and the Great-Depression, Technol and Culture, Vol 0038, 97. **CONTACT ADDRESS** Dept of Hist, Univ Wis, 455 North Park St, Madison, WI, 53706-1483.

LINDUFF, KATHERYN MCALLISTER
PERSONAL Born 10/16/1941, Beaver, PA **DISCIPLINE** ART HISTORY, ARCHEOLOGY **EDUCATION** Dickinson Col, BA, 63; Univ Pittsburgh, MA, 66, PhD(art hist), 72. **CAREER** Instr art hist, Univ Wis-Madison, 69-72; asst dean, Col Arts and Sci, 73-74, asst prof, 72-79, ASSOC PROF ART HIST, UNIV PITTSBURGH, 79-, Assoc cur, Jay C Leff Collections, 71-76. **MEMBERSHIPS** Asn for Asian Studies; Am Orient Soc; Archaeol Inst Am; Early China Soc; Col Art Asn. **RESEARCH** Ancient Chinese art and archaeology; art and archaeology of Central Asia; prehistoric art of the Old World and Asia. **SELECTED PUBLICATIONS** Auth, Zhukaigou, Steppe Culture and the Rise of Chinese Civilization, Antiquity, Vol 0069, 95. **CONTACT ADDRESS** Dept of Fine Arts, Univ of Pittsburgh, 104 Frick Fine Arts, Pittsburgh, PA, 15260-7601.

LINENTHAL, EDWARD TABOR
PERSONAL Born 11/06/1947, Boston, MA, m, 1974, 1 child **DISCIPLINE** RELIGIOUS STUDIES, AMERICAN HISTORY **EDUCATION** Western Mich Univ, BA, 69; PACIFIC Sch Relig, MDiv, 73; Univ Calif, Santa Barbara, PhD(relig studies), 79. **CAREER** Lectr Am relig, Univ Calif, Santa Barbara, 78-79; ASST PROF RELIG STUDIES, UNIV WIS-OSHKOSH, 79-, asst ed bk rev sect, Relig Studies Rev, 81-. **MEMBERSHIPS** Am Soc Church Hist; Am Acad Relig. **RESEARCH** Religion and war; religion and American culture; history of religions. **SELECTED PUBLICATIONS** Auth, Iwo Jima--Monuments, Memories, and the American Hero, Rev(s) in Amer Hist, Vol 0021, 93; Committing History in Public, J Amer Hist, Vol 0081, 94; The Boundaries of Memory--the United States Holocaust Memorial Museum, Amer Quart, Vol 0046, 94; American Samurai--Myth, Imagination, and the Conduct of Battle in the 1st Marine Division, 1941-1951, J Amer Hist, Vol 0082, 95; Struggling With History and Memory, J Amer Hist, Vol 0082, 95; The A Bomb Controversy at the National Air and Space Museum, Historian, Vol 0057, 95; Remembering War the American Way, J Amer Hist, Vol 0083, 96; Responses to Glassberg,David 'Public History and the Study of Memory'--Problems and Promise in Public History, Public Historian, Vol 0019, 97. **CONTACT ADDRESS** Dept of Relig, Univ of Wis, 800 Algoma Blvd, Oshkosh, WI, 54901-8601.

LINK, ARTHUR S.
PERSONAL Born 08/08/1920, New Market, VA, m, 1945, 4 children **DISCIPLINE** AMERICAN HISTORY **EDUCATION** Univ NC, AB, 41, AM, 42, PhD, 45; Oxford Univ, MA, 58. **CAREER** Instr, NC State Col, 43-44; from instr to asst prof, Princeton Univ, 45-49; from assoc prof to prof hist, Northwestern Univ, 49-60; Harmsworth prof, Oxford Univ, 58-59; prof hist, 60-65, Edwards prof Am hist, 65-76, GEORGE H DAVIS PROF AM HIST, PRINCETON UNIV, 76-, DIR WILSON PAPERS, 60-, Rosenwald, Guggenheim and Rockefeller fel, 41-42, 44-45, 50-51, 62-63; mem Inst Advan Studies, 49, 54-55; Shaw lectr diplomatic hist, Johns Hopkins Univ, 56; mem, Nat Hist Publ Comn, 68-72. **HONORS AND AWARDS** Julian P Boyd Award, Asn Doc Ed, 81., LittD, Bucknell Univ, 61, Univ NC, 62, Washington and Lee Univ, 65; LHD, Wash Col, 62; DHum, Davidson Col, 65. **MEMBERSHIPS** AHA: Southern Hist Asn (vpres, 67-68; pres, 68-69); Orgn Am Historians; Am Philos Soc; Asn Doc Ed (pres, 79-80). **RESEARCH** United States history since 1890; the Wilson era. **SELECTED PUBLICATIONS** Auth, Use of Force and Wilsonian Foreign Policy, Int Hist Rev, Vol 0016, 94; Grayson Predicament, Proc Amer Philos Soc, Vol 0138, 94. **CONTACT ADDRESS** Princeton Univ, Firestone Libr, Princeton, NJ, 08544.

LINSTONE, HAROLD A.
PERSONAL Born 06/15/1924, Hamburg, Germany, m, 1947, 2 children **DISCIPLINE** MATHEMATICS **EDUCATION** Columbia Univ, MA, 47; Univ of Southern Calif, PhD, 54. **CA-**

REER Sr scientist, The RAND Corp, 61-63; assoc dir of corporate development planning, Lockheed Aircraft Corp, 63-70; Ed-in-Chief, Tech Forecasting and Social Change J, 69-; Prof of Systems Sci, Portland State Univ, 70-. **HONORS AND AWARDS** Phi Beta Kappa, 44; Dart Award, Univ of Southern Calif, 70. **MEMBERSHIPS** Pres, Int Soc for the Systems Sci, 93-94. **RESEARCH** Multiple perspective concept for complex systems; technological forecasting. **SELECTED PUBLICATIONS** Co-ed, The Delphi Method, 75; Technological Substitution, 76; Futures Research: New Directions, 77; coauth, The Unbounded Mind, 93 & 95; The Challenge of the 21st Century, 94; auth, Multiple Perspectives for Decision Making, 77; Technologist and Executive: Using Multiple Perspectives to Bridge the Gap, 99. **CONTACT ADDRESS** Systems Sci PhD Prog, Portland State Univ, PO Box 751, Portland, OR, 97207. **EMAIL** hwhl@odin.cc.pdx.edu

LINT, GREGG LEWIS
PERSONAL Born 12/21/1943, South Bend, IN, m, 1971 **DISCIPLINE** DIPLOMATIC HISTORY **EDUCATION** Central Mich Univ, BA, 65, Ma, 68; Mich State Univ, PhD(diplomatic hist), 75. **CAREER** Teacher, Benton Harbor Public Sch, Mich, 65-67 and Durand Public Sch, Mich, 68-70; instr diplomatic hist and arch, Mich State Univ, 74-75; asst ed, 75-78, ASSOC ED, ADAMS PAPERS, 78-. **MEMBERSHIPS** Soc Historians Am Foreign Rel; AHA; Orgn Am Historians; Asn Doc Editing. **RESEARCH** American foreign policy and the law of nations, 1776-1815; John Adams. **SELECTED PUBLICATIONS** Auth, The Origins of Jeffersonian Commercial Policy and Diplomacy, William and Mary Quart, Vol 0051, 94; Federal Union, Modern World--the Law of Nations in an Age of Revolutions, 1776-1814, J Southern Hist, Vol 0062, 96. **CONTACT ADDRESS** Adams Papers Mass Hist Soc, 1154 Boylston St, Boston, MA, 02215.

LINTELMAN, JOY
PERSONAL Born 10/16/1957, Fairmont, MN, m, 1984, 3 children **DISCIPLINE** HISTORY **EDUCATION** Gustavus Adolphus Col, BA, 80; Univ Minn, MA, 83, PhD, 91. **CAREER** Tchg asst Hist Dept, 82-84, instr Hon Div, 86, instr Hist Dept, 88, instr Dept Independent Study, 84-91, Univ Minn; instr Hist Dept, Macalester Col, 88; ASSOC PROF HIST DEPT, CONCORDIA COL, 89-; diss fel, 87-88, Stout fel, 85-86, NW Area Stud For Lang fel, 84-85, Grad School fel, 81-82, Un iv Minn; Fulbright res scholar, 86-87; Lilly Lorenzen scholar, 86-87; Bush Fac Grant, Native Am Pedag, 94-95, Gender & Technol, 95-96; Nils William & Dagmar Olsson Scholar Fund, 97; Concordia Emigrant Inst grant, 97; Swedish Emigrant Inst Grant, 97. **MEMBERSHIPS** Am Hist Asn; Orgn Am Hist; Soc Sci Hist Asn; Immigration Hist Soc; Swed Am Hist Soc; Minn Hist Soc. **RESEARCH** Immigration; Women; Children; Native Americans. **SELECTED PUBLICATIONS** Auth On My Own: Single, Swedish, and Female in Turn-of-the-Century Chicago, Swedish-American L ife in Chicago: Cultural and Urban Aspects of an Immigrant People, 1850-1930, Univ Ill Press, 92; She did not whimper of complain: Case Records and Swedish American Working Class Women in Minneapolis, 1910-1930, Swed Am Hist Quart, 94; Making Service Serve Themselves: Immigrant Women and Domestic Service in N America, 1820-1930, Cambridge Univ Press, 95; An 'In-Progress' Report: The Crow Seminar and Teaching Indian History, Essays from Teaching and Writing Local and Reservation History: The Crows, Newberry Library, 95. **CONTACT ADDRESS** Concordia Col, Minnesota, 901 S 8th St, Moorhead, MN, 56562. **EMAIL** lintelma@cord.edu

LIPE, WILLIAM DAVID
PERSONAL Born 05/05/1935, Struggleville, OK, m, 1962, 3 children **DISCIPLINE** ARCHAEOLOGY **EDUCATION** Univ Okla, BA 57; Yale Univ, PhD(anthrop), 66. **CAREER** Res asst archaeol, Univ Utah, 58-60; instr anthrop, Univ Okla, 63-64; actg asst prof, State Univ NY Binghamton, 64-66, from asst prof to assoc prof, 66-72, actg chmn dept anthrop, 69-70, Nat Geog Soc res grant, 69-70; asst dir, Mus Northern Ariz, 72-76; assoc prof, 76-79, PROF ANTHROP, WASH STATE UNIV, 79-, NSF res grants, 72-76; Wash State Univ fac res grant, 77. **MEMBERSHIPS** Fel AAAS; fel Am Anthrop Asn; Soc Am Archaeol. **RESEARCH** Cultural adaptation to the environment; prehistory of Indians of Southwestern United States. **SELECTED PUBLICATIONS** Auth, The Depopulation of the Northern San Juan--Conditions in the Turbulent 1200s, J Anthropol Archaeol, Vol 0014, 95. **CONTACT ADDRESS** Dept of Anthrop, Wash State Univ, P O Box 644910, Pullman, WA, 99164-4910.

LIPPMAN, EDWARD
PERSONAL Born 05/24/1920, New York, NY, m, 1942, 2 children **DISCIPLINE** HISTORY OF MUSIC **EDUCATION** City Col NY, BS, 42; NY Univ, MA, 45; Columbia Univ, PhD(musicol), 52. **CAREER** From instr to assoc prof, 54-69, PROF MUSIC, COLUMBIA UNIV, 69-, Guggenheim fel, 58-59; Columbia Univ Coun Res Humanities grants, 60, 63, 65; Am Coun Learned Soc fel, 67-68; lectr, Bryn Mawr Col, 72-73. **HONORS AND AWARDS** Harriet Cohen Int Music Award, 54. **MEMBERSHIPS** Am Musicol Soc. **RESEARCH** Philosophy and aesthetics of music; 19th century history of music; ancient Greek conceptions of music. **SELECTED PUBLICATIONS** Auth, Wagner and Beethoven--Wagner, Richard Reception of Beethoven, Opera Quart, Vol 0009, 93. **CONTACT ADDRESS** Dept of Music, Columbia Univ, New York, NY, 10027.

LIPSETT-RIVERA, SONYA
DISCIPLINE HISTORY **EDUCATION** Univ Ottawa, BA, 82; Tulane Univ, MA, 84, PhD, 88. **CAREER** Assoc prof. **HONORS AND AWARDS** Hon(s) Degree adv. **RESEARCH** Late colonial and early national Mexico. **SELECTED PUBLICATIONS** Auth, Indigenous Communities and Water Rights in Colonial Puebla: Patterns of Resistance, The Americas, 48:4, 92; "Water and Bureaucracy in Colonial Puebla de los Angeles," Jour Latin Amer Stud, 25:1, 93; coauth, Columbus Takes on the Forces of Darkness: Film and Historical Myth in 1492: The Conquest of Paradise, Based on a True Story, Latin Amer Hist at the Movies, Delaware, Scholarly Resources Press, 97. **CONTACT ADDRESS** Dept of Hist, Carleton Univ, 1125 Colonel By Dr, Ottawa, ON, K1S 5B6. **EMAIL** sonya_lipsett-rivera@carleton.ca

LIPSEY, ROBERT E.
PERSONAL Born 08/14/1926, New York, NY, m, 1948, 3 children **DISCIPLINE** ECONOMICS **EDUCATION** Columbia Univ, BA, 44, MA, 46, PhD, 61. **CAREER** Res assoc, 60-, dir NY off, 77-, Natl Bur Econ Res; prof econ, 67-95, emer, 95-, Queens Col and Grad Ctr, CUNY. **HONORS AND AWARDS** Fulbright fel, 83; fel, Am Statist Asn; fel, NY Acad Sci. **MEMBERSHIPS** Am Econ Asn; Acad Int Bus; Eastern Econ Asn; Econometric Soc; Cliometric Soc; European Econ Asn; Conf on Income and Wealth; Western Econ Asn; Int Asn for Res in Income and Wealth. **RESEARCH** Foreign direct investment; price measurement; international comparisons of prices, output and investment; prices and international trade. **SELECTED PUBLICATIONS** Auth, Price and Quantity Trends in The Foreign Trade of The United States, Princeton, 63; coauth, Studies in The National Balance Sheet of the United States, Princeton, 63; coauth, Source Book of Statistics Relating to Construction, National Bureau of Economic Research, 66; coauth, Price Competitiveness in World Trade, National Bureau of Economic Research, 71; coauth, The Financial Effects of Inflation, National Bureau of Economic Research, 78. **CONTACT ADDRESS** Dept of Economics, National Bureau of Economic Research, 50 E 42nd St, 17th Fl, New York, NY, 10017-5405. **EMAIL** rlipsey@email.gc.cuny.edu

LISIO, DONALD JOHN
PERSONAL Born 05/27/1934, Oak Park, IL, m, 1958, 2 children **DISCIPLINE** RECENT AMERICAN HISTORY **EDUCATION** Knox Col BA, 56; Ohio Univ, MA, 58; Univ Wis, PhD(hist), 65. **CAREER** Asst prof Am hist, 64-69, assoc prof, 69-74, chmn dept hist, 73-81, HENRIETTA ARNOLD PROF HIST, 75-, Nat Endowment for Humanities younger scholar res fel, 69-70; Am Coun Learned Soc res grant, 71-72, res fel, 77-78. **MEMBERSHIPS** Orgn Am Historians; AHA. **RESEARCH** Herbert Hoover; recent America. **SELECTED PUBLICATIONS** Auth, The Colonel--the Life and Wars of Stimson,Henry, 1867-1950, Amer Hist Rev, Vol 0098, 93. **CONTACT ADDRESS** 4203 Twin Ridge Ct SE, Cedar Rapids, IA, 52402.

LISS, PEGGY K KORN
PERSONAL Born 10/03/1927, Philadelphia, PA, m, 1949, 2 children **DISCIPLINE** LATIN AMERICAN HISTORY **EDUCATION** Beaver Col, BA, 60; Univ Pa, Ma, 61, PhD(hist), 65. **CAREER** Lectr hist, Swarthmore Col. 66-70; lectr Latin Am hist, Hiram Col, 73-75. Lectr, Univ Pa, 67 and Case Western Reserve Univ, fall, 72; CHMN COMT MEX STUDIES, CONF LA HIST, 76-, mem exec comt, 78-79. **MEMBERSHIPS** Conf Latin Am Hist. **RESEARCH** Spain in America; the Americas from 1713 to 1826; Isabel I of Spain. **SELECTED PUBLICATIONS** Auth, The 'Buried Mirror' + Maxwell,Kenneth Criticism of the Television-Series on Spain and the New World--Comment, Ny Rev Bk(S), Vol 0040, 93; To Make America--European Emigration in the Early-Modern Period, Amer Hist Rev, Vol 0099, 94; Emigrants and Society--Extremadura and America in the 16th-Century, Amer Hist Rev, Vol 0099, 94 . **CONTACT ADDRESS** 501 D St SE, Washington, DC, 20003.

LISS, SHELDON BARNETT
PERSONAL Born 11/03/1936, Philadelphia, PA, m, 1959, 2 children **DISCIPLINE** LATIN AMERICAN HISTORY **EDUCATION** Am Univ, AB, 58, PhD(hist), 64; Duquesne Univ, MA, 62. **CAREER** Exec, pvt indust, 59-61; asst prof hist and co-chmn Latin Am Studies, Ind State Univ, 64-66; vis asst prof hist, Univ Notre Dame, 66-67; assoc prof, 67-69, dir doctoral studies, 69-70, PROF HIST, UNIV AKRON, 69-, Consult, Latin Am Inst, 65- and US Peace Corps, Latin Am, 66; adv, US Comt Panamanian Sovereignty, 76-77; consult, Nat Sci Found, 80 and Ohio Endowment Humanities, 80- **MEMBERSHIPS** AHA; Conf Latin Am Hist; Latin Am Studies Asn; Pan-Am Inst Geog and Hist; Soc Iberian and Latin Am Thought. **RESEARCH** Inter-American diplomacy; 20th century political history of Latin America; Marxist political and social thought in Latin America. **SELECTED PUBLICATIONS** Auth, Marxism in Latin America From 1909 to the Present--an Anthology, Hisp Amer Hist Rev, Vol 0073, 93; Panama and the United States--the Forced Alliance, J Amer Hist, Vol 0079, 93; The Latin-American Left--From the Fall of Allende to Perestroika, Hisp Amer Hist Rev, Vol 0074, 94; Law and Religion in Marxist Cuba--a Human-Rights Inquiry, Cath Hist Rev, Vol 0080, 94; Prize Possession--the United States and the Panama Canal, 1903-1979, J Latin Amer Stud, Vol 0027, 95. **CONTACT ADDRESS** Dept of Hist, Univ of Akron, Akron, OH, 44325.

LITCHFIELD, ROBERT BURR
PERSONAL Born 08/16/1936 **DISCIPLINE** EUROPEAN HISTORY **EDUCATION** Harvard Univ, AB, 58; Princton Univ, AM, 61, PhD(hist), 66. **CAREER** From instr to asst prof hist, Dartmouth Col, 63-68; asst prof, 68-72, ASSOC PROF HIST, BROWN UNIV, 72-, Am Coun Learned Soc grant-in-aid, 66-67. **MEMBERSHIPS** AHA **RESEARCH** France and Italy, 16th-19th centuries, old regime, revolutionary period and early 19th century; economic and social history. **SELECTED PUBLICATIONS** Auth, Feuds and Clans--the Genoese State in the Society of Fontanabuona, Amer Hist Rev, Vol 0098, 93; The Continuity of Feudal Power--the Caracciolo Di Brienza in Spanish Naples, Cath Hist Rev, Vol 0079, 93; The English Translation of 'Settecento Riformatore' and its Anglo-American Reception, Rivista Storica Italiana, Vol 0108, 96; Siena and the Sienese in the 13th Century, J Urban Hist, Vol 0023, 97; Turin 1564-1680--Urban Design, Military Culture, and Creation of the Absolutist Capital, J Urban Hist, Vol 0023, 97; A Provincial Elite in Early-Modern Tuscany--Family and Power in the Creation of the State, J Interdisciplinary Hist, Vol 0028, 97; Civic Politics in the Rome of Urban-Viii, J Urban Hist, Vol 0023, 97. **CONTACT ADDRESS** Dept of Hist, Brown Univ, 1 Prospect St, Providence, RI, 02912-9127.

LITOFF, JUDY BARRETT
PERSONAL Born 12/23/1944, Atlanta, GA, m, 1966, 2 children **DISCIPLINE** HISTORY **EDUCATION** Emory Univ, BA, 67, MA, 68; Univ Maine, PhD(hist), 75. **CAREER** ASSOC PROF HIST, BRYANT COL, 75-, Consult humanities, RI TV prod Anne Hutchinson, 76-77; hist consult, doc film, Daughters of Time, 78-80. **MEMBERSHIPS** Am Asn Univ Women; AHA; Nat Trust Hist Preserv; Orgn Am Historians. **RESEARCH** American women's history; American minority history; American social history. **SELECTED PUBLICATIONS** Auth, To the Rescue of the Crops--the Womens Land Army During World War II, Prologue-Quart National Arch, Vol 0025, 93; Cajun Country--Ancelet, Bj, Edwards, J, Pitre, G, J Amer Culture, Vol 0017, 94; Childrens Health in America--a History, Amer Hist Rev, Vol 0100, 95; United States Women on the Home Front in World War II, Historian, Vol 0057, 95; Goodbye, Piccadilly--British War Brides in America, J Amer Hist, Vol 0084, 97. **CONTACT ADDRESS** Bryant Col, 1150 Douglas Pike, Smithfield, RI, 02917-1291.

LITTLE, DOUGLAS JAMES
PERSONAL Born 05/24/1950, Lincoln, NE, m, 1974, 2 children **DISCIPLINE** AMERICAN HISTORY **EDUCATION** Univ Wis-Madison, BA, 72; Cornell Univ, MA, 75, PhD(hist), 78 **CAREER** ASST PROF TO PROF AM HIST, CLARK UNIV, 78-; vis prof Am Hist, Cornell Univ, 88-89. **HONORS AND AWARDS** Bernath Article Prize, Soc Historians Am Foreign Rel, 81. **MEMBERSHIPS** AHA; Orgn Am Historians; Soc Historians Am Foreign Rel **RESEARCH** American foreign relations with the Middle East; multinational corporations. **SELECTED PUBLICATIONS** Auth, Twenty years of turmoil: ITT, the State Department, and Spain 1924-1944, Bus Hist Rev, 79; Malevolent Neutrality: The United States, Great Britain, and the Origins of the Spanish Civil War, Cornell Univ Press, 85; New frontier on the Nile: JFK, Nasser, and Arab nationalism, Jour Am Hist, 88; Cold War and covert action: The United States and Syria 1945-1958, Middle East Jour, 93; Gideon's band: America and the Middle East since 1945, Diplomatic Hist, 94; His finest hour? Eisenhower, Lebanon, and the 1958 crisis in the Middle East, Diplomatic Hist, 96. **CONTACT ADDRESS** Dept Hist, Clark Univ, 950 Main St, Worcester, MA, 01610-1473. **EMAIL** dlittle@clarku.edu

LITTLE, ELIZABETH A.
PERSONAL 4 children **DISCIPLINE** ARCHAEOLOGY, ANTHROPOLOGY **EDUCATION** Wellesley Col, BA (Physics, Durant Scholar with high honors), 48; MIT, D Phil (Physics), 54; Univ MA, MA (Anthropology), 85. **CAREER** Nantucket Hist Asn Archaeological Field Dir, 76-77; coord, MA Hist Commission survey grant, 78-79, res dir, 79-84, curator of Prehistoric Artifacts, 85-95; MA Archaeologiocal Soc, trustee, 79-96, pres, 84-86, ed of the Bul of the MA Archaeological Soc, 86-96; res assoc, R S Peabody Museum of Archaeology, Philips Academy, Andover, MA; res fel, Archaeology, Nantucket Hist Asn. **HONORS AND AWARDS** Phi Beta Kappa, Sigma Xi, IBM fel, 47-54; Preservation Awards, MA Hist Commission, 79, 88. **MEMBERSHIPS** Soc for Am Archaeology; Soc for Archaeological Sciences. **RESEARCH** Radiocarbon dating; stable isotope studies of prehistoric diet; ethnohistory. **SELECTED PUBLICATIONS** Auth, Radiocarbon Age Calibration at Archaeological Sites of Coastal Massachusetts and Vicinity, J of Archaeological Science, 93; with Margaret J Schoeninger, The Late Woodland Diet on Nantucket Island and the Problem of Maize in Coastal New England, Am Antiquity,

95; Daniel Spotso: A Sachem at Nantucket Island, Massachusetts, circa 1691-1741, in Northeastern Indian Lives, 1632-1816, R S Grumet, ed, Univ MA Press, 96; Analyzing Prehistoric Diets by Linear Programming, with John D C Little, J of Archaeological Science, 97. **CONTACT ADDRESS** 37 Conant Road, Lincoln, MA, 01773. **EMAIL** ealittle@alum.mit.edu

LITTLE, JOHN IRVINE
PERSONAL Born 01/06/1947, Thetford Mines, PQ, Canada, m, 1978 **DISCIPLINE** CANADIAN HISTORY **EDUCATION** Bishop's Univ, BA, 68; Univ NB, Ma, 70; Univ Ottawa, PhD(French-Can hist), 77. **CAREER** Lectr Can hist, Univ PEI, 74-75 and St Thomas Univ, 75-76; ASST PROF CAN HIST, SIMON FRASER UNIV, 76-. **RESEARCH** Nineteenth century Quebec--social, economic, political; late 19th century Canadian political. **SELECTED PUBLICATIONS** Auth, Death in the Lower St John River Valley--the Diary of Machum, Jr., Alexander, 1845-1849, Acadiensis, Vol 0022, 92; The Short Life of a Local Protest Movement--the Annexation Crisis of 1849-50 in the Eastern Townships, J Can Hist Asn-Revue De La Societe Historique Du Canada, Vol 0003, 92; Patrons, Clients, Brokers--Ontario Society and Politics, 1791-1896, Can Hist Rev, Vol 0073, 92; The Development of the Quebecois Identity, Literary and Historical Images, Colby Quart, Vol 0029, 93; Popular Voices in Print, the Local Newspaper Correspondents of an Extended Scots Canadian Community, 1894, J Can Stud-Revue D Etudes Canadiennes, Vol 0030, 95; A New Lease on Life--Landlords, Tenants and Immigrants in Ireland and Canada, Histoire Sociale-Soc Hist, Vol 0029, 96. **CONTACT ADDRESS** Simon Fraser Univ, Burnaby, BC, V5A 1S6.

LITTLE, LESTER KNOX
PERSONAL Born 10/21/1935, Providence, RI **DISCIPLINE** MEDIEVAL HISTORY **EDUCATION** Dartmouth Col, BA, 57; Princton Univ, MA, 60, PhD, 62. **CAREER** Instr hist, Princeton Univ, 61-63; from asst prof to assoc prof, Univ Chicago 63-71; assoc prof, 71-76, prof hist, 76- , Dwight W. Morton Prof Hist, 83- , Smith Col; dir, American Academy in Rome, 98- . **HONORS AND AWARDS** Mem, Inst Advan Studies, 69-70; Am Coun Learned Socs fel, 70-71; Guggenheim fel, 83-84; NEH fel, 95-96. **MEMBERSHIPS** AHA: Mediaeval Acad Am; Int Soc Franciscan Studies. **RESEARCH** Social history of religious phenomena. **SELECTED PUBLICATIONS** Co-ed, Nature, Man and Society in the Twelfth Century, Univ Chicago, 68; auth, Pride Goes Before Avarice: Social Change and the Vices, Am Hist Rev, 71; coauth, Social Meaning in the Monastic and Mendicant Spiritualities, Past & Present, 74; Religious Poverty and the Profit Economy in Medieval Europe, Cornell Univ, 78; auth, Liberty, Charity, Fraternity: Lay Confraternities at Bergamo, Lubrina, 88; auth, Benedictine Maledictions, Cornell, 93; co-auth, Debating the Middle Ages, Blackwell, 98. **CONTACT ADDRESS** American Acad in Rome, Via Angelo Masina, 5, Rome, ., 00153. **EMAIL** little@librs6k.vatlib.it

LITTLE, MONROE HENRY
PERSONAL Born 06/30/1950, St Louis, Missouri, m **DISCIPLINE** HISTORY **EDUCATION** Denison Univ, BA 1971 (magna cum laude); Princeton Univ, MA 1973, PhD 1977. **CAREER** MIT, instructor 1976-77, asst prof 1977-80; Indiana Univ-Purdue Univ, Indianapolis, asst prof 1980-81, asst prof dir afro-amer studies 1981-. **HONORS AND AWARDS** Elected Omicron Delta Kappa Men's Leadership Honorary 1971; Fellowship Rockefeller Fellowship in Afro-Amer Studies 1972-75. **MEMBERSHIPS** Mem Amer Historical Assn; mem Organization of American Historians; mem Natl Urban League; mem Assoc for Study of Afro-Amer Life & History; consultant Educ Develop Ctr 1980; consultant CSR Inc US Dept of Labor 1981; consultant Black Women in the Mid-West Project Purdue Univ 1983. **CONTACT ADDRESS** Purdue Univ Indiana Univ-Indianapolis, Indianapolis, IN, 46206.

LITTLEFIELD, DAN F.
DISCIPLINE NATIVE AMERICAN LITERATURE & HISTORY **EDUCATION** SUNY, PhD. **CAREER** English and Lit, Univ Ark **SELECTED PUBLICATIONS** Auth, Alex Posey: Creek poet, journalist and humorist; The Life of Okah Tubbee; Coauth, A Biobibliography of Native American Writers; Coed: The Heath Anthology of American Literature; Kamaha Omaha Stories by Francis LaFlesche; The Fus Fixico Letters by Alex Posey. **CONTACT ADDRESS** Univ Ark Little Rock, 2801 S University Ave., Little Rock, AR, 72204-1099. **EMAIL** dflittlefiel@ualr.edu

LITTLEFIELD, DANIEL
DISCIPLINE HISTORY **EDUCATION** Johns Hopkins Univ, PhD, 77. **CAREER** Prof, Univ Ill Urbana Champaign **RESEARCH** American colonial history; comparative plantation societies; African American history. **SELECTED PUBLICATIONS** Auth, Rice and Slaves: Ethnicity and the Slave Trade in Colonial South Carolina, La State Univ, 81; Rice and the Making of South Carolina: An Introductory Essay, 95; Blacks, John Brown, and a Theory of Manhood, Univ Va, 95. **CONTACT ADDRESS** History Dept, Univ Ill Urbana Champaign, 52 E Gregory Dr, Champaign, IL, 61820. **EMAIL** dlittle@uiuc.edu

LITTLEJOHN, WALTER L.
PERSONAL Born 03/05/1932, Pine Bluff, AR, m **DISCIPLINE** EDUCATION **EDUCATION** BS 1954; MEd 1957; EdD 1966. **CAREER** Magnolia, AR, teacher 1954; Magnolia AR, principal 1965-58; Magnolia, AR, public school supt 1958-64; AM&N, prof 1966-74, dean of educ 1975-91, coordinator of graduate programs, 1991-. **MEMBERSHIPS** Mem Phi Delta Kappa; Alpha Kappa Mu; life mem Omega Psi Phi Frat; Natl Educ Assn; past pres State Tchrn Assn. **CONTACT ADDRESS** Coord Grad Programs, Sch Educ, Univ of Arizona, Pine Bluff, University Dr, Pine Bluff, AR, 71601.

LITTMAN, ROBERT J.
PERSONAL Born 08/23/1943, Newark, NJ, m, 1966, 3 children **DISCIPLINE** ANCIENT HISTORY, CLASSICS **EDUCATION** Columbia Univ, BA, 64, PhD(class philol), 70; Oxford Univ, BLitt, 68. **CAREER** Instr hist, Rutgers Univ, 67-68; instr classics, Brandeis Univ, 68-70; asst prof, 70-75, assoc prof, 75-79, PROF CLASSICS, UNIV HAWAII, MANOA, 79-, Herodotus fel and vis mem, Inst Advan Study, Princeton, 77. **MEMBERSHIPS** Am Philol Asn; Am Hist Asn; Soc Prom Hellenic Studies, Friends Ancient Hist. **RESEARCH** Greek history; historiography; Greek literature. **SELECTED PUBLICATIONS** Auth, Epidemiology of the Plague of Athens, Transactions of the American Philol Asn, Vol 0122, 92; Athens, Persia and the Book of Ezra, Transactions of the Amer Philol Asn, Vol 0125, 95; Kinship and Politics in Athens, 90; Jewish History in 100 Nutshells, 96. **CONTACT ADDRESS** Dept of Europ Lang and Lit, Univ of Hawaii Manoa, 1890 E. West Rd., Honolulu, HI, 96822-2362. **EMAIL** littman@hawaii.edu

LITWACK, LEON F.
PERSONAL Born 12/02/1929, Santa Barbara, CA, m, 1952, 2 children **DISCIPLINE** UNITED STATES HISTORY **EDUCATION** Univ Calif, BA, 51, MA, 52, PhD, 58 **CAREER** From instr to assoc prof hist, Univ Wis-Madison, 58-65; assoc prof, 65-71, prof, 71-87 A F & MAY T MORRISON PROF HIST, UNIV CALIF, BERKELEY, 87-, Soc Sci Res Coun fac fel, 61-62; Guggenheim fel, 67-68; humanities res fel, Univ Calif, Berkeley, 76 & 80; Fulbright lectr, Moscow State Univ, 80, Beijing Univ, China, 82, Univ Helsinki, 90, Univ Sydney, Australia, 91; lectr Am hist, Peking Univ, 82. **HONORS AND AWARDS** Distinguished Teaching Award, Univ Calif, Berkeley, 71; Francis Parkman Prize, Soc Am Historians, 79; Pulitzer Prize in Hist, 80; Am Book Award, History, 81; Pres, Orgn Am Hist, 86-87; Am Acad Arts & Sci, 87. **MEMBERSHIPS** AHA; Orgn Am Historians; Southern Hist Asn; Am Antiq Soc; Soc Am Hist **RESEARCH** Slavery, abolitionism, and the American Negro; 19th century United States history **SELECTED PUBLICATIONS** Auth, North of Slavery: The Negro in the Free States, 1789-1860, Univ Chicago, 61; ed, American Labor Movement, Prentice-Hall, 62; auth, The emancipation of the Negro abolitionist, In: The Antislavery Vanguard, Princeton Univ, 65; co-ed, Reconstruction: An Anthology of Revisionist Writings, La State Univ, 69; auth, Free at last, In: Anonymous Americans, Prentice-Hall, 71; co-ed, To Look for America (film), Nat Educ TV, 72; coauth, The United States, 4th ed, 76 & 5th ed, 82, Prentice-Hall; auth, Been in the Storm So Long, The Aftermath of Slavery, Knopf, 79; Trouble in Mind: Black Southerners in the Age of Jim Crow, Knopf, 98. **CONTACT ADDRESS** Dept of Hist, Univ of Calif, 3229 Dwinelle Hall, Berkeley, CA, 94720-2551.

LIU, CATHERINE
DISCIPLINE EARLY MODERN FRENCH NOVEL **EDUCATION** CUNY, PhD. **CAREER** Instr, Univ Minn, Twin Cities. **RESEARCH** The fiction of Lafayette. **SELECTED PUBLICATIONS** Published in the fields of psychoanalytic theory and art criticism. **CONTACT ADDRESS** Univ Minn, Twin Cities, Minneapolis, MN, 55455.

LIU, JUNG-CHAO
PERSONAL Born 02/09/1929, Taiwan, m, 1984, 5 children **DISCIPLINE** ECONOMICS **CAREER** McGill Univ, 64-70; SUNY, 70- . **MEMBERSHIPS** Am Econ Asn **CONTACT ADDRESS** SUNY-Binghamton, Vestal Pky E, Binghamton, NY, 13901. **EMAIL** jungliu@binghamton.edu

LIUZZA, ROY
DISCIPLINE ANGLO-SAXON LITERATURE, MEDIEVAL LITERATURE **EDUCATION** Northeast La Univ, BA, 78; Yale University, MA, 79, PhD, 88. **CAREER** Instr, 90, Tulane Univ. **SELECTED PUBLICATIONS** Auth, The Old English Version of the Gospels Early English Text Society, EETS O.S. 304, Oxford, 94; Representation and Readership in the Middle English Havelok, JEGP 93, 94; The Return of the Repressed: New and Old Theories in Old English Literary Criticism, Old English Shorter Poems: Basic Readings on Anglo-Saxon Lit 3, Garland Press, 94; On the Dating of Beowulf, Beowulf: Basic Readings on Anglo-Saxon Lit 1, Garland Press, 95; Orthography and Historical Linguistics, Jour Eng Ling 24, 96; co-ed, Anglo-Saxon Manuscripts in Microfiche, Facsimile vol 6: Gospels, MRTS, 95. **CONTACT ADDRESS** Dept of Eng, Tulane Univ, 6823 St Charles Ave, New Orleans, LA, 70118. **EMAIL** rliuzza@mailhost.tcs.tulane.edu

LIVEZEANU, I.
PERSONAL Born 10/18/1952, Bucharest, Romania **DISCIPLINE** EASTERN EUROPEAN HISTORY **EDUCATION** Swarthmore, BA, 74; Univ Mich, MA, 79; Univ Mich, PhD, 86. **CAREER** Asst prof, Colby Col, 87-91; **HONORS AND AWARDS** Phi Beta Kappa; FLAS-Russian; FLAS-Polish, IREX, ACLS Dissertation Fel; Mellon Post Doc, Univ Calif Berkeley; book award, Amer Romanian Acad; Heldt book prize. **MEMBERSHIPS** AAASS; Asn of Women in Slavic Studies; Soc for Romanian Studies; Asn for Jewish Studies; Asn for the Study of Nationalities. **RESEARCH** Culture; nationalism; Jews; intellectuals; identity. **SELECTED PUBLICATIONS** Auth, Defining Russian at the Margins, Russian Rev 95; A Jew from the Danube, Shvut: Jewish Problems in the USSR and Eastern Europe, 93; Moldavia, 1917-1990: Nationalism and Internationalism Then and Now, Armenian Rev, 90; Between State and Nation: Romania's Lower Middle Class Intellectuals in the Interwar Period, Splintered Classes: The European Lower Middle Classes in the Age of Fascism, 90; Fascists and Conservatives in Romania: Two Generations of Nationalists, Fascists and Conservatives in Europe, 90; Excerpts from a Troubled Book: An Episode in Romanian Literature, Cross Currents: A Yearbook of Central European Culture, 84; Urbanization in a Low Key and Linguistic Change in Soviet Moldavia Parts 1 and 2, Soviet Studies, 81; Cultural Politics in Greater Romania: Regionalism, Nation Building, and Ethnic Struggle, 1918-1930, Cornell Univ Press, 95; Cultura se Nationalism in Romania Mare, 1918-1930, Ed Humanitas, 98. **CONTACT ADDRESS** Univ of Pittsburgh, 3P01 Forbes Quadrangle, Pittsburgh, PA, 15260. **EMAIL** irinal@pitt.edu

LIVINGSTON, DONALD W.
DISCIPLINE HISTORY OF MODERN PHILOSOPHY **EDUCATION** WA Univ, PhD, 65. **CAREER** Philos, Emory Univ. **HONORS AND AWARDS** Nat Endowment Hum fel, 78-79. **SELECTED PUBLICATIONS** Auth, Hume's Philosophy of Common Life; Coed Hume, A Re-evaluation; Liberty in Hume's "History of England"; Hume as Philosopher of Society, Politics, and History. **CONTACT ADDRESS** Emory Univ, Atlanta, GA, 30322-1950.

LIVINGSTON, JOHN
PERSONAL Born 02/24/1935, New Haven, CT, m, 1961, 1 child **DISCIPLINE** AMERICAN HISTORY **EDUCATION** Harvard Univ, AB, 56; Univ WI, MA, 59, PhD(hist), 65. **CAREER** Vis asst prof hist, Univ Denver, 63-64; asst prof, Temple Buell Col, 64-68; assoc prof hist, Univ Denver, 68-. **MEMBERSHIPS** AHA; Orgn Am Historians. **RESEARCH** Late 19th and early 20th century American intellectual, social and political history; Am Jewish hist. **SELECTED PUBLICATIONS** The Industrial Removal Office and the Denver Jewish Community, Am Jewish Hist, 6/79; Clarence Darrow: The Mind of a Sentimental Rebel, 89. **CONTACT ADDRESS** Dept Hist, Univ Denver, 2199 S University, Denver, CO, 80210-4711. **EMAIL** jlivings@du.edu

LIVINGSTON, JOHN W.
DISCIPLINE OTTOMAN EMPIRE AND MOD ARAB STATES **EDUCATION** Princeton Univ, PhD, 68. **CAREER** Post Doctoral Res fel, Harvard Univ, 68-70; William Paterson Col, 87-; Temple Univ, Pa, 86-87; Amer Univ, Beirut, 70-85; Univ Fla, Orlando, 85-86; sr mem, Middle Eastern Stud Asn; serv, Fac Workshops; Hist Dept, Libr Rep, Activ Comt & Hon Soc Adv. **SELECTED PUBLICATIONS** Auth, Shaykh Muhammad Abduh and the Legitimation of Western Science, J Middle East Stud, 93; Shaykhs, Jabarti, and Attar: A Study of Science and Islam in Nineteenth Century Egypt, Studia Islamica, 93; Shaykh Rifa'a Rafi'i al-Tahtawi and the Islamic Response to Western Science, Der Islam; Science and the Occult in the Thinking of Ibn Qayyim al- Jawziyya, J Amer Orient Soc, 92; Bonaparte and Shaykh Bakri, Studia Islamica, fasicule 80, 94; On the Difference Between the Soul and the Spirit: Translation and Study of Qusta ibn Luqa's Psycho-physiological Treatise and its Place in Islamic Thought, Scripta Mediter vol 11, Soc for Mediter Stud, Univ Toronto, 82; rev(s), The Arab World, Wm Polk, The Hist Tchr, 93; Philosophy and Science in the Islamic World, J Amer Orient Soc, 93. **CONTACT ADDRESS** Dept of History, William Paterson Col, 300 Pompton Rd., Wayne, NJ, 07470. **EMAIL** jwl@frontier.wilpaterson.edu

LLOYD, ELISABETH A.
PERSONAL Born 03/03/1956 **DISCIPLINE** HISTORY, PHILOSOPHY OF SCIENCE **EDUCATION** Queen's Univ, 74-75; Univ Colo-Boulder, BA, Sci/Polit Theory, 76-80; Princeton Univ, PhD, 80-84. **CAREER** Vis instr, Exper Stud, Univ Colo-Boulder, 80; vis scholar, Genetics, Harvard Univ, 83-84; vis lectr, Philos, Univ Calif-San Diego, 84-85; asst prof, Philos, Univ Calif-San Diego, 85-88; asst prof, Univ Calif-Berkeley, 88-90; assoc prof, Univ Calif-Berkeley, 90-97; prof, Philos, Univ Calif-Berkeley, 97-; PROF, BIOL, IND UNIV, 98-. **MEMBERSHIPS** Nat Endow Hum; Nat Sci Found; Am Philos Asn; Philos Sci Asn; Int Soc Hist, Philos, & Soc Stud of Biol **SELECTED PUBLICATIONS** The Structure and Confirmation of Evolutionary Theory, Greenwood Press, 94; co-edr, Keywords in Evolutionary Biology, Harvard Univ Press, 92; "The Anachronistic Anarchist," Philosophical Studies 81, APA West Div Sympos, 96; "Science and Anti-Science: Objectivity

and its Real Enemies," Feminism, Science, and the Philosophy of Science, Kluwer, 96; "Feyerabend, Mill, and Pluralism," Philosophy of Science, Supplemental Issue: PSA 96 Symposium Papers, 97. **CONTACT ADDRESS** Hist & Philos Sci Dept, Indiana Univ, Bloomington, Goodbody Hall 130, Bloomington, IN, 47405-2401. **EMAIL** ealloyd@indiana.edu

LLOYD, JENNIFER
DISCIPLINE HISTORY **EDUCATION** Cambridge Univ, BA, MA; SUNY Brockport, MA; Univ Rochester, PhD. **CAREER** Vis asst prof. **RESEARCH** Women in Victorian Britain. **SELECTED PUBLICATIONS** Auth, Raising Lilies: Ruskin and Women, Jour British Hist, 95; Instructors' Manual for The Making of the Modern World, St Martin, 95. **CONTACT ADDRESS** Dept of History, State Univ NY Col Brockport, Brockport, NY, 14420. **EMAIL** jlloyd@acspr1.acs.brockport.edu

LO, WINSTON W.
PERSONAL Born 04/12/1938, China, m, 1967, 2 children **DISCIPLINE** HISTORY **EDUCATION** Harvard Univ, PhD, 70. **CAREER** PROF OF HIST, FLA STATE UNIV, 88-. **MEMBERSHIPS** Asn of Asian Studies. **RESEARCH** Chinese intellectual & institutional history (Song through the Qing period). **SELECTED PUBLICATIONS** Auth, Life and Thought of Yeh Shih, Chinese Univ of Hong Kong Press, 74; Szechwan in Sung Times, The Univ of Chinese Culture Press, Taipei, 82; An Introduction to the Civil Service of Sung China, Univ of Hawaii Press, 87. **CONTACT ADDRESS** Dept of Hist, Florida State Univ, Tallahassee, FL, 32306. **EMAIL** wlo@mailer.fsu.edu

LOACH, DONALD
DISCIPLINE MUSIC **EDUCATION** Yale Univ, MM; Univ Ca, PhD. **CAREER** Dept Music, Va Univ **RESEARCH** Choral conducting; counterpoint; medieval and renaissance music. **SELECTED PUBLICATIONS** Auth, A Stylistic Approach to Species Counterpoint, Journal Music Theory; Basic Counterpoint (rev), Jour Music Theory; The Study of Fugue (rev), Jour Music Theory. **CONTACT ADDRESS** Dept of Music, Virginia Univ, Charlottesville, VA, 22903. **EMAIL** dgl@virginia.edu

LOADER, COLIN T.
DISCIPLINE HISTORY **EDUCATION** Univ Calif Los Angeles, PhD, 74. **CAREER** Assoc prof, Univ Nev Las Vegas. **RESEARCH** German history; European intellectual history; 19th century Europe. **SELECTED PUBLICATIONS** Auth, The Intellectual Development of Karl Mannheim: Culture, Politics and Planning, Cambridge, 85. **CONTACT ADDRESS** History Dept, Univ Nev Las Vegas, 4505 Md Pky, Las Vegas, NV, 89154.

LOCKARD, CRAIG ALAN
PERSONAL Born 10/20/1942, Ft Madison, IA, m, 1970, 2 children **DISCIPLINE** ASIAN AND WORLD HISTORY **EDUCATION** Univ Redlands, BA, 64; Univ Hawaii, MA, 67; Univ Wis, PhD(hist), 73. **CAREER** Instr hist, Univ Bridgeport, 69-70; vis asst prof, State Univ NY Stony Brook, 72-73 and State Univ NY Buffalo, 73-74; asst prof, 75-79, ASSOC PROF HIST and SOCIAL CHANGE, UNIV WIS-GREEN BAY, 79-, Fulbright-Hays sr lectr, Univ Malaya, 77-78, grant, 77-78; fel, Univ Ky, 80; Am Ethnic Studies Coord Comt grant, 80-81; Univ Wis-Green Bay Outstanding Scholar Award, 81. **MEMBERSHIPS** Asn for Asin Studies; Borneo Res Coun; Royal Asiatic Soc; African Studies Asn. **RESEARCH** Modern Southeast Asian history especially Malaysia and Indonesia; overseas Chinese and Indonesians; comparative Third World socioeconomic history. **SELECTED PUBLICATIONS** Auth, The History of the Book in Canada--a Bibliography, Papers of the Bibliographical Soc Amer, Vol 0088, 94; Studies in Maritime Literary History, 1760-1930, Engl Stud in Can, Vol 0021, 95; From Folk to Computer Songs--the Evolution of Malaysian Popular Music, 1930-1990, J Popular Culture, Vol 0030, 96; Popular Musics and Politics in Modern Southeast Asia, a Comparative Analysis, Asian Music, Vol 0027, 96. **CONTACT ADDRESS** Dept of Hist and Social Change, Univ of Wisconsin, Green Bay, WI, 54302.

LOCKE, DON C.
PERSONAL Born 04/30/1943, Macon, Mississippi **DISCIPLINE** EDUCATION **EDUCATION** TN A&I State Univ, BS 1963, MEd 1964; Ball State Univ, EdD 1974. **CAREER** South Side HS, social studies teacher 1964-70; Wayne HS, school counselor 1971-73; Ball State Univ European Program, asst prof 1974-75; NC State Univ, asst/assoc prof/prof 1975-89, dept head 1987-93; Director, NCSU Doctoral Program at the Asheville Graduate Center, 1993-. **HONORS AND AWARDS** Summer Fellow Center for Advanced Study in Behaviorial Sciences 1979, 1992; ACA Professional Development Award, 1996. **MEMBERSHIPS** Mem Alpha Phi Alpha Fraternity Inc; mem New Bern Ave Day Care Center Bd, 1978-86; pres NC Counseling Assoc 1979-80; chairperson S Region Branch ACA 1983-84; mem Carroll Comm Schools Advisory Council 1984-87, ex director, 1987-1991; chairperson NC Bd of Registered Practicing Counselors 1984-87; sec Assn for Counselor Educ & Supervision 1985-86; pres Southern Association for counselor Educ and Supervision 1988-89, member board dir, Asheville -Buncombe United Way, 1997-. **SELECTED PUBLICATIONS** Co-author "Psychological Techniques for Teachers"; author Increasing Multicultural Understanding; author or co-author of more than 50 articles in professional journals. **CONTACT ADDRESS** Dir, Doctoral Program in ACCE, 143 Karpen Hall, Asheville, NC, 28804.

LOCKE, MAMIE EVELYN
PERSONAL Born 03/19/1954, Brandon, MS, s **DISCIPLINE** POLITICAL SCIENCE **EDUCATION** Tougaloo College, Tougaloo, MS, BA, 1976; Atlanta University, Atlanta, GA, MA, 1978, PhD, 1984. **CAREER** Dept of Archives & History, Jackson, MS, archivist, 1977-79; Atlanta Historical Society, Atlanta, GA, archivist, 1979-81; HAMPTON UNIVERSITY, HAMPTON, VA, associate professor, 1981-97, PROF, 1997-; assistant dean, 1991-96, DEAN, 1996-. **HONORS AND AWARDS** Lindback Award for Distinguished Teaching, Hampton University, 1990; Rodney Higgins Award, National Conference Black Political Scientists, 1986; Fulbright-Hays Award, Department of Education, 1986; Ford Foundation Grant, College of William & Mary, 1988; Ford Foundation Grant, Duke University, 1987; NEH Fellowship, National Endowment for the Humanities, 1985. **MEMBERSHIPS** National Conference of Black Political Scientists, 1976-, executive council, 1989-92, president elect, 1992-93, president, 1993-94; Alpha Kappa Alpha Sorority Inc; American Political Science Association, 1990-; Southeastern Women's Studies Association, 1987-; advisor, member, Alpha Kappa Mu National Honor Society, 1990-; editorial board, PS: Politics and Political Science, 1992-95; editorial board, National Political Science Review, 1994-; Hampton City Council; commissioner, Hampton Planning Commission; commissioner, Hampton Roads Planning District Commission; commissioner, Hampton Redevelopment & Housing Authority; VA Municipal League, Government Affairs Committee; National Black Caucus of Local Elected Officers; Women in Municipal Government, bd mem, 1998-99. **CONTACT ADDRESS** Hampton Univ, 119 Armstrong Hall, Hampton, VA, 23668.

LOCKE, RALPH PAUL
PERSONAL Born 03/09/1949, Boston, MA, m, 1979, 2 children **DISCIPLINE** MUSICOLOGY, MUSIC, HISTORY, SOCIOLOGY **EDUCATION** Harvard Univ, BA, 70; Univ Chicago, MA, 74, PhD, 80. **CAREER** Prof, Eastman School Music, 75-. **HONORS AND AWARDS** ASCAP Deems Taylor Award, 92 & 96. **MEMBERSHIPS** Am Musicol Soc; Sonneck Soc Am Music. **RESEARCH** Music and society; Music and gender; Music in France & Italy; Music patronage in the US; Musical exoticism and Orientalism. **SELECTED PUBLICATIONS** Auth Music, Musicians, and the Saint-Simonians, Univ Chicago Press, 86; Paris: Centre of Intellectual Ferment (1789-1852), Man & Music: The Early Romantic Era, Between Revelutions: 1789 and 1848, Prentice-Hall, 91; What Are These Women Doing in Opera? En travesti: Women, Gender Su bversion, Opera, Columbia Univ Press, 95; Cultivating Music in America: Women Patrons and Activists since 1860, Univ Cal Press, 97; Constructing the Oriental 'Other': Saint-Saens's Samson et Dalila, The Work of Opera: Genre, Nationhood, and Sexual Difference, Columbia Univ Press, 97; The French Symphony: David, Gounod, and Bizet to Saint-Saens, Franck, and Their Followers, The Nineteenth-Century Symphony, Schirmer Books, 97; Cutthroats and Casbah Dancers, Muezzins and Timeless Sands: Musical Images of the Middle East, The Exotic in Western Music, NE Univ Press, 98; Musicology and/as Social Concern: Imagining the Relevant Musicologist, Oxford Univ Press, 98. **CONTACT ADDRESS** Eastman Sch of Music, 26 Gibbs St, Rochester, NY, 14604-2599. **EMAIL** RLPH@UHURA.CC.ROCHESTER.EDU

LOCKHART, PHILIP N.
PERSONAL Born 05/03/1928, Smicksburg, PA, m, 1959, 2 children **DISCIPLINE** CLASSICAL STUDIES **EDUCATION** Univ Pa, BA, 50; Univ NC, MA, 51; Yale Univ, PhD(classical lang), 59. **CAREER** Teacher, Ezel Mission Sch, Ky, 51-52; instr class lang, Univ Mo, 54-56; instr class studies, Univ Pa, 57-61, asst prof, 61-63; assoc prof class lang and chmn dept, 63-68, prof, 68-71, ASBURY J CLARKE PROF LATIN and CHMN DEPT, DICKINSON COL, 71- Vis prof, Ohio State Univ, 69-70. **HONORS AND AWARDS** Ganoe Award Teaching, Dickinson Col, 69, 73. **MEMBERSHIPS** Am Philol Asn; Archaeol Inst Am; Am Class League; Vergilian Soc Am. **RESEARCH** Latin poetry; fourth century AD; Homeric background. **SELECTED PUBLICATIONS** Auth, Moser, Mary, E. 1950-1996--in Memoriam, Class World, Vol 0089, 96. **CONTACT ADDRESS** Dept of Class Lang, Dickinson Col, Carlisle, PA, 17013.

LOCKWOOD, LEWIS HENRY
PERSONAL Born 12/16/1930, New York, NY, m, 1977, 2 children **DISCIPLINE** MUSICOLOGY **EDUCATION** Queens Col, NY, BA, 52; Princeton Univ, MFA, 55, PhD(music), 60. **CAREER** From instr to prof, Princeton Univ, 58-72, chmn dept, 70-73, Robert Schirmer '21 prof music, 72-80; prof Music, Harvard Univ, 80-, Bicentennial preceptor, Princeton Univ, 62-65; coun humanities sr fel, 66-67; ed of jour, 63-66, Am Musicol Soc, Am Coun Learned Soc deleg, 66-68, fel, 68-69; consult ed, Grove's Dict of Music & Musicians, 70-; Nat Endowment for Humanities sr fel, 73-74; Guggenheim Found fel, 77-78; vis, Inst Advan Study, 77-78. **HONORS AND AWARDS** Einstein Award, Am Musicol Soc, 70; Hon Doctorate, Universita Degli Studi, Ferrara, 91; Hon Doctorate, New England Conservatory of Music, 97., MA, Harvard Univ. **MEMBERSHIPS** Am Musicol Soc (vpres, 70-72, pres, 87-88), Renaissance Soc Am. **RESEARCH** Renaissance music; music of Beethoven; history of opera. **SELECTED PUBLICATIONS** Auth, The autograph of Beethoven's Sonata for Violoncello and Piano, Op 69, Music Forum; The Counter-Reformation and the Masses of Vincenzo Ruffo, Fondazione Giorgio Cini, 70; On Beethoven's sketches and autographs: Some problems of definition and interpretation, Acta Musicol, 70; Music at Ferrara in the period of Ercole I d'Este, Studi Musicali, 72; Josquin at Ferrara: New documents and letters, Proc Int Josquin Festival-Conf, 73; Aspects of the L'homme Arme Tradition, Proc Royal Musical Asn, 73-74; ed, Palestrina: Pope Marcellus Mass, Norton Critical Scores, Norton, 75; auth, Dufay and Ferrara, Papers of the Dufay Quincentenary Conf, 76. **CONTACT ADDRESS** Dept of Music, Harvard Univ, Music Bldg, Cambridge, MA, 02138-3800. **EMAIL** llockw@fas.harvard.edu

LOENGARD, JANET SENDEROWITZ
PERSONAL Born 06/21/1935, Allentown, PA, m, 1964, 2 children **DISCIPLINE** MEDIEVAL EUROPEAN HISTORY **EDUCATION** Cornell Univ, BA, 55; Harvard Univ, LLB, 58; Columbia Univ, MA, 64; PhD(hist), 70. **CAREER** Instr hist, Rutgers Univ, Newark, 69-70; asst prof, City Col New York, 70-71; asst prof, 71-74; ASSOC PROF HIST, MORAVIAN COL, 74-, Co-chmn, Columbia Univ Sem on Hist of Legal and Polit Thought, 74-76; chmn mem comt, Am Soc Legal Hist, 75-77, bd dirs, 78-80; Am Philos Soc grant, 77; nominating comt, AHA, 78-80. **MEMBERSHIPS** Conf Brit Studies; Am Soc Legal Hist; AHA; Medieval Acad Am. **RESEARCH** Medieval English legal history; English legal history. **SELECTED PUBLICATIONS** Auth, Native Law and the Church in Medieval Wales. J Brit Stud, Vol 0034, 95; The Making of the Common Law, J Brit Stud, Vol 0034, 95; The Origins of the English Legal Profession, J Brit Stud, Vol 0034, 95; English Law in the Age of the Black Death, 1348-1381--a Transformation of Governance and Law, J Brit Stud, Vol 0034, 95; Women in England, C.1275-1525--Documentary Sources, Albion, Vol 0029, 97. **CONTACT ADDRESS** Dept of Hist, Moravian Col, 1200 Main St, Bethlehem, PA, 18018-6650.

LOERKW, WILLIAM
PERSONAL Born 08/13/1920, Toledo, OH, m, 1944, 7 children **DISCIPLINE** CLASSICAL ARCHAEOLOGY, ART HISTORY (ANCIENT-MEDIEVAL) **EDUCATION** Oberlin Col, BA, 42; Princeton Univ, MFA, 48; PhD, 56. **CAREER** Instr-asst prof, Brown Univ, 48-58; assoc prof, Bryn Mawr Col, 58-64; Prof of Art Hist, Univ Pittsburgh, 65-71, chmn Frick Fine Arts Dept, 65-68; Prof Byzantine Art, Harvard Univ at Dumbarton Oaks, Washington, DC, 71-88, dir, Center for Byzantine Studies, 71-78; vis prof, Hist of Architecture at School of Architecture, The Cath Univ of Am, Washington, DC, 78-88; lect in Hist of Architecture, The Cath Univ, Washington, DC, 88-91; lect in Hist of Architecture, School of Architecture, Univ MD, College Park, 91-93. **HONORS AND AWARDS** Miller scholar, Oberlin, 38-42; Phi Beta Kappa, Oberlin, 42; Jr fel, Princeton, 46-48; Fulbright res scholar at Am Academy Rome, 52-53; Danforth Teacher fel, 55-56. **MEMBERSHIPS** Med Academy of Am; Soc of Archit Historians; Soc of Fellows-Am Academy Rome; College Art Asn; Bd of Advisers, Center for Advanced Studies in the Visual Arts (CASVA), Nat Gallery, Washington, DC, 71-73, 81-83, 98-99. **RESEARCH** Roman Imperial Architecture (Pantheon); Early Christian Art. **SELECTED PUBLICATIONS** Auth, with G Cavallo and J Gribomont, Codex Purpureus Rossanensis, Commentarium, Salerno/Graz, 87; A Rereading of the Interior Elevation of Hadrian's Rotunda, JSAH, XLIX, 1, 90; contrib, Oxford Dictionary of Byzantium, Oxford Press, NYC, 91; Incipits and Author Portraits in Greek Gospel Books: Some Observations, in Byzantine East, Latin West, Art Historical Studies in Honor of Kurt Weitzmann, Princeton, 95; contrib, Dictionary of Early Christian Art & Archaeology, forthcoming. **CONTACT ADDRESS** 227 Gralan Rd, Catonsville, MD, 21228. **EMAIL** bloerke@aol.com

LOEWEN, JAMES W.
PERSONAL Born 02/06/1942, Decatur, IL, d, 2 children **DISCIPLINE** SOCIOLOGY **EDUCATION** Carlton Col, BA, 64; Harvard, PhD, 68. **CAREER** Tougaloo Col, assoc prof, sociol, 68-75; Univ VT, prof, sociol, 75-97, emeritus 97-; Catholic Univ Am, vis prof, 97-. **HONORS AND AWARDS** Lillian Smith Awd, best S non fict; Sydney Savack Awd, inter grp rel; Am book Awd; Oliver Cox Awd, anti racist schol. **MEMBERSHIPS** ASA; AS. **RESEARCH** Race relations; Am hist; Stand Test. **SELECTED PUBLICATIONS** Lies My Teacher Told Me: Everything Your High School History Text Book Got Wrong, NY, The New House Press, 95; The Mississippi Chinese: Between Black and White, Prospect Hts IL, Waveland Press, 88. **CONTACT ADDRESS** Life Cycle Inst, Catholic Univ of America, Washington, DC, 20064. **EMAIL** jloewen@zoo.uvm.edu

LOFGREN, CHARLES AUGUSTIN
PERSONAL Born 09/08/1939, Missoula, MT, m **DISCIPLINE** AMERICAN HISTORY **EDUCATION** Stanford Univ, AB, 61, AM, 62, PhD, 66. **CAREER** Instr hist, San Jose State Col, 65-66; Vis asst prof, Stanford Univ, 68-69; from asst prof to assoc prof, 66-76, prof his, Claremont McKenna Col, 76-, mem Claremont Grad Univ, Claremont Cols, 67-, Chmn Hist Claremont McKenna Col, 70-73, 76-80, Chmn Gov Dept, 84-86, 88-90, Crocker Prof Am Hist and Pol, 76. **MEMBERSHIPS** AHA; Orgn Am Historians; Am Soc Legal Hist. **RESEARCH** Am constitutional hist. **SELECTED PUBLICATIONS** Auth, Mr Truman's war: A debate and its aftermath, Rev Polit, 4/69; Warmaking under the constitution: The original understanding, Yale Law J, 3/72; United States vs Curtiss-Wright Export Corporation: An historical reassessment, Yale Law J, 11/73; Missouri vs Holland in historical perspective, Supreme Ct Rev, 75; Compulsory military service under the Constitution: The original understanding, William & Mary Quart, 1/76; National League of Cities versus Usery: Dual Federalism Reborn, Claremont J Pub Affairs, 77; contrib, Constitutional government in America, Carolina Acad Press, 80; To regulate commerce: Federal power under the Constitution, This Constitution, 86; Government from reflection and choice: Constitutional essays on war, foreign relations and federalism, Oxford Univ, 86; contr, The framing and ratification of the Constitution, Macmillan, 87; The original understanding of original intent?, Constitutional Commentrary, winter 88; auth, The Plessy Case: A legal-constitutional interpretation, Oxford Univ, 88; Madisonian limitations, Rev Am Hist, 3/92; contr, Benchmarks: Great constitutional controversies in the Supreme Court, Center for Ethics and Public Policy, 95; auth, Claremont pioneers: The founding of CMC, Gould Center, Claremont McKenna Col, 96. **CONTACT ADDRESS** Dept of Hist, Claremont McKenna Col, Pitzer Hall-850 Columbia, Claremont, CA, 91711-6420. **EMAIL** clofgren@mckenna.edu

LOGAN, FRENISE A.
PERSONAL Born 09/30/1920, Albany, GA, m **DISCIPLINE** HISTORY **EDUCATION** Fisk Univ, BA 1943; Case Western Reserve Univ, MA 1957, PhD 1953; Univ of Bombay India, Post-doctoral study 1954. **CAREER** Univ of Zambia, visiting prof 1968-70; Amer Embassy Lusaka Zambia, 1st sec Cultural Affairs 1968-70; Bur of Educ & Cultural Affairs US Dept of State Wash DC, chief East Central & So Africa 1970-73; Amer Embassy Nairobi Kenya, 1st sec cultural affairs 1973-77; Museum of African Art WA DC, assoc dir 1977-78; Amer Consulate Kaduna Nigeria, 1st consultant & br public affairs officer 1978-80; NC A&T State Univ, prof of history 1980-91. **HONORS AND AWARDS** Num hons, awds, fellowships & grants including Commendation for Outstanding Achievements in Intl & Educ/Cultural Exchanges from the United States Dept of State, Bureau of Educ and Cultural Affairs 1977. **MEMBERSHIPS** Mem Amer Hist Assoc, So Hist Assoc, Assoc for Study of Afro-Amer Life & Hist, Alpha Phi Alpha, East African Acad, Indian Hist Congress; mem Carolinas Symposium on British Studies. **SELECTED PUBLICATIONS** Author "Negro in NC 1876-1894"; num articles in scholarly publs in US & India.

LOGAN, SAMUEL TALBOT, JR.
DISCIPLINE CHURCH HISTORY **EDUCATION** Princeton Univ, BA, 65; Westminster Theol Sem, MDiv, 68; Emory Univ, PhD, 72. **CAREER** Tchg asst, Emory Univ, 69; instr, DeKalb Jr Col, 70; dir, Dept Amer Stud, Barrington Col, 70-79; asst prof, 1970-1978; prof, Barrington Col, 78-79; prof, Westminster Theol Sem, 79-. **SELECTED PUBLICATIONS** Auth, Academic Freedom at Christian Institutions, Christian Scholar's Rev; Shoulders to Stand On, Decision, 93; Theological Decline in Christian Institutions and the Value of Van Til's Epistemology, Westminster Theol Jour, 95; ed, The Preacher and Preaching: Reviving the Art in the Twentieth Century. **CONTACT ADDRESS** Westminister Theol Sem, PO Box 27009, Philadelphia, PA, 19118. **EMAIL** slogan@wts.edu

LOGAN, WENDELL
DISCIPLINE AFRICAN-AMERICAN MUSIC **EDUCATION** Fla A&M Univ, BS, 62; S Ill Univ, MM, 64; Univ Iowa, PhD 68. **CAREER** Ball State Univ, 67-69; Fla A&M, 68-70; Western Ill Univer, 70-73; Prof; Oberlin, 73, ch, jazz studies prog. **HONORS AND AWARDS** NEA grants, 73, 78, 85, 96; ASCAP awards, 80-96; Ohio Arts Coun grants, 84, 85, 93; Guggenheim award, 90; Cleveland Arts Prize, 91; fel, Rockefeller Study Ctr, Italy, 94., ASCAP awards, 86-90. **SELECTED PUBLICATIONS** Publ in, Perspectives of New Music , The Black Perspective in Music , NUMUS West, Black Music Res Jour and Field Magazine. **CONTACT ADDRESS** Dept of Mus, Oberlin Col, Oberlin, OH, 44074.

LOGSDON, JOSEPH
PERSONAL Born 03/12/1938, Chicago, IL, m, 1960, 2 children **DISCIPLINE** UNITED STATES HISTORY **EDUCATION** Univ Chicago, AB, 59, MA, 61; Univ Wis, PhD(hist), 66. **CAREER** From instr to asst prof hist, La State Univ, New Orleans, 64-69; assoc prof hist and urban studies, Lehigh Univ, 69-71; assoc prof, 71-72, PROF HIST, UNIV NEW ORLEANS, 73-, CHAIR, 80-, La State Univ res coun grant and Am Philos Soc grant, 68; Danforth fel black study, 70-71 and Danforth assoc, 72-. **MEMBERSHIPS** AHA; Asn Study Negro Life and Hist. **RESEARCH** Reconstruction; nineteenth century liberalism; Black history. **SELECTED PUBLICATIONS** Auth, Freedom at Risk--the Kidnapping of Free Blacks in America, 1780-1865, J Amer Hist, Vol 0082, 95; Where the River Runs Deep--the Story of a Mississippi River Pilot, J Southern Hist, Vol 0061, 95; Acadian to Cajun--Transformation of a People, J Amer Ethnic Hist, Vol 0015, 96; Durnford, Andrew--a Black Sugar Planter in the Antebellum South, J Southern Hist, Vol 0062, 96. **CONTACT ADDRESS** Dept of Hist, Univ of New Orleans, New Orleans, LA, 70148.

LOHMANN, CHRISTOPH KARL
PERSONAL Born 10/06/1935, Berlin, Germany, m, 1961, 2 children **DISCIPLINE** ENGLISH, AMERICAN STUDIES **EDUCATION** Swarthmore Col, BA, 58; Columbia Univ, MA, 61; Univ Pa, PhD(Am civilization), 68. **CAREER** Asst prof, 68-73, assoc prof, 73-81, PROF ENGLISH, IND UNIV, BLOOMINGTON and ASSOC DEAN FAC, 81-, Assoc ed, a Selected Edition of W D Howells, Ind Univ, 72-; Fulbright Comn sr res fel, Fed Repub Ger, 76-77. **MEMBERSHIPS** MLA; Am Studies Asn. **RESEARCH** Nineteenth century American literature; American studies. **SELECTED PUBLICATIONS** Auth, The Literary Context of Chopin,Kate the 'Awakening', Amer Lit Realism 1870-1910, Vol 0029, 97. **CONTACT ADDRESS** Dept of English, Indiana Univ, Bloomington, Bloomington, IN, 47401.

LOHOF, BRUCE ALAN
PERSONAL Born 02/29/1940, Billings, MT, m, 1964, 2 children **DISCIPLINE** AMERICAN STUDIES **EDUCATION** Stetson Univ, BA, 63, MA, 65; Syracuse Univ, PhD(Am studies), 68. **CAREER** Instr hist, Maria Regina Col, 66-68; asst prof Am studies, Heidelberg Col, 68-71, assoc prof, 71-72; asst prof hist and coordr Am studies, 72-75, chmn, Dept Hist, 75-76, ASSOC PROF HIST, UNIV MIAMI, 75-, Vis prof, Bowling Green State Univ, 72; Fulbright-Hays sr scholar and dir, Am Studies Res Centre, India, 76-78. **MEMBERSHIPS** Am Studies Asn; Orgn Am Historians; Popular Cult Asn. **RESEARCH** American studies; American history; popular culture. **SELECTED PUBLICATIONS** Auth, The Deeper Meaning of Marlboro, on Commercialization of a Metaphor, Neue Rundschau, Vol 0105, 94. **CONTACT ADDRESS** Univ of Miami, Box 248194, Coral Gables, FL, 33124.

LOHR, CHARLES HENRY
PERSONAL Born 06/24/1925, New York, NY **DISCIPLINE** HISTORY OF MEDIEVAL AND RENAISSANCE PHILOSOPHY **EDUCATION** Fordham Univ, BA, 47, PhL, 56; Woodstock Col, Md, STB, 61, STL, 62; Univ Freiburg, PhD(philos), 67, Dr phil habil, 72. **CAREER** Res asst, Raimundus-Lullus-Inst, Univ Freiburg, 63-67; from asst prof to assoc prof theol, Fordham Univ, 67-72; res fel philos, Raimundus-Lullus-Inst, Univ Freiburg, 72-74; Univ dozent theol, 74-76, PROF THEOL, ALBERT LUDWIGS UNIV, FREIBURG, 76-, Guggenheim Mem found fel, 71-72; dir, Raimundus-Lullus-Inst, Univ Freiburg, 75-; Nat Endowment Humanities grant, 76-77; dean, Theol Fac, Univ Freiburg, 77-78. **HONORS AND AWARDS** Mag Phil, Maioricensis Schola Lullistica, Palma, Majorca, 72; Dr phil, Univ Fribourg, 81. **MEMBERSHIPS** Mediaeval Acad Am; Am Hist Asn. **RESEARCH** History of medieval and Renaissance philosophy. **SELECTED PUBLICATIONS** Auth, Lull, Ramon and the Epistemic Theory of Lemyesier, Thomas, Isis, Vol 0086, 95; The Intellectual Activity in the Medieval Faculty of Arts at Paris--Texts and Masters, C. 1200-1500, Vol 1--Repertory of Names Beginning With the Letters A-B, Speculum-J Medieval Stud, Vol 0071, 96. **CONTACT ADDRESS** Raimundus-Lullus-Inst, Univ of Freiburg, Werthmannplatz D-78 Freiburg im Breisgan, Wreiburg, ., 7800.

LOMBARDO, STANLEY
DISCIPLINE GREEK AND LATIN LITERATURE **EDUCATION** Loyola Univ, BA; Tulane Univ, MA; Univ TX, PhD, 76. **CAREER** Dept ch; prof, Univ KS. **HONORS AND AWARDS** Kemper tchg fel; Nat Transl Ctr award. **RESEARCH** Transl of Homer's Odyssey. **SELECTED PUBLICATIONS** Transl, Greek poetry, including Homer's Iliad, Hackett, 97; Hesiod's Works & Daysand Theogony, Hackett, 93; Aratus' Phaenomena, N Atlantic, 82; Parmenides and Empedocles, The Fragments in Verse Translation, Grey Fox, 79; Horace's Odes in Latin Lyric and Elegiac Poetry, Garland, 95; Tao Te Ching, Hackett, 93; co-transl, Callimachus' Hymns, Epigrams & Select Fragments, Johns Hopkins, 88. **CONTACT ADDRESS** Dept of Class, Univ Kansas, Admin Building, Lawrence, KS, 66045. **EMAIL** LOMBARDO@KUHUB.CC.UKANS.EDU

LONDON, CLEMENT B. G.
PERSONAL Born 09/12/1928, m **DISCIPLINE** EDUCATION **EDUCATION** City Clg City Univ of NY, BA 1967, MA 1969; Tchr Clg Columbia Univ NY, EdM 1972, EdD 1973. **CAREER** Toco & Morvant EC Elem Schs Trinidad-Tobago Sch Systm Trinidad, W Indies, asst prncpl 1953-60; St Augustine Parochial Sch Brooklyn, NY, tchr 1960-61; Harlem Hosp Sch of Nrsng New York City, sec/registrar 1963-66; Development & Training Ctr Distrbtv Trades Inc NYC, instr math & engl 1967-70; Crossroads Alternative HS East 105th St NYC, assc prncl dean stdnt 1970-71; Tchr Clg Columbia Univ NYC, grad asst & instrctnl asst 1971-73; Intermediate Sch 136 Manhattan NYC, substitute tchr math 1974; Fordham Univ at Lincoln Center, Graduate School of Educ, asst prof of educ 1974-82, assoc prof of educ 1982-91, professor of education, currently. **HONORS AND AWARDS** Project Real, Special Recognition, Award for Outstanding Quality, 1983; Toco Anglican Elementary School, Clement London Day, Celebrant, 1977; Salem Community Service Council of New York City, 1981. **MEMBERSHIPS** Natl Alliance Black Sch EDUCATIONs 1975; Editorial Bd College Student Journal, editor Curriculum for a Career Ed & Dev Demonstration Proj for Youth 1978; editorial consultant Natl Council Negro Women 1978; Assn Teacher Educators 1979; summer chmn Div Curriculum & Teaching 1979; bd elders Council of Mwamko Wa Siasa Educ Institute 1980; Natl Sch Bd Assn 1980-; Org Amer Historians 1980; Assn Caribbean Studies 1980-; Amer Assn for Advancement of Humanities 1980; American Academy Political & Social Sci 1980-; rprtr bd dir Kappa Alpha Psi 1980-; faculty secretary Sch of Educ Fordham Univ 1981; Journal of Curiculum Theorizing 1982-; dir Project Real, 1984; bd dir Solidaridad Humana 1984; faculty adv, exec comm memPhi Delta Kappa; Kappa Delta Pi; adv bd, curriculum consultant La Nueva Raza Half House program; bd mem African Heritage Studies Assn; Schomburg Corp., Center for Research in Black Culture, board member, 1992-; ALL Bereavement Center, Ltd, bd mem, 1996-. **SELECTED PUBLICATIONS** Author, numerous research publications & professional activities including: On Wings of Changes, 1991; Through Caribbean Eyes, 1989; Test-taking Skills: Guidelines for Curricular & Instructional Practices, 1989; A Piagetian Constructivist Perspective on Curriculum, 1989; "Multicultural Curriculum Thought: A Perspective," 1992; "Multicultural Education and Curriculum Thought: One Perspective," 1992; "Curriculum as Transformation: A Case for the Inclusion of Multiculturality," 1992; "Afro-American Catholic School NYC", Black EDUCATION in the Univ Role as Moral Authority Clg Stdnt Jrnl Monograph 18(1 Pt 2), Career Ed for Educational Ldrs, A Focus on Decision Making 1983, "Crucibles of Caribbean Conditions, Factors of Understanding for Teachg & Learng Caribbean Stdnts Am Ed Settings" Jrnl of Caribbean Studies, 2&3, p 182-188, Autumn/Winter 1982; "Career & Emplymnt, Critical Factors in Ed Plng," African-American Jrnl Res & Ed, 1981; "Black Women of Valor," African Heritage Studies Assn Nwsltr, p 9, 1976; "Conf Call, The Caribbean & Latin Am," WABC Radio, 3 hr brdcst, 1979-80; 2 video-taped TV appearances: Natl TV Trinidad, W Indies, featuring emotionally oriented issues, 1976-77; Parents and Schools: A sourcebook, Garland Publishings, Inc, 1993; A critical perspective of multiculturality as a philosophy for educational change, Education, 114(3), p 368-383, 1994; Three Turtle Stories, New Mind Productions, Inc, 1994; Linking cultures through literacy: A perspective for the future, In NJ Ellsworth, CN Hedley and AN Baratta (Eds), Literacy: A redefinition, Lawrence Erlbaum Associates, 1994; Queens Public Access Television, discussing Fordham University Graduate School of Education and its leadership role in Language, Literacy, and Learning, 1994. **CONTACT ADDRESS** Graduate Sch Educ, Fordham Univ, 113 W 60th St, New York, NY, 10023-7478. **EMAIL** london@mary.fordham.edu

LONDON, HERBERT
PERSONAL Born 03/06/1939, New York, NY, d, 3 children **DISCIPLINE** MODERN HISTORY, SOCIAL SCIENCE **EDUCATION** Columbia Univ, BA, 60, MA, 61; NY Univ, PhD-(social studies), 66. **CAREER** Instr Am hist, New Sch Social Res, 63-64 & social studies, NY Univ, 65-66; Fulbright res scholar polit sci, Australian Nat Univ, 66-67; from asst prof to assoc prof, 67-73, dir exp progs, 72-73, PROF SOCIAL STUDIES, NY UNIV, 73-, Dean, Gallation Div, 76-92; Consult, 69-97, HUDSON INST, PRES, 97-; host, Myths That Rule America, Nat Broadcasting Co TV. **MEMBERSHIPS** Popular Cult Asn; AHA; Polit Sci Asn. **RESEARCH** Popular culture; contemporary American history; Australia Policy. **SELECTED PUBLICATIONS** Co-ed, Education in the Twenty-First Century, Interstate Press, 69; auth, Non-White Immigration and the White Australia Policy, NY Univ, 70; Fitting In: Crosswise at Generation Gap, Grosset, 74; The Overheated Decade, NY Univ, 76; The Seventies: Counterfeit Decade, 79 & Myths That Rule America, Univ Press Am, 81; auth, Why are They Lying to Our Children, Stein and Day, 86; auth, From the Empire State to the Vampire State, UPA, 94. **CONTACT ADDRESS** New York Univ, 113 University Pl, New York, NY, 10003.

LONG, ANTHONY ARTHUR
PERSONAL Born 08/17/1937, Manchester, England, m, 2 children **DISCIPLINE** CLASSICS **EDUCATION** Univ Col London, BA, 60, PhD 64. **CAREER** Pfof of Classic, Univ of California, Berkeley, 83; Dept Ch, 86-90; Prof of Greek (Gladstone), Univ of Liverpool, 73-83; Lectr & Reades in Greek and Latin, Univ Col London, 66-73; Lectr in Classio, Uni of Nottingham, 64-66; Lectr in Claaio, Univ of Otago, NZ, 61-64. **HONORS AND AWARDS** Irvin Sonte Prof of Lit, Verkeley, Fel of the Am Acad of Arts and Soc, 89-; Corr Fel of British Acad, 92-; Guggenheim Fellowship, 86-87; Membe Inst for Advan Study, Princeton, NJ, 70 & 79. **MEMBERSHIPS** Am Phislo Assoc, Aristotelion Soc. **RESEARCH** Greek Philos and Greek Lit. **SELECTED PUBLICATIONS** Auth, Language and Thought in Sophocles, London, 68; auth, Hellenistic Philosophy, London, 74, 86; coauth, The Hellenistic Philosophers,

Cambridge, 87; auth, Stoic Studio, Cambridge, 96. **CONTACT ADDRESS** Dept of Classics, Univ of California, Dwinelle Hall, Berkeley, CA, 94720. **EMAIL** aalong@uclink4.berkeley.edu

LONG, JAMES L.
PERSONAL Born 12/07/1937, Wintergarden, FL, s **DISCIPLINE** CRIMINAL JUSTICE **EDUCATION** San Jose State Coll, BA, 1960; Howard Univ Law School, JD, 1967. **CAREER** Legislative Counsel Bureau CA State Legislature, grad legal asst; Legal Aid Soc of Sacramento Co, grad legal asst; NAACP Western Region, special counsel; Private Practice, atty; Superior Court Bar Assn Liaison Comm, mem; SUPERIOR COURT, JUDGE; CALIFORNIA STATE UNIV, SACRAMENTO, CA, ASST PROF, CRIMINAL JUSTICE. **HONORS AND AWARDS** The Law and Justice Award Sacramento Branch NAACP; Outstanding Contribution Award in the Field of Civil Rights Riverside Branch NAACP; sat as Pro Tem Justice of the Supreme Court Dec 9, 1985; assigned Justice Pro Tem to the Court of Appeal Third Appellate Dist 1987. **MEMBERSHIPS** Hon mem, Wiley W Manual Bar Assn, Sacramento, CA; mem, Appellate Dept Superior Court of Sacramento Co, 1987; mem, Sacramento City/County Commn of the Bicentennial of the US Constitution. **SELECTED PUBLICATIONS** Co-author "Amer Minorities, The Justice Issue," Prentice Hall Inc, 1975. **CONTACT ADDRESS** Sacramento County Superior Court, 720 9th St, Sacramento, CA, 95814.

LONG, JEROME HERBERT
PERSONAL Born 00/00/1931, Little Rock, AR, m, 1959, 2 children **DISCIPLINE** HISTORY OF RELIGIONS **EDUCATION** Knox Col, AB, 56; Univ Chicago Divinity Sch, BD, 60, MA, 62, PhD(hist of relig), 73. **CAREER** From instr to assoc prof relig, Western Mich Univ, 64-70; vis assoc prof, 70-71, ASSOC PROF RELIG, WESLEYAN UNIV, 71-, Mem, Comt on Reorgn of Curric of Relig Dept, Western Mich Univ, 65-67, mem, African Studies Comt, 65-70, secy, 66-67, mediator, Black Am Studies Prog, 68-70; mem, African Studies Comt, Wesleyan Univ, 74-75, chmn, 75-76, chmn, Search Comt for Dir for Ctr for Afro-Am Studies and interim curric coordr, Ctr for Afro-Am Studies, 75-76; VIS SCHOLAR, INST AFRICAN STUDIES, LEGON, GHANA, WEST AFRICA, UNIV GHANA, 77-. **RESEARCH** Prehistoric and primitive religions; historical approaches to religion and culture; religions of African peoples. **SELECTED PUBLICATIONS** Auth, Symbol and reality among the Trobriand Islanders, in: Essays in Divinity, Vol 1: the History of Religion, Univ Chicago, 69. **CONTACT ADDRESS** Wesleyan Univ, Middletown, CT, 06457.

LONG, JOHN WENDELL
PERSONAL Born 11/30/1939, Hartford, CT, m, 1961, 1 child **DISCIPLINE** MODERN EUROPEAN HISTORY **EDUCATION** Univ Mass, Amherst, BA, 61; Columbia Univ, MA and cert, 65, PhD(hist), 72. **CAREER** Lectr hist, Manhattan Sch Music, 64-70; asst prof, 70-76, ASSOC PROF HIST, RIDER COL, 76-, Vis prof, Trenton State Col, 72; res assoc, Russ and E Europ Ctr, Univ Ill, 73; assoc Danforth Found, 74-; vis scholar, Kennan Inst Advan Russ Studies, Smithsonian Inst, 80. **MEMBERSHIPS** AHA; Am Asn Advan Slavic Studies; AAUP; Soc Hist Educ. **RESEARCH** History of Russia; modern history of Eastern Europe; modern history of Western Europe. **SELECTED PUBLICATIONS** Auth, The Russian Naval Museum, Slavic Rev, 6/71; Using the sources, Soviet Studies, 7/74; coauth, the Church and the Russian Revolution, St Vladimir's Theol Quart, 9/76; T G Masaryk and the Strategy of Czechoslovak Independence, Slavonic and E Europ Rev, 1/78; American Jews and the Root Mission to Russia in 1917, Am Jewish Hist, 3/80; auth, American Intervention in Russia: the North Russian Expedition, 1918-1919, Diplomatic Hist, 2/82. **CONTACT ADDRESS** Dept of Hist, Rider Col, 2083 Lawrenceville, Lawrenceville, NJ, 08648-3099.

LONG, R. JAMES
PERSONAL Born 12/15/1938, Rochester, NY, m, 1974, 3 children **DISCIPLINE** HISTORY OF MEDIEVAL PHILOSOPHY **EDUCATION** Pontif Inst Med Studies, LMS, 66; Univ Toronto, PhD(Medieval studies), 68. **CAREER** From asst prof to assoc prof, 69-78, prof philos, Fairfield Univ, 78-, Fulbright scholar medieval philos, Fulbright Comn, US Govt, 68-69; Can Coun fel philos, 68-69; Am Coun Learned Socs & Am Philos Soc grant-in-aid, 77; Nat Endowment for Humanities scholarly publ grant, 79; vis fac fel, Yale Univ, 82-83, dir hon prog, 82-91; liason faculty, program in Greek and Roman Studies, Ffld univ, 81-. **HONORS AND AWARDS** Fellow of Massey Col, Toronto, 65-68; Province of Ontario Graduate Fellowships, 66-68; Canada Council Doctoral Fellowship, 67-68; Fulbright Scholarship, Italy and U.K., 68-69; Canada Council Postdoctoral Fellowship, 69; NEH Summer Stipend, 74; Am Council of Learned Socs Grant-in-Aid, 77; Am Philos Soc Grant, 77; Assoc of Clare Hall, Cambridge Univ, 77; NEH Scholarly Publications Grant, 79; NEH Summer Seminar for College Teachers, Fordham Univ, 81; Yale Visiting Faculty Fellowship, 82-83; NEH Summer Seminar for College Teachers, Yeshiva Univ, 84; Am Philos Soc Grant, 84; Fairfield Univ Summer Stipends, 86, 89, 92; NEH Summer Seminar for College Teachers, Columbia Univ, 87; NEH Summer Stipend, 88; Warren W. Wooden Citation, PMR Conference, 89; NEH Editions/Texts Grant, ed of Richard Fishacre's Sentences-Commentary, 1-2, $130,000, 92-94; Yale Visiting Fellowship, Philosophy Dept, 96-98. **MEMBERSHIPS** Medieval Acad Am; Am Cath Philos Asn (life member); Soc Textual Scholarship; Soc Medieval & Renaissance Philos, secrt-treas, 91-; Catholic Comm on Intellectual and Cultural Affairs; Consociatio cultorum historiae Ordinis Praedicatorum; International Soc for Napoleanic Studies; Societe Internationale pour l'Etude de la Philosophie Medievale. **RESEARCH** Early thirteenth-century philosophy, particularly Oxford; 13th-century science, particularly medicine and botany; works of Richard Fishacre. **SELECTED PUBLICATIONS** Auth, Utrum iurista vel theologus plus proficiat ad regimen ecclesie . . ., 68; The Science of Theology according to Richard Fishacre: Ed of the Prologue to his Commentary on the Sentences, 72, Mediaeval Studies; In Defense of the Tournament: an ed of Pierre Dubois' De torneamentis . . ., 73; A Note on the Dating of MS Ashmole 1512, 74, Manuscripta ; Richard Fishacre and the Problem of the Soul, Mod Schoolman, 75; Richard Fishacre's Quaestio on the Ascension of Christ: An Edition, Mediaeval Studies, 78; ed, Bartholomaeus Anglicus, On the Properties of Soul and Body, Toronto Medieval Latin Texts IV, 79; auth, Botany in the High Middle Ages: An introduction, Res Publica Litterarum, 81; The Virgin as Olive-Tree: A Marian Sermon of Richard Fishacre and Science at Oxford, Archivum Fratrum Praedicatorum 52: 77-87, 82; Alfred of Sareshel's Commentary on the Pseudo-Aristotelian De plantis: A Critical Edition, Mediaeval Studies 47: 125-67, 85; The Question "'Whether the Church Could Better be Ruled by a Good Canonist than by a Theologian' and the Origins of Ecclesiology, Proceedings of the PMR Conference 10: 99-112, 85; Richard Fishacre, Dictionnaire de Spiritualite 13, cols 563-65, 87; Richard Fishacre's Way to God, A Straight Path: Studies in Medieval Philosophy and Culture, Essays in Honor of Arthur Hyman, eds Ruth Link-Salinger et al, 174-82, Washington, D.C.: The Catholic Univ of Am Press, 88: with Joseph Goering, Richard Fishacre's Treatise De fide, spe, et caritate, Bull de Philos Medievale 31: 103-11, 89; Adam of Buckfield and John Sackville: Some Notes on Philadelphia Free Library MS Lewis European 53, Traditio 45: 364-67, 89-90; The Reception and Interpretation of the Pseudo-Arostolian De Plantis at Oxford in the Thirteenth Century, Knowledge and the Sciences in Medieval Philosophy (proceedings of the Eighth Intnl Congress of Medieval Philos: S.I.E.P.M, eds Reijo Tyorinoja, Anja I. Lehtinen, & Dagfinn Follesdal: Annuals of the Finnish Soc for Missiology and Ecumenics, 55, pp 111-23, Helsinki, 90; The Moral and Spiritual Theory of Richard Fishacre: Edition of Trinity Col, MS 0.1.30, Archivum Fratrum Praedicatorum 60, 5-143, 90; The Anonymous Peterhouse Master and the Natural Philosophy of Plants, Traditio 46: 313-26, 91; Richard Fishacre, Medieval Philosophers, ed Jeremiah Hackett, Dictionary of Literary Biography, vol 115, pp 195-200, Detroit: Bruccoli Clark Layman, Inc, 92; A Thirteenth-Century Teaching Aid: An Edition of the Bodleian Abbreviatio of the Pseudo-Aristolian De Plantis, in Aspectus et Affectus: Essays and Editions in Grosseteste and Medieval Intellectual Life in Honor of Richard C. Dales, ed Gunar Freibergs with an intro by Richard Southern, AMS Studies in the Middle Ages: no 23: 87-103, New York: AMS Press, 93; Richard Fishacre's Super S. Augustini librum de haeresibus adnotationes: An Edition and Commentary, Archives d'histoire doctrinale et litteraire du moyen age 60: 207-79, 93; Botany, in Medieval Latin: An Introduction and Bibliographical Guide, ed F.A.C. Mantello and A.G. Rigg, 401-05, Washington, D.C.: The Catholic Univ of America Press, 96; Richard Fishacre's Treatise De libero arbitrio, Moral and Political Philosophies in the Middle Ages, proceedings of the 9th Itnl congress of Medieval Philos, ed B. Carlos Bazan, Eduardo Andujar, Leonard Sbrocchi, 2: 879-91, Ottawa, 17-22, Aug 92, Ottawa: Legas, 95; with Margaret Jewett, A Newly Discovered Witness of Fishacre's Sentences-Commentary: Univ of Chicago MS 156, Traditio 50: 342-45, 95; The Reception and Use of Aristotle by the Early English Dominicans, Aristotle in Britain During the Middle Ages, ed John Marenbon, pp 51-56, Turnhout (Belgium): Brepols, 96; Roger Bacon on the Nature and Place of Angels, Vivarium 35/2: 266-82, 97; Richard Fishacre, in the New Dictionary of National Biography, (in press); Adam de Buckfield, ibid; Geoffrey de Aspale, ibid; The Cosmic Christ: The Christology of Richard Fishacre, OP, Christ Among the Medieval Dominicans, UND Press (in press); Of Angels and Pinheads: The Contributions of the Early Oxford Masters to the Doctrine of Spiritual Matter, Franciscan Studies, Essays in Honor of Girard Etzkorn, ed Gordon A. Wilson and Timothy B. Noone, 56: 237-52, 98; The First Oxford Debate on the Eternity of the World, Recherches de Philosophie et Theologie Medievale 65/1: 54-98, 98; with Timothy B. Noone, Fishacre and Rufus on the Metaphysics of Light: Two Unedited Texts, Melanges Leonard Boyle (in press); The Role of Philosophy in Richard Fishacre's Theology of Creation, proceedings of the 10th Inl Congress of Medieval Philosophy, Erfurt, 25-30 August 97: 571-78, in press. **CONTACT ADDRESS** Dept of Philos, Fairfield Univ, 1073 N Benson Rd, Fairfield, CT, 06430-5195. **EMAIL** long@fair1.fairfield.edu

LONG, ROGER D.
DISCIPLINE HISTORY **EDUCATION** Univ Calif, Los Angeles, PhD. **CAREER** Assoc prof, Eastern Michigan Univ. **RESEARCH** Britain, British Empire, Canada, South Asia. **SELECTED PUBLICATIONS** Ed, The Man on the Spot: Essays on British Empire History. **CONTACT ADDRESS** Dept of History and Philosophy, Eastern Michigan Univ, 701 Pray-Harrold, Ypsilanti, MI, 48197. **EMAIL** his_long@online.emich.edu

LONG, RONALD WILSON
PERSONAL Born 04/05/1937, Pittsburgh, PA, m, 1965, 2 children **DISCIPLINE** UNITED STATES HISTORY **EDUCATION** Waynesburg Col, BA, 64; Univ GA, PhD, 68. **CAREER** Asst prof, 68-74, assoc prof, 74-82, prof hist, WVA Univ Inst Technol, 82. **MEMBERSHIPS** Southern Hist Asn; Inst Early Am Hist & Cult. **RESEARCH** Am colonial hist; Am soc and intellectual hist; Hist of technol. **SELECTED PUBLICATIONS** Auth, The Presbyterians in the Whiskey Rebillion, J Presby Hist, 3/65; Malcolm X, In: Encyclopedia of Contemporary Social Issues, 96; Gerhard Domagk, In: Biographical Encyclopeida of Science, 97; Daniel Blain, In: Dictionary of Virginia Biography, 98. **CONTACT ADDRESS** Hum Div, West Virginia Univ Inst of Tech, 405 Fayette Pike, Montgomery, WV, 25136-2436.

LONG, TIMOTHY
PERSONAL Born 01/31/1943, Cincinnati, OH, s **DISCIPLINE** CLASSICS **EDUCATION** Xavier Univ, BA, 65; Princeton Univ, MA, 67, PhD 71 **CAREER** Lect, 69-71, IN Univ; Asst Prof, 71-74; Assoc Prof, 74-88; Prof, 98-pres **HONORS AND AWARDS** Alexander von Humboldt Fellow, 77-78; Fulbright Senior Lctr, Univ Essen, Germany, 87-88 **MEMBERSHIPS** Am Philol Assoc; Am Assoc of Univ Profs **RESEARCH** Ancient Comedy **SELECTED PUBLICATIONS** Auth, Barbarians in Greek Comedy, Southern Illinois University Press, 86; Auth, Repetition and Variation in the Short Stories of Herodotus, Beitrhage zur Klassischen Philologie, 87, 179 **CONTACT ADDRESS** Dept of Classics, Indiana Univ, Bloomington, 547 Ballantine Hall, Bloomington, IN, 47405. **EMAIL** longt@indiana.edu

LONGFELLOW, DAVID LYMAN
PERSONAL Born 01/25/1949, Washington, DC **DISCIPLINE** EUROPEAN HISTORY **EDUCATION** Univ Va, AB, 70; Johns Hopkins Univ, MA, 72; PhD(hist), 80. **CAREER** Instr Europ hist, Hollins Col, 74-79, asst prof, 79-81; ASST PROF FRENCH HIST, BAYLOR UNIV, 81-, Lectr, Roanoke Col, 75-81. **MEMBERSHIPS** AHA; Soc Fr Hist Studies; Western Soc Fr Hist; Western Hist Asn; AAUP. **RESEARCH** French artisanal politics and organization, 18th century; French Revolution, social, economic and political; Western European artisanal politics and organization, 18th and 19th centuries. **SELECTED PUBLICATIONS** Auth, The End of an Elite--the French Bishops and the Coming of the Revolution, 1786-1790, J Church and State, Vol 0036, 94. **CONTACT ADDRESS** Dept of Hist, Baylor Univ, Waco, TX, 76798.

LONGYEAR, REY MORGAN
PERSONAL Born 12/10/1930, Boston, MA, m, 1959 **DISCIPLINE** MUSICOLOGY **EDUCATION** Calif State Col Los Angeles, AB, 51; Univ NC, MA, 54; Cornell Univ, PhD(musicol), 57. **CAREER** Teacher, High Sch, Md, 57-58; from asst prof to assoc prof music, Univ Southern Miss, 58-63; assoc prof, Univ Tenn, 63-64; assoc prof, 64-70, PROF MUSIC, UNIV KY, 70-, Bk rev ed, J Res Music Educ, 65-70; consult, Exploratory Comt for Assessing Progress in Educ, 67-68 and Nat Assessment of Educ Progress, 67-; Guggenheim fel, 71; bd mem, Univ Prof Acad Order, 81- **MEMBERSHIPS** Am Musicol Soc; Col Music Soc; Int Musicol Soc; Gesellschaft fur Musikforschung; Soc Ital Musicol. **RESEARCH** Eighteenth and 19th century music; music and German literature. **SELECTED PUBLICATIONS** Auth, Music and Musicians in 19th Century Italy, Notes, Vol 0049, 93. **CONTACT ADDRESS** Sch of Music, Univ of Ky, Lexington, KY, 40506.

LOOMIE, ALBERT J.
PERSONAL Born 07/29/1922, New York, NY **DISCIPLINE** MODERN EUROPEAN HISTORY **EDUCATION** Loyola Univ, Ill, BA, 44; W Baden Col, PhL, 46; Fordham Univ, MA, 49; Woodstock Col, STL, 53; Univ London, PhD(Tudor hist), 57. **CAREER** From instr to assoc prof, 58-69, chmn dept, 78-81, PROF HIST, FORDHAM UNIV, 69-, Am Philos Soc grants, 64 and 71; Guggenheim fel, 65; Huntington Libr grantee, 67-; Folger Libr grants, 61, 62 and 70. **HONORS AND AWARDS** Award of Merit, Am Asn State and Local Hist, 54. **MEMBERSHIPS** AHA; fel Royal Hist Soc; Am Cath Hist Asn; Renaissance Soc Am; Conf Brit Studies. **RESEARCH** Anglo-Spanish relations, 1580-1630; Tudor-Stuart history; Spain in the 16th and 17th centuries. **SELECTED PUBLICATIONS** Auth, Manuscripts of the Marquess of Downshire, Vol 5--Paper of Trumbull, William, September 1614, Revue Belge De Philologie Et D Hist, Vol 0070, 92; Lucretia Dreams--Politics and Prophecy in 16th-Century Spain, Revue Belge De Philologie Et D Hist, Vol 0070, 92; Elizabeth I--War and Politics, 1588-1603, Cath Hist Rev, Vol 0079, 93; Reading in Exile--the Libraries of Ramridge, John D 1568, Harding, Thomas D 1572 and Joliffe, Henry D 1573, Recusants in Louvain, Cath Hist Rev, Vol 0080, 94; Wills of the Archdeaconry of Sudbury, 1636-1638, Albion, Vol 0027, 95; Visitation Articles and Injunctions of the Early Stuart Church, Albion, Vol 0027, 95; Intelligence and Espionage in the Reign of Charles II, 1660-1685, Amer Hist Rev, Vol 0101, 96; The Return of the Armadas--the Last Years of the Elizabethan War Against Spain, 1595-1603,

Amer Hist Rev, Vol 0101, 96; St Gregorys College, Seville, 1592-1767, Cath Hist Rev, Vol 0082, 96. **CONTACT ADDRESS** Dept of Hist, Fordham Univ, Bronx, NY, 10458.

LOOS, JOHN LOUIS
PERSONAL Born 03/09/1918, Friend, NE, m, 1951, 2 children **DISCIPLINE** HISTORY **EDUCATION** Univ Nebr, AB, 39, MA, 40; Wash Univ, PhD, 53. **CAREER** Asst prof hist, Evansville Col, 48-51, instr, Wash Univ, 51-53; from instr to assoc prof, 55-66, PROF HIST, LA STATE UNIV, BATON ROUGE, 66-, CHMN DEPT, 63- **MEMBERSHIPS** AHA; Orgn Am Historians; Western Hist Asn. **RESEARCH** Biog of William Clark, 1770-1838; Western American history; business history. **SELECTED PUBLICATIONS** Auth, Davis, Edwin, Adams--Obituary, J Southern Hist, Vol 0061, 95. **CONTACT ADDRESS** Dept of Hist, Louisiana State Univ, Baton Rouge, LA, 70803.

LOPACH, JAMES L.
PERSONAL Born 06/23/1942, Great Falls, MT, d, 2 children **DISCIPLINE** POLITICAL SCIENCE **EDUCATION** Carroll Col, AB 64; Univ MT, law sch, 64; Univ Notre Dame, MA 67, MAT 68, PhD 73. **CAREER** John Adams HS, teacher 67-68; Pac Tele Co, asst mgr mgr 68-69; South Bend Manpwr asst dir and Admin Aide to Mayor 71-73; Univ Notre Dame, instr dir dept govt intl studies 72-73; Univ MT, asst prof 75-78, ch 77-84, 85-87, assoc prof 78-83, prof 83-, act dir 84-88, 91, assoc dean 87-88, spec asst to pres 88-92, assoc provost 92-95, spec asst to provost 95-96. **RESEARCH** Am Constitutional Law, Am Indian Govt and Law. **SELECTED PUBLICATIONS** Tribal Government Today: Politics on Montana Indian Reservations, Univ Press Colorado, rev ed, 98; Planning Small Town America-Observations, Sketches, and A Reform Proposal, with Kristina Ford and Dennis O'Donnell, Amer Plan Assn, 90; The Anomaly of Judicial Activism in Indian Country, Amer Ind Cult and Res Journal, 97. **CONTACT ADDRESS** Dept of Polit Sci, Univ Of MT, Missoula, MT, 59812. **EMAIL** lopach@selway.umt.edu

LOPATA, HELENA Z.
PERSONAL Born 10/01/1925, Poznan, Poland, w, 1946, 2 children **DISCIPLINE** SOCIOLOGY **EDUCATION** Univ Ill, BA, 46, MA, 47; Univ Chicago, PhD, 54. **CAREER** Asst Prof to Assoc Prof, Roosevelt Univ, 65-69; Prof Sociology, 69-97, Sr Prof Sociology, Loyola Univ Chicago, 97-, Dept Chair, 70-72, Dir, Ctr Comp Study Soc Roles, 72-; Vis Prof, Univ Southern Calif, 75; Vis Prof, Univ Minn, 80; Vis Prof, Boston Col, 82; Short-Term Vis Prof, Univ Guelph, 87; Landgrove Distinguished Vis Prof, Univ Victoria, 96. **HONORS AND AWARDS** Fac Mem of the Year, Loyola Univ Chicago, 75; Mieczyslaw Haiman Award for Sustained Scholarship Effort in the Field of Polish American Studies, Polish Am Hist Asn, 87; Distinguished Schol Award, Family Div Soc Study Soc Roles, 89; Burgess Award, Nat Coun Family Relations, 90; Distinguished Career Award, Section on Aging, Am Sociol Asn, 92; Distinguished Career Award, Soc Study Symbolic Interaction, 93; co-recipient, Bronislaw Malinowski Award of the Polish Inst Arts & Sci in Am, 95; Honorary Doctor of Science, Univ Guelph, 95. **MEMBERSHIPS** Int Sociol Asn; Int Sociol Inst; Int Gerontol Soc; Am Sociol Asn; Gerontol Soc Am; Soc Study Social Problems; Soc Study Symbolic Interaction; Sociol Women Soc; Nat Coun Family Relations; Midwest Sociol Soc; Polish Inst Arts & Sci Am; Polish Sociol Inst; Midwest Coun Social Res Aging. **RESEARCH** Cosmopolitan community of scholars; occupations and professions; widowhood; changing roles of American women. **SELECTED PUBLICATIONS** Auth, Widows: The Middle East, Asia and the Pacific, vol 1, Widows: North America, vol 2, Duke Univ Press, 87; coauth, Friendship in Context, JAI Press, 90; Polish Americans, Second, Revised Edition, Transaction, 94; auth, Circles and Settings: Role Changes of American Women, State Univ NY Press, 94; coauth, Current Widowhood: Myths and Realities, Sage, 96; series ed, Research on the Interweave of Social Roles. Renamed: Current Research on Occupations and Professions, JAI Press. **CONTACT ADDRESS** Sociology Dept, Loyola Univ, Chicago, 6525 N. Sheridan Rd., Chicago, IL, 60626. **EMAIL** Hlopata@luc.edu

LOPATA, ROY HAYWOOD
PERSONAL Born 02/26/1949, Bronx, NY, m, 1970, 2 children **DISCIPLINE** AMERICAN HISTORY **EDUCATION** Am Hist, BA, 70; Univ Del, MA, 72, PhD(hist), 75. **CAREER** Admin aide, 75-76, admin asst, 76-77, PLANNING DIR, CITY OF NEWARK, 77-, Asst prof, Hist Dept, Univ Del, 74-77. **MEMBERSHIPS** Nat Coun on Pub Hist. **RESEARCH** American urban and business history; urban planning and management. **SELECTED PUBLICATIONS** Auth, The Dome of the United States Capitol--an Architectural History, Public Historian, Vol 0017, 95. **CONTACT ADDRESS** PO Box 390, Newark, DE, 19711.

LOPES, WILLIAM H.
PERSONAL Born 10/25/1946, Providence, RI, m **DISCIPLINE** EDUCATION **EDUCATION** Providence Coll, BA 1967; Univ of CT, MA 1972; Univ of RI, MBA; Univ of CT, PhD Educ Admin 1976. **CAREER** McAlister Middle Sch, vice principal 1972-74; RI College, instr 1974-, exec asst to pres 1977-. **HONORS AND AWARDS** RI Educator of the Yr; IBA of RI; Phi Kappa Phi Hon Soc; other grants awds. **MEMBERSHIPS** Pub ASCD Annual Bulletin 1970; trustee Providence Public Library; bd dir OIC RI; bd dir RI Grp Health Assn; EPDA Fellow 1970-72; sev art in prof journals; doctoral dis felshp Univ of CT. **CONTACT ADDRESS** Rhode Island Col, 600 Mount Pleasant Ave, Providence, RI, 02908.

LOPEZ, DEBBIE
DISCIPLINE FINE ARTS AND HUMANITIES **EDUCATION** Univ S, BA; Middlebury College's Bread Loaf Sch Engl, MA; Harvard Univ, AM, PhD, 94. **CAREER** Asst prof; taught at, Univ AL at Birmingham, Birmingham-Southern Col & Harvard Univ; asst grad adv, Record & adv bd, McNair Stud Develop Comt, 96-. **HONORS AND AWARDS** UTSA Int Travel Grant, 96; Harvard's Howard Mumford Jones Prize, 94. **RESEARCH** Brit and Am Romanticism; 19th-century Brit poetry; late 19th and early 20th-century Am novels; ethnic minority lit. **SELECTED PUBLICATIONS** Presented invited papers at, Harvard University's Sem on Env Ethics, 94 & 95. **CONTACT ADDRESS** Col of Fine Arts and Hum, Univ Texas at San Antonio, 6900 N Loop 1604 W, San Antonio, TX, 78249.

LOPEZ, ROBERT SABATINO
PERSONAL Born 10/08/1910, Genoa, Italy, m, 1946, 2 children **DISCIPLINE** HISTORY **EDUCATION** Univ Milan, DLitt, 32; Univ Wis, PhD, 42. **CAREER** From assoc prof to prof hist, Teachers Cols Cagliari, Pavia and Genoa, Italy, 33-36; asst prof, Univ Genoa, 36-38; res asst, Univ Wis, 38-42; script ed, Ital sect, Off War Info, 42-43; lectr hist, Brooklyn Col, 43-44; foreign news ed, CBS, 44-45; lectr hist, Columbia Univ, 45-46; from asst prof to prof, 46-61, Durfee Prof, 61-70; chmn medieval studies, 63-70, Sterling prof, 70-71, EMER PROF HIST, YALE UNIV, 71-; FEL, CALHOUN COL, 47-, Vis assoc prof, Wesleyan Univ, 47-48, 49-50; Guggenheim fel, 48-49; De Bosis lectr Ital hist, Harvard Univ, 60-61; Nat Found for Humanities sr fel, 67-68. **HONORS AND AWARDS** Gautieri Prize, Acad Turin, Italy, 33; Lattes Prize, Univ Milan, 33., HLD, Hebrew Union Col, 64; Dr, Univ Montpellier, France, 77, Univ Rome, Italy, 78. **MEMBERSHIPS** Fel Mediaeval Acad Am; hon fel S Liguire di Storia Patria; hon fel S Pavese di Storia Patria; corresp mem Acad Inscriptions et Belles Lettres Inst, France; corresp fel, Royal Brit Acad, Eng. **RESEARCH** Mediaeval and economic history. **SELECTED PUBLICATIONS** Auth, Storia Delle Colonie Genovesi, Zanichelli, Bologna, 38; Mediaeval Trade in the Mediterranean World, Columbia Univ, 55; The Tenth Century: How Dark the Dark Ages?, Holt, 59; Naissance de l'Europe, Armand Colin, Paris, 62; The Birth of Europe, Evans-Lippincott, 67; The Three Ages of the Italian Renaissance, Univ Va, 69; The Commercial Revolution of the Middle Ages, Cambridge Univ Press, 70; Su e Gui per la Storia di Genoa, Inst Paleografia, Univ Genoa, 75; Byzantium and the World Around it, Variorum, 78. **CONTACT ADDRESS** 41 Richmond Ave, New Haven, CT, 06515.

LOPREATO, JOSEPH
PERSONAL Born 07/13/1928, Italy, d, 2 children **DISCIPLINE** SOCIOLOGY, ANTHROPOLOGY **EDUCATION** Univ of Conn, BA, 56; Yale Univ, PhD, 60. **CAREER** Asst prof, Univ of Mass, 60-62; res scholar, Univ of Rome, 62-64; assoc prof, Univ of Conn, 64-66; assoc prof, 66-68, prof, Univ Tex, Austin, 68-98. **HONORS AND AWARDS** Fulbright Res Scholar to Italy, 62-64 & 74; Soc Sci Res Coun Fac Res Fel, 63-64; Nat Sci Found Res Fel, 65-68; Univ of Tx Fac Res Fel, 73-74, spring 84 & spring 93; Italy's Guido Dorso 1992 Award for the U.S.A. **MEMBERSHIPS** Human Behavior and Evolution Soc; Int Soc for Human Ethology; Int Sociological Asn; Eurpean Sociobiological Soc. **RESEARCH** Ethnic assimilation; the evolution of gender roles; social inequality; the evolution of religion; politics and the economy; fertility; mortality. **SELECTED PUBLICATIONS** Auth, Italian Made Simple, 59; Peasants No More, 67; Italian Americans, 70; Class Conflict and Mobility Theories and Studies of Class Structure, 72; The Sociology of Vilfredo Pareto, 75; Human Nature and Biocultural Evolution, 84; Evoluzione e Natura Umana, 90; Crisis in Sociology: The Need for Darwin, 98. **CONTACT ADDRESS** Dept of Sociology, Univ of Texas, Austin, TX, 78712. **EMAIL** lopreato@mail.la.utexas.edu

LORA, RONALD GENE
PERSONAL Born 08/10/1938, Bluffton, OH, m, 1962, 4 children **DISCIPLINE** AMERICAN HISTORY **EDUCATION** Bluffton Col, BS, 60; Ohio State Univ, PhD, 67. **CAREER** Instr hist, Bluffton Col, 64-66; from asst prof to assoc prof Am hist, 67-75, prof hist, Univ Toledo, 75-; res leave, Univ Toledo, 73-74, 82. **HONORS AND AWARDS** Outstanding Teacher Award, Univ Toledo, 76 & Ohio Academy of Hist, 87; Master Teacher, Univ Toledo, 93-95; pres, Ohio Acad of Hist, 97-98. **MEMBERSHIPS** Orgn Am Historians; AHA; Southern Hist Asn; Ohio Acad Hist. **RESEARCH** Recent American history; American intellectual history; nineteen-sixties. **SELECTED PUBLICATIONS** Ed, The American West, Univ of Toledo, 80; auth, Education: Schools as crucible in Cold War America, Reshaping America, Ohio State Univ Press, 82; auth, Education, Public Policy and the State, American Choices, Ohio State, 86; auth, Jeffersonianism on Trial, For the General Welfare, 89; art, Russell Kirk: The Conservative Mind Three and One-Half Decades Later, Modern Age, 90; co-ed, The American Conservative Press, 99. **CONTACT ADDRESS** Dept of History, Univ of Toledo, 2801 W Bancroft St, Toledo, OH, 43606-3390. **EMAIL** rlora@uoft02.utoledo.edu

LORENCE, JAMES J.
PERSONAL Born 11/18/1937, Racine, WI, m, 1960, 2 children **DISCIPLINE** HISTORY **EDUCATION** Univ Wisc, BS, 60, MS, 64, PhD, 70. **CAREER** From asst prof to assoc prof to prof, Univ Wisc, 81-. **HONORS AND AWARDS** Emil Steijer Award for Excellence in Tchg, 70; State Historical Society Award of Merit, 78, 95; AASLH Comendation, 78; Hesseltine Award, 90; Carnegie- CASE Award, 94; Beueridge Family Tchg Prize, 98., Member, Univ Wisc, System Tchr Ed Task Force, 84; Chemn, Univ Wisc Col, 76-77, 78-81, 85-86. **MEMBERSHIPS** AHA; OAH; SHAFR; IAMHIST; SHE; SHSW; HFC; MCHS; WLHS **RESEARCH** US, 1900-; Great Depression; labor history; film history; US foreign relations. **SELECTED PUBLICATIONS** Coauth, Woodlot and Ballot Box: Marathon County in the Twentieth Century, 77; auth, Organized Business and the Myth of the China Market: The American Asiatic Association, 1898-1937, 81; auth, art, The Foreign Policy of Hollywood, 93; auth, Gerald J. Boileau and the Progressive-Farmer-Labor Alliance: Politics of the New Deal, 94; auth, Organizing the Unemployed: Community and Union Activists in the Industrial Heartland, 96. **CONTACT ADDRESS** Dept of History, Univ of Wisconsin-Marathon County, 518 S 7th Ave, Wausau, WI, 54401. **EMAIL** jlorence@uwc.edu

LORENZO, DAVID J.
PERSONAL Born 10/03/1961, Wynne, AR **DISCIPLINE** HISTORY & POLITICAL SCIENCE **EDUCATION** Univ Ar Fayetteville, BA, 84; Yale Univ, MA, 85, PhD, 93. **CAREER** Vis instr, 92-93, Univ Ar Fayetteville; policy spec, 95-97, U S Dept Educ; asst prof, 97-, Jamestown Col. **HONORS AND AWARDS** Phi Beta Kappa; Phi Beta Phi; Pi Sigma Alpha. **MEMBERSHIPS** Amer Polit Sci Assoc; Conf for Study of Polit Thought. **RESEARCH** Popular polit argument; polit tradition. **SELECTED PUBLICATIONS** Rev, Critical Pluralism, Democratic Performance, & Community Power, Midwest Polit Sci J, 92; rev, The Politics and Philosophy of Political correctness, Amer Rev Polit, 94; auth, Political Communications and the Study of Rhetoric: Persuasion from the Standpoint of Literary Theory and Anthropology, The Theory and Practice of Political Communication Research, SUNY Press, 96; art, The Portrayal of Similarities in the Justification of Empire: G A Henty and Late 19th Century Imperial Literature, McNeese Rev, 99; auth, Tradition and the Rhetoric of Right: Popular Political Argument in the Aurobindo Movement, Fairleigh Dickinson Univ Press, 99. **CONTACT ADDRESS** College Lane, Box 6075, Jamestown, ND. **EMAIL** lorenzo@acc.jc.edu

LORIMER, DOUGLAS
DISCIPLINE CANADIAN SOCIAL HISTORY **EDUCATION** British Columbia, PhD. **CAREER** Prof **SELECTED PUBLICATIONS** Auth, Colour, Class and the Victorians: English Attitudes to the Negro in the Mid-Nineteenth Century, Leicester Univ Press, 78. **CONTACT ADDRESS** Dept of History, Wilfrid Laurier Univ, 75 University Ave W, Waterloo, ON, N2L 3C5. **EMAIL** dlorimer@mach1.wlu.ca

LORIMER, JOYCE
DISCIPLINE EUROPEAN TRADE; SETTLEMENT IN GUAYANA **EDUCATION** Liverpool, PhD. **CAREER** Prof **SELECTED PUBLICATIONS** Auth, English and Irish Settlement on the River Amazon, 1550-1646 , Hakluyt Soc & Cambridge UP, 90 **CONTACT ADDRESS** Dept of History, Wilfrid Laurier Univ, 75 University Ave W, Waterloo, ON, N2L 3C5. **EMAIL** jlorimer@mach1.wlu.ca

LOSADA, LUIS ANTONIO
PERSONAL Born 01/07/1939, New York, NY, m, 1966 **DISCIPLINE** CLASSICS, ANCIENT HISTORY **EDUCATION** Hunter Col, AB, 60; Columbia Univ, MA, 62, PhD(Greek and Latin), 70. **CAREER** From lectr to asst prof classics, 68-74, ASSOC PROF CLASSICS, LEHMAN COL, 74-, Chmn Dept Class and Orient Lang, 73-, Assoc mem, Univ Sem Class Civilization, Columbia Univ, 72-. **MEMBERSHIPS** Am Philol Asn; Petronian Soc; Am Inst Archaeol. **RESEARCH** Greek history and numismatics; the teaching of classical languages. **SELECTED PUBLICATIONS** Auth, The Greeks in History, Phoenix-J Class Asn Can, Vol 0049, 95. **CONTACT ADDRESS** Lehman Col, CUNY, Bronx, NY, 10468.

LOSS, ARCHIE KRUG
PERSONAL Born 01/31/1939, Hanover, PA, m, 1967, 3 children **DISCIPLINE** MODERN LITERATURE, ART HISTORY **EDUCATION** Millersville State Col, BS, 60; Pa State Univ, MA, 66, PhD(English), 70. **CAREER** Asst prof English, Behrend Col, Pa State Univ, 70-72; asst prof, Wayne State Univ, 72-76; ASSOC PROF ENGLISH AND HEAD DIV ARTS AND HUMANITIES, BEHREND COL, PA STATE UNIV, 76-. **MEMBERSHIPS** MLA; Am Soc Aesthetics; James Joyce Found. **RESEARCH** Modern literature, modern art, and relations between the two; art history. **SELECTED PUBLICATIONS** Auth, Approaches to Teaching Joyce 'Ulysses', James Joyce Quart, Vol 0032, 94. **CONTACT ADDRESS** Dept of English, Pennsylvania State Univ, Erie, Station Rd, Erie, PA, 16563.

LOTCHIN, ROGER W.
PERSONAL Born 01/31/1935, Shelbyville, IL, m, 1958, 1 child **DISCIPLINE** HISTORY **EDUCATION** Millikin Univ, BS, 57; Univ Chicago, MA, 61, PhD, 69. **CAREER** Univ NC-Chapel Hill, 66-98. **MEMBERSHIPS** Urban Hist Asn; Western Hist Soc. **RESEARCH** Urban history; history of California cities; western US cities. **SELECTED PUBLICATIONS** Auth, Fortress California, The Martial Metropolis, San Francisco, 1846-1856. **CONTACT ADDRESS** Dept Hist, Univ N. Carolina, Hamilton Hall 562, Chapel Hill, NC, 27599-3195. **EMAIL** rlotchin@email.unc.edu

LOTZ, DAVID WALTER
PERSONAL Born 07/01/1937, Houston, TX, m, 1965 **DISCIPLINE** CHURCH AND EARLY MODERN EUROPEAN HISTORY **EDUCATION** Concordia Sr Col, BA, 59; Concordia Theol Sem, MDiv, 63; Wash Univ, MA, 64; Union Theol Sem, STM 65, ThD, 71. **CAREER** Instr relig, Concordia Sr Col, 63-64; from instr to assoc prof, 68-76, WASHBURN PROF CHURCH HIST, UNION THEOL SEM, 76-, Lectr church hist, Woodstock Col, NY, 71-74 and Gen Theol Sem, New York, 74-; consult, Inter-Lutheran Comn Worship, 73-74; theol consult, Atlantic Dist, Lutheran Church-Mo Synod, 74-. **MEMBERSHIPS** AHA; Am Acad Relig; Am Soc Church Hist; Am Soc Reformation Res; Am Cath Hist Asn. **RESEARCH** Reformation history and theology; 19th century religious thought; historiography. **SELECTED PUBLICATIONS** Auth, Christ Person and Life Work in the Theology of Ritschl,Albrecht With Special Attention to Munus Triplex, J Rel, Vol 0073, 93; The Harvest of Humanism in Central Europe--Essays in Honor of Spitz, Lewis, W, 16th Century J, Vol 0025, 94. **CONTACT ADDRESS** Dept of Church Hist, Union Theol Sem, 3061 Broadway, New York, NY, 10027-5710.

LOUD, PATRICIA CUMMINGS
PERSONAL Beaumont, TX, m, 3 children **DISCIPLINE** FINE ARTS **EDUCATION** Univ TX, Austin, BFA; Radcliffe Col, AM; Harvard Univ, PhD. **CAREER** Kimbell Art Museum, Fort Worth, TX, 81-, currently curator of Architecture and Museum Archivist. **HONORS AND AWARDS** Honorary memberships, AIA Fort Worth and TX Soc of Architects; 1998 John G Flowers Award by TSA for excellence in promotion of architecture through the media. **MEMBERSHIPS** Col Art Asn; Soc of Architectural Hist. **SELECTED PUBLICATIONS** Auth, The History of the Kimbell Art Museum, in Pursuit of Quality: The Kimbell Art Museum, An Illustrated History of the Art and Architecture, Kimbell Art Museum, 87; The Critical Fortune, (The Kimbell Art Museum), Design Rev, winter, 87; The Art Museum of Louis I Kahn, Dule Univ Museum of Art, 89; Louis I Kahn musei, Electra, 91; Yale Univ Art Gallery, Kimbell Art Museum, and Yale Center for British Art, in Louis I Kahn: In the Realm of Architecture, David Brownlee, David G de Long, Museum of Contemporary Art and New York: Rizzoli, 91; Louis I Kahn's Kimbell Art Museum, in The Construction of the Kimbell Art Museum, Accademia di architettura dell'Universita della Svizzera italiana, Mendrisio, and Milan: Skira, 97. **CONTACT ADDRESS** Kimbell Art Mus, 3333 Camp Bouie Blvd, Fort Worth, TX, 76107-2792. **EMAIL** ploud@kimballmuseum.org

LOUGEE, CAROLYN CHAPPELL
PERSONAL Born 02/02/1942, Detroit, MI, m, 1963, 2 children **DISCIPLINE** HISTORY **EDUCATION** Smith Col, AB, 63; Univ Mich, AM, 64, PhD(hist), 72. **CAREER** Lectr hist, Univ Mich, 72-73; asst prof, 73-78, ASSOC PROF HIST, STANFORD UNIV, 78-, Graves Found res fel, 76-77; dir, Inst Women's Hist, Stanford Univ, 78, chair, Comt Undergrad Studies, 79-81. **HONORS AND AWARDS** Dean's Award for Distinguished Teaching, Stanford Univ, 76; Dinkelspiel Award, Stanford Univ, 80. **MEMBERSHIPS** AHA; Soc French Hist Studies; Women's Hist Res Sem; Am Soc Eighteenth-Century Studies. **RESEARCH** Ancien regime France; women's history; history of education. **SELECTED PUBLICATIONS** Auth, Women in 17th-Century France, Amer Hist Rev, Vol 0097, 92; Birth of Intimacy--3000 Homes in Paris, 17th-18th-Centuries, Amer Hist Rev, Vol 0098, 93; Cartesian Women--Versions and Subversions of Rational Discourse in the Old Regime, Amer Hist Rev, Vol 0098, 93; Impolite Learning--Conduct and Community in the Republic of Letters, 1680-1750, J Interdisciplinary Hist, Vol 0027, 97. **CONTACT ADDRESS** Dept of Hist, Stanford Univ, Stanford, CA, 94305.

LOUGEE, ROBERT WAYNE
PERSONAL Born 05/04/1919, Reading, MA, m, 1941, 3 children **DISCIPLINE** EUROPEAN HISTORY **EDUCATION** Brown Univ, AB, 41, PhD(hist), 52. **CAREER** Asst hist, Brown Univ, 47-49; from instr to assoc prof, 49-62, dean col libr arts and sci, 71-74, head dept, 60-69, PROF HIST, UNIV CONN, 62-, Am Philos Soc grants, 56 and 65. **MEMBERSHIPS** AHA; New England Hist Asn (pres, 76-77). **RESEARCH** Modern German history; European social and intellectual movement, 1850-1914. **SELECTED PUBLICATIONS** Auth, Enlightenment, Revolution, and Romanticism--the Genesis of Modern German Political Thought, 1790-1800, Amer Hist Rev, Vol 0098, 93. **CONTACT ADDRESS** Dept of Hist, Univ of Conn, Storrs, CT, 06268.

LOUIS, JAMES PAUL
PERSONAL Born 05/13/1938, Brooklyn, NY, d, 3 children **DISCIPLINE** TWENTIETH CENTURY UNITED STATES **EDUCATION** Colgate Univ, AB, 60; Harvard Univ, AM, 62, PhD(hist), 68. **CAREER** From inst to asst prof, 64-74, asst dean, 74-81, assoc prof hist, Kent State Univ, 74-, assoc dean, Col Arts & Sci, 81-87; assoc provost fac affairs, 87-. **MEMBERSHIPS** AHA; Orgn Am Historians; Academy of Academic Personnel Administrators. **RESEARCH** Woman suffrage and the fight for the nineteenth amendment, 1913-1920; the progressive movement and progressive reform. **SELECTED PUBLICATIONS** Auth, The roots of feminism: a review essay, Civil War Hist, 6/71; Josephine Jewell Dodge, Mary Garret Hay & Sue Shelton White, In: Notable American Women, 1607-1950, (3 vols), 71; Ruth Hanna McCormick Simms, In: Dictionary of American Biography, (3rd suppl), 73; intro to F Chambers, Black Higher Education in the United States, 78. **CONTACT ADDRESS** Off Fac Affairs Exec Office, Kent State Univ, PO Box 5190, Kent, OH, 44242-0001. **EMAIL** jlouis@kentvm.kent.edu

LOUNSBURY, CARL
PERSONAL Born 01/05/1952, St. Paul, MN, m, 1 child **DISCIPLINE** AMERICAN STUDIES **EDUCATION** Univ NC, BA, 74; George Washington Univ, MA, 77, PhD, 83. **CAREER** Archit Hist, Colonial Williamsburg Fdn, 82-. **SELECTED PUBLICATIONS** Auth, Architects and Builders in North Carolina: A History of the Practice of Building; auth, An Illustrated Glossary of Early Southern Architecture and Landscape; auth, The Architecture of the Charleston County Courthouse. **CONTACT ADDRESS** Archit Res Dept, Colonial Williamsburg Foundation, PO Box 1776, Williamsburg, VA, 23187. **EMAIL** clounsbury@cwf.org

LOUNSBURY, MYRON
DISCIPLINE AMERICAN HISTORY/AMERICAN STUDIES **EDUCATION** Duke Univ, BA, 61; Univ PA, MA, 62, PhD, 66. **CAREER** Am Stud Dept, Univ Md **RESEARCH** Investigating film cult in NY City between 1940 and 1970. **SELECTED PUBLICATIONS** Auth, Flashes of Lightning: The Moving Picture in the Progressive Era, Jour Pop Cult, 70; The Origins of American Film Criticism, 1909-1939, Arno Press, 73; Against the American Game: The MStrenuous Life' of Willard Huntington Wright, Prospects: An Annual of Amer Cult Stud, 80; The Gathered Light: History, Criticism and the Rise of the American Film, Quart Rev of Film Stud, 80; The Progress and Poetry of the Movies: A Second Book of Film Criticism by Vachel Lindsay, Scarecrow Press, 95. **CONTACT ADDRESS** Am Stud Dept, Univ MD, Col Park, College Park, MD, 20742. **EMAIL** ml36@umail.umd.edu

LOUNSBURY, RICHARD CECIL
PERSONAL Born 01/03/1949, Yorkton, SK, Canada **DISCIPLINE** CLASSICAL LANGUAGES, CLASSICAL TRADITION, AMERICAN INTELLECTUAL HISTORY **EDUCATION** Univ Calgary, BA, 70; Univ Tex, Austin, MA, 72, PhD(classics), 79. **CAREER** Lectr classics, Univ Witwatersrand, 79-81; asst prof, Univ Victoria, 81-82; Prof Classics & Comp Lit, Brigham Young Univ, 82- **MEMBERSHIPS** Am Philol Asn; Class Asn Can; Am Comp Lit Asn; Int Soc Hist Rhetoric. **RESEARCH** Roman literature of the early Empire; classical rhetoric; intellectual history of the American South. **SELECTED PUBLICATIONS** Auth, The death of Domitius in the Pharsalia, Trans Am Philol Asn, 75; History and motive in book seven of Lucan's Pharsalia, Hermes, 76; Restoring the generous past: Recent books of rhetoric and criticism, Mich Quart Rev, 79; contribr, Intellectual Life in Antebellum Charleston, Tennessee, 86; auth, The Arts of Suetonius: An Introduction, peter Lang, 87; ed, Louisa S. McCord: Political and Social Essays, Univ Press of Virginia, 95; ed, Louisa S. McCord: Poems, Drama, Biography, Letters, Univ Press of Virginia, 96; ed, Louisa S. McCord: Selected Writings, Univ Press of Virginia, 97. **CONTACT ADDRESS** Dept of Humanities Classics & Comp Lit, Brigham Young Univ, 3010 Jhkb, Provo, UT, 84602-0002. **EMAIL** richard_lounsbury@byu.edu

LOUTHAN, HOWARD
DISCIPLINE HISTORY **EDUCATION** Emory Univ, BA, 86, MA 90, Princeton Univ, PhD, 94. **CAREER** Asst prof, 94-. **RESEARCH** Early modern cultural and intellectual history; Renaissance and Reformation history. **SELECTED PUBLICATIONS** Auth, Reforming a Counter-reform Court: Johannis Crato and the Austrian Habsburgs, 94; A Reappraisal of J. A. Comenius's The Labyrinth of the World in Light of his Subsequent Writings on Educational Reform, 96; Religion and Gender in Late Medieval England, 96; The Quest for Compromise: Peace Makers in Counter-Reformation Vienna, 97. **CONTACT ADDRESS** History and Philosophy of Science Dept, Univ of Notre Dame, Notre Dame, IN, 46556. **EMAIL** Howard.Louthan.2@nd.edu

LOVE, BARBARA
PERSONAL Born 04/13/1946, Dumas, AR **DISCIPLINE** EDUCATION **EDUCATION** AR AM & N, BA 1965; Univ of AR, MA 1967; Univ of MA, PhD, EdD 1972. **CAREER** Univ of MA Amherst Campus, assoc prof; Fellowship House, exec dir; Kansas City, teacher 1969-70; Center for Urban Educ, Univ of MA, grad asst 1970-71, instructor 1971-72, asso prof, chmn. **HONORS AND AWARDS** Leadership Found Scholarship 1965-66; Jr League Award 1967. **MEMBERSHIPS** Mem Phi Delta Kappa 1974; Nat Alliance Black Sch Educators 1973; Am Educ Studies Assn 1974; Panel Am Women 1968-70; Urban Coalition Task Force on Educ 1968-70; comm rep Nat Tchrs Corps 1969-70; tast force Nat Alternative Schs Prgm 1971-73. **CONTACT ADDRESS** Univ of Massachusetts, Furcolo Hall, Amherst, MA, 01002.

LOVE, JOSEPH L.
PERSONAL Born 02/28/1938, Austin, TX, 4 children **DISCIPLINE** LATIN AMERICAN HISTORY **EDUCATION** Harvard Univ, AB, 60; Stanford Univ, MA, 63; Columbia Univ, PhD(hist), 67. **CAREER** From instr to assoc prof, 66-78, PROF HIST, UNIV ILL, URBANA-CHAMPAIGN, 78-, Dir, Latin am Studies, 93-, Chmn, Brazilian Studies Comt, 73; mem, Bolton Prize Comt, 73-74; mem, Gen Comt, Conf Latin Am Hist, 81-83; sr res assoc, St Anthony's Col, Oxford Univ, 82. **HONORS AND AWARDS** Conf Prize, Conf Latin Am Hist, 71; Latin Am Hist Prize, Southwest Soc Sci Asn, 77; NEH, SSRC, IREX, Fulbright, and Guggenheim Fellowships; Vis Schol, Univ Sao Paulo, 89-90; Vis Schol, Inst Ortegoy Gasset, Madrid, 95-96. **MEMBERSHIPS** AHA; Conf Latin Am Hist; Latin Am Studies Asn. **RESEARCH** Regional politics and economics in 19th and 20th century Brazil; history of economic ideas and policies in Latin America and Eastern Europe. **SELECTED PUBLICATIONS** Auth, Rio Grande do Sul and Brazilian Regionalism, Stanford Univ, 71; co-ed, Quantitative Social Science Research on Latin America, Univ Ill, 73; auth, Sao Paulo in the Brazilian Federation, Stanford Univ, 80; co-ed, Guiding the Invisible Hand: Economic Liberalism and the State in Latin American History, Praeger, 88; auth, Crafting the Third World: Theorizing Underdevelopment in Rumania and Brazil, Stanford Univ, 96. **CONTACT ADDRESS** Dept of History, Univ of Illinois, Urbana-Champaign, 810 S Wright St, Urbana, IL, 61801-3611. **EMAIL** j-love2@uiuc.edu

LOVEJOY, DAVID SHERMAN
PERSONAL Born 11/30/1919, Pawtucket, RI, m, 1941, 1 child **DISCIPLINE** AMERICAN HISTORY **EDUCATION** Bowdoin Col, BS, 41; Brown Univ, AM, 47, PhD(Am civilization), 54. **CAREER** Fac Am hist and lit, Marlboro Col, 50-53; asst prof Am hist, Mich State Univ, 54-55 and Brown Univ, 55-59; vis asst prof, Northwestern Univ, 59-60; from asst prof to assoc prof, 60-65, PROF AM HIST, UNIV WIS-MADISON, 65-, Fulbright lectr, Univ Aberdeen, 64-65; Guggenheim fel, 67-68; coun mem, Inst Early Am Hist and Cult, Va, 75-78. **MEMBERSHIPS** AHA; Orgn Am Historians. **RESEARCH** American colonial history, American Revolution. **SELECTED PUBLICATIONS** Auth, Williams, Roger and Fox, George, the Arrogance of Self Righteousness, New Eng Quart-Hist Rev New Eng Life and Letters, Vol 0066, 93; Satanizing the American-Indian, New Eng Quart-Hist Rev of New England Life and Letters, Vol 0067, 94; Between Hell and Plum Island--Sewall, Samuel and the Legacy of the Witches, 1692-1697, New Eng Quart-Hist Rev of New Eng Life and Letters, Vol 0070, 97. **CONTACT ADDRESS** Dept of Hist, Univ of Wis, Madison, WI, 53706.

LOVEJOY, PAUL E.
PERSONAL Born 05/06/1943, Girard, PA, m, 1977, 3 children **DISCIPLINE** AFRICAN HISTORY **EDUCATION** Clarkson Col, BS, 65; Univ Wis, MS, 67, PhD(hist), 73. **CAREER** ASSOC PROF HIST, YORK UNIV, 71-, Hon lectr, Ahmadu Bello Univ, Nigeria, 75-76. **MEMBERSHIPS** African Studies Asn; Can Asn African Studies; Can Hist Asn. **RESEARCH** Slavery in Africa and the Americas; precolonial African economic history; trade, production and society in West Africa. **SELECTED PUBLICATIONS** Auth, The Human Commodity--Perspectives on the Trans-Saharan Slave Trade, Int J African Hist Stud, Vol 0026, 93; Africa in America--Slave Acculturation and Resistance in the American South and the British Caribbean, 1736-1831, Int J African Hist Stud, Vol 0028, 95; Competing Markets for Male and Female Slaves--Prices in the Interior of West Africa, 1780-1850, Int J African Hist Stud, Vol 0028, 95; British Abolition and its Impact on Slave Prices Along the Atlantic Coast of Africa, 1783-1850, J Econ Hist, Vol 0055, 95; Africa and Africans in the Making of the Atlantic World, 1400-1680, J Interdisciplinary Hist, Vol 0026, 95. **CONTACT ADDRESS** Dept of Hist, York Univ, N York, ON, M3J 1P3.

LOVELAND, ANNE CAROL
PERSONAL Born 12/23/1938, Jamaica, NY, m, 1991 **DISCIPLINE** AMERICAN INTELLECTUAL & SOCIAL HISTORY **EDUCATION** Univ Rochester, BA, 60; Cornell Univ, MA, 63, PhD(hist), 68. **CAREER** From instr to asst prof, 64-72, assoc prof, 72-80, Nat Endowment for Humanities Younger Humanist fel, 73-74, prof hist, LA State Univ,Baton Rouge, 80-93, T. Harry Williams Prof of Am Hist, LA State Univ, Baton Rouge, 93-. **HONORS AND AWARDS** Francis Mackemie Award, 80-82; Willie Lee Rose Publication Prize, 87. **MEMBERSHIPS** Orgn Am Historians; Southern Hist Asn. **RESEARCH** History of American religion; 19th and 20th century intellectual and social history. **SELECTED PUBLICATIONS** Auth, Evangelicalism and Immediate Emancipation in Ameri-

can Anti-Slavery Thought, J Southern Hist, 5/66; James Fenimore Cooper and the American Mission, Am Quart, summer 69; Emblem of Liberty: The Image of Lafayette in the American Mind, La State Univ Press, 71; Richard Furman's Questions on Slavery, Baptist Hist & Heritage, 7/75; The Southern Work of the Rev J C Hartzell, Pastor of Ames Church in New Orleans, 1870-73, La Hist, fall 75; Domesticity and Religion in the Ante-Bellum Period: The Career of Phoebe Palmer, Historian, 5/77; Presbyterians and Revivalism in the Old South, J Presby Hist, spring 79; Southern Evangelicals and the Social Order, 1800-1860, La State Univ Press, 80; Lillian Smith and the Problem of Segregation in the Roosevelt Era, Southern Studies, spring 83; Lillian Smith: A Southerner Confronting the South, LA State Univ Press, 86; American Evangelicals and the U.S. Military, 1942-1993, LA State Univ Press, 96; Later Stages of the Recovery of American Religious History, in Darryl Hart and Harry Stout, eds, New Directions in American Religious History, Oxford Univ Press, 97; Prophetic Ministry and the Military Chaplaincy during the Vietnam Era, in Lewis Perry and Karen Halttunen, ed., Moral Problems in American Life, Cornell Univ Press, 98. **CONTACT ADDRESS** Dept of Hist, Louisiana State Univ, Baton Rouge, LA, 70803-0001.

LOVERIDGE-SANBONMATSU, JOAN
PERSONAL Born 07/05/1938, Hartford, CT, m, 1964, 2 children **DISCIPLINE** RHETORIC AND COMMUNICATION; BRITISH AND IRISH HISTORY. **EDUCATION** Univ Vermont, BA, 60; Ohio Univ, MA, 63; Penn State Univ, PhD, 71. **CAREER** Tchg asst, Commun Stud, Ohio Univ, 62-63; instr Commun Stud & ESL, Penn State Univ, 66-67; vis asst prof Commun Stud, RIT, 71; adj prof Commun Stud, Monroe Commun Col, 72-76; asst prof Commun Stud & Womens Stud, SUNY Brockport, 63-77; Prof Commun Stud & Women,s Stud, SUNY Oswego, 77-. **HONORS AND AWARDS** Postdoctoral fel Multicult Womens Summer Sem, Univ Chicago, 83; Trailblazer Higher Educ Award, Nat Orgn Women, Cent NY State, 87; Womens Ctr Award Extraordinary Commitment Womens Issues, 96, Womens Ctr Award Outstanding Dedication to Womens Ctr, 98, SUNY Oswego ; SUNY Oswego Intensive Eng Prog, 95, 96; SEED Award, 98; Am Red Cross Overseas Asn Pres Citation Award Soc Change, 98. **MEMBERSHIPS** Nat Commun Asn; Nat Womens Stud Asn; E Commun Asn; NY State Speech Asn; Soc Int Educ, Trng & Res; Am Red Cross Overseas Asn; Speech Commun Asn Puerto Rico. **RESEARCH** Japanese American women interned at Poston in World War II; Womens studies, English as a second language; Rhetoric and social change. **SELECTED PUBLICATIONS** Auth, Multicultural Dilemnas of Language Usage, Why Don't You Talk Right, Multicultural Commun Perspectives, Kendall Hunt, 92; Benazir Bhutto: Feminist Voice for Democracy in Pakistan, Howard Jour Commun, 94; Helen Broinowski, Caldicott: pediatrician, peace activist, catalyst for the nuclear disarmament movement, Women Public Speakers in the United States, Greenwood Press, 94; coauth Feminism and Womans Life, Minerva Publ Co, 95. **CONTACT ADDRESS** 23 Mc-Cracken Dr., Oswego, NY, 13126. **EMAIL** sanbonma@oswego.edu

LOVIN, CLIFFORD R.
DISCIPLINE HISTORY **EDUCATION** Davidson Col, BA 57; Univ NC, Chapel Hill, MA 62, PhD, 65. **CAREER** Asst, 66-69, assoc, 69-72, PROF, 72-, W CAROLINA UNIV; dir, Mountain Heritage Ctr, W Carolina Univ, 77-81; dean, col arts scis, W Caroline Univ, 87-93. **SELECTED PUBLICATIONS** Auth, A School for Diplomats: The Paris Peace Conference of 1919, 97. **CONTACT ADDRESS** Dept of History, Western Carolina Univ, Cullowhee, NC, 28723. **EMAIL** lovin@wpoff.wcu.edu

LOVIN, HUGH TAYLOR
PERSONAL Born 12/10/1928, Pocatello, ID, m, 1956, 1 child **DISCIPLINE** COLONIAL AND RECENT AMERICAN HISTORY **EDUCATION** Idaho State Col, BA, 50; Wash State Univ, MA, 56; Univ Wash, PhD(hist), 63. **CAREER** Instr hist, Mil Br, Univ Alaska, 57-61; asst prof, Southwestern Ore Col, 63-64 and Kearney State Col, 64-65; assoc prof, 65-67, chmn dept, 68-71, PROF HIST, BOISE STATE UNIV, 68-. **RESEARCH** United States, 1900-1940; American labor history. **SELECTED PUBLICATIONS** Auth, The Politics of Righteousness--Idaho Christian Patriotism, J West, Vol 0032, 93; The Silver State--Nevadas Heritage Reinterpreted, J West, Vol 0032, 93; History of Idaho, Vols 1 and 2, J West, Vol 0035, 96; Farmers and Farm Workers Movements--Social Protest in American Agriculture, J West, Vol 0036, 97. **CONTACT ADDRESS** Dept Hist, Boise State Univ, 1310 S Gourley, Boise, ID, 83725.

LOVOLL, ODD SVERRE
PERSONAL Born 10/06/1934, Sande In Sunnmore, Norway, m, 1958, 2 children **DISCIPLINE** AMERICAN HISTORY **EDUCATION** Univ of Bergen, Bergen, Norway, Basic Examination in Norwegian lang and lit, 61; Univ of Oslo, Oslo, Norway, Basic and Intermediate Examinations in History, 65-67; Univ NDak, MA, 69; Univ Minn, Minneapolis, PhD(Am hist), 73. **CAREER** Instr Norweg, Univ NDak, 67-70; teaching asst, Univ Minn, 70-71; from Instr to Prof of Norwegian and History, 71-92, King Olav V Prof, Scandinavian-Am Studies, St Olaf Col, 92-; publ ed, Norweg-Am Hist Asn, 80-; Prof II Humanities, Univ of Oslo, 95-; Guest Prof of Am Hist at the Univ of Trondheim and Univ of Oslo, fall 93. **HONORS AND AWARDS** Phi Alpha Theta; Award of Merit for A Folk Epic, the State Hist Soc of Wis, 76; Norweg Govt res grant, 77-78; Knight's Cross of the Royal Order of Merit, 86; Award of Superior Achievement for A Century of Urban Life, Ill State Hist Soc, 89; inducted member, The Norweg Acad of Sci and Letters, 89-; The Am-Norway Heritage Fund Award, 90; Alf Mjoen Award "Honored Emigrants", 96. **MEMBERSHIPS** Soc Advan Scand Studies; Norweg-Am Hist Asn. **RESEARCH** European migration to America, primarily Scandinavian; American ethnic studies; Scandinavian history. **SELECTED PUBLICATIONS** Auth, A Century of Urban Life: The Norwegians in Chicago before 1930, The Norweg-Am Hist Asn, 88; coauth, Den store Chicagoreisen, Oslo, Universitetsforlaget, 88; ed, Nordics in America: The Future of Their Past, Norweg-Am Hist Asn, 93; auth, Det lofterike landet, En norskamerikansk historie, Universitetsforlaget, 97; The Promise Fulfilled: A Portrait of Norwegian Americans Today, Univ Minn Press, 98; Loftet infridd, Et norskamerikansk samtidsbilde, Vett & Viten (Oslo), forthcoming 98; The Promise of America: A Norwegian American History, Univ of Minn Press (forthcoming); author of numerous other journal articles and book chapters. **CONTACT ADDRESS** History Dept, St. Olaf Col, 1520 St Olaf Ave., Northfield, MN, 55057-1099. **EMAIL** loroll@stolaf.edu

LOWE, BENNO P.
DISCIPLINE HISTORY **EDUCATION** Georgetown Univ, PhD. **CAREER** Assoc prof. **MEMBERSHIPS** Am Hist Asn. **RESEARCH** Early modern Europe; Tudor-Stuart England. **SELECTED PUBLICATIONS** Auth, Imagining Peace: A History of Early English Pacifist Thought 1340-1560, 97; Religious Wars and the 'Common Peace': Anglican Anti-War Sentiment in Elizabethan England, Albion, 96. **CONTACT ADDRESS** History Dept, Florida Atlantic Univ, 777 Glades Rd, Boca Raton, FL, 33431. **EMAIL** bplowe@fau.edu

LOWE, DONALD M.
PERSONAL Born 12/27/1928, Shanghai, China, 2 children **DISCIPLINE** HISTORY **EDUCATION** Yale Univ, BA, 50; Univ Chicago, MA, 51; Univ Calif, Berekley, PhD(hist), 63. **CAREER** Asst prof hist, Duquesne Univ, 58-63 and Univ Calif, Riverside, 63-68; assoc prof, 68-72, PROF HIST, CALIF STATE UNIV, SAN FRANCISCO, 72-, Ford Found fel, 55-57; Fulbright-Hays grant, 64; Soc Sci Res Coun grant, 66-67. **MEMBERSHIPS** AHA; Asn Asian Studies; Soc Phenomenol and Existential Philos. **RESEARCH** Marxist thought; historiography; phenomenology. **SELECTED PUBLICATIONS** Auth, Engels and the Formation of Marxism--History, Dialectics and Revolution, Amer Hist Rev, Vol 0098, 93. **CONTACT ADDRESS** Dept of Hist, California State Univ, San Francisco, San Francisco, CA, 94132.

LOWE, EUGENE Y., JR.
PERSONAL Born 08/18/1949, New York, NY, m, 4 children **DISCIPLINE** RELIGION; CHURCH HISTORY **EDUCATION** Princeton Univ, AB, 71; Union Theol Sem, M Div, 78; Union Theol Sem, PhD, 87. **CAREER** Res assoc and consult, Andrew W. Mellon Found, 93-97; lectr, dept of relig, Princeton Univ, 93-95; dean of students, Princeton Univ, 83-93; assoc provost, Northwestern Univ, 95-. **HONORS AND AWARDS** Phi Beta Kappa; Protestant fel; fund for Theol Educ, 76-77; Harold Willis Dodds Prize, Princeton Univ, 71; grad fel, Episcopal Church Found, 78-81. **MEMBERSHIPS** Amer Acad of Relig; Amer Soc of Church Hist; Lilly Seminar on Relig and Higher Educ. **SELECTED PUBLICATIONS** Auth, Walter Righter, Dict of Heresy Trials in American Christianity, Greenwood Press, 320-326, 97; auth, Racial Ideology, Encycl of Amer Social Hist, 335-346, Charles Scribner's Sons, 93; auth, From Social Gospel to Social Science at the University of Wisconsin, The Church's Public Role: Retrospect and Prospect, 233-251, Eerdmans, 93; auth, Mordecai Kaplan, Twentieth-Century Shapers of American Popular Religion, 210-217, Greenwood, 89. **CONTACT ADDRESS** Office of the Provost, Northwestern Univ, Crown Center 2-154, Evanston, IL, 60208.

LOWE, RICHARD GRADY
PERSONAL Born 07/05/1942, Eunice, LA, m, 1962, 3 children **DISCIPLINE** AMERICAN HISTORY **EDUCATION** Univ Southwestern La, BA, 64; Harvard Univ, AM, 65; Univ Va, PhD(hist), 68. **CAREER** Asst prof to regents prof hist, Univ N Tex, 68-. **MEMBERSHIPS** Southern Hist Asn; Va Hist Soc; Tex State Hist Asn; La Hist Asn; Soc of Civil War Historians. **RESEARCH** Civil War and Reconstruction; Southern United States; quantitative history. **SELECTED PUBLICATIONS** Auth, Massachusetts and the Acadians, William & Mary Quart, 4/68; Virginia's Reconstruction Convention, 10/72 & The Republican Party in Antebellum Virginia, 7/73, Va Mag Hist & Biog; coauth, Wealthholding and Political Power in Antebellum Texas, Southwestern Hist Quart, 7/75; The Slave-breeding Hypothesis, J Southern Hist, 8/76; Slavery and the Distribution of Wealth in Texas, J Am Hist, 9/76; Wealth and Power in Antebellum Texas, Tex A&M Univ, 77; auth, Planters and Pain, Folk, SMU Press, 87; Republicans and Reconstruction in Virginia, Univ Va, 91; The Texas Overland Expedition of 1863, Ryan Place, 93; The Freedmen's Bureau and Local Black Leadership, J Am Hist, 12/93; The Freedmen's Bureau and Local White Leaders in Virginia, J Southern Hist, 8/98. **CONTACT ADDRESS** Dept of Hist, Univ of N Tex, PO Box 310650, Denton, TX, 76203-0650. **EMAIL** lowe@unt.edu

LOWE, WILLIAM J.
DISCIPLINE MODERN IRISH HISTORY **EDUCATION** Michigan State Univ, BA; Univ Dublin, Trinity Col, PhD. **CAREER** Dean, Col Liberal Arts, prof, 91-. **HONORS AND AWARDS** Fulbright scholar, Ireland. **RESEARCH** Irish plice in the period before 1922. **SELECTED PUBLICATIONS** Pub(s), book and series of articles on Irish immigration in Victorian England. **CONTACT ADDRESS** Dept of Hist, Univ Detroit Mercy, 4001 W McNichols Rd, PO BOX 19900, Detroit, MI, 48219-0900.

LOWENSTAM, STEVEN
PERSONAL Born 12/14/1945, Springfield, IL **DISCIPLINE** CLASSICAL LANGUAGES **EDUCATION** Univ Chicago, BA, 67; Harvard Univ, MA, 69, PhD(classics), 75. **CAREER** Asst prof, 75-81, ASSOC PROF CLASSICS, UNIV ORE, 81-. **MEMBERSHIPS** Am Philol Asn; Archaeol Inst Am; Philol Asn PACIFIC Coast. **RESEARCH** Archaic epic; literary criticism; glyptics. **SELECTED PUBLICATIONS** Auth, The Uses of Vase Depictions in Homeric Studies, Transactions of the Amer Philol Asn, Vol 0122, 92; The Dialogs of Plato, Vol 2, 'Symposium', Class World, Vol 0086, 92; The Arming of Achilleus on Early Greek Vases, Class Antiquity, Vol 0012, 93; Is Literary Criticism an Illegitimate Discipline--a Fallacious Argument in Plato 'Ion', Ramus Critical Studies in Greek and Roman Literature, Vol 0022, 93; The Pictures on Junos Temple in the 'Aeneid', Class World, Vol 0087, 93; Homer, the 'Odyssey', Class World, Vol 0088, 94; Sympotica, a Symposium on the Symposion, Class World, Vol 0087, 94; The 'Odyssey' of Homer, Class World, Vol 0088, 94; The 'Odyssey', an Epic of Return, Class World, Vol 0088, 94; Vatican 35617 and Iliad 16, Amer J Archaeol, Vol 0098, 94; The Bending of the Bow, Class World, Vol 0090, 97; Blood and Iron--Stories and Storytelling in Homer 'Odyssey', Class World, Vol 0090, 97. **CONTACT ADDRESS** Dept of Classics, Univ of Ore, Eugene, OR, 97403-1205.

LOWENSTEIN, STEVEN MARK
PERSONAL Born 02/26/1945, New York, NY, m, 1974, 2 children **DISCIPLINE** JEWISH HISTORY, EUROPEAN HISTORY **EDUCATION** City Col New York, BA, 66; Princeton Univ, MA, 69, PhD(hist), 72. **CAREER** Asst archivist & res assoc, YIVO Inst, 73-75; archivist, Leo Baeck Inst, 75-79; prof, Univ Of Judaism, 79-, Archivist, United Jewish Appeal, 75-77. **MEMBERSHIPS** AHA; Asn Jewish Studies; Soc Am Archivists. **RESEARCH** Modernization of German Jewry; Yiddish dialectology; Jewish folk traditions; social history of early modern France. **SELECTED PUBLICATIONS** Auth, The Rural Community and the urbanization of German Jewry, Cent Europ Hist, 80; The 1840's and the creation of the German Jewish Religious Reform movement, In: Revolution and Evolution, 1848, German Jewish History, 81; Voluntary and involuntary fertility limitations in nineteenth century Bavarian Jewry, In: Modern Jewish Fertility, 81; The Berlin Jewish Community 1770-1830: Enlightenment, Family, & Crisis, Oxford Univ Press, 94; The Mechanics of Change: Essays in German Jewish Social History, Scholars Press, 92; Frankfurt on the Hudson: The German Jewish Community of Washington heights 1933-1983, Wayne State Univ Press, 89; 4 chapters in German-Jewish History in Modern Times, Vol 3: Integration in Dispute 1871-1918, Columbia Univ Press, 98. **CONTACT ADDRESS** Univ of Judaism, 15600 Mulholland Dr, Los Angeles, CA, 90077-1599. **EMAIL** as155@lafn.org

LOWRIE, MICHELE
PERSONAL Born 04/24/1962, New Haven, CT, m, 1988, 1 child **DISCIPLINE** CLASSICS **EDUCATION** Yale Univ BA 84; Harvard Univ PhD 90. **CAREER** New York Univ, asst prof, assoc prof, 90 to 96-. **HONORS AND AWARDS** Presidential Fell NYU. **MEMBERSHIPS** CS **RESEARCH** Latin lit; Augustan poetry. **SELECTED PUBLICATIONS** Auth, Horace's Narrative Odes, Oxford, Clarendon Press, 97, rev by Bryn Mawr Classical Rev 98; Spleen and the Monumentum: Memory in Horace and Baudelaire, Comp Lit, 97; A Parade of Lyric Predecessors, Horace Odes, Phoenix, 95; Lyric's Elegos and the Aristotelian Mean: Horace Odes, Class World, 94; Myrrha's Second Taboo, Ovid Metamorphoses, Class Philology, 93. **CONTACT ADDRESS** Dept of Classics, New York Univ, 25 Waverly Pl, New York, NY, 10003. **EMAIL** michele.lowrie@nyu.edu

LOWRY, BULLITT
PERSONAL Born 06/17/1936, New York, NY, m, 1974, 2 children **DISCIPLINE** MODERN EUROPEAN HISTORY **EDUCATION** Transylvania Col, AB, 56; Duke Univ, AM, 59, PhD, 63. **CAREER** Asst prof hist, Converse Col, 60-64; assoc prof to prof hist, N TX State Univ, 64-; vis prof, Wiley Col, 68; res asst, US Congress, 78; prof and dir, TX-London semester, 89, 90. **HONORS AND AWARDS** Nat Endowment for Humanities grant, 76; John Ben Shepperd Award, TX Hist Comm, 88; Foreign assoc member, Royal Inst of Int Affairs, 90-; Chairs

lecturer, Tamkang Univ, Taiwan, 96. **MEMBERSHIPS** AHA; Soc for Military Hist; Eur His Sect of Southern Hist Asn. **RESEARCH** Modern European diplomatic and military history; nineteenth century European radicalism. **SELECTED PUBLICATIONS** Auth, Music under Stalin, fall 67 & The Historian and his Politics, spring 68, Arlington Quart; Pershing and the Armistice, J Am Hist, 9/68; El indefendible Penon: Inglaterra y la permuta de Gibraltar por Ceuta de 1917 a 1919, Revista Polit Int, 77; co-auth & trans, The Red Virgin: The Memoirs of Louise Michel, Univ AL Press, 81; coauth, World History, West Pub Co, 91; auth, War Experience and Armistice Conditions, in Facing Armageddon, ed, H Cecil and P H Liddle, Leo Cooper/Pen and Sword, 96; The Causes and Consequences of World War I, Tamkang Univ Press, 96; Armistice 1918, Kent State Univ Press, 96. **CONTACT ADDRESS** Dept Hist, Univ North Texas, PO Box 310650, Denton, TX, 76203-0650. **EMAIL** blowry@unt.edu

LOWRY, WILLIAM R.
DISCIPLINE POLITICAL SCIENCE **EDUCATION** IN Univ, BS 79; Univ IL, Chicago, MBA 83; Stanford Univ, MA 85, PhD 88. **CAREER** Dept Pol Sci, WA Univ **HONORS AND AWARDS** Polit Sci Prof of the Yr, 98, 96; Facul Res Gnt; Mortar Bd Tch Awd; Golden Key Nat Hon Soc; Women's Panhellenic Tch Awd; IFC tchr of the yr; MBT Awd; Brookings Inst Fell; Stanford Univ Fell; Univ IL Fell; Beta Gamma Sima Hon Bus Frat; Pi Sigma Alpha Hon PS Frat. **RESEARCH** Environmental policy, public lands. **SELECTED PUBLICATIONS** Preserving Public Lands for the Future: The Politics of Intergenerational Goods, Wash DC, Georgetown 98; The Capacity for Wonder: Preserving National Parks, Wash DC, Brookings Inst, 94; The Dimensions of Federalism: State Governments and Pollution Control Policies, Durham, Duke Univ Press, 92; Public Provision of Intergenerational Goods, in Amer Jour Pol Sci, 98; Paradise Lost?, Forum for Applied Res and Public Policy, 97; National Parks policy, in: Charles Davis, ed, Western Public Lands and Environ Pol, Lawrence KS, Univ Press KS, 97. **CONTACT ADDRESS** Dept of Polit Sci, Washington Univ, St Louis, MO, 63130. **EMAIL** lowry@artsci.wustl.edu

LOWTHER, LAWRENCE LELAND
PERSONAL Born 07/29/1927, Centralia, WA, m, 1947, 2 children **DISCIPLINE** COLONIAL AMERICAN HISTORY **EDUCATION** Univ Wash, BA, 52, MA, 59, PhD(Hist), 64. **CAREER** Assoc prof Am Hist, Gen Beadle State Col, 64-65; from asst prof to assoc prof, 65-74, prof Colonial & Revolutionary Am Hist, Cent Wash Univ, 74-, Col participant, Tri Univ Proj Elem Educ-Soc Sci, Univ Wash, 69-70; retired, prof emeritus, 92. **MEMBERSHIPS** AHA; Orgn Am Historians; Nat Coun Soc Studies. **RESEARCH** Colonial Rhode Island. **SELECTED PUBLICATIONS** Auth, Town and colony in early 18th century Rhode Island, Newport Hist, 7/64; coauth, History in the high school: A brief survey of Washington State, Pac Northwest Quart, 7/68; auth, Collingwood and historical inquiry, Univ Wash Col Educ Rec, 5/70. **CONTACT ADDRESS** Dept of History, Central Washington Univ, 400 E 8th Ave, Ellensburg, WA, 98926-7502.

LU, SUPING
DISCIPLINE LIBRARY SCIENCE, INTERNATIONAL RELATIONS **EDUCATION** Ohio Univ, MA, 92; Univ SC, MLIS, 94. **CAREER** ASST PROF, UNIV NEB, 94-. **CONTACT ADDRESS** Lincoln Love Libr, Univ of Nebraska, 201AB, Lincoln, NE, 68588-0410. **EMAIL** supingl@unllib.unl.edu

LUBBEN, JOSEPH
DISCIPLINE MUSIC THEORY **EDUCATION** Univ Notre Dame, BA, 85; Brandeis Univ, MFA, 89; Brandeis Univ, PhD, 95. **CAREER** Vis fac, Univ Notre Dame, 90-92; Brandeis Univ, 92-93; Visiting asst prof, Oberlin Coll, 95. **HONORS AND AWARDS** AMS50 Dissertation Fel, Am Musicol Soc, 93. **SELECTED PUBLICATIONS** Contribu, Mus Theory Spectrum, 93. **CONTACT ADDRESS** Dept of Mus, Oberlin Col, Oberlin, OH, 44074.

LUBBERS, JEFFREY S.
PERSONAL Born 01/26/1949, Madison, WI **DISCIPLINE** HISTORY AND GOVERNMENT **EDUCATION** Cornell Univ, BA, 71; Univ Chicago Law Sch, JD, 74. **CAREER** Instr, Univ Miami Sch of Law, 74-75; atty, 75-82; res dir, Admin Conf of US, 82-95; fel in Admin Law, Amer Univ Wash Col of Law, 95-. **HONORS AND AWARDS** Pres rank of meritorious exec, 91; outstanding govt svc award, Amer Bar Asn, 94; Walter Gellhorn award for admin law, Fed Bar Asn, 97. **MEMBERSHIPS** Amer Bar Asn; DC Bar. **RESEARCH** Administrative law; Regulation; Alternative dispute resolution. **SELECTED PUBLICATIONS** Auth, A Guide to Federal Agency Rulemaking, 3rd ed, Amer Bar Asn Book Publ, 98; If It Didn't Exit, it Would Have to Be Invented--Reviving the Administrative Conference, 30, Ariz State Law Jour, 147, 98; The ABA Section of the Administrative Law and Regulatory Practice--From Objector to Protector of the APA, 50, Admin Law Rev, 157, 98; The Administrative Law Agenda for the Next Decade, 49, Admin Law Rev, 159, 97; Testimony on H.R. 2592, The Private Trustee Reform Act of 1997, before the Subcomt of Com and Admin Law, Comt on the Judiciary, US House of Rep, 9 Oct, 97; Ombudsman Offices in the Federal Government--An Emerging Trend?, 22, Admin & Regulatory Law News, 6, summer, 97; Paperwork Redux: The Stronger Paperwork Reduction Act of 1995, 49, Admin Law Rev, 111, 97; APA Adjudication: Is the Quest for Uniformity Faltering?, 10, The Admin Law Jour of the Amer Univ, 65, 96; The Regulatory Reform Recommendations of the National Performance Review, 6, RISK: Health Safety and Environ, 145, Franklin Pierce Law Ctr, spring, 95; Justice Stephen Breyer: Purveyor of Common Sense in Many Forums, part of Symposium: Justice Stephen Breyer's Contribution to Administrative Law, 8, The Admin Law Jour of the Amer Univ, 775, 95; Reinventing Chinese Administrative Law, 19, Admin Law News, 1, spring, 94; Better Regulations: The National Performance Review's Regulatory Reform Recommendations, paper presented to the Duke Law Jour Twenty-Fifth Annual Admin Law Conf, Durham, NC, 20 Jan, 94, publ, 43, Duke Law Jour, 94; Anatomy of a Regulatory Program: Comments on Strategic Regulators and the Choice of Rulemaking Procedures, Hamilton and Schroeder, 56, Law and Contemporary Problems, 161, 94. **CONTACT ADDRESS** 4801 Massachusetts Av. NW, Washington, DC, 20016. **EMAIL** jsl26@aol.com

LUBENOW, WILLIAM CORNELIUS
PERSONAL Born 07/28/1939, Freeport, IL **DISCIPLINE** MODERN EUROPEAN HISTORY **EDUCATION** Cent Col, Iowa, BA, 61; Univ Iowa, MA, 62, PhD(hist), 68. **CAREER** Instr hist, Cent Col, Iowa, 62-64, from asst prof to assoc prof, 65-71; prof hist, Stockton State Col, 71-, Huntington Libr & Art Gallery fel hist, 74. **MEMBERSHIPS** AHA; Conf Brit Studies, Comn Study Parliamentary & Rep Insts; fel, Royal Historical Soc. **RESEARCH** British politics; voting behavior; parliamentary behavior. **SELECTED PUBLICATIONS** Auth, Politics of Government Growth, David & Charles, 71; Social recruitment and social attitudes, Huntington Libr Quart, 77; Ireland, the Great Depression and the railway rates, Proc Am Philos Soc, 78; The Cambridge Apostles, 1820-1914: Liberalism Imagination and Friendship in British Lateral and Professional Life, Cambridge University Press, 98. **CONTACT ADDRESS** Stockton State Col, Pomona, NJ, 08240-9999.

LUBENSKY, SOPHIA
DISCIPLINE RUSSIAN **EDUCATION** Kharkov Univ, MA, 63; Leningrad Univ, MA, 57, PhD, 72. **CAREER** From asst prof 77 to prof 96-, Univ Albany, State Univ NY. **SELECTED PUBLICATIONS** Russian-English Dictionary of Idioms, Random House, 95 and publ in Russia: Russko-angliiskii frazeologicheskii slovar, Iazyki russkoi kul'tury, 97; Approaches to a Russian-English Dictionary of Idioms, In Dictionaries, 91; Aspectual Properties of Verba Percipiendi, In The Scope of Slavic Aspect, UCLA Slavic Ser 12, Slavica, 85; coauth, Nachalo: When in Russia... a Basal Russian Textbook with a Video Component, McGraw-Hill, 96. **CONTACT ADDRESS** Dept of Languages, Literatures, and Cultures, Univ at Albany, SUNY, 1400 Washington Ave, Humanities 254, Albany, NY, 12222. **EMAIL** lubensky@cnsvax.albany.edu

LUBICK, GEORGE MICHAEL
PERSONAL Born 01/08/1943, Butte, MT, m, 1971, 1 child **DISCIPLINE** AMERICAN HISTORY **EDUCATION** Univ Mont, BA, 66, MA, 68; Univ Toledo, PhD(Am hist), 74. **CAREER** Asst prof hist, Mont Col Mineral Sci and Technol, 71-77; ASST PROF HIST, NORTHERN ARIZ UNIV, 77-, Nat Endowment Humanities fel, 76. **MEMBERSHIPS** AHA; Orgn Am Historians; Western Hist Asn; Nat Trust Hist Preserv. **RESEARCH** Conservation-environmental history; progressive movement in the Rocky Mountains. **SELECTED PUBLICATIONS** Auth, The Japanese-American Experience, J West, Vol 0032, 93; From Coastal Wilderness to Fruited Plain--A History of Environmental Change in Temperate North America, 1500 to the Present, Amer Hist Rev, Vol 0101, 96. **CONTACT ADDRESS** Dept of Hist and Polit Sci, No Arizona Univ, Flagstaff, AZ, 86011-0001.

LUBRANO, LINDA L.
DISCIPLINE RUSSIAN POLITICS AND SOCIETY **EDUCATION** Hunter Col, BA; Indiana Univ, MA, PhD. **CAREER** Prof, Am Univ. **HONORS AND AWARDS** Grants, Nat Sci Found; Am Coun Learned Socs; Ford Found; Smithsonian Inst., Dir, Div Comp Reg Studies, Sch Int Ser.. **RESEARCH** Comparative science studies with a focus on gender and the ethics of technique. **SELECTED PUBLICATIONS** Auth, Soviet Sociology of Science and The Social Context of Soviet Science. **CONTACT ADDRESS** American Univ, 4400 Massachusetts Ave, Washington, DC, 20016.

LUCAS, MARION BRUNSON
PERSONAL Born 09/09/1935, m, 1957, 3 children **DISCIPLINE** UNITED STATES HISTORY **EDUCATION** Univ SC, BA, 59, MA, 62, PhD, 65. **CAREER** Asst prof hist, Morehead State Univ, 64-66; prof hist, Western KY Univ, 66. **HONORS AND AWARDS** Phi Kappa Phi; Phi Alpha Theta. **MEMBERSHIPS** Southern Hist Asn; KY Hist Soc; Filson Club; KY Asn Tchr(s) Hist. **RESEARCH** Civil War Reconstruction hist; the Old South. **SELECTED PUBLICATIONS** Auth, Sherman and the Burning of Columbia, TX A&M Univ, 76; A History of Blacks in Kentucky, From Slavery to Segregation, 1760-1891, KY Hist Soc, 92. **CONTACT ADDRESS** Dept of Hist, Western Kentucky Univ, Bowling Green, KY, 42101-3576. **EMAIL** marion.lucas@wku.edu

LUCAS, PAUL
PERSONAL Born 09/22/1934, New York, NY **DISCIPLINE** EARLY MODERN AND MODERN EUROPEAN HISTORY **EDUCATION** Brandeis Univ, BA, 55; Princeton Univ, MA, 57, PhD, 63. **CAREER** From instr to assoc prof Europ hist, Wash Univ, 59-69; ASSOC PROF EUROP HIST, CLARK UNIV, 69-, Vis asst prof, Princeton Univ, 66-67; Am Coun Learned Soc fel, 67-68; vis lectr, Boston Univ, 73; mem, Inst Advan Studies, Princeton, NJ, 75-76. **MEMBERSHIPS** Int Comn Hist Rep and Parliamentary Insts; AHA; Conf Brit Studies. **RESEARCH** Quantitative analyses of French revolutionary assemblies, 1789-1799; French and English social and legal history, 1600-1850; European intellectual history, 1600-1850. **SELECTED PUBLICATIONS** Auth, Blackstone and the reform of the legal profession, English Hist Rev, 62; Blackstone and the natural law, Am J Legal Hist, 63; Edmund Burke's doctrine of prescription, Hist J, 68; Structure of politice in mid-eighteenth century Britain and its American colonies, William and Mary Quart, 71; Collective Biog of Lincoln's Inn, 1680-1804, J Mod Hist, 74. **CONTACT ADDRESS** Dept of Hist, Clark Univ, 950 Main St, Worcester, MA, 01610-1473.

LUCAS, PAUL ROBERT
PERSONAL Born 08/06/1940, Des Moines, IA, m, 1962, 2 children **DISCIPLINE** AMERICAN HISTORY **EDUCATION** Simpson Col, BA, 62; Univ Minn, PhD(hist), 70. **CAREER** Lectr, 67-70, asst prof, 70-76, ASSOC PROF AM HIST, IND UNIV, 76-, Assoc ed, Am Hist Rev, 78-80, actg ed, 80-81. **MEMBERSHIPS** Orgn Am Historians; AHA. **RESEARCH** American colonial history; American intellectual history; American social history. **SELECTED PUBLICATIONS** Auth, The Divine Dramatist--Whitefield, George and the Rise of Modern Evangelicalism, Amer Hist Rev, Vol 0098, 93; Congregational Communion--Clerical Friendship in the Anglo American Puritan Community, 1610-1692, J Amer Hist, Vol 0082, 95; Edwards, Jonathan--Puritan, Preacher, Philosopher, Amer Hist Rev, Vol 0100, 95; The Saving Remnant--Religion and the Settling of New-England, Amer Hist Rev, Vol 0102, 97; Stoddard, Solomon and the Origin of the Great Awakening in New England, Historian, Vol 0059, 97. **CONTACT ADDRESS** Dept of Hist, Indiana Univ, Bloomington, Bloomington, IN, 47405.

LUCAS, ROBERT HAROLD
PERSONAL Born 08/22/1933, Portland, OR **DISCIPLINE** MEDIEVAL HISTORY **EDUCATION** Univ Ore, BA, 54; Columbia Univ, MA, 58, PhD, 66. **CAREER** Instr medieval hist, Smith Col, 65-66; asst prof, Univ Calif, Irvine, 66-73; assoc prof, 73-80, prof hist, Williamette Univ, 80-, chmn dept, 81-. **HONORS AND AWARDS** Fulbright Scholarship, 59-60; res grant, Am Philos Soc, 70. **MEMBERSHIPS** Mediaeval Acad Am. **RESEARCH** Late medieval France and England. **SELECTED PUBLICATIONS** Auth, Two Notes on Jacques Legrand, Augustiniana, 62; ed, Le Livre du Corps de Policie par Christine de Pisan, Edition Critique, Droz, Geneva, 67; auth, Medieval French Translations of the Latin Classics, Speculum, 70; Ennoblement in Late Medieval France, Medieval Studies, 77. **CONTACT ADDRESS** Dept of History, Willamette Univ, 900 State St, Salem, OR, 97301-3931.

LUCKERT, KARL WILHELM
PERSONAL Born 11/18/1934, Winnenden-Hoefen, Germany, m, 1957, 3 children **DISCIPLINE** HISTORY OF RELIGIONS **EDUCATION** Univ Kans, BA, 63; Univ Chicago, MA, 67, PhD, 69. **CAREER** Vis lectr, rel, NCent Col, 68-69; asst prof humanities, Northern Ariz Univ, 69-79; assoc prof, 79-82, prof relig studies, Southwest Mo State Univ, 82-; gen ed, Am Tribal Relig series, Univ Nebr Press, 77-. **HONORS AND AWARDS** NEH res fel anthrop, Okla Univ, 72-73; Rockefeller Found Humanities res fel, 77-78; res assoc, Mus Northern Ariz, 77-; Burlington Northern Found Fac Achievement Award for Schol, 88; named hon prof, Univ Ningxia, China, 90; Excellence in Res Award, SMSU Found, 95. **MEMBERSHIPS** Am Acad Relig. **RESEARCH** American Indian religions; religion in evolution. **SELECTED PUBLICATIONS** Auth, The Navajo Hunter Tradition, Univ Ariz, 75; Olmec Religion: A Key to Middle America and Beyond, Okla Univ, 76; Navajo Mountain and Rainbow Bridge Religion, Mus Northern Ariz Press, 77; A Navajo Bringing-Home Ceremony, Mus Northern Ariz Univ, 78; Coyoteway, A Navajo Holyway Healing Ceremonial, Univ Ariz, 79; Egyptian Light and Hebrew Fire: Theological and Philosophical Roots of Christendom in Evolutionary Perspective, State Univ NY Press, 91; coauth, Myths and Legends of the Hui, a Muslim Chinese People, State Univ NY Press, 94; Kazakh Traditions in China, Univ Press Am, 98; Uighur Stories from Along the Silk Road, Univ Press Am, 98; author numerous journal articles. **CONTACT ADDRESS** Dept Relig Studies, Southwest Mo State Univ, 901 S National, Springfield, MO, 65804-0088. **EMAIL** luckert@dialnet.net

LUCKEY, EVELYN F.
PERSONAL Born 04/30/1926, Bellefonte, PA, d **DISCIPLINE** EDUCATION **EDUCATION** Central State Univ, 1945; OH State Univ, BA, BsEd, English, Psych 1947, MA English 1950, PhD Ed 1970. **CAREER** Columbus Public Schools, teacher 1957-66, evaluation asst 1965-67; OH State Univ, asst prof 1971-72; Columbus Public Schools, exec dir 1972-77, asst supt 1977-90; Otterbein College, Westerville, OH, asst prof, 1990-. **HONORS AND AWARDS** Outstanding Educator Awd Alpha Kappa Alpha 1978; Woman on the Move Moles 1978; Woman of the Year Omega Psi Phi 1980; Distinguished Kappan Awd Phi Delta Kappa 1981; Disting Alumnae Awd OH State Univ 1982; Certificate of Honor City of Columbus 1984; YWCA Woman of Achievement Award 1987, 1991; United Negro College Fund Eminent Scholar, 1990. **MEMBERSHIPS** Mem Amer Assoc of School Admin 1977-, Adv Bd of Urban Network of No Central Reg Ed Lab 1985-90, Assoc for Suprv & Curriculum Devel 1972-93, Natl Alliance of Black School Ed 1978-, Central OH Mktg Council 1984-89, Bd of Planned Parenthood of Central OH 1984-87; trustee, pres Bd of Public Libr of Columbus & Franklin Cty 1973-89; member, Links, Inc, 1988-; trustee, pres, board, Columbus Metropolitan Library, 1973-89; trustee, Central Ohio Marketing Council, 1984-89. **CONTACT ADDRESS** Otterbein Col, Westerville, OH, 43081.

LUCKINGHAM, BRADFORD FRANKLIN
PERSONAL Born 05/15/1934, Fitchburg, MA, m, 1963, 1 child **DISCIPLINE** AMERICAN HISTORY **EDUCATION** Northern Ariz Univ, BS, 61; Univ Mo, Columbia, MA, 62; Univ Calif, Davis, PhD(hist), 68. **CAREER** Asst prof hist, Ind Univ, Kokomo Campus, 68-70; asst prof, 70-74, ASSOC PROF HIST, ARIZ STATE UNIV, 74-. **RESEARCH** American urban history. **SELECTED PUBLICATIONS** Auth, Open Spaces, City Places, J West, Vol 0035, 96; Essays in 20th-Century New Mexico History, J West, Vol 0035, 96. **CONTACT ADDRESS** Dept of Hist, Arizona State Univ, Tempe, PO Box 872501, Tempe, AZ, 85287-2501.

LUDWIG, THEODORE MARK
PERSONAL Born 09/28/1936, Oxford, NE, m, 1960, 4 children **DISCIPLINE** HISTORY OF RELIGIONS, ASIAN RELIGIONS **EDUCATION** Concordia Sem St Louis, BA, 58, MDiv, 61, STM, 62, ThD, 63; Univ Chicago, PhD(Hist Relig), 75. **CAREER** Asst prof, 68-73, res prof, 79-80, assoc prof Theol, Valparaiso Univ, 74-, Missionary, Nihon Ruteru Kyokai, Japan, 63-67; res assoc Hist Relig, Univ Chicago, 73-75; dir Overseas Study Ctr Reutlingen, Ger, Valparaiso Univ, 76-78; Danforth assoc, 77-; Nat Endowment for Humanities fel, 81-82. **HONORS AND AWARDS** Distinguished teaching award, Valparaiso Univ, 79-80. **MEMBERSHIPS** Soc Bibl Lit; Am Acad Relig; Asn Asian Studies; Soc for Study of Japanese Religions. **RESEARCH** Ancient Near Eastern religions; Japanese religions; Japanese tea ceremony. **SELECTED PUBLICATIONS** Auth, Jeremiah's Book of Consolation, 68, Concordia Theol Monthly; The traditions of the establishing of the earth in Deutero-Isiah, J Bibl Lit, 73; The way of tea: a religioaesthetic mode of life, Hist Relig, 74; co-ed (with Frank Reynolds), Transitions and Transformations in the History of Religions: Essays in Honor of Joseph M Kitagawa, 80 & auth, Remember not the former things: Disjunction and transformation in Ancient Israel, In: Transitions and Transformations in the History of Religions: Essays in Honor of Joseph M Kitagawa, 80, E J Brill, Leiden; Christian self-understanding and other religions, Currents in Theol & Mission, 80; Before Rikyu: Religious and aesthetic influences in the early history of the tea ceremony, Monumenta Nipponica, 81; The Sacred Paths of the West, 94; The Sacred Paths: Understanding the Religions of the World, 96. **CONTACT ADDRESS** Dept of Theology, Valparaiso Univ, Valparaiso, IN, 46383-6493. **EMAIL** Ted.Ludwig@valpo.edu.

LUEBKE, FREDERICK CARL
PERSONAL Born 01/26/1927, Reedsburg, WI, m, 1951, 4 children **DISCIPLINE** AMERICAN HISTORY **EDUCATION** Concordia Col, Ill, BS, 50; Claremont Grad Sch, MA, 58; Univ Nebr, PhD(hist), 66. **CAREER** Prin, elem schs, 50-57; instr high sch, Calif, 57-61; from asst prof to assoc prof hist, Concordia Col, Nebr, 61-68; assoc prof, 68-72, PROF HIST, UNIV NEBR, LINCOLN, 72-, Danforth assoc, Danforth Found, 70-; sr Fulbright res fel, Univ Stuttgart, WGer, 74-75; fel state and local hist, Newberry Libr, Chicago, 77 and 78; ed, Great Plains Quart, 80-; nominating bd, Orgn Am Historians, 80-82; scholar-in-residence, Rockefeller Found Study Ctr, Bellagio, Italy, 82. **MEMBERSHIPS** Orgn Am Historians; Western Hist Asn; Immigration Hist Soc. **RESEARCH** American immigration history; Western frontier history; Nebraska history. **SELECTED PUBLICATIONS** Auth, The Mysteries of St Louis--a Novel, J Amer Ethnic Hist, Vol 0012, 93; Victorian West--Class and Culture in Kansas Cattle Towns, Great Plains Quart, Vol 0013, 93; Family, Church, and Market--a Mennonite Community in the Old and New World, Agr Hist, Vol 0068, 94; Under Western Skies--Nature and History in the American West, J West, Vol 0033, 94; Writing Western History--Essays on Major Western Historians, Great Plains Quart, Vol 0014, 94; The Persistence of Ethnicity--Dutch Calvinist Pioneers in Amsterdam, Montana, Great Plains Quart, Vol 0015, 95; The Progressive Context of the Nebraska Capitol + the Execution of Murals in the Nebraska State Capitol--the Collaboration of Goodhue and Tack, Great Plains Quart, Vol 0015, 95; Peopling the Plains--Who Settled Where in Frontier Kansas, Pac Hist Rev, Vol 0065, 96; Nebraska History--an Annotated Bibliography, Great Plains Quart, Vol 0017, 97. **CONTACT ADDRESS** Dept Hist, Univ Nebraska, Lincoln, NE, 68588.

LUEHRS, ROBERT BOICE
PERSONAL Born 10/05/1939, Portland, OR, m, 1965, 1 child **DISCIPLINE** EUROPEAN HISTORY **EDUCATION** Columbia Univ, AB, 61; WA Univ, AM, 63; Stanford Univ, PhD, 69. **CAREER** Instr Ger & mod Europ hist, Univ OR, 66-67; asst prof hist, 68-71, dir honors prog, 72-74, assoc prof, 71-80, prof hist, Ft Hays State Univ, 80, Ch of Hist Dept, 94-96. **MEMBERSHIPS** AAUP; Phi Kappa Phi. **RESEARCH** Am and Brit deism; the Scottish Enlightenment; Myth and magic in hist; Early twentieth-century children's lit. **SELECTED PUBLICATIONS** Auth, Franz Overbeck and the theologian as antichrist, Katallagete, summer 73; Christianity against history: Franz Overbeck's concept of the Finis Christianismi, Katallagete, summer 75; The problematic compromise: The early deism of Anthony Collins, In: Studies in Eighteenth Century Culture, Vol VI, Univ Wis, 77; L. Frank Baum and the Land of Oz: A children's author as social critic, Nineteenth Century, autumn 80; Reginald Scot and the witchcraft controversy of the Sixteenth Century, Fort Hays Studies, 85; Population and utopia in the thought of Robert Wallace, Eighteenth Century Studies; John Locke and Jean-Jacques Roussseau, In: Research Guide to European Historical Biography, 1500 to the Present, Beacham Publ, 92-93. **CONTACT ADDRESS** Dept of Hist, Fort Hays State Univ, 600 Park St, Hays, KS, 67601-4009. **EMAIL** hirl@fhsuvm.fhsu.edu

LUFRANO, RICHARD
DISCIPLINE MODERN CHINESE HISTORY **EDUCATION** SUNY, BA, 74; Columbia, PhD, 87. **CAREER** Hist, Columbia Univ **SELECTED PUBLICATIONS** Auth, Jolting the Age: Xu Zi and the Evolution of Qing Statecraft Thinking, 97, Honorable Merchants: Self Cultivation and Commerce in Late Imperial China, 97. **CONTACT ADDRESS** Columbia Univ, 2960 Broadway, New York, NY, 10027-6902.

LUFT, DAVID SHEERS
PERSONAL Born 05/06/1944, Youngstown, OH, m, 1967, 1 child **DISCIPLINE** MODERN EUROPEAN INTELLECTUAL HISTORY **EDUCATION** Wesleyan Univ, BA, 66; Harvard Univ, MA, 67, PhD(mod Europ hist), 72. **CAREER** ASST PROF MOD EUROP HIST, UNIV CALIF, SAN DIEGO, 72-. **HONORS AND AWARDS** Excellence in Teaching, Revelle Col, Univ Calif, San Diego, 75. **RESEARCH** German and Austrian intellectual and social history since the 18th century. **SELECTED PUBLICATIONS** Auth, Philosophy From Vienna, Mod Austrian Lit, Vol 0026, 93; The Jews Body, J Mod Hist, Vol 0066, 94; Being and German History--Historiographical Notes on the Heidegger Controversy, Cent Europ Hist, Vol 0027, 94. **CONTACT ADDRESS** Dept of Hist and Soc Sci, Univ of Calif San Diego, La Jolla, CA, 92093.

LUKACS, JOHN ADALBERT
PERSONAL Born 01/31/1924, Budapest, Hungary, 2 children **DISCIPLINE** HISTORY **EDUCATION** Univ Budapest, PhD, 46. **CAREER** Lectr, Hungarian Inst Int Affairs, 45-46 & Columbia Univ, 46-47; from lectr to assoc prof, 47-65, prof hist, Chestnut Hill Col, Penn, 65-93, vis lectr, La Salle Col, 49-83; vis assoc prof, Columbia Univ, 54-55; vis prof, Univ Pa, 64, 67 & 68, 94-96; Johns Hopkins Sch Advan Int Studies, 70-71, vis prof Fletcher Sch Law, 72 & 73; vis prof Princeton Univ, 88; vis prof, Kozgazdasagi Univ, and Eotvos Univ, Budapest, 91. **HONORS AND AWARDS** Elected pres Am Cath hist Asn, 77; fel Soc of Am Hist, 82; hon doctorate, la Salle Univ, 89; Ingersoll Prize, 91; Cross of Merit of the Republic of Hungary, 94. **MEMBERSHIPS** Am Cath Hist Asn (pres, 77). **RESEARCH** Modern European history; diplomatic history; historiography; American history. **SELECTED PUBLICATIONS** Auth, Outgrowing Democracy: A History of the United States in the Twentieth Century, Doubleday, 84; auth, Budapest 1900: A Historical Portrait of a City and Its Cultures, Weidenfeld & Nicolson, 89; auth, Confessions of An Original Sinner, Ticknor & Fields, 90; auth, The Duel: The Eighty-Day Struggle Between Churchill and Hitler, Ticknor & Fields, 91; auth, The End of the Twentieth Century (And the End of the Modern Age) Ticknor & Fields, 93; auth, Destinations Past, Missouri, 94; auth, George F. Kennan and the Origins of Containment, 1944-1946: The Kennan-Lukacs Correspondence, Missouri, 97; auth, The Hitler of History, Knopf, 97; auth, A Thread of Years, Yale, 98. **CONTACT ADDRESS** 129 Valley Park Rd, Phoenixville, PA, 19460.

LUMIN, BERNARD
PERSONAL Born 10/15/1923, Washington, DC, m, 1957 **DISCIPLINE** PSYCHOLOGY **EDUCATION** PA State Univ, PhD, 58; George Washington Univ, MA, 53; BA, 52. **CAREER** Prof Dept of Psychol, 76-; City Chm Dept Psychol, 76-83; Univ MO-Kansas, Dir Clin Training, Dept of Psychol, 74-76; Univ of Houston, Dir of Psychol, 67-74; Greater Kansas City Mental Health Found. **HONORS AND AWARDS** Curators Prof, Univ of MO, 88; N T Veatech Award for Res and Creative Activity, 81; Unic MO-Kansas City; Listed in Who's Who in the World; Who's Who in Amer. **MEMBERSHIPS** Amer Psychol Assoc; Amer Assoc for the Advacement of Sci. **RESEARCH** Measurement and Mgt of Mood. **SELECTED PUBLICATIONS** Ecological and community approaches to disaster response, Washington DC, forthcoming; Taylor & Fracis, Hanson P G & Lubin B, Answers to most frequently asked questions about organization development Newbury Park CA, Sage Publishing Co, 95; Psychological Aspects of Disaster, NY, Wiley and Sons, 89; Psychological Dimension in Personal Injury Cases, Estalblishin damages in catastrophic injury litigation, pp35-40, Tucson AZ Lawyers and Judges Publ, 94; The mental health of incaracerated persons, Greenwood Press, fprthcoming; Multiple Affect Adjective List-Revised 3rd ed, San Diego CA Edits, 98; Research in professional consultation and consultation for organizational change: An annotated bibilography, Grenwoood Press, 74-95. **CONTACT ADDRESS** Dept Psychol, Univ of MO, Kansas City, MO, 64110. **EMAIL** Lubin@cctr.umkc.edu

LUMSDEN, IAN G.
PERSONAL Born 06/08/1945, Montreal, PQ, Canada **DISCIPLINE** ART HISTORY **EDUCATION** McGill Univ, BA, 68; Mus Mgt Inst, Univ Calif Berkeley, 91. **CAREER** Cur art dept, NB Mus St John, 69; cur, 69-83, DIR, BEAVERBROOK ART GALLERY, 83-; dir, Artsatlantic, 94-. **MEMBERSHIPS** Art Mus Dirs Org; Material Hist Steering Comt Univ NB; adv comt, Atlantic Conserv Ctr, Can Conserv Inst; Can Mus Asn; Atlantic Prov Art Gallery Asn; Am Asn Mus. **SELECTED PUBLICATIONS** Auth, New Brunswick Landscape Artists of the 19th Century, 69; auth, From Sickert to Dali: International Portraits, 76; auth, Bloomsbury Painters and Their Circle, 76; auth, The Murray and Marguerite Vaughan Inuit Print Collection, 81; auth, Drawings by Carol Fraser 1948-1986, 87; auth, Gainsborough in Canada, 91; auth, Early Views of British North America, 94. **CONTACT ADDRESS** Beaverbrook Art Gallery, PO Box 605, Fredericton, NB, E3B 5A6.

LUND, JEROME A.
PERSONAL Born 09/12/1948, Willmar, MN, m, 1988, 3 children **DISCIPLINE** ANCIENT SEMITIC LANGUAGES **EDUCATION** Hebrew Univ, PhD, 89; LA Baptist Theol Sem, MDiv, 73. **CAREER** Assoc res scholar, 90-, Hebrew Union College. **HONORS AND AWARDS** James Montgomery fel. **MEMBERSHIPS** AOS; SBL; IBR. **RESEARCH** Aramaic and Hebrew Languages; Ancient Bible Versions. **SELECTED PUBLICATIONS** The Old Testament in Syriac according to the Peshitta Version, Concordance to the Pentateuch, prepared by PG Borbone, J Cook, KD Jenner, DM Walter in collaboration with JA Lund and MP Weitzman, Leiden Brill, 97; Sepher Bereshit Jerusalem: Caspari Center, 94, a study book on the book of Genesis; The Third and Forth Oracles of Balaam in the Peshitta and Targums, in: Targum Studies 2: Targum and Peshitta, ed, Paul V Flesher, Atlanta, Scholars Press, 98; The Noun mattar Prison: A possible Ghost Word in the Lexicon of Middle Western Aramaic, Orientalia, 97. **CONTACT ADDRESS** 3101 Clifton Ave, Cincinnati, OH, 45220. **EMAIL** JLund@cn.huc.edu

LUNDE, ERIK SHELDON
PERSONAL Born 10/16/1940, Hanover, NH, m, 1963, 2 children **DISCIPLINE** AMERICAN HISTORY, FILM HISTORY, FILM STUDIES **EDUCATION** Harvard Univ, AB, 63; Univ Md, MA, 66, PhD(Am Hist), 70. **CAREER** Asst prof Am Hist, Marquette Univ, 69-70; asst prof, 70-74, assoc prof, 74-79, prof Am Thought & Lang, Mich State Univ, 79-. **HONORS AND AWARDS** Outstanding Teacher Award, Mich State Univ Chapter, Golden Key National Honor Society, 94. **MEMBERSHIPS** Orgn Am Historians. **RESEARCH** Auth, Horace Greeley, G K Hall, 81; Civil War and Reconstruction; American intellectual history; American studies. **SELECTED PUBLICATIONS** Co-ed with Douglas Noverr, Film Studies and Film History, Markus Wiener, 89; **CONTACT ADDRESS** Dept of American Thought & Lang, Michigan State Univ, 289 Bessey Hall, East Lansing, MI, 48824-1033.

LUNENFELD, MARVIN
PERSONAL Born 09/10/1934, New York, NY, m, 1960, 1 child **DISCIPLINE** EARLY MODERN EUROPEAN & SPANISH HISTORY **EDUCATION** City Col NY, BBA, 57 NY Univ, MA, 63, PhD, 68. **CAREER** Lectr hist, Overseas Prog, Univ Md, 64; instr, City Col NY, 67-68; instr, Rutgers Univ, 68-70; Assoc Prof History, DISTINGUISHED TEACHING PROF EMER, DEPT OF HISTORY, STATE UNIV NY COL FREDONIA, 70. Lectr hist, New Sch Social Res, 68-; Rockeller fel, Villa Serbelloni Residence, 94; fel, Aston Magna Acad on Baroque Spain & Latin Am, 95; Malone fel, Nat Counc US-Arab Rel, 96; NEH fel, 96-97. **HONORS AND AWARDS** Acad World Star Int Acad Auth Educ Moscow, 98. **MEMBERSHIPS** Soc Span & Port Hist Studies; AHA. **RESEARCH** Urban history; police and the military; Spanish Inquisition. **SELECTED PUBLICATIONS** Auth, The Council of the Santa Hermandad: A Study of Ferdinand and Isabella's Pacification Forces, Univ Miami, 70; Keepers of the City: The Corregidores of Isabella I of Castile (1474-1504), Cambridge Univ Press, 87; Los Corregidores de Isabel La Catolica, Ed Labor, 89; The 1492 Reader, Newberry Library, 89; 1492: Discovery, Invasion, En-

counter, Heath & Co, 90; The Real World: How to Use College to Get Your Career Started, Semester Press, 89; College Basics: How to Start Right and Finish Strong, Kendall/Hunt Publ Co, 92. **CONTACT ADDRESS** 231 Norwood Ave, Buffalo, NY, 14222. **EMAIL** Mlunenfe@sescva.esc.edu

LUPIA, JOHN N.
PERSONAL Born 05/18/1952, Orange, NJ, d, 6 children **DISCIPLINE** ART HISTORY **EDUCATION** City Coll CUNY, MA, 82; Rutgers Univ, PhD candidate, 82-87, MLS, 93. **CAREER** Prof, 83-87, Ken Univ; Prof, 87-90, Seton Hall Univ; Prof, 91-96, Brookdale Comm Coll; Prof in library, 96-98, Kean Univ. **HONORS AND AWARDS** Rutgers Univ Fel, Headstart Sev Awd. **MEMBERSHIPS** CBAA, ASP. **RESEARCH** Biblical archaeology, Biblical textual criticism, philosophy, New Testament Studies, papyrology, information science, medieval & renaissance studies. **SELECTED PUBLICATIONS** Contrib auth, 21 articles for The Dictionary of Art, London Macmillan Pub Ltd, 95, Who's Minding the Church? A Brief Review of the Papacy 1100-1520, in: The Medieval & Renaissance Times, 94. **CONTACT ADDRESS** 501 North Ave, Apt B1, Elizabeth, NJ, 07208-1731.

LURIE, ALISON
PERSONAL Born 09/03/1926, Chicago, IL, m, 1996, 3 children **DISCIPLINE** CHILDREN'S LITERATURE, FOLKLORE **EDUCATION** Radcliffe Col, AB, 47. **CAREER** Lectr Eng, 69-73, adj assoc prof, 73-76, assoc prof, 76-79, Prof Eng, Cornell Univ, 79-, Frederic J Whiton Prof Am Lit, Cornell Univ, Yaddo Found fel, 63, 64 & 66; Guggenheim fel, 65; Rockefeller Found fel, 67. **HONORS AND AWARDS** New York State Cultural Coun Found Grant (CAPS), 72-73; Am Ac Arts & Lett Award, Fiction, 84; Pulitzer Prize, Fiction, 85; Radcliffe Col Alumnae Recognition Award, 87; Prix Femina Etranger, 89 **MEMBERSHIPS** MLA; Aaup; Children's Lit Asn; Pen Club; Author's Guild. **SELECTED PUBLICATIONS** Auth, Love and Friendship, Macmillan, 62; The Nowhere City, Coward McCann, 65; Imaginary Friends, 67, Coward McCann; Real People, 69 & The War Between the Tates, 74, Random House; V R Lang: Poems and Plays, with Memoir by Alison Lurie, Random House, 75; co-ed, The Garland Library of Children's Classics (73 vols), Garland Publ, 76; auth, Only Children, Random House, 79; Clever Gretchen and Other Forgotten Folk Tales, Crowell, 80; The Heavenly Zoo, Farrar Strauss, 81; The Language of Clothes, Random House, 81; Foreign Affairs, Random House, 84; The Truth abut Lorin Jones, Little Brown, 88; Don't Tell the Grownups: Subversive Children's Literature, Little Brown, 90; Women and Ghosts, Doubleday, 94; The Last Resort, Holt, 98; ed, The Oxford Book of Modern Fairy Tales. **CONTACT ADDRESS** Eng Dept, Cornell Univ, 252 Goldwin Smith Hall, Ithaca, NY, 14853-0001. **EMAIL** al28@cornell.edu

LUSIGNAN, SERGE
PERSONAL Born 10/22/1943, Montreal, PQ, Canada, m, 1967 **DISCIPLINE** MEDIEVAL INTELLECTUAL HISTORY **EDUCATION** Col Andre Grasset, BA, 64; Univ Montreal, MA, 67 and 68, PhD(medieval studies), 71. **CAREER** Res asst, 71-72, asst prof, 72-77, ASSOC PROF MEDIEVAL STUDIES, UNIV MONTREAL, 77-, CHMN DEPT, 77-. **MEMBERSHIPS** Medieval Acad Am; Int Soc Study Medieval Philos. **RESEARCH** Medieval encyclopedia; 13th century logic; text processing by computer. **SELECTED PUBLICATIONS** Auth, Imaging Aristotle--Verbal and Visual Representation in 14th-Century France, Moyen Age, Vol 0102, 96. **CONTACT ADDRESS** Inst of Medieval Studies, Univ of Montreal, Montreal, PQ, H3C 3J7.

LUTZ, JESSIE GREGORY
PERSONAL Born 08/06/1925, Halifax, NC, m, 1948 **DISCIPLINE** HISTORY **EDUCATION** Univ NC, BA, 46; Univ Chicago, MA, 48; Cornell Univ, PhD(Chinese hist), 55. **CAREER** From instr to assoc prof, 56-70, chmn dept, 72-75, PROF HIST, RUTGERS UNIV, 70-, ACTG DIR INT PROG, 75-, Am Asn Univ Women fel, 63-64; Soc Sci Res Coun and Am Coun Learned Socs fels, 70-71. **HONORS AND AWARDS** Lindback Found Award, 68; Bk Prize, Berkshire Conf Women Historians, 73. **MEMBERSHIPS** AHA; Asn Asian Studies; Berkshire Conf Women Historians. **RESEARCH** Modern Chinese nationalism, education, student movements, missions. **SELECTED PUBLICATIONS** Auth, A Phoenix Transformed--the Reconstruction of Education in Postwar Hong Kong, Amer Hist Rev, Vol 0100, 95. **CONTACT ADDRESS** Rutgers State Univ, New Brunswick, NJ, 08903.

LUZBETAK, LOUIS JOSEPH
PERSONAL Born 09/19/1918, Joliet, IL **DISCIPLINE** LINGUISTIC ANALYSIS, CULTURAL ANTHROPOLOGY **EDUCATION** Divine Word Sem, BA, 42; Pontif Gregorian Univ, STL, 46, JCB, 47; Univ Fribourg, PhD(anthrop), 51. **CAREER** Prof anthrop, ling and missiology, Divine Word Sem, Ill, 51-52, 56-58; lectr and summer asst prof appl anthrop, Cath Univ Am, 60-65; exec dir, Ctr Appl Res in Apostolate, Washington, DC, 65-73; pres, Divine Word Col, Iowa, 73-78; ED, ANTHROPOS, INT REV ETHNOLOGY AND LING, 79-, Dir, Anthropos Inst, St Augustin bei Sieberg, WGer, 51-; Ford Found fel, 52-54; cult anthrop and ling field work, New Guinea, 52-56; lectr appl anthrop, Ctr Intercult Formation, Cuernavaca, Mex, 60-65; Ctr for Intercult Commun, Cath Univ PR, 60-65; rector, Divine Word Col, DC, 68-73; Walsh-Price fel, Ctr Mission Studies, Maryknoll, NY, 78-79. **HONORS AND AWARDS** Pierre Charles Award, Fordham Univ, 64. **MEMBERSHIPS** Fel Am Anthrop Asn; Cath Anthrop Asn (vpres, 61-62, pres, 62-69); Ling Soc Am; Soc Appl Anthrop; Am Soc Missiology (pres, 75-76). **SELECTED PUBLICATIONS** Auth, Schmidt, Wilhelm, an Ethnologist for All Seasons, Cath Hist Rev, Vol 0079, 93. **CONTACT ADDRESS** 5205 Sankt Augustin 1, 52045.

LYDOLPH, PAUL E.
PERSONAL Born 01/04/1924, Bonaparte, IA, m, 1966, 5 children **DISCIPLINE** GEOGRAPHY **EDUCATION** Univ WI, PhD, 55. **CAREER** Assoc prof, 52-59, Los Angeles St Col; chmn, 59-96, geo dept, Univ WI. **HONORS AND AWARDS** Ford Found Fel; Festschrift pub in my honor. **MEMBERSHIPS** Asn of Amer Geographers, Amer Asn for the Advancement of Slavic Stud. **RESEARCH** Geography of the USSR; climatology **SELECTED PUBLICATIONS** Auth, Geography of the USSR: Topical Analysis, Misty Valley Pub, 64, 70, 79, 90; auth, The Climate of the Earth, Rowman & Allenheld, 85; auth, Climates of the Soviet Union, Vol 7, World Survey of Climatology, Elsevier, 77. **CONTACT ADDRESS** No 8328 Snake Rd, Elkhart Lake, WI, 53020-2011.

LYE, WILLIAM FRANK
PERSONAL Born 02/19/1930, Kimberley, BC, Canada, m, 1953, 4 children **DISCIPLINE** AFRICAN HISTORY **EDUCATION** Utah State Univ, BSc, 59; Univ Calif, Berkeley, MA, 59; Univ Calif, Los Angeles, PhD(African hist), 69. **CAREER** Prof hist and polit sci, Ricks Col, 59-63 and 67-68; from asst prof to assoc prof African hist, 68-73, actg head dept hist and geog, 69-70, head dept, 70-76, PROF AFRICAN HIST, UTAH STATE UNIV, 73-, DEAN COL HUMANITIES, ARTS AND SOC SCI, 76-. **MEMBERSHIPS** African Studies Asn; Western Asn Africanists. **RESEARCH** History of South African Bantu-Sotho; precolonial and early colonial South African history, particularly of the Sotho speaking peoples. **SELECTED PUBLICATIONS** Auth, A South African Kingdom--the Pursuit of Security in 19th-Century Lesotho, J Interdisciplinary Hist, Vol 0026, 95; The Dust Rose Like Smoke--the Subjugation of the Zulu and the Sioux, Amer Hist Rev, Vol 0100, 95. **CONTACT ADDRESS** Col of Humanities Arts and Soc Sci, Utah State Univ, Logan, UT, 84322.

LYMAN, J. REBECCA
DISCIPLINE CHURCH HISTORY **EDUCATION** W Mich Univ, BA; Cath Univ Am, MA; Univ Oxford, DPhil. **CAREER** Samuel M. Garrett prof, Church Divinity Sch Pacific **SELECTED PUBLICATIONS** Auth, The Making of a Heretic: The Life of Origen in Epiphanius' Panarion 64, Studia Patristica, 97; A Topography of Heresy: Mapping the Rhetorical Creation of Arianism, Arianism after Arius, Edinburgh, 93; Lex Orandi: Heresy, Orthodoxy, and Popular Religion, The Making and Remaking of Christian Doctrine, Oxford, 93; Christology and Cosmology: Models of Divine Action in Origen, Eusebius, and Athanasius, Oxford UP, 93. **CONTACT ADDRESS** Church Divinity Sch of the Pacific, 2451 Ridge Rd, Berkeley, CA, 94709-1217.

LYMAN, R. LEE
PERSONAL Born 01/13/1951, Dayton, WA, m, 1974, 2 children **DISCIPLINE** ANTHROPOLOGY **EDUCATION** WA State Univ, BA, 72, MA, 76; Univ WA, PhD, 82. **CAREER** Asst prof, OR State Univ, 82-86; asst prof, 86-89, assoc prof, 89-95, prof, Univ MO-Columbia, 95-. **RESEARCH** North Am archaeology; zooarchaeology. **SELECTED PUBLICATIONS** Auth, Vertebrate Taphonomy, Cambridge Univ Press, 94; sr ed with M J O'Brien and R C Dunnell, American Culture History: Fundamentals of Time, Space, and Form, Plenum Press, 97; The Rise and Fall of Culture History, sr author with M J O'Brien and R C Dunnell, 97; White Goats, White Lies: The Abuse of Science in Olympic National Park, Univ UT Press, 98; James A Ford and the Growth of Americanist Archaeology, coauth with M J O'Brien, Univ MO Press, 98; Seriation, Superposition, and Interdigitation: A History of Americanist Graphic Depictions of Cultural Change, Am Antiquity, sr auth with S Wolverton and M J O'Brien, 98; Basic Incompatabilities between Evolutionary and Behavioral Archaeology, Am Antiquity, co-auth with M J O'Brien and R Leonard, 98; Measuring Late Quaternary Ursid Dimunition in the Midwest, Quaternary Res, co-auth with S Wolverton, 98; The Goals of Evolutionary Archaeology: History and Explanation, Current Anthropol, in press, sr auth with M J O'Brien, 98; numerous other publications, several forthcoming. **CONTACT ADDRESS** Dept of Anthropology, Univ of Missouri, Columbia, 107 Swallow Hall, Columbia, MO, 65211. **EMAIL** anthrull@showme.missouri.edu

LYMAN, RICHARD B.
DISCIPLINE HISTORY **EDUCATION** Bowdoin Coll, BA, 57; Harvard Univ, MA, 60, PhD, 74. **CAREER** PROF, HIST, DEPT CH AND DIR, E ASIAN STUD, SIMMONS COLL **MEMBERSHIPS** Am Antiquarian Soc **RESEARCH** Lincoln Family, 1810-1840. **SELECTED PUBLICATIONS** Auth, "'What Is Done in My Absence?': Levi Lincoln's Oakman, Massachusetts, Farm Workers, 1807-20, 89. **CONTACT ADDRESS** Hist Dept, Simmons Coll, 300 The Fenway, Boston, MA, 02115. **EMAIL** rlyman@uvmsvax.simmons.edu

LYNCH, HOLLIS R.
PERSONAL Born 04/21/1935, Port-of-Spain, Trinidad and Tobago, d **DISCIPLINE** AFRICAN STUDIES **EDUCATION** British Columbia, BA 1960; Univ of London, PhD 1964. **CAREER** Univ of IFE Nigeria, lecturer 1964-66; Roosevelt Univ Chicago, assoc prof 1966-68; State Univ of NY at Buffalo, assoc prof 1968-69; Columbia Univ, prof 1969-; Inst of African Studies Columbia Univ, dir 1971-74, 1985-90. **HONORS AND AWARDS** Recipient Commonwealth Fellow London Univ 1961-64; Hoover Nat Fellow Stanford Univ 1973-74; fellow Woodrow Wilson Intl Ctr for Scholars 1976; ACLS (Am Council of Learned Soc) Fellowship 1978-79. **MEMBERSHIPS** Fmem African Studies Assn; Assn for Study of Afro-Am Life & History; Am Historical Assn. **SELECTED PUBLICATIONS** Apartheid in Historical Prespective: A Case For Divestment, Columbia College Today, 1985; The Foundation of American-Nigerian Ties: Nigerian Students in the United States, 1939-48, Black Ivory, The Pan-African Magazine, 1989; author Edward Wilmot Blyden Pan Negro Patriot 1967 & The Black Urban Condition 1973; Black Africa 1973; "Black Am Radicals & Liberaton of Africa" 1978; "Black Spokesman" 1970; "Selected Letters of Edward W Blyden" (with a foreword by Pres Leopold Sedar Senghor) 1978.. **CONTACT ADDRESS** Inst of African Studies, Columbia Univ, New York, NY, 10027.

LYNCH, JOHN EDWARD
PERSONAL Born 10/21/1924, New York, NY **DISCIPLINE** MEDIEVAL HISTORY **EDUCATION** St Paul's Col, AB, 47; Univ Toronto, MA, 56, PhD(philos), 65; Pontifical Inst Medieval Studies, Toronto, MSL, 59. **CAREER** Prof ecclesiastical hist, St Paul's Col, 59-73; PROF HIST, CATH UNIV AM, 66-, PROF HIST CANON LAW, 68-, CHMN DEPT HIST CANON LAW, 74-. **MEMBERSHIPS** AHA; Am Soc Church Hist; Am Cath Hist Asn; Canon Law Soc Am; AAUP. **RESEARCH** Early CHURCH HIST; Medieval Canon Law. **SELECTED PUBLICATIONS** Auth, The 73rd Annual Meeting of the American Catholic Historical Association, Cath Hist Rev, Vol 0079, 93; The 2 Cities - Medieval Europe, Ad-1050-1320, Church Hist, Vol 0063, 94: James of Viterbo--'De Regimine Christiano'--'On Christian Government', Church Hist, Vol 0065, 96. **CONTACT ADDRESS** Catholic Univ of America, 3015 Fourth St NE, Washington, DC, 20064.

LYNCH, JOSEPH HOWARD
PERSONAL Born 11/21/1943, Springfield, MA, m, 1965, 3 children **DISCIPLINE** MEDIEVAL & CHURCH HISTORY **EDUCATION** Boston Col, BA, 65; Harvard Univ, MA, 66, PhD, 71. **CAREER** Vis asst prof hist, Univ Ill, Urbana, 70-71; asst prof & asst dir Ctr Medieval & Renaissance Studies, 71-77, assoc prof hist, 77-85, dir ctr Medieval & Renaissance Studies, 78-83, prof hist, Ohio State Univ, 85. **HONORS AND AWARDS** Am Coun Learned Soc fel, 75, Inst Advanced Study, 88, NEH Fel, 87-88 **MEMBERSHIPS** Mediaeval Acad Am; Soc Relig Higher Educ; AHA; Am Cath Hist Assoc; Int Sermon Studies; Assoc Research History of monasticism; Medieval church hist. **RESEARCH** History of monasticism; Medieval church history. **SELECTED PUBLICATIONS** Auth, Spiritale Vinculum: the Vocabulary of Spiritual Kinship in Early Medieval Europe, 87; The Medieval Church: A Brief History, 92; auth, Christianizing Kinship: Ritual Sponsorship in Anglo-Saxon England, 98. **CONTACT ADDRESS** Dept of History, Ohio State Univ, 230 W 17th Ave, Columbus, OH, 43210-1361. **EMAIL** lynch.1@osu.edu

LYNN, JOHN A.
PERSONAL Born 03/18/1943, Glenview, IL, m, 1965, 2 children **DISCIPLINE** EARLY MODERN EUROPEAN HISTORY/MILITARY HISTORY **EDUCATION** Univ Ill Urbana Champaign, BA, 64; Univ Cal Davis, MA, 67; Univ Cal Los Angeles, PhD, 73. **CAREER** Vis Asst Prof, Ind Univ, 72-73; Asst Prof, Univ Maine, 73- 77; Asst Prof, Assoc Prof, PROF, UNIV ILL URBANA CHAMPAIGN, 78-. **HONORS AND AWARDS** Oppenheimer Prof of Marine Corps Warfighting Strategy, Univ Quantico, VA **MEMBERSHIPS** Soc Military Hist, Soc Fr Hist Studies, Am Hist Asn **RESEARCH** Early modern military hist. **SELECTED PUBLICATIONS** Auth, The Wars of Louis XIV, 1667-1714, 99, Longman, Ltd; auth, Giant of the Grand Siecle: the French Army, 1610-1715, 87, Cambridge Univ Press; auth, The Bayonets of the Republic: Motivation and Tactics in the Army of Revolutionary France, 1791- 94, rev ed 96, Westview Press; ed, Feeding Mars: Logistics in Western Warfare from the Middle Ages to the Present, 93, Westview Press; auth, "The Embattled Future of Academic Military History," Jour Military Hist, Oct 97; auth, The Evolution of Army Style in the Modern West, 800-2000," Int Hist Rev, Aug 96; auth, "War of Annihilation, War of Attrition, and War of Legitimacy: A New- Clausewitzian Approach to Twentieth-Century Conflicts," Marine Corps Gazette, Oct 96; auth, "Recalculating French Army Growth During the Gran Siecle, 1610-1715," Fr Hist Studies, Fall 94; auth, "How War Fed War:

The Tax of Violence and Contributions During the Gran Siecle," Jour Modern Hist, June 93. **CONTACT ADDRESS** Univ of Illinois, Urbana-Champaign, 810 S Wright, Urbana, IL, 61801. **EMAIL** j-lynn@uiuc.edu

LYNN, KENNETH SCHUYLER
PERSONAL Born 06/17/1923, Cleveland, OH, m, 1948, 3 children **DISCIPLINE** HISTORY **EDUCATION** Harvard Univ, AB, 47, MA, 50, PhD, 54. **CAREER** Instr, 54-55, Harvard Univ; from asst prof to prof Eng, 55-68, prof, 68-69, Am studies, Fed City Col; prof, 69-, Johns Hopkins Univ, vis prof, 58, Copenhagen Univ & Univ Madrid, 63-64; assoc ed, 62-, Daedalus & New Eng Quart. **MEMBERSHIPS** AHA; Am Studies Assn; MLA. **SELECTED PUBLICATIONS** Auth, Hemingway, 87; auth, Charlie Chaplin and His Times, 97. **CONTACT ADDRESS** 1709 Hoban Rd NW, Washington, DC, 20007.

LYNN, MARY CONSTANCE
PERSONAL Born 12/16/1943, Schnectady, NY, m, 1973, 2 children **DISCIPLINE** INTERDISCIPLINARY STUDIES **EDUCATION** Elmira Col, BA, 64; Univ Rochester, PhD(hist), 75. **CAREER** Lectr hist, Univ Col, Univ Rochester, 68-69; instr, 69-70, from instr to Assoc Prof, 70-92, PROF AM STUDIES, SKIDMORE COL, 92-, Chmn Dept, 77-87; Adv, Univ Without Walls, Skidmore Col, 71-74; consult, NY State Historian Residence Prog, 79-80; gov fac, Regents' External Degree, Univ State NY, 79-84. **HONORS AND AWARDS** Phi Beta Kappa. **MEMBERSHIPS** Am Studies Asn; Orgn Am Historians. **RESEARCH** History of women in America; popular culture and literature; 20th century United States. **SELECTED PUBLICATIONS** Auth, Women in 17th century New England, Empire State Col, 73; ed, Women's Liberation in the 20th Century, John Wiley & Sons, 75; co-ed, The Black Middle Class, Skidmore Col, 80; ed, An Eyewitness Account of the American Revolution and New England Life: The Journal of J.F. Wasmus, Greenwood Press, 90; auth, The American Revolution, Garrison Life in French Canada and New York: Journal of an Officer in the Prinz Friedrich Regiment, 1776-1783, Greenwood Press, 93; The Specht Journal: A Military Journal of the Burgoyne Campaign, Greenwood Press, 95. **CONTACT ADDRESS** Dept of Am Studies, Skidmore Col, 815 N Broadway, Saratoga Springs, NY, 12866-1698. **EMAIL** mcl@skidmore.edu

LYONS, BONNIE
DISCIPLINE FINE ARTS AND HUMANITIES **EDUCATION** Newcomb Col, BA; Tulane Univ, MA, PhD. **CAREER** Prof; taught at, Newcomb Col, Boston Univ; Fulbright vis prof, Inst for Am Stud in Rome, Univ Haifa & Univ Tel Aviv; Fulbright sr lectr, Aristotelian Univ, Thessaloniki, Greece, Ctr Univ & Autonoma Univ Barcelona, Spain. **HONORS AND AWARDS** UTSA Res Leave; 3 UTSA Fac Res Awd(s); 2 Fulbright Prof; UTSA President's Distinguished Achievement Awd, Tchg Excellence, 91; AMOCO Tchg Awd, 85. **RESEARCH** 19th and 20th-century Am lit; 20th-century Brit and Continental lit; mod drama; the Eng Novel; Am Jewish lit; women in lit; drama as a genre. **SELECTED PUBLICATIONS** Auth, Henry Roth: The Man and His Work, Cooper Square Publ, 77; publ in, Stud in Jewish Am Lit; on Roth, Hellman, Bellow, Schwartz, Olsen, Chopin, Atwood. **CONTACT ADDRESS** Col of Fine Arts and Hum, Univ Texas at San Antonio, 6900 N Loop 1604 W, San Antonio, TX, 78249. **EMAIL** blyons@lonestar.utsa.edu

LYONS, CLARE A.
DISCIPLINE HISTORY **EDUCATION** Lewis & Clark Coll, BS, 80; Univ Calif at Santa Barbara, MA, 89; Yale Univ, PhD, 96. **CAREER** ASST PROF, HIST, UNIV MARYLAND AT COLLEGE PARK **HONORS AND AWARDS** Eggleston Prize, Yale Univ, 97. **MEMBERSHIPS** Am Antiquarian Soc **SELECTED PUBLICATIONS** Auth, "Sex Among the 'Rabble': Gender Transitions in the Age of Revolution, Philadelphia 1750-1830," Yale, 96. **CONTACT ADDRESS** Hist Dept, Univ of Maryland, 2115 Francis Scott Key Blvd, College Park, MD, 20742. **EMAIL** cl130@umail.umd.edu

LYONS, DECLAN P.
PERSONAL Born 12/03/1961, Galway, Ireland **DISCIPLINE** ANCIENT CLASSICS, FRENCH **EDUCATION** Nat Univ Ireland, BA; Univ Dublin, MLitt, 90; SUNY-Buffalo, PhD, 98. **CAREER** Tchg asst, SUNY-Buffalo, 88-92; res scholar, Univ de Geneve-Suisse, 92-93; asst prof Classics, Franciscan Univ, 94- . **HONORS AND AWARDS** Coun Euro res fel, Switz, 92-93; Ital Cult inst res awd, 98. **MEMBERSHIPS** APA; CAAS. **RESEARCH** Hellenistic Philosophy; Neronian Rome; SENECA; Hellenistic Poetry; Psychology and Classics. **CONTACT ADDRESS** Dept of Modern and Ancient Language, Franciscan Univ of Steubenville, Franciscan Way, Steuberville, OH, 43952. **EMAIL** lyons@fran.u.edu

LYONS, JOSEPH
PERSONAL Born 08/17/1955, Wilkes-Barre, PA, m, 1979, 2 children **DISCIPLINE** ACCOUNTING **EDUCATION** BS, acctg, Univ Scranton, 77; MA, Univ Penn, 97. **CAREER** Vpres finance and internal auditor, Allied Services, 86-87; cert pub acct, McDonnell Smith & Assoc, 86-87; assoc exec dir finance, clinical pract, Univ Penn, 87-93; exec dir, Lehigh Valley Physician Grp, 94-. **HONORS AND AWARDS** Cert Pub Acct; Cert Internatl Auditor; Cert Info Systems Auditor; MLA degree. **MEMBERSHIPS** Amer Soc of Law; Med & Ethics; Amer Inst of CPAs; Penn Inst of CPAs; Info Syst Auditors Asn. **RESEARCH** Sociology of medicine; Medical & business ethics; Professions and society; Alternative medicine. **SELECTED PUBLICATIONS** Auth, The American Medical Doctor in the Current Milieu: A matter of trust, Perspectives in Bio and Med, 37, 3, 442-459, spring, 94. **CONTACT ADDRESS** 1007 Quill Ln., Oreland, PA, 19075. **EMAIL** lions4@earthlink.net

LYONS, SHERRIE L.
DISCIPLINE SCIENCE AND SOCIETY **EDUCATION** Univ Cal, BA, 69; Cal State Univ LA, MS, 73; Univ Chicago, PhD, 90. **CAREER** Asst Prof, 92-, Daemon College; Lectr, 88-89, 91, Univ Chicago; Asst Prof 90-91, Sonoma, State Univ; Instr 83, Mont Comm College; Instr 81, Freder Comm College; Instr 80-81, Marin College and San Quentin St Prison; Instr 78-81, Diablo Valley College. **HONORS AND AWARDS** Who's Who In Amer College Teachers; NEH Fel; NSF Fel; Sigma, Xi Res Gnt; U of Chi Overseas Fel; Morris Fishbein Fel; AEC Fel. **MEMBERSHIPS** HSS; ISH; PSSB. **SELECTED PUBLICATIONS** Auth, Spirits Skulls Serpents and Darwin: Approaches to Science in the 19th Century, John Hopkins Univ Press; forthcoming; The Evolution of Thomas Huxley's Scientific Views, Prometheus Press, forthcoming; Science or Pseudo-Science: Phrenology as a Cautionary Tale for Evolutionary Psychology, Perspectives in Bio and Med, 98; Convincing Men They are Monkeys, in: Thomas Henry Huxley's Place in Science and Letters, Centenary Essays, ed, Alan Barr, Univ GA Press, 97; The Origins of T H Huxley's Saltationalism: History in Darwin's Shadow, JHB 95; The World of Morality According to Darwin Huxley and De Waal, Between the Species, in press. **CONTACT ADDRESS** Humanities Division, Daemen Col, 4380 Main St, Amherst, NY, 14226. **EMAIL** slyons@daemen.edu

LYONS, TIMOTHY JAMES
PERSONAL Born 07/06/1944, Framingham, MA, m, 1967, 2 children **DISCIPLINE** FILM HISTORY AND HISTORIOGRAPHY **EDUCATION** Univ Calif, Santa Barbara, BA, 66, MA, 68; Univ Iowa, PhD(speech and dramatic art), 72. **CAREER** From instr to asst prof radio, TV and film, Temple Univ, 72-76, chmn dept, 76-78, assoc prof, 76-80. ED, J UNIV FILM ASN 76-. **MEMBERSHIPS** Soc Cinema Studies (secy, 75-77, pres, 77-79); Univ Film Asn. **RESEARCH** American silent film; Charles Chaplin. **SELECTED PUBLICATIONS** Auth, The Complete Guide to American Film Schools and Cinema and Television Programs, J Film and Video, Vol 0047, 95. **CONTACT ADDRESS** 2534 Poplar, Philadelphia, PA, 19130.

LYTLE, MARK HAMILTON
PERSONAL Born 01/05/1945, Buffalo, NY, m, 1968, 1 child **DISCIPLINE** AMERICAN HISTORY, AMERICAN STUDIES **EDUCATION** Cornell Univ, BA, 66; Yale Univ, MPhil, 71, PhD(hist), 73. **CAREER** Instr hist, Yale Univ, 72-74, asst prof, 74-80, ASSOC PROF HIST, BARD COL, 80-, CHMN AM STUDIES PROG, 80-, Co-chmn, Yale Univ, New Haven Hist Educ Proj, 71-74; consult social studies, Encycl Britannica Educ Corp, 72- and McGraw-Hill, 75- **MEMBERSHIPS** AHA; Orgn Am Historians; Am Studies Asn. **RESEARCH** United States diplomatic history--Cold War Era; history of conservation in America. **SELECTED PUBLICATIONS** Auth, Philosophical Foundations of Historical Knowledge, J Amer Hist, Vol 0082, 95; an Environmental Approach to American Diplomatic History, Diplomatic Hist, Vol 0020, 96; National Defense and the Environment, Env Hist, Vol 0002, 97. **CONTACT ADDRESS** Bard Col, P O Box 5000, Annandale, NY, 12504-5000.

M

MABRY, DONALD JOSEPH
PERSONAL Born 04/21/1941, Atlanta, GA, m, 1992, 2 children **DISCIPLINE** LATIN AMERICAN HISTORY **EDUCATION** Kenyon Col, AB, 63; Bowling Green State Univ, MEd, 64; Syracuse Univ, PhD (Latin Am hist), 70. **CAREER** Asst testing, Bowling Green State Univ, 63-64; mem fac hist, St Johns River Jr Col, 64-67; asst financial aids, Syracuse Univ, 67-68, US social hist, 68-69; from asst prof to assoc prof, 70-80, PROF HIST, MISS STATE UNIV, 80-, Assoc Dean, Arts & Sci, 91-, Creator and Archivist, The Hist Text Arch; Sr Fel, Ctr for Int Security, 81-. **HONORS AND AWARDS** Fel, Newberry Libr, 75. **MEMBERSHIPS** SECOLAS; CLAH; CCAS. **RESEARCH** Higher education and politics; United States-Latin American relations; Contemporary Mexico. **SELECTED PUBLICATIONS** Auth, Mexico's Accion Nacional: A Catholic Alternative to Revolution, Syracuse Univ, 73; Manuel Gomez Morin, In: Revolutionaries, Traditionalists, and Dictators in Latin America, Cooper, 73; Mexico, Am Ann, In: Encycl Am, Grolier, 73-92; Mexico's Party Deputy System, J Inter Am Studies & World Affairs, 74; Changing Models of Mexican Politics, New Scholar, 76; Mexican Anticlerics, Bishops, Cristeros and the Devout in the 1920's, J Church & State, 78; coauth, Neighbors-Mexico and the United States, Wetback and Oil, Nelson-Hall, 81; auth, The Mexican University and the State: Student Conflicts, 1910-1971, Tex A&M Univ, 82; ed, The Latin American Narcotics Trade and the United States National Security. **CONTACT ADDRESS** Drawer AS, Mississippi State Univ, MS, 39762-5508. **EMAIL** djm1@ra.msstate.edu

MACCAFFREY, WALLACE T.
PERSONAL Born 04/20/1920, LaGrande, OR, m, 1956 **DISCIPLINE** MODERN BRITISH HISTORY **EDUCATION** Reed Col, AB, 42; Harvard Univ, PhD, 50. **CAREER** From instr to asst prof hist, Univ Calif, Los Angeles, 50-53; from assoc prof to prof, Haverford Col, 53-68; prof hist, 68-80, FRANCIS LEE HIGGINSON PROF HIST, HARVARD UNIV, 80-, Guggenheim fel, 56-57; overseas res fel, Churchill Col, Cambridge, 68-69. **MEMBERSHIPS** AHA; Econ Hist Soc; fel Royal Hist Soc. **RESEARCH** Sixteenth and 17th century English history. **SELECTED PUBLICATIONS** Auth, Locality and Polity--a Study of Warwickshire Landed Society, 1401-1499, Amer Hist Rev, Vol 0098, 93; The European Dynastic State, 1494-1660, Renaissance Quart, Vol 0047, 94; The Newhaven Expedition, 1562-1563, Hist J, Vol 0040, 97. **CONTACT ADDRESS** Dept of Hist, Harvard Univ, Cambridge, MA, 02138.

MACCHIARULO, LOUIS
PERSONAL Born 01/04/1958, Queens, NY, m, 1983, 2 children **DISCIPLINE** CLASSICS **EDUCATION** Fordham Univ, PhD, 86. **CAREER** Instr Latin, Greek & Italian, Regis High School. **HONORS AND AWARDS** Assistantship, Fordham Univ, 79-81; Fordham Univ Fel, 81-83. **MEMBERSHIPS** APA; Virgilian Soc **RESEARCH** Homer; Virgil, Dante, Roman History **SELECTED PUBLICATIONS** The Life and Times of Fortunato, PhD Thesis. **CONTACT ADDRESS** 55 E 84th St, New York, NY, 10028.

MACCOULL, LESLIE
PERSONAL Born 08/07/1945, New London, CT, s **DISCIPLINE** CLASSICS; SEMITICS (COPTIC) **EDUCATION** Vassar Col, AB, 65, summa cum laude; Yale Univ, MA, 66; Catholic Univ of Amer, PhD with distinction, 73. **CAREER** Curator, 74-78, Inst of Christian Oriental Research, Catholic Univ; dir of studies, 78-84, Soc for Coptic Archaelogy (North Amer) Cairo; senior research scholar, 84- , adjunct, 97, AZ Ctr for Medieval and Renaissance Studies, AZ State Univ. **HONORS AND AWARDS** Phi Beta Kappa 64; jr fel 69-71; summer fel, 83; fel, 90-91; fel, Ameri Research Ctr in Egypt, 78-79; NEH Fel, 93-94. **MEMBERSHIPS** Amer Soc of Papyrologists; Intl Assn for Coptic Studies; US Natl Committee for Byzantine Studies, Mensa. **RESEARCH** Coptic papyrology; Byzantine papyrology; social and cultural hist of lat antiquity. **SELECTED PUBLICATIONS** Auth, Dated and datable Coptic documentary hands before A.D. 700, Le Museon, 97; auth, The Triadon: an English translation, Greek Orthodox Theological Review, 97; auth, Chant in Coptic pilgrimage, in Pilgrimage and Holy Space in Late Antique Egypt, 98; auth, BM 1075: A Sixth-Century Tax Register from the Hermopolite, in press; coauth, Catalogue of the Illustrated Manuscripts in the Coptic Museum, in press. **CONTACT ADDRESS** 914 E Lemon St, #137, Tempe, AZ, 85281. **EMAIL** haflele@imap4.asu.edu

MACDONALD, BURTON
PERSONAL Born 09/13/1939, Canada, m, 1980 **DISCIPLINE** BIBLE & ARCHAEOLOGY; NEAR EASTERN ARCHAEOLOGY; CHRISTIAN RELIGION **EDUCATION** Univ Ottawa, BA, 60; MA, 65; Cath Univ Am, PhD, 74. **CAREER** Sr Resident, Massey Col in Univ Tor, 95-96; prof & chair Dept Theolog & Relig Studies, St Francis Xavier Univ, Nova Scotia, 89-97; assoc prof Dept Theolog, St Francis Xavier Univ, 79-89; annual prof, Amer Center Oriental Res, Amman, Jordan, 79-80, 86-87; asst prof, St Francis Dept Theolog, St Francis Xavier Univ, 72-79; lctr Dept Theolog, St Francis Xavier Univ, 66-67; lctr Dept Theolog, Xavier Col, Sydney, Nova Scotia. **MEMBERSHIPS** Brit Inst at Amman for Archaeology & History; Can Mediter Inst; Cath Bibl Assoc Amer; Soc Bibl Lit; Amer Schools of Oriental Res. **RESEARCH** Ammonitties, Moabites, and Edomites: History & Archaeology; Biblical Site Identification East of the Jordan; Archaeological Survey of Southern Jordan. **SELECTED PUBLICATIONS** Co-ed, Ancient Ammon, EJ Brill Pub, forthcoming; Ammonite Territory and Sites, in Ancient Ammon, EJ Brill Pub, forthcoming; Ammon, Moab, and Edom: Early States/Nations of Jordan in the Biblical Period (End of the 2nd and During 1st Millennium BC), Al Kutba Pub, 94. **CONTACT ADDRESS** Dept of Religious Studies, St Francis Xavier Univ, PO Box 5000, Antigonish, NS, B2G 2W5. **EMAIL** bmacdona@stfx.ca

MACDONALD, J. FRED
PERSONAL Born 03/14/1941, New Waterford, NS, Canada, m, 1971 **DISCIPLINE** MODERN UNITED STATES HISTORY **EDUCATION** Univ Calif, Berkeley, BA, 63, MA, 64; Univ Calif, Los Angeles, PhD(hist), 69. **CAREER** Assoc prof, 69-78, prof hist, Northeastern Ill Univ, 78-, Chmn Inst Popular Cult Studies, 69-. **MEMBERSHIPS** Popular Cult Asn (pres, 80-82); Midwest Popular Cult Asn (vpres, pres, exec secy); Acad TV Arts & Sci; AHA. **RESEARCH** Social history of

television and radio programming; film and popular music. **SELECTED PUBLICATIONS** Auth, The Foreigner in Juvenile Series Fiction, 1900-1945, J Popular Cult, winter 74; Radio's Black Heritage: Destination Freedom, 1948-1950, Phylon, 3/78; The Cold War as Entertainment in Fifties Television, J Popular Film & TV, 78; Government Propaganda in Commercial Radio: The Case of Tresury Star Parade, 1942-1943, J Popular Cult, 78; Don't Touch That Dial! Radio Programming in American Life, 1920-1960, Nelson-Hall, 79; Black perimeters-Paul Robeson, Nat King Cole and the role of Blacks in American TV, J Popular Film & TV, 79; Radio and Television Studies and American Culture, Am Quart, 80; Blacks and White TV: Afro-Americans in Television Since 1948, Nelson-Hall (in prep); ed, An Interview with Bud Freeman, Popular Music & Soc, summer 74; auth, The Foreigner in Juvenile Series Fiction, 1900-1945, J Popular Cult, winter 74; Radio's Black Heritage: Destination Freedom, 1948-1950, Phylon, 3/78; Don't Touch That Dial! Radio Programming in American Life, 1920-1960, Nelson-Hall, 78. **CONTACT ADDRESS** Dept of Hist, Northeastern Illinois Univ, 5500 N St Louis Ave, Chicago, IL, 60625-4625.

MACDONALD, MARY N.
PERSONAL Born 12/29/1946, Maleny, Australia, s **DISCIPLINE** HISTORY OF RELIGION **EDUCATION** Univ Chicago, PhD, 88 **CAREER** Lctr, Melanesian Inst, New Guinea, 80-83; prof Hist Relig, LeMoyne Col, 88-98 **HONORS AND AWARDS** Newcombe Dissertation Fel, 87-88 **MEMBERSHIPS** Amer Acad Relig; Assoc Social Anthropology in Oceania **RESEARCH** Religions of Oceania; Religious Movements; Ecology and Religion **SELECTED PUBLICATIONS** "Magic and the Study of Religion in Melanesia," Religiologigues, 95; "Youth and Religion in Papua New Guinea," Catalyst, 96; "Religion and Human Experience," Introduction to the Study of Religion, Orbis, 98 **CONTACT ADDRESS** Relig Studies Dept, LeMoyne Col, Syracuse, NY, 13214. **EMAIL** macdonald@maple.lemoyne.edu

MACDONALD, RODERICK JAMES
PERSONAL Born 06/08/1933, Waltham, MA, m, 1964, 1 child **DISCIPLINE** HISTORY **EDUCATION** Univ Edinburgh, MA, 60, PhD(hist), 69. **CAREER** Press officer, Ghana Info Serv, New York, 61; sr researcher Africa, Libr Cong, 63-64; lectr hist, Univ Malawi, 65-67; vis lectr, 67-69, asst prof, 69-74, ASSOC PROF HIST, SYRACUSE UNIV, 74-, Am Coun Learned Socs study fel hist, 71-72. **MEMBERSHIPS** African Studies Asn. **RESEARCH** Blacks in London, 1919-1948; Central Africa in the 20th century; 20th century linkages within the African Diaspora. **SELECTED PUBLICATIONS** Auth, The Quanah Route--a History of the Quanah Acme and Pacific Railway, Southwestern Hist Quart, Vol 0097, 93. **CONTACT ADDRESS** Syracuse Univ, 119 College Pl, Syracuse, NY, 13210.

MACDONALD, WILLIAM L.
PERSONAL Born 12/02/1963, Columbus, OH, m, 1993, 2 children **DISCIPLINE** SOCIOLOGY **EDUCATION** Bowling Green State Univ, PhD, 92. **CAREER** Asst Prof, 92-98, Assoc Prof Sociol, Ohio State Univ at Newark, 98-. **HONORS AND AWARDS** Young Schol in Am Relig, 97-98; Newark Schol Achievement Award, Ohio State Univ. **MEMBERSHIPS** Am Sociol Asn; Soc Scientific Study Relig; Southern Sociol Soc; Nat Coun Family Relations. **RESEARCH** Religion; family; social movements; voluntary euthanasia; science. **SELECTED PUBLICATIONS** Coauth, Remarriage, Stepchildren, and Marital Conflict: Challenges to the Incomplete Institutionalization Hypothesis, J Marriage and the Family, 95; auth, The Effects of Religiosity and Structural Strain on Reported Paranormal Experiences, J Scientific Study Relig, 95; coauth, Parenting Stepchildren and Biological Children: The Effects of Stepparent's Gender and New Biological Children, J Family Issues, 96; auth, Situational Factors and Attitudes toward Voluntary Euthanasia, Soc Sci & Med, 98; The Difference Between Blacks' and Whites' Attitudes toward Voluntary Euthanasia, J Scientific Study Relig (forthcoming). **CONTACT ADDRESS** Sociology Dept, Ohio State Univ, Newark, OH, 43055. **EMAIL** macdonald.24@osu.edu

MACDONALD, WILLIAM L.
PERSONAL Born 07/12/1921, Putnam, CT, 3 children **DISCIPLINE** FINE ARTS, HISTORY OF ARCHITECTURE **EDUCATION** Harvard Univ, AB (history, high honors), 49, AM (fine arts), 53, PhD (fine arts, history of architecture), 56. **CAREER** Boston Architectural Center, 50-54; Wheaton Col, 53-54; Yale Univ, 56-65; A P Brown Prof, Smith Col, 65-80; vis prof at: Berkeley, Emory, Georgetown, Harvard, MIT, Minnesota, Penn, Williams, etc. **HONORS AND AWARDS** Veterans Nat Scholar; Emerton, Shaw awards; Rome Prize, Am Academy in Rome, 54-56; Morse fel (Yale, Am Academy in Rome), 62-63; Getty Scholar, The Getty Center for the Fine Arts and the Humanities, 85-86; Hitchcock Prize, 87, 96; AIA Int Book Award, 97; fel, Am Academy in Rome; fel, Am Academy of the Arts and Sciences. **MEMBERSHIPS** Soc of Architectural Historians; Soc for the Promotion of Roman Studies; Archaeological Inst of Am. **RESEARCH** Classical architecture in its various manifestations; the Roman Empire; fireworks as art; flying boats. **SELECTED PUBLICATIONS** Auth, Early Christian and Byzantine Architecture, 62; The Architecture of the Roman Empire: I: An Introductory Study, 65, rev ed, 82, II: An Urban Appraisal, 86 (Hitchcock Prize, Soc of Architectual Historians; Kevin Lynch Award, MIT Dept of Urban Studies, III: An Historical Reconnaissance, in prep; Northampton Massachusetts Architecture & Buildings, 75; The Pantheon-Design, Meaning, and Progency, 76; assoc ed and contrib, The Princeton Encyclopedia of Classical Sites, 76; Piranesi's Carceri: Sources of Invention, 79; Hadrian's Villa and Its Legacy, coauth with John A Pinto of Princeton, 95 (Hitchcock Prize, Soc of Architectural Historians; George Wittenborn Memorial Award; Book of the Year Award, Am Inst of Architects); Villa Adriana, La costruzione e il mito da Adriano a Louis Kahn, 97; Hadrian's World, in press; about 180 articles, reviews, chapters, and introductions in books, exhibitions catalogue essays, entries in reference works, etc. **CONTACT ADDRESS** 3811 39th St NW, Washington, DC, 20016-2835.

MACDOUGALL, ELISABETH BLAIR
PERSONAL Born 01/01/1925, Chicago, IL, m, 1949, 1 child **DISCIPLINE** HISTORY OF ART **EDUCATION** Vassar Col, BA, 46; NY Univ, MA, 54; Harvard Univ, PhD(art hist), 70. **CAREER** Instr art hist, Colo Col, 48-51; instr hist of archit, Boston Archit Ctr, 54-57; assoc surv dir, Cambridge Hist Dist Comn, 64-66; asst prof art hist, Boston Univ, 66-72; assoc prof, 72-76, PROF HIST LANDSCAPE ARCHIT, DUMBARTON OAKS, HARVARD UNIV, 76-, DIR STUDIES, 72-, Mem hist garden comt, Int Comn Monuments and Sites, 73-, exec comt mem, US Nat Comt, 75-. **MEMBERSHIPS** Soc Archit Historians (secy, 65-78). **RESEARCH** Italian Renaissance architecture; Italian Renaissance gardens; preservation of historic gardens. **SELECTED PUBLICATIONS** Gardens and Gardening in Papal Rome, Renaissance Quart, Vol 0045, 92. **CONTACT ADDRESS** Dumbarton Oaks, Harvard Univ, Cambridge, MA, 02138.

MACE, SARAH
DISCIPLINE CLASSICS **EDUCATION** Colby Col, BA, 82, Univ Penn, MA, 85; Yale Univ, PhD, 92. **CAREER** Lectr, Univ Penn, 92-93; vis asst prof, Columbia Univ, 93-94; vis asst prof, Dartmouth Col, 94-95; vis asst prof, 95-97, asst prof, 97-, Union Col. **HONORS AND AWARDS** Charles C Sherman fel, 86-87; Yale Univ fel, 87-89; 85-86; Whiting Diss Fel, 90-91. **RESEARCH** Homer, Hesiod and the epic tradition; Presocratica; Archaic Greek lyric; Epinician; Aeschylus; Lucretius. **SELECTED PUBLICATIONS** Auth, Utopian and Erotic Fusion in a New Elegy of Simonides, APE, 96; rev of Lesbian Desire in the Lyrics of Sappho by Snyder, AJP, forthcoming. **CONTACT ADDRESS** Dept of Classics, Union Col, Schenectady, NY, 12308. **EMAIL** maces@idol.union.edu

MACEY, DAVID A.J.
DISCIPLINE HISTORY **CAREER** Prof; Cornelius V. Starr prof, Russ and E Europ Stud; dir, Russ and E Europ Stud Prog; dir, Off of Off-Campus Study; teaching at Middlebury Col for 20 yrs. **RESEARCH** Agrarian reform in pre-Revolutionary Russia between 1857 and 1916, with particular interest in the Stolypin reforms, 1906-1916. **CONTACT ADDRESS** Dept of History, Middlebury Col, Middlebury, VT, 05753. **EMAIL** macey@middlebury.edu

MACFARQUER, RODERICK
PERSONAL Born 12/02/1930, LaHore, India, m, 1964, 2 children **DISCIPLINE** GOVERNMENT **EDUCATION** Oxford Univ, BA, 53; Harvard Univ, MA, 55; London Sch Economics, PhD, 81. **CAREER** Harvard Univ, ch Dept Gov, 98-, Walter Channing Cabot Fel, 93-94, FCEAR, Dir 86-92, Prof 84-; WWC WA Fel, 80-81; Member of Parliament, 74-79; RIIA Fel, 71-74; BBC 24 Hours, founding co-presenter, 71-74, 79-80; RICAEAI Fel, 69; BBC TV, Panorama, reporter, 63-64; The China Qtly, founding editor, 59-68; Daily Telegraph, Sunday Telegraph, China specialist, 55-61. **HONORS AND AWARDS** Smith Richardson Foun Gnt; Chiang Chin-kuo Foun Gnt; Walter Channing Cabot Fel; Leverhulme Res Fel; Ford Foun Gnt; Rockefeller Fun Res Gnt. **MEMBERSHIPS** AAAS; RIIA; AAS; BACS; APSA. **RESEARCH** China, Asia. **SELECTED PUBLICATIONS** Coed, contrib, The Politics of China 1949-89, 93, new edition, 97; coed, Perspectives on Modern China: Four Anniversaries, 91; coed, The Secret Speeches of Chairman Mao, 89; coed, The Cambridge History of China, 87. **CONTACT ADDRESS** Dept of Government, Harvard Univ, Cambridge, MA, 02138. **EMAIL** rKolodney@latte.harvard.edu

MACGILLIVRAY, ROYCE C.
PERSONAL Born 05/13/1936, Alexandria, ON, Canada **DISCIPLINE** HISTORY **EDUCATION** Queen's Univ, BA, 59; Harvard Univ, AM, 60, PhD, 65. **CAREER** PROF HISTORY, UNIV WATERLOO, 62-. **SELECTED PUBLICATIONS** Auth, Restoration Historians, 74; auth, The House of Ontario, 83; auth, The New Querist, 83; auth, The Mind of Ontario, 85; auth, The Slopes of the Andes, 90; auth, Bibliography of Glengarry County, 96; coauth, History of Glengarry County, 79; ed, Ontario History, 79-. **CONTACT ADDRESS** General Delivery, Maxville, ON, KOC 1TO.

MACH, THOMAS S.
PERSONAL Born 04/14/1966, Cleveland, OH, m, 1989, 1 child **DISCIPLINE** HISTORY **EDUCATION** Cedarville Col, BA, 88; Cleveland State Univ, MA, 89; Univ Akron, PhD, 96. **CAREER** Tchg asst, Cedarville Col, 86-87; res asst, 89, grad asst, 88-89, Cleveland State Univ; res asst, 92, grad asst, 89-94, lectr, 92-93, Univ Akron; asst prof hist, 94-98, dir honors prog, 96- , assoc prof hist, 98- , Mount Vernon Nazarene Col. **HONORS AND AWARDS** Phi Alpha Theta; William and Dora Martin Hist Endowment Scholar, 91-94; President's Award for Excellence in Tchg, 97-98. **MEMBERSHIPS** Conf on Faith and Hist; Nat Collegiate Honors Coun; Ohio Acad of Hist; Orgn of Am Hist. **RESEARCH** United States history; nineteench century United States history. **SELECTED PUBLICATIONS** Author, Calvin Stewart Brice, in American National Biography, Oxford, 99; auth, George Hunt Pendleton: The Ohio Idea and Political Continuity in Reconstruction America, Ohio Hist, forthcoming. **CONTACT ADDRESS** Dept of History, Mount Vernon Nazarene Col, 800 Martinsburg Rd, Mt Vernon, OH, 43050. **EMAIL** tmach@mvnc.edu

MACHAFFIE, BARBARA J.
PERSONAL Born 11/29/1949, Philadelphia, PA, m, 1972 **DISCIPLINE** RELIGIOUS STUDIES; ECCLESIASTICAL HISTORY **EDUCATION** Col of Wooster, BA, 71; Univ of Edinburgh, Scotland, BD, 74, PhD, 77. **CAREER** Ref Libr, Princeton Theol Sem, 77-80; vis asst prof, Cleveland State Univ, 81-83; instr, Marietta Col, 83-87; asst prof, Hist and Relig, Marietta Col, 92- . **HONORS AND AWARDS** Molly C. Putnam and Israel Ward Andrews Assoc prof Relig. **MEMBERSHIPS** Phi Beta Kappa; Scottish Ecclesiastical Hist Soc; Amer Acad Rel. **RESEARCH** 19th Century British Ecclesiastical History; Women and Religion. **SELECTED PUBLICATIONS** Auth, Her Story: Women in Christian Tradition, Fortress, 86; Readings in Her Story: Women in Christian Tradition, Fortress, 92. **CONTACT ADDRESS** Dept of History and Religion, Marietta Col, Marietta, OH, 45750. **EMAIL** machaffb@marietta.edu

MACIAS, ANNA
PERSONAL Born 05/20/1930, Sewaren, NJ **DISCIPLINE** LATIN AMERICAN HISTORY **EDUCATION** Hunter Col, BA, 52; Smith Col, MA, 54; Columbia Univ, PhD(hist), 65. **CAREER** Instr Am hist, Dana Hall Sch, Mass, 54-56; asst Am studies, Amherst Col, 57-59; instr Latin Am hist, Smith Col, 62-63; from instr to assoc prof, 63-75, PROF LATIN AM HIST, OHIO WESLEYAN UNIV, 75-, Foreign area fel individual res on Mex women, Am Coun Learned Soc-Soc Sci Res Coun grant, 73-74. **MEMBERSHIPS** AHA; Conf Latin Am Hist; Latin Am Studies Asn. **RESEARCH** Mexican women in the social revolution, 1900-1953; political developments in Mexico during the independence movement. **SELECTED PUBLICATIONS** Auth, Gathering Rage--the Failure of 20th-Century Revolutions to Develop a Feminist Agenda, Hisp Amer Hist Rev, Vol 0074, 94; Women of the Mexican Countryside, 1850-1990, Historian, Vol 0058, 96; The Secret History of Gender--Women, Men, and Power in Late Colonial Mexico, Historian, Vol 0059, 97; The Island of the Anishnaabeg--Thunderers and Water Monsters in the Traditional Ojibwe Life World, J West, Vol 0036, 97. **CONTACT ADDRESS** Dept of Hist, Ohio Wesleyan Univ, Delaware, OH, 43015.

MACISAAC, DAVID
PERSONAL Born 06/22/1935, Boston, MA, m, 1959, 4 children **DISCIPLINE** EUROPEAN AND MILITARY HISTORY **EDUCATION** Trinity Col, Conn, AB, 57; Yale Univ, AM, 58; Duke Univ, PhD(hist), 70. **CAREER** Instr hist, 64-66, asst prof, 68-70, assoc prof, 72-75, PROF HIST, US AIR FORCE ACAD, 76-, Vis prof strategy, US Naval War Col, 75-76; fel nat security affairs, Woodrow Wilson Int Ctr Scholars, 78-79. **MEMBERSHIPS** Inter-Univ Sem Armed Forces and Soc; Am Comt Hist Second World War. **RESEARCH** Air warfare, World War II to the present; history of military theory and strategy; European military affairs, ancient, medieval, modern. **SELECTED PUBLICATIONS** Auth, The Crucible of War, 1939-1945--the Official History of the Royal Canadian Air Force, Vol 3, J Mil Hist, Vol 0060, 96. **CONTACT ADDRESS** Dept of Hist, US Air Force Academy, CO, 80840.

MACIUIKA, BENEDICT VYTENIS
PERSONAL Born 11/16/1927, Kaunas, Lithuania, m, 1955, 3 children **DISCIPLINE** MODERN EUROPEAN AND SOVIET HISTORY **EDUCATION** Univ Chicago, MA, 54, PhD(int rels), 63. **CAREER** Res assoc, Soc Sci Div, Univ Chicago, 54-56, admin and res asst, Ctr Studies Am Foreign and Mil Policy, 56-58; from instr to assoc prof, 58-72, PROF HIST, UNIV CONN, 72-, Univ Conn Res Found res grant, 72. **MEMBERSHIPS** AHA; Am Polit Sci Asn; Am Asn Advan Slavic Studies; Asn Advan Baltic Studies; Inst Lithuanian Studies. **RESEARCH** History and institutions of Lithuania since 1940; Russian and Soviet history. **SELECTED PUBLICATIONS** Auth, Russia as a Multi-National Empire--Emergence, History, Collapse, J Baltic Stud, Vol 0024, 93; The Nordic Way--a Path to Baltic Equilibrium, J Baltic Stud, Vol 0026, 95; The Sorcerer as Apprentice--Stalin as Commissar of Nationalities, 1917-1924, J Baltic Stud Vol 0026, 95. **CONTACT ADDRESS** Univ Connecticut, Hartford, CT, 06112.

MACK, SARA
PERSONAL Born 05/01/1939, New Haven, CT, w, 2 children **DISCIPLINE** CLASSICS **EDUCATION** AM, 64, PhD, 74, Harvard Univ. **CAREER** Asst/Assoc/Full Prof, 76-, UNC-Chapel Hill. **HONORS AND AWARDS** Bowman and Gordon Gray Professorship, 94-97; Fellowship, Natl Humanities Ctr. **MEMBERSHIPS** Amer Philological Assoc; Assoc of Literary Scholars and Critics; Classics Assoc of the Midwest and South; NC Classical Assoc; Virgilian Soc. **RESEARCH** Latin Poetry; Greek and Latin epic **SELECTED PUBLICATIONS** Auth, Ovid (Hermes Books), 88; reviews, Allen Mandelbaum, The Metamorphoses of Ovid: A New Verse Translation, 94; Carole Newlands, Playing with Time, Ovid and the Fasti, 97. **CONTACT ADDRESS** UN. Carolina-Chapel Hill, 212 Murphy Hall, CB #3145, Chapel Hill, NC, 27599-3145. **EMAIL** smack@email.unc.edu

MACKENZIE, DAVID
PERSONAL Born 06/10/1927, Rochester, NY, m, 1953, 3 children **DISCIPLINE** MODERN HISTORY **EDUCATION** Univ Rochester, AB, 51; Columbia Univ, AM, 53, PhD, 62. **CAREER** Asst prof Russ lang & Europ hist, US Merchant Marine Acad, 53-58; lectr Russ & Europ hist, Princeton Univ, 59-61; from asst prof to assoc prof hist, Wells Col, 61-69; Prof Hist, Univ NC, Greensboro, 69-, Ford Found fel, Austria & Yugoslavia, 55-56; Inter-Univ Comt Travel Grants grant, USSR, 58-59; vis asst prof, Cornell Univ, 62; grants, Am Coun Learned Soc, 65-66, Am Philos Soc, 69, 74, 78 & 79 & Fulbright, 78 & 82. **MEMBERSHIPS** Am Asn Advan Slavic Studies; NAm Soc Serbian Studies; Southern Coun Slavic Studies. **RESEARCH** Russ mil hist, 19th century; Serbian and Yugoslav hist, 19th century; Russ for rel. **SELECTED PUBLICATIONS** Auth, The Serbs and Russian Pan-Slavism, 1875-1878, Cornell Univ, 67; Tashkent: Past and present, Russ Rev, 4/69; Expansion in Central Asia... 1863-1866, Can Slavic Studies, summer 69; Lion of Tashkent: The Career of General M G Cherniaev, Univ Ga, 74; A History of Russia and the Soviet Union, Dorsey, 77, rev ed, 82; contribr, Modern Encycl of Russian and Soviet Hist, Int Asn Scholarly Publ, 77-; Ilija Garasanin: Balkan Bismarck, 85; Apis: The Congenial Conspirator, 89, Serbian ed, 89, 96; Imperial Dreams, Harsh Realities: Tsarist Foreign Policy, 93; From Messianism to Collapse: Soviet Foreign Policy, 94; The Black Hand on Trial: Salonika 1917, 95; Serbs and Russians, 96; Violent Solutions, 96. **CONTACT ADDRESS** Dept of Hist, Univ of N. Carolina, 1000 Spring Garden, Greensboro, NC, 27412-0001.

MACKEY, THOMAS
PERSONAL Born 08/17/1956, Radford, VA **DISCIPLINE** AMERICAN CONSTITUTIONAL AND LEGAL HISTORY **EDUCATION** Beloit Coll, BA, 78; Rice Univ, PhD, 84. **CAREER** Samuel I. Golieb post doc fel in American legal history, NYU school of Law, 84-85; Visiting asst Prof, 85-86, MI State Univ; asst prof, 86-886, Univ Nebraska-Lincoln; asst prof, 88-89, Eastern Montana Coll; visiting asst prof, 89-90, asst prof, 90-91, Kansas State Univ; asst prof, assoc prof, 91-present, Univ Louisville. **HONORS AND AWARDS** Samuel I. Golies Postdoctural Fel; Finalist, Teaching Award, Coll of Arts and Sci, Univ Louisville, 94. **MEMBERSHIPS** Ogn of Amer Historians; Amer Soc for Legal Hist; Southern Historical Assn; Filson Club Historical Soc. **RESEARCH** Amer Constitutional and Legal History; vice control; first amendment issues. **SELECTED PUBLICATIONS** Auth, Red Lights Out: A Legal History of Prostitution, Disorderly Houses, and Vice districts, 1870-1917, 87; auth, They are Positively Dangerous Men: The Lost Court Documents of Benjamin Gitlow and James Larking Before the NY City Magistrate Court 1919, NYU Law Review, 94; Anti-Vice Funding and the Apple: The Business of Anti-Vice Reform and the Committee of Fourteen in NY City 1905-32, Essays in Economic and Business History, 94; chptr auth, The Stamp Act, Events that Changed America in the 18th Century, 98; chptr auth, Jacksonian Democracy, Events that Changed America in the 19th Century, 97. **CONTACT ADDRESS** Dept. Of History, Univ Louisville, Louisville, KY, 40292. **EMAIL** tcmack01@athena.louisville.edu

MACKIE, HILARY S.
DISCIPLINE CLASSICS **EDUCATION** BA, 87; Princeton Univ, PhD, 93. **CAREER** Vis prof, Stanford Univ. **RESEARCH** Archaic Greek poetry; lit theory; Augustan poetry. **SELECTED PUBLICATIONS** Auth, Talking Trojan: Difference and Conversational Style in the Iliad, 96. **CONTACT ADDRESS** Stanford Univ, Bldg 20, Main Quad, Stanford, CA, 94305.

MACKINNON, ARAN S.
PERSONAL Born 12/16/1965, Edinburgh, Scotland, s **DISCIPLINE** HISTORY **EDUCATION** Queen's Univ, BA with honors, 88; Univ of Natal, MA, 91; Univ of London, PhD, 96. **CAREER** Vis asst prof, Univ of NC at Charlotte, 96-97; ASST PROF OF HIST, STATE UNIV OF WEST GA, 97-. **HONORS AND AWARDS** Irwin Travelling Scholar Grant, 93; Univ of London Fees Scholar, 93, 94, & 95. **MEMBERSHIPS** African Studies Asn; Southeastern Regional Asn of African Studies; Royal African Soc. **RESEARCH** South Africa, Rural Africa, Aging. **SELECTED PUBLICATIONS** Auth, The Persistence of the Cattle Economy in Zululand, Canadian J of Africa Studies, 99. **CONTACT ADDRESS** Dept of History, State Univ of West Georgia, 1500 Maple St, Carrollton, GA, 30118. **EMAIL** amackinn@westga.edu

MACKINNON, STEPHEN ROBERT
PERSONAL Born 12/02/1940, Columbus, NE, m, 1967, 2 children **DISCIPLINE** EAST ASIAN & MODERN CHINESE HISTORY **EDUCATION** Yale Univ, AB, 63, MA, 64; Univ Calif, Davis, PhD(hist), 71. **CAREER** Vis instr hist, New Asia Col, Chinese Univ Hong Kong, 68-69; prof hist, Ariz State Univ, 71-, Dir of Asian Stud, 88-95; Fulbright scholar India, 77-78; vis scholar, Acad Soc Sci, Peoples Rep China, 79-81, 85. **HONORS AND AWARDS** Res Fellow Am Council of Learned Socs, 78; Fulbright Found, India, 77-78; Res Sr Comnr on Scholarly Comn, Peoples' Repub of China, 92. **MEMBERSHIPS** Asn Asian Studies (bd dirs 90-91); Soc Ch'ing Studies; Am Coun Learned Soc. **RESEARCH** Modern Chinese social and political history; twentieth century Chinese warlordism; American journalists in China during 1930's and 1940's. **SELECTED PUBLICATIONS** Auth, Power/Politics China, 80; Power and Politics in Late Imperial China, 80; Co-auth, China Reporting, 87; co-ed, Chinese Women Revolution, 76; ed, Portrait of chinese Women in Revolution, 76; Tragedy of Wuhan, 1938, Modern Asian Studies, 8/96; Toward a History of the Chinese Press in the Republican Period, Modern China, 1/97. **CONTACT ADDRESS** Dept of History, Arizona State Univ, Tempe, PO Box 872501, Tempe, AZ, 85287-2501. **EMAIL** icsrm@asuvm.inre.asu.edu

MACKINTOSH, BARRY
PERSONAL Born 12/24/1942, Hartford, CT, m, 1963, 2 children **DISCIPLINE** AMERICAN HISTORY **EDUCATION** Tufts Univ, BA, 64; Univ Md, MA, 74. **CAREER** HISTORIAN US HIST, NAT PARK SERV, DEPT INTERIOR, 65-. **HONORS AND AWARDS** Fletcher M Green Award, Southern Hist Asn, 78. **MEMBERSHIPS** Orgn Am Historians; Southern Hist Asn; Nat Trust Hist Preserv; Columbia Hist Soc. **RESEARCH** Historic preservation; Black history. **SELECTED PUBLICATIONS** Auth, The Historic Preservation Movement in California, 1940-1975, Pac Hist Rev, Vol 0063, 94; Petrified Forest National Park--a Wilderness Bound in Time, Pac Hist Rev, Vol 0066, 97. **CONTACT ADDRESS** Nat Park Serv, Dept of Interior, Washington, DC, 20240.

MACLEAN, ELIZABETH
DISCIPLINE HISTORY **EDUCATION** Conn Col, BA, 64; Univ Md, Col Pk, MA, 77, PhD, 86. **CAREER** Asst, 86-91. assoc, chair, 91-97, PROF, 97-, HIST/POL SCI, OTTERBEIN COL. **CONTACT ADDRESS** Dept of Hist/Pol Sci, Otterbein Col, 1 Otterbein, Westerville, OH, 43081. **EMAIL** EMacLean@Otterbein.edu

MACLENNAN, ROBERT S.
PERSONAL Born 05/20/1941, Los Angeles, CA, m, 1966 **DISCIPLINE** HISTORY; ANCIENT STUDIES - 2ND TEMPLE JUDAISM **EDUCATION** Occidental Col, BA, 63; Princeton Theol Seminary, BD, 66; Univ Minn, PhD, 88. **CAREER** Presbyterian Minister, Presbyterian Congregation Churches, 66-98; Adjunct Prof Classics, Macalester Col, 94-, Exec Dir Black Sea Archaeological Project, 94-; archaeological excavations, City of David (Jerusalem), 78; Dir, Black Sea Ventures Group, 96-; Mem, Bd of Moral Re-Armament, 98-. **SELECTED PUBLICATIONS** Auth, Early Christian Texts on Jew and Judaism, Schol Press, 90; coauth, Diaspora Jews and Judaism, Schol Press, 92; auth, In Search of the Jewish Diaspora: A First Century Synagogue in the Crimea?, Bibl Archaeol Rev, 96; coauth, To the Study of Jewish Antiquities From Chersonesus Tavrichesky, Archaeol, 97; auth, Diaspora Jews, Romans, Pagans, and Others in Sardis, Aphrodisias and the Crimea in the Greco-Roman Period, The Jewish Population in South Ukraine, Yearbook, Research, Memories and Documents, Jewish World, 98; author of several other articles and archaeological reports. **CONTACT ADDRESS** 6 Edgehill St., Princeton, NJ, 08540. **EMAIL** RSMacL@aol.com

MACLEOD, DAVID IRVING
PERSONAL Born 06/08/1943, Chatham, ON, Canada, m, 1970, 2 children **DISCIPLINE** HISTORY **EDUCATION** Univ Toronto, BA, 65; Univ Wisc, PhD, 73. **CAREER** Instr, prof, 70-, Central Mich Univ; vis asst prof, 74-75, Univ Toronto; ed, 98- Mich Hist Rev. **MEMBERSHIPS** Org of Amer Hist; Hist of Ed Soc. **RESEARCH** History of Amer childhood & youth; voluntary assns; progressive era. **SELECTED PUBLICATIONS** Auth, Carnegie Libraries in Wisconsin, St Hist Soc of Wisc, 68; auth, Building Character in the American Boy: The Boy Scouts, YMCA, and Their Forerunners, 1870-1920, Univ Wisc Press, 83; auth, The Age of the Child: Children in America, 1890-1920, Twayne Pub, 98. **CONTACT ADDRESS** Dept of History, Central Michigan Univ, Mt. Pleasant, MI, 48859. **EMAIL** David.Macleod@Cmich.edu

MACLEOD, MALCOLM K.
PERSONAL Born 10/10/1936, Lunenburg, NS, Canada **DISCIPLINE** HISTORY **EDUCATION** Dalhousie Univ, BA, 58; Univ Toronto, MA, 61; Univ Ottawa, PhD, 74. **CAREER** Tchr, Halifax Grammar Sch, 58; tchr, King's Col Sch, 61; tchr, Vaughan Rd Col Inst, 63-64; tchr, Navigation Sch, Can Forces & summer sch, Univ Ottawa, Univ Moncton, St. Mary's Univ, NS Tchrs Col, 73-78; PROF HISTORY, MEMORIAL UNIV NFLD, 68-70, 78-. **MEMBERSHIPS** Nfld Hist Soc (pres, 92-94) **SELECTED PUBLICATIONS** Auth, Nearer than Neighbours, 82; auth, Peace of the Continent, 86; auth, A Bridge Built Halfway, 90; auth, Kindred Countries, 94. **CONTACT ADDRESS** History Dept, Memorial Univ of Newfoundland, Elizabeth Ave, St. John's, NF, A1B 3X5. **EMAIL** mmacleod@morgan.ucs.mun.ca

MACLEOD, RODERICK CHARLES
PERSONAL Born 05/11/1940, Calgary, AB, Canada, m, 1962, 2 children **DISCIPLINE** HISTORY **EDUCATION** Univ Alta, BA, 61; Queen's Univ, MA, 67; Duke Univ, PhD(hist), 71. **CAREER** Asst prof, 69-75, assoc prof, 75-81, PROF HIST, UNIV ALTA, 81-. Can Coun leave fel, 76; gen ed, Alta Rec Publ Bd, 78-; chmn hist dept, 80- **MEMBERSHIPS** Can Hist Asn; Am Soc Legal Hist. **RESEARCH** Canadian legal history; Canadian social history; history of western Canada. **SELECTED PUBLICATIONS** Auth, Lord,Alex British Columbia--Recollections of a Rural School Inspector, 1915-36, Pac Northwest Quart, Vol 0084, 93; Pioneer Policing in Southern Alberta--Deane of the Mounties 1888-1914, Vol 9,, J Imperial and Commonwealth Hist, Vol 0023, 95. **CONTACT ADDRESS** Dept of Hist, Univ of Alta, Edmonton, AB, T6G 2E1.

MACMILLAN, MARGARET
PERSONAL Born 12/23/1943, Toronto, ON, Canada **DISCIPLINE** HISTORY **EDUCATION** Univ Toronto, BA, 62; Oxford Univ, Bphil, 68, Dphil, 74. **CAREER** Prof hist, Ryerson Polytech (former dept ch); Prof hist, Univ Toronto; BOARD & EXEC MEMBER, ONTARIO HERITAGE FOUNDATION. **MEMBERSHIPS** Can Inst Int Affairs; Victorian Stud Asn Can. **SELECTED PUBLICATIONS** Auth, Women of the Raj; co-ed, Canada and NATO: The Uneasy Century; co-ed, Int J. **CONTACT ADDRESS** 503 Sackville St, Toronto, ON, M4X 1T6.

MACMULLEN, RAMSAY
PERSONAL Born 03/03/1928, New York, NY, m, 1954, 4 children **DISCIPLINE** ANCIENT HISTORY **EDUCATION** Harvard Univ, AB, 50, AM, 53, PhD, 57. **CAREER** From instr to asst prof hist, Univ Ore, 56-61; from asst prof to assoc prof, Brandeis Univ, 61-65, 67-77, chmn dept classics, 67-67; chmn dept hist, 70-72, prof 67-79, DUNHAM PROF HIST AND CLASSICS, YALE UNIV, 79-, Fulbright res grant, Italy, 60-61; fel, Inst Advan Studies, 64-65; Guggenheim fel, 65; Nat Endowment for Humanities sr fel, 74-75; fel, Wolfson Col, Oxford Univ, 74-75. **MEMBERSHIPS** Soc Prom Roman Studies; AAUP; Asn Ancient Historians (pres, 78-81); Friends of Ancient Hist. **RESEARCH** Roman history. **SELECTED PUBLICATIONS** Auth, Religion and Society During the Roman Empire--a Colloquium in Honor of Vittinghoff, Friedrich, Gnomon Kritische Zeitschrift fur die Gesamte Klassische Altertumswissenschaft, Vol 0065, 93. **CONTACT ADDRESS** Dept of Hist, Yale Univ, New Haven, CT, 06520.

MACNEIL, ANNE
DISCIPLINE MUSIC HISTORY **EDUCATION** Univ Chicago, PhD. **CAREER** Asst prof; Am Acad fel in Rome, 92; ed, Socy for 17th-century Music Newsletter. **MEMBERSHIPS** Comt on the Status of Women, Am Musicol Soc. **RESEARCH** Renaissance; early mod studies. **SELECTED PUBLICATIONS** Auth, book on the Andreini family and music in the commedia dell'arte, Oxford UP, 99; The Divine Madness of Isabella Andreini, Proc Royal Musical Asn 120, 95 & The Virtue of Gender, La femme lettre la Renaissance: XIIth Colloque Int de L'Institut Interuniversitaire Renaissance et Humanisme, Bruxelles, 96, Brussels: Inst Interuniversitaire Renaissance et Humanisme, 97; coauth, The New International Dictionary of Music, NY, Meridian, 92. **CONTACT ADDRESS** School of Music, Univ of Texas at Austin, 2613 Wichita St, Austin, TX, 78705.

MACRO, ANTHONY DAVID
PERSONAL Born 07/10/1938, London, England, m, 1967, 2 children **DISCIPLINE** CLASSICAL PHILOLOGY, ANCIENT HISTORY **EDUCATION** Oxford Univ, BA, 61, MA, 64; Johns Hopkins Univ, PhD, 69. **CAREER** Teaching assoc classics, Ind Univ, Bloomington, 61-62; instr, Univ Md, College Park, 65-67; jr instr, Johns Hopkins Univ, 67-69; asst prof classics, 69-75, assoc prof, 75-85, prof, 85-, Hobart Prof Class Lang, 92-, Trinity Col. **HONORS AND AWARDS** Leverhulme Commonwealth fel, Univ Wales, 75-76. **MEMBERSHIPS** Am Philol Asn; Soc Prom Hellenic Studies; Soc Prom Roman Studies. **RESEARCH** Greek epigraphy; Roman imperial history; comparative linguistics. **SELECTED PUBLICATIONS** Auth, Sophocles, Trachiniai, 112-21, American Journal of Philology, 73; Imperial provisions for Pergamum: OGIS 484, Greek, Roman & Byzantine Studies, 76; "A Confirmed Asiarch," American Journal of Philology, 79; The Cities of Asia Minor under the Roman imperium, Aufstieg und Niedergang der romischen Welt, Vol 2, No 7, Berlin, 80; Applied classics: Using Latin and Greek in the modern world, Class Outlook, 81; auth, "Asiarch Reconfirmed," American Journal of Philology, 85; auth, Prolegemena to the Study of Galatian-Celtic Name

Formations, Celtic Connections, ACTA, 94. **CONTACT ADDRESS** Dept of Classics, Trinity Col, 300 Summit St, Hartford, CT, 06106-3186. **EMAIL** ad.macro@mail.trincoll.edu

MADDEN, DAVID WILLIAM

PERSONAL Born 09/10/1950, San Francisco, CA, m, 1977, 1 child **DISCIPLINE** AMERICAN AND ANGLO-IRISH LITERATURE **EDUCATION** Univ Calif, Davis, BA, 72, MA, 74, PhD(Am lit), 80. **CAREER** Lectr Am lit, Univ Pisa, Italy, 77-78; lectr compos and Am lit, Univ Calif, Davis, 79-82; instr compos, Am River Col, 81-82; ASST PROF AM LIT AND COMPOS, CALIF STATE UNIV, SACRAMENTO, 82-, Instr, Sacramento City Col, 80-82; instr, Am River Col, 80-81. **MEMBERSHIPS** Mod Lang Asn; Western Lit Asn. **RESEARCH** Contemporary American novel; modern American literature. **SELECTED PUBLICATIONS** Auth, Reading Carver, Raymond, Mod Fiction Stud, Vol 0040, 94; Cain, James, M. and the American Authors Authority, Mod Fiction Stud, Vol 0040, 94; The American Roman Noir--Hammett, Cain, and Chandler, Mod Fiction Stud, Vol 0042, 96; Fables of Subversion--Satire and the American Novel, 1930-1980, Mod Fiction Stud, Vol 0042, 96. **CONTACT ADDRESS** California State Univ, Sacramento, 800 Turnstone Dr, Sacramento, CA, 95819.

MADDEN, T.F.

PERSONAL Born 06/10/1960, Phoenix, AZ, m, 1994, 2 children **DISCIPLINE** MEDIEVAL HISTORY **EDUCATION** Univ IL, PhD 93, MA 90; Univ New Mexico, BA 86. **CAREER** St Louis Univ, asst prod, dept ch, assoc prof, 92 to 98-. **HONORS AND AWARDS** Gladys Krieble Delmas Foun Gnts; Laurence Marcellos Larson Prize **MEMBERSHIPS** CHA; HS; MAA; Us Nat Comm for Byzantine Study; Soc for the Stud of Crusades and the Latin East. **RESEARCH** Medieval Europe; The Crusades; Venice; Constantinople. **SELECTED PUBLICATIONS** Auth, The Forth Crusade: The Conquest of Constantinople, 1201-1204, coauth, Phil, U of Penn Press, 97; Medieval and Renaissance Venice, co-ed, Urbana, U of IL Press, 98; Outside and Inside the Forth Crusade, The Intl Hist Rev, 95; Venice and Constantinople in 1171 and 1172: Enrico Dandolo's Attitude Toward Byzantium, Med Hist Rev, 93; Vows and Contracts in the Forth Crusade: The Treaty of Zara and the Attack on Constantinople in 1204, Intl Hist Rev, 93; Father of the Bride: Father's Daughter's and Dowries in Late Medieval and Early Renaissance Venice, coauth, Renaissance Quart, 93. **CONTACT ADDRESS** Dept of History, St Louis Univ, 3800 Lindell Blvd, PO Box 56907, St Louis, MO, 63156-0907. **EMAIL** maddentf@slu.edu

MADDOX, ROBERT JAMES

PERSONAL Born 12/07/1931, Monroe, NY, m, 1958, 3 children **DISCIPLINE** AMERICAN DIPLOMATIC HISTORY **EDUCATION** Fairleigh Dickenson Univ, BS, 57; Univ Wis, MS, 58; Rutgers Univ, PhD(hist), 64. **CAREER** Instr hist, Paterson State Col, 62-64; asst prof, Mich State Univ, 64-66; from asst prof to assoc prof, 66-73, PROF HIST, PA STATE UNIV, 73-. **MEMBERSHIPS** AHA; Orgn Am Historians; Soc Hist Am Foreign Rels. **RESEARCH** American foreign policy, 1900-1940. **SELECTED PUBLICATIONS** Auth, Theres a War to Be Won--the United States Army in World War II, Historian, Vol 0055, 93; The Biggest Decision, Why We Had to Drop the Atomic Bomb, Amer Heritage, Vol 0046, 95; Operation Crossroads--the Atomic Tests at Bikini Atoll, Int Hist Rev, Vol 0017, 95; A-Bomb Scholarship, Amer Heritage, Vol 0046, 95; The View From Xanadu--Hearst,William,Randolph and United States Foreign Policy, Int Hist Rev, Vol 0019, 97; Lifeline to a Sinking Continent + the Marshall-Plan, Amer Heritage, Vol 0048, 97. **CONTACT ADDRESS** Dept of Hist, Pennsylvania State Univ, 108 Weaver Bldg, Univ Pk, PA, 16802-5500.

MADIGAN, MARY

PERSONAL Born 07/25/1922, Chicago, IL **DISCIPLINE** MEDIEVAL ENGLISH **EDUCATION** DePaul Univ, BA, 52; Univ Detroit, MA, 58; St Louis Univ, PhD(English), 67. **CAREER** Asst prof English, St Procopius Col, 65-69; assoc prof, Duquesne Univ, 69-72; ASSOC PROF ENGLISH, ST MICHAEL'S COL, UNIV TORONTO, 72-. **MEMBERSHIPS** Mediaeval Acad Am; MLA. **RESEARCH** Middle English prose; English drama; literary criticism. **SELECTED PUBLICATIONS** Auth, Sidney, Amer Scholar, Vol 0065, 96. **CONTACT ADDRESS** 2 S 304 Hawthorne Lane, Wheaton, IL, 60187.

MADISON, JAMES H.

PERSONAL Born 10/05/1944, York, PA, m, 1967, 2 children **DISCIPLINE** UNITED STATES HISTORY **EDUCATION** Gettysburg Col, BA, 66; Ind Univ, MA, 68, PhD(hist), 72. **CAREER** Fel bus hist, Harvard Univ, 72-73; vis asst prof, 73-76, asst prof, 76-81, ASSOC PROF HIST, IND UNIV, 81-, Assoc ed, J Am Hist, 73-76; ed, Ind Mag Hist, 76-; Newberry Libr fel, 78; Rockefeller Arch Ctr grant-in-aid, 81. **HONORS AND AWARDS** Herman Krooss Essay Award, Bus Hist Conf, 77. **MEMBERSHIPS** Orgn Am Historians; Bus Hist Conf; Am Asn State and Local Hist. **RESEARCH** Indiana, community and state history; business and economic history. **SELECTED PUBLICATIONS** Auth, Huntington, Henry, Edwards--a Biog, J Amer Hist, Vol 0082, 95; The War in American Culture--Society and Consciousness During World War II, Amer Hist Rev, Vol 0102, 97. **CONTACT ADDRESS** Dept of Hist, Indiana Univ, Bloomington, Ballantine Hall, Bloomington, IN, 47405.

MADISON, KENNETH GLENN

PERSONAL Born 01/11/1942, Washington, DC **DISCIPLINE** MEDIEVAL HISTORY **EDUCATION** Univ Ill, Urbana, AB, 62, AM, 63, PhD, 68. **CAREER** ASST PROF HIST, IA STATE UNIV, 67-. **MEMBERSHIPS** Mediaeval Acad Am, Richard III Soc. **RESEARCH** 14th and 15th century England and France **CONTACT ADDRESS** Dept of Hist, Iowa State Univ, Ames, IA, 50011-1202.

MADSEN, BRIGHAM DWAINE

PERSONAL Born 10/21/1914, Magna, UT, m, 1939, 4 children **DISCIPLINE** AMERICAN WESTERN HISTORY **EDUCATION** Univ Utah, BA, 38; Univ Calif, Berkeley, MA, 40, PhD(hist), 48. **CAREER** Assoc prof hist, Brigham Young Univ, 48-54 and Utah State Univ, 61-64; dean, Div Continuing Educ, Univ Utah, 66, deputy acad vpres admin, 67, admin vpres, 68-71, dir librs, 72-73, chmn dept hist, 74-75, PROF HIST, UNIV UTAH, 65-, Asst dir training, Peace Corps, Washington DC, 64; dir training, Vista, Washington DC, 65; dir Utah progs, Nat Endowment for humanities, 74-75. **MEMBERSHIPS** Western Hist Asn; Western Writers Am. **RESEARCH** Transportation in American West; American Indian history--PACIFIC Northwest and Utah; Utah history. **SELECTED PUBLICATIONS** Auth, Encounters With a Distant Land--Exploration and the Great-Northwest, Montana-Mag Western Hist, Vol 0046, 96. **CONTACT ADDRESS** 2181 Lincoln Lane, Salt Lake City, UT, 84117.

MADSEN, CAROL CORNWALL

PERSONAL Salt Lake City, UT **DISCIPLINE** AMERICAN AND WOMEN'S HISTORY **EDUCATION** Univ Utah, BA, 51, MA, 77. **CAREER** Res historian, Hist Div, Church of Jesus Christ of Latter-Day Saints, 77-78; RES HISTORIAN, JOSEPH FIELDING SMITH INST OF CHURCH HIST, BRIGHAM YOUNG UNIV, 78-. **MEMBERSHIPS** Mormon Hist Asn; Western Hist Asn; Orgn Am Historians; Coord Coun Women in the Hist Prof. **RESEARCH** Women in American history; women in Western American history; women in Mormon history. **SELECTED PUBLICATIONS** Auth, The so Called Power of Combination--Wells, Emmeline ,B. and the National and International Council of Women Church of Jesus Christ of Latter Day Saints, Brigham Young Univ Stud, Vol 0033, 93. **CONTACT ADDRESS** Joseph Fielding Smith Inst Church Hist, Brigham Young Univ, PROVO, UT, 84602.

MADSEN, DEBORAH

DISCIPLINE AMERICAN STUDIES & ENGLISH **EDUCATION** Univ Adelaide, BA, 81, MA, 84; Univ Sussex, DPhil, 88. **CAREER** Dir, Am stud prog, Univ Leicester; DEPT ENG, SO BANK UNIV, LONDON. **MEMBERSHIPS** Am Antiquarian Soc **RESEARCH** Hist of Pynchon & Hawthorne families **CONTACT ADDRESS** 2 Croft Close, Histon, ., CB4 4HU.

MAGEE, S.P.

PERSONAL Born 03/17/1943, Wichita, KS, m, 1988, 4 children **DISCIPLINE** ECONOMICS **EDUCATION** Tex Tech, BA, 65; MA, 66; MIT, PhD, 69. **CAREER** Asst prof, Univ Cal Berkeley, 69-71; assoc prof, Univ Chicago, 71-76; prof, Univ Tex, 76- . **HONORS AND AWARDS** Top Researcher, Grad Sch of Business, Univ Tex, 90; Who's Who in Am; Beasley Teaching Award and Best First-Year MBA Teacher, Univ Tex. **MEMBERSHIPS** Am Econ Asoc. **RESEARCH** International political economy (endogenous protection); the economic effects of lawyers; industrial organization. **CONTACT ADDRESS** Dept. of Finance, Univ of Texas, Austin, TX, 78712. **EMAIL** magee@mail.utexas.edu

MAGNAGHI, RUSSELL MARIO

PERSONAL Born 10/12/1943, San Francisco, CA, m, 1973 **DISCIPLINE** AMERICAN HISTORY **EDUCATION** Univ San Francisco, BA, 65; St Louis Univ, MA, 67, PhD(hist), 70. **CAREER** Instr Am hist, Florissant Valley Community Col, 67-68; instr, St Louis Univ, 68-69; from instr to asst prof, 69-74, assoc prof, 74-80, PROF AM HIST, NORTHERN MICH UNIV, 80-, Res grants, Northern Mich Univ, 76 and 78. **MEMBERSHIPS** AHA; Orgn Am Hist; Western Hist Asn. **RESEARCH** Spanish borderlands; American Indians; Trans-Mississippi West. **SELECTED PUBLICATIONS** Auth, Farmers, Hunters, and Colonist--Interaction Between the Southwest and Southern Plains, Great Plains Quart, Vol 0014, 94. **CONTACT ADDRESS** Dept of Hist, No Michigan Univ, 1401 Presque Isle Ave, Marquette, MI, 49855-5301.

MAGNUS, BERND

DISCIPLINE NINETEENTH AND TWENTIETH-CENTURY EUROPEAN PHILOSOPHY **EDUCATION** Columbia Univ, PhD. **CAREER** PROF, UNIV CALIF, RIVERSIDE. **RESEARCH** Critical literary theory; History of modern philosophy. **SELECTED PUBLICATIONS** Auth, Nietzsche's Case: Philosophy as/and Literature, Routledge, 93; "Reading Ascetic Reading: Toward the Genealogy of Morals and the Path Back to the World," Nietzsche, Genealogy, Morality, Univ Calif Press, 94; "Postmodern Pragmatism," Pragmatism: From Progressivism to Postmodernism, Praeger, 95; Postmodern Philosophy, The Cambridge Dictionary of Philos, Cambridge Univ Press, 95; "Holocaust Child," Contemp Continental Philos in the US: A Photogrammic Presentation, 96; ed, Specters of Marx, Routledge, 94; Whither Marxism?, Routledge, 95; co-ed, The Cambridge Companion to Nietzsche, Cambridge Univ Press, 96. **CONTACT ADDRESS** Dept of Philos, Univ Calif, 1156 Hinderaker Hall, Riverside, CA, 92521-0209. **EMAIL** magnus@ucracl.ucr.edu

MAHAN, HOWARD F.

PERSONAL Born 10/14/1923, New York, NY, m, 1946, 3 children **DISCIPLINE** HISTORY, POLITICAL SCIENCE **EDUCATION** Drew Univ, BA, 48; Columbia Univ, MA, 51, PhD(hist and govt), 58. **CAREER** Assoc prof hist, Univ Ala, 54-64; PROF HIST AND CHMN DEPT, UNIV S ALA, 64-. **MEMBERSHIPS** AHA; Orgn Am Historians; Am Studies Asn; Southern Hist Asn. **RESEARCH** Origins of United States declarations of war; early republic, intellectual history. **SELECTED PUBLICATIONS** Auth, Partisans of the Southern Press--Editorial Spokesmen of the 19th-Century, J Southern Hist, Vol 0062, 96. **CONTACT ADDRESS** 4158 Holly Springs Dr, Mobile, AL, 36688.

MAHAN, SUSAN

PERSONAL Born 04/13/1949, San Jose, CA, m, 1997, 3 children **DISCIPLINE** HISTORIC THEOLOGY **EDUCATION** Univ South FL, BA, 71, MA, 77; Marquette Univ, PhD, 88. **CAREER** Adjunct prof: San Jose State Univ, 88-97, Santa Clara Univ, 92-97, Univ of San Francisco, 92-98; ADJUNCT PROF, LOYOLA-MARYMOUNT, 98-. **MEMBERSHIPS** AAR; CTSA; CTS. **RESEARCH** Amer spirituality; women mystics; Asceticism; spirituality and work; spirituality and marriage. **CONTACT ADDRESS** 181 Rainbow Lane, Watsonville, CA, 95076. **EMAIL** smahan@got.net

MAHONEY, JOHN FRANCIS

PERSONAL Born 05/19/1929, Detroit, MI, m, 1980 **DISCIPLINE** ENGLISH, CLASSICS **EDUCATION** Univ Detroit, BA, 50, MA, 52; Univ NC, PhD, 56. **CAREER** Instr English, Univ NC, 53-56; instr Latin, Duke Univ, 54-56; asst prof Mid English, Duquesne Univ, 56-59, assoc prof English & chm grad studies, 59-61; assoc prof English & comp lit, Univ Detroit, 61-63, chm grad comt, 61-64, dean col arts & sci, 69-73, prof English & comp lit & chm dept, 64-73; dean, Walden Univ, 73-74; vpres acad affairs, William Paterson Col NJ, 74-78; Dean, Walden Univ, 79-, Southern Fels Fund fel, 56; mem bd, Am Grad & Prof Comn, 66-; pres, Vri, Inc, 79-; admin dir, Beli-Laddi farm, 80- ; ed & publ Imperial Beach & South County Times, 85-98; columnist, Imperial Beach Eagle & Times, 98- ; PROJECT DEVELOP OFFICER, B.E.L.I., Inc., 96- . **MEMBERSHIPS** MLA; Mediaeval Acad Am; Dante Soc Am; Soc Exceptional Children. **RESEARCH** Mixed media; mediaeval languages; Dante. **SELECTED PUBLICATIONS** Ed, The Structure of Purgatorio, Dante Soc Bull, 62; Chaucerian Tragedy and the Christian Tradition, Ann Mediaevale, 62; American Authors and Critics (12 vols), Holt, 62-; coauth, Studies in Honor of V T Holmes, Jr, Univ NC, Chapel Hill, 66; The Insistent Present, Houghton, 70; co-ed, New Poets, New Music, Winthrop, 71; coauth, Early Help (film), Medianovations, 73; The House of Tenure (play), Medianovations, 80. **CONTACT ADDRESS** PO Box 5429, Playa del Rey, CA, 92293. **EMAIL** mahwis@gte.net

MAHONEY, JOSEPH F.

PERSONAL Born 07/04/1927, Jersey City, NJ, m, 1953, 4 children **DISCIPLINE** AMERICAN HISTORY **EDUCATION** Duns Scotus Col, AB, 49; Seton Hall Univ, AM, 58; Columbia Univ, PhD(hist), 64. **CAREER** From asst prof to assoc prof, 59-69, prof hist, Seton Hall Univ, 69-97, prof emeritus, 98-, ed, NJ Hist, 69-80; dir, NJ Cath Hist Rec Comn, 76-. **MEMBERSHIPS** AHA; Am Cath Hist; Orgn Am Historians. **RESEARCH** New Jersey history; 20th century United States; late 19th century American history. **SELECTED PUBLICATIONS** Auth, Backsliding convert: Woodrow Wilson and the seven sisters, Am Quart, spring 66; Woman suffrage and the urban masses, NJ Hist, fall 69; Impact of industrialization on the New Jersey Legislature, 1870-1900, In: New Jersey Since 1860; New Findings and Interpretations, 72. **CONTACT ADDRESS** Dept of Hist, Seton Hall Univ, 400 S Orange Ave, South Orange, NJ, 07079-2697. **EMAIL** mahonejo@shu.edu

MAHONEY, MICHAEL SEAN

PERSONAL Born 06/30/1939, New York, NY, m, 1960, 2 children **DISCIPLINE** HISTORY OF SCIENCE AND TECHNOLOGY **EDUCATION** Harvard Univ, BA, 60; Princeton Univ, MA, 64, PhD(hist sci), 67. **CAREER** Instr hist, 65-67, asst prof, 67-72, assoc prof, 72-80, PROF HIST AND HIST OF SCI, PRINCETON UNIV, 80-, NSF-NATO fel, 69-70; Nat Humanities fac, 75-. **MEMBERSHIPS** Hist Sci Soc; Renaissance Soc Am; Soc Hist Tech. **RESEARCH** History of mathematics; scientific revolution. **SELECTED PUBLICATIONS** Auth, The Magic of Numbers and Motion--the Scientific Career of Descartes, Rene, Isis, Vol 0084, 93; Von Neumann,John and the Origins of Modern Computing, Isis, Vol 0084, 93; Toward a

History of Game Theory, Isis, Vol 0085, 94; The 4th Discontinuity--the Coevolution of Humans and Machines, Isis, Vol 0086, 95; De Quadratura Arithmetica Circuli Ellipseos Et Hyperbolae Cujus Corollarium Est Trigonometria Sine Tabulis, Isis, Vol 0086, 95; Index of British Mathematicians .3. 1701-1800, Isis, Vol 0086, 95; The 4th Discontinuity--the Coevolution of Humans and Machines, Isis, Vol 0086, 95; Landmarks in Digital Computing--a Smithsonian Pictorial History, Isis, Vol 0086, 95; The Investigation of Difficult Things--Essays on Newton and the History of the Exact Sciences in Honor of Whiteside, D.T., Isis, Vol 0087, 96; Penetralia Motus--Relativistic Foundation of Mechanics in Huygens,Christiaan With the Edition of the Codex-Hugenorium-7a, Isis, Vol 0087, 96; Fermat Theorem and his Readers, Isis, Vol 0088, 97; The Early History of Data Networks, Technol and Culture, Vol 0038, 97. **CONTACT ADDRESS** Dept of Hist, Princeton Univ, Princeton, NJ, 08544.

MAHONEY, TIMOTHY
DISCIPLINE 19TH CENTURY AMERICAN URBAN AND SOCIAL HISTORY **EDUCATION** Univ Chicago, PhD, 82. **CAREER** Assoc prof, Univ Nebr, Lincoln. **HONORS AND AWARDS** NEH fel, Newberry Libr, Chicago, 91-92; Mayers fel, Huntington Libr, 96. **RESEARCH** Middle class experience in the Antebellum Middle West. **SELECTED PUBLICATIONS** Auth, River Towns in the Great West: The Structure of Provincial Urbanization in the American Middle West, 1820-1870, Cambridge UP, 90. **CONTACT ADDRESS** Univ Nebr, Lincoln, 636 Oldfat, Lincoln, NE, 68588-0417. **EMAIL** tmahoney@unlinfo.unl.edu

MAIDMAN, MAYNARD PAUL
PERSONAL Born 08/07/1944, Philadelphia, PA, m, 1971, 2 children **DISCIPLINE** ANCIENT HISTORY, BIBLICAL STUDIES **EDUCATION** Columbia Univ, AB, 66; Univ Pa, PhD(Oriental studies), 76. **CAREER** Lectr, 72-76, asst prof, 76-78, ASSOC PROF HIST AND HEBREW, YORK UNIV, 78-. **MEMBERSHIPS** Am Oriental Soc; Soc Bibl Lit. **RESEARCH** Private economic records from Late Bronze Age Iraq and their significance; the dynamics of ancient archive keeping; ancient Israelite political history. **SELECTED PUBLICATIONS** Auth, Reallexikon of Assyriology and Near Eastern Archaeology, Vol 8, Fascicles 1-2, Meek Miete, Fascicles 3-4, Miete Moab, J Amer Oriental Soc, Vol 0116, 96; Uncovering Ancient Stones--Essays in Memory of Richardson, H. Neil, J Amer Oriental Soc, Vol 0116, 96. **CONTACT ADDRESS** York Univ, N York, ON, M3J 1P3.

MAIER, DONNA J. E.
PERSONAL Born 02/20/1948, St. Louis, MO, 2 children **DISCIPLINE** HISTORY, AFRICA **EDUCATION** Col Wooster, BA, 69; Northwestern Univ, MA, 72, PhD(hist), 75. **CAREER** Asst prof, Univ TX, Dallas, 75-78; asst prof, 78-81, asst prof, 78-81, assoc prof, 81-86, prof hist, Univ Northern IA, 86-; consult, Scott, Foresman, 75-82, Fulbright Hayes fel, 87; co-ed, Africa Economic Hist, 92-. **HONORS AND AWARDS** IA Board of Regents Faculty Excellence Award, 96. **MEMBERSHIPS** African Studies Asn; Ghana Studies Coun. **RESEARCH** Nineteenth century Asante (Ghana) history; African Islam; traditional African medicine. **SELECTED PUBLICATIONS** Coauth, History and Life, Scott, Foresman & Co, 77, 4nd ed, 90; auth, Nineteenth Century Asante Medical Practices, Comp Studies Soc & Hist, 79; Competition for Power and Profits in Kete-Krachi, West Africa, 1875-1900, Int African Hist Studies, 80; The Dente Oracle, the Bron Confederation, and Asante: Religion and the Politics of Secession, J African Hist, 81; History and Life: The World and Its Peoples, with T W Wallbank and A. Shrier, Scott Foresman, 1st ed, 77, 2nd ed, 82, 3rd ed, 86, 4th ed, 90; Priests and Power: The Case of the Dente Shrine in Nineteenth-Century Ghana, IN Univ Press, 83; Colonial Distortion of the Volta River Salt Trade, in African Economic Hist, 86; Slave Labor/Wage Labor in German Togoland, in Arthur Knoll and Lewis Gann, eds, Germans in the Tropics: Essays in German Colonial History, Greenwood Press, 87; Asante War Aims in the 1869 Invasion of Ewe, in Enid Schildkrout, ed, The Golden Stool: Studies of the Asante Center and Periphery, Am Museum of Nat Hist Press, 87; The Military Aquisition of Slaves in Asante, in D. Henige and T C McCaskie, eds, West African Economic and Social History, African Studies, Madison, 90; Treasures of the World: Literature and Source Readings for World History, with H Roupp, Scott Foresman, 91; Persistance of Precolonial Patterns of Production: Cotton in German Togoland 1800-1914, in A Issacman and R Roberts, eds, Cotton, Colonialism, and Social History in Sud-Sahara Africa, Heinemann, 95; Islam and the Idea of Asylum in Asanta, in J Humwick and N Lawlor, eds, The Cloths of Many-Colored Silks, Northwestern Univ Press, 96. **CONTACT ADDRESS** Dept Hist, Univ Northern IA, Cedar Falls, IA, 50614-0001. **EMAIL** donna.maier@uni.edu

MAIER, PAUL LUTHER
PERSONAL Born 05/31/1930, St. Louis, MO, 4 children **DISCIPLINE** ANCIENT HISTORY **EDUCATION** Concordia Sem, AB, 52, BD, 55; Harvard Univ, MA, 54; Univ Basel, PhD, 57. **CAREER** From asst prof to assoc prof, 59-68, prof hist, Western Mich Univ, 68-; Lutheran Campus Chaplain, Western Mich Univ, 58-. **HONORS AND AWARDS** Detur Award, 50;

Distinguished Fac Scholar Award, Western Mich Univ, 81; The Gold Medallion Book Award for Josephus -- The Essential Writings, Evan Christian Publishers Assoc, 89; Doctor of Letters Degree award honoris causa by Concordia Seminary, St Louis, 95. **MEMBERSHIPS** AHA **RESEARCH** Ancient history; Palestine and Rome in first century AD. **SELECTED PUBLICATIONS** Auth, Caspar Schwenckfeld on the Person and Work of Christ, VanGorcum, Neth, 59; A Man Spoke, A World Listened, McGraw, 63; Pontius Pilate, Doubleday, 68; First Christmas--The True and Unfamiliar Story, 61, First Easter--The True and Unfamiliar Story, 73 & First Christians--Pentecost and the Spread of Christianity, 76, Harper; ed, The Best of Walter A Maier, Concordia, 80; auth, The Flames of Rome, Doubleday, 81; A Skeleton in God's Closet, Thomas Nelson, 94; ed, trans, Josephus, The Essential Works, Kregel, 95; Eusebius, The Church History, Kregel, 98. **CONTACT ADDRESS** Dept of History, Western Michigan Univ, 1201 Oliver St, Kalamazoo, MI, 49008-3805. **EMAIL** paul.maier@wmich.edu

MAIER, PAULINE RUBBELKE
PERSONAL Born 04/27/1938, St. Paul, MN, m, 1961, 3 children **DISCIPLINE** AMERICAN HISTORY **EDUCATION** Radcliff Col, AB, 60; Harvard Univ, PhD(hist), 68. **CAREER** From asst prof to assoc prof hist, Univ MA, Boston, 68-77; Robinson-Edwards prof, Univ WI-Madison, 77-78; prof Hist, 78-89, Wm Rand prof Am Hist, MA Inst Technol, 90-; Chas Warren Ctr Study Am Hist fel, Harvard Univ, 74-75; Nat Endowment Humanities Younger Humanist fel, 74-75, 88-89; Guggenheim fel, 90. **HONORS AND AWARDS** Douglass G Adair Award, Inst Early Am Hist, 76; LLD (hon), Regis Col, 87; DHL (hon), Williams Col, 93. **MEMBERSHIPS** Soc Am Historians; Am Antiq Soc; Orgn Am Historians; AHA; SHEAR; Col Soc of MA; MA Hist Soc. **RESEARCH** The Colonial, Revolutionary, and Early National Periods of American history. **SELECTED PUBLICATIONS** Auth, Popular Uprisings and Civil Authority in 18th Century America, William & Mary Quart, 70; The Charleston Mob and the Development of Popular Politics in Revolutionary South Carolina, 1765-1784, Perspectives Am Hist, 70; From Resistance to Revolution: Colonial Radicals and the Development of American Opposition to Britain, 1765-1776, Knopf, 72; Coming to Terms with Samuel Adams, Am Hist Rev, 76; co-ed, Interdisciplinary Studies of the American Revolution, Sage, 76; The Old Revolutionaries: Political Lives in the Age of Samuel Adams, Knopf, 80; The Road Not Taken: Nullification John C Calhoun, and the Revolutionary Tradition in South Carolina, SC Hist Mag, 81; Boston and New York in the 18th Century, Proc Am Antiq Soc, 82; The American People: A History, DC Heath, 86; Revolutionary Origins of the American Corporation, William and Mary Quart, 93; American Scripture: Making the Declaration of Independence, Knopf, 97; intro, The Constitution, the Bill of Rights, and the Declaration of Independence, Bantam, 98. **CONTACT ADDRESS** History Faculty, Massachusetts Inst of Tech, 77 Massachusetts Ave, Cambridge, MA, 02139-4307. **EMAIL** pmaier@mit.edu

MAILLET, MARGUERITE
PERSONAL Born 03/17/1924, St. Norbert, NB, Canada **DISCIPLINE** CANADIAN/ACADIAN STUDIES **EDUCATION** Laval Univ, BPh, 57; Regina Mundi (Rome) & St Mary's Univ (Ind), MA (Sacred Stud), 66; Laval & Moncton Univ, MA (Fr), 71; Univ Ottawa, PhD, 82. **CAREER** Tchr, NB sch; prof, Ecole normale de Moncton, 68; prof, Univ Moncton, 73, dir Fr stud, 79-81, vice dean arts, 85, ch, d'etudes acadiennes, 87-90, PROF EMER, UNIV MONCTON, 94-. **RESEARCH** Acadian studies. **SELECTED PUBLICATIONS** Auth, Histoire de la litterature acadienne: de reve en reve, 83; auth, Bibliographie des publications d'Acadie 1609-1990: Sources premieres et sources secondes, 92; auth, Bibliographie des publications de l'Acadie des provinces Maritimes: livres et brochures 1609-1995, 97; coauth, Anthologie de textes litteraires acadiens, 79; coauth, The Bicentennial Lectures on New Brunswick Literature, 85; coauth, La Reception des oeuvres d'Antonine Maillet. **CONTACT ADDRESS** 101 Archibald St, Apt 3003, Moncton, NB, E1C 9J7.

MAIN, GLORIA L.
PERSONAL Born 06/01/1933, San Francisco, CA, m, 1956, 3 children **DISCIPLINE** AMERICAN HISTORY **EDUCATION** Columbia Univ, PhD 72. **CAREER** Univ Colorado, assoc prof, 83-. **MEMBERSHIPS** AHA; AHEHA; SSHA; AOI; EAHC; AAS; NEHGS. **RESEARCH** Early American History; Native Amer History; Hist of Slavery in the Americas; Family History. **SELECTED PUBLICATIONS** Auth, Naming Children in Early New England, The Jour of Interdisciplinary Hist, 96; Auth, Gender Work and Wages in Colonial New England, WM and Mary Quart, 94; Family Structures: The British Colonies, Encycl of the N Amer Colonies, 93; auth, The English Family in America: A Comparison of Chesapeake New England and Pennsylvania Quaker Families in the Colonial Period, Lois Green Carr, The Chesapeake and Beyond: A Celebration, Crownsville MD, 92. **CONTACT ADDRESS** Dept of History, Univ of Colorado, 2305 Dartmouth Ave, Boulder, CO, 80303. **EMAIL** maing@spot.colorado.edu

MAIN, JACKSON T.
DISCIPLINE HISTORY **EDUCATION** Univ Wis, BA, 39, MA, 40, PhD, 48. **CAREER** PROF, ADJ, UNIV COLO AT BOULDER **MEMBERSHIPS** AM Antiquarian Soc **SELECTED PUBLICATIONS** Auth, "Summary: The Hereafter," Forum; auth, Toward a History the Standard of Living in British America, Wm & Mary Quart 45, 88; auth, The Social Origins of Leaders, 2000 BC to 1845 AD, Brandywine Press. **CONTACT ADDRESS** 2305 Dartmouth Ave, Boulder, CO, 80303.

MAIRE-CARLS, ALICE-CATHERINE
PERSONAL Born 06/14/1950, Mulhouse, France, m, 1977, 3 children **DISCIPLINE** HISTORY, POLISH LITERATURE **EDUCATION** Univ de Paris IV-Sorbonne, BA, 70, MA, 72, BA, 73, Doctorat de Troisieme Cycle, 76. **CAREER** Eastern Europ corresp, 81-98, ed adv, 98- , Center for Public Justice, Washington DC; from asst prof, history, to assoc prof, 92- , chemn Dept of Hist and Polit Sci, Univ Tenn, Martin. **HONORS AND AWARDS** Listed, Who's Who in America, Who's Who among Polish-Americans, Who's Who in American Education, Who's Who in Polish America, Who's Who in the World, Who's Who among America's Teachers, Who's Who in the South and Southwest, International Authors and Writers Who's Who, Who's Who of American Women; Int Scholar Award nominee, Univ Tenn, 95. **MEMBERSHIPS** Phi Kappa Phi; Phi Alpha Theta; Pi Delta Phi; Polish-Am Hist Asn; Polish Inst of Arts and Sci; Am Asn for Adv of Slavic Stud; AHA; Ctr for Public Justice; So Asn for Slavic Stud; So Hist Asn. **RESEARCH** Translation; Eastern European literature; history; twentieth-century Polish literature, history, society and politics. **SELECTED PUBLICATIONS** Transl, Echapper a ma tombe, by Jozef M. Rostocki, with intro, Editions Editiner, 95; transl, Jozef Wittlin, with intro, Poesie Premiere, 97; transl, Clarte, grace, humour: l'intellect de Wislawa Szymborska, by Anna Frajlich, Poesie Premiere, 97; transl, Polyphonic, equilibre, couleur: la poesie vitale de Awaikta, by Marilou Awiakta, with intro, Poesie premiere, 97; transl, Aleksander Wat, a contricourant, with intro, Poesie Premiere, 98; transl, Devant l'autoportrait de Weimar, par Durer, Nocturnes, Devant Bonnard, Calligraphies, Les saules d'Alma-Ata, Nuit d'automne avec montagnes, oliviers et pleine lune, Poeme bucolique, by Aleksander Wat, with intro, le Journal des Poetes, Brusseld, 98; transl, Une mouche dans ma soupe, by Jozef M. Rostocki, Editions Editinter, 98; contribur, Encyclopedia of Modern East Europe, 1815-1989, Garland, forthcoming; auth, Jozef Wittlin's Passage Through France, in Proceedings of the Jozef Wittlin Conference, Columbia Univ, forthcoming. **CONTACT ADDRESS** 59 Lesa Dr, Jackson, TN, 38305. **EMAIL** accarls@utm.edu

MAISCH, CHRISTIAN
DISCIPLINE LATIN AMERICA **EDUCATION** Am Univ, PhD. **CAREER** Prof, Am Univ. **MEMBERSHIPS** Inter-American Develop Bank. **RESEARCH** International relations theory and international law and organization. **SELECTED PUBLICATIONS** Auth, A Legal and Historical Analysis of the Conflicting Anglo-Argentine Claims to the Falkland/Malvinas Islands,Universidad Inca Garcilaso, 95. **CONTACT ADDRESS** American Univ, 4400 Massachusetts Ave, Washington, DC, 20016.

MAIZLISH, STEPHEN E.
PERSONAL Born 12/13/1945, Los Angeles, CA **DISCIPLINE** AMERICAN HISTORY **EDUCATION** Univ Calif, Berkeley, BA, 67; Univ Mich, MA, 68; Univ Calif, Berkeley, PhD(hist), 78. **CAREER** Actg instr, Univ Calif, Berkeley, 76; ASST PROF HIST, UNIV TEX, ARLINGTON, 78- **MEMBERSHIPS** AHA; Orgn Am Historians. **RESEARCH** United States Civil War and reconstruction; United States political history; United States 19th century. **SELECTED PUBLICATIONS** Auth, Lincoln at Gettysburg--the Words That Remade America, Historian, Vol 0055, 93; The Market Revolution--Jacksonian America, 1815-1846, Amer Hist Rev, Vol 0098, 93. **CONTACT ADDRESS** Dept Hist, Univ Tex, Arlington, TX, 76019.

MAJOR, JAMES RUSSELL
PERSONAL Born 01/07/1921, Riverton, VA, m, 1945, 4 children **DISCIPLINE** HISTORY **EDUCATION** Va Mil Inst, AB, 42; Princeton Univ, AM, 48, PhD, 49. **CAREER** From instr to assoc prof, 49-61, prof, 61-80, CANDLER PROF RENAISSANCE HIST, EMORY UNIV, 80-. Fulbright fel, France, 52-53; Guggenheim fels, 53-54, 67-68; Soc Sci Res Coun fels, 55-58, 61-62; vis prof, Harvard Univ, 65-66; mem, Inst Advan Studies, 67-68, 79-80; Nat Endowment for Humanities sr fel, 73-74. **MEMBERSHIPS** Southern Hist Asn; AAUP; AHA; Renaissance Soc Am; Am Soc Reformation Res; Soc Hist France. **RESEARCH** European constitutional history, 1400-1700; French history, 1400-1700. **SELECTED PUBLICATIONS** Auth, Vertical Ties Through Time + Patronage, Language, and Political-Culture, Fr Hist Stud, Vol 0017, 92; War and Government in the French Provinces--Picardy 1470-1560, J Interdisciplinary Hist, Vol 0026, 95; Louis XII, Cath Hist Rev, Vol 0081, 95; Renaissance Warrior and Patron--the Reign of Francis-I, Amer Hist Rev, Vol 0101, 96; The State in Early Modern France, Historian, Vol 0059, 97. **CONTACT ADDRESS** Dept of Hist, Emory Univ, Atlanta, GA, 30322.

MAJOR, WILFRED E.
DISCIPLINE CLASSICS **EDUCATION** Southern IL Univ Carbondale, BA, 89; IN Univ, MA, 91; IN Univ, PhD, 96. **CAREER** Assoc instr, IN Univ, 90-94; instr, Hobart and William Smith Col, 94-96; instr, Loyola Univ New Orleans, 95-97; adj instr, Tulane Univ, 96-97; asst prof, St Anselm Col, 97-. **SELECTED PUBLICATIONS** Auth, Gorgias' Undeclared Theory of Arrangement Revisited, Southern Comm Jour, 97; Gorgias' "Undeclared" Theory of Arrangement: A Postscript to Smeltzer, Southern Comm Jour, 96; The Epistemic Music of Rhetoric: Toward the Temporal Dimension of Affect in Reader Response and Writing (rev), Southern Ill UP, 96, and Bryn Mawr Classical Rev, 97; ed, Euripides: Andromache in Aris and Phillips 1994, Didaskalia, 95. **CONTACT ADDRESS** Department of Class, St Anselm Col, 100 Saint Anselm Dr, Box 1701, Manchester, NH, 03102-1310. **EMAIL** wmajor@anselm.edu

MAKOWSKI, ELIZABETH
PERSONAL Born 03/13/1951, Milwaukee, WI **DISCIPLINE** HISTORY OF MEDIEVAL EUROPE **EDUCATION** Univ Wis-Milwaukee, BA, 73; MA, 76; Harvard Univ, AM, 77; Columbia Univ, PhD, 93. **CAREER** Asst prof, SW Tex State Univ, 93-98; assoc prof, 98-. **HONORS AND AWARDS** Columbia Univ President's Fel, 89-93; SWT Res Grants, 94, 96, 97; Sch of Lib Arts Award for Scholarly Activ, 97. **MEMBERSHIPS** Am Cath Hist Asoc; Tex Cath Hist Asoc; Tex Medieval Asoc. **RESEARCH** Canon law; Medieval religious women. **SELECTED PUBLICATIONS** Auth, The Conjugal Debt and Medieval Canon Law, Equally in God's Image, Women in the Middle Ages, 90; auth, with James A. Brundage, Enclosure of Nuns: The Decretal Periculoso and Its Commentators, J Medieval Hist, 94; auth, Tomas Sanchez on the Cloistering of Nuns: Canonical Theory and Spanich Cololnial Practice, Cath Southwest, 96; auth, Canon Law and Cloistered Women: Periculoso and Its Commentators 1298-1545, 97; Mulieres Religiosae, Strictly Speaking: Some Fourteenth-Century Canonical Opinions, The Cath Hist Rev, forthcoming. **CONTACT ADDRESS** Dept. of History, SW Texas State Univ, San Marcos, TX, 78666. **EMAIL** em13@swt.edu

MALAMUD, MARTHA A.
PERSONAL Boston, MA, m, 2 children **DISCIPLINE** CLASSICS **EDUCATION** Bryn Mawr, BA, 78; Cornell, PhD, 85. **CAREER** Asst, assoc prof, Univ of Southern Cal, 84-92; assoc prof, classics dept, Univ of Buffalo (SUNY), 92-. **HONORS AND AWARDS** Mellon fel; Rome prize: NEH sr fel, Amer Acad in Rome, 88-89; ACLS grant. **MEMBERSHIPS** Amer Philol Asn. **RESEARCH** Late antique lit; Latin epic. **SELECTED PUBLICATIONS** Ed, Arethusa. **CONTACT ADDRESS** Classics Dept., Univ of Buffalo (SUNY), Clemens Hall, Buffalo, NY, 14260. **EMAIL** malamud@acsu.buffalo.edu

MALANDRA, WILLIAM
DISCIPLINE CLASSICAL AND NEAR EASTERN STUDIES **EDUCATION** Haverford Col, BA, 64; Brown Univ, BA, 66; Univ Pa, PhD, 71. **CAREER** Assoc prof, Univ Minn, Twin Cities. **RESEARCH** Indo-Iranian philological studies. **SELECTED PUBLICATIONS** Auth, Avestan zanu-drajah: an Obscene Gesture, Indo-Iranian J 22, 80; An Introduction to Old Iranian Religion, Univ Minn Press, 83; Rasnu and the Office of Divine Judge: Comparative Reconstructions and the Varuna Problem, Festschrift for Ludo Rocher, Madras: Adyar Libr, 87. **CONTACT ADDRESS** Dept of Class and Near Eastern Stud, Univ Minn, Twin Cities, Minneapolis, MN, 55455.

MALBON, ELIZABETH STRUTHERS
PERSONAL Born 01/24/1947, Orlando, FL, m, 1979, 2 children **DISCIPLINE** BIBLICAL STUDIES, NEW TESTAMENT **EDUCATION** Fla State Univ, BA, 69, MA, 70, PhD(humanities), 80. **CAREER** Teaching asst humanities, Fla State Univ, 76-77; vis instr relig, Vassar Col, 78-79; adj lectr, Fla State Univ, 79-80; asst prof relig, Va Polytech Inst & State Univ, 80-85, assoc prof, 85-92, prof, 92-, dir Religious Studies Program, 94-. **HONORS AND AWARDS** ACLS Research Fellowship, 84; NEH Summer Seminar, 87; ACLS Travel Grant, 88. **MEMBERSHIPS** Soc Bibl Lit; Am Acad Relig; Cath Bibl Assoc; Soc Values in Higher Ed; Studiorum Novi Testamenti Societas. **RESEARCH** Gospel of Mark; literary approaches; gospels. **SELECTED PUBLICATIONS** Auth, Mythic Structure and Meaning in Mark: Elements of a Levi-Straussian Analysis, Semeia, Vol 16, 79; Galilee and Jerusalem: History and literature in Marcan interpretation, Cath Bibl Quart, 82; Structuralism, Hermeneutics and Contextual Meaning, J Am Acad Relig, 83; No need to have any one Write?: A Structural Exegesis of 1 Thessalonians, Semeia,Vol 26, 83; Fallible Followers: Women and Men in the Gospel of Mark, Semeia, Vol 28, 83; The spiral and the Square: Levi-Strauss's Mythic Formula and Greimas's Constitutional Model, Linguistica Biblica, 84; The Jesus of Mark and the Sea of Galilee, J Bibl Lit, 84; Auth, The Text and Time: Levi-Strauss and New Testament Studies, in Anthropology and the Study of Religions, ed Frank E. Reynolds and Robert L. Moore, Council for the Scientific Study of religion, 84. Joint Auth, Parabling as a via Negativa: A Critical Review of the work of John Dominic Crossan, J Relig, 84. Auth, The Theory and Practice of Structural Exegesis: A review article, Perspectives in Religious Stud, 84; Te oikia autou: Mark 2:15 in Context, New Testament Studies, 85; Mark: Myth and Parable, Bibl Theol Bul, 86; Disciples/Crowds/Whoever: Markan Characters and Readers, Novum Testamentum, 86; The Jewish Leaders in the Gospel of Mark: A Literary Study of N¤Marcan Characterizations, J Bibl Lit, 89; Ending at the Beginning: A response, Semeia, Vol 52, 90; Echoes and Foreshadowings in Mark 4-8: Reading and Rereading, J Bibl Lit, 93; Texts and Contexts: Interpreting the Disciples in Mark, Semeia, Vol 62, 93; The Poor Widow in Mark and Her Poor Rich Readers, Cath Bibl Quart, 91: Auth, Narrative Space and Mythic Meaning in Mark, Harper & Row, 86, Sheffield Academic Press, 91;Narrative Criticism: How Does the Story Mean?, in Mark and Method: New Approaches in Biblical Studies, ed Janice Capel Anderson and Stephen D. Moore, Fortress Press, 92. Joint ed, Characterization in Biblical Literature, Semeia, Vol 63, 93; Joint auth, Literary critical methods, in Searching the Scriptures, Vol 1, A Feminist Introduction, ed Elisabeth Schussler Fiorenza, Crossroad Press, 93. Auth, Echoes and foreshadowings in Mark 4-8: Reading and rereading, J Bibl Lit, 93; Texts and contexts: Interpreting the disciples in Mark, Semeia, Vol 62, 93; The New Literary Criticism and the New Testament, Sheffield Academic Press, 94, Trinity Press Int, 94; The Major Importance of the Minor Characters in Mark, in The New Literary Criticism and the New Testament, ed Elizabeth Struthers Malbon and Edgar V. McKnight, Sheffield Academic Press, 94, Trinity Press Int, 94; Literary Contexts of Mark 13, in Biblical and Humane: A Festschrift for John F. Priest, ed Linda Bennett-Elder, David Barr, and Elizabeth Struthers Malbon, Scholars Press, 96; Biblical and Humane: A Festschrift for John F. Priest, Scholars Press, 96. Auth, Fourteen entries on New Testament topics for The Harper Collins Dictionary of Religion, 95; Twelve entries for Women in Scripture: A Dictionary of Named and Unnamed Women in the Hebrew Bible, Apocrypha, and New Testament, ed by Carol Meyers, Toni Craven, and Ross Kraemer, in press. **CONTACT ADDRESS** Religious Studies Program, Center for Interdiscipl, Va Polytech Inst & State Univ, 100 Virginia Tech, Blacksburg, VA, 24061-0135. **EMAIL** Malbon@vtvm1.cc.vt.edu

MALEFAKIS, EDWARD
DISCIPLINE MODERN EUROPEAN HISTORY **EDUCATION** Bates Col, BA, 53; Columbia Univ, PhD, 65. **CAREER** Prof. **RESEARCH** Comparative history of Spain, Portugal, Italy and Greece since 1800. **SELECTED PUBLICATIONS** Auth, Agrarian Reform and Peasant Revolution in Spain, 70; Southern Europe in the 19th and 20th Centuries, 92. **CONTACT ADDRESS** Dept of Hist, Columbia Col, New York, 2960 Broadway, New York, NY, 10027-6902.

MALEFAKIS, EDWARD EMANUEL
PERSONAL Born 01/02/1932, Springfield, MA, m, 2 children **DISCIPLINE** EUROPEAN HISTORY **EDUCATION** Bates Col, AB, 53; Johns Hopkins Sch Advan Int Studies, DC, MA, 55; Columbia Univ, PhD(hist), 65. **CAREER** Vis instr hist, Northwestern Univ, Evanston, 62-63; asst prof, Wayne State Univ, 63-64; asst prof, Columbia Univ, 64-68; assoc prof, Northwestern Univ, Evanston, 68-71; prof, Univ Mich, Ann Arbor, 71-74; PROF HIST, COLUMBIA UNIV, 74-, Soc Sci Res Coun fac res grant, 67-68; dir, Prog Comp Studies in Hist, Univ Mich, 72-74; John Simon Guggenheim Mem Found fel, 74-75; Nat Endowment for Humanities res grant, 77-78. **HONORS AND AWARDS** Herbert Baxter Adams Prize, AHA, 71; Orden de Merito Civil, Spain, 88. **MEMBERSHIPS** AHA; Soc Span & Port Hist Studies; Soc Ital Hist Studies; Mod Greek Studies Asn. **RESEARCH** Spanish and Southern European history since 1750; social and quantitative history. **SELECTED PUBLICATIONS** Auth, Agrarian Reform and Peasant Revolution in Spain: Origins of the Civil War, Yale Univ, 70; contribr, The Republic and the Civil War in Spain, Macmillan, 71; Modern European Social History, Heath, 72; Civil Wars in the Twentieth Century, Univ Ky, 72; ed, Indalecio Prieto: Discursos Fundamentales, Turner, Madrid, 75; ed, La Guerra de Espana, 1936-1939, Taurus, 86; auth, Southern Europe in the 19th and 20th Centuries: An Historical Overview, Juan March, 92. **CONTACT ADDRESS** Dept of Hist, Columbia Univ, 2960 Broadway, New York, NY, 10027-6900. **EMAIL** eem1@Columbia.edu

MALIK, HAFEEZ
PERSONAL Lahore, Pakistan, m, 2 children **DISCIPLINE** POLITICAL SCIENCE **EDUCATION** BA Govt Col, Lahore Pakistan, 49; Graduate Diploma, Jour Univ of the Punjab, 52; MS 55, Syracuse Univ, MA 57, PhD 61. **CAREER** Asst Prof, 61-63, Polit Sci Villanova Univ, Assoc Prof, 63-67, Prof, 67-. **MEMBERSHIPS** Assoc Asian Studies; Pi Sigma Alpha-Natl Polit Sci Hon Soc; Am Assoc Univ Profs; Am Polit Sci Assoc; Am Hist Assoc; Pakistan Council, Asia Soc, NY Chm; Member Nstl Seminar on Pakistan/Bangladesh Columbia Univ. **SELECTED PUBLICATIONS** Central Asia: Its Strategic Importanc and Future Prospect, London: Macmillan and NY: St Martin's Pres, 93-94; Soviet_Pakistan Relations and Current Dynamics London: Macmillan and NY: St Martin's Press, 93; Encyclopedia of the Modern Islamic World, 93-94; Interests and Influence in the Gulf, Brookings Inst Wash DC, 87; Conf ib Relations Between Sussia, the Commonwealth of Independent States as a Whole and Pakistan in Moscow, 92; Interview with Assoc Press corresp on the UN-US challenge to Iraq to remove missiles from the no-fly zone, 93; Channel 3 taping for Newsmakers regarding the peace process in the Middle East. **CONTACT ADDRESS** Villanova Univ, 416-421 SAC, Villanova, PA, 19085. **EMAIL** Hmalik@email.vill.edu

MALIK, SALAHUDDIN
DISCIPLINE HISTORY **EDUCATION** Punjab Univ, BA, MA; McGill Univ, PhD. **CAREER** Prof. **RESEARCH** British imperialism in India; Nineteenth Century Muslims; Middle East history. **SELECTED PUBLICATIONS** Auth, Changing Emphasis on American Muslims with Emphasis on Pakistani Americans; God, England and the Indian Mutiny: Victorian Perspectives, Jour Islam, 83; Nineteenth Century Approaches to the Indian Mutiny, Jour Asian Hist, 80; Pakistanis in the American Melting Pot: History of Rochester NY, Islamic Studies, 93. **CONTACT ADDRESS** Dept of History, State Univ NY Col Brockport, Brockport, NY, 14420. **EMAIL** smalik@acspr1.acs.brockport.edu

MALINO, FRANCES
PERSONAL Born 03/06/1940, Danbury, CT, d, 2 children **DISCIPLINE** EARLY MODERN FRENCH & JEWISH HISTORY **EDUCATION** Skidmore Col, BA, 61; Brandeis Univ, MA, 63, PhD(Judaic studies), 71. **CAREER** From asst prof to prof hist, Univ Mass, Boston, 70-89; assoc prof hist, Harbor Camput, Univ Mass, 70; Vis prof, Brandeis Univ, 71 & Yale Univ, 74; mem, Commission Francaise des Archives Juives, 77-; fel, Mary Ingraham Bunting Inst, Radcliff Col, 79-80, scholar-in-residence, Tauber Inst, Brandeis Univ, spring 83; vis prof Jewish Studies, Mount Holyoke Col, 86-87; Ecole des Haute Etudes en Sciences Sociales, Paris, 89; SOPHIA MOSES ROBINSON PROF JEWISH STUDIES AND HIST, WELLSLEY COL, 89-. **HONORS AND AWARDS** ACLS res grant, 79-80; ACLS travel grant, 87; Healey res grant, 88; guest fel, Wolfson Col, Oxford, 88; Wellsley Col res grant, 91, 96; Littauer Fdn res grant, 93, 96; Alumni Periclean schol award, Skidmore Col, 97; Barnett Miller Fac Dev grant for Int Studies, 98. **MEMBERSHIPS** AHA; Asn Jewish Studies; Soc French Hist Studies; Edit Bd, Jewish Soc Studies; Acad Adv Bd, Int Res Inst on Jewish Women. **RESEARCH** Jewish autonomy and citizenship in 18th century France; nationalism and modern national movements; contemporary Middle East; Jewish women teachers of the Alliance Israelite Universelle. **SELECTED PUBLICATIONS** Auth, Memoires d'un Patriole Proscrit, In: Michael IV, Diaspora Res Inst, Tel Aviv, 76; The Sephardic Jews of Bordeaux: Assimilation and Emancipation in Revolutionary and Napoleonic France, Univ Ala Press, 78; Furtado et les Portugais, Annales Hist Revolution Francaise, 1-3/79; Zalkind Hourwitz-Juif Polonais, Dix-Huitieme Siecle, 81; From patriot to Israelite: Abrahkam Furtado in revolutionary France, In: Essays in Jewish Intellectual History in Honor of Alexander Altmann, Duke Univ Press, 82; Attitudes toward Jewish communal autonomy in pre-revolutionary France, In: Essays in Modern Jewish History: A Tribute to Ben Halpern, Fairleigh Dickinson Univ Press, 82 & ed, Essays in Modern Jewish History; co-ed, The Jews in Modern France, Univ Press New England, 85; co-ed, From East and West: Jews in a changing Europe, Basil Blackwell, 90; ed, Profiles in Diversity: Jews in a Changing Europe, Wayne State Univ Press, 98; auth, A Jew in the French Revolution: The Life of Zalkind Hourwitz, Basil Blackwell, 96; auth, "Women teachers of the Alliance Israelite Universelle," in Jewish Women in Historical Perspective, Wayne State Univ Press, 98; auth, "Jewish Emancipation in France," in Religious Minorities, State and Society in Nineteenth-Century Europe, Manchester Univ Press, 98; auth, "Resistance and Rebellion: The Jews in Eighteenth Century France," in Jewish Historical Studies, No. 30, 89; auth, "Jewish Women in Early Modern Europe," in Women's Studies Encyclopedia, Greenwood Press, 91. **CONTACT ADDRESS** Dept Hist, Wellesley Col, Wellesley, MA, 02481. **EMAIL** fmalino@wellesley.edu

MALINOWSKI, MICHAEL J.
DISCIPLINE GOVERNMENT **EDUCATION** Tufts Univ, BA, 87; Yale Law School, JD, 91. **CAREER** Adj prof law, Univ Houston Law Ctr, 93; assoc, Kirkpatrick & Lockhart LLP, 93-97; mem, Special Comn Genetic Info Policy, Mass Leg, 95-97; mgr gov affairs & commun, Mass Biotech Counc, 97-98; counselm, Foley, Hoag & Eliot LLP, 98-. **HONORS AND AWARDS** Phi Beta Kappa **MEMBERSHIPS** Ethics Comn & Biomedical Working Group: Biotech Ind Org; Res fel: Eunice Shriver Ctr for Mental Retardation: Genome Radoio Proj. **RESEARCH** Bioethcis; Commercialization of Life Scis; Health law and policy. **SELECTED PUBLICATIONS** various **CONTACT ADDRESS** Foley Hoag & Eliot LLP, 1 Post Office Square, Boston, MA, 02109. **EMAIL** mmalinow@fhe.com

MALKIEL, BURTON GORDON
PERSONAL Born 08/28/1932 **DISCIPLINE** ECONOMICS **EDUCATION** Boston Latin Sch, 43-49; Harvard Col, BA 49-53; Harvard Grad Sch of Bus, MBA 53-55; Princeton Univ, PhD 60-64. **CAREER** Smith Barney & Co, assoc 58-60; Council Econ Adv, mem 75-77; Princeton Univ, asst prof 64-66, dir fin res 66-81, assoc prof 66-68, prof 68-81, Gordon S Rentschler Memorial Prof 69-81, chair 74-75, chair 77-81; Yale School of Org Mgmt, dean 81-88; Princeton Univ, Chem Bank Chmn Prof 88. **HONORS AND AWARDS** H D Humane Letters; Phi Beta Kappa; Alumni Achv Awd. **MEMBERSHIPS** AFA; AEA. **SELECTED PUBLICATIONS** A Random Walk

Down Wall Street, W W Norton & Co, NY, 73, rev, 75, 81, 85, 90, 93, 96, translated into several languages; Global Bargain Hunting: An Investors Guide to Profits in Emerging Markets, with J P Mei, Simon & Schuster, NY 98; The Inflation Beaters Guide, W W Norton & Co, NY 80, rev paperback ed, Winning Investment Strategies, 82; numerous pub articles. **CONTACT ADDRESS** Dept Economics, Princeton Univ, Princeton, NJ, 08544.

MALLARD, HARRY
DISCIPLINE MUSIC HISTORY **EDUCATION** Sam Houston State Univ, BM, MA; Univ Tex, PhD. **CAREER** Coordr, Hist and Lit Stud; prof, Sam Houston State Univ. **HONORS AND AWARDS** NEH grant recipient. **RESEARCH** 18th-century musical thought. **CONTACT ADDRESS** Dept of Music, Sam Houston State Univ, Huntsville, TX, 77341.

MALLORY, MICHAEL
PERSONAL Born 11/01/1936, Buffalo, NY, m, 2 children **DISCIPLINE** ART **EDUCATION** Yale Univ, BA, 59; Columbia Univ, MA, 62, PhD, 65. **CAREER** Prof, Brooklyn Col, CUNY, 65- **HONORS AND AWARDS** Fulbright Fel, 63-64; NEH, 67; CUNY Res Found Grants, 82-92. **SELECTED PUBLICATIONS** Coauth, Guido Riccio and the Resistance to Critical Thinking, Syracuse Scholar, 91; Sano di Pietro's Bernardino Triptych for the compagnia della Uergine, Burlington Mag, 91; Did Siena Get its Carta Before its Horse? J of Art, 91; auth, The Guido Riccio Controversy in Art History, in Confronting the Experts, St Univ NY Press, 96. **CONTACT ADDRESS** Art Dept, Brooklyn Col, CUNY, Brooklyn, NY, 11210-2889.

MALM, WILLIAM P.
PERSONAL Born 03/06/1928, LaGrange, IL, m, 1954, 3 children **DISCIPLINE** ETHNOMUSICOLOGY **EDUCATION** Northwestern Univ, BA, 49, MM, 50; Univ Calif, Los Angeles, PhD, 59. **CAREER** Instr music, Univ Ill, 50-51; instr, US Naval Sch Music, 51-52; lectr, Univ Calif, Los Angeles, 57-60; from asst prof to assoc prof, 60-66, PROF MUSIC, UNIV MICH, ANN ARBOR, 66-, Am Coun Learned Soc grant, 63; sr fel, Cult Learning Inst, EAst-West Ctr, Hawaii, 73; Ernest Bloch prof music, Univ Calif, Berkeley, 80; dir, Stearns Collection, 81- **MEMBERSHIPS** Soc Ethnomusicol (pres, 77-79); Soc Asian Music; Asn Asian Studies; Int Folk Music Coun. **RESEARCH** Japanese music; holography; computer data banks in organology. **SELECTED PUBLICATIONS** Auth, Comparative Musicology and Anthropology of Music--Essays on the History of Ethnomusicology, Music and Letters, Vol 0074, 93. **CONTACT ADDRESS** Sch of Music, Univ of Mich, Ann Arbor, MI, 48109.

MALONE, BARBARA S. (BOBBIE)
PERSONAL Born 01/02/1944, San Antonio, TX, m, 1977, 2 children **DISCIPLINE** AMERICAN HISTORY **EDUCATION** Newcomb College, BA 75; Tulane Univ, MS 79, MA 90, PhD 94. **CAREER** State Hist Soc of Wisconsin, dir off sch ser, 95. **MEMBERSHIPS** ASLH; NCSS; SJHS; WCSS **RESEARCH** Amer southern and other regional Jewish histories; WI hist; regional hist; materials related to hist for edu purposes; late 19th-20th century social and cultural hist **SELECTED PUBLICATIONS** Auth, Rabbi Max Heller: Reformer Zionist Southerner 1860-1929, Univ Alabama Press, 97; Rabbi Max Heller and the Negro Question New Orleans 1891-1911, in: The Quiet Voices: Southern Rabbis and Black Civil Rights, eds, Mark Bauman, Berkley Kalin, Univ Ala Press, 97; Jews in Christian America, by Naomi W. Cohen for Amer Jour of Legal Hist, 94; Back to Beginnings: The Early Days of Dane County, Dane Cty Cultural Affs Comm, 98; Learning for the Land: Wisconsin Land Use for 4th graders, coauth, accompanying teachers guide, 98; Wisconsin's Built Environment, coauth, classroom resource kit, 98. **CONTACT ADDRESS** Office of School Services, State Historical Soc of Wisconsin, 816 State St, Madison, WI, 53706-1488. **EMAIL** bobbis.s.malone@ccmail.adp.wisc.edu

MALONE, BILL CHARLES
PERSONAL Born 08/25/1934, Smith County, TX, m, 1971, 3 children **DISCIPLINE** UNITED STATES CULTURAL HISTORY **EDUCATION** Univ Tex, Austin, BA, 56, MA 58, PhD(US hist), 65. **CAREER** Instr US hist, Southwest Tex State Col, 62-64, asst prof Southern hist, 64-67; assoc prof Southern and Black hist, Murray State Univ, 67-69; assoc prof Black hist, Univ Wis-Whitewater, 69-71; assoc prof, 71-80, PROF SOCIAL AND CULT HIST, TULANE UNIV, 80-. **MEMBERSHIPS** Orgn Am Historians; Southern Hist Asn. **RESEARCH** United States social and cultural history; Southern United States history; rural history. **SELECTED PUBLICATIONS** Auth, Writing the History of Southern Music--a Rev-Essay, Miss Quart, Vol 0045, 92; Everybody Says Freedom, J Southern Hist, Vol 0059, 93; Sing for Freedom--the Story of the Civil Rights Movement Through its Songs, J Southern Hist, Vol 0059, 93; Well Understand It Better by and by--Pioneering African-American Gospel Composers, J Southern Hist, Vol 0060, 94; You Wrote My Life--Lyrical Themes in Country Music, J Amer Hist, Vol 0080, 94; Country-Music Seriously--an Interview With Malone, Bill, C., South Atlantic Quart, Vol 0094, 95; 'Times Aint Like What They Used to Be, Early Rural and Popular American Music, 1928-1935' + Dunner, S, J Amer Folklore, Vol 0108, 95; The 'Mandolin of Bill Monroe, One-on-One With the Master' + Monroe, B, J Amer Folklore, Vol 0108, 95; 'Docs Guitar, Fingerpicking and Flatpicking' + Watson, D, J Amer Folklore, Vol 0108, 95; The 'Banjo of Ralph Stanley' + Stanley, R, J Amer Folklore, Vol 0108, 95; Transforming Tradition--Folk-Music Revivals Examined, J Southern Hist, Vol 0062, 96; The Comprehensive Country Music Encyclopedia, J Southern Hist, Vol 0062, 96; Tubb, Ernest--the Texas Troubadour, J Country Music, Vol 0019, 97; Main Street Amusements--Movies and Commercial Entertainment in a Southern City, 1896-1930, Amer Hist Rev, Vol 0102, 97. **CONTACT ADDRESS** Div of Arts and Sci Dept of Hist, Tulane Univ, New Orleans, LA, 70118.

MALONE, CAROLYN
DISCIPLINE MEDIEVAL ART AND ARCHAEOLOGY **EDUCATION** Univ Calif ,Berkeley, PhD, 73. **CAREER** Assoc prof; Univ Southern Calif; lect, Kalamozoo, 96. **HONORS AND AWARDS** NEH grants, late 70s; Courtland-Elliot prize, Medieval Acad Am, 95; **RESEARCH** French Romanesque and English Gothic architecture and sculpture. **SELECTED PUBLICATIONS** Auth, Les Fouilles de Saint-Benigne de Dijon 1976-1978 et le probleme de l'eglise de l'an mil in the Bulletin Monumental; **CONTACT ADDRESS** Col Letters, Arts & Sciences, Univ Southern Calif, University Park Campus, Los Angeles, CA, 90089.

MALONE, DUMAS
PERSONAL Born 01/10/1902, Coldwater, MS, m, 1925, 2 children **DISCIPLINE** HISTORY, BIOGRAPHY **EDUCATION** Emory Univ, BA, 10; Yale Univ, BA, 16, MA, 21, PhD, 23. **CAREER** Instr hist, Yale Univ, 19-23, asst prof, 23; from assoc prof to prof, Univ Va, 23-29; ed, Dict Am Biog, 29-31, ed-in-chief, 31-36; dir and chmn bd Syndics, Harvard Univ Press, 36-43; prof hist, Columbia Univ, 45-59; Jefferson Found prof hist, 59-62, BIOGRAPHER IN RESIDENCE, UNIV VA, 62-, Vis prof, Yale Univ, 27, Sterling sr fel, 27-28; ed, Hist Bk Club, 48-; Guggenheim fels, 51-52 and 58-59; managing ed, Polit Sci Quart, 53-58; hon consult, Am hist, Libr Congr, 68. **HONORS AND AWARDS** Porter Prize, Yale Univ, 23, Wilbur L Cross Medal, 72; Thomas Jefferson Award, Univ Va, 64; John F Kennedy Medal, Mass Hist Soc, 72; Pulitzer Prize in Hist, 75., DLitt, Emory Univ and Rochester Univ, 36, Dartmouth Col, 37 and Col William and Mary, 77; LLD, Northwestern Univ, 35 and Univ Chattanooga, 62. **MEMBERSHIPS** AHA; Southern Hist Asn(pres, 67-68); Am Antiq Soc; Am Acad Arts and Sci; Soc Am Hist. **RESEARCH** Early American history. **SELECTED PUBLICATIONS** Auth, A Linguistic Approach to the Bakhtinian Hero in Martin, Steve 'Roxanne', Lit-Film Quart, Vol 0024, 96. **CONTACT ADDRESS** Alderman Libr, Univ of Va, Charlottesville, VA, 22901.

MALONE, GLORIA S.
PERSONAL Born 05/12/1928, Pittsburgh, PA, m **DISCIPLINE** EDUCATION **EDUCATION** Central State Wilberforce OH, BS 1949; Kent State, ME 1956, MA 1969, PHD 1979. **CAREER** Alliance OH Public Schools, elementary teacher, 1949-53, high school teacher, 1953-69; Mt Union Coll, prof of English 1969-90; Ohio Northern Univ, visiting professor, 1990-91; Stark County Head Start Program, education coordinator, 1991-93. **HONORS AND AWARDS** State Scholarship Awards, Delta Kappa Gamma, 1967, 1974; Teacher of the Year, Alliance High School, 1969; Outstanding Member, Al Kaf Court Dts of Isis Akron, 1970; frequent speaker, Religious Civic Fraternity Groups; Citizen of the Year, 1986; Martin Luther King Award, 1996. **MEMBERSHIPS** Member, NAACP; Second Baptist Church; Natl Educ Assn; Amer Assn of Univ Prof; Delta Kappa Gamma Soc; grand worthy matron, Amaranth Grand Chapter OES PHA 1972-74; bd of dir, Alliance United Way; bd of dir, Alliance Community Conc Assn; bd of dir, Alpha Kappa Alpha Sorority; table leader, ETS essay readings, consultant, evaluator, North Central Assn of Schools & Coll, 1987-91.

MALONE, MICHAEL PETER
PERSONAL Born 04/18/1940, Pomeroy, WA, m, 1962, 2 children **DISCIPLINE** RECENT AND WESTERN AMERICAN HISTORY **EDUCATION** Gonzaga Univ, BA, 62; Wash State Univ, PhD(Am studies), 66. **CAREER** Asst prof hist, Tex AandM Univ, 66-67; asst prof, 60-70, assoc prof, 70-73, PROF HIST, MONT STATE UNIV, 73-, DEAN GRAD STUDIES, 79-; REV ED, MONT: THE MAG WESTERN HIST, 78-, Exec coun, Western Hist Asn, 75-77. **MEMBERSHIPS** Orgn Am Historians; Western Hist Asn; AHA. **RESEARCH** Recent Western and Northwestern history; history of Montana and the West. **SELECTED PUBLICATIONS** Auth, Politics and Public Policy in the Contemporary American West, Southwestern Hist Quart, Vol 0097, 93; Rocky Mountain West--Colorado, Wyoming, and Montana, 1859-1915, Pac Hist Rev, Vol 0062, 93; The Montana University System the 1st Half-Century, Montana-Mag Western Hist, Vol 0044, 94; In Commemoration--Burlingame, Merrill, G. 1901-1994, Montana-Mag Western Hist, Vol 0045, 95; Roeder, Richard, B., 1930-1995--in Commemoration, Montana-Mag Western Hist, Vol 0046, 96. **CONTACT ADDRESS** Dept of Hist and Philos, Montana State Univ, Bozeman, MT, 59715.

MALONEY, THOMAS
DISCIPLINE MEDIEVAL PHILOSOPHY AND THE PHILOSOPHY OF RELIGION **EDUCATION** Gregorian Univ, Rome, PhD. **CAREER** Dept Philos, Univ Louisville **RESEARCH** 13th-century logic, espec semantics. **SELECTED PUBLICATIONS** Publ(s), transl on of three treatises on universals by Roger Bacon along with an edition and annotated transl of Bacon's Compendium studii theologiae; transl, Bacon's Summulae dialectices. **CONTACT ADDRESS** Dept of Philos, Univ Louisville, 2301 S 3rd St, Louisville, KY, 40292. **EMAIL** tsmalo01@ulkyvm.louisville.edu

MALPASS, LESLIE FREDERICK
PERSONAL Born 05/16/1922, Hartford, CT, m, 1946, 4 children **DISCIPLINE** PSYCHOLOGY **EDUCATION** Syracuse Univ, BA, 47, MA, 49, PhD, 52. **CAREER** Asst to assoc prof, Southern Ill Univ, 52-60; visiting prof, Univ of Fl, 59-60; prof, chemn, Behavioral Sci, Univ of South Fl, 60-65; post-doctoral fel, UNC-Chapel Hill, 62-63; prof of Psychology, 65-74, 74-87, dean, Col of Arts & Sci, 65-68, VP, Acad Affairs, 68-74, Va Tech; pres emeritus, Western Ill Univ. **HONORS AND AWARDS** Honorary Doctorate in Humanities, Carl Sandburg Col, 74. **MEMBERSHIPS** Am Psychological Asn; Asn of Higher Ed; Nat Asn of State Univ/Land Grand Cols. **RESEARCH** Learning-bright, normal, retarded children (awards from Kennedy Found and more). **SELECTED PUBLICATIONS** Auth, nine books and 30-plus scholarly articles including: Individual Behavior, McGraw-Hill, 65; Social Behavior, McGraw-Hill, 66; Chapter 19, Handbook of Mental Deficiency, McGraw-Hill; What's Past is Prologue, Western Ill Univ Press, 88. **CONTACT ADDRESS** President Emeritus, Western Illinois Univ, 3927 Swarthmore Rd., Durham, NC, 27707.

MALSBARY, GERALD HENRY
PERSONAL Born 11/06/1952, Oakland, CA, m, 1979, 5 children **DISCIPLINE** CLASSICS **EDUCATION** Univ Calif, Berkeley, BA, 74, MA, 76; Univ Toronto, PhD, 88. **CAREER** Asst prof, St. Michael's Col, 87-89; res, Thesaurus Linguae Latinae, Munich, 89-91; prof, St. Charles Borromeo Sem, 91- . **HONORS AND AWARDS** Am Philol Asn, TLL fel, 89. **MEMBERSHIPS** APA; NAMLA. **RESEARCH** Trivium; ethics; metaphysics; education history; Vatican II doctrines; Chinese and Indian philosophy. **SELECTED PUBLICATIONS** Three articles on Early Christian Latin; four books translated from German and Italian. **CONTACT ADDRESS** 260 Ballymore Rd, Springfield, PA, 19064. **EMAIL** drmalsbary@juno.com

MALSBERGER, JOHN WILLIAM
PERSONAL Born 01/18/1951, Allentown, PA, m, 1978, 1 child **DISCIPLINE** AMERICAN HISTORY **EDUCATION** Temple Univ, AB, 72, PhD, 80. **CAREER** Tchg asst US hist, Temple Univ, 74-76, res asst, 76-78; from Instr to Assoc Prof, 78-96, prof US hist, Muhlenberg Col, 96. **MEMBERSHIPS** AHA; Orgn Am Historians; Social Sci Hist Asn. **RESEARCH** US Congress in 20th Century; polit theory; Am conservatism. **SELECTED PUBLICATIONS** Auth, The political thought of Fisher Ames, J Early Repub, spring 82; The Transformation of Republican Conservatism: The US Senate, 1938-1952, Congress & the Presidency, Spring 87; From Obstruction to Moderation: The Transformation of Senate Conservatism, 1938-1952, Susquehanna Univ Press. **CONTACT ADDRESS** Dept of Hist, Muhlenberg Col, 2400 W Chew St, Allentown, PA, 18104-5586. **EMAIL** malsberg@muhlenberg.edu

MALTBY, WILLIAM SAUNDERS
PERSONAL Born 10/23/1940, Cleveland, OH **DISCIPLINE** EARLY MODERN HISTORY **EDUCATION** Hiram Col, BA, 62; Duke Univ, MA, 65, PhD(hist), 67. **CAREER** Asst prof hist, Ohio Univ, 66-68; asst prof, 68-70, assoc prof, 70-82, PROF HIST, UNIV MO ST LOUIS, 82-, Exec dir, Ctr Reformation Res, 77-. **MEMBERSHIPS** AHA; Soc Relig Higher Educ; Renaissance Soc Am; Am Soc Reformation Res. **RESEARCH** Sixteenth century Spain; the revolt of the Netherlands; 16th century Anglo-Spanish relations. **SELECTED PUBLICATIONS** Auth, The Admirable Year 1492, Amer Hist Rev, Vol 0097, 92; England, Spain, and the Gran Armada, 1585-1604--Essays From the Anglo-Spanish Conferences, London and Madrid, 1988, Albion, Vol 0024, 92; The Tudor Navy--an Administrative, Political, and Military History, J Mil Hist, Vol 0057, 93; The Muslims of Valencia in the Age of Ferdinand and Isabel--Between Coexistence and Crusade, 16th Century J, Vol 0024, 93; Herrera, Juan, De, Architect to Philip-II of Spain, 16th Century J, Vol 0025, 94; Crown and Cortez--Government, Institutions and Representation in Early Modern Castille, 16th Century J, Vol 0025, 94; The Decoration of the Royal Basilica of El Escorial, 16th Century J, Vol 0026, 95; The Return of the Armadas--the Last Years of the Elizabethan War Against Spain, 1595-1603, Albion, Vol 0027, 95; The Courtier and the King--Gomezdesilva, Ruy, Philip-II, and the Court of Spain, 16th Century J, Vol 0027, 96; Letters of Portuguese Sovereigns to Charles-V and the Empress 1528-1532 Preserved in the Simancas-Archives, 16th Century J, Vol 0027, 96; Complete Works of Sepulveda, Juan, Gines, De Vol 1--'Historia De Carlos V'-Bk(S) 1-4, 16th Century J, Vol 0027, 96; The Making of an Enterprise--the Society of Jesus in Portugal, its Empire, and Beyond, 1540-1750, J Interdisciplinary Hist, Vol 0028, 97; Lords

of All the World--Ideologies of Empire in Spain, Britain, and France, C.1500 C.1800, Historian, Vol 0059, 97. **CONTACT ADDRESS** Dept of Hist, Univ of Mo, St Louis, MO, 63121.

MAMOOJEE, ABDOOL-HACK
DISCIPLINE CLASSICS **EDUCATION** Merton Col, Oxford, BA, 65, MA, 68; Univ Ottawa, PhD, 78. **CAREER** Instr, Royal Col, Port-Louis, Mauritius; Univ Quebec, Univ Ottawa; prof, 69-. **HONORS AND AWARDS** Ch, dept lang; deputy-dean, Fac Arts; corresponding mem, Can Fed for the Hum; act mem, Class Assn Can. **RESEARCH** Works of Cicero and the history of the Late Roman Republic. **SELECTED PUBLICATIONS** Auth, "The purpose of Q. Cicero's legateship in Gaul," Ancient Hist Bulletin, 92; "The date of the trial of Q. Gallius," Ancient Hist Bulletin, 93; Le proconsulat de Q. Ciceron en Asie, Echos du monde classique, 94; Cicero, In toga candida fr 8, Class Views, 95. **CONTACT ADDRESS** Dept of Lang, Lakehead Univ, 955 Oliver Rd, Thunder Bay, ON, P7B 5E1. **EMAIL** aketonen@sky.lakeheadu.ca

MANCKE, ELIZABETH
DISCIPLINE HISTORY **EDUCATION** Johns Hopkins Univ, PhD, 90. **CAREER** Asst Prof, Dept Hist, Univ Akron. **RESEARCH** Early modern British America. **CONTACT ADDRESS** Univ of Akron, Dept of History, Akron, OH, 44325-1902. **EMAIL** emancke@uakron.edu

MANDAVILLE, JON ELLIOTT
PERSONAL Born 10/09/1937, Inglewood, CA, m, 1997, 3 children **DISCIPLINE** MIDDLE EAST HISTORY, ISLAMIC STUDIES **EDUCATION** Dartmouth Col, BA, 59; Univ Edinburgh, dipl Islamic studies, 61; Princeton Univ, MA, 64, PhD(Orient studies), 69. **CAREER** Asst prof, 65-69, assoc prof, 69-79, co-dir, Pub Hist Prog, 77-78, Prof Hist, Portland State Univ, 79-, Dir, Middle East Studies Ctr, 95-; dir, Am Inst Yemeni Studies, Yemen, 78-80. **HONORS AND AWARDS** Fulbright-Hays fac res fel, 70-71; fel, Am Res Inst, Turkey, 71; Soc Sci Res Coun res fel in Yemen, 76-. **MEMBERSHIPS** Am Orient Soc; fel Mid East Studies Asn NAm; Turkish Studies Asn. **RESEARCH** Ottoman Arab lands; Arabian Peninsula; Islamic law. **SELECTED PUBLICATIONS** Auth, Ottoman court records of Syria and Jordan, 66 & Ottoman province of al-Hasa, 70, J Am Orient Soc; Usurious piety: Cash trusts law in Ottoman Empire, Int J Mid Eastern Studies, 78; The New Historians, 80 & Yemen, 81, Aramco World. **CONTACT ADDRESS** Dept of Hist, Portland State Univ, PO Box 751, Portland, OR, 97207-0751. **EMAIL** mandavillej@pdx.edu

MANEY, PATRICK J.
PERSONAL Born 12/09/1946, Warsau, WI, m, 1970, 3 children **DISCIPLINE** HISTORY **EDUCATION** Univ of WI, BS, 69; Univ of MD, PhD, 76 **CAREER** Asst Prof, Prof, 80-98, Tulane Univ **RESEARCH** US Political Hist **SELECTED PUBLICATIONS** Auth, Young Bob LaFollette: A biography of Robert M. La Follette, Jr. 1895-1953, Univ of Missouri Press, 78; The Roosevelt Presence: The Life and Legacy of FDR, Univ of CA Press, 98 **CONTACT ADDRESS** Dept of History, Univ of So Carolina, Columbia, SC, 29208. **EMAIL** maney@sc.edu

MANFRA, JO ANN
PERSONAL Schenectady, NY, m, 1980 **DISCIPLINE** AMERICAN HISTORY, LAW **EDUCATION** State Univ NY at Cortland, BS, 63, MS, 67; Univ Iowa, PhD(hist), 75; Suffolk Univ Law Sch, JD, 77; Harvard Law Sch, LLM, 79. **CAREER** Teacher hist, Kingston High Sch, 64-66; instr Am hist, Ball State Univ, 66-67; asst prof, 72-75, ASSOC PROF AM HIST, WORCESTER POLYTECH INST, 76-, Res fel, Nat Endowment for Humanities, summer 76, Mary Ingraham Bunting Inst, 77-79. **MEMBERSHIPS** Am Soc Legal Hist; Orgn Early Am Historians; Orgn Am Historians; Am Cath Studies Asn. **RESEARCH** American religious history; American social history; American legal history. **SELECTED PUBLICATIONS** Auth, A Biog of Flaget, Benedict, Joseph, B-1763-D-1850--1st Bishop of the Dioceses of Bardstown and Louisville, Kentucky, 1811-1850, Cath Hist Rev, Vol 0079, 93. **CONTACT ADDRESS** Worcester Polytech Inst, 39 Waterford Dr, Worcester, MA, 01602.

MANGRUM, ROBERT G.
PERSONAL Born 05/06/1948, Abilene, TX, m, 1980 **DISCIPLINE** HISTORY **EDUCATION** Hardin-Simmons Univ, BA, 70; Univ N Tex, MA, 75, PhD, 78. **CAREER** Commissioned off, Lt. Col, 70-98, US Army; chem, asst prof 78-80, Clarke Col; chemn, assoc prof, asst dir, dir, Robert D. Coley Distinguished prof, Univ hist, 80-, Howard Payne Univ. **HONORS AND AWARDS** Who's Who South Southwest, 80-98; Outstand Young Men Am, 81; Who's Who Tex, 85-86; pres, 86-87, treas, 90-92, Kiwanis Club Brownwood; Who's Who Among Am Tchrs, 94-95, 98-99; Who's Who World, 95-96, Who's Who Am Educ, 96-97; Council Member, Early City Council, 98-., Grad, US Army Command, General Staff Col, 81; grad, Nat Defense Univ, 87; grad fac, MA prog, US Army Command, General Staff Col, 89-98; US Military acad, post grad, workshop Military History for ROTC, 89. **MEMBERSHIPS** Am Hist Asn, Southern Hist Asn; Org Am Hist; Soc Military Hist; Tex State Hist Asn; Tex Oral Hist Asn; Nat Soc, Sons Am Revolution; Sons Confederate Veterans; Asn US Army; Nat Railway Hist Soc. **RESEARCH** US history; civil war; military; institutional history of Howard Payne University. **SELECTED PUBLICATIONS** Rev, Civil War History, 83-85; rev, Journal of Southern History, 85, 89, 91, 93; rev, Military Affair, 85; rev, Locus, 89; rev, American Historical Review, 94, 97. **CONTACT ADDRESS** 112 Broken Arrow St, Early, TX, 76802-2531. **EMAIL** rmangrum@hputx.edu

MANGUSSO, MARY C.
DISCIPLINE ALASKA **EDUCATION** TX Tech Univ, PhD, 78. **CAREER** Univ Alaska **SELECTED PUBLICATIONS** Coed, Alaskan Anthology: Interpreting the Past, Univ Wash Press, 96. **CONTACT ADDRESS** Univ AK Fairbanks, PO Box 757480, Fairbanks, AK, 99775-7480. **EMAIL** fyhist@aurora.aluaska.edu

MANIATES, MARIA RIKA
PERSONAL Born 03/30/1937, Toronto, ON, Canada **DISCIPLINE** MUSICOLOGY, PHILOSOPHY **EDUCATION** Univ Toronto, BA, 60; Columbia Univ, MA, 62, PhD(musicol), 65. **CAREER** From lectr to assoc prof, 65-74, chmn dept, 73-78, PROF MUSICOL, UNIV TORONTO, 74-, Am Coun Learned Socs grant-in-aid musicol, 66-67; vis prof music, Columbia Univ, 67 and 76; appln appraiser musicol, Can Coun, 69-, res fel, 70-72; Einstein Award Comt, Am Musicol Soc, 76-79; Can Coun travel grants, 73, 75, 77, 78, 79, and 80; Univ Toronto humanities res grants, 78-79 and 79-80. **MEMBERSHIPS** Int Musicol Soc; Am Musicol Soc; Renaissance Soc Am; Can Renaissance Soc; Int Soc Hist Rhetoric. **RESEARCH** Renaissance music and culture; mannerism; philosophy and aesthetics. **SELECTED PUBLICATIONS** Auth, Musica Scientia--Musical Scholarship in the Italian Renaissance, Notes, Vol 0050, 93; The Politicized Muse--Music for Medici Festivals, 1512-1537, Renaissance and Reformation, Vol 0018, 94; Music in Renaissance Magic--Toward a Historiography of Others, J Amer Musicol Soc, Vol 0048, 95; **CONTACT ADDRESS** Fac of Music, Univ of Toronto, Toronto, ON, M5S 1A1.

MANN, ALFRED
PERSONAL Born 04/28/1917, Hamburg, Germany, m, 3 children **DISCIPLINE** MUSIC **EDUCATION** State Acad Music, dipl, 37; Curtis Inst Music, dipl, 42; Columbia Univ, AM, 50, PhD, 55. **CAREER** Instr, State Acad, Berlin, 37; instr and res asst, Curtis Inst Music, 39-41; from asst prof to assoc prof, 47-56, prof, 56-79, EMER PROF MUSIC, RUTGERS UNIV, 80-; PROF MUSICOL, EASTMAN SCH MUSIC, UNIV ROCHESTER, 80-, Conductor, Cantata Singers, NY, 52-59; dir publ, Am Choral Found, Inc and ed, Am Choral Rev, 61-; mem bd dirs, Georg Friedrich Handel Ges, Halle, 67-; Gottinger Handelges, 67-; mem, Bach Choir of Bethlehem, 69-81. **HONORS AND AWARDS** MusD, Spokane Conserv Music, 47, Baldwin-Wallace Col, 81. **MEMBERSHIPS** Am Musicol Soc; Int Musicol Soc; Neve Bachgesellschaft (secy, Am Chap, 72-). **RESEARCH** History of music theory and choral music. **SELECTED PUBLICATIONS** Coauth, Thomas Attwoods Theorie--und Kompositionsstudien bei Mozart, 65 and auth, J J Fux, Gradus ad Parnassum, 67, Barenreiter; coauth, the present state of Handel research, Acta Musicologica, 69; auth, Beethoven's contrapuntal studies with Haydn, Musical Quart, 70; Haydn's Elementarbuch, Music Forum, 73; Hanuel's Composition Lessons, Bareureiter, 79; Zur Kontrapunktlehre Haydons Und Mozarts, Mozart-Jahrbuch, 78, 79; Zu Schubert's Studien im Strengen Satz, Schuburt Congr Report, 78. **CONTACT ADDRESS** Eastman Sch of Music, Rochester, NY, 14604.

MANN, ARTHUR
PERSONAL Born 01/03/1922, New York, NY, m, 1943, 2 children **DISCIPLINE** HISTORY **EDUCATION** Brooklyn Col, BA, 44; Harvard Univ, MA, 47, PhD, 52. **CAREER** Instr Fr, US Army Port of Embarkation Sch, Le Havre, 45; tutor hist, Brooklyn Col, 46; from instr to asst prof, Mass Inst Technol, 48-55; from asst prof to prof, Smith Col, 55-66; prof, 66-70, PRESTON AND STERLING MORTON PROF AM HIST, UNIV CHICAGO, 70-, Lectr, Columbia Univ, 56, Salzburg Sem Am Studies, 58, Univ Mich, 61, Univ Wyo, 62, Williams Col, 63, Harvard Univ, 65 and US State Dept, Venezuela, 70; Soc Sci Res Coun grant-in-aid, 59; Am Coun Learned Soc fel, 63; adv, Am Hist Ser, McGraw-Hill Films, 67-73; educ collab, Minorities Ser, Coronet Instruct Films, 69-73; adv-ed Am hist, Univ Chicago Press, 69-; panelist, Nat Endowment for Humanities, 72; Fulbright-Hays sr scholar, Univ Sydney, 74; co-adv, Oral Hist Proj of Holocaust Survivors, Am Jewish Comt's William E Wiener Oral Hist Libr, 74-76; lectr, USIA, Fiji, Indonesia, Malaysia, NZ, and Singapore, 74, Portugal, Ger, Yugoslavia and Rumania, 76, Hong Kong and Japan, 79. **MEMBERSHIPS** AHA; Orgn Am Historians; fel Soc Am Hist. **RESEARCH** American history. **SELECTED PUBLICATIONS** Auth, an Unknown Detail of Handel Biog, Bach, Vol 0025, 94; The 'Lions of Change', Stand Mag, Vol 0038, 97. **CONTACT ADDRESS** Dept of Hist, Univ of Chicago, Chicago, IL, 60637.

MANN, BRIAN
PERSONAL San Francisco, CA **DISCIPLINE** MUSIC HISTORY **EDUCATION** Univ Edinburgh, BMus; Univ Calif, Berkeley, MA, PhD. **CAREER** Assoc prof, Vassar fac, 87-. **RESEARCH** Vocal music of the Italian Renaissance. **SELECTED PUBLICATIONS** Auth, monograph on the secular madrigals of the Flemish composer Filippo di Monte, 1521-1603, UMI Press, 83; res, Jagellonian Library, Kracow, Poland; Mus Libry Asn Notes, 92; ed, Complete Works, Filippo di Monte; Univ Leuven Press; Ensemble Mus of Paolo Quagliati, 94. **CONTACT ADDRESS** Classic Dept, Vassar Col, 124 Raymond Ave., Poughkeepsie, NY, 12604. **EMAIL** mann@vassar.edu

MANN, KRISTIN
DISCIPLINE HISTORY **EDUCATION** Stanford Univ, BA, 68, MA, 70, PhD, 77. **CAREER** Assoc prof **RESEARCH** 18th through 20th-century African social and economic history; history of marriage and the family; history of slavery, emancipation, and the slave trade; history of colonial political and legal changes; history of West African commercial and agricultural transformations. **SELECTED PUBLICATIONS** Auth, Marrying Well: Marriage, Status and Social Change among the Educated Elite in Colonial Lagos; co-ed, Law in Colonial Africa. **CONTACT ADDRESS** Dept History, Emory Univ, 221 Bowden Hall, 561 Kilgo Cir, Atlanta, GA, 30322-1950. **EMAIL** kmann@socsci.ss.emory.edu

MANN, RALPH
DISCIPLINE HISTORY **EDUCATION** Duke Univ, BA, 65; Stanford Univ, MA, 66; PhD, 70. **CAREER** Prof, Univ Colo, 92-. **SELECTED PUBLICATIONS** Auth, After the Gold Rush: Society in Grass Valley and Nevada City, California, 1849-1870, Stanford, 82; Mountain Settlement: Appalalachian and National Modes of Migration, J Appalachian Studies, 96; Diversity in the Antebellum Appalachian South: Four Farm Communities in Tazewell County, Virginia, Univ NC, 95. **CONTACT ADDRESS** History Dept, Univ of Colorado, Boulder, Boulder, CO, 80309. **EMAIL** ralph.mann@colorado.edu

MANN, WILLIAM EDWARD
PERSONAL Born 05/06/1940, Los Angeles, CA, m, 1966, 2 children **DISCIPLINE** HISTORY OF PHILOSOPHY, PHILOSOPHY OF RELIGION **EDUCATION** Stanford Univ, BA, 62, MA, 64; Univ Minn, Minneapolis, PhD(Philos), 71. **CAREER** From instr to asst prof Philos, St Olaf Col, 67-72; asst prof, Ill State Univ, 72-74; assoc prof, 74-80, prof Philos, Univ VT & chmn dept, 80-. **HONORS AND AWARDS** 1971 Dissertation Essay Competition, The Rev of Metaphys, 72. **MEMBERSHIPS** Am Philos Asn, div sec-treas, 94; Soc Ancient Greek Philos; Soc Medieval Renaissance Philos. **RESEARCH** Philosophical theology; medieval philosophy, ancient philosophy. **SELECTED PUBLICATIONS** Auth, The ontological presuppositions of the ontological argument, Rev Metaphysics, 72; The divine attributes, Am Philos Quart, 75; The perfect island, Mind, 76; The theft of the pears, Apeiron, 77; The third man--the man who never was, Am Philos Quart, 79; Anaxagoras and the homoiomere, Phronesis, 80; Divine simplicity, Relig Studies, 82; Dreams of immortality, Philos, 83; Hope in Eleonore Stump, ed, Reasoned Faith: Essays in Philosophical Theology in Honor of Norman Kretzmann, Ithaca, NY: Cornell University Press, 93; Piety: Lending a Hand to Euthyphro, Philosophy and Phenomenological Research, 98. **CONTACT ADDRESS** Dept of Philosophy, Univ of Vermont, 70 S Williams St, Burlington, VT, 05401-3404.

MANNING, CHRISTEL
PERSONAL Born 11/11/1961, Long Beach, CA **DISCIPLINE** HISTORY OF AMERICAN RELIGION **EDUCATION** Tufts Univ, BA, economics (Magna cum laude), 84; Univ CA, Santa Barbara, MA, relig studies, 91, PhD, relig studies, 95. **CAREER** Teacher, Social Studies, Noble and Greenough School, 86-89; lect, Elderhostel, Santa Barbara, 94; instr, dept of philos and relig, Hollins Col, 94-95; ASST PROF, DEPT OF PHILOS AND RELIGIOUS STUDIES, SACRED HEART UNIV, 95-. **HONORS AND AWARDS** Omnicron Delta Epsilon (Int Honor Soc in Economics), 84; Phi Beta Kappa, 84; Distinguished Scholars fel, 89-90; CA State grad fel, 91-92, 92-93; nominated for UCSB Outstanding Teaching Asst Award, 94; Thomas O'Day Award for the Study of Religion and Soc, 94; Soc for the Scientific Study of Religion, Res Award, 94. **MEMBERSHIPS** Am Academy Relig; Asn for Soc of Relig; Soc for the Scientific Study of Relig, Nat prog chair, 97. **RESEARCH** Gender and religion; fundamentalism; new religions. **SELECTED PUBLICATIONS** Auth, Review of Margaret Lamberts Bendroth, Fundamentalism and Gender, J for the Scientific Study of Religion 33.3, 94; Cultural Conflicts and Identity: Second Generation Hispanic Catholics in the United States, with Wade Clark Roof, Social Compass, 94; Embracing Jesus and the Goddess: Towards a Reconceptualizing of Conversion to Syncretistic Religion, in Magical Religion and Modern Witchcraft, ed by James Lewis, State Univ NY Press, 95; Review of Miriam Therese Winter, Defecting in Place: Women Claiming Responsibility for Their Own Spiritual Lives, J for the Scientific Study of Relig, 96; Women in a Divided Church: Liberal and Conservative Catholic Women Negotiate Changing Gender Roles, Sociology of Relig, 97; Review of Martin Marty & Scott Appleby, Fundamentalisms Comprehended, Review of Relig Res, 97; Women in New Religious Movements, in Encyclopedia of Women and World Religions, ed by Serinity Young, Macmillan, forthcoming, 98; Return to

Mother Nature: The Politics of Paganism in America and Western Europe, in The Encyclopedia of Politics and Religion, ed by Robert Wuthnow, Congressional Quart Books, forthcoming, 98; God Gave Us the Right: The Impact of Feminism on Conservative Christian and Orthodox Jewish Women, Rutgers Univ Press, forthcoming, 98; Conversations Among Women: Gender as a Bridge between Religious and Ideological Cultures, in Reflexive Ethnography: Remembering for Whom We Speak, ed by Lewis Carter, JAI Press, forthcoming, 99. **CONTACT ADDRESS** Dept Philos & Relig Studies, Sacred Heart Univ, 5151 Park Ave., Fairfield, CT, 06432. **EMAIL** manningc@sacredheart.edu

MANNING, JEAN BELL

PERSONAL Born 08/14/1937, LaMarque, TX, m **DISCIPLINE** EDUCATION **EDUCATION** Bishop Coll, BA (hon student Valedictoria Scholarship) 1958; N TX State Univ, MEd 1964, EDd 1970. **CAREER** Douglas HS Ardmore OK, instr 1958-60; Reading Lab Jarvis Coll Hawkins TX; instr & dir 1961-64; TX So Univ Houston, vis prof 1964-65; Douglas HS OK, instr 1964-65, 1965-67; Univ of Liberia, Liberia, W Africa, prof of English 1973-74; Paul Quinn Coll Waco TX, chmn dept educ 1970-73, 1974-78; Langston Univ OK, assoc prof/dir resources 1978-86, vice pres for academic affairs 1986-. **HONORS AND AWARDS** Ford Found Doctoral Grant 1969; Outstanding Sor of SW Phi Delta Kappa Sor 1978. **MEMBERSHIPS** Educ for Leadership in Black Ch Lilly Found Sponsored Houston TX 1975-77; curriculum devel Wiley Coll Marshall TX 1978; competency based educ Dallas Independent S Dist 1979; mem Alpha Kappa Alpha Sor 1956-; mem Links Inc 1974-; mem Phi Delta Kappa Sor 1956-. **CONTACT ADDRESS** Langston Univ, PO Box 907, Langston, OK, 73050.

MANNING, JOSEPH G.

DISCIPLINE CLASSICS **EDUCATION** BA, 81; Univ Chicago, PhD, 92. **CAREER** Asst prof, Stanford Univ. **RESEARCH** Papyrology; Hellenistic, Near Eastern, and Egyptian hist. **SELECTED PUBLICATIONS** Auth, Land and Social Status in Hellenistic Egypt in Grund und Boden in Altagypten, Tubingen, 95; Demotic Egyptian Instruments of Conveyance as Evidence of Ownershwip of Real Property in Chicago-Kent Law Review, 96; The Hauswaldt Papyri: A Third Century Family Archive from Edfu, Upper Egypt , Demotische Studien, 96. **CONTACT ADDRESS** Stanford Univ, Bldg 20, Main Quad, Stanford, CA, 94305.

MANNING, PETER K.

PERSONAL Born 09/27/1940, Salem, OR, d, 3 children **DISCIPLINE** SOCIOLOGY **CAREER** Vis Prof, Univ Victoria, 68, Portland State Univ, 76, Purdue Univ, 77, SUNY Albany, 82, MIT Sloan Sch, 82, Univ Mich, 93. **HONORS AND AWARDS** Pi Gamma Mu Soc Sci Hon; NDEA Fellow, Duke Univ, 62-64; NSF Summer Fellow, Duke, 63, 64; Alumni Citiation, Williamette Univ, 81; Vis Fellow, Wolfson Col, Oxford, 81, 82; Fellow, Balliol Col, Oxford, 82-83; Res Fellow, Wolfson Col, Oxford, 84-86; Beto Lecturer, Sam Houston State Univ, 90; Bruce W Smith Award, ACJS, 94; OW Wilson Award, ACJS, 97. **CONTACT ADDRESS** Dept Sociol, Michigan State Univ, 201 Berkey Hall, E Lansing, MI, 48824-1111.

MANNING, ROBERTA THOMPSON

PERSONAL Born 01/24/1940, Austin, TX, m, 1964, 1 child **DISCIPLINE** RUSSIAN-SOVIET HISTORY **EDUCATION** Rice Univ, BA, 62; Columbia Univ, MA, 67, PhD(hist), 75. **CAREER** Asst prof, 75-81, ASSOC PROF HIST, BOSTON COL, 81-, Actg asst prof hist, Univ Calif, San Diego, 75; mem, Nat Seminar in the Hist of Russian Soc in the 20th Century, 81-. **MEMBERSHIPS** Nat Hist Soc; Am Asn Advan Slavic Studies. **RESEARCH** Russian-Soviet history, 1861 the to present; Soviet politics and society 1920's and 1930's; agrarian politics and policies, 1905-1940. **SELECTED PUBLICATIONS** Auth, Reforming Rural Russia, 1855-1914, J Mod Hist, Vol 0065, 93; Politics and Society in Provincial Russia--Saraatov, 1590-1917, Russ Rev, Vol 0052, 93. **CONTACT ADDRESS** Boston Col, Chestnut Hill, MA, 02167.

MANNING, ROGER B.

PERSONAL Born 01/23/1932, Washington, DC, m, 1961, 2 children **DISCIPLINE** MODERN ENGLISH HISTORY **EDUCATION** Georgetown Univ, BS, 54, MA, 59, PhD, 61. **CAREER** From instr to asst prof hist, Ohio State Univ, 60-66; from asst prof to assoc prof, 66-73, chmn dept, 74-79, PROF HIST, CLEVELAND STATE UNIV, 73-, Vis lectr, Case Western Reserve Univ, 65 and 67, vis prof, 74. **HONORS AND AWARDS** Harlaxton Prize, Albion and Univ Evansville, Ind, 74. **MEMBERSHIPS** Conf Brit Studies; Conf 16th Century Studies; fel Royal Hist Soc; AHA. **RESEARCH** Tudor-Stuart England; Reformation Europe; 20th-century Great Britain. **SELECTED PUBLICATIONS** Auth, The Pursuit of Stability, Social-Relations in Elizabethan London, Albion, Vol 0024, 92; The Townshends and Their World--Gentry, Law and Land in Norfolk, C.1450-1551, Albion, Vol 0025, 93; Fire From Heaven--Life in an English Town in the 17th-Century, Amer Hist Rev, Vol 0098, 93; Going to the Wars--the Experience of the British Civil Wars, 1638-1651, 16th Century J, Vol 0024, 93; Prosecution and Punishment--Petty Crime and the Law in London and Rural Middlesex, 1660-1725, Amer Hist Rev, Vol 0098, 93; Political Thought and the Tudor Commonwealth--Deep Structure, Discourse and Disguise, 16th Century J, Vol 0025, 94; Faith and Fire--Popular and Unpopular Religion, 1350-1600, Amer Hist Rev, Vol 0100, 95; The Merchant Adventurers of England--the Company and the Crown, 1474-1564, Amer Hist Rev, Vol 0100, 95; The English Rural Community--Image and Analysis, J Interdisciplinary Hist, Vol 0025, 95; The Gentry in England and Wales, 1500-1700, Albion, Vol 0028, 96; The Nerves of State--Taxation and the Financing of the English State, 1558-1714, 16th Century J, Vol 0028, 97. **CONTACT ADDRESS** Cleveland State Univ, 2848 Coleridge Rd, Cleveland Heights, OH, 44115.

MANSON TOMASEK, KATHRYN

DISCIPLINE AMERICAN REVOLUTION AND CIVIL WAR **EDUCATION** Rice Univ, BA; Univ Wisconsin-Madison, MA, PhD,95. **CAREER** Ch. **RESEARCH** US women's history, 19th-century US, African-American history. **SELECTED PUBLICATIONS** Publ, on women and utopia, Alcott's March family trilogy; Children and family, Fourierist communities. **CONTACT ADDRESS** Dept of Mus, Wheaton Col, 26 East Main St, Norton, MA, 02766. **EMAIL** ktomasek@wheatonma.edu

MARABLE, MANNING

DISCIPLINE UNITED STATES HISTORY **EDUCATION** Earlham Univ, BA, 71; Md Univ, PhD, 76. **CAREER** Prof. **RESEARCH** African American history. **SELECTED PUBLICATIONS** Auth, Black Liberation in Conservative America, 97; Speaking Truth to Power: Essays on Race, Radicalism and Resistance, 96; Beyond Black and White, 95; The Crisis of Color and Democracy, 92; Race, Reform, and Rebellion: The Second Reconstruction in Black America 1945-1990, 91. **CONTACT ADDRESS** Dept of History, Columbia Col, New York, 2960 Broadway, New York, NY, 10027-6902.

MARCELLO, RONALD E.

PERSONAL Born 12/31/1939, Wrightsville, PA **DISCIPLINE** HISTORY **EDUCATION** Millersville State Col, BS, 61; Duke Univ, MA, 65, PhD, 69. **CAREER** From asst prof to prof, 67- , coordr, Oral Hist Prog, 67-, North Tex State Univ. **HONORS AND AWARDS** H. Bailey Carroll Award, 92, Tex State Hist Asn., Univ Scholar, 64-65, 66-67, Southern Res Fel, 65-66, Duke Univ. **MEMBERSHIPS** Oral Hist Asn; Tex Oral Hist Asn; Tex State Hist Asn. **RESEARCH** New Deal; WW II. **SELECTED PUBLICATIONS** Coauth, With Only the Will to Live: Accounts of Americans in Japanese Prison Camps, 94; coauth, Building The Death Railway: The Ordeal of American Prisoners in Burma, 92; coauth, Remembing Pearl Harbor Eyewitnes Accounts by US Military Men and Women, 91; auth, art, Lone Star POWs: Texas National Guardsmen and the Building of the Burma-Thailand Railroad, 1942-1945, 92; auth, art, Reluctance Versus Reality: The Desegregation of North Texas State College, 1954-1956, 96. **CONTACT ADDRESS** Univ N Texas, Box 311214, Denton, TX, 76203. **EMAIL** marcello@unt.edu

MARCOPOULOS, GEORGE JOHN

PERSONAL Born 06/30/1931, Salem, MA **DISCIPLINE** BALKAN & BYZANTINE HISTORY **EDUCATION** Bowdoin Col, AB, 53; Harvard Univ, AM, 55, PhD, 66. **CAREER** From instr to asst prof, 61-71, Assoc Prof Hist, Tufts Univ, 71-92; prof hist, Tufts Univ, 92. **HONORS AND AWARDS** Seymour O. Simcues Award for Distinguished Tchg Advising, 97. **MEMBERSHIPS** AHA; New Eng Hist Asn. **RESEARCH** The reign of Greece's King George I, 1863-1913; 19th and 20th century Europ royalty and monarchic institutions. **SELECTED PUBLICATIONS** Auth, King George I and the expansion of Greece, 1875-1881, 6/68 & The selection of Prince George of Greece as High Commissioner in Crete, 69, Balkan Studies; Cyprus and Greece, In: Americana Annual, Grolier, 98; Capodistrias, Ioannes Antoniou, Vol V, 606-607, Chios, Vol VI, 601-602, Constantine I, King of the Hellenes, Vol VII, 651 & Iraklion, Vol XV, 367, Marco Dozzaris, Vol IV, p394, Cephalonia, vol VI, p192, Constantine II King of the Hellenes, vol VIII, p651, COrfu, vol VII, p791, The Encyclopedia Americana. **CONTACT ADDRESS** Dept of Hist, Tufts Univ, East Hall, Medford, MA, 02155-5555. **EMAIL** gmarcopo@emerald.tufts.edu

MARCUS, DAVID

PERSONAL Dublin, Ireland **DISCIPLINE** BIBLE AND ANCIENT SEMITIC LANGUAGES **EDUCATION** Cambridge Univ, BA; Columbia Univ, PhD. **CAREER** Fac, Columbia Univ; prof, chr, Bible and Ancient Semitic Languages, Jewish Theol Sem Am. **RESEARCH** The Bible and the Ancient Near East; presently working with an international team of scholars revising the critical edition of the Hebrew Bible. **SELECTED PUBLICATIONS** Auth, From Balaam to Jonah: Anti-prophetic Satire in the Hebrew Bible, Brown Judaic Studies series; numerous scholarly articles; two language manuals, Akkadian, the ancient language of Mesopotamia, Tthe Aramaic of the Babylonian Talmud. **CONTACT ADDRESS** Jewish Theol Sem of America, 3080 Broadway, New York, NY, 10027. **EMAIL** damarcus@jtsa.edu

MARCUS, HAROLD G.

PERSONAL Born 04/08/1936, Worcester, MA, 1 child **DISCIPLINE** AFRICAN HISTORY **EDUCATION** Clark Univ, BA, 58; Boston Univ, MA, 59, PhD, 64. **CAREER** Asst prof history, Addis Ababa Univ, 61-63; asst prof African hist, Howard Univ, 63-68; assoc prof, 68-75, prof history and African studies, 74-, assoc ch dir grad studies, dept history, 88-92; dist prof hist & African studies, 94-, Mich State Univ, 75-, vis asst prof hist, Johns Hopkins Univ, 68; Hoover Inst res award bibliog, 66-67; Smithsonian Inst res award bibliog, 67-68; Soc Sci Res Coun res grant, Ethiopia, 68-69; NDEA Area Ctr fac res grant, Ethiopia, 69-70; Soc Sci Res Coun fel, 76; vis prof African history, Univ Khartoum. 81; Fulbright-Hays, 81-82; NEH Fel Univ Tchr, 92-93; vis distinguished prof comp history, Osaka Gaidai Univ, 97; Fulbright-Hays grant, 98. **HONORS AND AWARDS** Mich State Univ Completion Grant, 82; Soc Sci Res Coun, 82 & 85; Am Philos Soc, 85; Nat Hum Ctr, 85-86; USIS Travel Grant, 87; CICALS Travel Grant, 90; USIA grants for 12th Int Conf Ethiopian Stud, 94; Rockafeller Grant res Ethiopia, 96. **MEMBERSHIPS** African Studies Asn; AHA. **RESEARCH** Ethiopian history from 1850 to present, particularly the reigns of Menilek II, 1889-1913, and Haile Sellassie I, regent, 1916-1928, king, 1928-30, emperor, 1930-1974, died, 1975; Africa, Sudan, Somaliland; colonial & national records. **SELECTED PUBLICATIONS** Auth, A History of Ethiopia, Univ Calif Press, 94; ed, Haile Sellassie, My Life and Ethiopia's Progress, Mich State Univ Press, 94; General Mohammed Farah Aidid and Ethiopia, Ethiopia Rev, 94; Haile Sellassie's Development Policies and Views 1916-1960, Etudes ethiopiennes, 94; Haile Selassie's Leadership, New Trends in Ethiopian Studies, 94; Papers of the 12th International Conference of Ethiopian Studies, Red Sea Press, 94; The Loss of Erutrea as a Consequence of Ethiopia's Victory at Adwa, Ethiopian Regist, 96. **CONTACT ADDRESS** Dept of History, Michigan State Univ, 319 Morrill Hall, East Lansing, MI, 48824-1036. **EMAIL** ethiopia @hs1.hst.msu.edu

MARCUS, IRWIN MURRAY

PERSONAL Born 11/19/1935, New York, NY **DISCIPLINE** MODERN UNITED STATES HISTORY **EDUCATION** Pa State Univ, BS, 58; Lehigh Univ, MA, 59, PhD(hist), 65. **CAREER** Asst prof hist, Harrisburg Area Community Col, 64-65; assoc prof, 65-68, PROF HIST, INDIANA UNIV PA, 68-. **MEMBERSHIPS** Middle Atlantic Racial Historians Asn. **RESEARCH** History of the American labor movement; history of Black America; history of American radicalism. **SELECTED PUBLICATIONS** Auth, Cloud by Day--the Story of Coal and Coke and People, Pa Mag Hist and Biog, Vol 0117, 93; Out of This Furnace, Pa Mag Hist and Biog, Vol 0117, 93; Langham, Jonathan and the Use of Labor Injunction in Indiana County, 1919-1931, Pa Mag Hist and Biog, Vol 0118, 94; Can Workers Have a Voice--the Politics of Deindustrialization in Pittsburgh--Hathaway, Da, Vol 119, 95 and Pa Mag Hist and Biog, Vol 0119, 95. **CONTACT ADDRESS** Dept of Hist, Indiana Univ of Pennsylvania, Indiana, PA, 15701.

MARCUS, JACOB RADER

PERSONAL Born 03/05/1906, Connellsville, PA, m, 1925, 1 child **DISCIPLINE** AMERICAN AND JEWISH HISTORY **EDUCATION** Univ Cincinnati, AB, 17; Univ Berlin, PhD(hist), 25. **CAREER** Instr Bible and Rabbinics, 20-26, from asst prof to prof Jewish hist, 26-46, Ochs prof, 46-65, MILTON AND HATTIE KUTZ DISTINGUISHED SERV PROF AM JEWISH HIST, HEBREW UNION COL, OHIO, 65-, JEWISH ARCH, 47-, DIR, AM JEWISH PERIODICAL CTR, 56-. **HONORS AND AWARDS** Weil Award, Nat Jewish Welfare Bd, 55; Lee M Friedman Medal, Am Jewish Hist Soc, 61., LLD, Univ Cincinnati, 50, Dropsie Col, 55; DHL, Spertus Col Judaics, 77, Brandeis Univ and Gratz Col, 78. **MEMBERSHIPS** Am Jewish Hist Soc (pres, 56-59, hon pres, 59-); Jewish Publ Soc Am (vpres, 55); Cent Conf Am Rabbis (pres, 49, hon pres, 78-); AHA. **RESEARCH** American Jewish history. **SELECTED PUBLICATIONS** Auth, Yivo Annual, Vol 20, Amer Jewish Arch, Vol 0044, 92; Angles of Vision--a Memoir of My Lives, Amer Jewish Arch, Vol 0044, 92; Jewish Polemics, Amer Jewish Arch, Vol 0044, 92; Saving Remnants--Feeling Jewish in America, Amer Jewish Arch, Vol 0044, 92; The Luckiest Orphans--a History of the Hebrew Orphan Asylum of New York, Amer Jewish Arch, Vol 0044, 92; Jews in Christian America--the Pursuit of Religious Equality, Amer Jewish Arch, Vol 0044, 92; Shtetl in the Adirondacks--the Story of Gloversville and its Jews, Amer Jewish Arch, Vol 0044, 92; an Unillustrious Alliance--the African American and Jewish American Communities, Amer Jewish Arch, Vol 0044, 92; Stern ,Malcolm, H.--January 29, 1915 January 5, 1994-in Memoriam, Amer Jewish Arch, Vol 0045, 93. **CONTACT ADDRESS** Hebrew Union Col, Cincinnati, OH, 45220.

MARCUS, PAUL

PERSONAL Born 02/26/1953, New York, NY, m, 1987, 2 children **DISCIPLINE** CLINICAL PSYCHOLOGY **EDUCATION** Univ London, PhD, 80. **CAREER** Psychologist and psychoanalyst. **MEMBERSHIPS** APA, Amer Col of Forensic Psychology. **RESEARCH** Trauma, Ethnic conflict, Child custody. **SELECTED PUBLICATIONS** Auth, Autonomy in the Extreme Situation: Bruno Bettelheim, the Nazi Concentration Camps and the Mass Society, Praeger, 98; Co-ed, Psychoanalytic Versions of the Human Condition: Philosophies of Life and

Their Impact on Practice, New York Univ, 98. **CONTACT ADDRESS** 115 Wooleys Ln, Great Neck, NY, 11023.

MARDER, TOD A.
DISCIPLINE RENAISSANCE-MODERN ARCHITECTURE **EDUCATION** Columbia Univ, PhD. **CAREER** Prof, Rutgers, The State Univ NJ, Univ Col-Camden. **RESEARCH** Bernini's architecture; urban planning in Rome;classical traditions in architecture. **SELECTED PUBLICATIONS** Auth, Alexander VII, Bernini and the Urban Setting of the Pantheon, J of the Soc of Architectural Historians, Sept 91; Bernini's Commission for the Equestian Statue of Constantine in St. Peter's, in An Architectural Progress in the Renaissance and Baroque, eds Henry A. Millon and Susan S. Munshowe, Papers in Art Hist from the Pa State Univ, VIII, 92; Sisto V e la fontana del Mose (Sixtus V and the Fountain of Moses), in Sisto V. Roma e Lazio, eds Marcello Fagiolo and Maria Luisa Madonna, 92; Review of Manfredo Tafuri, Ricerca del rinascimento: Principi, citta, archtetti, Art Bull, Mar 95; Gianlorenzo Bernini's Scala Regia and the Equestrian Statue of Constantine, Cambridge UP, 97. **CONTACT ADDRESS** Dept of Art Hist, Rutgers, The State Univ NJ, Univ Col-Camden, Voorhees Hall, 71 Hamilton St, New Brunswick, NJ, 08903. **EMAIL** marder@rci.rutgers.edu

MARDIN, SERIF
DISCIPLINE INTERNATIONAL STUDIES **EDUCATION** Stanford Univ, BA, Johns Hopkins Sch Adv Int Studies, MA; Stanford Univ, PhD. **CAREER** Prof, Am Univ; Vis Prof, Columbia; Vis Prof, Princeton; Vis Prof, UCLA. **HONORS AND AWARDS** Islamic Chair, Am Univ. **RESEARCH** Middle East. **SELECTED PUBLICATIONS** Auth, Religion and Social Change in Modern Turkey, State Univ NY Press, 89. **CONTACT ADDRESS** American Univ, 4400 Massachusetts Ave, Washington, DC, 20016.

MARGERISON, KENNETH
PERSONAL Born 03/22/1946, Philadelphia, PA, m, 1967, 1 child **DISCIPLINE** HISTORY **EDUCATION** Univ of NC, BA, 67; Duke Univ, MA, 69, PhD, 73 **CAREER** Inst, 69-72, Sacred Heart Col; Inst, 72-73, Asst Prof, 73-83, Assoc Prof, 83-87, Prof, 87-, SW TX St Univ **MEMBERSHIPS** Am hist Asn **RESEARCH** Political pamphlets and public opinion during French Revolution **SELECTED PUBLICATIONS** Auth, Political Thought and Practice During the French Revolution, The American Philosophical Society, 83; Pamphlets and Public Opinion: The campaign to Create a Union of Orders in the Early French Revolution, Purdue Univ Press, 98 **CONTACT ADDRESS** Dept of History, Southwest Texas State Univ, San Marcos, TX, 78666. **EMAIL** km04@swt.edu

MARGOLIN, VICTOR
DISCIPLINE ART HISTORY **EDUCATION** Union Inst, PhD. **CAREER** Assoc prof, Univ IL at Chicago. **RESEARCH** Design hist; theories of mod and contemp art and soc. **SELECTED PUBLICATIONS** Ed, Design Discourse: History, Thought, Criticism; co-ed, Discovering Design: Explorations in Design Studies. **CONTACT ADDRESS** Art Hist Dept, Univ Illinois Chicago, S Halsted St, PO Box 705, Chicago, IL, 60607.

MARGOLIS, GARY
PERSONAL Born 05/24/1945, Great Falls, MT, m, 1975, 2 children **DISCIPLINE** SOCIOLOGY **EDUCATION** Middlebury College, BA; SUNY Buffalo, PhD. **CAREER** Middlebury College, assoc prof, dir Cen for Counseling and Human Rel. **HONORS AND AWARDS** Robert Frost Fell; VT Counc Arts Gnt; Bread Loaf Winter's Conf. **SELECTED PUBLICATIONS** Auth, The Day We Still Stand Here Falling Awake, in: College Student Psychotherapy: Dev Opportunities. **CONTACT ADDRESS** Carr Hall, Middlebury Col, Middlebury, VT, 05753. **EMAIL** margolis@middlebury.edu

MARGOLIS, MAXINE LUANNA
PERSONAL Born 08/02/1942, New York, NY, m, 1970, 1 child **DISCIPLINE** ANTHROPOLOGY **EDUCATION** New York Univ, BA, 64; Columbia Univ, PhD, 70. **CAREER** ASST PROF, 70-74, ASSOC PROF, 74-83, PROF, 84-, UNIV OF FL, 84. **HONORS AND AWARDS** Fulbright Senior Res/Lectr, Rio de Janeiro, 97. **MEMBERSHIPS** Am Anthropological Asn; Latin Am Studies Asn. **RESEARCH** Gender roles; transnational migration; Brazilian immigrants. **SELECTED PUBLICATIONS** Auth, Little Brazil: An Ethnography of Brazilian Immigrants in New York City, Princeton Univ Press, 94; auth, An Invisible Minority: Brazilian Immigrants in New York City, Allyn & Bacon, 98; auth, A Minoria Invisivel: Imigrantes Brasileiros em Nova York, Travessia: Revista do Migrante, 95; auth, Brazilians and the 1990 United States Census: Immigrants, Ethnicity and the Undercount, Human Org, 95; auth, Social Class, Education and the Brain Drain among Brazilian Immigrants to the United States, Network, 95; auth, Transnationalism and Popular Culture: The Case of Brazilian Immigrants in the United States, J of Popular Culture, 95; auth, Brazilians, Encycl of Am Immigrant Cultures, Macmillan, 97. co-ed, Science, Materialism, and the Study of Culture: Readings in Cultural Materialism, Univ Pres of FL. **CONTACT ADDRESS** Dept of Anthropology, Univ of Fl, Gainesville, FL, 32611. **EMAIL** maxinem@nersp.nerdc.ufl.edu

MARINA, WILLIAM F.
DISCIPLINE HISTORY **EDUCATION** Univ Denver, PhD. **CAREER** Prof. **RESEARCH** Modern American history; business history; Florida history; evolution of civilizations; international relations; Southeast Asia history. **SELECTED PUBLICATIONS** Co-auth, American Statesman on Slavery and the Negro; A History of Florida; ed, News of the Nation. **CONTACT ADDRESS** History Dept, Florida Atlantic Univ, 777 Glades Rd, Boca Raton, FL, 33431. **EMAIL** rinaldi@acc.fau.edu

MARINO, JOHN ANTHONY
PERSONAL Born 05/18/1946, Chicago, IL, m, 2 children **DISCIPLINE** EARLY MODERN EUROPEAN HISTORY **EDUCATION** Univ Chicago, BA, 68, MA, 70, PhD(hist), 77. **CAREER** Instr humanities, Kennedy-King Col, 73-74; vis asst prof hist, Fla Int Univ, 76-77; asst prof hist, Univ Calif, San Diego, 78-86; assc prof, 86-; Fulbright, 74-75; Fel, Fondazione Luigi Einaudi, 77-79; Newberry Library Exxon fel, 85-86; Newberry Lib/NEH, 92-93. **MEMBERSHIPS** Am Hist Asn; Econ Hist Asn; Renaissance Soc Am; Sixteenth Century Studies Conference. **RESEARCH** Italian history; economic history. **SELECTED PUBLICATIONS** Auth, La Crisi di Venezia e la New Economic History, Studi Storici, 78; Professazione Voluntaria e Pecore in Aerea: Ragione Economica e Meccanismi de Mercato Nella Dogana de Foggia del Secolo Sedicesimo, Rivista Storica Italiana, 82; Economic Idylls and Pastoral Realities: The Trickster Economy in the Kingdom of Naples, Comparative Studies in Soc & Hist, 82; Pastoral Economics in the Kingdom of Naples, John Hopkins, 88. **CONTACT ADDRESS** Dept of Hist, 0104, Univ of Calif, 9500 Gilman Dr, La Jolla, CA, 92093-0104. **EMAIL** jmarino@ucsd.edu

MARION, CLAUD COLLIER
PERSONAL Fort Pierce, Florida, m **DISCIPLINE** EDUCATION **EDUCATION** FL A&M Univ, BS 1936; Univ of MN, MS 1941; Cornell Univ, PhD 1948. **CAREER** TN A&I Univ, guest prof of educ 1951-52, 1956-70; Univ of MD Eastern Shore, asst dir and coordinator of 1890 extension programs 1972-77, prof agricultural educ and teacher training, beginning 1948, administrator of 1890 extension programs 1977-80. **HONORS AND AWARDS** Certificate of Appreciation for Serv to the Office of Admin by Pres Harry S Truman 1946; Honorary American Farmer degree Natl Org of FFA 1975; Teacher of Teachers Gold Award Natl Vocational Agriculture Teachers Assoc Inc 1976; Certificate of Award for Outstanding Citizenship Princess Anne Chapter of Links Inc 1976; member of Maryland agri team to Soviet Union, 1990. **MEMBERSHIPS** Mem UMES Extension Comm, Administrative Conf Comm, Personnel Coord Comm, Publications Comm; mem Foreign Relations Comm Amer Vocational Assoc; commissioner of Higher Educ Peninsula Conf United Methodist Church Dover DE 1970-; advisor Alpha Tau Alpha; mem Masonic Lodge, Elks Lodge, Alpha Phi Alpha Frat. **CONTACT ADDRESS** Professor Emeritus, Univ of Maryland Eastern Shore.

MARISSEN, MICHAEL
DISCIPLINE MUSIC HISTORY **EDUCATION** Calvin Col, BA; Brandeis Univ, PhD. **CAREER** Vis prof, Princeton Univ; vis prof, Oberlin Col Conserv Music; assoc prof, Swarthmore Col, 89. **RESEARCH** Music hist; early music performance. **SELECTED PUBLICATIONS** Auth, The Social and Religious Designs of J. S. Bach's Brandenburg Concertos, Princeton UP, 95; Lutheranism, Anti-Judaism, and Bach's St John Passion, Oxford UP, 98; coauth, An Introduction to Bach Studies, Oxford UP, 98; ed, Creative Responses to the Music of J. S. Bach from Mozart to Hindemith, U Neb P, 98. **CONTACT ADDRESS** Swarthmore Col, Swarthmore, PA, 19081-1397. **EMAIL** jlord1@cc.swarthmore.edu

MARKEL, STEPHEN
PERSONAL Born 04/30/1954, Pittsburgh, PA, s **DISCIPLINE** ASIAN ART HISTORY AND MUSEUM PRACTICE **EDUCATION** Univ Fla, BA, 76; MA, 80; Univ Mich, PhD, 89. **CAREER** Cur asst grad intern, asst cur, assoc cur, Los Angeles City Mus Art, 83-98; cur and dept head, South and Southeast Asian Art, 98- . **MEMBERSHIPS** Am Coun for Southern Asian Art; Asoc for Asian Studies. **RESEARCH** Art of India, especially Hindu Sculpture and Mughal Decorative Arts. **SELECTED PUBLICATIONS** Auth, Origins of the Indian Planetary Deities, Studies in Asian Thought and Religion, 95; auth, A Jaipur Ragamala in the ¤University of Michiganl Museum of Art, Bull of The Univ of Mich Mus of Art and Archael, 95; auth, Unpublished Ragmala in the Michigan Museum of Art, Roopankan: Recent Studies in Indian Pictorial Heritage, 95; auth, The Use of Flora and Fauna Imagery in Mughal Decorative Arts, Flora and Fauna in Mughal Art, forthcoming; A New Masterwork by Mir Kalan Khan, New Discoveries in Indian Art: Essays in Honor of Anand Krishna, forthcoming. **CONTACT ADDRESS** South and Southeast Asian Art, 5905 Wilshire Blvd, Los Angeles, CA, 90036. **EMAIL** smarkel@lacma.org

MARKOFF, JOHN
PERSONAL Born 03/19/1942, New York, NY, m, 1995, 1 child **DISCIPLINE** SOCIOLOGY **EDUCATION** Columbia Col, BA, 62; Johns Hopkins, PhD, 72. **CAREER** Prof, sociol, hist, polit sci, Univ Pittsburgh. **HONORS AND AWARDS** Pinkney Prize, Soc for Fr Hist Stud; co-winner Sharlin Prize, Soc Sci Hist Asn; Distinguished Scholarly Pub Award, Am Sociol Asn; election to Sociol Res Asn. **RESEARCH** Social movements; democracy. **SELECTED PUBLICATIONS** Coauth, Democrats and Technocrats: professional Economists and Regime Transitions in Latin America, in Can J of Develop Stud, 93; auth, Frontier Societies, in Encycl of Soc Hist, 94; auth, Violence, Emancipation and Democracy: The Countryside and the French Revolution, in Am Hist Rev, 95; auth, The Great Wave of Democracy in Historical Perspective, Cornell Univ, 95; auth, Waves of Democracy: Social Movements and Political Change, Pine Forge Pr, 96; auth, The Abolition of Feudalism: Peasants, Lords and Legislators in The French Revolution, Penn St Univ Pr, 97; auth, Peasants Help Destroy an Old Regime and Defy a New One: Lessons from (and for) the Study of Social Movements, in Am J of Sociol, 97; coauth, A Matter of Definition, in Textual Analysis for the Social Sciences: Methods for Drawing Statistical Inferences from Texts and Transcripts, Lawrence Erlbaum, 97; auth, Really Existing Democracy: Latin America in the 1990s, New Left Review, 97; coauth with Shapiro, Revolutionary Demands: A Content Analysis of the Cahiers de Doleances of 1789, Stanford, 98. **CONTACT ADDRESS** Dept of Sociology, Univ of Pittsburgh, Pittsburgh, PA, 15260. **EMAIL** jm2@vms.cis.pitt.edu

MARKOVITZ, IRVING L.
DISCIPLINE POLITICAL SCIENCE **EDUCATION** Brandeis Univ, BA, 56; Boston Univ, MA, 58; Univ of Calif at Berkeley, PhD, 67. **CAREER** Teaching asst, 59-60, head teaching asst, Dept of Political Sci, Univ of Calif at Berkeley, 60-61; res asst for prof Peter Odegarde, N.B.C. Television, 61-62; vis asst prof, NY Univ, 62-63; fel of the Foreign Area Prog, 64-66; LECTR, DEPT OF POLITICAL SCI, 66-67, ASST PROF, 67-70, ASSOC PROF, 70-71, PROF, QUEENS COL, 72-; affiliated res scholar, Inst of African Studies, 68; Univ of Ghana, 73; vis adjunct prof, Dept of Political Sci & Inst of African Studies, Columbia Univ, 96. **HONORS AND AWARDS** Doctoral Res Grant, 68-69 & 69-70 (declined), Summer Res Grant, CUNY, 69; grants 80-81, 82-83, 84-85, 85-86, 89-90, & 94-95, Jr Fac Grant, Nat Endowment for the Humanities, 69; presidential res award, Queens Col, 86; Ford Fel, Am Coun of Learned Soc, 89-90 & 93; Presidential Innovation in Teaching Award, 92-93; Fac Res Award, CUNY, 72-74, 83-84, 85, 86, & 90; Mellon Fel, 83-84. **MEMBERSHIPS** Fel of the African Studies Asn; Am Political Sci Asn. **SELECTED PUBLICATIONS** Auth, An Uncivil View of Civil Society in Africa, forthcoming; Constitutions, Civil Society, and the Federalist Papers, Constitutionalism: Reflections and Recommendations, The InterAfrica Group, 94; Camels, Intellectuals, Origins, and Dance in the Invention of Somalia: A Commentary, The Invention of Somalia, The Red Sea Press, 95; Checks and Balances, Civil Society and the Federalist Papers, Constitutions and Constitution-Making in Eritrea, Univ of NC Press, forthcoming; coauth, African Literature and Social Science in the Teaching of World Studies, Soc Studies, 93. **CONTACT ADDRESS** Dept of Political Sci, Queens Col, CUNY, 6530 Kissena Blvd, Flushing, NY, 11367.

MARKS, ARTHUR S.
DISCIPLINE ART HISTORY **EDUCATION** Univ London, PhD. **CAREER** Prof, Univ NC, Chapel Hill. **RESEARCH** Am and Brit art and archit; mod archit. **SELECTED PUBLICATIONS** Articles and essays in var jour, including Am Art J, Apollo, Burlington Mag, Art Quart, J of the Warburg and Courtauld Inst, and exhibition catalogs. **CONTACT ADDRESS** Univ N. Carolina, Chapel Hill, Chapel Hill, NC, 27599. **EMAIL** amarks@email.unc.edu

MARKS, ROBERT B.
PERSONAL Born 06/08/1949, Rhinelander, WI, m **DISCIPLINE** HISTORY **EDUCATION** Univ Wis-Madison, BA, 71, MA, 73, PhD, 78. **CAREER** From asst prof to assoc prof to prof, 78-, VP acad affairs, 86-92, Whittier Col. **HONORS AND AWARDS** Aldo Leopold Prize, Am Soc Environ Hist, 96. **MEMBERSHIPS** Asn Asian Stud; Am Soc Environ Hist. **SELECTED PUBLICATIONS** Auth, "Commercialization without Capitalism: Processes of Environmental Change in Late Imperial China," Environ Hist, 96; "Are We Concerned Yet?: Environmental Crisis and Economic Development in China," Bulletin of Concerned Asian Scholars, 96; "'It Never Used to Snow': Climate Change and Agricultural Productivity in South China, 1650-1850," in Sediments of Time, Environment and Society in China, Cambridge Univ Press, 97; Tigers, Rice, Silk and Silt: Environment and Economy in Late Imperial South China, Cambridge University Press, 98; "Maritime Trade and the Agro-Ecology of South China, 1685-1850," in Pacific Centuries, Routledge, 99. **CONTACT ADDRESS** Dept of History, Whittier Col, PO Box 634, Whittier, CA, 90608. **EMAIL** rmarks@whittier.edu

MARKS, SALLY JEAN
PERSONAL Born 01/18/1931, New Haven, CT **DISCIPLINE** MODERN INTERNATIONAL & EUROPEAN HISTORY **EDUCATION** Wellesley Col, AB, 52; Univ NC Chapel Hill, MA, 61; Univ London, PhD, 68. **CAREER** Instr, Woman's Col, Univ NC, 60-62; from instr to prof hist, Rhode Island Col, 62-88. **HONORS AND AWARDS** Am Coun Learned Soc res fel, 77-78; G L Beer Prize, AHA, 81; Phi Alpha Theta Book

Award, 83; Bernadotte E. Schmitt Award of AHA, 88. **MEMBERSHIPS** AHA; Am Coun Learned Soc; Institut Royal des Relations Internationales, Brussels; Conf Group Cent Europ Hist; Soc for French Hist Stud. **RESEARCH** Interwar Europe; Belgian history; diplomatic and financial history of the post World War I era. **SELECTED PUBLICATIONS** Auth, My Name is Ozymandias: The Kaiser in Exile, Cent Europ Hist, 83; art, Black Watch on the Rhine: A Study in Propaganda, Prejudice, and Prurience, Europ Stud Rev, 83; art, Diplomacy, Ency Britannica, 15th ed, Macropaedia, 91; art, Smoke and Mirrors in Smoke-Filled Rooms and the Galerie des Glaces, The Versailles Treaty: A Reassessment after Seventy-Five years, Cambridge, 98. **CONTACT ADDRESS** 603 Hope St, Providence, RI, 02906. **EMAIL** smarks@grog.ric.edu

MARLIN-BENNETT, RENE
DISCIPLINE INTERNATIONAL POLITICAL ECONOMY **EDUCATION** Pomona Col, BA; Mass Inst Technol, PhD. **CAREER** Prof, Am Univ. **RESEARCH** Intellectual property rights, trade relations, conflict resolution. **SELECTED PUBLICATIONS** Auth, Foodfights: International Regimes and the Politics of Agricultural Trade Disputes, Gordon & Breach, 93. **CONTACT ADDRESS** American Univ, 4400 Massachusetts Ave, Washington, DC, 20016.

MARM, MICHAEL
DISCIPLINE ASIAN HISTORY AND MODERN EUROPEAN HISTORY **EDUCATION** Univ, CA-Berkeley, PhD. **CAREER** Ch, Columbia Univ sem on traditional China; asst prof. **SELECTED PUBLICATIONS** Auth, Population and Possibility in Ming Suzhou: A Quantified Model, Ming Studies 12, 81; Heaven on Earth: The Rise of Suzhou, 1127-1550, Cities of Jiangnan in Late Imperial China, SUNY, 93. **CONTACT ADDRESS** Dept of Hist, Fordham Univ, 113 W 60th St, New York, NY, 10023.

MARONEY, JAMES C.
PERSONAL Born 10/06/1936, Houston, TX, m, 1957, 3 children **DISCIPLINE** UNITED STATES HISTORY **EDUCATION** Sam Houston State Univ, BA, 61, MA, 63; Univ Houston, PhD, 75. **CAREER** Instr hist, Sam Houston State Univ, 62-63 & Amarillo Col, 63-64; MEM FAC HIST, LEE COL, 64-, chmn dept Soc Sci, 78-92; vis scholar, New Handbook of Texas project, TX State Hist Asn, spring 94; co-managing ed, Touchstone (student journal), Walter Prescott Webb Soc, TX State Hist Asn, 95-. **MEMBERSHIPS** Orgn Am Historians; Southern Hist Asn; Labor Hist Asn. **RESEARCH** Early 20th century United States history; American labor history; Texas History. **SELECTED PUBLICATIONS** Auth, The Negro and Organized Labor: Selected Views, 1880-1920, Community Col Social Sci Quart, spring 76; coauth, Teaching College History: A Critique and Historiographical Analysis, Teaching Hist, spring 77; Survey United States history courses: Two and four-year institutions in Texas as a case study, Community Col Social Sci J, 8/77; auth, The Texas-Louisiana oil field strike of 1917, In: Essays in Southern Labor History, Greenwood, 77; The International Longshoremen's Association in the Gulf States during the Progressive Era, Southern Studies, summer 77; The Galveston Longshoremen's Strike of 1920, ETex Hist J, spring 78; The Unionization of Thurber, 1903, Red River Valley Hist Rev, spring 79; co-auth, The Heritage of Texas Labor, 1838-1980, TX AFL-CIO, 82; Labor's Struggle for Acceptance: The Houston Worker in a Changing Society, 1900-1929, Houston Rev 6, no 1, 84; co-ed, From Humble Beginnings, Exxon USA, 95. **CONTACT ADDRESS** Dept of Soc Sci, Lee Col, PO Box 818, Baytown, TX, 77522-0818. **EMAIL** jmaroney@lee.edu

MARQUARDT-CHERRY, JANET TERESA
DISCIPLINE ART HISTORY **EDUCATION** UCLA, BA, MA, PhD. **CAREER** Art Dept, Eastern Ill Univ **HONORS AND AWARDS** Res Assistantship, UCLA; Tchg Assistantship, UCLA; Edward A. Dickson Hist Art fel, UCLA; Grad div grant, UCLA; Edward A. Dickson, Special Opportunity Grant, UCLA; Edward A. Dickson res grant, UCLA; Fac res grant, Eastern IL Univ; Tenure, Eastern IL Univ, FL State Univ. **SELECTED PUBLICATIONS** Auth, Ottonian Imperial Saints in the Pruem Troper Manuscripta, 89; Ascension Sunday in Tropers: Innovative Scenes in the Pruem and Canterbury Tropers and Their Relationship to the Accompanying Texts, Proceedings Ill Medieval Asn, 89; King David In Germany: Royal Traditions at Pruem, Proceedings Ill Medieval Asn, 92; Rethinking the Cultural Context of Foundations, FATE Jour, 93-94; Katja Oxman: Working in the Tradition of the Woman Artist, Woman's Art Jour, 94. **CONTACT ADDRESS** Eastern Illinois Univ, 600 Lincoln Ave, Charleston, IL, 61920-3099.

MARQUIS, ALICE GOLDFARB
PERSONAL Born 03/30/1930, Munich, Germany, 1 child **DISCIPLINE** MODERN EUROPEAN AND CULTURAL HISTORY **EDUCATION** San Diego State Univ, BA, 66, MA, 69; Univ Calif, San Diego, PhD(hist), 78. **CAREER** Co-publ, PACIFIC Calif Tribune, 54-59 and Star-News Publ, San Diego, Calif, 61-72; instr hist, Univ Calif, San Diego, 78-81; RES AND WRITING, 81-, Instr art hist, San Diego Evening Col, 70-74; planning commr, San Diego County, 72-76. **HONORS AND AWARDS** Suburban Journalist of the Year, Suburban Newpapers of Am, 72. **MEMBERSHIPS** AHA **RESEARCH** Western culture between the two world wars; history of media and propaganda; Biog of 20th century cultural figures. **SELECTED PUBLICATIONS** Auth, Patron Saints--5 Rebels Who Opened America to a New Art, 1928-1943, Amer Hist Rev, Vol 0098, 93; The Private Worlds of Duchamp, Marcel--Desire, Liberation, and the Self in Modern Culture, Amer Hist Rev, Vol 0102, 97. **CONTACT ADDRESS** Univ California, San Diego, CA, 92103.

MARR, WILLIAM L.
PERSONAL Born 03/25/1944, Hamilton, ON, Canada **DISCIPLINE** ECONOMIC HISTORY **EDUCATION** McMaster Univ, BA, 66; Univ Western Ont, MA, 67, PhD, 73. **CAREER** Instr, Univ Western Ont, 68-70; lectr, Waterloo Lutheran Univ, 70; asst prof, 73-75, assoc prof, 75-82, PROF ECONOMICS, WILFRID LAURIER UNIV, 82-, asst dean, grad stud & assoc dir instruct develop, 88-92, 94-; vis scholar, Duke Univ; vis prof, Univ Western Ont; vis prof, Mcmaster Univ; consult, Citizenship & Immigration Can. **HONORS AND AWARDS** Ont Grad fels; Can Coun fels; Hurd Medal; SSHRCC res grant; Ont Econ Coun res grant; Citizenship & Immigration Can res grant; Inst Res Public Policy, res grant; Can Mortgage & Housing Corp res grant. **MEMBERSHIPS** Can Econ Asn; Can Pop Soc (secy-tres, 90-92); Econ Hist Asn; Asn Can Stud; Can Reg Sci Asn. **SELECTED PUBLICATIONS** Auth, Labour Market and Other Implications of Immigration Policy for Ontario, 76; coauth, An Economic History, 80; co-ed, How Economists Explain, 83. **CONTACT ADDRESS** Dept of Economics, Wilfrid Laurier Univ, Waterloo, ON, N2L 3C5.

MARRIN, ALBERT
DISCIPLINE HISTORY **EDUCATION** CUNY, BA, 58; Yeshiva Univ, MS, 59; Columbia Univ, MA, 61, PhD, 68. **CAREER** Lectr, 67, asst 68, assoc, 74, PROF, 79-, CHAIR HISTORY, 79- , YESHIVA UNIV. **CONTACT ADDRESS** 750 Kappock St, New York, NY, 10463.

MARRONE, STEVEN PHILLIP
PERSONAL Born 08/16/1947, Frederick, MD, 2 children **DISCIPLINE** MEDIEVAL HISTORY **EDUCATION** Harvard Univ, BA, 69, PhD, 78. **CAREER** Asst prof hist, 78-95, prof hist, Tufts Univ, MA, 96-. **MEMBERSHIPS** Medieaval Acad Am; AHA; Soc Medieval & Renaissance Philos. **RESEARCH** Medieval philosophy; history of medieval science. **SELECTED PUBLICATIONS** Auth, William of Auvergne and Robert Grosseteste: New Ideas of Truth in the Early Thirteenth Century, Princeton Univ Press, 83; Truth and Scientific Knowledge in the Thought of Henry of Ghent, Medieval Academy, 85. **CONTACT ADDRESS** Dept Hist, Tufts Univ, Medford, MA, 02155-5555. **EMAIL** smarrone@emerald.tufts.edu

MARRUS, MICHAEL R.
PERSONAL Born 02/03/1941, Toronto, ON, Canada **DISCIPLINE** HISTORY **EDUCATION** Univ Toronto, BA, 63; Univ Calif Berkeley, MA, 64, PhD, 68. **CAREER** Asst prof to prof, 68-78, DEAN SCH GRADUATE STUDIES & PROF HISTORY, UNIV TORONTO, 78-, sr cont fel, Massey Col, 86-, fel, Trinity Col, 87-; sr assoc mem, St. Antony's Col, Oxford Univ, 78-80; vis prof, Univ Calif Los Angeles, 82; acad comt, Int Ctr Stud Anti-Semitism, 83-, fel, Inst Advan Stud, Hebrew Univ(-Jerusalem), 84-85; adv bd, Ctr Refugee Stud, York Univ, 86-. **HONORS AND AWARDS** Connaught Found fel, 77-79; Killam sr res fel, Can Coun, 78-79; Guggenheim fel, 84-85; FRSC, 87; FRHS, 94. **MEMBERSHIPS** Int adv comt, Tauber Inst, 87-; int adv bd, Holocaust Ser, Pargamon Press & Inst Contemporary Jewry, 88-; int adv bd, Anti-Defamation League, Braun Ctr Holocaust Stud, 90-; acad adv bd, Holocaust Educ Found, 92-. **RESEARCH** Holocaust; Jewish studies; refugee studies. **SELECTED PUBLICATIONS** Auth, The Politics of Assimilation, 71, 80; auth, The Unwanted: European Refugees in the Twentieth Century, 85; auth, The Holocaust in History, 87; auth, Mr. Sam: The Life and Times of Samuel Bronfman, 91; auth, The Nuremburg War Crimes Trial, 1945-46: A Documentary History, 97; coauth, Vichy, France and the Jews, 81, 96; ed adv bd, Holocaust & Genocide Stud, 85-; assoc ed, J Refugee Stud, 87-. **CONTACT ADDRESS** Sch Grad Stud, Univ of Toronto, 65 St. George St, Toronto, ON, M5S 2Z9.

MARSCHALL, JOHN PETER
PERSONAL Born 12/11/1933, Chicago, IL **DISCIPLINE** AMERICAN RELIGIOUS HISTORY **EDUCATION** Loyola Univ, Ill, AB, 56; St Louis Univ, MA, 61; Cath Univ Am, PhD(hist), 65. **CAREER** Lectr relig hist, Cath Univ Am, 65; asst prof, Viatorian Sem, Washington, DC, 61-65; asst prof Am relig hist, Loyola Univ, Ill, 66-69, mem grad fac, 68; dir, Ctr Relig and Life, 69-72, prog coordr, Ctr Relig and Life, 73-76; lectr, 69-80, ASSOC PROF AM HIST, UNIV NEV, RENO, 80-, Schmitt Found travel grant, Europe, 63-64; dir, Self-Studies Sisters of Charity, BVM, 66-68; co-dir, Self-Studies New Melleray Trappist Abbey, 68-69; mem subcomt hist, life and ministry priests, Nat Coun Bishops, 68-72; Western dir, Nat Inst for Campus Ministries, 75-79; ed consult, NICM J for Christian and Jews in Higher Educ, 75-79; asst to pres, Univ Nev, Reno, 80-. **MEMBERSHIPS** Cath Campus Ministry Asn (pres, 75-76); Am Acad Relig; Orgn Am Historians; Am Cath Hist Asn; Am Acad Polit and Soc Sci. **RESEARCH** Nineteenth century American Catholic history; history of religion in Nevada. **SELECTED PUBLICATIONS** Auth, The Premier See--a History of the Archdiocese-of-Baltimore, Church Hist, Vol 0065, 96. **CONTACT ADDRESS** Dept of Hist, Univ of Nev, Reno, NV, 89557-0001.

MARSDEN, G.M.
PERSONAL Born 02/25/1939, m, 1969, 2 children **DISCIPLINE** HISTORY OF CHRISTIANITY **EDUCATION** Haverford College, BA, honors, 59; Westminster Theol Sem, BD, 63; Yale Univ MA, 61, PhD, 65. **CAREER** Francis A McAnaney Prof of Hist, 92-, Univ Notre Dame; Prof 86-92, Duke Univ; vis Prof 86, 90, Univ Cal Berkeley; vis Prof 76-77, Trinity Evang Div Schl; Dir 80-83, Calvin College; Instr, Asst Prof, Assoc Prof, Prof, 65-86, Calvin College; Asst Instr, 64-65, Yale Univ. **HONORS AND AWARDS** Lippincott Prize; YHF for NEH; Calvin Cen Christ Schl fel; Eternity Book of the Year; Calvin Res Fel; J Howard Pew Freedom Gnt; Guggenheim Fel. **MEMBERSHIPS** ASCH. **SELECTED PUBLICATIONS** Auth, The Outrageous Idea of Christian Scholarship, NY, Oxford Univ Press, 97; The Soul of the American University: From Protestant Establishment to Established Nonbelief, NY, Oxford Univ Press, 94; coed, The Secularization of the Academy, NY, Oxford Univ Press, 92; Understanding Fundamentalism and Evangelicalism, Grand Rapids, W B Eerdmans, 91, collection of previously pub essays; Reforming Fundamentalism: Fuller Seminary and the New Evangelicalism, Grand Rapids, W b Eerdmans, 87, reissued pbk, 95. **CONTACT ADDRESS** Dept of History, Univ Notre Dame, Notre Dame, IN, 46556. **EMAIL** marsden.1@nd.edu

MARSH, PETER T.
PERSONAL Born 12/08/1935, Toronto, ON, Canada, m, 1962, 3 children **DISCIPLINE** MODERN BRITISH HISTORY **EDUCATION** Univ Toronto, BA, 58; Cambridge Univ, PhD(19th century Brit hist), 62. **CAREER** From inst to asst prof hist, Univ Sask, 62-67; chmn dept, 68-70, assoc prof, 67-78, PROF HIST, SYRACUSE UNIV, 78-, DIR, UNIV HONORS PROG, 78-, Can Coun res grant, 65 and res fel, 66-67; vis fel, All Souls Col, Oxford Univ, 66-67; vis prof, Victorian Studies Ctr, Univ Leicester, 70; vis fel, Emmanuel Col, Cambridge Univ, 73-74; Nat Prog Chmn, Conf Brit Studies, 75-77; Guggenheim fel, 80-81; hon res fel, Univ Birmingham, 80-81. **MEMBERSHIPS** Can Hist Asn; Anglo-Am Hist Conf; AHA; fel Royal Hist Soc. **RESEARCH** Modern British history. **SELECTED PUBLICATIONS** Auth, Victorian Liberalism, 19th Century Prose, Vol 0019, 92; Palmerston and Liberalism, 1855-1865, Victorian Stud, Vol 0036, 92; After Chartism, Class and Nation in English Radical Politics, 1848-1874, Albion, Vol 0026, 94; Entrepreneurial Politics in Mid-Victorian Britain, Albion, Vol 0026, 94; Disraeli, a Biog, Historian, Vol 0057, 94; Paths Not Taken, J Mod Hist, Vol 0069, 97. **CONTACT ADDRESS** Dept of Hist, Syracuse Univ, Syracuse, NY, 13244.

MARSH, VINCENT
DISCIPLINE HISTORIC PRESERVATION; CITY AND REGIONAL PLANNING **EDUCATION** SUNY Buffalo, BS 70; Univ Connecticut, MSW 74; MIT Cambridge, MA 79-81; Cornell Univ, MRP 81. **CAREER** Planning Dept, CCSF, pres plan, 97-, sec plan 89-96, plan 86-89; United Way Sf, assoc 85; Democ Nat Conv, trans sch mgr 84; Earth Metrics Inc/ Revoir Devel Co, plan consul 82-83; Nat Trust Hist Pres, field rep/plan 81-82; Cornell Univ, tchg asst 80-81; Lane Frenchman MA, planner 80; Boston Landmarks Ex Off MA, res adv/consul 80; North End Union Inc MA, exec dir 74-79; Children's Museum MA, consul 77; Metro Plan Proj MA, consul 77; Greater Hartford Process Inc MA, planner 73-74. **HONORS AND AWARDS** Calif Pres Foun Awd; Mast Thesis Support Awd; NEH Fel. **MEMBERSHIPS** BAHA; CHS; NTHP; APA; OHA; AIA; SAH; AANC; HPPA; SPURA; San Francisco Tomorrow; FSFAH; United Way SF; VAF; Vict Alliance SF. **RESEARCH** American Architecture 19th and 20th centuries; California and San Francisco history and architecture. **SELECTED PUBLICATIONS** Auth, San Francisco Planning Dept, Neighborhood Commercial Issues Paper, coauth, The Planning Dept, 98; Preservation, An Element of the General Plan of the City and County of San Francisco, Proposal for Adoption, Implementation Program Document and Appendices, coauth, The Planning Dept, 98; Revisions to Article 10, Landmarks Preservation, amending Part II Ch II of the San Francisco Municipal Code by repealing Article 10 thereof and adding a new Article 10, secs 1001-1024. Thereto creating a Landmarks Board, describing the power and the duties of the Landmarks Bd, re-designing previously designated Landmarks and Historic Districts, requiring Certificates of Appropriateness for alterations of Landmarks and Hist Districts, est guidelines doe decisions and imposing penalties for violations of Article 10, coauth, Text Amend for Adoption, 96; Thirty City Landmark Case Report Nominations, Appen to Article 10, coauth, ed, List of Designated Landmarks, 88-; Pocket Guide to the Historic Districts of San Francisco, coauth, SF Visitors Bureau and Vict Alliance, 93. **CONTACT ADDRESS** The Planning Dept, 1660 Mission St 5th Floor, San Francisco, CA, 94123-4761. **EMAIL** VincentMarsh@ci.sf.ca.us

MARSHALL, BYRON K.
DISCIPLINE HISTORY **EDUCATION** Stanford Univ, PhD, 66. **CAREER** Prof emer. **HONORS AND AWARDS** Ed, J Asian Studies. **RESEARCH** Japanese history; ideology and social change in late nineteenth- and early twentieth-century Japan. **SELECTED PUBLICATIONS** Auth, Capitalism and Nationalism in Prewar Japan: The Ideology of the Business Elite 1868-1941, Stanford, 97; Learning To the Modern: Education in Japanese Political Discourse, 94; Academic Freedom and the Japanese Imperial University 1868-1939, Univ Calif, 92; co-auth, A Comparative History of Civilizations in Asia, Westview, 86. **CONTACT ADDRESS** History Dept, Univ of Minnesota, Twin Cities, 614 Social Sciences Tower, 267 19th Ave S, Minneapolis, MN, 55455. **EMAIL** marsh004@tc.umn.edu

MARSHALL, DOMINIQUE
DISCIPLINE HISTORY **EDUCATION** Univ de Montreal, BA, 83, MA, 85, PhD, 89. **CAREER** Assoc prof. **RESEARCH** Quebec and Canadian families and social politicies in the twentieth century. **SELECTED PUBLICATIONS** Auth, Family Allowances and Family Autonomy: Quebec 1945-1955, Can Family Hist: Selected Readings, Toronto, Copp Clark, 92; "The Language of Children's Rights, the Formation of the Welfare State and the Democratic Experience of poor Families, Quebec, 1940-1955," Can Hist Rev Vol 78, 97; Le recul du travail des enfants au Quebec entre 1940 et 1960: une explication des conflits entre les familles pauvres et l'Etat providence, Labour/Le Travail, 89; reprinted and transl as The Decline of Child Labour in Quebec, 1940-1960: Conflict Between Poor Families and the State, Hist Perspectives on Law and Soc in Canada, Copp Clark, 94; "Nationalisme et politiques sociales au Quebec depuis 1867: Un siecle de rendez-vous manques entre l'Etat, l'Eglise et les familles," Brit Jour of Can Stud, 94. **CONTACT ADDRESS** Dept of Hist, Carleton Univ, 1125 Colonel By Dr, Ottawa, ON, K1S 5B6. **EMAIL** dmarsha2@ccs.carleton.ca

MARSHALL, HOWARD WIGHT
DISCIPLINE AMERICAN ARCHITECTURE, MATERIAL CULTURE, HISTORIC PRESERVATION **EDUCATION** Univ Mo, BA; Ind Univ, MA, PhD, 76. **CAREER** Prof; vis fel, Europ Ethnol Res Cte, Edinburgh; ch, dept Art Hist and Archaeol. **HONORS AND AWARDS** Cofinalist for 2 Grammy awd(s). **RESEARCH** Vernacular architecture and cultural/historical monuments in Missouri; historic farm buildings in the central lowlands of Scotland. **SELECTED PUBLICATIONS** Auth, Little Dixie; British Isles Subregion Upper Avon River Valley, Central Scotland; Estate Worker's Housing, Scotland; & other chap in Encycl Vernacular Archit of the World, Cambridge UP, 98; Paradise Valley, Nevada: The People and Buildings of an American Place, Tucson: Univ Ariz Press, 95; Vernacular Architecture in Rural and Small Town Missouri: An Introduction, Columbia: Univ Mo Exten Div, 94; Architecture, Folk, chap in Folklore: An Encyclopedia of Forms, Methods, and History, NY, Garland, 97; Vernacular Architecture, chap in Amer Folklore: An Encycl, NY and London, Garland Publ, Inc, 95; Vernacular Housing and American Culture, lead chap in Amer Popular Housing, NY, Greenwood, 95 & Milestones and Stumbling Blocks, Continued, J Cult Geog 15 1, 94; coauth, Now That's a Good Tune: Masters of Traditional Missouri Fiddling, Columbia, Publ Univ Mo Cult Heritage Ctr, 89; co-ed, The German-American Experience in Missouri: Essays in Celebration of the Tricentennial of German Immigration to Ameria, 1683-1983, Columbia, Publ Univ Mo Cult l Heritage Ctr, 86. **CONTACT ADDRESS** Dept of Art History and Archaeology, Univ of Missouri-Columbia, 109 Pickard Hall, Columbia, MO, 65211. **EMAIL** ahahm@showme.missouri.edu

MARSHALL, PETER K.
PERSONAL Born 07/02/1934, Cardiff, Wales, d, 2 children **DISCIPLINE** CLASSICAL LANGUAGES, MEDIEVAL LITERATURE **EDUCATION** Univ SWales, BA, 54; Oxford Univ BA, 56, MA, 60. **CAREER** Instr classics, 59-61, asst prof, 62-68, assoc prof, 68-73, Prof Classics, Amherst Col, 73-, Asst lectr Latin & Greek, Univ Liverpool, England, 61-62. **HONORS AND AWARDS** ACLS fel, 76-77; Guggenheim fel, 80-81, MA, Amherst Col, 73. **MEMBERSHIPS** Class Asn Gt Brit; Am Philol Asn; Medieval Acad Am. **RESEARCH** The textual transmission of classical Latin authors; the Commentarii of Servius; the De Proprietatibus Rerum of Bartholomaeus Anglicus. **SELECTED PUBLICATIONS** Auth, Utopia, Sir Thomas More, Washington Sq Press, 65; ed, A Gellii Noctes Atticae, 2 vols, Oxford Univ Press, 68; auth, The Manuscript Tradition of Cornelius Nepos, Univ London, 77; ed, Cornelii Nepotis Vitae cum Fragmentis, Teubner, Leipzig, 77; Isidore, Etymologies Book II, Les Belles Lett, Paris, 82; coauth, Texts and Transmission, Clarendon Press, 83; auth, Servati Lupi Epistulae, Teubner, 84; Hyginus Fabulae, Teubner, 93; Servius and Commentary on Virgil, CEMERS, 97. **CONTACT ADDRESS** Dept of Classics, Amherst Col, Amherst, MA, 01002-5000. **EMAIL** pkmarshall@amherst.edu

MARSHMAN, MICHELLE
PERSONAL Born 03/31/1968, Seattle, WA, m, 1989 **DISCIPLINE** HISTORY **EDUCATION** Univ CA, Riverside, PhD, 97. **CAREER** Asst prof, 97-, European And Women's Hist, Northwest Nazarene Col **MEMBERSHIPS** French Hist Soc; AAR. **RESEARCH** Catholic women in 17th century France. **CONTACT ADDRESS** Northwest Nazerene Col, 623 Holly St, Nampa, ID, 83686. **EMAIL** m/marshman@exodus.nnc.edu

MARSZALEK, JOHN FRANCIS
PERSONAL Born 07/05/1939, Buffalo, NY, m, 1965, 3 children **DISCIPLINE** UNITED STATES HISTORY **EDUCATION** Canisius Col, BA, 61; Univ Notre Dame, MA, 63, PhD, 68. **CAREER** Teaching asst hist, Univ Notre Dame, 62-64; Capt, U.S. Army, 65-67; instr, Canisius Col, 67-68; from asst prof to assoc prof, Gannon Col, 68-73; from Assoc Prof to Prof Hist, 73-94, William L. Giles Distinguished Prof, Miss State Univ, 94. **HONORS AND AWARDS** NEH res grant, 71; Am Coun Learned Soc grant-in-aid, 73-74; travel grants, Cushwa Ctr, Univ Notre Dame, 84, Am Philos Soc, 88; Miss State Univ Alum Asn Grad Level Teaching Award, 90; Ohioana Libr Non-Fiction Award, 93; Non-Fiction Award, Miss Libr Asn, 94; res grant, Criss Found, Miss State Univ, 96; Miss Legislature Outstanding Teacher Award, 97. **MEMBERSHIPS** Orgn Am Historians; Southern Hist Asn; Miss Hist Soc; Soc Civil War Hist; Lincoln Forum; Hist Civil War Western Theatre; Golden Triangle Civil War Roundtable. **RESEARCH** Civil War and Reconstruction; U.S. Middle Period; U.S. race relations. **SELECTED PUBLICATIONS** Auth, Court-Martial: A Black Man in America, Scribner, 72, paperback ed titled: Assault at West Point, 94; coauth, A Black Businessman in White Mississippi 1886-1974, Univ Miss, 77; ed, The Diary of Miss Emma Holmes, 1861-1866, La State Univ Press, 79; Shermans Other War: The General and the Civil War Press, Memphis State Univ Press, 81; coauth, A Black Physician's Story, Bringing Hope in Mississippi, 85; co-ed, Grover Cleveland, A Bibliography, 88; Encyclopedia of African-American Civil Rights, From Emancipation to the Present, 92; auth, Sherman, A Soldier's Passion for Order, 93; co-ed, American Political History, The State of the Discipline, 97; auth, The Petticoat Affair: Manners, Mutiny, and Sex in Andrew Jackson's White House, 98; author of numerous journal articles and book reviews. **CONTACT ADDRESS** Dept of Hist, Mississippi Col, Drawer H, Ms State Univ, MS, 39762-5508. **EMAIL** jfm1@ra.msstate.edu

MARTEN, JAMES
PERSONAL Born 09/10/1956, Madison, SD, m, 1977, 2 children **DISCIPLINE** AMERICAN HISTORY **EDUCATION** S Dakota St Univ, BA, 78; Univ S Dakota, MA, 81; Univ Texas, Austin, PhD, 86. **CAREER** Tchr, Eng, 78-80, Woodbine High Schl, IA; asst prof, 86-92, assoc prof, 92-, Marquette Univ. **HONORS AND AWARDS** Fulbright Lect People's Rep of China, 99. **MEMBERSHIPS** Org of Amer Hist; So Hist Assn, Soc of Civil War Hist. **RESEARCH** Civil war era; children; soc hist; African Amer. **SELECTED PUBLICATIONS** Auth, Texas Divided: Loyalty and Dissent in the Lone Star State, 1856-1874, Univ Press KY, 90; auth, Texas, World Bibliog Ser, Oxford Clio Bks, 92; art, For the Army, the People, and Abraham Lincoln: A Yankee Newspaper in Occupied Texas; Civil War Hist 39, 93; art, In the Best Interests of the Parent: Children, Material Culture, and the Law, Rev in Amer Hist 23, 95; art, Stern Realities: The Children of Chancellorsville and Beyond, Chancellorsville: The Battle & Its Aftermath, Univ NC Press, 96; art, Fatherhood in the Confederacy: Southern Soldiers and Their Children, J of S Hist 63, 97; auth, The Children's Civil War, Univ NC Press, 98; auth, Lessons of War: The Civil War in Children's Magazines, SR Bks, 98. **CONTACT ADDRESS** History Dept, Marquette Univ, PO Box 1881, Milwaukee, WI, 53201-1881. **EMAIL** james.marten@marquette.edu

MARTER, JOAN
DISCIPLINE TWENTIETH CENTURY ART **EDUCATION** Univ Delaware, PhD. **CAREER** Prof, Rutgers, The State Univ NJ, Univ Col-Camden. **RESEARCH** Twentieth-century painting and sculpture in Europe and America; American sculpture from 1930 to the present. **SELECTED PUBLICATIONS** Auth, Alexander Calder, Cambridge UP, 91; Theodore Roszak: The Drawings, Univ Wash Press, 92; Dorothy Dehner: Sixty Years of Art, Univ Wash Press, 93; Sculpture in Postwar Europe and America, in Art J 53, 94; The Ascendancy of Abstraction for Public Art: The Monument to the Unknown Political Prisoner Competition. **CONTACT ADDRESS** Dept of Art Hist, Rutgers, The State Univ NJ, Univ Col-Camden, Voorhees Hall, 71 Hamilton St, New Brunswick, NJ, 08903. **EMAIL** joanmarter@aol.com

MARTI, DONALD B.
DISCIPLINE HISTORY **EDUCATION** Univ Minn, BA, 61; Univ Wis, MS, 63, PhD, 66. **CAREER** ASSOC PROF, HISTORY, UNIV INDIANA SOUTH BEND **MEMBERSHIPS** AM Antiquarian Soc **SELECTED PUBLICATIONS** Auth, "The Rev Henry Colman's Agricultural Ministry," Agr Hist 51, 77; auth, "Agricultural Journalism and the Diffusion of Knowledge: The First Half-Century in America," Agr Hist 54, 80; auth, "Woman's Work in the Grange: Mary Ann Mayo of Michigan, 1882-1903," Agr Hist 56, 82; auth, "Francis William Bird: A Radical's Progress through the Republican Party," Hist Jour of Mass 11, 83; ed, Historical Directory of American Agricultural Fairs, Greenwood Press, 86; auth, Women of the Grange: Mutuality and Sisterhood in Rural America, 1866-1920, Greenwood Press, 91; auth, "Answering the Agrarian Question: Socialists, Farmers, and Algie Martin Simons, Agr Hist 65; auth, Rich Methodists: The Rise and Consequences of Lay Philanthropy in the Mid Nineteenth-Century, in Perspectives on American Methodism, Kingswood Books, 93. **CONTACT ADDRESS** 1322 E. South St, South Bend, IN, 46615.

MARTIN, AUSTIN LYNN
PERSONAL Born 10/05/1942, Onawa, IA, m, 1963, 3 children **DISCIPLINE** RENAISSANCE AND REFORMATION HISTORY **EDUCATION** Univ Ore, BA, 65; Univ Wis-Madison, MA, 68, PhD(hist), 71. **CAREER** Specialist hist, Univ Wis, 71; asst prof, Lakehead Univ, 71-73; lectr, 74-80, SR LECTR, UNIV ADELAIDE, 80-, Mem coun, Sixteenth Century Studies Conf, 72-73; Am Coun Learned Soc grant-in-aid, 73; exec secy, Australasian Historians of Medieval and Early Mod Europe, 74-76; res grant, Australian Res Grants Coun, 76. **MEMBERSHIPS** Australian Hist Asn; Am Soc Reformation Res; AHA; Am Soc Church Hist. **RESEARCH** Society of Jesus. **SELECTED PUBLICATIONS** Auth, Student Views about the Contribution of Literary and Cultural Content to Language Learning at Intermediate Level, For Lang Annals, Vol 0026, 93; Venice, a Documentary History, 1450-1630, Parergon, Vol 0011, 93; Julius II, Parergon, Vol 0012, 94; The 1st Jesuits, Cath Hist Rev, Vol 0080, 94; Pius V, Saint, Parergon, Vol 0012, 94; Fernando of Cordova, Parergon, Vol 0012, 94; Nadal, Jerome, 1507-1580,, Church Hist, Vol 0064, 95; Pastoral Visitations and Elaboration of Computer Data, Church Hist, Vol 0064, 95; Words and Deeds in Renaissance Rome, Parergon, Vol 0012, 95; Pastoral Visitations and Elaboration of Computer Data, Church Hist, Vol 0064, 95; For Matters of Greater Moment--the First 30 Jesuit General-Congregations--a Brief History and a Translation of the Decrees, Cath Hist Rev, Vol 0082, 96; Classes, Estates, and Order in Early Modern Brittany, J Mod Hist, Vol 0068, 96; Apostolic Traditions and Conscientious Citizen of Medieval Milan--the Legend of Barnabas, Church Hist, Vol 0065, 96; Right Thinking and Sacred Oratory in Counter-reformation Rome, Parergon, Vol 0014, 96; Together as a Companionship--a History of the 31st, 32nd and 33rd General Congregations of the Society of Jesus, Cath Hist Rev, Vol 0083, 97; King Death, 16th Century J, Vol 0028, 97; Galileo and the Church, Cath Hist Rev, Vol 0083, 97; The Medieval Hall, Parergon, Vol 0014, 97. **CONTACT ADDRESS** Dept of Hist, Univ of Adelaide, Adelaide, SA, 5005.

MARTIN, JAMES KIRBY
PERSONAL Born 05/26/1943, Akron, OH, m, 1965, 3 children **DISCIPLINE** HISTORY **EDUCATION** Hiram Col, BA, 65; Univ Wisc, Madison, MA, 67, PhD, 69. **CAREER** From asst prof to prof, hist, 69-80, Rutgers Univ; prof, hist, 80-97, dept chemn, 80-83, acting dept chemn 90, Distinguished Univ Prof of Hist, 97- , Scholar-In Residence and Res Fel, David Lib of the Am Revolution, and Res Fel, Philadelphia Ctr for Early Am Stud, Univ Penn, 88; adj and vis assoc prof and Prof of Alcohol Stud, Rutgers Univ, 78-88; vis prof hist, Rice Univ, 92. **HONORS AND AWARDS** R.P. McCormick Prize, NJ Hist Comn, 84; NJ Soc of the Cincinnati Prize, 95; Homer D. Babbidge, Jr. Award, Soc for the Stud of Conn Hist, 98. **MEMBERSHIPS** Phi Beta Kappa; Phi Kappa Phi; Phi Alpha Theta; Pi Gamma Mu; Omicron Delta Kappa; AHA; Org of Am Hist; So Hist Asn; Soc for Military Hist; Soc for Hist of the Early Am Republic; Inst of Early Am Hist and Culture; Eastern Natl Park and Monument Asn; Texas State Hist Asn; NJ Hist Soc. **RESEARCH** United States history: social, military, and early American. **SELECTED PUBLICATIONS** Coauth, A Respectable Army: The Military Origins of the Republic, 1763-1789, Harlan Davidson, 82; coauth, Drinking in America: A History, 1620-1980, Free Press, 82; ed, Ordinary Courage: The Revolutionary War Adventures of Joseph Plumb Martin, Brandywine Press, 93; coauth, America and Its Peoples: A Mosaic in the Making, 3rd ed, Longman, 97; auth, Benedict Arnold, Revolutionary Hero: An American Warrior Reconsidered, NY Univ, 97. **CONTACT ADDRESS** History Dept, Univ of Houston, Houston, TX, 77204-3785.

MARTIN, JAMES KIRBY
PERSONAL Born 05/26/1943, Akron, OH, m, 1965, 3 children **DISCIPLINE** UNITED STATES HISTORY **EDUCATION** Hiram Col, BA, 65; Univ Wis-Madison, MA, 67, PhD(hist), 69. **CAREER** From asst prof to assoc prof hist, Rutgers Univ, New Brunswick, 69-78, asst provost admin affairs, 72-74, vpres acad affairs, 77-79, prof hist, 78-80; PROF HIST & CHMN DEPT, UNIV HOUSTON, 80-, Adj prof alcohol studies, Rutgers Univ Ctr Alcohol Studies, 78- **MEMBERSHIPS** AHA; Orgn Am Historians; Southern Hist Asn; Soc Historians Early Am Repub. **RESEARCH** Early American political, social, and military history. **SELECTED PUBLICATIONS** Auth, Washington, George War, J Amer Hist, vol 0080, 93; Gentry and Common Folk, Political Culture on a Virginia Frontier, 1740-1789, Miss Quart, vol 0046, 93; The Destructive War, J Soc Hist, vol 0026, 93; Patriarch, J Southern Hist, vol 0060, 94; North Country Captives, Ethnohist, vol 0041, 94; The Mohicans of Stockbridge, Ethnohist, vol 0042, 95; Plunder, Profit, and Paroles, J Soc Hist, vol 0028, 95; Deadly Medicine, J Soc Hist, vol 0030, 96; The American Revolution in Indian Country, Ethnohist, vol 0044, 97; Religion and Wine, Amer Hist Rev, vol 0102, 97. **CONTACT ADDRESS** Dept of Hist, Univ Houston, Central, Houston, TX, 77004.

MARTIN, JANET MARION
PERSONAL Born 10/24/1938, Bogalusa, LA **DISCIPLINE** CLASSICS **EDUCATION** Radcliffe Col, AB, 61; Univ MI, MA, 63; Harvard Univ, PhD, 68. **CAREER** From instr to asst prof classics, Harvard Univ, 68-72; asst prof, 73-76, Assoc Prof Classics, Princeton Univ, 76-, Fel Post-classical & humanistic studies, Am Acad Rome, 71-73. **MEMBERSHIPS** Am Philol Asn; Mediaeval Acad Am. **RESEARCH** Medieval Latin lit: ancient and medieval rhetoric and poetics; the class tradition. **SELECTED PUBLICATIONS** Ed, Peter the Venerable: Selected Letters, Pontifical Inst Mediaeval Studies, 74; auth, John of Salisbury's manuscripts of Frontinus and of Gellius, J Warburg & Courtauld Insts, 77; Uses of tradition: Gellius, Petronius, and John of Salisbury, Viator, 79; contribr, chap, In: The Renaissance of the Twelfth Century, Harvard Univ, 82. **CONTACT ADDRESS** Dept of Class, Princeton Univ, 104 E Pyne, Princeton, NJ, 08544-1098. **EMAIL** jmmartin@princeton.edu

MARTIN, JAY H.
PERSONAL Born 10/30/1935, Newark, NJ, m, 1956, 3 children **DISCIPLINE** ENGLISH, AMERICAN STUDIES **EDUCATION** Columbia Col, AB, 56; Ohio State Univ, MA, 57, PhD, 60; Southern Calif Psychoanal Inst, PhD, 83. **CAREER** Instr English, Pa State Univ, 57-58; from instr to assoc prof English & Am studies, Yale Univ, 60-68; dir prog comp, cult, 68-71, dir educ abroad, 71-74, prof English & comp lit, 68-79, LECTR PSYCHIAT, DEPT PSYCHIAT & HUMAN BEHAV, UNIV CALIF, IRVINE, 78-, LEO S BING PROF ENGLISH, 79-; CONSULT PSYCHOANAL, VET ADMIN HOSP, LONG BEACH, 78-, Fel, Silliman Col, Yale Univ, 61-68; Yale Univ fac club lectr, 63; Morse fel, 63-64; Am Philos Soc grant, 66; Guggenheim fel, 66-67; mem panels, Nat Endowment for Humanities, 74-; Rockefeller Found sr fel humanities, 75; res clin assoc, Southern Calif Psychoanal Inst, 77-81. **MEMBERSHIPS** English Inst; MLA; Auth Guild; Pen. **RESEARCH** Biography; literary history; American literature; psychoanalysis. **SELECTED PUBLICATIONS** Auth, Harvests of Change: American Literature, 1865-1914, 67 & ed, A Collection of Critical Essays on the Waste land, 68, Prentice-Hall; auth, Nathanael West: The Art of His Life, Farrar, 70; ed, Twentieth Century Views of Nathanael West, Prentice-Hall, 71; A Singer in the Dawn: Reinterpretations of Paul Laurence Dunbar, 74 & The Dunbar Reader, 74, Dodd; Always Merry and Bright: The Life of Henry Miller, Capra, 78; Winter Dreams: An American in Moscow, Houghton, 79. **CONTACT ADDRESS** Univ Calif, 18651 Via Palatino, Irvine, CA, 92715.

MARTIN, JOHN STEPHEN
PERSONAL Born 04/29/1933, New York, NY, m, 1961, 2 children **DISCIPLINE** ENGLISH, AMERICAN STUDIES **EDUCATION** Hofstra Univ, BA, 55; Univ Ga, MA, 61; Univ Wis, PhD(English), 65. **CAREER** Asst prof English & Am studies, Univ NMex, 65-68; assoc prof, 70-79, PROF ENGLISH & AM STUDIES, UNIV CALGARY, 79-, Fulbright lectr, Univ Salaburg, 68-69; reader Am lit & Am studies, Free Univ, Amsterdam, 69-70; ed, Rocky Mountain Am Studies Newslett, 72-; assoc ed, Ariel, 73-81. **MEMBERSHIPS** MLA; Am Studies Asn; Rocky Mountain Am Studies Asn (secy-treas, 72-74, vpres, 74-76, pres, 76-78); Can Asn Am Studies (vpres, 81-); Asn Can Univ Teachers English. **RESEARCH** American literature since 1607; American studies; modern literature, English, American and continental. **SELECTED PUBLICATIONS** Auth, Emerson and Thoreau--Contemporary Reviews, Can Rev Amer Stud, vol 0023, 93; The Return of Thematic Criticism, Ariel-Rev Int Eng Lit, vol 0024, 93; The Genteel Tradition and the Sacred Rage, Can Rev Amer Stud, vol 0023, 93; The Problem of American Realism, Studies in the Cultural History of a Literary Idea, Can Rev Amer Stud, vol 0024, 94; The Emerson Effect, Can Rev Amer Stud, vol 0027, 97; Academic and Clinical Preparation and Practices of School Speech-Language Pathologists With People Who Stutter, Lan Speech and Hearing Serv in Sch(S), vol 0028, 97. **CONTACT ADDRESS** Univ Calgary, 3323 Breton Close NW Calgary, Calgary, AB, T2N 1N4.

MARTIN, KENNETH R.
PERSONAL Born 02/12/1938, Upper Darby, PA **DISCIPLINE** MODERN EUROPEAN & AMERICAN HISTORY **EDUCATION** Dickinson Col, AB, 59; Univ Pa, MA, 51, PhD, 65. **CAREER** Readership, 64, Univ Pa; from instr to asst prof hist, 65-68, Gettysburg Col; assoc prof, 68-74, Slippery Rock State Col; Dir, 74-80, Kendall Whaling Mus; assoc, Hist Assoc Inc, 81-84; ed, 70-71, Mercer County Hist; Eleutherian Mills/Hagley Found grant-in-aid, 72; instr, 76-78, Univ Calif, Berkeley; self employed, author, hist, 85-. **MEMBERSHIPS** Melville Soc **RESEARCH** American maritime history; 19th century whaling; business history. **SELECTED PUBLICATIONS** Auth, Phase One: A History of Thomas Group, Inc, TGI, 92; coauth, Time Warrior, Mcgraw-Hill, 92; coauth, Quality Alone is Not Enough, Am Mng Assn, 92; coauth, Survival at Nodulex, TGI/Heritage, 94; coauth, The Pattens of Bath: A Seagoing Dynasty, Maine Maritime Mus, 96; auth, A Life of It's Own... Nova Scotia Folk Art, 1975-1995, Art Gal of Nova Scotia, 97; auth, Heavy Weather and Hard Luck: Portsmouth Goes Whaling, Portsmouth Marine Soc, 98. **CONTACT ADDRESS** PO Box 284, Woolwich, ME, 04579.

MARTIN, MARTY
PERSONAL Born 02/05/1928, West Point, NE, m, 1982, 7 children **DISCIPLINE** RELIGIOUS HISTORY **EDUCATION** Lutheran School of Theol, Chicago, STM, 54; Univ of Chicago, PhD, 56. **CAREER** Lutheran Pastor, 49-63, Washington, DC; Prof, 63-98, Univ of Chicago; Sr, Ed, Christian Century, 56-98; George B. Caldwell Sr Scholar in Residence, Park Ridge Center for Health, Faith and Ethics, 81-. **HONORS AND AWARDS** Natl Medal of Hum; Natl Book Award; Medal of the Amer Acad of Arts and Sci; 60 honorary degrees. **MEMBERSHIPS** Past Pres Amer Acad of Rel; Amer Soc of Church Hist; Amer Catholic Hist Assoc. **RESEARCH** American Religious History, 18th and 20th centuries; comparative internatioal studies of movements such as fundamentalism and ethnonationalism. **SELECTED PUBLICATIONS** Auth, Righteous Empire: The Protestant Experience in America, Dial, 70; Pilgrims in Their Own Land: 500 Years of Religion in America, Little Brown, 84; Religion and Republic: The American Circumstance, Beacon, 87; The One and the Many: America's Struggle for the Common Good, Harvard, 97; 3 volume Modern American Religion: The Irony of It All: 1893-1919, Univ of Chicago, 86; The Noise of Conflict, 1919-1941, Univ of Chicago, 91; Under God, Indivisible, 1941-1960, Univ of Chicago, 96. **CONTACT ADDRESS** 239 Scottswood Rd, Riverside, IL, 60546.

MARTIN, RICHARD
PERSONAL Born 12/04/1945, Bryn Mawr, PA, s **DISCIPLINE** ART HISTORY **EDUCATION** Swarthmore Col, BA, 67; Columbia Univ, MA, 69, MPhil, 71; Otis Col Art & Design, DFA, 97. **CAREER** Instr to Assoc Prof, 73-84, Prof Hist Art, Fashion Inst Technol, 84-92, Dean Grad Studies, 88-90, Exec Dir, Shirley Goodman Resource Ctr, 80-92; Instr, Sch Visual Arts, 75-80, 93-; Asst Prof to Assoc Prof, 77-84, Adj Prof Art, NY Univ, 84-; Critic-in-Residence, Md Inst, Col Art, 85, 86, 87; Whitney Halstead Vis Prof, Sch Art Inst Chicago, 86; Adj Prof, Painting & Sculpture, Sch Arts, Columbia Univ, 87-89; Prof, MFA in Visual Art, Vermont Col, 91-97; Instr, Juilliard Sch, 94-96; Instr, Parsons Sch Design, 95-; Adj Prof, Art Hist & Archaeol, Columbia Univ, 95-; Instr, NY Acad Art, Grad Sch figurative Art, 97-98; Ed & Publ, Textile & Text, 88-92; Ed, 74-88, Ed & Publ, Arts Mag, 85-87; Exec Dir, Educ Found Fashion Industries, 91-92; Curator, Costume Inst, Metropolitan Museum Art, 93-. **MEMBERSHIPS** Col Art Asn (Dir 98-02). **RESEARCH** Fashion history. **SELECTED PUBLICATIONS** Coauth, Madame Grs, Metropolitan Museum Art, 94; Orientalism; Visions of the East in Western Dress, Metropolitan Museum Art/Abrams, 94; ed & contribr, Contemporary Fashion, St. James Press/Gale Res, 95; coauth, Tango!, Thames & Hudson, 95; Bloom, Metropolitan Museum Art, 95; auth, La Dernire Mode 1995, Metropolitan Museum Art, 96; ed, St. James Fashion Encyclopedia, Visible Ink, 96; The Four Seasons, Metropolitan Museum Art, 97; Wordrobe, Metropolitan Museum Art, 97; Gianni Versace, Metropolitan Museum Art/Abrams, 97; American Ingenuity, Metropolitan Museum Art, 98; author of numerous journal articles and other publications. **CONTACT ADDRESS** The Costume Inst, Metropolitan Mus of Art, 1000 Fifth Ave, New York, NY, 10028-0198.

MARTIN, RICHARD C.
PERSONAL Born 07/24/1938, Des Moines, IA, m, 1980, 1 child **DISCIPLINE** MIDDLE EASTERN STUDIES **EDUCATION** Princeton Theol Sem, ThM, 66; NY Univ, PhD, 75. **CAREER** Chmn 83-89, Dept of Religious Stud, 75-95, Ariz State Univ; Chmn Relig Stud Prog, 95-96 Iowa State Univ; Prof, Chmn dept of Relig, 96-, Emory Univ. **MEMBERSHIPS** ASSR **RESEARCH** Islamic religious thought, comparative religions. **SELECTED PUBLICATIONS** Co-auth, Defenders of Reason in Islam, Mu'tazilism from Medieval School to Modern Symbol, London, Oneworld, 97; auth, Islamic Studies, A History of Religious Approach, Englewood Cliffs NJ, Prentice Hall, 95; Public Aspects of Theology in Medieval Islam, The Role of Kalam in Conflict Definition and Resolution, in: J for Islamic Studies, 93. **CONTACT ADDRESS** Dept of Religion, Emory Univ, Atlanta, GA, 30322. **EMAIL** rcmartin@emory.edu

MARTIN, RICHARD PETER
PERSONAL Born 05/19/1954, Dorchester, MA **DISCIPLINE** GREEK AND LATIN: LANGUAGE COURSES **EDUCATION** Harvard, AB, 76, AM, 78; PhD, 81. **CAREER** The Boston Globe, gen assignment reporter, 74-78; Harvard, tchg fellow, 78-81; asst prof, 81-88, assoc prof, 89-94 Princeton Univ; Vis assoc prof, Univ Calif, 91; Prof, Princeton Univ, 94-. **HONORS AND AWARDS** Harvard, Bowdoin Prize, 79; Howard Behrman tchg fel, 96-00; Grants, Stanley Seeger fel res Cyclades,94; Stanley Seeger fel res, Ionian islands, 95; Onassis Found grant, fieldwork in oral tradition Crete, 96; Princeton 250th anniversary Award for Innovative Tchg, 97. **RESEARCH** Latin poetry; Hesiod; Greek hymns; Pindar. **SELECTED PUBLICATIONS** Auth, The Language of Heroes: Speech and Performance in the Iliad. Cornell Univ Press, 89; Bulfinch's Mythology, Harper Collins, 91; Similes in Performance; The Scythian Accent: Anacharsis and the Cynics, Univ Calif Press 97. **CONTACT ADDRESS** Princeton Univ, 1 Nassau Hall, Princeton, NJ, 08544. **EMAIL** rpmartin@princeton.edu

MARTIN, RUSSELL E.
DISCIPLINE RUSSIA, EARLY MODERN EUROPE **EDUCATION** Univ Pittsburgh, BA, 86; Harvard Univ, AM, 89, PhD, 96. **CAREER** Head tchg fel, Harvard Univ, 90-91; grad wrtg fel, Harvard Univ, 91-92; instr, Harvard Univ, 90-92, 93-94; tchg fel, Harvard Univ, 93-94, 94-95; instr, Harvar Univ, 94-95; asst prof, 96-. **HONORS AND AWARDS** Undergrad tchg fel, Univ Pittsburgh, 85-86; David L. Lawrence Nationalities Room fel, 86; Richard Hunt prize, Univ Pittsburgh, 86; Univ Serv award, Univ Pittsburgh, 87; Univ scholar, Univ Pittsburgh, 87; res grant, Univ Pittsburgh, 87; FLAS fel, 87; traveling grant, 91; res initiative grant, Soc Sci Res Coun, 92; distinction in tchg awards, Derek Bok Ctr Tchg, 93-94, 94-95; dissertaition write-up grant, Soc Sci Res Coun, 96., Expert commentator, Ivan IV the Terrible, 97; co-founder, co-dir, Muscovite Biog Database, 91-.; consult, Expert Witness, 93-; res asst, Harvard Univ, 89-94. **MEMBERSHIPS** Mem, Amer Hist Assn; Amer Assn Advancement Slavic Stud; N Amer Vexillogical Assn. **SELECTED PUBLICATIONS** Auth, Royal Weddings and Crimean Diplomacy: New Sources on Muscovite Chancellery Practice during the reign of Vasilii III, Rhetoric of the Medieval Slavic World, Harvard Ukrainian Stud, vol 19, 95; co-auth, Opyt sozdaniia istoriograficheskogo banka dannykh sostava Boiarskoi dumy XV nachala XVII vv" in Istochnikovedenie i komparativnyi metod v gumanitarnom znanii, Moscow, 96; Nekotorye itogi komp iuternoi obrabotki istochnikov po istorii Boiarskoi Dumy XVII v, Sosloviia i gosudarstvennaia vlast v Rossii XV-seredina XIX vv, Moscow, 94; rev, Ludwig Steindorff, Memoria in Altrualand, Harvard Ukrainian Stud, 94. **CONTACT ADDRESS** Dept Hist, Westminister Col, New Wilmington, PA, 16172-0001. **EMAIL** MartinRE@Westminster.edu

MARTIN, SHERRILL V.
DISCIPLINE MUSTIC HISTORY **EDUCATION** Univ NC, Chapel Hill, PhD. **CAREER** Prof, Univ NC, Wilmington; nat musicol ed, Am Mus Tchr; nat bk rev ed, Sonneck Soc Bull. **SELECTED PUBLICATIONS** Auth, Feel the Spirit, 88; Henry Gilbert: A Bio-Bibliography; one essay in Time, Talent, Tradition. **CONTACT ADDRESS** Univ N. Carolina, Wilmington, Kenan Hall, Wilmington, NC, 28403-3297. **EMAIL** martins@uncwil.edu

MARTIN, TONY
PERSONAL Trinidad and Tobago **DISCIPLINE** HISTORY **EDUCATION** Hon Soc of Gray's Inn, London, England, Barrister-at-Law, 65; Mich State Univ, PhD, 73. **CAREER** Asst prof, Univ Mich-Flint, 71-73; assoc prof, Wellesly Col, 73-79; prof, 79- . **HONORS AND AWARDS** Am Phiolos Soc, res grant, 90. **MEMBERSHIPS** Asoc of Caribbean Historians; Asoc for the Study of Classical African Civilizations. **RESEARCH** Marcus Garvey; Pan-Africanism; Black intellectual history. **SELECTED PUBLICATIONS** Auth, Race First: The Ideological and Organizational Struggles of Marcus Garvey and the UNIA, 76; Literary Garveyism: Garvey, Black Arts and the Harlem Renaissance, 83; The Pan-African Connection, 83; The Jewish Onslaught, 93. **CONTACT ADDRESS** Dept of Africana Studies, Wellesley Col, Wellesley, MA, 02181. **EMAIL** amartin@wellesley.edu

MARTIN, VIRGINIA
PERSONAL Born 05/04/1962, Milwaukee, WI, m, 1989, 1 child **DISCIPLINE** HISTORY **EDUCATION** Wassar Col, BA, 84; Univ Wis, MA, 87; Univ S Calif, PhD, 96. **CAREER** ASST PROF, HIST, UNIV ALA, HUNTSVILLE, 96-. **HONORS AND AWARDS** IREX res fel, Kazakhstan, Rus, 93-94; Soc Sci Res Counc fel, 92-93; IREX fel, 92-93. **MEMBERSHIPS** AHA, AAASS, World Hist Asn, S Slavic Conf. **RESEARCH** Hist, soc, cult; anthrop; Kazakhstan; Rus Empire. **SELECTED PUBLICATIONS** Auth, Akhmet Baitursin, in The Supplement to the Modern Encyclopedia of Russian, Soviet, and Eurasian History, Acad Int Press, forthcoming; auth, Barimta, in The Supplement to the Modern Encyclopedia of Russian, Soviet, and Eurasian History, Acad Int Press, forthcoming; auth, Barymta: Nomadic Custom, Imperial Crime, in Russia's Orient: Imperial Borderlands and Peoples, 1700-1917, Ind Univ Press, 97; auth, Nomads, Borders and the Resolution of Land Disputes in the Kazakh Steppe, Bull Am Asn Central Asian Res, IX, no 1, Spring 96. **CONTACT ADDRESS** Dept of History, Univ of Alabama, Huntsville, 402 Roberts Hall, Huntsville, AL, 35801. **EMAIL** martinvi@email.uah.edu

MARTIN, WAYNE M.
DISCIPLINE HISTORY OF PHILOSOPHY **EDUCATION** Univ Calif-Berkeley, PhD, 93. **CAREER** UNDERGRAD ADV, UNIV CALIF, SAN DIEGO. **RESEARCH** Post-Kantian idealists; Phenomenology. **SELECTED PUBLICATIONS** Auth, "Without a Striving, No Object is Possible: Fichte's Striving Doctrine and the Primacy of Practice," New Perspectives on Fichte, Hum Press, 96; Fichte's Anti-Dogmatism, Ratio V:2,92. **CONTACT ADDRESS** Dept of Philos, Univ Calif, San Diego, 9500 Gilman Dr, La Jolla, CA, 92093.

MARTINES, LAURO
PERSONAL Born 11/22/1927, Chicago, IL, m, 1957, 1 child **DISCIPLINE** RENAISSANCE HISTORY, ENGLISH LIT-

ERATURE **EDUCATION** Drake Univ, AB, 50; Harvard Univ, PhD(hist), 60. **CAREER** From instr to asst prof hist, Reed Col, 58-62; PROF HIST, UNIV CALIF, LOS ANGELES, 66-, Am Philos Soc grants, 60, 61, 66; Am Counc Learned Soc fel, 62-63; Harvard Ctr Ital Renaissance Studies fel, Villa I Tatti, Florence, Italy, 62-65; John Simon Guggenheim Mem Found fel, 64-65; Ford Found grant, 68-69; Nat Endowment for Humanities sr fel, 71, fel, 78-79. **MEMBERSHIPS** AHA; Renaissance Soc Am; fel Mediaeval Acad Am. **RESEARCH** Seventeenth century Europe; the Italian Renaissance; the social analysis of English Renaissance verse. **SELECTED PUBLICATIONS** Auth, Law, Family, and Women, J Mod Hist, vol 0066, 94; On the Practice or Art of Dancing, J Mod Hist, vol 0067, 95; The Revolt of the Ciompi, Amer Hist Rev, vol 0100, 95; Love and History--The Renaissance Italian Connection, Annales-Hist Sci Sociales, vol 0051, 96; Family Memoirs--The Castellani Family of 14th Century Florence, Speculum-J Medieval Stud, vol 0071, 96; The District of Green Dragon, J Interdisciplinary Hist, vol 0027, 97; The Fortunes of the Courtier--The European Reception of Castiglione Cortegiano, Amer Hist Rev, vol 0102, 97. **CONTACT ADDRESS** Dept of Hist, Univ of Calif, Los Angeles, CA, 90024.

MARTINEZ, OSCAR J.
DISCIPLINE HISTORY **EDUCATION** Calif State Univ, Los Angeles, BA, 69; Stanford Univ, MA, 70; Univ Calif, Los Angeles, PhD, 75. **CAREER** Instr, Foothill Comm Col, Calif, 70-71; lectr, Calif State Univ, Hayward, 70; from asst prof to prof, Hist Dept, 75-88, dir, Inst of Oral Hist, 75-82, dir, Ctr for Inter-Am and Border Stud, 82-87, Univ Texas, El Paso; prof, Hist Dept, 88- , dir Grad Stud, Hist Dept, 90-92, interim dir, Latin Am Area Ctr, 94-95, Univ Arizona; vis prof, Yale Univ, 95. **HONORS AND AWARDS** Fel, Ctr for Advanc Stud in Behavioral Sci, Stanford, 81-82; Fulbright Study Fel, S Am, 85; Border Regional Lib Asn, Southwest Book Awards, 78, 83, 88, 95; pres, Asn for Borderlands Scholars, 85-87; award for Outstanding Scholarship and Service, Asn of Borderlands Scholars, 92; book award, Fac of Soc and Behavioral Sci, Univ Arizona, 95; nom for Five-Star Tchg Award, Univ Arizona, 96; inducted El Paso Writers Hall of Fame, 97. **MEMBERSHIPS** Asn for Borderlands Scholars; Latin Am Stud Asn; Natl Asn for Chicano Stud. **SELECTED PUBLICATIONS** Auth, Border Boom Town: Ciudad Juarez Since 1848, Texas, 78; auth, ed, Fragments of the Mexican Revolution: Personal Accounts from the Border, New Mexico, 83; auth, Across Boundaries: Transborder Interaction in Comparative Perspective, Texas Western, 86; auth, Troublesome Border, Arizona, 88; auth, Border People: Life and Society in the U.S.-Mexico Borderlands, Arizona, 94; ed, The U.S.-Mexico Borderlands: Historical and Contemporary Perspectives, Scholarly Resources, 95. **CONTACT ADDRESS** History Dept, Univ of Arizona, Tucson, AZ, 85721. **EMAIL** oscar-martinez@ns.arizona.edu

MARTINSON, FRED
DISCIPLINE ART **EDUCATION** Univ Chicago, PhD, 68. **CAREER** Prof. **SELECTED PUBLICATIONS** Auth, The Great Buddha Bend in Eastern Sichuan: The Ancient Stone Carvings at Dazu; Instructional and Research Uses of Multimedia as Learning Empowerment for Faculty and Students: Teaching Chinese Art History with AVC, Charlottesville, 93; Stone Sculptures of Dazu, 91. **CONTACT ADDRESS** Dept of Art, Knoxville, TN, 37996.

MARTY, MARTIN EMIL
PERSONAL Born 02/05/1928, West Point, NE, m, 1952, 5 children **DISCIPLINE** MODERN RELIGIOUS HISTORY **EDUCATION** Concordia Sem, BA, 49, MDiv, 52; Lutheran Sch Theol, Chicago, STM, 54; Univ Chicago, PhD(church hist), 56. **CAREER** From assoc prof to prof relig hist, 63-78, assoc dean divinity sch, 70-75, F M CONE DISTINGUISHED SERV PROF, UNIV CHICAGO, 78-, Vis assoc prof, Lutheran Sch Theol, Chicago, 61 & Union Theol Sem, New York, 65; bd mem, Nat Humanities Ctr, 76-; assoc ed, Christian Century, ed newslet, Context & coed, Church Hist. **HONORS AND AWARDS** Nat Bk Award, 72., Nineteen from US cols & univs. **MEMBERSHIPS** Fel Am Acad Arts & Sci; Soc Am Historians; Soc Values Higher Educ. **RESEARCH** Nineteenth century religious history of United States, Great Britain and Western Europe; effects of political-industrial revolutions on religion; history of religious behavior in America. **SELECTED PUBLICATIONS** Auth, American Religious History in the 80s, Church Hist, vol 0062, 93; Dictionary of American Religious Biography, 2nd ed, Cath Hist Rev, vol 0079, 93; From the Centripetal to the Centrifugal in Culture ind Religion, Theol Today, vol 0051, 94; Religion and Radical Politics, J Relig, vol 0074, 94; Defending the Faith, J Amer Hist, vol 0082, 95; Evangelicalism, J Southern Hist, vol 0061, 95; God in the Wasteland, J Relig, vol 0076, 96; Neale, J.M. and the Quest for Sobornost, J Relig, vol 0076, 96; Religion, Public Life, and the American Polity, J Relig, vol 0077, 97. **CONTACT ADDRESS** Divinity Sch Swift Hall, Univ of Chicago, Chicago, IL, 60637.

MARTY, MYRON AUGUST
PERSONAL Born 04/10/1932, West Point, NE, m, 1954, 4 children **DISCIPLINE** AMERICAN HISTORY **EDUCATION** Concordia Teachers Col, Ill, BS, 54; Wash Univ, MEd, 60; St Louis Univ, MA, 65, PhD(hist), 67. **CAREER** Teacher, Lutheran High Sch, St Louis, Mo, 57-65; from asst prof to assoc prof hist, Florissant Valley Community Col, 67-72, chmn div soc sci, 66-75, prof, 72-80; DEP DIR, EDUC PROG, NAT ENDOWMENT FOR HUMANITIES, 80-, Mem Comt exam soc sci-hist, Col Level Exam Prog, Educ Testing Serv, 67-76, consult-examr, NCent Asn Cols & Schs, 69-80; Nat Endowment for Humanities fel, 72-73; vis lectr, Univ Md, 72-73; bk reviewer, St Louis Post-Dispatch, 72-; mem exec bd, NCent Asn Cols & Schs, Comn Inst Higher Educ, 77-80: mem, Nat Bd Consults Nat Endowment for Humanities, 78-80. **MEMBERSHIPS** AHA; Orgn Am Historians; Am Soc Church Hist; Am Studies Asn; Am Asn State & Local Hist. **RESEARCH** Recent America; American nationality and ethnicity; family and community history. **SELECTED PUBLICATIONS** Auth, Lutherans and Roman Catholicism: The Changing Conflict, 1917-1963, Univ Notre Dame, 68; coauth, Retracing Our Steps: Studies in Documents from the American Past (2 vols), Harper, 72; Your Family History: A Handbook for Research and Writing, AHM, 78; auth, Nearby history: Exploring the past around you, Am Asn State & Local Hist, 82. **CONTACT ADDRESS** Educ Prog, National Endowment for the Humanities, Washington, DC, 20506.

MARX, ANTHONY W.
PERSONAL Born 02/28/1959, New York, NY, m, 1992, 2 children **DISCIPLINE** POLITICAL SCIENCE **EDUCATION** Yale Univ, BA, 81; Princeton Univ, MPA, 84, MA, 86, PhD, 90. **CAREER** Asst Prof of Polit Sci, Columbia Univ, 90-96; Assoc Prof, 96-. **HONORS AND AWARDS** Guggenheim Fellow, 94, 98; US Inst of Peace Grant, 92-93; Nat Hum Ctr Fellow, 97-98; Howard Foundation Fellow, 97-98. **MEMBERSHIPS** APSA; ASA; SSHA. **RESEARCH** Comparative politics. **SELECTED PUBLICATIONS** Auth, Contested Images and Implications of South African Nationhood, The Violence Within: Cultural and Political Analyses of National Conflicts, Westview Press, 93; The State, Economy and Self-Determination in South Africa, Polit Sci Quart, 107:4, 93; auth, Contested Citizenship The Dynamics of Racial Identity and Social Movements, Int Rev of Soc Hist, vol 40, 95; auth, Race Making and the Nation-State, World Polit, vol 48, 1/96; auth, Apartheid's End: South Africa's Transition from Racial Domination, Ethnic and Racial Stud, 20:3, 7/97; auth, Making Race and Nation: A Comparison of the United States, South Africa and Brazil, Cambridge Univ Press, 98. **CONTACT ADDRESS** 420 W 118th St, Rm 701, NY, NY, 10027. **EMAIL** awm4@columbia.edu

MARZIK, THOMAS DAVID
PERSONAL Born 12/15/1941, Bridgeport, CT **DISCIPLINE** HISTORY **EDUCATION** Col Holy Cross, AB, 63; Columbia Univ, MA & Cert, 66, PhD, 76. **CAREER** Instr, 70-75, asst prof, 75-81, assoc prof, 81-97, PROF HIST, 97- , ST JOSEPH'S COL, PA, 81- ; Book review ed, Slovakia, East Central Europe, 81-91. **HONORS AND AWARDS** Gold Medal of Pres of Slovak Repub, 98. **MEMBERSHIPS** AHA; Am Asn Advan Slavic Studies; Czechoslovak Hist Conf; Czechoslovak Soc Arts & Sci; Slovak Studies Asn; Immigration & Ethnic Hist Soc. **RESEARCH** Modern Slovak and Czech history. **SELECTED PUBLICATIONS** Auth, T G Masaryk and the Slovaks, 1882-1914, In: Columbia Essays in International Affairs: The Dean's Papers, 1965, Columbia Univ, 66; Masaryk's national background, In: The Czech National Renascence of the Nineteenth Century: Essays Presented to Otakar Odlozilik in Honour of His Seventieth Birthday, Univ Toronto, 70; co-ed, Immigrants and Religion in Urban America, Temple Univ, 77; The Slovakophile Relationship of T G Masaryk and Karel Kalal prior to 1914, T G Masaryk (1850-1937, Thinker and Politician, St Martin Press, 90; coauth R W Seton-Watson and His Relations with the Czechs and Slovaks: Documents 1906-1951, 95-96. **CONTACT ADDRESS** Dept of Hist, St Joseph's Univ, 5600 City Ave, Philadelphia, PA, 19131-1395. **EMAIL** tmarzik@sjuphil.sju.edu

MARZOLF, MARION TUTTLE
PERSONAL Born 07/06/1930, Greenville, MI, m, 1953 **DISCIPLINE** AMERICAN HISTORY **EDUCATION** Mich State Univ, BA, 52; Univ Mich, MA, 63, PhD(Am cult), 72. **CAREER** Copywriter, Wallace-Lindeman, 52-53; reporter & asst, Washington Post, 55-57; ed asst, Nat Geog Mag, 57-63; lectr English jour, Eastern Mich Univ, 64-68; asst prof, 68-73, ASSOC PROF JOUR, UNIV MICH, 73-, Reporter, Biloxi Bull, Miss, 52-53. **MEMBERSHIPS** Asn for Educ Jour; Women in Communications, Inc; Immigration Hist Soc; Danish Am Heritage Soc; Soc Advan Scandinavian Studies. **RESEARCH** History of women in Jism; development of professional Jist in America, 1890-1920 era; immigrant press, especially Scandinavian. **SELECTED PUBLICATIONS** Auth, Bly, Nellie, J Amer Hist, vol 0082, 95. **CONTACT ADDRESS** Univ Michigan, 1420 Granger, Ann Arbor, MI, 48109.

MASLOWSKI, PETER
DISCIPLINE U.S. MILITARY HISTORY **EDUCATION** Ohio State Univ, PhD, 72. **CAREER** Prof, Univ Nebr, Lincoln. **RESEARCH** The Vietnam War. **SELECTED PUBLICATIONS** Auth, Treason Must Be Made Odious: Military Occupation and Wartime Reconstruction in Nashville, Tennessee, 1862-1865, KTO Press, 78; Armed with Cameras: The American Military Photographers of World War II, Free Press, 93; coauth, For the Common Defense: A Military History of the United States of America, Free Press, 84. **CONTACT ADDRESS** Univ Nebr, Lincoln, 624 Oldfat, Lincoln, NE, 68588-0417. **EMAIL** pm@unlinfo.unl.edu

MASON, DONNA S.
PERSONAL Born 01/15/1947, Mount Vernon, New York, m, 1973 **DISCIPLINE** EDUCATION **EDUCATION** Howard Univ, BA, 1969, MEd, 1972; Univ of Maryland, Colllege Park, AGS, 1975, PhD, 1987. **CAREER** District of Columbia Public Schools, classroom teacher, building resource teacher, computer camp teacher, computer curriculum writer, computer teacher trainer, computer education instructor/lab coordinator, 1969-. **HONORS AND AWARDS** Electronic Learning's, Educator of the Decade, 10 Who Made A Difference Award, 1991; Washington Post, Agnes Meyer Outstanding Teacher Award, 1991; Learning Magazine/Oldsmobile, Professional Best Teacher Excellence Award, 1991; Apple Computer, Thanks to Teachers Award, 1990; Business Week, Award for Innovative Teaching, 1990; University of MD Distinguished Alumni Award, 1995; Freedom Foundation at Valley Forge Award, 1995. **MEMBERSHIPS** Maryland Instructional Computer Coordinators Assn; Univ of Maryland Alumni Assn; International Society for Technology in Education; Special Interest Group for Computing Coordinators. **SELECTED PUBLICATIONS** US Office of Education, Christa McAuliffe Fellowship, 1988, 1994; IBM/Classroom Computer Learning, Teacher of the Year for the District of Columbia, 1988; The Cafritz Foundation, Cafritz Foundation Teacher Fellowship, 1988; The Washington Post, The Washington Post Mini-Grant Award, 1986; "A Teacher's Place To Work and Learn," Teaching & Computers 1986; "Multimedia Applications in the Curriculum: Are Schools Preparing Students for the 21st Century?" NASSP Curriculum Report, 1997; "Display Word Processing Terms" The Computing Teacher, 1986; "Ten Computers-One Thousand Students" Sigcc Bulletin for Computing Coordinators, 1987; "Factors that Influence Computer Laboratory Use in Exemplary Junior High/Middle schools in the District of Columbia" UMI's Dissertation Abstracts, 1988. **CONTACT ADDRESS** Alice Deal Junior High Sch, Fort Drive & Nebraska Ave, NW, Room 201, Washington, VT, 20016-1886.

MASON, FRANCIS M.
DISCIPLINE HISTORY **EDUCATION** Univ CA Riverside, AB, 57; Wake Forest Univ, MA, 66; Univ CT, PhD, 74. **CAREER** Prof, 67-, St Anselm Col. **RESEARCH** Edwardian women's suffrage; the life of Sylvia Pankhurst; Manchester, NH hist. **SELECTED PUBLICATIONS** Auth, Charles Masterman and National Health Insurance, Albion, 78; The Newer Eve: The Catholic Women's Suffage Society in England 1911-1923, Cath Hist Rev, 86; bk revs in Albion, Hist NH, Historian, and Studies in Soviet Thought; ed, Childish Things: Reminiscences of Susan B. Blount, Thompson and Rutter, 88. **CONTACT ADDRESS** St Anselm Col, 100 Saint Anselm Dr, Manchester, NH, 03102-1310. **EMAIL** frmason@anselm.edu

MASON, H.J.
PERSONAL Born 07/29/1943, Norwich, United Kingdom, m, 1970, 3 children **DISCIPLINE** CLASSICS **EDUCATION** McGill Univ, BA, 64; AM, 65, PhD, 68, Harvard Univ. **CAREER** Teaching Fel, Harvard Univ, 65-66, 67-68; Asst Prof, 68-72, Assoc Prof, 72-, Undergrad coordinator, 95-, Univ Toronto. **RESEARCH** Ancient novel; classical linguistics; topography **SELECTED PUBLICATIONS** Auth, Salmonella typhi and the Throne of Spain, Canadian Bulletin of Medical History, 90; Ancient Novels and Opera libretti, The Ancient Novel: Classical Paradigms and Modern Perspectives, 90; Mytilene and Methymna: Quarrels, borders and topography, EMC, 93; Greek and Latin Versions of the Ass-Story, ANRW, 94; Romance in a Limestone Landscape, CP, 95; The End of Antissa, AJP, 95. **CONTACT ADDRESS** Dept of Classics, Univ of Toronto, 16 Hart House Circle, Toronto, ON, M5S 3J9. **EMAIL** hmason@chass.utoronto.ca

MASON, HERBERT WARREN
PERSONAL Born 04/20/1932, Wilmington, DE, m, 1954, 3 children **DISCIPLINE** ISLAMIC HISTORY & RELIGION **EDUCATION** Harvard Univ, AB, 55, AM, 65, PhD, 69. **CAREER** Teaching fel & lectr, Harvard Univ, 62-67; UNIV PROF, BOSTON UNIV, 72-; Lectr English lit, St Joseph's Col, 60-62; vis lectr, Simmons Col, 62-63; vis lectr Islamic hist, Tufts Univ, 65-66; tranls & ed, Bollingen Found, 68-72; coed, Humaniora Islamica, 72-76; guest lectr various univ, 73-79 & Libr of Congress, 79. **MEMBERSHIPS** Am Oriental Soc; Mark Twain Soc; Medieval Acad Am; Am Acad Relig; PEN; Am Hist Asn; Am Academy of Poets. **RESEARCH** Islamic history, literature and religion, especially Sufism; Arabic: translation of sources; comparative medieval studies: Islamic, Latin European & Byzantine sources. **SELECTED PUBLICATIONS** Ed, Reflections on the Middle East Crisis, Mouton & Co, 70; auth, Gilgamesh, A Verse Narrative, Houghton Mifflin Co, 71; Two Statesmen of Medieval Islam, Mouton & Co, 72; En Parlant de Gilgamesh Avec Louis Massignon, L'Herne, Paris, 75; The Death of al-Hallaj, Notre Dame Univ Press, 79; Summer Light, Farrar, Straus and Giroux, 80; Gilpins Point, Sewanee Rev, 80; ed & transl, The Passion of al-Hallaj, Princeton

Univ Press, 82; A Legend of Alexander, Notre Dame Univ Press, 86; Memoir of a Friend: Louis Massignon, Notre Dame Univ Press, 88; Testimonies and Reflections, Notre Dame Univ Press, 89; Al-Hallaj, Curzon Press, UK, 95; Haythu Taltaqi al-Anhar, novel in Arabic, Abu Dhabi Press, 98. **CONTACT ADDRESS** 745 Commonwealth Ave, Boston, MA, 02215-1401.

MASON, PHILIP P.
PERSONAL Born 04/28/1927, Salem, MA, m, 1951, 5 children **DISCIPLINE** AMERICAN HISTORY **EDUCATION** Boston Univ, BA, 50; Univ Mich, MA, 51, PhD, 56. **CAREER** Res assoc hist collections, Univ Mich, 51-53; dir, State Arch MI, 53-58; assoc prof, 58-65, prof hist, Wayne State Univ, 65, Univ Archivist, 58, dir, labor hist arch, 59; Distinguished Prof Hist, 90; Distinguished Graduate Faculty Award, 85. **HONORS AND AWARDS** Fellow, Soc Am Archivists. **MEMBERSHIPS** Orgn Am Historians; fel Soc Am Archivists (exec secy, 63-70, pres, 70-71); Oral Hist Assoc; Detroit Historical Commision; William L Clements Library Board Of Governors. **RESEARCH** Am Indian; labor hist; Am archival administration. **SELECTED PUBLICATIONS** Auth, Schoolcraft's Expedition to Lake Itasca: The Discovery of the Source of the Mississippi, Mich State Univ, 58; School craft, The Literary Voyager or Muzzeniegun, Mich State Univ, 62; coauth, Harper of Detroit, The Origin and Growth of a Great Metropolitan Hospital, 64 & auth, Detroit, Fort Lernoult, and the American Revolution, 64, Wayne State Univ; A History of American Roads, Rand McNally, 67; auth, Working in America, Am Asn State & Local Hist, 75;Copper Country Journal, Wayne State univ Press, MI Bureau of Hist, 90; Rum Running and the Roaring Twenties: Prohibition on the Michigan/Ontario Waterways, WSU Press, 95; Schoolcrafts Ojibwa Lodge Stories: Life on the Lake Superior Fronteer, MI State Univ Press, 97; co auth, The Ambassador Bridge: A Monument to Progress, Wayne State univ Press, 92. **CONTACT ADDRESS** Fac Admin Bldg, Rm 3109, Wayne State Univ, 838 Mackenzie, Detroit, MI, 48202-3919.

MASON, STEVE
PERSONAL Born 09/14/1957, Toronto, ON, Canada **DISCIPLINE** EARLY JUDAISM AND CHRISTIAN ORIGINS **EDUCATION** McMaster Univ, BA, 80, MA, 81; Univ St Michaels Col, PhD, 86. **CAREER** Vis asst prof, Mem Univ NF, 87-89; prof and head, Dept Classics & Ancient Mediter Stud, Penn State Univ, 96-96; asst prof, 89-92, assoc prof, 92-98, prof, 98-, York Univ-Toronto. **MEMBERSHIPS** Soc Bibl Lit; Am Philol Asn; Studiorum Novi Testamenti Soc; Can Soc Bibl Stud. **RESEARCH** Philosophy and religion in the Greco-Roman world, especially Judaism (specialization: Flavius Josephus) and early Christianity. **SELECTED PUBLICATIONS** Coed An Early Christian Reader, Can Scholars Press, 90; auth Flavius Josephus on the Pharisees, E J Brill, 91; Josephus and the New Testament, Hendrickson, 92; ed Understanding Josephus: Seven Perspectives, Sheffield Acad Press, 98. **CONTACT ADDRESS** York Univ, 219 Vanier Col, Toronto, ON, M3J 1P3. **EMAIL** smason@yorku.ca

MASS, JEFFREY PAUL
PERSONAL Born 06/29/1940, New York, NY, m, 1963, 2 children **DISCIPLINE** JAPANESE HISTORY **EDUCATION** Hamilton Col, BA, 62; New York Univ, MA, 65; Yale Univ, MPhil, 69, PhD(Japanese hist), 71. **CAREER** Lectr hist, Yale Univ, 72-73; asst prof, 73-76, ASSOC PROF HIST, STANFORD UNIV, 76-, Stanford Mellen fel, Stanford Univ, 75-76; Social Sci Res Coun fel, 76-76; Guggenheim Found fel, 78-79. **MEMBERSHIPS** Asn Asian Studies. **RESEARCH** Japanese medieval history. **SELECTED PUBLICATIONS** Auth, Takeuchi, Rizo, 1907-1997--in Memoriam, Monumenta Nipponica, vol 0052, 97. **CONTACT ADDRESS** Dept of Hist, Stanford Univ, Stanford, CA, 94305-1926.

MASSANARI, RONALD LEE
PERSONAL Born 06/04/1941, Champaign, IL, m, 1963, 2 children **DISCIPLINE** HISTORY OF CHRISTIAN THOUGHT **EDUCATION** Goshen Col, BA, 63; Univ Wis-Madison, MA, 65; Garrett Theol Sem, BD, 66; Duke Univ, PhD(relig), 69. **CAREER** Vis asst prof church hist, Divinity Sch, Duke Univ, 69-70; from asst prof to assoc prof, 70-80, PROF RELIG, ALMA COL, 80-, Adj prof, San Francisco Theol Sem, 77-. **MEMBERSHIPS** Am Soc Church Hist; Am Acad Relig **RESEARCH** Religion and imagination; myth and ritual; political theology. **SELECTED PUBLICATIONS** Auth, True or false socialism: Adolf Stoecker's critique of Marxism from a Christian socialist perspective, Church Hist, 72; Christian socialism in nineteenth century Germany: A case study of a shift in anthropological perspective, Union Sem Theol Quart, 73; Vision and praxis, 77 & The politics of imagination, 77, Cross Currents; An exploration into religious symbolism, Relig in Life, 77; Time line, circle time, beneath and beyond, 78 & In the image of the father, but ..., 80, Relig in Life; A Journey with the Great Mother, Anima, 81. **CONTACT ADDRESS** Dept of Relig, Alma Col, 614 W Superior St, Alma, MI, 48801-1511.

MASTELLER, RICHARD N.
DISCIPLINE TWENTIETH-CENTURY AMERICAN LITERATURE **EDUCATION** Univ Rochester, BA; Univ Va, MA; Univ Minn, PhD. **CAREER** Instr, Univ Minn; Ill State Univ; prof, 78-. **HONORS AND AWARDS** Postdoc fel, Smithsonian's Nat Mus Amer Art., Cur, exhib photography and of satiric graphic art of the 30s. **RESEARCH** Relations between literature and visual art in an American studies context. **SELECTED PUBLICATIONS** Publ, essays on the vision of the American purveyed by western stereographs of the late nineteenth century; satiric vision of Reginald Marsh and John Dos Passos in the era of the 30s. **CONTACT ADDRESS** Dept of Eng, Whitman Col, 345 Boyer Ave, Walla Walla, WA, 99362-2038. **EMAIL** mastellerr@whitman.edu

MASTERS, DONALD C.
PERSONAL Born 02/08/1908, Shelburne, ON, Canada **DISCIPLINE** HISTORY **EDUCATION** Univ Toronto, BA, 30, MA, 31; Oxford Univ, PhD, 45; Bishop's Univ, DCl, 75. **CAREER** Lectr hist, Queen's Univ, 38-39; asst prof, 41-44, prof hist, Bishop's Univ, 44-66; prof Can hist, 66-74, PROF EMER, UNIV GUELPH, 77-. **MEMBERSHIPS** Can Hist Asn; Can Inst Int Affairs. **SELECTED PUBLICATIONS** Auth, The Reciprocity Treaty of 1854, 37; auth, The Rise of Toronto, 47; auth, The Winnipeg General Strike, 50; auth, A Short History of Canada, 58; auth, Protestant Church Colleges in Canada, 66; coauth, Ten Rings on the Oak: Mountain-Nicolls Family Story, 87; coauth, Henry John Cody: An Outstanding Life, 95. **CONTACT ADDRESS** 19 Monticello Cres, Guelph, ON, N1G 2M1.

MASTERS, ROGER D.
PERSONAL Born 05/08/1933, Boston, MA, m, 1984, 3 children **DISCIPLINE** POLITICAL SCIENCE **EDUCATION** Harvard Col, AB, 55; Univ Chicago, MA, 58, PhD, 61. **CAREER** Asst prof, Yale Univ, 61-67; Assoc to full prof, Dartmouth Col, 67-98; Nelson A Rockefeller Prof Emeritus, 98-. **HONORS AND AWARDS** Fulbright Fellowship to France, 58-59; Joint Yale-SSRC Fellow, 64-65; John Simon Guggenheim Fellow, 67-68; John Sloan Dickey Third Cent Prof of Govt, Dartmouth Col, 79-85; Dir d'Etudes Assoc, Ecole des Hautes Etudes en Sci Soc, Paris France, 86. **MEMBERSHIPS** Am Asn Adv of Sci; Am Polit Sci Asn. **RESEARCH** Political philosophy. **SELECTED PUBLICATIONS** Auth, Beyond Relativism: Science, Philosophy, and Human Nature, Univ Press of NE, 93; co-ed, The Neurotransmitter Revolution, S Ill Univ Press, 93; co-ed, Rousseau's Social Contract, with Discourse on Virtue of Heroes, Geneva Manuscript and Fragments Collected Writings of Rousseau, vol 4, Univ Press of NE, 94; gen ed, Gruter Institute Reader: Biology, Human Social Behavior, and Law, McGraw Hill, primis; auth, Machiavelli, Leonardo and the Science of Power, Univ Notre Dame Press, 96; auth, Fortune is a River: Leonardo da Vinci and Niccolo Machiavelli's Magnificent Dream to Change the Course of Florentine History, Free Press, 98. **CONTACT ADDRESS** Dept of Govt, Dartmouth Col, Silsby 6108, Hanover, NH, 03755.

MASTIN, CATHARINE M.
PERSONAL Born 08/01/1963, Toronto, ON, Canada **DISCIPLINE** CURATOR/ART HISTORY **EDUCATION** York Univ, BA, 86, MA, 88. **CAREER** Educ off, 85-88, cur, McMichael Can Art Coll, 87; course dir, Can art, York Univ, 88-89; Can hist art, Art Gallery Windsor, 89-95; CURATOR OF ART, GLENBOW MUSEUM, CALGARY, 95-. **RESEARCH** Canadian art **SELECTED PUBLICATIONS** Auth, William G.R. Hind: The Pictou Sketchbook, 90; auth, The Talented Intruder: Wyndham Lewis in Canada 1939-1945, 92; auth, Kenneth Saltmarche: A Retrospective, 94; auth, The Life and Art of Franklin Carmichael. **CONTACT ADDRESS** Glenbow Mus, 130 9th Ave SE, Calgary, AB, T2G 0P3.

MASTRONARDE, DONALD JOHN
PERSONAL Born 11/13/1948, Hartford, CT, m, 1971, 2 children **DISCIPLINE** CLASSICAL PHILOLOGY **EDUCATION** Amherst Col, BA, 69; Oxford Univ, BA, 71; Univ Toronto, PhD(classical studies), 74. **CAREER** From Asst Prof to Assoc Prof, 73-84, Prof Classics, Univ Calif, Berkeley, 84-, Dept Chair, 93-99. **HONORS AND AWARDS** Am Coun Learned Soc, fel, 78-79, 96-97; Guggenheim Fel, 84-85; Charles J. Goodwin Award of Merit, Am Philol Asn, 97. **MEMBERSHIPS** Am Philol Asn. **RESEARCH** Greek tragedy; Greek and Latin poetry. **SELECTED PUBLICATIONS** Auth, Theocritus' Idyll 13: love and the hero, Trans Am Philol Asn, 99, 68; Seneca's Oedipus: the drama in the word, Trans Am Philol Asn 101, 70; Iconography and imagery in Euripides' Ion, Calif Studies in Class Antiquity 8, 75; Are Euripides' Phoinissai 1104-1140 interpolated?, Phoenix, Vol 32; Contact and Discontinuity: Some conventions of speech and action on the Greek tragic stage, Univ Calif Publ Class Studies, Vol 21, 79; P Strasbourg WG 307 re-examined (Eur Phoin 1499-1581, 1710-1736), Zeitschrift fuer Papyrologie und Epigraphik 38, 1; coauth, The Textual Tradition of Euripides' Phoinissai, Univ Calif Publ Class Studies, Vol 27, 82; auth, Euripides, Phoenissae, Teubner editon, 88; Introduction to Attic Greek, Univ Calif Press, 93; Euripides, Phoenissae, Cambridge Classical Texts and Commentaries, 29, 94. **CONTACT ADDRESS** Dept of Class, Univ of California, Berkeley, 7303 Dwinelle Hall, Berkeley, CA, 94720-2520. **EMAIL** pinax@socrates.berkeley.edu

MASUR, LOUIS P.
DISCIPLINE HISTORY **EDUCATION** SUNY-Buffalo, BA, 78; Princeton Univ, MA, 81, PhD, 85. **CAREER** PROF, HIST, CITY COLL NY **MEMBERSHIPS** Am Antiquarian Soc **SELECTED PUBLICATIONS** Auth, "The Revision of the Criminal Law in Post-Revolutionary America," Criminal Justice Hist 7, 87; auth, Rites of Execution: Capital Punishment and the Transformation of American Culture, 1776-1865, Oxford Univ Press, 89. **EMAIL** masur@mail.humanities.ccny.cuny.edu

MATE, MAVIS
PERSONAL Born 11/12/1933, London, England, m, 1956, 2 children **DISCIPLINE** MEDIEVAL HISTORY **EDUCATION** Oxford Univ, BA, 56, MA, 61; Ohio State Univ, PhD, 67. **CAREER** Am Asn Univ Women fel, 67-68; Nat Endowment for Hum tchg resident, Denison Univ, 68-69; instr hist, OH State Univ, 69-72, lectr, 72-74; asst prof, 74-77, assoc prof hist, Univ OR, 77-84, Prof, 84-98, Am Coun Learned Soc fel, 81-82. **MEMBERSHIPS** Mediaeval Acad Am; AHA; Econ Hist Soc; Fellow of the Royal Hist soc. **RESEARCH** Monetary problems of 13th and 14th century Europe; the soc and economic position of Canterbury Cathedral priory; souteast Engl in late mid ages; Soc and Economic position of women in Engl. **SELECTED PUBLICATIONS** Auth, A mint of trouble, 1279-1307, Speculum, 69; Monetary policies of Edward I, 1272-1307, Brit Numis J, 72; The indebtedness of Canterbury Cathedral Priory, 1215-1290, 2nd ser, 73 & High prices in early fourteenth England: causes and consequences, 2nd ser, 75, Econ Hist Rev; Coping with inflation: a fourteenth century English example, J Medieval Hist, 78; The role of gold coinage in the English economy, 1338-1400, Numis Chronicle, 78; Profit and productivity on the estates of Isabella de Forz, 1260-92, Econ Hist Rev, 80; The impact of war on the economy of Canterbury Cathedral Priory, 1294-1340, Speculum, 82; 2 sections on Kent and Sussex in The Agarian History of England and Wales, v III (1350-1500), Cambridge, 91; ed, Daughters Wives and Widows of the Black Death (1350-1535), Boyhill and Bower, 98. **CONTACT ADDRESS** Dept of Hist, Univ of OR, Eugene, OR, 97403-1205. **EMAIL** memate@oregon.uoregon.edu

MATHENY, WILLIAM EDWARD
PERSONAL Born 12/23/1932, Sterling, IL, m, 1960, 4 children **DISCIPLINE** EUROPEAN HISTORY, LATIN AMERICAN STUDIES **EDUCATION** Univ IL, Urbana, BS, 56; Southwestern Baptist Sem, MDiv, 61; TX Christian Univ, MA, PhD(hist), 72. **CAREER** Prof, Baptist Theol Sem of Peru, 72-78; prof hist, Liberty Univ & Sem, 78-, chm, dept cross cultural studies, 82-. **MEMBERSHIPS** Am Soc Church Hist. **RESEARCH** The major themes and fate of dissenters in 16th century Spain; The origins and spread of Protestant Christianity in Latin America; Possible pre-Columbian arrival of Europeans in the Americas. **SELECTED PUBLICATIONS** Auth, La Multiplicacion de Iglesias en America Latina, Baptist Sem of Peru, 73; La Capacitacion de Obreros Cristianos en America Latina, Casa Bautista de Publ, El Paso, 75; Job, in Liberty Old Testament Commentary, Nelson, 82. **CONTACT ADDRESS** Dept Hist, Liberty Univ, PO Box 20000, Lynchburg, VA, 24506-8001.

MATHES, WILLIAM LLOYD
PERSONAL Born 11/25/1932, Chapman, KS **DISCIPLINE** RUSSIAN HISTORY **EDUCATION** Univ Witchita, BA, 54; Ohio State Univ, MA, 55; Columbia Univ, cert Russ Inst & MA, 57, PhD(Russ hist), 66. **CAREER** Asst, Ohio State Univ, 55; from instr to asst prof Europ hist, Fairleigh Dickinson Univ, 60-66; from asst prof to assoc prof, 66-75, PROF RUSS HIST, SETON HALL UNIV, 75-, DIR, RUSS AREA STUDIES PROG, 66-, Inter univ travel grant, Leningrad State Univ, 67-68; Dept Health, Educ & Welfare Group Projs Abroad fac exchange travel grant, Warsaw, Poland, 72-73; contrib ed, Slavic & Europ Educ Rev, 77- **MEMBERSHIPS** AHA; Am Asn Advan Slavic Studies; AAUP. **RESEARCH** The student movement during the reign of Alexander II; history of Russian universities, 1755-1917. **SELECTED PUBLICATIONS** Auth, Steeltown, USSR--Soviet Society in the Gorbachev Era, Labor Hist, vol 0035, 94. **CONTACT ADDRESS** Dept of Hist, Seton Hall Univ, 400 S Orange Ave, South Orange, NJ, 07079-2697.

MATHEWS, DONALD G.
PERSONAL Born 04/15/1932, Caldwell, ID, m, 1959 **DISCIPLINE** AMERICAN HISTORY **EDUCATION** Col Idaho, BA, 54; Yale Univ, BD, 57; Duke Univ, PhD(Am hist), 62. **CAREER** Instr hist, Duke Univ, 61-62; instr, Princeton Univ, 62-65, asst prof Am social hist, 65-68; assoc prof, 68-73, PROF AM SOCIAL HIST, UNIV NC, CHAPEL HILL, 73-, Soc Sci Res Coun fac res grant, 67-68; Nat Endowment for Humanities grant, 75-76. **HONORS AND AWARDS** Fel, Nat Endowment Humanities, 79-80; Bicentennial Chair Am Studies, Univ Helsinki, 81-82. **MEMBERSHIPS** AHA; Orgn Am Historians. **RESEARCH** American religious history; United States history, 1780-1850; American social history. **SELECTED PUBLICATIONS** Auth, The Slaveholders Dilemma--Freedom and Progress in Southern Conservative Thought, 1820-1860, J Southern Hist, vol 0059, 93; Awash in a Sea of Faith, Church Hist, vol 0063, 94; The Sanctified South--Brasher, John, Lakin and the Holiness Movement, Southern Cultures, vol 0002, 95; Fundamentalisms Comprehended, J Church and State, vol

0038, 96; Appalachian Mountain Religion, Church Hist, vol 0065, 96; The Sound of the Dove, Church Hist, vol 0066, 97. **CONTACT ADDRESS** Dept of Hist, Univ of NC, Hamilton Hall 070-A, Chapel Hill, NC, 27514.

MATHIESEN, THOMAS J.
PERSONAL Born 04/30/1947, Roslyn Heights, NY, m, 1971 **DISCIPLINE** MUSIC **EDUCATION** Willamette Univ, BA, 68; Univ South Cal, MM, 70, DMA, 71. **CAREER** Willamette Univ, tchg asst, 66; Univ S Cal, tchg asst, 69-71, lectr, 71-72; Brigham Young Univ, inst, asst prof, assoc prof, prof, assoc dean, head musicology, 72-88; Indiana Univ, Sch of Mus, prof, dist prof, 88-. **HONORS AND AWARDS** NEH, sr fel, 85-86; MLA, Vincent Duckles Award, 90; Guggenheim fel, 90-91; AMS & IMS Awards 96-. **MEMBERSHIPS** IMS, AMS, MLA, APA, AAUP. **RESEARCH** Musicology; ancient Greek music and music theory **SELECTED PUBLICATIONS** Auth, Greek Views of Music, in: Source Readings in Music History, ed by Leo Treitler, NY: W.W. Norton, 97; Ancient Greek Music Theory: A Catalogue raisonne of Manuscripts, G. Henle Verlag, 88; Aristides Quintilianus on Music in Three Books: Translation, with Introduction, Commentary, and Annotations, ed by Claude V. Palisca, Yale Univ Press, 83;A Bibliography of Sources for the Study of Ancient Greek Music, ed by G.R. Hill, Boonin, 74; Greek and Latin Music Theory, Founding & Gen Editor, Univ Nebraska Press, 92-. **CONTACT ADDRESS** School of Music, Indiana Univ, Bloomington, Bloomington, IN, 47405. **EMAIL** mathiese@indiana.edu

MATHIOT, MADELEINE
PERSONAL Born 06/11/1927, Saulxures-sur-Moselotte, France, m, 1960, 1 child **DISCIPLINE** LINGUISTICS, ANTHROPOLOGY **EDUCATION** Georgetown Univ, BS, 54, MS, 55; Cath Univ Am, PhD(anthrop), 66. **CAREER** Asst prof anthrop, Univ Calif, Los Angeles, 67-69; assoc prof ling, 69-74, Prof Ling & Anthrop, State Univ NY Buffalo, 74-, Dir, Ctr Studies Cult Transmission, 74- **MEMBERSHIPS** Am Anthrop Asn; Ling Soc Am; Semiotic Soc Am. **RESEARCH** Lexicology; ethnosemantics; face-to-face interaction. **SELECTED PUBLICATIONS** Auth, An Approach to the Cognitive Study of Language, 68 & A Papago Dictionary of Usage, vol 1, 73, vol 2, 78, Ind Univ; ed, Approaches to the Analysis of Face-to-Face Interaction, Semiotica, 78; Ethnolinguistics: Boas, Sapir, Whorf Revisited, Mouton, 79; A meaning based theory of face to face interaction, Int J Soc Ling (in prep). **CONTACT ADDRESS** Dept Ling, State Univ NY, Buffalo, NY, 14260.

MATHISEN, RALPH WHITNEY
PERSONAL Born 02/17/1947, Ashland, WI, m, 1979 **DISCIPLINE** ANCIENT HISTORY, CLASSICS **EDUCATION** Univ Wis, BS, 69, MA, 73, PhD(hist), 79; Rensselaer Polytech Inst, MS, 72. **CAREER** Vis asst prof Roman hist, Univ Ill, Chicago Circle, 79-80; ASST PROF ANCIENT & BYZANTINE HIST, UNIV SC, 80-. **MEMBERSHIPS** Asn Ancient Historians; Am Philol Asn; Am Hist Asn; Soc Ancient Numis. **RESEARCH** Late Roman society and religion; late Roman prosopography; Greek and Roman numismatics. **SELECTED PUBLICATIONS** Auth, The Role of the Church and Church Hierarchy in the Development of Episcopal and Monastic Institutions in Early-Medieval Europe, Speculum-J Medieval Stud, vol 0067, 92; Barbarian Bishops and the Churches in Barbaricus Gentibus During Late Antiquity + The Development, Organization and Hierarchy of the Arian Germanic Churches Beyond the Imperial Frontiers 4th Century 6th Century, Speculum-J Medieval Stud; Agrestius of Lugo, Eparchius Avitus, and a Curious 5th Century Statement of Faith, J Early Christian Stud, vol 0002, 94; Ambrosiana Ecclesia, Speculum-J Medieval Stud, vol 0070, 95; Caesarius of Arles--The Making of a Christian Community in Late Antique Gaul, Amer Hist Rev, vol 0101, 96. **CONTACT ADDRESS** Dept of Hist, Univ of SC, Columbia, SC, 29208.

MATILSKY, BARBARA C.
DISCIPLINE ART HISTORY **EDUCATION** NY Univ, PhD. **CAREER** Adj asst prof, Univ NC, Chapel Hill. **RESEARCH** Asian & 19th century French painting. **SELECTED PUBLICATIONS** Auth, Francois-August Biard: Artist, Naturalist, Explorer, Gazette de Beaux Arts, 85; Classical Myth and Imagery in Contemporary Art, Exhib Cat, Queens Mus, 88; Fragile Ecologies: Artists' Interpretations and Solutions, Rizzoli Int, 92; The Survival of Culture and Nature: Perspectives on the History of Environmental Art, Art and Design, 94. **CONTACT ADDRESS** Univ N. Carolina, Chapel Hill, Chapel Hill, NC, 27599.

MATOSSIAN, MARY KILBOURNE
PERSONAL Born 07/09/1930, Los Angeles, CA, m, 1954, 4 children **DISCIPLINE** MODERN HISTORY **EDUCATION** Stanford Univ, BA, 51, PhD(hist), 55; Univ Beirut, MA, 52. **CAREER** Res assoc USSR hist, Columbia Univ, 55-56; res fel Kemalism, Ctr Mid Eastern Studies, Harvard Univ, 57-58; asst prof hist, State Univ NY Col Buffalo, 60-62; lectr, 63-67, asst prof, 67-72, ASSOC PROF HIST, UNIV MD, COLLEGE PARK, 72-. **MEMBERSHIPS** AHA: Am Asn Advan Slavic Studies. **RESEARCH** History of the family; European health history. **SELECTED PUBLICATIONS** Auth, Fevered Lives--Tuberculosis in American Culture Since 1870, J Amer Hist, vol 0084, 97. **CONTACT ADDRESS** Dept of Hist, Univ of Md, College Park, MD, 20742.

MATRAY, JAMES IRVING
PERSONAL Born 12/06/1948, Evergreen Park, IL, m, 1971, 2 children **DISCIPLINE** AMERICAN HISTORY **EDUCATION** Lake Forest Col, BA, 70; Univ VA, MA, 73, PhD, 77. **CAREER** One year replacement appointments: Univ TX, Arlington, CA State Col, Bakersfield, Glenville State Col, WV, one semester at DE State Col, 75-80; vis assoc prof hist, Univ Southen CA, 88-89; Distinguished vis scholar, Grad Inst of Peace Studies, Kyung Hee Univ, Seoul, Korea, 90; vis asst prof, 80-81, asst prof, 82-86, assoc prof, 87-91, prof Hist, NM State Univ, 92-. **HONORS AND AWARDS** IL State scholarship recipient, 66-70; nominated for a Woodrow Wilson fel, 69; Phi Beta Kappa, 70; Harry S Truman Lib Found res grant, 75, 82; MacArthur Memorial Lib res grant, 84; nominee, Burlington Northern Outstanding Teacher Award, 85; Donald C Roush Award for Teaching Excellence, NMSU, 88; Fulbright Lecture Award recipient, Univ Warsaw, 88-89 (declined); Gold Key Student Soc honorary membership for outstanding teaching, 90; NEH grant, 90; Outstanding Teacher, Academic-Athletics Awards Banquet, 94; finalist, El Paso Natural Gas Fac Achievement Award, 96; numerous grants from the NM State Univ. **MEMBERSHIPS** Am Hist Asn; Soc for Historians of Am Foreign Relations. **SELECTED PUBLICATIONS** Auth, Hodge Podge: US Occupation Policy in Korea, 1945-1948, Korean Studies, XIX, 95; Civil is a Dumb Name for War, SHAFR Newsletter, XXXVII, 4, Dec 95; Foreword in We Will Not Be Strangers: Korean War Letters Between a MASH Surgeon and His Wife, ed Dorothy Horwitz, Univ Il Press, 97; Civil War of a Sort: the International Origins of the Korean War, in The Korean War in Retrospect, ed Daniel Meador, Univ Press Am, forthcoming 98; Korea's Partition: Soviet-American Pursuit of Reunification, 1945-1948, Parameters, forthcoming 98; Japan's Emergence as a Global Power, Greenwood Press, forthcoming; Historical Dictionary of US-East Asian Relations, Greenwood Press, forthcoming; The Uncivil War: Korea, 1945-1953, M E Sharpe Inc, forthcoming 2000; The Price of Intervention: American Foreign Policy in Korea, 1950-1953, in progress; numerous reviews and review essays, articles, books, book chapters, and dictionary entries. **CONTACT ADDRESS** Dept of History, New Mexico State Univ, La Cruces, NM, 88003. **EMAIL** jmatray@nmsu.edu

MATTER, EDITH ANN
PERSONAL Born 12/29/1949, Ft Smith, AR **DISCIPLINE** HISTORY OF CHRISTIANITY **EDUCATION** Oberline Col, BA, 71; Yale Univ, MA, 75, PhD(relig studies), 76. **CAREER** Lectr, 76, ASST PROF RELIG STUDIES, UNIV PA, 77-, Grant-in-aid text studies, Univ Pa, 78. **MEMBERSHIPS** Am Acad Relig, Women's Caucus; Mediaeval Acad Am; Am Soc Church Hist; Southeastern Medieval Asn. **RESEARCH** Biblical study in the Early Middle Ages; women in Medieval monasticism; textual editing. **SELECTED PUBLICATIONS** Auth, Paulinus of Aquileia, Opera Omnia, vol 1--Contra Felicem Libri Tres, Speculum-J Medieval Stud, vol 0068, 93; The Letters of Catherine of Siena, vol 1, Church Hist, vol 0062, 93; Friendship and Community--The Monastic Experience, 350-1250, Speculum-J Medieval Stud, vol 0068, 93; The Cult of the Virgin Mary in Anglo Saxon England, Church Hist, vol 0062, 93; Readings on the Song of Songs, Jewish Quart Rev, vol 0083, 93; Andreas De Sancto Victore, vol 6--Expositio in Ezechielem 'Exposition on Ezekiel', Speculum-J Medieval Stud, vol 0069, 94; Meanings of Sex Difference in the Middle Ages, J Interdisciplinary Hist, vol 0026, 95; Egyptian Obelisks--Politics and Culture in Rome During the Baroque Period, 16th Century J, vol 0026, 95; Angela of Foligno, Church Hist, vol 0064, 95; Eriugena--East and West, Church Hist, vol 0064, 95; Through a Speculum that Shines, Church Hist, vol 0065, 96; Eros and Allegory--Medieval Exegesis of the 'Song of Songs', Theol Stud, vol 0057, 96; A Conflict of Traditions--Women in Religion in the Early Middle Ages Ad500-840, Church Hist, vol 0065, 96; Biblical Commentaries from the Canterbury-School of Theodore and Hadrian, Speculum-J Medieval Stud, vol 0072, 97. **CONTACT ADDRESS** Dept of Relig Studies, Univ Pa, 236 S 34th St, Philadelphia, PA, 19104-3804.

MATTESON, LYNN ROBERT
DISCIPLINE ART HISTORY **EDUCATION** Univ Calif, Berkeley, PhD, 75. **CAREER** Assoc prof, Univ Southern Calif; correspondent for Pantheon; dean, Sch Fine Arts, 88-93. **RESEARCH** 18th & 19th Century European art. **SELECTED PUBLICATIONS** Auth, The Sense of an Ending: Apocalyptic Imagery in British Romantic Painting, Proceedings Conf on the Apocalypse, Missiac, France, 97; contribur, International Dictionary of Art, 92. **CONTACT ADDRESS** Col Letters, Arts & Sciences, Univ Southern Calif, University Park Campus, Los Angeles, CA, 90089.

MATTHEWS, J. ROSSER
PERSONAL Born 09/27/1964, Williamsburg, VA, s **DISCIPLINE** HISTORY **EDUCATION** Col of William and Mary, BA 85; Duke Univ, MA 88, PhD 92; Col Wm And Mary, MPP 97. **CAREER** N Carolina State Univ, vis lectr, 92,93; Duke Univ, asst prof 93; Univ Oklahoma, asst prof 94; College William and Mary, adj prof 97, 99. **MEMBERSHIPS** HSS; AAHM. **RESEARCH** Historical and philosophical issues raised by appeals to quantitative evidence in medicine including ethical aspects. **SELECTED PUBLICATIONS** Auth, Qualification and the Quest for Medical Certainty, Princeton, Princeton U Press, 95; auth, Practice Guidelines and Tort Reform: The Legal System Confronts the Technocratic Wish, Jour of Health Politics Policy and Law, forthcoming; Why Should the Stroke Prevention Policy Model be Used?, coauth, in: The Stroke Prevention Policy Model: Linking Evidence and Clinical Decisions, coauth, Annals of Internal Medicine, 97; auth, History of Biostatistics, entries on J. Gavarret, PCA Louis, P Pinel, A Quetelet, in: Encyc of Biostatistics, Chichester UK, John Wiley & Sons, 98; auth, Alfred W Crosby, The Measure of Reality: Quantification and Western Society, 1250-1600. In: The Amer Hist Rev, 98; Marc Berg, Rationalizing Medical Work: Decision-Support Techniques and Medical Practices, in: Isis: An Intellectual Rev Devoted to the Hist of Science and it Cultural Influences, 97. **CONTACT ADDRESS** William & Mary Col, 200 Captain Newport Circle, Williamsburg, VA, 23185. **EMAIL** rmatthews@widomaker.com

MATTHEWS, JOHN F.
PERSONAL Born 02/15/1940, Leicester, England, m, 1995, 2 children **DISCIPLINE** CLASSICS, ANCIENT HISTORY **EDUCATION** Oxford Univ, BA, 63; MA, 67; PhD, 70. **CAREER** Res Fel, Balliol Coll, Oxford, 65-69; lectr, fel, Corpus Christi Coll, 69-76; lectr, Queen's Coll Oxford, 76-90; reader, 90-92; prof; prof, yale Univ, 96-. **HONORS AND AWARDS** Fel of Brit Acad; Fel of Royal Hist soc; Fel of Soc of Antiquaries of London. **MEMBERSHIPS** Soc for the Promotion of Roman Stuides London; Am Philol Asn. **RESEARCH** Late Roman History. **SELECTED PUBLICATIONS** Auth, Western and Imperial Court, 90; Political Life and Culture in Late Roman Society, 85; Laying down the Law: a Study of the Theodosian Code, 99; coauth, Atlas of Roman World, 82; The Goths in the Fourth Century, 91. **CONTACT ADDRESS** 160 McKinley Ave, New Haven, CT, 06515. **EMAIL** john.matthews@yale.edu

MATTHEWS, ROY T.
PERSONAL Born 02/14/1932, Franklin, VA, m, 1959, 2 children **DISCIPLINE** MODERN EUROPEAN AND DIPLOMATIC HISTORY **EDUCATION** Wash & Lee Univ, BA, 54; Duke Univ, MA, 56; Univ NC, Chapel Hill, PhD(Europ hist), 66. **CAREER** Instr soc studies, Womans' Col Ga, 58-60; mod civilization, Univ NC, 61-64; instr Europ hist, Univ Houston, 64-65; from instr to asst prof humanities, 65-71, staff, Justin Morrill Col, 69-71, dept hist, 69-73, 76 & 81-82; assoc prof, 71-76, PROF HUMANITIES, MICH STATE UNIV, 76- **MEMBERSHIPS** AAUP; North Am Conf Brit Studies; Victorian Soc Am. **RESEARCH** History of caricature and cartooning; 19th century English social and cultural history; influence of caricaturists. **SELECTED PUBLICATIONS** Auth, F.C.G. + Gould, Francis, Carruthers, 19th Century Prose, vol 0019, 92; Rank, Arthur, J. and the British Film Industry, Albion, vol 0026, 94; The Victorians Biography of Bull, John, 19th Century Prose, vol 0022, 95; Dictionary of British Cartoonists and Caricaturists, 1730-1980, Albion, vol 0027, 95. **CONTACT ADDRESS** Michigan State Univ, E LANSING, MI, 48824.

MATTHEWS, VICTOR J.
PERSONAL Born 01/29/1941, Londonderry, Northern Ireland, m, 1967, 1 child **DISCIPLINE** CLASSICS **EDUCATION** Queen's Univ, Belfast, BA, 63; Queen's Univ, Belfast, Dip Educ, 64; McMaster Univ, Hamilton, Ontario, MA, 65; Queen's Univ, Belfast, PhD, 68. **CAREER** Lectr, 65-69, asst prof, 69-74, assoc prof, 74-94, prof, 94-, classics, Univ Guelph. **HONORS AND AWARDS** Nat Humanities Ctr fel, 86-87; SSHRC leave fel, 86-87. **MEMBERSHIPS** Ontario Class Asn; The Class Asn of Can; The Amer Philol Asn; The Israel Soc for the Promotion of Class Studies. **RESEARCH** Greek epic; Hellenistic literature; Greek athletics. **SELECTED PUBLICATIONS** Auth, Antimachus of Colophon: Text and Commentary, Leiden, 96; auth, Aphrodite's Hair: Colluthus and Hairstyles in the Epic Tradition, Eranos 94, 96; auth, The Greek Pentathlon Again, Zeitschrift fur Papyrologie und Epigraphik 100, 94; auth, In Defense of the Artemis of Antimachos, Liverpool Class Mth, 18.6, 93. **CONTACT ADDRESS** School of Languages & Lits, Univ of Guelph, Guelph, ON, N1G2W1. **EMAIL** vjmatthe@uoguelph.ca

MATTINGLY, CAROL
DISCIPLINE HISTORY OF RHETORIC, COMPOSITION THEORY AND PRACTICE, AMERICAN LITERATURE **EDUCATION** Univ Louisville, PhD, 92. **CAREER** Assoc prof, dir, Nat Writing Proj, La State Univ. **HONORS AND AWARDS** Phi Kappa Phi Award, 97. **RESEARCH** 19th century American women writers; 19th-century women and rhetoric. **SELECTED PUBLICATIONS** Auth, Women in Louisville: Moving Toward Equal Rights, The Filson Club Hist Quart 55, 81; Valuing the Personal: Feminist Concerns for the Writing Classroom: Gender and Academe: Feminist Pedagogy and Politics, Rowman and Littlefield, 94; Pin-the Condom-on the Man: Strategies for Selling Safe Sex, Popular Cult Rev VI.2, 95; Women-Tempered Rhetoric: Public Presentation and the WCTU, Rhet Rev 14.1, 95. **CONTACT ADDRESS** Dept of Eng, Louisiana State Univ, 232B Allen Hall, Baton Rouge, LA, 70803. **EMAIL** enmatt@unix1.sncc.lsu.edu

MATTINGLY, PAUL HAVEY
PERSONAL Born 02/04/1941, Washington, DC, m, 1964, 2 children **DISCIPLINE** AMERICAN HISTORY **EDUCATION** Georgetown Univ, AB, 62; Univ Wis, MA, 64, PhD, 68. **CAREER** Instr, Dept of Hist, Univ Wis, 67-68; asst to assoc prof, 68-76, prof, 76-81, Dept Of Cultural Foundations, Chemn,74-81, Ed, Hist of Education Quart, 71-85; PROF OF HIST, DIR, PROGRAM IN PUBLIC HIST, NYU 81-. **HONORS AND AWARDS** NEH, summer 85; Nat Res Coun Grant, 70-71; Spencer Fel, 74-79. **MEMBERSHIPS** Am Hist Asn; Org of Am Historians; Nat Coun on Public Hist; Social Sci Hist Asn; Hist of Ed Soc. **RESEARCH** American higher education; suburbanization & community formation; philanthropy & professionalization. **SELECTED PUBLICATIONS** Auth, Suburban Landscapes: Culture and Politics in a Metropolitan Community, forthcoming; Old Suburbia, Invisible Am, Henry Holt and Co, 95; Politics and Ideology in a Metropolitan Suburb, Contested Terrain: Power, Politics and Participation in Suburbia, Greenwood Press, 95; The Suburban Canon Over Time, Suburban Discipline, Princeton Architectural Press, 97; The Political Culture of Antebellum American Colleges, Hist of Higher Ed Annual, 97; coauth, The Pedagogy of Public History, J of Am Ethnic Hist, 98. **CONTACT ADDRESS** 19 University Pl., No. 525, New York, NY, 10003.

MATTISON, ROBERT S.
DISCIPLINE HISTORY OF ART **EDUCATION** Middlebury Col, BA, 74; Williams Col, MA, 77; Princeton Univ, MFA, 79, PhD, 85. **CAREER** Asst prof, 81-86, assoc prof, 87-94, PROF, 95-, LAFAYETTE COL. **CONTACT ADDRESS** Art Dept, Lafayette Col, Easton, PA, 18042. **EMAIL** mattison@lafayette.edu

MATTSON, VERNON E.
DISCIPLINE HISTORY **EDUCATION** Univ Kans, PhD, 71. **CAREER** Assoc prof, Univ Nev Las Vegas. **RESEARCH** American intellectual history; American religious history; Holocaust studies. **SELECTED PUBLICATIONS** Auth, Frederick Jackson Turner: A Reference Guide, Boston, 85. **CONTACT ADDRESS** History Dept, Univ Nev Las Vegas, 4505 Md Pky, Las Vegas, NV, 89154.

MATUSOW, ALLEN JOSEPH
PERSONAL Born 05/18/1937, Philadelphia, PA **DISCIPLINE** AMERICAN HISTORY **EDUCATION** Ursinus Col, BA, 58; Harvard Univ, MA, 59, PhD(hist), 63. **CAREER** From asst prof to assoc prof, 63-70, PROF HIST, RICE UNIV, 70-, DEAN SCH HUMANITIES, 80-, Vis asst prof, Stanford Univ, 67-68. **MEMBERSHIPS** AHA; Orgn Am Historians. **SELECTED PUBLICATIONS** Auth, From Opportunity to Entitlement--The Transformation and Decline of Great Society Liberalism, Amer Hist Rev, vol 0102, 97. **CONTACT ADDRESS** Dept of Hist, Rice Univ, Houston, TX, 77251.

MATZKO, JOHN AUSTIN
PERSONAL Born 09/18/1946, Audubon, NJ, m, 1976, 1 child **DISCIPLINE** AMERICAN LEGAL HISTORY **EDUCATION** Bob Jones Univ, BA, 68; Univ Cinncinati, MA, 72; Univ VA, PhD (Am Legal Hist), 84. **CAREER** Teaching asst, Univ Cinncinati, 68, 71; teahcing asst and acting asst prof, Univ VA, 76-78; MEMBER OF HIST FACULTY (UNRANKED), BOB JONES UNIV, 71-74, 78-, CHAIRMAN, DIV OF SOCIAL SCIENCE, 97-. **MEMBERSHIPS** OAH; ASLH. **RESEARCH** Presenting hist to the public; cultural resource management. **SELECTED PUBLICATIONS** Auth, President Theodore Roosevelt and Army Reform, Proceedings of the SC Hist Asn, 73; Ideological Chaff, review of Jerold Auerbach, Unequal Justice, Nat Rev, 29, Jan. 7, 77; The Best Men of the Bar: The Founding of the American Bar Association, in Gerald Gawalt, ed, The New High Priests, Greenwood Press, 84; review of Michael J. Powell, From Patrician to Professional Elite: The Transformation of the New York City Bar Association, in Am J of Legal Hist, 34, Oct 90; review of William P. LaPiana, Logic and Experience: The Origin of Modern American Legal Education, Oxford Univ Press, 94, in Am J of Legal Hist, 39, April 95; Ralph Budd and Early Attempts to Reconstruct Fort Union, 1925-1941, North Dakota Hist, 64, summer 97; contributor of three entries to D. R. Woolf, ed, A Global Encyclopedia of Historical Writing, Garland Pub, Inc., 98; Reconstructing Fort Union: The Interplay of Citizens and Their Government in the Development of a Historical Park, forthcoming. **CONTACT ADDRESS** Bob Jones Univ, Box 34561, Greenville, SC, 29614. **EMAIL** jmatzko@bju.edu

MAUGHAN, STEVEN
DISCIPLINE MODERN EUROPEAN AND NON-WESTERN HISTORY **EDUCATION** Col ID, BA, summa cum laude; Harvard Univ, MA, PhD. **CAREER** Prof, Albertson Col, 92. **HONORS AND AWARDS** Mellon fel, King's Col, London; Fulbright grant, King's Col, London. **SELECTED PUBLICATIONS** Auth, 'Mighty England Do Good': the Major English Denominations and Organisation for the Support of Foreign Missions in the Nineteenth Century, in Missionary Encounters: Sources and Issues, ed, R Bickers and R Seton, Curzon, 96; Women'sForeign Missions, Civic Culture, and the British Imperial Imagination,1860-1914, The Making of Civil society in Modern Germany and Britain: NewCultural, Political and Theoretical Perspectives, ed, F Trentmann, Berghahn, 98. **CONTACT ADDRESS** Albertson Col, Idaho, Caldwell, ID, 83605. **EMAIL** smaughan@stimpy.acofi.edu

MAULTSBY, PORTIA K.
PERSONAL Born 06/11/1947, Orlando, Florida, s **DISCIPLINE** MUSIC **EDUCATION** Mount St Scholastica Coll, Atchison, KS, BM, piano/theory composition, 1968; Univ of WI, Madison, WI, MM, musicology, 1969, PhD, ethnomusicology, 1974. **CAREER** IN Univ, Bloomington, IN, prof, Afro-American Studies, 1971-. **HONORS AND AWARDS** Selected as one of 8 American performers/scholars to participate in workshop/conference on African American Sacred Music in Havana, Cuba, 1990; selected as one of 6 American ethnomusicologists to participate in an American-Soviet Research Conference in the Soviet Union, 1988; Awarded Honorary Doctor of Music Degree, Benedictine, KS, 1985; Portia K Maultsby Day proclaimed by the Mayor of Orlando, FL, 1975; Utrecht Univ, Netherlands, apptd prof to "Belle van Zuylen" Chair, Distinguished Visiting Professor, 1997-98. **MEMBERSHIPS** Exec bd, Int Assn for the Study of Popular Music, 1987-95, editorial bd, 1989-; council mem, Society for ethnomusicology, 1973-76, 1977-80, 1988-91. **SELECTED PUBLICATIONS** Delivered keynote address for GATT Conference on the exchange of culture between America and Europe in Tilburg, The Netherlands, 1994. **CONTACT ADDRESS** Dept of Afro-American Studies, Indiana Univ, Bloomington, Memorial Hall East, Bloomington, IN, 47405.

MAUS, FRED EVERETT
DISCIPLINE MUSIC HISTORY **EDUCATION** Oxford Univ, ML; Princeton Univ, PhD. **CAREER** Dept Music, Va Univ **RESEARCH** Dramatic and narrative aspects of instrumental music; relations between musical analysis and musical aesthetics; gender studies; recent American music. **SELECTED PUBLICATIONS** Auth, Music as Drama, 88; Recent Ideas and Activities of James K. Randall and Benjamin Boretz, 88; Music as Narrative, Ind Theory Rev, 91; Hanslickos Animism, Jour Musicol, 92; Masculine Discourse in Music Theory, 93. **CONTACT ADDRESS** Dept of Music, Virginia Univ, Charlottesville, VA, 22903. **EMAIL** fem2x@virginia.edu

MAUSKOPF, SEYMOUR HAROLD
PERSONAL Born 11/11/1938, Cleveland, OH, m, 1961, 3 children **DISCIPLINE** HISTORY OF CHEMISTRY **EDUCATION** Cornell Univ, BA, 60; Princeton Univ, PhD, 66. **CAREER** Instr to asst prof to assoc to PROF, DUKE UNIV, 64-. **HONORS AND AWARDS** Dexter Award, Am Chem Soc, 98. **MEMBERSHIPS** Hist of Science Soc **RESEARCH** Hist 18th-19th century science, hist chem. **SELECTED PUBLICATIONS** Auth, Crystals and Compounds, 76; The Elusive Science, 80; ed, Chemical Sciences in the Modern World, 93. **CONTACT ADDRESS** Dept History, Duke Univ, Box 90719, Durham, NC, 27708-0719. **EMAIL** shmaus@acpur.duke.edu

MAUSS, ARMAND
PERSONAL Born 06/05/1928, Salt Lake City, UT, m, 1951, 8 children **DISCIPLINE** HISTORY; SOCIOLOGY **EDUCATION** Sophia Univ, Tokyo, BA, 54; Univ CA Berkeley, MA, 57, PhD, 70. **CAREER** Inst, 63-67, Diablo Valley coll; assoc prof, 67-69, Utah State Univ; prof, 69-99, Washington State Univ. **HONORS AND AWARDS** Ed, Journal for the Scientific Study of Religion, 89-92; pres, Mormon History Assn, 97-98; Chipman Award for best book (MHA), 94; Arrington Career Award, (MHA), 94. **MEMBERSHIPS** Soc for the Scientific Study of Religion; Assn for the Sociology of Religion; Religion Research Assn; Mormon History Assn; Mormon Social Science Assn. **RESEARCH** Sociology of Religion; deviant behavior and social problems **SELECTED PUBLICATIONS** Auth, Neither White nor Black: Mormon Scholars Confront the Race Issue in a Universal Church, Signature Books, Salt Lk City, 84; The Angel and the Beehive: The Mormon Struggle with Assimilation, Univ of Ill Press, 94; Marketing for Miracles: Mormonism in the Twenty-First Century, Dialogue: A Journal of Mormon Thought, Spring 96; The Impact Of Feminism and Religious Involvement on Sentiment toward God, Review of Religious Research, March 96; In Search of Ephraim: Tradition Mormon Conceptions of Lineage and Race, Journal of Mormon History, Spring 99. **CONTACT ADDRESS** 2061 C.S., Pullman, WA, 99165.

MAVOR, CAROL
DISCIPLINE ART HISTORY **EDUCATION** Univ CA, Santa Cruz, PhD. **CAREER** Asst prof, Univ NC, Chapel Hill. **RESEARCH** Critical theory; Victorian cult. **SELECTED PUBLICATIONS** Auth, Pleasures Taken: Performances of Sexuality and Loss in Victorian Culture, Duke UP, 95; Becoming: The Photographs of Clementina Hawarden, Genre, 96; Collecting Loss, Cult Stud, 97. **CONTACT ADDRESS** Univ N. Carolina, Chapel Hill, Chapel Hill, NC, 27599.

MAXMIN, JODY
DISCIPLINE CLASSICS **EDUCATION** BA, 71; Oxford, DPhil, 79. **CAREER** Assoc prof art/class, Stanford Univ. **RESEARCH** Greek and Roman art; Greek vase-painting and sculpture. **SELECTED PUBLICATIONS** Auth, A Hellenistic Echo in Daumier's Penelope? Art International, 84; A New Amphora by the Painter of Berlin 1686 in Studien zur Mythologie und Vasenmalerei, Festschrift for Konrad Schauenburg, 86; coauth, Euphronios: A Presbyope in Ancient Athens?, The Eye of the Artist, 96. **CONTACT ADDRESS** Stanford Univ, Bldg 20, Main Quad, Stanford, CA, 94305.

MAXON, ROBERT MEAD
PERSONAL Born 12/10/1939, Oneonta, NY, m, 1968, 2 children **DISCIPLINE** HISTORY **EDUCATION** Duke Univ, BA, 61; Syracuse Univ, PhD(hist), 72. **CAREER** Asst prof, 69-74, ASSOC PROF HIST, W VA UNIV, 74-. **MEMBERSHIPS** African Studies Asn; Hist Asn of Kenya. **RESEARCH** Colonial history of Kenya; the traditional history of the Bunyore of Western Kenya. **SELECTED PUBLICATIONS** Auth, A History of East Africa, 1592-1902, Amer Hist Rev, vol 0102, 97. **CONTACT ADDRESS** Dept of Hist, West Virginia Univ, P O Box 6303, Morgantown, WV, 26506-6303.

MAXWELL, KENNETH R.
PERSONAL Born 03/02/1941, Wellington, United Kingdom, s **DISCIPLINE** HISTORY **EDUCATION** Cambridge Univ St John's, BA 63, MA 67; Princeton Univ, MA 67, PhD 70. **CAREER** Coun on For Rels, Rockefeller Sr Fel, 95-, vpres, Dir, 96; Tirke Found Inc, prog dir, 79-85; Columbia Univ, assoc prof, 76-84; Princeton Univ Menke, adv stud, 71-75. **HONORS AND AWARDS** Order of Rio Branco; Order of Sci Merit; Guggenheim Fel. **MEMBERSHIPS** AHA; IHG. **RESEARCH** Latin America and Southern Europe; Spain and Portugal. **SELECTED PUBLICATIONS** Auth, Pombol, Paradox of the Enlightenment, Cambridge, 95; auth, The Making of Portuguese Democracy, Cambridge, 95; auth, The New Spain, coauth, Council On Foreign Relations, 94; auth, Conflicts and Conspiracies, Brazil and Portugal, 1750-1808, Cambridge, 73. **CONTACT ADDRESS** Council on Foreign Relations, 58 East 68th St, New York, NY, 10021. **EMAIL** kmaxwell@email.cfr.org

MAY, CHRISTOPHER N.
PERSONAL Born 03/05/1943, Evanston, IL, m **DISCIPLINE** AMERICAN LAW **EDUCATION** Harvard Univ, AB, 65; Yale Univ, LLB, 68. **CAREER** Dir res, Nat Inst Educ Law & Poverty, Sch Law, Northwestern Univ, 68-69; Staff atty, San Francisco Neighborhood Legal Assistance Found, 70-73; instr, Sch Law, Golden Gate Univ, 71-73; prof Law, Loyola Law Sch, Ca, 73-. **HONORS AND AWARDS** Alpha Sigma Nu Natl Jesuit Book Award, 89. **RESEARCH** Supreme Court & congressional exercises of the war powers; Presidential noncompliance with the law. **SELECTED PUBLICATIONS** Auth, A Manual on the Laws & Administrative Regulations of the General Assistance & ADC Programs in the State of Illinois, Am Civil Liberties Union, 67; Withdrawal of Public Welfare: The right to a prior hearing, 76 Yale Law J 1234, 67; coauth (with Daniel William Fessler), Amicus Curiae brief in Goldberg versus Kelly, 397 US 254, 70; auth, Supreme Court holds residency test unconstitutional, Vol 3, No 1, Administration unveils welfare reform package: Recipients must work, Vol 3, No 89 & Supreme Court approves maximum grants, Vol 3, No 321, Clearinghouse Rev; coauth (with Daniel William Fessler), The Municipal Services Equalization Suit: A Cause of Action in Quest of a Forum, Public Needs, Private Behavior, and the Metropolitan Political Economy, Resources Future, Cambridge Univ, 75; In The Name of War: Judicial Review and the War Powers since 1918, Harvard Univ, 89; coauth, The Law of Prime Numbers, NY Univ Law Rev, 73; auth, Presidential Defiance of Unconstitutional Laws: Reviving the Royal Prerogative, Hastings Const Law Quart, 94; What Do We Do Now?: Helping Juries Apply the Instructions, Loyola Los Angeles Law Jour, 95; coauth, The Jurisprudence of Yogi Berra, Emory Law Jour, 97; Constitutional Law: National Power and Federalism, Aspen Law and Bus, 98; Constitutional Law: Individual Rights, Aspen Law and Bus, 98; auth, Presidential Defiance ofUnconstitutional Laws: Reviving the Royal Prerogative, Greenwood, 98. **CONTACT ADDRESS** Law Sch, Loyola Marymount Univ, 919 S Albany St, Los Angeles, CA, 90015-0019. **EMAIL** cmay@lmulaw.lmu.edu

MAY, ELAINE TYLER
PERSONAL Born 09/17/1947, Los Angeles, CA, m, 1970, 3 children **DISCIPLINE** AMERICAN HISTORY **EDUCATION** Univ Calif, Los Angeles, AB, 69, MA, 70, PhD(US hist), 75. **CAREER** Asst prof hist, Princeton Univ, 74-78; asst prof Am studies, 78-81, ASSOC PROF AM STUDIES, UNIV MINN, 81-, Mellon Fac fel humanities, Harvard Univ, 81-82; Radcliffe res scholar, 82. **MEMBERSHIPS** AHA; Orgn Am Historians; Women Hist Midwest. **RESEARCH** American social history; United States women's history; history of marriage and the family. **SELECTED PUBLICATIONS** Auth, Rosie the Riveter Gets Married + American Women and World War II, Mid America-Hist Rev, vol 0075, 93; Ideology and Foreign Policy, Diplomatic Hist, vol 0018, 94; The Radical Roots of American Studies, Amer Quart, vol 0048, 96; Grand Expectations--The United States, 1945-1974, Amer Hist Rev, vol 0102, 97. **CONTACT ADDRESS** Univ Minn, 88 Arthur Ave SE, Minneapolis, MN, 55455.

MAY, ERNEST
DISCIPLINE MUSIC **EDUCATION** Harvard Univ, BA; Princeton Univ, PhD. **CAREER** Prof. **HONORS AND AWARDS** Pres, Am Musicol Soc, 88-90. **SELECTED PUBLICATIONS** Auth, pubs on Bach organ music; ed, New Bach Edition; co-ed, J. S. Bach as Organist, Univ Ind, 86. zGEN **CONTACT ADDRESS** Music and Dance Dept, Univ of Massachusetts, Amherst, 720 Massachusetts Ave, Amherst, MA, 01003.

MAY, HENRY FARNHAM
PERSONAL Born 03/27/1915, Denver, CO **DISCIPLINE** AMERICAN HISTORY **EDUCATION** Univ Calif, AB, 37; Harvard Univ, AM, 38, PhD, 47. **CAREER** From asst prof to assoc prof hist, Scripps Col, 47-52; from assoc prof to prof, 52-63, Margaret Byrne prof, 63-80, EMER MARGARET BYRNE PROF HIST, UNIV CALIF, BERKELEY, 80-, Vis assoc prof, Bowdoin Col, 50-51; Pitt prof Am hist & inst, Cambridge Univ, 71-72; vis prof, Univ Leuvon, Belgium, 81; Berkeley Citatin, 80. **HONORS AND AWARDS** Merle Curti Award, Orgn Am Historians & Beveridge Prize, Am Hist Asn, 77. **MEMBERSHIPS** AHA; Orgn Am Historians; Am Acad Arts & Sci; Am Soc Church Hist. **RESEARCH** American intellectual and religious history. **SELECTED PUBLICATIONS** Auth, The American Religion--The Emergence of the Post Christian Nation, Rev(s) in Amer Hist, vol 0021, 93. **CONTACT ADDRESS** Dept of Hist, Univ of Calif, Berkeley, CA, 94720.

MAY, JAMES M.
DISCIPLINE GREEK AND ROMAN RHETORIC **EDUCATION** Kent State Univ, BS, 73; Univ NC, PhD, 77. **CAREER** Drama, St. Olaf Col. **SELECTED PUBLICATIONS** Auth, Trials of Character: The Eloquence of Ciceronian Ethos, Univ N Carolina Press, 88. **CONTACT ADDRESS** St Olaf Col, 1520 St Olaf Ave, Northfield, MN, 55057. **EMAIL** may@stolaf.edu

MAY, JUDE THOMAS
PERSONAL Born 06/07/1936, Grand Forks, ND, m, 1964, 2 children **DISCIPLINE** HISTORY OF MEDICINE **EDUCATION** St Mary's Univ, Tex, BS & BA, 58; Univ Pittsburgh, MA, 62; Tulane Univ, PhD(hist), 70. **CAREER** Res asst, Univ Pittsburgh, 61-62; asst prof, 68-76, assoc prof Hist of Med & Human Ecol, Univ OK, 76-; consult, Nat Study Consumer Participation Neighborhood Health Ctrs, Health Servs & Ment Health Admin, USPHS, 69-71 & Nat Ctr Health Servs Res & Develop, 71-; Am Philos Soc grant-in-aid, 71; consult, State-based Humanities Prog, Nat Endowment for Humanities, 73-. **HONORS AND AWARDS** David Ross Boyd Prof, Univ of OK, 95; Assoc Dean, Col of Public Health, Univ of OK, 90-93. **MEMBERSHIPS** AHA; Orgn Am Historians; Am Asn Hist Med; Southern Hist Asn; Am Pub Health Asn. **RESEARCH** History of health care delivery; sociology of health and medicine; social implications of patterns of the distribution of health services. **SELECTED PUBLICATIONS** Auth, Continuity and Change in the Labor Policies of the Union Army and the Freedmen's Bureau, Civil War Hist, 9/71; Conflict and Resolution in a Health Care Program: The Function of Historical Analysis, Anthrop Quart, 7/73; coauth, The Neighborhood Health Center Program, Washington, DC, 76; Professional Control and Innovation, In: New Research in the Sociology of Health Care, JAI Press, 80; Conflict, Consensus, and Exchange, Social Problems, 2/80; auth, The Professionalization of Neighborhood Health Centers, Health/PAC Bull, Vol 12, No 2. **CONTACT ADDRESS** Col of Public Health, Univ of Oklahoma, Box 26901, Oklahoma City, OK, 73190.

MAY, LARY L.
DISCIPLINE HISTORY **EDUCATION** Univ Calif Los Angeles, PhD, 76. **CAREER** Assoc prof **RESEARCH** American cultural history. **SELECTED PUBLICATIONS** Auth, Screening Out the Past: The Birth of Mass Culture and the Motion Picture Industry, Oxford, 80; pubs on popular culture and modern society. **CONTACT ADDRESS** History Dept, Univ of Minnesota, Twin Cities, 614 Social Sciences Tower, 267 19th Ave S, Minneapolis, MN, 55455. **EMAIL** mayxx001@tc.umn.edu

MAY, ROBERT EVAN
PERSONAL Born 07/06/1943, Brooklyn, NY, m, 1967, 2 children **DISCIPLINE** AMERICAN HISTORY **EDUCATION** Union Col, NY, BA, 65; Univ Wis-Madison, MA, 66, PhD(hist), 69. **CAREER** Asst prof, 69-75, ASSOC PROF HIST, PURDUE UNIV, WEST LAFAYETTE, 75-. **HONORS AND AWARDS** Grant-in-Aid, Am Coun Learned Soc, 80; McLemore Prize, Miss Hist Soc, 86; Willie D. Halsell Prize, Miss Hist Soc, 89; Frederick W. Beinecke Fel in Western Americana, Beinecke Rare Book and Manuscript Library, Yale Univ, 97-98. **MEMBERSHIPS** Orgn Am Historians; Southern Hist Asn; Soc for Hist of the Early Republic; Miss Hist Soc. **RESEARCH** Southern history; American expansionism. **SELECTED PUBLICATIONS** Auth, The Southern Dream of a Caribbean Empire, 1854-1861, La State Univ, 73; Dixie's Martial Image: A Continuing Historiographical Enigma, Historian, 2/78; Lobbyists for commercial empire: Jane Cazneau, William Cazneau and US Caribbean Policy, 1846-1878, Pac Hist Rev, 8/79; John A. Quitman: Old South Crusader, LSU Press, 85; ed, The Union, the Confederacy, and the Atlantic Rim, Purdue Univ Press, 95; auth, The Slave Power Conspiracy Revisited: United States Presidents and Filibustering, 1848-1861, In: Union & Emancipation: Essays on Politics and Race in the Civil War Era, Kent State Univ Press, 97; auth, Manifest Destiny's Filibusters, In: Manifest Destiny and Empire: American Antebellum Expansionism, College Station, 97; author of several other books and journal articles. **CONTACT ADDRESS** Dept of Hist, Purdue Univ, West Lafayette, IN, 47907-1358.

MAYER, ARNO JOSEPH
PERSONAL Born 06/19/1926, Luxembourg, 2 children **DISCIPLINE** MODERN EUROPEAN HISTORY **EDUCATION** City Col New York, BBA, 49; Yale Univ, MA, 50, PhD, 54. **CAREER** Teaching fel, Wesleyan Univ, 52-53; res consult, Found World Govt, 53-54; from instr to asst prof polit, Brandeis Univ, 54-58; asst prof hist, Harvard Univ, 58-61; assoc prof, 61-63, PROF HIST, PRINCETON UNIV, 63-, Am Coun Learned Soc fel, 60-61; Soc Sci Res Coun auxiliary res award, 62; Rockefeller Found res grant, 63-64; vis Prof, Columbia Univ, 66-70; Guggenheim fel, 67-68; res assoc, Inst War & Peace, Columbia Univ, 71-72; res fel, Lehrman Inst, 76-77. **MEMBERSHIPS** AHA; fel Am Acad Arts Sci. **RESEARCH** Modern European politics. **SELECTED PUBLICATIONS** Politics and Diplomacy of Peacemaking, Knopf, 67; coauth, Historical Thought and American Foreign Policy in the Era of World War I, In: The Historian and the Diplomat, Harper, 67; Churchill: Power Politician and Counterrevolutionary, In: The Responsibility of Power, Doubleday, 67; Domestic Causes of the First World War, In: The Responsibility of Power, Doubleday, 67; auth, Dynamics of Counterrevolution, Touch, 71; contribr, The Lower Middle Class as Historical Problem, J Mod Hist, 75; Internal Crisis and War Since 1870, In: Revolutionary Situations in Europe, 1917-1922, Inter-Univ Ctr Europ Studies, Montreal, 77; auth, Persistence of the Old Regime, Pantheon, 81. **CONTACT ADDRESS** Dept of Hist, Princeton Univ, Princeton, NJ, 08544.

MAYER, HENRI ANDRE VAN HUYSEN
DISCIPLINE HISTORY **EDUCATION** Harvard Univ, BA, 70; Univ Calif, Berkeley, MA, 71, PhD, 73. **CAREER** MEMBER, BD REGENTS, COMM MASS **MEMBERSHIPS** Am Antiquarian Soc **SELECTED PUBLICATIONS** Auth, "Agriculture: The Island Empire," Daedalus, 74; auth, King's Chapel: The First Century, 76; auth, The Crocodile Man: A Case of Brain Chemistry and Criminal Violence, 76. **CONTACT ADDRESS** McCormack Bldg, Rm 619, Boston, MA, 02108.

MAYER, THOMAS F.
PERSONAL Born 09/10/1951, McLeansboro, IL, m, 1983, 1 child **DISCIPLINE** HISTORY **EDUCATION** Mich State Univ, BA, 73, MA, 77; Univ Minn, PhD, 83. **CAREER** Asst prof, Southwest Mo State Univ, 83-85; vis asst prof, Harvard Univ, 89-90; from asst prof to assoc prof to dir, 85-, Augustana Col. **HONORS AND AWARDS** Carl S. Meyer Prize, 78; Exxon Found Fel, 81, 85; Am Counc Learned Societies, Grant in Aid, 87; Gladys Krieble Delmas Found Grant, 92-93; NEH Fel, 92-93; Am Philos Society Grant, 97. **MEMBERSHIPS** Am Hist Asn, 78-; Sixteenth Century Stud Conference, 76-; Society for Reformation Res, 77-; Renaissance Society Am, 80-81, 88-; North Am Conference British Stud, 84-. **RESEARCH** Italian Renaissance and Reformation; comparative European intellectual and cultural history. **SELECTED PUBLICATIONS** Auth, art, A Sticking -plaster Saint: Autobiography and Hagiography in the Making of Reginald Pole, 95; auth, art, A Test of Wills: Cardinal Pole, Ignatius Loyola, and the Jesuits in England, 96; auth, art, Marcello Who? Un Unknown Italian Painter in Cardinal Pole's Entourage, 96; Auth, art, When Maecenas was Broke: Cardinal Pole's Spiritual Patronage, 96; auth, art, Heretics be not in All Things Heretics: Cardinal Pole and the Potential for Toleration, 97. **CONTACT ADDRESS** Dept of History, Augustana Col, Rock Island, IL, 61201-2296. **EMAIL** himayer@augustana.edu

MAYERFELD, JAMIE
DISCIPLINE POLITICAL SCIENCE **EDUCATION** Princeton Univ, PhD, 92. **CONTACT ADDRESS** Political Science, Univ of Washington, PO Box 353530, Seattle, WA, 98195.

MAYERSON, PHILIP
PERSONAL Born 05/20/1918, New York, NY, 2 children **DISCIPLINE** CLASSICS **EDUCATION** NY Univ, AB, 47, PhD, 56. **CAREER** From instr to assoc prof, 48-66, vdean, 70-71, acting dean, 71-73, dean, 73-78, Wash Sq Col & Univ Col; prof, 66-, NY Univ; Rockefeller Found grant-in-aid, 56-57; Am Coun Learned Soc fel, 61-62; adv ed, J Am Res Ctr in Egypt, 69-. **MEMBERSHIPS** Colt Archaeol Inst; Am Philol Assn; Am Res Ctr in Egypt; Am Schls of Oriental Res. **RESEARCH** Ancient history, papyrology, literature and archeology; late antiquity in Egypt lands of the Bible. **SELECTED PUBLICATIONS** Art, A Confusion of Indias: Asian India and African India in the Byzantine Sources, J of Am Oriental Soc 113, 93; art, The Use of Ascalon Wine in the Medical Writers of the Fourth to the Seventh Centuries, Israel Exploration J 43, 93; auth, Aelius Gallus at Cleopatris (Suez) and on the Red Sea, Greek, Roman & Byzantine Stud, Duke Univ, 95; auth, Solving riddles and Untying Knots, Bibl, Epigraphic, and Semitic Stud, in honor Jonas C Greenfield, Eisenbrauns, 95; auth, The Port of Clysma (Suez) in Transition From Roman to Arab Rule, JNES 55, 96; auth, The Role of Flax in Roman and Fatimid Egypt, JNES 56, 97; art, Egeria and Peter the Deacon on the Site of Clysma (Suez), J of Am Res Ctr Egypt, 96; auth, Periplus Maris Erythraei 4: Where Was The Port of Adulis?, Eretz-Israel, Archaeol, Hist & Geographie Stud, vol 25, 96. **CONTACT ADDRESS** Dept of Classics, New York Univ, 25 Waverley Pl, New York, NY, 10003. **EMAIL** pm2@is.nyu.edu

MAYFIELD, JOHN
PERSONAL Born 11/06/1945, TX, m, 1984, 1 child **DISCIPLINE** HISTORY **EDUCATION** Columbia Univ, AB, 68; Johns Hopkins, PhD, 73. **CAREER** Univ Ky, 72-82; Univ Baltimore, 85-95; Samford Univ, 95-. **HONORS AND AWARDS** Ford Found Fel, 72., Cum Laude, Columbia Univ; distinguished dissertation. **MEMBERSHIPS** SHA; SHEAR. **RESEARCH** Old south; southern lit. **SELECTED PUBLICATIONS** Auth, Rehearsal for Republicanism, 80; auth, The New Nation, 1800-1845, 82. **CONTACT ADDRESS** Dept of History, Samford Univ, Birmingham, AL, 35229.

MAYNES, MARY JO
DISCIPLINE HISTORY **EDUCATION** Univ Pa, BA, 71; Univ Mich, PhD, 77. **CAREER** Prof **RESEARCH** German history. **SELECTED PUBLICATIONS** Auth, Schooling For the People, Comparative Local Studies of Schooling History in France and Germany, 1750-1850, Holmes and Meier, 851 Schooling in Western Europe: A Social History, SUNY, 85; Taking the Hard Road: Lifecourse in French and German Workers' Autobiographies of the Industrial Era, Univ NC, 95; coauth, Interpreting Women's Lives, Feminist Theory and Personal Narratives; The European Experience of Declining Fertility, Blackwell, 92; co-ed, German Women in the Eighteenth and Nineteenth Centuries, A Social and Literary History, Univ Ind, 86; Fraun im Osterreich; Gender, Kinship and Power: A Comparative and Interdisciplinary History. **CONTACT ADDRESS** History Dept, Univ of Minnesota, Twin Cities, 614 Social Sciences Tower, 267 19th Ave. S, Minneapolis, MN, 55455. **EMAIL** mayne001@tc.umn.edu

MAZLISH, BRUCE
PERSONAL Born 09/15/1923, New York, NY, m, 4 children **DISCIPLINE** HISTORY, POLITICAL SCIENCE **EDUCATION** Columbia Univ, BA, 44, MA, 47, PhD(hist), 55. **CAREER** Instr hist, Univ Maine, 46-48; lectr, Columbia Univ, 49-50; instr, 50-53, 55-56, from asst prof to assoc prof, 56-65, chmn sect, 65-70, head dept humanities, 74-79, PROF HIST, MASS INST TECHNOL, 65-. Assoc ed, Hist & Theory, 60-70; Soc Sci Res Coun fac fel, 67-68; assoc ed, J Interdisciplinary Hist, 69-; vis mem, Inst Advan Studies, 72-73; mem, Nat Sci Found adv panel, Worcester Polytech Inst, 72-75. **MEMBERSHIPS** Fel Am Acad Arts & Sci; AHA; Int Soc Polit Psych; Group Applied Psychoanal. **RESEARCH** Modern intellectual and social history; personality and politics; psychoanalysis and history. **SELECTED PUBLICATIONS** Auth, A Triptych--Freud the Interpretation of Dreams, Haggard, Rider She, and Bulwerlytton the Coming Race, Comp Stud in Soc and Hist, vol 0035, 93; Inventing Human Science, Amer Hist Rev, vol 0102, 97; Comparing Global History to World History, J Interdisciplinary Hist, vol 0028, 98. **CONTACT ADDRESS** Massachusetts Inst of Tech, 77 Massachusetts Ave, CAMBRIDGE, MA, 02139.

MAZON, MAURICIO
DISCIPLINE HISTORY **EDUCATION** UCLA, PhD, 76; Southern California Psychoanalytic Inst, PhD. **CAREER** Assoc prof & ch; dir, Amer Stud and Ethnicity Prog, Univ Southern Calif. **RESEARCH** Chicano/a History; Psychohistory; American political biography. **SELECTED PUBLICATIONS** Auth, The Zoot-Suit Riots: The Psychology of Symbolic Annihilation, Univ Tex, 84. **CONTACT ADDRESS** Dept of History, Univ Southern Calif, University Park Campus, Los Angeles, CA, 90089. **EMAIL** mazon@bcf.usc.edu

MAZOR, LESTER JAY
PERSONAL Born 12/12/1936, Chicago, IL, m, 1992, 3 children **DISCIPLINE** PHILOSOPHY OF LAW, LEGAL HISTORY **EDUCATION** Stanford Univ, AB, 57, JD, 60. **CAREER** Instr law, Univ Va, 61-62; from asst prof to prof, Univ Utah, 62-70; Henry R Luce prof, 70-75, Prof Law, Hampshire Col, 75-, Reporter, Am Bar Asn Proj Standards Criminal Justice, 65-69; vis assoc prof law, Stanford Univ, 67-68; vis prof, State Univ NY Buffalo, 73-74; proj dir mat study, Am Bar Found Study Legal Educ, 74-. **MEMBERSHIPS** Law & Soc Asn; Int Soc Asn; Am Legal Studies Asn; Int Asn Philos Law & Soc Philos. **RESEARCH** Legal hist; legal and polit theory; future studies. **SELECTED PUBLICATIONS** Ed, Prosecution and Defense Functions, 67 & Providing Defense Services, 70, American Bar Asn; coauth, Introduction to the Study of Law, Found Press, 70; auth, Power and responsibility in the attorney-client relation, Stanford Law Rev, 68; The crisis of liberal legalism, Yale Law J, 72; Disrespect for law, In: Anarchism, NY Univ, 78. **CONTACT ADDRESS** Sch of Soc Sci, Hampshire Col, 893 West St, Amherst, MA, 01002-3359. **EMAIL** lmazor@hampshire.edu

MAZRUI, ALI AL'AMIN
PERSONAL Born 02/24/1933, Mombasa, Kenya, 5 children **DISCIPLINE** POLITICAL SCIENCE; COMPARATIVE POLITICS; AFRICAN POLITICS; ISLAMIC POLITICS; POLITICS & CULTURE **EDUCATION** Univ Manchester, BA, 60; Columbia Univ, MA, 61; Oxford Univ, DPhil, 66. **CAREER** Dir inst Global Cult Studies, Albert Sshweitzer Prof Hum, Prof Polit Sci & Afrincan stud, SUNY-Binghamton; Albert Luthuli Prof-at-large, Univ Jos, Nigeria; Sr scholar Afrocana stud, & Andrew D White Prof-at-latge Emer, Cornell Univ; Ibn Khaldun Ptof-at-large, School of Islamic & soc sci, VA; Walter Rodney prof hist & Governance, Univ Guyana. **HONORS AND AWARDS** Distinguished Africanist Award, 95; 50th Anniversary Distinguished Award, Nat Univ Lesotho, S Af, 95; Distinguished Global Cult Hum Award, 97; DuBois-Garvey Award for Pan-African Unity, Morgan State Univ, 98; Icon of Twentieth Century Award, Lincoln Univ, 98. **RESEARCH** The role of culture, particularly religion and language, in the formation and operation of politics. **SELECTED PUBLICATIONS** Coauth, Swahili, State and Society: The Political Economy of an African Language, E African Educ Publ, 95; Islam and Western Values, Foreign Affairs, 97; Three Stages of Globalization: Mombasa, Cities Fit for People UNDP, 97; The African Diaspora: African Origins and New World Identities, Ind Univ Press, 98; The Power of Babel: Language and Goverance in the African Experience, Iniv Chicago Press, 98; The Scottish Factor in the African Experience: Between Negritude and Scottitude, Jour African Stud, 98; The Failed State and Political Collapse in Africa, Peacemaking and Peacekeeping for the New Century, Rowman & Littlefield Publ, 98; Islam and Afrocentricity: The Triple Heritage School, The Post-colonial Crescent, Peter Lang Publ, 98. **CONTACT ADDRESS** Inst of Global Cult Stud, SUNY, Binghamton, PO Box 6000, Binghamton, NY, 13902-6000. **EMAIL** amazrui@binghamton.edu

MAZZAOUI, MAUREEN FENNELL
PERSONAL Born 08/06/1938, New York, NY **DISCIPLINE** MEDIEVAL AND RENAISSANCE ITALIAN ECONOMIC HISTORY **EDUCATION** Hunter Col, BA, 58; Bryn Mawr Col, MA, 60, PhD(hist), 66. **CAREER** Asst prof hist, Ind Univ, Bloomington, 70-73; asst prof, 73-77, assoc, 77-84, PROF HIST, UNIV WIS-MADISON, 84-. **HONORS AND AWARDS** Fulbright-Hays fel, 67-69; Inst Res Hum fel, 72-73; Villa I tatti fel, 80-81; Div Hist & Philos Sci, NSF, summer fel, 81; ACLS fel, 83-84; mem, Sch Hist Stud, Inst Adv Stud, 83-84. **MEMBERSHIPS** Medieval Acad Am; Soc Ital Hist Studies. **RESEARCH** Medieval, Renaissance Italy; hist textile industry. **SELECTED PUBLICATIONS** Auth, The Weavers Art Revealed--Facsimile, Translation, and Study of the 1st 2 Published Books on Weaving, vol 1, Ziegler, Marx Weber Kunst und Bild Buch, Isis, vol 0084, 93; The Weavers Art Revealed--Facsimile, Translation, and Study of the 1st 2 Published Books on Weaving, vol 2, Lumscher, Nathaniel Neu Eingerichtetes Weber Kunst und Bild Buch, Isis, vol 0084, 93; co- auth, Prospettive nella Storia dell'Industria Tessile Veneta, Trieste, 72; auth, The Italian Cotton Industry in the Later Middle Ages, 1100-1600, Cambridge Univ Press, 81; co-ed, The Other Tuscany: Essays in the History of Lucca, Pisa and Siena during the Thirteenth, Fourteenth and Fifteenth Centuries, The Medieval Inst (Kalamazoo), 94; ed, An Expanding World: Textiles, Production, Trade and Demand, 1450-1800, Ashgate VAriorum, 98.. **CONTACT ADDRESS** Dept of Hist, Univ of Wis, 455 North Park St, Madison, WI, 53706-1483. **EMAIL** Mazzaoui@Facstaff.Wis.Edu

MBODJ, MOHAMED
DISCIPLINE AFRICAN HISTORY **EDUCATION** Univ Dakar, BA, 73; Univ Paris, PhD, 78. **CAREER** Assoc prof. **SELECTED PUBLICATIONS** Auth, The Abolition of Slavery in Senegal, 1820-1890: Crisis or the Rise of a New Entrepreneurial Class?, Slavery, Bondage, and Emancipation in Modern Africa and Asia, 93; Perspectives Historiques, and Dynamiques Regionales, La Population du Senegal, 94; La terre ne ment pas. Exploitation de donnes imparfaites sur l'agriculture ouest-africaine durant la priode coloniale, Conf on the 100th Anniversary Establishment of Fr W Africa, 95. **CONTACT ADDRESS** Dept of Hist, Columbia Col, New York, 2960 Broadway, New York, NY, 10027-6902.

MCAFEE, WARD MERNER
PERSONAL Born 09/20/1939, Salem, OR, m, 1962, 3 children **DISCIPLINE** AMERICAN HISTORY **EDUCATION** Stanford Univ, BA, 61, MA, 62, PhD, 66. **CAREER** From asst prof to assoc prof, 65-73, prof hist, 76-, Dean Soc & Behav Sci 71-74, 75-84; act vice pres, 84-85, Calif State Col, San Bernardino. **HONORS AND AWARDS** CSUSB outstanding prof, 93; **MEMBERSHIPS** Orgn Am Historians; Phi Kappa Phi, **RESEARCH** California history; Civil War and Reconstruction, World Religions. **SELECTED PUBLICATIONS** Auth, Religion, Race and Reconstruction: The Public School in the Politics of the 1870's, SUNY Press, 98. **CONTACT ADDRESS** Dept of History, California State Univ, San Bernardino, 5500 University Pky, San Bernardino, CA, 92407-7500. **EMAIL** wmcafee@wiley.csusb.edu

MCALEER, J. PHILIP
PERSONAL Born 06/16/1935, New York, NY **DISCIPLINE** ARCHITECTURAL HISTORIAN **EDUCATION** Columbia Univ, BA, 56; Princeton Unif, MFA, 59; Univ London, PhD, 63. **CAREER** Tchr, 61-; prof, Dalhousie Univ. **HONORS AND AWARDS** Fel, Soc of Antiq of London. **MEMBERSHIPS** CAA; ICMA; SAH; SAH-GB; RAI; BAA; Avista. **RESEARCH** Medieval architecture. **SELECTED PUBLICATIONS** Auth, A Pictorial History of St. Paul's Anglican Church, Halifax, Nova Scotia, Technical Univ of Nova Scotia, 93; "The Former Benedictine Abbey Church of St. Mary and St. Modwen (Modwenna) at Burton-on Trent and the Problem of a West Transept There," Staffordshire Stud, 93; "The Facade of Norwich Cathedral," Norfolk Arch, 93; "Rochester Cathedral: The North Choir Aisle and the Space between it and 'Gundulf's' Tower," Archaeologia Cantiana, 93; "The Romanesque Facade of Winchester Cathedral," Proc of the Hampshire Field Club and Archaeol Soc, 96; "Some Observations about the Romanesque Choir of Ely Cathedral," Jrnl of the Soc of Archit Historians, 94; "Encore Lindisfarne Priory and the Problems of Its Nave Vault," The Antiq Jrnl, 94; "Towards an Architectural History of Kilwinning Abbey," Proc of the Soc of Antiq of Scotland, 95; "The Facade of Norwich Cathedral as It Might Have Been," Norfolk Archaeol, 97; "L.N. Cottingham's Central Tower for Rochester Cathedral: A Question of Style," Archaeol Jrnl, 97; "The So-called Gundulf's Tower at Rochester Cathedral. A Reconsideration of its History," Antiq Jrnl, 98. **CONTACT ADDRESS** 98 Bedford Hills Rd, Bedford, NS, B4A 1J9.

MCBETH, HARRY LEON
PERSONAL m **DISCIPLINE** CHURCH HISTORY **EDUCATION** Wayland Baptist Univ, BA, 54; Southwestern Baptist Theol Sem, MDiv, 57, ThD, 61. **CAREER** Distinguished prof, Southwestern Baptist Theol sem, 60-. **HONORS AND AWARDS** Outstanding Young Men Am, 66, Pastor, First Baptist Church, 55-60. **MEMBERSHIPS** S Baptist Hist Soc; Amer Soc Church Hist. **SELECTED PUBLICATIONS** Auth, The Baptist Heritage: Four Centuries of Baptist Witness, Broadman Press, 87; A Sourcebook for Baptist Heritage, Broadman Press, 90; Texas Baptists: A Sesquicentennial History, Baptist Way Press, 98. **CONTACT ADDRESS** Sch Theol, Southwestern Baptist Theol Sem, PO Box 22000, Fort Worth, TX, 76122-0418. **EMAIL** hlm@swbts.swbts.edu

MCBRIDE, MARGARET
DISCIPLINE FINE ARTS AND HUMANITIES **EDUCATION** Univ KS, BA; Univ PA, MA, PhD. **CAREER** Assoc prof; dir, Grad Prog & Grad Adv Record, 78-81 & 88-. **HONORS AND AWARDS** Facu Res Leave, 97; UTSA Fac Res Awd, 83; Col of Fine Arts Awd, 92; Hum Travel Grant, 93; AMOCO Awd, 87. **RESEARCH** James Joyce. **SELECTED PUBLICATIONS** Publ on James Joyce, in The James Joyce Quart, Joyce Stud Annual, JEGP. **CONTACT ADDRESS** Col of Fine Arts and Hum, Univ Texas at San Antonio, 6900 N Loop 1604 W, San Antonio, TX, 78249.

MCBRIDE, PAUL WILBERT
PERSONAL Born 05/23/1940, Youngstown, OH, m, 1962, 3 children **DISCIPLINE** UNITED STATES HISTORY, ETHNIC STUDIES **EDUCATION** Youngstown State Univ, BA, 63; Kans State Univ, MA, 65; Univ Ga, PhD(hist), 72. **CAREER** Instr hist, Augusta Col, 67; asst prof, 70-74, assoc prof Hist, Ithaca Col, 74-, Dana Teaching fel, 82. **MEMBERSHIPS** Orgn Am Historians; Immigration Hist Asn; Hist Educ Asn. **RESEARCH** Twentieth-century United States history; United States ethnic history; Italian American studies. **SELECTED PUBLICATIONS** Auth, The co-op industrial education experiment, Hist Educ Quart, summer 74; Culture Clash: Immigrants and Reformers 1880-1920, R & E Res Assocs, 75; Peter Roberts and the YMCA Americanization Program, Pa Hist, 4/77; Daniel Bell and the permissive society, summer 77, Occas Rev; Manipulated schools, manipulated history, Hist Educ Quart, spring 79; Masters of their fate, J Ethnic Studies, 11/79; The solitary Christians: Italian Americans and their church, 12/81 & Reflections on dreams and memories, summer 82, Ethnic Groups. **CONTACT ADDRESS** Dept of History, Ithaca Col, Ithaca, NY, 14850-7002. **EMAIL** McBride@Ithaca.edu

MCBRIDE, THERESA MARIE
PERSONAL Born 11/07/1947, Seattle, WA **DISCIPLINE** EUROPEAN SOCIAL AND MODERN FRENCH HISTORY **EDUCATION** Seattle Univ, BA, 69; Rutgers Univ, New Brunswick, MA, 70, PhD(hist), 73. **CAREER** Asst prof, 73-79, ASSOC PROF HIST, COL OF THE HOLY CROSS, 79-, Fel, Nat Endowment Humanities, 81-82. **MEMBERSHIPS** AHA; Europ Labor & Working Class Hist; Marxist Historians Asn; Fr Hist Studies Asn. **RESEARCH** French history, 19th and 20th centuries; comparative social history. **SELECTED PUBLICATIONS** Auth, Taste and Power--Furnishing Modern France, J Soc Hist, vol 0031, 97; Country House Life--Family and Servants, 1815-1914, Amer Hist Rev, vol 0102, 97. **CONTACT ADDRESS** Dept of Hist, Col of the Holy Cross, 1 College St, Worcester, MA, 01610-2322.

MCBRIER, VIVIAN FLAGG
PERSONAL Lynchburg, VA, w **DISCIPLINE** MUSIC **EDUCATION** VA State Coll, BS Music, BS El Educ 1937; Columbia U, MA Music 1941; Cath Univ of Am, PhD Musicology 1967. **CAREER** DC Tchr Coll, prof, mnr Tchr 1944-72; Hampton Inst, tchr 1945-46; Pub Sch Lynchburg, VA, 1937-44; Cath Univ, lecturer 1971-72; Sch of Religion Howard U, lectr 1973-76. **HONORS AND AWARDS** Alpha Kappa Alpha Achvmnt Award. **MEMBERSHIPS** Dir Coll Choir & num ch choirs in DC; lecturer Niagara Falls NY & Canada. **SELECTED PUBLICATIONS** R Nathaniel Dett His Life & Works, 1974; numerous articles.

MCCAA, ROBERT
DISCIPLINE HISTORY **EDUCATION** Univ Calif Los Angeles, PhD, 78. **CAREER** Prof **RESEARCH** Latin American history; sexual violence; changing status of Mexican women; quantitative history and demography. **SELECTED PUBLICATIONS** Auth, Marriage and Fertility in Chile: Demographic Turning Points in the Petorca Valley, 1840-1976, 83; ed, Latin American Population History Bulletin. **CONTACT ADDRESS** History Dept, Univ of Minnesota, Twin Cities, 614 Social Sciences Tower, 267 19th Ave. S, Minneapolis, MN, 55455. **EMAIL** rmccaa@tc.umn.edu

MCCAFFREY, DANIEL
DISCIPLINE DEPARTMENT OF CLASSICS **EDUCATION** Fordham Univ, AB, 68; Pa State Univ, MA, 69; Univ Mich, PhD, 74. **CAREER** Vis asst prof, Hope Col, 74-75; prof, Randolph-Macon Col, 75-. **HONORS AND AWARDS** NEH Summer Inst, Ohio State Univ, 83; NEH Summer Inst, Univ Southern Calif, 87; Dana fel, Carnegie Mellon Univ, 88-89., Mem, Va's Lat textbk adoption comt, 90. **MEMBERSHIPS** Mem, Bd of Dir, Class Asn of Va 91-95; mem, APA Comt on Comput Activ, 91-94; mem, APA Subcomt on Assessment, 91-95; Comt mem, For Lang Asn of Va, 96-97. **SELECTED PUBLICATIONS** Auth, Some Dangers in the Uncritical Use of CAI in the Classroom, in Computer-Aided Instruction in the Humanities, ed by Solveig Olsen, MLA, 85; Teaching Ancient Languages with the Computer, Prospects, Summer, 92; coauth, Building Collegiality through Co-operative Programs, CJ 83, 88. **CONTACT ADDRESS** Dept of Class, Randolph-Macon Col, Ashland, VA, 23005-5505.

MCCAFFREY, JAMES M.
PERSONAL Born 05/10/1946, Springfield, IL, m **DISCIPLINE** CIVIL ENGINEERING **EDUCATION** Univ of Mo at Rolla, BS, 70; Univ of Houston, ME, 74, MA, 87, PhD, 90. **CAREER** Lectr, 89-91, asst prof, 91-95, assoc prof, Univ Houston, 95-. **HONORS AND AWARDS** USMA/ROTC Fel IN Military Hist, 91. **MEMBERSHIPS** Soc for Military Hist. **RESEARCH** American military history. **SELECTED PUBLICATIONS** Auth, This Band of Heroes: Granbury's Texas Brigade, C.S.A., Eakin Press, 85, Tx A&M Univ Press, 96; Army of Manifest Destiny: The American Soldier in the Mexican War, 1846-1848, NY Univ Press, 92; Surrounded by Dangers of All Kinds: The Mexican War Letters of Lieutenant Theodore Laidley, Univ of N Tex Press, 97; coauth, Wake Island Pilot: A World War II Memoir, Brassey's, 95. **CONTACT ADDRESS** History Dept, Univ of Houston--Downtown, 1 Main St, Houston, TX, 77002. **EMAIL** McCaffreyJ@zeus.dt.uh.edu

MCCAFFREY, LAWRENCE JOHN
PERSONAL Born 08/10/1925, Riverdale, IL, m, 1949, 3 children **DISCIPLINE** HISTORY **EDUCATION** St Ambrose Col, BA, 49; Ind Univ, MA, 50; Univ Iowa, PhD(hist), 54. **CAREER** Instr hist, Univ Iowa, 50-54, vis lectr, 58-59; instr humanities, Mich State Univ, 54-55; assoc prof hist, Col St Catherine, 55-58; from asst prof to assoc prof, Univ Ill, 59-64; prof, Marquette Univ, 64-69; prof, Univ Maine, Orono, 69-70; chmn dept, 70-73, PROF HIST, LOYOLA UNIV CHICAGO 70-, Ed, Regnery-Gateway's Irish Studies ser. **MEMBERSHIPS** AHA; Am Cath Hist Asn; Am Comt Irish Studies (secy, 58-68, vpres, 72-75, pres, 75-78); Conf Brit Studies. **RESEARCH** Irish nationalism and Irish literature, 1800 to the present; politics and culture of Irish Catholicism; the Irish-American experience. **SELECTED PUBLICATIONS** Auth, Ideology and the Irish Question--Ulster Unionism and Irish Nationalism, Albion, vol 0027, 95; Piety and Nationalism--Lay Voluntary Associations and the Creation of an Irish Catholic Community in Toronto, 1850-1895, J Ecclesiastical Hist, vol 0046, 95; The Orange Riots--Irish Political Violence in New York City, 1870 and 1871, Cath Hist Rev, vol 0081, 95. **CONTACT ADDRESS** Dept of Hist, Loyola Univ, Chicago, IL, 60611.

MCCALL, MARSH H., JR.
DISCIPLINE CLASSICS **EDUCATION** BA, 60; Harvard Univ, PhD, 65. **CAREER** Prof class and dean cont studies/ summer sess, Stanford Univ. **RESEARCH** Greek lit; Greek tragedy; rhetoric; lit and textual criticism. **SELECTED PUBLICATIONS** Auth, Ancient Rhetorical Theories of Simile and Comparison,69; The Chorus of Aeschylus' Choephori in Cabinet of Muses: Essays in Honor of Thomas G. Rosenmeyer, 90; ed, Aeschylus, A Collection of Critical Essays, 72. **CONTACT ADDRESS** Stanford Univ, Bldg 20, Main Quad, Stanford, CA, 94305.

MCCALMAN, IAIN

DISCIPLINE CULTURAL HISTORY **EDUCATION** Australian Natl Univ; Monash Univ. **CAREER** Dep dir, Ctr Cross-Cult Res; dir, Hum Res Ctr, Australian Natl Univ; vis fels, Manchester Univ, Oxford, Inst Advanced Studies in the Humanities, Edinburgh Univ, Wash Univ, St Louis, and Res Sch Social Sciences, Australian Natl Univ. In 1992 he received the Vice-Chancellor's Award for Teaching Excellence (ANU). **HONORS AND AWARDS** Vice-Chancellor's Award for Teaching Excellence, Australian Natl Univ, 92., FRHS, FASSA, FAHA. **RESEARCH** 18th and 19th century cultural history. **SELECTED PUBLICATIONS** Auth, Radical Underworld: prophets, revolutionaries and pornographers in London, 1795-1840, Cambridge Univ, 88, repr, Clarendon Oxford Univ, 93; Horrors of Slavery: the life and writings of Robert Wedderburn, Edinburgh Univ, Martin Wiener Press, 92; The Oxford Companion to the Romantic Age, pending; Newgate Romanticism, Clarendon Press, pending; co-ed, Literature of Travel and Empires, pending; ed, The Age of Romanticism and Revolution: An Oxford Companion to British Culture, 1776-1832, pending; auth, Grub Street in Revolution: romanticism, popular politics and culture, 1780-1848, Oxford Univ, pending; co-ed, Axe to the Root: an anthology of popular political satire, 1789-1822, Oxford Univ, pending. **CONTACT ADDRESS** Dept of Education, Australian National Univ. **EMAIL** Iain.McCalman@anu.edu.au

MCCANN, FRANCIS D., JR.

PERSONAL Born 12/15/1938, Lackawanna, NY, 2 children **DISCIPLINE** HISTORY **EDUCATION** Ind Univ, PhD. **CAREER** Prof, Univ NH, 71-. **HONORS AND AWARDS** Fulbright-Hays fel; Nat Hist Publ Comn fel; Am Philos Soc grants; Joint Soc Sci Res Coun and Am Coun of Learned Soc fel; vis scholar, Woodrow Wilson Int Ctr for Scholars; Heinz Endowment Grant; Herbert E. Bolton Mem Honorable Mention Award, Conf on Latin Am Hist; Stuart L Bernath Prize, Soc for Hist of Am For Rel; New Eng Coun on Latin Am Stud Prize; Nat Univ Cont Educ Asn Prize; Pacificador Medal, Brazil. **MEMBERSHIPS** Corresp mem, Inst de Geografia e Hist Militar do Brasil and Inst do Ceara Comendador Order of Rio Branco, Brazil. **RESEARCH** Brazil and the United States. **SELECTED PUBLICATIONS** Auth, The Brazilian-American Alliance, 1937-1945, 73; A Nacao Armada: Ensaios Sobre a Historia do Exercito Brasileiro, 82; ed and contribur, Modern Brazil: Elites and masses in Historical Perspective, 89-91. **CONTACT ADDRESS** Univ NH, Durham, NH, 03824. **EMAIL** fdm@christa.unh.edu

MCCARL, MARY F.R.

DISCIPLINE HISTORY **EDUCATION** Radcliffe, BA, 61; Harvard Univ, MA, 66; Simmons, MLS, 79; Univ Mass Boston, MA, 82. **CAREER** IND SCHOLAR **MEMBERSHIPS** Am Antiquarian Soc **RESEARCH** Thomas Shepard **SELECTED PUBLICATIONS** Auth, "Thomas Shepard's Record of Religious Experiences, 1648-1649," Wm and Mary Q, 91; auth, "Spreading the News of Satan's Malignity in Salem: Benjamin Harris, Printer and Publisher of the Witchcraft Narratives," Essex Inst Hist Colls 129, 93; auth, The Plowman's Tale: The circa 1532 and 1606 editions of a spurious Canterbury Tale, Garland, 97; auth, "Publishing the Works of Nicholas Culpeper in Seventeenth Century London," Canad Bulletin Med Hist. **CONTACT ADDRESS** 1828 Mission Rd., Vestabia Hills, AL, 35216-2229. **EMAIL** mrmccarl@mail.business.uab.edu

MCCARREN, VINCENT PAUL

PERSONAL Born 03/22/1939, New York, NY, m, 1968 **DISCIPLINE** CLASSICAL STUDIES, MEDIEVAL LITERATURE **EDUCATION** Fordham Univ, AB, 60; Columbia Univ, AM, 67; Univ Mich, PhD(class studies), 75. **CAREER** Lectr Greek & Latin, Brooklyn Col, 63-68; instr, Hunter Col, 68-69, class lang & lit, Herbert H Lehman Col, 69-70; Icctr Greek & Latin, 75-76, acad coun gen acad areas, 77-78, RESEARCHER, MIDDLE ENGLISH DICT, UNIV MICH, 79-. **MEMBERSHIPS** Am Soc Papyrologists; Am Philol Soc. **RESEARCH** Documentary papyrology; Greek and Latin etymological studies. **SELECTED PUBLICATIONS** Aith, The Tanner Bede--The Old English Version of Bede 'Historia Ecclesiastica', Oxford Bodleian Library Tanner 10, Together With the Mediaeval Binding Leaves, Oxford Bodleian Library 10, and the Domitian Extracts, London British Libra, Speculum; Bristol University Ms Dm 1, a Fragment of the 'Medulla Grammaticae'--an dd, Traditio Stud in Ancient and Medieval Hist Thought and Relig, vol 0048, 93. **CONTACT ADDRESS** Middle English Dict, Univ Michigan, 555 S Forest, Ann Arbor, MI, 48109.

MCCARTHY, DENNIS MICHAEL PATRICK

PERSONAL Born 01/02/1944, East Cleveland, OH **DISCIPLINE** ECONOMIC HISTORY, BUSINESS HISTORY **EDUCATION** Boston Col, BA, 66; Yale Univ, MA, 70, PhD(econ hist prog), 72. **CAREER** Asst prof, 72-79, ASSOC PROF HIST, IOWA STATE UNIV, 79-. **MEMBERSHIPS** Econ Hist Asn; Econ Hist Soc; African Studies Asn; AHA. **RESEARCH** Comparative African colonial bureaucracies; implications for economic change past and present; history of under development. **SELECTED PUBLICATIONS** Auth, Media as ends: money and the under-development of Tanganyika to 1940, J Econ Hist, 9/76; Organizing Under-Development from the inside: The Bureaucratic Economy in Tanganyika, 1919-40, Int J African Hist Studies, 10/77; Language Manipulation in Colonial Tanganyika, 1919-40, J African Studies, 6/79; Colonial Bureaucracy and Creating Underdevelopment: Tanganyika, 1919-1940, Iowa State Univ Press, 82. **CONTACT ADDRESS** Dept of Hist, Iowa State Univ, Ames, IA, 50011-0002.

MCCAUGHEY, ROBERT ANTHONY

PERSONAL Born 04/13/1939, Pawtucket, RI, m, 2 children **DISCIPLINE** AMERICAN HISTORY **EDUCATION** Univ Rochester, BA, 61; Univ NC, MA, 65; Harvard Univ, PhD(hist), 70. **CAREER** Asst prof, 69-74, assoc prof, 74-80, PROF HIST, 80- , DEAN OF FACULTY, 87-93, BARNARD COL, COLUMBIA UNIV;fel, Charles Warren Ctr Studies Am Hist, 72-73; Guggenheim fel, 75-76. **MEMBERSHIPS** AHA **RESEARCH** History of American higher education; intellectual history. **SELECTED PUBLICATIONS** Auth, From Town to City: Boston in the 1820's, Polit Sci Quart, 73; Josiah Quincy: The Last Federalist, Harvard Univ, 74; The Transformation of American Academic life: Harvard University, 1821-1892, Perspectives Am Hist, 74; American University Teachers and Opposition to the Vietnam War: A Reconsideration, Minerva, 76; Four Academic Ambassadors: International Studies and the American University Before the Second World War, Perspectives in Am Hist, 79; In the Land of the Blind: American International Studies in the 1930s, The Annals of the Am Acad Polit & Soc Sci, 80; The Current Stake of International Studies: Special Consideration Reconsidered, J Higher Educ, 80; Am International Studies: The History of an Intellectual Enterprise, Columbia Univ, 84; auth, Scholars and Teachers: The Faculties of Select Liberal Arts Colleges and Their Place in American Higher Learning, Mellon Found, 95. **CONTACT ADDRESS** Dept of History, Barnard Col, 3009 Broadway, New York, NY, 10027-6598.

MCCLAIN, ANDREW BRADLEY

PERSONAL Born 11/12/1948, Akron, OH **DISCIPLINE** EDUCATION **EDUCATION** Univ of Akron, Akron, OH JD 1984-88; Kent State Univ Kent, OH, M Ed 1976-78; Univ of Akron Akron, OH, BA 1966-70. **CAREER** Akron Bd of Educ, English teacher 1970-73; Western Reserve Acad, dir upward bound 1973-87; The Univ of Akron, dir upward bound 1987; Western Reserve Academy, Hudson, OH, dir Upward Bound 1973-87; UNIV OF AKRON, dir pre college programs, 1988, DIR OF ACADEMIC ACHIEVEMENT PROGRAMS, currently; PRIVATE PRACTICE, ATTY. **HONORS AND AWARDS** Fellowship Natl Assoc of Independent Schools 1982; Fellowship Inst for Educational Leadership 1982-; Ohio Assn of Educational Opportunity Program Personnel OAEOPP, James Rankin Award, 1990. **MEMBERSHIPS** Consultant A Better Chance 1975-86; dir School Scholarship Serv 1979-84; consultant Mid-South Assoc of Independent Schools 1981-83, Marquette Univ 1984; mem former dir and pres state chap MAEOPP; mem NAACP; consultant, Natl Council of Educational Opportunity Assn, (NCEOA); parlamentarian, NCEOA, 1993-94; treasurer, Education Foundation Mid American Assn, Educ Opportunity Probram Personnel (MAEOPP), 1992-95; mem, African Amer Male Commission, 1989-. **CONTACT ADDRESS** Academic Achievement Program, Univ of Akron, Gallucci Hall 112, Akron, OH, 44325-7908.

MCCLAIN, JOHN O.

DISCIPLINE OPERATIONS RESEARCH **EDUCATION** Yale Univ, PhD, 70. **CAREER** Sch Management, Cornell Univ **CONTACT ADDRESS** SC Johnson Grad Sch of Management, Cornell Univ, Sage Hall, Ithaca, NY, 14853.

MCCLAIN, MOLLY A.

PERSONAL Born 10/19/1966, San Diego, CA **DISCIPLINE** HISTORY **EDUCATION** Univ Chicago, BA, 87; Yale, PhD, 94. **CAREER** Asst prof, Univ San Diego, 95-. **HONORS AND AWARDS** Andrew W. Mellon Dissertation Fel; Mellon Found Res Fel; Jacob K. Javits Grad Fel. **MEMBERSHIPS** AHA; ASECS; NACBS; Phi Alpha Theta **RESEARCH** Britain and colonial American; history of science. **SELECTED PUBLICATIONS** Auth, art, The Wentwood Forest Riot: Property Rights and Political Culture in Restoration England, 95; auth, art, The Duke of Beaufort's Tory Progress Through Wales, 1684, 97; co-auth, Schaum's Quick Guide to Writing Great Essays, 98. **CONTACT ADDRESS** Dept of History, Univ of San Diego, 5998 Alcala Pk, San Diego, CA, 92110. **EMAIL** mmcclain@acusd.edu

MCCLAIN, SHIRLA R.

PERSONAL Born 02/04/1935, Akron, Ohio, m, 1957 **DISCIPLINE** EDUCATION **EDUCATION** Univ of Akron, Akron OH, BS, 1956, MS, 1970, PhD, 1975. **CAREER** Akron Public School, Akron OH, teacher and supervisor, 1956-76; Kent State University, Kent OH, prof of education, 1976-87; Walsh University, North Canton OH, prof of education, 1987-; asst director of teacher preparation, 1990-. **HONORS AND AWARDS** Achievement award, Akron Urban League, 1975; distinguished black alumna award, Black Alumna Assoc of Univ of Akron, 1986; lifetime achievement award, Black United Students, Walsh College, 1988; distinguished educator award, Multicultural Education Special Interest Group of the Assn of Teacher Educators, 1989; Akron Grassroots Activist Award, University of Akron's Afro-American Studies, 1991; Alumni Honor Award for Excellence in Professional Achievement, Univ of Akron, 1994; Inducted into the Consortium of Doctors, Savannah GA, 1994. **MEMBERSHIPS** Mem, Assn of Teacher Educators, 1984-87, 1989-; mem, Univ of Akron Black Cultural Center advisory board, 1987. **SELECTED PUBLICATIONS** Author of numerous monographs, book chapters, and reviews. **CONTACT ADDRESS** Professor of Education, Walsh Univ, 2020 Easton St N W, Farrell Hall 212, Canton, OH, 44720.

MCCLAY, WILFRED M.

PERSONAL Born 07/12/1951, Champaign, IL, m, 1983, 2 children **DISCIPLINE** UNITED STATES HISTORY **EDUCATION** St John's Col, BA, 74; Johns Hopkins Univ, PhD, 87. **CAREER** Vis instr, Towson State Univ, 85-86; asst prof, Univ of Dallas, 86-87; from asst prof to assoc prof, Tulane Univ, 87- ; vis prof, Georgetown Univ, 98-99. **HONORS AND AWARDS** Danforth Grad fel, 80-84; Nat Acad of Educ, Spencer Postdoctoral fel, 93-94; Merle Curti Award in Intellectual Hist, Org of Am Hists, 95; Fac Res Award, Tulane Univ, 96; Univ Profs fel, Nat Endowment for the Hums, 97-98; Woodrow Wilson fel, Int Ctr for Scholars, 97-98; Templeton Honor Rolls, J.Templeton Found, 97-98; app to Royden B. Davis Ch in Interdisciplinary Studies, Georgetown Univ, 98. **MEMBERSHIPS** Am Hist Asn; Org of Am Hists; The Hist Soc. **RESEARCH** The intellectual and cultural history of the United States. **SELECTED PUBLICATIONS** Auth, The Strange Career of The Lonely Crowd: Or, The Antinomies of Automomy, The Culture of the Market: Historical Essays, eds T. L. Haskell and R. F. Teichgraeber, 93; John W. Burgess and the Search for Cohesion in American Political Thought, Polity, vol 26, no 1, 93; The Hipster and the Organization Man, First Things, no 43, 94; The Masterless: Self and Society in Modern America, 94; The Socialization of Desire, Society, vol 32, no 4, 95; Edward Bellamy and the Politics of Meaning, Am Scholar, vol 64, no 2, 95; Where Have We Come Since the 1950s? Thoughts on Materialism and American Social Character, Rethinking Materialism: Perspectives on the Spiritual Dimension of Economic Behavior, ed R. Wuthnow, 95; The Soul of Man Under Federalism, First Things, no 64, 96; Filling the Hollow Core: Religious Faith and the Postmodern University, The New Religious Humanists: A Reader, ed G. Wolfe, 97; Mr Emerson's Tombstone, First Things, no 83, 98; The Lonely Crowd at Fifty, Wilson Quart, vol 22, no 3, 98; Is America an Experiment, The Public Interest, no 133, 98. **CONTACT ADDRESS** Dept of History, Tulane Univ, New Orleans, LA, 70118. **EMAIL** mcclay@mailhost.tcs.tulane.edu

MCCLEARY, ANN

DISCIPLINE HISTORY **EDUCATION** Brown Univ, PhD, 96. **CAREER** Asst prof. **RESEARCH** American women history; early American history; American architecture; American material culture. **SELECTED PUBLICATIONS** Auth, pubs on vernacular architecture. **CONTACT ADDRESS** History Dept, State Univ of West Georgia, Carrollton, GA, 30118. **EMAIL** amcclear@westga.edu

MCCLELLAN, CHARLES W.

PERSONAL Born 06/16/1945, Brooklyn, NY **DISCIPLINE** AFRICAN & THIRD WORLD HISTORY **EDUCATION** Emporia State Univ, BSE, 67; Michigan State Univ, MA, 71, PhD(hist), 78. **CAREER** Asst prof hist, Murray State Univ, Ky, 79; asst prof, State Univ NY, Plattsburgh, 79-80; prof hist, Radford Univ, 80-98; Africa bk rev ed, Int J Oral Hist, 82. **HONORS AND AWARDS** Am Council of Learned Societies grant in Aid, 89; Fulbright-Hays Research Award, 90; 2nd Vpres and member of Board of Trustees, Pi Gamma Mu, 90; Int observer for Ethiopian elections, 92. **MEMBERSHIPS** African Studies Asn; Am Assoc Univ Profs; National Council of Returned Peace Corps Volunteers. **RESEARCH** History 19th and 20th century Ethiopia, with special interest in the south; history and social anthropology of East Africa; underdevelopment theory as related to Africa. **SELECTED PUBLICATIONS** Coauth, A note on Ethiopianist source material in Chicago's Field Museum of Natural History, Ethiopianist Notes, Vol II, 78; auth, Perspective on the Neftenya-Gabbar system--the example of Darasa, Africa, Rome, Vol XXXIII, 78; The Ethiopian occupation of northern Sidamo--recruitment and motivation, Proc 5th Int Conf Ethiopian Studies, 79; Land, labor and coffee--the South's role in Ethiopian self-reliance, 1889-1935, African Econ Hist, Vol IX, 80; Observations on the Ethiopian Nation, Its Nationalism, and the Italo-Ethiopian War, Northeast African Studies, New Series, 96; The Tales of Yoseph & Woransa: Gedeo Experiences in the Era of the Italo-Ethopian War, (in press). **CONTACT ADDRESS** Dept of History, Radford Univ, PO Box 6941, Radford, VA, 24142-6941. **EMAIL** cmcclell@runet.edu

MCCLELLAN, WOODFORD

PERSONAL Born 03/20/1934, Martinsville, IL, d, 3 children **DISCIPLINE** MODERN RUSSIAN & EASTERN EUROPEAN HISTORY **EDUCATION** Stanford Univ, AB, 57, MA, 58; Univ Calif, Berkeley, PhD, 63. **CAREER** From instr to asst prof hist, US Mil Acad, 61-65; assoc prof, 65-72, fel, Ctr Advan Studies, 71-72, PROF HIST, UNIV VA, 72-, Am Coun Learned Soc grant, 67-68; Nat Endowment for Humanities fel, 67-68; Am Coun Learned Soc & Acad Sci USSR exchange scholar humanities & soc sci, 73-74. **MEMBERSHIPS** AHA; Am Asn Advan Slavic Studies. **RESEARCH** History of Russia; history of socialist thought and movements. **SELECTED PUBLICATIONS** Auth, Svetozar Markovic, Princeton Univ, 64; Serbia and social democracy, Int Rev Social Hist, 66; Postwar political evolution of Yugoslavia, Contemporary Yugoslavia, Univ Calif, 69; Nechaevshchina: An unknown chapter, Slavic Rev, 9/73; Revolutionary Exiles: The Russians in the First International and the Paris Commune, Frank Cass, London, 78; Russia: The Soviet Period and After, 4th Ed, Prentice Hall, 98. **CONTACT ADDRESS** Dept Hist, Univ Va, 1 Randall Hall, Charlottesville, VA, 22903-3244. **EMAIL** wdm@virginia.edu

MCCLELLAND, CHARLES E.
DISCIPLINE GERMAN HISTORY **EDUCATION** Princeton Univ, AB, 62; Yale Univ, MA, 63, PhD, 67. **CAREER** Instr, Princeton Univ, 66-68; asst prof, Univ Pa, 68-74; assoc to full, 74-97, PROF EMER, 98-, UNIV NMEX. **CONTACT ADDRESS** 1002 Richmond Dr NE, Albuquerque, NM, 87106. **EMAIL** cemcc@unm.edu

MCCLELLAND, JAMES
DISCIPLINE HISTORY OF MODERN RUSSIA **EDUCATION** Princeton Univ, PhD, 70. **CAREER** Assoc prof, Univ Nebr, Lincoln. **RESEARCH** The relationship between the Russian revolution and education. **SELECTED PUBLICATIONS** Auth, Autocrats and Academics: Education, Culture and Society in Tsarist Russia, Univ Chicago Press, 79. **CONTACT ADDRESS** Univ Nebr, Lincoln, 604 Oldfat, Lincoln, NE, 68588-0417. **EMAIL** jcm@unlinfo.unl.edu

MCCLELLAND, WILLIAM LESTER
PERSONAL Born 08/25/1924 **DISCIPLINE** HISTORY OF CHRISTIANITY **EDUCATION** Westminster Col, BA, 48; Pittsburgh Theol Sem, BD, 51, ThM, 56; Princeton Theol Sem, PhD(hist theol), 67. **CAREER** Pastor, Knox United Presby Church, Des Moines, 51-53; pastor, Avalon United Presby Church, Pittsburgh, 53-56; from asst prof to assoc prof, 56-71, dir honors, 67-72, trustee, Bd Trustees, 76-77, chmn dept, 68-74, PROF RELIG, MUSKINGUM COL, 71, CHMN DEPT RELIG & PHILOS, 77, Coordr, Div Arts & Humanities, 81-, Vis lectr, Westminster Col, Eng, 67; Am Col Switz, 69. **MEMBERSHIPS** Am Soc Church Hist; Am Acad Relig; Soc Liturgica; AAUP. **RESEARCH** American religious experience as compared with European religious experience; Reformation history; liturgical history. **SELECTED PUBLICATIONS** Auth, Underhill, Evelyn--Artist of the Infinite Life, Church Hist, vol 0063, 94. **CONTACT ADDRESS** Dept of Relig & Philos, Muskingum Col, New Concord, OH, 43762.

MCCLESKY, TURK
DISCIPLINE HISTORY **EDUCATION** Univ Texas Austin, 75; Col of William and Mary, PhD 90. **CAREER** Oakland Univ, asst prof 90-93; Virginia Military Inst, asst prof, assoc prof, 94 to 98-. **CONTACT ADDRESS** Dept of History, Virginia Military Institute, 103 Ivy Dr Apt 6, Charlottesville, VA, 22903.

MCCLINTOCK, THOMAS COSHOW
PERSONAL Born 10/06/1923, Lebanon, OR, m, 1954, 3 children **DISCIPLINE** UNITED STATES HISTORY **EDUCATION** Stanford Univ, AB, 49; Columbia Univ, MA, 50; Univ Wash, PhD(US intellectual hist), 59. **CAREER** From instr to assoc prof US Hist, 59-70, actg chmn dept hist, 67-68 & 71-72, PROF US HIST, ORE STATE UNIV, 70-, CHMN DEPT HIST, 72-, Danforth assoc, 69-; vis prof, Univ Manchester, 70 & Univ Stirling, 71; mem, Ore Comt for Humanities, 75-81. **MEMBERSHIPS** Orgn Am Historians; Western Hist Asn. **RESEARCH** The American frontier; the progressive movement; Oregon history. **SELECTED PUBLICATIONS** Auth, An Arrow in the Earth, J West, vol 0032, 93; Saules, James, Burnett, Peter, and the Oregon Black Exclusion Law of June 1844, Pac Northwest Quart, vol 0086, 95; Astorian Adventure--Journal of Seton, Alfred, 1811-1815, J West, vol 0035, 96; Fire at Edens Gate--Mccall, Tony and the Oregon Story, Pac Northwest Quart, vol 0088, 97. **CONTACT ADDRESS** Dept of Hist, Oregon State Univ, Corvallis, OR, 97331.

MCCLOSKEY, DEIRDRE
PERSONAL Born 09/11/1942, Ann Arbor, MI, d, 2 children **DISCIPLINE** ECONOMICS **EDUCATION** Harvard Col, BA, 64; Harvard Univ, PhD, 70. **CAREER** From asst prof to assoc prof, Univ Chicago, 68-80; prof hist & econ, Univ Iowa, 80-. **HONORS AND AWARDS** Guggenheim and NEH Fel; David A. Wells Prize for "Economic Maturity". **MEMBERSHIPS** Econ Hist Asn. **RESEARCH** British history; rhetoric of history. **SELECTED PUBLICATIONS** Auth, Economic Maturity and Entrepreneurial Decline: British Iron and Steel, 1870-1913, Harvard Univ Press, 73; auth, Enterprise and Trade in Victorian Britain: Essays in Historical Economics, Allen and Unwin, 81; auth, The Rhetoric of Economics, Univ Wis Press, 85; auth, Econometric History, Macmillan, 87; auth, If You're So Smart: The Narrative of Economic Expertise, Univ Chicago Press, 90. **CONTACT ADDRESS** Dept Econ, Univ Iowa, 108 Pappajohn Bus Admin Bldg., Ste. 5336, Iowa City, IA, 52242. **EMAIL** deirdre-mccloskey@uiowa.edu

MCCLURE, LAURA KATHLEEN
PERSONAL Born 12/26/1959, Wichita Falls, TX, m, 1988, 2 children **DISCIPLINE** CLASSICS **EDUCATION** Bard Col, BA, 82; St. John's Col, MA, 84; Univ Chicago, MA, 86, PhD, 91. **CAREER** Univ Wisconsin, Madison, asst prof, classics, 91-. **MEMBERSHIPS** APA, CAMS, WCC **RESEARCH** Athenian drama; women in antiquity; classical tradition. **SELECTED PUBLICATIONS** Auth, Spoken Like a Woman: Speech and Gender in Athenian Drama, Princeton Univ Press, forthcoming/99; co-edit, Making Silence Speak: Women's Voices in Ancient Greece, PUP, fc; He Is and Is Not: Euripides as a Comic Character, in: Approaches to Teaching World Literature, ed R. Mitchell-Boyask, fc; Gunaikos Logos: Speech, Gender and Spectatorship in Aeschylus' Agamemnon, Helios, 97; Teaching a Course on Gender in the Classical World, Class Jour, 97; Clytemnestra's Binding Song, Class Jour, 97; Female Speech and Characterization in Euripides, in: Lo spettacolo delle voci, ed A.H. Sommerstein and F. de Martino, Bari, 95; On Knowing Greek: George Eliot and the Classical Tradition, in: Clas & Mod Lit, 93. **CONTACT ADDRESS** Dept of Classics, Univ of Wisconsin, Madison, 1220 Linden Dr, Madison, WI, 53706. **EMAIL** lmcclure@facstaff.wisc.edu

MCCLURE, WESLEY CORNELIOUS
DISCIPLINE EDUCATION **CAREER** Virginia State University, Petersburg, VA, president; LANE COLLEGE, PRES, 1992-. **CONTACT ADDRESS** Lane Col, 545 Lane Ave, Jackson, TN, 38301-4598.

MCCLUSKEY, STEPHEN C.
PERSONAL Chicago, IL, m, 2 children **DISCIPLINE** HISTORY OF SCIENCE, MEDEIVAL HISTORY **EDUCATION** IL Inst Technol, BS, 61; Univ WI-Madison, PhD, 74. **CAREER** Vis asst prof hist, KS Univ, 74-75; vis asst prof hist of sci, Univ Notre Dame, 75-76; vis asst prof, 76-80, prof hist, WVA Univ, 80, NSF res grant, 78-80. **MEMBERSHIPS** Hist Sci Soc; Mediaeval Acad Am; Sigma Xi. **RESEARCH** Am astronomy soc; Medieval sci; hist of the physical sci(s). **SELECTED PUBLICATIONS** Auth, Astronomy of the Hopi Indians, J Hist Astron, 8/77; Astronauts and Cultures in Early Medieval Europe, cambridge univ press, 98. **CONTACT ADDRESS** Dept of Hist, West Virginia Univ, PO Box 6303, Morgantown, WV, 26506-6303. **EMAIL** scmcc@wvnvm.edu

MCCLYMER, JOHN FRANCIS
PERSONAL Born 03/04/1945, Brooklyn, NY, m, 1969, 1 child **DISCIPLINE** AMERICAN HISTORY **EDUCATION** Fordham Col, AB, 66; State Univ NY Stony Brook, MA, 67, PhD(Am hist), 73. **CAREER** Instr, 70-73, asst prof, 73-77, ASSOC PROF HIST, ASSUMPTION COL, 77-, Fel, Nat Endowment for the Humanities summer sem, Vanderbilt Univ, 75 & Immigration Hist Res Ctr, Univ Minn, summer 77; Nat Endowment for the Humanities res fel, Washington, summer 76 & 79-80; reviewer & referee, J Urban Hist & J Am Ethnic Hist, 76-; teaching res fel, Newberry Libr, Chicago, summer 78. **MEMBERSHIPS** Am Hist Asn; Orgn Am Historians; Soc Hist Educ. **RESEARCH** Ethnic studies; community studies; women's studies. **SELECTED PUBLICATIONS** Auth, In the Floating Army--Mills, F.C. on Itinerant Life in California, 1914, Historian, vol 0055, 93; American Xenophobia and the Slav Immigrant, a Living Legacy of Mind and Spirit, Int Hist Rev, vol 0016, 94; Education and the Immigrant, vol 10, of American Immigration and Ethnicity, J Amer Ethnic Hist, vol 0013, 94; The United States and its Immigrants, J Amer Ethnic Hist, vol 0015, 96; French America--Mobility, Identity, and Minority Experience Across the Continent, J Amer Ethnic Hist, vol 0015, 96; Pittsburgh Surveyed--Social Science and Social Reform in the Early 20th-Century, J Amer Hist, vol 0084, 97; Making Men Moral, J Amer Hist, vol 0083, 97. **CONTACT ADDRESS** Dept of Hist, Assumption Col, Worcester, MA, 01609.

MCCLYMONDS, MARITA P.
DISCIPLINE MUSIC **EDUCATION** Univ Ca, PhD. **CAREER** Dept Music, Va Univ **RESEARCH** 18th century opera. **SELECTED PUBLICATIONS** Auth, La morte di Semiramide ossia La vendetta di Nino and the Restoration of Death and Tragedy to the Italian Operatic Stage in the 1780s and 90s, 87; The Venetian Role in the Transformation of Italian Opera Seria during the 1790s, 89. **CONTACT ADDRESS** Dept of Music, Virginia Univ, Charlottesville, VA, 22903. **EMAIL** mpm3c@virginia.edu

MCCOLLEY, ROBERT
DISCIPLINE HISTORY **EDUCATION** Univ Calif Berkeley, PhD, 60. **CAREER** Prof, Univ Ill Urbana Champaign. **RESEARCH** Early American history to 1830; high culture in the United States. **SELECTED PUBLICATIONS** Auth, Slavery and Jeffersonian Virginia, Univ Ill, 73; Classical Music in Chicago and the Founding of the Symphony, 1850-1905, Ill Hist J, 85. **CONTACT ADDRESS** History Dept, Univ Ill Urbana Champaign, 52 E Gregory Dr, Champaign, IL, 61820. **EMAIL** rmcolle@uiuc.edu

MCCOMB, DAVID GLENDINNING
PERSONAL Born 10/26/1934, Kokomo, IN, m, 1957, 3 children **DISCIPLINE** URBAN HISTORY **EDUCATION** Southern Methodist Univ, BA, 56; Stanford Univ, MBA, 58; Rice Univ, MA, 62; Univ Tex, PhD(hist), 68. **CAREER** Instr hist, STex Jr Col, 62; asst prof, San Antonio Col, 62-66; instr, Univ Houston, 66-68; spec res assoc oral hist proj, Univ Tex, Austin, 68-69, consult, 69-72; from asst prof to assoc prof, 69-77, chmn dept, 75-80, PROF HIST, COLO STATE UNIV, 77-, Nat Endowment Humanities younger humanist fel, 70-71; vis instr, Univ Pittsburgh, 82. **MEMBERSHIPS** Orgn Am Historians; Am Asn State & Local Hist; Oral Hist Asn. **RESEARCH** United States urban history; world urban history; history of technology. **SELECTED PUBLICATIONS** Auth, In Memory of Frantz, Joe, B., Southwestern Hist Quart, vol 0097, 94; 900 Miles on the Butterfield Trail, J Amer Hist, vol 0083, 96; The American West in the 20th Century--A Bibliography, Montana-Mag Western Hist, vol 0046, 96; The Bay Shrimpers of Texas--Rural Fishermen in a Global Economy, Southwestern Hist Quart, vol 0100, 97; Galveston as a Tourist City, Southwestern Hist Quart, vol 0100, 97. **CONTACT ADDRESS** Dept of Hist, Colorado State Univ, Ft Collins, CO, 80523.

MCCONNELL, ROLAND CALHOUN
PERSONAL Born 03/27/1910, Amherst, NS, Canada, m, 1996 **DISCIPLINE** HISTORY **EDUCATION** Howard Univ, AB, 31, AM, 33; NY Univ, PhD, 45. **CAREER** Instr soc sci, Elizabeth City State Teachers Col, NC, 38-39 & 41-42; archivist, Nat Arch, 43-47; assoc prof hist, 47-48, prof hist, 48-79, chmn div soc sci, 53-55, chmn dept hist, polit sci & geog, 68-79, prof emeritus, Morgan State cuniv; Consult, Afro-Am Bicentennial Corp, Washington, DC, 72-76; chmn, Md State Comn Afro-Am Hist & Cult, 77- . **MEMBERSHIPS** AHA; Soc Am Archivists; Asn Study Negro Life & Hist. **RESEARCH** Archives. **SELECTED PUBLICATIONS** Auth, Negro Troops of Antebellum Louisiana, A History of the Battalion of Free Men of Color, La State Univ, 68; Records in the National Archives Pertaining to the History of North Carolina, 1775-1943, NC Hist Rev; Importance of records in the National Archives on the history of the Negro & Isaiah Dorman and the Custer Expedition, J Negro Hist; The Black experience in Maryland, 1634-1900, In: The Old Line State, A History of Maryland, Annapolis, 71; Biographical sketches on Robert Purvis, Archibald Grimke, Thurgood Marshall, Louis Stokes and Roy Wilkins, In: Encycl of World Biography, Vols 1-12, McGraw-Hill, 73; Black life and activities in West Florida, 1762-1763, In: Eighteenth Century Florida, Life on the Frontier, Univ Fla, 76; co-ed, J of the Afro-Am Hist and Geneal Soc, special issue, African Americans in the Military, 91. **CONTACT ADDRESS** 2406 College Ave, Baltimore, MD, 21214.

MCCORISON, MARCUS ALLEN
PERSONAL Born 07/17/1926, Lancaster, WI, m, 1950, 6 children **DISCIPLINE** AMERICAN HISTORY **EDUCATION** Ripon Col AB, 50; Univ Vt, MA, 51; Columbia Univ MS, 54. **CAREER** Librn, Kellogg-Hubbard Libr, Montpelier, Vt, 54-55; chief, Rare Bks Dept, Dartmouth Col Libr, 55-59; head spec collections, State Univ Iowa, 59-60; LIBRN, AM ANTIQ SOC, 60-, DIR, 67-, Lectr colonial Am hist, Clark Univ, 67-; chmn, Independent Res Libr Asn, 72-73 & 78-79; adv comt, US Newspaper Proj, Orgn Am Historians, 75; mem, NAm Comt for 18th Century Short Title Catalogue of English Bks, 78-. **HONORS AND AWARDS** Pepys Medal, Ephemera Soc, London, 80. **MEMBERSHIPS** Orgn Am Historians; Asn Col & Res Libr; Am Antiq Soc; Bibliog Soc Am(pres, 80). **RESEARCH** American bibliography; American printing history. **SELECTED PUBLICATIONS** Auth, Towner, Lawrence, William--In Memoriam, Proc Amer Antiquarian Soc, vol 0102, 92; Report of the Council + Semiannual Meeting of the American Antiquarian Society, Providence, Rhode Island, Apr 15, 1992, Proc Amer Antiquarian Soc, vol 0102, 92; Dealing, Collecting, and the Marketplace + Rare Books and Manuscripts--Discussion, Harvard Libr Bull, vol 0004, 93; Peterson, Hall, James + Obituary, Proc Amer Antiquarian Soc, vol 0104, 94; Fessenden, Thomas, Green 1771-1837--Not in Bal, Papers of the Bibliographical Soc Am, vol 0089, 95; A Checklist of the Works of Author Fessenden, Thomas, Green 1771-1837, vol 89, Pg 5, 1995, Papers of the Bibliographical Soc Am, vol 0089, 95; Adomeit, Ruth, Elizabeth--Obituary, Proc Amer Antiquarian Soc, vol 0106, 96. **CONTACT ADDRESS** Salisbury Green, 3601 Knightsbridge Close, Worcester, MA, 01609.

MCCORMICK, RICHARD P.
PERSONAL Born 12/24/1916, New York, NY **DISCIPLINE** AMERICAN HISTORY **EDUCATION** Rutgers Univ, AB, 38, AM, 40; Univ Pa, PhD, 48. **CAREER** Historian, Philadelphia Qm Dept, 42-44; instr, Univ Del, 44-45; from instr to prof hist, 45-74, univ historian, 48-82, chmn dept, 66-69, dean col, 74-77, univ prof, 74-82, EMER UNIV PROF HIST, RUTGERS UNIV, 82-, Soc Sci Res Coun fel, 57-58; lectr Am hist, Cambridge Univ, 61; Commonwealth lectr, Univ London, 71. **HONORS AND AWARDS** LittD, Rutgers Univ, 82. **MEMBERSHIPS** AHA; Am Asn State & Local Hist; Orgn Am Historians. **RESEARCH** History of American politics; New Jersey history. **SELECTED PUBLICATIONS** Auth, The Ordinance of 1784, William and Mary Quart, vol 0050, 93. **CONTACT ADDRESS** Rutgers Univ, 111 Grad Sch Libr Serv, New Brunswick, NJ, 08903.

MCCORMICK, ROBERT B.
PERSONAL NC **DISCIPLINE** HISTORY **EDUCATION** Wake Univ, BA, 86; Univ SC, MA, 92; PhD, 96. **CAREER** Asst prof, chair, Newman Univ, 96- **MEMBERSHIPS** AAASS; NACBS. **RESEARCH** Ante Pavelic; Croatia during World War II. **CONTACT ADDRESS** Newman Univ, 3100 McCormick Ave, Wichita, KS, 67213.

MCCOUBREY, JOHN W.
PERSONAL Born 11/04/1923, Boston, MA, m, 1948, 6 children **DISCIPLINE** HISTORY OF ART **EDUCATION** Harvard Univ, BA, 47; Ecole du Louvre, 52-53; Inst Fine Arts, NY Univ, PhD, 58. **CAREER** From instr to asst prof hist of art, Yale Univ, 53-60, Univ Pa, 60-96; Farquhar Prof Emer Hist Art. **HONORS AND AWARDS** Fulbright fel, Paris, 52-53 & London, 64-65; Guggenheim fel, 64-65. **MEMBERSHIPS** Adv bd, Pa Acad Fine Arts; mem various comts, Philadelphia Mus Art; Col Art Asn Am. **RESEARCH** Nineteenth and twentieth century painting; J M W Turner; Cezanne. **SELECTED PUBLICATIONS** Auth, Baron Gros' battle of Eylau and Roman Imperial art, Art Bull, 6/61; American Tradition in Painting, Braziller, 63; The revival of Chardin in French still life, Art Bull, 3/64; ed, American Art 1700-1960, Prentice-Hall, 65; coauth, The Colonial Arts, Scribner, 67; Parliament on Fire, Turner's Burnings, Art in Am, 94; War and Peace in 1842: Turner Haydon and Wilkie, Turner Studies, 84; Time's Railway, Turner and teh Great Western, Turner Studies, 86; The Hero of a Hundred Fights, Turner Studies, 91; Turner's Slaveship, Abolition, Ruskin and Reception, Word & Image, 98. **CONTACT ADDRESS** Dept of Hist of Art, Univ Pa, 3405 Woodland Walk, Philadelphia, PA, 19104. **EMAIL** mccoubre@mailsas.upenn.edu

MCCOY, DONALD RICHARD
PERSONAL Born 01/18/1928, Chicago, IL, m, 1949, 3 children **DISCIPLINE** UNITED STATES HISTORY **EDUCATION** Univ Denver, BA, 49; Univ Chicago, MA, 49; Am Univ, DC, PhD(hist), 54. **CAREER** Archivist, Nat Arch, 51-52; from instr to assoc prof hist, State Univ NY Col Cortland, 52-57; from asst prof to prof, 57-74, UNIV DISTINGUISHED PROF HIST, UNIV KANS, 74-, Lectr, Am Univ, DC, 50-52; alderman, City of Cortland, NY, 55-57; Fulbright vis prof, Univ Bonn, 62; dir spec res proj, Harry S Truman Libr Inst, 67-72; Nat Endowment for Humanities res grants, 68-70, 73-74 & 81-82; mem, US Adv Comt for Protection Arch & Records Ctrs, 74-76 & US Nat Arch Adv Coun, 76-79; Mary Ball Washington Prof hist, Univ Col, Dublin, 76-77. **HONORS AND AWARDS** Waldo Gifford Leland Prize, Soc Am Archivists, 79. **MEMBERSHIPS** AHA; Orgn Am Historians; Soc Am Archivists. **RESEARCH** Recent American history; American political history. **SELECTED PUBLICATIONS** Auth, Angry Voices: Left-of-Center Movements in the New Deal Era, Univ Kans, 58; coauth, Readings in 20th Century American History, MacMillan, 63; auth, Landon of Kansas, Univ Nebr, 66; Calvin Coolidge: The Quiet President, Macmillan, 67; Coming of Age: America During the 1920s and 1930s, Penguin, 73; coauth, Quest and Response: Minority Rights and the Truman Administration, Univ Kans, 73; auth, prologue, The Beginnings of the Franklin D. Roosevelt Library, J Nat Archives, fall 75; Charles Gates Dawes, suppl 5, Dict Am Biog, 77; The National Archives: America's Ministry of Documents, Univ NC, 78; Herbert Hoover and foreign policy, 1939-1945, Cong Rec, 7/79. **CONTACT ADDRESS** Dept of Hist, Univ of Kans, Lawrence, KS, 66045.

MCCOY, GARY W.
PERSONAL m, 3 children **DISCIPLINE** CHURCH MUSIC **EDUCATION** Cent Mo State Univ, BME; Southwestern Baptist Theol Sem, MCM; Southwestern Baptist Theol Sem, DMA; addn stud, Midwestern Baptist Theol Sem; Myong Dong Inst, Seoul, degree Korean Lang Stud. **CAREER** Prof, Korea Baptist Col/Sem, 85-89; dir, Area Mus Dept, Korea Baptist Col/Sem, 86-89; church mus consult, 75-79; assoc prof, 91; dir, Bill and Pat Dixon Sch of Church Mus, Golden Gate Baptist Theol Sem. **HONORS AND AWARDS** Missionary, For Mission Bd, 74; minister of mus, Concord Korean Baptist Church. **SELECTED PUBLICATIONS** Auth, Come to the Manger; Easter Praises and Jesus; the Very Thought of Thee, Jordan Press Seoul, Korea; Hymn Arrangements for the Korean Church Pianist and His Only Son: God's Gift at Christmas; pub(s), S Baptist keyboard mag; Pedalpoint. **CONTACT ADDRESS** Golden Gate Baptist Theol Sem, 201 Sem Dr, Mill Valley, CA, 94941-3197. **EMAIL** GaryMcCoy@ggbts.edu

MCCRAY, JAMES
DISCIPLINE MUSIC **EDUCATION** Univ Ill, BME; Southern Ill Univ, MM; Univ Iowa, PhD. **CAREER** Prof. **SELECTED PUBLICATIONS** Auth, pubs on composition, choral methods, and conducting. **CONTACT ADDRESS** Music, Theatre, and Dance Dept, Colorado State Univ, Fort Collins, CO, 80523. **EMAIL** jmccray@vines.colostate.edu

MCCREADY, WILLIAM DAVID
PERSONAL Born 07/29/1943, Guelph, ON, Canada, m, 1976 **DISCIPLINE** MEDIEVAL AND INTELLECTUAL HISTORY **EDUCATION** Univ Waterloo, BA, 66, MA, 67; Univ Toronto, PhD(medieval studies), 71. **CAREER** Lectr, 69-71, asst prof, 71-75, ASSOC PROF HIST, QUEEN'S UNIV, ONT, 75-. **MEMBERSHIPS** Mediaeval Acad Am. **RESEARCH** Late medieval political theory and ecclesiology. **SELECTED PUBLICATIONS** Auth, An Interpretation of the 'Dialogues' II of Gregory the Great, J Ecclesiastical Hist, vol 0045, 94; Bede, Isidore, and the 'Epistola Cuthberti' + A Study of Early Medieval Anglo Latin Literature, Traditio Stud in Ancient and Medieval Hist Thought and Relig, vol 0050, 95; Isidore, the Antipodeans, and the Shape of the Earth, Isis, vol 0087, 96; To the Editor--Reply, Isis, vol 0087, 96. **CONTACT ADDRESS** Dept of Hist, Queen's Univ, Kingston, ON, K7L 3N6.

MCCRONE, KATHLEEN E.
PERSONAL Regina, Canada **DISCIPLINE** HISTORY **EDUCATION** Univ Sask, BA, 63; New York Univ, MA, 67, PhD, 71. **CAREER** Lectr, 68-72, asst prof, 72-76, head dept, 78-81, PROF HIST, UNIV WINDSOR, 84-, DEAN SOCIAL SCIENCES 90-. **MEMBERSHIPS** Can Conf Deans Arts Hum Soc Sci; Soc Sci Fedn Can; Can Hist Asn. **SELECTED PUBLICATIONS** Auth, Sport And The Physical Emancipation Of Women, 1870-1914, 88; auth, Class, Gender and English Women's Sport, 1890-1914, in J Sport Hist, 91. **CONTACT ADDRESS** Dept of History, Univ of Windsor, Windsor, ON, N9B 3P4. **EMAIL** kem@uwindsor.ca

MCCUE, ROBERT J.
PERSONAL Born 02/17/1932, Cardston, AB, Canada, m, 1956, 7 children **DISCIPLINE** SIXTEENTH CENTURY EUROPE **EDUCATION** Univ Alta, BA, 57, BEd, 60; Brigham Young Univ, MA, 59, PhD(hist), 70. **CAREER** Instr hist, Brigham Young Univ, 64-65; lectr, 68-70, ASST PROF HIST, UNIV VICTORIA, BC, 70-. **MEMBERSHIPS** Can Asn Univ Teachers, Historians of Early Mod Europe. **RESEARCH** Religious history, particularly on the 16th and 19th centuries. **SELECTED PUBLICATIONS** Auth, Crossing the Boundaries--Christian Piety and the Arts in Medieval and Renaissance Confraternities, Quaderni d Italianistica, vol 0013, 92. **CONTACT ADDRESS** Dept of Hist, Univ of Victoria, Victoria, BC, V8W 2Y2.

MCCULLAGH, SUZANNE FOLDS
PERSONAL Born 01/30/1951, Evanston, IL, m, 1975, 2 children **DISCIPLINE** ART HISTORY **EDUCATION** Williams Col, 71-72; Smith Col, BA (cum laude), 73; Harvard Univ, MA, 74, PhD (fine arts), 81. **CAREER** Intern, Metropolitan Museum Art, 72; curatorial asst in charge, print dept, Harvard Univ, Fogg Art Museum, 74-75; curatorial asst, 75-79, asst curator, 79-84, co-coor, self-study & long range plan, 80-82, assoc curator, 85-87, curator of Earlier Prints and Drawings, Dept of Prints and Drawings, The Art Institute of Chicago, 87-; adjunct prof, Northwestern Univ, 83-; Connoisseurship seminars, The Art Institute of Chicago, 85, 87, 94; vis prof, Univ Chicago, Dept Art, 94. **HONORS AND AWARDS** Phi Beta Kappa; Agnes Mongan Traveling fel, 77; Kemper Educational and Charitable Trust grant, 87-89, 90-; NEH Arts Documentation grant, 87-90; Getty Grant for Vis Scholars, 89-91; Art Hist Information prog, Getty Trust, 93-94; NEH Humanities grant reviewer, 94. **MEMBERSHIPS** Snite Art Museum, Notre Dame Univ (vis comm, 85-); Print Coun of Am (bd, 82-85); The North Shore Country Day School, Winnetka (trustee, 88-, chmn, art comm, 87-); Landmarks Preservation Coun of IL (dir, 95-); Harvard Club of Chicago (dir, 95-). **RESEARCH** French and Italian drawings. **SELECTED PUBLICATIONS** Auth, Nicholas Lancret 1690-1743, book rev with Margaret Morgan Grasselli, Master Drawings 32, no 2, summer 94; The Golden Age of Florentine Drawing: Two Centuries of Disegno from Leonardo to Volterrano, exhibition coord, AIC 5/26-7/17/94; The Extraordinary Eye, Erudition, Energy, and Example of Agnes Mongan, Drawing 16, July-Aug 94, Harvard Univ Art Museums Rev 3, no 2, spring 94; European Master Drawings from the Collection of Peter Jay Sharp, exhibition catalogue, Nat Academy of Design, 5/24-8/28/94, entry on Federico Barocci; preparing the Drawing Collection Catalogues, Print Coun of Am Newsletter, no 17, spring 95; The Touch of the Artist: Drawings in the Woodner Collection, exhibition catalogue, Nat Gallery of Art, Washington, entries on V Carpaccio and G de Saint-Aubin, 95; Gabriel de Saint-Aubin's Debt to Antoine Watteau and Francois Boucher, in Correspondances: Festschrift fur Margret Stuffmann zum 24, November 1996, Mainz, 96; Recent Acquisitions of Florentine Drawings in the Art Institute of Chicago, in L'Arte del Disegno: Festschrift fur Christel Thiem, Stuttgart, 97; Michelangelo and His Influence: Drawings from Windsor Castle, exhibition organizer, AIC 4/12-6/22/97; Italian Drawings before 1600 in The Art Institute of Chicago, proj dir and co-auth with Laura M Giles, AIC 4/12-6/22/97. **CONTACT ADDRESS** Curator of Earlier Prints and Drawings., Art Inst of Chicago, 111 S Michigan Ave, Chicago, IL, 60603. **EMAIL** smcculla@artic.edu

MCCULLOCH, SAMUEL CLYDE
PERSONAL Born 09/03/1916, Aarat, Australia, m, 1944, 3 children **DISCIPLINE** HISTORY **EDUCATION** Univ Calif, AB, 40 AM, 42, PhD, 44. **CAREER** Teaching asst hist, Univ Calif, Los Angeles, 43-44; instr, Oberlin Col, 44-45; asst prof, Amherst Col, 45-46; vis asst prof, Univ Mich, 46-47; from asst prof to assoc prof, Rutgers Univ, 47-58; prof hist & assoc dean, Col Arts & Sci, 58-60, asst dean, 50-58; prof hist & dean, San Francisco State Col, 60-64; dean sch humanities, 64-70, actg chmn dept hist, 72-73, coordr, Educ abroad Prog, 75-, PROF HIST, UNIV CALIF, IRVINE, 64-, Fulbright res fel, Univ Sydney, 54-55; assoc ed, J Brit Studies, 62-68; Fulbright res prof, Univ Melbourne & Monash Univ, Australia, 70. **MEMBERSHIPS** AHA; Royal Australian Hist Soc; Conf Brit Studies (exec secy, 68-73, pres, 75-77); Am Soc Church Hist; fel Royal Hist Soc. **RESEARCH** English history and the British Empire; British humanitarian movement of the 18th and 19th centuries; Australian political and economic history of 19th century. **SELECTED PUBLICATIONS** Auth, A History of Tasmania, vol 2, Colony and the State from 1856 to the 1980s, Amer Hist Rev, vol 0098, 93. **CONTACT ADDRESS** Univ Calif Irvine, Irvine, CA, 92717.

MCCULLOH, JOHN MARSHALL
PERSONAL Born 09/13/1943, Abilene, KS, m, 1965 **DISCIPLINE** MEDIEVAL HISTORY **EDUCATION** Univ Kans, BA, 65; Univ Calif, Berkeley, MA, 66, PhD(hist), 71. **CAREER** Actg asst prof hist, Univ Calif, San Diego, 71-72 & Univ Calif, Los Angeles, 72-73; asst prof, 73-76, ASSOC PROF HIST, KANS STATE UNIV, 76-, Alexander von Humboldt Found fel, 77, 80; Fulbright fel, Ger, 80-81. **MEMBERSHIPS** AHA; Mediaeval Acad Am. **RESEARCH** Church history; hagiography; monasticism. **SELECTED PUBLICATIONS** Auth, Wessex and England from Alfred to Edgar, Albion, vol 0025, 93; In the Footsteps of Mabillon--22 Miscellaneous Essays in Association With the Institut fur Historische Hilfswissenschaften at the Philipps Universitat Marburg, on the 80th Anniversary of the Birth of Heinemeyer, Walter, Speculum; The Last Christology of the West--Adoptionism in Spain, 783-820, Speculum-J Medieval Stud, vol 0070, 95; Guibert of Gembloux, 'Epistolae' Codex B.R.Brux.5527-5534 Inueniuntur, vol 1--Epistolae-I-XXIV, vol 2--Epistolae-XXV-LVI, Speculum-J Medieval Stud, vol 0068, 93; Lives of Catherine, Saint 2 Vols, Speculum-J Medieval Stud, vol 0070, 95; Medieval Hagiographies--An International History of Latin and Vernacular Hagiographical Literature from the East from the Beginnings to 1550, vol 2, Speculum-J Medieval Stud, vol 0071, 96; Jewish Ritual Murder + Medieval Christian Hostility and Anti Semitism in Western Europe--William of Norwich, Thomas of Monmouth, and the Early Dissemination of the Myth, Speculum-J Medieval Stud, vol 0072, 97; Books and Manuscripts from the Monasteries of Helmarshausen and Corvey, Speculum-J Medieval Stud, vol 0072, 97. **CONTACT ADDRESS** Dept of Hist, Kansas State Univ, 208 Eisenhower Hall, Manhattan, KS, 66506-1000.

MCCULLOH, WILLIAM EZRA
PERSONAL Born 09/08/1931, McPherson, KS, m, 1956, 2 children **DISCIPLINE** CLASSICAL LANGUAGES & LITERATURES **EDUCATION** Ohio Wesleyan Univ, AB, 53; Oxford Univ, BA, 56; Yale Univ, PhD, 62. **CAREER** Instr classics, Wesleyan Univ, 56-61; from instr to assoc prof, 61-68, prof classics, Kenyon Col, 68-. **HONORS AND AWARDS** Am Philological Assoc Award for Excellence in Teaching, 85; Nat Endowment for the Humanitites Fel for Col Teachers, 84-85; Ohio Prof of the Year, Carnegie Found for the Advancement of Teaching and Council for Advancement and Support of Educ, 95. **MEMBERSHIPS** Am Philol Asn; Class Asn Mid W & S; Soc Ancient Greek Philos; NAm Patristics Soc; Int Soc for Neoplatonic Studies. **RESEARCH** Greek poetry and philosophy; the ancient novel; Greek patristics. **SELECTED PUBLICATIONS** Auth, Introduction to Greek Lyric Poetry, Bantam, 62; Metaphysical solace in Greek tragedy, Class J, 12/63; Aristophanes seen whole, Sewanee Rev, fall 65; Longus, Twayne, 70. **CONTACT ADDRESS** Dept of Classics, Kenyon Col, Ascension Hall, Gambier, OH, 43022-9623. **EMAIL** mcculloh@kenyon.edu

MCCUMMINGS, LEVERNE
PERSONAL Born 10/28/1932, Marion, SC, m **DISCIPLINE** EDUCATION **EDUCATION** St Augustine's, BA 1960; Univ of PA, MSW 1966; Ohio State Univ, PhD 1975. **CAREER** Competency Certification Bd, Bd of Health & Human Svcs, Futures Think Tank, chmn 1981-82; Natl Conf of Grad Deans/Dirs & Off Soc Work Progs, pres 1982-85; CHEYNEY UNIV OF PA, PRES, currently. **HONORS AND AWARDS** Outstanding Educators Awd Univ of KY 1971; Recognition Awd NASW Sixth Biennial Prof Symposium 1980; Distinguished Alumni Awd Univ of PA 1980; Recognition Awd Council of Intl Prog 1981; Institute for Educational Management, Harvard University, 1989. **CONTACT ADDRESS** Cheyney Univ of Pennsylvania, Cheyney, PA, 19319.

MCCURDY, CHARLES WILLIAM
PERSONAL Born 09/28/1948, Pasadena, CA, m, 1973 **DISCIPLINE** AMERICAN LEGAL HISTORY **EDUCATION** Univ Calif, San Diego, BA, 70, PhD, 76. **CAREER** Asst prof hist, 75-79; assoc prof hist & law, Univ Va, 79-. **HONORS AND AWARDS** Louis Pelzer Award, Orgn Am Historians, 73; Arthur Cole Award, Econ Hist Asn, 79. **MEMBERSHIPS** Orgn Am Historians; Am Soc Legal Hist; Econ Hist Asn. **SELECTED PUBLICATIONS** Auth, "Justice Field and the Jurisprudence of Government-Business Relations," Journal of American History, 75; "Stephen J. Field and Public Land Law Development in California, 1850-1866," Law & Society Review, 76; "American Law and the Marketing Structure of the

Large Corporation," Journal of Economic History, 78; "The Knight Sugar Decision of 1895 and the Modernization of American Corporation Law," Business History Review, 79. **CONTACT ADDRESS** Dept of History, Univ of Virginia, 1 Randall Hall, Charlottesville, VA, 22903-3244. **EMAIL** cwm@virginia.edu

MCCURDY, HOWARD EARL
PERSONAL Atascadero, CA **DISCIPLINE** PUBLIC ADMINISTRATION AND POLITICAL SCIENCE **EDUCATION** Univ Wash, BA, 62; Univ Wash, MA, 65; Cornell Univ, PhD, 69. **CAREER** Prof, Amer Univ, 68-. **RESEARCH** Public policy; Public management; Space exploration. **SELECTED PUBLICATIONS** Auth, Space and the American Imagination, Smithsonian Inst Press, 97; auth, Spaceflight and the Myth of Presidential leadership, Univ Ill Press, 97; auth, Inside NASA, Johns Hopkins univ Press. **CONTACT ADDRESS** School of Public Affairs, American Univ, Washington, DC, 20016. **EMAIL** mccurdy@american.edu

MCCUSKER, JOHN J.
DISCIPLINE HISTORY; ECONOMICS **EDUCATION** Saint Bernards Sem and Col, BA, 61; Univ Rochester, Mass, 63; Univ Pittsburgh, PhD, 70. **CAREER** Vis lectr, Mount Allison Univ, 63; lectr, St Francis Xavier Univ, 65-66; from lectr to asst prof to assoc prof to prof, Univ Md, 68-92; lectr, Univ Md, Univ Col, European Div, 71-72, 76-77; vis asst prof, Col William and Mary Va, 72-73; vis res prof, Katholieke Univ, 84-85; dist prof, prof, Trinity Univ, 92-; adj prof, Univ TX, 94-. **HONORS AND AWARDS** Vis res assoc, 69-70, Smithsonian Inst; Grants in Aid, Am Philos Soc, 69, 70, 72, 75, 82; res grants, Economic Hist Asn, 69, 72, 77; fac res fel and awards, Univ Md, 71, 74, 80, 81, 84, 85, 88, 89, 90; fel, Omohundro Inst, 71-73; Vis Senior Mellon Scholar, Univ Cambridge, 96-97; John Adams Fel, Univ London, 96-97; fel, The British Libr, 96-97; Leverhulme Trust vis fel, Univ Cambridge, 96-97; Helen Cam vis fel, Univ Cambridge, 96-97; Fulbright Senior Scholar, Great Britian, 96-97; Scholar in Residence, Rockefellow Ctr 97., New York State Scholar, 57-61, 62-63; Grad Tchg Fel, Univ Pittsburgh, 63-65; Andrew Mellon Pre-Doctoral Fel, Univ Pittsburgh, 66-67. **MEMBERSHIPS** Am Hist Asn; Organization Am Historians; Am Antiquarian Soc; Va Hist Soc; NY State Hist Asn; Pa Hist Soc; Economic Hist Soc; Bibliographical Soc; Md Hist Soc. **RESEARCH** Economic history of the Atlantic World during the seventeenth and eighteenth centurys. **SELECTED PUBLICATIONS** Coauth, The Beginnings of Commercial and Financial Journalism: The Commodity Price Currents, Exchange Rate Currents, and Money Currents of Early Modern Europe, 91; auth, The Italian Business Press in Early Modern Europe, 92; auth, Money and Exchange in Europe and America, 1600-1775: A Handbook, 92; auth, The Role of Antwerp in the Emergence of Commercial and Financial Newspapers in Early Modern Europe, 96; auth, Essays in the Economic History in the Atlantic World, 97. **CONTACT ADDRESS** Dept of History, Trinity Univ, 715 Stadium Dr, San Antonio, TX, 78212. **EMAIL** jmccuske@trinity.edu

MCCUTCHEON, JAMES MILLER
PERSONAL Born 10/31/1932, New York, NY, m, 1959, 2 children **DISCIPLINE** AMERICAN HISTORY & STUDIES **EDUCATION** Hobart Col, BA, 54; Univ Wis-Madison, MS, 55, PhD, 59. **CAREER** Asst prof hist, Simpson Col, 61-62; from asst prof to assoc prof, 62-73, PROF HIST & AM STUDIES, UNIV HAWAII, MANOA, 73-, spec asst pres, 79, Chair Am Studies Dept, 84-88; Fulbright fel, Univ London, 59-60; deleg, Cong Orient, Canberra, Australia, 71; Fulbright lectr, Beijing Inst Foreign Lang, 81-82. **HONORS AND AWARDS** Robert W Clopton Award Distinguished Community Service, 78. **MEMBERSHIPS** AHA; Orgn Am Historians; Am Studies Asn; Urban Studies Asn. **RESEARCH** City in American history; Asian influences in American life; China and America. **SELECTED PUBLICATIONS** Auth, Missionary archives in England for East and Southeast Asia, J Asian Studies, 5/69; Tremblingly obey: British and other western responses to China, Historian, 8/71; China and America: A Bibliography of Interactions Foreign and Domestic, Univ Hawaii, 73; The Asian dimension in the American revolutionary period, In: The American Revolution: Its Meaning to Asians and Americans, 77; The Idea of Community in America, In: Educational Perspectives, 78; Sino-American Political Relations Since 1911, In: Proc of Int Am Studies Conf, 81; The Chinese People's Cultural Adjustment to the United States, Proceedings of the Conference on Sino-American Cultural and Educational Relations, Taipei, 88; The American City,Univ of the Air, Tokyo, 89; Making China Christian, Cousins, More's Utopia and the Utopian Inheritance, 95. **CONTACT ADDRESS** Dept of Am Studies, Univ of Hawaii at Manoa, 1890 E West Rd, Honolulu, HI, 96822-2318. **EMAIL** jmcc@hawaii.edu

MCDANIEL, GEORGE WILLIAM
PERSONAL Born 05/04/1942, Washington, IA, s **DISCIPLINE** HISTORY **EDUCATION** St. Ambrose Univ, BA, 66; Mt. St. Bernard Sem & Aquinas Inst of Theol, 66-69; Cath Univ Am, 69-70; Aquinas Inst of Theol, MA, 74; Univ Iowa, MA, 77; PhD, 85. **CAREER** Ordained, Roman Catholic Priest, 70; assoc pastor, St. Peter's Parish & fac, Cardinal Stritch Jr-Sr High Sch, 70-73; assoc pastor, St. Patrick's Parish, Ottumwa, 73-74; Dean of Students, ST. AMBROSE UNIV, 74-76; assoc dir dev, 76-77; PROF HIST, 77-. **HONORS AND AWARDS** Throne/Aldrich Award Outstadning Article, Annals of Iowa, 97; Benjamin F. Chambaugh Award, Outstanding Book in Iowa Hist, 96; Throne/Aldrich Award, Hon Men, 95; Baecke Chair of Hum, St. Ambrose Univ, 93; Hoover Scholar, 82, 85, Herbert Hoover Libr. **MEMBERSHIPS** Org Am Historians; US Capitol Hist Asn; The Natl Trust for Hist Pres; The Hoover Pres Library Asn; St Hist Soc Iowa; Phi Alpha Theta; Soc Midland Authors. **RESEARCH** Iowa hist; populism; progressivism; Cath social action, local civil rights. **SELECTED PUBLICATIONS** Auth, Smith Wildman Brookhart: Iowa's Renegade Republican, 95; "Catholic Action in Davenport: St. Ambrose College and The League for Social Justice," The Annals of Iowa, 96. **CONTACT ADDRESS** St. Ambrose Univ, 518 W. Locust St., Davenport, IA, 52803. **EMAIL** gmcdanil@saunix.sau.edu

MCDONALD, ARCHIE PHILIP
PERSONAL Born 11/29/1935, Beaumont, TX, m, 1957, 2 children **DISCIPLINE** AMERICAN HISTORY **EDUCATION** Lamar State Col, BS, 58; Rice Univ, MA, 60; La State Univ, PhD(Hist), 65. **CAREER** Asst prof, Murray State Col, 63-64; from asst prof to assoc prof, 64-72, prof Hist, Stephen F Austin State Univ, 72-, executive bd, Tex County Records Inventory Proj, 78-; Tex Comt for Humanities, 79-85; Tex Sesquicentennial Comn, 81-86. **HONORS AND AWARDS** Distinguished Prof Award, Stephen F Austin Alumni Asn, 76; Regents Prof, 86. **MEMBERSHIPS** Southern Hist Assn; Texas State Hist Assn. **RESEARCH** Civil War, Texas and Southern history. **SELECTED PUBLICATIONS** Auth, Recollections of a Long Life, Blue & Gray, 73; Make Me a Map of the Valley: The Journal of Jedidiah Hotchkiss, Southern Methodist Univ, 73; The War with Mexico, Health; Travis, 77 & Eastern Texas History, 78, Pemberton; On This Day of New Beginnings, Tex State Libr, 79; The Texas Heritage, Forum, 80-; Texas, A Sesquicentennial Presentation, Dallas Times-Herald, 82; Nacogdoches with James G Partin, and Joe and Carolyn Ericson, Best of East Texas Publishers, Lufkin, TX, 95; Nacogdoches, Texas--A Pictorial History, with R G and Ouida Whitaker Dean, The Donning Company Publishers, Virginia Beach, VA, 96; Historic Texas: An Illustrated Chronicle of Texas' Past, Published for Preservation Texas, Inc, Lammert Publications, Inc, San Antonio Tx, 96. **CONTACT ADDRESS** Dept of History, Stephen F. Austin State Univ, 1936 North St, Nacogdoches, TX, 75961-3940. **EMAIL** AMcDonald@SFA.edu

MCDONALD, FORREST
PERSONAL Born 01/07/1927, Orange, TX, m, 1963, 5 children **DISCIPLINE** AMERICAN HISTORY **EDUCATION** Univ Texas, BA, 49; Univ Texas, MA, 49; Univ Texas, PhD, 55 **CAREER** Assoc prof, Brown Univ, 59-64; prof, Brown Univ, 64-67; prof, Wayne State Univ, 67-76; prof, Univ Alabama, 76-87; distinguished univ res prof, Univ Alabama, 87- **HONORS AND AWARDS** Guggenheim Fel, 62-63; Board For Scholar, 85-87; Pulitzer Prize Finalist, 86; Ingersoll Prize, 90; Salvatori Award, 92 **SELECTED PUBLICATIONS** The American Presidency: An Intellectual History, 94; Novus Ordo Seclorum: The Intellectual Origins of the Constitution, 85; Alexander Hamilton: A Biography, 79; The Presidency of Thomas Jefferson, 76 **CONTACT ADDRESS** Dept Hist, Univ Alabama, Box 155, Coker, AL, 35452.

MCDONALD, ROBERT M.S.
PERSONAL Born 07/18/1970, Stratford, CT, s **DISCIPLINE** HISTORY **EDUCATION** Univ Virginia, BA, 92; Univ N Carolina, Chapel Hill, MA, 94, PhD, 98; Oxford Univ, MSt, 97. **CAREER** Asst prof, 98-, US Mil Acad. **RESEARCH** Colonial Anglo-Amer, revolutionary & early republican US, Thomas Jefferson. **CONTACT ADDRESS** Dept of History, US Military Acad, West Point, NY, 10996. **EMAIL** kr6691@exmail.usma.edu.

MCDONALD, WILLIAM ANDREW
PERSONAL Born 04/26/1913, Warkworth, ON, Canada, m, 1941, 2 children **DISCIPLINE** GREEK HISTORY, ARCHEOLOGY **EDUCATION** Univ Toronto, BA, 35, MA, 36; Johns Hopkins Univ, PhD, 40. **CAREER** Mem staff, Excavations, Olynthus, 38, Pylos, 39, 53; mem fac, Lehigh Univ, 39-43, Univ Tex, 45-46 & Moravian Col, 46-48; from assoc prof to prof classics, 48-73, dir excavation, Nichoria, 69-73, dir honors div, Col Lib Arts, 64-67, Regents' prof class studies & dir Ctr Ancient Studies, 73-80, DIR MINN MESSENIA EXPED, UNIV MINN, MINNEAPOLIS, 61-, Guggenheim fel, 58-59 & 67-68; Nat Geog Soc res fel, 72-73; trustee, Whittlesey Found, Inc, 73-. **HONORS AND AWARDS** Gold Medal, Archaeol Inst Am, 81. **MEMBERSHIPS** Archaeol Inst Am; Am Philol Asn; Asn Field Archaeol; Soc Prof Archeologists. **RESEARCH** Prehistoric archaeology; toponymy; Greek history and prehistory. **SELECTED PUBLICATIONS** Auth, Two Quarters, Kenyon Rev, vol 0017, 95. **CONTACT ADDRESS** Univ of Minn, 310 Folwell Hall, Minneapolis, MN, 55455.

MCDONOUGH, C.J.
PERSONAL Born 04/10/1942, United Kingdom, m, 1967, 2 children **DISCIPLINE** CLASSICS **EDUCATION** Univ Col London, BA, 63, MA, 65; Univ Toronto, PhD, 68. **CAREER** Prof, Univ Toronto, 67- **MEMBERSHIPS** APA, Medieval Acad Am. **RESEARCH** Latin satire; medieval latin literature. **SELECTED PUBLICATIONS** ed, Warner of Rouen, Pims, 95. **CONTACT ADDRESS** Dept of Classics, Univ of Toronto, 97 St. George St., Toronto, ON, M5S 2E8. **EMAIL** christopher.mcdonough@utoronto.ca

MCDONOUGH, CHRISTOPHER MICHAEL
PERSONAL Born 12/28/1963, Boston, MA, m, 1990 **DISCIPLINE** CLASSICAL PHILOLOGY **EDUCATION** Tufts Univ, BA, 86; Univ North Carolina, MA, 91, PhD, 96. **CAREER** Adj prof, Univ North Carolina, Greensboro, 92-96; vis asst prof, Princeton Univ, 96-97; asst prof, Boston Col, 97- . **MEMBERSHIPS** APA; CAMWS; Am Soc of Lit Critics; Am Acad in Rome. **RESEARCH** Roman religion; social history. **CONTACT ADDRESS** Dept of Classics, Boston Col, 158 Carney, Chestnut Hill, MA, 02167. **EMAIL** mcdonoch@bc.edu

MCDOUGALL, IAIN
DISCIPLINE ANCIENT GREEK HISTORY **EDUCATION** St. Andrews Univ, Scotland, BA, 64;, PhD, 81. **CAREER** Prof; dept ch. **RESEARCH** An historical commentary on Cassius Dio's Roman History books. **SELECTED PUBLICATIONS** Auth, A Lexicon to Diodorus Siculus, Hildesheim, 83. **CONTACT ADDRESS** Dept of Classics, Univ of Winnipeg, 515 Portage Ave, Winnipeg, MB, R3B 2E9. **EMAIL** mcdougall@uwpg02.uwinnipeg.ca

MCDOWALL, DUNCAN L.
DISCIPLINE MODERN CANADIAN BUSINESS AND POLITICAL HISTORY **EDUCATION** Queen's Univ, BA, 72, MA, 73; Carleton Univ, PhD, 78. **CAREER** Prof. **RESEARCH** History of Bermuda. **SELECTED PUBLICATIONS** Auth, Quick to the Frontier: Canada's Royal Bank, McClelland & Stewart, Toronto, 93; Trading Places: The Trade Policies of Canada's Grits and Tories, 1840-1988, The NAFTA Puzzle: Politics, Parties, and Trade in North America, Westview Press, 94; Business as Usual: Some Recent Business History, Acadiensis, 94; "From Pesthole to 'Nature's Fairyland': The Aesthetic and Practical Origins of Bermuda Tourism, 1800-1914," Bermuda Jour Archaeol and Maritime Hist, 96. **CONTACT ADDRESS** Dept of Hist, Carleton Univ, 1125 Colonel By Dr, Ottawa, ON, K1S 5B6. **EMAIL** grad_history@carleton.ca

MCDOWELL, JOHN H.
PERSONAL Born 05/25/1903, Tiffin, OH, m, 1935, 3 children **DISCIPLINE** THEATRE HISTORY AND CRITICISM **EDUCATION** Boston Univ, BS, 29; Univ Wash, MA, 33; Yale Univ, PhD(theatre), 37. **CAREER** Instr theatre speech, Cornish Sch Theatre, Seattle, 30-34; asst prof, Wellesley Col, 36; asst prof hist theatre, Smith Col, 37-44; asst prof theatre speech, Manhattanville Col, 44-45; from asst prof to prof, 45-73, EMER PROF HIST THEATRE, OHIO STATE UNIV, 73-, Nat Theatre Conf fel, 50; Ohio State Univ res found grants-in-aid, 50-68; Ohio State Univ develop fund grant, 55-65; mem, Int Cong Libr Performing Arts, 61-; US mem, Comn Bibliog Iconographique Opera, 65- **HONORS AND AWARDS** Award of Excellence, Am Col Theatre Festival, 74. **MEMBERSHIPS** Int Soc Theatre Res. **RESEARCH** The early history of the box set; Filippo Juvarra's theatre in the Palazzo della Cancelleria in Rome; Pierre Dumont's theatre in a Jesuit seminary in Rome. **SELECTED PUBLICATIONS** Auth, The Renaissance Stage: Documents of Serlio, Sabbattini, and Furttenbach, Univ Miami, 58; Original scenery and documents for productions of Uncle Tom's Cabin, Rev Hist Theatre, Paris, 63; The Ottoboni Theatre: A Research Adventure, Ohio State Univ Theatre Collection Bull, 64: The Ohio State University Theatre Collection: A Working and Teaching Collection, Acts VIIIe Congres Int Bibliot Muses Arts Spectacle, Amsterdam, 65; I'm Going There, Uncle Tom: A promptbook production, Theatre Studies, Ohio State Univ, 79. **CONTACT ADDRESS** 1977 Gulf Shore Blvd, Naples, FL, 33940.

MCELVAINE, ROBERT S.
DISCIPLINE HISTORY **EDUCATION** Rutgers Univ, BA, 86; SUNY at Binghamton, MA, PhD, 74. **CAREER** Elizabeth Chisholm prof Arts and Letters & dept ch. **HONORS AND AWARDS** Millsaps' Distinguished prof, 83. **SELECTED PUBLICATIONS** Auth, Down and Out in the Great Depression: Letters from the Forgetten Man, NC, 83; The Great Depression: America, 1929-1941. Times Books 84, 93; The End of the Conservative Era: Liberalism After Reagan, Arbor House, 87; Mario Cuomo: A Biography, Scribners, 88; What's Left; A New Democratic Vision for America, Adams, 96; Sex: Women, Men, and History, 98 or 99. **CONTACT ADDRESS** Dept of History, Millsaps Col, 1701 N State St, Jackson, MS, 39210. **EMAIL** mcelvrs@okra.millsaps.edu

MCFARLAND, GERALD W.
PERSONAL Born 11/07/1938, Oakland, CA, m, 1964 **DISCIPLINE** AMERICAN HISTORY **EDUCATION** Univ CA, Berkeley, AB, 60; Columbia Univ, MA, 62, PhD, 65. **CAREER** Instr Am hist, 64-65, from asst prof to assoc prof hist, 65-75, chmn dept, 75-78, prof hist Univ MA, Amherst, 75. **HONORS AND AWARDS** Am Coun Learned Soc grant-in-

aid, 71-72; John Simon Guggenheim Mem found fel, 78-79, Conti Research Fellow, 92-93; Am Philos Soc Research Grant, 95. **MEMBERSHIPS** AHA; Orgn Am Historians. **RESEARCH** Late 19th century Am polit and cult. **SELECTED PUBLICATIONS** Ed, Mugwumps, Morals and Politics, 1884-1920, Univ Mass, 75; A Scattered People: An American Family Moves West, Pantheon, 85; The Counterfeit Man: The True Story of the Boorn-Colvin Murder Case, Pantheon, 91. **CONTACT ADDRESS** Dept of Hist, Univ of Massachusetts, Amherst, MA, 01003-3930. **EMAIL** geraldm@history.umass.edu

MCFARLANE, LARRY ALLAN
PERSONAL Born 04/02/1934, Independence, MO, m, 1958 **DISCIPLINE** AMERICAN HISTORY **EDUCATION** Univ Mo, BA, 56, MA, 59, PhD, 63. **CAREER** From asst prof to assoc prof hist, Northern Ariz Univ, 62-70; assoc prof Am hist, Purdue Univ, Lafayette, 70-71; assoc prof, 71-73, PROF AM HIST, NORTHERN ARIZ UNIV, 73-, Am Philos Soc res grant, 72. **MEMBERSHIPS** AHA; Orgn Am Historians; Econ Hist Asn; Agr Hist Soc; Bus Hist Conf. **RESEARCH** American economic, business and agricultural history. **SELECTED PUBLICATIONS** Auth, The Finishing Touch, NMex Hist Rev, vol 0069, 94; Prince Charming Goes West, Great Plains Quart, vol 0014, 94. **CONTACT ADDRESS** Dept of Hist, No Arizona Univ, Box 5810, Flagstaff, AZ, 86011-0001.

MCGEE, JAMES SEARS
PERSONAL Born 07/12/1942, Houston, TX, m, 1966, 2 children **DISCIPLINE** TUDOR-STUART ENGLAND **EDUCATION** Rice Univ, BA, 64; Yale Univ, MA, 66, MPhil, 68, PhD(hist), 71. **CAREER** Asst prof hist, Ga Southern Col, 69-71; asst prof, 71-78, ASSOC PROF HIST, UNIV CALIF, SANTA BARBARA, 78-. **MEMBERSHIPS** AHA; Conf Brit Studies; Past & Present Soc, Eng; Am Soc Church Hist. **RESEARCH** Tudor-Stuart England; early modern European history. **SELECTED PUBLICATIONS** Auth, The Political Career of St-john, Oliver, 1637-1649, Church Hist, vol 0063, 94; Predestination, Policy and Polemic, Albion, vol 0026, 94; Philosophy and Government 1572-1651, 16th Century J, vol 0025, 94; Preaching in the Last Days, Church Hist, vol 0064, 95. **CONTACT ADDRESS** Dept of Hist, Univ of Calif, 552 University Rd, Santa Barbara, CA, 93106-0001.

MCGEE, PATRICK
DISCIPLINE CULTURAL STUDIES, POSTCOLONIAL THEORY **EDUCATION** Univ Calif, Santa Cruz, PhD, 84. **CAREER** Prof, La State Univ. **HONORS AND AWARDS** Fulbright grad res grant for Fr, 82-83; NEH summer stipend, 88; LSU res coun summer grant, 92, 94. **RESEARCH** Modernism (Joyce); Shakespeare; film; African-American literature. **SELECTED PUBLICATIONS** Auth, Telling the Other: The Question of Value in Modern and Postcolonial Writing, 92; The Politics of Modernist Form, or, Who Rules the Waves?, in Mod Fiction Stud, 92; Decolonization and the Curriculum of English, Race, Identity, and Representation in Educ, 93; When Is a Man Not a Man? or, The Male Feminist Approaches 'Nausicaa,' in Joyce in the Hibernian Metropolis, 96; Ishmael Reed and the Ends of Race, 97; Cinema, Theory, and Political Responsibility in Contemporary Culture, 97. **CONTACT ADDRESS** Dept of Eng, Louisiana State Univ, 212T Allen Hall, Baton Rouge, LA, 70803. **EMAIL** pmcgee@unixl.sncc.lsu.edu

MCGEE, REECE JEROME
PERSONAL Born 10/19/1929, St. Paul, MN, m, 1978, 3 children **DISCIPLINE** SOCIOLOGY **EDUCATION** Univ Minn, BA, 52, MA, 53, PhD, 56 **CAREER** Asst prof, 56, Humboldt St Col; res assoc, 57, Univ Minn; asst prof, 57-61, assoc prof, 61-64, Univ Texas Austin; vis assoc prof, 64-65, prof, 65-67, Macalester Col; prof, master tchr, 67-94, prof emeritus, 94-, dept head, sociology & anthropology, 87-92, Purdue Univ. **CONTACT ADDRESS** Dept of Sociology & Antropol, Purdue Univ, Stone Hall 1365, West Lafayette, IN, 47907-1365.

MCGEHEE, ABBY
PERSONAL Born 02/19/1964, Denver, CO, m **DISCIPLINE** ART HISTORY **EDUCATION** Unic Cal Berk, PhD 97, MA 91; Pomona Col, BA 86. **CAREER** Oregon Col, asst prof 97-. **HONORS AND AWARDS** Fulbright fel; Mellon fel; CASVA; de Tocqueulle Sch. **MEMBERSHIPS** CAA; SAH; ICMA; AVISTA **RESEARCH** Medieval art and architecture. **CONTACT ADDRESS** Dept of Art and Craft, Oregon Col of Arts and Crafts, 3954 SE ASH ST, Portland, OR.

MCGEHEE, R.V.
PERSONAL Born 08/01/1934, Tyler, TX, s, 2 children **DISCIPLINE** KINESIOLOGY AND SPORT HISTORY **EDUCATION** Univ Texas, BA, 55; Yale Univ, MA, 56; Texas A&M Univ, MA, 78; Univ Texas Austin, PhD, 63. **CAREER** Span lang ed transl, Journ ICHPER-SD, 91-; sport hist res in Guatemala Mex Nicaragua Costa Rica La, 90-; Fulbright prof, Phys Educ and Geology, Univ Liberia Monrovia, 82-83; Fulbright prof, phys educ, Nat Teachers Col Honduras, 88; Vis prof of phys educ, Natl Univ of Honduras Tegucigalpa, 88; prof, SE Ls Univ, 78-; tchr, Tx A&M Univ, Univ Tx San Antonio, Nat Autonomous Univ Mex, W Mich Univ, SDak Sch Mines & Tech, Univ Ks, Univ Tx Austin, Yale Univ. **HONORS AND AWARDS** Fulbright scholar, Univ Liberia Monrovia, 82-83; scholar, Escuela Superior del Prof Francisco Morazan Tegucigalpa Honduras, 88; La Asn Health Phys Educ Rec Dance, 95-96; Sturgis Leavitt Prize, SE Coun Latin Amer Studies, 96; fel, AAHPERD Res Consortium, 97; ICHPER-SD Outstanding Contrib Serv Award, 97. **MEMBERSHIPS** AAHPERD, 78-; hist acad chair, NASPE, 96-97; chair, S Dist Intl Rel Coun, 93-94; La AHPERD, 78-; chair, arch comt, 94-; Tx AHPERD, 78-; N Amer Soc Sport Hist, 89-; Sport Lit Asn, 89-; exec bd, Listserv, 96-; Intl Coun HPER-SD, 91-; hist phys educ and sport comn, 94-; Intl Soc Comparative Phys Educ and Sport, 91-; SE Coun on Latin Amer Studies, 93-; N Amer Soc Sociol of Sport, 95-. **SELECTED PUBLICATIONS** El papel del deporte en la cultura popular nicaraguense, 1889-1926, Revista de Historia de Nicaragua; The Impact of Imported Sports on the Popular Culture of Nineteenth and Twentieth Century Latin America, Karen Racine and Ingrid Fey eds, Strange Pilgrimages: Travel, Exile, and Foreign Residency in the Creation of Identity in Latin America, 1800-1990; Carreras, Patrias y Caudillos: Sport/Spectacle in Mexico and Guatemala, 1926-1943, S Eastern Latin Americanist, vol 41, pp 19-32, 98; The Virtual Wall: A Key to Learning the Basic Tennis Serve, Journ Phys Educ, Rec and Dance, vol 68, 7, pp 10-12, 97; Vollyball - The Latin American Connection, ICHPER-SD Journ, vol 33, n 4, pp 31-35, 97; El lugar del nino en el desarrollo inicial del deporte moderno en Centro America y Mexico, principios del siglo veinte, Memoria del XVI Congreso Panamericano de Educacion Fisica, vol 2, 97; Sergio Ramirez's Jeugo Perfecto and Tarde de Sol, Aethlon, v 13, 2, pp 121-123, 96; Pan American Games, David Levinson and Karen Christensen eds, Encycl World Sport, Santa Barbara, CA, ABC-CLIO, vol 2, pp 715-719, 96; Gymnastics, David Levinson and Karen Christensen eds, Encycl World Sport, Santa Barbara, CA, ABC-CLIO, vol 1, pp 388-397, 96; Baseball, Latin America, David Levinson and Karen Christensen eds, Encycl World Sport, Santa Barbara, CA, ABC-CLIO, v1, pp 84-91, 96 **CONTACT ADDRESS** SLU 677, Hammond, LA, 70402. **EMAIL** rmcgehee@selu.edu

MCGEOCH, LYLE ARCHIBALD
PERSONAL Born 03/25/1931, Tanta, Egypt, m, 1958, 3 children **DISCIPLINE** MODERN EUROPEAN HISTORY **EDUCATION** Westminster Col, Pa, AB, 53; Univ Pa, MA, 56, PhD(hist), 64. **CAREER** Instr hist, Kent State Univ, 59-63; asst prof, Univ Dubuque, 63-66; asst prof, 66-70, ASSOC PROF HIST, OHIO UNIV, 70-, Grants, Am Philos Soc, 68 & 78, Baker Fund, Ohio Univ, 69-70. **MEMBERSHIPS** AHA; Brit Polit Group. **RESEARCH** Nineteenth century European diplomatic history; British foreign policy; British political biography. **SELECTED PUBLICATIONS** Auth, The Limits of British Influence--South Asia and the Anglo American Relationship, 1947-56, Historian, vol 0057, 94; Channel Tunnel Visions, 1850-1945--Dreams and Nightmares, Amer Hist Rev, vol 0101, 96; After Liberalism, Historian, vol 0059, 97. **CONTACT ADDRESS** Dept of Hist, Ohio Univ, Athens, OH, 45701.

MCGERR, M.
PERSONAL Born 01/15/1955, New Rochelle, NY, m, 1978, 2 children **DISCIPLINE** HISTORY **EDUCATION** Yale, BA, 76, MA, 78, MPhil, 79, PhD, 84. **CAREER** Asst Prof, 84-89, Mass Inst of Tech; assoc prof, 89-, Indiana Univ. **HONORS AND AWARDS** NEH Fel for College Tchrs, 86. **MEMBERSHIPS** AHA; Org of Amer Historians. **RESEARCH** US since the Civil War. **SELECTED PUBLICATIONS** Auth, The Decline of Popular Politics The American North, 1865-1928, Oxford Univ Press, 86. **CONTACT ADDRESS** Dept of History, Indiana Univ, Bloomington, Ballantine 742, Bloomington, IN, 47405. **EMAIL** mmcgerr@indiana.edu

MCGHEE, ROBERT J.
PERSONAL Born 02/27/1941, Wiarton, ON, Canada **DISCIPLINE** HISTORY/ARCHAEOLOGY **EDUCATION** Univ Toronto, BA, 64, MA, 66; Univ Calgary, PhD, 68. **CAREER** Arctic archaeol, Nat Mus Can, 68-72; assoc prof, Memorial Univ Nfld, 72-76; CURATOR ARCTIC ARCHAEOLOGY, ARCHAEOLOGICAL SURVEY OF CANADA, CANADIAN MUSEUM OF CIVILIZATION, 76-. **HONORS AND AWARDS** Fel, Royal Soc Can. **MEMBERSHIPS** Arctic Inst N Am; pres, Can Archaeol Asn, 87-90. **RESEARCH** Canadian prehistory; arctic prehistory. **SELECTED PUBLICATIONS** Auth, Canadian Arctic Prehistory, 78; auth, Ancient Canada, 89; auth, Canada Rediscovered, 91; auth, Ancient People of the Arctic, 96. **CONTACT ADDRESS** Canadian Mus of Civilization, Hull, PQ, J8X 4H2.

MCGIFFERT, MICHAEL
PERSONAL Born 10/05/1928, Chicago, IL, m, 1960 **DISCIPLINE** AMERICAN HISTORY **EDUCATION** Harvard Univ, BA, 49; Yale Univ, BD, 52, PhD(Am studies), 58. **CAREER** Instr hist, Colgate Univ, 54-55, Univ MD, 55-56 & Colgate Univ, 56-60; from asst prof to prof, Univ Denver, 60-72; Prof hist, Col William & Mary & Ed, William & Mary Quart, 72-97, Nat Endowment for Hum fel, 77-78; Col William & Mary fac res grant, 81,89. **HONORS AND AWARDS** Fac Research Grants, Col of William and Mary, 81,89; Fel, Natl Endowment for the Hum, 77-78; Fac research grant, Univ of Denver, 1970. **MEMBERSHIPS** AHA; Orgn Am Historians; Am Studies Asn; AAUP. **RESEARCH** Early Am hist; Puritanism; Am intellectual hist. **SELECTED PUBLICATIONS** Auth, The Higher Learning in Colorado: An Historical Study, 1860-1940, Sage, 64; ed, The Character of Americans, Dorsey, 64, rev ed, 69; Puritanism and the American Experience, 69 & co-ed, American Social Thought: Sources and Interpretations (2 vols), 72, Addison-Wesley; ed, God's Plot: The Paradoxes of Puritan Piety: Being the Autobiography and Journal of Thomas Shepard, Univ Mass, 72; God's Plot: Puritan Spirituality in Thomas Shepard's Cambridge, Univ Mass, 94. **CONTACT ADDRESS** 102 Old Glory Ct, Williamsburg, VA, 23185-4914. **EMAIL** mcgiff@factstaff.wm.edu

MCGINN, BERNARD JOHN
PERSONAL Born 08/19/1937, Yonkers, NY, m, 1971, 2 children **DISCIPLINE** HISTORY OF CHRISTIANITY **EDUCATION** St Joseph's Sem, BA, 59; Pontif Gregorian Univ, STL, 63; Brandeis Univ, PhD, 70. **CAREER** Instr theol, Cath Univ Am, 68-69; instr theol & hist Christiantiy, 69-70, asst prof hist Christianity, 70-75, assoc prof, 75-78, Prof Hist Theol & Christianity, Univ Chicago, 78-, Am Asn Theol Schs res fel, 71. **MEMBERSHIPS** AHA; Medieval Acad Am; Am Cath Hist Asn; Am Acad Relig; Am Soc Church Hist. **RESEARCH** Hist of theol; intellectual and cult hist of the Middle Ages. **SELECTED PUBLICATIONS** Auth, The abbot and the doctors, Church Hist, 71; The Golden Chain, Cistercian Publ, 72; The Crusades, Gen Learning Press, 73; Apocalypticism in the Middle Ages, Mediaeval Studies, 75; ed, Three Treatises on Man, Cistercian Publ, 77; auth, Visions of the End, Columbia, 79; transl, Apocalyptic Spirituality, 79 & coauth (with E Colledge), Meister Eckhart, 81, Paulist; Foundations of Mysticism, Crossroad, 91; Growth of Mysticism, Crossroad, 94; Flowering of Mysticism, Crossroad, 98. **CONTACT ADDRESS** Divinity Sch, Univ of Chicago, 1025-35 E 58th St, Chicago, IL, 60637-1577. **EMAIL** bmcginn@midway.uchicago.edu

MCGINNIS, DAVID PRENTICE
PERSONAL Born 09/21/1937, Chicago, IL, m, 1972 **DISCIPLINE** HISTORY **EDUCATION** Univ Ore, BA, 59; Univ Calif, Berkeley, MA, 60, PhD(hist), 68. **CAREER** Asst prof, 66-70, ASSOC PROF HIST, UNIV CALGARY, 70-. **RESEARCH** European economic history. **SELECTED PUBLICATIONS** Auth, Making America Corporate 1870-1920, Australian J Politics and Hist, vol 0039, 93. **CONTACT ADDRESS** Dept of Hist, Univ of Calgary, Calgary, AB, T2N 1N4.

MCGOLDRICK, JAMES EDWARD
PERSONAL Born 01/05/1936, Philadelphia, PA **DISCIPLINE** RENAISSANCE & REFORMATION HISTORY **EDUCATION** Temple Univ, BS, 61, MA, 64; WVa Univ, PhD(hist), 74. **CAREER** From instr to asst prof hist, John Brown Univ, 66-70; instr, WVa Univ, 70-73; from asst prof to assoc prof, Cedarvill Col, 73-75, prof hist, Cedarville Col, 75-. **HONORS AND AWARDS** Faculty Scholar of the Year, 94, Cedarville Col; elected a Fellow of Early Modern Studies by the Sixteenth Century Studies Conference, 98. **MEMBERSHIPS** AHA; Am Soc Church Hist; Am Soc Reformation Res; Sixteenth Century Studies Conf. **RESEARCH** Lutheran reformation; Tudor England, ecclesiastical biography. **SELECTED PUBLICATIONS** Auth, Edmund Burke; Christian activist, Mod Age, summer 73; Mussolini and the Vatican, Univ Dayton Rev, summer 76; 1776: a Christian Loyalist view, Fides et Historia, 11/77; Luther's English Connection, Northwestern Publ House, 79; Was William Tyndale a Synergist?, Westminster Theological Journal, 44 (58-70), 82; Baptists and the Reformation, Reformation Today, 68 (14-20), 82; Three Principles of Protestantism, Banner of Truth, 232 (1-12), 83; Luther in Life Without Dichotomy, Grace Theol J, 5 (3-11), 84; Patrick Hamilton, Luther's Scottish Disciple, Sixteenth Century J, 18 (81-88), 87; E.B. Pursey, Great Lives From History, British and Commonwealth Series, Pasadena, Ca: Salem Press, 88; St. Benedict of Nursia, Great Lives From History, Ancient and Medieval Series, Pasadena, Ca: Salem Press, 88; The Trail of Blood, Reformation Today, 75 (2-9), 88; Luther's Scottish Connection, Madison, NJ: Fairleigh Dickinson Univ Press, 89; Frederick the great, Great Lives From History, Renaissance to 1900 Series, Pasadena, Ca: Salem Press, 89; King Henry IV of France, Great Lives From History, Renaissance to 1900 Series, Pasadena, Ca: Salem Press, 89; Robert Barnes, Historical Dictionary of Tudor England, Westport, Ct: Greenwood Press, 91; Lollardy, Hist Dict of Tudor England, Westport, Ct: Greenwood Press, 91; Lutheranism in England, Hist Dict of Tudor England, Westport, Ct: Greenwood Press, 91; Lenin and the Communists Impose the 'Red Terror, Great Events from History, Human Rights Series II (218-24), Pasadena, Ca: Salem Press, 92; Stepping Beyond the Law, The Standard, 83 (10-11), May 93; Czar Nicholas Executed and Red Terror Begins, Great Events From Hist, Human Rights Series, Pasadena, Ca: Salem Press, 93; Lutheranism in Scotland, Dict of Scottish Church Hist and Theology, London: Hodder and Stoughton, 93; Baptist Successionism: A Crucial Question in Baptist History, Metuchen, NJ: Scarecrow Press, 94; Ellen Gould Harmon White, Great Lives From Hist, American Women Series, Pasadena, Ca: Salem Press, 94; Every Inch for Christ: Abraham Kuyper on the Reform of the Church, Reformation and Revival 3, 94; Robert Barnes, Encyclopedia of the Reformation, New York: Oxford Univ Press, 96; Henry Balnaves, Encyclopedia of the Reformation, New York: Oxford

Univ Press, 96; many publications forthcoming. **CONTACT ADDRESS** Cedarville Col, PO Box 601, Cedarville, OH, 45314-0601. **EMAIL** McGold@Cedarville.edu

MCGOVERN, PATRICK E.
PERSONAL Born 12/09/1944 **DISCIPLINE** NEAR EASTERN ARCHAEOLOGY AND LITERATURE. **EDUCATION** Univ Penn, PhD, 80. **CAREER** Sr res sci & res assoc Near Eeast Sect, Adj assoc prof anthrop, Univ Penn, 79-. **HONORS AND AWARDS** Fullbright fel, Sweden, 93-94. **MEMBERSHIPS** Am Schools Oriental Res; Archaeol Inst Am. **RESEARCH** Archaeological chemistry. **SELECTED PUBLICATIONS** Coauth, The Late Bronze Egyptian Garrison at Beth Shan: A Study of Levels VII and VIII, Univ Penn Mus, 93; The Origins and Ancient History of Wine, Gordon & Breach, 95; auth Science in Archaeology: A Review, Am Jour Archaeol, 95; Technological Innovation and Artistic Achievement in the Late Bronze and Iron Ages of Central Transjordan, Studies in the History and Archaeology of Jordan V, 95; Neolithic Resinated Wine, Nature, 96; Vin Extraordinaire, The Sciences, 96; The Beginnings of Winemaking and Viniculture in the Ancient Near East and Egypt, Expedition, 97; Wine of Egypts Golden Age: An Archaeochemical Perspective, Jour of Egyptian Archaeol, 97; Wine for Eternity, Archaeol, 98. **CONTACT ADDRESS** Univ of Pennsylvania Museum, 33rd and Spruce Sts, Philadelphia, PA, 19104. **EMAIL** mcgovern@sas.upenn.edu

MCGRATH, ROBERT
DISCIPLINE ART HISTORY **EDUCATION** Middlebury Col, AB; Princeton Univ, MFA, PhD. **CAREER** Prof, Dartmouth Col. **RESEARCH** Rt of the Adirondacks and White Mountains; Western Am art. **SELECTED PUBLICATIONS** Auth, Facing North and East: The Ideology of the Gaze in Scenes of Placid Lake (exh cat), 93; Sacred Spaces: The Adirondack Vision of Nathan Farb, (exh cat), 93; 'Everlasting and Unfallen': New Hampshire and the State of Redemption, (exh cat), 92; A Wild Sort of Beauty: Public Places and Private Visions (exh cat), 92; The Space of Morality: Death and Transfiguration in the Adirondacs, (exh cat), 91; Curator and essayist for numerous exhib of art of the White Mountains and Adirondacks, and var articles. **CONTACT ADDRESS** Dartmouth Col, 3529 N Main St, Ste. 207, Hanover, NH, 03755. **EMAIL** robert.mcgrath@dartmouth.edu

MCGRATH, SYLVIA WALLACE
PERSONAL Born 02/27/1937, Montpelier, VT, m, 1966, 2 children **DISCIPLINE** AMERICAN HISTORY, HISTORY OF SCIENCE **EDUCATION** Mich State Univ, BA, 59; Radcliffe Col, MA, 60; Univ Wis-Madison, PhD(Am hist & hist of sci), 66. **CAREER** Teacher pub schs, 60-62; res, proj & teaching asst hist, Univ Wis, 62-66, proj assoc, 66-67; asst prof, 68-73, ASSOC PROF HIST, STEPHEN F AUSTIN STATE UNIV, 73-. **MEMBERSHIPS** Orgn Am Historians; Southern Hist Asn; Hist Sci Soc; Coord Comt Women in the Hist Profession. **RESEARCH** History of American science; history of women. **SELECTED PUBLICATIONS** Auth, Women in the Field--America Pioneering Women Naturalists, Isis, vol 0084, 93. **CONTACT ADDRESS** Dept of Hist, Stephen F Austin State Univ, Box 13013, Nacogdoches, TX, 75962.

MCGREW, RODERICK ERLE
PERSONAL Born 09/06/1928, Mankato, MN, m, 1948, 2 children **DISCIPLINE** MODERN RUSSIAN HISTORY **EDUCATION** Ripon Col, BA, 50; Univ Minn, MA, 51, PhD(hist), 55. **CAREER** Asst, Univ Minn, 51-54; instr hist, Mass Inst Technol, 54-55; instr, Univ Mo, Columbia, 55, from asst prof to prof, 55-67, chmn dept, 62-65; PROF HIST, TEMPLE UNIV, 67-, Am Coun Learned Soc sr res fel, 61-62; vis prof hist, Univ Rochester, 69-70; Am Philos Soc grant-in-aid, 71-72; Am ed, Jahrbucher fur Geschichte Osteuropas, 76- **MEMBERSHIPS** AHA; Am Asn Advan Slavic Studies; Midwest Conf Asian Affairs(vpres, 59); AAUP; Study Group 18th Century Russia, Britain. **RESEARCH** Russian social and intellectual history, 18th and 19th centuries; history of development and modernization; medical history. **SELECTED PUBLICATIONS** Auth, Catherine the Great, the Autocrat of All the Russians, Jahrbucher fur Geschichte Osteuropas, vol 0040, 92; Rhubarb--The Wondrous Drug, Amer Hist Rev, vol 0098, 93; Catherine-II Charters of 1785 to the Nobility and the Towns, Jahrbucher fur Geschichte Osteuropas, vol 0041, 93; A Man of Honor--Czartoryski, Adam as a Statesman of Russia and Poland 1795-1831, Amer Hist Rev, vol 0099, 94; Imperial Russian Foreign Policy, Slavonic and East Europ Rev, vol 0073, 95; Alexander-I, Amer Hist Rev, vol 0101, 96; The Year 1812 as Remembered by Contemporaries, Jahrbucher fur Geschichte Osteuropas, vol 0045, 97. **CONTACT ADDRESS** Dept of Hist, Temple Univ, Philadelphia, PA, 19122.

MCGUIRE, CHARLES
PERSONAL Born 11/24/1969, Minneapolis, MN, m **DISCIPLINE** MUSICOLOGY **EDUCATION** Oberlin Col, BA, 92; Oberlin Conserv, BMus, 92; Harvard Univ, AM, 95, PhD, 98. **CAREER** Vis Lectr Mus, Harvard Univ. **HONORS AND AWARDS** Grad Soc Diss Comp Fellow, 97-98; Pirotta Res Fellow, Summer 97; Harvard Univ Cert Distinction Tchg, 94-96; Oscar Schafer Fellow, 96-97; Ctr Euro Stud Travel Grant, 96; John Knowles Paine Travel Fellow, 95; Thorvald Otterstrom Mem Scholar, 92; Alwin M. Pappenheimer Scholar, 92-93, 96-97; High Honors in Hist, Oberlin Col, 92; Charles Martin Hall Award, Mus Hist, 92; Arion Award for Mus Excel, 87. **MEMBERSHIPS** Am Musicol Soc; Col Mus Soc; Elgar Soc. **RESEARCH** 19th and 20th century music, focusing on cantatas, oratorios, and the music of Edward Elgar; British Music Education of the 19th and 20th centuries; Wagner and Wagnerism in England and America; aesthetics of music; medieval polyphony; American folk and popular music. **SELECTED PUBLICATIONS** Epic Narration: The Oratorios of Edward Elgar, PhD Thesis, Harvard Univ, 98; Cultural Patronage in Fifteenth-Century England, honors thesis, Oberlin Col, 92. **CONTACT ADDRESS** Harvard Univ, Music Dept, Cambridge, MA, 02138. **EMAIL** mcguire@fas.harvard.edu

MCGUIRE JR., DONALD T.
DISCIPLINE CLASSICS **EDUCATION** Brown Univ, BA; Cornell Univ, MA; PhD. **CAREER** Asst prof, Univ Southern CA, 84-92; to dir summer progr Greece, 86-88; asst prof, SUNY Buffalo, 92. **RESEARCH** Latin imperial poetry; epic poetry; Greek and Roman hist and historiography; hist of archit; and mod popular cult and the ancient world. **SELECTED PUBLICATIONS** Auth, Textual Strategies and Political Suicide in Flavian Epic in The Imperial Muse: Ramus Essays on Roman Literature of the Empire, vol 2; History Compressed: The Roman Names of Silius' Cannae Episode, Latomus, 95. **CONTACT ADDRESS** Dept Classics, SUNY Buffalo, 712 Clemens Hall, Buffalo, NY, 14260.

MCHALE, VINCENT EDWARD
PERSONAL Born 04/17/1939, Jenkins Twp, PA, m, 1963, 1 child **DISCIPLINE** POLITICAL SCIENCE/ INTERNATIONAL RELATIONS **EDUCATION** Wilkes Univ, BA, Polit Sci, 64; Pa State Univ, MA, 66, PhD, 69. **CAREER** Asst prof, polit sci, Univ of Pa, 69-75; assoc prof. Polit sci, Case Western Reserve Univ, 75-84; PROF, POLIT SCI, CASE WESTERN RESERVE UNIV, 84-. **HONORS AND AWARDS** Nominee Wittke Undergraduate Tchg Award., Ch, Case Western Reserve Univ Polit Sci Dept, 77-. **RESEARCH** European mass politics **SELECTED PUBLICATIONS** Vote, Clivages Socio - Politiques et Developpment Regional en Belgique, 74; Political Parties of Europe, 83; Evaluating Transnational Programs in Government and Business, 80. **CONTACT ADDRESS** Dept of Polit Sci, Case Western Reserve Univ, Cleveland, OH, 44106. **EMAIL** vem@po.cwru.edu

MCHUGH, MICHAEL P.
PERSONAL Born 06/07/1933, Lackawanna, NY, m, 1961, 4 children **DISCIPLINE** CLASSICAL PHILOLOGY, PATRISTIC STUDIES **EDUCATION** Cath Univ Am, AB, 55, MA, 56, PhD(classics), 65. **CAREER** From instr to asst prof classics & humanities, Howard Univ, 58-68; from asst prof to assoc prof, 68-77, PROF CLASSICS, UNIV CONN, STORRS, 77-. **MEMBERSHIPS** NAm Patristic Soc; Am Philol Asn; Vergilian Soc; Am Class League; Medieval Acad Am. **RESEARCH** St Ambrose; Prosper of Aquitaine; textual studies. **SELECTED PUBLICATIONS** Auth, Christianity and the Rhetoric of Empire--The Development of Christian Discourse, J Early Christian Stud, vol 0001, 93. **CONTACT ADDRESS** Univ of Conn, Box U-57, Storrs, CT, 06268.

MCINERNEY, DANIEL J.
DISCIPLINE HISTORY **EDUCATION** Manhattan Col, BA, 72; Purdue Univ, MA, 75, PhD, 84. **CAREER** Vis instr, Purdue Univ, 84-86; asst prof, Utah State Univ, 86-93; ASSOC PROF, UTAH STATE UNIV, 93-. **CONTACT ADDRESS** History Dept, Utah State Univ, 0710 Old Main Hill, Logan, UT, 84322-0710. **EMAIL** danielj@hass.usu.edu

MCINTIRE, CARL THOMAS
PERSONAL Born 10/04/1939, Philadelphia, PA, 2 children **DISCIPLINE** MODERN HISTORY, PHILOSOPHY OF HISTORY **EDUCATION** Univ Pa, MA, 62, PhD(hist), 76; Faith Theol Sem, MDiv, 66. **CAREER** Instr hist, Shelton Col, 65-67; asst prof hist, Trinity Christian Col, 67-71; vis scholar, Cambridge Univ, 71-73; SR MEM HIST, INST CHRISTIAN STUDIES, TORONTO, 73-, Am Philos Soc res grant, 81; Soc Sci & Humanities Res Coun Can res grant, 81-82; lectr, Trinity Col, Univ Toronto, 82- **MEMBERSHIPS** AHA; Conf Faith & Hist; Am Cath Hist Asn; Am Soc Church Hist. **RESEARCH** Secularization of modern thought and society; comparative views of history: Christian, Hindu, Jewish, Marxist, Liberal and African Tribal; English politics in relation to the papacy, especially 19th century. **SELECTED PUBLICATIONS** Auth, The Knights Monks of Vichy France--Uriage, 1940-1945, Stud in Relig-Sciences Religieuses, vol 0024, 95. **CONTACT ADDRESS** Univ Toronto, 229 College St, Toronto, ON, M5S 1A1.

MCINTYRE, JERILYN S.
DISCIPLINE COMMUNICATION HISTORY **EDUCATION** Univ Wash, PhD, 73. **CAREER** Prof. **MEMBERSHIPS** Asn Edu in Jour and Mass Commun; Am Hist Asn; Org Am Hist. **SELECTED PUBLICATIONS** Auth, Transportation Developments in a Mid-Nineteenth Century Frontier Community, Jour W, 95; Rituals of Disorder: A Dramatistic Interpretation of Radical Dissent, 89; The Avvisi of Venice: Toward an Archaeology of Media Forms, Jour Hist, 87; Repositioning a Landmark: The Hutchins Commission and Freedom of the Press, 87. **CONTACT ADDRESS** Dept of Communication, Utah Univ, 100 S 1350 E, Salt Lake City, UT, 84112. **EMAIL** mcintyre@admin.comm.utah.edu

MCJIMSEY, GEORGE TILDEN
PERSONAL Born 03/09/1936, Dallas, TX, m, 1970 **DISCIPLINE** UNITED STATES HISTORY **EDUCATION** Grinnell Col, BA, 58; Columbia Univ, MA, 59; Univ WI, PhD, 68. **CAREER** Instr hist, Portland State Col, 64-65; from instr to asst prof, 65-71, assoc prof hist, 71-81, PROF, 81-, IA STATE UNIV, DEPT CHAIR, 92-. **HONORS AND AWARDS** Doctor of Humane Letters, Grinnell Col, 98. **RESEARCH** Political history of the United States, 1850-1900. **SELECTED PUBLICATIONS** Auth, Genteel Partisan: Manton Marble, 1834-1917, IA State Univ, 71; Dividing and Reuniting of America, 1848-1877; Harry Hopkins, Ally of the Poor and Defender of Democracy. **CONTACT ADDRESS** Dept of Hist, Iowa State Univ, Ames, IA, 50011-0002. **EMAIL** gmcjimse@iastate.edu

MCJIMSEY, ROBERT
PERSONAL Born 03/09/1936, Dallas, TX, m, 1961, 3 children **DISCIPLINE** MODERN HISTORY **EDUCATION** Grinnell Col, AB, 58; Univ Wis, AM, 61, PhD, 68. **CAREER** Instr hist, Oberlin Col, 65-66; instr, Ohio Wesleyan Univ, 66-68; asst prof, 68-75, assoc prof hist, CO Col, 75-83, prof 83. **MEMBERSHIPS** NACBS **RESEARCH** Seventeenth century Engl; Eng opinion and for policy during the reign of William III. **CONTACT ADDRESS** Dept of Hist, Colorado Col, 14 E Cache La Poudre, Colorado Springs, CO, 80903-3294.

MCKALE, DONALD MARSHALL
PERSONAL Born 10/24/1943, Clay Center, KS, m, 1966, 3 children **DISCIPLINE** MODERN EUROPEAN HISTORY **EDUCATION** Iowa State Univ, BS, 66; Univ MoColumbia, MA, 67; Kent State Univ, PhD(hist), 70. **CAREER** Asst prof mod Europ hist, Ga Col, 70-74, assoc prof, 74-78, prof, 78-79; PROF MOD EUROP HIST, CLEMSON UNIV, 79-, Study visit to West Ger, Ger Acad Exchange Serv, 75; vis assoc prof mod Europ hist, Univ Nebr-Lincoln, 75-76. **MEMBERSHIPS** AHA; Conf Group Cent Europ Hist. **RESEARCH** Nazi Germany. **SELECTED PUBLICATIONS** Auth, German Policy Toward the Sharif of Mecca, 1914-1916, Historian, vol 0055, 93; The Nazi Menace in Argentina, 1931-1947, Ger Stud Rev, vol 0016, 93; 2 Against Hitler--Stealing the Nazis Best-Kept Secrets, Amer Hist Rev, vol 0098, 93; Hitler Japanese Confidant--Hiroshi, Oshima and Magic Intelligence, 1941-1945, Amer Hist Rev, vol 0099, 94; Germany and the Arab Question Before World War I, Historian, vol 0059, 97; The Kaisers Spy--Oppenheim, Max, Von and the Anglo German Rivalry Before and During the First World War, Europ Hist Quart, vol 0027, 97. **CONTACT ADDRESS** Dept of Hist, Clemson Univ, Clemson, SC, 29631.

MCKAY, ALEXANDER G.
PERSONAL Born 12/24/1924, Toronto, ON, Canada **DISCIPLINE** CLASSICS **EDUCATION** Univ Toronto, BA, 46; Yale Univ, MA, 47; Princeton Univ, PhD, 50. **CAREER** Instr, Princeton Univ, 47-49; instr, Wells Col, 49-50; instr, Univ Pa, 50-51; instr, Univ Man, 51-52; asst prof, Mt Allison Univ, 52-53; asst prof, Waterloo Col, 53-55; Dir, Classical Sumer Sch Italy, Vergilian Soc Am, 55-97; asst prof, Univ Man, 55-57; asst prof, 57-59, assoc prof, 59-61, prof, 61-90, PROF EMER CLASSICS, McMASTER UNIV, 90-, chmn, 62-68, 76-79, dean hum, 68-73; adj prof hum, York Univ, 90-96; vis lectr, Concordia Univ, 92-93. **HONORS AND AWARDS** Off, Order Can; Queen's Silver Jubilee Medal; Centenary Medal, Royal Soc Can; Canada 125 Medal; Woodrow Wilson fel; Killam sr res fel; LLD(hon), Univ Man, 86; LLD(hon), Brock Univ, 90; LLD(hon), Queen's Univ, 91; DLitt (hon), McMaster Univ, 92; DLitt(hon), Waterloo Univ, 93. **MEMBERSHIPS** Acad Hum Soc Sci; Class Asn Can; Vergilian Soc; Int Acad Union **RESEARCH** Ancient Roman architecture and literature. **SELECTED PUBLICATIONS** Auth, Naples and Campania, 62; auth, Victorian Architecture in Hamilton, 67; auth, Vergil's Italy, 70; auth, Ancient Campania, 72; auth, Houses, Villas and Palaces in the Roman World, 75; auth, Vitruvius, Architect and Engineer, 78, 85; auth, Romische Hauser, Villen und Palaste, 80; auth, Roma Antiqua, Latium & Erturia, 86; coauth, Roman Lyric Poetry: Catullus and Horace, 69, 74; coauth, Roman Satire: Horace, Juvenal, Persius et al, 76; coauth, Selections from Vergil's Aeneid, Books I, IV, VI (Dido and Aeneas), 88; coauth, The Two Worlds of the Poet: New Perspectives on Vergil, 92; coauth, Tragedy, Love and Change: Roman Poetic Themes and Variations, 94. **CONTACT ADDRESS** Classics Dept, McMaster Univ, Hamilton, ON, L8S 4L5.

MCKAY, JOHN PATRICK
PERSONAL Born 08/28/1938, St. Louis, MO, m, 1961, 2 children **DISCIPLINE** EUROPEAN ECONOMIC/SOCIAL HISTORY **EDUCATION** Wesleyan Univ, BA, 61; Fletcher Sch Law, MA, 62; Univ Calif, Berkeley, PhD, 68. **CAREER** From instr to assoc prof, 66-76, prof hist, 76-, Univ Ill; Guggenheim Found fel, 70-71; Fulbright-Hays fel, Soviet Union, 74. **HONORS AND AWARDS** Herbert Baxter Adams Award, AHA, 70. **MEMBERSHIPS** AHA; Econ Hist Assn; Bus Hist Conf;

Am Assn Advan Slavic Studies; Fr Hist Assn. **RESEARCH** Russian economic history; West European economic and social history; history of urban transportation, world history. **SELECTED PUBLICATIONS** Auth, John Cockerill in Southern Russia, 1885-1905: A Study of Aggressive Foreign Entrepreneurship, Bus Hist Rev, 67; auth, Pioneers for Profit: Foreign Entrepreneurship and Russian Industrialization, 1885-1913, Univ Chicago, 70; ed & transl, Jules Michelet's The People, Univ Ill, 73; auth, Foreign Enterprise in Russian and Soviet Industry: A Long Term Perspective, Bus Hist Rev, 74; contrib, The Rich, The Well Born and The Powerful: Elites and Upper Classes in History, Univ Ill, 74; auth, Tramways and Trolleys: The Rise of Urban Mass Transport in Europe, Princeton Univ, 76; auth, A History of Western Society, Vol II, Houghton Mifflin, 99; auth, A History of World Societies, 96. **CONTACT ADDRESS** Dept of History, Univ of Illinois, Urbana-Champaign, 810 S Wright St, Urbana, IL, 61801-3611. **EMAIL** j-mckay2@uiuc.edu

MCKEEN, WILLIAM

PERSONAL Born 09/16/1954, Indianapolis, IN, d, 3 children **DISCIPLINE** HISTORY; MASS COMMUNICATION; EDUCATION **EDUCATION** Indiana Univ, BA, 74, MA, 77; Univ OK, PhD, 86. **CAREER** Educator, 77-; Prof and ch, jour dept, Univ Florida. **HONORS AND AWARDS** Various teaching Awds **MEMBERSHIPS** Pop culture asn; SO book critics cir; AJHA; asn for edu in journ and mass comm. **RESEARCH** Pop cult; journ hist; music. **SELECTED PUBLICATIONS** The Norton Book of Rock and Roll, 99; Good Stories, Well Told, 99; Tom Wolfe, 95; Bob Dylan: A Bio-Bibliography, 93; Hunter S Thompson, 91; The Beatles: A Bio-Bibliography, 90. **CONTACT ADDRESS** Univ Florida, 2089 Weimer Hall, Gainsville, FL, 32611. **EMAIL** wmckeen@jou.ufl.edu

MCKENNA, JOHN WILLIAM

PERSONAL Born 07/23/1938, West Warwick, RI, m, 1961, 2 children **DISCIPLINE** MEDIEVAL AND ENGLISH CONSTITUTIONAL HISTORY **EDUCATION** Amherst Col, AB, 60; Columbia Univ, MA, 62; Cambridge Univ, PhD(medieval hist), 65. **CAREER** Instr hist, Brooklyn Col, 65-66; asst prof, Univ Calif, Riverside, 66-69; WALTER D & EDITH M L SCULL ASSOC PROF ENGLISH CONSTITUTIONAL HIST, HAVERFORD COL, 69-. **MEMBERSHIPS** Mediaeval Acad Am; AHA; Conf Brit Studies; fel Royal Hist Soc. **RESEARCH** Royal political propaganda in Northern Europe; late medieval and early modern government and politics; medieval kingship and sovereignty. **SELECTED PUBLICATIONS** Auth, Holocaust Memorial Museum, Smithsonian, vol 0024, 93. **CONTACT ADDRESS** Dept of Hist, Haverford Col, Haverford, PA, 19041.

MCKENNA, MARIAN CECILIA

PERSONAL Born 07/03/1926, Scarsdale, NY **DISCIPLINE** AMERICAN HISTORY **EDUCATION** Columbia Univ, BS, 49, MA, 50, PhD, 53. **CAREER** Instr hist, Hunter Col, 53-59; asst prof, Manhattanville Col, 59-66; assoc prof, 66-68, PROF HIST, UNIV CALGARY, 68-, Danforth fel, 64-65; Can Coun awards, 67, 68, 69, res fel, 72-73. **HONORS AND AWARDS** Penrose Award, Am Philos Soc, 56. **MEMBERSHIPS** Orgn Am Historians; Immigration Hist Soc; Can Asn Am Studies; Can Hist Asn; Can Ethnic Studies Asn. **RESEARCH** Canadian-American immigration; American Civil War and Reconstruction; American political history post 1850. **SELECTED PUBLICATIONS** Auth, Prelude to Tyranny--Wheeler, Roosevelt, F.D. and the 1937 Court Fight, Pac Hist Rev, vol 0062, 93; The Peace Progressives and American Foreign Relations, Pac Hist Rev, vol 0065, 96; Managing Local Uncertainty--Elite Lawyers in the New Deal, Can Rev Amer Stud, vol 0027, 97. **CONTACT ADDRESS** Dept of Hist, Univ of Calgary, 2920 24th Ave NW, Calgary, AB, T2N 1N4.

MCKENNA, MARY OLGA

DISCIPLINE EDUCATION/HISTORY **EDUCATION** Mt St Vincent Univ, BA, 47; Boston Col, Mass, MA, 57, PhD, 64; Univ London, ALE, 77; Univ PEI, LLD, 90. **CAREER** Sch tchr, 39-61; super educ, Archdiocese Boston, 61-64; PROF EMER EDUC, MT ST VINCENT UNIV 64-86; congregational hist, Sisters Charity, Halifax, 86-. **MEMBERSHIPS** Am Conf Relig Women; Can Cath Hist Asn; Can Soc Stud Educ. **SELECTED PUBLICATIONS** Auth, Micmac by Choice: An Island Legend, 90; auth, Paradigm Shifts in a Women's Religious Institution: The Sisters of Charity, Halifax, 1950-79, in CCHA Hist Studs 61, 95. **CONTACT ADDRESS** Mount Saint Vincent Univ, 106 Shore Dr, Halifax, ON, B3M 3J5.

MCKEOWN, JAMES C.

DISCIPLINE CLASSICAL STUDIES **EDUCATION** Cambridge Univ, PhD, 78. **CAREER** Dept Classics, Wisc Univ **RESEARCH** Latin literature. **SELECTED PUBLICATIONS** Auth, pubs on Latin poetry, and Ovid's Amores. **CONTACT ADDRESS** Dept of Classics, Univ of Wisconsin, Madison, 500 Lincoln Drive, Madison, WI, 53706. **EMAIL** jmckeown@macc.wisc.edu

MCKEVITT, GERALD

PERSONAL Born 07/03/1939, Longview, WA **DISCIPLINE** AMERICAN HISTORY, THEOLOGY **EDUCATION** Univ San Fancisco, AB, 61; Univ Southern CA, MA, 64; Univ CA, Los Angeles, PhD(hist), 72; Pontif Gregorian Univ, Rome, STB, 75. **CAREER** Res asst prof hist, 75-77, asst prof, 77-92, prof hist, Univ Santa Clara, 93-, dir Univ Arch, 75-85. **HONORS AND AWARDS** Oscar O Wither Award, 91. **MEMBERSHIPS** Soc Am Archivists. **RESEARCH** California history; Jesuit education in California; Italian Jesuit exiles in America, 19th century. **SELECTED PUBLICATIONS** Auth, Gold Lake myth, J West, 10/64; The Jesuit Arrival in California and the Founding of Santa Clara College, Records Am Cath Hist Soc, 9-12/74; From Franciscan Mission to Jesuit College: a Troubled Transition at Mission Santa Clara, Southern CA Quart, summer 76; Progress Amid Poverty, Santa Clara College in the 1870s, Pac Hist, winter 76; The Beginning of Santa Clara University, San Jose Studies, 2/77; The University of Santa Clara, A History, 1851-1977, Stanford Univ, 79; Jump That Saved Rocky Mountain Mission, Pacific Hist Rev, 86; Jesuit Missionary Linguistics, Western Hist Quart, 90; Hispanic Californians and Catholic Higher education, CA Hist, 90-91; Jesuit Higher Education in US, Mis-America, 91; Italian Jesuits in New Mexico, NM Hist Rev, 92; Christopher Columbus as Civic Saint, CA Hist, winter 92-93; Art of Conversion: Jesuits and Flatheads, US Cath Hist, 94. **CONTACT ADDRESS** Dept Hist, Univ Santa Clara, 500 El Camino Real, Santa Clara, CA, 95053-0001. **EMAIL** gmckevitt@mailer.scu.edu

MCKILLOP, A.B.

DISCIPLINE HISTORY **EDUCATION** Univ Manitoba, BA, 68, MA, 70; Queen's Univ, PhD, 77. **CAREER** Prof. **RESEARCH** Historiography of Canada. **SELECTED PUBLICATIONS** Auth, Contours of Canadian Thought, Univ Toronto Press, 87; Marching as to war: Elements of Ontario Undergraduate Culture, 1880-1914, Univ, Youth and Soc, McGill-Queen's UP, 89; "Culture, Intellect and Context," Jour Can Stud 24, 89; Matters of Mind: the University in Ontario 1791-1951, Univ Toronto Press, 94; co-ed, God's Peculiar Peoples, Essay on Polit Cult in Nineteenth-Century Can, Carleton UP, 93. **CONTACT ADDRESS** Dept of Hist, Carleton Univ, 1125 Colonel By Dr, Ottawa, ON, K1S 5B6. **EMAIL** brian_mckillop@carleton.ca

MCKITRICK, ERIC LOUIS

PERSONAL Born 07/05/1919, Battle Creek, MI, m, 1946, 4 children **DISCIPLINE** AMERICAN HISTORY **EDUCATION** Columbia Univ, BS, 49, MA, 51, PhD, 59. **CAREER** Lectr hist, Sch Gen Studies, Columbia Univ, 52-54; asst prof, Univ Chicago, 55-59; asst prof, Douglass Col, Rutgers Univ, 59-60; assoc prof, 60-65, PROF HIST, COLUMBIA UNIV, 65-, Fel, Rockefeller Found, 54-55; Soc Sci Res Coun fel, 54; Ford Found grant, 56; Rockefeller Found grant, 62-63; Nat Endowment for Humanities grant, 67-68; fel, Inst Advan Studies, 70-71 & 76-77; Guggenheim fel, 70-71 & 76-77; Pitt prof Am hist & instr, Cambridge Univ, 73-74; Harmsworth prof, Am Hist Inst, Oxford Univ, 79-80. **HONORS AND AWARDS** Dunning Prize, AHA, 60. **MEMBERSHIPS** Am Studies Asn; AHA; Orgn Am Historians; Acad Polit Sci. **RESEARCH** Late 18th and 19th century political, social and intellectual American history. **SELECTED PUBLICATIONS** Auth, Arguing About Slavery--The Great Battle in the United States Congress, New York Review of Books, vol 0043, 96; American Sphinx--The Character of Jefferson, Thomas, NY Rev Bks, vol 0044, 97. **CONTACT ADDRESS** Dept of Hist Grad Sch of Arts & Sci, Columbia Univ, New York, NY, 10027.

MCKIVEN, HENRY M., JR.

DISCIPLINE HISTORY **EDUCATION** Auburn Univ at Montgomery, BA; Va Polytech Inst, MA; Vanderbilt Univ, PhD. **CAREER** Assoc prof; Univ W Al, 90-91; prof, Univ South Al, 89-90 & 91-. **RESEARCH** U.S. South, Civil War and reconstruction, labor **SELECTED PUBLICATIONS** Auth, Iron and Steel: Class, Race, and Community in Birmingham, Alabama 1870-1920, Chapel Hill, Univ NC Press, 95 & White Workers, White Capital, and the Struggle for Shop Floor Control in Birmingham, Alabama, 1880-1895, Locus 6 1, 93, Southern Hist. **CONTACT ADDRESS** Dept of History, Univ South Alabama, 370 Humanities, Mobile, AL, 36688-0002. **EMAIL** hmckiven@jaguar1.usouthal.edu

MCKNIGHT, EDGAR VERNON

PERSONAL Born 11/21/1931, Wilson, SC, m, 1955, 2 children **DISCIPLINE** RELIGION, CLASSICAL LANGUAGES **EDUCATION** Col Charleston, BS, 53; Southern Baptist Theol Sem, BD, 56, PhD, 60; Oxford Univ, MLitt, 78. **CAREER** Chaplain, Chowan Col, 60-63; from asst prof to assoc prof, 63-74, assoc dean acad affairs, 70-73, prof relig & classics, 74-82, chemn, dept classics, 78-80, chemn, dept relig, 91-95, William R Kenan Prof Relig, Furman Univ, 82-; vis prof, Southern Baptist Theol Sem, 66-67; Fulbright sr res prof, Univ Tubingen, 81-82, Univ Muenster, 95-96; NEH study grant, Yale Univ, summer, 80; Bye-fel Robinson Col, Univ Cambridge, 88-89. **HONORS AND AWARDS** Bk of Year Award, MLA, 78. **MEMBERSHIPS** Soc Bibl Lit; Am Acad Relig; Am Schs Orient Res; Studiorum Novi Testamenti Soc. **RESEARCH** Biblical scholarship among American and Baptist scholars, espec A T Robertson; Biblical hermeneutics; structuralism and semiotics. **SELECTED PUBLICATIONS** Coauth, A History of Chowan College, Graphic Arts, 64; auth, Opening the Bible: A Guide to Understanding the Scriptures, Broadman, 67; coauth, Introd to the New Testament, Ronald 69; auth, What is Form Criticism?, In: Series on Introduction to Biblical Scholarship, Fortress, 69; coauth, Can the Griesbach Hypothesis be Falsified?, J Bibl Lit, 9/72; auth, Structure and Meaning in Biblical Narrative, Perspectives Relig Studies, spring 76; Meaning in Texts: The Historical Shaping of a Narrative Hermeneutics, Fortress, 78; The Bible and the Reader, Fortress, 85; Postmodern Use of the Bible, Abringdon, 88; ed, Reader Perspectives on the New Testament, Semeia 48, 89; NT ed, Mercer Dictionary of the Bible, 90; NT ed, Mercer Commentary on the Bible, Mercer, 94; co-ed, The New Literary Criticism and the New Testament, Sheffield and Trinity, 94. **CONTACT ADDRESS** Dept of Relig, Furman Univ, 3300 Poinsett Hwy, Greenville, SC, 29613-1218. **EMAIL** edgar.mcknight@furman.edu

MCKNIGHT, JOSEPH WEBB

PERSONAL Born 02/17/1925, San Angelo, TX, m, 2 children **DISCIPLINE** LEGAL HISTORY, FAMILY LAW **EDUCATION** Univ Tex, Austin, BA, 47; Oxford Univ, BA, 49, BCL, 50, MA, 54; Columbia Univ, LLM, 59. **CAREER** Legal pract, Cravath, Swaine & Moore, New York, 51-55; from asst prof to prof, 55-63, assoc dean, 77-80, Prof Law, Sch Law, Southern Methodist Univ, 63-, Consult, Hemisfair, 67-69; dir, Family Code Proj, State Bar Tex, 66-75. **HONORS AND AWARDS** Phi Beta Kappa; Rhodes Scholar; Kent fel, 58-59; Academia Mexicana de Derecho Int, 88; State Bar of Texas Family Law Section Hall of Legends, 97. **MEMBERSHIPS** Am Soc Legal Hist (vpres, 67-69); Am Soc Int Law; Nat Legal Aid & Defenders Asn. **SELECTED PUBLICATIONS** Auth, Family Law: Husband and Wife, Annual Survey of Texas Law, SMU L Rev, 93, 94, 95, 96, 97, 98; auth, Texas Community Property Law: Conservative Attitudes, reluctant Change, Law & Contemp Prob, 93; auth, The Mysteries of Spanish Surnames, El Campanario, 94; auth, Spanish Legitim in the United States: Its Survival and Decline, Am J Comp L, 96; auth, Survival and Decline of the Spanish Law of Descendent Succession on the Anglo-Hispanic Frontier of North America: Homenaje al Professor Alfonso Garcia-Gallo, 96; contribur, Tyler, ed, The New Handbook of Texas, 96; auth, Eugene L. Smith, 1933-1997, An Appreciation of His Achievements, Family Law Section Rept, 97; coauth, Texas Matrimonial Property Law, 2d ed, Lupus, 98. **CONTACT ADDRESS** Sch of Law, Southern Methodist Univ, Dallas, TX, 75275. **EMAIL** suzannes@mail.smu.edu

MCLAREN, ANGUS

PERSONAL Born 12/20/1942, Vancouver, ON, Canada **DISCIPLINE** HISTORY OF MEDICINE **EDUCATION** Univ BC, BA, 65; Harvard Univ, MA, 66, PhD, 71. **CAREER** Asst prof, Univ Calgary, 70-71; Grinnell Col, 71-73; sr assoc fel, St. Anthony's Col, Oxford, 73-75; assoc prof, 75-83, PROF HISTORY, UNIV VICTORIA, 83-; vis Hannah Prof Hist Med, Univ Toronto, 85. **MEMBERSHIPS** Soc Social Hist Med; Can Soc Hist Med; Can Hist Asn. **SELECTED PUBLICATIONS** Auth, Birth Control in Nineteenth Century England, 78; auth, Sexuality and Social Order, 83; auth, Reproductive Rituals, 84; auth, Our Own Master Race, 90; auth, A History of Contraception, 90; auth, A Prescription for Murder, 93; auth, The Trials of Masculinity: Policing Sexual Boundaries, 1870-1930, 97; coauth, The Bedroom and the State, 86. **CONTACT ADDRESS** History Dept, Univ of Victoria, Victoria, BC, V8W 2Y2.

MCLAUGHLIN, ANDREE NICOLA

PERSONAL Born 02/12/1948, White Plains, New York **DISCIPLINE** EDUCATION **EDUCATION** Cornell Univ, BS 1970; Univ of MA-Amherst, MEd 1971, EdD 1974. **CAREER** Medgar Evers College/CUNY, asst prof/project dir 1974-77, chairperson 1977-79, dean of administration and assoc prof, 1979-82, planning coord of Women's Studies Rsch & Develop 1984-89, professor of Humanities, 1986-; University of London Institute of Education, distinguished visiting scholar, 1986; Hamilton Coll, Jane Watson Irwin Visiting Prof of Women's Studies, 1989-91; Medgar Evers College/CUNY, prof of literature & language/prof of interdisciplinary studies, 1992-, Office of International Women's Affairs, director, 1996-. **HONORS AND AWARDS** Natl Endowment for the Humanities Fellow, 1976, 1979, 1984, 1989, 1993; 25 articles published; Amer Council on Educ, Fellow in Acad Admin, 1980-81; Andrew W Mellon Fellow, CUNY Graduate School & Univ Center, 1987; **MEMBERSHIPS** Bd mem, Where We At, Black Women Artists, 1979-87; mem Natl Women's Studies Assoc 1980-84, Amer Assoc of Univ Profs 1982-; founding intl coord, Intl Resource Network of Women of African Descent, 1982-85, founding mem Sisterhood in Support of Sisters in South Africa 1984-; adv bd mem Sisterhood of Black Single Mothers 1984-86; founding intl coordinator, Cross-Cultural Black Women's Studies Inst, 1987-; chair, Editorial Bd, Network: A Pan African Women's Forum (journal), 1987-91; mem, Policy & Publication Comm, The Feminist Press, CUNY, 1988-. **SELECTED PUBLICATIONS** Co-editor, Wild Women in the Whirlwind: Afra-American Culture & the Contemporary Literary Renaissance, Rutgers Univ Press, 1990; Author, Double Dutch, poetry, 1989; author, "Black Women's Studies in America," 1989; author, "Urban Politics in the Higher Education of Black

Women," 1988; author, "The International Nature of the Southern African Women's Struggles," 1988; author, "Unfinished Business of the Sixties: Black Women on the Front Line," 1990; author, "Black Women, Identity and the Quest for Humanhood and Wholeness," 1990; author, Through the Barrel of Her Consciousness: Contemporary Black Women's Literature and Activism in Cross Cultural Perspective, 1994. Susan Koppelman Book Award for Best Edited Feminist work in Popular/American Culture Studies, 1990; author The Impact of the Black Consciousness and Women's Movements on Black Women's Identity: Intercontinental Empowerment, 1995. **CONTACT ADDRESS** Professor, Medgar Evers Col, CUNY, 1650 Bedford Ave, Brooklyn, NY, 11225.

MCLAUGHLIN, KEN
DISCIPLINE HISTORY **EDUCATION** Univ Waterloo, BA, 65; Dalhousie Univ, MA, 67; Univ Toronto, PhD, 74. **CAREER** Prof **HONORS AND AWARDS** Arts Awd, 94; Outstanding Achievement Awd, 84; Awd Honour, 82. **SELECTED PUBLICATIONS** Auth, Allen Huber: Berlin's Stangest Mayor; Bishops and Politics: A Canadian Example; Cambridge: The making of a Canadian City; Donald Grant Creighton 1902-1979; Doon Pioneer Village: Master Plan. **CONTACT ADDRESS** Dept of History, St. Jerome's Univ, Waterloo, ON, N2L 3G3. **EMAIL** kmclaugh@watarts.uwaterloo.ca

MCLAUGHLIN, KEVIN P.
PERSONAL Born 08/15/1960, Seattle, WA **DISCIPLINE** MUSIC **EDUCATION** Univ of MN, DAM, 92; Yale Univ, MM, 85; Univ of MI, BM, 83 **CAREER** Inst, 92-95, St Olaf Col; Asst Prof, 95-96, NE MO St Univ **HONORS AND AWARDS** Phi Kappa Phi, 9 1 **MEMBERSHIPS** Am Libr Asn; Asn of Col & Res Librs **RESEARCH** Music hist; Hist of Opera **SELECTED PUBLICATIONS** Auth, The Mirror of Justice, 97; Das Wunderjahr in Jena, 98; The View from the Tower, 98 **CONTACT ADDRESS** Dept of German, Princeton Univ, Princeton, NJ, 08544. **EMAIL** tjz@princeton.edu

MCLAUGHLIN, MARY MARTIN
PERSONAL Born 04/15/1919, Grand Island, NE **DISCIPLINE** MEDIEVAL HISTORY **EDUCATION** Univ Nebr, AB, 40, MA, 41; Columbia Univ, PhD, 52. **CAREER** Instr hist, Wellesley Col, 43-46; instr, Vassar Col, 46-48; vis asst prof, Univ Nebr, 52-52, 54-55; asst prof, Vassar Col, 59-67; Ingram Merrill Found fel, 65-66; RES & WRITING, 66-, Am Philos Soc travel grant, Europe, 55. **MEMBERSHIPS** AHA; Medieval Acad Am; Renaissance Soc Am; Am Cath Hist Asn. **RESEARCH** Medieval social and intellectual history, 10th-15th centuries, especially Abelard; history of women, especially religious life. **SELECTED PUBLICATIONS** Auth, The Oldest Vocation--Christian Motherhood in the Middle Ages, Cath Hist Rev, vol 0081, 95; Male Authors, Female Readers--Representation and Subjectivity in Middle English Devotional Literature, Amer Hist Rev, vol 0102, 97; Women in Christian History--A Bibliography, Church Hist, vol 0066, 97. **CONTACT ADDRESS** Valley Farm Rd, Millbrook, NY, 12545.

MCLAUGHLIN, MEGAN
DISCIPLINE HISTORY **EDUCATION** Stanford Univ, PhD, 85. **CAREER** Assoc prof, Univ Ill Urbana Champaign. **RESEARCH** European religion and society to 1200; history of women and gender; sexuality, gender and politics in eleventh-century Europe. **SELECTED PUBLICATIONS** Auth, On Communion with the Dead, J Medieval Hist, 91; Gender Paradox and the Otherness of God, Gender Hist, 91; Consorting with Saints: Prayer for the Dead in Early Medieval France, Cornell, 94. **CONTACT ADDRESS** History Dept, Univ Ill Urbana Champaign, 52 E Gregory Dr, Champaign, IL, 61820. **EMAIL** megmclau@uiuc.edu

MCLAURIN, MELTON ALONZA
PERSONAL Born 07/11/1941, Fayetteville, NC, m, 1961, 3 children **DISCIPLINE** UNITED STATES & LABOR HISTORY **EDUCATION** E Carolina Univ, BS, 62, MA, 64; Univ SC, PhD(US hist), 67. **CAREER** Prof hist, Univ S AL, 67-77; prof hist & chemn dept, Univ NC, Wilmington, 77-. **MEMBERSHIPS** Southern Hist Asn; Orgn Am Historians. **RESEARCH** The American South; race relations. **SELECTED PUBLICATIONS** Auth, Paternalism and Protest, Southern Cotton Mill Workers and Organized Labor, 1875-1905, Greenwood, 71; auth, The Knights of Labor in the South, 78, Greenwood; coauth, The Image of Progress, Alabama Photographs, 1872-1917, Univ AL, 80; Separate Pasts, Growing Up White in the Segregated South, Univ GA, 87; Celia, A Slave, Univ GA, 91; co-ed, You Wrote My Life, Lyrical Themes in Country Music, Gordon & Breach, 92. **CONTACT ADDRESS** Dept Hist, Univ N. Carolina, 601 S College Rd, Wilmington, NC, 28403-3201. **EMAIL** mclaurin@uncwil.edu

MCLEAN, ANDREW MILLER
PERSONAL Born 05/25/1941, Brooklyn, NY, 1 child **DISCIPLINE** ENGLISH RENAISSANCE LITERATURE & HISTORY **EDUCATION** St Olaf Col, BA, 63; Brooklyn Col, MA, 67; Univ NC, Chapel Hill, PhD(English), 71. **CAREER** Asst prof, 71-76, Assoc Prof English, 77-82, prof, 82- ,Univ Wis-Parkside; Rev ed, Clio: An Interdisciplinary Jour of Lit, Hist, and Philos of Hist, 71-93; res prof, Catholic Univ Louvain, 75-76. **MEMBERSHIPS** MLA; Soc Studies Midwestern Lit; Renaissance Soc Am; Shakespeare Asn Am. **RESEARCH** Sixteenth century English literature; interdisciplinary studies, film-Shakespeare. **SELECTED PUBLICATIONS** Auth, Emerson's Brahma, New England Quart, 3/69; James Joyce & A Doblin, Comp Lit, spring 73; English translation of Erasmus, Moreana, 11/74; Castiglione, Cicero & English dialogues, Romance Notes, 75; Barlow, More & the Anglican episcopacy, Moreana, 2/76; contribr, Bibliography on teaching Shakespeare, In: Teaching Shakespeare, Princeton Univ, 77; Barlow & the Lutheran Factions, Renaissance Quart, summer 78; auth, Shakespeare: Annotated Bibliographies and Media Guide for Teachers, MCTE, 80; ed, Work of William Barlowe, Sutton Courtenay press, 81; co-ed, Redefining Shakespeare: Literary Theory and Theater Practice in the German Democratic Republic. Univ Delaware, 98. **CONTACT ADDRESS** Dept of English, Univ of Wiscosin, Parkside, Box 2000, Kenosha, WI, 53141-2000. **EMAIL** andrew.mclean@uwp.edu

MCLEAN, MABLE PARKER
PERSONAL Cameron, NC, w **DISCIPLINE** EDUCATION **EDUCATION** Barber Scotia Coll; Johnson C Smith U; Howard U; NW U; Cath Univ of Am; Inst for Educ Mgmt Harvard Univ 1972; Johnson C Smith U, LHD 1976; Rust Coll, LHS 1976; Coll of Granada, LlD; Barber-Scotia, Pedu. **CAREER** Barber-Scotia Coll, prof of educ and psychology, coordinator of student teaching 1969-71, chairman dept of elementary educ 1970-71, dean of college 1971-74, apptd interim president 1974, apptd acting president of college 1974, apptd president of the college 1974-. **HONORS AND AWARDS** 7 Honorary Degrees; numerous awds and citations among which are Johnson C Smith Alumni Outstanding Achievement Awd 1977; Disting Alumna Awd 1977; Alumna of the Year Johnson C Smith Univ 1980; Dedicated Service Citation-Consortium on Rsch Training 1982; Disting Service Awd Grambling State Univ 1984; Presidential Scroll for devotion to higher educ by promoting achievement of excellence 1986. **MEMBERSHIPS** Mem Assn for Childhood Edn; Assn for Student Teaching; Nat & St NC Assn for Supr & Curriculum Devel; St Coun on Early Childhood Edn; Delta Kappa Gamma Soc of Women Edn; NC Adminstrv Women in Edn; Am Assn of Univ Adminstr; Nat Coun of Adminstrv Women in Edn; mem exec com Metrolina Lung Assn; Dem Women's Org of Cabarrus Co; Alpha Kappa Alpha Sorority Inc; elder John Hall Presb Ch; elected bd of dir Children's Home Soc of NC; past pres United Presb Women's Org of John Hall United Presb Ch; pres Presidents Roundtable of UPC USA; bd dir NAFEO; mem United Bd for Coll Develop; mem United Way of Cabarrus Co; mem exec com NC Assn of Independent Colleges & U; mem exec com NC Assn of Colleges & U. **CONTACT ADDRESS** Barber-Scotia Col, Concord, NC, 28025.

MCLEOD, JANE
DISCIPLINE EVENTEENTH AND EIGHTEENTH-CENTURY EUROPEAN HISTORY **EDUCATION** Brock Col; Univ York, MA, PhD. **CAREER** Assoc prof. **RESEARCH** Social and political history in seventeenth and eighteenth-century France. **SELECTED PUBLICATIONS** Coauth, Amiraute de Guyenne: Source de l'histoire de la Nouvelle France, Ottawa: Nat Archv Can. **CONTACT ADDRESS** Dept of Hist, Brock Univ, 500 Glenridge Ave, St Catharines, ON, L2S 3A1. **EMAIL** jmcleod@spartan.ac.BrockU.CA

MCLOUD, MELISSA
PERSONAL Born 03/27/1954, Okinawa, Japan, m, 1982 **DISCIPLINE** HISTORY **EDUCATION** George Washington Univ, PhD 88; Brown Univ, BA 76. **CAREER** Chesapeake Bay Maritime Museum, dir , 96-; NEH Museums prog officer, 94-96; Natl Building Museum, curator, 88-94; Smithsonian Inst NMAH, edu consul, 85-86, admin asst, res fel, 81-83. **HONORS AND AWARDS** Smthsn Inst NMAH, pre-doc fel; Preservation Tst, fel; NMAH AACP, res fel; CO Women's fel; Phi Delta Beta sch; Myron Loe fel., Exhibits: Visions of Home 94; Making it Work: Pittsburgh Defines a City 93; Visions, Revisions 92; Washington: Symbol and City 92; Ideal Place: Rockefeller Visions for America 92. **SELECTED PUBLICATIONS** Auth, Craftsmen and Entrepreneurs: Washington DC Builders, in progress; Urban Water Technology: An Alexandria Cistern and Filter System, 95; Washington: Symbol and the City, An Educator's Guide, coauth, 94; In a Workmanlike Manner, The Building of Residential Washington, coauth, 84. **CONTACT ADDRESS** Center for Chesapeake Studies, Chesapeake Bay Maritime Mus, PO Box 636, St Michaels, MD, 21663-0636. **EMAIL** mmcloud@cbmm.org

MCLUCAS, ANNE DHU
PERSONAL Born 07/26/1941, Denver, CO, d, 1 child **DISCIPLINE** MUSICOLOGY **EDUCATION** Harvard Univ, PhD, 75. **CAREER** Music Dept, Univ Oregon **HONORS AND AWARDS** Dir, NEH-sponsored Summer Inst Col Tchrs, 92; NEH Summer Stipend, Scotland, Brit, 87-88; Am Antiquarian Soc Res Grant, 86-87; NEH Res Grant, 85-86; Clark Fund Res Grant, Harvard Univ, 81-85; Danforth Found Fellow Grad Stud; 65-68; Phi Beta Kappa, Univ Colo, 65; Boettcher Found Scholar, 59; Nat Merit Scholar, 59. **RESEARCH** American Music and its social contexts; British-American folksong; Native-American music; Music of Wilhelm Friedemann Bach. **SELECTED PUBLICATIONS** Ed, Music and Context: Essays for John M. Ward, Cambridge, MA, Harvard Univ, 85; Ed, Charles Dibdin's The Touchstone, or Harlequin Traveller, 1779, 90; Nineteenth Century Melodrama: from A Tale of Mystery to Monte Cristo, Bits and Pieces: Music for Theatre, Harvard Lib Bull, New Series, V 2, n4, 92; Black Sacred Song and the Tune-Family Concept, In Search of New Perspectives in Music: Festschrift Eileen Southern, Warren, MI, Harmonie Pk Press, 92; The Multi-Layered Concept of 'Folk Song' in American Music: The Case of Jean Ritchie's 'The Two Sisters', Themes and Variations: Writings on Music in Honor of Rulan Chao Pian, Cambridge, MA, Harvard Univ Mus Dept, 94, 212-230; Ed, Monte Cristo 1884, Nineteenth-Century Am Mus Theater, NY, Garland Press, 95; From Ballads to Broadway: A Very Brief History of American Musical Theater,1735-1931, Ore Fest of Am Mus Prog Book, 96; On the Importance of Music and Music Education, Tuning up for a Second Century, Portland, OR, Ore Council for the Human, 96; Samuel Preston Bayard: 1908-1997, Folk Mus Jour, 97, 392-393; Louis Moreau Gottschalk and the American Obstacle Course, Ore Festival of Am Mus Prog Book, 97, 12-14; Monodrama, Schetky, Taylor, Pelissier, Tune Families, in The New Grove Dict of Music and Musicians, MacMillan Publ, rev ed, 98; Musical Theater as a Link Between Folk and Popular Traditions, in Vistas of Am Mus: Essays and Compositions in Honor of William K. Kearns, Detroit, Harmonie Pk Press, 98. **CONTACT ADDRESS** Univ of Oregon, 1225 School of Music, Eugene, OR, 97403-1225. **EMAIL** amclucas@oregon.uoregon.edu

MCLURE, CHARLES E., JR.
PERSONAL Born 04/14/1940, Van Horn, TX, m, 1962 **DISCIPLINE** ECONOMICS **EDUCATION** Univ Kans, BA, 62; Princeton Univ, MA, 64, PhD, 66. **CAREER** Vice pres, Natl Bureau of econ res, 77-81, Cline Prof, 65-77, Rice Univ; dep asst sec treasury, 83-85, US Treasure Dept; sr fel, presently, Hoover Inst, Stanford Univ. **RESEARCH** Intergovernmental fiscal relations; consumption-based taxes; and taxation of electronic commerce. **SELECTED PUBLICATIONS** Auth, Must Corporate Income Be Taxed Twice?, 79; ed, Tax Assignment in Federal Countries, 83; co-ed, Fiscal Federalism and the Taxation of Natural Resources, 83; ed, State Corporation Income Tax: Issues in Worldwide Unitary Taxation, 84; auth, Economic Perspectives on State Taxation of Multijurisdictional Corporations, 86; auth, The Value Added Tax: Key to Deficit Reduction, 87; co-ed, World Tax Reform, 90; coauth, The Taxation of Income from Business and Capital in Colombia, 90. **CONTACT ADDRESS** Hover Inst, Stanford Univ, Stanford, CA, 94022. **EMAIL** mclure@hoover.stanford.edu

MCMAHON, GREGORY
DISCIPLINE HISTORY **EDUCATION** Univ Chicago, PhD. **CAREER** Assoc prof, Univ NH, 88; assoc dir, Alisar Hoyuk Excavations, Turkey. **HONORS AND AWARDS** Fulbright-Hays fel. **RESEARCH** Hittite magical ritual. **SELECTED PUBLICATIONS** Auth, The Hittite State Cult of the Tutelary Deities, 91. **CONTACT ADDRESS** Univ NH, Durham, NH, 03824. **EMAIL** gmcmahon@christa.unh.edu

MCMAHON, ROBERT J.
PERSONAL Born 05/13/1949, Bayside, NY, m, 1976, 2 children **DISCIPLINE** HISTORY **EDUCATION** Fairfield Univ, BA, 71; Univ of Conn, PhD, 77. **CAREER** Historian, U.S. Dept of State, 78-82; PROF OF HIST, UNIV OF FL, 82-. **HONORS AND AWARDS** Teaching Excellence Award, Univ of FL, 95; Stuart L. Bernath Article Prize, 89, Bernath Lecture Award, 91, Soc for Historians of Am Foreign Relations. **MEMBERSHIPS** Am Hist Asn; Org of Am Historians; Soc for Historians of Am Foreign Relations. **RESEARCH** U.S. history; U.S. foreign relations, especially during the 20th century. **SELECTED PUBLICATIONS** Auth, The Limits of Empire: The United States and Southeast Asia Since World War II, Columbia Univ Press, 99; auth, The Cold War on the Periphery: The United States, India, and Pakistan, Columbia Univ Press, 94; auth, Colonialism and Cold War: The United States and the Struggle for Indonesian Independence 1945-49, Cornell Univ Press, 81; co-ed, The Origins of the Cold War, Houghton-Mifflin, 99; ed, Major Problems in the History of the Vietnam War, Houghton-Mifflin, 92; auth, numerous articles in J of Am Hist, Political Sci Quarterly, Int Hist Rev, Pacific His Rev, and Diplomatic Hist. **CONTACT ADDRESS** Dept of History, Univ of Florida, 4131 Turlington Hall, Gainesville, FL, 32611. **EMAIL** rmcmahon@history.ufl.edu

MCMANAMON, JOHN
DISCIPLINE HISTORY **EDUCATION** NC Chapel Hill, PhD, 84. **CAREER** Hist, Loyola Univ. **RESEARCH** Late Medieval-Renaissance European history. **SELECTED PUBLICATIONS** Auth, Continuity and Change in the Ideals fo Humanism: The Evidence from Florentine Funeral Oratory, In Life and Death in Fifteenth-Century Florence, Durham: Duke UP, 89; The Sinking fo the Wells Burt, Inland Seas 46, 90; Marketing a Medici Regime: The Funeral Oration of Marcello Virgilio Adriani for Giuliano de' Medici 1516, Renaissance Quart 44, 91. **CONTACT ADDRESS** Fine Arts Dept, Loyola Univ, Chicago, 6525 N. Sheridan Rd., Chicago, IL, 60626. **EMAIL** jmcmana@wpo.it.luc.edu

MCMANUS, EDGAR J.
PERSONAL Born 03/04/1924, New York, NY, m, 1956 **DISCIPLINE** AMERICAN COLONIAL, LEGAL & CONSTITUTIONAL HISTORY **EDUCATION** Columbia Univ, BS, 52, MA, 53, PhD, 59. **CAREER** Lectr hist, Columbia Univ, 53-56; from lectr to assoc prof, 57-73, prof hist, Queens Col, NY, 73, Adj prof law, NY Law Sch, 62-66; Am Coun Learned Soc fel, 68-69. **HONORS AND AWARDS** JD, NY Univ, 59. **MEMBERSHIPS** AHA **RESEARCH** Am Negro slavery; legal origins of Am Negro slavery. **SELECTED PUBLICATIONS** Auth, The status of res ipsa loquitor in New York, NY Univ Intramural Law Rev, 11/47; Antislavery legislation in New York, J Negro Hist, 10/61; The enforcement of acceleration clauses in New York, NY Law Forum, 12/62; A History of Negro Slavery in New York, 66, Black Bondage in the North, 73, Syracuse Univ; Law and Libery in Early New England, Univ of MA, 93. **CONTACT ADDRESS** Dept of Hist, Queens Col, CUNY, 6530 Kissena Blvd, Flushing, NY, 11367-1597.

MCMICHAEL, ANDREW
DISCIPLINE HISTORY **EDUCATION** George Mason Univ, MA; Vanderbilt Univ, PhD cand. **CAREER** Commun assoc, Am Hist Asn. **MEMBERSHIPS** Am Hist Asn. **RESEARCH** Migration of slaves and slaveholders in the 1830s. **CONTACT ADDRESS** American Historical Assn.

MCMILLAN, WILLIAM ASBURY, SR.
PERSONAL Born 02/29/1920, Winnabow, NC, m **DISCIPLINE** EDUCATION **EDUCATION** Johnson C Smith Univ, BA 1942; University of Michigan, MA 1945, PhD 1954. **CAREER** Gatesville NC, tchr 1942-44, 1946-47; Johnson C Smith Univ, asst dean of instr 1947-48; Pomeroy PA, counselor 1948-49; Wiley Coll, dir 1949-58; Bethune-Cookman Coll, acad dean 1958-64, 1966-67; Rust Coll, pres 1967-93, pres emeritus, 1993-. **HONORS AND AWARDS** Hon LLD: Cornell Coll, Johnson C Smith Univ, Bethune-Cookman Coll; Pres of Yr, MS Tchrs Assn 1973-74. **MEMBERSHIPS** Life mem NEA; ATA; Mid-S Med Assn; pres MS Assn of Pvt Coll 1977-78; Alpha Phi Omega; NAACP; Boy Scout Leader; chmn bd of educ N MS; Conf of United Meth Ch; Omega Psi Phi; UNCF chairman, membership & visitation committee, board of directors, vice chair of the members; board of directors Mississippi Methodist Hospital & Rehabilitation Center; Phi Delta Kappa.

MCMILLEN, NEIL RAYMOND
PERSONAL Born 01/02/1939, m, 1960, 2 children **DISCIPLINE** RECENT UNITED STATES HISTORY **EDUCATION** Univ Southern Miss, BA, 61, MA, 63; Vanderbilt Univ, PhD(hist), 69. **CAREER** Asst prof hist, Ball State Univ, 67-69; dean Basic Col, 70-71; from asst prof to assoc prof, 69-78, PROF HIST, UNIV SOUTHERN MISS, 78-, Danforth assoc, 73; vis assoc prof hist, Univ Mo-Columbia, 74-75; Moorman Distinguished Prof, 93-95. **HONORS AND AWARDS** Grant, Nat Endowment for Humanities, 75 & 81; Bancroft Prize, 90; McLemore Prize, 90; Gustavus Myers Outstanding Book award, 90. **MEMBERSHIPS** Southern Hist Asn; Orgn Am Historians. **RESEARCH** Recent South; black history. **SELECTED PUBLICATIONS** Auth, The Citizens' Council, Univ Ill, 71; coauth, Synopsis of American History, Rand McNally, 3d-7th ed, 77-98; auth, Dark Journey, Univ Ill, 89. **CONTACT ADDRESS** Dept of History, Univ Southern Miss, Hattiesburg, MS, 39401.

MCMORDIE, MICHAEL J.
PERSONAL Born 04/23/1935, Toronto, ON, Canada **DISCIPLINE** ARCHITECTURE/HISTORY **EDUCATION** Univ Toronto, BArch, 62; Univ Edinburgh, PhD, 72. **CAREER** Staff mem, Gordon S. Adamson & Assoc, 62-65; lectr, Univ Edinburgh; ASSOC PROF TO PROF, UNIV CALGARY, 74-, prog dir archit, 79-82, dean gen stud, 90-98; vis assoc, 74-75, life mem, Clare Hall, Cambridge Univ, 76-. **MEMBERSHIPS** Soc Stud Archit Can; Asn Can Stud; Soc Archit Hist. **RESEARCH** History and theory of architecture. **SELECTED PUBLICATIONS** Coauth, Twelve Houses, 95; contribur, The Canadian Encyclopedia; ed bd, TRACE, 79-82; ed bd, Urban Hist Rev, 83-; ed bd, Interchange, 95-. **CONTACT ADDRESS** Dept of Architecture, Univ Calgary, Calgary, AB, T2N 1N4. **EMAIL** mcmordie@acs.ucalgary.ca

MCMULLIN, STAN
DISCIPLINE HISTORY **EDUCATION** Univ Dalhousie, PhD. **CAREER** Assoc prof, Carleton Univ. **HONORS AND AWARDS** Coord, Cult and Cult Policy Prog Area. **RESEARCH** Canadian regionalism; history of spiritualism and psychic research in Canada; popular culture; provinvial parks; and public policy. **SELECTED PUBLICATIONS** Auth, A Matter of Attitude: The Subversive Margin in Canada, Post-Colonial Formations a special number of Cultural Policy (Australia), Vol 6, 94; The Canadian Perspective on Mexico, Mexico: Ante el bloque Norteamericano, Memorias, Univ Monterrey, 92. **CONTACT ADDRESS** Dept of Canadian Studies, Carleton Univ, 1125 Colonel By Dr, Ottawa, ON, K1S 5B6.

MCMULLIN, THOMAS AUSTIN
PERSONAL Born 08/12/1942, Boston, MA, m, 1968, 2 children **DISCIPLINE** HISTORY **EDUCATION** Univ Mass, Amherst, BA, 64; Univ Wis, Madison, MA, 66, PhD Hist, 76. **CAREER** Instr hist, Boston State Col, 64-73, asst prof, 74-78, assoc prof, 78-82; assoc prof hist, Univ Mass-Boston, 82-, grad sch lectr, Northeastern Univ, 80. **MEMBERSHIPS** Orgn Am Historians; Urban Hist Assoc. **RESEARCH** American urban and political history. **SELECTED PUBLICATIONS** Auth, Lost Alternative: The Urban Industrial Utopia of William D Howland, New England Quart, 3/82; Part I: The Struggle For Power In Massachusetts, Introduction in Massachusetts Politics: Selected Historical Essays, Institute For Massachusetts Studies, 98. **CONTACT ADDRESS** Dept of History, Univ of Massachusetts, 100 Morrissey Blvd, Boston, MA, 02125-3300.

MCMURRY, LINDA O.
PERSONAL Born 10/24/1945, Montgomery, AL, m, 1 child **DISCIPLINE** HISTORY **EDUCATION** Oxford Col of Emory Univ, AA, 64; Auburn Univ, BA, 68, MA, 72, PhD, 76. **CAREER** Asst prof, 76-79, assoc prof, Valdosta State Col, 79-81; ASSOC PROF, 81-87, PROF, 87-, NC STATE UNIV. **HONORS AND AWARDS** Rockefeller Found Humanities Fel, 85-86; Ala Authors Award for Nonfiction, 84; Auburn Univ Humanities Alumni Award, 96. **MEMBERSHIPS** Org of Am Historians; Southern Hist Asn; Asn for the Study of Afro-American Life & Hist. **RESEARCH** African American history, 1865-1940. **SELECTED PUBLICATIONS** Auth, To Keep the Waters Troubled: The Life of Ida B. Wells, 99, Oxford Univ Press; auth, Recorder of the Black Experience: A Biography of Monroe Nathan Work, La State Univ Press, 85; auth, George Washington Carver: Scientist and Symbol, Oxford Univ Press, 81; coauth, American and Its Peoples, Longman Green, 97. **CONTACT ADDRESS** 1505 Village Glen Dr., Raleigh, NC, 27612. **EMAIL** lomcmurry@aol.com

MCMURRY, RICHARD MANNING
PERSONAL Born 09/13/1939, DeKalb Co, GA, m, 3 children **DISCIPLINE** UNITED STATES HISTORY **EDUCATION** Va Mil Inst, BA, 61; Emory Univ, MA, 64, PhD, 67. **CAREER** Lectr hist, Emory Univ, 66-67; from asst prof to prof hist, Valdosta State Col, 67-81; MEM FAC, NC STATE UNIV, 81-. **MEMBERSHIPS** Orgn Am Historians; Southern Hist Asn. **RESEARCH** Civil War and Reconstruction; Old South; American military history. **SELECTED PUBLICATIONS** Auth, Why the Confederacy Lost, Civil War Hist, vol 0038, 92; Pemberton--A Biography, J Southern Hist, vol 0059, 93; Lee Considered, Southwestern Hist Quart, vol 0096, 93; Embrace an Angry Wind, J Amer Hist, vol 0079, 93; They Followed the Plume, J Southern Hist, vol 0060, 94; The Union Army--Organization and Operations, vol 2, the Western Theater, Civil War Hist, vol 0040, 94; With Pen and Saber, J Southern Hist, vol 0062, 96; Portraits of Conflict, Miss Quart, vol 0047, 94 and vol 0049, 96; More Generals in Gray, Civil War Hist, vol 0042, 96; The Civil War Memoir of Stephenson, Philip, Daingerfield, Ark Hist Quart, vol 0055, 96. **CONTACT ADDRESS** 3212 Caldwell Dr, Raleigh, NC, 27607.

MCNABB, DEBRA
PERSONAL Glace Bay, NS, Canada **DISCIPLINE** MUSEUM STUDIES **EDUCATION** Mt Allison Univ, BA, 79; Univ BC, MA, 86. **CAREER** REGISTRAR, NOVA SCOTIA MUSEUM INDUST. **HONORS AND AWARDS** MA fel, Soc Sci & Humanities, Res Coun Can. **SELECTED PUBLICATIONS** Auth, Working Worlds, plate 37, in Historical Atlas of Canada; auth, Old Sydney Town: Historic Buildings in Sydney's North End, 86. **CONTACT ADDRESS** Nova Scotia Mus of Industry, 147 N Foord St, Box 2590, Stellarton, NS, BOK 1SO. **EMAIL** dmcnabb@fox.nstn.ca

MCNAIRY, FRANCINE G.
PERSONAL Born 11/13/1946, Pittsburgh, PA **DISCIPLINE** EDUCATION **EDUCATION** Univ of Pittsburgh, BA, Sociology, 1968, MSW, 1970, PhD, Comm, 1978. **CAREER** Allegheny Co Child Welfare Servs supvr & soc worker, 1970-72; Comm Action Regional training, tech asst specialist, 1972; Clarion Univ of PA, assoc prof/counselor 1973-82, coord of academic devel & retention 1983, dean of acad support serv & asst to the acad vice pres, 1983-88; WEST CHESTER UNIV, ASSOC PROVOST, 1988-. **MEMBERSHIPS** Presenter Natl Conf on the Freshmen Yr Experience Univ of SC 1982-86; advisor Clarion Univ Black Student Union 1973-; vice chair Clarion Co Human Resources Develop Comm 1983-86; presenter, Intl Conf on the First Year Experience England, 1986, Creative Mgmt in Higher Educ, Boston 1986; consultant, Univ of NE, Briar Cliff Coll, Marshall Univ 1986; St Lawrence Coll 1984, Wesleyan Coll 1983; mem, PA Advisory Bd to ACT; member, AAHE; member, National Assn of Black Women in Higher Education. **SELECTED PUBLICATIONS** Publications "Clarion Univ Increases Black Student Retention"; co-authored "Taking the Library to Freshman Students via Freshman Seminar Concept" 1986, "The Minority Student on Campus" 1985. **CONTACT ADDRESS** West Chester Univ, 151 E O Bull Center, West Chester, PA, 19383.

MCNALLY, MICHAEL
DISCIPLINE HISTORY **EDUCATION** Harvard Univ, PhD. **CAREER** Asst prof, Eastern Michigan Univ. **RESEARCH** History of Native American religious traditions. **SELECTED PUBLICATIONS** Auth, A History of Russia, 2 vol, McGraw-Hill, 97; coauth, The Twentieth Century: A Brief Global History, 4th ed, McGraw-Hill, 94, 5th ed, 97; The Uses of Hymn Singing at White Earth: Toward a History of Practice, in Lived Religion in America, Princeton UP, 97. **CONTACT ADDRESS** Dept of History and Philosophy, Eastern Michigan Univ, 701 Pray-Harrold, Ypsilanti, MI, 48197.

MCNALLY, RAYMOND T.
PERSONAL Born 04/15/1931, Cleveland, OH, m, 1957, 3 children **DISCIPLINE** RUSSIAN HISTORY **EDUCATION** Fordham Univ, AB, 53; Free Univ Berlin, PhD(Russian hist), 56. **CAREER** Instr Europ & Russ hist, John Carroll Univ, 56-58; from asst prof to assoc prof Russ hist, 58-71, PROF RUSS HIST, BOSTON COL, 71-, DIR SLAVIC & E EUROP CTR, 64-, InterUniv Comt travel grant, Leningrad State Univ, 61; Fulbright res exchange prof hist, Univ Bucharest, 69-70. **MEMBERSHIPS** AHA; Am Asn Advan Slavic Studies. **RESEARCH** Russian intellectual history in the first half of the nineteenth century. **SELECTED PUBLICATIONS** Auth, An Introduction to 19th-Century Russian Slavophilism, Samarin, Y.F., Russ Hist-Histoire Russe, vol 0020, 93; The Grand Duchess Elena of Russia and Baron Haxthausen, August, Von--2 Conservative Reformists in the Age of Abolition of Russian Serfdom, Slavic Rev, vol 0052, 93; Reinterpreting Russian History, Readings, 860-1860s, Russ Hist-Histoire Russe, vol 0022, 95. **CONTACT ADDRESS** Dept of Hist, Boston Col, 140 Commonwealth Ave, Chestnut Hill, MA, 02167.

MCNALLY, SHEILA
DISCIPLINE ART AND ARCHAEOLOGY OF LATE ANTIQUITY **EDUCATION** Vassar Col, AB, 53; Harvard Univ,PhD, 65. **CAREER** Prof, Univ Minn, Twin Cities. **RESEARCH** Architectural decoration in the time of Diocletian. **SELECTED PUBLICATIONS** Auth, The Architectural Decoration of Diocletian's Palace: Ornament in Context, BAR Int Ser, 96; coauth, Excavations in Akhmim, Egypt: Continuity and change in city life from late antiquity to the present, BAR Int Ser 590, 93; coauth & ed, Diocletian's Palace: Report on the Joint Excavations, Southeast Quart 1-6, 72-96. **CONTACT ADDRESS** Dept of Class and Near Eastern Stud, Univ Minn, Twin Cities, Minneapolis, MN, 55455. **EMAIL** mcnal001@tc.umn.edu

MCNAMEE, KATHLEEN
PERSONAL Born 11/27/1949, Cambridge, MA, m, 1986, 2 children **DISCIPLINE** CLASSICS **EDUCATION** Duke Univ, PhD, 77. **CAREER** From instr to prof to ch, Dept Classics, Greek, &Latin, Wayne State Univ, 76-; interim dean, Col Lib Arts, Wayne State Univ, 92-94. **MEMBERSHIPS** Am Philos Asn. **RESEARCH** Greek literature; Latin poetry. **SELECTED PUBLICATIONS** Auth, Abbreviations in Greek Literary Papyri and Ostraca, 81; auth, Sigla and Select Marginalia in Greek Literary Papyri: Papyrologica Bruxellensia, Aug, 92; auth, Classical Studies Presented to William Hailey Willis, Bulletin of the Am Soc Papyrologists, 85; auth, Another Chapter in the History of Scholia, Class Quart, 98; auth, An Innovation in Annotated Codices on Papyrus, Akten des 21, Internationalen Papyrologenkongresses, Berlin, 1995, 97; auth, Missing Links in the Development of Scholia, Greek, Roman, & Byzantine Studies, July, 96. **CONTACT ADDRESS** Dept of Classics, Greek & Latin, Wayne State Univ, 431 Manoogian Hall, Detroit, MI, 48202. **EMAIL** k.mcnamee@wayne.edu

MCNAUGHTON, PATRICK
DISCIPLINE AFRICAN, OCEANIC, AND PRE COLUMBIAN ART **EDUCATION** Yale Univ, PhD. **CAREER** Prof. **RESEARCH** Aesthetics; technology and expertise; social roles of art; historical problems in African art; critical issues of theory and methodology. **SELECTED PUBLICATIONS** Auth, The Mande Blacksmiths: Knowledge, Power, and Art in West Africa. **CONTACT ADDRESS** Dept of History and Art, Indiana Univ, Bloomington, 300 N Jordan Ave, Bloomington, IN, 47405. **EMAIL** mcnaught@indiana.edu

MCNEIL, DAVID O.
PERSONAL 3 children **DISCIPLINE** EARLY MODERN EUROPE **EDUCATION** Antioch Col, BA, 65; Stanford Univ, MA, 66, PhD(hist), 72. **CAREER** Asst prof, 70-75, assoc prof, 75-80, PROF HIST, SAN JOSE STATE UNIV, 75- **MEMBERSHIPS** AHA; World History Assoc. Renaissance Society of America. **RESEARCH** Early modern French and Italian social and intellectual history. **SELECTED PUBLICATIONS** Guillaume Bude and Humanism in the Reign of Francis I, Droz, Geneva, 75. **CONTACT ADDRESS** Dept of Hist, San Jose State Univ, 1 Washington Sq, San Jose, CA, 95192-0117. **EMAIL** dmcneil@sjsu.euj

MCNEIL, WILLIAM KINNETH
PERSONAL Born 08/13/1940, Canton, NC **DISCIPLINE** AMERICAN FOLKLORE AND HISTORY **EDUCATION** Carson-Newman Col, BA, 62; Okla State Univ, MA, 63; State Univ NY, Oneonta, MA, 67; Ind Univ, PhD(Am folklore), 80. **CAREER** Historian, Off State Hist, Albany, NY, 67-70; adminr & folklorist, Smithsonian Inst, 75-76; FOLKLORIST, OZARK FOLK CTR, 76-, Adv & consult, Fr Cult Proj, Old Mines, Mo, 78-80; bd mem, Nat Coun Traditional Arts, 79-;

chief consult, Echoes of Ozarks, 82. **MEMBERSHIPS** Am Folklore Soc; Am Asn State & Local Hist; Ozark States Folklore Soc; Southern Folklore Soc. **RESEARCH** American music, particularly 19th century popular and 20th century country; American theater; American folklore, particulary folklore of the Southern mountains. **SELECTED PUBLICATIONS** Auth, Stories from Home, J Country Mus, vol 0015, 93 ; Lift Up Your Head Tom Dooley, Appalachian J, vol 0021, 94; Death and Dying in Central Appalachia, Appalachian J, vol 0022, 95; Rip--Memorial Wall Art, NY Folklore, vol 0022, 96; The Quest of the Folk, NY Folklore, vol 0022, 96. **CONTACT ADDRESS** Ozark Folk Ctr, Mountain View, AR, 72560.

MCNEILL, JOHN R.
PERSONAL Born 10/06/1954, Chicago, IL, m, 1985, 4 children **DISCIPLINE** HISTORY **EDUCATION** Duke Univ, PhD, 81. **CAREER** Asst prof, 83-85, Goucher Col; asst prof to prof, 85-, Georgetown Univ. **HONORS AND AWARDS** Fulbright Fel, 87-88, 92-93; Woodrow Wilson Center Fel, 96-97; Guggenheim Fel, 97-98. **MEMBERSHIPS** Amer Hist Assoc; Amer Soc for Environmental Hist; World Hist Assoc. **RESEARCH** Environmental hist **SELECTED PUBLICATIONS** Auth, The Atlantic Empires of France and Spain, UNC Press, 85; auth, The Mountains of the Mediterranean World: An Environmental History, Cambridge Univ Press, 93; art, Of Rats and Men: A Synoptic Environmental History of the Island Pacific, J of World Hist; coed, Atlantic American Societies from Columbus through Abolition, 1492-1800, Routledge, 92. **CONTACT ADDRESS** History Dept, Georgetown Univ, Washington, DC, 20007.

MCNEILL, PAULA L.
PERSONAL Fort Lauderdale, FL, 1 child **DISCIPLINE** DEPARTMENT OF ART **EDUCATION** Ariz State Univ, BA; Univ of NMex, MA; Univ Mo-Columbia, PhD. **CAREER** Prof, Valdosta State Univ Instr, Navajo Reservation in Ganado; instr, archv, Univ Mo-Columbia. **RESEARCH** The history of art education; the history of technology in art education. **SELECTED PUBLICATIONS** Published works in the area of the history of art education. **CONTACT ADDRESS** Dept of Art, Valdosta State Univ, 1500 N. Patterson St, Valdosta, GA, 31698.

MCNEILL, WILLIAM HARDY
PERSONAL Born 10/31/1917, Vancouver, BC, Canada, m, 1946, 4 children **DISCIPLINE** HISTORY **EDUCATION** Univ Chicago, BA, 38, MA, 39; Cornell Univ, PhD(hist), 47. **CAREER** From instr to prof hist, 47-69, chmn dept, 61-67, ROBERT A MILLIKEN DISTINGUISHED SERV PROF HIST, UNIV CHICAGO, 69-, Vis prof, Univ Hawaii, winter, 80; George Eastman vis prof, Oxford Univ, 80-81. **HONORS AND AWARDS** Nat Bk Award 63., DHL, Washington Col, Md, 75, Lawrence Univ, 77, RI Col, 78 & Swarthmore Col, 79; DSc, Chicago Med Col, 77; DL, Franklin Col, 80. **MEMBERSHIPS** AHA; Am Acad Arts & Sci; Am Philos Soc; Asn Comp Hist & Law. **RESEARCH** Universal history; contemporary history; modern Greek and Balkan history. **SELECTED PUBLICATIONS** Auth, Politics and War--European Conflict from Philip-II to Hitler, J Mod Hist, vol 0064, 92; Surviving Trench Warfare, Technol and Culture, vol 0034, 93; Salt and Civilization, Amer Hist Rev, vol 0098, 93; International Theory--The 3 Traditions, Historian, vol 0055, 93;Epidemics and Ideas, J Soc Hist, vol 0027, 93; Geopolitics and Geoculture, Diplomatic Hist, vol 0018, 94; Arms and the State--Patterns of Military Production and Trade, Int Hist Rev, vol 0016, 94; Inside Hitler Greece, J Mod Hist, vol 0067, 95; The Changing Shape of World History, Hist and Theory, vol 0034, 95; Inventing Europe, Int Hist Rev, vol 0018, 96; Cultures in Conflict, NY Rev Bks, vol 0043, 96; The Middle East, NY Rev Bks, vol 0043, 96; On the Origins of War and the Preservation of Peace, J Mil Hist, vol 0060, 96; The Clash of Civilizations and the Remaking of World Order, NY Rev Bks, vol 0044, 97; Millennium, J World Hist, vol 0008, 97; The Origins of Western Warfare, J Mil Hist, vol 0061, 97; Guns, Germs, and Steel--The Fates of Human Societies, NY Rev Bks, vol 0044, 97. **CONTACT ADDRESS** Dept of Hist, Univ of Chicago, 1126 E 59th St, Chicago, IL, 60637.

MCNUTT, JAMES CHARLES
PERSONAL Born 08/10/1950, Denison, TX, m, 1971, 2 children **DISCIPLINE** AMERICAN STUDIES, FOLKLORE **EDUCATION** Harvard Univ, BA, 72; Univ Tex, Austin, MA, 77, PhD(Am civilization), 82. **CAREER** Asst instr Am studies, Univ Tex, Austin, 80-82; RES ASSOC, INST TEXAN CULTURES, UNIV TEX, SAN ANTONIO, 82-. **MEMBERSHIPS** Am Studies Asn; Am Folklore Soc. **RESEARCH** Regionalism. **SELECTED PUBLICATIONS** Auth, The Enormous Vogue of Things Mexican--Cultural Relations Between the United States and Mexico, 1920-1935, Southwestern Hist Quart, vol 0097, 94. **CONTACT ADDRESS** Inst Texan Cultures, Univ of Texas, PO Box 1226, San Antonio, TX, 78294.

MCNUTT, PAULA M.
PERSONAL Born 03/12/1955, Denver, CO, s **DISCIPLINE** HEBREW BIBLE, ANTHROPOLOGY AND ARCHAEOLOGY **EDUCATION** Univ Colorado, BA, 78; Univ Montana, MA, 83; Vanderbilt Univ, PhD, 89. **CAREER** Prof, Canisius Col, 87-. **HONORS AND AWARDS** NEH Fel for Col Tchr, 94-95. **MEMBERSHIPS** Amer Acad Relig; Soc Bibl Lit, Cath Bibl Asn, Amer Sch Oriental Res, Archaeol Inst Amer **RESEARCH** Social world of ancient Israel; social roles and statuses of artisans; religion and technology. **SELECTED PUBLICATIONS** Reconstructing the Society of Ancient Israel, Libr of Ancient Israel Series, Louisville, Westminster John Knox Press, 99; The Kenites, the Midianites, and the Rechabites as Marginal Mediators in Ancient Israelite Tradition, Semeia 67, p 109-132, 94; coauth with James W. Flanagan, David W. McCreery and Khair Yassin, Preliminary Report of the 1993 Excavations at Tell Nimrin, Jordan, Ann of the Dept of Antiquities of Jordan, XXXVIII, pp 205-244, 94; Kenites, P. 407 in The Oxford Companion to the Bible, Bruce M. Metzger and Michael D. Coogan eds, Oxford Univ Press, 93; The Development and Adoption of Iron Technology in the Ancient Near East, Proceedings: The Eastern Great Lakes Bibilical Society, 12, pp 47-66, 92; The African Ironsmith as Marginal Mediator: A Symbolic Analysis, Journ of Ritual Studies, 5/2, pp 75-98, 91; The Forging of Israel: Iron Technology, Symbolism, and Tradition in Ancient Society, The Social World of Biblical Antiquity Series, 8, Sheffield, Almond Press, 90; Sociology of the Old Testament, pp 835-839, Mercer Dict of the Bible, Macon, GA, Mercer Univ Press, 90; Egypt as an Iron Furnace: A Metaphor of Transformation, pp 293-301, Society of Biblical Literature 1988 Seminar Papers, David J. Lull ed, Atlanta, Schol Press, 88; Interpreting Ancient Israel's Fold Traditions, Journ for the Study of the Old Testament, 39, pp 44-52, 87. **CONTACT ADDRESS** Canisius Col, 2001 Main St., Buffalo, NY, 14208. **EMAIL** mcnutt@canisius.edu

MCPHEE, SARAH
DISCIPLINE 17TH AND 18TH CENTURY ITALIAN ARCHITECTURE AND URBANISM **EDUCATION** Columbia Univ, PhD, 96. **CAREER** Archit, Emory Univ. **SELECTED PUBLICATIONS** Auth, Bernini's Bell Towers for St. Peter's: Architectural Competition at the Vatican. **CONTACT ADDRESS** Emory Univ, Atlanta, GA, 30322-1950. **EMAIL** smcphee@emory.edu

MCPHERSON, JAMES ALAN
PERSONAL Born 09/16/1943, Savannah, GA, d, 1 child **DISCIPLINE** LITERATURE, HISTORY, LAW **EDUCATION** Morris Brown Col, BA, 65; Harvard Law School, LLB, 68; Writers Workshop, Univ IA, MFA, 71. **CAREER** Lect, Univ CA at Santa Cruz, 69-71; asst prof, Morgan State Univ, 75-76; assoc prof, Univ VA, 76-81; prof, Univ IA, 81-. **HONORS AND AWARDS** Pulitzer Prize, 78; MacArthur Prize Fellows Award, 81. **MEMBERSHIPS** ACLU; NAACP; Authors Guild; Am Academy of Arts and Sciences; fel, Center for Advanced Studies, Stanford Univ, 97-98. **RESEARCH** Law. **SELECTED PUBLICATIONS** Auth, Crabcakes, 98; Fatherly Daughter, 98. **CONTACT ADDRESS** Dept of English, Univ of Iowa, Iowa City, IA, 52242.

MCPHERSON, JAMES MUNRO
PERSONAL Born 10/11/1936, Valley City, ND, m, 1957 **DISCIPLINE** AMERICAN HISTORY **EDUCATION** Gustavus Adolphus Col, BA, 58; Johns Hopkins Univ, PhD(hist), 63. **CAREER** From instr to assoc prof, 62-72, prof hist, 72-82, Edwards prof Am hist, 82-91, DAVIS PROF AM HIST, PRINCETON UNIV, 91-; Commonwealth Fund Lectr Am Hist, Univ Col London, 82; Fel Proctor & Gamble Fdn, 64-65; NEH 67-68; Guggenheim Fdn, 67-68; Huntington Libr, 77-78, 87-88, 95-96; Stanford Ctr Advan Study Behav Sci, 82-83; Rollins Fdn, 91-92. **HONORS AND AWARDS** Anisfield-Wolf Award, 65, Pulitzer Prize, 89; Lincoln Prize, 98. **MEMBERSHIPS** AHA; Orgn Am Historians; Southern Hist Asn. **RESEARCH** Civil War and Reconstruction; slavery and antislavery; United States Reconstruction to World War I. **SELECTED PUBLICATIONS** auth, The Struggle for Equality, 64; auth, The Negro's Civil War, 65; auth, The Abolitionist Legacy from Reconstruction to the NAACP, Princeton Univ, 75; aauth, Ordeal by Fire: The Civil War and Reconstruction, Knopf, 82, 92; Batle Cry of Freedom: The Civil War Era, 88; auth, Abraham Lincoln and the Second American Revolution, 91; auth, Drawn with the Sword: Reflections on the American Civil War, 96; auth, For Cause and Comrades: Why Men Fought in the Civil War, 97; ed, Lamson of the Gettysburg: The Civil War Letters of Roswell H. Lamson, U.S. Navy, 97; ed, Writing and the Civil War: The Quest to Understand, 98. **CONTACT ADDRESS** Dept Hist, Princeton Univ, Princeton, NJ, 08544.

MCQUAID, KIM
PERSONAL Born 11/02/1947, Boothbay, ME **DISCIPLINE** AMERICAN HISTORY, ECONOMIC HISTORY **EDUCATION** Antioch Col, BA, 70; Northwestern Univ, MA, 73, PhD, 75. **CAREER** Asst prof hist, Lake Erie Col, 77- **HONORS AND AWARDS** Woodrow Wilson Fel, 70; Marv Ball Wash Prof Am Hist, Univ Col Dublin, 85-86; Fulbright Overseas Teaching Award, Malaysia, 95-96. **MEMBERSHIPS** Econ Hist Asn; Bus Hist Conf; Soc Hist Technol; Am Hist Asn. **RESEARCH** American economic history; 20th century American business; evolution of United States welfare policies; science, technology, and society. **SELECTED PUBLICATIONS** Coauth, Creating the Welfare State: The Political Economy of Twentieth Century Reform, Praeger Spec Studies, 80, rev ed, Univ Press Kans, 92; The Roundtable: Getting Results in Washington, Harvard Bus Rev, 5-6/81; Big Business and Presidential Power: from Roosevelt to Reagan, William Morrow & Co, autumn 82; Bureaucrats as Social Engineers: Federal Welfare Programs in Herbert Hoover's America, Am J Econ & Sociol, 10/80; Welfare Reform in the 1950's, The Social Serv Rev, 3/80; Big Business and Government Policy in Post-New Deal America: From Depression to Detente, Antitrust Law & Econ Rev, 79; Big Business and Public Policy in the Contemporary United States, Quart Rev Econ & Bus, summer 80; auth, The Anxious Years: America in the Vietnam-Watergate Era, Basic Books, 89; Uneasy Partners: Big Business in American Politics, 1945-1990, Johns Hopkins Univ Press, 94. **CONTACT ADDRESS** Lake Erie Col, 391 W Washington St, Painesville, OH, 44077-3389.

MCSEVENEY, SAMUEL THOMPSON
PERSONAL Born 10/03/1930, New York, NY, m, 1958, 1 child **DISCIPLINE** RECENT AMERICAN HISTORY **EDUCATION** Brooklyn Col, BA, 51; Univ Conn, MA, 53; Univ Iowa, PhD(hist), 65. **CAREER** From instr to asst prof hist, Calif State Col Los Angeles, 60-66; from asst prof to assoc prof, Brooklyn Col, 66-72; ASSOC PROF HIST, VANDERBILT UNIV, 72-, Res grants, Nat Endowment for Humanities, 70-71. **HONORS AND AWARDS** Outstanding Prof Award, Calif State Col Los Angeles, 66. **MEMBERSHIPS** AHA; Orgn Am Historians. **RESEARCH** American politics, 1850-1900. **SELECTED PUBLICATIONS** Auth, Voting and the Spirit of American Democracy, J Interdisciplinary Hist, vol 0024, 94; Dimensions of Law in the Service of Order, Amer Hist Rev, vol 0100, 95; Davies, Keith, A. 1941-1994 + In Memoriam, Hisp Amer Hist Rev, vol 0075, 95; Running for President--The Candidates and Their Images, vol 1, 1789-1896, vol 2, 1900-1992, J Amer Hist, vol 0082, 96. **CONTACT ADDRESS** Dept of Hist, Vanderbilt Univ, Nashville, TN, 37240.

MCSHEA, WILLIAM PATRICK
PERSONAL Born 08/16/1930, Pittsburgh, PA, m, 1955, 3 children **DISCIPLINE** HISTORY, LATIN CLASSICS **EDUCATION** St Vincent Col, BA, 52; Duquesne Univ, MA, 54. **CAREER** From instr to assoc prof hist, Mt Mercy Col, 53-70; PROF & CHMN, DEPT HIST, CARLOW COL, 70-, DIR, PEACE STUDIES PROG, 76-, Prof, Comp Communism Consortia, var univs in Pa, 73-; mem adv coun, Int Poetry Forum, 77-. **MEMBERSHIPS** Int Soc Psycho Historians. **RESEARCH** Reformation; psycho history; recent American history. **SELECTED PUBLICATIONS** Auth, The Christian Tradition--Beyond Its European Captivity, J Ecumenical Stud, vol 0030, 93; Luther Legacy--Salvation and English Reformers 1525-1556, Theol Stud, vol 0056, 95; Lutheran Identity and Mission--Evangelical and Evangelistic, J Ecumenical Stud, vol 0032, 95; A Common Calling--The Witness of Our Reformation Churches in North America Today, J Ecumenical Stud, vol 0032, 95; Nothing Beyond the Necessary--Roman Catholicism and the Ecumenical Future, Theol Stud, vol 0057, 96; **CONTACT ADDRESS** Carlow Col, 3333 Fifth Ave, Pittsburgh, PA, 15213.

MCSHEFFREY, SHANNON
DISCIPLINE HISTORY **EDUCATION** Carleton Univ, BA; Univ Toronto, MA, PhD. **CAREER** Assoc prof. **RESEARCH** Gender, marriage, literacy, heresy, and popular religion in late medieval England. **SELECTED PUBLICATIONS** Auth, Gender and Heresy: Women and Men in Lollard Communities, 1420-1530, Univ Pa Press, 95; Love and Marriage in Late Medieval London, Medieval Inst Publ, 95. **CONTACT ADDRESS** Dept of Hist, Concordia Univ, Montreal, 1455 de Maisonneuve W, Montreal, PQ, H3G 1M8. **EMAIL** mcsheff@vax2.concordia.ca

MCSPADDEN, LUCIA
PERSONAL Born 02/14/1934, NJ, m, 1961, 3 children **DISCIPLINE** CULTURAL ANTHROPOLOGY; CULTURAL FOUNDATIONS OF EDUCATION **EDUCATION** Univ CA, Davis-BA, 56; Univ Nebraska, MA, 68; Univ Utah, PhD, 78, PhD, 89. **CAREER** Supervision of Doctor of Ministry and Master of Arts candidates, 88-94, CA and San Francisco Theological Seminary; adjunct prof, 89-94, Pacific Sch of Religion; researcher and consultant, 90-92, United Methodist Committee on Relief; organizer and principal investigator, From Token to Colleague, an inter-denominational team funded by the Fund for Theological Education to research barriers to multi-ethnic/racial/immigrant inclusiveness in United Methodist, American Baptist and Roman Catholic denominations in Northern California and to develop training models to overcome such barriers, 91-93; coordinator seminary intern study cluster, 92-93, Fund for Theological Education; project dir, 94, Negotiations between UNHCR and the Eritrean government for Repatriation of Eritrean Refugees; principal investigator, 96, Eritrea: NGOs and Repatriation (in process). **HONORS AND AWARDS** Phi Beta Kappa; Phi Kappa Phi; graduate research fel; Rockefeller Found Grant; Fund for Theological Education in Grant. **MEMBERSHIPS** Amer Anthropological Assn, fel; Soc for Applied Anthropology,fel; Intl Assn for the Study of Forced Migration; Soc of Christian Ethics; Intl Peace Research. **RESEARCH** Forced migration; social place theory; ethnicity; applied anthropology, development; non-government organization; anthropol-

ogy of relig; peace research. **SELECTED PUBLICATIONS** Auth, Eritrean Repatriation, Return or Development?, 98 (publication pending); auth, Contradictions and Control in Repatriation: Negotiations for the Return of Eritrean Refugee, Refugee Repatriation and Reconstruction, 98 (publication pending); auth, Negotiating Masculinity in the Reconstruction of Social Place: Eritrean and Ethiopian Refugees in the United States and Sweden, in Engendering Forced Migration: Theory and Practice, 98 (publication pending); auth, I Must Have My Rights! The Presence of State Power in the Resettlement of Ethiopian and Eritrean Refugees: Research and Programmatic Considerations, in Research and Human Rights, 98, publication pending. **CONTACT ADDRESS** 66 Sandpoint Dr, Richmond, CA, 94804. **EMAIL** lmespad@igc.org

MCTAGUE, ROBERT
PERSONAL Born 01/10/1968, Charleston, SC, m, 1995 **DISCIPLINE** HISTORY **EDUCATION** Loyola Univ, BA, 90; Drew Univ, MA, 93, MPhil, 96, PhD, 99. **CAREER** Hist adj, Essex Commun Col, 93; tchg asst, Drew Univ, 94-95; hist adj, Kean Univ, 94; hist adj, William Paterson Univ, 97; hist adj, 95-97, hist lectr, 98- , Fairleigh Dickinson Univ. **MEMBERSHIPS** Am Hist Asn. **RESEARCH** European intellectual history; Europe 1789-present; American political history; American intellectual history. **SELECTED PUBLICATIONS** Auth, Modern Physics, Kandinsky, and Klee, The European Legacy, 97; rev, The Land Arms Race and World War II, J of Conflict Stud, 98; rev of Ron Arnold's Ecoterror: The Violent Agenda to Save Nature: The World of the Unabomber, J of Conflict Studies, 99. **CONTACT ADDRESS** Dept of Social Sciences & History, Fairleigh Dickinson Univ, 285 Madison Ave, Madison, NJ, 07940.

MCVAUGH, MICHAEL ROGERS
PERSONAL Born 12/09/1938, Washington, DC, m, 1961 **DISCIPLINE** HISTORY OF SCIENCE, MEDIEVAL HISTORY **EDUCATION** Harvard Univ, AB, 60; Princeton Univ, MA, 62, PhD(hist), 65. **CAREER** From asst prof to assoc prof, 64-76, PROF HIST, UNIV NC, CHAPEL HILL, 76-, Nat Sci Found fel & mem, Sch Hist Studies, Inst Advan Study, 68-69. **MEMBERSHIPS** Hist Sci Soc; Mediaeval Acad Am. **RESEARCH** Medieval medical theory; 20th century experimental parapsychology. **SELECTED PUBLICATIONS** Auth, History of Science Society Distinguished Lecture--Introduction, Isis, vol 0085, 94; The Beginnings of Western Science--The European Scientific Tradition in Philosophical, Religious, and Institutional Context, 600 BC to AD 1450, J Interdisciplinary Hist, vol 0025, 95; Mondino of Liuzzi 'Expositio Super Capitulum de Generatione Embrionis Canonis Avicennae Cum Quibusdam Quaestionibus', Speculum-J Medieval Stud, vol 0071, 96; Historia Naturalis, Isis, vol 0087, 96; Avicenna Latinus--Codices, Isis, vol 0087, 96; Bedside Manners in the Middle Ages, Bull Hist of Med, vol 0071, 97. **CONTACT ADDRESS** Dept of Hist, Univ of NC, Chapel Hill, NC, 27515.

MCWILLIAMS, ALFRED E., JR.
PERSONAL Born 02/03/1938, Wewoka, OK, m **DISCIPLINE** EDUCATION **EDUCATION** CO State Coll, BA 1959, MA 1960; Univ No CO, PhD 1970. **CAREER** Denver Public School CO, teacher, counselor & admin asst 1960-68; Proj Upward Bound Univ No CO, dir 1968-70; Univ No CO, asst dean-special educ & rehabilitation 1970-72; Fed of Rocky Mt States Inc, consultant & career educ content coord 1972-76; Univ No CO, dir personnel AA/EEO 1976-79, asst vice pres admin serv personnel 1979-82; Univ of CO, asst to vice pres for admin 1982-84; Atlanta Univ, vice pres for admin 1984-85; Atlanta Univ, dean, School of Educ, 1985-87; GA State Univ, professor, educational policy studies, 1987-, coordinator, educational leadership program, 1995-. **HONORS AND AWARDS** Appreciation Award Natl Brotherhood of Skiers 1979; Leadership Styles & Management Strategies, Management Education, series at Atlanta Univ, 1986; Review of KA Heller, et al Placing Children in Special Education: A Strategy for Equity, Natl Academy Press, 1987. **MEMBERSHIPS** Chmn/co-founder Black Educators United 1967-68; asst prof 1970-72, assoc prof educ 1976-82 Univ of No CO; bd mem CO Christian Home Denver 1977-; sec 1977-, chmn 1980-84 Aurora CO Career Serv Comm; bd mem Natl Brotherhood of Skiers 1978-79; mem 1978-, bd mem 1980-85 Amer Assn of Univ Admin; mem 1978-, Gov Lamm appointed chmn 1980-84 CO Merit System Council; council mem 1978-, chmn elect 1981-82 (EEO) Coll & Univ Personnel Assn; mem Am Soc for Personnel Admin 1979-; cons, trainer Natl Center for Leadership Development Atlanta Univ 1979-80; cons, trainer Leadership Develop Training Prog Howard Univ 1981-82; mem, Rotary Club of West End Atlanta, 1984-87, 1989-; mem & army committeeman, Greater Atlanta Chapter reserve Officers Assn of US, 1985-; mem & chairman ofbd of dir, APPLE Corps, 1986; mem, Professional Journal Committee, Assn of Teacher Educators, 1987-; member, Amer Assn for Higher Education, 1989-; member, Assn for Supervision and Curriculum Development, 1989-; Amer Assn of Univ Professors, 1995-. **CONTACT ADDRESS** Educ Policy Studies, Georgia State Univ, University Plaza, Atlanta, GA, 30303.

MCWILLIAMS, TENNANT S.
PERSONAL Born 09/12/1943, Birmingham, AL, m, 1975, 1 child **DISCIPLINE** AMERICAN HISTORY **EDUCATION** Birmingham-Southern Col, AB, 65; Univ Ala, MA, 67; Univ Ga, PhD(hist), 73. **CAREER** Instr Am lit, Walker Col, 67-68, instr Am hist, 68-69; teaching fel, Univ Ga, 69-73; asst prof, Tidewater Col, 73-74; asst prof, 74-78, ASSOC PROF HIST, UNIV ALA, BIRMINGHAM, 78-, CHMN DEPT, 81-. **MEMBERSHIPS** Southern Hist Asn; Am Hist Asn. **RESEARCH** Recent America; American diplomatic history; Southern history. **SELECTED PUBLICATIONS** Auth, Morgan, John, Tyler and the Search for Southern Autonomy, Va Quart Rev, vol 0070, 94. **CONTACT ADDRESS** Dept of Hist, Univ of Ala, 1530 3rd Ave S, Birmingham, AL, 35294-0001.

MCWORTER, GERALD A.
PERSONAL Born 11/21/1942, Chicago, IL, d **DISCIPLINE** SOCIOLOGY **EDUCATION** Ottawa Univ, BA Soc & Philosophy, 1963; Univ of Chicago, MA, 1966, PhD, 1974. **CAREER** Ottawa Univ Dept of Philosophy, teaching asst, 1962-63; Univ of Chicago Natl Opinion Research Center, research asst, asst study dir, 1963-67; Fisk Univ Center for Afro-Amer Studies, asst prof of sociology, 1967-68; Inst of the Black World, asst prof of sociology, 1967-68; Fisk Univ, asst prof, assoc prof of sociology & Afro-Amer studies, 1969-75, dir, Afro-Amer Studies Program, 1969-75; Univ of Illinois at Chicago, assoc prof of Black studies, 1975-79; Univ of Illinois at Urbana-Champaign, assoc prof of sociology & Afro-Amer studies, 1979-87, dir Afro-Am Studies & Research Program, 1979-84; Twenty-First Century Books & Publications, sr editor, currently; State Univ of New York at Stony Brook, assoc prof of Africana studies, currently. **MEMBERSHIPS** Founder & dir, Cooperative Research Network in Black Studies, 1984-; ed bd, Malcolm X Studies Newsletter, 1987-, Afro Scholar Newsletter, 1983-, Western Journal of Black Studies, 1983-, Black Scholar, 1969-; founder, chair, Org of Black Amer Culture, 1965-67 **CONTACT ADDRESS** SUNY, Stony Brook, Stony Brook, NY, 11794.

MEACHAM, STANDISH
PERSONAL Born 03/12/1932, Cincinnati, OH, m, 1957, 3 children **DISCIPLINE** MODERN ENGLISH HISTORY **EDUCATION** Yale Univ, BA, 54; Harvard Univ, PhD(hist), 61-**CAREER** From instr to asst prof hist, Harvard Univ, 61-67; assoc prof, 67-70, chmn dept, 70-73, PROF HIST, UNIV TEX, AUSTIN, 70-, Am Coun Learned Soc fel, 65-66; Guggenheim fel, 72-73. **MEMBERSHIPS** AHA; Conf Brit Studies. **RESEARCH** Nineteenth century English church history; modern English labor history. **SELECTED PUBLICATIONS** Auth, Religion and Urban Change--Croydon, 1840-1914, Amer Hist Rev, vol 0099, 94; Architecture and Social Reform in Late Victorian London, Amer Hist Rev, vol 0101, 96. **CONTACT ADDRESS** Dept of Hist, Univ of Tex, 0 Univ of Texas, Austin, TX, 78712.

MEAD, CHRISTOPHER CURTIS
PERSONAL Born 04/30/1953, New Haven, CT, m, 1990 **DISCIPLINE** HISTORY OF ART & ARCHITECTURE **EDUCATION** Univ CA, Riverside, BA (summa cum laude), 75; Univ PA, MA, 78, PhD, 86. **CAREER** To full prof with joint appointment in Dept of Art & Art History and School of Architecture & Planning, Univ NM, 80-. **HONORS AND AWARDS** Phi Beta Kappa, 75; Penfield Res Scholarship, 78-79; Samuel H Kress Advanced Res fel, 88; Burlington Resources Found Fac Achievement Award, 92. **MEMBERSHIPS** Soc of Architectural Historians. **RESEARCH** History of architecture and urbanism in Europe and North America 1750-present. **SELECTED PUBLICATIONS** Auth, Space for the Continuous Present in the Residential Architecture of Bart Prince, Univ NM Art Museum, 89; ed, with an intro to, The Architecture of Robert Venturi, Univ NM Press, 89; Houses by Bart Prince, An American Architecture for the Continuous Present, Univ NM Pres, 91; Charles Garnier's Paris Opera: Architectural Empathy and the Renaissance of French Classicism, The Architectural Hist Found/ MIT press, 91; Shinen'kan, A Collaboration in L A, Cite, fall 92-winter 93; Urban Contingency and the Problem of Representation in Second Empire Paris, J of the Soc of Architectural Historians, LIV, no 2, June 95; The Architecture of Bart Prince: A Pragmatics of Place, W W Norton, 99. **CONTACT ADDRESS** Dept of Art & Art Hist, Univ of New Mexico, Albequerque, NM, 98131. **EMAIL** ccmead@unm.edu

MEADE, CATHERINE M.
PERSONAL Boston, MA **DISCIPLINE** AMERICAN HISTORY **EDUCATION** Regis Col, AB, 54; Boston Col, PhD(hist), 72. **CAREER** Instr, 67-72, asst prof, 72-74, dean freshmen, 76-80, ASSOC PROF HIST, REGIS COL, 74-, CHMN, HIST DEPT, 81- **MEMBERSHIPS** AHA; Orgn Am Historians; Nat Women's Studies Asn. **RESEARCH** Social and intellectual history; woman's history; American culture and architecture; medieval history; medieval women. **SELECTED PUBLICATIONS** Auth, My Nature is Fire: Catherine of Siena, Alba House, 91. **CONTACT ADDRESS** Dept of History, Regis Col, 235 Wellesley St, Weston, MA, 02193-1505.

MEADE, WADE C.
DISCIPLINE HISTORY **EDUCATION** La Tech Univ, BS, 59, MS, 61; Univ TX at Austin, 69. **CAREER** Asst and instr geol, 60-61, asst prof hist,67-70, assoc prof hist and archaeol, 70-76, prof hist and archaeol, La Tech Univ, 76-; hist asst, Univ TX at Austin, 64-66; geog instr, 65-66, hist and anthrop instr, SW TX state Univ, 66. **HONORS AND AWARDS** Outstanding Research Award for Col of Arts & Sci(s), La Tech Univ, 80-81. **MEMBERSHIPS** Am Asn Univ Prof; Am Hist Asn; Archaeol Inst Am; Class Asn Midwest & South; Class Soc Am Acad Rome; Int Asn Class Archaeol; Soc Prom Roman Studies; Soc Pressional Archeol; Soc Vertebrate Paleontol; SW Soc Sci Asn; Vergilian Soc. **RESEARCH** Rome hist; Near East hist; Greece; and Roman hist; Etruscan, Greek, Egyptian, and Indian Archeol. **SELECTED PUBLICATIONS** Auth, Pericles of Athens and the Birth of Democracy, by Donald Kagan, Historian, 91-92; The Early History of the Ancient Near East, 9000-2000 B.C., by Hans J. Nissen, Am Hist Rev, 90. **CONTACT ADDRESS** Dept of Hist, Louisiana Tech Univ, PO Box 3178, Ruston, LA, 71272.

MEADERS, DANIEL
DISCIPLINE HISTORY **EDUCATION** CUNY, Staten island, BA, 74; Yale Univ, MA, 79; PhD, 90. **CAREER** Asst prof, William Paterson State Col, 91- & adj prof, 91; adj prof, Manhattan Community Cole, NY City, 91; assoc ed, Frederick Douglass Papers, Yale Univ, 89-90 & res asst, 86-89. **HONORS AND AWARDS** Woodrow Wilson-Martin Luther King, fel, 74. **SELECTED PUBLICATIONS** Auth, South Carolina Fugitives as Viewed Through Local Colonial Newspapers with Emphasis on Runaway Notices, 1732-1801, J Negro Hist, 76; Dead or Alive: Fugitive Slaves and White Indentured Servants before 1830, Garland, 93. **CONTACT ADDRESS** Dept of History, William Paterson Col, 300 Pompton Rd., Wayne, NJ, 07470. **EMAIL** meaders@frontier.wilpaterson.edu

MEADORS, GARY T.
PERSONAL Born 06/03/1945, Connersville, IN, m, 1967 **DISCIPLINE** GREEK, NEW TESTAMENT **EDUCATION** Grace Coll and Theol Sem. ThD, 83. **CAREER** Asst Prof, 79-83, Piedmont Baptist Coll; Prof of NT, 83-93, Grace Theol Sem; Prof of NT, 93-95, Baptist Sem of PA; Prof of NT, 95-, Grand Rapids Baptist Sem. **MEMBERSHIPS** ETS, IBR, SBL. **RESEARCH** New Testament; Ethics. **SELECTED PUBLICATIONS** Auth, Can a Believer Fall from Grace?, Spire 14:2, 86; Discipleship-Another Nuance to Consider, Exposition 4:3, 93; Evangelical Dictionary of Biblical Theology, ed by Walter Elwell, Grand Rapids, Baker Book House, 96; Love is the Law of Spiritual Formation, Presidential address to the Midwest Region Meeting of the Evangelical Theological Society, 98; Why Are They Looking At Jesus?, The Jesus Seminar, Baptist Bulletin, 97; Craig Blomberg, 1 Corinthians, The Application Series, JETS41, 98. **CONTACT ADDRESS** Grand Rapids Baptist Sem, 1001 E Beltline NE, Grand Rapids, MI, 49525. **EMAIL** gmeadors@cornerstone.edu

MEADOWS, EDDIE
DISCIPLINE ETHNOMUSICOLOGY **EDUCATION** TN State Univ, BA; Univ IL, MS; MI State Univ, PhD; Univ CA, postdoc stud. **CAREER** Instr, Univ CA, Berkeley; Univ Ghana, W Africa; vis prof, UCLA; prof-. **HONORS AND AWARDS** Martin Luther King distinguished vis profship, MI State Univ; Meritorious Performance and Professional Promise awards, CA State Univ. **RESEARCH** African-am music and jazz studies areas. **SELECTED PUBLICATIONS** Auth, Afro-America Music, 76; Theses and Dissertations on Black and American Music, 80; Jazz Reference and Research Materials, 81; Jazz Research and Performance Materials: A Select Annotated Bibliography, 95. **CONTACT ADDRESS** Sch Mus and Dance, San Diego State Univ, 5500 Campanile Dr, San Diego, CA, 92182. **EMAIL** meadows@mail.sdsu.edu

MEARS, JOHN A.
PERSONAL Born 01/26/1938, St. Paul, MN, m, 1960, 2 children **DISCIPLINE** EARLY MODERN EUROPEAN HISTORY **EDUCATION** Univ Minn, BA, 60; Univ Chicago, MA, 62, PhD(hist), 64. **CAREER** Asst prof hist, NMex State Univ, 64-67; asst prof, 67-70, ASSOC PROF HIST, SOUTHERN METHODIST UNIV, 70-. **MEMBERSHIPS** AHA; Conf Group Cent Europ Hist. **RESEARCH** Seventeenth century Germany, especially the Habsburg monarchy; seventeenth-century European military history; comparative revolutions. **SELECTED PUBLICATIONS** Auth, Politics and War, Amer Hist Rev, vol 0099, 94; World Historians and Their Goals, J World Hist, vol 0005, 94; European Warfare 1660-1815, Amer Hist Rev, vol 0101, 96; Holland and the Dutch Republic in the 17th-Century, Historian, vol 0058, 96. **CONTACT ADDRESS** Dept of Hist, Southern Methodist Univ, P O Box 750001, Dallas, TX, 75275-0001.

MEERBOTE, RALF
PERSONAL Born 05/08/1942, Merseburg, Germany **DISCIPLINE** HISTORY OF MODERN PHILOSOPHY **EDUCATION** Univ Chicago, BS, 64; Harvard Univ, MA, 67, PhD(philos), 70. **CAREER** Asst prof philos, Univ Ill, Chicago Circle, 69-73, assoc prof, 73-80; ASSOC PROF PHILOS, UNIV ROCHESTER, 80-, Fulbright sr res fel, 76-77. **MEM-**

BERSHIPS Am Philos Asn; Kantgesellschaft. **RESEARCH** Kant's theory of knowledge; theory of knowledge; aesthetics. **SELECTED PUBLICATIONS** Auth, Kant and Jobs Comforters, J Amer Acad Relig, vol 0060, 92. **CONTACT ADDRESS** Dept of Philosophy, Univ of Rochester, Rochester, NY, 14627.

MEHLER, BARRY ALAN
PERSONAL Born 03/18/1947, Brooklyn, NY **DISCIPLINE** AMERICAN HISTORY **EDUCATION** Yeshiva Univ, BA, 70; City Col, MA, 72; Univ Ill, PhD, 88. **CAREER** Instr, Wash Univ, 77; res assoc, Nat Hist Found, 80; Instr, Univ Ill, 81-88; instr, 88-90; asst prof, 90-93; assoc prof, 94-. **HONORS AND AWARDS** Grant-in-Aid, Rockefeller found, 77; Joseph Ward Swain prize, Univ Ill, 84; Babcock fel, Univ Ill, 85-86; fac devel grant, 88; instructional develop grant, 88; Ferris State Bd Ctrl Cert of Recognition, 94., Founder, exec dir, ISAR. **RESEARCH** History of science, behavior-genetic analysis, history of racism. **SELECTED PUBLICATIONS** Auth, In Genes We Trust: When Science Bows to Racism, Reform Judaism, 94; rev, republ, The Pub Eye, 95, RaceFile, 95; Networking: A Publication of the Fight The Right Network, 95; Israel Diary, 1996, Israel Horizons, 96; Heredity and Hereditarianism, Philos Education: An Encyclopedia, Garland Publ, 96; Beyondism: Raymond B. Cattell and the New Eugenics, Genetica, 97. **CONTACT ADDRESS** Dept of Hum, Ferris State Univ, 901 S State St, Big Rapids, MI, 49307. **EMAIL** mehlerb@ferris.edu

MEHLINGER, HOWARD DEAN
PERSONAL Born 08/22/1931, Hillsboro, KS, m, 1952, 3 children **DISCIPLINE** MODERN RUSSIAN HISTORY **EDUCATION** McPherson Col, AB, 53; Univ Kans, MS, 59, PhD(hist), 64. **CAREER** High sch teacher, Kans, 53-63; co-dir social studies curric develop ctr, Pittsburgh Pub Schs, 63-64; asst dir, NCent Asn Schs and Cols Foreign Rels Proj, 64-65; asst prof hist, 65-70, assoc prof hist and educ, 70-74, dep chmn inter-univ comt on travel grants, 65-66, dir high sch curric ctr govt, 66-71, PROF HIST and EDUC, IND UNIV, BLOOMINGTON, 74-, DIR SOCIAL STUDIES DEVELOP CTR, 68-, DEAN, SCH EDUC, 81-, Consult social studies curric ctr, Northwestern Univ, 64-65; dir, Educ Prof Develop Assistance Civics Dissemination Inst, 69-70; co-dir, Social Studies Field Agt Training Proj, 70-73; Am Polit Sci Asn polit sci course mem, 72-77; pres, Nat Coun Social Studies, 77. **MEMBERSHIPS** Am Educ Res Asn; Am Polit Sci Asn; Am Asn Advan Slavic Studies; Asn Supv and Curric Develop; Nat Coun Social Studies. **RESEARCH** Russian revolution of 1905; instructional development. **SELECTED PUBLICATIONS** Auth, Soviet Education Under Perestroika, Slavic Rev, Vol 53, 94. **CONTACT ADDRESS** 3606 Park Lane, Bloomington, IN, 47401.

MEIER, AUGUST
PERSONAL Born 04/20/1923, New York, NY **DISCIPLINE** AMERICAN NEGRO STUDIES **EDUCATION** Oberlin Col, AB, 45; Columbia Univ, AM, 48, PhD, 57. **CAREER** Asst prof hist, Tougaloo Col, 45-49; asst prof, Fisk Univ, 53-56, asst to pres, 53-54; from asst prof to assoc prof hist, Morgan State Col, 57-64; prof, Roosevelt Univ, 64-67; UNIV PROF HIST, KENT STATE UNIV, 67-, Ed, Negro in Am Life Ser, Atheneum, 66-74; Guggenheim fel, 71-72; GEN ED, SER ON BLACKS IN NEW WORLD, UNIV ILL PRESS, 72-; Nat Endowment for Humanities fel, 75-76; Ctr for Advan Studies Behav Sci fel, 76-77. **MEMBERSHIPS** Am Anthrop Asn; Am Studies Asn; Southern Hist Asn; Asn Study Negro Life and Hist; Orgn Am Historians. **SELECTED PUBLICATIONS** Auth, Black on the Poetic Function of Reality Shock in Hoffmann, E. T. A. Fantasy Novella Don Juan, Zeitschrift Deutsch Philol, Vol 0111, 92; Untitled, Jour Am Hist, Vol 81, 94; The Forging of a Black Community, Seattles Central District from 1870 Through the Civil Rights Era, W Am Quart, Vol 26, 95; The Papers of King, Martin, Luther, Vol 1, Called to Serve--January 1929 June 1951, J Am Hist, Vol 80, 93;Towards a Research Agenda on Blacks and Jews in United States History, J Am Ethnic Hist, Vol 12, 93; The Douglass, Frederick Papers--Speeches, Debates, and Interviews, Vol 4, 1864-80, J Southern Hist, Vol 59, 93; Poets and Non Poets, Literary Political Background of Andersch, Alfred Interest for Vittorini, Elio, Zeitschrift Germanistik, Vol 3, 93; The Douglas, Frederick Papers, Series 1, Speeches, Debates, and Interviews, Vol 5, 1881-95, J Southern Hist, Vol 60, 94. **CONTACT ADDRESS** Dept of Hist, Kent State Univ, Kent, OH, 44242.

MEIKLE, JEFFREY L.
PERSONAL Born 07/02/1949, m, 2 children **DISCIPLINE** AMERICAN STUDIES **EDUCATION** Brown Univ, AB and AM, 71; Univ Tex, Austin, PhD(Am studies), 77. **CAREER** Asst instr Am studies, Univ Tex, Austin, 73-77; instr, Colby-Sawyer Col, 77-78; Nat Hist Publ and Records Comn fel hist ed, Charles Willson Peale Papers, Nat Portrait Gallery, Smithsonian Inst, 78-79; asst prof English, 79-80, ASST PROF AM STUDIES, UNIV TEX, AUSTIN, 79-, ASST PROF ART HIST, 80-, Consult, Gillespie County Hist Soc, 75 and WGBH Educ Found, 80; hist consult, Dorian Walker Prod, Inc, 79 and Laybourne and Lemle Inc, 80; CHMN, UNIV TEX AND UNIV WURZBURG EXCHANGE COMT, 80-; fel, Design Arts Prog, Nat Endowment for Arts, 81. **HONORS AND AWARDS** DeGolyer Prize, DeGolyer Inst, Southern Methodist Univ, 81. **MEMBERSHIPS** Am Studies Asn; AHA; Col Art Asn; Soc Hist Technol. **SELECTED PUBLICATIONS** Auth of Bicycles, Bakelites, and Bulbs--Toward a Theory of Sociotechnical Change, TechCult, Vol 37, 96; American Technological Sublime, Tech Cult, Vol 36, 95; The Portable Radio in American Life, Tech Cult, Vol 34, 93; The Portable Radio in American Life, Tec Cult, Vol 34, 93; Steinway and Sons, J Am Hist, Vol 83, 96; Material Doubts--The Consequences of Plastic, Environmental Hist, Vol 2, 97; Of Bicycles, Bakelites, and Bulbs--Toward AaTheory of Sociotechnical Change, Tech Cult, Vol 37, 96; Auto Opium--A Social History of American Automobile Design, Am Hist Rev, Vol 0101, 96; American Technological Sublime, Tech Cult, Vol 36, 95. **CONTACT ADDRESS** Dept of Am Studies, Univ of Tex, Austin, TX, 78704.

MEISEL, JANET ANNE
PERSONAL Born 01/30/1944, Dallas, TX **DISCIPLINE** MEDIEVAL ENGLISH & FRENCH HISTORY **EDUCATION** Oberlin Col, AB, 67; Univ Calif, Berkeley, MA, 71; PhD(Hist) 74. **CAREER** Asst prof, 74-81, assoc prof Hist, Univ Tex, Austin, 81-, Am Coun Learned Soc fel Hist, 77. **MEMBERSHIPS** AHA; Mediaeval Acad Am. **RESEARCH** Medieval frontier societies; medieval law; medieval nobilities. **SELECTED PUBLICATIONS** Auth, Barons of the Welsh Frontier: The Corbet, Pantulf, and Fitzwarin Families, 1066-1272, Univ Nebr Press, 80. **CONTACT ADDRESS** Dept of History, Univ of Texas, Austin, TX, 78712-1026. **EMAIL** jmeisel@mail.utexas.edu

MEISTER, MAUREEN
PERSONAL Born 08/25/1953, Spokane, WA, m, 1979, 2 children **DISCIPLINE** ART AND ARCHITECTURAL HISTORIAN **EDUCATION** Mt. Holyoke, AB, 75; Univ Pittsburgh, BA, 80; Brown Univ, AM, 83, PhD candidate present. **CAREER** Visiting lectr, fall 85, Sch of the Museum of Fine Arts; lectr, fall 89, Northeastern Univ; visiting lectr, spring 98, Tufts Univ; instr, 82-86, adjunct asst prof, 86-91, assoc prof, 91-present, Art Inst of Boston. **HONORS AND AWARDS** Newspaper Fund award, 74; Univ Fel, Brown Univ, 80-81; Graham Found grant to edit symposium papers on HH Richardson for publication. **MEMBERSHIPS** Soc of Architectural Historians; Coll Art Assn; Soc of Architectural Historians-New England chapter, Victorian Soc in Amer; Gibson House Museum (president), Winchester Historical Soc (dir and ed of architects series). **RESEARCH** 19th and early 20th century art and architecture. **SELECTED PUBLICATIONS** Auth, weekly exhibition reviews and interviews with artists, 77-79; Sulptures-cape, Art News, Feb 78; Coauth, All the Banners Wave: Art and War in the Romantic Era, 82; Ed, The Architects of Winchester, Massachusetts, Winchester Historical Society, Winchester, MA, 94; Auth, Rand & Taylor, A Biographical Dictionary of Architects in Maine, Architects in Maine, 95; The Selling of Winslow Homer, Visual Resources: An International Journal of Documentation, 97; Rangeley: A Romantic Residential Park in Winchester, Massachusetts, Antiques, 97; **CONTACT ADDRESS** 38 Rangeley Rd., Winchester, MA, 01890. **EMAIL** meisterm@interserv.com

MEISTER, MICHAEL WILLIAM
PERSONAL Born 08/20/1942, West Palm Beach, FL, m, 1970 **DISCIPLINE** HISTORY OF ART **EDUCATION** Harvard Univ, BA, 64, MA, 72, PhD, 74. **CAREER** Asst prof hist art, Univ Tex, Austin, 74-76; asst prof hist art and SAsia studies, 76-79, ASSOC PROF HIST ART, UNIV PA, 79-, Ed, Encycl Indian Temple Archit. **HONORS AND AWARDS** MA, Univ Pa, 79. **MEMBERSHIPS** Asn Asian Studies; Am Comt SAsian Art; SAsian Relig Art Studies. **RESEARCH** South Asian architecture, particularly the Hindu temple; Indian sculpture, questions of style and idiom; icons and narrative in Indian imagery. **SELECTED PUBLICATIONS** Auth, The Queen Stepwell at Patan, Artibus Asiae, Vol 53, 93; Man and Man Lion, The Philadelphia Narasimha, Artibus Asiae, Vol 56, 96. **CONTACT ADDRESS** Asian Regional Studies, Univ of Pa, Philadelphia, PA, 19139.

MELANCON, DONALD
PERSONAL Born 11/12/1939, Franklin, LA, m **DISCIPLINE** EDUCATION **EDUCATION** Southern Univ, BS, 1963; Univ of IL, MEd 1971, PhD 1976. **CAREER** Kankakee Sch Dist, cent off adminstr 1971-72, sch psychol couns 1970; St Anne HS, tchr 1964-70; MO, tchr 1963; Nympum Mini-bike Prgm YMCA, consult 1972; Pembroke Consol Sch Dist, 1972; Opport Ind Ctr, 1972; Kankakee Boys Camp, 1972; UofIL, lab trainer 1972; Ofc of Edn,1979; Union Grad Sch, 1979; St Ann Sch Bd of Educ 1976; Kankakee Sch Dist, elem sch prin; Lemoyne-Owen College, professor, 1994-. **HONORS AND AWARDS** Sel Phi Delta Kappa-Hon Soc in Edn; Bicent Declar for Serv to Cub Sct 1976; Ebony Esteem Aw 1976; Men of prgss Outst Edecator Award 1978. **MEMBERSHIPS** Bd of dir Kankakee Drug Abuse; Old Fair Pk Day Care; Kankakee Cult Prgm; YMCA Exten Dept; Cub Sct Mstr; Appt by Gov of IL Reg Manpwr Comm for CETA; mem NEA; IL Educ Assn; Humanist Assn; Sch Bd Assn of IL; Kankakee Co Adminstr Assn. **SELECTED PUBLICATIONS** "As Students See Things" IL Educ Assn Jour 1969; "Staff Dev on a Shoestring" IL Princ Journl 1973; "A System Apprch to Tension Monit & Tension Reduct in an Educ Setting" Journl of Rsrch in Educ 1973; "Model for Sch Commun Relat" Phi Delta Kappan 1974. **CONTACT ADDRESS** Lemoyne-Owen Col, Memphis, TN, 38126.

MELE, ALFRED R.
DISCIPLINE CLASSICS AND PHILOSOPHY **EDUCATION** Wayne State Univ, BA, 73; Univ MI, PhD, 79. **CAREER** Vail Prof Philos, 79. **RESEARCH** Cognitive philos; hist of ancient philos. **SELECTED PUBLICATIONS** Auth, Irrationality, Oxford UP, 87; Springs of Action, Oxford UP, 92; Autonomous Agents, Oxford UP, 95; co-edr, Mental Causation, Clarendon, 93. **CONTACT ADDRESS** Davidson Col, 102 N Main St, PO Box 1719, Davidson, NC, 28036. **EMAIL** almele@davidson.edu

MELENDEZ, GABRIEL
DISCIPLINE AMERICAN STUDIES **EDUCATION** Univ NMex, PhD, 84. **CAREER** Assoc prof, res assoc, Ctr for Reg Stud, Univ NMex; bd, Acad/El Norte Publ; res assoc, Southwest Hisp Res Inst. **HONORS AND AWARDS** Rockefeller Hum fel, 91; Ctr for Reg Stud grant, 92; Sr Res fel, NMEx Endowment for Hum, 93. **MEMBERSHIPS** Nat Asn for Chicano Stud; Am Stud Asn. **RESEARCH** Ethnic and cultural representation. **SELECTED PUBLICATIONS** Auth, So All is Not Lost: The Poetics of Print in Nuevomexicano Communities, 1834-1950, UNM Press, 97; coauth, Reflexiones del Corazon, 93. **CONTACT ADDRESS** Univ NMex, Albuquerque, NM, 87131.

MELENDY, HOWARD BRETT
PERSONAL Born 05/03/1924, Eureka, CA, m, 1952 **DISCIPLINE** HISTORY **EDUCATION** Stanford Univ, AB, 46, MA, 48, PhD(hist), 52. **CAREER** High sch teacher, Calif, 50-54; instr hist, Fresno Jr Col, 54-55; from instr to prof, San Jose State Col, 55-70, head dept, 58-69, asst acad vpres, 68-70, actg acad vpres, 70; prof hist, Univ Hawaii, Manoa, 70-79; dean undergraduate studies, 79-81, PROF HIST, SAN JOSE STATE UNIV, 79-, ASSOC ACAD VPRES UNDERGRAD STUDIES, 81-, Reader Am hist, Educ Testing Serv, Princeton, NJ, 61-74; Am Philos Soc grants, 62 and 74; vis rep, Col Entrance Exam Bd, 65-66; fel, Am Coun Educ Acad Admin Internship Prog, 67-68; vpres, Community Cols, Univ Hawaii, 70-73; fel, Danforth Assoc, 74; Nat Endowment Humanities grant, 80-83. **MEMBERSHIPS** AHA; NEA; Am Asn Higher Educ. **RESEARCH** Asian immigration; West in twentieth century. **SELECTED PUBLICATIONS** Asian American Panethnicity--Bridging Institutions and Identities, J Am Hist, Vol 80, 94; The New Asian Immigration in Los Angeles and Global Restructuring, Pac Hist Rev, Vol 66, 97; Asian Americans, Cal Hist, Vol 71, 92; The City and County of Honolulu--A Governmental Chronicle, Pac Hist Rev, Vol 62, 93. **CONTACT ADDRESS** Dept of Hist, San Jose State Univ, San Jose, CA, 95114.

MELLINI, PETER JOHN DREYFUS
PERSONAL Born 08/16/1935, Hermosa Beach, CA, m, 1977 **DISCIPLINE** MODERN EUROPEAN HISTORY **EDUCATION** Stanford Univ, BA, 62, MA, 65, PhD, 71. **CAREER** Tutor hist & polit, Stanford Univ; 66, instr hist, 68-70; asst prof, 70-73, assoc prof, 73-80, dir hist preserv prog, 75-80, prof hist, Sonoma State Univ, 80-, Jr Humanist fel, 71-; vis prof, San Francisco State Univ, 81; dir, Inst Hist Study, Victorian Soc, 80-82; lect Hist Jour, San Fran State Univ, 85-90. **HONORS AND AWARDS** NEH Fel, 83; Fel Royal Hist Soc; Preserv Award, Calif Coun Hist Soc, 80. **MEMBERSHIPS** AHA; Conf Brit Studies; Nat Trust for Hist Preserv; Victorian Soc. **RESEARCH** Nineteenth and 20th century caricature and cartoons; British social history; National symbols; A biography of Punch. **SELECTED PUBLICATIONS** Auth, Sir Eldon Gorst: The Overshadowed Proconsul, Hoover, 77; coauth, (with K L Seavey), The rural field school: Jolon, California, Monterey Dept Parks, 79; auth 21 articles on Brit & Eur Hist coauth (with R T Matthews), In Vanity Fair, Scholar Press London & Univ Calif Berkeley, 82. **CONTACT ADDRESS** Dept Hist, Sonoma State Univ, Rohnert Park, CA, 94928-3609. **EMAIL** peter.mellini@sonoma.edu

MELLINK, MACHTELD JOHANNA
PERSONAL Born 10/26/1917, Amsterdam, Netherlands **DISCIPLINE** CLASSICAL AND NEAR EASTERN ARCHEOLOGY **EDUCATION** Univ Amsterdam, BA, 38, MA, 41; Univ Utrecht, PhD, 43. **CAREER** Field asst Tarsus excavations, Inst Advan Study, 47-49; from asst prof to assoc prof, 49-62, PROF CLASS ARCHAEOL, BRYN MAWR COL, 62-, FIELD DIR, COL EXCAVATIONS, KARATAS, TURKEY, 63-, MEM STAFF, UNIV MUS EXCAVATIONS, GORDION; VPRES, AM RES INST IN TURKEY, 80-; PRES, ARCHAEOL INST AM, 81- **MEMBERSHIPS** Sch Orient Res; Am Orient Soc; corp mem Royal Neth Acad Sci; fel Am Acad Arts and Sci; Am Philos Soc. **RESEARCH** Anatolian and Aegean archaeology. **SELECTED PUBLICATIONS** Auth Archaeology in Anatolia, Am J Archaeol, Vol 97, 93. **CONTACT ADDRESS** Dept of Class and Near Eastern Archaeol, Bryn Mawr Col, Bryn Mawr, PA, 19010.

MELLON, STANLEY
PERSONAL Born 01/16/1927, Brooklyn, NY **DISCIPLINE** MODERN EUROPEAN AND FRENCH HISTORY **EDUCATION** Columbia Col, AB, 50; Princeton Univ, MA, 52, PhD, 54. **CAREER** Instr hist, Univ Mich, 54-58; asst prof, Univ Calif, Berkeley, 58-60; from asst prof to assoc prof, Yale Univ, 60-69; PROF HIST, UNIV ILL, CHICAGO CIRCLE, 69-, Vis

assoc prof hist, Columbia Univ, 68-69. **MEMBERSHIPS** AHA; Soc Fr Hist Studies. **RESEARCH** Nineteenth century French history; intellectual history. **SELECTED PUBLICATIONS** Auth, Individual Choice And The Structures Of History - Detocqueville,Alexis As Historian Reappraised - Mitchell,H/, American Historical Review, Vol 0102, 97 An Intellectual History of Liberalism, Am Hist Rev, Vol 0101, 96; Guizot, Francois and the Political Culture of his Times, J Mod Hist, Vol 66, 94; The Humane Comedy--Constant, Tocqueville, and French Liberalism, Am Hist Rev, Vol 98, 93; The Inside of History--Daubigne, Jean, Henri, Merle and Romantic Historiography, Am Hist Rev, Vol 0102, 97; The Rhetoric of Historical Representation--3 Narrative Histories of the French Revolution, Am Hist Rev, Vol 97, 92. **CONTACT ADDRESS** Dept of Hist, Univ of Ill at Chicago Circle, Chicago, IL, 60680.

MELLOR, RONALD
PERSONAL Born 09/30/1940, New York, NY, m, 1969, 1 child **DISCIPLINE** CLASSICS **EDUCATION** Fordham Col, BA, 62; Princeton Univ, MA, 64, PhD, 68. **CAREER** Stanford Univ, asst prof, 65-75; UCLA, Assoc prof, prof, dept ch, 76-. **HONORS AND AWARDS** NEH fel, ACLS fel, Australian Nat Univ Fel. **MEMBERSHIPS** AHA, APA, AAH, SPRS. **RESEARCH** Roman studies; ancient religion; historiography. **SELECTED PUBLICATIONS** Auth, Thea Rhome: The Worship of the Goddess Roma in the Greek World, Gottingen, 75; auth, From Augustus to Nero: The First Dynasty of Imperial Rome, ed., MSU Pr, 90; auth, Tacitus, Routledge, 93; auth, Tacitus: The Classical Tradition, Garland Books, 95; auth, The Historians of Rome, ed., Routledge, 97; auth, The Roman Historians, Routledge, 99. **CONTACT ADDRESS** Dept of History, Univ of California, Los Angeles, Los Angeles, CA, 90095-1473. **EMAIL** rmellor@ucla.edu

MELOSI, MARTIN V.
PERSONAL Born 04/27/1947, San Jose, CA, m, 1971, 2 children **DISCIPLINE** HISTORY **EDUCATION** Univ Montana, BA, 69, MA, 71; Univ Texas, PhD, 75. **CAREER** From instr to prof, Texas A&M Univ, 75-84; prof Hist, dir, Inst for Public Hist, 84- , Univ Houston; vis prof, Univ Paris VIII, 93; vis scholar, The Sea and the Cities Program, Univ Helsinki, 97, 98. **HONORS AND AWARDS** Ford Found fel, 74; Rockefeller Found fel, 76-77; Nat Hum Ctr, 82-83; NEH fel, 88-92; vis scholar, Smithsonian Inst, 91. **MEMBERSHIPS** Orgn of Am Hist; Am Soc for Environ Hist; Nat Coun on Public Hist; Public Works Hist Soc. **RESEARCH** Urban history; environmental history; public history; history of energy and technology. **SELECTED PUBLICATIONS** Auth, Thomas A. Edison and the Modernization of America, Addison, Wesley, Longman, 90; ed and contribur, Urban Public Policy: Historical Modes and Methods, Penn State, 93; auth, The Sanitary City: Urban Infrastructure in America from Colonial Times to the Present, Johns Hopkins, 99. **CONTACT ADDRESS** Dept of History, Univ of Houston, Houston, TX, 77204-3785. **EMAIL** mmelosi@uh.edu

MELTON, JAMES V.H.
DISCIPLINE HISTORY **EDUCATION** Vanderbilt Univ, BA, 74; Univ Chicago, MA, 75, PhD, 82. **CAREER** Assoc prof **HONORS AND AWARDS** Biennial Bk Prize, Conf Group Cent Europ Hist. **RESEARCH** Enlightenment Europe; early modern German and Habsburg History; politics, culture, and the public sphere in Enlightenment Europe. **SELECTED PUBLICATIONS** Auth, Absolutism and the Eighteenth-Century Origins of Compulsory Schooling in Prussia and Austria; co-ed/ trans, Land and Lordship: Structures of Governance in Medieval Austria; co-ed, Paths of Continuity: Historical Scholarship in Central Europe, 1933-1960. **CONTACT ADDRESS** Dept History, Emory Univ, 221 Bowden Hall, 561 Kilgo Cir, Atlanta, GA, 30322-1950. **EMAIL** jmelt01@emory.edu

MELTZER, ALLAN H.
PERSONAL Born 02/06/1928, Boston, MA, m, 1950, 3 children **DISCIPLINE** ECONOMICS **EDUCATION** Duke Univ, AB, 48; Univ Cal, Los Angeles, MA 55, PhD 58. **CAREER** Carnegie Mellon Univ, assoc prof, prof, 57-; The Bank of Japan, Hon Advis, 86-; Am Ent Inst for Pub Pol Res, Vis Schol, 89-; The Allan Meltzer Univ Prof of Pol Econ, 97-. **HONORS AND AWARDS** Medal Outstanding Prof Ach Awd; Fellow, Nat Asn Bus Econ; Man Of The Year In fin; Templeton Honor Roll, Edu in a Free Soc; Distg Ach Awd Money Mkteers NY Univ. **MEMBERSHIPS** AEA; WEA; Nat Asn Bus. **RESEARCH** Monetary econo; Pol Econ; Hist Fed Reserve. **SELECTED PUBLICATIONS** Money Credit and Policy, Edward Elgar Pub, 95; Money and the Economy: Issues in Monetary Analysis, with K Brunner, Cambridge Press, 91. **CONTACT ADDRESS** Carnegie Mellon Univ, Pittsburgh, PA, 15213. **EMAIL** am05@andrew.cmu.edu

MENARD, RUSSELL R.
DISCIPLINE HISTORY **EDUCATION** Univ Iowa, MA, PhD. **CAREER** Prof **RESEARCH** Economic, demographic, and social history of the Chesapeake region during early Colonial period; plantation slavery in British America; economic development of lower South in the eighteenth century; late nineteenth-century U.S. social history. **SELECTED PUBLICATIONS** Auth, Economy and Society in Early Colonial Maryland, Garland, 85; co-auth, The Economy of British America, 1607-1789, Univ NC, 91; Robert Cole's World: Agriculture and Society in Early Maryland, Univ NC, 91; co-ed The Economy of Early America: The Revolution Period, 1763-7190, Univ Va, 88. **CONTACT ADDRESS** History Dept, Univ of Minnesota, Twin Cities, 614 Social Sciences Tower, 267 19th Ave. S, Minneapolis, MN, 55455. **EMAIL** menar001@tc.umn.edu

MENASHE, LOUIS
PERSONAL Born 12/10/1935, Brooklyn, NY, m, 1958, 2 children **DISCIPLINE** RUSSIAN AND SOVIET HISTORY **EDUCATION** City Col New York, BA, 59; NY Univ, MA, 63, PhD(hist), 66. **CAREER** Asst prof, 65-68, ASSOC PROF HIST, POLYTECH INST NY, 68-, Adj prof hist, NY Univ, 70-73; communist affairs ed, Marxist Perspectives, 78-80. **MEMBERSHIPS** Am Asn Advan Slavic Studies; AHA. **RESEARCH** Social and political history of the Russian Revolution; Soviet politics and society; international affairs. **SELECTED PUBLICATIONS** Auth, Theremin, Cineaste, Vol 21, 95; Visions of the Past--The Challenge of Film to our Idea of History, Hist J Film Radio TV, Vol 16, 96; Shadows on the Past--Studies in the Historical Fiction Film, Hist Jour Film Radio TV, Vol 16, 96; Burnt By The Sun, Cineaste, Vol 21, 95; Film Posters of the Russian Avant Garde, Cineaste, Vol 23, 97; Art, History and Politics in the Former Yugoslavia--An Interview With Benson, Michael, Cineaste, Vol 22, 96; Kinoglasnost--Soviet Cinema in our Time, Russ Rev, Vol 53, 94; Sideburns, Cineaste, Vol 20, 93; Prisoner of the Mountains, Cineaste, Vol 23, 97; Kolya , Cineaste, Vol 22, 97; Requiem for Soviet Cinema, 1917-1991k, Cineaste, Vol 21, 95; The Films of Tarkovsky, Andrei--A Visual Fugue, Cineaste, Vol 22, 97; Wild Reeds, Cineaste, Vol 22, 96. **CONTACT ADDRESS** Dept of Hist, Polytech Inst of New York, 6 Metro Tech Ctr, Brooklyn, NY, 11201-3840.

MENDELSOHN, EVERETT IRWIN
PERSONAL Born 10/28/1931, Yonkers, NY, m, 1954, 3 children **DISCIPLINE** HISTORY OF SCIENCE **EDUCATION** Antioch Col, AB, 53; Harvard Univ, PhD, 60. **CAREER** From instr to assoc prof, 60-69, PROF HIST SCI, HARVARD UNIV, 69- CHMN DEPT, 71-, Dir prog, Technol & Soc, Harvard Univ, 66-68; Macy sr fac fel, 68-69; overseas fel, Churchill Col, Cambridge Univ, 68-69; mem comt life sci & soc policy, Nat Acad Sci, 68-73; ed, J Hist Biol; fel, Zentrum fur Interdiszplinare Forschung, Bielefeld, 78-79 fel, Wissonschaftskslleg zu Berlin, 83-84; Prof Invitee, Conservatoire Nat Des Arts et Metiers, 89-90; Olaf Palme Prof, Sweden SCASSS, 94; co-ed, Sociol of Sci Yearbk; Ed Jour of Hist Of Biol. **HONORS AND AWARDS** Gregor Mendel Medal, Czech Acad Sci., DHL, RI Col, 77. **MEMBERSHIPS** Hist Sci Soc; fel AAAS (vpres, 73-74); Int Acad Hist Sci; fel Am Acad Arts & Sci; Int Acad hist Med. **RESEARCH** Development of modern biological sciences; aspects of the social relations of science; social assessment of science. **SELECTED PUBLICATIONS** Auth, Heat and Life, Harvard Univ, 64; Physical models and physiological concepts: Explanation in nineteenth century biology, Brit J Hist Sci, 66; ed, Human aspects of Biomedical Innovation, Harvard Univ, 71; auth, Should science survive its success?, Boston Study Philos Sci, 74; co-ed, Science and Values, Humanities, 74; auth, Revolution and rejunction, Rels Between Sci & Philos, Humanities, 76; co-ed & contribr, Topics in the Philosophy of Biology, 76 & Social Production of Scientific Knowledge, 77, Reidel; coed Technology, Pessimism, and Postmodernism, Soc of Sci Yearbk, Kluwer Acad Publ, 95; Biology as Society, Society as Biology: Metaphors, Soc of Sci Yearbk, Kluwer Acad Publ, 95; coauth Negotiating Jerusalem, Am Acad Arts & Sci, 97. **CONTACT ADDRESS** Dept of Hist of Sci, Harvard Univ, Science Ctr 235, Cambridge, MA, 02138-3800. **EMAIL** emendels@FAS.Harvard.edu

MENDELSON, JOHANNA
DISCIPLINE POLITICAL SCIENCE **EDUCATION** Wash Univ, PhD; Am Univ, JD. **CAREER** Prof, Am Univ. **RESEARCH** Democracy and civil-military relations. **SELECTED PUBLICATIONS** Coauth, Lesson of the Venezuelan Experience, Johns Hopkins Press, 95. **CONTACT ADDRESS** American Univ, 4400 Massachusetts Ave, Washington, DC, 20016.

MENDEZ, JESUS
PERSONAL Born 10/03/1951, Havana, Cuba **DISCIPLINE** LATIN AMERICAN HISTORY **EDUCATION** Univ Miami, BS, 72, MA, 74; Univ Tex, Austin, PhD(hist), 80. **CAREER** Instr hist, State Univ NY Binghamton, 81; ASST PROF HIST, BARRY UNIV, 81-, Jr fel, Fulbright Comn, 83. **MEMBERSHIPS** AHA; Am Cath Hist Asn; Latin Am Studies Asn; Conf Latin Am Historians. **RESEARCH** Argentine intellectual history; Spanish intellectual history. **SELECTED PUBLICATIONS** Auth, El Imperio Desierto, Insula Revista Letras Ciencias Humanas, Vol 48, 93. **CONTACT ADDRESS** Dept of Hist, Barry Univ, 11300 N E 2nd Ave, Miami, FL, 33161-6695.

MENDLE, MICHAEL J.
DISCIPLINE HISTORY OF BRITISH POLITICAL THOUGHT **EDUCATION** WA Univ, PhD. **CAREER** Music Dept, Univ Ala **SELECTED PUBLICATIONS** Auth, Dangerous Positions: Mixed Government, the Estates of the Realm, and the Making of the Answer to the XIX Propositions, 85; Henry Parker and the English Civil War: The Political Thought of the Public's Privado, 95. **CONTACT ADDRESS** Univ AL, Box 870000, Tuscaloosa, AL, 35487. **EMAIL** mmendle@tenhoor.as.ua.edu

MENDOZA, LOUIS
DISCIPLINE FINE ARTS AND HUMANITIES **EDUCATION** Univ TX at Austin, MA, PhD. **CAREER** Asst prof; taught at, Univf Houston-Downtown & Brown Univ; fac adv, Chicana-Chicano Student Union, UTSA; bd-mem, La Pena Arts organization of Austin & Red Salmon Press; mem ed-bd, San Anto Cult Arts. **RESEARCH** Cult studies; contemp lit theory; Chicano/a lit and film; ethnic studies; gender studies; postcolonial lit and theory. **SELECTED PUBLICATIONS** Publ on, computer pedagogy, border lit, poetry of Sara Estela Ramirez and Raul Salinas; ed, East of the Freeway, a collection of poems. **CONTACT ADDRESS** Col of Fine Arts and Hum, Univ Texas at San Antonio, 6900 N Loop 1604 W, San Antonio, TX, 78249. **EMAIL** lmendoza@pclan.utsa.edu

MENK, PATRICIA HOLBERT
PERSONAL Born 06/04/1921, Rutherford, NJ, m, 1943, 3 children **DISCIPLINE** MODERN HISTORY OF WESTERN CIVILIZATION **EDUCATION** Fla State Univ, AB, 41; Univ Va, MA, 42, PhD(hist), 45. **CAREER** Instr hist, Univ Va Exten, 44-50; from instr to assoc prof, 52-66, actg pres, 75-76, prof and chmn dept, 66-81, EMER PROF HIST, MARY BALDWIN COL, 81-, Researcher, Va Hist Comn World War II, 46-47; mem city coun, Staunton, Va, 62-66 and 69, mayor, 64-66; vis prof, Univ Va, 69. **MEMBERSHIPS** Southern Hist Asn; Orgn Am Historians. **RESEARCH** Twentieth century United States urban history; 19th century Valley of Virginia history; United States history. **SELECTED PUBLICATIONS** Auth, Hat Makes a Church Related College, Mary Baldwin College and the Synod of Virginia, 1842-92, Am Presbyterians J Presbyterian Hist, Vol 71, 93; The College of William and Mary--A History, Va Mag Hist Biog Vol 0102, 94. **CONTACT ADDRESS** Dept of Hist, Mary Baldwin Col, Staunton, VA, 24401.

MENNEL, ROBERT MCKISSON
PERSONAL Born 10/18/1938, Toledo, OH **DISCIPLINE** AMERICAN HISTORY **EDUCATION** Denison Univ, BA, 60; Ohio State Univ, MA, 65, PhD(Am hist), 69. **CAREER** Instr hist, Denison Univ, 66-67; asst prof, 69-73, chmn dept, 74-77, assoc prof, 73-79, Prof Am Hist, Univ NH, 79-, Dir, Honors Prog, 85-. **HONORS AND AWARDS** Am Philos Soc grant, 75; Charles Warren fel, 77-78. **MEMBERSHIPS** Orgn Am Historians. **RESEARCH** History of children and youth; social welfare history; comparative social history. **SELECTED PUBLICATIONS** Co-ed, Children and Youth in America, Harvard Univ, Vols I, II & III, 70, 71 & 74; auth, Origins of the Juvenile Court-Changing Perspectives on the Legal Rights of Juvenile Delinquents, Crime & Delinq, 1/72; Juvenile Delinquency in Perspective, Hist Educ Quart, fall 73; Thorns and Thistles: Juvenile Delinquents in the United States, 1825-1940, Univ New Eng, 73; Family System of Common Farmers: The Ohio Reform School for Boys, 1858-1880, Ohio Hist, spring & summer 80; Attitudes and Policies Toward Juvenile Delinquency in the United States: A Historiographical Review, In: Crime and Justice: An Annual Review of Research, Univ Chicago Press, 82; co-ed, Holmes and Frankfurter: Their Correspondence, 1912-34, Univ New Eng, 96. **CONTACT ADDRESS** Honors Prog, Univ of New Hampshire, Hood House, Durham, NH, 03824-4724.

MENTZER, RAYMOND A.
PERSONAL Born 09/20/1945, Pittsburgh, PA, m, 1968, 2 children **DISCIPLINE** HISTORY **EDUCATION** Fordham Univ, AB, 67, MA, 70; Univ Wisc, 73. **CAREER** From asst prof to assoc prof 73-83, prof, 83- , Montana St Univ. **HONORS AND AWARDS** Phi Beta Kappa, 67; Phi Kappa Phi, 71; Harold J. Grimm Prize, 87; Natl Huguenot Soc Book Prize, 95. **MEMBERSHIPS** AHA; Am Soc of Church Hist; Am Catholic Hist Asn; French Hist Stud; Renaissance Soc of Am; Sixteenth Century Stud Soc; Soc for Reformation Res. **RESEARCH** Early modern European history. **SELECTED PUBLICATIONS** Auth, Heresy Proceedings in Languedoc, 1500-1560, Am Philos Soc, 84; auth, Sin and the Calvinists: Morals Control and the Consistory in the Reformed Tradition, Sixteenth Century J Pub, 94; auth, Blood and Belief: Family Survival and confessional Identity among the Provincial Huguenot Nobility, Purdue Univ, 94; auth, The Persistence of Superstition and Idolatry among Rural French Calvinists, Church Hist, 96; auth, The Reformed Churches of France and the Visual Arts, Calvinism and the Visual Arts, Eerdmans, 98. **CONTACT ADDRESS** Dept of History, Montana State Univ, Bozeman, MT, 59717. **EMAIL** uhirm@montana.edu

MERCADO, JUAN CARLOS
DISCIPLINE CULTURAL STUDIES **EDUCATION** Univ Comahue, BS; Queens Col, MA; CUNY, PhD. **CAREER** Eastern Stroudsburg Univ PA **HONORS AND AWARDS** NEH grant. **SELECTED PUBLICATIONS** Auth, Esteban Echeverrea: Building a Nation: The Case of Echeverrea. **CONTACT ADDRESS** East Stroudsburg Univ of Pennsylvania, 200 Prospect Street, E Stroudsburg, PA, 18301-2999.

MERCHANT, CAROLYN
PERSONAL Born 07/12/1936, Rochester, NY, 2 children **DISCIPLINE** ENVIRONMENTAL HISTORY, PHILOSOPHY & ETHICS **EDUCATION** Vassar Col, AB, 58; Univ Wis, MA, 62, PhD, 67. **CAREER** Lectr hist of sci, Univ San Francisco, 69-74, asst prof, 74-78; asst prof environ hist, 79-80, assoc prof 80-, CHANCELLOR PROF ENVIRON HIST, PHILOS & ETHICS, UNIV CALIF, BERKELEY, former chmn, Dept Conserv & Resource Studies; Vis prof, Ecole Normale Superieure, Paris, 6/86. **HONORS AND AWARDS** NSF, 76-78; NEH grant, 77, 81-83; Am Counc Learned Soc fel, 78; Center Advan Studies, Behavioral Sci, 78; Fulbright sr scholar, Umea Univ, Sweden, 84; Agr Exp Station, Univ Calif, Berkeley, 80-86, 86-92, 92-; Nathan Cummings Found, 92; Am Cultures fel, Univ Calif, Berkeley, 6/90; Vis fel, School Soc Sci, Murdoch Univ, Perth, Australia, 91; John Simon Guggenheim fel, 95; Doctor Honoris Causa, Umea Univ, Sweden, 95. **MEMBERSHIPS** Hist Sci Soc; West Coast Hist Sci Soc; British Soc Hist Sci; Soc Hist Technol; Am Soc Environ Hist. **RESEARCH** Scientific revolution; American environmental history; women and nature. **SELECTED PUBLICATIONS** Auth, D'Alembert and the vis viva controversy, Studies in Hist and Philos of Sci, 8/70; Leibniz and the vis viva controversy, Isis, spring 71; The Leibnizian-Newtonian debates: Natural philosophy and social psychology, British J for the Hist of Sci, 12/73; Madame du Chatelet's metaphysics and mechanics, Studies in Hist and Philos of Sci, 5/77; The Death of Nature: Women, Ecology, and the Scientific Revolution, Harper and Row, San Francisco, 80, 2nd ed, 90; Earthcare: Women and the environmental movement, Environment, 6/81; Isis' consciousness raised, Isis, fall 82; Ecological Revolutions: Nature, Gender, and Science in New England, Univ NC Press, 89; Radical Ecology: The Search for a Liveable World, Routledge, 92; Major Problems in American Environmental History: Ecology, Humanities Press, 94; Earthcare: Women and the Environment, Routledge, 96; ed, Green Versus Gold: Sources in California's Environmental History, Island Press, 98; Reinventing Eden: Women, Nature, and Narrative, in progress. **CONTACT ADDRESS** Dept of Environ Sci, Policy & Mgt, Univ Calif, Berkeley, CA, 94720-3310. **EMAIL** merchant@nature.berkeley.edu

MERITT, LUCY
PERSONAL Born 08/07/1906, Camden, NJ, m, 1964 **DISCIPLINE** CLASSICS **EDUCATION** Bryn Mawr Coll, AB, 27, MA, 28, PhD, 35; Brown Univ, LHD, 74; Hamilton Coll, LHD, 94. **CAREER** Asst prof, 37-41, assoc prof, 41-50, counsellor, then chief counsellor of students, Mount Holyoke Coll; member of Institue for Advanced Study, 48-49, 50-73, Princeton; ed of publications, 50-72, Amer Sch of Classical Studies at Athens; visiting prof, 58, 60, Washington Univ; visiting lect, 59, Princeton Univ; prof, 73-74, 75-76, 90, Univ of Texas at Austin, visiting scholar, 73- **HONORS AND AWARDS** Gold Medal of the Archaeological Inst of Amer for Distinguished Archaeological Achievement, 76; Outstanding Woman of Texas Humanities AAUW, 80; Pro Bene Meritis Award, Univ of Texas at Austin, 97 **MEMBERSHIPS** Member of the managing committee of the Amer sch of classical studies at Athens; pres pathfinders club Austin, 76-77, 91-92; thankful hubbard chapter DAR, vice-regent 84-86, regent 90-92, honorary regent 92-; Austin Woman's Club **SELECTED PUBLICATIONS** Auth, History of the American School of classical Studies at Athens, 1939-1980, 84; The Athenian Ionic Capital, Eius Virtutis Studiosi, classical and Post-Classical Studies in Memory of Frank Edward Brown, 1908-1988, Studies in the Histry of Art, 93; Athenian Ionic Capitals from the Athenian Agora, Hesperia, 96. **CONTACT ADDRESS** Dept Class, Univ Texas, Austin, TX, 78712. **EMAIL** IEMEB@mail.utexas.edu

MERKELY, PAUL B.
DISCIPLINE MUSIC HISTORY **EDUCATION** Harvard Univ, PhD. **CAREER** Prof, Univ Ottawa. **RESEARCH** Musicology (Medieval Music, Twentieth-Century Music). **SELECTED PUBLICATIONS** Auth, Modal Assignment in Northern Tonaries, Inst of Medieval Mus, 92; Italian Tonaries, Inst Medieval Mus, 88; coauth, The Melodic Tradition of Ambrosian Office Antiphons, Inst Medieval Mus, 90; The Antiphons of the Ambrosian Office, Inst Medieval Mus, 89. **CONTACT ADDRESS** Dept of Music, Univ Ottawa, 70 Laurier Ave, PO Box 450, Ottawa, ON, K1N 6N5.

MERKL, PETER HANS
PERSONAL Born 01/29/1932, Munich, Germany, m, 1954, 2 children **DISCIPLINE** POLITICAL SCIENCE **EDUCATION** Univ Cal Berkeley, PhD, 59. **CAREER** Lectr, Asst Prof, Assoc Prof, Prof, 58-92, Dept Chmn, 72-73, EmeritusProf, 93-, Univ Cal; vis Prof, 83, Univ Augsburg, 87, U of Istanbul, 88 Bogazici U, 90, U of Gottingen, 91, Free U of Berlin. **HONORS AND AWARDS** Rockefeller Fel; Ford Fnd Fel; DAAD Gnt; Volkswagen Fnd Gnt; NEH; Japan Soc Gnt; UCSB Fac Res Lectshp; West German Fed Order of Merit; Japan Soc Promotion Sci Gnt. **MEMBERSHIPS** APSA; IPSA; ISA; CES; CGGP. **RESEARCH** Comparative and European Politics; political parties; elections; right radicalism; political violence and terror. **SELECTED PUBLICATIONS** Auth, German Unification in the European Context, Penn State Press, 93; Coed, Encounters with the Contemporary Radical Right, Boulder CO, Westview, 93; ed, The Federal Rep At Forty-Five, London, Macmillan and NYU Press, 95; coed, The Revival of Rightwing Extremism in the Nineties, London, Frank Cass; ed, The Federal Rep at Fifty, London, Macmillan, NYU Press, forthcoming; **CONTACT ADDRESS** Dept of Political Science, Univ Calif Santa Barbara, Santa Barbara, CA, 93106. **EMAIL** merkl@sscf.ucsb.edu

MERKLEY, PAUL C.
DISCIPLINE HISTORY **EDUCATION** Univ Toronto, BA, 56, MA, 57, PhD, 65. **CAREER** Prof. **RESEARCH** Religion in the history of the United States. **SELECTED PUBLICATIONS** Auth, The Greek and Hebrew Origins of Our Idea of History, Lewiston: Mellen Press, 88; "Religion and Political Prosperity: Recent Historiography in American Religious Studies," Can Jour Hist, 91; Theodore Roosevelt Was Right!, The New Federation, 95. **CONTACT ADDRESS** Dept of Hist, Carleton Univ, 1125 Colonel By Dr, Ottawa, ON, K1S 5B6. **EMAIL** pmerkley@ccs.carleton.ca

MERLI, FRANK JOHN
PERSONAL Born 03/29/1929, New York, NY, m, 1964, 2 children **DISCIPLINE** AMERICAN DIPLOMACY **EDUCATION** State Univ NY Albany, BA, 57; Ind Univ, MA, 59, PhD, 64. **CAREER** Instr hist, Kent State Univ, 61-62; guest lectr, Birmingham Univ, 63-64; asst prof, Ind Univ, 64-68; asst prof, 68-72, assoc prof hist, Queens Col, NY, 72-, Am Philos Soc grant, 72. **MEMBERSHIPS** AHA; Orgn Am Historians; Soc Historians Am Foreign Rels; Conf Brit Studies. **RESEARCH** Nineteenth-century Anglo-American relations; Anglo-American relations, 1856-72; 19th century neutrality, 1819-1919. **SELECTED PUBLICATIONS** Auth, Curious case of Alexandra, Civil War Hist, 6/63; Great Britain and the Confederate Navy, 1861-1865, Ind Univ, 70; co-ed, Makers of American Diplomacy, Scribner, 74; Civil war diplomacy, in Guide to American Foreign Relations Since 1700, Clio Press, 83. **CONTACT ADDRESS** Dept of Hist, Queens Col, CUNY, 6530 Kissena Blvd, Flushing, NY, 11367-1597.

MERLING, DAVID
PERSONAL Born 06/14/1948, Pittsburg, PA, m, 1969, 2 children **DISCIPLINE** OLD TESTAMENT STUDIES, ARCHAEOLOGY, HISTORY OF ANTIQUITY **EDUCATION** Andrews Univ, PhD, 96. **CAREER** Assoc prof of Archaeol and Hist of Antiquities, Andrews Univ, 86-; Curator, Siegfried H. Horn Archaeol Museum, 91- . **HONORS AND AWARDS** Andrews Univ Fac Res Grant, 91-92, 94; Who's Who in Bibl Stud and Archaeol, 93; Zion Res found travel grant, 84, Tell e-Umeyri, Jordan. **MEMBERSHIPS** Adventist Theol Soc; Amer Sch Oriental Res; Bibl Archaeol Soc; Evangelical Theol Soc; Inst Bibl Res; Israel Exploration Soc; Near Eastern Archaeol Soc; Soc Bibl Lit. **RESEARCH** Archaeology and the Book of Joshua. **CONTACT ADDRESS** Dept of Archaeology, Andrews Univ, Berrien Springs, MI, 49104-0990. **EMAIL** merling@andrews.edu

MERRIFIELD, WILLIAM R.
PERSONAL Born 09/28/1932, Chicago, IL, m, 1952, 4 children **DISCIPLINE** LINGUISTICS, ANTHROPOLOGY **EDUCATION** Wheaton Col, Ill BA, 54; Cornell Univ, MA, 63, PhD(cult anthrop), 65. **CAREER** Ling consult in Mex, 62-74, coordr anthrop res in Mex, 65-69, coordr ling res in Mex, 65-59, 72-74, dir sch, Univ Okla, 74-77, INT COORDR ANTHROP AND COMMUN DEVELOP, SUMMER INST LING, 72-, Dir, MUS ANTHROP, TEX, 74-, Vis asst prof ling, Univ Wash, 65-72; vis prof anthrop, Wheaton Col, 71-72; ADJ PROF LING, UNIV TEX, ARLINGTON, 74-; adj prof anthrop, Univ Okla, 75-77, adj prof ling, 77. **MEMBERSHIPS** Am Anthrop Asn; Ling Soc Am; Am Sci Affiliation; Am Asn Mus; Ling Asn Can and US. **RESEARCH** Cultural and applied anthropology; social organization; theory of grammar. **SELECTED PUBLICATIONS** Auth, Linguistic Theory and Grammatical Description Joseph, Je, Lan, Vol 70, 94. **CONTACT ADDRESS** Summer Inst of Ling, 7500 Camp Wisdom Rd, Dallas, TX, 75236.

MERRIMAN, JOHN M.
PERSONAL Born 06/15/1947, Battle Creek, MI, m, 1980, 2 children **DISCIPLINE** FRENCH, EUROPEAN & URBAN HISTORY **EDUCATION** Univ MI, BA, 68, MA, 69, PhD, 72. **CAREER** Lectr soc & hist, Univ MI, 72-73; asst prof, 73-78, Assoc Prof Hist, 78-82, Prof, 1983-95, Charles Seymour prof hist, Yale Univ, 96-, Guggenheim fel, 79-80. **MEMBERSHIPS** AHA; Fr Hist Studies. **RESEARCH** French soc hist, 19th century; French urban hist, 19th century; French labor hist, 19th to 20th century. **SELECTED PUBLICATIONS** Ed, 1830 in France & auth, Intro & The Demoiselles of the Ariege, 1829-31, In: 1830 in France, Franklin Watts, 75; auth, The Norman fires of 1830: Incendiaries and fear in rural France, Fr Hist Studies, spring 76; Agony of the Republic: The Repression of the Left in Revolutionary France, 1848-51, Yale Univ Press, 78; ed, Consciousness and Class Experience in Nineteenth Century Europe & auth, Intro & Incident at the statue of the Virgin Mary: The conflict of old and new in nineteenth century Limoges, In: Consciousness and Class Experience in Nineteenth Century Europe, Holmes & Meier, 79; ed, French Cities in the Nineteenth Century & auth, The changing image of the nineteenth century French city & Restoration town, bourgeois city, In: French Cities in the Nineteenth Century, Hutchison, London, 82; Ed, For Want of a Horse: Chance & Humor in History, Stephen Green Press, 85; The Red City: Limoges and the French Nineteenth City, Oxford Univ Press, 85 and French trans: Limoges, la ville rouge, Belini, 90; The Margins of City Life, Oxford Univ Press; 91, and French trans: Aux marges de la ville, Editions du Sevil, 94; Co-ed, Edo and Paris: Urban Life and the State in the Early Modern Period, Cornell Univ Press, 94; A History of Modern Europe, 2 vol, W W Norton & Co, 96. **CONTACT ADDRESS** Dept of Hist, Yale Univ, PO Box 208324, New Haven, CT, 06520-8324. **EMAIL** john.merriman@yale.edu

MERRIMAN, MIRA P.
DISCIPLINE ITALIAN RENAISSANCE AND BAROQUE ART **EDUCATION** Columbia Univ, PhD. **CAREER** Prof emer **SELECTED PUBLICATIONS** Auth, monograph and catalogue raisonne on Giuseppe Maria Crespi (1665-1747), Rizzoli; publ, The Burlington Mag, Paragone, Source; cat of exhib(s), London, Washington Nat Gallery, Bologna Pinacoteca, Kimbell Mus. **CONTACT ADDRESS** Dept of Art, Wichita State Univ, 1845 Fairmont, Wichita, KS, 67260-0062.

MERRITT, RAYMOND HARLAND
PERSONAL Born 03/29/1936, Sioux Falls, SD, m, 1956, 3 children **DISCIPLINE** AMERICAN URBAN AND TECHNOLOGICAL HISTORY **EDUCATION** St Olaf Col, BA, 58; Luther Theol Sem, BD, 62; Univ Minn, MA, 63, PhD(hist), 68. **CAREER** Instr soc sci, SDak Sch Mines and Technol, 63-64 and Wis State Univ, River Falls, 64-66; from instr to asst prof Am hist, NDak State Univ, 66-69; asst prof hist, Univ Wis-Milwaukee, 69-70, assoc prof hist and systs design, 70-80, dir, Cult and Technol Studies Prog, 73-80; Caroline Werner Gannett prof, Rochester Inst Technol, 80-81; PROF and CHMN, MINNEAPOLIS COL ART and DESIGN, 81- **MEMBERSHIPS** Orgn Am Historians; AHA; Soc Hist Technol; Am Studies Asn; Pub Works Hist Soc (vpres, 77-78, pres, 78-79). **RESEARCH** History of American technology and engineering. **SELECTED PUBLICATIONS** Auth, Structures in The Stream--Water, Science, and The Rise of the US Army Corps of Engineers, Tech Cult, Vol 37, 96; Reshaping National Water Politics--The Emergence of the Water Resources Development Act of 1986, Public Hist, Vol 15, 93; Building Air Bases in the Negev--The US Army Corps of Engineers in Israel, 1979-1982, Tech Cult, Vol 36, 95. **CONTACT ADDRESS** Minneapolis, MN, 55403.

MERRY, SALLY E.
DISCIPLINE ANTHROPOLOGY **EDUCATION** Wellesley Col, BA, 66; Yale Univ, MA, 67; Brandeis Univ, PhD, 78. **CAREER** Asst Prof to Prof Anthropol, 77-94, Class of 1949 Prof in Ethics, Wellesley Col, 94-; Vis Prof, Amherst Col, 93. **HONORS AND AWARDS** Durant Schol, Wellesley Col, 66; Phi Beta Kappa, 66; Distinguished Vis Schol, Ariz State Univ, 87; Class of 1949 Chair in Ethics, 94; Anna and Samuel Pinanski Prize for Excellence in Teaching, 94. **SELECTED PUBLICATIONS** Co-ed, The Possibility of Popular Justice: A Case Study of American Community Mediation, Univ Mich Press, 93; auth, Narrating Domestic Violence: Producing the Truth of Violence in 19th- and 20th-Century Hawaiian Courts, Law & Soc Inquiry, 94; Resistance and the Cultural Power of Law, Law and Soc Rev, 95; Gender Violence and Legally Engendered Selves, Identities: Global Studies in Culture and Power, 95; Global Human Rights and Local Social Movements in a Legally Plural World, Canadian J Law & Soc, 98; Law, Culture, and Cultural Appropriation, Yale J Law & Humanities, 98; The Criminalization of Everyday Life, Everyday Practices and Trouble Cases, Northwestern Univ Press, 98; The Culture of Mennonite Peacemaking, From the Ground Up, Syracuse Univ Press, 98; author of numerous other articles and publications. **CONTACT ADDRESS** Anthropology Dept, Wellesley Col, Wellesley, MA, 02181. **EMAIL** smerry@wellesley.edu

MERTINS, DETLEF
DISCIPLINE ARCHITECTURE; HISTORY AND THEORY **EDUCATION** Univ Toronto, BArch 80; Princeton Univ, MA, 91, PhD, 96. **CAREER** Architect, Private Pract, Toronto, 80-89; lectr to Assoc Prof, Univ Toronto, 91-. **HONORS AND AWARDS** Vis scholar Can Ctr Archit, 98, Medal of Serv City of Toronto, 82. **MEMBERSHIPS** On Asn Archit; Royal Archit Inst Can; Soc Archit Hist; Soc Study Archit Can. **RESEARCH** Architectural history, theory and criticism; 20th Century; German, American, Canadian. **SELECTED PUBLICATIONS** Ed, Metropolitan Mutations: The Architecture of Emerging Public Spaces, Little, Brown, & Co, 88; The Presence of Mies, Princeton Archit Press, 94; auth, System and Freedom, Autonomy and Ideology, Monicelli, 97; Anything But Literal, Architecture and Cubism, MIT Press, 97. **CONTACT ADDRESS** Fac of Archit, Landscape, & Design, Univ Toronto, 230 College St., Toronto, ON, M5T 1R2. **EMAIL** detlef.mertins@utoronto.ca

MERTZ, PAUL ERIC
PERSONAL Born 02/27/1943, Bartlesville, OK, m, 1966, 2 children **DISCIPLINE** AMERICAN HISTORY **EDUCATION** Phillips Univ, BA, 65; Univ Okla, MA, 67, PhD, 71. **CAREER** Instr, 69-72, asst prof, 72-77, assoc prof, 77-82, PROF HIST, UNIV WIS-STEVENS POINT, 82-, chmn, Hist Dept, 92-98. **HONORS AND AWARDS** Woodrow Wilson Nat fel, Univ Okla, 65-66. **MEMBERSHIPS** Orgn Am Historians; Southern Hist Asn. **RESEARCH** Recent south; New Deal era;

civil rights movement. **SELECTED PUBLICATIONS** Auth, New Deal Policy and Southern Rural Poverty, La State Univ Press, 78. **CONTACT ADDRESS** 2100 Main St, Stevens Point, WI, 54481-3897. **EMAIL** pmertz@uwsp.edu

MERWICK, DONNA
DISCIPLINE CULTURAL HISTORY **CAREER** Vis fel, Ctr Cross-Cult Res, 97-00. **RESEARCH** Dutch and English settlements in New York. **SELECTED PUBLICATIONS** Possessing Albany, 1630-1710: The Dutch and English Experiences, Cambridge Univ, 90. **CONTACT ADDRESS** Dept of Education, Australian National Univ. **EMAIL** Donna.Merrick@anu.edu.au.

MESCH, CLAUDIA
DISCIPLINE ART **EDUCATION** Yale Univ, BA, 82; Univ CA, MA, 89; Univ Chicago, PhD, 97. **CAREER** Instr, 97-. contrib(s) to Sculpt and Dialogue magazines. **RESEARCH** Post-war and contemp visual cult. **SELECTED PUBLICATIONS** Publ, The Chicago Reader; The New Art Examiner; Checkpoint, Ger. **CONTACT ADDRESS** Dept of Art, Cleveland State Univ, 83 E 24th St, Cleveland, OH, 44115.

MESSER, ROBERT LOUIS
PERSONAL Born 07/11/1944, Indianapolis, IN, m, 1967, 2 children **DISCIPLINE** UNITED STATES DIPLOMATIC HISTORY **EDUCATION** Ind Univ, BA, 66, MA, 68; Univ Calif, Berkeley, PhD(hist), 75. **CAREER** Asst prof, 75-81, ASSOC PROF, UNIV ILL, CHICAGO, 81-, CONSULT HUMAN RIGHTS, WORLD WITHOUT WAR COUN, MIDWEST, 77-, BD DIR PEACE ISSUES CTR, 78- **MEMBERSHIPS** Am Hist Asn; Orgn Am Historians; Soc Historians Am Foreign Rels. **RESEARCH** Twentieth century American foreign policy; origins of Cold War; human rights. **SELECTED PUBLICATIONS** Auth, Truman and the Hiroshima Cult, Am Hist Rev, Vol 0102, 97. **CONTACT ADDRESS** Dept of Hist, Univ of Ill, Chicago Circle, Box 4348, Chicago, IL, 60680.

MESSER-KRUSE, TIMOTHY
PERSONAL Born 03/13/1963, Tecumseh, NE, m, 1990, 3 children **DISCIPLINE** HISTORY **EDUCATION** Univ Wis-Madison, PhD, 94. **CAREER** Asst Prof Labor Hist, Univ Toledo, 95-. **HONORS AND AWARDS** William Hesseltine Award, 94. **RESEARCH** Hist Am Left; Knights of Labor; UAW; Great Depression. **SELECTED PUBLICATIONS** The Yankee International: Marxism and the American Reform Tradition, 1848-1876, Univ NC Press, 98; The Campus Klans of the Univ of Wisconsin: Tacit and Active Support for the Ku Klux Klan in a Culture of Intolerance, Wis Mag of Hist, 77, Autumn 93; The Best Dressed Workers in New York: Liveried Teamsters in the Gilded Age, Labor Hist, 95-96; The First International in America, The Greenback Labor Party, The Chinese Question, Richard Hinton, in the Encyclopedia of the American Left, Paul Buhle, ed, rev ed, 98; Socialism, The American Federation of Labor, The Knights of Labor, Eight Hour Day, Pullman Strike, in the Am Heritage Encyclopedia of Am Hist, forthcoming; The Bulldozing of Labor Hist: The Destruction of the Toledo's Historic Elm St Bridge, Northwest Ohio Quarterly, 96; Collaborative Publishing on the Net: Notes From Recent Experience, in Dennis Trinkle, ed, Writing, Teaching and Researching History in the Electronic Age, M E Sharpe, 98. **CONTACT ADDRESS** Dept of History, Univ of Toledo, Toledo, OH, 43606-3390. **EMAIL** tmesser@uoft02.utoledo.edu

MESSINGER, SHELDON L.
PERSONAL Born 08/26/1925, Chicago, IL, m, 1947, 2 children **DISCIPLINE** SOCIOLOGY **EDUCATION** UCLA, PhD, 69 **CAREER** Res Sociologist, Ctr for the Study of Law and Soc, Univ Calif Berkeley, 61-70; prof and dean, School of Criminology, Univ Calif Berkeley, 70-77; prof, School of Law, Univ Calif Berkeley, 77-91; prof emeritus, Univ Calif Berkeley, 91-. **HONORS AND AWARDS** A. McGee Award for Outstanding Contributions to Criminal Justice Research, Am Justice Inst; Award of Merit, Calif Bureau of Criminal Statistics; award for Outstanding Contributions to the Field of Criminology, Western Soc of Criminology; fel, Inst of Criminology, Univ Cambridge; fel, Ctr for Advanced Study in Behavioral Sciences; fel, Soc Sci Res Council. **MEMBERSHIPS** Asn for Criminal Justice Res. **RESEARCH** Health insurance, especially for elderly; experiences with chronic illness, especially among elderly. **CONTACT ADDRESS** School of Law, Univ of California, Berkeley, CA, 94720. **EMAIL** slm@uclink.berkeley.edu

METCALF, ALIDA C.
PERSONAL Born 04/05/1954, Albany, NY, m, 1996, 2 children **DISCIPLINE** HISTORY **EDUCATION** Smith Col, BA, 76; Univ Tex, MA, 78, PhD, 83. **CAREER** Vist asst prof, Ind Univ, 83-84; asst prof, Univ Tex, 84-86; from asst prof to assoc prof to prof, 86-, Trinity Univ. **HONORS AND AWARDS** Bolton Prize, 94; Harvey Johnson Book Award, 93., Fulbright Lecturing Award, 86; Fulbright-Hayes Doctoral Dissertation Award, 79-81. **MEMBERSHIPS** Am Hist Asn; Latin Am Std Asn. **RESEARCH** Colonial Latin America **SELECTED PUBLICATIONS** Auth, article, Women of Means: Women and Family Property in Colonial Brazil, 90; auth, Family and Frontier in Colonial Brazil: Santana de Parnaiba, 1580-1822, 92. **CONTACT ADDRESS** Dept of History, Trinity Univ, San Antonio, TX, 78212-7200. **EMAIL** ametcalf@trinity.edu

METCALF, MICHAEL F.
DISCIPLINE HISTORY **EDUCATION** Univ Stockholm, MA, PhD. **CAREER** Prof **RESEARCH** Development of Danish and Swedish absolutism during the seventeenth century; eighteenth-century Swedish party politics; emergence of the Scandinavian welfare state. **SELECTED PUBLICATIONS** Auth, Russia, England, and Swedish Party Politics, 1762-1766: The Interplay Between Great Power Diplomacy and Domestic Politics During Sweden's Age of Liberty, 77; ed, The Riksdag: A History of the Swedish Parliament, 87. **CONTACT ADDRESS** History Dept, Univ of Minnesota, Twin Cities, 614 Social Sciences Tower, 267 19th Ave. S, Minneapolis, MN, 55455. **EMAIL** mmetcalf@tc.umn.edu

METCALF, THOMAS R.
PERSONAL Born 05/31/1934, Schenectady, NY, 2 children **DISCIPLINE** MODERN HISTORY **EDUCATION** Amherst Col, BA, 55; Cambridge Univ, BA, 57, MA, 61; Harvard Univ, PhD, 60. **CAREER** Instr hist, Univ WI, 59-60; asst prof Univ CA, Santa Barbara, 61-62; from asst prof to assoc prof, 62-73, PROF HIST, UNIV CA, BERKELEY, 73-, Ford Found Foreign Area Training fel, IND, 60-61; Am Inst Indian Studies fac res fel, 64-65; Fulbright-Hays res fel, India, 69-70 & Pakistan, 73-74; trustee, Am Inst Indian Studies, 71-83. **HONORS AND AWARDS** Watumull Prize, AHA, 66. **MEMBERSHIPS** AHA; Asn Asian Studies. **RESEARCH** Nineteenth century India; the British Empire. **SELECTED PUBLICATIONS** Auth, The Aftermath of Revolt: India 1857-1870, Princeton Univ, 64; contribr, Social Structure and Land Control in Indian History, Univ WI, 69; A History of World Civilizations, Wiley, 72; Land, Landlords and British Raj, Univ CA, 78; An Imperial Vision, Univ Ca, 89; Ideologies of the Raj, Univ Cambridge, 95. **CONTACT ADDRESS** Dept of Hist, Univ of Calif, 3229 Dwinelle Hall, Berkeley, CA, 94720-2550. **EMAIL** metcalfe@socrates.berkeley.edu

METCALF, WILLIAM E.
PERSONAL Born 12/16/1947, East Grand Rapids, MI, m, 1991, 1 child **DISCIPLINE** CLASSIC STUDIES **EDUCATION** Univ Michigan, BA 69, MA 70, PhD 73. **CAREER** The American Numismatic Society, chief curator, curator, assoc curator, asst curator, 73 to 79-. **HONORS AND AWARDS** NEA Fel; Kraay and Robinson Fel; IAS mem. **MEMBERSHIPS** APA; AIA; RNS; ANS; SPRS. **RESEARCH** Roman imperial history and coinage. **SELECTED PUBLICATIONS** Auth, The Silver Coinage of Caesarea in Cappadocia Vespasian to Commodus, NY, Numis Notes and Mono, 96; A Primer of Roman Numismatics, E. J. Brill, 99; Regionalism in the imperial coinage of Asia Minor, in: Region in Asia Minor in the Hellenistic and Roman Periods, Hartford 98; Coins as Primary Evidence, in: Togo Salmon Studies, Ann Arbor, 98; Aurelian's reform at Alexandria, in: studies in Greek Numismatics in memory of Martin Jessop Price, eds, R. H. Ashton, S Hurter, London, 98; Byzantine Imperial Coinage, in: The Glory of Byzantine, art and Cultur of the Middle Byzantine Era A.D. 843-1261, eds, Helen C. Evans, William D. Wixom, New York, 97. **CONTACT ADDRESS** The American Numismatic Society, Broadway at 155th St, New York, NY, 10032.

METCALFE, WILLIAM CRAIG
PERSONAL Born 07/17/1935, Toronto, ON, Canada, m, 1958, 2 children **DISCIPLINE** EUROPEAN HISTORY & CANADIAN STUDIES **EDUCATION** Univ Toronto, BA, 58; Univ MN, MA, 59, PhD, 67. **CAREER** Asst hist, Univ MN, 59-61, instr, 62-63; from instr to assoc prof, 63-74, chmn dept music, 73-78, prof hist, Univ VT, 74-, assoc dir can studies, 63, dir Baroque Ensemble, 65-89, chmn dept hist, 80-87, Dir Canadian Studies, 87-97; prof hist emer, 98; Lectr, Inst Elizabethan Arts & Lett, 65-68; mem rev staff, Am Recorder, 69-; mem joint comt, Can Am Studies, AHA-Can Hist Asn, 72-74; ed, Am Rev Can Studies, 73-; Albert Corey Prize judge, AHA, 75-76; Ed, Am Rev Canadian Studies. **HONORS AND AWARDS** Douner Medal in Canadian Studies, 93. **MEMBERSHIPS** Can Hist Asn; Am Musicol Soc; Conf Brit Studies; Asn Can Studies US. **RESEARCH** Tudor-Stuart England; Can hist; music hist. **SELECTED PUBLICATIONS** Auth, Dolce or traverso? the flauto problem in Vivaldi's instrumental music, 8/65 & The recorder contatas of Telemann's Harmonischer Gottesdienst, 11/67, Am Recorder; Some aspects of the parliament of 1610, Historian, 11/72; contribr, Voices of Canada, Asn Can Studies in US, 78; ed, Understanding Canada: An Interdisciplinary Intro to Canadian Studies, New York Univ Press, 82; co-ed, Northern Approaches: Scholarship on Canada in the U S, Asn for Canadtion Studies in the U S, 93; co-auth, Canadian Culture in the Late 1990's, In: Introducing Canada, Nat Coun Soc Studies, 97. **CONTACT ADDRESS** 39 Brookes Ave, Burlington, VT, 05401-3327. **EMAIL** wmetcalf@zoo.uvm.edu

METZ, LEON CLAIRE
PERSONAL Born 11/06/1930, Parkersburg, WV, m, 1970, 4 children **DISCIPLINE** AMERICAN HISTORY **CAREER** Exec asst to Mayor of El Paso, 79-81; ASST TO PRES, UNIV TEX, EL PASO, 81-, LECTR WESTERN HIST, 68-; bk ed, El Paso Times, 71-79. **MEMBERSHIPS** Western Writers Am; Western Hist Asn; Coun Am Mil Past. **RESEARCH** Frontier military; frontier biography; Mexican history. **SELECTED PUBLICATIONS** Auth The Life of Horn, Tom Revisited, W Am Quart, Vol 24, 93; Desert Lawmen--The High Sheriffs of New Mexico and Arizona, 1846-1912, Montana Mag W Hist, Vol 44, 94; Judge Bean, Roy Country, Southw Am Quart, Vol 0100, 97; Border Cuates--A History of the United States Mexican Twin Cities, Southw Am Quart, Vol 99, 96; Billy The Kid--His Life and Legend, Montana Mag We Hist, Vol 45, 95. **CONTACT ADDRESS** Pres Off, Univ Tex, El Paso, TX, 79968.

METZGER, THOMAS ALBERT
PERSONAL Born 07/02/1933, Berlin, Germany, m, 1995, 2 children **DISCIPLINE** CHINESE HISTORY **EDUCATION** Harvard Univ, PhD(Hist, Far Eastern Lang), 67. **CAREER** PROF EMER, UNIV OF CALIF, SAN DIEGO, 90-; sr fel, Hoover Inst, Stanford Univ, 90-. **HONORS AND AWARDS** Award for Excellence in Res, 80; Ch'ien Mu Lecture in Hist and Cult, 94. **RESEARCH** Contemporary Chinese political thought **SELECTED PUBLICATIONS** Auth, The Internal Organization of Ch'ing Bureacracy, 73, Harvard Univ Pr; auth, Escape from Predicament, 77, Columbia Univ Pr. **CONTACT ADDRESS** Hoover Inst, Stanford Univ, Stanford, CA, 94305-6010.

MEVERS, FRANK CLEMENT
PERSONAL Born 10/10/1942, New Orleans, LA, m, 1967, 2 children **DISCIPLINE** UNITED STATES HISTORY **EDUCATION** La State Univ, Baton Rouge, BA, 65, MA, 67; Univ NC, Chapel HIll, PhD(Am hist), 72. **CAREER** Asst ed, Papers of James Madison, NH Hist Soc, 72-73, assoc ed, 73-74; ed, Papers of Josiah Bartlett, 74-77, ed, Papers of William Plumer, 77-79; DIR and STATE ARCHIVIST, NH DIV REC MGT and ARCH, 79- **HONORS AND AWARDS** Great Am Achievement, Bicentennial Coun of Thirteen Original States, 77. **MEMBERSHIPS** Orgn Am Historians; Soc Am Archivists; New Eng Archivists. **RESEARCH** American medical history; American Revolution and early national periods; military history. **SELECTED PUBLICATIONS** Auth, Celebrating the 4th-Independence Day and the Rites of Nationalism in the Early Republic, New England Quart Hist Rev New England Life Letters, Vol 70, 97; Wentworth, John and the American Revolution--The English Connection, New England Quart Hist Rev New England Life Letters, Vol 67, 94. **CONTACT ADDRESS** NH Hist Soc, 30 Park St, Concord, NH, 03301.

MEYER, ADOLPHE ERICH
PERSONAL New York, NY, m, 1942, 1 child **DISCIPLINE** HISTORY **EDUCATION** NY Univ, BS, 21, MA, 22, PhD, 26. **CAREER** High sch teacher French, NY, 21-22; instr Ger, 22-28, from instr to prof, 28-63, EMER PROF HIST OF EDUC, NY UNIV, 63-, Vis prof, Univ Ill, 65-67, vis lectr, 68; distinguished prof, Old Dom Univ, 67-68. **MEMBERSHIPS** Auth League Am. **SELECTED PUBLICATIONS** Auth, Tributes to Haddad, James, B, J Criminal Law Criminology, Vol 83, 92. **CONTACT ADDRESS** 3106 S First, Champaign, IL, 61820.

MEYER, DONALD
PERSONAL Born 10/29/1923, Lincoln, NE, m, 1965 **DISCIPLINE** HISTORY **EDUCATION** Univ Chicago, BA, 47; Harvard Univ, MA, 48, PhD, 53. **CAREER** Instr Am constitutional hist, Harvard Univ, 53-55; from asst prof to assoc prof Am intellectual and social hist, Univ Calif, Los Angeles, 55-65, prof US social hist, 65-67; PROF US SOCIAL HIST AND DIR AM STUDIES, WESLEYAN UNIV, 67-, Soc Sci Res Coun fac res grants, 58 and 62; Guggenheim fel, 66; Am Philos Soc grant, 70-71. **MEMBERSHIPS** AHA; Orgn Am Historians. **RESEARCH** American cultural and social history. **SELECTED PUBLICATIONS** Auth, Beyond Politics, J Am Hist, Vol 83, 96; To the Ends of the Earth--Womens Search for Education in Medicine, Am Hist Rev, Vol 98, 93; Saskatchewan River Rendezvous Centers and Trading Posts--Continuity in a Cree Social Geography, Ethnohistory, Vol 42, 95; Return to Essentials--Some Reflections on the Present State of Historical Study, Hist Theory, Vol 32, 93; A Chains Reaction, Preservation, Vol 49, 97; The Powers of the Past--Reflections on the Crisis and the Promise of History, Hist Theory, Vol 32, 93. **CONTACT ADDRESS** Dept of Hist, Wesleyan Univ, Middletown, CT, 06457.

MEYER, DONALD HARVEY
PERSONAL Born 06/28/1935, Rochester, NY, m, 1958 **DISCIPLINE** AMERICAN INTELLECTUAL HISTORY **EDUCATION** Univ Rochester, BA, 57; Univ Chicago, BD, 61; Univ Calif, Berkeley, PhD(Am hist), 67. **CAREER** Asst prof, 67-72, assoc prof, 72-80, PROF HIST, UNIV DEL, 80- **MEMBERSHIPS** AHA; Orgn Am Historians. **RESEARCH** American intellectual history, especially 19th century religious history. **SELECTED PUBLICATIONS** Auth, Franklin, Benjamin, Edwards, Jonathan, and the Representation of American Culture, William Mary Quart, Vol 51, 94. **CONTACT ADDRESS** Dept of Hist, Univ of Del, Newark, DE, 19711.

MEYER, GEORGE H.
PERSONAL Born 02/19/1928, Detroit, MI, m, 1988, 2 children **DISCIPLINE** POLITICAL SCIENCE **EDUCATION** Univ Mich, BA, 49; Harvard Law, JD, 52; Oxford Univ, Certif, 55; Wayne St Univ, LLM, 62 **CAREER** 1st Lt, USAF, 52-55; Fischer, Franklin & Ford (assoc, 56-63, partner, 63-74); sr. member, Meyer, Kirk, Snyder & Safford, 74-; **HONORS AND**

AWARDS Phi Betta Kappa; Pi Sigma Alpha; Wm Jennings Bryan Prize; Who's Who in Amer **MEMBERSHIPS** Amer Bar Assoc; Mich Bar Assoc; Amer Folk Art Soc **RESEARCH** American Folk Art **SELECTED PUBLICATIONS** "Folk Artists Biographical Index," Gale, 86 **CONTACT ADDRESS** 100 W Long Lake Rd., Suite 100, Bloomfield Hills, MI, 48304. **EMAIL** mkss@michbar.org

MEYER, JAMES S.
DISCIPLINE AMERICAN AND EUROPEAN ART **EDUCATION** Johns Hopkins Univ, PhD, 95. **CAREER** Art, Emory Univ. **SELECTED PUBLICATIONS** Auth, The Genealogy of Minimalism: Carl Andre, Dan Flavin, Donald Judd, Sol LeWitt, and Robert Morris. **CONTACT ADDRESS** Emory Univ, Atlanta, GA, 30322-1950. **EMAIL** jmeye03@emory.edu

MEYER, JERRY D.
PERSONAL Born 11/19/1939, Carbondale, IL, m, 1963, 2 children **DISCIPLINE** ART HISTORY **EDUCATION** SIU, BA, 62, NYU, PHD, 73 **CAREER** Col Sci Tech, 66-68, Brooklyn Col; Art Historian, 68-pres, N IL Univ **MEMBERSHIPS** Col Art Assoc; Midwst Art Hist Soc; Am Acad of Relig **RESEARCH** Late 18th-20th Century American, British, European Art; Religious Imagery; References; Contemporary Art **SELECTED PUBLICATIONS** Auth, "Profane and Sacred Religious Imagery and Prophetic Expression in Postmodern Art," Journ of the Am Acad of Relig, 97, 19-46; Auth, "The Woman Clothed with the Sun," Stud in Inconography, 88, 148-60 **CONTACT ADDRESS** 3030 N First St, De Kalb, IL, 60115. **EMAIL** jmeyer@niu.edu

MEYER, KATHRYN E.
DISCIPLINE ANCIENT HISTORY, MODERN EUROPE, AND WOMEN'S HISTORY **EDUCATION** Wash State Univ, PhD, 92. **CAREER** Asst prof, Washington State Univ. **SELECTED PUBLICATIONS** Auth, The Political Influence of Livia Drusilla during the Reign of Augustus, Selecta II, 90 & The Chinese Must Go! Anti-Chinese Sentiment in Columbia County, 1870-1910, Pacific Northwest Forum, 84. **CONTACT ADDRESS** Dept of History, Washington State Univ, 301 Wilson Hall, PO Box 644030, Pullman, WA, 99164-4030. **EMAIL** kemeyer@mail.wsu.edu

MEYER, KENNETH JOHN
PERSONAL Born 08/24/1930, Manitowoc, WI, m, 1953, 4 children **DISCIPLINE** ENGLISH, AMERICAN STUDIES **EDUCATION** Lawrence Col, BA, 53; Univ Minn, MA, 56, PhD (Am studies), 65. **CAREER** Instr English, Monmouth Col, Ill, 57-61; assoc prof English, 64-67, coordr, Res and Planning Develop Proj, 67-71, Prof English, Huron Col, Sdak, 67-, CHMN DEPT, 64- **MEMBERSHIPS** Am Studies Asn; NCTE; Conf Col Compos and Commun; Aaup. **RESEARCH** American literature and cultures, 1800-1900; curriculum in the small liberal arts college; the teaching of composition. **SELECTED PUBLICATIONS** Auth, The Availability of Fiction--Interpretations and Poetological Studies of 13th Century Works Based on the Arthurian and Dietrich Von Bern Traditions, J Eng Ger Philol, Vol 96, 97; A Concise Middle High German Dictionary, Germ Notes Revs, Vol 26, 95. **CONTACT ADDRESS** 1941 McClellan Dr, Huron, SD, 57350.

MEYER, LEONARD B.
PERSONAL Born 01/12/1918, New York, NY, m, 1975, 3 children **DISCIPLINE** MUSIC **EDUCATION** Columbia Univ, AB, 40, AM, 48; Univ Chicago, PhD(hist of cult), 54. **CAREER** From instr to prof music, Univ Chicago, 46-72, chmn dept music, 61-70, Phyllis Fay Horton prof humanities, 72-75; BENJAMIN FRANKLIN PROF MUSIC and UNIV PROF, UNIV PA, 75-, Fel, Ctr Advan Studies, Wesleyan Univ, 60-61; mem, Nat Humanities Fac, 70-71; Ernest Bloch prof music, Univ Calif, Berkeley, 71; Guggenheim fel, 71-72; VIS PROF, SCH MUSIC, UNIV MICH, ANN ARBOR, 73; SR FEL, SCH CRITICISM AND THEORY, 74- **HONORS AND AWARDS** DHL, Grinnell Col, 67, Loyola Univ, Chicago, 70 and Bard Col, 76. **MEMBERSHIPS** Fel Am Acad Arts and Sci; Am Musicol Soc; Am Soc Aesthet; fel AAAS; Soc Music Theory. **RESEARCH** Music theory and analysis; aesthetics; psychology. **SELECTED PUBLICATIONS** Auth, Participatory Discrepancies and Ethnomusical Theory, Ethnomusicology, Vol 39, 95; Anatomy of a Performance--Sources of Musical Expression, Mus Perception, Vol 13, 96. **CONTACT ADDRESS** Dept of Music, Univ of Pa, 201 S 34th St, Philadelphia, PA, 19174.

MEYER, MICHAEL
PERSONAL Born 04/07/1940, Magdeburg, Germany, m, 1966, 2 children **DISCIPLINE** MODERN EUROPEAN & INTELLECTUAL & CULTURAL HISTORY **EDUCATION** Univ Calif, Los Angeles, BA, 61, MA, 64, PhD(hist), 71. **CAREER** Assoc prof, 70-80, prof hist, Calif State, Northridge, 80-, chmn dept, 75-87. **HONORS AND AWARDS** Res grant, Univ Calif, Los Angeles, Calif State Univ, Northridge, 75, 78, 90, 93, 95, 97, 98, & Am Philol Soc, 78; DAAD Grant 96-97; Fulbright, 99; Univ Pub Award: The Politics of Music in the Third Reich, 91. **MEMBERSHIPS** AHA; Conf Group Cent Europ Studies; Coun European Studies; Ger Studies Asn. **RESEARCH** Anti-Semitism; music in the Third Reich; Ger Emisies in South Cal; modern ideologies and the arts. **SELECTED PUBLICATIONS** Auth, The Nazi Musicologist as Myth Maker in the Third Reich, J Contemp Hist, 10/75; Prospects of a New Music Culture in the Third Reich in Light of the Relationship between High and Popular Culture in European Musical Life, Hist Reflections, summer 77; The SA Song Literature: A Singing Ideological Posture, J Popular Cult, winter 77; Musicology in the Third Reich: A Gap in Historical Research, Europ Studies Rev, 78; A Reference in the Music Commentary of Theodor W Adorno: The Musicology of Volk and Race, Humanities in Soc, fall 79; Music on the Eve of the Third Reich, In: Towards the Holocaust: Fascism and Anti-Semitism in Weimar Germany, Greenwood Press, 83; The Politics of Music in the Third Reich, Peter Lang, 91; A Musical Facade for the Third Reich: 1933-1938, In: 1937: Modern Art and Politics in Prewar Germany, 91; Herr Linse Berichtet: Fotografien aus dem Magdeburger Umland 1933-1935 von Karl Meyer, Ziethan Verla Oscherschleben, 96; National Socialist Germany: Art, In: Encyclopedic History of Modern Germany, Garland Publ, 98. **CONTACT ADDRESS** Dept of Hist, California State Univ, Northridge, 18111 Nordhoff St, Northridge, CA, 91330-8200. **EMAIL** michael.meyer@csun.edu

MEYER, MICHAEL ALBERT
PERSONAL Born 11/15/1937, Berlin, Germany, m, 1961, 3 children **DISCIPLINE** JEWISH HISTORY **EDUCATION** Univ Calif, Los Angeles, BA, 59; Hebrew Union Col, Ohio, PhD(Jewish hist), 64. **CAREER** Asst prof Jewish hist, Hebrew Union Col, Calif, 64-67; from asst prof to assoc prof, 67-72, PROF JEWISH HIST, HEBREW UNION COL, OHIO, 72-, Vis asst prof, Univ Calif, Los Angeles, 65-67; vis lectr, Antioch Col, 68; FEL, LEO BAECK INST, 69-; vis sr lectr, Haifa Univ, 70-71 and Univ Negev, Israel, 71-72; vis prof, Hebrew Univ, Jerusalem, 77-78; Am Coun Learned Soc fel, 82. **HONORS AND AWARDS** Frank and Ethel Cohen Award, Jewish Bk Coun Am, 68. **MEMBERSHIPS** AHA; Asn Jewish Studies(-pres, 78-80). **RESEARCH** Jewish intellectual history of modern Europe; history of Reform Judaism. **SELECTED PUBLICATIONS** Auth, The Broken Staff--Judaism Through Christian Eyes, Central Europ Hist, Vol 25, 92; The Jews and Germany--From the Judeo German Symbiosis to the Memory of Auschwitz, Am Hist Rev, Vol 0101, 96; The Jewish Press in the Third Reich, Central Europ Hist, Vol 26, 93; The Berlin Jewish Community--Enlightenment, Family, and Crisis, 1770-1830, Am Hist Rev, Vol 0100, 95; Jews for Sale-Nazi Jewish Negotiations, 1933-1945, Central Europ Hist, Vol 28, 95; English Noblewomen in the Later Middle Ages, Albion, Vol 26, 94; Alternatives to Assimilation--The Response of Reform Judaism to American Culture, 1840-1930, J Am Hist, Vol 82, 95. **CONTACT ADDRESS** Dept of Hist, Hebrew Union Col, Cincinnati, OH, 45220.

MEYER, RICHARD
DISCIPLINE MODERN AND CONTEMPORARY ART **EDUCATION** Univ Calif, Berkeley, PhD. **CAREER** Asst prof, Univ Southern Calif; curated exhib on the early career of the realist painter Paul Cadmus for, Whitney Mus Amer Art. **RESEARCH** 20th-century art and cultural studies. **SELECTED PUBLICATIONS** Auth, Rock Hudson's Body, in Inside/Out: Lesbian Theories, Gay Theories, NY: 91; Robert Mapplethorpe and the Discipline of Photography, in The Lesbian and Gay Studies Reader, NY: 93; Warhol's Clones, in the Yale Journal of Criticism, 94; This Is To Enrage You: Gran Fury and the Graphics of AIDS Activism, in But Is It Art?: The Spirit of Art As Activism, Seattle: 95. **CONTACT ADDRESS** Col Letters, Arts & Sciences, Univ Southern Calif, University Park Campus, Los Angeles, CA, 90089.

MEYER, STEPHEN
DISCIPLINE AMERICAN SOCIAL AND LABOR HISTORY, AFRICAN AMERICAN HISTORY, HISTORY OF TECH **EDUCATION** SUNY at Stony Brook, BA, 67; Rutgers Univ, MA, 73, PhD, 77. **CAREER** Prof, Univ of WI, Parkside. **HONORS AND AWARDS** Rockefeller Hum fel in residence, Wayne State Univ, 85-86; NEH Summer Sem, Wayne State Univ, 81; NEH Summer Sem, Univ MS, 92; NEH Summer Sem, Univ WI, 96. **RESEARCH** Hist of automobile workers; hist of the Blues; hist of masculinity. **SELECTED PUBLICATIONS** Auth, The Five Dollar Day: Labor Management, and Social Control in the Ford Motor Company, 1908-1921, Albany, SUNY Press, 81; Stalin Over Wisconsin: The Making and Unmaking of Militant Unionism, 1900-1950, New Brunswick, Rutgers UP, 92; co-ed, On the Line: Essays in the History of Auto Work, Urbana, Univ Ill Press, 89. **CONTACT ADDRESS** Dept of Hist, Univ of Wisconsin, Parkside, 900 Wood Rd, Molinaro 1, PO Box 2000, Kenosha, WI, 53141-2000. **EMAIL** stephen.meyer@uwp.edu

MEYEROWITZ, JOANNE
PERSONAL Born 04/08/1954, Washington, DC **DISCIPLINE** HISTORY **EDUCATION** Univ Chicago, BA, 76; Stanford Univ, MA, 78; Stanford Univ, PhD, 83. **CAREER** Assoc prof Hist, Univ Cincinnati, 90- ; Asst prof, Univ Cincinnati, 85-90; Vis asst professor Hist, Claremont McKenna Col, 83-84. **HONORS AND AWARDS** Social Sci Res Coun, Sexuality Res Fellow, 96-97; McMicken Dean's Award for Disting Tchg, Univ Cincinnati, 94; Ohio State Univ, Univ Postdoc Fellow, 84-85; Am Hist Asn, Beveridge Grant, 84; Nat Endow Human, Summer Stipend, 84; Newberry Libr, Exxon Ed Found Fellow, 83. **RESEARCH** 20th-Century US Social/Cultural History; US Women's/Gender History; History of Sexuality; **SELECTED PUBLICATIONS** Women and Migration: Autonomous Female Migrants to Chicago, 1880-1930, Jour Urban Hist, 13:2, Feb, 87, 147-168; Women Adrift: Independent Wage Earners in Chicago, 1880-1930, Univ Chicago Press, 88; Sexual Geography and Gender Economy: The Furnished Room Districts of Chicago, 1890-1930, Gender and History, 2:3, Autumn, 90; American Women's History: The Fall of Women's Culture, Canadian Rev Am Stud, 92; Beyond the Feminine Mystique: A Reassessment of Postwar Mass Culture, 1946-1958, Jour Am Hist, 79:4, Mar 93; Not June Cleaver: Women and Gender in Postwar America, 1945-1960, Temple Univ Press, 94; 'Sex Change' and the Popular Press: Historical Notes on Transsexuality in the United States, 1930-1955, GLQ: A Journal of Lesbian and Gay Studies, 4:2, 98; Women, Cheesecake, and Borderline Material: Responses to Girlie Pictures in the Mid-Twentieth-Century US, Jour Women's Hist, 8:3, Fall, 96; **CONTACT ADDRESS** Univ of Cincinnati, Dept of History, PO Box 210373, Cincinnati, OH, 45221-0373. **EMAIL** Joanne.Meyerowitz@uc.edu

MEZA, PEDRO THOMAS
PERSONAL Born 09/02/1941, New York, NY, m, 1973, 2 children **DISCIPLINE** ENGLISH & EARLY MODERN HISTORY **EDUCATION** NY Univ, AB, 62, MA, 63, PhD(hist), 67. **CAREER** Lectr hist, Bronx Community Col, 66-67; asst prof, 67-74, assoc prof hist, 74-84, prof, 84-, Queensborough Community Col. **MEMBERSHIPS** Conf Brit Studies; AAUP; Soc Hist Technol. **RESEARCH** Early 18th century England--the Church of England. **SELECTED PUBLICATIONS** Co-ed, Readings in Western Civilization: The Early Modern Period, McCutchan, 70; The Question of Authority in the Church of England 1689-1717, 3/73 & Gilbert Burnet's Concept of Religious Tolerations, Hist Mag Protestant Episcopal Church, 9/81. **CONTACT ADDRESS** Queensborough Comm Col, CUNY, 22205 56th Ave, Flushing, NY, 11364-1432.

MEZNAR, JOAN E.
DISCIPLINE HISTORY **EDUCATION** Univ Tex, Austin, 86. **CAREER** Asst prof, Mount Holyoke Col, 86-89; asst prof, Univ SC, 89-95; assoc prof, Westmont Col, 95-. **HONORS AND AWARDS** Fulbright-Hays grant, 83-84; NEH, 87; Fulbright sr scolar lectr/res award, 93., Contrib ed, Handbook of Latin Amer Stud. **RESEARCH** Latin Am; Brazilian. **SELECTED PUBLICATIONS** Auth, Bound By Freedom: Peasants and the End of Slavery in Northeast Brazil, 1831-1888, Positivism, Survey of Social Science: Government and Politics, Salem Press, 95; Radioactive Powder Kills Four and Injures Hundreds in Goiania, Brazil, Brazilian President Announces Plans to Protect Rain Forest, Earth Summit Covenes in Rio de Janeiro, Brazil, Great Events from History II: Ecology and the Environment, Salem Press, 95. **CONTACT ADDRESS** Dept of Hist, Westmont Col, 955 La Paz Rd, Santa Barbara, CA, 93108-1099.

MEZZATESTA, MICHAEL P.
DISCIPLINE ART HISTORY **EDUCATION** The Inst of Fine Arts, PhD. **CAREER** Adj prof, Duke Univ. **RESEARCH** Baroque Italy **SELECTED PUBLICATIONS** Auth, The Art of Gianlorenzo Bernini: Selected Sculpture. **CONTACT ADDRESS** Dept of Art and Art Hist, Duke Univ, Duke Univ Mus of Art, Durham, NC, 27706.

MICCO, MELINDA
DISCIPLINE ETHNIC STUDIES **EDUCATION** Univ Calif at Berkeley, BA, 90, MA, 92, PhD, 95. **CAREER** Asst prof; Mills Col, 93-. **RESEARCH** American Indian history and literature; mixed race identity studies. **SELECTED PUBLICATIONS** Auth, Tribal Recreations: Buffalo Child Long Lance and Black Seminole Narratives, in Lit Stud E and W, Vol 16, Univ Hawai'i & E-W Ctr, 98; Racial Identity in the New Millenium: Black and Indian Communities, Nat Asn for Ethnic Stud, Inc, Fresno, 98; Isolation Of and Demands on Native American Faculty, Amer Indian/97 Alaska Native Prof Asn Conf, Lawrence, 97; Tribal Re-Creations: Buffalo Child Long Lance and Black Seminole Narratives, for the panel: Changing Paradigms: The Ethnic Self and Its Transvestisms, Multi-Ethnic Lit US, Honolulu, 97; Experiment in Domesticity: Native Women in Missionary and Boarding Schools, Western Soc Sci Asn, Oakland, 95; African Americans and American Indians: Historical Significance and Present Realities, Western Soc Scie Asn, Albuquerque, 94; co-ed, Pretending To Be Me: Ethnic Transvestism and Cross-Writing, Univ Ill Press, Encycl Amer Indian, African Americans and Amer Indians, Boston: Houghton Mifflin; 95. **CONTACT ADDRESS** Dept of Ethnic Studies, Mills Col, 5000 MacArthur Blvd, Oakland, CA, 94613-1301. **EMAIL** melinda@mills.edu

MICHAELS, PAULA A.
DISCIPLINE HISTORY **EDUCATION** Northwestern Univ, BA, 87; Univ NC Chapel Hill, MA, 91, PhD, 97. **CAREER** Asst prof, Univ Iowa, 97- . **HONORS AND AWARDS** IREX on-site lang training grant, 91-92; IREX advan res fel, 94-95;

SSRC dissertation fel, 96-97. **MEMBERSHIPS** AAASS; AHA. **RESEARCH** Russia/USSR; Central Asia **SELECTED PUBLICATIONS** Auth, Ninety Winds of Change: The 1985 Alma-Ata Riots and the Mobilization of Kazak Ethnic Identity, Mich Discussions in Anthrop, 96; Kazak Women: Living the Heritage of a Unique Past, in Women in Muslim Societies: Diversity within Unity, Lynne Rienner Publ, 98; Medical Traditions, Kazak Women, and Soviet Medical Politics to 1941, Nationalities Papers, 98; Shamans and Surgeons: Medicine as Politics In Soviet Kazakstan, 1917-53, forthcoming 2002. **CONTACT ADDRESS** Dept of History, Univ Iowa, Schaeffer Hall 280, Iowa City, IA, 52242.

MICHAUX, HENRY G.
PERSONAL Born 01/19/1934, Morganton, NC, s **DISCIPLINE** ART HISTORY **EDUCATION** TX So Univ, BFA (magna cum laude) 1959; PA State Univ, MEd 1960, DEd 1971, grad grant-in-aid 1959-60, grad asst 1966-67. **CAREER** VA State Univ, tchr fine arts & art educ 1960-62; So Univ in New Orleans, 1962-67; Cntrl State Univ, 1967-68; TX So Univ, 1968-70; Coll of the VI, 1970; Appalachian State Univ, assoc prof art educ 1972-76; NC Central Univ, assoc prof art educ 1977-78; SC STATE UNIVERSITY, ASSOC PROF ART EDUC 1978-. **HONORS AND AWARDS** Honorary mem Alpha Kappa Mu 1956-59; Jesse Jones Fine Arts Scholarship TX So Univ 1956-59; Selected Participant Japanese Seminar on Preserv of Cultural Continuity by SC Consortium for Intl Studies 1980; numerous exhibits; natl winner of competition for one-man shows; Madison Galleries, NY; work in Look Magazine; drawings owned by NC Arts Museum; "African American Artists, NC USA" NC Museum of Art 1980; interview and feature on "Carolina Camera" WBTV Charlotte 1981; apptd SC Acquisitions Comm a part of the SC Museum Commn 1982-84; NC Artist International, Hickory Museum of Art, 1987; Natl Invitationals "Dimensions and Directions, Black Artists of the South" Jackson MS 1983; "Changing Images,": Hickory Museum of Art, 1993 . **MEMBERSHIPS** National Association of Schools of Art and Design; National Sculpture Center; NC Coalition of Arts; mem Amer Craftsmen Council 1964-; National Council on Education for the Ceramic Arts; Seminar for Research in Art Education; Amer Assn of Univ Profs 1962-71; natl Art Educ Assn 1974-87; Black Art Festivals; first pres Caldwell Arts Council Lenoir, NC 1976; designed and coord first indoor/ outdoor regional (NC, GA, SC, TN, VA) Sculptors Competition Lenoir NC 1986 through Lenoir Parks & Recreational Dept & the Caldwell Arts Cncl; developed Black Studies (African-Amer Studies for Caldwell Comm Coll Lenoir NC) Project proposal; ETV (WXEX-TV) participant VA State Coll. **CONTACT ADDRESS** So Carolina State Col, 300 College St, NE, Orangeburg, SC, 29117-0001.

MICHEL, SONYA
DISCIPLINE HISTORY **EDUCATION** Brown Univ, PhD, 86. **CAREER** Assoc prof, Univ Ill Urbana Champaign. **RESEARCH** Women and gender in the United States; comparative perspective, gender and social welfare; popular culture. **SELECTED PUBLICATIONS** Co-ed, Mothers of a New World: Maternalist Politics and the Origins of Welfare States, Routledge, 93. **CONTACT ADDRESS** History Dept, Univ Ill Urbana Champaign, 52 E Gregory Dr, Champaign, IL, 61820. **EMAIL** s-michel@uiuc.edu

MICHELINI, ANN NORRIS
PERSONAL Born 03/14/1939, Baltimore, MD, m, 1958, 3 children **DISCIPLINE** CLASSICS **EDUCATION** Radcliff Col, AB, 60; Harvard Univ, PhD, 71. **CAREER** Asst prof, 71-73, Univ Mass Boston; asst prof, 73-78, Harvard Univ; asst, assoc, prof, 78-, Univ of Cincinnati. **MEMBERSHIPS** APA; AAUP; AAUW; Class Asn of Midwest & South. **RESEARCH** Greek tragedy; Plato **SELECTED PUBLICATIONS** Auth, Tradition and Dramatic Form in the Persians of Aeschylus, Cin Class Series 4, sec 1 & sec 2, Brill, 82; auth, Euripides and the Tragic Tradition, Part 1 & Part 2, Wisconsin Univ Press, 87; rev, Black Athena Journal of Womens History, 93; art, The Dance of the Elements Fragment B17 of Empedocles, Power and Spirit, Annalex Univ Turkuensis, 93; art, Political Themes in Euripides Suppliants, Amer Jour Of Phil, 94; rev, Euripides Conformist Deviant or Neoconservative, Arion, 97; art, Alcibiades and Theseus in Euripides Suppliants Colby Quart, 97; art, Rudeness and Irony in Platos Gorgias, Class Phil, 93. **CONTACT ADDRESS** Classics Dept, Univ of Cincinnati, ML 0226, Cincinnati, OH, 45221-0226. **EMAIL** ann.micheline@uc.edu

MICHELS, ANTHONY
PERSONAL Born 11/17/1967, Kingston, NY, s **DISCIPLINE** HISTORY **EDUCATION** Santa Cruz Univ, BA; Stanford Univ, PhD. **CAREER** Asst Prof, Univ of Wisconsin. **MEMBERSHIPS** Assoc for Jewish Stud; Amer Hist Assoc **RESEARCH** Amer Jewish history; European Jewish history; socialism; nationalism; Yiddish culture; popular culture. **CONTACT ADDRESS** Dept of Hist, Univ of Wisconsin-Madison, 1401 Observatory Drive, Madison, WI, 53706. **EMAIL** aemichels@facstaff.wisc.edu

MICHELS, EILEEN M.
PERSONAL Born 03/27/1926, Fargo, ND, m, 1955, 1 child **DISCIPLINE** ART HISTORY **EDUCATION** Univ Minn, BA, 47, MA, 53, MLS, 59, PhD, 71. **CAREER** Part time instr, lectr, art hist, Univ Minn, 63-71; asst prof, Univ Wisc, River Falls, 66-71; vis asst prof, Stanford Univ, 72-73; asst prof, art, Col of St Catherine, 74-78; vis prof, Univ Wisc, Milwaukee, 76; assoc prof and chemn 78-88, prof, 89-92, adj prof, 92-96, prof emerita, 92- , Dept of Art Hist, Univ St. Thomas. **HONORS AND AWARDS** Magna cum Laude, 47; Phi Beta Kappa, 47; Fulbright Award, 56-57; NEH Summer Sem, 80; Vincent Scully Jr res grant from Archit Hist Found, 94. **MEMBERSHIPS** Soc Archit Hist; Col Art Asn; Frank Lloyd Wright Home and Studio Found; Frank Lloyd Wright Found; Minn Hist Soc; Minn Preservation Alliance. **RESEARCH** American architecture, painting and sculpture, seventeenth century to present; European nineteenth and twentieth century architecture, painting and sculpture; decorative arts; prehistoric art; ancient art; medieval art. **SELECTED PUBLICATIONS** Auth, Edwin Lundie, in Mulfinger, ed, The Architecture of Edwin Lundie, Minn Hist Soc, 95; contribur, Dictionary of Art, Grove's Dictionaries, Macmillan, 97; auth, The Buildings of Minnesota, Oxford, forthcoming. **CONTACT ADDRESS** 2183 Hendon Ave, St Paul, MN, 55108. **EMAIL** epmichels@stthomas.edu

MICHELSEN, JOHN MAGNUS
PERSONAL Bergen, Norway **DISCIPLINE** GREEK PHILOSOPHY **EDUCATION** Univ Wash, BA, 60, MA, 64, PhD(philos), 70. **CAREER** Lectr philos, Univ Alta, 65-66; lectr, 66-70, asst prof, 70-77, ASSOC PROF PHILOS, UNIV VICTORIA, BC, 77- **MEMBERSHIPS** Can Philos Asn; Int Husserl and Phenomenol Res Soc; Hegel Soc Am; Soc for Advan Am Philos; Can Archaeol Inst at Athens. **RESEARCH** Aristotle, Plato and Santayana; post-Kantian European philosophy. **SELECTED PUBLICATIONS** Auth, Bmw Trouble, Aba Jour, Vol 83, 97. **CONTACT ADDRESS** Dept of Philosophy, Univ of Victoria, Victoria, BC, V8W 2Y2.

MICKIEWICZ, ELLEN PROPPER
DISCIPLINE POLITICAL SCIENCE **EDUCATION** Wellesley Col, BA; Yale Univ, PhD. **CAREER** James R Shepley Prof Pub Policy Studies, Duke Univ, 94-; dir, DeWitt Wallace Ctr for Com and Jour, Terry Sanford Inst of Pub Policy, Duke Univ, 94-; prof, dept polit sci, Duke Univ, 94-; fel, The Carter Ctr, 86-; prof polit sci, Emory Univ, 88-93; dir, int media com prog, Emory Univ, 86-93; prof, dept polit sci, Emory Univ, 85-88; dean, grad school of arts and sci, Emory Univ, 80-85; prof, dept polit sci, Mich State Univ, 73-80; assoc prof, Mich State Univ, 67-73. **HONORS AND AWARDS** Edelman Award for Distinguished Scholar in Polit Com, Amer Polit Sci Asn, 97; Outstanding Service to Promote Democratic Media in Russia, Union of Jour of Russia, 94; Elec Media Book of the Year, Nat Asn Broadcasters and Broadcast Educ Asn, 88; Guggenheim Fel, 73-74. **MEMBERSHIPS** Amer Polit Sci Asn; Int Com Asn; Amer Asn for the Advan of Slavic Studies; Dante Soc of Amer. **RESEARCH** Political communication; comparative politics; public policy. **SELECTED PUBLICATIONS** Auth, Changing Channels: Television and the Struggle for Power in Russia, Oxford, 97; After Soviet-era Rule: The Role of Journalists in Democratizing Societies, The Politics of News, the News of Politics, 98; Media, Transition, and Democracy: Television and the Transformation of Russia, Communications Cornucopia, 98; co-auth, Television, Campaigning, and Elections in the Soviet Union and Post-Soviet Russia, 96; auth, The Political Economy of Media Democratization, Russia in Transition, 95; Television and Political Change, Cambridge Encyclopedia of Russia and the Soviet Union, Cambridge Univ, 94; co-auth, Television/Radio News and Minorities, Emory Univ, 94. **CONTACT ADDRESS** Dept of Public Policy Studies, Duke Univ, Durham, NC, 27708-0241. **EMAIL** epm@pps.duke.edu

MICKOLUS, EDWARD F.
PERSONAL Born 12/28/1950, Cincinnati, OH, m, 1983, 1 child **DISCIPLINE** POLITICAL SCIENCE **EDUCATION** Georgetown Univ, AB, 73; Yale Univ, MA, 74, MPhil, 75, PhD, 81. **CAREER** Tchng Asst, Yale Univ, 74-76; Asst to Dir, Yale Univ, 74; Dir, Summer Inst, Georgetown Univ, 71-73. **HONORS AND AWARDS** Mgr of the Yr in a Fed Govt Agency, 93; Exceptional Performance Awards in a Fed Agency, 3/90, 1/91, 4/91, 8/95, 9/97, 5/98; Quality Step Increase, 89; Delta Tau Kappa Soc Sci Honors Soc, 75; Pi Sigma Alpha Polit Sci Honors Soc, Georgetown Univ, 72; Mensa., Founder & Pres, Vinyard Software, Inc; Granted Cocktail right C-458 by Bartender Magazine via Am Bartender Asn for Ciana Sunrise, 4/88. **MEMBERSHIPS** Acad of Polit Sci, 75-80; Am Acad of Polit & Soc Sci, 75-80; Am Polit Sci Asn; Am Soc for Int Law, 75-81; Int Soc for Contemp Legend Res, 91-93; Int Stud Asn, 73-81; Soc for Basic Irreproduceable Res, 73-; Disco Preservation Soc, 86-; Yale Int Relations Asn, Inc, (pres), 73-75. **RESEARCH** Terrorism & polit science; virtual communities. **SELECTED PUBLICATIONS** Auth, Terrorism, 1988-1991: A Chronology of Events and a Selectively Annotated Bibliography, Bibliographies & Indexes in Mil Stud, no 6, Greenwood Press, 93; co-auth, Terrorism, 1992-1995: A Chronology of Events and a Selectively Annotated Bibliography, Greenwood Press, 97; . **CONTACT ADDRESS** 2305 Sandburg St, Dunn Loring, VA, 22027-1124. **EMAIL** edward.mickolus.grd.poli@aya.yale.edu

MIDDLEKAUFF, ROBERT LAWRENCE
PERSONAL Born 07/05/1929, Yakima, WA, m, 1952, 2 children **DISCIPLINE** AMERICAN COLONIAL HISTORY **EDUCATION** Univ Wash, AB, 52, MA, 56; Yale Univ, PhD, 61. **CAREER** Instr hist, Yale Univ, 59-62; from Asst Prof to Prof, 62-81, Margaret Byrne Prof Hist, 81-88, Prof Hist, 88-91, Hutchks Prof, Univ Calif, Berkeley, 91-, Provost & Dean, Col Lett & Sci, 81-83; Dir, Henry E. Huntington Libr and Art Gallery, 83-88. **HONORS AND AWARDS** Am Coun Learned Soc fel, 65-66; Bancroft Prize Am Hist, Columbia Univ, 72. **MEMBERSHIPS** AHA; Orgn Am Historians; Soc Am Hist; Am Acad Arts & Sci; Am Philos Soc. **RESEARCH** Colonial education; Puritanism in New England; early American history. **SELECTED PUBLICATIONS** Auth, A Persistent Tradition: The Classical Curriculum in 18th Century New England, William & Mary Quart, 1/61; Ancients and Axioms, Yale Univ, 63; Pity and Intellect in Puritanism, William & Mary Quart, 7/65; The Mathers: Three Generations of Puritan Intellectuals, Oxford Univ, 71; Why Men Fought in the American Revolution, Huntington Libr Quart, spring 80; The Glorious Cause: The American Revolution, 1763-1789, Oxford Univ Press, 1982; Benjamin Franklin and his Enemies, Calif, 96. **CONTACT ADDRESS** Dept of Hist, Univ of Calif, 3229 Dwinelle Hall, Berkeley, CA, 94720-2551. **EMAIL** rlmiddlek@juno.com

MIDDLETON, CHARLES
PERSONAL Born 09/16/1944, Hays, 3 children **DISCIPLINE** HISTORY **EDUCATION** Florida State Univ, AB, 65; Duke Univ, MA, PhD, 69. **CAREER** Asst to Prof Hist Univ Col, Boulder, 69-96, Assoc Dean, Col Arts & Sciences, 80-88; Dean, 88-96; Prof Hist, Bowling Green State Univ 96-, Prov, vpres Acad Affairs, BGSU, 96-. **HONORS AND AWARDS** Phi Eta Sigma; Phi Alpha Theta; Phi Beta Kappa; Teaching Recognition Award Univ Col; Fel Royal Hist Soc; Robert L Stearns Award Univ Col; Univ Col Medal; Golden Key Nat Honor Soc; Phi Kappa Phi; numerous editions of Who's Who in West and Who's Who. **MEMBERSHIPS** Am Hist Asn; N Am Conf Brit Studies (life); Western Conf on Brit Studies; Southern Conf Brit Studies; Comt on Gay & Lesbian Hist AHA (life); Am Conf Irish Studies. **RESEARCH** Mod Brit soc hist; gay and lesbian hist. **SELECTED PUBLICATIONS** Administration of British Foreign Policy, 1782-1846, Duke Press, 77; Numerous Articles. **CONTACT ADDRESS** Bowling Green State Univ, McFall Center 230, Bowling Green, OH, 43403. **EMAIL** charlrm@bgnet.bgsu.edu

MIDDLETON, RICHARD TEMPLE, III
PERSONAL Born 01/17/1942, Jackson, Mississippi, m **DISCIPLINE** EDUCATION **EDUCATION** Lincoln Univ of MO, BS 1963, MEd 1965; Univ of Southern MO, EdD 1972. **CAREER** Tougaloo Coll, instructor of educ 1967-70; Jackson State Univ, asst & assoc prof 1970-76, dir student teaching 1976-97; Episcopal priest, 1995-. **HONORS AND AWARDS** Woodrow-Wilson King Fellowship Doctoral Study 1969; selected as mem of leadership, Jackson MS Chamber of Commerce 1987-88. **MEMBERSHIPS** Bd mem Ballet Mississippi 1983-85, Security Life Ins Co 1985; pres Beta Gamma Boule Sigma Pi Phi Frat 1985-87; bd mem Opera/South Co 1986-90, Catholic Charities 1986-90; vice pres Mississippi Religious Leadership Conference 1988-89; mem Natl Executive Council The Episcopal Church 1987-88; vice chairman, Jackson, MS Planning Board, 1990-94; NCATE Board of Examiners. **CONTACT ADDRESS** Dir of Student Teaching, Jackson State Univ, 1400 JR Lynch St, Jackson, MS, 39217.

MIDDLETON, STEPHEN
DISCIPLINE HISTORY **EDUCATION** Ohio State Univ, MA, 77; Miami Univ (OH), PhD, 87. **CAREER** ASSOC PROF, HIST, NC STATE UNIV **MEMBERSHIPS** Am Antiquarian Soc **SELECTED PUBLICATIONS** Auth, Ohio and the Antislavery Activities of Attorney S.P. Chase, Garland, 90; auth, "We Must Not Fail: Horace Sudduth," Queen City Heritage 49; auth, The Black Laws in the Old Northwest, Greenwood, 93; "Law and Ideology in Ohio and Kentucky," Filson Club Hist Quart 67, 93. **CONTACT ADDRESS** Dept of Hist, No Carolina State Univ, Box 8108, Raleigh, NC, 27695. **EMAIL** stephen_middleton@ncsu.edu

MIDELFORT, H.C. ERIK
PERSONAL Born 04/17/1942, Eau Claire, WI, 3 children **DISCIPLINE** REFORMATION & EARLY MODERN GERMAN HISTORY **EDUCATION** Yale Univ, BA, 64, MPhil, 67, PhD, 70. **CAREER** Instr Western civilization, Stanford Univ, 68-70; from Asst Prof to Assoc Prof. 70-87, Prof Hist, 87-, C. Julian Bishko Prof, Univ Va, 96-, Principal, Brown Col at Univ Va, 96-. **HONORS AND AWARDS** Gustave O Arlt Award, Coun Grad Sch of US, 73; Guggenheim Mem Found fel, 75-76; NEH Fel, 87-88; Roland H. Bainton Award, 16th Century Studies Conf, 95. **MEMBERSHIPS** Am Soc Reformation Res. **RESEARCH** History of insanity; the vulgar Renaissance in Germany. **SELECTED PUBLICATIONS** Auth, Witch Hunting in Southwestern Germany, 1562-1684, Stanford Univ, 72; co-ed & transl, Bernd Moeller, Imperial Cities and the Reformation, Fortress, 72; auth, The revolution of 1525?, Cent Europ Hist, 78; co-ed & transl, Peter Blickle, The Revolution of 1525, Johns Hopkins Univ Press, 81; Madness and Civilization in Early Modern Europe, A Reappraisal of Michel Fou-

cault, In: After the Reformation, Univ Pa, 80; auth, Mad Princes of Renaissance Germany, Univ Press Va, 94; A History of Madness in 16th Century Germany, Stanford Univ Press, 98; transl, Wolfgang Behringer, Shaman of Oberstdorf. Conrad Stoeckhlim and the Phantoms of the Night, Univ Press Va, 98; transl and co-ed, Johann Weyer, On Witchcraft, Pegasus Press, 98. **CONTACT ADDRESS** Dept of Hist, Univ of Va, Randall Hall, Charlottesville, VA, 22903-3284. **EMAIL** hem7e@virginia.edu

MIECZKOWSKI, BOGDON

PERSONAL Born 11/08/1924, Poland, m, 1961, 3 children **DISCIPLINE** ECONOMICS **EDUCATION** Univ London, BS, 50; Univ Ill, MA, 53; PhD, 54. **CAREER** Asst prof, Univ Vt, 54-57; res assoc, Columbia Univ, 58-62; asst prof, Boton Col, 62-65; ASSOC PROF AND PROF, ITHACA COL, 65- . **HONORS AND AWARDS** ODE; Distinguished Fel of the NY State Econ Asoc. **MEMBERSHIPS** NY State Econ Asoc. **RESEARCH** Comparative economic systems; dysfunctional bureaucracy. **SELECTED PUBLICATIONS** Auth, The Rot at the Top: Dysfunctional Bureacracy in Academia, 95. **CONTACT ADDRESS** Dept of Econ, Ithaca Col, Ithaca, NY, 14850. **EMAIL** bogdan@ithaca.edu

MIGLIAZZO, ARLIN C.

PERSONAL Born 09/20/1951, South Gate, CA, m, 1977, 2 children **DISCIPLINE** HISTORY **EDUCATION** Biola Col, BA, 74; Northern Az Univ, MA, 75; Washington St Univ, PhD, 82. **CAREER** Instr, 77-78, Biola Col; lectr, 79-81, Washington St Univ; instr, 81, Pac Lutheran Univ; asst prof, 82-83, Judson Baptist Col; lectr, 86, Univ Pittsburgh; adj prof, 88, Spokane Comm Col; Fulbright/Hays prof, 90, Keimyung Univ Daegu, Rep of Korea; asst to full prof, 83-, Whitworth Col. **HONORS AND AWARDS** Lily Fellows Grant, 96, 96, 97; Who's Who Among Amer Teachers, 96; Whitworth Col Teaching Excellence Award, 97., Who's Who Among Amer Univ & Col, 74; cum laude grad, Biola Col, 74; Phi Kappa Phi; Phi Alpha Theta. **MEMBERSHIPS** E Wa St Hist Soc; Conf on Faith & Hist. **RESEARCH** Race & ethnicity in Amer life; twentieth century Amer intellectual cult; hist of higher educ. **SELECTED PUBLICATIONS** Art, A Tarnished Legacy Revisited: Jean Pierre Purry and the Settlement of the Southern Frontier, 1718-1736, SC Hist Mag, 91; art, The Challenge of Educational Wholeness: Linking Beliefs, Values and Academics, Faculty Dialogue, 93; art, Korean Leadership in the Twenty-First Century: A Profile of the Corning Generation, Korea J, 93; art, Cultural Mimesis and Christian Higher Education: A personal Reconnaissance, Fides et Historia, 93; co-auth, Whitworth College: Evangelical in the Reformed Tradition, Models for Christian Higher Education: Strategies for Survival and Success in the Twenty-First Century, William B Eerdmans Press, 97. **CONTACT ADDRESS** Dept Hist/Polit & Int Stud, Whitworth Col, 300 W Hawthorne Rd, Spokane, WA, 99218. **EMAIL** amigliazzo@whitworth.edu

MIHELICH, DENNIS

PERSONAL Cleveland, OH **DISCIPLINE** UNITED STATES HISTORY **EDUCATION** Kent State Univ, BA, 66; Case Western Reserve Univ, MA, PhD, 72. **CAREER** Adv, career plan and public hist internships; prof. Creighton Univ. **MEMBERSHIPS** Past pres, Hist Soc Douglas Co, Nebr State Hist Soc; ch, Omaha Street Naming Adv bd; ch prog comt, Nat Conf Christians and Jews; mem, Nebr State Hist Records bd. **RESEARCH** African American history. **SELECTED PUBLICATIONS** Publ on res interest. **CONTACT ADDRESS** Dept of History, Creighton Univ, 2500 California Plaza, Omaha, NE, 68178. **EMAIL** dnm@creighton.edu

MIHESUAH, DEVON ABBOTT

PERSONAL Born 06/02/1957, Wichita Falls, TX, m, 1990, 2 children **DISCIPLINE** AMERICAN HISTORY **EDUCATION** Tx Christian Univ, BS, 81; MED, 82; MA, 86; PhD, 89. **CAREER** Assoc prof, N Ariz Univ, 95-; asst prof, N Ariz Univ, 89-95; Ed, Amer Indian Quart, 98-; assoc ed, Amer Indian Quart, 93-; Women of the West Museum Proj, Boulder, CO, 92-; Consultant, Exhibit Content Develop Proj at Women of West Museum 94-96; Consultant, Edge of the Rez, Arizona Daily Sun & KNAU Radio Series on Bordertown Race Relations, 96; Consultant, Texas Indian Commission's and Texas Historical Commission's Committee on the Acquisition & Disposition of Humanities Remains & Sacred Objects, 84-89; Consultant, Northeastern State Univ Archives & Special Collections, 88-89. **HONORS AND AWARDS** Ford Found Postdoctoral Fel; Critics' Choice Award of Amer Educ Studies Assoc for Cultivating the Rosebuds: The Education of Women at the Cherokee Female Seminary, 1851-1909; Native Amer Students United Award for Outstanding Fac, 94; NAU Pres Award for Outstanding Fac; NAU Organized Res Grant, 93; Ariz Humanities Council Studies Grant, 93; Amer Council of Learned Soc Fel; Amer Historical Assoc Albert Beveridge Res Grant, 92; Ntl Endowment Humanities Travel to Collections Grant, 92; NAU Outstanding Fac Woman of Year Award, 92; NAU Organized Res Grant, 92. **MEMBERSHIPS** Amer Historical Assoc; Amer Indian Historians' Assoc; Amer Soc for Ethnohistory; Okla Historical Soc; Phi Alpha Theta; Western History Assoc. **RESEARCH** American Indian History; Reparation Issues; Identity; Women **SELECTED PUBLICATIONS** Medicine Woman, Red Ink 5, 98; American Indian Racial and Ethnic Identities, Univ AZ Pr, forthcoming; ed, Natives and Academics: Discussions on Researching and Writing About American Indians, Univ Nebr Pr, 98; American Indians: Stereotypes and Realities, Clarity Intl, 98; Cultivating the Rosebuds: The Education of Women at the Cherokee Female Seminary, 1851-1909, Univ Ill, 93. **CONTACT ADDRESS** Dept of History, Devon Abbott Mihesuah, Northern AZ Univ, PO Box 6023, Flagstaff, AZ, 86011-6023. **EMAIL** devon.mihesuah@nau.edu

MILAC, METOD M.

PERSONAL Born 10/02/1924, Prevalje, Slovenia, m, 1951, 3 children **DISCIPLINE** LIBRARIANSHIP; MUSICOLOGY; EMIGRATION STUDIES **EDUCATION** Cleveland Inst Mus, BM, 57; Cleveland Inst Mus, MM, 60; Western Reserve Univ, MSLS, 62; Syracuse Univ, MPh, 87; Syracuse Univ, PhD, 91. **CAREER** Mus Libr, Syracuse Univ Lib, 62-65; Head, Ref Dept, SUL, 65-68; Asst Dir, SUL, 68-73; Actg Dir, SUL, 73-74; Assoc Dir, SUL, 74-92. **HONORS AND AWARDS** Post Std Award for Excel in Lib Serv, 82; Disting Serv Award, Syracuse Univ Lib, 89. **MEMBERSHIPS** Am Musicol Soc; Am Assoc Advance of Slavic Stud; Mus Lib Assoc; Soc Slovene Stud. **RESEARCH** Late 16th century music, composer Jacobus Gallus Carniolus (1550-1591); World War II, Central Europe. **SELECTED PUBLICATIONS** Anno Domini 1574: The Question of Jacobus Gallus and the Imperial Court Chapel, in Gallus Carniolus in Evropska Renesansa (Ljubljana: Slovene Acad of Sci and Arts, 91, 21-48; The War Years, 1941-1945: From My Experiences, Slovene Studies, v16, n2, 94, 31-47; Petje Druzi Nove Priseljence: Ustanovitev in Prva Leta Pevskega Zbora Korotan / Choral Singing Unifies New Immigrants: Founding and First Years of Singing Society Korotan, Dve Domovini/ Two Homelands, Migration Studies 8, Ljubljana, Ctr Sci Res of the Slovene Acad Sci and Arts, The Inst for Slovene Emigration Res, 97, 49-70; Porocilo Avstrijskega Centra Za Etnicne Manjsine 1996, Volksgruppen Report/Ethnic Group Report, Zapiski, Chron Am Slovene Congress, Issue III, Autumn 97, 8-13. **CONTACT ADDRESS** 259 Kensington Pl, Syracuse, NY, 13210-3307. **EMAIL** mmilac@syr.edu

MILBURN, CORINNE M.

PERSONAL Born 09/20/1930, Alexandria, LA, w, 1952 **DISCIPLINE** EDUCATION **EDUCATION** Marian Coll Indpls, BS 1950; Univ of SD, MA 1970, EdD 1976. **CAREER** IN Univ Med Ctr, lab tech (clin biochem) 1950-53; Carver Found-Tuskegee Inst, tissue culture tech 1954-57; Elk Point Pub Sch, high school teacher 1969-73, teacher corps team leader 1973-75; grad intern sci consult AEA 12-Sioux City 1975-76; proj writer-HEW grant Univ of SD 1976-77; Univ of SD, asst prof/dir of outreach beginning 1977; assoc prof, C/I, beginning 1988, assoc dean, school of education, 1990. **MEMBERSHIPS** State pres Epsilon Sigma Alpha Int 1977-78; chap pres Phi Delta Kappa (USD chpt) 1979-80; state pres Assn of Tchr EDUCATIONs 1979-80; exec director, South Dakota Assoc of Middle Level Education; international pres, Epsilon Sigma Alpha Int, 1986-87. **SELECTED PUBLICATIONS** "A Challenging Alternative for the Gifted/Talented Student" 1976; "A New Dimension for the Gifted/Talented Student" 1976; "Education-A Lifelong Process" ESA Jour 1980; Helping to make the transition from high school to College, 1988; The Effect of Assertive Discipline & Training, Reducing Anxiety and Stress in the Student Teaching Setting, The Teacher Educ Autumn, 1993; Implementing Middle School Concepts in Rural Areas, Problems & Solutions, Middle School Journal, Sept, 1994.

MILES, EDWIN ARTHUR

PERSONAL Born 02/02/1926, Birmingham, AL **DISCIPLINE** AMERICAN HISTORY **EDUCATION** Birmingham-Southern Col, AB, 48; Univ NC, MA, 49, PhD(hist), 54. **CAREER** Instr soc sci, Univ NC, 49-50; researcher, State Dept Arch and Hist, NC, 52-54; from asst prof to assoc prof, 54-62, chmn dept, 69-73, PROF HIST, UNIV HOUSTON, 62- **MEMBERSHIPS** AHA; Orgn Am Historians; Southern Hist Asn. **RESEARCH** Southern history; early national period; Jacksonian period. **SELECTED PUBLICATIONS** Auth, Correspondence of Polk, James,K., Vol 8--September December 1844, Jour Southern Hist, Vol 61, 95; The Founders and The Classics--Greece, Rome and the American Enlightenment, Jour Southern Hist, Vol 62, 96. **CONTACT ADDRESS** Dept of Hist, Univ of Houston, Houston, TX, 77004.

MILES, GARY B.

PERSONAL Born 07/21/1940, St. John, NB, Canada, m, 1962, 2 children **DISCIPLINE** CLASSICS **EDUCATION** Colby Col, BA, 62; Harvard Univ, AM, 64; Yale Univ, PhD, 71. **CAREER** Philips Acad, Andover, 64-66; Wesleyan Univ, 68-69; Univ Texas, 70-71; Univ Cal, Santa Cruz, 71-. **HONORS AND AWARDS** Danforth fel, 62-68; NEH fel 86, Excellence Tchg, Univ Cal, 98. **MEMBERSHIPS** AIA/APA; Virgilian Soc; AHA **RESEARCH** Roman literature and cultural history, especially of the Late Republic; Early Empire; Historiography. **SELECTED PUBLICATIONS** Auth, The First Roman Marriage and the Theft of the Sabine Women, Innovations of Antiquity, Routledge, 92; Virgil, Reference Guide to World Literature, St James Press, 95; Livy: Reconstructing Early Rome, Cornell Univ Press, 95. **CONTACT ADDRESS** Cowell Col, Univ Cal, Santa Cruz, CA, 95064. **EMAIL** miles@cats.ucsc.edu

MILES, MARGARET M.

PERSONAL Born 09/16/1952, Detroit, MI **DISCIPLINE** CLASSICAL ARCHAEOLOGY **EDUCATION** Wayne State Univ, 69-71; Univ Mich, AB, 73; MA, 76, PhD, 80, Princeton Univ. **CAREER** Visiting Asst Prof, 82-87, Univ California-Berkeley; Visiting Asst Prof, 88-90, Intercollegiate Center, Rome, Italy; Visiting Asst Prof, 91-92, Smith Col; Asst Prof, 92-94, Assoc Prof, 94-, Univ California-Irvine. **HONORS AND AWARDS** John Williams White Fellow 76-77; Olivia Damer Fellow, 89-90; Rome Prize Fellow, AAR, 87-88; Mellon Fellow, IAS, 90-91; NEH Fellow, 96-97. **MEMBERSHIPS** AIA; CAA; APA **RESEARCH** Greek and Roman art and architecture; ancient religion **SELECTED PUBLICATIONS** Auth, The Propylon to the Sanctuary of Demeter Malo phoros at Selinous, AJA, 98; auth, The Athenian Agora XXXI: The City Eleusinion, 98. **CONTACT ADDRESS** Dept of Art History, Univ of Cal-Irvine, Irvine, CA, 92697-2785. **EMAIL** mmmiles@uci.edu

MILHAM, MARY ELLA

PERSONAL Born 03/22/1922, Waukesha, WI **DISCIPLINE** CLASSICS **EDUCATION** Carroll Col, BA, 43; Univ Wis, MA, 44, PhD(classics, ling), 50. **CAREER** Instr classics and integrated lib studies, Univ Wis, 50-54; from asst prof to assoc prof, 54-68, PROF CLASSICS, UNIV NB, 68-, Can Coun sr res fel, 61-62, leave fel, 68-69; Soc Sci Human Res Coun leave fel, 81-82. **MEMBERSHIPS** Am Philol Asn; Ling Soc Am; Class Asn Can (vpres, 76-78); Humanities Asn Can (secy-treas, 66-68); Renaissance Soc Am. **RESEARCH** Late Latin; Renaissance Latin; textual criticism. **SELECTED PUBLICATIONS** Auth, Classical Latin Manuscripts From Public Libraries in France, Vol 1-Agen Evreux, Phoenix J Classical Assoc Can, Vol 45, 91. **CONTACT ADDRESS** 20900 W Cleveland Ave, New Berlin, WI, 53151.

MILLAR, GILBERT JOHN

PERSONAL Born 04/07/1939, Kilwinning, Scotland, m, 1989, 2 children **DISCIPLINE** TUDOR-STUART HISTORY **EDUCATION** Southeastern La Col, BA, 61; La State Univ, MA, 64, PhD(English hist), 74. **CAREER** Instr hist, Ark State Col, 65-67; asst prof, 70-76; Assoc to PROF PROF HIST, LONGWOOD COL, 76- **HONORS AND AWARDS** Maude Glenn Raiford Award, 96 **MEMBERSHIPS** Soc Army Hist Res; Am Mil Inst; Conf Brit Studies. **RESEARCH** Late medieval and early modern European history; Tudor England. **SELECTED PUBLICATIONS** Auth, The Landsknecht: His recruitment and organization with some reference to the reign of Henry VIII, Mil Affairs, 10/71; The Albanians: Sixteenth-century mercenaries, 7/76 & Mercenaries under Henry VIII, 3/77, Hist Today; The Lollards of Scotland, Va Soc Sci Asn J, 11/78; Henry VIII's Colonels, J Soc Army Hist, fall 79; Tudor Mercenaries and Auxiliaries, 1485-1547, Univ Press Va, 80; auth, Henry VIII's Preliminary Letter of Retainer to Colonel Frederick von Reiffenberg, J Soc Army Hist, winter 89, reviews of books, J Mil Hist, Am Hist Asn. **CONTACT ADDRESS** Dept of Hist & Polit Sci, Longwood Col, Farmville, VA, 23909.

MILLAR, JOHN F.

PERSONAL Born 01/19/1945, New York, NY, m, 1972, 1 child **DISCIPLINE** HISTORY **EDUCATION** Harvard Col, AB 66; Col of WM and Mary, MA 81. **CAREER** Lecturer in History, 1972 to present. **RESEARCH** Eighteenth Century American. **CONTACT ADDRESS** 710 South Henry St, Williamsburg, VA, 23185-4113.

MILLAR, STEVEN

DISCIPLINE ART **EDUCATION** Yale Univ, BA, 91; Washington Univ (St. Louis, MO), MFA, 95. **CAREER** Instr, St. Louis Comm Col, 96; Instr, Maryville Univ, 96; Lectr, Washington Univ, 96-97; Asst Prof, 97-, Fairfield Univ. **CONTACT ADDRESS** 48 Rayfield Rd, Westport, CT, 06880.

MILLE, DIANE

DISCIPLINE ART HISTORY **EDUCATION** Rutgers Univ, BA, 79; Hunter Col, MA, 82; Cuny Grad Ctr, PhD, 93. **CAREER** Dir, Thomas J. Walsh Art Gallery, Fairfield Univ, 87-89; Adj Prof, Fairfield Univ, 96-; Adj Prof, 93-, Sacred Heart Univ. **CONTACT ADDRESS** Thomas J. Walsh Art Gallery, Fairfield Univ, Fairfield, CT, 06430.

MILLEN, SHIRLEY A.

DISCIPLINE HISTORY **EDUCATION** Univ Minn, PhD, 85. **CAREER** Instr, Bethel Col, 79, 82-83; prof, Westmont Col, 84-. **RESEARCH** Philos of hist; ethics of David Hume; anti-semitism; Europ nationalism and liberalism; w civilization. **SELECTED PUBLICATIONS** Auth, Organized Freethought: the Religion of Unbelief in Victorian England, Garland, 87; Keeping the Faith: The Struggle for a Militant Atheist Press, 1839-62, Victorian Periodicals Rev, 92; Individualism in the Liberal Arts: Thoughts on Habits of the Heart, Fac Dialogue, 87; Women in History and Hannah More, Fides et Historia, 87. **CONTACT ADDRESS** Dept of Hist, Westmont Col, 955 La Paz Rd, Santa Barbara, CA, 93108-1099.

MILLER, ANDREW M.

PERSONAL Born 05/26/1947, CA **DISCIPLINE** CLASSICS **EDUCATION** Univ Calif, BA, anthrop, Greek, 69, MA, 71, PhD, 77, comparative lit. **CAREER** Asst prof classics, 77-83, assoc prof classics, 83-97, prof classics, 97-, Univ Pittsburgh. **HONORS AND AWARDS** NEH Fellowship for Study and Research, 81-82. **MEMBERSHIPS** Amer Philological Assn; Classical Assn Atlantic States. **RESEARCH** Greek and Roman poetry; translation studies. **SELECTED PUBLICATIONS** Auth, From Delos to Delphi: A Literary Study of the Homeric Hymn to Apollo, 86; auth, "Inventa Componere: Rhetorical Process and Poetic Composition in Pinder's Ninth Olympian Ode," Transactions of the American Philological Assn, vol 123, 93; auth, "Pindaric Mimesis: The Associative Mode," Classical Journ, vol 87, 93; auth, Greek Lyric: An Anthology in Translation, 96; auth, "Levels of Argument in Pinder's Second Nemean Ode," Hellas 7, 96. **CONTACT ADDRESS** Dept of Classics, Univ of Pittsburgh, Pittsburgh, PA, 15260. **EMAIL** amm2@ pitt.edu

MILLER, ANGELA L.

DISCIPLINE CULTURAL HISTORY 19TH- AND 20TH-C AM ART **EDUCATION** Yale Univ, PhD, 85. **CAREER** Hist, Washington Univ. **HONORS AND AWARDS** John Hope Franklin Profize; Charles Eldredge Profize. **SELECTED PUBLICATIONS** Auth, Empire the Eye: Landscape Reprofesentation and Am Cultural Politics, 1825-1875, Cornell Univ Profess, 93; Breaking Down the Profeserves Visual Profoduction, Am Art, 97; The Moving Panorama, in Wide Angle: A Film Quarterly, 96. **CONTACT ADDRESS** Washington Univ, 1 Brookings Dr, St. Louis, MO, 63130.

MILLER, BERNICE JOHNSON

PERSONAL Chicago, IL, m **DISCIPLINE** EDUCATION **EDUCATION** Roosevelt Univ Chicago IL, BA; Chicago Teachers Coll, MA 1965; CAS Harvard Univ Grad School of Ed, 1968-69, EdD 1972; Harvard Univ Grad School of Ed, 1972. **CAREER** Chicago Bd of Ed, teacher elem & hs 1950-66; The New School for Children Inc, headmistress 1966-68; Jackson Coll, assoc dean 1968-70; Radcliffe, instr1970-73; Harvard Grad School of Ed, assoc dir 1971-75; Boston Public Schools Lucy Stone School, principal 1977-78; Boston Public Schools, sr officer 1978-84; Harvard Grad School, dir high tech rsch proj 1983-84; CITY COLL OF CHGO, PRES, currently. **HONORS AND AWARDS** Educator's Award Boston 350th Anniv of Boston MA 1980; Educator of the Year Urban Bankers Ed Awd Boston 1982; Woman of the Year Awd Assoc of Mannequins 1984; Woman in Ed Business & Professional Women Boston & Vicinity 1984; Freedom Awd Roosevelt Univ 1985; Disting Alumni of Chicago State Univ NABSE 1985; Outstanding Achievement Awd in Educ YWCA 1986; Minority Networking Org of Focus & Seana Mag Serv Awd 1986. **MEMBERSHIPS** Bd mem, Children's World Day Care Ctr Boston 1972-84, Blue Cross/Blue Shield Boston, United Way; trustee, Brigham's & Women's Hosp Med Found; mem 1968-84, pres, United Commun Plng Corp 1983-85; bd mem, Chicago Metro History Fair Bd; mem, Mayor's Commiss on Women. **CONTACT ADDRESS** Harold Washington Col, President, 30 E Lake St, Chicago, IL, 60601.

MILLER, CARMAN I.

PERSONAL Born 05/31/1940, Moser's River, NS, Canada **DISCIPLINE** HISTORY **EDUCATION** Acadia Univ, BA, 60, BEd 61; Dalhousie Univ, MA, 64; Univ London, PhD, 70. **CAREER** Lectr, 67-70, asst prof, 70-76, assoc prof, 76-93, chmn, 78-81 & 90-93, prof history, McGill Univ, 94-, dean arts 95-; dir, Can Inst Hist Microreproduction, 86-89; ed bd, Can Rev Stud Nationalism, 73-78; Stud Hist Politics, 79-80; Int J, 92-; adv comt, Dict Can Biog, 93-. **HONORS AND AWARDS** Fels, Dalhousie Univ grad; Univ W Ont tchg; Can Coun doctoral; Can Coun leave; SSHRCC leave; schools, Ont govt, IODE over-seas postgrad; Can Coun res grant; SSHRCC aid to publ grant, res award, int conf award **MEMBERSHIPS** Can Hist Asn (coun, 71-73, chmn prog comt, 77) **SELECTED PUBLICATIONS** Auth, The Canadian Career of the Fourth Earl of Minto, 80; auth, Painting the Map Red, 94. **CONTACT ADDRESS** Dept of History, McGill Univ, 853 Sherbrooke St W, Montreal, PQ, H3A 2T6. **EMAIL** carman@artsci.lan.mcgill.ca

MILLER, CAROL

DISCIPLINE AMERICAN STUDIES AND AMERICAN INDIAN STUDIES **EDUCATION** Univ Okla, PhD, 80. **CAREER** Assoc prof, Morse Alumni Distinguished Prof Am Stud and Am Indian Stud, Univ Minn, Twin Cities. **MEMBERSHIPS** Cherokee Nat of Okla. **RESEARCH** Contemporary American Indian literatures. **SELECTED PUBLICATIONS** Published on the performance of students of color in composition and multicultural pedagogy; recently published articles or chapters in the field of American Studies and American Indian Studies have concerned the representation of urban Indian experience in Native fiction, how treatments of World War II by Native writers address the myth of assimilation, and issues of mediation in the writing of Mourning Dove and Ella Deloria. **CONTACT ADDRESS** Univ Minn, Twin Cities, 206 Scott, Minneapolis, MN, 55455. **EMAIL** mille004@maroon.tc.umn. edu

MILLER, CHAR

PERSONAL Born 11/23/1951, St. Louis, MO, m, 1977, 2 children **DISCIPLINE** HISTORY **EDUCATION** Pitzer Col, BA, 75; Johns Hopkins Univ, MA, 77, PhD, 81. **CAREER** Vis asst prof, Univ Miami, 80-81; asst to assoc to PROF, HIST, TRINITY COL, 81-. **HONORS AND AWARDS** Hon Gilman Fel, Johns Hopkins Univ, 78-79; Outstanding prof, Trinity Univ, 86; Curr Devel Grant, Trinity Univ, 87; Bell Fel, Forest Hist Soc, 92; Archie K. Davis Fel, N Carol Soc, 93; Hoffman Fac Advisor Res Award, Phi Alpha Theta, 93; Outstanding Prof, Hum & Arts Div, Trinity Univ, Mortar Board, 96-97; The Dr. and Mrs. Z. T. Scott Fac Fel, 97; Sen Fel, The Pinchot Inst for Conservation, 98., Sen Fel, The Pinchot Inst. for Conservation, 98. **MEMBERSHIPS** Am Hist Asn; Am Soc Environ Hist; Forest Hist. Soc; Org for Am Hist. **RESEARCH** Cultural, environmental, intellectual and social histories. **SELECTED PUBLICATIONS** Ed, To Raise the Lord's Banner" Selected Correspondence of Hiram Bingham, 88; co-ed, Urban Texas: Politics and Development, in Southwest Studies, 8, 90. **CONTACT ADDRESS** History Dept, Trinity Univ, San Antonio, TX, 78212-7200. **EMAIL** Fmiller@trinity.edu

MILLER, CHARLES J.

PERSONAL Born 03/18/1919, Scranton, PA **DISCIPLINE** HISTORY **EDUCATION** Wheaton Col, Ill, BS, 40; Northwestern Univ, PhD, 47. **CAREER** Instr hist, Northwestern Univ 47; from asst prof to assoc prof, Am Univ, Beirut, 47-54, actg dean arts and sci, 53-54; vis prof, 54-56, assoc prof, 56-58, asst dean acad affairs, 72-75, PROF HIST, CALVIN COL, 58-, DEAN ACAD PROG ADMIN, 75- **MEMBERSHIPS** AHA; Soc Fr Hist Studies; Church Hist Soc; Conf Faith and Hist. **RESEARCH** Cultural exchange as a fundamental phenomenon in modern history; relation of British and American Protestantism to French Protestantism during the first half of the 19th century. **SELECTED PUBLICATIONS** Auth, Consumer Protection Law in India, Int Comp Law Quart, Vol 42, 93; Reforming Products Liability, Int Comparative Law Quart, Vol 42, 93. **CONTACT ADDRESS** Calvin Col, Grand Rapids, MI, 49506.

MILLER, CLEMENT ALBIN

PERSONAL Born 01/29/1915, Cleveland, OH, m, 1937, 3 children **DISCIPLINE** MUSICOLOGY **EDUCATION** Cleveland Inst Music, BM, 36, MM, 37; Western Reserve Univ, MA, 42; Univ Mich, PhD, 51. **CAREER** Instr music theory, Cleveland Inst Music, 37-65, head, Dept Music Hist, 61-65, Dept Musicol, 55-65, from actg dean to dean fac, 52-65; PROF MUSIC, JOHN CARROLL UNIV, 67-, Instr, Western Reserve Univ, 42-43; Guggenheim Mem Found fel, 74-75. **HONORS AND AWARDS** Outstanding Educator, Outstanding Educators Am, 75. **MEMBERSHIPS** Am Musicol Soc; Music Libr Asn; Royal Music Asn; fel Int Inst Arts and Lett; Renaissance Soc Am. **RESEARCH** Philosophy; literature, particularly medieval and Renaissance; philology. **SELECTED PUBLICATIONS** Auth, The Environmental Imagination, Thoreau, Nature Writing, and the Formation of American Culture, New England Quart Hist Rev New England Life Letters, Vol 69, 96; Musica Enchiriadis and Scolica Enchiriadis,16th Century Jour, Vol 28, 97; The Theory of Music,16th Century Jour, Vol 26, 95; Acts of Discovery, Visions of America in the Lewis and Clark Journals, William Mary Quart, Vol 51, 94. **CONTACT ADDRESS** Apt 411 18975 Van Aken Blvd, Shaker Heights, OH, 44122.

MILLER, D. GARY

PERSONAL Born 12/12/1942, Allentown, PA, m, 1967, 2 children **DISCIPLINE** LINGUISTICS CLASSICS **EDUCATION** Moravian Col, AB, 64; Harvard Univ, PhD(ling), 69. **CAREER** Instr ling, Southern Ill Univ, 68-69; asst prof, Univ Ill, Urbana, 69-71 and McGill Univ, 71-72; asst prof ling and classics, 72-76, ASSOC PROF LING AND CLASSICS, UNIV FLA, 76-, Pres, Academics Plus, Inc. **MEMBERSHIPS** Ling Soc Am; Philol. Soc. **RESEARCH** Indo-European studies; linguistic theory. **SELECTED PUBLICATIONS** Auth, A Subharmonic Vibratory Pattern in Normal Vocal Folds, JSpeech Hearing Rsch, Vol 39, 96; The Birth of a Journal, Interpretation J Bible Theol, Vol 50, 96; A Structured Approach to Voice Range Profile Phonetogram Analysis, JSpeech Hearing Rsch, Vol 37, 94. **CONTACT ADDRESS** Dept of Classics, Univ of Fla, 3c Arts and Sciences, Gainesville, FL, 32611-9500.

MILLER, DAVID

PERSONAL Born 09/18/1951, East Chicago, IN, m, 1989, 1 child **DISCIPLINE** AMERICAN STUDIES **EDUCATION** Stanford Univ, BA, 74; MA 75, PhD, 82, Brown Univ **CAREER** Visiting prof, Binnington Coll, 81-82; tutor, 82-84, Harvard Univ; visiting asst prof, 84-85, Reed Coll; Mellen Fel, 86-88, Stanford Univ; assoc prof, Allegheny Coll, 85-98 **MEMBERSHIPS** Amer Studies Assn **RESEARCH** Amer Art and Lit, 19th century, landscape **SELECTED PUBLICATIONS** Auth, Review of Nathalia Wright, ed, The Correspondence of Washington Allston, New England Quarterly, June 94; Review of The Correspondence of Washington Allston, New England Quarterly, June 94; Washington Allston and the Sister Arts Tradition in America, European Romantic Review, Summer 94; Review of Robert K. Wallace, Melville & Turner: Spheres of Love and Fright, Journal of the Early Republic, Fall 94, Review of David M. Lubin, Picturing Nation: Art and Social Change in 19th-Century America, New England Quarterly, June 95. **CONTACT ADDRESS** Dept of English, Allegheny Col, Meadville, PA, 16335. **EMAIL** dmiller@alleg.edu

MILLER, DAVID B.

PERSONAL Born 01/01/1933, Ottumwa, IA, m, 1956, 3 children **DISCIPLINE** RUSSIAN HISTORY **EDUCATION** Univ Wis, BA, 54; Columbia Univ, MA, 59, PhD(hist), 67; cert, Russ Inst, 59. **CAREER** From Asst Prof to Prof, 61-98, PROF EMERITUS RUSS HIST, ROOSEVELT UNIV, 98-, CHMN DEPT HIST, 68-; vis lectr Russ hist, Univ Chicago, 65-66. **HONORS AND AWARDS** Inter-Univ Comt Travel Grants, US/USSR exchange fel, 63-64; Am Coun Learned Soc fel, Inst Hist, Acad Sci, USSR, 69-70. **MEMBERSHIPS** AHA; Am Asn Advan Slavic Studies. **RESEARCH** History and culture of medieval Russia. **SELECTED PUBLICATIONS** Auth, The coronation of Ivan IV as tsar, Jahrbucher Geschichte Osteuropas, 12/67; Legends of the icon of Our Lady of Vladimir, Speculum, 10/68; The Lubeckers Bartholomaus Ghotan and Nicolas Bulow in Novgorod and Moscow and the Problem of Early Western Influences on Russian Culture, Viator, 9/77; The Veli-kie Minei Chetii and the Stepennaia Kniga of Metropolitan Makarii and the Origins of Russian Nationa Consciousness, Forschungen zur osteuropaischen Geschichte, 26/79. **CONTACT ADDRESS** Dept of History, Roosevelt Univ, 430 S Michigan Ave, Chicago, IL, 60605-1394.

MILLER, DAVID H.

PERSONAL Born 08/26/1938, Spangler, PA, m, 1963 **DISCIPLINE** MEDIEVAL HISTORY **EDUCATION** Baldwin-Wallace Col, BA, 63; Mich State Univ, MA, 65, PhD(hist), 67. **CAREER** Asst prof, 67-72, asst chmn dept, 76-78, ASSOC PROF HIST, UNIV OKLA, 72-, DIR CTR COMP FRONTIER STUDIES, 82-, Nat Endowment for Humanities younger scholar res fel, Belg, 68-69. **MEMBERSHIPS** AHA; Mediaeval Acad Am; Am Cath Hist Asn; Soc Comp Study Civilizations; Mid-Am Medieval Asn (pres, 78). **RESEARCH** historical theory; comparative history of complex pre-industrial societies; medieval European history. **SELECTED PUBLICATIONS** Auth, Before the Normans--Southern Italy in the 9th and-10th Centuries, Speculum J Medieval Stud, Vol 69, 94; War in the Tribal Zone--Expanding States and Indigenous Warfare, J World Hist, Vol 4, 93; The Early State and the Towns--Forms of Integration in Lombard Italy, Ad568 774, Speculum J Medieval Stud, Vol 69, 94; Frontiers of the Roman Empire--A Social and Economic Study, Am Hist Rev, Vol 0100, 95; The Early State and the Towns--Forms of Integration in Lombard Italy, Ad568-774, Speculum J Medieval Stud, Vol 69, 94; Before the Normans--Southern Italy in the 9th and 10th Centuries, Speculum J Medieval Stud, Vol 69, 94; Ethnogenesis and Religious Revitalization Beyond the Roman Frontier,The Case of Frankish Origins, J World Hist, Vol 4, 93. **CONTACT ADDRESS** Dept of Hist, Univ of Okla, 455 W Lindsay, Norman, OK, 73069.

MILLER, DAVID WILLIAM

PERSONAL Born 07/09/1940, Coudersport, PA, m, 1964 **DISCIPLINE** MODERN HISTORY **EDUCATION** Rice Univ, BA, 62; Univ Wis-Madison, MA, 63; Univ Chicago, PhD(hist of cult), 68. **CAREER** From instr to asst prof, 67-73, assoc prof, 73-80, PROF HIST, CARNEGIE-MELLON UNIV, 80-, Sr res fel, Inst Irish Studies, Queen's Univ, Belfast, 75-76. **MEMBERSHIPS** AHA; Am Comt Irish Studies. **RESEARCH** Irish history, religion, computer applications in history. **SELECTED PUBLICATIONS** Auth, Church, State and Nation in Ireland, 1898-1921, Gill & MacMillan Ltd & Univ Pittsburgh, 73; Irish Catholicism and the Great Famine, J Social Hist, fall 75; Queen's Rebels: Ulster Loyoalism in Historical Perspective, 78 & Presbyterianism and Modernization in Ulster, Past and Present, 78, Gill & MacMillan Ltd & Barnes & Noble; auth, the Armaugh Troubles, 1784-95, in Irish Peasants, Univ Wis Press, 83; ed, Peep d'Day Boys and Defenders, Public Record Office Northern Ireland, 90; princ developer, The Great American History Machine, The ePress Project, Univ Md, 94; auth, Non-professional Soldiery, c 1600- 1800, in A Military History of Ireland, Cambridge Univ Press, 96. **CONTACT ADDRESS** Dept of Hist, Carnegie Mellon Univ, 5000 Forbes Ave, Pittsburgh, PA, 15213-3890. **EMAIL** dwmiller@cmu.edu

MILLER, DOUGLAS T.

PERSONAL Born 05/27/1938, Orange, NJ, 2 children **DISCIPLINE** AMERICAN INTELLECTUAL HISTORY **EDUCATION** Colby Col, BA, 58; Columbia Univ, MA, 59; Mich State Univ, PhD(hist), 65. **CAREER** From instr to asst prof Am intellectual hist, Univ Maine, 63-66; from asst prof to assoc prof, 66-75, PROF HIST, MICH STATE UNIV, 75-, Coe res grant, Univ Maine, 64-65; all univ res grant, Mich State Univ, 67-82, res term, 68-69; Danforth Found assoc, 70-72; Am Philos Soc grant, 72-73; Fulbright Hays fel, Denmark, 79-80. **MEMBERSHIPS** AHA; Orgn Am Historians; Am Studies Asn; Popular Cult Asn. **RESEARCH** American history, 1815-1860 and 1945-1975; American utopianism. **SELECTED PUBLICATIONS** Auth, Picturing an Exhibition--The Family of Man and 1950s America, Am Hist Rev, Vol 0102, 97. **CONTACT ADDRESS** Dept of Hist, Michigan State Univ, East Lansing, MI, 48824.

MILLER, GENEVIEVE

PERSONAL Born 10/15/1914, Butler, PA **DISCIPLINE** HISTORY OF MEDICINE **EDUCATION** Groucher College, BA, 35; John Hopkins Univ, MA, 39; Cornell Univ, PhD, 55. **CA-**

REER Research Sec to Dr. Henry E Sigerist Dir of JHIHM 37-42, Asst, 43-44, Instr, 45-48, research Assoc, Hist Med, 80-94, John Hopkins Inst Hist of Med; Curator, 62-67, Dir, 67-79, Howard Dittrick Museum Hist Med; Asst Prof 53-67, Assoc Prof 67-79, Emeritus, 79-, Case West Res Sch Med. **HONORS AND AWARDS** Phi Beta Kappa; Dean Van Meter Fel; Kate Campbell Hurd Mead Lectr, ; Wm H Welch Medal; Fielding H Garrison Lectr, ; Clendening Lectr, ; CMLA Hon Fel; Who' Who In: the Midwest, the East, the World, America, Among Amer Women. **MEMBERSHIPS** AAHM; OAMH; HMHS; AHA; ISHM; SAH; VSA; SSHM; MHSMS; GSHM; AHMBA. **SELECTED PUBLICATIONS** Auth, Wm Beaumont's Formative Years, Two Early Notebooks 1811-1821: With Annotations and an Introductory Essay, NY, Henry Schuman, 46; The Adoption of Inoculation for Smallpox in England and France, Philadelphia, Univ of Penn Press, 57; Bulletin of the History of Medicine, Index to vols I-XX, 1933-1950, Baltimore, John Hopkins Press, 64; ed, Yankee in Grey: The Civil War Memoirs of Henry E Handerson, with a selection of his war-time letters, Cleveland, Press of West Res Univ, 62; Bibliography of the Writings of Henry E Sigerist, Montreal, McGill Univ Press, 66; Letters of Edward Jenner and Other Documents concerning the Early History of Vaccination, Baltimore and London, John Hopkins Press, 83. **CONTACT ADDRESS** 1890 E 107th St, Apt 816, Cleveland, OH, 44106.

MILLER, GEORGE HALL
PERSONAL Born 08/05/1919, Evanston, IL **DISCIPLINE** AMERICAN HISTORY **EDUCATION** Univ Mich, AB, 41, PhD(hist), 51; Harvard Univ, MA, 49. **CAREER** Instr hist, Univ Mich, 51-54; from asst prof to assoc prof, 54-64, prof, 64-81, EMER PROF HIST, RIPON COL, 81-, Ford Found fel, 51-52. **MEMBERSHIPS** AHA; AAUP; Orgn Am Historians; Econ Hist Asn. **RESEARCH** American economic History; local history. **SELECTED PUBLICATIONS** Auth, Archaeological Applications of Amino Acid Racemization, Archaeometry, Vol 39, 97. **CONTACT ADDRESS** Dept of Hist, Ripon Col, Ripon, WI, 54971.

MILLER, HOWARD SMITH
PERSONAL Born 02/28/1936, Pontiac, IL, m, 1958, 3 children **DISCIPLINE** AMERICAN SOCIAL HISTORY, HISTORY OF SCIENCE **EDUCATION** Bradley Univ, AB, 58; Univ Wis, MS, 60, PhD(hist), 64. **CAREER** Asst prof hist, Univ Southern Calif, 64-71; ASSOC PROF HIST, UNIV MO-ST LOUIS, 71-, Graves Award fel humanities, 70-71; vis scholar, Piedmont Cols Vis Scholar Prog, Winston-Salem, NC, 71. **HONORS AND AWARDS** Univ Southern Calif Assocs Award, 70. **MEMBERSHIPS** Orgn Am Historians; Hist Sci Soc; Soc Hist Technol. **RESEARCH** American social history; history of science; history of technology. **SELECTED PUBLICATIONS** Auth, Children of Divorce--A Practical Guide for Parents, Attorneys, and Therapists, Bull Am Academy Psych Law, Vol 24, 96. **CONTACT ADDRESS** Dept of Hist, Univ of Mo, St Louis, MO, 63121.

MILLER, HUBERT J.
PERSONAL Born 12/09/1927, Hays, KS, m, 1957, 7 children **DISCIPLINE** LATIN AMERICAN HISTORY **EDUCATION** Univ Dayton, BA, 51; St Louis Univ, MA, 54; Loyola Univ, Ill, PhD(Hist), 65. **CAREER** Teacher, Acad Sacred Heart, Mo, 51-53 & St John's High Sch, 53-54; teacher, Am Sch & dir Night Sch, English inst, El Salvador, 55-56; fel lectr Hist, Loyola Univ, Ill, 56-59; from asst prof to assoc prof Latin Am Hist, St Mary's Univ, Tex, 60-71, chmn dept Hist, 63-69; assoc prof Mex Hist, Univ Tex-Pan American, 71-; prof, 82-93; prof Emeritus, 94; Tinker Found grant, 67. **HONORS AND AWARDS** Smith-Mundt Grant to Guatemala, 59-60; NEH Grants, 79, 86, 84. **MEMBERSHIPS** AHA; Latin Am Studies Asn; AAUP; Am Oral Hist Asn. **RESEARCH** Educational ideas of Thomas Jefferson; the church and the state in Latin America, especially in Guatemala; teaching methodology of Mexican-American heritage. **SELECTED PUBLICATIONS** Auth, Hernan Cortes, 72, Bartolome de las Casas, 72, Antonio de Mendoza, 73 & Juan de Zumarraga, 73, New Santander; El Estado y la Iglesia en Guatemala, 1871-1885, La Editorial de la Universidad de San Carlos, 76; ed, chap, In: The Texas Samplar, Tex Gov Comt Aging, 76; Jose Vasconcelos, 77 & Jose de Escandon, 80, New Santander; Three chapters in Historia General de Guatemala, 97-98, chapter in Central America, Historical Perspecitves on the Contemporary Crisis, ed, Ralph Lee Woodword, Greenwood Press, 88; chapter in Liberals, the Church and Indian Peasants, ed, Robert H Jackson, New Mexico Univ Press, 97. **CONTACT ADDRESS** Dept of Philosophy, Univ of Texas-Pan American Univ, 1201 W University Dr, Edinburg, TX, 78539-2970.

MILLER, JACQUELYN C.
DISCIPLINE AMERICAN HISTORY, EARLY MODERN EUROPEAN HISTORY **EDUCATION** Milligan Col, BA, 77; Rutgers Univ, MLS, 84, MA, 88; Doctorate, 95. **CAREER** Instr, fac adv, Stud Res Asn, Phi Alfpa Theta Nat Hist Honor Soc, mem, Sullivan Leadership Award comt; Women's Stud Bd, Seattle Univ. **MEMBERSHIPS** Am Asn of Univ Women; AHA; Am Stud Asn; Inst of Early Am Hist and Cult; Orgn of Am Hist; Soc for the Hist of the Early Am Repub. **RESEARCH** Emotional self-control and the problem of domestic violence in 18th-century middle-class households. **SELECTED PUBLICATIONS** Auth, Franklin and Friends: Benjamin Fraklin's Ties to Quakers and Quakerism, Pa Hist, 57, 90; Beach Over Troubled Waters: Special Interest Groups and Public Policy Formation--The Morris Canal Abandonment Controversy, NJ Hist 109, 91; 'A Most Melancholy Scene of Devastation': The Public Response to the 1793 Philadelphia Yellow Fever Epidemic, The Pub Hist 16, 94; An 'Uncommon Tranquility of Mind': Emotional Self-Control and the Construction of a Middle-Class Identity in Eighteenth-Century Philadelphia, J of Soc Hist 30, 96; Passions and Politics: The Multiple Meanings of Bejamin Rush's Treatment for Yellow Fever, in A Melancholy Scene of Devastaton, eds, Billy G. Smith and J. Worth Estes, Watson, 97; coauth, Benjamin Rush, M.D.: A Bibliographic Guide, Greenwood, 96. **CONTACT ADDRESS** Seattle Univ, Seattle, WA, 98122-4460. **EMAIL** jcmiller@seattleu.edu

MILLER, JAMES
PERSONAL Born 02/28/1947, Chicago, IL, m, 3 children **DISCIPLINE** POLITICAL SCIENCE **EDUCATION** Pomona Col, BA, 69; Brandeis Univ, PhD, 75. **CAREER** Inst, Univ Waterloo, 75-76; asst prof, Univ Tex at Austin, 76-80; vis asst prof, Boston Univ, 86, 88; lecturer, Harvard Univ, 87-89; vis asst prof, Brown Univ, 90; vis lamont prof, Union Col, 94; fac, Skidmore Col, 88, 92-; assoc prof & dir of Liberal Stud, grad fac of polit and soc sci, 92-94; prof, polit sci, dir liberal stud, NY School for Soc Res, 94-. **HONORS AND AWARDS** Woodrow Wilson Dissertation Fellow, 72-73; NEH Fellow, 79-80, 91; ASCAP_Deems Taylor Award, 83, 84; Nat Book Critics Circle Finalist, 87; Premio Letterario Giovanni Comisso Finalist, 94; Guggenheim Fellow, 97. **RESEARCH** Political & social science. **SELECTED PUBLICATIONS** Auth, The Passion of Michael Foucalt, Simon & Schuster, 93; auth, Foucalt's Politics in Biographical Perspective, Salmagundi, no 97, winter 93; auth, From Socrates to Foucalt: The Problem of the Philisophocal Life, new formations, no 25, summer 95. **CONTACT ADDRESS** Comm on Liberal Stud, New Sch for Social Research, 65 Fifth Ave, New York, NY, 10003.

MILLER, JAMES R.
PERSONAL Born 04/28/1943, Cornwall, ON, Canada **DISCIPLINE** HISTORY **EDUCATION** Univ Toronto, BA, 66, MA, 67, PhD, 72. **CAREER** Asst prof, 70-74, assoc prof, 75-79, PROF HISTORY, UNIV SASKATCHEWAN, 79. **HONORS AND AWARDS** Can Hist Asn (pres, 96-97) **SELECTED PUBLICATIONS** Auth, Equal Rights: The Jesuits' Estates Act Controversy, 79; auth, Skyscrapers Hide the Heavens: A History of Indian-White Relations in Canada, 89; auth, Mistahimusqua (Big Bear), 96; auth, Shingwauk's Vision: A History of Native Residential Schools, 96; ed, Sweet Promises: A Reader on Indian-White Relations in Canada, 91. **CONTACT ADDRESS** Dept of History, Univ Saskatchewan, 9 Campus Dr, Saskatoon, SK, S7N 5A5. **EMAIL** miller@sask.usask.ca

MILLER, JOHN EDWARD
PERSONAL Born 03/28/1945, Beloit, KS, m, 1972, 2 children **DISCIPLINE** HISTORY **EDUCATION** Univ MO, BA, 66; Univ WI, Madison, MA, 68, PhD(hist), 73. **CAREER** Instr hist, Univ MD, Overseas Prog, 69-70; asst prof, Univ Tulsa, 73-74; asst prof, 74-78, assoc prof, 78-83, PROF HIST, SDAK STATE UNIV, 83-. **HONORS AND AWARDS** Literary Contribution Award, Mountain Plains Library Asn, 93. **MEMBERSHIPS** Orgn Am Historians; Mid-Am Am Studies Asn. **RESEARCH** Recent American history; American cultural history; social epistemology. **SELECTED PUBLICATIONS** Auth, Governor Philip F La Follette, the Wisconsin Progressives, and the New Deal, Univ MO Press, 82; Looking for History on Highway 14, IA State Univ Press, 93; Laura Ingalls Wilder's Little Town: Where History and Literature Meet, Univ Press KS, 94; Becoming Laura Ingalls Wilder: The Woman Behind the Legend, Univ MO Press, 98. **CONTACT ADDRESS** Dept of Hist, SDak State Univ, Brookings, SD, 57007-0393. **EMAIL** MillerJ@mg.sdstate.edu

MILLER, JOHN F.
PERSONAL Born 02/04/1950, Washington, DC, m, 1972 **DISCIPLINE** CLASSICS **EDUCATION** Xavier Univ, HAB, 72; Univ North Carolina Chapel Hill, MA, 74, PhD, 79. **CAREER** Vis instr, N Carolina State Univ, 77-78; asst prof, Univ Minn, 78-84; asst to assoc prof, Univ Va, 84- . **HONORS AND AWARDS** Alexander von Humboldt-Stiftung fel, Heidelberg, 85-86; ed, Class J, 91-98; ovatio & pres-elect, Class Assoc of Middle West and South, 98. **MEMBERSHIPS** APA; Class Assoc of Middle West and South; Class Assoc of Va; Roman Soc. **RESEARCH** Latin literature; Roman religion; Hellenistic poetry. **SELECTED PUBLICATIONS** Auth, Ovid's Elegiac Festivals: Studies in the Fasti, Studien zur klassischen Philologie 55, NY, 91; auth, Ovidian Allusion and the Vocabulary of Memory, Materiali e discussioni per l'analisi dei testi classici, 93; auth, Virgil, Apollo, and Augustus, in Solomon, ed, Apollo, Origins and Influences, Tucson & London, 94; auth, Apostrophe, Aside and the Didactic Addressee: Poetic Strategies in Ars Amatoria III, Materiali e discussioni per l'analisi dei testi classici, 94; auth, The Memories of Ovid's Pythagoras, Mnemosyne, 94; auth, Lucretian Moments in Ovidian Elegy, Class J, 97. **CONTACT ADDRESS** Dept of Classics, Univ of Virginia, Charlottesville, VA, 22903. **EMAIL** JFM4J@virginia.edu

MILLER, JOSEPH CALDER
PERSONAL Born 04/30/1939, Cedar Rapids, IA, m, 3 children **DISCIPLINE** AFRICAN HISTORY **EDUCATION** Wesleyan Univ, BA, 61; Northwestern Univ, MBA, 63; Univ Wis-Madison, MA, 67, PhD(hist), 72. **CAREER** Ad hoc instr hist, Exten Div, Univ Wis-Madison, 71-72, vis asst prof, 71-72; asst prof, 72-75, assoc prof hist, Univ VA, 75-82, prof 82-89, Commonwealth prof, 89-96, T. Cary Johnson Jr. prof, 96-; dean, Col of Arts and Sciences, 90-95; Am Coun Learned Socs study fel, 74-75; Am Coun Learned Socs & Soc Sci Res Coun res grant, Africa, 77; Nat Endowment for Humanities fel, 78-79, 85; Co-ed, Journal of African History, Cambridge Univ Press, 90-97. **HONORS AND AWARDS** Member, Center for Advanced Studies, Univ of Va, 89; Melville J. Herskovits Award (African Studies Asn), 89; Special citation, Bolton Prize (Conference on Latin Am Hist), 89); Distinguished Vis Lect, Foreign Service Institute, 93; Research div, Am Hist Asn, 87-89; Catherine Gould Chism Visiting Lecturer, Univ of Puget Sound, 95; President-elect, AHA, 97-President, 98. **MEMBERSHIPS** Soc Sci Hist Asn; Int Conf Group Mod Portugal; African Studies Asn; AHA; Int African Inst. **RESEARCH** History of African verbal societies; Central African history, especially Portuguese Africa; history of slavery and the slave trade. **SELECTED PUBLICATIONS** Auth, The Imbangla and the Chronology of Early Central African History, Journal of African History 13: 549-74, 72; Requiem for the 'Jaga,' Cahiers d'etudes africaines 13:121-49, 73; Nzinga of Matamba in a New Perspective, Journal of African Hist 16: 201-16, 75; Kings and Kinsmen: Early Angola, in Martin L. Kilson and Robert I. Rotberg, eds, The African Diaspora: Interpretive Essays, Harvard Univ Press, pp 75-113, 76; Some aspects of the Commercial Organization of Slaving at Luanda, Angola-1760-1830, in H. Gemery and J. Hogendorn, eds, The Uncommon Market: Essays in the Economic History of the Atlantic Slave Trade, Academic Press, pp 77-106, 79; Mortality in the Atlantic Slave Trade: Statistical Evidence on Causality, Journal of Interdisciplinary Hist 11: 385-434, 80; ed, The African Past Speaks: Essays on Oral Tradition and History, Wm. Dawson and Sons and Archon Books, 80; auth, Lineages, Ideology, and the History of Slavery in Western Central Africa, in Paul E. Lovejoy, ed, The Ideology of Slavery in Africa, Sage Pubs, pp 40-71, 81; The Significance of Drought, Disease, and Famine in the Agriculturally Marginal Zones of West-Central Africa, Journal of African Hist 23: 17-61, 82; The Paradoxes of Impoverishment in the Atlantic Zone, in David Birmingham and Phyllis Martin, eds, History of Central Africa (Longmans), vol 1, pp118-59, 83; comp, Slavery: A Worldwide Bibliography, 1900-1982, Kraus Int, 85; auth, with John K. Thornton, The Chronicle as Source, History, and Hagiography: The 'Catalogo dos Governadores de angola,' Paideuma 33: 359-89, 87; with Dauril Alden, Unwanted Cargos: The Origins and Dissemination of Smallpox via the Slave Trade from Africa to Brazil, c. 1560-1830, in Kenneth F. Kiple, ed, The African Exchange, Duke Univ Press, pp 35-109, 88; Overcrowded and Undernourished: Techniques and Consequences of Tight-Packing in the Portuguese Southern Atlantic Slave Trade, in Serge Daget, ed, De la traite a l'esclavage (Societe Francaise d'Histoire du Monde Atlantique), vol 2, pp 395-424, 88; Way of Death: Merchant Capitalism and the Angolan Slave Trade, 1730-1830, Univ of Wisc Press, 88 (Winner, Melville J. Herskovits Prize, African Studies Asn, 89; Special Citation, Conference on Latin American History Bolton Prize Committee, 89); A Marginal Institution on the Margin of the Atlantic System: The Portuguese Southern Atlantic Slave Trade in the Eighteenth Century, in Barbara Solow, ed, Slavery and the Rise of the Atlantic System, Cambridge Univ Press, pp 120-50, 91; The Slave Trade, in Encyclopedia of the North American Colonies (Jacob Ernest Cooke, ed in chief), Charles Schribners' Sons, vol 2, pp 45-66, 93; Co-ed, with R. W. Harms, D. S. Newbury, and M. D. Wagner, Paths to the African Past: African Historical Essays in Honor of Jan Vansina, ASA Press, 94; auth, The Slave Trade, in Encyclopedia of Latin American History (Barbara Tenenbaum, ed), Charles Scribner's Sons, vol 5, pp 122-27, 95; History ed, Encyclopedia of Africa South of the Sahara, gen ed, John Middleton, Simon & Schuster, 4 vols, 97; Co-ed, with Paul Finkelman, Macmillan Encyclopedia of World Slavery, Macmillan, contrib, 10 articles, 98; Comp, Slavery and Slaving in World History, A Bibliography, 1900-1991, vol 1, Slavery and Slaving in World History: A Bibliography, 1902-1996, vol 2. M. E. Sharpe, 98. **CONTACT ADDRESS** Dept of Hist, Univ of Va, 1 Randall Hall, Charlottesville, VA, 22903-3244.

MILLER, JUDITH A.
DISCIPLINE HISTORY **EDUCATION** Coll Wooster, BA, 78; Duke Univ, PhD, 87. **CAREER** Assoc prof **HONORS AND AWARDS** Gershenkron Prize, Econ Hist Asn; Koren Prize, Soc Fr Histl Studies. **RESEARCH** 18th and 19th-century French history; opera and theater from 1789 to 1830; modern European economic history. **SELECTED PUBLICATIONS** Auth, Politics and Urban Provisioning Crises: Bakers, Police, and Parlements in France, 1750-1793. **CONTACT ADDRESS** Dept History, Emory Univ, 221 Bowden Hall, 561 Kilgo Cir, Atlanta, GA, 30322-1950. **EMAIL** histjam@emory.edu

MILLER, KERBY A.
PERSONAL Born 12/30/1944, Phoenix, AZ, m, 1979, 3 children **DISCIPLINE** AMERICAN & MODERN IRISH HISTORY **EDUCATION** Pomona Col, BA, 66; Univ Calif, Berkeley,

MA, 67, PhD(Hist), 76. **CAREER** Lectr Hist, Univ Calif, Berkeley, 76-77; sr fel, Inst Irish Studies, Queen's Univ Belfast, 77-78; asst prof Hist, Univ Mo-Columbia, 78-. **MEMBERSHIPS** AHA; Orgn Am Historians; Immigration Hist Soc; Irish Hist Soc; Am Comt Irish Studies. **RESEARCH** Irish immigration to North America; American social & urban history; modern Irish socio-economic and cultural history. **SELECTED PUBLICATIONS** Auth, Emigrants and exiles: Irish cultures and Irish emigration to North America, 1790-1922, Irish Hist Studies, 9/80; contribr, Irish emigration and the popular image of America in rural Ireland, In: Emigration: The Irish Experience, Educ Bk Co, Dublin, Ireland, 82. **CONTACT ADDRESS** Univ of Missouri, 101 Read Hall, Columbia, MO, 65211-0001. **EMAIL** histkm@showme.missouri.edu

MILLER, M. SAMMYE
PERSONAL Born 02/23/1947, Philadelphia, PA, m **DISCIPLINE** HISTORY **EDUCATION** Delaware State University, BA 1968; Trinity Coll Washington, MAT 1970; The Catholic Univ of Amer, PhD 1977; Stanford Univ, Post Doc Fellow 1983. **CAREER** Natl Endowment for the Humanities, humanist admin & policy analyst 1978-80; Assn for the Study of Afro-Amer Life & History Inc, exec dir 1983-84; BOWIE STATE UNIV, DEPT CHMN/PROF OF HIST, currently. **HONORS AND AWARDS** NAFEO Research Achievemnt Award Natl Assn for Equal Opportunity in Higher Educ 1984; fellowships Knights of Columbus 1970; Penfield Fellow; Bd Trustees Scholar, Catholic Univ. **MEMBERSHIPS** Southern History Assn; Org of Amer Historian; The Amer Historical Assn; life mem Kappa Alpha Psi Fraternity Phi Alpha Theta Intl; Hon Soc in History; ASALH; Knights of Columbus. **CONTACT ADDRESS** Dept of History & Government, Bowie State Univ, Bowie, MD, 20715. **EMAIL** millers@boedd.minc.umd.edu

MILLER, MARA
DISCIPLINE WOMEN'S VOICES AND IMAGES OF WOMEN IN JAPANESE ART **EDUCATION** Yale Univ, PhD, 87. **CAREER** Emory Univ. **SELECTED PUBLICATIONS** Auth, The Garden as an Art. **CONTACT ADDRESS** Emory Univ, Atlanta, GA, 30322-1950. **EMAIL** jmeye03@emory.edu

MILLER, MARLA R.
DISCIPLINE HISTORY **EDUCATION** Univ Wis - Madison, BA, 88; Univ N Carol at Chapel Hill, PhD, 97. **CAREER** HIST, UNIV NC CHAPEL HILL **MEMBERSHIPS** Am Antiquarian Soc **SELECTED PUBLICATIONS** Auth, My Daily Bread Depends Upon My Labor: Craftswomen, Community and the Marketplace in Rural Massachusetts, 1740-1820; coauth, "Common Parlors: Women and the Reservation Community Identity in Pittsfield, MA, 1870-1920," Gender & Hist 6, 94. **CONTACT ADDRESS** Dept of Hist, UN. Carolina-Chapel Hill, CB No. 3195, Chapel Hill, NC, 27599. **EMAIL** mrm@email.unc.edu

MILLER, MARTIN ALAN
PERSONAL Born 05/23/1938, Baltimore, MD, m, 1964, 2 children **DISCIPLINE** RUSSIAN & EUROPEAN HISTORY **EDUCATION** Univ Md, AB, 60; Univ Chicago, MA, 62, PhD(Russ hist), 67. **CAREER** Instr western civilization, Stanford Univ, 67-70; prof Russ hist, Duke Univ, 70-, vis prof, New Sch Soc Res, 79-80; US-USSR cult exchange, 65 & 76; Nat Inst Ment Health fel, 78-79; Nat Coun for Soviet Res fel, 82; sr fel, Russ Inst, Columbia Univ, 82. **HONORS AND AWARDS** Ford Found 88-89; Int Research & Exchanges Board, 90; Nat Endowment for the Humanities, 90-91. **MEMBERSHIPS** AHA; Am Asn Advan Slavic Studies; Labor Hist. **RESEARCH** Nineteenth century Russian intelligentsia, revolutionary movement, emigration; psychoanalysis; terrorism. **SELECTED PUBLICATIONS** Auth, Kropotkin, Univ Chicago Press, 76 & 79; The Russian Revolutionary Emigres, 1825-1870, Hopkins, 86; Freud and the Bolsheviks: Psychoanalysis in Russia and the Soviet Union, Yale, 98. **CONTACT ADDRESS** Dept of History, Duke Univ, PO Box 90719, Durham, NC, 27708-0719. **EMAIL** mmiller@acpub.duke.edu

MILLER, NAOMI
PERSONAL Born 02/28/1928, New York, NY, s **DISCIPLINE** HUMANITIES AND ART HISTORY **EDUCATION** City Col, NY, BS, 48; Columbia Univ, MA, 50; NY Univ, Inst of Fine Arts, MA, 60; PhD, 66. **CAREER** Vis prof, RI Sch of Design, Providence, RI, 63-64; Univ BC, Vancouver, 67; Hebrew Univ of Jerusalem, 80; asst, assoc, prof, art hist, Boston Univ, 63-80; Univ Calif Berkeley, 64-. **HONORS AND AWARDS** Fel, Nat Endow for the Humanities, 72-73; Dumbarton Oaks, Wash, DC, Harvard Univ Ctr for Landscape Studies, 76-77, 83-89; Villa I Tatti, Florence, 84-85; Ctr for Advan Studies in Visual Arts, Nat Gallery of Art, Wash, DC, Winter, 88, 95; Padua Facul Exchange Prog, Padua, Summer, 90. **MEMBERSHIPS** Col Art Asn; Soc of Archit Hist. **RESEARCH** Renaissance to modern: architecture and urbanism; Landscape studies. **SELECTED PUBLICATIONS** Coauth, Architecture in Boston, 1975-90, Munich, Prestel, 90; auth, Renaissance Bologna: A Study in Architectural Form and Content, Peter Lang, Univ Ks Humanistic Studies, 56, 89; Heavenly Caves: Reflections on the Garden Grotto, NY, Braziller, 82; coauth, Fons Sapientiae: Garden Fountains in Illustrated Books, Sixteenth-Eighteeth Centuries, Wash, DC, Dum Dumbarton Oaks, 77; auth, French Renaissance Fountains, NY, Garland, 77; **CONTACT ADDRESS** Art History Dept., Boston Univ, 725 Commonwealth Av., Boston, MA, 02215. **EMAIL** nmiller@bu.edu

MILLER, NAOMI F.
DISCIPLINE ANTHROPOLOGY **EDUCATION** Univ MI, BA 72, MA 73, PhD 82. **CAREER** Visiting Asst Prof, Washington Univ, St. Louis, 84-86; Research Specialist, Applied Sci Ctr for Archaeology, 87-97; Senior Research Scientist, Univ PA Museum, 97-present. **RESEARCH** Ancient environment and land use systems (especially in the Near East); complex societies (especially their economic base) **SELECTED PUBLICATIONS** Auth, Bulletin of the American Schools of Oriental Research, The Aspalathus Caper, 95; Current Anthropology, Seed Eaters of the Ancient Near East, 96; MASCA Research Papers in Science and Archaeology, Farming and Herding along the Euphrates: Environmental Constraint and Cultural Choice (Fourth to Second Millennia B.C.), 97; Paleorient, The Macrobotanical Evidence for Vegetation in the Near East, c. 18000/16000 bc to 4000 bc, 97. **CONTACT ADDRESS** Museum Applied Science Center for Archaeology, Univ of Pennsylvania Museum, 33rd and S, Philadelphia, PA, 19104. **EMAIL** nmiller0@sas.upenn.edu

MILLER, PATRICIA COX
PERSONAL Born 01/19/1947, Washington, DC, m **DISCIPLINE** RELIGION IN LATE ANTIQUITY **EDUCATION** Mary Washington Col of U Va, BA, 69; Univ Chicago, MA, 72; PhD, 79. **CAREER** Asst prof, Univ Wash, 75-76; asst prof, Syracuse Univ, 77-83; assoc prof, Syracuse Univ, 83-95; prof, Syracuse Univ, 95-; dir grad studies, dept relig, Syracuse Univ, 92-. **HONORS AND AWARDS** Pres, Namer Patristics Soc, 96-97; fel, NEH, 83; Kent fel, Univ Chicago, 72-75. **MEMBERSHIPS** Amer Acad Relig; Namer Patristics Soc. **RESEARCH** Religion and Aesthetics in Late Antiquity; Early Christian asceticism; Early Christian and Pagan hagiography. **SELECTED PUBLICATIONS** Auth, Dreams in Late Antiquity: Studies in the Imagination of a Culture, Princeton, Princeton Univ Press, 94; Biography in Late Antiquity: A Quest for the Holy Man, Berkeley, Univ Calif Press, 83; Articles, Differential Networks: Relics and Other Fragments in Late Antiquity, Jour of Early Christ Studies, 6, 113-38, 98; Strategies of Representation in Collective Biography: Constructing the Subject as Holy, Greek Biography and Panegyrics in Late Antiquity, ed Tomas Hagg and Philip Rousseau, Berkeley, Univ Calif Press, 98; Jerome's Centaur: A Hyper-Icon of the Desert, Jour of Early Christ Studies, 4, 209-33, 96; Dreaming the Body: An Aesthetics of Asceticism, Asceticism, ed Vincent Wimbush and Richard Valantasis, New York, Oxford Univ Press, 281-300, 95; Desert Asceticism and The Body from Nowhere, Jour of Early Christ Studies, 2, 137-53, 1994; The Blazing Body: Ascetic Desire in Jerome's Letter to Eustochium, Jour of Early Christian Studies, 1, 21-45, 93; The Devil's Gateway: An Eros of Difference in the Dreams of Perpetua, Dreaming, 2, 45-63, 92; Plenty Sleeps There: The Myth of Eros and Psyche in Plotinus and Gnosticism, Neoplatonism and Gnosticism, ed R. Wallis and J. Bregman, Stony Brook, State Univ of NY Press, 223-38, 92. **CONTACT ADDRESS** Dept. of Religion, Syracuse Univ, 501 Hall of Languages, Syracuse, NY, 13244-1170. **EMAIL** plmiller@syr.edu

MILLER, PATRICK
DISCIPLINE MUSIC **EDUCATION** Univ Kans, BM, MM; Univ Mich, PhD. **CAREER** Former fac, Pembroke State Univ; Univ Mi; Univ North Texas; Chairperson, Music Theory Department, Hartt, 1980-. **MEMBERSHIPS** Musical Heritage Soc. **SELECTED PUBLICATIONS** Auth, College Music Symposium; Perspectives of New Music; Theory & Practice; Gwynn S. McPeek Festschrift. **CONTACT ADDRESS** Hartt Sch Music, Univ Hartford, 200 Bloomfield Ave, West Hartford, CT, 06117.

MILLER, RANDALL MARTIN
PERSONAL Born 04/16/1945, Chicago, IL, m, 1968, 1 child **DISCIPLINE** AMERICAN HISTORY **EDUCATION** Hope Col, AB, 67; OH State Univ, MA, 68, PhD(Am hist), 71. **CAREER** Asst prof hist, Wesley Col, DE, 71-72; asst prof Am hist, 72-78, assoc prof hist, 78-82, prof hist, St Joseph's Univ, PA, 82-; Inst Ed Hist Doc fel, 73; Robert S Starobin Mem Libr fel, 75; Am Coun of Learned Soc fel, 75-76 & 80-81; Danforth assoc, 81-; ed, PA Magazine of Hist and Biography, 86-91. **HONORS AND AWARDS** Lindback Award, 79; Tengelman Award, 97. **MEMBERSHIPS** AHA; Orgn Am Historians; Southern Hist Asn. **RESEARCH** Ethnic studies; South and slavery; religion and politics. **SELECTED PUBLICATIONS** Auth, The Cotton Mill Movement in Alabama, Arno, 78; Kaleidoscopic Lens, Ozer, 80; auth, Afro-American Slaves, Krieger, 81; The Fabric of Control: Slavery in Antebellum Southern Textile Mills, Bus Hist Rev, 12/81; A Warm and Zealous Spirit: John J Zubly, Mercer Univ, 82; Dear Master: Letters of a Slavery Family, Cornell, 78, rev ed, GA, 90; Catholics in the Old South, Mercer, 83; Ethnic and Racial Images in American Film and Television, Garland, 87; co-ed, Dictionary of Afro-American Slavery, Greenwood, 88, rev ed, Praeger, 97; Book of American Diaries, AVon, 95; American Reform and Reformers, Greenwood, 97; Religion and the Civil War, Oxford, 98; and others. **CONTACT ADDRESS** Dept of Hist, St Joseph's Univ, 5600 City Ave, Philadelphia, PA, 19131-1376. **EMAIL** miller@sju.edu

MILLER, RICHARD G.
DISCIPLINE HISTORY **EDUCATION** Univ Nebr, PhD, 70. **CAREER** Prof. **RESEARCH** Urbanization as an agent of social change. **SELECTED PUBLICATIONS** Auth, pubs on city and social classes in 19th century America. **CONTACT ADDRESS** History Dept, State Univ of West Georgia, Carrollton, GA, 30118. **EMAIL** dmiller@westga.edu

MILLER, SALLY M.
PERSONAL Born 04/13/1937, Chicago, IL **DISCIPLINE** AMERICAN HISTORY **EDUCATION** Univ Ill, BA, 58; Univ Chicago, AM, 63; Univ Toronto, PhD, 66. **CAREER** From instr to asst prof Am thought & lang, Mich State Univ, 65-67; asst prof, 67-70, assoc prof, 70-75, PROF HIST, UNIV OF THE PAC, 75-, Res awards, Univ of the Pac, 70, 71, 72, 76, 78 & 81; Am Philos Soc travel grants, 71 & 76; vis sr lectr hist, Univ Warwick, 78-79; Am Coun Learned Soc travel grant, 79; Calif Coun Humanities grant, 81. **HONORS AND AWARDS** Distinguished Fac Award, Univ of the Pac, 76; Fulbright lectr, Univ Otago, NZ, 86; Fulbright lectr, Turku Univ, Finland, 96; newberry Lib Fel, 92; Missouri Hist Book Award, 94. **MEMBERSHIPS** AHA; Orgn Am Historians; Immigration Hist Soc; West Coast Asn Women Historians; Europ Labor & Working Class Hist Study Group. **RESEARCH** American intellectual history; progressive era; labor, immigration and women's history. **SELECTED PUBLICATIONS** Auth, Socialist Party Decline and World War I, Sci & Soc, winter 70; "The Socialist Party and the Negro, 1901-1920," Journal of Negro History, 7/71; Victor Berger and the Promise of Constructive Socialism, Greenwood, 73; The Radical Immigrant, 1820-1920, Twayne, 74; contribr, Milwaukee: Of Ethnicity and Labor, In: Socialism and the Cities, Kennikat, 75; auth, Americans and the Second International, Proc Am Philos Soc, 76; "From Sweatshop Worker to Labor Leader: Theresa Malkiel," American Jewish History Quarterly, 79; ed, Flawed Liberation: Socialism & Feminism, Greenwood, 81; The Writings and Speeches of Kate Richards O'Hare, La State Univ Press, 82; ed, The Ethnic Press in the United States; Historical Analysis and Sourcebook, Greenwood, 87; auth, From Prairie to Prison: The Life of Social Activist Kate Richards O'Hare, Missouri, 93; co-ed, American Labor in the Era of World War II, Greenwood, 93; auth, Race, Ethnicity and Gender in Early 20th Century American Socialism, Garland, 96. **CONTACT ADDRESS** Dept of History, Univ of the Pacific, Stockton, 3601 Pacific Ave, Stockton, CA, 95211-0197. **EMAIL** smiller3@uop.edu

MILLER, STEPHEN G.
PERSONAL Born 06/22/1942, Goshen, IN **DISCIPLINE** CLASSICAL ARCHAEOLOGY **EDUCATION** Wabash Col, BA (Greek), 64; Princeton Univ, MA, 67, PhD, 70. **CAREER** Res asst, Inst Advanced Study, Princeton, 72-73; Dir, Nemea Excavations, 73-; asst prof, 73-75, assoc prof, 75-81, PROF, DEPT OF CLASSICS, UNIV CA, BERKELEY, 81-; Dir, Am School of Classical Studies, Athens, 82-87; brd of dirs, Fulbright Found in Greece, 82-87; brd advisors to Minister of Culture, Greece, 95-. **HONORS AND AWARDS** Various fels, Dept Art and Archaeology, Princeton Univ, 64-68; Fulbright fel to Greece, 68-69; Agora Excavating fel, 69-72; Am Council Learned Socs, summer grant-in-aid, 72; principal investigator, NEH, 75-77, 77-79, 79-81; Humanities res fel, Univ CA, 76-77, 80-81; corresponding mem, Deutsches Archaologisches Institut, 79; Honorary citizen, Archaia Nemea, Greece, 81; Order of the Golden Bear, Univ CA, 91; Governor's Medal for Distinguished Service to the Korinthia, 91; active mem, Academia Scientarum et Artium Europaeae, 92; Phi Beta Kappa vis scholar, 92-93; President's res fel, Univ CA, 94-95; Honorary Citizen, Leontion, Greece, 95; Honorary President, Soc for the revival of the Nemean Games, 95; Honorary Doctorate, Univ Athens, 96; decorated by President K. Stephanopoulos of the Hellinic Republic, 96; other honorary awards, 97-98. **SELECTED PUBLICATIONS** Auth, Moschos the Beautiful: An Athletic Graffito in Nemea, B. R. Baker and J. E. Fischer, ed, Exegisti Monumentum Aere Perennius, Festschrift J. Charles, Indianapolis, 94; The New Nemean Games, video, prod and dir, 95; Nemea, A Brief Guide, Athens, 95; Old Metroon and Old Bouleterion in the Classical Agora of Athens, Historia Einzelschriften 95, 95; Architecture as Evidence for the Identity of a Polis, Acts of the Copenhagen Polis Centre II, 95; Nemea, Encyclopedia dell'Arte Antica, supp II, Rome, 95; A Day at the Races: Living the Olympic Idea, CA Monthly 107, 96; Nemea, An Encyclopedia of the History of Classical Archaeology, Westport, 96; Stadiums, The Oxford Encyclopedia of Archaeology in the Near East 5, Oxford, 97; There's No Place Like Home for Our Heritage, Mycenaean Treasures of the Aegean Bronze Age Repatriated, ed R. Howland, Washington, 97. **CONTACT ADDRESS** Dept of Classics, Univ California, MC #2520, Berkeley, CA, 94720-2520. **EMAIL** sgmnemea@socrates.berkeley.edu

MILLER, SUSAN
DISCIPLINE NATIVE AMERICAN HISTORY **EDUCATION** Univ Nebr, Lincoln, PhD, 97. **CAREER** Asst prof Hist

& Ethnic Stud, Univ Nebr, Lincoln. **HONORS AND AWARDS** Outstanding Dissertation on Okla Hist, Okla Hist Soc, 97; Distinguished Doctoral Dissertation, Univ Nebr, Lincoln, 98. **SELECTED PUBLICATIONS** Published several articles in the ethnohistory of native Americans and the American West. **CONTACT ADDRESS** Univ Nebr, Lincoln, 639 Oldfat, Lincoln, NE, 68588-0417. **EMAIL** smiller@unlinfo.unl.edu

MILLER, SUSAN P.
DISCIPLINE LEARNING DISABILITIES; LEARNING STRATEGIES, EDUCATIONAL ADMINISTRATION **EDUCATION** Univ Fla, PhD. **CAREER** Coordr, undergrad stud, grad generalist, Univ Nev, Las Vegas. **SELECTED PUBLICATIONS** Auth, Perspectives on mathematics instruction, in Deshler, D, Ellis, E S, & Lenz, B K, Teaching adolescents with learning disabilities (2nd ed), Love Publ Co, 96; coauth, Strategic Math Series, Edge Enterprises, 91-94; Teaching initial multiplication skills to students with disabilities in general education classrooms, Learning Disabilities Res and Pract, 10, 95. **CONTACT ADDRESS** Dept of Spec Educ, Univ Nev, Las Vegas, 4505 Maryland Pky, Las Vegas, NV, 89154-3014. **EMAIL** millersp@nevada.edu

MILLER, TICE LEWIS
PERSONAL Born 08/11/1938, Lexington, NE, m, 1963, 1 child **DISCIPLINE** THEATRE HISTORY **EDUCATION** Kearney State Col, BA, 60; Univ Nebr, Lincoln, MA, 61; Univ Ill, Urbana, PhD(Theatre), 68. **CAREER** Instr speech & theatre, Kansas City Jr Col, 61-62; asst prof theatre, Univ WFla, 68-72; assoc prof, 72-79, prof Theatre & Drama, Univ Nebr, Lincoln, 79-, fel, Ctr Great Plains Studies, 78. **HONORS AND AWARDS** Fellow, College of Fellows of American Theatre, JFK Center, Washington, D.C., 92; Sam Davidson Theatre Award, Lincoln Arts Council, 98. **MEMBERSHIPS** Am Soc Theatre Res; Am Theatre Asn; Univ & Col Theatre Asn; Mid-Am Theatre Conf. **RESEARCH** American theatre; 19th century American theatre; American theatre critics. **SELECTED PUBLICATIONS** Auth, John Ranken Towse: Last of the Victorian critics, Educ Theatre J, 5/70; Towse on Reform in the American Theatre, Cent States Speech Commun J, winter 72; Early Cultural History of Nebraska: The Role of the Opera House, Nebr Speech Commun J, 74; Alan Dale: The Hearst critic, Educ Theatre J, 3/74; From Winter to Nathan: The Critics Influence on the American Theatre, Southern Speech Commun J, winter 76; Identifying the Dramatic Writers for Wilkes's Spirit of the Times, 1859-1902, Theatre Survey, 5/79; Bohemians and Critics: Nineteenth Century Theatre Criticism, Scarecrow Press Inc, 81; Fitz-James O'Brien: Irish Playwright & Critic in New York, 1851-1862, Nineteenth Century Theatre Res, fall 82; co-ed, Cambridge Guide to American Theatre, 93; co-ed, The American Stage, Cambridge, 93; editorial advisory board & major contributor, Cambridge Guide to Theatre, 88, 92, 95. **CONTACT ADDRESS** Dept of Theatre Arts, Univ of Nebr, PO Box 880201, Lincoln, NE, 68588-0201. **EMAIL** tmiller@unlinfo.unl.edu

MILLER, TIMOTHY
PERSONAL Born 08/23/1944, Wichita, KS, m, 1982, 2 children **DISCIPLINE** AMERICAN STUDIES **EDUCATION** Univ Kans, PhD, 73. **CAREER** Lectr, relig, Univ Kans, 73-88; asst prof to assoc prof to prof and chair, relig, Univ Kans, 88-; visiting prof, Dartmouth Col, 95. **MEMBERSHIPS** Amer Acad of Relig; Communal Studies Asn; Soc for the Sci Study of Relig; Mid-Amer Amer Studies Asn. **RESEARCH** History of intentional communities; Alternative religions in America; American religious history. **SELECTED PUBLICATIONS** Auth, The Quest for Utopia in Twentieth-Century America, vol 1, 1900-1960, Syracuse Univ Press, 98; auth, The Hippies and American Values, Univ of Tenn Press, 91; auth, American Communes, 1860-1960: A Bibliography, Garland Publ Co, 90; auth, Following in His Steps: A Biography of Charles M. Sheldon, Univ Tenn Press, 87; ed, America's Alternative Religions, State Univ of NY Press, 95; ed, When Prophets Die: The Postcharismatic Fate of New Religious Movements, State Univ of NY Press, 91; article, Artists' Colonies as Communal Societies in the Arts and Crafts Era, Communal Soc, 16, 96; article, Two appendices to America's Alternative Religions, Albany, State Univ of NY Press, 417-442, 95; co-auth, article, Seven section introductions to America's Alternative Religions, Albany, State Univ of NY Press, 95; article, The Evolution of Hippie Communal Spirituality: The Farm and Other Hippies Who Didn't Give Up, America's Alternative Religions, Albany, State Univ of NY Press, 95; article, Black Jews and Black Muslims, America's Alternative Religions, Albany, State Univ of NY Press, 277-283, 95; article, Introduction to America's Alternative Religions, Albany, State Univ of NY Press, 1-10, 95; article, Peter Cornelius Plockhoy and the Beginnings of the American Communal Tradition, Gone to Croatan: Origins of North American Dropout Culture, NY, Autonomedia, 117-26, 93. **CONTACT ADDRESS** Dept of Religious Studies, Univ of Kansas, Lawrence, KS, 66045. **EMAIL** tkansas@ukans.edu

MILLER, VIRGINIA E.
DISCIPLINE ART HISTORY **EDUCATION** Univ TX Austin, PhD. **CAREER** Assoc prof, Univ IL at Chicago. **RESEARCH** Pre-Columbian and native Am art. **SELECTED PUBLICATIONS** Ed, The Role of Gender in Precolumbian Art and Architecture. **CONTACT ADDRESS** Art Hist Dept, Univ Illinois Chicago, S Halsted St, PO Box 705, Chicago, IL, 60607.

MILLER, WORTH ROBERT
PERSONAL Born 09/19/1943, Tucson, AZ **DISCIPLINE** HISTORY **CAREER** Instr, Univ Okla, 84-85; vis asst prof, E Texas State Univ, 85-86; vis asst prof, Texas A&M Univ, 86-87; ASST PROF TO PROF, SW MO STATE UNIV, 87-. **HONORS AND AWARDS** SMSU Found Fac Achievement Award for Excellence in Research, 91-92. **MEMBERSHIPS** Southern Hist Asn, Soc for the Hist of the Gilded Age and Progressive Era. **RESEARCH** Populism, progressivism, Okla, Texas. **SELECTED PUBLICATIONS** Auth, Oklahoma Populism: A History of the People's Part in the Oklahoma Territory, 87, Univ Okla Press; auth, "Farmers and Third-Party Politics in Late Nineteenth Century America," in The Gilded Age: Essays on the Origins of Modern America, 96, Scholarly Resources; auth, "The Republican Tradition," in American Populism, 94, D.C. Heath; coauth, "Ethnic Conflict and Machine Politics in San Antonio," Journal of Urban History, Aug 93; auth, "A Centennial Historiography of American Populism," Kansas History: A Journal of the Central Plains, Spring 93. **CONTACT ADDRESS** Dept of History, Southwest Missouri State Univ, Springfield, MO, 65804. **EMAIL** wrm043p@mail.smsu.edu

MILLER, ZANE L.
PERSONAL Born 05/19/1934, Lima, OH, m, 1955 **DISCIPLINE** AMERICAN URBAN HISTORY **EDUCATION** Miami Univ, BS, 56, MA, 59; Univ Chicago, PhD(hist), 66. **CAREER** Instr hist, Northwestern Univ, 64-65; from instr to assoc prof, 65-74, prof hist, Univ Cincinnati, 74-; Nat Coun for Humanities younger scholar fel, 68; NSF res grant, 68-70; res assoc, Ctr Urban Studies, Univ Chicago, 70-71; fel, Newberry Libr, Chicago, winter 76; vis scholar, Afro Am Curric, Univ NC, spring 81; co-dir, Ctr Neighborhood Community Studies, Univ Cincinnati, 81-. **MEMBERSHIPS** AHA; Southern Hist Asn; Orgn Am Historians. **RESEARCH** American urban and social history; American political history, 1865 to the present. **SELECTED PUBLICATIONS** Auth, Boss Cox's Cincinnati, J Am Hist, spring 68; Boss Cox's Cincinnati, Oxford Univ, 68; co-ed, Physician to the West, Univ Ky, 70; auth, Urbanization of Modern America: a Brief History, Harcourt, 73; contrib, The New Urban History, Princeton Univ, 75; The Urban History Yearbook, Leicester Univ, 77; auth, Scarcity, abundance and American urban history, J Urban Hist, 2/78; Suburb, Univ Tenn, 81; Changing Plans for America's Inner Cities: Cincinnatti's Over-the-Rhine and Twentieth Century Urbanism, Columbus: The Ohio State University Press, 98. **CONTACT ADDRESS** Dept of History, Univ of Cincinnati, PO Box 210373, Cincinnati, OH, 45221-0373. **EMAIL** millerzl@email.uc.edu

MILLER-JONES, DALTON
PERSONAL Born 07/06/1940, St. Louis, MO, m **DISCIPLINE** PSYCHOLOGY **EDUCATION** Rutgers Univ, BA & BS 1962; Tufts Univ, MS Experimental Psy 1965; Cornell Univ, PhD Psychology 1973. **CAREER** Cornell Univ Africana Studies, lecturer & rsch assoc 1969-73; Univ of Mass/Amherst, asst prof 1973-82; Williams Coll, Henry Luce assoc prof 1982-84; CITY UNIV OF NEW YORK GRAD SCHOOL, ASSOC PROF 1984-. **HONORS AND AWARDS** NSF & Office Education Fellowships 1966-69; NSF 1972; Carnegie Corp New York Grant 1972-73; articles and book chapters on Black children's language & thought in J of Black Studies and Academic Press 1979-84. **MEMBERSHIPS** Adjunct prof & fellow Inst Comparative Human Cognition Rockefeller Univ, NY 1974-76; member Soc for Rsch in Child Dev 1978-; empirical rsch consultant in Black psychology for New York Board of Ed, Am Can Co & Black community organizations 1980; Jean Piaget Society 1981-; Amer Psych Assn 1982-; Amer Ed Rsch Assn 1981-. **CONTACT ADDRESS** Psychology Dept, Graduate Sch and Univ Ctr, CUNY, 33 W 42nd St, New York, NY, 10036.

MILLETT, ALLAN REED
PERSONAL Born 10/22/1937, New York, NY, m, 1960, 2 children **DISCIPLINE** UNITED STATES MILITARY HISTORY **EDUCATION** DePauw Univ, BA, 59; OH State Univ, MA, 63, PhD(hist), 66. **CAREER** Asst prof hist, Univ MO-Columbia, 66-69; assoc prof & mem res fac, Mershon Ctr, 69-74, Prof hist & dir prog inter security & Mil affairs, Mershon Ctr, OH State Univ, 74-91, Univ MO Res Coun fel, 68; Nat Endowment for Hum fel, 69; Am Philos Soc fel, 69, Lec, Korea, 91; Korea Foundation, 96; General Raymond E. Mason, Jr. Prof of Mil Hist, OH State Univ, 91-. **HONORS AND AWARDS** Distinguished Fulbright **MEMBERSHIPS** Am Mil Inst; AHA; Orgn Am Historians; Inter-Univ Sem Armed Forces & Soc; US Commissions. **RESEARCH** US mil hist; Korean War; hist of the Marine Corps. **SELECTED PUBLICATIONS** Auth, 70; The United States and Cuba: The uncomfortable abrazo, 1898-1968, In: Twentieth Century American Foreign Policy, OH State Univ, 71; The politics of intervention: The military occupation of Cuba, 1906-1909, OH State Univ, 69; auth, The General: Robert L Bullard and Officership in the US Army, Greenwood, 75; Military Professionalism and Officership in America & Academic Education in National Security Policy, OH State Univ, 77; Semper Fidelis: History of the US Marine Corps, Macmillan, 80; In Many a Strife: Gerald C. Thomas and the US Marine Corps, Naval Inst Press, 93; co-auth, For the Common Defense: The Military History of the United States of America, Free Press, 94, rev ed, 94. **CONTACT ADDRESS** Dept of History, Ohio State Univ, 230 W 17th Ave, Columbus, OH, 43210-1361. **EMAIL** millett.2@osu.edu

MILLS, ERIC L.
PERSONAL Born 07/07/1936, Toronto, ON, Canada **DISCIPLINE** HISTORY OF SCIENCE **EDUCATION** Carleton Univ, BS, 59; Yale Univ, MS, 62; PhD, 64. **CAREER** Asst prof, Queen's Univ, 63-67; assoc prof, 67-71, PROF OCEANOGRAPHY & BIOL, 71-, PROF HIST SCIENCE, DALHOUSIE UNIV, 94-; vis fel, Cambridge Univ, 74-75; Nuffield fel, Univ Edinburgh, 81-82; guest prof, Univ Kiel, 84, 88; H Burr Steinbach Vis Scholar, Woods Hole Oceanographic Inst, 88; Ritter Mem Fel, Scripps Inst Oceanography, 90; Jack Ludwick Lectr, Old Dominion Univ, 91; vis scholar, Scripps Inst Oceanography, 95-96. **MEMBERSHIPS** NS Bird Soc; Hist Sci Soc; Soc Hist Natural Hist. **SELECTED PUBLICATIONS** Auth & ed, One Hundred Years of Oceanography, 75; Biological Oceanography: An Early History, 89. **CONTACT ADDRESS** Dalhousie Univ, Halifax, NS, B3H 4J1.

MILNER, CLYDE A., II
PERSONAL Born 10/19/1948, Durham, NC, m, 1977, 2 children **DISCIPLINE** AMERICAN STUDIES **EDUCATION** Univ NC Chapel Hill, BA, 71; Yale Univ, MA, 73, MPhil, 74, PhD, 79. **CAREER** Assoc ed to coed to ed to exec ed, Western Historical Quarterly, 84- ; instr to asst prof to assoc prof to prof, Utah St Univ, 76- . **HONORS AND AWARDS** Vivian A Paladin Writing Award, 87; Western Heritage Award, 95; Caughey W Hist Assoc Award, 95; Frederick W. Beinecke Fel, 97; Charles Redd Prize, 96. **MEMBERSHIPS** W Hist Assoc; W Lit Assoc; Org of Amer Hist; Amer Hist Assoc; Amer Stud Assoc; Amer Folklore Soc; Amer Soc for Environ Hist. **RESEARCH** History of N Amer West **SELECTED PUBLICATIONS** Coed, Trails: Toward a New Western History, Univ Press Ks, 91; The Oxford History of the American West, Oxford Univ Press, 94; Major Problems in the History of the American West, Houghton Mifflin, 97; ed, Major Problems in the History of the American West, Heath & Co, 89; A new Significance: Re-envisioning the History of the American West, Oxford Univ Press, 96. **CONTACT ADDRESS** Mountain West Center for Regional Stud, Ut St Univ, 0735 Old Main Hill, Logan, UT, 84322-0735. **EMAIL** cmilner@hass.usu.edu

MINAR, EDWARD
DISCIPLINE WITTGENSTEIN AND THE HISTORY OF ANALYTIC PHILOSOPHY **EDUCATION** Harvard Univ, PhD. **CAREER** Philos, Univ Ark **SELECTED PUBLICATIONS** Articles; Synthese, Philos & Phenomenological Res, Pacific Philos Quart. **CONTACT ADDRESS** Univ Ark, Fayetteville, AR, 72701. **EMAIL** eminar@comp.uark.edu

MINAULT, GAIL
PERSONAL Born 03/25/1939, Minneapolis, MN, m, 1992, 1 child **DISCIPLINE** HISTORY **EDUCATION** Smith Col, BA, 61; Univ Pa, MA, 66, PhD, 72. **CAREER** Asst prof to PROF, HIST, UNIV TEX, 72-. **HONORS AND AWARDS** NDFL For Lang Fel, 64-65, 65-66, 66-67; Fulbright-Hays fel, res India, 67-68; Nat Hum Ctr fel, 87-88; NEH fel, 94-95; SSRC, Am Inst Indian Studies fels. **MEMBERSHIPS** Asn Asian Stud; AHA; Berkshire Conf Women Historians. **RESEARCH** 19th, 20th cent India; women in S Asia; Islam in S Asia. **SELECTED PUBLICATIONS** Auth, Secluded Scholars: Women's Education and Muslim Social Reform in Colonial India, Oxford Univ Press, 98; auth, Sayyid Karamat Husain and Muslim Women's Education, in Lucknow:Memories of a City, Oxford Univ Press, 97; auth, Other Voices, Other Rooms: The View from the Xenana, in Women as Subjects, Stree (Calcutta) and Univ Press Va, 94. **CONTACT ADDRESS** Dept of History, Univ of Texas, H518 Ave C, Austin, TX, 78712. **EMAIL** gminault@utxvms.cc.utexas.edu

MINEAR, RICHARD H.
DISCIPLINE HISTORY **EDUCATION** Harvard Univ, PhD, 68. **CAREER** Prof, Univ MA Amherst . **RESEARCH** Japan hist **SELECTED PUBLICATIONS** Auth, Japanese Tradition and Western Law, 70; Victors' Justice: The Tokyo War Crimes Trial, 71; ed, Through Japanese Eyes, 94. **CONTACT ADDRESS** Dept of Hist, Univ Massachusetts Amherst, Mass Ave, Amherst, MA, 01003.

MINER, CRAIG
PERSONAL m, 2 children **DISCIPLINE** REGIONAL AND BUSINESS HISTORY **CAREER** Prof, 69-. **HONORS AND AWARDS** Willard W Garvey distinguished prof hist, 88; Public Hum award, Kans Comm Hum, 87; Choice mag award for best acad bk(s), 87; Lyon award, Kans Author's Club, 88; Kans Preservation Alliance award, 93; Governor's Aviation Hon(s) award, 95., Certificate of Commendation, Amer Assn for State and Local Hist, 86. **RESEARCH** Regional and business history, **SELECTED PUBLICATIONS** Publ, eleven bk(s), Univ presses; seventeen bk(s), non-acad presses; forty two jour arti-

cles, numerous book rev(s); Auth, West Wichita: Settling the High Plains of Kansas, 1865-1890, 86; Uncloistered Halls, history of Wichita State Univ; Harvesting the High Plains: John Kriss and the Business of Farming, 20-50, 98. **CONTACT ADDRESS** Dept of Hist, Wichita State Univ, 1845 Fairmont, Wichita, KS, 67260-0062.

MING LEE, HUGH
PERSONAL Honolulu, HI **DISCIPLINE** GREEK AND LATIN **EDUCATION** St Mary's Col, BA; Stanford University, MA, PhD. **CAREER** Instr, IN Univ; Univ OH; Howard Univ; assoc prof-. **HONORS AND AWARDS** Res fel(s), Fulbright Found, Rome; NEH, Amer Coun of Learned Soc(s)., Prog coord, DC Soc Archaeol Inst Am; mem, Bd of Governors. **RESEARCH** Ancient Greek and Roman athletics. **SELECTED PUBLICATIONS** Auth, Running and the Stadium, Archaeol, 96; Yet Another Scoring System for the Ancient Pentathlon, Nikephoros 8, 96. **CONTACT ADDRESS** Dept of Class, Univ MD, 4229 Art-Sociology Building, College Park, MD, 20742-1335. **EMAIL** hlee@deans.umd.edu

MINKEMA, KENNETH P.
PERSONAL Born 10/30/1958, Ridgewood, NJ, m, 1984, 2 children **DISCIPLINE** HISTORY **EDUCATION** Univ CT, Storrs, PhD, 88. **CAREER** EXEC ED, WORKS OF JONATHAN EDWARDS, YALE UNIV, 89-; LECT, CHURCH HIST, YALE DIVINITY SCHOOL, 96-. **MEMBERSHIPS** AHA; OAH; ASCH. **RESEARCH** US relig hist; colonial. **SELECTED PUBLICATIONS** Ed, with James F. Cooper, The Sermon Notebook of Samuel Parris, 1689-1694, Colonial Soc MA, 94; ed, with John E. Smith and Harry S. Stout, A Jonathan Edwards Reader, Yale Univ Press, 95; auth, The Lynn End 'Earthquake' Narratives of 1727, New England Quart LXIX, Sept 96; Jonathan Edwards, Messianic Prophecy, and the Other Unfinished 'Great Work': 'The Harmony of the Old and New Testaments,' in Jonathan Edward's Writings: Text, Context, Interpretation, ed, Stephen J. Stein, IN Univ Press, 96; Jonathan Edwards on Slavery and the Slave Trade, William and Mary Quart LIV, Oct 97; ed, The Works of Jonathan Edwards, 14, Sermons and Discourses, 1723-1729, Yale Univ Press, 97; auth, 'The Devil Will Roar in Me Anon': The Possession of Martha Roberson, Boston, 1741, in Spellbound: Women and Witchcraft in America, ed, Elizabeth S. Reis, Scholarly Resources, 98; ed, with Wilson H. Kimnach and Douglas A. Sweeney, The Jonathan Edwards Sermons Reader, Yale Univ Press, forthcoming, 99. **CONTACT ADDRESS** Works of Jonathan Edwards, Yale Univ, 409 Prospect St., Box 250, New Haven, CT, 06511. **EMAIL** Ken.Minkema@yale.edu

MINNICH, NELSON H.
DISCIPLINE CHURCH HISTORY **EDUCATION** Boston Col, AB, 65, MA, 66; Gregorian Univ, STB, 70; Harvard Univ, PhD, 77. **CAREER** Instr, Loyola Acad, 66-68; teach fel, asst, 72, 74; asst, 77-83, assoc 83-93, PROF, HIST, CHURCH HIST, 93-, act chair, 78, 85, chair 79, 87-89, 98-, CHURCH HIST, CATH UNIV AM, assoc ed, 77-90, ADVIS ED, CATHOLIC HIST REV, 91-; ED, MELLVILLE STUD IN CHURCH HIST; ASSOC ED, ENCYCLOPEDIA RENAISSANCE, 96. **CONTACT ADDRESS** Dept Church History, Catholic Univ of America, 417 Caldwell Hall, Washington, DC, 20064.

MINOR, CLIFFORD EDWARD
PERSONAL Born 01/11/1946, Bronxville, NY, m, 1966 **DISCIPLINE** GREEK & ROMAN HISTORY **EDUCATION** Univ WA, BA, 67, MA, 68, PhD, 72. **CAREER** Asst prof ancient hist, 71-75, assoc prof, 75-80, prof hist, CA State Univ, Chico 80. **MEMBERSHIPS** Asn Ancient Historians **RESEARCH** Graeco-Roman world of the third century CE; soc, relig and polit hist of the Later Roman Empire; Hellenistic hist. **SELECTED PUBLICATIONS** Auth, Bagaudae or Bacaudae?, Traditio, 75; The Robber Tribes of Isauria, Ancient World, 79; Lest We Forget: The Parthenon and an Overlooked Tricentennial, Ancient World, 89; Bacaudae: A Reconsideration, Traditio, 96; Classifying the Bacaudae: Some Reasons for Caution. Part I: Who were the Third Century Bacaudae?, Ancient World, 97. **CONTACT ADDRESS** Dept of Hist (735), California State Univ, Chico, 101 Orange St, Chico, CA, 95929-0001. **EMAIL** cminor@facultypo.csuchico.edu

MINTZ, DONALD
PERSONAL Born 05/09/1929, New York, NY, m, 1978, 2 children **DISCIPLINE** MUSIC **EDUCATION** Cornell Univ, BA, 49; Princton Univ, MFA, 51; Cornell Univ, PhD, 60. **CAREER** Ref Asst, Libr Cong, 56-57; instr, Wellesley Col, 57-58; vis asst prof, Cornell Univ, 59-60; Am ed, Int Inventory of Musical Sources, 61-63; staff writer, The Sunday Star, 63-69; vis lectr, Univ Md, 67-68; grad fac, Peabody Conserv Music, 68-72; exec dir, Md Arts Coun, 69-72; dean, Montclair State Col, 72-83; prof, Montclair State Univ, 72-. **HONORS AND AWARDS** Fulbright student grant; Jr Fel, Princeton Univ. **MEMBERSHIPS** Am Musicol Society; Int Musicol Society; Music Libr Asn; Int Music Libr Asn. **RESEARCH** Mendelssohn; Liszt; 19th century concerto. **SELECTED PUBLICATIONS** Transl, Melusine: ein Entwurf Mendelssohns, 82; auth, 1848, Anti-Semitism and the Mendelssohn Reception, Mendelssohn Studies, Cambridge, 92. **CONTACT ADDRESS** Dept of Music, Montclair State Univ, Montclair, NJ, 07043. **EMAIL** dmintz@alpha.montclair.edu

MINTZ, LAWRENCE E.
DISCIPLINE AMERICAN STUDIES/ENGLISH **EDUCATION** Univ SC, BA, 66; MI State Univ, MA, 67, PhD, 69. **CAREER** Am Stud Dept, Univ Md **RESEARCH** Am popular cult and Am humor. **SELECTED PUBLICATIONS** Auth, The Standup Comedian as Social and Cultural Mediator, Amer Quart, 85; Devil and Angel: Philip Roth's Humor, Stud in Amer Jewish Lit, 89; Ethos and Pathos in Chaplin's City Lights, Charles Chaplin: Approaches to Semiotics, Mouton deGryter, 91; Humor and Ethnic Stereotypes in Vaudeville and Burlesque, MELUS, 96; ed, Humor in America: A Research Guide to Genres and Topics, Greenwood Press, 88. **CONTACT ADDRESS** Am Stud Dept, Univ MD, Col Park, College Park, MD, 20742. **EMAIL** lm36@umail.umd.edu

MINTZ, STEVEN
DISCIPLINE HISTORY **EDUCATION** Oberlin Col, BA, 73; Yale Univ, PhD, 79. **CAREER** ASSOC DEAN, GRAD STUD, COL HUM, FINE ARTS, COMMUNIC, 98-, PROF HIST, 93-, UNIV HOUSTON. **CONTACT ADDRESS** History Dept, Univ of Houston, Houston, TX, 77204-3785. **EMAIL** smintz@uh.edu

MIQUELON, DALE B.
PERSONAL Born 09/27/1940, Wetaskiwin, AB, Canada **DISCIPLINE** HISTORY **EDUCATION** Univ Alta, BA, 63; Carleton Univ, MA, 66; Univ Toronto, PhD, 73. **CAREER** Hist res, Nat Hist Sites Div NA & NR, Ottawa, 63-64; asst prof, 70-75, assoc prof 75-79, PROF HISTORY, UNIV SASKATCHEWAN, 79-, assoc dean hum & fine art, 84-89, dept head 90-95. **HONORS AND AWARDS** Can Coun pre-doctoral fel, 66-70, doctoral thesis prize, 75, fel, 76-77; SSHRCC released time fel, 82-83. **SELECTED PUBLICATIONS** Auth, Dugard of Rouen: French Trade to Canada and the West Indies 1729-1770, 78; auth, New France 1701-1744: 'A Supplement to Europe,' 87; auth, The First Canada: to 1791, 94; ed, Society and Conquest: The Debate on the Bourgeoisie and Social Change in French Canada 1799-1850, 77. **CONTACT ADDRESS** Dept of History, Univ Saskatchewan, 9 Campus Dr, Saskatoon, SK, S7N 5A5. **EMAIL** miquelon@sask.usask.ca

MISKELL, JERRY
DISCIPLINE MUSIC **EDUCATION** Univ Akron, BM, 85, MM, 87; Univ SC, DMA, 95. **CAREER** Dept music, Mt Union Col **SELECTED PUBLICATIONS** Auth, Ode to a Painter's Friend, New Mmus Publ, San Rafael, 95; compos, Endless Summer Eternity Light and Fireworks, 97; Orchestral Piece, Of Summer and Eternity, 97; Piano Quartet, The Winds are Aloft in the Western Reserve, 96; Percussion duo, The Winds are Aloft in the Western Reserve, 96; Violin/Viola duo, Commercial Time Out, 96 Woodwind Quintet; Commissioned by the Tapestry Ensemble, Puzzles and Cannons, 96; Trio for Flexible Instrumentation; Ode to a Painter's Friend, 95; String quartet & 3 screaming women, Relentless Variations, 94. **CONTACT ADDRESS** Dept of Music, Mount Union Col, 1972 Clark Ave, Alliance, OH, 44601. **EMAIL** miskeljp@muc.edu

MITCHELL, BETTY L.
DISCIPLINE HISTORY **EDUCATION** Douglass, AB, 69; Univ Mass at Amherst, MA, 72, PhD, 79. **CAREER** Assoc, prof, hist, Univ SE Mass; PROF, HIST, UNIV MASS DARTMOUTH. **MEMBERSHIPS** AM Antiquarian Soc **SELECTED PUBLICATIONS** Auth, "Massachusetts Reacts to John Brown's Raid," Civil War Hist 19, 73; auth, "Realities Not Shadows," Civil War Hist 20, 74; auth, Edmund Ruffin: A Biography, 81; "Out of the Glass House: Robert Todd Lincoln's Crucial Decade, 1865-75," Timeline Mag, 88. **CONTACT ADDRESS** 56 Revell St, Northampton, MA, 01060.

MITCHELL, HELEN BUSS
PERSONAL Born 07/17/1941, New York, NY, m, 1964, 1 child **DISCIPLINE** INTELLECTUAL HISTORY, WOMEN'S HISTORY **EDUCATION** Hood Col, BA, 63; Loyola Col, MEd, 75, MMS, 79; Univ Md, PhD, 90. **CAREER** Asst dir cont educ, 74-79, dir cont educ, 79-87, assoc dean, 87-93, prof Philos, dir women's studs, 93-, Howard Commun Col. **HONORS AND AWARDS** Who's Who Among Amer Women; Who's Who Among Amer Educs; Phi Kappa Phi; Alpha Sigma Nu; NISOD excellence awd, 97-98; Howard Commun Col outstanding fac mem, 98. **MEMBERSHIPS** Amer Philos Asn; Natl Women's Studs Asn. **RESEARCH** World Philosophy, Women's Studies. **SELECTED PUBLICATIONS** Auth, Roots of Wisdom: Speaking the Language of Philosophy, Wadsworth Publ Co, 95; Roots of World Wisdom: A Multicultural Reader, Wadsworth Publ Co, 96; Taking Sides: Clashing Viewson Controversial Issues in World Civilizations, McGraw, 98. **CONTACT ADDRESS** Dept of Philosophy, Howard Comm Col, Columbia, MD, 21044. **EMAIL** hmitchel@howardcc.edu

MITCHELL, REID
DISCIPLINE HISTORY **EDUCATION** Univ CA, PhD. **CAREER** Assoc prof, Univ MD Baltimore County . **RESEARCH** Civil War; Southern hist. **SELECTED PUBLICATIONS** Auth, Civil War Soldiers; The Vacant Chair: The Northern Soldier Leaves Home. **CONTACT ADDRESS** Dept of Hist, Univ MD Baltimore County, Hilltop Circle, PO Box 1000, Baltimore, MD, 21250. **EMAIL** mitchell@gl.umbc.edu

MITCHELL, RICHARD E.
PERSONAL Born 06/02/1934, Rainelle, WV, m, 1958, 1 child **DISCIPLINE** ANCIENT HISTORY **EDUCATION** Olivet Col, BA, 57, Univ MI, MA, 58; Univ Cincinnati, PhD, 65. **CAREER** Instr hist, Olivet Col, 58-61; From Asst Prof to Prof Hist, Univ Ill, Urbana-Champaign, 65. **HONORS AND AWARDS** Am Coun Learned Soc fel, 70-71. **MEMBERSHIPS** AHA; Am Philol Asn; Archaeol Inst Am; Am Numis Soc; Royal Numis Soc. **RESEARCH** Hist of the Roman Republic; Roman numismatics. **SELECTED PUBLICATIONS** Auth, The fourth century origin of Roman didrachms, Mus Notes, 69; Roman Carthaginian treaties: 306 & 279/8 BC, Historia, 71; The aristocracy of the Roman Republic, In: The Rich, the Wellborn, and the Powerful: Elites and Upper Classes in History, Univ Ill, 73; Patricians and Plebeians: The Origin of the Roman State, Cornell Univ Press, 90. **CONTACT ADDRESS** Dept of Hist, Univ of Illinois, 810 S Wright St, Urbana, IL, 61801-3611. **EMAIL** rmitchell@uiuc.edu

MITCHELL, RICHARD HANKS
PERSONAL Born 04/16/1931, Jacksonville, IL, m, 1960 **DISCIPLINE** MODERN JAPANESE HISTORY **EDUCATION** Univ Wis, BS, 57, MS, 58, PhD(EAsian hist), 63. **CAREER** Lectr hist, Far East Div, Univ Md, 63-66 & 67-68; assoc prof EAsian hist, Col New Paltz, State Univ NY, 66-67; vis assoc, Univ Nebr, Lincoln, 68-69; vis assoc prof Japanese hist, Univ Rochester, 69-70; assoc prof, 70-76, prof Japanese Hist, Univ MO St Louis, 76-, Sem assoc, Columbia Univ Sem EAsia, Japan, 70-82; Univ Mo-St Louis fac res grants, Japan, 72, 74, 76; Nat Endowment for Humanities fel, summer, 78. **HONORS AND AWARDS** Res & Publ Award, Univ Md, Far East Div, 68. **MEMBERSHIPS** Asn Asian Studies. **RESEARCH** Japanese justice system. **SELECTED PUBLICATIONS** Auth, The Korean minority in Japan, Univ Calif, 67; Japan's peace preservation law of 1925: Its origins and significance, Monumenta Nipponica, fall 73; Thought Control in Prewar Japan, Cornell Univ, 76; Political Bribery in Japan, U Gtsezii, 96. **CONTACT ADDRESS** Dept of History, Univ Missouri, St. Louis, 8001 Natural Bridge, St. Louis, MO, 63121-4499.

MITCHELL, WILLIAM P.
PERSONAL Born 08/30/1937, Brooklyn, NY, m, 1998, 2 children **DISCIPLINE** ANTHROPOLOGY **EDUCATION** Brooklyn Col, BA, 61; Univ Pitt, PhD, 72 **CAREER** Freed prof Soc Sci, Monmouth Univ, 86-; prof Anthropology, Monmouth Univ, 78-; res assoc Anthropology, Universidad Catolica, 83, 96 **HONORS AND AWARDS** NY Acad Sci Fel; Intl Representative of Regional Assoc of Displaced People of Central Area of Peru, 96; Peace Maker of Year, Monmouth People for Peace and Disarmament, 95; Magna cum laude, Brooklyn Col; Phi Beta Kappa and Sigma Xi, Brooklyn Col, 61 **MEMBERSHIPS** Amer Anthropolog Assoc; NY Acad Sci; Sigma Xi; Phi Beta Kappa **RESEARCH** War and Peace; Social Evolution; Andes; Migration **SELECTED PUBLICATIONS** Auth, Peasants on the Edge: Crop, Cult, and Crisis in the Andes, Univ Tex, 91; auth, Picturing Faith: The Huntington Quechua Pictographic catechism, Huntington Free Library, forthcoming; ed, Irrigation at High Altitudes: The Social Organization of Water Control Systems in the Andes, Amer Anthropolog Assoc, 94 **CONTACT ADDRESS** Dept Hist/Anthropology, Monmouth Univ, 400 Cedar Ave, West Long Branch, NJ, 07764. **EMAIL** mitchell@mondec.monmouth.edu

MITCHINSON, WENDY
PERSONAL Born 12/28/1947, Hamliton, ON, Canada **DISCIPLINE** HISTORY **EDUCATION** York Univ, BA, 70, MA, 71, PhD, 77. **CAREER** Lectr & asst prof, Mt St Vincent Univ, 75-77; asst prof, 77-81, assoc prof, 81-85, Univ Windsor; assoc prof, 85-91, PROF HISTORY, UNIV WATERLOO, 91-; vis prof, McMaster Univ, Hannah Inst Hist Med, 88-89; scholar-in-residence, Rockefeller Stud Ctr, Bellagio, Italy, 94; Fudacion, Valparaiso, Spain, 97. **MEMBERSHIPS** Can Hist Asn; Ont Hist Asn; Ont Women's Hist Network; Can Soc Hist Med; Can Stud Asn; **SELECTED PUBLICATIONS** Auth, The Nature of Their Bodies: Women and Their Doctors in Victorian Canada, 91; coauth, Canadian Women: A History, 88, 2nd ed, 96; co-ed, The Proper Sphere, 76; co-ed, Essays in Canadian Medical History, 88; co-ed, Canadian Women: A Reader, 96. **CONTACT ADDRESS** Dept of History, Univ Waterloo, Waterloo, ON, N2L 3G1. **EMAIL** wlmitchi@watarts.uwaterloo.ca

MITTELMAN, JAMES
DISCIPLINE GLOBAL POLITICAL ECONOMY **EDUCATION** Mich State Univ, BA; Cornell Univ, MA, PhD. **CAREER** Prof, Am Univ. **HONORS AND AWARDS** Dean, Grad Sch Int Studies, Univ Denver; Dir, Soc Sci Found, Columbia Univ; Dean, div Soc Sci, Queens Col, CUNY. **RESEARCH** African politics, international organization. **SELECTED PUBLICATIONS** Contrib, Globalization: Critical Reflections, Lynne Rienner Publs, 96; co-auth, Out from Underdevelopment Revisited: Changing Global Structures and the Remaking of the Third World, St. Martin's Press, 97; Co-ed, Innovation and Transformation in International Studies, Cambridge Univ Press, 97. **CONTACT ADDRESS** American Univ, 4400 Massachusetts Ave, Washington, DC, 20016.

MIXON, WAYNE
PERSONAL Born 08/19/1945, Winnsboro, SC, m, 1967, 2 children **DISCIPLINE** HISTORY **EDUCATION** Univ SC, BA, 67, MA, 70; Univ NC, Chapel Hill, PhD, 74. **CAREER** Asst prof, Univ Southern MS, Natchez, 75-77; from asst prof to assoc prof to prof, 77-96, Mercer Univ; prof, Augusta State Univ, 96-. **HONORS AND AWARDS** NEH Summer Fel, 86. **MEMBERSHIPS** Am Hist Asn; Southern Hist Asn; South Atlantic Modern Language Asn. **RESEARCH** The American South; US social and intellectual history. **SELECTED PUBLICATIONS** Auth, Southern Writers and the New South Movement, 1865-1913, 80; ed, My Young Master: A Novel by Opie Read, 87; auth, art, The Ultimate Irrelevance of Race: Joel Chandler Harris and Uncle Remus in Their Time, 90; auth, The Adaptable South: Essays in Honor of Goerge Brown Tindall, 91; auth, The People's Writer: Erskine Caldwell and the South, 95. **CONTACT ADDRESS** Dept of History and Anthropology, Augusta State Univ, Augusta, GA, 30904. **EMAIL** wmixon@aug.edu

MOBERG, DAVID OSCAR
PERSONAL Born 02/13/1922, Montevideo, MN, m, 1994, 4 children **DISCIPLINE** HISTORY AND SOCIOLOGY **EDUCATION** Bethel Jr Col, AA, 42; Seattle Pacific Col, AB, 47; Univ Wash, MA, 49; Univ Minn, PhD, 52. **CAREER** US army, 42-46; student-pastor, Sylvan Way Bapt Church, Bremerton, Wash, 46-48; assoc instr, sociol, Univ Wash, 48-49; instr to prof, sociol, Bethel Col, St Paul, Minn, 49-68; Fulbright lectr, sociol, State Univ Groningen, Netherlands, 57-58; sr Fulbright lectr, sociol of relig, Muenster Univ, Ger, 64-65; chair, dept of sociol and anthrop, 68-77, prof, sociol, 68-91, Marquette Univ. **HONORS AND AWARDS** Alumnus of the year, Bethel Col and Sem, 76; Alpha Kappa Delta, 48; Pi Gamma Mu, 54; Fulbright lectr, H. Paul Douglass Lectr, Relig Res Asn, 86; Inaugural Kellogg Gerontology Lectr, Southwestern Baptist Theol Sem, 87; Inaugural lectr, Frederick Alexander Shippey lectures in the sociol of christ, Drew Univ Theol Sch, Madison, NJ, oct, 88. **RESEARCH** Spirituality; Religion; Aging. **SELECTED PUBLICATIONS** Articles, The history and meaning of Spiritual Well-Being as a concept, CARS Chronicle, no 1, p 4, 1 May, 95, also in Aging and Relig, 2, 1, winter, 97, Ctr for Aging, Relig and Spirituality, St Paul, Minn; A Response to spiritual well-being defined, Aging and Spirituality, 9, 1, 8, spring, 97; Applications of research methods, chap 37, ed Melvin A. Kimble, Susan H. McFadden, James W. Ellor and James J. Seeber, Aging, Spirituality and Relig, Minneapolis, Fortress Press, pp 541-557, 95; Religion in gerontology: From benign neglect to belated respect, The Gerontologist, 36, 2, 264-267, apr 96; Spiritual maturity and aging, Theol News and Notes, 42, 4, 3-5, 21, dec 95; The secularizing of Christian America, ed Ed Crawfor, Holy Living in a Post-Christian Age, Nampa, Id, Wesley Ctr for Applied Theol, Northwest Nazarene Col, pp 1-8, jun 95; Spiritual growth while life winds down, Seasons: The Inter-Faith Family Jour, pp 17-19, spring, 95; Religion and personal adjustment in old age: A replication and explication, RIE: Resources in Education, Ann Arbor, Mich, ERIC/CAPS Clearinghouse, Univ Mich, 90-91; Preparing for the graying of the church: Challenges from our changing society, Rev and Expositor, 88, 3, 179-193, summer 91; **CONTACT ADDRESS** 7120 W. Dove Ct., Milwaukee, WI, 53223. **EMAIL** domoberg@juno.com

MOCKLER, ROBERT J.
PERSONAL s **DISCIPLINE** BUSINESS **EDUCATION** Harvard Univ, BA, 54, MBA, 59; Columbia Univ, PhD, 61. **CAREER** St John's Univ, Col of Bus, Grad School, prof, 63-. **HONORS AND AWARDS** St. Johns Univ, Annual Merit Award, 89-98, Joseph F.Adams prof, 98; personal audience with Pope John-Paul II, St. John's Univ, Thirty year Distinguished Service Award., NYC Marathon, ran and finished, at age 65, 97; DSI, 5th Intl Conf, co-ch, Athens Greece, 99; NACRA, ed bd, of: Case Research Jour, 94-, Jour Strat Change, ed bd, 94-, NSF, lead review, 97; DSI, Creating a Strategic Res Plan, orig / organ, co-lead 95,96 & 97, APSMA, founder, 95; 25th Annual DSI Conf, MIS Track co-ch, 94; NACRA nominating commit, 93-94 **MEMBERSHIPS** DSI, NACRA, IRMA, ECWA, IEEE / ACM **RESEARCH** Multinational strategic alliances; CIS/MIS sys; intl bus strategies; cross-cult mgmt; knowledge based sys; innov tchg methods. **SELECTED PUBLICATIONS** Auth, Multinational Strategic Alliances, John Wiley and Sons, 99; The Case Study Development Program of the Management Department at St. John's University, Strat Man Res Group, 98; Developing Knowledge-Based Systems Using an Expert System Shell: A Guide for General Business Managers and Computer Information System Technicians, 19 Sample Prototype Systems and a Development Shell, Prentice Hall / MacMillan, 92, trans to Chinese, China Railway Pub Corp, 98; Strategic Management, Idea Group Pub, 93, trans to Chinese, Intl Cult Pub Comp, 97; Computer Software to Support Strategic Management Decision Making: A Comprehensive Review of Available Existing Conventional and Knowledge-Based Applications, Prentice Hall / MacMillan, 92; Contingency Approaches to Strategic Management: Integrating Basic and Applied Research, SMRG, 92. **CONTACT ADDRESS** Dept of Management, St. John's Univ, 114 East 90th St (1B), NYC, NY, 10128. **EMAIL** mocklerr@stjohns.edu

MOEHRING, EUGENE P.
DISCIPLINE HISTORY **EDUCATION** City Univ NY PhD, 76. **CAREER** Prof, Univ Nev Las Vegas. **RESEARCH** Modern American history; urban history; business history. **SELECTED PUBLICATIONS** Auth, Public Works and the Patterns of Urban Real Estate Growth in Manhattan, 1835-1894, 81; Resort City in the Sunbelt: Las Vegas, 1930-1970, 89. **CONTACT ADDRESS** History Dept, Univ Nev Las Vegas, 4505 Md Pky, Las Vegas, NV, 89154.

MOFFAT, FREDERICK
DISCIPLINE ART **EDUCATION** Univ Cahicago, PhD, 72. **CAREER** Assoc prof. **SELECTED PUBLICATIONS** Auth, Intemperate Patronage of Henry D. Cogswell, 92; Arthur Dow Pont Aven, Rennes Univ, 86; Carl Sublett, The Painter, 84; Clark Stewart, 82; Sandra Blain, 82; Philip Livingston, 82. **CONTACT ADDRESS** Dept of Art, Knoxville, TN, 37996.

MOFFETT, SAMUEL HUGH
PERSONAL Born 04/07/1916, Pyongyang, Korea, m, 1942 **DISCIPLINE** HISTORY OF MISSIONS, ASIAN CHURCH HISTORY **EDUCATION** Wheaton Col, Ill, AB, 38; Princeton Theol Sem, ThB, 42; Yale Univ, PhD, 45. **CAREER** Lectr English & church hist, Yenching Univ, Peking, 48-49; asst prof church hist, Nanking Theol Sem, 49-50; vis lectr ecumenics, Princeton Theol Sem, 53-55; prof church hist, 60-81, dean Grad Sch, 66-70, assoc pres, 70-81, Presby Theol Sem, Seoul, Korea; pres, Asian Ctr Theol Studies & Mission, 74-81; prof missions & ecumenics, 81-87, Henry Winters Luce Prof of Ecumenics and Mission, emeritus, Princeton Theol Sem; bd dir, Yonsei Univ, Seoul, 57-81, Soongjun Univ, Seoul, 69-81 & Whitworth Col, Spokane, Wash, 73-79; mem, US Educ Comn, Korea, 66-67. **HONORS AND AWARDS** Order Civil Merit, Repub Korea, 81; DD, King Col, TN, 85; DD, Gordon Conwell Theol Sem, 95; DD, Presbyterian Col and Theol Sem, 96; hon PhD Soongsil Univ, SEoul, 97., LittD, Yonsei Univ, Seoul, Korea, 81. **MEMBERSHIPS** Am Soc Missiology; Int Asn Missiological Studies; Korean Church History Soc; Royal Asiatic Soc (pres, Korean Br, 68-69). **RESEARCH** Asian church history; history of missions; Korean studies. **SELECTED PUBLICATIONS** Coauth, First Encounters: Korea 1880-1910, Dragon's Eye Press, Seoul, 82; auth, History of Christianity in Asia, Beginnings to 1500, Harper Collins, 92. **CONTACT ADDRESS** 150 Leabrook Ln, Princeton, NJ, 08540.

MOHR, CLARENCE L.
PERSONAL Born 10/03/1946, Almont, MI, m **DISCIPLINE** HISTORY **EDUCATION** Birmingham Southern Col, AB, 68; Univ Ga, MA, 70, PhD, 75. **CAREER** Prof & ch, Univ S Al, 98-; asst prof, 81-86, assoc chem, 84-86 & 89-90, assoc prof, 86-98; prof, 98-, Tulane Univ. **HONORS AND AWARDS** Avery O. Craven awd, Orgn Amer Historians, 87; listed in, Who's Who in the South and Southwest, 95-96; Contemp Authors; Directory Amer Scholars; Summer stipend, Nat Endowment for the Humanities, 87; grant-in-aid, Rockefeller Arch Ctr, Tarrytown, NY, 86; fel, Amer Coun Learned Soci, 79-80; grant-in-aid, Amer Philos Soc,78; fel in Advan Ed, Nat Hist Publ Comn, 75-76. **RESEARCH** Southern history,19th and 20th century; economic and social reform, higher education, Civil War,slavery and race relations. **SELECTED PUBLICATIONS** Auth, On the Threshold of Freedom: Masters and Slaves in Civil War Georgia, Athens and London: Univ Ga Press, 86; Schooling, Modernization, and Race: The Continuing Dilemma of The American South, Amer J Educ 106, 98 & Before Sherman: Georgia Blacks and the Union War Effort, 1861-1864, J Southern His XLV, 79, rep in, Major Problems in the History of the Civil War and Reconstruction, Lexington, Mass: D C Heath, 91 and The Day of Jubilee: The Civil War Experience of Black Southerners, NY: Garland Publ Inc, 94; contrib, The Impact of World War II on the American South, Jackson: UP Miss, 96; Dictionary of Afro-American Slavery, Westport: Greenwood Press, 88, paperback ed, 97; Dictionary of Georgia Biography, 2 vols, Athens: Univ Ga Press, 83 & Encyclopedia of the Confederacy, 93. **CONTACT ADDRESS** Dept of History, Univ South Alabama, 342 Humanities, Mobile, AL, 36688-0002. **EMAIL** cmohr@jaguar1.usouthal.edu

MOHR, JAMES CRAIL
PERSONAL Born 01/28/1943, Edgewood, MD, m, 1965, 2 children **DISCIPLINE** AMERICAN HISTORY **EDUCATION** Yale Univ, BA, 65; Stanford Univ, PhD(hist), 69. **CAREER** From asst prof to prof hist, 69-92, Univ Md, Baltimore County; assoc prof hist, Stanford Univ, 73-74 & Univ Va, 77; prof and dept head, hist, Univ Oregon, 92-98, ARTS & SCIENCES DIST PROF, HIST, UNIV OREGON, 98- . **HONORS AND AWARDS** Rockefeller-Ford Pop Policy fel, 75-76; Danforth assoc, 75-; Nat Endowment for Humanities, 79-80; Throne Aldrich Prize, 90. **MEMBERSHIPS** AHA; Org Am Historians; Southern Hist Asn. **RESEARCH** Nineteenth century United States political, social, legal, medical and policy history. **SELECTED PUBLICATIONS** Auth, The Radical Republicans and Reform in New York during Reconstruction, Cornell, 73; ed and contrib, Radical Republicans in the North: State Politics During Reconstruction, Johns Hopkins, 76; auth, Abortion in America: The Origins and Evolution of National Policy, 1800-1900, Oxford Univ, 78; ed, The Cormany Diaries: A Northern Family in the Civil War, Pittsburgh, 82; auth, Doctors and the Law: Medical Jurisprudence in Nineteenth-Century America, Oxford, 93. **CONTACT ADDRESS** Dept of History, Univ Oregon, Eugene, OR, 97403-1288.

MOKYR, JOEL
DISCIPLINE ECONOMICS **EDUCATION** Hebrew Univ-Jerusalem; Yale Univ, PhD, 74. **CAREER** Vis prof, Harvard; vis prof, Univ Chicago; vis prof, Stanford Univ; vis prof, Hebrew Univ-Jerusalem; vis prof, Univ Tel Aviv; vis prof, Univ Coll Dublin; vis prof, Univ Manchester; PROF, ECON & HIST, NORTHWESTERN UNIV, 74-. **SELECTED PUBLICATIONS** Why Ireland Starved: An Analytical and Quantitative Study of the Irish Economy; the Lever of Riches: Technological Creativity and Economic Progress; The British Industrial Revolution: An Economic Perspective; sen edr, Journal of Economic History. **CONTACT ADDRESS** Dept Econ, Northwestern Univ, Evanston, IL, 60208.

MOLFESE, D.L.
PERSONAL Born 03/18/1946, Tulsa, OK, m, 1971, 2 children **DISCIPLINE** PSYCHOLOGY **EDUCATION** OK City Univ, BA, 69; Penn St Univ, MS, 70, PhD, 72. **CAREER** Asst prof, 72-76, assoc prof, 76-80, Southern IL Univ; res assoc, Yerkes Regional Primate Res Center Emory Univ; prof, Dept of Pediatrics Physiology Behavioral & Social Sciences School of Med, 80, chmn Behavioral & Social Sciences, School of Med, 92-, Southern IL Univ. **HONORS AND AWARDS** Phi Kappa Phi Outstanding Scholar, 97; Univ Outstanding Scholar, 90; Southern IL Univ Sigma Xi Kaplan Res Award for Significant Contributions in Child Psychology, 87; vis res Scientist Univ of Konstanz West Germany, 73, 75, 81. **MEMBERSHIPS** APA; Sigma Xi; Midwestern Psychol Asn; Phi Kappa Phi; Soc for Neuroscience; Acoustical Soc of Amer; Psychonomic Soc; Aerospace Med Asn; Intl Neuropsychological Soc; Amer Psychol Soc; Soc for Res in Child Dev; New York Academy of Science; The Belgian Soc of Electromyography and Clinical Neurophysiology. **RESEARCH** Development changes in the neurophysiological correlates of linguistic and cognitive processes; predicting cognitive and linguistic skills from infancy; brain-language relationships in language trained chimpanzees; cognitive functions in head injured adults; factors underlying lateralization of language and cognitive functions; phonological and semantic confusions by aphasics; electrophysiological techniques to assess hearing abilities in infants; and children, neural network applications to neuropsychology. **SELECTED PUBLICATIONS** Coauth, Known Versus Unknown Word Discrimination In 12 Month Old Human Infants, Dev Neuropsychology 3-4, 93; coauth, Predicting Long-Term Development From Electrophysiological Measures Taken At Birth, Human Behavior and Brain Development, Guilford Press, **CONTACT ADDRESS** Behavioral and Social Scis, Southern IL Univ, Carbondale, IL, 62901-6517. **EMAIL** dmolfese@som.sie.edu

MONET, JACQUES
PERSONAL Born 01/26/1930, Saint-Jean, PQ, Canada **DISCIPLINE** HISTORY **EDUCATION** Univ Montreal, BA, 55; Immaculee-Conception, PhL, 56, ThL, 67; Univ Toronto, MA, 61, PhD, 64. **CAREER** Asst prof, Univ Toronto, 68; prof agrege, 69-80, prof titul, hist, 80-82, Univ d'Ottawa; pres, Regis Col, Toronto, 82-88; dir, Can Inst Jesuit Stud, 88-; RECTEUR, UNIV SUDBURY, 92-. **HONORS AND AWARDS** Chev l'ordre des Palmes acad, 74., O. pretre, Montreal, 66; derniers voeux dans la cie de Jesus (Jesuites) Montmartre, 71. **MEMBERSHIPS** Soc Royale Can; Soc Hist Can (pres, 75-76); conseil Nat pour l'evaluation des Archives, 79-83; Commission des lieux et monuments historiques du Canada, 95-. **SELECTED PUBLICATIONS** Auth, The Last Cannon Shot: A Study of French Canadian Nationalism, 69; auth, The Canadian Crown, 79; auth, La Monarchie au Canada, 79; auth, La Premiere Revolution Tranquille, 81. **CONTACT ADDRESS** Univ of Sudbury, Sudbury, ON, P3E 2C6.

MONEYHON, CARL HOFMANN
PERSONAL Born 06/07/1944, Brownwood, TX, m, 1978, 2 children **DISCIPLINE** CIVIL WAR & RECONSTRUCTION **EDUCATION** Univ TX, Austin, BA, 67, MA, 68; Univ Chicago, PhD(hist), 73. **CAREER** Asst prof, 74-78, assoc prof Hist, 78-82, prof hist, Univ AR, Little Rock, 83-. **MEMBERSHIPS** Southern Hist Asn; TX Hist Asn; AR Hist Asn. **RESEARCH** American Reconstruction politics; social history of the American South in the 19th century. **SELECTED PUBLICATIONS** Auth, Republicanism in Reconstruction Texas, Univ TX Press, 80; coauth, Portraits of Conflict: A Photographic History of Arkansas in the Civil War, Univ AR Press, 87; Historical Atlas of Arkansas, Univ OK Press, 89; Portraits of Conflict: A Photographic History of Louisiana in the Civil War, Univ AR Press, 90; Portraits of Conflict: A Photographic History of Mississippi in the Civil War, Univ AR Press, 93; auth, The Impact of the Civil War and Reconstruction in Arkansas, LA State Univ Press, 94; Arkansas and the New South, Univ AR Press, 97. **CONTACT ADDRESS** Dept Hist, Univ AR, 2801 S University Av, Little Rock, AR, 72204-1000. **EMAIL** CHMoneyhon@UALR.edu

MONHEIT, MICHAEL L.
DISCIPLINE REFORMATION AND EARLY MODERN EUROPEAN HISTORY **EDUCATION** Univ Calif Berkeley, BA, 76; Princeton Univ, PhD, 88. **CAREER** Assoc prof, Univ South Al. **RESEARCH** Formation of a reformer, 1528-41. **SELECTED PUBLICATIONS** Auth, Young Calvin, Textual Interpretation and Roman Law, Bibliotheque d'Humanisme et

Renaissance, Tome LIX, 97; The Origins of the edictalis-decretalis bonorum possessio Distinction in a Renaissance Defense of Scholastic Hermeneutics, Quaderni fiorentini per la storia del pensiero giuridico moderno, 96; Guillaume Bude, Andrea Alciato, and Pierre de l'Estoile: Renaissance Interpreters of Roman Law, J Hist Ideas, vol 58, 97 & The Ambition for an Illustrious Name: Humanism, Patronage, and Calvin's Doctrine of the Calling, Sixteenth Century J, Vol XXIII, 92. **CONTACT ADDRESS** Dept of History, Univ South Alabama, 376 Humanities, Mobile, AL, 36688-0002. **EMAIL** mmonheit@jaguar1.usouthal.edu

MONK, DENNIS
DISCIPLINE MUSICOLOGY AND MUSIC HISTORY **EDUCATION** San Francisko State Univ, BA, MA; UCLA, PhD. **CAREER** Music Dept, Univ Ala **HONORS AND AWARDS** Fulbright Fel. **SELECTED PUBLICATIONS** Area: Music Hist, Educ, and Administration. **CONTACT ADDRESS** Univ AL, Box 870000, Tuscaloosa, AL, 35487-0000. **EMAIL** dmonk@music.ua.edu

MONOD, PAUL
DISCIPLINE HISTORY **EDUCATION** Princeton Univ, AB; Yale Univ, MA, MPhil, PhD. **CAREER** Prof, 84-. **RESEARCH** Early modern Britain; early modern Europe; modern Britain & political, social and cultural history. **SELECTED PUBLICATIONS** Auth, Jacobitism and the English People, 1688-1788, Cambridge, 89. **CONTACT ADDRESS** Dept of History, Middlebury Col, Middlebury, VT, 05753. **EMAIL** monod@panther.middlebury.edu

MONOSON, S. SARA
DISCIPLINE CLASSICS AND POLITICAL SCIENCE **EDUCATION** Brandeis, BA, 81; London Sch Econ and Polit Sci, MSc, 82; Princeton Univ, PhD, 93. **CAREER** Asst prof, Northwestern Univ, 93-. **RESEARCH** Plato and Athenian democracy. **SELECTED PUBLICATIONS** Auth, Citizen as Erastes: Erotic Imagery and the Idea of Reciprocity in the Periclean Funeral Oration, Polit Theory, 94; Frank Speech, Democracy and Philosophy: Plato's Debt to a Democratic Strategy of Civic Discourse, Athenian Polit Thought and the Reconstruction of Am Democracy, Cornell, 94. **CONTACT ADDRESS** Dept of Classics, Northwestern Univ, 1801 Hinman, Evanston, IL, 60208. **EMAIL** s-monoson@nwu.edu

MONROE, BETTY I.
DISCIPLINE ART HISTORY **EDUCATION** Mich Univ, PhD. **CAREER** Prof emerita, Northwestern Univ. **RESEARCH** Indian sculpture and painting; Chinese painting; Chinese ceramics. **SELECTED PUBLICATIONS** Auth, Chinese Ceramics in Chicago Collections; transl, ed & adapted, Japanese Painting in the Literati Style. **CONTACT ADDRESS** Dept of Art History, Northwestern Univ, 1801 Hinman, Evanston, IL, 60208.

MONROE, WILLIAM S.
PERSONAL Born 03/15/1952, Pottstown, PA, m, 1978, 2 children **DISCIPLINE** HISTORY **EDUCATION** Temple Univ, BA, 79; Drexel Univ, MS, 84; MA, 88, Mphil, 91, Columbia Univ. **CAREER** Cataloger, Teachers Col, Columbia Univ, 84-86; Ref Libr, Humanities Bibliographer, NY Univ, 86-91; Head of Collection Devel, Brown Univ, 93-. **MEMBERSHIPS** ALA; Amer Historical Assoc; Medieval Acad of Amer; Amer Theological Library Assoc. **RESEARCH** Cultural and legal history; early middle ages **SELECTED PUBLICATIONS** Auth, Redefining the Library: The Year's Work in Collection Development 1991, Library Resources & Technical Services 36, 92; coauth, Western European Political Science: An Acquisition Study, College & Research Libraries, 94; coauth, A New Kind of Space for a New Kind of Collection, BiblioFile: Newsletter of Brown Univ Library, 96; auth, The Role of Selection in Collection Development: Past, Present, and Future, Collection Management for the 21st Century: A Handbook for Librarians, 97; auth, Via iustitiae: The Biblical Sources of Justice in Gregory of Tours, Gregory of Tours and His World, 99. **CONTACT ADDRESS** Library, Brown Univ, Box A, Providence, RI, 02912. **EMAIL** william_monroe@brown.edu

MONTEIRO, THOMAS
PERSONAL Born 10/06/1939, New York, NY, d **DISCIPLINE** EDUCATION **EDUCATION** Winston-Salem State University, Winston-Salem, NC, BS, 1961; Queens College of the City University of New York, New York NY, MA, 1966; Fordham University, New York, NY, professional diploma, 1968-69, PhD, 1971-74. **CAREER** Board of Education, New York, NY, teacher, 1961-68, district curriculum director, 1969-70; Brooklyn College of the City University of New York, New York, NY, professor, 1970-85, CHAIRPERSON, DEPT OF EDUC ADMIN AND SUPERVISION, DIR, THE PRINCIPAL'S CENTER AT BROOKLYN COLL, 1985-. **HONORS AND AWARDS** Congressional Achievement Award, Congressman Floyd Flake, 1990; Outstanding Educator Award, Success Guide George Fraser, Editor, 1991; Educator of the Year Award, New York Association of Black Educators, 1988; Educational Leadership Award, Council of Supervisors and Administrators of New York, 1991; Award of Excellence, New York, Alliance of Black School Educators, 1988. **MEMBERSHIPS** President, New York Jamaica Branch, NAACP, 1977, 1978; education co-chairperson, New York State, NAACP, 1976-1980. **CONTACT ADDRESS** Sch of Education, Brooklyn Col, CUNY, Ave H & Bedford Ave, Brooklyn, NY, 11210.

MONTGOMERY, TONI-MARIE
PERSONAL Born 06/25/1956, Philadelphia, Pennsylvania, s **DISCIPLINE** MUSIC **EDUCATION** Philadelphia College of Performing Arts, Philadelphia, PA, BM, 1980; University of Michigan, Ann Arbor, MI, MM, 1981, DMA, 1984. **CAREER** Western Michigan University, Kalamazoo, MI, asst director school of music, 1985-87; University of Connecticut, Storrs, CT, asst dean, 1987-89; Arizona State University, Tempe, AZ, assoc dean/asst professor, 1990-96; Arizona State Univ, School of Music, dir, 1996-. **HONORS AND AWARDS** Outstanding Keyboard Performer, American Keyboard Artists, 1988; Black Women's Task Force Arts Award, 1998. **MEMBERSHIPS** Phoenix Symphony Board, 1998-; member, Tempe Arts Commission, 1991-93; president, Sister Friends: African-American Women, 1990-; member, board of directors, president Faculty Women's Association, 1990-. **CONTACT ADDRESS** Director/Prof, School of Music, Arizona State Univ, Tempe, PO Box 870405, Tempe, AZ, 85287-0405.

MOODY, CHARLES DAVID, SR.
PERSONAL Born 08/30/1932, Baton Rouge, LA, m **DISCIPLINE** EDUCATION **EDUCATION** Central State Univ, BS Biology 1954; Chicago Tchrs Coll, MA Sci Ed 1961; Univ of Chicago, Cert Adv Study 1969; Northwestern Univ, PhD Ed Admin1971. **CAREER** Mentally Handicapped Chicago Schs, tchr of educable 1959-62; Dist #143 1/2 Posen-Robbins IL, tchr of sci & soc studies 1962-64; Sch Dist #65 Evanston, asst principal 1964-68; Sch Dist #147, supt 1968-70; Urban Fellows TTT Prog North WU, instr 1979-70; Div of Educ Specialist Univ MI, chmn 1973-77; Proj for Fair Admn Student Disc Univ MI, dir 1975-80; Univ MI, prof educ SOE 1970-, dir prog for educ oppor 1970-87, dir ctr for sex equity in schs 1981-87, vice provost for minority affairs 1987-. **HONORS AND AWARDS** Awd of Respect Washtenaw Comm Coll Ann Arbor MI 1984; Dr of Laws Degree Central State Univ 1981; Comm Leader Awd Ann Arbor Veterans Admn Med Ctr 1980; Professional of the Yr Awd Ann Arbor Chap of Natl Assn of Negro Businesses & Professional Women Inc 1979; Charter Inductee, Central State Univ, Wilberforce OH 1989. **MEMBERSHIPS** Fndr/ex bd NABSE 1970-; pres/fndr CD Moody & Assocs Inc 1981-; bd dirs Ann Arbor NAACP 1983-85; bd dirs NITV. **CONTACT ADDRESS** Vice Provost for Minority Affairs, Univ of Michigan, 503 Thompson St, 3052 Fleming Admin Building, Ann Arbor, MI, 48109-1340.

MOODY, J. CARROLL
PERSONAL Born 01/03/1934, Abilene, TX, m, 1953, 5 children **DISCIPLINE** UNITED STATES ECONOMIC & LABOR HISTORY **EDUCATION** Univ Corpus Christi, BS, 56; Tex A&I Univ, MS, 60; Univ Okla, PhD, 65. **CAREER** High sch teacher, Tex, 56-61; from instr to asst prof hist, 64-68, asst dean, Col Arts & Sci, Univ Toledo, 66-68; prof hist, Northern Ill Univ, 68-, chmn dept, 74-. **RESEARCH** Steel industry and the National Industrial Recovery Act; labor relations in the steel industry; history of the credit union in the United States. **SELECTED PUBLICATIONS** Coauth, The credit union movement: Origins and development, 1850-1970, Univ Nebr, 71;art, The transformation of the American economy, 1877-1900, The Reinterpretation of American History and Culture, Nat Coun Social Studies, 73. **CONTACT ADDRESS** Provost's Office, No Illinois Univ, De Kalb, IL, 60115-2825. **EMAIL** cmoody@niu.edu

MOODY, PETER R.
PERSONAL Born 10/13/1943, San Francisco, CA, m, 1966, 6 children **DISCIPLINE** POLITICAL SIENCE **EDUCATION** Vanderilt, AB, 65; Yale Univ, PhD, 71. **CAREER** Prof, Notre Dame, 83-. **HONORS AND AWARDS** Peace Fel, Hodver Inst, 75; Chiang Ching Kuo Res Fel, 78. **MEMBERSHIPS** APSA. **RESEARCH** Chinese Politics; Asian Politics; Asian International Relations; Chinese Political Thought. **SELECTED PUBLICATIONS** Auth, Trends in the Study of Chinese Political Culture, China Quart, 94; Asian Values, J of Int Affairs, 96; Introduction, China Doc Annual 93: The End of the Post-Mao Era, 97; Four Powers Are Good, Six May Be Better, Diplomacy, 97; The Politics of Presidentialism on Taiwan, 1988-1997, Working Papers in Taiwan Studies, 98. **CONTACT ADDRESS** Dept of Government and International Studies, Univ of Notre Dame, Notre Dame, IN, 46556. **EMAIL** Peter.R.Moody@nd.edu

MOOGK, PETER N.
PERSONAL Born 10/05/1943, Chiltington, England **DISCIPLINE** HISTORY **EDUCATION** Univ Toronto, BA, 65, MA, 66, PhD, 73. **CAREER** Asst prof Univ BC, 70-77; vis scholar, Darwin Col, Cambridge Univ, 82-83; ASSOC PROF HISTORY, UNIV BC, 77-. **HONORS AND AWARDS** Ste-Marie Prize Hist, 75; Can Asn Res Awards, 76, 87, 89; Daughters Colonial Wars Prize Early Am hist, 80. **MEMBERSHIPS** Fel, Can Numismatic Res Soc; Can Hist Asn; Fre Colonial Hist Soc; Vancouver Numismatic Soc. **SELECTED PUBLICATIONS** Auth, Building a House in New France, 77; auth, Vancouver Defended, 78; coauth, Berczy, 91. **CONTACT ADDRESS** Dept of History, Univ BC, Vancouver, BC, V6T 1Z1.

MOON, CYRIS HEE SUK
PERSONAL Born 09/04/1933, Korea, m, 1959, 3 children **DISCIPLINE** HISTORY **EDUCATION** Emory Univ, PhD, 71. **CAREER** Prof, San Franciso Theol Sem. **MEMBERSHIPS** AAP; SBL. **SELECTED PUBLICATIONS** Auth, A Cultural History of Korea, Seoul: Voice, 96. **CONTACT ADDRESS** 2915 Ballesteros Ln, Tustin, CA, 92782. **EMAIL** cyrismoon@aol.com

MOONEY, L.M.
DISCIPLINE MEDIEVAL STUDIES **EDUCATION** Univ Toronto, PhD, 81. **CAREER** Asst Prof, Assoc Prof, 86-99, Univ Maine. **MEMBERSHIPS** MAA; EBS; AMARC; EETS; New Chaucer Soc. **RESEARCH** Medieval English Manuscripts, Literature and History. **SELECTED PUBLICATIONS** Auth, Index of Middle English Prose, vol XI, Trinity College, Cambridge, 95; coauth, The Chronicle of John Somer, OFM, Camden Soc Miscellany 98. **CONTACT ADDRESS** Dept of English, Univ Maine, Orono, ME, 04473.

MOONEY-MELVIN, PATRICIA
DISCIPLINE HISTORY **EDUCATION** Cincinnati, PhD. **CAREER** Co-dir, Kingsley Hist Proj, Kingsley elem sch, Evanston, 95-96; prin investr, Guidebook to DoD-related World War II Sites and Mus, Legacy Res Management Prog, dept defense, 92-95; consult, Interpretive Strategy Proj, Lake County Mus, 95; proj dir, East Rogers Park Neighborhood Hist Proj, Loyola Univ, 92-94; proj dir, Agents of Change: the Jesuits and Mid-America, Traveling Exhibit, Loyola Univ, 92-93; ed & prin auth, Ark Preserv, Hist Preserv Alliance of Ark, 88-89; consult, Making Equal Opportunity a Reality: A History of the Urban League of Little Rock Proj, The Urban League of Little Rock, 87-89; consult, Civilian Conserv Corps Oral Hist Proj, Nat Asn of Civilian Conserv Corps Alumni, Little Rock, 81-86; guest cur, Behold Our Works Were Good exhib, in conjunction with the Ark Women's Hist Inst, The Old State House, Little Rock, 86; actg dir, UALR Archives and Special Collections, Univ Ark at Little Rock, 83-84; guest cur, Ohio Quilts and Quilters 1800-1981, exhib, Frick Art Gallery, Col Wooster, 81; cur, Ohio Labor Hist Proj, Ohio Hist Soc, 77-79. **RESEARCH** Neighborhoods; community organization; tourism. **SELECTED PUBLICATIONS** Auth, The Organic City: Urban Definition and Neighborhood Organization 1880-1920, Lexington: UP Ky, 87; The Path From Our Founding to Our Future: A City Tour of Loyola University Chicago's Historic Downtown Sites, Walking Tour Brochure, 95; Reading Your Neighborhood: A History of East Rogers Park, Chicago: Loyola Univ, 93; coauth, The Urbanization of Modern America, 2nd Ed, San Diego: Harcourt Brace Jovanovich, 87; ed & prin auth, American Community Organizations: A Historical Dictionary, Westport: Greenwood Press, 86; articles; Urban History, Local History, and Public History, History News 51, 96; Beyond the Book: Historians and the Interpretive Challenge, Public Historian 17, 95; Professional Historians and Destiny's Gate, Public Historian 17, 95; Harnessing the Romance of the Past: Preserv, Tourism, and History, Public Historian 13, 91. **CONTACT ADDRESS** Fine Arts Dept, Loyola Univ, Chicago, 6525 N. Sheridan Rd., Chicago, IL, 60626. **EMAIL** pmooney@luc.edu

MOORE, A. LLOYD
PERSONAL Born 03/22/1931, Hamilton, ON, Canada, m, 1956, 4 children **DISCIPLINE** MODERN HISTORY **EDUCATION** Univ Toronto, BA, 54; Univ Minn, MA, 56; PhD(hist), 58. **CAREER** Res asst, Univ Minn, 57-58; lectr hist, Univ Toronto, 58- 61; asst prof, Univ Cincinnati, 61-62; from asst prof to assoc prof, 62-71, Prof Hist, Univ Southern Calif, 71-, Vis assoc prof, Queen's Univ, Ont, 65-66; Nat Endowment for Humanities Younger Scholar fel, 69-70; Guggenheim fel, 77. **HONORS AND AWARDS** Koren Prize, Soc French Hist Studies, 62. **MEMBERSHIPS** AHA; Soc Fr Hist Studies; Past & Present Soc, England. **RESEARCH** Seventeenth century France. **SELECTED PUBLICATIONS** Auth, Law And Justice Under Louis XIV, In: Louis XIV and the Craft of Kingship, Ohio State Univ, 69; The Seventeenth Century: Europe in Ferment, Heath, 70; The Revolt of the Judges: The Parlement of Paris and the Fronde, 1643-1652, Princeton Univ, 71; coauth, Seventeenth century peasant furies: Some problems of comparative history, Past & Present, 571; auth, The preconditions of revolution in early modern Europe: Did they really exist?, Can J Hist, 1272; coauth, The World of Europe, Forum, 73; auth, The Annals Historians, Queen's Quart, Can, 78; The Myth Of Absolutism - Change And Continuity In Early-Modern Europe - Henshall,N, Sixteenth Century J, Vol 0025, 1994; The Emerging Intendants and French Political Change, Can J Hist, 79; Louis-Xvi - Hardman,J, American Historical Review, Vol 0099, 1994; The Deaths Of Louis-Xvi - Regicide And The French Political Imagination - Dunn,S, J Of Modern History, Vol 0068, 1996; Colbert Fortune - French - Villain,J, Sixteenth Century J, Vol 0027, 1996; Economics And Finance During The Ancien-Regime - A Research Guide 1523-1789 - French - Felix,J, Sixteenth Century J, Vol 0027, 1996; The Fronde - A French-Revolution, 1648-1652 - Ranum,O, American Historical Review, Vol 0100, 1995; Introduction - New Bottles And

New Wine - The Current State Of Early Modernist Biographical Writing, French Historical Studies, Vol 0019, 1996. **CONTACT ADDRESS** Dept of Hist, Univ of Southern Calif, Los Angeles, CA, 90007.

MOORE, CHRISTOPHER H.
PERSONAL Born 06/09/1950, Stoke-on-Trent, England **DISCIPLINE** HISTORY **EDUCATION** Univ BC, BA, 71; Univ Ottawa, MA, 77. **CAREER** Staff Hist, Parks Can, 72-75; sec bd gov, Heritage Can Found, 77-78; hist columnist, The Beaver, 91-; lectr, Univ Guelph, 85; lectr, Univ Toronto, 89-91; vis scholar, Univ Guelph, 90. **HONORS AND AWARDS** Gov Gen Lit Award, 82; Riddell Award, Ont Hist, 84; Sec State, Prize Exellence Can Stud, 85; IODE Toronto Bk Award, 93. **MEMBERSHIPS** Writers' Union of Can **SELECTED PUBLICATIONS** Auth, Louisbourg Portraits, 82; auth, The Loyalists, 84; auth, The Law Society of Upper Canada and Ontario's Lawyers, 97; auth, 1867: How the Fathers Made a Deal, 97; coauth, The Illustrated History of Canada, 87; coauth, The Story of Canada, 92. **CONTACT ADDRESS** 396 Pacific, No 202, Toronto, ON, M6P 2R1.

MOORE, DEBORAH DASH
PERSONAL Born 08/06/1946, New York, NY, m, 1967, 2 children **DISCIPLINE** HISTORY **EDUCATION** Brandeis Univ, BA, 67; Columbia Univ, MA, 68, PhD, 75. **CAREER** Asst prof, 76-84, assoc prof, 84-88, prof, Vassar Col, 88-, chair, dept of relig, 83-87, dir, prog in Am culture, 92-95; Fulbright-Hays Sr lect, dept of Am studies, Hebrew Univ, 84-85. **HONORS AND AWARDS** Nat Jewish Book Award Honor Book, 94; Dartmouth Medal of American Library Asn for best reference work in 1997. **MEMBERSHIPS** Am Academy of Jewish Res; Am Jewish Hist Soc; Asn for Jewish Studies; Am Studies Asn. **RESEARCH** Am Jewish hist; urban hist; relig in America. **SELECTED PUBLICATIONS** Auth, On Reading the Akedah as a Mother of Sons, SH'MA, Sept 94; Foreward, Greenwich Village, 1920-1930, by Caroline Ware, Classics in Urban History, Univ CA Press, 94; Trude Weiss-Rosmarin and The Jewish Spectator, The Other New York Jewish Intellectuals, ed Carole Kessner, NY Univ Press, 94; I'll Take Manhattan: Reflections on Jewish Studies, Judaism, fall 95; Judaism and Jewish Culture, Encyclopedia of the United States in the Twentieth Century, ed Stanley Kutler, Simon & Schuster, 95; To The Golden Cities: Pursuing the American Jewish Dream in Miami and LA, The Free Press, 94, paperback, Harvard Univ Press, 96, Chapter Four reprinted in Religion and American Culture, ed David G Hackett, Routledge, 95; Jewish Women on My Mind, Culturefront, winter 97; Identity Politics--Kosher Style, Sh'ma, May 97; Jewish Women in America: An Historical Encyclopedia, co-ed with Paula Hyman, 2 vols, Routledge, 97; Separate Paths: Blacks and Jews in the 20th Century South, in Struggles in the Promised Land: Toward a History of Black-Jewish Relations in the United States, ed Jack Salzman and Cornel West, Oxford Univ Press, 97; Zionism After Israel: Some Modest Proposals, The Reconstructionist, 62:2, spring 98; Jewish GI's and the Creation of the Judeo-Christian Tradition, Religion and American Culture, 8:1, winter 98; numerous other publications. **CONTACT ADDRESS** 620 Ft Washington Ave, New York, NY, 10040. **EMAIL** moored@vassar.edu

MOORE, EDGAR BENJAMIN
PERSONAL Born 07/17/1928, Spring Lake, NJ, m, 1952, 3 children **DISCIPLINE** EUROPEAN HISTORY **EDUCATION** Wesleyan Univ, BA, 50; Drew Univ, BD, 54, MSacred Theol, 58; Univ St Andrews, PhD, 65. **CAREER** Chaplain & asst prof relig, 62-64, from asst prof to assoc prof hist, 64-70, chmn dept 64-73, prof hist, Baldwin-Wallace Col, 70-. **MEMBERSHIPS** AAUP; African Studies Assn; Am Soc Church Hist; AHA. **RESEARCH** Reformation history; African studies. **CONTACT ADDRESS** Dept of History, Baldwin-Wallace Col, 275 Eastland Rd, Berea, OH, 44017-2088.

MOORE, GEORGE EAGLETON
PERSONAL Born 03/25/1927, Osaka, Japan, m, 1953, 3 children **DISCIPLINE** EASTERN ASIAN HISTORY **EDUCATION** Univ Calif, Berkeley, BA, 51, MA, 59, PhD(hist), 66. **CAREER** From assoc prof to prof, 64-68 San Jose State Univ, 73-. **HONORS AND AWARDS** Ford Foundation Fellowship 62-63; NEH Summer Fell, 79; Meritorious Serv Award, Coll of Social Sciences, San Jose State Univ, 98. **MEMBERSHIPS** Assn Asian Studies. **RESEARCH** Modernization of Japan; modernization of Asia; world history. **SELECTED PUBLICATIONS** Auth, Samurai conversion: The case of Kumamoto, Asian Studies, 4/66; coauth, Changing Japanese attitudes toward the military: Mitsuya Kenkyu and the Japanese self defense force, Asian Surv, 9/67. **CONTACT ADDRESS** Dept of History, San Jose State Univ, 1 Washington Sq, San Jose, CA, 95192-0117.

MOORE, GERALD L.
PERSONAL Born 07/31/1933, New York, NY **DISCIPLINE** SOCIOLOGY **EDUCATION** City Coll of NY, BA Sociology (honors) 1974; Wharton School Univ of PA, Certificate Finance & Acctg 1978; Grad School & Univ Center City Univ of NY, PhD Sociology 1982. **CAREER** Natl Urban League, proj dir 1965-67; Lance Moore Assoc, pres 1969-73; Consolidated Edison, sr training rep internal consultant 1973-77; Amer Express Co, mgr training 1977-79; NJ INST OF TECH, asst prof orgl behav 1979-82; CONSULTANT AND EDUCATOR 1982-. **HONORS AND AWARDS** . **MEMBERSHIPS** Metro Council OD Network 1968-69; Amer Soc of Training & Develop 1974-77; Amer Soc Assn 1982-85; Assn of Black Sociologists 1982-85; recruited, selected and made test-sophisticated the first Blacks and Hispanics to enter IBM, Pitney Bowes, Xerox and Bell Telephone in craft positions. **SELECTED PUBLICATIONS** Book "The Politics of Management Consulting" 1984.

MOORE, JAMES TALMADGE
PERSONAL Born 10/23/1936, Houston, TX, m, 1974, 4 children **DISCIPLINE** AMERICAN HISTORY **EDUCATION** Univ Houston, BS, 58; Episcopal Theol Sem Southwest, MDiv, 61; Tex A&M Univ, MA, 73, PhD, 80. **CAREER** Asst prof, Tex A&M Univ, 80-81; PROF, HIST, NORTH HARRIS COUNTY COMMUNITY COL, 81-; asst prof, Tex A & M Univ, 80-81. **HONORS AND AWARDS** Paul J Foik C S C Award, Hist res & writing, 94. **MEMBERSHIPS** Cath Hist Asn; Tex Cath Hist Soc (pres, 98-). **RESEARCH** Colonial American history; American Indian history; Indian and missionary relations. **SELECTED PUBLICATIONS** Auth, Indians and Jesuits: A Seventeenth Century Encounter, Loyola Univ Press, Chicago, 82; Through Fire and Flood, the Catholic Church in Frontier Texas, 1836-1900, Tex A & M Press, 92. **CONTACT ADDRESS** Hist Dept, No Harris County Comm Col, 21806 Galewood Ln, Houston, TX, 77073.

MOORE, JAMES TICE
PERSONAL Born 08/08/1945, Greenville, SC, m, 1965, 3 children **DISCIPLINE** AMERICAN HISTORY **EDUCATION** Univ SC, BA, 66; Univ VA, MA, 68, PhD(hist), 72. **CAREER** Instr, 70-72, asst prof, 72-78, actg chmn, 81-82, ASSOC PROF HIST, VA COMMONWEALTH UNIV, 78-, chmn dept, 82-86. **HONORS AND AWARDS** Lecturer's Award, Col Humanities & Sci, VA Commonwealth Univ, 82; Distinguished Teaching Award, Col Humanities and Sci, VA Commonwealth Univ, 95. **MEMBERSHIPS** Orgn Am Historians; Southern Hist Asn; VA Hist Soc. **RESEARCH** New South 1865-1920, political history; conservation history, especially in relation to the South; Southern intellectual history. **SELECTED PUBLICATIONS** Auth, The University of Virginia and the Readjusters, VA Mag Hist & Biog, 1/70; Two Paths to the New South: The Virginia Debt Controversy, 1870-1883, Univ Press KY, 74; Black Militancy in Readjuster Virginia, 1879-1883, J of Southern Hist, 5/75; The Death of the Duel: The Code Duello in Readjuster Virginia, 1879-1883, VA Mag of Hist & Biog, 7/75; Majority and Morality: John Taylor's Agrarianism, Agr Hist, 4/76; Redeemers Reconsidered: Change and Continuity in the Democratic South, 1870-1900, J of Southern Hist, 8/78; Gunfire on the Chesapeake: Governor Cameron and the Oyster Pirates, 1882-1885, VA Mag of Hist & Biog, 7/82; co-ed, The Governors of Virginia, 1860-1978, Univ Press of VA , 82; Secession and the States: A Review Essay, VA Mag of Hist and Biog, 1/86; Of Cavaliers and Yankees: Frederic W.M. Holliday and the Sectional Crisis, 1845-1861, VA Mag of Hist and Biog, 7/91; From Dynasty to Disenfranchisement: Some Reflections About Virginia History, 1820-1902, VA Mag of Hist and Biog, winter 96. **CONTACT ADDRESS** Dept of Hist, Virginia Commonwealth Univ, Box 2001, Richmond, VA, 23284-2001. **EMAIL** jmoore@atlas.vcu.edu

MOORE, JOHN CLARE
PERSONAL Born 05/17/1933, Wichita, KS, m, 1956, 4 children **DISCIPLINE** MEDIEVAL EUROPEAN HISTORY **EDUCATION** Rockhurst Col, AB, 55; Johns Hopkins Univ, PhD(Hist), 60. **CAREER** Instr Hist, Hofstra Col, 59-62; asst prof, Parsons Col, 62-63; from asst prof to assoc prof, 63-72, assoc dean, 71-74, prof Hist, Hofstra Univ, 72-98, chmn dept, 76-82, 87-93. **MEMBERSHIPS** AAUP; AHA; Medieval Acad Am. **RESEARCH** Medieval church; papacy; medieval love. **SELECTED PUBLICATIONS** Auth, Count Baldwin IX of Flanders, Philip Augustus, and the Papal power, Speculum, 1/62; Papal justice in France around the time of Pope Innocent III, Church Hist, 72; Love in Twelfth-Century France, Univ Pa, 72; Courtly love: A problem of terminology, J Hist of Ideas, 79; Innocent III's de miseria humanae conditionis: A speculum curiae?, Cath Hist Rev, 81; The Sermons of Pope Innocent II, Romische Historische Mitteilunger, 36, 94; Die Register Innocenz II, 6 Band, 6 Pontifikatsjahr (12-3-1204), one of three eds, Vienna: Verlag der Osterreichischen Akademie der Wissenschaften, 95. **CONTACT ADDRESS** Dept of History, Hofstra Univ, 1000 Fulton Ave, Hempstead, NY, 11550-1091. **EMAIL** jclaremoore@worldnet.att.net

MOORE, MARIAN J.
PERSONAL Saginaw, MI **DISCIPLINE** AFRICAN HISTORY, CURATOR **CAREER** National Afro-American Museum and Cultural Center, former director; Museum of African American History, Detroit, MI, director, 1988-93. **CONTACT ADDRESS** Museum of African American History, 301 Frederick Douglass, Detroit, MI, 48202.

MOORE, MICHAEL J.
PERSONAL Born 09/16/1940, Seattle, WA, m, 1963, 2 children **DISCIPLINE** HISTORY **EDUCATION** Univ of Wash, BA, 63, MA, 66, PhD, 71. **CAREER** Instr, Western Wash Univ, 65-70; instr, Skagit Valley col, 70-71; asst prof, 71-79, prof, Appalachian State Univ, 80- . **HONORS AND AWARDS** Fel, Royal Hist Soc., Ed & pub of Albion. **MEMBERSHIPS** Am Hist Asn; North Am Confr on British Studies. **RESEARCH** Modern Britain: social & economic. **CONTACT ADDRESS** Dept of Hist, Box 32072 ASLL, Boone, NC, 28608. **EMAIL** mooremj@conrad.appstate.edu

MOORE, ROBERT HENRY
PERSONAL Born 09/16/1940, Madisonville, KY, m, 1964, 2 children **DISCIPLINE** AMERICAN LITERATURE & HISTORY **EDUCATION** Davidson Col, AB, 62; Univ NC, Chapel Hill, MA, 64; Univ Wis-Madison, PhD(English), 70. **CAREER** Instr English, US Mil Acad, 68-70; asst prof, Univ Md, College Park, 70-76, assoc prof, 76-80. Contrib-reader, Dict Am Regional English, 68-; exec secy, Faulkner Concordance Proj, 70-, ed, Faulkner Concordance Newslett, 72-; reviewer, Nat Endowment for Humanities, 72; fel, Inter-Univ Sem Armed Forces & Soc, 73-. **MEMBERSHIPS** MLA; Am Studies Asn; Am Civil Liberties Union. **RESEARCH** twentieth century American language and literature, American studies; armed forces and society. **SELECTED PUBLICATIONS** Coauth, Black puritan, William & Mary Quart, 467; ed, Ellison at West Point, Contempt Lit, spring 74; coauth, School for Soldiers, Oxford Univ, 74; Cameras in state courts, An historical-perspective, judicature, vol 0078, 1994. **CONTACT ADDRESS** 9202 Saybrook Ave Branwell Park, Silver Spring, MD, 20901.

MOORE, ROBERT JOSEPH
PERSONAL Born 04/29/1934, Medina, TN, m, 1980, 4 children **DISCIPLINE** AMERICAN HISTORY **EDUCATION** Lambuth Col, BA, 55; Boston Univ, MA, 57, PhD, 61. **CAREER** From asst prof to assoc prof, 60-67, prof hist, Columbia Col, SC, 67-, Chmn Dept, 60-83; Duke Univ-Univ NC Coop Prog fac fel int studies, 68-69. **MEMBERSHIPS** AHA; AAUP; Southern Hist Asn. **RESEARCH** Reconstruction period in American history; 20th century America; civil rights movement. **SELECTED PUBLICATIONS** Auth, Robert C Winthrop: Conservative opponent of Lincoln, Proc SC Hist Asn, 61; Interpretations of Reconstruction, The Search, 4/62; Andrew Johnson: The second swing 'round the circle, Proc SC Hist Asn, 66; Governor Chamberlain and the end of reconstruction, Proc SC Hist Asn, 77. **CONTACT ADDRESS** Dept of Hist, Columbia Col, So Carolina, 1301 Columbia Col, Columbia, SC, 29203-5998. **EMAIL** bmoore@colucoll.edu

MOORE, ROBERT LAURENCE
PERSONAL Born 04/03/1940, Houston, TX, m, 1963, 3 children **DISCIPLINE** AMERICAN INTELLECTUAL & CULTURAL HISTORY **EDUCATION** Rice Univ, BA, 62; Yale Univ, MA, 64, PhD(hist), 68. **CAREER** Actg instr hist & Am studies, Yale Univ, 67-68, asst prof, 68-72; assoc prof, 72-78, Prof Hist, Cornell Univ, 78-, Chmn Dept, 80-; HOWARD A NEWMAN PROF AM STUD, CORNELL UNIV, 98-, chmn dept hist, 80-83, dir, Am Stud Prog, 98-. **HONORS AND AWARDS** Yale Univ Morse fel, 70-71; Nat Endowment for Humanities fel, 75-76; Rockefeller Found fel, 79-80; fel, Woodrow Wilson Ctr IntlScholars, 87-88; Fulbright lectr, India, 97. **MEMBERSHIPS** AHA; Orgn Am Historians; Am Studies Asn. **RESEARCH** Am radicalism; Am relig hist; 20th cent Am thought. **SELECTED PUBLICATIONS** Auth, European Socialists and the American Promised Land, Oxford Univ, 70; ed, The Emergence of an American Left: Civil War to World War I, Wiley, 73; auth, In Search of White Crows, Spiritualism, Parapsychology and American Culture, Oxford Univ, 77; auth, Modern American Religion, Vol 2 - The Noise Of Conflict, 1919-1941 - Marty,Me, J Of The American Academy Of Religion, Vol 0061, 1993; auth, The Shaker Experience In America - A History Of The United-Society-Of-Believers - Stein,SJ, New England Quarterly-A Historical Review Of New England Life And Letters, Vol 0066, 1993; Right Center-Left - Essays In American History - Ribuffo,LP, American Historical Review, Vol 0098, 1993; The Shaker Experience In America - A History Of The United- Society-Of-Believers - Stein,SJ, New England Quarterly-A Historical Review Of New England Life And Letters, Vol 0066, 1993; American Socialists And Evolutionary Thought, 1870-1920 - Pittenger,M, Reviews In American History, Vol 0022, 1994; Spreading The Word - The Bible Business In 19th-Century America - Wosh,PJ, J Of American History, Vol 0082, 1995; auth, Religious Outsider and the Making of Americans, Oxford Univ Press, 86; auth, Selling God: American Religion in the Marketplace of Culture, Oxfored Univ Press, 94; co-auth, The Godless Constitution, The Case Against Religious Correctness, Norton, 96. **CONTACT ADDRESS** Dept of Hist, Cornell Univ, McGraw Hal, Ithaca, NY, 14853-0001.

MOORE, SALLY F.
PERSONAL Born 01/18/1924, New York, NY, m, 1951, 2 children **DISCIPLINE** ANTHROPOLOGY **EDUCATION** Barnard Col, BA, 43; Columbia Law School, LLB, 45; Columbia Univ, PhD, 57. **CAREER** Assoc attorney, Spence Hotchkiss, Parker and Duryea, 45-46; staff attorney, War Dept, Nuremberg Trials, 46; dept asst, Dept of Anthropology, Columbia Univ, 50-52; asst prof, 63-65, part-time lectr in the Law School,

70-75, prof on Anthrop, 70-77, chmn, Anthrop Section, Dept of Sociology and Anthrop, Univ of Southern Calif, 72-77; res assoc, Univ Col, Univ of East Africa, 68-69; res assoc, Univ of Dar es Salaam, 73-74; vis prof, Dept of Anthrop, Yale Univ, 75-76; prof of Anthrop, Univ of Calif, 77-81; VIS PROF OF LAW AND ANTHROP, 78, DEAN OF GRAD SCHOOL OF ARTS AND SCI, 85-89, PROF OF ANTHROP, HARVARD UNIV, 81-; consult, A.I.D., U.S. State Dept, 91-96. **HONORS AND AWARDS** Ansley Prize, Columbia Univ, 57; Post-doctoral res scholar, 67-68; res grant, Soc Sci Res Coun, 68-69; Dart Award for Innovative Teaching, 71; res grant, Nat Sci Found, 72-75 & 79; honorary res fel, Dept of Anthropology, Univ of London, 73-; co-chair, Wenner Gren Conf, 74; award for creativ scholar and res, Assoc of U.S.C, 75; honorary membership, Iota Chapter, Phi Beat Kappa, Radcliffe, 83-; res grant, Wenner Gren Found, 83; Barnard Col Medal of Distinction, Columbia Univ, 87; Guggenheim Fel, 94; Huxley Memorial Medallist and Lectr for 1999, Coun of Royal Anthrop Inst of Great Britain and Ireland, 97. **MEMBERSHIPS** Bar of the State of NY; Am Anthrop Asn; Royal Anthrop Inst of Great Britain and Ireland; Int African Inst, London; African Studies Asn; Asn of Social Anthropologists; Law and Soc Asn; Comn of Folk Law and Pluralism; Am Acad of Arts and Sci; Am Ethnological Soc; Asn for Legal and Political Anthrop; Asn for Africanist Anthrop. **SELECTED PUBLICATIONS** Auth, Anthropology and Africa: Changing Perspectives on a Changing Scene, The Univ of Va Press, 94; Law in Unstable Settings: The Dilemma of Migration, Focaal, 94; Imperfect Communications, Understanding Disputes: The Politics of Argument, Berg Pub, 95; Introduction to O.F. Raum's Chaga Childhood, 96, Int African Inst, 96; Doctrine as Determinism, Rechthistorisches J, 96; Post-socialist Micropolitics: Kilimanjaro 1993, Int African Inst, 96; Concerning Archie Mafeje's Reinvention of Anthropology and Africa, Codesria Bulletin, 96; Archie Mafeje's Prescriptions for the Academic Future, Af Sociological Rev, 98; Cusomary Law, Encyclo of Africa, Simon and Schuster, 98. **CONTACT ADDRESS** Harvard Univ, 348 William James Hall, Cambridge, MA, 02138. **EMAIL** moore@wjh.harvard.edu

MOORE, WILLIAM HOWARD
PERSONAL Born 06/26/1942, Harriman, TN, m, 1986, 1 child **DISCIPLINE** AMERICAN HISTORY **EDUCATION** Univ Tenn, Knoxville, BS, 64, MA, 65; Univ Tex, Austin, PhD, 71. **CAREER** Instr hist, Southwest Tex State Univ, 71-72; asst prof, Ohio Univ, 72-73; asst prof, 73-78, assoc prof hist, 78-, prof, 89, chmn hist dept, 92, Univ Wyo. **HONORS AND AWARDS** NEH grant, 77, 90; travel grant, Herbert C Hoover Pres Lib Assoc; travel grant, Eisenhower World Affairs Inst, 90; Wyoming Coun for Hum Grants, 81; **MEMBERSHIPS** AHA; Orgn Am Historians; Ctr for Study of Presidency. **RESEARCH** Twentieth century United States; American social history; American labor history. **SELECTED PUBLICATIONS** Auth, Do We Like Ike?: Historians and the Eisenhower Presidency, Kansas History, 90; art, Crime and Justice, Encyclopedia of United States Congress, 95. **CONTACT ADDRESS** Dept of History, Univ of Wyoming, PO Box 3198, Laramie, WY, 82071-3198. **EMAIL** budmoore@uwyo.edu

MOORE, WINFRED B., JR.
DISCIPLINE HISTORY **EDUCATION** Furman Univ, BA, 71; Duke Univ, MA, 72, PhD, 75. **CAREER** Asst prof, 76-81, assoc prof, 81-89, PROF, 90-, THE CITADEL. **CONTACT ADDRESS** Dept of History, The Citadel, Charleston, SC, 29409. **EMAIL** bo.moore@citadel.edu

MOORHEAD, JAMES HOWELL
PERSONAL Born 01/16/1947, Harrisburg, PA, m, 1969, 2 children **DISCIPLINE** AMERICAN RELIGIOUS HISTORY **EDUCATION** Westminster Col, PA, BA, 68; Princeton Theol Sem, MDiv, 71; Yale Univ, MPhil, 73, PhD(relig studies), 75. **CAREER** Asst prof, 75-80, Assoc Prof Relig, NC State Univ, 80-, Fel independent study & res, Nat Endowment for Humanities, 81-82. **HONORS AND AWARDS** Brewer Prize, Am Soc Church Hist, 76. **MEMBERSHIPS** Am Soc Church Hist; Am Acad Relig; Am Hist Asn. **RESEARCH** Nineteenth century and early twentieth century American Protestantism; Millennialism; views of death and after life. **SELECTED PUBLICATIONS** Auth, Joseph Addison Alexander: Common sense, romanticism and Biblical criticism at Princeton, J Presbyterian Hist, spring 75; American Apocalypse: Yankee Protestants and the Civil War, 1860-1869, Yale Univ Press, 78; Social reform and the divided conscience of antebellum Protestantism, Church Hist, 79; Softly And Tenderly Jesus Is Calling - Heaven And Hell In American Revivalism, 1870-1920 - Butler,Jm, Church History, Vol 0062, 1993; Glorious Contentment - The Grand Army Of The Republic, 1865-1900 - Mcconnell,S, J Of American History, Vol 0080, 1993; A Field Of Divine Wonders - The New-Divinity And Village Revivals In Northwestern Connecticut, 1792-1822 - Kling,Dw, Theology Today, Vol 0051, 1994; A Friend To Gods Poor - Smith,Edward,Parmalee - Armstrong,Wh, J Of American History, Vol 0081, 1995; Church People In The Struggle - The National- Council-Of-Churches And The Black-Freedom Movement, 1950-1970 - Findlay,JF, J Of Interdisciplinary History, Vol 0026, 95; Peddler In Divinity - Whitefield, George And The Transatlantic-Revivals, 1737-1770 - Lambert,F, Theology Today, Vol 0051, 1995; Arguing The Apocalypse - A Theory Of Millennial Rhetoric - Oleary,Sd, Theology Today, Vol 0051, 1994; No Sorrow Like Our Sorrow Northern Protestant Ministers And The Assassination Of Lincoln - Chesebrough,Db, American Historical Review, Vol 0100, 1995; auth, Consumer Rites - The Buying And Selling Of American Holidays - Schmidt,LE, Theology Today, Vol 0053, 1996; The Myth Of American Individualism - The Protestant Origins Of American Political-Thought - Shain,BA, J Of Religion, Vol 0076, 1996; Our Southern Zion - A History Of Calvinism In The South-Carolina Low Country, 1690-1990 - Clarke,E, J Of Presbyterian History, Vol 0075, 1997; Law And Providence In Bellamy, Joseph New-England - Valeri,M, American Presbyterians-J Of Presbyterian History, Vol 0074, 1996; Spreading The Word - The Bible Business In 19th- Century America - Wosh,PJ, American Presbyterians, J Of Presbyterian History, Vol 0074, 1996. **CONTACT ADDRESS** Dept of Philos & Relig, No Carolina State Univ, PO Box 5688, Raleigh, NC, 27650.

MORAN, DIANE D.
DISCIPLINE ART HISTORY **EDUCATION** Univ ND, BS; Univ VA, PhD. **CAREER** Fac, 77-; prof, Sweet Briar Col. **RESEARCH** Feminist inquiry of 19th century mourning portraits in France and England and a new interpretation of a painting by Courbet. **SELECTED PUBLICATIONS** Auth, publ(s) which include articles and exhibition catalog essays on California artists Lorser Feitelson and Helen Lundeberg. **CONTACT ADDRESS** Sweet Briar Col, Sweet Briar, VA, 24595. **EMAIL** witcombe@sbc.edu

MORAN CRUZ, JO ANN HOEPPNER
PERSONAL Born 05/12/1944, Eau Claire, WI, m, 3 children **DISCIPLINE** MEDIEVAL HISTORY **EDUCATION** Harvard Univ, BA, 66; Brandeis Univ, MA, 69, PhD(hist ideas), 75. **CAREER** Lectr hist, Boston Col, 71-72; assoc prof lectr, George Washington Univ, 75-78; Asst Prof Hist, 78-84, assoc prof, 84-, chair, Georgetown Univ, 97-. **HONORS AND AWARDS** Alpha Sigma Nu Hon fel; Brown Bk Prize, Med Acad of Am; Exec Cmt, N Am Conf on British Stu; Councillor, Med Acad Am. **MEMBERSHIPS** Mediaeval Acad Am; Am Hist Asn. **RESEARCH** Education and literacy in late medieval Britain; ecclesiastical history in late medieval Britain; use of wills as a historical source. **SELECTED PUBLICATIONS** Auth, Education and Learning in the City of York, 1300- 1548, Univ York, 79; Literacy and education in Northern England, 1350-1550: A methodological inquiry, Northern Hist, 81; Clerical recruitment in the Diocese of York, 1340-1530: Data and commentary, J Ecclesiastical Hist, 82; The 73rd Annual-Meeting Of The American-Catholic-Historical-Association, Catholic Historical Review, Vol 0079, 1993;. **CONTACT ADDRESS** Dept of Hist, Georgetown Univ, 1421 37th St N W, Washington, DC, 20057-0001. **EMAIL** moranj@gunet.georgetown.edu

MORBY, JOHN EDWIN
PERSONAL Born 03/19/1939, Berkeley, CA, d, 1 child **DISCIPLINE** EUROPEAN HISTORY **EDUCATION** Univ Calif, Berkeley, AB, 60, PhD(Europ hist), 71; Harvard Univ, MA, 61. **CAREER** Instr Europ hist, Univ Tex, Austin, 65-68; asst prof, Chico State Univ, 68-69; from asst prof to assoc prof, 69-80, prof Europ Hist, Calif State Univ, Hayward, 80-. **RESEARCH** Musical institutions of 17th and 18th century France. **SELECTED PUBLICATIONS** Auth, The Great Chapel-Chamber Controversy, Musical Quart, 7/72; Biography of a Grand Motet: The Jean Gilles Requiem in Eighteenth Century Paris and Versailles, Proc Western Soc French Hist, 75; The French Classical Repertory in the 18th Century, Proc Western Soc Fr Hist, 78; The Sobriquets of Medieval European Princes, Can J Hist, 78; Dynasties of the World: A Chronological and Geneological Handbook, Oxford Univ Press, 89. **CONTACT ADDRESS** Dept of Hist, California State Univ, Hayward, 25800 Carlos Bee Bvd, Hayward, CA, 94542-3001.

MORE, ELLEN SINGER
PERSONAL New York, NY **DISCIPLINE** BRITISH HISTORY, AMERICAN MEDICAL HISTORY **EDUCATION** State Univ NY New Paltz, BA, 68; Univ Rochester, MA, 70, PhD(hist), 80. **CAREER** Instr hist, Harley Sch, 78-79; Asst Prof Hist, Univ Rochester, 80-, Vis Asst Prof Preventive Med, Sch Of Med, 82-, Consult, Sch of Nursing, Univ Rochester, 80-83; lectr, Nursing Asn of the Am Col of Obstet & Gynecol, 82. **MEMBERSHIPS** AHA; Conf British Studies. **RESEARCH** The new Arminians in Mid-Seventeenth Century England; women and the radical sects in seventeenth century England; women and the history of American health care. **SELECTED PUBLICATIONS** Contribr, A Biographical Dict of British Radicals in the 17th Century, Harvester Press, 82; John Goodwin and the origins of the new Arminianism, J Brit Studies, 82; Jexblake,Sophia - A Woman Pioneer In 19th-Century Medical Reform - Roberts,S, Social History Of Medicine, Vol 0007, 1994; Jexblake,Sophia - A Woman Pioneer In 19th-Century Medical Reform - Roberts,S, Social History Of Medicine, Vol 0007, 1994; Medicine In America - A Short History - Cassedy,Jh, Reviews In American History, Vol 0022, 1994. **CONTACT ADDRESS** Dept of Hist, Univ of Rochester, Rochester, NY, 14627.

MOREHEAD, JOSEPH HYDE
PERSONAL Born 01/30/1931, New York, NY, m, 1966, 1 child **DISCIPLINE** SOCIAL FOUNDATIONS OF EDUCATION **EDUCATION** Univ Calif-Berkeley, BA, MA, MLS, EdD, 73. **CAREER** PROF, SCH INFO SCI & POLICY, UNIV ALBANY, 70-. **MEMBERSHIPS** Am Libr Asn **RESEARCH** Access to governmentt information as a First Right Amendment. **SELECTED PUBLICATIONS** coauth, Introduction to United States Government Information Sources, 4th ed, Libr Unlimited, 92; Introduction to United States Government Information Sources, 5th ed, Libr Unlimited, 96. **CONTACT ADDRESS** Sch Info Sci & Policy, SUNY-Albany, Albany, NY, 12222. **EMAIL** jhm@cnsvax.albany.edu

MORELAND-YOUNG, CURTINA
PERSONAL Born 03/05/1949, Columbia, South Carolina, d, 1978 **DISCIPLINE** POLITICAL SCIENCE **EDUCATION** Fisk University, Nashville, TN, BA, 1969; University of Illinois, Urbana, Il, MA, 1975, PhD, 1976; Harvard University, Cambridge, MA, post-doctoral, 1982. **CAREER** Ohio State University, Dept of Black Studies, Columbus, OH, instructor asst prof, 1971-78; Jackson State University, Mississippi College & University Consortium for International Study, Dept of Political Science, coord for MA program, assoc prof, 1978-84, chair, public policy & administration dept, 1984-. **HONORS AND AWARDS** Kellogg National Fellow, Kellogg Foundation, 1989-92; Rockefeller Foundation Feller, Rockefeller Foundation, 1983; DuBois Scholar, DuBois Institute, Harvard University, 1983; John Oliver Killen Writing Award, Fisk University, 1969; Lilly Fellow, Lilly Foundation, 1979-80. **MEMBERSHIPS** Chair, pres, The Conference of Minority Public Administrators, 1989-90; member, exec board, National Conference of Black Political Scientist, 1989; member, National Council of American Society for Public Administrators, 1989-90; chair, The Committee on Organization Review & Evaluation, ASPA, 1990-91; member, exec board, Jackson International Visitors Center. **CONTACT ADDRESS** Public Policy & Administration Dept, Jackson State Univ, 3825 Ridgewood Rd, Box 18, Jackson, MS, 39211.

MORELLO, JOHN
DISCIPLINE HISTORY **EDUCATION** George Washington Univ, BA, 73, MA, 77; Univ Ill, PhD, 98-. **CAREER** Prof, Devry Inst Tech. **HONORS AND AWARDS** Best Prof Series; West Suburban Post Secondary Consortium. **MEMBERSHIPS** AHA; ISHS **RESEARCH** Advertising history **CONTACT ADDRESS** 1221 N Swift Rd, Addison, IL, 60101. **EMAIL** morello@dpg.devry.edu

MORGAN, ANNE LEE
PERSONAL Born 01/12/1941, Minneapolis, MN, m, 1976, 2 children **DISCIPLINE** ART HISTORY **EDUCATION** Knox Col, BA, 62; Florida State Univ, MA, 63; Univ of Iowa, PhD, 73. **CAREER** Instr,Univ of Ill at Urbana, 68-73, asst prof, Dept of Art and Design, 73-78; ed, New Art Examiner, 79-95; ed, St James Pr, 82-85; vis asst prof, Univ of Ill at Chicago, Hist of Archit and Art Dept, 85-86; ed Twenty One/Art and Culture, Univ of Ill at Chicago, 87-90. **HONORS AND AWARDS** Phi Beta Kappa, 62; Yale Univ grant, 76; Who's Who in the East, 98. **MEMBERSHIPS** Coll Art Asn; Soc of Archit Hist; Am Stud Asn; Natl Coalition of Independent Scholars. **RESEARCH** American art. **SELECTED PUBLICATIONS** Auth, Arthur Dove: Life and Work, with a Catalogue Raisonne, Delaware, 84; ed, auth, Contemporary designers, Gale, 84; ed, International Contemporary Arts Directory, St. James, 85; coauth, Contemporary Architects, 2d ed., St. James, 87; ed, Dear Stieglitz, Dear Dove, Delaware, 88; auth, Dictionary of American Art and Artists, Oxford, forthcoming; auth of numerous articles. **CONTACT ADDRESS** 17 Honey Brook Dr, Princeton, NJ, 08540-7408. **EMAIL** ALM@research.nj.nec.com

MORGAN, DAVID
PERSONAL Born 12/21/1957, m, 1980, 3 children **DISCIPLINE** HISTORY **EDUCATION** Concordia Col, BA, 80; Univ AR, MA, 84; Univ Chicago, PhD, 90. **CAREER** Assoc prof, Valparaiso Univ, 90-. **HONORS AND AWARDS** Fel, Yale Univ; Fel, Getty Program; Fel, Am Antiquarian Society., Alpha Lambda Delta Nat Honors Society; Award for Tchg Excellence, Valparaiso Univ, 92. **MEMBERSHIPS** Col Art Asn; Am Acad of Religion; Org of Am Hist. **RESEARCH** Popular Religious Art **SELECTED PUBLICATIONS** Auth, Icons of American Protestantism: The Art of Warner Sallman, 96; auth,article, Ambiguous Icons: The Art of Ed Paschke, 97; auth,article, Domestic Devotion and Ritual: Visual Piety in the Modern American Home, 98; auth, Visual Piety A History and Theory of Popular Religious Images, 98; auth, Protestants and Pictures: Religion, Visual Culture, and the Age of American Mass Production, 99. **CONTACT ADDRESS** Art Dept, Valparaiso Univ, Valparaiso, IN, 46383. **EMAIL** dmorgan@exodus.valpo.edu

MORGAN, DAVID TAFT
PERSONAL Born 01/05/1937, Fayetteville, NC, m, 1958, 2 children **DISCIPLINE** AMERICAN HISTORY **EDUCATION** BA Baylor Univ, 59; CH, MA 64, PhD 68, Univ NC. **CAREER** Asst Prof, Patrick Henry Col, 64-68; Asst Prof, TX

A&M Univ, 68-73; Vis Assoc Prof Rhode Island Col, 70-71; Prof Univ Montevallo, 73-97. **HONORS AND AWARDS** Natl Pres, Phi Alpha Theta, 98-99. **MEMBERSHIPS** Southern Historical Assoc, Phi Alpha Theta. **RESEARCH** Colonial & Revolutionary Am; 2nd Hist of Am Rel. **SELECTED PUBLICATIONS** The New Crusade, the New Holy Land: Conflict in the Southern Baptist Convention, 69-91, Univ Alabama Press, 96; The Devious Dr Franklin, Colonail Agent: Benjamin Franklin's Years in London. **CONTACT ADDRESS** Dept of Soc Sci, Univ of Montevallo, Montevallo, AL, 35115. **EMAIL** morgan2@ix.netcom.com

MORGAN, H. WAYNE
PERSONAL Born 05/16/1934, Ashland, OK **DISCIPLINE** UNITED STATES HISTORY **EDUCATION** Ariz State Univ, BA, 55; Claremont Grad Sch, MA, 56; Univ Calif, Los Angeles, PhD, 60. **CAREER** Instr hist, San Jose State Col, 60-61; from asst prof to prof, Univ Tex, Austin, 61-72; prof, 72-76, George Lynn Cross Res Prof, Univ Okla, 76-, Am Philos Soc fel, 63. **MEMBERSHIPS** Orgn Am Historians. **RESEARCH** United States history, 1877-1914; American literary criticism, 1877-1932; art history. **SELECTED PUBLICATIONS** Auth, Eugene V Debs: Socialist for President, 62 & William McKinley and his America, 63, Syracuse Univ; coauth, The Gilded Age: A reappraisal, Syracuse Univ, 63, 70; ed, American Socialism, 1900-1964, Prentice-Hall, 64; auth, America's Road to Empire, Wiley, 65; From Hayes to McKinley: National Party Politics 1877-1896, Syracuse Univ, 69; Yesterday's Addicts: American Society and Drug Abuse, 1865-1920, Univ Okla, 74; coauth, Oklahoma: A Bicentennial History, Norton, 77; auth, New Muses: Art and American Society, 1865-1920, Univ Okla, 78; A Ship To Remember - The Maine And The Spanish-American War - Blow,M, Historian, Vol 0055, 1993; Drugs in America: A Social History, 1800-1980, Syracuse Univ, 81; Better In Darkness - A Biography Of Adams,Henry, His 2nd Life, 1862-1891 - Chalfant,E, Historian, Vol 0057, 1995. **CONTACT ADDRESS** Dept of Hist, Univ of Oklahoma, Norman, OK, 73069.

MORGAN, JOHN D.
PERSONAL Born 04/10/1955, Washington, DC **DISCIPLINE** CHEMISTRY **EDUCATION** Univ CA, Berkeley, PhD (chemistry), 78. **CAREER** Postdoctoral fel, Dept of Physics, Princeton Univ, 78-81. **HONORS AND AWARDS** NEH Fellowships, 93, 98-99. **MEMBERSHIPS** Am Philol Asn; Archaeological Inst of Am. **RESEARCH** Greek and Roman history and lit; epigraphy; textual criticism; ancient astronomy. **SELECTED PUBLICATIONS** Auth, Palaepharsalus-the Battle and the Town, Am J of Archaeology 87, 83; Cruces Propertianae, Classical Quart, 36, 86; The Calendar and the Chronology of Athens, Am J of Archaeology 100, 96; IG II2-1714: An Acephalous List of Athenian Archins from Around the Time of the First Mithridatic War, with Kevin M Clinton, Am J of Archaeology 101, 97; Polyeuktos, the Soteria, and the Chronology of Athens and Delphi, Am J of Archaeology 102, 98; Determination of the Calendar Equation of Ii2-689 MA 14906, Horos, forthcoming 99; numerous other publications. **CONTACT ADDRESS** Dept of Physics and Astronomy, Univ of Delaware, Newark, DE, 19716-2570. **EMAIL** JDMorgan@udel.edu

MORGAN, KATHRYN A.
PERSONAL Born 04/15/1962, Montreal, PQ, Canada **DISCIPLINE** CLASSICS **EDUCATION** Univ Calif, Berkeley, PhD, 91. **CAREER** Asst prof classics, Ohio State Univ, 91-95; asst to assoc prof classics, Univ Calif, Los Angeles, 95- . **HONORS AND AWARDS** Jr fel, Ctr for Hellenic Stud, 95-96. **MEMBERSHIPS** APA. **RESEARCH** Archaic and classical Greek literature; intellectual history; archaeology. **SELECTED PUBLICATIONS** Coauth, A Trophy from the Battle of Chaironeia of 86 BC, Am J of Archaeol, 92; auth, Socrates and Gorgias at Delphi and Olympia, Phaedrus 235d6-236b4, Class Q, 94; auth, Apollo's Favorites, Greek, Roman, and Byzantine Stud, 94; coauth, An Athenian Dedication to Herakles at Panopeus, Hesperia, 97. **CONTACT ADDRESS** Classics Dept, Univ California, Los Angeles, Dodd 100, 141702, PO Box 951417, Los Angeles, CA, 90095-1417. **EMAIL** kmorgan@humnet.ucla.edu

MORGAN, KATHRYN L.
PERSONAL Philadelphia, PA, 1 child **DISCIPLINE** HISTORY, FOLKLORE **EDUCATION** VA State Col, BA, 46; Howard Univ, MA, 52; Univ Pa, MA, 68, PhD(folklore-folklife), 70. **CAREER** Asst prof folklore, Univ Del, 71-72; Assoc Prof Hist & Folklore, Swarthmore Col, 72-, Guest lectr, Bryn Mawr Col, 71-73 & Haverford Col, 71-73; consult, Smithsonian Inst, 73-; assoc, Danforth Found. **MEMBERSHIPS** Am Folklore Soc; Am Soc Ethnohist; Oral Hist Asn. **RESEARCH** Folklife history; Black studies. **SELECTED PUBLICATIONS** Contribr, Mother Wit from the Laughing Barrel Caddy Buffers: Legends of a Middle Class Negro Family in Philadelphia, Prentice-Hall, 73; In Search of the Miraculous, Bryn Mawr Col, 73; auth, Jokes among urban Blacks, In: Black Folk, 73; auth, Social Distance From Jews In Russia And Ukraine, Slavic Review, Vol 0053, 1994. **CONTACT ADDRESS** Swarthmore Col, Swarthmore, PA, 19081.

MORGAN, KENNETH
DISCIPLINE HISTORY **EDUCATION** Leicester (Eng), BA, 74; Cambridge, PGCE, 81; Oxford, D Phil, 84. **CAREER** Instr, hist, Hyde Sixth Form Coll, Cheshire, Eng; PRIN LECT, HIST, BRUNEL UNIV COLL, MIDDDLESEX, ENG. **HONORS AND AWARDS** Beit Prize, Oxford Univ Press, 84. **MEMBERSHIPS** Am Antiquarian Soc **SELECTED PUBLICATIONS** Auth, "The Organization of the Convict Trade to Maryland: Stevenson, Randolph, and Cheston, 1768-1775," Wm & Mary Quart 42, 85; auth, "English and American Attitudes towards Convict Transportation, 1718-1775," Hist 72, 87; auth, "Shipping Patterns and the Atlantic Trade of Bristol, 1749-1770," Wm & Mary Quart 46, 89; auth, An American Quaker in the British Isles: The Travel Journals of Jabez Maud Fisher, 1775-1779, Oxford Univ Press, 92; auth, Bristol and the Atlantic Trade in the Eighteenth Century, Cambridge Univ Press, 93; "The Organization of the Colonial Rice Trade, Wm & Mary Quart 52, 95. **CONTACT ADDRESS** Park Rd, East Twickenham, ., TW1 2QB.

MORGAN, PHILLIP D.
DISCIPLINE HISTORY **EDUCATION** Cambridge, BA, MA, 81; Univ Coll London, PhD, 78. **CAREER** Prof hist, Fla State Univ; ED, WM & MARY QUARTERLY AND PROF, HIST, COLL OF WM & MARY. **MEMBERSHIPS** AM Antiquarian Soc **CONTACT ADDRESS** OIEAHC, PO Box 8781, Williamsburg, VA, 23187-8781.

MORGAN, THOMAS SELLERS
PERSONAL Born 12/13/1934, Jackson, MS, m, 1960, 3 children **DISCIPLINE** UNITED STATES HISTORY **EDUCATION** Davidson Col, AB, 57; Duke Univ, MA, 62; Univ NC, Chapel Hill, PhD(hist), 69. **CAREER** Teacher social studies, Edmondson High Sch, Md, 59-62; instr hist, Wake Forest Univ, 64-65; instr hist & mod civilization, Univ NC, Chapel Hill, 66-67; from asst prof to assoc prof, 67-75, asst dean, Col Arts & Sci, 74-76, assoc dean, 76-80, Prof Hist, Winthrop Col, 75-, Dean, Col Arts & Sci, 80-, Danforth assoc, 72-. **MEMBERSHIPS** AHA; Southern Hist Asn; Orgn Am Historians; Social Welfare Hist Group; Am Asn Higher Educ. **RESEARCH** Recent United States; social welfare in the New Deal; post Civil War North Carolina. **SELECTED PUBLICATIONS** Auth, A folly ... manifest to everyone: The movement to enact unemployment insurance legislation in North Carolina, 1935-1936, NC Hist Rev, 775; contrib several biographies in Dict NC Biog, 78; Conservative Constraints - North-Carolina And The New Deal. - Abrams,Dc, J Of American History, Vol 0080, 1993; Byrnes,James,F. And The Politics Of Segregation, Historian, Vol 0056, 1994. **CONTACT ADDRESS** Col of Arts & Sci, Winthrop Univ, Rock Hill, SC, 29733.

MORGAN, WILLIAM
PERSONAL Born 06/13/1944, Princeton, NJ, m, 1978, 4 children **DISCIPLINE** ARCHITECTURAL HISTORY **EDUCATION** Dartmouth, AB, 66; Columbia Univ, MA, certif. in archit, 68; Univ Delaware, PhD, 71 **CAREER** Lect, Princeton Univ, 71-74; Archit Critic, The Courier-Journal, 75-80; Chmn, Kentucky Historic Preservation Rev Bd, 75-90; Book Rev Ed, Landscape Archit, 76-78; Nat Endowment for the Humanities Sr Res Fel, 84-85; Ed Board, Competitions, 1990-; DISTINGUISHED TEACHING PROF, UNIV LOUISVILLE, 1974-. **HONORS AND AWARDS** Nomination for Pulitzer Prize in Criticism; President's Award for Outstanding Scholar, Res, & Creative Activity. **MEMBERSHIPS** Soc of Archit Historians. **RESEARCH** Amer Archit, Scandinavian Archit, Amer Arts, Cities. **SELECTED PUBLICATIONS** Coauth, Bucks County, Horizon, 74; coauth, Old Louisville: The Victorian Ear, Courier-Journal, 75; auth, Louisville: Architecture and the Urban Environment, WL Bauhan, 79; auth, Collegiate Gothic: The Architecture of Rhodes College, Missouri, 89; auth, The Almighty Wall: The Architecture of Henry Vaughan, MIT, 93; auth, Heikkinen & Komonen Architects, Monacelli, 98. **CONTACT ADDRESS** Allen R. Hite Art Inst, Univ of Louisville, Louisville, KY, 40292. **EMAIL** w0morg01@ulkyvm.louisville.edu

MORGANSTERN, ANNE MCGEE
PERSONAL Born 02/05/1936, Morgan, GA, m, 1966 **DISCIPLINE** HISTORY OF ART **EDUCATION** Wesleyan Col, Ga, BFA, 58; NY Univ, MA, 61, PhD(Hist of Art), 70. **CAREER** Instr Hist of Art, Manhattanville Col Sacred Heart, 61 & Vassar Col, 65-66; lectr, Univ Wis-Milwaukee, 70-73; asst prof, 73-79, assoc prof History of Art, Ohio State Univ, 79-; Historians of Neth, Europe. **MEMBERSHIPS** Col Art Asn Am; Medieval Acad Am; Int Ctr Medieval Art. **RESEARCH** Late Gothic sculpture in France; Northern Renaissance painting; relation of the arts to social and political history. **SELECTED PUBLICATIONS** Auth, Quelques observations a propos de l'architecture du tombeau du Cardinal Jean de la Grange, Bull Monumental, 70; The La Grange tomb and choir, Speculum, 1/73; Pierre Morel, master of works in Avignon, Art Bull, 76; The Pawns in Bosch's Death and the Miser, Nat Gal Art Studies in the Hist of Art, 82; The Bishop, the Lion and the Two-headed Dragon: The Burghersh Memorial in Lincoln Cathedral, Acts of the XXIVth Intern Congress of the History of Art, 96. **CONTACT ADDRESS** Div of Hist of Art, Ohio State Univ, 100 Hayes Hall, Columbus, OH, 43210-1318. **EMAIL** morganstern.z@osu.edu

MORGANSTERN, JAMES
PERSONAL Born 10/16/1936, Pittsburgh, PA, m, 1966 **DISCIPLINE** HISTORY ART; ARCHITECTURE **EDUCATION** Williams College, BA 58; Yale Univ, Sch Archit 58-60; Univ Cal Berk, 61-62; NY Univ Inst Fine Arts, MA 64, PhD 73. **CAREER** Univ Wisconsin, asst prof, 70-73; Ohio State Univ, asst prof, assoc prof, prof, 73 to 90-; Univ VA, vis lect, 87. **HONORS AND AWARDS** Dumbarton Oaks Cen Byzantine Stud Fel; ARI Turkey Fel; NEH; Outstanding Tchr OSU; Samuel Kress Foun Gnt; APS Gnt; Fulbright Fel; NEH; Florence Gould Foun Gnt **MEMBERSHIPS** AIA; BSC; CAA; ICMA; MAA; SAH; US Ntl Comm Byzan Stud; Soc Antiquaries Normandy; Soc Fran d'Archeologie **RESEARCH** Early Christine and Byzantine Art and Architecture; Western Medieval Art and Architecture. **SELECTED PUBLICATIONS** Auth, Reading Medieval Buildings: The Question of Diaphragm Arches at Notre-Dame de Jumieges, ed C. L. Striker, Archit Stud in Memory of Richard Krautheimer, Mainz, 96; The Fort at Dereagzi and Other Material remains in Its Vicinity: From Antiquity to the Middle Ages, coauth, Istanbuler Forschungen, Tubingen, 93; et al. **CONTACT ADDRESS** Dept History of Art, Ohio State Univ, 108 North Oval Mall, Columbus, OH, 43210.

MORGENTHALER, HANS RUDOLF
PERSONAL Born 06/07/1952, Switzerland, m **DISCIPLINE** ART HISTORY **EDUCATION** Univ Zurich, 80; Stanford Univ, MA, 84; PhD, 88. **CAREER** Asst prof, Conn Col, New London, 86; asst prof, Univ Ore, Eugene, 87-89; assoc prof, Univ Colo Denver, 89-. **MEMBERSHIPS** JSAH; CAA; GSA; ACSA. **RESEARCH** Architectural History of the 20th Century; Architectural Theory. **SELECTED PUBLICATIONS** Auth, Chronology versus System: Unleashing the Creative Potential of Architectural History, Journ Archit Educ, 48, May, 218-226, 95; The Early Sketches of German Architect Erich Mendelsohn: No Compromise with Reality, Edwin Mellen Press, 92; Erich Mendelsohn in the USA: Nuclear Physics and Urban Design, Selected Works: Coun of Educ in Landscape Archit, 1990 Conf, Washington, pp 59-65, 91; Pittsburgh's Golden Triangle: Opportunity Lost and Found?, Avant Garde, 4, Summer, 58-71, 90; coauth, Hansruedi Morgenthaler, Univ Zurich, Basel: Gesellschaft fur Schweizerische Kunstgeschichte, 80. **CONTACT ADDRESS** Univ of Colorado at Denver, Campus Box 126, PO Box 173364, Denver, CO, 80217-3364. **EMAIL** hmorgent@carbon.cudenver.edu

MORI, AKANE
DISCIPLINE MUSIC **EDUCATION** Toho Gakuen Sch Music, BA; Yale Univ, MA, PhD. **CAREER** Former lectr music theory, Yale Univ; Hartt. 1994-. **SELECTED PUBLICATIONS** Auth, In Theory Only & Jour of Music Theory **CONTACT ADDRESS** Hartt Sch Music, Univ Hartford, 200 Bloomfield Ave, West Hartford, CT, 06117.

MORIARTY, THOMAS FRANCIS
PERSONAL Born 07/21/1934, Holyoke, MA, m, 1975, 1 child **DISCIPLINE** MODERN IRELAND **EDUCATION** Holy Cross Col, BA, 56; Univ Notre Dame, MA, 58, PhD(hist), 64. **CAREER** Instr & asst prof hist, Fordham Univ, 61-68; vis prof, Talladega Col, 68-69; ASSOC PROF HIST, COL OF OUR LADY OF THE ELMS, 69- **MEMBERSHIPS** Am Cath Hist Soc; Am Conf for Irish Studies. **RESEARCH** Eighteenth and 19th century Ireland; Irish American history. **SELECTED PUBLICATIONS** Auth, The Truth-Teller and Irish Americana of the 1820's, Rec Am Cath Hist Soc Philos, 3/69; The Irish absentee tax controversy of 1773: A study in Anglo-Irish politics on the eve of the American Revolution, Proc Am Philos Soc, 74; The Irish American response to the struggle for Catholic Emancipation, Cath Hist Rev, 7/80. **CONTACT ADDRESS** Dept of Hist, Col of Our Lady of the Elms, 291 Springfield St, Chicopee, MA, 01013-2839. **EMAIL** moriartyt@elms.edu

MORK, GORDON ROBERT
PERSONAL Born 05/06/1938, St. Cloud, MN, m, 1963, 3 children **DISCIPLINE** MODERN HISTORY, GERMAN HISTORY **EDUCATION** Yale Univ, BA, 60; Univ Minn, MA, 63, PhD, 66. **CAREER** Lectr Hist, Univ Calif, Davis, 66-68, asst prof, 68-70; asst prof, 70-73, from assoc prof to prof; 73-94, Hist, Purdue Univ, West Lafayette, 73-, fel, inst res in Humanities, Univ Wis-Madison, 69-70. **MEMBERSHIPS** AHA; Conf Group Cent Europ Hist; Conf Group Ger Polit; Intl Soc for Hist Didactics, Vice Pres, 95-. **RESEARCH** Nineteenth and twentieth century Germany; Western civilization. **SELECTED PUBLICATIONS** Auth, Flint and Steel...Military Technology and Tactics in 17th Century Europe, Smithsonian J Hist, 67; The Archives of the German Democratic Republic, Cent Europ Hist, 69; Bismarck and the Capitulation of German Liberalism, J Mod Hist, 71; Modern Western Civilization, Dorsey, 76, rev ed, Univ Press Am, 81, USMC edition, 94; German Nationalism and Jewish Assimilation, Leo Baeck Inst, 77; Teaching the Hitler Period: History and Morality, History Teacher, 80; Schindler's List: The Book and the Film, Informations/Mitteilungen/Communications, 16/2, 95. **CONTACT ADDRESS** Dept of History, Purdue Univ, West Lafayette, IN, 47907-1968. **EMAIL** gmork@purdue.edu

MORRIS, IAN
DISCIPLINE CLASSICS **EDUCATION** BA, 81; Cambridge Univ, PhD, 86. **CAREER** Ch dept class and prof class/hist, Stanford Univ. **RESEARCH** Greek hist; archaeol. **SELECTED PUBLICATIONS** Auth, Death-Ritual and Social Structure in Classical Antiquity, 92; Classical Greece: Ancient History and Modern Archaeologies, 94. **CONTACT ADDRESS** Stanford Univ, Bldg 20, Main Quad, Stanford, CA, 94305.

MORRIS, JAMES MATTHEW
PERSONAL Born 07/13/1935, Reed City, MI, m, 1958, 6 children **DISCIPLINE** AMERICAN MILITARY AND NAVAL HISTORY, AMERICAN UTOPIANISM **EDUCATION** Aquinas Col, AB, 57; Cent MI Univ, MA, 62; Univ Cincinnati, PhD, 69. **CAREER** Instr hist, Col Steubenville, 62-64; from instr to asst prof, Providence Col, 67-71; from asst prof to assoc prof, 71-77, prof hist, Christopher Newport Univ, 77. **HONORS AND AWARDS** US Dept Educ Certificate of Appreciation for Promoting Education and Education Reform, 85; First Honoree, Alpha Chi, Va Zeta Chapter, Distinguished Prof Award, 85; Inductee, The Honorable Order of St. Barbara, 93. **MEMBERSHIPS** US Naval Inst; NAm Soc Oceanic Hist; Soc Mil Hist. **RESEARCH** Nineteenth and twentieth century Am mil and naval hist. **SELECTED PUBLICATIONS** Auth, Our Maritime Heritage: Maritime Developments and Their Impact on American Life, Univ Press Am, 79; sr res ed, America's Maritime Legacy: A History of the United States Shipping and shipuilding Industries form Colonial Times to the Present, Westview, 79; auth, History of the U.S. Navy, Bison Books, 84, 93, 97; History of the U.S. Army, Brompton Books, 86, 92, 97; America's Armed Forces: A History, Prentice Hall, 91, 96; coauth, Historical Dictionary of the U.S. Navy, Scarecrow Press, 98. **CONTACT ADDRESS** Dept of Hist, Christopher Newport Univ, 50 Shoe Lane, Newport News, VA, 23606-2949. **EMAIL** cnewton@cnu.edu

MORRIS, KENNETH EARL
PERSONAL Born 03/19/1955, Baltimore, s, 1 child **DISCIPLINE** SOCIAL STUDIES **EDUCATION** Ind Univ, BS, 76; Stanford Univ, AM, 77; Univ Ga, PhD, 83. **CAREER** Instructor at various colleges and universities. **HONORS AND AWARDS** NEH summer fel, 87, 94, 97. **MEMBERSHIPS** Am Studies Asn. **RESEARCH** Social thought. **SELECTED PUBLICATIONS** Auth, Bonhoeffer's Ethic of Discipleship, 86; Jimmy Carter, American Moralist, 96. **CONTACT ADDRESS** 187 Chattooga Ave., Athens, GA, 30601. **EMAIL** kemorris@arches.uga.edu

MORRIS, RICHARD J.
PERSONAL Born 01/13/1947, Boston, MA, m, 1970, 3 children **DISCIPLINE** AMERICAN HISTORY **EDUCATION** Boston State Col, BA, 68; Ohio Univ, MA, 70; NY Univ, PhD, 75. **CAREER** Nat Hist Publ & Rec Comn fel, The Papers of Alexander Hamilton, 75-76; asst prof, 76-85, ASSOC PROF HIST, LYCOMING COL, 86-. **MEMBERSHIPS** Essex Inst; AHA. **RESEARCH** Colonial; revolutionary and early national American history. **SELECTED PUBLICATIONS** Auth, Wealth distribution in Salem, MA 1759-99, Essex Inst Hist Col, 78; assoc-ed, The Papers of Alexander Hamilton XXVI, Columbia Univ Press, 79; Urban migration in Revolutionary America: The case of Salem, Mass, J Urban Hist, 82; co-auth, Williamsport: Frontier Village to Regional Center, 84; Social change, Republican rhetoric and the American Revolution: The case of Salem, Mass, J Soc Hist, 97. **CONTACT ADDRESS** Lycoming Col, 700 College Pl, Box 19, Williamsport, PA, 17701-5192. **EMAIL** morris@lycoming.edu

MORRIS, THOMAS DEAN
PERSONAL Born 11/01/1938, Eugene, OR, m, 1960, 3 children **DISCIPLINE** AMERICAN CONSTITUTIONAL HISTORY **EDUCATION** Univ Wash, BA, 60, MA, 66, PhD(hist), 69. **CAREER** From instr to asst prof, 67-74, Assoc Prof Hist, Portland State Univ, 74-, Vis asst prof hist, Univ Wash, 73. **MEMBERSHIPS** Am Soc Legal Hist; Orgn Am Historians. **RESEARCH** Nineteenth century American constitutional and legal history. **SELECTED PUBLICATIONS** Auth, Free Men All: The Personal Liberty Laws of the North, 1780-1861, John Hopkins Univ, 74; Practicing Law In Frontier California - Bakken,Gm, Pacific Northwest Quarterly, Vol 0084, 1993; The Facts Of Reconstruction - Essays In Honor Of Franklin,John,Hope - Anderson,E, Moss,Aa, J Of Southern History, Vol 0059, 1993; Texas, New-Mexico, And The Compromise Of 1850 - Boundary-Dispute And Sectional Crisis - Stegmaier,Mj, Civil War History, Vol 0042, 1996; New South-New Law - The Legal Foundations Of Credit And Labor-Relations In The Postbellum Agricultural South - Woodman,Hd, J Of Economic History, Vol 0056, 1996; Slavery And The Founders - Race And Liberty In The Age Of Jefferson - Finkelman,P, J Of Southern History, Vol 0063, 1997; Slavery, Capitalism, And Politics In The Antebellum Repubic, Vol-1, Commerce And Compromise, 1820-1850 - Ashworth,J, American Historical Review, Vol 0102, 1997. **CONTACT ADDRESS** Dept of Hist, Portland State Univ, Portland, OR, 97207.

MORRIS-HALE, WALTER
PERSONAL Born 01/30/1933, Chicago, Illinois **DISCIPLINE** BRITISH HISTORY **EDUCATION** Univ of CA Berkeley, 1957; Univ of Stockholm Sweden, MA 1962; Univ of Geneva Switzerland, PhD 1969. **CAREER** Smith Coll, asst prof 1969-75, assoc prof, full prof, currently. **SELECTED PUBLICATIONS** Publs "British Admin in Tanganyika from 1920-45, with Spec Reference to the Preparation of Africans for Admin Positions" 1969, "From Empire to Nation, the African Experience" in Aftermath of Empire Smith Coll Studies in History XIVII 1973; Conflict & Harmony in Multi-Ethnic Societies: An International Perspective, 1996. **CONTACT ADDRESS** Full Professor, Smith Col, Northampton, MA, 01063.

MORRISON, ALEX
PERSONAL Born 01/23/1941, Sydney, NS, Canada **DISCIPLINE** MILITARY HISTORY **EDUCATION** Mt Allison Univ, BA, 68; Royal Mil Col Can, MA, 80. **CAREER** Can Forces, 56-90, retired rank Lt Col; lectr, Can mil hist, Royal Mil Col, 82-83; lectr, Columbia Univ, 88; lectr, York Univ, 87-94; PRES, LESTER B. PEARSON CAN INT PEACEKEEPING TRAINING CTR, 94-; PRES, CAN INST STRATEGIC STUD, 98-. **HONORS AND AWARDS** Meritorious Serv Cross, 89; Award Merit, Secy State External Affairs, 91. **SELECTED PUBLICATIONS** Auth, The Voice of Defence: The History of the Conference of Defence Associations, 82; auth, The Breed of Manly Men: the History of the Cape Breton Highlanders, 94; coauth, The New Peacekeeping Partnership, 95; ed, Peacekeeping, Peacemaking or War: International Security Enforcement, 91; ed, Divided We Fall: The National Security Implications of Canadian Constitutional Issues, 92; ed, A Continuing Commitment: Canada and North Atlantic Security, 92; ed, The Changing Face of Peacekeeping, 93. **CONTACT ADDRESS** Can Inst Strategic Stud, 2300 Yonge St, Ste. 402, Box 2321, Toronto, ON, M4P 1E4.

MORRISON, DENNIS L.
PERSONAL Born 10/29/1949, Miami, FL, d **DISCIPLINE** HISTORICAL, SOCIAL, CULTURAL FOUNDATIONS OF EDUCATION **EDUCATION** Univ Houston, EdD, 93. **CAREER** PROF HIST AND GEOGRAPHY, UNIV HOUSTON, 90-, division chair, Social and Behavioral Sciences, 93-96. **MEMBERSHIPS** Phi Alpha Theta; Phi Kappa Phi; Pi Kappa Delta; Asn of Pacific Coast Geographers; Am Asn of Geographers; South Central Women Studies Asn. **RESEARCH** Black hist; women's hist. **SELECTED PUBLICATIONS** Auth, et al, American History Reader, Vol I, 91, Vol II, 92, Kendall-Hunt Pub; auth, Woman of Conscience: Senator Margaret Chase Smith of Maine, Brandywine Press, 94; Up, Down, and Out: Henry A. Wallace and Democratic Party Politics, 1940-1946, Emancipation Press, 95; with Mark S. Saka, Silent No More!: Forgotten Voices of the American Past, Emancipation Press, 96; Our Moral Duty: Educating Minority Students in the United States, Vol I, Emancipation Press, 96; et al, Our Legacy; Articles and Documents in American History, Vols I and II, Am Heritage Custom Pub, 96; with Sara C. Mayfield, World Geography: A Study Guide, Emancipation Press, 97. **CONTACT ADDRESS** 3514 Scott, #1, Houston, TX, 77004.

MORRISON, G. GRANT
PERSONAL Born 09/12/1936, Live Oak, FL, m, 1961, 2 children **DISCIPLINE** AMERICAN HISTORY **EDUCATION** Univ FL, AB, 60; City Univ New York, PhD, 74. **CAREER** Lectr hist, Queens Col, City Univ NY, 68-73; asst prof hist, 73-79, assoc prof hist, C W Post Col, Long Island Univ, 79-86, prof hist, Long Island Univ, 86. **MEMBERSHIPS** Orgn Am Historians; Am Studies Asn. **RESEARCH** US Early Nat Period; US soc hist. **SELECTED PUBLICATIONS** Auth, Isaac Bronson and the Search for System in American Capitalism, 1789-1838, Arno, 78; A New York City Creditor and His Upstate Debtors, New York Hist, 7/80; Interregional Entrepreneurship in the 1830's: The Role of New Yorkers in the Founding of an Ohio Corporation, Old Northwest, spring 81; Boundlessness and Limits in America's Self-Images, Ventures in Research, fall 85; James Fenimore Cooper and American Republicanism, Modern Age, spring 92. **CONTACT ADDRESS** Dept of Hist, Long Island Univ, 720 Northern Blvd, Greenvale, NY, 11548-1300.

MORRISON, JAMES V.
DISCIPLINE CLASSICS **EDUCATION** Oberlin Col, BA; Univ Wash, MA; Univ Mich, PhD. **CAREER** Vis fac, Davidson Col; vis fac, Georgetown Univ; fac, Centre Col, 93-; assoc prof, current. **RESEARCH** Homer and ancient epic; Greek literature and philosophy; late republican and Augustan literature; and history and classical tradition in 20th-century literature and culture. **SELECTED PUBLICATIONS** Auth, Homeric Misdirection: False Predictions in the Iliad, Univ Mich Press, 92; contribu, Latomus, Jour Am Cult, Relig Studies Rev. **CONTACT ADDRESS** Centre Col, 600 W Walnut St, Danville, KY, 40422. **EMAIL** morrison@centre.edu

MORRISON, KARL FREDERICK
PERSONAL Born 11/03/1936, Birmingham, AL, m, 1964, 2 children **DISCIPLINE** MEDIEVAL & CHURCH HISTORY **EDUCATION** Univ Miss, BA, 56; Cornell Univ, MA, 57, PhD(hist), 61. **CAREER** Actg instr hist, Stanford Univ, 60-61; from instr to asst prof, Univ Minn, 61-64; asst prof, Harvard Univ, 64-65; assoc prof, 65-68, chmn dept hist, 70-76, Prof Medieval Hist, Univ Chicago, 68-, McKnight Found award, 63; Am Coun Learned Socs fels, 63-64 & 66-67; mem, Inst Advan Study, 66-67 & 76-77; consult, Time-Life Bks, 66-68; pres, Midwest Medieval Conf, 77- 78. **MEMBERSHIPS** AHA; Mediaeval Acad Am; Midwest Asn Medieval Studies (pres, 76-78); Medieval Asn Midwest (pres, 77-78). **RESEARCH** History of political thought; church history. **SELECTED PUBLICATIONS** Auth, The Two Kingdoms, Princeton Univ, 64; Rome and the City of God, Am Philos Soc, 64; Tradition and Authority in the Western Church: 300-1140, Princeton Univ, 67; Carolingian coinage, Am Numis Soc, 68; Europe's Middle Ages: 565-1500, Scott, 70; ed, The Investiture Controversy: Issues, Ideals and Results, Holt, 71 & Ferdinand Gregorovius, Rome and Medieval Culture, Univ Chicago, 71; auth, The Mimetic Tradition of Reform in Western Culture, Princeton, 82; The Letters Of Damian,Peter, Vol 3 - Letters-91-150 - German - Reindel,K, Editor, Speculum-A J Of Medieval Studies, Vol 0068, 1993. **CONTACT ADDRESS** Dept of Hist, Univ of Chicago, Chicago, IL, 60637.

MORRISON, SIMON
PERSONAL Born 12/30/1964, London, England, m **DISCIPLINE** MUSIC HISTORY **EDUCATION** Univ Toronto, BM, 87; McGill Univ, MA, 93; Princeton Univ, MFA, 94, PhD, 97. **CAREER** Asst prof, lecturer, Princeton Univ, 1998- **HONORS AND AWARDS** Charlotte Elizabeth Proctor Hon Fel, 95; Am Musicol Soc Diss Fel 96 **MEMBERSHIPS** Am Musicol Soc; Col Mus Soc; Am Assoc Teachers of Slavic and East Europ Lang. **RESEARCH** Russian 19th and 20th Century Music, French and Russian Symbolism, Neoclassicism, Ballet **SELECTED PUBLICATIONS** Skryabin and the Impossible, Jour Am Musicol Soc 51:2, 98, p201-48. **CONTACT ADDRESS** Princeton Univ, Woolworth Bldg, Princeton, NJ, 08544. **EMAIL** simonm@phoenix.princeton.edu

MORRISON, WILLIAM R.
PERSONAL Born 01/26/1942, Hamilton, ON, Canada **DISCIPLINE** HISTORY **EDUCATION** McMaster Univ, BA, 63, MA, 64; Univ Western Ont, PhD, 73. **CAREER** Fac mem, 69-85, prof history, Brandon Univ, 85-89; fac mem, 89-92, dir, Ctr Northern Stud, Lakehead Univ, 90-92; dean, res & grad stud, 92-97, PROF HISTORY, UNIV NORTHERN BRITISH COLUMBIA, 92-. **SELECTED PUBLICATIONS** Auth, A Survey of the History and Claims of the Native People of Northern Canada, 84; auth, Showing the Flag, 85; coauth, Land of the Midnight Sun: A History of the Yukon, 88; coauth, The Sinking of the Princess Sophia: Taking the North Down With Her, 90; coauth, The Alaska Highway in World War II: The U.S. Army of Occupation in Canada's Northwest, 92; coauth, The Forgotten North, 92; coauth, Working the North: Labor and the Northwest Defense Projects, 94; co-ed, For Purposes of Dominion: Essays in Honour of Morris Zaslow, 89; co-ed, Interpreting the North: Selected Readings, 89; co-ed, My Dear Maggie: Letters from a Western Manitoba Pioneer, 91; co-ed, The Historiography of the Provincial Norths, 96. **CONTACT ADDRESS** Dept of History, Univ Northern BC, 3333 University Way, Prince George, BC, V2N 4Z9. **EMAIL** morrison@unbc.ca

MORROW, JOHN HOWARD, JR.
PERSONAL Born 05/27/1944, Trenton, New Jersey, m **DISCIPLINE** HISTORY **EDUCATION** Swarthmore Coll, BA, (with honors), 1966; Univ of PA Philadelphia, PhD history 1971. **CAREER** Univ of TN Knoxville, asst prof to full prof & dept head 1971-; Natl Aerospace Museum Washington DC, Lindbergh prof of history 1989-90; University of Georgia Athens, GA Franklin prof of history 1989-, department chr, 1991-93, assoc dean of arts & science's, 1993-95 **HONORS AND AWARDS** Hon Soc Phi Kappa Phi 1980; Lindsay Young Professorship 1982-83; Outstanding Teacher UT Natl Alumni Assn 1983; UT Macebearer 1983-84; Univ Distinguished Serv Professorship 1985-88. **MEMBERSHIPS** Mem Amer Historical Assn 1971-; consult Coll Bd & Ed Testing Serv 1980-84, 1990-; chr, Coll Board Natl Academic ASN, 1993-95, mem Coll Board, bod of trustees, 1993-; mem AHA Comm on Committees 1982-85, AHA Prog Comm for 1984 Meeting 1983-84; mem edit adv bds Aerospace Historian 1984-87; and Military Affairs 1987-90; Smithsonian Inst Pr, 1987-93; chairman History Advisory Committee to the Secretary of the Air Force 1988-92. **SELECTED PUBLICATIONS** Author: Building German Airpower 1909-1914, 1976, German Airpower in World War I, 1982; The Great War in the Air, 1993; A Yankee Ace in the RAF, co-ed, 1996. **CONTACT ADDRESS** Department of History, Univ of Georgia, Athens, GA, 30602.

MORSE, CHARLOTTE COOK
PERSONAL Born 10/26/1942, Washington, DC **DISCIPLINE** ENGLISH LITERATURE, MEDIEVAL STUDIES **EDUCATION** Brown Univ, AB, 64; Stanford Univ, MA, 68, PhD(English), 70. **CAREER** From instr to asst prof English, Yale Univ, 68-76, Assoc Prof English, VA Commonwealth Univ, 76-, Morse fel English, Yale Univ, 72-73; prog officer div res grants, Nat Endowment for Humanities, 75-76. **MEMBERSHIPS** Mediaeval Acad Am; MLA; Southeastern Medieval Asn. **RESEARCH** Middle English literature; Old French literature; medieval intellectual history. **SELECTED PUBLICATIONS** Auth, The image of the vessel in Cleanness, Univ Toronto Quart, 71; The Pattern of Judgment in the Queste and Cleanness, Univ Mo, 78; The Manuscripts Of The 'Canterbury Tales', Notes And Queries, Vol 0040, 1993; Women Defamed

And Women Defended - An Anthology Of Medieval Texts - Blamires,A, Pratt,K, Marx,Cw, Editors, Medium Aevum, Vol 0063, 1994; The Shorter Poems - Minnis,Aj, Notes And Queries, Vol 0043, 1996; Gender And Romance In Chaucer,Geoffrey 'Canterbury Tales' - Crane,S, Speculum-A J Of Medieval Studies, Vol 0071, 1996; Gender And Romance In Chaucer,Geoffrey 'Canterbury Tales' - Crane,S, Speculum-A J Of Medieval Studies, Vol 0071, 1996; Chaucer 'Clerks Tale' - The Griselda Story Received, Rewritten, Illustrated - Bronfman,J, Notes And Queries, Vol 0043, 1996; From 'Pearl' To 'Gawain' - Form And Fynisment - Blanch,Rj, Wasserman,Jn, Speculum-A J Of Medieval Studies, Vol 0072, 1997; From 'Pearl' To 'Gawain' - Form And Fynisment - Blanch,Rj, Wasserman,Jn, Speculum-A J Of Medieval Studies, Vol 0072, 1997. **CONTACT ADDRESS** Dept of English, VA Commonwealth Univ, Box 2005, Richmond, VA, 23284-9004.

MORSTEIN-MARX, ROBERT
DISCIPLINE ROMAN HISTORY **EDUCATION** Univ Calif, Berkeley, PhD, 87. **CAREER** ASSOC PROF, UNIV CALIF, SANTA BARBARA. **RESEARCH** Roman history; Cocero; Roman oratory and rhetoric; Hellensitic epigraphy. **SELECTED PUBLICATIONS** Auth, "Athens, Thebes, and the Foundation of the Second Athenian League," Classical Antiquity 4, 85; "Asconius 14-15 C and the Date of Q, Mucius Scaevola's Command in Asia," Class Philol 84; "The Trial of Rutilius Rufus," Phoenix 44, 90; Hegemony to Empire, The Development of the Roman Imperium in the East, UC Press, 95; "Quintus Fabius Maximus and the Dyme Affair," CQ 45, 95; "Two Athenian Decrees Concerning Lemnos of the Late First Century B.C.," Chiron 27, 97; Publicity, Popularity and Patronage in the Commentariolum Petitionis, Class Antiquity, 98. **CONTACT ADDRESS** Dept of Classics, Univ Calif, Santa Barbara, CA, 93106-7150. **EMAIL** morstein@humanitas.ucsb.edu

MORTON, DESMOND D.P.
PERSONAL Born 09/10/1937, Calgary, AB, Canada **DISCIPLINE** CANADIAN HISTORY **EDUCATION** Royal Mil Col Can, BA, 59; Oxford Univ, BA, 61, MA, 66; London Sch Econ, Univ London, PhD, 68. **CAREER** Asst prof, Univ Ottawa, 68-69; Asst prof, 69-70, assoc prof, 71-75, prof hist, Univ Toronto, 75-; vis asst prof, Univ Western Ont, 70-71; vis assoc prof, Mich State Univ, 75; assoc dean, 75-59, vice prin (acad), 76-79, prin, Erindale Col, 86-94; dir, McGill Institute for the Study of Canada. **HONORS AND AWARDS** City Toronto Book Prize, 71; Univ Toronto Alumni Award, 83; Off, Order Can, 96. **MEMBERSHIPS** Can Hist Asn; Can Comn Mil Hist; Mem bd, Can Nat Hist Soc; mem bd, Inst Res Public Policy; ed bd, The Beaver. **SELECTED PUBLICATIONS** Auth, Working People: An Illustrated History of the Canadian Labour Movement, 90; auth, When Your Number's Up: The Canadian Soldier in the First World War, 93; auth, Victory 1945 Canadians From War to Peace, 95; coauth, A Military History of Canada, 85, 2nd ed, 90, 3rd ed A Military History of Canada: From Champlain to the Gulf War, 92; coauth, Winning the Second Battle: Canadian Veterans and the Return to Civilian Life, 87; coauth, Marching to Armageddon: Canada in the First World War, 89; coauth, Silent Battle: Canadian Prisoners of War in Germany, 1914-19, 92; coauth, A Short History of Canada, 95, rev ed 97. **CONTACT ADDRESS** McGill Inst for the Study of Can, 3463 Peel St, Montreal, PQ, H3A 1W7. **EMAIL** dmorton@leacock.lan.mcgill.ca

MORTON, MARIAN JOHNSON
PERSONAL Born 05/19/1937, Cambridge, MA, m, 1959, 4 children **DISCIPLINE** AMERICAN STUDIES & HISTORY **EDUCATION** Smith Col, BA, 59; Case Western Reserve Univ, MA, 63, PhD(Am studies), 70. **CAREER** Vis lectr, 70-72, asst prof, 72-77, assoc prof, 77-81, FULL PROF HIST, JOHN CARROLL UNIV, 82-. **MEMBERSHIPS** Am Studies Asn; Orgn Am Historians; Western Reserve Historical Soc. **RESEARCH** American historiography; women's history. **SELECTED PUBLICATIONS** Auth, The Terrors of Ideological Politics: Liberal Historians in a Conservative Mood, Case Western Reserve Univ, 72; coauth, Cowboy Without a Cause: His Image in Today's Popular Music, Antioch Rev, 6-7/77; As Mothers, as Sisters, as Daughters: Women Reformers in the Western Reserve, Western Reserve Mag, 3-4/81; My dear, I don't give a damn: Scarlett O'Hara and the Great Depression, Frontiers: J Women's Studies, fall 80; Fallen Women, Federated Charities, and Maternity Homes, 1913-1973, Social Service Rev, March 88; From Saving Souls to Saving Cities: Women and Reform in Cleveland, in Bitrh of Modern Cleveland, 1865-1930, ed by Thomas F. Campbell and Edward M. Miggins, London and Ontario: Assoc Univ Presses, 88; Homes for Poverty's Children: Cleveland Orphanages, 1851-1933, OH Hist, winter/spring 89; Emma Goldman and the American Left: Nowhere at Home, NY: Twayne, 92; Maternity Homes in Encyclopedia of Childbearing: Critical Perspectives,ed by Barbara Katz Rothman, Phoenix: Oryx Press, 93; And Sin No More: Social Policy and Unwed Mothers in Cleveland, 1855-1990, Columbus: The OH State Univ Press, 93; First Person Past: American Autobiographies, co-ed with Russell Duncan, two volumes, St James, NY: Brandywine Press, 94; Women in Cleveland: An Illustrated History, Bloomington: IN Univ Press, 95; Cleveland's Child Welfare System and the American Dilema, 1941-1965, Social Service Rev, March 98. **CONTACT ADDRESS** Dept of Hist, John Carroll Univ, 20700 N Park Blvd, Cleveland, OH, 44118-4581. **EMAIL** mmorton@jc.raxa.edu

MORTON, PATRICIA A.
PERSONAL Born 10/16/1955, ID, m, 1992 **DISCIPLINE** ARCHITECTURAL HISTORY **EDUCATION** Princeton Univ, PhD, 94. **CAREER** Asst prof, Art History, Univ Calif, Riverside, 93- . **HONORS AND AWARDS** DAAD scholar, Geothe Inst, Berlin, 88; Mellon Found grant, Princeton Univ, 88-90; Graham Found grant, 91-92; Predoctoral fel, The Getty Center for Hist of Art and Hum, Santa Monica CA, 92-93; Graham Found grant for WomEnhouse, WWW collaborative feminist proj, 95; res fel, Univ Calif Hum Res Inst, Irvine, 96; Fulbright Sr Scholar Prog, Umea Univ, Sweden, 99. **MEMBERSHIPS** AAUP; Col Art Assoc; Soc of Archit Hist. **RESEARCH** Twentieth century architecture and urbanism; contemporary architecture; theory of architecture; post-Colonial theory. **SELECTED PUBLICATIONS** Auth, The Building That Looks Back, in Angles of Incidence, Princeton Architec Pr, 92; auth, Arata Isozaki: A Report on the Postmodern Condition, in Casabella, 94; auth, Compare and Contrast: Mark Robbins' Borrowed Landscape, in Oz, 95; auth, The Apprehension of the City: Flanerie on the Margins of the Metropolis, in SURFACE: J of UCLA School of the Arts and Archit, 96; auth, Indochina at the 1931 Colonial Exposition in Paris, in Dialogue: An Internatl Forum for Archit Design and Culture, 97; auth, The Death of the Architect, in 1100 Architect: Work in Progress, Monacelli, 97; auth, A Visit to WomEnhouse, in Toward an Architecture of the Everyday: A Collection of Essays and Projects, Princeton Archit Pr, 97; auth, Notes on the Inside and Outside of Architecture, in From the Center: Design process at SCI-Arc, Monacelli, 98; auth, The Two Halves of the Orange, in Fabrications, San Francisco Museum of Modern Art, 98; auth, National and Colonial: The Musee des Colonies for the 1931 Colonial Exposition in Paris, in Art Bull, 98; auth, The Incommensurable and the Indissociable, in Practices, 98; auth, A Study in Hybridity: The Madagascar and Morocco Pavilions at the 1931 Colonial Exposition, in J of Archit Educ, 98; auth, Hybridity and Difference: The 1931 International Colonial Exposition in Paris, MIT, 99. **CONTACT ADDRESS** Art History Dept, Univ of California, Riverside, CA, 92521-0319. **EMAIL** pamorton@ix.netcom.com

MORVAN, JENNIFER
PERSONAL Binghamton, NY, m, 1996 **DISCIPLINE** ARCHITECTURAL HISTORY **EDUCATION** Dartmouth College, BA, 95; Univ Virginia, MA, 97. **CAREER** Architectural Historian, Heritage Consulting, private consul, one year. **MEMBERSHIPS** SAH; VAF. **RESEARCH** 16th Century French and Italian Architecture; Franco-Italian Studies of the Renaissance. **CONTACT ADDRESS** 26 Howe St, Medway, MA, 02053. **EMAIL** jenmorvan@norfolk-county.com

MOSELEY, MICHAEL EDWARD
PERSONAL Born 03/29/1941, Dayton, OH, m, 1963, 1 child **DISCIPLINE** ANTHROPOLOGY, ARCHAEOLOGY **EDUCATION** Univ Calif, Berkeley, BA, 63; Harvard Univ, MA & PhD(anthrop), 68. **CAREER** From instr to assoc prof anthrop, Harvard Univ, 68-76, asst cur SAm archaeol, 70-76; Assoc Cur Mid & S AM Archaeol & Ethnol, Field Mus of Natural Hist, 76-. **MEMBERSHIPS** Soc Am Archaeol. **RESEARCH** The development of agriculture and the functioning of pre- industrial cities in the New World. **SELECTED PUBLICATIONS** Coauth, Twenty-Four Architectural Plans of Chan Chan, Peur, Peabody Mus, 74; auth, The Maritime Foundations of Andean Civilization, Cummings, 75; contribr, Social and technological management in dry lands, Westview, 78; coauth, Peru's Golden Treasures, Field Mus of Natural Hist, 78; Preagricultural coastal civilization in Peru, Carolina Biological, 78; Doomed By Natural Disaster Archaeology, Vol 45, Pg 44, 1992, Archaeology, Vol 0046, 1993. **CONTACT ADDRESS** Field Mus of Natural History, Chicago, IL, 60605.

MOSER, HAROLD DEAN
PERSONAL Born 10/31/1938, Kannapolis, NC, m, 1964, 2 children **DISCIPLINE** AMERICAN HISTORY, AMERICAN LITERATURE **EDUCATION** Wake Forest Univ, BA, 61, MA, 63; Univ Wis-Madison, PhD(hist), 77. **CAREER** Instr hist, Chowan Col, 63-65; teaching asst, Univ Wis- Madison, 67-69; res asst, State Hist Soc Wis, 68-71; from asst ed to co-ed, Papers of Daniel Webster, Dartmouth Col, 71-78, ed corresp ser, Papers of Daniel Webster, 78-79; Ed & Dir, Papers of Andrew Jackson, Univ Tenn, 79-, Nat Hist Pub Comn fel, Dartmouth Col, 71-72. **HONORS AND AWARDS** Philip M Hamer Award, Soc Am Archivists, 75. **MEMBERSHIPS** Orgn Am Historians; Southern Hist Asn; AHA. **RESEARCH** Jacksonian America; the Old South; Daniel Webster. **SELECTED PUBLICATIONS** Auth, Reaction in North Carolina to the Emancipation Proclamation, NC Hist Rev, 67; New Hampshire and the ratification of the Twelfth Amendment, Dartmouth Libr Bull; co- ed, The Papers of Daniel Webster: Correspondence Series (Vols 1, 2 & 4), 75-78, ed, Vol 5, 82, Univ Press New Eng; The Papers of Andrew Jackson, Univ Tenn Press, Vol 2 (in prep); Liberty And Power - The Politics Of Jacksonian America - Watson,Hl, Virginia Magazine Of History And Biography, Vol 0101, 1993. **CONTACT ADDRESS** Papers of Andrew Jackson, Univ of Tenn, Hermitage, TN, 37066.

MOSES, CLAIRE GOLDBERG
PERSONAL Born 06/22/1941, Hartford, CT, m, 1966, 2 children **DISCIPLINE** WOMEN'S & FRENCH HISTORY **EDUCATION** Smith Col, AB, 63; George Washington Univ, MPhil, 72, PhD(hist), 78. **CAREER** Asst prof lectr hist, George Washington Univ, 71-76; Asst Prof Women's Studies, Univ MD, 77-, Managing ed, Feminist Studies, 77-. **MEMBERSHIPS** Nat Women's Studies Asn; Am Hist Asn; Soc French Hist Studies; Coord Comt Women in Hist Profession. **RESEARCH** Women's history in 19th century France; feminist theory; feminist history (intellectual, political, worldwide). **SELECTED PUBLICATIONS** Auth, Saint-Simonian men Saint-Simonian women: The transformation of feminist thought in 1830's France, J of Mod Hist, 682; Nineteenth-Century French Feminism, State Univ NY Press (in prep); Civilization Without Sexes - Reconstructing Gender In Postwar France, 1917-1927 - Roberts,Ml, American Historical Review, Vol 0100, 1995; The Notorious Life Of Gyp - Right-Wing Anarchist In Fin-De-Siecle France - Silverman,Wz, American Historical Review, Vol 0101, 1996. **CONTACT ADDRESS** 11658 Mediterranean Ct, Reston, VA, 22090.

MOSES, WILSON J.
PERSONAL Detroit, MI, m, 1963, 2 children **DISCIPLINE** HISTORY **EDUCATION** Wayne St Univ, AB, 65, MA, 67; Brown Univ, PhD, 75. **CAREER** Instr to asst prof, 71-76, Univ Iowa; assoc prof, 76-80, S Methodist Univ; assoc prof to prof, , 80-88 Brown Univ; prof, dir, 88-92, Boston Univ; prof, fel, 92-, Pa St Univ. **HONORS AND AWARDS** Nat Endow for the Humanities Summer Stipend, 78; ACLS Grant, 79; S Fel Fund/ Andrew Mellon Found Postdoctoral Grant, 78-79; Nat Res Conch/Ford Found Grant, 83-84; Nat Endow for the Humanities Fel, 87-88; Woodrow Wilson Scholar, 89, 90; Fulbright Professorships, 83-84; Pa St Univ Faculty Scholars Medal for Distinction, 94; Cert of Special Tribute, 98. **MEMBERSHIPS** Amer Hist Assoc; Org of Amer Hist; Amer Stud Assoc; Assoc for the Study of African Amer Life & Hist. **RESEARCH** 19th century Amer cultural & intellectual hist; African Amer leadership; Back to Africa movement. **SELECTED PUBLICATIONS** Auth, The Golden Age of Black Nationalism, 1850-1925, Oxford Univ Press, 88; auth, Black Messiahs and Uncle Toms: Social and Literary Interpretations of a Religious Myth, Pa St Univ Press, 82, 93; auth, Alexander Crummell: A Study in Civilization and Discontent, Oxford Univ Press, 89; auth, The Wings of Ethiopia: Studies in African American Life and Letters, Iowa St Univ Press, 90; auth, Afrotopia: Roots of African-American Popular History, Cambridge Univ Press, 98. **CONTACT ADDRESS** 272 Oakley Dr, State College, PA, 16803. **EMAIL** WJM12@Psu.edu

MOSKOS, CHARLES C.
PERSONAL Born 05/20/1934, Chicago, IL, m, 1966, 2 children **DISCIPLINE** SOCIOLOGY **EDUCATION** Princeton Univ, BA, 56; Univ Calif, LA, PhD, 63. **CAREER** Assoc prof, Northwestern Univ, 1966; PROF, SOC, NORTHWESTERN UNIV. **MEMBERSHIPS** Am Soc Asn; Am Polit Asn; Inter-Univ Sem Armed Forces & Soc **RESEARCH** Military Sociology; Greek Americans **SELECTED PUBLICATIONS** "Humanitarians or Warriors?: Race, Gender, and Combat Status in Operation Restore Hope," Armed Forces & Soc, 95; "Affirmative Action in the Army: Why it Works," The Aff Action Debate, 96; "The Army's Success," Double Exposure: Poverty and Race in America, 97; "Civil-Military Relations After the Cold War," Civil-Mil Relations in Post-Communist States, 97; "Black Leadership and Racial Integration: Army Lessons for American Society," Raceand& Ethnic Relations in the US: Readings for the 21st Century, 98. **CONTACT ADDRESS** Dept Sociol, Northwestern Univ, Evanston, IL, 60208. **EMAIL** c-moskos@nwu.edu

MOSKOVITZ, MARC
DISCIPLINE MUSIC **EDUCATION** NC Sch Arts, BA; IN Univ, MA, PhD. **CAREER** Asst prof, Univ Toledo. **SELECTED PUBLICATIONS** Auth, publ(s) on Berlioz and David Popper. **CONTACT ADDRESS** Dept of Music, Univ Toledo, Toledo, OH, 43606.

MOSS, BERNARD HAYM
PERSONAL Born 04/17/1943, New York, NY, m, 1967 **DISCIPLINE** MODERN FRENCH & EUROPEAN LABOR HISTORY **EDUCATION** Univ Paris, dipl etudes francaises, 63; Cornell Univ, BA, 64; Columbia Univ, MA & cert Europ studies, 66, PhD(hist), 72. **CAREER** Instr hist, Univ Southern Calif, University Park, 69-71, asst prof, 72-80. Alternate Comn Relief in Belgium Am study fel, Belg, 71-72; Am Philos Soc grant, 73; actg ed, Newslett Europ Labor Hist, Study Group Europ Labor & Working Class Hist, 73-; Am Coun Learned Socs study fel, 76. **MEMBERSHIPS** AHA; Fr Hist Soc; Study Group Europ Labor & Working Class Hist. **RESEARCH** French labor and socialist history; Marxism; Euro- communism. **SELECTED PUBLICATIONS** Auth, Parisian workers and the origins of republican socialism, In: The Revolution of 1830, Thomas Watts, 74; Producers' associations and the origins of French socialism: Ideology from below, J Mod Hist, 75; The Origins of the French Labor Movement: The Socialism of Skilled Workers, 1830-1914, Univ Calif, 76; Insurgent Identities - Class, Community, And Protest In Paris From 1848 To

The Commune - Gould,Rv, American Historical Review, Vol 0102, 1997. **CONTACT ADDRESS** 3835 W 59th, Los Angeles, CA, 90043.

MOSS, WALTER GERALD
PERSONAL Born 04/20/1938, Cincinnati, OH, m, 1963, 3 children **DISCIPLINE** RUSSIAN HISTORY **EDUCATION** Xavier Univ, OH, BS, 60; Georgetown Univ, PhD, 68. **CAREER** From instr hist to asst prof, Wheeling Col, 67-70; asst prof, 70-74, assoc prof, 74-79, prof hist, Eastern MI Univ, 79-, Grant, NDEA Inst Methods Soc; Nat Endowment for Humanities grant, proj dir Southeastern MI Consortium Geront & Humanities, 73-75; consult, Choice; exec dir, Pres Comn on Future of Eastern MI Univ, 75-76; consult/panelist, Nat Endowment for Hum, 76-77 & 79-80. **MEMBERSHIPS** AHA; Am Asn Advan Slavic Studies; AAUP. **RESEARCH** Russ hist; 20th century world hist. **SELECTED PUBLICATIONS** Auth, Vladimir Soloviev and the Jews in Russia, Russ Rev, 4/70; co-ed, Growing Old, Pocket Bks, 75; ed, Humanistic Perspectives on Aging, Univ Mich/Wayne State Univ, 76; auth, Why the anxious fear?, Aging and death in the works of Turgenev, In: Aging and the Elderly, Humanities, 78; co-auth, The Twentieth Century: A Brief Global History, 5th ed, McGraw-Hill, 98; auth, A History of Russia, 2 vol, McGraw-Hill, 97. **CONTACT ADDRESS** Dept of Hist & Philos, Eastern Michigan Univ, 701 Pray Harrold, Ypsilanti, MI, 48197-2201. **EMAIL** his_moss@online.emich.edu

MOSSE, GEORGE L.
PERSONAL Born 09/20/1918, Berlin, Germany **DISCIPLINE** HISTORY **EDUCATION** Haverford Col, BS, 41; Harvard Univ, PhD, 46. **CAREER** Lectr hist, Univ Mich, 44; from instr to assoc prof, Univ Iowa, 44-55; from assoc prof to prof, 55-67, Bascom Prof Hist, Univ Wismadison, 65-, Huntington Libr grant, 49; vis expert, US High Comn, Ger, 51 & 54; Soc Sci Res Coun grant, 62; vis prof, Stanford Univ, 63-64; co-ed, J Contemp Hist, 66-; vis prof hist, Hebrew Univ Jerusalem, 69-70, 72, 74, 76 & 78 & Jewish Theol Sem Am, 77-; sr fel hist ideas, Australian Nat Univ, 72 & 79; bd gov, Wiener Libr, London, 73- & Leobaeck Inst, 74-; bd overseers, Tauber Inst, Brandeis Univ, 79-; Koebner prof hist, Hebrew Univ, Jerusalem, 79-; vis prof, Kaplan Ctr Jewish Studies, Univ Capetown, 80 & Univ Munich, 82. **HONORS AND AWARDS** Harbison Award, Danforth Found, 70; Aqui Storia, Italy, 75., DLitt, Carthage Col, 73. **MEMBERSHIPS** Am Soc Church Hist; AHA; Am Soc Reformation Res (pres, 61- 62). **RESEARCH** European intellectual history. **SELECTED PUBLICATIONS** Auth, The Reformation, Holt, 63; Crisis of German Ideology, Grosset, 64 & Schocken, 81; Nazi Culture, Grosset, 66 & Schocken, 81; coauth, Europe in the Sixteenth Century, Longmans, 68; auth, Germans and Jews, Fertig, 70 & Grosset, 71; The Nationalization of the Masses, Fertig, 75 & New Am Libr, 77; Toward the Final Solution, Fertig, 78 & Harpers, 79; Nazism, Transaction, 78; Masses and Men, Fertig, 81; Homosexuality In The Nazi Era - Documents Of Discrimination And Persecution - German - Grau,G, Central European History, Vol 0026, 1993. **CONTACT ADDRESS** Dept of Hist, Univ of Wis, Madison, WI, 53706.

MOSSHAMMER, ALDEN ADAMS
PERSONAL Born 03/22/1941, Greenwich, CT, m, 1971 **DISCIPLINE** ANCIENT HISTORY, CLASSICS **EDUCATION** Amherst Col, BA, 62; Brown Univ, PhD(classics), 71. **CAREER** Instr Latin, Laconia High Sch, NH, 62-63; instr classics, Mercersburg Acad, Pa, 63-67, registr, 65-67; instr, Kenyon Col, 70-71; asst prof, Swarthmore Col, 71-72; asst prof, 72-77, Assoc Prof Hist, Univ Calif, San Diego, 77-. **MEMBERSHIPS** Am Philol Asn; AHA. **RESEARCH** Greek chronography; archaic Greek history; church history. **SELECTED PUBLICATIONS** Auth, The epoch of the seven sages, 76 & Phainias of eresos and chronology, 77, Calif Studies Class Antiq; The Chronicle of Eusebius and Greek Chronographic Tradition, Assoc Univ, 79; The Barberini manuscript of George Syncellus, Greek, Roman, Byzantine Studies, 80; Two fragments of Jerome's chronicle, Rheinisches Mus, 81; Thales' Eclipse, Am Philol Asn, 81; The date of the first pythiad-again, Greek, Roman, Byzantine Studies, 82; ed, Ecolga Chronographiae Georgii Syncelli, Teubner ; Agatharchides Of Cnidos 'On The Erythraean Sea' - Burstein,Sm, J Of The American Oriental Society, Vol 0112, 1992. **CONTACT ADDRESS** Dept of Hist B-007, Univ of Calif San Diego, 9500 Gilman Dr, La Jolla, CA, 92093-5003.

MOST, GLENN WARREN
PERSONAL Born 06/12/1952, Miami, FL **DISCIPLINE** COMPARATIVE LITERATURE, CLASSICAL LANGUAGES **EDUCATION** Harvard Univ, AB, 72; Yale Univ, MPhil, 78, PhD(comp lit), 80; Tubingen, WGer, DPhil, 80. **CAREER** Teaching asst philos, Yale Univ, 75, teaching asst lit, 76; teaching asst Latin, Univ Tubingen, 77-78; vis lectr lit theory, Yale Univ, 78-79; teaching asst classics, Univ Heidelberg, 79-80; Mellon Asst Prof Classics, Princeton Univ, 80-, Mellon fel, Am Acad Rome, 82-83. **RESEARCH** Literature; literary theory; philosophy. **SELECTED PUBLICATIONS** Auth, Principled reading, Diacritics, 79; Sappho Fr 16 6-7 LP, Class Quart, 81; Callimachus and Herophilus, Hermes, 81; On the arrangement of Catullus' Carmina Maiora, 81 & Neues Zur Geschichte des Terminus Epyllion, 82, Philologus; contribr, Geschichtsbewusstsein und Rationalitat: Zum Problem der Geschichtlichkeit in der Theoriebildung, Klett-Cotta Verlag, West Ger, 82; Ancient Writers: Greece and Rome, Charles Scribner's Sons, 82; co-ed, G W Leibniz, Specimen Dynamicum, Felix Meiner Verlag, Hamburg, West Ger, 82; Professionalizing Politics, Politicizing The Profession + Differences Between The Current State Of Classics In America And Europe, Transactions Of The American Philological Association, Vol 0122, 1992; A Seminar Held At The International Scholarly Forum In Heidelberg %June 16-18, 1995; On The Theme Of The Theory And History Of The Collection Of Literary Fragments, Organized By Most,Glen,W., Gnomon-Kritische Zeitschrift Fur Die Gesamte Klassische Al Schlegel,Friedrich, Schlegel,August,Wilhelm And The Birth Of The Tragic Paradigm, Poetica-Zeitschrift Fur Sprach-Und Literaturwissenschaft, Vol 0025, 1993; Reading Raphael - The 'School Of Athens' And Its Pre-Text, Critical Inquiry, Vol 0023, 1996. **CONTACT ADDRESS** Dept of Classics, Princeton Univ, Princeton, NJ, 08544.

MOTEN, CHAUNCEY DONALD
PERSONAL Born 07/02/1933, Kansas City, KS, m **DISCIPLINE** EDUCATION **EDUCATION** TX Coll, BA, 1955; Vandercook Coll, MA, 1959; Univ of MO, MA, 1969; Univ of MI, PhD, 1972. **CAREER** KS City Public School, teacher 1965-68; Univ of MO, dir 1968-70, 1971-73; Metro Comm Coll, exec & asst 1974-77; Metro Comm Coll Kansas City MO, exec dean ofc of human devel 1977-79; Penn Valley Comm Coll Kansas City MO, asst dean comm serv/instructional serv 1979-. **HONORS AND AWARDS** Mott Fellowship 1970-71; VFW VIP 1972; Man of the Yr 1972; Rockefeller Fellow 1973-74; Recog for Outstndg Srvc MO Assn for Affirmtv Actn 1977; Award of Apprec Am Assn for Affirmtv Actn 1978; Valuable Serv Award Spirit of Freedom Found 1978; Citation of Excellnc TX Coll 1980; Jefferson Award Am Inst for Public Serv 1980. **MEMBERSHIPS** Review panalist HEW 1977; consult IO Assn for Equal Emplymnt Oppor/Affirmtn Action Prof 1977; consult Univ Resrch Corp 1978; consult Nat Counc for Staff Prog & Organztnl Devel 1978; consult Mid-am Regnl Counc 1978; consult OR State Univ 1979; consult NW Coll Personnel Assn 1979; consult Am Assn for Affirmatv Action 1980; consult Thomas E Baker & Asso 1980; consult KCRCHE 1976; HEW 1976; Mott Found 1975; CBS 1974; Serengeti Res Inst 1972; KS & MO Bds of Educ pres MO Assn for Affirmatv Action 1980-81; exec bd mem Charlie Parker Mem Found 1978-80; mem MO Black Ldrshp Assn 1977-80; exec bd mem Kansas CitySpirit of Freedom Fountn Inc 1978-80; exec bd mem Yng Men's Christian Assn 1974-76; ofcr Natl Univ Ext Assn 1975-77; mem Am Affr Act Assn 1975-77; comm MO Affm Act Assn1976-80; exec bd mem Momm Educ Assn 1975-80; mem KCMO Serboma Club; NAACP; exec bd mem Black Archives of Mid-am 1974-80; bd mem AFRICARE KCMO 1975-80; mem Urban Leag; bd mem KS Assn for Blind 1977-80. **CONTACT ADDRESS** Dean, Pennsylvania Valley Comm Col, 3201 Southwest Trafficway, Kansas City, MO, 64111.

MOTT, MORRIS K.
DISCIPLINE HISTORY **EDUCATION** Univ Manitoba, BA, MA; Queen's Univ, PhD. **CAREER** Hist, Brandon Univ. **RESEARCH** History of sport. **SELECTED PUBLICATIONS** Auth, John B. Mather, Univ Toronto,, 90; Sports in Canada: Historical Readings, Mississauga, 89; co-auth, Curling Capital: Winnipeg and the Roarin' Game 1876-1988, Univ Maitoba, 89. **CONTACT ADDRESS** History Dept, Brandon Univ, 270-18th St, Brandon, MB, R7A 6A9. **EMAIL** mott@BrandonU.ca

MOTTO, ANNA LYDIA
PERSONAL New York, NY, m, 1959, 2 children **DISCIPLINE** CLASSICS **EDUCATION** Queen's Col, NY, BA, 46; NY Univ, MA, 48; Univ NC, PhD, 53. **CAREER** Asst, Univ NC, 49-50, part-time instr, 51-52; asst prof Latin, Greek & Span, Washington Col, 53-57; teacher Latin & French, Northport High Sch, NY, 57-58; asst prof Latin & Greek & chmn dept classics, Alfred Univ, 58-65; assoc prof Latin & Greek & chmn dept, Muhlenberg Col, 65-66; assoc prof, St John's Univ, NY, 66-68; from assoc prof to prof, Drew Univ, 68-73; chmn dept for lang, 74-78, Prof Classics, Univ South Fla, 73-, Fulbright grant, Am Acad Rome & Vergilian Soc, Cumae, 56; vis prof, Univ Mich, 69. **MEMBERSHIPS** Classic Asn Atlantic States (vp, 72-73); Am Philol Asn; Am Classic League; MLA; S Atlantic Mod Lang Asn. **RESEARCH** Seneca the philosopher; Roman Stoicism; Roman satire. **SELECTED PUBLICATIONS** Auth, Seneca Sourcebook: Guide to the Thought of Lucius Annaeus Seneca, Adolf Hakkert, Amsterdam, 70; Seneca's ironic art, Classic Philol, 470; Seneca's prose writings: A decade of scholarship, 1958-1968, Classic World, 1-271; Et terris iactatus et alto: The art of Seneca's Epistle 53, Am J Philol, 471; Seneca, Twayne, 73; co-ed, Satire: That Blasted Art (anthology), Putnam, 73; Philosophy and poetry: Seneca and Vergil, Classic Outlook, 9-1078; Art and ethic in the drama: Senecan pseudotragedy reconsidered, Ill Classic Studies, 82; Seneca On Friendship, Atene E Roma, Vol 0038, 1993; Oedipus And The Fabrication Of The Father - 'Oedipus Tyrannus' In Modern Criticism And Philosophy - Pucci,P, Classical Bulletin, Vol 0068, 1992; Seneca 'Phaedra' - English And Latin - Boyle,Aj, Editor-Translator, Classical Bulletin, Vol 0068, 1992; Seneca On Cruelty, Maia-Rivista Di Letterature Classiche, Vol 0046, 1994; The Monster In Seneca 'Hercules Furens' 926-939, Classical Philology, Vol 0089, 1994; Kill Em All - An Ancient And Modern Satiric Theme, Thalia-Studies In Literary Humor, Vol 0014, 1994. **CONTACT ADDRESS** Dept of Classics, Univ of S FL, 4202 Fowler Ave, Tampa, FL, 33620-9951.

MOULTON, EDWARD C.
DISCIPLINE HISTORY **EDUCATION** Memorial Univ, BA; MA; Univ London, PhD. **CAREER** Prof **RESEARCH** Asian history. **SELECTED PUBLICATIONS** Auth, Lord Northbrook's Indian Administration 1872-1876, 69; Indian Studies in Canada, 85; Problems of Municipal Self-Government and Urban Development in Nineteenth Century North India: Allan O. Hume and Municipal Beginnings in the Town of Etawah in the 1860s, 94. **CONTACT ADDRESS** Dept of History, Univ Manitoba, Winnipeg, MB, R3T 2N2. **EMAIL** emoultn@cc.umanitoba.ca

MOULTON, GARY EVAN
PERSONAL Born 02/21/1942, Tulsa, OK, m, 1969, 3 children **DISCIPLINE** AMERICAN HISTORY **EDUCATION** Northeastern OK State Univ, BA, 68; OK State Univ, MA, 70, PhD, 73. **CAREER** Instr hist, Southwestern OK State Univ, 73-74, asst prof, 74-79; assoc prof, 79-88, prof hist, Univ NE-Lincoln, 88-, ed, papers Chief John Ross, Nat Hist Publ & Rec Comn, 75-79; ed, J Lewis & Clark Expedition, Univ NE-Lincoln, 79. **HONORS AND AWARDS** Wrangler Award, Best Western Non-fiction, Nat Cowboy Hall of Fame, Okla City, 84; Award of Meritorius Achievement, Lewis & Clark Trail Heritage Found, 88; J Franklin Jemson Prize for Outstanding Ed Achievement, AHA, 90; Fulbright Scholar Award, lectr, Universitat Hannover, Ger, 94; Distinguished Tchg Award, Univ NE-Lincoln, 96. **MEMBERSHIPS** Asn Documentary Ed; Lewis & Clark Trail Heritage Found; NE State Hist Soc; Western Hist Asn. **RESEARCH** Lewis and Clark expedition; Am Indians; Am West. **SELECTED PUBLICATIONS** Auth, John Ross, Cherokee Chief, Univ GA Press, 78; The Specialized Journals of Lewis and Clark, Proc Am Philos Soc, 83; Papers of Chief John Ross, 2 vol, Univ OK Press, 85; On Reading Lewis and Clark: The Last Twenty Years, Montana, 88; Lewis and Clark: Meeting the Challenges of the Trail, In: Encounters with a Distant Land (Carlos A Schwantes, ed), Univ ID Press, 94; Journals of Lewis and Clard Expedition, 12 vol, Univ Nebr Press, 83; coauth, Prince Maximilian and new maps of the Missouri and Yellowstone rivers by William Clark, Western Historical Quart, 10/81. **CONTACT ADDRESS** Dept Hist, Univ NE-Lincoln, Lincoln, NE, 68588-0327. **EMAIL** gmoulton@unl.edu

MOUNT, GRAEME S.
PERSONAL Born 07/26/1939, Montreal, PQ, Canada **DISCIPLINE** HISTORY **EDUCATION** McGill Univ, BA, 61; Univ Toronto, MA, 67, PhD, 69. **CAREER** PROF HISTORY LAURENTIAN UNIV 1985-. **SELECTED PUBLICATIONS** Auth, Presbyterian Missins to Trinidad and Puerto Rico, 83; auth, The Sudbury Region: An Illustrated History, 86; auth, Spies and Spying in the Peaceable Kingdom, 93; coauth, An Introduction to Canadian-American Relations, 84, 89. **CONTACT ADDRESS** History Dept, Laurentian Univ, 935 Ramsey Lake Rd, Sudbury, ON, P3E 2C6. **EMAIL** GMOUNT@NICKEL.LAURENTIAN.CA

MOURELATOS, ALEXANDER PHOEBUS DIONYSIOU
PERSONAL Born 07/19/1936, Athens, Greece, m, 1962 **DISCIPLINE** PHILOSOPHY, CLASSICAL PHILOLOGY **EDUCATION** Yale Univ, BA, 58, MA, 61, PhD(philos), 64. **CAREER** Instr, Yale Univ, 62-64; from asst prof to assoc prof, 65-71, Prof Philos, Univ Tex Austin, 71-, Jr fel, Inst Res Humanities, Univ Wis, 64-65; mem, Inst Advan Study, Princeton, NJ, 67-68; Nat Endowment for Humanities fel, 68 & 82-83; jr fel, Ctr Hellenic Studies, Washington, DC, 73-74; Am Coun Learned Soc fel, 73-74; vis fel, Humanities Res Ctr, Australian Nat Univ, Canberra, 78. **MEMBERSHIPS** Am Philos Asn; Am Philol Asn; Can Philos Asn. **RESEARCH** Pre-Socratic philosophy; Plato; Aristotle. **SELECTED PUBLICATIONS** Auth, Aristotle's Powers and Modern Empiricism, Ratio, 67; The Route of Parmenides, Yale Univ, 70; co-ed, Exegesis and Argument: Studies Presented to Gregory Vlastos, Van Gorcum, Assen, Neth, 73; ed, The Pre-Socratics: A Collection of Critical Essays, Doubleday, 74; Events, processes, and states, Ling & Philos, 78; Astronomy and kinematics in Plato's project of rationalist explanation, Study Hist & Philos of Sci, 80; Vlastos,Gregory - In-Memoriam, Gnomon-Kritische Zeitschrift Fur Die Gesamte Klassische Altertumswissenschaft, Vol 0065, 1993. **CONTACT ADDRESS** Dept of Philos, Univ of Tex, Austin, TX, 78712-1026.

MOWAT, FARLEY
PERSONAL Born 05/12/1921, Belleville, ON, Canada **DISCIPLINE** HISTORY **EDUCATION** Univ Toronto, BA, 49. **HONORS AND AWARDS** DLitt(hon), Laurentian Univ, 70; DLaws(hon), Univ Lethbridge, 73; DLaws(hon), Univ Toronto, 73; DLaws(hon), Univ PEI, 79; off, Order Can, 81; DLitt(hon), Univ Victoria, 82; DLitt(hon), Lakehead Univ, 86; Can Achievers Award, Toshiba, Can, 90; Take Back Nat Award, Coun Can, 91; Author's Award, Can Found Advan Can Lett, 93; DLitt(hon), McMaster Univ, 94; DLaws(hon), Queen's Univ,

95; DLitt(hon), Univ Col Cape Breton, 96 **SELECTED PUBLICATIONS** Auth, Sibir, 70; auth, A Whale for the Killing, 72; auth, Wake of the Great Sealers, 73; auth, Tundra, 73; auth, The Snow Walker, 75; auth, Canada North Now, 76; auth, And No Birds Sang, 79; auth, Sea of Slaughter, 84; auth, My Discovery of America, 85; auth, Virunga, 87; auth, The New Founde Land, 89; auth, Rescue the Earth, 90; auth, My Father's Son, 92; auth, Born Naked, 93; auth, Aftermath, 95. **CONTACT ADDRESS** Key Porter Books, 70 The Esplanade, 3rd Fl, Toronto, ON, M5E 1R2.

MOYER, ALBERT EARL
PERSONAL Born 03/05/1945, Connellsville, PA, m, 1969, 2 children **DISCIPLINE** HISTORY OF SCIENCE **EDUCATION** Oberlin Col, BA, 67; Univ Colo, Boulder, MS, 69; Univ Wis- Madison, MA, 74, PhD(hist of sci), 77. **CAREER** Asst prof physics, Lees Jr Col, 69-72; Asst Prof Hist Of Sci, VA Tech, 77-. **MEMBERSHIPS** Hist Sci Soc; Am Asn Physics Teachers. **RESEARCH** History of physics, especially in the United States. **SELECTED PUBLICATIONS** Auth, Robert Hooke's ambiguous presentation of Hooke's Law, Isis, 677; Physics teaching and the learning theories of G S Hall and E L Thorndike, The Physics Teacher, 481; contribr, Percy Williams Bridgman, Dict of Am Biography, Scribner's Sons, 81; auth, American Physics in Transition: A History of Conceptual Change in the Late Nineteenth Century, Tomash Pub, 82; The Correspondence Of Faraday,Michael, Vol 1, 1811 December 1831, Letters 1-524 - Faraday,M, Isis, Vol 0086, 1995; The Correspondence Of Faraday,Michael, Vol 2, 1832 December 1840, Letters 525-1333 - Faraday,M, Isis, Vol 0086, 1995; The Correspondence Of Faraday,Michael, Vol 1, 1811 December 1831, Letters 1-524 - Faraday,M, Isis, Vol 0086, 1995; The Correspondence Of Faraday,Michael, Vol 2, 1832 December 1840, Letters 525-1333 - Faraday,M, Isis, Vol 0086, 1995. **CONTACT ADDRESS** Dept of Hist, VA Tech, Blacksburg, VA, 24061.

MOYER, JAMES CARROLL
PERSONAL Born 11/30/1941, Norristown, PA, m, 1965, 3 children **DISCIPLINE** OLD TESTAMENT, ANCIENT HISTORY **EDUCATION** Wheaton Col, BA, 63; Gordon Divinity Sch, MDiv, 66; Brandeis Univ, MA, 68, PhD(Mediter studies), 69. **CAREER** Sachar Int fel, Brandeis Univ, 69-70; asst prof, 70-75, assoc prof hist, 75-78, assoc prof religious studies, 78-79, Prof Relig Studies, Southwest MO State Univ, 79-, Fel archaeol, Hebrew Union Col Bibl & Archaeol Sch, Jerusalem, 69-70. **MEMBERSHIPS** Soc Bibl Lit; Am Orient Soc; Am Schs Orient Res; Cath Bibl Asn. **RESEARCH** Old Testament; Israelite historiography and chronology; Hittitology. **SELECTED PUBLICATIONS** Auth, Philistines and Samson, In: Zondervan Pictorial Encyclopedia of the Bible, 75; Review of Edwin Yamauchi, Pre Christian Gnosticism: a survey of the proposed evidences, Fides et Historia, VIII No 2, 76; contribr 14 articles for the revision of Eerdman's Int Standard Bible Encycl, Vol I, 79, Vol II, 82; co-ed, Hittite and Israelite cultic practices: A selected comparison, In: Scripture in Context II, 82; Ashkelon Discovered - From Canaanites And Philistines To Romans And Moslems - Stager,Le, J Of Biblical Literature, Vol 0112, 1993; History And Technology Of Olive-Oil In The Holy-Land - Frankel,R, Avitsur,S, Ayalon,E, Jacobson,J, Biblical Archaeologist, Vol 0059, 1996; Through The Ages In Palestinian Archaeology - An Introductory Handbook - Rast,We, Biblical Archaeologist, Vol 0057, 1994; Scripture And Other Artifacts - Essays On The Bible And Archaeology In Honor Of King,Philip,J. - Coogan,Md, Exum,Jc, Stager,Le, Biblical Archaeologist, Vol 0058, 1995. **CONTACT ADDRESS** Dept of Hist, Southwest MO State Univ, Springfield, MO, 65802.

MOYER, RONALD L.
DISCIPLINE THEATRE HISTORY, LITERATURE AND ACTINIG **EDUCATION** Univ IL, BA, 66, MA, 67; Univ Denver, PhD, 74. **CAREER** Prof & dir, Grad Stud; prof, Univ SD, 74-, dept ch, 78-83, 89-91, tenure, 80; dir, Black Hills Playhouse, 76- & assoc mng dir, 79 & 80; tchg fel, Univ Denver, 72-73; instr, Purdue Univ-Calumet, 67-71; grad asst, Univ IL, 66-67; local arrangements ch, SDHSAA One-Act Play Festival, 90 & 85; local arrangements supvr, Irene Ryan Competition, ACTF, Region V North, 89; hon mem, Bd Dir, The Black Hills Playhouse, 92-; second VP & mem, Bd Dir, The Black Hills Playhouse, 83-91; critic, Am Col Theatre Festival Region V N, 84; local arrangements ch, ACTF Region V North Festivention, 83; Univ/Col Theatre Asn Repr, Mid- Am Theatre Conf Coun, 81-83; treasurer, S Dakota Theatre Asn, 78-82, finance comt, 78-82 & nominating comt, 78; co-drafter, Const Rev, 78; local arrangements ch, SDHSAA One-Act Play Festival, 82; mem, Plan Comt, MATC Conv, 80-81; ch, Reg Theatre Auditions, MATC Conv, 81; critic & mem, Reg Screening Team, ACTF Region V North, 80-81; mem, Plan Comt, MATC Conv, 79-80; ch, Reg Theatre Auditions, MATC Conv, 80; local arrangements ch, SDHSAA One-Act Play Festival, 80; univ comt(s), Univ Graphics Rev Comt, 94-95; Grad Coun, 78-83,84-87, 89-; subcomt(s), Univ Senate, 77-78 & Rules and Nominating Comt, 87-89; Presidential-Alumni Scholar Selection Comt, 80, 81; Educ Media Comt, 76-77; Statewide Educ Serv Adv Comt, 75-77. **HONORS AND AWARDS** Sioux Falls Argus Leader, 95; USD Stud Theatre League Fac Appreciation Awd, 92; Courseware develop awd, IBM-Rochester, 91; The Divorce Colony, play won second prize, David Libr of the Am Revolution, 87; USD Stud Theatre League Fac Appreciation Awd, 86; first prize, 2 plays, David Libr Am Revolution nat contest, 76; NDEA Title IV fel, Univ Denver, 71-74; Bush Mini-Grant Prog, 95; USD fac develop prog, 93; vis prof, IBM-Rochester, 92 & 91; USD fac develop prog, 92; Bush Found grant, 89, 88 & 85; SD Arts Coun grant, 82-83. **RESEARCH** Use of the Internet for the study of theatre and drama; Shakespearean performance; methods of playscript analysis. **SELECTED PUBLICATIONS** Auth, American Actors, 1861-1910: An Annotated Bibliography of Books, Troy, NY, Whitston Publ Co, 79; coauth & ed advert brochure, IBM Ultimedia Video Delivery System/400, Rochester, MN, Int Bus Mach Corp, co 92. **CONTACT ADDRESS** Dept of Theatre, Univ SD, 414 E Clark St, Vermillion, SD, 57069. **EMAIL** rmoyer@charlie.usd.edu

MOYLAN, PRUDENCE A.
DISCIPLINE HISTORY **EDUCATION** Univ Ill-Urbana, PhD, 75. **CAREER** Hist, Loyola Univ. **RESEARCH** Modern British history; gender & peace Stud. **SELECTED PUBLICATIONS** Auth, The Form and Reform of County Government: Kent, 1889-1914, Leicester UP, 78; Local Government, in Victorian Britain: an Encyclopedia, 86. **CONTACT ADDRESS** Fine Arts Dept, Loyola Univ, Chicago, 6525 N. Sheridan Rd., Chicago, IL, 60626. **EMAIL** pmoylan@orion.it.luc.edu

MOYNIHAN, KENNETH J.
DISCIPLINE HISTORY **EDUCATION** Holy Cross, AB, 66; Clark, MA, 69, PhD, 73. **CAREER** PROF, HIST, ASSUMPTION COLL **MEMBERSHIPS** Am Antiquarian Soc **RESEARCH** Hist of Worcester **SELECTED PUBLICATIONS** Auth, "Meetinghouse vs. Courthouse: The Struggle for Legitimacy in Worcester, 1783- 1788," in Shays' Rebellion: Selected Essays, 87; auth, "The Importance of Being Protestant: The Swedish Role in Worcester, Massachusetts, 1868-1930," in Swedes in America: New Perspectives, 93; auth, "Can the Scholars' History be the Public History?" Procs of the AAS 105, 95. **CONTACT ADDRESS** Hist Dept, Assumption Col, 500 Salisbury St, Worcester, MA, 01615-0005. **EMAIL** kmoynihan@eve.assumption.edu

MOYNIHAN, RUTH BARNES
PERSONAL Born 08/19/1933, Wallingford, CT, m, 1953, 7 children **DISCIPLINE** AMERICAN HISTORY **EDUCATION** Univ Conn, BA, 73; Yale Univ, PhD(hist), 79. **CAREER** Lectr hist, Univ Conn, 77 & 82; vis asst prof, Univ Tex, Dallas, 79-80; vis lectr hist & women's studies, Yale Univ, 80-81; Res & Writing, 81-, Am Coun Learned Soc grant, 80. **HONORS AND AWARDS** Beinecke Prize in Western Hist, Yale Univ, 79. **MEMBERSHIPS** AHA; Orgn Am Historians. **RESEARCH** American women's Colonial history to 1900. **SELECTED PUBLICATIONS** Auth, Children and young people on the Overland Trail, Western Hist Quart, 75; co-ed, The Writings of Abigail Scott Duniway, Feminist Press; auth, Rebel for Rights: Abigail Scott Duniway of Oregon, Yale Univ Press (in prep); Wagon Wheel Kitchens - Food On The Oregon Trail - Williams,J, J Of American History, Vol 0081, 1994; Converting The West - A Biography Of Whitman,Narcissa - Jeffrey,Jr, American Historical Review, Vol 0098, 1993; Small Worlds, Children And Adolescents In America, 1850-1950 - West,E, Petrik,P, Pacific Historical Review, Vol 0063, 1994; Pioneer Children On The Journey West - Werner,Ee, Pacific Historical Review, Vol 0065, 1996; The Frontiers Of Womens Writing - Womens Narratives And The Rhetoric Of Westward Expansion - Georgifindlay,B, Western Historical Quarterly, Vol 0028, 1997. **CONTACT ADDRESS** 37 Farrell Rd RR 1, Storrs, CT, 06268.

MOYSEY, ROBERT ALLEN
PERSONAL Born 06/27/1949, Richmond, IN **DISCIPLINE** CLASSICAL LANGUAGES, ANCIENT HISTORY **EDUCATION** Univ Cincinnati, BA, 71; Princeton Univ, MA, 73, PhD(class), 75. **CAREER** Teaching asst class, Princeton Univ, 73-75; vis asst prof, Hamilton Col, 77-78; vis asst prof hist, Univ Del, 79-80; asst prof class, 80-85, assoc prof class, 85-90, prof class, 90-, chair and prof class, Univ Miss, 93-. **HONORS AND AWARDS** Phi Beta Kappa; Charles McMicken Honors Prize. **MEMBERSHIPS** Archaeol Inst Am; Am Philol Asn; Asn Ancient Historians; Am Numis Soc. **RESEARCH** Greek & Persian history, 4th century BC; Greek epigraphy; Greek numismatics. **SELECTED PUBLICATIONS** Auth, The Date of the Strato of Sidon Decree, Am J of Ancient Hist, 76; The Thirty and the Pnyx, Am J of Archaeol, 81; Greek Funerary Monuments in Mississippi, Zeitschrift fur Papyrologie und Epigraphik, 88; Three Fragmentary Attic Inscriptions, Zeitschrift fur Papyrologie und Epigraphik, 89; Observations on the Numismatic Evidence relating to the Great Satrapal Refolt of 362/1 BC, Revue des Etudes Anciennes, 89; Thucydides, Kimon and the Peace of Kallias, Ancient His Bulletin, 91; Diodoros, the Satraps and the Decline of the Persian Empire: A Book Review of Michael Weiskopf's The So-Called Great Satrapal Revolt 366-360 BC, Ancient Hist Bulletin, 91; A Brief History of Olynthus, Olynthus: An Overview, Univ Miss, 92; Plutarch, Nepos and the Satrapal Revolt of 362/1 BC, Historia, 92. **CONTACT ADDRESS** Dept of Classics, Univ of Mississippi, University, MS, 38677-9999. **EMAIL** clmoysey@olemiss.edu

MRUCK, ARMIN EINHARD
PERSONAL Born 06/06/1925, Osterode, Germany, m, 1952, 3 children **DISCIPLINE** MODERN HISTORY **EDUCATION** Univ Gottingen, DPhil, 51. **CAREER** Grant, Univ KY, 51-52; instr Ger, NY Univ, 53-55; from asst prof to assoc prof hist, Morgan State Col, 55-67, chmn div soc sci, 60-63; vp fac asn, 67-72, Prof Hist, Towson State Univ, 67- , Teacher, Gym & Lyceum, Ger, 61-62; sen, Fac Senate State Univs & Cols, 82-. **MEMBERSHIPS** AHA; AAUP **RESEARCH** Renaissance, reformation, national socialism and resistance against it. **SELECTED PUBLICATIONS** Auth, Deutschland im Europaeischen Spannungsfeld, 63; Der 29 Juli in amerikanischer Sicht, 65, Die amerikanische Ostpolitik, 66 & Deutsch-amerik Beziehungen im 20, Jahrhundert, 67, Europaeische Begegnung; coauth, An Austrian view of the US Navy, Am Neptune, 74; auth, Die Brucke zur Vergangenheit, Ostpreussenblat, 776; Neves aus der alten ostdtsch heimat, Washington J, 1076; Poland: An experiment in Eurocomms, Sun, 77; American Intelligence And The German Resistance To Hitler - A Documentary History - Heideking,J, Mauch,C, German Studies Review, Vol 0020, 1997; Frontsoldaten - The German Soldier In World-War-Ii - Fritz,Sg, International History Review, Vol 0019, 1997. **CONTACT ADDRESS** Dept of Hist, Towson State Univ, Baltimore, MD, 21204.

MUCCIGROSSO, ROBERT HENRY
PERSONAL Born 07/13/1939, Elmira Heights, NY, m **DISCIPLINE** HISTORY **EDUCATION** Syracuse Univ, BA, 60; Columbia Univ, MA, 61, PhD, 66. **CAREER** From instr to asst prof, 66-75, assoc prof, 75-80, PROF HIST, BROOKLYN COL, 81-98, prof emer, 98-; Fulbright jr lectr, Rome, 72-73. **MEMBERSHIPS** AHA; Orgn Am Historians; Soc Hist Educ. **RESEARCH** Late 19th and 20th century United States intellectual and cultural history. **SELECTED PUBLICATIONS** Auth, The city reform club: a study in late 19th century reform, NY Hist Soc Quart, 7/68; American gothic: Ralph Adams Cram, Thought, spring 72; Richard Ward Greene Welling, Dictionary of Am Biog, 74; Ambrose Bierce & Wallace Stevens, Encycl Am Biog, 74; Ralph Adams Cram: the architect as communitarian, Prospects, 75; Corruption and the Alienation of the Intellectuals, in Before Watergate, Brooklyn Col, 78; Television and the Urban Crisis, in The Impact of Television upon Aspects of Contemporary Civilization, Nelson-Hall, 79; American Gothic: The Mind and Art of Ralph Adams Cram, Univ Press Am, 80; co-auth, America in the Twentieth Century: Coming of Age, Harper & Row, 88; ed, Research Guide to American Historical Biography, 3 vol, Beacham Publ, 88; co-ed, Henry Adams and His World, Transactions of the Am Philos Soc, 93; Celebrating the New World: Chicago's Columbian Exposition of 1893, Ivan R Dee, 93; co-auth, Manufacturing in America: A Legacy of Excellence, Greenwich Publ Group, 95. **CONTACT ADDRESS** 10704 Baylark Ave, Las Vegas, NV, 89134.

MUELLER, CLAUS
PERSONAL Born 07/23/1948, Berlin, Germany, m, 1984, 2 children **DISCIPLINE** SOCIOLOGY **EDUCATION** Univ of Cologne, BA (equiv), 64; New Schl for Soc Res, MA, 60, PhD, 70; Inst dEtudes Politiques, Paris, 77. **CAREER** Sr Part, Media Resource Assoc, 75-85; Pres, Intl Film and TV Exchange Inc, 85-, Adv, 89/95-, Assoc Prof, 76-80, Dir, 85-, Hunter Col, CUNY. **HONORS AND AWARDS** Brd Mem/Off, Intl Film and TV Exchange, NY Film/video Coun; Taiwan Intl Cult Exchange. **MEMBERSHIPS** New York Film and Video Coun, Assoc of Independent Video and Film Prof, Carnegie Coun on Intl Relation, New York Film/Video Coun, Intl Radio and TV Soc **RESEARCH** International Communications; information and the class structure; contemporary documentaries. **SELECTED PUBLICATIONS** Development Communication in the USA, Media Sup and Develop Comm in a World of Change, Bad Honnef: 95; The Refracted Mirror, Intl Jour of Group Tensions, 96; The Cologne Medien Forum, The Ind, 98; Third World Television Access to US Media, F Naumann Found, 89. **CONTACT ADDRESS** 420 East 64th W2H, New York, NY, 10021. **EMAIL** cmueller@hunter.cuny.edu

MUELLER, HOWARD ERNEST
PERSONAL Born 08/04/1936, Danube, MN, m, 1959, 2 children **DISCIPLINE** HISTORY OF RELIGIONS **EDUCATION** NCent Col, BA, 58; Evangel Theol Sem, BD, 61; Yale Univ, Stm, 62; Northwestern Univ, PhD(relig), 73. **CAREER** Asst prof relig, Carleton Col, 73-76; asst prof Relig, 76-80, assoc prof, 81-85, PROF RELIG, NCENT COL, 85-, CHMN DEPT, 90-. **HONORS AND AWARDS** Toenniges Prof of Religious Studies, 92. **MEMBERSHIPS** Am Acad Relig. **RESEARCH** African traditional religions; death and dying; biblical studies. **CONTACT ADDRESS** Dept of Religious Studies, No Central Col, 30 N Brainard St, Naperville, IL, 60566. **EMAIL** hem@noctrl.edu

MUELLER, MARTIN
DISCIPLINE CLASSICS AND ENGLISH **EDUCATION** Ind Univ, MA, PhD, 66. **CAREER** Prof, Northwestern Univ, 76-. **RESEARCH** Repertorium Homericum, A Relational Database Tool for the Study of Homer. **SELECTED PUBLICATIONS** Auth, Children of Oedipus and Other Essays on the Imitation of Greek Tragedy, 1550-1800, Toronto, 80; The Iliad, London, 84. **CONTACT ADDRESS** Dept of Classics, Northwestern Univ, 1801 Hinman, Evanston, IL, 60208. **EMAIL** martinmueller@nwu.edu

MUELLER, ROLAND MARTIN
PERSONAL Born 06/16/1929, Athens, WI, m, 1951, 2 children **DISCIPLINE** AMERICAN & EUROPEAN HISTORY **EDUCATION** Concordia Teachers Col, Ill, BS, 51; Colo State Col, MA, 55; Univ Kans, PhD(US hist), 78. **CAREER** Asst prof hist, 56-64, assoc prof, 64-79, Prof Soc Sci, St John's Col, Kans, 79-. **MEMBERSHIPS** Orgn Am Historians; Nat Coun Geog Educ; Concordia Hist Inst. **RESEARCH** Clergy in the pre-Revolution period of Colonial history; the Chautauqua movement in Kansas. **SELECTED PUBLICATIONS** Auth, Reasons for seasons, 66 & Social studies and the local scene, + 72, Lutheran Educ; Teaching Beyond The Quincentennial + The 500th Anniversary Of Columbus Landfall In The America And The Dearth Of Reference Material Concerning It, Hispania-A J Devoted To The Teaching Of Spanish And Portuguese, Vol 0076, 1993. **CONTACT ADDRESS** 1714 E 11th, Winfield, KS, 67156.

MUHLBERGER, STEVEN
DISCIPLINE HISTORY **EDUCATION** Mich State Univ, BA, 72; Univ Toronto, MA, 74, PhD, 81. **CAREER** Asst prof, 89-93 to assoc prof, 93-, Nipissing Univ; asst prof, Trent Univ, Peterborough, Ont & Brock Univ, St Catharines, Ont, 88-89; asst prof, Univ Toronto, 82-84 and 85-88. **SELECTED PUBLICATIONS** Auth, The Fifth-Century Chroniclers: Prosper, Hydatius and the Chronicler of 452, Francis Cairns Publications, Ltd, 90; War, Warlords and Christian Historians from the Fifth to the Seventh Century, After Rome's Fall: Narratives and Sources of Early Medieval Hist, Univ Toronto Press, 98; Eugippius and the Life of St Severinus, Medieval Prosopography 17, 96; Looking back from from mid-century: The Gallic Chronicler of 452 and the crisis of Honorius' reign, Fifth-Century Gaul: A Crisis of Identity, Cambridge UP, 92; coauth, Democracy's Place in World History, J World Hist 4, 93. **CONTACT ADDRESS** Dept of History, Nipissing Univ, 100 College Dr, Box 5002, North Bay, ON, P1B 8L7. **EMAIL** stevem@faculty.unipissing.ca

MUIR, EDWARD
PERSONAL Born 12/02/1946, Cambridge, MA, d **DISCIPLINE** HISTORY **EDUCATION** Univ Utah, BA, 64; Rutgers Univ, MA, 70, PhD, 75. **CAREER** Asst prof, Stockton State Col, 73-77; asst to assoc prof, Syracuse Univ, 77-86; assoc to prof, La State Univ, 86-93; CLARENCE L VER STENG PROF ARTS, SCIS, NORTHWESTERN UNIV, 93-. **HONORS AND AWARDS** Herbert Baxter Adams Prize, 82; Howard R Marraro Prize, 82, 93; Harold J Grimm Prize, 89. **MEMBERSHIPS** AHA; Renaissance Soc Am; Soc Italian Hist Stud. **RESEARCH** Italian Renaissance **SELECTED PUBLICATIONS** Auth, Mad Blood Stirring: Vendetta and Factions in Friuli during the Renaissance, Johns Hopkins Univ, 93; auth, The Italian Renaissance in America, Am Hist Rev 100, 95; auth, Ritual in Early Modern Europe, Cambridge Univ Press, 97. **CONTACT ADDRESS** Dept Hist, Northwestern Univ, 1881 Sheridan Rd, Evanston, IL, 60208-2220. **EMAIL** e-muir@nwu.edu

MUIR, MALCOLM, JR.
PERSONAL Born 04/24/1943, Williamsport, PA, m, 1965, 2 children **DISCIPLINE** HISTORY **EDUCATION** Emory Univ, BA, 65; Fla State Univ, MA, 66; Ohio State Univ, PhD, 76. **CAREER** From prof to chemn, 77-, Austin Peay State Univ; Secy, Naval Hist Ctr, 87-88; vis prof, US Military Acad, 88-90; vis prof, Air War Col, 96-97. **HONORS AND AWARDS** John Lyman Prize, 96. **MEMBERSHIPS** Air Force Asn; Am Asn Univ Prof; Army Hist Found; Hist Society; Nat Asn Scholars; Phi Alpha Theta; Phi Kappa Phi; Society Military Hist; US Naval Inst. **RESEARCH** Military **SELECTED PUBLICATIONS** Auth, The Iowa-Class Battleships: Iowa, New Jersey, Missouri, and Wisconsin, 87; auth, Black Shoes and Blue Water: Surface Warfare in the United States Navy, 1945-1975, 96. **CONTACT ADDRESS** Dept of History, Austin Peay State Univ, Clarksville, TN, 37044. **EMAIL** muirm@apsu01.apsu.edu

MUIR, WILLIAM KER
DISCIPLINE POLITICAL SCIENCE **EDUCATION** Yale, PhD, 65. **CAREER** Prof Political Science, Univ Calif Berkeley, 68-. **HONORS AND AWARDS** Hadley Cantril Award; Edward S Corben Award; Distinguished Tchg Award. **MEMBERSHIPS** Am Polit Sci Asn. **RESEARCH** Democracy; Power, American society and government. **SELECTED PUBLICATIONS** The Bully Pulpit; Legislature: California's School for Politics; Police: Street Corner Politicians; Law and Attitude Change. **CONTACT ADDRESS** Dept of Political Science, Univ Calif Berkeley, Berkeley, CA, 94720-1950. **EMAIL** sandymuir@aol.com

MUISE, D.A.
DISCIPLINE HISTORY **EDUCATION** Carleton Univ, MA, 64; Univ W Ontario, PhD, 70. **CAREER** Prof. **RESEARCH** Social and economic history of the Maritime Province. **SELECTED PUBLICATIONS** Coauth, "Coal Mining in Canada: A Historical and Comparative Study," Nat Mus Of Sci and Tech, 96; auth, The Industrial context of Inequality: Female Participation in Nova Scotia's Paid Workforce, 1871-1921, Acadiensis XX, 91; reprinted, Farm, Factory and Fortune: New Studies in the Economic History of the Maritime Provinces, Acadiensis Press, 93; Labour and Working Class History in Atlantic Canada: A Reader, ISER press, 95; co-ed, The Atlantic Provinces in Confederation, Univ Toronto Press and Acadiensis Press, 93; Urbanization in Atlantic Canada, 1867-1991: Demographic Change and Community Development, Canadian Museum of Civilization, Mercury Series, 93. **CONTACT ADDRESS** Dept of Hist, Carleton Univ, 1125 Colonel By Dr, Ottawa, ON, K1S 5B6. **EMAIL** dmuise@ccs.carleton.ca

MULCAHEY, DONALD C.
DISCIPLINE HISTORY **EDUCATION** St. Paul Seminary, BA; Catholic Univ Am, MA, PhD; Univ Baltimore, JD. **CAREER** Assoc dir, Evening and Summer Prog, Towson State Univ, 71-74; Dean Col Continuing Educ, Univ Baltimore, 74-76; Assoc prof, dept hist & philos, 76-85; Dir Master of Arts in Legal Studies, 85-91, 95-; prof, Division of Legal, Ethical, Hist Studies, 86-; Dir, Jurisprudence Major, 83-85; 92-94. **MEMBERSHIPS** Baltimore County Bar Asn; Past & Present Univ Comt Mem; Provost's Task Force on Curriculum; Fac Mediation Commt; Provost's Commt Ethics Curriculum; Univ Acad Integrity Comt; Univ Fac Appeals Comt. **SELECTED PUBLICATIONS** Coauth, Advertising: Ethical Reflections, Md Hum, 96. **CONTACT ADDRESS** Univ Baltimore, 1420 N. Charles Street, Baltimore, MD, 21201.

MULDER, JOHN MARK
PERSONAL Born 03/20/1946, Chicago, IL, m, 1968, 1 child **DISCIPLINE** AMERICAN CHURCH HISTORY **EDUCATION** Hope Col, AB, 67; Princeton Theol Sem, MDiv, 70; Princeton Univ, PhD, 74. **CAREER** From ed asst to asst ed, Papers of Woodrow Wilson, 71-74; instr Am church hist, Princeton Theol Sem, 74-75, asst prof, 75-80, assoc prof, 80-81; Pres, Louisville Presby theol sem, 81-, Asst ed, Theology Today, 69-; fels hist, Asn Theol Schs in US & Can, 76 & Am Coun Learned Soc, 77. **MEMBERSHIPS** AHA; Orgn Am Historians; Am Soc Church Hist; Presby Hist Soc; Am Acad Relig. **RESEARCH** Woodrow Wilson; relig and polit in Am; relig in the Revolutionary and early national periods; 20th century Am relig. **SELECTED PUBLICATIONS** Auth, William Livingston: Presbyterian propagandist against Episcopacy, J Presby Hist, 76; Heavenly cities and human cities: Washington Gladden and urban reform, Ohio Hist, 78; Calvinism, politics, and the ironies of history, Relig & Life, 78; co-ed, Religion in American History: Interpretive Essays, Prentice Hall, 78; auth, Woodrow Wilson: The Years of Preparation, Princeton Univ, 78; intro to Horace Bushnell's Christian Nurture, Baker, 79; ed, Our Life in God's Light, Westminster, 79; The Papers of David Avery, 1746-1818, Princeton Univ, 80. **CONTACT ADDRESS** Louisville Presbyterian Theol Sem, 1044 Alta Vista Rd, Louisville, KY, 40205-1758. **EMAIL** jmmulder@lpts.edu

MULLANEY, MARIE
PERSONAL Born 09/21/1953, Newark, NJ, m, 1977, 3 children **DISCIPLINE** HISTORY **EDUCATION** Seton Hall Univ, BA, 75; Rutgers Univ, MA, 77, PhD, 80 **CAREER** Prof, 80-, Caldwell Col **HONORS AND AWARDS** Danforth Fel, 75-80, Steering Com Chair **MEMBERSHIPS** Am hist Asn; Nat Asn of Scholars **RESEARCH** Hist of Feminism **SELECTED PUBLICATIONS** Auth, Revolutionary women: Gender and the Socialist revolutionary role, New York: Praeger, 83; Biographical Directory of the Governors of the United States, 1988-1994, Westport, Ct: Greenwood Press, 94 **CONTACT ADDRESS** Livingston, NJ, 07039. **EMAIL** mmullane@caldwell.edu

MULLEN, PIERCE C.
PERSONAL Born 03/04/1934, Hastings, NE, m, 1958, 2 children **DISCIPLINE** HISTORY OF SCIENCE **EDUCATION** Hastings Col, BA, 57; Univ Nebr, Lincoln, MA, 58; Univ Calif, Berkeley, PhD(hist), 64. **CAREER** Asst prof hist, San Francisco State Col, 63; from asst prof to assoc prof, 63-72, PROF HIST, Mont State Univ, 72-. **MEMBERSHIPS** Hist Sci Soc. **RESEARCH** History of biology and medicine. **SELECTED PUBLICATIONS** Auth, The scientist as romantic: Lorenz Oken, Studies in Romanticism, 77; Educating In The American-West - 100 Years At Lewis-Clark-State-College, 1893-1993 - Petersen,K, Pacific Northwest Quarterly, Vol 0085, 1994; Commemoration - Burlingame,Merrill,G. 1901-1994, Montana-The Magazine Of Western History, Vol 0045, 1995; Roeder,Richard,B., 1930-1995 - In Commemoration, Montana-The Magazine Of Western History, Vol 0046, 1996. **CONTACT ADDRESS** Dept of Hist, Montana State Univ, Bozeman, MT, 59715.

MULLER, EDWARD K.
PERSONAL Born 03/03/1943, Pittsburgh, PA **DISCIPLINE** AMERICAN HISTORY, HISTORICAL GEOGRAPHY **EDUCATION** Dartmouth Col, BA, 65; Univ Wis-Madison, MA, 68, PhD(geog), 72. **CAREER** Lectr geog, Univ Md, College Park, 70-72, asst prof, 72-77; Assoc Prof Hist, Univ Pittsburgh, 77-, Dir, Urban Studies, 78-. **MEMBERSHIPS** Asn Am Geogr; Social Sci Hist Asn. **RESEARCH** United States urban history; United States frontier settlement; United States settlement landscape. **SELECTED PUBLICATIONS** Coauth, The process of Black residential concentration: Baltimore and Washington in the late 19th century, J Hist Geog, 75; The changing location of the clothing industry: A link to the social geography of Baltimore in the late 19th century, Md Hist Mag, 76; auth, Selective urban growth in the Middle Ohio Valley, 1800-1860, Geog Rev, 76; Regional urbanization and the selective growth of towns, J Hist Geog, 77; co-ed, Geographical perspectives on Maryland's past, Dept Geog, Univ Md, No 4, 79; coauth, Industrial districts in mid-nineteenth century Baltimore, Geog Rev, 79; auth, Spatial order before industrialization: Baltimore's central district, 1833-1860, In: Working Papers, Regional Econ Hist Res Ctr, Eleutherian Mills- Hagley Found, 80; Lubove,Roy 1934-1995 - Tribute, J Of Urban History, Vol 0022, 1996; The Geography Of Nowhere - The Rise And Decline Of America Man-Made Landscape - Kunstler,Jh, J Of The West, Vol 0035, 1996. **CONTACT ADDRESS** Dept of Hist, Univ of Pittsburgh, 3p38 Forbes Quad, Pittsburgh, PA, 15260-0001.

MULLER, JERRY Z.
PERSONAL Born 06/07/1954, Niagara Falls, ON, Canada, m, 1976, 3 children **DISCIPLINE** MODERN EURO HISTORY **EDUCATION** Brandeis Univ, BA, 77; Columbia Univ, Phd, 84. **CAREER** Catholic Univ Am, asst prof 84, assoc prof 90, prof 96; advisory editor, Society, 97-. **MEMBERSHIPS** AHA; Conf Gp on Cen Euro Hist; German Stud Asn; Jewish Stud Asn; Intl Soc for Intellec Hist; Historical Soc; Conf for the Stud Polit Thought. **RESEARCH** Modern europ intellect hist. **SELECTED PUBLICATIONS** Conservatism:AN Anthology of Social and Political Thought From David Hume to the Present, Princeton Univ Press, 97; Fritz Stern at Seventy: An Appreciation, co ed with Marion Deshmukh, Washington, German Hist Inst, 97; Adam Smith in His Time and Ours: Designing the Decent Society, The Free Press 93, Princeton Univ Press, 97; The Other God That Failed: Hans Freyer and the Deradicalization of German Conservatism, Princeton Univ Press, 87. **CONTACT ADDRESS** Dept Hist, Catholic Univ of America, Washington, DC, 20064.

MULLER, PETER O.
PERSONAL Born 05/10/1942, England, m, 1966, 2 children **DISCIPLINE** GEOGRAPHY **EDUCATION** Rutgers Univ, PhD, 71. **CAREER** Asst prof, geog, Villanova Univ, 66-70; asst to assoc prof, Temple Univ, 70-80; PROF/CHP, GEOG, UNIV MIAMI, 80-. **HONORS AND AWARDS** Phi Beta Kappa, 63; Urban Land Inst Fel, 88-94. **MEMBERSHIPS** Asn Am Geogs; Am Geog Soc. **RESEARCH** Urban geography; Economic geography **SELECTED PUBLICATIONS** coauth, "Beyond the Beltway: Suburban Downtowns in Northern Virginia," in the Capital Region, Rutgers Univ Pr, 92; coauth, "The Suburban Downtown and Urban Economic Development Today, in Sources of Metropolitan Growth, Rutgers Univ, 92; ed, "Transportation and Urban Form: Stages in the Spatial Evolution of the American Metropolis," in The Geog of Urban Transp, Guilford Press, 95; coauth, Physical Geography of the Global Environment, John Wiley & Sons, 96; auth, "The Suburban Transformation of the Globalizing American City," in Annals of the Am Acad of Polit Soc Sci, 97; coauth, Geography: Realms, Regions, and Concepts, John Wiley & Sons, 98; coauth, Economic Geography, John Wiley & Sons, 98. **CONTACT ADDRESS** Dept Geog, Univ Miami, Po Box 8067, Coral Gables, FL, 33124-2060. **EMAIL** pmuller@miami.edu

MULLER, PRISCILLA ELKOW
PERSONAL Born 02/15/1930, New York, NY, m **DISCIPLINE** ART HISTORY **EDUCATION** Brooklyn Col, BA, 51; NY Univ, MA, 59, PhD(art hist), 63. **CAREER** Asst cur metalwork, 64-68, lectr, Brooklyn Col, 66; CUR PAINTINGS & METALWORK, HISPANIC SOC AM, 68-, CUR MUS, 70-, CUR EMER, 95. **HONORS AND AWARDS** Elected mem Real Acad de Ciencias, Bellas Letras y Nobles Artes de Cordoba; elected mem Real Acad de Bellas Artes de San Fernando; elected mem The Hispanic Soc of Am. **MEMBERSHIPS** Am Soc Hispanic Art Hist Studies; Int Found Art Res; Renaissance Soc Am; Asn Latin Am Art. **RESEARCH** Spanish painting; graphic arts; metalwork. **SELECTED PUBLICATIONS** Auth, The Prophet David by Francisco Pacheco, Art Bull, 63; Francisco Pacheco as a Painter, Marsyas, 63; The Drawings of Antonio del Castillo, 64; Goya's The Family of Charles IV, Apollo, 70; coauth, Francisco Goya's Portraits, 72; auth, Jewels in Spain, 1500-1800, 72; Sorolla in America, Am Artist, 74; Francisco Bayeu, Tiepolo La Granja, Pantheon, 77; auth, Goya's Black Paintings: Truth and Reason in Light and Liberty, 84. **CONTACT ADDRESS** Hispanic Society of America, 613 W 155th St, New York, NY, 10032.

MULLIN, ROBERT BRUCE
PERSONAL Born 10/24/1953, Plainfield, NJ, m, 1960, 1 child **DISCIPLINE** RELIGIOUS HISTORY **EDUCATION** Col of William & Mary, AB, 75; Yale Divinity School, MAR, 79; Yale Univ, PhD. **CAREER** Instr, Yale Univ, 84-85; asst prof to prof, North Carolina State Univ, 85-98; LEARNING PROF OF HIST & WORLD MISSION, GENERAL THEOLOGICAL SEMINARY, 98-. **MEMBERSHIPS** Soc for the Promotion of Religion, General Theological Seminary; AAR; ASCH; Hist Soc of the Episcopal Church. **RESEARCH** American religious history; modern intellectual history; Anglicanism. **SELECTED PUBLICATIONS** Auth, Episcopal Vision/American Reality: High Church Theology and Social Thought in Evangelical America, Yale Univ Press, 86; The Scientific Theist: A Life of

Francis Ellingwood Abbot, Mercer Univ Press, 87; Moneygripe's Apprentice: The Personal Narrative of Samuel Seabury III, Yale Univ Press, 89; Reimagining Denominationalism: Interpretive Essays, Oxford Univ Press, 94; Miracles and the Modern Religious Imagination, Yale Univ Press, 96. **CONTACT ADDRESS** The General Theological Sem, 175 Ninth Ave, New York, NY, 10011-4977.

MULTHAUF, ROBERT PHILLIP
PERSONAL Born 06/08/1919, Sioux Falls, SD, m, 1948 **DISCIPLINE** HISTORY OF SCIENCE **EDUCATION** Iowa State Col, BS, 41; Univ Calif, MA, 50, PhD(hist), 53. **CAREER** Chem engr, Hercules Powder Co, 41-42, US Rubber Co, 42-43 & US Govt, Japan, 46-48; from cur div eng to head cur dept sci & technol, US Nat Mus, 54-67, dir mus hist & technol, 67-69, Sr Researcher Mus Hist & Techol, Smithsonian Inst, 70-, Fel, Inst Hist Med, Johns Hopkins Univ, 53-54; prof lectr, George Washington Univ, 64-; ed, Isis, Hist Sci Soc, 64-. **MEMBERSHIPS** AHA; Hist Sci Soc; Soc Hist Technol. **RESEARCH** History of chemistry and technology. **SELECTED PUBLICATIONS** Auth, Catalogue of instruments and models, Am Philos Soc; The origins of chemistry, Oldbourne, London, 67; Neptune's Gift: A History of Common Salt, Johns Hopkins Univ, 78; Science Has No National Borders - Kelly,Harry,C. And The Reconstruction Of Science And Technology In Postwar Japan - Yoshikawa,H, Kauffman,J, Technology And Culture, Vol 0036, 1995; Science And Civilization In China, Vol 5, Chemistry And Chemical-Technology .6. Military Technology - Missiles And Sieges - Needham,J, Yates,Rds, Technology And Culture, Vol 0037, 1996. **CONTACT ADDRESS** Mus of Hist & Technol, Smithsonian Inst, Washington, DC, 20560.

MUMFORD, ERIC
PERSONAL Born 07/14/1958, Sandusky, OH, m, 1989 **DISCIPLINE** ARCHITECTURAL HISTORY & THEORY **EDUCATION** Princeton Univ, PhD, 96. **CAREER** Adjunct asst prof, Columbia Univ Sch of Archit, 90-93; visiting lectr, Harvard Grad Sch of Design, 95-96; asst prof of archit hist and theory, Wash Univ Sch of Archit, 94-. **HONORS AND AWARDS** Graham Found grant, 97; Butler prize, Princeton Univ, 92. **MEMBERSHIPS** ACSA; SAH. **RESEARCH** Architecture, 1880-present; Urban design. **SELECTED PUBLICATIONS** Auth, The Discourse of CIAM Urbanism, MIT Press, 99; dict entries, Dictionnaire de l'architecture moderne et comtemporaine, Paris, 96; book rev, Erno Goldfinger, Soc of Archit Hist Jour, dec, 97; book rev, Architects and the City: Holabird and Roche of Chicago, 1880-1918, Chicago Tribune, 4 jan, 98; book rev, Building a New Boston, Planning Perspectives 10, 95; auth, CIAM Urbanism After the Athens Charter, Planning Perspectives, 7, 391-417, 92; auth, The Tower in a Park in America: Theory and Practice 1920-1960, Planning Perspectives, 10, 17-41, 95; auth, CIAM and Latin America/Els CIAM I America Llatina, Sert: Arquitecte a Nova York, Barcelona, 97. **CONTACT ADDRESS** 1 Brookings Dr., Campus box, St. Louis, MO, 63130. **EMAIL** epm@arch.wustl.edu

MUNDY, JOHN HINE
PERSONAL Born 12/29/1917, London, England, m, 1942, 2 children **DISCIPLINE** HISTORY **EDUCATION** Columbia Univ, BA, 40,MA, 41, PhD(hist), 50. **CAREER** Instr hist, Shrivenham Army Univ, Eng, 45 & NY Univ, 46; instr gen studies, 47-50, asst prof, 50-52, asst prof, Barnard Col, 52-56, assoc prof grad sch, 56-62, PROF HIST, COLUMBIA UNIV, 62-, Guggenheim Mem Found fel, 77-78; Am Acad Arts & Sci fel, 81. **MEMBERSHIPS** AHA; fel Mediaeval Acad Am. **RESEARCH** Medieval urban, military and ecclesiastical history. **SELECTED PUBLICATIONS** Auth, Liberty and Political Power in Toulouse, 1050-1230, Columbia Univ, 54; coauth, The Medieval Town, Van Nostrand, 58; The Council of Constance, Columbia Univ, 61; co-ed, Essays in Honor of Austin P Evans; auth, Charity and Social Work in Toulouse, 1100-1250, Traditio, 66; Europe in the High Middle Ages: 1150-1309, Longmans Canada & Basic Bks, 73; The Parishes Of Toulouse From 1150 To 1250 + An Examination Of Ecclesiastical Districts In France Following The 12th-Century Gregorian Reform, Traditio-Studies In Ancient And Medieval History Thought And Religion, Vol 0046, 1991; Histories Of A Historian - Kantorowicz - French - Boureau,A, J Of Modern History, Vol 0065, 1993; Pelhisson,Guillaume, 'Chronique' 1229-1244, Narrative Sources On The Troubles At Albi 1234 - French - Duvernoy,J, Speculum-A J Of Medieval Studies, Vol 0072, 1997. **CONTACT ADDRESS** Columbia Univ, 621 Fayerweather Hall, New York, NY, 10027.

MUNGELLO, DAVID EMIL
PERSONAL Born 11/20/1943, Washington, PA, m, 1966, 2 children **DISCIPLINE** CHINESE & EUROPEAN HISTORY **EDUCATION** George Washington Univ, AB, 65; Univ Calif, Berkeley, MA, 69, PhD(hist), 73. **CAREER** Asst prof Chinese studies, Lingnan Col, 73-74; asst prof hist & relig, Briarcliff Col, 74-77; Humboldt res fel, Leibniz Arch, Niedersachsische Landesbibliot, Hannover, 78-80; Asst Prof Hist, Coe Col, 80-, Ed, China Mission Studies (1550-1800) Bull, 80- **MEMBERSHIPS** Leibniz Ges **RESEARCH** Confucianism; Western interpretations of Confucianism; Sin- Western cultural contacts. **SELECTED PUBLICATIONS** Auth, Neo-Confucianism and Wen-Jen aesthetic theory, 69 & On the significance of the question: Did China have science?, 72-73, Philos E & W; Reconciliation of neo-Confucianism with Christianity in writings of JPremare, Philos E & W, 76; Leibniz and Confucianism: The Search for Accord, Univ Press Hawaii, 77; Seventeenth century missionary interpretations of Confucianism, Philos E & W, 78; On understanding the confluence of Chinese & western intellectual history, J Hist Ideas, 79; auth, Malebranche and Chinese philosophy, J Hist Ideas, 80; Jesuits' use of Chang Chu-cheng (Zhang Juzheng's) commentary in their translation of the Confucian four Books (1687), China Mission Studies (1550-1800) Bull, 81; A Question Of Rites - Navarrete,Domingo And The Jesuits In China - Cummins,Js, Bulletin Of The School Of Oriental And African Studies- University Of London, Vol 0057, 1994. **CONTACT ADDRESS** Dept of Hist, Coe Col, Cedar Rapids, IA, 52402.

MUNHOLLAND, JOHN KIM
DISCIPLINE HISTORY **EDUCATION** Princeton Univ, MA, 61; PhD, 64. **RESEARCH** Twentieth-century and modern French history; U.S.-French cultural conflicts during WWII. **SELECTED PUBLICATIONS** Auth, Origins of Contemporary Europe, 70; The Trials of the Free French in New Caledonia, 1940-1942, 86; The French Army and Intervention in Ukraine, 88; World War II and the End of Indentured Labor in New Caledonia, 91; L'image traditionnelle de la France et politique des Etats-Unis vers Charles de Gaulle, 1940-1944, 92; The United States and the Free French, 94; Wartime France: Remembering Vichy, 94; Michaud's Histoire des croisade and the French Crusade in Algeria, 94. **CONTACT ADDRESS** History Dept, Univ of Minnesota, Twin Cities, 614 Social Sciences Tower, 267 19th Ave. S, Minneapolis, MN, 55455. **EMAIL** munho001@tc.umn.edu

MUNN, MARK H.
DISCIPLINE ANCIENT HISTORY (GREEK) **EDUCATION** Univ Calif, BA, 74; Univ Penn, PhD, 83. **CAREER** Asst prof, classics, Stanford Univ, 83-92; asst prof, history, Univ Calif-Santa Barbara, 94-95; asst prof, 95-98, ASSOC PROF, HISTORY AND CLASSICAL AND ANCIENT MEDITER STUDIES, PENN STATE UNIV, 98-. **SELECTED PUBLICATIONS** Auth, The Defense of Attica: The Deuna Wall and Boiotian War 378-375 B.C., Univ Calif Press, 93; auth, Athens in the Age of Socrates, Univ Calif Press, forthcoming. **CONTACT ADDRESS** 663 Exeter Ct, State College, CA, 16803. **EMAIL** mxm20@psu.edu

MUNROE, JOHN ANDREW
PERSONAL Born 03/15/1914, Wilmington, DE, m, 1945, 3 children **DISCIPLINE** AMERICAN HISTORY **EDUCATION** Univ Del, AB, 36, AM, 41; Univ Pa, PhD, 47. **CAREER** From instr to prof, 42-62, alumni secy, 43-45, asst to dean arts & sci, 49-51, chm dept hist, 52-69, SHARP PROF HIST, UNIV DEL, 62-, **HONORS AND AWARDS** Phi Kappa Phi; Phi Beta Kappa; Fund Advan Educ fel, 51-52; vis prof, Univ Wis, 60; mem hist adv comt, Eleutherian Mills-Hagley Found, 62-64 & 65-68, trustee, 73-93. **MEMBERSHIPS** AHA; Org Am Historians; Soc Hist of Early Am Repub. **RESEARCH** Revolutionary and early national periods. **SELECTED PUBLICATIONS** Auth, Nonresident Representation in the Continental Congress, William & Mary Quart, 4/52; Federalist Delaware, 1775-1815, Rutgers Univ, 54; ed, Timoleon's Biographical History of Dionysius, Tyrant of Delaware, Univ Del, 58; auth, Delaware, a Student's Guide to Localized History, Columbia Univ, 65; Louis McLane, Federalist and Jacksonian, Rutgers Univ, 74; ed, Delaware History, Hist Soc Del, 69-; auth, Colonial Delaware, KTO, 78; History of Delaware, Univ Del, 79, 3d ed, 93; coauth, Books, Bricks and Bibliophiles: The University of Delaware Library, Delaware, 84; auth, The University of Delaware: A History, Delaware, 86. **CONTACT ADDRESS** 215 Cheltenham Rd, Newark, DE, 19711.

MUNSELL, FLOYD DARRELL
PERSONAL Born 12/30/1934, Gorham, KS, m, 1962, 1 child **DISCIPLINE** BRITISH AND MODERN EUROPEAN HISTORY **EDUCATION** Ft Hays Kans State Col, BA, 57, MA, 60; Univ Kans, PhD(hist), 67. **CAREER** Asst prof, 65-66, assoc prof, 66-78, prof hist, 78-97 West Texas A & M Univ. **HONORS AND AWARDS** Phi Alpha Theta; Pi Sigma Alpha; fac res award, 86. **MEMBERSHIPS** N Am Conf on British Stud; SW Conf on British Stud; SW Social Sci Asn; Consortium on Revolutionary Europe. **RESEARCH** Early and mid-Victorian England; Crimean War; Irish famine; Peelite Party (Gt Britain); Liberal Party (Gt Britain). **SELECTED PUBLICATIONS** Auth, The Unfortunate Duke: Henry Pelham, Fifth Duke of Newcastle, 1811-1864, Missouri, 85; contribur, Mitchell, ed, Victorian Britain: An Encyclopedia, Garland, 88; auth, The Victorian Controversy Surrounding the Wellington War Memorial: The Archduke of Hyde Park Corner, Edwin Mellen, 91. **CONTACT ADDRESS** PO Box 1485, Carbondale, CO, 81623. **EMAIL** dmunsell@snowcap.net

MUNSON, HENRY LEE
PERSONAL Born 03/01/1946, New York, NY, m, 1971, 4 children **DISCIPLINE** ANTHROPOLOGY **EDUCATION** Columbia Col, BA 70; Univ Chicago, MA 73, PhD. **CAREER** Univ CA, Santa Barb, vis lectr 80-81; Univ ME, asst prof 82-88, assoc prof 88-94;prof 94-, chair 98. **HONORS AND AWARDS** Woodrow Wilson Fell; John D and Catherine T MacArthur Gnt. **MEMBERSHIPS** AAA; Middle East Stud Assn. **RESEARCH** Relig and polit, Comp Relig. **SELECTED PUBLICATIONS** Religion and Power in Morocco, Yale Univ Press, 93; Islam and Revolution in the Middle East, Yale Univ Press, 88; The House of S Abd Allah, Yale Univ Press, 84 **CONTACT ADDRESS** Dept of Anthrop, Univ of ME, Orono, ME, 04469. **EMAIL** henry-munson@umit.maine.edu

MURDOCH, JAMES MURRAY
PERSONAL Born 07/08/1937, Belpre, OH, m, 1958, 2 children **DISCIPLINE** EARLY AMERICAN HISTORY **EDUCATION** Baptist Bible Col, BTh, 60; Northwestern Univ, Evanston, MA, 62, PhD, 71. **CAREER** Teaching asst Western civilization, Northwestern Univ, 63-64, lectr, 64-65; instr Am hist, Jewish Theol Sem Am, 64-65; assoc prof, 65-70; prof hist, Cedarville Col, 70-, coordr interdisplinary stud, 72-, chemn soc sci dept, 74-; lectr, Ohio Bicentennial Comn, 73-76. **MEMBERSHIPS** AHA; Orgn Am Historians; Conf Faith & Hist; Southern Hist Soc. **RESEARCH** Early 19th century history. **SELECTED PUBLICATIONS** Auth, Portrait of Obedience: A Biography of R T Ketcham, Regular Baptist Press, Chicago, 79. **CONTACT ADDRESS** Dept of History, Cedarville Col, PO Box 601, Cedarville, OH, 45314-0601. **EMAIL** murdochm@cedarville.edu

MURDOCK, KATHERINE
DISCIPLINE MUSICOLOGY-COMPOSITION **EDUCATION** Humboldt State Univ, BA; SF State Univ, MA; Eastman Sch Mus, PhD. **CAREER** Instr, Univ Tex-Austin; SF State Univ; Eastman Sch Mus; dir, WSU Contemp Mus Fest; assoc prof. **SELECTED PUBLICATIONS** Publ, Dorn Publ Inc. **CONTACT ADDRESS** Dept of Mus, Wichita State Univ, 1845 Fairmont, Wichita, KS, 67260-0062.

MURGIA, CHARLES EDWARD
PERSONAL Born 02/18/1935, Boston, MA **DISCIPLINE** CLASSICS **EDUCATION** Boston Col, AB, 56; Harvard Univ, MA, 60, PhD(Class Philol), 66. **CAREER** Instr Classics, Franklin & Marshall Col, 60-61; vis instr, Dartmouth Col, 64-65; asst prof, 66-72, assoc prof, 72-78, prof Classics, Univ Calif, Berkeley, 78-94, chmn, 80-83, Am Coun Learned Soc grant-in-aid, 68; appointed to edit Vol V of Editio Harvardiana of Servius; Univ Calif Humanities Res Comt res fels, Fall 70; Am Coun Learned Soc fel, 74-75; Nat Endowment for Humanities fel, 78-79; prof Emeritus, 94-; prof grad school, Univ Calif, Berkeley, 95-99. **MEMBERSHIPS** Am Philol Asn; Philol Asn Pac Coast. **RESEARCH** Latin textual criticism; Latin paleography; classical literature. **SELECTED PUBLICATIONS** Auth, Critical notes on the text of Servius' commentary on Aeneid III-V, Harvard Studies Class Philol, 67; Avienus' supposed iambic version of Livy, 70 & More on the Helen episode, 71, The Donatian life of Virgil, DS, and D, 74, Calif Studies Class Antiq; Prolegomena to Servius V--the manuscripts, Vol 11, Class Studies Ser, Univ Calif, 75; The minor works of Tacitus--a study in textual criticism, Class Philol, 77; The length of the lacuna in Tacitus' Dialogus, Calif Studies Class Antiq, 79; The date of Tacitus' Dialogus, Harvard Studies Class Philol, 80. **CONTACT ADDRESS** Dept of Classics, Univ of California, Berkeley, 7303 Dwinelle Hall, Berkeley, CA, 94720-2521. **EMAIL** cem@socrates.berkeley.edu

MURNION, PHILIP JOSEPH
PERSONAL Born 03/01/1938, New York, NY **DISCIPLINE** SOCIOLOGY **EDUCATION** Columbia Univ, MA, PhD, Theol. **CAREER** Priest **CONTACT ADDRESS** 309 Elizabeth St, New York, NY, 10012.

MURPHEY, MURRAY GRIFFIN
PERSONAL Born 02/22/1928, Colorado Springs, CO, 3 children **DISCIPLINE** AMERICAN CIVILIZATION **EDUCATION** Harvard Univ, AB, 49; Yale Univ, PhD, 54. **CAREER** Fel, 54-56, from asst prof to assoc prof, 56-67, Prof Am Civilization, Univ PA, 67-, Fulbright fel, Cambridge, 53-54; Rockefeller fel, 54-56. **MEMBERSHIPS** AHA; Am Studies Asn; Peirce Soc (pres, 68-69). **RESEARCH** History of philosophy; social history. **SELECTED PUBLICATIONS** Auth, Development of Pierce's Philosophy, Harvard Univ, 61; coauth, Principals Tendencias de la Filosofia Norteamericana, Pan-Am Union, 63; auth, Our Knowledge of the Historical Past, Bobbs, 73; coauth, A History of Philosophy in America (2 vols), Putnam, 77; Deweys Ethical Thought - Welchman,J, J Of American History, Vol 0082, 1996; The Logic Of Historical Explanation - Roberts,C, American Historical Review, Vol 0102, 1997. **CONTACT ADDRESS** 200 Rhyl Lane, Bala-Cynwyd, PA, 19004.

MURPHY, FRANCIS JOSEPH
PERSONAL Born 07/11/1935, Boston, MA **DISCIPLINE** MODERN EUROPEAN & CHURCH HISTORY **EDUCATION** Col of the Holy Cross, AB, 57; St Johns Sem, STB, 62; Cath Univ Am, MA, 70, PhD, 71. **CAREER** Assoc prof hist, Boston Col, 71-. **MEMBERSHIPS** AHA; Soc Fr Hist Studies; Am Cath Hist Asn. **RESEARCH** Twentieth century France; Christian-Marxist dialogue; Vatican diplomacy. **SELECTED PUBLICATIONS** Auth, La Main tendue: Prelude to Christian-

Marxist dialogue in France, 1936-1939, Cath Hist Rev, 7/74; Milestones of Christian-Communist dialogue in France, J Ecumenical Studies, winter 78; Communists and Catholics in France, 1936-1939: The Politics of the Outstretched Hand, Univ Fla, 89; Pere Jacques: Resplendent in Victory, ICS Publ, 98. **CONTACT ADDRESS** Dept of History, Boston Col, 140 Commonwealth Ave, Chestnut Hill, MA, 02467.

MURPHY, JOHN C.
PERSONAL Born 11/16/1927, Buffalo, NY **DISCIPLINE** MEDIEVAL HISTORY **EDUCATION** St Bonaventure Univ, BA, 51; Univ Notre Dame, MSM, 61, DSM(mediaeval studies), 65. **CAREER** From Instr To Assoc Prof, 55-72, Prof Hist, Siena Col, Ny, 72-, Dean Col Of Arts, 77-, Prof Fine Arts & Vp Acad Affairs, 80-. **MEMBERSHIPS** Renaissance Soc Am. **RESEARCH** Franciscan College at the University of Paris in the 15th century. **SELECTED PUBLICATIONS** Auth, The early Franciscan Studium at the University of Paris, In: Studium Generale: Studies Offered to Astrik L Gabriel (Texts and Studies in the History of Mediaeval Education), Univ Notre Dame, 67; Pacific Sketchbook - From Training Camp To V-Jday, A Young Officers Crisp, Confident Drawings Of World-War-II Army Life, American Heritage, Vol 0044, 1993. **CONTACT ADDRESS** Dean Col of Arts Dept of Hist, Siena Col, Loudonville, NY, 12211.

MURPHY, KEVIN
DISCIPLINE ARCHITECTURAL HISTORY **EDUCATION** Swarthmore Col, BA, 82; Boston Univ, MA, 85; Northwestern Univ, PhD, 92. **CAREER** Asst prof. **RESEARCH** Modern European architecture. **SELECTED PUBLICATIONS** Co-ed, A Noble and Dignified Stream: The Piscataqua Region in the Colonial Revival, 92. **CONTACT ADDRESS** Dept of Architectural History., Virginia Univ, Charlottesville, VA, 22903. **EMAIL** kdm2g@virginia.edu

MURPHY, LARRY G.
PERSONAL Born 11/07/1946, Detroit, MI, m, 1967, 1 child **DISCIPLINE** AMERICAN AND AFRICAN AMERICAN RELIGIOUS HISTORY **CAREER** Lectr, African Amer studies, Univ Calif Berkeley, 72; lectr, hist dept, St. Mary's Col of Calif, 72-74; assoc prof, hist of christ, Garrett-Evangelical Sem, 74-. **HONORS AND AWARDS** Henry McNeal Turner centennial lectr, Capetown, South Africa, 96. **MEMBERSHIPS** Soc for the Study of Black Relig; Oral Hist Asn; Amer Acad of Relig. **SELECTED PUBLICATIONS** Co-ed, Encyclopedia of African American Religions, Garland Press. **CONTACT ADDRESS** 2121 Sheridan Rd., Evanston, IL, 60201. **EMAIL** l-murphya@nwu.edu

MURPHY, ORVILLE THEODORE
PERSONAL Born 10/09/1926, Louisville, KY, m, 1949, 2 children **DISCIPLINE** MODERN EUROPEAN HISTORY & DIPLOMACY **EDUCATION** Univ Louisville, BA, 50; Univ Minn, Minneapolis, MA, 51, PhD(hist), 57. **CAREER** Lectr hist, Univ Caen, 55-56; from instr to asst prof, Williams Col, 56-62; assoc prof, 62-70, asst to pres, 66-67, Prof Hist, State Univ NY Buffalo, 70-, Am Philos Soc grant, 61. **MEMBERSHIPS** AHA; Soc Fr Hist Studies; Soc Mod Hist, France. **RESEARCH** French diplomacy of the Old Regime; Charles Gravier de Vergennes, 1719-1787; the teaching of history. **SELECTED PUBLICATIONS** Auth, The Comte de Vergennes, the Newfoundland fisheries and the peace of 1783, Can Hist Rev, 365; DuPont de Nemours and the Anglo-French commercial treaty of 1786, Econ Hist Rev, 1266; Introducing the arts into a history course, Soc Sci Rec, 67; Spanish Observers And The American-Revolution, 1775-1783 - Cummins,Lt, J Of Southern History, Vol 0059, 1993; Preserving The Monarchy - The Comte-De-Vergennes, 1774-1787 - Price,M, American Historical Review, Vol 0102, 1997. **CONTACT ADDRESS** 63 Little Robin Rd, Getzville, NY, 14068.

MURPHY, PAUL LLOYD
PERSONAL Born 09/05/1923, Caldwell, ID, m, 1946, 2 children **DISCIPLINE** HISTORY **EDUCATION** Col Idaho, BA, 47; Univ Calif, MA, 48, PhD(hist), 53. **CAREER** Asst prof US hist, Colo State Univ, 53; instr, Ohio State Univ, 53-57; asst prof hist, 57-60, assoc prof hist & Am studies, 60-70, Prof Hist & Am Studies, Univ Minn, Minneapolis, 70-, Vis prof, Northwestern Univ, 58-59; res fel, Ctr Studies Hist Liberty Am, Harvard Univ, 61-62; Guggenheim fel, 65-66; Fulbright sr lectr, Univ Lagos, 71-72; Danforth Found assoc, 73- ; Robert Lee Bailey prof hist,' Univ NC, Charlotte, 77; mem steering comt, Proj 87, AHAAm Polit Sci Asn, 77-80; chmn, comt bicentennial era, AHA, 79-81; Nat Endowment for Humanities fel, 81-82; Near vs Minnesota in The Context of Historical Developments, Minn Law Rev, 81. **HONORS AND AWARDS** LLD, Col Idaho, 76. **MEMBERSHIPS** AHA; Orgn Am Historians; Am Soc Legal Hist; Am Studies Asn; Southern Hist Asn. **RESEARCH** American constitutional and legal history; history of civil liberties and civil rights; United States political history. **SELECTED PUBLICATIONS** Co-ed, Liberty and Justice, Knopf, 58; auth, Sources and nature of intolerance in the 1920's, J Am Hist, 664; The Meaning of Freedom of Speech, Greenwood, 72; The Constitution in Crisis Times, 1918-1969, Harper, 72; ed, Political Parties in American History: 1890-present, Putnam, 74; co-ed, The Passaic Textile Strike of 1926, Wadsworth, 74; contribr, The Pulse of Freedom: American Liberties: 1920-1970's, 75 & auth, World War I and the Origin of Civil Liberties in the United States, 79; Hate Speech - The History Of An American Controversy - Walker,S, American Historical Review, Vol 0100, 1995; The Supreme-Court Reborn - The Constitution Revolution In The Age Of Roosevelt - Leuchtenburg,We, J Of American History, Vol 0082, 1996; The Kingfish And The Constitution - Long,Huey, The First-Amendment, And The Emergence Of Modern Press Freedom In America - Cortner,Rc, J Of Southern History, Vol 0063, 1997. **CONTACT ADDRESS** 2159 Folwell St Flacon Heights, St Paul, MN, 55108.

MURRAY, JACQUELINE
PERSONAL Trail, BC, Canada **DISCIPLINE** HISTORY/ HUMANITIES **EDUCATION** Univ BC, BA, 78; Univ Toronto, MA, 79, PhD, 87. **CAREER** Cur, Ctr Reformation & Renaissance Studs, Vic Col, 85-87, sr fel, 88-92, Univ Toronto; asst prof, dept hist, 88-91, ASSOC PROF, UNIV WINDSOR, 91-; dir, Humanities Res Gp 91-. **MEMBERSHIPS** Am Hist Asn; Can Soc Medieval Stud; Medieval Acad Am; Soc Medieval Feminist Scholar; Can Soc Renaissance Stud **SELECTED PUBLICATIONS** Auth, Domestic Society in Medieval Europe: A Selected Bibliography, 90; auth, Agnolo Firenzuola's On the Beauty of Women, 92; auth, Constructing Sexualities, 93; auth, Our Secret Weapon: The Humanities Must Be Brought Back from the Margins in Bull Can Fed Humanities, 93. **CONTACT ADDRESS** Dept of History, Univ of Windsor, Windsor, ON, N9B 3P4. **EMAIL** jmurray@uwindsor.ca

MURRAY, JAMES
PERSONAL Born 03/27/1954, Baltimore, MD, m, 1977, 1 child **DISCIPLINE** MEDIEVAL EUROPEAN HISTORY **EDUCATION** Northwestern Univ, PhD, 83. **CAREER** Assoc prof, Univ of Cincinnati, 90-present asst prof, Univ of Cincinnati, 84-90, lectr dept of hist, Stanford Univ, 82-84. **HONORS AND AWARDS** Fulbright fel to Belgium; NEH Summer fel; Am Council of Learned Soc Fel; Belgian Am Educ Found Fel. **MEMBERSHIPS** Medieval Acad of Am. **RESEARCH** Economic and urban hist, Flanders and the Low Countries, Diplomatics and Palaegraphy. **SELECTED PUBLICATIONS** A History of Business in Medieval Europe, 1200-1500, with E.S. Hunt, forthcoming from Cambridge University Press in 1999; Notarial Instruments in Flanders between 1280 and 1452, Commission royale d'histoire, Brussels, 1995; The Liturgy of the Count's Advent in Bruges, from Galbert to Van Eyck, in City and Spectacle in Medieval Europe, Univ of MN, 94 pp.137-152; The Profession of Notary Public in Medieval Flanders, Jour of Legal History, 61, 93:1-29. **CONTACT ADDRESS** Univ of Cincinnati, PO Box 210373, Cincinnati, OH, 45221-0373. **EMAIL** murrayjm@email.uc.edu

MURRAY, JOAN
PERSONAL Born 08/12/1943 **DISCIPLINE** ART HISTORY **EDUCATION** Univ Toronto, BA, 65; Columbia Univ, MA, 66. **CAREER** Lectr, York Univ, 70-71, 73-75; cur, Can Art, Art Gall Ont, 70-73; cons, Ont Arts Counc, 72-75; coun, Can Mus Asn, 74-76; dir, Ont Heritage Found, 75-78; DIR, THE ROBERT MCLAUGHLIN GALLERY 1974-. **HONORS AND AWARDS** Asn Cult Exec Award, outstanding contrib in cult mgt, 93. **MEMBERSHIPS** Adv bd, Artmagazine, 74-78; fel, Royal Can Acad, 92. **SELECTED PUBLICATIONS** Auth, Letters Home: 1859-1906, The Letters of William Blair Bruce, 82; auth, The Beginning of Vision: The Drawings of Lauren Harris, 82; auth, Kurelek's Vision of Canada, 83; auth, Frederick Arthur Verner: The Last Buffalo, 84; auth, Daffodils in Winter: The Life and Letters of Pegi Nicol MacLeod, 84; auth, The Best of the Group of Seven, 84; auth, Northern Lights: Masterpieces of Tom Thomson and the Group of Seven, 94; auth, The Last Spring: Confessions of a Curator, 96. **CONTACT ADDRESS** 400 St. John St W, Whitby, ON, L1N 1N7.

MURRAY, MABEL LAKE
PERSONAL Born 02/24/1935, Baltimore, Maryland, m, 1968 **DISCIPLINE** EDUCATION **EDUCATION** Coppin State Teachers Coll, Baltimore MD, BS, 1956; Loyola Coll, Baltimore MD, MED, 1969; Virginia Polytechnic Institute, Blacksburg VA, Case, 1978-81, EdD, 1982. **CAREER** Baltimore City Public Schools, teacher, 1956-68; Prince Georges County Public Schools, reading specialist, 1968-70; Project KAPS, Baltimore MD, reading coordinator, 1970-72; Univ of MD, reading coordinator, 1972-76; Johns Hopkins Univ, adjunct professor, 1972-76; Carroll County Public Schools, supervisor, 1976-87; Sojourner Douglass Coll, Baltimore MD, professor, beginning 1987-, supervisor, Student Teaching, currently; NAACP Education Dept, natl coordinator NTE; Sojourner-Douglass Coll, Human Growth Dev, coord, currently. **HONORS AND AWARDS** Designed curriculum material for two school systems, 1968-72; Conducted numerous workshops, 1969-89; Guest speaker at variety of educ/human relations activities, 1969-89; Outstanding Educator, State of MD Intl Reading Assn, 1979; Guest Lecturer, Baltimore City Schools Special Educ, 1979; Developed reading program for state mental hospital, 1981; Mayor's Citation, 1982; Service Award, Baltimore City Chapter, Delta Sigma Theta, 1983; Mem of Congressman Louis Stokes Committee on Black Health Issues, 1989. **MEMBERSHIPS** Mem, Delta Sigma Theta Sorority, 1972-; Baltimore County Alumnae Chapter, Delta Sigma Theta; advisor, Lambda Kappa and Mu Psi Chapters, Delta Sigma Theta; consultant, Piney Woods School, 1984-89; commission chair-instruction, Natl Alliance of Black School Educators, 1987-96; executive board, Natl Alliance of Black School Educators, 1987-; consultant, AIDS Project MSDE, 1988; consultant, Dunbar Middle School, 1989; consultant, Des Moines Iowa Schools; Natl Council on Educating Black Children; pres, Maryland Council of Deltas; natl pres, Pinochle Bugs Social and Civic Club; natl treas, The Societas Doctas; Baho Chap, The Society. **CONTACT ADDRESS** Coordinator, Human Growth & Development, Sojourner-Douglass Col, 500 N Caroline St, Baltimore, MD, 21205.

MURRAY, ROBERT KEITH
PERSONAL Born 04/09/1922, Union City, IN, m, 1943, 3 children **DISCIPLINE** HISTORY **EDUCATION** Ohio State Univ, BA & BS, 43, MA, 47, PhD(mod Am hist), 49. **CAREER** Res assoc, Nat Red Cross Hq, 48; instr Am hist, Ohio State Univ, 48-49; from instr to assoc prof hist, 49-59, head dept hist, 59-69, asst dean grad sch, 60-64, PROF AM HIST, PA STATE UNIV, UNIVERSITY PARK, 59-, Mem comt expanding opportunities in educ, Am Coun Educ, 65-67; mem, Nat Arch Comn, US Govt, 71-74; mem, Nat Hist Adv Comt Bicentennial lectr, State of Pa, 75-76; CBS & PBS hist consult electrons, 76 & 80. **HONORS AND AWARDS** Nat Bk Award, Phi Alpha Theta, 69; McKnight Distinguished Bk Award, Univ Minn Regents, 69; Distinguished Res Serv Award, State of Ohio, 69. **MEMBERSHIPS** AHA; Orgn Am Historians (treas, 76-); NEA; AAUP. **RESEARCH** Twentieth century history, especially social and political; the 1920's; presidential history and evaluation. **SELECTED PUBLICATIONS** Auth, Red Scare: A Study in National Hysteria, Minn Press, 55 & McGraw, 60; The Harding Era: Warren G Harding and his Administration, Univ Minn, 69; The twenties, In: Interpreting American History: Conversations with Historians, Macmillan, 70; The Politics of Normalcy: Governmental Theory and Practice in the Harding-Coolidge Era, Norton, 73; The 103rd Ballot: Democrats and the Disaster in Madison Square Garden, Harper, 76; Democrats vs frustration city, Smithsonian, 4/76; Trapped: The Saga of Floyd Collins, Putman's, 79; Hoover and the Harding Cabinet, Hoover as Secretary of Commerce, Univ Iowa, 81. **CONTACT ADDRESS** Pennsylvania State Univ, 816 Liberal Arts Tower, University Park, PA, 16802.

MURRAY, SHOON
DISCIPLINE U.S. FOREIGN POLICY **EDUCATION** Oberlin Col, BA; Yale Univ, MA, MPhil, PhD. **CAREER** Prof, Am Univ. **RESEARCH** Public opinion, political psychology, andAmerican politics. **SELECTED PUBLICATIONS** Auth, Anchors Against Change: American Opinion Leaders' Beliefs After the Cold War, Univ Mich Press, 96. **CONTACT ADDRESS** American Univ, 4400 Massachusetts Ave, Washington, DC, 20016.

MURRAY, STEPHEN O.
PERSONAL Born 05/04/1950, St. Paul, MN **DISCIPLINE** SOCIOLOGY **EDUCATION** James Madison Col, BA, 72; Univ AZ, MA, 75; Univ Toronto, PhD, 79; Univ CA, Berkeley, post-doctoral study, 80-82. **CAREER** Res dir, El Instituto Obregon, 82-. **HONORS AND AWARDS** Theory Development award, Int Gay Academic Union, 82; Academy for the Study of Male Homosexualities, 95; Ong Iotek Award, Taiwan Found, 95. **MEMBERSHIPS** Am Anthropology Asn; Am Sociol Asn. **RESEARCH** Ethnology of sexuality; science of studies. **SELECTED PUBLICATIONS** Auth, Theory Groups in the Study of Language in North America: A Social History, Studies in the History of the Language Sciences 69, John Benjamins, 94; Taiwanese Society, Taiwanese Culture, with Keelung Hong, Univ Press of Am, 94; Latin American Male Homosexualities, Univ NM Press, 95; American Gay, Univ Chicago Press, 96; Angkor Life, Bangkok: Bua Luang, 96; Islamic Homosexualities, with Will Roscoe, NY Univ Press, 97; Boy Wives and Female Husbands: Studies in African Homosexualities, St Martin's Press, 98; American Sociolinguistics: A Social NetworkHistory, John Bemjamins, 98; Homosexualities, Univ Chicago Press, 99. **CONTACT ADDRESS** El Instituto Obregon, 1360 De Haro, San Francisco, CA, 94107. **EMAIL** keelung@ITSA.UCSF.EDU

MURRIN, JOHN MATTHEW
PERSONAL Born 08/20/1935, Minneapolis, MN, m, 1967 **DISCIPLINE** AMERICAN HISTORY **EDUCATION** Col St Thomas, BA, 57; Univ Notre Dame, AM, 60; Yale Univ, PhD(hist), 66. **CAREER** From asst prof to assoc prof hist, Washington Univ, 63-73; assoc prof, 73-80, Prof Hist, Princeton Univ, 80-, Nat Endowment for Humanities jr scholar fel, 69. **MEMBERSHIPS** AHA; Orgn Am Historians; Southern Hist Asn. **RESEARCH** American colonial and revolutionary history; United States in the early national period, 1789-1861; 18th century Britain. **SELECTED PUBLICATIONS** Auth, review essay, Hist & Theory, 72; The French and Indian War, the American Revolution and the counterfactual hypothesis: Reflections on Lawrence Henry Gipson and John Shy, Rev Am Hist, 73; coauth, Feudalism, Communalism and the Yeoman Freeholder: The American Revolution considered as a Social Accident, Univ NC, 73; Launching Mcgiffert Quarter-century,

William and Mary Quarterly, Vol 0054, 1997. **CONTACT ADDRESS** Dept of Hist, Princeton Univ, Princeton, NJ, 08544-1098.

MURSTEIN, BERNARD I.
PERSONAL Born 04/29/1929, Vilnius, Lithuania, m, 1954, 2 children **DISCIPLINE** PSYCHOLOGY **EDUCATION** Col of City of NY, BSS, 50; Univ Miami, MS, 51; Univ Tex, PhD, 55. **CAREER** Endowed Ch, May Buckley Sadowski Prof Psychology, Conn Col, 94-; chairperson Dept Psychology, Conn Col, 76-79; 90-91; Fulbright Prof, Institut de Psychologie, Universite de Louvain, 68-69; prof Psychology, Conn Col, 65-. **HONORS AND AWARDS** Amer Psycholog Assoc Convention Invited Address, 91; Honored in Twentieth Century Psychologists series, October 1987 issue of Papeles Psicologos del Colegio; George I Alden Trust Acad Bus Integration Prog Grant, 82; Mellon Grant, 78, 80; Ntl Sci Found Grant, 70; Ntl Sci Found Grant Consultant; Editorial Consultant to various psychological journals; Amer Psychol Fel, 63, 77, 93; ABPP Diplomate in Clinical Psychol, 61; Soc for Projective Techniques Fel, 59; US Pub Health Fel Stipend, 54-55. **MEMBERSHIPS** Amer Psychol Assoc; Soc for Personality Assessment; Ntl Council on Family Relations; Intl Council of Psychologists; Intl Soc for Study of Interpersonal Relationships. **SELECTED PUBLICATIONS** Auth, The psychology of investment, Conn Col Mag, 98; coauth, Gender differences in love, sex, and motivation for sex, Psychol Reports, 98; auth, On exchange theory, androcentrism, and sex stereotypy, Psychol Reports, 97; coauth, "Paranoia assessment with the SIS-II: In a college student sample, Jour of Projective Psychol and Mental Health, 96. **CONTACT ADDRESS** Dept of Psychology, Univ of Connecticut, 46 Beacon Hill Dr, Waterford, CT, 06385-4110. **EMAIL** bimur@conncoll.edu

MURZAKU, INES A.
PERSONAL Born 06/02/1964, Tirana, Albania, m, 1987, 1 child **DISCIPLINE** ORIENTAL CHURCH HISTORY **EDUCATION** Ponitfical Oriental Institute, PhD, 95. **CAREER** Asst prof, Acad Arts, Tirana-Albania, 86-91; journalist, East Europe - Vatican Radio, 92-94; ADJ PROF, ST. JOHN FISHER COL, 96- . **MEMBERSHIPS** AAR; AHA; ACHA; AAASS; ASN. **RESEARCH** East Europe: religion, history and culture; Jesuit history; Albanian history; religious values and contemporary society; women in the church. **SELECTED PUBLICATIONS** Auth, Angazhimi yne Shoqeror, 94; auth, Religion in Post-Communist Albania, Missioni e Popoli, 94; auth, The Activity and the Role of the Jesuits in the Albanian History and Culture 1841-1946, 96; The Flying Mission (Missione Volante), Diakonia; The Beginning of the Jesuit Albanian Mission, Diakonia. **CONTACT ADDRESS** 3242 Leeward Cir., Walworth, NY, 14568. **EMAIL** murzaku@sjfc.edu

MUSCARELLA, OSCAR WHITE
PERSONAL Born 03/26/1931, New York, NY, m, 1957, 2 children **DISCIPLINE** ARCHAEOLOGY **EDUCATION** City Col New York, BA, 55; Univ Pa, MA, 58, PhD(class archaeol), 65. **CAREER** Lectr hist, City Col New York, 60-64; Assoc Cur, Dept Ancient Near Eastern Art, Metrop Mus Art, 64-, Sr Res Fel, 78-, Ed bds, Archaeol J Field Archaeol & Source. **MEMBERSHIPS** Archaeol Inst Am; Brit Inst Persian Studies; Asn Field Archaeol (secy, 74-). **RESEARCH** Greek-Near East relations; Iron Age Greece and Near East; Ancient Iran. **SELECTED PUBLICATIONS** Auth, Phrygian Fibulae from Gordion, B Quaritch, London, 67; The Tumuli at Se Girdan, Metrop Mus J, 69 & 71; Excavations at Agrab Tepe, Iran, 873 & The Iron Age at Dinkha Tepe, Iran, 974, Metrop Mus Art J; ed, Ancient Art, The Norbert Schimmel Collection, Mainz, 74; Ziwiye and Ziwiye the Forgery of a Provenience, J Field Archaeol, IV, 277; Un excavated Objects and Ancient Near Eastern Art, Bibliot Mesopotamica, VII, 77; The catalogue of ivories from Hasanlu, Iran, Phila, 80; Achaemenid History-iv - Center and Periphery - Sancisiweerdenburg,h, Kuhrt,a, American J of Archaeology, Vol 0097, 1993; Achaemenian Ornaments - German - Rehm,e, J of The American Oriental Society, Vol 0115, 1995; b Near-eastern Ornaments From The Beginnings to The Achaemenian Period C.10000-300bc - German - Musche,b, J of The American Oriental Society, Vol 0115, 1995. **CONTACT ADDRESS** Metropolitan Mus of Art, New York, NY, 10028.

MUSGROVE, PHILIP
PERSONAL Born 09/04/1940, Dallas, TX, m, 1989, 2 children **DISCIPLINE** MATHEMATICS, ECONOMICS **EDUCATION** Haverford Coll, BA, summa cum laude, 62; Princeton Univ, MPA, 64; MIT, PhD, 74. **CAREER** Res asst , 64-68, res assoc, 71-76, 78-81, Brookings Institution; tech coordinator, ECIEL Program of Joint Studies of Latin Amer Integration, 66-68, 71-80; consultant, Banco Central de Venezuela and Corporacion Venezolana de Guayana, 75-79; assoc prof lecturer, Dept of Econ, George Wash Univ, 74, 76-78; visiting asst prof, Dept of Economics, Univ Fla, 75; staff assoc, Resources for the Future, 77-78; adjunct prof, Latin Amer Program, applied economics, Amer Univ, 78-84; consultant, US Dept of Agriculture, Office of Nutrition Economics, 79-82; regional advisor in health economics, 82-90, Pan Amer Health Orgn; consultant, Development Res Center, 71-73, 74, Living Standards Measurement Study, 81, Tech Dept, Latin Am and Caribbean Region, 90-93, World Development Report, 92-93, , health economist to sr economist to principal economist, 90-, Resident Mission in Brasilia, Brazil, 96-98, World Bank. **MEMBERSHIPS** Scientific and Tech Advisory Coun, Natl Food and Nutrition Inst, 86-90; Advisory Coun on Scientific Publications, Pan Amer Health Org, 87-91, chm, 89-90; Advisory Coun to Pres of the Maternal and Child Health Inst of Pernambuco (Recife), 89-. **RESEARCH** Health economics, with emphasis on Latin America. **SELECTED PUBLICATIONS** Auth, "Economic Crisis and Health Policy Response," in Demographic Responses to Economic Adjustment in Latin America, 97; "Equitable Allocation of Ceilings on Public Investment," Human Capital Development Working Paper, World Bank, 96; "Public and Private Roles in Health: Theory and Financing Patterns," Discussion Paper no. 339, World Bank, 96; "Cost-Effectiveness and the Socialization of Health Care," Health Policy 32, 95; "Reformas al Sector Salud en Chile: Contexto, Logica y Posibles Caminos," in La Salud en el Siglo Veintiuno, Cambios Necesarios, 95. **CONTACT ADDRESS** The World Bank, 1818 H St, NW, Washington, DC, 20433. **EMAIL** pmusgrove@worldbank.org

MUSHKAT, JEROME
PERSONAL Born 05/05/1931, Livingston Manor, NY, m, 1961, 2 children **DISCIPLINE** AMERICAN & URBAN HISTORY **EDUCATION** Syracuse Univ, BA, 53, PhD, 64. **CAREER** From Instr to Assoc Prof, 62-76, prof hist, Univ Akron, 76. **HONORS AND AWARDS** Grant, Asn for Study State & Local Hist, 65. **MEMBERSHIPS** Am Asn Univ Professors; Orgn Am Historians; Am Studies Asn. **RESEARCH** Nineteenth century Am hist; NY hist; urban polit machines. **SELECTED PUBLICATIONS** Auth, The impeachment of Andrew Johnson: A contemporary view, NY Hist, 7/67; Epitaphs by Mordecai M Noah, NY Hist Soc Quart, 7/71; Tammany: The Evolution of a Political Machine: 1789-1865, Syracuse Univ Press, 71; Mineral and timber prospects in upper Michigan, Inland Seas, 74; Matthew Livingston Davis and the political legacy of Aaron Burr, NY Hist Soc Quart, 75; Ben Wood's Fort Lafayette as a peace democratic source, Civil War Hist, 75; The Reconstruction of the New York Democracy, 1861-1874, Fairleigh-Dickinson Press, 81; Fernando Wood and the Commercial Growth of New York City, Univ Va Press, 90; Fernando Wood: A Political Biography, Kent State Univ Press, 90; Martin Van Buren: Law, Politics, and the Shaping of Republican Ideology, Northern IL Univ Press, 98. **CONTACT ADDRESS** Dept of Hist, Univ of Akron, 302 Buchtel Mall, Akron, OH, 44325-1902.

MUSTO, DAVID FRANKLIN
PERSONAL Born 01/08/1936, Tacoma, WA, m, 1961, 4 children **DISCIPLINE** HISTORY & SOCIAL SCIENCES **EDUCATION** Univ Wash, BA, 56, MD, 63; Yale Univ, MA, 61. **CAREER** Spec asst to dir, Nat Inst Mental Health, 67-69; from asst prof to assoc prof hist & psychiat, 69-78, sr res scientist, Child Study Ctr, 78-80, Lectr Hist & Am Studies, Yale Univ, 78-, Prof Psychiat, Child Study Ctr & Prof Hist Med, 81-, Head, Sect Hist & Social Policy, Child Study Ctr & Bush Ctr, 81-, Residency psychiat, Yale Univ, 64-67; vis asst prof, Johns Hopkins Univ, 68-69; fel, Drug Abuse Coun, 72-73; consult, Nat Comn Marijuana & Drug Abuse, 72-73; prog dir, Nat Humanities Inst, 77-78; hist consult, President's Comn Ment Health, 77-78; mem US deleg, UN Comn Narcotic Drugs, 78 & 79; mem, White House Strategy Coun, Off Pres US, 77-81; mem, Nat Coun Smithsonian Inst, 81-; mem panel on alcohol policy, Nat Res Coun, 78-81. **HONORS AND AWARDS** William Osler Medal, Am Asn Hist Med, 60; Edward Kremers Award, Am Inst Hist Pharmacy, 74. **MEMBERSHIPS** AHA; Am Psychiat Asn; Am Asn Hist Med. **RESEARCH** History of the family; application of psychology to history; history of drug control in America. **SELECTED PUBLICATIONS** Coauth, Strange encounter, Psychiatry, 868; auth, Youth of John Quincy Adams, Proc Am Philos Soc, 869; The American Disease: Origins of Narcotic Control, Yale Univ, 73; coauth, Historical perspectives on mental health and racism in the United States, In: Racism and Mental Health, Univ Pittsburgh, 73; Whatever happened to community mental health?, Pub Interest, spring 75; Continuity Across Generations, Smithsonian Inst Press, 79; Temperance and prohibition in America, In: Alcohol and Pubic Policy, Nat Acad Press, 81; Adams family, Proc Mass Hist Soc, 82; Drugs And Narcotics in History - Porter,r, Teich,m, J of Interdisciplinary History, Vol 0028, 1997. **CONTACT ADDRESS** Child Study Ctr, Yale Univ, New Haven, CT, 06510.

MUSTO, RONALD G.
PERSONAL Born 05/24/1948, New York, NY, m, 1970 **DISCIPLINE** HISTORY **EDUCATION** Fordham Univ, BA, Hist, 69; Columbia Univ, MA, Hist, 70, PhD, 77. **CAREER** Vis lectr, New York Univ, Hist, 76; fell, Am Acad Rome, 78-79; vis prof, Columbia Univ, 80; asst prof, Duke Univ, Hist, 80-81; writer & ed, New York City Hum Ref, 81-85; PUBL, ITALICA PRESS, MEDIEVAL & RENAISSANCE STUDIES, 85-. **MEMBERSHIPS** Am Hist Asn; Am Catholic Hist Asn; Medieval Acad Am; Renaissance Soc Am; Am Acad Rome Soc Fellows **RESEARCH** Interaction of religious belief and civil life in the Middle Ages and modern period. **SELECTED PUBLICATIONS** Marvels of Rome for the Macintosh, New York: Italica Press, 97; co-edr, The Holy Land on Disk, New York: Italica Press, 97; co-edr, The Road to Compostela, New York: Italica Press; Apocalypse in rome: Cola di Rienzo and the Politics of the New Age, Univ Calif Press, 99. **CONTACT ADDRESS** Italica Press, 595 Main St, Apt 605, New York, NY, 10044. **EMAIL** italica@idt.met

MUTCHLER, DAVID EDWARD
PERSONAL Born 06/21/1941, Lexington, KY, m, 1979, 3 children **DISCIPLINE** SOCIAL SCIENCE **EDUCATION** PhD WA Univ (ST Louis) 70. **CAREER** Sr Foreign Service Offical US Agency for Intl Devel USAID 27yrs Incl Sr Adv Cord for Cuba, 97-98; Mission Dir for Panama, 94-96. **MEMBERSHIPS** Assoc for the Study of the Cuban. **CONTACT ADDRESS** Sr Adv/Coordinator for Cuba, Ronald Regan Building, 1300 Pennsylvania Ave. N.W. Fifth Floor 5 8A, Washington, DC, 20523. **EMAIL** damutchler@usaid.gov

MUTSCHLER, BEN
DISCIPLINE HISTORY **EDUCATION** Harvard Univ, AB, 88; Columbia Univ, MA, 92; MPhil, 94. **CAREER** PHD CAND IN HIST, COLUMBIA UNIV **RESEARCH** Illness in New Eng, 1690-1820. **CONTACT ADDRESS** 72 Powder House Blvd, No. 2, Somerville, MA, 02144. **EMAIL** bm35@columbia.edu

MUYUMBA, FRANCOIS N.
PERSONAL Born 12/29/1939, Luputa Kasai-orien, Zaire, m **DISCIPLINE** AFRICAN-AMERICAN STUDIES **EDUCATION** David & Elkins Coll Elkins WV, BA 1963-67; Portland State U, MS 1969-70; IN Univ Boomington, MA & PhD 1977. **CAREER** IN State Univ, asst prof 1977-; Univ Libre duCongo, asst prof/adminstrn asst 1968-69; Usaid-Kinshasa, asst training officer 1967-68; Youth Center (Carrefour deJeunes) Kinshasa Zaire, dir 1967. **HONORS AND AWARDS** Soccer Letters & Trophies Davis & Elkins Coll Elkins WV 1963-67; Travel Grant Intl Peace Research Assn 1975; Consult Grant Gilmore Sloane Presbyterian Center 1975. **MEMBERSHIPS** Mem Tchrs of Engl as Second Lang 1973-80; mem Intl Peace Research Assn 1975-80; consult Inst for World Order's Sch Progs 1975-78; mem World Council for Curriculum & Instr 1974-80; mem Peache Educ Council 1978-80; mem Nat Council for Black Studies 1976-80. **CONTACT ADDRESS** Afro-American Studies Dept, Indiana State Univ, Terre Haute, IN, 47809.

MWAMBA, ZUBERI I.
PERSONAL Born 01/03/1937, Tanzania **DISCIPLINE** AFRICAN STUDIES **EDUCATION** Univ WI, BS 1968; Univ Pitts, MA 1968; Howard U, PhD 1972. **CAREER** Govt Tanzania, radio announcer, court clerk, interpreter, information asst 1957-62; Howard U, instr 1968-72; US State Dept 1969-70; African Studies TX So U, prof dir 1982-. **HONORS AND AWARDS** Fellows Fulbright 1965-68; WI Legislature 1965-67; Howard Univ Trust 1969-70; International Election Observer at the general elections in South Africa, 1994; TX Southern Univ, Distinguished Service of the Year Award, 1997. **MEMBERSHIPS** Mem Am Political Sci Assn 1971-; Nat Council Black Political Scientists 1971-; Educator to Africa Assn 1972-; pres Pan African Students Orgn 1965-67; Tanzania Students Union 1968-70 1971-72; exec com East African Students Orgn 1968-70; adv TX So Univ Student Gov Assn 1974-75; faculty sponsor TSU YoungDemo 1974-75. **CONTACT ADDRESS** Texas So Univ, 3100 Cleburne Ave, Houston, TX, 77004.

MYERS, CHARLES BENNETT
PERSONAL Born 06/08/1939, Columbia, PA, m, 1959, 3 children **DISCIPLINE** AMERICAN HISTORY AND SOCIAL SCIENCE EDUCATION **EDUCATION** Pa State Univ, BS, 61; George Peabody Col Teachers, MA, 63, PhD, 68. **CAREER** Hist teacher, Jr High Sch, Pa, 61-62; teacher demonstration sch, Peabody Col, 64; asst prof educ & hist, Rider Col, 65-68; soc sci specialist, Speedier Proj, Palmyra, Pa, 68-70; from asst prof to assoc prof, 70-78, prof hist & soc sci educ, George Peabody Col, 78-79, dir, Progs for Educ Youth, 74-79, adminr, Ctr Econ & Soc Studies Educ, 77-79; prof social studies educ, George Peabody Col, Vanderbilt Univ, 79-86; chmn, dept teaching and learning, 79-86; Prog develop specialist, Teacher Educ Alliance Proj, Tenn, 68-70; mem bd dir, Nat Coun for Social Studies, 76-81. **MEMBERSHIPS** Nat Coun Social Studies; Coun for Advan Citizenship; NEA; Asn Pvt Enterprise Educ (secy-treas, 78-79, vpres, 79-80, pres, 80-81); Am Edu Res Asn; Am Asn of Col for Teacher Edu; Nat Coun for the Accred of Teacher Educ; Soc Sci Cons; Phi Delt Kap; Kap Delt Pi; Pi Gam Mu; Phi Alph Thet; Phi Kap Phi. **RESEARCH** Teacher education and learning; school reform; accreditation of teacher education institutions and programs. **SELECTED PUBLICATIONS** Contrib, Teaching strategies for developing children's thinking (4 vols), Inst Staff Develop, 70; coauth, Cooperative teacher education programs: Old acquaintances create new partnerships, Peabody J Educ, 10/71; auth, The Environmental Crisis, Prentice-Hall, 72, coauth 2nd ed, 76; ed, Taba Program in Social Science, Addison-Wesley, 73-75; coauth, The effects of a training program in the Taba teaching strategies on teaching methods and teacher perceptions, Peabody J Educ, 4/77; auth, The disseminator's bias and instructional change, Counterpoint, 5/81; Teachers for the Social Studies, in Social Studies for the 80's, Nat Educ Asn, 80; Diffusion does not equal instructional change, Social Educ, 10/79; A Response to Needs for Diffusion and Implementation of Economic Education Pro-

grams, in Perspective on Economic Education, Joint Council on Economic Education, 77; coauth, Peope, Time, and Change, 83; coauth, An Introduction to Teaching and Schools, Holt, Rinehart, and Winston, 90; coauth Testbank for the Professional Teacher: A New Introduction to Teaching and Schools, Wadsworth, 95; coauth, A Student Study Guide for the Professional Teacher: A New Introduction to Teaching and Schools, Wadsworth, 95; coauth, Re-Creating Schools: Places Where Everyone Learns and Likes It, Crowin, 98. **CONTACT ADDRESS** Col for Teachers, Vanderbilt Univ, Peabody Col Sta, PO Box 330, Nashville, TN, 37203-2402. **EMAIL** charles.b.meyers@vanderbilt.edu

MYERS, DAVID
DISCIPLINE RELIGIOUS HISTORY **EDUCATION** Yale Univ, PhD. **CAREER** Assoc prof, Fordham Univ. **HONORS AND AWARDS** Reviewer, Chicago Tribune Bk Rev. **RESEARCH** Hist of sin and crime in early mod Europe. **SELECTED PUBLICATIONS** Auth, Poor, Sinning Folk: Confession and the Making of Consciences in Counter-Reformation Germany, Cornell UP, 96; Die Jesuiten die Beichte, und die katholische Reformation in Bayern, Beitge zur altbayerischen Kirchengeschichte 96; Ritual, Confession, and Religion in Early Sixteenth-Century Germany, Arch fur Reformationsgeschichte, 97. **CONTACT ADDRESS** Dept of Hist, Fordham Univ, 113 W 60th St, New York, NY, 10023.

MYERS, JOHN L.
PERSONAL Born 06/13/1929, Findlay, OH, m, 1957, 3 children **DISCIPLINE** AMERICAN HISTORY **EDUCATION** Bowling Green State Univ, BS, 51; Univ Mich, MA, 54, PhD, 61. **CAREER** From asst prof to assoc prof hist, Southeast Mo State Col, 58-64; assoc prof, 64-68, PROF HIST, STATE UNIV NY COL PLATTSBURGH, 68-; mem comt on status hist in schs, Orgn Am Historians, 74-80. **HONORS AND AWARDS** State Univ NY Res Found fel, 68 & 69. **MEMBERSHIPS** Orgn Am Historians; Soc Hist Early Am Rep. **RESEARCH** The antislavery movement; career of Henry Wilson. **SELECTED PUBLICATIONS** Auth, The beginning of antislavery agencies in New York State, NY Hist, 4/62; Antislavery activities of five Lane Seminary boys in 1835-1836, Hist & Philos Soc Ohio, 4/63; Organization of the seventy, Mid-Am, 1/66; American antislavery society agents and the free Negro, 1833-1838, J Negro Hist, 7/67; The major effect of antislavery agents in Neew Hampshire, 1835-1837, Hist NH, fall 71. **CONTACT ADDRESS** Dept of Hist, State Univ of NY, 95 Broad St, Plattsburgh, NY, 12901.

MYERS, LENA WRIGHT
PERSONAL w **DISCIPLINE** SOCIOLOGY **EDUCATION** Tougaloo Coll, BA Sociology; MI State Univ, MA Sociology & Anthropology 1964, PhD Sociology & Social Psychology 1973. **CAREER** Utica Jr Coll, instructor of soc & psych 1962-68; Washtenaw Comm Coll, asst prof of psychology 1968; Center for Urban Affairs MI State Univ, urban rsch 1970-73; Jackson State Univ, prof of sociology 1973-. **HONORS AND AWARDS** State of MS House of Rep Concurrent Resolution No 70 Commendation 1981; Disting Amer Awd 1981. **MEMBERSHIPS** Mem of comm on status of women in sociology Amer Sociol Assoc 1974-77; rsch/consul TIDE 1975-78; pres Assn of Social/Behavioral Scientists Inc 1976-77; rsch/consul KOBA 1979-80; mem bd of dirs Soc for the Study of Social Problems 1980-83; rsch/consul Natl Sci Foundation 1983; pres Assn of Black Sociologists 1983-84. **CONTACT ADDRESS** Prof of Sociology, Jackson State Univ, Jackson, MS, 39217.

MYERS, SAMUEL L., JR.
PERSONAL Born 03/09/1949, Boston, MA **DISCIPLINE** AFRICAN-AMERICAN STUDIES **EDUCATION** Morgan State Coll, BA 1971; MIT, PhD 1976. **CAREER** Univ of Minnesota, Roy Wilkins Chair prof, 1992-; Univ of Maryland, prof; Univ of Texas at Austin, asst prof of economics; Boston Coll, instr 1973; Bowie State Coll, visiting instr 1972. **HONORS AND AWARDS** Alpha Kappa Mu Merit Award, 1970; Inst Fellow, MIT, 1971-73; Natl Fellowship Fund Fellow, 1973-75; Fulbright Lecturer in Economics, Cuttington Coll, Liberia, 1975-76; Fulbright Scholar, Univ of South Australia, Faculty of Aboriginal and Islander Studies, 1997. **MEMBERSHIPS** Amer Economics Assn; Natl Economics Assn; Amer Acad of Political & Social Science; Amer Assn for the Advancement of Science; Alpha Phi Alpha; co-coordinator, Black Grad Economics Assn 1973; Assn for Public Policy Analysis & Mgt, vp, 1997-99. **SELECTED PUBLICATIONS** Co-author: Bittersweet Success: Faculty of Color in Academe; Persistent Disparity: Race & Economic Inequality in the US 1998; The Black Underclass: Critical Essays on Race and Unwantedness, 1994; Editor: Civil Rights and Race Relations in the Post Reagan-Bush Era 1997; Co-editor: Economics of Race and Crime, Transaction Press, 1988; author, editor, and contributor of articles, chapters, and reviews to newspaper, periodicals, books, and journals. **CONTACT ADDRESS** H H Humphrey Institute of Public Affairs, Univ of Minnesota, 301 19th Ave S, Minneapolis, MN, 55455.

MYRICK, HOWARD A., JR.
PERSONAL Born 06/22/1934, Dawson, Georgia, m, 1955 **DISCIPLINE** EDUCATION **EDUCATION** Florida A&M University, Tallahassee, FL, BS, 1955; University of Southern California, Los Angeles, CA, MA, 1966, PhD, 1967. **CAREER** Corp for Public Broadcasting, Washington, DC, director of research, 1977-82; Clark-Atlanta University, Atlanta, GA, professor, 1982-83; Howard University, Washington, DC, chairman, radio/tv/film dept, 1983-89. **HONORS AND AWARDS** Legion of Merit, Dept of Defense, 1977; Distinguished Graduate, Florida A&M University, 1989; Soldier's Medal, Republic of China, 1969. **MEMBERSHIPS** Editorial board, National Academy of Television Arts & Sciences, 1989-91; chairman, commission on minorities, Broadcast Education Association, 1988-90; board of directors, International Association of Knowledge Engineers, 1988-91; consultant, National Telecom and Info Agency, 1986-90; board of experts, National Endowment for the Arts, 1988-91. **CONTACT ADDRESS** Dept of Radio, Television and Film, Temple Univ School of Communication, #15 Annenberg Hall, Philadelphia, PA, 19122.

N

NADEL, STANLEY
PERSONAL Born 11/08/1944, New York, NY, 2 children **DISCIPLINE** HISTORY **EDUCATION** Univ Mich, BA, 66; Mich State Univ, Grad Stud, 66-67; Columbia Univ, MA, 74, PhD, 81. **CAREER** Col asst, Lehman Col, City Univ New York, 74-76; lectr, Marymount Manhattan Col, 77; vis asst prof, SUNY, 81-82, 83-84; vis asst prof, St Lawrence Univ, 82-83; vis asst prof, Univ Ill, Champaign-Urbana, 85-87; vis asst prof, Pa State Univ, 88; vis asst prof, Austin Peay State Univ, 88-91; vis asst prof, Central Conn State Univ, 91-92; adj assoc prof, St Marys Col, vis asst prof, Winona State Univ, 92-93; vist asst prof, SUNY, Plattsburgh, 93-94; asst prof, Mo State Univ, 94-95; assoc prof, dept chemn, Southwestern Okla State University, 95-. **HONORS AND AWARDS** Columbian Univ Readership Hist, 73-75; NEH Summer Stipend, Fac Res Fel, SUNY, 82; NEH Summer Sem, UCLA, 95. **RESEARCH** Am Social Hist; immigration and ethnicity; racial and ethnic minoritys; suicide and infanticide. **SELECTED PUBLICATIONS** Auth, Little Germany: Ethnicity, Religion and Class in New York City, 1845-1880, 90; auth, art, Those Who Would Be Free: the Eight-hour Day Strikes of 1872, 90; auth, art, German's in New York, 95; auth, art, Immigration Restrictionists: Historical Context and Critique, 95; auth, art, The German-American Left, 96. **CONTACT ADDRESS** Dept of Socal Sci, Southwestern Oklahoma State Univ, Weatherford, OK, 73096. **EMAIL** nadels@swosu.edu

NADEL, STANLEY
PERSONAL Born 11/08/1944, New York, NY, 2 children **DISCIPLINE** HISTORY **EDUCATION** Univ Mich, BA, 66; Mich State Univ, Grad Stud, 66-67; Columbia Univ, MA, 74, PhD, 81. **CAREER** Col asst, Lehman Col, City Univ New York, 74-76; lectr, Marymount Manhattan Col, 77; vis asst prof, SUNY, 81-82, 83-84; vis asst prof, St Lawrence Univ, 82-83; vis asst prof, Univ Ill, Champaign-Urbana, 85-87; vis asst prof, Pa State Univ, 88; vis asst prof, Austin Peay State Univ, 88-91; vis asst prof, Central Conn State Univ, 91-92; adj assoc prof, St Marys Col, vis asst prof, Winona State Univ, 92-93; vist asst prof, SUNY, Plattsburgh, 93-94; asst prof, Mo State Univ, 94-95; assoc prof, dept chemn, Southwestern Okla State University, 95-. **HONORS AND AWARDS** Columbian Univ Readership Hist, 73-75; NEH Summer Stipend, Fac Res Fel, SUNY, 82; NEH Summer Sem, UCLA, 95. **RESEARCH** Am Social Hist; immigration and ethnicity; racial and ethnic minoritys; suicide and infanticide. **SELECTED PUBLICATIONS** Auth, Little Germany: Ethnicity, Religion and Class in New York City, 1845-1880, 90; auth, art, Those Who Would Be Free: the Eight-hour Day Strikes of 1872, 90; auth, art, German's in New York, 95; auth, art, Immigration Restrictionists: Historical Context and Critique, 95; auth, art, The German-American Left, 96. **CONTACT ADDRESS** Dept of Socal Sciences, Southwestern Oklahoma State Univ, Weatherford, OK, 73096. **EMAIL** nadels@swosu.edu

NADELL, PAMELA
PERSONAL Born 12/13/1951, Newark, NJ, m, 1976, 2 children **DISCIPLINE** HISTORY **EDUCATION** OH State Univ, PhD. **CAREER** Assoc prof of History, dir, Jewish Studies Program, American Univ, 82-. **RESEARCH** American Jewish history. **SELECTED PUBLICATIONS** Auth, Women Who Would Be Rabbis: A History of Women's Ordination, 1889-1985, 98; Conservative Judaism in America: A Biographical Dictionary and Sourcebook. **CONTACT ADDRESS** Jewish Studies Program, American Univ, 4400 Massachusetts Ave NW, Washington, DC, 20016. **EMAIL** pnadell@american.edu

NADER, HELEN
PERSONAL Born 04/29/1936, Miami, AZ **DISCIPLINE** RENAISSANCE & REFORMATION HISTORY **EDUCATION** Univ Ariz, BA, 58; Smith Col, MA, 59; Univ Calif, Berkeley, PhD(hist), 72. **CAREER** Actg instr hist, Univ Calif, Berkeley, 67-68; asst prof, Univ Hawaii, 71-75; asst prof, Stanford Univ, 75-76; asst prof, 76-79, Assoc Prof Hist, Ind Univ, 79-, Am Coun Learned Soc fel, 74-75, grant-in-aid, 76; Lilly Libr res fel, 76; consult, Nat Endowment for Humanities & ed, Bull Soc Span & Port Hist Studies, 77-79; Tinker Found Inc fel, 78; vis scholar, Stanford Univ Food Res Inst, 78-79; Nat Endowment for Humanities res fel, 82-83; assoc ed, Am Hist Rev, 82-. **MEMBERSHIPS** Soc Ital Hist Studies; Acad Am Res Historians Medieval Spain; AHA; Renaissance Soc Am; Soc Span & Port Hist Studies. **RESEARCH** Spain 1350-1700; humanism in southern Europe; the Mendoza Family. **SELECTED PUBLICATIONS** Auth, Josephus and Don Diego Hurtado de Mendoza, Romance Philol, 73; Noble income in sixteenth-century Castile: The case of the Marquises of Mondejar, Econ Hist Rev, 77; The Greek Commander Hernan Nunez de Toledo, Spanish humanist and civic leader, Renaissance Quart, 78; The Mendoza Family in the Spanish Renaissance, 1350-1550, Rutgers Univ, 79; Spanish Reaction to the Introduction of Habsburg Ceremonial, In: Arts, Letters and Ceremonial at the Court of the Spanish Habsburgs, Duke Univ (in prep); The End of The Oldworld + Assessing The Impact of Columbus on The America And Europe, Renaissance Quarterly, Vol 0045, 1992; The Avila of Teresa,saint - Religious Reform in a 16th-century City - Bilinkoff,j, Renaissance Quarterly, Vol 0046, 1993; The Golden-age of Painting in Spain - Brown,j, Renaissance Quarterly, Vol 0048, 1995. **CONTACT ADDRESS** Dept of Hist, Indiana Univ, Bloomington, Ballantine Hall, Bloomington, IN, 47401.

NAFZIGER, E. WAYNE
PERSONAL Born 08/14/1938, Bloomington, IL, m, 1966, 2 children **DISCIPLINE** ECONOMICS **EDUCATION** Goshen Col, BA, 60; Univ Mich, MA, 62; Univ Ill, PhD, 67. **CAREER** Commerce Bank Distinguished Grad Fac, Kans St Univ, 96-; prof, Kans St Univ, 78-; assoc prof, Kans St Univ, 73-78; asst prof, Kans St Univ, 66-73; Sen Res Fel, UN Univ/World Inst for Develop Economics Res, 96-98; Hewlett Vis Fel, Carter Center Emory Univ, 91; vis prof, Intl Univ Japan, 83; East-West Center Fel, 72-73; Fulbright prof, Andhra Univ, India, 70-71; Res Assoc, Univ Nigeria, 64-65. **HONORS AND AWARDS** Mid_Amer Univ Assoc Honor Lctr, Kans St Univ, 84-85; Commerce Bank Distinguished Grad Fac, Kans St Univ, 96-; Choice Outstanding Acad Book Award, 89-90. **MEMBERSHIPS** Amer Econ Assoc; Amer Assoc Univ Professors; Assoc Evolutionary Econ; Assoc Indian Economics Studies; Assoc Asian Studies; Fulbright Assoc **RESEARCH** Economics of Conflict; Economic Development and Income Distribution; Comparative Economic Development. **SELECTED PUBLICATIONS** Auth, Fathers, Sons, and Daughters: Industrial Entrepreneus During India's Liberalization, JAI Pr, 98; auth, The Economics of Developing Countries, Prentice Hall, 97; auth, Learning from the Japanese: Japan's Prewar Development and the Third World, ME Sharpe, 95; auth, Poverty and Wealth: Comparing Afro-Asian Development, JAI Pr, 94. **CONTACT ADDRESS** Dept of Economics, Kansas State Univ, 327 Waters Hall, Manhattan, KS, 66506. **EMAIL** nafwayne@ksu.edu

NAG, MONI
PERSONAL Born 04/01/1925, India, m, 1964, 1 child **DISCIPLINE** ANTHROPOLOGY; PUBLIC HEALTH; POPULATION; STATISTICS **EDUCATION** Calcutta Univ, M.SC, 46; Yale Univ, MA, 59, Yale Univ, PhD, 61 **CAREER** Adjunct prof Anthropol, Columbia Univ, 76-; senior assoc, Johns Hopkins Univ, 96-; senior assoc, Population Council, 76-92 **HONORS AND AWARDS** Fyfe Scholar, Scottish Church Col Calcutta, 42-44; Fulbright Travel Grant, 57-61; Brady, Boies Fel, Yale Univ, 57-58; Univ Fel, Yale Univ, 58-59; Boies Fel, Yale Univ, 59-60; Fel from Committee of Res on Sex, National Res Coun, 60-61 **RESEARCH** Statistics; Anthropology; Mathematics **SELECTED PUBLICATIONS** Auth, Sexual Behavior and AIDS in India, Vikas, 96; auth, "Sexual behaviour in India with risk of HIV/AIDS transmission," Health Transmission Rev; coauth, Listening to Women Talk about Their Health: Issues and Evidence from India, Har-Anand, 94 **CONTACT ADDRESS** 260 Garth Rd., 5Es, Scarsdale, NY, 10583-4051. **EMAIL** mn7@columbia.edu

NAGARAJAN, VIJAYA
PERSONAL Born 06/02/1961, Ewangudi, India, m, 1991 **DISCIPLINE** ANTHROPOLOGY **EDUCATION** Univ Calif, Berkeley, PhD. **CAREER** Asst prof, theol & rel stud, 96-, Univ San Francisco. **HONORS AND AWARDS** Fulbright Res Fel , 92-94; Chancellors Dissert Writing Fel, 95-96. **MEMBERSHIPS** AAR; Amer Anthrop Assn. **RESEARCH** Gender; ecology; art; nonviolence; memory. **SELECTED PUBLICATIONS** Auth, The Earth as Goddess Blui Devi, Toward a Theory of Embedded Ecologies, L Folle Hinduism, Purifying the Earthly Body of God: Religion & Ecology in Hindu India, SUNY Press, 98. **CONTACT ADDRESS** Dept of Theology and Religious Studies, Univ of San Francisco, 2130 Fulton St., San Francisco, CA, 94117-1080. **EMAIL** nagarajan@usfca.edu

NAGLE, BETTY ROSE
DISCIPLINE CLASSICAL STUDIES **EDUCATION** Univ Pa, BA, 70; Univ Ind, PhD, 75. **CAREER** Prof. **SELECTED PUBLICATIONS** Auth, Ovid's Fasti: Roman Holidays, Ind Univ, 95; Ovid: Fasti V, Bryn Mawr, 96. **CONTACT ADDRESS** Dept of Classical Studies, Indiana Univ, Bloomington, 300 N Jordan Ave, Bloomington, IN, 47405.

NAGLE, D. BRENDAN
DISCIPLINE HISTORY **EDUCATION** Cath Univ Am, STB; USC, AM, PhD. **CAREER** National Endowment for the Humanities fel, Amer Acad in Rome, 70; dept chem, 76-83; prof, Univ Southern Calif. **HONORS AND AWARDS** CINE Golden Eagle. **RESEARCH** Social, cultural & political historian of the ancient world, with a special interest in Greece and Rome. **SELECTED PUBLICATIONS** Auth, The Ancient World: A Social and Cultural History, Prentice-Hall, 96, 3rd ed; coauth, The Ancient World: Readings in Social and Cultural History, Prentice-Hall, 95; **CONTACT ADDRESS** Dept of History, Univ Southern Calif, University Park Campus, Los Angeles, CA, 90089. **EMAIL** nagle@usc.edu

NAGLER, MICHAEL NICHOLAS
PERSONAL Born 01/20/1937, New York, NY, m, 1959, 2 children **DISCIPLINE** CLASSICAL LITERATURE AND SOCIETY **EDUCATION** NY Univ, BA, 60; Univ Calif, Berkeley, MA, 62, PhD(comp lit), 66. **CAREER** Instr foreign lang, San Francisco State Col, 63-65; asst prof, 65-73, humanities res fel, 68-69, Assoc Prof Classics & Comp Lit, Univ Calif, Berkeley, 73-, Am Coun Learned Soc study grant, Sanskrit lang & lit, 71-72. **MEMBERSHIPS** Am Philol Asn; Int Comp Lit Asn. **RESEARCH** Oral poetry, chiefly Homer, Old English and Sanskirt; myth and religion; peace and conflict studies. **SELECTED PUBLICATIONS** Auth, Towards a generative view of the Homeric formula, Trans Am Philol Asn, 67; Oral poetry and the question of originality in literature, Proc Vth Cong Int Comp Lit Asn, 67; Spontaneity and Tradition: A Study of Homer's Oral Art, Univ Calif, 74; Dread goddess endowed with speech, Archaeol News, 77; Mysticism: A hardheaded definition for a romantic age, Study Mystica, 78; Peace as a paradigm shift, Bull Atom Scientists, 81; America Without Violence, Island Press, 82; Epic Singers And Oral Tradition - Lord,ab, Classical J, Vol 0087, 1992; Discourse And Conflict Hesiod - Eris And The Erides, Ramus- critical Studies in Greek And Roman Literature, Vol 0021, 1992; Penelope Male Hand - Gender And Violence in The 'Odyssey', Colby Quarterly, Vol 0029, 1993. **CONTACT ADDRESS** Dept of Classics, Univ of Calif, Berkeley, CA, 94720.

NAGY, GREGORY JOHN
PERSONAL Born 10/22/1942, Budapest, Hungary **DISCIPLINE** CLASSICS, LINGUISTICS **EDUCATION** Ind Univ, AB, 62; Harvard Univ, PhD(classics), 66. **CAREER** Instr classics & ling, Harvard Univ, 66-69, asst prof classics, 69-73; from assoc prof to prof, Johns Hopkins Univ, 73-75; Prof Classics, Harvard Univ, 75- **MEMBERSHIPS** Am Philol Asn; Ling Soc Am. **RESEARCH** Greek literature; Indo-European linguistics; poetics. **SELECTED PUBLICATIONS** Auth, Observations on the sign-grouping and vocabulary of linear A, Am J Archaeol, 65; On dialectal anomalies in Pylian texts, Atti Memorie 1st Cong Int Micenologia, 68; Greek Dialects and the Transformation of an Indo-European Process, Harvard Univ, 70; coauth, Greek: A Survey of Recent Work, Mouton, The Hague: 73; auth, Phaethon, Sappho's Phaon, and the White Rock of Leukas, Harvard Studies Class Philol, 73; Comparative Studies in Greek and Indic Meter, Harvard Univ, 74. **CONTACT ADDRESS** Dept of Classics, Harvard Univ, 204 Boylston Hall, Cambridge, MA, 02138-3800. **EMAIL** gnagy@fas.harvard.edu

NAIDITCH, P.G.
PERSONAL Los Angeles, CA **DISCIPLINE** CLASSICS **EDUCATION** Santa Monica City Col, AA, 69; Univ Southern Calif, BA, 71; Univ London, MA, 76; Ind Univ, MLS, 80. **CAREER** Publ ed, Dept Spec Collections, 87-; classics bibliogr, Charles E. Young Res Libr, Univ Calif, , 91-. **MEMBERSHIPS** Am Philos Asn; Bibliog Soc. **RESEARCH** A.E. Housman; history of classical scholarship; history of the book. **SELECTED PUBLICATIONS** Coauth, Philodemus and Greek Papyri, 94; auth, Problems in the Life and Writings of A.E. Housman, 95. **CONTACT ADDRESS** Special Collections, Charles E. Young Research Lib, Univ Calif, Los Angeles, Box 951575, Los Angeles, CA, 90095-1575. **EMAIL** naiditch@library.ucla.edu

NAIR, SUPRYIA
DISCIPLINE POSTCOLONIAL LITERATURE AND THEORY, AFRICAN AND DIASPORA STUDIES **EDUCATION** St Joseph's Col, Vizag, India, BA, 82; Univ Hyderabad, India, MA, 84; Baylor Univ, MA, 86; Univ TX at Austin, PhD, 92. **CAREER** Instr, 92, Tulane Univ. **RESEARCH** Women studies, Carribean lit. **SELECTED PUBLICATIONS** Auth, Melancholic Women: The Intellectual Hysteric(s) in Nervous Conditions, Res African Lit 26.2, 95. **CONTACT ADDRESS** Dept of Eng, Tulane Univ, 6823 St Charles Ave, New Orleans, LA, 70118. **EMAIL** supriya@mailhost.tcs.tulane.edu

NAISON, MARK
DISCIPLINE AFRICAN-AMERICAN HISTORY **EDUCATION** Columbia Univ, PhD. **CAREER** Prof, Fordham Univ. **HONORS AND AWARDS** Founder, Bronx Youth Employ Proj. **SELECTED PUBLICATIONS** Auth, Communists in Harlem during the Depression, Univ Ill Press, 83; Outlaw Culture in Black Culture, Reconstruction, 94; African-Americans and the Rise of Buffalo's Post-Industrial City, Urban League's anthology, 90; co-auth, The Tenant Movement in New York City, 1940-1984, Rutgers UP, 86. **CONTACT ADDRESS** Dept of Hist, Fordham Univ, 113 W 60th St, New York, NY, 10023.

NAJEMY, JOHN MICHAEL
PERSONAL Born 09/09/1943, Worcester, MA **DISCIPLINE** RENAISSANCE HISTORY **EDUCATION** Princeton Univ, BA, 65; Harvard Univ, PhD(hist), 72. **CAREER** From instr to asst prof hist, Harvard Univ, 71-75; from Asst Prof to Assoc Prof, 75-92, PROF HIST, CORNELL UNIV, 92-. **HONORS AND AWARDS** Fels hist, Villa I Tatti, Harvard Univ Ctr Ital Renaissance Studies & Leopold Schepp Found, 74-75; fac fel, Soc for Humanities, Cornell Univ, 82-83; Marraro Prize of the Am Hist Asn, for Corporatism and Consensus, 83; Marraro Prize of the Soc for Ital Hist Studies, for Between Friends, 95; Guggenheim fel, 85-86; NEH fel, 98-99. **MEMBERSHIPS** AHA; Renaissance Soc Am. **RESEARCH** Florence: politics, society, guilds, political thought, historiography, Machiavelli, Alberti; Medieval and Renaissance Italy. **SELECTED PUBLICATIONS** Contribr, The Dialogue of Power in Florentine Politics, In: City-States in Classical Antiquity and Medieval Italy, Franz Steiner Verlag, 91; Dante and Florence, In: The Cambridge Companion to Dante, Canbridge Univ Press, 93; Machiavelli and Geta: Men of Letters, In: Machiavelli and the Discourse of Literature, Cornell Univ Press, 93; auth, Between Friends: Discourses of Power and Desire in the Machiavelli-Vettori Letters of 1513-1515, Princeton Univ Press, 93; Brunetto Latini's Politica, Dante Studies, 94; Stato, comune e "universitas", Annali dell'Istituto Storico Italo-germanico in Trento, 94; contribr, Language and The Prince, In: Niccol¤ Machiavelli's The Prince: New Interdisciplinary Essays, Manchester Univ Press, 95; The Republic's Two Bodies: Body Metaphors in Italian Renaissance Political Thought, In: Language and Images of Renaissance Italy, Clarendon Press, 95; Baron's Machiavelli and Renaissance Republicanism, Am Hist Rev, 96; Contribr, Gianozzo and His Elders: Alberti's Critique of Renaissance Patriarchy, In: Culture and Self in Renaissance Europe, Univ Calif Press (forthcoming). **CONTACT ADDRESS** Dept of History, Cornell Univ, Mcgraw Hall, Ithaca, NY, 14853-4601. **EMAIL** jmn4@cornell.edu

NAKHAI, BETH ALPERT
PERSONAL Born 07/05/1951, New York, NY, m, 1986, 1 child **DISCIPLINE** NEAR EASTERN ARCHAEOLOGY, BIBLICAL STUDIES **EDUCATION** Conn Col, BA, 72; Harvard Div Sch, MTS, 79; Univ Ariz, MA, 85, PhD, 93. **CAREER** Tchg asst, Univ Ariz, 83-86, 88-89; adj instr, Prescott Col, 95; Lectr, Univ Ariz, 94- . **HONORS AND AWARDS** Robert H. Pfeiffer Found Trust, 78; Zion Res Found Travel Scholar, 79; Univ Ariz Grad Tuition Scholar, 82-83; Maurice Cohen Awd in Judaic Stud, 83; Bernard Ivan Amster Mem Awd, 83; tchg asst, Dept Oriental Stud, 1st yr Hebrew, 83-87; Samuel H. Kress found fel, 86-87; Univ Ariz Grad Acad Scholar, 87-89; Dorot Found doctoral fel, 88-89; Tchg asst, Dept Near East Stud, Ancient Civilizations Near East, 88-89; Res Asst, Dept Near East Stud, 90; Mem found Jewish Cult Doctoral Scholar, 86-91; Amer Sch Oriental Res Comm Archaeol Policy Endow Bibl Archaeol grant, 97; Amer Sch Oriental Res Comm Archaelo Policy Endow Bibl Archael grant, 97; Assoc Women fac travel grant, Univ Ariz, 97-98. **MEMBERSHIPS** Amer Sch Oriental Res; Soc Bibl Lit; Ctr Middle East Stud; Assn Women Fac, Univ Ariz. **RESEARCH** Canaanite and Israelite Religion; women's issues. **SELECTED PUBLICATIONS** Auth, Tell el-Wawiyat, Israel Exploration Jour, 37, 2-3, 87, 181-185; Tell el-Wawiyat, 1986, in Excavations and Surveys in Israel 1987-1988 vol 6, Jerusalem, Hadashot Archaeologiyot, 88, 100-102; Tell el-Wawiyat, Revue biblique, 95/2, 88, 247-251; Tell el-Wawiyat, 1987 Israel Exploration Jour, 39.1-2, 102-104, 89; Tell el-wawiyat (Bet Netofa Valley)-1987, in Excavations and Surveys in Israel 1988/89 vol 7-8, Jerusalem, Hadashot Archaelolgiyot, 90; Tell el-Wawiyat, Encyclopedia of Archaelolgical Excavations in the Holy Land, 2nd ed, E. Stern, ed, Jerusalem, Israel Exploration Soc, 92; What's a Bamah? How Sacred Space Functioned in Ancient Israel, Bibl Archaeol Rev, 20, 18-19, 77-78; Wawiyat, Jell el-, Encyclopedia of Archaeology in the Bibl World, vol 5, 333-334, Eric M. Meyers, ed, New York, Oxford UP, 97; Syro-Palestinian Temples, Encyclopedia of Near Eastern Archaelolgy, vol 5, E.M. Meyers, ed, New York, Oxford UP, 169-174, 97; Locus, Encyclopedia of Near Eastern Archaeology, vol 3, E.M. Meyers, ed, NY, Oxford UP, 97, 383-384; Kitan, Tel., Encyclopedia of Near Eastern Archaeology, vol 3, E.M. Meyers, ed, New York, Oxford Univ Press, 97, 300; Furniture and Furnishings: Furnishings of the Bronze and Iron Ages, Encyclopedia of Near eastern Archaeology, vol 2, E.M. Meyers, ed, NY, Oxford UP, 97, 354-356; Beth Zur, Encyclopedia of near Eastern Archaeology vol 1, E.M. Meyers, ed, NY, Oxford UP, 97, 314; Featured in Written in Stones, People, Places and Society: A Publication for Alumni and Friends of the College of Social and Behavioral Sciences, Univ Ariz, Spring, 3, 98; Rev article, Jerusalem: An Archaeological Biography, Shofar, 16,3, 98, 174-176. **CONTACT ADDRESS** Univ of Arizona, 905 N Tenth Ave, Tucson, AZ, 85705-7623. **EMAIL** bnakhai@u.arizona.edu

NALL, GARRY LYNN
PERSONAL Born 08/12/1936, Loving, TX **DISCIPLINE** UNITED STATES HISTORY **EDUCATION** Univ Tex, Austin, BA, 58, MA, 59; Univ Okla, PhD(hist), 72. **CAREER** From instr to asst prof, 63-74, assoc prof, 74-81, Prof Hist, W TX State Univ, 81-. **MEMBERSHIPS** Orgn Am Historians; Agr Hist Soc; Western Hist Asn. **RESEARCH** United States agricultural history; the Great Plains; United States, 1876-1914. **SELECTED PUBLICATIONS** Auth, The farmers' frontier in the Texas Panhandle, 72, Panhandle farming in the golden era of American agriculture, 73, Specialization and expansion: Panhandle farming in the 1920's, 74 & Dust bowl days: Panhandle farming in the 1930's, 75, Panhandle-Plains Hist Rev; Rural Oklahoma, Okla Hist Soc, 77; The struggle to save the land, the soil conservation effort in the dust bowl, In: The Depression in the Southwest, Kennikat Press, 80; Land of Plenty - Oklahomans in The Cotton Fields of Arizona, 1933-1942 - Weisiger,ml, J of American History, Vol 0083, 1997. **CONTACT ADDRESS** Dept of Hist, W TX State Univ, 2501 4th Ave, Canyon, TX, 79016-0001.

NALLE, SARA TIGHMAN
DISCIPLINE HISTORY **EDUCATION** Bryn Mawr Col, BA, 75; Johns Hopkins Univ, MA, 78; PhD, 83. **CAREER** Assoc prof, William Paterson Col, 91-; dept exec coun, Col-wide GE reform comt, Search Comt & Provost and VP for Acad Aff, 94-95; dept exec coun, Promotions Comt & Western Civ Comm, 93-94; dept exec coun, Western Civ Comt ch, mem-search comt for WPC Distinguished Hisp Scholar, 91-92; dept curric comt, Western Civ Comt & Col Res Awd(s) Comt, 90-91; ch, dept curric comt, 88-89; Sch of Humanities Gen Educ Comt, All-Col Acad Comput Comt & dept curric comt, 87-88; vis assoc prof, Inst for Shipboard Educ, Univ Pittsburgh, 92; asst prof, William Paterson Col, 86-91; asst prof, Rhode Island Cole, Providence, 84-86; postdr tchg fel, Boston Col, Chestnut Hill, 82-84; asst prof, US Naval Acad, Annapolis, 81-82; tchg asst, Johns Hopkins Univ, Baltimore, 80-81 & 77-78. **HONORS AND AWARDS** Mem, Inst Advan Stud, 95; visitor, 96; Roland Bainton Bk Prize, 93; NJ Gov's fel in the Humanities, 89-90; Harold J Grimm Prize, 88; Career develop, travel, and/or assigned res time grants, William Paterson Col; postdoctoral res grant, Treaty for Friendship, Defense, and Coop between the USA and the Kingdom of Spain, 85 & 86; grad fel, Johns Hopkins Univ, 79-80; Fulbright-Hays Dissertation Scholar, Spain, 78-79; finalist, Woodrow Wilson tchg fel, 75. **MEMBERSHIPS** Soc Span and Port Hist Stud, 80-, membership secy, 89-95; Nominating Comt, 85-88 & ch, 90 Prog Comt; AHA, 81-; Int Inst Found in Spain, corporator 83- & mem, Plan comt 95-; 16th century Stud Asn, 87-. **RESEARCH** Connections between religious radicalism, rebellion, and perceptions of sanity in 16th-century Spain. **SELECTED PUBLICATIONS** Auth, Bones and Crosses: Recent Trends in Early Mod Spanish Historiography, Bul of the Soc for Span and Port Hist Stud, 94; God in La Mancha: Religious Reform and the People of Cuenca, 1500-1650, Baltimore: Johns Hopkins Univ Press, 92; A Saint for All Seasons, in Culture and Control in Counter-Reformation Spain, Hisp Issues Ser, Minneapolis: Univ Minn Press, 91; Literacy and Culture in Early Mod Castile, Past and Present, No 125, 89; Inquisitors, Priests and the People during the Catholic Reformation in Spain, 16th century J, 87; rev(s), The Phoenix and the Flame. Catalonia and the Counter Reformation in the J Mod Hist 95; El mundo del libro en la iglesia catedral de Sevilla en el siglo XVI, in Libr(s) and Cult 29, 94; Heresy and Mysticism in Spain: The Alumbrados, in the Amer Hist Rev, 94; Moving Crucifixes in Mod Spain, J Mod Hist, 94; Passional Culture: Emotion, Religion, and Society in Southern Spain. Hist of Europ Ideas, 93; Sacred Charity, Confraternities and Social Welfare in Spain, 1400-1700, The Renaissance Quart, 90; Keepers of the City, The Corregidores of Isabella I of Castile 1474-1504,The Renaissance Quart, 89; Inquisition in The Relig Stud Rev, 89. **CONTACT ADDRESS** Dept of History, William Paterson Col, 300 Pompton Rd., Wayne, NJ, 07470. **EMAIL** nalle@frontier.wilpaterson.edu

NANCE, JOSEPH MILTON
PERSONAL Born 09/18/1913, Kyle, TX, m, 1944, 3 children **DISCIPLINE** UNITED STATES & TEXAS HISTORY **EDUCATION** Univ Tex, BA, 35, MA, 36, PhD, 41. **CAREER** State supvr Am imprints, manuscripts & newspaper inventory, Hist Rec Surv, Works Prog Admin, 38-40; instr hist, Agr & Mech Col Tex, 41-42; instr radio code & typing, US Naval Training Sch, Tex, 42-43; head dept hist & govt, 58-68, head dept hist, 68-73, from instr to assoc prof, 46-57, Prof Hist, Tex A&m Univ, 57-, Fund Improvement Tex res grant, 57; mem Pub bd, Arizona & The West, 79-; mem Pub adv comt, Tex Hist Found, 79-. **HONORS AND AWARDS** Tex Inst Lett Award, 63; Walter Prescott Award, 66; Amoco Distinguish Award in Res & Writing, 79; Col Law, Baylor Univ established Joseph Milton Nance Scholarships, 79; Dept Hist, Tex A&M Univ established J Milton Nance Lectures, 80-. **MEMBERSHIPS** AHA; Orgn Am Historians; Southern Hist Asn; Am Studies Asn; Western Hist Asn. **RESEARCH** Texas history; United States history before 1865; early Hawaiian history to 1860. **SELECTED PUBLICATIONS** Auth, Checklist of Texas Newspapers, 1813-1939, San Jacinto Mus of Hist, 41; Early history of Bryan and the surrounding area, Hood's Brigade-Bryan Centennial Comt, 62; After San Jacinto: Texas-Mexican Frontier Relations, 1836-1841, 63 & Attack and Counterattack: The Texas-Mexican Frontier, 1842, 64, Univ Tex; ed, Some Reflections Upon Modern America, Tex A&M Univ, 69; auth, Instructor's manual, 70 & Student's guide, 71, to accompany Graebner, Fite, White, A History of the American People, McGraw; The Gulf Coast and

the Texas question during the presidential campaign of 1844, In: Americanization of the Gulf Coast, 1803-1850, Hist Peninsula Preserv Bd, 72; ed, Joseph D McCutchan's Narrative of the Texian Mier Expedition of 1842, Univ Tex, Austin, 78; Papers Concerning Robertson Colony in Texas, Vol 18, August 11, 1840 Through March 4, 1842, The End of an Era - Mclean,md, Western Historical Quarterly, Vol 0024, 1993. **CONTACT ADDRESS** 1403 Post Oak Circle, College Station, TX, 77840.

NAPPA, CHRISTOPHER
DISCIPLINE CLASSICAL STUDIES **EDUCATION** Univ Tex, BA, 90; Univ Va, MA, 92, PhD, 96. **CAREER** Instr. **SELECTED PUBLICATIONS** Auth, Agamemnon 717-36: The Parable of the Lion Cub, 94; Catullan Provocations (rev), Univ Ca, 93; Virgil, New Haven, 91. **CONTACT ADDRESS** Dept of Classics, Knoxville, TN, 37996.

NAQUIN, SUSAN
PERSONAL Born 00/00/1944, Chicago, IL **DISCIPLINE** CHINESE HISTORY **EDUCATION** Stanford Univ, BA, 66; Yale Univ, MA, 69, PhD(hist), 74. **CAREER** Asst prof, 76-81, Assoc Prof Hist, Univ PA, 81-, Co-ed, Ching-shih wen-ti. **RESEARCH** Ching social history; popular movements. **SELECTED PUBLICATIONS** Auth, Millenarian Rebellion in China: The Eight Trigrams Uprising of 1813, 76 & Shantung Rebellion: The Wang Lun Uprising of 1774, 81, Yale Univ Press; Chinese Local Elites And Patterns of Dominance - Esherick,j, Rankin,mb, American Historical Review, Vol 0098, 1993. **CONTACT ADDRESS** Dept of Hist, Univ PA, Philadelphia, PA, 19104.

NARDONE, RICHARD MORTON
PERSONAL Born 06/21/1929, Orange, NJ **DISCIPLINE** HISTORICAL THEOLOGY **EDUCATION** Seton Hall Univ, BA, 50; Cath Univ Am, STL, 54; Univ St Michael's Col, PhD(-theol), 72. **CAREER** Assoc Prof Relig Studies, Seton Hall Univ, 68-, Judge, Matrimonial Tribunal-Archdiocese of Newark, NJ, 77-. **MEMBERSHIPS** Cath Theol Soc Am; Am Acad Relig. **RESEARCH** Patristics; liturgical studies; ecumenical studies. **SELECTED PUBLICATIONS** Auth, The Roman calender in ecumenical perspective, Worship, 5/76; coauth, The Church of Jerusalem and the Christian Calender, Standing Before God, KTAV Publ House, 81; auth, Liturgical change: A reappraisal, Homiletic & Pastoral Rev, 11/81; The Story of the Christian Year, Paulist Press, 91. **CONTACT ADDRESS** Dept of Relig Studies, Seton Hall Univ, 400 S Orange Ave., South Orange, NJ, 07079-2697.

NASGAARD, ROALD
PERSONAL Born 10/14/1941, Denmark **DISCIPLINE** ART HISTORY **EDUCATION** Univ BC, BA, 65, MA, 67; Inst Fine Art, NY Univ, PhD, 73. **CAREER** Lectr, fine art, 71-74, asst prof, 74-75, Univ Guelph; cur contemp art, 75-78, dep dir & chief cur, 78-93, AGO; vis lectr, 83-92, adj prof, 92-95, Univ Toronto; prof & chair, dept art, Florida State Univ, 95-; co-dir prog, Inst Mod & Contemporary Art, Calgary, 95-. **MEMBERSHIPS** Trustee, Gershon Iskowitz Found, 91-; Toronto Pub Art Comn, 86-88; Col Art Asn; Univ Art Asn Can; Int Art Critics Asn. **SELECTED PUBLICATIONS** Auth, various articles in Artscanada, Vie des Art, Arts Magazine, Northern J. **CONTACT ADDRESS** Dept of Art, Florida State Univ, Tallahassee, FL, 32306-2037.

NASH, ANEDITH
DISCIPLINE ART AND DESIGN **EDUCATION** Baylor Univ, BA, 64; Wash State Univ, MA, 70; Univ Minn, PhD, 83. **CAREER** Assoc acad dean, Minneapolis Col Art and Design, 97-; prof & ch, Liberal Arts Div, Minneapolis Col Art and Design, 92 & 96; coordr, Grad Prog, Minneapolis Col Art and Design, 93-; adj fac, Hamline Univ Grad Sch, 87-95; dean cont stud, Minneapolis Col Art and Design, 89-92; prog dir & primary fac, Metro Urban Stud Term and City Arts Prog, Higher Educ Consortium for Urban Aff, HECUA Hamline Univ, 82-89; lectr, Dept Soc, Macalester Col, 83-87. **SELECTED PUBLICATIONS** Coauth, The Skyway System and Urban Space: Vitality in Enclosed Public Places, The Community of the Streets, Greenwich, Conn, and London: JAI Press, Inc, 94. **CONTACT ADDRESS** Minneapolis Col of Art and Design, 2501 Stevens Ave S, Minneapolis, MN, 55404. **EMAIL** anedith_nash@mn.mcad.edu

NASH, GARY B.
PERSONAL Born 07/27/1933, Philadelphia, PA, m, 1955, 4 children **DISCIPLINE** AMERICAN HISTORY **EDUCATION** Princeton Univ, AB, 55, PhD(hist), 64. **CAREER** From instr to asst prof hist, 64-66; from asst prof to assoc prof, 66-72, Prof Hist, Univ Calif, Los Angeles, 72-, Guggenheim Found fel, 70-71; Am Coun Learned Soc fel, 73-74. **MEMBERSHIPS** Orgn Am Historians; Am Studies Asn; Inst Early Am Hist & Cult. **RESEARCH** Colonial American history. **SELECTED PUBLICATIONS** Auth, Auth, Slaves and slave holders in prerevolutionary Philadelphia, William & Mary Quart, 73; The transformation of urban politics, 1700-1765, J Am Hist, 1273; Red, White and Black: The People of Early America, Prentice-Hall, 74, 2nd ed, 82; Poverty and poor relief in prerevolutionary Philadelphia, William & Mary Quart, 176; Urban wealth and poverty in pre revolutionary America, J Interdisciplinary Hist, spring 76; Up from the bottom in Franklin's Philadelphia, Past & Present, 1177; The Urban Crucible, Harvard Univ Press, 79; Struggle and Survival in Colonial America, Univ Calif Press, 81; Gabriel Rebellion - The Virginia Slave Conspiracies of 1800 And 1802 - Egerton,dr, Arkansas Historical Quarterly, Vol 0054, 1995; Dorsey,william Philadelphia And Ours - on The Past And Future of The Black City in America - Lane,r, J of Interdisciplinary History, Vol 0025, 1995; The Price of Nationhood, The American- revolution in Charlescounty - Lee,jb, William And Mary Quarterly, Vol 0052, 1995; On United-States History Standards, Historian, Vol 0057, 1995; Free People of Color - Inside The African-American Community - Horton,jo, African American Review, Vol 0030, 1996; Molding The Good Citizen - The Politics of High- school History Texts - Lerner,r, Nagai,ak, Rothman,s, J of American History, Vol 0083, 1997; Early American History And The National History Standards, William And Mary Quarterly, Vol 0054, 1997. **CONTACT ADDRESS** Dept of Hist, Univ of Calif, Los Angeles, CA, 90024.

NASH, GERALD DAVID
PERSONAL Born 07/16/1928, Berlin, Germany, m, 1967, 1 child **DISCIPLINE** HISTORY **EDUCATION** NY Univ, BA, 50; Columbia Univ, MA, 52; Univ Calif, Berkeley, PhD, 57. **CAREER** Instr, 57-58 asst prof, 59-60, Stanford Univ; asst prof, 58-59, Northern Ill Univ; post dr fel, 60-61, Harvard Univ; asst prof, 61-63, Univ N Mex; assoc prof, 63-68, prof, 68-, chmn, 74-80, dist prof, 85-94, prof emeritus, 94-, vis assoc prof, 65-66, New York Univ; George Bancroft Prof, 90-91, Goettingen Univ, Germany. **RESEARCH** US 20th century, West in 20th century, US economic policies. **SELECTED PUBLICATIONS** Auth, Issues in American Economic History, Heath, 63, ed, 2nd ed, 72 & 3rd ed, 80; Franklin Delanor Roosevelt, Prentice- Hall, 67; Introduction to Administrative History, Univ Calif, 68; US Oil Policy, 1890-1964, Univ Pittsburgh, 68; The Great Transition, Allyn & Bacon, 71; The American West in the Twentieth Century, Prentice-Hall, 73; Organizing America, St Martin's (in press); The Urban West, Sunflower, 79; The Great Depression and World War II, St Martin's, 79; The West Transformed, 1941-1945, Ind Univ, 83; Its Your Misfortune And None of My Own - a New History of The American-west - White,r, California History, Vol 0072, 1993; The End of American Exceptionalism, Frontier Anxiety From The Old-west to The New- deal - Wrobel,dm, Western Historical Quarterly, Vol 0024, 1993; American-Indians And World-War-2 - Toward a New Era in Indian Affairs - Bernstein,ar, Ethno history, Vol 0039, 1992; Gunfighter Nation - The Myth of The Frontier in 20th-century America - Slotkin,r, J of The West, Vol 0034, 1995; The 2nd Gold-rush - Oakland And The East-Bay in World-War-II - Johnson,ms, California History, Vol 0074, 1995; Railroad Crossing - Californians And The Railroad, 1850-1910 - Deverell,w, Pacific Historical Review, Vol 0064, 1995; Trading in Santa-fe - Kingsbury,john,m. Correspondence With Webb,j Ames,josiah, 1853-1861 - Elder,jl, Weber,dj, Western Historical Quarterly, Vol 0028, 1997. **CONTACT ADDRESS** 8809 New Hampton Rd, NE, Albuquerque, NM, 87111. **EMAIL** gnash@unm.edu

NASH, JUNE C.
DISCIPLINE ANTHROPOLOGY **EDUCATION** Barnard Col, BA, 48; Univ Chicago, MA, 53, PhD, 60. **CAREER** Yale Univ, asst prof, 63-68; NYU, assoc prof, 69-72; City Col CUNY, prof, distinguished prof, 72-. **HONORS AND AWARDS** C. Wright Mills Award, AAA Distinguished Svc Award. **MEMBERSHIPS** AAA, AES, LASA, Sigma Phi. **RESEARCH** Latin America; Industry; Artisan Prosecution; Indigenous social organization. **CONTACT ADDRESS** Dept of Anthropology, New York Univ, New York, NY, 10031.

NASH, LEE
PERSONAL Born 09/10/1927, North Bend, OR, m, 1951, 3 children **DISCIPLINE** HISTORY **EDUCATION** Cascade Col, AB, 50; Univ Wash, MA, 51; Univ Ore, PhD(hist), 61. **CAREER** Asst prof hist & English, Cascade Col, 51-56, assoc prof hist, 59-60, prof & chmn div soc sci, 60-67, dean, 62-67; from assoc prof to prof hist, Northern Ariz Univ, 67-75; Prof Hist & Chmn Div Soc Sci, George Fox Col, 75-, Develop Fund res grant, Univ Ore, 61, res assoc, 61-62; Am Asn State & Local Hist grant- in-aid, 69; Autzen Found res grant, 70. **HONORS AND AWARDS** Marion F McClain Award, 62. **MEMBERSHIPS** AHA; Orgn Am Historians; Am Soc Church Hist; Western Lit Asn; Conf Faith & Hist. **RESEARCH** United States, 1865-1915; American thought and culture; American biography. **SELECTED PUBLICATIONS** Auth, Portland's first history, Call Number, spring 60; Kenneth Scott Latourette: 1888-1968, Fides et Historia, spring 69; Scott of the Oregonian: The editor as historian, Ore Hist Quart, 69; Liberalism in America, In: Westminster Dictionary of Church History, Westminster Press, 71; Evangelism and social concern, In: The Cross and the Flag, Creation House, 72; coauth, Alienation in The Great Gatsby, Rocky Mountain Soc Sci J, 73; auth, Harvey Scott's cure for drones: An Oregon alternative to Pubic higher schools, Pac Northwest Quart, 473; Scott of the Oregonian: Literary frontiersman, Pac Hist Rev, 76; Free-thought on The American Frontier - Whitehead,f, Muhrer,v, Western American Literature, Vol 0028, 1993; Many Faces - an Anthology of Oregon Autobiography - Beckham,sd, Oregon Historical Quarterly, Vol 0095, 1994; Landes,Bertha,Knight of Seattle - Big-city Mayor - Haarsager,s, Western Historical Quarterly, Vol 0027, 1996; Washington County - Politics And Community in Antebellum America - Bourke,p, Debats,d, Oregon Historical Quarterly, Vol 0098, 1997. **CONTACT ADDRESS** Dept of Hist, George Fox Univ, Newberg, OR, 97132.

NASH, ROBERT N., JR.
DISCIPLINE CHURCH HISTORY, THEOLOGY, WORLD RELIGIONS **EDUCATION** GA Col, BA, MA; Southern Baptist Theol Sem, MDiv, PhD. **CAREER** Asst prof, dir, Relig Act, Shorter Col. **SELECTED PUBLICATIONS** Auth, An 8-Track Church in a CD World: The Modern Church in the Post-modern World, Smyth & Helwys. **CONTACT ADDRESS** Shorter Col, Rome, GA, 30165-9901.

NASH, RODERICK W.
PERSONAL Born 01/07/1939, New York, NY, m, 1960, 2 children **DISCIPLINE** AMERICAN ENVIRONMENTAL HISTORY **EDUCATION** Harvard Univ, BA, 60; Univ Wis, MA, 61, PhD(hist), 64. **CAREER** Instr Am hist, Dartmouth Col, 64-66; asst prof Am intellectual hist, 66-71, assoc prof, 71-73, Prof Hist & Environ Studies, Univ Calif, Santa Barbara, 73-, Chmn Dept Environ Studies, 71-, Resources for Future fac grant, 67-70; consult, US Off Educ, 70-; mem bd dirs, Yosemite Inst, 71-; mem adv comt, US Nat Park Serv, 72-; consult, Rockefeller Found, 73- & State of Alaska, 80-; Lindbergh fel, 82. **MEMBERSHIPS** Am Studies Asn; Forest Hist Soc; Orgn Am Historians; AHA. **RESEARCH** American social and intellectual history; wilderness history and management; popular cultural history. **SELECTED PUBLICATIONS** Coauth, Philanthropy in the Shaping of American Higher Education, Rutgers Univ, 65; auth, Wilderness and the American Mind, Yale Univ, 67, rev ed, 73, 3rd ed, 82; The American Environment, Addison-Wesley, 68, rev ed, 76; ed, The American Culture: The Call of the Wild, Braziller, 70; Grand Canyon of the Living Colorado, Sierra Club, 70; Environment and Americans, Holt, 72; auth, From These Beginnings: A Biographical Approach to American History, Harper, 73; coauth, The Big Drops: Ten Legendary Rapids of the American West, Sierra Club, 78; The Sierra-club Centennial in Historical-perspective - Introduction to The Special Issue, California History, Vol 0071, 1992. **CONTACT ADDRESS** Dept of Hist, Univ of Calif, Santa Barbara, CA, 93106.

NASKE, CLAUS-M.
PERSONAL Born 12/08/1935, Stettin, Germany, m, 1960, 2 children **DISCIPLINE** HISTORY **EDUCATION** Univ of AK, BA, 61; Univ of MI, MA, 64; WA St Univ, PhD, 70 **CAREER** Inst, 65-67, Univ of AK; Tch Asst, 67-69, WA St Univ; Asst Prof, 69-72, Univ of AK, Fairbanks; Exec Dir, 88-, UA Press **HONORS AND AWARDS** Ten books **MEMBERSHIPS** Western Hist Asn **RESEARCH** Alaska **SELECTED PUBLICATIONS** Auth, Alaska, A History of the 49th State, 87 **CONTACT ADDRESS** Dept of History, Univ of Alaska, Fairbanks, Fairbanks, AK, 99775. **EMAIL** ffcmn@aurora.alaska.edu

NATHAN, ANDREW J.
PERSONAL Born 04/03/1943, New York, NY **DISCIPLINE** ASIA **EDUCATION** Harvard Univ, BA, 63, MA, 65, PhD(-Polit Sci), 71. **CAREER** Teaching fel, Harvard Univ, 66; lectr hist, Univ Mich, 71; from asst prof to assoc prof, 71-82, prof polit sci, 82, dir grad studies, 97-, Columbia Univ. **HONORS AND AWARDS** Guggenheim Fel, 73-74; NEH Fel, 86-87, 92-93; Levenson Prize for best book on 20th century China, for Chinese Democracy, 87; recipient of numerous grants. **MEMBERSHIPS** Coun For Relations; Am Polit Sci Asn; Asn Asian Studies. **SELECTED PUBLICATIONS** Auth, MFN and the Human Rights Issue, in Beyond MFN: Trade with China and American Interests, The AEI Press, 94; auth, The Mao Era and After, In: Spotlight on China: Traditions Old and New, The Am Forum for Global Educ, 97; coauth, The Great Wall and the Empty Fortress: China's Search for Security, W.W. Norton, 97; auth, China's Transition, Columbia Univ Press, 97; author of numerous articles and other publications. **CONTACT ADDRESS** East Asian Inst, Columbia Univ, New York, NY, 10027. **EMAIL** ajni@columbia.edu

NATUNEWICZ, MARY ANN T.
PERSONAL Born 12/16/1937, NJ, m, 1966, 2 children **DISCIPLINE** CLASSICS **EDUCATION** Wellesley Col, BA, 58; Univ Wis, MA, 61; Univ Wis, 78. **CAREER** Wells Col, 64-67; Houston Independent School District, 86-. **MEMBERSHIPS** Amer Philol Assoc; J Classical League **RESEARCH** Cicero; Homer **CONTACT ADDRESS** 2107 Teague Rd, Houston, TX, 77088.

NAUERT, CHARLES G.
PERSONAL Born 07/26/1928, Quincy, IL, m, 1964, 2 children **DISCIPLINE** HISTORY **EDUCATION** Quincy Col, AB, 50; Univ of Ill, AM, 51, PhD, 55. **CAREER** Instr, Bowdoin Col, 55-56; asst prof of hist, Williams Col, 56-61; ASST PROF TO PROF OF HIST, UNIV OF MO-COLUMBIA, 61-, DEPT CHEMN, 65-68. **HONORS AND AWARDS** ACLS sr fel, 68-69; Thomas Jefferson Awd, Univ of Mo System. **MEMBERSHIPS** Phi Alpha Theta; Phi Kappa Phi; Am Hist Asn; Renais-

sance Soc of Am; Sixteenth Century Studies Confr; Am Soc for Reformation Res; Am Asn of Univ Prof. **RESEARCH** European intellectual and cultural history in the Renaissance-Reformation period; Humanism and Scholasticism. **SELECTED PUBLICATIONS** Auth, Introductions and annotations for Collected Works of Erasmus vol 11: Letters 1535 to 1657, January-December 1525, Univ of Toronto Press, 94; Humanism and the Culture of Renaissance Europe, Cambridge Univ Press, 95; The Humanist Challenge to Medieval German Culture, Daphnis: Zeitschrift fur mittlere deutsche Literatur, 86; Humanist Infiltration into the Academic World: Some Studies of Northern Humanism, Renaissance Quart, 90; Humanism as Method: Roots of Conflict with the Scholastics, Sixteenth Century J, 98. **CONTACT ADDRESS** Dept of Hist, Univ of Missouri, Columbia, 101 Read Hall, Columbia, MO, 65211. **EMAIL** histcgn@showme.missouri.edu

NAYLOR, JOHN FRANCIS
PERSONAL Born 04/03/1937, Newburgh, NY, m, 1960, 2 children **DISCIPLINE** MODERN BRITISH HISTORY **EDUCATION** Hamilton Col, AB, 59; Harvard Univ, MA, 60, PhD(hist), 64. **CAREER** Asst sr tutor, Quincy House & instr hist, Harvard Univ, 64- 67; from asst prof to assoc prof hist, 67-77, v chmn dept, 68- 71, assoc dean, fac Soc Sci, 78-81, Prof Hist, State Univ Ny, Buffalo, 77-, Actg Dean, Fac Soc Sci, 81-, Canada Fund grant, Harvard Univ, 66; State Univ NY Res Found fac res fels, 69, 73 & 75. **MEMBERSHIPS** Conf Brit Studies. **RESEARCH** Victorian England; 20th century British history; the Cabinet Secretariat, 1916-1976. **SELECTED PUBLICATIONS** Ed, The British Aristocracy and the Peerage Bill of 1719, Oxford Univ, 68; auth, Labour's International Policy: The Labour Party in the 1930s, Weidenfeld, London & Houghton, 69; ed, Britain, 1919-1970, Quadrangle, 71; auth, The establishment of the Cabinet Secretariat, Hist J, United Kingdom, 71; Eden,anthony - a Political-biography, 1931-1957 - Rothwell,v, Albion, Vol 0025, 1993; Keynes,john,maynard, Vol 2, The Economist as Savior, 1920-1937 - Skidelsky,r, Albion, Vol 0026, 1994; Wilson,Harold - Morgan,A, American Historical Review, Vol 0099, 1994; Collision of Empires - Britain in 3 World-wars, 1793-1945 - Harvey,ad, J of Modern History, Vol 0067, 1995; Turncoats, Changing Party Allegiance by British Politicians - Leach,r, Albion, Vol 0028, 1996; From Salisbury to Major - Continuity And Change in Conservative Politics - Evans,b, Taylor,a, Albion, Vol 0029, 1997. **CONTACT ADDRESS** 24 Fenwick Rd, Tonawanda, NY, 14150.

NAYLOR, NATALIE A.
PERSONAL Born 08/20/1937, Peekskill, NY **DISCIPLINE** AMERICAN HISTORY, WOMEN'S STUDIES **EDUCATION** Bryn Mawr Col AB, 59; Columbia Univ, MA, 62, EdD, 71. **CAREER** Res asst, Nat Bur Econ Res, 59-62; teacher social studies, Tuckahoe High Sch, 62-65; instr hist & found educ, 68-71, asst prof, 71-77, Assoc Prof & Teaching Fel Am Hist, New College, Hofstra Univ, 76-. **MEMBERSHIPS** Am Educ Studies Asn; Orgn Am Historians; Am Studies Asn. **RESEARCH** History of education; women and education; Long Island history. **SELECTED PUBLICATIONS** Auth, The antebellum College movement: A reappraisal of Tewksbury's Founding of American Colleges and Universities, Hist Educ Quart, fall 73; Paul Monroe, In: Dict of American Biography, Supplement Four, Charles Scribner's Sons, 74; The theological seminary in the configuration of American higher education: The antebellum years, Hist Educ Quart, spring 77; Horace Mann, In: American Renaissance in New England Vol I, In: Dict of Literary Biography, Gale Res, 78; Hilda Taba In: Notable American Women: Modern Period, Belknap Press, 80; coauth, Teaching Today and Tomorrow, Charles E Merrill, 81; Hudson- valley Lives - Writings From The 17th-century to The Present - Marranca,b, New York History, Vol 0073, 1992; The Orphan Trains - Placing Out in America - Holt,mi, New York History, Vol 0075, 1994; America And The Americans in 1833-4 - by an Emigrant, Gooch,richard - Widdicombe,rt, New York History, Vol 0078, 1997; J of a Revolutionary-war Woman - Greenberg,je, Mckeever,hc, New York History, Vol 0078, 1997. **CONTACT ADDRESS** Hofstra Univ, 107 Barnard Hall, Hempstead, NY, 11550.

NEARY, PETER F.
PERSONAL Born 08/15/1938, Bell Island, NF, Canada **DISCIPLINE** CANADIAN HISTORY **EDUCATION** Memorial Univ Nfld, BS, 59, MA, 62; London Sch Econ & Polit Sci, Univ London, PhD, 65. **CAREER** Asst prof, 65-71, assoc prof, 71-82, chmn, 78-81, PROF HISTORY, 82-, DEAN, FACULTY OF SOCIAL SCIENCE, UNIV WESTERN ONT, 95-; Winthrop Pickard Bell Lectr, Mt Allison Univ, 89; WS MacNutt Lectr, Univ NB, 91. **HONORS AND AWARDS** Heritage Award, Nfld Hist Soc, 95 **MEMBERSHIPS** Can Hist Asn (mem coun, 71-74, 87-90) **SELECTED PUBLICATIONS** Auth, Newfoundland in the North Atlantic World, 1929-1949, 88; coauth, Part of the Main: An Illustrated History of Newfoundland and Labrador, 83; ed, The Political Economy of Newfoundland, 1929-1972, 73; ed, White Tie and Decorations: Sir John and Lady Hope Simpson in Newfoundland, 1934-1936, 96; co-ed, By Great Waters: A Newfoundland and Labrador Anthology, 74; co-ed, Newfoundland in the Nineteenth and Twentieth Centuries: Essays in Interpretation, 80; co-ed, Twentieth Century Newfoundland: Explorations, 94; co-ed, The Good Fight: Canadians and World War II, 95; co-ed, The Veterans Charter and Post-World War II Canada, 98. **CONTACT ADDRESS** Faculty Soc Sci, Univ Western Ont, London, ON, N6A 5C2. **EMAIL** neary@sscl.uwo.ca

NEATBY, H. BLAIR
PERSONAL Born 12/11/1924, Renown, SK, Canada **DISCIPLINE** CANADIAN HISTORY **EDUCATION** Univ Sask, BA, 50; Oxford Univ, MA, 55; Univ Toronto, PhD, 56. **CAREER** PROF EMER HISTORY, CARLETON UNIV. **SELECTED PUBLICATIONS** Auth, W.L. MacKenzie King, vol I 1923-32, 63, vol II 1932-39, 76; auth, Laurier and a Liberal Quebec, 72; auth, The Politics of Chaos, 72. **CONTACT ADDRESS** Dept of History, Carleton Univ, 1125 Colonel By Dr, Ottawa, ON, K1S 5B6.

NECHELES-JANSYN, RUTH F.
PERSONAL Born 04/20/1936, Chicago, IL **DISCIPLINE** MODERN HISTORY **EDUCATION** Univ Chicago, MA, 56, PhD(hist), 63. **CAREER** Asst prof hist, Mary Washington Col, Univ Va, 62-64; from asst prof to assoc prof, 64-73, dir Jewish studies prog, 72-76, chmn dept, 76-82, assoc dir, Univ Honors Prog, 88-92, co-dir, 92-94, prof hist, 73-94, PROF EMER, 94-, LONG ISLAND UNIV, BROOKLYN CTR. **HONORS AND AWARDS** Am Philos Soc grant, 66 **MEMBERSHIPS** AHA; Soc For Hist Studies; AAUP; Am Soc 18th Century Studies; Soc Hist Mod. **RESEARCH** French Revolution; emancipation era; church in a revolutionary era. **SELECTED PUBLICATIONS** Auth, The Abbe Gregoire's Work in Behalf of Jews, 1788-1791, Fr Hist Studies, 69; The Abbe Gregoire, 1787-1831, The Odyssey of an Egalitarian, Greenwood, 71; The Abbe Gregoire and the Jews, Jewish Social Studies, 71; The Abbe Gregoire and the Egalitarian Movement, Studies 18th Century Cult, 73; The Cures in the Estates General of 1789, J Mod Hist, 9/74; L'Emancipation des Juifs, 1787-1795-Aspects Intellectuels et Politiques, In: Les Juifs et la Revolution Francaise, 1976, Edouard Privat, 76; The Constitutional Church, 1794-1802: An Essay in Voluntarism, Proc of Consortium on Revolutionary Europe, Fla Univ Press, 76; Linguistic Nationalism or Ecclesiastical Universalism: The Controversy Over a French Sacramentary, Enlightenment Studies in Honour of Lester G Crocker, The Voltaire Found, 79; auth, French Dialect or Latin Mass? A Final Crisis Within the Revolutionary Church, in, Consortium on Revolutionary Europe: 1750-1850, Proceedings, 89; contrib, Horward, ed, Bicentennial of the French Revolution, Inst on Napoleon & the French Revolution, FSU, 90. **CONTACT ADDRESS** 70 Valentine St, Highland Park, NJ, 08904.

NEEDELL, ALLAN A.
PERSONAL Born 07/02/1950, Paterson, NJ, m, 1987, 2 children **DISCIPLINE** HISTORY OF SCIENCE, TECHNOLGOY & PUBLIC POLICY **EDUCATION** Cornell Univ, BA, 72; Yale Univ, PhD, 80. **CAREER** Assoc hist, Ctr Hist of Physics, Am Inst Physics, 78-81; Curator, Space Sci & Exploration, Nat Air & Space Mus, Smithsonian Inst, 81-. **HONORS AND AWARDS** Am Phys Soc fel **MEMBERSHIPS** Am Phys Soc, Hist Sci Soc; Am Hist Asn. **RESEARCH** Am federal sci policy; gov/acad relations/ hist sci and tech. **SELECTED PUBLICATIONS** Auth, From Military Research to Big Science: Lloyd Berkner and Science-statesmanship in the Postwar Era, in Big Science: The Growth of Large-scale Research, Stanford Univ Press, 92; auth, Truth is Our Weapon: Project TROY, Political Warfare, and Government/Academic Relations in the National Security State, Diplomatic History, 17:3, 93; auth, Rabi, Berkner, and the Rehabilitation of Science in Europe: The Cold War Context of American Support for International Science 1945-1958, Chapter 13 of The United States and the Integration of Europe: Legacies of the Post War Era, St. Martin's Press, 96; co-auth, Science, Scientists and the CIA: Balancing International Ideals, National Needs, and Professional Opportunities, Intelligence and National Security, 12:1, 97; auth, Project Troy and the Cold War Annexation of the Social Sciences" in Universities and Empire: Money and Politics in the Social Sciences during the Cold War, The New Press, 98. **CONTACT ADDRESS** Space Hist Div, Nat Air & Space Mus, Smithsonian Inst, Washington, DC, 20560-0311. **EMAIL** allan.needell@nasm.si.edu

NEEL, CAROL
DISCIPLINE HISTORY **EDUCATION** Bryn Mawr Col, BA; Cornell Univ, MA, 78, PhD, 81. **CAREER** Prof. **SELECTED PUBLICATIONS** Auth, A Philip of Harvengts Vita Augustini: The Medieval Premonstratensians and the Patristic Model, 95; Philip of Harvengt and Anselm of Havelberg: The Premonstratensian Vision of Time, 93. **CONTACT ADDRESS** Dept of History, Columbia Col, New York, 14 E Cache La Poudre St, Colorado Springs, CO, 80903. **EMAIL** cneel@cc.colorado.edu

NEFF, AMY
DISCIPLINE ART **EDUCATION** Univ Pa, PhD, 77. **CAREER** Assoc prof. **HONORS AND AWARDS** Rome Prize. **SELECTED PUBLICATIONS** Auth, Manuscript Illuminators and the arte dei cristallari in Late Thirteenth-Century Venice, 92; Wicked Children on Calvary and the Baldness of St. Francis, 90; The Dialogus Beatae Mariae et Anselmi de Passione Domini: Toward an Attribution, 86; A New Interpretation of the Supplicationes Variae Miniatures, 82. **CONTACT ADDRESS** Dept of Art, Knoxville, TN, 37996.

NEFF, HECTOR
PERSONAL Born 12/19/1952, Los Angeles, CA, m, 1984, 2 children **DISCIPLINE** ANTHROPOLOGY **EDUCATION** Stanford Univ, AB, 75; Univ Calif, MA, 79; PhD, 84. British Coun Archaeol Study Tour to Northern Ireland, 93; completed MIT Center for Materials Res in Archaeol and Ethnology Summer Inst Course, 84; trainee in neutron activation analysis and statistical modeling, Brookhaven Nat Lab, 10/82-12/82. **CAREER** Archaeologist, Center for Archaeol Studies, 80-84 & 85-86, asst res archaeologist, Mesoamerican Res Center, Univ of Calif, 86-90; programmer/analyst, Univ of San Francisco, 84-85; postdoctoral fel, res collaborator & consult database programmer, Conservation Analytical Lab, Smithsonian Inst, 86-90; res scientist, 90-93, SR RES SCIENTIST, MO UNIV RES REACTOR, 93-; adjunct asst prof, anthropology, 90-97, ADJUNCT ASSOC PROF, ANTHROPOLOGY, UNIV OF MO, COLUMBIA, 97-. **HONORS AND AWARDS** UCSB Humanities Grant, 81; postdoctoral fel, 86 & 87, res opportunity fund grant, Smithsonian Inst, 87, 88, & 89; NSF Grants, 89, 91, 95, 96, & 99-2000; grant, Univ Houston-Clear Lake, 90 & 92; Weldon Springs Fund, 91, fac res grant, 91, res board grant, Univ Mo, 94; British Council Grant, 93; grant, Nat Park Service, 93 & 94; **MEMBERSHIPS** SAA Excellence in Ceramic Studies Award Comm; Soc for Am Archaeol; Am Anthropological Asn; Asn for Field Archaeol. **RESEARCH** Archaeological Method and Theory; Mesoamerican Archaeology; Quantitative Methods; Ceramic Analysis; Neutron Activation Analysis; Southwest Archaeology. **SELECTED PUBLICATIONS** Coauth, Methodology of Comparison in Evolutionary Archaeology, Rediscovering Darwin: Evolutionary Theory in Archaeol Explanation, 97; The Evolution of Anasazi Ceramic Production and Distribution: Compositional Evidence from a Pueblo-III Site in South-Central Utah, J of Field Archaeol, 97; A Reassessment of the Acid-Extraction Approach to Compositional Characterization of Archaeological Ceramics, Am Antiquity, 96; The Current State of Nuclear Archaeology, J of Radioanalytical and Nuclear Chemistry, 95; A Ceramic Compositional Perspective on the Formative to Classic Transition in Southern Mesoamerica, Latin Am Antiquity, 94; auth, The Development of Plumbate Ceramic Ware in Southern Mesoamerica, JOM, 95; RQ-mode Principal Components Analysis of Ceramic Compositional Data, Archaeometry, 94; Theory, Sampling, and Technical Studies in Archeological Pottery Analysis, Am Antiquity, 93. **CONTACT ADDRESS** Research Reactor, Univ Mo, Columbia, MO, 65211.

NEIHOFF, ARTHUR H.
PERSONAL Born 12/30/1921, Indianapolis, IN, 1 child **DISCIPLINE** ANTHROPOLOGY **EDUCATION** BA, IN Univ, 49; PhD Columbia Univ, 57. **CAREER** Mtlw Museum-Curator, 51-54; WS State Dept Comm Develop, Harvard, 59-61; Univ Wisc, 62-64; Univ Washington, 64-70; Calif State Univ, LA, 70-90, Retired 91. **HONORS AND AWARDS** Fullbright 51-52, India. **MEMBERSHIPS** Am Anthro Assoc; PMA **RESEARCH** Humankind-in all places, all times. **SELECTED PUBLICATIONS** On Becoming Human, 420pp, The Human Press, 96; Take over: How Eeroman Changed the World, 250pp, Human Press, 96; On Being a Cultural Animal, 310 pp, The Human Press, 97; An Anthropologist Winter, The Bad, 400pp, The Human Press, 99. **CONTACT ADDRESS** 31765 Rooking Rd, Escondida, CA, 92026. **EMAIL** neihoff@accessl.net

NEILS, JENIFER
DISCIPLINE EUROPEAN AND AMERICAN MODERN ART **EDUCATION** Bryn Mawr Col, AB, 72; Princeton Univ, MFA, 77; Sydney Univ, MA, 78; Princeton Univ PhD, 80; dept ch 86. **CAREER** Curatorial/teaching app, Cleveland Mus Art; Whitehead Vis prof Am Sch Classical Studies CWRU. **HONORS AND AWARDS** Mus Exhib Comt Archaeol Inst Am. **SELECTED PUBLICATIONS** Auth, The Youthful Deeds of Theseus, 87; Goddess and Polis: The Panathenaic Festival in Ancient Athens, 92; Worshipping Athena: Panathenaia and Parthenon, 96. **CONTACT ADDRESS** Case Western Reserve Univ, 10900 Euclid Ave, Cleveland, OH, 44106. **EMAIL** jxn4@po.cwru.edu

NEILSON, JAMES WARREN
PERSONAL Born 06/19/1933, St. Louis, MO **DISCIPLINE** AMERICAN HISTORY **EDUCATION** Northeast MO State Tchr(s) Col, BS, 54, MA, 55; Univ IL, PhD, 58. **CAREER** Assoc prof, 58-59, chmn dept soc sci, 68-81, prof hist, Mayville State Col, 59-98; Prof Emeritus, May 98. **MEMBERSHIPS** AHA; Orgn Am Historians. **RESEARCH** Am hist, 1865-1930; railroad hist. **SELECTED PUBLICATIONS** Auth, Shelby M Cullom: Prairie State Republican, Univ IL, 62; From Protest to Preservation: What Republicans Have Believed, Christopher, 68; The School of Personal Service: A History of Mayville State College, private publ, 80. **CONTACT ADDRESS** Dept of Hist, Mayville State Col, 330 3rd St NE, Mayville, ND, 58257-1299.

NELLES, HENRY V.
PERSONAL Born 11/09/1942, Cambridge, ON, Canada **DISCIPLINE** HISTORY **EDUCATION** Univ Toronto, BA, 64, MA, 65; PhD, 70. **CAREER** PROF HISTORY, YORK UNIV, 70-; vis prof Can stud, Tsukuba Univ, Keio Univ, Int Christian

Univ 76-77; WLM King Prof Can stud, Harvard Univ, 81-82; chmn, Ont Coun Univ Affairs, 88-92; co-ed, Can Hist Rev, 88-92. **HONORS AND AWARDS** Newcomen Award, 73; Toronto Bk Award, 77; Fel, Royal Soc, 85; Sir John A. Macdonald Prize, 86. **MEMBERSHIPS** Can Hist Asn **SELECTED PUBLICATIONS** Auth, Politics of Development, 74; coauth, The Revenge of the Methodist Bicycle Company, 77; coauth, Monopoly's Moment, 86; coauth, Southern Exposure, 88; ed, The Philosophy of Railroads, 72; ed, Nationalism or Local Control, 72; ed, But This Is Our War, 81; gen ed, Social History of Canada, 78-88. **CONTACT ADDRESS** History Dept, York Univ, 4700 Keele St, North York, ON, M3J 1P3.

NELSON, DANIEL
PERSONAL Born 08/28/1941, Indianapolis, IN, m, 1963, 2 children **DISCIPLINE** UNITED STATES HISTORY **EDUCATION** OH Wesleyan Univ, BA, 63; OH State Univ, MA, 64; Univ WI, PhD, 67. **CAREER** Specialist indust collections, Eleutherian Mills Hist Libr, 67-69; coordr Hagley prog, Eleutherian Mills-Hagley Found, 69-70; assoc prof, 70-77, prof hist, Univ Akron, 77, Asst prof, Univ Del, 67-70. **HONORS AND AWARDS** C.A. Kulp Mem Award, 71; Outstanding Res Award, 81. **RESEARCH** Economic and business hist; labor hist; recent US hist. **SELECTED PUBLICATIONS** Auth, Unemployment Insurance: The American Experience, Univ WI, 69; Managers and Workers, Univ Wis, 75, 95; Frederick W Taylor and the Rise of Scientific Management, Univ Wis, 80; American Rubber Workers and Organized Labor, 88; ed, A Mental Revolution, 92; auth, Farm and Factory, 95; Shifting Fortunes, 97. **CONTACT ADDRESS** Dept of Hist, Univ of Akron, Olin Hall, Akron, OH, 44325-1902. **EMAIL** nelson@uakron.edu

NELSON, GERSHAM
DISCIPLINE HISTORY **EDUCATION** Univ Ill, PhD. **CAREER** Prof & dept head, Eastern Michigan Univ. **RESEARCH** Latin America, Africa, South of the Sahara. **SELECTED PUBLICATIONS** Auth, The Life and Works of Rudolph James: Founder of Black Adventism in Canada; co-ed, From Outside of Western Civilization Legacy of 1492. **CONTACT ADDRESS** Dept of History and Philosophy, Eastern Michigan Univ, 701 Pray-Harrold, Ypsilanti, MI, 48197. **EMAIL** Gersham.Nelson@emich.edu

NELSON, J. DOUGLAS
PERSONAL Born 07/23/1941, Billings, MT, m, 1964, 2 children **DISCIPLINE** HISTORY OF AFRICA **EDUCATION** Linfield Col, BA, 63; Geo Wash Univ, AM 66, PhD, 74 **CAREER** Asst Prof, 66-68, KS St Univ; Assoc Dir, 70-72, Geo Wash Univ; Asst Prof, Dir, 72-75, Baldwin-Wallace col; Prof, 75-, Anderson Univ **HONORS AND AWARDS** Delegate, Internatl Human Rights conf, Capetown South Africa, 79, Malone Fel, 92 **MEMBERSHIPS** Midw Polit Sci Assn **RESEARCH** Eastern and Southern Africa **CONTACT ADDRESS** Anderson, IN, 46011. **EMAIL** dnelson@anderson.edu

NELSON, JAMES DAVID
PERSONAL Born 02/13/1930, Luray, KS, m, 1957, 2 children **DISCIPLINE** HISTORY OF CHRISTIAN THOUGHT **EDUCATION** Westmar Col, AB, 52; United Theol Sem, BD, 59; Univ Chicago, MA, 61, PhD(church hist), 63. **CAREER** Asst prof & librn, 63-65, from asst prof to prof hist theol, 65-77, Prof Church Hist, United Theol Sem, 77-, Mem comn arch & hist, United Methodist Church, 72-78. **MEMBERSHIPS** Am Acad Relig; Am Hist Asn; Am Soc Church Hist. **RESEARCH** German Lutehran Pietism; theological enlightenment in Germany; German romanticism. **SELECTED PUBLICATIONS** Auth, Piety and invention, In: The Impact of Christianity on its Environment, Univ Chicago, 68; Responsible Grace - Wesley,john Practical Theology - Maddox,rl, Theological Studies, Vol 0056, 1995. **CONTACT ADDRESS** 20 Greenmount Blvd, Dayton, OH, 45419.

NELSON, KEITH LEBAHN
PERSONAL Born 05/24/1932, Omaha, NE, m, 1975, 1 child **DISCIPLINE** HISTORY **EDUCATION** Stanford Univ, BA, 53, MA, 54; Univ Calif, Berkeley, PhD(hist), 65. **CAREER** Instr hist, Univ Tex, Austin, 63-65; asst prof, 65-72, Assoc Prof Hist, Univ Calif, Irvine, 72-, Danforth assoc, Danforth Found, 68-. **MEMBERSHIPS** AHA; Soc Historians Am Foreign Rel; Conf Peace Res Hist; Soc Sci Hist Asn. **RESEARCH** Twentieth century United States history; American relations with Europe; war and social change. **SELECTED PUBLICATIONS** Ed, C Hartley Grattan's Why We Fought, Bobbs Merrill, 69; auth, What Colonel House overlooked in the Armistice, Mid-America, 469; The black horror on the Rhine: Racism in post World War I diplomacy, J Mod Hist, 1270; The warfare state: History of a concept, Pac Hist Rev, 571, reprint, Bobbs Merrill; ed, The Impact of War on American Life: The Twentieth Century Experience, Holt, Rinehart, & Winston, 71; auth, Victors Divided: America and the Allies in Germany, 1918-23, 75 & coauth, Why War?, Ideology, Theory, and History, 78, Univ Calif; Nixon - Ruin And Recovery, 1973-1990 - Ambrose,se, Reviews in American History, Vol 0021, 1993; Johnson, Vietnam, And The West - Transatlantic Burdens, 1963-1969 - German - Arenth,j, J of American History, Vol 0083, 96; Century of War - Politics, Conflict, And Society Since 1914 - Kolko,g, American Historical Review, Vol 0102, 1997. **CONTACT ADDRESS** Dept of Hist, Univ of Calif, Irvine, CA, 92717.

NELSON, LYNN HARRY
PERSONAL Born 09/21/1931, Harvey, IL, m, 1962, 1 child **DISCIPLINE** MEDIEVAL HISTORY **EDUCATION** Univ Chicago, BA, 48; Univ Tex, BA, 58, PhD(medieval hist), 63. **CAREER** From instr to assoc prof, 63-74, Prof Medieval Hist, Univ Kans, 74-, Fulbright Res Fel, Spain, 65-66. **HONORS AND AWARDS** H Bernard Fink Award Outstanding Teaching, 68. **MEMBERSHIPS** Medieval Acad Am; Am Acad Res Historians of Medieval Spain; Soc Span & Port Hist Studies; Soc Comp Frontier Studies; Soc Sci Hist Asn. **RESEARCH** Twelfth century Britain; Aragon and Cataluna in the 11th and 12th centuries. **SELECTED PUBLICATIONS** Coauth, A lost fragment of the Defensio iuris domus Lancastriae, Speculum, 465; auth, The Normans in South Wales, 1070-1171, Univ Tex, 66; Rotrou of Perche and the Aragonese reconquest, Traditio, 70; Land use in early Aragon: the organization of a medieval society, Societas, 73; The Aragonese pardina: Its etymology and function, Bull Fac Arts & Lett, Univ Garyounis, 75; coauth, Orosius' commentary on the fall of Roman Spain, Classical Folia, 77; auth, The foundation of Jaca (1076): urban growth in early Aragon, Speculum 78; coauth, Occident 42 of the Notitia Dignitatum's Dating and Structure, Res Pub Literarum, 81; Medieval Seals From The Kingdom of Navarre - Documentation And Description - Spanish - Menendezpidaldenavascues,f, Ramosaguirre,m, Ochoadeolzaeguiraun,e, Speculum-a J of Medieval Studies, Vol 0071, 1996. **CONTACT ADDRESS** Dept of Hist, Univ of Kans, Lawrence, KS, 66045-0001.

NELSON, OTTO MILLARD
PERSONAL Born 05/31/1935, Owatonna, MN, m, 1959, 4 children **DISCIPLINE** MODERN EUROPEAN HISTORY **EDUCATION** Univ Ore, BS, 56, MA, 61; Ohio State Univ, PhD(hist), 68. **CAREER** Instr hist, Ohio State Univ, 64-65; asst prof to assoc prof Hist, Tex Tech Univ, 65-, dir honors, 81-83, assoc dean, Col of Arts and Sci, 83-. **HONORS AND AWARDS** Distinguished Teaching Award, AMOCO Foundation, 74. **MEMBERSHIPS** AHA; AAUP; Ger Studies Asn; Leo Baeck Inst; SW Soc Sci Asn. **RESEARCH** History of Caricature; modern Germany; European socialism. **SELECTED PUBLICATIONS** Auth, Thomas Theodor Heine: His Expatriate Correspondence, Libr Chroncicle Univ Tex, Austin, fall 74; Simplicissimus and the Rise of National Socialism, Historian, 5/78; co-ed, War and Peace: Perspectives in the Nuclear Age, Lubbock, 88. **CONTACT ADDRESS** Dept of Hist, Tex Tech Univ, Lubbock, TX, 79409-0001.

NELSON, PAUL DAVID
PERSONAL Born 05/15/1941, Patrick Co, VA, m, 1964, 2 children **DISCIPLINE** AMERICAN REVOLUTIONARY, MILITARY HISTORY, HISPANIC AMERICAN HISTORY **EDUCATION** Berea Col, BA, 65; Duke Univ, MA, 68, PhD(Am revolutionary hist), 69. **CAREER** Asst prof Am revolutionary hist, Villanova Univ, 69-70; asst prof, 70-76, Assoc Prof Hist, Berea Col, 76-, Julian-Van Dusen Prof of Am Hist, 93. **HONORS AND AWARDS** Hist Essay Prize, NY State Hist Asn, 76. **MEMBERSHIPS** AHA; Southern Hist Asn; Orgn Am Historians. **RESEARCH** Mil hist. **SELECTED PUBLICATIONS** Auth, Horatio Gates at Newburgh, 1783: A misunderstood role, William & Mary Quart, 1/72; Legacy of controversy: Gates, Schuyler, and Arnold at Saratoga, 1777, Mil Affairs, 4/73; From intolerance to moderation: The evolution of Abraham Lincoln's racial views, Register Ky Hist Soc, 1/74; Experiment in interracial education at Berea College, 1858-1908, J Negro Hist, 1/74; General Horatio Gates: A Biography, La State Univ, 76; Guy Carleton vs Benedict Arnold: The campaign of 1776 in Canada and on Lake Champlain, NY Hist, 7/76; James Fenimore Cooper's maritime nationalism, 1828-1850, Mil Affairs, 10/77; British conduct of the American Revolutionary War: A review of interpretations, J Am Hist, 12/78; Citizen Soldiers as Regulars, Mil Affairs, 79; Anthony Wayne, IN Univ, 85; William Alexander, Lord Stirling, Univ of AL, 87; William Tryon, Univ of NC, 90; Gen James Grant, Univ Press of FL, 93; Sir Charles Grey, First Earl Grey, Fairleigh Dickinson Univ Press, 96; Gen Sir Guy Carleton, FDU Press, 99. **CONTACT ADDRESS** Dept of History, Berea Col, Berea, KY, 40404. **EMAIL** david_necsom@berea.edu

NELSON, RANDOLPH A.
DISCIPLINE CONTEXTUAL EDUCATION **EDUCATION** Gustavus Adolphus Col, BA; Lutheran Sch Theol, MDiv, 68; Univ Chicago Divinity Sch, MA, 70, PhD, 78. **CAREER** Instr, Lutheran Sch Theol, 69-71; act dean of stud (s), Lutheran Sch Theol, 71-73; asst to the dir, Lutheran Sch Theol, 73-75; asst prof, 75; Melvin A. Hammarberg prof, 82-. **HONORS AND AWARDS** Scholar, Bavarian State Government; Fulbright Travel grant; Lutheran Brotherhood Grad Stud grant., Pastor, Resurrection Lutheran Church, 68-75; 5 **SELECTED PUBLICATIONS** Auth, Making Faithful Choices: How Do I Decide?, Cross Signs, 93. **CONTACT ADDRESS** Dept of Contextual Education, Luther Sem, 2481 Como Ave, St. Paul, MN, 55108. **EMAIL** rnelson@luthersem.edu

NELSON, ROBERT S.
PERSONAL Born 10/27/1947, Temple, TX, 2 children **DISCIPLINE** ART HISTORY **EDUCATION** Rice Univ, BA, 69; New York Univ, MA, 73, PhD(art hist), 78. **CAREER** Asst prof art hist, Univ Chicago, 77-. **MEMBERSHIPS** US Nat Comt Byzantine Studies; Int Ctr Medieval Art; Medieval Acad. **RESEARCH** Byzantine art. **SELECTED PUBLICATIONS** Auth, The Iconography of Preface and Miniature in the Byzantine Gospel Book, New York Univ Press, 80; Theodore Hagiopetrites, A Late Byzantine Scribe and Illuminator, Vienna, 91; co-ed, Critical Terms for Art History, Chigago, 96. **CONTACT ADDRESS** 5540 Greenwood Ave, Chicago, IL, 60637-1506. **EMAIL** olin@midway.uchicago.edu

NELSON, SUSAN
DISCIPLINE EAST ASIAN ART **EDUCATION** Harvard Univ, PhD. **CAREER** Assoc prof. **RESEARCH** Chinese painting and literary culture. **SELECTED PUBLICATIONS** Auth, pubs on Chinese art theory and criticism. **CONTACT ADDRESS** Dept of History and Art, Indiana Univ, Bloomington, 300 N Jordan Ave, Bloomington, IN, 47405. **EMAIL** senelson@indiana.edu

NELSON, WANDA LEE
PERSONAL Born 11/16/1952, Franklin, LA, m **DISCIPLINE** EDUCATION **EDUCATION** Grambling State Univ, BA 1973; Ball State Univ, MA 1975; Natl Cert Counselor 1984; Louisiana State Univ, Ed S 1985; Northern Illinois Univ DeKalb Il Ed.D 1989. **CAREER** Bicester Amer Elem School, England, learning specialist 1974-76; Summer Enrichment Program LSUE, music teacher 1984; LSUE, counselor; Northern Illinois Univ, counselor & minority programs coordinator, 1985-89; UNIV OF TEXAS, AUSTIN TX, asst dean of students 1989-92; aaoc dean of students, 1992-95, EXECUTIVE DIRECTOR UNIVERSITY OUTREACH CENTERS, 1995-. **HONORS AND AWARDS** Magna Cum Laude Grambling State Univ 1973; President's Award Little Zion BC Matrons, Opelousas, LA 1985; Alpha Kappa Mu Honor Society, Grambling State Univ; Kappa Delta Pi Honor Society, Northern Illinois Univ 1988; Best Advisor of the Year, 1989; Alpha Golden Image Award, Northern ILL Univ; Outstanding Educator, Texas Employees Retirement System, 1991; African-American Faculty/Staff of the Year, 1995; Pan-Hellenic Image Award, Univ of Texas; Leadership Austin Class, 1997-98; Governor's Executive Development Program, 1998. **MEMBERSHIPS** Advisor Awareness of Culture, Ed & Soc Student Club 1978-85; Anti-Grammateus Epsilon Alpha Sigma Chap, 1979-80; organized Mu Upsilon Chap, 1992; Basileus Alpha Kappa Sigma, Chapter 1994-; life mem, Sigma Gamma Rho Sorority, Inc; Jack and Jill of America Inc, 1996-; advisor, Innervisions Gospel Choir, Univ of Texas, 1993-95; advisor, Zeta Nu Chap, 1984-89; life member Grambling State Univ Alumni Assn; member Amer Assn for Counseling & Dev; American Assn of Higher Education; Amer college Personnel Assn. **CONTACT ADDRESS** University Outreach Ctrs, Univ of Texas, Austin, 600 W 24th St, Austin, TX, 78705.

NELSON LIMERICK, PATRICIA
DISCIPLINE HISTORY **EDUCATION** Univ Calif Santa Cruz, BA, 72; Yale Univ, PhD, 80. **CAREER** Lectr, Univ Calif, 70-71; vis asst prof, 71-73, asst prof, 73-78, assoc prof, Univ Colo, 78-. **SELECTED PUBLICATIONS** Auth, The Adventures of the Frontier in the Twentieth Century, Univ Calif, 94; Turnerians All: The Hope for a Helpful History in an Intelligible World, Am Hist Rev, 95; Reason and Region, Johns Hopkins, 95; The Shadows of Heaven Itself, Norton, 97. **CONTACT ADDRESS** History Dept, Univ of Colorado, Boulder, Boulder, CO, 80309. **EMAIL** limerick@stripe.colorado.edu

NENNER, HOWARD ALLEN
PERSONAL Born 09/18/1935, New York, NY, m, 1990, 2 children **DISCIPLINE** ENGLISH & LEGAL HISTORY **EDUCATION** Queens Col, BA, 56; Columbia Univ, LLB, 59; Univ Calif, Berkeley, PhD, 71. **CAREER** Pvt pract, 60-63; lectr hist, 68-71, asst prof, 71-75, assoc prof, 75-81, prof hist & Roe/Straut Prof, Smith Col, 81-, Am Bar Found fel legal hist, 78-79. **MEMBERSHIPS** AHA; Am Soc Legal Hist; Conf Brit Studies. **RESEARCH** Tudor and Stuart legal and constitutional history. **SELECTED PUBLICATIONS** Auth By Colour of Law, Univ Chicago, 77; The Right To Be King, MacMillan & Univ NC, 95; Ed, Politics and the Political Imagination in Later Stuart Britain, Univ Rochester, 97. **CONTACT ADDRESS** Dept Hist, Smith Col, 98 Green St, Northampton, MA, 01063-0001. **EMAIL** hnenner@sophia.smith.edu

NESS, ARTHUR J.
PERSONAL Born 01/27/1936, Chicago, IL, m, 1984 **DISCIPLINE** MUSIC **EDUCATION** Univ S Cal, BM Music Theory, 58; Harvard Univ, AM, 63; New York Univ, PhD, 84. **CAREER** Univ S Cal, asst prof, 63-76; Daemen Col, assoc prof, dept chair, 76-84; SUNY/Buffalo, prof music, 83-85. **HONORS AND AWARDS** Charles Healey Award, Outstanding Diss in Humanities; Fulbright Fel Univ Munich **MEMBERSHIPS** Am Musicol Soc; Int Musicol Soc; Lute Soc, UK; Nederlandse Luitvereniging Int; Asn of Mozart & Music Libraries. **RESEARCH** Music for LuteWind; Music of Mozart & Contemporaries. **SELECTED PUBLICATIONS** The Lute Music of Francesco Canova da Milano, 1497-1543, Harvard Univ Press, 70. **CONTACT ADDRESS** 2039 Commonwealth Ave, Ste 10, Boston, MA, 02135. **EMAIL** 71162.751@Compuserve.com

NESS, GARY CLIFFORD
PERSONAL Born 04/08/1940, Sioux City, IA, m, 1963, 2 children **DISCIPLINE** RECENT AMERICAN & SOUTHERN HISTORY **EDUCATION** Iowa State Univ, BS, 63; Duke Univ, AM, 69, PhD(hist, 72. **CAREER** Asst prof hist, Univ Cincinnati, 70-; consult, Am Tel & Tel Soc Sci Workshop, spring 71. **MEMBERSHIPS** AHA; Southern Hist Asn; Orgn Am Historians; AAUP. **RESEARCH** Recent United States politics; the South; historical methodology. **CONTACT ADDRESS** 700 Gatehouse Lane, Worthington, OH, 43085.

NESS, GAYL DEFORREST
PERSONAL Born 03/19/1929, Los Angeles, CA, m, 1955, 4 children **DISCIPLINE** SOCIOLOGY **EDUCATION** Univ Calif Berkeley, MA, 57; PhD, 61. **CAREER** Asst prof Sociology, 64-66, Assoc prof Sociology, 66-72, prof Sociology, 72-96, PROF EMER, 96-, UNIV MICH, 64- . **HONORS AND AWARDS** Univ Mich Fac Governance Award, 95. **MEMBERSHIPS** Am Soc Assoc; Am Assoc Asian Studies; Pop Assoc Am. **RESEARCH** Population, Development, and Environment, Especially in Asia. **SELECTED PUBLICATIONS** coauth, Population-Environment Dynamics: Ideas and Observations, Univ Mich Press, 93; "People, Parks, and Biodiversity, People, Parks, and Biodiversity," Am Assoc Advan Sci, 95; World Population Growth, The Global Environ: Science, Technology and management, Scand Sci Press, 96; Population and Strategies for National Sustainable Development: A guidebook to assist environmental planners in dealing with population issues, Earthscan Press, 97; Environment for People: Building Bridges for Sustainable Development, UNFPA, 97. **CONTACT ADDRESS** Dept of Sociology, Univ of Mich, 3012 Literature, Science, & the Arts Building, Ann Arbor, MI, 48109-1382. **EMAIL** gaylness@umich.edu

NESS, LAWRENCE
PERSONAL Born 08/09/1946, Chicago, IL **DISCIPLINE** ART HISTORY **EDUCATION** Univ Chicago, BA, 66-70; Harvard Univ, MA, 74; PhD, 77. **CAREER** Vis sessional lectr, Univ Victoria (Canada), 76-77; lectr, Univ Mass, 77-78; vis asst prof, Harvard Univ, 80; vis prof, Bryn Mawr Col, 89; adj prof, art conservation dept, 96-; asst prof, 78-82; assoc prof, 82-88; prof, 88-; assoc ch, 86-87. **HONORS AND AWARDS** Gen Univ res grant, 93; grant-in-aid for res, Amer Philos Soc, 93; summer stipend, NEH, 95; grant, Samuel H Kress, 96. **SELECTED PUBLICATIONS** Auth, From Justinian to Charlemagne, European Art, A.D. 565-787, G K Hall Critical Bibliographies, Historical Art, G K Hall, 85; The Gundohinus Gospels, Medieval Acad Am Bk(s), 87; A Tainted Mantle:Hercules and the Classical Tradition at the Carolingian Court, Pa Univ Press, 91; ed, Approaches to Early-Medieval Art, 97; auth, Introduction, Approaches to Early-Medieval Art, ed. Lawrence Nees, Medieval Acad Am, 98; Art and Architecture, The New Cambridge Mediaeval Hist, Cambridge, 95; rev, Carolingian Art, Merovingian Art, Migrations Art, Medieval France: An Encyclopedia, NY and London, 95. **CONTACT ADDRESS** Dept of Art Hist, Univ Delaware, 162 Ctr Mall, Newark, DE, 19716.

NESS, SALLY A.
PERSONAL Born 10/29/1959, Washington, DC **DISCIPLINE** CULTURAL ANTHROPOLOGY **EDUCATION** Univ Washington, PhD 87. **CAREER** Univ Cal Riverside, assoc prof 93-. **HONORS AND AWARDS** SSRC S E Asia Adv Res Gnt. **MEMBERSHIPS** AAA **RESEARCH** Philippine studies; tourism; dance. **SELECTED PUBLICATIONS** Auth, Body Movement and Culture: Kinesthetic and Visual Symbolism in a Philippine Community, Philadelphia PA, Univ Penn Press, 92. **CONTACT ADDRESS** Dept of Dance, Univ of California, Riverside, Riverside, CA, 92521.

NESTINGEN, JAMES A.
DISCIPLINE CHURCH HISTORY **EDUCATION** Concordia Col, BA, 67; Luther Sem, MDiv, 71; MTh, 78; St. Michael's Col, Univ Toronto, ThD, 84. **CAREER** Instr, 76-78; asst prof, 80; prof, 92-. **HONORS AND AWARDS** Bruce prize in New Testament, 71., Pastor, Faith Lutheran Church, 71-74; curriculum ed, Augsburg Publ House, 74-76; asst to the pastor, St. Ansgar Lutheran Church, Can, 78-80. **SELECTED PUBLICATIONS** Auth, The Faith We Hold, 83; Martin Luther: His Life and His Writings, 82; Roots of Our Faith, 78; coauth, Free to Be, 75. **CONTACT ADDRESS** Dept of Church History, Luther Sem, 2481 Como Ave, St. Paul, MN, 55108. **EMAIL** jnesting@luthersem.edu

NETHERCUT, WILLIAM ROBERT
PERSONAL Born 01/11/1936, Rockford, IL **DISCIPLINE** CLASSICS **EDUCATION** Harvard Univ, AB, 58; Columbia Univ, MA, 60, PhD(Classics), 63. **CAREER** From instr to asst prof Greek & Latin, Columbia Univ, 61-67; from assoc prof to prof Classics, Univ Ga, 67-75; prof Classics, Univ Tex, Austin, 75-, Lawrence Chamberlain fel, Columbia Univ, 67; lectr, First Int Conf on Ovid, Constanta, Romania, 72, Int Soc Homeric Studies, Athens, 73, 74, Int Congr Cypriot Studies, 74 & Int Congr SE Europ Studies, 74. **MEMBERSHIPS** Am Philol Asn; Class Asn Mid W & S; Archaeol Inst Am; Vergilian Soc Am; Petronian Soc. **RESEARCH** Propertius; Vergil; Greek poetry. **SELECTED PUBLICATIONS** Auth, The conclusion of Lucretius' fifth book, Class J, 12/67; Notes on the structure of Propertius, book IV, Am J Philol, 10/68; Apuleius' literary art, Class J, 69; The ironic priest: Propertius' Roman elegies, Am J Philol, 10/70; Propertius, 3/11, Trans Am Philol Asn, 71; The imagery of the Aeneid, Class J, 71-72; Vergil's De Return Natura, 73 & The epic journey of Achilles, 76, Ramus; Recent Scholarship on Propertius, Aufstieg und Noedergang cler Romischer Welt, 83. **CONTACT ADDRESS** Dept of Classics, Univ of Texas, Austin, TX, 78712-1026. **EMAIL** nethercut@mailutexas.edu

NETTL, BRUNO
PERSONAL Born 03/14/1930, Prague, Czechslovakia, m, 1952, 2 children **DISCIPLINE** ETHNOMUSICOLOGY, ANTHROPOLOGY **EDUCATION** Ind Univ, AB, 50, PhD(musicol), 53; Univ Mich, MA, 60. **CAREER** From instr to asst prof music, Wayne State Univ, 53-56, asst librn, 58-64; lectr musicol, Univ Kiel, 56-58; assoc prof, 65-67, chmn div musicol, 66-72 & 75-77, prof, 67-92, prof emeritus, Univ Ill, 92-, Fulbright lectr, Ger, 56-58; Fulbright res scholar, Iran, 68-69; sr fel, Am Inst Indian Studies, 81-82. **HONORS AND AWARDS** Honoryary Doctorate, Dist Alumni Service Awd, Koizumi Prizel Am Acad of Arts and Scis fel, Am Musicological Soc, hon mem. **MEMBERSHIPS** Soc Ethnomusicol (pres, 69-71); Am Musicol Soc; Col Music Soc. **RESEARCH** Ethnomusicology; musical cultures of Iran; native American music; intellectual history of ethnomusicology. **SELECTED PUBLICATIONS** Auth, Music in Primitive Culture, Harvard Univ, 56; Theory and Method in Ethnomusicology, Free Press, 64; Folk and Traditional Music of the Western Continents, Prentice-Hall, 65; Daramad of Chahargah, A Study in the Performance Practice of Persian Music, Inform Coord, 72; Folk Music in the United States, 3rd ed, Wayne State Univ, 76; Eight Urban Musical Culture, Univ Ill, 78; co-ed, Comparative Musicology and Anthropology of Music: Essays on the History of Ethnomusicology, Univ Chicago, 91; coauth, Excursions in World Music, Prentice Hall, 92, end ed 96; co-ed, Community of Music: An Ethnographic Seminar in Champaign-Urbana, 93; auth, Heartland Excursions: Ethnomusicological Reflections on Schools of Music, Univ Il, 95; co-ed, In the Course of Performance: Studies in the World of Musical Improvisiation, Univ of Chicago, 98. **CONTACT ADDRESS** Sch of Music, Univ of Ill, Urbana, IL, 61801. **EMAIL** b-nettl@uiuc.edu

NETTL, BRUNO
PERSONAL Born 03/14/1930, Prague, Czechoslovakia, m, 1952, 2 children **DISCIPLINE** MUSICOLOGY **EDUCATION** Indiana Univ, AB, 50, PhD, 53; Univ of Mich, MA, 60. **CAREER** Instr, asst prof and music libn, Wayne State Univ, 53-56; lectr, Univ of Kiel, Germany, 56-58; from assoc prof to prof, Univ of Ill, 64-92; prof emer, Univ of Ill , 92-. **HONORS AND AWARDS** Distinguished Alumni Serv Award, Ind Univ, 86; Hon Doctorate, Univ of Chicago, 93; Koizumi Prize for Ethnomusicology, Japan, 94; Hon mem, Am Musicological Soc, 95; Hon Doctorate, Univ of Ill, 96; Fel, Am Acad of Arts and Scis, 97. **MEMBERSHIPS** Soc for Ethnomusicology; Am Musicological Soc; Sonneck Soc; Soc for Asian Music; Int Coun for Traditional Music. **RESEARCH** Ethnomusicology; musical cultures of Iran; Native American music; intellectual history of ethnomusicology. **SELECTED PUBLICATIONS** Auth, North American Indian Musical Styles, 54; Music in Primitive Culture, 56; An Introduction to Folk Music in the United States, 60; Cheremis Musical Styles, 60; Theory and Method in Ethnomusicology, 64; Folk and Traditional Music of the Western Continents, 65; The Study of Ethnomusicology: 29 Issues and Concepts, 83; The Western Impact on World Music, 85; The Radif of Persian Music: Studies of Structure and Cultural Context, 87; Blackfoot Musical Thought: Comparative Perspectives, 89; Heartland Excursions: Ethnomusicological Reflections on Schs of Music, 95; coauth, Folk Music in the United States, 3rd ed of Introd to Folk Music in the United States, 76; Daramad of Chahargah, 72; Contemporary Music and Music Cultures, 73; Excursions in World Music, 92; ed, Reference Materials in Ethnomusicology, 61; Eight Urban Musical Cultures, 78; coed, Comparative Musicology and Anthropology of Music: Essays on the History of Ethnomusicology, 91; Community of Music: An Ethnographic Seminar in Champaign-Urbana, 93; In the Course of Performance: Studies in the World of Musical Improvisation, 98. **CONTACT ADDRESS** Sch of Music, Univ of Illinois, 1114 West Nevada, Urbana, IL, 61801. **EMAIL** b-nettl@uiuc.edu

NEU, CHARLES ERIC
PERSONAL Born 04/10/1936, Carroll, IA, d, 2 children **DISCIPLINE** AMERICAN HISTORY **EDUCATION** Northwestern Univ, BA, 58; Harvard Univ, PhD, 64. **CAREER** From instr to assoc prof hist, Rice Univ, 63-70; assoc prof, 70-76, prof hist, Brown Univ, 76-, Chair, 95-98; Comt Am Far Eastern Policy Studies res grant, Harvard Univ, 64-65; NEH Younger Scholar fel, 68-69; fel, Charles Warren Ctr Study Am Hist, 71-72; Am Coun Learned Socs fel, 75-76 & Howard Found fel, 76-77; dir, NEH summer sem, 79, 86, 87, 89, 92; Guggenheim fel, 81-82; guest schol, Woodrow Wilson Ctr, Summer 88. **MEMBERSHIPS** AHA; Orgn Am Historians; Soc Hist Am Foreign Rels. **RESEARCH** American foreign relations. **SELECTED PUBLICATIONS** Auth, An Uncertain Friendship: Theodore Roosevelt and Japan, 1906-1909, Harvard Univ, 67; contrib, Twentieth-Century American Foreign Policy, Ohio State Univ, 71; American-East Asian Relations: A Survey, Harvard Univ, 72; auth, The Troubled Encounter: The United States and Japan, Wiley, 75; contribr, The New American State, 87; contribr and co-ed, The Wilson Era: Essays in Honor of Arthur S. Link, 91; contribr, Essays in Honor of Ernest R. May, 99. **CONTACT ADDRESS** Dept of Hist, Brown Univ, 142 Angell St, Providence, RI, 02912-9127.

NEUHOUSER, FREDERICK
DISCIPLINE 19TH CENTURY GERMAN PHILOSOPHY **EDUCATION** Columbia Univ, PhD, 88. **CAREER** Instr, Harvard Univ; PROF, PHILOS, UNIV CALIF, SAN DIEGO. **HONORS AND AWARDS** Humboldt fel. **RESEARCH** Philosophical foundations of Hegel's social theory. **SELECTED PUBLICATIONS** Auth, Fichte's Theory of Subjectivity, Cambridge Univ Press, 90; "Freedom, Dependence, and the General Will," The Philos Rev, 93; "Fichte and the Relation between Right and Morality," Fichte: Historical Context/ Contemporary Controverseries, Hum Press, 94; "The First Presentation of Fichte's Wissenschaftslehre (94/95)," The Cambridge Companion to Fichte, Cambridge Univ Press, 96. **CONTACT ADDRESS** Dept of Philos, Univ Calif, San Diego, 9500 Gilman Dr, La Jolla, CA, 92093.

NEUMANN, FREDERICK
PERSONAL Born 12/15/1907, Czechoslovakia, m, 1957, 1 child **DISCIPLINE** MUSIC HISTORY **EDUCATION** Univ Berlin, PhD(polit sci), 34; Columbia Univ, MA, 47, PhD, 52. **CAREER** Prof violin & music lit, Univ Miami, 48-51; prof music hist, strings & orchestra, Univ Richmond, 55-78. Am Philos Soc grant-in-aid, 64; Am Coun Learned Soc grants-in-aid, 65, 66 & 71; Guggenheim Mem Found fel, 67-68 & 74-76; vis prof music & sr fel, Coun Humanities, Princeton Univ, 70-71; Nat Endowment for Humanities fel, 77-78. **MEMBERSHIPS** Am Musicol Soc; Fr Musicol Soc; Am String Teachers Asn; New Bach Soc; Int Musicol Soc. **RESEARCH** Economics; violin technique; historical performance. **SELECTED PUBLICATIONS** Auth, The French Inegales, Quantz, and Bach, J Am Musicol Soc, fall 65; La note pointee, Rev Musicol, 65; External evidence and uneven notes, Musical Quart, 66; The use of Barogue Treatises on musical performance, Music & Lett, 1067; Couperin and the Downbeat Doctrine for appoggiatures, Acta Musicol, 71; The question of rhythm in Bach's French Overture, BWV 831, In: Studies in Renaissance and Barogue Music in Honor of Arthur Mendel, Barenreiter, 74; Facts and fiction about overdotting, Musical Quart, 77; Ornamentation in Barague and Post Barogue Music, Princeton Univ, 78; Improper Appoggiaturas in The 'Neue Mozart Ausgabe' + The Cataloging And Presentation of Musical Texts, J of Musicology, Vol 0010, 1992; Performance-practice in Mozart, Music & Letters, Vol 0074, 1993; Performance-practice in Mozart + Response to Maunder,richard on The Unwritten Appoggiaturas, Music & Letters, Vol 0075, 1994. **CONTACT ADDRESS** 4102 W Franklin St, Richmond, VA, 23221.

NEUMANN, KLAUS
DISCIPLINE CULTURAL HISTORY **CAREER** Sr res assoc, Ctr Cross-Cult Res, Australia Natl Univ. **RESEARCH** Colonialism and historiography; relationship between history and social memory. **SELECTED PUBLICATIONS** Auth, Rabaul Yu Swit Moa Yet: Surviving the 1994 Volcanic Eruption, Oxford Univ, 96. **CONTACT ADDRESS** Dept of Education, Australian National Univ. **EMAIL** Klaus.Neumann@anu.edu.au

NEVERDON-MORTON, CYNTHIA
PERSONAL Born 01/23/1944, Baltimore, MD, m **DISCIPLINE** AFRICAN-AMERICAN STUDIES **EDUCATION** Morgan State Univ, BA 1965, MS 1967; Howard Univ, PhD 1974. **CAREER** Baltimore Public School Syst, tchr of history 1965-68; Peale Museum, rschr/jr archivist 1965; Inst of Afro-Amer Studies, instructor curr develop 1968; MN Lutheran Synod Priority Prog, consultant 1969; Univ of MN, admissions assoc 1968-69, coordinator special programs 1969-71; Coppin State Coll, asst dean of students prof of hist 1971-72, assoc prof of history 1972-81, chairperson dept of history, geography, international studies 1978-81; prof of history, 1981-; Historically Black Colleges and Universities (HBCU) Fellow, EEO/Special Emphasis Programs, summer 1989-93, Dept of Defense, 50th Anniversary of WWII Commemoration Comm, 1993-95; MI State Univ, Research for CD-ROM on Immigration and Migration in US 1900-1920, consultant, 1996; MD Museum of African American History and Culture, head of academic team, 1998-. **HONORS AND AWARDS** Publ "The Impact of Christianity Upon Traditional Family Values" 1978; "The Black Woman's Struggle for Equality in the South" 1978; NEH Fellowship for College Teachers 1981-82; publ "Self-Help Programs as Educative Activities of Black Women in the South 1895-1925, Focus on Four Key Areas" 1982; "Blacks in Baltimore 1950-1980, An Overview" with Bettye Gardner 1982; "Black Housing Patterns in Baltimore 1895-1925" publ MD Historian 1985; Annual Historical Review 1982-83, 1983-84; Ordnance Center & School Aberdeen Proving Ground 1986; mem consult ed bd Twentieth Century Black Amer Officials & Leaders publ Greenwood Press. **MEMBERSHIPS** Study grant to selected W African Nations 1974; participant Caribbean-Amer Scholars Exchange Program 1974; mem adv bd MD Commn of Afro-Amer Life 1977-; mem Assn of Black Female

Historians 1979-; mem adv bd Multicultural Educ Coalition Com 1980-; mem Assn for the Study of Afro-Amer Life & History; reader & panelist Natl Endowment for the Humanities Smithsonian Inst Fellow 1986; Natl Forum for History Standards, 1992-94; reviewer, history dept, Howard Univ, 1995; mem MD State Dept of Educ Task Force on the Teacher of Social Studies, 1991, mem Accreditation Team; Nonstandard English and the School Environment Task Force, Baltimore County Public Schools, 1990; bd of editors Twentieth Century Black American Officials and Leaders; Great Blacks In Wax, bd mem. **SELECTED PUBLICATIONS** "Afro-American Women of the South and the Advancement of the Race 1895-1925" Univ of TN Press 1989; essay,"Through the Looking Glass: Reviewing the African American Female Exerience" in Feminist Studies 1988; wrote eight chapters, African American History in the Press, 1851-1899, Gale Press, 1996; "Securing the Double V: African-American and Japanese-american Women in the Military During World War II" in A Woman's War Too: US Women in the Military in World War II, 1996; "In Search of Equality: Maryland and the Civil Rights Movement, 1940-1970," Black Classic Press, 1997; guest editor, Negro History Bulletin, 1995-98; "Interracial Cooperation Movement," The Readers Companion to US Women's History, Houghton Mifflin, 1998 **CONTACT ADDRESS** Coppin State Col, 2500 W North Ave, Baltimore, MD, 21216.

NEVILLE, DON
DISCIPLINE MUSIC **EDUCATION** Cambridge Univ, PhD, 86. **CAREER** Assoc prof **HONORS AND AWARDS** Vis fel, Oxford, 96; dir, Metastasio. **RESEARCH** History of opera; history of the American musical theatre; 18th century opera. **SELECTED PUBLICATIONS** Auth, Metastasio: Beyond the Stage in Vienna, 97; From Simplicity to Complexity in La clemenza di Tito, Oxford, 95; The rondo in Mozart's Late Operas, 95; Semiramide in Vienna: beyond Metastasian Metastasis, 95; From Myth to Libretto, Cambridge, 93; Metastasio's Reinterpretation of Aristotle, 91; Cartesian Principles in Mozart's La clemenza di Tito, Broude, 88. **CONTACT ADDRESS** Dept of Music, Western Ontario Univ, London, ON, N6A 5B8. **EMAIL** dneville@uwovax.uwo.ca

NEVILLE, GWEN K.
PERSONAL Born 03/23/1938, Taylor, TX, m, 1975, 3 children **DISCIPLINE** ANTHROPOLOGY **EDUCATION** Mary Baldwin Col, BA, 59; Univ of Fla, MA, 68, PhD, 71. **CAREER** Asst prof to assoc prof, Emory Univ, 71-79; assoc prof to full prof, Southwestern Univ, 79-. **HONORS AND AWARDS** Phi Beta kappa; William Carrington Finch Award, Southwestern univ; NEH fellowships. **MEMBERSHIPS** Am Anthrop Asn; Am Ethnological Soc; Soc for the Anthrop of Europe; Soc for Cultural Anthrop. **RESEARCH** Symbolic anthropology; ritual; religion; family; Scotland; USA. **SELECTED PUBLICATIONS** Auth, Kinship and Pilgrimage: Rituals of Reunion in American Protestant Culture, Oxford Univ Press, 87; The Mother Town: Civic Ritual, Symbol, and Experience in the Scottish Borders, 94. **CONTACT ADDRESS** Dept of Sociology and Anthropology, Southwestern Univ, University Ave., Georgetown, TX, 78626.

NEWBY, GORDON D.
DISCIPLINE HISTORY AND NEAR EASTERN/JUDAIC LANGUAGES AND LITERATURE **EDUCATION** Univ Utah, BA, 62; Brandeis Univ, MA, 64, PhD, 66. **CAREER** Affl prof hist dept/chemn dept Near Eastern Judaic Langs Lits. **HONORS AND AWARDS** Founding ed, Medieval Encounters. **RESEARCH** Islamic history; medieval Jewish history; Muslim/non-Muslim relations. **SELECTED PUBLICATIONS** Auth, A History of the Jews of Arabia; The Making of the Last Prophet. **CONTACT ADDRESS** Dept History, Emory Univ, 221 Bowden Hall, 561 Kilgo Cir, Atlanta, GA, 30322-1950. **EMAIL** gdnewby@emory.edu

NEWBY, I.A.
PERSONAL Born 10/03/1931, Hawkinsville, GA **DISCIPLINE** UNITED STATES HISTORY **EDUCATION** GA Southern Col, BS, 51; Univ Sc, MA, 57; Univ Calif, Los Angeles, PhD(hist), 62. **CAREER** Asst prof hist, Western Wash State Col, 62-63 & Calif State Col, Fullerton, 63-66; assoc prof, Univ Hawaii, 66-67 & Calif State Col, Fullerton, 67-68; assoc prof, 68-70, Prof Hist, Univ Hawaii, 70-. **MEMBERSHIPS** AHA; Orgn Am Historians; Southern Hist Asn; Asn Study Negro Life & Hist. **RESEARCH** History of the South; Negro history; racism. **SELECTED PUBLICATIONS** Auth, Jim Crow's Defense, 65; & Challenge to the Court, 67, La State Univ; ed, The Development of Segregationist Thought, Dorsey, 68; The Civil War and Reconstruction, Appleton, 71; auth, Black Carolinians, Univ SC, 73; The South: A History, Holt, Rinehart & Winston, 78; The Meaning of South-carolina History - Essays in Honor of Rogers,george,c. Jr - Chesnutt,dr, Wilson,cn, J of Southern History, Vol 0059, 1993; African- americans at Mars Bluff, South-carolina - Vernon,aw, J of American History, Vol 0082, 1995; Behind The Mash of Chivalry - The Making of The 2nd Ku-klux-klan - Maclean,n, American Historical Review, Vol 0100, 1995; Under Their Own Vine And Fig Tree - The African-american Church in The South, 1865-1900 - Montgomery,we, J of Church And State, Vol 0036, 1994; The Specter of Communism in Hawaii - Holmes,tm, Pacific Historical Review, Vol 0064, 1995; One Blood - The Death And Resurrection of Drew,charles,r. - Love,s, J of American History, Vol 0083, 1996. **CONTACT ADDRESS** Dept of Hist, Univ of Hawaii, Honolulu, HI, 96822.

NEWCOMB, BENJAMIN H.
PERSONAL Born 07/01/1938, Philadelphia, PA, 2 children **DISCIPLINE** COLONIAL AMERICAN HISTORY **EDUCATION** Haverford Col, BA, 60; Univ PA, MA, 61, PhD, 64. **CAREER** Asst prof, 64-72, assoc prof hist, 72-93, PROF, TX TECH UNIV 93-. **MEMBERSHIPS** AHA; Orgn Am Historians; AAUP. **RESEARCH** America in the 18th century; early American politics and religions. **SELECTED PUBLICATIONS** Auth, Effects of the Stamp Act on Colonial Pennsylvania politics, William & Mary Quart, 4/66; Franklin and Galloway: A Political Partnership, Yale Univ, 72; Political Partisanship in the Middle American Colonies, LSU, 95; English Puritan Clergy: Acceptence of Political Parties, J Religious Hist, 8/95. **CONTACT ADDRESS** Dept of Hist, Texas Tech Univ, Box 41013, Lubbock, TX, 79409-0001. **EMAIL** fjbhn@ttacs.ttu.edu

NEWELL, MARGARET E.
DISCIPLINE HISTORY **EDUCATION** Brown Univ, AB, 84; Univ Va, MA, 86, PhD, 91. **CAREER** ASSOC PROF, HIST, OHIO STATE UNIV **MEMBERSHIPS** Am Antiquarian Soc **SELECTED PUBLICATIONS** Auth, "Robert Child and the Entrepreneurial Vision: Economic Ideology and Development in Early New England," NEQ 58; "Merchants and Miners: Economic Culture in Seventeenth Century Massachusetts and Peru," Revista de Indias 21, May-Sept 94; auth, "A Revolution in Economic Thought: From the Currency Act to the Imperial Crisis in Massachusetts," in Entrepreneurs: The Boston Business Community, 1750-1850, 97; auth, "Massachusetts Body of Liberties," and "John Leland," in Encyclopedia of Religion and the Law; auth, The Drove of Adam's Degenerate Seed: Indian Slavery in Colonial New England, Cornell Univ Press; auth, From Dependency to Independence: Economic Revolution in Colonial New England, Cornell Univ Press. **CONTACT ADDRESS** Dept of Hist, Ohio State Univ, 230 W 17th Ave, Columbus, OH, 43210. **EMAIL** newell.20@osu.edu

NEWHALL, DAVID SOWLE
PERSONAL Born 07/26/1929, Burlington, VT, m, 1952, 5 children **DISCIPLINE** MODERN HISTORY **EDUCATION** Univ Vt, BA, 51; Harvard Univ, MA, 56, PhD, 63. **CAREER** From instr to asst prof hist, Univ Vt, 59-66; from asst prof to assoc prof, 66-70, prof hist, 70-95, POTTINGER DISTINGUISHED PROF OF HIST EMER, 95- , CENTRE COL, 70- ; Phi Beta Kappa, 51; **HONORS AND AWARDS** Acorn Award Ky Advocates for Higher Educ, 94. **MEMBERSHIPS** Soc Fr Hist Studies. **RESEARCH** Political history of the Third French Republic; Georges Clemenceau. **SELECTED PUBLICATIONS** Clemenceau: A Life at War, 91. **CONTACT ADDRESS** Dept of Hist, Centre Col, Danville, KY, 40422.

NEWMAN, EDGAR LEON
PERSONAL Born 01/21/1939, New Orleans, LA, m, 1963, 2 children **DISCIPLINE** EUROPEAN HISTORY **EDUCATION** Ecole du Louvre, Paris, dipl, 59; Yale Univ, BA, 62; Univ Chicago, PhD, 69. **CAREER** Res asst hist, Univ Chicago, 63-64; teaching asst, Univ Ill, Chicago Circle, 66-67; asst prof, 69-75, ASSOC PROF HIST, NM STATE UNIV, 75-, NEH fels, Sem Hist Socialism, 74 & Sem High Cult & Popular Cult in 19th Century Europe, 77; NEH res grant, 75-76; res grant, NM State Univ, 78. **MEMBERSHIPS** AHA; Soc Fr Hist Studies; Southern Hist Asn; Western Soc Fr Hist (pres, 77-78); Dir, Soc Hist Revolution 1848. **RESEARCH** The intellectual and social aftermath of the French Revolutions of 1789 and 1830; the French worker-poets of the July Monarchy, 1830-50; workers and the liberal leadership of the July Revolution in France, 1830. **SELECTED PUBLICATIONS** Auth, What the Crowd Wanted in the French Revolution of 1830, In: 1830 and the Origins of the Social Question in France, Watts, 74; The Popular Idea of Liberty in the French Revolution of 1830, Proc Consortium Revolutionary Europe, 74; The Blouse and the Frock Coat: The Alliance Between the Common People and the Liberal Leadership During the Last Years of the Bourbon Restoration, 3/74; La blouse et la redingote, Ann Hist Revolution Francaise, 76; The French Women Worker Poets 1830-48, 19th Century Soc & Cult, 78; The Revolutionary Mentality of the French Worker-Poets, 1830-48, J Mod Hist; ed, Historical Dictionary of France From the Bourbon Restoration to the Second Empire, 1815-52, 2 vols, 87; auth, Franenstein, Les Lumineres et la Revolution comme monstre, Annales historiques de la Revolution francaise, 92; The Historian on Apostle: Romanticism, Religion, and the First Socialist History of the World, Jnal of the Hist of Ideas, 95; contrib to: Dictionaire de biographie francaise, Dictionnaire biographique du mouvement ouvier francais, Am Hist Asn Giude to Hist Lit. **CONTACT ADDRESS** Dept of Hist, State Univ, PO Box 30001, Las Cruces, NM, 88003-8001. **EMAIL** enewman@nmsu.edu

NEWMAN, GERALD GORDON
PERSONAL Born 12/08/1938, Singapore, Malaya **DISCIPLINE** MODERN BRITISH INTELLECTUAL AND SOCIAL HISTORY **EDUCATION** Univ Wash, BA, 60, MA, 64; Harvard Univ, PhD, 71. **CAREER** Instr hist, W Wa State Col, 65-66; asst prof, 70-78, Assoc prof hist to prof Kent State Univ, 78-. **HONORS AND AWARDS** Distinguished Teaching Award, Kent State Univ Alumnae Asn, 76. **MEMBERSHIPS** AHA; Conf Brit Studies; Res Soc Victorian Periodicals; World Hist Asn. **RESEARCH** Modern British intellectual and social history. **SELECTED PUBLICATIONS** Armchair History and the writings of Macaulay, Studies in Hist & Soc, spring 74; Anti-French propaganda and British liber nationalism in the early nineteenth century: Suggestions toward a general interpretation, Victorian Studies, 6/75; The vindication of Voltaire in the British periodical press, 1850-1900, J Popular Cult, spring 77; Voltaire in Victorian historiography, J Mod Hist, 12/77; Aspects of British Nationalism during the later eighteenth century, Consortium Revolutionary Europe: Proc 1981, 81; The Rise of English Nationalism, 87; Britain in the Hanoverian Age, 1714-1837: An Encycl, 97. **CONTACT ADDRESS** Dept Hist, Kent State Univ, PO Box 5190, Kent, OH, 44242-0001. **EMAIL** gnewman@kent.edu

NEWMAN, J.R.
PERSONAL Born 03/26/1954, Chicago, IL, m, 1995, 1 child **DISCIPLINE** ANTHROPOLOGY, ARCHAEOLOGY **EDUCATION** Triton Col, AA, 74; Grinnell Col, BA, 76; Southern Methodist Univ, MA, 84, PhD, 97. **CAREER** Archaeologist, Southern Methodist Univ, 78-87; archaeologist, U.S. Army Corps of Engineers, 87-98. **HONORS AND AWARDS** Certificate of Appreciation, Office of the Secretary of Defense, 90; Achievement Medal for Civilian Service, 92; Design & Environmental Excellence Award, 93, Commendations, 89, 90, 91, & 92, Certificate of Achievement, 90, 91, Dept of Army; Fort Burgwin Res Fel, 81 & 82; Grant, Inst for the Study of Earth and Man, 83 & 85; Weber Grant, 87, multiple small grants, 82-85, Southern Methodist Univ. **MEMBERSHIPS** Soc of Professional Archaeologists; Register of Professional Archaeologists; Tx Archeological Soc; Soc for Am Archaeology; Coun of Tx Archeologists. **RESEARCH** Lithic sourcing & analysis; Lithic economic procurement patterns & use; statistical analysis; cultural resources management. **SELECTED PUBLICATIONS** Contributing auth, Shoreline Survey of Lewisville Lake, Denton County, Texas, 1986, Univ of Tx, 90; auth, A Cultural Resources Survey of the Proposed Central Distribution Center (CDC) Construction Site and Sanitary Landfill Area at the Red River Army Depot, Bowie County, Texas, U.S. Army Corps of Engineers, 88; coauth, An Archeological Inventory of a Proposed Incinerator Construction Site at the Louisiana Army Ammunition Plant, Webster Parish, Louisiana, U.S. Army Corps of Engineers, 88; auth, A Cultural Resources Survey of Proposed Actions Related to Test Area Expansions, Longhorn Army Ammunition Plant, Harrison County, Texas, U.S. Army Corps of Engineers, 88; auth, Notes On the XRF Artifact Sourcing & Characterization of Six Rhyodacite Sources On the Taos Plateau, Northern Rio Grande Region, New Mexico, 90; auth, Effects of Source Distance on Lithic Reduction Technology, 94; auth, Initial Nots On the X-ray Flourescence Characterization of the Rhyodacite Sources of the Taos Plateau, Mexico, Archaeometry, Oxford Univ, 87; auth, The Effects of Source Distance on Lithic Material Reduction Technology, J of Field Archaeology, 94; auth, Task Selection of Lithic Raw Materials in the Northern Rio Grande Valley, New Mexico, Bulletin of the Tx Archaeological Soc, 98. **CONTACT ADDRESS** CESWF-EV-EC, U.S. Army Corps of Engineers, PO Box 17300, Fort Worth, TX, 76102-0300. **EMAIL** jay.r.newman@swf02.usace.army.mil

NEWMAN, JOHN KEVIN
PERSONAL Born 08/17/1928, Yorkshire, England, m, 1970, 3 children **DISCIPLINE** CLASSICAL PHILOLOGY, COMPARATIVE LITERATURE **EDUCATION** Oxford Univ, BA (Lit Humaniores), 50, BA(Russ), 52, MA, 53; Bristol Univ, PhD (Classics), 67. **CAREER** Master classics, Downside Sch, Bath, England, 55-69; assoc prof, 70-80, prof Classics, Univ Ill, Urbana, 80-, chmn dept, 81-85, Ed, Ill Class Studies, 81-87. **HONORS AND AWARDS** Awards, Vatican Int Latin Poetry Competition, 60, 63, 66, 97; Certamen Capitolinum, 68 & 80; assoc mem. **RESEARCH** Greek and Latin poetic traditions. **SELECTED PUBLICATIONS** Auth, Augustus and the new poetry, 67 & The concept of Vates in Augustan poetry, 67, Collection Latomus; Pushkin's Bronze horseman and the epic tradition, Comp Lit Studies, 72; co-ed, Serta Turyniana, 74; Univ Ill; Latin Compositions, 76, Golden Violence, 76 & Dislocated: An American Carnival, 77, Ex Aedibus, Urbana, Ill; De Novo Galli Fragmento in Nubia Eruto, Latinitas, 80. **CONTACT ADDRESS** 707 S Mathews Ave, Urbana, IL, 61801-3625. **EMAIL** j-newman@uiuc.edu

NEWMAN, KATHLEEN
DISCIPLINE AMERICAN STUDIES **EDUCATION** Yale Univ, PhD. **CAREER** History, Carnegie Mellon. **SELECTED PUBLICATIONS** Areas: Civil War medical photographs. **CONTACT ADDRESS** Carnegie Mellon Univ, 5000 Forbes Ave, Pittsburgh, PA, 15213.

NEWMAN, LEX
DISCIPLINE THE HISTORY OF MODERN PHILOSOPHY **EDUCATION** Irvine, PhD, 94. **CAREER** Asst prof, Univ Nebr, Lincoln, 94-; vis asst prof, Univ Pittsburgh, 96. **SE-**

LECTED PUBLICATIONS Auth, Descartes on Unknown Faculties and Our Knowledge of the External World, Philos Rev 103, 94; Descartes' epistemology, in The Stanford Encyclopedia of Philosophy, ed, Edward N Zalta, an online publication of Ctr for Stud of Lang and Infor, Stanford Univ, http://plato.stanford.edu/entries/descartes-epistemology, 97. **CONTACT ADDRESS** Univ Nebr, Lincoln, Lincoln, NE, 68588-0417.

NEWMAN, PETER C.

PERSONAL Born 05/10/1929, Vienna, Austria **DISCIPLINE** HISTORY/POLITICAL SCIENCE **EDUCATION** Univ Toronto, BA, 50, Inst Bus Admin, MCom, 54. **CAREER** Asst ed to prod ed, Financial Post, 51-55; asst ed to nat affairs ed, 56-63, ed, Maclean's mag, 71-83; ed to ed-in-chief, Toronto Star, 64-71; vis prof, polit sci, McMaster Univ, 69-71; vis prof, polit sci, York Univ, 79-80. **HONORS AND AWARDS** Nat Newspaper Award Jour, 71; Achievement Life Award, Encycl Britannia Publs, 77; off, 79, companion, Order Can, 90; Can Authors Asn Lit Award Non-fiction, 86. **RESEARCH** Canadian economic and political history. **SELECTED PUBLICATIONS** Auth, Flame of Power, 59; auth, Renegade in Power: The Diefenbaker Years, 63; auth, The Distemper of Our Times, 68; auth, Home Country-People, Places and Power Politics, 73; auth, The Canadian Establishment-Vol I, The Great Business Dynasties, 75; auth, Bronfman Dynasty: The Rothschilds of the New World, 78; auth, The Acquisitors: The Canadian Establishment, Vol II, 81; auth, The Establishment Man: A Portrait of Power, 82; auth, True North: Not Strong and Free-Defending the Peaceable Kingdom in the Nuclear Age, 83; auth, Company of Adventurers: An Unauthorized History of the Hudson's Bay Company, 3 vols, 85-91; auth, Sometimes A Great Nation: Will Canada belong to the 21st Century?, 88; auth, Empire of Bay, 89; auth, Portrait of a Promised Land: The Canadian Revolution from Deference to Defiance, 95; auth, Defining Moments: Dispatches from an Unfinished Revolution, 97; gen ed, Debrett's Illustrated Guide to the Canadian Establishment, 83. **CONTACT ADDRESS** 2568 W 1st Ave, Vancouver, BC, V6K 1G7.

NEWMAN, WILLIAM S.

PERSONAL Born 04/06/1912, Cleveland, OH, m, 1947, 1 child **DISCIPLINE** HISTORY OF MUSIC **EDUCATION** Western Reserve Univ, BS, 33, AM, 35, PhD, 39; Cleveland Inst Music, BS, 33. **CAREER** Asst choral dir, Western Reserv Univ, 34-36; teacher, sec schs, Ohio, 35-40 & 41-42; from asst prof to prof, 46-62, alumni distinguished prof, 62-77, Emer Prof Music, Univ Nc, Chapel Hill, 77-, Instr, Cleveland Music Sch Settlement, 37-38; lectr, Teachers Col, Columbia Univ, 40; Carnegie res grants, 47 & 48; Guggenheim fel, 60-61; Am Coun Learned Soc grants-in-aid, 60-62; Nat Endowment for Humanities sr fel, 72-73, 75 & 77-78. **MEMBERSHIPS** Music Teachers Nat Asn; Music Educ Nat Cong; Am Musicol Soc (vp, 68-69, pres, 69-70); Music Libr Asn; Int Musicol Soc. **RESEARCH** History of the sonata; piano playing; music appreciation. **SELECTED PUBLICATIONS** Auth, The Pianist's Problems, Harper, rev ed, 56 & 74; Sonata in the Barogue Era, Univ NC, 59, 2nd ed, 66, rev ed, 72 & 82; Understanding Music, Harper, rev ed, 61 & 82; Sonata in the Classic Era, Univ NC, 63, rev ed, 72 & 82; Sonata Since Beethoven, Univ NC, 68, rev ed, 72 & 82; Performance Practices in Beethoven's Piano Sonatas, 71; Communications + Review of 'Beethoven on Beethoven' And Piano Playing in His Day - Comment, Notes, Vol 0050, 1993. **CONTACT ADDRESS** Dept of Music, Univ of NC, Chapel Hill, NC, 27514.

NEWMYER, STEPHEN THOMAS

PERSONAL Born 07/10/1948, Pittsburgh, PA, m, 1978 **DISCIPLINE** CLASSICS **EDUCATION** Duquesne Univ, BA, 70; Univ NC, Chapel Hill, PhD(classics), 76. **CAREER** Asst prof, 76-80, Assoc Prof Classics, Duquesne Univ, 80-, Fel, Inst Teaching Post-Bibl Found Western Civilization, Jewish Theol Sem Am, 78. **MEMBERSHIPS** Am Philol Asn; Vergilian Soc; Class Asn Middle West & South; Class Asn Atlantic States. **RESEARCH** Roman epic poetry; classical influence on later literature; medicine. **SELECTED PUBLICATIONS** Auth, Pessimistic Prometheus: A Comparison of Aeschylus and Robert Lowell, Helios, fall-winter 78-79, The Silvae of Statius: Structure and Theme, Brill, Leiden, 79; Ancient and Talmudic Medicine: A Course Description, Helios, winter-spring 79-80; Talmudic medicine: A Classicist's perspective, Judaism, 29: 360- 367; Robert Lowell and the weeping philosopher, Class and Mod Lit, winter 80; Talmudic medicine, Jewish Digest, 81; Charles Anthon: Knickerbocker scholar, Class Outlook, 12-181-82; Statius, 'Thebaid Ix' - English And Latin - Dewar,m, Editor- translator, American J of Philology, Vol 0113, 1992. **CONTACT ADDRESS** 119 S 21st St, Pittsburgh, PA, 15203.

NEWTON, ESTHER

PERSONAL Born 11/28/1940, New York, NY **DISCIPLINE** ANTHROPOLOGY **EDUCATION** Univ Mich, BA, 62; Univ Chicago, MA, 64, PhD, 68. **CAREER** Assoc Prof, Prof, 72 to 93-, SUNY Purchase; Asst Prof, 68-71, Queens College. **HONORS AND AWARDS** Ruth Benedict Prize; Gustavus Meyer Prize. **MEMBERSHIPS** AAA **RESEARCH** Gay and Lesbian History and Culture. **SELECTED PUBLICATIONS** Auth, Cherry Grove, Fire Island: Sixty Years in America's First Gay and Lesbian Town, Boston, Beacon Press, 93; coauth, Women-friends, NY, Friends Press, 76; Dick(less) Tracys' and the Homecoming Queen: Lesbian Power and Representation In Gay Male Cherry Grove, in: Ellen Lewin, ed, Inventing Lesbian Cultures in America, Beacon Press, 96; My Best Informant's Dress: The Erotic Equation in Fieldwork, in: Cultural Anthropology, 93, reprinted in Ellen Lewin and Wm Leap, eds, Out In the Field: Reflections of Lesbian and Gay Anthropologists, Urbana IL, U of IL Press, 94. **CONTACT ADDRESS** Division of Social Science, SUNY Purchase, 735 Anderson Hill Rd, Purchase, NY, 10577. **EMAIL** newton@purchase.edu

NEWTON, JAMES E.

PERSONAL Born 07/03/1941, Bridgeton, NJ, m, 1967 **DISCIPLINE** AFRICAN-AMERICAN STUDIES **EDUCATION** NC Central Univ, BA 1966; Univ of NC, MFA 1968; IL State Univ, PhD 1972. **CAREER** Univ of NC, art instr 1967-68; W Chester State Coll PA, asst prof art 1968-69; IL State Univ Normal, asst prof art 1969-71; Western IL Univ Macomb, asst prof art 1971-72; Univ of DE Newark, asst prof ed 1972-73; UNIV OF DE NEWARD, PROF, DIR BLACK AMER STUDIES 1973-. **HONORS AND AWARDS** Exhibitions, Natl Print & Drawing Show 11th Midwest Bienniel Exhib 1972; 1st prize Sculpture & Graphics 19th Annual Exhib of Afro-Amer Artists 1972; 23rd Annual Mid-States Art Exhibit 1972; Purchase Awd 13th Reg Art Exhibit Univ of DE 1974; DE Afro-Amer Art Exhib 1980; Exhibited Lincoln Univ, West Chester State Coll, FL A&M Univ, DE State Coll, Dover DE; Excellence in Teaching Award Univ of Delaware 1988; EasternRegion Citation Award Phi Deltappa National Sorority 1989; Wilmington News Journal, Hometown Hero Award 1990; Jefferson Award, Amer Inst for Public Service. **MEMBERSHIPS** Mem edit bd, Natl Art Ed Assoc; Editorial board Education 1974-; mem exec counselor Assoc Study Afro-Amer Life & History 1976-77; bd mem Western Journal of Black Studies 1983-; bd mem past chairman Walnut St YMCA Delaware 1983-; State Dir Assn for the Study of Afro-American Life & History 1988-. **SELECTED PUBLICATIONS** Publ, College Student Jrnl, Jrnl of Negro Ed, Negro History Bulletin, Crisis, Education, Clearing House; books, A Curriculum Eval of Black Amer Studies in Relation to Student Knowledge of Afro-Amer History & Culture R&E Assoc Inc 1976, Roots of Black Amer; aduio-tapes Slave Aritsans & Craftsmen, Contemporary Afro-Amer Art Miami-Dade Comm Coll 1976. **CONTACT ADDRESS** Col of Urban Affairs & Public Policy & Professor of Black American Studies, Univ of Delaware, 417 Ewing Bldg, Newark, DE, 19711.

NEWTON, MERLIN OWEN

PERSONAL Born 02/16/1935, Ashland, AL, m, 1958, 3 children **DISCIPLINE** POLITICAL HISTORY **EDUCATION** Tulane Univ, MA, Hist, 58; Univ Ala, PhD, 92. **CAREER** RETIRED, HUNTINGDON COLL, 95. **MEMBERSHIPS** Ala Hist Soc; Souther Hist Soc **RESEARCH** Constitutional issues. **SELECTED PUBLICATIONS** Armed With the Constitution: Jehovah's Witnesses in Alabama and the U.S. Supreme Court, 1939-1946, Univ Ala Press, 95; "Roscoe Jones and Alabama Judiciary," Ala Rev, 96. **CONTACT ADDRESS** 4519 W Terict, Montgomery, AL, 36106.

NEWTON, WESLEY PHILLIPS

PERSONAL Born 04/02/1925, Montgomery, AL, m, 1958, 3 children **DISCIPLINE** HISTORY **EDUCATION** Univ Mo, AB, 49; Univ Ala, MA, 53, PhD(hist), 64. **CAREER** Asst prof soc sci, Ala Col, 64; from asst prof to assoc prof, 64-74, Prof Hist, Auburn Univ, 74-. **MEMBERSHIPS** Latin Am Studies Asn; Southern Hist Asn; Southeastern Coun Latin Am Studies (pres, 80-81). **RESEARCH** United States-Latin American diplomatic history; history of aviation in Latin America and the United States; military history. **SELECTED PUBLICATIONS** Coauth, Air Force Combat Units of World War II, Watts, 64; auth, International aviation rivalry in Latin America, 1919- 1927, JInter-Am Studies, 65; The role of the Army air arm in Latin America, 1922-1931, Air Univ Rev, 967; Lindbergh comes to Alabama, Ala Rev, 73; The third flight: Charles A Lindbergh and aviation diplomacy in Latin America, J Am Aviation Hist Soc, summer 75; Bertram (Bert) Blanchard Acosta, In: Dictionary of American Biography, Supplement Five, 1951-1955, 77; The Perilous Sky: United States Aviation Diplomacy and Latin America, 1919- 1931, Univ Miami, 78; coauth (with W David Lewis), Delta: The History of an Airline, Univ Ga, 79; Storm Over Iraq - Air Power And The Gulf-war - Hallion,rp, Technology And Culture, Vol 0035, 1994. **CONTACT ADDRESS** Dept of Hist, Auburn Univ, Auburn, AL, 36830.

NEYLAND, LEEDELL WALLACE

PERSONAL Born 08/04/1921, Gloster, MS, m **DISCIPLINE** HISTORY **EDUCATION** Virginia State College, AB, 1949; New York University, MA, 1950, PhD, 1959. **CAREER** Leland Coll Baker LA, professor of social science, dean of college, 1950-52; Grambling Coll, associate professor of social sciences, 1952-58; Elizabeth City Coll, dean, 1958-59; Florida A&M University, professor of history, dean of humanities/social science, 1959-84, College of Arts and Sciences, dean, 1968-82, vice pres for academic affairs, 1982-85; CONSULTANT, LECTURER ON BLACK HISTORY AND EDUCATION, currently. **HONORS AND AWARDS** Carnegie Grant, 1965. **MEMBERSHIPS** Co-chairman, Governor's Dr Martin Luther King Jr Commemorative Celebration Commission, 1985-87; member, board of directors, Leon County/Tallahassee Chamber of Commerce, 1984-86; vice chairman, Tallahassee Preservation Board, 1984-88; member, Presbyterian National Committee on the Self-Development of People, currently; member, Florida Historial Records Advisory Board, currently; member, Phi Beta Sigma; member, Sigma Pi Phi; member, 32 Degree Mason, Modern Free and Accepted Masons of the World. **SELECTED PUBLICATIONS** Author, Unquenchable Black Fires, Leney Educational and Publishing Inc, 1994. Co-author: History of Florida A&M University, 1963; Twelve Black Floridians, 1970; History of the Florida State Teachers Assn, 1977; History of the Florida Interscholastic Assn, 1982; Florida A&M University: A Centennial History, 1887-1987, 1987; Historical Black Land-Grant Institutions and the Development of Agriculture and Home Economics, 1890-1990, 1990; author of numerous articles appearing in professional publications. **CONTACT ADDRESS** Florida A&M Univ, Tallahassee, FL, 32307.

NG, ON-CHO

PERSONAL Born 01/29/1953, Hong Kong, m, 1995 **DISCIPLINE** HISTORY, RELIGIOUS STUDIES **EDUCATION** Univ HI, PhD, 86. **CAREER** Vis asst prof, Univ CA, Riverside, 86-89; asst prof, 89-95, assoc prof, PA State Univ, 95-. **MEMBERSHIPS** Am Academy of Relig; Asn for Asian Studies; Soc for Comparative and Asian Philos; Soc of Chinese Religions. **RESEARCH** Intellectual hist of late Imperial China; 16th-18th centuries; Confucian tradition. **SELECTED PUBLICATIONS** Auth, Revisiting Kung Tzu-chen's (1792-1841) Chin-wen (New Text) Precepts: An Excursion in the History of Ideas, J of Oriental Studies, 31-2, fall 93; A Tension in Ch'ing Thought: Historicism in Seventeenth and Eighteenth Century Chinese Thought, J of the History of Ideas, 54-4, Oct 93; Hsing (Nature) as the Ontological Basis of Practicality in Early Ch'ing Ch'eng-Chu Confucianism: Li Kuang-ti's (1642-1718) Philosophy, Philos East and West 44-1, Jan 94; Mystical Oneness and Meditational Praxis: Religiousness in Li Yong's (1627-1703) Confucian Thought, J of Chinese Religions, no 22, fall 94; Mid-Ch'ing New Text (Chin-wen) Classical Learning and Its Han Provenance: The Dynamics of a Tradition of Ideas, East Asian History, no 8, Dec 94; Interpreting Qing Thought in China as a Period Concept: On the Construction of an Epochal System of Ideas, Semiotica: J of the Int Asn for Semiotic Studies, 107-3/4, 95; Is Emotion (Qing) the Source of a Confucian Antimony?, J of Chinese Philos, 98; Imagining Boundaries: Changing Confucian Doctrines, Texts, and Hermeneutics, co-ed with Kai-wing Chow and John Henderson, SUNY, March 99; and two book chapters. **CONTACT ADDRESS** History Dept, Pennsylvania State Univ, University Park, PA, 16802. **EMAIL** oxn1@psu.edu

NICHOL, TODD W.

DISCIPLINE CHURCH HISTORY **EDUCATION** St. Olaf Col, BA, 74; Luther Sem, MDiv, 78; Grad Theol Union, ThD, 88. **CAREER** Instr, 83; assoc prof, 91-; dir grad stud (s), 91-93. **HONORS AND AWARDS** Grad fel, Univ Minn; awd of commendation, Concordia Hist Inst., Asst pastor, Christ Eng Lutheran Church, 79-80; assoc pastor, interim sr pastor, St. Philip's Lutheran Church, 84-86. **SELECTED PUBLICATIONS** Ed, transl, Vivacious Daughter: Seven Lectures on the Religious Situation Among the Norwegians in America, by H.A. Preus, 90; co-ed, Called and Ordained: Lutheran Perspectives on the Office of the Ministry, 90. **CONTACT ADDRESS** Dept of Church History, Luther Sem, 2481 Como Ave, St. Paul, MN, 55108. **EMAIL** tnichol@luthersem.edu

NICHOLLS, DAVID

PERSONAL Born 11/19/1955, Birmingham, England, m, 1984, 2 children **DISCIPLINE** MUSIC **EDUCATION** Cambridge Univ BA 78, MA, 82, PhD, 86. **CAREER** 84-87 Keasbey Fel, Am Stud, Selwyn Col, Cambridge; Keele Univ 87-, prof, 95-. **HONORS AND AWARDS** 1st class honours, 78. **MEMBERSHIPS** Sonneck Soc Am Music, 87-; Am Musicol Soc, 97-. **RESEARCH** 20th-Century Am Radical Music. **CONTACT ADDRESS** Dept of Music, Keele Univ, Staffordshire, ., ST5 5BG. **EMAIL** mua02@cc.keele.ac.uk

NICHOLLS, MICHAEL LEE

PERSONAL Born 09/10/1944, Des Moines, IA, m, 1966 **DISCIPLINE** AMERICAN HISTORY **EDUCATION** Cedarville Col, BA, 66; Univ Dayton, MA, 67; Col William & Mary, PhD(Am hist), 72. **CAREER** Asst prof, 70-80, Assoc Prof Am Hist, Utah State Univ, 80-. **MEMBERSHIPS** Orgn Am Historians; Southern Hist Asn. **RESEARCH** Early American history; American social history; American economic history. **SELECTED PUBLICATIONS** Co-auth, The Mormon Genealogical Society and Research Opportunities in Early American History, William & Mary Quart, 75; ed, News from Monrovia, VA Mag Hist & Biog, 77; co-ed, Legacies of the American Revolution, Utah State Univ, 78; auth, In the Light of Human Beings, VA Mag Hist & Biog, 81; Old Southampton - Politics And Society in a Virginia County, 1834- 1869 - Crofts,dw, J of Southern History, Vol 0060, 1994; Encyclopedia of The North-American Colonies - Cooke,je, Western Historical Quarterly, Vol 0026, 1995; Slavery in North- carolina, 1748-1775 - Kay,mlm, Cary,ll, William And Mary Quarterly, Vol 0053, 1996. **CONTACT ADDRESS** Dept of Hist, Utah State Univ, Logan, UT, 84321.

NICHOLS, JALDEN
PERSONAL Born 02/28/1919, Westerly, RI, m, 1946, 3 children **DISCIPLINE** MODERN EUROPEAN HISTORY **EDUCATION** Wesleyan Univ, BA, 41; Columbia Univ, MA, 48, PhD(mod Europ hist), 51. **CAREER** From instr to asst prof hist, Wesleyan Univ, 48-61; asst prof, Skidmore Col, 50-51; Ford Found Fund Advan Educ fac fel, 51-52; ed soc sci & humanities, Col Dept, Ginn & Co, Boston, 52- 59; assoc prof, 61-67, Prof Hist, Univ IL, Urbanachampaign, 67-, Managing ed, Daedalus, 59-61. **MEMBERSHIPS** AHA **RESEARCH** German history, 1890-1914. **SELECTED PUBLICATIONS** Auth, Germany After Bismarck: The Caprivi Era, 1890-1894, Harvard Univ, 58; Bismarck, In: Vol II, Interpreting European History, Dorsey, 67; German Foreign-policy, 1890-1894 - From Bismarck Balance-of-power Policy to Caprivi Alliance Strategy - German - Lahme,r, J of Modern History, Vol 0066, 1994. **CONTACT ADDRESS** Dept of Hist, Univ of Ill Urbana-Champaign, Urbana, IL, 61801.

NICHOLS, JOHN A.
PERSONAL Born 09/13/1939, New Kensington, PA, m, 1963, 1 child **DISCIPLINE** HISTORY **EDUCATION** Geneva Col, BA, 62; Fairleigh Dickinson Univ, MA, 66; Kent State Univ, PhD(medieval hist), 74. **CAREER** Teacher English, Franklin High Sch, NJ, 62-63; teacher hist, Mt Lakes High Sch, 63-66; from instr to assoc prof, 66-79, dean chemn soc sci & behav sci, 77-78, prof 79-, chemn hist, Slippery Rock Univ, 98-; vis prof, Mansfield Col, Oxford Univ, 84-85; pres, Conf Medieval & Renaissance cultures, 85-97, int summer prog dir, Florence, Italy, 89, Istanbul, Turkey, 93; fel Centre Europeen de Recherches sur les Congregations ed Ordres Religieux, 87. **HONORS AND AWARDS** Nat Endowment for Humanities grant, 76 & 80; SRU Learning Tech Award, 98; Fac Prof Development Coun Grant, 96, Honors Course, 94, Pa State System of Higher Ed; SRU Apple Polishing Award for Best Prof, 95; IBM Multimedia Teaching Award, 92; SRU Int Studies Prof Travel Award, 92, SRU Int Prof Developmental Award, 90. **MEMBERSHIPS** Am Catholic Hist Asn, 87-; Am Hist Asn, 83-; Asn of Cistercian Scholars, 73-; Medieval Acad of Am, 67-. **RESEARCH** Women's studies; medieval history. **SELECTED PUBLICATIONS** Auth, The architectural and physical features of an English Cistercian nunnery, Cistercian Ideals & Reality, 78; The internal organization of English Cistercian nunneries, Citeaux: Commentarii Cistercienses, 78; Why found a Cistercian Nunnery?, Mediaevalia, 79; Medieval English Cistercian Nunneries Their Art and Physical Remains, Melanges Dimier, 81; Distant Echoes: Medieval Religious Women, 84; Peaceweavers: Medieval Religious Women, 87; Why found a medieval Cistercian Nunnery?, Medieval Prosopography, 91; Cistercian Monastic Women: And Introduction to Hidden Springs, Cistercian Studies Quarterly, 93; Medieval Art of Sinningthwaite Nunnery, Studies in Cistercian Art & Archit; Cistercian nuns in Twelfe and Thirteenth Century England, Hidden Springs, 95; The cistercian Nunnery of Swine Priory: Its Church and Choir Stalls, Studiosorum Speculum, 93; co-ed, Hidden Springs: Cistercian Monastic Women, 95. **CONTACT ADDRESS** History Dept, Slippery Rock State Univ, 14 Maltby Dr, Slippery Rock, PA, 16057-1326. **EMAIL** john.nichols@sru.edu

NICHOLS, MARY P.
DISCIPLINE CLASSICS **EDUCATION** Chicago Univ, PhD. **CAREER** Prof, Fordham Univ. **SELECTED PUBLICATIONS** Auth, Socrates and the Political Community: An Ancient Debate, 87; Citizens and Statesmen: A Study of Aristotle's Politics, 92. **CONTACT ADDRESS** Dept of Class Lang and Lit, Fordham Univ, 113 W 60th St, New York, NY, 10023.

NICHOLS, ROGER L.
PERSONAL Born 06/13/1933, Racine, WI, m, 1959, 4 children **DISCIPLINE** UNITED STATES HISTORY **EDUCATION** Wis State Col, La Crosse, BS, 56; Univ Wis, MS, 59, PhD(US hist), 64. **CAREER** From instr to asst prof hist, Wis State Univ, Oshkosh, 63-65; assoc prof, Univ Ga, 65-69; assoc prof, 69-70, prof hist, Univ Az, 70-, res fel, Henry E. Huntington Libr & Art Gallery, 73; vis lectr hist, Univ Md, 75-76. **HONORS AND AWARDS** Senior Fulbright Lecturer, Martin Luther Univ, Halle, Germany, 97. **MEMBERSHIPS** AHA; Orgn Am Historians; Western Hist Asn; fel Am Philos Soc; Soc Hist Early Am Repub. **RESEARCH** American westward movement; 19th century United States frontier military history; American Indian history. **SELECTED PUBLICATIONS** Auth, General Henry Atkinson, 65 & Missouri Expedition, 1818-1820, 69, Univ Okla; co-ed, The American Indian: Past and Present, Xerox, 71; coauth, Stephen Long and American Scientific Exploration, Univ Del, 80; Natives and Strangers: Ethnic Groups and the Rise of Modern America, Oxford Univ, 79; ed, The American Indian: Past and Present, Wiley, 81; ed, The American Indian: Past and Present, Knopf, 86; McGraw-Hill, 92; ed, American Frontier and Western Issues: A Historigraphical Review, Greenwood, 86; co-auth, Natives and Strangers: Blacks, Indians, and Immigrants in America, Oxford Univ, 90; auth, Black Hawk and the Warrior's Path, Harlan Davidson, 92; co-auth, Natives and Strangers: A Multicultural History of Americans, Oxford Univ, 96; auth, Indians in the United States and Canada: A Comparative History, Univ Nebr, 98. **CONTACT ADDRESS** Dept of Hist, Univ of Ariz, Tucson, AZ, 85721-0001. **EMAIL** Roger-Nichols@ns.Arizona.edu

NICHOLSON, JOHN H.
PERSONAL Born 01/11/1958, Atlanta, GA **DISCIPLINE** CLASSICS **EDUCATION** Univ South, BA, 80; Univ Ga, MA, 86; Univ NC, PhD, 91. **CAREER** Asst prof, Univ Del, 91-98; instr, Univ Ga, 98-. **HONORS AND AWARDS** Fourmy Classical Scholar, 86-89. **MEMBERSHIPS** Am Philol Asn **RESEARCH** Latin literature **SELECTED PUBLICATIONS** Auth, Cicero's Return from Exile, 92; auth, The Delivery and Confidentiality of Cicero's Letters, 94; auth, Goats and Gout in Catullus 71, 97; auth, The Survival of Cicero's Letters, 98. **CONTACT ADDRESS** Dept of Classics, Univ of Georgia, Park Hall, Athens, GA, 30602. **EMAIL** jhn@arches.uga.edu

NICHOLSON, NIGEL
PERSONAL Born 10/30/1968, Aldershot, United Kingdom, m, 1996 **DISCIPLINE** CLASSICS **EDUCATION** Oxford Univ, BA, 90; Univ Penn, MA, PhD, 94. **CAREER** Asst prof, Wellesley Col, 94-95; asst prof, Reed Col, 95- . **HONORS AND AWARDS** Sunderland Prize, 90; first class honors, 90; William Penn Fel, 90-93; Dean's Scholar, 91; Andrew W. Mellon Diss Fel, 93-94. **MEMBERSHIPS** Am Philol Asn; Class Asn of the Pacific Northwest. **RESEARCH** Archaic Greek lyric poetry. **SELECTED PUBLICATIONS** Auth, The Truth of Pederasty: A Supplement to Foucault's Genealogy of the Relation between Truth and Desire in Ancient Greece, Intertexts, 98; auth, Victory without Defeat? Carnival Laughter and its Appropriation in Pindar's Victory Odes, in Barta, ed, Carnivalizing Difference: Bakhtin and the Other, Harwood, 98; auth, Bodies Without Names, Names Without Bodies: Propertius 1.21-22, Class J, forthcoming. **CONTACT ADDRESS** Classics Dept, Reed Col, 3203 SE Woodstock Blvd, Portland, OR, 97202. **EMAIL** nigel.nicholson@reed.edu

NICKELS, CAMERON C.
PERSONAL Born 08/20/1941, Sabetha, KS, 2 children **DISCIPLINE** AMERICAN SUTDIES, LITERATURE **EDUCATION** Ft Hays State Univ, Ba, 62; Southern IL Univ, MA, 64; Univ MN, PhD, 71. **CAREER** Instr Eng, Cent MO State Univ, 64-67; assoc prof, 71-82, Prof Eng, James Madison Univ, 82, Nat Endowment for Hum, summer sem, 79. **MEMBERSHIPS** MLA; Am Studies Asn; SAtlantic Mod Lang Asn; Am Humor Studies Asn. **RESEARCH** Am humor; early Am lit; nineteenth-century Am cult. **SELECTED PUBLICATIONS** Auth, Seba Smith embattled, Maine Hist Soc Quart, 73; contribr, The Oldest Revolutionary: Essays on Benjamin Franklin, Univ Pa, 76; ed, An early version of The Tar Baby story, J Am Folklore, 81; The idology of early New England Humor, Early Am Lit, 82; auth, New England Humor, From the Revolutionalry war to the civil war, 93; ed, To Wit, newsltr, 91. **CONTACT ADDRESS** Dept of Eng, James Madison Univ, 800 S Main St, Harrisonburg, VA, 22807-0002. **EMAIL** nickelcc@jmu.edu

NICKELSBURG, GEORGE WILLIAM ELMER
PERSONAL Born 03/15/1934, San Jose, CA, m, 1965, 2 children **DISCIPLINE** NEW TESTAMENT & CHRISTIAN ORIGINS, EARLY JUDAISM **EDUCATION** Valparaiso Univ, BA, 55; Concordia Sem, St Louis, BD, 60, STM, 62; Harvard Div Sch, ThD, 68. **CAREER** From Asst Prof to Prof Relig, 69-98, Daniel J. Krumm Distinguished Prof New Testament and Reformation Studies, Univ Iowa, 98-; Guest lectr, Concordia Sem, St Louis, 68, instr, 69; guest prof, Christ-Sem-Seminex, 79; vis scholar, Univ Munster, 74; assoc ed, Cath Bibl Quart, 79-. **HONORS AND AWARDS** Fel, John Simon Guggenheim Mem Found, 77-78; Fel, Netherlands Inst Advan Study, 80-81; Fel, Human Sci Res Coun of SAfrica, 93. **MEMBERSHIPS** Soc Bibl Lit; Studiorum Novi Testamenti Societas; Cath Bibl Asn. **RESEARCH** The synoptic gospels; New Testament christology; history and literature of early post-biblical Judaism. **SELECTED PUBLICATIONS** Auth, Resurrection, Immortality and Eternal Life in Intertestamental Judaism, Harvard/Oxford, 72; ed, Studies on the Testament of Abraham, Scholars Press, 76; auth, Apocalyptic and myth in 1 Enoch 6-11, J Bibl Lit, 77; collabr, A Complete Concordance to Flavius Josephus, Vol 3, Brill, 79; auth, The genre and function of the markan passion narrative, Harvard Theol Rev, 80; Jewish Literature between the Bible and the Mishnah, Fortress, 81; Enoch, Levi and Peter, recipients of revelation in Upper Galilee, J Bibl Lit, 81; coauth, Faith and Piety in Early Judaism, Fortress, 83. **CONTACT ADDRESS** Sch of Relig, Univ of Iowa, Gilmore Hall, Iowa City, IA, 52242-1376. **EMAIL** george-nickelsburg@uiowa.edu

NICKLES, THOMAS
DISCIPLINE HISTORY AND PHILOSOPHY OF SCIENCE **EDUCATION** Princeton Univ, PhD, 69. **CAREER** Prof, Univ Nev, Reno. **RESEARCH** Knowledge pollution; historicism. **SELECTED PUBLICATIONS** Contributed to How to Take the Naturalistic Turn, Univ Chicago, 93; recent publications in Soc Stud of Sci; Isis; Brit J for the Philos of Sci; Biol and Philos. **CONTACT ADDRESS** Univ Nev, Reno, Reno, NV, 89557. **EMAIL** nickles@unr.edu

NIEMEYER, GLENN ALAN
PERSONAL Born 01/14/1934, Muskegon, MI, m, 1955, 3 children **DISCIPLINE** MODERN AMERICAN HISTORY **EDUCATION** Calvin Col, BA, 55; Mich State Univ, MA, 59, PhD, 62. **CAREER** Teacher, Grand Haven Christian Sch, 55-58; asst instr, 59-62, Mich State Univ; asst instr Am hist, 62-63, from asst prof to prof, 63-70, dean col arts & sci, 70-73, vpres cols, 73-76, prof Am Hist, 70-, vpres acad affairs, 76-, provost, 80-, Grand Valley State Univ. **MEMBERSHIPS** AHA; Orgn Am Historians; Am Assn Higher Educ. **RESEARCH** Twentieth century American political and economic history; biography. **SELECTED PUBLICATIONS** Auth, Automotive Career of Ransom E. Olds, Mich State Univ, 63; art, The Curved Dash Oldsmobile, Bus Topics, autumn 63; art, Oldsmar for Health, Wealth, Happiness, Fla Hist Quart, 7/76; coauth, The General of General Motors, Am Heritage, 8-73. **CONTACT ADDRESS** Dept of History, Grand Valley State Univ, 1 Campus Dr, Allendale, MI, 49401-9401. **EMAIL** niemeyeg@gvsu.edu

NIEMI, BOB
DISCIPLINE AMERICAN POPULAR CULTURE AND FILM **EDUCATION** Univ MA, PhD. **CAREER** Eng, St. Michaels Col. **SELECTED PUBLICATIONS** Auth, Bibliography of Weldon Kees. **CONTACT ADDRESS** St. Michael's Col, Winooski Park, Colchester, VT, 05439. **EMAIL** rniemi@smcvt.edu

NIESSEN, JAMES P.
PERSONAL Born 12/26/1952, Nutley, NJ, s **DISCIPLINE** HISTORY **EDUCATION** Notre Dame, BA, 75; Univ Indiana, MA, 79, PhD, 89; Univ Texas, M Lis, 94. **CAREER** Vis asst prof, 88-91, Univ S Miss; libr, history & foreign lang, 94-, Texas Tech Univ. **RESEARCH** East European hist, libraries & archives. **CONTACT ADDRESS** Libr, Texas Tech Univ, Lubbock, TX, 79409-0002. **EMAIL** lijpn@lib.ttu.edu

NIETO, JOSE CONSTANTINO
PERSONAL Born 04/07/1929, El Ferrol, Spain, m, 1959, 2 children **DISCIPLINE** HISTORY OF RELIGIOUS THOUGHT **EDUCATION** Univ Santiago, BS, 49; United Evangel Sem, Madrid, BD, 56; Princeton Theol Sem, ThM, 62, PhD(relig), 67. **CAREER** Pastor, Span Evangel Church, 58-61; from asst prof to assoc prof, 67-78, prof relig, 78-82, Mary S Geiger Prof Relig & Hist, Juniata Col, 82-. **MEMBERSHIPS** Am Soc Reformation Res; Sixteenth Century Studies Conf; Am Acad Relig; AAUP. **RESEARCH** Spanish 16th century religious thought, particularly reformation, humanism and mysticism. **SELECTED PUBLICATIONS** Auth, Juan de Valdes and the Origins of the Spanish and Italian Reformation, Librairie Droz, Geneva, 70 & transl, Madrid-Mexico, Fondo de Cultura Economica, 79; Mystic, Rebel, Saint: A study of St John of the Cross, Geneva, Droz, 79 & Spanish ed, Mistico, poeta, rebelde, Santo, En torno a San Juan de Cruz, Marid-Mexico, Fondo de Cultura Economica, 82; ed and auth introd notes, Valdes Two Catechisms, The Dialogue on Christian Doctrine and the Christian Instruction for Children, Coronado Press, 81; Sexuality And Confession - Sexual Solicitation on Trial Before The Holy-office 16th-century to The 19th-century - Spanish - Sarrionmora,a, Sixteenth Century J, Vol 0026, 1995; Correspondence of Enzinas,francisco,de - Spanish, Latin - Enzinas,fd, Garciapinilla,ij, Sixteenth Century J, Vol 0027, 1996. **CONTACT ADDRESS** Dept History, Juniata Col, 1700 Moore St, Huntingdon, PA, 16652-2196.

NIEWYK, DONALD LEE
PERSONAL Born 12/21/1940, Grand Rapids, MI **DISCIPLINE** MODERN EUROPEAN HISTORY **EDUCATION** Western Mich Univ, BA, 62; Tulane Univ, MA 64, PhD(hist), 68. **CAREER** Asst prof hist, Ithaca Col 68-72; Assoc Prof Hist, Southern Methodist Univ, 72-, Res grants, Col Ctr Finger Lakes, 69 & Southern Methodist Univ, 73; Am Philos Soc res grant, 74-. **MEMBERSHIPS** AHA; Southern Hist Asn. **RESEARCH** German political and social history since 1871; 20th century Europe; Jewish history. **SELECTED PUBLICATIONS** Auth, Socialist, Anti-Semite, and Jew, La State Univ, 71; The Economic and Cultural Role of the Jews in the Weimar RePubic, Yearbk XVI, Leo Baeck Inst, 71; Jews and the courts in Weimar Germany, Jewish Social Studies, 75; transl & ed, History and Criticism of the Marcan Hypothesis, T&T Clark, 80; auth, The Jews in Weimar Germany, La State Univ, 80; The Impact of Inflation and Depression on the German Jews, Yearbk XXVII, Leo Baeck Inst, 82; Anti-semitism - The Longest Hatred - Wistrich,rs, Historian, Vol 0055, 1993; The Renaissance of Jewish Culture in Weimar Germany - Brenner,m, American Historical Review, Vol 0102, 1997; Anatomy of The Auschwitz Death Camp - Gutman,y, Berenbaum,m, Holocaust And Genocide Studies, Vol 0011, 1997. **CONTACT ADDRESS** Dept of Hist, Southern Methodist Univ, P O Box 750001, Dallas, TX, 75275-0001.

NIGHTENGALE, ANDREA WILSON
DISCIPLINE CLASSICS **EDUCATION** BA, 81; Oxford Univ, MA, 84; Univ CA Berkeley, MA, 85; PhD, 89. **CAREER** Assc prof, Stanford Univ. **RESEARCH** Ancient philos, Greek and Latin lit, lit and philos of ecology. **SELECTED PUBLICATIONS** Auth, Writing/Reading a Sacred Text: A Literary Interpretation of Plato's Laws, Class Philol, 93; Towards an Ecological Eschatology: Plato and Bakhtin on Other Worlds and Times in Bakhtin and the Classics, Northwestern UP, 97; Aristotle on the 'Liberal' and 'Illiberal' Arts, Proceedings Boston Area Colloq Ancient Philos, 97; Genres in Dialogue: Plato

and the Construct of Philosophy, Cambridge, 95. **CONTACT ADDRESS** Stanford Univ, Bldg 20, Main Quad, Stanford, CA, 94305.

NIGHTINGALE, CARL
DISCIPLINE HISTORY **EDUCATION** Princeton Univ, PhD, 92. **CAREER** Asst prof, Univ MA Amherst. **RESEARCH** Recent Am hist. **SELECTED PUBLICATIONS** Auth, On the Edge: A History of Poor Black Children and their American Dreams, 93. **CONTACT ADDRESS** Dept of Hist, Univ Massachusetts Amherst, Mass Ave, Amherst, MA, 01003.

NIGOSIAN, SOLOMON ALEXANDER
PERSONAL Born 04/23/1932, Alexandria, Egypt **DISCIPLINE** HISTORY OF RELIGION **EDUCATION** Univ Toronto, BA, 68; McMaster Univ, MA, 70, PhD(relig), 75. **CAREER** Teaching asst relig, McMaster Univ, 69-71; lectr, 72-75, Asst Prof Relig, Univ Toronto, 75-, Lectr relig, Ctr Christian Studies, Toronto, 71-74 & York Univ, 71-73; consult films relig, Ont Educ Commun Authority, Toronto, 72-73; assoc ed, Armenian Missionary Asn Am, Inc, Paramus, NJ, 72-76; asst prof, Ont Col Art, Toronto, 78-79. **MEMBERSHIPS** Int Asn Hist Relig; Can Soc Study Relig; Am Acad Relig. **RESEARCH** History of interreligious interactions with specialization in the Near East. **SELECTED PUBLICATIONS** Auth, World Religions, Clark, Can, 74, Arnold, England, 75 & McDougall, Littel, 76; World Religions: An Idea Book for Teachers, Clark, Can, 74; The religions in Achaemenid Persia, 74-75 & Zoroastrianism in Fifth Century Armenia, 78, Studies Relig; Occultism in the Old Testament, Dorrance, 78; The challenge of religious pluralism, Ecumenist, 78; Dialoguing For Differences, al Mushin, 79; Modes of Worship, Bk Soc, Can, 81; What Is Scripture - Cantwellsmith,w, Studies in Religion- sciences Religieuses, Vol 0023, 1994. **CONTACT ADDRESS** Dept of Relig Studies, Univ of Toronto, Toronto, ON, M5S 1A1.

NIKELLY, ARTHUR G.
DISCIPLINE PSYCHOLOGY **EDUCATION** Roosevelt Univ, Chicago, BA 54, MA 55; Univ Ottawa CA, PhD 59. **CAREER** Univ IL Health Cen, assoc prof clin psychol 59. **MEMBERSHIPS** APA; IPA; NA Soc of Adlerian Psychol. **SELECTED PUBLICATIONS** Cultural Babel: The challenge of immigrants to the helping professions, Cultur Div and Mental Health, 97; Alternatives to the androcentric bias of personality disorders, Clinical Psychol and Psychotherapy; Drug Advertisements and the medicalization of unipolar depression in women, Health Care for Women Intl, 95; Alcoholism: Social as well as Psycho-medical problem: the missing big picture, Journal of Alcohol and Drug Education, 94. **CONTACT ADDRESS** Univ of Illinois Health Service, Urbana, IL, 61801.

NISCHAN, BODO
PERSONAL Born 05/03/1939, Berlin, Germany, m, 1968, 1 child **DISCIPLINE** RENAISSANCE AND REFORMATION HISTORY **EDUCATION** Yale Univ, BA, 61; Lutheran Theol Seminary, Philadelphia, BD, 65; Univ Pa, PhD(hist), 71. **CAREER** Asst prof, 69-77, Assoc Prof Hist, E Carolina Univ, 77-, Danforth Found assoc, 74; Am Philos Soc res grant hist, 76; Ger Acad Exchange Serv res grant, 77; grant, Herzog August Bibliothek, 78 & 81. **MEMBERSHIPS** AHA; Am Soc for Reformation Res; Am Soc Church Hist; Conf Group Cent Europ Hist; Sixteenth Century Studies Conf. **RESEARCH** History of the Reformation in Germany; the Thirty Years War; Calvinism in Brandenburg. **SELECTED PUBLICATIONS** Auth, Reformed Irenicism and the Leipzig Colloquy of 1631, Cent Europ Hist, 9: 3-26; Propaganda in an age of ideological division: The case of Saxony in the Thirty Years War, Jour Hist, 4: 23-29; Brandenburg's reformed rate and the Leipzig Manifesto of 1631, JRelig Hist, Vol 4, No 1; John Bergius: Irenicism and the beginning of official religious toleration in Brandenburg- Prussia, Church Hist (in prep); Civic Calvinism in Northwestern Germany and the Netherlands - 16th-century to the 19th-century - Schilling,h, Sixteenth Century J, Vol 0023, 1992; Lutheran Confessionalization in Germany - German - Rublack,hc, Editor, Archiv Fur Reformationsgeschichte-archive for Reformation History, Vol 0085, 1994; Religion and Governmental Power in the Palatinate Around the Year 1600 - the Chronicle by Lamm,marcus,zum 1544-1606, a Member of the Heidelberg Church Council 1544-1606 - German - Hepp,f, Sixteenth Century J, Vol 0025, 1994; Political Correspondence of the Duke and Elector Maurice-of-saxony, Vol 4 - May-26,1548 to January-8,1551 - German - Herrmann,j, Wartenberg,g, Editors, Sixteenth Century J, Vol 0026, 1995; Voracious Idols and Violent Hands - Iconoclasm in Reformation Zurich, Strasbourg, and Basel - Wandel,lp, Church History, Vol 0065, 1996; Village and Religion - Reformed Moral Discipline in Bern Communities During the Early-modern Era - German - Schmidt,hr, Central European History, Vol 0029, 1996; Demarcating Boundaries - Lutheran Pericopic Sermons in the Age of Confessionalization, Archiv Fur Reformationsgeschichte- archive for Reformation History, Vol 0088, 1997. **CONTACT ADDRESS** Dept of Hist, East Carolina Univ, Greenville, NC, 27834.

NISETICH, FRANK
PERSONAL Born 05/29/1942, Sacramento, CA, 2 children **DISCIPLINE** CLASSICAL PHILOLOGY **EDUCATION** Univ Calif, Berkeley, BA, 65, MA, 67; Harvard Univ, PhD(-class philol), 73. **CAREER** From instr to asst prof, 71-78, fac growth grant, 77, assoc to prof and chmn Classics, Univ Mass, Boston, 78-, vis asst classics, Yale Univ, 73-74. **HONORS AND AWARDS** Translation Award, 78; Chancellor's Distinguished Scholar Award, 81. **MEMBERSHIPS** Am Philol Asn. **RESEARCH** Classical philology; ancient Greek lyric poetry; tragedy; Callimachus. **SELECTED PUBLICATIONS** Auth, Olympian 1.8-11: An Epinician Metaphor, Harvard Studies Class Philol, 75; The Leaves of Triumph and Mortality, Trans Am Philol Asn, 77; Convention and Occasion in Isthm.2, Calif Studies in Class Antiquity, 77; Pindar's Victory Songs, Johns Hopkins Univ, 80; Immortality in Heragas, Class Philol, 88; Euripides, Orestes, Oxford Univ, 95. **CONTACT ADDRESS** Dept of Classics, Univ of Mass, 100 Morrissey Blvd, Boston, MA, 02125-3300. **EMAIL** Nisetich@umbsky.cc.umb.edu

NISH, CAMERON
PERSONAL Born 07/05/1927, Montreal, PQ, Canada, m, 1948, 1 child **DISCIPLINE** CANADIAN HISTORY **EDUCATION** Sir George Williams Univ, BA, 57; Univ Montreal, MA, 59; Univ Laval, DHist, 66. **CAREER** Lectr hist, Sir George Williams Univ, 60-62; charge of hist course, Royal Mil Col, 62-65; from asst prof to assoc prof, 65- 72, Prof Hist, Concordia Univ, 72-, Res dir Ctr rech hist econ du Can francais, 66-; Can Coun grant, 67-68; dir, Ctr Etud Quebec, 67-. **MEMBERSHIPS** Can Hist Asn; AHA. **RESEARCH** Economic and social history of New France; social structures of New France; ideologies in French Canada. **SELECTED PUBLICATIONS** Auth, The French Regime, 65 & Le Regime Francais, 67, Prentice-Hall; The Canadian bourgeoisis: Composition, character and functions, Report Can Hist Asn, 67; The French Canadians: Conquered? Half-Conquered or Liberated?, 67 & coauth, The Social Structure of New France, 68, Copp Clark; Education in New France - Magnuson,r, American Historical Review, Vol 0098, 1993. **CONTACT ADDRESS** Hist Dept, Concordia Univ, Montreal, Montreal, PQ, H3G 1M8.

NISHIMURA-JENSEN, JULIE M.
PERSONAL Born 07/26/1965, Berkeley, CA, m, 1993, 1 child **DISCIPLINE** CLASSICS **EDUCATION** Univ WI, Madison, PhD, 96. **CAREER** Asst prof of Classical Languages, AZ State Univ, 97-. **HONORS AND AWARDS** Col of Liberal Arts and Sciences Undergraduate Teaching Development Grant, ASU, 97-98; fac grant-in-aid of res, ASU, 97. **MEMBERSHIPS** Am Philol Asn; Classical Asn of the Middle West and South; Women's Classical Caucus. **RESEARCH** Hellenistic poetry; genre studies. **SELECTED PUBLICATIONS** Auth, The Poetics of Aethalides: Silence and Poikilia in Apollonius' Argonautica, Classical Quart, 98. **CONTACT ADDRESS** 445 Rogers Lane, Wallingford, PA, 19086. **EMAIL** jnishjen@hven.swartmore.edu

NISSENBAUM, STEPHEN W.
DISCIPLINE HISTORY **EDUCATION** Harvard Univ, BA, 61; Columbia Univ, MA, 63; Univ Wis, PhD, 68. **CAREER** PROF, HIST, UNIV MASS AMHERST **HONORS AND AWARDS** Finalist, Pulitzer Prize in Hist, 97. **MEMBERSHIPS** Am Antiquarian Soc **SELECTED PUBLICATIONS** Coauth, Salem Possessed: The Social Origins of Witchcraft, Harvard Univ Press, 74; auth, Sex, Diet, and Debility in Jacksonian America: Sylvester Graham and Health Reform, 80; auth, The Pursuit of Liberty, 84; auth, Introduction to Nathaniel Hawthorne, The Scarlet Letter and Other Writings, Modern Library Coll Edition, 84; auth, "Sexual Radicalism and the Contested Norm," in Making, Unmaking, and Remaking America: Popular Ideology before the Civil War, Quaderno I, 87; auth, "Christmas in Early New England, 1620-1820: Puritanism, Popular Culture, and the Printed Word," Procs of the AAS 106, 96; The Battle for Christmas, 96; auth, "Christmas Church Music in Early New England," Dublin Seminar in NE Folklife. **CONTACT ADDRESS** Dept Hist, Univ of Mass, Amherst, MA, 01003. **EMAIL** snissenbaum@history.umass.edu

NISSENBAUM, STEPHEN WILLNER
PERSONAL Born 01/13/1941, Jersey City, NJ, m, 1962, 4 children **DISCIPLINE** AMERICAN HISTORY **EDUCATION** Harvard Univ, AB, 61; Columbia Univ, MA, 63; Univ Wis-Madison, PhD, 68. **CAREER** Asst prof, 68-72, assoc prof, 72-79, prof hist, 79-, Univ Mass, Amherst; vis lectr, Smith Col, 73 & 76; vis lectr, Hampshire Col, 79, 94, 97; vis lectr, Mt Holyoke Col, 80, 98; NEH fel, 76-77, 91-92 & Charles Warren Ctr for Studies in Am Hist fel, Harvard Univ, 76-77, 94-95; Coun Am Studies Asn, 79-81, 97-00; New England Am Studies, vpres 78-81, pres 95-97; pres, Mass Found for the Hum, 87-89; Fulbright distinguished chair, Germany, 98-99. **HONORS AND AWARDS** John H Dunning Prize, Am Hist Asn, 74; finalist, Pulitzer Prize, history, 97. **MEMBERSHIPS** AHA; Orgn Am Historians; Am Studies Asn. **RESEARCH** American cultural history; American social history; history of the book. **SELECTED PUBLICATIONS** Ed, The Great Awakening at Yale College, 72; co-ed, Salem-Village Witchcraft: A Documentary Record of Local Conflict in Colonial New England, Wadsworth, 72; coauth, Salem Possessed: The Social Origins of Witchcraft, Harvard Univ, 74; co-ed, The Salem Witchcraft Papers, Da Cap Press, 77; auth, The Firing of Nathaniel Hawthorne, Essex Institute Historical Collections, 78; art, Sex, Diet, and Debility, Jacksonian America: Sylvester Graham and Health Reform, Greenwood Press, 80; coauth, All Over the Map: Rethinking American Region, Johns Hopkins, 95; auth, The Battle for Christmas, Knopf, 96. **CONTACT ADDRESS** Dept of History, Univ of Mass, Amherst, MA, 01003. **EMAIL** snissenbaum@history.umass.edu

NOBLE, DAVID WATSON
PERSONAL Born 03/17/1925, Princeton, NJ, m, 1944, 4 children **DISCIPLINE** AMERICAN INTELLECTUAL HISTORY **EDUCATION** Princeton Univ, AB, 48; Univ WI, MA, 49, PhD 52. **CAREER** From instr to assoc prof, 52-65, prof hist, Univ MN, Minneapolis, 65-, Lectr, Am Studies summer sem, Kyoto, Japan, 80. **HONORS AND AWARDS** Horace T Morse Award, Standard Oil Co Ind, 68. **MEMBERSHIPS** Am Studies Asn. **RESEARCH** Am intellectual and cult hist. **SELECTED PUBLICATIONS** Auth, The Paradox of Progressive Thought, 58 & Historians Against History, 65, Univ Minn; Eternal Adam and New World Garden, Braziller, 68; The Progressive Mind, Rand McNally, 70 & Burgess, 81; coauth, The Restless Centuries, Burgess, 73, 2nd ed, 79; The Free and the Unfree, Penquin, 77; Twentieth Century Limited, Houghton Mifflin, 80; The End of American History, 85. **CONTACT ADDRESS** Am Studies Program, Univ of MN, 72 Pleasant St S E, Minneapolis, MN, 55455-0270.

NOBLE, THOMAS FRANCIS XAVIER
PERSONAL Born 05/10/1947, Chicago, IL, m, 1967, 2 children **DISCIPLINE** MEDIEVAL HISTORY **EDUCATION** Ohio Univ, BA, 69; Mich State Univ, MA, 71, PhD(hist), 74. **CAREER** Instr hist, Albion Col, 75; instr humanities, Mich State Univ, 75-76; asst prof hist, Tex Tech Univ, 76-80; Asst Prof Hist, Univ VA, 80-. **MEMBERSHIPS** AHA; Medieval Acad Am; Am Cath Hist Asn; Archaeol Inst Am; Am Soc Church Hist. **RESEARCH** Carolingian history; early medieval Ecclesiastical history. **SELECTED PUBLICATIONS** Auth, The revolt of King Bernard of Italy in 817, Studi Medievali, 74; The Monastic Ideal as a model for empire, Rev Benedictine, 76; The place in Papal history of the Roman Synod of 826, Church Hist, 76; The Danish Frontier under Charlemagne and Louis the Pious, In: The Frontier: Comparative Studies, Vol IV, Univ Okla, 79; Louis the Pious and His Piety Re- reconsidered, Revue belge, 80; Papal Records in the Early- middle-ages - Diplomatic and Legal-historical Studies of the Letters of Gregory-the-great - German - Pitz,e, Speculum-a J of Medieval Studies, Vol 0068, 1993; The Formation of Europe, Ad840-1046 - German - Fried,j, Speculum-a J of Medieval Studies, Vol 0069, 1994; the Complete Works of Rather-of-verona - Reid,pld, Translator, Speculum-a J of Medieval Studies, Vol 0069, 1994; Emperor, Prefects and Kings - the Roman West, Ad395- 565 - Barnwell,ps, Speculum-a J of Medieval Studies, Vol 0069, 1994; The Peace of God - Social Violence and Religious Response in France Around the Year 1000 - Head,t, Landes,r, J of Interdisciplinary History, Vol 0025, 1995; The Ambiguity of the Book - Prince, Power, and People in Medieval Biblical Commentary - French - Buc,p, Church History, Vol 0064, 1995; The Germanization of Early-medieval Christianity - a Sociohistorical Approach to Religious Transformation - Russell,jc, American Historical Review, Vol 0100, 1995; History of Christianity from Apostolic Times to the Present, Vol 4 - Bishops, Monks, and Emperors Ad610-1054- French - Dagron,g, Riche,p, Vauchez,a, Editors, Speculum-a J of Medieval Studies, Vol 0071, 1996; Medieval France - an Encyclopedia - Kibler,ww, Zinn,g, Church History, Vol 0065, 1996; the Resurrection of the Body in Western Christianity, 240-1336 - Bynum,cw, American Historical Review, Vol 0101, 1996; The Church Triumphant - a History of Christianity up to Ad1300 - Hinson,eg, Church History, Vol 0066, 1997; Institutional Life in Medieval Europe - an Introduction - Italian - Ascheri,m, Speculum-a J of Medieval Studies, Vol 0072, 1997; Church Triumphant - a History of Christianity up to Ad1300 - Hinson,eg, Church History, Vol 0066, 1997; the 'Lives of the Ninth-century Popes' 'Liber Pontificalis' - the Ancient Biographies to 10 Popes from Ad817-891 - English, Latin - Davis,r, J of Ecclesiastical History, Vol 0048, 1997; The 'Lives of the Ninth-century Popes','Liber Pontificalis' - the Ancient Biographies to 10 Popes from Ad817-891 - English, Latin - Davis,r, J of Ecclesiastical History, Vol 0048, 1997; Institutional Life in Medieval Europe - an Introduction - Italian - Ascheri,m, Speculum-a J of Medieval Studies, Vol 0072, 1997. **CONTACT ADDRESS** Dept of Hist, Univ VA, 1 Cocke Hall, Charlottesville, VA, 22903-3248.

NOBLE, WILLIAM P.
PERSONAL Born 01/25/1932, New York, NY, m, 1998, 2 children **DISCIPLINE** LAW & HISTORY **EDUCATION** Lehigh Univ, BA, 54; Univ Penn, JD, 61. **CAREER** Instr, 86- , writing assessment mentor, 94- , Commun Col of Vermont; Ver Hum Scholar, Ver Coun on Hum, 91- ; adj fac, external degree prog, Johnson State Col, 93- . **HONORS AND AWARDS** Nominated for Eli Oboler Award, ALA Intellectual Freedom Roundtable, 92. **MEMBERSHIPS** Authors Guild; Freedom to Read Comt. **RESEARCH** Law; history; writing. **SELECTED PUBLICATIONS** Auth, Bookbanning in America, Eriksson, 90; auth, Show Don't Tell, Eriksson, 91; auth, Twenty-Eight

Most Common Writing Blunders, Writer's Digest, 92; auth, Conflict, Action & Suspense, Writer's Digest, 94; auth, The Complete Guide to Writers' Conferences and Workshops, Eriksson, 95; auth, Three Rules for Writing a Novel, Eriksson, 97. **CONTACT ADDRESS** PO Box 57, Salisbury, VT, 05769.

NOBLES, GREGORY H.
DISCIPLINE HISTORY **EDUCATION** Princeton Univ, BA, 70; Univ Mich, MA, 74, PhD, 79. **CAREER** Assoc prof, hist, tech & soc, and PROF & CHAIR, SCH HIST, TECH & SOC, GEORGIA TECH **MEMBERSHIPS** Am Antiquarian Soc **SELECTED PUBLICATIONS** Auth, Divisions Throughout the Whole: Politics and Society in Hampshire County, Massachusetts, 1740-1775, Cambridge Univ Press, 83; auth, "Breaking into the Backcountry: New Approaches to the Early American Frontier," Wm & Mary Quart 46, 89; auth, "Straight Lines and Stability: Mapping the Political Order of the Anglo-American Frontier," Jour of Am Hist 80, 93; auth, American Frontiers: Cultural Encounters and Continental Conquest, Hill & Wang, 97. **CONTACT ADDRESS** Hist, Tech, and Soc, Georgia Inst of Tech, Atlanta, GA, 30332-0345. **EMAIL** gregory.nobles@hts.gatech.edu

NODES, DANIEL J.
PERSONAL Born 11/01/1951, Hoboken, NJ, m, 1972, 2 children **DISCIPLINE** MEDIEVAL STUDIES **EDUCATION** St. Peter's Col, BA, 74; Univ NH, MA, 76; Univ Toronto, PhD, 82. **CAREER** Prof & dir, Grad Lib Studies, Hamline Univ, 96-; assoc prof & ch, Dept Class & Hum, Conception Sem Col, 87-96; asst prof, Sch Hum, Old Col, 82-87. **HONORS AND AWARDS** Andrew Mellon Fel, 96; NEH Fel, 95; NEH Summer Stipend, Villanova Univ, 94; NEH Summer Seminar, Univ Penn, 93. **MEMBERSHIPS** Medieval Acad Am; N Am Patristic Soc; Renaissance Soc Am; Am Philol Asn; Class Asn Minn; Am Asn Univ Prof. **RESEARCH** Late Antiquity; Patristic theology; poetry based on biblical themes; Classical Tradition; Medieval scholasticism; Renaissance humanism. **SELECTED PUBLICATIONS** Auth, Doctrine and Exegesis in Biblical Latin Poetry, 93; auth, Origin of Alexandria Among the Renaissance Humanists and Their Twentieth-Century Historians, Vetus Doctrina: Studies in Early Christianity in Honor of Fredric W, Schlatter, SJ, 98; auth, Homeric Allegory in Egidio of Viterbo's Reflections on the Human Soul, Recherches de Theol et Philos Medievales, 98; auth, Rhetoric and Cultural Synthesis in the Hexaemeron of George of Pisidia, Virgiliae Christianae, 96; auth, Humanism in the Commentary ad mentem Platonis of Giles of Viterbo, Augustiniana, 95; auth, Salvation by Abduction in Giles of Viterbo's Commentary ad mentem Platonis, Studi Umanistici Piceni, 93. **CONTACT ADDRESS** Graduate Liberal Studies, Hamline Univ, 1536 Hewitt Ave., MS A-1730, St. Paul, MN, 55104. **EMAIL** djnodes@hamline.edu

NOE, KENNETH W.
PERSONAL Born 11/09/1957, Richmond, VA, m, 1985, 1 child **DISCIPLINE** HISTORY **EDUCATION** Emory & Henry Col, BA, 79; Virginia Tech, MA, 81; Univ Kentucky, MSLS, 83; Univ of Ill, PhD, 90. **CAREER** Librn, Blue Ridge Regional Librn Martinsville, VA, 83-85; instr, Berea Col, 87-88; arch, Ill Hist Survey, Urbana, IL, 88-90; asst prof History, 90-95, ASSOC PROF HISTORY, 95-98, STATE UNIV W GA, 90-; Beta Phi Mu; Phi Alpha Theta; Phi Kappa Phi. **HONORS AND AWARDS** Tenn Hist Book Award, 96; Stud Govt Asn Fac Mem Yr, 96-97; J. David Griffin Tchg Award, 93. **MEMBERSHIPS** Orgn Am Hist; S Hist Asn; Appalachian Stud Asn; Ga Hist Asn. **RESEARCH** American Civil War in the Upper South especially Appalachia. **SELECTED PUBLICATIONS** Southwest Virginia's Railroad: Modernization and the Sectional Crisis, Urbana, 92; A Southern Boy in Blue, 96; The Civil War in Appalachia, Knoxville, 97. **CONTACT ADDRESS** History Dept, State Univ W Ga, Carrollton, GA, 30118. **EMAIL** knoe@westga.edu

NOEL, THOMAS JACOB
PERSONAL Born 05/06/1945, Cambridge, MA, m, 1973 **DISCIPLINE** AMERICAN HISTORY **EDUCATION** Univ Denver, BA, 66, MA, 69; Univ Colo, Boulder, PhD(hist), 78. **CAREER** Librn, Univ Calif, Riverside, 69; instr, Univ Denver, 75-78; Asst Prof Hist, Univ Colo, Denver, 81- & Dir Colo Studies Ctr, 81-. **MEMBERSHIPS** Western Hist Asn. **RESEARCH** Denver history; Colorado history; Rocky Mountain region history. **SELECTED PUBLICATIONS** Auth, Richthofen's Montclair: A Pioneer Denver Suburb, Pruett Pub, 78; Denver: Rocky Mountain Gold, Continental Heritage, 80; Denver Larimer Street: Main Street, skid row & urban renaissance, Hist Denver, Inc, 81; The City and The Saloon: Denver, 1858-1916, Univ Nebr Press, 82; coauth, A Colorado History, Pruett Pub Co (in press); Great Mysteries of the West - Szasz,fm, Western Historical Quarterly, Vol 0025, 1994; Seeking Pleasure in the Old West - Dary,d, New Mexico Historical Review, Vol 0071, 1996; From Skisport to Skiing - 100 Years of an American Sport, 1840-1940 - Allen,ejb, J of American History, Vol 0081, 1995; Strange Genius - the Life of Hayden,ferdinand,vandeveer - Foster,m, Western Historical Quarterly, Vol 0027, 1996. **CONTACT ADDRESS** 1245 Newport St, Denver, CO, 80220.

NOER, THOMAS JOHN
PERSONAL Born 11/29/1944, Emmetsburg, IA, m, 1968, 1 child **DISCIPLINE** AMERICAN HISTORY **EDUCATION** Gustavus Adolphus Col, BA, 66; Wash State Univ, MA, 68; Univ Minn, Phd(hist), 72. **CAREER** Asst prof hist, Univ Minn, Minneapolis, 72-73; asst prof, 73-77, ASSOC PROF HIST, CARTHAGE COL, 78-, Acad consult, Wis Humanities Comn, 77-; fel, Charles Warren Ctr Am Hist, Harvard Univ, 79-80; res grants, Am Philos Soc, 79 & Harry S Truman Inst, 79. **MEMBERSHIPS** AHA; Orgn Am Historians; Soc Hist Am Foreign Rel. **RESEARCH** American foreign policy; comparative racial attitudes, United States and Africa. **SELECTED PUBLICATIONS** Auth, The American government and the Irish question during World War I, S Atlantic Quart, winter 73; Commodore R W Shufeldt and America's South African strategy, Am Neptune, fall 74; Henry Kissinger's philosophy of history, Mod Age, spring 75; Briton, Boer, and Yankee: The US and Southern Africa, 1870-1914, Kent State Univ, 78; Segregation and the origins of Apartheid, Phylon, fall 78; The United States and black Africa, In: American Foreign Relations: A Historiographic Approach, Greenwood Press, 81; the Peace-corps in Cameroon - Amin,ja, J of American History, Vol 0079, 1993; Apartheid Reluctant Uncle - the United-states and Southern Africa in the Early Cold-war - Borstelmann,t, American Historical Review, Vol 0099, 1994; Foreign-relations of the United-states, 1955-1957, Vol 18, Africa - Glennon,jp, Shaloff,s, J of American History, Vol 0081, 1994; Rising Wind - Black-americans and Us Foreign-affairs, 1935-1960 - Plummer,bg, J of American History, Vol 0084, 1997. **CONTACT ADDRESS** Dept of Hist, Carthage Col, 2001 Alford Park Dr, Kenosha, WI, 53140-1994.

NOF, SHIMON Y.
PERSONAL Haifa, Israel, m, 1972, 2 children **DISCIPLINE** INDUSTRIAL ENGINEERING/ MANAGEMENT **EDUCATION** Technion, Israel Inst of Tech, BSC, 69, MSC, 72; Univ Mich, PhD, 76. **CAREER** Instr, 71-72 Shenkar Col, Israil; instr, 74-75, asst prof, 76, Univ Mich; sr lectr, 80-81, Tel Aviv Univ; vis res scholar, 89, MIT; Mendes France Vis Prof, 96-97, Technion; prof, 88-, Purdue Univ. **HONORS AND AWARDS** B.Sc & M.Sc with dist; Most Outstanding Book in Engineering, 85; Most Outstanding Ref Book in Science & Engineering, 88; Fel IIE; Omega Rho Intl Honor Soc. **MEMBERSHIPS** ACM; IIE; EFPR; IFAC; IFIP; SME. **RESEARCH** Design & control of prod systems, info technologies for indust systems; robotics & artificial intell in manuf. **SELECTED PUBLICATIONS** Auth and ed, Integration and Collaboration Models, Info & Collab Models of Integration, Kluwer Acad Pub, 94; ed, Information and Collaboration Models of Integration, Kluwer Acad Pub, 94; coauth, Cooperation Requirement Planning for Multiprocessors, Info & Collab Models of Integ, Kluwer Acad Pub, 94; coauth, Coordination and Integration Models for CIM Information, Knowledge Based Systems, World Scientific Pub, 97; coauth, Industrial Assembly, Chapman & Hall, 97; coauth, A Formalism to Structure and Parallelize the Integration of Cooperative Engineering Design Tasks, IIE Trans on Design and Manuf, 98; coauth, CIM Flexibility Measures: A Review and a Framework for Analysis and Applicability Assessment, Intl Jour of CIM, 97; coauth, A Client-Server Model for Integration and Collaboration in Production Testing, Inst Jour of Prod Res, 98; coauth, Application of Design and Control Tools in a Multi-Robot Cell, Computers & IE, 97; coauth, Object-Oriented Integration of Design and Manufacturing in a Laser Processing Cell, Intl Jour of CIM, 97; coauth, Integration and Adaptability Issues, Intl Jour of CIM, 97; coauth, Information Management for FMS and Non-FS Decision Support Integratio, Intl Jour of IE Applications and Practice, 98; auth, Book Review: Force and Touch Feedback for Virtual Reality, IIE Transaction on Operation Engg, 98; auth, Next Generation of Production Research: Wisdom, Collaboration and Society, Intl Jour of Prod Econ, 98; coauth, Communication Based Coordination Modeling in Distributed Manufacturing Systems, Intl Jour of Prod Econ, 98; coauth, Models of Material Handling and Robotics, Modeling Manufacturing Systems: From Aggregate Planning to Real Time Control, Springer-Verlag, 99; auth, handbook of Industrial Robotics, Wiley, 99; coauth, Computational, AI and Multi-Agent Techniques for Planning Robot Operations, Handbook of Indus Robotics, Wiley, 99; ed, Handbook of Industrial Robotics + CD-ROM, John Wiley & Sons, 99. **CONTACT ADDRESS** School of Industrial Eng, Purdue Univ, 1287 Grissom Hall, West Lafayette, IN, 47907-1287. **EMAIL** nof@ecn.purdue.edu

NOGEE, JOSEPH LIPPMAN
PERSONAL Born 06/16/1929, Schenectady, NY, m, 1960, 2 children **DISCIPLINE** POLITICAL SCIENCE **EDUCATION** Georgetown Sch of Foreign Serv, BSFS, 50; Univ Chicago, MA, 52; Yale Univ, PhD, 58. **CAREER** Prof, polit sci, Univ Houston, 58- ; vis prof NY Univ, 63, 64, Vanderbilt Univ, 69-70, US Army War Col, 79, 80, 84, 85, Rice Univ 82, 86, 87, 90, Univ Va, 88, 89. **HONORS AND AWARDS** NY State Regents fel; Overbrook Fel & Sterling Fel, Yale; Rockefeller grant; Carnegie Endowment grant; tchg excellence award, Univ Houston. **MEMBERSHIPS** Am Polit Sci Asn; Am Asn for Advanc Slavic Stud. **RESEARCH** Russian foreign policy. **SELECTED PUBLICATIONS** Auth, Soviet Policy Toward International Control of Atomic Energy, Notre Dame, 61; coauth, The Politics of Disarmament, Praeger, 62; ed, Man, State, and Society in the Soviet Union, Praeger, 72; co-ed, Congress, The Presidency, and American Foreign Policy, Pergamon, 81; ed, Soviet Politics: Russia after Brezhnev, Praeger, 85; coauth, Peace Impossible/War Unlikely, Little Brown, 88; coauth, Soviet Foreign Policy since World War II, Macmillan, 92; coauth, Russian Politics: The Struggle for a New Order, Allyn & Bacon, 97; coauth, Russian Foreign Policy, ME Sharpe, 98. **CONTACT ADDRESS** Dept of Political Science, Univ of Houston, Houston, TX, 77204. **EMAIL** jnogee@uh.edu

NOLAN, JANET
DISCIPLINE HISTORY **EDUCATION** Conn Univ, PhD, 86. **CAREER** Hist, Loyola Univ. **RESEARCH** Irish, Irish-American & oral history. **SELECTED PUBLICATIONS** Auth, The Great Famine and Women's Emigration from Ireland, in The Hungry Stream: Essays on Famine and Emigration, Belfast: Inst of Irish Stud/Queen's UP, 97; St. Patrick's Daughter: Amelia Dunne Hookway and Chicago's Public Schools, in At the Crossroads: Old St. Patrick's and the Chicago Irish, Chicago: Loyola UP, 97; The National Schools and Irish Women's Mobility in the Late Nineteenth and Early Twentieth Centuries, Irish Stud Review 18, 97; Patrick Henry in the Classroom: Margaret Haley and the Chicago Teachers' Federation, Eire-Ireland XXX:2, 95; L'extraordinaire aventure de l'emigration des femmes irlandaises 1885-1920, in Vers un ailleurs prometteur... l'emigration, une response universelle a une situation de crise, Paris and Geneva: Presses Universitaires de France, 93; Irish-American Teachers and the Struggle Over American Urban Education, 1890-1920, Rec Am Catholic Hist Soc Pa 103:3-4, 92. **CONTACT ADDRESS** Fine Arts Dept, Loyola Univ, Chicago, 6525 N. Sheridan Rd., Chicago, IL, 60626. **EMAIL** jnolan@luccpua.it.luc.edu

NOLAN, MARY
PERSONAL Born 01/17/1944, Chicago, IL, 2 children **DISCIPLINE** MODERN EUROPEAN & WOMEN'S HISTORY **EDUCATION** Smith Col, BA, 66; Columbia Univ, MA, 69, PhD, 75. **CAREER** Asst prof, Harvard Univ, 75-80; from Asst Prof to Assoc Prof, 80-92, prof hist, NY Univ, 92-. **RESEARCH** Modern German history; comparative working-class history. **SELECTED PUBLICATIONS** Auth, Social policy, economic mobilization and the working class in the Third Reich: A review of the literature, Radical Hist Rev, No 39, 77; Proletarischer anti-feminismus, Frauen und Wissenschaft Courage, Verlag, 77; coauth, The social democratic reform cycle in Germany, Polit Power & Social Theory, 81; auth, Social Democracy and Society: Working-class Radicalism in Dusseldorf, 1890-1920, Cambridge Univ Press, 82; The Historikenstreit & Social History, New Ger Critique 44, 88; Housework Made Easy: The Taylorized Housewife in Weimar Germany's Rationalized Economy, Feminist Studies, Fall 90; Vision of Modernity: American Business & The Modernization of Germany. Oxford, 94; Is Liberalism Really the Answer?, Int Labor & Working Class Hist 46, 94; Anti-Fascism Under Fascism: German Vision & Voices, New Ger Critique, 96. **CONTACT ADDRESS** Dept Hist, New York Univ, 53 Washington Square S, New York, NY, 10003-4556. **EMAIL** mn4@is2.nyu.edu

NOLL, MARK ALLAN
PERSONAL Born 07/18/1946, Iowa City, IA, m, 1969, 3 children **DISCIPLINE** HISTORY OF CHRISTIANITY (NORTH AMERICAN) **EDUCATION** Wheaton Col, Ill, BA, 68; Univ Iowa, MA, 70, Trinity Evangel Divinity Sch, MA, 72; Vanderbilt Univ, PhD(church hist), 75. **CAREER** Asst prof hist, Trinity Col, Ill, 75-78; from assoc prof hist to McManis prof of Christian Thought, Wheaton Col, Ill, 78-, vis prof Regent Col, Vancouver, 90, 95, 97; vis prof Harvard Divinity School, spring 98. **HONORS AND AWARDS** Fels, Nat Endowment for Humanities 78-79, 87-88, Pew Charitable Trusts, 93-94. **MEMBERSHIPS** Am Cath Hist Asn; AHA; Am Soc Church Hist; Canadian Soc of Church Hist; Conf Faith & Hist; OAH. **RESEARCH** Theology, politics, society in America 1730-1860; Protestants in the North Atlantic region; cultural history of the Bible. **SELECTED PUBLICATIONS** Auth, Christians in the American Revolution, Eerdmans, 77; Between Faith and Criticism: Evangelicals, Scholarship, and the Bible in America, Harper & Row, 86; One Nation Under God? Christian Faith and Political Action in America, Harper & Row, 88; Princeton and the Republic, 1768-1822, Princeton Univ Press, 89; A History of Christianity in the United States and Canada, Eerdmans, 92; The Scandal of the Evangelical Mind, Eerdmans, 92; Turnung Points: Decisive Moments in the History of Christianity, Baker Books, 98. Co-ed and contrib, The Bible in America, Oxford Univ Press, 82; Religion and American Politics, Oxford Univ Press, 89; Evangelicalism: Comparative Studies of Popular Protestantism in North America, the British Isles, and Beyond, Oxford Univ Press, 93; Evangelicals and Science in Historical Perspective, Oxford Univ Press, 98; co-auth, The Search for Christian America, 2nd ed, Helmers & Howard, 89. **CONTACT ADDRESS** Hist Dept, Wheaton Col, Wheaton, IL, 60187-5593. **EMAIL** Mark.Noll@wheaton.edu

NOONAN, THOMAS S.
DISCIPLINE HISTORY **EDUCATION** Univ Ind, PhD, 66. **CAREER** Prof **RESEARCH** Economic history of ancient and medieval Russia; Russian archaeology and numismatics. **SELECTED PUBLICATIONS** Auth, pubs on archaic Greek colonization in the northern Black Sea, medieval Russian-Estonian

relations, impact of Mongol rule on Russian attitudes toward the West, Suzdalia's oriental trade in the pre-Mongol era, and relations between Arabs, Khazars, Rus', and Vikings in the nineteenth centuries. **CONTACT ADDRESS** History Dept, Univ of Minnesota, Twin Cities, 614 Social Sciences Tower, 267 19th Ave. S, Minneapolis, MN, 55455. **EMAIL** noona001@tc.umn.edu

NOONE, TIMOTHY
PERSONAL Born 09/21/1957, Baltimore, MD, m, 1979, 3 children **DISCIPLINE** MEDIEVAL STUDIES **EDUCATION** Lock Haven State Univ, BA 79; Univ Toronto, MA 80; Pontifical Inst Medieval Studies Toronto ON CA, MSL 87; Univ Toronto, PhD 88. **CAREER** Cath Univ Am Sch Philos, asst dean, 97-; Cath Univ Am, asst prof, assoc prof, 94 to 96-; St Bonaventure Univ, asst prof, assoc prof, 89-94; St. John's Univ, asst prof, 88-89; St. Bonaventure Univ, instr, 87. **HONORS AND AWARDS** NEH; 3 SBU Fac Res Gnts; Bradley Foun Gnt; 3 CUA Res Awds. **MEMBERSHIPS** ACPA; APA; SMRP. **RESEARCH** Metaphysics in the high Middle Ages; History of Franciscan Philos; Albert the Great; Latin Commentaries on Aristotle's Metaphysics. **SELECTED PUBLICATIONS** Auth, Franciscan Studies: Essays in Honor of Dr Girard Etzkorn, co-ed, St Bonaventure NY, Franciscan Inst, 98; auth, Questions in libros Metaphysicorum Aristotelis Opera Philosophica III-IV, co-ed, St Bonaventure NY, Franciscan Inst, 97; auth, A Century of Medieval Scholarship, Philosophy in the Last One Hundred Years, ed, Rev Brian Shanley, Washington DC, Cath U Press of Am, forthcoming; Aquinas on Divine Ideas: Scotus's Evaluation, Franciscan Stud, 98; auth, The Originality of St. Thomas's Position on the Philosophers and Creation, The Thomist, 96; rev, William A. Frank, Allan B. Wolter, Duns Scotus, Metaphysician, Purdue, Purdue Univ Press, 96, Amer Cath Philos Quart; forthcoming; translation of, Thomas Celano's Vita prima Beati francisci, The New Omnibus of Franciscan Sources, NY, New City Press, forthcoming. **CONTACT ADDRESS** 2899 Chalet Court, Woodbridge, VA, 22192. **EMAIL** noonet@cua.edu

NORDLING, JOHN G.
PERSONAL Born 03/17/1957, Portland, OR, m, 1985 **DISCIPLINE** CLASSICS AND LATIN LITERATURE **EDUCATION** Univ Wisc Madison, PhD, 91. **CAREER** Asst prof, dept foreign lang & lit, Valparaiso Univ, 94-. **MEMBERSHIPS** Amer Philol Asn; Soc of Bibl Lit; Archaeol Inst of Amer. **RESEARCH** Ancient epistelography; Paul - life and theology; Ancient slavery. **SELECTED PUBLICATIONS** Rev, G. Clark, Augustine Confessions: Books I-IV, Concordia Theol Quart, 61, 318-319, 97; rev, D. E. Goatley, Were You There?: Godforsakenness in Slave Religion, Concordia Jour, 23, 265-266, 97; rev, C. Hill, The Scriptures Jesus Knew, Concordia Jour, 22, 70-71, 97; rev, T. Cahill, How the Irish Saved Civilization, Concordia Jour, 22, 121-122, 96; rev, D. W. J. Gill and C. Gempf, The Book of Acts in its First Century Setting. Volume 2: Greco-Roman Setting, Logia4, 68-70, 95; rev, Robert Grant, Heresy and Criticism, Logia3, 65-66, 94; rev, Wayne Meeks, The First Urban Christians, Condordia Jour, 19, 277-80, 93; article, Christ Leavens Culture: St. Paul on Slavery, Concordia Jour, 24, 43-52, 98; article, Onesimus Fugitivus: a Defense of the Runaway Slave Hypothesis in Philemon, Jour for the Study of the New Testament, 41, 97-119, 91. **CONTACT ADDRESS** Valparaiso Univ, 108 Meier Hall, Valparaiso, IN, 46383. **EMAIL** jnorfdling@exodus.valpo.edu

NORDQUIST, BARBARA K.
PERSONAL Born 08/29/1940, Oxnard, CA, m, 1963, 3 children **DISCIPLINE** FASHION; HUMAN BEHAVIOR **EDUCATION** Ore State Univ, BS, 62; Cornell Univ, MS, 63; US Int Univ, San Diego, PhD, 69. **CAREER** Asst prof, San Diego State Univ, 63-70; Assoc Prof to Prof, Howard Univ, 70-. **HONORS AND AWARDS** Phi Kappa Phi; Alpha Omicron Nu; Alpha Lambda Delta. **MEMBERSHIPS** ITAA. **RESEARCH** Cultural textiles & dress. **SELECTED PUBLICATIONS** Ed, Proceedings: Clean Coal Technology Meeting, E Mont Col, 90; co-auth, Cosmetics in the African American Market, African American Dress and Adornment, Kendall/Hunt, 90; auth, Traditional African Textiles and Dress, Unbroken Threads from an African Past, Black Fashion Mus, 3/95. **CONTACT ADDRESS** Dept of Art, Howard Univ, 6th & Howard Place, Washington, DC, 20059. **EMAIL** bnordquist@fac.howard.edu

NORDSTROM, BYRON JOHN
PERSONAL Born 08/30/1943, Minneapolis, MN, m, 1968, 2 children **DISCIPLINE** SCANDINAVIAN & EUROPEAN DIPLOMATIC HISTORY **EDUCATION** Lawrence Univ, Wis, BA, 65; Univ Minn, Minneapolis, MA, 68, PhD(hist), 72. **CAREER** Asst prof hist, Mankato State Univ, 71-73; res specialist, Minn Hist Soc, 73-74; asst prof area studies, Gustavus Adolphus Col, 74-76; asst prof Scand hist, Pac Lutheran Univ & Univ Wash, 76-77; asst prof to prof hist, Gustavus Adolphus Col, 77-. **MEMBERSHIPS** Upper Midwest Ethnic Studies Asn; Soc Advan Scand Study; Swed Pioneer Hist Soc. **RESEARCH** Swedish foreign policy and interest group influence in policy determination; Scandinavian immigration; Scandinavian immigrant communities in urban areas of the Midwest. **SELECTED PUBLICATIONS** Ed, The Swedes in Minnesota, Dennison, 76; auth, The Sixth Ward: A Minneapolis Swede Town in 1905, Proc Conf Swed Heritage, 78; auth, Swedish-American Bibliography, Swed Pioneer Hist Quart, 78-; Evelina Mansson and the Memoir of an Urban Labor Migrant, Swed Pioneer Hist Quart, 7/80; ed, Dict Scand Hist, Greenwood Press, 86; auth, Dict Scand Hist, 86; ed, Swed-Am Hist Quart, 97-; auth, A History of Modern Scandinavia, 99. **CONTACT ADDRESS** Gustavus Adolphus Col, 800 W College Ave, Saint Peter, MN, 56082-1498. **EMAIL** byron@gustavus.edu

NORE, ELLEN
PERSONAL Born 01/15/1942, Loup City, NE, 2 children **DISCIPLINE** AMERICAN HISTORY **EDUCATION** Univ Nebr, Lincoln, BA, 63; Stanford Univ, MA, 64, PhD(hist), 80. **CAREER** Woodrow Wilson teaching intern hist, Lamar State Col Technol, 65-66; instr, San Jose State Col, 67-69; instr, 79-80, Asst Prof Hist, Southern Ill Univ, 80-. **MEMBERSHIPS** AHA; Orgn Am Historians; Concerned Asian Scholars; Soc Historians of the Early Am Repub. **RESEARCH** Intellectual history of the United States; biography; United States diplomatic history since 1945. **SELECTED PUBLICATIONS** Auth, Charles A Beard's Act of faith: Context and content, J Am Hist, 80; Veblen,thorstein and His Critics, 1891-1963 - Conservative, Liberal, and Radical Perspectives - Tilman,r, American Historical Review, Vol 0098, 1993; Parrington,v.l. - Through the Avenue of Art - Hall,hl, J of American History, Vol 0082, 1995; Charles A Beard: An Intellectual Biography, Southern Ill Univ Press (in prep); Modernist Impulses in the Human- sciences, 1870-1930 - Ross,d, Reviews in American History, Vol 0023, 1995. **CONTACT ADDRESS** Dept of Hist Studies, Southern Ill Univ, 6 Hairpin Dr, Edwardsville, IL, 62026-0001.

NORLING, LISA A.
DISCIPLINE HISTORY **EDUCATION** Rutgers Univ, PhD, 92. **CAREER** Asst prof **RESEARCH** American women's history; early American social history; maritime history. **SELECTED PUBLICATIONS** Auth, 'How Frought With Sorrow and Heartpangs': Mariners' Wives and the Ideology of Domesticity in New England, New England Quarterly, 92; The Sentimentalization of American Seafaring, 1790-1870, Acadiensus, 91. **CONTACT ADDRESS** History Dept, Univ of Minnesota, Twin Cities, 614 Social Sciences Tower, 267 19th Ave. S, Minneapolis, MN, 55455. **EMAIL** norli001@tc.umn.edu

NORMORE, CALVIN GERARD
PERSONAL Corner Brook, NF, Canada **DISCIPLINE** PHILOSOPHY, MEDIEVAL STUDIES **EDUCATION** McGill Univ, BA, 68; Univ Toronto, MA, 69, PhD(philos), 76. **CAREER** Lectr philos, York Univ, 72-74; Killam fel, Univ Alta, 76- 77; Mellon Asst Prof Philos, Princeton Univ, 77-. **MEMBERSHIPS** Am Philos Asn; Can Medieval Acad Am; Soc Medieval & Renaissance Philos. **RESEARCH** Medieval philosophy; social and political philosophy; philosophy of time. **SELECTED PUBLICATIONS** Auth, Future contingents, In: Cambridge History of Later Medieval Philosophy, 82; Walter Burley on continuity, In: Infinity & Continuity in Ancient & Medieval Thought, 82; the Necessity in Deduction - Cartesian Inference and its Medieval Background, Synthese, Vol 0096, 1993. **CONTACT ADDRESS** Dept Philosophy, Univ Toronto, Toronto, ON, M5S 1A1.

NORRELL, ROBERT J.
DISCIPLINE HISTORY **EDUCATION** Univ Va, PhD. **CAREER** Prof. **RESEARCH** Modern South and American race relations. **SELECTED PUBLICATIONS** Auth, Reaping the Whirlwind: The Civil Rights Movement, Knopf, 85; James Bowron: The Autobiography of a New South Industrialist, Univ Ca. **CONTACT ADDRESS** Dept of History, Knoxville, TN, 37996.

NORRIS, ETHEL MAUREEN
PERSONAL Born 03/03/1956, Petersburg, Virginia, s **DISCIPLINE** MUSIC **EDUCATION** East Carolina Univ, B Mus 1977; OH State Univ, MA 1978; summer study, Westminster Choir Coll 1985-86; Ohio State Univ, doctoral study in music history 1987-; Ohio State Univ, PhD, 1994. **CAREER** St Pauls Coll, instructor of music; Virginia State Univ, asst prof of music, currently. **HONORS AND AWARDS** Finalist Natl Achievement Scholarship Program for Outstanding Negro Students 1973; One-Year Minority Fellowship OH State Univ 1977-78; Graduate Teaching Assistantship OH State Univ 1987-88; Grant, UNCF, 1987-88; Grant, National Endowment for the Humanities, 1989-90; OSU Presidential Fellowship, 1993-94. **MEMBERSHIPS** Instr Piano Lessons 1979-; mem Sigma Alpha Iota, Coll Music Soc, Amer Guild of Organists, Phi Kappa Phi; Sonneck Society. **CONTACT ADDRESS** Instructor of Music, 6901 Sudley Rd, Petersburg, VA, 23806.

NORRIS, JAMES D.
PERSONAL Born 11/02/1930, Richmond, MO, m, 1957, 3 children **DISCIPLINE** AMERICAN FRONTIER & ECONOMIC HISTORY **EDUCATION** Univ Mo-Columbia, BS, 56, MA, 58, PhD, 61. **CAREER** Asst prof hist, Hiram Col, 61-65; vis assoc prof, Univ Wis, 65-66; assoc prof hist, Univ Mo-St Louis, 66-69, prof, 69-79; Dean, Col Lib Arts & Sci, 79-95, Prof Hist, Northern Ill Univ, 95-; Am lectr, Fulbright-Hays prog, Univ Ghana, 72-73. **MEMBERSHIPS** Orgn Am Historians; Bus Hist Asn. **RESEARCH** Business history; American frontier; American economic history. **SELECTED PUBLICATIONS** Auth, One price policy in antebellum country stores, Bus Hist Rev, 62; Frontier Iron: The Meramec Iron Works 1826-1876, 64; Business longevity and the frontier iron industry, Ann Bus Hist, 65; The Missouri and Kansas Zinc Miner's Association, Bus Hist, 66; History of American Zinc, 68, co-ed, Politics and Patronage in the Gilded Age, 70 & R G Dun & Co, 1841-1900: The Development of Credit Reporting in 19th Century America, 78; coauth, Advertising & the Transformation of the American Economy, 1865-1920, Building a Tradition of Excellence, 91; The James Foundation in Missouri, 1941-1991, 96. **CONTACT ADDRESS** Col Lib Arts & Sci, No Illinois Univ, 1425 W Lincoln Hwy, De Kalb, IL, 60115-2825.

NORTH, HELEN FLORENCE
PERSONAL Born 01/31/1921, Utica, NY **DISCIPLINE** CLASSICAL LITERATURE, RHETORIC **EDUCATION** Cornell Univ, AB, 42, AM, 43, PhD(classics), 45. **CAREER** Sibley fel, 45-46; instr class lang, Rosary Col, 46-48; asst prof Greek & Latin, 48-53, assoc prof, 53-62, William J Kenan prof, 73-78, Prof Classics, Swarthmore Col, 62-, Chmn Dept, 59-, Centennial Prof, 78-, Ford & Fulbright fels, Rome, 53-54; vis assoc prof, Barnard Col, Columbia Univ, 54-55; Guggenheim fel, Rome, 58-59; secy adv coun, Sch Class Studies, Am Acad Rome, 60-62 & 64, mem bd trustees, 72-75 & 77-91; Asn Univ Women res fel, Rome, 62-63; Nat Endowment for Hum sr fel, Rome, 67-68; chmn, Cath Comn on Intellectual & Cult Affairs, 68-69; mem bd dir, King's Col, Pa, 69-71 & 73-75; Am Coun Learned Soc fel, Rome, 71-72; Martin class lectr, Oberlin Col, 72; mem bd trustees, La Salle Col, 73-; Guggenheim fel, 75-76. **HONORS AND AWARDS** Harbison Tchg Prize, Danforth Found, 69; Charles A Goodwin Award for Sophrosyne, Am Philol Asn, 69. **MEMBERSHIPS** Am Philol Asn (2nd vpres, 74, pres, 76); Class Asn Atlantic States; Class Soc Am Acad Rome (pres, 60-61); AAAS. **RESEARCH** Concept of Sophrosyne in Greek lit; Plato's rhetoric; Roman rhetoric. **SELECTED PUBLICATIONS** Trans Milton's Second Defence of the English people, In: Vol IV, Complete Prose Works of John Milton, Yale Univ, 66; Sophrosyne: Self-Knowledge and Self-Restraint in Greek Literature, 66 & coed, Of Eloquence; Studies in Ancient and Mediaeval Rhetoric, Cornell Univ, 70; auth, Ancient Salt: The New Rhetoric and the Old, J Hist Ideas, 74; ed, Interpretations of Plato: A Swarthmore Symposium, Brill, 77; auth, The Yoke of necessity: Aulis and beyond, Class World, 77; From Myth to Icon, Cornell Univ, 79; auth, Opening Socrates, Ill Class Stud, 94; auth, The Dacian Walls Speak, Festschrift fur Paul MacKendrick, 98. **CONTACT ADDRESS** 604 Ogden Ave, Swarthmore, PA, 19081.

NORTH, JAMES BROWNLEE
PERSONAL Born 01/21/1941, Hammond, IN, m, 1962, 2 children **DISCIPLINE** AMERICAN HISTORY **EDUCATION** Lincoln Christian Col, BA, 62; Lincoln Christian Sem, MA, 63; Univ Chicago Div Sch, MA, 67; Univ Il, PhD, 73. **CAREER** Prof, 72-77, San Jose Christian Col; prof to chair, interim dean, vice-pres, 77-, Cincinnati Bible Col & Sem; **HONORS AND AWARDS** Teacher of the Year, 88. **MEMBERSHIPS** Amer Soc of Church Hist; Conf on Faith & Hist; Disciples of Christ Hist Soc; Oh Acad of Hist. **RESEARCH** Amer relig hist; hist of Christian churches, churches of Christ. **SELECTED PUBLICATIONS** Auth, The Church of the New Testament; From Pentecost to the Present: A Short History of Christianity, Col Press Publ Co, 83; auth, Union in Truth: An Interpretive History of the Restoration Movement, Std Publ, 94; coauth, Coming Together in Christ: Pioneering a New Testament Way to Christian Unity, Col press Publ Co, 97. **CONTACT ADDRESS** Cincinnati Bible Col and Sem, 2700 Glenway Ave, Cincinnati, OH, 45204. **EMAIL** Jim.North@cincybible.edu

NORTH, ROBERT
PERSONAL Born 03/25/1916, Iowa City, IA **DISCIPLINE** BIBLICAL ARCHEOLOGY **EDUCATION** St Louis Univ, MA, 39; Pontif Bibl Inst, Rome, SSD, 54. **CAREER** Instr Greek, Marquette Univ High Sch, 39-41; prof archaeol & Arabic, Pontif Bibl Inst, Rome, 51-56; prof archaeol, Arabic & Hebrew & dir, Pontif Bibl Inst, Jerusalem, 56-59; dir, Excavation of Ghassul, Jericho, 59-60; from assoc prof to prof theol, Marquette Univ, 61-72; Prof Old Testament & Archaeol, Pontif Bibl Inst, Rome, 63-, Cath Bibl Asn Am scholar, 46-51; vis prof theol, Sch Divinity, St Louis Univ, 60-64 & Gonzaga Univ, 74; assoc in coun, Soc Bibl Lit, 63-66. **MEMBERSHIPS** Cath Bibl Asn Am (vp, 68-69); Soc Old Testament Studies; Soc Bibl Lit. **SELECTED PUBLICATIONS** Auth, Ghassul 1960 Excavation Report, Pontif Bibl Inst, Rome, 61; Leviticus, In: Encycl Britannica, 65; Archeo-Biblical Egypt, Pontif Bibl Inst, Rome, 67; Teilhard and the Creation of the Soul, Bruce, 67; Byblos . . ., In: New Catholic Encyclopedia, McGraw, 67; The chronicler: geography, In: Jerome Catholic Commentary, Prentice-Hall, 68; In Search of the Human Jesus, Corpus Bks, 70; Yobel etc, In: Theological Dictionary to the Old Testament, 74; Umm-al-rasas-mayfaah, Vol 1 - Excavation of the Church-of-saint-stephen - Italian - Piccirillo,m, Alliata,e, Biblica, Vol 0077, 1996; The Anchor Bible Dictionary, Vols-1-6 - Freedman,dn, Biblica, Vol 0075, 1994; One and Many - Essays on Change and Variety in Late Norse Heathenism - Mckinnell,j, Medium Aevum, Vol 0066, 1997. **CONTACT ADDRESS** Pontifical Biblical Inst, Via Pilotta 25, Rome, ..

NORTHRUP, DAVID ARTHUR
PERSONAL Born 05/01/1941, Rochester, NY, m, 3 children **DISCIPLINE** AFRICAN HISTORY **EDUCATION** Fordham Univ, BS, 63, MA, 65; Univ Calif, Los Angeles, MA, 69, Ph-D(hist), 74. **CAREER** Instr, Tuskegee Inst, 68-70 & 72; from Asst Prof to Assoc Prof, 74-89, PROF HIST, BOSTON COL, 89-. **HONORS AND AWARDS** Phi Beta Kappa, 63; NY State Teaching Fel, 63-64; Fulbright-Hays Doctoral Dissertation Res Abroad Grant, 72-73; Fulbright-Hays Fac Res Abroad Grant, African Studies Grant, Soc Sci Res Coun, Mellon Fund Grant, Boston Col, 80-81; Boston Col Fac Fel, 84; Development Grant, Boston Col Women's Studies Comt/Ford Found, 87; Travel Grant (London), Am Coun of Learned Soc, 88; Cult Diversity Core Grant, Ford Found/Xocomil, 92; Fac Teaching and Advising Grants, Boston Col, 91, 94; NEH Summer Stipends, 80, 95. **MEMBERSHIPS** African Studies Asn; Am Asn Univ Prof; Am Hist Asn; World Hist Asn. **RESEARCH** French indentured labor trade from Africa and India to the French Carribean; Africa's discovery of Europe 1450-1800: changing impressions and perceptions. **SELECTED PUBLICATIONS** Auth, The growth of trade among the Igbo before 1800, 72 & The compatibility of the slave and palm oil trades in the bight of Biafra, 76 J Africa Hist; African mortality in the suppression of the slave trade, J Interdisciplinary Hist, 78; Trade without rulers: Pre-colonial economic development in South-Eastern Nigeria, Clarendon Press, 78; Nineteenth-century patterns of slavery and economic growth in Southeastern Nigeria, Int J African Hist Studies, 79; The Ideological Context of Slavery in Southeastern Nigeria in the 19th Century, In: The Ideology of Slavery in Africa, Sage Publ, 81; A Church in Search of a State: Catholic Missions in Eastern Zaire, 1879-1930, J of Church and State, Spring 88; The Ending of Slavery in Eastern Zaire, 1870-1930, In: The End of Slavery in Africa, Univ Wis Press, 88; Beyond the Bend in the River: A Labor History of Eastern Zaire, 1870-1940, Ohio Univ Press, 88; ed and compiler, The Atlantic Slave Trade, D.C. Heath and Co, 94; auth, Indentured Labor in the Age of Imperialism, 1834-1922, Cambridge Univ Press, 95; coauth, The Earth and Its Peoples: A Global History, Houghton Mifflin Co, 97. **CONTACT ADDRESS** Dept of History, Boston Col, 140 Commonwealth Ave, Chestnut Hill, MA, 02167-3806. **EMAIL** northrup@bc.edu

NORTON, KAY
DISCIPLINE MUSIC HISTORY **EDUCATION** Univ Colo, PhD. **CAREER** Asst prof, Brenau Women's Col; assoc prof, Univ Mo, Kansas City. **RESEARCH** Art music traditions of the 19th and 20th centuries. **SELECTED PUBLICATIONS** Recently completed a monograph on the American composer Normand Lockwood, published by the Scarecrow Press, 93; her work has also been published in the Sonneck Soc Bull, MLA Notes, 18th Century: A Current Bibliography, Music Res Forum, and Int Fedn for Choral Mus Bull. **CONTACT ADDRESS** Univ Mo, Kansas City, Kansas City, MO, 64110-2499. **EMAIL** knorton@cctr.umkc.edu

NORTON, MARY BETH
DISCIPLINE HISTORY **EDUCATION** Univ Mich, BA; Harvard Univ, MA, 65, Phd, 69. **CAREER** Asst prof, Univ Conn, 69-71; asst prof, 71-87; Mary Donlon Alger prof, 87-. **HONORS AND AWARDS** Allan Nevins Prize, 70; Alice and Edith Hamilton Prize, 80; Douglass Adair Prize, 80; Berkshire Conf Prize, 81;Francis Parkman Prize, 92; Bancroft Prize, 98., Finalist, Pulitzer Prize, 97. **MEMBERSHIPS** Soc Am Hist; Am Antiquarian Soc; Mass Hist Soc; Am Hist Asn; Org Am Hist; Coordinating Coun Women Hist; Inst Early Am Hist Cult; Upstate NY Women's Hist Org. **RESEARCH** Early American history; American women's gender history. **SELECTED PUBLICATIONS** Auth, Rethinking American History Textbooks, 94; Founding Mothers & Fathers: Gendered Power and The Forming of American Society (rev), 96; coauth, A People and a Nation, 82; ed, The American Historical Association's Guide to Historical Literature, Oxford, 95; Major Problems in American Women's History, 95. **CONTACT ADDRESS** Dept of History, Cornell Univ, Ithaca, NY, 14853-2801. **EMAIL** mbn1@cornell.edu

NORTON, MARY BETH
PERSONAL Born 03/25/1943, Ann Arbor, MI **DISCIPLINE** AMERICAN HISTORY **EDUCATION** Univ Mich, Ann Arbor, AB, 64; Harvard Univ, AM, 65, PhD(hist), 69. **CAREER** Asst prof hist, Univ Conn, 69-71; asst prof 71-74, assoc prof, 75-81, PROF HIST, CORNELL UNIV, 81-, MARY DONLON ALGER PROF, CORNELL UNIV, 87-; Nat Endowment for Humanities Younger Humanists fel, 74-75; Charles Warren Ctr fel, Harvard Univ, 74-75; fel, Shelby Cullom Davis Ctr, Princeton Univ, 77-78; mem, Nat Coun on Humanities, 78-84; Rockefeller Fdn fel, 86-87; Cornell Soc Hum fel, 89-90; John Simon Guggenheim Fdn fel, 93-94. **HONORS AND AWARDS** Allan Nevins Prize, Soc Am Historians, 69; Book Prize, Berkshire Conf Women Historians, 80; finalist, Pulitzer Prize Hist, 97. **MEMBERSHIPS** AHA; Orgn Am Historians; Soc Am Historians; Coord Comt Women in Hist Prof; Berkshire Conf Women Historians. **RESEARCH** American Revolution; American women. **SELECTED PUBLICATIONS** Auth, The British-Americans, Little, 72; co-ed & contribr, Women of America, Houghton Mifflin, 79; auth, Liberty's Daughters, Little, 80, Cornell, 96; coauth, A People and a Nation, Houghton Mifflin, 82, 5th ed, 96; co-ed, To Toil the Livelong Day, Cornell, 87; co-ed, Major Problems in American Women's History, Heath, 89, Houghton Mifflin, 95; ed, The American Historical Association's Guide to Historical Literature, 3rd ed, Oxford, 95; auth, Founding Mothers & Fathers, Knopf, 96. **CONTACT ADDRESS** Dept of Hist, Cornell Univ, Mcgraw Hall, Ithaca, NY, 14853-4601. **EMAIL** mbn1@cornell.edu

NORTON, PAUL F.
PERSONAL Born 01/23/1917, Newton, MA, m, 1942, 3 children **DISCIPLINE** ART HISTORY **EDUCATION** Oberlin Coll, BA, 38; Princeton Univ, PhD, 52. **CAREER** Asst prof to assoc prof, 47-58, Penn State Univ; prof, 58-93, chairman, 58-71, Art Dept, Univ Mass Amherst. **HONORS AND AWARDS** Fulbright Res Award to England, 53-54; grant, NEH; grant, Graham Found; fellowship, Brown Univ, Center for Amer Historical Soc, 93-96; fellowship, Rhode Island Historical Soc, 98-99. **MEMBERSHIPS** Soc Archit Historians (U.S.) ; Soc of Archit Hist (England); Pioneer Am Soc; Victorian Soc. **RESEARCH** American and European archit (19th and 20th c); American stained glass windows. **SELECTED PUBLICATIONS** "Oudinot's Windows for Trinity Church, Boston," Victorian Soc Journ, 93; "Life and Stained Glass Windows of Robert Barrie," Stained Glass Quarterly, summer, 97. **CONTACT ADDRESS** Art Dept., Univ of Massachusetts, 57 Woodside Ave., Amherst, MA, 01002-2524. **EMAIL** pnorton@arthist.umass.edu

NORWOOD, VERA
DISCIPLINE AMERICAN STUDIES **EDUCATION** Univ NMex, PhD, 74. **CAREER** Prof, ch, dept Am Stud, Univ NMex. **HONORS AND AWARDS** Grant, Rockefeller Found, Am Coun of Learned Soc, Nat Endowment for Arts, NMex Hum Coun. **RESEARCH** Women's responses to nature and the built environment. **SELECTED PUBLICATIONS** Auth, Made From This Earth: American Women and Nature, 93; ed, The Desert is No Lady: Women Writers and Artists of the Southwest, 87. **CONTACT ADDRESS** Univ NMex, Albuquerque, NM, 87131.

NOSCO, PETER
PERSONAL New York, NY, m, 1976, 2 children **DISCIPLINE** HISTORY **EDUCATION** Cambridge Univ, BA/MA, 73/77; BA, 71, PhD, 78, Columbia Univ. **CAREER** Asst Prof, St. John's Univ, 79-85; Asst Prof, 86-89, Assoc Prof, 89-93, Prof, 93-, Univ Southern California. **HONORS AND AWARDS** DHEW Fulbright Fel, 75-76; Fulbright Senior Research Award, 86, Historiographical Inst Tokyo Univ; Fulbright-Hays Group Projects Abroad Project Dir of Japan Field Study, 98. **MEMBERSHIPS** Assoc for Asian Studies; Amer Acad of Religion; Amer Soc for Eighteenth Century Studies **RESEARCH** Intellectual and social history of Japan; popular culture; confucianism; nativism; underground religious movements **SELECTED PUBLICATIONS** Auth, Remembering Paradise: Nativism and Nostalgia in 18th Century Japan, Harvard-Yenching Institute Monograph Series, 90; ed, Confucianism and Tokugawa Culture, 96 (revised ed); Japanese Identity: Cultural Analyses, 97; guest ed, Philosophy East and West, special issue on theme of Religious Dimension of Confucianism in Japan, 98. **CONTACT ADDRESS** Univ of Southern California, 226 Taper Hall, Los Angeles, CA, 90089-0357. **EMAIL** nosco@usc.edu

NOTEHELFER, FRED G.
PERSONAL Born 04/13/1939, Tokyo, Japan, m, 1966 **DISCIPLINE** MODERN JAPANESE HISTORY **EDUCATION** Harvard Univ, AB, 62; Princeton Univ, PhD(hist), 68. **CAREER** Instr hist, Princeton Univ, 66-67, vis lectr, 67-68, lectr, 68-69; asst prof, 69-71, Assoc Prof Hist, Univ Calif, Los Angeles, 71-, Fulbright-Hays res grant, vis prof, Doshisha Univ & res fel, Inst Humanistic Studies, Kyoto Univ, Japan, 71-72; dir, Univ Calif, Educ Abroad Tokyo Study Ctr, 79-81; vis prof, Univ BC, 82. **MEMBERSHIPS** Asn Asian Studies. **RESEARCH** Meiji period socialist and Christian movements. **CONTACT ADDRESS** Dept of Hist, Univ of Calif, Los Angeles, CA, 90024.

NOVICK, PETER
PERSONAL Born 07/26/1934, Jersey City, NJ, m, 1964, 1 child **DISCIPLINE** MODERN HISTORY **EDUCATION** Columbia Univ, BS, 57, PhD(hist), 65. **CAREER** Lectr hist, Rutgers Univ, 61-62; lectr, Columbia Univ, 61- 65; asst prof, Univ Calif, Santa Barbara, 65-66; asst prof, 66- 72, Assoc Prof Europ Hist & Soc Sci, 72-. **HONORS AND AWARDS** Clark M Ansley Award, 65. **MEMBERSHIPS** AHA **RESEARCH** Twentieth Century United States and Europe. **SELECTED PUBLICATIONS** Auth, The Resistance vs Vichy, Columbia Univ, 68; That Noble Dream - Haskell,tl Vol 29, Pg 143, 1990, History And Theory, Vol 0032, 1993; Godforsaken Scholarship + Response to Wolfe,Alan Article on My Work on Ways of Knowing, Lingua Franca, Vol 0006, 1996. **CONTACT ADDRESS** Dept of Hist, Univ of Chicago, 1126 E 59th St, Chicago, IL, 60637-1539.

NUGENT, DONALD CHROSTOPHER
PERSONAL Born 12/31/1930, Lousiville, KY, s **DISCIPLINE** HISTORY/THEOLOGY **EDUCATION** PhD Univ of IA, 65; MA Theol, Univ of San Francisco, 82. **CAREER** Asst Prof, Univ KY, 66-95; Vis Prof, Univ Col Dublin, 72-73; Univ Alberta, 61-62. **RESEARCH** Msyticism; Spirituality, esp St John of the Cross. **SELECTED PUBLICATIONS** Ecummenism in the Age of the Reformation, Harvard, 74; Masks of Satan: The Demonic in History, Sheed & Ward, 83; Mysticism, Deathe and Dying, Albany: SUNY, 94; Satori in St John of the Cross: The Eastern Buddhist, Kyoto, 95; Pax Sexuals: The Month, London, 98. **CONTACT ADDRESS** Dept Hist, Univ Kentucky, Lexington, KY, 40506.

NUGENT, PAULINE
PERSONAL Born 06/28/1938, Ireland **DISCIPLINE** CLASSICAL STUDIES **EDUCATION** Univ Incarnate Word, BA, 64; Univ Tex Austin, MA, 71, PhD 92. **CAREER** Instr, Incarnate Word Col, 75-79; asst prof, Southwest Mo State Univ, 92-97; assoc prof, 98-. **MEMBERSHIPS** Am Philol Asn; Class Asn of Middle West and South; North Am Patristic Soc; Vergilian Soc of Am; Am Asn of Teachers of French; Int Soc for the Class Traditions. **RESEARCH** Patristics; Classical studies; Antiquity; Biblical Hebrew. **SELECTED PUBLICATIONS** Auth, "Prefaces for Profit Without Prophets" in Studia Patristica, 97. **CONTACT ADDRESS** 1830 S Fremont Ave, Springfield, MO, 65804. **EMAIL** PAN851F@mail.smsu.edu

NULL, ELISABETH M.
PERSONAL Born 12/01/1942, Wercester, MA, 2 children **DISCIPLINE** FOLKLORE, HISTORY, LIBRARY SCIENCE **EDUCATION** Sarah lawrence Col, BA, MA, 85, Mphil, 89 **CAREER** Appoint, Lib of Congress, 95, Librn, 91-98, Georgetown Univ **MEMBERSHIPS** Am Folklore Soc **RESEARCH** Am Musical life **CONTACT ADDRESS** Silver Spring, MD, 20910-5534. **EMAIL** elisabeth.null@tcs.wap.org

NUMBERS, RONALD LESLIE
PERSONAL Born 06/03/1942, Boulder, CO, m, 1999, 1 child **DISCIPLINE** HISTORY, SCIENCE & MEDICINE **EDUCATION** Southern Missionary Col, BA, 63; Fla State Univ, MA, 65; Univ Calif, Berkeley, PhD(hist), 69. **CAREER** Asst prof hist, Andrews Univ, 69-70; asst prof humanities, Sch Med, Loma Linda Univ, 70-74; asst prof, 74-76, chmn dept hist med, 77-81, assoc prof, 76-79, prof 79-91, William Coleman Prof, 91, Hilldale Prof Hist Sci & Med, 97, Univ Wisc, Madison; Macy Found fel, Inst Hist of Med, Johns Hopkins Univ, 73-74. **HONORS AND AWARDS** Guggenheim fel, 83-84; fel, Am Acad of Arts & Sci, 95; pres, Am Soc of Church Hist, 99-00; pres, Hist of Sci Soc, 00-01. **MEMBERSHIPS** AHA; Hist Sci Soc; Am Asn Hist Med; Orgn Am Historians; Am Soc Church Hist. **RESEARCH** Science and medicine in America; science, medicine, and religion. **SELECTED PUBLICATIONS** Auth, Prophetess of Health: A Study of Ellen G White, Harper & Row, 76; Creation by Natural Law: Laplace's Nebular Hypothesis in American Thought, Univ Wash, 77; auth, Almost Persuaded: American Physicians and Compulsory Health Insurance, 1912-1920, Johns Hopkins Univ, 78; auth, The Creationists, Knopf, 92; auth, Darwinism Comes to America, Harvard, 98. **CONTACT ADDRESS** Dept of Hist of Med, Univ of Wis, 1300 University Ave, Madison, WI, 53706-1510. **EMAIL** RNumbers@macc.wisc.edu

NUNIS, DOYCE BLACKMAN
PERSONAL Born 05/30/1924, Cedartown, GA **DISCIPLINE** HISTORY, EDUCATION **EDUCATION** BA, UCLA, 47; MS in Ed, USC,50; M Ed, USC, 52; PhD Hist, USC,58. **CAREER** Univ Southern Cal, Prof Emer, 89-, Hist Prof, 68-89, Assoc Prof, 65-68; UCLA, Assoc Prof, Edu, Assoc Research Hist, Office Oral Hist, 64-65, Asst Prof, Ed Hist, 61-64, Lectr, Hist Edu, 60-61; El Camino Col, Instr, 56-59; Los Angeles City Col, Instr, 52-57; Univ Southern Cal, Lectr, 53-56, Teaching Asst, Dept Am Civilizations Institutions, 51-53. **HONORS AND AWARDS** Doyce B Nunis Jr Award, est by the Historical Soc Southern Cal to honor 37 yrs as editor of its pub, Southern California Quarterly, 96; Knight Commander St Gregory, pontifical honor, 94; Distinguished Emer Award, USC, 94; Benemerinti Medal, pontifical honor, 84; five distinguished teaching awards, USC; Henry R Wagner Mem Award, CHS, 88; Fel Cal Hist Soc, 81; Am Philos Soc, Fel, 81; Guggenheim Foundation, Fel, 63-64; Huntington Library, Fel, 60. **RESEARCH** Hist of Am West; California; Los Angeles; Hist of Medicine. **SELECTED PUBLICATIONS** Southern California Local Hist: A Gathering of the Writings of W W Robinson, ed, 93; From Mexican Days to the Gold Rush, ed, 93; Tales of Mexican California by Antonio Coronel, ed, 94; Land Policy and Land Use in Southern California, ed, 94; The St Francis Dam Disaster Revisited, ed, 95; Women in the Life of Southern California, ed, 96; Hispanic California Revisited: Essays by Francis F Guest, ed, 96; El Presidio de San Francisco: A History Under Spain and Mexico, 1776-1846, ed, 96; Mission San Fernando Rey de Espana: A Bicentennial Salute, 97. **CONTACT ADDRESS** Univ Southern Cal, Dept Hist, Los Angeles, CA, 90027-1250.

NUNN, FREDERICK MCKINLEY
PERSONAL Born 10/29/1937, Portland, OR, m, 1960, 1 child **DISCIPLINE** LATIN AMERICAN HISTORY **EDUCA-**

TION Univ Ore, BA, 59; Univ NMEX, MA & PhD, 63. **CAREER** Asst prof hist, Elbert Covell Col, Univ of the Pac, 63-65; from asst prof to assoc prof, 65-72, fac res grants, 65-68, asst dir Pac Rim Studies Ctr, 72-73; prof 72-80, HEAD DEPT HIST, PORTLAND STATE UNIV 80-; Lectr & consult, Univ NMex Peace Corps Training Ctr, 65-66; Am Philos Soc fel, 69; Soc Sci Res Coun-Am Coun Learned Soc fel, 78; hon res fel, Inst Lat Amer Studies, Univ London 77-78. **HONORS AND AWARDS** Hubee & Herring Mem Award, 80. **MEMBERSHIPS** AHA; Conf Latin Am Hist; Latin Am Studies Asn; Pac Coast Coun Latin Am Studies; Am Franciscan Hist. **RESEARCH** Modern Latin American history; historical role of the military in Latin America; Chilean political history. **SELECTED PUBLICATIONS** Auth, Military rule in Chile: The revolutions of September 5, 1924 and January 23, 1925, Hisp Am Hist Rev, 2/67; Chilean Politics, 1920-1931: The Honorable Mission of the Armed Forces, Univ NMex, 70; Emi! Korner and the Prussianization of the Chilean army: Origins, process and consequences 1885-1920, Hisp Am Hist Rev, 70; Military professionalism and professional militarism in Brazil: Historical perspectives and political consequences 1870-1970, J Latin Am Studies, 72; The Military in Chilean History: Essays on Civil-Military Relations, 1810-1973, NMex Univ, 76; Latin American military lore: The introduction and a case study, The Americas, 4/79; Professional militarism in twentieth-century Peru: Historical and theoretical background to the Golpe de Esbedo of 1968, Hisp Am Hist Rev, 8/79. **CONTACT ADDRESS** Dept of Hist, Portland State Univ, PO Box 751, Portland, OR, 97207-0751.

NUNNALLY, DAVID H., SR.
PERSONAL Born 10/16/1929, Athens Clarke Co, GA, m **DISCIPLINE** EDUCATION **EDUCATION** Union Bapt Inst; Tuskegee Inst; Atlanta U; Univ of GA; Gov State U, MS; Loyal Univ of Chicago, PhD. **CAREER** Kennedy-Ing Coll, counselor; teacher; Jr HS counselor; HS counselor; residential counselor; Sutdent Personnel Ser, dir; Comm Adult HS, asst dir; athletic coach; employment counselor; camp counselor; Georgia Dome, personnel asst. **HONORS AND AWARDS** BSA Outstanding Male Tchr Am Tchr Assn 1964; Martin Luther King Hum Rel Award Eta Iota Lambda Chap 1970; Man of Yr Eta Iota Lambda Chap & GA Alpha Phi Alpha 1970. **MEMBERSHIPS** Mem PTA; AFT; NEA; Phi Delta Kappa; VFW; APGA; IGPA; ICPA; GAE; past dir Dist IX Assn of Educators; past mem Assn of Educ Bd of Dir; Chicago Hghts Ldrshp Forum; founder Athens Chap Ita Iota Lambda; mem Lions Intl Club; Alpha Phi Alpha; Masonic Lodge; sponsor Comm Ser Club; troop scout master. **CONTACT ADDRESS** 3394 Charlemagne Dr, Decatur, GA, 30034.

NUTT, R.
PERSONAL Born 07/31/1953, Kansas City, MO, m, 1978, 2 children **DISCIPLINE** US RELIGIOUS HISTORY **EDUCATION** Vanderbilt Univ, PhD, 86 **CAREER** Asst prof, 88-94, Assoc prof, 94-, Muskingum Coll. **HONORS AND AWARDS** Wm Rainey Harper Award for Outstanding Scholarship, 94, 98 **MEMBERSHIPS** Amer Soc of Church Hist; Presbyterian Historical Soc; Amer Acad of Relig **RESEARCH** American Religious Hist; Church-State Issues; Presbyterian Hist **SELECTED PUBLICATIONS** Auth, Contending for the Faith: The First Two Centuries of the Presbyterian Church in Cincinnati Area, 91; Toward Peacemaking: Presbyterians in the South and National Security, 1945-1983, 94; Presbyterians and Nuclear Weapons: Fifty Years of a Life-and-Death Issue, American Presbyterians, Summer 95; The Whole Gospel for the Whole World: G Sherwood Eddy and American Protestant Social Mission, 97; G. Sherwood Eddy and Attitudes of the Protestants in the US toward Global Mission, Church History, 97. **CONTACT ADDRESS** Brown Chapel, Muskingum Col, New Concord, OH, 43762. **EMAIL** rnutt@muskingum.edu

NWAUWA, APOLLOS O.
DISCIPLINE AFRICAN HISTORY, BRITISH IMPERIAL HISTORY **EDUCATION** Bendel State Univ, Nigeria, BA; Dalhousie Univ, Can, MA, PhD. **CAREER** Instr, RI Col. **RESEARCH** African chronology and state formation; Britain and the politics of African Univ educ. **SELECTED PUBLICATIONS** Auth, The British Establishment of Universities in Africa, 1920-1948: A Reaction Against the Spread of American 'Radical' Influence, Cahiers d'Etudes Africaines; The British Abolition of the Slave Trade: A Reappraisal of the Economic and Humanitarian Controversy, African Quart; coed, Fundamentals of African History. **CONTACT ADDRESS** Rhode Island Col, Providence, RI, 02908.

NYBAKKEN, ELIZABETH I.
PERSONAL Born 11/26/1940, Iowa City, IA, m, 1977, 1 child **DISCIPLINE** HISTORY **EDUCATION** Carleton Col, BA, 62; Univ Del, MA, 70, PhD(Am Hist), 74. **CAREER** Teacher Hist, Montclair High Sch, 63-64 & H C Conrad High Sch, 64-67; instr, Univ Del, Wilmington, 72-74; asst prof, West Chester State Col, 74-76; asst prof, 76-81, assoc prof Hist, Miss State Univ, 81-. **HONORS AND AWARDS** Excellence in Teaching Award; Outstanding Woman Professional Award; American Society for Eighteenth-Century Studies. **MEMBERSHIPS** Orgn Am Historians; Inst Early Am Hist & Culture; Southern Hist Asn. **RESEARCH** Colonial & revolutionary America; women in American history; American Family History. **SELECTED PUBLICATIONS** Ed, The Centinel: Warnings of a Revolution, Univ Del Pres, 80; auth, New Light on the Old Side: Irish Influences on Colonial Presbyterianism, J Am Hist, 3/82; The Enlightenment and Calvinism: Mutual Support Systems for the Eighteenth-Century American Wilderness, Studies Voltaire & 18th Cent, 9/80; In the Irish Tradition: Pre-Revolutionary Academics in America, History of Education Quarterly, Summer, 97. **CONTACT ADDRESS** Dept of History, Mississippi State Univ, PO Box H, Mississippi State, MS, 39762-5508. **EMAIL** ean1@ra.msstate.edu

NYE, MARY JO
PERSONAL Born 12/05/1944, Nashville, TN, m, 1968, 1 child **DISCIPLINE** HISTORY OF SCIENCE **EDUCATION** Univ Wisc, PhD, 70. **CAREER** Vis asst prof, to prof, hist of sci 70-91, G.L. Cross res prof hist of sci, 91-94, Univ Okla; Horning prof of hum and prof of hist, Oregon State Univ, 94-; vis prof of hist of sci, Harvard Univ, 88. **HONORS AND AWARDS** Phi Beta Kappa, 65; fel, Am Acad of Arts and Sci; pres, Hist of Sci Soc, 88-89; by-fel, Churchill Col, Cambridge, UK, 95. **MEMBERSHIPS** Am Hist Asn; Hist of Sci Soc; AAAS; Am Chem Soc. **RESEARCH** History of modern physical sciences; social and cultural history of science; science and politics. **SELECTED PUBLICATIONS** Auth, Molecular Reality: A Perspective on the Scientific Work on Jean Perrin, Elsevier, 72; ed, The Question of the Atom: From the Karlsruhe Congress to the First Solvan Conference, 1860-1911, A Selection of Primary Sources, Erwin Tomash, 84; auth, Science in the Provinces: Scientific Communities and Provincial Leadership in France, 1860-1930, California, 86; co-ed, The Invention of Physical Science: Intersections of Mathematics, Theology and Natural Philosophy Since the Seventeenth Century: Essays in Honor of Erwin N. Hiebert, Kluwer Academic, 92. auth, From Chemical Philosophy to Theoretical Chemistry: Dynamics of Matter and Dynamics of Disciplines, 1800-1950, California, 93; auth, Before Big Science: The Pursuit of Modern Chemistry and Physics, 1800-1940, Twayne, 96. **CONTACT ADDRESS** Dept of History, Oregon State Univ, Milam Hall 306, Corvalis, OR, 97331.

NYE, ROBERT ALLEN
PERSONAL Born 06/15/1942, Concord, CA, m, 1968, 1 child **DISCIPLINE** MODERN EUROPEAN & FRENCH HISTORY **EDUCATION** San Jose State Col, BA, 64; Univ Wis, MA, 65, PhD(hist), 69. **CAREER** Assoc prof, 69-79, PROF HIST, UNIV OKLA, 80-, Am Philos Soc fel, 70 & 77; Nat Endowment of Humanities Jr Humanities fel, 72. **HONORS AND AWARDS** Zeitlin-Verbrugge Prize, Hist of Sci Soc, 79. **MEMBERSHIPS** AHA; AAUP **RESEARCH** Modern French history since 1800; European intellectual history since 1700; the history of the social sciences since 1700. **SELECTED PUBLICATIONS** Auth, Two paths to a psychology of social action: Gustave LeBon and Georges Sorel, J Mod Hist, 973; The Origins of Crowd Psychology: Gustave LeBon and the Crisis of Mass Democracy in the Third RePubic, Sage, 75; Heredity or milieu: The foundations of Modern European criminological theory, Isis, 976; The Anti- Democratic Sources of Elite Theory: Pareto, Mosca, Michels, Sage, 77; Crime in Modern Societies: Some Research Strategies for Historians, JSocial Hist, 678; Gustave LeBon's Psychology of Revolution: History, Social Science and Politics in Nineteenth and Early Twentieth Century France, introduction to LeBon's La Revolution Francaise et la psychologie des revolutions, Classics Social Sci, Transaction Bks, 80; Degeneration, Neurasthenia, and the Culture of Sport in Belle Epoque, JContemp Hist, 182; Degeneration and the Medical Model of Cultural Crisis in the French Belle Epoque, Political Symbolism in Modern Europe: Essays in Honor of George L Mosse, Transaction Press, 82; Madness And Social Representations - Living With The Mad in One French Community - Jodelet,d, American Historical Review, Vol 0097, 1992; The Rise And Fall of The Eugenics Empire - Recent Perspectives on The Impact of Biomedical Thought in Modern Society, Historical J, Vol 0036, 1993. **CONTACT ADDRESS** Dept of Hist, Univ of Okla, Norman, OK, 73069.

NYSTROM, BRADLEY
DISCIPLINE HISTORY **EDUCATION** Univ Calif, Davis, BA, 74, MA, 77, PhD, 81. **CAREER** Assoc prof, Calif St Univ, Sacramento, 91- . **MEMBERSHIPS** Soc of Bibl Lit; Assoc of Ancient Hist. **RESEARCH** Early Christianity; Greek poetry. **SELECTED PUBLICATIONS** Transl, ed, Ancient Greece, Kendall/Hunt, 90; The Song of Eros, Southern Ill, 91; auth, "Women, Priests and the Jewish Instriptions of Crete," Ariadne, 95. **CONTACT ADDRESS** Dept of Humanities and Religious Studies, California State Univ, Sacramento, Sacramento, CA, 95819-6083. **EMAIL** nystrom@csus.edu

NZEGWU, NKIRU
DISCIPLINE ART HISTORY **EDUCATION** Univ Ottowa, PhD, 88. **CAREER** Assoc prof, SUNY Binghamton. **RESEARCH** Philos of art; traditional African art and cult hist; colonialism and postcolonial influences in contemp African art; Black Canadian art. **SELECTED PUBLICATIONS** Auth, Questions of Identity and Inheritance: A Critical Review of Anthony Appiah's 'In My Father's House', Hypatia: Jour Feminist Philos, 96; Bypassing New York in Representing EKO: Production of Space in a Nigerian City in Re-Presenting the City: Ethnicity, Capital and Culture in the 21st Century Metropolis, Macmillan and NY UP, 96. **CONTACT ADDRESS** SUNY Binghamton, PO Box 6000, Binghamton, NY, 13902-6000. **EMAIL** panap@binghamton.edu

O

O'BOYLE, CRONELIUS
DISCIPLINE HISTORY **EDUCATION** Cambridge Univ, BA, 82, Mphil, 83, PhD, 87. **CAREER** Asst prof, 90. **RESEARCH** Medieval natural philosophy and medicine; early history of universities; historiography of science. **SELECTED PUBLICATIONS** Auth, Medieval Prognosis and Astrology, 91; Medicine, God and Aristotle in the Early Universities, 92; Surgical Texts and Social Contexts: Physicians and Surgeons in Paris 1270-1430, 94. **CONTACT ADDRESS** History and Philosophy of Science Dept, Univ of Notre Dame, Notre Dame, IN, 46556. **EMAIL** Cornelius.O.Boyle.1@nd.edu

O'BRIEN, J. WILLARD
DISCIPLINE AMERICAN LEGAL SYSTEM **EDUCATION** Fordham Univ, BS, 52; Fordham Univ Sch Law, JD, 57. **CAREER** Prof; Villanova Univ, 65- & dean, Law Sch, 72-83. **MEMBERSHIPS** Canon Law Soc; Order of the Coif; Amer Bar Asn; Pa Bar Asn; bd dir, Interfaith Coun on the Holocaust. **RESEARCH** Human rights, holocaust. **SELECTED PUBLICATIONS** Contrib, The Subversion of Justice: Lessons in Legal Ethics, in the Holocaust Forty Years Later, 89 & The Obligation of a Law School to Instruct Students on Morality, in Holocaust Education, 85. **CONTACT ADDRESS** Law School, Villanova Univ, 800 Lancaster Ave, Villanova, PA, 19085-1692. **EMAIL** obrien@law.vill.edu

O'BRIEN, JEAN M.
DISCIPLINE HISTORY **EDUCATION** Bemidji State Univ, BA, 80; Univ Chicago, MA, 82; PhD, 90. **CAREER** ASSOC PROF, HIST, UNIV MINN **MEMBERSHIPS** Am Antiquarian Soc **SELECTED PUBLICATIONS** Coauth, "Guide to Historical Sources: An Annotated Bibliography," in The Illinois and Michigan Canal National Heritage Corridor: A Guide to History and Sources, N Ill Univ Press, 88; auth, Dispossession by Degrees: Indian Land and Identity in Natick, Massachusetts, 1650-1790, Cambridge Univ Press, 97. **CONTACT ADDRESS** 16A Grove St, Minneapolis, MN, 55401.

O'BRIEN, THOMAS F.
PERSONAL Born 02/16/1947, Boston, MA, m, 1968, 3 children **DISCIPLINE** HISTORY **EDUCATION** Boston Col, BA, 68; Univ Conn, MA, 70, PhD, 76. **CAREER** From asst prof to assoc prof to prof, to chemn, 77-99, Univ Houston. **HONORS AND AWARDS** Robertson Prize, 80, Honorable Mention Boltin Prize, 98, Conference on Latin American Hist. **MEMBERSHIPS** Conference on Latin Am Hist; Latin Am Stud Asn. **RESEARCH** US business in Latin America. **SELECTED PUBLICATIONS** Auth, art, The Antofagasta Co: A Case Study of Peripheral Capitalism, 80; auth, The Nitrate Industry and Chile's Crucial Transition, 82; auth, art, Rich Beyond the Dream of Avarice: The Guggenheim Brothers in Chile, 89; auth, art, The Revolutionary Mission: American Enterprise in Cuba, 93; auth, The Revolutionary Mission: American Enterprise in Latin America, 1900-1945, 96. **CONTACT ADDRESS** Dept of History, Univ of Houston, Houston, TX, 77204-3785. **EMAIL** tobrien@uh.edu

O'BRIEN-KEHOE, JEAN
DISCIPLINE AMERICAN INDIAN HISTORY AND UNITED STATES COLONIAL HISTORY **EDUCATION** Univ Chicago, PhD, 90. **CAREER** Asst prof Hist and Am Indian Stud, Univ Minn, Twin Cities, 90-. **HONORS AND AWARDS** Res grant, Newberry Libr, Am Antiq Soc, and Mass Hist Soc; McKnight Land-Grant Professorship, 92; Recognition Award for Emerging Scholars, Am Asn Univ Women. **RESEARCH** 19th century New Englanders' representations of local and regional Indian history. **SELECTED PUBLICATIONS** Auth, Divorced from the Land: Accomodation Strategies of Indian Women in 18th Century New England, in Gender, Kinship, and Power, Routledge, 96; Dispossession by Degrees: Indian Land and Identity in Natick, Massachusetts, 1650-1790, Cambridge UP, 97. **CONTACT ADDRESS** Univ Minn, Twin Cities, 614 Soc Sci Bldg, Minneapolis, MN, 55455. **EMAIL** obrie002@maroon.tc.umn.edu

O'CONELL, ROBERT J.
DISCIPLINE CLASSICS **EDUCATION** Sorbonne, PhD. **CAREER** Prof emer, Fordham Univ. **SELECTED PUBLICATIONS** Auth, Augustine's Early Theory of Man, 68; St Augustine's Confessions: The Odyssey of Soul, 69; Soundings in St Augustine's Imagination, 94. **CONTACT ADDRESS** Dept of Class Lang and Lit, Fordham Univ, 113 W 60th St, New York, NY, 10023.

O'CONNELL, DANIEL C.
PERSONAL Born 05/20/1928, Sand Springs, OK, s **DISCIPLINE** EXPERIMENTAL PSYCHOLOGY **EDUCATION** St Louis Univ, AB, 51; St Louis Univ, AM, 53; St Louis Univ, PhL, 52; St Louis Univ, STL, 60; Univ Illinois, PhD, 63 **CAREER** Prof, Georgetown Univ, 90-98; chmn, Dept Pyschol, 91-96; visiting prof, Georgetown Univ, 86, 89, 90; dir, Graduate Prog Cognitive Pyschol, Loyola Univ, 85-89; prof, Loyola Univ, 80-90, 98- **HONORS AND AWARDS** Georgetown Univ Grad School Grant, 97; Georgetown Univ Fac Grant, 91; Humboldt-Stiftung Grant to Germany, 90, 91; Fulbright Fel, Univ Kassel, 79-80; Alpha Sigma Nu Ntl Jesuit Honor Soc, 75; Phi Beta Kappa, 74 **MEMBERSHIPS** Amer Psychol Soc; Amer Psychol Assoc; Midwestern Psychol Assoc; Missouri Psychol Assoc; Illinois Psychol Assoc; Southwestern Psychol Assoc; Eastern Psychol Assoc; Psychonomic Soc; Soc Scientific Study Relig; Amer Assoc Advancement Sci; Amer Assoc Univ Professors **RESEARCH** Psycholinguistics; Temporal Organization of Speech **SELECTED PUBLICATIONS** Coauth, "Theoretical ideals and their violation: Princess Diana and Martin Bashir in the BBC interview," Pragmatics, 97; coauth, "Language use and time," KODIKAS/CODE, 96; coauth, "Language use and dialogue from a psychological perspective," Der Dialogbegriff am Ende des 20. Johrhunderts, 96 **CONTACT ADDRESS** Pyschol Dept, Loyola Univ, Damen Hall 615, Chicago, IL, 60626. **EMAIL** doconnel@luc.edu

O'CONNOR, CAROL A.
PERSONAL Born 02/14/1946, Evanston, IL, m, 1977, 2 children **DISCIPLINE** HISTORY **EDUCATION** Manhattanville Col, BA, 67; Yale Univ, MPhil, 70; PhD, 76. **CAREER** Instr, 74-76, asst prof, Knox Col, 76-77; ASST PROF, 77-80, ASSOC PROF, 80-86, PROF, UTAH STATE UNIV, 86-. **HONORS AND AWARDS** Caughey Prize, WHA, 94; Western Heritage Wrangler Awd, 94; Bradley Fel, Mont Hist Soc, 97. **MEMBERSHIPS** Org of Am Historians; Urban Hist Asn; Western Hist Asn. **RESEARCH** U.S. West. **SELECTED PUBLICATIONS** Co-ed & contribur, The Oxford History of the American West, Oxford Univ Press, 94; auth, A Sort of Utopia: Scarsdale 1891-1981, State Univ of NY press, 83; From Scarsdale to the Nation: Finding the Meaning in Local History, Working Papers of the Seminar of NY State Hist, NY State Ed Dept, Division of His and Anthrop Services, 85; Setting a Standard for Suburbia: Innovation in the Scarsdale Schools 1920-30, Hist of Ed Quart, 80. **CONTACT ADDRESS** Dept of Hist, Utah State Univ, Logan, UT, 84322-0710. **EMAIL** coconnor@hass.usu.edu

O'CONNOR, EUGENE
PERSONAL Born 09/03/1948, Buffalo, NY **DISCIPLINE** CLASSICS **EDUCATION** Univ Cal Santa Barbara, PhD 84. **CAREER** Prometheus Book, editor 89-; Univ Montana, vis asst prof 88-89; The Col of Wooster, vis asst prof 87-88; Univ Cal Irvine, vis lect 85-87; Univ Cal Santa Barbara, vis lectr 84-85. **HONORS AND AWARDS** BA Cum Laude **MEMBERSHIPS** APA **RESEARCH** Greek and Roman satire and epigram; neo latin; gay studies. **SELECTED PUBLICATIONS** Auth, Martial the Moral Jester: Priapic Motifs and the Restoration of Order in the Epigrams, in: Martial, ed, F. Grewing, N. Holzberg, Stuttgart: Franz Syeiner Verlag, 98; Panormita's Reply to His Critics: The Hermaphroditus and the Literary Defense, Renaissance Quart, 97; Hell's Pit and Heaven's Rose: The Typology of Female Sights and Smells in Panormita's Hermaphroditus, Medievalia et Humanistica, 96; The Essential Epicurus: Letters, Principal Doctrines, Vatican Sayings and Fragments, translated with an introduction by Eugene O'Connor, Amherst NY, Prometheus Books, 93. **CONTACT ADDRESS** Prometheus Books, Apt B30, Buffalo, NY, 14201. **EMAIL** pontano@aol.com

O'CONNOR, JOHN E.
PERSONAL Born 08/13/1943, New York, NY, m, 1965, 2 children **DISCIPLINE** AMERICAN HISTORY, CINEMA **EDUCATION** St Johns Univ, NY, BA, 65; Queens Col, NY, MA, 67; City Univ New York, PhD(early Am hist), 74. **CAREER** Lectr hist, Queens Col, NY, 66-69; asst prof, 69-79, assoc prof hist, NJ Inst Technol, 79-89; coordr Man & Technol Prog, 77-89, assoc chmn, 70-76, chemn, 76- , Historians Film Comt, 70-76; co-ed, Film & Hist J, 71- . **HONORS AND AWARDS** AHA created John E. O'Connor Award for Best Film or TV Production about History, 91. **MEMBERSHIPS** AHA; Orgn Am Historians; Am Studies Asn; Soc Cinema Studies. **RESEARCH** Early American history; history and technology; motion pictures and television. **SELECTED PUBLICATIONS** Coauth, Teaching History With Film, AHA, 74; ed, Film & the Humanities, Rockefeller Found, 77; auth, Legal reform in the Early Republic: The New Jersey Experience, Am J Legal Hist, 78; William Paterson: Lawyer and Statesman 1745-1806, Rutgers Univ Press, 79; ed, American History/American Film: Interpreting the Hollywood Image, Frederick Ungar Publ, 79; ed, I am a Fugitive From a Chain Gang, Univ Wis Press, 81; auth, Image as Artifact: The Historical Analysis of Film and Television, Kreiger, 91. **CONTACT ADDRESS** Dept of Humanities, New Jersey Inst of Tech, 323 M L King Jr Blvd, Newark, NJ, 07102-1824.

O'CONNOR, JOSEPH E.
DISCIPLINE HISTORY **EDUCATION** Univ Notre Dame, BA; Univ Va, MA, PhD. **CAREER** Prof, 67-; Asso provost; former dept chair. **HONORS AND AWARDS** Alumni ass Dist Tchng Award; Archivist, interviewer, JFK Oral Hist Proj.. **RESEARCH** Development op civilization, Russian-Soviet history; 20 Century Europe. **SELECTED PUBLICATIONS** Areas: Yugoslavian sculptor Ivan Mestrovic and on faculty development, instructional improvement programs, career planning and career change, and faculty re-direction; ed,Teaching in Higher Education. **CONTACT ADDRESS** Wittenberg Univ, Springfield, OH, 45501-0720.

O'CONNOR, MICHAEL PATRICK
PERSONAL Born 04/07/1950, Lackawanna, NY **DISCIPLINE** ANCIENT NEAR EASTERN LANGUAGES; LITERATURE **EDUCATION** Univ Michigan, PhD 78, AM 74; Univ of British Columbia, MA 72; Univ Notre Dame, BA 70. **CAREER** Catholic Univ of Amer, assoc prof 97-; Union Theol Sem, assoc prof 95-97; Univ St Thomas St Paul Sem, asst prof 92-95; Editing 80-93; Eisenbrauns IN, Sr consul editor 85-; Boston Univ Med Sch, neuro consul 85-89; The Anchor Bible, DoubleDay & Co NY, asst gen editor 77-80. **MEMBERSHIPS** AOS; CBA; SBL; Biblical Colloquium. **RESEARCH** Poetry **SELECTED PUBLICATIONS** Auth, Hebrew Verse Structure, Winona Lake IN, Eisenbrauns, 80, 2nd print, 97; auth, An Introduction to Biblical Hebrew Syntax, coauth, Winona Lake IN, Eisenbrauns, 90, 6th print 97. **CONTACT ADDRESS** Languages and Literatures, The Catholic Univ of America, Washington, DC, 20064. **EMAIL** oconnorm@cua.edu

O'CONNOR, THOMAS H.
PERSONAL Born 12/09/1922, South Boston, MA, m, 1949, 3 children **DISCIPLINE** AMERICAN HISTORY **EDUCATION** Boston Col, AB, 49, MA, 50; Boston Univ, PhD, 58. **CAREER** From instr to assoc prof, 50-70, chmn dept, 62-70, fac asst to pres, 70-71, chmn coun libr educ, 71-75, prof hist, 70-93, emeritus, 93-, Boston Col; lectr, 67-, Harvard Univ. **HONORS AND AWARDS** Irish Charitable Soc of Boston: Dist Irish-Amer Award, 88; Shattuch Award: tchng Excel, Harvard Univ, 90; Dr of Humane Lett, hon, Boston Col, 93; Dr of Humane Lett, hon, Merrimack Col, 95. **MEMBERSHIPS** AHA; AAUP; Am Cath Hist Assn; Orgn Am Historians; Bostonian Soc, res fel; Mass Archives Comm. **RESEARCH** Boston hist, New England hist, 1820-1860; the age of Jackson; the Civil War. **SELECTED PUBLICATIONS** Auth, Fitzpatrick's Boston: 1846-1866, Northeastern, 84; auth, South Boston: My Home Town, Northeastern, 94, Little Brown, 97; auth, Civil War Boston, Northeastern, 98; auth, Boston Catholics, Northeastern, 98. **CONTACT ADDRESS** Dept of History, Boston Col, 140 Commonwealth Ave, Chestnut Hill, MA, 02167-3800. **EMAIL** OCONNORT:thomas.oconnor.1@bc.edu

O'DAY, EDWARD FRANCIS
PERSONAL Born 04/27/1925, Portsmouth, VA, m, 1961, 5 children **DISCIPLINE** PSYCHOLOGY **EDUCATION** Univ of Florida, PhD 56, MA 54, BS 52. **CAREER** San Diego State Univ, prof, assoc prof, asst prof, 57-86. **HONORS AND AWARDS** Phi Beta Kappa; Phi Beta Phi **CONTACT ADDRESS** Apt# 8093, Livingston, TX, 77351-9330.

O'DELL, LESLIE
DISCIPLINE PERFORMANCE THEORY **EDUCATION** Queen's, BA; Toronto, MA, PhD. **CAREER** Assoc Prof **SELECTED PUBLICATIONS** Auth, Garrison Theatre; Amateurs of the Regiment, 1815-1870. **CONTACT ADDRESS** Dept of English, Wilfrid Laurier Univ, 75 University Ave W, Waterloo, ON, N2L 3C5. **EMAIL** lodell@mach1.wlu.ca

O'DONNELL, JAMES
PERSONAL Born 10/11/1937, Memphis, TN, m, 1972, 3 children **DISCIPLINE** HISTORY **EDUCATION** Lambuth Col, BA, 59; Duke Univ, MA, 61, PhD, 63. **CAREER** Prof, Radford Col, 63-69; Thomas prof, Marietta Col, 69-. **HONORS AND AWARDS** Harness Fellow, McCoy Prof, 96-99. **MEMBERSHIPS** Ohio Acad Hist; Southern Hist Asn; Org Am Historians. **RESEARCH** Southern Indians before 1820; northern Indians before 1820; 19th century liberal arts Cols. **SELECTED PUBLICATIONS** Auth, Southern Indians in the American Revolution, 72; auth, Southeastern Frontiers, 83. **CONTACT ADDRESS** Marietta Col, 215 Fifth St, Marietta, OH, 45750. **EMAIL** odonnelj@marietta.edu

O'DONNELL, JAMES JOSEPH
PERSONAL Born 02/26/1950, Giessen, Germany, s **DISCIPLINE** CLASSICAL AND MEDIEVAL STUDIES **EDUCATION** Princeton Univ, BA, 72; Yale Univ, PhD, 75. **CAREER** Lectr, Bryn Mowr Col, 75-76; asst prof, Catholic Univ of Am, 76-77; asst prof, Cornell Univ, 77-81; ASSOC PROF, 81-90, PROF, 90-, VICE PROVOST, 96-, UNIV OF PA. **HONORS AND AWARDS** Guggenheim Fel, 89. **MEMBERSHIPS** Am Philological Asn; Medieval Acad of Am. **RESEARCH** Cultural history of late antiquity. **SELECTED PUBLICATIONS** Auth, Cassiodorus, Univ of Calif Press, 79; auth, Boethius, Consolatio Philosophiae: Text and Commentary, Bryn Mawr Commentaries, 84; auth, Augustine, Twayne Publishers, 85; auth, Augustine, Confessions: Text and Commentary, Clarendon Press, 92; auth, Avatars of the Word, Harvard Univ Press, 98; co-ed, Scholarly Journals at the Crossroads: A Subversive Proposal for Electronic Publishing, Asn for Res Libr, 95. **CONTACT ADDRESS** 3401 Walnut St, Ste 230A, Philadelphia, PA, 19104. **EMAIL** jod@sas.upenn.edu

O'DONNELL, KIM
PERSONAL Born 06/05/1965, Brooklyn, NY, m, 1990, 3 children **DISCIPLINE** PSYCHOLOGY **EDUCATION** New York Univ, BA, 87; Temple Univ, PhD, 95. **CAREER** Psychol Fel, Yale Univ, 92-94; staff psychol, Elmcrest Psychiatric Inst, 94-97; chemn, Naugatuck Valley Com Tech Col, 97-. **HONORS AND AWARDS** Presidential Scholar, New York Univ, 83-87. **MEMBERSHIPS** Am Psychol Asn **RESEARCH** Adolescence; autonomy develop; substance abuse; personality disorders. **SELECTED PUBLICATIONS** Coauth, art, Discrepancies between perceptions of decision making and behavioral autonomy, 91; coauth, art, Toddler language and play in the second year: Stability, covariation and influences of parenting, 92. **CONTACT ADDRESS** Naugatuck Valley Comm-Tech Col, 750 Chase Pky, Waterbury, CT, 06708. **EMAIL** kodonnell@nvctc5.commnet.edu

O'DONNELL, KRISTA E.
DISCIPLINE HISTORY **EDUCATION** SUNY, Oneonta, BS, 88; SUNY, Binghamton, MA, 91; PhD, 96. **CAREER** Asst prof, William Paterson Univ, 97-; vis asst prof, Southwest State Univ, 96-97; asst, Workshop and Technical Support Staff, Humanities On Line H-Net, 94-95; tchg asst & lectr, Binghamton Univ, 90-95. **HONORS AND AWARDS** Distinguished Dissertation Soc Sci Awd, Binghamton Univ, 96; Alternate, Amer Asn Univ Women Dissertation fel, 94-95; Fulbright res fel, Universitat Bielefeld, Ger, 92-93; DAAD, Ger Acad Exchange Serv, res grant. **SELECTED PUBLICATIONS** Auth, Making War with Poison: Gendering Danger, Illicit Violence, and Domestic Work in German Southwest Africa, 96; **CONTACT ADDRESS** Dept of History, William Paterson Col, 300 Pompton Rd., Atrium 202, Wayne, NJ, 07470. **EMAIL** mollyod@frontier.wilpaterson.edu

O'GORMAN, JAMES F.
PERSONAL Born 09/19/1933, St. Louis, MO, m, 1998, 3 children **DISCIPLINE** HISTORY OF ART **EDUCATION** Wash Univ, BA, 56; Univ IL, MArch 61; Harvard Univ, PhD, 66. **CAREER** Grace Slack McNeil Prof, 75-, Wellesley College. **HONORS AND AWARDS** Henry Russell Hitchcock Prize; SAH Awd. **SELECTED PUBLICATIONS** Auth, Accomplished in All Departments of Art: Hammatt Billings of Boston 1818-1874, Amherst MA, U of Mass Press, 98; ABC of Architecture, Philadelphia, U of Penn Press, 98; Living Architecture: A Biography of H H Richardson, NY, Simon & Schuster, 97; The Perspective of Anglo-American Architecture: Notes on some graphic attempts at three-dimensional representation in the colonies and early republic, Philadelphia, The Athenaeum, 95. **CONTACT ADDRESS** Dept of Art, Wellesley Col, 106 Central St, Wellesley, MA, 02181-8257. **EMAIL** jogorman@wellesley.edu

O'HARA, JAMES J.
DISCIPLINE AUGUSTAN POETRY **EDUCATION** Col Holy Cross, AB; Univ Mich, PhD. **CAREER** Vis asst prof, 86-87; asst prof, 87-92; assoc prof, 92-97; Professor, 97-. **HONORS AND AWARDS** Holy Cross, Nat Merit Scholar; Henry Bean four-year full-tuition Classics Sch; Philip A. Conniff Clas Prize; Valedictorian Mich: Sci & Arts First-year Fel; dept Clas Studies, Dissertatoion fel, Horace H. Rackham Predoctoral Fel. Nat Endowment Hum Rome Prize fel, Proj grants. **SELECTED PUBLICATIONS** Auth, Death and the Optimistic Prophecy in Vergil's Aeneid, Princeton, 90. **CONTACT ADDRESS** Wesleyan Univ, Middletown, CT, 06459. **EMAIL** johara@wesleyan.edu

O'KEIFE, J. PAUL
PERSONAL Born 11/30/1939, Boston, MA, s **DISCIPLINE** HISTORY **EDUCATION** Boston Col, BA, 61, MA, 63; Univ Wis, PhD, 79. **CAREER** Prof, Northland Col, 86-. **RESEARCH** Papacy; social-intellectual history. **CONTACT ADDRESS** 1650 Monroe St #G, Madison, WI, 53711. **EMAIL** po'keife@wheeler.northland.edu

O'MALLEY, JOHN WILLIAM
PERSONAL Born 06/11/1927, Tiltonsville, OH **DISCIPLINE** RENAISSANCE & REFORMATION HISTORY **EDUCATION** Loyola Univ, Ill, AB, 51, MA, 57, STL, 60; Harvard Univ, PhD, 66; DLitt, Loyola Univ, Ill, 82. **CAREER** From asst prof to prof hist, Univ Detroit, 65-79; prof hist, Weston Sch Theol, 79-; Harvard Ctr Ital Renaissance Studies fel, Italy, 66-68; vis assoc prof hist, Univ Mich, Ann Arbor, 72-73. **HONORS AND AWARDS** Guggenheim fel, 75-76; NEH fel, 83. **MEMBERSHIPS** Renaissance Soc Am; Am Cath Hist Assn; pres Am Cath Hist Assoc, 90; Fel Am Acad of Arts & Sci, 96; Mem Am Philos Soc, 97; pres, Renaissance Soc of Am, 98-2000. **RESEARCH** Religious culture of early modern Europe, especially Giles of Viterbo; Erasmus; Renaissance and reformation history; rhetoric and Renaissance oratory. **SE-**

LECTED PUBLICATIONS Auth, Giles of Viterbo on Church and Reform, E J Brill, Leiden, 68; auth, Praise and Blame in Renaissance Rome, 79; auth, The First Jesuits, 93. CONTACT ADDRESS 3 Phillips Pl, Cambridge, MA, 02138-3495. EMAIL jomalley@wjst.edu

O'NEIL, PATRICK M.
PERSONAL Born 12/03/1947, Norwich, NY, s **DISCIPLINE** HISTORY; MODERN EUROPE; MODERN BRITAIN; BRITISH EMPIRE **EDUCATION** NY State Univ, BA, 69;MA in English Lit, 73;MA in Philos, 79; MA History, 81; MA Soc Sci,89; PhD History, 93. **CAREER** Assoc prof, Broome Comm Col, 97-; asst prof, Broome Comm Col, 95-97; adjunct instr, Broome Comm Col, 85-95; adjunct lctr, SUNY, 91; instr Comm Educ Prog, Broome Comm Col, 86-; adjunct instr, St Univ NY at Morrisville, 85-91. **HONORS AND AWARDS** Notary Public, St of NY, 77-92; SUNY Tchg Assistanceship, 68-70; General Foods Scholar, 83-84; NY St Regents Scholar, 65-70. **MEMBERSHIPS** Amer Acad Polit Sci; Amer Intl Assoc for Philos of Law; Amer Assoc for Philos Study of Soc; Amer Historical Assoc; Amer Philos Assoc; Federalist Soc for Law & Pub Safety; Intercollegiate Studies Institute; NY St Assoc of European Historians; NY St Philos Assoc; Soc of Cath Social Scientists; Soc of Christian Philosophers; Intl Churchill Soc; Modern Lang Assoc. **RESEARCH** British Empire History; Winston S Churchill; American Constitutional Law; Ethical Philosophy; Philosophy of Law. **SELECTED PUBLICATIONS** Winston's S. Churchill's Philosophy of Empire: Mind of the Imperialist, Peter Lang, 99; A Reconciliation of the Humean Is/Ought Problem to an Objective Moral Order, Cath Social Sci Rev, Villanove Univ, 98; Encycl of Int Slavery, Macmillan, 98. **CONTACT ADDRESS** Depts of Humanities and Social Sciences, Broome Comm Col, 75 Colfax Ave, Binghamton, NY, 13905. **EMAIL** oneil_p@sunybroome.edu

O'NEILL, JAMES E.
PERSONAL Born 02/02/1929, Renovo, PA, m, 1953, 5 children **DISCIPLINE** MODERN HISTORY **EDUCATION** Univ Detroit, AB, 52, MA, 54; Univ Chicago, PhD, 61. **CAREER** Ref librn, Univ Detroit, 56-57; from instr to asst prof hist, Univ Notre Dame, 57-63; Europ manuscript specialist, Libr Congr, 63-65; assoc prof hist, Loyola Univ, Ill, 65-69; dir, Franklin D Roosevelt Libr, 69-71; dep archivist of US, Nat Arch & Rec Serv, 72-80; ASST ARCHIVIST FOR PRESIDENTIAL LIBR, 80-, Am Coun Learned Soc res grant, 63; mem adv bd, US Army Mil Hist Res Collection, 73-78; mem bd dirs, Eleanor Roosevelt Inst, 73-; mem, Adv Comt, Senate Hist Off, 76, Exec Comt, Int Coun Arch, 80- & Dept Army Hist Adv Comn, 78-; ed, Int J Arch, 78-81. **HONORS AND AWARDS** LHD, St Edward's Univ, 75. **MEMBERSHIPS** AHA; fel Soc Am Archivists. **RESEARCH** Modern United States and British history; archives and historical manuscripts; social history. **SELECTED PUBLICATIONS** Auth, The Victorian background to the British welfare state, S Atlantic Quart, spring 67; Will success spoil the presidential libraries?, Am Archivist, summer 73; coauth, Episodes in American History, Ginn, 73; auth, The security classification of records in the United States, Indian Archivist, 74; co-ed, World War II: An Account of Its Documents, Howard Univ, 76; contribr, Access to the Papers of Recent Public Figures, Orgn Am Historians, 77; Replevin, Col & Res Libr, 79. **CONTACT ADDRESS** Nat Archives Bldg, Washington, DC, 20408.

O'NEILL, KERILL
PERSONAL Born 06/30/1965, Dublin, Ireland **DISCIPLINE** CLASSICS **EDUCATION** Trinity Col, BA, 87; Cornell Univ, PhD, 95. **CAREER** Vis asst prof, 92-94, Taylor asst prof, 94-98, Colby Col. **RESEARCH** Latin love elegy; Greek tragedy, intertextuality. **SELECTED PUBLICATIONS** Coauth, Neolithic Chipped Stone, an appendix to John E. Coleman, Excavations at Halai, Hesperia, 92; auth, Propertius 4.4: Tarpeia and the Burden of Aetiology, Hermathena, 95;auth, Aeschylus, Homer, and the Snake at the Breast, forthcoming, 98; auth, Symbolism and Sympathetic Magic in Propertius 4.5, forthcoming, 94; auth, Ovid and Propertius: Reflexive Annotation in Amores1.8, forthcoming, 99. **CONTACT ADDRESS** Dept of Classics, Colby Col, 4161 Mayflower Hill, Waterville, ME, 04901. **EMAIL** knoneill@colby.edu

O'SHAUGHNESSY, ANDREW J.
DISCIPLINE HISTORY **EDUCATION** Oxford Univ, BA, 82, MA, 87, DPhil, 88. **CAREER** Lect, Lincoln Coll, Oxford; ASST PROF, UNIV OF WIS-OSHKOSH. **MEMBERSHIPS** Am Antiquarian Soc **RESEARCH** British West Indies and the Am Revolution **SELECTED PUBLICATIONS** Coauth, "Accounting for Slaves in the British West Indies," Accounting Hist Rev; sub-ed, History Sixth. **CONTACT ADDRESS** 207 E Irving Ave., No. 203, Oshkosh, WI, 54901.

O'SULLIVAN, JOHN
DISCIPLINE HISTORY **EDUCATION** Columbia Univ, PhD. **CAREER** Prof. **HONORS AND AWARDS** Tchg Incentive Prog Awd. **RESEARCH** 20th century American history; war and peace. **SELECTED PUBLICATIONS** Co-auth, From Volunteerism to Conscription: Congress and the Selective Service 1940-1945, 82; The Draft and Its Enemies, 74; American Economic History, 89; We Have Just Begun Not to Fight: An Oral History of Conscientious Objectors in Civilian Public Service During World War Two, 96. **CONTACT ADDRESS** History Dept, Florida Atlantic Univ, 777 Glades Rd, Boca Raton, FL, 33431. **EMAIL** rinaldi@acc.fau.edu

OAKLEY, FRANCIS
PERSONAL Born 10/06/1931, Liverpool, England, m, 1958, 4 children **DISCIPLINE** MEDIEVAL & RENAISSANCE HISTORY **EDUCATION** Oxford Univ, BA, 53, MA, 57; Yale Univ, MA, 58, PhD(medieval hist), 60. **CAREER** Instr hist, Yale Univ, 59-61; lectr, 61-62, from asst prof to assoc prof, 62-70, chmn hist of ideas prog, 74-76, Prof Hist, Williams Col, 70-, Dean Fac, 77-, Soc Sci Res Coun fel, 63; Am Coun Learned Soc grant-in-aid, 65, sr fel, 69-70; vis lectr, Bennington Col, 67; Nat Endowment for Humanities sr res fel, 76; mem, Sch Hist Studies, Inst Advan Study, Princeton Univ, 81-82. **HONORS AND AWARDS** B K Smith Lectr, Univ St Thomas, 68; Mead-Swing lectr, Oberlin Col, 81. **MEMBERSHIPS** Am Cath Hist Asn; Mediaeval Acad Am; Am Church Hist Soc; Am Hist Asn. **RESEARCH** Medieval political theory; conciliar studies; late medieval legal theory. **SELECTED PUBLICATIONS** Auth, The Political Thought of Pierre d'Ailly, Yale Univ, 64; Kingship and the Gods: The Western Apostasy, Univ St Thomas, 68; Jacobean political theology, J Hist Ideas, 68; coauth, Creation: The Impact of an Idea, Scribner's, 69; auth, Council over Pope, Herder, 69; Walter Ullmann's vision of medieval politics, Past & Present, 73; The Medieval Experience, Scribner's, 74; The Western Church in the Later Middle Ages, Cornell Univ, 79; The Crucial Centuries, Terra Nova, rev ed, 79, Span transl, Los Siglos Decisivos, Alianza Ed, 80; Capacity And Volition - a History of The Distinction of Absolute And Ordained Power - Courtenay,wj, Speculum-a J of Medieval Studies, Vol 0068, 1993; Church, State And Christian Society at The Time of The Investiture-contest - Tellenbach,g, Church History, Vol 0063, 1994; Dailly,pierre 'Tractatus Super De Consolatione Philosophiae Boethii', Quaestio-primus - French And Latin - Chappuis,m, Editor, Speculum-a J of Medieval Studies, Vol 0071, 1996; Nederman, Gerson, Conciliar Theory And Constitutionalism - Sed-contra, History of Political Thought, Vol 0016, 1995; b Complexities of Context - Gerson, Bellarmine, Sarpi, Richer, And The Venetian-interdict of 1606-1607, Catholic Historical Review, Vol 0082, 1996; Divine Power - The Medieval Power Distinction up to Its Adoption by Albert, Bonaventure, And Aquinas - Moonan,l, Speculum-a J of Medieval Studies, Vol 0071, 1996; Divine Power - The Medieval Power Distinction up to Its Adoption by Albert, Bonaventure, And Aquinas - Moonan,l, Speculum-a J of Medieval Studies, Vol 0071, 1996; Dailly,pierre 'Tractatus Super De Consolatione Philosophiae Boethii', Quaestio-primus - French And Latin - Chappuis,m, Editor, Speculum-a J of Medieval Studies, Vol 0071, 1996; The Elusive Academic Profession - Complexity And Change, Daedalus, Vol 0126, 1997. **CONTACT ADDRESS** Dept of Hist, Williams Col, 880 Main St, Williamstown, MA, 01267-2600.

OAKLEY, JOHN H.
DISCIPLINE CLASSICAL ART & ARCHAEOLOGY **EDUCATION** Rutgers Univ, BA, 72, MA, 76, PhD, 80. **CAREER** Asst prof, 80-86, assoc prof, 86-93, Col Wm & Mary; PROF, CHANCELLOR, COL WM & MARY, 93-; vis prof, Univ Canterbury, Christchurch, New Zealand, 97; Elizabeth G. WHitehead vis prof, Am Sch Class Stud, Athens, 97-98. **CONTACT ADDRESS** Dept of Class Stud, Col of William and Mary, Williamsburg, VA, 23187. **EMAIL** jxoakl@facstaff.wm.edu

OATES, JOHN FRANCIS
PERSONAL Born 08/07/1934, Holyoke, MA, m, 1957, 4 children **DISCIPLINE** ANCIENT HISTORY **EDUCATION** Yale Univ, BA, 56, MA, 58, PhD(Classics, Ancient Hist), 60. **CAREER** From instr to asst prof Classics, Yale Univ, 60-67; assoc prof Ancient Hist, 67-71, chmn Dept Class Studies, 71-80, prof Ancient Hist, Duke Univ, 71-72, Morse fel, 65-66; hon res asst Greek, Univ Col, Univ London, 65-66; mem Managing Comt, Intercollegiate Ctr, Rome, 72-76 & Am Sch Class Studies, Athens, 73-; Am Coun Learned Socs fel, 73-74; mem Adv Coun, Sch Class Studies, Am Acad in Rome, 76-; vpres & trustee, Triangle Univs Ctr for Advan Studies, Inc, 76-90; trustee, Nat Humanities Ctr, 77-90; dir, Nat Fedn State Humanities Coun, 80-83; dir Duke Papyrus Archive 92. **MEMBERSHIPS** Archaeol Inst Am; AHA; Class Asn MidW & South; Am Soc Papyrologists (pres, 75-); Am Philol Asn. **RESEARCH** Ancient history; papyrology. **SELECTED PUBLICATIONS** Auth, A Christian inscription in Greek from Armenna in Nubia, J Egyptian Archaeol, 63; coauth, Papyri in the Beinecke Library at Yale, Vol I, Am Soc Papyrologists, 67; auth, A Rhodian auction sale of a slave girl, J Egyptian Archaeol, 69; coauth, Checklist of papyrological editions, Bull Am Soc Papyrologists, 74, 2nd ed, 78. **CONTACT ADDRESS** Dept of Classical Studies, Duke Univ, PO Box 90103, Durham, NC, 27708-0103. **EMAIL** joates@duke.edu

OBER, JOSIAH
PERSONAL Born 02/27/1953, Brunswick, ME, m, 1986 **DISCIPLINE** HISTORY **EDUCATION** Univ Minn, BA, 75; Univ Mich, PhD, 80. **CAREER** Asst Prof to full Prof Hist, 80-90, Montana State Univ; Prof of Classics 90-, dept Chmn Classics 93-, Princeton Univ. **HONORS AND AWARDS** APA Goodwin Awd of Merit, Guggenheim Fel, Martin Lect Oberlin Coll. **MEMBERSHIPS** APA **RESEARCH** Greek history, political theory, comparative democracy. **SELECTED PUBLICATIONS** Auth, The Athenian Revolution, Essays on Ancient Greek Democracy and Political Theory, Princeton Univ Press, 96; Political Dissent in Democratic Athens, Intellectual Critics of Popular Rule, Princeton Univ Press, 98; Co-ed, The Craft of the Ancient Historian, Essays in Honor of Chester G Starr, Univ Press of Amer, Lanham MD, 85; co-ed, The Birth of Democracy, Amer School of Classical Stud, Princeton, 93; co-ed, Athenian Political Thought and the Reconstruction of American Democracy, Cornell Univ Press Ithaca, 94; co-ed, Demokratia, A Conversation on Democracies Ancient and Modern, Princeton Univ Press Princeton, 96. **CONTACT ADDRESS** Dept of Classics, Princeton Univ, 104 Pyne, Princeton, NJ, 08544. **EMAIL** jober@princeton.edu

OBERDECK, KATHRYN J.
DISCIPLINE HISTORY **EDUCATION** Yale Univ, PhD, 91. **CAREER** Asst prof, Univ Ill Urbana Champaign. **RESEARCH** American cultural and intellectual history popular culture; cultural criticism. **SELECTED PUBLICATIONS** Auth, 'Not Pink Teas': The Working-Class Women's Movement in Seattle, 1905-1918, Labor Hist, 91; Religion, Culture, and the Politics of Class: Alexander Irvine's Mission to Turn-of-the-Century New Haven, Am Quarterly, 95. **CONTACT ADDRESS** History Dept, Univ Ill Urbana Champaign, 52 E Gregory Dr, Champaign, IL, 61820. **EMAIL** k-oberd@uiuc.edu

OBY, JASON B.
PERSONAL Born 08/13/1963, Baton Rouge, LA, s **DISCIPLINE** MUSIC **EDUCATION** Manhattan Sch of Music, BM, 88, MM, 90; FL St Univ, DM, 96 **CAREER** Asst prof, 91-93, AL St Univ; Asst prof, 94-95, E KY Univ; Asst Prof, 96-, TX S univ **HONORS AND AWARDS** Artist-scholar, 94; Phi Kappa Phi, Univ Fel at FSU; Fels to Aspen Music Fest **MEMBERSHIPS** Nat Asn of Teachers **SELECTED PUBLICATIONS** Auth, Equity in Operatio Casting as Perceived by African American Male Singers, Edwin Mellan Press, 98 **CONTACT ADDRESS** Houston, TX, 77004. **EMAIL** jbo813@aol.com

OCHSNER, JEFFREY KARL
PERSONAL Born 08/25/1950, Milwaukee, WI, m, 1979 **DISCIPLINE** ARCHITECTURE **EDUCATION** Rice Univ, BA, 73, MArch, 76. **CAREER** Instr, part-time, School of Archit, Rice Univ, 80-86; owner, Ochsner Assoc, 84-87; from lectr, asst prof, assoc prof, Dept of Archit, Univ Washington, 88- , chemn dept, 96- . **HONORS AND AWARDS** Am Inst Archit fel, 96; Lionel Pries Tchg Award, 90, 92. **MEMBERSHIPS** AIA; Soc of Archit Hist; Col Art Asn; Vernacular Archit Forum; Nat Trust for Hist Preservation; Congress for the New Urbanism. **RESEARCH** H.H. Richardson; nineteenth and twentieth century American architecture; Pacific Northwest architecture; urban design; preservation. **SELECTED PUBLICATIONS** Auth, H.H. Richardson: Complete Architectural Works, MIT, 82; ed and coauth, Shaping Seattle Architecture: A Historical Guide to the Architects, Univ Washington, 94; auth, Understanding the Holocaust through the United States Holocaust Memorial Museum, J of Archit Educ, 95; auth, In Search of Regional Expression: The Washington State Building at the World's Columbian Exposition, Chicago, 1893, Pacific NW Q, 95; auth, Willis A Ritchie and Public Architecture in Washington, 1889-1905, Pacific NW Q, 96; auth, Henry Hobson Richardson, in Dictionary of Art, Grove, 96; auth, A Space of Loss: The Vietnam Veterans Memorial, J of Archit Educ, 97. **CONTACT ADDRESS** Dept of Architecture, Univ of Washington, PO Box 355720, Seattle, WA, 98195-5720. **EMAIL** jochsner@u.washington.edu

ODEM, MARY E.
DISCIPLINE HISTORY **EDUCATION** Wash Univ, BA, 80; Univ Calif Berkeley, MA, 84, PhD, 89. **CAREER** Assoc prof hist dept/Inst Women's Studies. **HONORS AND AWARDS** Pres Bk Awd, Soc Sci Hist Assn. **RESEARCH** US social history; women's history; history of sexuality; Progressive-era history; multi-cultural approaches to history and women's studies. **SELECTED PUBLICATIONS** Auth, Delinquent Daughters: Protecting and Policing Adolescent Female Sexuality in the United States, 1885-1920; ed, Confronting Rape and Sexual Assault. **CONTACT ADDRESS** Dept History, Emory Univ, 221 Bowden Hall, 561 Kilgo Cir, Atlanta, GA, 30322-1950. **EMAIL** modem@emory.edu

ODOM, EDWIN DALE
PERSONAL Born 07/10/1929, Sanger, TX, m, 1949, 3 children **DISCIPLINE** UNITED STATES HISTORY **EDUCATION** NTex State Col, BA, 55, MA, 56; Tulane Univ, PhD(hist), 61. **CAREER** Instr hist, NTex State Col, 55-56; instr econ hist, Victoria Col, Tex, 56-57; instr hist, Tulane Univ, 57-59; from instr to asst prof, 59-64, Assoc Prof Hist, N Tex State Univ, 64-. **MEMBERSHIPS** Orgn Am Historians; Southern Hist Asn; Econ Hist Asn; Agr Hist Soc; Bus Hist Found. **RESEARCH** Local history; agricultural history since 1865; 20th century United States dairy industry. **SELECTED PUBLICATIONS** Auth, The Vicksburg, Shreveport and Texas: the for-

tunes of a scalawag railroad, Southwestern Soc Sci Quart, 63; auth & ed, The 1934 attack on mainstream history and the establishment, Soc Sci Quart, 570; coauth, A brief history of Denton County, Texas, Denton County Hist Comn, 75; Texas Through Time - Evolving Interpretations - Buenger,wl, Calvert,ra, Southwestern Historical Quarterly, Vol 0096, 1993. **CONTACT ADDRESS** 420 Headlee Lane, Denton, TX, 76201.

OESTREICHER, RICHARD JULES
PERSONAL Born 08/09/1947, Morristown, NJ, m, 1972, 2 children **DISCIPLINE** AMERICAN HISTORY **EDUCATION** Mich State Univ, BA, 69, MA, 73, PhD, 79. **CAREER** Instr social sci, 76-77, asst prof, 79-80, Mich State Univ, 76-80; instr hist, Ariz State Univ, 77-79; asst prof history, 80-84, assoc prof history, Univ Pittsburgh, 84- ; Am Counc Learned Soc Fel, 81; **HONORS AND AWARDS** Arizona Hum Coun Grant, 78-79; Fac Arts Sci Summer Res Grant Univ Pittsburgh, 81, 84, & 89; Res Develop Grant, 87; Brinkley-Stephenson Award, 89. **MEMBERSHIPS** Orgn Am Historians. **RESEARCH** United States working class history; comparative labor history; photographic history. **SELECTED PUBLICATIONS** Auth Labor: the Jacksonian Era through Reconstruction, Encycl Am Soc Hist, Charles Scribner's Sons, 93; The Counted and the Uncounted: The Occupational Structure of Early Am Cities, Jour Soc Hist, 94; The Two Souls of American Democracy, The Social Construction of Democracy, 1870-1990, NY Univ Press, 95; The Spirit of "92: Popular Opposition in Homestead's Politics and Culture, 1892-1937, Pittsburgh Surv Revisited, 96. **CONTACT ADDRESS** History Dept, Univ of Pittsburgh, 3p38 Forbes Quad, Pittsburgh, PA, 15260-0001.

OFFNER, JOHN L.
PERSONAL Born 04/11/1930, Richland, PA, m, 1950, 3 children **DISCIPLINE** MODERN AMERICAN DIPLOMATIC HISTORY **EDUCATION** PA State Univ, BEd, 51, MA, 52, PhD(hist), 57. **CAREER** Foreign serv officer, US Dept State, Washington, DC, 56-65; assoc prof hist, 65-67, Prof Hist, Shippensburg State Col, 67-. **MEMBERSHIPS** AHA; Orgn Am Historians. **SELECTED PUBLICATIONS** United-states Expansionism And Cuban Annexationism in The 1850s - Opatrny,j, J of American History, Vol 0080, 1993; Crucible of Empire - The Spanish-American War And Its Aftermath - Bradford,jc, J of American History, Vol 0081, 1995. **CONTACT ADDRESS** Dept of Hist, Shippensburg State Col, Shippensburg, PA, 17252.

OGASAPIAN, JOHN
PERSONAL Born 10/01/1940, Worcester, MA, m, 1967, 1 child **DISCIPLINE** MUSICOLOGY **EDUCATION** Boston Univ, B. Mus, 62, M.Mus 64, PhD, 77. **CAREER** Lowell State Col, Instr, 65-69, asst prof, 69-76; Univ of Lowell, asst prof, 76-79; Univ of MA, prof, 79; Lowell ch, acad studies dept, Col of Fine Arts, 77-80, 92-96 ed. **HONORS AND AWARDS** Organ Hist Soc, Distinguished Ser Award, 94. **MEMBERSHIPS** Organ Hist Soc Am Musicological Soc Sonneck Soc for Am Music Am Guild of Organists. **RESEARCH** 19th-century Am organ building, organ music and urban church music. **CONTACT ADDRESS** Univ of Massachusetts, 217 Durgin Hall, Lowell, MA, 01854.

OGILVIE, LEON PARKER
PERSONAL Born 10/28/1931, Kansas City, MO, 2 children **DISCIPLINE** AMERICAN HISTORY **EDUCATION** Cent Mo State Col, BS, 53; La State Univ, MA, 56; Univ Mo, Columbia, PhD(hist), 67. **CAREER** Instr hist, Metrop Jr Col, 62-67; asst prof, Cent Mo State Col, 67-69; assoc prof, Nicholls State Univ, 69-70; instr hist, Penn Valley Community Col, 70-81; chm, Soc Sci Dept, Maplewoods Community Col, 82-, Chm, Comt V on Jr & Community Cols, AAUP, 79-82. **MEMBERSHIPS** AHA; Orgn Am Historians; Southern Hist Asn; AAUP. **RESEARCH** American South; Missouri history; recent American history. **SELECTED PUBLICATIONS** Auth, Governmental efforts of reclamation in the southeast Missouri lowlands, 1/70 & Populism and socialism in the southeast Missouri lowlands, 1/70 & Populism and socialism in the southeast Missouri lowlands, 1/70, Mo Hist Rev. **CONTACT ADDRESS** Soc Sci Dept, Maple Woods Comm Col, 2601 NE Barry Rd, Kansas City, MO, 64156-1254.

OGLESBY, JAMES ROBERT
PERSONAL Born 05/30/1941, m **DISCIPLINE** EDUCATION **EDUCATION** SC State Coll, BS 1966; Univ of Missouri-Columbia, MEd 1969, PhD 1972. **CAREER** Jefferson Jr High School, classroom teacher; UNIV OF MISSOURI-COLUMBIA, graduate research asst 1969-70, graduate teaching asst 1970-71, coord of space & facilities and asst prof of educ 1972-74, asst prof of educ and asst provost for admin 1974-80, asst prof of educ and dir facilities utilization, beginning 1980, ASST TO THE CHANCELLOR, currently. **HONORS AND AWARDS** grant received, Boone County Comm Serv Council (to partially fund a building addition for Columbia Day Care Corp), City of Columbia (to fund a summer youth employment prog titled CARE). **MEMBERSHIPS** Guest lecturer for educ courses Univ of MO-Columbia 1972-; bd dirs Columbia Day Care Corp 1973-; mem Bd of Educ Columbia MO 1974-; mem MO State Teacher's Assn 1974-; mem, 1976-, pres, 1989, Natl Sch Bds Assn; MO School Bd Assn 1977- (holding various positions and serving on numerous bds in both assocs); sec Bd of Trustees Columbia Coll 1978-; mem Ambassador Club 1982-; comm develop consultant on Educ and Politics for Minneapolis MN; consultant Task Force on Governance-Natl Sci Foundation; consultant site visitor Secondary Sch Recognition Program US Dept of Educ. **SELECTED PUBLICATIONS** Published material includes "Education for the Twenty First Century," Natl Science Foundation Comm on Public Educ 1983. **CONTACT ADDRESS** Univ of Missouri, 105 Jesse Hall, Columbia, MO, 65211.

OGLESBY, RICHARD E.
PERSONAL Born 03/27/1931, Waukegan, IL, m, 1957, 1 child **DISCIPLINE** AMERICAN HISTORY **EDUCATION** Northwestern Univ, BS, 53, MA, 57, PhD(hist), 62. **CAREER** Asst prof hist, Eastern Ill Univ, 61-65; chmn dept, 73-76, asst prof, 65-80, Prof Hist, Univ Calif, Santa Barbara, 80-. **MEMBERSHIPS** Western Hist Asn; Orgn Am Historians. **RESEARCH** American western history; California history. **SELECTED PUBLICATIONS** Auth, Manuel Lisa and the Opening of the Missouri Fur Trade, Univ Okla, 63; The fur trade as business, In: The Frontier Re-examined, Univ Ill, 67; Manuel Lisa, In: The Fur Trade and the Mountain Men, Arthur Clark, 67; coauth, American Profile, Heath, 69; auth, Smoke gets in your eyes, MO Hist Soc Bull, 470; coauth, Vol II, Portrait of a Nation, Heath, 72; News of The Plains And Rockies, 1803-1865 - White,da, Pacific Historical Review, Vol 0066, 1997. **CONTACT ADDRESS** Dept of Hist, Univ of Calif, Santa Barbara, CA, 93106.

OGREN, KATHY J.
DISCIPLINE HISTORY **EDUCATION** Scripps Col, BA, 77; Johns Hopkins Univ, PhD, 86. **CAREER** Prof, Redlands Univ. **HONORS AND AWARDS** Outstanding Tchg Awd, 96; Outstanding Res Awd, 90; Graves Foundation Res Awd, 92. **RESEARCH** Late 19th and 20th century social and cultural history of US. **SELECTED PUBLICATIONS** Auth, The Jazz Revolution: Twenties America and the Meaning of Jazz, Oxford, 89; Coming Full Circle in the Land of Northern Mysteries, Dry Crik Rev, 94; Debating With Beethoven: Understanding the Fear of Early Jazz, Greenwood, 92; What Is Africa To Me? African Strategies in the Harlem Renaissance, Verso, 94; Jazz Isn't Just Me: Jazz Autobiographies as Performance Personas, Wayne State Univ, 91. **CONTACT ADDRESS** History Dept, Univ Redlands, 1200 E Colton Ave, Box 3090, Redlands, CA, 92373-0999. **EMAIL** ogren@uor.edu

OHLINE, HOWARD ALBERT
PERSONAL Born 08/13/1936, St. Louis, MO, m, 1961, 3 children **DISCIPLINE** EARLY AMERICAN HISTORY **EDUCATION** Grinnell Col, AB, 58; Univ Mo, MA, 61, PhD(hist), 69. **CAREER** Instr hist, Kansas City Mo Jr Col, 61-63; asst prof, 66-80, Assoc Prof Hist, Temple Univ, 80-. **MEMBERSHIPS** Orgn Am Historians; Southern Hist Asn; assoc Inst Early Am Hist & Cult. **RESEARCH** Slavery in early American politics. **SELECTED PUBLICATIONS** Auth, Republicanism and slavery: Origins of the three- fifths clause in the US Constitution, William & Mary Quart, 71; Georgetown, SC: Racial anxieties and militant behavior, 1802, SC Hist Mag, 72; Jefferson and slavery, Forum Press Ser Am Hist, 75; Slavery, economics, and congressional politics, 1790, J Southern Hist, 80; Constitutional History of The American- revolution - The Authority to Legislate - Reid,jp, Pennsylvania Magazine of History And Biography, Vol 0117, 1993; A Necessary Evil - Slavery And The Debate Over The Constitution - Kaminski,jp, J of Southern History, Vol 0062, 1996. **CONTACT ADDRESS** Dept of Hist Soc Sci, Temple Univ, 1114 W Berks St, Philadelphia, PA, 19122-6029.

OHNUMA, REIKO
PERSONAL Born 04/10/1963, New Haven, CT, m, 1993, 1 child **DISCIPLINE** ASIAN STUDIES, BUDDHIST STUDIES **EDUCATION** Univ of Michigan, Ann Arbor, PhD, 97. **CAREER** Vis lectr, 96-98, Univ of TX, Austin; Asst Prof, 98-99, Univ of AL, Tuscaloosa. **HONORS AND AWARDS** Charlotte Newcombe Doctoral Dissertation Fellowship. **MEMBERSHIPS** Intl Assoc of Buddhist Stud; Amer Acad of Rel. **RESEARCH** Indian Buddhist Literature, especially narrative literature; Women and Literature. **SELECTED PUBLICATIONS** Auth, The Gift of the Body and the Gift of Dharma, History of Religions, 98. **CONTACT ADDRESS** 11 Dubois Terrace, Tuscaloosa, AL, 35401. **EMAIL** rohnuma@bama.ua.edu

OKENFUSS, MAX JOSEPH
PERSONAL Born 09/14/1938, Ste. Genevieve, MO, m, 1 child **DISCIPLINE** RUSSIAN HIST **EDUCATION** Univ Mo, BA, 63, MA, 64; Harvard Univ, PhD, 71. **CAREER** Asst prof, 70-77, assoc prof hist, Wash Univ, 77-. **HONORS AND AWARDS** NEH fel, 74; Delmas Found, 83; Fulbright, 89; NEH, 94. **MEMBERSHIPS** AHA; Hist Early Mod Europe; Am Assn Advan Slavic Studies; Cent Slavic Conf. **RESEARCH** History of education and social change in 18th century Russia. **SELECTED PUBLICATIONS** Art, The Ages of Man on the Muscovite Frontiers of Early-Modern Europe, The Historian, 93; auth, The Rise and Fall of Latin Humanism in Early-Modern Russia: Pagan Authors, Ukrainians, and the Resiliency of Muscovy Brill's Series in Intellectual History, Leiden/New York/Koln, 95; co-auth & ed, Reemerging Russia: Search for Identity, Simon and Schuster, 95. **CONTACT ADDRESS** Dept of History, Washington Univ, 1 Brookings Dr, St. Louis, MO, 63130-4899. **EMAIL** okenfuss@artsci.wustl.edu

OKIHIRO, GARY Y.
PERSONAL Born 10/14/1945, Aiea, HI, m, 1971, 2 children **DISCIPLINE** HISTORY **EDUCATION** Univ Calif, Los Angeles, PhD, 76. **CAREER** Asst Prof, Humboldt State Univ, 76-80; Assoc Prof, Santa Clara Univ, 80-89; Prof, Cornell Univ, 89-. **MEMBERSHIPS** Am Hist Asn; Org of Am Hist; Am Stud Asn; Asn for Asian-Am Stud. **RESEARCH** Asian Am; S Africa. **SELECTED PUBLICATIONS** Auth, Margins and mainstreams: Asians in American History and Culture, 94; auth, Whispered Silences: Japanese Americans and World War II, 97. **CONTACT ADDRESS** Dept of Hist, Cornell Univ, Ithaca, NY, 14853. **EMAIL** gyo1@cornell.edu

OKIN, LOUIS A.
PERSONAL Born 04/27/1940, Detroit, MI, m, 1966, 1 child **DISCIPLINE** HISTORY **EDUCATION** UCLA, BA, 62, MA, 65, PhD, 74. **CAREER** Lect, Univ of the Pacific, 68-69; Asst Prof, 69-75, Assoc Prof, 75-82, Prof, 82-, Chmn History Humboldt Univ. **HONORS AND AWARDS** NEH Sum Sem, Archaic Greece, Havard Univ, 81; NEH Sum Sem, Classical Greece, Stanford Univ, 76. **MEMBERSHIPS** APA, Archaeological Inst of Amer, Amer Hist Assoc, Amer Res Center in Egypt. **RESEARCH** Greek Historiography, Hellenistic Greek History, Classical Greek History. **SELECTED PUBLICATIONS** Auth, Panhellenica: Essays in Ancient History and Historiography in Honor of Truesdell S. Brown, Coronado Press, 80; art, Herodotus and Panyassis Ethnics in Duris of Samos, Class View, Echos du Monde Classique, 82; art, Theognis of Megara and the sources for the History of Archaic Megara, in: Theognis of Megara, Poetry and the Polis, John Hopkins Univ Press, 85. **CONTACT ADDRESS** Humboldt State Univ, Dept of History, 1 Harpst S, Arcata, CA, 95521. **EMAIL** 1ao2@axe.humboldt.edu

OKOYE, IKEM
DISCIPLINE HISTORY OF ART IN WEST AFRICA, CARABBEAN, AMERICAN SOUTH **EDUCATION** Mass Inst Tech, PhD. **CAREER** Prof, Northwestern Univ; Rockefeller fel, Inst for Advan Study and Res; fel, Advan Study Center, Univ Michigan. **MEMBERSHIPS** Inst for Advan Study, Princeton Univ. **RESEARCH** Historical interrogation of modernity; gender theory; race theory; contemporary art historiography. **SELECTED PUBLICATIONS** Auth, Shamanic Penumbra: Houston Conwill's Art of Color; History, Aesthetics, and the Political in Igbo Spatial Heterotopias; Tribe and Art History. **CONTACT ADDRESS** Dept of Art History, Northwestern Univ, 1801 Hinman, Evanston, IL, 60208.

OKUNOR, SHIAME
PERSONAL Born 06/02/1937, Accra, Ghana, d **DISCIPLINE** AFRICAN-AMERICAN STUDIES **EDUCATION** New York Univ, Certificate 1968; Grahm Jr College, AAS 1971; The Univ of NM, BA Speech Communications 1973, MPA 1975, PhD 1981; Yale Divinity School, MDiv, 1995. **CAREER** The University of NM, Afro-Amer studies 1981-82, dir academic affairs Afro-Amer studies 1982-, acting dean univ coll 1985-86, dean general coll 1986-87, asst prof educ found, Acting Assoc Dean Graduate Studies 1988-89. **HONORS AND AWARDS** Outstanding Sr Awd 1971; Outstanding Intl Awd 1971; Pres Recognition Awd Univ of NM 1981-85; AP Appreciation Awd Albuquerque Public Schools 1981; Comm Serv Awd NAACP 1982; WM Civitan Merit Awd 1984; Black Communication Serv Awd 1984; Presidency Awd Schomburg Ctr New York City 1985-86; NM Sec of State Cert of Apprec 1985; NM Assoc of Bilingual Teachers Awd 1986; US Military Airlift Command Cert of Recognition 1987; Cert of Apprec US Corps of Engrs 1987; Yvonne Ochillo, Southern Conference on African American Studies, 1990. **MEMBERSHIPS** Mem exec bd NAACP 1975-86; mem Affirmative Action Policy Comm; bd of dirs, pres NM Sickle Cell 1981-91; secretary, treasurer, New Mexico Endowment for the Humanities, 1987-92; member, New Mexico Jazz Workshop, 1991-92. **CONTACT ADDRESS** Director, African-American Studies, Univ of New Mexico, 4025 Mesa Vista Hall, Albuquerque, NM, 87131.

OLCOTT, MARTHA
DISCIPLINE NATIONALISM, ETHNIC POLITICS, AND ETHNO-NATIONALISM **EDUCATION** SUNY Buffalo; Univ Chicago, PhD, 78. **CAREER** Vis instr, UC Berkeley; dept ch, prof-. **HONORS AND AWARDS** Res fel, Truman Inst, Hebrew Univ, Jerusalem; Bunting Inst, Radcliffe; Russ Res Ctr, Harvard Univ, East-West Ctr, Duke Univ; sr assoc, Carnegie Endowment for Intl Peace, Moscow; dir, Moscow Study Group, 96, 97. **SELECTED PUBLICATIONS** Publ, articles in scholar jour(s), bk(s); auth, The Kazakhs, Hoover Inst, 96; Central Asias New States, USIP, 96. **CONTACT ADDRESS** Dept of Russ Stud, Colgate Univ, 13 Oak Drive, Hamilton, NY, 13346.

OLDSON, WILLIAM O.
PERSONAL Born 01/23/1940, Hampton, VA, m, 1967, 2 children **DISCIPLINE** EAST EUROPEAN HISTORY **EDUCATION** Spring Hall Col, BA, 65; Ind Univ, Bloomington, MA, 66, PhD (hist), 70. **CAREER** Asst prof, 69-74, assoc chemn of undergraduate affairs, 73-75, 83-84, assoc chemn of graduate affairs, 94, assoc prof, 74-79, prof hist, Fla State Univ, 79-, dir, hist admin and public hist prog, 87-, hist computer progs and res, 93-, dir, Inst on WWII & The Human Experience, 97-, Int Res & Exchanges Bd res fel, Romania, 73; chief negotiator, United Fac Fla, 80-81. **HONORS AND AWARDS** Rus and East Europ Inst Fel, Indiana Univ, 65-66; Nat Defense Foreign Lang Fel, Indiana Univ, 66-67; Flubright-Hays Fel, 67-68; Romanian State Fel, 67-68; Rus and East Europ Inst Grantee, 67-68; Int Res & Exchanges Board Fel, 73; FLA State Univ Found Travel Grantee, 82; Phi Alpha Theta Prof of the Year, 88; Comt on Faculty Res Support Grantee, 72-73, 90; John Frederick Louis Award, 91; Holocaust Project Microfilming Grant, 93; Teaching Incentive Program Award, 94; Coun on Res & Creativity Planning Grant, 94-95; Univ Teaching Award, 88, 95; Louis E & Patrice J Wolfson Found Grant, 95; Holocaust Educ Foundation Grant, 94, 96; Wolfson Family Found Grant, 96; Int Res and Exchanges Board Short-Term Travel Grant, 96. **RESEARCH** Cultural and intellectual history, especially the Balkans; ethnicity and nationalism; Anti-Semitism; The Holocaust. **SELECTED PUBLICATIONS** Auth, Faculty Relations Before and After Collective Bargaining, Ctr Employ Rels & Law Rev, 81; The Enlightenment and the Romanian National Revival (Moldvia, Wallachia, Transylvania), Can Rev Studies in Nationalism, 82; The Boyars Golesti: The Impact of French Revolutionary Thought in Romania, Proceedings of the Consortium on Revolutionary Europ, 1750-1850, Inst on Napolean and the French Revolution, 90; Rationalizing Anti-Semitism: The Romanian Gambit, Proceedings of the Am Philos Soc, 25-30, 94; Background to Catastrophe: Romanian Modernization to policies and the Environment, East Europ Quart, 517-27, 97. **CONTACT ADDRESS** Dept of History, Florida State Univ, 481 Bellamy, Tallahassee, FL, 32306-2200. **EMAIL** woldson@garnet.acns.fsu.edu

OLENIK, JOHN KENNETH
PERSONAL Born 05/07/1941, Cleveland, OH, m **DISCIPLINE** MODERN CHINESE HISTORY AND LITERATURE **EDUCATION** John Carroll Univ, BSS, 63; Seton Hall Univ, MA, 66; Cornell Univ, MA, 70, PhD(hist China), 73. **CAREER** Asst prof, 71-78, Assoc Prof Hist E Asia, Montclair State Col, 78-, Am Coun Learned SocNat Endowment for Humanities lang & res fel, Japan, 76-77; vis scholar, Fac Law, Keio Univ, Japan, 76-77. **MEMBERSHIPS** AHA; Asn Asian Studies. **RESEARCH** China, Repubican Period; China, political parties and movements; China, poetry of the Six Dynasties Period. **SELECTED PUBLICATIONS** Mountain Fires - The Red-army 3-year War in South China, 1934-1938 - Benton,g, J of Asian History, Vol 0028, 1994; Mountain Fires - The Red-army 3-year War in South China, 1934- 1938 - Benton,g, J of Asian History, Vol 0028, 1994. **CONTACT ADDRESS** 1 Normal Ave, Montclair, NJ, 07043-1699.

OLESON, JOHN P.
PERSONAL Born 11/24/1946, Hackensack, NJ, m, 1970, 2 children **DISCIPLINE** CLASSICAL ARCHAEOLOGY **EDUCATION** Harvard Univ, BA, 67, MA, 71, PhD, 73. **CAREER** Asst prof, Florida State Univ, 73-76; assoc prof, prof, Univ of Victoria, 76-. **HONORS AND AWARDS** Fel of Royal Soc of Can. **MEMBERSHIPS** Archaeol Inst of Am; Am Sch of Oriental Res; Am Ctr of Oriental Res. **RESEARCH** Ancient technology; underwater archaeology; Roman Near East. **SELECTED PUBLICATIONS** Auth, The Humeima Excavation Project, Jordan: Preliminary Report of the 1992 Season, Echos du Monde Classique/Class Views, 93; auth, Humeima Hydraulic Survey, 1989, in, Chronique Archeologique Jordanie, Syria, 93; auth, An Ancient Lead Sounding-Weight in the National Maritime Museum, Sefunim: Bull of the Nat Maritime Mus, Haifa, 94; coauth, The Harbours of Caesarea Maritima, vol 2: The Finds and the Ship, British Archaeological Reports, 94; auth, The Origins and Design of Nabataean Water-Supply Systems, in Studies in the History and Archaeology of Jordan, Amman, Dept of Antiquities, 95; coauth, The Origins, Early History, And Applications of the Pyoulkos (Syringe), in Argoud, ed, Science et Vie Intellectuelle a Alexandrie (Ier-IIIe siecle apres JC), Saint-Etienne, 95; auth, Water-Lifting Devices at Herculaneum and Pompeii in the Context of Roman Technology, Bull Antieke Beschaving, 96; coauth, Artifactual Evidence for the History of the Harbors of Caesarea, in Raban, ed, Caesarea Maritima: A Retrospective after Two Millennia, Brill, 96; coauth, Baths of the Hisma Desert, Balnearia, 97; coauth, Greek and Roman Technology: A Sourcebook, Routledge, 97; auth, Humeima, in Bikai, ed, Archaeology in Jordan, Am Jour of Archaeol, 97. **CONTACT ADDRESS** Dept of Greek and Roman Studies, Victoria Univ, PO Box 3045, Victoria, BC, V8W 3P4. **EMAIL** jpoleson@uvic.ca

OLIEN, DIANA DAVIDS
PERSONAL Born 02/24/1943, Oceanside, NY, m, 1970, 1 child **DISCIPLINE** HISTORY **EDUCATION** Swarthmore Col, BA, 64; Yale Univ, MA, 66; M Phil, 67; PhD, 69. **CAREER** Asst prof, Southern Meth Univ, 69-73; Sr lectr, Univ Tex of the Permian Basin, 86- . **HONORS AND AWARDS** High Honors, Phi Beta Kappa, Swarthmore Col. **MEMBERSHIPS** Bus Hist Conf; Tex State Hist Asoc; West Tex Hist Soc; Permian Basin Hist soc. **RESEARCH** U.S. petroleum industry, especially Texas; women's history. **SELECTED PUBLICATIONS** Co-auth with Roger M. Olien, Oil Booms: Social Change in Five Texas Towns, 82; auth, Wildcatters: Texas Independent Oilmen, 84; auth, Life in the Oil Fields, 86; Easy Money: Promoters and Investors in the Jazz Age, 90; auth, Morpeth: A Victorian Public Career, 93. **CONTACT ADDRESS** Univ of Texas of the Permian Basin, 4901 E. University, Odessa, TX, 79762.

OLIN, JOHN C.
PERSONAL Born 10/07/1915, Buffalo, NY, m, 1942, 4 children **DISCIPLINE** HISTORY **EDUCATION** Canisius Col, BA, 37; Fordham Univ, MA, 41; Columbia Univ, PhD, 60. **CAREER** From asst prof to assoc prof medieval & mod Europ hist, 46- 69, Prof Hist, Fordham Univ, 69-. **MEMBERSHIPS** Renaissance Soc Am; Am Cath Hist Asn; Amici Thomae Mori. **RESEARCH** Renaissance and Reformation; Erasmus. **SELECTED PUBLICATIONS** Edtranslr, Christian Humanism and the Reformation: Selected Writing of Erasmus, 65, ed, Calvin and Sadoleto: A Reformation Debate, 66, The Catholic Reformation: Savonarola to Ignatius Loyola, 69, ed, The Autobiography of St Ignatius Loyola, 74 & Six Essays on Erasmus, 79, Harper; The Correspondence of Erasmus - Letters 1535 to 1657, January-december 1525 - Dalzell,a, Translator, Nauert,cg, Annotator, Catholic Historical Review, Vol 0081, 1995; Utopia, an Elusive Vision - Fox,a, Renaissance Quarterly, Vol 0048, 1995. **CONTACT ADDRESS** Van Houten Fields, West Nyack, NY, 10994.

OLIN, MARGARET
DISCIPLINE ART HISTORY **EDUCATION** Univ Chicago, MA, 77, PhD, 82. **CAREER** Instr, Univ IL; Northwestern Univ; assoc prof, 85-. **HONORS AND AWARDS** Fulbright fel. **SELECTED PUBLICATIONS** Pub(s), Art Bulletin; Critical Inquiry; Forms of Representation in Alois Riegl's Theory of Art; **CONTACT ADDRESS** Dept of Art Hist, Sch of the Art Inst of Chicago, 37 S Wabash Ave, Chicago, IL, 60603. **EMAIL** molin@artic.edu

OLIVA, L. JAY
PERSONAL Born 09/23/1933, Walden, NY, m, 1961, 2 children **DISCIPLINE** MODERN EUROPEAN HISTORY **EDUCATION** Manhattan Col, BA, 55; Syracuse Univ, MA, 57, PhD, 60. **CAREER** Res assoc intel, Res Inst, Syracuse Univ, 57-58 & 59-60; from instr to assoc prof, 60-69, actg dean, Univ Col Arts & Sci, 72-73, vpres acad affairs, 77-80, prof Rus Hist, 69-, provost & exec vp acad aff, 80-83, chancel and exec vp acad aff, 83-91, pres, NY Univ, 91. **HONORS AND AWARDS** Chevalier of the French Leg of Hon; Medal of the Sorbonne, Univ of Paris; Man in Educ Awd, Ital Welfare. **MEMBERSHIPS** AAU; Campus Compact; Royal Inst of Int Aff; CICU; Coun of For Rels; Coun for US and Italy; Nat Col Ath Assn; NY St New Compact for Learn; NY St Comm on Nat and Comm Svc; UNA NY; UAA; ABNY; Irish Am Cult Inst; **RESEARCH** Eighteenth century Russia; Franco-Russian relations; continuity in Russo-Soviet history. **SELECTED PUBLICATIONS** Auth, Misalliance: A Study of French Policy in Russia During the Seven Years' War, NYU, 64; cotransl, A Medical Journey in California, Zeithlin and ver Brugge, 67; auth, Russia in the Era of Peter the Great, Prentice Hall, 69, rev ed, Holmes and Meier, 92; ed, Peter the Great, Prentice Hall, 70; ed, Catherine the Great, Prentice Hall, 71; auth, Maxim Gorky Discovers America, NY Hist Soc Qrt, 66; auth, The Dorming of New York City, NY Times, 89; auth, Do the Right Thing About Athletucsm AGB Reports, 89; auth, What Trustees Should Know About Intercollegoate Athletics, AGB Spec Rpt, 89; auth, Academic Affairs at New York University, University, 89; auth, NYU's Networking: Historically Black Colleges Make A Difference, 90; auth, Showdown in Dallas, AGB, 90; auth, Presidents' Ten Commandments, The Charoltte Observ, 91; aut, Big Time or Not, Reform Starts at Home, The Washington Post, 91. **CONTACT ADDRESS** NY Univ, New York, NY, 10003.

OLIVER, DAILY E.
PERSONAL Born 08/05/1942, Ft. Devons, MA, m **DISCIPLINE** ETHNIC STUDIES **EDUCATION** Univ of Utah, BS 1965; Univ of Utah, MEd 1973; Univ of Utah, PhD 1978. **CAREER** Utah Board of Pardons, member 1979-83; Weber State College, dir Ethnic Studies 1985. **HONORS AND AWARDS** Skiing Magazine, The Skiing 100, Sept 1996. **MEMBERSHIPS** Member, Prof Ski Instructors of America, 1964-. **CONTACT ADDRESS** Ethnic Studies, Weber State Col, 3750 Harrison Blvd, Ogden, UT, 84408.

OLIVER, LISI
DISCIPLINE ANGLO-SAXON STUDIES **EDUCATION** Harvard Univ, PhD, 95. **CAREER** Asst prof, La State Univ. **HONORS AND AWARDS** Directing grant, Nat Opera Inst, 78; Socialist Activist Award, Berlin DDR, 79; MLA-Whiting fel, Harvard Univ, 94-95., Listed in Int Who's Who in Mus. **RESEARCH** Medieval literature; historical linguistics; opera libretti/translation. **SELECTED PUBLICATIONS** Auth, Spilled Wine and Lost Resonance in Chretien's Perceval; The Representation of the Dental Fricative in Early Kent; "Cyninges fedesl": The feeding of the king in Aethelberht 12; ed, Selected Writings of Calvert Watkins. **CONTACT ADDRESS** Dept of Eng, Louisiana State Univ, 236C Allen Hall, Baton Rouge, LA, 70803. **EMAIL** lolivel@unix1.sncc.lsu.edu

OLIVIA, LEONORA
DISCIPLINE GREEK AND LATIN LANGUAGES AND LITERATURES **EDUCATION** Brown Univ, PhD. **CAREER** Dept Classics, Millsaps Col **SELECTED PUBLICATIONS** Publ on, comp lit. **CONTACT ADDRESS** Dept of Classics, Millsaps Col, 1701 N State St, Jackson, MS, 39210. **EMAIL** olivil@okra.millsaps.edu

OLM, LEE ELMER
PERSONAL Born 07/17/1928, Appleton, WI, m, 1954, 1 child **DISCIPLINE** COLONIAL-REVOLUTIONARY AMERICAN HISTORY **EDUCATION** Western Mich Univ, BA, 52; Cornell Univ, MA, 53; Univ Mich, PhD, 60. **CAREER** Instr high sch, Mich, 53-55; from asst prof to assoc prof, 59-64, PROF HIST, SAM HOUSTON STATE UNIV, 64-, CHMN DEPT, 76-88, PROF EMER, 88-. **MEMBERSHIPS** AHA; Inst Early Am Hist & Cult; Orgn Am Historians. **RESEARCH** Revolutionary and Colonial America; 18th century England. **SELECTED PUBLICATIONS** Auth, The Mutiny Act for America: New York's Noncompliance, NY Hist Soc Quart, 7/74. **CONTACT ADDRESS** Dept of Hist, Sam Houston State Univ, P O Box 2239, Huntsville, TX, 77341-2239.

OLSEN, DONALD J. AMES
PERSONAL Born 01/08/1929, Seattle, WA **DISCIPLINE** HISTORY **EDUCATION** Yale Univ, BA, 49, MA, 51, PhD(hist), 54. **CAREER** Actg lectr hist, Univ Col Hull, Eng, 52-53; instr, Univ Mass, 54-55; from instr to prof, 55-72, chmn dept, 71-74, Prof Hist on The Eloise Ellery Chair, Vassar Col, 72-, Fac fel, Vassar Col, 59-60; Guggenheim fel, 67-68 & 79-80; vis prof Victorian studies, Univ Leicester, 70. **MEMBERSHIPS** AHA; Conf Brit Studies; Soc Archit Hist; Am Soc Eighteenth Century Studies. **RESEARCH** Landed estates in London, 17th century to the present; a comparative study of London, Paris, and Vienna; growth and structure of modern cities. **SELECTED PUBLICATIONS** Auth, Town Planning in London: The 18th and 19th Centuries, Yale Univ, 64; House upon house, In: The Victorian City, Routledge & Kegan Paul, 73; Victorian London: Specialization, segregation and privacy, Victorian Studies, 74; The Growth of Victorian London, BT Batsford, 76 & Penguin, 79; Peoples Parks, The Design And Development of Victorian Parks in Britain - Conway,h, Victorian Studies, Vol 0036, 1993; Gardens And The Picturesque, Studies in The History of Landscape-architecture - Hunt,jd, Victorian Studies, Vol 0036, 1993; Pennethorne,james And The Making of Victorian London - Tyack,g, Albion, Vol 0026, 1994; Architecture And Power - The Town Hall And The English Urban-community, C 1500-1640 - Tittler,r, American Historical Review, Vol 0098, 1993; Budapest And New-york - Studies in Metropolitan Transformation, 1870-1930 - Bender,t, Schorske,ce, J of Social History, Vol 0029, 1995. **CONTACT ADDRESS** Dept of Hist, Vassar Col, Poughkeepsie, NY, 12601.

OLSEN, GERALD WAYNE
PERSONAL Born 09/16/1939, Windsor, ON, Canada, m, 1968, 1 child **DISCIPLINE** BRITISH & EUROPEAN HISTORY **EDUCATION** Univ Windsor, Ont, BA Hons, 61, MA, 62; Univ Western Ont, PhD(hist), 72. **CAREER** From lectr to asst prof hist, King's Col, Univ Western Ont, 67-70, asst prof, Exten Dept, 71-73; asst prof, 73-76, Assoc Prof, Nipissing Univ Col, 76-. **MEMBERSHIPS** Can Cath Hist Asn; Can Hist Asn; Can Asn Univ Teachers. **RESEARCH** Anglican temperance movements; religion and revolution; early industrial England. **SELECTED PUBLICATIONS** Auth, Anglican temperance movements, 1859-1873: An example of practical ecumenism, Can Cath Hist Asn Study Sessions, 73; The Church of England temperance magazine, 1862-1873, Victorian Periodicals Newslett, 678; The Halevy thesis: What it owes to Marxism and liberal idealism, Hist Reflections, winter 78; The Evangelist of Desire - Wesley,john And The Methodists - Abelove,h, Histoire Sociale-social History, Vol 0025, 1992. **CONTACT ADDRESS** RR #4 Comp 16, North Bay, ON, P1B 8G5.

OLSEN, GLENN WARREN
PERSONAL Born 11/27/1938, Minneapolis, MN, m, 1966, 4 children **DISCIPLINE** MEDIEVAL HISTORY **EDUCATION** North Park Col, BA, 60; Univ Wis, MA, 62, PhD, 65. **CAREER** Asst prof hist, Seattle Univ, 65-66 & Fordham Univ, 66-69; assoc prof medieval hist & dir hon prog, Seattle Univ, 69-72; Assoc Prof Medieval Hist, Univ Utah, 72-, Seattle Univ fac res grant, 65-66; adv ed, Cath Hist Rev, 71-81; Univ Utah fac res grant, 73; mem bd regents, St Mary's Col, Ind, 73-79; D P Gardner fel, Univ Utah, 77-78; Inst for Ecumenical & Cult Res fel, 78-79; Am Coun Learned Soc grant, 79. **MEMBERSHIPS** Medieval Asn of Pac; Soc Ital Hist Studies; Mediaeval Acad Am; AHA; Am Cath Hist Asn. **RESEARCH** Medieval intellectual history, canon law and philosophy; medieval church and cultural history. **SELECTED PUBLICATIONS** Auth, The definition of the ecclesiastical benefice in the twelfth century: The canonists' discussion of spiritualis, Studia Gratiana, Vol 11, 67; The idea of the ecclesia primitiva in the writings of the

twelfth century canonists, Traditio 25, 69; Italian merchants and the performance of papal banking functions in the early thirteenth century, Explor Econ Hist, 69- 70; contribr, The investiture contest, In: Religion in the making of western man, St John's Univ, 74; auth, Allegory, typology and symbol: The sensus spiritalis, Communio 4, 77; Reference to the ecclesia primitiva in Eighth Century Irish Gospel Exegesis, Thought, Vol 54, 79; St Boniface and the vita apostolica, Am Benediction Rev, Vol 31, 80; Hans Urs Von Balthasar and the rehabilitation of St Anselm's doctrine of the atonement, Scottish J Theol, Vol 34, 81. **CONTACT ADDRESS** Dept of Hist, Univ of Utah, 217 Carlson Hall, Salt Lake City, UT, 84112-3124.

OLSON, ALISON GILBERT
PERSONAL Born 10/10/1931, Oakland, CA, m, 1959 **DISCIPLINE** MODERN HISTORY **EDUCATION** Univ Calif, Berkeley, BA, 52, MA, 53; Oxford Univ, DPhil, 56. **CAREER** From instr to asst prof hist, Smith Col, 57-60; lectr, asst prof, 63-67, Douglass Col; lectr, asst prof, 63-67, Rutgers Univ; assoc prof, Am Univ, 67-73; prof hist, univ MD, College Park, 73-. **HONORS AND AWARDS** Am Philos Soc grants, 60 & 67-68; fels, Am Coun Learned Soc, 60-61, Am Assn Univ Women, 61-62 & Folger Libr, 67Guggen Hum Fel, 83-94; Outstanding Teacher, 88; Distinguished Scholastic Teacher, 87-88; Distinguished Fac Fel, 91-92. **MEMBERSHIPS** Conf Brit Studies. **RESEARCH** English and American history in the 17th and 18th centuries. **SELECTED PUBLICATIONS** Auth, The Radical Duke: Career and Correspondence of Charles Lennox, Third Duke of Richmond, Oxford Univ, 61; co-ed, Anglo-American Political Relations, 1675-1775, Rutgers Univ, 70; auth, Anglo-American Politics, Oxford Univ, 73. **CONTACT ADDRESS** Dept of History, Univ of Maryland, College Park, MD, 20742-0001.

OLSON, GARY DUANE
PERSONAL Born 07/30/1939, Spring Grove, MN, m, 1960, 3 children **DISCIPLINE** AMERICAN HISTORY **EDUCATION** Luther Col, Iowa, BA, 61; Univ Nebr, Lincoln, MA, 65, PhD(hist), 68. **CAREER** Instr high sch, Minn, 61-63; asst prof, 68-74, assoc prof, 74-79, prof hist, Agustana Col, S Dak, 79-, dean acad serv, 81-87, dean of the Col and Vice Pres, 87-95, ex dir, ctr western studies, Augustana Col, 71-74. **MEMBERSHIPS** Orgn Am Historians; AHA; Inst Early Am Hist & Cult. **RESEARCH** American colonial and confederation periods and Sioux Falls. **SELECTED PUBLICATIONS** Auth, Relief for Nebraska grasshopper victims: The official journal of Lt Theo E True, Nebr Hist, summer 67; Loyalists and the American Revolution: Thomas Brown and the South Carolina backcountry (2 parts), 1775-1776, SC Hist Mag, 10/67 & 1/68; The Soderstrom incident: A reflection upon Federal-State relations under the Articles of Cofederation, NY Hist Soc Quart, 4/71; coauth, Prelude to Glory: A Newspaper Accounting of Custer's 1874 Expedition to the Black Hills, Brevet, 74; auth, David Ramsay Thomas Brown: Patriot historian & loyalist critic, SC Hist Mag, 10/76; Thomas Brown and the East Florida rangers, Proc Fourth Ann Fla Bicentennial Symp, 78; ed, Microfilm edition of the Richard F Pettigrew papers, Augustana Col, 78; The historical background of land settlement in eastern South Dakota, In: Big Sioux Pioneers, Sioux Falls, 80; Dakota Resources: The Richard F. Pettigrew Papers, So Dak Hist, summer/fall, 82; co-auth, Sioux Falls, South Dakota, A Pictorial History, 85. **CONTACT ADDRESS** Dept of Hist, Augustana Col, 2001 S Summit Ave, Sioux Falls, SD, 57197-0002.

OLSON, JAMES S.
DISCIPLINE HISTORY **EDUCATION** Brigham Young Univ, BA; State Univ NY-Stony Brook, PhD. **CAREER** Distinguished prof; dept ch, Sam Houston State Univ, 88-. **HONORS AND AWARDS** Recipient, Excellence in Tchg, Excellence in Res awd(s); Nat Bk awd, Popular Culture Asn. **RESEARCH** Recent America, Vietnam war, American immigration. **SELECTED PUBLICATIONS** Coauth, Ethnic Dimension in American History; Saving Capitalism: The Reconstruction Finance Corporation and the New Deal, 1933-1940; Catholic Immigrants in America; Winning is the Only Thing: Sports in America since 1945; Where the Domino Fell: America and Vietnam, 1945 to 1990; John Wayne: American. **CONTACT ADDRESS** Dept of History, Sam Houston State Univ, Huntsville, TX, 77341. **EMAIL** his_jso@shsu.edu

OLSON, JEANINE
DISCIPLINE RENNAISSANCE AND REFORMATION **EDUCATION** St Olaf Col, BA; Stanford Univ, AM, PhD. **CAREER** Instr, RI Col. **RESEARCH** The Reformation; 16th century Europe. **SELECTED PUBLICATIONS** Auth, Calvin and Social Welfare: Deacons and the Bourse Francaise; Deacons and Deaconesses through the Centuries; Histoire de l'Eglise, vingt siecles et six continents; Jean Crespin, Humanist Printer Among the Reformation Martyrologists, in The Harvest of Humanism in Central Europe: Essays in Honor of Lewis W. Spitz; Reformation and Revolution in Calvin's Geneva, Halcyon: A J of the Hum. **CONTACT ADDRESS** Rhode Island Col, Providence, RI, 02908.

OLSON, KEITH WALDEMAR
PERSONAL Born 08/04/1931, Poughkeepsie, NY, m, 1955, 2 children **DISCIPLINE** AMERICAN HISTORY **EDUCATION** State Univ NY, Albany, BA, 57, MA, 59; Univ Wis-Madison, PhD(hist), 64. **CAREER** From instr to asst prof hist, Syracuse Univ, 63-66; asst prof, 66-72, assoc prof, 72-79, PROF HIST, UNIV MD, COLLEGE PARK, 79- **HONORS AND AWARDS** Fulbright Prof, Finland. **MEMBERSHIPS** AHA; Org Am Hist; Soc for Hist in Am For Rels; State Hist Soc of Wis; Swedish-Am For Rels; Finnish Hist Soc; Ctr for the Stu of the Pres. **RESEARCH** 20th century United States; poltical and foreign relations; modern Scandinavia. **SELECTED PUBLICATIONS** Auth, Woodrow Wilson, Franklin K. Lane, and the Wilson Cabinet Meetings, The Historian, 70; auth, The G.I. Bill and Higher Education: Success and Surprise, Am Quart, 73; auth The G.I. Bill, The Veterans, and the College, Univ Ky, 74; auth, Biography of a Progressive: Franklin K. Lane, 1864-1921, Greenwood, 79; auth, The American Beveridge Plan, Mid-America, 83; auth, Finland: Between East and West, Wilson Qrt, 86; auth, Franklin D. Roosevelt, The Ghost of Woodrow Wilson, and Wold War II, The Road to War, Univ Tampre, 93; auth, American Historians and the History of Finland Since 1939, Charting and Independent Course: Finalnd's Place in the Cold War and in U.S. Foreign Policy, Regina, 98. **CONTACT ADDRESS** Dept of History, Univ of Maryland, College Park, MD, 20742-0001.

OLSON, ROBERT
PERSONAL Born 12/14/1940, Devil's Lake, ND, m, 1970, 2 children **DISCIPLINE** HISTORY **EDUCATION** Ind Univ, PhD, 73 **CAREER** Asst prof to assoc prof to prof, Univ Ky, 73- **HONORS AND AWARDS** Sr Fulbright Res Fel, 90-91 **MEMBERSHIPS** Middle East Stud Assoc; Turkish Stud Assoc; Middle East Inst; Third World Stud Assoc. **RESEARCH** Turkey; Kurds; Syria; Iran & Iraq. **SELECTED PUBLICATIONS** Auth, The Ba'th in Syria, 1947-1982: The Evolution of Ideology, Party and State from the French Withdrawal to the Era of Hafiz al-Asad, Kingston Pres, 83; The Emergence of Kurdish Nationalism and the Sheikh Said Rebellion: 1880-1925, Univ of Tx Press, 89, 91; Imperial Meanderings and Republican By-Ways: Essays on Eighteenth Century Ottoman History and Twentieth Century History of Turkey, Isis Press, 97; The Kurdish Question And Turkish-Iranian Relations: From World War to 1998, Mazda Press, 98. **CONTACT ADDRESS** 3717 Higbee Woods Ct, Lexington, KY, 40503. **EMAIL** hisposta@pop.uky.edu

OLUGEBEFOLA, ADEMOLA
PERSONAL Born 10/02/1941, Charlotte Amalie, St Thomas, Virgin Islands of the United States **DISCIPLINE** ART HISTORY **CAREER** Artist lectr works include hundreds of vibrant cover designs & illustrations for leading authors pub by Doubleday, Broadside, William Morrow, Harper & Row, Am Museum of Natrl History and others; has been in numerous major exhibitions over 30 yr period; had over 50 one man exhibitions; work is in collections throughout US, S Am, Africa, Caribbean; Gumbs & Thomas Publishers, vp, currently. **HONORS AND AWARDS** Won critical acclaim for innovative set designs for Lew Lafayette Theatre, NY Shakespeare Fest, Nat Black Theatre; design comm, NY Urban Coalition, 1990; design comm, Literary Assistance Ctr, 1989; design comm, Chase Bank, 1997; Banco Popular de Puerto Rico, 1996. **MEMBERSHIPS** Vice Pres, International Communications Association; vp, Harlem Artists & Scholars Interests Consortium; chmn Educ Dept of Weusi Acad of Arts & Studies; served as consultant to Mtro Museum of Art, NY Urban Coalition and is co-dir of Grinnell Fine Art Collection. **CONTACT ADDRESS** 800 Riverside Dr, #5E, New York, NY, 10032.

OMMER, ROSEMARY
PERSONAL Glasgow, Scotland **DISCIPLINE** HISTORY **EDUCATION** Glasgow Univ, MA, 64; Memorial Univ, MA, 74; McGill Univ, PhD, 79. **CAREER** High sch tchr, Scotland, 65-66; McConnell fel, McGill Univ, 74; asst prof, 78-83, econ hist, 83-85, PROF HISTORY, MEMORIAL UNIV 85-. **MEMBERSHIPS** SSHRCC; Vanier Inst Family; Can Hist Found. **SELECTED PUBLICATIONS** Auth, From Outpost to Outport, 91; co-ed, Volumes Not Values, 79; co-ed, Working Men Who Got Wet, 80. **CONTACT ADDRESS** Dept of History, Memorial Univ of Newfoundland, St. John's, NF, A1C 5S7. **EMAIL** iser@morgan.ucs,mun.ca

OMOLADE, BARBARA
PERSONAL Born 10/29/1942, Brooklyn, New York **DISCIPLINE** EDUCATION **EDUCATION** Queens Coll, BA 1964; Goddard Coll, MA 1980; City University of New York, New York, NY, PhD, Sociology, 1997. **CAREER** Ctr for the Elimination of Violence in the Family, co-dir 1977-78; Women's Action Alliance, 1979-81; Empire State Coll Ctr for Labor Studies, instructor 1980-81; WBAI Radio, producer/commentator 1981-83; CCNY-CWE, higher educ officer/adjunct faculty 1981-,assoc prof, , currently; freelance writer 1979-; City University of New York, New York, NY, coordinator curriculum change faculty development seminars, 1988-. **HONORS AND AWARDS** Unit Awds in Media Lincoln Univ of MO 1981; Malcolm X Awd The East 1982; Susan B Anthony Awd New York City Natl Org of Women 1987. **MEMBERSHIPS** Bd mem Sisterhood of Black Single Mothers 1983-, co-founder CUNY Friends of Women Studies 1984-; Career Faculty Member CCNY-CWE. **SELECTED PUBLICATIONS** Author, The Rising Song of African American Women.

ONORATO, MICHAEL P.
PERSONAL Born 08/03/1934, New York, NY, m, 1962 **DISCIPLINE** SOUTHEAST ASIAN HISTORY **EDUCATION** St Peter's Col, BS, 56; Georgetown Univ, MA, 59, PhD(hist), 60. **CAREER** From instr to asst prof, SE Asian hist, Canisius Col, 60- 65; from asst prof to assoc prof, 65-70, Prof Hist, Calif State Univ, Fullerton, 70-, Vis prof, Ateneo de Manila Univ, 63-64; Am Philos Soc grant-in-aid, 64-65, 68-69 & 71-72; exec secy, Philippine Studies Coun, 72-75. **MEMBERSHIPS** Asn Asian Studies; Asn Asian Studies Pac Coast (chairperson, 77-78). **RESEARCH** Philippines; comparative imperial institutions in Southeast Asia. **SELECTED PUBLICATIONS** Auth, Leonard Wood and the Philippine Cabinet Crisis of 1923, Univ Manila, 67; Independence rejected: The Philippines, 1924, Philippine Studies, 67; Leonard Wood as Governor General: A Calendar of Selected Correspondence, MCS Enterprises, 68; The United States and Philippine Independence, A Reappraisal, Solidarity, 70; A Brief Review of American Interest in Philippine Development and Other Essays (rev ed), MCS Enterprises, 72; Manuel Luis Quezon and His Modus Operandi, Asian Forum, 73; ed, Origins of the Philippine Republic: Extracts From the Diaries and Records of Francis Burton Harrison, Cornell Univ, 74; auth, Francis Burton Harrison: Liberal proconsul: The Filipinazation of the Philippine Islands, Bull Am Hist Collection, 76; Veracruz,philip - a Personal History of Filipino Immigrants And The Farmworkers Movement - Scharlin,c, Villanueva,lv, Pacific Historical Review, Vol 0062, 1993; Bound to Empire - The United-states And The Philippines - Brands,hw, American Historical Review, Vol 0098, 1993; Battle For Batangas - a Philippine Province at War - May,ga, Pacific Historical Review, Vol 0062, 1993. **CONTACT ADDRESS** Dept of Hist, California State Univ, Fullerton, Fullerton, CA, 92634.

ONUF, PETER S.
DISCIPLINE HISTORY **EDUCATION** Johns Hopkins, AB, 67, PhD, 73. **CAREER** Asst prof, hist, Worcester Polytechnic Inst; THOMAS JEFFERSON MEM FDN PROF, HIST, UNIV VA. **MEMBERSHIPS** Am Antiquarian Soc **SELECTED PUBLICATIONS** Auth, "From Constitution to Higher Law: The Reinterpretation of the Northwest Ordinance, Ohio Hist 94, 85; auth, "Liberty, Development, and Union: Visions of the West in the 1780's," Wm & Mary Quart 43, 86; coauth, "Toward a Republican Empire: Interest and Ideology in Revolutionary America," Am Quart 37, 85; auth, Statehood and Union: A History of the Northwest Ordinance, 87; auth, essays on land policy, territorial policy, and federalism, The Origins of the Federal Republic: Juris Contros. in the United States, 1775-1787, 87; coauth, The Midwestern Nation, 90; coauth, A Union of Interests: Politics and Economics in Revolutionary America, 90; coauth, Federal Union, Modern World: The Law of Nations in an Age of Revolutions, 1776-1814, Madison House, 93; ed, Jefferson Legacies, Univ Press Va, 93. **CONTACT ADDRESS** Dept of Hist, Univ of Virginia, Randall Hall, Charlottesville, VA, 22903. **EMAIL** dude@virginia.edu

OPPENHEIM, JANET
PERSONAL Born 05/05/1948, New York, NY, m, 1971, 1 child **DISCIPLINE** BRITISH HISTORY **EDUCATION** Bryn Mawr Col, BA, 70; Columbia Univ, MA, 71, PhD(hist), 75. **CAREER** Instr hist, Mary Washington Col, Fredericksburg, 74-75; asst prof, 75-80, Assoc Prof Hist, Am Univ, Washington, DC, 80-, Vis asst prof hist, Princeton Univ, 79. **MEMBERSHIPS** AHA; Conf Brit Studies; Northeast Victorian Studies Asn. **RESEARCH** Modern British cultural and intellectual history. **SELECTED PUBLICATIONS** Auth, The Nationalization of Culture: The Development of State Subsidies to the Arts in Great Britain, Hamish Hamilton & NY Univ, 77; Class Formation And Urban Industrial-society - Bradford, 1750-1850 - Koditschek,t, J of Social History, Vol 0026, 1993; Besant,annie - a Biography - Taylor,a, American Historical Review, Vol 0098, 1993; Psychiatry For The Rich - a History of Ticehurst, Private Asylum - Mackenzie,c, American Historical Review, Vol 0099, 1994; Women in English Social- history, 1800-1914 - a Guide to Research in 3 Volumes - Kanner,b, J of Modern History, Vol 0066, 1994; High Society, The English Social Elite, 1880-1914 - Horn,p, Albion, Vol 0026, 1994; Women And Social-action in Victorian And Edwardian England - Lewis,j, J of Modern History, Vol 0066, 1994; a Mothers Role, A Daughters Duty, Balfour,blanche, Sidgwick,eleanor, And Feminist Perspectives, J of British Studies, Vol 0034, 1995. **CONTACT ADDRESS** Dept of Hist, American Univ, Washington, DC, 20016.

OPPENHEIM, SAMUEL AARON
PERSONAL Born 11/11/1940, New York, NY, m, 1965, 3 children **DISCIPLINE** RUSSIAN & MODERN EUROPEAN HISTORY **EDUCATION** Univ Ariz, BA, 62; Harvard Univ, AM, 64; Ind Univ, PhD (Russ & mod Europ hist), 72. **CAREER** Instr Russ & hist, Bishop Col, 64-67; asst prof, 71-74, assoc prof, 74-79, Prof Hist, Calif State Col, Stanislaus, 79-, Instr Russ & hist, Austin Col, 65-67. **MEMBERSHIPS** AAUP; Am Asn Advan Slavic Studies; AHA. **RESEARCH** Twentieth century Russian Soviet history. **SELECTED PUBLICATIONS** Auth, Rehabilitation in the post-Stalinist Soviet Union, Western Polit Quart, 367; The Supreme Economic Council, 1917- 1921, Soviet Studies, 773; The soviet semester: An historical interdisciplinary experience, Hist Teacher, 577; The making of a Right Communist--A I Rykov to 1917, Slavic Rev,

977; The Practical Bolshevik: A I Rykov and Russian Communism, 1881-1938, Hoover Inst Press, 79; Forty articles, In: Modern Encyclopedia of Russian and Soviet History, Acad Int, 76; The Ghost of The Executed Engineer - Technology And The Fall of The Soviet-union - Graham,lr, Russian Review, Vol 0053, 1994. **CONTACT ADDRESS** 3008 Prince Valiant Lane, Modesto, CA, 95350.

ORBACH, ALEXANDER
PERSONAL Born 02/16/1945, Dzalal Abad, USSR, m, 1967, 2 children **DISCIPLINE** MODERN JEWISH HISTORY **EDUCATION** Queens Col, New York, BA, 66; Univ Wis, MA, 69, PhD Hist, 75. **CAREER** Asst prof Relig, Oberlin Col, 73-76; asst prof Hist, Ind Univ, Bloomington, 76-77; assoc prof Relig Studies, Hist, Univ Pittsburgh, 77-. **MEMBERSHIPS** AHA; Am Asn Advan Slavic Studies; Asn Jewish Studies. **RESEARCH** Russian Jewry 19th century; modern Jewish thought. **SELECTED PUBLICATIONS** Auth, Jewish intellectuals in Odessa in the late 19th century: The nationalist theories of Ahad Ha'am and Simon Dubnov, Nationalities Papers, VI: 109-123; The Jewishness of Soviet-Jewish culture: Historical considerations, J Jewish Communal Serv, Vol L VII, No 2; New Voices of Russian Jewry: A Study of the Russian-Jewish Press in the Era of the Great Reforms, 1860-1871, Brill Press, Leiden, Holland, 80; The Saul M Ginsburg Archival Collection: A major source for the study of Russian-Jewish life and letters, Soviet Jewish Affairs, Vol XI, No 2. **CONTACT ADDRESS** Dept of Relig Studies, Univ of Pittsburgh, 2604 Cathedral/Learn, Pittsburgh, PA, 15260-0001. **EMAIL** orbach@vms.cis.pih.edu

ORDOWER, HENRY M.
PERSONAL Chicago, IL, 3 children **DISCIPLINE** TAXATION LAW, MEDIEVAL LITERATURE **EDUCATION** Washington Univ, St Louis, AB, 67; Univ Chicago, MA, 70, JD, 75. **CAREER** Instr law, Univ Chicago Law Sch, 75-76; assoc atty, Sonnenschein, Calin, Nath & Rosenthal, 75-77; asst prof, 77-80, assoc prof Law, St Louis Univ Law Sch, 80-83. **MEMBERSHIPS** Soc Advan Scand Studies. **RESEARCH** United States taxation of income, estates and gifts; the Icelandic family saga. **SELECTED PUBLICATIONS** Art, Separating Statutory Frameworks: Incompatibility of the Complete Liquidation & Reorganization Provisions of the Internal Revenue Code, St Louis Univ Law J, 81; auth, Tax Act Offers New Choices: Planning the Large Estate, Trusts & Estates, 82. **CONTACT ADDRESS** Law School, St. Louis Univ, 3700 Lindell Blvd, St. Louis, MO, 63108-3412. **EMAIL** ordoweh@slu.edu

OREL, SARA E.
DISCIPLINE ART HISTORY **EDUCATION** Bryn Mawr Col, BA; Univ Toronto, MA, PhD. **CAREER** Asst prof; ch, Art Hist Fac Comm, Truman State Univ. **SELECTED PUBLICATIONS** Co-auth, Murder in Ancient Egypt, in Death and Taxes in the Ancient Near East, 92; From Cave to Monastery: Changes at the Nome Frontier of Gebel el-Haridi in Upper Egypt, Shifting Frontiers in Late Antiquity: Proc of the First Intl Interdisciplinary Conf on Late Antiquity, 96; ed, Death and Taxes in the Ancient Near East, Edwin Mellen Press, 92; auth, Two Unpublished Stelae from Beni Hasan, Jour Egyptian Archaeol, 96; John Garstang/Excavations at Beni Hasan, KMT, 96. **CONTACT ADDRESS** Dept of Art, Truman State Univ, 100 E Normal St, Kirksville, MO, 63501-4221.

ORLIN, ERIC
PERSONAL Born 02/22/1964, Boston, MA, m **DISCIPLINE** ANCIENT HISTORY **EDUCATION** Yale Univ, BA 86; Univ Cal Berk, PhD 94. **CAREER** Cal State Univ Fresno, lect 94-96; Bard Col, asst prof 96-. **MEMBERSHIPS** APA; AAH **RESEARCH** Roman Religion and politica; Roman Imperialism; Greek Hist. **SELECTED PUBLICATIONS** Auth, Temples, Religion and Politics in the Roman Republic, Brill, 96. **CONTACT ADDRESS** Dept of History, Bard Col, 3 Salisbury Ct, Rhinebeck, NY, 12572. **EMAIL** orlin@bard.edu

ORLOW, DIETRICH OTTO
PERSONAL Born 06/02/1937, Hamburg, Germany, m, 1959, 1 child **DISCIPLINE** MODERN EUROPEAN HISTORY **EDUCATION** Ohio Univ, AB, 58; Univ Mich, MA, 59, PhD, 62. **CAREER** From instr to asst prof, 62-67 Col William & Mary; assoc prof, 67-71, Syracuse Univ; prof hist, 71-, dept chmn, 79-84, Boston Univ; Duke Univ-Univ NC Coop Prog in Humanities fel, 66-67; Alexander von Humboldt Stiftung sr res fel, 74-75, fel, 78-79; vis prof, 75, Univ Hamburg, Ger; fel, Netherlands Inst for Advan Stud; Fulbright Europe, Reg Res Fel, 85, 86, 93. **MEMBERSHIPS** AHA; pres, 95-96, Conf Group Cent Europ Hist. **RESEARCH** History of National Socialist Germany; 20th century totalitarianism; history of the Weimar Republic. **SELECTED PUBLICATIONS** Auth, Weimar Prussia, 1925-1933: The Illusion of Strength, Univ Pitt Press, 91; auth, A History of Modern Germany, 1870 to the Present, Prentice-Hall, 98; auth, Common Destiny: A Comparative History of the Dutch, French, and German Social Democratic Parties 1945-1969, Berghahn Bks, 99. **CONTACT ADDRESS** Dept of History, Boston Univ, 226 Bay State Rd, Boston, MA, 02215-1403. **EMAIL** dorlow@bu.edu

ORMAND, KIRK
PERSONAL Born 11/05/1962, Traverse City, MI, m, 1984, 1 child **DISCIPLINE** CLASSICAL STUDIES **EDUCATION** Stanford Univ, PhD, 92. **CAREER** Vis Asst Prof, Oberlin Col, 92-93; Asst Prof, Loyola Univ Chicago, 93-97. **HONORS AND AWARDS** John J. Winkler Memorial Prize, 91; Gildersleeve Prize, Am J Philol, 96; Solmsen Fel, Inst Res Humanities, 98-99. **MEMBERSHIPS** Am Philol Asn; Women's Classical Caucus; Lesbian Gay and Bisexual Classical Caucus. **RESEARCH** Ancient Greek literature and culture; modern critical theory. **SELECTED PUBLICATIONS** Auth, Trachiniae 1055ff: More Wedding Imagery, Mnemosyne 67, 93; Lucan's auctor vix fidelis, Classical Antiquity, 94; Silent by Convention? Sophocles' Tekmessa, AJP, 96; Exchange and the Maiden: Marriage in Sophoclean Tragedy, Univ Tex Press (forthcoming 99). **CONTACT ADDRESS** Washburn Observatory, Univ Wisconsin Madison, 1401 Observatory Dr., Madison, WI, 53706. **EMAIL** kormand@facstaff.wisc.edu

ORMSBY, MARGARET A.
PERSONAL Quesnel, BC, Canada **DISCIPLINE** HISTORY **EDUCATION** Univ BC, BA, 29, MA, 31; Bryn Mawr Col, PhD, 37. **CAREER** Lectr, McMaster Univ, 40-43; lectr, 43-46, asst prof, 46-49, assoc prof, 49-52, PROF EMER HISTORY, UNIV BC, 65-. **HONORS AND AWARDS** DLitt, Univ BC, 74; LLD, Univ Manitoba, 60; LLD, Univ Notre Dame, Nelson BC; LLD, Simon Fraser Univ, 71; LLD, Univ Victoria, 76; LLD, Univ North BC, 95. **MEMBERSHIPS** Can Hist Asn; BC Hist Asn; Royal Soc Can; BC Heritage. **SELECTED PUBLICATIONS** Auth, British Columbia: A History, 58, 62, 64, 71; auth, A Pioneer Gentlewoman in British Columbia: the Recollections of Susan Allison, 76, 94; auth, Coldstream-Nulli Secundus, 90. **CONTACT ADDRESS** Dept of History, Univ BC, Vancouver, BC, V6T 1Z1.

OROZCO, CYNTHIA E.
DISCIPLINE HISTORY, CHICANA/O STUDIES **EDUCATION** Univ Calif, Los Angeles, PhD, 92 **CAREER** Res assoc, Tex State Hist Assoc, 88-92; res assoc, Inst Texan Cultures, 92-93; vis prof, Univ Tex, San Antonia, 93-94; Instr, Eastern NMex State Univ, Ruidoso, 97-98; vis asst prof, 97-98, VIS ASST PROF HIST, CHICANA/O STUD, UNIV NMEX, 98-. **CONTACT ADDRESS** Dept of History, Univ of New Mexico, Albuquerque, NM, 87131-1181. **EMAIL** corozco@unm.edu

ORR, LESLIE
PERSONAL Born 04/29/1948, Ann Arbor, MI **DISCIPLINE** HISTORY OF RELIGIONS, ASIAN RELIGIONS **EDUCATION** McGill Univ, BS, 70, MA, 81-82, PhD, 93. **CAREER** Full-time lectr, asst, assoc prof, 91-; full-time lect, McGill Univ, 89-91; part-time lectr, McGill Univ, 84-89; tchg asst, McGill Univ, 82-83. **RESEARCH** Women in the religions of India (Hinduism, Buddhism, and Jainism). **SELECTED PUBLICATIONS** Auth, "Jain Worship in Medieval Tamilnadu," Proc Intl Conf on Approaches to Jaina Stud: Philosophy, Logic, Rituals and Symbols, Ctr S Asian Stud, Univ Toronto, 97; "The Vaisnava Community at Srirangam: The Testimony of the Early Medieval Inscriptions," Jour of Vaisnava Stud, 95; The Concept of Time in Sankara's Brahma-sutra-bhasya, Hermeneutical Paths to the Sacred Worlds of India, Scholar's Press, 94; Women of Medieval South India in Hindu Temple Ritual: Text and Practice, Annual Rev of Women in World Religions 3, 94. **CONTACT ADDRESS** Dept of Rel, Concordia Univ, Montreal, 1455 de Maisonneuve W, Montreal, PQ, H3G 1M8.

ORTH, JOHN VICTOR
PERSONAL Born 02/07/1947, Lancaster, PA, m, 1972, 2 children **DISCIPLINE** HISTORY OF LAW, PROPERTY LAW **EDUCATION** Oberlin Col, AB, 69; Harvard Univ, JD, 74, PhD(hist), 77. **CAREER** Law clerk, US Ct Appeals, 77-78; asst prof, 78-81, Assoc Prof Law, Univ NC, 81-. **MEMBERSHIPS** AAUP; Am Soc Legal Hist; Am Bar Asn; Selden Soc; Conf Brit Studies. **RESEARCH** American constitutional history; history of labor law. **SELECTED PUBLICATIONS** Auth, Doing legal history, Irish Jurist, 79; The fair fame and name of Louisiana: The Eleventh Amendment and the end of reconstruction, Tulane Lawyer, 80; Sir William Blackstone: Hero of the common law, Am Bar Asn J, 80; contribr, Law-Making and Law-Makers in British History, Royal Hist Soc, 80; auth, English law and striking workmen: The Molestation of Workmen Act, 1859, J Legal Hist, 81; The Eleventh Amendment and the North Carolina state debt, NC Law Rev, 81; Jeremy Bentham: The common law's severest critic, Am Bar Asn J, 82; On the relation between the rule of law and Pubic opinion, Mich Law Rev, 82; a Bibliography of 19th-century Legal Literature - Adams,jn, Davies,mj, American J of Legal History, Vol 0038, 1994; Currents of Radicalism - Popular Radicalism, Organized-labor And Party Politics in Britain 1850-1914 - Biagini,ef, Reid,aj, American J of Legal History, Vol 0037, 1993; Law, Politics And The Church-of- england, The Career of Lushington,stephen, 1782-1873 - Waddams,sm, Albion, Vol 0025, 1993; The Independence of The Judiciary, The View From The Lord-chancellor Office - Stevens,r, Albion, Vol 0026, 1994; Judicial Enigma - The First Justice Harlan - Yarbrough,te, American J of Legal History, Vol 0040, 1996; The Republican Crown - Lawyers And The Making of The State in 20th-century Britain - Jacob,jm, Albion, Vol 0029, 1997; Leading Cases in The Common-law - Simpson,awb, American Historical Review, Vol 0102, 1997. **CONTACT ADDRESS** Sch of Law, Univ of NC, Chapel Hill, NC, 27514.

ORTNER, SHERRY B.
DISCIPLINE ANTHROPOLOGY **EDUCATION** Bryn Mawr Col, AB, 62; Univ Chicago, MA, 66, PhD, 70. **CAREER** Lectr, 69-70, vis fel, 70-71, Princeton Univ; fac, Sarah Lawrence Col, 71-77; assoc prof, 77-84, prof anthropol, 84-95, chair anthropol, 86-89, prof women's stud, 88-95m, Sylvia L Thrupp prof anthropol & women's stud, 92-94, Univ Mich; prof anthropol, Univ Calif, Berkeley, 94-96; PROF ANTHROPOL, COLUMBIA UNIV, 96-. **CONTACT ADDRESS** Dept of Anthropol, Columbia Univ, 1200 Amsterdam Ave, New York, NY, 10027. **EMAIL** sbo3@columbia.edu

ORTQUIST, RICHARD THEODORE
PERSONAL Born 12/22/1933, Muskegon, MI, m, 1958, 2 children **DISCIPLINE** RECENT UNITED STATES HISTORY **EDUCATION** Hope Col, BA, 56; Univ Mich, Ann Arbor, MA, 61, PhD(hist), 68. **CAREER** From instr to asst prof, 64-71, assoc prof, 71-80, Prof Hist, Wittenberg Univ, 80-, Chmn Dept, 80-. **MEMBERSHIPS** AHA; Orgn Am Historians. **RESEARCH** Recent American political history; depression and New Deal period. **SELECTED PUBLICATIONS** Auth, Depression politics in Michigan: The election of 1932, Mich Acad, spring 70; Unemployment and relief: Michigan's response to the depression during the Hoover years, fall 73 & Tax crisis and politics early Depression Michigan, spring-summer 75, Mich Hist; Depression Politics in Michigan, 1929-1933, Garland Pub, Inc, 82; Exemplar of Americanism - The Philippine Career of Worcester,dean,c. - Sullivan,rj, Michigan Historical Review, Vol 0018, 1992. **CONTACT ADDRESS** Dept of Hist, Wittenberg Univ, Springfield, OH, 45501.

OSBORN, RONALD EDWIN
PERSONAL Born 09/05/1917, Chicago, IL, m, 1940, 1 child **DISCIPLINE** CHURCH HISTORY **EDUCATION** Phillips Univ, BA, 38, MA, 39, BD, 42; Univ Ore, PhD(hist), 55. **CAREER** Ed youth Pub, Christian Bd of Pub, St Louis, Mo, 43-45; prof church hist & relig, educ, NW Christian Col, 46-50; from asst prof to prof church hist, Christian Theol Sem, 50-73, dean, 59-70; Prof Church Hist, Disciples Found Chair, Sch Theol & Claremont Grad Sch & Univ Ctr, 73-, Deleg, World Conf Faith & Order, Lund, Sweden, 52 & Montreal, Can, 63; vis lectr, Grad Sch Ecumenical Studies, Celigny, Vaud, Switz, 54-55; mem, Consultation Church Union, 63-79; vis prof church hist & ecumenics, Union Theol Sem Philippines, 65; pres, Int Convention Christian Churches, 67-68; moderator, Christian Church, 68. **HONORS AND AWARDS** LittD, Phillips Univ, 69. **MEMBERSHIPS** AHA; Am Soc Church Hist; Disciples Christ Hist Soc (pres, 50-53). **RESEARCH** History of preaching; religion in Western America. **SELECTED PUBLICATIONS** Auth, The Spirit of American Christianity, Harper, 57; coauth & ed, The Reformation of Tradition, Bethany, 63; auth, A Church for These Times, Abingdon, 65; In Christ's Place: Christian Ministry in Today's World, Bethany, 67; coauth, Disciples and the Church Universal, Disciples of Christ Hist Soc, 67; auth, Religious freedom and the form of the church, Lexington Theol Quart, 76; Experiment in Liberty, 78 & The Faith We Affirm, 79, Bethany; a Case-study of Mainstream Protestantism - The Disciples Relation to American Culture, 1880-1989 - Williams,dn, Ecumenical Review, Vol 0045, 1993. **CONTACT ADDRESS** Dept of Church Hist, Sch of Theol Claremont Grad Sch, 1325 N College, Claremont, CA, 91711.

OSBORNE, JOHN
DISCIPLINE ART HISTORY **EDUCATION** Univ Carleton, BA; Univ Toronto, MA; Univ London, PhD. **CAREER** Prof **RESEARCH** Material culture of medieval Europe and Byzantium; cities of Rome and Venice in the Middle Ages. **SELECTED PUBLICATIONS** Auth, The Paper Museum of Cassiano dal Pozzo, Series A, Part II, Early Christian and Medieval Antiquities, 2 vols, Harvey Miller Press, London, 96-98; A Tale of Two Cities: Sacred Geography in Christian Jerusalem, Queen's Quart 103, 96; The early medieval sculpture, Excavations at the Mola di Monte Gelato: A Roman and Medieval Settlement in South Etruria, Archaeol Monogr(s) of the Brit Sch at Rome, 11, 97; The hagiographic programme of the mosaics in the south dome of San Marco at Venice, RACAR 22, 95; The cross-under-arch motif in ninth-century Venetian sculpture: an imperial reading, Thesaurismata 27, 97; Proclamations of Power and Presence: The Setting and Function of Two Eleventh-Century Murals in the Lower Church of San Clemente, Rome, Mediaeval Stud 59, 97. **CONTACT ADDRESS** Dept of Hist in Art, Victoria Univ, PO Box 1700, Victoria, BC, V8W 2Y2. **EMAIL** josborne@finearts.uvic.ca

OSBORNE, JOHN WALTER
PERSONAL Born 08/19/1927, Brooklyn, NY, m, 1958, 1 child **DISCIPLINE** HISTORY **EDUCATION** Rutgers Univ, AB, 57, AM, 59, PhD(hist), 61. **CAREER** Asst hist, Rutgers Univ, 57-59; consult grad rec exam in hist, Educ Testing Serv, NJ, 59; asst prof hist, Newark State Col, 62-63; asst prof, Newark Col Eng, 63-64; from asst prof to assoc prof, 64-69, Prof Hist, Rutgers Univ, New Brunswick, 69-, Am Philos Soc grant, 66 & 75; consult ed, Irish Univ Press, 69- 71; ed, J Rutgers Univ Libr,

75-80. **MEMBERSHIPS** AHA; Conf Brit Studies. **RESEARCH** British history. **SELECTED PUBLICATIONS** Auth, Parliamentary career (1614-1621) of Sir Edwin Sandys, Bermuda Hist Quart, 62; William Cobbett and the Catholic emancipation crisis, 1823-1829, Cath Hist Rev, 63; William Cobbett: His Thought and His Times, Rutgers Univ, 66; The Silent Revolution: The Industrial Revolution in England as a Source of Cultural Change, Scribner, 70; John Cartwright, Cambridge, 72; The endurance of literary history in Great Britain: Charles Oman, G M Trevelyan and the genteel tradition, Clio, 1072; Henry Hunt's career in Parliament, Historian, 76; William Cobbett and Ireland, Studies, 81; Trevelyan,george,macaulay - a Life in History - Cannadine,d, Clio-a J of Literature History And The Philosophy of History, Vol 0022, 1993; Cobbett,william And Rural Popular-culture - Dyck,i, Albion, Vol 0025, 1993; Morison,samuel,eliot Historical World - Pfitzer,gm, Clio-a J of Literature History And The Philosophy of History, Vol 0023, 1993; Interests And Obsessions - Historical Essays - Skidelsky,r, Clio-a J of Literature History And The Philosophy of History, Vol 0024, 1995. **CONTACT ADDRESS** 24 Helen Ave, West Orange, NJ, 07052.

OSBORNE, THOMAS ROBERT
PERSONAL Born 12/16/1943, Rochester, NY, m, 1963, 2 children **DISCIPLINE** HISTORY **EDUCATION** Univ Conn, BA, 64, MA, 68, PhD(Mod Europ hist), 74. **CAREER** Lectr hist, Cent Conn State Col, 72-73; adJasst prof, New York Inst Technol, 75-78; Asst Prof Hist, Univ N Ala, 78-. **MEMBERSHIPS** AHA; Soc Fr Hist Studies; Soc Hist Educ. **RESEARCH** Nineteenth & 20th century Europe; Modern France. **SELECTED PUBLICATIONS** Auth, Sciences Po and the Concours: The recruitment of the bureaucratic elite in the early Third RePubic, Third RepubTroisieme RePubique, fall 76; Social Science at the Sciences Po: Training the bureaucratic elite in the early Third RePubic, Hist Reflections, spring 81; Religion, Politics And Preferment in France Since 1890 - La-belle-epoque And Its Legacy - Larkin,m, American Historical Review, Vol 0102, 1997. **CONTACT ADDRESS** Dept of Hist, Univ of N Ala, Florence, AL, 35630.

OSHEIM, DUANE JEFFREY
PERSONAL Born 05/28/1942, Roland, IA, m, 1968 **DISCIPLINE** MEDIEVAL & RENAISSANCE HISTORY **EDUCATION** Luther Col, BA, 64; Univ Nebr, Lincoln, MA, 67; Univ Calif, Davis, PhD(hist), 72. **CAREER** Asst prof, 76-82, ASSOC PROF HIST, UNIV VA, 82-, Am Acad in Rome, Rome Prize fel hist, 74-76. **MEMBERSHIPS** AHA; Mediaeval Acad Am; Soc Ital Hist Studies. **RESEARCH** Social and economic history; church history; institutional history. **SELECTED PUBLICATIONS** Auth, The Episcopal archive of Lucca in the Middle Ages, Manuscripta, 73; Rural population and the Tuscan economy in the Middle Ages, Viator, 76; An Italian Lordship, the Bishopric of Lucca in the Late Middle Ages, Univ Calif, 77; Conversion, Conversi and the Christian Life in Late Medieval Tuscany, Speculum, 82. **CONTACT ADDRESS** Corcoran Dept of Hist, Univ of Va, Randall Hall, Charlottesville, VA, 22903-3244. **EMAIL** djo@virginia.edu

OSLER, MARGARET JO
PERSONAL Born 11/27/1942, New York, NY **DISCIPLINE** HISTORY & PHILOSOPHY OF SCIENCE **EDUCATION** Swarthmore Col, BA, 63; Ind Univ, MA, 66, PhD(hist & philos of sci), 68. **CAREER** Asst prof hist of sci, Ore State Univ, 68-70; asst prof hist, Harvey Mudd Col, 70-74; asst prof, Wake Forest Univ, 74- 75; Assoc Prof Hist, Univ Calgary, 75-. **MEMBERSHIPS** Hist of Sci Soc; West Coast Hist Sci Soc; Can Soc Hist & Philos of Sci. **RESEARCH** Locke's relation to 17th century science; philosophical problems of 17th century science; theories of matter and scientific method in the 17th century. **SELECTED PUBLICATIONS** Auth, John Locke and the ideal certainty in 17th century science, J Hist Ideas, 70; Galileo, motion, and essences, Isis, 74; coauth, Physical sciences, history of, In: Encycl Britannica; Certainty, scepticism, and scientific optimism, In: Probability, Time, and Space, AMS Press, 78; Descartes and Charleton on nature, God, and the mechanical philosophy, J Hist of Ideas, 79; Renaissance And Revolution - Humanists, Scholars, Craftsmen, And Natural Philosophers in Early Modern Europe - Field,jv, J Ames,fajl, Isis, Vol 0086, 1995; Gassendi - Scientific Explorer - a Catalog of The Exhibition on The Occasion of Gassendi,pierre 400th Birthday at The Musee-de- digne, May 19 to October 18, 1992 - French - Turner,a, Gomez,n, Annals of Science, Vol 0051, 1994; Gassendi - Scientific Explorer - a Catalog of The Exhibition on The Occasion of Gassendi,pierre 400th Birthday at The Musee-de-digne, May 19 to October 18, 1992 - French - Turner,a, Gomez,n, Annals of Science, Vol 0051, 1994; an Overview of Gassendi Philosophy - French - Bernier,f, Annals of Science, Vol 0051, 1994; An Overview of Gassendi Philosophy - French - Bernier,f, Annals of Science, Vol 0051, 1994; Providence and divine will in Gassendi's views on scientific knowledge, J Hist Ideas (in prep); The Matter of Revolution - Science, Poetry And Politics in The Age of Milton - Rogers,j, Isis, Vol 0088, 1997; The Matter of Revolution - Science, Poetry And Politics in The Age of Milton - Rogers,j, Isis, Vol 0088, 1997; Westfall,richard,s., 22 April 1924-21 August 1996, Isis, Vol 0088, 1997. **CONTACT ADDRESS** Dept of Hist, Univ of Calgary, Calgary, AB, T2N 1N4.

OSTHAUS, CARL RICHARD
PERSONAL Born 06/02/1943, Sandusky, OH, m, 1965, 2 children **DISCIPLINE** HISTORY **EDUCATION** Kalamazoo Col, BA, 65; Univ Chicago, MA, 66, PhD(hist), 71. **CAREER** From instr to asst prof, 70-77, Assoc Prof Am Hist, Oakland Univ, 77-. **MEMBERSHIPS** Orgn Am Historians; Southern Hist Asn. **RESEARCH** Civil War and Reconstruction; the American South. **SELECTED PUBLICATIONS** Auth, The rise and fall of Jesse Binga, Black Financier, J Negro Hist, 173; From the Old South to the New South: The editorial career of William Tappan Thompson of the Savannah Morning News, Southern Quart, 376; Freedmen, Philanthropy, and Fraud: A History of the Freedman's Savings Bank, Univ Ill, 76; Francis Warrington Dawson and South Carolina's spirit of 1876: A case study of the perils of Jistic heresy, Hayes Hist J, fall 77; An affair of honor--not an honorable affair: The Ritchie- Pleasants duel and the press, VA Cavalcade, winter 77; Inner World of Lincoln,abraham - Burlingame,m, Michigan Historical Review, Vol 0021, 1995; Pulling The Temple Down - The Fire- eaters And The Destruction of The Union - Heidler,ds, J of American History, Vol 0082, 1995. **CONTACT ADDRESS** Dept of Hist, Oakland Univ, Rochester, MI, 48063.

OSTROW, STEVEN F.
PERSONAL Born 06/23/1954, Dallas, TX, m, 1994, 1 child **DISCIPLINE** ART HISTORY **EDUCATION** Princeton Univ, PhD, 87; MFA, 81; McGill Univ, BA, 76 **CAREER** Chair, 94-, Assoc prof, 94-, Asst Prof, 92-94, Univ of CA, Riverside; Assoc prof with tenure, 92, Asst Prof, 87-92, Inst, 85-87, Vassar Col **HONORS AND AWARDS** Samuel H Kress Found Subvent Grant **MEMBERSHIPS** Art hist of Southrn CA, Col Art Asn **RESEARCH** Italian art and culture **SELECTED PUBLICATIONS** Auth, Paolo Sanquirico: A Forgotten Virtuoso of Seicento Rome, Storia dell'arte, 99; **CONTACT ADDRESS** Dept of Hist of Art, Univ of California, Riverside, Riverside, CA, 92521-0319. **EMAIL** steveo@mail.ucr.edu

OSTROWER, GARY BERT
PERSONAL Born 10/11/1939, New York, NY **DISCIPLINE** DIPLOMATIC HISTORY **EDUCATION** Alfred Univ, BA, 61; Univ Rochester, MA, 62, PhD(hist), 70. **CAREER** Instr hist, Vassar Col, 67-68; asst prof, 69-75, Assoc Prof Hist, Alfred Univ, 75-, Lyndon Baines Johnson Found Moody grant, 77; vis prof, Univ Pa, 79-80; Advan Placement reader, Educ Testing Serv, 77-82. **MEMBERSHIPS** AHA; Soc Hist Am Foreign Rels; Orgn Am Historians. **RESEARCH** International organization; interwar diplomacy, 1919-39; modern political history. **SELECTED PUBLICATIONS** Auth, American ambassador to the League of Nations: A proposal postponed, 71 & Historical studies in American internationalism, 71, Int Orgn; Revising revisionist historians, Alfred News, 71; American decision to join the ILO, Labor Hist, 975; Collective Insecurity: The US and the League of Nations During the Early Thirties, Bucknell Univ Press, 79; Henry L Stimson and international organization, The Historian, 79; to End All Wars - Wilson,woodrow And The Quest For a New-world Order - Knock,tj, American Historical Review, Vol 0099, 1994; America Secret War Against Bolshevism - Us Intervention in The Russian Civil-war, 1917-1920 - Foglesong,ds, American Historical Review, Vol 0102, 1997. **CONTACT ADDRESS** Div of Human Studies, Alfred Univ, 26 N Main St, Alfred, NY, 14802-1222.

OSTWALD, MARTIN
PERSONAL Born 01/15/1922, Dortmund, Germany, m, 1948, 2 children **DISCIPLINE** CLASSICAL PHILOLOGY **EDUCATION** Univ Toronto, BA 46; Univ Chicago, AM, 48; Columbia Univ, PhD, 52. **CAREER** Instr class philol, 50-51, Wesleyan Univ; lectr & assoc Greek & Latin, 51-54, Columbia Univ; asst prof, 54-58, assoc prof, 58-66, prof classics, 66-92, Swarthmore Col; prof class studies, 68-92, prof emeritus, 92-Univ Pa; Fulbright res fel, Greece, 61-62; Am Coun Learned Soc res fel, 65-66; NEH sr fel, 70-71; vis fel, 70-71, Balliol Col Oxford Univ; mem, Inst Adv Study, 74-75 & 81-82, Princeton Univ; dir, NEH fel-in-residence in classics, 76-77; Guggenheim fel, 77-78. **HONORS AND AWARDS** Goodwin award of Merit of Amer Philol Assn, 90; fel, Amer acad of Arts & Sci, 91; Amer Philos Soc, 93; hon mem, Soc for Promotion of Hellenic Stud, 95; Dr Honuris Causa, Fribourg, Suisse, 95. **MEMBERSHIPS** Soc Prom Hellenic Studies; Am Philol Assn; Class Assn Can; Archaeol Inst Am. **RESEARCH** Greek social and political thought and institutions; Greek history, philosophy and literature. **SELECTED PUBLICATIONS** Auth, Autonomia: Its Genesis and Early History, Scholars, 82; auth, From Popular Sovereignty to the Sovereignty of Law, Univ Calif Press, 86. **CONTACT ADDRESS** 408 Walnut Ln, Swarthmore, PA, 19081. **EMAIL** mostwal1@swarthmore.edu

OSZUSCIK, PHILIPPE
PERSONAL Born 03/17/1941, Hattiesburg, MS, m, 1964 **DISCIPLINE** ART, ARCHITECTURAL HISTORY **EDUCATION** Univ Iowa, PhD , art and archit history, 79. **CAREER** Asst prof, Northwestern State Univ La, Natchitoches, 68-70; asst prof, Augustana Coll, 70-77; assoc prof, 77-, Univ South Ala. **HONORS AND AWARDS** Who's Who in the Humanities, 92; fellow, NEH summer seminar, Amer Folklife, 81; fellow, Amer Fed Art, Art Criticism, NYC, 68. **MEMBERSHIPS** Bd mem, 84-89, Pioneer Amer Soc; Vernacular Archit Forum; Soc Art Historians; pres, 89, newsletter ed, 88-95, Soc of Archit Historians, SE Chap, Soc of Archit Historians; SE Coll Art Conf; SE Amer Soc 18th-Century Studies; Art History Assn. **RESEARCH** Creole housing; ethnicities in vernacular archit; southeastern archit; postmodern archit; African-American archit. **SELECTED PUBLICATIONS** Auth, "Passage of the Gallery and Other Caribbean Elements from the French and Spanish to the British in the United States," Pioneer America Transactions, vol. 14, 92; "French Creoles on the Gulf Coast," "African-Americans in the American South," in To Build a New Land, 92; "A Postmodern Public Public Monument: Design Elements Make Reference to Older Structures," in Renaissance by the River (special section), Mobile Register, 19 Sept 93; "Comparisons Between Rural and Urban French Creole Housing," Material Culture, fall 94. **CONTACT ADDRESS** Dept of Art and Art History, Univ of S. Alabama, UAB 152, Mobile, AL, 36688-0002.

OTTENBERG, SIMON
PERSONAL Born 06/06/1923, New York, NY, m, 1986 **DISCIPLINE** CULTURAL ANTHROPOLOGY **EDUCATION** Univ WI, Madison, BA (anthropology), 48; Northwestern Univ, PhD (anthropology), PhD, 57. **CAREER** Instr, anthropol, Univ Chicago, 54; instr, anthropology, WA State Col, 54-55; instr to prof, Univ WA, 55-90, Emeritus prof, 90-. **HONORS AND AWARDS** Guggenheim fel, 70-71; NSF grant, 59-60; Social Science res Coun fel, 51-53, 62-63; NEH fel, 78-79; Honorary D of Lit, Univ Nigeria, 92; Leadership award, Arts Coun of the African Studies Asn, 92; Regents fel, Smithsonian Inst, 93-94. **MEMBERSHIPS** Am Anthropological Asn; African Studies Asn; Royal Anthropological Inst. **RESEARCH** Traditional and contemporary African art, ethnicity, change. **SELECTED PUBLICATIONS** Auth, Boyhood Rituals in an African Society: An Interpretation, Univ WA Press, 89; Seeing With Music: The Lives of 3 Blind African Musicians, Univ WA Press, 96; New Traditions from Nigeria: Seven Artists of the Nsukka Group, Smithsonian Inst Press, 97. **CONTACT ADDRESS** 2317 22nd Ave E, Seattle, WA, 98112-2604. **EMAIL** otten@homer.u.washington.edu

OUELLET, FERNAND
PERSONAL Born 11/06/1926, Lac-Bouchette, PQ, Canada **DISCIPLINE** HISTORY **EDUCATION** Univ Laval, BA, 48, LL, 50, DL, 65. **CAREER** Asst archv, prov Que, 56-61; prof, Univ Laval, 61-65; prof, Carleton Univ, 65-75; prof, Univ Ottawa, 75-85; prof, 86-95, PROF EMER HISTOIRE, YORK UNIV, 95-. **HONORS AND AWARDS** Grand prix litteraire de la ville de Montreal, 67; Laureat des concours litteraires de la prov Que, 67; Prix David, 67; Medaille Tyrrell, soc royale Can; Prix gov gen Can, 77; Prix Sir John A. Macdonald, 77; off, ordre Can, 79; Medaille du centenaire Can, 67; Medaille du jubilee de la Reine, 77. **MEMBERSHIPS** Soc hist Can; soc royale Can. **SELECTED PUBLICATIONS** Auth, Histoire economique et sociale du Quebec (1760-1850), 66; auth, Le Bas-Canada 1771-1840, 76; dir, Histoire sociale/Social History, 71-88. **CONTACT ADDRESS** 92A Alcorn Ave, Toronto, ON, M4V 1E4.

OURADA, PATRICIA K.
PERSONAL Born 04/20/1926, Menominee, MI **DISCIPLINE** AMERICAN INDIAN HISTORY **EDUCATION** Col St Catherine, BA, 47; Univ Colo, MA, 53; Univ Okla, PhD(Am Indian hist), 73. **CAREER** Teacher hist, Pub High Schs, NDak & Minn, 47-60; from instr to assoc prof US hist, 62-73, Prof Us & Indian Hist, Boise State Univ, 73-. **RESEARCH** American Indian history and history of sports in America. **SELECTED PUBLICATIONS** Auth, The Chinese in Colorado, Colo Hist Quart, fall 52; ed, The hat Sitting Bull wore, Ann Wyo, 1069; auth, Mr Lincoln goes to war, Lincoln Herald, winter 69; Idaho Indian reservations, Idaho Heritage 1077; Biographies of Dillon Myer and Glenn Emmons in Kvasnicka and Viola, Commissioners of Indian Affairs, 1824-1977, Univ Nebr Press, 79; The Minominee Indians: A History, Univ Okla Press, 79; Migrant Workers in Idaho, Boise State Univ Print Shop, 80; Native-american Communities in Wisconsin, 1600-1960 - a Study of Tradition And Change - Bieder,re, American Historical Review, Vol 0102, 1997. **CONTACT ADDRESS** Dept of Hist, Boise State Univ, Boise, ID, 83725.

OVERBECK, JAMES A.
PERSONAL Born 09/11/1940, Eau Claire, WI, m, 1966, 3 children **DISCIPLINE** ECCLESIASTICAL HISTORY **EDUCATION** Univ of Chicago, MA, PhD, Grad Library Sch, MALS. **CAREER** Librarian, professor. **MEMBERSHIPS** Amer Library Assn, Amer Acad of Religion. **RESEARCH** History of Religious Journalism **SELECTED PUBLICATIONS** Auth, The Rise and Fall of Presbyterian Official Journals 1925-1985, Diversity of Fellowship, Westminister Press, 91. **CONTACT ADDRESS** 517 Ridgecrest Rd, NE, Atlanta, GA, 30307-1845. **EMAIL** Joverbec@ce1.af.public.lib.ga.us

OVERBECK, JOHN CLARENCE
PERSONAL Born 11/04/1933, Tulsa, OK, m, 1972, 1 child **DISCIPLINE** CLASSICAL ARCHEOLOGY, ANCIENT GREEK **EDUCATION** Univ Okla, AB, 55; Univ Cincinnati, PhD(classics), 63. **CAREER** Asst prof, 63-66, Assoc Prof

Classics, State Univ NY Albany, 66-, Mem managing comt, Am Sch Class Studies, Athens, 66-75; dir archaeol surv, Dept of Antiquities, Repub of Cyprus, 70. **MEMBERSHIPS** Archaeol Inst Am; Soc Prom Hellenic Studies; Asn Field Archaeol; Mod Greek Studies Asn. **RESEARCH** Cycladic Bronze Age; early Greek literature. **SELECTED PUBLICATIONS** Auth, Tacitus and Dio on Boudicca's rebellion, Am J Philol, 4/69; Greek towns of the Early Bronze Age, Class J, 10/69; Some notes on the interior of the Erechtheum, Athens Ann Archaeol, 4/72; coauth, Two Cypriot Bronze Age Sites at Kafkallia, Paul Astrom, Goteborg, Sweden, 72; The date of the last palace at Knossos, Am J Archaeol, spring 76; auth, Pioneers of Attic Vase Painting, In: The Greek Vase, Hudson-Mohawk Asn Cols & Univs, 81; The hub of commerce: Keos and Middle Helladic Greece, In: Temple University Aegean Symposium, Betancourt, 82; coauth, Consistency and diversity in the Middle Cycladic Era, In: Papers in Cycladic Prehistory, Univ Calif, Los Angeles, 79. **CONTACT ADDRESS** Dept of Classics, State Univ of NY, 1400 Washington Ave, Albany, NY, 12222-1000.

OVERHOLT, THOMAS WILLIAM
PERSONAL Born 08/09/1935, Bucyrus, OH, m, 1957, 2 children **DISCIPLINE** BIBLICAL STUDIES, HISTORY OF RELIGIONS **EDUCATION** Heidelberg Col, BA 57; Chicago Theol Sem, BD, 61; Univ Chicago, MA, 63, PhD, 67. **CAREER** Prof relig studies, Yankton Col, 64-75; assoc prof, 75-80, prof relig studies, Univ Wis-Stevens Point, 80-99. **HONORS AND AWARDS** Soc Values Higher Educ fel anthrop, Univ Ariz, 73-74. **MEMBERSHIPS** Am Acad Relig; Soc Bibl Lit; Soc Values Higher Educ. **RESEARCH** Old Testament; American Indian religions. **SELECTED PUBLICATIONS** Auth, Prophecy in Cross-Cultural Perspective: A Sourcebook for Biblical Researchers, Atlanta: Scholars Press, 86; auth, Jeremiah, Harper's Bible Commentary, San Francisco: Harper and Row, 88; auth, Channels of Prophecy: The Social Dynamics of Prophetic Activity, Minneapolis: Fortress Press, 89; auth, Cultural Anthropology and the Old Testament, Minneapolis: Fortress Press, 96. **CONTACT ADDRESS** Dept of Philosophy, Univ of Wisconsin, Stevens Point, 2100 Main St, Stevens Point, WI, 54481-3897. **EMAIL** toverhol@uwsp.edu

OWEN, CHRISTOPHER H.
PERSONAL Born 06/22/1959, Bryan, TX, m, 4 children **DISCIPLINE** HISTORY **EDUCATION** Univ Ga, AB, 81; Baylor Univ, MA, 86; Emory Univ, PhD, 91. **CAREER** From asst prof to assoc prof, Northeastern State Univ, 92-. **RESEARCH** American south; American religion. **SELECTED PUBLICATIONS** Auth, art, To Refrain From Political Affairs: Southern Evangelical, Cherokee Missions, and the Spirituality of the Church, 94; auth, art, Heaven's Gate, American Religious History, and the Culture of Death, 97; auth, art, To Keep the Way Open for Methodism: Georgia Weseylan Neutrality Towards Slavery, 1844-1861, 98; auth, The Sacred Flame of Love: Methodism and Society in Nineteenth-Century Georgia, 98. **CONTACT ADDRESS** Dept of History, Northeastern State Univ, Tahlequah, OK, 74464. **EMAIL** owen@cherokee.nsuok.edu

OWEN, DAVID I.
PERSONAL Born 10/28/1940, Boston, MA, m, 1964, 2 children **DISCIPLINE** ASSYRIOLOGY, ARCHEOLOGY **EDUCATION** Boston Univ, AB, 62; Brandeis Univ, MA, 63, PhD, 69. **CAREER** Res asst archaeol, Univ Mus, Univ PA, 64-65, asst cur archaeol, 69-71, res assoc Assyriol, 71-75; asst prof Ancient Near Eastern studies, Dropsie Univ, 71-74; asst prof, 74-77, assoc prof, 77-82, chmn dept, 75-79, prof ancient near eastern hist & archaeol, dept dept near eastern studies, Cornell Univ, 83, Fulbright scholar, Ankara Univ, 66-68; adj prof Ancient Near Eastern Studies, Inst Nautical Archaeol, TX A&M Univ. **HONORS AND AWARDS** NEH Sr Fel, Am Sch Oriental Res, Jerusalem, 88-89. **MEMBERSHIPS** Archaeol Inst Am; Am Orient Soc; Israel Exploration Soc; Fondation assyriologique George Dossin. **RESEARCH** Assyriology; hist and archaeol of the Ancient Near East. **SELECTED PUBLICATIONS** Auth, The John Frederick Lewis Collection: Texts from the Third Millennium in the Free Library of Philadelphia, Materiali per il Vocabolario Neosumerico, Multigrafica Editrice, Rome, 75; A Sumerian letter from an angry housewife(?), In: The Bible World, Studies in Honor of Cyrus H Gordon, KTAV, New York, 80; Widow's rights in Ur III Sumer, In: Zeitschrift for Assyriologie, Berlin, 80; An Akkadian letter from Ugarit at Tel Aphek, In: Tel Aviv, Tel Aviv, 81; Of birds, eggs and turtles, In: Zeitschrift for Assyriologie, Berlin, 81; co-ed (with M A Morrison), Studies on the Civilization and Culture of Nuzi and the Hurrians in Honor of Ernest R Lacheman, 81 &; Neo-Sumerian Archival Texts Primarily from Nippur in the University Museum, the Oriental Institute and the Iraq Museum, 82, Eisenbrauns; Selected Ur III Texts from the Harvard Semitic Museum, Materiali per il Vocabolario Neosumerico, Vol 11, Multigrafica Editrice, Rome, 82. **CONTACT ADDRESS** Dept of Near Eastern Studies, Cornell Univ, Rockefeller Hall, Ithaca, NY, 14853-2502. **EMAIL** dio1@cornell.edu

OWENS, KENNETH NELSON
PERSONAL Born 06/06/1933, Tacoma, WA, m, 1954, 2 children **DISCIPLINE** AMERICAN HISTORY **EDUCATION** Lewis & Clark Col, BA, 55; Univ Minn, PhD, 59. **CAREER** From asst prof to assoc prof hist, Northern Ill Univ, 59- 68; assoc prof, 68-70, dir native Am studies, 69-70, Prof Hist & Ethnic Studies, Calif State Univ, Sacramento, 70. Consult, Sacramento Hist Ctr, 78-80, City of Sacramento, 79-81, Bur Land Mgt, 80-81 & Western Water Educ Found, 80-82. **MEMBERSHIPS** AHA; Orgn Am Historians; Western Hist Asn; Am Indian Hist Soc. **RESEARCH** American West; American Indian ethnohistory; Pubic history. **SELECTED PUBLICATIONS** Auth, Galena, Grant and the Fortunes of War, Northern Ill Univ, 63; Research opportunities in Western territorial history, Ariz & West, 66; Pattern and structure in Western Territorial politics, Western Hist Quart, 70; contribr, Reader's Encycl of American West, Crowell, 77; The California Mother Lode Region: Historical Overview, Folsom District, Bur Land Mgt, US Dept Interior, 79; The Sacramento Past: An Exhibition Document for the Sacramento History Center (2 vols), Sacramento Hist Ctr, 80; Government & Politics in the Nineteenth Century, In: Essays in Western Historiography, Nebr Univ Press, 82; The Historic Preservation Movement in California, 1940-1976 - Hata,ni, Pubic Historian, Vol 0016, 1994; ed, Wreck of the Sv Nikolai, Ore Hist Soc Press (in prep); Great American Outlaw - a Legacy of Fact And Fiction - Prassel,fr, Montana-the Magazine of Western History, Vol 0046, 1996; Overland - The California Emigrant Trail of 1841-1870 - Macgregor,g, Pubic Historian, Vol 0019, 1997. **CONTACT ADDRESS** Dept of Hist, California State Univ, Sacramento, Sacramento, CA, 95819.

OWENS, LARRY
DISCIPLINE HISTORY **EDUCATION** Princeton Univ, PhD, 87; Rutgers Univ, PhD, 72. **CAREER** Prof, Univ MA Amherst. **RESEARCH** Hist of sci and tech. **SELECTED PUBLICATIONS** Auth, The Counterproductive Management of Science during WWII, Bus Hist, 94; Where are We Going, Phil Morse? Changing Agendas and the Rhetoric of Obviousness in the Transformation of Computing at MIT 1939-1957; Science in the U.S.-The Last Century, 97. **CONTACT ADDRESS** Dept of Hist, Univ Massachusetts Amherst, Mass Ave, Amherst, MA, 01003.

OWENS, NORA ESTELLE
PERSONAL Born 09/16/1948, Buna, TX **DISCIPLINE** AMERICAN HISTORY **EDUCATION** Wayland Baptist Col, BA, 71; Baylor Univ, MA, 73; Auburn Univ, PhD, 83. **CAREER** Asst prof hist, Wayland Baptist Univ, 74-, Consult, Educ Serv Div, Tex State Hist Asn 79-. **HONORS AND AWARDS** Tchr of the year,86, 87, 90; Sears Found Award for Excellence in Tchg; Who's Who Among Am Tchr.. **MEMBERSHIPS** Southern Hist Asn. **RESEARCH** Civil War and reconstruction; Texas; American women. **SELECTED PUBLICATIONS** Coauth, Colonial America: A Handbook for Teachers & Civil War and Reconstruction: A Handbook for Teachers, Wayland Press, 70; auth, Have tape recorder will travel: Organizing an oral history program, Tex Historian, 81; Preachers and politics: Texas Baptists and reconstruction, Tex Baptist Hist, 82, Holding Forth the Word of Life; A Hist Of the Panhandle Pastor's and Laymen's Conf 96. **CONTACT ADDRESS** 1906 Ennis, Plainview, TX, 79072. **EMAIL** owensest@wbu1.wbu.edu

OWENS, WILLIAM M.
DISCIPLINE CLASSICS **EDUCATION** Cornell Univ, BA, 76; Yale Univ, PhD, 86. **RESEARCH** Social hist; anc slavery; Roman comedy; the Greek novel. **CONTACT ADDRESS** Dept of Classics, Ohio Univ, Athens, OH, 45701. **EMAIL** owensb@ohio.edu

OWRAM, DOUGLAS R.
PERSONAL Born 11/08/1947, Aurora, ON, Canada **DISCIPLINE** HISTORY **EDUCATION** Queen's Univ, BA, 70, MA, 72; Univ Toronto, PhD, 76. **CAREER** Asst prof, 76-80, assoc prof hist, 80-85, assoc dean Arts 88-90, assoc dean Grad Stud, 92-94, assoc vice pres Acad, 94-95, VICE PRES ACADEMIC, UNIV ALBERTA, 95-. **HONORS AND AWARDS** Fel, Royal Soc Can, 90; Kaplan Award Res Excellence, Univ Alta, 94. **SELECTED PUBLICATIONS** Auth, Building for Canada, 79; Promise of Eden 80; Government Generation, 86; Born at the Right Time, 96; coauth, Imperial Dreams and Colonial Realities, 88; A History of the Canadian Economy, 91; 2nd ed 96. **CONTACT ADDRESS** Univ of Alberta, 3-4 University Hall, Edmonton, AB, T6G 2E1.

OZORAK, ELIZABETH WEISS
PERSONAL Born 06/12/1957, Tacoma Park, MD, m, 1 child **DISCIPLINE** PSYCHOLOGY **EDUCATION** Wesleyan Univ, BA, 78; Harvard Univ, MA, 83, PhD, 87. **CAREER** Assoc prof of Psychology, chair, Dept of Psychol, Allegheny Col. **HONORS AND AWARDS** Phi Beta Kappa, 77; Psi Chi, 90. **MEMBERSHIPS** APS; SSSR. **RESEARCH** Religious beliefs, practices and commitment; religious identity. **SELECTED PUBLICATIONS** Auth, Social and Cognitive Influences on the Development of Religious Beliefs and Commitment in Adolescence, J for the Scientific Study of Relig, 28, 89; The Power, But Not the Glory: How Women Empower Themselves Through Religion, J for the Scientific Study of Relig, 35, 96; Women's Faith and Women's Lives: The Connections Between Psychology and Theology, Explorations, 14, 96; In the Eye of the Beholder: A Social-Cognitive Model of Religious Belief, in B Spilka & D McIntosh, eds, The Psychology of Religion: Theoretical Approaches, Westview, 96. **CONTACT ADDRESS** Dept of Psychology, Allegheny Col, 520 N Main St, Meadville, PA, 16335. **EMAIL** eozorak@alleg.edu

P

PACA, BARBARA
PERSONAL Born 11/21/1959, CA, d **DISCIPLINE** ARCHITECTURE **EDUCATION** Bachelor of Landscape Archit, Univ Ore, Eugene, 84; hist of archit, Princeton Univ, MFA, 92, PhD, 95. **CAREER** Private practice in landscape archit; res in the hist of landscape archit. **HONORS AND AWARDS** Postdoctoral Fulbright, Rep of Ireland, 95; visitor, Inst for Advan Study, Princeton Univ, 97. **MEMBERSHIPS** Soc of Archit Hist; Intl Coun on Monuments and Sites; Amer Soc of Landscape Archit; Intl Soc of Arboriculture; Royal Horticulture Soc; Garden Hist Soc; Royal Oak Soc. **RESEARCH** History of Landscape Architecture; Sculpture; Iconography. **SELECTED PUBLICATIONS** Auth, Miscellanea Structurea Curiosa: The Cross-Curvenives of Vitruvius Hibernicus, Jour of Garden Hist, 97; The Mathematics of an 18th century American Wilderness Garden, Jour of Garden Hist, 96. **CONTACT ADDRESS** 103 E. 84th St., New York, NY, 10028.

PACE, KAY ROBERTINE
PERSONAL Mobile, Alabama **DISCIPLINE** MUSIC **EDUCATION** Xavier Univ LA, BA 1968; Southern IL Univ Carbondale, MM 1970; Peabody Conservatory of Johns Hopkins Univ Baltimore, DMA 1984. **CAREER** Southern IL Univ, instr music & coord of accompanying 1970-73; AL State Univ, asst prof of piano. **HONORS AND AWARDS** Elected mem Phi Kappa Phi Natl Honor Soc 1969, Pi Kappa Lambda Music Honor Soc 1970; Solo piano concerts throughout US 1970-; 1st Place Winner IL State Music Teachers Young Artist Comp 1972, St Louis Artist Presentation Comp 1973; Spec Study Grant Van Cliburn Intl Piano Comp 1977; Otto Ortmann Theory Awd Peabody Conserv of Music 1978; Fellowship Ford Foundation for Doctoral Study 1978-81; SE Reg Winner Natl Black Music Comp 1979; A Portrait of Kay Pace AL Public TV 30 min spec 1979. **MEMBERSHIPS** Coord Univ Piano Guild 1975-; mem Delta Omicron Music Frat for Women 1976-; coord of keyboard AL State Univ 1979-; pres & founder Soc of Friends of Music Montgomery 1979; mem AL Theory Teachers Assoc 1981-; chairperson Dean Selection Comm Music ASU 1982-83; mem Delta Sigma Theta Sor 1983. **CONTACT ADDRESS** Alabama State Univ, 915 S Jackson St, Montgomery, AL, 36195.

PACKARD, RANDALL M.
DISCIPLINE HISTORY **EDUCATION** Wesleyan Univ, BA, 67; Northwestern Univ, MA, 68; Univ Wis Madison, PhD, 76. **CAREER** Asa G. Candler Prof African Hist. **HONORS AND AWARDS** CHOICE Outstanding Bk Awd. **RESEARCH** African history; social history of health and disease. **SELECTED PUBLICATIONS** Auth, White Plague, Black Labour: the Political Economy of Health and Disease in South Africa; Chiefship and Cosmology: A Study of Political Competition; **CONTACT ADDRESS** Dept History, Emory Univ, 221 Bowden Hall, 561 Kilgo Cir, Atlanta, GA, 30322-1950. **EMAIL** packard@fox.sph.emory.edu

PACKER, JAMES
DISCIPLINE CLASSICS **EDUCATION** UC Berkeley, BA, 59, MA, 60, PhD, 64. **CAREER** Prof, Northwestern Univ, 66-. **RESEARCH** The Temple of the Divine Trajan, Rome; The Theatre of Pompey, Rome. **SELECTED PUBLICATIONS** Auth, The West Library of the Forum of Trajan: the Problems and Some Solutions, Nat Gallery Art, 92; The Forum of Trajan: A Study of the Monuments, Calif, 94. **CONTACT ADDRESS** Dept of Classics, Northwestern Univ, 1801 Hinman, Kresge 12, Evanston, IL, 60208. **EMAIL** j-packer@nwu.edu

PACKULL, WERNER O.
DISCIPLINE HISTORY **EDUCATION** University Guelph, BA, 69; Emmanuel Bible Col, BTh, 69; University Waterloo, MA, 70; Queen's Univ, PhD, 74. **CAREER** Prof **SELECTED PUBLICATIONS** Auth, Denck's Alleged Baptism by Hubmaier: Its Significance for the Origin of South German-Austrian Anabaptism, 73, Gottfried Seebass on Hans Hut: A Discussion, 75 & coauth, From Monogenesis to Polygenesis: The Historical Discussion of Anabaptist Origins, 75, Mennonite Quart Rev, 75; auth, Zur Entwicklung des Suddentschen Taufertums in: Umstrittenes. **CONTACT ADDRESS** Dept of History, Conrad Grebel Col, 200 Westmount Rd, Waterloo, ON, N2L 3G6.

PADILLA, MARK
DISCIPLINE CLASSICS **EDUCATION** Princeton, PhD, 87. **CAREER** Asst prof, 85-92, assoc prof, 93-present, associate dean/faculty arts & sciences, 97-present, Bucknell Univ. **HONORS AND AWARDS** Summer NEH Fel **MEMBERSHIPS** Amer Philogical Assn **RESEARCH** Greek drama; Greek myth. **CONTACT ADDRESS** Classics Dept, Bucknell Univ, Lewisburg, PA, 17837.

PAGE, JAMES E.
PERSONAL Born 08/03/1942, Woodstock, ON, Canada **DISCIPLINE** CANADIAN STUDIES **EDUCATION** Queen's Univ, BA, 67, MA, 68. **CAREER** Dir, Can stud, Secy State Can, 84-89; dir gen, educ sup, 89-94, EXEC SECY, NATIONAL LITERACY SECRETARIAT, HUMAN RESOURCES DEVELOPMENT CANADA, 94-; adj res prof, Inst Can Stud, Carleton Univ, 91-. **MEMBERSHIPS** Can Asn Curric Stud; Champlain Soc; Australian & NZ Asn Can Stud; Brit Asn Can Stud; Gesellschaft fur Kanada-Studien; Asn francaise d'etudes canadiennes. **RESEARCH** Canadian studies; education. **SELECTED PUBLICATIONS** Auth, Canadian Studies in Community Colleges, 73; auth, Seeing Ourselves, 79; auth, A Canadian Context for Science Education, 80; auth, Reflections on the Symons' Report: The State of Canadian Studies in 1980, 81; coauth, Some Questions of Balance: Human Resources, Higher Education and Canadian Studies, 84; contribur, To Know Ourselves: The Report of the Commission on Canadian Studies, 76; ed bd, J Can Stud, 79-93. **CONTACT ADDRESS** National Literacy Secretariat, 15 Eddy St, Ottawa, ON, K1A 1K5.

PAGE, STANLEY W.
PERSONAL Born 11/18/1913, Chicago, IL, m, 1966 **DISCIPLINE** MODERN RUSSIAN HISTORY **EDUCATION** City Col New York, BSS, 35; Harvard Univ, PhD(hist), 47. **CAREER** Instr hist, Simmons Col, 45-46; from instr to assoc prof, 47-65, Prof Hist, City Col New York, 65-, Instr, Harvard Univ, 47; prof hist, City Univ New York, 66-; Am Philos Soc grant, 68. **MEMBERSHIPS** AHA; Am Asn Advan Slavic Studies; Asn Advan Baltic Studies. **RESEARCH** Lenin; Russian revolution; Baltic states. **SELECTED PUBLICATIONS** Auth, Lenin's assumption of international proletarian leadership, J Mod Hist, 954; Lenin and World Revolution, NY Univ, 59; The Formation of the Baltic States, Harvard Univ, 59; Russia in Revolution, Van Nostrand, 65; ed, Lenin, Dedicated Marxist or Revolutionary Pragmatist? Heath, 70; Lenin and peasant Bolshevism in Latvia, 1903-1915, summer 72 & The year 1919 in the Baltic, fall-winter 72, J Baltic Studies; The Communists - The Story of Power And Lost Illusions, 1948-1991 - Ulam,ab, Historian, Vol 0055, 1993; Lenin Tomb - The Last Days of The Soviet Empire - Remnick,d, Historian, Vol 0057, 1994. **CONTACT ADDRESS** Dept of Hist, City Col, CUNY, New York, NY, 10031.

PAGE, WILLIE F.
PERSONAL Born 01/02/1929, Dothan, AL, m **DISCIPLINE** AFRICAN-AMERICAN STUDIES **EDUCATION** Wayne State University, BSME, 1961; Adelphi University, MBA, 1970; NY University, PhD, 1975. **CAREER** Brooklyn Coll, CUNY, asso prof, 1979-; Dept of Africana Studies, Brooklyn Coll, chmn, asso prof, 1974-79; Nassau-Suffolk CHES, exec dir, 1972-74; Glen Cove Coop Coll Center, SUNY, dir, lectr, 1971-72; Grumman Aerospace, asst to dir prodn, 1967-70; The Boeing Co, engr, 1961-63; New York City Head Start Regional Training Office, consult, 1975-79; Natl Endowment for the Humanities, consult, 1977-78; NY State Educ Dept, consult, 1977-79. **HONORS AND AWARDS** EPDA Fellowship, USOE, NYU, 1973; Dissertation Year Fellowship Nat Fellowships Fund Atlanta, 1975; Henry Meissner Research Award, Phi Delta Kappa, NYU, 1975; NEH, Fellowship Seminar on Slavery, Harvard Univ, 1978. **MEMBERSHIPS** African Heritage Studies Assn, 1974-80; Am Educ Research Assn, 1974-80; Weeksville Soc Brooklyn, board member, 1979-80. **CONTACT ADDRESS** Afro-American Studies, Brooklyn Col, CUNY, 2901 Bedford Ave, Brooklyn, NY, 11210-2813.

PAINTER, KAREN
PERSONAL Born 07/13/1965, Stanford, CA, m **DISCIPLINE** MUSICOLOGY **EDUCATION** Yale Univ, BA, 87; Univ Calif Berkeley, MPhil, 96, MA, 90; Columbia Univ, PhD, 96. **CAREER** Asst prof, Dartmouth Col, 95-97; asst prof, Harvard Univ, July, 97; vis asst prof, Univ Ore Sch Music, 97. **RESEARCH** Am Musicol Soc. **SELECTED PUBLICATIONS** Reception history, cultural history, aesthetics, German music from the late 18th through the mid 20th century. **CONTACT ADDRESS** Dept of Music, Harvard Univ, Cambridge, MA.

PAINTER, NELL IRVIN
PERSONAL Born 08/02/1942, Houston, TX, m, 1989 **DISCIPLINE** HISTORY **EDUCATION** Univ of CA Berkeley, BA 1964; Univ of CA Los Angeles, MA 1967; Harvard Univ, PhD 1974. **CAREER** Harvard Univ, teaching fellow 1969-70, 1972-74; Univ of PA, asst prof 1974-77, assoc prof 1977-80; Univ of NC Chapel Hill, prof of history 1980-88; Princeton Univ, professor of history, 1988-91, Edwards professor of American history, 1991-, dir, program In African-American Studies, 1997-. **HONORS AND AWARDS** Fellow Natl Humanities Ctr NC 1978-79; Fellow John Simon Guggenheim Foundation 1982-83; Candace Awd Natl Coalition of 100 Black Women 1986; Fellow, Center for Advanced Study in the Behavioral Science, 1988-89; 1989 Alumnus of the Year, Black Alumni Club, Univ of California, Berkeley, 1989; Peterson Fellowship, American Antiquarian Society, 1991; National Endowment for the Humanities, Fellow, 1992-93; Wesleyan Univ, hon doctorate, 1996; Dartmouth Coll, hon doctorate, 1997; SUNY New Paltz, hon doctorate, 1998. **MEMBERSHIPS** Natl dir Association Black Women Historians 1982-84; amer studies comm Amer Council of Learned Societies 1982-; exec bd Organization of Amer Historians 1984-87; mem NOW, The Nation Assocs; mem Harvard and Radcliffe Alumni/ae Against Apartheid; national council, American Historical Association, 1990-94; national council, American Studies Association, 1989-92; Southern Historical Association, Syndor prize committee, chair, 1991-92. **SELECTED PUBLICATIONS** Author, 50 publications, 35 reveiws and review essays, 4 books. **CONTACT ADDRESS** History Dept, Princeton Univ, 129 Dickinson Hall, Princeton, NJ, 08544-1017.

PAJAKOWSKI, PHILIP E.
DISCIPLINE HISTORY **EDUCATION** PhD,History IN Univ, 89; MA, Hist IN Univ, 82; BA History Manchester Col 80. **CAREER** Assoc prof, 89, St Anselm Col. **RESEARCH** Polit thought and policies of Polish conservative landowners in the empire in the last half of the 19th century and their participation in the parliament in Vienna; soc order and perceptions of polit radicalism among Central Europ elite groups. **SELECTED PUBLICATIONS** Auth, The Polish, Club, Badeni, and the Austrian Parliamentary Crisis of 1897, Canadian Slavonic Papers, 93; Dynamics of Galician Polish Conservatism in the Late Nineteenth Century, Jahrbucher Geschichte Osteuropas, 95; Austrian Legislation against Social Radicalism 1886, Historian, 95. **CONTACT ADDRESS** St Anselm Col, 100 Saint Anselm Dr, Manchester, NH, 03102-1310. **EMAIL** ppajakow@anselm.edu

PAL, PRATAPADITYA
PERSONAL Born 09/01/1935, Sylhet, Bangladesh, m, 1968 **DISCIPLINE** HISTORY OF ART **EDUCATION** Univ Delhi, BA, 56; Univ Calcutta, MA, 58, DPhil(archit of Nepal), 62; Cambridge Univ, PhD(sculpture & painting of Nepal), 65. **CAREER** Lectr Indian studies, Cambridge Univ, 63-64; res assoc, Am Acad Benares, India, 66-67; keeper Indian collections, Mus Fine Arts, 67-69; Cur Indian & Islamic Art, Los Angeles County Mus Art, 70-; Prof Fine Arts, Univ Southern Calif, 70-, JD Rockefeller Third Fund grants, 64 & 66; lectr, Harvard Univ, 68- ; dir, Tibetan Found, NY; dir, Int Doc Ctr, San Bernadino, Calif; Baldwin lectr, Oberlin Col, Ohio, 70-71; Sir George Birdwood Mem Lect, Royal Soc Arts, Brit, 74; Nat Endowment for Arts fel, 74; vis prof, Univ Columbia, 80-81 & Univ Calif, Santa Barbara, 80; d. **HONORS AND AWARDS** Distinguished Achievement Award, Assoc Indians in N Am, 80. **MEMBERSHIPS** Asia Soc; Asiatic Soc, India. **RESEARCH** The art and architecture of Nepal; the art of Tibet, India and South Asia. **SELECTED PUBLICATIONS** Auth, Nepal Where the Gods are Young, Asia Soc, NY, 75; The Sensuous Line, Los Angeles County Mus Art, 76; The Sensuous Immortals, Los Angeles County Mus Art & Mass Inst Technol, 77; The Ideal Image, Asia Soc, NY, 78; In Her Image, Univ Calif, Santa Barbara, 80; Hindu Religion and Iconology, Vichitra Press, 81; Elephants and Ivories, 81 & Tibetan Art, 82, Los Angeles County Mus Art; From The Northwest of The Indian Subcontinent, Arts of Asia, Vol 0024, 1994; Herukahevajra in Khmer Art + a Comparison of Sculptures - a Preliminary-study, Oriental Art, Vol 0040, 1994. **CONTACT ADDRESS** Los Angeles County Mus of Art, 5905 Wilshire Blvd, Los Angeles, CA, 90036.

PALAIS, JAMES BERNARD
PERSONAL Born 03/08/1934, Cambridge, MA, m, 1959, 2 children **DISCIPLINE** HISTORY **EDUCATION** Harvard Univ, BA, 55, PhD(Far East lang), 68; Yale Univ, MA, 60. **CAREER** Asst prof hist, Norfolk State Col, 66-67; asst prof, Univ Maine, Portland-Gorham, 67-68; asst prof, 68-75, Assoc Prof Hist, Univ Wash, 75-, Assoc Prof E Asian Studies, 79-, Nat Defense Foreign Lang grant, Korean, 60-62; Foreign Area fel, 63-65; mem joint comt Korean studies, Soc Sci Res Coun-Am Coun Learned Soc, 71-; Nat Endowment for Humanities res fel, 75-76. **MEMBERSHIPS** Asn Asian Studies. **RESEARCH** Korean history, especially the 17th through the 20th centuries. **SELECTED PUBLICATIONS** Auth, Records and record-keeping in nineteenth century Korea, J Asian Studies, 571; contribr, Stability in the Yi Dynasty (in Korean), Tradition & Change in Korea, Seoul, 73 & Democracy in South Korea, 1948-72, In: Without Parallel: Essay on Korea, Pantheon, 74; ed, Occasional Papers on Korea, Nos 1-5, 74-77; auth, Political leadership in the Yi Dynasty, In: Political Leadership in Korea, Univ Wash, 76; a Search For Korean Uniqueness, Harvard J of Asiatic Studies, Vol 0055, 1995; Korea Since 1850 - Lone,s, Mccormack,g, American Historical Review, Vol 0100, 1995. **CONTACT ADDRESS** Inst for Comp & Foreign Area Studies, Univ of Wash, Seattle, WA, 98195.

PALEY, SAMUEL M.
DISCIPLINE CLASSICS **EDUCATION** Columbia Univ, PhD, 74. **CAREER** Fac, 77; prof, present, SUNY Buffalo. **HONORS AND AWARDS** Asst dir Alishar Hoyuk Res Proj, Sorgun, Turkey; dir Emeq Hefer Proj, Univ Buffalo. **RESEARCH** The ancient Near East and Egypt; Judaism; Hebrew. **SELECTED PUBLICATIONS** Auth, King of the World: Ashurnasirpal II of Assyria (833-859 B.C.), Brooklyn Mus, 76; coauth, The Reconstruction of the Relief Representations and Their Positions in the Northwest Palace of Kalhu (Nimrud), vols II/III, Philipp von Zabern, 87 and 92. **CONTACT ADDRESS** Dept Classics, SUNY Buffalo, 712 Clemens Hall, Buffalo, NY, 14260.

PALISCA, CLAUDE VICTOR
PERSONAL Born 11/24/1921, Fiume, Italy, m, 1960, 2 children **DISCIPLINE** MUSIC EDUCATION Queens Col, BA, 43; Harvard Univ, MA, 48, PhD(music), 54. **CAREER** From instr to asst prof music, Univ Ill, 53-59; assoc prof hist of music, 59-64, chmn dept music, 69-75, dir grad studies music, 67-70, chmn & dir grad studies Renaissance studies, 77- 80, prof hist of music, 64-80, Henry L & Lucy G Moses Prof Music, Yale Univ, 80-, Guggenheim fel, 60 & 80; vis assoc prof & sr fel, Princeton Univ, 61; dir sem on music educ, US Off Educ, 63, consult, 63-; sr fac fel, Yale Univ, 66-67; consult, Nat Endowment for Humanities, 67-, sr fel, 72-73. **HONORS AND AWARDS** MA, Yale Univ, 64. **MEMBERSHIPS** Am Musicol Soc (1st vp, 65-67, pres, 70-72); Renaissance Soc Am; Col Music Soc; fel Am Coun Arts in Educ (pres, 67-69); Int Musicol Soc (vp, 77-82). **RESEARCH** Musicology, history of Renaissance and baroque music; history of music theory. **SELECTED PUBLICATIONS** Auth, Baroque Music, Prentice-Hall, 68, 2nd ed, 81; co- transl, G Zarlino, the Art of Counterpoint, Yale Univ, 68; The Artusi-Monteverdi controversy, In: The Monteverdi Companion, Faber & Faber, 68; The Alterati of Florence, pioneers in the theory of dramatic music, In: New Looks at Italian Opera, Cornell Univ, 68; auth, Ut oratoria musica: The rhetorical basis of musical mannerism, In: The Meaning of Mannerism, Univ New England, 72; ed & auth of introd, Hucbald, Guido and John on Music: Three Medieval Treatises, Yale Univ, 78; coauth, History of Western Music, 80 & ed, Norton Anthology of Western Music, 80, Norton; The Court Musicians in Florence During The Principate of The Medici, With a Reconstruction of The Artistic Establishment - Kirkendale,w, Notes, Vol 0051, 1995; Doni,giovanni,battista Interpretation of The Greek Modal System, J of Musicology, Vol 0015, 1997. **CONTACT ADDRESS** 68 Spring Rock Rd Pine, Orchard Branford, CT, 06405.

PALMA, RONALD B.
PERSONAL Born 11/18/1946, Suffern, NY, m, 1967, 2 children **DISCIPLINE** CLASSICS **EDUCATION** Cornell Univ, BA, 68; Univ Cincinnati, MA, 72, and work completed to PhD. **CAREER** Tchr, classics, acting chemn, Dept of Lang, Holland Hall Sch, Tulsa, Okla, 73- . **HONORS AND AWARDS** Merit Scholar, Cornell Univ, 64-68; Semple fel, Univ Cincinnatti, 68-73; Fulbright fel, 81; Rockefeller Found fel, 87; tchr of the year, 82; citation, Comt on Pres Scholars, 83; Col Bd Advanced Placement Special Recognition Award, 91. **MEMBERSHIPS** Am Philol Asn; Am Class League; Vergilian Soc. **RESEARCH** The connection between high school and college teaching in Classics and establishing national standards in teaching Latin and Greek. **SELECTED PUBLICATIONS** Coauth, Ecce Romani: A Latin Reading Program, Addison-Wesley, 84, 95; ed, Review and Test Preparation Guide for the Beginning Student, Addison- Wesley, 95; ed, Review and Test Preparation Guide for the Intermediate Student, Addison-Wesley, 95; articles in The Class Outlook, The New England Class Newsl, The Longman Latin Newsl. **CONTACT ADDRESS** 1112 W Queens Pl, Broken Arrow, OK, 74012. **EMAIL** ronpalma@iamerica.net

PALMEGIANO, EUGENIA M.
PERSONAL Born 03/09/1939, Lawrence, MA **DISCIPLINE** MODERN BRITISH HISTORY **EDUCATION** Georgian Court Col, AB, 60; Rutgers Univ, MA, 61, PhD(mod Brit hist), 66, JD, 79. **CAREER** Lectr mod Europ hist, Col Notre Dame, Md, 61-62; teaching asst, Rutgers Univ, 62-64; from instr to assoc prof, 66-77, dir honors prog, 70-77, Prof Mod Brit Hist, St Peter's Col, NJ, 77-, Fac fel, St Peter's Col, 72 & 82; mem, Fulbright-Hays Nat Selection Comt, UK, 77-81, chair, 78 & 79; consult, Nat Endowment for Humanities, 79- & NJ Comt Humanities, 80-; summer sem fel, Nat Endowment for Humanities, 81. **MEMBERSHIPS** AHA; Conf Brit Studies; Am Bar Asn. **RESEARCH** Victorian cultural history; history of Victorian periodical press. **SELECTED PUBLICATIONS** Auth, Feminist propaganda in the 1850's and 1860's, RSVP Newslett, 71; The Statues of Women in Honors Programs, Forum for Honors, 74; Women and British Periodicals, Garland Pub, 76; Jists For Empire - The Imperial Debate in The Edwardian Stately Press, 1903-1913 - Startt,jd, American Historical Review, Vol 0097, 1992. **CONTACT ADDRESS** Dept of Hist, St Peter's Col, 2641 Kennedy Blvd, Jersey City, NJ, 07306-5997.

PALMER, PHYLLIS MARYNICK
PERSONAL Born 04/05/1944, Dallas, TX **DISCIPLINE** AMERICAN HISTORY **EDUCATION** Oberlin Col, AB, 66; Ohio State Univ, MA, 67, PhD(hist), 73. **CAREER** Asst prof hist, Mt Holyoke Col, 72-77; assoc prof Am studies, women's studies, George Washington Univ, 77-. **HONORS AND AWARDS** ACLS res fel 93. **MEMBERSHIPS** AHA; Orgn Am Historians; Am Studies Asn; Nat Women's Studies Asn. **RESEARCH** Women in United States; Race Studies and Postwar intercivilism **SELECTED PUBLICATIONS** Auth, Domesticity and dirt: Domestic service in the nineteenth century, In: Quantification and Psychology; Toward a New History, Univ Press of Am, 80; White women/Black women: The dualism of female identity and experience, Feminist Studies 83. **CONTACT ADDRESS** American Studies Dept, George Washington Univ, 2108G St NW, Washington, DC, 20052-0001. **EMAIL** ppalmer@gwu.edu

PALMER, ROBERT L., II
PERSONAL Born 03/01/1943, Tuscaloosa, AL, m, 1990 DISCIPLINE EDUCATION EDUCATION Indiana University, Bloomington, IN, BS, 1969, MS, 1973; State University of New York at Buffalo, Buffalo, NY, PhD, 1979. CAREER State University College at Buffalo, Buffalo, NY, counselor education opportunity program, 1972-74, assistant director educational opportunity program, 1973-74; STATE UNIV OF NY AT BUFFALO, assistant vice president of student affairs, 1974-82, associate provost, 1982-87; PROVOST OF STUDENT AFFAIRS, 1987-. HONORS AND AWARDS Outstanding Service Award, Buffalo Urban League, 1989; Buffalo Black Achievers Award, Buffalo 1840 Enterprise Inc, 1985; Outstanding Leadership Award, University at Buffalo Campus Ministry, 1985; Award of Excellence, United Way of Buffalo & Erie County, 1989; Human Relations Award, Buffalo NAACP, 1988. MEMBERSHIPS Co-chair, United Negro College Fund, Buffalo & Western New York Campaign, 1989-; board of directors, Coordinated Care, 1989-; chairman, board of directors, Buffalo Urban League, 1987-90; member, board of directors, Buffalo Area Engineering Awareness, 1982-; member, The Western New York Health Science Consortium Minority Manpower Task Force for Minorities, 1989-. CONTACT ADDRESS SUNY, Buffalo, 542 Capen Hall, Buffalo, NY, 14260.

PALMER, RUSS
PERSONAL Detroit, MI DISCIPLINE BIBLICAL STUDIES, THE HISTORY OF CHRISTIAN THOUGHT, AND CHRISTIAN ETHICS EDUCATION Wayne State Univ, BA; Dallas Theol Sem, MA; Univ Iowa, PhD. CAREER Instr, Univ Nebr, Omaha, 65-; ed, Karl Barth Soc Newsl. MEMBERSHIPS Exec bd, Karl Barth Soc of N Am; steering comt, Reformed Theol and Hist Consultation, Am Acad of Relig. SELECTED PUBLICATIONS Auth, Introduction to World Religions Study Guide, Kendall-Hunt Publ. CONTACT ADDRESS Univ Nebr, Omaha, Omaha, NE, 68182.

PALMER, SCOTT W.
DISCIPLINE HISTORY EDUCATION Univ Kansas, BA, 89; Univ Ill, PhD, 97 CAREER Adjunct asst prof, Univ Ill, 97-98; asst prof, Western Ill Univ, 98- HONORS AND AWARDS Fulbright-Hays Res Fel; IREX Fel; Kennon Inst Grant; Center for Russian & East European Studies, Univ Kansas, 98- MEMBERSHIPS AAASS; Historical Soc RESEARCH Russian Intellectual & Cultural History; Technology; Culture & Process of Moderation SELECTED PUBLICATIONS Auth, "On Wings of Courage: Public Air-Mindedness and National Identity in Late Imperial Russia," Russian Rev, 95; auth, "O vliianii transatlanticheskogo pereleta Ch. Lindberga na amerikanskoe I evropeiskoe obshchestvo," Iz istorii aviatsii I kosmonavtiki, 95; auth, "A Crisis of Faith: Boris Savinkov and the Fighting Organization, 1903-1912," Scottish Slavonic Rev, 92 CONTACT ADDRESS Dept Hist, Western Illinois Univ, 438 Morgan Hall, Macomb, IL, 61455. EMAIL SW-palmer@wiu.edu

PALMER, STANLEY HOWARD
PERSONAL Born 10/22/1944, Washington, DC, m, 1975, 4 children DISCIPLINE HISTORY EDUCATION Brown Univ, BA, 66; Harvard Univ, MA, 72, PhD(hist), 73. CAREER Asst prof, 73-80, Assoc Prof Brit Hist, Univ Tex, Arlington, 80-, Fel, Woodrow Wilson Int Ctr for Scholars, 81. MEMBERSHIPS AHA; Conf Brit Studies; Am Comt Irish Studies; Irish Am Cult Inst. RESEARCH Eighteenth, nineteenth century; British economic history; police in England and Ireland. SELECTED PUBLICATIONS Auth, The Irish Police experiment: the beginnings of modern police in the British Isles, 1785-1795, Soc Sci Quart, 1275; contribr, Essays in Modern European Revolutionary History, Univ Tex, 77; auth, Before the bobbies: the Caroline riots of 1821, Hist Today, 1077; Economic Arithmetic: A Guide to the Statistical Source of English Commerce, Industry, and Finance, 1700-1850, Garland, 77; Cops and guns: Arming the American police, Hist Today, 678; Calling out the troops: The military, the law, and police order in England, 1650-1850, J Soc Army Hist Res, winter 78; Sir George Cornwall Lewis: A Different Kind of Englishman, Eire Ireland, fall 81; The London Hanged - Crime And Civil-society in The 18th-century - Linebaugh,p, American J of Legal History, Vol 0037, 1993; b English Laundresses - a Social- history, 1850-1930 - Malcolmson,pe, Labor History, Vol 0035, 1994; Making The Peace - Pubic-order And Pubic Security in Modern Britain - Townshend,c, American Historical Review, Vol 0100, 1995; Race, Discourse, And The Origin of The America - a New-world View - Hyatt,vl, Nettleford,r, American Historical Review, Vol 0102, 1997. CONTACT ADDRESS Dept of Hist, Univ of Tex, Arlington, TX, 76019.

PALMER, STUART
PERSONAL Born 04/29/1924, New York, NY, m, 1946, 1 child DISCIPLINE SOCIOLOGY EDUCATION Yale Univ, BA, 49, MA 51, PhD, 55 CAREER Instr, 55-68, prof, 64-81, prof, 82-97, prof emeritus of sociology and dean emeritus of coll of liberian arts, 97-, Univ NH. HONORS AND AWARDS Phi Beta Kappa; Sigma Chi MEMBERSHIPS Amer Sociological Assoc; NY Acad of Sci RESEARCH Criminology; Social institutions SELECTED PUBLICATIONS The Universities Today, 98. CONTACT ADDRESS Dept of Sociology and Anthropology, Univ of New Hampshire, PO Box 904, Durham, NH, 03824.

PALMER, WILLIAM
PERSONAL Born 06/15/1951, Ames, IA, m, 1983, 2 children DISCIPLINE HISTORY EDUCATION Iowa State Univ, BS, 73; Univ Maine, PhD, 81. CAREER Asst prof his, Marshall Univ, 84-88; assoc prof his, Marshall Univ, 88-92; prof his, Marshall Univ, 92-. HONORS AND AWARDS Fel, Royal Historical Society; Reynolds Outstanding Teacher Award; Who's Who in American Colleges and Universities. MEMBERSHIPS Am Hist Asn; North Am Conference on British Studies; Royal Hist Society. RESEARCH Early modern England and Ireland; historiography. SELECTED PUBLICATIONS Auth, The Political Career of Oliver St. John, 1637-1649, Univ of Delaware Press, 93; auth, "That 'Insolent Liberty': Honor, Rites of Power, and Persuasion in Sixteenth Century Ireland", in Renaissance Quart 44 2, 93; auth, The Problems of Ireland in Tudor Foreign Policy, 1485-1603, Boydell Press, 94; auth, "Borderlands and Colonies: Tudor Ireland in the Perspective of Colonial America", in Eire: Ireland 3, 94; auth, "Ireland and Tudor Foreign Policy in the 1570s", in The Historian 58 1, 95; auth, "Sir Richard Southern Looks Back: a Portrait of the Medievalist as a Young Man", Va Quart Review 74 1, 98; auth, "High Officeholding, Foreign Policy, and the British Dimension in the Tudor Far North, 1525-1563", in Albion 29 4, 97. CONTACT ADDRESS Department of History, Marshall Univ, Huntington, WV, 25755. EMAIL Palmer@marshall.edu

PALUDAN, PHILLIP SHAW
PERSONAL Born 01/26/1938, St. Cloud, MN, m, 1963, 2 children DISCIPLINE UNITED STATES HISTORY EDUCATION Occidental Col, BA, 60, MA, 63; Univ Ill, Urbana-Champaign, PhD(hist), 68. CAREER Assoc prof, 68-80, Prof Hist, Univ Kans, 80-, Fel, Harvard Law Sch, 73-74; Am Coun Learned Soc study fel, 73-74 & res fel, 75; Guggenheim fel, 79-80. MEMBERSHIPS Orgn Am Historians. RESEARCH Civil War and Reconstruction; United States legal and constitutional history; 19th century social history. SELECTED PUBLICATIONS Auth, John Norton Pomeroy, state right nationalist, Am J Legal Hist, 1068; Law and the failure of Reconstruction: The case of T M Cooley, J Hist Ideas, 1072; American Civil War considered as a crisis in law and order, Am Hist Rev, 1072; American Civil War: Triumph through tragedy, Civil War Hist, 974; A Covenant with Death, Univ Ill, 75; Lincoln, the rule of law and the American Revolution, J Ill State Hist Soc, 277; ed, Issues Past and Present, Heath, 77; Victims: A True Story of the Civil War, Univ Tenn; Let Us Have Peace - Grant,ulysses,s. And The Politics of War And Reconstruction, 1861-1868 - Simpson,bd, Pennsylvania Magazine of History And Biography, Vol 0117, 1993; Lincoln in American Memory - Peterson,md, Historian, Vol 0057, 1995. CONTACT ADDRESS Dept of Hist, Univ of Kans, Lawrence, KS, 66044.

PANAITESCU, ADRIAN
PERSONAL Born 03/07/1937, Bucharest, Romania, m, 1969, 7 children DISCIPLINE ARCHITECTURE EDUCATION School of Architecture, Romania, architect 63, PhD 75. CAREER School of Arch, Romania, prof 64-75. HONORS AND AWARDS 1st Prize Arch 75; 1st Prize Exequo Church Switzerland, 84 MEMBERSHIPS SAH RESEARCH Hist and theory of arch; painting. CONTACT ADDRESS 35 Scott Rd, Greenwich, CT, 06831-2832.

PANELLA, ROBERT J.
DISCIPLINE ROMAN HISTORY AND HISTORIOGRAPHY EDUCATION Harvard, PhD. CAREER Prof, Fordham Univ. SELECTED PUBLICATIONS Auth, The Letters of Apollonius of Tyana: A Critical Text with Prolegomena, Translation, and Commentary, 79; Greek Philosophers and Sophists in the Fourth Century A.D.: Studies in Eunapius of Sardis, 90. CONTACT ADDRESS Dept of Class Lang and Lit, Fordham Univ, 113 W 60th St, New York, NY, 10023.

PANKAKE, MARCIA J.
DISCIPLINE AMERICAN STUDIES EDUCATION Univ Minn, BA, 67, MA, 71, PhD, 75. CAREER PROF & BIBLIOGR, WILSON LIB, UNIV MINN MEMBERSHIPS Am Antiquarian Soc RESEARCH Am travel SELECTED PUBLICATIONS Coauth, "A Guide to Coordinated and Cooperative Collection Development," Lib Res & Tech Ser 27, 83; auth, "From Book Selection to Collection Management," Advan in Librnship 13, 83; coauth, "English and American Literature," in Selection of Library Materials in the Humanities, Social Sciences, and Sciences, Am Lib Asn, 85; co-ed, English and American Literature: Sources and Strategies for Collection Development, Am Lib Asn, 87; co-ed, The Prairie Home Companion Folk Song Book, Viking, 88. CONTACT ADDRESS Univ of Minn, 309 19th Ave So, Minneapolis, MN, 55455. EMAIL m-pank@tc.umn.edu

PAOLETTI, JO
DISCIPLINE AMERICAN CULTURE EDUCATION Syracuse Univ, BS, 71; Univ RI, MS, 76; Univ MD, PhD, 80. CAREER Am Stud Dept, Univ Md RESEARCH 1970s unisex trends, on-line exhibition and publ. SELECTED PUBLICATIONS Co-auth, Conclusion" in Men and Women: Dressing the Part, Smithsonian Inst Press, 89; The Children's Department,Men and Women: Dressing the Part, Smithsonian Inst Press, 89; auth, Little Lord Fauntleroy and His Dad, Hope and Glory, 91; The Value of Conversation in Teaching and Learning, Essays on Teaching, Univ MD IBM-TQ Project, 97; The Gendering of Infants' and Toddlers' Clothing in America, The Material Culture of Gender/The Gender of Material Culture, Winterthur Mus, 97. CONTACT ADDRESS Am Stud Dept, Univ MD, Col Park, College Park, MD, 20742. EMAIL jp4@umail.umd.edu

PAPACOSMA, SOLON VICTOR
PERSONAL Born 07/11/1942, Freepost, NY DISCIPLINE BALKAN & MODERN EUROPEAN HISTORY EDUCATION Bowdoin Col, AB, 64; Ind Univ, Bloomington, MA, 66, PhD(hist), 71. CAREER Asst prof, 69-77, Assoc Prof Hist, Kent State Univ, 77-, Coordr Hellenic Studies, 76-, Am Coun Learned Soc grant res in Greece & Eng, 72-73; managing ed mat on Greece, Southeastern EuropeEurope du Sud-Est, 73-76; Fulbright-Hays fac res abroad grant, 78-79. MEMBERSHIPS AHA; Am Asn Advan Slavic Studies; Mod Greek Studies Asn; Am Asn Southeast Europ Studies. RESEARCH Politics in modern Greece. SELECTED PUBLICATIONS Auth, The Military in Greek Politics: The 1909 Coup d'Etat, Kent State Univ, 77; Greek transl ten articles, Hestia, Athens, 81; Inside Hitler Greece - The Experience of Occupation, 1941-44 - Mazower,m, American Historical Review, Vol 0100, 1995; Modern Greek Lessons - a Primer in Historical Constructivism - Faubion,jd, American Historical Review, Vol 0100, 1995; Metaxas Dictatorship - Aspects of Greece, 1936-1940 - Higham,r, Veremis,t, J of Modern Greek Studies, Vol 0015, 1997. CONTACT ADDRESS Dept of Hist, Kent State Univ, PO Box 5190, Kent, OH, 44242-0001.

PAPADAKIS, ARISTEIDES
DISCIPLINE HISTORY EDUCATION Fordham Univ, PhD. CAREER Prof, Univ MD Baltimore County . RESEARCH Byzantine and medieval hist; relig hist. SELECTED PUBLICATIONS Auth, Crisis in Byzantium; The Christian East and the Rise of the Papacy 1071-1453. CONTACT ADDRESS Dept of Hist, Univ MD Baltimore County, Hilltop Circle, PO Box 1000, Baltimore, MD, 21250. EMAIL papadaki@research.umbc.edu

PAPADOPOULOS, JOHN K.
PERSONAL Born 08/29/1958, Sydney, Australia, m, 1991 DISCIPLINE ARCHAEOLOGY EDUCATION Univ Sydney, BA, 80; Univ Sydney, MA, 83; Univ Sydney, PhD, 88 CAREER Deputy dir, Australian Archaeol Inst Athens, 87-91; asst prof, Univ Sydney, 91-93; assoc curator, J Paul Getty Museum, 94- HONORS AND AWARDS Fel Athens Archaeol Soc MEMBERSHIPS Archaeol Inst Amer; Australian Archaeol Inst Athens RESEARCH Aegean Archaeology SELECTED PUBLICATIONS Auth, The Early Iron Age Cemetery at Torone, forthcoming; coauth, Torone I: The Excavations of 1975-1978, Athens Archaeol Soc, 98; auth, "Drawing Circles: Experimental Archaeology and the Pivoted Multiple Brush," Amer Jrnl Archaeol, 98 CONTACT ADDRESS J. Paul Getty Mus, 1200 Getty Center Dr, Suite 1000, Los Angeles, CA, 90049-1687. EMAIL jpapadopoulos@getty.edu

PAPALAS, ANTHONY JOHN
PERSONAL Born 06/17/1939, Detroit, MI DISCIPLINE HISTORY EDUCATION Wayne State Univ, BA, 61, MA, 63; Univ Chicago, PhD(hist), 69. CAREER Asst prof hist, Carthage Col, 69-70; Assoc Prof Hist, E Carolina Univ, 70-. MEMBERSHIPS AHA; Am Philol Asn; Am Asn Ancient Historians. RESEARCH Roman Athens; Greece under Roman rule. SELECTED PUBLICATIONS Auth, Herodes Atticus and His Son, Platon, 73; Hipparchus the Tyrant, Ellinika, 75; Lucius Verus and the Hospitality of Herodes Atticus, Athenaeum, 78; Sports And Games of Ancient- egypt - Decker,w, Guttmann,a, Translator, Classical Bulletin, Vol 0069, 1993; Early Hellenistic Coinage From The Accession of Alexander to The Peace of Apamea 336-188-bc - Morkholm,o, Classical World, Vol 0088, 1994; Palmyra And Its Empire - Zenobia Revolt Against Rome - Stoneman,r, Classical Bulletin, Vol 0070, 1994; Water Management in Ancient-greek Cities - Crouch,dp, Classical Bulletin, Vol 0071, 1995; The Development of The Trireme, Mariners Mirror, Vol 0083, 1997. CONTACT ADDRESS Dept of Hist, East Carolina Univ, Greenville, NC, 27834.

PAPAYANIS, NICHOLAS
PERSONAL Born 03/09/1940, New York, NY DISCIPLINE MODERN FRENCH SOCIAL AND URBAN HISTORY EDUCATION NY Univ, BA, 61; Harvard Univ, MA, 63; Univ WI, PhD, 69; Fulbright Fel, Univ Paris, 65-66. CAREER From lectr to asst prof, 68-78, prof hist, Brooklyn Col, 78-, Fac res grant, Res Found City Univ NY, 72-73. HONORS AND AWARDS Prof Staff Congess-City Univ NY Research Award, 90, 93, 95, 97; Dir, Natl Endowment Hum Summer Seminar 94, 96; fel, Natl Endowment Hum, 91-92. MEMBERSHIPS Phi Beta Kappa; Soc French Hist Studies; AHA; NY City Area Seminar French Hist; Western Soc French Hist. RESEARCH Mod French labor and soc hist. SELECTED PUBLICATIONS Auth, Alphonse Merrheim and the strike of Hennebont: The struggle for the 8-hour day in France, Int Rev Social Hist, 71; Revolutionary Syndicalism in France, Arch Sozialgeschichte, 72; Les masses revolutionnaires et les chefs reformistes, Mouvement Social, 74; Collaboration and Pacifism in France

During World War I, Francia, 78; Horse Drawn Cabs and Omnibuses in Paris: The Idea of Circulation and the Business of Public Transit, LA State Univ Press, 96; The Coachmen of Nineteenth-Century Paris: Service Workers and Class Consciousness, LA State Univ Press, 93; Alphonse Merrheim: The Emergence of Reformism in Revolutionary Syndicalism 1871-1925, Dordrecht Boston lancaster, 85. **CONTACT ADDRESS** Dept of Hist, Brooklyn Col, CUNY, 2900 Bedford Ave, Brooklyn, NY, 11210-2899.

PAPAZIAN, DENNIS RICHARD
PERSONAL Born 12/15/1931, Augusta, GA, m, 2 children **DISCIPLINE** RUSSIAN & SOVIET HISTORY **EDUCATION** Wayne State Univ, BA, 54, MA, 56 Univ Mich, MA, 58, PhD(hist), 66. **CAREER** Lectr, 62-66,assoc prof, 66-71, PROF HIST, UNIV MICH, DEARBORN, 71-, chair, div LS & A, assoc dean acad affairs, 73-74, dir grad studies, 79-85, dir Armenian Res Center, 85-; mem bd dirs, Nat Asn Armenian Studies & Res, 69-79 & Armenian Assembly Am, Inc, 68-88; mem, exec counc, Soc Armenian Studies, 88-, pres, 88-93, 95-; ed, Jour Soc Armenian Studies, 95-. **MEMBERSHIPS** AHA; Am Asn Advan Slavic Studies; Nat Asn Armenian Studies & Res; AAUP; Soc Armenian Studies; Middle East Studies Asn **RESEARCH** Ukranian nationalism; 20th century Soviet and Russian history; Armenia and the Caucasus. **SELECTED PUBLICATIONS** Auth numerous articles & publications **CONTACT ADDRESS** Univ of Mich, 4901 Evergreen Rd, Dearborn, MI, 48128-1491. **EMAIL** papazian@umich.edu

PAPER, JORDAN
PERSONAL Born 12/03/1938, Baltimore, MD **DISCIPLINE** HISTORY OF RELIGIONS, EAST ASIA **EDUCATION** Univ Chicago, AB, 60; Univ Wis-Madison, MA, 65, PhD(Chinese), 71. **CAREER** Asst prof hist, Ind State Univ, 67-72; asst prof, 72-78, Assoc Prof Humanities, York Univ, 78-, Vis prof Am lit, Ching I Col, Taiwan, 73-74. **MEMBERSHIPS** Asn Asian Studies; Am Orient Soc; Soc Studies Pre-Han China; Soc Study Chinese Relig; Can Soc Study Relig. **RESEARCH** East Asian aesthetics; Chinese intellectual history; East Asian and Amerindian religion. **SELECTED PUBLICATIONS** Auth, The Ch'un meng so yen, an erotic Chinese literary tale, Nachrichten, Hamburg, 71; Index to Short Stories in the Fa Yuan Chu Lin, CMRASC, Inc, Taipei, 72; Guide to Chinese Prose, Twayne, 73; Confucianism in the Post-Han Era, Chinese Cult, 75; A Shaman in contemporary Toronto, Relig & Cult Can, 77; The meaning of the T'ao-t'ieh, Hist Relig, 78; From Shaman to mystic in Ojibwa religion, Studies Relig, 80; From Shaman to mystic in the Chuang-Tzu, Scottish J Relig Studies, 82; Methodological Controversies in The Study of Native-american Religions + Authors Response to Review of His Book 'Offering Smoke - The Sacred Pipe And Native American Religion' by Parkhill,thom, Studies in Religion-sciences Religieuses, Vol 0022, 1993; Ethnophilosophical And Ethnolinguistic Perspectives on The Huron Indian Soul - Pomedli,mm, Studies in Religion-sciences Religieuses, Vol 0022, 1994; Mystic Endowment - Religious Ethnography of The Warao Indians - Wilbert,j, Studies in Religion-sciences Religieuses, Vol 0024, 1995; Prophecy And Power Among The Dogrib Indians - Helm,j, J of Religion, Vol 0076, 1996. **CONTACT ADDRESS** Div of Humanities, York Univ, 4700 Keele St, Downsview, ON, M3J1P3.

PAPPAS, NICHOLAS C.J.
PERSONAL m **DISCIPLINE** HISTORY **EDUCATION** Stanford Univ, AB, AM, PhD. **CAREER** Assoc prof, Sam Houston State Univ, 90-. **RESEARCH** Ancient history, Eastern Europe, the Balkans, and Russia. **SELECTED PUBLICATIONS** Auth, Greeks in Russian Military Service in the Late Eighteenth and Early Nineteenth Centuries, Inst Balkan Stud, 91; Between Two Empires: Serbian Survival in the Years After Kosovo, Serbia's Hist Heritage, 94. **CONTACT ADDRESS** Dept of History, Sam Houston State Univ, Huntsville, TX, 77341.

PARCHMENT, STEVEN
DISCIPLINE HISTORY OF MODERN PHILOSOPHY, SPINOZA, ANCIENT AND MEDIEVAL PHILOSOPHY, MET **EDUCATION** Emory Univ, PhD, 96. **CAREER** Lectr, Ga State Univ. **SELECTED PUBLICATIONS** Published an article on Spinoza in Hist of Philos Quart. **CONTACT ADDRESS** Georgia State Univ, Atlanta, GA, 30303. **EMAIL** phlsgp@panther.gsu.edu

PARET, PETER
PERSONAL Born 04/13/1924, Berlin, Germany, m, 1961, 2 children **DISCIPLINE** HISTORY **EDUCATION** Univ Calif - Berkeley, BA, 49; King's Col, Univ London, PhD, 60. **CAREER** Resident Tutor, Oxford Univ, 59-60; Res Assoc, Princeton Univ, 60-62, 63; Vis Asst Prof, 62-63, Assoc Prof Hist, Univ Calif - Davis, 63-66; Prof Hist, Univ Calif - Davis, 66-69; Vis Res Fe Fel, London Sch Econ & Polit Sci, 71-72; Prof Hist, 69-77, Raymond A. Spruance Prof Int Hist, Stanford Univ, 77-86; Andrew W. Mellon Prof Humanities, Sch Hist Studies, Inst Advanced Study, Princeton Univ, 86-97, emeritus, 97-. **HONORS AND AWARDS** Fel, Ctr Advanced Study Behavioral Sci, 68-69; NEH Sr Fel, 80-81; Sr Fel by Courtesy, Hoover Inst, Stanford Univ, 88-93; Sr Fel, Ctr Hist Analysis, Rutgers Univ, 93-95; Thomas Jefferson Medal, Am Philos Soc; LittD, Univ London; DLitt, Univ SC; HHD, Col Wooster; Fel, Am Acad Arts & Letters; Honorary Fel, London Sch Econ & Polit Sci; Fel, Leo Baeck Inst. **MEMBERSHIPS** Am Philos Soc. **RESEARCH** European cultural history, 18th-20th century; the history of war. **SELECTED PUBLICATIONS** Auth, The Berlin Secession, Harvard, 80; ed, Makers of Modern Strategy from Machiavelli to the Nuclear Age, Princeton, 86; auth, Art as History, Princeton, 88, rev ed, 89; Understanding War, Princeton, 92; coauth, Persuasive Images, Princeton, 92; co-ed, Sammler, Stifter und Museen, Bohlau, 93; auth, Imagined Battles: Reflections of War in European Art, NC, 97. **CONTACT ADDRESS** Dept of History, Inst for Advanced Studies, Princeton, NJ, 08540. **EMAIL** collinrf@cua.edu

PAREZO, NANCY JEAN
PERSONAL Born 01/08/1951, Buffalo, NY, m, 1982 **DISCIPLINE** ANTHROPOLOGY **EDUCATION** Univ Arizona, PhD 81, MA 76; Miami Univ, BA cum laude, 73. **CAREER** Univ Arizona, Bureau Ethnic Research, grad res asst, Dept Land Architecture, inst, Women's Studies Faculty, aff fac mem, Dept of Anthropology, grad res asst/assoc, grad tchg asst, inst, ethnologist, dir, lect, assoc res prof, res prof, 74 to 92-; AZ BD Regents, loaned exec 90-91; AZ State Museum, assoc curator, curator 85 to 90-; Ntl Sci foun, assoc prog dir 87-88; UA Women's Stud Fac, aff fac mem, 85-; Prima Comm Col, inst, 83, 79-81; Smithsonian Inst Ntl Museum Nat Hist, inst 81-82; Prima Coll, inst 79-81; AZ State Museum, res 76; Miami Univ, lab tech, tchg asst, student register 70-73; Musee de'Etat Luxembourg, ceramic rest 71-72. **HONORS AND AWARDS** D'Arcy McNickle Ind Voices Fel; Post doc Fel Smithsonian; Weatherhead Res Sch; Sigma Xi schshp; UZ Grad schshp; Miami U Alum schshp; NPA schshp; NYS Regent schshp; 9 Wenner-Gren Foun Gnts; APSR Gnt; 3 NEH Fel; Comins Fel; et al. **MEMBERSHIPS** Coun Preservation of Anthro records; NICCP; CMA; Phi Beta Kappa; AAA; WFA; AES; SAA; HAC; AAAS; AEA; SFA; AAM; HAN; AAUW. **SELECTED PUBLICATIONS** Auth, Bureau of American Ethnology, in: The History of Science in the United States: An Encycl, ed Marc Rothenberg, NY, Garland Pub, in press; Matilda Coxe Stevenson, in: American National Biography, eds John A. Garraty, Mark C. Carnes, NY, ACLS and Oxford Press, 99; Community Motherhood and Health: Issues in Lesbian; Gay Life, in: Reviews in Anthropology, coauth, in press; Paths of Life: American Indians of the Southwest and Northern Mexico, co-ed, Tucson, Univ AZ Press, 96; Preserving the Anthropological Record, co-ed, 2nd ed, NY, Wenner-Gren Foun AR, 95; Hidden Scholars, Women Anthrop and the Native American Southwest, ed, Albuquerque, Univ N Mexico Press, 93; Indian Chic: The Denver Art Museum's Indian Style Show, coauth, Amer Ind Art Mag, 97; Matthews and the Discovery of Navajo Dry Paintings, in: Washington Matthews, Studies of Navajo Culture, eds, Katherine Spencer Halpern, Susan Brown McGreevy, Albuquerque, U of N Mexico Press, 97; Southwestern Art Worlds, Jour of Southwest, 96; Indian Trade Blankets, coauth, arti-FACT, 97; Wealth Concealed, coauth, Common Ground, 96; Southwest Native Amer Painting, Southwest Native Amer Metalwork, Southwest Native Amer Dress and Adornment, Southwest Native Amer Carving and Sculpture, in: Dictionary of Art, London, Macmillan, 96; Painting a Local Landscape, rev of High Art Down Home, An Economic Anthropology of a Local art Market, by Stuart Plattner, Current Anthrop, 98; et al. **CONTACT ADDRESS** Dept of American Indian Studies, Univ of Arizona, American State Museum, Tucson, AZ, 85721. **EMAIL** parezo@u.arizona.edu

PARINS, MARYLYN
DISCIPLINE ARTHURIAN LITERATURE **EDUCATION** Univ Mich, PhD. **CAREER** English and Lit, Univ Ark **SELECTED PUBLICATIONS** Auth, Malory: The critical heritage; Looking for Arthur: Theories of origin and historicity; King Arthur; Scholarship, Modern Arthurian, The New Arthurian Encyclopedia; Malory's Expurgations, Arthurian Tradition: Essays in Convergence. **CONTACT ADDRESS** Univ Ark Little Rock, 2801 S University Ave., Little Rock, AR, 72204-1099. **EMAIL** mjparins@ualr.edu

PARK, DAVID ALLEN
PERSONAL Born 10/13/1919, New York, NY, m, 1945, 4 children **DISCIPLINE** THEORETICAL PHYSICS, HISTORY OF SCIENCE **EDUCATION** Harvard Univ, AB, 41; Univ Mich, Ann Arbor, PhD(physics), 50. **CAREER** From asst prof to assoc prof, 51-59, Prof Physics, Williams Col, 59-, Lloyd fel, Inst Advan Study, 50-51; vis lectr physics, Univ Sri Lanka, 55-56, 72 & Cambridge Univ, 62-63; vis prof, Univ NC, 64. **HONORS AND AWARDS** Bk Award, Phi Beta Kappa, 80, 88. **MEMBERSHIPS** Fel Am Phys Soc; Int Soc Study Time (pres, 73-76). **RESEARCH** Quantum theory; natural philosophy of time; history of science. **SELECTED PUBLICATIONS** Auth, Introduction to the Quantum Theory, McGraw, 64, 74, 92; Contemporary Physics, Harcourt, 64; Introduction to Strong Interactions, Benjamin, 67; Classical Dynamics and Its Quantum Analogues, Springer, 79, 90; The Image of Eternity, Univ Mass, 80; The How and the Why, 88; The Fire Within the Eye, 97. **CONTACT ADDRESS** Dept of Physics, Williams Col, Williamstown, MA, 01267. **EMAIL** dpark@williams.edu

PARKER, HENRY H.
PERSONAL Born 09/11/1933, Memphis, TN **DISCIPLINE** EDUCATION **EDUCATION** St Thomas Coll, BA 1956; Univ of MN, MA 1959; Univ of IL, PhD 1975. **CAREER** Univ of MN, asst prof 1961-65; Univ of N Iowa, asst prof 1965-68, Univ of IL, asst prof 1968-71; Univ of N Iowa, asst prof 1971-84, full prof 1984-; Univ of Tennessee, Martin, professor, Dept of Psychology, Philosophy & Religion, 1990-. **HONORS AND AWARDS** NDEA Lecturer in Rhetoric 1965; Danforth Assoc Danforth Found; Iowa's Most Outstanding Prof Awd 1972; Geo Wash Carver Disting Lecturer Awd 1975; Ford Foundation Fellow, 1969. **MEMBERSHIPS** Pres the Off-Campus Univ consulting firm; founder & principal Waterloo-Pre-Sch Acad; pres The Parker Reading Co; pub The Parker Reader Elem Sch Newspaper; producer & star the Hank Parker Show Ch 7; co-dir with Marilyn Crist of CP Collegians Gifted Children's Prog; National Director of Curriculum, Jesse Jackson's PUSH-Excel. **CONTACT ADDRESS** Dept of Psych, Philos & Rel, Univ of Tennessee, Martin, Martin, TN, 38237.

PARKER, HOLT
DISCIPLINE CLASSICS **EDUCATION** Tulane Univ, BA, 78; Yale Univ, MA, 80, MPhil, 82, PhD, 86. **CAREER** Assoc prof, Univ Cincinnati. **HONORS AND AWARDS** Rome Prize; Women's Classical Caucus Prize; NEH Fel; Res Granr, Univ Ariz; Provost's Tchng Improvement Award, Univ Ariz. **MEMBERSHIPS** Am Philol Asn; Soc Ancient Med; Women's Classical Caucus; Screen Actor's Guild. **RESEARCH** Gender studies; Augustan poetry; Greek lyric poetry; Roman comedy; linguistics; literary theory; ancient medicine. **SELECTED PUBLICATIONS** Auth, Crucially Funny or Tranio on the Couch, TAPA, 89; auth, Another Go at the Text of Philaenis, ZPE, 89; auth, The Bones: Propertius 1.21.9-10, Clas Philol, 91; auth, In the Mood: Prop. 2. 26. 1-3, Mnemosyne, 92; auth, The Fertile Fields of Umbria: Propertius 1. 22. 10, Mnemosyne, 92; auth, Love 's Body Anatomized: The Ancient Erotic Manuals and the Rhetoric of Sexuality, Oxford Univ Press, 92; auth, Fish in Trees and Tie-Dyed Sheep: A Function of the Surreal in Roman Poetry, Arethusa, 92; auth, Other Remarks on the Other Sulpicia, CW, 92; auth, Sappho Schoolmistress, TAPA, 93; auth, Sulpicia, the Auctor de Sulpicia and the Authorship of 3.9 and 3.11 of the Corpus Tibullianum, Helios, 94; auth, Innocent on the Face of it: An Overlooked Obscenity in Martial, Mnemosyne, 94; auth, A Curiously Persistent Error: Satyricon 43.4, Clas Philol, 94; auth, Heterosexuality, Oxford Univ Press, 96; auth, Women Physicians in Greece, Rome, and the Byzantine Empire, Univ Press Ky, 97; auth, Latin and Greek Poetry by Five Renaissance Italian Women Humanists, SUNY Press, 97; auth, Plautus vs. Terence: Audience and Popularity Reexamined, AJP, 96; auth, The Teratogenic Grid, Princeton Univ Press, 97. **CONTACT ADDRESS** Dept of Classics, Univ Cincinnati, PO Box 0226, Cincinnati, OH, 45210-0226. **EMAIL** parkerhn@ucbeh.san.uc.edu

PARKER, KEITH ALFRED
PERSONAL Born 06/01/1933, Hull, England, m, 1966, 1 child **DISCIPLINE** BRITISH & UNITED STATES RELATIONS **EDUCATION** Fairleigh Dickenson Univ, BA, 59; Univ Md, MA, 62, PhD(hist), 65. **CAREER** Instr hist, Univ Md, 62-63; asst prof, NY State Univ Col Oswego, 65-66; asst prof, 66-80, Assoc Prof Hist, Univ S Fla, 80-, Can studies proj dir, Univ SFla. **MEMBERSHIPS** Asn Can Studies US; AHA. **RESEARCH** North Atlantic community, Britain, United States and Canada; Canadian labor history. **SELECTED PUBLICATIONS** Coauth, Student in society, Littlefield, fall 68; Colonization roads and commercial policy, Ont Hist, 75; The making of a radical, Alta Hist, 78; British Evacuees in America During World-War-II, J of American Culture, Vol 0017, 1994. **CONTACT ADDRESS** Dept of Hist, Univ of S FL, 4202 Fowler Ave, Tampa, FL, 33620-9951.

PARKER, LISA S.
DISCIPLINE HISTORY OF SCIENCE **EDUCATION** Univ Pittsburgh, PhD, 90. **CAREER** Asst prof, Univ Tenn, 90-91; asst prof, Univ Pittsburgh, 91-98; assoc prof, Univ Pittsburgh, 98-. **HONORS AND AWARDS** Nellie Westerrman Prize in Ethics, 90. **MEMBERSHIPS** Am Soc of Bioethics and Humanities; Am Philos Asn; Sigma Xi. **RESEARCH** Bioethics. **SELECTED PUBLICATIONS** Auth, Social Justice, federal paternalism, and feminism: Breast implantation in the cultural context of femaule beauty, Kennedy Inst of Ethics J, 93; Bioethics for human geneticists: Models for reasoning and methods for teaching, Am J of Human Genetics, 94; Beauty and breast implantation: How candidate selection affects autonomy and informed consent, Hypatia, 95; Breast cancer genetic screening and bioethics' critical gaze, J of Med and Philos, 95; coauth, Standards of care and ethical concerns in genetic testing and screening, Clinical Obstetrics and Gynecology, 96. **CONTACT ADDRESS** Ctr for Health Louisianaward and Bioethics, 3708 Fifth Ave, Pittsburgh, PA, 15213. **EMAIL** lsp@med.pitt.edu

PARKER, MARK M.
PERSONAL Born 08/14/1952, Royal Oak, MI, m, 1980, 3 children **DISCIPLINE** MUSIC THEORY **EDUCATION** Bob Jones Univ, BA, 74; Univ Rochester, MA, 76; Univ N Tex, PhD, 88. **CAREER** BOB JONES UNIV, 76-86, 85-. **MEMBERSHIPS** Soc for Mus Theory, Mus Theory Southeast, Tech

Inst Mus Educators. **RESEARCH** Hist mus theory, Schenkerian analysis, mus tech. **SELECTED PUBLICATIONS** various **CONTACT ADDRESS** Bob Jones Univ, Box 34441, Greenville, SC, 29614. **EMAIL** mparker@bju.edu

PARKER, RICHARD W.
DISCIPLINE CLASSICS **EDUCATION** Univ British Columbia, PhD, 86. **CAREER** Lect, Univ of Saskatchewan, 84-85, 86-87; lect, Brock Univ, 85-86; asst prof, Univ Western Ontario, 87-88; asst prof, 88-96, ASSOC PROF, 96-, DEPT CHAIR, BROCK UNIV, 93-98. **MEMBERSHIPS** Archaeological Inst of Am, brd of governors (AIA-Canada); Can Archaeological Inst in Athens; Am Philol Asn; Classical Asn Can; Asn Internationale d'Epigraphie Grec et Latine. **RESEARCH** Greek hist; Greek epigraphy; Greek lit. **SELECTED PUBLICATIONS** Auth, A Greek Inscription from Honoring a Julio-Claudian, Zeitschrift fur Papyrologie und Epigraphik 75, 88; Potamon of Mytilene and His Family, Zeitschrift fur Papyrologie und Epigraphik 85, 91; with E. H. Williams, A Fragment of a Diocletianic Tax Assessment from Mytilene, Echos du Monde Classique XXXIX, New Series 14, 95. **CONTACT ADDRESS** Dept of Classics, Brock Univ, St. Catherines, ON, L2S 3A1. **EMAIL** rparker@spartan.ac.brocku.ca

PARKER, SIDNEY BAYNES
PERSONAL Born 07/13/1922, Jamaica, West Indies, m, 1978 **DISCIPLINE** EDUCATION **EDUCATION** Mico Teachers' College, attended, 1941-43; Howard University, BS, MA, 1949, MDiv, 1953; Geneva Theological College, EdD, 1970; LaSalle University, LLB, 1970. **CAREER** Excelsior High School, teacher, 1944-45; St Michael's Episcopal Church, vicar, 1953-57; Leland College, instructor, 1953-57; Trinity Episcopal Church, rector, 1957-70; Newark Public School System, instructor, 1960-70; St Mary's Anglican Church, interim rector, 1967; St Philip's Episcopal Church, rector, 1970-78; ST GABRIEL'S EPISCOPAL CHURCH, VICAR, 1970-; EDWARD WATERS COLLEGE, PROF, 1976-. **HONORS AND AWARDS** Howard University, Homiletic Award, 1952; City of Jacksonville, Mayor's Award, 1979; University of North Florida, Achievement Award, 1990. **MEMBERSHIPS** Montclair Mayor's Committee, president, 1969-70; Diocese of Florida Standing Committee, 1976-79; Jacksonville Library, bd of trustees, 1987-. **CONTACT ADDRESS** St. Gabriel Episcopal Church, 5235 Moncrief Rd W, Jacksonville, FL, 32209.

PARKER, SIMON B.
PERSONAL Born 02/23/1940, Manchester, England, m, 1961, 2 children **DISCIPLINE** ANCIENT NEAR EASTERN STUDIES, SEMITIC LANGUAGES, HEBREW BIBLE **EDUCATION** Univ Manchester, BA, 60; Asbury Theol Sem, BD, 63; Johns Hopkins Univ, PhD, 67. **CAREER** Asst prof of Humanities and Relig, Reed Col, 67-75; asst to the Pres, Boston Univ, 77-78, asst provost, 78-81, assoc dean and assoc prof, Boston Univ School of Theol, 81-88, assoc prof of Hebrew Bible, 88-97, prof of Hebrew Bible, Boston Univ School of Theol, 97-. **HONORS AND AWARDS** Graves Award, 72; Named First Harrell F Beck Scholar of Hebrew Scripture, Boston Univ. **MEMBERSHIPS** Am Oriental Soc; Am Schools of Oriental Res; Soc of Biblical Lit; Soc for Old Testament Study, UK. **RESEARCH** Continuities and discontinuities in the lit and relig of ancient Israel; Canaan Israelite culture and social hist. **SELECTED PUBLICATIONS** Auth, The Pre-Biblical Narrative Tradition: Essays on the Ugaritic Poems Keret and Aqhat, Resources for Biblical Study 24, Scholar Press, 89; Official Attitudes Toward Prophecy at Mari and in Israel, Vetus Testamentum 45, 93; The Beginning of the Reign of God--Psalm 82 an Myth and Liturgy, Revue Biblique 102, 95; Stories in Scripture and Inscriptions, Oxford Univ Press, 97; ed and trans, Ugaritic Narrative poetry, Writings From the Ancient World, Scholars Press, 97; gen ed since 1994 of Writings From the Ancient World, Scholars Press; numerous scholarly articles in books and journals. **CONTACT ADDRESS** School of Theology, Boston Univ, 745 Commonwealth Ave, Boston, MA, 02215. **EMAIL** sbparker@bu.edu

PARKER MCLACHLAN, ELIZABETH
DISCIPLINE MEDIEVAL ART **EDUCATION** Courtauld Inst of Art, PhD. **CAREER** Assoc prof, Rutgers, The State Univ NJ, Univ Col-Camden. **RESEARCH** Medieval manuscripts and iconography, especially English, 12th-century and earlier; influence of the liturgy and liturgical drama on medieval art; pictorial cycles in medieval psalters. **SELECTED PUBLICATIONS** Auth, The Scriptorium of Bury St. Edmunds in the Twelfth Century, Garland Publ, 86; coauth, Romanesque Reassembled in England: A Review, in Gesta 2 4;1, 85; coed, The Carver's Art: Medieval Sculpture in Ivory, Bone, and Horn, exh cat, The Jane Voorhees Zimmerli Art Mus, Rutgers Univ, 89. **CONTACT ADDRESS** Dept of Art Hist, Rutgers, The State Univ NJ, Univ Col-Camden, Voorhees Hall, 71 Hamilton St, New Brunswick, NJ, 08903. **EMAIL** epmcl@rci.rutgers.edu

PARMAN, DONALD L.
DISCIPLINE HISTORY **EDUCATION** Central Mo State Col, BSEd, 58; Ohio Univ, MA, 63; Univ Okla, PhD, 67. **CAREER** Asst prof, 63; assoc prof, 75; PROF, 93-, PURDUE UNIV. **CONTACT ADDRESS** Dept of History, Purdue Univ, West Lafayette, IN, 47907-1358.

PARMAN, DONALD LEE
PERSONAL Born 10/10/1932, New Point, MO, m, 1953, 2 children **DISCIPLINE** AMERICAN HISTORY **EDUCATION** Cent Mo State Col, BSEd, 58; Ohio Univ, MA, 62; Univ Okla, PhD (Am hist), 67. **CAREER** Instr soc studies, Cent Mo State Col, 61-62; from Asst Prof to Assoc Prof, 66-93, PROF AM HIST, PURDUE UNIV, WEST LAFAYETTE, 93-; Consult, Proj Impact, Off Educ, 68; Consult, U.S. Dept Justice as expert witness in Navajo claims case, 84-87; Consult, Mudd Libr of Manuscripts, Princeton Univ, to evaluate the Asn Am Indians Affairs papers. **HONORS AND AWARDS** Nat Endowment for Humanities grant, 72-73; recipient of numerous grants, 73-96. **MEMBERSHIPS** Ind Hist Soc; Ind Asn Hist; Western Hist Asn. **RESEARCH** Twentieth century Indians of the United States. **SELECTED PUBLICATIONS** Auth, The Indian and the Civilian Conservation Corps, Pac Hist Rev, 2/71; J C Morgan: Navajo apostle of assimilation, Prologue, J Nat Arch, summer 72; coed, The American Search (2 vols), Forum, 73; auth, The Navajos and the New Deal, Yale Univ, 76; American Indians and the bicentennial, NMex Hist Rev, 7/76; auth, The Big Stick in Indian affairs, The Bai-a-lil-le incident in 1909, Ariz & the West, Vol 20, winter 78; Francis E Leupp, Commissioner of Indian Affairs, 1905-1909, In: The Commissioners of Indian Affairs, 1824-1977, Univ Nebraska Press, 79; A Whites Man's Fight: The Crow Scandal, 1906-1913, In: The American West: Essays in Honor of W Eugene Hollon, Univ Toledo, 80; Indians of the Modern West, In: Major Issues in Twentieth Century Western History, Univ New Mex Press, 89; Indians and the American West in the Twentieth Century, Ind Univ Press, 94; The Indian Reorganization Act of 1934, In: Classroom Activities on Wisconsin Indian History: Treaties and Tribal Sovereignty, Wis Dept Public Educ, 96; Window to a Changed World: The Personal Memoirs of William Graham, Ind Hist Soc, 98; author of numerous journal and encyclopedia articles. **CONTACT ADDRESS** Dept of History, Purdue Univ, West Lafayette, IN, 47907-1968. **EMAIL** history@sla.purdue.edu

PARMET, HERBERT S.
PERSONAL Born 09/28/1929, New York, NY, m, 1948, 1 child **DISCIPLINE** AMERICAN HISTORY **EDUCATION** State Univ NY Col Oswego, BS, 51; Queens Col, NY, MA, 57. **CAREER** Instr hist, Fairleigh Dickinson Univ, 58-64; from asst prof to assoc prof, 68-75, Prof Hist, Queensborough Community Col, City Univ, NY, 75-, Prof Grad Sch, 77-, Fac res fel, State Univ NY, 74; secy-treas bd dirs, Acad Humanities & Sci, City Univ NY. **MEMBERSHIPS** AHA; Orgn Am Historians. **RESEARCH** Recent American history. **SELECTED PUBLICATIONS** Coauth, Aaron Burr: Portrait of an Ambitious Man, 67, Never Again: A President Runs for a Third Term, 68, contribr, Our Presidents, 69 & auth, Eisenhower and the American Crusades, 72, Macmillan; contrib, Makers of American Diplomacy, 74 & Pinnacle of Power, 76, Scribners; auth, The Democrats: The Years After FDR, Macmillan, 76; Jack: The Struggles of John F Kennedy, Dial, 80; The La-folletes of Wisconsin, Love And Politics in Progressive America - Weisberger,ba, Western Historical Quarterly, Vol 0026, 1995. **CONTACT ADDRESS** 18-40 211th St, Bayside, NY, 11360.

PARMET, ROBERT DAVID
PERSONAL Born 12/11/1938, Bronx, NY, m, 1963, 1 child **DISCIPLINE** MODERN AMERICAN HISTORY **EDUCATION** City Col NY, BA, 60; Columbia Univ, MA, 61, PhD, 66. **CAREER** Lectr hist, 62-65, City Col NY; asst prof, 65-67, Newark State Col; from asst prof to assoc prof, 67-77, chmn dept hist & philos, 72-75, prof hist, 78-, York Col, CUNY. **MEMBERSHIPS** AHA; Southern Hist Assn; Orgn Am Historians; Acad Polit Sci. **RESEARCH** US Labor and Immigration history. **SELECTED PUBLICATIONS** Auth, The Presidential Fever of Chauncey Depew, NY Hist Soc Quart, 70; art, Schools for the Freedmen, Negro Hist Bull, 71; coauth, American Nativism, 1830-1860, Van Nostrand Reinhold, 71; art, Competition for the World's Columbian Exposition: The New York Campaign, J Ill State Hist Soc, 72; auth, Labor and Immigration in Industrial America, Twayne Publ, 81. **CONTACT ADDRESS** One Highland Pl, Great Neck, NY, 11020. **EMAIL** pdrmet@york.cuny.edu

PAROT, JOSEPH JOHN
PERSONAL Born 06/04/1940, Hammond, IN, m, 1962, 2 children **DISCIPLINE** AMERICAN RELIGIOUS & URBAN/ETHNIC HISTORY **EDUCATION** Maryknoll College, 58; IN Univ, 59-60; St Joseph's Col, Ind, BA, 63; DePaul Univ, MA, 67; Northern IL Univ, PhD, 71. **CAREER** Instr hist, St Augustine High Sch, Chicago, 63-67; from instr to asst prof hist & bibliog, 67-74, assoc prof, 75-82, prof hist & head hist ctr, Northern IL Univ, 82-, prof hist & head soc sci dept, 84; Instr soc sci, Chicago Comt Urban Opportunity Prog, 66-67; vis prof urban/ethnic studies, George Williams Col, 72-73; assoc ed, Polish-Am Studies, 73. **HONORS AND AWARDS** Ed Emer Award, St Joseph's Col, 63; Lions Int, Outstanding Teacher Award, Chicago rea, 66; Pi Gamma Mu, DePaul Univ, 67; Oscar Halecki Award from Polish Am Hist Asn for outstanding book, 83; grants from Am Philos Soc, NEH; Honorariums from Multicultural Hist Soc of Ontario, 78; Pa Hist Comm, 76; Univ Notre Dame 82; Multicultural Curr Trnasformation Ins, 95. **MEMBERSHIPS** AHA; Polish-Am Hist Asn. **RESEARCH** Immigration hist; urban hist; religious hist in Am. **SELECTED PUBLICATIONS** Auth, Ethnic versus Black metropolis: Origins of Polish Black housing tensions in Chicago, 71, Unthinkable thoughts on unmeltable ethnics, 74 & Racial dilemma in Chicago's Polish neighborhoods, 1920-1970, 75, Polish Am Studies; contribr, Bishop Francis Hodur, suppl five, In: Dict of American Biography, 77; Strangers in the city: Immigrant Catholics and the black community in Twentieth century Chicago, Black History Conference, Lincoln Univ Press, 4/78; Immigrant Labor and the Paradox of Pluralism in American Urban Society, 1860-1930: A Comparative Study and Census Analysis of Polish, German, Irish, Bohemian, Italian and Jewish Workers in Chicago, Polish Res Inst of the Jagiellonian Univ, Cracow, 79; Sources of community conflict in Chicago Polonia: A comparative analysis and historigraphical appraisal, Ethnicity, vol 7, winter 80; Polish Catholics in Chicago, 1850-1920: A Religious History, Northern Ill Univ Press, 81; The Serdeczna Matko of the sweatshops: Marital and family crises of immigrant working-class women in late nineteenth century Chicago, Poles in North America Conference, Multicult Hist Soc of Ont, 82; Steelmills, sweatshops, stockyards, and slums: The social fabric of the immigrant Catholic working class in Chicago, 1870-1930, Perspectives in American Catholicism, Univ Notre Dame, 11/82; Catholic manuscript and archival sources in the Greater Chicago area, Mdwest Archives Conf, Chicago 5/83; The urbanization and suburbanization of the ethnic working class in Chicago, 1870-1980, Celebrate Illinois: Its Cultural Heritage, Ill Humantities Counc, 4/85; Family and social history in the immigrant community, Polish Genealogical Soc, 11/88; co-ed (with James Pula, et al), Polish History in America to 1908, vol 1-4; Catholic Univ of Am Press, 94-98, Kruszka Transl Proj; ed board of Ill Hist Jour, 95-98; The German immigrant in Illinois, 1840-1930, Elmhurst Hist Soc, 3/98; Reverend Vincent Barzynski, In: American National Biography, 99; Multicultural difficulties in the Polish Catholic community in Chicago, Ill Hist Teacher, 99. **CONTACT ADDRESS** Founders Libr, No Illinois Univ, Soc Sci Dept, De Kalb, IL, 60115-2825.

PARR, JOY
PERSONAL Toronto, ON, Canada **DISCIPLINE** HISTORY **EDUCATION** McGill Univ, BA, 71; Yale Univ, MPhil, 73, PhD, 77. **CAREER** Asst prof, Univ BC, 76-78; asst to assoc prof, Queen's Univ, 79-92; coordr Women's Stud, 89-90, FARLEY PROF HIST, SIMON FRASER UNIV, 92-. **HONORS AND AWARDS** Harold Innis Award; Macdonald Prize; Berkshire Prize; Laura Jamieson Prize; Fred Landon Award. **MEMBERSHIPS** Uppsala Univ; Radcliff Col; Royal Soc Can; All Souls Col, Oxford. **SELECTED PUBLICATIONS** Auth, Labouring Children, 80; auth, Childhood and Family in Canadian History, 82; auth, Canadian Women on the Move, 83; auth, Still Running, 86; auth, The Gender of Breadwinners, 90; auth, A Diversity of Women 1945-80, 95; auth, Gender and History in Canada, 96. **CONTACT ADDRESS** Dept of History, Simon Fraser Univ, Burnaby, BC, V5A 1S6. **EMAIL** joy-parr@sfu.ca

PARRISH, MICHAEL EMERSON
PERSONAL Born 03/04/1942, Huntington Park, CA, 2 children **DISCIPLINE** AMERICAN HISTORY **EDUCATION** Univ Calif, Riverside, BA, 64; Yale Univ, PhD(hist), 68. **CAREER** Asst prof, 68-73, assoc prof, 73-80, Prof Hist, Univ Calif, San Diego, 80-. **SELECTED PUBLICATIONS** Auth, Securities Regulation and the New Deal, Yale Univ Press, 70; Cold war justice: The Supreme Court and the Rosenbergs, Am Hist Rev, 77; The Hughes Court, the Great Depression, and the historians, The Historian, 78; Felix Frankfurter and His Times: The Reform Years, Free Press, 82; The New-dealers - Power-politics in The Age of Roosevelt - Schwarz,ja, Reviews in American History, Vol 0022, 1994; Justice Holmes,oliver,wendell - Law And The Inner Self - White,ge, American Historical Review, Vol 0100, 1995; In The Shadow of War - The United-states Since The 1930s - Sherry,ms, Reviews in American History, Vol 0024, 1996; The Return of Sutherland,george - Restoring a Jurisprudence of Natural Rights - Arkes,h, American Historical Review, Vol 0101, 1996; Battles on The Bench - Conflict Inside The Supreme-court - Cooper,pj, American Historical Review, Vol 0102, 1997; b The Hidden Holmes - His Theory of Torts in History - Rosenberg,d, J of American History, Vol 0083, 1997; The Amerasia Spy Case - Prelude to Mccarthyism - Klehr,h, Radosh,r, Reviews in American History, Vol 0025, 1997. **CONTACT ADDRESS** Dept of Hist, Univ of Calif, San Diego, CA, 92039.

PARRISH, WILLIAM E.
PERSONAL Born 04/07/1931, Garden City, KS, m, 1972, 2 children **DISCIPLINE** AMERICAN HISTORY **EDUCATION** Kans State Univ, BS, 52; Univ Mo, MA, 53, PhD(hist), 55. **CAREER** From asst prof to prof, Westminster Col, Mo, 55-71, dean col, 73-75, Truman prof Am hist, 71-78; prof & head, dept hist, Miss State Univ, 78-85, prof, 85-96, PROF EMER, 96- . **HONORS AND AWARDS** Ed, Sesquicentennial Hist Mo, 71; mem, Mo Adv Coun on Hist Preserv, 67-78; Award of Merit, Am Asn State & Local Hist, 74; chm, Mo Am Rev Bicentennial Comt, 74-77. **MEMBERSHIPS** Org Am Historians; Southern Hist Asn; Nat Trust Hist Preserv; Western Hist Asn. **RESEARCH** Sectionalism, Civil War and Reconstruction; American West. **SELECTED PUBLICATIONS** Auth, David Rice Atchison of Missouri: Border Politican, 61, Turbulent Partnership: Missouri and the Union, 1861-1865, 63 & Missouri Under Radical Rule, 1865-1870, 65, Univ Mo; ed, The Union:

State and Local Studies, In: Vol II, Civil War Books: A Critical Bibliography, La State Univ, 68; contrib, Radicalism, Racism and Party Realignment: The Border States During Reconstruction, Johns Hopkins Univ, 69; ed, The Civil War: A Second American Revolution?, Dryden, 70 & Kreiger, 77; auth, A History of Missouri, Vol 3, Univ Mo, 73; auth, Missouri: The Heart of the Nation, Forum, 80, 2d ed, Harlan Davidson, 92; auth, Frank Blair: Lincoln's Conservative, Missouri, 98. **CONTACT ADDRESS** Dept of History, Mississippi State Univ, Mississippi State, MS, 39762.

PARRY, JOSEPH D.
PERSONAL Born 12/02/1960, Salt Lake City, UT, m, 1989, 1 child **DISCIPLINE** HISTORY **EDUCATION** Brigham Young Univ, BA, 85, MA, 87; Univ Utah, PhD, 95. **CAREER** Lectr, 87-88, ASST PROF, 93-, GRAD COORD, 95-, BRIGHAM YOUNG UNIV. **HONORS AND AWARDS** Clark-Harris Outstanding Grad Stud Award, 87; Allan D Breck Award, Rocky Mountain Medieval and Renaissance Asn, 95; Col Hum Res, Travel Grants, Brigham Young Univ, 94-99., Grad Student Instr, Brigham Young Univ, 85-87; Teaching Fel, Univ Utah, 88-93. **MEMBERSHIPS** Renaissance Soc Am; Medieval Acad Am; Rocky Mtn Medieval, Renaissance Asn. **RESEARCH** Medieval and Renaissance literary and visual narratives, espec Lawman, Chaucer, Malory and Spenser. **SELECTED PUBLICATIONS** Auth, "Margery Kempe's Inarticulate Narration," Magistra 1.2, 95; "Dorigen, Narration and Coming Home in the Franklin's Tale," Chaucer Rev 30, 96; "Narration and Quattrocento Annunciation Paintings," JRMMRA 17, 96; "Following Malory out of Arthur's World," Mod Philol 95, 97; "Exploring the Middle Ages with the Medieval May," Interdisciplinary Humanities, 15.1, 98; "Narrators, Messengers and Lawman's Brut," Arthuriana 8.3, 98; **CONTACT ADDRESS** Dept of Hum, Classics and Comp Lit, Brigham Young Univ, Provo, UT, 84602. **EMAIL** joseph_parry@byu.edu

PARSONS, JAMES
DISCIPLINE MUSICOLOGY **EDUCATION** Fla State Univ, BachMus, 78; Univ N Texas, PhD Musicol, 92. **CAREER** Vis asst prof, Univ Mo, 92-95; ASST PROF, COORD MUSIC HIST, SOUTHWEST MO STATE UNIV, 99-. **CONTACT ADDRESS** 4355 S National Ave, #1209, Springfield, MO, 1209. **EMAIL** jap614f@mail.smsu.edu

PARSONS, JED
PERSONAL Born 02/02/1971, New York, NY, m, 1997 **DISCIPLINE** CLASSICS **EDUCATION** Harvard Univ, BA, 93; Univ Calif Berk, MA, 95, PhD, 99. **RESEARCH** Roman comedy. **SELECTED PUBLICATIONS** Auth, A New Approach to the Saturnian Verse, Trans of the APA, forthcoming. **CONTACT ADDRESS** Univ of California, Berkeley, 7303 Dwinelle Hall, Berkeley, CA, 94705. **EMAIL** jed@scorates.berkeley.edu

PARSONS, KEITH M.
PERSONAL Born 08/31/1952, Macon, GA, s **DISCIPLINE** HISTORY & PHILOSOPHY OF SCIENCE; PHILOSOPHY OF RELIGION **EDUCATION** Queens Univ, PhD, 86; Univ Pitts, PhD, 96. **CAREER** Asst Prof Univ Houston-Clear Lake; Ed, Philo, Jour Soc Humanist Phil **MEMBERSHIPS** Philos Sci Asn; Am Philos Asn. **RESEARCH** Rationality & theory change in science; history of the earth sciences; Darwinism; science and religion. **SELECTED PUBLICATIONS** Auth, God and the Burden of Proof, Prometheus Books, 89; Drawing Out Leviathan: What do we Really Know About Dinosaurs? Ind Univ Press. **CONTACT ADDRESS** Univ Houston-Clear Lake, 2700 Bay Area Blvd., Houston, TX, 77058-1098. **EMAIL** parsons@cl.uh.edu

PARSONS, LYNN
DISCIPLINE HISTORY **EDUCATION** Grinnell Col, BA, 58; Johns Hopkins Univ, MA, 64, PhD, 67. **CAREER** Prof. **RESEARCH** American history **SELECTED PUBLICATIONS** Auth, John Quincy Adams: An American Profile, Madison, 98; European Offshoot or Unique Experiment: The United States in World History, St Martin, 95; co-ed, The Home Front, Greenwood, 95. **CONTACT ADDRESS** Dept of History, State Univ NY Col Brockport, Brockport, NY, 14420. **EMAIL** lparsons@acspr1.acs.brockport.edu

PARSSINEN, TERRY
DISCIPLINE HISTORY OF NARCOTIC DRUGS AND THEIR IMPACT ON SOCIETY **EDUCATION** Grinnell Col, BA, 65; Brandeis Univ, MA, 63, PhD, 68. **CAREER** Prof; dean, clas, 92-95, Univ of Tampa. **SELECTED PUBLICATIONS** Auth, Secret Passions, Secret Remedies: Narcotic Drugs and British Society, 1820-1930, ISHI Publ & Manchester UP, 83. **CONTACT ADDRESS** Dept of Hist, Univ of Tampa, 401 W. Kennedy Blvd, Tampa, FL, 33606-1490.

PASCAL, CECIL BENNETT
PERSONAL Born 05/04/1926, Chicago, IL, m, 1959, 1 child **DISCIPLINE** CLASSICAL PHILOLOGY **EDUCATION** Univ Calif, Los Angeles, AB, 48, MA, 50; Harvard Univ, MA, 53, PhD, 56. **CAREER** Instr classics, Univ Ill, 55-56; instr, Cornell Univ, 57- 60; asst prof classic lang, 60-65, head dept classics, Chinese & Japanese, 65-67 & 72-73, assoc prof, 65-76, Prof Classics, Univ Ore, 76-, Head Dept Classics, 78-, William Amory Gardner traveling fel, Harvard Univ, 56-57; Fulbright-Hays res fel, Univ Rome, 67-68. **MEMBERSHIPS** Am Philol Asn; Philol Asn Pac Coast; Classic Asn Pac Northwest; Archaeol Inst Am; AAUP. **RESEARCH** Latin and Greek literature; Roman religion. **SELECTED PUBLICATIONS** Auth, Horatian Chiaroscuro, In: Hommages a Marcel Renard, Latomus, 69; Rex Nemorensis, Numen, 76; October Horse, Harvard State Col Philol, 81; The Dubious Devotion of Turnus + Vergil 'Aeneid', Book-11, Transactions of The American Philological Association, Vol 0120, 1990. **CONTACT ADDRESS** Dept of Classics, Univ of Ore, Eugene, OR, 97403.

PASCAL, PAUL
PERSONAL Born 03/26/1925, New York, NY, m, 1948, 2 children **DISCIPLINE** CLASSICS, MEDIEVAL LATIN **EDUCATION** Univ VT, BA, 48; Univ NC, PHD(classics), 53. **CAREER** Prof Classics, Univ Wash, 53-. **MEMBERSHIPS** Am Philol Asn. **RESEARCH** Mediaeval Latin literature. **SELECTED PUBLICATIONS** Coauth, The Institutionum Disciplinae of Isidore of Seville, Traditio, 57; Notes on Missus Sum in Vineam of Walter of Chatillon, Studies in Honor of B L Ullman, Rome, 64; The Conclusion of the Pervigilium Veneris, Neophilologus, 65; The Julius Exclusus of Erasmus, Ind Univ, 68; The Poetry of Boethius - Odaly,g, Classical J, Vol 0087, 1992. **CONTACT ADDRESS** Dept of Classics, Univ of Wash, Seattle, WA, 98105.

PASCOE, LOUIS B.
PERSONAL Born 05/26/1930, Carbondale, PA **DISCIPLINE** MEDIEVAL HISTORY **EDUCATION** Univ Scranton, BA, 52; Woodstock Col, Md, PhL, 58, STL, 65; Fordham Univ, MA, 60; Univ Calif, Los Angeles, PhD(hist), 70. **CAREER** Asst prof, Woodstock Col, 71-73; asst prof to prof hist, Fordham Univ, 73-; Fel, Woodstock Col, 70-71; lectr hist, Union Theol Sem, 71-73; fel, Fordham Univ, 78-79; vis prof hist, Jesuit Sch Theol at Berkeley, 81-82. **MEMBERSHIPS** AHA; Mediaeval Acad Am; Cath Hist Asn; Cusanus Soc of Am. **RESEARCH** Medieval ecclesiastical and intellectual history. **SELECTED PUBLICATIONS** Auth, The Council of Trent and Bible study: Humanism and Scripture, Cath Hist Rev, 66; Jean Gerson: Principles of Church Reform, Brill, 73; Gerson and the Donation of Constantine, Viator, 74; Jean Gerson: The Ecclesia Primitiva and Reform, Traditio, 74; Jean Gerson: Mysticism, Conciliarism, and Reform, Annuarium Hist Conciliarum, 74; Nobility and Ecclesiastical Office in Fifteenth-Century Lyons, Mediaeval Studies, 76; Theological Dimensions of Pierre d'Ailly's Teaching on the Papal Plenitude of Power, Annarium Hist Conciliarum, 789; Pierre d'Ailly: Histoire, Schisme et Antechrist, Genese et debuts du Grand Schisme d'Occident, 80; Jean Gerson, Dictionary of the Middle Ages, 85; Law and Evangelical Liberty in the Thought of Jean Gerson, 85; Religious Orders, Evangelical Liberty, and Reform in the Thought of Jean Gerson, 89. **CONTACT ADDRESS** Dept of Hist, Fordham Univ, 441 E Fordham Rd, Bronx, NY, 10458-5191.

PASHA, MUSTAPHA
DISCIPLINE POLITICAL ECONOMICS **EDUCATION** Forman Christian Col, BA; Punjab Univ, Pakistan LLB; Univ Denver, MA, PhD. **CAREER** Prof, Am Univ. **HONORS AND AWARDS** Wilma and Roswell Messing Jr. Faculty Award, Webster Univ. **RESEARCH** Global political economy and the comparative politics of the Third World. **SELECTED PUBLICATIONS** Auth, Colonial Political Economy: State-Building and Underdevelopment in the Punjab, Oxford Univ Press, 97. **CONTACT ADDRESS** American Univ, 4400 Massachusetts Ave, Washington, DC, 20016.

PASLER, JANN C.
PERSONAL Born 07/06/1951, Milwaukee, WI **DISCIPLINE** MUSIC **EDUCATION** Vanderbilt Univ, BA, 73; Univ Chicago, MA, 74, PhD, 81. **CAREER** Actg asst prof, Univ Va, 78-80; prof, Univ Calif, San Diego, 81- . **HONORS AND AWARDS** Magna Cum Laude, 73; NEH grant, 82; NEH fel, 85, 88-89; Univ Calif Pres Fel, 88-89; Stanford fel, 93-94; Univ Calif Hum Res Inst, co-dir res residency, 94. **SELECTED PUBLICATIONS** Auth, Concert Programs and Their Narratives as Emblems of Ideology, Int J of Musicol, 93; auth, John Cage: Releasing Spirit in Life and Music, Music Today, 93; auth, Reinterpreting Indian Music: Delage and Roussel, in Music-Cultures in Contact, Currency Press, 94; auth, Inventing a Tradition: John Cage's Composition in Retrospect, in Perloff, ed, John Cage: Composed in America, Univ Chicago, 94; auth, Directions in Musicology, Acta Musicol, 97; contribur, New Grove Dictionary of Music and Musicians, 97; auth, Material Culture and Postmodern Positivism: Understanding the Popular in Late 19th Century French Music, in Marvin, ed, Reading Texts: The Interpretation of Sources in Musical Scholarship, Oxford, 99; auth, Useful Music, 1871-1903, Univ Calif, in progress. **CONTACT ADDRESS** Univ of California, San Diego, La Jolla, CA, 92093. **EMAIL** jpasler@ucsd.edu

PASTAN, ELIZABETH C.
PERSONAL Born 05/03/1955, Philadelphia, PA, m, 1980, 3 children **DISCIPLINE** ART HISTORY; MEDIEVAL FIELD **EDUCATION** Smith Col, BA, 77; Columbia Univ, MA, 79; Brown Univ, PhD, 86. **CAREER** Visit asst prof, Wellesley Col, 85-88; asst prof, Indiana Univ, Bloomington, 88-95; Assoc Prof, Emory Univ, 95-. **HONORS AND AWARDS** Kross Fnd Pub Subsidy, 97-98; Col Art Asn Millard Meiss Pub Subsidy, 95-96; NEH Summer Travel Stipend, 94; Indiana Univ Summer Fac Fel, 94. **MEMBERSHIPS** Societe academique de l'Aube; Int Ctr of Medieval Art; Medieval Acad of Am; Col Art Asn. **RESEARCH** Cult of relics; hagiography; stained glass representation of Jews and Heretics; Champagne (France). **SELECTED PUBLICATIONS** Coauth, The Torture of the Saint George Medallion from Chartres Cathedral in Princeton, Record of The Art Museum, Princeton Univ, 56, 10-34, 97; auth,Tam haereticos quam Judaeos: Shifting Symbols Themes in the Glazing of Troyes Cathedral, Word and Image, 10, 66-83, 94; auth, Process and Patronage in the Decorative Arts of the Early Campaigns of Troyes Cathedral, c. 1200-1220s, Jou of the Soc of Arch Hist, 53, 215-231, 94; auth, Restoring the Stained Glass of Troyes Cathedral: The Ambiguous Legacy of Viollet-le-Duc, Gesta, 29/2, 155-166; 90; auth, Fit for a Count: The Twelfth-Century Stained Glass Panels from Troyes, Speculum, 64, 338-372, 89. **CONTACT ADDRESS** Dept of Art History, Emory Univ, Atlanta, GA, 30322. **EMAIL** epastan@empry.edu

PASTEUR, ALFRED BERNARD
PERSONAL Born 04/14/1947, Ocala, FL **DISCIPLINE** EDUCATION **EDUCATION** FL A&M Univ, AB; IN Univ, MS; Northwestern Univ, PhD. **CAREER** Temple Univ, asst prof; Chicago Bd of Educ, counselor admins; Hunter Coll, prof, currently. **MEMBERSHIPS** Mem Dayton OH Model Cities, Morgan State Coll, Bethune Cookman Coll, MN State Dept of Educ, Kennedy Found, Atlanta Univ, Chicago Career Oppor Prog, Southern Univ, Savannah State Coll, OIC Phila, Princeton Univ, Univ of Delaware, Univ of TX Austin, Virgin Islands Univ; mem Amer Personnel & Guidance Assn, Amer Psychol Assn, Assn of Black Psychol, Phi Delta Kappa, Assn for Non-White Concerns in Personnel & Guidance; devel stages of Black Self-Discovery Journal of Negro Educ 1972; soul music technique for therapeutic intervention Journal of Non-White Concerns 1972; rsch travel to Nigeria, W Africa, Senegal, Ghana, Haiti, Trinidad, Barbados, Brazil, Jamaica, Virgin Islands. **SELECTED PUBLICATIONS** Therapeutic Dimensions of the Black Aesthetic Journal of Non-White Concerns 1976; publication "Roots of Soul, A Psychology of Black Expressiveness" Doubleday Press 1982; "Black Academic & Cultural Excellence" Alliance for Black Educatorss 1984. **CONTACT ADDRESS** Hunter Col, CUNY, 695 Park Avenue, New York, NY, 10021.

PASTOR, BEATRIZ
PERSONAL Born 07/25/1948, Seo de Urgel, Spain, m, 1978, 2 children **DISCIPLINE** LATIN AMERICAN & SPANISH LITERATURE **EDUCATION** Univ Barcelona, BA, 68; Univ Minn, Minneapolis, MA, 71, PhD(Latin Am lit), 77. **CAREER** Asst Prof Latin Am, Span & Comp Lit, Dartmouth Col, 76-. **MEMBERSHIPS** Latin Am Studies Asn; MLA. **RESEARCH** Contemporary Latin American literature; colonial Latin American literature. **SELECTED PUBLICATIONS** Auth, Rupture y Limiles and la narrative de Roberto Arlt, Revista de Critica Lit Latinam, 80; Los 7 Locos y Los Lanfallamas: De le rebelion al Jascismo, Hisp Rev, spring 81; Roberto Arlt y la Rebelion Alienada, Hispamerica, 81; El Mib en la Historie: Camino de Santiago de A Carpenter, Cuadernos Hispanoam, 82; Utopia And Conquest - Utopian Dynamics And Colonial Identity, Revista De Critica Literaria Latinoamericana, Vol 0019, 1993. **CONTACT ADDRESS** Dept of Span & Port, Dartmouth Col, 6072 Dartmouth Hall, Hanover, NH, 03755-3511.

PASTOR, LESLIE P.
PERSONAL Born 05/08/1925, 2 children **DISCIPLINE** EUROPEAN HISTORY, GERMAN **EDUCATION** Educ: Seton Hall Univ, AB, 56; Columbia Univ, MA, 59, PhD, 67; Inst E Cent Europe, cert, 60. **CAREER** Instr Seton Hall Prep Sch, 56-60; from instr to asst prof, 60-68, Assoc Prof Ger, Seton Hall Univ, 68-. **MEMBERSHIPS** Am Asn Advan Slavic Studies; Am Asn Tchr(s) Ger; Am Asn for Study Hungarian Hist. **RESEARCH** Ger lang and lit; 18th and 19th century Hungarian hist; hist of East Central Europe; mod East Europ hist. **CONTACT ADDRESS** Dept of Mod Lang, Seton Hall Univ, 400 S Orange Ave, South Orange, NJ, 07079-2697. **EMAIL** pastorle@shu.edu

PASZTOR, SUZANNE B.
DISCIPLINE HISTORY **EDUCATION** Adams State Col, BA, 86; TX Univ, MA, 88; NM Univ, PhD, 94. **CAREER** Asst prof, Univ Pacific. **SELECTED PUBLICATIONS** Auth, Modern Mexico, Libr Congress. **CONTACT ADDRESS** Hist Dept, Univ Pacific, Pacific Ave, PO Box 3601, Stockton, CA, 95211.

PATE, J'NELL L.
PERSONAL Born 07/31/1938, Jacksboro, TX, m, 1960 **DISCIPLINE** HISTORY **EDUCATION** TX Christian Univ, BA,

60, MA, 64; Univ of N TX, PhD, 82 **CAREER** Tchr, 60-67, Fort Worth Pub Schs; Tchr, 68-72, Tchr, 72-, Tarrant County Jr. Col **HONORS AND AWARDS** Outstanding Centennial Alumni, 90; Most outstanding book in the field of TX Hist for the year 88, Summa Cum Laude, TCU, 60; Outstanding Grad Student in History, UNT 77-78; Phi Kappa Phi Honor Soc, UNT, 82 **MEMBERSHIPS** TX Comm Col Tchrs Asn; TX St Hist Asn **RESEARCH** Local Fort Worth hist, TX hist; livestock indus **SELECTED PUBLICATIONS** Auth, Livestock Legacy: The Fort Worth Stockyards, 1887-1987, 88; Document Sets for Texas and the Southwest for US History, DC Heath & Co., 91; Ranald Slidell mackenzie Brave Cavalry Colonel, Eakin Press, 94; North of the River: a brief history of North fort Worth, Texas Christian Univ Press, 94 **CONTACT ADDRESS** Dept of History, Tarrant County Jr Col, Hurst, TX, 76054-3299. **EMAIL** jpate@tcjc.cc.tx.us

PATE, JAMES PAUL
PERSONAL Born 09/01/1942, Tremont, MS, m, 1963, 2 children **DISCIPLINE** EARLY AMERICAN HISTORY **EDUCATION** Delta State Univ, BSEd, 64; Miss State Univ, MA, 65, PhD (Am hist), 69. **CAREER** Teaching asst Am hist surv, Miss State Univ, 65-67; from asst prof to assoc prof, 67-76, chmn div hist & soc sci, 72-74, Prof Hist, Livingston Univ, 76-, Dean, Col Gen Studies, 74-. **MEMBERSHIPS** AHA; Orgn Am Historians; Southern Hist Asn. **RESEARCH** American Indians; Alabama History; Southern frontier. **SELECTED PUBLICATIONS** Colonial Alabama, Ala News Mag, 76; Women of the revolution & the road to revolution, Sumter County J, Bicentennial Spec, 76; John Sevier, Catawba Indians, Chickamauga Indians, & Battle of Mauvilla, In: Encycl of Southern History, La State Univ, 79; The Fort Tombecbe Historical Research & Documentation Project, Livingston Univ, 80; Deerskins And Duffels - The Creek Indian Trade With Anglo-america, 1685-1815 - Braund,keh, J of Southern History, Vol 0061, 1995. **CONTACT ADDRESS** Dean Col of Gen Studies, Livingston Univ, Livingston, AL, 35470.

PATERSON, THOMAS GRAHAM
PERSONAL Born 03/04/1941, Oregon City, OR **DISCIPLINE** AMERICAN HISTORY **EDUCATION** Univ NH, BA, 63; Univ Calif, Berkeley, MA, 64, PhD (hist), 68. **CAREER** From asst prof to assoc prof, 67-73, Prof Hist, Univ Conn, 73-, Harry S Truman Inst grants-in-aid, 67-68, 72 & 75; Am Philos Soc res grant, 72; Eleanor Roosevelt Inst grant-in-aid, 75; Nat Endowment for Humanities fel, 76-77; dir, Nat Endowment Humanities summer sem, 80. **MEMBERSHIPS** Soc Historians of Am Foreign Rels; Orgn Am Historians; AHA; AAUP. **RESEARCH** Twentieth century United States; history of American foreign policy; the Cold War. **SELECTED PUBLICATIONS** Ed, Cold War Critics, Quadrangle, 71; Containment and the Cold War, Addison-Wesley, 73; auth, Soviet-American Confrontation, Johns Hopkins Univ, 73; The Search for Meaning: George F Kennan, In: Makers of American Diplomacy, Scribners, 74; ed, Origins of the Cold War, 74, Major Problems in American Foreign Policy, 78 & coauth, American Foreign Policy: A History, 82, Heath; auth, On Every Front: The Making of the Cold War, 79, Norton; coauth, A People and a Nation: A History of the United States, Houghton Mifflin, 82; Behind The Throne - Servants of Power to Imperial Presidents, 1898-1968 - Mccormick,tj, Lafeber,w, J of Interdisciplinary History, Vol 0026, 1995; The Spy Who Saved The World - How a Soviet Colonel Changed The Course of The Cold-war - Schecter,jl, Deriabin,ps, J of American History, Vol 0080, 1993. **CONTACT ADDRESS** Dept of Hist, Univ of Conn, Storrs, CT, 06268.

PATRIARCA, SILVANA
DISCIPLINE MODERN WESTERN EUROPE HISTORY **EDUCATION** Johns Hopkins Univ, PhD, 92. **CAREER** Assoc prof. **RESEARCH** Italy, history of quantification and the social sciences. **SELECTED PUBLICATIONS** Auth, Numbers and Nationhood: Writing and Statistics in 19th Century Italy, 96. **CONTACT ADDRESS** Dept of Hist, Columbia Col, New York, 2960 Broadway, New York, NY, 10027-6902.

PATRIAS, CARMELA
DISCIPLINE CANADIAN LABOUR AND IMMIGRATION HISTORY **EDUCATION** Brit Columbia Univ, BA; Sussex Col, MA; Univ Toronto, PhD. **CAREER** Asst prof. **RESEARCH** Studies of immigrant labor in the Niagara Peninsula. **SELECTED PUBLICATIONS** Auth, Patriots and Proletarians; Politicizing Hungarian Immigrants in Interwar Canada, McGill-Queen's UP. **CONTACT ADDRESS** Dept of Hist, Brock Univ, 500 Glenridge Ave, St Catharines, ON, L2S 3A1. **EMAIL** cpatrias@spartan.ac.BrockU.CA

PATRICK, OPAL LEE YOUNG
PERSONAL Born 07/16/1929, Tatums, OK, m **DISCIPLINE** EDUCATION **EDUCATION** Langston Univ, BA 1951; Univ of NM, MA 1963; Univ of UT, PhD 1974. **CAREER** Public School OK, teacher 1951-56; Bur Ind Affairs, inst counselor 1956-63; Univ of MD Educ Centers Deptnd School, 1963-66; USAFE W Germany, instr lecturer teacher; Clearfield Job Corp, inst counselor adminstr 1966-70; Univ of UT, inst of educ 1971-74, asst prof of educ 1974-77; guest lecturer, coordinator, consultant, tutor, 1979-91. **MEMBERSHIPS** Presenter various conf; participant presenter Natl Organ; guest lectr coord of various projects & research activities; mem State Mental Health Assn, 1973-; UT Acad of Sci 1974-; Natl Coll of Soc Studies 1976-; Assn of Teach Educ 1974-; Natl Cncl Tchrs of Eng 1973-; vice pres Natl Cncl Tchrs of Eng 1973; Assn of Sch & Currs Develop 1975-; pres Davis Co NAACP 1978. **SELECTED PUBLICATIONS** "A Recipe for Effective Teaching" 1977; "The Culturally Unique" 1973; "Mental Health & the Cultural Differ" 1975; "Blacks in Edn" 1976; article, "Ethnic Student's Perceptions of Effective Teachers," Educational Research Quarterly, Vol. 3, No. 2, Summer 1978.

PATSOURAS, LOUIS
PERSONAL Born 05/05/1931, Steubenville, OH, d, 1 child **DISCIPLINE** HISTORY **EDUCATION** Kent State Univ, BA, 53, MA, 59; Ohio State Univ, PhD, 66. **CAREER** Inst, Asst, Assoc, Prof, 63-88-, Kent State Univ. **MEMBERSHIPS** OAH **RESEARCH** French social History; Socialism. **SELECTED PUBLICATIONS** Auth, Jean Grave and the Anarchist Tradition in France, Middletown NJ, Caslon Press, 95; coed, Rebels Against the Old Order: Essays in Honor of Morris Salvin, Youngstown OH, YSU Press, 94; ed, Debating Marx, San Francisco, Mellen Res Univ Press, 93; coed, Essays On Socialism, San Fran, Mellen Res Univ Press, 93. **CONTACT ADDRESS** 494 Moore RD, Akron, OH, 44319.

PATTERSON, CYNTHIA
DISCIPLINE HISTORY **EDUCATION** Stanford Univ, BA, 71; Univ Penn, PhD, 76. **CAREER** Assoc prof **RESEARCH** Greek history, particularly social and family history; Greek historians. **SELECTED PUBLICATIONS** Auth, articles on marriage law, family structures, and the relation of family and state in the Greek polis. **CONTACT ADDRESS** Dept History, Emory Univ, 221 Bowden Hall, 561 Kilgo Cir, Atlanta, GA, 30322-1950. **EMAIL** cpatt01@emory.edu

PATTERSON, DAVID SANDS
PERSONAL Born 04/26/1937, Bridgeport, CT, m, 1968, 1 child **DISCIPLINE** AMERICAN DIPLOMATIC HISTORY, INTERNATIONAL RELATIONS **EDUCATION** Yale Univ, BA, 59; Univ Calif, Berkeley, MA, 63, PhD(hist), 68. **CAREER** Instr hist, Ohio State Univ, 65-69; asst prof, Univ Ill, Chicago Circle, 69-71; asst prof, Rice Univ, 71-76; vis assoc prof US hist, Colgate Univ, 76-78; HISTORIAN, DEPT OF STATE, 80-, Dep Hist & Gen Ed Foreign Relations Series, 96-; Mershon soc sci fel, 66; Nat Endowment for Humanities summer fel, 71-; Johns Hopkins-Nanjing Univ Ctr, 90-91. **HONORS AND AWARDS** Bernath lectr Am diplomatic hist, Soc Hist Am Foreign Rel, 78. **MEMBERSHIPS** Peace Hist Soc, pres 86-89; Soc Hist Am Foreign Rel, council 98-. **RESEARCH** American diplomatic history; national security affairs; arms control. **SELECTED PUBLICATIONS** Auth, Woodrow Wilson and the mediation movement, 1914-17, Historian, 8/71; auth, Toward a Warless World: The Travail of the American Peace Movement, 1887-1914, Ind Univ, 76; The United States and the origins of the world court, Polit Sci Quart, summer 76; What's wrong (and right) with American diplomatic history: A diagnosis and prescription, Soc Hist Am Foreign Rel Newslett, 78; A historical view of American security, Peace & Change, fall 81; auth, President Eisenhower and Arms Control, Peace & Courage, No 3/4, 86; auth, The Department of State: The Formative Years, 1775-1800, Prologue, winter 92; auth, The Legacy of President Eisenhower's Arms Control Policies, The Military-Industrial Complex: Eisenhower's Warning Three Decades Later, Peter Lang, 92; auth, Pacifism and Arms Limitation, Encyclopedia of the United States in the Twentieth Century, Scribner's, 96. **CONTACT ADDRESS** 9011 Montgomery Ave, Chevy Chase, MD, 20815. **EMAIL** pattersond@panet.us-state.gov

PATTERSON, H. ORLANDO L.
PERSONAL Born 05/05/1940, Jamaica, m, 1995, 2 children **DISCIPLINE** SOCIOLOGY **EDUCATION** Univ Coll of W Indies, BS, 62; UCWI, London, Honors External; London Sch of Econ: Sociol, PhD, 65. **CAREER** John Cowles Prof of Soc, Harvard Univ, 71-. **HONORS AND AWARDS** AM, Harvard Univ, 71; Dr of Humane Letters, Trinity Col, 92; UCLA Medal, 92; Walter Channing Cabot Fac Prize, Harvard, 97. **MEMBERSHIPS** Am Acad of Arts & Sci; Am Sociol Asn. **RESEARCH** Race relations (contemporary); historical sociology; freedom & slavery. **SELECTED PUBLICATIONS** Auth, Freedom in the Making of Western Culture, Basic Books, 91; auth, About Freedom, Earth Stars & Writers, Lib of Cong, 93; auth, The New Puritanism, Salmagundi, 94; auth, The Crisis of Gender Relations in the African American Community, Race, Gender, and Power in America, Oxford Univ Press, 94; auth, For Whom the Bell Curves, The Bell Curve Wars, Basic Books, 95; auth, The Ordeal of Integration: Progress and Resentment in America's Racial Crisis, Counterpoint/Civitas, 97; auth, Rituals of Blood: Redefining the Color Line in Modern America, Counterpoint/Civitas, (in press), 98. **CONTACT ADDRESS** Dept Sociol, Harvard Univ, 33 Kirkland St, Cambridge, MA, 02138. **EMAIL** op@wjh.harvard.edu

PATTERSON, JAMES TYLER
PERSONAL Born 02/12/1935, Bridgeport, CT, 2 children **DISCIPLINE** HISTORY **EDUCATION** Williams Col, AB, 57; Harvard Univ, AM, 61, PhD, 64. **CAREER** From asst prof to prof hist, 64-72 chmn dept, 76-79, Ind Univ, Bloomington; Guggenheim fel, 69-70; NEH jr fel, 69, consult, 75-77; Am Hist Assn rep, Adv Comt to Nat Arch, 75-77; consult/reviewer, 75-80, Hist Bk Club; NEH fel, 79-80; Harmsworth prof Am hist, Univ Oxford, 81-82; prof hist, 90-, Ford Found, Brown Univ; John Adams Prof, Am Hist, 88-89, Univ Amsterdam; Pitt Prof of Amer Inst, 99-00, Cambridge Univ. **HONORS AND AWARDS** Frederick Jackson Turner Award, Orgn Am Historians, 66; Ohioana Award, Martha Kinney Cooper Ohioana Libr Assn, 73; Dr of Let, LaTrobe Univ, Melbourne, Australia, 97; Bancroft Prize in History, 97; Amer Acad of Arts & Sci, 97. **MEMBERSHIPS** AHA; Orgn Am Historians; Soc Am Historians. **SELECTED PUBLICATIONS** Auth, The Welfare State in America, 1930-1980, Brit Assn Am Studies, Pamphlet No 7, 81; auth, The Dread Disease: Cancer and Modern American Culture, Harvard Univ Press, 87; auth, Grand Expectations: The Unites States, 1945-1974, Oxford Univ Press, 96. **CONTACT ADDRESS** Dept of History, Brown Univ, Providence, RI, 02912. **EMAIL** james_patterson@brown.edu

PATTERSON, JOBY
PERSONAL Born 01/01/1942, Cheyenne, WY, m, 3 children **DISCIPLINE** ART HISTORY **EDUCATION** Univ CO, Boulder, BA (French & Psychol), 64, MA (Art Hist), 70; Babes-Bolyai Univ of Cluj, Romania, PhD (Art Hist), 98. **CAREER** Part-time, art history (adjunct fac), Eastern OR Univ, La Grande, OR, 80-95. **HONORS AND AWARDS** Smithsonian Res fel, Nat Museum of Am Art, Washington, DC, 90; Fulbright Res fel, Romania, 80-95. **MEMBERSHIPS** Soc of Architectural Hists; Nat and local (Marion D Ross) chapters, Soc for Romanian Studies. **RESEARCH** History of Am and European prints; Old Master prints; Mediaeval European Art/City Planning; history of Am and European architecture, esp vernacular and wooden architecture; Islamic architecture; Byzantine architecture and art. **SELECTED PUBLICATIONS** Auth, Hesychastic Thought as Revealed in Byzantine Greek and Romanian Frescoes: A Theory of Origin and Diffusion, Revue des Etudes Sud-Est Europeennnes, XVI:4 (Oct-Dec), 78; A Mediaeval Buddhist Bronze from Swat and Its Connections with Kashmir, Art and Archaeol Res Papers, vol 13, June 78; Romanian Folk Architecture: the Wood tradition, Festschrift (for Marion D Ross): A Collection of Essays on Architectural History, Northern Pacific Coast Chapter, Soc of Architectural Hists, 78; the Palace of the Lascarids at Nymphaeum, Abstracts of Papers, Fourth Annual Byzantine Studies Conference, 78; Contemporary Wooden Church Building in Maramures: Revision, Revival, or Renaissance?, Transylvanian Rev, V:1, spring 96; Bertha E Jacques and the Chicago Society of Etchers, Assoc Univ Presses, forthcoming 99; Romanian Wooden Churches from Mediaeval Maramures, East European Monographs, Columbia Univ Press, forthcoming 99; numerous other articles. **CONTACT ADDRESS** 402 Walnut St, La Grande, OR, 97850. **EMAIL** patterj@eou.edu

PATTERSON, KARL DAVID
PERSONAL Born 04/06/1941, Newport News, VA, m, 1963, 3 children **DISCIPLINE** AFRICAN HISTORY, MEDICAL HISTORY **EDUCATION** Syracuse Univ, BS, 63, MA, 67; Stanford Univ, PhD(hist), 71; Univ NC, Chapel Hill, MSPH, 82. **CAREER** Asst prof, 71-76, assoc prof, 76-80, Prof Hist, Univ NC, Charlotte, 80-. **MEMBERSHIPS** Am Asn Hist Med; African Studies Asn. **RESEARCH** Nineteenth and twentieth century western Africa; medical and demographic history; modern Ghana. **SELECTED PUBLICATIONS** Auth, The Northern Gabon Coast to 1875, Oxford Univ, 75; The vanishing Mpongwe: European contact and demographic change in the Gabon River, JAfrican Hist, Vol XVI, 75; The influenza epidemic of 1918-19 in the Gold Coast, Trans Hist Soc Ghana, Vol XVI, No 2; co-ed, History and Disease in Africa, 78 & auth, River blindness in the Northern Gold Coast, 1900-1950, In: History and Disease in Africa, 78, Duke Univ; Health in Urban Ghana: The case of Accra, 1900-1940, Soc Sci & Med, Vol 13; Veterinary dept and animal industry in the Gold Coast, 1909-1955, Int JAfrican Hist Studies, Vol 13, 80; Stalinism in The Ukraine in The 1940s - Marples,dr, Russian History-histoire Russe, Vol 0021, 1994; Health in Colonial Ghana: Disease, medicine and socio-economic change, 1900-1955, 81; Yellow-fever And Pubic-health in The New South - Ellis,jh, J of American History, Vol 0080, 1994; Mortality in Late Czarist Russia - a Reconnaissance, Social History of Medicine, Vol 0008, 1995; 1st Demographic Portraits of Russia, 1951-1990, Slavic Review, Vol 0054, 1995; Swing Low, Sweet Chariot - The Mortality Cost of Colonizing Liberia in The 19th-century - Mcdaniel,a, American Historical Review, Vol 0101, 1996. **CONTACT ADDRESS** Dept of Hist, Univ of NC, Charlotte, NC, 28213.

PATTERSON, RICHARD
DISCIPLINE ANCIENT PHILOSOPHY **EDUCATION** Univ PA, PhD, 75. **CAREER** Philos, Emory Univ. **HONORS AND AWARDS** Assoc mem, Am Sch Clas Studies, Athens, 74-75; Fel, Ctr Hellenic Studies, 78-79; Nat Ctr Hum Fel, 85-86; Fel, Inst Adv Study, 89; Dir, Prog Clas Studies, Emory Univ, 87-93. **SELECTED PUBLICATIONS** Auth, Image and Reality in Plato's Metaphysics; Aristotle's Modal Logic: Essence and Entailment in the Organon. **CONTACT ADDRESS** Emory Univ, Atlanta, GA, 30322-1950.

PATTERSON, ROBERT BENJAMIN
PERSONAL Born 04/30/1934, West Hartford, CT, m, 1960, 2 children **DISCIPLINE** MEDIEVAL HISTORY **EDUCATION** St Bernard's Sem & Col, BA, 56; Trinity Col, Conn, MA, 58; Johns Hopkins Univ, PhD(medieval hist), 62. **CAREER** From asst prof to assoc prof, 62-71, Prof Hist, Univ SC, 71-, Vis assoc prof, Univ Conn, 65-66; consult, Nat Endowment for Humanities, 71-73 & 76-77; lectr hist, Merton Col, Oxford Univ, 75-76. **MEMBERSHIPS** Conf Brit Studies; Pipe Roll Soc; Southern Hist Asn; AHA; Mediaeval Acad Am. **RESEARCH** The medieval Mediterranean and the Crusades; Anglo-Norman history in the 11th and 12th centuries. **SELECTED PUBLICATIONS** Ed, The early existence of the Funda and Catena in the twelfth-century Latin Kingdom of Jerusalem, Speculum, 64; William of Malmesbury's Robert of Gloucester: A reevaluation of the Historia Novella, Am Hist Rev, 65; Stephen's Shaftsbury Charter: Another case against William of Malmesbury, Speculum, 68; auth, An un-edited charter of Henry Fitz Empress and Earl William of Gloucester's comital status, English Hist Rev, 72; ed, Earldom of Gloucester to AD 1717, Clarendon, 73; auth, Anarchy in England 1135-54: the theory of the constitution, Albion, fall 74; Vassals and the earldom of Gloucester's scriptorium, J Nat Libr Wales, 78; Llandaff Episcopal Acta, 1140-1287 - Crouch,d, Editor, Speculum-a J of Medieval Studies, Vol 0067, 1992; Scribes And Scholars at Salisbury Cathedral, C.1075-c.1125 - Weber,t, American Historical Review, Vol 0099, 1994; King-john - Turner,rv, American Historical Review, Vol 0101, 1996. **CONTACT ADDRESS** Dept of Hist, Univ of SC, Columbia, SC, 29208.

PATTERSON, ROBERT LEYBURNE
PERSONAL Born 06/01/1932, Camden, NJ, m, 1960 **DISCIPLINE** HISTORY **EDUCATION** Yale Univ, BA, 53, MA, 55, PhD(hist), 60. **CAREER** From asst prof to assoc prof, 60-70, chmn dept soc sci, 63-69, coordr, 72-75; vis assoc prof hist, Dartmouth Col, 66-67; Nat Endowment for Humanities fel, 70-71; prof hist, 70-87, emeritus, 87-, Castleton State Col. **MEMBERSHIPS** Conf Brit Studies. **RESEARCH** Historiography and mythology of the Whig party; modern British intellectual class; social mobility. **CONTACT ADDRESS** Castleton, VT, 05735. **EMAIL** pattersr@sparrow.csc.vsc.edu

PATTERSON, SAMUEL C.
PERSONAL Born 11/20/1931, Omaha, NE, m, 1956, 3 children **DISCIPLINE** POLITICAL SCIENCE **EDUCATION** Univ SD, BA 53; Univ WI, MS 56, PhD 59. **CAREER** OH State Univ, prof emer 98-, prof 86-98; Univ IA, Carver Distg prof 85-86, asst prof 61-85; OK State Univ, asst prof 59-61. **HONORS AND AWARDS** Phi Eta Sigma; Phi Beta Kappa; Phi Kappa Phi; M l Huit teach Awd; Hon Deg Doctor Of Humane Letters; Richard F Fenno Prize; Distg Scholar Awd; Fulbright Bologna Italy; Listed in Who's Who in Am; Amer Men and Women of Sci; Who's Who in the Midwest; Contemporary Authors; World Who's Who of Authors. **MEMBERSHIPS** IPSA; APSA; MPSA. **RESEARCH** Comp polit institutions, parliaments and legislatures, polit leadership. **SELECTED PUBLICATIONS** Senates and the Theory of Bicameralism, in: S C Patterson & A Mughan, eds, Senates: Bicameralism in the Contemporary World, OH State Univ Press, forthcoming; Parliaments and Legislatures, in: G T Kurian, ed, World Encyclopedia of Parliaments and Legislatures, Congress Quart Press, Wash, forthcoming; Congress and Gun Control, in: J M Bruce & C Wilcox, eds, The Changing Politics of Gun Control, Rowman and Littlefield, MD, 98; many publ(s). **CONTACT ADDRESS** Dept of Polit Sci, Ohio State Univ, 2140 Derby Hall, Columbus, OH, 43210-1373. **EMAIL** spatte@ohstmvsa.acs.ohio-state.edu

PATTERSON, STEPHEN EVERETT
PERSONAL Born 02/15/1937, Fredericton, NB, Canada, m, 1963, 2 children **DISCIPLINE** AMERICAN HISTORY **EDUCATION** Univ NB, Fredericton, BA, 59; Univ Wis, Madison, MA, 61, PhD(hist), 68. **CAREER** Lectr hist, Univ NB, St John, 64-66; from asst prof to assoc prof, 66-78, Prof Hist, Univ NB, Fredericton, 78-. **MEMBERSHIPS** Can Asn Am Studies; Orgn Am Historians; Can Asn Univ Teachers; Atlantic Asn Hist. **RESEARCH** American Revolution; Colonial America. **SELECTED PUBLICATIONS** Auth, Political Parties in Revolutionary Massachusetts, Univ Wis, 73; Ratification of The Constitution by The States - Virginia - Kaminski,jp, Saladino,gj, Canadian Review of American Studies, Vol 0023, 1993; Indian-white Relations in Nova-scotia, 1749-61 - a Study in Political Interaction, Acadiensis, Vol 0023, 1993; Ratifying The Constitution - Gillespie,ma, Lienesch,m, Canadian Review of American Studies, Vol 0023, 1993. **CONTACT ADDRESS** Dept of Hist, Univ of NB, Fredericton, NB, E3B 5A3.

PATTERSON, WAYNE KIEF
PERSONAL Born 12/20/1946, Philadelphia, PA, m, 1977 **DISCIPLINE** HISTORY, INTERNATIONAL RELATIONS **EDUCATION** Swarthmore Col, BA, 68; Univ Pa, MA, 69 & 74, PhD(int rels), 77. **CAREER** Teaching fel hist, Univ Pa, 69-71 & int rels, 71-73; lectr hist & polit sci, Univ Md, 74-75; asst prof hist, St Norbert Col, 77-. **MEMBERSHIPS** Asn Asian Studies; Int Studies Asn; Immigration Hist Soc; AHA; Soc Historians of Am Foreign Relat. **RESEARCH** Korean immigration to, and Koreans in, America; Korean-American relations; modern Korean and East Asian history. **SELECTED PUBLICATIONS** Co-ed, The Koreans in America, 1882-1974: A Chronology and Fact Book, Oceana, 74; coauth, The Koreans in America, Lerner, 77; auth, The First Attempt to Obtain Korean Laborers for Hawaii, 1896-1897, Korean Diaspora, 77; The Divided East Asian Nations: A Comparative Approach to Partition in China, Korea and Vietnama Research Note, Asian Forum, 79; Horace Allen and Korean Immigration to Hawaii, In: The United States and Korea, Western Mich Univ, 79; Upward social Mobility of the Koreans in Hawaii, Korean Studies, 79; Sugar-Coated Diplomacy: Horace Allen and Korean Immigration to Hawaii, 1902-1905, Diplomatic Hist, 79; Chosenjin no Hawai iju to Nihon, Sanzenri, 80; Japan in Transition: The Meiji Mind in Thought and Action, 1868-1912, Assoc Univ Presses, Inc, 82. **CONTACT ADDRESS** Dept of Hist, St Norbert Col, 100 Grant St, De Pere, WI, 54115-2099. **EMAIL** pattwk@sucac.suc.edu

PATTERSON, WILLIS CHARLES
PERSONAL Born 11/27/1930, Ann Arbor, MI, m **DISCIPLINE** MUSIC **EDUCATION** University of Michigan, MusB, M Mus; PhD, Higher Education. **CAREER** Southern Univ, Baton Rouge, LA, 1959-61; Virginia State College, associate professor, 1962-68; Univ of Michigan, professor, 1977; Univ of Michigan, School of Music, associate dean, 1979; Major, Our Own Thing Inc, performer; Univ of Michigan School of Music, associate dean/prof of voice. **HONORS AND AWARDS** Compiled "Anthology of Art Songs by Black Amer Composers", Edward B Marks Music Corp, 1977; Recorded with: RCA Victor, Philips Records, NBC, BBC. **MEMBERSHIPS** National Opera Assn; National Assn Teachers Singing; Alpha Phi Alpha; NAACP; Natl Assn of Negro Musicians; Natl Black Music Caucus. **CONTACT ADDRESS** Univ of Michigan, Ann Arbor, 3028 Moore - Music Bldg, Ann Arbor, MI, 48109-2085.

PATTON, GERALD WILSON
PERSONAL Born 11/13/1947, Chattanooga, Tennessee, m **DISCIPLINE** EDUCATION **EDUCATION** Kentucky State Univ, BA 1969; Western Illinois Univ, MA 1973; Univ of Iowa, PhD 1978. **CAREER** North Carolina State Univ, asst prof history 1978; Washington Univ, asst dean of graduate school of arts & science 1978-81; North Central Assn of Colleges & Schools, assoc dir, commission on institutions of higher education, currently. **HONORS AND AWARDS** Congressional Black Caucus Found Scholars lecturer 1984. **MEMBERSHIPS** Coordinator "St Louis A Policy Framework for Racial Justice, an Agenda for the 80's" sponsored by the Danforth Found 1984-85; chmn Educ Comm 100 Black Men of St Louis 1983-; chmn MO Comm of Black Studies 1984-. **SELECTED PUBLICATIONS** "War and Race, Black Officer in the Amer Military" 1981; **CONTACT ADDRESS** Commission on Institutions of Higher Education, North Central Association of Cols & Schools, 159 N Dearborn, Chicago, IL, 60601.

PAUL, GEORGE MACKAY
PERSONAL Born 07/16/1927, Glasgow, Scotland, m, 1956, 3 children **DISCIPLINE** CLASSICS, ANCIENT HISTORY **EDUCATION** Oxford Univ, BA & MA, 54; Univ London, PhD(classics), 63. **CAREER** From asst lectr to lectr classics, Univ W Indies, 55-64; from asst prof to assoc prof, 64-70, chmn dept, 73-76, Prof Classics, McMaster Univ, 70, Mem, Comt Coord Acad Libr Serv Ont Univs, 66-67; Can Coun leave fel, 71-72. **MEMBERSHIPS** Class Asn Can (treas, 67-69); Am Philol Asn; Soc Prom Roman Studies; Asn Ancient Historians; Soc Prom Hellenic Studies. **RESEARCH** Greek and Roman historiography; Roman history. **SELECTED PUBLICATIONS** Auth, Sallust, In: Latin Historians, Routledge & Kegan Paul, 66; Oxford Classical Dictionary, Oxford Univ, 70 & Encycl Britannica, 74; Josephus And Judaean Politics - Schwartz,s, American J of Philology, Vol 0114, 1993. **CONTACT ADDRESS** Dept of Classics, McMaster Univ, 1280 Main St W, Hamilton, ON, L8S 4M2.

PAUL, HARRY W.
PERSONAL Born 09/21/1933, m, 1958, 2 children **DISCIPLINE** MODERN EUROPEAN RELIGIOUS & INTELLECTUAL HISTORY **EDUCATION** Univ Nfld, BA, 54; Columbia Univ, MA, 58, PhD(hist), 62. **CAREER** Asst prof hist, Md State Col, 62-63 & Newark State Col, 63- 66; assoc prof, 66-73, Prof Hist, Univ FL, 73-, Nat Endowment for Humanities fel, 71-72; NSF grants soc sci, 77 & 81. **MEMBERSHIPS** Soc Fr Hist Studies; AHA; Soc Mod Hist, France; Am Cath Hist Asn; Hist Sci Soc. **RESEARCH** Intellectual history; religious history; history of science. **SELECTED PUBLICATIONS** Auth, The Second Ralliement: The Rapprochement Between Church and State in France in the 20th Century, Cath Univ Am, 67; The Sorcerer's Apprentice: The French Scientist's Image of German Science, 1840-1919, Univ Fla, 72; Religion and Darwinism, In: The Comparative Reception of Darwinism, Univ Tex, 74; The Edge of Contingency: French Catholic Reactions to Scientific Change from Darwin to Duhem, Univ Fla, 79; Apollo courts the Vulcans: The applied science institutes in nineteenth-century French science faculties, In: The Organization of Science and Technology in France, 1808-1914, Cambridge Univ Press, 80; The role and reception of monographs in nineteenth-century French science, In: Development of Science Pubishing in Europe, Elsevier, 80; coauth (with T W Shinn), The state and structure of science in France, Contemp Fr Civilization, fall 81-winter 82; The Urban Wine Growers - Maconnais And Chalonnais 1848-1914 - French - Goujon,p, American Historical Review, Vol 0099, 1994; Nature, The Exotic, And The Science of French Colonialism - Osborne,ma, American Historical Review, Vol 0100, 1995; Approaching Hysteria - Disease And Its Interpretations - Micale,ms, J of Modern History, Vol 0068, 1996. **CONTACT ADDRESS** Dept of Hist, Univ of Fla, Gainesville, FL, 32611.

PAUL, JUSTUS F.
PERSONAL Born 05/27/1938, Boonville, MO, m, 1960, 3 children **DISCIPLINE** RECENT UNITED STATES HISTORY **EDUCATION** Doane Col, AB, 59; Univ Wis-Madison, MA, 60; Univ Nebr, PhD(hist), 66. **CAREER** Instr, High Sch, Wis, 60-62; instr hist, Univ Nebr, 63-64 & 65-66; from asst prof to assoc prof, 66-75, prof hist, Univ Wis-Stevens Point, 75-, chemn dept, 69-86, dean Col Of Letters & Sci, 86-, Res grants, Univ Wis, 66-67, 68-69, 76 & 77 & 79-79; Am Asn State & Local Hist res grant, 68-69; Nat Endowment for Humanities, summer 78. **HONORS AND AWARDS** Univ Sci Award, 84; Win Rothman Local Hist Award, 96; Paul Kersenbrok Humanitarian Ward, 96. **MEMBERSHIPS** AHA; Orgn Am Historians; State Hist Soc Wis; Nebr State Hist Soc. **RESEARCH** Political history; Midwestern state and local history. **SELECTED PUBLICATIONS** Auth, Senator Hugh Butler and Nebraska Republicanism, Nebr State Hist Soc, 76; The World is Ours: A History of the University of Wisconsin-Stevens Point, 1894-1994, UWSP Foundation, 94; ed, Selected Writings of Rhys W Hays, Palmer Printers, 77; co-ed, The Badger State: A Documentary History of Wisconsin, Wm B Eerdmans, 79. **CONTACT ADDRESS** Dept of History, Univ Wisconsin, Stevens Point, 2100 Main St, Stevens Point, WI, 54481-3897. **EMAIL** jpaul@wsp.edu

PAULEY, BRUCE F
PERSONAL Born 11/04/1937, Lincoln, NE, m, 1963, 2 children **DISCIPLINE** CENTRAL EUROPEAN HISTORY **EDUCATION** Grinnell Col, BA, 59; Univ Nebr, MA, 61; Univ Rochester, PhD(hist), 66. **CAREER** Instr hist, Col Wooster, 64-65 & Univ Nebr, 65-66; asst prof, Univ Wyo, 66-71; assoc prof, 71-77, Prof Hist, Univ Cent FL, 77-, Vis instr hist, Col William & Mary, 75. **MEMBERSHIPS** Conf Group Cent Europ Hist; AHA; Western Asn Ger Studies. **RESEARCH** Hahnenschwanz and Swastika; The Styrian Heimatschutz and Austrian National Socialism, 1918-1934. **SELECTED PUBLICATIONS** Auth, The Habsburg Legacy, 1867-1939, Holt, 72 & Krieger, 77; Hahnenschwanz und Hakensreuz: der Steirische Heimatschutz und der Osterreichisch Nationalsozialismus, 1918-1934, Europa, 72; The Patchwork Treaties: St Germain and Trianon reconsidered, Rocky Mountain Soc Sci J, 72; A case study in Fascism: The Styrian Heimatschutz and Austrian National Socialism, In: Austrian History Yearbook, 78; Nazis and Fascists: The struggle for Austria, 1918-1938, In: Who Were the Fascists? Social Roots of European and the Forgotten Nazis, Univ NC, Chapel Hill, 79; From splinter party to mass movement: The Austrian Nazi breakthrough, Ger Studies Rev, 79; Fascism and the Fuehrerprinzip: The Austrian example, Cent Europ Hist, 79; Hitler and the forgotten Nazis: A history of Austrian National Socialism, Macmillan & NC, 82; Himmler Auxiliaries - The Volksdeutsche-mittelstelle And The German National Minorities of Europe, 1933-1945 - Lumans,vo, American Historical Review, Vol 0099, 1994; For The Soul of The People - Protestant Protest Against Hitler - Barnett,v, German Studies Review, Vol 0017, 1994. **CONTACT ADDRESS** Dept of Hist, Univ Cent Fla, P O Box 161350, Orlando, FL, 32816-1350.

PAULI, LORI
PERSONAL Guelph, ON, Canada **DISCIPLINE** ARTS HISTORIAN **EDUCATION** Univ Waterloo, BA, 82; Queen's Univ, MA, 90. **CAREER** Cur, York Sunbury Hist Soc Mus; tchr, dept art, Queen's Univ; asst cur, Photographs, Nat Gallery Can. **SELECTED PUBLICATIONS** Auth, Disciple of the American Dream: Listte Model in The World and I 4 vol.7; auth, Silent Communion: Christel Gang and Edward Weston in History of Photography 2 vol.19; auth, A Few Hellers: Women at the Clarence H. White School of Photography in Margaret Watkins 1884-1969 Photographs, 94. **CONTACT ADDRESS** Photographs Collection, National Gallery of Canada, 380 Sussex Dr, Ottawa, ON, K1N 9N4. **EMAIL** lpauli@ngc.cwn.gc.ca

PAUWELS, HEIDI
PERSONAL Belgium **DISCIPLINE** ASIAN STUDIES **EDUCATION** Univ Washington, PhD, 94. **CAREER** Lectr, School of Oriental and African Studies, 94-97; Asst Prof, Univ Washington, 97-. **HONORS AND AWARDS** Fulbright to study at Univ Wash; Grant from Belgian Embassy for 1 yr field work in India. **MEMBERSHIPS** AAR; AOS; AAS **RESEARCH** Hinduism (Bhakti/Hagiography/Reworking of Scripture); Gender issues; Hindi Lit. **SELECTED PUBLICATIONS** Auth, Krishna's Round Dance Reconsidered **CONTACT ADDRESS** Dept Asian Language & Literature, Univ of Washington, Seattle, WA, 98195-3521.

PAXTON, FREDERICK S.
DISCIPLINE HISTORY **EDUCATION** Michigan State Univ, BA; Univ Wash, MA; Univ Calif at Berkeley, PhD. **CAREER** Assoc prof; Conn Col, 85-; vis prof, Chalice of Repose Proj in Missoula, Mont. **MEMBERSHIPS** Amer Coun Learned Soc, Yale Univ, Mellon Found, Fulbright Comn & Camargo Found, grants and fel(s). **RESEARCH** Medieval European cultural history; Ritual, Medicine, and Religion; Historical context of Music-Thanatology. **SELECTED PUBLICATIONS** Auth, Christianizing Death: The Creation of a Ritual Process in Early Medieval Europe, 90; A Medieval Latin Death Ritual: The Monastic Customaries of Bernard and Ulrich of Cluny, 93; Liturgy and Anthropology, 93. **CONTACT ADDRESS** Dept of History, Connecticut Col, 270 Mohegan Ave, Box 5063, New London, CT, 06320. **EMAIL** fspax@conncoll.edu

PAXTON, ROBERT O.
DISCIPLINE MODERN EUROPEAN AND FRENCH HISTORY **EDUCATION** Univ Wash, BA, 54; Oxford Univ, BA, 56; Harvard Univ, PhD, 63. **CAREER** Prof. **SELECTED PUBLICATIONS** Auth, Parades and Politics, in Vichy, 66; Vichy France: Old Guard and New Order, 72; co-auth, Vichy and the Jews, 81; co-ed, United States, 95; Europe in the Twentieth Century, 97. **CONTACT ADDRESS** Dept of Hist, Columbia Col, New York, 2960 Broadway, New York, NY, 10027-6902.

PAXTON, ROBERT OWEN
PERSONAL Born 06/15/1932, Lexington, VA, m **DISCIPLINE** EUROPEAN HISTORY **EDUCATION** Washington & Lee Univ, AB, 54; Oxford Univ, BA, 56, MA, 61; Harvard Univ, PhD, 63. **CAREER** From acting instr to asst prof hist, Univ Calif, Berkeley, 61-67; assoc prof, State Univ NY Stony Brook, 67-69; PROF HIST, COLUMBIA UNIV, 69-, chmn dept, 80-82; Am Coun Learned Soc fel, 74-75; Rockefeller Found fel, 78-79; German Marshall Fund fel, 85. **HONORS AND AWARDS** DLitt, Washington & Lee Univ, 74. **MEMBERSHIPS** Fel Am Acad Arts & Lett. **RESEARCH** Modern France; Fascism. **SELECTED PUBLICATIONS** Auth, Parades and Politics at Vichy, Princeton Univ, 66; Vichy France: Old Guard and New Order, 1940-44, Knopf, 72, Fr ed & Span ed, 73; Europe Since 1914, Harcourt, Brace & Jovanovich, 75, 3rd ed, 96; Vichy France and the Jews, Basic Bks, 81, Fr ed, 81; DeGaulle and the United States, 95; French Peasant Fascism, Oxford, 96. **CONTACT ADDRESS** Dept of Hist, Columbia Univ, 2960 Broadway, New York, NY, 10027-6900. **EMAIL** rop1@columbia.edu

PAYNE, DEBORAH C.
DISCIPLINE SEVENTEENTH- AND EIGHTEENTH-CENTURY STUDIES **EDUCATION** UCLA, PhD. **CAREER** Assoc prof, Am Univ; univ rep, Folger Institute. **HONORS AND AWARDS** Distinguished Tchg Award, Am Univ, 92. **RESEARCH** Seventeenth- and eighteenth-century studies **SELECTED PUBLICATIONS** Co-ed, Cult Readings Restoration & Eighteenth-Century Eng Theatre, 96. **CONTACT ADDRESS** American Univ, 4400 Massachusetts Ave, Washington, DC, 20016. **EMAIL** dcpayne@ibm.net

PAYNE, HARRY CHARLES
PERSONAL Born 03/25/1947, Worcester, MA **DISCIPLINE** MODERN EUROPEAN & EUROPEAN INTELLECTUAL HISTORY **EDUCATION** Yale Univ, BA & MA, 69, MPhil, 70, PhD, 73. **CAREER** From instr to asst prof, 73-78, assoc prof, 78-82, Prof Hist, Colgate Univ, 82-, Adv ed Europ hist, Eighteenth-Century Studies, 77; assoc ed, Eighteenth-Century Life, 77; overseas fel, Churchill Col, Cambridge Univ, 77. **HONORS AND AWARDS** Article Prize, Am Soc Eighteenth-Century Studies, 77. **MEMBERSHIPS** Am Soc Eighteenth-Century Studies. **RESEARCH** French enlightenment; European intellectual history, 1880- 1914; ritual in modernizing Europe, 1800-1945. **SELECTED PUBLICATIONS** Auth, Elite vs popular mentality in the eighteenth century, Hist Reflections, 75; Pauvrete, misere and the aims of enlightened economics, Studies on Voltaire & the 18th Century, 76; The Philosophes and the People, Yale Univ, 76; Modernizing the Ancients: The Reconstruction of Ritual Drama 1870-1920, Proc Am Philos Soc, 77; The novel as social history: A methodological reflection, Hist Teacher, 77; Rituals of balance and silence: The ideal Theater of Gordon Craig, Bull Res Humanities, 79; ed, Studies in Eighteenth-Century Culture, Vols 10-12, Univ Wis Press, 81-83; Malinowski's Style, Proc Am Philos Soc, 81. **CONTACT ADDRESS** Dept of Hist, Colgate Univ, Hamilton, NY, 13346.

PAYNE, STANLEY GEORGE
PERSONAL Born 09/09/1934, Denton, TX, m, 1961 **DISCIPLINE** MODERN EUROPEAN HISTORY **EDUCATION** Pac Union Col, BA, 55; Claremont Grad Sch, MA, 57; Columbia Univ, PhD, 60. **CAREER** Instr mod Europ hist, Univ Minn, 60-62; from asst prof to prof, Univ Calif, Los Angeles, 62-68; PROF MOD EUROP HIST, UNIV WIS-MADISON, 68-; Lectr, Columbia Col, 59-60; instr, Hunter Col, 60; Am Philos Soc grant, 61, 67; Soc Sci Res Coun grant, 61; Guggenheim fel, 62-63; mem exec comt, Coun Europ Studies, 76-78. **MEMBERSHIPS** Soc Span & Port Hist Studies; Ital Hist Soc; AHA. **RESEARCH** Modern west European history; Spanish history. **SELECTED PUBLICATIONS** Auth, Falange: A History of Spanish Fascism, Stanford Univ, 61; coauth, Modern Times: Europe since 1815, Heath, 64; auth, Politics and the Military in Modern Spain, Stanford Univ, 67; Franco's Spain, Crowell, 67; The Spanish Revolution, Norton, 70; A History of Spain and Portugal (2 vols), Univ Wis, 73; Basque Nationalism, Univ Nev, 75; Fascism: Comparison and Definition, Univ Wis, 80; The Franco Regime 1936-1975, Univ Wis, 87; A History of Fascism, 1914-1945, Univ Wis, 95. **CONTACT ADDRESS** Dept of Hist, Univ of Wis, 455 North Park St, Madison, WI, 53706-1483. **EMAIL** spayn@macc.wisc.edu

PAZDERNIK, CHARLES
PERSONAL Born 07/03/1968, Breckenridge, MN, m, 1996 **DISCIPLINE** CLASSICS **EDUCATION** Cornell Univ, BA summa cum laude 90; Oxford Univ, Mphil 92; Princeton Univ, MA 95, PhD 97. **CAREER** NY Univ Law Sch, Samuel I. Golieb Fel, 97-98; Brooklyn College, adj prof, 98; Emory Univ Law Sch, Mellon post doc fel, 98-. **HONORS AND AWARDS** Phi Beta Kappa; Telluride Sch; Stanley Seeger Fel; Princeton Grad Fel. **MEMBERSHIPS** APA. **RESEARCH** Ancient law; classical historiography; late antiquity; epic poetry. **SELECTED PUBLICATIONS** Auth, Justinian's Novels and the law of succession, in: The Transformation in Law and Society in Late Antiquity Proceedings of Shifting Frontiers II, ed, R. Mathisen, forthcoming; Odysseus and his audience: Odyssey 9.30-40 and its formulatic resonance's, The Amer Jour of Philology, 95; Our most pious consort given us by God': Dissident reactions to the partnership of Justinian and Theodora AD 525-48, Classical Antiquity, 94. **CONTACT ADDRESS** Dept of Classics, Emory Univ, N404G Callaway Ct, Atlanta, GA, 30322. **EMAIL** cpazder@emory.edu

PEABODY, SUSAN
DISCIPLINE EARLY MODERN EUROPEAN **EDUCATION** Univ Iowa, PhD, 93. **CAREER** Asst prof, Washington State Univ. **RESEARCH** Comparative history of slavery, history and multimedia. **SELECTED PUBLICATIONS** Auth, There are No Slaves in France: The Political Culture of Race and Slavery in the Ancient Regime, Oxford UP, 96. **CONTACT ADDRESS** Dept of History, Washington State Univ, 301 Wilson Hall, PO Box 644030, Pullman, WA, 99164-4030. **EMAIL** peabody@vancouver.wsu.edu

PEARCE, JAMES
DISCIPLINE GREEK AND LATIN LANGUAGE AND LITERATURE **EDUCATION** Baylor Univ, BA; Univ TX-Austin, MA, PhD. **CAREER** Prof,68-, Trinity Univ. **RESEARCH** Pastoral poetry. **SELECTED PUBLICATIONS** Auth, The Eclogues of Calpurnius Siculus, 90; The Eclogues of Nemesian and the Einsiedeln Manuscript, 92. **CONTACT ADDRESS** Dept of Class, Trinity Univ, 715 Stadium Dr, San Antonio, TX, 78212.

PEARSON, BIRGER ALBERT
PERSONAL Born 09/17/1934, Turlock, CA, m, 1966, 5 children **DISCIPLINE** HISTORY OF RELIGION **EDUCATION** Upsala Col, BA, 57; Univ Calif, Berkeley, MA, 59; Pac Lutheran Sem, BDiv, 62; Harvard Univ, PhD(Christian origins), 68. **CAREER** Instr Greek, chmn dept, 76-79, Pac Lutheran Sem, 59-62; lectr New Testament, Episcopal Theol Sch, 65-66; from instr to asst prof relig, Duke Univ, 66-69; from asst prof to assoc prof relig studies, 69-75, assoc dir, Educ Abroad Prog, 74-76, chmn dept, 76-80, Prof Relig Studies, Univ Calif, Santa Barbara, 75-, Fel, Humanities Inst, Univ Calif, 70-71, 72-73; Am Philos Asn grant, 72; dir, Univ Calif Study Ctr, Lund, Sweden,79-81. **MEMBERSHIPS** Soc Bibl Lit; Am Acad Relig; Archaeol Inst Am; Soc New Testament Studies; Soc Coptic Archaeol. **RESEARCH** Gnosticism; Early Christianity; Hellenistic religions. **SELECTED PUBLICATIONS** Auth, I Thessalonians 2:13-16: A Deutero-Pauline interpretation, Harvard Theol Rev, 71; Jewish Haggadic traditions in The Testimony of Truth From Nag Hammandi, In: Ex Orbe Religionum, Brill, 72; The Pneumatikos-Psychikos Terminology in I Corinthians, Soc Bibl Lit, 73, Scholars, 76; ed & transl, The Gnostic Attitude, Univ Calif Inst Relig Studies, 73; ed & contribr, Religious Syncretism in Antiquity, Scholars, 75; contribr, The Nag Hammadi Library in English, BrillHarper, 77; auth, The figure of Norea in Gnostic literature, In: Proceedings of the International Colloquium on Gnosticism, Stockholm, 1973, Almqvist & Wiksell, 77; Nag Hammadi Codices IX and X, Brill, 81; The New Alexandria Library - Promise or Threat, Biblical Archaeologist, Vol 0056, 1993; The New Alexandria Library - an Update, Biblical Archaeologist, Vol 0056, 1993; The Gospel According to The Jesus-seminar + a Methodological Assessment of The Quest For The Historical Jesus, Religion, Vol 0025, 1995; 2-peter, Jude - a New Translation With Introduction And Commentary - Neyrey,jh, J of Biblical Literature, Vol 0114, 1995. **CONTACT ADDRESS** Dept of Relig Studies, Univ of Calif, Santa Barbara, CA, 93106.

PEARSON, EDWARD
DISCIPLINE HISTORY **EDUCATION** Birmingham, BA, 80; Bowling Green State, MA, 83; Univ Wis-Madison, PhD, 92. **CAREER** ASST PROF, HIST, FRANKLIN & MARSHALL **MEMBERSHIPS** Am Antiquarian Soc **CONTACT ADDRESS** 303 N West End Dr, Lancaster, PA, 17603.

PEARSON, SAMUEL C.
PERSONAL Born 12/10/1931, Dallas, TX, m, 1955, 2 children **DISCIPLINE** HISTORY OF CHRISTIANITY **EDUCATION** TX Christian Univ, AB, 51; Univ Chicago, DB, 53, MA, 60, PhD, 64. **CAREER** Asst prof, 64-69, assoc prof, 69-74, prof, hist stud, 74-, dept chmn, 72-77 & 81-83, act dir, 86-87, Reg Res & Develop Serv, Dean, Sch of Soc Sci, 83-95, dean emeritus, 95-, Southern Ill Univ. **HONORS AND AWARDS** Phi Eta Sigma; Phi Kappa Phi (Emeritus Lifetime Member); Phi Alpha Theta; Outstanding Foreign Expert Northeast Normal Univ, 95, appointed vis prof, 96; Nat Endowment for the Hum Sum Sem grants to Yale Univ, 76, and Univ Hawaii, 98. **MEMBERSHIPS** Am Soc Church Hist; Am Hist Asn; Org of Am Hist; Am Academy of Relig. **RESEARCH** Religions in the modern world. **SELECTED PUBLICATIONS** Auth, From Church to Denomination: American Congregationalism in the Nineteenth Century, Church Hist, XXXVIII, 69; auth, Enlightenment Influence on Protestant Thought in Early National America, Encounter, XXXVII, 77; auth, The Great Awakening and Its Impact on American History, Forum Press, 78; auth, The Campbell Institute: Herald of the Transformation of an American Religious Tradition, The Scroll, LXII, 78; auth, Rationalism in an Age of Enthusiasm: The Anomalous Career of Robert Cave, The Bul of MO Hist Soc, XXXV, 79; auth, The Cave Affair: Protestant Thought in the Guilded Age, Encounter, XLI, 80; auth, The Religion of John Locke and the Character of His Thought, John Locke: Critical Assessments, 4 vols, Routledge, 91; Alexander Campbell, 1788-1866, Makers of Christian Theology in America, Abingdon Press, 97. **CONTACT ADDRESS** Dept of Historical Studies, Southern Illinois Univ, Edwardsville, IL, 62026-1454. **EMAIL** spearso@siue.edu

PEARSON, THOMAS SPENCER
PERSONAL Born 09/19/1949, Rockville Center, NY, m, 1971 **DISCIPLINE** RUSSIAN HISTORY, NINETEENTH CENTURY EUROPE **EDUCATION** Univ Santa Clara, BA, 71; Univ NC, MA, 73, PhD(Russ hist), 77. **CAREER** Asst prof Russ & world hist, Auburn Univ, 77-78; Asst Prof Russ & Europ Hist, Monmouth Col, 78-. **MEMBERSHIPS** AHA; Am Asn Advan Slavic Studies; Southern Conf Slavic Studies. **RESEARCH** Imperial Russian administrative and social history; Russian intellectual history. **SELECTED PUBLICATIONS** Soviet State And Society Between Revolutions, 1918-1929 - Siegelbaum,lh, Historian, Vol 0056, 1994. **CONTACT ADDRESS** Dept of Hist, Monmouth Univ, 400 Cedar Ave, West Long Branch, NJ, 07764-1898.

PEASE, JANE HANNA
PERSONAL Born 11/26/1929, Waukegan, IL, m, 1950 **DISCIPLINE** AMERICAN HISTORY **EDUCATION** Smith Col, AB, Univ Rochester, MA, 57, PhD(hist), 69; Western Reserve Univ, MS, 58. **CAREER** Instr hist, Emma Willard Sch, 55-64, chmn dept, 63-64; lectr, Univ Calgary, 64-65, instr, 65-66; from instr to assoc prof, 66-79, Prof Hist, Univ Maine, Orono, 79-, Am Coun Learned Soc grant-in-aid, 65; Am Philos Soc grants-in-aid, 66 & 73; Nat Endowment for Humanities res grant, 80-82; Nat Sci Found res grant, 81-82. **MEMBERSHIPS** AHA; Orgn Am Historians; Southern Hist Asn; New Eng Hist Asn (pres, 75-76); Soc Historians Early Am Republic. **RESEARCH** Nineteenth century American social history; antebellum urban history. **SELECTED PUBLICATIONS** Coauth, Black Utopia: Negro communal experiments in America, Wis State Hist Soc, 63; co-ed, Anti-Slavery Argument, Bobbs, 65; coauth, Bound With Them In Chains: A Biographical History of the Antislavery Movement, Greenwood, 72; They Who Would Be Free: Blacks' Search for Freedom, 1830-1861, Athenum, 74; The Fugitive Slave Law and Anthony Burns: A Problem in Law Enforcement, Lippincott, 75; Paternal Dilemmas: Education, property, and patrician persistence in Jacksonian Boston, New England Quart, 80; The economics and politics of Charleston's nullification crisis, J Southern Hist, 881; Social structure and the potential for urban change: Boston and Charleston in the 1830's, J Urban Hist, 82; The Advocates of Peace in Antebellum America - Ziegler,vh, J of Southern History, Vol 0059, 1993; Fuller,margaret - an American Romantic Life, Vol 1, The Private Years - Capper,c, American Historical Review, Vol 0099, 1994; The 1st Woman in The Repubic - a Cultural Biography of Child,lydia,maria - Karcher,cl, Reviews in American History, Vol 0023, 1995. **CONTACT ADDRESS** Dept of Hist, Univ of Maine, 205 E Annex, Orono, ME, 04473.

PEASE, OTIS ARNOLD
PERSONAL Born 07/31/1925, Pittsfield, MA, m, 1949, 4 children **DISCIPLINE** HISTORY **EDUCATION** Yale Univ, BA, 49, PhD, 54. **CAREER** Instr hist, Univ Tex, 53-55; asst prof, Univ Wash, 55-56; from asst prof to assoc prof, Stanford Univ, 56-64, W R Coe prof hist & Am studies, 64-66; chmn dept hist, 67-72, Prof Am Hist, Univ Wash, 66-, Soc Sci Res Coun res fel, 62-63; Phi Beta Kappa scholar, 68-69, lectr, 76-; mem bd trustees, Stanford Univ, 69-; mem, Nat Advert Rev Bd, 71-75. **MEMBERSHIPS** AHA (vp prof div, 78-); Orgn Am Historians; Am Studies Asn. **RESEARCH** American political, social and intellectual history; American historiography. **SELECTED PUBLICATIONS** Auth, Parkman's History: The Historian as Literary Artist, 53 & Responsibilities of American Advertising, 1920-1940, 58, Yale Univ; ed, Progressive Years, Braziller, 62; The City, Univ Wash, 67; auth, Leland Stanford, Stanford Mag, No 2, 674; Teaching Americans to Consume, In: Advertising

and the Pubic, Univ Ill, 79; Parkman,francis, Historian as Hero - The Formative Years - Jacobs,wr, Pacific Northwest Quarterly, Vol 0084, 1993. **CONTACT ADDRESS** Dept of Hist DP-20, Univ of Wash, Seattle, WA, 98195.

PECK, WILLIAM HENRY
PERSONAL Born 10/02/1932, Savannah, GA, m, 1967, 3 children **DISCIPLINE** ART & EGYPTIAN HISTORY **EDUCATION** Wayne State Univ, BFA, 60, MA, 61. **CAREER** Jr cur, 60-62, from asst cur to assoc cur, 62-68, Cur Ancient Art, Detroit Inst Arts, 68-, Lectr art hist, Cranbrook Acad, Bloomfield Hills, Mich, 62-65; field archaeologist, Inst Fine Arts, NY Univ-Am Res Ctr Egypt, excavation at Mendes, Egypt, 64-66; adJprof art hist, Wayne State Univ, 66-; vis lectr, Univ Mich, 70; field archaeologist, Brooklyn Mus Theban Exped-Mut Temple Project, Egypt, 78-. **MEMBERSHIPS** Archaeol Inst Am; Am Asn Mus; Int Asn Egyptologists. **SELECTED PUBLICATIONS** Auth, Mummy Portraits from Roman Egypt, Detroit Inst Arts, 67; The present state of Egyptian art in Detroit, Connoisseur, 1270; A seated statue of Amun, J Egyptian Archaeol, 71; A ramesside ruler offers incense, J Near Eastern Studies, 172; Drawings from Ancient Egypt, Thames & Hudson, 78, Ger trans, 79 & Fr trans, 80; Ancient art in Detroit, Archaeol, 578; ; The constant lure, In: Ancient Egypt: Discovering its Splendors, Nat Geog Soc, 78; contribr, Mummies of ancient Egypt, In: Mummies of the World, Cambridge Univ, 81; After Tutankhamun - Research And Excavation in The Royal Necropolis at Thebes - Reeves,cn, American J of Archaeology, Vol 0097, 1993; The Private Chapel in Ancient-egypt - a Study of The Chapels in The Workmens Village at El-amarna With Special Reference to Deir-el-medina And Other Sites - Bowman,ah, Classical World, Vol 0086, 1992; Reading Egyptian Art - a Hieroglyphic Guide to Ancient Egyptian Painting And Sculpture - Wilkinson,rh, American J of Archaeology, Vol 0097, 1993; Mesopotamia - Writing, Reasoning, And The Gods - Bottero,j, Classical World, Vol 0087, 1994; Carter,howard The Path to Tutankhamun - J Ames,tgh, American J of Archaeology, Vol 0097, 1993;The Offering Chapel of Kayemnofret in The Museum-of- fine-arts, Boston - Simpson,wk, J of Near Eastern Studies, Vol 0055, 1996; The Offering Chapel of Kayemnofret in The Museum-of- fine-arts, Boston - Simpson,wk, J of Near Eastern Studies, Vol 0055, 1996. **CONTACT ADDRESS** Dept of Ancient Art, Detroit Inst of Arts, 5200 Woodward Ave, Detroit, MI, 48202.

PEDERSEN, DIANA
DISCIPLINE HISTORY **EDUCATION** Univ Brit Columbia, BA; Carleton Univ, MA, PhD. **CAREER** Instr, Queen's Univ; Univ W Ontario; asst prof, 91-. **SELECTED PUBLICATIONS** Auth, articles on Can middle-class women's organizations and social reform movements, and on the uses of photographs as documents for women's history; bibliography on Can women's history. **CONTACT ADDRESS** Dept of Hist, Concordia Univ, Montreal, 1455 de Maisonneuve W, Montreal, PQ, H3G 1M8. **EMAIL** dpeders@vax2.concordia.ca

PEDERSON, WILLIAM DAVID
PERSONAL Born 03/17/1946, Eugene, OR **DISCIPLINE** AMERICAN HISTORY & GOVERNMENT **EDUCATION** Univ Ore, BS, 67, MA, 72, PhD(polit sci), 79. **CAREER** Teaching & res asst polit sci, Univ Ore, Eugene, 75-77; instr govt, Lamar Univ, Beaumont, Tex, 77-79; asst prof polit sci, Westminster Col, Fulton, Mo, 79-80; asst prof & head, dept polit sci, Yankton Col, Univ SDak, 80-81; prof, coordr polit sci, dir am studies, dept soc sci, La State Univ, Shreveport, 81-; Intern, Operations Ctr, Dept State, Washington, DC, summer, 71; prog analyst, off of the dir, Nat Inst Health, Bethesda, Md, summer, 74; vis res prof, NY Univ, summer, 81; res assoc, Russian & East Europ Ctr, Univ Ill, Urbana, summer, 82. **HONORS AND AWARDS** Westcoast Lumbermen's Assoc Scholar, 65; Eugene Educ Assoc Scholar, 65; Oregon State Scholar Comn Scholars, 65; Nat Inst of Health Training Award, 74; Deutsche Sommerschule am Pazifik Scholar, 75; Coun for Eurpoean Studies/DAAD Grant, 75; Kosciuszko Found Grant, 79; Westminster Col Student Gov Assoc Outstanding Leadership and Service Award, 80; NY Univ, 81, Harvard Univ, 85, Nat Endowment for the Humanities Fel; Fac Res Grant on Soviet and Russian Military Amnesties, 82; Kappa Alpha Fraternity Prof of the Month, 9/85; Fac Excellence Award, 94-95, La State Univ in Shreveport; Essay Competition for Colum on the Bicentennial of the US Constitution, 87; Special Humanities Award, 98, La Endowment for the Humanities; Annual Award of Achievement, Abraham Lincoln Assoc, Springfield, IL, 2/94; Cultural Olympiad, Regional Designation Award in the Humanities, 95-96; The Times Journal page Shreveport Rose Award, 9/95; Phi Kappa Phi, 96. **MEMBERSHIPS** Am Asn Advan Slavic Studies; Am Polit Sci Asn; Int Soc Polit Psychol; Int Lincoln Assoc; La Hist Asn; North La Hist Asn; Acad of Criminal Justice Sci; Lincoln Fel of Wisconsin; Center for the Study of the Presidency; Presidency Res Group; Ger Studies Asn; Amnesty Int; Am Studies Prog; Am Soc Public Admin; Smithsonian Inst. **RESEARCH** American politics; presidental behavior; human rights. **SELECTED PUBLICATIONS** Co-ed, Abraham Lincoln: Sources and Style of Leadership, Greenwood Press, 94, 95; Ambraham Lincoln: Contemporary, Savas Woodbury, 95; FDR and the Modern Presidency. Leadership and Legacy, Praeger, 97; Journal of Contemporary Thought, 97; The New Deal and Public Policy, St Martin's Press, 98; A Comparative Test of Jimmy Carter's Character, The Presidency and Domestic Policies of Jimmy Carter, Greenwood Press, 94; Preface to Lincoln and Leadership Summer Teachers Institute, The 1993 ILA Annals, International Lincoln Assoc, 94; Preface in Abraham Lincoln: Sources and Style of Leadership, Greenwood Press, 94; Congressman Thomas Hale Boggs, Encyclopedia of the US Congress Vol 3, Simon and Schuster, 95; guest ed, Quarterly Journal of Ideology, 6/94; **CONTACT ADDRESS** Dept of Soc Sci, Louisiana State Univ, 1 University Pl, Shreveport, LA, 71115-2301.

PEDLEY, JOHN GRIFFITHS
PERSONAL Born 07/19/1931, Burnley, England **DISCIPLINE** CLASSICAL ARCHEOLOGY **EDUCATION** Cambridge Univ, BA, 53, MA, 59; Harvard Univ, PhD(class archaeol), 65. **CAREER** From asst prof to prof, 65-74, actg chmn dept classical studies, 71-72 & 75-76, Dir Kelsey Mus Ancient & Medieval Archaeol, 73-86; PROF CLASS ARCHAEOL & GREEK, UNIV MICH, ANN ARBOR, 74- . **HONORS AND AWARDS** Julia Lockwood Award, 94; NES Fel, 86-87; Am Philos Soc grant, 79; NEH grants, 75, 77, 83, 84; Nat Endowment for Arts grants, 74, 75, 77, 79, 80; Am Coun Learned Socs Fel, 72-73; James Loeb Res Fel class Archaeol, Harvard Univ, 69-70; Nat Found Arts and Humanities grahs, 67-68. **MEMBERSHIPS** Int Asn Class Archaeol; Soc Promotion Hellenic Studies; Archaeol Inst Am; Asn Field Archaeol; Soc Libyan Studies. **RESEARCH** Archaeology of Asia Minor and North Africa; Greek sculpture. **SELECTED PUBLICATIONS** Coauth, The statue of Meleager, Antike Plastik, 64; auth, Sardis in the Age of Croesus, Univ Okla, 68; auth, The archaic Favissa at Cyrene, Am J Archaeol, 71; Ancient Literary Sources on Sardis, Harvard Univ, 72; Carians in Sardis, J Hellenic Studies, 74; Greek Sculpture of the Archaic Period: The Island Workshops, Philipp von Zabern, Mainz, 76; coauth, Apollonia, the Port of Cyrene, suppl vol to Libya Antiqua IV, 77; ed, New Light on Ancient Carthage, Univ Mich Press, 80; auth, Paestum: Greeks & Romans in Southern Italy, 90; Greek Art & Archaeology, 92; coauth, Sanctuary of Santa Venera at Paestum, 93; coauth, Corpus des Mosaiques de Tunisie, III, Thysdrus, 96. **CONTACT ADDRESS** Dept of Classical Studies, Univ of Michigan, Ann Arbor, MI, 48109-1003. **EMAIL** jpedley@umich.com

PEEK, MARVIN E.
PERSONAL Born 08/21/1940, Cleveland, OH, m **DISCIPLINE** HISTORY **EDUCATION** Allen Univ, BA History 1964-65; IN Univ, MA History 1965-67; Univ of TN, PhD History 1971. **CAREER** US Park Service, park ranger 1963-65; Lane Coll, chair social scis div 1970-71; Univ of TN Afro-Amer Studies, dir 1971-86, asst to the provost 1987-. **HONORS AND AWARDS** Alpha Phi Alpha Scholarship; Ford Found Educ Study Grant; Faculty Develop Grant. **MEMBERSHIPS** Sec Natl Cncl for Black Studies 1984-86; pres elect Assn of Social & Behavorial Scientists 1986; consul Memphis State Univ Wm Patterson Coll Comm for the Humanities; reader Natl Endowment for the Humanities; LSU Press; Univ TN Press. **CONTACT ADDRESS** Univ of Tennessee, 812 Volunteer Blvd, Knoxville, TN, 37916.

PEGRAM, THOMAS R.
PERSONAL Born 11/29/1955, Hammond, IN, m, 1986, 2 children **DISCIPLINE** AMERICAN HISTORY **EDUCATION** Brandeis Univ, PhD, 88. **CAREER** Instr in History, 88-90, Ohio State Univ; asst prof History, 90-94, ASSOC PROF, 95-, & CHR HIST DEPT, 98-, LOYOLA COL, 90-; Phi Beta Kappa. 78, Santa Clara Univ; Irving & Rose Crown fel, Brandeis Univ, 78-84. **HONORS AND AWARDS** Choice Outstanding Acad Book, 94; Award Super Achievement **MEMBERSHIPS** OAH; SHGAPE **RESEARCH** 19th and 20th century American political and social history; Progressive literature; Temperance reform and prohibition. **SELECTED PUBLICATIONS** auth "The Dry Machine: The Formation of the Anti-Saloon League of Illinois," IL Hist Jour, 90; "Public Health and Progressive Dairying in Illinois," Agric Hist, 91; Partisans and Progressives: Private Interest and Public Policy in Illinois, 1870-1922, Urbana: Univ IL Press; "Temperance Politics and Regional Political Culture: The Anti-Saloon League in Maryland and the South, 1907-1915," Jour S Hist, 97; Battling Demon Rum: The Struggle for a Dry America, 1800-1933, Chicago: Ivan Dee, 98. **CONTACT ADDRESS** Dept of History, Loyola Col, 4501 N Charles St, Baltimore, MD, 21210-2699. **EMAIL** PEGRAM@LOYOLA.EDU

PEGUES, FRANKLIN J.
PERSONAL Born 04/29/1924, Cheraw, SC, m, 1952, 3 children **DISCIPLINE** MEDIEVAL HISTORY **EDUCATION** Duke Univ, AB, 47; Cornell Univ, MA, 48, PhD, 51. **CAREER** Instr hist, Univ Colo, 52-54; from asst prof to assoc prof, 54-63, Prof Hist, Ohio State Univ, 63-, Fulbright grant, France, 51-52; mem nat selection comt France, Fulbright Found, 58-59; Guggenheim fel, 61-62; ed, J Higher Educ, 64-66. **MEMBERSHIPS** AHA; Mediaeval Acad Am; Conf Brit Studies; Soc Fr Hist Studies. **RESEARCH** Administrative and legal history of medieval England and France; history of philanthropy in medieval education; medieval French and English social and economic history. **SELECTED PUBLICATIONS** Auth, Lawyers of the Last Captains, Princeton Univ, 62; The Origins of The English Legal Profession - Brand,p, American Historical Review, Vol 0098, 1993; English Law in The Age of The Blackdeath, 1348-1381 - a Transformation of Governance And Law - Palmer,rc, American Historical Review, Vol 0100, 1995. **CONTACT ADDRESS** Dept of Hist, Ohio State Univ, Columbus, OH, 43210.

PEIRCE, SARAH
DISCIPLINE GREEK RELIGION, DRAMA, HISTORY **EDUCATION** Bryn Mawr Univ, PhD. **CAREER** Dir, summer session, Amer Sch Class Stud, Athens, 98; assoc prof, Fordham Univ. **HONORS AND AWARDS** Fel, Ctr Hellenic Stud Wash DC, 96-97. **SELECTED PUBLICATIONS** Auth, Death, Revelry, and Thysia, Class Antiquity, 93; Visual Language and Concepts of Cult on the 'Lenaia Vases, Class World, 97. **CONTACT ADDRESS** Dept of Class Lang and Lit, Fordham Univ, 113 W 60th St, New York, NY, 10023.

PEISS, KATHY
DISCIPLINE HISTORY **EDUCATION** Carleton Col, BA, 75; MA, 77, PhD, 82, Brown Univ. **CAREER** Asst Prof, Univ Maryland, 81-86; Assoc Prof, 86-91, Prof, 91-, Univ Massachusetts (Amherst). **SELECTED PUBLICATIONS** Auth, Cheap Amusements: Working Women and Leisure in Turn-of-the-Century New York, 86; Passion and Power: Sexuality in History, 89; Love Across the Color Line, 96. **CONTACT ADDRESS** History Dept, Univ of Massachusetts, Amherst, MA, 01003-3930. **EMAIL** peiss@history.umass.edu

PEJOVICH, SVETOZAR
PERSONAL Born 03/22/1931, Yugoslavia, m, 1982, 4 children **DISCIPLINE** ECONOMICS **EDUCATION** Univ Belgrade, LLB, 55; Georgetown Univ, PhD (economics), 63. **CAREER** Prof of Economics, TX A&M; fel, Int Center of Economics Res, Turin, Italy; vis prof, Univ of Podgorica. **HONORS AND AWARDS** Templeton Award of Excellence in Higher Ed, 97. **MEMBERSHIPS** AEA. **RESEARCH** Economics of property rights; economics of systems. **SELECTED PUBLICATIONS** Auth, A Property Rights Analysis of Alternative Methods of Organizing Production, Communist Economies, 6, summer 94; The Market for Institutions vs Capitalism by Fiat: The Case of Eastern Europe, Kyklos, 47, Dec 94; Zwischen Liberalismus und Nationalismus, Transit, Europaische Revue, 9, summer 95; Privitizing the Process of Institutional Change in Eastern Europe, J of Transition Management, 1, spring 96; IL Mutamento Instituzionale Nei Paesi dell'Est: Publico et Privato, Biblioteca della Liberta, 31, May-June 96; The Prospects of Liberalism in Eastern Europe, Economia delle Scelte Pubbliche, 14, Jan-April, 96; Law, Tradition and the Transition Process in Eastern Europe: The Case for the Mafia, IB Rev, 1, winter 97; Law, Tradition, and the Transition in Eastern Europe, Independent Rev, 2, Sept 97; ed, The Economic Foundations of Property Rights, Edward Elgar Pub, 97; auth, Economic Analysis of Institutions and Systems, Kluwer Academic Pubs, Dordrecht, Netherlands, 2nd ed, 98; numerous other publications. **CONTACT ADDRESS** Dept of Economics, Texas A&M Univ, College Station, TX, 77843. **EMAIL** s-pejovich@tamu-edu

PELIKAN, JAROSLAV
PERSONAL Born 12/17/1923, Akron, OH, m, 1946, 3 children **DISCIPLINE** HISTORY **EDUCATION** Concordia Sem, BD, 46; Univ Chicago, PhD, 46. **CAREER** Mem fac hist & philos, Valparaiso Univ, 46-49, Concordia Sem, 49-53, Univ Chicago, 53-62; Titus Street prof ecclesiastical hist, 62-72, actg dean grad sch, 73-74, chmn medieval studies, 74-75 & 78-80, Sterling Prof Relig Studies, Yale Univ, 72-, Relig ed, Encycl Britannica, 55-68; ed, Makers of Mod Theol, 66-68; Nat Endowment for Humanities sr fel, 67-68; pres, IV Int Congr Luther Res, 71. **HONORS AND AWARDS** Abingdon Award, 59; Pax Christi Award, St John's Univ, Minn, 66; John Gilmary Shea Prize, Am Cath Hist Asn, 71; Nat Award, World Slovak Cong, 73., DD, Concordia Col, Moorhead, Minn, 60, Concordia Sem, 67; LittD, Wittenberg Univ, 60, Wheeling Col, 66, Pac Lutheran Univ, 67 & Gettysburg Col, 67; MA, Yale Univ, 61; LHD, Valparaiso Univ, 66, Rockhurst Col, 67 & Albertus Magnus Col, 73; DH, Providence Col, 66, LLD, Keuka Col, 67; DTheol, Univ Hamburg, 71; ThD, St Olaf Col, 72. **MEMBERSHIPS** Am Soc Church Hist (pres, 65); AHA; Mediaeval Acad Am. **SELECTED PUBLICATIONS** Ed, Interpreters of Luther, Fortress, 68; auth, Development of Christian Doctrine, Yale Univ, 69; ed, Twentieth Century Theology in the Making, (3 vols), Harper & Collins, 69-71; auth, Historical Theology: Continuity and Change in Christian Doctrine, Westminster, 71; The emergency of the Catholic tradition (100-600), Vol I, 71, The spirit of Eastern Christendom (600-1700), Vol II, 1974 & The growth of medieval theology (600-1300), Vol III, 78, In: The Christian Tradition: A History of the Development of Doctrine, Univ Chicago; ed, The Preaching of Augustine: Our Lord's Sermon the Mount, Fortress, 73; The Historian as Polyglot, Proceedings of The American Philosophical Society, Vol 0137, 1993; Giamatti,a.bartlett April 4,1938 September 1,1989, Proceedings of The American Philosophical Society, Vol 0139, 1995. **CONTACT ADDRESS** Dept of Hist, Yale Univ, New Haven, CT, 06520.

PELLECCHIA, LINDA
DISCIPLINE ART HISTORY **EDUCATION** Harvard Univ, PhD 83. **CAREER** Univ Delaware, assoc prof. **HONORS AND AWARDS** Amer Acad Rome; Vela I tath Harv U Cen Ren Stud. **MEMBERSHIPS** CAA; SAH; IAS. **RESEARCH** Renaissance art and architecture. **SELECTED PUBLICATIONS** Auth, Property and Identity in Renaissance Florence: The Gandi Palace, in progress; articles in: Renaissance Quart, Jour of Soc Architectural Histories. **CONTACT ADDRESS** Dept of Art History, Univ of Delaware, Old College, Newark, DE, 19711. **EMAIL** lpell@udel.edu

PELLER HALLETT, JUDITH
DISCIPLINE LATIN LANGUAGE AND LITERATURE **EDUCATION** Wellesley Col, AB; Harvard Univ, MA, PhD; postdoc stud, Am Acad, Rome; Inst Classical Stud, Univ London. **HONORS AND AWARDS** Distinguished scholar-tchr, 92-93; award for excellence tchg, Col of Arts and Hum. **RESEARCH** Women, sexuality and the family in class antiquity. **SELECTED PUBLICATIONS** Auth, Fathers and Daughters in Roman Society: Women and the Elite Family, Princeton 84; co-ed, Compromising Traditions: the Personal Voice in Classical Scholarship, Routledge, 96. **CONTACT ADDRESS** Dept of Class, Univ MD, 4229 Art-Sociology Building, College Park, MD, 20742-1335. **EMAIL** jh10@umail.umd.edu

PELLS, RICHARD HENRY
PERSONAL Born 11/06/1941, Kansas City, MO, m, 1966, 2 children **DISCIPLINE** HISTORY **EDUCATION** Rutgers Univ, BA, 63; Harvard Univ, MA, 64, PhD, 69. **CAREER** Lectr hist, Harvard Univ, 68-71; asst prof, 71-74, assoc prof hist, Univ TX, Austin, 75, prof Hist, univ Hist, 85-; Fel, Charles Warren Ctr Studies Am Hist, Harvard Univ, 70-71; Rockefeller humanities fel, 76; Fulbright sr lectr, Univ Amsterdam, 79 & Univ Copenhagen, 82-83; fellow, Woodrow Wilson Intl Center for scholars, 86-87; Guggenheim Fel, 93-94; 50th anniv, fulbright ch, Amer Studies, Ger, 97-98. **RESEARCH** Twentieth century Am intellectual hist; Am lit period since 1920; popular cult, films, radio and television. **SELECTED PUBLICATIONS** Auth, Radical Visions and American Dreams; Culture and Social Thought in the Depression Years, Harper, 73; The Liberal Mind in a Conservative Age: American Intellectuals in the 1940s and 1950s, Harper, 85; Not Like Us: How Europeans Have Loved Hated and Transformed American Culture Since World War II, Basic Books, 97. **CONTACT ADDRESS** Dept of Hist, Univ of Texas, Austin, TX, 78712-1026. **EMAIL** rpells@aol.com

PELTO, WILLIAM
DISCIPLINE MUSIC THEORY **EDUCATION** Yale Univ, BA; San Francisco State Univ, MA; Univ Tex, PhD. **CAREER** Assoc prof. **MEMBERSHIPS** Col Music Soc; Soc Music Theory. **SELECTED PUBLICATIONS** Auth, pubs on musical analysis and music theory pedagogy. **CONTACT ADDRESS** Dept of Music History, Theory and Composition, Ithaca Col, 100 Job Hall, Ithaca, NY, 14850. **EMAIL** pelto@ithaca.edu

PELZ, STEPHEN ERNEST
PERSONAL Born 12/01/1942, New Haven, CT, m, 1966, 2 children **DISCIPLINE** HISTORY **EDUCATION** Johns Hopkins Univ, BA, 64; Harvard Univ, MA, 66, PhD, 71. **CAREER** Asst prof, 71-76, asoc prof hist, Univ Mass, Amherst, 76-81, Nat fel, Hoover Inst War, Revolution & Peace, Stanford Univ, 73-74; Nat Security Studies fel, Woodrow Wilson Int Ctr Scholars, Washington, DC, 78-79; fel, East Asian Inst, Columbia Univ, 79-80. **HONORS AND AWARDS** Stuart L Bernath Prize, Soc Hist Am Foreign Rel, 75. **MEMBERSHIPS** AHA; Soc Hist Am Foreign Rels. **RESEARCH** American diplomatic history; American-East Asian relations; international relations. **SELECTED PUBLICATIONS** Auth, Race to Pearl Harbor: The failure of the Second London Naval Conference and the onset of World War II, In: Am East Asian Rel Ser, Harvard Univ, 74; contribr, Japanese Attitudes Toward the Outside World, Tokyo Univ, 74. **CONTACT ADDRESS** Dept of History, Univ of Massachusetts, Amherst, MA, 01003-0002.

PEMBERTON, GAYLE R.
PERSONAL Born 06/29/1948, St. Paul, MN, s **DISCIPLINE** AFRICAN-AMERICAN STUDIES **EDUCATION** Lake Forest College, attended, 1966-68; University of Michigan, BA, 1969; Harvard University, MA, 1971, PhD, 1981. **CAREER** Columbia University, lecturer, 1974-77; Middlebury College, instructor, 1977-80; Northwestern University, assistant professor, 1980-83; Reed College, visiting associate professor, 1983-84; Bowdoin College, African-American Studies, visiting associate professor, acting director, 1986-88, Minority Affairs, director, 1988-90; PRINCETON UNIV, AFRICAN-AMERICAN STUDIES, ASSOC DIR, 1990-. **HONORS AND AWARDS** W E B DuBois Foundation, 1975; Ford Foundation, Doctoral Fellowship, 1969-74; Southwest Review, Margaret Hartley Memorial Award, 1992. **MEMBERSHIPS** Modern Language Assn. **SELECTED PUBLICATIONS** Author: "A Sentimental Journey," Race-ing Justice En-Gendering Power, 1992; The Hottest Water in Chicago, 1992; "It's The Thing That Counts," State of Black America, 1991; John Simon Guggenheim Fellow, 1993; New Jersey Committee for the Humanities, Book of the Year Award, for Hottest Water. **CONTACT ADDRESS** African-American Studies, Princeton Univ, 112 Dickinson Hall, Princeton, NJ, 08544-1017.

PEMBERTON, WILLIAM ERWIN
PERSONAL Born 03/26/1940, Duncan, OK, m, 1967, 1 child **DISCIPLINE** RECENT UNITED STATES HISTORY **EDUCATION** Univ Okla, BA, 63; Univ Mo, MA, 65, PhD, 74. **CAREER** Prof US Hist, Univ WI-LaCrosse, 66-. **MEMBERSHIPS** Orgn Am Historians; Ctr Study Presidency; Am Soc Pub Admin. **RESEARCH** Recent United States political history; administrative history; United States economic history. **SELECTED PUBLICATIONS** Auth, The Politics of Bureaucracy: Executive Reorganization During the Truman Administration, Univ Mo, 78; Harry S Truman: Fair Dealer and Cold Warrior, Twayne, 89; Exit with Honor: The Life and Presidency of Ronald Reagan; M E Shupe, 97. **CONTACT ADDRESS** Dept Hist, Univ Wisconsin, 1725 State St, La Crosse, WI, 54601-3788. **EMAIL** BillPember@aol.com

PENDERGRAFT, MARY L.B.
PERSONAL Born 02/14/1953, Charlotte, NC, m, 1975, 3 children **DISCIPLINE** CLASSICS **EDUCATION** Univ of N Carolina, AB, 75; UNC Chapel Hill, PhD, 82 **CAREER** Vis Asst Prof, 84-86, UNC; Vis Asst Prof, 87-88, Duke Univ; Vis Asst Prof, 83-84, Wake Forest Univ; Asst. Prof, 88-94, Wake Forest Univ; Assoc Prof, 94-pres, Wake Forest Univ **HONORS AND AWARDS** Nat Merit Schol; Phi Beta Kappa; Univ Fel **MEMBERSHIPS** Am Philo Assoc; Classical Assoc of Middle West & South; Am Inst of Archeol; Am Class League **RESEARCH** Greek Poetry; Latin Poetry **SELECTED PUBLICATIONS** Auth, "Aratean Echoes in Theocritus," Quaderni Urbinati di Cultura Classica, 86, 47-54; Auth, "On the Nature of the Constellations: Aratus, Ph. 367-85," Eranos 88, 90, 99-106 **CONTACT ADDRESS** Wake Forest Univ, Box 7343, Winston-Salem, NC, 27109. **EMAIL** pender@wfu.edu

PENELLA, ROBERT JOSEPH
PERSONAL Born 02/16/1947, Boston, MA, m, 1968, 1 child **DISCIPLINE** CLASSICS, ROMAN HISTORY **EDUCATION** Boston Col, AB, 67; Harvard Univ, MA, 69, PhD(classics), 71. **CAREER** Asst prof, 71-78, chemn dept, 77-83, assoc p, 78-91, prof classics, Fordham Univ, 91-. **HONORS AND AWARDS** Grant-in-aid, ACLS, 84; NEH Fellowship for Univ Teachers, 93. **MEMBERSHIPS** Am Philol Asn; Asn Ancient Historians. **RESEARCH** Late Antiquity; Imperial Greek prose; Roman historyand historiography. **SELECTED PUBLICATIONS** Auth, The Letters of Apollonius of Tyana, Mnemosyne Supplements, 56, E J Brill, 79; Greek Philosophers and Sophists in the Fourth Century AD: Studies in Eunapius of Sardis, Leeds: F Cairns, 90; The Private Orations of Themistius, Berkeley: Univ CA Press, 99. **CONTACT ADDRESS** Dept of Classics, Fordham Univ, 501 E Fordham Rd, Bronx, NY, 10458-5191. **EMAIL** rpenella@murray.fordham.edu

PENHALL, MICHELE M.
PERSONAL Born 07/30/1953, CA, m, 1990 **DISCIPLINE** ART HISTORY **EDUCATION** Univ Hawaii, BFA, 80; CUNY Queens College, MA, 87; Univ New Mexico, PhD. **CAREER** Independent Scholar. **HONORS AND AWARDS** Phi Kappa Phi; UNM Regents Fel; Samuel H Kress Fel; UNM Grad res Gnt; UNM MFA Awd; Mellon Res Gnt; Bainbridge Bunting Fel; UNM Res Gnt. **MEMBERSHIPS** SAH; Phi Beta Kappa. **RESEARCH** Latin American Photography; Vernacular Photography. **SELECTED PUBLICATIONS** Martin Chambi as Artist, Hist of Photography, guest ed, Hist Photog Latin Amer, Hist of Photog, 99; ed, Betty Hahn: Photography or Maybe Not, Albuquerque, UNM Press, 95; rev Stones in the Road: Photographs of Peru, by Nubar Alexanian, Hist of Photog, 93; contrib, Christopher Curtis Mead, The Architecture of Bart Prince: A Pragmatics of Place, preface by David Van Zanten, NY, London, WW Norton & Co, 99; Michael Webb, Architecture: Twist and Shout-A Dynamically Expressive House for the Coast of N Cal, Archit Digest, NY, Conde Nast, 97; Space Design Art and Architecture, Tokyo, Kajima, Pub 97; Philip Jodido, New Forms: Architecture in the 1990's, Koln, Taschen Verlag, 97; Christopher Mead, When Architects Serve Their Clients, Designer/Builder, Santa Fe, Fine Adds Inc, 97; Contemporary American Architects, vol II, Koln, Taschen Verlag, 96. **CONTACT ADDRESS** 4504 Sunningdale Ave NE, Albuquerque, NM, 87110. **EMAIL** kapu@unm.edu

PENKOWER, MONTY NOAM
PERSONAL Born 07/15/1942, New York, NY, m, 1969, 4 children **DISCIPLINE** HISTORY, JEWISH STUDIES **EDUCATION** Yeshiva Univ, BA, 63; Columbia Univ, MA, 64, PhD(hist), 70. **CAREER** Asst prof, Bard Col, NY, 70-74; vis assoc prof, 73-74, chmn dept, 76-79, Assoc Prof Hist, Touro Col, NY, 74-. Eleanor Roosevelt Inst grant hist, 71-73 & 78-79 & Harry S Truman Libr, 73-75; Mem Found Jewish Cult fel hist, 74-75 & 77-78; Nat Found Jewish Cult fel hist, 75-76; acad coun, World Jewish Cong. **MEMBERSHIPS** AHA; Am Jewish Hist Asn; Orgn Am Historians. **RESEARCH** American political history; diplomacy of the Holocaust; Palestine and the Anglo-American alliance. **SELECTED PUBLICATIONS** Auth, The Federal Writer's Project: A Study in Government Patronage of the Arts, Univ Ill, 77; The 1943 joint Anglo- American statement on Palestine, Herzl Yearbk, 78; Reluctant Ally - United-states-foreign-policy Toward The Jews From Wilson to Roosevelt - Brecher,fw, American Jewish History, Vol 0081, 1993. **CONTACT ADDRESS** Touro Col, 30 W 44 St, New York, NY, 10036.

PENNER, HANS HENRY
PERSONAL Born 01/29/1934, Sacramento, CA, m, 1959 **DISCIPLINE** HISTORY OF RELIGIONS **EDUCATION** Univ Chicago, DB, 58, MA, 62, PhD, 65. **CAREER** Instr hist of relig, Univ VT, 62-65; asst prof, 65-72, assoc prof relig, 72-74, John Phillips prof, & chmn dept, 74-79, Dean Fac, Dartmouth Col, 81-, Fulbright res scholar, India, 66; Soc Relig Higher Educ-Danforth Cross-disciplinary fel, 68-69; Dartmouth fac fel, 68-69. **MEMBERSHIPS** Asn Asian Studies; Soc Sci Studies Relig; Am Acad Relig; Int Asn Hist Relig. **RESEARCH** Methodological approaches to understanding relig; myth and ritual-phenomenology; relig traditions of India. **SELECTED PUBLICATIONS** Auth, Cosmogony as Myth in Vishnu Purana, Hist Relig, 66; The Study of Religion According to Jan de Vries, J Relig, 1/69; Myth and Ritual: Wasteland or Forest of Symbols, Hist & Theory, 69; The poverty of functionalism, Hist Relig, 71; Ritual, In: Encyl Britannica; Creating a Brahman & The problem of semantics in the study of religion, Method Issues Relig Studies, 75; Impasse & Resolution: A Critique of the Study of Religion, 89; Why Does Semantics Matter to the Study of Religion, Method and Theory in the Study of Religion, 7/95. **CONTACT ADDRESS** Dept Relig, Dartmouth Col, 6036 Thornton Hall, Hanover, NH, 03755-3592. **EMAIL** Hans.Penner@Dartmouth.edu

PENNISTON, JOYCE K.
PERSONAL Born 12/22/1939, Buffalo, NY, m, 1960, 2 children **DISCIPLINE** CLASSICS **EDUCATION** Radcliffe, BA, 61; Harvard Grad Sch of Educ, MAT, 62; Univ NC Chapel Hill, MA, 76; Univ Mn, PhD, 83. **CAREER** Instr, St. Olaf Col, 79-81; instr, Mn Bible Col, 81- ; instr, St. Mary's Univ Mn, 93- . **HONORS AND AWARDS** Summer stud, Amer Sch for Classical Stud, Athens, Greece, 81, Rome, Italy, 78; NEH Summer Sem, Harvard with Gregory Nagy, 84. **MEMBERSHIPS** Amer Philol Assoc; Classical Assoc of the Midwest & South; Vergilian Soc; Classical Assoc of Mn. **RESEARCH** Ancient comedy. **SELECTED PUBLICATIONS** Auth, Quot Homines Tot Sententiae: Off-Stage Acquaintances in Ancient Comedy, Classical J, 91; Pragma and process in Greek and Roman Comedy, Syllecta Classica, 96; Commentary on the Acts of the Apostles in Study Bible for Women, Baker books, Grand Rapids, Mich, 96; Translation of Cicero's De Finibus, Hackett, 99-00; Translation of Latin passages in Anatomy of Radical Prostatectomy as defined by Magnetic Resonance Imaging, The J of Urology, 98. **CONTACT ADDRESS** 835 10 1/2 St SW, Rochester, MN, 55902. **EMAIL** joyce.penniston@swix.com

PENNY, BENJAMIN
DISCIPLINE CULTURAL HISTORY **EDUCATION** Univ of Sydney; Univ of Cambridge; Australian Natl Univ. **CAREER** Proj off Hum Res Ctr, Australian Natl Univ, 96-; postdoctoral fel, Australian Natl Univ. **RESEARCH** History of Chinese religions; Daoism; fate calculation; hagiography; qigong. **SELECTED PUBLICATIONS** Auth, The Celestial Master: Zhang Daoling and the origins of Daoism, pending; ed, Religion and Biography in China and Tibet, pending.

PENNY SMALL, JOCELYN
DISCIPLINE GREEK, ETRUSCAN AND ROMAN ART **EDUCATION** Princeton Univ, PhD. **CAREER** Prof, Rutgers, The State Univ NJ, Univ Col-Camden. **RESEARCH** Etruscan and Roman art, mythology and iconography; cognitive studies. **SELECTED PUBLICATIONS** Auth, SIBYL: The US Database of Classical Iconography: Issues of Simplicity and Complexity of Design, in Rev Informatique et Statistique dans les Sci humaines 29, 93; The Etruscan View of Greek Art, in Boreas 14/15, 94; Scholars, Etruscans, and Attic Painted Vases, J of Roman Archaeol 7, 94; Wax Tablets of the Mind: Cognitive Studies of Literacy and Memory in Classical Antiquity, Routledge, 97; coed, Murlo and Etruscan Studies. Essays in Memory of Kyle Meredith Phillips, Jr, Univ of Wis Press, 94. **CONTACT ADDRESS** Dept of Art Hist, Rutgers, The State Univ NJ, Univ Col-Camden, Voorhees Hall, 71 Hamilton St, New Brunswick, NJ, 08903. **EMAIL** jpsmall@rci.rutgers.edu

PENTON, MARVIN J.
PERSONAL Born 04/27/1932, Clarkbridge, SK, Canada **DISCIPLINE** HISTORY **EDUCATION** Univ Arizona, BA, 56; Univ Iowa, MA, 58, PhD, 65. **CAREER** Asst prof, Univ Puerto Rico, 59-60; asst prof, Univ Wisconsin, 64-65; asst prof, Univ Calgary, 65-67; asst prof, 67-76, prof, 76-89, PROF EMER HISTORY, UNIV LETHBRIDGE, 89-. **MEMBERSHIPS** Mem, Christian Renewal Ministries; past pres, Can Soc Church Hist **RESEARCH** Religion; Jehovah's Witnesses **SELECTED PUBLICATIONS** Auth, Jehovah's Witnesses in Canada, 76; auth, The Story of Jehovah's Witnesses, 85, 97; ed, Eng edition The Gentile Times Reconsidered, 83; ed, The Bible Examiner, 82-84; ed, The Christian Quest, 86-91. **CONTACT ADDRESS** 58 Coachwood Point W, Lethbridge, AB, T1K 6A9.

PEOPLES, VERJANIS ANDREWS
PERSONAL Born 08/08/1955, Monroe, LA, m, 1975 **DISCIPLINE** EDUCATION **EDUCATION** Grambling St University, BS, 1976, MS, 1978; Kansas St University, PhD, 1990. **CAREER** Bienville Parish School System, teacher, 1976-79; Grambling St University, lab school, teacher, 1979-88, College of Education, professor, 1989-90; SOUTHERN UNIVERSITY,

COLLEGE OF EDUC, professor, 1991-92, assistant dean, 1992-95, INTERIM DEAN, 1995-. **HONORS AND AWARDS** Teacher of the Year, Grambling Lab School, 1989. **MEMBERSHIPS** LA Association of Teacher Educators, 1996; Association of Teacher Educators, 1996; Association for Supervision & Curriculum Dev, 1996; LA Alliance for Education Reform, 1996; LA Council for Teacher Education, 1996; American Association of Colleges for Teacher Education, 1996. Created proposal for Teachers Alumni As-Partners Program (TAAP); Instituted "First Class Teachers Program;" Dev Partnership programs with surrounding parishes. **SELECTED PUBLICATIONS** Published article, "Restoring Human Dignity: A Model for Prevention & Intervention;" Published chapter, "Teacher Preparation Programs at Historically Black Colleges." **CONTACT ADDRESS** Col of Education, So Univ, PO Box 9983, Baton Rouge, LA, 70813. **EMAIL** vpeoples@subrum.subr.edu

PERADOTTO, JOHN JOSEPH
PERSONAL Born 05/11/1933, Ottawa, IL, m, 1959, 4 children **DISCIPLINE** GREEK & LATIN LANGUAGES & LITERATURE **EDUCATION** St Louis Univ, AB, 57, MA, 58; Northwestern Univ, PhD(Greek & Latin), 63. **CAREER** Instr Greek, Latin & English, Western Wash State Col, 60-61; from instr to asst prof Greek & Latin, Georgetown Univ, 61-66; from asst prof to assoc prof classics, State Univ NY Buffalo, 66-73; prof & chmn dept, Univ Tex, Austin, 73-74; chmn dept, 74-77, Prof Classics, State Univ NY Buffalo, 74-, Dean, 78-, Nat Endowment for Humanities fel, Ctr Hellenic Studies, 72-73; ed-in-chief, Arethusa, 75-. **HONORS AND AWARDS** Chancellor's Award for Excellence in Teaching, State Univ NY, 75. **MEMBERSHIPS** Am Philol Asn; Class Asn Atlantic States. **RESEARCH** Greek literature; Greek mythology and religion; narrative analysis. **SELECTED PUBLICATIONS** Auth, The omen of the eagles and the ethos of Agamemnon, Phoenix, 69; Classical Mythology, Am Philol Asn, 73; Odyssey 8 564-671: Verisimilitude, narrative analysis, and bricolarge, Tex Studies Lit & Lang, 74; co-ed, Population Policy in Plato and Aristotle, 75; ed, Classical Literature and Contemporary Literary Theory, 77, Women in the Ancient World, 78, co-ed, Virgil 2000 Years, 81 & Semiotics and Classical Studies, 83, Arethusa; Rethinking the Classical Caon, 94; ed, Horace: 2000 Years, 95; co-ed, The NewSimonides, 96; The Iliad and its Contexts, 97, Arethusa. **CONTACT ADDRESS** Dept of Classics, SUNY, Buffalo, PO Box 604650, Buffalo, NY, 14260-4650. **EMAIL** peradott@acsu.buffalo.edu

PERAINO, JUDITH A.
DISCIPLINE MUSIC **EDUCATION** Univ Chicago, BA, 87; Univ Calif at Berkeley, MA, 90, PhD, 95. **CAREER** Asst prof **MEMBERSHIPS** Amer Musicol Soc; Soc for Ethnomusicol. **RESEARCH** 13th-century French secular music; music and queer identity; Rock music. **SELECTED PUBLICATIONS** Auth, Et pui conmencha a canter: Refrains, Motes, and Melody in the Thirteenth-century Narritive Renart le nouvel, Plainsong and Medieval Music, 97; PJ Harvey's 'Man-size Sextet' and the Inaccessible, Inescapable Gender," Women and Music: A Journal of Gender and Culture, Spring, 98; Courtly Obsessions: Music and Masculine Identity in Gottfried von Strassburg's Tristan, Repercussions 4:2 95; I am an Opera: Identifying with Henry Purcell's Dido and Aeneas, En Travesti: Women, Gender Subversion, Opera, NY: Columbia UP, 95. **CONTACT ADDRESS** Dept of Music, Cornell Univ, 104 Lincoln Hall, Ithaca, NY, 14853. **EMAIL** jap28@cornell.edu

PERDICOYIANAI-PALEOLOGOU, HELENE
PERSONAL Born 02/12/1959, Greece **DISCIPLINE** CLASSICS **EDUCATION** Sorbonne Univ, PhD, 92. **CAREER** From vis prof to lectr, Hellenic Col, 96-; vis scholar, Harvard Univ, 98; guest vis scholar, Harvard Divinity Sch, 97-99, vis scholar, Brown Univ, 97-99. **MEMBERSHIPS** Can Asn Univ Tchrs; Int Asn Papyrology; Int Asn Greek & Latin Epigraphy; Asn Linguistics Paris; Grammatical Info; Asn Guillaume Bude; Am Philol Asn; Chronicle High Educ; VITA LATINA; Int Soc Class Tradition; Am Soc Papyrologists; Ling Soc Am. **RESEARCH** Greek and Latin Philology and Linguistics. **SELECTED PUBLICATIONS** Auth, Etude Lexicologique des Familles de Daenai, de Didaskein et de Paideuein d'Homere a Hippocrate, 94; auth, L'enonciation dans l'Hecube d'Euripide, Miscellanea Linguistica Graeco-latina, 93; auth, Le vocabulaire de l'education d'Homere a Euripide. Eytude lexicologique: les familles de daenai de didaskein et de paideuein d'Homere a Euripide, IG, 93; auth, Le Vocabulaire de la douleur dans l'Hecube et les Troyennes d'Euripide, LEC, 93; auth, Le vocabulaire de l'habitation chez Euripide, LEC, 96; auth, Philos chez Euripide, RB Ph. H, 96. **CONTACT ADDRESS** Dept of Classics, Hellenic Col, 50 Goddard Ave., Brookline, MA, 02146.

PERDUE, CHARLES L.
PERSONAL Born 12/01/1930, DeKalb, GA, m, 1954, 4 children **DISCIPLINE** ANTHROPOLOGY **EDUCATION** North Ga Coll, 48-49; Santa Rosa Jun Coll, 53; Univ Calif-Berkeley, AB, Geol, 55-59; Univ Penn, MA, Folklore, MA, 67-68, PhD, 68-71. **CAREER** Engg writer, Convair astronautics, Vandenberg Air Force Base, CA, 59-60; Geol, Branch Mineral Class, US Geol Survey, 60-67; asst prof, Eng, Univ Va, 71-76; assoc prof, Univ Va, 76-92; PROF, ENG & FOLKLORE, ENG & ANTHROP, 92-. **HONORS AND AWARDS** Ntl Oral Hist Assoc Award, 97 **MEMBERSHIPS** Am Folklore Soc; Middle Atlantic Folklife Asn; Nat Coun Traditional Arts; Va Folklore Soc **SELECTED PUBLICATIONS** "The Madison County, Virginia FSA Photographs of Arthur Rothstein," Madison County Bicentennial Commission, 93; foreward, The Negro in Virginia, John F. Blair Publ, 94; coauth, "Shenandoah Removals," The Appalachian Trail Reader, Oxford Univ Press, 96; coauth, "An Abiding Haven," Virginia Cavalcade, 97; coauth, "Talk About Trouble: The Virginia Writers' Project," Virginia Cavalcade, 97; "What Made Little Sister Die?: The Core Aesthetic and Personal Culture of a Traditional Singer," Western Folklore, 95; coauth, Talk Trouble: A New Protrait of Virginians in the Great Depression," Univ North Carolina Press, 96. **CONTACT ADDRESS** Dept Anthrop, Univ Va, 100 Brooks Hall, Charlottesville, VA, 22903. **EMAIL** clpsa@virginia.edu

PERELMUTER, HAYIM GOREN
PERSONAL Born 06/02/1914, Montreal, PQ, Canada, m, 1940, 2 children **DISCIPLINE** JEWISH HISTORY **EDUCATION** McGill Univ, BA, 35; Jewish Inst Relig, MHL, 39; Hebrew Union Col Jewish Inst Relig, DHL, 79. **CAREER** Rabbi, Beth Israel, Waltham MAss, 39-41; rabbi, Beth Zion Temple, Johnstown Penn, 41-57; rabbi, KAM Isaiah Israel, 57-79; prof Jewish Stud, Catholic Theol Union, 49- . **MEMBERSHIPS** Am Acad Relig; Conf of Am Rabbis; North Am Acad of Liturgy; Soc of Bibl Lit; Am Jewish Hist Soc. **SELECTED PUBLICATIONS** Trans, Song of the Steps and In Defense of Preachers, Hebrew Union Col, 84; auth, This Immortal People: A Short History of the Jews, Paulist, 85; coauth, Von Kanaah nach Israel, Deutsche Tascherbuch Verlag, 86; auth, Siblings: Rabbinic Judaism and Early Christianity at Their Beginnings, Paulist, 89; coauth, Paul the Jew: Jewish-Christian Dialogue, Center for Hermeneutical Stud, Grad Theol Union, 90; auth, Do Not Destroy in the Ecological Challenge, Liturgical, 94; coauth, Harvest of a Dialogue, Ktav, 97. **CONTACT ADDRESS** Catholic Theol Union at Chicago, 5401 S Cornell Ave, Chicago, IL, 60615. **EMAIL** foodper@ctu.edu

PERERA, NIHAL
PERSONAL Born 12/14/1953, Sri Lanka, m, 1976, 3 children **DISCIPLINE** HISTORY AND THEORY OF URBANISM **EDUCATION** SUNY, Binghamton, PhD, 95. **CAREER** Regional and Physical Planner, Transmigration Project, Indonesia, 88; Chief Archit-Planner, Mahaweli Authority of Sri Lanka, 83-89; Adj Lectr, Binghamton Univ, 91-95; Asst Prof Urban Planning, Ball State Univ, 95-. **HONORS AND AWARDS** Univ Fel, SUNY, 89-91; Dissertation Year Fel, SUNY, 91-92; Grad Student Award for Excellence in Teaching, SUNY, 95; Wings Int grant for the Virtual International Education project, 97; Graham Found Fel, 97. **MEMBERSHIPS** Am Planning Asn; Int Planning Hist Soc; Royal Inst British Archit; Inst Town Planners, Sri Lanka; Asn Asian Studies. **RESEARCH** Society and space: investigating the crucial correlation between transformations in urban and regional spatial structures and landscapes, and economic, political, and cultural developments. **SELECTED PUBLICATIONS** Auth, Critical Vernacularism: The Subversion of Universalizing Trends in Architecture, Proceedings of the 83rd ACSA Annual Meeting, 95; Exploring Columbo: The Relevance of a Knowledge of New York, Representing the City: Ethnicity, Capital, and Culture in the 21st Century Metropolis, Macmillan, 96; coauth, Winning on the Net: Virtual International Design Education, Proceedings of the Asn Collegiate Sch Archit Int Conf, 97; auth, Society and Space: Colonialism, Nationalism, and Postcolonial Identity in Sri Lanka, Westview Press, 98. **CONTACT ADDRESS** Dept Urban Planning, Ball State Univ, Muncie, IN, 47306. **EMAIL** 00mnperera@bsuvc.bsu.edu

PERKINS, BRADFORD
PERSONAL Born 03/06/1925, Rochester, NY, m, 1949, 4 children **DISCIPLINE** HISTORY **EDUCATION** Harvard Univ, AB, 47, PhD(hist), 52. **CAREER** From instr to assoc prof hist, Univ Calif, Los Angeles, 52- 62; Prof Hist, Univ Mich, Ann Arbor, 62-, Soc Sci Res Coun fac res fel, 57-60; Guggenheim fel, 62-63; Commonwealth Fund lectr, Univ Col, Univ London, 64; mem counc, Inst Early Am Hist & Cult, Williamsburg, Va, 68-71. **HONORS AND AWARDS** Bancroft Prize, 65; Albert Shaw lectr, Johns Hopkins Univ, 80. **MEMBERSHIPS** AHA; Orgn Am Historians; Soc Historians of Am Foreign Rels (pres, 73). **RESEARCH** American diplomatic history; Anglo-American relations. **SELECTED PUBLICATIONS** Auth, First Rapprochement: England and the United States, 1795-1805, Univ Pa, 55; Youthful America, 60, Prologue to War: England and the United States, 1805-1812, 61 & Castlereagh and Adams: England and the United States, 1812-1823, 74, Univ Calif; The Great Rapprochement: England and the United States, 1895- 1914, Atheneum, 68; Adams,john,quincy And The Pubic Virtues of Diplomacy - Russell,g, William And Mary Quarterly, Vol 0053, 1996. **CONTACT ADDRESS** 1335 W Huron River Dr, Ann Arbor, MI, 48103.

PERKINS, DWIGHT HEALD
PERSONAL Born 10/20/1934, Chicago, IL, m, 1957, 3 children **DISCIPLINE** ECONOMICS **EDUCATION** BA, Cornell Univ, 56; AM, 61, PhD, 64, Harvard Univ. **CAREER** Inst, Asst Prof Econ, 63-66; Assoc Prof Modern China Studies and Econ, 66-69, Assoc Dir EARC, 73-77, Prof Modern China Studies and Econ, Assoc of the East Asian Res Center, 69-77; Chm Dept of Econ, 77-80; Harold Hitchings Burbank Prof of Poli Econ, 81-; Dir Harvard Inst for Intl Devel HUD, 80-95; Harold Hitchings Burbank Prof Poli Econ, 95-. **HONORS AND AWARDS** Phi Beta Kappa; Pi Kappa Phi; BA with Distinction and High Hon; Woodrow Wilson Fel(honorary). **MEMBERSHIPS** Phi Beta Kappa Vis Scholar, 92-93; Soc Sci Res Council(NY); Mem Bd Dir, 79-82. **RESEARCH** Econ Hist and Contemporary Devel of East and SEast Asia. **SELECTED PUBLICATIONS** China: Asia's Economic Giant, Univ Wash Press, 86; Agricultural Development in China, 1368-1968, Aldine, 69; Industrialization and the State: Korea's Heavy and Chemical Industry Drive, with J Stern, Ji-Hong Kim and Jung-Ho Yoo, Harvard Institute for Intl Devel, 97; Reforming Economic Systems in Deveoloping Countries,ed With M Roemer, Cambridge: Harvard Univ Press, 91. **CONTACT ADDRESS** Dept Econ, Harvard Univ, Cambridge, MA, 02138. **EMAIL** dperkins@hiid.harvard.edu

PERKINS, EDWARD JOSEPH
PERSONAL Born 1928, Sterlington, LA, m, 1962 **DISCIPLINE** POLITICAL SCIENCE **EDUCATION** Univ of MD, BA 1968; Univ of Southern CA, MPA 1972, PhD 1978. **CAREER** AID Far East Bureau Washington, asst general serv officer; US Operations Mission to Thailand Bangkok, asst genl serv officer 1967-69, mgmt analyst 1969-70, deputy asst dir for mgmt 1970-72; Office of the Dir General of the Foreign Serv Washington, staff assistant 1972, personnel officer; Bureau of Near Eastern & South Asian Affairs, admin officer 1974-75; Office of Mgmt & Opers, mgmt analysis officer 1975-78; Accra, counselor for polit affairs 1978-81; Monrovia, deputy chief of mission 1981-83; Bureau Of African Affairs Office of West African Affairs, dir 1983-85; Dept of State, ambassador to Liberia 1985-86, ambassador to South Africa 1986-89, dir general The Foreign Service 1989-92; United Nations and UN Security Council, ambassador, 1992-93; US ambassador to Australia, 1993-96; UNIV OF OKLAHOMA, EXEC DIR, INTERNATIONAL PROGRAMS CENTER, WILLIAM J CROWE CHAIR PROFESSOR OF GEOPOLITICS, 1996-. **HONORS AND AWARDS** Honoree of the Beta Gamma Sigma Chapter of the Univ of Oklahoma, 1998; Univ of Southern California, Distinguished Alumni Award, 1991; Southern Univ, Achievement Award, 1991; Kappa Alpha Psi, C Rodger Wilson Leadership Conference Award, 1990; The Links, Inc, Living Legend Award, 1989; Eastern Province, Kappa Alpha Psi, Award for Distinguished Service as US Ambassador to South Africa, 1989; Presidential Distinguished Service Award, 1989; Una Chapman Cox Foundation Award, 1989; Presidential Meritorious Service Award, 1987; Kappa Alpha Psi Fraternity Award for Outstanding Achievement in the Foreign Service, 1986; Dept of State, Superior Honor Award, 1983; Agency for Intl Development, Meritorious Honor Award, 1967; National Academy of Public Administration, fellow; Statesman of the Year, George Washington Univ, 1992; Distinguished Honor Award, Department of State, 1992; St Augustine College, Doctor of Humane Laws, Honoris Causa, 1993; Beloit College, Doctor of Humanities, 1990; and numerous other honorary degrees. **MEMBERSHIPS** Epsilon Boule of Sigma Pi Phi Fraternity; Kappa Alpha Psi Fraternity; Navy League; Honor Society of Phi Kappa Phi; American Society for Public Administration, 1971-; Veterans of Foreign Wars, Chevy Chase Chapter; American Academy of Diplomacy; American Foreign Service Assn; American Political Science Assn; World Affairs Councils of Central OK and Washington, DC; Cranlana Programme, bd; Asia Society, bd of trustees; Joint Center for Political and Economic Studies, bd of govs; numerous other organizations, councils, and boards; American Legion, Chester A. Arthur Society, Council on Foreign Relations, Foreign Policy Assn, Intl Studies Assn, Pacific Council on Intl Policy, Public Service Commission, American Consortium for Intl Public Administration, Center for the Study of the Presidency bd of dirs, Assn for Diplomatic Studies & Training; bd of trustees, Inst of Intl Education; adv bd, Inst for Intl Public Policy; bd of trustees, Lewis & Clark College; adv council Univ Ofc of Intl Programs, Pennsylvania State Univ. **SELECTED PUBLICATIONS** Author, "New Dimensions in Foreign Affairs: Public Administration Theory in Practice," Public Administration Review, July-August 1990; "Divsersity in US Diplomacy," The Bureaucrat, Vol 20, No 4, 1991-92; "The United States and the UN", Yale Univ Law Journal, 1993; "Global Institutions (Action for the Future)," U.S. Catholic Conference, 1995; "Resolution of Conflict, the Attainment of Peace", University of Sydney, Centre for Peace and Conflict Studies, 1996; "An International Agenda for Change," American Behavioral Scientist, Vol 40, Number 3, Sage Publishers, 1997; "The Psychology of Diplomacy: Conflict Resolution in a Time of Minimal or Unusual Small-Scale Conflicts, "Chapter 4, The Psychology of Peacekeeping, edited by Harvey J. Langholtz, Westport, CT: Praeger, 1998. Distinguished Jerry Collins Lecturer in Public Administration, Florida State Univ; presidential appointment to the Presidential/Congressional Commission on Public Service, 1992-93. **CONTACT ADDRESS** International Programs Ctr, Univ of Oklahoma, 339 W Boyd St, Rm 400, Norman, OK, 73019-5144.

PERKINS, KENNETH J AMES
PERSONAL Born 03/27/1946, Weehawken, NJ, m, 1971, 2 children **DISCIPLINE** HISTORY **EDUCATION** VA Mil

Inst, BA, 68; Princeton Univ, MA, 71, PhD(Mid E studies), 73. **CAREER** Res assoc, Inst Islamic Studies, McGill Univ, 73-74; asst prof, 74-80, Assoc Prof Islamic Hist, Univ SC, 80-. **MEMBERSHIPS** Mid E Studies Asn N Am; Mid E Inst; French Colonial Hist Soc. **RESEARCH** Nineteenth and 20th century North Africa; colonial military administrative structures. **SELECTED PUBLICATIONS** Auth, Pressure and persuasion in the policies of the French Military in Colonial North Africa, Mil Affairs, 76; North African propaganda and the United States, 1946-1956, African Studies Rev, 76; Qaids, Captains, and Colons: French Military Administration in the Colonial Maghrib, 1844-1934, New York, 80; In the twilight of Imperialism: Great Britain and the Egyptian Frontier Districts Administration, 1919-1939, Middle East Studies, 82; to Be a Caid in Colonial Algeria - French - Establet,c, International J of African Historical Studies, Vol 0026, 1993; Morocco in The Reign of Sulayman,mawley - Elmansour,m, American Historical Review, Vol 0098, 1993; The French Communist-party And The Algerian War - Joly,d, International J of African Historical Studies, Vol 0025, 1992; The Hundred-years-war For Morocco - Gunpowder And The Military Revolution in The Early-modern Muslim World - Cook,wf, American Historical Review, Vol 0100, 1995; The Caliphate in The West - an Islamic Political Institution in The Iberian Peninsula - Wasserstein,dj, Historian, Vol 0057, 1995; The Hajj- The Muslim Pilgrimage to Mecca And The Holy Places - Peters,fe, Historian, Vol 0057, 1995; an Historical Encyclopedia of The Arab-israeli Conflict - Reich,b, J of Military History, Vol 0061, 1997. **CONTACT ADDRESS** Dept of Hist, Univ of SC, Columbia, SC, 29208.

PERKINS, LEEMAN LLOYD

PERSONAL Born 03/27/1932, Salina, UT, 4 children **DISCIPLINE** MUSICOLOGY **EDUCATION** Univ Utah, BFA, Phi Beta Kappa, 54; Yale Univ, PhD, 65. **CAREER** From instr to asst prof musicol, Yale Univ, 64-71; assoc prof, Univ Tex, Austin, 71-76; PROF MUSICOL, COLUMBIA UNIV, 76-, Morse fel, Yale Univ, 67-68; Am Coun Learned Socs fel & grant, Univ Res Inst, Univ Tex, Austin, 73-74; Nat Endowment for Humanities fel, 79. **HONORS AND AWARDS** Otto Kinkeldey Award, Am Musicol Soc, 80; La Medaillo de la Ville de Tours, 97. **MEMBERSHIPS** Am Musicol Soc; Int Musicol Soc; Renaissance Soc Am; Amici Thomae Mori. **RESEARCH** The history of the music of the Renaissance, the 15th and 16th centuries, with special interest in primary sources, musical institutions, and the development of musical style. **SELECTED PUBLICATIONS** Ed, Johannis Lheritier Opera Ominia, Am Inst Musicol 69; auth, Notes bibliographiques au sujet de l'ancien fond musical de l'eglise de St Louis des Francais a Rome, Fontes Artis Musicae, 69; Mode and structure in the masses of Josquin, J Am Musicol Soc, 73; contribr, Grove's Dict of Music and Musicians; co-ed, The Mellon Chansonnier, Yale Univ, 79; gen ed, Masters and Monuments of the Renaissance, Broude Bros Ltd, Music in the Age of Renaissance, W W Norton and Co, 98. **CONTACT ADDRESS** Dept Music, Columbia Univ, 2960 Broadway, New York, NY, 10027-6900. **EMAIL** LLPI@columbia.edu

PERKINS, LINDA MARIE

PERSONAL Born 11/22/1950, Mobile, Alabama, m **DISCIPLINE** AFRICAN-AMERICAN STUDIES **EDUCATION** Kentucky State University, BS, 1971; Univ of Illinois, C-U, MS, 1973, PhD, 1978. **CAREER** Univ of Ill-Champaign Urbana, Asst Dir of Minority Affrs, 1973-75; William Paterson Coll Dir of Affirmative Action, 1978-79; Radcliffe College, The Mary Bunting Institute, Research Fellow, Asst Dir, 1979-83; The Claremont Coll, asst vice pres, 1983-86; Center for Afro-Amer Studies, UCLA, visiting scholar, 1986-. **HONORS AND AWARDS** Research Grant, Natl Inst of Educ, 1979-81; Natl Endowment for the Humanities, 1984; Spencer Foundation, 1986- . **MEMBERSHIPS** Big Sisters of Boston, 1981-83; Pomona Valley YWCA, Board Member, 1984-; Los Angeles United Way, Allocation Team, 1984-86. **CONTACT ADDRESS** Visiting Scholar, UCLA, 738 Santa Barbara Drive, Los Angeles, CA, 90024.

PERLIS, VIVIAN

PERSONAL Born 04/26/1928, Brooklyn, NY, w, 1949, 3 children **DISCIPLINE** MUSIC LITERATURE, HISTORY **EDUCATION** Univ Mich, BA, 49, MA, 52; Columbia Univ, PhD, 65-67. **CAREER** Vis lectr, USC, Eastman, Duke, Smith, Cornell, Wesleyan; sr res assoc, lectr, Dir Oral History & Am Music, Yale School Music & Library, 73-. **HONORS AND AWARDS** Am Inst Acad Arts & Lectrs Ines Award, 71; Kinkeldey Awards, 75; ASCAP Book Award, 85; Sovneck Soc Book Award, 89. **MEMBERSHIPS** Am Musicol Soc; Sovneck Soc; Oral Hist Asn. **RESEARCH** Contemporary composition; 20th Century music history. **SELECTED PUBLICATIONS** Auth Charles Ives, Remembered, 74; coed An Ives Celebration, 75; Copeland 1900-'942, 84; Copeland since 1943, 89. **CONTACT ADDRESS** School of Music and Library, Yale Univ, 425 College St, New Haven, CT, 06520. **EMAIL** vivian.perlis@yale.edu

PERMAN, MICHEAL

PERSONAL Born 03/07/1942, London, England, m, 2 children **DISCIPLINE** HISTORY **EDUCATION** Hartford Col, BA, 63; Univ Ill, Urbana - Champaign, MA, 65, PhD, 69. **CAREER** Lect, 68-70, Manchester Univ, UK; asst prof, 70-74, assoc prof, 74-84, prof, 84-90, res prof, human, 90-, Univ Ill Chicago. **RESEARCH** Southern hist, civil war & reconstruction **SELECTED PUBLICATIONS** Auth, The South and Congress' reconstruction policy 1866- 67, J Am Studies, 71; Reunion Without Compromise: The South and Reconstruction 1865-68, Cambridge Univ, 73; The Haymarket affair, 1886, In: Nations and Empires, Vol 9 of Milestones of History, Weidenfeld & Nicolson, 75; Reconstruction the nation, Reconstruction and the American Negro, Vol 8, In: The American Destiny, Danbury Press; The Lincoln Persuasion - Remaking American Liberalism - Greenstone,jd, Reviews in American History, Vol 0022, 1994; Southern Stories - Slaveholders in Peace And War - Faust,dg, Reviews in American History, Vol 0022, 1994; Black-belt Scalawag - Hays,charles And The Southern Republicans in The Era of Reconstruction - Rogers,wn, J of American History, Vol 0081, 1994; Entrepreneur For Equality - Governor Bullock,rufus, Commerce, And Race in Post-civil War Georgia - Duncan,r, American Historical Review, Vol 0100, 1995. **CONTACT ADDRESS** Dept of History, Univ of Illinois, Chicago, 601 S. Morgan, Chicago, IL, 60607-7109. **EMAIL** mperman@uic.edu

PERNAL, ANDREW B.

DISCIPLINE HISTORY **EDUCATION** Assumption Univ, BA; Windsor Univ, MA; Univ Ottawa, PhD. **CAREER** Hist, Brandon Univ. **RESEARCH** History of Poland, Russia and Ukraine; diplomatic relations; historiography; historical cartography. **SELECTED PUBLICATIONS** Auth, An Analysis of Disbursements for Diplomacy during the Ratification of the Hadiach Union Treaty at the Warsaw Diet of 1659, Harvard, 93; Echoes of the 3 May 1791 Polish Constitution in the Contemporary Canadian Press, 93; co-auth, Beauplan's A Description of Ukraine, Cambridge, 93; Guillaume Le Vasseur, Sieur de Beauplan, 93. **CONTACT ADDRESS** History Dept, Brandon Univ, 270-18th St, Brandon, MB, R7A 6A9.

PERNICK, MARTIN STEVEN

PERSONAL Born 06/02/1948, New York, NY, m, 1 child **DISCIPLINE** HISTORY OF MEDICINE, AMERICAN HISTORY **EDUCATION** Brandeis Univ, BA, 68; Columbia Univ, MA, 69, PhD(hist), 79. **CAREER** Instr hist of med, Pa State Univ, 72-79; vis lectr, Harvard Univ, 75-76; from Asst Prof to Assoc Prof, 79-92, PROF HIST, UNIV MICH, ANN ARBOR, 92-, Assoc Dir, Prog Soc & Med, 92-. **HONORS AND AWARDS** NEH Fel, 79-83; Fel, Spencer Found, 82-83; Nat Libr Med grant, 84-85, 98; NEH grant, 85-88; Excellence in Education Award, Univ Mich, 94; Rackham Fac Recognition Award, Univ Mich, 97-2000; Burroughs Welcome Fund grant, 97-99. **MEMBERSHIPS** Am Asn Hist of Med; Orgn Am Historians; AHA; Hist Sci Soc. **RESEARCH** History of disease, health, and the body; film and the mediation of professional and popular culture; history of ethics and value issues in medicine; histories of eugenics, euthanasia, and suffering. **SELECTED PUBLICATIONS** Contribr, Medical professionalism, In: Encycl of Bioethics, Free Press, Macmillan, 78; auth, A Calculus of Suffering: Pain, Professionalism, and Anesthesia in Nineteenth Century America, Columbia Univ Press, 85; The Black Stork: Eugenics and the Death of "Defective" Babies in American Medicine and Motion Pictures since 1915, Oxford Univ Press, 96; Eugenic Euthanasia in Early-Twentieth-Century America and Medically-Assisted Suicide Today, In: New Perspectives on Assisted Suicide (tentative title), Univ Mich Press (in press 98); historical consultant on script and archival film project, Fit: Episodes in the History of the Body, Straight Ahead Films, 92, syndicated on PBS, 94; The People's Plague: Tuberculosis in America, Florentine Films, 95, PBS broadcast, 10/2/95; author of numerous articles and other publications. **CONTACT ADDRESS** Dept of Hist, Univ Mich, 435 S State St, Ann Arbor, MI, 48109-1003. **EMAIL** mpernick@umich.edu

PERRICONE, JACK

PERSONAL Born 03/19/1940, New Haven, CT, m, 1987, 2 children **DISCIPLINE** MUSIC **EDUCATION** Haitt Col Music, PM, 61; Ind Univ, MM, 68. **CAREER** Writer, pop, country, R & B songs; teacher, chair, founder, Songwriting Dept, Berklee Col Music. **HONORS AND AWARDS** ASCAP awards, Songwriters Guild **MEMBERSHIPS** ASCAP **SELECTED PUBLICATIONS** Auth, Melody In Songwriting: A Study of its Components and Relationship to Harmony, Berklee Press. **CONTACT ADDRESS** Berklee Col of Music, 1140 Boylston St, Boston, MA, 01701. **EMAIL** JPerricon@berklee.edu

PERRY, CHARLES RICHARD

PERSONAL Born 09/29/1946, Atlanta, GA, m, 1968, 2 children **DISCIPLINE** BRITISH HISTORY **EDUCATION** Davidson Col, AB, 68; Harvard Univ, MA, 69, PhD(hist), 76. **CAREER** Teaching fel hist & lit, Harvard Univ, 70-74; instr hist, 74-77, Asst Prof Hist, Univ of The South, 77-, Nat Endowment for Humanities fel, Univ NC, 78-79; tutor British studies, St John's Col, Oxford Univ, 81. **MEMBERSHIPS** AHA; Conf British Studies; Carolinas Symposium Brit Studies. **RESEARCH** Victorian administrative history; modern British political history; modern European economic history. **SELECTED PUBLICATIONS** Contribr, The Social Impact of the Telephone, Mass Inst Technol Press, 77; auth, Frank Ives Scudamore and the post office telegraphs, Albion, 80; The general post office's Zanzibar shipping contracts, 1860-1914, Mariner's Mirror, 82; British History 1815-1906 - Mccord,n, Albion, Vol 0025, 1993; Liberty And Morality - a Political-biography of Bulwerlytton,edward - Snyder,cw, Albion, Vol 0028, 1996. **CONTACT ADDRESS** Dept Hist, Univ of the South, Sewanee, TN, 37375.

PERRY, EDMUND

PERSONAL Born 05/18/1923, GA, m, 3 children **DISCIPLINE** HISTORY OF RELIGIONS **EDUCATION** Univ Ga, AB, 44; Emory Univ, BD, 46; Northwestern Univ, PhD(bibl theol, hist of relig), 50. **CAREER** Dir Wesley Found, GA State Col Women, 46-48; from instr to asst prof Bible & hist of relig, Duke Univ, 50-54; assoc prof, 54-62, Prof Hist Of Relig, Northwestern Univ, 62-, Chmn Dept, 54-, Mem univ senate, Methodist Church, 54-60; educ consult, Am Tel & Tel Co, 60-62; Fulbright prof, Vidyodaya Univ Ceylon, 67- 68. **HONORS AND AWARDS** DLitt, Vidyodaya Univ Ceylon, 68. **MEMBERSHIPS** Am Orient Soc; Am Theol Soc; Am Acad Relig; Soc Bibl Lit; Int Soc Buddhist-Christian Friends (exec secy, 68-). **RESEARCH** History and methods of studying religions; history and the history of religions; a Christian theology of religion. **SELECTED PUBLICATIONS** Coauth, Jews and Christians in North America, Westminster, 65; auth, The Study and Practice of Religion Today, Vidyodaya Univ Ceylon, 68; Buddhist Studies in Honour of Walpola Rahula, Fraser, London, 80; Theravada Buddhism - a Social-history From Ancient Benares to Modern Colombo - Gombrich,rf, J of The American Oriental Society, Vol 0117, 1997. **CONTACT ADDRESS** Dept of Hist & Relig, Northwestern Univ, Evanston, IL, 60201.

PERRY, JOHN CURTIS

PERSONAL Born 07/18/1930, Orange, NJ, M, 1957, 5 children **DISCIPLINE** MODERN HISTORY **EDUCATION** Yale Univ, BA, 52, MA, 53; Harvard Univ, PhD(hist), 62. **CAREER** From instr to asst prof hist, Conn Col, 62-66; from asst prof to assoc prof hist, Carleton Col, 66-74, dir Asian studies prog, 66-73, chm dept hist, 71-74, acting dir of libr, 75-76, prof, 74-80; vis prof diplomacy, 80-81, HENRY WILLARD DENISON PROF HIST, FLETCHER SCH LAW & DIPLOMACY, TUFTS UNIV, 81-, Vis res assoc, Fairbank E Asia Res Ctr, Harvard Univ, 76-77 & Japan Inst, Harvard Univ, 77-80. **HONORS AND AWARDS** Japanese Imperial Decoration, Order of the Sacred Treasure, 91 **MEMBERSHIPS** AHA; Japan Soc. **RESEARCH** Oceanic history. **SELECTED PUBLICATIONS** Auth, Beneath the Eagle's Wings: Americans in Occupied Japan, 80; coauth, Sentimental Imperialists: The American Experience in East Asia, 81; Facing West: Americans and the Opening of the Pacific, 95. **CONTACT ADDRESS** Fletcher Sch of Law and Diplomacy, Tufts Univ, Packard Ave., Medford, MA, 02155-5555. **EMAIL** blackships@aol.com

PERRY, MARILYN

PERSONAL Born 04/03/1940, Glendale, CA **DISCIPLINE** HISTORY OF ART **EDUCATION** Stanford Univ, BA, 62, MA, 63; Univ NC, Chapel Hill, MA, 66; Univ London, MPhil, 68, PhD(hist Europ art), 75. **CAREER** Lectr hist of art, Am, Brit & Can univ & col progs abroad, Italy & England, 58-82; Exec VP, S H Kress Found, 82-, Fel, Villa I Tatti, Harvard Univ Ctr for Ital Renaissance Studies, 76-77; fel, Gladys Krieble Delmas Found for res in Venice, 77- 78. **RESEARCH** Italian Renaissance art; collections of art and antiquities in Renaissance Venice; Stendhal in Rome. **SELECTED PUBLICATIONS** Auth, The pride of Venice, Aquileia nostra, 74-75; A Greek bronze in Renaissance Venice, 75 & Candor Illaesus: the impresa of Clement VII and other Medici devices in the Vatican Stanze, 77, Burlington Mag; Saint Mark's trophies: legend, superstition and archaeology in Renaissance Venice, 77 & Cardinal Domenico Grimani's legacy of ancient art to Venice, 78, J Warburg & Courtauld Inst; La pauvre Miss Bathurst: memorials to a tragedy in Stendhal's Rome, Connoisseur, 78; On Titian's borrowings from ancient art: A cautionary case, Tiziano e Venezia, 76; A Renaissance showplace of art: The Palazzo Grimani at Santa Maria Formosa, Venice, Apollo, 81. **CONTACT ADDRESS** S H Kress Found, 221 W 57th, New York, NY, 10019.

PERRY, ROBERT LEE

PERSONAL Born 12/06/1932, Toledo, OH, m **DISCIPLINE** ETHNOHISTORY **EDUCATION** Bowling Green St Univ, BA sociology 1959, MA sociology 1965; Wayne St Univ, PhD sociology 1978. **CAREER** Lucas Cnty Juv Ct Toledo, OH, probation counselor 1960-64, juvenile ct referee 1964-67; Detroit Inst Techn, asst prof 1967-70; DEPARTMENT OF ETHNIC STUDIES, BOWLING GREEN STATE UNIV CHMN, 1970-; licensed professional counselor, 1988; Ohio certified prevention consultant, 1989-. **HONORS AND AWARDS** Sigma Delta Pi natl Spanish Hon Soc 1958; Alpha Kappa Delta Natl Soc Honor Soc 1976; $37,000 Grant, Dept HEW 1979; Post Doct Fellowship Amer Social Soc Inst for Soc Research UCLA 1980; Charles C Irby National Association of Ethnic Studies (NAES), Distinguished Service Award, 1994. **MEMBERSHIPS** Consult Natl Inst of Law Enf and Crimin Just 1978-82; consult Div Soc Law and Econ Scis Natl Sci Found 1980; consult Children's Def Fund Task Force on Adoption Assist 1980; chair Status of Women & Minorities Comm N Cent Sociol Soc 1983-

85; bd mem Citizens Review Bd Lucas Cnty Juv Ct Toledo, OH 1979-91; bd mem Inst for Child Advocacy Cleveland, OH 1981-85. **CONTACT ADDRESS** African American Studies Dept, Eastern Michigan Univ, 620 Pray Harrold, Ypsilanti, MI, 48197.

PERSON, DAWN RENEE
PERSONAL Born 12/10/1956, Sewickley, PA, m, 1986 **DISCIPLINE** EDUCATION **EDUCATION** Slippery Rock Univ, BS Educ 1977, M Educ 1979; Teachers College, Columbia Univ, EdD, 1990. **CAREER** Slippery Rock Univ, human relations counselor 1978-79, minority affairs coord 1979-80, advisor to black & intl students 1980-81; CO State Univ, dir black student services 1981-85; Lafayette College, asst dean of academic services, 1985-90; Teachers College, Columbia Univ, asst prof of higher educ, 1990-97; STUDENT DEVELOPMENT IN HIGHER EDUCATION, ASSOC PROF. **HONORS AND AWARDS** Outstanding Black Achiever in Pennsylvania, Black Opinions, 1989; Service Award, Lafayette College Alumni Chapter of Black Collegians, 1988; Excellence in Higher Education, Lafayette College Minority Students, 1990; Publication & Research in Minority Student Retention, Student Cultures, & Multicultural Issues in Higher Educ. **MEMBERSHIPS** Workshop facilitator Male/Female Relation 1978-; mem ACPA; mem NAACP Easton PA Chap 1985-87; mem Black Conference-Higher Educ PA 1986-87; NASPA; Leadership Lehigh Valley 1989-90. **CONTACT ADDRESS** Student Devt in Higher Educ, California State Univ, Long Beach, Bellflower Blvd, Ed Bu II, No. 214, Long Beach, CA, 90840.

PERSON, WILLIAM ALFRED
PERSONAL Born 08/29/1945, Henderson, North Carolina, m **DISCIPLINE** EDUCATION **EDUCATION** Johnson C Smith University, BA, 1963-67; University of Georgia, MEd, 1972-73, EdD, 1973-77. **CAREER** Wilkes City Board of Education, teacher, 1967-72; University of Georgia, Grad Asst/Admin Asst, 1973-77; Mississippi State Univ, asst prof, 1977-80, assoc professor, 1980-. **HONORS AND AWARDS** Two academic scholarships, 1963-65; Sigma Man of the Year, Phi Beta Sigma, 1979. **MEMBERSHIPS** Treasurer, Phi Delta Kappa, 1982-83; vice pres, Phi Beta Sigma, 1982-83; president, Phi Beta Sigma, 1983-; bd of directors, Starkville Kiwanis Breakfast Club, 1984-. **CONTACT ADDRESS** Mississippi State Univ, P O Box 6331, Mississippi State, MS, 39762-6331.

PESEK, THOMAS G.
DISCIPLINE RUSSIA AND CENTRAL EUROPE **EDUCATION** Ind Univ, PhD, 70. **CAREER** Assoc prof, Washington State Univ. **CONTACT ADDRESS** Dept of History, Washington State Univ, 301 Wilson Hall, PO Box 644030, Pullman, WA, 99164-4030. **EMAIL** pesek@wsu.edu

PESELY, GEORGE E.
PERSONAL Born 01/24/1949, Quantico, VA **DISCIPLINE** ANCIENT HISTORY **EDUCATION** San Diego State Univ, AB, 70; Univ of IL, Urbana-Champaign, MA, 71; Univ of CA, Berkeley, PhD, 83. **CAREER** Lectr, Class, 83-84, State Univ NY at Buffalo; Asst Prof, Hist, 84-85, Arkansas Tech Univ; Asst Prof, Hist, 85-86, Univ of IL, Urbana-Champaign; Asst Prof, Class, 86-87, Memphis State Univ; Asst Prof, Hist, 87-88, Clarion Univ; Asst Prof, Hist, 88-90, Univ of Northern Iowa; Asst Prof to Assoc Prof, Hist, 90-, AustinPeay State Univ. **MEMBERSHIPS** Amer Philo Assoc; Archaeol Inst of Amer; Assoc of Ancient Hist; Class Assoc of the Middle West and South; Class Assoc of Canada; Amer Numismatic Soc; Amer Soc of Greek and Latin Epigraphy. **RESEARCH** Greek Political and Construction History; Greek History. **SELECTED PUBLICATIONS** Auth, Did Aristotle use Androtion's Atthis?, Klio 76, 94; Aristotle's Source for the Tyranny of Peisistratos, Athenaeum 83, 95; Andron and the Four Hundred, Illinois Classical Studies 20, 95; Poredak Platonichih dijaloga prema Frani Petricu, Filozofska Istrazivanja, 98; Hangon, Athenaeum, 89; The Speech of Endius in Diodorus Siculus, Classical Philology, 85. **CONTACT ADDRESS** Dept History, Austin Peay State Univ, Box 4486, Clarksville, TN, 37044. **EMAIL** peselyg@apsu.edu

PESKIN, ALLAN
PERSONAL Born 03/16/1933, Cumberland, MD, m, 1963, 2 children **DISCIPLINE** AMERICAN HISTORY **EDUCATION** Univ Chicago, AB, 53; Western Reserve Univ, AB, 55, MA, 56, PhD(Hist), 65. **CAREER** Instr Hist & Govt, Fenn Col, 62-64; asst prof, 64-67, assoc prof, 67-81, prof Hist, Cleveland State Univ, 81-. **HONORS AND AWARDS** Outstanding Publication Award, Ohio Acad Hist, 78; Ohioana Book Award--Biography, Ohioana Libr Asn, 79. **MEMBERSHIPS** Orgn Am Historians; Southern Hist Asn. **RESEARCH** Nineteenth century America. **SELECTED PUBLICATIONS** Auth, North into Freedom: The Autobiography of John Malvin, Free Negro, 1795-1880, Western Reserve Univ, 66; contrib, For the Union: Ohio Leaders in the Civil War, Ohio State Univ, 68; auth, The put-up job: Wisconsin and the Republican National Convention of 1880, Wis Mag Hist, Summer 72; Was there a compromise of 1877?, J Am Hist, 6/73; Garfield, Kent State Univ, 78; The historiography of reconstruction, Encycl Southern Hist, La State Univ Press, 79; James A Garfield, Historian, The Historian, 8/81; Who Were the Stalwarts? Who Were Their Rivals? Poli Sci Q, Winter, 84-85; Volunteers, The Mexican War Journals of Private Richard Coulter & Sergeant Thomas Barelay, Kent State Univ, 91. **CONTACT ADDRESS** Dept of History, Cleveland State Univ, 1983 E 24th St, Cleveland, OH, 44115-2440. **EMAIL** a.peskin@csuohio.edu

PESSEN, EDWARD
PERSONAL Born 12/31/1920, New York, NY, m, 1940, 5 children **DISCIPLINE** HISTORY **EDUCATION** Columbia Univ, BA, 47, MA, 48, PhD(hist), 54. **CAREER** Lectr hist, City Col NY, 48-54; assoc prof, Fisk Univ, 54- 56; prof hist & chmn dept hist & div lib arts & sci, Staten Island Community Col 56-70; Distinguished Prof Hist, Baruch Col & City Univ NY Grad Ctr, 70-, Vis prof, New Sch Soc Res, 65-66; State Univ NY Res Found fel grant, 65-66; mem adv bd, Martin Van Buren Papers Proj, 69-; Guggenheim fel, 77-78; Rockefeller Found fel, 78. **MEMBERSHIPS** AHA; Soc Am Historians; Orgn Am Historians; Soc Historians of Early Am Repub. **RESEARCH** American social and intellectual history; politics and political history; Jacksonian era. **SELECTED PUBLICATIONS** Auth, Most Uncommon Jacksonians, State Univ NY, 67; The egalitarian myth and the American social reality: Wealth, equality, and mobility in the era of the common man, Am Hist Rev, 1071; Who governed the nation's cities in the era of the common man?, Polit Sci Quart, 1272; Riches, Class and Power Before the Civil War, 73 & ed, Three Centuries of Social Mobility in America, 74, Heath; auth, Jacksonian Panorama, Bobbs, 76; Prologue to Who rules America? Power and politics in the Democratic Era, 1825-1975, J Nat Arch, spring 77; Jacksonian America: Society, Personality and Politics, Dorsey, rev ed, 78; How different from each other were the Antebellum North & South?, Am Hist Rev, 80; The Market Revolution - Jacksonian America, 1815-1846 - Sellers,c, J of Southern History, Vol 0059, 1993. **CONTACT ADDRESS** Dept of Hist, Baruch Col, CUNY, New York, NY, 10010.

PESSIN, SARAH
PERSONAL Born 07/23/1970, New York, NY **DISCIPLINE** MEDIEVAL PHILOSOPHY **EDUCATION** Yeshiva Univ, BA, 91; Columbia Univ, MA, 94; OH State Univ, doctoral candidate, 2000. **CAREER** Graduate student/fellow, OH State Univ. **HONORS AND AWARDS** Melton Center for Jewish Studies Graduate Fellowship. **RESEARCH** Neoplatonism; Jewish and Islamic Medieval Philosophy. **CONTACT ADDRESS** Dept of Philos, Ohio State Univ, 230 N. Oval Mall, 350 Univ H, Columbus, OH, 43209. **EMAIL** pessin.4@osu.edu

PESTANA, CARLA
PERSONAL Born 10/24/1958, Burbank, CA, m, 1981, 2 children **DISCIPLINE** HISTORY **EDUCATION** Loyola Marymount Univ, BA; 80, UCLA, MA, 83, PhD, 87. **CAREER** John Carter Brown Library, res assoc, 85-86; OH State, asst prof, 87-93, assoc prof, 93 -. **HONORS AND AWARDS** Walter Muir Whitehill Prize in Colonial Hist, 83; NEH-Huntington Senior Fel, 97-98 ; Am Philos Soc Research Grant, 94-95; Fletcher Jones Research Fel, Huntington Library, 94-95; Huntington Library-Brit Acad Exchange, 92-93, 87: Lilly Tchg Fel, OH State Univ, 91-93; Recent Recipients of the PhD Fel, Am Council of Learned Soc, 89-90; Kate B. and Hall J. Peterson Fel, Am Antiquarian Soc, 88-89; Graduate Woman of the Year Award, UCLA Assoc of Acad Women 87; Charlotte W. Newcombe Doctoral Dissertation Fel, Woodrow Wilson National Fel Found 86-87; Huntington-Frank Hideo Kono Memorial Fel, Huntington Library 85-86; Distinguished Scholar Award, UCLA Alumni Assoc 84; Research Fel, John Carter Brown Library 83. **MEMBERSHIPS** AHA, OAH Assoc of the Omohundro Institute of Early Am Hist and Cult, Colonial Soc of MA, coord council for women in hist, North Am Conference on Brit Studies. **RESEARCH** Anglo-Atlantic in the 17th century; Quakers. **SELECTED PUBLICATIONS** Quakers and Baptists in Colonial Massachusetts, 91; Liberty of Conscience and the Growth of Religious Deversity in Early America, 1636-1786, 86; The Quaker Executions as Myth and hist, Jour of Amer Hist, 93; The City upon the Hill under siege: Puritan Perceptions of the Quaker threat to Massachusetts Bay, New England Quarterly 84, The Social World for Salem: William King's 1681 Blasphemy Trial, Amer Qrt 89. **CONTACT ADDRESS** Ohio State Univ, 230 W 17th Ave, Columbus, OH, 43210-1367. **EMAIL** Pestana.1@osu.edu

PETERS, EDWARD MURRAY
PERSONAL New Haven, Conn, m, 3 children **DISCIPLINE** MEDIEVAL HISTORY **EDUCATION** Yale Univ, BA, 63, MA, 65, PhD(medieval studies), 67. **CAREER** Instr English, Quinnipiac Col, 64-66; asst prof hist, Univ Calif, San Diego, 67-68; Henry C Lea asst prof, 68-70, Henry C Lea assoc prof, 70-81, HENRY C LEA PROF MEDIEVAL HIST, UNIV PA, 81-; CUR, HENRY C LEA LIBR, 68-. **HONORS AND AWARDS** John Simon Guggenheim Fel 88-89; Am Coun Learned Soc fel, 81-82., MA, Univ Pa, 72. **MEMBERSHIPS** Mediaeval Acad Am; AHA; fel Royal Hist Soc, London; Dante Soc Am; ICMAC; Am Soc Legal Hist; Ren Soc Am. **RESEARCH** Medieval legal and political theory; medieval kingship and governance; medieval and Renaissance cultural history. **SELECTED PUBLICATIONS** Auth, The Shadow King: Rex Inutilis in Medieval Law and Literature, 751-1327, Yale Univ, 70; co-ed, Witchcraft in Europe, 1100-1700: A Documentary, 72 & The World of Piers Plowman, 75, Univ Pa; auth, Europe: The World of the Middle Ages, Prentice-Hall, 77; The Magician, the Witch and the Law, Univ Pa, 78; Heresy and Authority in Medieval Europe, Univ Pa, 80; Europe and the Middle Ages: A Short History, Prentice-Hall, 82; auth, Europe and the Middle Ages, 3rd ed, 96; auth, Torture, 85; auth, Inquisition, 89; auth, The First Crusade, 2nd ed 98. **CONTACT ADDRESS** Dept of Hist, Univ of Pa, 3401 Walnut St, Ste 352B, Philadelphia, PA, 19104-6228. **EMAIL** empeters@sas.upenn.edu

PETERS, FRANCIS EDWARD
PERSONAL Born 06/23/1927, New York, NY, m, 1957, 1 child **DISCIPLINE** CLASSICS, ISLAMIC STUDIES **EDUCATION** St Louis Univ, AB, 50, MA, 52; Princeton Univ, PhD(Orient studies), 61. **CAREER** Instr English, Latin & Greek, Canisius High Sch, Buffalo, NY, 52-54; instr English, Scarborough Country Day Sch, NY, 55- 56; from asst prof to assoc prof classics, 61-69, Prof Hist & Near Eastern Lang & Lit & Chmn Dept Near Eastern Lang & Lit, New York Univ, 70-. **MEMBERSHIPS** Am Orient Soc; Mid E Studies Asn. **RESEARCH** Social and intellectual history of Late Antiquity and Early Islam; Near Eastern urbanism. **SELECTED PUBLICATIONS** Auth, Greek Philosophical Terms, 67 & Aristotle and the Arabs, 68, New York Univ; Aristoteles Arabus, Brill, 68; The Harvest of Hellenism, 71 & Allah's Commonwealth, 74, Simon & Schuster; Ours, R Mareck, 81; The Children of Abraham: Judaism, Christianity, Islam, Princeton Univ Press, 82; Jesus And Muhammad - a Historians Reflections, Muslim World, Vol 0086, 1996; Ritual, Politics And The City in Fatimid Cairo, Sanders,p, Speculum-a J of Medieval Studies, Vol 0071, 1996; Ritual, Politics And The City in Fatimid Cairo, Sanders,p, Speculum-a J of Medieval Studies, Vol 0071, 1996; Abraham, Sign of Hope For Jews, Christians And Muslims - Kuschel,kj, J of Religion, Vol 0077, 1997. **CONTACT ADDRESS** Dept of Near Eastern Lang & Lit, New York Univ, New York, NY, 10003.

PETERS, ISSA
PERSONAL Born 03/15/1935, Mishtaya, Syria, m, 1965, 1 child **DISCIPLINE** ARABIC, MIDDLE EAST HISTORY **EDUCATION** Univ Damascus, BA, 58; Mich State Univ, MA, 60; Columbia Univ, PhD(Arabic), 74. **CAREER** Teacher English, Midway Jr Col, 64-65; instr English, Northern Ill Univ, 65-68; assoc prof Arabic, Defense Lang Inst, 71-76; assoc prof, 76-80, Prof Arabic & Middle East Studies, Am Grad Sch Int Mgt, 80- **MEMBERSHIPS** Am Asn Teachers Arabic; Am Orient Soc; Middle E Studies Asn. **RESEARCH** Contemporary Arabic literature and thought; Middle East history. **CONTACT ADDRESS** Dept of Int Studies, American Grad Sch of Intl Mgt, 15249 N 59th Ave, Glendale, AZ, 85306-3236. **EMAIL** petersi@t-bird.edu

PETERS, JULIE
DISCIPLINE DRAMA AND THEATRE HISTORY **EDUCATION** Yale Univ, AB, 81; Princeton Univ, PhD, 87. **CAREER** Asoc prof. **HONORS AND AWARDS** Fel, Fulbright found; fel, Folger Library; fel, Amer Coun Learned Soc; fel, Humboldt found. **RESEARCH** Law and literature. **SELECTED PUBLICATIONS** Auth, Congreve, the Drama, and the Printed Word, Stanford, 90; co-ed, Women's Rights, Human Rights: International Feminist Perspectives, Routledge, 95. **CONTACT ADDRESS** Dept of Eng, Columbia Col, New York, 2960 Broadway, New York, NY, 10027-6902.

PETERS, TOM F.
DISCIPLINE HISTORY OF ARCHITECTURAL AND CIVIL ENGINEERING TECHNOLOGY AND THE CULTURE O **EDUCATION** Dr. Sc. Techn., ETH Zurich **CAREER** Prof, Lehigh Univ **HONORS AND AWARDS** Dir, Inst Study Highrise Habitat. **RESEARCH** Current and historical topics in building. **SELECTED PUBLICATIONS** The Evolution of Long-span Bridge Building, Transitions In Engineering and Building the 19th Century. **CONTACT ADDRESS** Lehigh Univ, Bethlehem, PA, 18015.

PETERSEN, PETER LEWIS
PERSONAL Born 02/07/1935, Shelby County, IA, m, 1962, 2 children **DISCIPLINE** HISTORY **EDUCATION** Dana Col, BS, 62; Univ SD, MA, 63; Univ Iowa, PhD(hist), 71. **CAREER** From asst prof to assoc prof, 67-78, Prof Hist, West Tex State Univ, 78-, Ed consult hist, Annals Iowa, 78. **MEMBERSHIPS** AHA; Orgn Am Historians; Agr Hist Soc; Immigration Hist Soc. **RESEARCH** American political history, 1896-present; 20th century American agriculture; Scandinavian migration to the United States. **SELECTED PUBLICATIONS** Auth, Some research opportunities in the papers of Edwin T Meredith, 1876-1928, Books Iowa, 67; Edwin T Meredith: Iowa's other secretary of agriculture, Iowan, spring 73; Language and loyality: Governor Harding & Iowa's Danish-Americans during World War I, Annals Iowa, fall 74; Stopping Al Smith, SD Hist, fall 74; The reluctant candidate: Edwin T Meredith and the 1924 Democratic national convention, Palimpsest, 76; A new Oslo on the plains: The Anders L Mordt Land Company and Norwegian migration to the Texas Panhandle, Panhandle-Plains Hist Rev, 76; The making of an agricultural Publisher, In: Agricultural Literature: Proud Heritage--Future Promise, USDA Grad Sch, 77; coauth, Square deal for Eschiti, a footnote from the progressive era, In: Railroads in Oklahoma, Okla Hist Soc, 77; Canyon

Visions - Photographs And Pastels of The Texas Plains - Flores,d, Winton,ag, Southwestern Historical Quarterly, Vol 0097, 1994. **CONTACT ADDRESS** Dept of Hist, W Tex State Univ, 2501 4th Ave, Canyon, TX, 79016-0001.

PETERSON, CHARLES S.
PERSONAL Born 01/30/1927, Snowflake, AZ, m, 1953, 5 children **DISCIPLINE** HISTORY OF AMERICAN WEST **EDUCATION** Brigham Young Univ, BA, 52, MA, 58; Univ Utah, PhD(hist), 67. **CAREER** Instr hist, Col Eastern Utah, 58-66, dean instr, 66-68; asst prof hist, Univ Utah, 68-69; dir Utah State Hist Soc 69-71; assoc prof, 71-74, Prof Hist & Geog, Utah State Univ, 74-, Ed, Utah Hist Quart, 69-71; coed, Western Hist Quart, 71-; dir, Man & His Bread Mus, 71-; Nat Endowment for Humanities fel, Huntington Libr, 78. **MEMBERSHIPS** Western Hist Asn; Orgn Am Historians (asst secy-treas, 68-69); Am Asn State & Local Hist; Agr Hist Soc; Forest Hist Soc. **RESEARCH** Frontier history; agricultural and conservationist related topics; Mormon history with emphasis on the colonizing process of the church. **SELECTED PUBLICATIONS** Contribr, A Trail Guide to the Trail of the Mormon Battalion, Utah Hist Soc, 72; auth, Take Up Your Mission: Mormon Colonizing Along the Little Colorado 1870-1900, Univ Ariz, 73; Small holding land patterns in Utah and the problem of forest watershed management, Forest Hist, 773; ed, A Levi Mathers Savage: The look of Utah in 1873, Utah Hist Quart, 73; Look to the Mountains: Southeastern Utah and the La Sal National Forest, 75 & contribr, Utah's History: A College Text, 77, Brigham Young Univ; auth, Utah: A Bicentennial History, Norton, 77; Quest For The Golden Circle - The Four-corners And The Metropolitan West, 1945-1970 - Gomez,ar, Western Historical Quarterly, Vol 0027, 1996. **CONTACT ADDRESS** Dept of Hist & Geog, Utah State Univ, Logan, UT, 84322.

PETERSON, EDWARD NORMAN
PERSONAL Born 08/27/1925, St. Joseph, MO, m, 1946, 2 children **DISCIPLINE** HISTORY **EDUCATION** Univ Wis, PhD(hist), 53. **CAREER** Teaching asst, Univ Wis, 52-53; asst prof Eastern Ky State Col, 53-54; chmn dept soc sci, 63, Prof Hist, Univ Wis-river Falls, 54-, Chmn Dept, 62-, Humboldt Found fel, 63-64; State Univ Regents grant, 66; fels, Nat Endowment for Humanities, 69- 70 & Soc Sci Res Coun, 69-71; consult, Nat Endowment for Humanities, 72-. **MEMBERSHIPS** AHA; Conf Ger Politics. **RESEARCH** Source and use of power; World War II; 20th century Germany. **SELECTED PUBLICATIONS** Auth, Hjalmar Schacht, Christopher, 54; Geographic dichotomy, Soc Studies, 62; The bureaucracy and the Nazi party, Rev Polit, 66; Die Burokratie und die NSDAP, Der Staat, 67; The Limits of Hitler's Power, Princeton Univ, 69; Beurteilung der einwirkung Amerikas auf Deutschland 1945-52, In: Tradition und Neubeginn, Heymanns, Koln, 76; American Occupation of Germany, Wayne State Univ, 78; Die-spd-aber-aufgehoert-hat-zu-existieren - Social-democrats Under Soviet Occupation - German - Bouvier,bw, Schulz,hp, German Studies Review, Vol 0017, 1994; Flight And Defection From The Sbzddr 1945, 1949, 1961, Refugee Policy of The Federal-repubic-of-germany Before The Berlin-wall - German - Heidemeyer,h, American Historical Review, Vol 0100, 1995; The Russians in Germany - a History of The Soviet-zone-of- occupation, 1945-1949 - Naimark,nm, German Studies Review, Vol 0019, 1996; a Blitzkrieg Legend - The Military Campaign in The West - German - Frieser,kh, German Studies Review, Vol 0020, 1997; The Soviet-union And The Origins of The Second-world-war - Russo-german Relations And The Road to War, 1933-1941 - Roberts,g, German Studies Review, Vol 0020, 1997. **CONTACT ADDRESS** Dept of Hist, Univ of Wis, 410 S 3rd St, River Falls, WI, 54022-5013.

PETERSON, FRANK ROSS
PERSONAL Born 09/07/1941, Montpelier, ID, m, 1963, 3 children **DISCIPLINE** CONTEMPORARY AMERICAN HISTORY **EDUCATION** Utah State Univ, BA, 65; Wash State Univ, PhD(Am studies), 68. **CAREER** Asst prof hist, Univ Tex, Arlington, 68-71; from asst prof to assoc prof, 71-78, Prof Hist, Utah State Univ, 78-, Chmn Dept Hist & Geog, 76-, Nat Endowment for Humanities Younger Humanist fel, 72-73; lectr, Fulbright-Hays Fel, New Zealand, 78. **MEMBERSHIPS** Orgn Am Historians; Western Hist Asn; Asn Studies Afro-Am Life & Hist. **RESEARCH** Contemporary political history; school integration; conservation history. **SELECTED PUBLICATIONS** Contribr, Essays on Radicalism in Contemporary America, Univ Tex, 72; auth, Prophet Without Honor, Univ Ky, 74; Idaho: A Bicentennial History, Norton, 76; contribr, Utah's History, Brigham Young Univ, 79; Fighting The Odds, The Life of Church,frank - Ashby,l, Gramer,r, Western Historical Quarterly, Vol 0026, 1995; River of Life, Channel of Death - Fish And Dams on The Lower-snake - Petersen,kc, Pubic Historian, Vol 0019, 1997; Church,frank, Dc And Me - Hall,b, Pacific Northwest Quarterly, Vol 0088, 1997; Long,george,s - Timber Statesman - Twining,ce, J of The West, Vol 0036, 1997; Controversy, Conflict and Compromise - a History of the Lower-snake-river Development - Petersen,kc, Reed,me, Pubic Historian, Vol 0019, 1997. **CONTACT ADDRESS** Dept of Hist & Geog, Utah State Univ, 710 University Blvd, Logan, UT, 84322-0710.

PETERSON, JACQUELINE
DISCIPLINE NATIVE AMERICAN, NORTH AMERICAN HISTORY **EDUCATION** Univ Ill, Chicago, PhD, 81. **CAREER** Prof, Washington State Univ. **SELECTED PUBLICATIONS** Auth, Sacred Encounters: Father De Smet and the Indians of the Rocky Mountain West, Univ Okla Press, 93; ed, The New Peoples: Being and Becoming Metis in North America, Univ Manitoba Press, 91. **CONTACT ADDRESS** Dept of History, Washington State Univ, 301 Wilson Hall, PO Box 644030, Pullman, WA, 99164-4030. **EMAIL** peterson@vancouver.wsu.edu

PETERSON, JON ALVAH
PERSONAL Born 09/21/1935, Columbus, OH, m, 1963 **DISCIPLINE** AMERICAN HISTORY **EDUCATION** Swarthmore Col, BA, 57; Ohio State Univ, MA, 59; Harvard Univ, PhD(Am hist), 67. **CAREER** Lectr, 66-67, asst prof, 67-81, asst chmn dept hist, 74-76, Assoc Prof US Urban & Immigration Hist, Queens Col, NY, 81-, Adj asst prof, Fordham Univ, 68, 70; grants-in-aid, Am Coun Learned Soc, 76-77 & Am Philos Soc, 76-77; fel, Charles Warren Ctr Studies Am Hist, 76-77. **MEMBERSHIPS** AHA; Orgn Am Historians; Soc Welfare Hist Group; Immigration Hist Group; Soc Archit Historians. **RESEARCH** Urban history; history of city planning in the United States. **SELECTED PUBLICATIONS** Auth, From social settlement to social agency: settlement work in Columbus, Ohio, 1898-1958, Soc Serv Rev, 65; The city beautiful movement: forgotten origins and lost meanings, J Urban Hist, 76; The impact of sanitary reform upon American urban planning, 1840-1890, J Soc Hist, fall 79; Company Town - Architecture and Society in the Early Industrial-age - Garner,js, J of American History, Vol 0081, 1994; the Nation and its City - Politics, Corruption, and Progress in Washington, Dc, 1861-1902 - Lessoff,a, American Studies International, Vol 0032, 1994. **CONTACT ADDRESS** 11 Baker Hill Rd, Great Neck, NY, 11023.

PETERSON, JOYCE SHAW
PERSONAL Born 06/18/1939, Greenport, NY, m, 1967, 2 children **DISCIPLINE** HISTORY **EDUCATION** Denison Univ, BA, 61; Boston Univ, MA, 63; Univ Wis- Madison, PhD(hist), 76. **CAREER** Asst Prof Hist, Fla Int Univ, 77-. **MEMBERSHIPS** AHA; Orgn Am Historians. **RESEARCH** Labor history; women's history; social history. **SELECTED PUBLICATIONS** Auth, Black automobile workers in Detroit, 1910-1930, J Negro Hist, summer 79; Robbins,matilda - a Womans Life in the Labor-movement, 1900-1920, Labor History, Vol 0034, 1993; American automobile workers and their work, 1897-1933, Labor Hist, spring 81; Heroes of Unwritten Story - the Uaw, 1934-1939 - Kraus,h, J of American History, Vol 0082, 1995; The Gentle General - Pesotta,rose, Anarchist and Labor Organizer - Leeder,e, American Historical Review, Vol 0100, 1995. **CONTACT ADDRESS** Dept of Hist, Florida Intl Univ, Tamiami Trail, Miami, FL, 33199.

PETERSON, LARRY
PERSONAL Born 12/10/1941, Wichita, KS, m, 1965, 2 children **DISCIPLINE** MUSICOLOGY **EDUCATION** Texas Christian Univ, BM, 64, MM, 69; Univ NC-Chapel Hill, PhD, 73. **CAREER** Inst mus, Jersey State Col, 73-75; assoc prof music, 75-77, dir, Sch Mus, 78-80, George Peabody Col; Chair, Dept Mus, 80-85, prof mus, 85- , Univ Del. **HONORS AND AWARDS** Masters of Innovation Award, 2nd pl, Zenith Data Systems Nat Compet, 91; EDUCOM's Joe Wyatt Challenge Award, 91; Nat Endow Human Summer Sem, Mus and Tech, 87; Gold CINDY Award; Univ Nebr Merit award, 86; Nat Endow Human grant, 82-84; Woodrow Wilson Fellow, 71. **MEMBERSHIPS** Am Guild of Organists; Am Musicol Soc; Assoc Develop of Computer-based Inst Syst; Asn Tech Mus Instr; Col Mus Soc; Comp Mus Asn; Int Soc Tech Ed; Mus Ed Nat Conf; Phi Mu Alpha Sinfonia. **RESEARCH** Music and Poetry of Olivier Messiaen; Uses of new technologies to teach music; The lament tradition. **SELECTED PUBLICATIONS** The Complete Organ Works of Simon Lohet, Am Inst Musicol, 75; Handel's 'He Was Despised:' The Tradition of Laments, Nats Bulletin, Spr, 89; The Information Highway: Computer Networking for Choral Musicians, The Choral Jour, April 94; Music Literature Instruction and Multimedia: A Delaware Perspective, in Musicus: Computer Applications in Music Education, v4, June 95; Messiaen and Surrealism: A Study of His Poetry, in Messiaesn's Language of Mystical Love, Siglind Bruhn, ed., Garland Publ, 98; **CONTACT ADDRESS** Univ of Delaware, Dept of Music, Newark, DE, 19711. **EMAIL** peterson@udel.edu

PETERSON, LUTHER D.
DISCIPLINE HISTORY **EDUCATION** Univ WI Madison, MS; PhD. **CAREER** Prof, SUNY Oswego. **HONORS AND AWARDS** Vollstipendium, Govt Niedersachsen and Volkswagenstiftung, 81. **RESEARCH** Renaissance and Reformation; hist of Judaism and Christianity. **SELECTED PUBLICATIONS** Auth, Melanchthon on Resisting the Emperor in Regnum, Religio et Ratio, 87; Justus Menius, Philipp Melanchthon and the Writing of the 1547 Treatise, Von der Notwehr Unterricht in Archiv fuerReformationsgeschichte 81, 90; Philippism, Justus Menius, and Synergistic Controversy, in The Encyclopedia of the Reformation, Oxford UP, 95. **CONTACT ADDRESS** Dept Hist, SUNY Oswego, 101 Mahar Hall, Oswego, NY, 13126.

PETERSON, M. JEANNE
PERSONAL Born 11/26/1937, Hibbing, MN **DISCIPLINE** MODERN BRITISH HISTORY **EDUCATION** Univ Calif, Berkeley, BA, 66, PhD, 72. **CAREER** Lectr, 71-72, asst prof, 72-78, Assoc Prof Hist, Ind Univ, Bloomington, 78-, Assoc Mem Dept Hist & Philos Sci, 76-, Woodrow Wilson fel, 66-67; Univ Calif-Berkeley grad career prize, 66-71; Am Asn Univ Women fel, 69-70; Am Coun Learned Soc grant-in-aid, 75; Nat Endowment for Humanities fel, 78-79. **MEMBERSHIPS** AHA; Conf British Studies; Soc Social Hist Med. **RESEARCH** Victorian social history; history of professions; family history. **SELECTED PUBLICATIONS** Auth, The Victorian governess: Status incongruence in family and society, Victorian Studies, 70; The Medical Profession in Mid-Victorian London, Univ Calif, 78; Sir George Paget and Cambridge Medical Education, 1851-1892, Med Educ Proc of the 6th Int Symposium on the Comp Hist of Med, Taniguchi Found, 82; Cruelty and Companionship - Conflict in 19th-century Married Life - Hammerton,aj, American Historical Review, Vol 0100, 1995. **CONTACT ADDRESS** Dept of Hist, Indiana Univ, Bloomington, 742 Ballantine Hall, Bloomington, IN, 47401.

PETERSON, MERRILL DANIEL
PERSONAL Born 03/31/1921, Manhattan, KS, m, 1944, 2 children **DISCIPLINE** HISTORY **EDUCATION** Univ Kans, AB, 43; Harvard Univ, PhD(hist Am civilization), 50. **CAREER** From instr to asst prof Am civilization, Brandeis Univ, 49- 55, from asst prof to prof, 58-63, dean students, 60-62; asst prof hist, Princeton Univ, 55-58; Jefferson Prof Hist, Univ VA, 63-, Dean Fac, 81-, Guggenheim fel, 62-63; fel, Ctr Advan Studies Behav Sci, 68-69; Nat Endowment for Humanities fel, 80- 81. **HONORS AND AWARDS** Bancroft Prize, 61., DHM, Washington Col, 76. **MEMBERSHIPS** AHA; Orgn Am Historians; Southern Hist Asn; Soc Am Historians. **RESEARCH** Jefferson; middle period; American intellectual history. **SELECTED PUBLICATIONS** Auth, Jefferson Image in the American Mind, Oxford Univ, 60; coauth, Major Crises in American History (2 vols), Harcourt, 62; ed, Democracy, Liberty and Property, Bobbs, 66; Thomas Jefferson: A Profile, Hill & Wang, 67; auth, Thomas Jefferson and the New Nation: A Biography, Oxford Univ, 70; James Madison: A Biography in His Own Words, Harper, 74; ed, The Portable Jefferson, Viking, 75; auth, Adams and Jefferson: A Revolutionary Dialogue, Univ Ga, 76; Olive Branch and Sword: The Compromise of 1833, La State Univ Press, 82; Commemorations - the Politics of National Identity - Gillis,jr, J of American History, Vol 0082, 1995. **CONTACT ADDRESS** Dept of Hist, Univ of VA, Charlottesville, VA, 22901.

PETERSON, NORMA LOIS
PERSONAL Born 12/22/1922, Roseau, MN **DISCIPLINE** AMERICAN HISTORY **EDUCATION** Colo Col, BA, 49; Univ Mo, MA, 51; PhD, 53. **CAREER** From Asst prof to assoc prof, 53-57, chmn div soc studies, 57-71, chmn div hist, govt & philos, 71-79, Prof Hist, Adams State Col, 57-, Chmn Div Arts and Letters, 79-, Am Asn Univ Women Florence Sabin fel, 57-58; vis lectr, Univ Va, 67-68. **HONORS AND AWARDS** LLD, Colo Col, 78. **MEMBERSHIPS** Orgn Am Historians; Southern Hist Asn: AHA. **RESEARCH** American intellectual history, 1850-1940; early 19th century America. **SELECTED PUBLICATIONS** Auth, Freedom and Franchise, Univ Mo, 65; coauth, Letters of William S Stewart, Mo Hist Rev, 167, 467 & 767; auth, The Defence of Norfolk, Norfolk Co Hist Soc, 70; Littleton Waller Taxewell, VA Cavalcade, spring 73; Clay,henry - Statesman for the Union - Remini,rv, J of Southern History, Vol 0059, 1993. **CONTACT ADDRESS** Div of Hist Govt & Philos, Adams State Col, Alamosa, CO, 81102.

PETERSON, RICHARD HERMANN
PERSONAL Born 01/16/1942, Berkeley, CA, m, 1970, 1 child **DISCIPLINE** AMERICAN & WESTERN AMERICAN HISTORY **EDUCATION** Univ Calif, Berkeley, AB, 63; Calif State Univ, San Francisco, MA, 66; Univ Calif, Davis, PhD(hist), 71. **CAREER** Asst prof US hist, Ind Univ, Kokomo, 71-76; Col Redwoods, 76-78; Assoc Prof Hist, San Diego State Univ, 78-, San Diego State Univ summer fac fel, 80. **MEMBERSHIPS** Orgn Am Historians; Western Hist Asn. **RESEARCH** Trans-Mississippi West; 19th century United States; entrepreneurial history. **SELECTED PUBLICATIONS** Auth, Conflict and consensus: Labor relations in Western mining, J West, 173; The failure to reclaim: California state swamp land policy and the Sacramento Valley, 1850-1866, Southern Calif Quart, spring 74; Manifest Destiny in the Mines: A Cultural Interpretation of Anti-Mexican Nativism in California, 1848-53, R&E Res Assoc, 75; The frontier thesis and social mobility on the mining frontier, Pac Hist Rev, 75; The Bonanza Kings: The Social Origins and Business Behavior of Western Mining Entrepreneurs, 1870-1900, Univ Nebr, 77; Simeon Gannett Reed and the Bunker Hill and Sullivan: The frustrations of a mining investor, fall 79 & Pacific northwest entrepreneur: The social and political behavior of Simeon Gannett Reed, fall 80, Idaho Yesterdays; Anti-Mexican nativism in California, 1848- 1853: A study of cultural conflict, Southern Calif Quart, winter 80; California History, Vol 0073, 1994; Giannini,a.p. and the Bank of America - Nash,gd, Western Historical Quarterly, Vol 0024, 1993; the United-states-sanitary-commission and King,thomas,starr in California, 1861-1864, California History, Vol 0072, 1993; The Life and Personality of

Hearst,phoebe,apperson - Bonfils,wb, California History, Vol 0073, 1994; Gold Seeking - Victoria and California in the 1850s - Goodman,d, Western Historical Quarterly, Vol 0026, 1995; The Western Rides Again, J of the West, Vol 0035, 1996. **CONTACT ADDRESS** Dept of Hist, San Diego State Univ, San Diego, CA, 92182.

PETERSON, WILLARD JAMES

PERSONAL Born 08/01/1938, Oak Park, IL, m **DISCIPLINE** CHINESE HISTORY **EDUCATION** Harvard Univ, PhD, 70 **CAREER** Asst Prof, Dartmouth Col, 70-71; Asst Prof to Prof, Princeton Univ, 71-. **MEMBERSHIPS** Asn Asian Studies **RESEARCH** Chinese intellectual history. **SELECTED PUBLICATIONS** Auth, Life of Yen-Wu (1613-1682), Harvard J Asiatic Studies 28 & 29, 68-69; auth, Bitter Gourd: Fang I-Chih and the Impetus for Intellectual Change, Yale Univ Press, 79; auth, Power of Culture, Chinese Univ Press, Hong Kong, 91. **CONTACT ADDRESS** Dept East Asian Studies, Princeton Univ, 211 Jones Hall, Princeton, NJ, 08544.

PETILLO, CAROL MORRIS

PERSONAL Born 09/05/1940, Clarksburg, WV, 4 children **DISCIPLINE** AMERICAN HISTORY **EDUCATION** Montclair State Col, BA, 74; Rutgers Univ, MA, 76, PhD(Am hist), 79. **CAREER** Instr Am hist, Douglass Col, Rutgers Univ, 75-79; asst prof, 79-82, Assoc Prof Am Hist, Boston Col, 82-, consult, Round Hill Prod, Inc, 81. **MEMBERSHIPS** Orgn Am Historians; Am Mil Inst; Soc Historians Am Foreign Relations. **RESEARCH** United States relations with developing nations, particularly Southeast Asia; phychobiography of national and international leaders; the role of military in the third world. **SELECTED PUBLICATIONS** Auth, Douglas MacArthur and Manuel Quezon: A note on an imperial bond, Pac Hist Rev, 279; On the importance of a central archival repository, Prologue, summer 80; Douglas MacArthur: The Philippine Years, Ind Univ Press, 81; American Women and the United-states Armed-forces - a Guide to the Records of Military Agencies in the National-archives Relating to American Women - Seeley,cp, J of Military History, Vol 0057, 1993; Biography - an Annotated-bibliography - Rollyson,c, Biography-an Interdisciplinary Quarterly, Vol 0018, 1995; Old Soldiers Never Die - the Life of Macarthur,douglas - Perret,g, J of American History, Vol 0083, 1997. **CONTACT ADDRESS** Hist Dept, Boston Col, 140 Commonwealth Ave, Chestnut Hill, MA, 02167-3800.

PETRAGLIA, MICHAEL

PERSONAL Born 10/06/1960, New York, NY, m, 1994 **DISCIPLINE** ANTHROPOLOGY AND ARCHAEOLOGY **EDUCATION** Univ NY, BA, anthrop, 82; Univ Nmex, anthrop, MA, 84, PhD, 87. **CAREER** Dir, Cultural Resources Dept, Parsons, 88-; res, Nat Mus of Natural Hist; Smithsonian Inst, 88-. **HONORS AND AWARDS** Postdoctoral fel, Smithsonian Inst. **MEMBERSHIPS** Soc for Amer Archaeol; Amer Anthrop Asn. **RESEARCH** Early human behavior; Hunter-gatherers; Lithic technology; Site formation. **SELECTED PUBLICATIONS** Co-ed, with R. Koresettar, Early Human Behavior in Global Context: the Rise and Development of the Lower Paleolithic Record, London, Routledge Press, 98; monogr, with R. Potts, The Old World Paleolithic Collections of the National Museum of Natural History, Smithsonian Inst, Smithsonian Press, 98; with D. Knepper, J. Rutherford, P. LaPorta, K. Puseman, J. Schuldenrein, N. Tuross, The Prehistory of Lums Pond: The Formation of a Woodland Site in Delaware, vols I and II, Del Dept of Transp Archaeol Series, 98; co-ed, with R. Korisettar, The Lower Paleolithic of India and its Bearing on the Asian Record, in Early Human Behavior in Global Context: the Rise and Diversity of the Lower Paleolithic Record, London, Routledge Press, 98; with R. Potts, L. Straus, P. Vandiver, Upper Paleolithic Collections from the Salat Valley of Pyrenean France, 98; with D. Knepper, P. LaPorta, J. Schuldenrein, J. Risetto, Specialized Occupations on Kettle Creek, a Tributary of the West Branch of the Susquehanna, Archaeol of Eastern N Amer, 98; symposia papers, with J. Schuldenrein, The Formation of Paleolandscapes in India, to Soc for Amer Archaeol Mtg, Seattle, Wash, Mar, 98; with P. LaPorta, Acheulian Quarrying in India, to Soc for Amer Archaeol Mtg, Seattle, Wash, mar, 98; article, with D. Knepper, Assessing Prehistoric Chronology in Piedmont Contexts, N Amer Archaeol, 17, 37-59, 96; with D. Knepper, P. Glumac, M. Newman, C. Sussman, Immunological and Microwear Analysis of Chipped-stone Artifacts from Piedmont Contexts, Amer Antiquity, 61, 127-135, 96; with D. Knepper, Prehistoric Occupation at the Connoquenessing Site, an Upland Setting in the Upper Ohio River Valley, Archaeol of Eastern N Amer, 24, 29-57, 96; Reassembling the Quarry: Quartzite Procurement and Reduction along the Potomac, N Amer, Archaeol, 15, 283-319, 94; with J. Bedell, T. Plummer, Status, Technology, and Rural Traditions in Western Pennsylvania: Excavations at the Shaeffer Farm Site, Northeast Hist Archaeol, 23, 29-58, 94. **CONTACT ADDRESS** 4557 Sawgrass Ct., Alexandria, VA, 22312. **EMAIL** mike_petraglia@parsons.com

PETRAS, JAMES FRANK

PERSONAL Born 01/17/1937, Lynn, MA, m, 1959, 2 children **DISCIPLINE** POLITICAL SCIENCE **EDUCATION** Boston Univ, BA 58; Univ CA Berkeley, MA 63, PhD 67. **CAREER** PA State Univ, asst prof 67-70, assoc prof 70-72; SUNY Binghamton, prof 73. **HONORS AND AWARDS** Ford Found; Vis Scholar Chinese Academy. **MEMBERSHIPS** Latin Am Stud Assn. **RESEARCH** Latin Am, US fire arm policy. **SELECTED PUBLICATIONS** Class Conflict in Neoliberalism in Latin America, co auth, Macmillan, 97; Empire or Republic, co auth, Pontledge, 95; The Left Strikes Back, Westview, 98; Poverty and Democracy in Chile, Westview, 94; Latin America in the Time Of Cholera, Pontledge, 93. **CONTACT ADDRESS** Dept of Sociology, State Univ of NY, Binghamton, NY, 13901.

PETRIK, PAULA E.

DISCIPLINE HISTORY **EDUCATION** Cornell Univ, BA, 69; Univ Mont, MFA, 73; SUNY-Binghampton, MA, 79, PhD, 82. **CAREER** Assoc prof, hist, Montana State Univ; PROF, HIST, UNIV MAINE. **MEMBERSHIPS** Am Antiquarian Soc **SELECTED PUBLICATIONS** Auth, No Step Backward: Women and Family on the Rocky Mountain Mining Frontier, Helena, Montana, 1865-1900; auth, "The House that Parcheese Built," Bus Hist Rev, 86; auth, If She Be Content: The Development of Montana Divorce Law, 1865-1907, Western Hist Quart, 87; auth, "Desk-Top Publishing: The Making of the American Dream," Hist Today 39, 89; auth, "The Youngest Fourth Estate: Race, Gender, and the Novelty Toy Printing Press," in Small Worlds: Children and Adolescents in America, Univ Kans Press, 92. **CONTACT ADDRESS** Dept of Hist, Univ of Maine, Orono, ME, 04469.

PETRONE, KAREN

DISCIPLINE HISTORY **EDUCATION** Harvard Univ, BA, 87; Univ Mich, MA, 90, PhD, 94. **CAREER** Asst prof, 94-, Univ Ky. **HONORS AND AWARDS** Nat Endow for the Humanities Summer Stipend, 97; Chancellor's Award for Outstanding Teaching-Univ Ky, 98., Int Res & Exchanges Bd-Res Fel, 91-92; Fulbright-Hays Dissertation Res Fel, 91-92; Soc Sci Res Coun-Dissertation Fel, 92-93. **MEMBERSHIPS** AHA; AAASS. **RESEARCH** Soviet celebrations in the 1930s; Imperial & Soviet military heroes & patriotic cultures, 1900-1950. **SELECTED PUBLICATIONS** Auth, Soviet Celebrations Against a Backdrop of Terror: Holidays in 1937, Konets stoletiia: predvaritel'nye itogi Kul'turologicheskie zapiski, 93; art, Parading the Nation: Physical Culture Celebrations and the Construction of Soviet Identities, Michigan Discussions in Anthropology: Post Soviet Eurasia, 96; art, Family, Masculinity, and Heroism in Russian Posters of the First World War, Borderlines: Genders and Identities in War and Peace, 1880-1930, Routledge, 98; art, Gender and Heroes: The Exploits of Soviet Pilots and Arctic Explorers in the 1930s, Women and Political Change: Perspectives from East-Central Europe, St Martin's Press, 98. **CONTACT ADDRESS** Dept of History, Univ Ky, Lexington, KY, 40506-0027. **EMAIL** petrone@pop.uky.edu

PETRONE, SERAFINA

PERSONAL Thunder Bay, ON, Canada **DISCIPLINE** EDUCATION **EDUCATION** Univ Toronto, ATCM, 42; Univ Western Ont, BA, 51; Lakehead Univ, MA, 70; Univ Alta, PhD, 77. **CAREER** Tchr, rural, elementary, secondary, Tchrs Col, univ; PROF EMER, LAKEHEAD UNIV. **HONORS AND AWARDS** Can 125 Medal, 92; Order Ont, 92; Excellence Tchg, Lakehead Univ, 89; Citizens of Exceptional Achievement Award, Thunder Bay, 81, 84, 89; Hon Chief, Tibaajimowowinan Kaababaamaawadoonany, Gatherer of Legends and Stories. **MEMBERSHIPS** Can Coun; Can Fedn Univ Women; Thunder Bay Regional Arts Coun. **SELECTED PUBLICATIONS** Auth, Selected Short Stories of Isabella Valancy Crawford, 75; auth, the Fairy Tales of Isabella Valancy Crawford, 77; auth, First People, First Voices, 83; auth, Northern Voices, 88; auth, Breaking the Mould: A Memoir, 95. **CONTACT ADDRESS** Lakehead Univ, Thunder Bay, ON, P7B 5E1.

PETROPULOS, JOHN ANTHONY

PERSONAL Born 12/19/1929, Lewiston, ME, m, 1958, 3 children **DISCIPLINE** BALKANS & MIDDLE EAST HISTORY **EDUCATION** Yale Univ, BA, 51, Harvard Univ, PhD, 63. **CAREER** From instr to assoc prof, 58-73, prof, 73-90, E. Dwight Salmon prof hist, Amherst Col, 90-, NDEA fel, Mid E Inst, Columbia Univ, 64-65 & Am Res Inst, Turkey, 65-66; Nat Endowment for Hum sr fel, Greece, 73-74. **MEMBERSHIPS** AHA; Mid E Inst; Mid E Studies Asn NAm; Mod Greek Studies Asn (vpres, 72-73, pres, 74-76). **RESEARCH** The Ottoman Empire; Greek-Turkish rel(s); medieval and mod Greece, nat liberation movements. **SELECTED PUBLICATIONS** Auth, Politics and Statecraft in the Kingdom of Greece 1833-1843, Princeton Univ, 68; Co-auth, Hellenism and the First Greek War of Libertation 1821-1830, Institute of Balkan Studies, 76; Foreign Interference in Greek Politics, Pella, 76. **CONTACT ADDRESS** Dept of Hist, Amherst Col, Amherst, MA, 01002-5003. **EMAIL** japetropulos@amherst.edu

PETRY, CARL FORBES

PERSONAL Born 06/29/1943 **DISCIPLINE** MIDDLE EASTERN HISTORY **EDUCATION** Carleton Col, BA, 65; Univ Mich, MA, 66, PhD(Mid East hist), 74. **CAREER** Lectr, Univ Mich, 73-74; asst prof, 74-80, Assoc Prof mid East Hist, Northwestern Univ, 80-, Nat Endowment for Humanities sr fel, Egypt, 80-81. **MEMBERSHIPS** Mediaeval Acad Am; Mid East Studies Asn North Am; Am Res Ctr in Egypt. **RESEARCH** Medieval Egyptian history; social history of the ulama' (civilian elite) of Cairo; computerized data retrieval--medieval biographical sources. **SELECTED PUBLICATIONS** Auth, Geographic origins of the Civil Judiciary of Cairo in the fifteenth century, XXI: 52-73, Geographic origins of Diwan Officials in Cairo during the fifteenth century, XXI: 165-183, Geographic origins of academicians in Cairo during the fifteenth century, XXIII: 119-141 & Geographic origins of religious functionaries in Cairo during the fifteenth century, XXIII: 240- 264, J Econ & Social Hist of Orient; The Civilian Elite of Cairo in the Later Middle Ages, Princeton Univ Press, 82; Scholastic Stasis in Medieval Islam Reconsidered, Mamluk Patronage in Cairo, Poetics Today, Vol 0014, 1993; Islamic History - a Framework for Inquiry - Humphreys,rs, Speculum-a J of Medieval Studies, Vol 0069, 1994; Islamic History - a Framework for Inquiry - Humphreys,rs, Speculum-a J of Medieval Studies, Vol 0069, 1994; Majnun - the Madman in Medieval Islamic Society - Dols,mw, J of the American Oriental Society, Vol 0117, 1997; Popular-culture in Medieval Cairo - Shoshan,b, Speculum-a J of Medieval Studies, Vol 0071, 1996; Popular-culture in Medieval Cairo - Shoshan,b, Speculum-a J of Medieval Studies, Vol 0071, 1996; Majnun - the Madman in Medieval Islamic Society - Dols,mw, J of the American Oriental Society, Vol 0117, 1997; Mongols and Mamluks - the Mamluk-ilkhanid-war, 1260-1281 - Amitaipreiss,r, American Historical Review, Vol 0102, 1997. **CONTACT ADDRESS** Dept of Hist, Northwestern Univ, Evanston, IL, 60201.

PEYROUX, CATHERINE

DISCIPLINE HISTORY **EDUCATION** Princeton Univ, PhD, 91. **CAREER** Asst prof, Duke Univ. **RESEARCH** Notion and process of the Christianization of Europe from Late Antiquity through the Middle Ages; hist and historiography of medieval Ireland; intersection of poverty and leprosy in the medieval Europ imagination. **SELECTED PUBLICATIONS** Ed, Gertrude's Furor: Reading Anger in an Early Medieval Saint's Life, Anger's Past, 98. **CONTACT ADDRESS** Dept of Hist, Duke Univ, Carr Bldg, Durham, NC, 27706. **EMAIL** peyroux@acpub.duke.edu

PFAFF, RICHARD WILLIAM

PERSONAL Born 08/06/1936, Oklahoma City, OK, m, 1962, 1 child **DISCIPLINE** MEDIEVAL & ENGLISH HISTORY **EDUCATION** Harvard Univ, AB, 57; Oxford Univ, BA, 59, MA, 63, DPhil, 65. **CAREER** Teacher Eng, Pembroke Country Day Sch, Mo, 59-60; asst to pres, Swarthmore Col & to Am secy, Rhodes Scholars, 60-62; curate, Christ Church, Suffern, NY, 66-67; from asst prof to assoc prof, 67-75, Prof Hist, Univ NC, Chapel Hill, 75-. **MEMBERSHIPS** Medieval Acad Am; Am Soc Church Hist. **RESEARCH** Medieval church; medieval England; history of scholarship. **SELECTED PUBLICATIONS** Auth, New Liturgical Feasts in Later Medieval England, Oxford Univ, 70; The Library of the Fathers, Studies in Philol, 73; The English Devotion of St Gregory's Trental, Speculum, 74; Anglo-American patristic translations 1886-1900, J Ecclesiastical Hist, 77; M R James on cataloguing of manuscripts, Scriptorium, 77; Montague Rhodes James, Scholar Press, 80; William of Malmesbury's Abbreviatio Amalarii, Recherches de Theologie ancienne et medieval,, commentary 80, text 81; Medieval Latin liturgy: A select bibliography, Toronto Univ, 82; Inventing the Middle-ages - the Lives, Works, and Ideas of the Great Medievalists of the 20th-century - Cantor,nf, Speculum-a J of Medieval Studies, Vol 0068, 1993; Church and City 1000-1500 - Essays in Honor of Brooke,christopher - Abulafia,d, Franklin,m, Rubin,m, J of Interdisciplinary History, Vol 0024, 1994; Early-christian Baptism and the Catechumenate, Vol 1 - West and East Syria, Vol 2 - Italy, North-africa, and Egypt - Finn,tm, J of Ecclesiastical History, Vol 0045, 1994; Baptism and Change in the Early-middle-ages, C.ad200-c.ad1150 - Cramer,p, J of Ecclesiastical History, Vol 0046, 1995; The Middle-ages - from its Origins to the 13th-century - French - Palazzo,e, J of Ecclesiastical History, Vol 0046, 1995; The Responsories and Versicles of the Latin Office-of-the-dead - Ottosen,k, Speculum-a J of Medieval Studies, Vol 0070, 1995; Religion and Devotion in Europe, C.1215-c.1515 - Swanson,rn, Church History, Vol 0065, 1996; A History of Lincoln-minster - Owen,d, Editor, Church History, Vol 0065, 1996; Likeness and Presence - a History of the Image Before the Era of Art - Belting,h, Church History, Vol 0065, 1996; the Quest for Becket Bones - the Mystery of the Relics of Thomas-becket-of-canterbury - Butler,j, Church History, Vol 0065, 1996; Manuscripts and Libraries in the Age of Charlemagne - Bischoff,b, Papers of the Bibliographical Society of America, Vol 0091, 1997; The Register of Kirkby,john, Bishop-of-carlisle 1332-1352, and the Register of Ross,john, Bishop-of-carlisle, 1325-1332 Vol 2 - Storey,rl, Church History, Vol 0066, 1997; Theodore,archbishop - Commemorative Studies on His Life and Influence - Lapidge,m, Speculum-a J of Medieval Studies, Vol 0072, 1997; English Benedictine Libraries - the Shorter Catalogs - Sharpe,r, Carley,jp, Thomson,rm, Watson,ag, Library, Vol 0019, 1997. **CONTACT ADDRESS** Dept of Hist, Univ of NC, Chapel Hill, NC, 27514.

PFEFFER, PAULA F.

PERSONAL Chicago, IL, m, 3 children **DISCIPLINE** HISTORY **EDUCATION** Northwestern Univ, PhD, 90. **CAREER** Assoc prof, Mundelein Col, 74-91; Assoc Prof, Loyola Univ Chicago, 91- . **HONORS AND AWARDS** Human Rights Award, 91. **MEMBERSHIPS** Am Hist Asn; Orgn Am Hist; Ill Labor Hist Soc; Soc Welfare Hist Group; Am Asn Univ

Women. **RESEARCH** American social welfare & social reform; labor history; womens history; ethnic history. **SELECTED PUBLICATIONS** Auth, Homeless Children, Childless Homes, Chicago Hist, 88; James Farmer, Contemporary American Activists, Greenwood Press, 94; Anna Arnold Hedgeman, Black Women in the United States: An Historical Encyclopedia, Carlson Publ, 93; Halena Wilson, African American Women: A Biographical Dictionary, Garland Publ, 93; Frank Crosswaith, Encycl of African-Am Cult and Hist, Macmillan Publ, 95; Brotherhood of Sleeping Car Porters, Encycl of African-Am Cult and Hist, Macmillan Publ, 95; The Women Behind the Union: Halena Wilson, Rosina Tucker, and the Ladies Auxiliary to the Brotherhood of Sleeping Car Porters, Labor History, 95; A Philip Randolph: Pioneer of the Civil Rights Movement, Lousiana State Univ Press, 90; Eleanor Roosevelt, the National and World Women's Parties, The Historian, 96; Esther Loeb Kohn, Jewish Women in America: An Hist Encycl, Routledge, 97. **CONTACT ADDRESS** History Dept, Loyola Univ, Chicago, 6363 N Sheridan Rd., Chicago, IL, 60626. **EMAIL** ppfeffe@orion.it.luc.edu

PFLUGFELDER, GREGORY
DISCIPLINE JAPANESE HISTORY **EDUCATION** Harvard Univ, BA, 81, Stanford Univ, PhD, 96. **CAREER** Asst prof. **SELECTED PUBLICATIONS** Auth, Seiji to daidokoro: Akita-ken joshi sanseiken undoshi (Politics and the kitchen: a history of the women's suffrage movement in Akita prefecture), 86; Strange Fates: Sex, Gender, and Sexuality, in Torikaebaya Monogatari, Monumenta Nipponica 47, 92. **CONTACT ADDRESS** Dept of Hist, Columbia Col, New York, 2960 Broadway, New York, NY, 10027-6902.

PFUND, PETER H.
PERSONAL Born 10/06/1932, Bryn Mawr, PA, m, 1959, 2 children **DISCIPLINE** HISTORY, LAW **EDUCATION** Amherst Col, BA, 54; Union PA Law Sch, JD, 59. **CAREER** US Dept of St, Officer of the Legal Advisor, full-time, 59-97; asst legal advisor for private int law, 79-97; special advisor for pvt int law, 97-. **HONORS AND AWARDS** Am Bar Asn, Sect for Int Law & Pract, Leonard J. Theberge Prize for Pvt Int Law, 87. **MEMBERSHIPS** Am Law Inst; German-American Lawyers Asn, Bonn, Ger. **SELECTED PUBLICATIONS** Auth, Contributing to Professional Development of Private International Law: The International Process and the United States Approach, 249 Recusil des cours 9-144, 94-V **CONTACT ADDRESS** 10419 Pearl St, Fairfax, VA, 22032-3824. **EMAIL** pildb@his.com; lphildos@aol.com

PHILIPPIDES, MARIOS
PERSONAL Born 08/05/1950, Athens, Greece, m, 1973 **DISCIPLINE** GREEK, LATIN **EDUCATION** Queens Col, BA, 73; State Univ NY Buffalo, MA, 76, PhD(classics), 78. **CAREER** Asst prof, Union Col, 77-78; Asst Prof Classics, Univ Mass, Amherst, 78- **MEMBERSHIPS** Am Philol Asn; Class Asn New England; Modern Greek Studies Asn; Am Inst Archaeol; Am Class League. **RESEARCH** Palaeologan period of the Byzantine empire; ancient Greek religion and Mediterranean ritual and myth; the ancient novel. **SELECTED PUBLICATIONS** Auth, A note on Longus' Lesbiaka, The Class World, 78; The foundation of Taras and the Spartan partheniai, The Ancient World, 79; The Fall of the Byzantine Empire, Univ Mass Press, 80; The digressive aitia in Longus, The Class World, 80; The characters in Freedom or Death, The Charioteer, 80; The pronunciation of Greek, Phone, 81; The fall of Constantinople 1453, Greek, Roman & Byzantine Studies, 81; the prooemium in Lorgus, The Class Bull, 82; Late 15th-century Euboea - the Economy, Population, and Registers of 1474 - French - Balta,e, Speculum-a J of Medieval Studies, Vol 0068, 1993; Byzantium Last Imperial Offensive in Asia-minor - the Documentary Evidence for and Hagiographical Lore about John-iii-ducas-vatatzes Crusade Against the Turks, Ad-1222 or 1225 to 1231 - Langdon,js, Speculum-a J of Medieval Studies, Vol 0069, 1994; Byzantium and the Bulgars 7th-century to the 10th-century - a Study of Byzantine Foreign-policy - Greek and German - Kyriakis,ek, Speculum-a J of Medieval Studies, Vol 0070, 1995; Nicephorus-ii- phocas 63-69, His Reforms as Military Commander and Emperor - German - Kolias,tg, Speculum-a J of Medieval Studies, Vol 0070, 1995; the Church and Social-reform - the Policies of the Patriarch Athanasios-of-constantinople - Boojamra,jl, Speculum-a J of Medieval Studies, Vol 0071, 1996; Greeks, Westerners and Turks from Ad1054 to 1453 - 4 Centuries of History and International-relations - French - Spiridonakis,bg, Catholic Historical Review, Vol 0082, 1996; Church and Social-reform - the Policies of the Patriarch Athanasios-of-constantinople - Boojamra,jl, Speculum-a J of Medieval Studies, Vol 0071, 1996; the Last Centuries of Byzantium, Ad 1261-1453 - Nicol,dm, Speculum-a J of Medieval Studies, Vol 0071, 1996; Church and Society in Byzantium under the Comneni, 1081-1261 - Angold,m, Speculum-a J of Medieval Studies, Vol 0072, 1997. **CONTACT ADDRESS** Dept of Classics, Univ Mass, Amherst, MA, 01003-0002.

PHILLIPS, ANN
DISCIPLINE EUROPEAN POLITICS **EDUCATION** Denison Univ, BA; John Hopkins Univ, MA; Georgetown Univ, PhD. **CAREER** Prof, Am Univ. **RESEARCH** Transferability of institutions from west to east in the democratization of Central-East Europe. **SELECTED PUBLICATIONS** Auth, Soviet Policy Toward East Germany Reconsidered: The Postwar Decade, Greenwood Press, 86; An Island of Stability? The German Political Party System and the Elections of 1994, W Europ Pol, 95. **CONTACT ADDRESS** American Univ, 4400 Massachusetts Ave, Washington, DC, 20016.

PHILLIPS, CARLA RAHN
PERSONAL Born 11/14/1943, Los Angeles, CA, m, 1970 **DISCIPLINE** HISTORY **EDUCATION** Pomona Col, BA, 65; NY Univ, MA, 66, PhD, 72. **CAREER** Instr, 70, Rhode Island Col; instr, 70-72, San Diego City Col & San Diego Mesa Col; asst prof, 72-78, assoc prof, 78-86, prof, 86-, Univ Minn; vis prof, 87, Univ Calif San Diego. **RESEARCH** European hist, 1300-1800; Spain; economy & soc; exploration & discovery, maritime hist. **SELECTED PUBLICATIONS** Auth, Urban control of the Castilian countryside: Additional evidence from 17th century Ciudad Real, Societas, autumn 73; Ciudad Real no periodo dos Habsburgos: Um estudo demografico, Anais de Historia, 12/75; coauth, Spanish wool and Dutch rebels: The Middleburg Incident of 1574, Am Hist Rev, 4/77; The Castilian fairs in Burgos, 1601-1604, J of Europ Econ Hist, fall 77; Moriscos of La Mancha, 1570-1614, J Mod Hist, 6/78; auth, Ciudad Real, 1500-1750: Growth, Crisis and Readjustment in the Spanish Economy, Harvard Univ, 79; Columbus - an Annotated Guide to the Scholarship on His Life and Writings, 1750 to 1988 - Provost,f, J of American History, Vol 0079, 1993; Isabel-the-queen - Life and Times - Liss,pk/, Hispanic American Historical Review, Vol 0073, 1993; Vanguard of Empire - Ships of Exploration in the Age of Columbus - Smith,rc, American Neptune, Vol 0054, 1994; The Exploration of the Atlantic - Spanish - Cespedesdelcastillo,g, Hispanic American Historical Review, Vol 0074, 1994; Magellan - Joyner,t, J of the West, Vol 0034, 1995; The Courtier and the King - Gomezdesilva,ruy, Philip-ii, and the Court of Spain - Boyden,jm/, Renaissance Quarterly, Vol 0050, 1997; From Madrid to Purgatory - the Art and Craft of Dying in 16th-century Spain - Eire,cmn/, Hispanic American Historical Review, Vol 0077, 1997; Spain, Europe, and the Spanish Miracle, 1700-1900 - Ringrose,dr, J of Interdisciplinary History, Vol 0028, 1997. **CONTACT ADDRESS** Dept of History, Univ of Minnesota, 614 Social Sciences, 267 19th Ave S., Minneapolis, MN, 55455. **EMAIL** phill002@tc.umn.edu

PHILLIPS, GLENN OWEN
PERSONAL Born 09/26/1946, Bridgetown, Barbados, m, 1972 **DISCIPLINE** HISTORY **EDUCATION** Atlantic Union College, BA 1967; Andrews Univ, MA 1969; Howard Univ, PhD 1976. **CAREER** Caribbean Union Coll, lecturer 1969-71, Howard Univ, asst prof history 1981-82, Morgan State Univ, asst prof history 1978-, asst dir Univ Honors Program 1981-82, research assoc 1982-92, acting dir of Institute for Urban Research 1986-89, asst prof 1989-90; Morgan State Univ, Baltimore, MD, acting chair, dept of history, 1989-90, 1995-96, assoc prof, 1990-. **HONORS AND AWARDS** HBCU Faculty Fellshp United Negro Coll Fund/US Dept of Lab 1980; Morgan State Univ Honorary Member (Promethean Kappa Tau) 1982; Cited Nat'l Dir Latin Americans; Assoc Editor Afro- Hispanic Rev, 1982-84; Books, The Making of Christian College, 1988; "The Caribbean Basin Initiative" co-editor 1987; Over a Century of Adventism, 1991, Fulbright Summer Scholar, Cairo, Egypt, 1994. **MEMBERSHIPS** MSU Liaison Officer to NAFEO, DC 1985-94; president, Barbados National Association of Washington District of Columbia, 1985-89; Comm Council of Caribbean Organizations, DC 1985-89; School Bd Chair, 1991-94; G E Peters Elementary School 1987-; bd of trustees, Caribbean Union Coll, 1989-94; Assn of Amer Univ Professors, 1995-97. **CONTACT ADDRESS** Department of History, Morgan State Univ, Cold Spring Ln & Hillen Rd, Baltimore, MD, 21239.

PHILLIPS, JANE ELLEN
PERSONAL Born 09/27/1943, Philadelphia, PA **DISCIPLINE** CLASSICS **EDUCATION** Millersville State Col, BA, 65; Univ NC, Chapel Hill, PhD(classics), 69. **CAREER** Asst prof classics, Univ NC, Chapel Hill, 69-71; adj instr, Dickinson Col, 71-72; adj instr, Franklin & Marshall Col, 71-72, vis asst prof, 72-73; asst prof, 73-80, Assoc Prof Classics, Univ KY, 80-, Fel in residence for col teachers, Nat Endowment for Humanities, 75-76. **MEMBERSHIPS** Am Philol Asn; Class Asn Midwest & South; Archaeol Inst Am; Am Class League; Vergilian Soc. **RESEARCH** Latin historiography; age of Augustus; Latin poetry. **SELECTED PUBLICATIONS** Auth, Verbs compounded with trans in Livy's triumph reports, 74 & Form and language in Livy's triumph notices, 74, Class Philol; The pattern of images in Catullus, Am J Philol, 76; Juno in Aeneid, Vergilius, 77; Roman mothers and the lives of their adult daughters, Helios, 78; Livy and the beginning of a new society, Class Bull, 79; Lucretian echoes in Shelley's Mont Blanc, Class & Mod Lit, 82; Roman Marriage - Iusti-coniuges from the Time of Cicero to the Time of Ulpian - Treggiari,s/, Classical World, Vol 0087, 1994. **CONTACT ADDRESS** Dept of Classics, Univ of Ky, 500 S Limestone St, Lexington, KY, 40506-0003.

PHILLIPS, JOANNE HIGGINS
PERSONAL Born 08/26/1946, Boston, MA **DISCIPLINE** CLASSICAL PHILOLOGY **EDUCATION** Boston Univ, AB, 68; Harvard Univ, MA, 71, PhD(class philol), 77. **CAREER** Assoc Prof Classics, Tufts Univ, 77-. **MEMBERSHIPS** Am Philol Asn; Am Asn Hist Med. **RESEARCH** History of Greek and Roman medicine. **SELECTED PUBLICATIONS** Auth, The boneless one in Hesiod, Phiologus, 80; Early Greek medicine and poetry of Solon, Clio Medica, 80; The emergence of the Greek medical profession in the Roman Republic, Trans and Studies of Col of Physicians Philadelphia, 80; Juxtaposed medical traditions: Pliny NH 27 106 131, 81 & Lucretius on the inefficacy of the medical art: 6 1179 and 6 1226-1238, 82, Class Philol; The Hippocratic physician and astronomy, Proc of the IVth Int Colloquium on Hippocratic Med, Lausanne, Switz, 81, 82. **CONTACT ADDRESS** Dept of Classics, Tufts Univ, 318 Eaton Hall, Medford, MA, 02155-0000. **EMAIL** jphillip@emerald.tufts.edu

PHILLIPS, JOHN ALLEN
PERSONAL Born 09/22/1949, Dahlonega, GA, m, 1980, 1 child **DISCIPLINE** HANOVERIAN AND VICTORIAN ENGLAND **EDUCATION** Univ Ga, BA, 71; Univ Iowa, MA, 72, PhD(hist), 76. **CAREER** Asst prof, 76-82, Assoc Prof Hist, Univ Calif, Riverside, 82-, Regent's fac fel, Univ Calif, 77 & 80. **MEMBERSHIPS** Conf Brit Studies. **RESEARCH** Electoral behavior in unreformed and reformed Britain; English social history. **SELECTED PUBLICATIONS** Auth, Nominal Record Linkage, Univ Iowa, 76; Achieving a critical mass while avoiding an explosion: Letter-cluster sampling, J Interdisciplinary Hist, 79; The structure of the unreformed electorate, J Brit Studies, 79; Popular politics in unreformed England, J Mod Hist, 80; Electoral Behavior in Unreformed England, Princeton Univ Press, 82; Britons, Forging the Nation, 1707-1837 - Colley,L, Albion, Vol 0025, 1993; The Great-reform-act of 1832 and the Political Modernization of England, American Historical Review, Vol 0100, 1995; The Origins of Middle-class Culture - Halifax, Yorkshire, 1660-1780 - Smail,J, American Historical Review, Vol 0101, 1996; The Politics of the People in 18th-century Britain - Dickinson,T, J of Modern History, Vol 0069, 1997. **CONTACT ADDRESS** Dept of Hist, Univ Calif, Riverside, CA, 92521.

PHILLIPS, RICHARD E.
PERSONAL Born 12/13/1950, Los Angeles, CA, d, 2 children **DISCIPLINE** ART HISTORY **EDUCATION** Univ Texas, PhD 93. **CAREER** VA Commonwealth Univ, asst prof 95-; Savannah Col, prof 92-93. **HONORS AND AWARDS** Samuel H. Kress Gnt. **MEMBERSHIPS** CAA; SAH; ALAA; ASHAHS. **RESEARCH** Spanish colonial architecture and its decoration in Latin America. **SELECTED PUBLICATIONS** Auth, Prilidiano Pueyrredon: The Pampas Landscapes, Latin Amer Art Mag, 90. **CONTACT ADDRESS** Dept of Art History, Virginia Commonwealth Univ, 2331 W Grace St Apt 1, Richmond, VA, 23220-1968. **EMAIL** rphillip@hibbs.vcu.edu

PHILLIPS, RODERICK
DISCIPLINE MODERN HISTORY **EDUCATION** Trent Univ, BA, 71; Univ Otago, New Zealand, post grad dipl with credit, 72; Univ Oxford, PhD, 76. **CAREER** Prof. **RESEARCH** French Revolution. **SELECTED PUBLICATIONS** Auth, Putting Asunder: A History of Divorce in Western Society, Cambridge UP, 88; Une Perspectiva sobre la historia de la paternidad, int La Figura del padre en las Familias de la Sociedades Desarrolladas, Gobierno de Canarias, 95; Untying the Knot: A Short History of Divorce, Cambridge UP, 91; Portuguese language edition: Lisbon: Terramar, 96; Chinese language edition: Beijing: China Transl and Publ Corp, 96; Society, State and Nation in Twentieth-Century Europe, Upper Sallde River, NJ: Prentice Hall 96. **CONTACT ADDRESS** Dept of Hist, Carleton Univ, 1125 Colonel By Dr, Ottawa, ON, K1S 5B6. **EMAIL** rodphill@ccs.carleton.ca

PHILLIPS, ROMEO ELDRIDGE
PERSONAL Born 03/11/1928, Chicago, Illinois, m **DISCIPLINE** MUSIC EDUCATION **EDUCATION** Chicago Conservatory Coll, MusB 1949; Chicago Musical Coll, MusM 1951; Eastern MI Univ, MA 1963; Wayne State Univ, PhD 1966. **CAREER** Chicago IL Public Schools, teacher 1949-55; Detroit MI Public Schools, teacher 1955-57; Inkster MI Public Schools, teacher 1957-66; Kalamazoo Coll, chmn dept of educ 1974-86, tenured prof of educ/music 1968-93, prof emeritus, 1993-; Portage MI, city councilman, 1991-. **HONORS AND AWARDS** Invited by the govt of the Republic of Nigeria West Africa to be a guest to the World Festival of Black and African Art 1977; Omega Psi Phi Leadership Awd 1982; Committee of Scholars for the Accreditation of MI Colls 1982-84; Kalamazoo NAACP Appreciation Awd 1982; Fulbright Scholar to Liberia West Africa 1984-85; **MEMBERSHIPS** Mem Amer Assoc of Coll for Teacher Educ, Music Educators Natl Conf, MI Sch Vocal Assoc, Assoc for Supervison & Curriculum Develop, MI Assoc for Supervision & Curriculum Develop, MI Assoc for Improvement of Sch Legislation, Natl Alliance of Black School Educators, Natl Assoc of Negro Musicians, Phi Delta Kappa, Kappa Alpha Psi; conductor AfraAmerican Chorale. **SELECTED PUBLICATIONS** article; 2 book reviews; chapters contributed to or credit given in 6 books. **CONTACT ADDRESS** Prof Emeritus, Kalamazoo Col, 1200 Academy, Kalamazoo, MI, 49006.

PHILLIPS, WILLIAM
DISCIPLINE HISTORY **EDUCATION** Univ NY, PhD, 71. **CAREER** Prof **RESEARCH** History of medieval Spain; Mediterranean world in the Middle Ages; global cross-cultural contacts from the eleventh century to the present. **SELECTED PUBLICATIONS** Auth, Enrique Iv and the Crisis of Fifteenth-Century Castle, 1425-1480, Medieval Acad Am, 78; Slavery From Roman Times to the Early Transatlantic Trade, Univ Minn, 85; co-auth, The Worlds of Christopher Columbus, Cambridge, 92. **CONTACT ADDRESS** History Dept, Univ of Minnesota, Twin Cities, 614 Social Sciences Tower, 267 19th Ave S, Minneapolis, MN, 55455. **EMAIL** phill004@tc.umn.edu

PHILLIPS, III, C. ROBERT
DISCIPLINE ANCIENT HISTORY AND LITERATURE **EDUCATION** PhD, Brown Univ. **CAREER** Prof, Lehigh Univ **RESEARCH** Social history and Greco-Roman religion. **SELECTED PUBLICATIONS** Areas: Roman religion, early christianity, and magic. **CONTACT ADDRESS** Lehigh Univ, Bethlehem, PA, 18015.

PHILP, KENNETH
PERSONAL Born 12/06/1941, Pontiac, MI, m, 1968, 1 child **DISCIPLINE** RECENT AMERICAN HISTORY **EDUCATION** Mich State Univ, BA, 63, PhD, 68; Univ Mich, MA, 64. **CAREER** Asst prof, 68-73, assoc prof, 73-80, prof hist, Univ Tx, 80-, mem, Region 7 Nat Arch Adv Coun, 76-78. **MEMBERSHIPS** AHA; Orgn Am Historians; Western Hist Asn. **RESEARCH** American Indian history. **SELECTED PUBLICATIONS** Auth, Albert Fall and the protest from the Pueblos, 1921-1923, Ariz & the West, fall 70; Herbert Hoover's new era: A false dawn for the American Indian, 1929-1932, Rocky Mountain Soc Sci J, 4/72; John Collier's crusade to protect Indian religious freedom, J Ethnic Studies, spring 73; contribr, Indian-White Relations: A Persistent Paradox, Howard Univ, 76; auth, Turmoil at Big Cypress: Seminole deer and the Florida cattle tick controversy, Fla Hist Quart, 7/77; John Collier's Crusade For Indian Reform, 1920-1954, Univ Ariz, 77; John Collier and the Indians of the Americas: The dream and the reality, Prologue: The J Nat Arch, spring 79; New Deal for Alaska natives, Pac Hist Rev, 8/81; Termination: A Legacy of the Indian New Deal, W Hist Quart, 83; Stride Toward Freedom: The Relocation of Indians to Cities, 1952-1960, W Hist Quart, 85; Dillon S Myer and the Advent of Termination, West Hist Quart, 88; Ed, Indian Self-Rule: First-Hand Accounts of Indian-White Relations from Roosevelt to Reagan, Howe Bros, 86; Termination Revisited Native Americans on the Trail to Self-Determination, 1933-1953, Univ Ne, 99. **CONTACT ADDRESS** Dept Hist, Univ Texas, Arlington, TX, 76019.

PHILYAW, SCOTT L.
DISCIPLINE HISTORY **EDUCATION** Univ NC, PhD. **CAREER** Hist, W Carolina Univ. **SELECTED PUBLICATIONS** Auth, After the Backcountry: Rural Life and Society, Nineteenth-Century Valley of VA, 98. **CONTACT ADDRESS** Dept of Hist, W Carolina Univ, Cullowhee, NC, 28723. **EMAIL** registrar@wcu.edu

PIAN, RULAN CHAO
PERSONAL Born 04/20/1922, Cambridge, MA, m, 1945, 1 child **DISCIPLINE** ETHNO-MUSICOLOGY **EDUCATION** Radcliffe Col, BA, 44, MA, 46, PhD, 60. **CAREER** Tchng asst Chinese, 47-58, instr, 59-61, lectr, 61-74, prof East Asian lang & civilizations of music, 74-92, Harvard Univ; Yenching Inst grant travel & res Orient music in Japan, Hong Kong, Taiwan & Korea, 58-59; Am Coun Learned Socs-J D Rockefeller III Fund travel & res grant Peking opera, US, Asia & Europe, 65-66; NEH grant res abroad, 78-79; vis prof, music, 75, 78-79, 82, 94, Chinese Univ Hong Kong; vis prof, 90-, Inst Lit Natl Tsing Hua Univ Taiwan; vis prof, 92-, Schl Human Natl Central Univ Taiwan. **HONORS AND AWARDS** Caroline I Wilby Prize, Radcliffe Col, 60; Otto Kinkeldy Award, Am Musicol Soc, 68; Radcliffe Grad Soc Medal, 80; Academician, Acad Sinica Taiwan ROC, 90. **MEMBERSHIPS** Am Musicol Soc; Soc Ethnomusicol; Intl Musicol Soc; Soc for Asian Music; Assn for Asian Stud; Int Coun for Trad Music; Chinese Lang Tchrs Assn; Assn for Chinese Music Res. **RESEARCH** Chinese modern language; Chinese music history; interpretation of Sonq dynasty musical sources; present day Chinese musical dramatic and narrative arts. **SELECTED PUBLICATIONS** Auth, A Syllabus for the Mandarin Primer, 61; auth, Sonq Dynasty Musical Sources and Their Interpretation, Harvard Univ, 67; auth, The Function of Rhythm in the Peking Opera, The Musics of Asis, Nat Music Coun Philippines-UNESCO Nat Comn Philippines, 71; auth, Aria Structural Patterns in the Peking Opera, 71; auth, Text Setting with the Shipyi Animated Aria, Words and Music, the Scholar's View: A Medley of Problems and Solutions, Harvard Univ, 72; auth, Modes, Transposed Scales, Melody Types and Tune Types, Proc 12th Cong Int Musicol Soc; auth, Transcription and Study of the Medley Song, The Couresan's Jewel Box, Chinoperl Papers, Vol 9, No 10, Cornell Univ. **CONTACT ADDRESS** Dept of East Asian Lang & Civilizations, Harvard Univ, 2 Divinity Ave, Cambridge, MA, 02138. **EMAIL** thhpian@ail.com

PICCATO, PABLO
DISCIPLINE LATIN AMERICAN HISTORY **EDUCATION** La Universidad Nacional Autonoma de Mexico, BA, 90; Univ Tex, PhD, 97. **CAREER** Hist, Columbia Univ **SELECTED PUBLICATIONS** Auth, Understanding Society: Porfirian Discourse about Criminality and Alcolohism; Los intentos de establecer el parlamentarismo desde la Camara de Diputados, 1912-1921: Entre la opinion publica y los grupos de choque; La experiencia penal en la ciudad de Mexico: cambios y permanencias tras la revolucion. **CONTACT ADDRESS** Columbia Univ, 2960 Broadway, New York, NY, 10027-6902.

PICKENS, DONALD KENNETH
PERSONAL Born 05/28/1934, FOSS, OK, m, 1957, 2 children **DISCIPLINE** UNITED STATES SOCIAL & INTELLECTUAL HISTORY **EDUCATION** Univ Okla, BA, 56, MA, 57; Univ Tex, PhD(hist), 64. **CAREER** Asst prof US hist, Tarleton State Col, 57-58; assoc prof, Southwestern State Col, 62-65; assoc prof, 65-76, Prof Us Hist, North Tex State Univ, 76-. **MEMBERSHIPS** Orgn Am Historians; Am Studies Asn. **RESEARCH** Women in United States history; United States historiography; history of ideas. **SELECTED PUBLICATIONS** Auth, The sterilization movement, Phylon, 67; Eugenics and the Progressives, Vanderbilt Univ, 68; coauth, America in Process, Winston, 73; auth, Infinite desires in a finite world, Soc Sci Quart, 9/76; Henry Adams's failures: A success story, Am Quart, fall 81; Westward expansion and the end of American exceptionalism: Sumner, Turner, and Webb, Western Hist Quart, 10/81; The historical images in Republican campaign songs, 1860- 1900, J Popular Cult, winter 81; Walter Prescott Webb's tomorrow, Red River Hist Rev, winter 81; the End of American Exceptionalism - Frontier Anxiety from the Old West to the New- deal - Wrobel,dm, J of the West, Vol 0034, 1995; Race and Labor in Western Copper - the Fight for Equality, 1896-1918 - Mellinger,pj, J of the West, Vol 0035, 1996. **CONTACT ADDRESS** Dept of Hist, No Texas State Univ, Denton, TX, 76201.

PICKER, MARTIN
PERSONAL Born 04/03/1929, Chicago, IL, m, 1956, 3 children **DISCIPLINE** MUSICOLOGY **EDUCATION** Univ of Chicago, PhB, 74, MA, 51; Univ of Calif, PhD, 60. **CAREER** Instr, Univ of Ill, 59-61; from asst prof to prof, Rutgers Univ, 61-. **HONORS AND AWARDS** Harvard Univ, I Tatti Fel, 66-67; NEH Sen Fel, 72-73. **MEMBERSHIPS** Am Musicological Soc; Int Musicological Soc; Royal Soc for Dutch Music Hist **RESEARCH** Renaissance Music **SELECTED PUBLICATIONS** Auth, Johannes Ockeghem and Jacob Obrecht, in A Guide to Research, 88; The Habsburg Courts in the Netherlands andAustria, in The Renaissance: From the 1470s to the End of the 16th Century, 90; Henricus Isaac, in A Guide to Research, 91; The Career of Marbriano de Orto, in Collectanea II, Studien zur Geschichte der Paepstlichen Kapelle, 94; Isaac in Flanders: The Early Works of Henricus Isaac, in From Ciconia to Sweelinck, donum natalicium Willem Elders, 94; ed, The Chanson Albums of Marguerite of Austria, 65; Fors Seulement: Thirty Compositions, 81; The Motet Books fo Andrea Antico, 87. **CONTACT ADDRESS** Music Dept, Rutgers Univ, Douglass Campus, New Brunswick, NJ, 08903-0270. **EMAIL** mpicker@rci.rutgers.edu

PICKETT, TERRY H.
PERSONAL Born 04/19/1941, Washington, GA, m, 1961, 2 children **DISCIPLINE** GERMAN LITERATURE & HISTORY **EDUCATION** Univ GA, AB, 66; Vanderbilt Univ, PhD(Ger lit), 70. **CAREER** Asst prof, 70-79, Prof Ger, Univ Ala, 80-, Chmn Dept Ger & Russ, 78-, Fulbright-Exchange Teacher, Hans-Sachs-Gym & Univ of Erlangen-Nurnberg, 72-73. **MEMBERSHIPS** MLA; Southeastern Mod Lang Asn; Am Asn Teaciers Ger. **RESEARCH** Nineteenth century German literature; Tenacious literature 1800-1850; Varnhagen von Ense. **SELECTED PUBLICATIONS** Auth, Varnhagen's mistaken identity in two recent works, Germanic Notes, 71; Heinrich Boll's plea for civilization, Southern Humanities Rev, 73; Varnhagen von Ense & his mistaken identity, Ger Life & Lett, 4/74; coauth, Varnhagen von Ense and the reception of Russian literature in Germany, Germano-Slavica, fall 74;Masters and Lords - Mid-19th-century United-states Planters and Prussian Junkers - Bowman,sd, Germanic Notes and Reviews, Vol 0025, 1994; the Biedermeier Novel and the Corporatist Order Crisis - Studies on Literary Conservatism - German - Brandmeyer,r, Germanic Notes and Reviews, Vol 0025, 1994; the Faces of Physiognomy - Interdisciplinary Approaches to Lavater,johann,caspar - Shookman,e, Germanic Notes and Reviews, Vol 0026, 1995; Terrible Sociability - the Text of Manners in Laclos, Goethe, and James - Winnett,s, Germanic Notes and Reviews, Vol 0028, 1997; a Grand Illusion - an Essay on Europe - Judt,t/, Germanic Notes and Reviews, Vol 0028, 1997; Fascist Italy and Nazi Germany - the Fascist Style of Rule - Degrand,aj/, Germanic Notes and Reviews, Vol 0028, 1997; Terrible Sociability - the Text of Manners in Laclos, Goethe, and James - Winnett,s, Germanic Notes and Reviews, Vol 0028, 1997. **CONTACT ADDRESS** Dept of Ger, Univ of Ala, University, AL, 35486.

PICKLESIMER, DORMAN
DISCIPLINE COMMUNICATION/HISTORY **EDUCATION** Morehead State Univ, AB, 60; Bowling Green State Univ, MA, 65; Ind Univ, PhD, 69. **CAREER** Prof, Boston Col, 69-. **HONORS AND AWARDS** Phi Kappa Delta; Gold Key Honor Soc. **MEMBERSHIPS** Nat Communication Asn; Eastern Communication Asn; World Communication Asn. **RESEARCH** History of American public address; classical rhetoric. **CONTACT ADDRESS** Dept of Communcations, Boston Col, Lyons Hall 215, Chestnut Hill, MA, 02167. **EMAIL** picklesi@bC.edu

PICO, FERNANDO
PERSONAL Born 08/15/1941, Santurce, PR **DISCIPLINE** MEDIEVAL HISTORY **EDUCATION** Fordham Univ, AB, 65, MA, 66; Johns Hopkins Univ, PhD(hist), 70; Woodstock Col, MDiv, 72. **CAREER** Asst prof, 72-78, Assoc Prof Hist, Univ Pr, Rio Piedras, 78-, Coordr hist grad prog, Univ PR, Rio Piedras, 81. **MEMBERSHIPS** AHA; Medieval Acad Am; Cath Hist Asn; Fr Hist Soc. **RESEARCH** Social and professional composition of French medieval clergy; Formation of rural peonage--19th century Puerto Rico; Small holders: 18th century Mexico and 19th century Puerto Rico. **SELECTED PUBLICATIONS** Auth, Membership in the Cathedral Chapter of Laon, 1217- 1238, Cath Hist Rev, 75; Changements dans la composition du chapitre cathedrale de Laon 1155-1318, Rev Hist Eccleciastique, 76; ed, Registro general de Jeros de Utuado, 1849-50, Ediciones Huracan, 77; Cosificacion de la naturaleza, deshumanizacion del trabajo: Los comienzos del cafe en Utuado, Cuadernos Facultad de Humanidades, 79; Libertad y servidumbre en el Puerto Rico del siglo XIX, 79 & Amargo cafe: los pequenos y medianos preductores agricolas de Utuado, 81, Ediciones Huracan; Non-aristocratic bishops in the France of Louis IX (1226-1270), Medieval Prosopography, 82; Los pequenos y medianos productores agricolas de Irapuato en los siglos 17 y 18, In: Vol II de Historia de la agricultura en Mexico, 82; Puerto-rican and Cuban Catholics in the United-states, 1900-1965 - Dolan,jp, Vidal,jr/, Catholic Historical Review, Vol 0082, 1996. **CONTACT ADDRESS** RFD 3 Buzon 1498, Rio Piedras, PR, 00928.

PIEHLER, G. KURT
DISCIPLINE HISTORY **EDUCATION** Rutgers Univ, PhD. **CAREER** Asst prof. **SELECTED PUBLICATIONS** Auth, Remembering War the American Way, Smithsonian Inst, 95; co-ed, Major Problems in American Military History, Houghton Mifflin, 98. **CONTACT ADDRESS** Dept of History, Knoxville, TN, 37996.

PIERARD, RICHARD VICTOR
PERSONAL Born 05/29/1934, Chicago, IL, m, 1957, 2 children **DISCIPLINE** MODERN EUPOPEAN HISTORY, HISTORY OF CHRISTIANITY **EDUCATION** CA State Univ, Los Angeles, BA, 58, MA, 59; Univ IA, PhD, 64. **CAREER** Tchg asst Western civilization, Univ IA, 59-64; from asst prof to assoc prof, 64-72, prof hist, IN State Univ, Terre Haute, 72-, Vis prof, Greenville Col, 72-73; vis prof, Fuller Theol Seminary, 88, 91; Fulbright prof, Univ Frankfurt, Ger, 84-85; Univ Halle-Wittenberg, Ger, 89-98. **MEMBERSHIPS** AHA; Conf Group Cent Europ Hist; Conf Faith & Hist (secy-treas, 67-); Am Soc Church Hist; Am Soc Missiology. **RESEARCH** Europ polit and relig expansion into Africa since 1800; mod Germany; conservative relig and polit ideas. **SELECTED PUBLICATIONS** Coauth, Civil Religion and the Presidency, Zondervan, 88; coauth, Two Kingdoms: The Church and Culture Through the Ages, Moody, 93; Ed, The Revolution of the Candles, Mercer, 96; Religion and New Right in the 1980s, in Religion and the State, Baylor, 85; Separation of Church and State: Figment of an Infidels Imagination?, in Faith and Freedom, Pergamon, 85; Pax Americana and the Evangical Missionary Advance, In Earthern Vessels: American Evangelicals and Foreign Missions, Erdmans, 90; President Eisenhower, die Amerikanische Rechte und die Internatinalen Krisen von 1956, Berliner Debate, 95; Stephen Neil, In Historians of the Christian Tradition, broadman $ Holman, 95; Shaking the Foundations : World War I, The Western Allies, and German Protesant Missions, International Bulliten of Missionary Research, 98; Informers or Resisters? The East German Secret Police and the Church, Christian Scholar Review, 98. **CONTACT ADDRESS** Dept of Hist, Indiana State Univ, 210 N 7th St, Terre Haute, IN, 47809-0002. **EMAIL** hipier@ruby.indstate.edu

PIERCE, RICHARD A.
DISCIPLINE RUSSIAN AMERICA **EDUCATION** Univ CA, PhD, 56. **CAREER** Univ Alaska **SELECTED PUBLICATIONS** Auth, Russian America: A Biographical Dictionary; Ed, G.H. van Langsdorff, Remarks and Observations on a Voyage Around the World, 1803-1807; K.T. Khlebnikov. Notes on Russian America. **CONTACT ADDRESS** Univ AK Fairbanks, PO Box 757480, Fairbanks, AK, 99775-7480. **EMAIL** fyhist@aurora.alaska.edu

PIERCE, THOMAS B.
DISCIPLINE MENTAL RETARDATION **EDUCATION** Univ NMex, PhD, 89. **CAREER** Coordr, ment retardation transition prog, Univ Nev, Las Vegas. **HONORS AND AWARDS** Lilly Fong Distinguished Prof, 95; pres, Div of Legal Proc and

Advocacy, Am Asn on Ment Retardation, 96. **SELECTED PUBLICATIONS** Auth, Teaching functional skills to people with developmental disabilities, Korean Inst of Spec Educ, Nov, 95; coauth, Effects of self-determined, data-determined and supervisor-determined goals on student teacher behavior, Prof Educ, 17 (2), 95; The state of special education leadership training and college and university faculty: What we know and what we don't, Tchr Educ and Spec Educ, 18, 96. **CONTACT ADDRESS** Dept of Spec Educ, Univ Nev, Las Vegas, 4505 Maryland Pky, Las Vegas, NV, 89154-3014. **EMAIL** pierce@ nevada.edu

PIERSON, PETER O'MALLEY
PERSONAL Born 10/04/1932, Indianapolis, IN **DISCIPLINE** EARLY MODERN EUROPEAN HISTORY **EDUCATION** UCLA, BA, 54, MA, 63, PhD, 66. **CAREER** From instr to asst prof, 66-77, assoc prof 77-89, prof hist, Univ Santa Clara, 89, Dept Ch, 88-92; Fulbright Fel, Spain, 64-66; Nat Endowment for Hum fel, 74. **HONORS AND AWARDS** Lee and Seymour Graff Prof, 93; Fac Senate Prof. **MEMBERSHIPS** Soc Span & Port Hist Studies; Historians Early Mod Europe. **RESEARCH** Span government and nobility of the period of Philip II. **SELECTED PUBLICATIONS** Auth, A commander for the Armada, Mariner's Mirror, 11/69; Philip II of Spain, Thames & Hudson, 75; Commander of the Armada: The Seventh Duke of Medina Sidonia, Yale, 89; Brethren of the Coast, MHQ: Quart Jour Military Hist, autumn 94; Elizabeth's Pirate Admiral, MHQ, summer 96; Lepanto, MHQ, winter 97; History of Spain, Greenwood, 98. **CONTACT ADDRESS** Dept of Hist, Univ of Santa Clara, 500 El Camino Real, Santa Clara, CA, 95053-0001. **EMAIL** ppierson@mailer.scu.edu

PIERSON, RUTH
PERSONAL Seattle, WA **DISCIPLINE** HISTORY **EDUCATION** Univ Wash, BA, 60, MA, 63; Yale Univ, PhD, 70. **CAREER** Tchg asst, Univ Wash, 61-63; asst instr, Yale Univ, 66-67; lectr, Univ Maryland, Col Park, 68-69; asst prof, 70-76, assoc prof, 76-80, Memorial Univ Newfoundland; assoc prof, 80-90, PROF, ONT INST STUD EDUC, UNIV TORONTO, 90-. **MEMBERSHIPS** Can Hist Asn; Can Comt Women's Hist; Can Women's Stud Asn; Int Fedn Res Women Hist. **SELECTED PUBLICATIONS** Auth, They're Still Women After All: the Second World War and Canadian Womanhood, 86; auth, Women and Peace: Theoretical, Historical and Practical Perspectives, 87; auth, No Easy Road: Women in Canada 1920s to 1960s, 90; coauth, Strong Voices, Vol 1 in Can Women's Issues, 93. **CONTACT ADDRESS** OISE, Univ Toronto, Toronto, ON, M5S 1V6. **EMAIL** rrpierson@oise.utoronto.ca

PIGG, KENNETH E.
DISCIPLINE DEVELOMENT SOCIOLOGY **EDUCATION** Cornell Univ, PhD, 76. **CAREER** Assoc prof, Univ Ky, 75-83; extension prog dir and assoc dean, Univ Mo, 83-87; assoc prof, Univ Mo, 87- . **RESEARCH** Community development; program evaluation **CONTACT ADDRESS** Univ Mo - Columbia, 204 Sociology Bldg., Columbia, MO, 65211. **EMAIL** piggk@ missouri.edu

PIKE, FREDRICK BRAUN
PERSONAL Born 12/23/1924, Los Angeles, CA, m, 1949, 3 children **DISCIPLINE** HISTORY **EDUCATION** Loyola Univ, Los Angeles, BA, 49; Univ Tex, MA, 51, PhD, 56. **CAREER** From asst prof to assoc prof, 53-69, Prof Hist, Univ Notre Dame, 69-; Grants, Doherty Found, Chile, 59-60 & Soc Sci Res Coun, Peru, 63-. **RESEARCH** Colonial Latin American institutions; United States-Latin American relations. **SELECTED PUBLICATIONS** Auth, Chile and the United States, 1880-1962, 62 & ed, Freedom and Reform in Latin America, 59, Univ Notre Dame; Peru Apra, Parties, Politics, and the Elusive Quest for Democracy - Graham,c/, Hispanic American Historical Review, Vol 0073, 1993. **CONTACT ADDRESS** Dept of Hist, Univ of Notre Dame, Notre Dame, IN, 46556.

PIKE, RUTH
PERSONAL Born 07/26/1931, New York, NY **DISCIPLINE** MODERN EUROPEAN HISTORY **EDUCATION** Columbia Univ, BS, 53, MA, 54, PhD(Span hist), 59. **CAREER** Lectr, Brooklyn Col, 55-56; instr, Douglass Col, Rutgers Univ, 55-57; lectr Europ hist, Hunter Col, 57-58 & 59-60; instr Europ & Latin Am hist, Rutgers Univ, 60-61; from asst prof to assoc prof, 61-71, Prof Europ & Span Hist, Hunter Col, 72-, Am Coun Learned Soc grant-in-aid, 63-64; mem PhD prog in hist, City Univ NY, 67-; vis assoc prof hist, Johns Hopkins Univ, 69-; City Univ NY Res Found fac res award, 70-71 & 79-80. **HONORS AND AWARDS** John A Krout Prize Hist, Columbia Univ, 53; Newcomen Award Bus Hist, 65. **MEMBERSHIPS** AHA; Econ Hist Asn; Conf Latin Am Hist; Am Asn Teachers Span & Port; Soc Span & Port Hist Studies. **SELECTED PUBLICATIONS** Auth, Enterprise and Adventure: The Genoese in Seville and the Opening of the New World, Cornell Univ, 66; The Converso family of Baltasar del Alcazar, Ky Romance Quart, 69; Slavery in Seville at the time of Columbus, In: From Reconquest to Empire: The Iberian Background of Latin American History, Knopf, 70; An urban minority: The Moriscos of Seville, Int J Mid E Studies, 71; Aristocrats and Traders: Sevillian Society in the Sixteenth Century, Cornell Univ, 72; Penal

labor in sixteenth-century Spain: The mines of Almaden, Societas-Rev Soc Hist, 73; Crime and punishment in sixteenth-century Spain, J Europ Econ Hist, 76; Penal servitude in the Spanish Empire: Presidio labor in the eighteenth century, Hisp Am Hist Rev, 78; the Dramatist Jimenezdeenciso,diego and the Linajudos of Seville/, Bulletin of Hispanic Studies, Vol 0070, 1993; Andalusia in 1492 - Spanish - Ladero,ma/, Hispanic American Historical Review, Vol 0073, 1993; New Light on the Biography of Lacueva,juan,de/, Romance Quarterly, Vol 0041, 1994. **CONTACT ADDRESS** Dept of Hist, Hunter Col, CUNY, 695 Park Ave, New York, NY, 10021.

PILANT, CRAIG WESLEY
PERSONAL Born 08/26/1952, San Francisco, CA **DISCIPLINE** THEOLOGY, AMERICAN RELIGIOUS STUDIES, HISTORICAL THEOLOGY **EDUCATION** Loyola Univ, Chicago, BA, 74; Univ Ill, Chicago, MA, 83; Fordham Univ, MSEd, 87, PhD, 97. **CAREER** Dir of admissions, GSAS, 90-97, asst dean, GSAS, 97-, Fordham Univ. **MEMBERSHIPS** AAR; CHS; NAGAP. **RESEARCH** American religious history; hagiography; music and theology; Social Gospel; Orestes A. Brownson. **SELECTED PUBLICATIONS** Auth, Inward Promptings: Orestes A. Brownson, Outsidership and Roman Catholicism in the United States, 96. **CONTACT ADDRESS** 838 Wesley Ave., 1-K, New Rochelle, NY, 10801. **EMAIL** cwphd@aol.com

PILE, JOHN F.
PERSONAL Born 12/03/1924, Philadelphia, PA, m, 1965, 2 children **DISCIPLINE** ARCHITECTURE **EDUCATION** Univ Penn, BA; Beaux Arts Inst of Design, cert; Friends Design School, Philadelphia. **CAREER** Prof of Design, Pratt Inst, 48-; assoc, George Nelson and Co., 51-61; independent design consult, 61- . **MEMBERSHIPS** Soc of Archit Hist. **RESEARCH** Architecture; design. **SELECTED PUBLICATIONS** Auth, Interior Design, Abrams; auth, Dictionary of 20th Century Design, Facts on File; auth, Furniture, Modern and Post Modern, Wiley; auth, perspective for Interior Designers, Whitney Library; auth, Open Office Planning, Whitney Library; auth, Design: Purpose, Form and Meaning, Univ Mass Press; coauth, Sketching Interior Architecture, Whitney Library; coauth, Drawing Interior Architecture, Whitney Library; auth, Interiors Third Book of Offices, Whitney Library; auth, Interiors Second Book of Offices, Whitney Library. **CONTACT ADDRESS** 13 Grace Court Alley, Brooklyn, NY, 11201.

PILLSBURY, JOANNE
DISCIPLINE ART HISTORY, ARCHAEOLOGY **EDUCATION** Univ CA, Berkeley, BA (anthropology), 82; Columbia Univ, MA (art hist/anthropoplgy), 86, M Phil (art hist/ anthropol), 87, PhD (art hist/anthropol), 93. **CAREER** Asst Dean, Center for Advanced Study in the Visual Arts, Nat Gallery of Art; lect (asst prof), Sainsbury Research Unit for the Arts of Africa, Oceania and the Americas, Univ of East Anglia, 91-; vis prof, The Johns Hopkins Univ, spring, 98, spring, 99. **HONORS AND AWARDS** Am Asn of Univ Women Fel, 89-90; Dumbarton Oaks Jr Fel in Pre-Columbian Studies, Washington, DC, 89-90; Samuel H Kress Found Project grant, 90; Fulbright Scholarship, Peru, 90-91; Andrew W Mellon, The Metropolitan Museum of Art, New York, 94-95. **MEMBERSHIPS** Asn for Latin Am Art (officer); Col Art Asn; Acive member, Inst of Andrean Studies, Berkeley (elected); Fel, Royal Anthropol Inst, London (elected); Soc for Am Archaeology. **RESEARCH** Pre-Columbian Art Hist: Archaeology. **SELECTED PUBLICATIONS** Auth, Technical Evidence for Temporal Placement: Sculpted Adobe Friezes of Chan Chan, Peru, in Materials Issues in Art and Archaeology III, eds, Pamela Vandiver, James Druzik, George Wheeler and Ian Freestone, Materials Res Soc Symposium Proceedings vol 267, 92; Los Relieves de Chan Chan: Nuevos Datos para el Estudio de la Sequencia y Ocupacion de la Ciudad, Revista del Museo Arqueologico de la Universidad Nacional de Trujillo, 95; Pre-Columbian Shellwork of South America, in The Dictionary of Art, ed, Jane Shoaf Turner, Macmillan, 96; The Thorny Oyster and the Origins of Empire: Implications of Recently Uncovered Spondylus Imagery from Chan Chan, Peru, Latin Am Antiquity, 7 (4), 96; Inka and Chimu entries, in The Spirit of Ancient Peru: Treasures from the Mudeo Arqueologico Rafael Larco Herrera, ed, Kathleen Berrin, Fine Arts Museums of San Francisco, 97; The Arts of Ancient Mesoamerica, with T Leyenaar, in Catalogue of the Robert and Lisa Sainsbury Collection, eds Steven Hooper, Yale Univ Press, 97. **CONTACT ADDRESS** Center for Advanced Study in the Visual Arts, National Gallery of Art, Washington, DC, 20565.

PINA, LESLIE
DISCIPLINE INTERIOR DESIGN **EDUCATION** Case Western Reserve Univ, BA, MA, PhD. **CAREER** Assoc prof. **SELECTED PUBLICATIONS** Auth, pubs on 20th century decorative arts. **CONTACT ADDRESS** Dept of Interior Design, Ursuline Col, 2550 Lander Road, Pepper Pike, OH, 44124. **EMAIL** lfelder@ursuline.edu

PINDER, KYMBERLY
DISCIPLINE ART HISTORY **EDUCATION** Middlebury Col, BA; Yale Univ, PhD. **CAREER** Instr, Middlebury Col; Saint Michael's Col; asst prof, 96-. **HONORS AND AWARDS**

Henry Luce foundation fel; Sumner, McKnight, Crosby res grant. **SELECTED PUBLICATIONS** Pub(s), numerous critical essays. **CONTACT ADDRESS** Dept of Art Hist, Sch of the Art Inst of Chicago, 37 S Wabash Ave, Chicago, IL, 60603. **EMAIL** kpinder@artic.edu

PINKETT, HAROLD THOMAS
PERSONAL Born 04/07/1914, Salisbury, MD, m, 1943 **DISCIPLINE** ARCHIVES, HISTORY **EDUCATION** Morgan Col, AB, 35; Univ Pa, AM, 38; Am Univ, PhD, 53. **CAREER** Teacher, High Sch, Md, 36-38; prof hist, Livingstone Col, 38-39 & 41-42; archivist, Nat Archs, 42-79; consult archivist & historian, 80-, Coun Libr Resources fel, 72-73; lectr hist & archival admin, Howard Univ, 70-76; lectr, Am Univ, Washington, DC, 76-77. **HONORS AND AWARDS** Bancroft Hist Prize, 47 & 48; book award, agric hist soc, 68. **MEMBERSHIPS** Fel Soc Am Archivists; AHA; Orgn Am Historians; Forest Hist Soc (pres, 76-78); Agr Hist Soc (pres, 82-). **RESEARCH** Archival administration, history and use; American conservation history; progressive era. **SELECTED PUBLICATIONS** Art, American Archival Theory: The State of the Art, American Archivist, summer 81; auth, National Church of Zion Methodism, 89; auth, Conservationists at the Cosmos Club, 90. **CONTACT ADDRESS** 5741 27th Street NW, Washington, DC, 20015.

PINNELL, RICHARD
DISCIPLINE MUSIC HISTORY **EDUCATION** Univ Utah, BA; Univ Ca, PhD, 76. **CAREER** Dept Music, Wisc Univ **RESEARCH** Latin American music. **SELECTED PUBLICATIONS** Auth, Francesco Corbetta and the Baroque Guitar, UMI Res, 80; The Rioplatense Guitar, Bold Strummer, 93. **CONTACT ADDRESS** Dept of Music, Univ of Wisconsin, La Crosse, 1725 State St, La Crosse, WI, 54601. **EMAIL** pinnell@ mail.uwlax.edu

PINO, JULIO CESAR
PERSONAL Born 12/30/1960, Havana, Cuba, m, 1992 **DISCIPLINE** HISTORY **EDUCATION** Univ Calif, Los Angeles, BA, 84, MA, 87, PhD, 91. **CAREER** Vis prof, Univ Calif, Los Angeles, 91; vis prof, Bowdoin Col, 91-92; ASSOC PROF, HISTORY, KENT STATE UNIV, 92-. **HONORS AND AWARDS** Fulbright-Hays fel, 89-90; Kent State Univ summer grants, 93, 97, 99. **MEMBERSHIPS** AHA; Lat Am Stud Asn; Third World Studies Asn. **RESEARCH** Brazil; Cuba; African diaspora. **SELECTED PUBLICATIONS** Auth, Family and Favela: Reproduction of Poverty in Rio de Janeiro, Greenwood Press, 97; auth, Labor in the Favelas of Rio de Janeiro, Latin American Research Review 32:3, Nov 97; auth, Urban Squatter Households in Rio de Janeiro, 1940-1969, Locus: Regional and Local History of the Americas 8:2, May 96; auth, Teaching the History of Race in Latin America, Perspectives: Newsletter of the AHA 35:7, Oct 97; auth, Bay of Pigs Invasion, in Great Events from History: North American Series, Salem Press, 97. **CONTACT ADDRESS** Dept of History, Kent State Univ, Kent, OH, 44242-0001. **EMAIL** jpino@phoenix.kent.edu

PINTNER, WALTER MCKENZIE
PERSONAL Born 06/19/1931, Yonkers, NY, m, 1958, 2 children **DISCIPLINE** RUSSIAN HISTORY **EDUCATION** Univ Chicago, AB, 51, MA, 57; Harvard Univ, MA, 55, PhD, 62. **CAREER** Res specialist econ, US Dept State, 56-58; instr hist, Princeton Univ, 61-62; asst prof, 62-68, assoc prof, 68-79, prof hist, Cornell Univ, 79-; vis schol, USSR Acad Sci, Moscow, 81; vis prof, Univ London, 87-88; vis schol, Saitama Univ, Japan, 96. **HONORS AND AWARDS** Inter-Univ Comt Travel Grants fel, Leningrad State Univ, 66 & Int Res & Exchanges Bd travel fel, 70; res fel, Russ Res Ctr, Harvard Univ, 65-66; fel, Woodrow Wilson Ctr, Smithsonian Inst, 77-78. **MEMBERSHIPS** Am Asn Advan Slavic Studies; Study Group 18th Century Russia. **RESEARCH** Eighteenth and 19th century Russian economic, administrative and military history. **SELECTED PUBLICATIONS** Auth, Inflation in Russia During the Crimean War, in Am Slavic & East Europ Rev, 1/59; Russian Economic Policy Under Nicholas I, Ithaca Univ, 67; Social Characteristics of the Early 19th Century Russian Bureaucracy, in Slavic Rev, 3/70; The Russian Higher Civil Service on the Eve of the Great Reforms, in J Soc Hist, spring 75; ed (with D K Rowney), Russian Officialdom, Chapel Hill, 80. **CONTACT ADDRESS** Dept of Hist, Cornell Univ, McGraw Hall, Ithaca, NY, 14853-8703. **EMAIL** wmp1@cornell.edu

PIPER, JON KINGSBURY
PERSONAL Born 09/06/1957, m, 1980, 3 children **DISCIPLINE** BOTANY **EDUCATION** Bates Col, BS, biology, 79; Wash St Univ, PhD, Botany, 84, **CAREER** Grad tchng asst, 80, 81, 83, & 84, grad res asst, dept zoology, 85, vis asst prof, gen biology, 85, Wash St Univ; res assoc, The Land Inst, Salina KS, 85-97; adj fac, 89, Benedictine Col at Marymount; assoc prof, biology, 97-, Bethel Col, KS; adj res, 98-, The Land Institute. **HONORS AND AWARDS** Wash St Univ, grad stud travel grant, 80; Sigma Xi, res grant, 82; Wash Native Plant Soc grant, 82; Natl Sci found, diss improv grant, 82; Eppley Found for res, 88, 91, 96; The Charles A. & Anne Morrow Lindbergh Found, 95; Julius A. & Agatha Dyck Franz Fac Devel Award, 98. **MEMBERSHIPS** Ecol Soc Amer. **RESEARCH** Ecology; botany; environ sci; gen biology; agroecology **SELECTED PUB-**

LICATIONS Coauth, Farming in Nature's Image: An Ecological Approach to Agriculture, Island Press, 92; art, Nature As A Model for Sustainability, Rural Comm Survival, 1994 Conf Proc, 96; art, Density of Anomoea Flavokansiensis on Desmanthus Illinoensis, Entomologia Experimentalis et Applicata 81:105, 96; art, Natural Systems Agricultural Research, Ecol of Our Landscape: The Botany of Where We Live, 1995 Conf Proc, 96; art, Diversity in Sustainable Agriculture, Field Crops Res 48:235, 96; coauth, Incidence and Severity of Viral Disease Symptoms On Eastern Gamagrass Within Monoculture and Polycultures, Agriculture, Ecosystems & Environ 59:139, 96; art, The Last Harvest, Culture & Agriculture 19:57, 97; art, Growth and Seed Yield of Three Perennial Grains Within Monocultures and Mixed Stands, Agriculture, Ecosystems & Environ 68:1, 98; art, Natural Systems Agriculture, Biodiversity in Agroecosystems, CRC Press, FL, 98; art, Farming Practices, Sustainable, & Farmland & Farming Communities, Conservation, Encycl of Ecology & Environ Mgt, Oxford, 98; art, Another Modest Proposal For the Great Plains, Ecology 79:2574, 98. **CONTACT ADDRESS** Dept of Biology, Bethel Col, North Newton, KS, 67117. **EMAIL** smilax@bethelks.edu

PIPER, LINDA JANE
PERSONAL Born 04/10/1935, Blairsville, PA **DISCIPLINE** ANCIENT HISTORY **EDUCATION** Univ Pittsburgh, AB, 57; Ohio State Univ, MA, 60, PhD(class hist), 66. **CAREER** Asst prof hist, Univ GA, 66-81. **MEMBERSHIPS** AHA; Am Philol Asn; Archaeol Inst Am; AAUP. **RESEARCH** Hellenistic Sparta. **SELECTED PUBLICATIONS** Auth, Livy's portray of early Roman women, Class J, 12/71; War, Women and Children in Ancient-rome - Evans,jk/, Histoire Sociale-social History, Vol 0026, 1993. **CONTACT ADDRESS** 310 S Church St, Athens, GA, 30605.

PIPES, DANIEL
PERSONAL Born 09/09/1949, Boston, MA, d, 2 children **DISCIPLINE** HISTORY **EDUCATION** Harvard Univ, BA 71, PhD 78. **CAREER** Univ Chicago, tch 78-82; State Dept, 82-83; Harvard Univ, lectr 83-84; Navel War Col, prof 84-86; For Policy Research Inst, director 86-93; Middle East Forum, director 94. **HONORS AND AWARDS** Vice Chmn of J Fulbright Bd of Foreign Scholarships; Who's Who in the East; Who's Who in Entertainment; Who's Who in America; Who's Who in the World., Has served twice on the Bush for pres campaigns and recently helped Bob Dole, Testified before five Senate and House committees. **SELECTED PUBLICATIONS** Conspiracy: How the Paranoid Style Flourishes, and Where it Comes From, 97; The Rushdie Affair, 90; In the Path of God: Islam and Political Power, 83; Slave Soldiers and Islam, 81; Syria Beyond the Peace Process, 96; The Hidden hand: Middle East Fears of Conspiracy, 96; The Long Shadow: Culture and Politics in the Middle East, 89; Articles in major newspapers and other publ. **CONTACT ADDRESS** Middle East Forum, 1920 Chestnut St, Philadelphia, PA, 19103. **EMAIL** mcgmef@aol.com

PIPKIN, HARRY WAYNE
PERSONAL Born 08/10/1939, Houston, TX, m, 1965, 2 children **DISCIPLINE** HISTORY OF CHRISTIANITY **EDUCATION** Baylor Univ, BA, 61; Univ Conn, MA, 63; Hartford Sem Found, PhD(hist Christianity), 68. **CAREER** Asst in instr church hist, Hartford Sem Found, 67-68; Fulbright scholar Renaissance hist, Univ Vienna, 68-69; asst prof church hist, Baylor Univ, 69-74; assoc dir consortium higher educ relig studies, Pontif Col Josephinum, 74-76; dir, Univ Without Walls, Ohio, 76-78; Assoc Prof Church Hist, Baptist Theol Sem, Switz, 78-, Dir, Inst Baptist & Anabaptist Studies; Reporter & coordr, The Primary Source: Int Newslett Baptist Hist. **MEMBERSHIPS** Am Soc Church Hist; Zwingli Verein; Am Soc Reformation Res. **RESEARCH** Reformation studies and theology; Huldrych Zwingli; Balthasar Hubmaier. **SELECTED PUBLICATIONS** Auth, Zwingli, The Laity and the Orders: From the Cloister Into the World, Hartford Quart, winter 68; The Preaching and Sermons of Huldrych Zwingli, In: 20 Centuries of Great Preaching, Word Bks, 71; A Zwingli Bibliography: Bibliographia Tripotamopolitana, Clifford E Barbour Libr, 72; transl, The Gospel of Liberation by Jurgen Moltmann, Word Bks, 73; auth, Huldrych Zwingli and True Religion, AD 1974, 10/74; Christian Meditation, Its Art and Practice, Hawthorn, 77; Marpeck,pilgram - His Life and Theology - Boyd,sb/, Sixteenth Century J, Vol 0024, 1993; Spiritual Legacy of Denck,hans - Interpretation and Translation of Key Texts - Bauman,c/, Sixteenth Century J, Vol 0024, 1993. **CONTACT ADDRESS** Dept Church Hist, Baptist Theol Sem, Ruschlikon, ..

PISANI, MICHAEL
DISCIPLINE MUSIC HISTORY **EDUCATION** Univ Rochester, PhD. **CAREER** Asst prof. **HONORS AND AWARDS** Conductor & cast preparation for Houston Grand Opera, Seattle Opera, and Opera Company of Boston; asst, Leonard Bernstein, 85, 86 on Europ productions of his opera, A Quiet Place at La Scala, Vienna State Opera. **RESEARCH** Opera, theater and film music, musical exoticism. **SELECTED PUBLICATIONS** Cintrubu, The Exotic in Western Music, Northeast Univ Pres, 98. **CONTACT ADDRESS** Classic Dept, Vassar Col, 124 Raymond Ave., Poughkeepsie, NY, 12604. **EMAIL** mipisani@vassar.edu

PITMAN, GROVER A.
DISCIPLINE MUSICOLOGY **EDUCATION** Univ Tex, Austin, BM, MM; The Catholic Univ Am, PhD; Postdoc, Monastery of Solesmes, France, Biblioteque Nationale in Paris, the Brit Mus, London, Old Sarum, Eng. **CAREER** Instr, Muskingum Col, Winthrop Col; prof, 78-. **MEMBERSHIPS** Mem, Mus Edu Nat Conf; Westminister Commun People. **RESEARCH** French horn; Gregorian chant. **SELECTED PUBLICATIONS** Co-Auth, Philosophy and Purposes, Undergrad Bulletin. **CONTACT ADDRESS** Dept of Mus, Westminister Col, New Wilmington, PA, 16172-0001. **EMAIL** pitmanga@westminster.edu

PITRE, MERLINE
PERSONAL Opelousas, LA **DISCIPLINE** AMERICAN SOCIAL & CULTURAL HISTORY **EDUCATION** Southern Univ, BS, 66; Atlanta Univ, MA, 67; Temple Univ, PhD, 76. **CAREER** Instr French, St Augustine's Col, 67-70; teacher, St Landry Parish Sch, 71-72; asst prof hist, Tex Southern Univ, 76- **MEMBERSHIPS** Asn Study Afro-Am Life & Hist; Orgn Am Historians. **RESEARCH** Afro-American political history; Frederick Douglass 1870-1895; The Black Press in Houston, Texas, 1920-1950. **SELECTED PUBLICATIONS** Auth, Frederick Douglass and the Annexation of Santo Domingo, J Negro Hist, 10/77; Frederick Douglas: The Politician vs the Social Reformer, Phylon, 9/79; The Economic Philosophy of Martin Luther King, Jr., J Black Polit Econ, Winter 79; The Evolution of a Black University in Texas, Western J Black Studies, 79; The Partisan Politics of Frederick Douglass, J Soc and Behavioral Sci, Fall 80; Scholar's Reaction to Bakke, Western J Black Studies, Summer 81; Frederick Douglass and Republican Presidents, Girot, Summer 83; Black Houstonians and the Doctrine of Separate But Equal: Lulu White v Carter Wesley, Houston Rev, 7/90; Barbara Jordan, in Black Women in America: Historical, Carlson Publ Co, 93; author numerous other articles and book reviews. **CONTACT ADDRESS** Dept of Hist, Tex Southern Univ, 3100 Cleburne St, Houston, TX, 77004-4597.

PITTENGER, MARK A.
DISCIPLINE HISTORY **EDUCATION** Denison Univ, BA, 74; Univ Mich, MA, 77; PhD, 84. **CAREER** Prof. **SELECTED PUBLICATIONS** Auth, American Socialists and Evolutionary Thought, 1870-1920, Univ Wis, 93; A World of Difference: Constructing the 'Underclass' in Progressive America, Am Quarterly, 97; Imagining Genocide in the Progressive Era: The Socialist Science Fiction of George Allan England, Am Studies, 94. **CONTACT ADDRESS** History Dept, Univ of Colorado, Boulder, Boulder, CO, 80309. **EMAIL** mark.pittenger@spot.colorado.edu

PITTS, BILL
PERSONAL Born 12/27/1937, Winfield, KS, m, 1961, 2 children **DISCIPLINE** RELIGION; CHURCH HISTORY **EDUCATION** Baylor Univ, BA, 60; Vanderbilt Divinity School, MD, 63; Vanderbilt, PhD, 69. **CAREER** Instr, Mercer Univ, 66-69; asst prof, Houston Baptist Univ, 69-70; assoc prof, Dallas Baptist Univ, 70-75; assoc prof & prof, Baylor Univ, 75- . **HONORS AND AWARDS** Luke Acts Prize & Hist Prize, Vanderbilt, 73; Lilly Scholar, 64-65; Piper Prof Nominee, 74; Mortar Bd Distinguished Prof, 93. **MEMBERSHIPS** Soc Study Christian Spirituality; Am Acad Relig; Am Soc Church Hist; Nat Asn Baptist Prof Relig; Conf Faith & Hist. **RESEARCH** New religious movements; historiography; spirituality; Baptist history. **SELECTED PUBLICATIONS** Auth, Millennial Spirituality of the Branch Davidians, Christian Spirituality Bull, 93; The Mount Carmel Davidians: Adventist Reformers, 1935-1959, Syzgy, 93; The Davidian Tradition, The Coun Soc for Study Relig Bull, 93; The Davidian Tradition, From the Ashes: Making Sense of Waco, Rowman & Littlefield Publ, 94; Davidians and Branch Dividians: 1929-1987, Armageddon in Waco, Univ Chicago Press, 95; Davidians and Branch Davidians, New Cath Encycl, Cath Univ Press, 95; The Persistence of the Millennium, Medieval Perspectives, 97. **CONTACT ADDRESS** Religion Dept, Baylor Univ, Waco, TX, 76798. **EMAIL** william_pitts@baylor.edu

PITTS, VERA L.
PERSONAL Born 01/23/1931, Wichita, KS, w **DISCIPLINE** EDUCATION **EDUCATION** Mills Coll, AA 1950; NC Berkeley, BA 1953; Sacramento State Univ, MA 1962; MI State Univ, PhD 1969. **CAREER** Stockton Unified School Dist, teacher, counselor, admin 1954-65; City Coll NY, asst prof 1967-69; Palmer Handwriting Co, consult 1975-; CA State Univ Hayward, prof, dept chair ed admin 1969-; program mgr, Dept of Educ, 1986-87; assoc supt, Oakland Unified School District 1987-88; Oakland Public Schools, Oakland, CA, interim supt, 1989; Natl Hispanic Univ, San Jose, CA, provost, 1990-91. **HONORS AND AWARDS** Mott Fellowship Natl Awd MI 1965-67; Danforth Assoc Found 1974-; Vstg Professorships Univ Houston, Univ MI, Pepperdine Univ 1974-; Rockefeller Postdoctoral Fellowship 1978-80; Natl Faculty Exchange to US Dept of Ed 1986-87. **MEMBERSHIPS** Mem bd dir League of Women Voters 1975-; mem Western Assoc Accrediting Teams 1975-; pres San Mateo Br Amer Assoc Univ Women 1976-77; vice pres CA State Div Amer Assoc Univ Women 1978-82; mem Foster City Ed Facilities Comm 1983; counselor Univ of CA Alumni Assoc 1979-83; Natl Urban League Ed Adv Comm 1979-; dir-at-large Natl Council Admin Women in Ed 1982-; Phi Delta Kappa 1982-85; Pacific School of Religion Bd of Trustees, 1989-; Rotary Intl, 1988-. **CONTACT ADDRESS** Dept Chair, California State Univ, Hayward, 25800 Carlos Bee Blvd, Hayward, CA, 94542.

PITZER, DONALD ELDEN
PERSONAL Born 05/06/1936, Springfield, OH, m, 1960, 2 children **DISCIPLINE** AMERICAN SOCIAL & INTELLECTUAL HISTORY **EDUCATION** Wittenberg Univ, AB, 58; Ohio State Univ, MA, 62, PhD(hist), 66. **CAREER** Instr social studies, Messiah Col, 59-61; asst prof hist, Taylor Univ, 66-67; from asst prof to assoc prof, 67-74, Prof Hist, Ind State Univ Evansville, 74-, Mem & historian, Ind New Harmony Comn, 72-; ed, Nat Hist Communal Socs Asn Newsletter, 74-; dir, Ctr Communal Studies, Ind State Univ Evansville, 76-; exec dir, Nat Hist Communal Socs Asn, 77-. **MEMBERSHIPS** Orgn Am Historians; AHA; Conf Faith & Hist; Nat Hist Communal Socs Asn (pres, 74-77). **RESEARCH** Communal societies; effects of modern physics and existentialism on American thought; Mayan civilization. **SELECTED PUBLICATIONS** Ed, Robert Owen's American Legacy, Ind Hist Soc, 72; Organizing historic communes for preservation and scholarship, Communal Studies Newsletter, 7/76; coauth, New Harmony's Fourth of July Tradition, Raintree Bks, 76; auth, The Harmonist heritage of three towns, 10-12/77 & Harmonist folk art discovered, 10/12/77, Hist Preserv; Education in Utopia: The New Harmony experience, In: The History of Education in the Middle West, Ind Hist Soc, 78; New Harmony's First Utopians, Ind Mag Hist, 9/79; All Things New - American Communes and Utopian Movements, 1860-1914 - Fogarty,rs/, J of American History, Vol 0079, 1993. **CONTACT ADDRESS** Dept of Hist, Indiana State Univ, 8600 University Blvd, Evansville, IN, 47712-3591.

PIVAR, DAVID J.
PERSONAL Born 06/06/1933, Philadelphia, PA, m, 1960, 1 child **DISCIPLINE** AMERICAN SOCIAL HISTORY **EDUCATION** Millersville State Col, MSEd, 57; Temple Univ, MA, 61; Univ Pa, PhD(hist), 65. **CAREER** Teaching asst hist, Univ Pa, 63-64; assoc prof Am Hist, 65- 71, Prof Hist & Am Studies, Calif State Univ, Fullerton, 71-. **MEMBERSHIPS** AHA; Am Studies Asn. **RESEARCH** American social history. **SELECTED PUBLICATIONS** Auth, The hosiery workers and the Philadelphia Third Party impulse, 1927-35, Labor Hist, winter 64; Theocratic businessmen and Philadelphia municipal reform, 1870-1900, PA Hist, 10/66; Purity Crusade: Sexual Morality and Social Control, 1868-1900, Greenwood, 73; Cleansing the Nation: The War on Prostitution, 1917-21, Prologue, spring 80; The Military Prostitution and Colonial Peoples: India and the Philippines, 1885-1917, J Sex Res, 8/81; City of Eros - New-york-city, Prostitution, and the Commercialization of Sex, 1790-1920 - Gilfoyle,tj, Reviews in American History, Vol 0021, 1993; Unsubmissive Women - Chinese Prostitutes in 19th-century San-francisco - Tong,b/, American Historical Review, Vol 0101, 1996; Sin and Censorship - the Catholic-church and the Motion-picture Industry - Walsh,f, American Historical Review, Vol 0102, 1997. **CONTACT ADDRESS** Dept of Hist, California State Univ, Fullerton, Fullerton, CA, 92631.

PIXTON, PAUL BREWER
PERSONAL Born 06/22/1940, Salt Lake City, UT, m, 1965, 3 children **DISCIPLINE** MEDIEVAL HISTORY **EDUCATION** Univ Utah, BA, 65, MA, 67; Univ Iowa, PhD(hist), 72. **CAREER** Asst prof hist, Univ Wis-Superior, 71-74; asst prof, 74-78, Assoc Prof Hist, Brigham Young Univ, 78-. **MEMBERSHIPS** AHA; Medieval Acad Am. **RESEARCH** Medieval ecclesiastical reform in Germany; German cathedral schools; crusade recruitment. **SELECTED PUBLICATIONS** Auth, Dietrich von Wied: Geistlicher ehrgeiz und politischer opportunismus im fruhen dreizehnten jahrhundert, Archiv fur mittelrheinische Kirchengeschichte, 74; Auf Gottes Wachturm: Ein erzbischofliches Reformprogramm im Trier des fruher 13 Jahrhunderts, Trierisches Jahrbuch, 77; Das Anwerben des Heeres Christi: Prediger des funften Kreuzzuges in Deutschland, Deutsches Archiv, 78; Reform of Head and Members - Study on the Development and Application of this Formulation During the High and Later Middle-ages - German - Frech,ka, Catholic Historical Review, Vol 0079, 1993. **CONTACT ADDRESS** Dept of Hist, Brigham Young Univ, Provo, UT, 84601.

PLAKANS, ANDREJS
PERSONAL Born 12/31/1940, Riga, Latvia, m, 1964, 2 children **DISCIPLINE** EUROPEAN SOCIAL HISTORY **EDUCATION** Franklin & Marshall Col, BA, 63; Harvard Univ, MA, 64, PhD(hist), 69. **CAREER** Asst prof, Boston Col, 69-74; assoc prof, 75-82, Prof Hist, Iowa State Univ, 82-, Res assoc, Dept Anthrop, Univ Mass, Amherst, 74-75. **MEMBERSHIPS** AHA; Social Sci Hist Asn; Am Asn Advan Slavic Studies; Asn Advan Baltic Studies; Int Union Sci Study Pop. **RESEARCH** Social structure of pre-industrial Eastern European peasantries; history of family and kinship; history of the Baltic area. **SELECTED PUBLICATIONS** Auth, Peasant, intellectuals and nationalism in Russian Baltic provinces, J Mod Hist, 74; Peasant farmsteads and households in Baltic littoral, Comp Studies Soc & Hist, 75; Seigneurial authority and peasant family life, J Interdisciplinary Hist, 75; contribr, Sozialgesch-

ichte der Familie in der Neuzeit Europas, Klettverlag, 76; auth, Identifying kinfolk beyond the household, J Famly Hist, 77; contribr, Family In Imperial Russia, Univ Ill Press, 78; coauth, Russification in Baltic Provinces and Finland in 19th Century, Princeton Univ Press, 81; Kinship and kinship roles in East European peasant communities, J Family Hist, 82; European Population Country Analysis - Rally,J, and Blum,A, J of Interdisciplinary History, Vol 0024, 1993; Social Networks, Kinship, and Community in Eastern-europe, J of Interdisciplinary History, Vol 0024, 1994; Peasant Russia - Family and Community in the Post-emancipation Period - Worobec,C, Slavic Review, Vol 0054, 1995; the Nordic Way - Killham,E, Slavic Review, Vol 0055, 1996; a 'Tale of Two Nations' - North,D, Russian Review, Vol 0054, 1995; The Baltic World 1772-1993 - Europe Northern Periphery in an Age of Change - Kirby,d, American Historical Review, Vol 0101, 1996. **CONTACT ADDRESS** Dept Hist, Iowa State Univ, Ames, IA, 50011-0002.

PLANEAUX, CHRISTOPHER
PERSONAL Born 04/10/1967, Atlanta, GA, m, 1996 **DISCIPLINE** PHILOSOPHY; HISTORY; CLASSICS GREEK **EDUCATION** Ind Univ, AB, 93, AB, 94; Univ Cambridge, MPhil, 97. **CAREER** Dept For Lang, Purdue Univ **HONORS AND AWARDS** Fac Develop Mentorship grant, Ind Univ, 94; Univ Cambridge res grant, 94. Thelander Mem Award, Ind Univ, 94. **MEMBERSHIPS** Amer Philol Asn; Class Asn Mid W & S; Asn Ancient Hist; Soc Greek Philos; Univ London Inst Class Studies; Cambridge Philol Soc; Darwin Col Soc. **RESEARCH** Dramatic settings of Platos Dialogues; Athens (ca. 470-40413 BCE); Peloponnesioan War; Thirty tyrants; Greek poets; Athenian calendar; AtticCultic societies; Philosophical schools; Alcibiades. **SELECTED PUBLICATIONS** Auth, Socrates, Alcibiades, and Plato's: Does the Charmides Have an Historical setting?, Mnemosyne, 99. **CONTACT ADDRESS** Dept of Foreign Languages & Cultures, Indiana Univ-Purdue Univ, Indianapolis, 425 Univ Blvd, Indianapolis, IN, 46202. **EMAIL** cplaneau@iupui.edu

PLANK, GEOFFREY
DISCIPLINE HISTORY **EDUCATION** Swarthmore, BA, 80; Univ Conn, JD, 84; Princeton Univ, PhD, 94. **CAREER** ASSOC PROF, HIST, UNIV CINCINNATI **MEMBERSHIPS** Am Antiquarian Soc **SELECTED PUBLICATIONS** Auth, "The Changing Country of Anthony Casteel: Language, Religion, Geography, Political Co and Nationalism in Mid-Eighteenth Century Nova Scotia," Studies in Eighteenth- Century Culture, vol 27, 97; auth, The Two Majors Cope: The Boundaries of Nationality in Mid-Eighteenth Century Nova Scotia, Acadiensis, 97. **CONTACT ADDRESS** Dept of Hist, Univ of Cincinnati, ML 373, Cincinnati, OH, 45221. **EMAIL** geoffrey.plank@uc.edu

PLANK, STEVEN E.
DISCIPLINE MUSICOLOGY **EDUCATION** Univ Louisville, BM, 73, MM, 74; Wash Univ, PhD, 80. **CAREER** Visiting ass, prof, Univ Mass, 75; tchg asst, Wash Univ, 77-79; affil tchr, St Louis Univ, 78-79; prof, Oberlin Coll, 80-.. **MEMBERSHIPS** Mem, Hist Perf Prog; fac mem: Louisville Orchestra, 70-76; Early Mus Ensemble of St. Louis, 78-79 **RESEARCH** Early music performance, 17th century music. **SELECTED PUBLICATIONS** co-transl, Edward Tarr's TheTrumpet, 88; author, The Way to Heaven's Doors: An Introduction to Liturgical Process and Musical Style, 94; assoc ed, Historical Brass Soc Jour; contrib, Early Music, Musical Times, Music and Letters, Rel Stud. Rev.. **CONTACT ADDRESS** Dept of Mus, Oberlin Col, Oberlin, OH, 44074.

PLATA, FERNANDO
DISCIPLINE RENAISSANCE AND BAROQUE SPANISH LITERATURE **EDUCATION** Univ de Navarra, Pamplona, Spain, licenciado, 87; Univ MI, MA, 89, PhD, 94. **CAREER** Asst prof, Colgate Univ. **HONORS AND AWARDS** Rackham predoctoral fel, Univ MI, 92-93; dissertation scholar, prog for cult coop, Spain Ministry of Cult and US Univ(s), 92; Tercer Premio Nacional de Terminacion de Estudios de Filologia, 87; scholar, Universidad Internacional Menendez Pelayo, Santander, 86. **MEMBERSHIPS** Mem, Univ student disciplinary syst. **SELECTED PUBLICATIONS** Auth, Ocho poemas satericos de Quevedo, EUNSA, 97; Inquisicion y censura en el siglo XVIII: El Parnaso espanol de Quevedo, La Perinola. Revista de investigacion quevediana, 97; rev, Robert L. Hathaway, Not Necessarily Cervantes: Readings of the 'Quixote', Juan de la Cuesta, 95; Una nota sobre Lope de Vega y las 'leneas del amor' de Terencio, Romance Notes 32, 92; Hacia una edicion cretica de la comedia La inclinacion espanola de Bances Candamo, RILCE, Revista de Filologea Hispanica 8, 92. **CONTACT ADDRESS** Dept of Romance Lang, Colgate Univ, 13 Oak Drive, Hamilton, NY, 13346. **EMAIL** fplata@center.colgate.edu

PLATT, FRANKLIN DEWITT
PERSONAL Born 11/15/1932, Marion, LA, m, 1956, 1 child **DISCIPLINE** HUMANITIES & BRITISH HISTORY **EDUCATION** La State Univ, BA, 55; Wash Univ, AM, 63, PhD(hist), 69. **CAREER** From instr to asst prof, 64-72, asst chmn dept humanities, Mich State Univ, 71-, assoc prof, 72-. **MEMBERSHIPS** AHA **RESEARCH** Contemporary humanities; 19th century England. **SELECTED PUBLICATIONS** Auth, Reflections on a new breed of student, Bull Res Humanities Educ, I:8-11. **CONTACT ADDRESS** Dept of Humanities, Michigan State Univ, East Lansing, MI, 48824.

PLATT, GERALD M.
PERSONAL Born 02/13/1933, Brooklyn, NY, s, 2 children **DISCIPLINE** SOCIAL PSYCHOLOGY **EDUCATION** Brooklyn College, BA 55, MA 57; Univ Cal LA, PhD 64. **CAREER** Univ Cal LA, inst 61-63; Harvard Univ, lect 64-70; Univ Mass, assoc prof 70-74; John Hopkins Univ, vis assoc prof 73; London Sch Econ Pol Sci, acad vis 77; Univ Cal Santa Cruz, vis prof 78; Univ Cal LA, vis prof 79-80; Univ Mass, prof 74-. **HONORS AND AWARDS** NSF Fel; Carnegie Corp Fel; SSRC Fel; NIH Fel; Inst ASH Fel; Albert Einstein Fel **MEMBERSHIPS** ASA; ESS **RESEARCH** Social movements; social change; the Amer Civil Rights Movement, 1954-1970. **SELECTED PUBLICATIONS** Auth, Race and Gender Discourse Strategies: Creating Solidarity and Framing the Civil Rights Movement, coauth, Social Prob, 98; Correspondents' Images of Martin Luther King Jr: An Interpretive Theory of Movement Leadership, coauth, in: Constructing the Social, eds Theodore R. Sarbin John I. Kitsues, Sage Pub, 94, reprint Leadership : Classical Contemporary and Critical Approaches, ed Keith Grint, Oxford, OUP, 97; Religion Ideology and Electoral Politics, Society, 88, reprint, in: Cultural Wars in Amer Politics: Crit Revs of a Popular Myth, ed, Rhys H. Williams, NY, Aldine De Gruyter, 97; Multiple Images of a Charismatic: An Interpretive Concept of Martin Luther King Jr's Leadership, coauth, in: Self Collected Behavior and Society: Essays Honoring the Contributions of Ralph H Turner, eds, Gerald M Platt Chad Gordon, Contemp Stud in Sociol, Theoretical and Empirical Monos, Greenwich CT, JAI Press, 94. **CONTACT ADDRESS** Dept of Sociology, Univ of Massachusetts, Thompson Hall, Amherst, MA, 01003. **EMAIL** platt@soc.umass.edu

PLATT, HAROLD L.
DISCIPLINE HISTORY **EDUCATION** Rice, PhD. **CAREER** Hist, Loyola Univ. **RESEARCH** Urban history; Civil War & reconstruction. **SELECTED PUBLICATIONS** Auth, The Electric City: Energy and the Growth of the Chicago Area, 1880-1930, Univ Chicago Press, 91. **CONTACT ADDRESS** Fine Arts Dept, Loyola Univ, Chicago, 6525 N. Sheridan Rd., Chicago, IL, 60626.

PLECK, ELIZABETH
DISCIPLINE HISTORY **EDUCATION** Brandeis Univ, PhD, 73. **CAREER** Assoc prof, Univ Ill Urbana Champaign. **RESEARCH** American family history. **SELECTED PUBLICATIONS** Auth, Black Migration and Poverty: Boston 1865-1900, Acad, 79; Domestic Tyranny: The Making of Social Policy Against Family Violence from Colonial Times to the Present, Oxford, 87; co-ed, A Heritage of Her Own: Toward a New Social History of American Women, Simon and Schuster, 79. **CONTACT ADDRESS** History Dept, Univ Ill Urbana Champaign, 52 E Gregory Dr, Champaign, IL, 61820. **EMAIL** epleck@uiuc.edu

PLESCIA, JOSEPH
PERSONAL Born 08/23/1928, Italy, d, 2 children **DISCIPLINE** GREEK HISTORY & PHILOSOPHY, ROMAN HISTORY & LAW **EDUCATION** Gregorian Univ, Baccalaureatum in Philos, 50; Univ CA, Berkeley, BA, 58; Stanford Univ, MA, 60, PhD, 65. **CAREER** From instr to assoc prof, 62-78, prof classics, FL State Univ, 78. **HONORS AND AWARDS** Richardson Latin Composition Prize, Univ Calif, Berkeley, 57-58; Woodrow Wilson Fel, 59; Summer Award, Am Coun Learned Soc, Univ Calif, Berkeley, 72, 73; Vis Schol, Yale Law Sch, 76-77; mem Governor's Challenge Prog Fla 2000: Creative Crime Control, 82; mem Conf on Agreement Between Ital and Am Universities Related to Doctoral Programs, Study and Conf Ctr of the Rockefeller Found, Villa Serbelloni, Bellagio (Lago di Como), 83. **RESEARCH** Greek and Roman law. **SELECTED PUBLICATIONS** Auth, Oath and Perjury in Ancient Greece, Fla State Univ Press, 70, sold out, Cited in the Oxford Classical Dictionary, 3rd ed, 96; Roman Law on Water, Index 21, 93; Ius Pacis in Roman Law, RIDA 41, 94; The Bill of Rights and Roman Law, Austin & Winfield, 95, 2nd printing, 97, 2nd ed (in prep); The Doctrine of Liability in Roman Law, Studies in Roman Law (opuscula series), Frederic II Univ, Italy (in press); International Law in Ancient Rome (submitted for publication); author of numerous articles. **CONTACT ADDRESS** Dept of Class, Florida State Univ, 205H Dodd Hall, Tallahassee, FL, 32306-1096. **EMAIL** jplescia@mailer.fsu.edu

PLESTINA, DIJANA
DISCIPLINE POLITICAL SCIENCE **EDUCATION** Carleton Univ, Canada, BA, 70, MA, 73; Univ Calif-Berkeley, PhD, 87. **CAREER** Assoc prof. **RESEARCH** Economic development and democratization in East and West Europe, and the former Soviet Union. **SELECTED PUBLICATIONS** Auth, Regional Development in Communist Yugoslavia: Success, Failure and Consequences. **CONTACT ADDRESS** Dept of Russ, Col of Wooster, Wooster, OH, 44691.

PLETCHER, DAVID MITCHELL
PERSONAL Born 06/14/1920, Faribault, MN **DISCIPLINE** HISTORY **EDUCATION** Univ Chicago, AB & AM, 41, PhD, 46. **CAREER** Instr hist, State Univ Iowa, 44-46; assoc prof, Knox Col, 45-56; from assoc prof to prof, Hamline Univ, 56-65; Prof Hist, Ind Univ, Bloomington, 65-, Lectr, Inst Int Affairs, Grinnell Col, 47; Fulbright sr res grant, London, 53-54; Soc Sci Res Coun grant 62-63; assoc ed, Hisp Am Hist Rev, 65-70. **HONORS AND AWARDS** Albert J Beveridge Mem Prize, AHA, 57; McKnight Found award in humanities, 62. **MEMBERSHIPS** AHA; Soc Historians of Am Foreign Rels (pres, 80). **RESEARCH** United States diplomatic history; United States-Latin American relations. **SELECTED PUBLICATIONS** Auth, The fall of silver in Mexico and its effect on American investments, J Econ Hist, 3/58; Rails, Mines and Progress: Seven American Promoters in Mexico, 1867-1911, Cornell Univ, 58; Mexico opens the door to American capital, 1877-1880, Americas, 7/59; The Awkward Years: American Foreign Relations Under Garfield and Arthur, 62 & The Diplomacy of Annexation: Texas, Oregon, and the Mexican War, 73, Univ Mo; Rhetoric and Results: A pragmatic view of American Expansionism, 1865-1898, Diplomatic Hist, spring 81; a Mexican View of America in the 1860s - a Foreign Diplomat Describes the Civil-war and Reconstruction - Schoonover,T, Pacific Historical Review, Vol 0062, 1993; Army of Manifest Destiny - the American Soldier in the Mexican-war, 1846-1848 - Mccaffrey,J, J of American History, Vol 0079, 1993; Most-favored-nation - the Republican Revisionists and United-states Tariff Policy, 1897-1912 - Wolman,P, American Historical Review, Vol 0098, 1993; Mexico and the United-states - Ambivalent Vistas - Raat,W, Pacific Historical Review, Vol 0063, 1994; the United-states and Latin- america - Myths and Stereotypes of Civilization and Nature - Pike,F, Diplomatic History, Vol 0018, 1994. **CONTACT ADDRESS** Dept of Hist, Indiana Univ, Bloomington, Bloomington, IN, 47401.

POCOCK, EMIL
DISCIPLINE AMERICAN STUDIES **EDUCATION** Univ MD, BA, 68; NY Univ MA, 71; IN Univ, MA, PhD. **CAREER** Eng Dept, Eastern Conn State Univ **MEMBERSHIPS** Asn Study Conn Hist; Conn Rev; Jour Am Hist. **SELECTED PUBLICATIONS** Auth, Popular Roots of Jacksonian Democracy: The Case of Dayton, Ohio, 1815-1830, Jour, Early Republic, 89; 'I enjoy but little sunshine on my path': Reverend James Welsh on Three Frontiers, 1790-1825, IN Mag Hist, 90; 'A Candidate I'll Surely Be': Election Practices in Early Ohio, 1798-1825, Kent State Univ Press, 94. **CONTACT ADDRESS** Eastern Connecticut State Univ, 83 Windham Street, Willimantic, CT, 06226.

PODET, ALLEN HOWARD
PERSONAL Cleveland, OH **DISCIPLINE** MODERN JEWISH HISTORY **EDUCATION** Univ Ill, Urbana, BA, 56; Hebrew Union Col, BHL, 58, MA, 62, DHL, 64; Univ Wash, PhD(hist), 79 **CAREER** Lectr, Dept Near Eastern Lang & Lit, Univ Wash, Seattle, 70-73; asst prof, 69-73, PROF, DEPT PHILOS & RELIG STUDIES, STATE UNIV NY COL BUFFALO, 80-, Consult, Jewish Collection, Folklore Archives, Buffalo, 80-; contrib ed, Am Books by Europ Judaism J, 77-; Univ lectr, Univ Vienna, Austria, 98. **HONORS AND AWARDS** Fulbright-Hays fel, Jerusalem, 95-96 **MEMBERSHIPS** Cent Conf Am Rabbis; Asn Jewish Studies **RESEARCH** Rabbinics **SELECTED PUBLICATIONS** Auth, The Sephardim of Seattle, Jewish Digest, 9/68; Secular studies and religious uniqueness: A view of Hanukkah, Relig Educ, Vol 71, No 6, 11-12/76; The Jew as witness to history, Europ Judaism, Vol II, No 1, winter 77; Ein historischer Zuzang zu einem Philsophen: Moses Maimonides in seiner Zeit, Emuna, Vol 4, No 77, winter 77; The unwilling midwife: Ernest Bevin and the birth of Israel, Europ Judaism, Vol II, No 2, winter 77; Anti-Zionism in a key United States Diplomat: Loy Henderson at the end of World War II, Am Jewish Archives, Vol 30, No 2, 11/78; The Al-Barazi Testimony: a Secret Syrian Peace Proposal Recognizing the State of Israel, Mid East Studies Anthology; The Soviet Jewish problem, J Assembly of Rabbis. **CONTACT ADDRESS** Dept of Philos & Relig Studies, State Univ NY Col, 1300 Elmwood Ave, Buffalo, NY, 14222-1095. **EMAIL** podetah@buffalostate.edu

PODLECKI, ANTHONY JOSEPH
PERSONAL Born 01/00/1936, Buffalo, NY, m, 1962 **DISCIPLINE** CLASSICS **EDUCATION** Col Holy Cross, AB, 57; Oxford Univ, BA, 60, MA, 63; Univ Toronto, MA, 61, PhD, 63. **CAREER** From instr to asst prof classics, Northwestern Univ, 63-66; from assoc prof to prof, PA State Univ, University Park, 66-75, head dept, 66-75; Prof Classics & Head Dept, Univ BC, 75-, Mem managing comt, Am Sch Class Studies, Athens, 70-; chmn, aid to Pub comt, Can Fed for Humanities, 76-. **MEMBERSHIPS** Class Asn Can West; Class Asn Pac Northwest (pres, 77-78); Joint Asn Class Teachers; Am Philol Asn; Claudel Soc. **RESEARCH** Greek history and literature and their interrelations; Roman historiography. **SELECTED PUBLICATIONS** Auth, The Political Background of Aeschylean Tragedy, Univ Mich, 66; The peripatetics as literary critics, Phoenix, 69; Reciprocity in Prometheus Bound, Greek, Roman & Byzantine Studies, 69; transl, Aeschylus' The Persians, Prentice-Hall, 70; auth, Some Odyssean similes, Greece & Rome, 71; The Life of Themistocles, McGill-Queens, 75; Themisto-

cles in Alexandrian and 18th century drama, Restoration & 18th century Theater Res, 76; Plutarch, the 'Lives of Aristeides and Cato' - English and Greek - Sansone,D, Editor-translator, Phoenix-the J of the Classical Association of Canada, Vol 0046, 1992; The Letters of Themistocles, Vol 1, Critical Edition, Translation, Textual Notes and Indexes, Vol 2, the Historical Problem - the Witness and the Tradition - Italian and Greek - Cortassa,G, Editor- translator, Culassogastaldi,E, Co, Classical Review; A Commentary on Plutarch 'Pericles' - English and Greek - Stadter,pa, Phoenix-the J of the Classical Association of Canada, Vol 0046, 1992; Plutarch, 'Life of Kimon' - English and Greek - Blamire,A, Translator-commentator, Phoenix-the J of the Classical Association of Canada, Vol 0046, 1992. **CONTACT ADDRESS** Univ British Columbia, Vancouver, BC, V6T 1W5.

PODUSKA, DONALD MILES
PERSONAL Born 12/02/1934, Chicago, IL, m, 1958, 3 children **DISCIPLINE** CLASSICAL LANGUAGES **EDUCATION** Loyola Univ, Ill, AB, 56; Univ Ky, MA, 57; Ohio State Univ, PhD, 63. **CAREER** From instr to assoc prof, 60-73, prof class lang, John Carroll Univ, 73-; vis assoc prof class lang, 70-71, vis prof class lang, 85-86, Rome Ctr, Loyola Univ, Ill. **MEMBERSHIPS** Am Philol Assn; Am Class League; Vergilian Soc; Class Assn Mid W & S. **RESEARCH** Roman comedy; Roman historians; Vergil. **CONTACT ADDRESS** Dept of Class Lang, John Carroll Univ, 20700 N Park Blvd, Cleveland, OH, 44118-4581. **EMAIL** poduska@jcvaxa.jcu.edu

POE, JOE PARK
DISCIPLINE GREEK AND LATIN LITERATURE **CAREER** Instr, NY Univ, 60-62; lectr, Brooklyn Col, 62; instr, Univ TX, 62-64; act asst prof, Univ CA-Barkeley, 64-65; asst prof, 65-70; assoc prof, 70-89; prof, 89-; dept ch, 71-74, 77-88. **RESEARCH** Theatrical antiquities. **SELECTED PUBLICATIONS** The Determination of Episodes in Greek Tragedy, Amer Jour Philol 114, 93; The Periaktoi and Actors' Entrances, Hermes 121, 93; Pollux and the Klision, Philologus 138, 94; The Supposed Conventional Meanings of Dramatic Masks: A Re-examination of Pollux 4. 133-54, Philologus 140, 96. **CONTACT ADDRESS** Dept of Class Stud, Tulane Univ, 6823 St Charles Ave, New Orleans, LA, 70118. **EMAIL** jpoe@mailhost.tcs.tulane.edu

POEN, MONTE MAC
PERSONAL Born 11/25/1930, Lake City, IA, 3 children **DISCIPLINE** RECENT UNITED STATES HISTORY **EDUCATION** San Jose State Col, BA, 61; Univ Mo, MA, 64, PhD(recent US hist), 67. **CAREER** Instr US hist, Univ Mo, 64-66; asst prof, 66-70, assoc prof, 70-79, PROF RECENT US HIST, NORTHERN ARIZ UNIV, 79-; ed, Mary W Lasker Oral Hist Proj, Albert D Lasker Found, 67- **MEMBERSHIPS** Org Am Historians; Oral Hist Asn; Ctr Study Presidency's. **RESEARCH** Recent United States social and political development; medical politics, history of the national health insurance movement; Harry S Truman. **SELECTED PUBLICATIONS** Auth, Harry S Truman vs The Medical Lobby, Univ Mo, 79; ed, Strictly Personal and Confidential: The Letters Harry Truman Never Mailed, Little, Brown & Co, 82. **CONTACT ADDRESS** 3703 N Grandview Dr, Flagstaff, AZ, 86001.

POGEMILLER, LEROY
DISCIPLINE MUSIC HISTORY **EDUCATION** Conserv Mus, Kansas City, Bachelor of Mus, 57, Master of Mus, 57; Univ Mo, Kansas City, Doctor of Mus Arts, 67. **CAREER** Asst prof, 59-61, tchg assoc, 64-67, assoc prof, 67-70, prof, 70-, prin grad adv, 77-84, 87-, actg assoc dean, grad stud, 88-90, assoc dean, grad stud, 90-97, interim dean, 93-94, Prof Emer, Univ Mo, Kansas City, 97-; pvt piano tchr, New Rochelle, NY, 61-62; vocal mus tchr, Pub Sch, East Liverpool, Ohio, 62-64. **HONORS AND AWARDS** AMOCO Good Tchg Award, 78, 84; Conserv Bd of Trustees Good Tchg Award, 87; Weldon Spg Presidential Outstanding Tchg Award, 91; UKC Bd of Trustees Tchg Award, 91. **MEMBERSHIPS** UMKC Alumni Asn; UMKC Retirees Asn. **RESEARCH** A computer software program to analyze figured bass progressions. **SELECTED PUBLICATIONS** Auth, Some Observations on College T eaching Vacancies, Newsl, Col Mus Soc, Mar, 91; College Teaching Jobs and the Marketplace, Am Mus Tchr, Dec/Jan, 91/92. **CONTACT ADDRESS** Univ Mo, Kansas City, Kansas City, MO, 64110-2499. **EMAIL** lpogemiller@cctr.umkc.edu

POGUE, SAMUEL FRANKLIN
PERSONAL Born 04/11/1919, Cincinnati, OH, 1 child **DISCIPLINE** MUSICOLOGY **EDUCATION** Princeton Univ, AB, 41, MFA, 63, PhD(music), 68. **CAREER** From asst prof to assoc prof, 68-77, Prof Music, Col Conserv Music, Univ Cincinnati, 77-. **HONORS AND AWARDS** LLD, Edgecliff Col, 73. **MEMBERSHIPS** Am Musicol Soc; Int Musicol Soc; New Bach Soc. **RESEARCH** Early music printing. **SELECTED PUBLICATIONS** Auth, Jacques Moderne, Lyons Music Printer of the Sixteenth Century, Editions Droz, Geneva, 69; contribr, articles, In: Grove's Dictionary of Music and Musicians, 74-75; Further notes on Jacques Moderne, Bibliotheque D'Humanisme et Renaissance, 75; A sixteenth century editor at work: Gardana and Moderne, J of Musicol, 82; Catalog of Editions of Music Pubished in Louvain by Phalese,Pierre and His Sons 1545-1578 - French - Vanhulst,H, Notes, Vol 0049, 1993. **CONTACT ADDRESS** Col Conserv of Music, Univ of Cincinnati, Cincinnati, OH, 45221.

POHL, JAMES WILLIAM
PERSONAL Born 07/26/1931, Dubuque, IA, m, 1965, 2 children **DISCIPLINE** MILITARY HISTORY **EDUCATION** Univ N Tex, BA, 53, MA, 55; Univ Tex, PhD, 67. **CAREER** Instr hist, Univ Tex, 60-63; from instr to assoc prof, 64-74, prof, Hist, Southwest Tex State Univ, 74-; visit prof, Univ Tex, 85-86; Durm Tex State Hist Asn, 85-86; Dir, Ctr for Stu of Hist, Univ Tex, 85-86; Res Fel, Mosher Inst for Defense Stu, Tex A & M Univ 88-; pres, Tex State hist Asn, 87-88; visit prof, US Army Command and Gen Staff Col, 98. **HONORS AND AWARDS** Dist Svc Awd, Tex State Hist Asn, 86, 88, 96; Gov's Letter of Commendation for Svc to the State of Tex, 86, 87; John Bell Hood Awd, H.B. Simpson Res Ctr, 90; Outstanding Centennial Alumnus Awd, Univ of N Tex, 90; Fel, Tex State Hist Asn, 94; Jefferson Davis Awd, UDC, 96. **MEMBERSHIPS** Am Mil Inst; Tex State Hist Asn **RESEARCH** Military history, particularly United States and European. **SELECTED PUBLICATIONS** Auth, The congress and the secretary of war, 1915: An instance of political pressure, NJ Hist, fall 71; coauth, People of America, Benson, 73; auth, The influence of Antoine Henri de Jomini on Winfield Scott's campaign in Mexico, Southwestern Hist Quart, 7/73; The American Revolution and the Vietnam War: Pertinent military analogies, Hist Teacher, 2/74; auth, The Military History of the Texas Revolution, Southwestern, Hist Qrt, 86; ed, Southwestern Historical Quarterly, 85-86; auth, Battle of San Jacinto, 89; co-ed, The New Texas, 6 vols, 96. **CONTACT ADDRESS** Dept of History, Southwest Texas State Univ, 601 University Dr, San Marcos, TX, 78666-4685. **EMAIL** JP19@swt.edu

POHLSANDER, HANS ACHIM
PERSONAL Born 10/10/1927, Celle, Germany, m, 1956, 3 children **DISCIPLINE** CLASSICS **EDUCATION** Univ Utah, BA, 54; Univ Calif, Berkeley, MA, 55; Univ Mich, PhD, 61. **CAREER** Teacher Latin & Ger, Carmel High Sch, Calif, 56-58; asst prof Classics, Wash Univ, 61-62; asst prof to prof Classics, 62-95, prof Relig Studies, 91-95, emeritus 95-, State Univ NY Albany; vis assoc prof classics & cult studies, Am Univ Beirut, 68-69; vis prof Classics, Ohio State Univ, Columbus, 83-83. **HONORS AND AWARDS** Am Coun Learned Soc grant-in-aid, 62; Ger Acad Exchange Serv study grant, 82; Am Philos Soc res grants, 83, 88; NEH res grant, 86. **MEMBERSHIPS** Am Philol Asn; Archaeol Inst Am; Hagiographic soc. **RESEARCH** Later Roman Empire; early Christianity; Trier. **SELECTED PUBLICATIONS** Auth, Metrical Studies in the Lyrics of Sophocles, Brill, Leiden, 64; Helena: Empress and Saint, Ares, Chicago, 95; The Emperor Constantine, Routledge, London, 96; Maximinus und Paulinus: Two Bishops of Trier in the Fourth Century, Trierer Zeitschrift, 96; Die Anfunge des Christentums in der Stadt Trier, Trierer Zeitschrift, 97. **CONTACT ADDRESS** Dept of Classics, Univ at Albany, Albany, NY, 12222-1000. **EMAIL** pohlsander@global2000.net

POINTER, RICHARD W.
DISCIPLINE HISTORY **EDUCATION** Johns Hopkins Univ, PhD, 82; post doc res, Univ Pa, 85-86. **CAREER** Vis asst, Wheaton Col, 82-83; assoc prof, Trinity Col, 83-84; assoc prof, Westmont Col, 94-. **HONORS AND AWARDS** Kerr prize, NY State Hist Assn, 86., Assoc ed, Hist and Polit Sci, 95-. **RESEARCH** Colonial & revoluationary hist; native Am hist; relig in Am. **SELECTED PUBLICATIONS** Auth, Poor Indians, Poor in Spirit: The Indian Impact on David Brainerd, The New Eng Quart 67, 94; Kenneth S. Latourette, Handbook of Church Historians, Broadman Press, 95; The New York Review, The Amer Conservative Press, Greenwood Press, 95; Recycling Early American Religion: Some Historiographical Problems and Prospects, Fides et Historia 23, 91. **CONTACT ADDRESS** Dept of Hist, Westmont Col, 955 La Paz Rd, Santa Barbara, CA, 93108-1099.

POINTER, STEVEN R.
DISCIPLINE AMERICAN AND BRITISH CHURCH HISTORY **EDUCATION** Duke Univ, BA, 72, PhD, 71; Trinity Evangelical Divinity Sch, MA, 76. **CAREER** History, Trinity Int Univ **SELECTED PUBLICATIONS** Auth, Joseph Cook, Boston Lecturer and Evangelical Apologist, 91. **CONTACT ADDRESS** Trinity Int Univ, 2065 Half Day Road, Deerfield, IL, 60015.

POLAK, EMIL JOSEPH
PERSONAL Born 08/16/1936, Bayshore, NY, m, 1968 **DISCIPLINE** MEDIEVAL AND ANCIENT HISTORY **EDUCATION** State Univ NY Albany, AB, 57; Columbia Univ, AM, 58, PhD(Medieval hist), 70. **CAREER** Lectr hist, Brooklyn Col, 61-65; instr, hist, St John's Univ, NY, 65-66; lectr, Staten Island Community Col, 66-67 & City Col New York, 67-70; instr, 70, asst prof, 71-76, assoc prof hist, 76-82, prof, 82-, Queensborough Community Col. **HONORS AND AWARDS** Fel post-class humanistic studies, Am Acad in Rome, 62-; Res Found City Univ New York awards, 77-98; fel hist, Int Res & Exchanges Bd, 78-79, 81, 96; Am Coun Learned Soc/USSR Acad Sci exchange fel, 81; Gladys Krieble Delmas Found grant, 95; NEH sum stipend, 97; Distinguished Alumnus Award, SUNY Albany, 95. **MEMBERSHIPS** AHA; Medieval Acad Am; Am Philol Asn; Int Soc Hist of Rhetoric; Int Asn Neo-Latin Studies. **RESEARCH** Tradition of letter-writing and secular oratory in the Middle Ages and Renaissance. **SELECTED PUBLICATIONS** Auth, A Textual Study of Jacques de Dinant's Summa dictaminis, Etudes de Philologie et d'Histoire, 28, Librairie Droz, Geneva, 75; auth, Medieval and Renaissance Letter Treatises and Form Letters: A Census of Manuscripts Found in Eastern Europe and the Former USSR, E.J. Brill, 93; auth, Medieval and Renaissance Letter Treatises and Form Letters: A Census of Manuscripts Found in Part of Western Europe, Japan, and the United States of America, E.J. Brill, 94. **CONTACT ADDRESS** Dept of History, Queensborough Comm Col, CUNY, 222-05 56th Ave, Bayside, NY, 11364-1497.

POLAKOFF, KEITH IAN
PERSONAL Born 12/12/1941, New York, NY, m, 1964 **DISCIPLINE** AMERICAN HISTORY **EDUCATION** Clark Univ, BA, 63; Northwestern Univ, MA, 66, PhD, 68. **CAREER** Lectr US hist, Lehman Col, 67-69; from asst prof to assoc prof, 69-78, Prof US Hist, CALIF STATE UNIV, LONG BEACH, 78-, Ed, Hist Teacher, 72-77, prod mgr, 77-80; assoc dean, Sch Soc & Behav Sci, Cal State Univ, Long Beach, 80-84; Dean, School Fine Arts, 84-85; Dean School Soc Behav Sci, 85-86; ASSOC VPRES ACAD AFFAIRS, 86- , CALIF STATE UNIV. **MEMBERSHIPS** Orgn Am Historians. **RESEARCH** Reconstruction; post Civil War politics; history of American political parties. **SELECTED PUBLICATIONS** Auth, The Politics of Inertia, La State Univ, 73; coauth, Generations of Americans, St Martin's, 76; Political Parties in American History, John Wiley & Sons, 81. **CONTACT ADDRESS** Off of Acad Affairs, California State Univ, Long Beach, 1250 N Bellflower, Long Beach, CA, 90840-0118. **EMAIL** kip@csulb.edu

POLENBERG, RICHARD
PERSONAL Born 07/21/1937, New York, NY, m, 1988, 4 children **DISCIPLINE** AMERICAN HISTORY **EDUCATION** Brooklyn Col, BA, 58; Columbia Univ, MA, 59, PhD, 64. **CAREER** Lectr hist, Queens Col, 60-61; lectr, Brooklyn Col, 61-64, from instr to asst prof, 64-66; from asst prof to prof, 66-86, Goldwin Smith prof Am hist, Cornell Univ, 86-, Grants, Soc Sci Res Coun & Am Coun Learned Soc, 70-71. **HONORS AND AWARDS** Clark Distinguished Tchg Award, 79; Am Bar Asn Silver Gavel Award, 88. **RESEARCH** Twentieth century Am hist. **SELECTED PUBLICATIONS** Auth, Reorganizing Roosevelt's Government: 1936-1939, Harvard Univ, 66; ed, America at War: The Home Front, 1941-1945, Prentice-Hall, 68; Radicalism and Reform in the New Deal, Addison-Wesley, 72; auth, War and Society: The United States, 1941-1945, Lippincott, 72; coauth, The American Century, Wiley, 75; One Nation Divisible: Class, Race and Ethnicity in the United States Since 1938, Viking, 80; Fighting Faiths: The Abrams Case, The Supreme Court, and Free Speech, Viking, 87; The World of Benjamin Cardozo: Personal Values anda the Judicial Process, Harvard Univ, 97. **CONTACT ADDRESS** Dept of Hist, Cornell Univ, Mcgraw Hall, Ithaca, NY, 14853-0001. **EMAIL** rp19@cornell.edu

POLING, CLARK V.
PERSONAL 2 children **DISCIPLINE** ART HISTORY **EDUCATION** Yale Univ, BA, 62; Columbia Univ, MA, 66, PhD(art hist), 73 **CAREER** Asst prof, 73-79, assoc prof, 79-88, PROF ART HIST, EMORY UNIV, 88-; dir, Emory Univ Mus Fine Art and Archaeol, 1/82-12/86. **HONORS AND AWARDS** Ger Acad Exchange Serv grants, 77 & 81; NEH grant 78. **MEMBERSHIPS** Col Art Asn Am **RESEARCH** Bauhaus theories of art and design; Wassily Kandinsky; color theories of modern artists; surrealism; Andre Masson. **SELECTED PUBLICATIONS** Auth, Bauhaus Color, 76 & Contemporary Art in Atlanta Collections, 76, Atlanta High Mus Art; Contemporary Art in Southern California, 80; auth, Kandinsky au Bauhaus: Theories de la couleur et grammaire picturale, Change, Paris, spec issue, La Peinture, 2/76; auth, Kadinsky's Teaching at the Bauhaus: Color Theory and Analytical Drawing, Rizzoli, 87; Kadinsky: Russian and Bauhaus Years, 1815-1933, Solomon R Guggenheim Mus, 83; Henry Hornbostel/Michael Graves, Emory Univ Mus of Art & Archaeol, 85; Surrealist Vision and Technique: Drawings and Collages from the Pompidou Center and the Picasso Museum, Paris, Michel C Carlos Mus, Emory Univ, 96. **CONTACT ADDRESS** Art Hist Dept, Emory Univ, Carlos Hall, Atlanta, GA, 30322. **EMAIL** cpoling@emory.edu

POLING, CLARK V.
PERSONAL 2 children **DISCIPLINE** ART HISTORY **EDUCATION** Yale Univ, BA, 62; Columbia Univ, MA, 66, PhD(art hist), 73. **CAREER** Asst prof, 73-79, assoc prof, 79-88, prof, art hist, Emory Univ, 88-; dir, Emory Univ Museum of Art and Archaeology, 82-86. **HONORS AND AWARDS** Ger Acad Exchange Serv grants, NEH grants. **MEMBERSHIPS** Col Art Asn Am. **RESEARCH** Bauhaus theories of art and design; Wassily Kandinsky; color theories of modern artists; surrealism; Andre Masson **SELECTED PUBLICATIONS** Auth, Bauhaus Color, 76 & Contemporary Art in Atlanta Collections, 76, Atlanta High Mus Art; auth, Kandinsky's Teagcing at the Bauhaus: Color Theory and Analytical Drawing, Rizzoli, 87; auth, Kandinsky: Russian and Bauhaus Years, 1915-1933, Gug-

genheim Museum, 83; auth, Henry Hornbostel/Michael Graves, Emory Univ, 85; auth, Surrealist Vision and Technique: Drawings and Collages from the Pompidou Center and the Picasso Museum, Paris, Emory Univ, 96 **CONTACT ADDRESS** Dept of Art Hist, Emory Univ, 1364 Clifton Rd N E, Atlanta, GA, 30322-0001. **EMAIL** cpoling@emory.edu

POLK, ROBERT L.
PERSONAL Born 05/08/1928, Chicago, IL, d **DISCIPLINE** EDUCATION **EDUCATION** Doane Coll, BA 1952; Hartford Theol Sem, MDiv 1955; Doane Coll, Hon Dr of Div 1971; Huston-Tillotson, Hon Dr of Div 1984. **CAREER** 1st Congregational Church Berthold ND, pastor 1955-57; YMCA Minot ND, youth prog coord 1957-60; Riverside Church, minister to youth 1960-66; Dillard Univ New Orleans, dean of chapel & dean of students 1966-68; Riverside Church, minister of urban affairs 1969-76; Edwin Gould Serv for Children, exec dir 1976-80; Council of Churches City of NY, exec dir, 1980-88; CITY COLL OF NEW YORK, CITY UNIV OF NEW YORK, ACTING VICE PRES EXTERNAL RELATIONS & COMMUNITY AFFAIRS, 1988-. **HONORS AND AWARDS** Distinguished Service Award, Black Christian Caucus Riverside Church 1983; Sam Levinson Memorial Award, Jewish Community Relations Council, New York City 1984. **MEMBERSHIPS** Chmn CUNY Constr Fund; Mayor's Comm of Religious Leaders, Assoc Black Charities, Hole-in-the-Wall-Gang Camp Inc; New York City Bd of Educ, Capital Task Force on Construction & Renovation of Public Schools; New York State Dept of Educ Interfaith Educ Advisory Council to the Commr of Educ; Governor's Comm on Scholastic Achievement; Health Watch Advisory Bd. **CONTACT ADDRESS** External Relations & Community Affairs, City Col, CUNY, 138th St & Convent Ave, A-2050, New York, NY, 10031.

POLLACK, NORMAN
PERSONAL Born 05/29/1933, Bridgeport, CT, m, 1957, 1 child **DISCIPLINE** AMERICAN HISTORY **EDUCATION** Univ Fal, BA, 54; Harvard Univ, AM, 58, PhD(Am civilization), 61. **CAREER** From instr to asst prof hist, Yale Univ, 61-65; assoc prof, Wayne State Univ, 65-68; Prof Hist, Mich State Univ, 68-, Morse fac fel, Yale Univ, 64-65; Guggenheim fel, 68-69. **RESEARCH** American political and cultural history. **SELECTED PUBLICATIONS** Auth, Hofstadter on Populism: a critique of the age of reform, J Southern Hist, 60; The myth of Populist Anti-Semitism, Am Hist Rev, 62; The Populist Response to Industrial America, Harvard Univ, 62; coed, Builders of American Institutions, Rand McNally, 63; auth, Fear of man: Populism, authoritarianism and the historian, Agr Hist, 65; The Populist Mind, Bobbs, 67; coed, American Issues in the Twentieth Century, Rand McNally, 67; American Populism, a Social-history, 1877-1898 - Mcmath,RC, Western Historical Quarterly, Vol 0024, 1993; Prairie Populism - the Fate of Agrarian Radicalism in Kansas, Nebraska, and Iowa, 1880-1892 - Ostler,J, American Historical Review, Vol 0100, 1995. **CONTACT ADDRESS** Dept of Hist, Michigan State Univ, East Lansing, MI, 48823.

POLLACK, ROBERT HARVEY
PERSONAL Born 06/26/1927, New York, NY, m, 1948, 3 children **DISCIPLINE** PSYCHOLOGY **EDUCATION** CUNY, BS, 48; Clark Univ, MA, 50, PhD, 53. **CAREER** Lect, Univ Sydney, Australia, 53-61; NIH fel, Columbia Univ, 61; Deputy dir of res, Inst for Jouvenile Res, 61-69; Prof, 69-96, prof Emeritus, Univ GA, 96-. **HONORS AND AWARDS** Higo G Beiger Award by the Soc for the Scientific Study of Sexuality, for best paper published by the J of Sex Res 1982; certifird sex educator since 1975 by the Am Asn of Sex Educators, Counselors, and Therapists. **MEMBERSHIPS** Fel, Am Asn for the Advancement of Science; fel, Am Psychol Asn, div 3, 7; Am Asn of sex Educators, Counselors, and Therapists; **RESEARCH** Human sexual behavior; perceptual aging. **SELECTED PUBLICATIONS** Co-auth, with K P Kyes and I S Brown, The Effect of Exposure to a Common Script on Attitudes Toward Condoms, J of Psychol and Human Sexality, 4, 91; with T B Gouger, The Effect of Lightness Contrast on the Colored Mealier-Lyes Illusion, Perception & Psychopysics, 50, 91; with C R Hally, The Effects of Self-Esteem, Variety of Sexual Experience, and Erotophilia on Sexual Satisfaction in Sexually Active Heterosexuals, J of Sex Ed and Therapy, 19, 93; auth, A Developmental Framework for Contraception in Unmarried Adolescents, Sexuality and Health Forum, Issue #9, 93; co-auth, with S L Andersen, The Making of an Oral Sex Questionaire, J of Sex Ed and Therapy, 20, 94; with A Raj, Factors Predicting High-Risk Sexual Behavior in Heterosexual College Females, J of Sex and Marital Therapy, 21, 95; with Lara Blackford and Shannon Doty, Differences in Subjective Sexual Arousal in Heterosexual, Bisexual, & Lesbian Women, Can J of Human Sexuality, 5, 96; with T J Corley, Sex Role Ideology: Do Changes in the Stereotypic Depiction of a Lesbian Couple Effect Heterosexuals' Attitudes Towards Lesbianism?, J of Homosexuality, 32, 96; with S F Pearson, Female Response to Sexually Explicit Films, J of Psychol and Human Sexuality, 9, 97; numerous other scholarly articles, book chapters, books, and other publications. **CONTACT ADDRESS** Psychology Dept, Univ of Georgia, Athens, GA, 30602-3013. **EMAIL** bpollack@arches.uga.edu

POLLAK, MARTHA
PERSONAL Born 07/14/1951, Sighet, Romania **DISCIPLINE** ARCHITECTURE AND ARCHITECTURAL HISTORY **EDUCATION** Cornell Univ, BA, 75; MIT, PhD, 85. **CAREER** Assoc prof, Univ Ill, 91- . **HONORS AND AWARDS** Univ scholar, Unvi Ill; Visiting fel, CASUA, Nat Gallery of Art. **MEMBERSHIPS** SAH; CAA; Renaissance Soc of Am. **RESEARCH** Seventeenth century Italian architecture and urbanism. **SELECTED PUBLICATIONS** Auth, Turin, 1560-1680: Urban Design, Military Culture and the Creation of the Absoltist Capital, 91; ed, The Education of the Architect, 97. **CONTACT ADDRESS** Dept. of History, Univeristy of Illinois, 935 W. Harrison, Chicago, IL, 60607-7039. **EMAIL** m.pollak@uic.edu

POLLAK, OLIVER BURT
PERSONAL Born 11/10/1943, London, England, m, 1966, 2 children **DISCIPLINE** HISTORY **EDUCATION** Calif State Univ, Los Angeles, BA, 65; Univ Calif, Los Angeles, MA, 68, PhD(hist), 73; Creighton Univ Law, JD, 82. **CAREER** Lectr, Univ Rhodesia, 71-74; asst prof, Univ Nebr, Omaha, 74-77 & Univ Calif, Los Angeles, 77-78; asst prof, 78-80, Assoc Prof Hist, Univ Nebr, Omaha, 80-. **RESEARCH** Comparative colonialism and imperialism; British 19th century history; legal history. **SELECTED PUBLICATIONS** Auth, Recent trends in nineteenth century Burmese historiography, J Oriental Studies, 176; Dynasticism and revolt: Crisis of kingship in Burma, 1837-1851, J Southeast Asian Studies, 976; Candour and confidentiality: Textual criticism of two Greek letters on Anglo-Burmese relations, 1838, Southeast Asian Studies, 976; co-ed, Rhodesia Zimbabwe: An International Bibliography, G K Hall, 77; Empires in Collision: Anglo-Burmese Relations in the Mid-Nineteenth Century, Greenwood, 79; Rhodesia Zimbabwe, ABC Clio, 79; Efficiency, preparedness and conservation, Hist Today, 381; Administrative law, Creighton Law Rev, 81; Reaffirmation and Retention in Bankruptcy - Conflict in the Circuits over Protecting the Secured Creditor, Banking Law J, Vol 0111, 1994. **CONTACT ADDRESS** Dept of Hist, Univ of Nebr, Box 688, Omaha, NE, 68101.

POLLARD, DIANE S.
PERSONAL Born 10/31/1944, Richmond, VA, m **DISCIPLINE** EDUCATION **EDUCATION** Wellesley Coll, BA 1966; Univ of Chicago, MA 1967, PhD 1972. **CAREER** Roosevelt Univ, instructor 1969-72; Univ of WI, asst prof 1972-76, assoc prof 1976-, assoc prof of educ psychology & dir ctr for study of minorities & disadvantaged 1979-85; prof, 1993-. **HONORS AND AWARDS** AERA/SIG Research on Women & Education, Willystine Goodsell Awd, 1996; Faculty Distinguished Public Service Award, 1993. **MEMBERSHIPS** Mem Amer Educ Rsch Assn 1972-; mem Assn of Black Psychologists 1973-; mem Eta Phi Beta Inc 1978-; mem Soc for the Psychological Study of Social Issues; mem Alpha Kappa Alpha, Inc. **SELECTED PUBLICATIONS** Author: "A Profile of Black Professional Women in Educ, Psychology and Sociology"; "Perceptions of Black Parents Regarding the Socialization of their Children"; "Against the Odds: A Profile of Academic Achievers from the Urban Underclass," Journal of Negro Education, 1989; "Patterns of Coping in Black School Children;" Motivational Factors Underlying Achievement; book chapter, Black Women, Interpersonal Support and Institutional Change in Changing Education: Woman as Radicals and Conservators; "Reducing the Impact of Racism on Students," in Educational Leadership, 1990; "Toward a Pluralistic Perspective on Equity," WEEA Digest, 1992; co-author, book, Gender and Achievement, 1993; "Perspectives on Gender & Race," Educational Leadership, 1996; "Race, Gender & Educational Leadership," Educational Policy, 1997. **CONTACT ADDRESS** Educ Psych, Univ of Wisconsin, Milwaukee, Milwaukee, WI, 53201.

POLLINI, JOHN
PERSONAL Born 10/15/1945, Boston, MA, m, 1967, 2 children **DISCIPLINE** ART AND ARCHAEOLOGY **EDUCATION** Univ Washington, BA, 68; Univ Calif, Berkeley, MA, 73, PhD, 78. **CAREER** Asst prof, Johns Hopkins, Dept of Classics, Curator of Archaeol Mus, 80-87; assoc prof, 87-91, prof, 91- , Dept of Art Hist, Univ Southern Calif, Dean, School of Fine Arts, 93-96. **HONORS AND AWARDS** Magna Cum Laude, 68; Fulbright Fel, 75-76; NEH Fel, 83-84, 95-96; ACLS Fel, 87-88. **MEMBERSHIPS** Archaeol Inst Am; Col Art Asn; Am Philol Asn; Soc for the Promotion of Roman Stud; Asn of Ancient Hist. **RESEARCH** Greek, Etruscan and Roman art and archaeology; ancient religion, mythology, narratology, rhetoric, propaganda and gender issues. **SELECTED PUBLICATIONS** Auth, The Cartoceto Bronzes: Portraits of a Roman Aristocratic Family of the Late First Century BC, in Am J of Archaeol, 93; auth, The Gemma Augustea: Ideology, Rhetorical Imagery, and the Construction of a Dynastic Narrative, in Narrative and Event in Ancient Art, Cambridge, 93; auth, The Acanthus of the Ara Pacis as an Apolline and Dionysiac Symbol of Anamorphosis, Anakyklosis and Numen Mixtum, in Von der Bauforschumg zur Denkmalpflege, 93; auth, The Augustus from Prima Porta and the Transformation of the Polykleitan Heroic Ideal, in Polykleitos, the Doryphoros, and Tradition, 95; auth, The Dart Aphrodite: A New Replica of the Arles Aphrodite Type, The Cult Image of Venus Victrix in Pompey's Theater at Rome, and Venusian Ideology and Politics in the Late Republic-Early Principate, in Latomus, 97; coauth, Parian Lychnites and the Statue of Augustus from Prima Porta: New Scientific Tests and the Symbolic Value of the Marble, in J of Roman Archaeol, 98; auth, Two Gallo-Roman Bronze Portraits of Sacrificial Ministrants in the J Paul Getty Museum, in Acts of the 13th Int Bronze Cong, 98; auth, Parian Marble and its Possible Symbolic Value in Early Roman Imperial Art, in Acts of First Int Conf on Marble Stud on Paros, 98; auth, The Warren Cup: Homoerotic Love and Sympotic Rhetoric in Silver, in Art Bull, 99. **CONTACT ADDRESS** Dept of Art History, Univ of Southern California, Los Angles, CA, 90089-0293. **EMAIL** pollini@rcf.usc.edu

POLLITT, JEROME J.
PERSONAL Born 11/26/1934, Fair Lawn, NJ **DISCIPLINE** HISTORY OF ART, CLASSICAL PHILOLOGY **EDUCATION** Yale Univ, BA, 57; Columbia Univ, PhD(hist of art), 63. **CAREER** Instr classics, 62-65, from asst prof to assoc prof class art & archaeol, 65-73, chmn, Dept Classics, 75-77, PROF CLASS ARCHAEOL & HIST OF ART, YALE UNIV, 73-, Chmn, Dept Hist of Art, 81-, Dean, 86-91; Morse fel, 67-68; ed, Am J Archaeol, 73-77. **MEMBERSHIPS** Archaeol Inst Am **RESEARCH** Greek art and archaeology; art criticism. **SELECTED PUBLICATIONS** Auth, The Art of Greece: 1400-31 BC, 65 & The Art of Rome: c 753 BC-337 AD, 66, Prentice-Hall; Art and Experience in Classical Greece, Cambridge Univ, 72; The Ancient View of Greek Art, Yale Univ, 74; The impact of Greek art on Rome, Trans Am Philol Asn, 78; Kernoi from the Athenian Agora, Hesperia, 79; Art in the Hellenistic Age, Cambridge Univ, 86; The Art of Greece, Sources and Documents, Cambridge Univ, 90; Personal Styles in Greek Sculpture, Cambridge Univ, 96. **CONTACT ADDRESS** Dept of Classics, Yale Univ, PO Box 208272, New Haven, CT, 06520-8272. **EMAIL** jerome.pollitt@yale.edu

POLOMA, MARGARET MARY
PERSONAL Born 08/27/1943, Los Angeles, CA, d **DISCIPLINE** SOCIOLOGY **EDUCATION** Case Western Reserve Univ, PhD, 70. **CAREER** Prof emer, sociol, Univ Akron, Oh, 70-; visiting prof, grad relig and sociol, Southern Calif Col, Costa Mesa, 97-. **MEMBERSHIPS** Soc for the Sci Study of Relig; Relig Res Asn; Asn for the Sociol of Relig. **RESEARCH** Sociology of Religion, Spirituality and Health; Pentecostal/charismatic movement; Prayer. **SELECTED PUBLICATIONS** Coauth, with John C. Green, James L. Guth & Corwin E. Smidt, The Politics of Protestant Preachers, Univ Ks Press, Lawrence, Ks, 97; monogr, The Toronto Report, Terra Nova Publ, Wiltshire, UK, 96; jour articles, Routinization and Reality: Reflections on Serpents and the Spirit, Intl Jour for the Psychol of Relig, 8, 101-105, 98; coauth, with Lynette F. Hoelter, The Toronto Blessing: A Holistic Model of Healing, Jour for the Sci Study of Relig, vol 37, no 2, 258-273, fall, 98; The Spirit Movement in North America at the Millennium: From Azusa Street to Toronto, Pensacola and Beyond, Jour of Pentecostal Theol, 12, 83-107, 98; The Toronto Blessing: Charisma, Institutionalization, and Revival, Jour for the Sci Study of Relig, vol 36, no 2, 257-271, jun, 97; Charisma, Institutionalization and Social Change, Pneuma, Jour of the Soc for Pentecostal Studies, vol 17, no 2, 245-253, fall, 95. **CONTACT ADDRESS** 2872 Silver Lake Blvd., Silver Lake, OH, 44224. **EMAIL** mpoloma@uakron.edu

POMEROY, EARL
PERSONAL Born 12/27/1915, Capitola, CA, m, 1940, 4 children **DISCIPLINE** HISTORY **EDUCATION** San Jose State Col, AB, 36; Univ Calif, AM, 37, PhD, 40. **CAREER** Instr hist, Univ Wis, 40-42; asst prof hist, Univ NC, 42-45 & Ohio State Univ, 45-49; from assoc prof to prof hist, Univ Ore, 49-61, Beekman prof, 61-76; Prof Hist, Univ Calif, San Diego, 76-, Ford fel, 53-54; Guggenheim fel, 56-57 & 72; Huntington Libr fel, 58; lectr, Bologna Ctr, Johns Hopkins Univ, 63-64; Coe vis prof, Stanford Univ, 67-68; Nat Endowment for Humanities fel, 68; fel, Ctr Advan Study Behav Sci, 74-75; vis prof hist, Univ Calif, San Diego, 75-76. **MEMBERSHIPS** AHA; Orgn Am Historians; Agr Hist Soc; Western Hist Asn. **RESEARCH** American Far West, especially in the 20th century. **SELECTED PUBLICATIONS** Auth, The Territories and the United States, 1861-1890, 47 & 69; Pacific Outpost, American Strategy in Guam and Micronesia, 51; In Search of the Golden West: The Tourist in Western America, Knopf, 57; The Pacific Slope: A History of California, Oregon, Washington, Idaho, Utah and Nevada, Knopf, 65 & Univ Wash, 74; Computers in the Desert + Technology in Undeveloped Places - Transforming the Simple Life, Western Historical Quarterly, Vol 0025, 1994. **CONTACT ADDRESS** Dept of Hist, Univ of Calif San Diego, La Jolla, CA, 92093.

POMEROY, SARAH B.
PERSONAL Born 03/13/1938, New York, NY, 3 children **DISCIPLINE** CLASSICAL PHILOLOGY **EDUCATION** Barnard Col, BA, 57; Columbia Univ, MA, 59, PhD, 61. **CAREER** Instr class lang, Univ Tex, 61-62; lectr classics, 63-68, asst prof, 68-75, Assoc Prof Classics, 75-97, distinguished prof, 97- , Hunter Col; Coordr, Women's Studies Prog, 75-, Lectr classics, Brooklyn Col, 66-67; Am Coun Learned Soc grant-in-aid, 73-74; Nat Endowment for Humanities summer stipend, 73; fel, 81-82; Ford Found fel, 74-75; res grant, Fac Res Award Prog, City Univ New York, 75-79 & 82-83; Danforth assoc, 76-

HONORS AND AWARDS ACLS grant, 73, 74; NEH summer stipend, 73; Hunter Col grant, 73-74; Ford Found fel, 74-75; fac res award CUNY 75-77, 82-83, 85-86; NEH fel 76; Danforth Assoc, 76-82; NEH grant, 79-81; NEH fel, 81-82; NEH, dir, Hum Inst on Women in Classical Antiquity, 83; fel, Hum Res Ctr, Australian Natl Univ, 86; NEH, dir, Summer Sem, 87, 89; NEH sr fel, 87-88; Scholars Incentive Award, CUNY, 87; Pres Award for Excellence in Scholarship, 95; Guggenheim fel, 99. **MEMBERSHIPS** Am Philol Asn; Archaeol Inst Am; Am Soc Papryologists; Friends Ancient Hist; Asn Ancient Historians. **RESEARCH** Greek literature; women in classical antiquity; social history. **SELECTED PUBLICATIONS** Auth, Women in hellenistic Egypt from Alexander to Cleopatra, Wayne State Univ, reissue, 90; ed, Women's History and Ancient History, Univ North Carolina, 91; auth, Goddesses, Whores, Wives, and Slaves: Women in Classical Antiquity, Schocken, reissue 94; coauth, Women in the Classical World: Image and Text, Oxford, 94; auth, Xenophon Oeconomicus: A Social and Historical Commentary, Oxford, 94; coauth, Women's Realities, Women's Choices: An Introduction to Women's Studies, 2d ed, Oxford, 95; auth, Families in Classical and Hellenistic Greece: Representations and Realities, Oxford, 97; coauth, Ancient Greece, Oxford, 98. **CONTACT ADDRESS** Dept of Classics, Hunter Col, CUNY, 695 Park Ave, New York, NY, 10021-5085.

POMPER, PHILIP
DISCIPLINE RUSSIAN REVOLUTIONARY MOVEMENT **EDUCATION** Univ Chicago, BA, MA, PhD; Wesleyan Univ, MAAE. **CAREER** Wesleyan Univ. **HONORS AND AWARDS** Assoc ed, History and Theory. **SELECTED PUBLICATIONS** Auth, The Structure Of Mind In History. **CONTACT ADDRESS** Wesleyan Univ, Middletown, CT, 06459. **EMAIL** ppomper@wesleyan.edu

PONG, DAVID B.P.T.
PERSONAL Born 09/28/1939, Hong Kong, m, 1973, 3 children **DISCIPLINE** HISTORY **EDUCATION** Univ London, Sch of Oriental & African Stud, BA, 63, PhD, 69. **CAREER** Fellow, Far E Hist, Univ London, 66-69; Res Fellow, Inst of Adv Stud, Australian Nat Univ, 78-81; Dept of Hist, Univ Del, Asst Prof, 69-73, Assoc Prof, 73-89, Prof, 89-, Ch, 92-98. **HONORS AND AWARDS** Res Fellow, Univ London, 65-66; Res Fellow, Australian Nat Univ, 78-81; Am Coun of Learned Soc, 74-75. **MEMBERSHIPS** Asn for Asian Stud; Soc for Qing Stud; Am Hist Asn; Mid-Atl Region, Asn of Asian Stud. **RESEARCH** Modern Chinese history; naval development. **SELECTED PUBLICATIONS** Auth, Shen Pao-chen and China's Modernization in the Nineteenth Century, Cambridge Univ Press, 94; auth, Li Hung-chang and Shen Pao-chen: The Politics of Modernization, Li Hung-chang and China's Early Modernization, Sharpe, 79-107, 94; auth, China's First Modern Naval Officers: Training and Development at Mawei, 1866-1875, Marine Hist Res, 10, 213-232, 12/96; auth, Imperial Maritime Customs Service Personnel and China's Modern Defence Industry in the Nineteenth Century, Stud on the Hist of the Chinese Maritime Customs, Univ of HKG, 553-572, 98; auth, The Disbursement of the Maritime Customs Receipts and China's Defence Modernization, 1875-79, Tradition and Metamorphosis in Modern Chinese History, Inst of Modern Hist, vol 2, 98. **CONTACT ADDRESS** Dept Hist, Univ Del, Newark, DE, 19716. **EMAIL** david.pong@mvs.udel.edu

POOS, L.R.
PERSONAL Born 02/08/1954, Richmond, IN, s **DISCIPLINE** HISTORY **EDUCATION** AB, Harvard Univ, 76; PhD, Cambridge Univ, UK, 84. **CAREER** Fel, Fitzwilliam Col, Cambridge Univ, UK, 80-83; asst prof, 83-89, assoc prof, 89-95, prof and chair, 95-, dept of hist, The Cath Univ of Amer. **HONORS AND AWARDS** Fel, Royal Hist Soc, UK. **MEMBERSHIPS** Social Sci Hist Asn; Selden Soc. **RESEARCH** English history 1300-1600; Social, economic, demographic, and legal history. **SELECTED PUBLICATIONS** Coauth, with Lloyd Bonfield, Select cases in manorial courts 1250-1550: Property and family law, cxiv, Selden Soc, London, 98; articles, The heavy-handed marriage counsellor: Regulating marriage in some later-medieval English local ecclesiastical-court jurisdictions, Amer Jour of Legal Hist, xxxix, 291-309, 95; Sec, lies and the church courts of pre-Reformation England, Jour of Interdisciplinary Hist, xxv, 585-607, 95; with Sandra Lee Parker, A Consistory court from the Diocese of Rochester 1363-4, The Eng Hist Rev, cvi, 652-65; 91. **CONTACT ADDRESS** Dept. of History, The Catholic Univ of America, Washington, DC, 20064. **EMAIL** poos@cua.edu

POPE, DANIEL
PERSONAL Born 01/13/1946, Brooklyn, NY, m, 1970, 1 child **DISCIPLINE** AMERICAN HISTORY **EDUCATION** Columbia Univ, PhD, 73. **CAREER** Vis Asst Prof, 73-75, Carleton College; Asst Prof, Assoc Prof, 75 to 83-, Univ Oregon. **HONORS AND AWARDS** Fulbright Sr Lectr, Phi Beta Kappa; Harvard Postdoc Fel; Burlington-Northern Dist Teaching Awd. **MEMBERSHIPS** AHA; OAH. **RESEARCH** Business and Economic History, history of nuclear power, advertising, marketing and consumer culture. **SELECTED PUBLICATIONS** Auth, The Making of Modern Advertising, NY, Basic Books, 83, Japanese, Tokyo, Dentsu, 87; We Can Wait, We Should wait, Eugene's Nuclear Power Controversy 1968-70, Pacific Hist Rev, 90; Advertising as a Consumer Issue: An Historical View, J Social Issues, 91; Utilities and WPPSS Nuclear Plants 4 and 5: Seduced and Abandoned?, Columbia, 91; Antinuclear Activism in the Pacific Northwest: WPPSS and Its Enemies, in: John Findlay, ed, The Atomic West, Seattle, Univ WA Press, 98. **CONTACT ADDRESS** Dept of History, Univ Oregon, Eugene, OR, 97403. **EMAIL** dapope@oregon.uoregon.edu

POPE, ROBERT G.
DISCIPLINE HISTORY **EDUCATION** Yale Univ, PhD. **CAREER** RETIRED, ASSOC PROF, HIST, STATE UNIV NY-BUFFALO **MEMBERSHIPS** Am Antiquarian Soc **SELECTED PUBLICATIONS** The Halfway Covenant, 69; The Notebook of the Reverend John Fiske, Colonial Soc, 74. **CONTACT ADDRESS** PO Box 728, Pine, AZ, 85544.

POPENOE, DAVID
PERSONAL Born 10/01/1932, Los Angeles, CA, m, 1959, 2 children **DISCIPLINE** URBAN STUDIES; SOCIOLOGY **EDUCATION** Univ of Pa, MA, PhD. **CAREER** Prof, Sociol, Rutgers Univ. **HONORS AND AWARDS** Sr Fulbright Res Sch; Vis Fulbright Lecturer in Greece, Israel, & Spain; Fellow, Am Coun Learned Soc; Fellow, Am Scandinavian Foundation., Co-dir, Nat Marriage Project. **MEMBERSHIPS** Coun on Families in Am (founder & co-ch 92-96) **RESEARCH** Sociology of the family. **SELECTED PUBLICATIONS** Ed, The Urban-Industrial Frontier, 69; co-ed, Neighboorhood, Sociology, and Metropolis, 70; auth, Private Pleasure, Public Plight: American Metropolitan Community Life in Comparative Perspective, 85, 89; co-ed, Housing and Neighboorhoods, 87; auth, Disturbing the Nest: Family Change and Decline in Modern Societies, 88; co-ed, Promises to Keep: Decline and Renewal of Marriage in America, 96; auth, Life Without Father: Compelling New Evidence that Fatherhood and Marriage are Indispensable for the Good of Children and Society, 96. **CONTACT ADDRESS** 92 Moore St, Princeton, NJ, 08540.

POPKIN, JEREMY D.
PERSONAL Born 12/19/1948, Iowa City, IA, m, 1980, 2 children **DISCIPLINE** HISTORY **EDUCATION** Univ CA, Berkeley, BA 70, PhD 77; Harvard Univ, AM 71. **CAREER** Univ KY, asst prof to prof 78-; Univ Pitts, vis asst prof 77-78. **HONORS AND AWARDS** Guggenheim Fell; Fulbright Fell; NEH res; NEH lib. **MEMBERSHIPS** AHA; Soc French Hist Stud; ASECS. **RESEARCH** French hist, hist of press, historians and autobiography. **SELECTED PUBLICATIONS** A History of Modern France, Englewood Cliffs NJ, Prentice Hall, 94; A Short History of the French Revolution, Eng NJ, Pren Hall, 95, 2d ed, 98; Media and revolution, Lex KY, Univ Press KY, 95; The Memoires Secrets' and the Culture of Publicity, with Bernadette Fort, Oxford, Voltaire Found, 98; Revolutionary News: The Press in France, 1789-1799, Durham NC, Duke Univ Press, 90. **CONTACT ADDRESS** Dept of Hist, Univ of Kentucky, Lexington, KY, 40506. **EMAIL** popkin@pop.uky.edu

POPPINO, ROLLIE EDWARD
PERSONAL Born 10/04/1922, Portland, OR, m, 1950, 3 children **DISCIPLINE** LATIN AMERICAN HISTORY **EDUCATION** Stanford Univ, AB, 48, MA, 49, PhD(Brazilian hist), 53. **CAREER** Instr hist, Stanford Univ, 53-54; intel res spec Latin Am Off Res & Anal, US Dept State, 54-61; from asst prof to assoc prof, 61-67, Prof Hist, Univ Calif, Davis, 67-, Chmn Dept, 78-, Lectr, Am Univ, 59-61; consult, US Dept State, 62-74; Soc Sci Res Coun res grant, Brazil, 63, travel grant, Brazil, 67-68; Nat Endowment for Humanities sr fel, Brazil, 67-68; Fulbright lectr, Brazil, 74. **HONORS AND AWARDS** Color D Pedro Award, Sao Paulo Hist & Geog Inst. **MEMBERSHIPS** Am Hist Asn; Conf Latin Am Hist; Inst Hist Geografico Brasileiro. **RESEARCH** History of Brazil; Latin American international relations; Communism in Latin America. **SELECTED PUBLICATIONS** Auth, O processo politico no Brasil, 1929-45, Rev Brasileira Estud Polit, 64; International Communism in Latin America, Free Press, 64; coauth, A History of Modern Brazil, 1889-1964, Stanford Univ, 66; auth, Brazil: The Land and People, 68 & 73; Feira de Santana, Editora Itapua Salvador, 68; Las fuerzas armadas en la politica Brasilena, Estrategia, 71; contribr World Communism, A Handbook, 1918-1965, Hoover Inst, Stanford, 73; auth, Brazil after a decade of revolution, Current Hist, 74; Strategies of an Illusion - the World Revolution and Brazil 1922-1935 - Portuguese - Pinheiro,ps, American Historical Review, Vol 0097, 1992. **CONTACT ADDRESS** Dept of Hist, Univ of Calif, Davis, CA, 95616.

PORADA, EDITH
PERSONAL Born 08/22/1912, Vienna, Austria **DISCIPLINE** ART HISTORY, ARCHEOLOGY **EDUCATION** Univ Vienna, PhD, 35 Hon Degree: LittD, Smith Col, 67. **CAREER** Am Philos Soc fel, 40-42; Am Schs Orient Res, 43-44; instr hist of art, Queens Col, NY, 49-55, asst prof, 55-58; assoc prof, 58-63, Prof Art Hist & Archaeol, Columbia Univ, 63-, Guggenheim fel, 50-51; hon cur seals & tablets, Pierpont Morgan Libr, 55-; chmn, Columbia Univ Sem Archaeol of Eastern Mediter, Eastern Europ & Near E, 66-; Norton lectr, Archaeol Inst Am, 67. **MEMBERSHIPS** Soc Am Archaeol; Am Orient Soc; Am Acad Arts & Sci; corresp fel Brit Acad; Am Philos Soc. **RESEARCH** Ancient Near Eastern art and archaeology. **SELECTED PUBLICATIONS** Auth, Seal Impressions of Nuzi, Am Schs Orient Res; Corpus of Ancien Near Eastern Seals in North American Collections, Bollingen, 48; Alt-Iran, Holle, 62; The Art of Ancient Iran, Crown, 65; Tchoga Zambil IV, La Glyptique, Mem Del Arch Iran, 70; Studies of the Stamp Seals of Palestineisrael, Vol 2 - German - Keel,o, Leu,hk, Schroer,s, J of the American Oriental Society, Vol 0112, 1992; Bronze-working Centers of Western Asia C.1000-539bc - Curtis,J, J of the American Oriental Society, Vol 0114, 1994. **CONTACT ADDRESS** Dept of Art Hist & Archael, Columbia Univ, New York, NY, 10027.

PORSILD, CHARLENE
DISCIPLINE U.S. AND CANADIAN HISTORY **EDUCATION** Carleton Univ, Ottawa, Can, PhD, 94. **CAREER** Vis asst prof, Univ Nebr, Lincoln; ed, Great Plains Quart. **HONORS AND AWARDS** Vis Fulbright fel, Univ Col, Boulder, 93-94; Oral hist fel, Charles Redd Ctr, 95; Northern Inst res fel, 96. **SELECTED PUBLICATIONS** Auth, Universite d'Ottawa: Un heritage pour demain/Univeristy of Ottawa: A Tradition for Tomorrow, Ottawa UP, 90; Gamblers and Dreamers: Women, Men and Community in the Klondike, Univ Brit Columbia Press, 98. **CONTACT ADDRESS** Univ Nebr, Lincoln, 631 Oldfat, Lincoln, NE, 68588-0417. **EMAIL** nuhusker@unl.edu

PORTER, CURTISS E.
PERSONAL Born 12/29/1939, Braddock, PA, d **DISCIPLINE** EDUCATION **EDUCATION** Univ Pgh, BA; Univ Pgh, PhD. **CAREER** Univ Pittsburgh, chmn dept of black comm educ research & devel; DBCERD/PITT, asso dir 1969-72; DBCERD-PITT, dir program devel 1972-74. **MEMBERSHIPS** Chmn Reg 3 Nat Counc of Black Studies; consult Def Race Rels Inst; spl guest 6th Pan African Congress; mem Commn on Educ & Rsrch African Heritage Studies Assn; exec bd Nat Coun of Black Studies; mem Assn for the Study of Afro-Am Life & Hist; part Kuntu Writers Workshop; fdr Black Horizons Theatre; fdr Black Action Soc; mem Adv EST; mem EST Hunger Proj Com. **CONTACT ADDRESS** 3804 Forbes Ave, Pittsburgh, PA, 15260.

PORTER, DAVID H.
PERSONAL Born 10/29/1935, New York, NY, m, 1987, 4 children **DISCIPLINE** CLASSICS; MUSIC. **EDUCATION** Swarthmore College, BA, 58; Princeton Univ, PhD, 62; Philadelphia Conserv Music, 55-62. **CAREER** Instr, Carleton Col 62-63; asst prof, 63-68; assoc prof, 68-73; prof, 73-87; pres, 74-87; pres and prof, Skidmore Col, 87- . **HONORS AND AWARDS** NEH fel, 69-70, 83-84; ACLS fel, 76-77. **MEMBERSHIPS** Am Philol Asoc; Classical Asoc of the Atalantic States. **RESEARCH** Greek tragedy; Latin poetry, especially Horace; contemporary music. **SELECTED PUBLICATIONS** Auth, Horace's Poetic Journey: A Reading of Odes 1-3, 87; auth, Only Connect: Three Studies in Greek Tragedy, 87; auth, A Note on Aeschylus, Agamemnon 332, Classical Philol, 88; auth, The Structure of Beethoven's Diabellil Variations, op. 120-Again, Music Rev, 93; auth, Quo, quo scelesti ruitis: The Downward Momentum of Horace's Epodes, Ill Classical Studies, 95. **CONTACT ADDRESS** Skidmore Col, Saratoga Springs, NY, 12866. **EMAIL** bryan@skidmore.edu

PORTER, DAVID L.
PERSONAL Born 02/18/1941, Holyoke, MA, m, 1970, 2 children **DISCIPLINE** HISTORY, POLITICAL SCIENCE **EDUCATION** Franklin Col, BA, 63; Ohio Univ, MA, 65; Pa State Univ, PhD(hist), 70. **CAREER** Asst prof hist, Rensselaer Polytech Inst, 70-75; educ admin asst, Troy Civil Ser Comn, NY, 75-76; from asst prof to prof, 77-86, Louis Tuttle Shangle Prof Hist, William Penn Col, 86-, Dir Pre-Law Prog, 79-; Co-dir Am studies, Rensselaer Polytech Inst, 72-74; chmn hist, Troy Area Bicentennial Comt, 75-76; consult, Midwest Rev, 77-78. **HONORS AND AWARDS** President's Schol, 59-63; Frankin's Schol, 62-63; Lancers; Blue Key; Alpha; Phi Alpha Theta; Kappa Delta Phi; Nat Sci Found Grant, 67; Fac Travel Grants, 74, 77, 81, 86; NEH grant, 89; Eleanor Roosevelt Inst Grant, 81; Distinguished Service Award, United Nations Asn, 81; Prof Development Grant, 86, 89, 92; Choice Outstanding Academic Book, 88, 89. **MEMBERSHIPS** AHA; Orgn Am Historians; Soc Hist Am Foreign Rels; North Am Soc Sport Hist; Soc Am Baseball Res; Ctr for the Study of the Presidency; State Hist Soc Iowa; Professional Football Res Asn; Col Football Res Asn. **RESEARCH** United States political history; United States diplomatic history; United States sport history. **SELECTED PUBLICATIONS** Auth, The Seventy-Sixth Congress and World War II, 1939-1940, Univ Mo Press, 79; Congress and the Waning of the New Deal, Kennikat Press, 80; Biographical Dictionary of American Sports: Baseball, Greenwood Press, 87; Biographical Dictionary of American Sports: Football, Greenwood Press, 87; Biographical Dictionary of American Sports: Outdoor Sports, Greenwood Press, 88; Biographical Dictionary of American Sports: Basketball and Other Indoor Sports, Greenwood Press, 89; Biographical Dictionary of American S ports: 1989-1992 Supplement for Baseball, Football, Basketball, and Other Sports, Greenwood Press, 92, (92-95 supplement, 95);

compiler, A Cumulative Index to the Biographical Dictionary of American Sports, Greenwood Press, 93; auth, African-American Sports Greats, Greenwood Press, 95; author of numerous journal articles and book reviews. **CONTACT ADDRESS** Dept of Soc Sci, William Penn Col, 201 Trueblood Ave, 110C Penn , Oskaloosa, IA, 52577-1799. **EMAIL** porterd@wmpenn.edu

PORTER, ELLEN-JANE LORENZ
DISCIPLINE HISTORY OF MUSIC **EDUCATION** Wellesley, BA, 29; Wittenberg, MSM, 71; Union Grad Sch, PhD, 78. **CAREER** IND LECT, AUTHOR, COMPOSER. **MEMBERSHIPS** Am Antiquarian Soc **RESEARCH** Spirituals **SELECTED PUBLICATIONS** Auth, Folk Hymns for Handbells, 75; auth, Music Our Forefathers Sang, 78; auth, articles on Am mus; comp, for choruses, chamber groups; auth, Glory Hallelujah: The Story of the Campmeeting Spiritual, 80; comp, anthem arr of Am folk hymns, The Hymn 41; auth, "The Hymnody of the Evangelical United Brethren Church," Jour of Theol 91, 87. **CONTACT ADDRESS** 6369 Pebble Court, Dayton, OH, 45459.

PORTER, GLENN
PERSONAL Born 04/02/1944, New Boston, TX, m, 1987 **DISCIPLINE** HISTORY **EDUCATION** Rice Univ , BA 66; John Hopkins Univ, MA 68, PhD 70. **CAREER** Harvard Grad Sch of Bus, asst prof 70-76; Hagley Museum and Lib, dir Reg Ec Hist Res Cen, 76-83, dir 84. **HONORS AND AWARDS** Pres, Bus Hist Con; Pres, Ind Res Lib Assn. **MEMBERSHIPS** BHC; SHT; SAH; AAM **RESEARCH** Hist of Am Business; the business use of design and archit. **SELECTED PUBLICATIONS** Cultural Forces and Commercial Constraints: Designing Packaging in the Twentieth Century United States, forth coming in: Journal of Design History, 98; Industrialization and the Rise in Big Business, in: Charles W Calhoun, ed, The Gilded Age, 96; Troubled Marriage: Raymond Loewy and the Pennsylvania Railroad, in Amer Herit of Invention and Technology, 96; The Rise of Big Business, 73, revised 92. **CONTACT ADDRESS** Hagley Mus and Libr, Wilmington, DE, 19807.

PORTER, JACK NUSAN
PERSONAL Born 12/02/1944, Rovno, Ukraine, d, 2 children **DISCIPLINE** SOCIOLOGY **EDUCATION** Univ Wisconsin, BA 67; Northwestern Univ, MA PhD, 67-71. **CAREER** Harvard Univ, res assoc 82-84; The Spencer Group, pres 84-; Spencer Sch of RE, exe dir 86-; Spencer Inst for Bus & Soc, 84-; Boston Univ, asst prof 89-90, vis lect 87-88; Bryant Col, vis lect 91; Univ Mass, adj prof. **HONORS AND AWARDS** John Atherton Fel; Nom Natl Jewish Bk Awd; Who's Who in America., VP Assoc of Genocide Scholars; Advisory Bd Cen for Comparative Genocide; Ed Bd of the Encycl of Genocide; Ntl Steering Comm Black Fam Stud. **MEMBERSHIPS** PEN; Harvard Club; ASA; Bnai Brith Realty Lodge; AAAS. **SELECTED PUBLICATIONS** Auth, The Jew as Outsider: Historical and Contemporary Perspectives: Collected Essays; Genocide and Human Rights: A Global Anthology; Jewish Partisans: A Documentary of Jewish Resistance in the Soviet Union; Jews in Cults; Kids in Cults; Handbook of Cults, Sects and Alternative Religious Groups; The Sociology of Jewry; Women in Chains: A Source Book on the Agunah; Sexual Politics in Nazi Germany: The Persecution of the Homosexuals. **CONTACT ADDRESS** The Spencer Inst for Business, 40 Hartford St, Newton, MA, 02161.

PORTER, JEANNE CHENAULT
PERSONAL Born 03/18/1944, New York, NY, m, 1977, 1 child **DISCIPLINE** ART HISTORY **EDUCATION** Columbia Univ, BA, 65; Univ Mich, Ann Arbor, MA, 66, PhD, 71. **CAREER** Asst prof Baroque, Univ Tenn, Knoxville, 69-72; from asst prof to assoc prof Baroque & Renaissance, Finch Col, 72-74; assoc prof Baroque art, Pa State Univ, University Park, 74-, Adj asst prof surv, Hunter Col, 74. **MEMBERSHIPS** Col Art Asn Am. **RESEARCH** Italian, Spanish and French Baroque painting; Rococo painting; modern American painting. **SELECTED PUBLICATIONS** Contributing auth, Raffuello e l'Europa, Accademia Nazionale dei Lincei, Centro di Studi cultura e l'imagine a Roma, Rome, 92; co-ed, Pantheuope's Splendor, Art of the Golden Age in Naples, Papers in Art Hist from the Penn State Univ, Vol VII, 94; A Documentary History of Naples, 1600-1800, Italica Press, Vol IV of a 5 vol anthology, 98-99; James Brooks, Am Nat Biog, 98. **CONTACT ADDRESS** Pennsylvania State Univ, 229 Arts Bldg, University Park, PA, 16802-2901. **EMAIL** jcp1@psu.edu

PORTER, JOHN R.
PERSONAL Born 04/28/1949, Levis, PQ, Canada **DISCIPLINE** ART HISTORY **EDUCATION** Laval Univ, LL, 71, MA, 72; Univ Montreal, PhD, 82. **CAREER** Asst cur, Can art, Nat Gallery Can, 72-78; prof, art hist, Laval Univ; chief cur, Montreal Mus Fine Arts, 90-93; DIR, MUSEE DU QUEBEC, 93-. **SELECTED PUBLICATIONS** Auth, number of books on the history of early painting, sculpture and furniture production in Quebec. **CONTACT ADDRESS** Musee du Quebec, Parc des Champs de Bataille, Quebec, PQ, G1R 5H3.

PORTER, JONATHAN
PERSONAL Born 03/25/1938, Boston, MA, m, 1959 **DISCIPLINE** HISTORY, ASTRONOMY **EDUCATION** Harvard Univ, AB, 60; Univ Colo, MA, 63; Univ Calif-Berkeley, PhD, 71. **CAREER** Instr, Univ Colo, Hist, 64-65; instr. Univ NMex, Hist, 69-71; asst prof, Univ NMex. 71-74; assoc prof, Univ Nmex, 74-87; PROF, UNIV NMEX, HIST, 87-. **MEMBERSHIPS** Asn Asian Stud **RESEARCH** Early modern China; European expansion in Asia; Macau. **SELECTED PUBLICATIONS** Macau: The Imaginary City: Culture and Society, 1557 to the Present, Westview Press, 96. **CONTACT ADDRESS** Dept Hist, Univ NMex, Albuquerque, NM, 87131. **EMAIL** jporter@unm.edu

PORTER, MICHAEL LEROY
PERSONAL Born 11/23/1947, Newport News, VI, s **DISCIPLINE** LITERATURE, HISTORY **EDUCATION** VA State Univ, BA, (hon) sociology 1969; Atlanta Univ, MA, hist 1972; Leonardo DaVinci Acad, Rome, Italy, MCP Contem 1983-84; Emory Univ, PhD hist/Amer studies 1974; Sorbonne Univ, postpoet, hist, Paris France, 1979; Thomas Nelson Community Coll, cert crim justice 1981; US Armed Forces Staff Coll, Norfolk VA, US Pres Appt, 1987. **CAREER** WA State Univ, asst prof of history, black studies prog 1974-75; Mohegan Comm Coll, Dept History lectr 1975-76; Newport News VA, asst education coord, education comp, target proj prog 1977; Hampton Univ, asst prof history 1977-80; NC Mutual Ins Co, life ins underwriter 1980-81; Mullins Prot Serv VA Bch, private investigator, 1981-83; Amer Biographical Inst Raleigh, media freelancer 1984-85, publications dir/deputy governor 1985-; Old Dominion Univ, Norfolk VA, consultant 1985; Michael Porter Enterprises International, president, founder, 1985-88; INTL BIOGRAPHICAL CTR, CAMBRIDGE ENGLAND, DEPUTY DIR GEN 1986-. **HONORS AND AWARDS** 1st Black Concert Pianist to play Carnegie Hall, 1963; Lyon Dissertation Prize, 1974; Ebony Magazine, Eligible Bachelor, 1975; Outstanding Black, 1992; Hero, 1992; International Honors Cup, 1992; Abira Genius Grant, 1992; World Greetings, 1992; Pioneer Award, 1992; Great American, 1991; World Intellectual, 1993; Golden Academy Award, 1991; One of 500 Leaders of Influence in the 20th Century; Intl Hall of Leaders, Amer Biographical Inst, 1988; participant (exhibit), DuSable Museum of Black History, 1988; honoree, Intl Exhibit, Singapore, Malaysia, 1988; Outstanding Man of the World, Ormiston Palace, Tasmania, Australia, 1989; Exhibit, Intl Music Museum, London, ENG, 1989; Poetry Reading, Royal Palace, Lisbon, Portugal, 1998; Michael Porter Poetry Exhibit, Internet Intl Poetry Hall of Fame, 1997-2002; Lecture, Oxford Univ, Oxford, ENG, 1997; Famous Quote, Leningrad, Russia, 1998; 20th Century Award for Achievement, 1990; Black History Maker, 1992; International Man of the Year, 1992; Most Admired Person of the Decade, 1990-99; Recipient, Grant For Exceptionally Gifted Poets, 1998; US Congress, Certificate of Appreciation, 1991; Honorary US Congressman, 1993; Hampton History Center, Historical Marker, 1992; Appearances before US President's Council of Economic Advisors & Senate Finance Committee, 1992; Honorary Knighthood, 1997; US Presidential Medal of Freedom, 1993. **MEMBERSHIPS** Life patron World Inst of Achievement 1985; curator "Michael L Porter Historical & Literary Collection"; World Literary Acad 1984-85; World Biographical Hall of Fame 1985; Federal Braintrust, 1990; Intl Advisory Council, 1989-; African American Hall of Fame, 1994; Elite International, 1992; bd of governors, Amer Biog Inst, 1986; Phi Beta Kappa; Intl Academy of Intellectuals, 1993; Famous Poet's Society, 1996; chairman, US Selective Service Bd #32, 1986-92; chief delegate, Intl Congress on Arts & Communications, Nairobi, Kenya, 1990. **SELECTED PUBLICATIONS** "African Leadership Ideology" (w/Ukandi Damachi) Praeger 1976; "Sacrificing Qual Lang Learn for Pol Exped" 1977;Television Programs: Cited On World News Tonight; Hard Copy; 60 Minutes; Current Affairs; Entertainment Tonight; CBS Evening News; The Remarkable Journey; Journey of African American Athelete, 1995; Eve's Bayou, 1997; 4 Little Girls; NBC Nightly News; Film: The Making of Black Atlanta, 1974; 1st Black Elected to Intl Academy of Intellectuals, Paris, France, 1993; Radio: Empire State Bldg Broadcasting Ctr, WRIN, 1997; Publications: Ebony, Jet, Intl, Digest, Talent; Contemporary Authors. **CONTACT ADDRESS** Archives Administrator, 3 Adrian Circle, Hampton, VA, 23669-3814.

PORTERFIELD, RICHARD MAURICE
PERSONAL Born 07/19/1933, Baltimore, MD, m, 1960, 2 children **DISCIPLINE** EUROPEAN EXPANSION **EDUCATION** Johns Hopkins Univ, BA, 55; Univ Pa, MA, 57; Temple Univ, PhD, 78. **CAREER** Asst prof, 61-71, assoc prof hist, 71-, Chrmn Dept, 79-92, Glassboro St. Col. **MEMBERSHIPS** AHA; Conf Brit Studies; Asn Can Studies US. **RESEARCH** Canada and British Empire; Imperialism; European expansion. **SELECTED PUBLICATIONS** Auth, British Imperial Policy and the Quebecois in the Nineteenth Century, Quebec Studies, Vol I 17-43, 83; auth, Cecil Rhodes, Historic World Leaders, 94; auth, H.H. Kitchener, Historic World Leaders, 94. **CONTACT ADDRESS** Dept of History, Rowan Col of New Jersey, 201 Mullica Hill Rd, Glassboro, NJ, 08028-1702. **EMAIL** richport@bellatlantic.net

PORTON, GARY GILBERT
PERSONAL Born 03/12/1945, Reedley, CA, m, 1968, 2 children **DISCIPLINE** HISTORY OF JUDAISM **EDUCATION** UCLA, BA, 67; Hebrew Union Col, MA, 69; Brown Univ, PhD, 73. **CAREER** Asst prof, 73-80, assoc prof Relig Studies, 80-84, prof relig studies, Univ IL, 84-, prof Dept Hist, 91, prof Prog Comp Lit, Guggenheim fel, 82-83; assoc, Ctr Advan Study, Univ Ill, 82-83. **MEMBERSHIPS** Soc Bibl Lit; Europ Asn Jewish Studies. **RESEARCH** Rabbinic lit; Jewish Bibl exegesis; hist of Rabbinic Judaism. **SELECTED PUBLICATIONS** Auth, The Traditions of Rabbi Ishmael I, 76, II, 77, III, 78 & IV, 82, E J Brill; The Grape Cluster in Jewish art and literature in late antiquity, J Jewish Studies, 76; Midrash: The Bible and the Palestinian Jews in the Greco-Roman period, Aufsteig Niedergang Romischen Welt, 78; Understanding Rabbaic Midrash, KTAU, 85; Goyim: Gentiles and Israelites in Moshrah-Csefla, Scholars Press, 88; The Stranger within Your Gates: Converts and Conversion in Rabbinic Literature, Chicago, 94. **CONTACT ADDRESS** Univ of Illinois, 707 S Mathews Ave, Urbana, IL, 61801-3625. **EMAIL** g_porton@uiuc.edu

POSADAS, BARBARA MERCEDES
PERSONAL Born 10/02/1945, Chicago, IL, m, 1982 **DISCIPLINE** AMERICAN HISTORY **EDUCATION** DePaul Univ, BA, 67; Northwestern Univ, MA, 71, PhD(US hist), 76. **CAREER** Instr, 74-76, asst prof , 76-89, assoc prof Hist, Northern Ill Univ, 89-. **HONORS AND AWARDS** Senior Fulbright Research Award, 82-83, Phillipines; Postdoctoral Research Fellowship, Asian American Studies Center, Institute of American Cultures, U.C.L.A., 87-88; Harry E. Pratt Memorial Award, Il State Historical Society, 92 (given annually for the best article in the Il Historical Journal; VIP Gold Award, Filipino American National Historical Society, 94; Fil-Am Image Magazine 1996-97 Twenty Outstanding Filipino-Americans in the United States and Canada Award; Summer research Grant, Northern Il Univ, 97; Summer Research Stipend, National Endowment for the Humanities, 97. **MEMBERSHIPS** Orgn Am Historians, Am Hist Asn, Urban Hist Asn, Immigration Hist Soc, Asn for Asian American Studies, Filipino Am National Hist Soc, Filipino Am Hist Soc of Chicago, Il State Hist Soc, Chicago Hist Soc. **RESEARCH** United States urban history; United States women's history; United States social history. **SELECTED PUBLICATIONS** Auth, A home in the country: Suburbanization in Jefferson Township, 1870-1889, Chicago Hist, fall 78; Crossed Boundaries in Interracial Chicago: Philipino American families since 1925, Amerasia J, fall/ winter 81; The Hierarchy of Color and Psychological Adjustment in an Industrial Environment: Filipinos, the Pullman Company and the Brotherhood of Sleeping Car Porters, Labor Hist, summer 82; Suburb into Neighborhood: The Transformation of Urban Identity on Chicago's Periphery--Irving Park as a Case Study, 1970-1910, J Il State Hist Soc, autumn 83; To Preserve the Home: Reform, Suffrage, and the Changing Role of Illinois Club Women, in Roger D. Bridges & Rodney O. Davis, eds, Illinois:Its History and Legacy, 84; Hancock County's Cambre House, A Rare Survivor of Icarian Community, Historic Ill, Feb 85, written with Wm. B. Coney; Will the Real Pinoy Please Stand Up? Filipino Immigration to America: A Review Article, Pilipinas: J of Philipine Studies, fall 85, written with Roland Guyotte; At a Crossroad: Filipino American History and the Old-Timer' Generation, Amerasia J, 86-87; Concrete in Illinois: Its History and Preservation, Ill Preservation Series Number 8, 87, written with William B. Coney; Mestiza Girlhood: Interracial Families in Chicago's Filipino American Community Since 1930, in Judy Yung, ed, Making Waves: Writings About Asian American Women (89); Ethnic Life and Labor in Chicago'sPre-World War II Filipino Community, in Robert Asher and Charles Stephenson, eds, Labor Divided: Race and Ethnicity in United States Labor Struggles, 1940-1960 , 90; Unintentional Immigrants: Chicago's Filipino Foreign Students Become Settlers, 1900-1941, J Amer Ethnic Hist, spring 90, written with Roland L. Guyotte; Jose Rizal and the Changing Nature of Filipino Identity in an American Setting: Filipinos in Twentieth Century Chicago, Revue Francais d'Etudes Americaines, Feb 92, written with Roland L. Guyotte; Aspiration and Reality: Occupational and Educational Choice among Filipino Migrants to Chicago, 1900-1935, Ill Hist J, summer 92, written with Roland L. Guyotte; Northern Illinois University, in Gary Y. Okihiro and Lee C. Lee, eds, East of California: New Perspectives in Asian American Studies, 92; Celebrating Rizal Day: The Emergence of a Filipino Tradition in Twentieth Century Chicago, in Genevieve Fabre and Ramon A. Gutierrez, eds, Feasts and Celebrations in North American Ethnic Communities, 95, written with Roland L. Guyotte; Teaching About Chicago's Filipino Americans, OAH Magazine of History, summer 96; Filipino Americans, in Cynthia Linton, ed, The Ethnic Handbook: A guide to the Cultures and Traditions of Chicago's Diverse Communities, 96; Crossing the Collar Line: Working Women at Desks, Swithboards, and Tables, J Urban Hist, Sept 97; Filipinas, in Wilma Mankiller, et al, eds, The Reader's Companion to U.S. Women's History, 98; America's History, Vol 1 to 1877: Student Guide, 93, written with Stephen J. Kneeshaw, Timothy R. Mahoney, Gerald J. Goodwin, and Linda Moore; Refracting America: Gender, Race, Ethnicity, and Environment in American History to 1877, 93, ed with Robert McColley. **CONTACT ADDRESS** Dept of Hist, No Illinois Univ, 1425 W Lincoln Hwy, De Kalb, IL, 60115-2825. **EMAIL** bposadas@niu.edu

POSEN, BARRY R
DISCIPLINE POLITICAL SCIENCE **EDUCATION** Univ Calif, Berkeley, PhD, 81. **CAREER** Prof, Polit Sci, Mass Inst of Tech, 87-. **HONORS AND AWARDS** Edward J Furniss Jr Book Award, Ohio State univ, 84; Woodrow Wilson Found Book Award, APSA, 85; Levitan Prize in Hum, MIT, 91., Ed Bd for Security Studies, International Security, and Orbis. **MEMBERSHIPS** Int Inst for Strategic Stud; Coun on For Rel. **RESEARCH** US military strategy and force structure; nationalism. **SELECTED PUBLICATIONS** Auth, The Sources of Military Doctrine: France, Britain, and Germany Between the World Wars, Cornell Univ Press, 84; auth, Inadvertent Escalation: Conventional War and Nuclear Risks, Cornell Univ Press, 91; auth, The Security Dilemma and Ethnic Conflict, Survival, 35(1), 27-47, 93; auth, Nationalism, the Mass Army and Military Power, Int Sec, 18(2), 80-124, 93; auth, A Defense Concept for Ukraine, Ukraine: Issue of Security, 85-136, 96; auth, Military Responses to Refugee Disasters, Int Sec, 21(1), 72-111, 96; Competing Visions for U.S. Grand Strategy, Int Sec, 21(3), 5-53, 97; auth, U.S. Security Policy in a Nuclear Armed World, Sec Stud, 6(3), 1+31, 97. **CONTACT ADDRESS** CIS/DACS E38-616, Massachusetts Inst of Tech, 292 Main St, Cambridge, MA, 02139. **EMAIL** posen@mit.edu

POSPIELOVSKY, DIMITRY VLADIMIROVICH
PERSONAL Born 01/13/1935, Rovno, Ukraine, m, 1960, 3 children **DISCIPLINE** RUSSIAN HISTORY **EDUCATION** Sir George Williams Univ, BA, 57; Univ London, MA, 61, MPhil, 67. **CAREER** Prog asst Russ broadcasting, Brit Broadcasting Corp, 59-65, res asst Soviet & East Europ Soc, 65-67; res assoc Soviet Union, Hoover Inst, Stanford Univ, 67-69; sr res analyst Soviet soc, ideology & thought, Radio Liberty Cent Res Dept, WGer, 69-72; asst prof, 72-74, assoc prof, 75-80, PROF HIST, UNIV WESTERN ONT, 81- **MEMBERSHIPS** Am Asn Advan Slavic Studies; Can Asn Slavists; Asn Russ-Am Scholars in USA. **RESEARCH** Post-Stalin development of Russian society and dissent; historical development of public opinion and political and religio-philosophic thought in Russia; economic history of the immediately pre-revolutionary Russia. **SELECTED PUBLICATIONS** Auth, A Comparative Enquiry Into Neo-Slavophilism And Its Antecedents In The Russian Hist Of Ideas, Soviet Studies, Vol XXXI, No 3; Ethnocentrism, Ethnic Tensions And Marxism-Leninism, In: Ethnic Russia In The Ussr: The Dilemma Of Dominance, Pergamon Press & Columbia Univ, 79; History Of The Renovationist Schism In The Russian Orthodox Church, Russian Hist; The Russian Orthodox Church And The Soviet State, 1917-1982, St Vladimir's Sem Press; Intelligentsia And Religion: Aspects Of Religious Revival In The Contemporary Soviet Union, In: Religion And Communist Society: Selected Papers From The Second World Congress For Soviet And East European Studies, Berkeley Slavic Specialists; Theology In The Russian Diaspora--Church, Fathers, Eucharist In Afanasev,Nikolai: 1893-1966, Russian Hist-Histoire Russe, Vol 21, 94; The History Of The Church In Carpathian Russia, J Of Church and State, Vol 37, 95. **CONTACT ADDRESS** Dept of Hist, Univ of Western Ont, London, ON, N6A 5C2.

POST, GAINES
PERSONAL Born 09/22/1937, Madison, WI, m, 1969, 2 children **DISCIPLINE** HISTORY **EDUCATION** Cornell Univ, BA, 59; Oxford Univ, BA, 63; Stanford Univ, PhD, 69. **CAREER** Asst prof, 69-73, assoc prof, 73-83, Univ Texas Austin; exec dir, Rockefeller Found Comn on the Humanities, 78-80; dean of faculty and sr vpres, 83-, assoc prof hist, 83-88, prof hist, 88-, Claremont McKenna Col. **HONORS AND AWARDS** Rhodes scholar, 61-63. **MEMBERSHIPS** Amer Hist Asn, Inter-Univ Sem on Armed Forces and Soc. **RESEARCH** Twentieth century European diplomatic and military history; twentieth century Germany **SELECTED PUBLICATIONS** The Civil-Military Fabric of Weimar Foreign Policy, Princeton, Princeton Univ Press, 73; Co-ed, Essays in Honour of Gordon Craig, The Intl Hist Rev, v1, n4, Oct, 79; The Humanities in American Life: Report of the Commission on the Humanities, Berkeley, Univ Calif Press, 80; Ed, German Unification: Problems and Prospects, Claremont, Keck Ctr for Intl and Strat Studies, 92; Dilemmas of Appeasement: British Deterrence and Defense, 1934-1937, Ithaca, Cornell Univ Press, 93. **CONTACT ADDRESS** Claremont McKenna Col, 850 Columbia Ave., Claremont, CA, 91711. **EMAIL** gpost@mckenna.edu

POST, ROBERT C.
PERSONAL Born 03/24/1937, Pasadena, CA, m, 1971 **DISCIPLINE** U.S. HISTORY **EDUCATION** UCLA, PhD, 73. **CAREER** Historian, National Park Service, 72-73; historian, National Museum of History & Technology, 74-80; curator, National Museum of Am History, 80-95; assoc dir, Lemelson Ctr for the Study of Invention and Innovation, 96; adjunct prof, Univ Maryland, 97-. **HONORS AND AWARDS** President, Soc for the History of Technology; Distinguished Retiring Ed Award, Council of Editors of Learned Journals; Resident Fel, Dibner Inst for the History of Science and Technology; Awards in Recognition of Exceptional Services, Smithsonian Inst; Certificate of Merit, Art Directors Club of Metropolitan Washington; Res Fel, Smithsonian Res Foundation. **MEMBERSHIPS** Soc for the History of Technology; Am Historical Asn; Org of Am Historians; Soc for Industrial Archaeology; Railway and Locomotive Historical Soc. **RESEARCH** History and historiography of technology; technical museums; urban history; social construction of technological systems. **SELECTED PUBLICATIONS** Auth, Physics, Patents, and Politics, Science History Publications, 76; ed, 1876: A Centennial Exhibition, National Museum of History and Technology, 76; ed, Every Four Years: The American Presidency, Smithsonian Books, 84; auth, The Tancook Whalers: Origins, Rediscovery, Revival, Maine Maritime Museum, 86; ed, In Context: History and the History of Technology, Lehigh Univ Press, 89; auth, Street Railways and the Growth of Los Angeles, Golden West Books, 89; ed, Yankee Enterprise: The Rise of the American System of Manufacturers, Smithsonian Inst Press, 95; auth, High Performance: The Culture and Technology of Drag Racing, Johns Hopkins Univ Press, 96. **CONTACT ADDRESS** National Museum of American History, Smithsonian Institution, Washington, DC, 20560. **EMAIL** 75762.2476@compuserve.com

POSTLE, MARTIN J.
DISCIPLINE BRITISH PAINTING **EDUCATION** Univ London, PhD. **CAREER** Adj asst prof; dir, London prog. **SELECTED PUBLICATIONS** Co-auth, The Artist's Model: Its Role, British Art from Lely to Etty, Nottingham, 91; auth, Sir Joshua Reynolds and the Great Style, Cambridge, 93. **CONTACT ADDRESS** Dept of Art Hist, Univ Delaware, 162 Ctr Mall, Newark, DE, 19716.

POSTMA, JOHANNES
PERSONAL Born 01/14/1935, Netherlands, m, 1961, 2 children **DISCIPLINE** MODERN HISTORY **EDUCATION** Graceland Col, BA, 62; Univ Kans, MA, 64; Mich State Univ, PhD(hist), 70. **CAREER** Instr hist, Western Mich Univ, 64-66; from asst prof to assoc prof, 68-76, PROF HIST, MANKATO STATE UNIV, 76-, Am Coun Learned Soc fel, 72-73. **MEMBERSHIPS** AHA **RESEARCH** Atlantic slave trade; European social history; Dutch colonial empire. **SELECTED PUBLICATIONS** Auth, The Dimension Of The Dutch Slave Trade From Western Africa, J African Hist, 72; West African Exports And The Dutch West India Company, 1675-1731, Econ & Soc Hist J, 73; The Origin Of African Slaves, In: Race And Slavery In The Western Hemisphere, Princeton Univ, 74; The Dutch Slave Trade, Revue Francaise D'outre-Mer, 75; Mortality In The Dutch Slave Trade, In: The Uncommon Market, Acad Press, 79; Blacks In The Dutch World--The Evolution Of Racial Imagery In A Modern Society, J Of Interdisciplinary Hist, Vol 26, 96; Slave Society In The Danish West-Indies--St-Thomas, St-John, And St-Croix-Nat Hall, J Of Am Hist, Vol 80, 94; The Merchant-Warrior Pacified--The Voc: The Dutch-East-India-Company And Its Changing Political-Economy In India, Am Hist Rev, Vol 99, 94. **CONTACT ADDRESS** Dept of Hist, Mankato State Univ, Mankato, MN, 56001.

POTASH, ROBERT AARON
PERSONAL Born 01/02/1921, Boston, MA, m, 1946, 2 children **DISCIPLINE** HISTORY **EDUCATION** Harvard Univ, PhD(hist), 53. **CAREER** Vis lectr regional studies, Boston Univ, 49; instr Latin Am hist, 50-55, from asst prof to assoc prof, 55-61, acting head dept, 66-67, head, 68-69, chmn Latin Am Studies Comt, 68-76, PROF HIST, UNIV MASS, AMHERST, 61-, Foreign serv reserve officer, US Dept State, 55-57, consult, 62-; Am Coun Learned Soc-Soc Sci Res Coun Joint Comt Latin Am Studies fel, 62, 65 & 69-70; Orgn Am States fel, Arg, 61-62; mem, Latin Am Adv Comt Soc Sci, 66-68; chmn nat steering comt, Consortium Latin Am Studies Prog, 71-72; mem nat screening comt, Foreign Area Fel Prog, 72-75; mem, Five Col Latin Am Studies Coun, 80-82. **MEMBERSHIPS** AHA; Conf Latin Am Hist; Latin Am Studies Asn; New Eng Coun Latin Am Studies (pres, 73-74). **RESEARCH** Mexican economic history; Mexican historiography; contemporary Argentina. **SELECTED PUBLICATIONS** Auth, El Banco De Avio De Mexico, Fondo Cult Econ, 59; Historiography Of Mexico Since 1821, Hisp Am Hist Rev, 8/60; The Army And Politics In Argentina, 1928-1945, Stanford Univ Press, 69, Transl, Editorial Sudamerica, 71; The Military And The Policy Making Process, 1946-1958, In: New Perspectives On Modern Argentina, Ind Univ, 72; The Impact Of Professionalism On The Twentieth Century Argentine Military, Prog Latin Am Studies, Occasional Papers Ser No 3, Univ Mass, 4/77; The Army And Politics In Argentina, 1945-1962, Stanford Univ Press, 80, Transl, Editorial Sudamerica, 81; Argentina Lost Patrol--Armed Struggle, 1969-1979, Hispanic Am Hist Rev, Vol 76, 96. **CONTACT ADDRESS** Dept of Hist, Univ of Mass, Amherst, MA, 01002.

POTHECARY, SARAH
PERSONAL Born 05/10/1958, Trinidad and Tobago, m, 1986, 1 child **DISCIPLINE** CLASSICS **EDUCATION** St Anne's Col, Oxford Univ, BA, 81; Univ Toronto, MA, 89, PhD, 95. **CAREER** Author **RESEARCH** Shrabo; ancient geography. **CONTACT ADDRESS** 117 Lytton Blvd, Toronto, ON, M4R 1L5. **EMAIL** spothecary@aol.com

POTTS, CASSANDRA W.
DISCIPLINE HISTORY **EDUCATION** Pomona Col AB; Univ Cali at Santa Barbara, PhD. **CAREER** Assoc prof, 90-. **RESEARCH** Monasticism and hagiography. **SELECTED PUBLICATIONS** Auth, Monastic Revival and Regional Identity in Early Medieval Normandy, 97; Normandy or Brittany? A Conflict of Interests at Mont-Saint-Michel 996-1035, Anglo-Norman Stud, 89, 12, 90; Atque unum ex diversis gentibus populum effecit: Historical Tradition and the Norman Identity, Anglo-Norman Stud, 95, 18, 96. **CONTACT ADDRESS** Dept of History, Middlebury Col, Middlebury, VT, 05753. **EMAIL** potts@panther.middlebury.edu

POTTS, LOUIS WATSON
PERSONAL Born 05/23/1944, Waterbury, CT, m, 1966, 3 children **DISCIPLINE** EARLY AMERICAN HISTORY; HISTORY OF TECHNOLOGY **EDUCATION** Lafayette Col, BA, 66; Duke Univ MA, 68, PhD(hist), 70. **CAREER** Instr Am hist, Duke Univ, 70-71; from asst prof to assoc prof, 71-97, PROF AM HIST, UNIV MO, KANSAS CITY, 97-, Assoc Dean Grad Studies, 76-83. **HONORS AND AWARDS** USIA Lectr on Am Soc and Values, in Russia. **MEMBERSHIPS** Soc for Hist of the Early Am Repub; Soc for Indust Archael; Russian Asn for Am Studies. **RESEARCH** Nature of American Revolution; U.S. Constitution. **SELECTED PUBLICATIONS** Auth, Arthur Lee: A Virtuos Revolutionary, LSU, 81; series co-ed, Russian American Dialogues on American History, Univ Mo, 95-. **CONTACT ADDRESS** Dept of Hist, Univ of Mo, 5100 Rockhill Rd., Kansas City, MO, 64110-2499. **EMAIL** lwpotts@cctr.umkc.edu

POTVIN, GILLES E.J.
PERSONAL Born 10/23/1923, Montreal, PQ, Canada **DISCIPLINE** MUSIC/HISTORY **CAREER** Journalist, Le Canada, 46-48; librn, 48-50, public relations, 50-53, radio/TV producer 54-58, dir casting, CBC, 62-65; instr, McGill opera stud, 57; critic, Nouveau Journal, 61; critic, Le Devoir, 61-66; critic, La Presse, 66-70; instr, Can music, Ecole Normale de Musique, 70-71; critic, Le Devoir, 73-89. **HONORS AND AWARDS** Canada 125 Medal; mem, Royal Soc Can; Order Can. **MEMBERSHIPS** CMC Coun (bd mem), 68-77; Jeunesses Musicales (pres, 76-80); Asn des retraites de Radio-Can. **SELECTED PUBLICATIONS** Ed, Canada Music Book, 70-76; Fr ed, Encyclopedia of Music in Canada, 81. **CONTACT ADDRESS** 208 Bloomfield Rd, Outremont, PQ, H2V 3R4.

POWELL, BARRY
PERSONAL Born 04/30/1942, Sacramento, CA, m, 1967, 2 children **DISCIPLINE** CLASSICS **EDUCATION** Berkeley Univ, BA, 63, PhD, 70; Harvard, MA, 65. **CAREER** Asst Prof, 69-73, Northern Arizona Univ; Asst, Assoc to Full Prof, 73-. **MEMBERSHIPS** Amer Philos Assoc. **RESEARCH** Homer; Writing; Egyptology. **SELECTED PUBLICATIONS** Auth, Classical Myth, 2nd ed, 97; A New Companion to Homer, 97; Homer and the Origin of the Greek Alphabet. **CONTACT ADDRESS** Dept Classics, Univ of Wis, 1220 Linden Dr, Madison, WI, 53706. **EMAIL** BBPowell@facstaff.wisc.edu

POWELL, JAMES MATTHEW
PERSONAL Born 06/09/1930, Cincinnati, OH, m, 1954, 5 children **DISCIPLINE** MEDIEVAL HISTORY **EDUCATION** Xavier Univ, Ohio, AB, 53, MA, 55; Ind Univ PhD, 60. **CAREER** Instr hist, Kent State Univ, 59-61; asst prof, Univ Ill, Urbana, 61-65; from asst prof to assoc prof, 65-72, acting chmn dept, 72-73 & 80, PROF HIST, SYRACUSE UNIV, 72-, Vis lectr medieval hist, Univ Wis, Milwaukee, 63-64; res fel, Pontif Inst Mediaeval Studies, Toronto, 70; resident chmn, Syracuse Univ Semester in Italy, Florence, 70-71; Nat Endowment for Humanities res grant, 77-83. **MEMBERSHIPS** AHA; Mediaeval Acad Am; Mid W Medieval Conf (pres, 65-66); Soc Ital Hist Studies; Am Cath Hist Asn. **RESEARCH** Medieval society and culture. **SELECTED PUBLICATIONS** Auth, Medieval Monarchy And Trade, Studi Medievali, 62; Innocent III: Vicar Of Christ Or Lord Of The World?, Heath, 63; Genoese Policy And The Kingdom Of Sicily, 1220-1240, Mediaeval Studies, 66; The Civilization Of The West, Macmillan, 67; The Liber Augustalis Or Constitutions Of Melfi, 71 & Ed, Medieval Studies: An Introduction, 76, Syracuse Univ; Auth, Pastor Bonus: Some Evidence Of The Use Of The Sermons Of Innocent Iii By Pope Honorius III, Speculum, 77; Honorius Iii And The Leadership Of The Crusade, Cath Hist Rev, 77; Report Of The Chairman Of The Committee-On-Recruitment, Catholic Hist Rev, Vol 81, 95; The Norman Kingdom Of Sicily, Int Hist Rev, Vol 15, 93; Understanding Conversion, Catholic Hist Rev, Vol 80, 94. **CONTACT ADDRESS** Dept of Hist, Syracuse Univ, Syracuse, NY, 13210.

POWELL, THOMAS F.
PERSONAL Born 08/27/1933, Watertown, NY, m, 1957, 2 children **DISCIPLINE** AMERICAN STUDIES **EDUCATION** NY State Col Potsdam, BS, 59; Syracuse Univ, MA, 61, PhD(soc -ci), 64. **CAREER** From instr to asst prof hist, Univ Akron, 62-65; asst prof soc sci, Syracuse Univ, 65-67; assoc prof, 67-68, dean arts & sci, 68-71, PROF HIST, STATE UNIV NY COL OSWEGO, 71-, Regents col teaching fel, 59-62; dir, State Univ NY prog & guest prof, Univ Wuerzburg, WGer, 79-81. **HONORS AND AWARDS** Chancellor's Award for Excellence in Teaching, State Univ NY Col Oswego, 76. **RESEARCH** American intellectual history; American biography. **SELECTED PUBLICATIONS** Auth, Josiah Royce, Wash Sq, 67 & Twayne, 2nd Ed, 74; Ed, Humanities And The Social Studies, Nat Coun Soc Studies, 70; Auth, Penet's Square, N Country Bks, 76; Sozialismus In Amerika, Geschichte In

Wissenschaft Und Unterricht, 78; Towards A New American Nation--Redefinitions And Construction, Journal Of America History, Vol 83, 96. **CONTACT ADDRESS** Dept of Hist, State Univ NY Col, 7060 State Route 104, Oswego, NY, 13126-3599.

POWERS, DAVID STEPHEN
PERSONAL Born 07/23/1951, Cleveland, OH, 3 children **DISCIPLINE** ISLAMIC HISTORY, LAW **EDUCATION** Yale Univ, BA, 73; Princeton Univ, MA & PhD(Islamic hist), 79. **CAREER** Prof Arabic & Islamics, Cornell Univ, 79-. **MEMBERSHIPS** Am Oriental Soc; Mid Eastern Studies Asn. **RESEARCH** Islamic law; Islamic history; medieval social history. **SELECTED PUBLICATIONS** Auth, Studies in Quran and Hadith: The Formation of the Islamic Law of Inheritance, Berkeley, 86; Islamic Legal Interpretation: Muftis and Their Fatwas, Harvard, 86; The History of al-Tabari, volume XXIV The Empire in Transition, tras, David Stephen Powers, Suny Press, 89. **CONTACT ADDRESS** Cornell Univ, Rockefeller Hall, Ithaca, NY, 14853-0001. **EMAIL** dsp4@cornell.edu

POWERS, DORIS BOSWORTH
PERSONAL Born 09/17/1938, Seattle, WA, m, 2 children **DISCIPLINE** MUSICOLOGY **EDUCATION** Univ Wash, BA; Kans State Univ, MM; Univ NC--Chapel Hill, MA, PhD. **CAREER** Inst, mus hist, violin, Sterling Col, 80-83, 74-78; adj prof, Hutchinson Comm Jr Col, 76-78; tchr, mus supvr, Amherst Pub Schs, 62-63. **HONORS AND AWARDS** Phi Beta Kappa **MEMBERSHIPS** Am Musicol Soc; Col Mus Soc; Am String Tchr Asn. **RESEARCH** Late 18th Century: C.P.E. Bach, Johann Nikolaus Forkel **SELECTED PUBLICATIONS** Review of John Christian Bach: Mozart's Friend and Mentor, by Heinz Gartner, Notes 53/1, 96, 70-71; A Bow and A Beautiful Art in the Late Eighteenth Century, Continuo 15/5, 91, 12-14. **CONTACT ADDRESS** 301 Hickory Dr., Chapel Hill, NC, 27514. **EMAIL** dbpowers@juno.com

POWERS, JAMES FRANCIS
PERSONAL Born 06/16/1935, Washington, DC, m, 1958, 3 children **DISCIPLINE** MEDIEVAL & SPANISH HISTORY **EDUCATION** Univ Va, BA, 57, MA, 61, PhD(medieval hist), 66. **CAREER** Instr Europ hist, 63-66, from asst prof to assoc prof, 66-78, PROF HIST, COL HOLY CROSS, 78-, Mem bd corporators, Int Inst in Madrid. **MEMBERSHIPS** AHA; Mediaeval Acad Am; Am Acad Res Historians on Medieval Spain (secy-treas, 73-75); Soc Span & Port Hist Studies. **RESEARCH** Medieval Spain; military history; urban history. **SELECTED PUBLICATIONS** Medieval Spain, 1031-1250: Recent Research And Continuing Problems, Class Folia, 7/77; Frontier Competition And Legal Creativity: A Castilian-Aragonese Case Study Based On Twelfth-Century Municipal Military Law, Speculum, 7/77; Frontier Municipal Baths And Social Interaction In Thirteenth-Century Spain, Am Hist Rev, 79; Frontier Military Service And Exemption In The Municipalities Of Aragon And Castile, Mil Affairs, 4/81; The Military Orders--From The 12th-Century To The Early 14th-Century, Speculum-A J Of Medieval Studies, Vol 69, 94; Jews, Visigoths And Muslims In Medieval Spain--Cooperation And Conflict, Catholic Hist Rev, Vol 82, 96; The Medieval Spain, Catholic Hist Rev, Vol 80, 94; Latin Siege Warfare In The 12th-Century, Historian, Vol 57, 94; The Military Orders--From The 12th-Century To The Early 14th-Century, Speculum-A J Of Medieval Studies, Vol 69, 94. **CONTACT ADDRESS** Dept of Hist, Col of the Holy Cross, 1 College St, Worcester, MA, 01610-2322.

POWICKE, MICHAEL RHYS
PERSONAL Born 10/02/1920, Manchester, England, m, 1948, 3 children **DISCIPLINE** HISTORY **EDUCATION** Oxford Univ, MA, 43. **CAREER** Lectr, 46-52, from asst prof to assoc prof, 52-63, PROF HIST, UNIV TORONTO, 63- **MEMBERSHIPS** Mediaeval Acad Am; fel Royal Hist Soc. **RESEARCH** Medieval history; religion and history; Medieval war and politics. **SELECTED PUBLICATIONS** Auth, Military Obligation In Medieval England, Oxford Univ, 62; Coauth, The Hundred Year War, Macmillan, 69; Coauth & Coed, Essays In Medieval History Presented To Bertie Wilkinson, Univ Toronto, 71; auth, The Community Of The Realm, Random, 73; Warfare Under The Anglo-Norman Kings, 1066-1135, Albion, Vol 27, 95. **CONTACT ADDRESS** 67 Lee Ave, Toronto, ON, M4E 2P1.

POWNALL, FRANCES SKOCZYLAS
PERSONAL Born 10/17/1963, Sarnia, ON, Canada, m, 1994, 1 child **DISCIPLINE** CLASSICS **EDUCATION** McGill, BA, 85; Univ British Columbia, MA, 87; Univ Toronto, PhD, 93. **CAREER** Lectr, Memorial Univ, Newfoundland, 92-93; asst prof, Univ Alberta, 93- . **HONORS AND AWARDS** Summer scholar, Center for Hellenic Stud, 94. **MEMBERSHIPS** APA; Class Asn of Can; Class Asn of the Can West; Class Asn of the Middle West and South; Vergilian Soc. **RESEARCH** Greek history and historiography; Greek religion; Greek oratory. **SELECTED PUBLICATIONS** Auth, Presbeis Autokratores: Andocides' De Pace, Phoenix, 95; auth, Condemnation of the Impious in Xenophon's Hellenica, Harvard Theol Rev, 98; auth, What Makes A War A Sacred War, Class Views, 98; auth, Shifting Viewpoints in Xenophon's Helenica: The Arginusae Episode, Athenaeum, forthcoming. **CONTACT ADDRESS** Dept of History and Classics, Univ of Alberta, 2-28 Tory, Edmonton, AB, T6G 2H4. **EMAIL** frances.pownall@ualberta.ca

POZZETTA, GEORGE ENRICO
PERSONAL Born 10/29/1942, Great Barrington, MA, m, 1966, 2 children **DISCIPLINE** AMERICAN HISTORY **EDUCATION** Providence Col, BA, 64, MA, 65; Univ NC, Chapel Hill, PhD(hist), 71. **CAREER** Instr hist, Providence Col, 65-66 & Far East Ext Div, Univ Md, 68; teaching asst, Univ NC, Chapel Hill, 69-71; asst prof, 71-76, ASSOC PROF HIST & SOC SCI, UNIV FLA, 76- **MEMBERSHIPS** Am Ital Hist Asn (pres, 78-80); Orgn Am Historians; Southern Hist Asn; AHA; Immigration Hist Soc. **RESEARCH** History of immigration; ethnicity in American Life; social problems in urban America. **SELECTED PUBLICATIONS** Such Hardworking People--Italian Immigrants In Postwar Toronto, Canadian Hist Rev, Vol 74, 93; Italian Am Material Culture--A Dictionary Of Collections, Sites, And Festivals In The United-States And Canada, J Of Am Hist, Vol 79, 93; A Trade For Leaving--Tradition, Migration, Work, And Community In An Alpine Valley, Revs In Am Hist, Vol 21, 93; Indifferent Socialism--Italian Immigrants And The Socialist-Party In The United-States During The Early-20th-Century, Revs In Am Hist, Vol 21, 93; Dictionary Of Am Immigration History, J Of Am Ethnic Hist, Vol 12, 93; The Immigration History Research-Center--A Guide To Collections, J Of Am Hist, Vol 79, 93. **CONTACT ADDRESS** Dept of Hist, Univ of Fla, Gainesville, FL, 32611.

PRAGER, JONAS
DISCIPLINE ECONOMICS **EDUCATION** Yeshiva Col, NY City, AB (magna cum laude), 59; Columbia Univ, PhD, 64. **CAREER** Instr, 62-64, asst prof, 64-69, assoc prof, New York Univ, 69-, Dir Graduate Studies, Dept of Economics, 81, 86-89; vis sr economist, res dept, The Bank of Israel, 65-67; observer, US Delegation, CENTO Symposium on Central Banking, Monetary Policy, and Economic Development, 71; consult, United Nations Development prog; lect, US Information Service, India, 83, Yugoslavia, West Germany, 84, France, Hungary, 89; part, Fed Reserve Bank of NY, Central Banking Sem, 70, 74, 86; vis scholar, The Bank of Israel, 80, 82-83; vis prof, Hebrew Univ of Jerusalem, 82-83. **HONORS AND AWARDS** New York State Regents Teaching Fel, 59-61; Columbia Univ Fac Scholarship, 61-62; Am Philos Soc grant, 74-75, 75-76; Fulbright-Hays Fac Res Fel, 71, 82-83. **MEMBERSHIPS** Am Economic Asn; Hagop Kervorkian Center for Near Eastern Studies, NY Univ; C V Starr Center for Applied Economics, NY Univ; United Nations Development Program, Interregional Network on Privatization; Center for the Study of Central Banks. **SELECTED PUBLICATIONS** Auth, Applied Microeconomics: An Intermediate Text, Irwin, 93; Comment in M Klausner and L J S White, eds, Structural Changes in Banking, Business One Irwin, 93; Contracting Out Government Services, Public Administration Rev, March/April 94; Banking Privatization in Israel, 198301994: A Case Study in Political Economy, Banco Nazionale del Lavoro Quart Rev, June 96; Privatizing Local Government Operations: Lessons from Federal Contracting Out Methodology, with S Desai, Public Productivity and Management Rev, Dec 96; Contracting Out: Half Speed Ahead, J of Int Affairs, winter 97; Banking Privatization: How Compelling is the Case? in Anthony Bennett, ed, How Does Privatization Work? Essays in Honor of V V Ramanadham, Routledge, 97; Balancing the Scales: Halakha (Jewish Law), The Firm, and Information Asymmetries, in A Levine and M Pava, Jewish Business Ethics: The Firm and Its Stakeholders, Aronson, forthcoming; numerous other publications. **CONTACT ADDRESS** Dept of Ecomonics, New York Univ, 269 Mercer St, New York, NY, 10003. **EMAIL** pragerj@fasecon.econ.nyu.edu

PRANG, MARGARET E.
PERSONAL Born 01/23/1921, Stratford, ON, Canada **DISCIPLINE** HISTORY **EDUCATION** Univ Man, BA, 45; Univ Toronto, MA, 53, PhD, 59; Univ Winnipeg, LLD, 78; Univ BC, DLitt, 90. **CAREER** Mem, dept hist, 58-86, head dept, 74-79, 82-83, Univ BC. **HONORS AND AWARDS** UBC Medal Biog, 75. **MEMBERSHIPS** Coun Trustees, Inst Res Pub Policy 1973-79; bd Gov, Vancouver Sch Theol, 84-87; pres, Can Hist Asn, 76-77. **SELECTED PUBLICATIONS** Auth, N.W. Rowell: Ontario Nationalist, 75; auth, A Heart at Leisure from Itself: Caroline Macdonald of Japan, 95. **CONTACT ADDRESS** 2409 W 43rd Ave, No 401, Vancouver, BC, V6M 2E6.

PRATT, L.
PERSONAL Born 11/24/1960, New York, NY, m, 1988, 1 child **DISCIPLINE** CLASSICAL STUDIES **EDUCATION** Williams Col, BA 82; Univ Michigan, AM 84, PhD 88. **CAREER** Bowdoin Col, vis asst prof, 88-89; Emory Univ, asst prof, assoc prof, 89 to 95-. **HONORS AND AWARDS** OBK **MEMBERSHIPS** APA; CA of Midwest and S; WCC; GCA; ACL. **RESEARCH** Ancient Greek and Roman Lang; Literature and Culture. **SELECTED PUBLICATIONS** Auth, Lying and Poetry for Homer to Pindar: Falsehood and Deception in Archaic Greek Poetics, Univ Mich Press, 93; auth, Odyssey: On the Interpretations of Dreams and Signs in Homer, Classical Philos, 94; auth, The Seal of Theognis Writing and the Oral Poetry, Amer Jour of Philos, 95. **CONTACT ADDRESS** Dept of Classics, Emory Univ, 404 D Callaway Cen North, Atlanta, GA, 30322. **EMAIL** lpratt@emory.edu

PRATT, WILLIAM C.
PERSONAL Born 12/15/1941, Reading, PA, m, 1969 **DISCIPLINE** AMERICAN HISTORY **EDUCATION** Ursinus Col, BA, 63; Univ Md, College Park, MA, 65; Emory Univ, PhD(hist), 69. **CAREER** Instr hist & polit sci, Philadelphia Col Textiles & Sci, 65-66; instr hist, Hope Col, 68-69; asst prof, 69-72, chmn dept, 75-78, ASSOC PROF HIST, UNIV NEBR AT OMAHA, 72- **MEMBERSHIPS** AHA **RESEARCH** The American left. **SELECTED PUBLICATIONS** Auth, Glen H Taylor: Public Image And Reality, Pac Northwest Quart, 1/69; Contribr, Senator Glen H Taylor: Questioning American Unilateralism, In: Cold War Critics, Quadrangle, 71; Auth, Women And American Socialism: The Reading Experience, Pa Mag Hist & Biog, 1/75; Contribr, Jimmie Higgins' And The Reading Socialist Community: An Exploration Of The Socialist Rank And File, In: Socialism And The Cities, Kennikat, 75; Workers, Unions And Historians On The Northern Plains, Great Plains Quart, Vol 16, 96; The Farmers-Union, Mccarthyism And The Demise Of The Agrarian Left, Historian, Vol 58, 96; Women And The Farm Revolt Of The 1930s, Agricultural Hist, Vol 67, 93. **CONTACT ADDRESS** Dept of Hist, Univ of Nebr, 6001 Dodge St, Omaha, NE, 68182-0002.

PREISSER, THOMAS M.
PERSONAL New Orleans, LA, m, 1964, 2 children **DISCIPLINE** HISTORY **EDUCATION** Mt San Antonio Col, AA, 62; Stanford Univ, BA, 64; Northwestern Univ, MA, 68; Col William and Mary, PhD, 77. **CAREER** Prof and chemn, Sinclair Commun Col, 73-. **MEMBERSHIPS** Am Hist Asn; Ohio Acad Hist. **RESEARCH** Reformation and Twentieth-Century European History. **SELECTED PUBLICATIONS** Auth, The Precarious Trade of a Virginia Tobacco Merchant: Harry Piper of Alexandria, 78; auth, Alexandria and the Evolution of the Northern Virginia Economy, 81; auth, White Servant Labor in Colonial Alexandria, 82; auth, Working on the Hot Side of the Lights: Several Techniques for Effective Television Instruction, 89; auth, Strengthening our Community Ties: Corporate Training Programs, 94. **CONTACT ADDRESS** 550 Brassfield Cir, Dayton, OH, 45459. **EMAIL** tpreisse@sinclair.edu

PRENTICE, ALISON
PERSONAL Wilmington, DE **DISCIPLINE** EDUCATION/HISTORY **EDUCATION** Smith Col, BA, 55; Univ Toronto, MA, 58, PhD, 74. **CAREER** Tch, hist, Bishop Strachan Sch, 55-57; tchg asst, hist, Univ Toronto, 58-59; tchr, Harbord Col Inst, 59-61, 63; tchg asst, Univ Toronto, 64-67; lectr, asst prof, York Univ, 72-73; assoc prof, 75-83, PROF HISTORY & PHILOS, ONT INST SRUD EDUC, UNIV TORONTO, 83-, found head, Ctr Women's Studs, 83-85. **SELECTED PUBLICATIONS** Auth, the School Promoters: Education and Social Class in Mid-Nineteenth Century Upper Canada, 77; coauth, Schooling and Scholars in Nineteenth Century Ontario, 88; coauth, Gender and Education in Ontario: An Historical Reader, 91. **CONTACT ADDRESS** Dept of Theory & Policy Stud in Educ, OISE, Univ Toronto, Toronto, ON, M5S 1V6. **EMAIL** aprentice@oise.on.ca

PRESLEY, PAULA
PERSONAL Born 06/08/1938, Des Arc, AR, 3 children **DISCIPLINE** HISTORY **EDUCATION** Truman St Univ, BA, 85, MA, 87; Univ of IA, MLIS, 91 **CAREER** Prod ed, 82-, Sixteenth Cent Journ; Asst Ed, 86-91, Asoc Ed, 91-98, Dir, Ed in Chief, 98-, Truman St Univ **MEMBERSHIPS** Am Lib Asn; Am Soc of Indexers; Soc for Schol Pub; Calvin Studies Soc **RESEARCH** Incunabula **CONTACT ADDRESS** Truman State Univ, Kirksville, MO, 63501-4221. **EMAIL** ppresley@truman.edu

PRESSLY, WILLIAM L.
DISCIPLINE ART HISTORY, ARCHAEOLOGY **EDUCATION** Princeton Univ, AB, 66; Inst Fine Arts, NY Univ, PhD, 74. **CAREER** Asst prof, 73-79, assoc prof, 79-82, Yale Univ; sen lectr, Univ Tex, Austin, 82, 83; assoc prof, Duke Univ, 85-87; assoc prof, 87-93, PROF, 93, CHAIR, DEPT ART HIST, ARCHAEOLOGY, 96-99, UNIV MD. **CONTACT ADDRESS** Dept of Art Hist, Archaeol, Univ of Maryland, 1211B Art/Sociology Bldg, College Park, MD, 20742. **EMAIL** wp12@umail.umd.edu

PRESTON, CAROL
PERSONAL Brandon, MB, Canada **DISCIPLINE** HISTORY **EDUCATION** Univ Man, BA, 66; Univ Toronto, MLS, 75. **CAREER** Librn, Winnipeg, 66-73; librn, Hist Res Libr, Hudson's Bay Co, 75-77; asst ed, The Beaver, 77-85, mgr ed, 85-95, assoc ed, 95-. **MEMBERSHIPS** Can Club Winnipeg; Women & Hist Asn Manitoba; Can Mag Publs Asn. **SELECTED PUBLICATIONS** Contribur, Manitoba: 125, Vol 1, 93; ed, A Brief History of the Hudson's Bay Company, 89, 90, 94. **CONTACT ADDRESS** The Beaver: Exploring Canada's History, 167 Lombard Ave, Ste 478, Winnipeg, MB, R3B 0T6.

PRESTON, GEORGE NELSON
PERSONAL Born 12/14/1938, New York, NY, m **DISCIPLINE** EDUCATION **EDUCATION** City College of New York, BA, 1962; Columbia University, MA, 1967, PhD, 1973. **CAREER** Dept of art, City Coll, City Univ, NY, assoc prof, art

& art hist, 1980-, asst prof art & art history, 1973-80; dept of art, Livingston College, Rutgers University, asst prof, art & art hist, 1970-73. **HONORS AND AWARDS** Foreign area fellow, Joint Comm of the American Council of Learned Soc & the Soc Science Rsch Council, 1968-70, 1972. **MEMBERSHIPS** Special consultant, New York State Commn on the Arts, 1967-68; special consultant, New World Cultures, Brooklyn Museum, 1968; associate, Columbia Univ Seminar on Primitive & Precolumbian Art, 1973-80; bd of dir, Bd of Adult Educ, Museum of African Art, Washington, DC, 1972-80; Roger Morris-Jumel Hist Soc, 1973-80; bd of dir, Cinque Gallery, New York, NY, 1977-79. **SELECTED PUBLICATIONS** numerous publications **CONTACT ADDRESS** Art Dept, City Col, CUNY, 160 Convent Ave, New York, NY, 10031-9101.

PRESTON, KATHERINE K.
DISCIPLINE HISTORY OF MUSIC **EDUCATION** Evergreen State Coll, BA, 71; Univ Maryland, MM, 81; CUNY, PhD, 89. **CAREER** ASSOC PROF, MUS, COLL WM & MARY **MEMBERSHIPS** Am Antiquarian Soc **SELECTED PUBLICATIONS** Auth, articles for New Grove Dictionary of American Music; auth, "Popular Music in the Gilded Age," Popular Music: A Year Book, 85; auth, Music for Hire: The Working Journeyman Musicians in Washington, DC 1875-1900, Pendragon Press, 92; auth, Opera on the Road: Traveling Opera Troupes in the United States, 1820-1860, Univ Ill Press, 93; consult ed/auth on itinerant opera companies for New Grove Dictionary of Opera, Macmillan Press, 93; auth, "Antebellum Concert-Giving and Opera-Singing: The Triumphant 1838-1840 American Tour by Jane Shereff and John Umlson, British Vocal Stars," in American Musical Life in Context and Practice to 1865, Garland, 94; coauth, The Mulligan Guard Ball and Reilly and the 400, in Nineteenth- Century : American Musical Theater, Garland, 94; auth, bibliog entries, American National Biography, Oxford Univ Press; auth, "The Development of Art Music in the United States, 1800-1865," in The Cambridge History of American Music, Cambridge Univ Press. **CONTACT ADDRESS** Dept of Music, Col of William and Mary, Williamsburg, VA, 23185. **EMAIL** kkpres@facstaff.wm.edu

PRETE, ROY A.
DISCIPLINE HISTORY **EDUCATION** Saskatchewan, BA; Brigham Young Univ, MA; Alberta, PhD, 79. **CAREER** Assoc Prof, Royal Milit Col. **RESEARCH** Modern European and Canadian History; European diplomatic and military history. **SELECTED PUBLICATIONS** Auth, Strategy and Command: the Anglo-French Coalition on the Western Front, 1914-1918. **CONTACT ADDRESS** Royal Military Col Canada, PO Box 17000, Kingston, ON, K7K 7B4. **EMAIL** prete_r@rmc.ca

PREVOTS, NAIMA
PERSONAL Born 05/27/1935, NY, m, 1979, 2 children **DISCIPLINE** DANCE **EDUCATION** Brooklyn Coll, BA 55; Univ WI, MA 60; Univ S CA, PhD 83. **CAREER** Performer, Choreographer, Tchr, free lance, 55-67; Am Univ, 67-83; Hollywood Museum Dir 83-88; Am Univ, ch 88. **HONORS AND AWARDS** Fulbright fellow; NEH; Phi Beta Kappa. **MEMBERSHIPS** Phi Delta Kappa; CORD; SDHS; MDEA. **RESEARCH** 20th Century cult hist, mainly Am. **SELECTED PUBLICATIONS** Dance for Export: Cultural Diplomacy and the Cold War, Univ Press New Eng, 98; American Pageantry: A Movement for Art and Democracy, UMI Press, 90; Dancing in the Sun; Hollywood Choreographers 1915-1937, UMI Press, 87; Benjamin Zemach, Ballet Rev, 98. **CONTACT ADDRESS** Dept of Performing Arts, American Univ, 4400 Massachusetts Ave NW, Washington, DC, 20016. **EMAIL** prevots@american.edu

PRICE, DON CRAVENS
PERSONAL Born 02/28/1937, Washington, DC, m, 1970 **DISCIPLINE** HISTORY **EDUCATION** Amherst Col, BA, 58; Harvard Univ, AM, 60, PhD(hist), 68. **CAREER** Asst prof Hist, Johns Hopkins Sch Advan Int Studies, 67-68; asst prof, Yale Univ, 68-72; asst prof, 73-80, prof Hist, Univ Calif, Davis, 80-, Soc Sci Res Coun exchange res assoc, Inst Mod Hist, Acad Sinica, 71-72. **MEMBERSHIPS** Asn Asian Studies; Soc Ch'ing Studies. **RESEARCH** Modern Chinese intellectual history. **SELECTED PUBLICATIONS** Auth, Russia and the Roots of the Chinese Revolution, Harvard Univ, 74; Sung Chiao-Jen, Confucianism and revolution, Ch'ing-Shih Wen-T'i, 11/77; From Civil Society to Party Government: Models of the Citizens Role in the Late Qing, Imaginning the People Chinese Intellectuals and the Concept of Citizenship, 1890-1920, Sharpe, 97. **CONTACT ADDRESS** Dept of History, Univ of California, Davis, Davis, CA, 95616-5200. **EMAIL** deprice@ucdavis.edu

PRICE, GLENN WARREN
PERSONAL Born 10/16/1918, Libertyville, IA, m, 1940, 2 children **DISCIPLINE** UNITED STATES HISTORY **EDUCATION** LaVerne Col, AB, 40; Univ Southern Calif, AM, 50, PhD(hist), 66. **CAREER** Cur hist, Calif State Park Syst, 48-58; asst prof, Univ Pac, 58-66; assoc prof, 67-71, chmn dept, 71-74, chmn, Div Soc Sci, 77-80, prof hist, 71- , prof emeritus, Sonoma State Univ. **MEMBERSHIPS** AHA; Orgn Am Historians; Pac Hist Asn. **RESEARCH** United States foreign relations, midnineteenth century; cultural & intellectual history of American far West, 19th century; restoration of historic structures. **SELECTED PUBLICATIONS** Auth, Restoration of historic structures, Proc Conf Calif Hist Soc, 57; ed, From Hannibal to the gold fields in 1849, 11/60, 2-5/61 & auth, A golden age in Western history, 8/64, Pac Hist; Origins of the War with Mexico: The Polk-Stockton Intrigue, Univ Tex, 67. **CONTACT ADDRESS** 1320 Darby Rd, Sebastopol, CA, 95472.

PRICE, RICHARD
PERSONAL Born 11/11/1944, Ashford, England, d, 1 child **DISCIPLINE** HISTORY **EDUCATION** Univ Sussex, BA, 65; Univ Sussex, PhD, 68 **CAREER** Asst Prof, N Illinois Univ, 68-82; Prof, Maryland Col Park, 82-; Chair, Dept Hist, Univ Maryland, 86-92 **HONORS AND AWARDS** AELS Fel, 74 **RESEARCH** Modern British history **SELECTED PUBLICATIONS** co-ed, History of Labour Law in Comparative Perspective, Lang, 99; Dynamism Bounded: Containment and Change in Britain 1680-1880, 99; "Postmodernism and History," Language and Labour, Ashgate, 97; "Languages of Revisionism," Jour Soc Hist, 96 **CONTACT ADDRESS** Dept Hist, Univ Maryland, College Park, MD, 20742.

PRICE, ROBERT GEORGE
PERSONAL Born 06/01/1934, New York, NY, m, 1955, 2 children **DISCIPLINE** HISTORY OF LOGIC, ETHICS **EDUCATION** Yale Univ, BA, 55, MA, 57, PhD(philos), 63. **CAREER** From instr to asst prof, 59-66, Assoc Prof Philos, PA State Univ, University Park, 66- **MEMBERSHIPS** Am Philos Asn; Asn Symbolic Logic; Mind Asn. **RESEARCH** History of logic; moral and political philosophy; Greek philosophy. **SELECTED PUBLICATIONS** Auth, Some Antistrophes To The Rhetoric, Philos & Rhet, 68; Ockham And Supposito Personalis, Franciscan Studies, 71; A Refutative Demonstration In Metaphysics Gamma, Philos And Rhetoric, Vol 29, 96. **CONTACT ADDRESS** Dept Philos, Pennsylvania State Univ, 240 Sparks Bldg, University Park, PA, 16802-5201.

PRIMACK, MAXWELL
PERSONAL Born 06/04/1934, Brooklyn, NY, m, 1955, 4 children **DISCIPLINE** PHILOSOPHY; INTELLECTUAL HISTORY **EDUCATION** Brandeis Univ, BA, 56; John Hopkins Univ, PhD, 62. **CAREER** Erie Community Col, 26 years; Univ Buffalo (SUNYAB); Lincoln Univ in Pennsylvania; Illinois Inst Tech; Bloomsburg State College. **HONORS AND AWARDS** Cume Laude; Phi Betta Kappa **MEMBERSHIPS** Amer Phil Assoc. **RESEARCH** Marx; Lenin; The Bible **SELECTED PUBLICATIONS** Auth, A Reinterpretation of Francis Bacon's Philosophy, 68; The Last American Frontier: Education, 72. **CONTACT ADDRESS** 20 Marjann Ter., Buffalo, NY, 14223. **EMAIL** mprinted@aol.com

PRIMM, JAMES NEAL
PERSONAL Born 02/05/1918, Edina, MO, m, 1946 **DISCIPLINE** HISTORY **EDUCATION** Northeast Mo State Teachers Col, BS, 41; Univ Mo, MA, 49, PhD(hist), 51. **CAREER** From asst dir to dir, Western Hist Manuscripts Collection, Univ Mo, 51-58, from asst prof to assoc prof hist, 54-58; dean, Hiram Col 58-64, pres, 64-65; chmn dept, 65-70, prof hist, Univ Mo St Louis, 65-. **HONORS AND AWARDS** Thomas Jefferson Award, Univ Mo, 76. **MEMBERSHIPS** Econ Hist Asn; Orgn Am Historians; Southern Hist Asn. **RESEARCH** State economic policy; history of St Louis. **SELECTED PUBLICATIONS** Auth, The GAR in Missouri, 1866-1870, J Southern Hist; Economic Policy in the Development of a Western State--Missouri, 1820-1860, Harvard Univ, 54; The Haywood Case, Chandler Publ, 63; The American Experience, Forum, 72; Lion of the Valley: St Louis, 1764-1980, Pruett Publ, 81, 2nd ed, 91, 3rd ed, 98; A Foregone Conclusion: Founding of the Federal Reserve Bank of St. Louis, published by the Federal Reserve Bank, 91. **CONTACT ADDRESS** Dept of Hist, Univ of Mo, 8001 Natural Bridge, Saint Louis, MO, 63121-4499.

PRINCE, CARL E.
PERSONAL Born 12/08/1934, Newark, NJ, m, 1959, 2 children **DISCIPLINE** AMERICAN HISTORY **EDUCATION** Rutgers Univ, BA, 56, MA, 58, PhD(hist), 63. **CAREER** Instr hist, Fairleigh Dickinson Univ, 60-63; from asst prof to assoc prof, Seton Hall Univ, 63-68; assoc prof, 68-74, acting chmn dept, 76-77, PROF HIST, NY UNIV, 74-, CHMN DEPT, 78-, Nat Endowment for Humanities younger scholar fel, 68-69; Fulbright Scholar, Hebrew Univ, Jerusalem & Haifa Univ, 72-73. **HONORS AND AWARDS** Pres, SHEAR, 84-85. **MEMBERSHIPS** AHA; Orgn Am Historians; Inst Early Am Hist & Cult, SHEAR. **RESEARCH** Early American political behavior; early national American history, sports history. **SELECTED PUBLICATIONS** Auth, New Jersey's Jeffersonian Republicans, Inst Early Am Hist & Cult, Univ NC, 67; auth, Federalists and the Origins of the U.S. Civil Service, NY Univ, 78; ed, Papers of William Livingston, 5 vols, 79-88; auth, The U.S. Customs Service: A Bicentennial History, 89; auth, Brooklyn's Dodgers, 96,97. **CONTACT ADDRESS** Dept of Hist, New York Univ, 53 Washington Sq S, New York, NY, 10012. **EMAIL** cp2@is7.nyu.edu

PRINCE, SUSAN H.
DISCIPLINE ANCIENT GREEK **EDUCATION** Yale Univ, BA, 86; Oxford Univ, BA, 89; Univ MI, PhD, 97. **CAREER** Author **HONORS AND AWARDS** Distinguished Dissetation Award, 97, Univ MI. **MEMBERSHIPS** APA; Classical Assn of the Middle West and South; Soc for Ancient Greek Philosophy; Phi Beta Kappa. **RESEARCH** Greek prose; Greek philosophy; Mythology. **CONTACT ADDRESS** Dept of Classics, Boulder, CO, 80309-0348. **EMAIL** princes@stripe.colorado.edu

PRINDLE, DAVID F.
PERSONAL Born 04/10/1948, Los Angeles, CA, m, 1983, 1 child **DISCIPLINE** POLITICAL SCIENCE **EDUCATION** Univ CA, Santa Cruz, BA 70; UCLA, MA 72; MIT, PhD 77. **CAREER** Univ TX, 76. **HONORS AND AWARDS** V O Key Jr Awd for best bk on south, 82. **MEMBERSHIPS** APSA **RESEARCH** Am politics. **SELECTED PUBLICATIONS** Petroleum Politics and the Texas Railroad Commission, 81; The Politics of Glamour: Ideology and Democracy in the Screen Actors Guild, 88; Risky Business: The Political Economy of Hollywood, 93. **CONTACT ADDRESS** Dept of Govt, Univ of Texas, Austin, TX, 78712.

PRISCO, SALVATORE
PERSONAL Born 10/01/1943, Jersey City, NJ, m, 1976, 1 child **DISCIPLINE** HISTORY **EDUCATION** St Peter's Col, BSc, 64; Rutgers Univ, MA, 65, PhD, 69. **CAREER** Univ Alabama, assoc prof, hist, 69-74; Stevens Inst techno, prof hist, 75-, hd humani, 93-96. **HONORS AND AWARDS** Woodrow Wilson fel, 88-89; Freedoms Found fel, 84; NEH, 79; Windham Found Gnt, 72-73. **MEMBERSHIPS** Soc Stud Internationalism; Org Am Hist. **RESEARCH** Us diplom hist; econo hist; psychohistory intl pol. **SELECTED PUBLICATIONS** The Essentials of United States History, 1877-1912, Industrialism, Foreign Expansion and the Progressive Era, res and edu asn, 90; An Introduction to Psychohistory: Theories and case Studies, Univ Press of Am, 80; John Barrett, Progressive Era Diplomat, Univ Alabam Press, 73; many articles. **CONTACT ADDRESS** Stevens Institute Technology, Dept Humanities and Social Sciences, Hoboken, NJ, 07030. **EMAIL** SPRISCO@attila.stevens-tech.edu

PROCHASKA, DAVID
DISCIPLINE HISTORY **EDUCATION** Univ Calif Berkeley, PhD, 81. **CAREER** Assoc prof, Univ Ill Urbana Champaign. **RESEARCH** Comparative colonial history; postcolonial studies. **SELECTED PUBLICATIONS** Auth, Making Algeria French: Colonialism in Bone, 1870-1920, Cambridge, 90; Art of Colonialism, Colonialism of Art: the Description de l'Egypte (1809-1828), 94; History as Literature, Literature as History: Cagayous of Algiers, Am Hist Rev, 96. **CONTACT ADDRESS** History Dept, Univ Ill Urbana Champaign, 52 E Gregory Dr, Champaign, IL, 61820. **EMAIL** dprochas@uiuc.edu

PROCKO, BOHDAN P
PERSONAL Born 07/18/1922, Poland, m, 1954, 5 children **DISCIPLINE** RUSSIAN HISTORY **EDUCATION** Albright Col, BS, 45; Columbia Univ, MA, 46; Univ Ottawa, PhD(hist), 64. **CAREER** From instr to assoc prof, 49-69, PROF HIST, VILLANOVAUNIV, 69- **MEMBERSHIPS** AHA; Am Asn Advan Slavic Studies. **RESEARCH** East European nationalism; Byzantine rite churches. **SELECTED PUBLICATIONS** Auth, American Ukrainian Catholic Church: Humanitarian And Patriotic Activities, World War I, Summer 67 & Ukraine, 1967: A Historian's Personal Impressions, Fall 68, Ukrainian Quart; Soter Ortynsky: First Ruthenian Bishop In The United States, 1907-1916, Cath Hist Rev, 1/73; Contribr, Chap, In: The Ethnic Experience In Pennsylvania, Bucknell Univ, 73; Auth, The Establishment Of The Ruthenian Church In The United States, 1884-1907, Pa Hist, 4/75; Chap, In: The Ukrainian Experience In The United States, Harvard Ukrainian Res Inst, 79; Auth, Ukrainian Catholics In America: A History, Univ Press Of Am, 82; Wedded To The Cause--Ukrainian-Canadian Women And Ethnic-Identity 1891-1991, American Hist Rev, Vol 99, 94. **CONTACT ADDRESS** Dept of Hist, Villanova Univ, Villanova, PA, 19085.

PROCTER, BEN
PERSONAL Born 02/21/1927, Temple, Tex, m, 1951, 1 child **DISCIPLINE** AMERICAN HISTORY **EDUCATION** Univ Tex, BA, 51, MA, 52; Harvard Univ, PhD, 61. **CAREER** From instr to assoc prof, 57-68, Piper prof, 73, PROF HIST, TEX CHRISTIAN UNIV, 68-, Consult, St Marks Sch, Dallas, 62. **HONORS AND AWARDS** Summerfield G. Roberts Awd; Minnie Piper Fel; Sons of the Rep of TX; Longhorn Hall of Fame, Univ of TX; Phi Alpha Theta. **MEMBERSHIPS** Phi Beta Kappa; Phi Alpha Theta; W Hist Asn; SW Social Sci Assn; Am Hist Assn; Am Assn of Univ Profs; S Hist Assn; TX St Hist Assn **RESEARCH** American history from 1877-1941; the American frontier; Texas history, 1835 to the present. **SELECTED PUBLICATIONS** Auth, Not Without Honor: The Life of John H Reagan, Univ Tex, 62; The modern day Texas Rangers, In: Reflections by Western Historians, Univ Ariz, 69 & In: The Mexican-Americans: An Awakening Minority, Glencoe, 69; Ben McCulloch, In: Rangers of Texas, 69 & Washington-on-the Brazos, In: Capitols of Texas, 70, Texian; coauth,

The Land and its People, Hendrick-Long, 71; Texas Under a Cloud, Pemberton, 72; coauth, The Texas Heritage, Forum, 80; coauth, Texas Under a Cloud, Pemberton, 72; auth, Battle of the Alamo, Texas State Hist Asn, 86; auth, Just One Riot: Episodes of 20th Century Texas Rangers, Eakin, 91; ed, A Texas Ranger, R.R. Donnelley & Sons, 92; auth, The Texas Gubernatorial Election of 1990: Claytie vs. the Lady, Essays by Western Historians on the Twentieth Century West, Univ of Okla, 94; coauth, The Texas Heritage, Harlan Davidson, 97; auth, William Randolph Hearst: The Early Years 1863-1910, Oxford Univ, 98. **CONTACT ADDRESS** Dept of Hist, Tex Christian Univ, Fort Worth, TX, 76129-0002.

PROMEY, SALLY M.
DISCIPLINE AMERICAN ART **EDUCATION** Univ Chicago, PhD. **CAREER** Prof, Univ MD. **HONORS AND AWARDS** Charles C Eldredge prize, Nat Mus Amer Art, 93; Ailsa Mellon Bruce sr fel, Ctr for Advan Stud Visual Arts; fel, NEH; summer res fel(s), NEH., Adv Comm, Archiv Am Art; ed bd, Am Art. **RESEARCH** Relationships between visual cult and relig experience. **SELECTED PUBLICATIONS** Auth, Spiritual Spectacles: Vision and Image in Mid-Nineteenth-Century Shakerism, Ind, 93; publ(s), articles in Art Bulletin, Am Art, and Am Art Jour. **CONTACT ADDRESS** Dept Of Art and Archeol, Univ MD, 4229 Art-Sociology Building, College Park, MD, 20742-1335. **EMAIL** sp80@umail.umd.edu

PROROK, CAROLYN
PERSONAL Born 02/17/1956, Pittsburgh, PA **DISCIPLINE** GEOGRAPHY **EDUCATION** Louisiana State Univ, PhD 88; Univ Pittsburgh, MA 82; Slippery Rock Univ, BS 78. **CAREER** Slippery Rock Univ, asst, assoc, prof 97-; Louisiana State Univ, grad asst, inst 82-87; Moniteau School PA, teacher 78-82. **HONORS AND AWARDS** 2 NEH; Acad Adv Awd. **MEMBERSHIPS** NCGE; PGS; CLAG; CSA; NAG; AAG; AGS; SWG; Sigma Xi SRS; AAA; AAR; PHLF; RAS; AJG. **RESEARCH** Geography of Religions **SELECTED PUBLICATIONS** Auth, Asian Women and Their Work: A Geography of Gender and Development, coed, Path in Geog Ser, Ntl Coun Geo EDU , 98; The Significance of Material Culture in Historical Geography: A Case Study of the Church as School in the Diffusion of the Presbyterian Mission to Trinidad, Hist Reflec/Reflex Hist, 97; Women at Work, Soc EDU , with Barbara Cruz, 97; forthcoming, The Hindu Temple Gods of Trinidad, Penn Geog, 97; The Materiality of Identity, Intl Jour of Hin Stud; Boundaries are Made for Crossing, Gen, Place Cult; Dancing in the Fire, Jour of Cult Geog. **CONTACT ADDRESS** Dept of Geography and Environmental Studies, Slippery Rock Univ, PO Box 111, Slippery Rock, PA, 16057-2188. **EMAIL** carolyn.prorok@sru.edu

PROSSER, PETER E.
PERSONAL Born 12/16/1946, Birmingham, England, m, 1970, 2 children **DISCIPLINE** CHURCH HISTORY **EDUCATION** Univ Montreal, MDiv, 75, MA, 78, PhD, 89. **CAREER** Lectr, Inst Biblione Beree, Montreal, 72-75; fel, Univ Montreal, 82-83; asst prof, Church Hist, Regent Univ, 83-90; prof, 98- . **HONORS AND AWARDS** Who's Who in Am, 79, 84, 90-92, 98; Int Men of Distinction, 79. **MEMBERSHIPS** AAR/SBL; SPS; ETS. **RESEARCH** Millennialism; Reformation; apocalypticism; Methodist history. **SELECTED PUBLICATIONS** Auth, Prophecy: A Vital Gift to the Church, Including Yours, Acts 29 Mag, 92; Spirit-Filled Life Bible, Sections on 1 and 2 John, Thomas Nelson publ. **CONTACT ADDRESS** School of Divinity, Regent Univ, 1000 Regent Dr, Virginia Beach, VA, 23464-9800. **EMAIL** petepro@regent.edu

PROWE, DIETHELM MANFRED-HARTMUT
PERSONAL Born 01/04/1941, Bonn, Germany, m, 1968, 2 children **DISCIPLINE** MODERN & GERMAN HISTORY **EDUCATION** Kent State Univ, BA, 62; Stanford Univ, MA, 63, PhD(hist) 67. **CAREER** From instr to assoc prof, 66-78, prof hist, Carleton Col, 78-, Humboldt Found res fel, 75-76 & 79-80. **MEMBERSHIPS** AHA; Conf Group Cent Europ Hist; Ger Studies Asn. **RESEARCH** Germany; topics in foreign policy; post-World War II Germany. **SELECTED PUBLICATIONS** Auth, Berlin--Weltstadt in Krisen, 1949-1958, Gruyter, 73; Die Anf¤nge der Brandtschen Ostpolitik in Berlin 1961-1963, Schriftenreihe der Vierteljahrshefte fur Zeitgeschichte, 76; The new Nachkriegsgeschichte, 1945-49: West Germans in search of their historical origins, Cent Europ Hist, 12/77; Wirtschaftsdemokratische Ans¤tze 1945-49, WSI-Mitteilungen, 7/81; The Evolution and New Research Agenda of Postwar German History: A Historian's View, Working Papers of theVolkswagen-Foundation Seminars in Post-War German History, Working Paper 1, Washington, DC: American Institute for Contemporary German Studies and German Historical Institute, 95; The Making of ein Berliner, Kennedy, Brandt, and the Origins of Detente Policy in Germany, David Wetzel, ed, From the Berlin Museum to the Berlin Wall: essays on the Cultural and Political History of Modern Germany, Festschrift for Gordon A. Craig, Vol 1, New York, Praeger, 96; Ordnungsmacht and Mitbestimmung: The Postwar Labor Unions and the Politics of Reconstruction, David E. Barclay and Eric D Weitz, eds, Between Reform and Revolution: German Socialism and Communicsm from 1840 to 1990, Providence, RI and Oxford, Berghahn Publishers, 98. **CONTACT ADDRESS** Dept of History, Carleton Col, 1 N College St, Northfield, MN, 55057-4044. **EMAIL** dprowe@Carleton.edu

PROWN, JULES D.
PERSONAL Born 03/14/1930, Freehold, NJ, m, 1956, 5 children **DISCIPLINE** HISTORY OF ART **EDUCATION** Lafayette Col, AB, 51; Harvard Univ, AM, 53, PhD(fine arts), 61; Univ Del, AM, 56. **CAREER** Asst to dir, Fogg Art Mus, Harvard Univ, 59-61; from instr to assoc prof, 61-71, cur designate, Garvan Collection Am Art, 63-64, cur, 64-68, dir, Yale Ctr Brit Art & Brit Studies, 68-76, prof hist of art, 71, Paul Mellon prof hist of art, Yale Univ, 86; Guggenheim fel, 64-65; vis lectr, Smith Col, 66-67; mem adv comt, Fulbright Scholars 67-68; mem adv comn, Nat Portrait Gallery, DC, 69-76; mem bd gov, Yale Univ Press, 69-76; chief exec off, Paul Mellon Ctr Studies in Brit Art, London, 70-76; mem adv comt, Yale Ed of Horace Walpole's Corresp, 71-76; mem adv coun, Inst Early Am Hist & Cult, Va, 72-75; Benjamin Franklin fel, Royal Soc Arts, 72-; mem bd trustees, Whitney Mus Art, 75-94; mem exec bd, Nat Humanities Inst, New Haven, Ct, 75-78; mem coun, Am Antiquarian Soc, 77-94, mem adv comt, Am Art Journ, 77-. **HONORS AND AWARDS** Robert C. Smith Award, 83; Distinguished Teaching of Art Hist Award, Col Art Asn Am, 95; Fel, Whitney Humanities Center, Yale Univ, 92-94; George Washington Kidd, Class of 1836, Award, Lafayette Col Alumni Asn, 86., AM, Yale Univ, 71; DFA, Lafayette Col, 79. **MEMBERSHIPS** Col Art Asn Am; Am Studies Asn; Conf Brit Studies; Am Asn Mus; Am Soc 18th Century Studies. **RESEARCH** American and British painting. **SELECTED PUBLICATIONS** Auth, Text for John Singleton Copley Catalogue, October House, 65; John Singleton Copley, (2 vols), Harvard Univ, 66; co-auth, The Visual Arts in Higher Education, Yale Univ, 66; auth, American Painting from Its Beginnings to the Armory Show, Skira, 69; The Truth of Material Culture: History of Fiction?, History from Things: Essays on material Culture, Smithsonian Inst Press, 93; Benjamin West and The Use of Antiquity, Am Art Vol 10, no.2, 96; A Course of Antiquities at Rome 1764, Reading Am Art, Yale Univer Press, 98; contribur, Thomas Eakins Winslow Homer, Encycl Britannica; auth, The Architecture of the Yale Center for British Art, New Haven, Conn, 77; Style as Evidence, 80 & Mind in Matter, 82, Winterthur Portfolio. **CONTACT ADDRESS** Dept of Hist Art, PO Box 208272, New Haven, CT, 06520-8272. **EMAIL** jules.prown@yale.edu

PRUCHA, FRANCIS PAUL
PERSONAL Born 01/04/1921, River Falls, WI **DISCIPLINE** AMERICAN HISTORY **EDUCATION** Wis State Col, River Falls, BS, 41; Univ Minn, MA, 47; Harvard Univ, PhD(hist), 50. **CAREER** From asst prof to assoc prof, 60-66, chmn dept hist, 62-69, PROF AM HIST, MARQUETTE UNIV, 66-, Soc Sci Res Coun fac res grant, 59; Guggenheim fel, 67-68; sr fel, Nat Endowment for Humanities, 70-71 & 81-82. **MEMBERSHIPS** AHA; Orgn Am Historians; Western Hist Asn. **RESEARCH** Western military frontier; federal Indian policy. **SELECTED PUBLICATIONS** Auth, Broadax And Bayonet, Wis State Hist Soc, 53; American Indian Policy In The Formative Years, Harvard Univ, 62; The Sword Of The Republic, Macmillan, 69; Indian Peace Medals In American History, Wis State Hist Soc, 71; Ed, Americanizing The American Indians, Harvard Univ, 73; Auth, American Indian Policy In Crisis, Univ Okla, 76; A Bibliographical Guide To The History Of Indian-White Relations In The United States, Univ Chicago, 77; The Churches And The Indian Schools, Univ Nebr, 79; An Unspeakable Sadness--The Dispossession Of The Nebraska Indians, Great Plains Quart, Vol 15, 95; Indians And The Amn-West In The 20th-Century, Ethnohistory, Vol 43, 96; The Northern Cheyenne Indian Reservation, 1877-1900, Pacific Hist Rev, Vol 63, 94. **CONTACT ADDRESS** Dept of Hist, Marquette Univ, Milwaukee, WI, 53233.

PRUDE, JONATHAN
DISCIPLINE HISTORY **EDUCATION** Amherst, BA, 68; Harvard Univ, PhD, 76. **CAREER** Asst prof to ASSOC PROF, HIST, EMORY UNIV **HONORS AND AWARDS** E. Harold Hugo Prize **MEMBERSHIPS** Am Antiquarian Soc **SELECTED PUBLICATIONS** Auth, "The Social System of Early New England Textile Mills," in Working-Class America, 83; auth, The Coming of Industrial Order: Town and Factory Life in Rural Massachusetts, 1810-1860; auth, "Town-Factory Conflicts in Antebellum Rural Massachusetts," in The Countryside in the Age of Capitalist Transformation: Essays in the Social History of Rural America, 85; auth, "To Look Upon the Lower Sort: Runaway Ads and the Appearance of Unfree Laborers in America, 1750-1800," Jour of Am Hist, June 91; auth, "Capitalism, Industrialization, and the Factory in Post- Revolutionary America," in Jour of the Early Rep 16, 96, repr, in Wages of Independence: Capitalism in the Early American Republic, 97. **CONTACT ADDRESS** Dept of Hist, Emory Univ, Atlanta, GA, 30322. **EMAIL** histjp@emory.edu

PRUETT, GORDON EARL
PERSONAL Born 10/16/1941, Raton, NM, m, 1966, 1 child **DISCIPLINE** HISTORY OF RELIGION **EDUCATION** Yale Univ, BA, 63; Oxford Univ, BA & MA, 65; Princeton Univ, PhD, 68. **CAREER** Asst prof relig, Lehigh Univ, 68-69; asst prof, 69-74; acting chmn dept eng, 76-80; assoc prof philos & relig, Northeastern Univ, 74- . **RESEARCH** History of Christianity; Sociology of religion; Mysticism and psychoanalysis. **SELECTED PUBLICATIONS** Auth, A note on Robert Bellah's theory of religious evolution: The early modern period, Sociol Analysis, 73; History, transcendence, and world community in the work of Wilfred Cantwell Smith, Jour Am Acad Relig, 73; Christianity, history and culture in Nagaland, Contribs to Indian Sociol, 74; A Protestant doctrine of the Eucharistic presence, Calvin Theol Jour, 75; Thomas Cranmer's progress in the doctrine of the Eucharist, 1535-1548, Hist Mag Protestant Episcopal Church, 76; Will and freedom: Psychoanalytic themes in the work of Jacob Boehme, Studies Relig & Sci Relig, 77; Religion in higher education, Int Encycl Higher Educ, 78; The escape from the Seraglio: Anti-orientalist trends in modern religious studies, Arab Studies Quart, 80; Preparatio Evangelii: Religious Studies and Secondary Education, Nat Asn of Episcopal Schools Jour 1:1, 84; Islam and Orientalism, Orientalism, Islamists and Islam, ed Asaf Hussain, Robert Olson, and Jamil Qureshi, Amana, 84; Through a Glass Darkly: Knowledge of the Self in Dreams in Ibn Khaldun's Mugaddima, The Muslim World LXXV:1, 85; The Meaning and End of Suffering for Freud and the Buddhist Tradition, 87; World Theology and World Community: The Vision of Wilfred Cantwell Smith, Studies in Religion 19:4, 1990; Theravadin Buddhist Commentary on the Current State of Western Epistemology, Buddhist-Christian Studies 10, 1990; As a Father Loves His Children: The Image of the Supreme Being as Loving Father in Judaism, Christianity and Islam, 94. **CONTACT ADDRESS** Dept of Philosophy and Religion, Northeastern Univ, 360 Huntington Ave, Boston, MA, 02115-5000.

PRUETT, JOHN H.
DISCIPLINE HISTORY **EDUCATION** Princeton Univ, PhD, 78. **CAREER** Assoc prof, Univ Ill Urbana Champaign. **RESEARCH** Colonial and revolutionary America. **SELECTED PUBLICATIONS** Auth, Career Patterns among the Clergy of Lincoln Cathedral, 1660-1750, Church Hist, 75; The Parish Clergy under the Later Stuarts, Univ Ill, 78; A Late Stuart Leicestershire Parson (rev), J Relig Hist, 79. **CONTACT ADDRESS** History Dept, Univ Ill Urbana Champaign, 52 E Gregory Dr, Champaign, IL, 61820. **EMAIL** j-pruett@uiuc.edu

PRUITT, ANNE SMITH
PERSONAL Bainbridge, GA, m **DISCIPLINE** EDUCATION **EDUCATION** Howard Univ, BS (cum laude), 1949; Teachers Coll Columbia Univ, MA 1950, EdD 1964. **CAREER** Howard Univ, counselor 1950-52; Hutto HS, dir of guidance 1952-55; Albany State Coll, dean of students 1955-59; Fisk Univ, dean of students 1959-61; Case Western Reserve Univ, prof of educ 1963-79; OH State Univ, assoc dean grad school 1979-84, assoc provost 1984-86, dir Center for Teaching Excellence 1986-94, prof of Educ Policy and Leadership 1979-95; COUNCIL OF GRADUATE SCHOOLS, dean in residence, 1994-96, SCHOLAR IN RESIDENCE, 1996-. **HONORS AND AWARDS** Outstanding Alumnus Howard Univ 1975; Amer Council on Educ Fellow 1977-78; honorary degree DHum Central State Univ 1982; Named one of America's Top 100 Black Business & Professional Women, Dollars & Sense Magazine 1986; Ohio State Univ Distinguished Affirmative Action Award 1988; Amer Coll Personnel Assn Senior Scholar Award 1989, Dipolmate, 1996; Phi Beta Delta Honor Soc for Intl Scholars 1989. **MEMBERSHIPS** Mem Alpha Kappa Alpha Sor; mem Links Inc; consultant Women's Job Corps creation Pres Lyndon Johnson's War on Poverty 1964; mem bd of trustees Cleveland Urban League 1965-71; consultant Southern Regional Educ Bd 1968-81; mem Bd of Trustees Central State Univ 1973-82; moderator Mt Zion Congregational Church 1975-78; Research Task Force Southern Educ Found 1978-87; mem Adv Comm US Coast Guard Acad 1980-83; Amer Assn for Counseling and Devel; sec, Journal bd mem, pres-elect, pres 1976-77, 1st Black Amer Coll Personnel Assn; Amer Educ Research Assn; Amer Assn for Higher Educ; Amer Assn of Univ Professors; mem Columbus, OH, Mayor's Task Force on Private Sector Initiatives 1986-88, bd of trustees, Case Western Reserve Univ 1987-; member, board of directors, Columbus Area Leadership Program, 1988-92; member, Columbus 1992 Education Committee, 1988-92; co-chairperson, Ohio State Univ United Way Campaign, 1990-91; member, National Science Foundation, Committee on Equal Opportunities in Science and Engineering, 1989-95; coordinator, CIC Alliance for Success Planning Committee, 1989-90; Black Women's Agenda, pres, 1998-. **CONTACT ADDRESS** Scholar in Res, Council of Graduate Schools, One Dupont Circle NW, Ste 430, Washington, DC, 20036-1173.

PSATHAS, GEORGE
PERSONAL Born 02/22/1929, New Haven, CT, m, 1951, 3 children **DISCIPLINE** SOCIOLOGY **EDUCATION** Yale Univ, BA, 1950; Univ Michigan, MA, 51; Yale Univ, PhD, 56; New England School Photography, MA 78-79 **CAREER** Emeritus prof, Boston Univ, 97-; editor-in-chief, Human Studies, 78-; guest prof, Institute Human Sciences, Vienna, April 96; visiting prof, Manchester Univ, March 96; prof Sociology, Boston Univ, 68- **HONORS AND AWARDS** Postdoctoral fel, National Inst Mental Health, 61-62; Science Faculty Prof Develop Award, National Sci Found 78-79; Fulbright Grant, 82; British Academy for Res in Gt Brit, 95-96 **MEMBERSHIPS** Amer Sociol Assoc; Eastern Sociol Soc; Amer Assoc Univ Professors; Int Visual Sociol Assoc; Soc Phenomenol Existential Philos; Soc Phenomenol Human Sci **RESEARCH** Social Interaction; Phenomenological Sociology; Qualitative Methods; Ethnomethodology; Visual Sociology

SELECTED PUBLICATIONS "On Zaner's Methods for Becoming an Ethicist," Human Studies, 98; On multiple realities and the world of film," Sociol Aspect Lit, 97; "Phenomenology in Sociology in the United States," Encycl Phenomenol, 97; co-ed, Alfred Schultz Collected Papers, Kluwer, 96; ed, "Ethnomethodology: Discussions and Contributions," Human Studies, 95 **CONTACT ADDRESS** Dept Sociol, Boston Univ, 100 Cummington St., Boston, MA, 02215. **EMAIL** Geops1@acs.bu.edu

PUCCI, PIETRO

PERSONAL Born 11/27/1927, Modena, Italy **DISCIPLINE** CLASSICS **EDUCATION** Liceo Muratori, BA (Classics), 45; Univ Pisa, PhD (Classics), 49; Univ Florence, Libera Docenza (Classics), 60. **CAREER** Asst prof, Classics, Univ Florence, 51-52; asst prof, Classics, Univ Ottawa; asst prof, Classics, Univ KS, 61-62; vis prof, Classics, Santa Cruz Univ, 69; vis prof, Classics, Univ Florence, 70; Directeur d'Etudes, Ecole des Hautes Etudes Paris, 84, 89; asst prof, 62-67, assoc prof, 67-72, prof, dept of Classics, 72-91, chmn, 83-87, 90-91, 92-93, Golwin Smith prof of Classics, Cornell Univ, 91-. **HONORS AND AWARDS** Fel of the French govt, 55-57; fel of the German govt, 57-58; Jr fel at the Center for Hellenic Studies, Washington, 70; fel of the ACLS, 72; fel of the Guggenheim Memorial Found, 80-81; fel of the NEH, 89; resident of the Am Academy in Rome, 96. **SELECTED PUBLICATIONS** Auth, Oedipus and the Fabrication of the Father, Johns Hopkins Univ Press, 92; Human Sacrifice in the Oresteia, in Innovations in Antiquity, Ralph Hexter and Daniel Seldon, eds, Routledge, 92; Io e l'altro nel racconto di Odisseo sui Ciclopi, SIFC XI, 93; Antiphonal Lament between Achilles and Briseis in Colby Quart, XXXIX, 93; God's Intervention and Epiphany in Sophocles, AJP 115, 94; Persuasione nell' Orestea di Eschilo, Museum Criticum, XXXIX, 94; Ulysse Polytropos, French trans of Odysseus Polytropos, Septentrion, Presses Univ, Lille, 95; Enigma Segreto Oracolo, Instituto Editoriale: Roma, 96; L'Apologie d'Appollon, METIS, 96; Auteur et Destinataires dans le Travaux d'Hesiode, in Le Metier du Mythe, Lectures d'Hesiode, Septentrion, Presses Univ, Lille, 96; The Song of the Sirens and Other Essays, a book of old and new Homeric essays, Rowman & Littlefield, 97; numerous other publications. **CONTACT ADDRESS** Dept of Classics, Cornell Univ, 125 Goldwin Smith Hall, Ithaca, NY, 14853.

PUGACH, NOEL H.

PERSONAL Born 04/13/1939, Brooklyn, NY, m, 1955, 2 children **DISCIPLINE** HISTORY **EDUCATION** Brooklyn Col, BA, 60; Univ of Wis, MA, 62, PhD, 67. **CAREER** Instr, Kent State Univ, 65-68; ASST PROF TO PROF, UNIV OF NMEX, 68-. **HONORS AND AWARDS** Phi Alpha Theta; Wis State Hist Awd of Merit, 80. **MEMBERSHIPS** Am Hist Asn; Org of Am Hist; Soc for Hist of Am Foreign Relations. **RESEARCH** U.S.-East Asian relations in the 20th Century. **SELECTED PUBLICATIONS** Auth, Same Bed, Different Dreams: A History of the Chinese American Bank of Commerce, Univ of Hong Kong, 97; Paul S. Reinsch: Open Door Diplomat in action, KTO Press, 79; The Sinicization of the Chinese American Bank of Commerce: Causes and Consequences, Sino-Am Relations Since 1900, Centre of Asian Studies, Univ of Hong Kong, 91; Second Career: James A. Thomas and the Chinese American Bank of Commerce, Pacific Hist Rev, 87. **CONTACT ADDRESS** Dept of Hist, Univ of New Mexico, Albuquerque, NM, 87131-1181. **EMAIL** npugach@unm.edu

PUGLISI, CATHERINE

DISCIPLINE ART HISTORY **EDUCATION** NY Univ, PhD. **CAREER** Assoc prof, grad dir, Rutgers Univ. **RESEARCH** Baroque art; Bolognese painting; painting and sculpture in 17th-century Rome; 18th-century Venice. **SELECTED PUBLICATIONS** Auth, Francesco Albani, Yale UP, 97; Guido Reni's "Pallione del Voto" and the Plague of 1630, Art Bulletin, 95. **CONTACT ADDRESS** Dept of Art Hist, Rutgers Univ/Rutgers Col, Hamilton St., New Brunswick, NJ, 08903.

PULHAM, CAROL ANN

DISCIPLINE MEDIEVAL PERIOD **EDUCATION** Cedar Crest Col, BA, Lehigh Univ, MA, PhD. **CAREER** English Lit, Cedar Crest Col. **SELECTED PUBLICATIONS** Auth, Promises, Promises: Dorigen's Dilemma Revisited, Chaucer Rev. **CONTACT ADDRESS** Cedar Crest Col, 100 College Drive, Allentown, PA, 18104.

PULLEN, DANIEL J.

PERSONAL Born 05/19/1954, Pittsburg, KS **DISCIPLINE** CLASSICAL ARCHAEOLOGY; ANTHROPOLOGY **EDUCATION** Univ Kansas, BA, 76; Indiana Univ, MA, 78,PhD, 85. **CAREER** Administrator, Sardis Expedition, Harvard Univ Art Museums; asst prof, classics dept, 88-93, assoc prof, 93- , FL State Univ. **HONORS AND AWARDS** Univ Teaching Award, FL State Univ, 98. **MEMBERSHIPS** Archaeological Institute of Amer; Soc for Amer Archaeology; Amer Sch of Aegean Prehistory; Classical Archaeology; Complex Societies. **SELECTED PUBLICATIONS** Auth, Modelling Mortuary Behavior on a Regional Scale: A Case Study from Mainland Greece in the Early Bronze Age, Beyond The Site: Regional Studies in the Aegean Area, 94; auth, A lead seal from Tsoungiza Hill, Ancient Nemea, and Early Bronze Age Sealing Systems, American Journal of Archaeology, 94; auth, Artifact and Assemblage: The Finds from a Regional Survey of the Southern Argolid, Greece, vol I: The Prehistoric and Early Iron Age Pottery and the Lithic Artifacts, 95. **CONTACT ADDRESS** Dept of Classics, Florida State Univ, Tallahassee, FL, 32306-1510.

PURCELL, E.A.

PERSONAL Born 07/20/1941, Kansas City, MO, m, 1982, 2 children **DISCIPLINE** HISTORY **EDUCATION** Rockhurst Col, AB 62; Univ Kansas, MA 64; Univ Wisconsin, PhD 68; Harvard Law, JD 79. **CAREER** Univ Cal Berk, asst prof, 67-69; Univ Missouri Col, asst prof, assoc prof 69-77; New York Law Sch, prof law, 89-. **HONORS AND AWARDS** Louis Peltzer Awd; Frederick Jackson Turner Prize. **MEMBERSHIPS** OAH; ASLH; ABNY **RESEARCH** 19th, 20th Century Amer Social Intellectual and Legal Hist. **SELECTED PUBLICATIONS** Auth, The Crisis of Democratic Theory, 73; Litigation and Inequality, 92; Constitutional Visions and the Politics of the Federal Courts. **CONTACT ADDRESS** New York Law Sch, 57 Worth St, NYC, NY, 10013-2960.

PUREFOY MORRIS, SARAH

DISCIPLINE CLASSICAL ARCHAEOLOGY **EDUCATION** Univ N Carolina, BA, 76; Amer Sch Class Stud, Athens, Greece, 78-80; Harvard Univ, MA, MPhil, PhD, 81. **CAREER** Asst prof, 81-86; assoc prof, 89-93; PROF, UCLA, 93-, DEPT CH, 97-. **HONORS AND AWARDS** Eben Alexander Greek Translation prize, Univ NC, 76; Sinclair Kennedy Travelling fel, Harvard Univ, 78-79; Arthur W Parsons fel, Amer Sch Class Stud, Greece, 79; Charles Eliot Norton fel, Harvard Univ, 80; Olivia James fel, Archaeol Inst Am, 80; A Whitney Griswold fac res grant, Yale univ, 82, 84; res grant, Kress Found, 83; Susan Hilles Morse jr fac fel, Yale Univ, 84-85; res grant, Grant-in-Aid, Amer Coun Learned Soc, 88; James R Wiseman bk award, Archaeol Inst Amer, 93. **SELECTED PUBLICATIONS** Auth, The Black and White Style: Athens and Aigina in the Orientalizing Period, Yale Class Monogr 6, Yale Univ Press, 84; Daidalos and the Origins of Greek Art, Princeton Univ Press, 92, 95; The Ages of Homer, A Tribute to Emily Townsend Vermeule, Austin, 95, 97; "Greek and Near Eastern Art in the Age of Homer," New Light on a Dark Age, Exploring the Culture of Geometric Greece, Columbia, Mo, 97; "Homer and the Near East," A New Companion to Homer, Leiden: Brill, 97; co-ed, "Ancient Towers on Leukas, Greece," Structures Rurales et Societes Anciennes, Besancon, 94; "The Sacrifice of Astyanax: Near Eastern Contributions to the Trojan War," The Ages of Homer, Austin, Texas, 95; "The Legacy of Black Athena," Black Athena Revisited, Chapel Hill, NC, 96; rev(s), "From Modernism to Manure: Perspectives on Classical Archaeology," review of Classical Greece: Ancient Histories & Modern Archaeologies, Antiquity 69, 95; Ex Oriente Books: Near Eastern Resources for Classicists, AJA 101, 97. **CONTACT ADDRESS** Dept of Classics, Univ Calif, PO Box 951436, Los Angeles, CA, 90095-1436. **EMAIL** sarahm@humnet.ucla.edu

PURINTON, JEFFREY S.

PERSONAL Born 05/08/1960, Wilmington, DE **DISCIPLINE** CLASSICS **EDUCATION** Princeton Univ, PhD, 92. **CAREER** Vis asst prof philos, Univ Okla, 93- . **MEMBERSHIPS** APA. **RESEARCH** Epicureanism. **SELECTED PUBLICATIONS** Auth, Epicurus on the Telos, Phronesis, 93; auth, Magnifying Epicurean Minima, Ancient Philos, 94; auth, Aristotle's Definition of Happiness, Oxford Stud in Ancient Philos, 98. **CONTACT ADDRESS** Dept of Philosophy, Univ of Oklahoma, Dale Hall Tower 622, Norman, OK, 73019. **EMAIL** Jeffrey.S.Purinton_1@ou.edu

PURTLE, CAROL JEAN

DISCIPLINE ART HISTORY **EDUCATION** Maryville Col, St Louis, BA, 60; Manhattanville Col, NY, MA, 66; Washington Univ, PhD, 76. **CAREER** Advan res fel, Belgian-Am Educ Found, 74-75; Danforth assoc, 75-79; fac develop award, Memphis State Univ, 80, 85, 95; prof and coord art hist, Univ Memphis, 79-; **HONORS AND AWARDS** Alum Awd Prof Achievement 87; Nat Endowment for Hum Fel, 82, 88. **MEMBERSHIPS** Hist of Netherlandish Art; Col Art Asoc **SELECTED PUBLICATIONS** Auth, The Marian Paintings of Jan van Eyck, Princeton Univ Press, 82; auth, St. Luke Drawing the Virgin: Selected Essays in Context, Brepols, 97; auth, Narrative Time and Metaphoric Tradition in the Development of Jan van Eyck's Washington Annunciation, Art Bulletin, 99; auth, Le Sacerdoce de la Vierge et l'enigma d'un Parti leonographique Exceptionnel, Revue de Louvre, 96; The Iconography of Campin's Madonnes in Interiors: A Search for Common Ground, New Directory in Scholarship, National Gallery of Art, 171-182, 96; auth, The Iconography of Prayer, Jean de Berry and the Origin of the Annunciation in a Church, Simiolus, 227-239, 90. **CONTACT ADDRESS** Dept of Art, Univ of Memphis, 3706 Alumni St, Memphis, TN, 38152-0001. **EMAIL** cpurtle@cc.memphis.edu

PURVIS, THOMAS L.

DISCIPLINE HISTORY **EDUCATION** Wash Univ, AB, 71; Johns Hopkins Univ, MA, 77, PhD, 79. **CAREER** Asst prof, hist, Auburn at Montgomery; ASSOC ED, AMERICAN NATIONAL BIOGRAPHY. **MEMBERSHIPS** Am Antiquarian Soc **SELECTED PUBLICATIONS** Auth, Proprietors, Patronage and Paper Money: Legislative Politics in New Jersey, 1703-1776, 86; coauth, The Enduring Vision: A History of the American People, Heath, 90; Historical Almanac of Revolutionary America, 1763-1800, Facts on File, 95; Dictionary of American History, Basil Blackwell, 95; auth, Newport, Kentucky: A Bicentennial History, Zimmerman Printers, 96; Historical Almanacs of Colonial America, 1500-1763, Facts on File of New York, 98. **CONTACT ADDRESS** 328 E 9th St, Newport, KY, 41071-1980.

PUTNAM, JACKSON K.

PERSONAL Born 02/10/1929, Emmons Co, ND **DISCIPLINE** AMERICAN HISTORY **EDUCATION** Univ NDak, BS, 52, MA, 55; Stanford Univ, PhD(hist), 64. **CAREER** From instr to asst prof hist, Ore State Univ, 58-65; from asst prof to assoc prof, 65-73, PROF HIST, CALIF STATE UNIV, FULLERTON, 73- **HONORS AND AWARDS** Oscar O Winter Award, Western Hist Asn 77. **MEMBERSHIPS** AHA: Orgn Am Historians; Western Hist Asn; Western Lit Asn. **RESEARCH** Westward movement in United States history; California history. **SELECTED PUBLICATIONS** Auth, The Role Of The Socialist Party In North Dakota History, Ndak Quart, Fall 56; The Presistence Of Progressivism In The 1920's: The Case Of California, Pac Hist Rev, 11/66; Old Age Politics In California, From Richardson To Reagan, Stanford Univ, 70; Down To Earth: A B Guthrie's Quest For Moral And Historical Truth, Ndak Quart, Summer 71; The Turner Thesis And The Westward Movement: A Reappraisal, Western Hist Quart, 10/76; Historical Fact And Literary Truth: The Problem Of Authenticity In Western American Literature, Western Am Lit, 5/80; Modern California Politics, 1917-1980, Boyd & Fraser, 80; On Turners Trail--100 Years Of Writing Western History, Am Hist Rev, Vol 101, 96. **CONTACT ADDRESS** Dept of Hist, California State Univ, Fullerton, Fullerton, CA, 92634.

PUTNAM, MICHAEL C.J.

PERSONAL Born 09/20/1933, Springfield, MA **DISCIPLINE** CLASSICS **EDUCATION** Harvard Univ, AB, 54, MA, 56, PhD, 59 **CAREER** Instr, 59-60, Smith Col; instr to prof to MacMillan Prof, 60-, Brown Univ; act dir, 61-62, Harvard Univ; Townsend Prof, 85, Cornell Univ. **HONORS AND AWARDS** Rome Prize Fel, Amer Acad in Rome, 63-64; Guggenheim Mem Found Fel, 66-67; Nat Endowment for the Humanities, Sr Fel, 73-74; Amer Coun of Learned Soc Fel, 83-84; Inst for Adv Study; 87-88; Mellon Prof-in-Charge, 89-91., Charles J Goodwin Award of Merit, Amer Philol Assoc, 71. **MEMBERSHIPS** Amer Philol Assoc; Classical Assoc of New England; Medieval Acad of Amer. **RESEARCH** Latin poetry **SELECTED PUBLICATIONS** Ed with intro, Virgil: 2000 Years, Arethusa, 81; auth, Essays on Latin Lyric, Elegy, and Epic, Princeton Univ Press, 82; auth, Artifices of Eternity: Horace's Fourth Book of Odes, Cornell Univ Press, 86, 90; auth, Virgil's Aeneid: Interpretation and Influence, Univ NC Press, 95; auth, Virgil's Epic Designs: Ekphrasis in the Aeneid, Yale Univ Press, 98. **CONTACT ADDRESS** Dept of Classics, Brown Univ, Providence, RI, 02912-1856. **EMAIL** Michael_Putnam@brown.edu

PYNN, RONALD

PERSONAL Born 09/11/1942, Eau Claire, WI, m, 1961, 3 children **DISCIPLINE** POLITICAL SCIENCE **EDUCATION** Univ Mich. PhD, 70. **CAREER** Asst prof, Lake Super State Col, 70-71; PROF, UNIV N DAKOTA, 71-. **HONORS AND AWARDS** Univ Outstanding Tchg Award, 75; Michael Keedy Award, 94; Spirit of Sioux Award, 95. **MEMBERSHIPS** Am Polit Sci Asn; Midwst Polit Sci Asn; Text Acad Auth Asn. **RESEARCH** American government; Political theory. **SELECTED PUBLICATIONS** auth Watergate and the American Political Process, Praeger, 75; American Political Economy, Brooks/Cole, 88; American Politics: Changing Expectations, Simon & Schuster, 97. **CONTACT ADDRESS** Dept of Political Science, Univ N Dakota, Grand Forks, ND, 58201. **EMAIL** Pynn@badlands.nodak.edu

Q

QIAN, WEN-YUAN

PERSONAL Born 04/14/1936, Shanghai, China, d **DISCIPLINE** HISTORY **EDUCATION** Beijing Univ, BS, 59; Northwestern Univ, MA, 84; Univ Mich, PhD, 88. **CAREER** Asst prof, hist, Blackburn Col, 88-92; asst prof, hist, 92- 98, ASSOC PROF, MACMURRAY COL, 98-. **HONORS AND AWARDS** Dist Dept Hist Scholarship, Univ Mich, 84-87., NEH Inst, 92, 94. **RESEARCH** History sci, tech; Chinese hist; world hist. **SELECTED PUBLICATIONS** Auth, The Great Inertia: Scientific Stagnation in Traditional China, 85; "A Definition of Science as an Antidote Against Either Mystifying or Demystifying Science, Organon, 22/23: 86, 87. **CONTACT ADDRESS** Dept of History, MacMurray Col, 447 E. College, Jacksonville, FL, 62650.

QUANDT, RICHARD E.
PERSONAL Born 06/01/1930, Hungary, m, 1955, 1 child **DISCIPLINE** ECONOMICS **EDUCATION** Princeton, BA 52; Harvard Univ, MA 55, PhD 57. **CAREER** Princeton Univ, asst prof 56-59, assoc prof 59-64, prof 64-95, prof emeritus 95; A W Mellon Fond, Sr Advisor 90. **HONORS AND AWARDS** Guggenheim Fell, McCosh Fel; Ford Found Fell; Econometric Soc Fell; Nat Sci fell; Hugh-Rogers Fell; ASA Fell; APS Fell; Hon Doc Budapest; Gold Medal Budapest; Merit Cit Jagiellonian Univ; AAAS Fell; Medal of Merit Copernicus Univ; Hon Doc Comenius Univ; Hon Doc Queens Univ; Order of Merit Govt Hungary. **MEMBERSHIPS** ASA; AES; ESI. **RESEARCH** Economies **SELECTED PUBLICATIONS** Electronic Publishing and Virtual Libraries: Issues and an Agenda for the Andrew W Mellon Foundation, Serials Review, 96; Betting Bias and Market Equilibrium in Racetrack Betting, with S Chadha, Applied Financial Economics, 96; The Kornai Effect with Partial Bailouts and Taxes, with Karen L Magee, Economics of Planninf, 94; Optimal Decisions in Markets and Planned Economies, ed with D Triska, Boulder CO, WestView Press, 90; numerous books and articles. **CONTACT ADDRESS** Dept of Economics, Princeton Univ, Princeton, NJ, 08544-1017. **EMAIL** reg@quandt.com

QUATAERT, DONALD GEORGE
PERSONAL Born 09/10/1941, Rochester, NY, m, 1970, 2 children **DISCIPLINE** MIDDLE EAST HISTORY **EDUCATION** Boston Univ, AB, 66; Harvard Univ, AM, 68; Univ Calif, Los Angeles, PhD(hist), 73. **CAREER** Scholar hist, Near East Ctr, Univ Calif, Los Angeles, 73-74; asst prof, 74-79, asst to assoc prof, Univ Houston, 74-87; assoc to PROF, BINGHAMTON UNIV, 87; Mem, Am Coun Learned Soc Comt Teaching Mat Islamic Civilization, 76- **MEMBERSHIPS** AHA; Mideast Studies Asn; Turkish Studies Asn. **RESEARCH** Social, economic and labor history of the Ottoman Middle East, 1700-1922. **SELECTED PUBLICATIONS** Auth, Social Disintergration and Popular Resistance in the Ottoman Empire 1881-1908, 83; auth, Ottoman Manufacturing in the Age of the Idustrial Revolution, 93; auth, Technnology Transfer in the Ottoman Empire, 92; co-ed, An Economic and Social History of the Ottoman Empire, 1300-1914, 94. **CONTACT ADDRESS** Dept of Hist, SUNY, Binghamton, Binghamton, NY, 13902-6000. **EMAIL** dquataer@binghamton.edu

QUERE, RALPH WALTER
PERSONAL Born 09/26/1935, Cleveland, OH, m, 1957, 3 children **DISCIPLINE** HISTORY OF CHRISTIAN THOUGHT **EDUCATION** Princeton Univ, AB, 57; Trinity Sem, Columbus Ohio, BD, 64; Princeton Theol Sem,, 70. **CAREER** From instr to assoc prof, 69-84, Prof Hist & Theol, Wartburg Theol Sem, 84-. **MEMBERSHIPS** Am Soc Reformation Res; Am Soc Church Hist; Acad Evangel Theol Educ; Sixteenth Century Cong; Concordia Acad. **RESEARCH** Melanchthon's eucharistic thought; history of Christological thought; history of worship. **SELECTED PUBLICATIONS** Auth, Confrontation at Marburg, Harvard Case Study Inst, 73; Superstar and Godspell, Dialogue, summer 73; Evangelical Witness, Augsburg, 75; The spirit and the gifts are ours..., ordination rites, Lutheran Quart, 11/75; Melanchthonian motifs in the formula, in Dialogue, Discord and Concord, Fortress, 77; Melanchthon's Christum Cognoscere, DeGraaf, 77; Christ's efficacious presence in The Lord's Supper, Lutheran Quart, 2/77. **CONTACT ADDRESS** Wartburg Theol Sem, 333 Wartburg Pl, Dubuque, IA, 52004-5004. **EMAIL** quere@mwci.com

QUIN, CAROLYN L.
PERSONAL Born 10/12/1947, Yazoo City, MS **DISCIPLINE** MUSICOLOGY, MUSIC HISTORY AND LITERATURE, PIANO **EDUCATION** Millsaps Col, Jackson, Miss, BA, 70; Univ Ark, MM, 74; Univ Ky, PhD, 81. **CAREER** 79-92, Ch, Div of Liberal Stud; assoc Prof Music; Dir Honors Program; Co **HONORS AND AWARDS** Grants for res and travel from: Andrew W. Mellon Found; United Negro Col Fund; NEH; US Dept of Education; Jeannie E Lane Award for Teaching Excellence (Lane Col); Outstanding Teaching asn (Univ Kentucky); sabbatical leave to complete a book, Winthrop Univ. **MEMBERSHIPS** Col Music Soc; Am Musicol Soc; Music Asn Cal Comm Col. **RESEARCH** William Grant Still, 1895-1978, African Am class composer; Fanny Mendelssohn Hensel, 1805-1847, Ger composer; women composers; piano & harpsichord performance. **SELECTED PUBLICATIONS** Co-author, William Grant Still: A Bio-Bibliography, Greenwood Press, 96; Fusion of Cultures in the Piano Music of William Grant Still, in William Grant Still and the Fusion of Cult in Am Mus, Master-Player Library, 95, Classical Music Trivia, Lisa Huffman (musicol consult to author), Master-Player Library, 97; Fanny Mendelssohn Hensel: Her Contributions to Nineteenth-Century Musical Life, UMI, 81. **CONTACT ADDRESS** Riverside Community Col, 4800 Magnolia Ave, Riverside, CA, 92506. **EMAIL** quinc@cyberg8t.com

QUINAN, JACK
DISCIPLINE ART HISTORY **EDUCATION** Brown Univ, PhD. **CAREER** Fac, SUNY Buffalo, present; adj prof archit, Frank Lloyd Wright Schl Archit, concurrent. **HONORS AND AWARDS** Fellow, NEH., Curator of the Darwin D. Martin House restoration **RESEARCH** 19th- and 20th-century archit hist, Am archit. **SELECTED PUBLICATIONS** Auth, Frank Lloyd Wright's Larkin Building: Myth and Fact, AHF/MIT, 87. **CONTACT ADDRESS** Dept Art, SUNY Buffalo, 202 Center for the Arts, Buffalo, NY, 14260-6010.

QUINLIVAN, MARY E.
DISCIPLINE HISTORY **EDUCATION** St. Scholastica, BA, 54; Loyola, MA, 64; Univ Wis, PhD, 71. **CAREER** Assoc prof, hist, Univ Texas at Permian Basin; PROF, HIST, UNIV WIS WHITEWATER. **MEMBERSHIPS** Am Antiquarian Soc **SELECTED PUBLICATIONS** Auth, "Race Relations in the Antebellum Children's Literature of Jacob Abbott," Jour of Pop Cult, 82; auth, entries in American Writers Before 1800, Greenwood, 83. **CONTACT ADDRESS** PO Box 74, Whitewater, WI, 53190.

QUINN, JOHN F.
DISCIPLINE BUSINESS ETHICS, PHILOSOPHY OF LAW, MEDIEVAL PHILOSOPHY **EDUCATION** Univ Dayton, JD, 82. **CAREER** Dept Philos, Univ Dayton **SELECTED PUBLICATIONS** Co-auth, Indonesian Deforestation: A Policy Framework for Sustainable Development, Jour of Asian Bus, 94; Development in the Underdeveloped World: A New Challenge for Business Ethics, Who's Business Values?: Some Asian and Cross-Cultural Perspectives, Hong Kong UP, 95; Anthropocentric Modernism and the Search for a Universal Environmental Philosophy, Dialogue and Universalism, 95. **CONTACT ADDRESS** Dept of Philos, Univ Dayton, 300 Col Park, Dayton, OH, 75062. **EMAIL** quinn@checkov.hm.udayton.edu

QUIST, JOHN W.
PERSONAL Born 04/08/1960, Santa Monica, CA, m, 1982, 2 children **DISCIPLINE** HISTORY **EDUCATION** Univ of Mich, AM, 86, PhD, 92. **CAREER** Grad student tchg fel, Univ of Mich, 85-91; lectr, Eastern Mich Univ, 92-95; asst prof, D'Youville Col, 95-97; ASST PROF, SHIPPENSBURG UNIV, 97-. **HONORS AND AWARDS** Ralph D. Gray Article Prize, SHEAR, 95. **MEMBERSHIPS** SHEAR; SHA; OAH; AHA. **RESEARCH** Antebellum United States. **SELECTED PUBLICATIONS** Auth, Restless Visionaries: The Social Roots of Antebellum Reform in Alabama and Michigan, La State Univ Press, 98; Slaveholding Operatives of the Benevolent Empire: Bible, Tract, and Sunday School Societies in Antebellum Tuscaloosa County Alabama, J of Southern Hist, 96; The Great Majority of our Subscribers are Farmers: The Michigan Abolitionist Constituency of the 1840s, J of the Early Republic, 94; Polygamy among James Strang and his Followers, The John Whitmer Hist Asn J, 89; John e. Page: An Apostle of Uncertainty, J of Mormon Hist, 85. **CONTACT ADDRESS** Dept of Hist, Shippensburg Univ, Shippensburg, PA, 17257-2299. **EMAIL** jwquis@ship.edu

QUITT, MARTIN HERBERT
PERSONAL Born 11/22/1940, Boston, MA, m, 1971 **DISCIPLINE** AMERICAN COLONIAL HISTORY **EDUCATION** Brandeis Univ, BA, 62; Washington Univ, MA, 66, PhD(hist), 70. **CAREER** Instr hist, Tex A&M Univ, 67-68; from instr to asst prof, 68-75, assoc prof, 74-80, PROF HIST, BOSTON STATE COL, 80-, CO-DIR, CTR FAMILY STUDIES, 74-, Co-ed, Psychohistory, Bull Int Psychohist Asn, 76- **MEMBERSHIPS** Orgn Am Historians; Southern Hist Asn; Int Psychohist Asn; Assoc of Inst Early Am Hist & Cult. **RESEARCH** Psychohistory; institutional and demographic history of colonial Virginia; the family in the early modern era. **SELECTED PUBLICATIONS** Auth, Jackson, Indians And Psychohistory, Hist Of Childhood Quart, 76; Contemporary Crisis Of American Family, J Psychohistory, 76; Schism And Narcissism At Stockton, Psychohistory, 77; Adapting To A New-World - English Society In The 17th-Century Chesapeake, William And Mary Quarterly, Vol 52, 95; The Pleasure Gardens Of Virginia--From Jamestown To Jefferson, Va Magazine Of Hist And Biography, Vol 101, 93; Trade And Acculturation At Jamestown, 1607-1609--The Limits Of Understanding, William And Mary Quart, Vol 52, 95. **CONTACT ADDRESS** Dept of Hist, Boston Univ, 174 Ipswich St, Boston, MA, 02215.

QUIVIK, FREDRIC L.
PERSONAL Born 08/10/1949, Northfield, MN, m, 1971 **DISCIPLINE** HISTORY, SOCIOLOGY OF SCIENCE **EDUCATION** Univ Pa, PhD, 98 **CAREER** Archit hist, 82-90; Consulting Hist Tech, 94-. **MEMBERSHIPS** Soc Ind Archeol; Soc Hist Tech; Soc Archit Historians. **RESEARCH** Hist tech; Am West, 19th, 20th cent especially hist of metallurgical engg. **SELECTED PUBLICATIONS** Auth, The Industrial Landscape of Butte and Anaconda, in Images of an American Land, Univ NM, 97. **CONTACT ADDRESS** 2830 Pearl Harbor, Alameda, CA, 94501.

R

RAABE, WILLIAM A.
PERSONAL Born 12/14/1953, Milwaukee, WI, m, 2 children **DISCIPLINE** ACCOUNTING, TAXATION, PUBLIC FINANCE, LAW, ECONOMICS **EDUCATION** Univ of Ill, PhD, 79. **CAREER** Prof, Samford, 97- ; prof, Univ Wis-Milwaukee, 79-97; Ariz State Univ, 84. **HONORS AND AWARDS** Wis Disting Prof, 89-97; Amer Acctg Assn Fellow; Ernst & Young Fellow; Deloitte & Touche Fellow; Natl Ctr for Tax Ed and Res; Ed of the Yr, WI Soc of CPAs, 87. **MEMBERSHIPS** AAUP, Am Acctg Asn, Am Taxation Asn. **RESEARCH** Economic Impact of Arts, and of Sports/Stadiums; Tax Policy; Taxpayer Behavior; Federal, State, Local, International Tax Issues; Adult Learning Styles and Techniques; Integration of Technology into Adult Learning Systems. **SELECTED PUBLICATIONS** Books: West's Federal Taxation; West's Federal Tax Research; Income Tax Fundamentals; Multistate Corporate Tax Guide; The Capital Asset Pricing Model in Tax Litigation; Talking Tax; Eliminating Writing Errors by Professsionals; Taxation of the Virtual Office; Combined Reporting for the Alabama Corporate Income Tax. **CONTACT ADDRESS** Samford Univ School of Business, 800 Lake Shore Dr, Birmingham, AL, 35229. **EMAIL** waraabe@samford.edu

RAACK, RICHARD C.
PERSONAL Born 07/10/1928, Los Angeles, CA, 1 child **DISCIPLINE** MODERN EUROPEAN HISTORY **EDUCATION** Univ Calif, Los Angeles, BA, 50, MA, 53; Harvard Univ, PhD, 57. **CAREER** Instr hist, RI Sch Design, 56-57; instr, Mass Inst Technol, 57-59; asst prof, Long Beach State Col, 61-65; from asst prof to assoc prof, 65-70, PROF HIST, CALIF STATE UNIV, HAYWARD, 70- **MEMBERSHIPS** AHA; Am Asn Advan Slavic Studies. **RESEARCH** History of East Central Europe; historiography; film as history. **SELECTED PUBLICATIONS** Auth, The Fall Of Stein, Harvard Univ, 65; Coauth, Script & Co-Producer, Goodbye Billy, America Goes To War, 1917-1918, Churchill Films, 72; Producer, The Frozen War, America Intervenes In Russia, 1918-1920, Cadre Films, 73; Co-Producer, Will Rogers' 1920's: A Cowboy's Guide To The Times, Churchill Films, 75; Producer, Script, Sound & Film Editor, Storm Of Fire, World War II And The Destruction Of Dresden, Churchill Films, 78; Stalin Plans For World-War-2 Told By A High Comintern Source, Historical J, Vol 38, 95. **CONTACT ADDRESS** Dept of Hist, California State Univ, Hayward, Hayward, CA, 94542.

RAAFLAUB, KURT A.
PERSONAL Born 02/15/1941, Buea, Cameroon, m, 1978 **DISCIPLINE** CLASSICS **EDUCATION** Univ of Bard, PhD, 70. **CAREER** Asst prof, 72-78, Freic Univ, Berlin; asst, assoc, prof, 78-, Brown Univ; joint dir, 92-00, Ctrs for Hellenic Stud, Wash, DC. **RESEARCH** Social political and intellectual hist of archaic and classical Greece and of the Roman Rep **CONTACT ADDRESS** Dept of Classics, Brown Univ, Providence, RI, 02912-1856. **EMAIL** kurt_raaflaub@brown.edu

RAAT, WILLIAM D.
PERSONAL Born 07/01/1939, Ogden, UT, m, 1971, 2 children **DISCIPLINE** WORLD, LATIN AMERICAN & MEXICAN HISTORY **EDUCATION** Univ Utah, BS, 61, PhD, 67. **CAREER** Teaching assoc hist, Univ Utah, 65-66; from asst prof to assoc prof, Moorhead State Col, 66-70; assoc prof, 70-77, chmn dept, 73-74, prof hist State Univ NY Col Fredonia, 77-, Grant-in-aid, State Univ NY, 73, 75 & 79; Am Coun Learned Soc fel, 76-77. **HONORS AND AWARDS** James A Robertson Award, Conf Latin Am Hist, 68; Edwin Lieuwen Mem Prize, RMCLAS for Excellence in Teaching, 88. **MEMBERSHIPS** AHA; Conf Latin Am Hist; Latin Am Studies Asn. **RESEARCH** Mexican intellectual and social history; inter-American relations; American Southwest and Mexico's northern frontier. **SELECTED PUBLICATIONS** Auth, Leopoldo Zea and Mexican positivism, in Hisp Am Hist Rev, 2/68; Ideas & History in Mexico, Univ Tex & Nat Univ Mex, 71; Ideas & Society in Don Porfirio's Mexico, in Americas, 7/73; El positivismo durante el Porfiriato, Sep Setentas, 75; The Diplomacy of Suppression: Revoltosos, in Hisp Am Hist Rev, 11/76; Revoltosos, Mexico's Rebels in the US, 1903-1923, Tex A&M Univ Press, 81; Mexico: From Independence to Revolution, 1810-1910, Nebr, 82; The Mexican Revolution: Historiography and Bibliography, G K Hall, 82; Mexico and the United States: Ambivalent Vistas, Univ Ga, 92, 96; Mexico's Sierra Tarahumsia: A Photo-History of the People of the Edge, Univ Okla, 96. **CONTACT ADDRESS** Dept of Hist, State Univ of New York Col, 1 Suny at Fredonia, Fredonia, NY, 14063-1143. **EMAIL** raat@ait.fredonia.edu

RABB, THEODORE K.
PERSONAL Born 03/05/1937, Teplice-Sanov, Czechoslovakia, m, 1959, 3 children **DISCIPLINE** MODERN HISTORY **EDUCATION** Oxford Univ, BA, 58, MA, 62; Princeton Univ, PhD, 61. **CAREER** Asst hist, Princeton Univ, 61; instr, Stanford Univ, 61-62; instr, Northwestern Univ, 62-63; asst prof, Harvard Univ, 63-67; assoc prof, 67-76, PROF HIST, PRINCETON UNIV, 76-, Folger Shakespeare Libr vis fel, 60; Soc Sci Res Coun fel, 65; Am Philos Soc fel, 66 & 76; mem comt info technol, Am Coun Learned Soc, 68-71; vis assoc prof hist, Johns Hopkins Univ, 69 & State Univ Ny Binghamton, 73-74; Guggenheim Found fel, 70; co-ed, J Interdisciplinary Hist, 70-; mem, Nat Res Coun, 72-; mem nat bd consult, Nat Endowment for Humanities, 76-; dir, Community Col Internship Prog, Princeton Univ, 74- & Mid-Career Fel Prog, 77- **MEMBERSHIPS** AHA; Conf Brit Studies; fel Royal Hist Soc; Soc Sci

Hist Asn (treas, 77-); Am Asn Advan Humanities (secy/treas, 77-). **RESEARCH** English history; sixteenth and seventeenth centuries; interdisciplinary history. **SELECTED PUBLICATIONS** Co-ed, J of Interdisciplinary Hist, 70- ; auth, Renaissance Lives, Pantheon, 93; auth, Origins of the Modern West: Essays and Sources in Renaissance & Early Modern European History, McGraw-Hill, 93; auth, The Future of Opera, II: The Historian's Viewpoint, Lyric Opera of Chicago Stagebill, 93; auth, Whither History? Reflections on the Comparison Between Historians and Scientists, in Kozicki, ed, Developments in Modern Historiography, St Martin's, 93; auth, Religious Toleration During the Age of Reformation, in Thorp, ed, Politics, Religion, and Diplomacy in Early Modern Europe: Essays in Honor of De Lamar Jensen, Kirksville, 94; auth, Play, Not Politics: Who Really Understood the Symbolism of Renaissance Art? Times Literary Suppl, 95; auth, Historians and Art Historians: A Lowering of Sights? J of Interdisciplinary Hist, 96; auth, Jacobean gentleman, Sir Edwin Sandys, 1561-1629, Princeton, 98; auth, The Western Experience, 7th ed, Knopf, 98. **CONTACT ADDRESS** Dept of History, Princeton Univ, Princeton, NJ, 08540. **EMAIL** tkrabb@princeton.edu

RABBAT, NASSER O.
PERSONAL Born 05/21/1956, Damascus, Syria, m **DISCIPLINE** HISTORY OF ARCHITECTURE **EDUCATION** MIT, PhD 91; UCLA, M Arch 84; Univ Damascus Syria, BArch 79. **CAREER** MIT, asst prof, assoc prof, 91 to 95-. **HONORS AND AWARDS** Getty Postdoc Fel; Malcolm H. Kerr Diss Awd. **MEMBERSHIPS** SAH; CAA; MESA; ARCE; HIA. **RESEARCH** History of medieval Islamic architecture; Ancient and medieval urban history; 19th century Orientalism. **SELECTED PUBLICATIONS** Auth, The Citadel of Cairo: A New Interpretation of Royal Mamluk Architecture, Leiden NY, EJ Brill, 95; auth, Architects and Artists in Mamluk Society: The Perspective of the Sources, Jour of Archi Edu, 98; auth, The Formation of Neo-Mamluk Style in Modern Egypt, The Education of the Architect: Historiography Urbanism and the Growth of Arch Knowledge, ed Martha Pollack, Cambridge MA, MIT Press, 97; auth, My Life With Salah-al-Din: The Memoirs of Imad al-Din al-Katib al-Isfahani, Edebiyat. 96; auth, Al-Azhar Mosque: An Architectural Chronicle of Cairo's History, Muqarnas, 96; auth, The Art and Architecture of Islam 1250-1800, Sheila S. Blair, Jonathan M. Bloom, rev, Design Bk Rev, 96; auth, A Guide to the Late Antique World, eds GW Bowersock, P. Brown, O. Graber, Harvard Univ Press, 97; auth, Encycl of the Qur'an, Leiden Nthlnds, EJ Brill Pub, 98 cont, article The City. **CONTACT ADDRESS** Dept of Architecture, Massachusetts Inst of Tech, 77 Massachusetts Ave, Cambridge, MA, 02139. **EMAIL** nasser@mit.edu

RABE, STEPHEN
DISCIPLINE HISTORY **EDUCATION** Univ Conn, PhD, 77. **CAREER** Prof. **RESEARCH** American foreign relations; American slavery. **SELECTED PUBLICATIONS** Auth, The Road to OPEC: United States Relations with Venezuela 1919-1976, Univ Tex, 82; Eisenhower and Latin America: The Foreign Policy of Anticommunism, Univ NC, 88; coauth, Imperial Surge: The United States Abroad, The 1890-Early 1900's, D.C. Heath, 92; Slavery in American Society, D.C. Heath, 93. **CONTACT ADDRESS** Dept of History, Richardson, TX, 75083-0688. **EMAIL** rabe@utdallas.edu

RABINOWITCH, ALEXANDER
PERSONAL Born 08/30/1934, London, England, m, 1962, 2 children **DISCIPLINE** EUROPEAN & MODERN RUSSIAN HISTORY **EDUCATION** Knox Col, BA, 56; Univ Chicago, MA, 61; Ind Univ, PhD(hist), 65. **CAREER** US-USSR exchange res scholar hist, Moscow State Univ, 63-64; asst prof, Univ Southern Calif, 65-67; from asst prof to assoc prof, 67-75, dir grad studies hist, 71-73, PROF HIST & DIR RUSS & E EUROP INST, IND UNIV, BLOOMINGTON, 75-, Univ Southern Calif res grant, 65-66; Nat Endowment for Humanities fel, 67-68; Am Coun Learned Soc fel & US-USSR exchange sr scholar, Moscow State Univ, 70-71; mem, Inst Advan Study, Princeton Univ, 73-74; mem coun, Int Exchange of Scholars Adv Comt for EEurope & USSR, 77-; mem, Nat Coun Soviet & EEurop Res, 78. **MEMBERSHIPS** AHA; Midwest Slavic Conf; Am Asn Advan Slavic Studies. **RESEARCH** Nineteenth century Russian history; The Russian Revolution; Soviet history. **SELECTED PUBLICATIONS** Auth, Prelude To Revolution: The Petrograd Bolsheviks And The July 1917 Uprising, 68, Co-Ed, Revolution And Politics In Russia: Essays In Memory Of B I Nicolaevsky, 72 & Auth, The Petrograd Garrison And The Bolshevik Seizure Of Power, In: Revolution And Politics In Russia: Essays In Memory Of B I Nicolaevsky, 72, Ind Univ; Auth, The Bolsheviks Come To Power: The Revolution Of 1917 In Petrograd, Norton, 76; I Bolscevichi Al Potere: La Rivoluzione Del 1917 A Pietrogrado, Feltrinelli, 78.; Revolutionary Terrorist In Late Czarist Russia, Leader Of The Radical Agrarian Left-Socialist-Revolutionaries Party After The October 1917 Revolution, Russian Review, Vol 54, 95. **CONTACT ADDRESS** Dept of Hist, Indiana Univ, Bloomington, Bloomington, IN, 47401.

RABINOWITZ, HOWARD
DISCIPLINE U.S. URBAN HISTORY, SOUTHERN HISTORY **EDUCATION** Univ Chicago, PhD, 73. **CAREER** Prof, Univ NMex. **HONORS AND AWARDS** Fel, Ctr for Adv Stud in Behav Sci, Stanford Univ; grant and fel, NEH. **RESEARCH** American urban history; Southern history. **SELECTED PUBLICATIONS** Auth, Race Relations in the Urban South, 1865-1890, 78, 80, 96; Southern Black Leaders of the Reconstruction Era, 82; The First New South, 1865-1920, 92; Race, Ethnicity, and Urbanization, 94. **CONTACT ADDRESS** Univ NMex, Albuquerque, NM, 87131.

RABLE, GEORGE CALVIN
PERSONAL Born 06/08/1950, Lima, OH, m, 1972, 1 child **DISCIPLINE** AMERICAN HISTORY **EDUCATION** Bluffton Col, BA, 72; La State Univ, MA, 73, PhD(hist), 78. **CAREER** Asst prof hist, La State Univ, Alexandria, 79; ASST PROF HIST & DIR AM STUDIES, ANDERSON COL, 79-, Mem Nat Endowment for the Humanities summer sem, 82. **MEMBERSHIPS** Orgn Am Historians; Southern Hist Asn. **RESEARCH** Nineteenth century United States history; Civil War and Reconstruction; women's history. **SELECTED PUBLICATIONS** Auth, Anatomy of a unionist: Andrew Johnson in the secession crisis, Tenn Hist Quart, winter 73; Slavery, politics and the South: The gag rule as a case study, Capitol Studies, fall 75; Memphis: The first modern race riot, Geosci & Man, Vol XIX, 123-127; Forces of darkness, forces of light: The impeachment of Andrew Johnson and the paranoid style, Southern Studies, summer 78; Southern interests and the election of 1876: A re-appraisal, Civil War Hist, 12/80; Patriotism, platitudes and politics: Baseball and the American Presidency, Am Heritage (in prep); Republican Albatross: The Louisiana question, national politics and the failure of reconstruction, La Hist; Lynching In The New South - Georgia And Virginia, 1880-1930 , J of Am Hist, Vol 81, 95. **CONTACT ADDRESS** 1100 E 5th St, Anderson, IN, 46012-3495.

RACE, JEFFERY
PERSONAL Born 07/29/1943, Norwalk, CT **DISCIPLINE** POLITICAL SCIENCE **EDUCATION** Harvard College, BA 65; Harvard Univ, MA 71, PhD 73. **CAREER** Inst of Current World Affairs, Fellow, 72-76; Industry, Government, and Intl Orgs, Consultant, 77-. **RESEARCH** Technology transfer; econ political development; legal systems. **SELECTED PUBLICATIONS** Auth, War Comes to Long An: Revolutionary Conflict in a Vietnamese Province, Univ Cal Press, 72; Toward an Exchange Theory of Revolution, in: Peasant Rebellion and Communist Revolution in Asia, ed, John W Lewis, Stanford Univ Press, 74. **CONTACT ADDRESS** 20 Chester St, Somerville, MA, 02144.

RACE, WILLIAM H.
PERSONAL Born 03/24/1943, Wooster, OH, m, 1969, 2 children **DISCIPLINE** CLASSICS **EDUCATION** Univ Mich, BA, 65; Stanford Univ, MA, 72, PhD, 73. **CAREER** Tchr Latin & English, Detroit Country Day Sch, 68-69; asst prof Classics, Univ Calif Berkeley, 73-76; from asst prof to assoc prof to prof Classics, Vanderbilt Univ, 76-96; George L. Paddison prof Classics, Univ NC Chapel Hill, 96-. **HONORS AND AWARDS** Nat Endowment Hum grant, 85, 91; Outstanding Grad Tchr Award, Vanderbilt Univ, 92. **MEMBERSHIPS** Phi Beta Kappa; Am Philos Asn; Class Asn Mid W & S; Am Inst Archeol; Am Class League; Vergilian Soc; Int Soc Class Trad; Int Plutarch Soc; ed bd, Am Jour Philol. **RESEARCH** Classical Greek poetry; Augustan Poetry; rhetoric; classical tradition. **SELECTED PUBLICATIONS** Auth, The Classical Priamel from Homer to Boethius, 82; auth, Pindar, Twayne World Auth Ser, 86; auth, Classical Genres and English Poetry, 88; auth, Style and Rhetoric in Pindar's Odes, 90; auth, Pindar, Loeb Class Libr, 97. **CONTACT ADDRESS** Dept of Classics, Univ North Carolina, CB 3145, Chapel Hill, NC, 27599-3145. **EMAIL** whrace@email.unc.edu

RACHLEFF, PETER J.
PERSONAL Born 03/09/1951, New London, CT, m, 1997 **DISCIPLINE** HISTORY **EDUCATION** Univ Pitts, PhD 81, MA 76; Amherst Coll, BA 73. **CAREER** Macalester Col, prof hist 95-, assoc prof 87-95, asst prof 82-87. **HONORS AND AWARDS** Phi Beta Kappa **MEMBERSHIPS** OAH; Nat Writers Union; Workers Ed Loc 189. **RESEARCH** US labor, race immigration **SELECTED PUBLICATIONS** The Failure of Minnesota Farmer-Laborism, in: Kevin Boyle, ed, Organized Labor and Amer Politics, Albany State, Univ NY Press, forthcoming; The Dynamics of Americanization: The Croatian Fraternal Union in the 30's, in: Eric Arnesen, Julie Greene, Bruce Laurie, eds, Labor Histories: Class Politics and the Working Class Experience, Urbana IL, Univ IL Press, 98; Unbroken Mirror: One Hundred Years of the St Paul Union Advocate, with Barb Kucera, Labor's Heritage, 98; Organizing Wall to Wall: The Independent Union of All Workers 1933-37,in: Shelton Stromquist and Marvin Bergman, eds, Unionizing the Jungles: Labor and Community in the Twentieth Century Meatpacking Industry, IA City, Univ of IA Press, 97; numerous other pub. **CONTACT ADDRESS** Dept of Hist, Macalester Col, 1600 Grand Ave, St Paul, MN, 55105. **EMAIL** rachleff@macalester.edu

RACINE, PHILIP N.
PERSONAL Born 12/25/1941, Brunswick, ME, m, 1968, 2 children **DISCIPLINE** AMERICAN HISTORY **EDUCATION** Bowdoin Col, AB, 64; MA, 65; Emory Univ, PhD, 69. **CAREER** PROF, WOFFORD COL, 69-. **HONORS AND AWARDS** Founders Award, Mus of the Confederacy, 86; Phi Beta Kappa, 91. **MEMBERSHIPS** Am Hist Asn; Southern Hist Asn; Org of Am Historians. **RESEARCH** History of the American South; American Civil War. **CONTACT ADDRESS** Wofford Col, 429 N. Church St., Spartanburg, SC, 29303-3363. **EMAIL** racinepn@wofford.edu

RADAN, GEORGE T.
PERSONAL Born 12/31/1923, Budapest, Hungary, m, 1958, 2 children **DISCIPLINE** ARCHAEOLOGY; ART HISTORY **EDUCATION** Ecole du Louvre, Paris, AEM, 67; Univ Budapest, Hungary, MA PhD, 78-79. **CAREER** Haifa Marine Museum, Haifa, Israel, assoc dir, 54-59; Institute of Mediterranean Archaeol, assoc pres, 70-79; Villanova Univ, prof, dept art, hist, 60-. **HONORS AND AWARDS** Fr Nat Schol; Post-Doctoral, Univ Penna; IREX ACLS; ACLS; Israel Nat Maritime Res. **MEMBERSHIPS** Renaissance Scholars; Ancient Historians **RESEARCH** Medieval Archaeology **SELECTED PUBLICATIONS** Augustine In Iconography: History and Legend, with others, Lang, 98; Archaeological Excavations at San Leonardo al Lag and Santa Lucia di Rosia, Analecta Augustiniana, LX, 97; Lecceto e gli eremi Agostiniani in terra di Siena, w/o, Milano, 93; and more. **CONTACT ADDRESS** Dept History, Villanova Univ, Villanova, PA, 19085-1699. **EMAIL** tapiki@aol.com

RADDING, CYNTHIA
DISCIPLINE HISTORY **EDUCATION** Univ Calif San Diego, PhD, 90. **CAREER** Asst prof, Univ Ill Urbana Champaign. **RESEARCH** History of Latin America; history of Mexico; ethnohistory; peasant studies. **SELECTED PUBLICATIONS** Auth, Wandering Peoples: Colonialism, Ethnic Spaces, and Ecological Frontiers in Northwestern Mexico, 1700-1850, Duke, 97; Work, Labor and the Market: The Responses of Farmers and Semi-Nomadic Peoples to Colonialism in Northwest Mexico, Slavery Abolition, 94; Entre el desierto y la sierra. Las naciones o'odham y teguima de Sonora, 1530-1840, Inst Nat Indigenista, 95. **CONTACT ADDRESS** History Dept, Univ Ill Urbana Champaign, 52 E Gregory Dr, Champaign, IL, 61820.

RADER, BENJAMIN G.
PERSONAL Born 08/25/1935, Delaware, MO, m, 1961, 2 children **DISCIPLINE** AMERICAN HISTORY **EDUCATION** Southwest Mo State Col, BA, 58; Okla State Univ, MA, 59; Univ Md, PhD, 64. **CAREER** Instr Hist, Okla State Univ, 61-62; from instr to asst prof, 62-67; assoc prof, 67-72, prof History, Univ Nebr, Lincoln, 72-, Nat Humanities Found jr fel, 69; James L Sellers prof, 97. **MEMBERSHIPS** Orgn Am Historians; AHA. **RESEARCH** American intellectual history; history of economic ideas; history of American sport. **SELECTED PUBLICATIONS** Auth, Academic Mind and Reform: The Influence of Richard T Ely in American Life, Univ Ky, 66; Richard T Ely: Lay spokesman for the social gospel, J Am Hist, 4/66; Montana lumber strike of 1917, Pac Hist Rev, 5/67; Federal taxation in the 1920's, Historian, 5/71; Quest for subcommunities and the rise of American Sport, Am Quart, Fall 77; American Sports: From the Age of Folk Games to the Age of the Spectator, Prentice-Hall, 82; Baseball: A History of America's Game, Univ Illinois, 95. **CONTACT ADDRESS** Dept of History, Univ of Nebraska, PO Box 880327, Lincoln, NE, 68588-0327. **EMAIL** brader@unlinfo.unl.edu

RADER, ROSEMARY
DISCIPLINE HISTORY OF CHRISTIANITY **EDUCATION** Col St Catherine, BA; Univ Minn, MA; Stanford Univ, PhD. **CAREER** Religion, Carleton Univ. **SELECTED PUBLICATIONS** Auth, Breaking Boundaries: Male/Female Friendship in Early Christian Communities; Coauth, Women Writers of the Early Church. **CONTACT ADDRESS** Carleton Col, 100 S College St., Northfield, MN, 55057-4016.

RADICE, MARK A.
DISCIPLINE MUSIC HISTORY **EDUCATION** Boston Univ, BM; Univ Cincinnati, MM; Eastman Sch Music, PhD. **CAREER** Assoc prof. **SELECTED PUBLICATIONS** Auth, pubs on music of the 18th century. **CONTACT ADDRESS** Dept of Music History, Theory and Composition, Ithaca Col, 100 Job Hall, Ithaca, NY, 14850. **EMAIL** mradice@ithaca.edu

RADISICH, PAULA
DISCIPLINE ART AND ART HISTORY **EDUCATION** Univ Calif, Santa Barbara, 65-67; Univ Calif, Los Angeles, BA, 69; MA, 72; PhD, 77. **CAREER** Tchg asst, Univ Calif, 70-72; pt time instr, La Fashion Inst, 73; Calif Univ, 78; instr, UCLA, 78; Claremont Grad Sch, 79, 80, 81; LA County Mus, 80, 81; adj asst prof, 78-82; asst prof, 82; assoc prof, 87; prof, 95-. **HONORS AND AWARDS** Borchard grant, 96; Irvine grant award, 93; grants, 86, 90, 95 NEH; fac res grant, 86, Whittier col; four-yr Chancellor's tchg fel, 69., Ed, Eighteenth-Century Stud, 89-92; 93-94; co-winner, ASECS tchg competition award, 90. **RESEARCH** Women and the visual arts; visual arts of the eighteenth century, age of impressionism, age of DADA and Surrealism. **SELECTED PUBLICATIONS** Co-auth, Decon-

structing Dissipation, Eighteenth-Century Stud, 95-96; auth, La Chose Publique: Hubert Robert's Decorations for the petit salon at Mereville, The Consumption of Culture: Word, Image, and Object in the 17th and 18th Centuries, Routledge, 95; Evolution and Salvation: The Iconic Origins of Druellet's Monstrious Combatants ofthe Night, Flights of Fancy, Univ of Ga Press, 93. **CONTACT ADDRESS** Dept of Art, Whitter Col, 13406 Philadelphia St, Whitter, CA, 90608.

RADYCKI, DIANE
PERSONAL Born 12/04/1946, Chicago, IL, m, 1998 **DISCIPLINE** HISTORY **EDUCATION** Univ Ill, BA; Hunter Col/CUNY, MA; Harvard Univ, PhD, 93. **CAREER** Tchng fel, 87, Harvard Univ; dir, 99, Payne Gallery of Moravian Col; vis lectr, 97, Rutgers Univ; asst prof, 92-96, Univ Houston; asst prof, 98-, Moravian Col. **RESEARCH** paula Modersohn-Becker: translated journals. **CONTACT ADDRESS** Art Dept, Moravian Col, 1200 Main, Bethlehem, PA, 18018. **EMAIL** medjr01@moravian.edu

RAEFF, MARC
PERSONAL Born 07/28/1923, Moscow, Russia **DISCIPLINE** HISTORY **EDUCATION** Harvard Univ, PhD, 50. **CAREER** From assoc prof to prof Russ hist, 61-73, BAKHMETEFF PROF RUSS STUDIES, COLUMBIA UNIV, 73- **MEMBERSHIPS** Modern and intellectual Russian history; eighteenth century European history. **SELECTED PUBLICATIONS** Auth, We Fall And Rise--Russian-Language Newspapers In New-York-City, 1889-1914, Jahrbucher Fur Geschichte Osteuropas, Vol 40, 92; Russia As A Multinational Empire--Origins, Hist, Collapse, Jahrbucher Fur Geschichte Osteuropas, Vol 40, 92; Fleeing To Switzerland--The Swiss Asylum System In The 19th-Century And 20th-Century, Jahrbucher Fur Geschichte Osteuropas, Vol 43, 95; V.O. Kliuchevskii, Historian Of Russia, J Of Modern Hist, Vol 69, 97; Reform And Regicide--The Reign Of Peter-Iii Of Russia, Am Hist Rev, Vol 98, 93; The 'Legacy Of Genghis-Khan' And Other Essays On Russia Identity, Slavic Rev, Vol 51, 92. **CONTACT ADDRESS** Dept of Hist, Columbia Univ, New York, NY, 10027.

RAELIN, JOSEPH A.
PERSONAL Born 04/10/1948, Cambridge, MA, m, 1974, 2 children **DISCIPLINE** POLICY STUDIES **EDUCATION** SUNY Buff, PhD, 77. **CAREER** Prof, 76-, Boston College; vis Prof, 90, Lancaster Univ. **HONORS AND AWARDS** John Wiley Best Paper Awd; Who's Who Intl Authors and Writers; Dir Intl Bus & Mgmt Schls; Dir of Intl Biography. **MEMBERSHIPS** Acad of Mgmt. **RESEARCH** Developing the emerging field of work-based learning. **SELECTED PUBLICATIONS** Auth, Work-Based Learning: The New Frontier of Management Development, The OD Series, Addison Wesley Longman, forthcoming; Work-Based Learning in Practice, J Workplace Learn, forthcoming; A Model of Work-Based Learning, Org Science, 97; Action Learning and Action Science: Are They Different?, Org Dynamics, 97; Internal Career Development in the Age of Insecurity, Bus Forum, 97; Executive Professionalism and Executive Selection, Human Resource Plan, 97; Individual and Situational Precursors of Successful Action Learning, J Mgmt Edu, 97; coauth, Open the Door for Joint Ventures with Business, Sch Admin, 94; coauth, Regenerating Performance Appraisal for Scientists and Engineers, Res Techno Mgmt, 94; The Persean Ethic: Consistency of Belief and Action in Managerial Practice, Human Relations, 93. **CONTACT ADDRESS** Carroll Sch of Management, Boston Col, Chestnut Hill, MA, 02467. **EMAIL** raelin@bc.edu

RAGAN JR, BRYANT T.
DISCIPLINE FRENCH HISTORY **EDUCATION** Univ, CA-Berkeley, PhD. **CAREER** Asst prof, Fordham Univ. **HONORS AND AWARDS** Grant, Florence Gould found. **RESEARCH** Hist of sexuality, gender hist. **SELECTED PUBLICATIONS** Co-ed, Re-creating Authority in Revolutionary France, Rutgers UP, 92; Homosexuality in Modern France, Oxford UP, 97 **CONTACT ADDRESS** Dept of Hist, Fordham Univ, 113 W 60th St, New York, NY, 10023.

RAHN PHILLIPS, CARLA
DISCIPLINE HISTORY **EDUCATION** Univ NY, PhD, 72. **CAREER** Prof **HONORS AND AWARDS** Leo Gershoy Prize, 87. **RESEARCH** Social and economic history in western Europe; European trade and empire. **SELECTED PUBLICATIONS** Auth, Ciudad Real, 1500-1750: Growth, Crisis and Readjustment in the Spanish Economy, Harvard, 79; Six Galleons For the King of Spain: Imperial Defense in the Early Seventeenth Century, John Hopkins Univ, 86; pubs on population, landownership, trade, merchants, and society; co-auth, The Worlds of Christopher Columbus, Cambridge, 92; Spain's Golden Fleece: Wool Production and the Wool Trade From the Middle Ages to the Nineteenth Century, John Hopkins, 97. **CONTACT ADDRESS** History Dept, Univ of Minnesota, Twin Cities, 614 Social Sciences Tower, 267 19th Ave. S, Minneapolis, MN, 55455. **EMAIL** phill002@tc.umn.edu

RAINEY, PENELOPE
PERSONAL Born 12/06/1940, New York, NY, m, 1986, 2 children **DISCIPLINE** CLASSICS **EDUCATION** Harvard, BA, 62; Columbia, MA, PhD, 72 **CAREER** Germantown Friends Sch, 74-present. **HONORS AND AWARDS** Phi Beta Kappa, NEH Research grant **MEMBERSHIPS** APA, ALA, Vergehan Soc **RESEARCH** Medieval Latin poetry; classical Latin poetry; Plato **SELECTED PUBLICATIONS** Plato Laches Bryan Manor Commentaries, Medieval Latin Verse **CONTACT ADDRESS** 20 W. Willow Grove Ave., Philadelphia, PA, 19118.

RAJAGOPAL, ARVIND
DISCIPLINE CULTURAL STUDIES, MASS MEDIA, POSTCOLONIAL STUDIES **EDUCATION** UCLA, Berkeley, PhD, 92. **CAREER** Asst prof, Purdue Univ. **SELECTED PUBLICATIONS** Auth, And the Poor Get Gassed: Multinational-aided Development and the State: The Case of Bhopal, 87; The Rise of National Programming: The Case of Indian Television, Media, Cult, and Soc, 93; coauth, Mapping Hegemony: Television News and Industrial Conflict, Ablex, 91. **CONTACT ADDRESS** Dept of Commun, Purdue Univ, 1080 Schleman Hall, West Lafayette, IN, 47907-1080. **EMAIL** arvind@purdue.edu

RAKOVE, JACK NORMAN
PERSONAL Born 06/04/1947, Chicago, IL, m, 1969, 1 child **DISCIPLINE** AMERICAN HISTORY **EDUCATION** Haverford Col, AB, 68; Harvard Univ, PhD(hist), 75. **CAREER** Asst prof hist, Colgate Univ, 75-80; ASSOC PROF HIST, STANFORD UNIV, 80- **HONORS AND AWARDS** Delancey K Jay Prize, Harvard Univ, 76. **MEMBERSHIPS** Orgn Am Historians; AHA. **RESEARCH** American Revolution. **SELECTED PUBLICATIONS** Auth, Spreading The News--The American Postal System From Franklin To Morse, J Of Interdisciplinary Hist, Vol 28, 97; Devising Liberty--Preserving And Creating Freedom In The New Am Republic, Revs In Am Hist, Vol 24, 96; Understanding The Am-Revolution--Issues And Actors, New England Quarterly-A Hist Rev Of New England Life And Letters, Vol 69, 96; The Papers Of Robert Morris ,Vol 7, November 1, 1782 May 4, 1783 Vol 8, May 5, 1783 December 31, 1783, J Of Military Hist, Vol 61, 97; To Secure The Blessings Of Liberty--Rights In American History, J Of Am Hist, Vol 81, 94; Republics Ancient And Modern--Classical Republicanism And The Am-Revolution, Am Hist Rev, Vol 98, 93. **CONTACT ADDRESS** Dept of Hist, Stanford Univ, Stanford, CA, 94305-1926.

RALPH, JAMES R.
PERSONAL Born 07/04/1960, Akron, OH **DISCIPLINE** HISTORY **EDUCATION** Middlebury Col, BA 82; Harvard Univ, MA 84, PhD 90. **CAREER** Middlebury Col, asst prof, assoc prof, 89 to 96-. **HONORS AND AWARDS** Fulbright Fel; Lectr DeMontFort Univ UK. **MEMBERSHIPS** OAH; AHA; VHS; SHA. **RESEARCH** Civil rights movement. **SELECTED PUBLICATIONS** Auth, Northern Protest: Martin Luther King Jr, Chicago, and the Civil Rights Movement, Cambridge MA, Harvard Univ Press, 93. **CONTACT ADDRESS** Dept of History, Middlebury Col, Middlebury, VT, 05753. **EMAIL** ralph@panther.middlebury.edu

RAMAGE, JAMES ALFRED
PERSONAL Born 05/06/1940, Paducah, KY, m, 1964, 1 child **DISCIPLINE** AMERICAN HISTORY **EDUCATION** Murray State Univ, BS, 65, MA, 68; Univ Ky, PhD(hist), 72. **CAREER** Teacher social studies, Mehlville High Sch, Mo, 65-67; teaching asst hist, Univ Ky, 68-70; From asst prof to assoc prof, 72-76, asst to pres, 72-76, PROF HIST, NORTHERN KY UNIV, 76- **MEMBERSHIPS** Southern Hist Asn; Soc Historians Early Am Repub. **RESEARCH** Pioneer merchants; General John Hunt Morgan; the Hunts and Morgans, a prominent Kentucky family. **SELECTED PUBLICATIONS** Auth, When This Cruel War Is Over--The Civil-War Letters Of Charles Harvey Brewster, J Of Am Hist, Vol 80, 93; April 65--Confederate Covert Action In The American-Civil-War, J Of Southern Hist, Vol 62, 96; Life And Wars Of Gideon J. Pillow, Am Hist Rev, Vol 100, 95; Island No.10--Struggle For The Mississippi Valley, Civil War History, Vol 43, 97; Soldiering In The Army Of Tennessee--A Portrait Of Life In A Confederate Army, Civil War Hist, Vol 39, 93. **CONTACT ADDRESS** Dept of Hist, No Kentucky Univ, Highland Heights, KY, 41076.

RAMAGE, NANCY HIRSCHLAND
PERSONAL Born 03/29/1942, New York, NY, m, 1969, 2 children **DISCIPLINE** HISTORY OF ART, CLASSICAL ARCHAEOLOGY **EDUCATION** Wheaton Col, Mass, BA, 63; Harvard Univ, MA, 65, PhD, 69. **CAREER** Asst prof Greek & archaeol, Boston Univ, 70-71; asst prof art hist, State Univ NY Binghamton, 77; asst prof art hist, Cornell Univ, 78-; draftsman ancient pottery, Brit Sch at Rome, 66-68; res asst ancient sculpture, Harvard Univ/Cornell Univ Sardis Expedition, 66-71; prof art hist, Ithaca Col, 72-. **HONORS AND AWARDS** Phi Beta Kappa; NEH summer grant; NEH summer seminar. **MEMBERSHIPS** Archaeol Inst Am; Col Art Asn; Int Asn Class Archaeol. **RESEARCH** Greek and Roman sculpture; Greek pottery; Etruscan pottery. **SELECTED PUBLICATIONS** Auth, The head capitals of Sardis, Papers of Brit Sch at Rome, 67; art, Studies in early Etruscan Bucchero, Papers of Brit Sch at Rome, 70; coauth, The Siting of Lydian Burial Mounds, Studies Presented to George M A Hanfmann, 71; auth, A Draped Herm from Sardis, Harvard Studies in Class Philol, 74; coauth, Sculpture from Sardis: The Finds through 1975, Harvard Univ, 78; coauth, Roman Art: Romulus to Constantine, 96; coauth, Corinthian, Attic, and Laconian Pottery from Sardis, 97. **CONTACT ADDRESS** Dept of Art History, Ithaca Col, 953 Danby Rd, Ithaca, NY, 14850. **EMAIL** ramage@ithaca.edu

RAMOS, DONALD
PERSONAL Born 07/12/1942, New Bedford, MA, m, 1964, 1 child **DISCIPLINE** LATIN AMERICAN HISTORY **EDUCATION** Univ Mass, BA, 64; Univ Fla, PhD(hist), 72. **CAREER** From instr to asst prof, 71-76, ASSOC PROF HIST, CLEVELAND STATE UNIV, 76-, DIR, FIRST COL, 78- **MEMBERSHIPS** Latin Am Studies Asn. **RESEARCH** Demographic history; social history, particularly family history; race relations. **SELECTED PUBLICATIONS** Life And Death In Early Colonial Ecuador, Colonial Latin Am Hist Rev, Vol 5, 96; Slave Rebellions In Brazil--The Muslim Uprising Of 1835 In Bahia, Hispanic Am Hist Rev, Vol 74, 94; From Minho To Minas--The Portuguese Roots Of The Mineiro Family, Hispanic Am Hist Rev, Vol 73, 93. **CONTACT ADDRESS** Dept of Hist, Cleveland State Univ, 1983 E 24th St, Cleveland, OH, 44115-2440.

RAMSBOTTOM, MARY MACMANUS
DISCIPLINE HISTORY **EDUCATION** Mt Holyoke, BA, 75; Yale Univ, MA, 76; MPhil, 78; PhD, 87. **CAREER** ASSOF PROF, HIST, TRUMAN STATE UNIV **MEMBERSHIPS** Am Antiquarian Soc **RESEARCH** Rel Experience, 17th Century New Eng. **SELECTED PUBLICATIONS** Auth, "Religious Society and the Family in Charlestown, Massachusetts, 1630-1740." **CONTACT ADDRESS** 2314 York St, Kirksville, MO, 63501. **EMAIL** mmacrams@truman.edu

RAMSEY, JEFF
DISCIPLINE HISTORY AND PHILOSOPHY OF SCIENCE **EDUCATION** Kans State Univ, BA; Univ Chicago, MS (chem), PhD (hist & plilos science). **CAREER** Philos, Oregon St Univ. **RESEARCH** Three-dimensional molecular shape. **SELECTED PUBLICATIONS** Area: how approximations and idealizations affect our notions of justification and reduction. **CONTACT ADDRESS** Dept Philos, Oregon State Univ, Corvallis, OR, 97331-4501. **EMAIL** jramsey@orst.edu

RAMSEY, JOHN T.
PERSONAL Auburn, NY, m, 1976, 1 child **DISCIPLINE** CLASSICS **EDUCATION** Harvard Col, AB, 68; Balliol Col, BA, 70, MA, 80; Harvard Univ, PhD, 75. **CAREER** Vis assoc prof, Univ Chicago, 82; from asst prof to assoc prof to prof, UIC, 75-. **HONORS AND AWARDS** Phi Beta Kappa, 68; Phi Kappa Phi, 93; NEH Fel, 93-94; AB, summa cum laude., Chemn, UIC, 97-2000. **MEMBERSHIPS** Am Philological Asn; Asn Ancient Historians; Classical Asn Canada. **RESEARCH** Roman republican history; Roman prose authors; ancient astronomy. **SELECTED PUBLICATIONS** Auth, Studies in Asconius, 76; auth, The Prosecution of C. Manilius in 66 B.C. and Cicero's pro Manilio, 80; auth, Sallusts BELLUM CATILINAE, 84; auth, Cicero & Sallust on the Conspiracy of Catiline, 88; coauth, The Comet of 44 B.C. and Caesar's Funeral Games, 97. **CONTACT ADDRESS** Dept of Classics, Univ of Illinois, Chicago, 601 S Morgan, Chicago, IL, 60607-7112. **EMAIL** j-ramsey@uic.edu

RAMUSACK, BARBARA N.
PERSONAL Born 11/05/1937, Gary, IN, s **DISCIPLINE** HISTORY **EDUCATION** Alverno Col, BA, 60; Univ Mich, MA, 62, PhD, 69. **CAREER** Asst prof to prof, Univ Cincinnati, 67-; Dir Graduate Studies Hist, 79-83, 89-94; head, 99-2003. **HONORS AND AWARDS** Phi Beta Kappa, 63; Outstanding Alumnae Award, Alverno Col, 75; McMicken Dean's Award for Dist Service, 91. **MEMBERSHIPS** Am Coun Southern Asian Art; Am Hist Asn; Asn Asian Studies. **RESEARCH** Princes of India; Interaction among Brit & South Asian Women; Maternal & Infant Welfare in Colonial India. **SELECTED PUBLICATIONS** The Princes of India in the Twilight of Empire: Dissolution of a Patron-Client System, 1914-1939, Columbus, 78; Embattled Advocates: The Debate over Birth Control in India, 1920-1940, J Women's Hist, 89; Cultural Missionaries, Maternal Imperialists, Feminist Allies: Brit Women Activists in India, 1865-1945, Women's Studies Int Forum, 90; Indian Princes as Fantasy: Palace Hotels, Palace Museums, Palace-on-Wheels, in Consuming Modernity: Public Culture in a South Asian World, 66-89, ed Carol A Breckenridge, Minneapolis, 95. **CONTACT ADDRESS** Dept of History, Univ of Cincinnati, PO Box 210373, Cincinnati, OH, 45221-0373. **EMAIL** barbara.ramusack@uc.edu

RAND, HARRY
PERSONAL Born 01/10/1947, New York, NY, m, 1988, 1 child **DISCIPLINE** HISTORY **EDUCATION** CUNY, BA, 69; Harvard Univ, AM, 71, PhD, 74. **CAREER** Assoc Curator, 77-79, chmn, 78-84, dept 20th century painting & sculpture, curator, 79-93, sr curator, 93-97, painting & sculpture, Natl Museum of Amer Art, curator, 97-, cultural hist, Smithsonian Institution. **RESEARCH** Methodology of art hist; human stud; relig/theol in modern life. **CONTACT ADDRESS** NMAH, Smithsonian Inst, Washington, DC, 20560-0616. **EMAIL** rand@nmah.si.edu

RANDALL, FRANCIS BALLARD
PERSONAL Born 12/17/1931, New York, NY, m, 1957, 2 children **DISCIPLINE** HISTORY **EDUCATION** Amherst Col, BA, 52, Columbia Univ, MA, 54, PhD, 60. **CAREER** Instr hist, Amherst Col, 56-59; from instr to asst prof, Columbia Univ, 59-61; trustee, 71-76, Mem hum fac, Sarah Lawrence Col, 61-, Fulbright fel, India, 65; vis prof, Columbia Univ, 67-68. **MEMBERSHIPS** AHA; Am Asn Advan Slavic Studies. **RESEARCH** Hist of Communism; hist of Russ; hist of Russ art. **SELECTED PUBLICATIONS** Coauth, Essays in Russian and Soviet history, Columbia Univ, 63; Stalin's Russia: An Historical Reconsideration, Free Press, 65; N G Chernyshevskii, Twayne, 67; Vissarion Belinskii, Oriental Research Partner, 87; Articles: Grandiosity and overdecoration in Russian art, summer 72 & History as icon: the Tret'iakov Gallery of Russian Art, 2/73, Art News; Maoism is dead, Nat Rev, 3/77, Ten days that shook China: the October revolution in Shanghai, Contemp China, 3/77. **CONTACT ADDRESS** 425 Riverside Dr, Apt 10-I, New York, NY, 10025-7730.

RANDOLPH, ADRIAN W. B.
DISCIPLINE ART HISTORY **EDUCATION** Princeton Univ, AB; Courtauld Inst Art, MA; Harvard Univ, MA, PhD. **CAREER** Asst prof, Dartmouth Col. **RESEARCH** Italian 15th-century cult; gender studies. **SELECTED PUBLICATIONS** Auth, Regarding Women in Sacred Space, Picturing Women in Renaissance and Baroque Italy, Cambridge UP, 97; Black Male Suspect? Auseinandersetzungen mit Stereotypen afro-amerikanischer Mannlichkeit in der zeitgenossischen US-Kunst, Kritische Berichte, 95; various other articles; coauth, The Bastides of Southwest France, Art Bulletin, 95. **CONTACT ADDRESS** Dartmouth Col, 3529 N Main St, #207, Hanover, NH, 03755. **EMAIL** adrian.randolph@dartmouth.edu

RANSBY, BARBARA
PERSONAL Born 05/12/1957, Detroit, MI, m **DISCIPLINE** AFRICAN-AMERICAN HISTORY **EDUCATION** Columbia Univ, BA, 1984; Univ of MI, MA, 1987, PhD, 1996. **CAREER** Institute for African Affairs and Department of History, Columbia University, research asst, 1982-84; Univ of MI, instructor, 1986-87, 1989, teaching asst, 1987, research asst, 1988; Museum of African American History, curator of Nineteenth and Twentieth Century special projects, 1989-90; Chicago Clergy and Laity Concerned, group trainer, 1992; Crossroads Foundation, group trainer, 1992; DePaul Univ, instructor, 1992-95, director, asst prof, 1995-96; Ancona School, consultant, group facilitator, 1993; Chicago Historical Society, consultant, panelist, 1993; Mac Arthur Foundation, consultant, 1994; American College Testing, consultant, 1996; UNIV OF IL AT CHICAGO, ASST PROF, 1996-; Northwestern University, manuscript reviewer, 1997. **HONORS AND AWARDS** Univ of MI, Student Recognition Award for Leadership, 1987; Women's Action for Nuclear Disarmament, Annual Peace Award, 1988; Columbia University, Herman Ausubel Student Award for Achievement in History, 1983; Univ of MI, Women Studies Program fellow, 1986; Univ of MI, Student Essay Competition Award, 1986; Woodrow Wilson Fellowships Foundation, National Mellon Fellowship, 1984-86; Univ of MI Rackham Graduate School Fellowships, Michigan Minority Merit Fellowship, 1986-90; Ford Foundation and Center for Afro-American and African Studies, Grad Student Research grant, 1990; DePaul Univ School of Liberal Arts and Sciences, Summer Faculty Research Award, 1993; Univ of IL at Chicago, Office of Social Science Research Seed Fund Initiative, grant, 1996. **MEMBERSHIPS** Anti-Racism Institute, Clergy and Laity Concerned, bd mem; Chicago Coalition in Solidarity with Southern Africa, bd mem; Univ of MI, History Dept Search Committee, student mem; Editorial Board of the Journal Race and Class; Ella Baker-Nelson Mandela Center for Anti-Racist Education, Univ of MI, bd mem; Association for the Study of Afro-American Life and History; Association of Black Women Historians; Coordinating Committee for Women in the Historical Profession; Organization of American Historians; United Coalition Against Racism, co-founder; Free South Africa Coordinating Committee, co-founder, co-chair. **SELECTED PUBLICATIONS** Author, works include: "Ella Baker and the Black Radical Tradition," U of NC Press, 1999; "Black Women and the Black Freedom Movement: Following Ella Baker's Path", 1998; "US: The Black Poor and the Politics of Expendability", Race and Class, 1996; numerous articles and essays. **CONTACT ADDRESS** African American Studies and History, Univ of Illinois, Chicago, 601 S Morgan, M/C 069, Chicago, IL, 60607.

RANUM, OREST
PERSONAL Born 02/18/1933, Lyle, MN, m, 1955, 2 children **DISCIPLINE** HISTORY **EDUCATION** Macalester Col, BA, 55; Univ Minn, MA, 57, PhD, 60. **CAREER** Instr hist, Univ Southern Calif, 60-61; from instr to assoc prof, Columbia Univ, 61-69; chmn dept, 72-76, PROF HIST, JOHNS HOPKINS UNIV, 69-, Guggenheim fel, 68-69; fel, Inst Advan Studies, 73-74. **MEMBERSHIPS** AHA; Soc Fr Hist Studies (vpres, 73-74). **RESEARCH** Early modern French history. **SELECTED PUBLICATIONS** Auth, Richelieu and the Councillors of Louis XIII, Clarendon, 63; Paris in the Age of Absolutism, Wiley, 68; La Rochefoucauld And The Language Of Unmasking In 17th-Century France, Am Hist Rev, Vol 101, 96; Donatien Alphonse Francois, Marquis-De-Sade, Am Hist Rev, Vol 98, 93; The Gentry In England And Wales, 1500-1700, Renaissance Quart, Vol 50, 97; Beneath The Cross--Catholics And Huguenots In 16th-Century Paris, J Of Modern Hist, Vol 66, 94; The Huguenots And French Opinion, 1685-1787--The Enlightenment Debate On Toleration, J Of Modern Hist, Vol 66, 94; A Company Of Scientists--Botany, Patronage, And Community At The 17th-Century Parisian-Royal-Academy-Of-Sciences, J Of Modern Hist, Vol 64, 92. **CONTACT ADDRESS** Dept of Hist, Johns Hopkins Univ, 3400 N Charles St, Baltimore, MD, 21218-2680.

RAPPAPORT, RHODA
PERSONAL Born 08/10/1935, New York, NY **DISCIPLINE** HISTORY OF SCIENCE **EDUCATION** Goucher Col, 55; Cornell Univ, MA, 58, PhD(hist sci), 64. **CAREER** From instr to assoc prof, 61-76, PROF HIST, VASSAR COL, 76-, Am Coun Learned Soc fel & Nat Sci Found grant, 66-67. **MEMBERSHIPS** AHA; Hist Sci Soc; Brit Soc Hist Sci; Soc Fr Hist Studies. **RESEARCH** History of geology and chemistry in the 18th century; 18th century France. **SELECTED PUBLICATIONS** Auth, Rouelle And Stahl: The Philogistic Revolution In France, In: Chymia, Univ Pa, 61; Problems And Sources in the Hist Of Geology, 1749-1810, Hist Of Science, Cambridge Univ, 64; Lavoisier's Geologic Activities, 1763-1792, Isis, 67; James Hutton And The Hist Of Geology, Isis, Vol 85, 94; Questions Of Evidence--An Anonymous Tract Attributed To John Toland, J Of The Hist Of Ideas, Vol 58, 97; James Hutton And The Hist Of Geology, Isis, Vol 85, 94. **CONTACT ADDRESS** Dept of Hist, Vassar Col, Poughkeepsie, NY, 12601.

RAPSON, RICHARD L.
PERSONAL Born 03/08/1937, New York, NY, m, 1982, 2 children **DISCIPLINE** HISTORY **EDUCATION** Amherst Col, BA, 58; Columbia Univ, PhD, 66. **CAREER** Instr hist, 61-65, fac res, 62-65, Stanford Univ; asst prof hist Univ Calif, Santa Barbara, 65-66; from asst to assoc prof, 66-72, prof, 72-, hist, Univ Hawaii; dir, Hum Prog, 68-70, found and dir, New Col, Univ Hawaii, 70-73. **HONORS AND AWARDS** Phi Beta Kappa; Woodrow Wilson fel, 58-59, Amherst-Columbia fel, 59-60; Danforth Assoc, 67- ; nat finalist, Danforth Found E. Harris Harbison Award for Gifted Tchg, 72; Outstanding Teacher Award, Stanfor Univ, 92. **MEMBERSHIPS** Ed Bd, Univ Press of Am; Acad Adv Bd, Semester at Sea. **RESEARCH** Psychological history (love, marriage, sex, family, emotions); cultural history. **SELECTED PUBLICATIONS** Coauth, Love, Sex, and Intimacy: Their Psychology, Biology, and History, HarperCollins, 93; coauth, Emotional Contagion, Cambridge, 94; coauth, Love and Sex: Cross-Cultural Perspectives, Allyn & Bacon, 96. **CONTACT ADDRESS** Dept of History, Univ of Hawaii, Honolulu, HI, 96822. **EMAIL** rapson@hawaii.edu

RASMUSSEN, CHRIS
DISCIPLINE HISTORY **EDUCATION** Rutgers Univ, PhD, 92. **CAREER** Asst prof, Univ Nev Las Vegas. **RESEARCH** Intellectual history; environmental history. **SELECTED PUBLICATIONS** Auth, pubs on American Culture History. **CONTACT ADDRESS** History Dept, Univ Nev Las Vegas, 4505 Md Pky, Las Vegas, NV, 89154.

RASMUSSEN, S.J.
PERSONAL Born 05/19/1949, Chicago, IL, m, 1986 **DISCIPLINE** ANTHROPOLOGY **EDUCATION** Univ of Chicago, MA, 72; Indiana Univ, PhD, 86. **CAREER** Assoc prof, Dept of Anthrop, Univ of Houston, 90- . **HONORS AND AWARDS** Fulbright Fel; Social Sci Res Coun. **MEMBERSHIPS** Am Anthrop Asn; Af Stud Asn. **RESEARCH** Anthropology of religion; gender; life cycle and aging. **SELECTED PUBLICATIONS** Auth, Joking in Researcher-Resident Dialogue: Ethnography of Hierarchy amoung Tuareg, in Anthropological Q, 93; auth, Speech by Allusion: Voice and Authority in Tuareg Verbal Art, in J of Anthrop and Humanism, 93; auth, The Head Dance, Contested Self, and Art as a Balancing Act in Female Possession among the Tuareg, in Africa: J of the Internatl African Inst, 94; auth, The Poetics of Childhood and Politics of Resistance in Tuareg Society, in Ethos, 94; auth, Female Sexuality, Social Reproduction, and Medical Intervention: Kel Ewey Tuareg Perspectives, in Culture, Medicine, and Psychiatry, 94; auth, Zarraf, A Tuareg Women's Wedding Dance, in Ethnology, 95; auth, Art as Process and Product: Patronage and Change in Tuareg Smith/Artisan Roles, in Africa: J of Internatl African Inst, 95; auth, Spirit Possession and Personhood among the Kel Ewey Tuareg, Cambridge Univ Pr, 95; auth, The Tuareg, in HRAF Encycl of World Cultures, 96; auth, Matters of Tasted: Food, Eating, and Reflections on 'the Body Politic' in Tuareg Society, in J of Anthrop Res, 96; auth, Tuareg Tent as Field Space and Cultural Symbol, in Anthrop Q, 96; auth, Knowledge and Power amoung the Tuareg, in Oral Tradition, 96; auth, The Tuareg, in Eastwood Encycl of Cultures and Daily Life, 97; auth, African Myth and Cosmology, in Scribner Encycl of African South of the Sahara, 97; auth, Between Ritual, Theatre, and Play: Blacksmith Praise at Tuareg Marriage, in J of Am Folklore, 97; auth, Gender and health Care: The Case of Tuareg Women in Niger, in the Political Economy of Health Care in Sub-Saharan Africa, 97; auth, The Poetics and Politics of Tuareg Aging: Life Course and Personal Destiny in Niger, Northern Ill Univ Pr, 97. **CONTACT ADDRESS** Dept of Anthropology, Univ of Houston, McElding Hall, Houston, TX, 77204-5882. **EMAIL** srasmussen@uh.edu

RASPORICH, ANTHONY W.
PERSONAL Born 01/09/1940, Port Arthur, ON, Canada **DISCIPLINE** HISTORY **EDUCATION** Queen's Univ, BA, 62, MA, 65; Univ Manitoba, PhD, 70. **CAREER** Asst prof, 66-71, assoc prof, 71-76, head dept, 73-76, assoc dean, soc sci, 76-81, PROF HISTORY, UNIV CALGARY, 77-; CD Howe Postdoct Fel, 70-71; Killiam Res Fel, 79; SSHRC Leave Fel, 81-82; exec, Alta Hist Soc Pub Bd, 75-81; exec, Can Ethnic Stud Asn, 79-83. **SELECTED PUBLICATIONS** Auth, For a Better Life, 82; ed, adv bd, Encyclopedia of Canada's Peoples, 92-97; ed, William Lyon Mackenzie, 72; ed, Western Canada: Past and Present, 75; ed, The Making of the Modern West, 84; co-ed, Prairie Perspectives II, 73; co-ed, Can Ethnic Studies, 80-98; co-ed, Winter Sports in the West, 90. **CONTACT ADDRESS** Dept of History, Univ Calgary, Calgary, AB, T2N 1N4. **EMAIL** awraspor@acs.ucalgary.ca

RAST, WALTER EMIL
PERSONAL Born 07/03/1930, San Antonio, TX, m, 1955, 4 children **DISCIPLINE** OLD TESTAMENT, ARCHEOLOGY **EDUCATION** St John's Col, BA, 52; Concordia Theol Sem, MDiv, 55, STM, 56; Univ Chicago, MA, 64, PhD(Old Testament), 66. **CAREER** From asst prof to assoc prof, 61-73; Prof Old Testament & Archaeol, Valparaiso Univ, 73-, James Alan Montgomery fel, Am Schs Orient Res, Jerusalem, 66-67; res prof, Albright Inst Archaeol Res, Jerusalem, 71-72; Danforth assoc, 73-; co-dir, Excavations at Bab edh-Dhra & Numeira, 75-; Nat Endowment for Humanities res grants, 75, 77, 79 & 81; Univ Chicago fel, 76; vis prof Old Testament, Univ Notre Dame, 77-78 & 82; pres, Am Ctr of Orental Res Amman, 78-82; prof, Albright Inst Archaeol Res, Jerusalem, 82-83; Am Coun Learned Soc fel, 71-72; Nat Endowment for Humanities fel, 82. **MEMBERSHIPS** Archaeol Inst Am; Am Schs Orient Res; Soc Bibl Lit; Israel Explor Soc. **RESEARCH** Old Testament; Syro-Palestinian archeology; Semitic languages. **SELECTED PUBLICATIONS** Auth, Tradition History and the Old Testament, Fortress, 72; coauth, Survey of the Southeastern plain of the Dead Sea, Ann Dept Antiq Jordan, 74; A preliminary report of excavations at Bab edh, Dhra, 1975, Ann Am Schs Orient Res, 76; auth, Tannach I: Studies in the Iron Age Pottery, Am Scholars Orient Res, 78; Joshua, Judges, Samuel and Kings, Fortress, 78; An Ostracon from Tell el-Ful, 78 &; co-ed, The Southeastern Dead Sea Plain Expedition: An Interim Report of the 1977 Season, 79, Annals Am Scholars Orient Res; coauth, Preliminary Report of the 1979 Expedition to the Dead Sea Plain, Jordan, Bull Am Scholars Orient Res, 240; Studies In The Archaeology And History Of Ancient-Israel In Honor Of Moshe Dothan--English, French, German, Italian, Hebrew, J Of Near Eastern Studies, Vol 56, 97; The Archaeology Of The Israelite Settlement, J Of Near Eastern Studies, Vol 52, 93. **CONTACT ADDRESS** Dept of Theol, Valparaiso Univ, Valparaiso, IN, 46383.

RATCLIFFE, DONALD JOHN
DISCIPLINE HISTORY **EDUCATION** Oxford, BA, 63; Bristol, PCGE, 64; Oxford & Univ Calif, Berkeley, DPhil, 66; Oxford, MA, 67; Durham, PhD, 85. **CAREER** SR LECT, HIST, DURHAM **MEMBERSHIPS** Am Antiquarian Soc **SELECTED PUBLICATIONS** Auth, "The Role of Voters and Issues in Party Formation: Ohio, 1824," Jour of Am Hist, 73; auth, "The Experience of Revolution and the Beginnings of Party Politics in Ohio, 1776-1816," Ohio Hist, 76; auth, Voter Turnout in Ohio," Jour of Early Rep 7, 87, repr in New Perspectives on the Early Republic, 94; auth, "Antimasonry and Partisanship in Greater New England, 1826-1836," Jour Early Rep 15, 95; auth, Party Spirit in a Frontier Republic: Democratic Politics in Ohio, 1793-1821, Ohio State Univ Press. **CONTACT ADDRESS** Dept of Hist, 43 N Bailey, Durham, ., DH1 3EX. **EMAIL** d.j.ratcliffe@durham.ac.uk

RATHER, SUSAN
DISCIPLINE ART AND ART HISTORY **EDUCATION** Univ DE, PhD. **CAREER** Assoc prof; adv, Art Hist Grad, Univ of TX at Austin. **HONORS AND AWARDS** Nat Endowment for the Hum, Winterthur Mus, Am Coun Learned Soc, Yale Ctr for Brit Art, Mass Hist Soc & Univ TX. **RESEARCH** 18th-century Brit and Am portraiture, specifically, the representation of the artist. **SELECTED PUBLICATIONS** Auth, Archaism, Modernism, and the Art of Paul Manship, early 20th-century sculpture, 93 & several exhibition catalogue essays; publ in, Archives Amer Art J, Art Bulletin, Art J, Arts Mag, 18th-century Stud, Metropolitan Mus J, Pa Mag Hist and Biog & Winterthur Portfolio. **CONTACT ADDRESS** Dept of Art and Art Hist, Univ of Texas at Austin, 2613 Wichita St, FAB 2.130, Austin, TX, 78705.

RATLIFF, CHARLES EDWARD
PERSONAL Born 10/13/1926, Morven, NC, m, 1945, 3 children **DISCIPLINE** ECONOMICS **EDUCATION** Davidson Col, BA, 47; Duke Univ, AM, 51, PhD, 55. **CAREER** V-12, 44-45, aviation supply officer, U.S. Navy, 45-46; prof, 63-66, prof of economics, Forman Christian Col, 69-70; Kenan prof of economics, 47-92, Kenan prof emeritus, Davidson Col; United Methodist Bd Global Ministries. **HONORS AND AWARDS** Ford Found award; Fulbright-Hays award; CASE Prof of the Year, 85. **MEMBERSHIPS** Nat Tax Asn; Southern Economic Asn; Am Economic Asn. **RESEARCH** Idea of a world devel-

opment fund, an approach to financing world development. **SELECTED PUBLICATIONS** Auth, Interstate Apportionment: Business Income, UNC Press, 62, Oxford Univ Press, 63; auth, A World Development Fund, World Acad of Development & Cooperation, 87; auth, Economics at Davidson: A Serguicentenial History, Davidson Col, 87; contribur, Rural Development in Pakistan, Carolina Acad Press, 80. **CONTACT ADDRESS** PO Box 597, Davidson, NC, 28036-0597.

RATNER, LARRY
DISCIPLINE HISTORY **EDUCATION** Cornell Univ, PhD. **CAREER** Prof. **SELECTED PUBLICATIONS** Auth, Pre Civil War Reform, Antimasonry, Powder Keg: Northern Opposition to Antislavery, 1831-1840; co-ed, The Development of An American Culture; Multi-Culturalism in the United States. **CONTACT ADDRESS** Dept of History, Knoxville, TN, 37996.

RAUABITSCHEK, ANTONY E.
DISCIPLINE CLASSICS **EDUCATION** Univ Vienna, DPhil, 35. **CAREER** Prof emer class, Stanford Univ. **RESEARCH** Epigraphy; Greek hist. **SELECTED PUBLICATIONS** Auth, Dedications from the Athenian Akropolis, 49; Supplementum Epigraphicum Graecum X, 49; Early Cretan Armorers, 72; The School of Hellas, Essays on Greek History, Archaeology, and Literature, 91. **CONTACT ADDRESS** Stanford Univ, Bldg 20, Main Quad, Stanford, CA, 94305.

RAUCH, ALAN
DISCIPLINE CULTURAL STUDIES OF SCIENCE **EDUCATION** Rutgers Univ, PhD, 89. **CAREER** Assoc ch, assoc prof, Ga Inst of Technol; bk rev ed, Configurations: A J of Lit, Sci, and Technol, Johns Hopkins UP. **RESEARCH** The dissemination of knowledge in the 19th century. **SELECTED PUBLICATIONS** Ed, The Mummy! A Tale of the Twenty-Second Century (1827), Univ Mich Press, 94; coed, One Culture: Essays in Science and Literature, Univ Wis, 87. **CONTACT ADDRESS** Sch of Lit, Commun & Cult, Georgia Inst of Tech, Skiles Cla, Atlanta, GA, 30332. **EMAIL** alan.rauch@lcc.gatech.edu

RAUCHER, ALAN R.
PERSONAL Born 01/27/1939, New York, NY, 1 child **DISCIPLINE** AMERICAN BUSINESS HISTORY, AMERICAN SOCIAL & INTELLECTUAL HISTORY **EDUCATION** Univ Calif, Los Angeles, BA, 60; MA, 61, PhD, 64. **CAREER** Vis asst prof hist, Univ Pittsburgh, 64-65; vis asst prof, Rice Univ, 65-66; vis asst prof, Univ Ariz, 66-67; asst prof, 67-68, asst prof, 68-74, assoc prof hist, 74-86, chmn hist, 86-95, act dean, coll lib arts, 96-97, act assoc dean, coll lib arts, 96-97, Wayne State Univ. **MEMBERSHIPS** Orgn Am Historians. **RESEARCH** Recent American history. **SELECTED PUBLICATIONS** Auth, Employee Relations at General Motors, Labor History, 87; art, Dime Store Chains, Business Hist Rev, 91; art, Sunday Business and the Decline of Sunday Closing Laws, Journal of Church and State, 94. **CONTACT ADDRESS** Dept of History, Wayne State Univ, 838 Mackenzie, Detroit, MI, 48202-3919. **EMAIL** a-raucher@wayne.edu

RAUSCH, JANE M.
PERSONAL Born 12/12/1940, Indianapolis, IN, m, 1983 **DISCIPLINE** LATIN AMERICAN HISTORY **EDUCATION** DePauw Univ, BA, 62; Univ Wis-Madison, MA, 64; PhD, 69. **CAREER** Lecturer, Mount St. Mary's Col, 68-69; lecturer, UCLA, 68-69; instr, Univ Mass-Amherst, 69-71; asst prof, 71-76; assoc prof, 76-84; PROF, 84- . **HONORS AND AWARDS** Alpha Lambda Delta, Phi Beta Kappa, Fulbright-Hays Sr Lectureship, 87; Conf on Latin Am Hist Robertson Prize, 81; Corresp Mem, Acad de Hist del Meta (Columbia), 87; Hon Mem, Centro de Hist de Casanare, 89. **MEMBERSHIPS** Am Hist Asoc; Latin Am Studies Asoc; Conf on Latin Am Hist; New England Coun of Latin Am Studies; Asoc de Colombianistas Norteamericanos. **RESEARCH** Columbian history; comparative frontier history; colonial Latin Am history; Latin Am hist, 19th and 20th centuries. **SELECTED PUBLICATIONS** Auth, People and Issues in Latin American History: The Colonial Experience, 93; ed with David J. Weber, Where Cultures Meet: Frontiers in Latin American History, 94; auth, Una Frontera de la sabana tropical: Los Ilanos de Columbia, 1531-1831, 94; auth, Fronteras en crisis: la desintegracion de las misiones en el extremo norte de Mexico y en la Nueva Granada: 1821-1849, Boletin Cultural y Bibiografico, 96; auth, La comuneros olvidados: La insurreccion de 1781 en los Ilanos del Casanare, Boletin Cultural y Bibliografico, 96. **CONTACT ADDRESS** Dept of Hist, Univ Mass at Amherst, Amherst, MA, 01003. **EMAIL** jrausch@history.umass.edu

RAVEN, JAMES R.
DISCIPLINE HISTORY **EDUCATION** Cambridge Univ, MA, 81, PhD, 85. **CAREER** Fel, Pembroke Coll, Cambridge Univ; fel & dir stud in hist, Magdalene Coll, Cambridge; UNIV LECT MOD HIST & TUTORIAL FEL, MANSFIELD COLL. **MEMBERSHIPS** Am Antiquarian Soc **SELECTED PUBLICATIONS** Auth, "Commercial Marts and Early Newspapers in Britain and the American Colonies," Jour of Newspaper and Per Hist 2, 86; auth, British Fiction 1750-1770: A Chronological Checklilst of Prose Fiction Printed in Britain and Ireland, Univ Delaware Press, 87; auth, Judging New Wealth: Popular Publishing and Responses to Commerce in England, 1750-1800, Oxford Univ Press, 92; auth, The Practice and Representation of Reading in England, Cambridge Univ Press, 95; auth, "I viaggi dei libri: realt...e raffigurazioni," in Gli spazi del libro nell'Europa del XVIII secolo, Sassi, 96; auth, "The Representation of Philanthropy and Reading in the Eighteenth-Century Library," Libr and Cult 31, Spring, 96; auth, "Gentlemen, Pirates, and Really Respectable Booksellers: Some Charleston Customers for Lackington, Allen & Co," in Booksellers and their Customers, 97; auth, "Establishing and Maintaining Credit Lines Overseas: The Case of the Export Book Trade from London in the Eighteenth Century, Mechanisms and Personnel," in Des Personnes aux institutions: R, seaux et culture du credit du XVIe au XXe siecle en Europe, Fucam, 97; auth, "The Importation of Books in the Eighteenth Century," in The Colonial Book in the Transatlantic World; auth, "Sent to the Wilderness: Mission Literature in Colonial America," in Print for Free: Non-commercial Publishing in Comparative Perspective; auth, "The Export ofBooks to Colonial North America," Publ Hist, 98. **CONTACT ADDRESS** Mansfield Col, Oxford, ., OX1 3TF.

RAVERTY, DENNIS
DISCIPLINE TWENTIETH CENTURY EUROPEAN AND AMERICAN ART AND ARCHITECTURE **EDUCATION** Univ Minn, BA, 90; Univ Iowa; MA, 92; Rutgers Univ, PhD, 96. **CAREER** Instr, Boston Inst Contemp Art, 82-83; Boston Ctr Adult Edu, 86-87; tchg asst, Univ Iowa, 90-92; lectr, Univ Konstanz, 94; Rutgers Univ, 94-96; asst prof, Pittsburg State Univ, 96-. **HONORS AND AWARDS** Grad scholar, Univ Iowa, 90-91; Russell scholar, Rutgers Univ, 93-94; grad asstship, Rutgers Univ, 95-96. **SELECTED PUBLICATIONS** Auth, A Split in the American Avant Garde, Rutgers Art Rev 14, 96; Critical Perspectives on New Images of Man, Art Jour 53, 95; Rob Moore and the Limitations of Style, The Art of Rob Moore, exhib cat, Mass Col Art Gallery, 94 **CONTACT ADDRESS** Art Dept, Pittsburg State Univ, 1701 S Broadway St, Pittsburg, KS, 66762. **EMAIL** bparker-@mail.pittstate.edu

RAVINA, MARK
DISCIPLINE HISTORY **EDUCATION** Columbia Univ, AB 83; Stanford Univ, MA, 88, PhD, 91. **CAREER** Assoc prof **RESEARCH** Japanese history; political activism in the 1870s and 1880s--linking the jiyu minken undo with Tokugawa-era political thought. **SELECTED PUBLICATIONS** Auth, Wasan and the Physics that Wasn't; State-building and Political Economy in Early Modern Japan. **CONTACT ADDRESS** Dept History, Emory Univ, 221 Bowden Hall, 561 Kilgo Cir, Atlanta, GA, 30322-1950. **EMAIL** histmr@emory.edu

RAWLEY, JAMES A.
PERSONAL Born 11/09/1916, Terre Haute, IN, m, 1945, 2 children **DISCIPLINE** HISTORY **EDUCATION** Univ Mich, AB, 38, AM, 39; Columbia Univ, PhD, 49. **CAREER** Instr hist, NY Univ, 46-51; instr, Hunter Col, 51-53; assoc prof, Sweet Briar Col, 53-58, chmn dept hist, 53-57, prof, 58-64, chmn div social studies, 61-64; chmn dept, 66-67, PROF HIST, UNIV NEBR, LINCOLN, 64-, CHMN DEPT, 73-, Scholar-in-residence, Rockefeller Found Study & Conf Ctr, Bellagio, Italy, 77; Huntington-Nat Endowment for Humanities fel, Huntington Libr, 79; Huntington Libr fel, 81. **MEMBERSHIPS** AHA; Orgn Am Historians: fel Royal Hist Soc; Southern Hist Asn. **RESEARCH** American Civil War era; Atlantic slave trade; the Gilded Age. **SELECTED PUBLICATIONS** Auth, Edwin D Morgan, Columbia Univ, 55; The nationalism of Abraham Lincoln, Civil War Hist, 9/63; The American Civil War: An English View, Univ Va, 65; Turning Points of the Civil War, Univ Nebr, 66; Race and Politics, Lippincott, 69; ed, Lincoln and Civil War Politics, Holt, 69; The Politics of Union, Dryden, 74; The Transatlantic Slave Trade, Norton, 81; Gordon,Nathaniel The Only American Executed For Violating The Slave-Trade Laws, Civil War Hist, Vol 39, 93; The Culture Of English Antislavery, 1780-1860, Am Hist Rev, Vol 97, 92. **CONTACT ADDRESS** Dept of Hist, Univ of Nebr, Lincoln, NE, 68588.

RAWLS, JAMES J.
PERSONAL Born 11/10/1945, Washington, DC, m, 1967, 2 children **DISCIPLINE** HISTORY **EDUCATION** Stanford Univ, BA, 67; Univ Calif-Berkeley, MA, 69, PhD, 75. **CAREER** Instr, San Francisco State Univ, 71-75; Instr, Diablo Valley Col, 75-; Vis Lectr, 77-81, Vis As Assoc Prof, Univ Calif-Berkeley, 89. **HONORS AND AWARDS** Honors in Hist, Stanford Univ, 67; Schol-in-Residence, Calif State Univ, 87; Fac Lectr Award, Diablo Valley Col, 88; Fel, Calif Hist Soc, 88; Nat Teaching Excellence Award, Univ Tex, 89; Award of Merit, League for Hist Preservation, 93. **MEMBERSHIPS** Am Hist Asn; Calif Hist Soc; Calif Coun Humanities. **RESEARCH** California history; Native American history. **SELECTED PUBLICATIONS** Auth, Dr. History's Sampler: More Stories of California's Past, McGraw-Hill Bk Co, 94; California Dreaming: More Stories from Dr. History, McGraw-Hill Bk Co, 95; Chief Red Fox is Dead: A History of Native Americans Since 1945, Harcourt Brace Publ, 96; A Voyage through the Sea of Cortez, Special Expeditions, 97; co-ed, A Golden State: Mining and the Development of California, Univ Calif Press (forthcoming 98); author of numerous other publications and articles. **CONTACT ADDRESS** History Dept, Diablo Valley Col, Pleasant Hill, CA, 94523. **EMAIL** rawls@netdex.com

RAWSKI, EVELYN SAKAKIDA
PERSONAL Born 02/02/1939, Honolulu, HI, m, 1967 **DISCIPLINE** CHINESE HISTORY **EDUCATION** Cornell Univ, AB, 61; Radcliffe Col, AM, 62; Harvard Univ, PhD, 68. **CAREER** Asst prof, 67-72, assoc prof, 73-79, prof cultural hist, Univ Pittsburgh, 79-. **HONORS AND AWARDS** Nat Endowment for Humanities grant, 79-80; Am Coun Learned Soc grant, 73-74 **MEMBERSHIPS** Assn Asian Studies (bd dirs, 76-79); Econ Hist Assn. **RESEARCH** Chinese economic and social history. **SELECTED PUBLICATIONS** Auth, Agricultural Change and the Peasant Economy of South China, Harvard Univ, 72; auth, Education and Popular Literacy in Ch'ing China, Univ Mich, 78; auth, The Last Emperors: A Social History of Ch'ing Imperial Institutions, 98. **CONTACT ADDRESS** Dept of History, Univ of Pittsburgh, 3M38 Forbes Quad, Pittsburgh, PA, 15260-0001. **EMAIL** esrx@pitt.edu

REA, KENNETH W.
DISCIPLINE HISTORY **EDUCATION** La Tech Univ, BA, 66; Univ CO at Boulder, MA, 68; PhD, 70. **CAREER** Hist, LA Tech, Univ. **HONORS AND AWARDS** Outstanding Research Award, 79. **MEMBERSHIPS** Am Asn Chinese Studies; Asn Asian Studies. **RESEARCH** Mod China; Sino-Am rel; Pacific Rim; Am for policy. **SELECTED PUBLICATIONS** Ed, Canton in Revolution, 1925-1928,Westview, 77; Early Sino-American Relations, 1841-1912, Westview, 78; Dr. John Leighton Stuart and United States Policy Toward China, 1946-1949, ME Sharpe, 90; co-ed, The Forgotten Ambassador: John Leighton Stuart, 1946-1949, Westview, 81;China: An Analytic Reader, Milburn: RF, 75. **CONTACT ADDRESS** Dept of Hist, Louisiana Tech Univ, PO Box 3178, Ruston, LA, 71272.

REAGAN, LESLIE J.
DISCIPLINE HISTORY **EDUCATION** Univ Wis Madison, PhD, 91. **CAREER** Asst prof, Univ Ill Urbana Champaign. **RESEARCH** History of medicine; American women's history; sexuality; twentieth century American social history. **SELECTED PUBLICATIONS** Auth, 'About to Meet Her Maker': Women, Doctors, Dying Declarations, and the State's Investigation of Abortion, Chicago, 1867-1940, J Am Hist, 91; Linking Midwives and Abortion in the Progressive Era, Bul Hist Medicine, 95; When Abortion was a Crime: Women, Medicine, and Law in the United States, 1867-1975, Univ Calif, 96. **CONTACT ADDRESS** History Dept, Univ Ill Urbana Champaign, 52 E Gregory Dr, Champaign, IL, 61820. **EMAIL** lreagan@uiuc.edu

REAGAN, MARY JANE
PERSONAL Born 08/27/1921, Brainerd, MN, d, 1 child **DISCIPLINE** EDUCATION **EDUCATION** Univ Minn, PhD, 68. **CAREER** Dir Remedial Reading Ctr, Minneapolis,MN Public Sch Sys. **MEMBERSHIPS** Am Philos Asn **SELECTED PUBLICATIONS** Auth, Getting It Right for K-12 Schooling, Huntington House, 98. **CONTACT ADDRESS** 1917 Pinehurst Ave., St. Paul, MN, 55116-1340.

REAGON, BERNICE JOHNSON
PERSONAL Born 10/04/1942, Albany, GA **DISCIPLINE** AFRICAN HISTORY **EDUCATION** Albany State College, Albany, GA, BA, 1959-; Spelman College, Atlanta, GA, BA, 1970; Howard University, Washington, DC, PhD, 1975. **CAREER** Student Non-Violent Coordinating Comm, civil rights activist, 1961-62, field sec & freedom singer, 1962-64; AFRICAN AMERICAN FOLKLORE, FIELD RESEARCHER, 1965-; SWEET HONEY IN THE ROCK, WASHINGTON, DC, FOUNDER/ARTISTIC DIRECTOR, 1973-; Smithsonian Institution, Museum of American History, Program in Black American Culture, program director and cultural historian, 1976-88; SMITHSONIAN INSTITUTION, MUSEUM OF AMERICAN HISTORY, DIVISION OF COMMUNITY LIFE, CURATOR, 1988-; AMER UNIV, DISTINGUISHED PROF OF HISTORY, 1993-. **HONORS AND AWARDS** MacArthur Fellowship, 1989; Charles E. Frankel Prize, 1995. **SELECTED PUBLICATIONS** Publications: Voices of the Civil Rights Movement: Black American Freedom Songs, 1960-1966. **CONTACT ADDRESS** Dept of History, American Univ, 4400 Massachusetts Ave NW, Washington, DC, 20016.

REARDON, COLLEEN
DISCIPLINE MUSIC HISTORY **EDUCATION** UCLA, AB; MA; PhD. **CAREER** Assoc prof and dir undergrad studies, 93. **HONORS AND AWARDS** NEH Summer Stipend; Fulbright Fellow. **RESEARCH** Music in seventeenth-century Siena; convent music. **SELECTED PUBLICATIONS** Auth, Musica franca: Essays in Honor of Frank A. D'Accone, Pendragon, 96; Agostino Agazzari and Music at Siena Cathedral 1597-1641, Oxford UP, 93; Music as Leitmotif in Louisa May Alcott's Little Women, Children's Literature, 96; Insegniar la zolfa ai gittatelli: Music and Teaching at Santa Maria della Scala, Siena, during the Late Sixteenth and Early Seventeenth Centuries in Musica franca: Essays in Honor of Frank A. D'Accone, Pendragon, 96;, Music and Musicians at Santa Maria di Provenzano, Siena, 1595-1640, Jour Musicol, 93; Two Parody Magnificats on Palestrina's Vestiva i colli, Studi musicali, 86. **CONTACT ADDRESS** Dept Music, SUNY Binghamton, PO Box 6000, Binghamton, NY, 13902-6000.

REARDON, JOHN J.
DISCIPLINE HISTORY **EDUCATION** Georgetown Univ, PhD. **CAREER** Hist, Loyola Univ. **RESEARCH** Thematic research into the cosmopolitan dimensions in American history. **SELECTED PUBLICATIONS** Auth, Edmund Randolph: A Biography, NY: Macmillan, 75; Payton Randolph: 1721-1775 One Who Presided, NC: Carolina Acad Press, 82; America and the Multinational Corporation: The History of a Troubled Partnership 1945-1990, Praeger, 92. **CONTACT ADDRESS** Fine Arts Dept, Loyola Univ, Chicago, 6525 N. Sheridan Rd., Chicago, IL, 60626. **EMAIL** jreardo@wpo.it.luc.edu

REARICK, CHARLES
PERSONAL Born 08/02/1942, St. James, MO, 3 children **DISCIPLINE** MODERN EUROPEAN HISTORY **EDUCATION** Col Idaho, BA, 64; Harvard Univ, MA, 65, PhD, 68. **CAREER** Asst prof 68-74, assoc prof hist 74-83, prof hist 83-, Univ Ma, Amherst, 74- **MEMBERSHIPS** Soc Fr Hist Studies. **RESEARCH** Modern French history; modern European cultural history. **SELECTED PUBLICATIONS** Auth, Symbol, legend, and history: Michelet as folklorist-historian, Fr Hist Studies, spring 71; Henri Martin--from Druidic traditions to Republican politics, J Contemp Hist, 10/72; Beyond the Enlightenment: Historians and Folklore in Nineteenth Century France, Ind Univ, 74; Festivals and politics: The Michelet centennial of 1898, Historians in Politics, Sage, 74; Festivals in modern France: The experience of the Third Republic, J Contemp Hist, 7/77; Pleasures of the Belle Epoque: Entertainment and Festivity in Turn-of-the-Century France, 85; The French in Love and War: Popular Culture in the Era of the World Wars, 97. **CONTACT ADDRESS** Dept Hist, Univ Massachusetts, Amherst, MA, 01003-0002.

REAVES, BENJAMIN FRANKLIN
PERSONAL Born 11/22/1932, New York, NY, m, 1955 **DISCIPLINE** EDUCATION **EDUCATION** Oakwood Coll Huntsville AL, BA, 1955; Andrews Univ, MA, M Div; Chicago Theological Seminary. **CAREER** MI Conference of Seventh-Day Adventist, pastor, 1956-68; Westside Hospital, Chicago IL, counselor, 1968-72; Andrews Univ, Berrien Springs MI, youth pastor, 1972-73, assoc prof, 1973-77; US Army, instr for homeletics, 1977-85; OAKWOOD COLL, HUNTSVILLE AL, PRES, 1985-. **HONORS AND AWARDS** Distinguished Alumnus Award, Oakwood Coll, 1973; Teacher of the Year, Oakwood Coll, 1983; Music Humanitarian Award, Oakwood Coll, 1984; Outstanding Leadership Award, Oakwood Coll, 1986; **MEMBERSHIPS** Mem, Advisory Board of Andrews Univ; mem, Advisory Board of Loma Linda Univ; mem, United Negro College Fund; mem, Natl Assn for Equal Opportunity in Higher Educ; mem, Council for the Advancement of Private Colleges in AL; mem, Huntsville Chamber of Commerce Board; mem, Vision 2000; mem, Rotary club; mem, Urban Ministries Program; board of directors, UNCF; Chicago Sunday Evening Club, speaker. **SELECTED PUBLICATIONS** Author of articles in numerous journals such as: Message, The Review and Herald, Ministry, The Adventist Laymen, Collegiate Quarterly, South African Signs of the Times. **CONTACT ADDRESS** Oakwood Col, Oakwood Road, Huntsville, AL, 35896.

REBER, VERA BLINN
PERSONAL Born 05/23/1941, Hong Kong, m, 1979, 1 child **DISCIPLINE** LATIN AMERICA AND AFRICAN HISTORY **EDUCATION** Univ Indianapolis, BA, 63 (History and Social Science); Univ WI, Madison, MA, 67 (Comparative Tropical Hist); PhD, 72 (Latin America and African Hist). **CAREER** Asst prof, 70-72, assoc prof, 72-78, PROF, SHIPPENSBURG UNIV, 78-. **HONORS AND AWARDS** Tinker Found, 79; NEH Summer Seminar, 76, 82, 93; Social Science Res grant, 86; Arthur P. Whitaker Prize, Honorable Mention, 88; NEH Institute, History of Medicine, 95. **MEMBERSHIPS** Am Hist Asn; Conference on Latin Am Hist; Latin Am Studies Asn; World Hist Asn. **RESEARCH** 19th Century Argentina and Paraguay-economic, medieval and social history. **SELECTED PUBLICATIONS** Auth, The Demographics of Paraguay: A Reinterpretation of the Great War, 1864-1870, The Hispanic Am Hist Rev 68: 2, May 88; Teaching Undergraduates to Think Like Historians, in History Anew: Innovations in the Teaching of History Today, ed Robert Blackey, The Univ Press, CA State Univ, 93; A Nineteenth Century Development Model with Lessons for the 1990's: The Case of Paraguay 1810-1864, Latin American Essays, Vol VII, ed Alvin Cohen, Juan Espadas and Vera Reber, Middle Atlantic Council of Latin Am Studies, 94; El Comercio Exterior en la Economica del Paraguay (1810-1860), Investigationes y Ensayos, Vol 44, Buenos Aires, Argentina; Small Farmers in the Economy: The Paraguayan Example, 1810-1865, The Americas, April 95; Pocket Folders and Discussion Participation, The Teaching Professor, 12:2, May 98; Blood, Coughs, and Fever: Tuberculosis and the Working Class of Buenos Aires, Argentina, 1885-1915, forthcoming in Social Hist of Medicine, 12:1, April 99. **CONTACT ADDRESS** 314 E. King St., Shippensburg, PA, 17257. **EMAIL** vbrebe@ark.ship.edu

RECK, DAVID
PERSONAL Born 01/12/1935, Rising Star, TX, m, 1968, 2 children **DISCIPLINE** ETHNOMUSICOLGY; COMPOSITION **EDUCATION** Univ of Houston, BM, 58; Univ of Texas, MM, 59; Wesleyan Univ, PhD, 84. **CAREER** Prof, Amherst Col, 74-. **HONORS AND AWARDS** Guggenheim fel. **RESEARCH** Music of South India **SELECTED PUBLICATIONS** Coauth, Worlds of Music, 97; auth, Music of the Whole Earth, 97. **CONTACT ADDRESS** Dept of Music, Amherst Col, Amherst, MA, 01002. **EMAIL** dbreck@amherst.edu

REDFIELD, JAMES M.
PERSONAL Chicago, IL, m, 4 children **DISCIPLINE** CLASSICAL LANGUAGE AND LITERATURE **EDUCATION** Univ Chicago, BA, 54, PhD, 61. **CAREER** Instr, Comt Soc Thought, 60-62; Asst prof, 62-65; Assoc prof, 65-75; Prof, Univ Chicago, 76-. **HONORS AND AWARDS** Woodrow Wilson Fel; NEH Younger Sch; Am Coun Learned Socs; Martha Sutton Weeks Fel; NEH Grant. **SELECTED PUBLICATIONS** Auth, Anthropology and the Classics, Arion, 91; auth, The Politics of Immortality, Recherches et Rencontres, 91; auth, The Sexes in Hesiod, Reinterpreting the Classics, 93; auth, Homo Domesticus, the Greeks, Univ Chicago Press, 94. **CONTACT ADDRESS** Univ Chicago, 1126 E 59th St, SS Box 94, Chicago, IL, 60637.

REDMOUNT, CAROL A.
PERSONAL Born 09/15/1952, Indianapolis, IN, m **DISCIPLINE** ARCHAEOLOGY **EDUCATION** Oberlin Col, BA, 70; Harvard Div Sch, MTS, 74; Univ Chicago, PhD, 89. **CAREER** Lectr, asst and assoc prof, Near East Studies, Univ Calif, Berkeley, 90- . **HONORS AND AWARDS** Phi Beta Kappa; Hellman Family Fac Fund Award. **MEMBERSHIPS** Am Sch of Oriental Res; Am Res Ctr in Egypt; Soc for Stud of Egyptian Antiquities; ICOMOS. **RESEARCH** Egyptian archaeology; Syro-Palestinian archaeology; interrelations among the Aegean, Egypt and The Levant; pottery studies. **SELECTED PUBLICATIONS** Coauth, The City of the Lions: New Explorations at Tell el-Muqdam, Bull of the Egyptian Exploration Soc, 93; coauth, The 1993 Field Season of the Berkeley Tell el-Muqdam Project: Preliminary Report, Newsl of the Am Res Ctr in Egypt, 94; auth, Ethnicity, Pottery and the Hyksos at Tell el-Maskhuta in the Egyptian Delta, Bibl Archaeol, 95; auth, The Wadi Tumilat and the Canal of the Pharaohs, J of Near Eastern Stud, 95; auth, Of Silts and Marls and Mixes: Analysis of Modern Egyptian Pottery, Gottinger Miszellen, 95; auth, Major and Trace Element Analysis of Modern Egyptian Pottery, J of Archaeol Sci, 96; coauth, Tales of a Delta Site: Preliminary Report on the 1995 Field Season at Tell el-Muqdam, J of the Am Res Ctr in Egypt, 97; auth, Bitter Lives: Israel In and Out of Egypt, in Coogan, ed, Oxford History of the Biblical World, Oxford, 98. **CONTACT ADDRESS** Near East Studies Dept, Univ of California, Berkeley, CA, 94720-1940. **EMAIL** redmount@socrates.berkeley.edu

REECE, STEVE
DISCIPLINE GREEK AND ROMAN EPIC **EDUCATION** Univ HI, BA, 82, MA, 84; UCLA, PhD, 90. **CAREER** Drama, St. Olaf Col. **SELECTED PUBLICATIONS** Auth, The Stranger's Welcome: Oral Theory and the Aesthetics of the Homeric Hospitality Scene, Univ Mich Press, 93. **CONTACT ADDRESS** St Olaf Col, 1520 St Olaf Ave, Northfield, MN, 55057. **EMAIL** reece@stolaf.edu

REED, CHRISTOPHER A.
DISCIPLINE HISTORY **EDUCATION** McGill Univ, BA, 78; Univ Glasgow, M.Phil, 84; Univ Calif, Berkeley, PhD, 96. **CAREER** Vis asst prof, Reed Col, 96-97; asst prof, Ohio State Univ, 97-. **HONORS AND AWARDS** Glasgow Exchange Fel, 80-82, McGill Univ; Joseph R. Levenson Award in Chinese Studies, 85-86; Fulbright Hays Grad Award, 90-91; Committee for Scholarly Correspondence with China, 91-93. **MEMBERSHIPS** Am Hist Asn; Asn Asian Stud; Midwest Conference Asian Affairs. **RESEARCH** Modern Chinese political, social, urban, cultural history. **SELECTED PUBLICATIONS** Auth, art, Sooty Sons of Vulcan': Shanghai's Printing Machine Manufacturers, 1895-1932, 95. **CONTACT ADDRESS** Dept of History, Ohio State Univ, 230 W 17th Ave, Columbus, OH, 43202. **EMAIL** reed.434@osu.edu

REED, DAISY FRYE
PERSONAL Washington, DC, d **DISCIPLINE** EDUCATION **EDUCATION** DC Teachers Coll, BS 1953-56; George Washington Univ, MA 1957-61; Teachers Coll Columbia Univ, MEd, EdD 1973-75; Loyola Univ, MRE, 1992-94. **CAREER** Washington DC Publ Schools, teacher 1956-73; Teachers Coll Columbia Univ, asst prof, dir of teacher corps proj 1975-76; Publ School Syst VA, consult; State Department of Education, consultant; School of Ed VA Commonwealth Univ, professor, 1976-. **HONORS AND AWARDS** Innovation Awd DC Publ Schools Washington; Minority Student Scholarship Teachers Coll Columbia Univ; Reise-Melton Award for Promoting Cross-Cultural Understanding, Virginia Commonwealth University, 1990-91; Outstanding Service Award, 1991-92; Outstanding Teacher Award, 1994-95; Phi Kappa Phi; Bd of Visitors, teaching fellow, 1998-2000. **MEMBERSHIPS** President, Assn of Teacher Educatorss in Virginia, 1988-91; ATE, 1978-; Phi Delta Kappa; Zeta Phi Beta Sorority, 1955-. **SELECTED PUBLICATIONS** Co-Author: Classroom Management for the Realities of Today's Schools; Author of book chapter in J Wood's Mainstreaming; articles published in Action in Teacher Education; NASSP Journal; Middle School Journal; research studies: Resilient At-Risk Children; Teaching in Culturally Diverse Classrooms; Overage & Disruptive Students in the Middle School. **CONTACT ADDRESS** Sch Educ, Virginia Commonwealth Univ, Box 842020, Richmond, VA, 23284-2020.

REED, JAMES WESLEY
PERSONAL Born 10/17/1944, New Orleans, LA, m, 1962, 2 children **DISCIPLINE** SOCIAL HISTORY **EDUCATION** Univ New Orleans, BA, 67; Harvard Univ, AM, 68, PhD, 74. **CAREER** Res fel hist, Schlesinger Libr, 73-75; prof hist, Rugers Univ, 75-, Dean, Rutgers Col, 85-94. **RESEARCH** Soc hist; hist of med; hist of behavioral sci. **SELECTED PUBLICATIONS** Auth, From Private Vice to Public Virtue: The Birth Control Movement and American Society Since 1830, Basic Bks, 78. **CONTACT ADDRESS** Dept of Hist, Rutgers Univ, 16 Seminary Place, New Brunswick, NJ, 08901-1108. **EMAIL** jwr@rci.rutgers.edu

REED, JOHN JULIUS
PERSONAL Born 01/16/1913, Rochester, NY, m, 1941, 2 children **DISCIPLINE** AMERICAN HISTORY **EDUCATION** Univ Rochester, BA, 34, MA, 40; Univ PA, PhD(US hist), 53. **CAREER** Teacher, High Sch, NY, 35-41; instr hist & math, Univ PA, 42-45; from instr to assoc prof hist, 48-63, prof hist, 63-78, chmn dept, 71-78, dir Am studies, 72-78, emer prof hist, Muhlenberg Col, 78-; lectr, Trenton Ctr, Rutgers Univ, 47-48; La State Univ New Orleans, 64; Lehigh Univ, 79; Moravian Col, 80 & 81; Temple Univ, 81. **HONORS AND AWARDS** Lindback Found Award, 61. **MEMBERSHIPS** AHA; Orgn Am Historians; Am Studies Asn; Soc Sci Hist Asn. **RESEARCH** History of United States political parties; the origins, early development, and quantitative analysis of the Whig party; Thaddeus Stevens and early history of the Whig party. **CONTACT ADDRESS** 320 S 23rd St, Allentown, PA, 18104.

REED, LINDA
DISCIPLINE AMERICAN HISTORY, POST-1865 **EDUCATION** Ind Univ at Bloomington, PhD, 86. **CAREER** Assoc instr, Ind Univ, 80-81; asst prof of Hist, UNC-Chapel Hill, 88; Martin Luther King, Jr/Cesar Chavez/Rosa Parks visiting prof, Mich State Univ, 89; ed asst, J of Am Hist, Ind Univ, 81-83; ASST PROF OF HIST, 88-92, DIR, AFRICAN-AM STUDIES PROG, 92-, ASSOC PROF OF HIST, 92-, UNIV OF HOUSTON. **HONORS AND AWARDS** Greenwood Award, Univ of Houston/Houston City Coun, 93; Young Black Achievers of Houston Award, 92; Carter G. Woodson Inst for Afro-Am and African Studies Res Fel, Univ of Va, 83-85; Hist Dept Scholar, 82, Foundation Grant, 82, W.E.B. Du Bois Writing Contest Winner, 81, Black Hist Month Scholar Award, 83, Ind Univ; CIC Minorities Fel, 78-80; B.S. awarded with great honors, 77; Alpha Kappa Mu Honor Soc, 76-77; Acad achievement awards and acad scholar, 73-77; Ford Found Fel, Univ of Va, 91-92; Res Initiation Grant, Univ of Houston, 90. **MEMBERSHIPS** Asn for the Study of Afro-Am Life and Hist; Asn of Black Women Historians; Org of Am Historians; Southern Hist Asn; Southern Asn for Women Historians. **RESEARCH** Twentieth Century U.S.; Women's History; the Civil Rights Era. **SELECTED PUBLICATIONS** Auth, Montgomery Bus Boycott, Mississippi Freedom Democratic Party, & Mississippi Freedom Summer, The Reader's Companion to U.S. Women's Hist, Houghton Mifflin Co, 98; auth, The Brown Decision: Historical Context in a Historian's Refl'ctions, Extensions, 94; auth, Simple Decency and Common Sense: The Southern Conference Movement 1938-1963, Ind Univ Press, 91; auth, Fannie Lou Hamer: Civil Rights Leader, Black Women in Am: An Historical Encycl, 93; ed, We Spcialize in the Wholly Impossible: A Reader in Black Women's History, Carlson Pub Co, 95. **CONTACT ADDRESS** Univ of Houston, Univ Park, 4800 Calhoun Rd., Houston, TX, 77004.

REED, MERL E.
PERSONAL Born 08/14/1925, Syracuse, NY, m, 1958 **DISCIPLINE** AMERICAN HISTORY **EDUCATION** Syracuse Univ, AB, 50, MA, 52; La State Univ, PhD, 57. **CAREER** Asst, La State Univ, 52-57; instr hist, Tex Woman's Univ, 57-58; instr, Del Mar Col, 58-60, assoc prof & chmn dept, 60-61; asst prof soc sci, Ball State Teachers Col, 61-65; assoc prof hist, 65-72, PROF HIST, GA STATE UNIV, 72- **MEMBERSHIPS** Orgn Am Historians; Southern Hist Asn; Labor Hist Asn. **RESEARCH** United States economic history; labor history; Jackson period. **SELECTED PUBLICATIONS** Auth, New Orleans and the Railroads, La State Univ, 66; Lumberjacks and longshoremen: The SWW in Louisiana, 72 & The Augusta textile mills and the strike of 1886, 73, Labor Hist; coauth, Surveying the records of a city: The history of Atlanta Project, Am Archivist, 73; auth, FEPC, the Black worker and the Southern shipyards, S Atlantic Quart, 75; co-ed, Essays in Southern Labor History, Greenwood, 77; auth, FEPC and the federal agencies in the South, J Negro Hist, 80; co-ed, Southern Workers and Their Unions, Greenwood, 81; Jacksonville After The Fire, 1901-1919 - A New South City, J Of Southern Hist, Vol 59, 93; The North-Carolina Railroad, 1849-1871, And The Modernization Of North-Carolina, J Of Southern Hist, Vol 59, 93. **CONTACT ADDRESS** Dept of Hist, Georgia State Univ, 33 Gilmer St SE, Atlanta, GA, 30303-3080.

REED, T.V.
DISCIPLINE CULTURAL THEORY, CONTEMPORARY AMERICAN FICTION, AND THE 1960S **EDUCATION** Univ Calif, Santa Cruz, PhD. **CAREER** Assoc prof & dir Amer Stud, Washington State Univ. **RESEARCH** Various art forms as they have helped to shape social movement cultures from the Civil Rights era to the 1990s. **SELECTED PUBLICATIONS** Auth, Fifteen Jugglers, Five Believers: Literary Politics and the Poetics of American Social Movements, 92. **CONTACT ADDRESS** Dept of English, Washington State Univ, 1 SE Stadium Way, PO Box 645020, Pullman, WA, 99164-5020. **EMAIL** reedtv@wsu.edu

REEDY, CHANDRA L.
PERSONAL Born 12/11/1953, NM, m, 1975, 1 child **DISCIPLINE** ARCHAEOLOGY **EDUCATION** Univ Calif, BA, 75, MA, 82, PhD, 86. **CAREER** Vis lectr, 88, asst prof, art cons dept, 89-94, Univ Calif; fel, Inst Transforming Undergrad Ed, dir, PhD prog in art cons res, 89-, sr staff mem, Ctr for Hist Archit & Design, 98-, assoc prof, Museum Stud Prog, Art Cons Dept, 94-, Univ Del. **HONORS AND AWARDS** Fel, Amer Anthrop Assn; Fel, Inst for Transforming Undergrad Ed. **MEMBERSHIPS** Amer Anthrop Assn; Amer Inst for Conser of Hist & Artistic Works; Amer Com for South Asian Art; Col Art Assn of Amer; Intl Inst for Conser of Hist & Artistic Works; Soc for Amer Archaeol; Soc for Archaeol Sci. **RESEARCH** South Asian art; history of cultural materials & technology; art & architectural conservation research. **SELECTED PUBLICATIONS** Coauth, Statistical Analysis in Art Conservation Research, Res in Conser ser no 1, J Paul Getty Trust, 88; coauth, Principles of Experimental Design for Art Conservation Research, GCI Sci Prog Rep, J Paul Getty Trust, 92; auth, The Role of a PhD Degree in the Education of a Conservator, ICOM Com for Conser 10th Triennial Mtg Preprints, ICOMCC, 93; coauth, Relating Visual and Technological Styles in Tibetan Sculpture Analysis, World Archaeol vol 25, 94; art, Thin Section Petrography in Studies of Cultural materials, J of Amer Inst for Conser vol 33, 94; coauth, Statistical Analysis in Conservation Science, Archaeometry vol 36, 94; coauth, Interdisciplinary Research on Provenance of Eastern Indian Bronzes: Preliminary Findings, S Asian Stud, vol 10, 94; co-ed, Research Priorities in Art and Architectural Conservation, Amer Inst for Conser, Wash, 94; auth, Optical Mineralogy, in Excavations at Anshan (Tal-e Malyan): The Middle Elamite Period, Univ Penn Museum, Phil, 96; coauth, Application of PIXE to the Study of Renaissance Style Enamelled Gold Jewelry, Nuclear Instrumental Methods in Physics Res, B: Beam Interactions with Materials & Atoms, vol 109/10, 96; auth, Tibetan Bronzes: Technical Observations, Marg vol XLVII, 96; auth, Tibetan Sculpture, Dict of Art, MacMillan, 96; auth, "Introduction" to Thin-Layer Chromatography for Binding Media Analysis, Getty Conser Inst, LA, 96; auth, Himalayan Bronzes: Technology, Style, and Choices, Univ Del Press, 97; coauth, The Sacred Sculpture of Thailand, Walter Art Gallery Baltimore, 97; auth, Technical Studies of Gandharan Art, Gandharan Art in Context: East-West Exchanges at the Crossroads of Asia, Cambridge & New Delhi, 97; coauth, Electrochemical Tests as Alternatives to Current Methods for Assessing Effects of Exhibition Materials on Metal Artifacts, Stud in Conser, vol 43, 98. **CONTACT ADDRESS** Museum Studies Prog, Univ of Delaware, 301 Old College, Newark, DE, 19716. **EMAIL** clreedy@udel.edu

REEDY, WILLIAM T.
PERSONAL Born 08/19/1932, Reading, PA **DISCIPLINE** MEDIEVAL ENGLISH HISTORY **EDUCATION** Yale Univ, BA, 54; Johns Hopkins Univ, PhD(hist), 63. **CAREER** Instr hist, State Univ NY Col New Paltz, 63-64; asst prof, 64-72, assoc, 72-96, PROF HIST, STATE UNIV NY ALBANY, 96-, Am Coun Learned Soc fel, 76-77. **MEMBERSHIPS** AHA; Mediaeval Acad Am; Conf British Studies; Haskins Soc. **SELECTED PUBLICATIONS** Auth, The origins of the general eyre in the reign of Henry I, Speculum, 10/66; The first two Bassets of Weldon--Novi Barones in the early and mid-twelfth century, Northamptonshire Past & Present, 69-70; Were Ralph and Richard Basset really chief justiciars of England in the reign of Henry I?, Acta, Vol II, The Twelfth Century, 75; English Episcopal Acta-X--Bath And Wells, 1061-1205, Albion, Vol 28, 96; Charters Of The Medieval Hospitals Of Bury-St-Edmunds, Albion, Vol 27, 95; auth, Basset Charters, c1120-1250, Pipe Roll Soc London, 95. **CONTACT ADDRESS** Dept of Hist, State Univ of New York, 1400 Washington Ave, Albany, NY, 12222-1000. **EMAIL** wreedy@csc.albany.edu

REESE, JAMES VERDO
PERSONAL Born 12/23/1934, Itasca, TX, m, 1958, 2 children **DISCIPLINE** UNITED STATES HISTORY **EDUCATION** Rice Univ, BA, 57; Univ Tex, Austin, MA, 61, PhD(hist), 64. **CAREER** From instr to assoc prof hist, Tex Tech Univ, 62-77, assoc dean grad sch, 73-76, dir mus, 76-77; PROF HIST & DEAN SCH LIB ARTS, STEPHEN F AUSTIN STATE UNIV, 77-, Vis assoc prof hist, Univ Tex, Austin, 72. **MEMBERSHIPS** AHA; Orgn Am Historians; Southern Hist Asn; AAUP. **RESEARCH** Jacksonian era of United States history; American labor history; Texas history. **SELECTED PUBLICATIONS** Coauth, Texas: Land of Contrast, Benson, 72, 2nd ed, 78; auth, Early history of labor organizations in Texas, 68 & The evolution of an early Texas union, 71, Southwestern Hist Quart; Race And Labor In Western Copper--The Fight For Equality 1896-1918, Am Hist Rev, Vol 101, 96; Creating The Modern South--Millhands And Managers In Dalton, Georgia, 1884-1984, Am Hist Rev, Vol 99, 94. **CONTACT ADDRESS** Off of the Dean of Lib Arts, Stephen F Austin State Univ, Nacoqdoches, TX, 75962.

REEVES, ALBERT COMPTON
PERSONAL Born 11/04/1940, Kansas City, KS, d, 2 children **DISCIPLINE** MEDIEVAL HISTORY **EDUCATION** Univ Kans, BA, 62, MA, 64; Emory Univ, PhD(Hist), 67. **CAREER** Asst prof Medieval Hist, Univ Ga, 67-70; asst prof, 70-73, assoc prof, 73-81, prof Hist, Ohio Univ, 81-. **MEMBERSHIPS** AHA; Medieval Acad Am; fel Royal Hist Soc; Canterbury & York Soc. **RESEARCH** Medieval Wales; later medieval England. **SELECTED PUBLICATIONS** Auth, Some of Humphrey Safford's military indentures, Nottingham Medieval Studies, 72; Thomas Hoccleve, bureaucrat, Medievalia & Humanistica, 74; The Great Sessions in the Lordship of Newport in 1503, 75 & The Custumal of Rumney Manor, 77, Bull Bd Celtic Studies; contribr, Newport, In: Boroughs of Medieval Wales, Univ of Wales, 78; ed, The Wyclyf Tradition, Ohio Univ, 79; auth, Newport Lordship, 1317-1536, Univ Microfilms Int, 79; Lancastrian Englishman, Univ Press of Am, 81; Pleasures and Pastimes in Medieval England (Stroud: Alan Sutton Publishing, Ltd, 95, United Kingdom paperback ed: Stroud: Sutton Publishing, 97, non european paperback ed: New York: Oxford Univ Press, 98. **CONTACT ADDRESS** Dept of History, Ohio Univ, Athens, OH, 45701-2979. **EMAIL** reevesc@oak.cats.ohiou.edu

REEVES, THOMAS C.
PERSONAL Born 08/25/1936, Tacoma, WA, m, 1958, 3 children **DISCIPLINE** RECENT AMERICAN HISTORY **EDUCATION** Pac Lutheran Univ, BA, 58; Univ Wash, MA, 61; Univ Calif, Santa Barbara, PhD, 66. **CAREER** Asst prof hist, Univ Colo, 66-70, assoc prof, 70-73, prof hist, Univ of Wis Parkside, 73-; hist consult, WHA-TV, Madison, 76-78; historiographer, Episcopal diocese of Milwaukee, 81-85; historical adviser, PBS series on the American Presidency, 98. **HONORS AND AWARDS** Numerous research grants; Eleanor Roosevelt Inst fel, 74; Nat Endowment for Humanities fel, 76; Excellence in Res Award, Univ Wis-Parkside, 92. **MEMBERSHIPS** Nat Asn Schol; Fel Cath Schol. **RESEARCH** The U.S. from 1877; politics and religion. **SELECTED PUBLICATIONS** Auth, Freedom and the Foundation: The Fund for the Republic in the Era of McCarthyism, Knopf, 69; ed, Foundations under Fire, Cornell Univ, 70 & McCarthyism, Dryden, 73; auth, Gentleman Boss: The Life of Chester Alan Arthur, Knopf, 75; ed, James de Koven, Anglican Saint, 78; auth, The Life and Times of Joe McCarthy, Stein and Day, 82; A Question of Character: A Life of John F. Kennedy, 91; ed, James Lloyd Breck, Apostle of the Wilderness, 92; auth, The Empty Church: the Suicide of Liberal Christianity, 96. **CONTACT ADDRESS** Dept of Hist, Univ Wis-Parkside, Box 2000, Kenosha, WI, 53141-2000. **EMAIL** tcreeves@execpc.com

REEVES, WILLAIM DALE
PERSONAL Born 08/16/1941, New Orleans, LA, m, 1980, 2 children **DISCIPLINE** US HISTORY **EDUCATION** Williams Col, BA, 63; Tulane Univ, MA, 65, PhD (US Hist), 68. **CAREER** Independent scholar last ten years. **MEMBERSHIPS** LA Hist Soc (pres); LA Hist Asn. **RESEARCH** Louisiana hist, plantations, towns. **SELECTED PUBLICATIONS** Auth, PWA and the Competitive Theory of Administration, J of Am Hist, 73; De La Barre: Life of a French Creole Family in Louisiana, vol IV in Jefferson Parish Hist series, Polyanthos, 80; Public Works Administration in Government Agencies, Greenwood Encyclopedia of American Institutions, 82; Historic City Park: New Orleans, Friends of City Park, 82; Westgo: From Cheniere to Canal, vol XIV in Jefferson Parish Hist series, Dan Alario, 96; Manresa on the Mississippi: for the Greater Glory of God, Manresa, 96; A Transitional Plantation House in Louisiana Architecture, Arris, the J of the Southeast Chapter of the Soc of Architectural Hists, forthcoming 98; At Home in the Nation: From James White to Edward Douglass White, a three-generational biography, forthcoming 99. **CONTACT ADDRESS** 5801 St Charles, New Orleans, LA, 70115. **EMAIL** wdr@acadiacom.net

REFAI, SHAHID
PERSONAL Born 12/17/1936, Baroda, India, m, 1998, 3 children **DISCIPLINE** ASIAN STUDIES **EDUCATION** Baroda Univ, MA, 61; Cambridge Univ, PhD, 68. **CAREER** Asst librn, British Museum Lib, 68-69; vis lectr, Univ Calif, Los Angeles, 69-70; vis lectr, Univ Calif, Berkeley, 71; asst prof, 71-77, assoc prof, 77-83, Central Washington Univ; prof Hist, Col of Saint Rose, 84- . **HONORS AND AWARDS** Summa cum laude, 61; Cambridge Soc Scholar, 64-68; Lady Mountbatton Scholar, 67-68; Col of Saint Rose teaching awards. **MEMBERSHIPS** Exec Bd, NY Conf on Asian Stud; Asn for Asian Stud; Soc for Sci Study of Relig. **RESEARCH** Educational and social activism of American women missionaries in India in the nineteenth and twentieth centuries. **SELECTED PUBLICATIONS** Rev of Cynthia Hoehler-Fatton's Women of Fire and Spirit, Rev of Relig Res, 97; rev of Omar Khalidi's Indian Muslims Since Independence, Rev of Relig Res, 98. **CONTACT ADDRESS** Col of Saint Rose, PO Box 123, Albany, NY, 12203. **EMAIL** refais@rosnet.strose.edu

REFF, THEODORE FRANKLIN
PERSONAL Born 08/18/1930, New York, NY, m, 1990, 2 children **DISCIPLINE** HISTORY OF ART **EDUCATION** Columbia Col, AB, 52; Harvard Univ, AM, 53, PhD, 58. **CAREER** From instr to assoc prof art hist, 57-67, grants from coun on res hum, 59, 61 & 63, Prof of Art Hist, Columbia Univ, 67-, Mem, Inst Advan Studies, 63; Am Coun Learned Soc & Am Philos Soc grants, 63 & 64; chmn nominating comt, Porter Prize, 66-67, chmn selection comt, 71-72; Guggenheim fel, 67-68 & 74-75; consult, Libr Art Ser, Time-Life Bks, 68-70; vis prof art hist, Johns Hopkins Univ, 70, City Univ NY, 71-72, Princeton Univ, 73 & NY Univ, 74; Am Philos Soc grant, 72; guest cur, Metrop Mus Art, 76-77; dir Sem Col Tchrs, Nat Endowment for Hum, 77-78; Am Coun Learned Soc fel, 81-82; Nat Endow for Hum fel, 88-89; Chevalier, Ordre des Arts & des Lettres, 89. **MEMBERSHIPS** Col Art Asn Am. **RESEARCH** Mod Art; esp Manet, Degas, Cezanne, Picasso. **SELECTED PUBLICATIONS** Auth, Love and death in Picasso's early work, Artforum, 5/73 & In: Picasso: 1881-1973, London, 73; Matisse: Meditations on a statuette and goldfish, Arts Mag, 11/76; Manet: Olympia, Penguin Bks, London, 76 & Viking, 77; Degas: The Artist's Mind, Metrop Mus Art & Harper, 76 & Thames & Hudson, London, 76; The Notebooks of Edgar Degas (2 vols), Clarendon, 76; Duchamp and Leonardo: L H O O Q-alikes, Art in America, 1-2/ 77; Degas: A master among masters, Metrop Mus Art Bull, spring 77; Painting and theory in the final decade, In: Cezanne: The Late Work, 77; ed, Modern Art in Paris, 1850-1900, Garland,81; Manet & Modern Paris, Nat Gal Art, 83; Degas et Son Oeuvre: A Supplement, Garland, 84, Paul Cezanne: Two Sketchbooks, Phila Mus Art, 89, Jean Louis Forain: The Impressionist Years, Dixon Gal, Memphis, 95. **CONTACT ADDRESS** Dept of Art History, Columbia Univ, 2960 Broadway, New York, NY, 10027-6900.

REGALDO, SAMUEL O.
PERSONAL Born 03/22/1953, Glendale, CA **DISCIPLINE** HISTORY **EDUCATION** Calif State Univ, Northridge, BA, 80; Washington State Univ, MA, 83, PhD, 87. **CAREER** Calif State Univ, Stanislaus, visiting lecturer of history, 87, asst prof of history, 88-92, assoc prof of history, 92-97, prof of history, 97-. **HONORS AND AWARDS** Louise M. Davies Fellow, 1998; Smithsonian Institution Faculty Fellow, 94. **MEMBERSHIPS** Organization of Amer Historians; Amer Historical Assn; North Amer Soc for Sport History; Phi Alpha Theta; Western History Assn. **RESEARCH** Amer Sport History; Ethnic and Immigration History; Amer Social History. **SELECTED PUBLICATIONS** Auth, Viva Baseball!: Latin Major Leaguers and Their Special Hunger, 98; "Jackie Robinson and the Emancipitation of Latin American Baseball Players," in Jackie Robinson: Race, Sports, and the American Dream, 98; review of Sol White's History of Colored Base Ball with Other Documents on the Early Black Game, 1886-1936, in Sport History Review, no. 28, 97; "Play Ball! Baseball and the Seattle's Japanese American 'Courier League,' 1928-1941," Pacific Northwest Quarterly, winter, 95-96; "Dodgers Beisbol is on the Air: The Development and Impact of the Dodgers Spanish-Language Broadcasts, 1958-1994," California History, fall 95. **CONTACT ADDRESS** Dept of History, California State Univ, Stanislaus, 801 W Monte Vista Ave., Turlock, CA, 95382. **EMAIL** regalado@toto.csutan.edu

REGELSKI, THOMAS ADAM
PERSONAL Born 05/04/1941, m, 1993 **DISCIPLINE** MUSIC EDUCATION **EDUCATION** State Univ Col, Fredonia, BM (Music Ed), 58; Columbia Univ, MA (Choral and Vocal Music), 63; State Univ Col, Fredonia graduate studies, 63-64; OH Univ, Athens, PhD (Comparative Arts), 70. **CAREER** Public schools, New York City, 62-63; central schools, Bemus Point, NY, 63-65; public schools, Middletown, NY, 65-66; School of Music, State Univ Col, Fredonia, 66-68; OH Univ at Athens and Zanesville, 68-70; School of Music, State Univ Col, Fredonia, NY, 70-; vis prof, Aichi Univ, Nagoya, Japan, 84-85; assoc in ed, Harvard Univ, fall 91. **HONORS AND AWARDS** Danforth Found Leadership Award, SS Seward Inst, 58; Kappa Delta Pi, SUNY Fredonia, 62; cum laude, SUNY Fredonia, 62; Honors Award, Written Comprehensive Exams, OH State Univ, 70; Dean Earl C Siegfred Award, OH Univ, 70; Phi Kappa Phi, OH State Univ, 70; Outstanding Educators of Am, 73-74; Distinguished Prof Award and rank, SUNY Board of Trustees, 83; vis teaching and res scholar, Aichi Univ , Nagoya, Japan, 84-85; vis scholar, Philos of Ed Res Center, Harvard Graduate School of Ed, fall 91. **RESEARCH** Philos of music; philos of ed; sociol of music; sociol of ed. **SELECTED PUBLICATIONS** Auth, Action Research and Critical Theory: Empowering Music Teachers to Professionalize Praxis, Bul of the Coun for Res in Music Ed, no 123, winter 94-95; Scientism in Experimantal Music Research, Philos of Music Ed Rec, vol 4, no 1, spring 96; Taking the Art of Music for Granted: A Critical Sociology of the Aesthetic Philosophy of Music, in Critical Reflections on Music Education, ed L R Bartel and D J Elliott, Univ of Toronto, Can Music Ed Res Center, 96; Action for Change in Music Education-Guiding Ideals of the MayDay Group, with J T Gates, Univ Buffalo, postion paper of the MayDay Group, fall 96 (www.members.aol.com/jtgates/maydaygroup/); Critical Theory as a Basis for Critical Thinking in Music Education, in Studies in Music from the Univ of Western Ontario, vol 17, 98; A Prolegomenon to a Praxial Theory of Music and Music Education, Finnish J of Music Ed, vol 1 no

1, fall, 96, reprinted and expanded in Can Music Educator, vol 38, no 3, spring 97; A Critical Pagmatism of Creativity for General Music, General Music Today, vol 10, no 3, spring 97; Action Learning: Curriculum as and for Praxis, Proceedings of the Charles Fowler Conference on Arts Education, Univ MD, College Park, May 97; Critical Theory and Praxis: Professionalizing Music Education, MayDay Group, web page(see above); The Aristotelian Bases of Music and Music Education, The Philos of Music Ed Rev, spring 98; numerous other publications. **CONTACT ADDRESS** School of Music, SUNY, Fredonia, Mason Hall, Fredonia, NY, 14063. **EMAIL** regelski@cecomet.net

REGINALD, ALLEN
DISCIPLINE CLASSICS **EDUCATION** Haverford, AB, 53; Yale Univ, MA, 55; St Andrews, BPhil, 57; Yale Univ, PhD, 58. **CAREER** Prof, Northwestern Univ, 78-. **RESEARCH** Socratic Ethics; Plato's Ion; Hippias Minor; Laches; Protagoras; Lysias. **SELECTED PUBLICATIONS** Auth, Collected Dialogues of Plato, v.II, Yale, 91; ed, R. E. Allen, Plato's Parmineds, trans and analysis, Univ Minn. **CONTACT ADDRESS** Dept of Classics, Northwestern Univ, 1801 Hinman, Kresge 15, Evanston, IL, 60208. **EMAIL** r-allen2@nwu.edu

REGUER, SARA
PERSONAL Brooklyn, NY, 2 children **DISCIPLINE** MIDDLE EAST & JEWISH HISTORY **EDUCATION** City Col New York, BA, 66; Yeshiva Univ, BReligEduc, 66; Columbia Univ, MA, 69, PhD(MidE hist), 76. **CAREER** Instr, 74-77, asst prof to prof Judaic Studies, Brooklyn Col, 77-, chp, 87-; Consult, Fed Off Educ, 76-; vis asst prof Jewish hist, Yeshiva Univ, 77-78; vis distinguished prof, Univ Naples, 97. **HONORS AND AWARDS** Res fel, City Univ New York, 78-79. **MEMBERSHIPS** AHA; MidE Studies Asn; Asn for Jewish Studies; Coord Comt Women Hist Prof. **RESEARCH** Contemporary Middle East; Jews of the Middle East. **CONTACT ADDRESS** Dept of Judaic Studies, Brooklyn Col, CUNY, 2901 Bedford Ave, Brooklyn, NY, 11210-2813.

REHER, MARGARET MARY
PERSONAL Reading, PA **DISCIPLINE** HISTORICAL THEOLOGY, CHURCH HISTORY **EDUCATION** Immaculata Col, BA, 60; Providence Col, MA, 64; Fordham Univ, PhD, 72. **CAREER** Asst prof theol, Immaculata Col, 60-64; asst prof, 73-76, assoc prof, 76-80, Prof Relig, Cabrini Col, 80-93, Prof Emerita, 93. **MEMBERSHIPS** Col Theol Soc Am; Cath Hist Soc; Am Cath Hist Asn. **RESEARCH** Domestic and for outreach of communities of women relig established in Philadelphia. **SELECTED PUBLICATIONS** Auth, Pope Leo XIII and Americanism, In: The Inculcation of American Catholicism 1820-1900, Garland Publ Inc, 88; Americanism and Modernism -- Continuity or Discontinuity?, In: Modern American Catholicism, 1900-1965, Garland Publ Inc 88; Catholic Intellectual Life in America: A History of Persons and Movements, Macmillan Co, 89; Den¤nlis J Dougherty and Anna M Dengle: The Missionary Alliance, Records Am Cath Hist Soc of Philadelphia, spring 90; Bishop John Carroll and Women, Archbishop Gerety Lectures, 1988-89, Seton Hall Univ, 89; Get Thee to a ¤Peruvianl Nunnery: Cardinal Dougherty and the Philadelpha IHM's, Records Am Cath Hist Soc of Philadelphia, winter 92; Phantom Heresy: A Twice-Told Tale, U S Cath Hist, summer 93; Review Symposium on Begin Catholic: Commonweal from the Seventies to the Nineties, Loyola Univ Press, 93, Horizons, spring 94; co-auth, From St Edward's School to Providence Center: A Story of Commitment, Records Am Cath Hist Soc of Philadelphia, spring-summer, 96; Mission of America: John J Burke in Peru, U S Cath His, fall 97. **CONTACT ADDRESS** Dept of Relig, Cabrini Col, 610 King of Prussia, Radnor, PA, 19087-3698. **EMAIL** margaret.mcguinness@cabrini.edu

REHM, MAURICE
DISCIPLINE CLASSICS **EDUCATION** BA, 73; MA, 75; Stanford Univ, PhD, 85. **CAREER** Assoc prof, Stanforf Univ. **RESEARCH** Greek tragedy. **SELECTED PUBLICATIONS** Auth, Greek Tragic Theatre, 92; Marriage to Death: The Conflation of Marriage and Funeral Rituals in Greek Tragedy, 94. **CONTACT ADDRESS** Stanford Univ, Bldg 20, Main Quad, Stanford, CA, 94305.

REID, DONALD MALCOLM
PERSONAL Born 12/24/1940, Manhattan, KS, m, 1964, 2 children **DISCIPLINE** MIDDLE EASTERN HISTORY **EDUCATION** Muskingum Col, BA, 62; Princeton Univ, PhD(Mid Eastern & Europ hist), 69. **CAREER** Asst prof hist, Ohio Univ, 68-69; asst prof, 69-76, assoc prof hist, Ga State Univ, 76-83, prof, 83-, Nat Endowment for Humanities fel, 71-72; Am Res Ctr in Egypt fel, 77-78. **HONORS AND AWARDS** Fulbright Islamic Civ Res Fel, 82-83; Fulbright-Hays Fac Res Abroad Fel, 87-88; Fulbright Res Fel, 98-99; Am Res Center in Eng Fel, 99. **MEMBERSHIPS** MidE Studies Asn; AHA; Am Res Ctr, Egypt. **RESEARCH** Modern Middle Eastern history. **SELECTED PUBLICATIONS** Auth, The return of the Egyptian Wafd--1978, Int J African Hist Studies, Vol XII, 79; Fu'ad Siraj al-Din and the Egyptian Wafd, J Contemp Hist, Vol XV, 80; Lawyers and Politics in the Arab World, 1880-1960, Biblotheca Islamica, 81; Dawr Jamiat al-Qahira fi Bina Misr al-Haditha, Cairo: Markaz al-Mahrusa, 97; Cairo University and the Making of Modern Egypt, Cambridge Univ Press, 90, 91; Cromer and the Classics: Imperialism, Nationalism, and the Greek and Roman past in Modern Egypt, Middle Eastern Studies, 32, 1-29, 96; French Egyptology and the Architecture of Orientalism: Deciphering the Facade of Cairo's Egyptian museum, Franco-Arab Encounters: Studies in Memory of David C. Gordon, eds. Mathew Gordon and L. Carl Brown, Am Univ-Beirut, 35-69, 96. **CONTACT ADDRESS** Dept of History, Georgia State Univ, 33 Gilmer St SE, Atlanta, GA, 30303-3080. **EMAIL** dreid@gsu.edu

REID, JOEL OTTO
PERSONAL Born 05/17/1936, Newark, NJ **DISCIPLINE** SOCIOLOGY **EDUCATION** New York University School of Education, BS, 1959; Montclair State College, MA, 1965; Claremont Graduate School, Claremont, CA, PhD, 1973. **CAREER** Elizabeth Public School System, Elizabeth, NJ, teacher; White Plaines High School, counselor, teacher, 1962-65; White Plaines Board of Education, professional recruiter, 1965-67; National Teachers Corps, Migrant University, Southern California, teacher, leader, 1967-68; Claremont Graduate School, staff member, 1971-72; Social Science Department, professor, 1978; Pasadena City College, dean of continuing education, 1968-78, professor of social science, 1978-. **HONORS AND AWARDS** Two year Scholarship to College; Kiwanis Rotary Club Scholarship; Valley Settlement House Scholarship, West Orange, NJ; Womens Aux Scholarship, West Orange, NJ. **MEMBERSHIPS** Pasadena Education Association; Pasadena City College Faculty Association; NEA; Los Angeles Co Adult Education Adminstrators Association; chairman, Eval Com for Western Associations Schools & Colleges, 1969, 1970, 1974; board of directors, Urban League Com for Educ Fund Dr; Fair Hsg Com of Westchester Co, New York; Am Friends Ser Com on Hsg, Pasadena; counseled Neighborhod Youth Center; worked with economically educationally deprived areas; lectured at educational, civic, & religious organizations; consultant to schools, pvt groups & Comm agencies. **CONTACT ADDRESS** Social Science Dept, Pasadena City Col, 1570 E Colorado Blvd, Pasadena, CA, 91106.

REID, JOHN PHILLIP
PERSONAL Born 05/17/1930, Weehawken, NJ **DISCIPLINE** HISTORY, LAW **EDUCATION** Georgetown Univ, BSS, 52; Harvard Univ, LLB, 55; Univ NH, MA, 57; New York Univ, LLM, 60, JSD, 62. **CAREER** From instr to assoc prof, 60-66, Prof legal hist, NY Univ, 66-, Guggenheim Found fel, 80; fel, Henry E. Huntington Libr, 80. **RESEARCH** Am legal hist. **SELECTED PUBLICATIONS** Auth, Chief Justice: Judicial World of Charles Doe, Harvard Univ, 67; A Law of Blood: The Primitive Law of the Cherokee Nation, New York Univ, 70; A Better Kind of Hatchet: Law, Trade and Diplomacy in the Cherokee Nation During the Early Years of European Contact, 76, In a Defiant Stance: The Conditions of Law in Massachusetts Bay, The Irish Comparison and the Coming of the American Revolution, 77 & In a Rebellious Spirit: The Argument of Facts, the Liberty Riot, and the Coming of the American Revolution, 78, Pa State Univ; Law for the Elephant: Property and Social Behavior on the Overland Trail, Huntington Libr, 80; In Defiance of the Law: The Standing-Army Controversy, the Two Constitutions, and the Coming of the American Revolution, Univ NC, 81; The Briefs of the American Revolution: Constitutional Arguments between Thomas Hutchinson, Governor of Massachusetts Bay, and James Bowdoin for the Council, and John Adams for the House of Representatives, NY Univ, 81. **CONTACT ADDRESS** Sch of Law, New York Univ, New York, NY, 10003. **EMAIL** reidj@tuving.law.nyu.edu

REID, PETER L.D.
PERSONAL Born 01/30/1937, Edinburgh, Scotland, m, 1995, 2 children **DISCIPLINE** CLASSICS **EDUCATION** Cambridge Univ, BA, 60, MA, 64; UCLA, PhD, 74. **CAREER** Tchr, 60-70; Sec Sch in Scotland, NZ, USA; Asst Prof, Assoc Prof, Chr, 73-, Class, Tufts Univ. **HONORS AND AWARDS** NEH Inst for Tchr. **MEMBERSHIPS** APA. **RESEARCH** Medieval Latin **SELECTED PUBLICATIONS** Auth, Ratherii Veronensis: Opera Minora, Brepols, Corpus Christianorum, Cont Mediaevalis XLVI, 76; Tenth Century Latinity, Undena, 81; Ratherii Veronensis: Opera Maiora, Brepols, Corpus Christianorum, Cont Med XLVIA, 84; Rather of Verona: Complete Works in Translation, CEMERS, Binghamton, 91; Reviewed in; Church History, 95; Speculum, 94; Manuscripta, 92; Ecclesiastical History, 93. **CONTACT ADDRESS** Dept of the Classics, Tufts Univ, Medford, MA, 02155. **EMAIL** preid@infonet.tufts.edu

REIFF, DANIEL D.
PERSONAL Born 08/17/1941, Potsdam, NY, m, 1975, 2 children **DISCIPLINE** ART AND ARCHITECTURAL HISTORY **EDUCATION** Harvard Col, BA, 63; Harvard Univ, MA, 64, PhD, 70. **CAREER** Instr, Art Hist, Baylor Univ, 64-65, 66-67; acting asst sec, US Commission of Fine Arts, Washington, DC, 69-70; prof, Art Hist, State Univ of New York Col, 70-. **HONORS AND AWARDS** Kasling Memorial Lect, SUNY, Fredonia, 75; NEH fel for College Teachers, 84; Preservation League of NY State Architectural Heritage Honor Award, 86; Graham Found for Advanced Studies in the Fine Arts fel grant, 91. **MEMBERSHIPS** Soc of Architectural Historians; Col Art Asn; Nat Trust for Historic Preservation; Soc for the Preservation of New England Antiquities; Victorian Soc in Am; Preservation League of NY State. **RESEARCH** Am architecture, 18th-20th centuries. **SELECTED PUBLICATIONS** Auth, Washington Architecture, 1791-1861: Problems in Development, US Commission of Fine Arts, 71, reprinted 77; Architecture in Fredonia, 1811-1972: Sources, Context, Development, Thorner-Sidney Press, 72; Small Georgian Houses in England and Virginia: Origins and Development through the 1750's, Univ of DE Press, 86; Historic Camps of Mt Arab and Eagle Crag Lakes, Mt Arab Preserve Asn, 95; Architecture in Fredonia, New York, 1811-1997: From Log Cabin to I M Pei, White Pine Press, 97; Houses from Books: The Influence of Treatises, Pattern Books, and Catalogs in America, 1738-1950, PA State Univ Press, forthcoming fall 2000. **CONTACT ADDRESS** Dept of Art, SUNY, Fredonia, Fredonia, NY, 14063-1198. **EMAIL** reiff@fredonia.edu

REIGSTAD, RUTH
PERSONAL Born 04/24/1923, Minneapolis, MN **DISCIPLINE** CLINICAL PHYSICAL THERAPY, HISTORY OF ENGLISH, SCIENCE **EDUCATION** St Olef Coll, BA, 45; Univ Minn, RTP, 47. **CAREER** Consultant, Wash State Health Dept, 41-73; clin phys therapist, 47-61; volunteer activities. **HONORS AND AWARDS** Stipends for Post Grad Study, UCLA, USC, NYU; Children's Bureau; US Public Health. **MEMBERSHIPS** Public Health Asn; Am Phys Therapy Asn; Am Acad of Rel; AF Asn. **RESEARCH** Correlations between studies of science and religion; Early childhood development. **CONTACT ADDRESS** Box 4237, Tacoma, WA, 98438-0001.

REILL, PETER HANNS
PERSONAL Born 12/11/1938, New York, NY, m, 1968 **DISCIPLINE** GERMAN & INTELLECTUAL HISTORY **EDUCATION** NY Univ, BA, 60; Northwestern Univ, Evanston, MA, 61, PhD(hist), 69. **CAREER** Lectr hist, Northwestern Univ, 65-66; asst prof, 66-73, ASSOC PROF HIST, UNIV CALIF, LOS ANGELES, 73-, Consult ed, Jour Hist of Ideas, 77-80; Guggenheim grant, 78; Fulbright res grant, 79-80. **MEMBERSHIPS** AHA; Am Soc 18th Century Studies; Western Asn Ger Studies; Goethe Soc. **RESEARCH** Philosophy of history. **SELECTED PUBLICATIONS** Auth, History and hermeneutics in the Afklarung, J Mod Hist, 3/73; The German Enlightenment and the Rise of Historicism, Univ Calif, 74; Philology, culture and politics in early 19th century Germany, Romance Philol, suppl, 11/76; Johann Christoph Gatterer, Deutsche Historiker, 80; Barthold Georg Niebuhr and the enlightenment tradition, Ger Studies Rev, 2/80; Science And The Construction Of The Cultural Sciences In Late Enlightenment Germany - The Case Of Humboldt, Hist And Theory, Vol 33, 94. **CONTACT ADDRESS** Dept of Hist, Univ of Calif, Los Angeles, CA, 90290.

REILLY, BERNARD F
PERSONAL Born 06/08/1925, Audubon, NJ, m, 1948, 9 children **DISCIPLINE** MEDIEVAL HISPANIC & CHURCH HISTORY **EDUCATION** Villanova Univ, BA, 50; Univ Pa, MA, 55; Bryn Mawr Col, PhD(medieval hist), 66. **CAREER** From instr to assoc prof, 55-71, PROF HIST, VILLANOVA UNIV, 72- **MEMBERSHIPS** Mediaeval Acad Am; AHA; Am Cath Hist Asn. **RESEARCH** French influence in eleventh and twelfth century Spain; Leon-Castile in the eleventh and twelfth centuries; medieval Spanish historiography. **SELECTED PUBLICATIONS** Auth, Santiago and Saint Denis: The French Presence in twelfth-century Spain, Cath Hist Rev, 10/68; The Historia Compostelana: The genesis and composition of a twelfth-century Spanish Gesta, Speculum, 1/69; Existing manuscripts of the Historia Compostelana, notes toward a critical edition, Manuscripta, 7/71; The Court Bishops of Alfonso VII of Leon-Castilla, Medieval Studies, 7/74; The Chancery of Alfonso VII of Leon-Castilla: The period 1115-1135 reconsidered, Speculum, 4/76; Sources of the fourth book of Lucas of Tuy's Chronicon Mundi, Classical Folia, 12/76; On getting to be a bishop in Leon-Castilla: The emperor Alfonso VII and the post-Gregorian church, Studies in Medieval and Renaissance History, Vol 1, 78; The kingdom of Leon-Castilla under Queen Urraca: 1109-1126, Princeton Univ Press, 82; History Of The Iberian Peninsula In The Middle-Ages: 711-1480 Kingdoms, Crowns, Regions, Catholic Hist Rev, Vol 80, 94. **CONTACT ADDRESS** Dept of Hist, Villanova Univ, 845 E Lancaster Ave, Villanova, PA, 19085.

REILLY, LINDA
DISCIPLINE CLASSICAL STUDIES **EDUCATION** Vassar Col, AB, 65; Johns Hopkins Univ, MA, 66, PhD, 69. **CAREER** Assoc prof, 74-; ch, 92-95; asst prof, 69-74; assoc provest, 81-86 & dean Undergrad Progr and asst VP for Acad Aff, Col William and Mary; Abby Leach fel, low, Amer Sch Class Stud, Athens, Greece, 66-67; Ctr Hellenistic Stud, Wash, 74-75; sr res assoc, Amer Sch Class Stud, Athens, Greece, 86-87 & 95-96. **RESEARCH** Ancient dogs; Ancient city; Neoclassical traditions in North America. **SELECTED PUBLICATIONS** Auth, Slaves in Ancient Greece, Ares Publishers, 78, repr, 84; The Dogs from the Hunting Frieze at Vergina, J Hellenic Stud, Vol 113, 93; A Greek Inscription at Williamsburg, Amer J Archaeol, 74; New Inscriptions from Echinos, Amer J Philol, 71; Who Stole the Sphinx's Nose, Mediter Soc Am, Richmond, 96;

participant and guest lecturer, La State Semr for High Sch Humanities Teachers, Northwestern State Univ, Natchidoches, 91; A Protogemometric Naiskos From Crete CAMWS, Boulder, 97; Neo-Classical Achitecture in Williamsburg, VA, CAMWS-SS, Richmond, 92; Kerberos and Orthos: Two Monstrous Brothers, given at CAMWS in Austin, 92; Rumpus: One of A Kind, Dog World, 86 & Rumpus: A Full Life for a Deaf Corgi, Dog World, 90. **CONTACT ADDRESS** Dept of Classical Studies, Col of William and Mary, Morton Hall, Williamsburg, VA, 23187-8795. **EMAIL** lcreil@morton.wm.edu

REILLY, LISA
DISCIPLINE ARCHITECTURAL HISTORY **EDUCATION** Vassar Col, BA, 78; York Univ, MA, 80; Univ NY, PhD, 91. **CAREER** Asst prof. **RESEARCH** Medieval architecture. **SELECTED PUBLICATIONS** Auth, pubs on Peterborough Cathedral, Oxford. **CONTACT ADDRESS** Dept of Architectural History., Virginia Univ, Charlottesville, VA, 22903. **EMAIL** lar2f@virginia.edu

REINER, ERICA
PERSONAL Budapest, Hungary **DISCIPLINE** ASSYRIOLOGY **EDUCATION** Sorbonne, Dipl Assyriol, 51; Univ Chicago, PhD(Assyriol), 55. **CAREER** From res asst to res assoc Assyriol, 52-56, from asst prof to prof, 56-73, John A. Wilson Prof Assyriol, Univ Chicago, 73-, Distinguished Serv Prof, 83-; Assoc ed, Assyrian Dictionary, Orient Inst, Univ Chicago, 57-62, ed, 62-, ed-in-charge, 73-96. **HONORS AND AWARDS** Guggenheim fel, 74. **MEMBERSHIPS** Am Orient Soc; Ling Soc Am; Am Philos Soc; fel Am Acad Arts & Sci. **RESEARCH** Linguistics; Babylonian literature. **SELECTED PUBLICATIONS** Auth, Surpu: A Collection of Sumerian and Akkadian Incantations, Weidner, Graz, 58; A Linguistic Analysis of Akkadian, Mouton, The Hague, 66; Elamite language, In: Handbuch der Orientalistik, Brill, Leiden, 69; Akkadian, In: Current Trends in Linguistics, Mouton, The Hague, 69; Babylonian Planetary Omens: Parts 1 & 2, Undena, 75 & 81; Astral Magic in Babylonia, Transactions Am Philos Soc, 85/4, 95. **CONTACT ADDRESS** Orient Inst, Univ of Chicago, 1155 E 58th St, Chicago, IL, 60637-1540.

REINERMAN, ALAN JEROME
PERSONAL Born 03/22/1935, Cincinnati, OH, m, 1967, 1 child **DISCIPLINE** MODERN EUROPEAN HISTORY **EDUCATION** Xavier Univ, OH, BS, 57, MA, 58; Loyola Univ Chicago, PhD, 64. **CAREER** Instr hist, Loyola Univ Chicago, 62-63; from asst prof to assoc prof, Sacred Heart Univ, 63-70; prof, Appalachian State Univ, 70-73; prof hist, Boston Col, 73. **MEMBERSHIPS** AHA; Am Cath Hist Asn; Southern Hist Asn; Soc Ital Hist Studies (secytreas, 75-); Conf Group Cent Europ Hist. **RESEARCH** Metternich and the Papacy; Austria and the risorgimento; peasant unrest in Southern Italy. **SELECTED PUBLICATIONS** Auth, Austria and the papal election of 1823, Cent Europ Hist, 9/70; Metternich and reform: The case of the papal state, J Mod Hist, 12/70; Metternich, Italy, and the Congress of Verona, Hist J, 6/71; Metternich, Alexander I, and the Russian Challenge in Italy 1815-1820, J Mod Hist, 6/74; Metternich, the Powers and the 1831 Italian Crisis, Cent Europ Hist, 9/77; Metternich vs Chateaubriand, Austrian Hist Yearbk, 77; Austria and the Papacy in the Age of Metternich: Between Conflict and Cooperation, 1809-1830, Vol I, Cath Univ Am Press, 79; Austria and the Papacy in the Age of Metternich, In: Revolution and Reaction, 1830-1838, vol 2, 89. **CONTACT ADDRESS** Dept of Hist, Boston Col, 140 Commonwealth Ave, Chestnut Hill, MA, 02167-3800.

REINHARTZ, DENNIS PAUL
PERSONAL Born 04/29/1944, Irvington, NJ, m, 1966 **DISCIPLINE** RUSSIAN & EAST EUROPEAN HISTORY **EDUCATION** Rutgers Univ, AB, 66, AM, 67; NY Univ, PhD, 70. **CAREER** Instr hist, Newark Col Eng, 68-70; from asst prof to assoc prof, Madison Col, 70-73; from asst prof to assoc prof, 73-98, asst dean lib arts, 76-79, prof hist & Russ, Univ Tex, Arlington, 98-; Reviewer, NEH, 74-; assoc ed, Red River Valley Hist J, 75-. **HONORS AND AWARDS** NY Univ Founders Day Award for Acad Schol Achievement, 70; Col Lib Arts Constituency Coun Award for Excellence in Teaching, 76; Notable NJ Author Citation for Milovan Djilas, 83; Presidio La Bahia Award for The Mapping of the American Southwest, 87; The Adele Mellen Prize for The Cartographer and the Literati, Friends of the UTA Libr Fac Award, 96; Fort Worth Country Day Sch Mack Family Schol; recipient of numerous grants and fellowships. **MEMBERSHIPS** Southwestern Asn Slavic Studies(pres, 76-77); AHA; Am Asn Advan Slavic Studies; Hist Film Comt; Southern Conf Slavic Studies. **RESEARCH** Pre-Marxist 19th century Russian intellectual history; the Yugoslav Revolution; 20th century Balkan history. **SELECTED PUBLICATIONS** Auth, Milovan Djilas: A Revolutionary as a Writer, Columbia Univ Press, 81; coauth, Teach-Practice-Apply: The TPA Instructional Model, Nat Educ Asn, 88; Geography Across the School Curriculum, Nat Educ Asn, 90; Tabula Terra Nova, The Somesuch Press, 92; auth, The Cartographer and the Literati: Herman Moll and his Intellectual Circle, The Edwin Mellen Press, 97; author of numerous journal articles, book essays, reviews, and other scholarly publications. **CONTACT ADDRESS** Dept of Hist, Univ of Tex, Arlington, TX, 76019. **EMAIL** dprein@utarlg.uta.edu

REINHARZ, JEHUDA
PERSONAL Born 08/01/1944, Haifa, Israel, m, 1967, 2 children **DISCIPLINE** MODERN JEWISH & EUROPEAN HISTORY **EDUCATION** Jewish Theol Sem Am, BRE, 67; Columbia Univ, BS, 67; Harvard Univ, MA, 68; Brandeis Univ, PhD(Jewish hist), 72. **CAREER** Asst prof Jewish hist, Univ Mich, 72-76, assoc prof, 76-81, prof, 81-82; RICHARD KORET PROF MOD JEWISH HIST, BRANDEIS UNIV, 82-, Sr res fel, Nat Endownment for the Humanities, 79-80. **MEMBERSHIPS** AHA; Asn Jewish Studies; Leo Baeck Inst; World Union Jewish Studies. **RESEARCH** German Jewish history; history of Zionism. **SELECTED PUBLICATIONS** Auth, Fatherland or Promised Land, The Dilemma of the German Jew 1893-1914, Univ Mich Press, 75; ed, The Letters and Papers of Chaim Weizmann 1918-1920, Rutgers Univ Press, 77; co-ed, The Jew in the Modern World, Oxford Univ Press, 80; ed, Dokumente zur Geschichte des Deutschen Zionismus, J C B Mohr, Tuebingen, 81; co-ed, Mystics, Philosophers & Politicians, Duke Univ Press, 82; Israel in the Middle East, Oxford Univ Press; 2nd Chance--2 Centuries Of German-Speaking Jews In The United-Kingdom, J Of Modern Hist, Vol 65, 93. **CONTACT ADDRESS** Dept of Near Eastern & Judaic Studies, Brandeis Univ, 415 South St, Waltham, MA, 02154-2700.

REINSHAGEN-JOHO, LIANE
DISCIPLINE LATIN-AMERICAN AND SPANISH LITERATURES AND SPANISH LANGUAGE **EDUCATION** Univ Wash, Seattle, PhD. **CAREER** Vis prof Span, Univ Nev, Reno. **RESEARCH** The phenomenology of the non-monolingual speaker; 19th Century Mexican and German literatures. **SELECTED PUBLICATIONS** Published translations of Graham Greene and Edna St. Vincent Millay. **CONTACT ADDRESS** Univ Nev, Reno, Reno, NV, 89557. **EMAIL** reinshag@scs.unr.edu

REISCH, GEORGE
PERSONAL Born 12/25/1962, NJ **DISCIPLINE** HISTORY AND PHILOSOPHY OF SCIENCE **EDUCATION** Univ Chicago, MA, 90, PhD, 95. **CAREER** Vis asst prof, Il Inst Tech, 96-97; res fel, Northwestern Univ, 95-96. **MEMBERSHIPS** Philos of Sci Assoc. **SELECTED PUBLICATIONS** Auth, "Planning Science: Otto Neurath and the International Encyclopedia of Unified Science," Brit Jrnl for the Hist of Sci, 94; "Scientism Without Tears," Hist and Theory, 95; "Terminology in Action," in Encyclopedia and Utopia, Kluwer, 96; "How Postmodern was Neurath's Idea of Unified Science," Stud in Hist and Philos of Sci, 97; "Epistemologist, Economist...and Censor: On Otto Neurath's Infamous Index Verborum Prhibitorum," Perspectives on Sci, 97. **CONTACT ADDRESS** 5246 N. Kenmore Ave., 1N, Chicago, IL, 60640. **EMAIL** greisch@tezcat.com

REITZ, MIRIAM
PERSONAL Born 12/25/1935, Canada, w, 1985 **DISCIPLINE** SOCIAL WORK **EDUCATION** School of Soc Scv Admin, Univ Chicago, PhD, 82; MA, 62. **CAREER** Independent practice of therapy and consultation re family relationships, 89-present, Part-time Sr staff member at CFS/FIC, Inst of psych, NW Memorial Hosp and Medical School, Coordinator of Consult and Comm Ser CFS/FIC, 82-86; Part-time staff member CFS/FIC, 76-82; Edith Abbott Teaching Fellow at the School of Soc Scv Admin, Univ Chicago, 79-80; Dir of Prof Edu, Family Inst of Chicago, 73-76; Assoc Dir, Prof Edu, FIC, 72-73; Chief Soc Worker, 68, Commun Family Svc and Mental Health Center, LaGrange IL, 66-72. **MEMBERSHIPS** Natl Assoc of Soc Worker; IL Soc for Clin Soc Work; Clin Member Amer Assoc for Marriage and Family Therapy; Amer Family Therapy Academy; Alumni Assoc The Family Inst of Chicago. **SELECTED PUBLICATIONS** Reitz, Miriam and Watson, Kenneth W, Adoption and the Family System: Strategies fo Treatment, Guilford Publ, 92; Reitz, Miriam, The Groundswell of Change in Adoption Requires Anchoring by Resarch, forthcoming, Journal of Child & Adolescnt Social Work, 99. **CONTACT ADDRESS** 401 East Illinois St., Ste 320, Chicago, IL, 60611.

REITZES, LISA B.
DISCIPLINE EIGHTEENTH TO TWENTIETH-CENTURY ARCHITECTURE AND AMERICAN ART **EDUCATION** Univ DE, PhD. **CAREER** Assoc prof, Truman State Univ. **SELECTED PUBLICATIONS** Pub(s), early twentieth-century Am pub arch, nineteenth-century Am sculpt, and women in arch. **CONTACT ADDRESS** Dept of Art Hist, Trinity Univ, 715 Stadium Dr, San Antonio, TX, 78212. **EMAIL** lreitzes@trinity.edu

REJAI, MOSTAFA
PERSONAL Born 03/11/1931, Tehran, Iran **DISCIPLINE** POLITICAL SCIENCE **EDUCATION** Calif State Univ, BA, 59, MS, 61; UCLA, PHD, 64. **CAREER** Tchg fel UCLA, 63-64; asst prof, polit sci, 64-67, assoc prof, 67-70, prof, 70-83, distinguished prof, 83- , Miami Univ; vis scholar Ctr for Int Affairs, Harvard Univ, 72, Hoover Inst on War, Revolution and Peace, Stanford Univ, 73, Inst Int Stud, Iran, 74-75; vis prof Western Col, Oxford, 71, 72. **HONORS AND AWARDS** Assoc ed, J Polit and MilSociol, 73- ; contribur articles to prof journals & book chapters; Outstanding Teaching award, 70. **MEMBERSHIPS** Am Polit Sci Asn; Am Sociol Asn; Int Polit Sci Asn; Int Soc Polit Psychol; Int Stud Asn; Inter-Univ Sem on Armed Forces and Soc; Conf for Study Polit Thought; Midwest Polit Sci Asn; So Polit Sci Asn; Western Polit Sci Asn; Pi Gamma Mu; Pi Sigma Alpha. **SELECTED PUBLICATIONS** Auth, World Military Leaders: A Collective and Comparative Analysis, 66; auth, The Strategy of Political Revolution, 73; auth, The Comparative Study of Revolutionary Strategy, 77; auth, Comparative Political Ideologies, 84; coauth, Loyalists and Revolutionaries: Political Leaders Compared, 88; coauth, Demythogizing an Elite: American Presidents in Empirical, Comparative, and Historical Perspectives, 93; auth, World Military Leaders: A Collective and Comparative Analysis, 96; auth, Leaders and Leadership: An Appraisal of Theory and Research, 97. **CONTACT ADDRESS** Department of Political Science, Miami Univ, Oxford, OH, 45056.

RELIHAN, JOEL C.
DISCIPLINE CLASSICS **EDUCATION** Univ Ill, BA, 76; Univ Wis, MA, PhD,85. **CAREER** Class, Wheaton Col. **RESEARCH** Augustine; Boethius; myth; Egyptian lang & cult; ancient ecology; **SELECTED PUBLICATIONS** Auth, Ancient Menippean Satire, Johns Hopkins UP, 93. **CONTACT ADDRESS** Dept of Class, Wheaton Col, 26 East Main St, Norton, MA, 02766. **EMAIL** Joel_Relihan@wheatonma.edu

REMAK, JOACHIM
PERSONAL Born 12/04/1920, m, 1948, 2 children **DISCIPLINE** MODERN EUROPEAN HISTORY **EDUCATION** Univ Calif, Berkeley, BA, 42, MA, 46; Stanford Univ, PhD, 55. **CAREER** Instr hist, Stanford Univ, 54-58; from asst prof to assoc prof, Lewis & Clark Col, 58-65, chmn dept, 62-63; assoc prof, 65-67, PROF HIST, UNIV CALIF, SANTA BARBARA, 67-, CHMN DEPT, 77-, Danforth fac res grant, 60; vis assoc prof, Ind Univ, 63-64; Guggenheim fel, 66-67; Humanities Inst grant, 68; dir, Nat Endowment for Humanities Sem for Col Teachers, 75 & 77-78. **HONORS AND AWARDS** Borden award, Hoover Libr, Stanford Univ, 60; Higby Prize, J Mod Hist, 70. **MEMBERSHIPS** AHA **RESEARCH** German history; diplomatic history; Southeastern Europe. **SELECTED PUBLICATIONS** Co-ed, Documents on German Foreign Policy, 1918-1945, US Govt Printing Off, 49-51; auth, Sarajevo, Criterion, NY & Weidenfeld & Nicolson, London, 59; ed, The case of the fraudulent dust jacket, Harper's, 11/62; The emperor's old clothes, Yale Rev, 12/62; co-ed, The Gentle Critic, Theodor Fontane and German Politics, Syracuse Univ, 64; The Origins of World War I, Holt, 67; ed, Journey to Sarajevo, Commentary, 7/68; The Nazi Years, A Documentary History, 69 & The Origins of the Second World War, 76, Prentice-Hall; Tannenberg - Clash Of Empires, J Of Modern Hist, Vol 65, 93; The Naval Policy Of Austria-Hungary, 1867-1918--Navalism, Industrial-Development, And The Politics Of Dualism, Ame Hist Rev, Vol 100, 95. **CONTACT ADDRESS** Dept of Hist, Univ of Calif, Santa Barbara, CA, 93106.

REMER, ROSALIND
DISCIPLINE HISTORY **EDUCATION** Univ Calif at Berkeley, BA, 84; UCLA, MA, 86, PhD, 91. **CAREER** ASST PROF, HIST, MORAVIAN COLL **MEMBERSHIPS** Am Antiquarian Soc **RESEARCH** Philadelphia Publishers, 1790-1830. **SELECTED PUBLICATIONS** Auth, "Old Lights and New Money: A Note on Religion, Economics, and the Social Order in Boston, 1740," Wm & Mary Quart 48, Oct 90; auth, "Preachers, Peddlers, and Publishers: Philadelphia's Backcountry Book Trades, 1800-1830," Jour of the Early Rep 14, Winter, 94; auth, "Building an American Book Trade: Philadelphia Publishing in the New Republic," Bus & Econ Hist 23, Fall, 94; auth, Printers and the Men of the Capital: The Philadelphia Book Trade in the New Republic, Univ Penn Press, 96; auth, "A Scottish Printer in Late Eighteenth-Century Philadelphia: Robert Simpson's Journey from Apprentice to Entrepeneur," Penn Mag of Hist & Biog, Jan/Apr 97; auth, "Capturing the Bard: An Episode in the American Publication of Shakespeare's Plays, 1822-1851," Papers of the Bibliog Soc of Am 91, June 97. **CONTACT ADDRESS** Dept of Hist, Moravian Coll, 1200 Main St, Bethlehem, PA, 18018. **EMAIL** mernr01@moravian.edu

REMINI, ROBERT VINCENT
PERSONAL Born 07/17/1921, New York, NY, m, 1948, 3 children **DISCIPLINE** AMERICAN HISTORY **EDUCATION** Fordham Univ, BS, 43; Columbia Univ, MA, 47, PhD(hist), 51. **CAREER** From instr to assoc prof hist, Fordham Univ, 47-65; chmn dept, 65-66, 67-71, PROF HIST, UNIV ILL, CHICAGO CIRCLE, 65-, Vis lectr, Columbia Univ, 59-60; Am Coun Learned Soc grant-in-aid, 60; Am Philos Soc grant-in-aid, 65-66 & 80; consult ed, Papers of Andrew Jackson, 72-; res prof humanities, Univ Ill, 77-; Guggenheim Mem Found fel, 78. **HONORS AND AWARDS** Encaenia Award, Fordham Col, 63; Award of Merit, Friends of Am Writers, 77; Silver Circle Award for Excellence in Teaching, Univ Ill, Chicago Circle, 81. **MEMBERSHIPS** AHA; Orgn Am Historians; Southern Hist Asn. **RESEARCH** American history, 1789-1877; early national period; Jacksonian era. **SELECTED PUBLICATIONS** Auth, Martin Van Buren and the Making of the Democratic Party, Columbia Univ, 59; Election of Andrew Jackson, Lippincott, 63; Andrew Jackson, Twayne, 66; Andrew Jackson and the

Bank War, Norton, 68; ed, The Age of Jackson, Harper, 72; auth, The Revolutionary Age of Andrew Jackson, 76, Andrew Jackson and the Course of American Empire, 1767-1821, 78 & Andrew Jackson and the Course of American Freedom, 1822-1832, Vol II, 81, Harper & Row; Correspondence Of James K. Polk, Vol 8--September-December 1844, J Of Am Hist, Vol 81, 94. **CONTACT ADDRESS** Dept of Hist, Univ of Ill Chicago Circle, Chicago, IL, 60680.

REMPEL, RICHARD A.
DISCIPLINE HISTORY **EDUCATION** Saskatchewan Univ, BA; Oxford Univ, MA, PhD. **RESEARCH** Victorian and 20th century British political, social and intellectual hist. **SELECTED PUBLICATIONS** Auth, Unionists Divided: Joseph Chamberlain, Arthur Balfour and the Unionist Free Traders 1903-1914; auth, Prophecy and Dissent 1914-1916; auth, Pacifism and Revolution 1916-1918. **CONTACT ADDRESS** History Dept, McMaster Univ, 1280 Main St W, Hamilton, ON, L8S 4L9.

RENEHAN, ROBERT
DISCIPLINE GREEK AND LATIN LITERATURE **EDUCATION** Harvard Univ, PhD, 63. **CAREER** PROF, UNIV CALIF, SANTA BARBARA. **RESEARCH** Ancient medicine; philos; hist of class scholar; textual criticism; lexicography. **SELECTED PUBLICATIONS** Auth, Greek Textual Criticism, Harvard Univ Press, 69; Leo Medicus, De Natura Hominis, Akademie Verlag, Berlin, 69; Greek Lexicographical Notes I and II, Gottingen, 75, 82; Studies in Greek Texts, Gottingen, 76; The Staunching of Odysseus' Blood: The Healing Power of Magic, AJP 92; "Some Special Problems in the Editing of Aristotle," SIFC, 3rd series, 92; "Plato, Apology 27A-B," CP 88, 93; "Of Mice and Men in Aristotle," CP 89, 94; "Polus, Plato, and Aristotle," CQ 45, 95; "On Some Genitives and a Few Accusatives in Aristotle: A Study in Style," Hermes 125, 97; rev(s), The New Oxford Sophocles, CP 87, 92; "Avotins, On the Greek of the Novels of Justinian," Phoenix 49, 95. **CONTACT ADDRESS** Dept of Classics, Univ Calif, Santa Barbara, CA, 93106-7150. **EMAIL** renehan@humanitas.ucsb.edu

RENNA, THOMAS JULIUS
PERSONAL Born 08/18/1937, Old Forge, PA, m, 1969, 3 children **DISCIPLINE** MEDIEVAL HISTORY **EDUCATION** Univ Scranton, BA, 65; Univ Nebr-Lincoln, MA, 67; Brown Univ, PhD(medieval hist), 70. **CAREER** Asst prof, 70-74, assoc prof, 74-79, prof hist, Saginaw Valley State Univ, 79-, Am Philos Soc res grant, 74. **MEMBERSHIPS** AHA; Mediaeval Acad Am; Am Soc Church Hist; Cath Hist Asn. **RESEARCH** Political thought; Franciscan history; monasticism; France 800-1500. **SELECTED PUBLICATIONS** Auth, over 70 articles dealing with political theory, St. Augustine, monastic thought, and early Franciscan hist; Church and State in Medieval Europe 1050-1314, Kendall/Hunt, 74; The West in the Early Middle Ages, Univ Press Am, 77; The Idea of Jerusalem in Monastic Thought 400-1400, in press. **CONTACT ADDRESS** Dept of History, Saginaw Valley State Univ, 7400 Bay Rd, University Center, MI, 48710-0001. **EMAIL** renna@tardis.svsu.edu

RENNIE, BRYAN S.
PERSONAL Born 12/13/1954, Ayr, Scotland, m **DISCIPLINE** HISTORY; PHILOSOPHY OF RELIGION **EDUCATION** Edinburgh Univ, Scotland, BA, 77, MA, 88, PhD, 91. **CAREER** Instr, Youngstown S Univ, 91; instr, Allegheny Col, 92; instr, Westminster Col, 92-93; asst prof, Westminster Col, 93- . **MEMBERSHIPS** AAR; Amer Philos Asn; SSSR; NASR. **RESEARCH** Mircea Eliade; Theory and method in the study of religion; The broad application of philosophy to the study of religion. **SELECTED PUBLICATIONS** Auth, Kali: the Terrible Goddess of Hindu Tantra, The Jour Rel Stud (s), Patiala, Univ Punjab, 12, 2, Autumn 89, 27-34; Rev of Other Peoples' Myths by Wendy Doniger and Metaphorical Worlds by Samuel R. Levin, 24, 4, Winter 90; The Diplomatic Career of mircea Eliade: a Response to Adriana Berger, Rel, 22, 4, 92, 375-392; The Religious Creativity of Modern Humanity: Some Observations on Eliade's Unfinished Thought, Rel Stud (s), June 95; Mircea Eliade: coupable jusqu'a preuve du contraire? Jurnalul Literar, 13-16, May-June 94, 2; Reconstructing Eliade: Making Sense of Religion, New York, State U of New York P, 96; Memory, Identity, and Imagination: Imagining the Past and Remembering Destiny, in Memory, History, and Critique, European Identity at the Millenium, Proceedings of the 6th International ISSEI Conference at the University for Humanist Studies, Utrecht, The Netherlands, Aug 96; Actualitatea lui Mircea Eliade, Origini: A Review of Literature, Ideas, and the Arts, vo1, 5-6, Nov-Dec 97, vii, ix; Mircea Eliade in The Routledge Encycl of Philos, ed Edward Craig, Routledge, 98. **CONTACT ADDRESS** Dept of Religion and Philosophy, Westminster Col, New Wilmington, PA, 16172. **EMAIL** brennie@westminster.edu

RESCH, JOHN P.
DISCIPLINE HISTORY **EDUCATION** Denison, BA, 62; Ohio State, MA, 65, PhD, 69. **CAREER** ASSOC PROF, HIST, UNIV NEW HAMPSHIRE MANCHESTER **MEMBERSHIPS** Am Antiquarian Soc **SELECTED PUBLICATIONS** Auth, "Peterborough, New Hampshire: After the Revolution," in New Hampshire: The State that Made us a Nation, Peter Randall, 89; auth, "Politics and Public Culture: The 1818 Revolutionary War Pension Act," Jour of the Early Rep, Summer 88; auth, "Peterborough, New Hampshire, 1750-1800: A Case Study of the Transformation of a Frontier Agricultural Community," in Themes on Rural History of the Western World, Iowa State Univ Press, 93. **CONTACT ADDRESS** Univ of New Hampshire, 220 Hackett Hill Rd, Manchester, NH, 03102. **EMAIL** jpr@christa.unh.edu

RESINSKI, REBECCA
PERSONAL Born 11/19/1968, Johnstown, PA **DISCIPLINE** CLASSICS **EDUCATION** Bucknell Univ, BA, 90; Univ CA, Los Angeles, MA, 93, PhD, 98. **CAREER** Asst prof Classics, Dept of Relig and Classics, Univ Rochester, 98-. **HONORS AND AWARDS** William Bucknell Prize, 90; A D White fel at Cornell Univ, 90-92; Chancellor's fel at UCLA, 92-93; Luckman Award for Distinguished Teaching, UCLA, 97. **MEMBERSHIPS** Am Philol Asn; Women's Classical Caucus. **RESEARCH** Ancient poetry; ancient social thought; representations of women in antiquity; the classical tradition in 20th century lit. **SELECTED PUBLICATIONS** Auth, Cosmos and Cosmetics: Constituting an Adorned Female Body in Ancient Greek Literature, UCLA dissertation, 98. **CONTACT ADDRESS** Univ of Rochester, 430 Rush Rhees Library, Rochester, NY, 14627. **EMAIL** beci@troi.cc.rochester.edu

RESIS, ALBERT
PERSONAL Born 12/16/1921, Joliet, IL **DISCIPLINE** RUSSIAN HISTORY **EDUCATION** Northwestern Univ, BS, 47, MA, 48; Russian Inst, Columbia Univ, cert, 50, PhD(hist), 64. **CAREER** Teacher hist, Joliet Twp High Sch & Jr Col, 50-53; field rep, Am Found Polit Educ, 53-54; lectr, univ col, Rutgers Univ, 56-58; asst prof hist, Paterson State Col, 58-64; asst prof, 64-67, ASSOC PROF HIST, NORTHERN ILL UNIV, 67-**MEMBERSHIPS** AHA; Am Assoc Advan Slavic Studies. **RESEARCH** Communist policy toward world trade union movement; Lenin and the Russian revolutionary movement; Soviet foreign policy. **SELECTED PUBLICATIONS** Auth, The Profintern, In: Soviet Foreign Relations and World Communism, Princeton Univ, 63; Das Kapital comes to Russia, Slavic Rev, 6/70; Lenin, Valdimir Ilich, In: Encycl Britannica, 74; Lenin on Freedom of the press, Russ Rev, 7/77; The Churchill-Stalin Secret Percentages Agreement on the Balkans: Moscow, October, 1944, Am Hist Rev, 4/78; Lenin, In: Enciclopedico Dizionario, 78; Collectivization of agriculture in the USSR, In: Mod Encycl Russ & Soviet Hist, 78; Spheres of influence in Soviet wartime diplomacy, J Mod Hist, 3/81; 1939, On The Eve Of World-War-II--The Unleashing Of World-War-I and the International System, Jahrbucher Fur Geschichte Osteuropas, Vol 40, 92; Cold-War And Revolution--Soviet-Amn Rivalry And The Origins Of The Chinese Civil-War, 1944-1946, Russian Hist-Histoire Russe, Vol 21, 94. **CONTACT ADDRESS** Dept of Hist, No Illinois Univ, De Kalb, IL, 60115.

RESTIVO, SAL
PERSONAL Brooklyn, NY, 2 children **DISCIPLINE** SOCIOLOGY AND ANTHROPOLOGY **EDUCATION** CCNY, hon BA, 65; MSU, MA, __; MSU, PhD with Distinction, 71. **CAREER** Inst Dept of Sociol, Michigan State, 67-70; Inst to Asst Prof Dep of Sociol, Wellesley Col, 70-72; Asst Prof and Dir of the Graduate Prog in Sociol Sep of Sociol, Univ of Hartford, 72-74; Asst to Assoc Prof, Dept Anthro and Sociol, Center for the Study of the Hum Dimensions of Sci and Tech, RPI, 74-82, Prof Sociol and Sci Studies, Dept Sci and Tech Studies, 83-, Dir Grad Prog in STS, 88-90;. **HONORS AND AWARDS** Fellowship, Res Inst for the Study of Man, NDEA Fellowship in Comarative Soc Structures, Michigan State, Natl Sci Found Fellowships, NSF Grants; Phi Kappa Phi, Belgian Natl Res Found Professorship, Hon Res Prof, Univ Birmingham, UK, Special Prof of Math Edu, Nottingham Univ, UK. **MEMBERSHIPS** Soc for Soc Studies of Sci (Pres) 93-95. **RESEARCH** Soc and Anthro of Mind, Math and Sci. **SELECTED PUBLICATIONS** Comparative Studies in Science and Society(CE Merril, Coloumbus, 74) co-ed with CK Vanderpool; The Social Relations of Physics, Mysticism and Mathematics(D Reidel, Dordrecht, 88, Pallas paperback; The Sociological Worldview, B Blackwell Oxford, 91; Mathematics in Society and History(-Kluwer Academic Publishers, Dordrecht, 92, nominated for the Morris D, Forkosch Book Award of the J of the History of Ideas, Science, Society and Values: Toward a Socilogy of Objectivity, Leigh Univ Press, Bethelem PA, 94; Degrees of Compromise: Industrial Interests and Academic Values, Suny Press Albany, 98. **CONTACT ADDRESS** Rensselaer Polytech Inst, Troy, NY, 12181. **EMAIL** restis@rpi.edu

REUSHER, JAY
DISCIPLINE CLASSICS **EDUCATION** Fordham Univ, PhD, 69. **CAREER** Assoc prof, 69-, Georgetown Univ. **RESEARCH** Kant **CONTACT ADDRESS** 900 10th St NE, Washington, DC, 20002-3718.

REUTER, WILLIAM C.
PERSONAL Born 08/14/1933, Yosemite National Park, CA, m, 1954, 2 children **DISCIPLINE** UNITED STATES HISTORY **EDUCATION** Univ Calif, Berkeley, AB, 55, MA, 59, PhD(US hist), 66. **CAREER** Assoc prof, 65-74, PROF US HIST, CALIF STATE UNIV, HAYWARD, 74- **MEMBERSHIPS** AHA; Orgn Am Historians. **RESEARCH** United States political and social history, 1865-1920. **SELECTED PUBLICATIONS** Auth, The Anatomy of Political Anglophobia in the United States, 1865-1900, Mid-America, 61 & 5-7/79; Business Journals And Gilded Age Politics, Historian, Vol 56, 93. **CONTACT ADDRESS** Dept of Hist, California State Univ, Hayward, Hayward, CA, 94542.

REXINE, JOHN EFSTRATIOS
PERSONAL Born 06/06/1929, Boston, MA, m, 1957, 3 children **DISCIPLINE** CLASSICS **EDUCATION** Harvard Univ, AB, 51, AM, 53, PhD, 64. **CAREER** Res asst, inst class studies, Harvard Univ, 54-55; from actg instr to instr humanities, Brandeis Univ, 55-57; from instr to prof classics, 57-68, chmn dept, 64-73, Asian studies fel, 65-66, dir div univ studies, 69-72, dir, IBM Corp Inst Liberal Arts for Exec, 69-71, assoc dean fac, 73-74, actg dean fac, 77-78, Charles a Dana Prof Classics, Colgate Univ, 77-, Dir Div Humanities, 72-, Contrib ed, Hellenic Chronicle, 52-; bk rev ed, Athene, 57-67 & Orthodox Observer, 57-72; managing ed, Greek Orthodox Theol Rev, 59-60, assoc ed, 60-67; bk rev columnist, Orthodox Observer, 72-; asst ed, Helios: Class J Southwest US, 76-79; ed, Classical Outlook, 77-79; bk rev ed, Classics & Modern Greek, Mod Lang J, 77-79; Fulbright-Hays sr res scholar, Am Sch Classical Studies, Athens, 79-80. **HONORS AND AWARDS** Helicon Phoutrides Gold Medal, 62., LittD, Hellenic Col, 81. **MEMBERSHIPS** Am Class League; Mediaeval Acad Am; Am Philol Asn; Modern Greek Studies Asn; Inst for Byzantine & Mod Greek Studies (vpres, 74-). **RESEARCH** Classical Greek and Roman literature; modern Greek literature; Byzantine civilization and the Greek Orthodox Church. **SELECTED PUBLICATIONS** Auth, Lectiones-Primae--A Graded Reader--Artes-Latinae Level 1--English And Latin, Classical Bullet, Vol 69, 93; The Immortal Emperor--The Life And Legend Of Constantine-Palaiologos, Last Emperor Of The Romans, Classical Bullet, Vol 68, 92; Creatures Of Speech--Lion Herding and Hunting Similes In The Ilia, Classical World, Vol 86, 93; L Ennemi Du Poete, World Literature Today, Vol 66, 92; Ancient Icaria, Classical Bullet, Vol 70, 94; The Illyrians--The Peoples Of Europe, Classical Bullet, Vol 70, 94; Poetry And Civil-War In Lucan Bellum Civile, Classical Bullet, Vol 69, 93; Am Rome, Vol 1, Classical Rome, Classical Bullet, Vol 69, 93; Lectiones-Secundae--A Graded Reader--Artes-Latinae Level-2, Classical Bullet, Vol 69, 93. **CONTACT ADDRESS** Div of the Humanities, Colgate Univ, Hamilton, NY, 13346.

REYDAMS-SCHILS, GRETCHEN
PERSONAL m, 3 children **DISCIPLINE** CLASSICS; ANCIENT PHILOSOPHY **EDUCATION** Katholieke Universiteit Leuven, Belgium, AB (classics, magna cum laude), 87; Univ Cincinnati, MA, 89; KU Leuven, Belgium, Inst of Philos, res, 91-92; Univ CA, Berkeley, Candidate Philos, 91, PhD, 94. **CAREER** Prog dir, Int House, Berkeley, 89-91; teaching asst, Univ Cincinnati, 88-89; press & info office, European Parliament, Brussels, summer 90; post-graduate sem moderator, KU Leuven, Inst for Philos, 91-92; grad student instr, Univ CA, Berkeley, 92-93; press office Brussels, Council of the European Communities, spring 94; ASST PROF, PROG LIBERAL STUDIES, UNIV NOTRE DAME, 94-; vis prof, Spiritan Missionary Sem, Arusha, Tanzania, spring 98 (sabbatical). **HONORS AND AWARDS** Fulbright fel, 87-92; Louise Semple-Taft fel, Univ Cincinnati, 87-89; Sather Assist, Univ CA, Berkeley, 89-91; Louise McKay Prize in Latin Prose Composition, Univ CA, Berkeley, 91; Mellon Dissertation Res grant, 91; fel, Center of Western European Studies, spring 93; Chancellor's Dissertation Year fel, Univ CA, Berkeley, 93-94; Scientific Council of the Found Hardt, Geneva, 96; Belgian Univ Found pub grant, 96. **SELECTED PUBLICATIONS** Auth, Solon and the Hektemoroi, Ancient Soc 22, Leuven, 91; Plato's Myth of Er: the Light and the Spindle, l'Antiquite Classique 62, 93; Stoicized Readings of Plato's Timaeus in Philo of Alexandria, Soc Bib Lit, sem papers 94, Studia Philonica Annual 7, 95; The European Union and Cultural Policy, European Intergration and American Federalism: A Comparative Perspective, Richard Herr and Steven Weber, eds, Berkeley, 96; Plato's World Soul: Grasping Sensibles without Sense-Perception, Interpreting the Timaeus-Critias: Proceedings of the IV Symposium Platonicum, selected papers, Int Plato Studies 9, ed L. Brisson and T. Calvo, Sankt Augustin, 97; Posidonius and Plato's Timaeus: Off to Rhodes and Back to Plato?, Classical Quart 47, 97; Romand and Stoic, the Self as a Mediator, Dionysius, forthcoming; Demiurge and Providence, Stoic and Platonist Readings of Plato's Timaeus, Monotheismes et Philosophie 2, Brepols, forthcoming 98; An Anthology of Snakebites, Philosophy/Gender Studies, Seven Bridges Press, forthcoming 99. **CONTACT ADDRESS** Prog Liberal Studies, Univ Notre Dame, Notre Dame, IN, 46556. **EMAIL** gretchen.j.reydams-schils.1@nd.edu

REYERSON, KATHRYN L.
DISCIPLINE HISTORY **EDUCATION** Radcliffe Univ, PhD, 74. **CAREER** Prof **RESEARCH** Social and economic history of France in the twelfth through the fourteenth centuries. **SELECTED PUBLICATIONS** Auth, Business, Banking and Finance in Medieval Montpellier, 85; co-ed, The Medieval Castle: Romance and Reality, 84; The Medieval Mediterranean: Cross-Cultural Contacts, 89; City and Spectacle in Medieval Europe,

94. **CONTACT ADDRESS** History Dept, Univ of Minnesota, Twin Cities, 614 Social Sciences Tower, 267 19th Ave. S, Minneapolis, MN, 55455. **EMAIL** reyer001@tc.umn.edu

REYNOLDS, ANN
DISCIPLINE ART AND ART HISTORY **EDUCATION** CUNY, PhD. **CAREER** Asst prof; taught at, Hunter Cole, Queens Cole, Ramapo Col & Fordham Univ. **HONORS AND AWARDS** Univ Tchg Excellence awd, Students' Asn. **RESEARCH** Post 1945 visual cult in the US and Europe; mod archit; museum exhibition practice; feminist theory. **SELECTED PUBLICATIONS** Publ in, Oct, Ctr & Art and Text. **CONTACT ADDRESS** Dept of Art and Art Hist, Univ of Texas at Austin, 2613 Wichita St, FAB 2.130, Austin, TX, 78705.

REYNOLDS, DONALD E.
PERSONAL Born 07/20/1931, Munday, TX, m, 1960, 2 children **DISCIPLINE** AMERICAN HISTORY **EDUCATION** N Tex State Col, BA, 57, MA, 58; Tulane Univ, PhD(hist), 66. **CAREER** Instr hist & govt, Decatur Baptist Col, 58-61; assoc prof, 65-72, PROF HIST, E TEX STATE UNIV, 72- **HONORS AND AWARDS** Tex Writer's Roundup Award, 71. **MEMBERSHIPS** AHA; Southern Hist Asn; Orgn Am Historians. **RESEARCH** Southern history; Civil War and Reconstruction; military history. **SELECTED PUBLICATIONS** Coauth, Arkansas and the Vicksburg Campaign, Civil War Hist, 12-59; auth, The New Orleans riot of 1866, reconsidered, La Hist, winter 64; Ammunition supply in revolutionary Virginia, Va Mag Hist & Biog, 1/65; coed, Yank in the Carolinas Campaign: The diary of James W Chapin, Eighth Indiana Cavalry, NC Hist Rev, 1/69; auth, Union strategy in Arkansas during the Vicksburg Campaign, Ark Hist Quart, spring 70; Editors Make War: Southern Newspapers in the Secession Crisis, Vanderbilt Univ, 70; ed, A Mississippian in Lee's army: The letters of Leander Huckaby (3 parts), J Miss Hist, 2/74, 5/74, 8/74; co-ed, With the Army of the Cumberland in the Chickamauga Campaign, Ga Hist Quart, summer 75; Glory, Glory, Glorieta, The Gettysburg Of The West - Scott,R/, Western Historical Quarterly, Vol 24, 93; Reluctant Martyr--Anthony Bewley And The Texas Slave Insurrection Panic Of 1860/, Southwestern Hist Quart, Vol 96, 93. **CONTACT ADDRESS** Dept of Hist, East Texas State Univ, Commerce, TX, 75428.

REYNOLDS, E. BRUCE
PERSONAL Born 05/29/1947, Kansas City, KS, m, 1982 **DISCIPLINE** HISTORY **EDUCATION** Cent Mo St Univ, BS, 69, MA, 77; Univ Hawaii Manoa, PhD, 88. **CAREER** Lectr, 79-82, Chulalongkorn Univ, Thailand; asst prof to assoc prof to prof, 88-, San Jose St Univ. **HONORS AND AWARDS** Crown Prince Akihito Scholar, 85; Fulbright Fel, 86, 87. **MEMBERSHIPS** Assoc for Asian Stud; Asian Stud on the Pacific Coast; Amer Hist Assoc; Soc for Hist of Amer. Foreign Rel; World War II Stud Assoc; World Hist Assoc. **RESEARCH** Politics & int relations in East and Southeast Asia, 190-1950 **SELECTED PUBLICATIONS** Art, Aftermath of Alliance: The Wartime Legacy in Thai-Japanese Relations, J of SE Asian Stud, 90; art, International Orphans: The Chinese in Thailand During World War II, J of SE Asian Stud, 97; auth, Thailand and Japan's Southern Advance 1940-1945, St. Martin's Press, 94. **CONTACT ADDRESS** Dept of History, San Jose St Univ, San Jose, CA, 95192-0117. **EMAIL** ereynold@email.sjsu.edu

REYNOLDS, FRANK E.
PERSONAL Born 11/13/1930, Hartford, CT, m, 1997, 3 children **DISCIPLINE** HISTORY OF RELIGION, BUDDHIST STUDIES **EDUCATION** Oberlin Col, BA, 52; Yale Univ, BD, 55; Univ Chicago, MA, 64, PhD, 71. **CAREER** Prog dir, Student Christian Ctr, Bangkok, 56-59; minister to foreign students, Univ Chicago, 62-65, from instr to asst prof, 67-71, assoc prof, 72-79, PROF HIST RELIG & BUDDHIST STUDIES, UNIV CHICAGO, 79-, chmn, Comt Asian Southern Asian Studies, 78-83, prog dir, Inst Advan Studies Relig, 92-98; Lectr hist, Chulalonkorn Univ, 57-59; vis prof, Stanford Univ, 70-71; ed, Hist Relig J, 76-; Asn Asian Studies Monograph Series, 77-83; Fulbright sr fel, 73-74; NEH res fel, 78-79; assoc ed, J Relig Ethics, 90-, assoc ed, J Relig, 88-. **MEMBERSHIPS** Am Soc Study Relig; Am Acad Relig; Asn Asian Studies; NAm Soc Buddhist Studies; Int Asn Buddhist Studies; Law & Soc. **RESEARCH** Therauada Buddhism; Thailand; comparative ethics. **SELECTED PUBLICATIONS** Coauth, Two Wheels of Dhamma, Am Acad Relig, 72; co-ed, Religious Encounters with Death, Pa State Univ, 77; co-ed & contribr, The Biographical Process, Mouton, 76; Transitions and Transformations in the History of Religion, E J Brill, 80; auth, Guide to Buddhist Religion, 80; co-ed & transl, Those Worlds according to King Buang: A Thai Buddhists Cosmology, Asian Humanities Press, 82; co-ed, Cosmogony and Ethical Order, Chicago, 85; co-ed, Myth and Philosophy, SUNY, 90; co-ed, Discourse and Practice, SUNY, 92; co-ed, Religion and Practical Reason, 94. **CONTACT ADDRESS** Swift Hall, Univ of Chicago, 1025-35 E 58th St, Chicago, IL, 60637-1577. **EMAIL** mgp2@midway.uchicago.edu

REYNOLDS, ROGER EDWARD
PERSONAL Denver, CO **DISCIPLINE** MEDIEVAL INTELLECTUAL HISTORY **EDUCATION** Harvard Univ, AB, 58, PhD, 69; Univ Chicago, JD, 61. **CAREER** From asst prof to prof hist, Carleton Univ, 68-77; PROF MEDIEVAL STUDIES, UNIV TORONTO, 77-, Pontif Inst Mediaeval Studies sr fel, 77- **MEMBERSHIPS** Mediaeval Acad Am; Int Ctr Medieval Art; Henry Bradshaw Soc. **RESEARCH** Early medieval liturgy; canon law; iconography. **SELECTED PUBLICATIONS** The Carolingians And The Written Word, Speculum-A J Of Medieval Studies, Vol 67, 92; The Carolingians And The Written Word, Speculum-A J Of Medieval Studies, Vol 67, 92; The Uses Of Literacy In Early Medieval Europe, Speculum-A J Of Medieval Studies, Vol 67, 92; Instruction In Paleography And Diplomatics--Goals And Objectives, Speculum-A J Of Medieval Studies, Vol 72, 97; Fountain Of Life--In Memory Of Niels K. Rasmussen, Speculum-A J Of Medieval Studies, Vol 69, 94; The Uses Of Literacy In Early Medieval Europe, Speculum-A J Of Medieval Studies, Vol 67, 92; Instruction In Paleography And Diplomatics--Goals And Objectives, Speculum-A J Of Medieval Studies, Vol 72, 97. **CONTACT ADDRESS** Pontif Inst of Mediaeval Studies, 59 Queen's Park Crescent E, Toronto, ON, M5S 2C4.

REYNOLDS, TERRY S.
PERSONAL Born 01/15/1946, Sioux Falls, SD, m, 1967, 4 children **DISCIPLINE** HISTORY **EDUCATION** Southern State Col, BS, 66; Univ Kans, MA, 68, PhD, 73. **CAREER** From asst prof to assoc prof, 73-83, Univ Wisc; from assoc prof to prof to dir to chemn, 83-. **HONORS AND AWARDS** Norton Prize, Society for Indust Archeol; Pres, Society Hist Technol. **MEMBERSHIPS** Society Hist Tech; Society Indust Archeol; Nat Assoc Science, Technol, Society; Newcomen Society; Intl Comm Hist Technol. **RESEARCH** History of technology; history of engineering; industrial archeology **SELECTED PUBLICATIONS** Ed, The Engineer in America, 91; auth, art, The Education of Engineers in American Before the Morrill Act of 1962, 92; coed, Technology and the West, 97; coed, Technology and American History, 97; auth, art, Good Engineering, Poor Management: The Battle Creek Hydroelectric System, 95. **CONTACT ADDRESS** Dept of Social Sciences, Michigan Tech Univ, Program in Industrial History and Archeology, Houghton, MI, 49931. **EMAIL** treynold@mtu.edu

RHIE, MARYLIN
DISCIPLINE ART HISTORY **EDUCATION** Univ Chicago, MA, PhD. **CAREER** Dir, Prog E Asian Stud; Jessie Wells Post Prof. **RESEARCH** Chinese Buddhist art. **SELECTED PUBLICATIONS** Collab as curator of a major exhibition of Tibetan art, Wisdom and Compassion, the Sacred Art of Tibet & coauth, bk of the exhibition, 91. **CONTACT ADDRESS** Dept of Art, Smith Col, Hillyer Hall 111, Northampton, MA, 01063.

RHOADS, WILLIAM B.
PERSONAL Born 03/11/1944, Harrisburg, PA, m, 1966, 2 children **DISCIPLINE** ART HISTORY **EDUCATION** Princeton Univ, PhD, 75. **CAREER** SUNY New Paltz, currently Prof, Art Hist Dept, since 1970. **RESEARCH** Colonial Revival; FDR's sponsorship of art and architecture; art and architecture of the Hudson Valley; street and inter urban railways in America art and culture. **SELECTED PUBLICATIONS** Auth, The Architecture of the Catskill Mountain Heritage Trail, Hudson Valley Reg Rev, 97; Colonial Revival in American Craft, in: revivals Diverse Traditions, NY, Abrams, 94; Franklin D Roosevelt and Washington Architecture, Records of the Columbia Historical Soc, 89. **CONTACT ADDRESS** 34 Plattekill Ave, New Paltz, NY, 12561.

RHODES, RANDALL
PERSONAL Born 02/01/1959, Rochester, NY, s **DISCIPLINE** ART HISTORY **EDUCATION** Univ Chicago, BA, 79; Univ Chicago, MA, 81; Univ Chicago, PhD, 91. **CAREER** Buffalo State Col, 93-96; asst prof, Frostburg State Univ, 96-. **MEMBERSHIPS** CAA; AAH. **RESEARCH** Art hist; postmodernism; gender studies. **CONTACT ADDRESS** Frostburg State Univ, 101 Braddock Rd., Frostburg, MD, 21532. **EMAIL** R_RHODES@fre.fsu.umd.edu

RIASANOVSKY, NICHOLAS
PERSONAL Born 12/21/1923, Harbin, China, m, 1955, 3 children **DISCIPLINE** MODERN HISTORY **EDUCATION** Univ OR, BA, 42; Harvard Univ, AM, 47; Oxford Univ, DPhil, 49. **CAREER** From Asst prof to assoc prof hist, Univ IA, 49-57; from assoc prof to prof, 57-69, Sidney Hellman Ehrman prof Europ hist, Univ CA, Berkeley, 69-, Fulbright grant, 54-55; Guggenheim fel, 69; sr fel, Nat Endowment for Hum, 75; Fulbright sr scholar, 79. **HONORS AND AWARDS** Am Asn Advan Slavic Studies Distinguished Contributor Award, 93; AHA Award for Scholarly Distinction, 95. **MEMBERSHIPS** AHA; Am Asn Advan Slavic Studies. **RESEARCH** Russ intellectual hist in the first half of the nineteenth century. **SELECTED PUBLICATIONS** Auth, Russia and the West in the Teaching of the Slavophiles, Harvard Univ, 52; Nicholas 1st and Official Nationality in Russia, 1825-1855, Univ Calif, 59; History of Russia, Oxford Univ, 63; The Teaching of Charles Fourier, Univ Calif, 69; A Parting of Ways: Government and the Educated Public in Russia, 1801-1855, Clarendon, 10/76; The Image of Peter the Great in Russian History and Thought, Oxford Univ, 85; The Emergence of Romanticism, Oxford Univ, 92; Collected Writings, Charles Schlacks, Jr. Publ, 93. **CONTACT ADDRESS** Dept of Hist, Univ of California, 3229 Dwinelle Hall, Berkeley, CA, 94720-2551.

RICE, ALBERT R.
PERSONAL Born 06/09/1951, Pasadena, CA, m, 1987, 2 children **DISCIPLINE** MUSICOLOGY; LIBRARY SCIENCE **EDUCATION** Calif State Univ-Fullerton, BA, 74; Claremont Grad Univ, MA, 77, PhD, 87; San Jose Univ, MLS, 94. **CAREER** Curator, Kenneth G. Fiske Mus of Musical Instruments at Claremont Col, 86-; Libn, Los Angelas Public Lib, 98-. **HONORS AND AWARDS** NEA Travel to Collections res grant, 90-91; referee on the Music Hist panel for the Travel to Collections Grants, 92-93. **MEMBERSHIPS** Am Mus Instrument Soc; Galpin Soc; Am Lib Asn. **RESEARCH** 18th & 19th century clarinets, flutes, and pianos; 18th & 19th century musical literature for the clarinet. **SELECTED PUBLICATIONS** Auth, The Clarinet d'amour: A request for additional information, FoMHRI Quart, no 70, 17-17, 1/93; auth, The earliest clarinet concertos: Johann Valentin Rathgeber's Chelys Sonora (1728), The Clarinet, vol XX, no 4, 24-28, 93; auth, Some Performance Practice Aspects of American Sheet Music, 1793-1830, Music in Performance and Society: Essays in Honor of Roland Jackson, Harmonie Pk Press, 229-247, 97. **CONTACT ADDRESS** 495 St Augustine Ave, Claremont, CA, 91711. **EMAIL** al_rice@cucmail.claremont.edu

RICE, ARNOLD SANFORD
PERSONAL Born 05/09/1928, Albany, NY, m, 1954, 1 child **DISCIPLINE** AMERICAN HISTORY **EDUCATION** State Univ NY Albany, BA, 50; Columbia Univ, MA, 51; Ind Univ, PhD, 59. **CAREER** From instr to assoc prof Am hist, 58-66, chmn dept hist, 71-77, PROF AM HIST, KEAN COL NJ, 67-, Adj prof, Rutgers Univ, 59-63; Fulbright exchange prof, Netherlands, 64-65; Fulbright scholar, Dept Health, Educ & Welfare, 64-65; consult on minority hist & cult approx fifty sch districts in NJ, 67-73; res grantee, NJ Hist Comn, 71-72. **HONORS AND AWARDS** Distinguished alumnus award, SUNY Albany; distinguished tchg award, Kean Univ; Tchr of the Year, Kean Univ; Presidential Excellence Award for Distinguished Scholarship, Kean Univ. **MEMBERSHIPS** Am Hist Asn; Pi Gamma Mu; Phi Alpha Theta; Alpha Sigma Lambda; Phi Kappa Phi. **RESEARCH** Ku Klux Klan in the 20th century; 20th century American social and cultural history. **SELECTED PUBLICATIONS** Auth, The Ku Klux Klan in American Politics, Pub Affairs, 62; The American Political Right Wing, Algemeen Dagblad, 4/65; Herbert Hoover, 1874-1964, 71 & Newark, 1666-1970, 77, Oceana; coauth, United States since 1865, Harper, 77; auth, American Civilization since 1900, Harper, 83; auth, The Warren Court, Assoc Faculty Press, 87; auth, United States History to 1977, HarperCollins, 91; auth, United States History from 1865, HarperCollins, 91. **CONTACT ADDRESS** Dept of History, Kean Univ, Union, NJ, 07083-7131.

RICE, EILEEN F.
PERSONAL Born 10/04/1914, Chicago, IL **DISCIPLINE** AMERICAN DIPLOMATIC HISTORY **EDUCATION** Siena Heights Col, BA, 39; Univ Detroit, MA, 46; St Xavier Col, Ill, cert theol, 51; Cath Univ AM, PhD, 59. **CAREER** Instr elem sch, MI & NM, 35-46; instr hist, Aquinas High Sch, Ill, 46-49; instr, St Ambrose High Sch, Mich, 49-50; instr, Cath Cent High Sch, 50-53; instr, Hoban Dominican High Sch, Ohio, 57-62; from asst prof to assoc prof, 62-69, chmn dept hist, 69-75, prof hist, Barry Univ, 69-, chmn soc sci, 75. **MEMBERSHIPS** AHA; Am Cath Hist Asn; Southern Hist Asn. **RESEARCH** US-Mex diplomacy. **SELECTED PUBLICATIONS** Auth, Diplomatic relations between the United States and Mexico as effected by the problem of religious liberty in Mexico 1925-1929, 59. **CONTACT ADDRESS** Dept of Hist, Barry Univ, 11300 N E 2nd Ave, Miami, FL, 33161-6695.

RICE, LOUISE
DISCIPLINE ART HISTORY **EDUCATION** Harvard Univ, BA; Columbia Univ, PhD. **CAREER** Asst prof, Duke Univ. **RESEARCH** Renaissance and Baroque art and archit. **SELECTED PUBLICATIONS** Auth, The Altars and Altarpieces of New St. Peter's; pubs on seventeenth century Roman topics. **CONTACT ADDRESS** Dept of Art and Art Hist, Duke Univ, East Duke Building, Durham, NC, 27706. **EMAIL** lrice@acpub.duke.edu

RICE, RICHARD
DISCIPLINE HISTORY **EDUCATION** Portland State Univ, BA, 66; Univ Ill, MA, 67; Harvard Univ, MA, 67, PhD, 74. **CAREER** Prof. **SELECTED PUBLICATIONS** Auth, The Role of Meiji Militarism in Japan's Technological Progress (rev), Jour Econ Hist, 77; Economic Mobilization in Wartime Japan: Business, Bureaucracy, and Military in Conflict, Jour Asian Studies, 79. **CONTACT ADDRESS** Dept of History, 615 McCallie, Chattanooga, TN, 37403. **EMAIL** Richard-Rice@utc.edu

RICE, STEPHEN P.
DISCIPLINE AMERICAN STUDIES, HISTORY **EDUCATION** Conzaga, BA, 86; Yale Univ, MA, 93, PhD, 96. **CAREER** ASST PROF, AM STUD & HIST, RAMOPO COLL **MEMBERSHIPS** Am Antiquarian Soc **SELECTED PUBLICATIONS** Auth, "Minding the Machine: Languages of Class in Early Industrial America, 1820-1860." **CONTACT ADDRESS** Am/Intl Stud, Ramapo Col, New Jersey, 505 Ramopo Valley Rd, Mahwah, NJ, 10960. **EMAIL** srice@ramapo.edu

RICH, NORMAN
PERSONAL Born 04/19/1921, Cleveland, OH, m, 1952, 3 children **DISCIPLINE** MODERN HISTORY **EDUCATION** Oberlin Col, BA, 42; Univ CA, Berkeley, MA, 43, PhD, 49. **CAREER** Ed, Captured Ger For Ministry Archs, US Dept State, 49-54; res fel hist, Princeton Univ, 54-55; lectr, Bryn Mawr Col, 55-56; from asst prof to prof, Mich State Univ, 56-68; Prof hist, Brown Univ, 68-85, Emer Prof, 85- Res fel, St Antony's Col, Oxford Univ, 62-63; Guggenheim fel, 63-64. **HONORS AND AWARDS** Flbright fel, 80-81. **RESEARCH** Nineteenth and twentieth century Ger and Europ diplomatic hist, Baroque cult. **SELECTED PUBLICATIONS** Coauth, The Holstein Papers (4 vols), 56-63 & Friedrich von Holstein: Politics and Diplomacy in the era of Bismarck and Kaiser Wilhelm II, 64, Cambridge Univ; Age of Nationalism and Reform, 1850-1890, first ed, 70, sec ed, 77, & Ideology, the Nazi State, and the Course of Expansion, Vol I & The Establishment of the New Order, Vol II, In: Hitler's War Aims, 73-74, Norton; Why the Crimean War? A Cautionary Tale, New England Press, 90; Great Power Diplomacy, 1814-1914, McGraw Hill, 92. **CONTACT ADDRESS** 230 Arlington Ave, Providence, RI, 02906.

RICHARD, CARL J.
PERSONAL Born 12/16/1962, Gueydan, LA, m, 1997, 2 children **DISCIPLINE** HISTORY **EDUCATION** Univ of Southwestern La, BA, 83, MA, 85; Vanderbilt Univ, PhD, 88. **CAREER** Vis asst prof, Univ of Tx at Arlington, 88-89; asst prof, Univ of Southern Miss, 89-91; Assoc prof, Univ Southwestern La, 91-. **HONORS AND AWARDS** Found Distinguished Prof Award, Univ of Southwestern La, 97;Fraunces Tavern Museum Book Award, 95; Honorable Mention in Hist, Asn of Am Pub, 94. **MEMBERSHIPS** Org Am Historians; Southern Hist Asn; Soc HIst Early Am Republic. **RESEARCH** U.S. Intellectual Hist; U.S., American Revolution and early American history; ancient Greece and Rome. **SELECTED PUBLICATIONS** Auth, The Founders and the Classics: Greece, Rome, and the American Enlightenment, Havard, 94; The Louisiana Purchase, Center for La Studies, 95. **CONTACT ADDRESS** History Dept, Univ of Southwestern La, Lafayette, LA, 70504. **EMAIL** cjrichard@usl.edu

RICHARDS, JOAN LIVINGSTON
PERSONAL Boston, MA, 2 children **DISCIPLINE** HISTORY OF SCIENCE **EDUCATION** Radcliffe Col, BA, 71; Harvard Col, MA, 79, PhD, 80. **CAREER** Tutor hist of sci, Harvard Univ, 75-78; lectr, Cornell Univ, fall, 79 & Harvard Univ, spring, 80; vis asst prof, Cornell Univ, 80-81, fel, 81-82; asst prof, 82-90, assoc prof hist of sci, Brown Univ, 90. **RESEARCH** Hist of mathematics; hist of Victorian sci; philos of mathematics. **SELECTED PUBLICATIONS** Auth, Evolution of empiricism: The non-euclidean geometry of Hermann von Helmholt, Brit J Philos Sci, 9/77; The reception of a mathematical theory non-euclidean geometry in England 1868-1883, In: Natural Order: Historical Studies of Scientific Culture, Sage Publ Inc, 79; The art and the science of British algebra: A study in the perception of mathematical truth, Hist Math, 80; Mathematical Visions, Academic Press, 89. **CONTACT ADDRESS** Hist Dept, Brown Univ, 42 Angell St, Providence, RI, 02912-9127.

RICHARDS, JOHNETTA GLADYS
PERSONAL Born 07/18/1950, Bronx, NY, s **DISCIPLINE** AFRICAN-AMERICAN STUDIES **EDUCATION** Virginia State Coll, BA 1972; Univ of Cincinnati, MA 1974, PhD 1987. **CAREER** Trinity Coll, asst prof of history 1979-84; Univ of California Santa Barbara, lecturer Afro-Amer history 1977-78; Univ of Cincinatti, lecturer Amer history 1976-77; Northeastern Univ, adjunct instructor Afro-Am history 1971; Women's Studies California State Univ at Fresno, assoc prof 1984-88; San Francisco State Univ, assoc prof Black Studies 1988-. **HONORS AND AWARDS** Doctoral Fellowship, Natl Fellowship Fund, Atlanta GA 1978-79; Dissertation Fellowship, Center for Black Studies Univ of California 1977-78; Graduate Research Grant, Univ of Grad 1977; Danforth Fellowship, Univ of Cincinnati 1972-73; Mellon Research Grant 1981. **MEMBERSHIPS** Mem Assn for the Study of Afro-Am Life & History 1978-; mem Phi Alpha Theta Natl Honorary Frat of Historians 1974-; mem NAACP Hartford CT 1979-80;life mem Assn of Black Women Historians, 1983-; chair Far Western Region of the Assn of Black Women Historians 1986-88; Amer Historical Assoc, Pacific Coast Branch; national director, Assn of Black Women Historians, 1990-92; African American Museum and Library, Oakland, life member. **CONTACT ADDRESS** San Francisco State Univ, 1600 Holloway Ave, San Francisco, CA, 94132.

RICHARDS, LEON
PERSONAL Born 06/07/1945, Montgomery, Alabama, m, 1969 **DISCIPLINE** EDUCATION **EDUCATION** Alabama State University, BS (summa cum laude), 1968; University of Hawaii-Manoa, MA, 1970, PhD, 1974. **CAREER** East-West Center, University of Hawaii, Honolulu, HI, research assistant, 1970-71, 1974-75; Leeward Community College, Pearl City, HI, staff development specialist, 1975-77; Kapiolani Community College, Honolulu, HI, assistant dean of instruction, 1977-81, acting provost, 1983-84, dean of instruction, 1983-. **HONORS AND AWARDS** Alpha Kappa Mu Scholastic Honorary Society, 1966-68; Sigma Rho Sigma Scholastic Honorary Society for History Majors, 1966-68; American Council on Education Fellow in Academic Administratiion, 1981-82; Summer In-Residence Fellowship at National Center for Research in Vocational Education, 1979; East-West Ctr Fellows, 1993-97; Field Study Fellows to Peking University; Fulbright Study Abroad, Korea Foundation, for Field Study in China and Korea; Field Study Fellow to Peking Univ. **MEMBERSHIPS** Vice president, Hawaii Assn of Staff, Program & Organizational Development, 1978-90; member, National Committee of Black Political Scientist, 1979-; member, National Council of Resource Development, 1980-. **CONTACT ADDRESS** Dean of Instruction, Univ of Hawaii, 4303 Diamond Head Road, Honolulu, HI, 96816.

RICHARDS, LEONARD
DISCIPLINE HISTORY **EDUCATION** Univ CA, PhD, 68. **CAREER** Prof, Univ MA Amherst. **SELECTED PUBLICATIONS** Auth, Gentlemen of Property and Standing: Anti-Abolition Mobs in Jacksonian America, 70; The Advent of American Democracy, 77; The Life and Times of Congressman John Quincy Adams, 86. **CONTACT ADDRESS** Dept of Hist, Univ Massachusetts Amherst, Mass Ave, Amherst, MA, 01003.

RICHARDS, MICHAEL DULANY
PERSONAL Born 11/03/1941, Great Bend, KS, m, 1961, 3 children **DISCIPLINE** HISTORY **EDUCATION** Univ Tulsa, BA, 62; Duke Univ, AM, 64, PhD, 69. **CAREER** From instr to asst prof hist, 66-74, assoc prof hist, Sweet Briar Col, 74, Nat Endowment for Hum fel hist, 75-76. **MEMBERSHIPS** Eur hist sec southern historical asn; Ger Stu Asn; Southeastern World Hist Asn; World Hist Asn. **RESEARCH** Popular cult in Europe; revolutions and revolutionary movements; 20th Century World. **SELECTED PUBLICATIONS** Auth, Rosa Luxemburg, heroine of the left, Hist Today, 2/72; Leiden relieved, Holland saved, Mankind, 12/74; Revolution in the twentieth century, Forum, 76; The lower classes and politics, 1800-1850, Int Labor & Working Class Hist, 11/77; Europe, 1900-1980: A Brief History, Forum, 82; Co ed, Makers of Modern Europe, 87, Twentieth Century Europe: A Brief History, 98, Tamina As Alter Ego: Autobiography and History in: The Book of Laughter and Forgetting, 92, Ed. European History Newsletter, 97-02. **CONTACT ADDRESS** Box F, Box 14, Sweet Briar, VA, 24595-1056. **EMAIL** richards@sbc.edu

RICHARDSON, CHARLES O.
PERSONAL Born 03/13/1928, Reading, PA, m, 1969, 2 children **DISCIPLINE** MODERN HISTORY **EDUCATION** Lafayette Col, BA, 51; Univ Pa, MA, 55; Georgetown Univ, PhD, 63. **CAREER** Instr Hist, Otterbein Col, 61-62; instr, Albright Col, 62-64; asst prof, Rutgers Univ, 64-67; asst prof, 67-71, assoc prof Hist, Rider Col, 72-83; prof Hist, Rider Univ, 83-. **MEMBERSHIPS** AHA; Soc Fr Hist Studies; Am Acad Polit & Soc Sci. **RESEARCH** French diplomatic history, 1933-1940. **SELECTED PUBLICATIONS** Auth, French plans for allied attacks on the Caucasus oil fields, January-April, 1940, Fr Hist Studies, Spring 73; The Rome Accords of January 1935 and the coming of the Italian-Ethiopian War, The Historian, 11/78. **CONTACT ADDRESS** Rider Col, 2083 Lawrenceville, Lawrenceville, NJ, 08648-3099.

RICHARDSON, CORDELL
PERSONAL Born 11/10/1946, Pittsburgh, PA, m **DISCIPLINE** EDUCATION **EDUCATION** Lincoln U, BS 1968; Univ of Pitts, MS 1970, PhD 1974. **CAREER** Carnegie Mellon U, conslr asst dir & dir of upwrd bnd dir of Stud servs; Exclnc Prgm PUSH, natl dir. **MEMBERSHIPS** Mem Omega Psi Phi Frat; Am Soc for Engr Educs; Am Prpsychl Rsrch Fnd; Prince Hall Masons. **CONTACT ADDRESS** 5000 Forbes, Pittsburgh, PA, 15213.

RICHARDSON, DEAN M.
DISCIPLINE AMERICAN INDIAN LAW, CIVIL RIGHTS, PRODUCTS LIABILITY **EDUCATION** Univ Rochester, BA, 66; Syracuse Univ, JD, 69. **CAREER** Willamette Univ, Sch Law **HONORS AND AWARDS** NEH fel, Harvard Univ, 80., Ch, Northwest Afrikan Amer Ballet, Portland, Oregon, 94. **MEMBERSHIPS** Mem, Justinian Hon Law Soc. **SELECTED PUBLICATIONS** articles ed, Syracuse Law Rev. **CONTACT ADDRESS** Sch of Law, Willamette Univ, 900 State St, Salem, OR, 97301. **EMAIL** drichard@willamette.edu

RICHARDSON, DONALD
DISCIPLINE GREEK AND ROMAN CLASSICS, WORLD CLASSICS **EDUCATION** Univ Minn, PhD; post-doc work, Stanford Univ; Univ Oslo. **CAREER** Ex dept ch; prof. **SELECTED PUBLICATIONS** Transl, Euripides' Iphigenia At Aulis; auth, Great Zeus And All His Children; Eyewitnesses; Stories of the Greeks and Romans. **CONTACT ADDRESS** Dept of Eng, Univ Evansville, 1800 Lincoln Ave, Evansville, IN, 47714. **EMAIL** dr26@evansville.edu.

RICHARDSON, JOE M.
PERSONAL Born 12/17/1934, Stella, MO, m, 1966 **DISCIPLINE** UNITED STATES HISTORY **EDUCATION** Southwest Mo State Col, BS, 58; Fla State Univ, MS, 59, PhD(hist), 63. **CAREER** Asst prof hist, Univ Miss, 62-64; from asst prof to assoc prof, 64-71, PROF HIST, FLA STATE UNIV, 71-, Sr fel, Inst Southern & Negro Hist, Johns Hopkins Univ, 68-69. **MEMBERSHIPS** Asn Study Afro-Am Life & Hist; Southern Hist Asn. **RESEARCH** Black history; Post civil war; history of education. **SELECTED PUBLICATIONS** Auth, A Negro success story: James Dallas Burrus, J Negro Hist, 10/65; The Negro in the Reconstruction of Florida, Fla State Univ, 65; Christian Abolitionism: The American MIssionary Association and the Florida Negro, J Negro Educ, 71; Trial and Imprisonment of Jonathan Walker, Univ Fla, 74; To Help a Brother On: The first years of Talladega College, Ala Hist Rev, 75; Francis L Cardozo: a Black educator during Reconstruction, J Negro Educ, 78; A History of Fisk University, 1865-1946, Univ Ala Press, 80; The failure of the American Missionary Association to expand congregationaliam among southern Blacks, Southern Studies XVIII, spring 79; The Freedmen Bureau And Black Texans, Southwestern Hist Quart, Vol 97, 93; New-Orleans Dockworkers--Race, Labor And Unionism, 1892-1923, Labor Hist, Vol 34, 93. **CONTACT ADDRESS** Dept of Hist, Florida State Univ, 600 W College Ave, Tallahassee, FL, 32306-1096.

RICHARDSON, JOHN
DISCIPLINE RELATIONSHIPS BETWEEN POPULATION, RESOURCES AND ENVIRONMENT **EDUCATION** Univ Minn, PhD. **CAREER** Prof, Am Univ. **RESEARCH** Prevention,management and resolution of political conflict. **SELECTED PUBLICATIONS** Co-auth, Making it Happen: A Positive Guide to the Future, U.S. Asn Club Rome, 84; Ending Hunger: An Idea whose Time Has Come, Praeger, 84, 85. **CONTACT ADDRESS** American Univ, 4400 Massachusetts Ave, Washington, DC, 20016.

RICHARDSON, LAUREL
PERSONAL Born 07/15/1936, Chicago, IL, m, 1980, 5 children **DISCIPLINE** SOCIOLOGY **EDUCATION** Univ Chicago, BA, 56; Univ Colorado, PhD, 63. **CAREER** Asst prof, Dept Sociology, Calif State Univ Los Angeles, 62-64; asst prof, Dept Sociology, Denison Univ, 65-70; post-doctoral fellow, Coll Medicine, Natl Inst Health, 64-65, visiting asst prof, Dept Sociology, 69-70, asst prof, Dept Sociology, 70-74, assoc prof, Dept Sociology, 74-77, prof, Dept Sociology, 78-94, prof emerita, Dept Sociology, 93-, Graduate Prof of Women's Studies, Dept Sociology, 88-, visiting prof, Cultural Studies Program, Educ Policy and Leadership, Coll Educ, 95-, Ohio State Univ. **HONORS AND AWARDS** Visiting Distinguished Prof, New Mexico State Univ, 94; fellow, Natl Endowment for Humanities, declined; grant, faculty research released time, Dept of Sociology, Ohio State Univ, 90, 93; grant, co-recipient, Ohio Dept Health, "Impact of Rape Educ Strategies on Coll Students, 87-88. **MEMBERSHIPS** Amer Sociological Assn; North Central Sociological Assn; Soc Study Symbolic Interaction; Natl Women's Studies Assn; Sociologists Women in Soc. **RESEARCH** Qualitative methodology; gender; contemporary theory; feminist theory; interpretive studies; science studies; sociology of knowledge. **SELECTED PUBLICATIONS** Auth, **CONTACT ADDRESS** Dept of Sociology, Ohio State Univ, 190 N. Oval Mall, Columbus, OH, 43210. **EMAIL** Richardson.9@osu.edu

RICHARDSON, LAWRENCE JR
PERSONAL Born 12/02/1920, Altoona, PA, m, 1952 **DISCIPLINE** LATIN ARCHAEOLOGY **EDUCATION** Yale Univ, BA, 42, PhD(classics), 52. **CAREER** Instr classics, Yale Univ, 46-47; field archaeologist, Am Acad Rome, 52-55; from instr to assoc prof, Yale Univ, 55-66; Prof to James B Duke Prof, 66-91, Prof Emeritus Latin, Duke Univ, 91-; Guggenheim fel, 58-59; mem, Inst Advan Studies, 67-68; Am Coun Learned Soc fels, 67-68 & 72-73; Nat Endowment for Humanities fel, 79-80; Mellon prof Am Acad Rome, 80-81. **MEMBERSHIPS** Corresp mem, Ger Archaeol Inst; Am Philol Asn; Archaeol Inst Am. **RESEARCH** Latin poetry; Roman archaeology. **SELECTED PUBLICATIONS** Auth, Pompeii: The House of the Dioscuri, Am Acad Rome, 55; Cosa and Rome: Comitium and curia, Archaeology, 57; coauth, Cosa: The Temples of the Arx, Am Acad Rome, 60; auth, Furi et Aureli, comites Catulli, Class Philol, 63; Catullus 67: Interpretation and form, Am J Philol, 68; The tribunals of the praetors of Rome, Roemische Mitteilungen 80, 73; ed, Propertius, Elegies I-IV, Univ Okla, 77; auth, Curia Julia and Janus Geminus, Roemische Mitteilungen 85, 78; Pompei, an Architectural History, The Johns Hopkins Univ Press, 88; A New Topographical Dictionary of Ancient Rome, The Johns Hopkins Univ Press, 92; coauth, The Buildings of the Forum, Am Acad Rome, 93. **CONTACT ADDRESS** Dept of Class Studies, Duke Univ, PO Box 90103, Durham, NC, 27708-0103.

RICHARDSON, RICHARD C., JR.
PERSONAL Born 09/10/1933, Burlington, VT, m, 1954, 3 children **DISCIPLINE** EDUCATION **EDUCATION** Castleton State Col, BS, 54; Mich State Univ, MA, 58; Univ Texas, PhD, 63. **CAREER** Comn Off, US Marine Corps Res, 54-57; res asst, Mich State Univ, 58; instr Soc Stud & Counr, Vermont Col, 58-61; Dean Stud Pers Serv, Meramec Commun Col, 63-64; Dean of Instr, Forest Pk Commun Col, 64-67; founding pres, Northampton County Area Commun Col, 67-77; prof &

chr Dept Higher & Adult Educ, 77-83, Assoc dir, Nat Ctr Postsecondary Goverance & Fin Res Ctr, 85-90, Prof Div Ecid Ldr & Policy Stud, 84- , Ariz State Univ. distinguished grad award, Col Educ Univ Texas-Austin, 82; distinguished serv award, Am Asn Commun & Jr Col, 84; res of Year Award, Col Educ Ariz State Univ, 88 & 93. Hon Litt.D, Lafayette Col, 72; **MEMBERSHIPS** AERA; ASHE; AACC; Acad Mgt; AAUP **RESEARCH** Access and equity; higher education governance; state higher education policy issues. **SELECTED PUBLICATIONS** Coauth, Achieving Quality and Diversity: Universities in a Multicultural Society, Macmillan, 91; auth, Creating Effective Learning Environments: State Policy and College Learning, 93; coauth Overcoming the Effects of Apartheid in South African Universities, The Rev of Higher Educ, 96; State Structures for the Governance of Higher Education: A Comparative Study, Calif Higher Educ Policy Ctr, 97; Designing State Higher Education Systems For a New Century, Oryx Press, 98. **CONTACT ADDRESS** 5654 E Wilshire Dr., Scottsdale, AZ, 85257-1950. **EMAIL** RRichardson@asu.edu

RICHARDSON, WILLIAM
DISCIPLINE MARRIAGE; FAMILY THERAPY **EDUCATION** Georgia State Univ, PhD. **CAREER** Prof; prof therapist. **HONORS AND AWARDS** Clinical dir, Ctr for Marriage and Family Therapy at RTS. **MEMBERSHIPS** Clinical mem, clinical supvr, Amer Assn of Marriage and Family Therapy. **RESEARCH** Christian therapy. **SELECTED PUBLICATIONS** Auth, Train Up A Child: A Christian Parent's Handbook. **CONTACT ADDRESS** Dept of Marriage and Family Therapy, Reformed Theol Sem, 5422 Clinton Blvd, Jackson, MS, 39209-3099.

RICHEY, RUSSELL EARLE
PERSONAL Born 10/19/1941, Asheville, NC, m, 1965, 2 children **DISCIPLINE** CHURCH HISTORY **EDUCATION** Wesleyan Univ, BA (high honors), 63; Union Theol Sem, BD (M Div), 66; Princeton Univ, MA, 68, PhD, 70. **CAREER** Instr, asst prof, assoc prof, prof of church history, Drew Univ Theol and Graduate Schools, 69-86; assoc dean for academic progs and res prof of church hist, The Divinity School, Duke Univ, 86-92, assoc dean for Academic Progs and prof Church Hist, 92-, prof Church Hist, Duke Univ, 97-. **HONORS AND AWARDS** Wesleyan: High Honors, Distinction in Hist, Phi Beta Kappa, Sophomore, Junior, and Senior Honor Societies, French Prize in Relig, Honorary Woodrow Wilson; Union Theol Sem: Int Fels Prog, Columbia, Prize in Church Hist, Senior Honor Society; Princeton: Rockefeller Doctoral Fel (withdrew to be Univ Teaching Fel, 68-69), Frelinghuysen Fel, dissertation received with distinction; Ecumenical fac assoc grant, Gen Comm on Christian Unity and Interreligious Concerns, for Bossey conf on Teaching Ecumenics and subsequent three-year service as liason from Commision to United Methodist seminaries, ended 92; Lilly Endowment grant, 91; planning and implementation grant from the Lilly Endowment for a major study of US United Methodism. **MEMBERSHIPS** Am Soc of Church Hist (member, Council 76-78, 95-97); Am Academy of Relig; Hist Soc of the United Methodist Church; adv bd: Quart Rev, Christian Hist, Church Hist, and J of Southern Relig. **SELECTED PUBLICATIONS** Co-ed with Donald Jones, American Civil Religion, Harper & Row, 74, Mellon Res Univ Press, 90; ed and co-auth, Denominationalism, Abingdon Press, 77; co-ed with Kenneth E Rowe, Rethinking Methodist History, United Methodist Pub House, 85; auth, Early American Methodism, IN Univ Press, 91; co-auth and ed, Ecumenical and Interreligious Perspectives: Globalization in Theological Education, Quart Rev Imprint, 92; co-ed with Kenneth E Rowe and Jean Miller Schmidt, Perspectives on American Methodism, IN Univ Press, Kingswood/Abingdon, 93; co-ed and co-auth with R Bruce Mullin, Reimagining Denominationalism, Oxford Univ Press, 94; auth, The Methodist Conference in America: A History, Kingswood/Abingdon, 96; The Methodists, with James Kirby and Kenneth Rowe, Greenwood, 96; Connectionalism: Ecclesiology, Mission, and Identity, primary co-ed with Dennis M Campbell and William B Lawrence, UMAC, I, Abingdon, 97; The People(s) Called Methodist: Forms and Reforms of Their Life, co-ed with Dennis M Campbell and William B Lawrence, UMAC, II, Abingdon, 98; Doctrines and Discipline, co-ed with Dennis M Campbell and William B Lawrence, UMAC, III, Abingdon, forthcoming 99; Questions for the Twenty-First Century Church, co-auth and primary co-ed with Dennis M Campbell and William B Lawrence, UMAC, IV, forthcoming 99. **CONTACT ADDRESS** Divinity School, Duke Univ, Durham, NC, 27708-0968. **EMAIL** rrichey@mail.duke.edu

RICHLIN, AMY
DISCIPLINE CLASSICS AND THE STUDY OF WOMEN AND MEN IN SOCIETY **EDUCATION** Yale Univ, PhD. **CAREER** Prof, Univ Southern Calif. **RESEARCH** Construction of masculinity in the Roman rhetorical schools. **SELECTED PUBLICATIONS** Auth, The Garden of Priapus: Sexuality and Aggression in Roman Humor, 83, rev 92; ed, Pornography & Representation in Greece & Rome, 92 & Feminist Theory & the Classics, co-edited with Nancy Sorkin Rabinowitz, 93. **CONTACT ADDRESS** Col Letters, Arts & Sciences, Univ Southern Calif, University Park Campus, Los Angeles, CA, 90089. **EMAIL** richlin@.usc.edu

RICHMOND, DOUGLAS WERTZ
PERSONAL Born 02/21/1946, Walla Walla, WA, 1 child **DISCIPLINE** HISTORY **EDUCATION** Univ Wash, BA, 68, MA, 71, PhD(hist), 76. **CAREER** Asst prof, 76-82, assoc prof hist, Univ Tex, Arlington, 82-92, prof, 92-, chemn, Latin Am studies comt, 76-89. **MEMBERSHIPS** AHA; Conf Latin Am Hist; Southwest Coun of Latin Am Stud. **RESEARCH** Nineteenth and twentieth century Mexico. **SELECTED PUBLICATIONS** Auth, The Venustiano Carranza Archive, Hispanic Am Hist Rev, 5/76; El nacionalismo de Carranza y los cambios socioeconomicos, 1915-1920, Historia Mexicana, 7-9/76; co-ed, Essays on the Mexican Revolution, Univ Tex, 79; auth, Mexican politics and society during the Carranza Epoch, 1913-1920, In: Essays on the Mexican Revolution, 79; Factional political strife in Coahuila, 1910-1920, Hispanic Am His Rev, 2/80; La guerra de Texas se renova: Mexican Insurrection and Carrancista Ambitions, 1900-1920, Aztlan, spring 80; Mexican immigration and border strategy during the revolution, 1920-1920, New Mex Hist Rev, 7/82; Venustiano Carranza's Nationalist Struggle, 1893-1920, Univ Nebr Press, 83; auth, Comparative Elite Systems in Latin Amica and the United States, 1876-1914, Revista de historia de Am, 114, 7/92-12/92; auth, Essays on the Mexican War, Texas A&M Press, 86; auth, Carlos Pellegrini and the Crisis of the Argentine Elites, 1880-1916, Praeger, 89. **CONTACT ADDRESS** Dept of History, Univ Texas, Arlington, Box 19529, Arlington, TX, 76019-0529. **EMAIL** richmond@uta.edu

RICHMOND, VELMA B.
PERSONAL Born 03/12/1931, New Orleans, LA, m, 1958, 2 children **DISCIPLINE** ENGLISH LITERATURE; MEDIEVAL STUDIES **EDUCATION** La State Univ, BA, 51, MA, 52; Oxford Univ, BLitt, 57; Univ NC, PhD, 59. **CAREER** Instr, La State Univ, 57-58; Instr to Prof, 58-96, Prof Emeritus English, Holy Names Col, 96-, Chmn English, 70-76, Dean Acad Affairs, 80-85. **HONORS AND AWARDS** Fulbright Schol, Oxford Univ, 55-57; ACLS Fel, 76; Project Dir, NEH Implementation Grant for Core Prog in Humanities Studies, 81-84. **MEMBERSHIPS** Medieval Acad; New Chaucer Soc; Medieval Asn Pac; Mod Lang Asn; Mod Humanities Res Asn; Christianity and Lit; Int Arthurian Soc. **RESEARCH** Chaucer; medieval romance; Shakespeare; children's literature; contemporary Catholic fiction. **SELECTED PUBLICATIONS** Auth, Laments for the Dead in Medieval Narrative, Duquesne Univ Press, 66; The Popularity of Middle English Romance, Bowling Green State Univ Press, 75; Muriel Spark, Frederick Ungar Publ Co, 84; Geoffrey Chaucer, Continuum, 92; The Legend of Guy of Warwick, Garland, 96; author of numerous articles and reviews. **CONTACT ADDRESS** 1280 Grizzly Peak Blvd., Berkeley, CA, 94708.

RICHTER, DANIEL K.
DISCIPLINE HISTORY **EDUCATION** Thomas More, BA, 76; Columbia Univ, MA, 77, MPhil, 79; PhD, 84. **CAREER** PROF, HIST, DICKINSON COLL **MEMBERSHIPS** Am Antiquarian Soc **SELECTED PUBLICATIONS** Coauth, "Crossing the Cultural Divide: Indians and New Englanders, 1605-1763," Procs of the AAS 80, 80; auth, "Rediscovered Links in the Covenant Chain: Previously Unpublished Transcripts of New York Indian Treaty Minutes, 1677-1691," Procs of the AAS 92, 82; auth, "War and Culture: The Iroquois Experience," Wm & Mary Quart 40, 83; auth, "Iroquois versus Iroquois: Jesuit Missions and Christianity in Village Politics, 1642-1686," Ethnohist 32, 85; co-ed, Beyond the Covenant Chain: The Iroquois and Their Neighbors in Indian North America, 1600-1800, Syracuse Univ Press, 87; auth, "Cultural Brokers and Intercultural Politics: New York-Iroquois Relations, 1664-1701," Jour of Am Hist 75, 88; auth, "A Framework for Pennsylvania Indian History," Penn Hist 57, 90; auth, The Ordeal of the Longhouse: The Peoples of the Iroquois League in the Era of European Colonization, Univ NC Press, 92; auth, "Some of Them Would Always Have a Minister with Them: Mohawk Protestantism, 1683-1719," Am Indian Quart XVI, 92; auth, "Whose Indian History?" Wm & Mary Quart, 93; auth, "Native Peoples of North America and the British Empire," in The Oxford History of the British Empire, vol II: The Eighteenth Century. **CONTACT ADDRESS** Dept of Hist, Dickinson Col, PO Box 1773, Carlisle, PA, 17013. **EMAIL** richter@dickinson.edu

RICHTER, DONALD CHARLES
PERSONAL Born 03/13/1934, New York, NY, m, 1962, 2 children **DISCIPLINE** ANCIENT HISTORY **EDUCATION** Atlantic Union Col, BA, 55; Andrews Univ, MA, 57; Univ Md, MA, 58, PhD(hist), 65. **CAREER** Asst prof hist, Chapman Col, World Campus Afloat, 65-66; asst prof, 64-71, ASSOC PROF HIST, OHIO UNIV, 71- **MEMBERSHIPS** AHA; Archaeol Inst Am. **SELECTED PUBLICATIONS** Battle Tactics Of The Western Front--The British Army Art Of Attack, Am Hist Rev, Vol 101, 96. **CONTACT ADDRESS** Dept of Hist, Ohio Univ, Athens, OH, 45701-2979.

RIDDEL, FRANK STEPHEN
PERSONAL Born 10/25/1940, Sistersville, WV, m, 1964, 2 children **DISCIPLINE** SOCIAL STUDIES EUROPEAN HISTORY **EDUCATION** Marshall Univ, AB, 62, MA, 65; Ohio State Univ, PhD, 71. **CAREER** Instr, 62-63 Gallia Acad High Sch; instr, 63-68, Barboursville High Sch; instr, 68-69, Marshall Univ; res assoc, 69-71, Ohio St Univ; asst prof, 71-78, assoc prof, 78-84, prof, soc stud, 84-94, prof, hist, 94-, Marshall Univ. **MEMBERSHIPS** Soc Spanish & Portuguese Hist Studies; Nat Coun Social Studies; AHA; Am Studies Assn. **RESEARCH** Spanish politics during the Franco Regime; history and culture of Appalachia; methods of teaching social studies. **SELECTED PUBLICATIONS** Art, Improving the Teaching of History: How Can The Social Studies Methods Class Contribute?, J Teaching & Learning, 80; auth, Defining and Shaping the Good Citizen in an Authoritarian Society: Civic Education in Franco's Spain, Clearinghouse for Soc Sci Ed, 80; coauth, West Virginia Government, WV Hist Ed Found, 83; coauth, American Government: The USA and West Virginia, WV Hist Ed Found, 90; coauth, Undermining Authoritarianism: The Colegio Estudio and the Preservation of Liberal Education in Franco's Spain, J WV Hist Assn, 93. **CONTACT ADDRESS** Dept of History, Marshall Univ, Huntington, WV, 25701. **EMAIL** riddell@marshall.edu

RIDGEL, GUS TOLVER
PERSONAL Born 07/01/1926, Poplar Bluff, m **DISCIPLINE** EDUCATION **EDUCATION** Lincoln Univ, BS, 1950; Univ of MO, Columbia, MO, MA, 1951; Univ of WI, Madison, PhD, 1956. **CAREER** Fort Valley State Coll, Ft Valley, GA, head dept of business, 1952-58; Wiley Coll, Marshall, TX, dean academic affairs, 1958-60; Kentucky State Univ, Frankfort, KY, dean, School of Business, 1960-84; Central State Univ, Wilberforce, OH, vice pres, academic affairs, 1972-74; Southern Univ, Baton Rouge, vice pres of academic affairs, beginning 1985; KENTUCKY STATE COLL, VICE PRES OF ADMIN AFFAIRS, currently. **HONORS AND AWARDS** Univ of Missouri-Columbia, The Gus T Ridgel Minority Graduate Fellowship, 1988. **MEMBERSHIPS** Advisory bd, Republic Savings Bank, 1983-86; mem of LA Univ, Marine Consortium Council, 1986-. **CONTACT ADDRESS** So Univ, J S Clark Admin Bldg, 3rd Fl, Baton Rouge, LA, 70813.

RIDGWAY, BRUNILDE (SISMONDTO)
PERSONAL Born 11/14/1929, Chieti, Italy, m, 1958, 4 children **DISCIPLINE** ARCHAEOLOGY **EDUCATION** Univ Messina, Dr Let, 53; Bryn Mawr Col, MA, 54, PhD, 58; Georgetown Univ, Dr of Humane Let, Honoris Causal, 92; Union Col, Dr of Let, Honoris Causa, 92. **CAREER** Instr archaeol, 58-60, Bryn Mawr Col; asst prof classics, 60-61, Hollins Col; asst prof class Near Eastern archaeol, 61-67, from assoc prof to prof archaeol, 67-77, Rhys Carpenter Prof Archaeol, 77-, Bryn Mawr Col; cor mem, Ger Archaeol Inst, 67-; dir summer session, Am Sch Class Studies, Athens, 67 & 71; consult & panelist, NEH, 72-; exec comt mem, Int Lexicon Classical Mythology, 74-; Guggenheim fel, 74-75; ed-in-chief, Am J Archaeol, 77-85; leader, 79-94, Archaeol Tours of Sicily, Alumnae Assn, Bryn Mawr/Haverford Cols; lectr, 81-82, Thomas Spencer Jerome Lectures, Univ Mich & Amer Acad Rome. **HONORS AND AWARDS** Christian R & Mary F Lindback Found Award Dist Tchng, 81; Gold Medal of Archaeol Inst of Am for Dist Archaeol Achievement; Natl Gold Medalist, prof of Year prog, 89, Coun for Advancement & Sup of Ed (CASE); Penn Prof Year, 89, CASE. **MEMBERSHIPS** Archaeol Inst Am; Inst Assn Class Archaeol; German Archaeol Inst; Alumni Assn Am Schl of Class Stud at Athens; ASMOSIA; Amer Phil Soc; Soc for the Promotion of Hellenic Stud, 97. **RESEARCH** Greek sculpture; Greek architecture. **SELECTED PUBLICATIONS** Auth, Fifth Century Styles in Greek Sculpture, Princeton Univ, 81; auth, Roman Copies of Greek Sculpture: The Problem of the Originals, Ann Arbor, 84; co-ed, Ancient Anatolia, Essays in Honor of Machteld J Mellink, Madison 86; coauth, The Porticello Shipwreck: A Mediterranean Merchant Vessel of 415-385 BC, Texas A&M Univ Press, 87; auth, Hellenistic Sculpture I: The Styles of ca 331-200 BC, Madison, 90; auth, Fourth-Century Styles in Greek Sculpture, Madison, 97. **CONTACT ADDRESS** Dept of Classics & Near Eastern Archaeol, Bryn Mawr Col, Bryn Mawr, PA, 19010. **EMAIL** bridgeway@brynmawr.edu

RIDGWAY, WHITMAN HAWLEY
PERSONAL Born 11/13/1941, Schenectady, NY, 4 children **DISCIPLINE** UNITED STATES HISTORY, 1760-1860 **EDUCATION** Kenyon Col, AB, 63; San Francisco State Univ, MA, 67; Univ Pa, PhD, 73; Univ Md, JD, 85. **CAREER** From lectr to assoc prof, 69-78, assoc prof hist, Univ Md, College Park, 78-, assoc chair, 93-97. **HONORS AND AWARDS** Soc Sci Res Coun Award, 79.Newberry Libr fels, 74 & 77; NEH summer grant, 76; hon fel, Dept Geog, Univ Wis-Madison, 79-80; Libr Congress fel, 88. **MEMBERSHIPS** Orgn Am Historians; DC Bar Asn; Am Asn for Legal Hist; Md Hist Asn; Pa Hist Soc. **RESEARCH** Early national to middle period political culture; Bill of Rights, constitutional. **SELECTED PUBLICATIONS** Auth, Community Leadership in Maryland, 1790-1840: A Comparative Analysis of Power in Society, Univ NC, Chapel Hill, 79; coauth, Maryland: A History of Its People, Johns Hopkins Press, 86; co-ed, The Bill of Rights: Our Written Legacy, Krieger Publ Co, 93; auth, Popular Sentiment and the Bill of Rights Controversy, in The Bill of Rights: Government Proscribed, Univ Press Va, 97. **CONTACT ADDRESS** Dept of Hist, Univ of Md, College Park, MD, 20742-7315. **EMAIL** wr9@umail.umd.edu

RIDLEY, JACK B.
DISCIPLINE HISTORY OF MODERN FRANCE, 19TH CENTURY EUROPE, HISTORY OF ENGINEERING EDUCA **EDUCATION** Southwestern Okla State Univ, BA, 62; Univ SDak, MA, 63; Univ Okla, PhD, 70. **CAREER** Grad asst, Univ SDak, 62-63; instr, Murray State Col, 63-65; instr, Univ New Orleans, 67-68; grad tchg asst, Univ Okla, 65-67, 68-69; instr, 69-70, asst prof, 70-74, sect hd, Hist Sect, 74-75, assoc prof, 75-84, actg chemn, dept Soc Sci, 79-80; sect hd, Hist/Polit Sci Sect, 81-82, prof, 84-, ch, dept Hist and Polit Sci, 89-92, Distinguished Tchg Prof, 92-, dir, Mo London Prog, 94, coordr, UMSL-UMR coop MA degree prog, Univ Mo, Rolla. **HONORS AND AWARDS** Gilbert C Fite Award for Excellence in Grad Work, Univ of SDak, 63; travel fel, Univ Okla, 68; 20 Outstanding Tchr Awards, 3 AMOCO Tchg Awards,Univ Mo, Rolla, 69-92; NEH summer sem fel, 78; Phi Kappa Phi, 84; Fac Excellence Awards, 87, 88, 90; Fac Achievement Award, Burlington Northern Found, 87; Phi Eta Sigma, 89; Hon Mem, exec comt, Fort Leonard Wood Hist Bd, 89-92; Hon Knight of St Patrick, Univ Mo, Rolla, 91; Distinguished Tchg Prof, Univ Mo, Rolla, 92; President's Outstanding Tchg Award, Univ Mo, 93; Governor's Award for Excellence in Tchg, 93; MSM-UMR Alumni Merit Award, 95; finalist, Eugene Asher Award for Distinguished Tchg, Am Hist Asn, 96; Weldon Spring Endowment res grant, Uni Mo. **MEMBERSHIPS** State Hist Soc Mo; Western Soc for Fr Hist; Am Asn of Higher Educ. **RESEARCH** History of mining in Missouri. **SELECTED PUBLICATIONS** Auth, Completing the Circuit: A History of Electrical Education at MSM-UMR, Univ Mo Printing Serv, 84; Spanning the Years: Civil Engineering the Rolla Way, Univ Mo Printing Serv, 86; coauth, UM-Rolla: A History of MSM/UMR, Univ Mo Printing Serv, 83. **CONTACT ADDRESS** Univ Mo, Rolla, Rolla, MO, 65409-1060. **EMAIL** ridley@umr.edu

RIEDINGER, EDWARD
PERSONAL Born 03/26/1944, Cincinatti, OH, s **DISCIPLINE** HISTORY; LIBRARY & INFORMATION SCIENCE **EDUCATION** Univ of Chicago, MA, 69, PhD, 78; Univ of Calif, MLIS, 89. **CAREER** Pvt secy for English Correspondence, Juscelino Kubitschek, Rio de Janeiro, 72-76; asst prof, Pontifical Cath Univ, Rio de Janeiro, 76-77; asst prof, Univ of the Americas, Puebla, Mexico, 78; educ advising off, Fulbright Comn of Brazil, Am Consulate Gen, Rio de Janeiro, 79-88; vis lectr, San Francisco State Univ, 90; acting bibliogr, Univ of Calif, 90; assoc prof, Ohio State Univ, 91-. **HONORS AND AWARDS** Res Travel Award, NEH, 92; Res Travel Award, Tinker Found/Ohio State Univ Latin Am Studies Prog, 92, 96; Commendation, US-Brazil Cult Inst, Rio de Janeiro, 96; Fulbright Scholar Award, 96. **MEMBERSHIPS** AHA; Brazilian Studies Asn; Latin Am Studies Asn; Sem on the Acquisition of Latin Am Libr Materials. **RESEARCH** Modern Brazilian cultural history and politics. **SELECTED PUBLICATIONS** Como se faz um presidente: A campanha de JK, 88; Proceedings of the Brazilian Studies Association (BRASA): First Conference, Atlanta, Georgia, 10-12 March 1994, 94; Where in the World to Learn: A Guide to Library and Information Science for International Education Advisers, 95; Turned-on Advising: Computer and Video Resources for Educational Advising, 95; Proceedings of the Brazilian Studies Association (BRASA): Second Conference, Univ of Minn, Minneapolis, 11-13 May 1995, 95. **CONTACT ADDRESS** Latin American Studies Library, Ohio State Univ, 1858 Neil Ave Mall, Rm 312, Columbus, OH, 43210-1286. **EMAIL** riedinger.4@osu.edu

RIELY, JOHN C.
PERSONAL Born 08/27/1945, Philadelphia, PA, m, 1969, 2 children **DISCIPLINE** ENGLISH LITERATURE; ART HISTORY **EDUCATION** Harvard Col, AB, 67; Univ Pa, MA, 68, PhD, 71. **CAREER** Assoc res ed, Yale Addition Horace Walpoles Correspondence, 71-79; lectr, Yale Univ, 73-79; asst prof, Columbia Univ, 79-80; vis prof, Univ Minn, 80-81; from asst to assoc prof, Boston Univ, 81-. **HONORS AND AWARDS** Huntington Lib Fel, 73; ACLS Grant; Vis Fel, 82-83, Yale Ctr for Brittish Art; NEH Senior Fel, 88-89, Boston Public Libr Fel, 95-96; Fel Soc Antiquanes London and Royal Soc Arts. **MEMBERSHIPS** ASECS; NEASECS; Asn Lit Scholar Critics; Col Art Asn; Walpole Soc; Johnsonines US and UK. **RESEARCH** Late 17th thru early 19th early literature and art history; Johnson and his circle; Sir Joshua Reynolds; Horace Walpole; Alex Pope; Biography and Portraiture; caricature and comic art; English country house and landscape garden. **SELECTED PUBLICATIONS** Auth, Rowlandson Drawings From the Paul Mellon Collection, 77; auth, The Age of Horace Walpole and Caricature 73, 90. **CONTACT ADDRESS** Dept of English, Boston Univ, 236 Bay State Rd, Boston, MA, 02215. **EMAIL** jriely@bu.edu

RIES, NANCY
DISCIPLINE RUSSIAN CULTURE AND SOCIETY **EDUCATION** Cornell Univ, PhD, 93. **CAREER** Asst prof, Colgate Univ. **RESEARCH** Modes of discourse, and how they reproduce cult forms and soc value syst. **SELECTED PUBLICATIONS** Auth, Culture and Conversation during Perestroika, Cornell UP, 97. **CONTACT ADDRESS** Dept of Russ Stud, Colgate Univ, 13 Oak Drive, Hamilton, NY, 13346.

RIESENBERG, PETER
PERSONAL Born 11/17/1925, New York, NY, m, 1951, 2 children **DISCIPLINE** MEDIEVAL HISTORY **EDUCATION** Rutgers Univ, AB, 47; Univ Wis, MA, 49; Columbia Univ, PhD(medieval hist), 54. **CAREER** Instr hist, Rutgers Univ, 53-54; from instr to asst prof, Swarthmore Col, 54-60; from asst prof to assoc prof, 60-66, PROF HIST, WASH UNIV, 66-, Soc Sci Res Coun fel, Italy, 57-58; fel, I Tatti, Harvard Ctr Renaissance Studies, 64-65; Guggenheim fel, 64-65; mem, Col Entrance Exam Bd Examining Comt Europ Hist & World Cult, 67-70, chmn, 70-72; vis prof, Univ Calif, Berkeley, 68; fel, Nat Humanities Ctr, 78-79. **MEMBERSHIPS** Mediaeval Acad Am; Int Comn Hist Rep & Parliamentary Insts; Renaissance Soc Am. **RESEARCH** Medieval political thought and institutions; medieval urban history; medieval legal history. **SELECTED PUBLICATIONS** Auth, Inalienability of Sovereignty in Medieval Political Thought, Columbia Univ, 56; coauth, Medieval Town, Van Nostrand, 58; The Traditions of the Western World, Rand McNally, 67; auth, Civilism and Roman law in fourteenth century Italian society, Explor Econ Hist, fall 69; Citizenship and equality in late Medieval Italy, Studia Gratiana, 72; Citizenship at law in late Medieval Italy, Viator, 74; Violence, social control and community planning in medieval Italian city states, Washington Univ Law Quart, 75; The Jews in the structure of Western institutions, Judaism, 79; From Politics To Reason-Of-State--The Acquisition And Transformation Of The Language Of Politics, 1250-1600, Speculum-A J Of Medieval Studies, Vol 69, 94; From Politics To Reason-Of-State--The Acquisition And Transformation Of The Language Of Politics, 1250-1600, Speculum-A J Of Medieval Studies, Vol 69, 94. **CONTACT ADDRESS** Dept of Hist, Wash Univ, St Louis, MO, 63130.

RIESS, STEVE ALLEN
PERSONAL Born 08/26/1947, New York, NY, 3 children **DISCIPLINE** AMERICAN HISTORY **EDUCATION** NY Univ, BA, 68; Univ Chicago, MA, 69, PhD(Am hist), 74. **CAREER** Asst prof hist, State Univ NY, Brockport, 74-75; lectr social sci, Univ Mich, Dearborn, 75-76; asst prof, 76-80, assoc prof hist, 80-84, prof hist, Northeastern Ill Univ, 84-. **HONORS AND AWARDS** Presidential Merit Award, Northeastern Ill Univ, 81, 85, 89-93, 95-98; Fel for Col Teachers, Nat Endowment for the Humanities, 83-84; Webb-Smith Essay Prize, Univ Tex, 89; Outstanding Acad Book, City Games, 90-91; Summer Stipend for Independent Res, Nat Endowment for the Humanities, 92; Honorary Fel, Prog on Sports Studies, DeMontfort Univ, 96. **MEMBERSHIPS** Orgn Am Historians; NAm Soc Sport Hist; Soc for Am Baseball Res; Chicago Seminar on Sport and Culture. **RESEARCH** United States social history; United States urban history; American sport history. **SELECTED PUBLICATIONS** Ed, The American Sporting Experience: Essays and Documents, Leisure Press, 84; Major Problems in American Sport History, Houghton mifflin, 97; Sports and the American Jew, Syracuse Univ Press, 98; Sports in North America: A Documentary History Vol 6: Sports in the Progressive Erea, 1900-1920, Acad Int Press, 98; auth, Touching Base: Professional Baseball and American Culture in the Progressive Era, Greenwood Press, 80; City Games: The Evolution of American Society and the Rise of Sports, Univ Ill Press, 89, 91; Sports in the Industrial Age 1850-1920, Harlan Davidson, 95. **CONTACT ADDRESS** Dept of History, Northeastern Illinois Univ, 5500 N St Louis Ave, Chicago, IL, 60625-4625. **EMAIL** s-riess@neiu.edu

RIFE, JERRY E.
DISCIPLINE MUSIC HISTORY **EDUCATION** Kans State Univ, BS, MM; Mich State Univ, PhD. **CAREER** Ch, Rider Univ; contrib writer, The Saxophone Jour, 89;assoc producer, dir, If You Knew Sousa, doc film, 92-; conductor, Rider Univ Concert Band, 92; instr, Rider Univ, 84-; Westminister, 92-. **HONORS AND AWARDS** Hon, NJ State Senate, 93; cert appreciation, Somerset County, 93; Lindback award, 93. **MEMBERSHIPS** Am Musicol Soc. **RESEARCH** Life and music of Florent Schmitt, Igor Stravinsky, John Philip Sousa, Carl Nielsen, improvisation, single reed acoustics. **SELECTED PUBLICATIONS** Publ, numerous articles on Florent Schmitt, Sousa. **CONTACT ADDRESS** Dept of Theory and Mus Hist, Westfield State Col, 577 Western Ave., Westfield, MA, 01085.

RIGG, ARTHUR GEORGE
PERSONAL Born 02/17/1937, Wigan, England, m, 1964 **DISCIPLINE** MEDIEVAL ENGLISH & LATIN **EDUCATION** Oxford Univ, BA, 59, MA, 62, DPhil. **CAREER** Lectr English, Merton Col, Oxford Univ, 61-63, Merton & Balliol Cols, 63-66 & Oxford Univ, 65-66; vis asst prof, Stanford Univ, 66-68; assoc prof, 68-76, actg dir ctr, 76-78; Prof English & Medieval Latin, Ctr Medieval Studies, Univ Toronto, 76-. **MEMBERSHIPS** Mediaeval Acad Am. **SELECTED PUBLICATIONS** Auth, English Language; A Historical Reader, Appleton, 68; A Glastonbury Miscellany of the Fifteenth Century, Clarendon, Oxford Univ, 68; contribr, Medium Aevum, Anglia, English Lang Notes & Med Studies; ed, Editing Medieval Texts Written in England, Garland, 77; auth, Golias and other pseudonyms, Studi Medievali, 77; Medieval Latin poetic anthologies I, Mediaeval Studies, 77; Poems of Walter of Wimborne, Pontif Inst, Toronto, 78; Primas,Hugh And The Archpoet--Adcock,F/, Speculum-A J Of Medieval Studies, Vol 71, 96; Registrum-Anglie-De-Libris-Doctorum-Et-Auctorum-Veterum, Speculum-A J Of Medieval Studies, Vol 69, 94; John-Of-Hauville, Architrenius, Speculum-A J Of Medieval Studies, Vol 72, 97. **CONTACT ADDRESS** Ctr for Medieval Studies, Univ of Toronto, Toronto, ON, M5S 1A1.

RIGGS, ROBERT
DISCIPLINE MUSIC HISTORY **EDUCATION** Harvard Univ, PhD. **CAREER** Instr, 87-, actg ch, dept Mus, Univ MS, 96-; vis assoc prof, Univ UT, 94-96. **SELECTED PUBLICATIONS** Wrote numerous articles on the music of Mozart, Haydn, and Beethoven. **CONTACT ADDRESS** Univ MS, Oxford, MS, 38677. **EMAIL** muriggs@olemiss.edu

RIGGS, TIMOTHY A.
DISCIPLINE ART HISTORY **EDUCATION** Yale Univ, PhD. **CAREER** Asst prof, Univ NC, Chapel Hill. **RESEARCH** Prints and photographs. **SELECTED PUBLICATIONS** Auth, Hieronymus Cock, Printmaker and Publisher, Garland Publ Co, 77; Visions of City and Country: Prints and Photographs of Nineteenth-Century France, Worcester Art Museum and American Federation of Arts, 82; The Rise of Professional Printmakers in Antwerp and Haarlem, 1540-1640, in The Print Council Index to Oeuvre-Catalogues of Prints by European and American Artists, Kraus Int Publ, 83. **CONTACT ADDRESS** Univ N. Carolina, Chapel Hill, Chapel Hill, NC, 27599.

RIGSBY, KENT JEFFERSON
PERSONAL Born 02/25/1945, Tulsa, OK, m, 1969, 2 children **DISCIPLINE** CLASSICAL LANGUAGES, ANCIENT HISTORY **EDUCATION** Yale Univ, BA, 66; Univ Toronto, MA, 68. **CAREER** Asst prof, 71-77, Assoc Prof Classics, Duke Univ, 77-, Asst ed, Greek, Roman & Byzantine Studies, 72-77, assoc ed, 77-79, Roman ed, 79 & sr ed, 80- **MEMBERSHIPS** Am Philol Asn. **RESEARCH** Greek epigraphy; Hellenistic history; ancient religion. **SELECTED PUBLICATIONS** Auth, Cnossus and Capua, Trans Am Philol Asn, 76; Sacred Ephebic games at Oxyrhynchus, Chronique D'Egypte, 77; The era of the Province of Asia, Phoenix, 79; Seleucid Notes, Trans Am Philol Asn, 80; Missing Places + Confused And Erroneous Readings Of Toponyms In Greek And Coptic Texts/, Classical Philology, Vol 91, 96; Greek And Latin Inscriptions In The Manisa-Museum, Vienna, Am J Of Philology, Vol 117, 96; Missing Places + Confused And Erroneous Readings Of Toponyms In Greek And Coptic Texts, Classical Philology, Vol 91, 96. **CONTACT ADDRESS** Dept Class Studies, Duke Univ, Durham, NC, 27706.

RIKARD, MARLENE HUNT
PERSONAL TN, m, 1961, 2 children **DISCIPLINE** HISTORY **EDUCATION** Auburn Univ, BAA, 60; Samford Univ, MA, 71; Univ Ala, PhD, 83. **CAREER** From asst prof to prof, 79-, Samford Univ. **HONORS AND AWARDS** AAUW Fel, 80-81; John E. Rovensky Fel, Business, Economic Hist, 84, Ec Hy Asn; Sears Found Campus Leadership, Tchg, Res, 90, Samford Univ; Danforth Assoc; Phi Kappa Phi., Ed, The Newsletter of the Ala Hist Asn, 84-89; chemn, Ala Baptist Hist Commission, 84-88; chemn, Sov Baptist Hist Commission; 92-93; pres, Sov Asn women Historians, 90-91; pres, Ala Asn Historians, 90-92. **MEMBERSHIPS** Southern Hist Asn; Southern Asn Women's Historians; OAH; Asn Ala Historians; Ala Hist Asn. **RESEARCH** Southern history; Southern labor history; women's history. **SELECTED PUBLICATIONS** Auth, art, Goerge Gordon Crawford: Man of the New South, 87; auth, art, Alabama Enterprise, 87; auth, art, Company Towns, 89; auth, art, The Influence of Laywomen on Baptist Life, 89; auth, art, Henry DeBardeleben, 98. **CONTACT ADDRESS** Dept of Hist & Pol Sci, Samford Univ, Birmingham, AL, 35229. **EMAIL** mhrikard@samford.edu

RILEY, J.C.
PERSONAL Born 09/02/1943, Raleigh, NC, m, 1966, 2 children **DISCIPLINE** HISTORY **EDUCATION** NCU Chapel Hill, PhD, 71. **CAREER** Asst, Assoc, Prof, 75-, Indiana Univ; Asst, Assoc Prof, 70-75, Univ S. **HONORS AND AWARDS** NIH Shannon Awd; Guggenheim Fel; Ernest Meyer Prize. **MEMBERSHIPS** SSH; PAA; AAHM; IUSSP. **RESEARCH** Health; Mortality; Historical Demography; Old Regime Europe. **SELECTED PUBLICATIONS** Auth, Sick Not Dead: The Health of British Workingmen During the Mortality Decline, John Hopkins Univ Press, 97; Sickness Recovery and Death: A History and Forecast of Ill Health, MacMillan, London, U of Iowa, 89; The Eighteenth-Century Campaign to Avoid Disease, MacMillan London, St Martin's Press, 87; Seven Years War and the Old Regime in France: The Economic and Financial Toll, Princeton Univ Press, 86; Population Thought in the Age of the Demographic Revolution, Carolina Acad Press, 85. **CONTACT ADDRESS** History Dept, Indiana Univ, Bloomington, Bloomington, IN, 47405. **EMAIL** rileyj@indiana.edu

RILEY, JAMES DENSON
PERSONAL Born 10/11/1943, Oakland, CA, m, 1966, 3 children **DISCIPLINE** LATIN AMERICAN HISTORY **EDUCATION** St Mary's Col Calif, BA, 65; Tulane Univ, MA, 67, PhD(Latin Am hist), 72. **CAREER** Asst prof hist, Benedictine

Col, 70-76; asst prof, 76-80, ASSOC PROF HIST, CATH UNIV AM, 81- **MEMBERSHIPS** AHA; Conf Latin Am Hist; Latin Am Studies Asn. **RESEARCH** Colonial rural history in Mexico. **SELECTED PUBLICATIONS** Auth, Hacendados Jesuitas En Mexico, SepSetentas, Mexico, 76; Jesuit wealth in Mexico, 1675-1767, The Americas, 10/76; Santa Lucia: Desarrollo y administracion de una hacienda jesuita en el siglo XVIII, Historica Mexicana, 10/73; Landlords, Laborers and Royal Government: The Administration of Labor in Tlaxcala, 1680-1750, In: El trabajo y lost trabajadores en la historia de Mexico, Univ Ariz Press, 79; 2 Worlds Merging--The Transformation Of Society In The Valley-Of-Puebla, 1570-1640, Americas, Vol 54, 97; Mex Merchant Elite, 1590-1660--Silver, State And Soc, Americas, Vol 52, 96. **CONTACT ADDRESS** Dept of Hist, Catholic Univ of America, Washington, DC, 20017.

RILEY, PHILIP FERDINAND
PERSONAL Born 08/21/1941, South Bend, IN, m, 1967, 4 children **DISCIPLINE** EARLY MODERN EUROPE, OLD REGIME FRANCE **EDUCATION** Univ Notre Dame, AB, 63, AM, 64, PhD, 71. **CAREER** From Assoc Prof to Prof Hist, James Madison Univ, 71-. **HONORS AND AWARDS** Distinguished Teaching Award, James Madison Univ. **MEMBERSHIPS** Soc Fr Hist Studies; AHA; WHA. **RESEARCH** Louis XIV's Paris; world history. **SELECTED PUBLICATIONS** Auth, Louis XIII 1601-1643, Research Guide to European Historical Biography 1450 to the Present, Beacham Publ Inc, 92; Louis XIV, 1638-1715, Research Guide to European Historical Biography 1450 to the Present, Beacham Publ Inc, 92; Madame de Maintenon Francoise d'Aubigne, 1635-1719, Research Guide to European Historical Biography 1450 to the Present, Beacham Publ Inc, 92; Mr. Madison's University, Va 18, Winter 95; The Global Experience: Readings in World History, 2 vols, Prentice-Hall, 87, 3rd ed, 98; author of other articles. **CONTACT ADDRESS** Dept of Hist, James Madison Univ, Harrisonburg, VA, 22807-0002. **EMAIL** rileypf@jmu.edu

RILEY, TERENCE
PERSONAL Born 11/06/1954, IL, s **DISCIPLINE** ARCHITECTURE/DESIGN **EDUCATION** Univ Notre Dame, BA, 78; Columbia Univ, MS, 82. **CAREER** Gen partner, 84-91, limited partner, 91-, Keenen/Riley Architects; curator, 91-92, chief curator, 92-, Dept of Architecture and Design. **SELECTED PUBLICATIONS** Auth, Between the Museum and the Marketplace: Selling Good Design, Stud in Modern Art 4: The Museum of Modern Art at Mid-Century at Home and Abroad, Museum of Modern Art, NY, 94; coed, Frank Lloyd Wright: Architect, Museum of Modern Art, NY, 94; auth, Light Construction, Museum of Modern Art, NY, 95; auth, The Architectural Competition, Studies in Modern Art 7: Imagining the Future of the Museum of Modern Art, Museum of Modern Art, NY 95; auth, The Charette, Studies in Modern Art 7: Imagining the Future of the Museum of Modern Art, Museum of Modern Art, NY, 98; auth, Portrait of the Curator as a Young Man, Studies in Modern Art 6: Philip Johnson and the Museum of Modern Art, Museum of Modern Art, NY, 98. **CONTACT ADDRESS** Dept of Architecture and Design, Mus of Modern Art, 11 W 53rd St, New York, NY, 10019. **EMAIL** Terence_Riley@moma.org

RILLING, JOHN R.
PERSONAL Born 04/28/1932, Wausau, WI, m, 1953, 2 children **DISCIPLINE** HISTORY **EDUCATION** Univ Mn, BA, 53; Harvard Univ, AM, 57, PhD, 59. **CAREER** Asst prof to assoc prof to prof, chair, 59-, Univ Richmond; chair, 65-71, Westhampton Col. **HONORS AND AWARDS** Phi Beta Kappa, 53; Omicron Delta Kappa, 72; Woodrow Wilson Fel, 53; Archibald Coolidge Fel, 55-58; Harvard Traveling Fel, 58-59; Fel Folger Libr, 60., Distinguished Educ Award, 75, 76, 77, 80, 87; finalist, Prof of the Year, 81. **MEMBERSHIPS** Amer Hist Assoc; N Amer Conf on British Hist; Carolinas Symp on British Stud. **RESEARCH** Tudor/Stuart: late Tudor & early Stuart; admin & soc hist. **SELECTED PUBLICATIONS** Art, Amer Hist Rev; art, Renaissance News; art, Historian; art, J of Church & State. **CONTACT ADDRESS** History Dept, Univ Richmond, Richmond, VA, 23227. **EMAIL** jrilling@richmond.edu

RIMBY MEO, SUSAN
DISCIPLINE HISTORY **EDUCATION** Univ of Pittsburgh, PhD, 92; Kutztown St Col, MA, 81; Bloomsburg St Col, BS Ed, 76 **CAREER** Assoc/Asst Prof, 92-, Shippensburg Univ; Inst, 88-91, Millersville Univ; Tch Fel, 83-87, Univ of Pittsburgh; Soc Stud Tchr, 77-81, Gov Mifflin Sch Dist **HONORS AND AWARDS** Acad Achievmt Awd, 76, Magna cum laude, Bloomsburg **MEMBERSHIPS** Am Hist Asn; Orgn of Am Hist **SELECTED PUBLICATIONS** Coauth, The Antebellum Women's Movement: A Curriculum Unit for Grades 5-8, National Center for History in the Schools, 98; Auth, Lavina Lloyd Dock, Greenwood Press, 97 **CONTACT ADDRESS** Dept of History, Shippensburg Univ, Shippensburg, PA, 17257. **EMAIL** srleig@ark.ship.edu

RINDERLE, WALTER
PERSONAL Born 08/31/1940, Vincennes, IN, m, 1974, 2 children **DISCIPLINE** CHURCH HISTORY, THEOLOGY, EURO HISTORY **EDUCATION** St Meinrad Col, AB 62; State Univ Innsbruck, Austria, STL 66, MA 67; Univ Notre Dame, MA 73, PhD 76. **CAREER** Vincennes Univ, asst prof 90-94; Univ Southern IN, asst prof 94-97; Univ St Francis, instr 98. **HONORS AND AWARDS** 2 NEH awds. **MEMBERSHIPS** Indiana Hist Soc; Catholic Hist Soc. **RESEARCH** Role of the Lutheran Church in the collapse of East Germany; Medical hist; Nazi Germany. **SELECTED PUBLICATIONS** Nazi Impact on a German Village; 200 Years of Catholic Education; Permanent Pastors in Knox County. **CONTACT ADDRESS** RR 6, E-2, Vincennes, IN, 47591. **EMAIL** rinderle@bestonline.net

RINEHART, JOHN
DISCIPLINE MUSIC **EDUCATION** Kent State Univ, AB; Cleveland Inst of Mus, MM; OH State Univ, PhD. **CAREER** Assoc prof, Antioch Col; ed, CIM Notes. **HONORS AND AWARDS** ASCAP Ernest Bloch Award in compos, 60; grant, Am Mus Ctr, Nat Endowment for Arts, NY Coun of Arts, Margaret Jory Fund, Jerome Found, Bascom Little Found., Founding mem, Res Musica Am; founder, CIM Notes. **MEMBERSHIPS** Nat Coun of Am Soc of Univ Composers. **SELECTED PUBLICATIONS** Publ research in collaboration with behaviorist Carl Charnetski and geneticist Lester Turoczi on the effect of music on the production of immunoglobulin A (IgA) in hum(s). **CONTACT ADDRESS** Antioch Col, Yellow Springs, OH, 45387.

RINGENBERG, WILLIAM CAREY
PERSONAL Born 08/18/1939, Fort Wayne, IN, m, 1962, 4 children **DISCIPLINE** HISTORY **EDUCATION** Taylor Univ, BS, 61; Ind Univ, MAT, 64; Mich State Univ, Phd, 70. **CAREER** From asst prof to assoc prof to prof, 68-, assoc dean, 74-79, dept chemn, 82-, dir, honors prog, 83-94, 96-98, Taylor Univ. **HONORS AND AWARDS** Chi Alpha Omega Scholastic Honor Soc, 61, Taylor Univ; Lilly Fel Am Hist, 62, 63, Ind Univ; Inst Adv Christian Stud, Scholar, 81., VP, 87-88, pres, 89-90, Conference on Faith and Hist. **MEMBERSHIPS** Orgn Am Hist; Am Soc Church Hist; Conference Faith & Hist. **RESEARCH** History of Protestant higher education in America; Mennonite history in America. **SELECTED PUBLICATIONS** Auth, A Brief History of Fort Wayne Bible College,in Mennonite Q Rev, 80; auth, The Religious Thought and Practice of James A. Garfield, in The Old Northwest, 83; auth, The Christian College: A History of Protestant Higher Education in America, 84; auth, Benjamin Harrison: The Religious Thought and Practice of a Presbyterian President, in Am Presbyterians: J of Presbyterian Hist, 86; auth, Taylor University: The First 150 Years, 96. **CONTACT ADDRESS** Dept of History, Taylor Univ, Upland, IN, 46989. **EMAIL** wlringenb@tayloru.edu

RINGER, ALEXANDER
DISCIPLINE MUSIC **EDUCATION** New Sch Soc Res, MA; Columbia Univ, PhD. **CAREER** Prof emer, 58-, Univ IL Urbana Champaign. **RESEARCH** Medieval organum; music of the French Revolution; nineteenth-century music; and contemp Am compos(s); Middle Eastern music; Hebrew music; aesthetics and sociology of music; and music in educ. **SELECTED PUBLICATIONS** Auth, Arnold Schoenberg The Composer as Jew,90; The Early Romantic Era Between Revolutions: 1789 and 1848, 90; Musik als Geschichte,93; co-auth, Beethoven Interpretationen seiner Werke, 94. **CONTACT ADDRESS** Dept of Music, Univ Illinois Urbana Champaign, E Gregory Dr, PO Box 52, Champaign, IL, 61820. **EMAIL** a-ringer@uiuc.edu

RINGROSE, DAVID R.
PERSONAL Born 06/01/1938, Minneapolis, MN, m, 1961, 1 child **DISCIPLINE** EUROPEAN ECONOMIC HISTORY, HISTORY OF SPAIN **EDUCATION** Carleton Col, BA, 60; Univ Wis, MA, 62, PhD(hist), 66. **CAREER** From asst prof to assoc prof hist, Rutgers Univ, New Brunswick, 65-74; assoc prof, 74-80, assoc dir, Ctr Iberian & Latin Am Studies, 77-80, PROF HIST, UNIV CALIF, SAN DIEGO, 80-, CHMN, 81-. Rutgers res coun fac fel, 68-69; Fulbright res fel, Spain, 68-69; Nat Endowment for Humanities fel, 73-74. **MEMBERSHIPS** Econ Hist Asn; AHA; Soc Span & Port Hist Studies (gen secy, 73-75); Social Sci Hist Asn; Assoc Hist Economica Espana. **RESEARCH** Spanish economic history of the 17th to the 19th centuries; pre-industrial Europe; urban history. **SELECTED PUBLICATIONS** State, Geometry And Property--Origins Of The Cadastral Register In Spain: 1715-1941, J Of Interdisciplinary Hist, Vol 25, 95; Bayonne In Andalusia--The Bonapartist State In The Prefecture Of Jerez, J Of Modern Hist, Vol 66, 94; A Stagnating Metropolis--The Economy And Demography Of Stockholm, 1750-1850, European Hist Quart, Vol 23, 93; Ancient Road Networks And Settlement Hierarchies In The New-World, Hispanic Am Hist Rev, Vol 73, 93; In The Shadow Of The Crown--Local-Power And Urban Oligarchy: Madrid, 1606-1808, Am Hist Rev, Vol 102, 97; The Role Of Transportation In The Industrial-Revolution--A Comparison Of England And France, Am Hist Rev, Vol 98, 93. **CONTACT ADDRESS** Dept of Hist, Univ of Calif, 9500 Gilman Dr, La Jolla, CA, 92093-5003.

RINK, OLIVER A
PERSONAL Born 12/12/1947, Monahans, TX, m, 1969, 3 children **DISCIPLINE** AMERICAN HISTORY **EDUCATION** Univ Southern Calif, AB, 70, AM, 73, PhD(hist), 76. **CAREER** Lectr, 75-76, asst prof, 76-79, ASSOC PROF HIST, CALIF STATE COL, BAKERSFIELD, 79- **MEMBERSHIPS** AHA; Orgn Am Historians; Werkgroep voor Europaische Expansie. **RESEARCH** New Netherland (nee New York) 1609-1700; North Atlantic trade 1600-1800. **SELECTED PUBLICATIONS** Auth, Company management or private trade: The two patroonship plans for New Netherland, NY Hist, 1/78; The people of New Netherland: Notes on non-English immigration to New York in the seventeenth century, NY Hist, 1/81; Private Interest And Godly Gain--The West-India-Company And The Dutch-Reformed-Church In New-Netherland, 1624-1664/, New York Hist, Vol 75, 94; Inheritance And Family-Life In Colonial New-York-City, William And Mary Quart, Vol 52, 95; The Origins Of Amn Capitalism--Collected Essays, Am Hist Rev, Vol 98, 93. **CONTACT ADDRESS** California State Univ, Bakersfield, 9001 Stockdale Hwy, Bakersfield, CA, 93309.

RINKEVICH, THOMAS E.
DISCIPLINE GREEK AND LATIN LANGUAGES, GREEK AND LATIN POETRY, EGYPTIAN LANGUAGE, ANCIE **EDUCATION** Xavier Univ, BA, 64; Ohio State Univ, MA, 66, PhD, 73. **CAREER** Instr, 67-73, asst prof, 73-96, assoc prof, 96-, actg ch, Classics, Univ Nebr, Lincoln. **MEMBERSHIPS** APA, (CAMWS, ACL, CML); MAM. **SELECTED PUBLICATIONS** Auth, A KWIC Concordance to Lucretius, De Rerum Natura. **CONTACT ADDRESS** Univ Nebr, Lincoln, Lincoln, NE, 68588-0417. **EMAIL** rgorman@unlinfo.unl.edu

RIPLEY WOLFE, MARGARET
PERSONAL Born 02/03/1947, Kingsport, TN, m, 1966, 1 child **DISCIPLINE** HISTORY **EDUCATION** E Tenn State Univ, BS, 67, MA, 69; Univ Ky, PhD, 74. **CAREER** Senior res fel, 77-, from instr to asst prof to assoc prof to prof, 69-, E Tenn State Univ. **HONORS AND AWARDS** Distinguished Fac Award, 77, Found Res Award, 79, Alumni Cert Merit, 84, E Tenn State Univ., Haggin Fel, 72-73, Univ Ky; Outstanding Grad Stud Hist, 68, E Tenn State Univ. **RESEARCH** American social history; American urban; South; Appalachia; Women. **SELECTED PUBLICATIONS** Auth, Daughters of Cannan, Univ Ky. **CONTACT ADDRESS** 175 Ripley Ln, Church Hill, TN, 37642. **EMAIL** wolfem@etsu.edu

RIPPLEY, LA VERN J.
PERSONAL Born 03/02/1935, Waumandee, WI, m, 1960, 2 children **DISCIPLINE** GERMAN ROMANTICISM & IMMIGRATION HISTORY **EDUCATION** Col Holy Cross, BA, 56; Univ Wis, BS, 58; Kent State Univ, MA, 61; Ohio State Univ, PhD(Ger), 65. **CAREER** Teacher, River Falls Sr High Sch, 58-60; teaching asst, Ohio State Univ, 61-63; asst prof Ger, Ohio Wesleyan Univ, 64-67; assoc prof, 67-71, chmn dept, 67-74, Prof Ger, St Olaf Col, 71-, Ed, Newsletter Soc Ger-Am Studies; Fulbright fel, 63-64 & Deutscher Akademischer Austauschdienst Fulbright, 82. **MEMBERSHIPS** Cent States Mod Lang Asn; MLA; Am Asn Teachers Ger; Am Hist Soc Ger from Russia; Norweg Am Hist Asn. **RESEARCH** German-Americana; German Romanticism; modern German literature. **SELECTED PUBLICATIONS** Transit, Excursion through America, R.R. Donnelley, 73; auth, The German-Americans, Twayne, 74; Germans from Russia, In: Harvard Encycl of American Ethnic Groups, Harvard Univ Press, 80; Immigrant Wisconsin, Twayne, 85; German Place Names in Minnesota / Deutsche Ortsnamen in Minnesota, St. Olaf Col / Rainer Schmeissner, 89; co-transl, The German Colonies on the Lower Volga, Their Origin and Early Development, Am Hist Soc of Germans from Russia, 91; auth, The Whoopee John Wilfahrt Dance Band. His Bohemian-German Roots, Northfield, 92; coauth, The German-American Experience, Ind-Purdue Univ at Indianapolis, 93; auth, German-Bohemians: The Quiet Immigrants, Northfield, 93; co-ed, Emigration and Settlement Patterns of German Communities in North America, Ind-Purdue Univ at Indianapolis, 95; Noble Women, Restless Men. The Rippley (Rieple, Ripley, Ripli, Rippli) Family in Wisconsin, North Dakota, Minnesota and Montana, St. Olaf Col Press, 96; author of numerous articles. **CONTACT ADDRESS** 1520 St Olaf Ave, Northfield, MN, 55057-1098. **EMAIL** rippleyl@stolaf.edu

RISCHIN, MOSES
PERSONAL Born 10/16/1925, New York, NY, m, 1959, 3 children **DISCIPLINE** AMERICAN HISTORY **EDUCATION** Brooklyn Col, AB, 47; Harvard Univ, AM, 48, PhD, 57. **CAREER** Lectr hist, Brooklyn Col, 49-53; instr Am civilization, Brandeis Univ, 53-54; res Am Hist, Am Jewish Comt, 56-58; asst prof, Long Island Univ, 58-59; asst ed, Notable American women, 1607-1950, Radvliffe Col, 59-60; lectr, Univ Calif, Los Angeles, 62-64; assoc prof hist, 64-67, PROF HIST, SAN FRANCISCO STATE UNIV, 67-, Tercentenary fel, Am Jewish hist, 54-55; Am Philos Soc Penrose Fund grant, 62-64; Am Coun Learned Soc grant, 64 & fel, 66-67; Guggenheim fel, 68; Fulbright Hays lectr, Univ Uppsala, 69; mem, Am Issues Forum, San Francisco Bicentennial Comn, 74-76; consult, Nat Endowment Humanities, 74-, fel 77-78; consult, Calif Coun Humanities, 77-, San Diego Found, 80- **MEMBERSHIPS** AHA; Am Jewish Hist Soc; Orgn Am Historians; Immigration Hist Soc (vpres, 73, pres, 76-79). **RESEARCH** American social history; American immigration history; American urban history. **SELECTED PUBLICATIONS** Sea-Changes--British Emigration And Am Literature, Am Hist Rev, Vol 99, 94; Crossings--The Great Transatlantic Migrations, 1870-1914, J

Of Am Ethnic Hist, Vol 15, 96; United-States Jewry 1776-1985--Vol 1--The Sephardic Period, Am Jewish Hist, Vol 85, 97; The Warburgs--The 20th-Century Odyssey Of A Remarkable Jewish Family, J Of Am Hist, Vol 81, 94; Round-Trip To Am--The Immigrants Return To Europe, 1880-1930, J Of Am Ethnic Hist, Vol 15, 96; In The Shadow Of The Statue Of Liberty--Immigrants, Workers, And Citizens In The American Republic, 1880-1920, J Of Am Ethnic Hist, Vol 15, 96; This I Believe--Documents Of American Jewish Life, Am Jewish Hist, Vol 85, 97; The Jew In The American World--A Source-Book, Am Jewish Hist, Vol 85, 97. **CONTACT ADDRESS** Dept of Hist, San Francisco State Univ, 1600 Holloway Ave, San Francisco, CA, 94132-1740.

RISJORD, NORMAN KURT
PERSONAL Born 11/25/1931, Manitowoc, WI, m, 1959, 2 children **DISCIPLINE** AMERICAN HISTORY **EDUCATION** Col William & Mary, AB, 53; Univ Va, MA, 57, PhD, 60. **CAREER** Asst prof hist, DePauw Univ, 60-64; from asst prof to assoc prof, 64-69, PROF HIST, UNIV WIS-MADISON, 69- **RESEARCH** American history, early national period; the Old South. **SELECTED PUBLICATIONS** Principle And Interest--Thomas Jefferson And The Problem Of Debt, J Of Am Hist, Vol 83, 96; American Politics In The Early Republic--The New Nation In Crisis--Sharp,Jr/, Virginia Magazine Of Hist And Biography, Vol 103, 95; The Creation Of Washington, Dc--The Idea And Location Of The American Capital, J Of Southern Hist, Vol 59, 93; The Inner Jefferson--Portrait Of A Grieving Optimist, J Of Am Hist, Vol 83, 96; The Age Of Federalism, J Of Southern Hist, Vol 61, 95. **CONTACT ADDRESS** Dept of Hist, Univ of Wis, Madison, WI, 53706.

RISSO, PATRICIA
DISCIPLINE MIDDLE EAST, ISLAM, SOUTH ASIA **EDUCATION** McGill Univ, PhD, 82. **CAREER** Assoc prof, Univ NMex. **RESEARCH** The construct of piracy in the Indian Ocean. **SELECTED PUBLICATIONS** Auth, Oman and Muscat: an early modern history, 86; Muslim Identity in Maritime Trade: General Observations and Some Evidence from the 18th-century Persian Gulf/Indian Ocean Region, Int J of Mid Eastern Stud, 89; Indian Muslim Legal Status, 1964-1986, J of S Asian and Mid Eastern Stud, 92; Merchants and Faith: Muslim Commerce and Culture in the Indian Ocean, 95. **CONTACT ADDRESS** Univ NMex, Albuquerque, NM, 87131.

RITCHIE, DONALD ARTHUR
PERSONAL Born 12/23/1945, New York, NY, m, 1988, 2 children **DISCIPLINE** AMERICAN HISTORY **EDUCATION** City Col NY, BA, 67; Univ Md, MA, 69, PhD, 75. **CAREER** Ed, Md Historian, 72-73; instr hist, 74-76 Univ Col, Univ Md; assoc historian, 76-, US Senate Hist Off; Eleanor Roosevelt Inst res grant, 74; investr bibliog surv, AHA, 75-76; adj fac, 90-, Cornell Wash; ed, Twayne's Oral Hist Ser, 88-98. **HONORS AND AWARDS** Richard W. Leopold Prize, Orgn Am Hist, 92; Henry Adams Prize, Soc Hist in Fed Govt, 92; Letitia Woods Brown Mem Lectr, Hist Soc of Wash DC, 90; Forrest C. Pogue Award, Oral hist Mid-Atlantic Reg, 84 **MEMBERSHIPS** AHA; Orgn Am Historians; Oral Hist Assn; Soc Hist in Fed Govt. **RESEARCH** 20th century United States political and economic history; United States Senate history. **SELECTED PUBLICATIONS** Auth, Press Gallery: Congress and the Washington Correspondents, Harvard Univ Press, 91; auth, The Young Oxford Companion to the Congress and the Washington Correspondents, Harvard Univ Press, 91; auth, Doing Oral History, Twayne, 95; auth, American Journalists: Getting the Story, Oxford Univ Press, 97; auth, History of a Free Nation, Glencoe/McGraw-Hill, 98. **CONTACT ADDRESS** US Senate, Hist Office, Washington, DC, 20510. **EMAIL** Don_Ritchie@sec.senate.gov

RITSCHEL, DANIEL
DISCIPLINE HISTORY **EDUCATION** Oxford Univ, PhD. **CAREER** Assoc prof, Univ MD Baltimore County. **RESEARCH** Europ hist; econ and polit hist of mod Britain. **SELECTED PUBLICATIONS** Auth, The Politics of Planning: The Debate on Economic Planning in Britain in the 1930s. **CONTACT ADDRESS** Dept of Hist, Univ MD Baltimore County, Hilltop Circle, PO Box 1000, Baltimore, MD, 21250. **EMAIL** connect@umbc.edu

RITSON, G. JOY
PERSONAL Born 12/18/1945, Highworth, England **DISCIPLINE** HISTORICAL THEOLOGY **EDUCATION** Graduate Theo Union, PhD, 97. **CAREER** Seeking first position. **MEMBERSHIPS** AAR/SBL, APA, SSSR. **RESEARCH** History of Christian Spirituality; Early and Medieval Church; Linguistic Issues involving Latin and Greek Text. **SELECTED PUBLICATIONS** Auth, Eros, Allegory and Spirituality, in preparation, based on PhD Dissertation; Shame in the Developing Though of Augustine, in preparation. **CONTACT ADDRESS** 1277 Sun Cir E, Melbourne, FL, 32935. **EMAIL** MINDOX@ix.NETCOM.COM

RITTER, HARRY R.
PERSONAL Born 02/19/1943, St. Louis, MO, m, 1972, 1 child **DISCIPLINE** MODERN EUROPEAN HISTORY **EDUCATION** Univ AZ, BA, 65; Univ VA, MA, 67, PhD, 69. **CAREER** From asst prof to assoc prof hist, 69-86, prof hist, Western WA Univ, 86, Woodrow Wilson fel, 65-66. **HONORS AND AWARDS** Am Philos Soc res grant, 85; Austrian Cult Inst Prize, 89. **MEMBERSHIPS** Ger Studies Asn. **RESEARCH** Nineteenth and 20th century central Europe. **SELECTED PUBLICATIONS** Auth, Hermann Neubacher and the Austrian Anschluss Movement, 1918-40, Cent Europ Hist, 12/75; Friedrich Engels and the East European nationality problem, East Europ Quart, 2/76; Science and the imagination in the thought of Schiller and Marx, In: The Quest for the New Science, Southern Ill Univ Press, 79; Progressive historians and the historical imagination in Austria: Heinrich Friedjung and Richard Charmate, Austiran History Yearbook, 83-84; Austro-German liberalism and the modern liberal tradition, Ger Studies Rev, 5/84; Dictionary of Concepts in History, Greenwood, 86; German policy in occupied Greece and its economic impact, In: Germany and Europe in the Era of the Two World Wars (Frank X J Homer and Larry Wilcox, ed), 86; Austria and the struggle for German identity, Ger Studies Rev, winter 92. **CONTACT ADDRESS** Dept of Hist, Western Washington Univ, M/S 9056, Bellingham, WA, 98225-5996. **EMAIL** harry@cc.wwu.edu

RITVO, HARRIET
DISCIPLINE HISTORY; ENGLISH **EDUCATION** Harvard Univ, AB, 68, PhD, 75. **CAREER** Arthur J. Conner Prof of Hist, MIT. **HONORS AND AWARDS** Guggenheim Fel; Nat Endowment for the Humanities Fel; Writing Writers Prize. **MEMBERSHIPS** AHA; SHNH; PEN; HSS. **RESEARCH** British cultural history; history of biology/natural history; human-animal relations. **SELECTED PUBLICATIONS** Auth, The Platypus and the Mermaid and Other Figments of Classifying Imagination, Harvard Univ Press, 97; The Animal Estate: The English and Other Creatures in the Victorian Age, Harvard Univ Press, 87, Penguin Books, 90; The Sincerest Form of Flattery, Dead or Alive: Animal Captives of Human Cultures, Princeton Univ Press, 99; The Roast Beef of Old England, Mad Cows and Modernity: Cross-disciplinary Reflections on the Crisis of Creutzfeldt-Jacob Disease, Humanities Res Centre, 98; Introduction, The Variation of Animals and Plants under Domestication, Johns Hopkins Univ Press, 98; Zoological Nomenclature and the Empire of Victorian Science, Contexts of Victorian Science, Univ of Chicago Press, 97; co-ed, The Macropolitics of Nineteenth-Century Literature: Nationalism, Imperialism, Exoticism, Univ of Pa Press, 91, Duke Univ Press, 95. **CONTACT ADDRESS** Massachusetts Inst of Tech, 77 Massachusettes Ave., E51-288, Cambridge, MA, 02139. **EMAIL** hnritvo@mit.edu

RITZER, GEORGE
PERSONAL Born 10/14/1940, New York, NY, m, 1964, 2 children **DISCIPLINE** SOCIOLOGY **EDUCATION** CCNY, BA, 62; Univ MI, MBA, 64; Cornell Univ, PhD, 68. **CAREER** Asst prof, Tulane Univ, 68-70; Assoc prof, Univ Kansas, 70-74; prof, Univ of Maryland, 74-present. **HONORS AND AWARDS** Fulbright-Hays Fel; Distinguished Scholar-Teacher; Teaching Excellence Award; Fel in Residence Russian Acad of Sci. **MEMBERSHIPS** Amer, Eastern, Southern Sociological Soc **RESEARCH** Sociological theory, sociology of consumption. **SELECTED PUBLICATIONS** Auth, The McDonaldization of Society, 93, 96 (revised edition); co auth, McDisneyization and Post-Tourism: Complementary Perspectives on Tourism in Touring Cultures: Transformations in Travel and Theory, 97; Fast Food, in Gotterspeisen, 97; McDonaldization and Globalization, The Student's Companion to Sociology, 97; Postmodern Social Theory, 97; The McDonaldization Thesis: Extensions and Explorations, 98; Enchanting a Disenchanted World: Revolutionizing the Means of Consumption, forthcoming. **CONTACT ADDRESS** Dept. of Sociology, Univ Maryland, College Park, MD, 20740. **EMAIL** ritzer@bss2.umd.edu

RIVES, JAMES
DISCIPLINE ANCIENT HISTORY **EDUCATION** Univ Wash, BA, 83; Stanford Univ, PhD, 90. **CAREER** Assoc prof. **RESEARCH** Social and religious history of the Roman Empire. **SELECTED PUBLICATIONS** Auth, Religion and Authority in Roman Carthage: From Augustus to Constantine, 95. **CONTACT ADDRESS** Dept of Hist, Columbia Col, New York, 2960 Broadway, New York, NY, 10027-6902.

RIVEST, JOHANNE
PERSONAL Born 01/25/1956, Ormstown, PQ, Canada, s **DISCIPLINE** MUSICOLOGY **EDUCATION** Univ Montreal, CA, BM 80, Mmus 87, PhD 96. **CAREER** Univ IL, Urbana, vis schol 98-2000; Can Univ Music Soc, secre 97-99; Indepen Sch 96-98; Univ Montreal, guest lectr 95; Les Cahiers de la Soc PQ de res music, ed 93-98; Univ Montreal, teach asst 92-93; Univ of Quebec, Montreal, res asst 89-91. **HONORS AND AWARDS** Hum post doct Gnt; doct Gnt Univ MT; Human Schlshp; George Proctor Prize. **MEMBERSHIPS** AMS; Sonneck Soc Am Mus; CMS; CUMS; SQRM. **RESEARCH** 20th century music; am music; John Cage; can music **SELECTED PUBLICATIONS** John Cage's Concert for Piano and Orchestra: Essays in Amer Music, ed James R Heintze Michael Saffle, Hamden CT, Garland Pub, 98; Atlas Eclipticalis, commande montrealaise, Circuit revue nor-americaine de musique du Xxe siecle, 97; Marie-Therese Lefebvre, Jean Vallerand et la vie musicale du Quebec, 1915-1994, Review, Can Univ Music Review, 97. **CONTACT ADDRESS** Univ Illinois at Urbana, 404 South New St, Champaign, IL, 61820. **EMAIL** rivestjo@dsuper.net

RIX, BRENDA
PERSONAL Belleville, ON, Canada **DISCIPLINE** ART HISTORY **EDUCATION** Univ Toronto, BA, 78, MA, 80. **CAREER** Librn, 79-81, tchg asst, 79-81, Univ Toronto; res asst, educ off, 80-81, asst cur, 82-87, guest cur, 88-, SUPERVISOR, PRINTS & DRAWINGS STUDY CENTRE, ART GALLERY ONTARIO, 93-. **MEMBERSHIPS** Print Coun Am; William Morris Soc Can; Friends Thomas Fisher Rare Book Libr. **SELECTED PUBLICATIONS** Auth, Pictures for the Parlour: The English Reproductive Print from 1775 to 1900, 83; auth, Our Old Friend Rolly: Watercolours, Prints, and Book Illustrations by Thomas Rowlandson in the Collection of the Art Gallery of Ontario, 87; auth, Prints in The Earthly Paradise: Arts and Crafts by William Morris and his Circle from Canadian Collections, 93. **CONTACT ADDRESS** Art Gallery of Ontario, 317 Dundas St W, Toronto, ON, M5T 1G4.

ROARK, JAMES L.
DISCIPLINE HISTORY **EDUCATION** Univ Calif Davis, BA, 63, MA, 64; Stanford Univ, PhD, 73. **CAREER** Samuel Candler Dobbs Prof Am Hist. **RESEARCH** Southern history; 19th-century American history. **SELECTED PUBLICATIONS** Auth, Masters without Slaves; Southern Planters in the Civil War and Reconstruction; The American Promise: A History of the United States; coauth, Black Masters: A Free Family of Color in the Old South ; co-ed, No Chariot Let Down Charleston's Free People of Color on the Eve of the Civil War. **CONTACT ADDRESS** Dept History, Emory Univ, 221 Bowden Hall, 561 Kilgo Cir, Atlanta, GA, 30322-1950. **EMAIL** jlroark@emory.edu

ROAZEN, PAUL
PERSONAL Born 08/14/1936, Boston, MA **DISCIPLINE** SOCIAL & POLITICAL SCIENCE (HISTORY) **EDUCATION** Harvard Col, AB, 58; Harvard Univ, PhD, 65. **CAREER** Instr & asst prof, dept govt, Harvard Col, 65-71; assoc prof, 71-74, prof, 74-95, PROF EMER SOCIAL & POLITICAL SCIENCE, YORK UNIV, 96-. **HONORS AND AWARDS** Fel, Royal Soc Can. **RESEARCH** Psychoanalysis; Freud; Deutsch; Lippmann. **SELECTED PUBLICATIONS** Auth, Freud: Political and Social Thought, 68, 86; auth, Brother Animal: The Story of Freud and Tausk, 69, 90; auth, Freud and His Followers, 75, 92; auth, Erik H. Erikson: The Power and Limits of a Vision, 76, 96; auth, Helene Deutsch: A Psychoanalyst's Life, 85, 92; auth, Encountering Freud: The Politics and Histories of Psychoanalysis, 90; auth, Meeting Freud's Family, 93; auth, How Freud Worked: First-Hand Accounts of Patients, 95; co-auth, Heresy: Sandor Rado and the Psychoanalytic Movement, 95; ed, Sigmund Freud, 73, 87; ed, Lippman's Public Philosophy, 89; ed, Hartz's The Necessity of Choice, 90; ed, Tausk's Sexuality, War and Schizophrenia, 91; ed, Deutsch's Psychoanalysis of the Sexual Function of Women, 91; ed, Deutsch's The Therapeutic Process, The Self and Female Psychology, 92; ed, Liberty & The News (Lippmann), 95. **CONTACT ADDRESS** 31 Whitehall Rd, Toronto, ON, M4W 2C5.

ROBB, GEORGE
DISCIPLINE EUROPEAN HISTORY **EDUCATION** Univ Tex at Austin, BA, 84; Northwestern Univ, PhD, 90. **CAREER** Dept Hist, William Paterson Univ **HONORS AND AWARDS** Mellon res fel at the Huntington Libr, 96; Amer Coun of Learned Soc, Summer Res Grant, 94; Fulbright, UK, 87-88. **RESEARCH** British Social and Cultural History during the 19th and 20th centuries; History of Crime; Women's History; British Eugenics Movement. **SELECTED PUBLICATIONS** Auth, White-Collar Crime in Mod England: Financial Fraud and Business Morality, 1845-1929, Cambridge Univ Press, 92; Out of the Doll's House: The Trial of Florence Maybrick and Anxiety Over the New Woman, Proteus, 96; The Way of All Flesh: Degeneration, Eugenics, and the Gospel of Free Love, J Hist Sexuality, 96; Popular Religion and the Christianization of the Scottish Highlands in the Eighteenth and Nineteenth Centuries, J Rel Hist, 90; rev(s), English Local Prisons 1860-1900, TLS, 95; The Hanging Tree, TLS, 94; Apprehending the Criminal: The Production of Deviance in Nineteenth-Century Discourse, Victorian Stud, 94; The Cambridge Social History of Britain, 1750-1950, 3 vols, J Econ Hist, 93. **CONTACT ADDRESS** Dept of History, William Paterson Col, 300 Pompton Rd., Wayne, NJ, 07470. **EMAIL** robb@frontier.wilpaterson.edu

ROBB, STEWART A.
PERSONAL Born 03/10/1943, Montreal, PQ, Canada **DISCIPLINE** HISTORY **EDUCATION** Univ BC, BA, 66; Simon Fraser Univ, MA, 69. **CAREER** PROF HISTORY, UNIV PEI, 71-; dir, PEI Mus Heritage Found. **MEMBERSHIPS** Exec mem, Asn Can Stud, 74-80; ch, Coun Can Stud Prog Admins, 80-82. **RESEARCH** Canadian studies. **SELECTED PUBLICATIONS** Contribur, Dictionary of Canadian Biography; contribur, New Canadian Encyclopedia; bk rev ed, Can Rev Stud Nationalism. **CONTACT ADDRESS** History Dept, Univ PEI, 550 University Ave, Charlottetown, PE, C1A 4P3.

ROBBERT, LOUISE BUENGER
PERSONAL Born 08/18/1925, St. Paul, MN, m, 1960, 1 child **DISCIPLINE** MEDIEVAL STUDIES **EDUCATION** Carleton Col, BA, 47; Univ of Cincinnati, MA, 48, BEd, 49; Univ of Wis-Madison, 55, PhD. **CAREER** Instr, Smith Col, 54-55; instr in hist, Hunter Col of the City of NY, 57-60; asst prof, 62-63, assoc prof of hist, Tex Tech Univ, 64-75; VIS ASSOC PROF, 78-79, ASSOC ADJUNCT PROF, 79-91, PROF, UNIV OF MO, 91-. **HONORS AND AWARDS** Fulbright Scholar, 55-57; Grant in Aid, ACLS, 60; Gladys Krieble Delmas Grant in Aid, 83 & 87; Grant in Aid, Newberry Libr, 91 & 92. **MEMBERSHIPS** Am Hist Asn; Medieval Acad of Am; Soc for the Study of the Crusades and the Latin East; Midwest Medieval Hist Confr. **RESEARCH** Medieval Venice, especially money, business, colonies, and Crusades. **SELECTED PUBLICATIONS** Auth, Money and prices in thirteenth-century Venice, J of Medieval Hist, 94; Rialto businessmen and Constantinople 1204-61, Dumbarton Oaks Papers, 95; Il Sistema monetario, Storia di Venezia dalle origini alla caduta della serenissima, 95; Donald E. Queller, Memoirs of Fellows and Corresponding Fellows of the Medieval Academy of America, Speculum, 96; Venetian Participation in the Crusade of Damietta, Studi Veneziani, 95. **CONTACT ADDRESS** Dept of Hist, Univ of Missouri, 8001 Natural Bridge Rd, St. Louis, MO, 63121.

ROBBINS, BRUCE
DISCIPLINE MARXIST THEORY, POSTCOLONIAL THEORY, THEORY OF PROFESSIONAL FORMATION, CULT **EDUCATION** Harvard Univ, BA, MA, PhD. **CAREER** Prof Eng, Rutgers, The State Univ NJ, Univ Col-Camden; coed, Soc Text. **RESEARCH** 19th & 20th century literature; Marxist theory. **SELECTED PUBLICATIONS** Auth, The Servant's Hand: English Fiction from Below; Secular Vocations: Intellectuals, Professionalism, Culture. **CONTACT ADDRESS** Dept of Lit in Eng, Rutgers, The State Univ New Jersey, Univ Col-Camde, Murray Hall 041, New Brunswick, NJ, 08903. **EMAIL** brobbins@interport.net

ROBBINS, PAUL RICHARD
PERSONAL Born 10/27/1930, Washington, DC, d **DISCIPLINE** SOCIAL PSYCHOLOGY **EDUCATION** Univ Chicago, BA, 50; Columbia Univ, PhD, 59. **CAREER** Res asst, NIMH, 55-58; res psychol, USPHS, 59-62; dir consult proj, Ca Dept Health, 62-65; psychol School Med George Wash Univ, 66-72; PSYCHOL PRIVATE PRACTICE, 75-96. **HONORS AND AWARDS** Fel Columbia Univ. **MEMBERSHIPS** Am Psychol Asn **RESEARCH** Issues relating to personality and clinical psychology ie coping behaviors, dreams, and depression. **SELECTED PUBLICATIONS** auth Adolescent Suicide, Understanding Depression, The Psychology of Dreams, McFarland & Co NC; Medieval Summer, Branden Press. **CONTACT ADDRESS** 8401 Park Crest Dr, Silver Spring, MD, 20910.

ROBBINS, RICHARD G., JR.
PERSONAL Born 03/06/1939, Buffalo, NY, m, 1966, 2 children **DISCIPLINE** HISTORY **EDUCATION** Williams Col, BA, 61; Columbia Univ, MA, 65, PhD, 70. **CAREER** From asst prof to assoc prof to prof to chemn, 69-, Univ New Mex. **HONORS AND AWARDS** Phi Beta Kappa, Fulbright-Hays Fel, 67-68, 81. **MEMBERSHIPS** Am Hist Asn; Am Asn for Advancement; Slavic Studies. **RESEARCH** Russiam History-Late Imperial Period; State and Administration. **SELECTED PUBLICATIONS** Auth, The Imperial Government Responds to a Crisis, 75; auth, The Tsar's Viceroys: Russian Provencial Governors in the Last Years of the Empire, 87. **CONTACT ADDRESS** Dept of History, Univ of New Mexico, Albuquerque, NM, 87131. **EMAIL** rrobbins@unm.edu

ROBBINS, WILLIAM GROVER
PERSONAL Born 09/20/1935, Torrington, CT, 4 children **DISCIPLINE** AMERICAN HISTORY **EDUCATION** Western Conn State Col, BS, 62; Univ Ore, MA, 65, PhD(hist), 69. **CAREER** Asst prof hist, Ore Col Educ, 69-71; asst prof, 71-77, ASSOC PROF HIST, ORE STATE UNIV, 77- **MEMBERSHIPS** Orgn Am Historians; AHA; Forest Hist Soc. **RESEARCH** Indian-white relations; conservation history; forest history. **SELECTED PUBLICATIONS** Auth, Creating A New West--Big Money Returns To The Hinterland/, Montana-The Magazine Of Western History, Vol 46, 96; The Northwest Coast--British Navigation, Trade And Discoveries To 1812, Oregon Hist Quart, Vol 93, 92; The United-States-Forest-Service And The Problem Of History, Public Historian, Vol 15, 93; Flooding The Courtrooms--Law And Water In The Far-West, Western Hist Quart, Vol 25, 94; Washington County--Politics And Community In Antebellum America, Pacific Hist Rev, Vol 65, 96; Kanaka--The Untold Story Of Hawaiian Pioneers In British-Columbia And The Pacific-Northwest, Am Neptune, Vol 57, 97; 3 Frontiers--Family, Land, And Society In The American-West, 1850-1900, J Of Am Hist, Vol 82, 95; Our Natural-Hist--The Lessons Of Lewis And Clark, Oregon Hist Quart, Vol 98, 97; Environment And Experience--Settlement Culture In 19th-Century Oregon, Pacific Northwest Quart, Vol 85, 94. **CONTACT ADDRESS** Dept of Hist, Oregon State Univ, 306 Milam Hall, Corvallis, OR, 97331-5104.

ROBERGE, RENE-MICHEL
PERSONAL Born 07/08/1944, Charny, PQ, Canada **DISCIPLINE** THEOLOGY/HISTORY **EDUCATION** Univ Laval, BA, 65, BTh, 67, LTh, 69, DTh, 71. **CAREER** PROF THEOLOGIE FONDAMENTALE ET D'HISTOIRE DE LA THEOLOGIE, UNIV LAVAL, 71-, prof titulaire, 83-, vice-doyen theol, 88-89, doyen, 89-97; dir de la revue Laval theologique et philosophique, 87-92. **MEMBERSHIPS** Int Asn Patristic Stud; Can Soc Patristic Stud; N Am Patristic Soc; Soc can de theologie. **SELECTED PUBLICATIONS** Auteur d'une cinquantaine de pubs et de nom communications en patristique, en theol fond et system, et en documentation spec. **CONTACT ADDRESS** Fac de Theologie, Laval Univ, Laval, PQ, G1K 7P4. **EMAIL** Rene-Michel.Roberge@ftsr.ulaval.ca

ROBERT, JEAN-CLAUDE
PERSONAL Born 04/27/1943, Montreal, PQ, Canada **DISCIPLINE** HISTORY **EDUCATION** Univ Montreal, BA, 66, LL, 69, MA, 71; Univ Paris, doctorat en histoire, 77. **CAREER** Hist tchr, sec sch Mont-de-Lasalle, 67-69; socio cult serv, CEGEP de Joliette, 69-71; instr, Univ Que Chicoutimi, 74; PROF REGULIER HISTOIRE, UNIV QUEBEC MONTREAL, 75-, dir dept, 77-79, 97-. **MEMBERSHIPS** Inst hist Am francaise; Can Hist Asn (coun, 80-83, 88-92, vice pres, 88-89, pres, 89-90); Comite Int des Sci Historiques. **SELECTED PUBLICATIONS** Auth, Du Canada francais au Quebec libre, 75; auth, Atlas historique de Montreal, 94; coauth, Histoire du Quebec contemporain, 79; coauth, Quebec: A History 1867-1929, 83; coauth, Le Quebec depuis 1930, 86; coauth, Quebec Since 1930, 91; coauth, Atlas historique du Quebec: le pays Laurentian au XIX siecle, 95. **CONTACT ADDRESS** Dept of history, Univ of Quebec Montral, CP 8888, Montreal, PQ, H3C 3P8.

ROBERTS, BARBARA A.
PERSONAL Riverside, CA **DISCIPLINE** HISTORY/WOMEN'S STUDIES **EDUCATION** Simon Fraser Univ, BA, 72, MA, 76; Univ Ottawa, PhD, 80. **CAREER** Vis prof, 80-82, lectr, Univ Winnipeg, 82-83; asst prof, Univ Sask, 83-84; asst prof, Concordia Univ, 87-88; assoc prof, 89-92, PROF WOMEN'S STUDIES, ATHABASKA UNIV 92-. **MEMBERSHIPS** Bd dir, Can Res Inst Advan Women; Voice of Women. **SELECTED PUBLICATIONS** Auth, Whence They Came: Deportation from Canada 1900-35, 88; auth, A Decent Living: Women in the Winnipeg Garment Industry, 91; auth, Strategies for the Year 2000: A Women's Handbook, 95; auth, A Reconstructed World: A Feminist Biography of Gertrude Richardson, 96. **CONTACT ADDRESS** Dept of Women's Studies, Athabasca Univ, Athabaska, AB, TOG 2RO. **EMAIL** barbara@cs.athabaska.ca

ROBERTS, BRYNDIS WYNETTE
PERSONAL Born 09/04/1957, Sylvania, GA, s **DISCIPLINE** EDUCATION **EDUCATION** Wesleyan Coll, Macon, GA, AB (magna cum laude), 1978; Univ of GA, Athens, Ga, JD (cum laude), 1981. **CAREER** State Law Dept, Atlanta, GA, asst attorney general, 1981-87; UNIV OF GA, ATHENS, GA, VICE PRES FOR LEGAL AFFAIRS, 1987-. **HONORS AND AWARDS** Business & Professional Women Young Careerist, DeKalb Business & Professional Women, 1985; Outstanding Woman Law Student, GA Assn of Women Lawyers, 1981. **MEMBERSHIPS** Mem, Classic City Pilot Club, 1991-92, sec, School & College Law Section, State Bar, 1988-89; mem, National Association of College & University Attorney's, 1987-92, 1986-, chairman, 1986-87; mem, GA State Board of Accountancy, 1988-; Wesleyan Board of Trustees, 1991. **CONTACT ADDRESS** Legal Affairs, Univ of Georgia, 310 Old College, Athens, GA, 30602.

ROBERTS, CHARLES EDWARD
PERSONAL Born 08/25/1941, Bennington, OK, m, 1971, 2 children **DISCIPLINE** AMERICAN INDIAN HISTORY **EDUCATION** Fresno State Col, BA, 62; Univ Ore, MA, 67, PhD(hist), 75. **CAREER** Asst prof, 70-76, assoc prof Hist, Califor State Univ, Sacremento, 82-. **MEMBERSHIPS** Am Indian Historians Asn; Orgn Am Historians; Western History Asn; Am Soc Ethnohist. **RESEARCH** Choctaw Indian hist; Northern California Indian history; American Indian literature. **SELECTED PUBLICATIONS** Coauth, The Choctaws: A Critical Bibliography, Ind Univ Press, 80; auth, The Second Choctaw Removal, 1903 in After Removal: the Choctaw in Mississippi, Univ Press of Mississippi, 86; the cushman Indian Trades School and World War I, American Indian Quarterly, 87; A Choctaw Odyssey: the Life of Lesa Phillip Roberts, American Indian Quarterly, 90. **CONTACT ADDRESS** Dept of History, California State Univ, Sacramento, 6000 J St, Sacramento, CA, 95819-2694.

ROBERTS, MARION ELIZABETH
PERSONAL Born 05/26/1939, Berwyn, IL, m, 1973 **DISCIPLINE** ART HISTORY **EDUCATION** Duke Univ, BA, 60; Columbia Univ, MA, 62; Univ Chicago, PhD(art hist), 70. **CAREER** Asst prof art hist, Northern IL Univ, 66-68; asst prof, 68-74, sesquicentennial assoc, Inst Advan Studies, 73, ASSOC PROF ART HISTORY, UNIV VA, 74-. **MEMBERSHIPS** British Archaeol Asn; Medieval Acad Am; Col Art Asn; Int Center for Medieval Art. **RESEARCH** Salisbury Catherdral; illustrated pubs of Sir William Dugdale; English 13th Century architecture and sculpure; English medievalist antiquaries. **SELECTED PUBLICATIONS** Auth, Towards a Literary Source for the Scenes in the Passion in Queen Mary's Psalter, J Warburg & Courtauld Insts, 73; The Ark, Friends of Wells Cathedral Report, 73; The Tomb of Bishop Giles de Bridport in Salisbury Cathedral, Art Bull, LXV, 83; The Relic of the Holy Blood and the Iconography of the 13th-century North Transept Portal of Westminster Abbey, England in the 13th century, Proceedings of the 1984 Harlaxton Symposium, Grantham, 86; John Carter at St Stephen's Chapel, Westminster: a Romantic turns Archaeologist, England in the 14th century, Proceedings of the 1985 Harlaxton Symposium, Grantham, 86; The Dictionary of Art, London, John Carter; The Effigy of Bishop Hugh de Northwold in Ely Cathedral, The Burlington Magazine, vol CXXX, no 1019, Feb 88; The Emergence of Clarity, Images of English Cathedrals 1640-1840, Charlottesville, VA, 88; The Dictionary of Art, London, French Painting; Architectural History, London, Thomas Gray's Contribution to the Study of Medieval Architecture, vol 36, 93; The Seventeenth-century Restoration (catalogue of an exhibition of rare books in Alderman Library), with Prof Everett Crosby, Charlottesville, 93. **CONTACT ADDRESS** McIntire Dept of Art, Univ of Virginia, 102 Fayerweather Hall, Charlottesville, VA, 22903.

ROBERTS, MICHAEL
PERSONAL Born 09/16/1947, Eccles, United Kingdom, m, 1970, 1 child **DISCIPLINE** CLASSICS **EDUCATION** Cambridge Univ BA, 69, MA, 73; Univ IL Urbana-Champaign, MA, 74, PhD, 78. **CAREER** Vis lectr, Univ WI-Milwaukee, 78-80; asst prof, 80-86, assoc prof, 86-91, prof, 91-, Robert Rich Prof of Lat, 92-, Wesleyan Univ. **HONORS AND AWARDS** NEH summer sem fel, 82 & 86; ACLS fel, 87; NEH fel, Jan-June, 92. **MEMBERSHIPS** Am Philol Asn; Am Inst Archaeol; Medieval Acad of Am; N Am Patristic Societe; Medieval Lat Asn N Am. **RESEARCH** Late antiquity; Latin literature; rhetoric. **SELECTED PUBLICATIONS** Auth, Poetry and the Cult of the Martyrs, Michigan, 93; St. Martin and the Leper, Jour of Medieval Lat, 94; The Description of Landscape in the Poetry of Venantius Fortunatus, Traditio, 94; Martin Meets Maximus, Rev des etudes augustiniennes, 95. **CONTACT ADDRESS** Dept of Classical Studies, Wesleyan Univ, Middletown, CT, 06459-0146. **EMAIL** mroberts@wesleyan.edu

ROBERTS, WARREN ERROL
PERSONAL Born 05/08/1933, Los Angeles, CA, m, 1957, 4 children **DISCIPLINE** MODERN HISTORY **EDUCATION** Univ Southern Calif, BS, 55; Univ Calif, Berkeley, BA, 59, MA, 60, PhD, 66. **CAREER** Asst prof, 63-71, assoc prof, 71-80, PROF HIST, STATE UNIV NY ALBANY, 80- **RESEARCH** England, France, 1780-1830 literature and history; Jane Austen. **SELECTED PUBLICATIONS** Auth, Literature and Painting, Morality and Society in 18th-Century France, Univ Toronto, 74; Jane Austen and the French Revolution, Macmillan, Gt Brit, 79. **CONTACT ADDRESS** Dept of Hist, State Univ NY, Albany, NY, 12203.

ROBERTS, JR., KENNETH C.
PERSONAL PA **DISCIPLINE** MUSIC **EDUCATION** Univ Mich, Ann Arbor, Bmus, Mmus, PhD. **CAREER** A Barton Hepburn prof, Williams Col, 62-; past fac, Univ Mich; consult, Amer symphony orchestras. **HONORS AND AWARDS** Ger govt DAAD Awd, 62., Founded, Williams Col Choral Soc and Chamber Singers & conducted them for 25 years; founding pianist, Williams Trio, 70. **SELECTED PUBLICATIONS** Auth, a book on choral music; contribur to, New Grove Dictionary of Music; rev(s) for, Notes, Mus Libr Asn jour. **CONTACT ADDRESS** Music Dept, Williams Col, Williamstown, MA, 01267.

ROBERTSON, JAMES IRVIN
PERSONAL Born 07/18/1930, Danville, VA, m, 1952, 3 children **DISCIPLINE** HISTORY **EDUCATION** Randolph-Macon Col, BA, 55; Emory Univ, MA, 56, PhD, 59; Randolph-Macon Col, Litt. D., 80. **CAREER** Ed, Civil War History, Univ of Iowa, 59-61; exec. dir U.S. Civil War Centennial Comn, Wash, D.C., 61-65; assoc prof, Univ Mont, 65-67; prof, Va Polytech Inst and State Univ, 67-. **HONORS AND AWARDS** Douglas Southall Freeman Award; Fletcher Pratt Lit. Award; Richard Barksdale Harwell Award; Jefferson Davis Award; Lit Achievement Award; Special resolution of thanks from both houses of the Va Gen Assembly, 97-98. **MEMBERSHIPS** Southern Hist Asn, Va Hist Soc, Museum of the Confederacy, Stonewall Jackson Found. **RESEARCH** Confed. States of Am; Confed. Va, Am Presidency. **SELECTED PUBLICATIONS** Coauth, Jackson & Lee: Legends in Gray, 95; ed, Four Years with General Lee, 96; auth, Stonewall Jackson: The Man, The Soldier, The Legend, 97; Soldiers Blue and Gray, 98. **CONTACT ADDRESS** Dept of History, Virginia Polytechnic Institute and State Univ, Blacksburg, VA, 24061.

ROBERTSON, PATRICIA C.
PERSONAL Born 03/30/1954, Newark, NJ, m, 1987 **DISCIPLINE** MUSIC **EDUCATION** Univ Ma, BS, 77, Ball St Univ, MA, 89; PhD, 98. **CAREER** Instr, Ball St Univ, 90-91; adj prof, Anderson Univ, 91-98; adj prof to asst prof, Taylor Univ, 91-99. **HONORS AND AWARDS** Doctoral recital-lecture entitled Selected Lieder of Fanny Mendelssohn Hensel, 1805-

1847, first place, Mu Phi Epsilon Int Res Competition, 90. **MEMBERSHIPS** NATS; Pi Kappa Lambda; Mu Phi Epsilon. **RESEARCH** Vocal literature **SELECTED PUBLICATIONS** Auth, Fanny Mendelssohn Hensel, Junior Keynotes, 91; The Artsong: A Practical Investigation of Artsong Literature, Composers and Musico-poetic Structure for the Collegiate Singer Accompanied by a Performance-based Interpretation workbook, Doctor of Arts dissertation, 98. **CONTACT ADDRESS** 1512 Lynnwood Dr, Anderson, IN, 46012. **EMAIL** ptrobertson@tayloru.edu

ROBINET, HARRIETTE GILLEM
PERSONAL Born 07/14/1931, Washington, DC, m, 1960, 6 children **DISCIPLINE** HISTORY OF SCIENCE **EDUCATION** Col New Rochelle, BS, 53; Catholic Univ Am, MS, 57, PhD, 63. **CAREER** Bacteriologist, Walter Reed Army Med Ctr, 53-63; writer, 63-. **HONORS AND AWARDS** Friends Am Writers; Carl Sandburg Award; Midwest Writers Award. **MEMBERSHIPS** Soc Children's Writers & Illusr; Children's Reading Roundtable. **SELECTED PUBLICATIONS** Auth Children of the Fire; Mississippi Chariot; If You Please, President Lincoln; Washington City is Burning; The Twins, The Pirates, and the Battle of New Orleans; Forty Acres and Maybe a Mule; Atheneum, Simon & Schuster. **CONTACT ADDRESS** 214 S Elmwood Ave, Oak Park, IL, 60302.

ROBINS, GAY
PERSONAL Born 06/28/1951, Fleet, England, m, 1980 **DISCIPLINE** EGYPTOLOGY **EDUCATION** Univ Durham, BA (honors), 75; Univ Oxford, DPhil, 81. **CAREER** Lady Wallis Budge Fellow in Egyptology, Christ's College, Cambridge, 79-83; honorary research fel, Univ Coll London, 84-88; asst prof, 88-94, assoc prof, 94-98, prof, 98-, Art History Dept, curator of Egyptian art, 88-94, faculty curator of ancient Egyptian art, 94-98, faculty consult for ancient Egyptian art, 98-, Michael C. Carlos Museum, Emory Univ. **HONORS AND AWARDS** Thomas Mulvey Fund grant, H.M. Chadwick Fund grant, Univ Cambridge, 85; Suzette Taylor Travelling Fellow, Lady Margaret Hall, Oxford, 85-86; Wainwright Near Eastern Archeol Fund grant, 87; Natl Endowment for the Humanities grant, 92; Univ Research Comm grant, Emory Univ, 95-96. **MEMBERSHIPS** Amer Res Center in Egypt; Coll Art Assn; Egyptian Exploration Soc; Egyptological Seminar of New York; Intl Assn of Egyptologists; Soc Study Egyptian Antiquities. **RESEARCH** The content and function of ancient Egyptian art; use of the squared grid and changes in the proportions of figures in ancient Egyptian art; the Amarna grid system; composition of whole scenes in ancient Egyptian art; hierarchies in ancient Egyptian art; status of women in ancient Egypt. **SELECTED PUBLICATIONS** Coauth, Egyptian Painting and Relief, 86; coauth, The Rhind Mathematical Papyrus, 87, reprinted, 90, 98; auth, Women in Ancient Egypt, 93, reprinted, 96; auth, Proportion and Style in Ancient Egyptian Art, 94; auth, The Art of Ancient Egypt, 97. **CONTACT ADDRESS** Art History Dept, Emory Univ, Carlos Hall, Atlanta, GA, 30322. **EMAIL** grobins@emory.edu

ROBINSON, ANDREW
PERSONAL Born 02/16/1939, Chicago, IL **DISCIPLINE** EDUCATION **EDUCATION** Chicago State U, BA 1966; Roosevelt U, MA 1970; Northwestern U, PhD 1973. **CAREER** Univ of KY, asst prof, asso dir Cntr for urban educ 1975-; Chicago City Colls, adminstr 1974-75; Urban & Ethnic Edn, Asst dir; Pub Inst Chicago, supt 1973-74; Chicago Urban League, educ dir 1970-73; Univ IL, visiting instr 1972-73; Chicago Pub Schs, tchr 1966-69. **MEMBERSHIPS** Mem Phi Delta Kappa; Am Assn Sch Adminstrs; Am Assn of Tchr Edn; Nat Alliance Black Sch Educators; Prog Planning Comm Am Assoc of Coll Tchr Edn. **CONTACT ADDRESS** Col of Educ Asst Dean, Univ of Kentucky, Lexington, KY, 40506.

ROBINSON, GENEVIEVE
PERSONAL Born 04/20/1940, Kansas City, Missouri, s **DISCIPLINE** HISTORY **EDUCATION** Mt St Scholastica Coll, BA history 1968; New Mexico Highlands Univ, MA history 1974; Catholic Univ of Amer, history 1978-79; Boston Coll, PhD history 1986. **CAREER** Lillis HS, history teacher 1969-73, 1974-75, history dept chairperson 1970-73, admin/curriculum dir 1974-75; Donnelly Comm Coll, instructor 1976-78; Boston Coll, instructor 1983; Rockhurst Coll, instr 1985-86, asst prof 1986-91, dir, honors program, 1990-, associate professor, 1991-, chair of dept of history, 1994-. **HONORS AND AWARDS** Gasson Fellowship Boston Coll 1984-85; Natl Endowment for the Humanities Coll Teachers Summer Seminar Grant 1987, Presidential Grant, Rockhurst Coll, 1988; Natl Endowment for the Humanities Summer Inst, NEH, 1990; Lilly Workshop on the Liberal Arts, Lilly Endowment, Inc, 1990; Rockhurst College, Presidential Grant, 1988, 1992. **MEMBERSHIPS** Mem Phi Alpha Theta, Kappa Mu Epsilon, Organization of Amer Historians, Immigration History Soc, Pi Gamma Mu; mem Ethical Review Board 1988-; Notre Dame de Sion Schools, board of directors, 1990-95; National Assn of Women in Catholic Higher Education, regional rep. **CONTACT ADDRESS** Chair/History Dept, Assoc Prof, Rockhurst Col, 1100 Rockhurst Rd, Kansas City, MO, 64110-2508.

ROBINSON, JIM C.
PERSONAL Born 02/09/1943, Ackerman, MS **DISCIPLINE** AFRICAN-AMERICAN STUDIES **EDUCATION** CA St, BA 1966; CA St, MA 1968; Stanford U, MA 1972; Stanford U, PhD 1973. **CAREER** CA St Univ Long Beach, assoc prof Black Studies; CA St, spec asst vice pres acad affrs; CA St, dean faculty & staff affairs; San Jose St Coll, teacher. **MEMBERSHIPS** Mem, Nat Alliance of Black Sch Educators; Am Assn of Univ & Prof; dir of Reg Programs in W for Am Assn for Higher Edn; chmn Assn of Black Faculty &Staff of So CA; mem Mayor's Task Force Fiscal Mgmt & Cntrl, Compton. **CONTACT ADDRESS** California State Univ, Long Beach, 1250 Bellflower Blvd, Long Beach, CA, 90840.

ROBINSON, JONTYLE THERESA
PERSONAL Born 07/22/1947, Atlanta, GA **DISCIPLINE** ART HISTORY **EDUCATION** Clark College, BA, Spanish, 1968; Univ of Georgia, MA, art history, 1971; Univ of Maryland, PhD, contemporary Caribbean and Latin American art history, 1983. **CAREER** University of Georgia, Study Abroad Program (Europe) Fellowship, research assistant, 1970; Atlanta University, instructor, summer 1971, 1972; Philander Smith College, acting chairperson, 1971-72; University of Maryland, Eastern Shore, instructor, 1972-75; Emory University, instructor, 1978-83, assistant professor, joint appointment in African-American and African Studies Program/art history, 1983-86, director, designer, African-American and African studies/art history, Summer Study Abroad Program, Haiti, Jamaica, 1984, 1986, Haiti, The Dominican Republic, Puerto Rico, 1985; West Virginia State College, associate professor, 1986-87; Smithsonian Institution/Archives of American Art, research for a retrospective exhibition, catalogue raisonne, American painter Archibald John Motley Jr, 1986-88; Kenkeleba Gallery, research fellow, cocurator, Three Masters: Cortor, Lee-Smith, Motley, 1987-88; Winthrop College, associate professor, 1989; SPELMAN COLLEGE, DEPARTMENT OF ART, ASSOCIATE PROF, 1989-. **HONORS AND AWARDS** Spelman College, Coca-Cola Fund Grant for presentation/lecture for the African Americans in Europe Conference, Paris, France, 1992, Department of Art, Amoco Faculty Award, nominee, 1992, Bush Faculty Development Grant, Research for African American Architects, City Planners, Artisans, and Designers 1619-1850, 1993; Bessie L Harper Estate, Grant for The Art of Archibald J Motley Jr, 1990-91; numerous others. **MEMBERSHIPS** Delta Sigma Theta; National Conference of Artists, national executive secretary, 1971-72; Phi Kappa Phi Natl Hon Society. **SELECTED PUBLICATIONS** Author, works include: Archibald John Motley Jr, Chicago Historical Society, 1991; "Archibald John Motley Jr: Painting Jazz and Blues," paper, College Art Association, Chicago, Feb 13-15, 1992; "Archibald John Motley Jr: The Artist in Paris, 1929-1930," paper, African-Americans and Europe International Conference, Paris, Feb 5-9, 1992; review: "Black Art-Ancestral Legacy: The African Impulse in African-American Art," African Arts Magazine, Jan 1991; judge: Contemporary Art Exhibition, National Black Arts Festival, Atlanta, 1988; consultant: Archibald John Motley Jr Exhibition, Your Heritage House, Detroit, 1988; curator: "VH-4 Decades: The Art of Varnette P Honeywood," Spelman College, 1992; numerous other television/public lectures, tours, panels, publications. **CONTACT ADDRESS** Spelman Col, 350 Spelman Ln SW, Atlanta, GA, 30314.

ROBINSON, JOYCE H.
DISCIPLINE AMERICAN AND AFRICAN AMERICAN ART **EDUCATION** Davidson Col, BA; Univ Va, MA, PhD. **CAREER** Asst prof, Pa State Univ, 96-; adj curator, Palmer Museum.. **RESEARCH** Modern European art. **SELECTED PUBLICATIONS** Articles: Winterthur Portfolio; Studies Decorative Arts; New Art Examiner **CONTACT ADDRESS** Pennsylvania State Univ, 201 Shields Bldg, University Park, PA, 16802.

ROBINSON, LILIEN F.
PERSONAL Liubljana, Yugoslavia, m **DISCIPLINE** FINE ARTS **EDUCATION** Johns Hopkins, PhD, 78; Geo Wash Univ, MA, 65, BA, 62 **CAREER** Prof, 79-, Chair, 77-91, Assoc Prof, 76-79, Asst Prof, 65-76, Geo Wash Univ **HONORS AND AWARDS** Trachtenberg Svc Prize; Geo Wash Awd, Phi Beta Kappa; Grad w/honors; fels, schols **MEMBERSHIPS** Col Art Asn; N Am Serbian Studies Asn **RESEARCH** Contemporary exhibit artists **SELECTED PUBLICATIONS** Auth, Clay Variance, Lyons Agency, 95; Anna Klumpke: In Context, AZ St Univ, 93 **CONTACT ADDRESS** Dept of Fine Arts, George Washington Univ, Washington, DC, 20052.

ROBINSON, RUTH
PERSONAL Born 12/17/1949, Chicago, IL **DISCIPLINE** EDUCATION **EDUCATION** No IL Univ DeKalb, BA Elem Educ 1971; Pacific Oaks Coll, MA Child Develop 1974; Univ of CA Berkeley, PhD 1980. **CAREER** Pacific Oaks Coll & Children's School, faculty/head teacher 1972-73; Harold E Jones Child Study Center, teacher 1976-77; CA State Polytechnic Univ, lectr 1974-75, 1977-78; IN State Univ, asst prof, assoc prof early childhood educ, asst dean school of educ 1984-. **HONORS AND AWARDS** Grad Minority Fellowship UC Berkeley 1977-79; Doctoral Fellowship Carnegie Corp 1975-76; Collective Monologues I Toward a Black Perspective in Educ Stage Seven Inc Pasadena CA 1976. **MEMBERSHIPS** Curriculum consult Merced Co Region III Child Develop & migrant Child Care Prog 1978; curriculum consult Oakland Comm Sch 1975-76; mem Natl Assn Educ of Young Children 1979-; bd of dir Stage Seven Inc Black Perspective in Early Childhood Educ 1973-80. **CONTACT ADDRESS** Indiana State Univ, Statesman Towers West, Terre Haute, IN, 47809.

ROBINSON, TOM
DISCIPLINE HISTORY **EDUCATION** Univ New Brunswick, BA; McMaster Univ, PhD. **RESEARCH** Development of Christianity in the second and third century; development of computer programs for language training. **SELECTED PUBLICATIONS** Auth, pubs on Greek and early Christianity. **CONTACT ADDRESS** Dept of History, Lethbridge Univ, 4401 University Dr W, Lethbridge, AB, T1K 3M4. **EMAIL** robinson@hg.uleth.ca

ROBSON, ANN W.
PERSONAL England **DISCIPLINE** HISTORY **EDUCATION** Univ Toronto, BA, 53, MA, 54; Univ London, Eng, PhD, 58. **CAREER** PROF HIST UNIV TORONTO 68-. **SELECTED PUBLICATIONS** Auth, A Moralist In and Out of Parliament; auth, Sexual Equality. **CONTACT ADDRESS** Victoria Col, Univ Toronto, Toronto, ON, M5S 1K9. **EMAIL** arobson@epas.utoronto.ca

ROBSON, DAVID
PERSONAL Born 11/02/1946, Miami, FL, m, 1995 **DISCIPLINE** AMERICAN HISTORY **EDUCATION** Yale Univ, PhD, 74. **CAREER** Asst prof, Agnes Scott Coll, 71-74; vis asst prof, St Mary;s Univ, Nova Scotia, 74-75; asst prof, Emory Univ, 75-76; asst prof, Univ Wyo, 76-84; asst prof, John Carroll Univ, 85-93; PROF, DIR GRAD STUD, JOHN CARROLL UNIV, 93-. **MEMBERSHIPS** Am Hist Asn; Org Am Hist; Assoc Omihundro Inst Early Am Hist & Cult; Soc Hist of Early Am Repub; South Hist Asn **RESEARCH** American politics, intellectual, & higher educational history of 1750-1815. **SELECTED PUBLICATIONS** "Enlightening the Wilderness: Charles Nisbet's Failure at Higher Education in Post-Revolutionary Pennsylvania," History of Education Quarterly, 97; "Anticipating the Brethren: The Reverend Charles Nisbet Critiques the French Revolution," The Pennsylvania Magazine of History and Biography, 97. **CONTACT ADDRESS** John Carroll Univ, 20700 N Park Blvd, Univ Heights, OH, 44118. **EMAIL** Robson@jcu.edu

ROBY, PAMELA A.
PERSONAL Born 11/17/1942, Milwaukee, WI, d **DISCIPLINE** SOCIOLOGY **EDUCATION** Denver Univ, BA, 63, Syracuse Univ, MA, 66; NYU, PhD, 71. **CAREER** George Washington Univ, asst prof, 70-71; Branders Univ, asst prof, 71-73; Univ of Cal SC, assoc prof, prof, dir soc doc prog, chemn dept soc, 73-. **HONORS AND AWARDS** ACLS/ITG, UofC Innov in Tchg Award, Andrew W. Mellon fel, NSF Dissert Fel **MEMBERSHIPS** SSSP, SWS, PSA, ISA, ASA, ESA. **RESEARCH** Soc of leadership; gender and emotion. **SELECTED PUBLICATIONS** Women in the Workplace, Schenkman Pub Co, 81; The Poverty Establishment, ed, Prentice-hall, 74, Child Care - Who Cares? Foreign and Domestic Infant and Early Childhood Development Policies, ed, Basic Books 73; The Future of Inequality, coauth, Basic Books, 70; art, Becoming a Shop Steward: Perspectives on Gender and Race in Ten Trade Unions, in: Labor Studies Jour, 95; Becoming an Active Feminist Academic: Gender, Class, Race and Intelligence, in: Individual Voices, Collective Visions: Fifty Years of Women in Sociology, Temple Univ Press, 95. **CONTACT ADDRESS** Dept of Sociology, Univ of California, Santa Cruz, Santa Cruz, CA, 95064. **EMAIL** roby@cats.ucsc.edu

ROCK, HOWARD BLAIR
PERSONAL Born 07/11/1944, Cleveland, OH, m, 1975, 2 children **DISCIPLINE** UNITED STATES HISTORY **EDUCATION** Brandeis Univ, BA, 66; NY Univ, MA, 69, PhD(hist), 74. **CAREER** Asst prof, 73-79, assoc prof hist, FL Int Univ, 79-; NEH res fel, colonial value systs, Northwestern Univ, 78-79. **MEMBERSHIPS** AHA; Orgn Am Historians; Soc Hist Early Am Repub. **SELECTED PUBLICATIONS** Auth, The Mechanics of New York City and the American Revolution: One Generation Later, NY Hist, 7/76; The Perils of Laissez-faire: The Aftermath of the New York Bakers Strike of 1801, Labor Hist, summer 76; Artisans of the New Republic: The Tradesmen of New York City in the Age of Jefferson, NY Univ, 79; A Delicate Balance: The Mechanics & the City in the Age of Jefferson, NY Hist Quart, 4/79; ed, The New York City Artisan, 1789-1825, 85; ed, Keepers of the Revolution, New Yorkers at Work in the New Republic, 93. **CONTACT ADDRESS** Dept of Hist, Florida Intl Univ, 1 F I U South Campus, Miami, FL, 33199-0001. **EMAIL** rockh@fiu.edu

ROCK, KENNETH WILLETT
PERSONAL Born 12/12/1938, Abilene, KS, m, 1964, 2 children **DISCIPLINE** EAST CENTRAL EUROPEAN & EUROPEAN DIPLOMATIC HISTORY **EDUCATION** Univ Kans, BA, 60; Stanford Univ, MA, 62, PhD(hist), 69. **CAREER** From instr to asst prof, 65-72, assoc prof Hist, Colo State Univ, 72-83,

Danforth assoc, 78-84; Univ Honor's Prog, RECES Prog Russian, East & Central European Studies coord; Passim; pres, Colo Delta Phi Beta Kappa, 88-90, PBK Screening Officer, 94-; act dir, CSU Office of Int Ed, 84-85; vis scholar, Tech Univ of Budapest, Hungary, 93; Bradley Univ Berlin Seminar, 93, 96. **HONORS AND AWARDS** Honors Prof, Colo State Univ, 78; Outstanding Hist Prof, 86; Eddy Teacher Award, 96. **MEMBERSHIPS** Phi Beta Kappa; Phi Alpha Theta; AHA; Am Asn Advan Slavic Studies; Conf Group Cent Europ Hist; Rocky Mountain Asn Slavic Studies; Am Hist Soc Germans from Russia. **RESEARCH** Habsburg monarchy; European diplomatic history; East Central Europe. **SELECTED PUBLICATIONS** Auth, Schwarzenberg versus Nicholas I, round one: The negotiation of the Habsburg-Romanov alliance against Hungary in 1849, In: Austrian History Yearbook, 70-71; Felix Schwarzenberg, military diplomat, In: Austrian History Yearbook, Vol II, 75; The Colorado Germans from Russia study project, Soc Sci J, 4/76; Germans from Russia in America; the first hundred years, Colo State Univ, Germans from Russia in Am, Vol 1, 76; Unsere Leute: Colorado's Germans from Russia, Colo Mag, Spring 78; Loyalty & legality: Austria and the Western Balkans, In: Nation & Ideology: Essays in Honor of Wayne S Vucinich, East Europ Monographs, 81; A Time for Deeds and Courage: The Austrian State after 1848, Proceedings 1986, Consortium on Revolutionary Europe, 87; Rejuvenation by Edict: Schwarzenberg, Stadion, and Bach in 1848-1849, Selected Papers 1995, Consortium on Revolutionary Europe, 96. **CONTACT ADDRESS** Dept of History, Colorado State Univ, Fort Collins, CO, 80523-0001. **EMAIL** krock@vines.colostate.edu

ROCKE, ALAN J.
PERSONAL Born 09/20/1948, Chicago, IL, m, 1976 **DISCIPLINE** HISTORY OF SCIENCE **EDUCATION** Beloit Col, BA, 69; Univ Wis-Madison, MA, 73, PhD(hist of sci), 75. **CAREER** Lectr hist, Univ WI-Milwaukee, 75-76; lectr interdisciplinary studies, Univ WI-Madison, 76-78; asst prof, 78-84, assoc prof Hist, 84-93, BOURNE PROF HIST, CASE WESTERN RESERVE UNIV, 93-, chair, dept of Hist, 95-98. **MEMBERSHIPS** Hist Sci Soc; Soc Hist Technol; AAAS; corresp, Fedn Am Scientists; Sci Res Soc NAm. **RESEARCH** History of chemistry; history of nuclear weapons; history of atomic theories. **SELECTED PUBLICATIONS** Auth, Atoms and equivalents: The early development of the chemical atom and theory, Hist Studies in the Phys Sci, 78; Gay-Lussac and Dumas: Adherents of the Avogadro-Ampere hypothesis, 79 & The reception of chemical atomism in Germany, 79, Isis; Salt II: A step forward, Cleveland Plain Dealer, 79; coauth, A badger chemist genealogy, J Chem Educ, 79; contribr, Geoge Barger & Walter Jacobs, In: Dict of Scientific Biography, 80; auth, Kekule, Butlerov and the historiography of the theory of chemical structure, Brit J for the Hist Sci, 81; Subatomoc Speculations and the Origin of Structure Theory, Ambix ; Chemical Atomism in the 19th Century, OH State Univ Press, 84; The Quiet Revolution, Univ CA Press, 93. **CONTACT ADDRESS** Dept Hist of Sci, Case Western Reserve Univ, 10900 Euclid Ave, Cleveland, OH, 44106-4901. **EMAIL** ajr@po.cwru.edu

ROCKEFELLER, STEVEN C.
DISCIPLINE HISTORY OF RELIGION, PHILOSOPHY OF RELIGION, AND RELIGION, ETHICS, AND THE **EDUCATION** Princeton Univ, AB; Union Theol Sem, MDiv; Columbia Univ, PhD. **CAREER** Prof; Middlebury Col, 71-. **SELECTED PUBLICATIONS** Auth, John Dewey: Religious Faith and Democratic Humanism; co-ed, Spirit and Nature: Why the Environment is a Religious Issue-An Interfaith Dialogue. **CONTACT ADDRESS** Dept of Religion, Middlebury Col, Middlebury, VT, 05753.

ROCKLAND, MICHAEL AARON
PERSONAL Born 07/14/1935, New York, NY, m, 5 children **DISCIPLINE** AMERICAN & LATIN AMERICAN STUDIES **EDUCATION** Hunter Col, BA, 55; Univ Minn, MA, 60, PhD(Am studies), 68. **CAREER** Teaching asst Am studies, Univ Minn, 57-59, instr, 60-61, counsel, Col Arts & Sci, 59-61; asst cult attache, Am Embassy, Buenos Aires, 62-63, asst cult attache & dir, Casa Am Cult Ctr, Am Embassy, Madrid, 63-67; exec asst to chancellor, NJ State Dept Higher Educ, 68-69; asst prof, 69-71, asst dean col, 69-72, assoc prof, 72-81, Prof Am Studies, Douglass Col, Rutgers Univ, 81-, Chm Dept, 69-; Lectr, Univ Santa Fe, Arg, 63; guest lectr, Span Univ Syst, 64-67; publ subventions, Rutgers Univ & Arg Embassy, 70; fac chm contemporary Am sem returning foreign serv officers, US Info Agency, 72-73, mem bd, Int Inst Women Studies, 72-; contrib ed, NJ Monthly, 77-; contrib reporter, NJ Nightly News, 78-. **HONORS AND AWARDS** Alumni Hall of Fame, Hunter Col, 73; NJ Pres Assoc Award, 80; Pulitzer Prize nominee, 80; First Prize for Feature Journalism, Am Soc of Jour, 92; The Nat Am Studies Prize for Distinguished Teaching, 97; The Warren Susman Award for Distinguished Teaching, 97; Teacher of the Year Award, Rutgers Col, 98. **MEMBERSHIPS** Am Studies Asn (pres, 71-72); Orgn Am Historians; hon mem Inst Sarmiento, Arg. **RESEARCH** Foreign commentators on the United States; ethnic affairs in the United States, especially the relationship between Jews and the other ethnic groups; mobility in America; Am Aesthetics. **SELECTED PUBLICATIONS** Auth, Sarmiento's Travels in the United States in 1847, Princeton Univ, 70; ed, America in the Fifties and Sixties: Julian Marias on the United States, Pa State Univ, 72; coauth, Three Days on Big City Waters (film), Nat Educ TV, 74; auth, The American Jewish Experience in Literature, Haifa Univ, 75; Homes on Wheels, Rutgers Univ Pres, 80; A Bliss Case, Coffee House Press, 89; coauth, Looking for America on the New Jersey Turnpike, Rutgers Univ Press, 80; auth, Snowshoeing Through Sewers, Rutgers Univ Press, 94. **CONTACT ADDRESS** Dept of Am Studies, Rutgers Univ, PO Box 270, New Brunswick, NJ, 08903-0270. **EMAIL** rockland@rci.rutgers.edu

RODNEY, WILLIAM
PERSONAL Born 01/01/1923, Drumheller, AB, Canada **DISCIPLINE** HISTORY **EDUCATION** Univ Alta, BA, 50; Univ Cambridge, BA, 52, MA, 56; Univ London, PhD, 61. **CAREER** Nato Fel, 63-64; Can Coun Leave Fel, 68-69; Can Coun Sr Leave Fel, 78-79; dean arts, 79-88, PROF EMER, ROYAL MILITARY COLLEGE, 88-. **HONORS AND AWARDS** Award Merit Distinction, Am Asn State Local Hist, 70; Univ BC Medal Popular Biog, 70. **MEMBERSHIPS** Life mem, Can Hist Asn; mem, Can Inst Int Affairs; Johnian Soc; Royal Commonwealth Soc; Fellow, Royal Geog Soc; Royal Hist Soc. **SELECTED PUBLICATIONS** Auth, Neutralism in the Northern Nato States, 65; auth, Soldiers of the International: A History of the Communist Party of Canada 1919-1929, 68; auth, Kootenai Brown His Life and Times, 69, 2nd ed, 95; auth, Joe Boyle King of the Klondike, 74. **CONTACT ADDRESS** 308 Denison Rd, Victoria, BC, V8S 4K3.

RODNITZKY, JEROME L.
PERSONAL Born 08/01/1936, Chicago, IL, m, 1966, 2 children **DISCIPLINE** UNITED STATES SOCIAL CULTURAL & INTELLECTUAL HISTORY **EDUCATION** Univ Chicago, BA, 59, MAT, 62; Univ Ill, PhD(Hist), 67. **CAREER** From instr to assoc prof, 66-76, prof History, Univ Texas, Arlington, 76-. **MEMBERSHIPS** Am Studies Asn; Popular Cult Asn. **RESEARCH** History of American popular culture; history of 1960s counterculture; history of American feminism. **SELECTED PUBLICATIONS** Coauth, A pacifist St Joan: The odyssey of Joan Baez, In: Heroes of Popular Culture, Bowling Green Univ, 72; David Kinley: A paternal university president in the roaring twenties, J Ill State Hist Soc, 73; Popular music and American studies, Hist Teacher, 74; The new revivalism: American protest songs, 1945-1968, In: American Vistas, Oxford Univ, 2nd ed, 75; Minstrels of the Dawn: The Folk-Protest Singer as a Cultural Hero, Nelson-Hall, 76; The Southwest unbound: Janis Joplin and the new feminism, Feminist Art J, 77; The Essentials of American History, Knopf, 2nd ed, 80; Henry David Thoreau: Nearsighted native son, Modern Age, 81; Jazz Age Boomtown, Texas Arm, University Press, 97. **CONTACT ADDRESS** Dept of History, Univ of Texas, Arlington, TX, 76019. **EMAIL** Jerry.Rodnitzley@uth.edu

RODRIGUEZ, CLEMENCIA
DISCIPLINE FINE ARTS AND HUMANITIES **EDUCATION** Univ Javeriana, Bogota, BA, 84; OH Univ, Athens, MA, 90, PhD, 94. **CAREER** Asst prof, Univ TX at San Antonio, 94-; instr, OH Univ, 93; vis prof, Univ Centroamericana, 91-92; educ material evaluator, UNICEF/Radio Neth, , Managua, 91; grad asoc, OH Univ, 89-90; dir Educ Commun Prog, Univ Javarima, Bogota, 88; Commun Proj Coordr, CINEP, Bogota, 84-88; prof, Univ Javarima, Bogota, 84-88; res asst, ACICS, Bogota, 83-84 & Univ Javarima, 88. **HONORS AND AWARDS** Fac Res Awd, Univ TX at San Antonio, 95-96; Nat Coun Churches Christ in US, Dissertation grant, 93; John Houk Memorial Grant, OH Univ, 93; Certificate of Achievement, Commun & Develop Stud Prog, OH Univ, 90; rad Associateship, Sch Telecommun, OH Univ, 89. **MEMBERSHIPS** Int Commun Asn; Union Democratic Commun; San Antonio Hisp Res Network. **SELECTED PUBLICATIONS** Auth, Shedding Useless Notions of Alternative Media, Peace Rev 8 1, 96; The Rise and Fall of the Popular Correspondents' Movement in Revolutionary Nicaragua, 1982-1990, Media Cult and Soc 16 3, 94; A Process of Identity Deconstruction: Latin American Women Producing Video Stories, Women in Grassroots Communication, Furthering Social Change, Thousand Oaks, Sage, 94; De Cristal a Sassa Mutema: la Trayectoria del Melodrama Televisivo, From Cristal to Sassa Mutema: the Historic Evolution of Television Melodrama, Suplemento Gente, Barricada, 91; "Media for Participation and Social Change: Local Television in Catalonia, Comm Dev News, 91; Cuando la C mara se Convirtio en Espejo Electronico. Cronicas del Video Participativo, When the Camera Transmutes into an Electronic Mirror, Tales of Participatory Video, Cinep Informa, 2 5, 90; coauth, La Telenovela en Colombia: Mucho m s que Amor y L grimas, Colombian Telenovelas: Much more than Love and Tears, Coleccion Controversia, #155, Bogota, CINEP, 89; Information Technology, Culture, and National Development in Latin America, Political Communication Research: Approaches, Studies, Assessments, Vol II, Norwood, Ablex Publ Co, 96; Propuesta para una Nueva Agenda de Investigacion sobre Comunicacion Internacional, Dialogos de la Comun, Colombia, 42, 95; Propuesta para una Nueva Agenda de Investigacion sobre Comunicacion Internacional, Comun y Sociedad, Mexico 24, 95; ed, Contando Historias, Tejiendo Identidades, Telling Stories, Weaving Identities, Bogota, CINEP, 87; **CONTACT ADDRESS** Col of Fine Arts and Hum, Univ Texas at San Antonio, 6900 N Loop 1604 W, San Antonio, TX, 78249.

RODRIGUEZ, SYLVIA
PERSONAL Born 08/16/1947, Taos, NM, s **DISCIPLINE** ANTHROPOLOGY **EDUCATION** Barnard Col, BA, 69; Stanford Univ, MA, PhD, 81. **CAREER** Instr to asst prof, Carleton Col, 77-81; asst prof, UCLA, 83-88; asst prof, 88-92, Assoc Prof, 92- , Univ New Mexico. **HONORS AND AWARDS** Snead-Wertheim Lectr, Univ New Mexico, 96-97. Edward Spicer Award, Jour SW, 90; Webb-Smith Essay Competition, 93; Chicago Folklore Prize, 97; Border Reg Libr Asn Book Award, 97. **MEMBERSHIPS** Am Anthrop Asn; Am Ethnol Soc; Cult Anthrop Asn; Asn Lat Anthrop; Am Folklore Soc; Sm Stud Asn. **RESEARCH** Interethnic relations; ethnicity; ethnic identity, particularly in US-Mexico borderlands, upper Rio Grande Valley; tourism; land and water issues. **SELECTED PUBLICATIONS** Auth, Land, Water, and Ethnic Identity in Taos, Latinos and the Law, Garland Publ, 94; Art, Tourism and Race Relations in Taos: Toward A Sociology of the Art Colony, Tourism and Survival in the American West, Stone Ladder Press, 94; The Tourist Gaze, Gentrification, and the Commodification of Subjectivity in Taos, Essays on the Changing Images of the Southwest, Texas A&M Univ Press, 94; Defended Boundaries, Precarious Elites: The Arroyo Seco Matachines Dance, Jour Am Folklore, 94; Subaltern Historiography on the Rio Grande, A Review Essay on Gutierrez,s When Jesus Came, the Corn Mothers Went Away, Am Ethnol, 94; Water Planning, Ethnic Politics, and the State: The Case of Taos, Mass, 94; The Matachines Dance: Ritual Symbolism and Interethnic Relations in the Upper Rio Grande Valley, Univ NM Press, 96; The Taos Fiesta: Invented Tradition and the Infrapolitics of Symbolic Reclamation, Jour of SW, 97; Fiesta Time and Plaza Space: Resistance and Accommodation in a Tourist Town, Jour Am Folklore, 98. **CONTACT ADDRESS** Anthropology Dept, Univ New Mexico, Albuquerque, NM, 87131. **EMAIL** sylrodri@unm.edu

ROE, MARK J.
DISCIPLINE AMERICAN HISTORY, LAW **EDUCATION** Columbia Col, BA (Am hist), 72; Harvard Law School, JD, 75. **CAREER** Prof Law, Columbia Law School, 88-. **RESEARCH** Political influence on the corporation. **SELECTED PUBLICATIONS** Auth, Strong Managers, Weak Owners: The Political Roots of American Corporate Finance, Princeton Univ Press, 94; From Antitrust to Corporate Governance: The Corporation and the Law, 1959-1995, in The American Corporation Today, Carl Kaysen, ed, 96; Chaos and Evolution in Law and Economics, 109 Harvard Law Rev, 641, 96; Lifetime Employment: Labor Peace and the Evolution of Japanese Corporate Governance, with Ron Gilson, Brookings Inst, forthcoming; Backlash, 98 Columbia Law Rev 217, 98; Comparative Corporate Governance, Palgrave Dictionary on Law and Economics, forthcoming; German Securities Markets and German Codetermination, 98 Columbia Business Law Rev 167, 98; Corporate Reorganization and Finance (casebook and teaching materials), Foundation Press, forthcoming; A Theory of Path Dependence in Corporate Ownership and Governance, with Lucian Bebchuk, 51 Stanford Law Rev, forthcoming 98. **CONTACT ADDRESS** School of Law, Columbia Univ, New York, NY, 10027.

ROEBER, ANTHONY G.
DISCIPLINE HISTORY **EDUCATION** Univ Denver, BA, 71, MA, 72; Brown Univ, AM, 73, PhD, 77. **CAREER** Instr, hist, Princeton Univ; PROF, HIST, UNIV ILL CHICAGO and ADJ LECTR, LAW, KENT LAW COLL. **MEMBERSHIPS** Am Antiquarian Soc **SELECTED PUBLICATIONS** Auth, A New England Women's Perspective on Norfolk, Virginia, 1801-1802: Excerpts from the Diary of Ruth Henshaw Bascom," Procs of the AAS 89, 79; auth, "Authority, Law, and Custom: The Rituals of Court Day in Tidewater Virginia, 1720-1750," Wm & Mary Quart 37, 80, and in Material Life in America, 1600-1860, Northeastern Univ Press, 88; auth, Faithful Magistrates and Republican Lawyers: Creators of Virginia Legal Culture, 1680-1810, 81; auth, "The Scrutiny of the Ill-Natured Ignorant Vulgar: Lawyers and Print Culture in Virginia, 1716-1774," Virginia Mag Hist and Biog 91, 83; auth, "He Read it to me from a Book of English Law: Germans, Bench, and Bar in the Colonial South, 1715-1770," in Ambivalent Legacy: A Legal History of the South, Univ Press of Miss, 84; auth, "Germans, Property, and the First Great Awakening: Rehearsal for a Revolution?" in The Transit of Civilization from Europe to America: Essays in Honor of Galinsky, Gunter Narr Verlag, 86; auth, "Subjects or Citizens? German Lutherans and the Federal Constitution in Pennsylvania, 1789-1800," Am Stud, 89; auth, Palatines, Liberty, and Property: German Lutherans in Colonial British America, 92; auth, "Der Pietismus in Nordamerika," in Die Geschichte des Pietismus, 95. **CONTACT ADDRESS** 515 N 3rd Ave, Maywood, IL, 60153.

ROEDER, GEORGE H.
DISCIPLINE HISTORY **EDUCATION** Univ MD, BA, 65, MA, 73; Univ WI, PhD, 77. **CAREER** Instr, Univ MO; Northwestern Univ; vis lectr, Univ MI; Stanford Univ; undergrad div ch; prof, 80-. **HONORS AND AWARDS** Fel, NEH. **SELECTED PUBLICATIONS** Auth, Forum of Uncertainty: Confrontations with Modern Painting in Twentieth-Century American Thought; The World Through a Bombsight: Censorship, Propoganda, and American Visual Experience During World War II. **CONTACT ADDRESS** Dept of Lib Arts, Sch

of the Art Inst of Chicago, 37 S Wabash Ave, Chicago, IL, 60603.

ROEDIGER, DAVID
PERSONAL Born 07/13/1952, East St. Louis, IL, m, 1979, 2 children **DISCIPLINE** U.S. HISTORY **EDUCATION** Northern IL, BS, 75; Northwestern, PhD, 80 **CAREER** Asst prof of history, 80-84, Northwestern; asst prof, assoc prof, full prof of hist, 85-94, Univ of MO; prof of hist, 94- , Univ of MN; Chair of Amer studies program, 96- , Univ of MN. **HONORS AND AWARDS** Merle Curti Prize, 92; Gustavus Myers Award, 92; Choice Outstanding Academic Book Award, 92; Northern IL Distinguished Alumni Award, 97. **MEMBERSHIPS** Organization of Amer Historians; Amer Studies Assn. **RESEARCH** Race in the U.S.; U.S. Working class hist. **SELECTED PUBLICATIONS** Auth, The Wages of Whiteness: Race and the Making of the American Working Class, Verso Books, 98; Black on White: Black Writers on What It Means to Be White, Schocken, 98; The North and Slavery, includes afterword, What Frederick Douglass Knew, Garland, 98. **CONTACT ADDRESS** 75 S. Victoria St., St. Paul, MN, 55105. **EMAIL** roedi001@tc.umn.edu

ROEDIGER, HENRY L.
PERSONAL Born 07/24/1947, Roanoke, VA, m, 1982, 2 children **DISCIPLINE** PSYCHOLOGY **EDUCATION** Washington & Lee Univ, BA, 69; Yale Univ, PhD, 73. **CAREER** Asst prof, 73-76, assoc prof, 78-82, prof, 82-88, Purdue Univ; vis asst prof, 76-78, vis assoc prof, 81-82, Univ Toronto; prof psych, Rice Univ, 88-96; prof, chemn dept, 96-, James S. McDonnell Dist Univ prof psych, 98-, Washington Univ. **HONORS AND AWARDS** NSF res fel, 67-69; Magna Cum Laude, 69; Phi Beta Kappa; Yale Univ fel, 72-73; Guggenheim fel, 94-95; fel, Canadian Psychol Asn; fel, Am Psychol Soc; fel, Am Psychol Asn; fel, AAAS; pres-elect, div 3, Am Psychol Asn, 2000-2001; elected, Soc of Exp Psychol. **MEMBERSHIPS** AAAS; Am Psychol Asn; Am Psychol Soc; Can Psychol Asn; Cognitive Neuroscience Soc; Coun of Grad Dept of Psychol; False Memory Syndrome Found, Sci Advisory Bd; Memory Disorders Res Soc; Sigma Xi; Soc for Applied Res in Memory and Cognition; Soc for Neuroscience; Psychonomic Soc. **RESEARCH** Human learning and memory; cognitive psychology; retrieval processes in memory; implicit memory; controversies in psychology; cognitive illusions. **SELECTED PUBLICATIONS** Co-ed Varieties of Memory and Consciousness: Essays in Honour of Endel Tulving, Erlbaum, 89; coauth, Psychology, 4th ed, West, 96; co-ed, Readings in Psychology, West, 97; coauth, Experimental Psychology: Understanding Psychological Research, 6th ed, West, 97; coauth, Research Methods in Psychology, 6th ed, Brooks-Cole, 98; coauth, Principles of Learning and Memory, 2d ed, Erlbaum, forthcoming. **CONTACT ADDRESS** Dept of Psychology, Washington Univ, One Brookings Dr, PO Box 1125, St Louis, MO, 63130-4899. **EMAIL** roediger@artsci.wustl.edu

ROESCH, RONALD
PERSONAL Born 05/25/1947, Montclair, NJ, m, 1976, 4 children **DISCIPLINE** PSYCHOLOGY **EDUCATION** Univ of IL, PhD, 77. **CAREER** Prof, SFU, 84-; Dir, Mental Health, Law, and Policy Inst, SFU 91-. **HONORS AND AWARDS** Consul Psych Res Award, Amer Psychol Assoc, 77; Social Issues Dissertation Award, Soc Psychol Stud of Soc Issues, 77; Cert of Merit, ABA Gavel Award Comp, 82; Pres APLS (Div 41 of APA) 93-94. **MEMBERSHIPS** Fel, CPA; Fel, APA, APLAS **RESEARCH** Law and Psychology; mentally disordered offenders **SELECTED PUBLICATIONS** Coauth, Fitness to stand trial: Characteristics of remands since the 1992 Criminal Code amendments, CA Jour of Psych, 98; Coauth, Defining and assessing competency to stand trial, Hndbk of Forensic Psych, 98; Contr, Comprehensive Clinical Psychology: Applications in Diverse Populations, Oxford, 98; Coauth, The Fitness Interview Test (rev ed), 98; Coauth, Psychology and Law: The State of the Discipline, Plenum, 98. **CONTACT ADDRESS** Prof, Dept of Psychol, Simon Fraser Univ, Burnaby, BC, V5A 1S6. **EMAIL** rroesch@arts.sfu.ca

ROGERS, CLIFFORD J.
PERSONAL Born 10/17/1967, Nairobi, Kenya **DISCIPLINE** HISTORY **EDUCATION** Rice Univ, BA, 89; Ohio St Univ, MA, 90, PhD, 94 **CAREER** Olin Post dr fel, mil & strategic hist, 94-95,Yale Univ; asst prof, 95-, US Mil Acad. **RESEARCH** Late Medieval England & France; medieval military; military revolutions **CONTACT ADDRESS** Dept History, US Military Acad, Thayer Hall, West Point, NY, 10996. **EMAIL** kc1870@exmail.usma.edu

ROGERS, DANIEL E.
DISCIPLINE WESTERN CIVILIZATION I, WESTERN CIVILIZATION II, MODERN GERMANY, THE HOLOCAUST, HITLER AND NAZI GERMANY, NAZI GERMANY **EDUCATION** Univ Ala, BA; Univ NC at Chapel Hill, MA, PhD; **CAREER** Assoc prof; Univ NC, 90; fac, Univ Md, 90-91; prof, Univ South Al, 91-. **RESEARCH** How politicians in western Germany moved Germans towards a broad acceptance of the need to commemorate the Holocaust. **SELECTED PUBLICATIONS** Auth, Politics After Hitler: The Western Allies and the German Party System, London: Macmillan; NY UP, 95 & Transforming the German Party System: The US and the Origins of Political Moderation, 1945-1949, J Modern Hist 65, 93. **CONTACT ADDRESS** Dept of History, Univ South Alabama, 372 Humanities, Mobile, AL, 36688-0002. **EMAIL** drogers@jaguar1.usouthal.edu

ROGERS, LYNNE
DISCIPLINE MUSIC THEORY **EDUCATION** Pomona Col, BA, 76; Univ of Wash, MA, 80; Princeton Univ, MFA, 83, PhD, 89. **CAREER** Fac, Univ Tex, Austin, 87-94; asst prof, Oberlin Coll, 94-; Visiting lectr, University of Wis, 84. **HONORS AND AWARDS** Fel, Pach Sacher Found, Switzerland, 97; Univ Res Inst Summer Res Award, Univ Tex, 91. **SELECTED PUBLICATIONS** Contribu, Intl Jour of Musicol and Jour Musicol. **CONTACT ADDRESS** Dept of Mus, Oberlin Col, Oberlin, OH, 44074.

ROGERS, OSCAR ALLAN, JR.
PERSONAL Born 09/10/1928, Natchez, MS, m **DISCIPLINE** EDUCATION **EDUCATION** Tougaloo Coll, AB (Summa Cum Laude) 1950; Harvard Divinity Sch, STB 1953; Harvard Univ, MAT 1954; Univ of AR, EdD 1960; Univ of Washington, Postdoctoral study 1968-69. **CAREER** Natchez Jr Coll, dean/registrar 1954-56; AR Baptist Coll, pres 1956-59; Jackson State Univ, dean of students/prof of social science 1960-69, dean of the grad school 1969-84; Claflin Coll, pres; Oklahoma City University, DHL, 1992; Claflin College, Pres, 1984-94. **MEMBERSHIPS** Pastor Bolton-Edward United Methodist Church 1961-84; dir Orangeburg Chamber of Commerce 1987-90. **SELECTED PUBLICATIONS** "My Mother Cooked My Way Through Harvard With These Creole Recipes," 1972; "Mississippi, The View From Tougaloo," 1979. **CONTACT ADDRESS** Claflin Col, 400 College Ave, Orangeburg, SC, 29115.

ROGLER, LLOYD H.
PERSONAL Born 07/21/1930, San Juan, PR, m, 2 children **DISCIPLINE** SOCIOLOGY **EDUCATION** Univ IA, PhD 57. **CAREER** Case Western Reserve Univ, prof sociol 68-74; Univ of Puerto Rico, vis prof 71-72; Fordham Univ, dir found of Hisp Res Cen 77-90; Fordham Univ, Albert Schweitzer Prof Human 74. **HONORS AND AWARDS** Fell Hubert Humphrey Intl Renown Sch; Distg Alumni Ach Awd; Simon Bolivar Awd. **MEMBERSHIPS** ASA; APA. **RESEARCH** Urban sociology, medical soci, soc psychia, soc psych of poverty and human migrations, polit dimensions of ethnic grp assim, cult in men health iss. **SELECTED PUBLICATIONS** Framing res on cult in psychiatric diagnosis: The case of the DSM-IV, Psychiatry, 96; International migrations: A framework for directing research, American Psychologist, 94; The mental health relevance of idioms of distress: Anger and perceptions of injustice among New York Puerto Ricans, The Journal of Nervous and Mental Disease, 94; Viewpoint, Culture in psychiatric diagnosis: An issue of scientific accuracy, Psychiatry, 93; Culturally sensitizing psychiatric diagnosis: A framework for research, The Journal of Nervous and Mental Diseases, 93; numerous pub. **CONTACT ADDRESS** Schweitzer Professor, Fordham Univ, Faculty Memorial Hall 417, Bronx, NY, 10458. **EMAIL** rogler@murray.fordham.edu

ROHRBOUGH, MALCOLM JUSTIN
PERSONAL Born 08/03/1932, Cambridge, MA, m, 3 children **DISCIPLINE** AMERICAN HISTORY **EDUCATION** Harvard Univ, AB, 54; Univ WI, MA, 58, PhD, 63. **CAREER** Instr Am hist, Princeton Univ, 62-64; from asst prof to assoc prof, 64-71, prof Am Hist, Univ IA, 71-. **MEMBERSHIPS** Orgn Am Historians; Western Hist Asn. **RESEARCH** The French in the CA Gold Rush. **SELECTED PUBLICATIONS** Auth, The Land Office Business: The Settlement and Administration of American Public Lands, 1789-1837, 68 & The Trans-Appalachian Frontier: People, Societies, and Institutions, 1775-1850, 78, Oxford Univ; auth, Aspen: The History of A Silver Mining Town, 1879-1893, Oxford, 86; auth, Days of Gold: The California Gold Rush and the American nation, California, 97. **CONTACT ADDRESS** Dept of History, Univ of IA, 280 Schaeffer Hall, Iowa City, IA, 52242-1409. **EMAIL** malcolm_rohrbough@uiowa.edu

ROHRER, JUDITH C.
DISCIPLINE EUROPEAN ARCHITECTURE **EDUCATION** Columbia Univ, PhD, 84. **CAREER** Archit, Emory Univ. **SELECTED PUBLICATIONS** Auth, La nova escola catalana: politica arquetectonica i regionalisme artistic a Barcelona, 1880-1910; Josep Puigi Cadafalch: Architecture between the House and the City. **CONTACT ADDRESS** Emory Univ, Atlanta, GA, 30322-1950. **EMAIL** jcrohre@emory.edu

ROHRS, RICHARD CARLTON
PERSONAL Born 02/01/1948, Brooklyn, NY, m, 1971, 2 children **DISCIPLINE** AMERICAN HISTORY **EDUCATION** Bucknell Univ, BA, 69; Univ NE, MA, 73, PhD(hist), 76. **CAREER** Vis asst prof, 76-77, asst prof, 77-82, assoc prof, 82-98, PROF HIST, OK STATE UNIV, 98-. **HONORS AND AWARDS** Phi Alpha Theta; Phi Kappa Phi. **MEMBERSHIPS** Orgn Am Historians; Soc Historians Am Foreign Rels; Soc Historians Early Am Repub. **RESEARCH** Nineteenth century American history. **SELECTED PUBLICATIONS** Auth, The Germans in Oklahoma, Univ OK Press, 80; Partisan Politics and the Attempted Assassination of Andrew Jackson, J Early Am Repub, summer 81; The Federalist Party and the Convention of 1800, Diplomatic History, summer 88; Antislavery Politics and the Pearl Incident of 1848, The Hist, summer 94; American Critics of the French Revolution of 1848, J of Early Am Repub, fall 94; A Guide to Quantitative History, Praeger, 95. **CONTACT ADDRESS** Dept of Hist, Oklahoma State Univ, Stillwater, OK, 74078-0002.

ROISMAN, HANNA M.
PERSONAL Wroclaw, Poland, m, 1971, 2 children **DISCIPLINE** CLASSICS **EDUCATION** Tel Aviv Univ, BA, 72, MA, 76; Univ Wash, PhD, 81. **CAREER** Lect, Tel Aviv Univ, 81-89; Assoc prof, Colby Col, 90-94, full prof, 94-. **HONORS AND AWARDS** Fel, Center Hellenic Studies **MEMBERSHIPS** APA **RESEARCH** Early Greek epic and tragedy; Greek and Latin lyric poetry. **SELECTED PUBLICATIONS** Auth, Nothing Is As It Seems: The Tragedy of the Implicit in Euripedes, 98; co-auth, The Odyssey Re-Formed, 96; auth, "A New Look at Seneca's Phaedra," 99; auth, Loyalty in Early Greek Epic and Tragedy, 84. **CONTACT ADDRESS** Dept of Classics, Colby Col, Waterville, ME, 04901. **EMAIL** h_roisma@colby.edu

ROJAS, CARLOS
PERSONAL Born 08/12/1928, Barcelona, Spain, m, 1966, 2 children **DISCIPLINE** SPANISH LITERATURE, HISTORY **EDUCATION** Barcelona Univ, MA, 51; Univ Cent, Madrid, PhD(Span lit), 55. **CAREER** Asst prof Romance lang, Rollins Col, 57-60; from asst prof to assoc prof, 60-68, prof, 68-80, Charles Howard Candler Prof Romance Lang, 80-, emeritus, Emory Univ. **HONORS AND AWARDS** Nat Prize for Lit, Govt Spain, 68; Planeta Prize, Ed Planeta, 73; Ateneo de Sevilla Prize, 77; Nadal Prize, 80. **MEMBERSHIPS** MLA; SAtlantic Mod Lang Asn. **RESEARCH** Contemporary Spanish; art history. **SELECTED PUBLICATIONS** Auth, Dialogos Para Otra Espana, Ariel, 66; Auto de Fe, Guadarrama, 68; Diez Figuras Ante la Guerra Civil, Nauta, 73; Azana, 73, La Guerra Civil Vista por los Exiliados, 75, Retratos Antifranquistas, 77 & Memorias Ineditas, 78, Planeta; El Ingenioso Hidalgo y Poeta Federico Garcia Lorca Asciende a los Infiernos, 80, La Barcelonade Picasso, 81. **CONTACT ADDRESS** Dept of Romance Lang, Emory Univ, Atlanta, GA, 30322.

ROLAND, ALEX
PERSONAL Born 04/07/1944, Providence, RI, m, 1979, 4 children **DISCIPLINE** HISTORY **EDUCATION** US Naval Acad, BS, 66; Univ Hawaii, MA, 70; Duke Univ, Phd, 74. **CAREER** Capt, US Marine Corps, 66-70; Historian, Nat Aeronautics & Space Admin, 73-81; Assoc prof to prof, Duke Univ, 87-. **HONORS AND AWARDS** Harold K Johnson vis prof of Military Hist, US Army War Col. **MEMBERSHIPS** Soc for the Hist of Technol; Soc of Milit Hist; Hist of Sci Soc. **RESEARCH** Military hist; hist of technol. **SELECTED PUBLICATIONS** Auth, Underwater Warfare in the Age of Sail, Bloomington, Univ Press, 78; art, Model Research: The National Advisory Committee for Aeronautice, 1915-1958, Washington: NASA, 85; ed, A Spacefaring People: Perspectives on Early Spaceflight, Washington: NASA, 85; co-auth, Men in Arms: A History of Warfare and Its Interrelationships with Western Society, New York: Holt, Rinehart and Winston, 91. **CONTACT ADDRESS** Dept of History, Duke Univ, Durham, NC, 27708. **EMAIL** alex.roland@duke.edu

ROLAND, CHARLES G.
PERSONAL Born 01/25/1933, Winnipeg, MB, Canada **DISCIPLINE** HISTORY OF MEDICINE **EDUCATION** Univ Toronto, pre-med, 52-54; Univ Man, MD, BS(Med), 58. **CAREER** Pvt med pract, Tillsonburg, Ont, 59-60; Grimsby, Ont, 60-64; sr ed, J Am Med Asn, 64-69; lectr, Northwestern Univ, 68-69; chmn, Biomed Commun, Mayo Clinic & Mayo Found, 69-77; assoc prof, 69, prof, Mayo Med Sch, 73-77; JASON A. HANNAH PROF HISTORY OF MEDICINE, McMASTER UNIV, 77-, assoc mem dept hist, 78-95; cur, Osler Libr, McGill Univ, 82-; Sid Richardson Vis Prof Med Hum, Univ Texas, 84. **HONORS AND AWARDS** Jason A. Hannah Medal, Royal Soc Can, 94 **MEMBERSHIPS** Am Osler Soc (pres, 86-87); Can Soc Hist Med (pres, 93-95); Int Soc Hist Med; Am Asn Hist Med; ed bd, Can Bull Hist Med; J Hist Med & Allied Sci; Scientia Can. **SELECTED PUBLICATIONS** Auth, Clarence Meredith Hincks: A Biography, 90; auth, Courage Under Siege: Disease, Starvation and Death in the Warsaw Ghetto, 92; auth, Harold N. Segall, Cardiologist and Historian, 96; coauth, An Annotated Checklist of Osleriana, 76; coauth, An Annotated Bibliography of Canadian Medical Periodicals 1826-1975, 79; ed, Health, Disease and Medicine: Essays in Canadian History, 83; co-ed, Secondary Sources in Canadian Medical History: A Bibliography, 84; co-ed, Sir William Osler: An Annotated Bibliography with Illustrations, 87. **CONTACT ADDRESS** Dept of Hist Med, McMaster Univ, 3N10-HSC, Hamilton, ON, L8N 3Z5.

ROLAND, CHARLES P.
PERSONAL Born 04/08/1918, Maury City, TN, m, 1948, 3 children **DISCIPLINE** UNITED STATES HISTORY **EDUCATION** Vanderbilt Univ, BA, 38; La State Univ, PhD, 51.

CAREER Teacher, High Sch, Tenn, 38-40; hist tech, Natl Park Serv, 40-42, 46-47; instr hist, La State Univ, 50-51; asst to chief historian, US Dept Army, 51-52; from instr to prof hist, Tulane Univ, 52-70, head arts & sci dept hist, 63-67, chmn dept hist, 67-70; Alumni prof Hist, 70-88, PROF EMER, 88- , UNIV KY, 70-, Guggenheim Found fel, 60-61; Harold Keith Johnson vis prof mil hist, US Army Mil Hist Inst, 81-82; vis prof Mil Hist, US Mil Acad, 85-86 & 91-92. **HONORS AND AWARDS** La Lit Award, 57; Dept of Army: Outstanding Civilian Serv Medal; Comdr Award Public Serv; Declaration Distinguished Civilian Serv. **MEMBERSHIPS** Kentucky Hist Soc; Southern Hist Asn (pres, 80-81). **RESEARCH** Civil War; modern South; Old South. **SELECTED PUBLICATIONS** Auth, Louisiana Sugar Plantations During the American Civil War, E J Brill, 57; The Confederacy, Univ Chicago, 60; Albert Sidney Johnston: Soldier of Three Republics, Univ Tex, 64; coauth, A History of the South, Knopf, 72; The Improbable Era: The South Since World War II, Univ Press Ky, 75; ed, New Perspectives on the South, Univ Press Ky; An American Iliad: The Story of the Civil War, McGraw-Hill, 91; Reflections on Lee: A Historians Assessment, Stackpole Books, 95. **CONTACT ADDRESS** 814 Sherwood Dr, Lexington, KY, 40502.

ROLATER, FREDERICK STRICKLAND
PERSONAL Born 07/22/1938, McKinney, TX, m, 1960 **DISCIPLINE** AMERICAN HISTORY, HISTORIOGRAPHY **EDUCATION** Wake Forest Univ, BA, 60; Univ Southern Calif, MA, 63, PhD, 70 **CAREER** Assoc prof soc sci, Blue Mountain Col, 63-64; assoc prof hist & soc sci & chmn dept, Grand Canyon Col, 64-67; asst prof, 67-70, assoc prof, 70-80, dir grad studies, Dept Hist, 72-80, PROF HIST, MID TENN STATE UNIV, 80-. **HONORS AND AWARDS** Fulbright lectr, Japan, 87; Comnr, Southern Baptist Hist Comn, 84-92. **MEMBERSHIPS** Tenn Hist Soc; West Tenn Hist Soc; Southern Baptist Hist Soc; Tenn Baptist Hist Comt (chmn). **RESEARCH** History of the American Indian; Tennessee history; Public administration during the American Revolution. **SELECTED PUBLICATIONS** Auth, Charles Thomson, Prime Minister of the United States, Penn Mag Hist & Biogr, 7/77; The Doctor of Arts Degree and its Development at MTSU, in Proceedings of the Fifth Intl Conf on Improving Univ Teaching, 79; The Time They Cried (in Japanese), J Am Studies (Japan), 88; Japanese Americans, Rourke Press, 91; The American Indian and the Origin of the Second American Party System, Wis Mag Hist, spring 93. **CONTACT ADDRESS** Middle Tennessee State Univ, Box 336, Murfreesboro, TN, 37132-0001. **EMAIL** frolater@mtsu.edu

ROLLER, MATTHEW B.
PERSONAL Born 07/27/1966, Denver, CO **DISCIPLINE** CLASSICS, ROMAN STUDIES **EDUCATION** Stanford Univ, BA, 88; Univ Cal-Berkeley, MA, 90; PhD, 94. **CAREER** Asst prof of Classics, Johns Hopkins Univ, 94-; Mellon fel Hum, 88-90 and 93; Mellon Diss fel, 92 & 94. **MEMBERSHIPS** Am Philol Asn; Archaeol Inst Am; Class Asn Atlantic Stud. **RESEARCH** Latin literature; Roman social and cultural history; Graeco-Roman philosophy. **SELECTED PUBLICATIONS** Auth Ethical Contradiction and the Fractured Community in Lucan's Bellum Civile, Class Antiquity, 96; Colorblindness: Cicero's death, declamation, and the production of history, Class Philol, 97; Pliny's Catullus: the politics of literary appropriation, Transactions of the Am Philol Asn; 98. **CONTACT ADDRESS** Dept of Classics, Johns Hopkins Univ, 3400 N Charles St, Baltimore, MD, 21218-2690. **EMAIL** mroller@jhu.edu

ROLLINGS, WILLARD H.
DISCIPLINE HISTORY **EDUCATION** Tex Tech Univ, PhD, 83. **CAREER** Assoc prof, Univ Nev Las Vegas. **MEMBERSHIPS** Native American history; ethnohistory. **SELECTED PUBLICATIONS** Auth, An Ethnohistorical Study of Hegemony on the Prairie Plains, Columbia, 92; The Comanche, Univ NY, 89. **CONTACT ADDRESS** History Dept, Univ Nev Las Vegas, 4505 Md Pky, Las Vegas, NV, 89154.

ROMAN, ERIC
PERSONAL Born 03/26/1926, Bekescsaba, Hungary, m, 1953, 2 children **DISCIPLINE** MODERN HISTORY, WESTERN PHILOSOPHY **EDUCATION** Hunter Col, BA, 58; NY Univ, MA, 59, PhD(Hist), 65. **CAREER** From instr to assoc prof, 65-77, prof Hist, Western Conn State Univ, 77-. **HONORS AND AWARDS** Americanism Medal, Nat Daughters Am Revolution, 70. **MEMBERSHIPS** AHA. **RESEARCH** Modern German history; immediate origins of World War II; diplomacy of interwar period. **SELECTED PUBLICATIONS** Auth, The Best Shall Die, Prentice-Hall, 61, Davies, London, 61 & Plaza & Janes, Madrid, 64; After the Trial, Citadel, 68 & Carl Scherz, Berne, 69; Munich and Hungary, Eastern Europ Quart, 74; Will, Hope and the Noumenon, J Philos, 2/75; A Year as a Lion, Stein & Day, 9/78; Hungary and the Victor Powers, New York, St Martin's Press, 96. **CONTACT ADDRESS** 181 White St, Danbury, CT, 06810-6826. **EMAIL** romane@wsu.ctstateu.edu

ROMANO, SUSAN
DISCIPLINE FINE ARTS AND HUMANITIES **EDUCATION** Univ TX at Austin, MA, PhD. **CAREER** Asst prof, Univ TX at San Antonio. **HONORS AND AWARDS** Ellen Nold awd, 93. **RESEARCH** Introduction of electronic conferencing to writing classrooms and the attendant transformations in writing pedag. **SELECTED PUBLICATIONS** Publ on, gender, ethnicity, idea of equity in electronic environ, writing prog admin, composition res on the World Wide Web. **CONTACT ADDRESS** Col of Fine Arts and Hum, Univ Texas at San Antonio, 6900 N Loop 1604 W, San Antonio, TX, 78249.

ROMANS, J. THOMAS
PERSONAL Born 12/26/1933, Yonkers, NY, m, 1979, 2 children **DISCIPLINE** ECONOMICS **EDUCATION** Cornell Univ, BS 55; Univ Tenn, MS 57; Brown Univ , PhD 63. **CAREER** State Univ of NY Buffalo, assoc prof. **HONORS AND AWARDS** New Eng Pub Prize **MEMBERSHIPS** AEA **RESEARCH** Law & Economics; Reg Economics. **SELECTED PUBLICATIONS** Auth, Incomplete Markets and the Calculation of Economic Loss, coauth, in: Jour of Forensic Econ, 96; The Annals of the Latin American Debt Crisis, coauth, in: Jour of For Ex and Intl Fin, 94; The Estimation of Retirement Age in the Calculation of Earning Loss, coauth, in: Jour of Leg Econ, 93. **CONTACT ADDRESS** Dept of Economics, SUNY, Buffalo, Amherst, NY, 14260. **EMAIL** roman@acsu.buffalo.edu

ROMER, F.E.
PERSONAL Born 02/24/1946, Brooklyn, NY, s **DISCIPLINE** CLASSICS **EDUCATION** NY Univ, BA, 68; Stanford Univ, MA, 71, PhD, 74. **CAREER** Asst prof, Univ Vt, Sept 74-jun 75; asst prof, Oh State Univ, Sept 77-jun 78; asst prof, Johns Hopkins Univ, Jul 78-jun 86; book rev ed, The Amer Jour of Philol, Jan 82-dec 86; assoc prof, Hobart and William Smith Col, Jul 86-jun 91; assoc prof, Univ Ariz, Aug 91-. **HONORS AND AWARDS** Sch of Hist Studies, Inst for Adv Study, Princeton, Aug 86-jun 87; jr fel, Ctr for Hellenic Studies, Sept 84-jun 85; Stanford Univ dissertation prize in humanities, Jun 74; NY Univ Maitland prize in classics, may 68. **MEMBERSHIPS** Amer Philol Asn; Archaeol Inst of Amer; Asn of Ancient Hist; Class Asn of the Midwest and South. **RESEARCH** Greek and Roman intellectual history, literature, and religion; Historical analysis for archaeological excavations at Chianciano Terme and Lugnano, Italy. **SELECTED PUBLICATIONS** Auth, Pomponius Mela's Description of the World, Univ Mich Press, 98; article, Good Intentions and the ..., The City As Comedy: Society and Representation in Athenian Comedy, Univ NC Press, 51-74, 97; article, Diagoras the Melian, CW, 89, 393-401, 95/96; article, Atheism, Impiety, and the Limos Melios at Aristoph, Birds, 186, AJP, 115, 351-365, 94; article, Pliny, Vesuvius, and the Troublesome Wind, CW, 78, 587-591, 85; article, A Case of Client-Kingship, AJP, 106, 75-100, 85; article, When is a Bird Not a Bird?, TAPA, 113, 135-142, 83; article, The Aesymneteia: A Problem in Aristotle's Historical Method, AJP, 103, 25-46, 82; article, Gaius Caesar's Military Diplomacy in the East, TAPA, 109, 199-214, 79; article, A Numismatic Date for the Departure of C. Caesar?, TAPA, 108, 187-202, 78. **CONTACT ADDRESS** Dept. of Classics - ML 371, Univ of Arizona, Tucson, AZ, 85721-0067. **EMAIL** feromer@u.arizona.edu

ROMEY, WILLIAM DOWDEN
PERSONAL Born 10/26/1930, Richmond, IN, m, 1955, 3 children **DISCIPLINE** GEOLOGY AND GEOGRAPHY **EDUCATION** IN Univ, AB, 52; Univ CA, Berkeley, PhD, 62. **CAREER** Asst to assoc prof, geology and science ed, Syracuse Univ, 62-69; exec dir, Earth Science Educational Progs, Am Geological Inst, 69-72; prof geology, 71-83, dept chair, 71-76, prof geography and dept chair, St Lawrence Univ, 83-93, prof Emeritus, 93-. **HONORS AND AWARDS** Phi Beta Kappa; Nat Science Found Science fac fel, Univ of Oslo, 67-68. **MEMBERSHIPS** Nat Asn Geoscience Teachers (pres, 73); Geological Soc Am (fel); Am Asn for Advancement of Science (fel); Geological Soc of Norway; Asn of Am Geographers; Can Geographers Asn; Nat Coun for Geog Ed; Am Geophysical Union; Int Asn for Volcanology and Chemistry of..... **RESEARCH** Literature and geography; art and geography and geology; the geology of travel; volcanology; structural geology. **SELECTED PUBLICATIONS** Auth, Consciousness and Creativity: Transcending Science, Humanities, and the Arts, Ash Lad Press, 75; Confluent Education in Science, Ash Lad Press, 76; Teaching the Gifted and Talented in the Science Classroom, Nat Ed Asn, 80; The Effects of Volcanoes on the Landscapes and Peoples of the Americas, in T Martinson and S Brooker-Gross, eds, Revisiting the Americas: Teaching and Learning the Geography of the Western Hemisphere, Nat Coun for Geographic Ed, 92; Teaching Geology Through a Porthole-Opportunities on a World Cruise, J of Geological Ed, vol 42, 94; Teaching Geography Aboard Ship, proceedings, meeting of the New England-St Lawrence Valley Geographical Soc (Nesval), vol 23, 94; Plus Ca Change...: For the Love of France, Ash Lad Press, 96; Volcanoes in Kamchatka, GSA Today, vol 6, no 4, April 96; Stop-off at Tristan da Cunha: Focus, Am Geographical Soc, Aug 98. **CONTACT ADDRESS** PO Box 294, East Orleans, MA, 02643.

ROMM, JAMES S.
DISCIPLINE GREEK HISTORIOGRAPHY, GREEK PROSE LITERATURE **EDUCATION** Princeton, PhD. **CAREER** Vis assoc prof, Fordham Univ. **SELECTED PUBLICATIONS** Auth, The Edges of the Earth in Ancient Thought: Geography, Exploration, and Fiction, Princeton, 92; Strabo, Greek Authors, Dictionary of Lit Biog, 97. **CONTACT ADDRESS** Dept of Class Lang and Lit, Fordham Univ, 113 W 60th St, New York, NY, 10023.

ROMO, RICARDO
PERSONAL Born 06/23/1943, San Antonio, TX, m, 1967, 2 children **DISCIPLINE** UNITED STATES SOCIAL HISTORY **EDUCATION** Univ Tex, Austin, BS, 67; Loyola Univ, Los Angeles, MA, 70; Univ Calif, Los Angeles, PhD, 75. **CAREER** Teacher social studies, Franklin High Sch, Los Angeles, 67-70; asst prof hist, Calif State Univ, Northridge, 70-73; asst prof hist, Univ Calif, San Diego, 73-80; Assoc Prof Hist, Univ Tex, Austin, 80-, Vice-Provost Undergrad Studies, 93-. **HONORS AND AWARDS** Chancellor's Distinguished Lectureship, Univ Calif, Berkeley, Spring 85; Fel, Ctr for Advanced Studies in the Behavioral Studies, Stanford Univ, 89-90. **MEMBERSHIPS** Nat Asn Chicano Studies; AHA; Orgn Am Historians; Am Asn Higher Educ; Tex State Hist Asn; Inst Latin Am Studies. **RESEARCH** American southwest; 20th century social history of the United States. **SELECTED PUBLICATIONS** Coauth, New Directions in Chicano Scholarship, Monographs in Chicano Studies No. 1, Ctr for Chicano Studies, Univ Calif, Santa Barbara, 84; co-ed, The Mexican Origin Experience in the United States, Social Science Quart, Vol 65, No 2, 84; auth, East Los Angeles: History of a Barrio, Univ Tex Press, 83, 4th printing, 92; author of numerous articles and book chapters. **CONTACT ADDRESS** Office of the Exec Vice Pres and Provost, Univ of Tex at Austin, Main Building 201, Austin, TX, 78712-1026.

RONEY, JOHN B.
DISCIPLINE HISTORY **EDUCATION** Univ Toronto, PhD, 89. **CAREER** Assoc prof, Sacred Heart Univ . **RESEARCH** Early Mod and Mod France and the Low Countries (1500-1900); historiography: Reformation, Calvinism, Catholicism, Romanticism, French Revolutionary Europe; relig and soc. **SELECTED PUBLICATIONS** Auth, The Inside of History: Jean Henri Merle d'Aubigne and Romantic Historiography, Greenwood, 96. **CONTACT ADDRESS** Sacred Heart Univ, 5151 Park Ave, Fairfield, CT, 06432. **EMAIL** ChengW@sacredheart.edu

RONNICK, MICHELE VALERIE
DISCIPLINE CLASSICS, GREEK, LATIN **EDUCATION** Boston Univ, PhD, 90. **CAREER** ASSOC PROF, DEPT OF CLASSICS, WAYNE STATE UNIV. **HONORS AND AWARDS** Award For Teaching Excellence, APA, 97; Award for Outstanding State VP, Classical Asn of the Middle West and South, 96; Award for the Most Significant Project, Vanderbilt Univ, 96; Incentive Award for Younger Scholars, Classical and Modern Literature, 94. **MEMBERSHIPS** Int Soc for the Classical Tradition; APA; Classical Asn of the Middle West and South; Classical Asn of the Atlantic States; Am Asn of Neo-Latin Studies. **RESEARCH** Latin literature; Classical tradition; Classical studies & people of African descent. **SELECTED PUBLICATIONS** Auth, Substructural Elements of Architectonic Rhetoric and Philosophical Thought in Fronto's Epistles, Roman Persuasion, 97; Aratus, Dictionary of Literary Biography: Ancient Greek Authors, Gale Research Co, 97; Cicero's Paradoxa Stoicorum: A Commentary, an Interpretation, and a Study of Its Influence, 91; referee, Bos, Fur, Sus, atque Sacerdoes: Additional Light on Kaiser's Solution of a Minor Mystery, Proceedings of the Mass Hist Sco, 95; Concerning the Dramatic Elements in Milton's Defensiones: Theater Without a Stage, Classical and Modern Lit, 95; Seneca's Medea and Ultima Thule in Poe's Dream-land, Poe Studies/Dark Romanticism, 94; David Paul Brown's Sertorius or The Roman Patriot (1830): Another Influence on John Wilkes Booth, J of Am Culture, 96; Seneca's Epistle 12 and Emerson's Circles, Emerson Soc Papers, 96; Further Evidence Concerning the Origin of Cromwell's Title Lord Protector: Milton's Pro Se Defensio, Cromwelliana, 97; After Lefkowitz and Bernal: Research Opportunities in Classica Africana, The Negro Hist Bull, 97. **CONTACT ADDRESS** Dept of Classics, Wayne State Univ, 431 Manoogian Hall, Detroit, MI, 48202.

ROOF, WADE CLARK
DISCIPLINE SOCIOLOGY **EDUCATION** Univ NC, PhD, 71. **CAREER** Asst prof, prof, Univ Mass; J.F. Rowny Prof, relig & soc, Univ Calif, Santa Barbara. **MEMBERSHIPS** Soc Sci Stud of Relig. **RESEARCH** Religion **SELECTED PUBLICATIONS** Auth, A Generation of Seekers: the Spiritual Journeys of the Baby Boom Generation, Harper San Francisco, 93; auth, Americans and Their Spiritual Quests: Reshaping the Religious Landscape, Princeton Univ Press, 99. **CONTACT ADDRESS** Dept Religious Studies, Univ of California Santa Barbara, Santa Barbara, CA, 93106. **EMAIL** wcroof@humanities.UCSB.edu

ROOP, EUGENE F.
PERSONAL Born 05/11/1942, South Bend, IN, m, 1963, 2 children **DISCIPLINE** HISTORY; BIBLE; OLD TESTAMENT/HEBREW BIBILE **EDUCATION** Manchester Col, BS, 64; Bethany Theological Seminary, MDiv 67; Claremont Graduate Univ, PhD, 72. **CAREER** Prof of Old Testament, 70-

77, Earlham Sch of Relig; prof of Biblical Studies, 77-92, president, 72- , Bethany Theological Seminary. **HONORS AND AWARDS** Wieaud professor of biblical studies, Bethany Theological Seminary; ordained minister, Church of the Brethren. **MEMBERSHIPS** Soc of Biblical Lit **RESEARCH** Narrative lit in the Hebrew bible. **SELECTED PUBLICATIONS** Coauth, A Declaration of Peace, 90; authm Master Dreamer, The Bible Today, January, 90; auth, Heard in Our Land, 91; auth, Let The Rivers Run, 91; auth, Esther, Covenant Bible Series, 97; auth, Commentary on Ruth, Jonah, and Esther, forthcoming. **CONTACT ADDRESS** Bethany Theol Sem, 615 National Rd W, Richmond, IN, 47374-4019. **EMAIL** roopge@earlham.edu

ROOSEVELT, A.C.
PERSONAL Born 05/24/1946, Glen Cove, NY **DISCIPLINE** HISTORY **EDUCATION** Stanford Univ, BA, 68; Columbia Univ, MA, 74, PhD, 77. **CAREER** Prof of Anthrop, 94-, Univ of Illinois; Curator of Archaeol, 91-, Field Museum of Natural Hist. **HONORS AND AWARDS** Order of Rio Branco; Bettendorf Medal; Explorers Medal; Fellow, Amer Acad of Art and Sci. **MEMBERSHIPS** AAA, AAAS, AAA&S, NYAS, RGS, SWG, AES, SAA. **RESEARCH** Human ecology & evolution, tropical forests, African neo-tropics. **SELECTED PUBLICATIONS** Ed, Amazonian Indians: From Prehistory to the Present, Arizona; Moundbuilders of the Amazon: Geophysical Archaeology on Marajo Island, Brazil, Parmana: Prehistoric Maize and Manioc Subsistence along the Amazon and Orinoco, Academic Press; co-ed, The Ancestors: Native Artisans of the Americas, Washington; Excavations at Corozal: Stratigraphy and Ceramic Seration, Yale Univ Publications in Anthropology; Articles in; Science, The Sciences, Nature, Natural History, Man, L'homme, Advances in Computer Archaeology, Food and Evolution. **CONTACT ADDRESS** 1028 Judson Ave, Evanston, IL, 60202.

ROOT, DEANE LESLIE
PERSONAL Born 08/09/1947, Wausau, WI, m, 1972, 2 children **DISCIPLINE** MUSIC, MUSICOLOGY **EDUCATION** Univ IL, Urbana, PhD, 77, M mus, 71; New Col, Sarasota, FL, BA, 68. **CAREER** Prof, Music, Univ Pittsburgh, 98-; Curator, Foster Hall Collection, 82-; Instr, Lake City Comm Col, FL, 81-82; Research Assoc, Univ IL, 76-80; ed, New Grove Dict Music Musicians, 74-76; Lectr, Univ WI, 73. **HONORS AND AWARDS** Am Lib Asn, Choice Award, 91-92; Music Lib Asn Award, 81; Hon Pi Kappa Lambda, 72; Woodrow Wilson Fellow, 68. **MEMBERSHIPS** Am Musicological Soc; Sonneck Soc Am Music; Music Lib Asn; Am Studies Asn. **RESEARCH** Am Music; Am Musical Theater; Music Bibliography; Am Pop Culture. **SELECTED PUBLICATIONS** The Music of Florida Historic Sites, Tallahassee: The FL State Univ Sch of Music, 83; Resources of American Music History: A Diary of Source Materials from Colonial Times to WW II, gen ed, co auth, with D W Krummel, Jean Geil, Doris J Dyen, Urbana, Chicago, London, Univ Press, 81; American Pop Stage Music, 1860- 1880, Ann Arbor, MI, UMI Res Press, 81, ppbk, 83; The Sketchbook of Stephen Collins Foster, in progress; Nineteen Cent American Musical Theater, gen ed, Deane L Root, 16 vols, NY, London, Garland Pub, 94; The Music of Stephen C Foster: A Critical Edition, ed with Steven Saunders, 2 vols, WA, London, Smithsonian Inst Press, 90; Music Research in Nineteen Cent Theater or the Case of a Burlesquer a Baker and a Pantomime Maker, Vista of American Music, Essays Compositions in Honor of William Kearns, ed Susan L Porter John Graziano, ch 13, pp181-96, Warren, MI, Harmonie Pk Press, expected 98; The Voices that are Gone: Themes in Nineteen Cen American Pop Song, by Jon W Finson, J Am Musicological Soc, XLIX/3, 96; The Stephen Foster-Antonin Dvorak Connection, Dvorak in America, 1892-1895, ed by John C Tibbets, ch 18,pp243-54, Portland OR, Amadeus Press, 93; The Mythstory of Stephen C Foster, Why His True Story Remains Untold, the Am Music Research Cen J I, 91; The Pan American Association of Composers, 1928-34, Yearbook for Inter-American Music Research VIII, 72. **CONTACT ADDRESS** Univ Pittsburgh, Center for Am Music, Pittsburgh, PA, 15260. **EMAIL** dlr@pitt.edu

RORLICH, AZADE-AYSE
DISCIPLINE HISTORY **EDUCATION** Univ Wisconsin, PhD, 76. **CAREER** Assoc prof, Univ Southern Calif. **RESEARCH** 19th and 20th Century Russia and Soviet Union Nationalities; Russian and Soviet Islam; Modern European Intellectual. **SELECTED PUBLICATIONS** Auth, The Volga Tartars, Hoover Inst, 86. **CONTACT ADDRESS** Dept of History, Univ Southern Calif, University Park Campus, Los Angeles, CA, 90089. **EMAIL** arorlich@usc.edu

ROSAND, DAVID
PERSONAL Born 09/06/1938, Brooklyn, NY, m, 1961, 2 children **DISCIPLINE** ART HISTORY **EDUCATION** Columbia Univ, BA, 59, PhD(art hist), 65. **CAREER** From instr to assoc prof, 64-73, prof art hist, 73-95, Meyer Schapiro Prof Art Hist, Columbia Univ, 95-; Nat Endowment for Humanities younger scholar fel, 71-72, fel for independent study, 85-86, 91-92; Am Coun Learned Socs grant-in-aid, 70 & 77; Fulbright travel grant, 71-72; John S Guggenheim Mem Found fel, 74-75; Rockefeller Found Bellagio Study Center fel, 92. **HONORS AND AWARDS** Premio Cultura, Citta di Bassano del Grappa, 92; Great Teacher Award, Soc of Columbia Graduates, 97. **MEMBERSHIPS** Col Art Asn Am; Renaissance Soc Am; Ateneo Veneto, Venice. **RESEARCH** History of drawings and prints; Renaissance and baroque art; Venetian painting; theory and criticism. **SELECTED PUBLICATIONS** Coauth, Titian and the Venetian Woodcut, Int Exhibs Found, 76; auth, Titian, Abrams, 78; Painting in Cinquecento Venice: Titian, Veronese, Tintoretto, Yale, 82; The Meaning of the Mark: Leonardo and Titian, Spenser Museum, 88; coauth, Places of Delight: The Pastoral Landscape, Philips Collection and National Gallery of Art, 88; coauth, Robert Motherwell on Paper: Drawings, Prints, Collages, Abrams, 97. **CONTACT ADDRESS** Dept of Art Hist & Archaeol, Columbia Univ, 826 Schermerhorn Hall-mail code 5517, New York, NY, 10027. **EMAIL** dr17@columbia.edu

ROSE, BRIAN
DISCIPLINE ART HISTORY AND ARCHAEOLOGY **EDUCATION** Haverford Col, BA, 78; Columbia Univ, MA, 80, MPhil, 82, PhD, 87. **CAREER** Asst Prof, Univ Cincinnati, 87-94; Assoc prof, Univ Cincinnati, 94-. **HONORS AND AWARDS** McMicken Dean's Award; Max Planck Res Prize; Storer Found Grant; NEH Matching Three-Year Grant Troy Excavation Proj; Helen M. Woodruff Fel; Samuel H. Kress Fel. **MEMBERSHIPS** Archaeol Inst Am; Am Res Inst in Turkey. **SELECTED PUBLICATIONS** Auth, The Theater of Ilion, Studia Troica 1, 91; auth, Greek and Roman Excavations at Troy, l991, Studia Troica 2, 92; auth, Greek and Roman Excavations at Troy, l992, Studia Troica 3, 93; auth, Greek and Roman Excavations at Troy 1993, Studia Troica 4, 94; auth, Greek and Roman Excavations at Troy 1994, Studia Troica 5, 95; auth, Greek and Roman Excavations at Troy 1995, Studia Troica 6, 96; auth, Dynastic Commemoration and Imperial Portraiture in the Julio-Claudian Period, Cambridge Univ Press, 97. **CONTACT ADDRESS** Dept of Classics, Univ Cincinnati, PO Box 0226, Cincinnati, OH, 45210-0226. **EMAIL** brian.rose@uc.edu

ROSE, GILBERT PAUL
PERSONAL Born 08/06/1939, New York, NY, m, 1961, 2 children **DISCIPLINE** GREEK & LATIN LITERATURE **EDUCATION** Univ CA, Berkeley, Ab, 63, PhD, 69. **CAREER** From instr to assoc prof, 67-81, Prof Classics, Swarthmore Col, 81-; Vis asst prof, OH State Univ, 69; vis assoc prof, Univ CA, Berkeley, 79. **HONORS AND AWARDS** Old Dominion Found fel, 70-71; Mellon Found fel, 74-75; Am Philol Asn Award for Excellence in the Tchg of the Classics, 83. **MEMBERSHIPS** Am Philol Asn. **RESEARCH** Homer; Greek tragedy; Latin epic poetry. **SELECTED PUBLICATIONS** Auth, The Quest of Telemachus, 67, The Unfriendly Phaeacians, 69 & Odyssey 15 143-82: A Narrative Inconsistency?, 71 & Odysseus' Barking Heart, 79, Trans Am Philol Asn; The Swineherd and the Beggar, Phoenix, 80; ed, Plato's Crito, Bryn Mawr Commentaries, 80; Plato's Symposium, Bryn Mawr Commentaries, 81; auth, Plato's Republic, Book I, Bryn Mawr Commentaries, 83; Sophocle's Oedipus at Colonus, Bryn Mawr Commentaries, 88; Plato's Apology, Bryn Mawr Commentaries, 89. **CONTACT ADDRESS** Dept of Class, Swarthmore Col, 500 College Ave, Swarthmore, PA, 19081-1306. **EMAIL** grose1@swarthmore.edu

ROSE, J.
PERSONAL Born 11/27/1952, New York, NY, m, 1995, 1 child **DISCIPLINE** HISTORY **EDUCATION** Princeton Univ, BA 74; Univ Penn, MA 75, PhD 81. **CAREER** Drew Univ, asst prof, assoc prof, ch grad prog, dir grad prog, 84 to 98-; editor Book History 97-. **HONORS AND AWARDS** Res Gnts from: NEH, APS, BIUS, AHA, ESU. **MEMBERSHIPS** SHA; NVSA; AHA; RSVP. **RESEARCH** Modern British intellectual history; the history of the book. **SELECTED PUBLICATIONS** Auth, The Intellectual Life of the British Working Class 1750-1945, in progress; The Holocaust and the Book: Destruction and Preservation, ed, in progress; The Edwardian temperament, 1895-1919, Athens, Ohio Univ Press, 86; the History of Books: revised and Enlarged, Studies on Voltaire and the Eighteenth Century, 98; Marx Jane Eyre Tarzan: Miners' Libraries in South Wales, 1923-1952, Leipziger Jahrbuch zur Buchgeschichte, 94; How Historians Study Reading, in: Literature in the Marketplace, eds, John O. Jordan, Robert Patten, Cambridge, Cambridge Univ Press, 95; Working-Class Journals, in: Vict periodicals and Vice Society, eds Rosemary VanArsdel, J. Don Vann, Toronto Univ Press, 94. **CONTACT ADDRESS** Dept of History, Drew Univ, Madison, NJ, 07940. **EMAIL** jerose@drew.edu

ROSE, LEO E.
PERSONAL Born 01/02/1926, Hanford, CA **DISCIPLINE** POLITICAL SCIENCE **EDUCATION** Univ CA, Berkeley, PhD 51. **CAREER** Himalayan Border Countries Project, 62-69; Adjunt Prof 70-97; Univ CA, Berkeley, Editor Asian Survey 62-67. **RESEARCH** South Asian Politics; International rels. **CONTACT ADDRESS** Dept of Polit Sci, Univ California, Berkeley, CA, 94720. **EMAIL** rosel@socrates.berkeley.edu

ROSE, MARK
DISCIPLINE HISTORY **EDUCATION** Ohio State Univ, PhD. **CAREER** Prof. **RESEARCH** 20th century American history. **SELECTED PUBLICATIONS** Auth, Cities of Light and Heat: Domesticating Gas and Electricity in Urban America, 95; pubs in Technology and Culture; Journal of Policy History. **CONTACT ADDRESS** History Dept, Florida Atlantic Univ, 777 Glades Rd, Boca Raton, FL, 33431. **EMAIL** mrose@fau.edu

ROSE, PAUL L.
PERSONAL Born 02/26/1944, Glasgow, Scotland, m, 1969, 4 children **DISCIPLINE** HISTORY **EDUCATION** Oxford, BA, MA, 68; Parus-Sorbonne, PhD, 73. **CAREER** Lectr, UCLA, 68-69; res assoc, Univ Toronto, 69-70; instr, St. Johns, 70-71; asst prof, NYU, 71-74; aps fel, Cambridge Univ, 74-75; res prof, James Cook Univ, 74-84; prof, Univ Maita, 83-92; prof, Pa State Univ, 92-. **HONORS AND AWARDS** Fel of the Royal Hist Soc; Inst Adv Stud, Princeton; Robarts prof, 90-92, York Univ. **RESEARCH** German history; intellectual history; Jewish studies. **SELECTED PUBLICATIONS** Auth, The Italian Renaissance of Mathematics. Studies on Humanists and Mathematicians from Petrarch to Galileo, 75; auth, Bodin and the Great God of Nature: The Moral and Religious Universe of a Judaiser, 80; auth, German Question/Jewish Question. Revolutionary Antisemitism in Germany from Kant to Wagner, 90; auth, Wagner: Race and Revolution, 96; auth, Heisenberg and the Nazi Atomic Bomb Project, 1939-1945: A Study in German Culture, 98. **CONTACT ADDRESS** Dept of History, Pennsylvania State Univ, Weaver 108, University Park, PA, 16802. **EMAIL** plr2@psu.edu

ROSE, PETER WIRES
PERSONAL Born 05/13/1936, Paterson, NJ **DISCIPLINE** CLASSICS **EDUCATION** Williams Col, BA, 57; Harvard Univ, MA, 58, PhD, 67. **CAREER** Lectr, 63-66, Yale Univ; asst prof, 66-71, assoc prof, 71-77, Univ Texas Austin; fac mem, 77-80, prof, 80-, chmn, classics dept, 80-, Miami Univ. **RESEARCH** Homer Greek tragedy; Pindar and Greek lyric poetry. **CONTACT ADDRESS** Dept of Classics, Miami Univ, Oxford, OH, 45056.

ROSELL, GARTH M.
PERSONAL m, 3 children **DISCIPLINE** CHURCH HISTORY **EDUCATION** Wheaton Col, BA; Princeton Theol Sem, MDiv, 64, ThM, 66; Univ Minn, PhD, 71. **CAREER** Instr, Bethel Theol Sem; acad dean, 78; prof, Gordon-Conwell Theol Sem -; dir, Ockenga Inst. **MEMBERSHIPS** Mem, Assn Theol Sch(s); Boston Theol Inst. **SELECTED PUBLICATIONS** Co-auth, The Memoirs of Charles G. Finney: The Complete Restored Text, Zondervan, 89; American Christianity, Eerdmans, 86; The Millionaire and The Scrublady and Other Parables by William E. Barton, Zondervan, 90; auth, Shoeleather Faith, Bruce, 62; Cases in Theological Education, ATS, 86. **CONTACT ADDRESS** Gordon-Conwell Theol Sem, 130 Essex St, South Hamilton, MA, 01982.

ROSEN, DAVID
DISCIPLINE MUSIC **EDUCATION** Reed Col, BA, 60; Univ Calif at Berkeley, MA, 64, PhD, 76. **CAREER** Prof **HONORS AND AWARDS** Amer Coun Learned Societies, Grant-in-Aid, 85; Nat Endowment for the Humanities felp for Independent Study and Res, 79; Amer Philos Soc Grant-in-Aid, 77; Martha Baird Rockefeller Found Grant-in-Aid, 68-69; Woodrow Wilson fel, 60-61. **MEMBERSHIPS** Exec bd, Amer Inst Verdi Stud; Fondo Ruggero Leoncavallo, Consiglio scientifico; Amer Musicol Soc. **RESEARCH** Verdi; music in 19th-century Italy; opera theory and criticism; Mozart. **SELECTED PUBLICATIONS** Auth, Verdi: Requiem, Cambridge Music Handbooks, Cambridge: Cambridge UP, 95; Critical edition of Verdi's Messa da Requiem, in The Works of Giuseppe Verdi, ser III, v 1, Chicago and London; Milan: Univ Chicago Press and Ricordi, 90; eter, Character, and Tinta in Verdi's Operas, in Verdi's Middle Period: Source Studies, Analysis, and Performance Practice 1849-1859, Chicago and London: Univ Chicago Press, 97; Unexpectedness' and 'Inevitability' in Mozart's Piano Concertos, in Mozart's Piano Concertos: Text, Context, Interpretation, Ann Arbor: Univ Mich Press, 96; Reprise as Resolution in Verdi's Requiem, Theory and Practice 19, 94; Cone's and Kivy's 'World of Opera', Cambridge Opera J 4, 92; How Verdi's Serious Operas End, in Atti del XIV Congresso della Societa internazionale di musicologia, Turin: EDT, 90; co-ed, Verdi's Macbeth: A Sourcebook, NY: Norton, 84; **CONTACT ADDRESS** Dept of Music, Cornell Univ, 104 Lincoln Hall, Ithaca, NY, 14853. **EMAIL** dbr2@cornell.edu

ROSEN, RUTH E.
PERSONAL Born 07/25/1945, m, 1996, 2 children **DISCIPLINE** HISTORY **EDUCATION** Univ of Rochester, Ba, 67; Univ of Calif at Berkely, MA, 69, PhD, 76. **CAREER** FULL PROF, HIST DEPT, UNIV OF CALIF AT DAVIS, 74-. **HONORS AND AWARDS** Distinguished teaching award; visiting scholar, European Peace Univ. **MEMBERSHIPS** Rockefeller Gender Roles Fel; Am Hist Asn; Bershire Confr on Women's Hist; Org of Am Historians. **RESEARCH** U.S. History, post 1945; Cold War culture; public policy; media; gender & culture; immigration. **SELECTED PUBLICATIONS** Auth, The

Maimie Papers, 78, 96; auth, The Lost Sisterhood, 82; auth, Through Their Own Eyes, forthcoming. **CONTACT ADDRESS** Dept of Hist, Univ of Calif, Davis, CA, 95616. **EMAIL** rerosen@ucdavis.edu

ROSEN, STANLEY H.
PERSONAL Born 07/29/1929, Warren, OH, m, 1955, 3 children **DISCIPLINE** SOCIAL THOUGHT **EDUCATION** Univ Chicago, BA, 49, PhD, 55. **CAREER** 55-93, Evan Pugh prof, 86-93, Penn State Univ; Borden Parker Bowne prof, 93- , Boston Univ. **HONORS AND AWARDS** Pres, Metaphysical Soc of Amer **MEMBERSHIPS** APA; MSA. **SELECTED PUBLICATIONS** Auth, The Question of Being, 93; auth, The Mask of Enlightenment, 95; auth, Plato Statermen, 95; auth, Metaphysics In Ordinary Language, 99. **CONTACT ADDRESS** Philosophy Dept, Boston Univ, 745 Commonwealth Ave, Boston, MA, 02215. **EMAIL** srosen@acs.bu.edu

ROSENBERG, BRUCE
PERSONAL Born 07/27/1934, New York, NY, m, 1981, 4 children **DISCIPLINE** ENGLISH; FOLKLORE **EDUCATION** Hofstra Univ, BA, 55; Pa State Univ, MA, 62; Ohio State Univ, PhD, 65. **CAREER** Instr English, Univ Wis-Milwaukee, 62; asst prof, Univ Calif, Santa Barbara, 65-67 & Univ Va, 67-69; prof English & comp lit, Pa State Univ, 69-77; prof English lit & American Civilization, Brown Univ, 77-. **HONORS AND AWARDS** Am Coun Learned Soc fel, 67-68; James Russell Lowell Prize, 70; Nat Endowment for Humanities fel, 72-73; Guggenheim fel, 82-83; **MEMBERSHIPS** MLA; Folklore Fel Int; Am Folklore Soc. **RESEARCH** Middle English literature; folklore; comparative literature. **SELECTED PUBLICATIONS** Auth, Annus Mirabilis distilled, PMLA, 6/64; Wandering Angus & Celtic renaissance, Philol Quart, fall 67; Lord of the fire Flies, Centennial Rev, winter 67; ed, The Folksongs of Virginia, Univ Va, 69; auth, The Art of the American Folk Preacher, Oxford Univ, 70; co-ed, Medieval Literature and Folklore Studies, Rutgers Univ, 71; auth, Custer and the Epic of Defeat, Penn State, 75; The Code of the West, Ind Univ, 82; Teh Neutral Ground, 94. **CONTACT ADDRESS** Dept English, Brown Univ, 82 Waterman St, Providence, RI, 02912-0001. **EMAIL** AC401000@brown.edu

ROSENBERG, EMILY SCHLAHT
PERSONAL Born 07/21/1944, Sheridan, WY, m, 1966, 4 children **DISCIPLINE** AMERICAN HISTORY, INTERNATIONAL RELATIONS **EDUCATION** Univ NE, BA, 66; State Univ NY Stony Brook, MA, 69, PhD, 73. **CAREER** Asst prof, Honors Prog, Cent Mich Univ, 73-74; asst prof, 74-80, assoc prof, Macalester Col, 80-85; prof hist, 86-93; Dewitt Wallace prof, 93-, Stanford prof hist, San Diego State Univ, 96-97. **HONORS AND AWARDS** Phi Beta Kappa, 66, AAUW Fel, 71-72; NEH Fel, 83-84; SSRC Fel, 91-92; Burlington-Northern Tchg Award, 93; Thomas Jefferson Award, 94. **MEMBERSHIPS** OHA; AHA; SHAFR. **RESEARCH** 20th century US for rel(s); US cult and economic rel(s). **SELECTED PUBLICATIONS** Auth, Dollar Diplomacy under Wilson: An Ecuadoran Case, Inter-American Econ Affairs, 71; Co-auth, America: A Portrait in History, Prentice-Hall, 73, rev ed, 78; World War I and Continental Solidarity, The Americas, 75; Economic Pressures in Anglo-American Diplomacy in Mexico, 1917-18, Jour of Inter-Am Studies and World Affairs, 75; Co-ed, Postwar America: Readings and Reminiscences, Prentice-Hall, 76; Anglo-American Economic Rivalry in Brazil during World War I, Diplomatic Hist, 78; Emergency Executive Controls over Foreign Comerce and United States Economic Pressure on Latin American during World War I, Inter-Am Econ Affairs, spring 78; Spreading the American Dream: American Economic and Cultural Expansion, 1890-1945, Hill and Wang, 82; Foundations of United States International Financial Power: Gold Standard Dipolmacy, 1900-1905, Bus Hist Rev, 85; The Invisible Protectorate: The United States, Liberia and the Evolution of Neocolonialism, 1909-1940, Diplomatic Hist, 85; World War I and the Growth of United States Predominance in Latin America, Garland, 86; Co-auth, From Colonialism to Professionalism: The Public-Private Dynamic in United States Foreign Financial Policy, 1898-1930, Jour Am Hist, 87; Gender in A Round Table: Explaining the History of American Foreign Relations, Jour Am Hist, 90; Walking the Borders, Diplomatic Hist, 90; Signifying the Vietnam Experience, Rev in Am Hist, 91; Walking the Borders, In: Explaining the History of American Foreign Relations, Cambridge Univ Press, 91; The Rocky Mountain West: Region in Transit, Mont Bus Quart, 92; NSC-68 and Cold War Culture, In: American Cold War Strategy: Interpreting NSC 68, St. Martin's Press, 93; The Cold War and the Discourse of National Security, Dplomatic Hist, 93; A Century of Exporting the American Dream, In: Exporting America: Essays on American Studies Abroad, Garland, 93; Economic Interest and US Foreign Policy, In: American Foreign Relations Reconsidered, Routledge, 94; Foreign Affairs after World War II: Connecting Sexual and International Politics, Diplomatic Hist, 94; Cultural Interactions, In: The Encyclopedia of the United States in the Twentieth Century, Scribners, 96; A Call to Revolution: A Roundtable on Early U.S. Foreign Relations, Diplomatic Hist, 98; Revisiting Dollar Diplomacy: Narratives on Money and Manliness, Diplomatic Hist, 98; Co-auth, In Our Times: America since 1945, Prentice-Hall, rev ed, 99; Co-auth, Liberty, Equality, Power: A History of the American People, Harcourt-Brace, rev ed, 99. **CONTACT ADDRESS** 1600 Grand Ave, Saint Paul, MN, 55105-1899. **EMAIL** rosenberg@macalester.edu

ROSENBERG, JONATHAN
DISCIPLINE HISTORY **EDUCATION** Harvard Univ, PhD. **CAREER** Asst prof. **MEMBERSHIPS** Am Hist Asn. **RESEARCH** 20th century American history; political history; race relations. **SELECTED PUBLICATIONS** Auth, pubs on race relations and international history. **CONTACT ADDRESS** History Dept, Florida Atlantic Univ, 777 Glades Rd, Boca Raton, FL, 33431. **EMAIL** rinaldi@acc.fau.edu

ROSENBERG, NORMAN LEWIS
PERSONAL Born 02/15/1942, Lincoln, NE, m, 1966, 4 children **DISCIPLINE** AMERICAN HISTORY **EDUCATION** Univ NE-Lincoln, BA, 64, MA, 67; State Univ NY Stony Brook, PhD, 72. **CAREER** Asst prof, Cent MI Univ, 71-74; from asst prof to assoc prof, 74-85, prof hist, Macalester Col, 86-93, Dewitt Wallace Prof, 93-; Mem fac, Dept Jour, Univ Calif, Berkeley, 76; San Diego State, 96-97, Univ MN, 98. **HONORS AND AWARDS** Phi Beta Kappa, 64; SUNY fel, 67-70; Burlington-Northern Distinguished Teaching Award, 93. **MEMBERSHIPS** Am Soc Legal Hist; Am Hist Assoc; Org Am Hist. **RESEARCH** US legal-constitutional hist; US 20th century; US popular cult and media. **SELECTED PUBLICATIONS** Auth, Protecting the Best Men: An Interpretive History of the Law of Libel, Univ NC Press, 90; Perry Mason: Above But Not Beyond the Law, In: Prime Time Law, 98; Law Noir, In: Legal Reelism, Univ Ill Press, 96; Professor Lightcap Goes to Washington: Re-reading Talk of the Town, Univ of San Francisco Law Rev, 96; The Popular First Amendment and Classical Hollywood, 1930-1960, In: Freeing the First Amendment, NYU Press, 95; Young Mr Lincoln: The Lawyer as Super-Hero, Legal Studies Forum, 91; Gideon's Trumpet: Sounding the Retreat from Legal Realism, In: Recasting America, Univ Chicago Press, 88; co-auth, In Our Times: America Since 1945, Prentice-Hall, 6th ed, 99; Liberty, Equality, Power: A History of the United States, 2nd ed, Harcourt Brace, 99; America Transformed, Harcourt Brace, 99; From Colonialism to Professionalism: The Public-Private Dynamic in U S Foreign Financial Advising, 1898-1929, Jour Am Hist, 87. **CONTACT ADDRESS** Dept of Hist, Macalester Col, 1600 Grand Ave, Saint Paul, MN, 55105-1899. **EMAIL** rosenbergn@macalester.edu

ROSENBERG, ROSALIND NAVIN
PERSONAL Born 06/15/1946, Boston, MA, m, 1967, 2 children **DISCIPLINE** AMERICAN HISTORY **EDUCATION** Stanford Univ, BA, 68, PhD(hist), 74. **CAREER** Asst prof Am hist, Columbia Univ, 74-82; Asst prof AM Hist, Wesleyan Univ, 82-. **MEMBERSHIPS** AHA; Orgn Am Historians. **RESEARCH** Women's hist; intellectual hist; legal hist. **SELECTED PUBLICATIONS** Auth, Beyond Separate Spheres: Intellectual Roots of Modern Feminism, Yale Univ Press, 82, Divided Lives: American Women in the Twentieth Century, 92; Pauli Murray and the Killing of Jane Crow, in Forgotton Heroes of the Past, 98. **CONTACT ADDRESS** 1192 Park Ave, 8A, New York, NY, 10028. **EMAIL** rosenberg@barnard.columbia.edu

ROSENBLOOM, JOSEPH R.
PERSONAL Born 12/05/1928, Rochester, NY, m, 1952, 3 children **DISCIPLINE** MIDDLE EASTERN HISTORY **EDUCATION** Univ Cincinnati, BA, 50; Hebrew Union Col, OH, BHL, 52, MHL, 54, DHL(hist), 57; Eden Theol Sem, St Louis, MO, 73. **CAREER** Instr Mid Eastern hist, Univ KY, 57-61; adj prof classics, Washington Univ, 61-; Am Philos Soc grant, 65. **HONORS AND AWARDS** DD, Hebrew Union Col, 79. **MEMBERSHIPS** AHA; Am Orient Soc; Am Asn Mid E Studies. **RESEARCH** Hebrew language and culture. **SELECTED PUBLICATIONS** Auth, Biographical Dictionary of Early American Jewry, Univ, KY, 60; Notes on Chinese Jewry, Chicago Jewish Forum, fall 60; An Ancient Controversy and its Modern Effects, America, 4/64; A Literary Analysis of the Dead Sea Isaiah Scroll, Eerdmans, 68; Social Science Concepts and Biblical History, J Am Acad Relig, 12/72; Conversion to Judaism, Hebrew Union Col Press, 78. **CONTACT ADDRESS** Dept Asian Languages & Lit, Washington Univ, Box 1111, Saint Louis, MO, 63130-4899.

ROSENBLUM, ROBERT
PERSONAL Born 07/24/1927, New York, NY, 2 children **DISCIPLINE** HISTORY OF ART **EDUCATION** Queens Col, BA, 48; Yale Univ, MA, 50; NY Univ, PhD, 56; Oxford Univ, MA, 71. **CAREER** Instr hist art, Univ Mich, 55-56; from instr to asst prof, Princeton Univ, 56-66; prof fine arts, NY Univ, 66-, Vis asst prof, Columbia Univ, 60-63; Am Coun Learned Soc fel, 62-63; Slade Prof fine arts, Oxford Univ, 72. **HONORS AND AWARDS** Frank Jewell Mather Award, 81. **RESEARCH** Contemporary art; neoclassic and romantic art and architecture. **SELECTED PUBLICATIONS** Auth, Cubism and Twentieth Century Art, 60 & Ingres, 67, Abrams; Transformations in Late Eighteenth Century Art, Princeton Univ, 67; Frank Stella, Penguin, 71; Modern Painting and the Northern Romatic Tradition: Friedrich to Tothko, Harper, 75; 19th-Century Art, Abrams, 84; Paintings in the Musee d'Orsay, Stewart, Tabon, Chang, 89; The Jeff Koons Handbook, Thames and Hudson, 92. **CONTACT ADDRESS** Dept of Fine Arts, New York Univ, 100 Washington Sq E, New York, NY, 10003-6688.

ROSENOF, THEODORE DIMON
PERSONAL Born 09/15/1943, Newark, NJ, m, 1985, 2 children **DISCIPLINE** AMERICAN HISTORY **EDUCATION** Rutgers Univ, BA, 65; Univ WI, MA, 66, PhD(hist), 70. **CAREER** Vis instr hist, TX Tech Univ, 75-76, vis asst prof, 76-77; vis asst prof, Pan Am Univ, 77-78; res assoc, Univ WI, 78-79; asst prof, 79-84, assoc prof, 84-89, prof hist, Mercy Col, 89-. **MEMBERSHIPS** Am Hist Asn; Orgn Am Historians. **RESEARCH** Political and economic analysis since 1929. **SELECTED PUBLICATIONS** Auth, The Political Education of an American Radical: Thomas R Amlie in the 1930's, autumn 74, Wis Mag Hist; Freedom, Planning and Totalitarianism: The Reception of F A Hayek's Road to Serfdom, Can Rev Am Studies, fall 74; Dogma, Depression and the New Deal: The Debate of Political Leaders Over Economic Recovery, Kennikat Press, 75; The American Democratic Left Looks at the British Labour Government 1945-1951, The Historian, 11/75; Patterns of Political Economy in America: The Failure to Develop a Democratic Left Synthesis 1933-1950, Garland Publ, 83; New Deal Pragmatism and Economic Systems: Concepts and Meanings, The Historian, 5/87; Economics in the Long Run: New Deal Theorists and Their Legacies, 1933-1993, Univ NC Press, 97. **CONTACT ADDRESS** Dept Hist & Polit Sci, Mercy Col, 555 Broadway, Dobbs Ferry, NY, 10522-1189.

ROSENSTONE, ROBERT ALLAN
PERSONAL Born 05/12/1936, Montreal, PQ, Canada, m, 1997 **DISCIPLINE** AMERICAN HISTORY **EDUCATION** Univ Calif, Los Angeles, BA, 57, PhD(hist), 65. **CAREER** Vis asst prof Hist, Univ Ore, 65-66; from asst prof to assoc prof, 66-76, prof Hist, Calif Inst Technol, 76-, Am Philos Soc travel grant, 70; vis prof Am Studies, Kyushu Univ & Seinan Gakuin Univ, Fukuoka, Japan, 74-75; Fulbright-Hays sr lectr, Japan, 74-75; Nat Endowment Humanities sr fel, 81-82; res fel, East-West Ctr, Honolulu, fall 81; vis scholar, Doshisha Univ, Kyoto, Japan, spring 82. **HONORS AND AWARDS** Silver Medal Lit Award, Commonwealth Club Calif, 76. **MEMBERSHIPS** AHA; Orgn Am Historians; Fulbright Alumni Asn. **RESEARCH** Radical movements; cultural history; biography. **SELECTED PUBLICATIONS** Auth, Protest from the Right, Glencoe, 68; Crusade of the Left: The Lincoln Battalion in the Spanish Civil War, Pegasus, 69; ed, Seasons of Rebellion: Protest and Radicalism in Recent America, Holt, 73; coauth, Los cantos de la conmocion: Veinte anos de rock, Tusquets, 74; auth, The counter culture in America, Am Studies Newslett, Tokyo, 5/75; Romantic Revolutionary: A Biography of John Reed, Knopf, 75, Ital transl, Riuniti, Rome, 76, Fr transl, Maspero, Paris, 77, Span transl, Ediciones Era, Mexico City, 79, Kossuth, Budapest, 80; Mabel Dodge: Evenings in New York, In: The Genius in the Drawing Room: The Salon in Europe and America from the 18th to the 20th Century, Widenfeld & Nicolson, London, 80; Learning from those imitative Japanese: Another side of the American experience in the Mikado's empire, Am Hist Rev, 6/80. **CONTACT ADDRESS** Div Humanities & Soc Sci, California Inst of Tech, 1201 E California, Pasadena, CA, 91125-0002. **EMAIL** rr@ucs.caltech.edu

ROSENTHAL, ANGELA
DISCIPLINE ART HISTORY **EDUCATION** Trier Univ, PhD. **CAREER** Asst prof, Dartmouth Col. **RESEARCH** Eighteenth-century Eng art and cult. **SELECTED PUBLICATIONS** Auth, She's Got the Look!: Eighteenth-Century Female Portrait Painters and the Psychology of a Potentially 'Dangerous Employment' in Portraiture: Facing the Subject, Manchester UP, 97; Double-Writing in Painting in Strategien der Selbstdarstellung von Kunstlerinnen im 18. Jahrhundert, Kritische Berichte, 93; Kauffman and Portraiture in Angelika Kauffman: a Continental Artist in Georgian England, Reaktion Bks, 92; Angelica Kauffman Ma(s)king Claims, Art Hist, 92; Die Zeichnungen der Angelika Kauffmann im Vorarlberger Landesmuseum in Bregenz, Jahrbuch des Vorarlberger Landesmuseumsvereins, Bregenz, 90; var other articles. **CONTACT ADDRESS** Dartmouth Col, 3529 N Main St, #207, Hanover, NH, 03755. **EMAIL** angela.rosenthal@dartmouth.edu

ROSENTHAL, LISA
DISCIPLINE RENAISSANCE AND BAROQUE ART **EDUCATION** Univ Calif, Berkeley, PhD. **CAREER** Asst prof **HONORS AND AWARDS** J Paul Getty postdoc fel. **RESEARCH** Representation of family and gender and its relationship to philosophical and political discourse in the Early Modern period, especially Peter paul Rubens. **SELECTED PUBLICATIONS** Publ, articles in Amer and Brit sch jour(s) on seventeenth-century Dutch and Flemish art. **CONTACT ADDRESS** Dept of Art, Wichita State Univ, 1845 Fairmont, Wichita, KS, 67260-0062.

ROSENWEIN, BARBARA HERSTEIN
PERSONAL Born 03/01/1945, Chicago, IL, m, 1966, 2 children **DISCIPLINE** MEDIEVAL HISTORY **EDUCATION** Univ Chicago, BA, 66, MA, 68, PhD(hist), 74. **CAREER** From instr to Assoc Prof, 71-88, PROF HIST, LOYOLA UNIV OF CHICAGO, 88-. **HONORS AND AWARDS** NEH Fel, 86-87, 97-98; Guggenheim Fel, 92. **MEMBERSHIPS** AHA; Mediaeval Acad Am. **RESEARCH** Medieval religion and society; medieval culture; Cluny. **SELECTED PUBLICATIONS** Coauth, Saint Maeul, Cluny et la Provence: Expansion d'une abbaye

l'aube du Moyen Age, Les Alpes de LumiSre, Mane 94; La question de l'immunit¤ clunisienne, Bulliten de la Societe¤ des Fouilles archeologiques et des monuments historiques de l'Yonne, no 12, 95; The Family Politics of Berengar I, Speculum 71, 96; Friends and Family, Politics and Privilege in the Kingship of Berengar I, In: Portraits of Medieval and Renaissance Living: Essays in Memory of David Herlihy, Univ Mich Press, 96; L'espace clos: Gregoire et l'exemption episcopale, In: Gregoire de Tours et l'espace gaulois, actes du congress international, Tours, 3-5 November 1994, 13th supplement to Revue Archeologique du Centre de la France, Tours, 97; Association through Exemption: St. Denis, Salonnes and Metz, In: Vom Kloster zum Klosterverband: Das Werkzeug der Schriftlichkeit, Wilhelm Fink, 97; Negotiating Space: Power, Restraint, and Privileges of Immunity in Early Medieval Europe, Cornell Univ Press, 98; Cluny's Immunities in the Tenth and Eleventh Centuries: Images and Narratives, In: Die Cluniazenser in ihrem politisch-sozialen Umfeld, Monster, 98; ed, Anger's Past: The Social Uses of an Emotion in the Middle Ages, Cornall Univ Press, 98; co-ed, Debating the Middle Ages: Issues and Readings, Blackwell (in press). **CONTACT ADDRESS** Dept of History, Loyola Univ, 6525 N Sheridan Rd, Chicago, IL, 60626-5385. **EMAIL** brosenw@cpua.it.luc.edu

ROSENZWEIG, ROY
PERSONAL Born 08/06/1950, New York, NY, m, 1981 **DISCIPLINE** HISTORY **EDUCATION** Columbia Col, BA, 71; res student, St. John's Col Cambridge Univ, 71-73; Harvard Univ, PhD, 78. **CAREER** Asst prof, Worcester Polytechnic Inst, 78-80; Mellon Postdoctoral Fel, Wesleyan Univ, 80-81; from asst prof to assoc prof to prof, 81-98, distinguished prof, 81-, George Mason Univ. **HONORS AND AWARDS** James Harvey Robinson Prize, Am Hist Asn; Interactive Media Festival Award; Urban Hist Asn Prize; Abel Wolman Prize; Abbott Cumming Lowell Prize, Vernacular Architecture Forum; Hist Preservation Book Prize, Ctr for Hist Preservation. New York His Asn Award; NEH Grants; Kellogg Found Grant; Fulbright Commission; John Simon Guggenheim Memorial Found Fel; Forrest G. Pogue Award; Albert J. Beveridge Res Grant, AHA; Distinguished Fac Award, GMU. **SELECTED PUBLICATIONS** Auth, Eight Hours for What We Will: Workers and Leisure in an Industrial City, 1870-1920, 83; coauth, The Park and the People: A History of Central Park, 92; coauth, art, Historians and the Web: A Guide, 96; coauth, art, Brave New World or Blind Alley? American History on the World Wide Web, 97; coauth, The Presence of the Past: Popular Uses of History in American Life, 98. **CONTACT ADDRESS** Dept of History, George Mason Univ, Fairfax, VA, 22030. **EMAIL** rrosenzw@gmu.edu

ROSIN, ROBERT L.
PERSONAL Born 02/12/1951, Lexington, MO, m, 1975 **DISCIPLINE** HISTORICAL THEOLOGY **EDUCATION** Concordia Tchrs Col, BA, 72; Concordia Sem, MDiv, 76; Stanford Univ, MA, 77, PhD, 86. **CAREER** From instr to assoc prof, 81-97, prof hist theol, 97- , chemn dept, 95- , Concordia Sem; guest instr, Martin Luther Sem, Papua New Guines, 83; actg dir lib services, 88-90, fac marshal, 89-97, ed, Concordia Sem Publ, 95- ; Exec dir Center for Reformation Res, 97- . **MEMBERSHIPS** Soc for Reformation Res; Sixteenth-Century Stud Conf; Renaissance Soc of Am; Luther-Gesellschaft; Am Soc of Church Hist; Lutheran Hist Conf; Am Friends of the Herzog August Biliothek. **RESEARCH** Reformation and education/curriculum in the sixteenth century. **SELECTED PUBLICATIONS** Auth, Christians and Culture: Finding Place in Clio's Mansions, in, Christ and Culture: The Church in Post-Christian(?) America, Concordia Sem, 96; auth, Bringing Forth Fruit: Luther on Social Welfare, in Rosin, ed, A Cup of Cold Water: A Look at Biblical Charity, Concordia Sem, 97; auth, Reformers, The Preacher, and Skepticism: Luther, Brenz, Melanchthon, and Ecclesiastes, Verlag Philipp von Zabern, 97. **CONTACT ADDRESS** Concordia Sem, 801 DeMun Ave, St. Louis, MO, 63105. **EMAIL** rosinr@csl.edu

ROSIVACH, VINCENT JOHN
PERSONAL Born 05/08/1940, Jersey City, NJ **DISCIPLINE** CLASSICAL PHILOLOGY **EDUCATION** Fordham Univ, AB, 61, MA, 64, PhD(classics), 66. **CAREER** Adj instr Latin, Sch Educ, Fordham Univ, 63-64; from instr to assoc prof, 65-76, Prof Classics, Fairfield Univ, 76-. **MEMBERSHIPS** Am Philol Asn; Class Asn New Eng. **RESEARCH** Greek and Roman drama; Greek history. **SELECTED PUBLICATIONS** Auth, Plautine stage settings, Trans & Proc Am Philol Soc, 70; Manuscripts of Matthias Corvinus in the Barberini Collection, Manuscripta, 71; Terence, Adelphoe 155-9, Class Quart, 73; Terence, Adelphoe 60-63, Class Philol, 75; The first stasimon of the Hecuba, Am J Philol, 75; Sophocles' Ajax, Class J, 76; Hector in the Rhesus, Hermes, 77; Earthborns and Olympians: The parodos of the Ion, Class Quart, 77; The System of Public Sacrifice in Fourth Century Athens, Scholars Press, 94; When a Young Man Falls in Love: The Sexual Exploitation of Women in New Comedy, Routledge, 98. **CONTACT ADDRESS** Greek and Roman Studies, Fairfield Univ, 1073 N Benson Rd, Fairfield, CT, 06430-5195. **EMAIL** Rosivach@fair1.fairfield.edu

ROSKILL, MARK
PERSONAL London, England, m, 3 children **DISCIPLINE** ART HISTORY **EDUCATION** Trinity Col, BA, 56, MA, 61; Harvard Univ, MA, 57; Princeton Univ, PhD, 61. **CAREER** Prof, 73-. **RESEARCH** English painting; Victorian studies; European art of 19th and 20th centuries; history of photography; theory of modern art; contemporary art; criticism of modern art. **SELECTED PUBLICATIONS** Auth, What is Art History?, 89; The Interpretation of Cubism, 85; The Interpretation of Pictures, 89; Klee, Kandinsky and the Thought of their Time: A Critical Perspective, 92; The Languages of Landscape, 97; co-auth, Truth and Falsehood in Visual Images, 83. **CONTACT ADDRESS** Art History Dept, Univ of Massachusetts, Amherst, 720 Massachusetts Ave, Amherst, MA, 01003. **EMAIL** mroskill@arthist.umass.edu

ROSNER, DAVID
DISCIPLINE UNITED STATES HISTORY **EDUCATION** Univ Mass, MS; Harvard Univ, PhD. **CAREER** Prof. **SELECTED PUBLICATIONS** Auth, Children, Race, and Power: Kenneth and Mamie Clark's Northside Center,Univ Va, 96; co-auth, Deadly Dust: Silicosis and the Politics of Occupational Disease in Twentieth Century America, Princeton Univ, 94; co-ed, Hives of Sickness, Rutgers, 95; Health Care in America: Essays in Social History: Dying for Work, Ind Univ, 87; Slaves of the Depression, Cornell Univ, 87. **CONTACT ADDRESS** Dept of History, Columbia Col, New York, 2960 Broadway, New York, NY, 10027-6902.

ROSNER, STANLEY
PERSONAL Born 07/06/1928, Yonkers, NY, m, 1955, 4 children **DISCIPLINE** PSYCHOLOGY **EDUCATION** New School for Social Research, Phd, 56. **CAREER** Clinical Psycologist-Private Practice. **HONORS AND AWARDS** Outstanding contribution to state Psychological Affairs; American Psychological Assoc. **MEMBERSHIPS** American Psychological Assoc; CT Psych Assoc; National Academy of Neuropsychology; Int Society Neuropsych. **RESEARCH** Psychoanalysis. **SELECTED PUBLICATIONS** Ophthalmology, optometry and learning difficulties, J. Learning Disabilities,1(8) p17-19, 68; Opthalmology, optometry and learning disabilities, J. Pediatric Opthalmomogy, p82-85; Emotional aspects of intensive care, J. Contemporary Psychotherapy, 6(1), p62-66, 72; Some aspects of marriage and divorce in Israel, Interaction 3(1), with Tamar Cohen, 80; Further considerations of the internalization process, Dynamic Psychhtherapy,1(2) p149-158, 83; Analytic neutrality, stimulus ambiguity and the projective hypothesis, Dynamic Psychotherapy 6(1) p51-54, 88; Pine's Four Psychologies of Psychoanalysis and the Rorschach Psychoanalysis and Psychotherapy 8(2) p103-118, 90; In preparation: The Family on the job. **CONTACT ADDRESS** Counseling and Psychotherapy Group, 1305 Post Rd., Fairfield, CT, 06430.

ROSNOW, RALPH LEON
PERSONAL Born 01/10/1936, Baltimore, MD, m, 1963 **DISCIPLINE** PSYCHOLOGY **EDUCATION** BS, Univ MD, 53-57; MA, George Wash Univ, 57-58; PhD Experimental Soc Psychol, Am Univ, 60-62. **CAREER** Asst Prof of Cumm Res Boston Univ, 63-67; Assoc Prof, 67-70, Prof Psychol, Temple Univ, 70-82, Thaddeus L Boltonj Prof of Psychol, 82-; Dir Div of Soc & Org Psychol; Vis Prof of London School Of Econ & Poli Sci, 73; Vis Prof Psychol, Harvard Univ, 74, 88-89. **HONORS AND AWARDS** Fel of AAAS, APA, APS; James McKeen Cattell Fel in Applied Arts; APS; Psi Chi Distinguished Lectr EPA; APA Invited Address in Gn Psychol Div. **MEMBERSHIPS** Am Assoc for the Advan of Sci; Am Psychol Assoc Div 1,2,5,8,24; Comm on Standards in Res Ch; Am Psychol Soc EPA; Soc of Experimental Soc Psychol. **SELECTED PUBLICATIONS** With Edward J Robinson eds, Experiments in Persuasion, NY:Academic Press, 67; with Robert Rosenthal, eds, Artifact in Behavioral Research, NY, Academic Press, 69; with Robert Rosenthal, Beginning Behavioral Research: A Conceptual Primer, NY: Macmillan, 93; with Mimi Rosnow, Writing Papers in Psychology: A Student Guide 3rd ed, Pacific Groves, CA: Brooks/Cole, 95; With Robert Rosenthal, Beginning Behavioral Research: A Conceptual Primer, 2nd ed, Upper Saddle River, NJ: Prentice Hall, 96; with Mimi Rosnow, Writing Papers in Psychology:Student Guide, 4th ed, Pacific Groves, CA, Brooks/Cole, 98. **CONTACT ADDRESS** Temple Univ, 517 Weiss Hall, Philadelphia, PA, 19122. **EMAIL** rrosnow@nimbus.ocis.temple.edu

ROSS, DAVID
DISCIPLINE MUSIC **EDUCATION** Oberlin Conservatory Music, PhD. **CAREER** Univ Ark-Monticello **MEMBERSHIPS** Int Clarinet Soc. **SELECTED PUBLICATIONS** Auth, pubs on eighteenth century clarinet and its literature. **CONTACT ADDRESS** Dept of Music, Texas Univ, El Paso, TX, 79968. **EMAIL** dross@utep.edu

ROSS, DOROTHY RABIN
PERSONAL Born 08/13/1936, Milwaukee, WI, m, 1958, 2 children **DISCIPLINE** AMERICAN HISTORY **EDUCATION** Smith Col, AB; Columbia Univ, MA, 59, PhD, 65. **CAREER** Res fel psychiat & hist psychiat, 65-67, Payne Whitney Clin, Med Col, Cornell Univ; res fel hist psychol, 67-68, lectr hist, 71, George Washington Univ; asst prof, 72-78, Princeton Univ; assoc prof, prof, 78-90, Univ Va, Charlottesville; spec asst to secy, 77, HEW; mem adv comt, 78-80, Prog Hist, Nat Sci Found; mem adv coun, 80-84, Prog Am Soc & Polit, Woodrow Wilson Ctr; Arthur O Lovejoy Prof Hist, 90-, chmn, dept hist, 93-96, Johns Hopkins Univ; exec bd, Orgn Am hist, 87-89; bd ed, 92-, Intl Hist Ideas; **HONORS AND AWARDS** Natl Sci Found res fel, 80-81; fel Ctr for Advanced Stud in Behavioral Sci, Stanford, 92-93; Elect, Soc of Am Hist, 93; fel Woodrow Wilson Intl Ctr for scholar, DC, 96-97; Spencer Found Mentor Award, 97-99. **MEMBERSHIPS** AHA; Orgn Am Historians; Int Soc Hist Behav & Soc Sci; Hist Sci Soc; Am Studies Assn. **RESEARCH** American intellectual, social and behavioral sciences history. **SELECTED PUBLICATIONS** Auth, Historical Consciousness in the 19th Century America, AHR 89, 84; auth, The Origins of American Social Science, Cambridge Univ Press, 91; ed, Modernist Impulses in the Human Sciences, 1870-1930, Johns Hopkins Univ Press, 94; auth, Grand Narrative in American Historical Writing, AHR 100, 95. **CONTACT ADDRESS** 2914 33rd Pl NW, Washington, DC, 20008. **EMAIL** ross_dr@jhunix.hcf.jhu.edu

ROSS, ELLEN
PERSONAL Born 06/06/1942, Detroit, MI, m, 1991, 2 children **DISCIPLINE** HISTORY **EDUCATION** Univ Chicago, BA, 64; Columbia Univ, MA, 65; Univ Chicago, PhD, 75. **CAREER** Asst prof, Conn Col, 71-76; asst prof, Ramapo Co., 76-82; assoc prof, 82-91; prof, 92- . **HONORS AND AWARDS** Phi Beta Kappa, 64; Woodrow Wilson Fel, 64-65; NEH fel, 90-91. **MEMBERSHIPS** Am Hist Asoc; Berkshire Conf of Women Hist. **RESEARCH** Britain, 1870-1940; social history. **SELECTED PUBLICATIONS** Co-auth with Rayna Rapp, Sex and Society: Notes from the Intersection of Anthropology and Social History, Comparative Studies in Soc and Hist, 81; auth, Love and Toil: Motherhood in Outcast London 1870-1918, 93; auth, Human Commnion or a Free Lunch: School Dinners in Victorian and Edwardian London, Giving: Western Ideas of Philanthropy, 96; auth, Lady Explorers In Darkest London, 98; auth, Ladies Write the London Slums, The Historical Archeology of Urban Slums, 99. **CONTACT ADDRESS** School of Social Sciences, Ramapo Col, New Jersey, Mahwah, NJ, 07430. **EMAIL** eross@ramapo.edu

ROSS, MARILYN A.
PERSONAL Born 09/06/1946, New York, NY, s **DISCIPLINE** CLASSICAL PHILOLOGY **EDUCATION** Cornell Univ, PhD, 73. **CAREER** Assoc prof and assoc dean of the col, Wells Col; assoc prof and asst to the pres, Sweet Briar Col; pres, Ross Associates. **HONORS AND AWARDS** Phi Beta Kappa. **MEMBERSHIPS** Am Philol Asoc. **CONTACT ADDRESS** 6324 Burning Tree Terrace, Fayettevielle, PA, 17222. **EMAIL** maross@mail.cvn.net

ROSS, RONALD JOHN
PERSONAL Born 09/24/1935, St. Paul, MN, m, 1971 **DISCIPLINE** MODERN EUROPEAN HISTORY **EDUCATION** Univ MN, Minneapolis, AB, 61, MA, 63; Univ CA, Berkeley, PhD(hist), 71. **CAREER** From instr to asst prof, 68-74, chm dept hist, 76-78, assoc prof, 74-95, prof hist, Univ WI-Milwaukee, 96-. **MEMBERSHIPS** AHA;German Studies Asn. **RESEARCH** Modern German history; political and social history of modern Europe. **SELECTED PUBLICATIONS** Auth, Heinrich Ritter von Srbik and Gesamtdeutsch History, Rev Politics, 1/69; Beleaguered Tower: The Dilemma of Political Catholicism in Wilhelmine Germany, Univ Notre Dame, 76; Critic of the Bismarckian Constitution: Ludwig Windthorst and the Relationship Between Church and State in Imperial Germany, J Church & State, 3/79; Enforcing the Kulturkampf: The Bismarckian State and the Limits of Coercion in Imperial Germany, J Modern Hist, 3/84; Catholic Plight in the Kaiserreich: A Reappraisal, in Another Germany: A Reconsideration of the Imperial Era, Westview, 88; The Kulturkampf and the Limitations of Power in Bismarck's Germany, J Ecclesiastical Hist, 4/95; The Kulturkampf: Restrictions and Controls on the Practice of Religion in Bismarck's Germany, in Freedom and Religion in the Nineteenth Century, Stanford, 97; The Failure of Bismarck's Kulturkampf: Catholicism and the State Power in Imperial Germany, 1871-1887, Catholic Univ Am Press, 98. **CONTACT ADDRESS** Dept Hist, Univ Wisconsin, PO Box 413, Milwaukee, WI, 53201-0413. **EMAIL** rjross@csd.uwm.edu

ROSS, STEPHANIE A.
DISCIPLINE AESTHETICS, FEMINISM **EDUCATION** Smith Col, BA, 71; Harvard Univ, MA, 74, PhD, 77. **CAREER** Assoc prof, Univ Mo, St Louis. **HONORS AND AWARDS** UMSL summer res fel, 78; NEH summer sem, 80; Weldon Spg grant, Univ Mo, St Louis, 81; UMSL summer res fel, 84; trustee, Am Soc for Aesthet, 86-89; Huntington Libr NEH fel, 89; fel, Yale Ctr for Brit Art, 90; Univ Mo Res Bd grant, 94; NEH summer inst, 95. **MEMBERSHIPS** Am Philos Asn; Am Soc for Aesthet; Soc for Women in Philos. **RESEARCH** Misguided marriage. **SELECTED PUBLICATIONS** Auth, Conducting and Musical Interpretation, Brit J of Aesthet, Vol 36, No 1, 96. **CONTACT ADDRESS** Univ Mo, St Louis, St Louis, MO, 63121.

ROSS, STEVEN J.
DISCIPLINE HISTORY **EDUCATION** Princeton Univ, PhD, 80. **CAREER** Prof, Univ Southern Calif. **RESEARCH** U.S., social, labor, popular culture, film history. **SELECTED PUBLICATIONS** Auth, Workers on the Edge: Work, Leisure, & Politics in Industrializing Cincinnati, 1788-1890, Columbia, 85. **CONTACT ADDRESS** Dept of History, Univ Southern Calif, University Park Campus, Los Angeles, CA, 90089. **EMAIL** sjross@bcf.usc.edu

ROSSI, JOHN P.
PERSONAL Born 04/07/1936, Philadelphia, PA, m, 1966, 1 child **DISCIPLINE** MODERN BRITISH HISTORY **EDUCATION** LaSalle Col, BA, 58; Univ Notre Dame, MA, 60; Univ Pa, PhD(19th century Brit hist), 65. **CAREER** Asst instr hist, Univ Pa, 60-62; from instr to assoc prof, 62-75,prof hist, La Salle Col, 75-, chmn dept, 74-81. **MEMBERSHIPS** AHA; Conf Brit Studies; Am Coun Irish Studies; Soc of Am Baseball Research (SABR). **RESEARCH** Internal history of the British Liberal party in 1870's; career of the 1st Marquis of Ripon; British reaction to McCarthyism; career of George Orwell; History of Baseball. **SELECTED PUBLICATIONS** Auth, Orwell's Reception in America, Four Quarters, winter 73; Liberal Leadership and the Second Afghan War, Can J Hist, 9/73; Home Rule and the Liverpool by Election of 1880, Irish Hist Studies, 9/74; Selection of Lord Hartington as Liberal leader, Proc Am Philos Soc, 8/75; Orwell and Catholicism, Commonweal, 6/76; Transformation of the Liberal Party 1873-1880, Transaction Am Philos Soc, 7/78; America's view of George Orwell, Rev Polit, 10/81; Catholic Opinion of the Eastern Question, 1876-1878, Church Hist, 3/82; Farewell to Fellow-Traveling: The Waldorf Conference of March 1949, Continuity, Nu 10, spring 85; Churchill's Iron Curtain Speech: the American Reception, Modern Age, XXX, Nu 2, spring 86; The British Reaction to McCarthyism, LXX, nu i, Mid-America, Jan 88; Orwell and Chesterton, LXIII, nu 251, Thought, Dec 88; A Glorified Form of Rounders: Baseball in Britain February 1914, in Alvin Hall, ed, Cooperstown: Symposium on Baseball and American Culture, 1990, Meckler Press, 91; The Iron Curtain: A Premature Anti-Communist Film, Film and History, XXIV, No 3-4, 101-112, 94; A Baseball Myth Exploded: Bill Veeck and the 1943 Sale of the Phillies, co-authored with David Jordan and Larry Gerlach, The National Pastime: A Review of Baseball History #18, 98; No Golden Age: Baseball from the End of World War II to the First Expansion, 2960, McFarland, 99. **CONTACT ADDRESS** Dept of Hist, LaSalle Univ, 1900 W Olney Ave, Philadelphia, PA, 19141-1199. **EMAIL** Rossi@lasalle.edu

ROSSITER, MARGARET W.
PERSONAL Born 07/08/1944, Malden, MA, s **DISCIPLINE** HISTORY OF SCIENCE & MEDICINE **EDUCATION** Radcliffe Col, Harvard Univ, AB, 66; Univ Wis, MS, 67; Yale Univ, MPhil, 69, PhD, 71; Regis Col, ScD, 97. **CAREER** Actg Asst Prof & Lectr, 73-74, 75-76, Res Assoc, Univ Calif - Berkeley, 76-82; Res Assoc, Am Acad Arts & Sci, 77-86; Dir, Hist & Philos Sci Prog, Nat Sci Found, 82-83; Vis Lectr & Vis Schol, Harvard Univ, 83-86; NSF Vis Prof, 86-88, Prof, 88-93, The Marie Underhill Noll Prof Hist & Sci, Cornell Univ, 93-; Ed, Osiris, 93-; Ed, Isis, 94-. **HONORS AND AWARDS** Silver Medal, Justus-Liebig Univ, 79; Berkshire Prize, 83; Wilbur Cross Medal, Yale Univ Grad Sch, 84; Hoopes Teaching Award, Harvard Univ, 84; Res Prize, Justus-Liebig Univ, 85; Kreeger-Wolf Distinguished Vis Prof, Northwestern Univ, 85; Regents Lectr, Univ Calif - Riverside, 86; Sarton Lectr, Am Asn Advancement Sci, 90; Phi Beta Kappa; Arthur Holly Compton Distinguished Lectr, Wash Univ, 97; Hist of Women in Sci Prize, Hist Sci Soc, 97; Pfizer Prize, Hist Sci Soc, 97; recipient of numerous grants and fellowships. **MEMBERSHIPS** Hist Sci Soc; Am Asn Univ Prof; Int Comn Hist Women Sci, Technol, & Med; Forum Hist Am Sci; Am Chemical Soc; Berkshire Conf Hist Women; Agricultural Hist Soc; Soc Hist Technol; Am Asn Advancement Sci. **RESEARCH** History of women in science; American science; history of agriculture. **SELECTED PUBLICATIONS** Auth, The Emergence of Agricultural Science -- Justus Liebig and the Americans, 1840-1880, Yale Univ Press, 75; Women Scientists in America, Struggles and Strategies to 1940, Johns Hopkins Univ Press, 82; co-ed, Historical Writing on American Science, Johns Hopkins Univ Press, 86; Science at Harvard, 1636-1945, Lehigh Univ Press, 92; auth, Women Scientists in America: Before Affirmative Action, 1940-1972, Johns Hopkins Univ Press, 95; author of numerous articles and other publications. **CONTACT ADDRESS** Cornell Univ, 726 University Ave., #201, Ithaca, NY, 14850. **EMAIL** li10@cornell.edu

ROSZAK, THEODORE
PERSONAL Born 11/15/1933, Chicago, IL, m, 1 child **DISCIPLINE** HISTORY **EDUCATION** UCLA, BA, 55; Princeton Univ, PhD, 58. **CAREER** Stanford Univ, 59-62; Calif State Univ, Hayward, 62-. **HONORS AND AWARDS** Guggenheim Fel, 71-72. **SELECTED PUBLICATIONS** Auth, Flicker, 90, The Memoirs of Elizabeth Frankenstein, 95; The Voice of the Earth, 92; America the Wise, 98. **CONTACT ADDRESS** History Dept, California State Univ, Hayward, Hayward, CA, 94542.

ROTH, JONATHAN
PERSONAL Born 12/06/1955, Redwood City, CA, m, 1993 **DISCIPLINE** ANCIENT HISTORY **EDUCATION** Columbia Univ, PhD, 91. **CAREER** Vis asst prof, Tulane Univ, 90-91; tchg fel, New York Univ, 91-94; asst prof, San Jose State Univ, 94- . **HONORS AND AWARDS** Fulbright-Hayes scholar, 79-80; Dorot fel, 91-94. **MEMBERSHIPS** APA; Soc of Ancient Mil Hist. **RESEARCH** Roman military history. **SELECTED PUBLICATIONS** Coauth, Nine Unpublished Inscriptions in the Collection of Columbia University, Zeitschrift fur Papyrologie und Epigraphik, 88; coauth, Greek Ostraka from Mons Porphyrites, Bull of the Am Soc of Papyrologists, 92; auth, The Size and Organization of the Imperial Roman Legion, Historia, 94; auth, The Length of the Siege of Masada, Scripta Classica Israelica, 95; auth, P.Col.263-264, Sales of Donkeys, in Bagnall, ed, Columbia Papyri X, Columbia Univ, 97; auth, Early Kingdoms of Western Asia and Northern Africa, and Greece, in Stearns, ed, Langer Encyclopedia of World History, Houghton Mifflin, forthcoming; auth, George Willis Botsford, in Kornegay, ed, American National Biography, Oxford Univ, forthcoming; auth, The Logistics of the Roman Army at War, (264 BC-AD 235), EJ Brill, forthcoming. **CONTACT ADDRESS** History Dept, San Jose State Univ, 1 Washington Sq, San Jose, CA, 95192-0117. **EMAIL** jroth@email.sjsu.edu

ROTH, MITCHEL
DISCIPLINE HISTORY **EDUCATION** Univ Md, BA; Univ Calif, Santa Barbara, MA, PhD. **CAREER** Asst prof, Sam Houston State Univ, 95-. **RESEARCH** History of the American west, history of criminal justice. **SELECTED PUBLICATIONS** Auth, Cholera Summer: Independence, St. Joseph, and the Path of Contagion, Gateway Heritage, 95; Courtesy, Service, and Protection: Texas Department of Public Safety, 95; forthcoming, Cholera in Gold Rush-Era San Francisco and Sacramento, Pacific Historical Review; The End of the Texas Outlaw Tradition, East Texas Historical Journal; Historical Dictionary of War Journalism, Greenwood Press. **CONTACT ADDRESS** Dept of History, Sam Houston State Univ, Huntsville, TX, 77341.

ROTH, MOIRA
PERSONAL Born 07/24/1933, London, England, d **DISCIPLINE** ART HISTORY **EDUCATION** New York Univ, BA, 59; Univ Calif, Berkeley, MA, 66, PhD, 74. **CAREER** Asst/assoc prof, Univ Calif, San Diego, 74-85; PROF, ART HIST, MILLS COLL, 85-. **MEMBERSHIPS** Coll Art Asn **RESEARCH** Contemporary American Art; Feminism; Multiculturalism. **SELECTED PUBLICATIONS** edr/contrib, Connecting Conversations: Interviews with 28 Bay area woemn Artists, Eucalyptus Press, 88; edr, We Flew Over the Bridge; the Memoirs of Faith Ringgold, LittleBrown, 95; edr, Rachel Rosenthal, John Hopkins Univ Press, 97. **CONTACT ADDRESS** Art Dept, Mills Col, 5000 MacArthur Blvd, Oakland, CA, 94613.

ROTH, RANDOLPH A.
DISCIPLINE HISTORY **EDUCATION** Stanford, Univ, BA, 73; Yale Univ, PhD, 81. **CAREER** Instr, hist Grinnell; ASSOC PROF, HIST OHIO STATE UNIV **MEMBERSHIPS** Am Antiquarian Soc **SELECTED PUBLICATIONS** Auth, "The First Radical Abolitionists: The Reverend James Milligan and the Reformed Presbyterians of Vermont," New Eng Quart 55, 82; auth, The Democratic Dilemma: Religion, Reform, and the Social Order in Vermont, 1791-1850, 87; auth, "Is History a Process? Revitalization Theory, Nonlinearity, and the Central Metaphor of Social Science History," Soc Sci Hist 16, Summer 92; auth, "The Other Masonic Outrage: The Death and Transfiguration of Joseph Burnham," Jour of the Early Rep 14, Spring 94; auth, "The Generation Conflict Reconsidered," in American Vistas, Oxford Univ Press, 95; auth, "Blood Calls for Vengeance!: The History of Capital Punishment in Vermont," Vermont Hist 65, 97. **CONTACT ADDRESS** Dept of Hist, Ohio State Univ, Columbus, OH, 43210. **EMAIL** roth.5@osu.edu

ROTH, WILLIAM
PERSONAL Born 06/01/1942, New Haven, CT, m, 1994, 1 child **DISCIPLINE** POLITICAL SCIENCE **EDUCATION** Yale Univ, BA, 64; Univ Calif, Berkeley, PhD, 70. **CAREER** Tchng Asst, Univ Calif, 67-68; Instr, San Francisco Art Inst, 69; Instr, Univ Calif, 69-70; Lectuerer, Dartmouth Col, 71; Asst Prof, Univ Vt, 71-72; Sr Res Assoc, Carnegie Counc on Children, 72-76; Res Assoc, Univ Wisc, 76-78; Ch, Dept of Public Aff & Policy, Grad Sch of Pub Aff, 82-84; Assoc, Inst for Govt & Policy Stud, 84-88; Exec Dir for Policy & res, 88-90; Founder & Dir, Ctr for Computing & Disability, SUNY, 84-88; Asn Prof, SUNY, 78-. **RESEARCH** Disability studies, children. **SELECTED PUBLICATIONS** Auth, Disability and Computer Technology, & Society, Disability, and Technology, Disabilities Stud Quart, 92; auth, Personal Computers for Persons with Disabilities, McFarland & Co, Inc, 92; co-auth, Job Analysis and The Americans With Disabilities Act, Business Horizons, Nov/Dec 96. **CONTACT ADDRESS** Dept of Soc Welfare, SUNY, 1400 Washington Ave, Albany, NY, 12222. **EMAIL** wroth@csc.albany.edu

ROTH-BURNETTE, JENNIFER
PERSONAL Born 01/20/1971, Baton Rouge, LA, m, 1995 **DISCIPLINE** MUSICOLOGY **EDUCATION** New York Univ, PhD Musicol; Univ Ala, MM Organ Performance, 94. **HONORS AND AWARDS** Fulbright Grant 94-95. **MEMBERSHIPS** Am Musicol Soc; Am Guild of Organists; Organ Hist Soc; Col Music Soc. **CONTACT ADDRESS** New York Univ, 24 Waverly Pl, Rm 268, New York, NY. **EMAIL** jlr207@is5.nyu.edu

ROTHBLATT, SHELDON
PERSONAL Born 12/14/1934, Los Angeles, CA, m, 1956, 3 children **DISCIPLINE** MODERN ENGLAND, GEORGIAN/VICTORIAN CULTURAL HISTORY **EDUCATION** Univ Calif, Berkeley, BA, 56, MA, 59, PhD(Hist), 65. **CAREER** From instr to assoc prof, 63-74, assoc dir, Ctr Study Higher Educ, 77-82, prof Hist, Univ Calif, Berkeley, 74-, dean Fresh & Soph Studies, Lett & Sci, 82-, King's Col, Cambridge Univ, 61-63; stint prof Hist, Royal Instit Tech, Stockholm, Sweden, 97; Soc Sci Res Coun fac res fel, 66-67; Davis fel, Princeton Univ, 69-70; Guggenheim fel, 72-73; visitor, Nuffield Col, Oxford Univ, 77; scholar in residence, Rockefeller Ctr, Bellagio, 79; Am Coun Learned Soc fel, 81-82. **MEMBERSHIPS** AHA; Conf Brit Studies (pres, Pac Coast Br, 78-80); Hist Educ Soc; Cambridge Hist Soc; Fel Royal Hist Soc. **RESEARCH** University history, elites, professional groups; cultural and intellectual history. **SELECTED PUBLICATIONS** Auth, The Revolution of the Dons: Cambridge and Society in Victorian England, Faber & Faber, London & Basic Bks, 68 & Univ Press, 81; coauth, French lieutenant's women: A discussion, Victorian Studies, Tradition and Change in English Liberal Education, Faber & Faber, 76; Nineteenth-Century London, In: People and Communities in the Western World, Dorsey Press, 79; G M Young: England's Historian of Culture, Victorian Studies, Summer 79; co-ed, The European and American University Since 1800, Cambridge University Press, 93; The Modern University and Its Discontents, Cambridge University Press, 97. **CONTACT ADDRESS** Dept of History, Univ of California, Berkeley, 3229 Dwinelle Hall, Berkeley, CA, 94720-2551.

ROTHENBERG, GUNTHER ERIC
PERSONAL Born 07/11/1923, Berlin, Germany, m, 1952 **DISCIPLINE** CENTRAL & EAST EUROPEAN HISTORY **EDUCATION** Univ Ill, BA, 54, PhD, 58; Univ Chicago, MA, 56. **CAREER** Instr hist, Ill State Normal Univ, 58; asst prof, Southern Ill Univ, 58-62; from assoc prof to prof, Univ NMex, 63-73; PROF MIL HIST, PURDUE UNIV, 73-, Am Philos Soc grants, 61, 65, 67, 70 & 75; Am Coun Learned Soc & Soc Sci Res Coun grants, 62, 68, 73 & 77; Guggenheim fel, 62-63; mem, Hist Evaluation & Res Orgn, 63-68; fel, Interuniv Sem Armed Forces & Soc, 72- **MEMBERSHIPS** AHA; Renaissance Soc Am; Am Asn Advan Slavic Studies; Conf Group Cent Europ Hist; Co Mil Hist. **RESEARCH** Habsburg military history; military history; national security affairs. **SELECTED PUBLICATIONS** Auth, The Austrian Military Border in Croatia, Univ Ill, 60; The Military Border in Croatia, 1740-1881, Univ Chicago, 66; The nationality problem in the Habsburg army, Austrian Hist Yearbk, 67; The Austrian army in the age of Metternich, J Mod Hist, 6/68; The Army of Francis Joseph, Purdue Univ, 76; The Art of Warfare in the Age of Napoleon, Batsford, 77 & Ind Univ, 78; The Anatomy of the Israeli Army, Batsford, 79 & Hippocrene, 79; Napoleon's Great Adversaries: The Archduke Charles and the Austrian Army, 1792-1814, Batsford, 82 & Ind Univ, 82; auth, The Austro-Hungarian Campaign afianst Serbia in 1914, The J of Milit Hist 53, 89; auth, Soldiers and the Revolution: The French Army, Society, and the State, 1788-1789, Hist J 32, 89; auth, The Austrian Military Response to the French Revolution and Napoleon, Essays in European Hist, 89; auth, Military Intelligence Gathering in the Second Half of the Eighteenth Century, Go Spy the Land: Military Intelligence and History, Praeger, 92; auth, Armies and Warfare during the Last Century of the Ancien Regime, Readings in Military Art and Science, Colo Springs, 92; auth, The Age of Napoleon, The Laws of War, Constraints on Wardare in the Western Wold, Yale Univ, 95. **CONTACT ADDRESS** Dept of Hist, Purdue Univ, West Lafayette, IN, 47907-1968. **EMAIL** gunther.rothenberg@arts.monash.edu.au

ROTHENBERG, MARC
PERSONAL Born 10/13/1949, Philadelphia, PA, m, 1985, 2 children **DISCIPLINE** HISTORY OF SCIENCE, HISTORY AND ASTRONOMY **EDUCATION** Villanova Univ, BA, 70; Bryn Mawr Col, PhD, 74. **CAREER** Res assoc, pub mus, Acad of Natural Sci of Philadelphia, 74-75; asst ed, Joseph Henry Papers, 75-83; assoc ed, Joseph Henry Papers, 83-85; ed, Joseph Henry Papers, Smithsonian Inst, 85-. **MEMBERSHIPS** Hist of Sci Soc; Soc for Hist in the Fed Govt; Soc for the Hist of Tech; Orgn of Amer Hist. **RESEARCH** History of American science; History of astronomy; Documentary Ed. **SELECTED PUBLICATIONS** Ed, The Papers of Joseph Henry, Volume 7: 1847-1849: The Smithsonian Years, Smithsonian Inst Press, 96; auth, The History of Science and Technology in the United States: A Critical and Selective Bibliography, vol 2, Garland Publ, 93; ed, The Papers of Joseph Henry. Vol 6: 1844-1846: The Princeton Years, Smithsonian Inst Press, 92; co-ed, Scientific Colonialism: A Cross Cultural Comparison, Smithsonian Inst Press, 87; assoc ed, The Papers of Joseph Henry. Vol 5: 1841-1843: The Princeton Years, Smithsonian Inst Press, 85; auth, The History

of Science and Technology in the United States: A Critical and Selective Bibliography, Garland Publ, 82; asst ed, The Papers of Joseph Henry. Vol 4: 1838-1840: The Princeton Years, Smithsonian Inst Press, 81; co-ed, A Scientist in American Life: Essays and Lectures of Joseph Henry, Smithsonian Inst Press, 80; asst ed, The Papers of Joseph Henry. Vol 3: 1836-1837: The Princeton Years, Smithsonian Inst Press, 79. **CONTACT ADDRESS** Arts and Industries 2188, Smithsonian Institution, Joseph Henry Papers, Washington, DC, 20560-0429. **EMAIL** rothenbergm@osia.si.edu

ROTHENBUSCH, ESTHER H.
DISCIPLINE CHURCH MUSIC **EDUCATION** Baldwin-Wallace Col, BM; Univ Mich, MA, PhD. **CAREER** Instr, Univ Mich, Adrian Col, Bowling Green State Univ; asst prof, S Baptist Theol Univ, 94-. **SELECTED PUBLICATIONS** Auth, The Joyful Sound: Women in the Nineteenth-Century United States Hymnody Tradition; Hallelujah! Handel Meets the Megachurch. **CONTACT ADDRESS** Sch Church Mus and Worship, Southern Baptist Theol Sem, 2825 Lexington Rd, Louisville, KY, 40280. **EMAIL** erothenbusch@sbts.edu

ROTHFELD, ANNE
PERSONAL Born 01/12/1967, MD, 1 child **DISCIPLINE** LIBRARY HISTORY **EDUCATION** Catholic Univ Am, MSLS, 98. **CAREER** Archives Techn, US Holocaust Memorial Museum, 93-98; Infor spec, Univ Md, 98-. **MEMBERSHIPS** Am Libr Asn; Special Libr Asn; Am Asn State and Local Hist; Society Hist Progressive and Gilded Age. **RESEARCH** Local and public history; late 19th/early 20th century American library history; archives and special collections. **SELECTED PUBLICATIONS** Auth, rev, Economics of Digital Information: Collection, Storage, and Delivery, 99; auth, rev, Louis Shores: Defining Educational Librarianship, 99; auth, rev, More Than the Facts: The Research Division of the National Education Association, 1922-1997; ed, Information Technology Newsletter. **CONTACT ADDRESS** 3806 Stepping Stone Ln, Burtonsville, MD, 20866. **EMAIL** aroth001@umaryland.edu

ROTHFORK, JOHN G.
PERSONAL Born 12/18/1946, Holstein, IA, m, 1966, 1 child **DISCIPLINE** AMERICAN STUDIES, LITERATURE **EDUCATION** Morningside Col, BA, 68; Univ Iowa, MA, 70; Truman Univ, MA, 73; Univ NMex, PhD(Am studies), 73. **CAREER** Assoc prof philos & English, NMex Inst Mining & Technol, 70-98, asst prof English, Cent Ark Univ, 74-75; ed, NMex Humanities Rev, 78-82; lectr, Univ NMex, 79-80; Fulbright lectr, Indian Inst Technol, 81-82; Fulbright lectr, Tokyo Univ, Keio Univ, 85; prof Am Lit, Mukogawa Women's Univ, Japan, 98-. **MEMBERSHIPS** MLA; Am Philos Asn; Rocky Mountain Mod Lang Asn. **RESEARCH** Technology and values; comparative religion. **SELECTED PUBLICATIONS** Auth, Grokking god: Phenomenology in NASA & Science Fiction, Res Studies, 76; Transcendentalism and Henry Barnard's School Architecture, J Gen Educ, 77; The Buddha Center in Conrad's Youth, Lit East & West, 77; Indians (poems), Northwoods Press, 80; Having Everything is Having Nothing, Southwest Rev, 81; Uber Stanislaw Lem, Suhrkamp, 81; auth, V S Naipaul and the Third World, Res Studies, 81; Hindu Mysticism in the Twentieth Century: R K Narayan's The Guide, Philol Quart (in prep). **CONTACT ADDRESS** English Dept, Muskogawa Women's Univ, 6-46 Ikebiraki-cho, Nishinomiya, ., 663. **EMAIL** rothfork@zdnetmail.com

ROTHMAN, DAVID
DISCIPLINE UNITED STATES HISTORY **EDUCATION** Columbia Univ, MA, 58; Harvard Univ, PhD, 64. **CAREER** Prof. **SELECTED PUBLICATIONS** Auth, The Discovery of the Asylum: Social Order and Disorder in the New Republic, 71; Conscience and Convenience: The Asylum and Its Alternatives in Progressive America, 80; The Willowbrook Wars, 84; Strangers at the Bedside: A History of How Law and Bioethics Transformed Medical Decision-making, 91; Beginnings Count: The Technological Imperative in American Health Care, 97. **CONTACT ADDRESS** Dept of History, Columbia Col, New York, 2960 Broadway, New York, NY, 10027-6902.

ROTHMAN, HAL K.
DISCIPLINE HISTORY **EDUCATION** Univ Tex Austin, PhD, 85. **CAREER** Prof, Univ Nev Las Vegas. **RESEARCH** Environmental history; public history. **SELECTED PUBLICATIONS** Auth, Devil's Bargains: Tourism in the Twentieth Century American West, 98; The Greening of Nation? Environmentalism in the U.S. Since 1945, 97; I'll Never Fight Fire With My Bare Hands Again, 94; On Rims and Ridges: The Los Alamos Area Since 1880, 92; Preserving Different Pasts The American National Monuments, 89; ed, Reopening the American West, 98; co-ed, Out of the Woods: Essays in Environmental History, 97. **CONTACT ADDRESS** History Dept, Univ Nev Las Vegas, 4505 Md Pky, Las Vegas, NV, 89154.

ROTHNEY, GORDON O.
PERSONAL Born 03/15/1912, Richmond, PQ, Canada **DISCIPLINE** HISTORY **EDUCATION** Univ Bishop's Col, BA, 32; Univ London, MA, 34, PhD, 39. **CAREER** Bishop's Col Sch, Lennoxvile, Que, 39-41; soc sci fac, 41-52, prof hist, Sir George Williams Col, 41-52; prof & head hist, Memorial Univ Nfld, 52-63; dean arts, Lakehead Univ, 63-68; vis prof hist, Univ Western Ont, 69-70; prof hist, Univ Man, 70-79 (RETIRED). **HONORS AND AWARDS** Que gov post-grad scholar, 32-34; Can Coun sr res fel, 59-60, 68-69; Centennial Medal, 67; fel, Royal Hist Soc, London, 69; LLD(hon), Memorial Univ Nfld, 87. **MEMBERSHIPS** Institut d'histoire de l'Amerique francaise; Can Hist Asn; Hum Res Coun. **SELECTED PUBLICATIONS** Auth, Newfoundland: A History; auth, Canada In One World. **CONTACT ADDRESS** 333 Vaughan St, Ste 904, Winnipeg, MB, R3B 3J9.

ROTHNEY, JOHN ALEXANDER
PERSONAL Born 09/27/1935, Boston, MA **DISCIPLINE** MODERN FRENCH HISTORY, WORLD HISTORY **EDUCATION** Johns Hopkins Univ, AB, 57; Harvard Univ, AM, 58, PhD(hist), 64. **CAREER** Teaching fel hist, Harvard Univ, 61-64, instr, 64-66; from asst prof to assoc prof, Univ MO, Columbia, 66-70; assoc prof, 70-74, PROF HIST, OH STATE UNIV, 74-; Sr resident fel, Humanities Res Inst, Reed Col, 68; Am Coun Learned Socs fel, 71-72; ed, Fr Hist Studies, 76-85. **HONORS AND AWARDS** Co-Pres, Soc for French Hist Studies, 90-91. **MEMBERSHIPS** AHA; Soc Fr Hist Studies; Soc Hist Mod, France. **RESEARCH** Right-wing movements in modern France; the Second Empire in France; modernization and political change; 20th-century world history. **SELECTED PUBLICATIONS** Auth, Bonapartism after Sedan, Cornell Univ, 69; ed, The Brittany Affair and the Crisis of the Ancien Regime, Oxford Univ, 69; auth, (with Carter V. Findley) 20th-Century World, Houghton Mifflin, 86, 4th ed, 98. **CONTACT ADDRESS** Dept of Hist, Ohio State Univ, 230 W 17th Ave, Columbus, OH, 43210-1361. **EMAIL** rothney.1@osu.edu

ROTHSTEIN, WILLIAM
DISCIPLINE MUSIC **EDUCATION** Northwestern Univ, BM, 74; Yale Univ, MPhil, 78, PhD, 81; Postgrad study, New England Conserv, 74-76. **CAREER** Fac mem, Amherst Coll, Univ of Mich; Assoc prof, Oberlin Col, 92-; Guest lectr, Britten-Pears Sch for Advanced Mus Studies, Eng, 93. **HONORS AND AWARDS** ASCAP-Deems Taylor Award, 90. **SELECTED PUBLICATIONS** Auth, Phrase Rhythm in Tonal Music, Schirmer Bk(s). **CONTACT ADDRESS** Dept of Mus, Oberlin Col, Oberlin, OH, 44074.

ROTHWELL, KENNETH S.
PERSONAL Born 03/27/1955, Rochester, NY, m, 1989, 2 children **DISCIPLINE** CLASSICS **EDUCATION** Univ Vt, BA, 77; Columbia Univ, PhD, 85. **CAREER** Asst prof, Holy Cross Coll, 84-91; asst prof, Wellesley Coll, 91-92; asst prof, Boston Coll, 92-94; asst prof, Univ Mass Boston, 95-. **MEMBERSHIPS** APA; CANE. **RESEARCH** Greek Comedy. **SELECTED PUBLICATIONS** Auth, Politics and Persuasion in Aristophanes' Ecclesiazusoe, 90. **CONTACT ADDRESS** Univ of Mass, 100 Morrissey Blvd, Boston, MA, 02125. **EMAIL** rothwell@umbstey.cc.umb.edu

ROUMAN, JOHN CHRIST
PERSONAL Born 05/01/1916, Tomahawk, WI **DISCIPLINE** CLASSICS, LINGUISTICS **EDUCATION** Carleton Col, BA, 50; Columbia Univ, MA, 51; Univ WI-Madison, PhD, 65. **CAREER** Tchr, Seton Hall Prep Sch, NJ, 54-56 & Malverne High Sch, NY, 57-59; res asst Greek epigraphy, Inst Advan Study, Princeton Univ, 62-63; asst prof, 65-71, chmn dept Span & class, 72-76, assoc prof, 71-91, prof class, Univ NH, 91-, Chair classics, 87-98, Coord classics, 98-; Pres, Strafford Cty Greco-Roman Found, Bd mem, Phi Kappa Theta Nat Found. **HONORS AND AWARDS** Noyse Prize for Greek, Carleton Col, 50; Fulbright Scholar, Univ Kiel, WGer, 56-57; UNH Alumni Asn, Distinguished Tchg Award, 85; Barlow-Beach Award for Serv, Cause of Class, Class Asn of New Engl, 91; Am Philol Asn Nat Award for Excellence in Tchg, Class, 91; AHEPA and Daughters of Penelope, Pericles Award, 93. **MEMBERSHIPS** Am Philol Asn; Medieval Acad Am; Mod Greek Studies Asn; Class Asn New Engl. **RESEARCH** Class philol, espec Pindar and Homer; mod Greek studies; Byzantine hist. **SELECTED PUBLICATIONS** Auth, Nominal-Compound Epithets in Pindar: A Linguistic Analysis, Univ Microfilms, 67; coauth, More still on the Trojan Horse, Class J, 4-5/72. **CONTACT ADDRESS** Dept of Langs, Lit and Cult, Univ of NH, 125 Technology Dr, Durham, NH, 03824-4724. **EMAIL** jcrouman@christa.unh.edu

ROUSE, DONALD E.
PERSONAL Born 05/30/1932, Philadelphia, Pennsylvania, m **DISCIPLINE** EDUCATION **EDUCATION** BS; MS; MEd; PhD Educ Admin. **CAREER** New Teacher's Elementary & Secondary Coordinator, Intergroup Educ, teacher/consultant; principal; assoc prof educ; educ consultant; Elementary Summer School Program, original instructor; Adult Educ Germany, instructor; New Teachers Clinic, coordinator; reading consultant; Urban Centers, dir. **HONORS AND AWARDS** W Philadelphia Comm Award 1972; Landreth Man Yr Award 1971; St Thomas Church Awd; Schoolmen's Club 1986. **MEMBERSHIPS** PSEA; NEA; Amer Assn of Univ Profs; Coll Grad Council; Natl AAU; Phi Delta Kappa; Philadelphia Assn of School Admins; bd dir Tribune Charities; Interested Negroes Inc; Am Assn, Afro-Amer Educators; NAACP; Masons; Amer Found Negro Affairs. **CONTACT ADDRESS** Dir, Urban Center, Univ Cheyney, Philadelphia, PA, 19139.

ROUSE, JACQUELINE ANNE
PERSONAL Born 02/01/1950, Roseland, Virginia, s **DISCIPLINE** HISTORY **EDUCATION** Howard University, Washington, DC,, 1968-72; Atlanta University, Atlanta, GA, MA, 1972-73; Emory University, Atlanta, GA, PhD, 1983. **CAREER** Pal, Beach Jr College, Lake Worth, Florida, senior instructor, 1973-80; Georgia Institute of Teachers, Atlanta, GA, guest lecturer, 1983; Morehouse College, Atlanta, GA, associate professor, 1983-; American University/Smithsonian Institute, Landmarks professor of history, beginning 1989; Georgia State Univ, prof of history, currently. **HONORS AND AWARDS** FIPSE, Curriculum on Black Women's History, Spellman College, 1983-84; NEH Summer Grant for College Teachers, 1984; UNCF Strengthening the Humanities Grant, 1985. **MEMBERSHIPS** Assistant editor, Journal of Negro History, 1983-89; advisor/reference, Harriet Tubman Historial & Cultural Museum, Macon, GA, 1985; panelist, American Association University of Women, 1985-; principal scholar/member, Steering Committee, National Conference of Women in Civil Rights Movement, 1988; panelist, Jacob Javits Fellowship, Department of Education, 1989; national vice director, Assistant of Black Women Historians, 1989-; first vice president, Association of Social & Behavorial Scientists, 1989-; consultant/advisor, Atlanta Historical Society, 1989; historian consultant, Apex Collection of Life & Heritage, 1989. **CONTACT ADDRESS** Dept. of History, Georgia State Univ, Atlanta, GA, 30303.

ROUTLEDGE, MARIE I.
PERSONAL Born 08/23/1951, Toronto, ON, Canada **DISCIPLINE** CURATOR/ART HISTORY **EDUCATION** Univ Toronto, BA, 75. **CAREER** Res & cur, 75-79, res & doc coordr, Inuit art sect, Indian & Northern Affairs Can, 81-84; mgr, Theo Waddington Gallery, NY, 79-81; asst cur, 85-93, ASSOC CURATOR INUIT ART, NAT GALLERY OF CANADA, 93-. **MEMBERSHIPS** Native Art Stud Asn Can; Ottawa Native Art Stud Gp. **RESEARCH** Inuit art. **SELECTED PUBLICATIONS** Auth, Inuit Art in the 1970's, 79; auth, Pudlo: Thirty Years of Drawing, 90; ed, Inuit Arts Crafts mag, 81-84. **CONTACT ADDRESS** National Gallery of Canada, PO Box 427, Stn A, Ottawa, ON, K1N 9N4.

ROWAN, STEVEN
PERSONAL Born 04/04/1943, Bremerton, WA, m, 1966, 2 children **DISCIPLINE** HISTORY **EDUCATION** Univ Wash, BA, 65; Harvard Univ, AM, 66, PhD, 70. **CAREER** Prof, Univ Mo, St. Louis, 70-; temp lectr, Kings Col, London, 75-76. **HONORS AND AWARDS** Phi Beta Kappa, 64; Humboldt Fel, 89-90. **MEMBERSHIPS** Am Hist Asn; Medieval Acad Am. **RESEARCH** Late-medieval Germany; Roman law; Germans in America. **SELECTED PUBLICATIONS** Auth, Germans for a Free Missouri: Translations from the St. Louis Radical Press, 1856-1862, 83; auth, Ulrich Zasius: A Jurist in the German Renaissance, 1561-1535, 87; auth, Religious Movements in the Middle Ages, 95; auth, Memoirs of a Nobody: The Missouri Years of an Austrian Radical, 98. **CONTACT ADDRESS** Dept of History, Univ of Missouri-St. Louis, 8001 Natural Bridge Rd, St. Louis, MO, 63121. **EMAIL** sswrowa@umslvma.umsl.edu

ROWE, D.L.
PERSONAL Born 05/05/1947, Syracuse, NY **DISCIPLINE** HISTORY **EDUCATION** Ithaca College, BA, 69; Univ Virginia, MA, 72, PhD, 72. **CAREER** Hist Prof, 81, Middle Tenn State Univ; exec Dir, 77-81, Landmarks Assoc NY; res writer, 74-77, County Hist Planner NY. **HONORS AND AWARDS** Outstanding Honors Fac Mem, 97,95,92; Cannonsburgh Awd for Res. **RESEARCH** Amer Religious History; Primitive Baptists; Millenarianism. **SELECTED PUBLICATIONS** Auth, Tending the Garden: The Stewardship Commission and the Southern Baptist Convention, 1961-1997, 98; auth, Thunder and Trumpets: The Millerite Movement and Apocalyptic Thought in Upstate NY, 1800-1850, Chico CA, Scholars Press, 85; auth, The Millerites: A Shadow Portrait, in: The Disappointed: Millerism and Millenarianism in the Nineteenth Century, ed by Ron Numbers, Jonathan M Butler, Knoxville, Univ of Tenn, 93. **CONTACT ADDRESS** 800 E Burton, Murfreesboro, TN, 37130. **EMAIL** drowe@acad1.mtsu.edu

ROWE, DAVID C.
PERSONAL Born 09/27/1949, Montclair, NJ, m, 1974, 1 child **DISCIPLINE** PSYCHOLOGY AND BEHAVIORAL GENETICS **EDUCATION** Harvard Univ, AB, 72; Univ Colo, PhD, 77. **CAREER** Asst prof, Oberlin Col, 77-82; assoc prof, Univ Okla, 82-88; full prof of family studies, Univ Ariz, 88-. **HONORS AND AWARDS** Magna Cum Laude, Harvard Univ, 72. **MEMBERSHIPS** Behavior Genetics Asn; Amer Psychol Soc. **RESEARCH** Behavioral genetics; Molecular genetics of behavior. **SELECTED PUBLICATIONS** Auth, Genes, environment, and psychological development, ed A. Campbell & S. Muncer, The social child, London, UCL Press, 98; coauth, with E. van den Oord, An examination of genotype-environment interactions for academic achievement in an U. S. longitudinal survey, Intelligence, 25, 205-228, 97; with S. Losoya, S. Callor & H. H. Goldsmith, The origins of familial similarity in parenting: A study of twins and adoptive siblings; Develop Psychol, 33, 1012-1024, 97; auth, Genetics, temperament and personality, ed R. Hogan, J. A. Johnson & S. R. Briggs, Handbook of

Personality Psychology, pp 367-386, NY, Acad Press, 97; Genetik und sozialisation: Die grenzen der erziehung, Beltz: Psychologie Verlags Union, Ger transl of The Limits of Family Influence, 97; book rev, Born to rebel: Birth order, family dynamics, and creative lives, by Frank J. Sulloway, Evolution and Human Behavior, 18, 1-7, 97; coauth, with J. L. Rodgers, Poverty and behavior: Are environmental measures nature and nurture?, Develop Rev, 17, 358-375, 97; with T. Vazsonyi & D. J. Flannery, No more than skin deep: Ethnic and racial similarity in development process, reprinted ed N. BaNikongo, Leading essays in Afro-American studies, NY, IAAS Publ, 97; with J. L. Rodgers, Poverty and behavior: A response to a critique of a critique of a special issue, Develop Rev, 17, 394-406, 97; with D. Kandel, In the eye of the beholder? Parental ratings of externalizing and internatlizing symptoms, Jour of Abnormal Child Psychol, 25, 265-275, 97; auth, A place at the policy table? Behavior genetics and estimates of family environmental effects on IQ, Intelligence, 24, 133-158, 97; Group differences in developmental processes The exception or the rule?, Psychol Inquiry, 8, 218-222, 97; coauth, with A. T. Vazsonyi & A. J. Figueredo, Mating effort in adolescence: Conditional or alternative strategy, Personality and Individual Differences, 23, 105-115, 97; Are parents to blame? A look at The Antisocial Personalities, Psychol Inquiry, 28, 251-260, 97. **CONTACT ADDRESS** Univ of Arizona, Campus Box 210033, Tucson, AZ, 85721. **EMAIL** dcr091@ag.arizona.edu

ROWE, GAIL STUART
PERSONAL Born 12/02/1936, Los Angeles, CA, m, 1957, 2 children **DISCIPLINE** AMERICAN HISTORY **EDUCATION** Fresno State Col, AB, 59; Stanford Univ, MA, 60, PhD(hist), 69. **CAREER** From asst prof to assoc prof, 69-77, prof hist, Univ Northern CO, 77-. **MEMBERSHIPS** Inst Early Am Hist & Cult; Orgn Am Historians; Soc Historians Early Am Repub. **RESEARCH** Early Am legal hist; Am colonial hist, soc & polit; Am Revolution. **SELECTED PUBLICATIONS** Auth, A Valuable Acquisition in Congress: Thomas McKean, Delegate from Delaware to the Continental Congress, 1774-1783, PA Hist, 7/71; Thomas McKean and the Coming of the Revolution, PA Mag Hist & Biog, 1/72; The Travail of John McKinley, First President of Delaware, Del Hist, spring-summer 76; Outlawry in Pennsylvania, 1782-88, and the Achievement of an Independent Judiciary, Am J Legal Hist, 7/76; Rev V John Clowes, Jr, and the Shape of Politics in Pre-Revolutionary Sussex, Del Hist, fall-winter, 77; Thomas McKean: The Shaping of an American Republican, CO Assoc Univ, 78; Alexander Addison: The Disillusionment of a Republican Schoolmaster, W Pa Hist Mag, 7/79; Power, Justice, and Foreign Relations in the Confederation Period: The Marbois-Longchamps Affair, 1784-1786, PA Mag Hist & Biog, 7/80; Infanticide, Its Judicial Resolution, and Criminal Code Revision in Early Pennsylvania, Proceedings of the Am Philos Soc, 135, 91; Judicial Tyrant and Vox Populi: Pennsylvanians View Their State Supreme Court, 1777-1799, PA Mag of Hist and Biog, 118, Jan/Apr 94; Embattled Bench: The Pennsylvania Supreme Court and the Forging of a Democratic Society, 1684-1809, DE Univ Press, 94. **CONTACT ADDRESS** Dept Hist, Univ Northern Colorado, 501 20th St, Greeley, CO, 80639-0001. **EMAIL** growe@bentley.univnorthco.edu

ROWE, M.W.
PERSONAL Born 07/06/1937, Amarillo, TX, d, 4 children **DISCIPLINE** CHEMISTRY **EDUCATION** NM Tech, BS, 59; Univ Ark, PhD, 66. **CAREER** Staff mem, Los Alamos Nat Lab, 59-63; grad asst, Univ Ark, 62-66; Miller fel, Univ Calif Berkeley, 66-68; asst prof, Univ Wash, 68-69; asst to assoc to full prof, Tex A&M Univ, 69-. **HONORS AND AWARDS** Col of Sci Teaching award, Former Students Asn, 91; ed, Annual Series, Adv in Analytical Geochem, 93-96; fel, Tex Acad of Sci, 83-; assoc ed, Tex Jour of Sci, 80-93; assoc ed, Geochem Jour, 75-80; fel, Meteoritical Soc, 68-; Nininger Meteorite award, 64, 66; Mobil Outstanding Petroleum Eng Student award, 59. **MEMBERSHIPS** Amer Chem Soc; Soc of Amer Archaeol; Amer Rock Art Res Asn; Australian Rock Art Res Asn. **RESEARCH** Archaeological chemistry. **SELECTED PUBLICATIONS** Co-auth, Effect of Water on Pictographs, Rock Art Res, 98; co-auth, Investigating Antiquity: Direct Dating of Ancient Rock Paintings, Sci Spectra, 98; co-auth, Hand Prints at Pace Bend Park: Not Prehistoric, Bull of the Tex Archeol Soc, 98; co-auth, Dating Ancient Rock Paintings, Zinj, 98; co-auth, Plasma Extraction and AMS C Dating of Rock Paintings, Techne, 97; co-auth, Ordering the Rock Paintings of the Mitchell-Palmer Limestone Zone (Australia) for AMS Dating, The Artefact, 97; co-auth, Rock Art Image in Fern Cave, Lava Beds National Monument, California: Not the A.D. 1054 (Crab Nebula) Supernova, Antiquity, 97; co-auth, Krypton and Xenon Fractionation in North American Tektites, Meteoritics, 97; co-auth, Plasma-chemical Extraction and AMS Radiocarbon Dating of Rock Paintings, Amer Indian Rock Art, 97; co-auth, Analysis of White Pigments from the Olary Region, South Australia, Rock Art Res, 96; co-auth, The Origin of Round Phyllosilicate Aggregates in CR2 and CI1 Chondrites, Lunar and Planetary Sci, 96; co-auth, Ancient DNA from Texas Pictographs, Archaeol Chem V, Adv in Chem Series, Amer Chem Soc, 96; co-auth, Radiocarbon Dating of Ancient Rock Paintings, Archaeol Chem V, Adv in Chem Series, Amer Chem Soc, 96; co-auth, Ancient DNA from Texas Pictographs, Archaeol Sci, 96; co-auth, Dating Pictographs with Radiocarbon, Radiocarbon, 95; co-auth, Source Materials for North American Tektites, Lunar & Planetary Sci Conf, 95; co-auth, Datation Radiocarbone de Deux Figures Parietales de la Grotte du Portel, Prehistoire Ariegeoise, 95. **CONTACT ADDRESS** Dept. of Chemistry, Texas A&M Univ, Box 30012, College Station, TX, 77842-3012. **EMAIL** mwrowe@tamu.edu

ROWE, PATSY BAXTER
PERSONAL Philadelphia, PA, m, 2 children **DISCIPLINE** MUSIC **EDUCATION** Philadelphia Musical Acad, BM & BME; Temple Univ, MM & PhD. **CAREER** Asst prof, Community Col of Philadelphia, 76-90; dir, Arts School, Freedom Theatre, 85-87; INTERIM DEAN OF WOMEN, 95-96, CHAIR, MUSIC DEPT, LINCOLUN UNIV, 90-91 & 93-. **HONORS AND AWARDS** Four year doctoral fel. **MEMBERSHIPS** Nat Asn for the Study and performance of African-Am Music; Nat Asn of Schools of Music. **RESEARCH** Music psychology; the African-American creative process. **SELECTED PUBLICATIONS** Auth, An Investigation of the Ability of Fourth Grade Students to Master the Rhythmic Intricacies of Traditional African-Derived Music, vol 21, 95/96. **CONTACT ADDRESS** Music Dept, Lincoln Univ, PO Box 179, Lincoln University, PA, 19352.

ROWLAND, RICK
PERSONAL Born 06/20/1952, m, 1974, 3 children **DISCIPLINE** BIBLICAL STUDIES, OLD TESTAMENT **EDUCATION** Univ CA, BA, 74; Pepperdine Univ, MA, 87; Princeton theol sem, Mdiv, 90, PhD, 97. **CAREER** Mgr, Hebrew Lexicon proj, Princeton theol sem, 88-95; Dead Sea Scrolls proj, Princeton theol sem, 87-93; tchg fel, Princeton theol sem, 87-93; res asst, Princeton theol sem, 93; instr, Princeton theol sem, 93; adjunct inst, Princeton theol sem, 93-94; vis instr, 94-95; mgr, Acad proj design, 97-. **HONORS AND AWARDS** Pres's award, 77-80, 83-85; Henry Snyder Gehman award, Princeton theol sem, 88; George S. Green fel, Princeton theol sem, 90-91; one-yr fel award, Christian Scholar Found, 92-93, 93-94. **SELECTED PUBLICATIONS** Auth, Job's Humble Reply: Is the Question Really the Answer?, Difficult Texts in Job, Pepperdine Univ Annual Bible Lectures, 96; Religion 101 The History and Religion of Ancient Israel: Course Reader, 94; The Character and Identity of God in the Old Testament: Significance for Contemporary Christian Worship, Pepperdine Univ Annual Bible Lectures, 93; rev, E. Achtemeier, The Old Testament and the Proclamation of the Gospel, Leaven 3/1, 95. **CONTACT ADDRESS** Dept of Relig, Pepperdine Univ, 24255 Pacific Coast Hwy, Malibu, CA, 90263. **EMAIL** rrowland@pepperdine.edu

ROYSTER, CHARLES WILLIAM
PERSONAL Born 11/27/1944, Nashville, TN **DISCIPLINE** HISTORY **EDUCATION** Univ Calif, Berkeley, AB, 66, MA, 67, PhD(hist), 77. **CAREER** Asst prof hist, Col William & Mary, 77-79; asst prof hist, Univ Tex, Arlington, 79-81; assoc prof hist, La State Univ, 81-83; prof hist, 84-85; T. Harry Williams Prof Am Hist, 85-92; Boyd Prof Hist, 92-; fel hist, Inst Early Am Hist & Cult, 77-79; John Simon Guggenheim Fellow, 82-83; National Humanities Center Fellow, 84-85; vis fel, Henry E. Huntington Library, 89, 96, 98. **HONORS AND AWARDS** Francis Parkman Prize, 80; Book Prize, Nat Hist Soc, 81; Bancroft Prize, 92; Lincoln Prize, 92; Charles S. Sydnor Award, 92. **MEMBERSHIPS** AHA **RESEARCH** United States Civil War; American Revolution; war and society. **SELECTED PUBLICATIONS** Auth, The Nature of Treason: Revolutionary Virtue and Americans' Reactions to Benedict Arnold, William & Mary Quart, 4/79; A Revolutionary People at War: The Continental Army and American Character, 1775-1783, Univ NC, Chapel Hill, Press, 79; Light-Horse Harry Lee and the Legacy of the American Revolution, Alfred A Knopf, 81; The Destructive War: William Tecumseh Sherman, Stonewall Jackson, and the Americans, Alfred A. Knopf, 91. **CONTACT ADDRESS** Dept of Hist, Louisiana State Univ, Baton Rouge, LA, 70803-0001.

ROYSTER, PHILIP M.
PERSONAL m **DISCIPLINE** AFRICAN-AMERICAN STUDIES **EDUCATION** University of Illinois, 1960-62; DePaul University, BA, 1965, MA, 1967; Roosevelt University, Black Cultures Seminar, 1969; Loyola University, PhD, American and British Literature, 1974. **CAREER** Dept of African/Afro-Amer Studies, SUNY Albany, asst prof, 1975-78; English Dept, Fisk Univ, asst prof, 1974-75, instructor, 1970-74; Syracuse University, Department of Afro-American Studies, associate professor, 1978-1981; Kansas State University, Department of English, associate professor, 1981-85, professor, 1985-88, American Ethnic Studies Program, coordinator, 1984-88; Bowling Green State University, Department of Ethnic Studies, professor, 1987-92, assistant chair, 1990-91; University of Illinois at Chicago, Department of English, professor, 1991-, Department of African-American Studies, professor, 1991-, African-American Cultural Center, director, 1991-. **HONORS AND AWARDS** Bowling Green State University, Faculty Research Committee Basic Grant Award, 1988, Black Student Union and Board of Black Cultural Activities, Certificate of Appreciation, 1988; the Seaton Third Poetry Award, 1983; Kansas State University, Faculty Research Grant, 1981, 1982; Mellon Foundation, Mellon Project, 1980; Syracuse University, Senate Research Committee Grant, 1979; Fisk University, Study Grant, 1971, 1974; Loyola University, Assistantship, 1967-68, Fellowship, 1968-69; DePaul University, Arthur J Schmitt Scholarship, 1967. **MEMBERSHIPS** Society for New Music, board member, 1979-81; The African-American Drum Ensemble, 1987-; Honor Society of Phi Kappa Phi, 1992-; Illinois Committee of Black Concerns in Higher Education, 1992-; University of Illinois at Chicago Black Alumni Association, 1992-; Association of Black Cultural Centers, 1991-, National Steering Committee, 1991-, Constitution Bylaws Subcommittee, 1991-; Popular Culture Association, 1976-; Modern Language Association; College Language Association; National Council of Black Studies; National Association of the Church of God Summit Meeting Task Force; Emerald Avenue Church of God, Historical Committee, chairperson. **SELECTED PUBLICATIONS** Author, "The Rapper as Shaman for a Band of Dancers of the Spirit: U Can't Touch This," The Emergency of Black and the Emergence of Rap Special Issue of Black Sacred Music: A Journal of Theomusicology, pages 60-67, 1991, "The Sky is Gray: An Analysis of the Story," American Short Stories on Film: A Series of Casebooks, Langenscheidt-Longman, "The Curse of Capitalism in the Caribbean: Purpose and Theme in Lindsay Barrett's Song for Mumu," Perspectives in Black Popular Culture, The Popular Press, pages 22-35, 1990; Literary & Cultural Criticism: "In Search of Our Fathers' Arms: Alice Walker's Persona of the Alienated Darling," Black American Literature Forum, 20.4, 347-70, 1986; "The Spirit Will Not Descend Without Song: Cultural Values of Afro-American Gospel Tradition," Folk Roots: An Exploration of the Folk Arts & Cultural Traqditions of Kansas, Ed Jennie A Chinn, Manhattan: Univ for Man, 19-24, 1982; "Contemporary Oral Folk Expression," Black Books Bulletin, 6.3, 24-30, 1979; "A Priest and a Witch Against the Spiders and the Snakes: Scapegoating in Toni Morrison's Sula," Umoja 2.2, 149-68, 1979; "The Bluest Eye: The Novels of Toni Morrision," First World, 1.4, 34-44, 1977; Suggestions for Instructors to Accompany Clayers' and Spencer's Context for Composition, Co-authored with Stanley A Clayes, New York: Appleton-Century-Crofts, 1969; Books of Poetry: Songs and Dances, Detroit, Lotus Press, 1981; The Back Door, Chicago, Third World Press, 1971; Photography: A Milestone Sampler: Fifteenth Ann Anthology, Detroit, Lotus Press, "Samuel Allen," 10, "Jill Witherspoon Boyer," 22, "Beverley Rose Enright," 40, "Naomi F Faust," 44, "Ray Fleming," 50, "Agnes Nasmith Johnston," 56, "Delores Kendrick," 68, "Pinkie Gordon Lane," 74, "Naomi Long Madgett," 80, "Haki R Madhubuti," 86, "Herbert Woodward Martin," 92, "May Miller," 104, "Mwatabu Okantah," 110, "Paulette Childress White," 122, 1988; Master Drummer & Percussionist: "Earth Blossom," The John Betsch Society, Strata-East Recording Co, #SES-19748, 1975; Received a four and a half star review in Downbeat, 24-26, May 1975; "A White Sport Coat and a Pink Crustacean," Jimmy Buffet, Dunhill ABC, DSX 50150, 1973; "Hanging Around the Observatory," John Hiatt, Epic KE 32688, 1973; "We Make Spirit (Dancing in the Moonlight)," John Hiatt, Epic, 5-10990, ZSS 157218, 1973; "Backwoods Woman," Dianne Davidson, Janus, JLS 3043, 1972; "The Knack," The Interpreters, Cadet LP 762, 1965. **CONTACT ADDRESS** African-American Cultural Center, Univ of Illinois at Chicago, Rm 208 Addams Hall, 830 S Halsted Street, Chicago, IL, 60607-7030.

ROZENZWEIG, ROY
PERSONAL Born 08/06/1950, New York, NY, m, 1981 **DISCIPLINE** HISTORY **EDUCATION** Columbia Col, BA, 71; res student, St. John's Col Cambridge Univ, 71-73; Harvard Univ, PhD, 78. **CAREER** Asst prof, Worcester Polytechnic Inst, 78-80; Mellon Postdoctoral Fel, Wesleyan Univ, 80-81; from asst prof to assoc prof to prof, 81-98, distinguished prof, 81-, George Mason Univ. **HONORS AND AWARDS** James Harvey Robinson Prize, Am Hist Asn; Interactive Media Festival Award; Urban Hist Asn Prize; Abel Wolman Prize; Abbott Cumming Lowell Prize, Vernacular Architecture Forum; Hist Preservation Book Prize, Ctr for Hist Preservation. New York His Asn Award; NEH Grants; Kellogg Found Grant; Fulbright Commission; John Simon Guggenheim Memorial Found Fel; Forrest G. Pogue Award; Albert J. Beveridge Res Grant, AHA; Distinguished Fac Award, GMU. **SELECTED PUBLICATIONS** Auth, Eight Hours for What We Will: Workers and Leisure in an Industrial City, 1870-1920, 83; coauth, The Park and the People: A History of Central Park, 92; coauth, art, Historians and the Web: A Guide, 96; coauth, art, Brave New World or Blind Alley? American History on the World Wide Web, 97; coauth, The Presence of the Past: Popular Uses of History in American Life, 98. **CONTACT ADDRESS** Dept of History, George Mason Univ, Fairfax, VA, 22030. **EMAIL** rrosenzw@gmu.edu

RUBIN, JAMES HENRY
PERSONAL Born 05/04/1944, Cambridge, MA **DISCIPLINE** HISTORY OF ART **EDUCATION** Yale Univ, BA, 65; Univ Paris, Institute d'art, license-es-lettres, 67; Harvard, PhD, 72. **CAREER** SUNY, Stony Brook, prof and chair. **MEMBERSHIPS** CAA; AHNCA. **RESEARCH** 19th century art. **SELECTED PUBLICATIONS** Impressionism, Art and Ideas, London Phaidon Press, forthcoming 99; Courbet, art and Ideas, London Phaidon Press, 97; Manet's Silence and the Poetics of Bouquets, essays in art and culture, London and Cambridge MA, Harvard Univ Press, 94. **CONTACT ADDRESS** Dept Art, State Univ NY at Stony Brook, 4213 Fine Arts Bldg, Stony Brook, NY, 11794. **EMAIL** jrubin@ccmail.sunysb.edu

RUBINCAM, CATHERINE I.
PERSONAL Born 08/23/1943, Belfast, Northern Ireland, m, 1974, 4 children **DISCIPLINE** CLASSICAL STUDIES **EDUCATION** Univ Toronto, BA, 64; Oxford Univ, BA, 66; Harvard Univ, PhD, 69. **CAREER** Asst prof then assoc prof, classics, Erindale Col, Univ Toronto, 69- . **MEMBERSHIPS** Am Philol Asn. **RESEARCH** Ancient Greek history and historiography; history of classical tradition; history of women in the professoriate. **SELECTED PUBLICATIONS** Auth, Mary White and Women Professors of Classics in Canadian Universities, Class World, 96-97; auth, The Organization of Material in Graeco-Roman World Histories, in, Pre-Modern Encyclopedic Texts: Proceedings of the Second COMERS Congress, 97; auth, Did Diodorus Siculus Take Over Cross-References from His Sources? Am J of Philol, 98; auth, How Many Books Did Diodorus Siculus Originally Intend to Write? Class Q, 98. **CONTACT ADDRESS** Dept of Classics, Univ of Toronto, Mississauga, ON, L5L 1C6. **EMAIL** rubincam@chass.utoronto.ca

RUCK, CARL ANTON PAUL
PERSONAL Born 12/08/1935, Bridgeport, CT **DISCIPLINE** GREEK LANGUAGE & LITERATURE **EDUCATION** Yale Univ, BA, 58; Univ Mich, Ann Arbor, MA, 59; Harvard Univ, PhD(classics), 65. **CAREER** From instr to assoc prof, 64-76, PROF CLASSICS, BOSTON UNIV, 76-. **MEMBERSHIPS** Am Philol Asn. **RESEARCH** Greek tragedy and comedy; Greek mythology; teaching methods for Greek and Latin; ethnobotany; ethnopharmacology; clinical mythologist. **SELECTED PUBLICATIONS** Auth, IG II 2323: The List of Victors in Comedy at the Dionysia, Brill, 67; coauth, Pindar: Selected Odes (transl & essays), Univ Mich, 68; auth, Ancient Greek: A New Approach, Mass Inst Technol, 68, 72 & 79; On the Sacred Names of Iamos and Ion: Ethnobotanical Referents in the Hero's Parentage, Class J, 76; Duality and the Madness of Herakles, Arethusa, 76; coauth, The Road to Eleusis: Unveiling the Secret of the Mysteries, Harcourt, 78 (later translated into Spanish, Italian, Greek, and German); Mushrooms and Philosophers, 81 & The Wild and the Cultivated: Wine in Euripides' Bacchae, 82, J Ethnopharmacology; auth, Marginalia Pindarica I-VI, Hermes, 68-72; Euripides' Mother: Vegetables and the Phallos in Aristophanes, Arion, 75; coauth, A Mythic Search for Identity in a Male to Female Transsexual, J of Analytical Psch, 79; coauth, Strategies in Teaching Greek and Latin: Two Decades of Experimentation(Reading Greek), Scholars press, 91; coauth, On Nature (The Wild and the Cultivated in Greek religion), Notre Dame, 84; coauth, Persephone's Quest: Entheogens and the Origins of Religion, Yale, 86; auth, Latin: A Concise Structural Course, Univ Press Am, 87; coauth, The Sacred Mushroom Seeker (Mr Wasson and the Greeks), Dioscorides, 90; coauth, The World of Classical Myth: Gods and Godesses, Heroines and Heros, Carolina Academic Press, 94; coauth, Ethnobotany: Evolution of a Discipline (Gods and Plants in the Classical World), Dioscorides, 95; auth, Intensive Latin: First Year and Review (with computer tutorial Vade Mecum), Carolina Academic Press, 97; coauth, Mistletoe, Centaurs, and Datura, Eleusis n s 1.2, 98; auth, entry on Myth in the Blackwell Dictionary of Anthropology. **CONTACT ADDRESS** Dept of Classics, Boston Univ, 745 Commonwealth Ave, Boston, MA, 02215-1401. **EMAIL** bacchus@bu.edu

RUDDY, T. MICHAEL
PERSONAL Born 07/17/1946, Kansas City, KS, m, 1970, 3 children **DISCIPLINE** TWENTIETH CENTURY UNITED STATES & DIPLOMATIC HISTORY **EDUCATION** Rockhurst Col, AB, 68; Creighton Univ, MA, 70; Kent State Univ, PhD(hist), 73. **CAREER** Asst prof, Kent State Univ, Tuscarawas Campus, 73-77; assoc prof to prof hist, St Louis Univ, 77-. **HONORS AND AWARDS** Fulbright Lectureship, Joensuu Finland, 83-84. **MEMBERSHIPS** Soc Historians Am Foreign Rels; Orgn Am Historians. **RESEARCH** US relations with Europe's neutrals, especially Finland and Sweden; NATO; European integration. **SELECTED PUBLICATIONS** The Cautious Diplomat: Charles E Bohlen and the Soviet Union, 1929-1969, Kent State Univ Press; Damning the Dam: The St Louis District Corps of Engineers and the Controversy over the Meramec Basin Project from Its Inception to Its Deauthorization (GPO); ed, Charting an Independent Course: Finland's Place in the Cold War and in US Foreign Policy; articles on US foreign policy in the Cold War. **CONTACT ADDRESS** Hist Dept, St Louis Univ, 3800 Lindell Blvd, PO Box 56907, Saint Louis, MO, 63156-0907. **EMAIL** ruddytm@slu.edu

RUDGE, DAVID W.
PERSONAL Born 11/29/1962, Syracuse, NY, s **DISCIPLINE** HISTORY AND PHILOSOPHY OF SCIENCE **EDUCATION** Duke Univ, BS, 86; Univ Pittsburgh, MS, 90; Univ Pittsburgh, MA, 92; Univ Pittsburgh, PhD, 96. **CAREER** Lectr, philos, Tex A&M Univ, 96-97; temp asst prof, philos, Iowa State Univ, 97-. **HONORS AND AWARDS** London Visiting Scholars fel, Centre for the Philos of the Natural and Soc Sci, London Sch of Econ and Polit Sci, summer, 97; Intl Res Travel Assistance grant, Office of the Asst Provost for Intl Prog, Tex A&M Univ, spring, 97; Pew teaching leadership award, fall, 93. **MEMBERSHIPS** Amer Asn of Philos Teachers; Amer Philos Asn; Central States Philos Asn; Hist of Sci Soc; Intl Soc for the Hist, Philos & Soc Studies of Bio; Philos of Sci Asn; Sigma Xi. **RESEARCH** Experiments in evolutionary biology; H. B. D. Kettlewell. **SELECTED PUBLICATIONS** Article, Classroom Videotaping: A Protocol for Camera Operators and Consultants, Jour of Grad Teaching Asst Develop, 2, 3, 113-123, 95; co-auth, article, Structure, Function and Variation in the Hindlimb Muscles of the Margarornis Assemblage, Annals of the Carnegie Mus, 61, 207-237, 92; co-auth, article, The Phylogenetic Relationships of the Margarornis Assemblage, Condor, 94, 760-766, 92; book rev, Scientific Thinking by Robert M. Martin, Philos in Rev/Comptes rendus philos, 17, 5, 350-352, 97. **CONTACT ADDRESS** Department of Philosophy, Iowa State Univ, Rm. 435 Catt Hall, Ames, IA, 50011-1036. **EMAIL** rudge@iastate.edu

RUDIN, RONALD
DISCIPLINE HISTORY **EDUCATION** Univ Pittsburgh, BA; Univ York, MA, PhD. **CAREER** Prof. **SELECTED PUBLICATIONS** Auth, four books and numerous articles dealing with the economic and social history of Quebec in the nineteenth and twentieth centuries; Making History in Twentieth-Century Quebec. **CONTACT ADDRESS** Dept of Hist, Concordia Univ, Montreal, 1455 de Maisonneuve W, Montreal, PQ, H3G 1M8. **EMAIL** rudin@vax2.concordia.ca

RUDNICK, LOIS P.
PERSONAL Born 06/18/1944, Boston, MA, m, 1965, 1 child **DISCIPLINE** AMERICAN STUDIES **EDUCATION** Tufts Univ, BA, 66, MA, 68; Brown Univ, PhD, 77. **CAREER** Asst to Assoc to Prof English & Am Stud, Univ Mass, 77-; Dir, Am Stud Prog, Univ Mass, 83-. **HONORS AND AWARDS** Phi Beta Kappa; Mary C Turpie Award, Am Stud Assoc, 97. **MEMBERSHIPS** Am Stud Asn; MELUS. **RESEARCH** Modern American culture; Southwest literature & culture. **SELECTED PUBLICATIONS** Auth, Mabel Dodge Luhan: New Woman, New Worlds, Univ NMex Press, 84; co-ed, 1915, The Cultural Moment: The New Politics, The New Woman, The New Psychology, The New Art, and The New Theatre in America, Rutgers Univ Press, 91; auth, Utopian Vistas: The Mabel Dodge Luhan House and the American Counterculture, Univ NMex Press, 96. **CONTACT ADDRESS** 220 Wolomolopoag St, Sharon, MA, 02067. **EMAIL** rudnick@umbsky.cc.umb.edu

RUDNICK LUFT, SANDRA
PERSONAL Born 07/22/1934, Los Angeles, CA, m, 2 children **DISCIPLINE** HISTORY OF IDEAS **EDUCATION** Brandeis Univ, PhD, 63. **CAREER** Prof, humanities, San Francisco State Univ. **RESEARCH** Giambattista vico; F. Nietzsche; Post modern theory. **SELECTED PUBLICATIONS** Auth, Embodying the Eye of Humanism: Biambattista Vico and the Eye of Ingenium, Sites of Vision: The Discursive Construction of Vision in the History of Philosophy, MIT Press, 97; auth, The Postmodern: Raising the Questions Philosophy Doesn't Ask, Mag, 96; auth, Philosophy as Poiesis in Vico and Nietzsche, Proceedings of the Intl Soc for the Study of Europ Ideas Conf, 96; auth, Situating Vico Between Modern and Postmodern, Hist Reflections/Reflexions Historiques, 96; auth, The Secularization of Origins in Vico and Nietzsche, Personalist Forum, 94; auth, Derrida, Vico, Genesis, and the Originary Power of Language, The Eighteenth Century: Theory and Interpretation, 93; rev, Golden Doves with Silver Dots: Semiology and Textuality in the Rabbinic Tradition, New Vico Studies, 92. **CONTACT ADDRESS** San Francisco State Univ, 1600 Hallaway Ave., San Francisco, CA, 94132. **EMAIL** srluft@sfsu.edu

RUDOLPH, CONRAD
DISCIPLINE HISTORY OF ART **EDUCATION** Univ Calif, Los Angeles, BA, 77, MA, 81, PhD, 85. **CAREER** Vis asst prof, Gustavus Adolphus Col, 85-86; Mellon fel, Univ Pittsburgh, 86-87; Getty fel Getty Ctr Hist Art and Hum, 87- 88; asst prof, Univ Notre Dame, 88-91; assoc prof, 91-97, PROF, UNIV CALIF, RIVERSIDE, 97-. **CONTACT ADDRESS** Dept Hist Art, Univ of California, Riverside, Riverside, CA, 92521-0319. **EMAIL** conrad.rudolph@ucr.edu

RUDOLPH, FREDERICK
PERSONAL Born 06/19/1920, Baltimore, MD, m, 1949, 2 children **DISCIPLINE** HISTORY **EDUCATION** Williams Col, BA, 42; Yale Univ, MA, 49, PhD(hist), 53. **CAREER** Instr, 46-47, 51-53, from asst prof to assoc prof, 53-61, prof hist 61-82, PROF EMER, 82- , WILLIAMS COL. vis lectr hist & educ, Harvard Univ, 60-61; vis prof Univ Calif, Berkeley, 83; exec ed, Change, 80- . **HONORS AND AWARDS** Guggenheim fel, 58-59, 68-69; Frederick W Ness Award, Asn Am Col, 78; LittD, Williams Col, 85; LHD, Univ Rochester, 94; LHD, Wilkes Univ, 98. **MEMBERSHIPS** Nat Acad Ed, AHA; Org Am Historians; Am Studies Asn. **RESEARCH** American intellectual history; higher education in the United States; American national character. **SELECTED PUBLICATIONS** Auth, Mark Hopkins and the Log, Yale Univ, 56; American College and University: A History, Knopf, 62; ed, Essays on Education in the Early Republic, Harvard Univ, 65; auth, Neglect of Students as a Historical Tradition, Col & Students, 66; Curriculum: A History of the American Undergraduate Course of Study Since 1636, Jossey-Bass, 77; Heritage and Tradition in Carnegie Foundation for the Advancement of Teaching, In: Common Learning: A Carnegie Colloquium on General Education, 81; ed, Perspectives: A Williams Anthology, 83. **CONTACT ADDRESS** PO Box 515, Williamstown, MA, 01267.

RUDY, WILLIS
PERSONAL Born 01/25/1920, New York, NY, m, 1948, 3 children **DISCIPLINE** HISTORY **EDUCATION** City Col New York, BSS, 39; Columbia Univ, MA, 40, PhD, 48. **CAREER** Instr hist, City Col New York, 39-49; instr hist educ, Harvard Univ, 49-52; prof hist, Mass State Col, Worcester, 52-63; prof hist, 63-, prof emeritus, Fairleigh Dickinson Univ; res historian, Qm Corps, US Dept Army, 52; res consult, Nat Citizens Comn Pub Schs, 52-53; vis prof, NY Univ, 53; consult, Educ Policies Comn, Nat Educ Asn, 55; vis lectr, Harvard Univ, 53, 57-58. **HONORS AND AWARDS** Cromwell Medal. **MEMBERSHIPS** AHA; Orgn Am Historians. **RESEARCH** History of higher education in America; social and intellectual history of the United States; history of learning. **SELECTED PUBLICATIONS** Auth, The Universities of Europe 1100-1914, Fairleigh Dickinson, 84; auth, Total War and Twentieth Century Higher Learning, Fairleigh Dickinson, 91; coauth, Higher Education in Transition: A History of American Higher Education, 1636-1976, Transaction, 96; auth, The Campus and a Nation in Crisis, Fairleigh Dickinson, 96. **CONTACT ADDRESS** 161 W Clinton Ave, Tenafly, NJ, 07670.

RUEBEL, JAMES
PERSONAL Born 08/18/1945, Cincinnati, OH, m, 1966, 2 children **DISCIPLINE** ANCIENT ROMAN HISTORY, CLASSICAL LANGUAGES **EDUCATION** Yale Univ, BA, 67; Univ Cincinnati, MA, 70, PhD, 72. **CAREER** Instr Greek & Latin, Classics Dept, Univ Cincinnati, 72-73; asst prof, Classics Dept, Univ MN, 73-78; asst prof, 78-81, Assoc Prof, 81-93, PROF CLASSICS, FOR LANG & LIT, IA STATE UNIV, 93-. **MEMBERSHIPS** Am Philol Asn; Asn Ancient Historians; Class Asn Midwest & South; Am Class League; Archaeol Inst Am. **RESEARCH** Roman republican history; Roman culture from Hannibal to Horace. **CONTACT ADDRESS** Dept of For Lang & Lit, Iowa State Univ, Ames, IA, 50011-2205. **EMAIL** jsruebel@iastate.edu

RUEDY, JOHN D.
PERSONAL Born 04/28/1927, Alameda, CA, m, 1953, 3 children **DISCIPLINE** MIDDLE EAST HISTORY **EDUCATION** Univ Calif, Berkeley, AB, 48; San Diego State Col, MA, 61; Univ Calif, Los Angeles, PhD(hist), 65. **CAREER** Asst English, Lycee Henri IV, Paris, France, 48-49; asst prof, 65-68, assoc prof, 68-92, PROF HIST, GEORGETOWN UNIV, 92-, CHMN ARAB STUDIES PROG, 75-88, Lectr, Johns Hopkins Univ Sch Advan Int Studies, 70-75; Fulbright scholar, Tunisia, 72-73. **MEMBERSHIPS** Mid E Inst; Mid E Studies Asn of N Am; AHA. **RESEARCH** Colonial North Africa; 20th century Syria and Palestine. **SELECTED PUBLICATIONS** Auth, Land Policy in Colonial Algeria, Univ Calif, 67; contrib, Palestine: A Search for Truth, Pub Affairs, 70; The Transformation of Palestine, Northwestern Univ, 71; auth, Modern Algeria: The Origins and Development of a Nation, Indiana; ed & contribr, Islamism & Secularism in North Africa, St Martins, 94. **CONTACT ADDRESS** Dept of History, Georgetown Univ, Washington, DC, 20007.

RUEL ROBINS, MARIANNE
DISCIPLINE EARLY MODERN EUROPE HISTORY **EDUCATION** Univ, Paris-Sorbonne, 97. **CAREER** Instr, Duke Univ, 91; instr, Calvin Col, 93-96; asst prof, Westmont Col, 96-. **RESEARCH** French civilization and culture **SELECTED PUBLICATIONS** Auth, Un prophete en son pays: la Lettre chretienne d'une dame de la noblesse d'Argula von Stauffen, Paroles d'Evangiles, Publ de la Sorbonne, 95; Les chretiens et la danse dans l'Europe du Nord-Ouest, Historiens et Geographes, 94. **CONTACT ADDRESS** Dept of Hist, Westmont Col, 955 La Paz Rd, Santa Barbara, CA, 93108-1099.

RUESTOW, EDWARD G.
DISCIPLINE HISTORY **EDUCATION** Univ Pa, BA, 59; MA, 60; George Wash Univ, MA, 65; Univ Ind Bloomington, PhD, 70. **CAREER** Prof. **SELECTED PUBLICATIONS** Auth, The Microscope in the Dutch Republic: The Shaping of Discovery, Cambridge, 96; Of a Man and His Microscopes: Widening the Perspectives on Early Modern Science, Tractrix, 91; Physics at 17th and 18th-Century Leiden: Philosophy and the New Science in the University, Martinus Nijhoff, 73. **CONTACT ADDRESS** History Dept, Univ of Colorado, Boulder, Boulder, CO, 80309.

RUGGIERO, GUIDO
PERSONAL Born 05/24/1944, Danbury, CT **DISCIPLINE** HISTORY **EDUCATION** Univ Co, MA, 66, Univ Calif Los Angeles, MA, 67, PhD, 72. **CAREER** Vis prof to assoc prof, Univ Cincinnati, 71-87; assoc prof to prof, Univ Ct, 87-94; prof, Univ Miami, 94-97; Josephine Berry Weiss Chair, prof, Pa St Univ, 97- . **HONORS AND AWARDS** Inst Adv Study, Princeton, 81-82, 91; Ateneo Veneto, Socio Straniero; Harvard Villa I Tatti Fel, 90-91; NEH Fel, 81-82,90-91; John Simon Guggenheim Mem Found Fel, 91. **MEMBERSHIPS** Amer Hist Assoc, Renaissance Soc of Amer; Sixteenth Century Stud Assoc. **RESEARCH** Renaissance & early modern Italy history & lit; premodern sex & gender; culture & early sci. **SELECTED PUBLICATIONS** Auth, Binding Passions: Tales of Magic, Marriage, and Power at the End of the Renaissance, Oxford Univ Press, 93; Deconstructing the Body, constructing the Body Poli-

tic: Ritual Execution in the Renaissance, in Riti e rituali nelle societa medievali, Centro Italiano di Studi sull'Alto Medioevo, 94; Sexuality, & The Italian Renaissance, entries in The Encyclopedia of Social History, Garland Press, 94; coauth, Introduction: The Crime of History, & Afterword: Crime and the Writing of History, in History from Crime, Selections from Quaderni Storici, Johns Hopkins Univ Press, 94; auth, Politica e giustizia, in Storia di Venezia dalle origini alla caduta della Serenissima, Istituto della Encilopedia Italiana fondata da Giovanni Trecanni, 97. **CONTACT ADDRESS** Dept of History, Pennsylvania State Univ, University Park, PA, 16802-5500. **EMAIL** gxr12@psu.edu

RUGGIERO FREIS, CATHERINE
PERSONAL Born 10/18/1940, New York, NY, m, 1964, 2 children **DISCIPLINE** CLASSICS **EDUCATION** UC Berkeley, PhD, 80 **CAREER** Prof, Millsaps Col **HONORS AND AWARDS** Am Philol Soc Awd for Excel in the Tching of Classics **MEMBERSHIPS** Am Philol Soc; Classical Assoc of Midwest & South **RESEARCH** Tragedy & East & South Asian Dance Drama **SELECTED PUBLICATIONS** Auth, Didaskalia, 97 **CONTACT ADDRESS** 749 Oakwood St, Jackson, MS, 39202-1121. **EMAIL** freiscr@millsaps.edu

RUGGLES, STEVEN
DISCIPLINE HISTORY **EDUCATION** Univ Pa, PhD, 84. **CAREER** Prof **HONORS AND AWARDS** Sharlin Prize, 88; William J. Goode Awd, 89. **RESEARCH** Historical demography. **SELECTED PUBLICATIONS** Auth, Prolonged Connections: The Rise of the Extended Family in Nineteenth Century England and America, Univ Wis, 87; pubs on fertility, living arrangements of the elderly, race and ethnicity, family reconstitution, life-course analysis, and demographic methods. **CONTACT ADDRESS** History Dept, Univ of Minnesota, Twin Cities, 614 Social Sciences Tower, 267 19th Ave S, Minneapolis, MN, 55455. **EMAIL** ruggles@atlas.socsci.umn.edu

RUGOFF, MILTON
PERSONAL Born 03/06/1913, New York, NY, m, 1937, 1 child **DISCIPLINE** HISTORY, ENGLISH **EDUCATION** Columbia Col, BA, 33; Columbia Univ, MA, 34, PhD, 40. **CAREER** Ed, Alfred E Knopf, Inc, 42-47; assoc ed, 47-48, Mag of the Year; ed, 53, Readers Subscription Bk Club; ed, vice pres, 48-93, Chanticleer Press, Inc, NY. **HONORS AND AWARDS** Literary Lion medal, NY Pub Lib, 90; Ohioana Bk Award, 82. **MEMBERSHIPS** Soc Amer Hist; Authors' Guild. **RESEARCH** American Biography; Elizabethan literature; history of traveland exploration. **SELECTED PUBLICATIONS** Auth, The Penguin Book of World Folk Tales, Viking, 49; ed & intro, The Great Travelers, S and S, 61; auth, Donne's Imagery: A Study in Creative Sources, Atheneum, 62; auth, Marco Polo's Adventures in China, Caravel Bks, 64; auth, Prudery and Passion: Sexuality in Victorian America, Putnam, 71; ed, Britannica Encycl of American Art, Simon, 73; auth, The Beechers: An American Family in the Nineteenth Century, Harper & Row, 81; auth, America's Gilded Age: Intimate Portraits from an Era of Extravagance and Change, Holt & Co, 89. **CONTACT ADDRESS** 18 Ox Ridge Rd, Elmsford, NY, 10523.

RUIZ, TEOFILO FABIAN
PERSONAL Born 01/02/1943, Habana, Cuba, m, 1964, 2 children **DISCIPLINE** HISTORY **EDUCATION** City Col NY, BA, 69; NY Univ, MA, 70; Princeton Univ, PhD, 74. **CAREER** Instr hist, 73-74, asst prof, 74-80, assoc prof hist, 81-85, prof hist, 85-98, Dir Ford Colloquium, 92-95, Brooklyn Col; 80-, Mellon fel humanities, Aspen Inst Humanistic Studies, 75-76; Res Found City Univ New York fac res award, 75-76 & 76-77; Danforth assoc, 78-84; Am Coun Learned Soc fel, 79-80; prof Span Medieval lit, 88-98, prof hist 95-98, CUNY; vis prof distinguished tchg, Princeton Univ, 97-98; prof hist UCLA, 98-. **HONORS AND AWARDS** Dir Studies, Ecole des Hautes Etudes en Science Sociales, (Paris), 93; Outstanding Master's Univ & Col Prof of Year, Carnegie Found for Advan Teaching, 94-95; Premio del Rey, Am Hist Asn Biennial Award for Best Bk Span Hist, 95; PSC-CUNY Res Award, 96-97; Wolfe Inst Fel, 96-97. **MEMBERSHIPS** Soc Span Port Hist Studies; Acad Res Historians Medieval Spain; Medieval Acad. **RESEARCH** Castilian history late medieval (social and economic). **SELECTED PUBLICATIONS** Representacion de uno mismo, representacion de otros y por otros: Castilla, Los castellanos y el Nuevo Mundo a finales de la edad media, Temas Medievales, 93; Goodby Columbus and All That: History and Textual Criticism, New W Indian Guide, 93; Jew, Conversos, and the Inquisition, 1391-1492: The Ambiguities of History, in Jewish-Christian Encounters Over the Centuries: Symbiosis, Prejudice, Holocaust, Dialogue, ed M Perry & F M Schweitzer, NY, Peter Lang Inc, 94; Elite and Popular Culture in Late Fifteenth-Century Castilian Festivals: The Case of Jaen, In City and Spectacle in Medieval Europe, ed B A Hanawalt & K L Reyerson (Minn: Univ Mn, 94; Judios y cristianos en el ambito urbano bajomedieval: Avila Y Burgos, 1200-1350 Xudeos e conversos na historia, Actas do Congreso Internacional de Judios Y Conversos en la Historia, 2 vols Santiago de Compostela: Deputacion de Orense, 94; Crisis and Continuity: Land and Town in Late Medieval Castile, Univ Pa: Phil, 94; La fromazione della monarchia non consacrata: simboli e realta di potere nella Castiglia mediovale, in Federico II e il mondo mediterraneo, a cura di Pierre Toubert e Agostino Paravicino Bagliani, 3 vols, Palermo:Sellerio editore, 95; Representacion: Castilla, los castellanos y el Nuevo Mundo a finales de la edad media y principios de la moderna, in Historia a debate, Medieval, Santiago de Compostela, 95; Violence in Late Medieval Castile: The Case of the Rioja, Revista de Historia, 95; Teaching as Subversion: in Inspiring Teaching: Carnegie Professors of the Year Speak, ed John K Roth, Jaffrey, NH: Anker, 96; Propietat i llengua: Canvis d valors a la Castella medieval, L'Avenc, 97;Women, Work and Daily Life in Late Medieval Castile, in Women at Work in Spain: From the Middle Ages to Early Modern Times, ed M Stone & C Benito-Vessels, NY, 98; The Peasantries of Iberia, 1400-1800, in The Peasantries of Europe, From the Fourteenth to the Eighteenth Centuries, ed Tom Scott, (Longman: London) 98; A Social History of Spain, 1400-1600, Longman, 98. **CONTACT ADDRESS** 11433 Rochester Ave, Los Angeles, CA, 90025. **EMAIL** tfruiz@history.ucla.edu

RUMMEL, ERIKA
DISCIPLINE SOCIAL; INTELLECTUAL HISTORY OF EARLY MODERN EUROPE **EDUCATION** Univ Toronto, PhD. **CAREER** Prof **SELECTED PUBLICATIONS** Auth, Erasmus and His Catholic Critics, De Graaf, 89; Erasmus on Women, U of Toronto P, 96; The Humanist-Scholastic Debate in the Renaissance and Reformation, Harvard UP, 95; Erasmus, 96; The Importance of Being Doctor: The Quarrel over Competency between Humanists and Theologians, 96. **CONTACT ADDRESS** Dept of History, Wilfrid Laurier Univ, 75 University Ave W, Waterloo, ON, N2L 3C5. **EMAIL** erummel@mach1.wlu.ca

RUNYON, RANDOLPH PAUL
PERSONAL Born 02/13/1947, Maysville, KY, 2 children **DISCIPLINE** FRENCH LITERATURE, AMERICAN STUDIES **EDUCATION** Johns Hopkins Univ, PhD(French), 73. **CAREER** Asst prof, Case Western Reserve Univ, 74-76; asst prof to assoc prof, 77-84, Prof French, Miami Univ, 84-. **MEMBERSHIPS** MLA; Soc des Amis de Montaigne; Am Studies Asn; SAtlantic Mod Lang Asn; Robert Penn Warren Circle. **RESEARCH** Sixteenth century French literature; 20th century French literature; literary criticism; 20th century American literature. **SELECTED PUBLICATIONS** Auth, Deliverance: Souffrir non souffrir, Mod Lang Notes, 5/73; La Parole genee: Genese et palinodie, Change, 11/73; The errors of desire, Diacritics, fall 74; Sceve's Aultre Troye, Mod Lang Notes, 5/75; Fragments of an amorous discourse: Canon in U-bis, Visible Lang, fall 77; Montaigne his, In: Resnaissance et Nouvelle Critique, State Univ NY, Albany, 78; Fowles, Irving, Barthes: Canonical Variations on an Apocryphal Theme, Ohio State Univ Press, 81; The Braided Dream: Robert Penn Warren's Late Poetry, Univ Press of Ky, 90; The Taciturn Text: The Fiction of Robert Penn Warren, Ohio State Univ Press, 90; Reading Raymond Carver, Syracuse Univ Press, 92; Delia Webster and the Underground Railroad, Univ Press of Ky, 96. **CONTACT ADDRESS** Dept of French & Ital, Miami Univ, Oxford, OH, 45056-1602. **EMAIL** runyonr@muohio.edu

RUPP, GARY
DISCIPLINE COUNSELING **EDUCATION** Georgia State Univ, MEd, PhD. **CAREER** Assoc prof **RESEARCH** Clinical psychology. **SELECTED PUBLICATIONS** Coauth, Enrichment: Skills Training on Family Life; contrib, Jour of Commun Psychol. **CONTACT ADDRESS** Dept of Counseling, Reformed Theol Sem, 1015 Maitland Ctr Commons, Maitland, FL, 32751.

RUPP, LEILA J.
PERSONAL Born 02/13/1950, Plainfield, NJ **DISCIPLINE** HISTORY, WOMEN'S STUDIES **EDUCATION** Bryn Mawr Col, AB, 72, PhD(hist), 76. **CAREER** Vis lectr hist, Univ Pa, 76-77; asst prof, 77-82, assoc prof, 82-87, prof, OHIO STATE UNIV, 87-. **HONORS AND AWARDS** Ohio Acad of Hist Outstand Tchg Awd **MEMBERSHIPS** Berkshire Conf Women Historians; AHA; OHA **RESEARCH** Women's history; modern German history; modern American history. **SELECTED PUBLICATIONS** Auth, Mother of the Volk: The image of women in Nazi ideology, Signs, winter 77; Mobilizing Women for War: German and American Propaganda, 1939-1945, Princeton Univ, 78; co-ed, Nazi Ideology Before 1933: A Documentation, Univ Tex, 78; coauth, Survival in the Doldrums: The American Women's Rights Movement, 1945 to the 1960s, Oxford Univ, 87; auth Wolrds of Women: The Making of an International Women's Movement, Princeton Univ, 97. **CONTACT ADDRESS** 230 W 17th Ave, Columbus, OH, 43210-1361. **EMAIL** rupp1@osu.edu

RUSCH, SCOTT M.
PERSONAL Born 11/28/1956, Ft. Rucker, AL **DISCIPLINE** ANCIENT HISTORY, GREECE, ROME **EDUCATION** State Univ New York, Albany, BA, 78; Univ PA, MA, 89, PhD, 97. **CAREER** Three semesters as teaching asst at Univ PA, 79-81. **HONORS AND AWARDS** New York State Regents Scholarship, 74; Univ Fel from Univ PA, 81. **MEMBERSHIPS** Am Philol Asn; Classical Asn of the Atlantic States; Am Hist Asn; Asn of Ancient Hist; Friends of Ancient Hist; Soc of Ancient Military Hist. **RESEARCH** Ancient warfare; Thucydides; the history of the Peloponnesian War. **SELECTED PUBLICATIONS** Auth, Poliorcetic Assault in the Peloponnesian War, Univ PA, dissertation, 97. **CONTACT ADDRESS** 4224 Osage Ave, Apt 43, Philadelphia, PA, 19104. **EMAIL** rusch@ccat.sas.upenn.edu

RUSCO, ELMER R.
PERSONAL Born 05/06/1928, Haviland, KS, m, 1955, 2 children **DISCIPLINE** POLITICAL SCIENCE **EDUCATION** Univ Kansas, Ba, 51, MA, 52; Univ Calif, Berkeley, PhD, 60. **CAREER** San Diego State Col, 57-58; Univ Idaho, 59-60; Parsons Col, 61-63; from asst prof to prof, 63-86, prof emer, 86-, Univ Nev, Reno; dir Bureau of Govt Res, 66-76; vis prof Univ Nev, Las Vegas, 84. **HONORS AND AWARDS** Phi Beta Kappa; Pi Sigma Alpha. **MEMBERSHIPS** Am Polit Sci Asn; Am Soc for Ethnohistory. **RESEARCH** Law and public policy affecting ethnic racial groups. **SELECTED PUBLICATIONS** Auth, The Great Books, Multiculturalism, Political Correctness and Related Matters, Halcyon, 93; auth, Campaign Finance Reform in the Silver Era: A Puzzle, parts 1 & 2, Nev Hist Soc Q, 95; auth, A Fateful Time: The Background and Legislative History of the Indian Reorganization Act, Univ Nev, forthcoming. **CONTACT ADDRESS** PO Box 8947, Reno, NV, 89507.

RUSSELL, DIANA ELIZABETH H.
PERSONAL Born 11/06/1938, CapeTown, South Africa, d **DISCIPLINE** SOCIOLOGY **EDUCATION** PhD, 70, MA, 67, Harvard Univ; Postgraduate Diploma London School of Econ and Poli Sci, Soc Sci and Admin; BA Univ of Capetown South Africa, Psychol, 58. **CAREER** Asst Prof, 69-75, Assoc Prof, 75-83, Prof Emerita Soc, Mills Col Oakland, CA, 91-present; Prof Soc, 83-91; Res Assoc Inst of Criminol, Univ Capetown, SAfrica, 92-93; Writer, Res, Intl, Consul and Pub Speaker, 91-92; Res Assoc Univ Capetown, South Africa, 91; Writer, Res, Intl Consul and Pub speaker, 94-. **RESEARCH** Sexual assault, pornography, sexual violence of all kinds, women in SAfrica. **SELECTED PUBLICATIONS** Russell, D E H, Dangeous Relationshops: Pornography, Misogyny, and Rape, Newbury Park CA, Sage Publications, Revised expanded ed of Against Pornography: The Evidence of Harm, Berkeley, CA, Russell Publications, 94; Russell, D E H, Behind Closed Doors in White South Africa: Incest Survivors Tell Their Stories, Basingstoke, Hampshire, UK, Macmillan Press, 97; Russell, D E H, Incestuous Abuse: Itls Long-Term Effects, Pretoria, South Africa: The Human Sciences, Research Council Publishers, 95; Russell, D E H, Against Pornography: The Evidence of Harm, Berkeley, CA, Russell Publications, 94; Numerous more publications. **CONTACT ADDRESS** Div Soc Sci, Mills Col, 5000 MacArthur Blvd, Oakland, CA, 94613.

RUSSELL, FREDERICK HOOKER
PERSONAL Born 11/01/1940, Syracuse, NY, m, 1968 **DISCIPLINE** HISTORY **EDUCATION** Swarthmore Col, BA, 62; Johns Hopkins Univ, MA, 64, PhD(hist), 69; Univ Chicago, MA, 75. **CAREER** Jr instr hist, Johns Hopkins Univ, 63-65 & 68-69; from instr to asst prof, 69-75, grad dir hist, 76-80 & 80-81, Assoc Prof Hist, Rutgers Univ, NewarkA, 75-, Actg Assoc Dean Grad Sch, 78, Assoc, Columbia Univ Sem on Hist Legal & Polit Thought, 73-82; fel, Univ Chicago, 74-75; vis scholar, Inst Medieval Canon Law, Univ CA, Berkeley, 79; vis scholar, Univ of Nottingham, 85; vis scholar, Duke Univ, 89-90; NEH fel, 93. **HONORS AND AWARDS** Herbert Baxter Adams Prize, AHA, 76. **MEMBERSHIPS** AHA; Am Soc Legal Hist; Inst Medieval Canon Law; AAUP; Medieval Acad Am. **RESEARCH** Medieval canon law; patristic theol; legal hist. **SELECTED PUBLICATIONS** Auth, The Just War in the Middle Ages, Cambridge Univ, 75; Innocent IV's proposal to limit warfare, Monumenta Iuris Canonici, 76; Paulus Vladmiri's attack upon the Just War, In: Authority and Power, Cambridge Univ, 80; Crusade, origin and development of the concept, In: Dict of the Middle Ages,84. Historical Perspective in Bishops' Pastoral Letter, In: Peace in a Nuclear Age, Catholic Univ, 86; Love and hate in Warfare, In: Nottingham Medieval Studies, 87; Only Something Good Can Be Evil, In: Theological Studies, 90; Bifurcation of Creation, In: Sewanee Medieval Studies, 95; Augustine: Conversion by the Book, In: Varieties of religious Conversion in the Middle Ages, Univ Press of FL, 97. **CONTACT ADDRESS** Dept of History, Rutgers Univ, 175 University Ave, Newark, NJ, 07102-1897. **EMAIL** frussell@andromeda.rutgers.edu

RUSSELL, GILLIAN
DISCIPLINE CULTURAL HISTORY **CAREER** Vis fel, Ctr Cross-Cult Res, Australian Natl Univ, 97. **RESEARCH** 18th and 19th century British cultural history. **SELECTED PUBLICATIONS** Auth, The Theatre of War: Performance, Politics and Society 1793-1815, Oxford Univ, 95. **CONTACT ADDRESS** Dept of English, Australian National Univ. **EMAIL** Gillian.Russell@anu.edu.au

RUSSELL, HILARY A.
PERSONAL Born 10/24/1947, Kingston, Jamaica **DISCIPLINE** HISTORY **EDUCATION** Carleton Univ, BA, 69. **CAREER** STAFF HISTORIAN, NAT HIST SITES DIRECTORATE, 70-; co-dir conf, Bethune: His Times and His Legacy/son epoque et son message, McGill Univ, 79; proj hist, Elgin and Winter Garden Theatres, 85-89. **HONORS AND AWARDS** City Toronto Bk Award, 90. **SELECTED PUBLICATIONS**

Auth, All That Glitters: A Memorial to Ottawa's Capitol Theatre and its Predecesors, 75; auth, Double Take: The Story of the Elgin and Winter Garden Theatres, 89; contribur, American National Biography; contribur, The Canadian Encyclopedia; contribur, The Dictionary of Canadian Biography; contribur, The Oxford Companion to Theatre History. **CONTACT ADDRESS** National Historical Sites Directorate, 25 Eddy St, F5, Hull, PQ, K1A 0M5.

RUSSELL, JAMES M.
DISCIPLINE HISTORY **EDUCATION** Wesleyan Univ, BA, 66; Princeton Univ, MA, 68, PhD, 72. **CAREER** Prof. **SELECTED PUBLICATIONS** Auth, International Cotton Exposition of 1 881, Greenwood, 90; The Phoenix City and the Civil War: Atlanta's Economic Miracle, Jour Ga and S, 90; Using the Computer to Teach Undergraduates Quantitative Methodologies in Historical Research, Int Jour Soc Edu, 90; Regional and National Perspectives on American Urban History, Can Rev Am Studies, 90; Depicting the Battle of Chancellorsville on a Macintosh Computer, Hist Microcomputer Rev, 94; Economic Factors as Causes of the Civil War, Westport, 96. **CONTACT ADDRESS** Dept of History, 615 McCallie, Chattanooga, TN, 37403. **EMAIL** univrel@cecasun.utc.edu

RUSSELL, TILDEN A.
DISCIPLINE MUSIC **EDUCATION** Univ NC, PhD, 83. **CAREER** Asst prof, 86-92; assoc prof, 92-, Southern CT State Univ. **SELECTED PUBLICATIONS** Auth, publ(s) on Baroque; Classic; Romantic Eras; Beethoven; chamber music; historical musicology. **CONTACT ADDRESS** Music Dept, Southern CT State Univ, Crescent St, PO Box 500, New Heaven, CT, 06515-1355. **EMAIL** Russell_T@scsu.ctstateu.edu

RUSSELL-WOOD, A.J.R.
PERSONAL Born 10/11/1939, Corbridge-on Tyne, England, m, 1972, 2 children **DISCIPLINE** HISTORY **EDUCATION** Lisbon Univ, dipl, 60; Oxford Univ, BA, 63, MA, Dphil, 67. **CAREER** Lectr, Oxford Univ, 63-64; res fel, St Antonys Col, 67-70; from vist assoc prof to assoc prof to prof to chemn, 71-. **HONORS AND AWARDS** Herbert E. Bolton Prize, 69; Albert J. Beveridge Award, 69; Arthur P. Whitaker Prize, 83; Dom Joao de Castro Int Prize, 92; Commander of the Order of Dom Henrique, 96. **MEMBERSHIPS** Royal Geog Society; Royal Hist Society; Europ Acad Arts & Sciences. **RESEARCH** Colonial Latin America; Portuguese Seaborne Empire. **SELECTED PUBLICATIONS** Auth, Society and Government in Colonial Brazil, 1500-1822, 92; auth, A World on the Move. The Portuguese in Africa, Asia, and America, 1415-1808, 92; auth, The Black Man in Slavery and Freedom in Colonial Brazil, 93; auth, Portugal and the Sea: A World Embraced, 97; ed, Local Government in European Overseas Empire, 1450-1800, 99. **CONTACT ADDRESS** Dept of History, The John Hopkins Univ, Baltimore, MD, 21218. **EMAIL** russwood@jhuvms.hcf.jhu.edu

RUSSO, DAVID J.
DISCIPLINE HISTORY **EDUCATION** Univ Mass, BA; Yale Univ, MA, PhD. **RESEARCH** United States hist **SELECTED PUBLICATIONS** Auth, Families and Communities: A New View of American History, 74; auth, Keeper's of our Past: Local Historical Writing in the United States, 1820's-1930's, 88; auth, Clio Confused, 95. **CONTACT ADDRESS** History Dept, McMaster Univ, 1280 Main St W, Hamilton, ON, L8S 4L9.

RUSSO, JOSEPH ANTHONY
PERSONAL Born 04/14/1937, Brooklyn, NY, m, 1960, 2 children **DISCIPLINE** CLASSICS **EDUCATION** Brooklyn Col, BA, 58; Yale Univ, MA, 60, PhD, 62. **CAREER** From instr to assoc prof classics, Yale Univ, 62-70; assoc prof, 70-76, prof classics, Haverford Col, 76-, chmn dept, 80-, fel, Ctr Hellenic Studies, Wash, DC, 65-66; Nat Endowment for Humanities younger humanist fel, 73-74; Am Coun Learned Soc grant-in-aid, 74; Nat Endowment Hum Summer Stipend, 82 & 90; vis prof class studies, Univ Mich, 77-78; Univ Ca Berkley, 83. **HONORS AND AWARDS** Distinguished Alumni Award, Brooklyn Col, 82. **MEMBERSHIPS** Class Asn Atlantic States; Am Philol Asn. **RESEARCH** Greek literature and metrics; Homeric poetry; oral literature and folklore. **SELECTED PUBLICATIONS** Auth, A Closer Look at Homeric Formulas, Trans Am Philol Asn, 64; The Structural Formula of Homeric Verse, Yale Class Studies, 66; coauth, Homeric Psychology and the Oral Epic Tradition, J Hist Ideas, 68; Homer Against his Tradition, Arion, 68; The Inner Man in Archilochus and the Odyssey, Greek, Roman & Byzantine Studies, 74; Reading the Greek Lyric Poets, Arion, 75; How, and what, does Homer communicate, Class J, 76; contribr, Is Aural or oral composition the cause of Homer's formulaic style?, Oral Literature and the Formula, Univ Mich, 76; co-auth, A Commentary on Homer's Odyssey, Oxford Univ, 92; auth, Omero, Odissea V, Libri XVII-XX, Mondadori, Roma, 92. **CONTACT ADDRESS** Dept of Classics, Haverford Col, 370 Lancaster Ave, Haverford, PA, 19041-1392. **EMAIL** jrusso@haverford.edu

RUST, EZRA GARDNER
DISCIPLINE MUSIC **EDUCATION** UCLA, BA; UCB, MA, PhD. **CAREER** Prof; campus coordr, Interdisciplinary Stud Prog; past ch, Mus Dept; Sonoma State Univ, 68-. **RESEARCH** World music; World religious music and dance; Voice. **SELECTED PUBLICATIONS** Music and Dance of the World's Religions: A Comprehensive, Annotated Bibliography of Materials in the English Language, Greenwood Press, 96. **CONTACT ADDRESS** Dept of Music, Sonoma State Univ, 1801 E. Cotati Ave., Rohnert Park, CA, 94928-3609. **EMAIL** gardner.rust@sonoma.edu

RUTHERFORD, DONALD P.
DISCIPLINE HISTORY OF MODERN PHILOSOPHY **EDUCATION** Univ CA, PhD, 88. **CAREER** Philos, Emory Univ. **SELECTED PUBLICATIONS** Auth, Leibniz and the Rational Order of Nature. **CONTACT ADDRESS** Emory Univ, Atlanta, GA, 30322-1950.

RUTHERFORD, PAUL F.W.
PERSONAL Born 02/22/1944, Middlesex, England **DISCIPLINE** HISTORY/MEDIA STUDIES **EDUCATION** Carleton Univ, BA, 65; Univ Toronto, MA, 66, PhD, 73. **CAREER** Lectr, 69-73, asst prof, 73-75, assoc prof, 75-82, chmn, 82-87, PROF HISTORY, UNIV TORONTO, 82-. **SELECTED PUBLICATIONS** Auth, The Making of the Canadian Media, 78; auth, A Victorian Authority: The Daily Press in Late Nineteenth Century Canada, 82; auth, When Television Was Young: Primetime Canada 1952-1967, 90; auth, The New Icons? The Art of Television Advertising, 94; ed, Saving the Canadian City: The First Phase 1880-1920, 74. **CONTACT ADDRESS** Dept of History, Univ Toronto, Toronto, ON, M5S 1A1. **EMAIL** pruther@chass.utoronto.ca

RUTKOFF, PETER
DISCIPLINE HISTORY **EDUCATION** St Lawrence Univ, AB, 64; Univ Pa, MA 65; PhD, 71. **CAREER** Prof hist, NEH Distinguished Tchg Prof Hist, 97; prof, 85-; assoc prof, 78-85; asst prof, 71-77, Kenyon Coll; visiting instr, Union Col, 70-71; visiting assoc prof, Grad Fac New School for Social Research, 79-82. **HONORS AND AWARDS** Dir, NEH Summer Sem, 97; prof yr, Carnegie Found and Coun Advancement and Support Educ, 93; dir, NEH Summer Sem Sec Tchg(s), 93; Outstanding Fac Award: Black Student Union, 90, 98; Martin Luther King, Jr. Award, , 90., Fel, Smithsonian, 87-88, 92-93; grant, NEH, 93; proj grant, NAH, 87-89; Mellon Grant coord, 87-88. **RESEARCH** Modern America, American studies, Western cultural history. **SELECTED PUBLICATIONS** Auth, Revanche and Revision: The Origins of the Radical Right in France 1880-1900, Ohio Univ Press, 81; New York Baseball, The City Speaks, Prospects, 96; contrib, New York Encyclopedia, Yale Univ Press, 95; Golemby's Running, Crab Orchard Rev, 97;coauth, Appalachian Spring: An Artistic Collaboration, Prospects, 96; The Origins of Bebop, Kenyon Rev, 96. **CONTACT ADDRESS** Dept of Hist, Kenyon Col, Gambier, OH, 43022. **EMAIL** rutkoff@kenyon.edu

RUTLAND, ROBERT ALLEN
PERSONAL Born 10/01/1922, Okmulgee, OK, m, 1947, 2 children **DISCIPLINE** HISTORY **EDUCATION** Univ Okla, BA, 47; Cornell Univ, AM, 50; Vanderbilt Univ, PhD, 53. **CAREER** Res assoc hist, State Hist Soc Iowa, 52-54; from instr to prof jour, Univ Calif, Los Angeles, 54-69; bicentennial coordr, Libr Congr, 69-71; ed-in-Chief, Papers James Madison, 71-87, prof hist, 77-87, Univ Va; prof hist, Univ Tulsa, 87-98; Fulbright prof, Univ Innsbruck, Austria, 60-61; vis prof, Univ E Anglia, 80. **MEMBERSHIPS** Orgn Am Historians; Am Antiq Soc. **RESEARCH** History of Constitution and Bill of Rights. **SELECTED PUBLICATIONS** Auth, James Madison and the Search for Nationhood, Libr Cong, 81; ed, Papers of James Madison, Vols 8-14, Univ Chicago & Univ Va, 73-86; auth, James Madison, The Founding Father, Macmillan, 87; auth, The Presidency of James Madison, Kansas, 90; auth, Boyhood in the Dust Bowl, Colorado, 95; auth, The Republicans, Missouri, 96. **CONTACT ADDRESS** History Dept, Univ of Tulsa, Tulsa, OK, 74104. **EMAIL** rutlan/t-kelley@utulsa.edu

RUTLEDGE, HARRY CARRACI
PERSONAL Born 01/23/1932, Chillicothe, OH **DISCIPLINE** CLASSICS **EDUCATION** OH State Univ, BScEd, 54, MA, 57, PhD, 60. **CAREER** From asst prof to assoc prof classics, Univ GA, 60-68; assoc prof, head Romance lang, 72-79, Prof Class, Univ TN, Knoxville, 69-96, Prof Emer, 96-, Head Dept, 68-91, Secy adv coun, Am Acad Rome, 71-75. **MEMBERSHIPS** Am Philol Asn; Archaeol Inst Am; Vergilian Soc(pres , 77-79); Southern Comp Lit Asn (pres, 78-79); Class Asn Mid West & South (pres, 79-80); Am Class League (pres, 90-94). **RESEARCH** Lit of the Augustan Age; Vergil; class tradition in the 20th century. **SELECTED PUBLICATIONS** Auth, Propertius' Tarpeia: The poem itself, Class J, 11/64; Eliot and Vergil: Parallels in the Sixth Aeneid and Four Quartets, Vergilius, 66; Classical Latin poetry: An art for our time, In: The Endless Fountain, Ohio State Univ, 72; Contest and possession: Classical imagery in Henry James' The Golden Bowl, Comparatist, 5/77; Vergil's Dido in modern literature, Class & Mod Lit, summer 81; The Guernica Bull: Studies in the Classical Tradition in the Twentieth Century, Univ Ga Press, 89. **CONTACT ADDRESS** Dept of Class, Univ of TN, 1101 McClung Tower, Knoxville, TN, 37996-0471.

RUTLEDGE, STEVEN H.
PERSONAL Born 06/28/1963, Fresno, CA, m, 1985 **DISCIPLINE** CLASSICS **EDUCATION** Univ Mass - Boston, BA, 89; Brown Univ, PhD, 96. **CAREER** Asst Prof, Univ Md - College Park, 96-. **HONORS AND AWARDS** Grad Res Bd Fel, Univ Md, 97. **MEMBERSHIPS** APA; CAAS; CAMWS. **RESEARCH** Roman social history; Roman literature of the Early Empire. **SELECTED PUBLICATIONS** Auth, Delatores and the Tradition of Violence in Roman Oratory, AJP (forthcoming). **CONTACT ADDRESS** Classics Dept, Univ of Maryland Col Park, 2407 Marie Mount Hall, College Park, MD, 20742. **EMAIL** srutled@deans.umd.edu

RUTTER, JEREMY B.
PERSONAL Born 06/23/1946, Boston, MA, m, 1970, 2 children **DISCIPLINE** CLASSICS **EDUCATION** Haverford Col, BA, 67; Univ Pa, PhD, 74. **CAREER** Vis asst prof, Univ Calif, Los Angeles, 75-76; from asst prof to assoc prof to prof to chemn, 76-, Dartmouth Col. **HONORS AND AWARDS** Phi Beta Kappa, 67; Woodrow Wilson Fel, 67; Olivia James Travelling Fel, 75; NEH Res Grant, 79-81; ACLS Travel Grant, 82. **MEMBERSHIPS** Archaeol Inst Am; Am Sch Classical Stud, Athens; British Sch Archaeol, Athens; Classical Asn, New England. **RESEARCH** Aegean Prehistory; Ceramic Production and Exchange; Greco-Roman Athletics. **SELECTED PUBLICATIONS** Auth, The Transition to Mycenaean, 76; auth, Ceramic Change in the Aegean Early Bronze Age, 79; auth, Review of Aegean Prehistory II: The Pre-Palatial Bronze Age of the Southern and Central Greek Mainland, 93; auth, Lerna III: The Pottery of Lerna IV, 95; **CONTACT ADDRESS** Dept of Classics, Dartmouth Col, Hanover, NH, 03755. **EMAIL** jeremy.rutter@dartmouth.edu

RYAN, HERBERT JOSEPH
PERSONAL Born 02/19/1931, Scarsdale, NY **DISCIPLINE** THEOLOGY, HISTORY **EDUCATION** Loyola Univ, Ill, AB, 54, MA, 60, PhL, 56; Woodstock Col, Md, STL, 63; Gregorian Univ, STD, 67. **CAREER** From asst prof to assoc prof hist theol, Woodstock Col, Md, 67- 74; assoc prof relig studies, 74-79, Prof Theol, Loyola Marymount Univ, 79-, Off Roman Cath observer, Lambeth Conf, 68; mem joint comn Anglican-Roman Cath relat, Roman Cath Bishops Comn Ecumenical, Affairs, 68-; convenor joint comn ministry & off observer Roman Cath Church, Gen Conv Episcopal Church, 69, 71 & 73; secretariat for promoting Christian unity, Anglican-Roman Cath Int Comn, 69-; vis lectr hist theol, Union Theol Sem, NY, 71-74; vis prof ecumenical & ascetical theol, Gen Theol Sem, 73-74. **HONORS AND AWARDS** Int Christian Unity Award, Graymoor Ecumenical Inst, 74; Medal Order St Augustine, Archbishop Canterbury, London, 81., STD, Gen Theol Sem, 73. **MEMBERSHIPS** Am Acad Relig; Cath Hist Soc; Cath Theol Soc Am; Church Hist Soc; N Am Acad Ecumenists; Mediaeval Acad Am. **RESEARCH** Anglican theological tradition; influence of St Augustine on Christian theology; methodology of ecumenical theology. **SELECTED PUBLICATIONS** Auth, Wolsey - Church, State And Art - Gunn,Sj, Lindley,Pg, Editors/, Theol Studies, Vol 0053, 1992; The Synods For The Carolingian Empire From Ad721 To Ad090 Held In France And In Italy - Ger - Hartmann,W/, Speculum-A J Of Medieval Studies, Vol 0067, 1992; The Renewal Of Anglicanism - Mcgrath,Ae/, Theol Studies, Vol 0055, 1994. **CONTACT ADDRESS** Dept of Relig Studies, Loyola Marymount Univ, 7900 Loyola Blvd, Los Angeles, CA, 90045.

RYAN, JAMES D.
PERSONAL Born 11/29/1938, Buffalo, NY, m, 1963, 3 children **DISCIPLINE** HISTORY **EDUCATION** NY Univ, PhD, 72. **CAREER** From Instr to prof, Bronx Commun Col, CUNY, 79- ; Chm Dept Hist, 91- . **HONORS AND AWARDS** NEH fel, 81; ACLS grant, 90; PCS/CUNY res awards, 91, 92, 96, 97, 98; BCC found res grant, 93; AAC/NEA award, 96. **MEMBERSHIPS** Medieval Acad of Am; Medieval Club of NY; Am Hist Asn; Am Catholic Hist Asn; World Hist Asn; Am Acad of Polit and Soc Sci; ECCSSA. **RESEARCH** History of Crusades and Mission; Church history; medieval travel; cross cultural contacts. **SELECTED PUBLICATIONS** Auth, Nicholas IV and the Evoloution of the Eastern Missionary Effort, in Archivum Pontificiae Historiae, 81; auth For Christ of Christendom: Contrasting Western Missionary Goals in the Morea and Asian Mission Lands in the Late Thirteenth and Early Fourteenth Centuries, in Transactions of the 17th Internatl Congress of Hist Sci, 92; auth, Missionary Objectives in China and India ain the Fourteenth Century, in Proceedings of the Am Hist Asn, 92; auth, European Travelers before Columbus: The Fourteenth Century's Discovery of India, in Cath Hist Rev, 93; auth, Conversion vs. Baptism? European Missionaries in Asia in the Thirteenth and Fourteenth Centuries, in Varieties of Religious Conversion in the Middle Ages, Univ Pr Florida, 97; auth, Christian Wives of Mongol Khans: Tartar Queens and Missionary Expectations in Asia, in J of Royal Asiatic Soc, 98; auth, Preaching Christianity along the Silk Route: Missionary Outposts in the Tartar Middle Kingdom, in J of Early Mod Hist, 98. **CONTACT ADDRESS** Dept of History, Bronx Comm Col, CUNY, University Ave & West 181st St, Bronx, NY, 10453. **EMAIL** jdrbx@cunyvm.cuny.edu

RYAN, KEVIN
PERSONAL Born 10/07/1932, Mt. Vernon, NY, m, 1964, 3 children **DISCIPLINE** EDUCATION **EDUCATION** Univ Toronto, BA, 55; Stanford Univ, MA, 60; Harvard Univ, PhD, 66. **CAREER** Teacher, Suffern High Sch, 59-63; Instr, Naval Officers Candidate Sch, 63; Supvr Intern Teachers, 63-64, Coordr Supvrs, 64-66, Instr & Fac Resident, Stanford Univ, 65-66; Alfred North Whitehead Fel, Harvard Univ, 70-71; Sr. Study Dir, Nat Opinion Res Ctr, 73-75; Vis Prof, Harvard Univ, 73-74; Asst Prof, 66-68, Assoc Prof , Univ Chicago, 68-75; Sr. Fulbright Hayes Schol, Ministry Educ, Lisbon, Portugal, 80; Prof Educ, Ohio State Univ, 75-82, Assoc Dean Prog Development, Col Educ, 75-78; Prof, Sch Educ, 82-, Dir, Ctr Advancement Ethics & Character, Boston Univ, 89-. **HONORS AND AWARDS** Wall Street Journal Award, Columbia Univ, 62; Alfred North Whitehead Fel, Harvard Univ, 70-71; Certificate of Recognition, Am Asn Col for Teacher Educ, 75; Fulbright-Hayes Sr. Schol, 80; Distinguished Service Medal, Univ Helsinki, 80; Boston Univ Schol-Teacher Award, 89-90; Outstanding Teacher Educr Award, Asn Teacher Educ, 90. **MEMBERSHIPS** Character Educ Partnership; Am Educ Res Asn; Asn Supervision & Curriculum Development; Asn Teacher Educr; Phi Delta Kappa; Nat Soc Study Educ; Network Educ Excellence. **RESEARCH** Character and moral education; teacher education. **SELECTED PUBLICATIONS** Coauth, Lenses on Teaching, Holt/Dryden/Saunders, 89, 2nd ed, 94; co-ed, The Art of Lo Loving Well, Boston Univ, 90; ed, The Roller Coaster Year: Accounts of First Year Teachers, Harper Collins, 91; coauth, Reclaiming Our Schools: A Handbook for Teaching Character, Academics and Discipline, Macmillan, 93, 2nd ed, Prentice Hall/Merrill, 97; Building Character in Schools, Jossey-Bass (in press 98); author of numerous other publications. **CONTACT ADDRESS** School of Education, Boston Univ, 127 Commonwealth Ave., Boston, MA, 02167. **EMAIL** kryan@bu.edu

RYAN, THOMAS JOSEPH
PERSONAL Born 05/28/1942, Brooklyn, NY **DISCIPLINE** LATIN AMERICAN & UNITED STATES HISTORY **EDUCATION** Fla Southern Col, BS, 63; Univ Ala, MA, 66; NOVA Southeastern Univ, EdD, 87. **CAREER** Teacher & coach hist, Charlotte Sr High, 64-65; prof hist, Broward Community Col, 66-; Dir Camp BCC, 79-94; lectr Latin Am, World Campus Afloat, 75; tour guide, Broward Community Col 74-98. **HONORS AND AWARDS** Salvation Army Family Award, 85; USMC Semper Fi Award, 89 & 91; J.C. Penny Volunteer of the Year, 90; South Fla Manufacturer's Exemplary Practice, 91; Buick Volunteer Spirit, 94; SPD History Grant, 94 & 95; Teach Learn CTN, 95 & 96; BCC Boyr Award, 97; Intercollegiate Hall of Fame, 97; Prof of the Year, 98. **MEMBERSHIPS** South Eastern Conf Latin Am; Nat Asn Student Personel Admin; Am Camp Asn; Fla State Elks Assoc. **RESEARCH** Latin American travel study programs; Mayan experience; Caribbean pirates, Fidel Castro. **CONTACT ADDRESS** Broward Comm Col, 3501 Davie Rd, Fort Lauderdale, FL, 33314-1604.

RYAVEC, KARL WILLIAM
PERSONAL Born 01/29/1936, Cleveland, OH, m, 1957, 2 children **DISCIPLINE** POLITICAL SCIENCE **EDUCATION** Mimai Univ (Ohio), BA, 57; Columbia Univ, MA, 62, PhD, 68. **CAREER** FAC MEMBER, POLITICAL SCI DEPT, 64-, FULL PROF, 78-, UNIV OF MASS AT AMHERST. **HONORS AND AWARDS** William C. Foster Fel, U.S. Arms Control and Disarmament Agency, 95-96; Fel, Russian Res Center, Harvard Univ, 70-71; senior exchange participant, U.S.-Soviet senior scholarly exchange, 77. **MEMBERSHIPS** Am Asn for the Advancement of Slavic Studies; Soc for Slovene Studies. **RESEARCH** Russian politics and foreign policy; Slovene politics and foreign policy. **SELECTED PUBLICATIONS** Auth, United States-Soviet Relations, Longman, 89; auth, Implementation of Soviet Economic Reforms: Political, Oranizational and Social Processes, Praeger, 75; auth, Nikita Khrushchev and Soviet Politics, Governments and Leaders, Houghton-Mifflin, 78; auth, Slovenia and United States Policy on NATO Enlargement, Slovene Studies, 98; auth, Russo-Soviet Bureaucratism, Soviet and Post-Soviet Review, 98; auth, Gorbachev, Khrushchev, and Economic Reform, The Sons of Sergei: Khrushchev and Gorbachev as Reformers, Praeger, 92; ed, A Scholar's Odyssey: The Memoirs of Ferenc A. Vali, Iowa State Univ Press, 89; ed, Soviet Society and the Communist Party, Univ of Mass Press, 78. **CONTACT ADDRESS** Dept of Political Science, Univ of Massachusetts, Thompson Hall, Amherst, MA, 01003-7520. **EMAIL** ryavec@polsci.umass.edu

RYDELL, ROBERT WILLIAM
PERSONAL Born 05/23/1952, Evanston, IL **DISCIPLINE** AMERICAN HISTORY & STUDIES **EDUCATION** Univ Calif, Berkeley, AB, 74, Los Angeles, MA, 75, CPhil, 77, Ph-D(hist), 80. **CAREER** ASST PROF HIST, MONT STATE UNIV, 80-, Vis asst prof, Univ Calif, Los Angeles, summer, 81; fel, Smithsonian Inst, 82-83. **RESEARCH** United States intellectual history; United States cultural history; history of technology. **SELECTED PUBLICATIONS** Auth, Natures Metropolis - Chicago And The Great-W - Cronon,W/, Southwestern Hist Quart, Vol 0097, 1993; Capitalism On The Frontier - Billings And The Yellowstone-Valley In The 19th-Century - Vanwest,C/, Montana-The Mag Of Western Hist, Vol 0044, 1994; The Birth Of The Museum - History, Theory, Politics - Bennett,T/, Cult Studies, Vol 0011, 1997; Wild W Shows And The Images Of Am-Indians, 1883-1933 - Moses,Lg/, Pac Hist Rev, Vol 0066, 1997. **CONTACT ADDRESS** Dept of Hist & Philos, Montana State Univ, Bozeman, MT, 59717-0001.

RYNDER, CONSTANCE
DISCIPLINE AMERICAN SOCIAL HISTORY AND BRITISH HISTORY **EDUCATION** Univ Toledo, BA, 67; Univ NE, MA,70, PhD, 73. **CAREER** Prof; past pres, AAUP, Fla Conf. **HONORS AND AWARDS** Louise Loy Hunter Awd, 92. **RESEARCH** Women in hist; Native Am; western civilization, US hist since 1877; ancient hist and Irish hist. **SELECTED PUBLICATIONS** Auth, The education of a Progressive Reformer: William and Amy Maher, NW Ohio Quart, 91. **CONTACT ADDRESS** Dept of Hist, Univ of Tampa, 401 W. Kennedy Blvd, Tampa, FL, 33606-1490.

RYON, RODERICK NAYLOR
PERSONAL Born 07/11/1938, Washington, DC **DISCIPLINE** AMERICAN HISTORY **EDUCATION** Western Md Col, AB, 60; Pa State Univ, AM, 63, PhD(hist), 66. **CAREER** From asst prof to assoc prof, 65-73, PROF HIST, TOWSON COL, 73- **RESEARCH** Society and politics of the Jacksonian era; labor and reform movements. **SELECTED PUBLICATIONS** Auth, Craftsmens Union Halls, Male Bonding, And Female Industrial-Labor - The Case Of Baltimore, 1880-1917/, Labor Hist, Vol 0036, 1995; The New S Comes To Wiregrass Georgia, 1860-1910 - Wetherington,Mv/, J Of Southern Hist, Vol 0062, 1996; Reading, Writing And Race - The Desegregation Of The Charlotte Schools - Douglas,Dm/, J Of Southern Hist, Vol 0062, 1996. **CONTACT ADDRESS** Dept of Hist, Towson State Col, Baltimore, MD, 21204.

S

SAAB, E. ANN POTTINGER
PERSONAL Born 12/18/1934, Boston, MA, m, 1966, 2 children **DISCIPLINE** MODERN EUROPEAN & MIDDLE EASTERN HISTORY **EDUCATION** Wellesley Col, BA, 55; Radcliffe Col, MA, 57, PhD(hist), 62. **CAREER** Instr hist, Middlebury Col, 62-64; lectr, 65-66, from asst prof to assoc prof, 66-75, PROF HIST, UNIV NC, GREENSBORO, 75-, Head Dept, 78-84, assoc Dean Grad School, 90-98; Soc Sci Res Coun fel, Turkey, 64-65. **MEMBERSHIPS** Mid E Studies Asn NAm; AHA. **RESEARCH** French policy towards the German states in the 1860's; origins of the Crimean War with relation to Ottoman politics; British attitudes toward the ottoman Empire. **SELECTED PUBLICATIONS** Auth, Napoleon III and the German Crisis, 1865-66, Harvard Univ, 66; The Origins of the Crimean Alliance, Univ VA, 77; transl, Winifred Baumgart, The Peace of Paris, 1856, ABC-Clio, 81; Reluctant Icon: Gladstone, Bulgaria, and the Working Classes, 1856-1878, Harvard Univ, 91. **CONTACT ADDRESS** Dept of Hist, Univ of N. Carolina, Greensboro, NC, 27412.

SAADOUN, MOHAMED
PERSONAL Born 01/14/1954, Lebanon, m, 1975, 2 children **DISCIPLINE** INTERNATIONAL RELATIONS **EDUCATION** FIU, BS, 84. **CAREER** Publisher **MEMBERSHIPS** MESA. **RESEARCH** Islamic Aqeedah-Hadith; Quran Sciences. **SELECTED PUBLICATIONS** Auth, Lebanon-The Crisis That Ceases To End. **CONTACT ADDRESS** 17 Hammond, #403, Irvine, CA, 92618.

SABATO, LARRY J.
PERSONAL Born 08/07/1952, Norfolk, VA **DISCIPLINE** POLITICAL SCIENCE **EDUCATION** Univ of Virginia, BA 74; Princeton Univ 75; Queen's Col Oxford, asst inst, 76-78; Univ Virginia, asst prof, assoc prof, prof, 78-. **CAREER** Univ Virginia, Robert Kent Gooch Prof. **HONORS AND AWARDS** Rhodes Sch; Danforth Fel; Phi Beta Kappa; NEH; Outstanding Young Teacher; Outstanding Prof Awd; Brookings Inst Guest sch; Downing College Cambridge Univ Eng, Thomas Jefferson Vis Fellow., Served on Many National and State Commissions. **SELECTED PUBLICATIONS** Auth, Toward the Millennium: The Elections of 1996, Allyn and Bacon, 97; Dirty Little Secrets: The Persistence of Corruption in American Politics, Random House/Times Books, 96; Feeding the Frenzy: How Attack Journalism Has Transformed American Politics, Free Press/ Macmillan, 91, 93. **CONTACT ADDRESS** Virginia Univ, 2020 Minor Rd, Charlottesville, VA, 22903.

SACHAR, HOWARD MORLEY
PERSONAL Born 02/10/1928, St. Louis, MO, m, 1964, 3 children **DISCIPLINE** MODERN EUROPEAN & NEAR EASTERN HISTORY. **EDUCATION** Swarthmore Col, BA, 47; Harvard Univ, MA, 50, PhD, 53. **CAREER** Lectr hist, Univ Mass, 53-54; dir Hillel Found, Univ Calif, Los Angeles, 54-57; Charles Brown fel Mid Eastern Studies, 57-59; dir Hillel Found, Stanford Univ, 59-61; dir Hiatt Inst, Brandeis Univ, 61-64, Lown Inst, 64-65; assoc prof, 65-67, PROF HIST, GEORGE WASHINGTON UNIV, 67-, Nat Endowment Humanities fel, 70; vis prof, Tel-Aviv Univ, 73; Phi Beta Kappa; Dr Hum Letters Honoris Caresa, Hebrew Unio Col. **MEMBERSHIPS** AHA; Am Jewish Hist Soc; Mid East Inst; Mid East Studies Asn. **RESEARCH** Near Eastern, modern European and Jewish history. **SELECTED PUBLICATIONS** Auth, The Course of Modern Jewish History, 58, Aliyah: The Peoples of Israel, 61 & From the Ends of the Earth, 64, World; The Emergence of the Middle East, 69, Europe Leaves the Middle East, 72 & A History of Israel, 76, Knopf; The Man on the Camel, 80; Egypt and Israel, 81; Diasporn, 85; A History of Israel During the Yom Kippur War, 87; A History of the Jews in America, 92; Farewell Espana, 94; A History of Israel, 96; Europeand Israel, 99. **CONTACT ADDRESS** Dept of Hist, George Washington Univ, Washington, DC, 20006. **EMAIL** sachar@gwls2.circ.gwu.edu

SACHS, WILLIAM L.
PERSONAL Born 08/23/1947, Richmond, VA, m, 1986, 1 child **DISCIPLINE** HISTORY OF CHRISTIANITY **EDUCATION** Baylor, BA, 69; Vanderbilt Univ, MDiv, 72; Yale Univ, STM, 73; Univ Chicago, PhD, 81. **CAREER** Adj fac of Union Sem and Univ Richmond; consult for Lilly Endowment and Episcopal Church Found; Episcopal parish priest, 73- . **RESEARCH** English and American evangelicism; religious leadership; Anglican communion. **SELECTED PUBLICATIONS** Auth, The Transformation of Anglicanism, Cambridge; auth, Of One Body, John Knox. **CONTACT ADDRESS** 36 New Canaan Rd, Wilton, CT, 06897. **EMAIL** wls@aol.com

SACK, JAMES J.
PERSONAL Born 12/04/1944, Monroe, MI **DISCIPLINE** HISTORY **EDUCATION** Univ Notre Dame, BA, 67; Univ Mich, PhD, 73. **CAREER** Prof Hist, Univ Ill, Chicago. **MEMBERSHIPS** AHA; N Am Conf on British Stud; Midwest Victorian Stud Asn. **RESEARCH** Eighteenth and nineteenth century British politics. **SELECTED PUBLICATIONS** Auth, The Grenvillites: Party Politics and Factionalism in the Age of Pitt and Liverpool, Illinois, 79; auth, From Jacobite to Conservative: Reaction and Orthodoxy in Britain, 1760-1832, Cambridge, 93. **CONTACT ADDRESS** History Dept, Univ of Illinois, Chicago, 601 S Morgan St, Chicago, IL, 60607. **EMAIL** JSack@uic.edu

SACK, RONALD HERBERT
PERSONAL Born 11/23/1943, Chicago, IL **DISCIPLINE** ANCIENT NEAR EASTERN HISTORY **EDUCATION** Wis State Univ, BA, 65; Univ Minn, MA, 67, PhD(hist), 70. **CAREER** Instr, Univ Minn, 66-67 & Wis State Univ, 68-69; asst prof, Col Idaho, 70-71; asst prof, 71-74, assoc prof, 74-82, PROF HIST, NC STATE UNIV, 82- **MEMBERSHIPS** Am Orient Soc. **RESEARCH** Chaldean Mesopotamia; folklore in Ancient Near East. **SELECTED PUBLICATIONS** Auth, Achaemenid Hist, Vol 7, Through Travelers Eyes, European Travelers On The Iranian Monuments - Sancisiweerdenburg,H, Drijvers,Jw/, J Of The Am Oriental Soc, Vol 0113, 1993; Asia-Minor And Egypt, Old Cultures In A New Empire - Proceedings Of The Groningen 1988 Achaemenid-History-Workshop - Sancisiweerdenburg,H, Kuhrt,A/, J Of The Am Oriental Soc, Vol 0113, 1993. **CONTACT ADDRESS** Dept of Hist, No Carolina State Univ, Raleigh, NC, 27650.

SADLER, WILBERT L., JR.
PERSONAL Atlanta, GA, m **DISCIPLINE** EDUCATION **EDUCATION** Paine Coll, BS 1970; Morgan State Univ, MS 1972; Boston Univ, EdD 1981; Univ of Pennsylvania, Post Doctorate study 1981; Columbia Univ, post doctorate study, 1988. **CAREER** Morgan State Coll, instructor 1970-74; Boston Univ, grad asst 1974-76; Livingstone Coll, asst prof 1976-82; WINSTON-SALEM STATE UNIV, assoc prof 1982-1992, PROF, 1992-. **HONORS AND AWARDS** Natl Endowment for Humanities Fellowship; Published 2 books, 5 articles; member, Alpha Upsilon Alpha, National Reading Honor Society, 1989-90; member, Phi Delta Kappa, National Education Honor Society, 1989-90. **MEMBERSHIPS** Mem Pinehurst Comm Club 1976-; mem Salisbury Rown Symphony Guild; mem Optimist Club; mem Assn of Coll & Univ Profs; NAACP; life mem, Alpha Upsilon Alpha (Read Honor Society), NC College Read; Coll Reading Assn, Intl Reading Assn, Alpha Kappa Mu Hon Soc; mem Beta Mu Lambda, Alpha Phi Alpha Frat Inc. **CONTACT ADDRESS** Education Dept, Winston-Salem State Univ, Martin Luther King Jr Dr, Winston-Salem, NC, 27101.

SADLIER, ROSEMARY
PERSONAL Toronto, ON, Canada **DISCIPLINE** HISTORY **EDUCATION** York Univ, BA; Univ Toronto, MSW, BEd. **CAREER** PRES, BD DIRS, ONTARIO BLACK HISTORY SOCIETY. **HONORS AND AWARDS** Cert Recognition, Women PACE-Project Advan Childhood Educ, 96; Volunteer Award 10 Years Serv, Min Citizenship, 94; Volunteer Award, Ont Black Hist Soc. **MEMBERSHIPS** Writers' Union Can; CAN:BAIA. **SELECTED PUBLICATIONS** Auth, Leading the Way: Black Women in Canada, 95; auth, Mary Ann Shadd: Publisher, Editor, Teacher, Lawyer, Suffragette, 95; auth, Harriet Tubman and the Underground Railroad, Her Life in Canada and the United States, 96. **CONTACT ADDRESS** Ontario Black Hist Society, 10 Adelaide St E, Toronto, ON, M5C 1J3.

SADRI, AHMAD
PERSONAL Born 11/17/1953, Tehran, Iran, s **DISCIPLINE** SOCIOLOGY **EDUCATION** Univ Tehran, BA, MA. **CAREER** Asst prof, 88-95, assoc prof, Lake Forest Col, 95-. **HONORS AND AWARDS** William L Dunn Awd, excel teach; Lake Forest Shclsp. **MEMBERSHIPS** ASA; Middle Eastern Inst, Univ Chicago. **RESEARCH** Sociology of religion, politics; study of civilizations. **SELECTED PUBLICATIONS** Max Weber's Sociology of Intellectuals, NY, Oxford Press, 94; Reason Freedom Democracy in Islam: Essays By Abdolkarim Soroush, NY, Oxford Univ Press, 99, trans, ed, intro, co auth Mahmoud Sadri; Civilization Imagination Ethnic Coexistence IN: Handbook of Interethnic Coexistence, Cotinuum Press, 98; Searchers: The New Iranian Film, Brochure of Chicago Film Festival, 97; The Making of Foreign Policy in the United States, Round Table Discussion, The Middle East Quarterly, 98; many more articles and publications. **CONTACT ADDRESS** Lake Forest Col, Dept Sociology Anthropology, Lake Forest, IL, 60045. **EMAIL** sadri@lfc.edu

SAEGER, JAMES SCHOFIELD
PERSONAL Born 08/19/1938, Columbus, OH, m, 1964, 2 children **DISCIPLINE** LATIN AMERICAN HISTORY **EDUCATION** Ohio State Univ, BA, 60, MA, 63, PhD(hist), 69. **CAREER** Asst hist, Ohio State Univ, 62-65; instr, NC State Univ, 65-67; from instr to asst prof, 67-75, ASSOC PROF HIST, LEHIGH UNIV, 75-, Orgn Am States res fel, 73-74; Fulbright Comt res fel, 81. **MEMBERSHIPS** AHA; Latin Am Studies Asn; Conf Latin Am Hist; Mid Atlantic Coun Latin Am Studies. **RESEARCH** History of Paraguay; Spanish-Indian relations. **SELECTED PUBLICATIONS** Auth, Trade, War And Revolution, Exports From Spain To Spa-Am, 1797-1820 - Fisher,J/, Americas, Vol 0050, 1993; The Politics Of River Trade - Tradition And Development In The Upper Plata, 1780-1870 - Whigham,T/, Americas, Vol 0049, 1993; Hist Dictionary Of Paraguay - Nickson,Ra/, Americas, Vol 0050, 1994; The 'Mission' And Hist Missions + Film By Director Joffe,Roland - Film And The Writing Of Hist/, Americas, Vol 0051, 1995; Mission Cult On The Upper Amazon, Native Tradition, Jesuit Enterprise, And Secular Policy In Moxos, 1660-1880 - Block,D/, Americas, Vol 0052, 1995; Political-Parties And Generations In Paraguays Liberal Era, 1869-1940 - Lewis,Ph/, Americas, Vol 0052, 1996; They Built Utopia The Jesuit-Missions In Paraguay 1610-1768 - Reiter,Fj/, Cath Hist Rev, Vol 0083, 1997. **CONTACT ADDRESS** 445 High St, Bethlehem, PA, 18018.

SAFFIRE, PAULA REINER
PERSONAL Born 09/05/1943, NJ, s, 2 children **DISCIPLINE** CLASSICS AND PHILOSOPHY **EDUCATION** Mount Holyoke Col, BA, 65; Harvard, PhD, 76. **CAREER** Assoc Prof, Butler Univ, 89-. **HONORS AND AWARDS** Writing Across the Curriculum Awd, Butler Univ; Creative Tchr Awd; Indiana Classical Conference. **MEMBERSHIPS** APA, CAMUS, ICC **RESEARCH** Sappho; tragedy; mythology; pedagogy; performance. **SELECTED PUBLICATIONS** Auth, Aristotle on Personality and Some Implications for Friendship, in: Ancient Phil, 91; auth, Ancient Greek Alive, Aldine Press, 92; Coauth, Deduke men a Selanna: The Pleiades Mid-Sky, Mnemosyne, 93; auth, Whip, Whipped and Doctors: Homers Iliad and Camus the Plague, Interpretations, 94. **CONTACT ADDRESS** Dept of Classics, Butler Univ, 4600 Sunset Ave, Indianapolis, IN, 46208. **EMAIL** psaffire@butler.edu

SAFFLE, MICHAEL
PERSONAL Born 12/03/1946, Salt Lake City, UT, m, 1977, 1 child **DISCIPLINE** MUSICOLOGY, INTERDISCIPLINARY STUDIES **EDUCATION** Univ of Utah, BA (honors), BMus, 68; Boston Univ, AM, 70; Harvard Univ Divinity School, STM, 71; Standford Univ, PhD, 77. **CAREER** Instr, Stanford Univ, 77-78; ASST PROF, 78-83,ASSOC PROF, 83-93, PROF, 93-, VA TECH. **HONORS AND AWARDS** Phi Beta Kappa, 68; Francis Boott Prize in Choral Composition, Harvard Univ, 70; DAAD Fel, Univ of Bonn, 74-75; Alexander von Humboldt-Stiftung Fel, 84-86 & 93; Senior Fulbright Res Fel, 89-90. **MEMBERSHIPS** Am Musicological Soc; Int Musicological Soc; Sonneck Soc for Am Music; Va Humanities Conf. **RESEARCH** Liszt; Wagner; American music of the 19th and early 20th centuries; interdisciplinary studies in the arts. **SELECTED PUBLICATIONS** Auth, Liszt in Germany: 1840-1845: A Study in Sources, Documents, and the History of Reception, Franz Liszt Studies Series, Pendragon Press, 94; auth, Franz Liszt: A Guide to Research, Garland Composers Resource Guide, Garland Pub, 91; general ed, Franz Liszt Studies Series, Pendragon Press, 91-; general ed, Perspectives in Music Criticism and Theory, Garland Pub, 93-; co-ed, Essays in American Music, Garland Pub, 94-; biographical entries for the revised edition of Die Musik in Geschichte und Gegenwart, Barenreiter, 94-; ed, Journal of the American Liszt Society, 87-91; auth, book chapters and conference papers published in the Proceedings of the XIV, XV, & XVI Int Musicological Soc Congresses and other publications. **CONTACT ADDRESS** Virginia Polytechnic Inst and State Univ, Blacksburg, VA, 24061-0227. **EMAIL** msaffle@vt.edu

SAFFORD, FRANK ROBINSON
PERSONAL Born 06/04/1935, El Paso, TX, m, 1959, 2 children **DISCIPLINE** LATIN AMERICAN HISTORY **EDUCATION** Harvard Univ, AB, 57; Columbia Univ, MA, 59, PhD(Latin Am hist), 65. **CAREER** From instr to asst prof Latin Am & US hist, Dartmouth Col, 62-66; from asst prof to assoc prof, 66-77, PROF LATIN AM HIST, NORTHWESTERN UNIV, EVANSTON, 77-, Vis assoc prof hist, Univ Tex, Austin, 72-73; assoc ed, Hisp Am Hist Rev, 72-73. **MEMBERSHIPS** Conf Latin Am Hist; Latin Am Studies Asn. **RESEARCH** Nineteenth-century Latin America; social and economic history of Latin America; Colombian history. **SELECTED PUBLICATIONS** Auth, America - The Changing Face Of Latin-America And The Caribbean - Winn,P/, Hisp Am Hist Rev, Vol 0076, 1996. **CONTACT ADDRESS** Dept of Hist, Northwestern Univ, Evanston, IL, 60201.

SAFFORD, JEFFREY JAEGER
PERSONAL Born 05/14/1934, Greenwich Village, NY, m, 1957, 4 children **DISCIPLINE** UNITED STATES HISTORY **EDUCATION** Wagner Col, AB, 56, MSEduc, 59; Rutgers Univ, PhD(hist), 68. **CAREER** Instr phys educ, Wagner Col, 56-57; instr lang arts social studies, Plainfield Pub Schs, NJ, 59-61; instr English & jour & asst dir pub rels, Susquehanna Univ, 61-62; dir pub rels, Wagner Col, 62-65; from asst prof to assoc prof, 68-77, PROF HIST, MONT STATE UNIV, 77-, Vis lectr hist, Munson Inst Maritime Hist, 70-73. **HONORS AND AWARDS** Wylie Meritorious Res Award, Montana State Univ, 80. **MEMBERSHIPS** NAtlantic Soc Oceanic Historians; Soc Historians Am Foreign Rels; Orgn Am Historians. **RESEARCH** United States foreign affairs; United States maritime history. **SELECTED PUBLICATIONS** Auth, BAITED BY A COLOR OF GOLD TO A MOUNTAIN OF GRANITE .2. CONNECTICUT CAPITAL AT WORK IN THE MONTANA GOLDFIELDS, 1865-1868/, MONTANA-THE MAGAZINE OF WESTERN HISTORY, Vol 0047, 1997; **CONTACT ADDRESS** Dept of Hist, Montana State Univ, Bozeman, MT, 59717.

SAFFORD, JOHN L.
PERSONAL Born 01/06/1947, Pasadena, CA, m, 1983, 2 children **DISCIPLINE** POLITICAL SCIENCE **EDUCATION** Univ Calif Riverside, PhD, 84. **CAREER** Prof, Univ S, 85. **MEMBERSHIPS** Am Polit Sci Asn; Am Philos Assoc. **RESEARCH** Political Theory. **SELECTED PUBLICATIONS** Auth, Pragmatics and The Progressive Movement, 87; co-auth, Bhagavad Gita: A Philosophical System, 90; PS: Politics and Political Science, 95. **CONTACT ADDRESS** US. Carolina Sumter, 200 Miller Rd, Sumter, SC, 29150-2498.

SAFRAN, WILLIAM
PERSONAL Born 07/08/1930, Dresden, Germany, m, 1961, 2 children **DISCIPLINE** POLITICAL SCIENCE **EDUCATION** Columbia Univ, PhD, 64. **CAREER** Lectr & instr, CUNY, 60-65; vis prof, Hebrew Univ, Jerusalem, 73-74; asst prof, 65-68, assoc prof, 68-73, PROF OF POLITICAL SCI, UNIV OF COLO, 73-; vis prof, Institut d'Etudes Politiques, Univ Grenoble, 91-92; vis prof, Institut d'Etudes Politiques, Univ of Bordeaux, spring 98. **HONORS AND AWARDS** Soc Sci Found, 66; Nat Endowment for Humanities, 80-81; Hanns-Seidel Found, 83; French Ministry of Culture, 86; Am Coun of Learned Socs, 88-89; Fulbright, 91-92; fac res fel, Univ Colo, 66, 69-70. **MEMBERSHIPS** Am Acad of Political Sci; Am Political Sci Asn; Asn Francaise de Sci Politique; Asn for the Study of Ethnicity and Nationalism; Conf Group on French Politics and Soc; Conf Group on German Politics; Sci Comm, Data Bank on Minorities, Centre National de Recherche Sci; Int Political Sci Asn; Int Studies Asn; Inter-Univ Consortium for Soc Res on France; Tocqueville Soc; Western Political Sci Asn. **RESEARCH** Comparative politics; industrial democracies; European politics; French politics; the politics of ethnicity; nationalism; language; citizenship; civil liberties. **SELECTED PUBLICATIONS** Auth, Veto-Group politics, 67; The French Polity, 77, 79, 85, 91, 95, & 98; coauth, Ideology and Politics: The Socialist Party of France, 79; Comparative Politics, 83; Politics in Western Europe, 93 & 98; co-ed, Ethnicity and Citizenship: The Canadian Case, 96; ed, Nationalism and Ethnoregional Indentities in China, in press; contribur, Divided Nations, 94; Political Leaders in Western Europe, 95; Encyclopedia of Democracy, 95; Union Europea Y Estado Del Bienestar, 97; Fremde Freunde: Deutsche Und Franzonsen Vor Dem 21. Jahrhundert, 97; How France Votes: The Parliamentary Elections of 1997, in press. **CONTACT ADDRESS** Dept of Political Sci, Univ Colo, Boulder, CO, 80309-0333.

SAGE, MICHAEL
PERSONAL Born 12/04/1944, New York, NY, m, 2 children **DISCIPLINE** ROMAN HISTORY & CLASSICS **EDUCATION** Univ Mich, BA, MA (hist); Univ Toronto, MA (classics), PhD. **CAREER** Univ Waterloo, asst prof (hist), 74-75; Univ Cincinnati, asst prof (classics), 75-81, assoc prof, 81-90, prof, 90-. **HONORS AND AWARDS** Canada Coun, Province of Ontario, Semple Fel. **MEMBERSHIPS** Am Philological Asn; Soc Promotion Roman Studies. **RESEARCH** Late Roman hist; Christianity; ancient mil hist. **SELECTED PUBLICATIONS** Ancient Greek Warfare, London, 96. **CONTACT ADDRESS** Univ of Cincinnati, 407 Blegen Libr, Cincinnati, OH, 45221. **EMAIL** Michael.Sage@uc.edu

SAID, ABDUL AZIZ
DISCIPLINE INTERNATIONAL RELATIONS **EDUCATION** School Intl Serv, Amer Univ, PhD. **CAREER** Mohammed Said Farsi Prof, Islamic Peace; dir, Ctr Global Peace. **RESEARCH** Islamic peace; Peace and conflict resolution; East and West reconciliation. **CONTACT ADDRESS** School of Intl Serv, American Univ, Washington, DC, 20016. **EMAIL** asaid@american.edu

SAINSBURY, JOHN
DISCIPLINE EARLY MODERN BRITISH HISTORY **EDUCATION** Cambridge Univ, BA, MA; McGill Univ, PhD. **CAREER** Assoc prof; ch. **RESEARCH** John Wilkes. **SELECTED PUBLICATIONS** Auth, Disaffected Patriots: London Supporters of Revolutionary America, McGill-Queen's UP. **CONTACT ADDRESS** Dept of Hist, Brock Univ, 500 Glenridge Ave, St Catharines, ON, L2S 3A1. **EMAIL** jsainsbu@spartan.ac.BrockU.CA

SAKMYSTER, THOMAS LAWRENCE
PERSONAL Born 10/06/1943, Perth Amboy, NJ, m, 1967, 2 children **DISCIPLINE** MODERN & DIPLOMATIC HISTORY **EDUCATION** Dartmouth Col, BA, 65; Ind Univ Bloomington, MA, 67, PhD, 71. **CAREER** From asst prof to prof hist, 71-97, Walter Langsam Prof Mod Europ Hist, Univ Cincinnati, 97-. **HONORS AND AWARDS** Article Prize, Am Asn Study Hungarian Hist, 76; Book Prize, Am Asn Study Hungarian Hist, 85. **MEMBERSHIPS** AHA; Am Asn Advan Slavic Studies; Am Asn Study Hungarian Hist (secy, 73-75, pres, 79-80). **RESEARCH** Modern Hungary; East European diplomatic history; European military elites; film and history. **SELECTED PUBLICATIONS** Auth, Hungary, the Great Powers, and the Danubian Crisis, 1936-1939, Univ Ga Press, 80; Hungary's Admiral on Horseback: Miklos Horthy, 1918-1944, Columbia Univ Press, 94. **CONTACT ADDRESS** Dept of Hist, Univ of Cincinnati, PO Box 210373, Cincinnati, OH, 45221-0373. **EMAIL** tom.sakmyster@uc.edu

SALAMON, SONYA
PERSONAL Born 11/01/1939, Pittsburgh, PA, m, 1960, 2 children **DISCIPLINE** ANTHROPOLOGY **EDUCATION** Carnegie Mellon Univ, BFA, 61; Univ of Calif at Berkeley, MA, 65; Univ of Ill at Urbana-Champaign, PhD, 74. **CAREER** ACTING DEPT HEAD, HUMAN DEVELOPMENT AND FAMILY ECOLOGY, 80-81, GRAD PROG COORD, DIVISION OF HUMAN DEVELOPMENT AND FAMILY STUDIES, 81-88 & 91-93, ASST TO FULL PROF, 74-, DEPT OF HUMAN AND COMMUNITY DEVELOPMENT, UNIV OF ILL AT URBANA-CHAMPAIGN. **HONORS AND AWARDS** Postdoctoral fel coun for European Studies/DAAD, German Acad Exchange Prog, 74-75; assoc, Center for Advanced Study, 80-81, Paul A. Funk Recognition Award, Univ of Ill, 98; rural sociological soc policy fel, 88-89; Ameritech res fel, 88-89; visiting scholar, Economic Res Service U.S. Dept of Agriculture, 88-89 & 95-96. **MEMBERSHIPS** Am Anthropological Asn; Rural Sociological Soc; Ill Coun on Family Relations; Soc for Applied Anthropology; Nat Coun on Family Relations; Soc for Economic Anthropology. **RESEARCH** Families and the rural community; rural and small town community change; ethnicity in rural North America; culture and the structure of agriculture; farm families and sustainable agriculture. **SELECTED PUBLICATIONS** Auth, Ethnic Communities and the Structure of Agriculture, Rural Sociology, 85; auth, Prairie Patrimony: Family, Farming and Community in the Midwest, Univ of NC Press, 92; auth, Culture and Agricultural Land Tenure, Rural Sociology, 93; coauth, Share and Share Alike: Inheritance Patterns in Two Illinois Farm Communities, J of Family Hist, 88; coauth, Territory Contested through Property in a Midwestern Post-Agricultural Community, Rural Sociology, 94; Family Factors Affecting Adoption of Sustainable Farming Systems, J of Soil and Water Conservation, 97; coauth, Is Locally Led Conservation Planning Working? A Farm Town Case Study, Rural Sociology, 98. **CONTACT ADDRESS** Dept of Human and Community Development, Univ of Ill, 905 S Goodwin Ave, Urbana, IL, 61801. **EMAIL** ssalamon@uiuc.edu

SALIH, HALIL IBRAHIM
PERSONAL Born 02/26/1939, Kyrenia, Cyprus, m, 1989, 4 children **DISCIPLINE** POLITICAL SCIENCE, GOVERNMENT, AREA STUDIES, MIDDLE EAST AREA STUDIES, INTERNATIONAL STUDIES, INTERNATIONAL ORGANIZATIONS AND LAW **EDUCATION** Univ of Pacific, BA, 63; Am Univ, MA, 65, PhD, 67. **CAREER** Asst prof, 68-71, assoc prof, 71-81, Chr Polit Sci Dept, 73-95, Chr Soc Sci Dept, 95, prof of Political Science, 81-, Texas Wesleyan Col, 68-; Hall of Nations Scholar, 65-66; Pi Sigma Alpha, 67; Danfort Assoc, 79; Malone fel, 95. **HONORS AND AWARDS** Outstanding Educ Am, 72; Texas Wesleyan Fac Recog Award, 81 & 94; Mortar Board, 96. **MEMBERSHIPS** Mid East Inst; Am Asn Univ Prof; W Soc Sci Asn; SW Sco Sci Asn; Int Studies Asn. **RESEARCH** International law and organizations; Middle East; Greco-Turkish crisis; Cyprus. **SELECTED PUBLICATIONS** Auth Cyprus: An Analysis of Cypriot Political Discord, 68; Cyprus: The Impact of Diverse Nationalism on a State, 78. **CONTACT ADDRESS** Dept of Social Science, Tex Wesleyan Univ, 1201 Wesleyan St, Fort Worth, TX, 76105. **EMAIL** salihi@txwes.edu

SALISBURY, FRANK BOYER
PERSONAL Born 08/03/1926, Provo, UT, m, 1991, 7 children **DISCIPLINE** BOTANY, BIOCHEMISTRY, PLANT PHYSIOLOGY AND GEOCHEMISTRY **EDUCATION** Univ Ut., BS, botany, MA, botany and biochemistry, 51, 52; PhD, Calif Inst of Tech, plant physiology and geochemistry, 55; Atomic Energy Comn Predoctoral Fel, 51-53; McCallum Fel, 53-54. **CAREER** US Army Air Force, 45; Church of Jesus Christ of Latter-Day Saints rep in Ger-speaking Switzerland, 46-49; photog, Boyart Studio, 49-50; part-time portrait-commercial photog, 50-; asst prof, bot, Pomona Col, 54-55; asst prof, plant physiol, Colo State Univ, 61-66; NSF Sr Postdoctoral fel, Tubingen, Ger, Innsbruck, Austria, 62-63; head of plant sci dept, 66-70; prof to emer, plant physiol, 66-97, prof to emer, bot, 68-97, Ut State Univ; Bd of trustees, Colo State Univ Res Found, 60-62; tech rep, plant physiol, US Atomic Energy Comn, Germantown, Md, 73-74; guest prof, Univ Innsbruck, Lady Davis fel, Hebrew Univ of Jerusalem, 83; Church of Jesus Christ of Latter-Day Saints missionary, with wife, Oh Columbus Mission, 97-99; distinguished prof to emer, agr, 87-97. **HONORS AND AWARDS** Cert of Merit, Botanical Soc of Amer, 82; Distinguished prof, Col of Agr, 87-88; Founders award, Amer Soc for Gravitational and Space Bio, 94; NASA Life Sci Adv Comt, 86-88; NASA Aerospace Med Adv Comt, 88-93; chair, NASA Controlled Ecol Life Support Syst Discipline Working Grp, 88-93; COSPAR comt ISC F F.4. chair, Plenary Session of the Intl Congress of Plant Physiol, New Delhi, India, 88; The William A. (Tex) Frazier Lect at the 87th Annual Mtg of the Amer Soc for Horticultural Sci, Tucson, Ariz, 4 Nov 90, Who's Who in Amer, Who's Who in the West. **MEMBERSHIPS** Amer Soc for Gravitational and Spce Bio; Amer Soc of Plant Physiol, Amer Inst of Bio Sci, Amer Asn for the Advan of Sci (fel); Botl Soc of Amer; Phi Kappa Phi; Planetary Soc; Sigma Xi; Ut Acad of Arts, Letters and Sci. **RESEARCH** Space-flight experiments with Super-Dwarf wheat in the Russian Space Station Mir; selection of CELSS (Controlled Ecological LIfe-Support Systems); Conceptual designs of bioregenerative life support systems; Gravitropism in stems; Physiol of flowering. **SELECTED PUBLICATIONS** Ed, Units, Symbols and Terminology for plant physiology, Oxford Univ Press, NY, 96; jour articles, The International System of Units SI, BioSci, Oct, 98; coauth, with Josef I. Gitelson and Genry M. Lisovsky, Bios-3: Siberian experiments in bioregenerative life support, BioSci, 47, 575-585, 97; with Gail E. Bingham, William F. Campbell, John G. Carman, David L. Bubenheim, Boris Yendler, Gary Jahns, Growing Super-Dward wheat in Svet on Mir, Life Support and Biosphere Sci, 2, 1, 31-39, 95; with Mary Ann Z. Clark, Suggestions for crops grown in controlled ecological life-support systems, based on attractive vegetarian diets, Adv in Space Res, 18, 4/5, 33-39, 95; chap in books, Life Sciences: Botany, Yearbook of Sci and the Future, Encycl Britannica Inc, 392-396, 95. **CONTACT ADDRESS** Ohio Columbus Mission, PO Box 20130, Columbus, OH, 43220. **EMAIL** franksals@aol.com

SALISBURY, NEAL
DISCIPLINE HISTORY **EDUCATION** Univ Of Calif at LA, BA, 63, MA, 66, PhD, 72. **CAREER** PROF, HIST, SMITH COLL **MEMBERSHIPS** Am Antiquarian Soc **SELECTED PUBLICATIONS** Auth, Manitoba and Providence: Indians, Europeans, and the Making of New England, 1500-1643, Oxford Univ Press, 82; auth, "The Indians' Old World: Native Americans and the Coming of Europeans," Wm & Mary Quart 53, 96; ed with introd, The Sovereignty and Goodness of God, Bedford Books, 97. **CONTACT ADDRESS** Dept of Hist, Smith Coll, Northampton, MA, 01063. **EMAIL** nsalisbu@sophia.smith.edu

SALISBURY, RICHARD VANALSTYNE
PERSONAL Born 10/12/1940, Oswego, NY, m, 1966, 3 children **DISCIPLINE** LATIN AMERICAN HISTORY **EDUCATION** Hamilton Col, AB, 62; Univ WI, MA, 63; Univ KS, PhD, 69. **CAREER** Asst prof hist, State Univ NY Col Geneseo, 69-76; assoc prof, 76-80; prof hist, Western KY Univ, 80, Vis asst prof hist, AZ State Univ, 73-74. **HONORS AND AWARDS** Distinguished Univ Prof. **MEMBERSHIPS** Latin Am Studies Asn; Conf Latin Am Hist; Soc Historians Am For Rels. **RESEARCH** Central Am international rel, espec in the 20th century; for influence in Central Am. **SELECTED PUBLICATIONS** Auth, The Anti-Imperialist Career of Alejandro Alvarado Quiros, Hisp Am Hist Rev, 11/77; Costa Rica and the 1924 Honduran Crisis, Revista de Historia, 1/78; Jorge Volio and Isthmian Revolutionary Politics, Red River Valley Hist J World Hist, summer, 80; Good Neighbors? The United States and Latin America in the Twentieth Century, In: American Foreign Relations, A Historiographical Review, Greenwood Press, 81; The Middle American Exile of Victor Raul Maya de La Torre, The Americas, 7/83; Mexico, The United States, and the 1926-1927 Nicaraguan Crisis, Hisp Am Hist Rev, 5/86; Revolution and Recognition: A British Perspective on Isthmian Affairs During the 1920's, The Americas, 1/92; Great Britain, The United States, and the 1909-1910 Nicaraguan Crisis, The Americas, 1/97; Costa Rica y el Istmo, 1900-1934, Editorial de Costa Rica, 84; Anti-Imperialism and International Competition in Central America, 1920-1929, Sch Resources, 89. **CONTACT ADDRESS** Dept of Hist, Western Kentucky Univ, 1 Big Red Way St, Bowling Green, KY, 42101-3576. **EMAIL** richard.salisbury@wku.edu

SALLER, RICHARD
PERSONAL Born 10/18/1952, NC, m, 1974, 2 children **DISCIPLINE** CLASSICAL HISTORY **EDUCATION** Univ Ill, BA, 74; Cambridge Univ, PhD, 78. **CAREER** Asst prof, Swarthmore Col, 79-84; assoc to full prof, Univ Chicago, 84-, DEAN, SOC SCI DIV, UNIV CHICAGO, 94-. **MEMBERSHIPS** Am Philol Asn, Am Hist Asn **RESEARCH** Roman soc and econ hist. **SELECTED PUBLICATIONS** Auth, Patriarchy, Property, and Death in the Roman Family, 94, Cambridge Press; co-ed, The Family in Italy from Antiquity to the Present, 91, Yale Univ Press; auth, "The Social Dynamics of Consent to Marriage and Sexual Relations: The Evidence of Roman Comedy," in Consent and Coercion to Sex and Marriage in Ancient and Medieval Societies, 93; coauth, "Foucault on Sexuality in Greco-Roman Antiquity," in Foucault and the Writing of History," 94; auth, "The Hierarchical Household in Roman Society: A Study of Domestic Slavery," in Serfdom and Slavery, 96; auth, "Roman Kinship: Structure and Sentiment," in The Roman Family in Italy: Status, Sentiment, Space, 97. **CONTACT ADDRESS** Dept of Classics, Univ of Chicago, 1126 E 59th St, Chicago, IL, 60637. **EMAIL** sall@midway.uchicago.edu

SALLIS, CHARLES
DISCIPLINE SOUTHERN HISTORY AND ETHNIC AND CULTURAL DIVERSITY **EDUCATION** Univ Ky, PhD. **CAREER** Prof & past dept ch and past dir, Heritage Prog; fac, Millsaps Col, 68-; past tutor, Brit Stud Prog, Oxford Univ, 5 summers sessions. **HONORS AND AWARDS** Millsaps Distinquished prof, 73; 2 Nat Endowment for the Humanities fel(s); Southern Reg Council's Lillian Smith awd, 75. **SELECTED PUBLICATIONS** Coauth, Mississippi: Conflict and Change. **CONTACT ADDRESS** Dept of History, Millsaps Col, 1701 N State St, Jackson, MS, 39210. **EMAIL** salliwc@okra.millsaps.edu

SALMON, JOHN HEARSEY MCMILLAN
PERSONAL Born 12/02/1925, Thames, New Zealand **DISCIPLINE** EARLY MODERN HISTORY, FRENCH LITERATURE **EDUCATION** Victoria Univ Wellington, BA, 50, MA, 52, LittD(hist), 70; MLitt, Cambridge Univ, 57. **CAREER** Approved lectr hist, Cambridge Univ, 55-57; lectr, Victoria Univ Wellington, 57-60; prof, Univ NSW, 60-65 & Univ Waikato, NZ, 65-69; prof, 69-71, MARJORIE WALTER GOODHART PROF HIST, BRYN MAWR COL, 71-, Ed bds, Fr Hist Studies, Sixteenth Century J & J Mod Hist. **MEMBERSHIPS** AHA; fel Royal Hist Soc; Soc Fr Hist Studies. **RESEARCH** Early modern French history; French literature in the early modern period; French political theory. **SELECTED PUBLICATIONS** Auth, Soc And Institutions In Early-Modern France - Holt,Mp, Editor/, Renaissance Quart, Vol 0046, 1993; Constitutions, Old And New, Henriondepansey Before And After The Fr-Revolution/, Hist J, Vol 0038, 1995; The Legacy Of Bodin,Jean - Absolutism, Populism Or Constitutionalism/, Hist Of Pol Thought, Vol 0017, 1996; The Inside Of Hist - Merledaubigne,Jean,Henri And Romantic Historiography - Roney,Jb/, Sixteenth Century J, Vol 0027, 1996; The Making Of The Fr Episcopate 1589-1661 - Bergin,J/, Sixteenth Century J, Vol 0028, 1997; Civic Agendas And Religion Passion - Chalons-Sur-Marne During The Fr Wars Of Reigion - Konnert,Mw/, Sixteenth Century J, Vol 0028, 1997; State And Status - The Rise Of The State And Aristocratic Power In Western-Europe - Clark,S/, Am Hist Rev, Vol 0102, 1997; The Afterlife Of Henry-Of-Navarre + A Look At How Subsequent Generations Portrayed France Very Human 16th-Century Ruler/, Hist Today, Vol 0047, 1997. **CONTACT ADDRESS** Dept of Hist, Bryn Mawr Col, Bryn Mawr, PA, 19010.

SALOMAN, ORA FRISHBERG
PERSONAL Born 11/14/1938, New York, NY, m, 1968 **DISCIPLINE** MUSICOLOGY **EDUCATION** Barnard College, AB 69; Columbia Univ, MA 63, PhD 70. **CAREER** City Univ NY Baruch Col, asst assoc prof 72-81, chair 78-84, prof 82-; Grad Sch, prof, 96-. **HONORS AND AWARDS** NEH; Fulbright fel; Vis sch Queens Univ Kingston ON. **MEMBERSHIPS** AMS; SSAM; ABS; CMS; FAA; Columbia Univ Grad Sch Alum Assoc. **RESEARCH** Music; reception history of Beethoven, Gluck, LeSuer, and Berlioz; hist of opera and of music criticism; 19th century genre theories of symphony and opera; Euro-Amer connections in aesthetics, social hist and concert life. **SELECTED PUBLICATIONS** Auth, Beethoven's Symphonies and J. S. Dwight: The Birth of American Music Criticism, Boston, Northeastern Univ Press, 95; Chretien Urhan and Beethoven's Ninth Symphony in Paris 1838, in: Mainzer Studien zur Musikwissenschaft: Festschrift Walter Wigora, eds, Christoph-Hellmut Mahling, Ruth Seiberts, Tutzing, Hans Schneider, 97; Continental and English Foundations of J. S. Dwight's Early American Criticism of Beethoven's Ninth Symphony, Jour of Royal Musical Assoc, 94; Origins Performances and Reception History of Beethoven's Late Quartets, rev of, Beethoven: Naissance et Reniassance des Derniers Quatuors, by Ivan Mahaim, Paris Desclee De Brouwer 64, Music Quart, 96. **CONTACT ADDRESS** Dept of Music, Baruch Col, CUNY, 14 Summit St, Englewood, NJ, 07631. **EMAIL** ora_saloman@baruch.cuny.edu

SALVAGGIO, RUTH
DISCIPLINE AMERICAN STUDIES **EDUCATION** Rice Univ, PhD, 79. **CAREER** Prof, Univ NMex. **HONORS AND AWARDS** Grant, NEH, Folger Found, Am Soc for 18th-Century Stud, Los Alamos Nat Lab. **MEMBERSHIPS** Am Stud Asn; MLA. **RESEARCH** Critical, cultural, and feminist theory. **SELECTED PUBLICATIONS** Auth, Dryden's Dualities, 83; A Reader's Guide to Octavia Butler, 85; Enlightened Absence: Neoclassical Configurations of the Feminine, 88; Univ NMex and Los Alamos Rpt on Women in Sci, 93; coed, Early Women Critics 1660-1820, 95. **CONTACT ADDRESS** Univ NMex, Albuquerque, NM, 87131.

SALVATORE, NICHOLAS ANTHONY
PERSONAL Born 11/14/1943, Brooklyn, NY, m, 1974, 2 children **DISCIPLINE** HISTORY **EDUCATION** Hunter Col, BA, 68; Univ Calif, Berkeley, MA, 69, PhD, 77. **CAREER** Instr, Col Holy Cross, 76-77, asst prof hist, 77-81; from Asst Prof to Assoc Prof Hist, 81-92, Prof Hist, NY State Sch Indust & Labor Res, Cornell Univ, 93-, Prof Am Studies, Cornell Univ, 95-. **HONORS AND AWARDS** Batchelor fel hist, Col Holy Cross, 78; NEH fel, 79-80; Bancroft Prize in American History, 83; Outstanding Academic Book, Choice Magazine, 83; John H. Dunning Prize, 84; NEH fel, 88-89; New England Hist Asn Outstanding Book Award, 96. **MEMBERSHIPS** AHA; Orgn Am Historians; Soc Am Hist. **RESEARCH** American labor history; American socialism; Afro-American history. **SELECTED PUBLICATIONS** Auth, Eugene V Debs: Citizen and Socialist, Univ Ill Press, 82; ed, Seventy Years of Life and Labor, ILR Press, 84; auth, We All Got History: The Memory Books of Amos Webber, Times Books/Random House, 96. **CONTACT ADDRESS** American Studies and ILR, Cornell Univ, 290 Ives Hall, Ithaca, NY, 14853-0001. **EMAIL** nas4@cornell.edu

SALVUCCI, LINDA KERRIGAN
PERSONAL Born 05/28/1951, Pittston, PA, m, 1973, 2 children **DISCIPLINE** HISTORY **EDUCATION** Villanova Univ, BA, 73; Princeton Univ, MA, 79, PhD, 85. **CAREER** Asst prof, 85-91, assoc prof, hist, 91- , Trinity Univ. **HONORS AND AWARDS** Hubert Herring Award, Pacific Coast Coun on Latin Am Stud, 85; NEH fel, 88-89; vis scholar, center for Latin Am Stud, Univ Calif, Berkeley, 88-89; Lydia Cabrera Award for Cuban Hist Stud, Conf on Latin Am Hist, 95; Am Philos Soc grant, 97. **MEMBERSHIPS** Am Hist Asn; Nat Counc on Hist Educ; Conf on Latin Am Hist; Omohundro Inst of Early Am Hist and Culture. **RESEARCH** Early America; Atlantic empires; colonial Cuba; U.S. history textbooks. **SELECTED PUBLICATIONS** Coauth, The Politics of Protection: Interpreting Commercial Policy in Late Bourbon and Early National Mexico, in Andrien, ed, The Political Economy of Spanish America in the Age of Revolution, 1750-1850, New Mexico, 94; auth, Did NAFTA Rewrite History? Recent Mexican Views of the United States Past, J of Am Hist, 95; coauth, Call to Freedom: Beginnings to 1914, Holt, Rinehart & Winston, 98. **CONTACT ADDRESS** Dept of History, Trinity Univ, 715 Stadium Dr, San Antonio, TX, 78212-7200. **EMAIL** lsalvucc@trinity.edu

SALYER, GREGORY
DISCIPLINE INTERDISCIPLINARY STUDIES **EDUCATION** Emory Univ, PhD, 92. **CAREER** Asst prof Humanities, Huntingdon Col, 93-. **HONORS AND AWARDS** Lilly Tchg Fel. **MEMBERSHIPS** AAR; MLA; SHC. **RESEARCH** Native American literature and culture. **SELECTED PUBLICATIONS** Auth, Leslie Marmon Silko; Literature and Theology at Century's End. **CONTACT ADDRESS** Dept of Humanities, Huntingdon Col, 1500 E Fairview Ave, Montgomery, AL, 36106. **EMAIL** gsalyer@huntingdon.edu

SALYER, LUCY
DISCIPLINE HISTORYHISTORY **EDUCATION** Univ Calif, Berkeley, PhD. **CAREER** Assoc prof, Univ NH, 89-. **HONORS AND AWARDS** NEH fel; Am Coun for Learned Soc fel; Louis Pelzer Mem Award, J of Am Hist; Theodore Saloutos Mem Award, Immigration Hist Soc, 96. **RESEARCH** Social and legal history of American citizenship. **SELECTED PUBLICATIONS** Auth, Captives of Law: Judicial Enforcement of the Chinese Exclusion Laws, J of Am Hist 76, 89; Laws harsh as Tigers: Chinese Immigrants and the Shaping of Modern Immigration Law, 95; contribur, Entry Denied: Exclusion and the Chinese Community in America, 1882-1943, 91. **CONTACT ADDRESS** Univ NH, Durham, NH, 03824. **EMAIL** les@kepler.unh.edu

SALZMAN, NEIL
PERSONAL Born 10/25/1940, Brooklyn, NY, m, 1986, 3 children **DISCIPLINE** HISTORY **EDUCATION** City Col NY, BA, 62, MA, 65; Grad Ctr CUNY, MA, 77; NY Univ, PhD, 73. **CAREER** Instr of Hist, 70-75, Asst prof Polit Sci, 75-80, Assoc prof Polit Sci, 80-91, PROF POLIT SCI & HIST, FAIRLEIGH DICKINSON UNIV, 91- . **HONORS AND AWARDS** NY State Regents Scholar, 58-62; NY State Scholar Incentive Awd, 65-69; Grad Fel, CUNY, 68; Univ Res Grant-in-Aid, 88-89; Tchg Released Time for Res, 88, 89, 93, 96, 97; Univ Res Grant-in-Aid, 93-94; Tchr of the Year, 94-95. **RESEARCH** Am Polit Sci Asn; Am Hist Asn; Am Asn Univ Prof; Orgn Am

Hist. **SELECTED PUBLICATIONS** Rev, Alternative Paths: Soviets and Americans, 1917-1920, 'Festschrift for N V Riasanovsky, Russian Hist, 93; rev, War Revolution and Peach in Russia: The Passages of Frank Golder, 1914-1917, "Festschrift for N V Riasanovsky, Russian Hist, 93; auth, Reform and Revolution: The Life and Times of Raymond Robins, Kent State Univ Press, 94; The Jewish Currents Reader: 1986-1996, Asn Promotion Jewish Secularism, 98; Russia in War and Revolution: General William V. Judson's Accounts from Petrograd, 1917-1918, Kent State Univ Press, 98. **CONTACT ADDRESS** 162B Old Camby Road, Verbank, NY, 12585-5215.

SAMAHA, JOEL
DISCIPLINE HISTORY **EDUCATION** Northwestern Univ, JD; PhD. **CAREER** Prof **RESEARCH** Criminal justice history. **SELECTED PUBLICATIONS** Auth, Law and Order in Historical Perspective, 74; Sedition in Elizabethan Essex, 79; A Case of Murder: The Rule of Law in Minnesota, 1860, 76; Hanging for Felony: The Rule of Law in Elizabethan Colchester, 79; The Recognizance in tudor Law Enforcement, 80; Decretion and the Anglo-Saxon Books of Penitentials, 83; John Winthrop and the Criminal Law, 89; Criminal Law, 90; Criminal Justice, 89; Criminal Procedure, 90. **CONTACT ADDRESS** History Dept, Univ of Minnesota, Twin Cities, 614 Social Sciences Tower, 267 19th Ave S, Minneapolis, MN, 55455. **EMAIL** jsamaha@tc.umn.edu

SAMARASINGHE, VIDYAMALI
DISCIPLINE GENDER AND DEVELOPMENT, POPULATION AND MIGRATION ISSUES **EDUCATION** Univ Ceylon, BA; Camridge Univ, PhD. **CAREER** Prof, Am Univ. **RESEARCH** Southeast Asia, tea plantation women in Sri Lanka; income inequalities among farming communities; and female adolescent food allocation patterns in Sri Lanka. **SELECTED PUBLICATIONS** Co-ed, Women at the Crossroads: A SriLankan Perspective, Vikas, 90; Women at the Center: Gender and Development Issues for the 1990's, Kumarian, 93. **CONTACT ADDRESS** American Univ, 4400 Massachusetts Ave, Washington, DC, 20016.

SAMARIN, WILLIAM J.
PERSONAL Born 02/07/1926, Los Angeles, CA, m, 1947, 2 children **DISCIPLINE** LINGUISTICS, ANTHROPOLOGY **EDUCATION** Bible Theol Sem Los Angeles, BTh, 48; Univ Calif, Berkeley, BA, 50, PhD(ling), 62. **CAREER** Missionary linguist, Foreign Missionary Soc, Brethren Church, 51-60; from asst prof to prof ling, Hartford Sem Found, 61-68, dir Sango grammar & dict proj, US Dept Health, Educ & Welfare, 62-68; assoc prof, 68-71, Prof Anthrop & Ling, Univ Toronto, 71-, Nat Sci Found travel gant, WAfrican Lang Surv Congr, Dakar, Senegal, 62; Am Coun Learned Soc travel grant, int colloquium on multilingualism in Africa, Brazzaville, Congo Repub, 62; consult, Africa educ, studies-math proj, Educ Serv Inc, 62; NCTE proj sec sch textbooks for teaching English as a second lang, Africa ed, 62-64; consult nat literacy prog, Repub of Mali, Agency Int Develop, 63; travel grant, chair ling session, African Studies Asn, San Francisco, Calif, 63; vis prof, Univ Leiden, 66-67; res grants, Can Coun, lang alternation among new Canadians, 70-71, Am Philos Soc, emergence of Sango as lingua franca, 72-73; mem ed bd, Lang in Soc, 72- **MEMBERSHIPS** Can Ling Asn; Ling Soc Am; African Studies Asn; Am Anthrop Asn; WAfrican Ling Soc. **RESEARCH** African languages; sociolinguistics; marginal linguistic phenomena. **SELECTED PUBLICATIONS** Auth, Soc Motivations For Codeswitching - Evidence From Africa - In The Series Oxford Studies In Language Contact - Myersscotton,C/, Can Jl Of Linguistics-Revue Canadienne De Linguistique, Vol 0040, 1995; Interlanguage Pragmatics - Requests, Complaints And Apologies - Trosborg,A/, Can J Of Linguistics-Revue Canadienne De Linguistique, Vol 0041, 1996; Sociolinguistic Theory - Linguistic Variation And Its Soc Significance - Chambers,Jk/, Jl Of Pidgin And Creole Languages, Vol 0012, 1997. **CONTACT ADDRESS** 24 Candleigh Ave, Toronto, ON, M4R 1T2.

SAMUDIO, JEFFREY
PERSONAL Born 10/03/1966, San Gabriel, CA, s **DISCIPLINE** ARCHITECTURE **EDUCATION** Univ of Southern Calif, Bachelor of Archit; Archit Licensing, 98; Nat Trust for Historic Preservation Leadership Training, 93. **CAREER** Student asst slide libr curator, Archit & Fine Arts Image Center, 84-87, Freeman House Fel, School of Archit Frank Lloyd Wright Historic Site, 92-93, guest lectr, School of Archit, 92-95, assoc dir &co-founder, Prog in Historic Preservation, 93-96, instr, School of Archit & School of Urban Planning and Development, USC; instr, Los Angeles Trad-Tech Col and Rio Hondo Col, 89-97; VP of Acquistions and Project Development, Northeast Design and Development Group, Inc, 89-90; INSTR, 95, ADVISORY BOARD MEMBER, 97-, CAL POLY POMONA SCHOOL OF ENVIRONMENTAL DESIGN, 97-; ASSOC PROF, 97-, ENVIROMENTAL DESIGN DEPT, AM INTERCONTINENTAL UNIV; DIR & FOUNDER, CENTER FOR PRESERVATION ED AND PLANNING, 94-; PARTNER, DESIGN AID, ARCHIT PLANNING PRESERVATION, 87-. **HONORS AND AWARDS** Award of Honor, Am Inst of Archits; 1995 Hist Preservation Award, Los Angeles Conservancy, 95; Certificate of Appreciation, City of Los Angeles, 84 & 89; Outstanding Service to the Profession Award, AIA, 91; Phi Kappa Phi Res Mentorship Award, USC Grad School, 91; Freeman House Res Grant, Graham Found, 91; Grants for Diversity, Nat Trust for Hist Preservation & Getty Found, 92 & 96; Nat Trust for Hist Preservation Grant, 93; Getty Grant, USC Prog in Hist Preservation, 93; Nat Trust for Hist Preservation Grant, 93; Nat Park Service, USC Prog in Hist Preservation-Training Center, 95-96; Loyola Found of Washington-Marist Convent Fiji, 97; World Monuments Fund-Preservation Management, 97; Co-Sponsor for Confr on His Roads in Am, Nat Park Service, 98. **MEMBERSHIPS** Am Inst of Archits; Am Planning Asn; Soc of Archit Historians/SCC; Los Angeles City Hist Soc; Int Commt on Monuments and Sites; Nat Main St Roundtable; Nat Preservation Forum of the Nat Trust for Hist Preservation; Los Angeles Conservancy Asn for Preservation Tech APT. **RESEARCH** Historic preservation. **SELECTED PUBLICATIONS** Auth, Why the Heritage of the South Pacific is Important in a Eurocentric World, Soc of Archit Historians Rev, 97; auth, Preservation in Culturally Diverse Communities, Diversity and Architects, 95. **CONTACT ADDRESS** Design Aid Architects, 1722 N Whitley Ave, Hollywood, CA, 90028.

SAMUEL, ALAN EDOUARD
PERSONAL Born 07/24/1932, Queens, NY, m, 1964, 7 children **DISCIPLINE** ANCIENT HISTORY **EDUCATION** Hamilton Col, BA, 53; Yale Univ, MA, 57, PhD(classics), 59. **CAREER** From instr to asst prof classics, Yale Univ, 59-66; assoc prof, 66-67, PROF ANCIENT HIST, UNIV COL, UNIV TORONTO, 67- **MEMBERSHIPS** Archaeol Inst Am; Am Philol Asn; Am Soc Papyrologists; Class Asn Can. **RESEARCH** Hellenistic history; papyrology; ancient chronology. **SELECTED PUBLICATIONS** Auth, Faces Of Power - Alexander Image And Hellenistic Politics - Stewart,A/, Phoenix-The J Of The Classical Asn Of Can, Vol 0050, 1996. **CONTACT ADDRESS** 64 Alexandra Blvd, Toronto, ON, M4R 1L9.

SANABRIA, SERGIO LUIS
PERSONAL Born 10/14/1944, Havana, Cuba **DISCIPLINE** ARCHITECTURAL HISTORY **EDUCATION** Princeton Univ, PhD, 84. **CAREER** Assoc prof, Miami Univ, 80- . **HONORS AND AWARDS** Samuel Kress Publication Award, Archit Hist Found; Miami Univ fac res grants. **MEMBERSHIPS** SAH, SHOT, CAA. **RESEARCH** Gothic and Renaissance architecture in France and Spain. **SELECTED PUBLICATIONS** Auth, From Gothic to Renaissance Sterotomy: Design Methods of Philibert de l'Orme and Alonso de Vandelvira, Technol and Cult, 89; auth, A Late Gothic Drawing of San Juan de los Reyes in Toledo at the Prado Museum in Madrid, Jour of the Soc of Archit Historians, 92; auth, La Lave de la Catedral Neuva de Salamanca, El Siglo de Oro en Salamanca, 95; auth with Kristina Luce, The Rayonnant Gothic Buttresses at Metz Cathedral, The Cathedral, the Mill, and the Mine: Essays on Medieval Technology, 97; Rodrigo Gil and the Classical Transformation of Gothic Architecture in the Spanish Golden Age, 99. **CONTACT ADDRESS** Dept of Archit, Miami Univ, Oxford, OH, 45056. **EMAIL** sanabrsl@muohio.edu

SANCHEZ, ELIZABETH D.
DISCIPLINE NINETEENTH-CENTURY REALISM AND NATURALISM **EDUCATION** Univ Tex, BA, 66; Smith Col, MA, 64-65; Univ Tex, PhD, 69; NEH Summer Sem, Cornell Univ, 83. **CAREER** Assoc prof Span. **MEMBERSHIPS** Mem, Mod Lang Assn; S Cent Mod Lang Assn. **RESEARCH** Nineteenth centure realism and naturalism; chaos theory and the novel. **SELECTED PUBLICATIONS** Auth, La Regenta as Fractals, Revista de Estudios Hispanicos, 92; Order/Disorder and Complexity in La Regenta: A Case for Spiraling Outward and Upward, S Cent Rev, 96. **CONTACT ADDRESS** Dept of Mod Lang and Lit, Univ Dallas, 1845 E Northgate Dr, Irving, TX, 75062. **EMAIL** sanchez@acad.udallas.edu

SANCHEZ, GEORGE J.
DISCIPLINE HISTORY **EDUCATION** Harvard Col, BA, 81; Stanford Univ, MA, 84, PhD, 89. **CAREER** Dir, Chicano/Latino Stud Prog; assoc prof, Univ Southern Calif, 97-; assoc prof, Univ Mich, 93-97; asst prof, UCLA, 88-93; Andrew Norman Lect, Colo Col, 96; William Andrews Clark Mem Libr prof, UCLA, 93-94; Ford Found post-doc fel, 90-91; dir, Prog in Amer Cult, Univ Mich, 94-97. **HONORS AND AWARDS** Local History awd, Southern Calif Hist Soc, 97; Theodore Saloutus Mem Bk awd, Immigration Hist Soc, 94; Bk awd, Pac Coast Branch, Amer Hist Asn, 94; Robert Athearn Bk prize, Western Hist Asn, 94; J.S. Holliday awd, Calif Hist Soc, 94; New Scholar awd, Amer Educ Res Asn, 95. **MEMBERSHIPS** Amer Stud Asn, 97-; Latino Adv Comt, National Mus of Amer Hist, Smithsonian Inst, 95-; Comt on Int Migration, Soc Sci Res Coun, 94-. **SELECTED PUBLICATIONS** Auth, Becoming Mexican American: Ethnicity, Culture and Identity in Chicano Los Angeles, 1900-1945, NY: Oxford UP, 93; Face the Nation: Race, Immigration, and the Rise of Nativism in Late Twentieth Century America, Int Migration Rev 31:4, 97; Ethnicity, in A Companion to American Thought, Blackwell, 97; Reading Reginald Denny: The Politics of Whiteness in Late Twentieth Century America, in Amer Quart 47:3, 95; The 'New Nationalism,' Mexican Style: Race and Progressivism in Chicano Political Development during the 1920s, in Calif Progressivism Revisited, Berkeley: Univ Calif Press, 94; Assessing Relations Between Mexican Americans and the Japanese, in Relations Between American Ethnic Groups and Japan, Tokyo: NIRA, 94; coauth, Contemporary Peoples/Contested Places, in The Oxford Hist of the Amer West, NY: Oxford UP, 94; ser co-ed, American Crossroads: New Works in Ethnic Studies, Univ Calif Press. With Earl Lewis, Univ Mich, George Lipsitz, UC, San Diego, Peggy Pascoe, Univ Oregon, and Dana Takagi, UC, Santa Cruz, 94-: Pages from History: Documentary Series for Secondary Schools, Oxford UP, With Sarah Deutsch, Clark Univ, Emily Honig, UC, Santa Cruz, Carol Karlsen, Univ Mich, and Robert Moeller, UC, Irvine. 94-. **CONTACT ADDRESS** Dept of History, Univ Southern Calif, University Park Campus, Los Angeles, CA, 90089. **EMAIL** georges@rcf.usc.edu

SANCHEZ, JOSE MARIANO
PERSONAL Born 11/01/1932, Santa Fe, NM, m, 1956, 5 children **DISCIPLINE** 20TH CENTURY EUROPEAN HISTORY **EDUCATION** St Louis Univ, BS, 54, AM, 57; Univ NMex, PhD, 61. **CAREER** From instr to assoc prof, 60-69, chmn dept, 71-74, prof hist, St. Lous Univ, 69-. **MEMBERSHIPS** AHA; Am Cath Hist Assn; Soc Span & Port Hist Studies. **RESEARCH** Modern Spanish history; 20th century Europe. **SELECTED PUBLICATIONS** Auth, Reform and Reaction: The Politico-Religious Background of the Spanish Civil War, Univ NC, 64;auth, Anticlericalism: A Brief History, Univ Notre Dame, 72; coauth & contribr, Great Events From History: Modern Europe, Salem, 73; auth, The Spanish Civil War As A Religious Tragedy, University of Notre Dame Press, 87. **CONTACT ADDRESS** Dept of History, St. Louis Univ, 221 N Grand Blvd, St. Louis, MO, 63103-2097. **EMAIL** sanchejm@slu.edu.

SANDAGE, SCOTT A.
DISCIPLINE HISTORY **EDUCATION** Univ Iowa, BA, 85; Rutgers Univ, MA, 92, PhD, 95. **CAREER** ASST PROF, HIST, CARNEGIE MELLON UNIV **HONORS AND AWARDS** NE Assn of Grad Schools Prize, 95-96. **MEMBERSHIPS** Am Antiquarian Soc **SELECTED PUBLICATIONS** Auth, "A Marble House Divided: The Lincoln Memorial, the Civil Rights Movement, and the Politics of Memory, 1939-1963," Jour of Am Hist 80, 93, repr in Race and the Invention of Modern Nationalism, Garland Press; auth, Defeats and Dreams: A Cultural History of Failure in Nineteenth-Century America, Harvard Univ Press; auth, "The Gaze of Success: Failed Men and the Sentimental Marketplace, 1873-1893," in Sentimental Men: Sentimentality and Masculinity in American Fiction and Culture. **CONTACT ADDRESS** Dept of Hist, Carnegie Mellon Univ, BH240, Pittsburgh, PA, 15213-2878. **EMAIL** sandage@andrew.cmu.edu

SANDERS, LIONEL
PERSONAL Born 05/21/1942, Hitchin, United Kingdom, d, 1 child **DISCIPLINE** HISTORY; CLASSICS **EDUCATION** McMaster, PHD **CAREER** Lect, 70-71, Univ Kingston, Ont; Asst Prof, 72-74, Loyola Col, Montreal; Assoc Prof, 76-96, Concordia Univ, Montreal; Full Prof, 96-pres, Concordia Univ **MEMBERSHIPS** Hellenic Soc; Canadian Class Assoc; Am Philol Assoc **RESEARCH** History and Historiography of Greek Sicily **SELECTED PUBLICATIONS** Auth, "Plato's First Visit to Sicily," Kokalos, 79, 207-19; Auth, "Dionysius I of Syracuse and the Validity of the Hostile Tradition," SCI, 79, 64-84; Auth, "Diodorus Siculus and Dionysius I of Syracuse," Historia, 81, 394-411 **CONTACT ADDRESS** Dept. Of Classics Modern Langs, Sir George Williams Campus, Concordia Univ, 1435 De Maisonneuve Blvd W, Montreal, PQ, H3G 1M8. **EMAIL** sanders@alcor.concordia.ca

SANDERSON, WARREN
PERSONAL Born 02/09/1931, Boston, MA, m, 1952, 2 children **DISCIPLINE** HISTORY OF ART & ARCHITECTURE **EDUCATION** Boston Univ, BA, 54, MA, 56; NY Univ, PhD(hist of art), 65. **CAREER** Asst prof hist of art, Southern Ill Univ, 60-62; instr, Boston Univ, 63-64; assoc prof, State Univ NY Col Buffalo, 64-66; from assoc prof to prof hist of art & archit, Univ Ill, Chicago Circle, 66-70; prof hist of art, Fla State Univ, 70-76; PROF ART HIST, CONCORDIA UNIV, MONTREAL, 76-, Vis prof, Sch Libr Sci, Rosary Col, Ill, 68 & 69-70; Am Philos Soc grant, 69; vis prof art hist, Univ Trier, WGer, 77-78; Fulbright grant, 82. **MEMBERSHIPS** Col Art Asn Am; Soc Archit Hist; Int Ctr Medieval Art; Univ Arts Asn Can. **RESEARCH** Western European and Modern American art and architecture; Early Medieval civilization in Europe. **SELECTED PUBLICATIONS** Auth, A Tainted Mantle - Hercules And The Classical-Tradition At The Carolingian Court - Nees,L/, Speculum-A J Of Medieval Studies, Vol 0068, 1993. **CONTACT ADDRESS** 1455 De Maisonneuve Blvd, Montreal, PQ, H3G 1M8.

SANDIFORD, KEITH ARLINGTON PATRICK
PERSONAL Born 03/02/1936, Barbados, WI, m, 1963, 1 child **DISCIPLINE** HISTORY **EDUCATION** Univ Col WI, BA, 60; Univ Toronto, MA, 61, PhD(hist), 66. **CAREER** Lectr hist, York Univ, Ont, 64-65; asst prof, 66-72, ASSOC PROF HIST, UNIV MAN, 72-, Can Coun fel, 68. **RESEARCH** Victorian thought and culture; Tudor-Stuart Britain; 19th century British politics and diplomacy. **SELECTED PUBLICATIONS** Auth, Sport And The Making Of Britain - Birley,D/, Albion, Vol

0026, 1994; Palmerston Foreign-Policy, 1848 - Billy,Gj/, Int Hist Rev, Vol 0018, 1996. **CONTACT ADDRESS** Dept of History, Univ of Manitoba, Winnipeg, MB, R3T 2N2.

SANDLER, LUCY FREEMAN
PERSONAL Born 06/07/1930, New York, NY, m, 1958, 1 child **DISCIPLINE** ART HISTORY **EDUCATION** Queens Col, BA, 51; Columbia Univ, MA, 57; NY Univ, PhD, 64. **CAREER** From asst prof to assoc prof, 64-75, prof, hist of art, Washington Sq Col, NY Univ, 75-; chmn, dept Fien Arts, 75-88, Asst ed, Art Bull, 63-67; Nat Found Arts & Humanities grant, 67-68; ed, Col Art Asn Am Monogr Ser, 70-75, 86-89. **HONORS AND AWARDS** Nat Endowment for Humanities fel for independent study & res, 67-68,77; Guggenheim fel, 88-89; Fel of the Soc of Antiquaries of London, 91-; fel, Medieval Acad of Am, 97-. **MEMBERSHIPS** Col Art Asn Am (secy, 78-80, vpres, 80-81, pres, 81-); Int Ctr Medieval Art; AAUP. **RESEARCH** Medieval art; illuminated manuscripts. **SELECTED PUBLICATIONS** Ed, Essays in Memory of Karl Lehmann, Marsyas, Suppl I, 64; auth, Petersborough Abbey and the Peterborough Psalter in Brussels, J Brit Archaeol Asn, 70; A follower of Jean Pucelle in England, Art Bull, 70; Christian Hebraism and the Ramsey Abbey Psalter, J Warburg & Courtauld Insts, 72; The Peterborough Psalter in Brussels and Other Fenland Manuscripts, Harvey Miller & Medcalf, London, 73; An Early Fourteenth Century English Breviary at Longleat, 76 & An early fourteenth English Psalter in the Escorial, 78, J Warburg & Courtauld Insts; auth, The Peterborough Psalter in Brussels and Other Fenland Manuscripts, London and NY, 74; auth, The Psalter of Robert de Lisle in the British Library, London and NY, 83; auth, Gothic Manuscripts, 1285-1385 (A Survey of Manuscripts Illuminated in the British Isles, Vol V), London and NY, 2 Vols, 86; auth, The Age of Chivalry, English Art 1200-1400, London Royal Acad, 87; auth, Omne bonum: A Fourteenth Century Encyclopedia of Universal Knowledge, London, 2 Vols, 96; auth, The Ramsey Psalter, Graz, 97; auth, A Late Carolingian Gospel Book in the Pierpont Morgan Library, Marsyas, VII, 57-63, 57; auth, A Series of Marginal Illustrations in the Rutland Psalter, Marsyas, VIII, 70-84, 84; auth, The Historical Miniatures of the Fourteenth-Century Ramsey Psalter, Burlington Mag, 103, 605-611, 69; auth, Reflections on the Construction of Hybrids in English Gothic marginal Illustrations, Art the Ape of Nature, Studies in Honor of HW Hjanson, NE, 51-66, 81; auth, A Fragment of the Chertsey Breviary in San Francisco, Bodleian Lib Record XI, 155-61, 83; auth, Jean Pucelle and the Lost Miniatures of the Belleville Breviary, The Art Bul, LXVI, 73-96, 84; auth, The Handclasp in the Arnolfini Wedding: A Manuscript Precedent, The Art Bul, LXVIm 488-491, 84; auth, A Note on the Illuminators of Bohun Manuscripts, Speculum, LX, 364-372,85; auth, A Bawdy Betrothal in the Ormesby Pasalter, Tribute to Lotte Brand Phillip, Art Historian and Detective, NY, 155-159,85; auth, Face to Face with God: A Pictoral Image of the Beatific Vision, England in the Fourteenth Century, Proceedings of the 1985 Harlaxton Symposium, Woodbridge, UK, 86; auth, Notes for the Illuminator: the Case of the Omne bonum, The Art Bulletin, LXXI, 89; auth, Omne bonim: Compilato and Ordinationin an English Illustrated Encyclopedia of the Fourteenth Century, Medieval Book Production, Assessing the Evidence, Los Altos Hills, 183-200, 90; auth, The Image of the Book-Owner in the Fourteenth Century: Three Cases of Self-Definition, Harlaxton Medieval Stu III, Stamford, UK, 58-80, 93; auth, Enciclopedia, Enciclopedia dell'arte medievale, V, Rome, 95; auth, The Canon Law Illustrations of the Omne Bonum, and English Encyclopedia of the Fourteenth Century, Proceedings of the Ninth Int Cong of Medieval Canon Law, Monumenta iuris canonici, Series C, Subsidia Vol 10, Vatican City, Biblioteca Apostolica Vatucana, 675-689, 97; auth, Manuscript Images of Devotion and the Wilton Diptych, The Regal Image of Richard II and the Wilton Diptych, London, 137-154, 318-320, 97; auth, The Word in the Text and the Image in the Margin: The Case of the Luttrell Psalter, Jou of the Walters Art Fal LIV, 87-99, 96; auth, Verbal and Pictorial Play in the Margins: The Case of Stowe 49, Illuminating the Book: Makers and Interpretersm Essays in Honour of Janet Backhouse, London, 52-68, 98; auth, The Study of Marginal Imagery, Past, Present, and Future, Stu in Iconography, XVIII, 1-49, 97. **CONTACT ADDRESS** Dept of Fine Arts, New York Univ, 100 Washington Sq E, New York, NY, 10003-6688. **EMAIL** ls5@is2.nyu.edu

SANDOS, JAMES A.
DISCIPLINE HISTORY **EDUCATION** Univ Calif Berkeley, PhD, 78. **CAREER** Prof, Univ Redlands. **RESEARCH** Latin America history; California Indian history; Vietnam and Guerrilla warfare in the 20th century. **SELECTED PUBLICATIONS** Auth, From 'Boltonlands' to 'Weberlands' The Borderlands Enter American History, Am Quarterly, 94; Rebellion in the Borderlands: Anarchism and the Plan of San Diego, 1904-1923, Univ Okla, 92; Christianization Among the Chumash: An Ethnohistoric Perspective, Am Indian Quarterly, 91. **CONTACT ADDRESS** History Dept, Univ Redlands, 1200 E Colton Ave, Box 3090, Redlands, CA, 92373-0999. **EMAIL** sandos@uor.edu

SANDOVAL, DOLORES S.
PERSONAL Born 09/30/1937, Montreal, Quebec, Canada **DISCIPLINE** EDUCATION **EDUCATION** Institute of Chicago, art, 1956-58; University of Michigan, BSD, 1958-60; Indiana Univ, MS, 1968, PhD, 1970; Harvard University Institute for Educational Management, IEM, 1975. **CAREER** University of Vermont, assoc prof of education, 1971-, Middle East studies, co-chair, 1994-, assistant to the president for human resources, 1972-77; State University College at Buffalo, assoc prof, 1970-71; Author/Illustrator of "Be Patient Abdul,", Margaret McElderry Books, 1996; Paintings and photography of Africa, Middle East & Latin America exhibited in Europe, Canada and USA, 1987-; Represented by program Corp. of America, 1994; consultant on Race Relations & Diversity Programming. **HONORS AND AWARDS** Elected Democratic candidate for Congress from VT, 1990; Primary candidate, 1988; President's Fellow, Rhode Island School of Design, 1981, mem board of trustees, 1976-82; University Senate, University of VT, chair, 1981-82; Fellowship Challenges to Unity: The European Community, 1995, Maastricht, 1995; Fellow, University of New Mexico College of Fine Arts National Arts Project, Daring To Do It, 1993-94; Malone Alumni Fellow to Jordan, Israel, Palestine and Syria, summer, 1991; Malone Fellow in Arab and Islamic Studies in Tunisia, summer, 1989; Award from Black American Heritage Foundation, NYC for Contributions to Duke Ellington Concert & Speech Series, 1989-92; Fellow, National Endowment for the Humanities Summer Institute on African & African-American Culture, 1987. **MEMBERSHIPS** Partners of the Americas, Vermont/Honduras, president, 1997-, vice pres, 1994-96, board member, 1992-; Sister Cities, Burlington, (VT) Arad (Israel & Bethlehem), board member, 1995-96; Public Access Government TV, Channel 17 (VT), board member, 1991-95. **CONTACT ADDRESS** Univ of Vermont, Burlington, VT, 05405-0001.

SANDWEISS, MARTHA
DISCIPLINE AMERICAN HISTORY **EDUCATION** Yale Univ, doctorate. **CAREER** Cur, Amon Carter Mus, Ft Worth, 79-89; instr, 89-, dir, Mead Art Mus, Amherst Col. **RESEARCH** The cult hist of photography in the Am West during the 19th-century. **SELECTED PUBLICATIONS** Auth, Laura Gilpin: An Enduring Grace, 86; coauth, Eyewitness to War: Prints and Daguerreotypes of the Mexican War,1846-1848, 89; ed, Photography in Nineteenth-Century America, 91; coed, Oxford History of the American West, 94. **CONTACT ADDRESS** Amherst Col, Amherst, MA, 01002-5000.

SANDY, KITY
PERSONAL Born 08/17/1950, Chicago, IL, s **DISCIPLINE** HISTORY OF ART **EDUCATION** Northwestern Univ, BA, 71; Univ Chicago, MA, 74, PhD, 81. **CAREER** Univ Md, Col Pk, 96-. **HONORS AND AWARDS** Curated, A Hidden Treasure: Japanese Woodblock Prints from the James Austin Collection, travelling exhibition, Carnegie Mus Art, Det Inst Art, Mus Middlebury Coll, opened Sep 97. **SELECTED PUBLICATIONS** Auth, A Hidden Treasure: Japanese Prints in the James Austin Collection, Carnegie Inst, 95; auth, The Last Tosa: Iwasa Katsumochi Matabei, Bridge to Ukiyo-e, Univ Hawaii Press, forthcoming; auth, Kaikoku michi no ki, a 17th cen travelogue by Iwasa Matabei, Monumenta Serica XLV, 97; auth, A Court Painting of a Fast Bull in the Cleveland Museum of Art, Orientations, Sept 91; entries on Hiroshige and Munakata Shiko in the Handbook of the Carnegie Museum of Art, Carnegie Museum of Art, 95; review of Ukiyo-e Paintings in the British Museum by Timothy Clark, J Asian Stud, 94. **CONTACT ADDRESS** 2601 Park Ctr Dr, Alexandria, VA, 22302.

SANFORD, DANIEL
DISCIPLINE INTERNATIONAL STUDIES **EDUCATION** Univ Denver, PhD. **CAREER** Dir, Grad Sch Intl Mg, Whitworth col; prof-. **HONORS AND AWARDS** Fulbright scholar, Univ Kiemyung, Daegu, Korea; res fel, Univ Calif, Berkeley.., Former pres, World Trade Coun; Northwest Intl Edu Assn. **MEMBERSHIPS** Mem, Spokane Mayor's Comm Intl Devel; Spokane Chamber of Com Intl Steering Comm. **RESEARCH** International political economy with focus on trade politics in Northeast Asia. **SELECTED PUBLICATIONS** Auth, South Korea and the Socialist Countries; The Politics of Trade. **CONTACT ADDRESS** Dept of Hist, Whitworth Col, 300 West Hawthorne Rd, Spokane, WA, 99251. **EMAIL** dsanford@whitworth.edu

SANNEH, LAMIN
PERSONAL Georgetown, m, 1973, 2 children **DISCIPLINE** HISTORY **EDUCATION** Univ Birmingham, England, MA, 68; Univ London, PhD, 74. **CAREER** Asst, assoc prof, 81-89, Harvard Divinity Schl; prof, 89-, Yale Divinity Schl. **HONORS AND AWARDS** Commandeur de l'Ordre Natl du Lion, Senegal. **MEMBERSHIPS** Amer Acad Religion; Royal African Soc, England. **RESEARCH** History of religion and culture. **SELECTED PUBLICATIONS** Auth, Can a House Divided Stand? Reflections on Christian-Muslim Relations in the West, Intl Bull of Missionary Res, 93; art, World Christianity from an African Perspective: An Interview, Amer, 94; art, Religious Agnostics and Cultural Believers: Comparative Soundings on the Lost Trails of Christendom, Insights, Jour Fac Austin Sem, 93; auth, Translatability in Islam and in Christianity in Africa: A Thematic Approach, Religion in Africa, Heinemann, 94; auth, The Gospel, Language and Culture: The Theological Method in Cultural Analysis, Intl Rev of Mission, vol 84, 95; art, Global Christianity and the Re-Education of the West, Christian Century, 95; auth, The Crown and the Turban: Muslims and West African Pluralism, Westview Press, 96; auth, Religion and the Variety of Culture: A Study in Origin and Practice, Trinity Press Intl, 96; auth, Piety and Power: Muslims and Christians in West Africa, Orbis Books, 96; auth, Theology of Mission, Modern Theol, Blackwell Pub, 97; art, A Plantation of Religion and the Enterprise Culture in Africa: History, Ex-Slaves and Religious Inevitability, Jour of Rel in Africa, vol 27, 97; auth, Christianity - Missionary Enterprise in Africa, Encycl of Africa So of the Sahara, Macmillan Lib Ref; art, Faith, Power, and the Separation of Church and State: African Examples, Muslim Pol Report, NY Council on Foreign Relations, 97; coauth, Faith and Power: Christianity and Islam in Secular Britain, London SPCK, 98; auth, Mission to the West: Lesslie Newbigin, 1909-1998, Christian Century, 98; auth, Time, Space and Prescriptive Marginality in Muslim Africa: Symbolic Action an Structural Change, World History: Ideologies, Structures, and Identities, Blackwell Pub, 98; auth, Ibn Khaldun, Encycl of Pol & Rel, vol 1, Cong Quart, 98; auth, Separation of Church and State: a Principle Advancing the Struggle for Human Rights, Encycl of Pol & Rel, vol 1, Cong Quart, 98; art, Religion, Politics and the Islamic Response in Africa, Newsl, Intl Inst for the Stud of Islam in Modern World, Leiden, The Netherlands, Inaugural Issue, 98. **CONTACT ADDRESS** 409 Prospect St, New Haven, CT, 06511-2167. **EMAIL** lamin.sanneh@yale.edu

SANSONE, DAVID
PERSONAL Born 09/23/1946, New York, NY, m, 1969, 2 children **DISCIPLINE** CLASSICS **EDUCATION** Hamilton Col, AB, 68; Univ WI, MA, 69, PhD, 72. **CAREER** Asst prof, Univ HI, 72-74; asst prof, 74-80, assoc prof, 80-88, PROF, UNIV IL, 88-, CHAIR, CLASSICS DEPT, 96-. **MEMBERSHIPS** Am Philol Asn; Soc for the Promotion of Hellenic Studies; Cambridge Philol Soc; Int Plutarch Soc. **RESEARCH** Greek tragedy; ancient biography; Greek and Roman sport. **SELECTED PUBLICATIONS** Auth, Aeschlean Metaphors for Intellectual Activity (Hermes Einzelschrifton 35), F. Steiner Verlag, Wiesbaden, 75; Euripides, Iphigenia in Tauris, B. G. Teubner Verlag, Leipzig, 81; Greek Athletics and the Genesis of Sport, Univ CA Press, Berkeley, 88; Plutarch: Lives of Aristeides and Cato, Aris & Phillips, Warminster, 89; Towards a New Doctrine of the Article in Greek: Some Observations on the Definite Article in Plato, Classical Philol 88, 93; Plato and Euripedes, IL Classical Studies 21, 96. **CONTACT ADDRESS** Dept of Classics 4072 For Lang, Univ Illinois, 707 S Mathews Ave., Urbana, IL, 61801. **EMAIL** dsansone@uiuc.edu

SANTANA, DEBORAH
DISCIPLINE ETHNIC STUDIES **EDUCATION** San Francisco State Univ, BA, 86; Univ Calif, Berkeley, MA, 89, PhD, 93. **CAREER** Asst prof; field and archival research on commun power and sustainable develop, funded by the Fac Res Awd Prog, SUNY-Albany, 94; ciriacy-wantrup postdr fel, Univ Calif, Berkeley, 94-95; res to create a curric on develop and the env, Title VI grant from the US Dept Educ, 93-94. **HONORS AND AWARDS** Current Reviews for Acad Libraries Outstanding Acad Bk awd, 97., Founding mem, 98 Gp, 94-. **RESEARCH** Sustainable development; Labor; trade; migration; env; political ecology of natural resources; population; development policies; historical legacy of racism and colonialism; race; class; gender and the env; local responses to global processes; latin America; African diaspora in the Americas; US current and former Pacific Island possessions; US communities of color. **SELECTED PUBLICATIONS** Auth, Kicking off the bootstraps: env, develop, and commun power in PR, ser Society, Env, and Place, Tucson: Univ Ariz Press, 96; Geographers, colonialism, and development strategies: the case of PR, Spec issue on env racism, In Urban Geog 17:5, 96; El desarrollo economico, la lucha ambiental y el podereo comunitario en PR, In Homines 17:2, 94; Colonialism, resistance, and the search for alternatives: the enval movement in PR, In Race, Poverty and the Env VI:1, 94; bk chap, Envalism and the charge of genocide, USA on trial: the int tribunal on indigenous and oppressed peoples, Chicago: Ed Coque, 96. **CONTACT ADDRESS** Dept of Ethnic Studies, Mills Col, 5000 MacArthur Blvd, Oakland, CA, 94613-1301.

SANTIAGO, MYRNA
PERSONAL Born 02/26/1960, Chula Vista, CA, m, 1998, 1 child **DISCIPLINE** HISTORY **EDUCATION** Princeton Univ, BA, 78; Univ of Calif at Berkeley, MA, 93, PhD, 97. **CAREER** Lectr, Mills Col, 98; lectr, Univ of Calif at Berkeley, 98; ASST PROF, ST. MARY'S COL. **HONORS AND AWARDS** Ford Found fel; fulbright scholar. **MEMBERSHIPS** LASA; AHA; ASEH. **RESEARCH** Latin American history; Environment; labor. **CONTACT ADDRESS** Hist Dept, St. Mary's Col, Morasa, CA, 94574. **EMAIL** msantiag@stmarys-ca.edu

SANTOSUOSSO, ALMA
DISCIPLINE MUSIC HISTORY **EDUCATION** British Columbia, Bmus, MMus; Univ Ill, PhD. **CAREER** Prof **SELECTED PUBLICATIONS** Auth, Letter Notations in the Middle Ages; Analysis, Inventory and Text. **CONTACT ADDRESS** Dept of Music, Wilfrid Laurier Univ, 75 University Ave W, Waterloo, ON, N2L 3C5.

SANTOSUOSSO, ANTONIO
PERSONAL Born 07/20/1936, Taurasi, Italy, m, 1964, 2 children **DISCIPLINE** HISTORY **EDUCATION** Univ Toronto, BA, 68, MA, 69, PhD(hist), 72. **CAREER** Lectr, 71-72, asst prof, 72-74, assoc prof, 74-81, PROF HIST, UNIV WESTERN ONT, 81-, Can Coun leave fel, 76-78; consult TV drama, The Newcomers, Nielsen-Ferns, 76-80. **MEMBERSHIPS** Renaissance Soc Am; Renaissance Soc Can. **RESEARCH** Cultural history of Italian sixteenth century. **SELECTED PUBLICATIONS** Auth, A Hist Of The Roman Inquisition In Italy - Archives, Methodological Problems, And New Research - Italian - Delcol,A, Paolin,G, Editors/, Renaissance Quart, Vol 0046, 1993; Anatomy Of A Defeat In Renaissance Italy - The Battle Of Fornovo In 1495/, Int Hist Rev, Vol 0016, 1994; Dellacasa,Giovanni And His Lost Portrait By Titian/, Bibliotheque D Humanisme Et Renaissance, Vol 0057, 1995; The Man Who Sacked Rome - Bourbon,Charles,De, Constable Of France, 1490-1527 - Pitts,Vj/, Int Hist Rev, Vol 0017, 1995; Kadesh Revisited - Reconstructing The Battle Between The Egyptians And The Hittites/, J Of Military Hist, Vol 0060, 1996; Hist And Warfare In Renaissance Epic - Murrin,M/, Int Hist Rev, Vol 0018, 1996; The Inquisitional Trial Of The Cardinal Morone,Giovanni, A Critical Edition, Vol 6, Appendix 2 - 'Summarium Processus Originalis', Documents - Italian, Latin - Firpo,M, Marcatto,D/, Bibliotheque D Humanisme Et Renaissance, Vol 0058, 1996; The Fr Descent Into Renaissance Italy, 1494-1495 - Abulafia,D/, Int Hist Rev, Vol 0019, 1997; Giovio,Paolo - The Historian And The Crisis Of 16th-Century Italy - Zimmermann,Tcp/, Am Hist Rev, Vol 0102, 1997. **CONTACT ADDRESS** 55 Balcarres Rd, London, ON, N5X 2H6.

SAPPER, NEIL GARY
PERSONAL Born 02/15/1941, Denver, CO, m, 1965, 2 children **DISCIPLINE** HISTORY **EDUCATION** Univ Denver, BA, 63; Eastern NMex Univ, MA, 65; Tex Tech Univ, PhD(hist), 72. **CAREER** Instr hist, Black Hawk Col, 65-67; asst prof, 72-76, assoc prof, 76-79, prof Soc Sci, Amarillo Col, 79-; co-ed, H-Survey, 95-; co-ed, H-Texas, 97-. **HONORS AND AWARDS** Grant recipient, Pub Policy & Inter-scholastic Athletics in Tex, Tex Comt Humanities & Pub Policy, 76. **MEMBERSHIPS** Orgn Am Historians; Tex State Hist Asn. **RESEARCH** United States social history; African-American people in Texas. **SELECTED PUBLICATIONS** Auth, Aboard the Wrong Ship in the Right Books: Doris Miller and Historical Accuracy, E Tex Hist Rev XVIII, Winter 80; Black Culture in Texas: A Lone Star Renaissance, Red River Valley Hist Rev, Spring 81; For a Graybeard, Things Change, Community and Jr Col J LIII, 10/82; The Fall of the NAACP in Texas, The Houston Rev VII, Winter 85; coauth, Amarillo's Centenial Plaza: Public/Private Funding, Tex Recreation and Park Soc J, 10-12/87; auth, Telecourses Serve the Gifted and the Talented in Two Small Texas High Schools, The Agenda VII, Fall 92; Antonio Maceo Smith, Doris Miller, and Lonnie E. Smith, In: The New Handbook of Texas, Austin: Tex State Hist Asn, 95. **CONTACT ADDRESS** Dept of Social Sci, Amarillo Col, PO Box 447, Amarillo, TX, 79178-0001. **EMAIL** ngsapper@actx.edu

SAPPOL, MICHAEL
DISCIPLINE HISTORY **EDUCATION** City Coll NY, BA, 78; Columbia Univ, PhD, 97. **CAREER** PROJ HIST, PRESS & PRESIDENCY PROJ **MEMBERSHIPS** Am Antiquarian Soc **SELECTED PUBLICATIONS** Auth, "Sammy Tubbs and Dr. Hubbs: Anatomical Dissection, Minstrelsy and the Technology of Self-Making in Postbellum America," Configurations 4, 96; auth, Anatomical America: Death, Dissection, and Embodied Social Identity in the Nineteenth-Century, Princeton Univ Press. GEN **CONTACT ADDRESS** 635 E 14th St, No. 2G, New York, NY, 10009-3229.

SARASON, RICHARD SAMUEL
PERSONAL Born 02/12/1948, Detroit, MI **DISCIPLINE** RELIGIOUS STUDIES, HISTORY OF RELIGIONS **EDUCATION** Brandeis Univ, AB, 69; Hebrew Union Col, MAHL, 74; Brown Univ, PhD(relig studies), 77. **CAREER** Instr relig studies, Brown Univ, 76-77, asst prof, 77-79; asst prof, 79-81, Assoc Prof Rabbinic Lit & Thought, Hebrew Union Col, 81- **MEMBERSHIPS** Am Acad Relig; Soc Bibl Lit; Asn Jewish Studies; Am Sch Orient Res; Soc Values Higher Educ. **RESEARCH** Judaism in late antiquity; early rabbinic Judaism, Mishnah-Tosefta, rabbinic midrash and liturgy. **SELECTED PUBLICATIONS** Auth, Intertextuality And The Reading Of Midrash - Boyarin,D/, J Of Rel, Vol 0074, 1994. **CONTACT ADDRESS** Hebrew Union Col, 3101 Clifton Ave, Cincinnati, OH, 45220.

SARBIN, THEODORE R.
PERSONAL Born 05/08/1911, Cleveland, OH, w, 1949, 3 children **DISCIPLINE** PSYCHOLOGY **EDUCATION** Ohio St Univ, BA, 36; Western Reserve Univ, MA, 37; Ohio St Univ, PhD, 41. **CAREER** Counr, 38-41, Univ Minn; post doc fel, 41-43, SSRC, Univ Chicago; supvr psychol, 43-44, Illinios St; indep practice, 44-49; clin psychol, 46-69, Veterans Admin; prof, psychol & criminol, 49-69, Berkley, 69-76, Santa Cruz, emer prof, 76-90, Univ Calif; res psychol, 87-98, Security Res Ctr, Monterey CA. **HONORS AND AWARDS** Sr Fulbright award, Oxford Univ, 61-62; fel, John Simon Guggenheim Found, 65-66; fel, Ctr for Advance Stud, Wesleyan Univ, 68-69; Clement Staff Essay Award, Psychoanalytic Rev,71; foe, Ctr for Hum, Wesleyan Univ, 75; APA, div 30 Award for dist contr to Scientific Hypnosis, 93. **MEMBERSHIPS** Fel Amer Psychol Assn; Fel Amer Psychol Soc; Amer Sociol Assn. **RESEARCH** Narrative stud; emotional life; deviance; imagining. **SELECTED PUBLICATIONS** Co-ed, Varieties of Scientific Contextualism, Context Press 93; auth, The Narrative as a Root Metaphor for Contextualism, Ibid, 93; auth, Whither Hypnosis? A Rhetorical Analysis, Contemp Hypnosis, 93; auth, Steps to the Narratory Principle: an Autobiographical Essay, Life & Story: Autobiographies for a Narrative Psychology, Greenwood, 93; co-ed, Constructing the Social, Sage Pub, 94; auth, Prologue to Constructing the Social, Ibid, 94; art, Dissociation: State, Trait, or Skill, Contemp Hypnosis, 94; co-ed, Citizen Espionage: Studies in Trust and Betrayal, Praeger, 94; auth, A Criminological Theory of Citizen Espionage, Ibid, 94; art, On the Belief That One Body May Be Host to Two or More Personalities, Intl J of Clin & Exper Hypnosis, 95; art, A narrative approach to "Repressed Memories", J of Narrative & Personal Hist, 95; art, Emotional Life, Rhetoric, and Roles, J of Narrative & Personal Hist, 95; auth, Deconstructing Stereotypes: Homosexuals and Military Policy, Out in Force: Sexual Orientation and the Military, Univ Chicago Press, 96; art, The Poetics of Identity, Theory & Psychol, 97; art, On the Futility of Psychiatric Dagnostic Manuals (DSMs) and the Return of Personal Agency, Applied & Prev Psychol, 97; art, Multiple Personality Disorder: Fact or Artifact?, Current Opinion in Psych, 97; art, Hypnosis as a Conversation: Believed-in imaginings, Contemp Hypnosis, 97; coauth, Conventional and Unconventional Narratives of Emotional Life, in Emotions in Psychopathology: Theory & Res, Oxford Univ Press, 98; coauth, Nontraditional Ways of Classifying Mental Disorders, Encycl of Mental Health vol 1, Acad Press, 98; coauth, The Narrative Construction of Emotional Life, What Develops in Emotional Development? Plenum Press, 98; co-ed, Believed-in Imaginings: The Narrative Construction of Reality, APA, 98; auth, Believing and Imagining: A Narrative Perspective, Ibid, 98; auth, The Poetic Construction of Reality and Other Explanatory Categories, Ibid, 98. **CONTACT ADDRESS** 25515 Hatton Rd, Carmel, CA, 93923. **EMAIL** 5211p@vm1.cc.nps.navy.mil

SARDESAI, DAMODAR RAMAJI
PERSONAL Born 01/05/1931, Goa, India, m, 1960, 2 children **DISCIPLINE** HISTORY OF INDIA, HISTORY OF SOUTHEAST ASIA. **EDUCATION** Univ Bombay, BA, 52, MA, 55; Univ Calif, Los Angeles, PhD(hist), 65. **CAREER** Lectr hist, Siddharth Col, Univ Bombay, 55-61; asst prof, Calif State Univ, Los Angeles, 65-66; from asst prof to assoc prof, 66-77, PROF HIST, UNIV CALIF, LOS ANGELES, 77-, Nat Endowment for Humanities grant, 68; Ford Found grant, 68-69; vis prof hist & chmn dept, Univ Bombay, 72-73; Am Inst Indian Studies sr fel, 80-81. **MEMBERSHIPS** AHA; Asn Asian Studies; fel Indian Inst Hist Studies; Asiatic Soc Bombay; fel Royal Hist Soc, Gt Brit. **RESEARCH** Indian foreign policy; trade and empire in Southeast Asia; Portuguese in Asia. **SELECTED PUBLICATIONS** Auth, The Tragedy Of Cambodian Hist - Politics, War, And Revolution Since 1945 - Chandler,Dp/, Am Hist Rev, Vol 0098, 1993; The Fall Of Imperial Britain In South-East Asia - Tarling,N/, Albion, Vol 0026, 1994; The Forgotten Army - India Armed Struggle For Independence, 1942-1945 - Fay,Pw/, Historian, Vol 0057, 1995; The Fr Wolf And The Siamese Lamb - The Fr Threat To Siamese Independence, 1858-1907 - Tuck,P/, Int Hist Rev, Vol 0019, 1997. **CONTACT ADDRESS** Dept of Hist, Univ of Calif, Los Angeles, CA, 90024.

SARLOS, ROBERT KAROLY
PERSONAL Born 06/06/1931, Budapest, Hungary, m, 1962, 2 children **DISCIPLINE** THEATRE HISTORY **EDUCATION** Occidental Col, BA, 59; Yale Univ, PhD(hist of theatre), 65. **CAREER** Instr English, Mitchell Col, 62-63; from lectr to acting asst prof, 63-65, asst prof, 66-70, assoc prof, 70-79, PROF DRAMATIC ART, UNIV CALIF, DAVIS, 79-, Vpres, Woodland Opera House Inc, 80- **MEMBERSHIPS** Int Fed Theatre Res; Am Soc Theatre Res. **RESEARCH** Elizabethan, Baroque and American theatre. **SELECTED PUBLICATIONS** Auth The Impact Of Working-Conditions Upon Acting Style/, Theatre Res Int, Vol 0020, 1995. **CONTACT ADDRESS** Dept of Dramatic Art, Univ of Calif, Davis, CA, 95616.

SARNA, JONATHAN D.
PERSONAL Born 01/10/1955, Philadelphia, PA, m, 1986, 2 children **DISCIPLINE** AMERICAN JEWISH HISTORY **EDUCATION** Brandeis Univ, BA, 75, MA, 75; Yale Univ, MA, 76, MPhil, 78, PhD, 79. **CAREER** Joseph H. & Belle R. Braun Prof Amer Jewish Hist, 90- , Dept ch, 92-95, 98, Brandeis Univ; Prof Amer Jewish Hist, 88-90, assoc prof, 84-88, asst prof, 80-84, vis lectr, 79-80, Hebrew Union Col-Jewish Inst Rel; Ch of the Board, Judaica On-Line Network (H-Judaic), 96- ; Ch, Acad Coun, Amer Jewish Hist Soc, 92-95; Dir Boston Jewish Hist Proj, 92-95; Dir, Ctr Stud The Amer Jewish Experience, 86-90, Acad dir, 84-86, acad adv, 81-84; vis assoc prof, Hebrew Univ, 86-87; vis asst prof Judaic Stud, Univ Cincinnati, 83-84; asst Amer Hist, Yale Univ, 78; Dir, Am Jewish Experience Curriculum Proj, 82-90; assoc ed, Amer Natl Biog, ed J. Garraty; Consultant, Amram Nowak Assoc, Amer Jewish Hist Film Proj, 94- ; Consulting ed, Am: The Jewish Experience, by Sondra Leiman, UAHC Press, 92-94; Publ Committee, Jewish Publ Soc, 85-90; Ed Board, Univ Press New England, 92- ; ed, North Amer Judaism sec, Rel Stud Rev, 84-94; ed comm, Queen City Heritage, 85- ; ed board, Am Jewish Hist, 88- ;ed board, Rel and Amer Cult, 89-96; ed board, Contemporary Jewry, 92- ; ed board, Patterns of Prejudice, 94- ; ed committee, Jewish Soc Stud, 93- ; acad comm, Touro Natl Heritage Trust, 93- ; adv comm, Ctr for Amer Jewish Hist, Temple Univ, 91; adv comm, Ctr Stud N Amer Jewry, Ben-Gurion Univ, Israel, 91- ; Wexner Found Grad Fel Comm, 89-92; Adv board, Maurice Amado Found, 90-95. **HONORS AND AWARDS** NEH Sr fel, 96; Lilly Endow grants, 84-93; Pew Endow grant, 91-94; Lady Davis Endow 86-87; Amer Coun Learned Soc, 82; Mem Found Jewish Cult, 82-83; Bernard and Audre Rapoport Fel in Amer Jewish Hist, Amer Jewish Archives, 79-80; Mem Found Jewish Cult, 77-79; Natl Found Jewish Cult, 77-79; Loewenstein-Wiener Fel, Amer Jewish Archives, 77; Howard F. Brinton Fel, Yale Univ, 77-78; Seltzer-Brodsky Prize Essay, YIVO Inst, 77; Charles Andrews Fel, Yale Univ, 76-77; Hebrew Free Loan Assn Fel, Amer Jewish Hist Soc, 74-75. **MEMBERSHIPS** Amer Acad Rel; Amer Hist Assn; Amer Jewish Hist Soc; Assn Jewish Stud; Can Jewish Hist Soc; Cincinnati Hist Soc; Immigration Hist Soc; Org Amer Hist; Phi Beta Kappa; Soc Hist Early Am Rep. **RESEARCH** Judaism. **SELECTED PUBLICATIONS** Ed, Jews in New Haven, Jewish Hist Soc New Haven, 78; Mordecai Manuel Noah: Jacksonian Politician and American Jewish Communal Leader-A Biographical Study, PhD Theis, Yale Univ, 79; Jacksonian Jew: The Two Worlds of Mordecai Noah, Holmes & Meier, 81; People Walk on Their Heads: Moses Weinberger's Jews and Judaism in New York, Holmes & Meier, 82; co-ed, Jews and the Founding of the Republic, Markus Wiener, 85; The American Jewish Experience: A Reader, Holmes and Meier, 86, 2nd ed, 97; American Synagogue History: A Bibliography and State-of-the-Field Survey, with Alexandria S. Korros, Markus Wiener, 88; Yahadut Amerika: American Jewry: An Annotated Bibliography of Publications in Hebrew, with Janet Liss, Hebrew Univ, 91; JPS: The Americaniztion of Jewish Culture (A history of the Jewish publication Soc, 1888-1988), JPS, 89; The Jews of Cincinnati, with Nancy H. Klein, Ctr for the Stud Am Jewish Experience, 89; A Double Bond: The Constitutional Documents of American Jewry, ed with Daniel J. Elazar and Rela Geffen Monson, Univ Press of Am, 92; Ethnic Diversity and Civic Identity: Patterns of Conflict and Cohesion in Cincinnati Since 1820, ed with Henry D. Shapiro, U of Illinois P, 92; Yehude Artsot Ha-Berit, ed with Lloyd Gartner, Merkaz Shazar, 92; Observing America's Jews by Marshall Sklare, ed, with forword and headnotes, UP of New England, 93; The Jews of Boston, with Ellen Smith, Combined Jewish Philanthropies/Northeastern Univ Press, 95; The Evolution of the American Synagogue, in The Americanization of the Jews, ed Robert M. Seltzer & Norman J. Cohen, New York, NYU Press, 95, 215-229; When Jews Were Bible Experts, Moments, Oct 95, 4, 55.80; Perched Between Continuity and Discontinuity: American Judaism at a Crossroads, Proceedings of the Rabbinical Assembly, 56, 95, 74-79; Current Trends and Issues in American Jewish Religious Life, Gesher, 42, 132, 95, 111-117, in Hebrew; contribution to Rebuilding Jewish Peoplehood: Where Do We Go From Here? A Symposium in the Wake of the Rabin Assassination, Amer Jewish Comm, 96, 86-87; The American Jewish Community's Crisis of Confidence, Pamphlet, World Jewish Congress, 96; From Antoinette Brown Blackwell to Sally Priesand: An Historical Perspective on the Emergence of Women in the American Rabbinate, Women Rabbis: Exploration and Celebration, ed Gary P. Zola, Cincinnati, American Jewish Archives, 96, 43-53; A Projection of America as it Ought to Be: Zion in the Mind's Eye of American Jews, in Allon Gal, ed, Envisioning Israel: The changing Ideals and Images of North American Jews, Jerusalem & Detroit, Magnes Press & Wayne State Univ Press, 96, 41-59; If You Lend Money to My People, Learning Torah With. ..3:18, Feb 8, 97, 1-4; Minority Faiths and the American Protestant Mainstream, ed. U of Illinois P, 97; Abba Hillel Silver and American Zionism, co-ed with Mark A. Raider and Ronald W. Zweig, Frank Cass, 97; Religion and State in the American Jewish Experience, with David G. Dalin, U of Notre Dame P, 97; Masterworks of Modern Jewish Writing, gen ed, 11 vol, Markus Wiener Publ; Amer Jewish Life, co-ed, 8 vol, Wayne State Univ Press; Brandeis Series in American Jewish History, Cult and Life, gen ed, 10 vol, Brandeis Univ Press/UP of New England; Contribution to One Year Later: The Rabin Symposium, Am Jewish Comm, 97; Two Traditions of Seminary Scholarship, in Jack Werheimer, ed, Tradition Renewed: A History of the Jewish Theological Seminary, Jewish Theol Sem, 97, 54-80; Structural Challenges to Jewish Continuity, American Jewry: Portrait and Prognosis, ed David M. Gordis and Dorit P. Gray, Wilstein Inst Behrman House, 97, 404-408; Back to the Center: The Plain Meaning of A Statement on Jewish Continuity, Am Jewish Comm, 97; Jacob Rader Marcus, Am Jewish Year Bk, 97, 97, 633-640; Martha Wolfenstein, in Paula Hyman and Deborah D. Moore, eds, Jewish Women in Am, Routledge, 97, 1486-1487; Foreword to Gerry Cristol, A Light in the Prairie: Temple Emanu-El of Dallas, 1872-1997, TCU Press, 98; Committed Today, Divorced Tomorrow, JTS Mag, 7, Winter 98, 12, 23; Ten Ways That Israel Liberated American Jewry, Hadassah Mag, 79, June 98, 14-15; American Jewish Education in Historical Perspective, Jour Jewish Ed, 64, Fall 98, 8-21; **CONTACT ADDRESS** Dept of Near East and Judaic Studies, Brandeis Univ, MS 054, Waltham, MA, 02454. **EMAIL** sarna@brandeis.edu

SARTI, ROLAND
DISCIPLINE HISTORY **EDUCATION** Rutgers Univ, PhD, 67. **CAREER** Prof, Univ MA Amherst . **HONORS AND AWARDS** Howard Marraro Prize, 86. **MEMBERSHIPS** New England Hist Asn, Soc Italian Hist Studies. **RESEARCH** Italian and Europ soc hist. **SELECTED PUBLICATIONS** Auth, Fascism and the Industrial Leadership in Italy 1919-1940, 71; HisLong Live the Strong: A History of Rural Society in The Appenine Mountains, 85; Giuseppe Mazzini entitled Mazzini: A Life for the Religion of Politics, 97; ed, The Ax Within: Italian Fascism in Action, 74. **CONTACT ADDRESS** Dept of Hist, Univ Massachusetts Amherst, Mass Ave, Amherst, MA, 01003.

SASSON, JACK MURAD
PERSONAL Born 10/01/1941, Aleppo, Syria **DISCIPLINE** FOREIGN LANGUAGES, HISTORY **EDUCATION** Brooklyn Col, BA, 62; Brandeis Univ, MA, 63, PhD, 66. **CAREER** From asst prof to assoc prof, 66-77, Prof Relig, Univ NC, Chapel Hill, 77-, Soc Relig Higher Educ fel, 69-70; assoc ed, J Am Orient Soc, 77. **MEMBERSHIPS** Soc Bibl Lit; Am Orient Soc; Israel Explor Soc; Dutch Orient Soc. **RESEARCH** Ancient Near Eastern societies. **SELECTED PUBLICATIONS** Auth, Albright As An Orientalist + Albright,William,Foxwell And Palestinian Archaeol/, Bibl Archaeol, Vol 0056, 1993; Jonah - A Commentary - Limburg,J/, Interpretation-A J Of Bible And Theol, Vol 0049, 1995. **CONTACT ADDRESS** Dept of Relig, Univ of NC, Chapel Hill, NC, 27514.

SASSON, SARAH DIANE HYDE
PERSONAL Born 08/27/1946, Asheville, NC, m, 1969, 3 children **DISCIPLINE** AMERICAN LITERATURE & HISTORY **EDUCATION** Univ NC, BA, 68, PhD(Eng), 80; Univ IL, Urbana, MA, 71. **CAREER** Instr Eng, 80-81, lectr Am studies, 81-82, Dir, Master of Arts in Lib Studies Prog, Duke Univ, 87-; Dir, Univ MAT Prog, Duke Univ, 91-95; Assoc of Graduate Lib Studies, Pres, 94-96. **HONORS AND AWARDS** Am Coun Learned Soc Fel. **MEMBERSHIPS** Am Folklore Soc; Am Studies Asn; MLA. **RESEARCH** Shaker lit; Am autobiography; Am relig lit. **SELECTED PUBLICATIONS** Auth, The Shaker Personal Narrative, Univ TN Press (in prep). **CONTACT ADDRESS** Duke Univ, Box 90095, Durham, NC, 27708.

SATO, ELIZABETH SELANDERS
PERSONAL Born 03/17/1942, Philadelphia, PA, m, 1966, 2 children **DISCIPLINE** HISTORY **EDUCATION** Muskingun Col, BA, 65; Univ Mich, MA, 67, PhD(hist), 76. **CAREER** Fulbright res fel, Historiographical Inst, Tokyo Univ, 70-71; teaching fel, East Asia, Univ Mich, 71-72; vis asst prof, Univ Cincinnati, 72-73, asst prof hist, 73-80. **MEMBERSHIPS** Asn Asian Studies; AAUP. **RESEARCH** Social and economic history of medieval Japan; Japanese cultural history; women in Japan. **SELECTED PUBLICATIONS** Auth, Hired Swords - The Rise Of Private Warrior Power In Early Japan - Friday,Kf/, Am Hist Rev, Vol 0098, 1993. **CONTACT ADDRESS** Dept of Hist, Univ of Cincinnati, Cincinnati, OH, 45221.

SATRE, LOWELL JOSEPH
PERSONAL Born 11/15/1942, Veblen, SD, m, 1965, 4 children **DISCIPLINE** MODERN ENGLISH HISTORY **EDUCATION** Augustana Col, SDak, BA, 64; Univ SC, MA, 67, PhD(hist), 68. **CAREER** Asst prof, 68-75, assoc prof hist, Youngstown State Univ, 75-82, prof hist 82-. **MEMBERSHIPS** AHA; Conf Brit Studies; World Hist Asn; Midwest Victorian Studies Asn. **RESEARCH** British empire history; English social history. **SELECTED PUBLICATIONS** Auth, St John Brodrick and Army reform 1901-1903, J Brit Studies, spring 76; Mafeking relieved, Brit Hist Illus, 10/75; After the Match Girls' Strike: Bryant and May in 1890's, in Victorian Studies, pp.7-31, autumn 82; Biographical entry of Thomas Burt, Vol II of Biographical Dictionary of Modern British Radicals, ed by Joseph Baylen and Norbert Gossman, pp. 111-115, 84; Thomas Burt and the Crisis of Late-Victorian Liberalism in the North-East, in Northern History, pp. 174-193, Univ of Leeds, England, 87; Education and Religion in the Shaping of Thomas Burt, Miner's Leader, Bulletin of the North East History Labour Society, Bulletin No 26, pp. 87-104, 92; Diamond Jubilee (Queen Victoria's) entry in England in the 1890's: An Encyclopedia of British Literature, Art, and Culture, Garland Press, 93; Biography/biographical entry on Lord Castlereagh in Statesmen Who Changed the World, pp 73-84, Greenwood Press, 93; Great Depression entry in Events That Changed the World, pp 67-80, Greenwood Press, 95; A Note on the Northumberland Miners' Association Annual Picnic, North East History, 97. **CONTACT ADDRESS** Dept of Hist, Youngstown State Univ, One University Plz, Youngstown, OH, 44555-3452. **EMAIL** lesatre@ix.netcom.com

SAUL, NORMAN EUGENE
PERSONAL Born 11/26/1932, La Fontaine, IN, m, 1959, 3 children **DISCIPLINE** MODERN HISTORY, SLAVIC STUDIES **EDUCATION** Ind Univ, Bloomington, BA, 54; Columbia Univ, MA, 59, PhD, 65. **CAREER** Instr hist, Purdue Univ, 62-65; asst prof, Brown Univ, 65-68; vis assoc prof, Northwestern Univ, 69-70; assoc prof, 70-, prof hist & slavic area, 75-81, chmn, dept of hist, Univ KS, 81-89, US Educ Found Finland Fulbright sr res fel, Univ Helsinki, 68-69; Int Res & Exchanges Bd sr scholar exchange, Univ Moscow, 73-74, 92. **HONORS AND AWARDS** Byron Caldwell Smith Bk Award, Univ of KS, 92; Robert H. Ferrell Bk Award, Soc of Hist of Am For Rel, 97, for Concord and Conflict; Higuchi Research Award, Univ of KS, 97; KS Hum Council Public Scholar Award, 97. **MEMBERSHIPS** AHA; Am Asn Advan Slavic Studies; Am Hist Soc of Ger from Russ. **RESEARCH** Russ Revolution; Russ-Am rel; Russ Navy. **SELECTED PUBLICATIONS** Auth, The beginnings of American-Russian trade, 1763-1766, William & Mary Quart, 10/69; Russia and the Mediterranean, 1797-1807, Univ Chicago, 70; Lenin's decision to seize power, Soviet Studies, 4/73; A Russian 'Yankee Doodle,' Slavic Rev, 3/74; The migration of the Russian-Germans to Kansas, Kans Hist Quart, spring 74; Sailors in Revolt: The Russian Baltic Fleet in 1917, Regents Press, 78; Distant Friends: The United States and Russia, 1763-1867, Univ Press of KS, 91; Concord and Conflict: The United States and Russia, 1867-1914, Univ Press of KS, 96, Ed Russian-American Dialogue on Cultural Relations, 1776-1914, Univ of MO Press, 97. **CONTACT ADDRESS** Dept of Hist, Univ of Kansas, Lawrence, KS, 66045-0001.

SAUNDERS, CLARK T.
DISCIPLINE MUSIC **EDUCATION** State Univ NY, Buffalo, BFA, MFA; Temple Univ, PhD. **CAREER** Asst prof, Lebanon Valley Col; asst prof, Univ of Maryland; ch, Graduate Music Ed; prof, Hartt School Music. **SELECTED PUBLICATIONS** Auth, pubs in J Research in Music Ed, Bulletin of the Council for Res in Music Ed, The Quarterly Update & Music Educators J. **CONTACT ADDRESS** Hartt Sch Music, Univ Hartford, 200 Bloomfield Ave, West Hartford, CT, 06117.

SAUNDERS, ELMO STEWART
PERSONAL Born 04/03/1936, Bradenton, FL, m, 1969, 2 children **DISCIPLINE** EARLY MODERN EUROPEAN HISTORY **EDUCATION** DePauw Univ, BA, 59; Ball State Univ, MA, 62; Ind Univ, MA, 64; Ohio State Univ, PhD(hist), 80. **CAREER** Instr bibliog, Ohio State Univ Libr, 65-77; ASST PROF HIST RES METHODS, PURDUE UNIV LIBR, 78-, Chercheur en Mission, Inst Nat de Recherche en Sci Humaines, Nigeria, 72-73. **MEMBERSHIPS** Soc French Hist Studies; Soc Hist Technol; Asn Col Res Libr; Asn Bibliog Hist. **RESEARCH** Science, technology and bureaucracy in 17th century France; bibliography of 17th century science and technology; cultural policies of early modern France. **SELECTED PUBLICATIONS** Auth, Library Circulation Of Univ Press Publ/, J Of Scholarly Publ, Vol 0027, 1996. **CONTACT ADDRESS** General Libr, Purdue Univ, West Lafayette, IN, 47907.

SAUNDERS, MAUDERIE HANCOCK
PERSONAL Born 06/13/1929, Bartlesville, Oklahoma **DISCIPLINE** EDUCATION **EDUCATION** Langston Univ Langston OK, BA 1947; Univ of OK Norman, MEd 1950; Univ of OK, PhD education & Psychology, 1961; Univ of Chicago, 1965. **CAREER** Howard Univ, coordinator special educ prof of educ 1979-, chmn & prof of educ psychoednl studies dept 1976-79, prof dir special educ 1974-76; Howard Univ Center for the Study of Handicapped Children, asst dir 1973-74; Eastern Il Univ Charleston IL, prof 1970-73; WV State Coll Inst, prof 1966-70; Minot State Coll Minot ND, prof 1963-66; So Univ Baton Rouge, asso prof 1960-62; OK City Public Schools, visiting counselor school psychology 1950-59; Child Serv State Dept of Welfare Minot ND, psychol 1963-66; WV State Dept Mental Health, psychology consultant 1966-70; WV St Dept of Health. **HONORS AND AWARDS** Listed in black OK res guide Archives of OK 1950; first black wom to rec PhD Univ of OK Norman 1961. **MEMBERSHIPS** Mem Am Psychol Assn 1961-; mem Alpha Kappa Alpha 1972; sponsor Chartered Chap Eta Gamma East IL campus 1972; spons Charter Chap #253 Counc of Except Child Howard Univ 1976. **SELECTED PUBLICATIONS** "Teach the Educ Mental Retard Reading" Curr The Pointer 1964; outst W Virginians 1969; analys of cult diff Jour of Negro Educ 1970, and other publications. **CONTACT ADDRESS** Professor of Education, Howard Univ, 2400 6th St, NW, Washington, VT, 20059.

SAUTTER, UDO
PERSONAL Born 06/17/1934, Wiesbaden, Germany, m, 1966, 3 children **DISCIPLINE** HISTORY **EDUCATION** Univ Tubingen, PhD, 61. **CAREER** Asst prof Ger lit, Loyola Col Montreal, 66-69; from asst prof to assoc prof, 69-76, PROF HIST, UNIV WINDSOR, 76-, Vis prof hist, McGill Univ, 67-69. **MEMBERSHIPS** AHA; Can Hist Asn. **RESEARCH** Modern social history; comparative history. **SELECTED PUBLICATIONS** Auth, The Discovery Of Am - From Columbus To Humboldt,Alexander,Von - Ger - Bitterli,U/, Zeitschrift Fur Geschichtswissenschaft, Vol 0041, 1993; Closing The Door To Destitution - The Shaping Of The Soc-Security Acts Of The United-States And New-Zealand - Richards,R/, J Of Am Hist, Vol 0082, 1995; Towards A Soc-Welfare State - The Government And Unemployment In The United-States Before The New-Deal/, Historisches Jahrbuch, Vol 0116, 1996. **CONTACT ADDRESS** Dept of Hist, Univ of Windsor, Windsor, ON, N9B 3P4.

SAVAGE, DAVID WILLIAM
PERSONAL Born 01/01/1937, Cincinnati, OH, m, 1959, 3 children **DISCIPLINE** MODERN BRITISH HISTORY **EDUCATION** Denison Univ, BA, 59; Princeton Univ, MA, 61, PhD, 63. **CAREER** Instr hist, 62-63, Princeton Univ & Stanford Univ, 63-65, asst prof, 65-67; asst prof, 67-73, dir spec progs, 72-73, Clark Univ; assoc dean fac, , 73- Lewis & Clark Col. **MEMBERSHIPS** AHA; Conf Brit Studies. **RESEARCH** 19th & 20th century Britain. **SELECTED PUBLICATIONS** Auth, The Attempted Home Rule Settlement of 1916, Eire-Ireland, 67; ed, The Imprint of Roman Institutions, Holt, 70; auth, The Parnell of Wales has Become the Chamberlain of England: auth, Lloyd George and the Irish Question, J Brit Studies, 72. **CONTACT ADDRESS** Lewis & Clark Col, 0615 SW Palatine Hill Rd, Portland, OR, 97219-7879.

SAVAGE, WILLIAM W.
DISCIPLINE HISTORY **EDUCATION** Univ of SC, BA, 64, MA, 66; Univ of Okla, PhD, 72. **CAREER** From asst prof to prof, Univ of Okla, 73-. **MEMBERSHIPS** Western Hist Asn; Okla Hist Soc. **RESEARCH** Am Frontier; Popular Culture. **SELECTED PUBLICATIONS** Auth, The Cherokee Strip Live Stock Association, 73; The Cowboy Hero, 79; Singing Cowboys And All That Jazz, 83; Comic Books And America, 1945-1954, 90; ed, Cowboy Life, 75; Indian Life, 77. **CONTACT ADDRESS** Dept of History, Univ of Oklahoma, Rm. 406, Norman, OK, 73069.

SAVARD, PIERRE
PERSONAL Born 06/10/1936, Quebec, PQ, Canada, m, 1960, 3 children **DISCIPLINE** MODERN & CULTURAL HISTORY **EDUCATION** Laval Univ, BA, 57, Lic es Lett, 60, Dr es Lett(hist), 65; Univ Lyons, dipl d'etudes super, 61. **CAREER** From lectr to assoc prof hist, Laval Univ, 61-72; assoc prof, 72-75, PROF HIST, UNIV OTTAWA, 75-, DIR FR CAN CIVILIZATION RES CTR, 73- **MEMBERSHIPS** Can Hist Asn; Soc Hist Fr Am; fel Royal Soc Can. **RESEARCH** French Canadian historiography; French Canadian relations with France; French Canadian religious history. **SELECTED PUBLICATIONS** Auth, The Priests Of The Societe-De-Saint-Sulpice In Can - Prominent Hist Figures, Revue D Histoire Ecclesiastique, Vol 0091, 1996; Literary-Life In Quebec, Vol 3, 1840-1869, A-People-Without-Hist-Or-Lit - Fr - Lemire,M, Saintjacques,D/, Revue D Histoire De L Amerique Francaise, Vol 0051, 1997; O-Can + The 8th World-Jamboree-Of-Scouts - 1955/, J Of Can Studies-Revue D Etudes Canadiennes, Vol 0032, 1997. **CONTACT ADDRESS** Dept of Hist, Univ of Ottawa, Ottawa, ON, K1N 6N5.

SAWATSKY, RODNEY JAMES
PERSONAL Born 12/05/1943, Altona, MB, Canada, m, 1965, 3 children **DISCIPLINE** RELIGION, HISTORY **EDUCATION** Can Mennonite Bible Col, Winnipeg, B Christian Ed, 64; Bethel Col, Kans, BA, 65; Univ Minn, MA, 72; Princeton Univ, MA, 73 & Phd(relig), 77. **CAREER** Instr hist, Can Mennonite Bible Col, Winnipeg, 67-70; asst prof relig, 74-80, Dir Acad Affairs, Conrad Grabel Col, Univ Waterloo, 74, Assoc Prof Relig, 81- **MEMBERSHIPS** Am Soc Church Hist; Am Acad Relig; Can Soc Study Relig; Can Protection Relig Freedom (pres, 78-). **RESEARCH** Mennonite history; evangelical and new religions; Canadian religious history. **SELECTED PUBLICATIONS** Auth, Limits On Liberty, The Experience Of Mennonite, Hutterite And Doukhobor Communities In Can - Janzen,W/, Studies In Rel-Sciences Religieuses, Vol 0021, 1992. **CONTACT ADDRESS** 55 Menno, Waterloo, ON, N2L 2A6.

SAWKINS, ANNEMARIE
PERSONAL Born 06/15/1965, Durham, England, m, 1996 **DISCIPLINE** ART HISTORY **EDUCATION** McGill Univ, MA 93; PhD 98; Colgate Univ, BA 88. **CAREER** Univ Wis Mil, lect, adj prof, 95-98; McGill Univ, instr 94. **HONORS AND AWARDS** Villard de Honnecourt Res Prize; 2 Max Binz Fel; Women's Cent McGill Fel; Max Stern Major Fel. **MEMBERSHIPS** CAA; AVISTA; ICMA; SAH; 16th Century Studies; MAM; AFM. **RESEARCH** Architecture; Late gothic; medieval; renaissance. **SELECTED PUBLICATIONS** Auth, A Renaissance Treasury: The Flagg Collection of European Decorative Arts and Sculpture, entries forthcoming, Hudson Hills Press, 98; auth, Royal and Imperial Emblematics in the Architecture of Francois I, Archi and the Emblem, ed, Peter M Daly, 98; Byzantine Influence at Saint-Front at Perigueux, The Avista Forum Jour, 98; auth, Giovanni Battista Piranesi, in: From Durer to Daumier: European Prints from the Collection of McGill Univ, ed Carol Solomon-Kiefer, Montreal, McGill Univ Press, 93. **CONTACT ADDRESS** Historic Milwaukee, Inc, 4100 North Morris Blvd, Shorewood, WI, 53211-1839. **EMAIL** asawkins@aol.com

SAWYER, JEFFREY K.
DISCIPLINE LEGAL HISTORY **EDUCATION** San Francisco Art Inst, BFA, 72; Univ Calif Berkley, AB, 75, MA, 78, PhD, History, 82. **CAREER** Part-time Fac, Univ Calif, 78-83; Asst prof, Univ Richmond, 83-86; Assoc prof, Univ Balt, Dir, Jurisprudence Prog, 96-; Div Chair, 95-; Dir, Master Arts Legal & Ethical Studies, 91-95; Assoc prof, 92. **SELECTED PUBLICATIONS** Coauth, Judicial Corruption and Legal Reform in

Early Seventeenth-Century France, Law & Hist Rev, 88; auth, 'Benefit of Clergy' in Maryland and Virginia, Am Jour Legal Hist, 90; auth, Printed Poison: Pamphlets, Faction Politics, and the Public Sphere in Early Seventeenth-Century France, Univ Calif Press, 90; auth, Distrust of the Legal Establishment in Perspective: Maryland During the Early National Years, GA Jour S Legal Hist, 93. **CONTACT ADDRESS** College of Liberal Arts, Univ Baltimore, 1420 N. Charles Street, Baltimore, MD, 21201. **EMAIL** jsawyer@ubmail.ubalt.edu

SAWYER, WILLIAM GREGORY

PERSONAL Born 11/06/1954, Columbus, OH, s **DISCIPLINE** EDUCATION **EDUCATION** Eastern MI Univ, Ypsilanti, MI, 1972; Mount Union Coll, Alliance, OH, BA, 1976; Eastern New Mexico Univ, Portales, NM, MA, 1978; Univ of North TX, Denton, TX, PhD, 1986. **CAREER** Amarillo Coll, Amarillo, TX, communication instructor, 1978-80; Univ of North TX, Denton, TX, teaching fellow, 1980-83, hall dir, 1983-85, coordinator of interculture services, 1985-86, asst dean of students, 1986-88, assoc dean of students, 1988-90, dean of students, 1990-; FL GULF COAST UNIV, CHIEF STUDENT AFFFAIRS OFFICER & DEAN OF STUDENTS 1995-. **HONORS AND AWARDS** "Top Prof," Mortar Bd Honors Society, 1987-92; Outstanding Contributions to the Minority Community, TX Woman's Univ; Outstanding Service to the African Community, The Progressive Black Student Org; The Texas Award for Outstanding Vision and Leadership in Education. **MEMBERSHIPS** Pres, TX Assn of Coll & Univ Personnel Administrators, 1991-92, pres elect, 1990-91, vice pres, 1989-90, minority comm chair, 1987-89; mem, TX Assn of Black Professionals, 1988-92; Texas State Sickle Cell Foundation, board member; Minority Caucus Advisor Unit, 1985-; Progressive Black Student Organization, University of North Texas, advisor, 1985-. **CONTACT ADDRESS** Student Affair Officer, Florida Gulf Coast Univ, 17595 Tamiami Trail, Ste 200, Fort Myers, FL, 33908.

SAYEED, KHALID B.

PERSONAL Born 11/20/1926, Bellary, India **DISCIPLINE** POLITICAL STUDIES/HISTORY **EDUCATION** Univ Madras, BA, 47, MA, 48; London Sch Econ & Polit Sci, BS, 51; McGill Univ, PhD, 56. **CAREER** Lectr, polit sci, Univ Dacca, 51-53; assoc instr, Islamic stud, McGill Univ, 57-59; asst prof, polit sci, Univ NB, 59-61; asst prof 61-64, assoc prof, 64-66, prof, 66-93, PROF EMER POLITICAL STUDIES & ADJ PROF HISTORY, QUEEN'S UNIV, 93-; vis assoc prof, Duke Univ, 65; vis res prof, Am Univ, 84-85. **MEMBERSHIPS** Int Asn Middle E Stud; Can Polit Sci Asn; Middle E Stud Assn; Indian Inst Public Admin; Asn Muslin Soc Sci. **SELECTED PUBLICATIONS** Auth, Pakistan the Formative Phase, 61, 2nd ed, 68; auth, The Political System of Pakistan, 67; auth, Politics in Pakistan: The Nature and Direction of Change, 80; auth, Western Dominance and Political Islam: Challenge and Response, 94. **CONTACT ADDRESS** Dept of History, Queen's Univ, Kingston, ON, K7L 3N6.

SAYLOR, CHARLES F.

DISCIPLINE LATIN LITERATURE **EDUCATION** Univ Wash, BA, MA; Univ Calif Berkeley, PhD. **CAREER** Prof & supv Grad tchg assistants; past dir, Undergrad Study & Grad Study & 3 terms, ch; Univ Mo, 68-; thaught at, St Mary's Col, Calif, UC Davis & San Diego State Univ. **RESEARCH** Roman Comedy; silver Latin literature. **SELECTED PUBLICATIONS** Publ on, Propertius, Plautus, Terence, Vergil, Lucan, Pliny, Horace, Lucretius & Petronius. **CONTACT ADDRESS** Dept of Classical Studies, Univ of Missouri-Columbia, 309 University Hall, Columbia, MO, 65211.

SAYWELL, JOHN T.

PERSONAL Born 04/03/1929, Weyburn, SK, Canada **DISCIPLINE** HISTORY, ENVIRONMENTAL STUDIES **EDUCATION** Victoria Col Univ BC, BA, MA; Harvard Univ, PhD. **CAREER** Lectr, Univ Toronto, 54; asst prof, 57, assoc prof, 62, Prof History & Environmental Stud, Dean, York Univ, 63-73. **MEMBERSHIPS** Mem, Can Hist Asn; mem, Can Pol Sci Asn **SELECTED PUBLICATIONS** Auth, The Office of Lieut-Gov, 57, 86; auth, The Canadian Journal of Lady Aberdeen, 60; auth, Lord Minto's Canadian Papers, 83; auth, Making the Law, 91; auth, Just Call Me Mitch, 91; auth, Pathways to the Present, 94. **CONTACT ADDRESS** 158 Fulton Ave, Toronto, ON, M4K 1Y3.

SBACCHI, ALBERTO

PERSONAL Palermo, Italy, m, 1963, 2 children **DISCIPLINE** AFRICAN AND MODERN EUROPEAN HISTORY **EDUCATION** Columbia Union Col, BA, 62; Pac Union Col, MA, 63; Univ Ill, Chicago Circle, PhD, 75. **CAREER** Head social sci dept hist, Ethiopian Adventist Col, 63-68; res asst hist, Univ Ill, Chicago Circle, 68-74; PROF HIST, ATLANTIC UNION COL, 74-, Fel hist, Univ Ill, Chicago Circle, 70-71; res grant, Am-Italy Soc, 70-71, Ital Ministry Foreign Affairs, Rome, 70-72, Am Coun Learned Soc, 76-77 & Atlantic Union Col Fac Res Grant, 78-79. **HONORS AND AWARDS** Knight of the Order of the Merit of the Italian Republic; Outstand Svc and Ded as Fac Adv, Phi Alpha Theta; Recognition for Acad Ach, Atlantic Union Col; Student Asn Awd for Teach Excel, Atlantic Union Col. **MEMBERSHIPS** AHA; African Studies Asn; Soc Ital Hist Studies; Asn Seventh Day Adventist Historians (exec secy, 75-77); Afro-Ital Inst; Clinton Hist Soc; Phi Alpha Theta; Inst Sterice della resistenza e dell'Eta Moderna' Asn des Amis des Archives Diplomatiques. **RESEARCH** Italian colonialism in Ethiopia; European expansion; imperialism. **SELECTED PUBLICATIONS** Auth, Legacy of bitterness: Poison gas and atrocities in the Italo-Ethiopian War 1935-1936, Geneva-Africa, 2/74; Secret talks for the submission of Haile Selassie and Asfaw Wassen, 1936-1939, Int J African Hist Studies, 4/74; Italian mandate or protectorate over Ethiopia, 1935-1936, Rivista di Studi Politici Internazionali, 4/75; The Italians and the Italo-Ethiopian War, 1935-1936, TransAfrican J Hist, 2/76; Italy and the treatment of the Ethiopian aristocracy, 1936-1939, Int J African Hist Studies, 2/77; Italian plans and projects for the colonization of Ethiopia, 1936-1940, Africa, 4/77; Governor John Clarkson's diary and the origin of Sierra Leone, J African Studies, 1/78; Il Colonialismo Italiano in Ethiopia, 1936-1940, Milan: Mursia, 80; auth, Legacy of Bitterness: Ethiopia and Fascist Italy, 1935-1941, Red Sea Press, 97; auth, Ethiopia Under Mussolini, Zed Books, 85, 2nd ed 89;auth, marcus Gravey and Ethiopia 1920-1940, Proced of the IX Int Conf of Ethiopian Stu, USSR Acad of Sci and African Inst, 86; auth, The Consolata Mission Archives and Italian Colonialism, Atti del Cenvegne Internazionale, Fonti e Problemi della Politica Coloniale Italiana, Messina-Taermina, 89; auth, Itale-Ethiopian Relations 1935-1941; Le Guerre Coloniali del Fascisme, Laterza, 91; auth, The Late R.L. Mess and the Memoirs of Giacome Maretti at the Court of Yohannes IV of Ethiopia, Proceedof the XII Int Conf of Ethiopian Stu, Mich St Univ, 95; auth, The Recognition of the Italian Empire 1936-1938, Proceed of the XIII Int Conf of Ethiopian Stu, Univ of Kyoto, 97. **CONTACT ADDRESS** Atlantic Union Col, PO Box 1000, South Lancaster, MA, 01561-9999.

SCAGLIA, GUSTINA

PERSONAL Glastonbury, CT **DISCIPLINE** HISTORY/ART **EDUCATION** NY Univ, Inst of Fine Art, MA, 52, PhD, 60. **CAREER** Asst prof, 62, prof, 70-90, Queens Col, CUNY. **HONORS AND AWARDS** Amer Asn of Univ Women Fulbright Grand to Rome. **RESEARCH** Drawings of machines; arch drawings of antiquities by XV-XVI century artists. **SELECTED PUBLICATIONS** Auth, Il Vitruvio Magliabechiano di Francesco di Giorgio, Documenti inediti di cultura Toscana, Vol VI, 85; auth, Francesco di Giorgio, Checklist and History of Manuscripts and Drawings in Autographs and Copies. Lehigh Univ Press, 92, Architectural Drawings of Antonio Da Sangallo - the Younger, 94. **CONTACT ADDRESS** 400 Central Park West, 5A, New York, NY, 10025.

SCALISE, CHARLES J.

PERSONAL Born 07/25/1950, Baltimore, MD, m, 1980, 2 children **DISCIPLINE** CHURCH HISTORY, CHRISTIAN THEOLOGY **EDUCATION** Princeton Univ, AB, summa cum laude, 72; Yale Div Sch, MDiv, magna cum laude, 75; S Baptist Theol Sem, PhD, 87; Univ Oxford, postgrad, 90-91. **CAREER** Baptist Chaplain, Yale, 75-82; lectr, Pastoral Theol, Yale Div Sch, 76-80; dir, dept Christian higher educ, Baptist Conven New Eng, 82-84; asst prof, S Baptist Theol Sem, 87-94; assoc and mang ed, Rev and expositor, 91-94. **HONORS AND AWARDS** Sloan Scholar, 68-72; Ger bk prize, 71; Albert G. Milband mem scholar prize, 71; Phi Beta Kappa, 72; Tew prize, 73; Oliver Ellsworth Daggett prize, 74; Julia A. Archibald high scholar prize, 75; Outstanding young men Am, 75; Who's Who S and SW, 93-94. **RESEARCH** Theological hermeneutics; History of exegesis; History of doctrine; pastoral Theology. **SELECTED PUBLICATIONS** Auth, Allegorical Flights of Fancy: The Problem of Origen's Exegesis, The Greek Orthodox Theol Rev, 32, 87, 69-88; Origen and the Sensus Literalis, in Origen of Alexandria, Notre Dame, 88, 117-129; Developing a Theological Rationale for Ministry: Some Reflections on the Process of Teaching Pastoral Theology to MDiv Students, Jour Pastoral Theol, 1, 91, 53-68; Hermeneutics as Theological Prolegomena: A Canonical Approach, Mercer UP, 94; Canonical Hermeneutics: Childs and Barth, Scotish Jour Theol, 47, 94, 61-88; Teresa of Avila: Teacher of Evangelical Women? Cross Currents: The Jour of the Asn for Rel and Intel Life, 46, 96, 244-249; From Scripture to Theology: A Canonical Journey into Hermeneutics, InterVarsity Press, 96; Agreeing on where We Disagree: Lindbeck's Postliberalism and Pastoral Theology, Jour Pastoral Theol, 8, 98, 43-51. **CONTACT ADDRESS** Fuller Theol Sem, 101 Nickerson St, Ste 330, Seattle, WA, 98109-1621. **EMAIL** cscalise@fuller.edu

SCALLEN, CATHERINE B.

DISCIPLINE NORTHERN BAROQUE ART **EDUCATION** Wellesley Col, BA; Williams Col, MA, Princeton Univ PhD, 90. **CAREER** Vis prof, CWRU, 91-92; Fairfield uviv, Conn, 92-95; assist prof, CWRU, 95-. **HONORS AND AWARDS** Co-cur, Cubism and American Photography, 1910-1930. **SELECTED PUBLICATIONS** Auth, Catalog ed, exhib catalog Passion and Patience: The Joys of Collecting; Old Masters from the Arnold;Seena Davis Collection. **CONTACT ADDRESS** Case Western Reserve Univ, 10900 Euclid Ave, Cleveland, OH, 44106. **EMAIL** cbs2@po.cwru.edu

SCAMEHORN, HOWARD LEE

PERSONAL Born 02/27/1926, Kalamazoo, MI **DISCIPLINE** UNITED STATES ECONOMIC HISTORY **EDUCATION** Western Mich Univ, AB, 49; Univ Ill, MA, 52, PhD(hist), 56. **CAREER** PROF HIST, UNIV COLO, 56-, Dir, Western Bus Hist Res Ctr, Denver, 67- **MEMBERSHIPS** Orgn Am Historians; Western Hist Asn. **RESEARCH** Business, industry, mining in the American west; mining; transportation. **SELECTED PUBLICATIONS** Auth, Colorado Gold - From The Pikes-Peak Rush To The Present - Voynick,Sm/, J Of The W, Vol 0034, 1995; Silver,Harold,F., Western Inventor, Businessman, And Civic Leader - Arrington,Lj, Alley,Jr/, J Of The W, Vol 0034, 1995; Rocky-Mountain Boom-Town - A Hist Of Durango, Colorado - Smith,Da/, J Of The W, Vol 0034, 1995; A Way Of Work And A Way Of Life - Coal-Mining In Thurber, Tex, 1888-1926 - Rhinehart,Md/, J Of The W, Vol 0034, 1995; The Economics Of Petroleum Supply - Adelman,Ma/, J Of The W, Vol 0035, 1996; Done In Oil - An Autobiography - Marshall,Jh/, J Of The W, Vol 0036, 1997; Boulder - Evolution Of A City - Pettem,S/, J Of The W, Vol 0036, 1997; Hist Atlas Of Colorado - Noel,Tj, Mahoney,Pf, Stevens,Re/, J Of The W, Vol 0036, 1997. **CONTACT ADDRESS** Dept of Hist, Univ of Colo, Boulder, CO, 80309.

SCAMMELL, MICHAEL

DISCIPLINE ART **EDUCATION** Univ Nottingham, BA, 58; Univ Columbia, PhD, 85. **CAREER** Prof, Columbia Col NY. **HONORS AND AWARDS** Los Angeles Times Bk Awd, 84. **SELECTED PUBLICATIONS** Ed, The Solzhenitsyn File, Unofficial Art from the Soviet Union and Russia's Other Writers. **CONTACT ADDRESS** Sch of Arts, Columbia Col, New York, 2960 Broadway, New York, NY, 10027-6902. **EMAIL** ms474@columbia.edu

SCANLAN, RICHARD T.

PERSONAL Born 05/30/1928, St. Paul, MN, m, 1951, 5 children **DISCIPLINE** CLASSICS **EDUCATION** Univ Minn, BS, 51, MA, 52. **CAREER** Teacher Latin, Edina High Sch, Minn, 55-67; assoc prof, 67-80, prof Classics, Univ Ill, Urbana, 80-, mem Latin Achievement Test Comt, Col Entrance Exam Bd, 60-65, chmn Latin Advan Placement Exam Comt, 67-72, chief examr, Classics Prog, 73-77. **MEMBERSHIPS** Am Philol Asn; Am Class League; Class Asn midwest & S; Am Coun Teaching Foreign Lang; Archives Asn Am. **RESEARCH** The teaching of Latin; computer applications to the teaching of Latin; teaching of classical humanities. **SELECTED PUBLICATIONS** Auth, A survey of Latin textbooks, Class J, 76; A computer-assisted instruction course in vocabulary building, Foreign Lang Ann, 76; Suggestions for a course in ancient and modern tragedy, Class Outlook, 77; Beginning Latin, 77, Word Power, 77 & Latin Composition, 77, Control Data Co; Some criteria for the evaluation of Latin textbooks, 78 & The grading of the 1977 advanced placement examination, 78, Class J. **CONTACT ADDRESS** Dept of Classic, Univ of Illinois, 707 S Mathews Ave, Urbana, IL, 61801-3625. **EMAIL** rscanlon@uiuc.edu

SCANLON, JAMES EDWARD

PERSONAL Born 05/20/1940, Steubenville, OH **DISCIPLINE** HISTORY **EDUCATION** Georgetown Univ, AB, 62; Univ Wis, MA, 65; Univ Va, PhD(hist), 69. **CAREER** PROF HIST, RANDOLPH-MACON COL, 79-, CHMN DEPT, 81-, Consult, Choice Mag, 69- **MEMBERSHIPS** Orgn Am Historians; AAUP. **RESEARCH** Colonial history, New York and West Indies. **SELECTED PUBLICATIONS** Auth, Jeffersonian Legacies - Onuf,Ps/, Va Mag Of Hist And Biog, Vol 0102, 1994. **CONTACT ADDRESS** Dept of Hist, Randolph-Macon Col, 200 Henry St, Ashland, VA, 23005-1697.

SCANLON, THOMAS FRANCIS

PERSONAL Born 09/26/1951, Pittsburgh, PA **DISCIPLINE** CLASSICAL LANGUAGES **EDUCATION** Duquesne Univ, BA, 72; Ohio State Univ, MA, 75, PhD(classics), 78. **CAREER** Asst prof classics, Univ Md, College Park, 79-80 & Univ Calif, Los Angeles, 80-81; Asst Prof Classics, Univ Calif, Riverside, 81-, Scholar, Univ Vienna, Austria, 78-79; Fulbright fel, Austrian Fulbright-Hays Prog, 78-79. **MEMBERSHIPS** Am Philol Asn. **RESEARCH** Greek and Roman historical writing, athletics and linguistics. **SELECTED PUBLICATIONS** Auth, Echoes Of Herodotus In Thucydides - Self-Sufficiency, Admiration, And Law/, Historia-Zeitschrift Fur Alte Geschichte, Vol 0043, 1994; Games For Girls/, Archaeol, Vol 0049, 1996. **CONTACT ADDRESS** Dept of Lit & Lang, Univ of Calif, 900 University Ave, Riverside, CA, 92521-0001.

SCARBOROUGH, WILLIAM KAUFFMAN

PERSONAL Born 01/17/1933, Baltimore, MD, m, 1954, 2 children **DISCIPLINE** AMERICAN HISTORY **EDUCATION** Univ NC, AB, 54, PhD, 62; Cornell Univ, MA, 57. **CAREER** Res asst, Inst Res Soc Sci, Univ NC, 57-60, teaching fel, 60-61; asst prof hist, Millsaps Col, 61-63 & Northeast La State Col, 63-64; assoc prof, 64-76, prof hist, Univ S MS, 76, Chmn Dept, 80-90, Charles W. Moorman Distinguished Alumni Prof in the Hum, 96-98. **HONORS AND AWARDS** Jules and Frances Landry Award, for: Diary of Edmund Ruffin, LSU Press, 89. **MEMBERSHIPS** Southern Hist Asn; Agr Hist Soc; Orgn Am Historians; St George Tucker Soc. **RESEARCH** Middle period of US hist; the old South, espec the plantation-slavery regime; Am Civil War. **SELECTED PUBLICATIONS** Auth, The Overseer: Plantation Management in the Old South, La State Univ, 66; contribr, The Changing Economic Order: Readings in American Business and Economic History, Harcourt, 68; ed, The Diary of Edmund Ruffin, Vol I, Toward Independence, 72, Vol II, The Years of Hope, 77, Vol III, A Dream Shattered, 89, La State Univ Press; contribr, A History of Mississippi, 73 & Perspectives and Irony in American Slavery, 76, Univ Press of Miss; Science and Medicine in the Old South, LSU Press, 89. **CONTACT ADDRESS** Dept of Hist, Univ of S MS, S S Box 5047, Hattiesburg, MS, 39406-1000.

SCARDAVILLE, MICHAEL CHARLES
PERSONAL Born 02/05/1948, Newark, NJ, m, 1970, 2 children **DISCIPLINE** APPLIED & LATIN AMERICAN HISTORY **EDUCATION** Rutgers Univ, BA, 70; Univ Fla, MA, 72, PhD(hist), 77. **CAREER** Oral historian, Nat Geographic, 74; historian, Hist St Augustine Preservation Bd, 77-81; ASSOC PROF & DIR APPL HIST PROG, UNIV SC, 81-, Consult, Fla Endowment for the Humanities, 79-80, Pub Broadcasting Syst, 79, Riverside-Avondale Preservation, 80-81, City of Palatka, 80-82 & City of Arcadia, 82. **MEMBERSHIPS** Nat Coun Pub Hist; Nat Trust for Hist Preservation; Am Asn for State & Local Hist; Conf of Latin Am Historians; Southeast Borderlands Asn. **RESEARCH** Historic preservation; the effect of urban development on the built environment; urban development of southeastern and circum-Caribbean coastal communities. **SELECTED PUBLICATIONS** Auth, The Conquest Of Paradise - Columbus,Christopher And The Columbian Legacy - Sale,K/, Public Historian, Vol 0014, 1992; Columbus - The Great Adventure, His Life, His Times, And His Voyage - Taviani,Pe/, Public Historian, Vol 0014, 1992; The Mysterious History Of Columbus - An Exploration Of The Man, The Myth, The Legacy - Wilford,Jn/, Public Historian, Vol 0014, 1992; The Worlds Of Columbus,Christopher - Phillips,Wd, Phillips,Cr/, Public Historian, Vol 0014, 1992; Columbus - Fernandezarmesto,F/, Public Historian, Vol 0014, 1992; Columbian Consequences, Vol 3, The Spa Borderlands In Pan-Am Perspective - Thomas,Dh/, Hisp Am Hist Rev, Vol 0074, 1994; Desoto,Hernando And The Indians Of Florida - Milanich,Jt, Hudson,C/, Pac Hist Rev, Vol 0063, 1994; Hapsburg Law And Bourbon Order, State Authority, Popular Unrest, And The Criminal-Justice System In Bourbon Mexico-City/, Americas, Vol 0050, 1994;Latin-Am Urbanization, Historical Profiles Of Major Cities - Greenfield,Gm/, Hisp Am Hist Rev, Vol 0075, 1995; The Limits Of Racial Domination - Plebeian Society In Colonial Mexico-City, 1660-1720 - Cope,Rd/, Ethnohistory, Vol 0043, 1996; Annotated Guide And Index Of Viceregal Decrees, 1548-1553 - Spa - Gerhard,P/, Hisp Am Hist Rev, Vol 0077, 1997. **CONTACT ADDRESS** Dept of Hist, Univ of SC, Columbia, SC, 29208.

SCATTERDAY, MARK DAVIS
DISCIPLINE MUSIC **EDUCATION** Univ Akron, BM, 81; Univ Mich, MM, 83; Eastman Sch Music, DMA, 89. **CAREER** Assoc prof **HONORS AND AWARDS** Martha Holden Jennings Tchg Scholar; Guest Clinician, Ohio Univ Wind Ensemble Symp, 96; Guest Clinician, Duke Univ Wind Ensemble Symp, 94; Guest Clinician, Col Band Director's Nat Asn, Eastern Div Conf, Wash DC, 94. **MEMBERSHIPS** Sec and treas-Col Band Director's Nat Asn, Eastern Div; Conductor's Guild; Music Educator's Nat Conf; World Asn Symphonic Bands and Wind Ensembles; Nat Fed Musicians Union Local 132-314. **RESEARCH** Contemporary Music; Renaissance Instrumental Music; Conducting; Wind Ensembles. **SELECTED PUBLICATIONS** Auth, Karel Husa's Music for Prague 1968, Band Director's Guide, 92; Karel Husa's Apotheosis of this Earth, Band Director's Guide, 93; assoc ed, WindWorks, Warner Brothers Publ, 97. **CONTACT ADDRESS** Dept of Music, Cornell Univ, 104 Lincoln Hall, Ithaca, NY, 14853. **EMAIL** mds27@cornell.edu

SCHAAR, STUART H.
PERSONAL Born 09/26/1937, New York, NY **DISCIPLINE** COMPARATIVE HISTORY **EDUCATION** City Col NY, BA, 58; Princeton Univ, PhD, 66. **CAREER** Asst prof hist, Univ WI, Madison, 64-69; Fac assoc, Am Univs Field Staff, 67-69; assoc prof hist, Brooklyn Col, 69-97, Prof, 96. **HONORS AND AWARDS** John D and Catherine T MacArthur, $23,600 Grant (June 95) to organize a conference at the Center of International Studies, Princeton Univ on the present Algerian crisis; John D and Catherine T MacArthur $22,500. Grant (June 95) to produce a film on the Algerian crisis with the Algerian film director Merzac Allouache, receipient of the 1994 International Film Critics Award at Cannes, Paris, Shown in Aug 97; Swiss Foundation for Peace and Development Grants-tot, $45,000, Jan 95, two conferences, one with 18 North African Women re violence against North African Women and the second, cosponsored by the Institute for the Transregional study of the Contemporary Middle East, North Africa and Central Asia, Princeton Univ; John D and Catherina T MacArthur Foundation $43,000, Dec 97, international conference on the present Algerian crisis, London, Feb 98; John D and Catherine T MacArthur Foundation $25,000 Grant, projects aimed at fortifying civil society in North Africa, Apr 98. **MEMBERSHIPS** Fel Mid E Studies Asn NAm; AHA; World Hist Assoc. **RESEARCH** Comp Islamic hist. **SELECTED PUBLICATIONS** Auth, Rebellion, revolution and religious intermediaries in some nineteenth century Islamic states; Co-ed, The Shaping of the Modern World from the Enlightenment to the Present, 3d ed, Minn St Paul, West Publishing Co, 95; In: Churches and States: The Religious Institution and Modernization, Am Univs Field Staff, 67; The Barbary Coast (c 500 BC-AD 639), In: The Horizon History of Africa, Am Heritage, 71; King Hassan's alternatives, In: Man, State and Society in the Contemporary Maghreb, Praeger, 73; Le jeu des forces politiques en Tunisie, Maghreb-Machrek, 10-12/77; coauth, M'hamed Ali and the Tunisian labour movement, Race & Class, winter 78. **CONTACT ADDRESS** Dept Hist, Brooklyn Col, CUNY, 2901 Bedford Ave, Brooklyn, NY, 11210-2813. **EMAIL** sschaar@brooklyn.cuny.edu

SCHACHT, JOHN N.
PERSONAL Born 02/24/1943, Chicago, IL, m, 1972, 2 children **DISCIPLINE** HISTORY **EDUCATION** Wesleyan Univ, BA, 1964; MA, 1966, PhD, 1977, Univ Iowa; Univ Illinois, MS, 1977. **CAREER** Researcher, Communication Workers of America-Univ Iowa Oral History Project, 68-72; Libr, Univ Iowa, 77-. **HONORS AND AWARDS** Robert Hoover Library Assoc Scholar, 89-90. **MEMBERSHIPS** ALA; Assoc for Bibliography of History **RESEARCH** U.S. labor history; Iowa history; World War II; bibliography of history. **SELECTED PUBLICATIONS** Auth, Labor History in the Academy: A Layman's Guide to a Century of Scholarship, Labor's Heritage, 94. **CONTACT ADDRESS** Reference Dept, Library, Univ of Iowa, Iowa City, IA, 52242. **EMAIL** john_schacht@uiowa.edu

SCHACHTER, ALBERT
PERSONAL Born 08/23/1932, Winnipeg, MB, Canada, m, 1960 **DISCIPLINE** CLASSICS **EDUCATION** McGill Univ, BA, 55; Oxford Univ, DPhil(classics), 68. **CAREER** From lectr to assoc prof, 59-72, chmn dept, 70-74, Prof Classics McGill Univ, 72-, Ford Found grant, 68-70; gen ed, Teiresias: Rev & Cont Bibliog of Boiotian Antiq, 71-; vis fel, Wolfson Col, Oxford, 82-83. **MEMBERSHIPS** Am Philol Asn; Hellenic Soc; Class Asn Can; Joint Asn Class Teachers; Soc Des Etudes Anciennes du Que. **RESEARCH** Greek cults; Greek language teaching. **SELECTED PUBLICATIONS** Auth, Hiera Kala - Images Of Animal Sacrifice In Archaic And Classical Greece - Vanstraten,Ft/, Am J Of Archaeol, Vol 0100, 1996. **CONTACT ADDRESS** Dept of Classics, McGill Univ, 855 Sherbrooke St W, Montreal, PQ, H3A 2T7.

SCHACHTER, GUSTAV
PERSONAL Born 05/27/1926, Botosani, Romania, m, 1958, 2 children **DISCIPLINE** ECONOMICS **EDUCATION** New York Univ, PhD 62, MA 56; City Col NY, BS 54. **CAREER** Northeastern Univ, prof 65-98; City Col NY, asst prof 60-65; B&G Inc NY, prod mgr 51-59; IRO Rome, off mgr 49-51. **HONORS AND AWARDS** United Nations Sr Vis Sch Euro Econ Cen; Lowell Tchg Inst Hon Doc; NYC Founders Day Awd; Fulbright Dist Ch; Fulbright Sr Sch; Fulbright Lectr; Ital Gov Awd and Fulbright Gnt. **MEMBERSHIPS** AEA; EEA; ACE; RSA; ECA. **RESEARCH** Europe; Italy; Input output methodology. **SELECTED PUBLICATIONS** Auth, Economic Development in Boston in the 1990's, co-ed, 94; pattern Regionali di Convergenza Nell'Unione Europea e Performance Delle Regioni Alpine, coauth, F Bosacci, L Senn eds, Montagna, Area di Integrazione, F Angeli, 97; auth, The Impact of Mega Infrastructure Projects on Urban Development: Boston USA and Messina Streets Italy, coauth, Euro Plan Studies, 96; auth, The Impact of Redirection on the Transfer to the Italian South on Input Output and Employment to 2000, coauth, Jour of Sys Analysis and Model Simulation, 96; auth, Ell Mezzogiorno: Cuando si vive al sur del Capitol, coauth, Horizonte Sindical, 95; auth, Structural Change and Regional Development, coauth, Jour of Sys Analysis and Model Simulations, 94; auth, Economic Growth Through Dependence in the Mezzogiorno: 1950-1990, Jour of Euro Econ History, 94. **CONTACT ADDRESS** Dept of Economics, Northwestern Univ, 301 Lake Hall, Boston, MA, 02115.

SCHADE, ROSEMARIE
DISCIPLINE HISTORY **EDUCATION** York Univ, BA, MA; Univ York, PhD. **CAREER** Assoc prof. **RESEARCH** German bourgeois feminist movement. **SELECTED PUBLICATIONS** Auth, co-ed, eight volume bibliography, Gender Balancing History: Towards an Inclusive Curriculum; Ein weibliches Utopia: Organisationen und Ideologien der Madchen und Frauen in der burgerlichen Jugendbewegung, 1905-1933. **CONTACT ADDRESS** Dept of Hist, Concordia Univ, Montreal, 1455 de Maisonneuve W, Montreal, PQ, H3G 1M8. **EMAIL** rschade@vax2.concordia.ca

SCHAEFER, JEAN OWENS
DISCIPLINE ART HISTORY **EDUCATION** Stanford Univ, BA, 68; Univ CA-Berkeley, MA, 71, PhD, 77. **CAREER** Prof, adj prof, Women's Stud, Univ of WI, Parkside. **SELECTED PUBLICATIONS** Auth, Kaethe Kollwitz in America: Tides in the Reception of the Work, Women's Art J, vol 15, 94; Gossaert's Vienna St. Luke Portraying the Virgin: An Early Response to Iconoclasm, Source: Notes in the Hist of Art, XII, 92; Restructuring for Innovative Undergraduate Education, J Prof Stud, 90. **CONTACT ADDRESS** Dept of Art, Univ WY, PO Box 3964, Laramie, WY, 82071-3964. **EMAIL** Jeans@uwyo.edu

SCHAEFFER, PETER MORITZ-FRIEDRICH
PERSONAL Born 05/14/1930, Breslau, Germany, m, 1968 **DISCIPLINE** GERMANIC STUDIES, CLASSICS, RELIGIOUS STUDIES. **EDUCATION** Univ Ottawa, Lic Theol, 59; Princeton Univ, PhD(Germanic studies), 71. **CAREER** From lectr to asst prof Germanic studies, Princeton Univ, 70-74; vis lectr Ger & comp lit, Univ CA, Berkeley, 74-76; ASSOC PROF TO PROF GER, UNIV CA, DAVIS, 76-. **MEMBERSHIPS** ALSC; Renaissance Soc Am; Erasmus Soc; Tyndale Soc. **RESEARCH** Renaissance; Neo-Latin literature; Classical tradition. **SELECTED PUBLICATIONS** Auth, Joachim Vadianus, De poetica, Text, Translation & Commentary, Wilhelm Fink, Munich, 73; Hoffmannswaldau, De curriculo studiorum, Peter Lano, Bern, 91; Sapidus Consulator, Annvaire de Selestat, 96. **CONTACT ADDRESS** German Dept, Univ of California, Davis, One Shields Ave, Davis, CA, 95616-5200. **EMAIL** pmschaeffer@ucdavis.edu

SCHAFER, ELIZABETH
PERSONAL Born 03/12/1962, Morgantown, WV, d **DISCIPLINE** HISTORY OF ARCHITECTURE, LANDSCAPE ARCHITECTURE **EDUCATION** Smith Coll, BA, 85; Univ Va, MA, 98; Harvard Univ, PhD student. **MEMBERSHIPS** SAH. **CONTACT ADDRESS** 107 Fayerweather St, Cambridge, MA, 02138. **EMAIL** eschafer@fas.harvard.edu

SCHAFER, ELIZABETH D.
PERSONAL Born 09/26/1965, Opelika, AL **DISCIPLINE** HISTORY **EDUCATION** Auburn Univ, BA, 86, MA, 88, PhD, 93. **CAREER** Independent Scholar, 93-. **HONORS AND AWARDS** Shirley Henn Memorial Award for Critical Scholar, 98, Hollins Univ; Four Honorable Mentions in Writer's Digest writing competition for poetry, fiction and non-fiction, 94, 97, 98. **MEMBERSHIPS** Am Hist Asn; Org Am Hist; Southern Hist Asn; Soc Hist Technol; Hist Science Soc; Childrens Lit Asn. **RESEARCH** History of science and technology; history of women; history of African Americans. **SELECTED PUBLICATIONS** Coauth, Women Who Made a Difference in Alabama, Tuscaloosa AL: Alabama League of Women Voters, 95; auth, entry, Biographical Encyclopedia of Mathematicians, 98; Biographical Encyclopedia of Scientists, 98; auth, entry, Science Supplement: Spring 1998, 98; **CONTACT ADDRESS** PO Box 57, Loachapoka, AL, 36865. **EMAIL** edschafer@reporters.net

SCHAFER, J.K.
PERSONAL Born 12/12/1942, New Orleans, LA, m, 1963, 2 children **DISCIPLINE** HISTORY **EDUCATION** Newcomb Col, BA, 63; Tulane Univ, MA, 78; Tulane Univ, PhD, 85. **CAREER** Assoc dir, Murphy Inst Polit Econ, Tulane Univ, 85-98; visiting prof of law, Tulane Law Sch, 86-98. **HONORS AND AWARDS** Francis Butler Simkins Award, 95; Kemper Williams Prize, 95; Harold and Margaret Rorschach Lecture in Legal Hist, 96. **MEMBERSHIPS** Orgn Amer Hist; Amer Soc Legal Hist; S Hist Asn; La Hist Asn. **RESEARCH** Legal and Constitutional history of the U.S.; U.S. South, African-American legal history; Louisiana. **SELECTED PUBLICATIONS** Auth, Slavery, the Civil Law, and the Supreme Court of Louisiana, Louisiana State Univ, 94; The Louisiana Constitution of 1845: Reform or Experiment?, 93; Details Are of a Most Revolting Character: Cruelty to Slaves as Seen in Appeals to the Supreme Court of Louisiana, 93; The Battle of Liberty Place: A Matter of Historical Perception, 94; Under the Present Mode of Trial, Improper Verdicts Are Very Often Given: Criminal Procedure in the Trial of Slaves in Antebellum Louisiana, 96; An Uncommon Experience: Law and Judicial Institutions in Louisiana, 1803-2003, 97; Roman Roots of Louisiana's Law of Slavery: Emancipation in Louisiana, 1803-1857, 95; coauth, Louisiana: A History, 96; Civil Law, Encarta, Microsoft CD-ROM online. **CONTACT ADDRESS** Murphy Inst of Political Economy, Tulane Uni, 108 Tilton Hall, New Orleans, LA, 70118. **EMAIL** jschafer@mailhost.tcs.tulane.edu

SCHAFFER, RONALD
PERSONAL Born 04/22/1932, New York, NY, m, 1957, 2 children **DISCIPLINE** MILITARY & AMERICAN HISTORY **EDUCATION** Columbia Col, BA, 53; Princeton Univ, AM, 55, PhD, 59. **CAREER** Instr hist, Columbia Col, 58-60; from instr to asst prof, Ind Univ, 60-65; from asst prof to assoc prof, 65-75, prof hist, CA State Univ, Northridge, 75-, Grants, Am Philos Soc, 60 & 78; res grants, CA State Univ, Northridge, 68, 78 & 81; Nat Endowment Hum fel, 82. **MEMBERSHIPS** Orgn Am Historians; Soc Military Hist **RESEARCH** Recent US hist, espec mil hist. **SELECTED PUBLICATIONS** Auth, The Montana Woman Suffrage Campaign, 1911-1914, Pac NW Quart, 1/64; The War Department's Defense of ROTC, 1920-1940, Wis Mag Hist, winter 69-70; The 1940 Small Wars Manual and the Lessons of History, 4/72 & General Stanley D Embick: Military Dissenter, 10/73, Mil Affairs; The Problem of Consciousness in the Woman Suffrage Movement: A California Perspective, Pac Hist Rev, 11/76; auth, The United States in World War I: A Selected Bibliography, Clio Press, 78; American Military Ethics in World War II: The Bombing of German Civilians, J Am Hist, 9/80; Wings of Judgment: American Bombing in World War II, Oxford Univ Press, 85; America in the Great World War: The Rise of the War Welfare State, Oxford Univ Press, 91. **CONTACT ADDRESS** Dept of Hist, California State Univ, Northridge, 18111 Nordhoff St, Northridge, CA, 91330-8250. **EMAIL** ronald.schaffer@csun.edu

SCHALLER, MICHAEL
PERSONAL Born 06/02/1947, New York, NY, 3 children **DISCIPLINE** HISTORY OF UNITED STATES FOREIGN RELATIONS **EDUCATION** State Univ NY, Binghamton, BA, 68 Univ Mich, MA, 69, PhD(hist), 74. **CAREER** Asst prof, 74-79, assoc prof hist, Univ Az, 79-84, prof hist 84-, Nat Endowment for Humanities fel, 80-81; Guggenheim Mem fel, 81-82; Fulbright Fellowship, 83-84. **HONORS AND AWARDS** Bernath Book Prize, Soc Historians Am Foreign Rel, 80. **MEMBERSHIPS** Orgn Am Historians; Soc Hist Am Foreign Rel. **RESEARCH** United States-China relation, World War II period; post World War II United States-East Asian policies; United States-Japan relations. **SELECTED PUBLICATIONS** Auth, The United States Crusade in China, 1938-1945, Columbia Univ, 79; The United States and China in the 20th Century, Oxford Univ, 79; The American Occupation of Japan, Oxford Univ Press, 85; Douglas MacArthur--The Far Eastern General, Oxford Univ Press, 89; Reckoning with Reagan, Oxford Univ Press, 92; Altered States--The U.S. and Japan Since the Occupation, Oxford Univ Press, 97. **CONTACT ADDRESS** Dept of Hist, Univ Ariz, Tucson, AZ, 85721-0001. **EMAIL** Michael-Schaller@ns.arizona.edu

SCHAMA, SIMON
DISCIPLINE HISTORY OF ART **EDUCATION** Cambrdge Univ, PhD, 69. **CAREER** Prof. **HONORS AND AWARDS** Art critic, New Yorker. **RESEARCH** Biography of Rembrandt. **SELECTED PUBLICATIONS** Auth, Patriots and Liberators: Revolution in the Netherlands, 1780-1813, 77; Two Rothschilds and the Land of Israel, 78; The Embarrassment of Riches: an Interpretation of Dutch Culture in the Golden Age, 87; Citizens: a Chronicle of the French Revolution, 89; Dead Certainties: Unwarranted Speculations, 91; Landscape and Memory, 95. **CONTACT ADDRESS** Dept of Hist, Columbia Col, New York, 2960 Broadway, New York, NY, 10027-6902.

SCHANTZ, MARK S.
DISCIPLINE HISTORY **EDUCATION** Geo Wash Univ, BA, 77; Yale Div Sch, MDiv, 81; Emory, PhD, 91. **CAREER** ASST PROF, HIST, HENDRIX COLL **MEMBERSHIPS** Am Antiquarian Soc **SELECTED PUBLICATIONS** Auth, "Religious Tracts, Evangelical Reform, and the Market Revolution in Antebellum America," Jour of the Early Rep, 97; auth, Piety in Providence: The Class Dimensions of Religious Experience in Providence, Rhode Island, 1790-1860, Cambridge Univ Press. **CONTACT ADDRESS** Dept of Hist, Hendrix Col, Conway, AR, 72031. **EMAIL** schantzms@alpha.hendrix.edu

SCHAPSMEIER, EDWARD LEWIS
PERSONAL Born 02/08/1927, Council Bluffs, IA **DISCIPLINE** RECENT AMERICAN & DIPLOMATIC HISTORY **EDUCATION** Concordia Teacher's Col, Nebr, BA, 49; Univ Nebr, Omaha, MA, 52; Univ Southern Calif, PhD(hist), 65. **CAREER** Lectr hist, Univ Southern Calif, 64-65; instr, Ohio State Univ, 65-66; assoc prof, 66-67, PROF HIST, ILL STATE UNIV, 67-, Vis prof hist, Ill Wesleyan Univ, 68-69; regional ed, J West, 70-78. **MEMBERSHIPS** AHA; Orgn Am Historians; Oral Hist Asn; Am Studies Asn; Agr Hist Soc. **RESEARCH** Recent American history; diplomatic and agricultural history. **SELECTED PUBLICATIONS** Auth, Dry Farming In The Northern Great-Plains - Years Of Readjustment, 1920-1990 - Hargreaves,Mwm/, Am Hist Rev, Vol 0099, 1994; Wallace,Henry,A - His Search For A New-World Order - White,G, Maze,J/, Am Hist Rev, Vol 0102, 1997. **CONTACT ADDRESS** Dept of Hist, Illinois State Univ, Normal, IL, 61761.

SCHARF, BERTRAM
PERSONAL Born 03/03/1931, New York, NY, m, 1965, 2 children **DISCIPLINE** EXPERIMENTAL PSYCHOLOGY **EDUCATION** Harvard, PhD. **CAREER** Prof of Pschology, Northeastern Univ, 58-98, res prof, Emeritus, 98-. **HONORS AND AWARDS** Fel, ASA, 71, AAAS, 76; Distinguished Service Award of MA Sp Hearing Asn, 77; Fechner Medal, ISP, 95. **MEMBERSHIPS** Acoust Soc Am; Int Soc Psychophysics (ISP); Psychonomics Soc. **RESEARCH** Hearing, auditory attention. **SELECTED PUBLICATIONS** Co-auth with M Floentine and C H Meiselman, Critical Band in Auditory Lateralization, Sensory Processes, 76; auth, Loudness, in E C Carterette and M P Friedman, eds, Handbook of Perception, vol 4, Hearing, 78; Loudness Adaptation, in J V Tobias & E D Schuber, eds, Hearing Research and Theory, vol 2, 83; with S Quigley, C Aoki, N Peachey, and A Reeves, Focused Auditory Attention and Frequency Selectivity, Perception and Psychophysics, 42, 87; with A Chays & J Magnum, The Role of the Olivocochlear Bundle in Hearing: Sixteen Case Studies, Hearing Res, 103, 97. **CONTACT ADDRESS** Dept of Psychology, Northeastern Univ, 413 MU, Boston, MA, 02115-5096. **EMAIL** scharf@neu.edu

SCHARNAU, RALPH WILLIAM
PERSONAL Born 10/22/1935, Woodstock, IL, m, 1960, 3 children **DISCIPLINE** UNITED STATES HISTORY **EDUCATION** Beloit Col, BA, 57; Univ Ill, MA, 59; Northern Ill Univ, PhD, 70. **CAREER** Instr hist, Northern Ill Univ, 63-64; asst prof, McKendree Col, 65-69, assoc prof, 69-70; assoc prof, 70-75, prof hist, 75- , Univ Dubuque. **HONORS AND AWARDS** Participant, Wye Fac Sem, 87; NEH summer inst for col and univ faculty, 94; Throne-Aldrich Award, 94. **MEMBERSHIPS** AHA; Orgn Am Historians. **RESEARCH** American social and cultural history; American labor history; American environmental history. **SELECTED PUBLICATIONS** Auth, Thomas J Morgan and the United Labor Party of Chicago, J Ill State Hist Soc, spring 73; Elizabeth Morgan, crusader for labor reform, Labor Hist, summer 73; auth, Workers and Politics: The Knights of Labor in Dubuque, Iowa, 1885-1890, Annals of IA, 87; auth, The Knights of Labor in Iowa, Annals of IA, 91; auth, Workers, Unions, and Workplaces in Dubuque, 1830-1990, annals of IA, 93; auth, Street Car Strike 1903: Dubuque Walks, Labor's Heritage, 95; auth, The Labor Movement in Iowa, 1900-1910, J of the West, 96. **CONTACT ADDRESS** Dept of History, Univ of Dubuque, 2000 University Ave, Dubuque, IA, 52001-5050. **EMAIL** rrscharnau@aol.com

SCHAUB, MARILYN MCNAMARA
PERSONAL Born 03/24/1928, Chicago, IL, m, 1969, 1 child **DISCIPLINE** RELIGIOUS STUDIES, CLASSICAL LANGUAGES **EDUCATION** Rosary Col, BA, 53; Univ Fribourg, PhD(class philos), 57. **CAREER** Asst prof class lang, 57-62, assoc prof relig studies & class lang, 62-69, Rosary Col; assoc prof, 73-80, prof theol, 80-, Duquesne Univ; hon assoc, Am Schs Orient Res, Jerusalem, 66-67; admin dir, expedition to the southeast end of the Dead Sea, Jordan, 77, 79, 81. **HONORS AND AWARDS** Pres Award for Faculty Excellence in Teaching, Duquesne Univ, 90. **MEMBERSHIPS** Soc Bibl Lit; Cath Bibl Asn; Am Acad Relig; Archaeol Inst Am. **RESEARCH** Old Testament; New Testament; early Bronze Age settlements at the southeast end of the Dead Sea, Jordan. **SELECTED PUBLICATIONS** Co-translr, Agape in the New Testament, Herder, 63-67; auth, Friends and Friendship in St Augustine, Alba, 65; contribr, Encyclopedic Dictionary of Religion, Corpus, 78; ed, Harper Collins Bible Dictionary, 96; auth, Collegeville Pastoral Dictionary of Biblical Theology, 96. **CONTACT ADDRESS** Theol Dept, Duquesne Univ, Pittsburgh, PA, 15282. **EMAIL** schaub@duq3.cc.duq.edu

SCHAUS, GERALD
DISCIPLINE GREEK ARCHAEOLOGY **EDUCATION** Alberta, PhD. **CAREER** Prof; Dept Ch. **MEMBERSHIPS** Greek Symposia Assn Waterloo. **SELECTED PUBLICATIONS** Auth, Notes on the Topography of Eresos; An Archaeological Field Survey at Eresos, Lesbos. **CONTACT ADDRESS** Dept of Classics, Wilfrid Laurier Univ, 75 University Ave W, Waterloo, ON, N2L 3C5. **EMAIL** gschaus@mach1.wlu.ca

SCHEIBER, HARRY N.
PERSONAL Born 00/00/1935, New York, NY, m, 1958, 2 children **DISCIPLINE** UNITED STATES HISTORY **EDUCATION** Columbia Univ, AB, 55; Cornell Univ, MA, 57, PhD, 62. **CAREER** From instr to prof hist, Dartmouth Col, 60-71; prof hist, Univ Calif, San Diego, 71-80; PROF LAW, UNIV CALIF, BERKELEY, 80-, Am Coun Learned Socs fel studies law, 66-67; fel, Ctr Advan Studies Behav Sci, 66-67, vis scholar, 70-71; pres, NH Civil Liberties Union, 69-70; mem, Beveridge-Dunning Prize Comn, AHA, 70-73, chmn, 73; mem comt US hist, Col Entrance Exam Bd, 70-80; pres, Coun Res Econ Hist, 72-75; Guggenheim fel, 70-71; dir, Nat Endowment for Humanities Sem, 78, 79 & 81; Rockefeller fel, 80; Project 87 fel, 80. **HONORS AND AWARDS** Moses Coit Tyler Prize, 59 & Messenger Prize, 60, Cornell Univ; Ohio Univ Press Award, 70., MA, Dartmouth, 65. **MEMBERSHIPS** Orgn Am Historians; Agr Hist Soc (pres, 77-78); Law & Soc Asn; Econ Hist Asn; AHA. **RESEARCH** American economic history; 19th century United States history; history of American law. **SELECTED PUBLICATIONS** Auth, Innovation, Resistance, And Change - A Hist Of Judicial Reform And The Calif Courts, 1960-1990/, Southern Calif Law Rev, Vol 0066, 1993; Arming Military-Justice, Vol 1, The Origins Of The United-States Court-Of-Military-Appeals, 1775-1950 - Lurie,J/, J Of Am Hist, Vol 0080, 1993; The Wheeling-Bridge Case - Its Significance In Am Law And Technol - Monroe,Eb/, J Of Southern Hist, Vol 0060, 1994; The Guardian Of Every Other Right - A Constitutional Hist Of Property-Rights - Ely,Jw/, Am Hist Rev, Vol 0099, 1994. **CONTACT ADDRESS** Sch of Law, Univ of Calif, Berkeley, CA, 94720.

SCHEIFELE, ELEANOR L.
DISCIPLINE MEDIEVAL ART **EDUCATION** Univ Wash, PhD. **CAREER** Vis asst prof. **RESEARCH** Sculpture at Moissac; Cluniac Patronage; Visigothic and Mozarabic Spain; images of beasts and demons; medieval iconography; medieval court art. **SELECTED PUBLICATIONS** Auth, pubs on French Romanesque sculpture and patronage of Richard II, Oxford. **CONTACT ADDRESS** Dept of History and Art, Indiana Univ, Bloomington, 300 N Jordan Ave, Bloomington, IN, 47405. **EMAIL** escheife@indiana.edu

SCHEIFFELE, EBERHARD
PERSONAL Born 09/10/1959, Wehr, Germany, s **DISCIPLINE** PSYCHOLOGY **EDUCATION** Universitat Freiburg, Germany, 82; Univ TX, Austin, MA, 85; Univ Calif, Grad cert, 91, PhD, 95. **CAREER** Tchng asst, 82-83, Univ Freiburg; tchng asst, 84-85, Univ TX; Tchng asst, 84-85, Univ Mich; tchng asst, 85-87, 89-90, 92, 95, grad stud instr, logic, 87-88, knowledge & its limits, 89, Univ Calif, Berkeley; tchng asst, 91, Univ Calif, Santa Cruz; tchng asst, guest presenter, Psychodrama/role playing for Hum Int, guest presenter, Dynamic Med for Psychol of Conscious, 98-, West Chester Univ. **HONORS AND AWARDS** Myrtle L. Judkins Mem Schol, 93-94; Wheeler Fel, 85-86; UC Berkeley; German Exchan Fel, Univ TX, Austin **MEMBERSHIPS** Amer Sc of Group Psychotherapy & Psychodrama; Assn for Theatre in Higher Ed; Intl Fed for Theare Res; Amer Soc Theatre Res; Natl Assn for Drama Therapy; Amer Phil Assn; Amer Psychol Assn; Natl Ed Assn. **RESEARCH** Psychodrama, spontaneity & improvisation; theatrical theories & influences of Jacob Levy Moreno. **SELECTED PUBLICATIONS** Coauth, Proof by Mathematical Induction, Discov Geometry Tchrs Res Book, Key Curr Press, 77; auth, Writing a Logic Puzzle, Discov Geometry Tchrs Res Book, Key Curr Press, 97; art, The Theatre of Truth, Res in Drama Ed, 97; art, Therapeutic Theatre and Spontaneity: Goethe and Moreno, J of Group Psychotherapy, Psychodrama & Sociometry, 96. **CONTACT ADDRESS** Group in Logic and Methodology of Sci, Univ of Calif, Berkeley, CA, 94720. **EMAIL** scheiffe@math.berkeley.edu

SCHEINBERG, STEPHEN
DISCIPLINE 20TH CENTURY U.S. HISTORY **EDUCATION** Chicago Univ, BS; Univ Wis, MA, PhD. **CAREER** Vis prof, San Diego State Univ; Northeastern Ill Univ; prof. **RESEARCH** Anti-semitism in North America. **SELECTED PUBLICATIONS** Auth, Right Wing Extremism: Threats to International Peace and Security, 97. **CONTACT ADDRESS** Dept of Hist, Concordia Univ, Montreal, 1455 de Maisonneuve W, Montreal, PQ, H3G 1M8. **EMAIL** drsteve@alcor.concordia.ca

SCHEINER, IRWIN
PERSONAL Born 05/22/1932, New York, NY, m, 1965, 2 children **DISCIPLINE** MODERN JAPANES HISTORY **EDUCATION** Queens Col, NY, BA, 53; Univ Mich, Ann Arbor, MA, 58, PhD(Hist), 66. **CAREER** Actg instr, 63-65, lectr, 65-66, from asst prof to assoc prof, 66-73, prof Japanese Hist, Univ Calif, Berkeley, 73-, Soc Sci res fel, 68 & 69; Fulbright res fel, Japan, 68-69; Soc Sci Res Coun travel grant, 73-74; Univ Humanities res prof grant, Univ Calif, Berkeley, 74; Nat Humanities Inst fel, Univ Chicago, 77-78; Japan Found Fel, 81-82; 87-88. **MEMBERSHIPS** Assn Asian Studies. **RESEARCH** Japanese social-intellectual history of Tokugwa and Meiji Periods; comparative social and intellectual history. **SELECTED PUBLICATIONS** Auth, Christian Samurai and Samurai values, In: Modern Japanese Leadership, Univ Ariz, 66; Christian Converts and Social Protest in Meiji Japan, Univ Calif, 70; The mindful peasant: A sketch for the study of peasant rebellion, J Asian Studies, 8/73; ed, Modern Japan: An Interpretive Anthology, Macmillan, 74; auth, Benevolent lords and honorable peasants, In: Japanese Thought in the Tokugawa Period, Univ Chicago, 78; The Japanese Village: Imagined, Real, contested, Mirror of Modernity, Stephan Vlastos, ed, University of California Press, 98. **CONTACT ADDRESS** Dept of History, Univ of California, Berkeley, 3229 Dwinelle Hall, Berkeley, CA, 94720-2551.

SCHELBERT, LEO
PERSONAL Born 03/16/1929, Kaltbrunn, Switzerland, m, 1965, 4 children **DISCIPLINE** AMERICAN IMMIGRATION HISTORY **EDUCATION** Fordham Univ, MA, 61; Columbia Univ, PhD(Am hist), 66. **CAREER** Asst instr western civilization, Rutgers Univ, 63-64, from instr to asst prof hist, 64-69; Swiss Nat Found scholar res fel, 69-70; lectr Swiss emigration, Univ Zurich, 70-71; asst prof, 71-73, chmn dept, 77-79, assoc prof Am immigration hist, 73-79, actg chmn dept, 81-82, PROF AM IMMIGRATION HIST, UNIV ILL, CHICAGO CIRCLE, 79-, Guest prof, Univ Dusseldorf, 76. **MEMBERSHIPS** Orgn Am Historians; Swiss Am Hist Soc (secy, 68-69, pres, 75-80). **RESEARCH** American immigration; European emigration. **SELECTED PUBLICATIONS** Auth, The Georgia Dutch - From The Rhine And Danube To The Savanna, 1733-1783 - Jones,Jf/, J Of Am Hist, Vol 0080, 1994; Int-Business Networks, Emigration And Exports To Latin-Am In The 19th-Century - Swiss Trade With The Am - Veyrasat,B/, Am Hist Rev, Vol 0100, 1995. **CONTACT ADDRESS** Dept of Hist, Univ of Ill at Chicago Circle, Chicago, IL, 60680.

SCHENKER, DAVID J.
DISCIPLINE GREEK PROSE AND POETRY **EDUCATION** Vanderbilt, BA; Univ Calif Berkeley, MA, PhD. **CAREER** Assoc prof & dir Undergrad Stud; Univ Mo, 91-; teach in, Honors Col; taught 2 yrs at, Allegheny Col, Pa. **RESEARCH** Greek drama. **SELECTED PUBLICATIONS** Publ in, Rheinisches Mus, 95; Mnemosyne, 95; Phoenix, 94 & TAPA, 91. **CONTACT ADDRESS** Dept of Classical Studies, Univ of Missouri-Columbia, 309 University Hall, Columbia, MO, 65211.

SCHERER, IMGARD S.
PERSONAL Born 01/14/1937, Berlin, Germany, m, 1958, 4 children **DISCIPLINE** HISTORY OF PHILOSOPHY **EDUCATION** Amer Univ, PhD, 91. **CAREER** Asst Prof, 92-, Loyola Coll, MD; Vis Prof, 92, Amer Univ; Vis Prof, 88-91, George Mason Univ. **HONORS AND AWARDS** Amer Philos Assoc; North Amer Kent Soc. **MEMBERSHIPS** ASA, Phi Sigma Tan,

IHSP. **RESEARCH** Science of Aesthetics, Theory of Judgement applied to Science, Morality and Art. **SELECTED PUBLICATIONS** Auth, The Crisis of Judgement in Kant's Three Critiques, In Search of a Science of Aesthetics, NY, Peter Lang Pub Co, 95; The Problem of the A Priori in Sensibility, Revisiting Kant's and Hegel's Theories of the Senses, forthcoming, The Review of Metaphysics; co-auth, Kant's Critique of Judgement and the Scientific Investigation of Matter, Universitat Karlsruhe, Germany, Inst Of Philos, Vol 3, 97; Kant's Eschatology in Zum ewigen Frieden: The Concept of Purposiveness to Guarantee Perpetual Peace, Proceedings of the 8th International Kant Congress, Memphis, 95. **CONTACT ADDRESS** Dept of Philosophy, Loyola Col, 4501 N Charles St, Baltimore, MD, 21210-2699. **EMAIL** ischerer@loyola.edu

SCHERER, PAUL HENRY
PERSONAL Born 10/12/1933, Sedalia, MO, m, 1959, 2 children **DISCIPLINE** MODERN EUROPEAN DIPLOMATIC HISTORY **EDUCATION** Midland Lutheran Col, AB, 55; Univ Wis, MS, 56, PhD(hist), 64. **CAREER** From instr to asst prof, Colo State Univ, 61-64; from asst prof to assoc prof, 64-77, asst chmn dept, 66-68, chmn, 70-73, PROF HIST, IND UNIV, SOUTH BEND, 77-, Colo State Univ fac res grants, 62-63; Ind Univ Found res grant, 66-67, 71-73; Am Philos Found grant, 68. **MEMBERSHIPS** AHA **RESEARCH** Lord John Russell; 19th century Anglo-French diplomacy; 20th century European diplomacy. **SELECTED PUBLICATIONS** Auth, Collision Of Empires - Britain In 3 World-Wars, 1793-1945 - Harvey,Ad/, Albion, Vol 0025, 1993; Palmerstons Foreign-Policy - 1848 - Billy,Gj/, Historian, Vol 0057, 1994; Defense And Diplomacy - Britain And The Great-Powers, 1815-1914 - Bartlett,Cj/, Albion, Vol 0026, 1994. **CONTACT ADDRESS** Dept of Hist, Indiana Univ, South Bend, South Bend, IN, 46615.

SCHERR, A.E.
PERSONAL Born 01/05/1963, Florence, Italy, s **DISCIPLINE** US HISTORY **EDUCATION** NY Univ, PhD, 98. **CAREER** Asst prof, hist dept, CUNY-BCC, 98-. **HONORS AND AWARDS** Mazzini Soc fel; Smith Col Amer Studies, Diploma fel; NY Univ Hist teaching award; NY Univ dean's dissertation award. **MEMBERSHIPS** OAH; AHA. **RESEARCH** U.S. twentieth century cultural history; Popular culture; Film studies; New Deal. **SELECTED PUBLICATIONS** Auth, Did Private Nolan Get His Glory? Movies Press and Audiences during the Spanish American War, Columbia Jour of Amer Studies, 98; auth, In the Land of Milk and Honey: European Anti-Fascist Exiles in Hollywood, Hist Jour of Film, Radio and Television, 98; co-auth, Ambiguous Sovereignties: Notes on the Suburbs in Italian Cinema, Suburban Discipline, Princeton Archit Press, 97; auth, Shoot the Right Thing: African American Filmmakers and the Contemporary American Public Discourse, Toward a New American nation?, Keele Univ Press, 95; auth, Fritz Lang, I Moguls e altri recent citizens, Lo straniero interno, Ponte all Grazie, 94; auth, Facsimili storici, Corsari del tempo, Ponte alle Grazie, 94. **CONTACT ADDRESS** History Dept, Bronx Comm Col, CUNY, University Ave. and W. 181st St., Bronx, NY, 10453. **EMAIL** sqg0700@isz.nyu.edu

SCHERZINGER, M.
DISCIPLINE MUSIC THEORY; MUSICOLOGY **EDUCATION** Columbia Univ, MPhil 97, MA 93; Wits Univ SA, BMus 87-91, BA 84-86. **CAREER** Dept Music, Columbia Univ **HONORS AND AWARDS** Pres Fel; Young Sch Awd; Herbert L Hutner Fel; Mellon Fel; FCA Intl Schsp for Music; Ntl Postgrad Schshp; Merit Awds for Best Student; Abraham and Olga Lipman Schshp; Tongaat Hullet Merit Schshp. **MEMBERSHIPS** SAMRO; MUNY; MSUW; ICTM; PNM. **RESEARCH** Music theory, musicology, ethnomusicology, African studies, German romanticism, philosophy, literary theory, cultural studies. **CONTACT ADDRESS** Dept of Music, Columbia Univ, 100 Morningside Dr # 5H, New York, NY, 10027. **EMAIL** mrs22@columbia.edu

SCHICK, JAMES BALDWIN MCDONALD
PERSONAL Born 10/03/1940, Lafayette, IN, m, 1963, 1 child **DISCIPLINE** HISTORY **EDUCATION** Univ Wis-Madison, BS, 62, MS, 63; Ind Univ, Bloomington, PhD(hist), 71. **CAREER** Asst prof, 67-71, assoc prof, 71-77, PROF HIST, PITTSBURG STATE UNIV, 77-, Ed, Practice of Hist J, 77-78; ed, Midwest Quart, 81-; ed, Hist Comput Rev, 85-. **MEMBERSHIPS** Orgn Am Historians; Southern Hist Soc; Inst Early Am Hist & Cult. **RESEARCH** Antifederalism and the Constitution; North Carolina in the revolution. **SELECTED PUBLICATIONS** Coauth, The future as history: An experimental approach to introductory history for the general student, Hist Teacher, 74; auth, Microfilmed newspapers in the classroom, Masthead, 77; Vehicular religion and the gasoline service station, Midwest Quart, 77; Using the microfilmed Virginia Gazette in class, History Teacher, 80; coauth, The Early American Republic revisited: Textbook perceptions of American history, 1789-1848, J Early Repub, 81; auth, Teaching History with a Computer, Lyceum Books, 90. **CONTACT ADDRESS** Dept of History, Pittsburg State Univ, 1701 S Broadway St, Pittsburg, KS, 66762-7500. **EMAIL** jschick@pittstate.edu

SCHIEFEN, RICHARD JOHN
PERSONAL Born 05/09/1932, Rochester, NY **DISCIPLINE** MODERN CHURCH HISTORY, HISTORY OF RELIGION **EDUCATION** Univ Toronto, BA, 56, MA, 62; Univ St Michael's Col, STB, 61; Univ Rochester, MEd, 58; Univ London, PhD, 70. **CAREER** From asst prof to assoc prof hist, Univ St Thomas, Tex, 65-72, chmn dept, 70-72; assoc prof church hist, St Michael's Col, Univ Toronto, 72-81; DEAN SCH THEOL, UNIV ST THOMAS, 81- **MEMBERSHIPS** AHA; Am Cath Hist Asn; Can Cath Hist Asn; Ecclesiastical Hist Soc. **RESEARCH** Victorian religion; 19th century Roman Catholicism. **SELECTED PUBLICATIONS** Auth, A Hist Commentary On The Major Catholic Works Of Newman,Cardinal - Griffin,Jr/, Cath Hist Rev, Vol 0080, 1994; Trial Of Strength, Furtwangler,Wilhelm In The Third-Reich - Prieberg,Fk/, Biog-An Interdisciplinary Quart, Vol 0018, 1995; Cath Devotion In Victorian Eng - Heimann,M/, Cath Hist Rev, Vol 0083, 1997. **CONTACT ADDRESS** Sch of Theol, Univ of St Thomas, Houston, TX, 77024.

SCHIERLE, GOTTHILF GOETZ
DISCIPLINE ARCHITECTURAL DESIGN, STRUCTURAL DESIGN AND ANALYSIS, BUILDING SCIENCE **EDUCATION** Stuttgart, Ger, Dipl-Ing, 59; Univ CA, Berkeley, MA, 75, PhD, 75. **CAREER** Prof, 92-, assoc prof, 78-92, vis assoc prof, 76-78, vis asst prof, 75-76, Univ Southern CA; found dir & dir, USC, Grad Bldg Sci Prog, 85-95; lectr & ch Struct Sequence, Univ CA, Berkeley, 66-78; vis prof, UCLA, 96-97; lectr, Stanford Univ, 68. **HONORS AND AWARDS** Fel, Am Inst Arch, 93; Bund Deutscher Baumeister, Ger., Found dir, Master Bldg Sci Prog, 85-96. **MEMBERSHIPS** Col fellows, Am Inst Arch; Am Inst Arch; Bund Deutscher Baumeister, Ger; ed bd, J for Arch Educ, 95-98 & Fabrics & Arch, 95-; sci comt, Int Symp, 96; mem, NSF workshop, seismic res policy plan, DC, 93; chr, CA State Comn, Arch License Exams for Gen & Long-Span Struct, 86-89. **RESEARCH** Consortium seismic. **SELECTED PUBLICATIONS** Auth, Membranes under Prestress, Fabrics in Architecture, 96; Quality Control in Seismic Design and Construction, J Performance Constructed Fac, 96; Span/Depth Tables for Structure Systems and Elements, Guidelines for the Design of Double-Layer Grids, 96; Quality Control for Seismic Safety, ATC US-Japan Workshop, 94; Quality Control for Seismic Safety, LA Architect, 94; Computer Aided Seismic Design, J Arch and Plan Res, 94; Computer Aided Design for Wind and Seismic Forces, Comput Supported Design in Arch, ACADIA, 92; Dynamic Editing Computer Aided Design, Symp Proc Baden-Baden, 91; Computer Aided Seismic Design, Developments in Structural Engg, 90; coauth, Computer-Aided Design of Membrane Structures, Proc Int Symp Conceptual Design of Structures, Stuttgart, Ger, 96; Vernacular Forms: Wind Tunnel Tests and Computer Simulation, Proc Int Conf on Wind Engg, New Delhi, 95. **CONTACT ADDRESS** School of Archit, Univ of Southern California, University Park Campus, Los Angeles, CA, 90089. **EMAIL** schierle@usc.edu

SCHIERLING, STEPHEN P.
DISCIPLINE ANCIENT GREEK AND LATIN LANGUAGE, GREEK AND ROMAN COMEDY **EDUCATION** St Louis Univ, PhD, 80. **CAREER** Assoc prof Lat and Ancient Greek, coordr, undergrad Lat instr, 80-88; sec hd, Class, 86-89; Arts and Sci fac senate, 87-91, 95-97; pres, Arts and Sci fac senate, 90-91; Prescott Hall comp network admin, 92-, La State Univ. **RESEARCH** Greek and Latin paleography; textual criticism; computer applications to textual criticism. **SELECTED PUBLICATIONS** Auth, Vaticanus Graecus 2203 in the Manuscript Tradition of Thucydides, in Rev d'Hist des Texts, 11, 81; Rossi 508 and the Text of Sallust, in Manuscripts, XXIX, 85; New Evidence for Diomedes in Two Passages of Sallust, in Hermes, 113, 2, 85; Bellum Jugurthinum 113.3: A Restoration of the Text, in Manuscripta, XXXI. 87; SPSS/PC As a Useful Tool in Determining the Text of Sallust's Jugurtha: A Text Critic's Point of View, in The Class Bull, 65, nos 1 & 2, 89; The Jugurtha Epitaphs: The Texts and Tradition, in Manuscripta, 93. **CONTACT ADDRESS** Dept of For Lang and Lit, Louisiana State Univ, 220 B Prescott Hall, Baton Rouge, LA, 70803. **EMAIL** sschierl@homer.forlang.lsu.edu

SCHIFERL, ELLEN
DISCIPLINE ART **EDUCATION** Grinnell Col, BA; Univ Minn, MA, PhD. **CAREER** Assoc prof. **RESEARCH** Interactive multimedia educational software; visual environment and visualization; visual representation of space and time. **SELECTED PUBLICATIONS** Auth, pubs on medieval and renaissance art history, computer based instruction and art criticism. **CONTACT ADDRESS** Dept of Art, 37 Col Ave, Gorham, MA, 04038-1083. **EMAIL** usmadm@maine.maine.edu

SCHIFFHORST, GERALD JOSEPH
PERSONAL Born 10/13/1940, St. Louis, MO **DISCIPLINE** ENGLISH, ART HISTORY **EDUCATION** St Louis Univ, BS, 62, MA, 63; Wash Univ, PhD(English), 73. **CAREER** Instr English, Univ Mo-St Louis, 66-67; asst prof to prof English, Univ Cent Fla, 70-, Nat Endowment for Humanities fel art hist, Southeastern Inst Medieval & Renaissance Studies, Duke Univ, 74; . **MEMBERSHIPS** MLA; Shakespeare Asn Am; Milton Soc Am; SAtlantic Mod Lang Asn. **RESEARCH** Milton; Renaissance iconography of patience; teaching English composition. **SELECTED PUBLICATIONS** Ed & coauth, The Triumph of Patience: Medieval and Renaissance Studies, Fla Univ, 78; coauth, Short English Handbook, Scott, 79, 2nd ed, 82, 3rd ed, 86; auth, Patience & the Humbly Exalted Heroism of Milton's Messiah (art), Milton Studies, XVI, 82; auth, John Milton, 90; Short Handbook for Writers, McGraw Hill, 91, 97; co-ed, The Witness of Times, Duquesne Univ Press, 93; assoc ed, Seventeenth-Century News, 96-99. **CONTACT ADDRESS** Dept of English, Univ Central Fla, PO Box 161346, Orlando, FL, 32816-1346. **EMAIL** gschiff@ucf1vm.cc.ucf.edu

SCHIFFMAN, JOSEPH
PERSONAL Born 06/13/1914, New York, NY, m, 1942, 2 children **DISCIPLINE** ENGLISH, AMERICAN STUDIES **EDUCATION** LI Univ, BA, 37; Columbia Univ, MA, 47; NY Univ, PhD, 51. **CAREER** From instr to assoc prof English, LI Univ, 45-58, coordr grad prog Am studies, 56-58; chmn dept English, 59-68, prof English, 58-68, James Hope Caldwell prof Am studies, 68-79, EMER PROF ENGLISH & PROF CONTINUING EDUC, DICKINSON COL, 79-86, 90-96; Acting ed, Am Quart, 60; head Am lit, Int Bibliog Comt, 61-64; founding dir, Am Studies Res Ctr, India, 64; vis Fulbright prof, Univ Bordeaux, France, 65-66; vis prof, Univ South Fla, 81; Fulbright-Hays vis prof, Univ of Indonesia, 81-82. **HONORS AND AWARDS** Lindback Found Distinguished Teaching Award, 62. **MEMBERSHIPS** MLA; Am Studies Asn. **RESEARCH** American literature and civilization. **SELECTED PUBLICATIONS** Auth, Introduction to Lindsay Swift's Brook Farm, Corinth, 61; ed, Three Shorter Novels of Herman Melville, Harper, 62; Edward Bellamy's Duke of Stockbridge, Harvard Univ, 62; coauth, A critical history of American literature: from its beginning to the present, In: Cassell's Encyclopedia of World Literature, 73. **CONTACT ADDRESS** Dickinson Col, Carlisle, PA, 17013.

SCHILCHER, LINDA
DISCIPLINE HISTORY **EDUCATION** Oxford Univ, DPhil. **CAREER** Assoc prof. **RESEARCH** Islamic history; modern Middle East history. **SELECTED PUBLICATIONS** Auth, Der Nahe Osten in the Zwischenkriegszeit 1919-1939, Steiner Verlag, 89; co-auth, Families in Politics, Steiner Verlag, 85. **CONTACT ADDRESS** History Dept, Univ of Arkansas, Fayetteville, 511 Old Main, Fayetteville, AR, 72701. **EMAIL** lschilch@comp.uark.edu

SCHILLING, DONALD
PERSONAL Born 01/04/1942, Stevens Point, WI, m, 2 children **DISCIPLINE** HISTORY **EDUCATION** DePauw Univ, BA, 64; Univ Wis-Madison, MA, 96, PhD, 72. **CAREER** Denison Univ, asst prof, 72-78, assoc prof, 79-87, prof, 88-, dean, first-year students, 97-. **HONORS AND AWARDS** Fel, Summer Inst on the Holocaust and Jewish Civilization, Northwestern Univ, June, 96; Inst of Europ Stud Fel, Berlin, June, 93; Holocaust Educ Found: course develop grant, 92; Fulbright-Hays sem abroad: Soc and Econ Change in S Africa, 91; Denison Univ res found grant 94, 87, 84, 72; Dension Univ fac develop grant, 91, 81, 79, 77, 74, 73; NEH, summer sem fel, 76. **MEMBERSHIPS** Am Hist Asn; German Studies Asn; Ohio Acad of Hist. **RESEARCH** Mod German hist; Holocaust; historiography; pedagogy; educ policy in Africa. **SELECTED PUBLICATIONS** The Dynamics of Educational Policy Formation in Kenya, 1928-1934, Hist of Ed Quart, 80, 51-76; Local Native Councils and the Politics of African Education in Kenya, 1924-1939, Int Jour African Hist Stud, IX, 2, 76, 218-247; How Much War Should Be Included in a Course on World War II?, Teaching Hist: A Jour of Methods, 18:1, 93, 14-21; Modernization and the Origins of National Socialism: the Case of Middle Franconia, in Proceedings of the Citadel Symposium on Hitler and National Socialism, Charleston: Citadel Univ Press, 81, 60-70; The Politics of Education in Colonial Algeria and Kenya, Athens: Ohio Univ Press, 83; Politics in a New Key: the Transformation of Politics in Northern Bavaria, 1890-1914, Ger Stud Rev, XVII:1, 94, 33-57; The Dead End of Demonizing: Dealing with the Perpetrators in Teaching the Holocaust, in Perspectives on the Holocaust: A Guide for Teachers and Scholars, NY Univ Press, 96; Histories of the War in Europe and the Pacific," in World War II in Europe, Africa, and the Americas, with General Sources: A Handbook of Literature and Research, Greenwood Press, 97, 3-21; Ed, Lessons and Legacies II: Teaching the Holocaust in a Changing World, Evanston: Northwestern Univ Press, 98. **CONTACT ADDRESS** Denison Univ, Granville, OH, 43023. **EMAIL** schilling@denison.edu

SCHKADE, LAWRENCE L.
PERSONAL Born 07/31/1931, Port Arthur, TX, s, 2 children **DISCIPLINE** INDUSTRIAL ENGINEERING **EDUCATION** Lamar Univ, BBA, 56; Louisiana St Univ, MBA, 57, PhD, 61; Post Dr Fel , Univ of Chicago, 62, Univ of Cal, 65. **CAREER** Assoc Dean, Bus Admin, 69-71, Dean Univ Grad Schl, Chmn, Dept of Info Sys and Manag Sciences, 80-85, Dir, Center for Info Tech Manag, 84-87, Assoc Dir, Center for Advanced Eng Res, 92-95, Dean, Col of Bus, 98-, Univ of Texas at Arlington. **HONORS AND AWARDS** Fel, Amer Assoc for the Advancement of Science; Fel and Past Pres, Decision Sciences Inst. **MEMBERSHIPS** Amer Assoc for the Advancement of Science; Assoc for Info Systems; Intl Soc for System Sciences **RE-**

SEARCH Electronic commerce; economics of information technologies; technology transfer; policy analysis to increase organ recovery for transplantation . **SELECTED PUBLICATIONS** Medical Examiner Issues Survey of OPOs, Assoc of Organ Procurement Org, 94; Impact of Medical Examiner/ Coroner Practices on Organ Recovery in the United States, Jour of the AMA, 94; Experts and Expertise An Identification Paradox, Indust Mgt and Data Sys, 94; An Expert System to Evaluate Product Liability Claims, Knowledge-Based Sys, 94; Computers Organizations and Power A Game Theoretic Perspective, Jour of Tech Mgt, 95; Quality Function Deployment Usage in Software Development, Comm of the ACM, 96; Projected Impact of CDC HIV Screening Criteria on Organ Transplantation, CDC and Prevention, 96; Management Support Systems for Multinational Business, Info Tech in a Global Bus Environ, 96; Toward and Informational Model of the Organization CommunicationTransmission Metrics, Bull of ACM Siggroup, 97; Diffusion of Technologies in the Cyberoroganization, IEEE, 98. **CONTACT ADDRESS** College of Business Admin, Univ of Texas at Arlington, Box 19377, Arlington, TX, 76019-0377. **EMAIL** schkade@uta.edu

SCHLAFLY, PHYLLIS STEWART

PERSONAL Born 08/15/1924, St. Louis, MO, w, 1949, 6 children **DISCIPLINE** POLITICAL SCIENCE **EDUCATION** Washington Univ, BA, 44; Harvard Univ, MA, 45; Washington Univ Law School, 78; Niagara Univ, LLD, 76. **CAREER** Broadcaster, CBS Radio Network, 73-78; commentator, Cable TV News Network, 80-83; host, Matters of Opinion, WBBM-AM, Chicago, 73-75; PRES, EAGLE FORUM, 75-; SYNDICATED COLUMNIST, COPLEY NEWS SERV, 76-. **HONORS AND AWARDS** Ten honor awards, Freedom Found; Brotherhood award, NCCJ, 75; Woman of Achievement in Public Affairs, St Louis Globe-Democrat, 63; voted one of the ten most admired women in the world, Good Housekeeping poll, 77-90., Ill Bar, 79; DC Bar, 84; Mo Bar, 85; U.S. Supreme Court, 87. **MEMBERSHIPS** ABA; DAR; Ill Bar Asn, Phi Beta Kappa; Pi Sigma Alpha. **RESEARCH** Education; national defense; feminism; politics. **SELECTED PUBLICATIONS** Auth, pub, Phyllis Schlafly Report, 67-; auth, A Choice Not an Echo, 64; auth, The Gravediggers, 64; auth, Strike From Space, 65; auth, Safe Not Sorry, 67; auth, The Betrayers, 68; auth, Mindszenty The Man, 72; auth, Kissinger on the Couch, 75; auth, Ambush at Vladivostok, 76; auth, The Power of the Positive Woman, 77; auth, First Reader, 94; ed, Child Abuse in the Classroom, 84; auth, Pornography's Victims, 87; auth, Equal Pay for Unequal Work, 84; auth, Who Will Rock the Cradle, 89; auth, Stronger Families or Bigger Government, 90; auth, Meddlesome Mandate: Rethinking Family Leave, 91. **CONTACT ADDRESS** Eagle Forum, 7800 Bonhomme Ave., St. Louis, MO, 63105. **EMAIL** phyllis@eagleforum.org

SCHLAM, CARL C.

PERSONAL Born 10/23/1936, New York, NY, m, 1967 **DISCIPLINE** CLASSICS **EDUCATION** Columbia Univ, BA, 56, MA, 58, PhD(Greek & Latin), 68. **CAREER** Instr classics, Rutgers Univ, 64-66; preceptor Greek & Latin, Columbia Col, 66-67; asst prof, 67-73, Assoc Prof Classics, Ohio State Univ, 73- **MEMBERSHIPS** Am Philol Asn. **RESEARCH** Ancient literature; neo-Latin; paleography. **SELECTED PUBLICATIONS** Auth, Lucian - Satirical Sketches - Turner,P/, Humor-Int J Of Humor Res, Vol 0005, 1992; The Greek 'Alexander Romance' - Stoneman,R, Translator-Annotator/, Classical World, Vol 0086, 1993. **CONTACT ADDRESS** Dept of Classics, Ohio State Univ, Columbus, OH, 43210.

SCHLATTER, FREDRIC WILLIAM

PERSONAL Born 06/16/1926, Tacoma, WA **DISCIPLINE** CLASSICAL LANGUAGES, HISTORY **EDUCATION** Gonzaga Univ, AB, 49, MA, 50; Alma Col, Calif, STL, 57; Princeton Univ, PhD(classics), 60. **CAREER** Instr classics, Gonzaga Prep, 50-52; instr, St Francis Xavier Div, 52-53, from asst prof to assoc prof, 61-74, dean, 62-65, Prof Classics, Gonzaga Univ, 74-, Chmn Dept Class Lang, 68-, Prof Hist, 76- **MEMBERSHIPS** Am Philol Asn; Archaeol Inst Am; Asn Ancient Historians. **RESEARCH** Justin's Epitome of Pompeius Trogus. **SELECTED PUBLICATIONS** Auth, A Mosaic Interpretation Of Jerome, 'In Hiezechielem'/, Vigiliae Christianae, Vol 0049, 1995; The 2 Women In The Mosaic Of Santa-Pudenziana + Exploring The Exegetical, Apologetic, And Illustrative Significance Of Roman Theodosian Classicism/, J Of Early Christian Studies, Vol 0003, 1995; The Clash Of Gods - A Reinterpretation Of Early-Christian Art - Mathews,Tf/, Heythrop J-A Quart Rev Of Philos And Theol, Vol 0037, 1996. **CONTACT ADDRESS** Dept of Class Lang, Gonzaga Univ, 502 E Boone Ave, Spokane, WA, 99258-0001.

SCHLAUCH, WOLFGANG T.

PERSONAL Born 07/05/1935, Plochingen, Germany, m, 1964, 2 children **DISCIPLINE** MODERN EUROPEAN HISTORY **EDUCATION** Univ Freiburg, Staatsexamen, 62, PhD, 65. **CAREER** Teacher Ger, 62-65; asst prof hist, Converse Col, 65-67; assoc prof, Univ Miss, 67-69; assoc prof, 69-73, PROF HIST, EASTERN ILL UNIV, 73-98, PROF EMER, 7/98-; Vis prof, Univ Southern Queensland, spring 96. **HONORS AND AWARDS** Oustanding Fac Award, Eastern Ill Univ, 85. **MEMBERSHIPS** Ger Studies Asn; Conf Group Ger Politics. **RESEARCH** Twentieth century Europe; modern Germany; diplomatic history. **SELECTED PUBLICATIONS** Co-auth, The United States and the Federal Republic of Germany, Contacts and Relations in Historical and Cultural Perspective, Am Asc of Teachers, 77; Dissent in Eastern Europe:Rudolfo Bahro's Criticism of Eastern European Communism, Nationalities Papers, 81; West Germany: Reliable Part ner? Perspectives on Recent American-German Relations, Ger Studies Rev, 85; Ruestungshilfe der USA 1939-1945, 2nd ed, Bernard & Graefe, 86; The Atlantic Alliance at the Crossroads: A Changing Relationship, in War and Peace, Perspective in the Nuclear Age, Tex Tech Univ Press, 88; Defense and Security: The SPD and East-West Relations and Society in Germany, Austria and Switzerland, 90; The German Social Demeocrats and the Greens: A Challenge to the Western Alliance, Peace and Change, 90; Foreign Minister Genscher's Foreign Policy: Continuity or Ambiguity, European Studies J, 94. **CONTACT ADDRESS** 821 Raleigh Rd, Las Cruces, NM, 88005. **EMAIL** cfwgs@eiu.edu

SCHLEIFER, JAMES THOMAS

PERSONAL Born 11/15/1942, Rochester, NY, m, 1964, 2 children **DISCIPLINE** AMERICAN HISTORY **EDUCATION** Hamilton Col, BA, 64; Yale Univ, MA, 66; MPhil, 68, PhD(hist), 72. **CAREER** From instr to assoc prof, 69-83, PROF AM HIST, COL NEW ROCHELLE, 83-; Dir Gill Library Col New Rochelle, 87-; vis prof, Univ Paris, 86; vis lect, Yale Univ, 83, 84, 95; Am Coun Learned Soc fel, 74-75 & 81-82; vis fel, Hist Dept, Yale Univ, 81-82; res grant, Am Philos Soc, 79, 85; Nat Endowment for Humanities res grant, 82-83. **HONORS AND AWARDS** George Washington Egleston Prize, Yale Univ, 72; Gilbert Chinard Incentive Award, Soc Fr Hist Studies, 74; Merle Curti Award, Orgn Am Hist, 81. **MEMBERSHIPS** French Nat Comm for Publication of Complete Works of Tocqueville, 86-; Am Hist Asn; Orgn Am Historians; Soc Fr Hist Studies; Tocqueville Soc; Soc Historians Early Repub. **RESEARCH** Alexis de Tocqueville; European-American intellectual and cultural relations; American intellectual history; hist Am Higher Educ. **SELECTED PUBLICATIONS** Contribr, Writing History, Appleton, 2nd ed, 67; auth, Alexis de Tocqueville describes the American character: two previously unpublished portraits, S Atlantic Quart, spring 75; Images of America after the Revolution: Tocqueville and Beaumont visit the early Republic, 1/77 & How democracy influences preaching: a previously unpublished chapter from Tocqueville's Democracy in America, 10/77 & Tocqueville and American literature: A newly acquired letter, 1/80, & Tocqueville and Centrailization, 10/83, Yale Univ Libr Gazette; The Making of Tocqueville's Democracy: How Alexis de Tocqueville's Famous Work on America Developed, Univ NC, 80; Spanish translation, Fondo de Cultura Economica, 85 and rev ed, Liberty Fund, 99; contribr, Dictionary of French History, Greenwood, 86; auth, Tocqueville, Bouquin ed, Laffont, 86; auth, Reconsidering Tocqueville's Democracy in America, Rutgers, 88; auth, A Passion for Liberty: Tocqueville in Democracy and Revolution, Library of Congress, 89; Liberty of Expression in America and in France, Wilson Center, 88; auth, Interpreting Tocqueville's Democracy in America, Univ Press of Am, 91; auth, Liberty/Liberte: The American and French Experiences, Johns Hopkins, 92; Liberty, Equality, Democracy, NY Univ Press, 92; co-ed, De la Democratie en Amerique, Pleiade Edition, Gallimard, 92; auth, The College of New Rochelle: An Extraordinary Story, Donning, 94. **CONTACT ADDRESS** Gill Library, Col of New Rochelle, New Rochelle, NY, 10805. **EMAIL** jschleifer@cnr.edu

SCHLEINER, WINFRIED H.

PERSONAL Born 10/19/1938, Mannheim, Germany, m, 1968, 2 children **DISCIPLINE** ENGLISH & COMPARITIVE LITERATURE **EDUCATION** Univ Kiel, Staatsexamen, 64; Brown Univ, MA, 65, PhD, 68. **CAREER** Asst master & schoolmaster Eng & French, Max-Planck-Schule, Kiel, Ger, 68-70; asst prof Eng, RI Col, 70-73; asst prof, 73-75, assoc prof eng, Univ CA, Davis, 75. **HONORS AND AWARDS** UC Pres Fel Hum; Neh; Foreign Lib; Wolfenbuttel Biblothek fel. **MEMBERSHIPS** MLA; 16th Century Conf; Renaissance Soc Am; Am soc Hist of Med. **RESEARCH** Renaissance lit; comp lit; linguistics; hist med; gender studies. **SELECTED PUBLICATIONS** Auth, The Imagery of John Donne's Sermons, Brown Univ, 70; Aeneas' flight from Troy, Comp Lit, 75; Franklin and the infant Hercules, 18th Century Studies, 76-77; coauth, New material from the Grimm-Emerson correspondence, Harvard Libr Bull, 77; The Imagery of John Donnes Sermons, Brown Univ Press, 70; Melancholy Genius and Utopia in the Renaissance, Harrassowitz, 91; Medical Ethics in the Renaissance, Georgetown Univ Press, 95; A plot to his mose and cares cutt of: Schoppe as seen by the Archbishop of Canterbury, Renaissance and Reformation, 95; Cross-Dressing, Gender Errors and Sexual Taboos in Renaissance Literature in: Gender Reversals and Gender Cultures, London, 96. **CONTACT ADDRESS** Dept of Eng, Univ of California, Davis, CA, 95616-5200. **EMAIL** whschleiner@ucdavis.edu

SCHLERETH, THOMAS J.

PERSONAL Born 03/23/1941, Pittsburgh, PA, m, 1973, 1 child **DISCIPLINE** AMERICAN HISTORY AND STUDIES **EDUCATION** Univ Notre Dame, BA, 63; Univ Wisc, MA, 65; Univ Iowa, PhD, 69. **CAREER** Newberry Libr jr fel hist, 67-69; asst prof, hist & amer studies, Grinnell Col, 69-72; asst prof, 72-77, assoc prof, amer studies & chairman dept, 77-78, Univ Notre Dame; Nat facul fel, Nat Facul Found, 94-. **HONORS AND AWARDS** Facul fel, The Reilly Ctr for Sci, Tech and Values, Univ Notre Dame; Newberry Libr facul fel hist, 70-71; Nat Endowment for Humanities fel archit hist, 77-78; assoc, Danforth Found, 77-83; Newberry Libr fel hist, 78; Henry Francis DuPont Winterthur Mus scholar, 77, 83; The Public Historian, 86; Best Scholarly Article, 85-86; Presidential award, Univ Notre Dame, 86; Nat Endow for the Humanities Res fel, 77, 87; Rodger D. Branigin Scholar award, Franklin Col, 87; sr res fel, Smithsonian Inst, 88; Elsie Crews Parson prize, Ctr for Amer Culture Studies, 90; Henry H. Douglas Distinguished Scholar award, 94. **MEMBERSHIPS** Amer Studies Asn; Soc Archit Hist; Orgn Amer Hist; Asn State & Local Hist; Amer Asn Advan Humanities. **RESEARCH** American cultural history; Material culture studies; Urban architectural history; Landscape history. **SELECTED PUBLICATIONS** Auth, Victorian America: Transformations in Everyday Life, 1876-1915, Harper & Row, 91; auth, Cultural History and Material Culture, UMI Res Press, 90; auth, Reading the Road, Univ Tenn Press, 97; auth, A Dome of Learning: The University of Notre Dame's Main Building, Univ Notre Dame Alumni Asn, 91; co-ed, American Home Life, 1890-1930: A Social History of Spaces and Services, Univ Tenn Press, 92, 94; co-auth, Sense of Place: American Regional Cultures, Univ Press of Ky, 90, 94; auth, The Industrial Belt, Garland Publ, 87; auth, U.S. 40: A Roadscape of the American Experience, Ind Univ Press, 84; auth, Material Culture Studies in America, Amer Asn for State and Local Hist, 82; auth, Artifacts and The American Past, Amer Asn for State and Local Hist, 82; auth, The Cosmopolitan Ideal in Enlightenment Thought, Univ Notre Dame Press, The University of Notre Dame, A Portrait of Its History and Campus, Univ Notre Dame Press, 76, 79, 92. **CONTACT ADDRESS** Dept. of American Studies, Univ of Notre Dame, 303 O'Shaughnessy Hall, Notre Dame, IN, 46556. **EMAIL** thomas.j.schlereth.2@nd.edu

SCHLESINGER, JOSEPH ABRAHAM

PERSONAL Born 01/04/1922, Boston, MA, m, 1951, 2 children **DISCIPLINE** POLITICAL SCIENCE **EDUCATION** Univ Chicago, Econ, AB, 42; Harvard Grad Sch Educ, Tchg, AM, 47; Yale Univ, Polit Sci, 55. **CAREER** Instr, Soc Sci, Boston Univ Gen Coll, 47-49; tchg fel, Pol Sci, Wesleyan Univ, 52-53; instr, Soc Sci/Polit Sci, Mich state Univ, 53-55; asst prof, Mich State Univ, 55-59; assoc prof, Mich State Univ, 59-63; vis prof, Polit Sci, Univ Calif, Berkeley, 64-65; prof, Mich State Univ, 63-91; EMER PROF, 91-. **MEMBERSHIPS** Am Polit sci Asn; Midwest Polit Sci Asn **RESEARCH** American and French political parties. **SELECTED PUBLICATIONS** Political Parties and the winning of Office, Univ Mich Press, 91; "Understanding Political Parties: Back to Basic," Am Rev Polit, 93; coauth, "French Parties and the Legislative Elections of 1993," Party Polit, 95; coauth, "Dual Ballot Elections and Political Parties, The French Presidential Election of 1995," Comp Polit Stud, 98; coauth, "The Stability of the French Party System: The Enduring Impact of the Two-Ballot Electoral Rules," How France Votes, 98. **CONTACT ADDRESS** Dept Polit Sci, Michigan State Univ, East Lansing, MI, 48824. **EMAIL** schlesi@pilot.msu.edu

SCHLESINGER, ROGER

PERSONAL Born 12/23/1943, London, England, m, 1998 **DISCIPLINE** HISTORY **EDUCATION** Univ Ill, PhD, 69. **CAREER** Prof & dept chair, Hist Dept, Washington State Univ, 1968-. **MEMBERSHIPS** Am Hist Asn; Soc Hist Discoveries. **RESEARCH** Renaissance exploration; European-American Indian contact. **SELECTED PUBLICATIONS** Coauth, Andre Thevet's North America: A Sixteenth Century View, McGill-Queens, 86; auth, Portraits from the Age of Exploration, Univ Ill Press, 93; auth, In the Wake of Columbus, Harlan-Davidson, 96. **CONTACT ADDRESS** Dept Hist, Wash State Univ, Pullman, WA, 99164-4030. **EMAIL** schlesin@wsu.edu

SCHLEUNES, KARL ALBERT

PERSONAL Born 04/21/1937, Kiel, WI, m, 1964 **DISCIPLINE** MODERN GERMAN HISTORY **EDUCATION** Lakeland Col, BA, 59; Univ Minn, MA, 61, PhD(Ger hist), 66. **CAREER** Asst prof mod Europ hist, Univ Ill, Chicago, 65-71, res fel, 67; ASSOC PROF MOD EUROP HIST, UNIV NC, GREENSBORO, 71-, Soc Sci Res Coun grant, 71-72; Nat Endowment for Humanities res grant, 73. **MEMBERSHIPS** AHA; Hist Kommission der Deutschen Ges fur Erziehungswissenschaft. **RESEARCH** Nineteenth- and 20th-century Germany; history of education. **SELECTED PUBLICATIONS** Auth, the Twisted Road to Auschwitz, 70; auth, Schooling and Society: the Politics of Education in Prussia and Bavaria, 89. **CONTACT ADDRESS** Dept of History, Univ of No Carolina, 1000 Spring Garden, Greensboro, NC, 27402-6170. **EMAIL** kaschleu@hamlet.uncg.edu

SCHLOTTERBECK, JOHN THOMAS

PERSONAL Born 02/29/1948, Lynn, MA, m, 1973, 1 child **DISCIPLINE** AMERICAN HISTORY **EDUCATION** Johns Hopkins Univ, BA, 70, MA, 74, PhD(Am hist), 80; Univ Mich, MA, 72. **CAREER** Instr Am hist, Western Md Col, 74-75, asst prof, 76; instr, Oberlin Col, 77-78; instr, 78-80, ASST PROF

AM HIST, DEPAUW UNIV, 80- **MEMBERSHIPS** Orgn Am Historians; Southern Hist Asn; Inst Early Am Hist & Cult. **RESEARCH** Nineteenth century Southern society; rural and agricultural history; American slavery. **SELECTED PUBLICATIONS** Auth, From Congregation Town To Industrial-City - Cult And Soc-Change In A Southern Community - Shirley,M/, J Of Southern Hist, Vol 0061, 1995; 1 South Or Many - Plantation Belt And Upcountry In Civil-War Era Tennessee - Mckenzie,Rt/, J Of Southern Hist, Vol 0062, 1996; Tobacco Merchant - The Story Of Universal-Leaf-Tobacco-Company - Duke,M, Jordan,Dp/, Va Mag Of Hist And Biog, Vol 0104, 1996. **CONTACT ADDRESS** Dept of Hist, DePauw Univ, 313 S Locust St, Greencastle, IN, 46135-1736.

SCHLUNZ, THOMAS PAUL
PERSONAL Born 08/15/1941, Clinton, IA **DISCIPLINE** MEDIEVAL EUROPEAN HISTORY **EDUCATION** Belmont Abbey Col, AB, 65; Univ Ill, Urbana, AM, 67, PhD(hist), 73. **CAREER** Instr hist, Ohio Univ, Portsmouth, 67-69; instr, 73-74, asst prof, assoc prof, 74-84, Univ New Orleans, 84-. **MEMBERSHIPS** Haskins Soc. **RESEARCH** Anglo-Norman ecclesiastical history. **SELECTED PUBLICATIONS** Auth, Church and state in Normandy at the time of the Becket controversy, McNeese Rev, Vol XXIV, 58 & 75-75. **CONTACT ADDRESS** Dept of History, Univ of New Orleans, 2000 Lakeshore Dr, New Orleans, LA, 70148-0001.

SCHMANDT, RAYMOND HENRY
PERSONAL Born 09/20/1925, Indianapolis, IN, m, 1949, 2 children **DISCIPLINE** EUROPEAN HISTORY **EDUCATION** St Louis Univ, AB, 47, AM, 49; Univ Mich, AM & PhD(hist), 52. **CAREER** Instr Ger, St Louis Univ, 46-50; from instr to asst prof hist, DePaul Univ, 52-58; from asst prof to assoc prof, Loyola Univ, Ill, 58-66; chmn dept, 73-76, PROF HIST, ST JOSEPH'S COL, PA, 66-, Ed, Records Am Cath Hist Soc Phila, 68-73. **MEMBERSHIPS** AHA; Am Cath Hist Asn; Mediaeval Acad Am; Am Soc Reformation Res; Am Soc Church Hist. **RESEARCH** Medieval German and ecclesiastical history. **SELECTED PUBLICATIONS** Auth, The Am-Cath-Hist-Assoc Spring Meeting/, Cath Hist Rev, Vol 0079, 1993; Christ,Gunter - Studies On The Imperial Church During The 17th- And 18th-Century - Ger - Huttl,L, Salzman,R, Ed/, Church Hist, Vol 0062, 1993; Janssens,Francis, 1843-1897 - A Dutch-Am Prelate - Kasteel,A/, J Of Southern Hist, Vol 0059, 1993; Count And Bishop In Medieval Germany - A Study Of Regional Power, 1100-1350 - Arnold,B/, Speculum-A J Of Medieval Studies, Vol 0069, 1994; Province And Empire - Brittany And The Carolingians - Smith,Jmh/, Church Hist, Vol 0064, 1995; Nolan,Hugh,Joseph - Obituary/, Cath Hist Rev, Vol 0081, 1995; Under Crescent And Cross - The Jews In The Middle-Ages - Cohen,Mr/, Church Hist, Vol 0065, 1996. **CONTACT ADDRESS** Dept of Hist, St Joseph's Col, Philadelphia, PA, 19131.

SCHMAUS, WARREN STANLEY
PERSONAL Born 04/02/1952, Staten Island, NY, m, 1979, 2 children **DISCIPLINE** PHILOSOPHY & HISTORY OF SCIENCE **EDUCATION** Princeton Univ, AB, 74; Univ Pittsburgh, MA, 75, PhD(Hist & Philos of Sci), 80. **CAREER** Asst prof Philos, Ill Inst Technol, 80-, res assoc, Study Ethics in Professions, Ill Inst Technol, 80-; asst prof Phil, Ill Inst Technol, 80-85; from assoc prof to prof, 85-95. **HONORS AND AWARDS** Vis fel, Center for Philosophy of Science, Univ of Pittsburgh, 96-97; vis scholar, Univ Chicago, 87-88. **MEMBERSHIPS** Am Philos Asn; Philos Sci Asn; Hist Sci Soc; Cheiron; Soc Social Studies Sci. **RESEARCH** History and philosophy of the social sciences; philosophy of history; ethics of research. **SELECTED PUBLICATIONS** Auth, Fraud and sloppiness in science, Perspectives on Professions, 9 & 12/81; A reappraisal of Comte's three-state law, Hist & Theory, 5/82; Durkheim's Philosophy of Science and the Cosiology of Knowledge, Univ of Chicago Press, 94; some 30 articles. **CONTACT ADDRESS** Dept of Humanities, Illinois Inst of Tech, 3300 S Federal St, Chicago, IL, 60616-3793. **EMAIL** schmaus@charlie.iit.edu

SCHMELING, GARETH LON
PERSONAL Born 05/28/1940, Algoma, Wis, m, 1963 **DISCIPLINE** GREEK & LATIN LITERATURE **EDUCATION** Northwestern Col, Wis, BA, 63; Univ Wis, MA, 64, PhD(Greek & Latin), 68. **CAREER** Asst prof Greek & Latin, Univ Va, 68-70; assoc prof, 70-75, Prof & Chmn Dept Classics, Univ Fla, 75-93, Dir, Humanities Ctr, 78-90, prof, Classics, 93-98, Disting prof, 98-, Am Philos Soc fel, 70-78; Univ Fla fel, 71-74; Nat Endowment for Humanities fel, 73-74; Am Coun Learned Soc grant-in-aid, 74; Rome prize, Am Acad, Rome, 77-78. **MEMBERSHIPS** Am Philos Asn; Am Class League; Class Asn Mid W & S; Vergilian Soc; Soc Studies Classics, France. **RESEARCH** Ancient prose fiction; Petronius; Apuleius, Chariton, Xenophon. **SELECTED PUBLICATIONS** Contribr, Exclusus Amator Motif in Petronius, Baccola & Gili, Turin, 71; ed, Cornelius Nepos: Lives of Famous Mem, Coronado, 71; auth, Chariton, Twayne, 74; coauth, TS Eliot and Petronius, Comp Lit Ser, 75; coauth, Bibliography of Petronius, Brill, Leiden, 77; auth, The satyricon: Forms in search of a genre, Class Bull, 71; Humanities perspectives on the professions, Lib Educ, 77; Xenophon of Ephesus, Twayne, 80; Authority of the Author: From Muse to Aesthetics, MCSN, 81; auth, Manners and Morality in the Historia Apollonii, Picolo Moando Antico, Univ Perugin, 89; auth, The Satyricon: Sense of an Ending, Rheisches Museum, 91; auth, Notes to the Text of the Historian Apollonii, Ramuz, 94; auth, Notes to the Text of the Historian Apollonii, Latomus, 94; auth, Quid attinet veritaten per interpretem quaerere, Ramus, 94; auth, The Novel in the Ancient World, Brill, Leinden, 96; Ed, A History of Roman Literature, Brill, Leiden, 97; auth, Qui Miscuit Utile Dulci, Bolchozy, 98. **CONTACT ADDRESS** Dept of Classics, Univ of Fla, 3c Arts and Sciences, Gainesville, FL, 32611-9500. **EMAIL** schemlin@classics.ufl.edu

SCHMELLER, HELMUT JOHN
PERSONAL Born 09/02/1932, Baernau, m, 1963, 2 children **DISCIPLINE** EUROPEAN HISTORY **EDUCATION** Univ Erlangen, AB, 58; Ft Hays State Univ, MA, 68; Kans State Univ, PhD(hist), 75. **CAREER** PROF HIST, FT HAYS STATE UNIV, 66- **MEMBERSHIPS** Western Asn Ger Studies; Soc Ger Am Studies (first vpres, 81-83). **RESEARCH** National socialism; anti-Semitism; German-American studies. **SELECTED PUBLICATIONS** Auth, The Nazi Menace In Argentina, 1931-1947 - Newton,Rc/, Historian, Vol 0055, 1993; The Price Of Freedom - A Hist Of East-Central-Europe From The Middle-Ages To The Present - Wandycz,Ps/, Historian, Vol 0056, 1994; Germans In Russia - Foreigners In The East - Hist, Present-Day Situation, Perspectives - Ger - Dietz,B, Hilkes,P/, Jahrbucher Fur Geschichte Osteuropas, Vol 0042, 1994. **CONTACT ADDRESS** Dept of Hist, Fort Hays State Univ, Hays, KS, 67601.

SCHMID, A. ALLAN
PERSONAL Born 02/12/1935, NE, m, 2 children **DISCIPLINE** AGRICULTURAL ECONOMICS **EDUCATION** Univ Nebr, BSc, 56; Univ Wis, PhD, 59. **CAREER** Asst prof, 59-64, assoc prof, 64-68, prof, 68-, Mich State Univ. **HONORS AND AWARDS** Distinguished Univ Prof. **MEMBERSHIPS** Amer Econ Assn; Amer Agric Econ Assn; Assn Evolutionary Econ. **RESEARCH** Institutional and behavioral economics. **SELECTED PUBLICATIONS** Ed, Beyond Agricultural and Economics, 97; coauth, The Economy As a Process of Evaluation, 97; coauth, "Costs and Power," in Nahid Aslanbeigui and Young Back Chois, 97; auth, "The Environmental and Property Rights," in Handbook of Environmental Economics, 95; coauth, "Interest Groups, Selective Incentives, Cleverness, History and Emotion: The case of the American Soybean Association," Journ of Economic Behavior and Organization, vol 31, 97. **CONTACT ADDRESS** Dept of Agricultural Economics, Michigan State Univ, East Lansing, MI, 48224. **EMAIL** schmid@pilot.msu.edu

SCHMIDHAUSER, JOHN RICHARD
PERSONAL Born 01/03/1922, Bronx, NY, m, 1952, 7 children **DISCIPLINE** POLITICAL SCIENCE **EDUCATION** Univ Del, BA, 49; Univ Va, MA, 52; PhD, 54; res fel, 58, inst, judicial process, Univ Wisc; sr fel, law & behavioral sci, 59-60, Law Schl Univ Chicago. **CAREER** Grad instr, 52-54, Dupont Fel, 50-53, Univ Va; instr, 54-55, asst prof, 55-60, res prof, 59, assoc prof, 60-63, prof, 63-65, 67-73, Univ Iowa; res prof, Natl Sci Found Grant, 70-72; prof, 73-92, chmn, 73-75, 77-80, Univ S Calif; Proj '87, grantee, 80-81; Frank Talbot Vis Prof of Govern, 82-83, Univ Va; Wormuth Dist Scholar, 84, Univ Utah; dist vis prof, 84, Simon Fraser Univ, BC; dist vis prof, 85, So Ill Univ. **HONORS AND AWARDS** Phi Kappa Phi, 49; Phi Beta Kappa, 54; Raven Soc, 54; Univ Va Sesquicentennial Award, pub svc, 69; Phi Sigma Alpha Fac Excel Award, 84; Golden key Award for Res, 91; Raubenheimer Award, dist tchng & res, 91. **SELECTED PUBLICATIONS** Coauth, Age and Political Behavior, Concepts & Issues in Gerontology, Von Nostrand, 75; coauth, Political Corruption and Congress, Gen Lrng Press, 76; auth, Whales and Salmon: The Interface of Pacific Ocean and Cross-National Policy-Making, The Law of the Sea: Issues in Ocean Rsrc Mgt, Praeger Pub, 77; coauth, Whaling in Japanese-American Relations, Westview Press, 78; auth, Future International Shocks Related to Ocean Food Resources, Whaling in Japanese-American Rel, Westview Press, 78; auth, Judges and Justices, Little Brown & Co, 79; auth, Constitutional Law in American Politics, Brooks/Cole Pub, 84; auth, Comparative Judicial Systems: Challenging Frontiers in Conceptual and Empirical Analysis, Butterworths, 87. **CONTACT ADDRESS** Dept of Political Science, Univ of Southern California, Los Angeles, CA, 90007.

SCHMIDT, GREG
DISCIPLINE AMERICAN HISTORY **EDUCATION** Univ Ill, BA, MA, PhD. **CAREER** Prof; **MEMBERSHIPS** NCTE, MLA, TESOL, Dep Comp Comt. **RESEARCH** American social, intellectual and Constitutional history. **SELECTED PUBLICATIONS** Rev, Colonial Life, Am Studies, 79; Book Culture in Post-Revolutionary Virginia, Jour Early Republic, 86. **CONTACT ADDRESS** Winona State Univ, PO Box 5838, Winona, MN, 55987-5838.

SCHMIDT, HENRY CONRAD
PERSONAL Born 05/07/1937, Southampton, NY, m, 1966 **DISCIPLINE** LATIN AMERICAN HISTORY **EDUCATION** Univ Tex, Austin, BA, 60, MA, 69, PhD(Latin Am hist), 72. **CAREER** Asst prof, 72-78, ASSOC PROF HIST, TEX A&M UNIV, 78- **MEMBERSHIPS** Latin Am Studies Asn. **RESEARCH** Latin American culture and thought. **SELECTED PUBLICATIONS** Auth, Toward The Innerscape Of Mexican Historiology - Liberalism And The History Of Ideas/, Mexican Studies-Estudios Mexicanos, Vol 0008, 1992; Heretic Texts - Spa - Krauze,E/, Historia Mexicana, Vol 0043, 1993; South Of The Border - Mexico In The Am Imagination, 1914-1947 - Oles,J/, Southwestern Hist Quart, Vol 0098, 1994; The Latin-Americans - Spirit And Ethos - Dealy,Gc/, Hisp Am Hist Rev, Vol 0074, 1994. **CONTACT ADDRESS** Dept of Hist, Tex A&M Univ Col, 1 Texas A and M Univ, College Station, TX, 77843.

SCHMIDT, KLAUS
DISCIPLINE AMERICAN STUDIES **EDUCATION** Univ Mainz, BA, 85, MA, 88, PhD, 94. **CAREER** ASST PROF, BRITISH & AM STUD, UNIV MAINZ **MEMBERSHIPS** Am Antiquarian Soc **SELECTED PUBLICATIONS** Auth, "The Outsider's Vision", Lang, 94; co-ed, New Critical Essays on American Literature, Lang, 95; co-ed, Blurred Boundaries: Critical Essays on American Literature, Language, and Culture, Lang, 96; auth, "Between Creativity and Conformity: Marginality and Gender in Toni Morrison's Sula," in Transfer: Ubersetzen-Dolmetschen-Interkulturalitat, Lang, 97; co-ed, "Anything But Well Explored": New Essays on Early American Culture, Lang; auth, "Teaching Native Son in a German Undergraduate Literature Class," in Approaches to Teaching Wright's Native Son. **CONTACT ADDRESS** Institut fur Anglistik und Amerikanistik, Universitat Mainz, Germersheim, ., D-76711. **EMAIL** Schmidtk@nfask1.fask.uni-mainz.de

SCHMIDT, MARTIN EDWARD
PERSONAL Born 04/24/1935, Hartford, CT, 2 children **DISCIPLINE** HISTORY **EDUCATION** Kent State Univ, BS, 59, MA, 60; Univ PA, PhD(Hist), 66. **CAREER** Asst prof hist, Univ WI-Oshkosh, 66-69; asst chemn grad affairs, 76-78, asst prof hist, 70-74, assoc prof hist, Univ WI-Milwaukee, 74-, asst chemn undergrad affairs, 81-, retired; Am Philos Soc res fel, 70 & 74. **MEMBERSHIPS** Western Soc Fr Hist. **RESEARCH** Modern France; European diplomatic. **SELECTED PUBLICATIONS** Auth, Prelude to intervention: Madagascar and the failure of Anglo-French diplomacy, 1890-95, Hist J, 4/72; Le Parlement and the definition of the liberal Third Republic, 1879-1883, Can J Hist, 2/74; Alexandre Ribot: Odyssey of a Liberal in the Third Republic, Martinus Nijhoff, 74. **CONTACT ADDRESS** Dept Hist, Univ Wisconsin, PO Box 413, Milwaukee, WI, 53201-0413.

SCHMIDT, WILLIAM JOHN
PERSONAL Born 05/22/1926, Green Bay, WI, m, 1949 **DISCIPLINE** CHURCH HISTORY **EDUCATION** N Cent Col, BA, 51; Evangel Theol Sem, BD, 54; Columbia Univ, PhD (church hist), 66. **CAREER** Pastor, Wis Conf Evangel United Brethren Church, 52-62; tutor, Union Theol Sem, 62-65; from asst prof to assoc prof church hist, NY Theol Sem, 67-70; adj assoc prof church hist, 67-70, assoc prof, 70-78, Prof Theol, St Peter's Col, NJ, 78-, Res writer with Samuel McCrea Cavert on The American Churches in the Ecumenical Movement, 1900-1968, 65-67; mem Gen Prog Coun, Reformed Church Am, 70-76. **MEMBERSHIPS** Am Soc Church Hist; N Am Acad Ecumenists (secy-treas, 68-72). **RESEARCH** American church history; history of the ecumenical movement; religous syncretism. **SELECTED PUBLICATIONS** Auth, Weigel,Gustave - A Pioneer Of Reform - Collins,Pw/, J Of Ecumenical Studies, Vol 0030, 1993; Between The Flood And The Rainbow - Interpreting The Conciliar Process Of Mutual Commitment Covenant To Justice, Peace, And The Integrity Of Creation - Niles,Dp, Editor/, J Of Ecumenical Studies, Vol 0030, 1993; The Cath-Church In Mission - Highlights Of Church Teaching Since 1891 - Daniels,E/, J Of Ecumenical Studies, Vol 0031, 1994; Directory For The Application Of Principles And Norms On Ecumenism - United-States-Cath-Conference/, J Of Ecumenical Studies, Vol 0031, 1994. **CONTACT ADDRESS** Dept of Theol, St Peter's Col, Kennedy Blvd, Jersey City, NJ, 07306.

SCHMITT, HANS ADOLF
PERSONAL Born 06/06/1921, Frankfurt am Main, Germany, m, 1944, 3 children **DISCIPLINE** HISTORY **EDUCATION** Washington & Lee Univ, AB, 40; Univ Chicago, MA, 43, PhD(hist), 53. **CAREER** Asst prof hist, Ala State Teachers Col, Florence, 48-50; from asst prof to assoc prof, Univ Okla, 53-59; from assoc prof to prof, Tulane Univ, 59-67; prof, NY Univ, 67-71; mem, Ctr Advan Studies, 71-73, PROF HIST, UNIV VA, 71-, Fulbright Scholar, Belgium & Luxembourg, 56-57; Tulane Univ Fac Res Coun fel, 63 & 65-66; Sesqui-centennial assoc, Ctr Advan Studies, Univ Va, 77. **HONORS AND AWARDS** Louis G Beer Prize, AHA, 63. **MEMBERSHIPS** AHA; Southern Hist Asn (exec coun, 74-77); Soc Mod Hist, France; Soc Fr Hist Studies (pres, 66-67); Conf Group Cent Europ Hist. **RESEARCH** French intellectual history; problems of political integration on the national and international level; German constitutional history. **SELECTED PUBLICATIONS** Auth, Ger Resistance Against Hitler - The Search For Allies Abroad, 1938-1945 - Vonklemperer,K/, J Of Mil Hist, Vol 0057, 1993; For Prince And Fatherland - Establishment Of Legitimacy In

Bavaria Between 1848 Revolution And Ger Unity - Ger - Hanisch,M/, J Of Modern Hist, Vol 0066, 1994; More, Not Less, Hist/, Va Quart Rev, Vol 0070, 1994; Postcolonial Criticism + Response To Jacoby,Russell Portrayal Of The Shortcomings Of Postcolonial Theorists/, Lingua Franca, Vol 0006, 1995; A Very Civil-War - The Swiss Sonderbund-War Of 1847 - Remak,J/, J Of Mil Hist, Vol 0059, 1995; To The Ed/, Am Hist Rev, Vol 0101, 1996; Wilhelm-Ii, Volume 2, Emperor And Exile, 1900-1941 - Cecil,L/, J Of Mil Hist, Vol 0061, 1997. **CONTACT ADDRESS** Dept of Hist, Univ of Va, Charlottesville, VA, 22903.

SCHMITTER, AMY
DISCIPLINE HISTORY OF EARLY MODERN PHILOSOPHY, HISTORY OF METAPHYSICS, PHILOSOPHY OF A **EDUCATION** Bryn Mawr Col, AB, 84; grad work, Univ Bonn, 88-89; Univ Pittsburgh, PhD, 93. **CAREER** Asst prof, Univ NMex. **SELECTED PUBLICATIONS** Auth, Representation, Self-Representation, and the Passions in Descartes, Rev of Metaphysics, Vol XVII, No 2, Dec 94; Formal Causation and the Explanation of Intentionality in Descartes, The Monist, Jl 96. **CONTACT ADDRESS** Univ NMex, Albuquerque, NM, 87131.

SCHNEIDER, CATHY
DISCIPLINE COMPARATIVE POLITICS AND POLITICAL THEORY **EDUCATION** SUNY Albany, BA, MA; Cornell Univ, MA, PhD. **CAREER** Prof, Am Univ. **HONORS AND AWARDS** Aaron Diamond Post-Doctoral Fel, 93-96. **RESEARCH** Past dependency in social movements in neighborhood organization. **SELECTED PUBLICATIONS** Auth, Shantytown Protest in Pinochet's Chile,Temple Univ Press, 95. **CONTACT ADDRESS** American Univ, 4400 Massachusetts Ave, Washington, DC, 20016.

SCHNEIDER, JOANNE
DISCIPLINE GERMAN HISTORY, MODERN EUROPEAN HISTORY, WOMEN'S HISTORY **EDUCATION** St Olaf Col, BA; Brown Univ, MA, PhD. **CAREER** Instr, RI Col. **RESEARCH** 18th and 19th century Ger soc, intellectual, cult hist. **SELECTED PUBLICATIONS** Co-comp, Women in Western European History. **CONTACT ADDRESS** Rhode Island Col, Providence, RI, 02908.

SCHNEIDER, LAURENCE
DISCIPLINE CHINA **EDUCATION** Wash Univ, AB, 58, Univ Calif, MA, 60, PhD, 68. **CAREER** Asst prof to prof, State Univ NY, Buffalo, 66-91; Assoc dean, soc sci, 87-91; Prof, Wash Univ, 91- ; Dir, Int Studies fice, 91-93; Chair, Hist Grad Comt, 94. **HONORS AND AWARDS** Nat Endowment Hum fel, 69-70; Soc Sci Res Coun grants, 73-74, 81-82; Nat Sci Found grant, 78-79; NY Coun Hum grant, 85. **SELECTED PUBLICATIONS** Auth, The Rockefeller Foundation, the China Foundation, and the Development Modern Science in China, Soc Sci & Med, 82; Ed, Lysenkoism In China: Profoceedings The 1956 Qingdao Genetics Symposium, Sharpe, 86; Genetics in Republican China, 1920-1949; Science And Medicine In Twentieth Century China: Research And Education, Univ Mich Ctr Chinese Studies, 88; Learning from Russia: Lysenkoism and the Fate Genetics in China, 1950-1986, Sci & Technol In Post-Mao China, Harvard Univ Profess,89. **CONTACT ADDRESS** Washington Univ, 1 Brookings Dr, St. Louis, MO, 63130.

SCHNEIDER, ROBERT J.
PERSONAL Born 02/28/1939, Saginaw, MI, m, 1997 **DISCIPLINE** GENERAL STUDIES-HUMANITIES; MEDIEVAL STUDIES. **EDUCATION** Univ of the South, BA, 61; Univ of Notre Dame, MSM, 63, DSM, 65. **CAREER** Asst prof, 65-68, Univ of Southern CA; asst prof, 68, assoc 72, prof, 81, distinguished prof of general studies, 98, Berea Col. **HONORS AND AWARDS** Seabury Award for Excellence in Teaching, 89; Acorn Award for excellence in teaching and scholarship, 93; Templeton Found Sci and Relig Course Prize, 97. **MEMBERSHIPS** Medieval Acad of Amer; Soc for Values in Higher Education; Episcopal Church Working Group on Science, Technology, and Faith. **RESEARCH** Issues in science and religion. **SELECTED PUBLICATIONS** Auth, Vincent of Beauvais' Opus universale de statu principis: A Reconstruction of Its History and Contents, in Vincent de Beauvais: intentions et receptions d'une oeuvre encyclopedique au moyen-age, 91; coauth, The Medieval Circulation of the De morali principis institutione of Vincent of Beauvais, Viator, 91; auth, Vincentii belvacensis De morali principis institutione, 95; auth, Vincent of Beauvais, Dominican Author: From Compilatio to Tractatus, in Lector et compilator, Vincent de Beauvais, Frere Precheur: un intellectuel et son milieu au XIIIe siecle, 97. **CONTACT ADDRESS** Dept of Foreign Lang, Berea Col, CPO 1860, Berea, KY, 40404. **EMAIL** robert_schneider@berea.edu

SCHNEIDER, ROBERT W.
PERSONAL Born 05/28/1933, Londonville, OH, m, 1955, 3 children **DISCIPLINE** INTELLECTUAL HISTORY **EDUCATION** Col Wooster, BA, 55; Western Reserve Univ, MA, 56; Univ Minn, PhD, 59. **CAREER** Asst hist, 56-58, instr, Univ Minn, 58-59; instr, Col Wooster, 59-61; from asst prof to assoc prof, 61-73, PROF HIST, NORTHERN ILL UNIV, 73-98; Freelance writer & res, 98; Am Philos Soc res grant, 62, 64; Fulbright teaching fel, Regensburg Univ, Ger, 93-94. **MEMBERSHIPS** AHA; Am Studies Asn; Orgn Am Historians. **RESEARCH** American concepts of man. **SELECTED PUBLICATIONS** Auth, Stephen Crane and the drama of transition: A study in historical continuity, J Cent Miss Valley Am Studies Asn, 61; Frank Norris: The naturalist as Victorian, Midcontinent Am Studies J, 62; The American Winston Churchill, Midwestern Quart, 62; Five Novelists of the Progressive Era, Columbia Univ, 65; Novelist to a Generation: The Life & thought of Winston Churchill, Popular Press, 76. **CONTACT ADDRESS** Dept of Hist, No Illinois Univ, 1425 W Lincoln Hwy, De Kalb, IL, 60115-2825. **EMAIL** td0rws1@corn.cso.niu.edu

SCHNEIDER, TAMMI J.
PERSONAL Born 12/28/1962, Detroit, MI, m, 1998 **DISCIPLINE** ANCIENT HISTORY **EDUCATION** Univ PA, PhD (Ancient Hist), 91. **CAREER** ASST PROF IN RELIG, CLAREMONT GRADUATE UNIV, 93-. **MEMBERSHIPS** ASOR; SBL **RESEARCH** Ancient history; bible; archaeology; Assyriology. **SELECTED PUBLICATIONS** Auth, New Dissertations: A New Look at the Campaign Annals of Shalmaneser III, Mar Shipri: News letter of the Comm on Mesopotamian Civilization, 94; Did King Jehu Kill His Own Family?, Biblical Archaeology Rev, 95; Rethinking Jehu, Biblica, 96; New Project: Tel Safi, Israel, 97; Review of Mesopotamian Civilizations: The Material Foundations, by D. T. Potts, Cornell Univ Press, 97, RSR 23/4, 97; Statistical Consulting in Archaeology: Digging for Real Data, with Jim Bentley and Donald Bentley, Proceedings of the Fifth International Conference on Teaching of Statistics, vol 1, ed, Lionel Pereira-Mendoza, Int Asn for Statistical Ed, Singapore: JCS Office Supplies & Services Pte Ltd, 98; Field Report for Area G, Part !, with William Krieger, The Eighth Season of Excavation at Tel Harassim (Nahal Barkai) 1997, ed Edith Shmuel Givon, preliminary report 8, Tel-Aviv: Bar-Ilan Univ, 98; Assyria, Assurbanipal, Assurnasirpal, and Sargon II, in Eerdmans Dictionary of the Bible, Wm B. Eerdmans Pub Co, forthcoming; Judges, The Everlasting Covenant: Studies in Hebrew Narrative and Poetry, Liturgical Press, forthcoming. **CONTACT ADDRESS** Inst Antiquity & Christianity, Claremont Graduate Sch, 831 N. Dartmouth Ave., Claremont, CA, 91711. **EMAIL** Tammi.Schneider@cgu.edu

SCHNELL, GEORGE ADAM
PERSONAL Born 07/13/1931, Philadelphia, PA, m, 1958, 3 children **DISCIPLINE** GEOGRAPHY, SOCIAL SCIENCE **EDUCATION** Pa State Coll, Soc Sci, BS, 58; Pa State Univ, MS, Geog, 60; Pa State Univ, PhD, 65. **CAREER** Lectr, Pa State Univ, 62; asst prof, SUNY-New Paltz, 62-65; assoc prof, SUNY-New Paltz, 65-68; vis assoc prof, Univ Hawaii, 66; prof, SUNY-New Paltz, 68; chm, Dept Geog, SUNY-New Paltz, 69-94; adj prof, Empire State Coll, 74-81; PROF, GEOG, SUNY-NEW PALTZ. **MEMBERSHIPS** Asn Am Geog; Pa Acad Sci; Pa Geog Soc; Nat Coun Geog Educ **RESEARCH** Population growth; Migration & mortality of the aging **SELECTED PUBLICATIONS** "Pennsylvania's Aged Population: Problems and Prospects," Proceedings of the Annual Mtg of the Pa Geog Soc, 97; "Physiography and Cultural Landscape, A Study of Carbon County, Pa," Jour Pa Acad Sci, 97; contribur, "Protecting Freshwater Wetlands in New York: State Mapping and Local Response," Ecology of Wetlands and Associated Systems, Pa Acad Sci, 98. **CONTACT ADDRESS** Dept Geog, SUNY-New Paltz, 75 S Manheim Blvd, New Paltz, NY, 12561-2499. **EMAIL** schnellg@npvm.newpaltz.edu

SCHNUCKER, ROBERT VICTOR
PERSONAL Born 09/30/1932, Waterloo, IA, m, 1955, 3 children **DISCIPLINE** EARLY MODERN EUROPEAN HISTORY **EDUCATION** Northeast Mo State Univ, AB, 53; Univ Bubuque, BD, 56; Univ Iowa, MA, 60, PhD, 69. **CAREER** Pastor, First Presby Church, Springville, Iowa & United Presby Church, US, 56-63; from asst prof to assoc prof soc sci, 63-70, admin intern, 70-71, prof hist & religion, Northeast Mo State Univ 70-, Chmn Dept Philos & Relig, 71-86; Europ hist consult, Educ Media Inc, 71-76; managing ed & bk rev ed, Sixteenth Century J, 72-97; ed, Network News Exchange, Soc Hist Educ, 76-86; ed, Historians of Early Mod Europe, 76-97; vpres, Learning-Instr Facilitators, 76-86. **HONORS AND AWARDS** Recipient of numerous grants from Mo Comt for the Humanities, NEH, J. Paul Getty Trust, Huguenot Soc Am, and Diefale Gout; Certificate of Appreciation from the Serials Industry Systems Comt, 87; Fel, Soc Sci Study of Relig, 90; Sixteenth Century Studies Conf Medal, 97. **MEMBERSHIPS** Fel Soc Values in Higher Educ; Sixteenth Century Studies Conf (secy, 70-72, pres, 72-73, exec secy, 75-97); AHA; Am Soc Church Hist; Soc Reformation Res; Am Acad Relig; Mo Hist Conf; Am Asn Univ Prof (organized local chapter); numerous other organizations. **RESEARCH** Social history of Puritan England to 1645; Reformation history; theory of learning. **SELECTED PUBLICATIONS** Auth, Child Raising Principles Among the Puritans, in Mothers in Pre-Industrial England, Routledge, 90; Using the Internet in Journal Publishing, Schol Publ, 90; ed, Early Osteopathy in the Words of A.T. Still, TJUP, 92; auth, Welcome to the Electronic World, SEMS, 95; author of numerous other journal articles and book chapters. **CONTACT ADDRESS** Dept of Philos & Relig, Northeast Missouri State Univ, 100 E Normal St, Kirksville, MO, 63501-4221. **EMAIL** rvs@truman.edu

SCHOENAUER, NORBERT
PERSONAL Born 01/02/1923, Reghin, Romania **DISCIPLINE** ARCHITECTURE/HISTORY **EDUCATION** Royal Hungarian Tech Univ, Budapest; Royal Acad Fine Arts, Copenhagen; McGill Univ, MArch, 59. **CAREER** Dir, Sch Arch, 72-75, MACDONALD EMER PROF ARCHITECTURE, McGILL UNIV; Can Del UN Econ Comn Europe, Budapest, 76, Ottawa, 77. **HONORS AND AWARDS** La Medaille du Merite, 95. **MEMBERSHIPS** Fel, Royal Arch Inst Can; Royal Acad Arts; Order Archs Que. **SELECTED PUBLICATIONS** Auth, Introduction to Contemporary Housing, 73; auth, 6000 Years of Housing Vols 1-3, 81; auth, History of Housing, 92; auth, Cities, Suburbs, Dwellings, 94; auth, Arts & Crafts and Art Nouveau Dwellings, 96; coauth, The Court-Garden House, 62; coauth, Grassroots Greystones & Glass Towers, 89; ed, John Bland at Eighty: A Tribute, 91. **CONTACT ADDRESS** 3220 Ridgewood Ave, Apt P-2, Montreal, PQ, H3V 1B9. **EMAIL** norbert@urbarc.lan.mcgill.ca

SCHOENBACH, PETER J.
DISCIPLINE MUSIC **EDUCATION** Swarthmore Univ, BA, 62; Columbia Univ, MA, 64; Rutgers Univ, PhD, 73. **CAREER** DIR, SCH MUSIC, CHAUTAUQUA INST, 97-; DIR, SCH MUSIC, SUNY, FREDONIA, 93-; chair, dept mus, Wayne State Univ, 84-92; dir, Sch Mus, Boston Univ, 82-84; assoc dean, New England Conserv, 78-82; dean Curtis Inst Mus, 73-77; Univ Minn; Temple Univ. **CONTACT ADDRESS** Sch Music, SUNY, Fredonia, Fredonia, NY, 14063. **EMAIL** schoenbach@fredonia.edu

SCHOENBRUN, D. L.
PERSONAL Born 10/25/1958, Boston, MA, m, 1989 **DISCIPLINE** HISTORY **EDUCATION** UCLA, MA 83, PhD 90; Lewis & Clark Col, BA 80. **CAREER** Univ Georgia, asst prof 90-95, assoc prof 95-98. **HONORS AND AWARDS** Fulbright-Hays Fel; Soc Sci Res Coun Fel; Amer Coun of LS Gnt. **MEMBERSHIPS** ASA; BIEA **RESEARCH** Precolonial African History. **SELECTED PUBLICATIONS** Auth, A Green Place, A Good Place: Agrarian Change, Gender, and Social Identity in the Great Lakes Region to the 15th Century, Social Hist of Africa, eds, A. Issacmanand J. Allman, Portsmouth, NH, Heinman and James Curry, 98; The Historical Reconstruction of Great Lakes Bantu Cultural Vocabulary: Etymologies and Distributions, Rudiger Koppe Verlag, Koln, 97; Special Issue of the African Archaeological Rev: Papers in Honor of Merrick Posnansky, co-ed, 93; The (IN)Visible Roots of Bunyoro-Kitara and Buganda in the Lakes Region: 800-1300, in: Susan K. McIntosh, Pathways To Complexity: Intermediate Societies in Africa, Cambridge, Cam UP,99; Some Thoughts on Ancient Historical Dimensions of Current Conflicts in the Greater Kivu Region, Uganda Jour, 96; An Intellectual History of Power: Usable Pasts From the Great Lakes Region, eds Gilbert Pwiti, Robert Soper, Aspects of African Archaeology, Harare Zim, U of Zimbabwe Press, 96; Gendered Histories Between the Great Lakes: Varieties and Limits, Intl Jour of African Hist Stud, 96. **CONTACT ADDRESS** Dept of History, Univ of Georgia, Athens, GA, 30602-1602. **EMAIL** dschoenb@arches.uga.edu

SCHOENL, WILLIAM JAMES
PERSONAL Born 02/15/1941, Buffalo, NY, m, 1966, 3 children **DISCIPLINE** MODERN HISTORY **EDUCATION** Canisius Col, BS, 63; Columbia Univ, MA, 64, PhD, 68. **CAREER** From Asst Prof to Prof Hum, 68-89, prof hist, MI State Univ, 89. **HONORS AND AWARDS** Nat Endowment for Hum res grant, 70; Am Philos Soc res grant, 75; 5,000 Personalities of the World, 96. **MEMBERSHIPS** Kiwanis **RESEARCH** C.G. Jung (1875-1961); The Vietnam War (1965-1973). **SELECTED PUBLICATIONS** Auth, Von Hugel after the Modernist Controversy, Clergy Rev, 6/78; The Intellectual Crisis in English Catholicism: Liberal Catholics, Modernists, and the Vatican in the Late Nineteenth and Early Twentieth Centuries, Garland Publ Co, 82; Major Issues in the Life and Work of C.G. Jung, Univ Press Am, 96; C.G. Jung: His Friendships with Mary Mellon and J.B. Priestley, Chiron Publ, 98. **CONTACT ADDRESS** Dept of Hist, Michigan State Univ, East Lansing, MI, 48824-1036. **EMAIL** schoenl@pilot.msu.edu

SCHOFIELD, KENT
PERSONAL Born 03/12/1938, San Bernardino, CA, m, 1960, 2 children **DISCIPLINE** MODERN AMERICAN HISTORY **EDUCATION** Univ Calif, Riverside, BA, 61, PhD(hist), 66; Claremont Grad Sch, MA, 62. **CAREER** Asst prof hist, Harvey Mudd Col, 65-66; from asst prof to assoc prof, 66-74, assoc dean acad planning, 72-76, PROF HIST, CALIF STATE COL, SAN BERNARDINO, 74-, CHMN DEPT, 77- **MEMBERSHIPS** AHA; Orgn Am Historians; Am Studies Asn. **RESEARCH** Modern American history. **SELECTED PUBLICATIONS** Auth, Boston Wayward Children - Soc-Services For Homeless Children, 1830-1930 - Holloran,Pc/, J Of Am Ethnic Hist, Vol 0012, 1993. **CONTACT ADDRESS** Dept of Hist, California State Univ, San Bernardino, 5500 University Pky, San Bernardino, CA, 92407-7500.

SCHOFIELD, ROBERT EDWIN
PERSONAL Born 06/01/1923, Milford, NE **DISCIPLINE** HISTORY OF SCIENCE **EDUCATION** Princeton Univ, AB, 44; Univ Minn, MS, 48; Harvard Univ, PhD(hist sci), 55. **CAREER** Res asst physics, Knolls Atomic Power Lab, Gen Elec Co, 48-50; teaching fel gen ed, Nat Sci, Harvard Univ, 50-53, 54-55; from asst prof to assoc prof hist & hist sci, Univ Kans, 55-59; from assoc prof to prof, 60-72, Lynn Thorndike prof, 72-79; PROF HIST TECH & SCI, IOWA STATE UNIV, 79-, Guggenheim fels, 59-60 & 67-68; mem sch hist studies, Inst Advan Studies, 67-68 & 74-75; assoc, Ctr d'Hist des idees dans LeMonde Angle-Am, Univ Paris-Sorbonne, 77- **HONORS AND AWARDS** Pfizer Prize, Hist Sci Soc, 64. **MEMBERSHIPS** Am Phys Soc; Hist Sci Soc; Soc Hist Technol; Am Soc 18th Century Studies; fel Royal Soc Arts. **RESEARCH** History of 18th century English science and technology; life and work of Joseph Priestly; scientific societies. **SELECTED PUBLICATIONS** Auth, Roller,Duane,Henry,Dubose, 14 March 1920 22 August 1994/, Isis, Vol 0086, 1995. **CONTACT ADDRESS** Dept of Hist, Iowa State Univ, Ames, IA, 50011.

SCHOONOVER, THOMAS DAVID
PERSONAL Born 05/27/1936, Winona, MN, m, 1966, 1 child **DISCIPLINE** AMERICAN HISTORY **EDUCATION** Univ Minn, BA, 59, PhD(hist), 70 La State Univ, MA, 61. **CAREER** Instr hist, Univ Wis-La Crosse, 62-63; lectr, Europ Div, Univ Md, 63-67; from instr to asst prof, 69-75, ASSOC PROF AM HIST, UNIV SOUTHWESTERN LA, 75-, Nat Endowment for Humanities younger humanist fel, 72-73; area ed, The Americas: A Quart Rev of Inter-Am Hist, 73-; Deutscher Akademischer Austauschdiens grant 75; Am Philos Soc grants, 79 & 80; Southern Regional Educ Bd grant, 80; Nat Endowment for Humanities, summer sem, 80; Fulbright sr lectr, Univ of Bielefeld, 81-82; Fritz Thyssen Stiftung grant, 82. **MEMBERSHIPS** AHA; Orgn Am Hist; Soc Historians Am Foreign Rel; Soc Sci Hist Asn. **RESEARCH** United States relations with Latin America; 19th century United States; United States foreign relations. **SELECTED PUBLICATIONS** Auth, Patzcuaro, Romanticism And Commercialism - Ger - Muller,G, Spies,S, Sulberg,H, Zimmer,M/, Hisp Am Hist Rev, Vol 0073, 1993; Vichy And Free-France In Mexico - War, Cultures And Propaganda During World-War-Ii - Fr - Rolland,D/, Hisp Ame Hist Rev, Vol 0073, 1993; To End All Wars - Wilson,Woodrow And The Quest For A New-World Order - Knock,Tj/, Revs In Am Hist, Vol 0021, 1993; The Challenge Of Integration, Europe And The America - Smith,Ph/, Hisp Am Hist Rev, Vol 0075, 1995. **CONTACT ADDRESS** Dept of Hist, Univ of Southwestern La, 200 Hebrard Blvd, Lafayette, LA, 70504-8401.

SCHOPPA, ROBERT KEITH
PERSONAL Born 11/20/1943, Vernon, TX, m, 1968, 2 children **DISCIPLINE** MODERN CHINESE HISTORY **EDUCATION** Valparaiso Univ, BA, 66; Univ Hawaii, MA, 68; Univ Mich, PhD(mod Chinese hist), 75. **CAREER** Instr, 68-71 & 74-75, asst prof, 75-80, ASSOC PROF HIST, VALPARAISO UNIV, 75-, CHMN, 80-, Assoc ctr, Ctr Far Eastern Studies, Univ Chicago, 76-; res prof, Valparaiso Univ, 77-79. **MEMBERSHIPS** Asn Asian Studies; Soc Ch'ing Studies; AHA; Social Sci Hist Asn. **RESEARCH** Twentieth century Chinese social and political elites and institutions; Chinese social and political development from 1850-1949. **SELECTED PUBLICATIONS** Auth, The Making Of A Hinterland - State, Society, And Economy In Inland N China, 1853-1937 - Pomeranz,K/, Am Hist Rev, Vol 0099, 1994; Mountain Of Fame - Portraits In Chinese Hist - Wills,Je/, Am Hist Rev, Vol 0101, 1996; Native Place, City, And Nation - Regional Networks And Identities In Shanghai, 1853-1937 - Goodman,B/, J Of Economic Hist, Vol 0057, 1997. **CONTACT ADDRESS** Dept of Hist, Valparaiso Univ, 651 College Ave, Valparaiso, IN, 46383-6493.

SCHORSCH, ISMAR
PERSONAL Born 11/03/1935, Hanover, Germany, m, 1960, 3 children **DISCIPLINE** JEWISH HISTORY **EDUCATION** Ursinus Col, BA, 57; Columbia Univ, MA, 61, PhD(hist), 69; Jewish Theol Sem, MHL, 62. **CAREER** Instr Jewish hist, Jewish Theol Sem Am, 67-68; instr, Columbia Univ, 68, asst prof, 68-70; assoc prof, 70-76, prof, 76-80, RABBI HERMAN ABRAMOVITZ PROF JEWISH HIST, JEWISH THEOL SEM AM, 80-, DEAN, GRAD SCH, 75-; Mem Found Jewish Cult grant, 73-76. **HONORS AND AWARDS** Ansley Award, Columbia Univ Press, 69; Litt D (hon), Wittenberg Univ, 89, Ursinus Col, 90, Gratz Col, 95, Russian State Univ, 96. **MEMBERSHIPS** Leo Baeck Inst (pres); fel Am Acad Jewish Res. **RESEARCH** Modern German Jewish history; Jewish historiography; modern Jewish history. **SELECTED PUBLICATIONS** Auth, The philosophy of history of Nachman Krochmal, Judaism, 61; Moritz Gudemann: Rabbi, historian and apologist, Leo Baeck Inst Yearbk, 66; Jewish Reactions to German Anti-Semitism, 1870-1914, Columbia Univ, 72; German antisemitism in the light of post-war historiography, Leo Baeck Inst Yearbk, Vol XIX, 74; translator & ed, Heinrich Graetz's, The Structure of Jewish History and Other Essays, Jewish Theol Sem Am, 75; auth, From Wolfenbuttel to Wissenschaft: The divergent careers of Isaac M Jost and Leopold Zunz, Leo Baeck Inst Yearbk, Vol XXI, 76; Historical reflections on the Holocaust, Conservative Judaism, fall-winter 76-77; auth, From Text to Context: The Turn to History in Modern Judaism, 94. **CONTACT ADDRESS** Dept of Hist, Jewish Theol Sem of America, 3080 Broadway, New York, NY, 10027-4650. **EMAIL** isschorsch@jtsa.edu

SCHRECKER, ELLEN WOLF
PERSONAL Born 08/04/1938, Philadelphia, PA, m, 1981, 6 children **DISCIPLINE** HISTORY **EDUCATION** Radcliffe Col, BA, 60; Harvard Univ, MA, 62, PhD, 74. **CAREER** Preceptor, Expository Writing, Harvard Univ, 75-81; instr, New School for Social Research, 82-83; adj asst prof, Hist Dept, NY Univ, 83-85; Program Officer, NY Coun Hum, 84-85; lectr, Dept Hist, Princeton Univ, 85-87; adj prof, The Union Inst, 91-95; Columbia Univ, 96; asst to FULL PROF, YESHIVA UNIV, 87- ; ED, ACADEME, 98- ; Nat Hum Ctr fel, 94-95; Bunting Inst fel Radcliffe Col, 77-78; Outstanding Book Award Hist Educ Soc, 87; lectr US Infor Agency Fr, 96. **MEMBERSHIPS** Am Hist Asn; Orgn Am Hist; AAUP. **RESEARCH** Recent US history (Post World War II). **SELECTED PUBLICATIONS** Auth, The Age of McCarthyism: A Brief History with Documents, Bedford Books, 94; Surfing with Nixon, Radical Hist Rev, 94; Before the Rosenbergs: Espionage Scenarios in the Early Cold War, Secret Agents: The Rosenberg Case and the McCarthy Era, Routledge, 95; Immigration and Internal Security: Political Deportations during the McCarthy Era, Science & Soc, 96-97; Will Technology Make Academis Freedom Obsolete? Will Teach for Food: Academic Labor in Crisis, Univ Minn Press, 97; Many Are the Crimes: McCarthyism in America, Little, Brown, NY, 98; 'The Chilling Case of Kate Bronfenbrenner, Academe, 98. **CONTACT ADDRESS** Yeshiva Univ, 500 W 185th St, New York, NY, 10033. **EMAIL** schreckr@ymail.yu.edu

SCHREIBER, MAE N.
PERSONAL Born 05/03/1941, Wahiawa, HI, m, 1964, 4 children **DISCIPLINE** GOVERNMENT INFORMATION SOURCES; INTERNATIONAL TRADE SOURCES **EDUCATION** Oh St Univ, BS, 63; Simmons Col, MLS, 88. **CAREER** Ref librn to asst prof to assoc prof, Univ Akron, 89- . **MEMBERSHIPS** Amer Libr Assoc, Assoc of Col & Res Libr; Amer Assoc of Univ Prof; Assoc for Bibliogr of Hist. **RESEARCH** Government infor sources; int trade sources; evacuation of Japanese Americans from the West coast. **SELECTED PUBLICATIONS** Auth, Big Emerging Markets: Best Prospects, Electonic Market Data Book, 96; Integrating and Advertising Government Publications Internally and Externally: A Guide for Documents Librarians, J of Interlibrary Loan, Document Delivery & Infor Supply, 97; Cataloging Government Publication, Technicalities, 98; International Trade Sources: A Research Guide, Garland Press, 97. **CONTACT ADDRESS** Bierce Library, Univ of Akron, Reference Dept, Akron, OH, 44325-1709. **EMAIL** mael@uakron.edu

SCHREIBER, ROY
PERSONAL Born 03/13/1941, Newark, NJ **DISCIPLINE** HISTORY **EDUCATION** Univ Calif at LA, BA, 64, MA, 65; Univ London, PhD, 67. **CAREER** Asst prof, hist, Upsala Col, 67-68; asst to assoc to PROF, HIST, INDIANA UNIV S BEND, 68- **HONORS AND AWARDS** Fel, Inst Hist Res, London, 66-67; co-ed, conf British Stud Bio Series, 77; fel, Royal Hist Soc, 81; Authors' Guild, 89; Indiana Univ, S Bend Teaching Award, 89; All Univ Fac Coloquim Exc in Teaching, 90; Dramatists Guild, 93. **MEMBERSHIPS** Am Hist Asn; N Am Conf British Stud **RESEARCH** 17th and 18th cent Great Britain, 18th cent Pacific exploration; Australia, 1789-1810. **SELECTED PUBLICATIONS** Auth, The Fortunate Adversities of William Bligh, 91; "Triumphant Reason," Authors, 94-95; "Indiana University History Departments Talk About Teaching," Perspectives, 36, 98; auth, Some Food for Thought in History, Teching History, forthcoming; auth, James Hay, Earl of Carlisle, New Dictionary of National Biogrpahy, Oxford Univ Press, forthcoming; Wayward Souls, Raconteur, 1:9, Apr 94; Triumphant Reason, Authors, July 94-Feb 95. **CONTACT ADDRESS** Dept of History, Indiana Univ, South Bend, South Bend, IN, 46634.

SCHRIER, ARNOLD
PERSONAL Born 05/30/1925, Bronx, NY, m, 1949, 4 children **DISCIPLINE** HISTORY **EDUCATION** Northwestern Univ, PhD 56. **CAREER** Univ Cincinnati, asst prof. assoc prof, prof, dir of studies, 56-78, Walter C Langsam Prof 72-95, Walter C Langsam Prof Emeritus 95-. **HONORS AND AWARDS** SSRC Fell 56 and 63; Vis Assoc Prof IN Univ; Vis Lect Duke Univ; Dist Vis Prof US Airforce Acad; Dist Ser Awd. **MEMBERSHIPS** AHA; WHA; AAASS; OAH; IHRA; NCSS. **RESEARCH** Russian Hist; World Hist; Immigration Hist **SELECTED PUBLICATIONS** Auth, Ireland and the American Emigration, 1850-1900, Univ Minnesota, 58, re-issued, Russell and Russell 70, pbk, Dufour 97; Living World History, coauth, Pub Scott, Foresman, 64, rev 93; History and Life: The World and Its People, Pub Scott, Foresman, 77, rev 93; a Russian Looks At America, Chicago, 79. **CONTACT ADDRESS** Dept of History, Univ of Cincinnati, 10 Diplomat Dr, Cincinnati, OH, 45215. **EMAIL** hope.earls@uc.edu

SCHROEDER, JOHN H.
PERSONAL Born 09/13/1943, Twin Falls, ID, m, 1965, 2 children **DISCIPLINE** AMERICAN HISTORY **EDUCATION** Lewis & Clark Col, BA, 65; Univ Va, MA, 67, PhD, 71. **CAREER** Asst Prof, 71-76; Assoc Prof, 76-86; Prof, Univ Wisc-Milwaukee, 86-; Univ Wisc System Univ Prof, 98-; Vice Chancellor, Univ Wisc-Milwaukee, 85-90; Chancellor, Univ Wisc-Milwaukee, 90-98. **HONORS AND AWARDS** Univ Wisc-Milw Uhrig Award for Teaching Excellence, 74; Univ Wisc-Milw AMOCO Tchng Award, 75; Lewis M Sears Memorial Tchng Award, Purdue Univ, 75. **MEMBERSHIPS** Org of Am Hist; Soc for the Hist of the Early; Soc of Hist of Am Foreign Relations; Wisc State Hist Soc. **RESEARCH** 19th century American naval & diplomatic history. **SELECTED PUBLICATIONS** Auth, Mr. Polk's War: American Opposition and Dissent, 1846-1848, Univ Wisc Press, 73; auth, Shaping a Mritime Empire: The Commercial and Diplomatic Role of the American Navy, 1829-1861, Greenwood Press, 85; auth, Matthew C Perry: Antebellum Precursor of the New Navy, Captains of the Old Steam Navy, US Nav Inst, 3-25, 86; auth, Annexation or Independence: The Texas Issue in United States Politics and Diplomacy, 1836-1845; SW Hist Soc Quart, 89, 137-164, 10/85; auth, Stephen Decatur: Heroic Ideal of the Young Navy, Command Under Sail: Makers of the American Naval Tradition, US Nav Inst Press, 199-219, 85; auth, Jacksonian Naval Policy, 1829-1837, New Aspects of Naval History, Naut & Aviation Pub Co of Am, 29, 85. **CONTACT ADDRESS** Dept Hist, Univ Wisc-Milwaukee, Bolton Hall, PO Box 413, Milwaukee, WI, 53201. **EMAIL** jhs@csd.uwm.edu

SCHROEDER, PAUL W.
DISCIPLINE HISTORY **EDUCATION** Univ Tex Austin, PhD, 58. **CAREER** Prof, Univ Ill Urbana Champaign. **RESEARCH** Late sixteenth to twentieth century European international politics; theory of history. **SELECTED PUBLICATIONS** Auth, Austria, Great Britain and the Crimean War: The Destruction of the European Concert, Cornell, 72; AHR Forum: Did the Vienna Settlement Rest on a Balance of Power?, Am Hist Rev, 92; The Transformation of European Politics, 1765-1848, Clarendon, 94. **CONTACT ADDRESS** History Dept, Univ Ill Urbana Champaign, 52 E Gregory Dr, Champaign, IL, 61820.

SCHROEDER, SUSAN P.
DISCIPLINE HISTORY **EDUCATION** UCLA, PhD. **CAREER** Hist, Loyola Univ. **RESEARCH** Latin American history; Mexico Cuba. **SELECTED PUBLICATIONS** Auth, Society and Politics in Mexico Tenochtitlan, Tlatelolco, Texcoco, Culhuacan, and Other Nahua Altepetl in Central Mexico, Codex Chimalpahin, 97; Indian Women in early Mexico, Univ Okla Press, 97; Encyclopedia of Mexico. Three items, biographies: Chimalpahin and Juan de Tovar, S J; essay: Indian Women, Chicago and London: Fitzroy Dearborn Pub, 97; The Pax Colonial and Native Resistance in New Spain, Univ Nebr Press, 98; Chimalpahin y los reinos de Chalco, Colegio Mexiquense, 94; Looking Back at the Conquest: Nahua Perceptions of Early Encounters from the Anns of Chimalpahin, in Chipping Away on Earth: Stud in Prehispanic and Colonial Mexico in Honor of Arthur J.O. and Charles E. Dibble, Labryinthos Press, 94; Father Jose Maria Luis Mora, Libism, and the British and Foreign Bible Society in Nineteenth-Century Mexico, The Americas, 94. **CONTACT ADDRESS** Fine Arts Dept, Loyola Univ, Chicago, 6525 N. Sheridan Rd., Chicago, IL, 60626. **EMAIL** sschroe@wpo.it.luc.edu

SCHROEDER-LEIN, GLENNA R.
PERSONAL Born 09/23/1951, Pasadena, CA, m, 1990 **DISCIPLINE** HISTORY **EDUCATION** Univ GA, PhD 91; Univ AZ, MLS 81; Cal State Univ, Fullerton, MA 78, BA 75. **CAREER** Univ TN, 90, asst ed, pprs of Andrew Johnson, 93-, adj lectr hist; Washington Coll, 90, vis asst prof; World Vision, CA, 82-84, phto lib; South W Museum, CA, 77-81, archivist. **HONORS AND AWARDS** McClung Awd, best journal art. **MEMBERSHIPS** SHA; Conf on Faith Hist; OAH. **RESEARCH** Antebellum, civil war, reconst US. **SELECTED PUBLICATIONS** Confederate Hospitals on the Move: Samuel H Stout & The Army of Tennessee, 94; The Papers of Andrew Johnson, asst ed, 92-; various artl and bk revs. **CONTACT ADDRESS** Andrew Johnson Papers Project., Univ of TN, Knoxville, TN, 37996-4000.

SCHROTH, SARAH W.
DISCIPLINE ART HISTORY **EDUCATION** NY Univ, PhD. **CAREER** Adj asst prof, Univ NC, Chapel Hill. **RESEARCH** Span baroque painting. **SELECTED PUBLICATIONS** Auth, 36 Women Artists: Dissolving the Separation Between Art and Life, Atlanta Women's Art Collective, 78; Burial of the Court of Orgaz, Stud in the Hist of Art, Vol II, 82; Early Collectors of Still-Life Painting in Castile, Spanish Still Life in the Golden Age, 85; David Roberts in Context, Duke UP, 96. **CONTACT ADDRESS** Univ N. Carolina, Chapel Hill, Chapel Hill, NC, 27599.

SCHUDSON, MICHAEL
PERSONAL Born 11/03/1946, m, 1982, 3 children **DISCIPLINE** SOCIOLOGY **EDUCATION** Swarthmore Col, BA, 69; Harvard, PhD, 76. **CAREER** Asst prof, Univ Chicago, 76-80; assoc to full prof, Univ Cal San Diego, 80-; Guggenheim fel, MacArthur Prize fel. **MEMBERSHIPS** Am Sociol Asn; Int Commun Asn; Orgn Am Hist. **RESEARCH** US political cul-

ture; News media; History of communication. **SELECTED PUBLICATIONS** Discovering the News, Basic, 78; Advertising, The Uneasy Persuasion, Basic, 84; Watergate in American Memory, Basic Books, 92; The Power of News, Harvard, 95; The Good Citizen, Free Press, 98. **CONTACT ADDRESS** Dept of Communication, Univ Calif San Diego, La Jolla, CA, 92093-0503. **EMAIL** mschudson@ucsd.edu

SCHUFREIDER, GREGORY
DISCIPLINE HISTORY OF PHILOSOPHY, RECENT CONTINENTAL PHILOSOPHY, THE PHILOSOPHY OF ART **EDUCATION** Northwestern Univ, BA, 69; Univ Calif, Santa Barbara, MA, PhD, 75. **CAREER** Prof, La State Univ. **RESEARCH** Heidegger. **SELECTED PUBLICATIONS** Auth, An Introduction to Anselm's Argument, Temple UP, 78; The Metaphysician as Poet-Magician, in Metaphilosophy, 79; Art and the Problem of Truth, Man and World, 81; Heidegger on Community, Man and World, 81; The Logic of the Absurd, in Philos and Phenomenol Res, 83; Overpowering the Center: Three Compositions by Modrian, in JAAC, 85; Heidegger Contribution to a Phenomenology of Culture, 86; Confessions of a Rational Mystic: Anselm's Early Writings, Purdue Univ ser, in the Hist of Philos, 94. **CONTACT ADDRESS** Dept of Philos and Relig Stud, Louisiana State Univ, 106 Coates Hall, Baton Rouge, LA, 70803.

SCHULTE, JOSEPHINE HELEN
PERSONAL Born 05/09/1929, Foley, AL **DISCIPLINE** COLONIAL & MODERN LATIN AMERICAN HISTORY **EDUCATION** Spring Hill Col, BS, 57; Univ Southern Miss, MA, 61; Loyola Univ Chicago, PhD(hist), 69; Trinity Univ, MA, 76. **CAREER** Transl, Gulf Steamship Agency, Ala, 49-58; res asst Mobile metrop area audit, Southern Inst Mgt, 59-60; spec lectr hist, Spring Hill Col, 60-62; asst prof, Univ of the Americas, 67-70; assoc prof, 70-79, PROF HIST, ST MARY'S UNIV, TEX, 79-, GRAD ADV HIST, 73-, DIR LATIN AM STUDIES PROG, 74-, Teacher Ger info & educ, Brookley Field AFB, Ala, 51-62; teacher English & Span, Prichard Jr High Sch, Ala, 62; mem bd dirs, Southwestern Conf Latin Am Studies, 77-82; Orgn Am States grant, Mexico, 66-67; Orgn Am States & Spanish government res fel, Spain, 81-82. **MEMBERSHIPS** Latin Am Studies Asn; Cath Hist Asn. **RESEARCH** Mexico in the 19th century; Spanish borderlands in North America; Colonial Latin America. **SELECTED PUBLICATIONS** Auth, Mission And Might - The Political Religious Clash Between The Dominican Order In Peru And The Viceroy Francisco De Toledo 1561-1581 - Ger - Hehrlein,Y/, Cath Hist Rev, Vol 0079, 1993; Ger-Bohemians - The Quiet Immigrants - Rippley,Lj, Paulson,Rj/, Cath Hist Rev, Vol 0082, 1996; Manuscript Sources For The Hist Of Iberian Am - A Guide To Research Tools - Spa - Hilton,Sl, Gonzalescasasnovas,I/, Hisp Ame Hist Rev, Vol 0076, 1996; Origins Of The Cath-Church In The Caribbean-Islands - The Hist Of The Dioceses Of Santo-Domingo, Concepcion-De-La-Vega, San-Juan-De-Puerto-Rico And Santiago-De-Cuba From Their Establishments Up To The Mid-17th-Century - Ger, Cath Hist Rev. **CONTACT ADDRESS** 6623 Callaghan Rd Apt 1703, San Antonio, TX, 78229.

SCHULTENOVER, DAVID
PERSONAL Born 08/19/1938, Sauk Rapids, MN, s **DISCIPLINE** HISTORICAL THEOLOGY **EDUCATION** Spring Hill Col, BS, 63; Loyola Univ, MS, 66; St. Louis Univ, PhD, 75 **CAREER** Prof, 94-pres, Assoc Prof, 85-94, Adj Asst Prof, 78-83, Creighton Univ; Asst Prof, 75-78, Marquette Univ **HONORS AND AWARDS** Nat Endowm for the Humanities Fel; Alpha Sigma Nu Ntl Bk Award; Deutscher Akademischer Austauschdienst Fel; Alpha Sigma Nu **MEMBERSHIPS** Am Acad of Relig; Am Soc Church History; Cath Theolog Soc of Am **RESEARCH** Christology; Roman Catholic Modernism; Models and Images of the Church **SELECTED PUBLICATIONS** Auth, George Tyrrell: In Search of Catholicism, Patmos Press, 81; Auth, A View from Rome: The Eve of the Modernist Crisis, Fordham University Press, 93 **CONTACT ADDRESS** 518 N 19th St, Omaha, NE, 68102-4612. **EMAIL** dnover@creighton.edu

SCHULTZ, REYNOLDS BARTON
PERSONAL Born 08/09/1951, Elmhurst, IL, m, 1985 **DISCIPLINE** POLITICAL SCIENCE **EDUCATION** Univ Chicago, PhD, 87. **CAREER** Lectr, Univ Chicago, 89- . **HONORS AND AWARDS** Dept nomination, Leo Strauss Award for dissertation; vice-pres, Sidgwick Soc. **MEMBERSHIPS** APSA; Sidgwick Soc. **RESEARCH** Nineteenth and twentieth century Anglo-American ethics and political theory; Henry Sidgwick. **SELECTED PUBLICATIONS** Ed, Essays on Henry Sidgwick, California, 92; auth, The Social and Political Philosophy of Bertrand Russell, Philos of the Soc Sci, 96; ed, Complete Works & Select Correspondence of Henry Sidgwick, InteLex, 97. **CONTACT ADDRESS** Social Sciences Collegiate Division, Univ of Chicago, 5845 South Ellis Ave, Chicago, IL, 60637-1404. **EMAIL** rschultz@midway.uchicago.edu

SCHULTZ, STANLEY KENTON
PERSONAL Born 07/12/1938, Los Angeles, CA, m, 1962, 3 children **DISCIPLINE** AMERICAN HISTORY, URBAN STUDIES **EDUCATION** Occidental Col, AB, 60; Univ Kans, MA, 63, PhD(Am hist), 70. **CAREER** From instr to assoc prof Am hist, 67-76, assoc prof, 76-80, PROF HIST, UNIV WISMADISON, 80-, CHMN AM INST PROG, 69-, Lib Arts fel, Harvard Law Sch, 71-72; Res Training fel, Soc Sci Res Coun, 71-72. **HONORS AND AWARDS** Pelzer Prize, Orgn Am Historians, 65. **MEMBERSHIPS** Am Studies Asn; Orgn Am Historians. **RESEARCH** Interdisciplinary urban studies; American social history; history of American education. **SELECTED PUBLICATIONS** Auth, The Mysteries Of The Great City - The Politics Of Urban Design, 1877-1937 - Fairfield,Jd/, J Of Am Hist, Vol 0081, 1995. **CONTACT ADDRESS** Dept of Hist, Univ of Wisc, 455 North Park St, Madison, WI, 53706-1483.

SCHULZ, ANNE MARKHAM
PERSONAL Born 03/03/1938, New York, NY, 1 child **DISCIPLINE** HISTORY OF ART **EDUCATION** Radcliffe Col, BA, 59; NY Univ, MA, 62, PhD, 68. **CAREER** Instr, 63-65, Smith Col; asst prof, 67-68, Univ Ill, Chicago Circle; lectr, 68-70 & 75, vis asst prof, 77-79, res assoc, 81-83, vis prof, 92-93, Brown Univ; vis prof, 87, Universita degli Studi, Naples Italy; asst cur, Mus Art, RI Sch Design, 68-69; Am Coun of Learned Socs & Am Philos Soc grants-in-aid, 74-75; Howard Found fel, 72-73; Kress Found fel, 74-75; Am Coun Learned Socs travel grant, 75; Delmas Found fel, 78; NEH fel, 82-83, res grant, 82-. **HONORS AND AWARDS** Assoc, Villa Itatti, Florence, 83-84; Am Coun Learned Soc Sr frl, 87-88; IREX Travel grants, 92, 96; Fulbright Sr Res Fel, 97-97; Pro Helvetia grant, 97; NEH Sr Indep Stud Grant, 98. **MEMBERSHIPS** Col Art Assn; Renaissance Soc Am; Soc of Archit Hist; Istituto di Storia dell'ante Lombarda. **RESEARCH** Italian painting and sculpture of the early Renaissance; Renaissance painting in Northern Europe. **SELECTED PUBLICATIONS** Auth, Giambatista and Lorenzo Bregno: Venetian Sculpture in the High Renaissance, Cambridge Univ Press, 91; auth, Nanni di Bartolo e il portale della Bisilica di San Nicola a Tolentino, Centro Di Florence, 97; auth, Giammario Mosca called Padovano: A Renaissance Sculptor in Italy and Poland, Penn St Press, 98. **CONTACT ADDRESS** Dept of Art, Brown Univ, Providence, RI, 02912.

SCHULZ, JUERGEN
PERSONAL Born 08/18/1927, Kiel, Germany, m, 1968, 3 children **DISCIPLINE** HISTORY OF ART **EDUCATION** Univ Calif, Berkeley, BA, 50; Univ London, PhD, 58. **CAREER** From instr to assoc prof hist of art, Univ Calif, Berkeley, 58-68; Prof hist art, 68-90, Andrea V. Rosenthal prof hist of art & archit, 90-94, Brown Univ, Providence; Guggenheim fel, 66-67; Inst Advan Study, 72-73; NEH fel 72-73 & 78-79, Fulbright res scholar (Comm Educ & Cult Exch between Italy & US, 82-83. **HONORS AND AWARDS** Grande Ufficiale, Stella della Solidarieta dell Repubblica Italiana, 69. **MEMBERSHIPS** Col Art Asn; Renaissance Soc Am; Kunsthist Inst Florenz; Soc Archit Historians; Centro Internaz Studi Architettura, Vicenza, membro Cons. Sci, 84- ; Ateneo Veneto, Venice, socio 89- . **RESEARCH** History of Italian Renaissance art and architecture. **SELECTED PUBLICATIONS** Auth, Vasari at Venice, Burlington Mag, 61; Pinturicchio and the revival of antiquity, J Warburg & Courtauld Insts, 62; Pordenone's cupolas, Study Renaissance & Baroque Art Presented to Anthony Blunt, 67; Venetian Painted Ceiling of the Renaissance, Univ Calif, 68; Printed plans ..., of Venice, 1486-1797, Saggi e Memorie di Storia dell' Arte VII, 70; Jacopo de Barbaris view of Venice, Art Bull, 78. **CONTACT ADDRESS** Dept of Art, Brown Univ, Box 1855, Providence, RI, 02912.

SCHULZE, FRANZ
DISCIPLINE ART; ARCHITECTURE **EDUCATION** Univ Chicago, PhB 45; Sch Art Inst Chicago, MFA 50. **CAREER** Lake Forest College, Hollender Prof, 52-91. **HONORS AND AWARDS** Graham Foun Fel; NEH; Ford Foun Fel; Skidmore Owings & Merrill Foun Fel; Magor Awd; Alice Hitchcock Davis Awd; Hon Mention biography of Mies Van der Rohe 1586. **MEMBERSHIPS** SAH **RESEARCH** Architectural history and biography. **SELECTED PUBLICATIONS** Auth, Mies Van der Rohe: A Critical Biography, 86; Mies Van der Rohe: Critical essays, ed, 89; Mies Van der Rohe Archive, Museum of Mod Art, ed, 93; Philip Johnson: Life and Work, 94. **CONTACT ADDRESS** Lake Forest Col, Lake Forest, IL, 60045. **EMAIL** schulze@lfc.edu

SCHULZINGER, ROBERT D.
DISCIPLINE HISTORY **EDUCATION** Columbia Univ, BA, 67; Yale Univ, MPhil, 69; PhD, 71. **CAREER** Prof. **SELECTED PUBLICATIONS** Auth, A Time for War: The United States and Vietnam, 1945-1975, Oxford, 97; American Diplomacy in the Twentieth Century, Oxford, 94; co-auth, Present Tense: The United States since 1945, Houghton-Mifflin, 92. **CONTACT ADDRESS** History Dept, Univ of Colorado, Boulder, Boulder, CO, 80309. **EMAIL** schulzin@spot.colorado.edu

SCHUMACHER, BROCKMAN
PERSONAL Born 08/26/1924, St Louis, Missouri, m **DISCIPLINE** EDUCATION **EDUCATION** State Univ of IA, BA 1949; Washington U, MAEd 1952, PhD 1969. **CAREER** So IL U, coord rehab couns training prog rehab inst 1968-; Human Devel Corp, dir comprehen manpower progs 1966-68; St Louis State Hosp, dir of reha serv 1957-66; Halfway House for Psychiatric Patients, dir res & demon 1959-62; Webster Coll, asst prof soc scis 1966-67; Counc on Rehab, pres 1971-97. **HONORS AND AWARDS** Recip St Louis Mental Hlth Assn Citation for comm serv in mental hlth 1963; awd for serv Human Develop Corp 1968; NRA Cert of apprec for serv on bd of dirs 1971-73; Am Rehab Couns Assn; Nat Assn of Non-White Rehab Wkrs; Nat Task Force for Rehab of the mentally ill Dept of Health Educ & Welfare;Ed Problems Uniue to the Rehab of Psychia Patients St Louis Hosp 1963; Intens Serv for the Disadvataged IL Div of Voc Rehab 1972 **MEMBERSHIPS** Mem bd dir Nat Rehab Assn 1971-; IL bd of Mental Hlth Commnrs 1974-; IL Mental Hlth Plann Bd 1970-73; chmn com on Accreditation of rehab couns training progs Am Rehab Couns Assn 1972-.

SCHUNK, THOM
DISCIPLINE MODERN BRITAIN AND IRELAND, ANCIENT AND MEDIEVAL, U.S. HISTORY **EDUCATION** Univ WI-Oshkosh, BA, 72; Univ WI-Whitewater, MA, 75; Marquette Univ, PhD, 86. **CAREER** Dept Hist, Univ of WI **HONORS AND AWARDS** Smith Family Res fel, 84-85 & 85-86 ;Ocean County Col Res Grant, 93-94. **RESEARCH** Anglo-Irish hist; Northern Ireland 1945-present. **SELECTED PUBLICATIONS** Auth, Irish-Americans, Pasadena, 92. **CONTACT ADDRESS** Dept of Hist, Univ of Wisconsin, Parkside, 900 Wood Rd, PO Box 2000, Kenosha, WI, 53141-2000.

SCHUSTER, LESLIE
DISCIPLINE EUROPEAN SOCIAL AND LABOR HISTORY, COMPARATIVE HISTORY **EDUCATION** Roosevelt Univ, BA; Northern IL Univ, MA, PhD. **CAREER** Instr, RI Col. **RESEARCH** French labor and soc hist. **SELECTED PUBLICATIONS** Auth, Workers and Community: The Case of the Peat-Cutters and the Shipbuilding Industry in Saint-Nazaire, J of Soc Hist. **CONTACT ADDRESS** Rhode Island Col, Providence, RI, 02908.

SCHUSTER-CRAIG, JOHN
PERSONAL Born 01/13/1949, St. Louis, MO, m, 1980, 2 children **DISCIPLINE** MUSIC THEORY **EDUCATION** Univ Louisville, BM, 71; Univ No Carolina, MA, 76; Univ Kentucky, PhD, 87. **CAREER** Vis asst prof, musicology, Indiana Univ, 89, 90; asst prof, Music Theory, 88-93, Univ Louisville; asst prof, Webster Univ, 93-96; assoc prof, head, Dept of Music, Clayton Col & State Univ, 96- . **HONORS AND AWARDS** Andrew W. Mellon res fel, Harry Ransom Hum Res Ctr, Univ Texas. **MEMBERSHIPS** Am Musicological Soc; Soc for Music Theory; Col Music Soc; Am Liszt Soc. **RESEARCH** Twentieth century music. **SELECTED PUBLICATIONS** Auth, Contrasting Collections in Scriabin's Etudes, Op. 65, Theoretically Speaking, 92; auth, Compositional Process in Clermont Pepin's Quasars, CONUS, 92; auth, Bizarre Harmony and the So-Called Newest Style: The Harmonic Language of Rimsky-Korsakov's Le Coq d'or, J of the Am Liszt Soc, 98; auth, Stravinsky's Scenes de ballet and Billy Rose's The Seven Lively Arts: The Abravanel Account, in Parisi, ed, Music in the Theater, Church, and Villa; Essays in Honor of Robert Lamar Weaver and Norma Wright Weaver, Harmonie Park Press, forthcoming. **CONTACT ADDRESS** 100 Waldrop Way, Fayetteville, GA, 30215. **EMAIL** schustercraig@iainc.net

SCHUYLER, DAVID
PERSONAL Born 04/09/1950, Albany, NY, m, 1 child **DISCIPLINE** AMERICAN HISTORY **EDUCATION** Am Univ, BA, 71; Univ NC, MA, 76; Univ DE, MA, 76; Columbia Univ, PhD(hist), 79. **CAREER** Asst prof to PROF AM STUDIES, FRANKLIN & MARSHALL COL, 79-. **HONORS AND AWARDS** Richard B Morris Prize, Columbia Univ, 81; Christian F. and Mary R. Lindback Found Award for Distinguished Teaching, Franklin & Marshall Col, 94. **MEMBERSHIPS** Orgn Am Historians; Am Studies Asn; Soc Archit Historians; Urban Hist Asn; PA Hist Asn (coun); Soc Am City and Regional Planning Hist (pres). **RESEARCH** Urban history; American cultural history. **SELECTED PUBLICATIONS** Auth, introd to Victorian Landscape Gardening, Am Life Found, 78; Inventing a Feminine past, New England Quart, 9/78; Home as a Castle: Architecture and the Ideology of Domesticity, Susquehanna, 7/81; introd to Village and Farm Cottages, 82 & introd to Art of Beautifying Suburban Home Grounds, 82, Am Life Found; The New Urban Landscape: The Redefinition of City Form in Nineteenth-Century America, Johns hopkins, 86; Apostle of Taste: Andrew Jackson Downing, 1815-1852, Johns Hopkins Univ Press, 96; co-ed, The Papers of Frederick Law Olmsted, vol II: Slavery and the South, 1852-1857, 81, vol III: Creating Central Park, 1857-1861, 83, vol IV: The Years of Olmsted, Vaux & Company 1865-1874, 92. **CONTACT ADDRESS** Am Studies Prog, Franklin and Marshall Col, PO Box 3003, Lancaster, PA, 17604-3003. **EMAIL** D_Schuyler@acad.fandm.edu

SCHUYLER, DAVID
PERSONAL Born 04/09/1950, Albany, NY **DISCIPLINE** AMERICAN HISTORY **EDUCATION** Am Univ, BA, 71; Univ NC, MA, 76; Univ Del, MA, 76; Columbia Univ, PhD(hist), 79. **CAREER** ASST PROF AM STUDIES, FRANKLIN & MARSHALL COL, 79-, Assoc ed, Frederick Law Olmsted Papers Publ Proj, 79- **HONORS AND AWARDS** Richard B

Morris Prize, Columbia Univ, 81; Christian F and Mary R Lindback Fdn Award Dist Teach, 94. **MEMBERSHIPS** Orgn Am Historians; Am Studies Asn; Soc Archit Historians; Urban Hist Asn; Pa Historical Asn; Soc Am City and Regional Palnning Hist. **RESEARCH** Urban history; American cultural history. **SELECTED PUBLICATIONS** Auth, introd to Victorian Landscape Gardening, Am Life Found, 78; Inventing a feminine past, New England Quart, 9/78; Home as a castle: Architecture and the ideology of domesticity, Susquehanna, 7/81; introd to Village and Farm Cottages, 82 & introd to Art of Beautifying Suburban Home Grounds, 82, Am Life Found; auth, The New Urban landscape: The Redefinition of City Form in Nineteenth-Century America, Johns Hopkins Univ Press, 86; auth, Apostle of Taste: Andrew Jackson Downing, 1815-1852, Johns Hopkins Univ Press, 96; co-ed, The Papers of Frederick Law Olmsted, vol II: Slavery and the South, 1852-1857 (1981), vol III: Creating Central Park, 1857-1861 (1983), vol VI: The Years of Olmsted, Vaux & Company 1865-1874 (1992). **CONTACT ADDRESS** Am Studies Prog, Franklin and Marshall Col, PO Box 3003, Lancaster, PA, 17604-3003.

SCHUYLER, MICHAEL WAYNE
PERSONAL Born 09/05/1941, Winfield, KS, m, 1969, 2 children **DISCIPLINE** AMERICAN HISTORY **EDUCATION** Southwestern Col, Kans, BA, 63; Univ Kans, MA, 65, PhD(Am hist), 69. **CAREER** From asst prof to assoc prof, 69-78, prof hist, Kearney State Col, 78-, chm dept, 82-, Humanist Am Agr, Buffalo County Hist Soc, 78-; vis prof, Southwest Tex State Univ, 80-81. **MEMBERSHIPS** Orgn Am Historians; Nat Educ Asn; Am Hist Asn; Buffalo County Hist Soc; Ctr for the Study of the Presidency; Nebr State Council for the Social Studies; Nebr State Educ Asn; Nebr State Hist Soc; Popular Cult Asn. **RESEARCH** The 1920's and 1930's; Great Plains agriculture 1920 to 1930; the Kennedy assassination. **SELECTED PUBLICATIONS** Auth, Watergate in Historical Perspective: Conservative Achievement or Liberal Failure, Platte Valley Rev, spring 74; Drought and Politics 1936: Kansas as a Test Case, Great Plains J, fall 75; The Hair-Splitters: Reno and Wallace, 1932-1933, Ann Iowa, fall 76; Drought Relief in Kansas, 1934, Kans Hist Quart, winter 76; auth & contribr, Great Plains Agriculture in the 1930's, in: The Great Plains Experience, Univ Mid-Am, 78; The Assassination of John F Kennedy: The Search for Conspiracies, Platte Valley Rev, 79; auth, The Politics of Change: The Battle for the Agricultural Adjustment Act of 1938, Prologue: A Jour of the Nat Arch, Fall 83; The Ku Klux Klan in Nebraska -- 1920-1930, Nebr Hist: A Quart Magazine, Fall 85; The Bitter Harvest: Lyndon B. Johnson and the Assassination of John F. Kennedy, J Am Cult, Fall 85; Ghosts in the White House: LBJ, RFK, and the assassination of JFK, Presidential Studies Quart, Summer 87; The Dread of Plenty: Agricultural Relief Activities of the Federal Government in the Middle West, 1933-1939, Sunflower Univ Press, 89; New Deal Farm Policy in the Middle West: A Retrospective View, J of the West, October 94. **CONTACT ADDRESS** Dept of Hist, Univ of Nebr at Kearney, 905 W 25th St, Kearney, NE, 68849-4238.

SCHUYLER, ROBERT L.
PERSONAL Born 09/13/1941, New Haven, CT **DISCIPLINE** ANTHROPOLOGY, HISTORICAL ANTHROPOLOGY **EDUCATION** Univ AZ, BA, 64; Univ CA, Santa Barbara, MA, 68, PhD, 74. **CAREER** Instr, Univ MD, 69-70; asst prof, CCNY-City Univ New York, 70-79; assoc prof to assoc Curator, Univ PA, 79-98. **HONORS AND AWARDS** Council for Hist Archaeology Northeast, Pres, 80; Soc for Hist Archaeology, Pres, 82. **MEMBERSHIPS** Am Anthropological Asn; Soc for Hist Archaeology; Am Studies Asn; Sigma Xi; etc. **RESEARCH** Theory and hist of anthropology and archaeology; hist archaeology (AD 1400-), North Am and Global. **SELECTED PUBLICATIONS** Ed, Historical Archaeology, A Guide to Substantive and Theorhetical Contributions, Baywood Pub Co, 78;ed, Archaeological Perspectives on Ethnicity in America, Baywood Pub Co, 80; Historical Archaeology in the American West: the View from Philadelphia, Historical Archaeology 25, 90; Frontier Sites of the American West, in Oxford Companion to Archaeology, Oxford Univ Press, 96; Culture Contact in Evolutionary Prespective, Chapter 4, in Studies in Culture Contact: Interaction, Culture Change, and Archaeology, ed by James G Cusnick, Southern IL Univ, 98. **CONTACT ADDRESS** Univ Museum, Univ of Pennsylvania, 33rd and Spruce Sts, Philadelphia, PA, 19104. **EMAIL** schuyler@sas.upenn.edu

SCHWAB, PETER
PERSONAL Born 11/15/1940, s **DISCIPLINE** POLITICAL SCIENCE **EDUCATION** New School for Social Res, MA, 66, PhD, 69. **CAREER** Asst prof, 71-73, assoc prof, 73-80, prof, Political Sci, Purchase Col, SUNY, 80-. **HONORS AND AWARDS** Fulbright Scholar, 67; U.N. Commission on Human Right-authored book, Human Rights, selected as primary debate, 86. **RESEARCH** Cuba-the U.S. embargo. **SELECTED PUBLICATIONS** Auth, Cuba: Confronting the U.S. Embargo, St Martin's Press, 98; Ethiopia, Politics, Economics, and Society, Lynne Rienner Pub, 85; coauth, Toward a Human Rights Framwork, Praeger Pub, 82; Human Rights: Cultural & Ideological Perspectives, Praeger Pub, 79. **CONTACT ADDRESS** Dept of Political Sci, State Univ of NY, Purchase, NY, 10577. **EMAIL** schwabsuny@aol.com

SCHWALM, LESLIE A.
PERSONAL Born 02/18/1956, Washington, DC **DISCIPLINE** HISTORY **EDUCATION** Univ Ms Amherst, BA, 79; Univ Wi Madison, PhD, 91. **CAREER** Assoc prof, Univ Iowa, 91- **HONORS AND AWARDS** Willie Lee Rose Book Award, 98; Letitia Woods Brown Publ Prize, 98; Univ Iowa Faculty Scholar Award, 99-02; Nat Endow for the Humanities Sr Fel, 99-00. **MEMBERSHIPS** Amer Hist Assoc; Org of Amer Hist; S Hist Assoc; S Assoc of Women Hist. **SELECTED PUBLICATIONS** Auth, A Hard Fight for We: Women's Transition from Slavery to Freedom in Lowcountry South Carolina, Univ Il Press, 97; Sweet Dreams of Freedom: Freedwomen's Reconstruction of Life and Labor in Lowcountry South Carolina, J of Women's Hist, 97. **CONTACT ADDRESS** Dept of History, Univ of Iowa, Iowa City, IA, 52242. **EMAIL** leslie-schwalm@uiowa.edu

SCHWARTZ, DOUGLAS W.
PERSONAL Born 07/29/1929, Erie, PA, m, 1950, 3 children **DISCIPLINE** ANTHROPOLOGY **EDUCATION** Univ Ky, BA, 50; Yale Univ, PhD, 55. **CAREER** Dir, Mus Anthrop, Univ Ky, 56-67; Asst Prof, Univ Ky, 56-67; Acad Asst to Pres, Univ Ky, 63-64; Pres & CEO, Sch of Am Res, 67-. **HONORS AND AWARDS** Hon Dr of Letters, Univ NMex, 81; Hin Dr of Letters, Univ Ky, 89; Dist Service Award, Soc for Am Archaeol, 90; Dist Service Award, Am Anthrop Asn, 92. **MEMBERSHIPS** Witter Bynner Foundation for Poetry, Inc (bd member); Am Anthrop Asn, Long Range Planning Committee; Bd Member, 1st Nat Bank of Santa Fe, 95-. **RESEARCH** Retracing Charles Darwin's voyage of the Beagle; Northern Rio Grande Valley, New Mexico; Grand Canyon Arizona; Southern Italy. **SELECTED PUBLICATIONS** Auth, On the Edge of Splendor: Exploring the Grand Canyon's Human Past, SAR Press, 89; forward, The Pottery of Arroyo Hondo Pueblo, New Mexico, SAR Press, 93; forward, The Architecture of Arroyo Hondo Peublo, New Mexico, SAR Press, 93; forward, The Men Who Made Kentucky's Past, Ky Archaeol, Univ Ky Press, 96; forward, rev Introduction to Southwestern Archaeology, Yale Univ Press, in press. **CONTACT ADDRESS** Sch of Am Res, PO Box 2188, Santa Fe, NM, 87504-2188. **EMAIL** dws@sarsf.org

SCHWARTZ, ELI
PERSONAL Born 04/02/1921, New York, NY, m, 1948, 2 children **DISCIPLINE** ECONOMICS **EDUCATION** BS Acctg Univ of Denver, 43; U.S. Army, 43-46; Special Student,Univ of Manchester England, 45; MA Econ Univ of CO, 48; PhD in Econ, Brown Univ 52; Thesis: Studies in Distribution of Tax Burdens by Income Groups-A Critique. **CAREER** Named to Charles W MacFarlane Chair of Econ, Lehigh Univ 80,(Emeritus,91); Cam Econ Dept, Lehigh Univ, 78-84; Vis Prof, Tel Aviv Univ, 75; Fulbright Lecturer and Consulting Prof Autonomous, Univ of Madrid, Spain, 72; Lecturer London School of Econ, 66; Prof of Ceoc and Finance, Lehigh Univ, 62; Lehigh Univ, 54-, Retired active Prof emeritus, 91; Lecturer, Michigan State Univ 53-54; Chief Dis Econ(G11) Providence Dis of O.P.S, 51-53; Inst, Brown Univ, Providence Rhode Island, 48-51; Inst, Univ of Rhode Island, 47-48. **RESEARCH** Valuation of lifetime incomes; Money and Banking; Macroeconomics; Finance. **SELECTED PUBLICATIONS** Ed,(with J.R. Aronson), Management Policies in Loval Government Finance, Intl City Managers Assoc, Washington DC, 75(2nd ed 81,3rd ed 87,4th ed 96); A Quick Market Interest Rates and the Total Offset Method Re-visited, (forthcoming JFE); Life Insurance as an Offset in Wrongful Death Cases, Journal of Forensic Economics, 94; Capacity Planning in Public Utilities: An Inventory Theoretic Approach, Journal of Land Economics, 84; Reforming Public Pension Plans to Avoid Unfunded Liability, Management Information Service, ICMA (with J.R. Aronson and V.G. Munley), 83; The Economics of Lifetime Income, (with R.J. Thornton), The Forum (published by the Amer Bar Assoc), 83; Note on Stability Conditions Applied to Particular Market, (with Donald A. Moore), Southern Economic Journal, 55. **CONTACT ADDRESS** Dept of Econ, Lehigh Univ, Bethlehem, PA, 18015.

SCHWARTZ, GERALD
DISCIPLINE MODERN AMERICAN HISTORY **EDUCATION** WA State Univ, PhD. **CAREER** Hist Dept, Western Carolina Univ **SELECTED PUBLICATIONS** Auth, A Woman Doctor's Civil War: Esther Hill Hawks' Diary, 89. **CONTACT ADDRESS** Western Carolina Univ, Cullowhee, NC, 28723.

SCHWARTZ, JOEL
PERSONAL Born 09/12/1942, New York, NY, m, 1969, 2 children **DISCIPLINE** URBAN & SOCIAL HISTORY **EDUCATION** Univ Chicago, BA, 62, MA, 65, PhD, 72. **CAREER** Asst prof, 69-77, assoc prof, 77-86; prof hist, Montclair State Univ, 86-, Assoc, Columbia Univ Sem in the City, 73. **MEMBERSHIPS** Orgn Am Historians. **RESEARCH** Nineteenth century urban neighborhoods and families; suburbanization; progressivism. **SELECTED PUBLICATIONS** Auth, Evolution of suburbs In: Suburbia: The American Dream and Dilemma, Doubleday, 76; ed, Cities of the Garden State, Kendall/Hunt, 77; The New York Approach, OH State Univ Pres, 93. **CONTACT ADDRESS** Dept of Hist, Montclair State Univ, 1 Normal Ave, Montclair, NJ, 07043-1699. **EMAIL** schwartzj@saturn.montclair.edu

SCHWARTZ, MARVIN
PERSONAL Born 07/28/1941, Boston, MA, m, 1984, 2 children **DISCIPLINE** HISTORY MODERM EUROPE **EDUCATION** AB, Princeton Uni, 63; MA, PhD, Yale Univ, 64, 69. **CAREER** Inst Hist, Univ Mass, Boston, 67-68; Asst Prof, Assoc Prof, Prof Hist, Univ Mass, Amherst, 70-. **HONORS AND AWARDS** Danforth Fel; Woodrow Wilson Fel; Univ Mass for Res and Tchg. **RESEARCH** Europe, 1870-1945; British Poli and Foreign Policy; the Holocaust. **SELECTED PUBLICATIONS** The Union of Democratic Control in British Politics during the First Workd War, Oxford: Clarendon Press, 71; Disraeli's Reminiscences, London: Hamish Hamilton, 75; NY: Stein & Day, co-ed, 76; The Policies of British Foreign Policy in the Era of Disraeli and Gladstone, London: Macmillan; NY: St Martin's Press, 85. **CONTACT ADDRESS** Dept Hist, Univ Massachusetts, Herter Hall, Amherst, MA, 01003. **EMAIL** mswartz@history.umass.edu

SCHWARTZ, NORMAN B.
PERSONAL Born 02/13/1932, New York, NY, m, 1955, 4 children **DISCIPLINE** ANTHROPOLOGY **EDUCATION** Univ Penn, PhD 68. **CAREER** Middlebury College, asst prof, 62-68; Univ Delaware, prof, 68-; Conservation Intl, consultant, 92-95. **HONORS AND AWARDS** Phi Beta Kappa **MEMBERSHIPS** AAA; SAA; SLAA; Anthrop Study Gp Agrarian Systems; Guatemalan Schls Network. **RESEARCH** Tropical forests productive systems; conservation of tropical forests; land tenure systems; aquaculture systems; Central Amer. **SELECTED PUBLICATIONS** Auth, IDB Resources Book on Participation, coauth, Washington DC, Inter-American Devel Bank, 96; Community Consultation, sustainable Development and the Inter-American Development Bank: A Concept Paper, coauth, Washington DC, Soc Progs and Sustainable Devel Bank and Inter-American Devel Bank, 96; Itazaj Maya, coauth, in: Encycl of World Cultures: Middle America and the Caribbean, eds, J. Dow, R. V. Kemper, NY, HRAF and Hall-Macmillan, 95; Re-Privatization and Privation: Traditional and Contemporary Land Tenure System in Peten Guatemala, Mesoamerica, 95; Colonization development and deforestation in Peten Guatemala, in: The Social Causes of Environmental Destruction in Latin America, eds, M Painter, W. H. Durham, East Lansing MI, U of Mich Press, 95. **CONTACT ADDRESS** Dept of Anthropology, Univ of Delaware, 53 East Park Place, Newark, DE, 19711. **EMAIL** nbsanth@udel.edu

SCHWARTZ, SHULY RUBIN
DISCIPLINE JEWISH HISTORY **EDUCATION** Barnard Col, BA; Jewish Theol Sem Am, MA, PhD. **CAREER** Rabbi Irving Lehrman Res Asst Prof Am Jewish Hist; dean, Albert A. List Col Jewish Studies. **RESEARCH** Image and role of the Rebbetzin, the "traditional" rabbi's wife, in American Jewish life, the changing image and role of the contemporary "rabbinic spouse." **SELECTED PUBLICATIONS** Auth, The Emergence of Jewish Scholarship in America: The Publication of the Jewish Encyclopedia, Hebrew Union Col Press, 91; Camp Ramah: The Early Years, 1947-1952, Conser Judaism, 87; Ramah Philosophy and the Newman Revolution, Studies in Jewish Education and Judaica in Honor of Louis Newman. **CONTACT ADDRESS** Jewish Theol Sem of America, 3080 Broadway, New York, NY, 10027. **EMAIL** shschwartz@jtsa.edu

SCHWARTZ, STUART B.
PERSONAL Born 09/04/1940, Springfield, MA **DISCIPLINE** COLONIAL LATIN AMERICA **EDUCATION** Middlebury Col, AB, 62; Columbia Univ, MA, 63, PhD(hist), 68. **CAREER** From instr to assoc prof Latin Am hist, 67-73, chmn dept, 76-79, PROF HIST, UNIV MINN, 73-, Vis asst prof Latin Am hist, Univ Calif, Berkeley, 69-70; adv, Conf Latin Am Soc Sci, Mex, 72-; vis prof, Fed Univ Bahia, Brazil, 74; Am Coun Learned Soc fel, 74-75; Guggenheim fel, 78-79. **MEMBERSHIPS** AHA; Conf Latin Am Hist; Latin Am Studies Asn. **RESEARCH** Colonial Latin America; Brazil; social history. **SELECTED PUBLICATIONS** Auth, Africa And The Africans In The Making Of The Atlantic World, 1400-1680 - Thornton,J/, Hisp Am Hist Rev, Vol 0073, 1993; Family, Inheritance And Power In Sao-Paulo - 1765-1855 - Port - Bacellar,Cda/, J Of Interdisciplinary Hist, Vol 0024, 1994. **CONTACT ADDRESS** Dept of Hist, Univ of Minn, Minneapolis, MN, 55455.

SCHWARZ, JORDAN A.
PERSONAL Born 09/13/1937, Chicago, IL, m, 1963, 2 children **DISCIPLINE** RECENT AMERICAN HISTORY **EDUCATION** City Col New York, BA, 59; Columbia Univ, MA, 60, PhD, 67. **CAREER** Instr hist, Cedar Crest Col, 64-65; from instr to asst prof, 65-70, assoc prof, 70-80, PROF HIST, NORTHERN ILL UNIV, 80-, Am Philos Soc grant, 70-71. **MEMBERSHIPS** AHA; Orgn Am Historians; Econ Hist Asn. **RESEARCH** Recent American history. **SELECTED PUBLICATIONS** Auth, After Wilson - The Struggle For The Democratic-Party, 1920-1934. - Craig,Db/, J Of Am Hist, Vol 0080, 1993; Conservative Restraints - NC And The New-Deal - Abrams,C/, Miss Quart, Vol 0047, 1994; Losing Time - The Industrial-Policy Debate - Graham,Ol/, Rev In Am Hist, Vol 0022, 1994. **CONTACT ADDRESS** Dept of Hist, No Illinois Univ, De Kalb, IL, 60115.

SCHWARZ, PHILIP JAMES
PERSONAL Born 11/12/1940, New York, NY, m, 1970, 2 children **DISCIPLINE** AMERICAN HISTORY **EDUCATION** Brown Univ, AB, 62; Univ Conn, MA, 65; Rutgers Univ, MLS, 65; Cornell Univ, PhD, 73. **CAREER** From Asst Prof to Assoc Prof, 72-90, prof Am hist, Va Commonwealth Univ, 90-. **HONORS AND AWARDS** Fel, Va Ctr for the Humanities, Spring 93. **MEMBERSHIPS** Am Soc Legal Hist; Southern Hist Asn; Am Hist Asn; Henrico County Hist Soc; Nat Coun Hist Educ; Org Am Hist; Phi Kappa Phi, VCU Chapter; Soc Hist Early Repub; Va Coun Hist Educ; Va Hist Soc. **RESEARCH** Colonial America; slavery; constitutional history. **SELECTED PUBLICATIONS** Auth, The Jarring Interests: New York's Boundary Makers, 1664-1776, State Univ NY Press, 79; Twice Condemned: Slaves and the Criminal Laws of Virginia, LSU Press, 88; Slave Laws in Virginia, Univ Ga Press, 96. **CONTACT ADDRESS** Dept of Hist, Va Commonwealth Univ, Box 842001, Richmond, VA, 23284-2001. **EMAIL** pjschwar@vcu.edu

SCHWEIKART, LARRY EARL
PERSONAL Born 04/21/1951, Mesa, AZ, m, 1987, 1 child **DISCIPLINE** HISTORY **EDUCATION** Ariz State Univ, BA, Polit Sci, 72, MA, 80; Univ Calif-Santa Barbara, PhD, 84. **CAREER** Asst prof, Univ Dayton, 85; assoc prof, Univ Dayton, 88; PROF, UNIV DAYTON, 95-. **RESEARCH** US economic, business, military & industrial relations. **SELECTED PUBLICATIONS** Edr, Encyclopedia of American Business History, "Banking and Finance to 1913," Calif Bankers, Simon & Schuster, 94; "Abraham Lincoln and Growth of Government in the Civil War Era," Continuity 21, 97; coauth, "Banking in the Golden State from the Gold Rush to the 1990's," Calif Hist, 97; "Banking and Finance in North America, 1607-1997," Banking, Trade & Industry, Cambridge Univ Press, 97. **CONTACT ADDRESS** Dept Hist, Univ Dayton, Dayton, OH, 45469. **EMAIL** schweika@checkov.hm.udayton.edu

SCHWENINGER, LOREN LANCE
PERSONAL Born 01/07/1941, Culver City, CA, m, 1965, 4 children **DISCIPLINE** AFRICAN AMERICAN HISTORY **EDUCATION** Univ of Colo, BA, 62, MA, 66; Univ of Chicago, PhD, 72. **CAREER** Instr, 71-73, asst prof, 73-78, assoc prof, 78-85, prof, 85-, Univ NC, Greensboro. **HONORS AND AWARDS** Fulbright Senior lectr, Univ of Geneva, Italy, 91; NEH Res Grant, 95-97, 97-99; NHPRC Res Grant, 91-99; Charles Stewart Mott Found Res Grant, 97-99. **MEMBERSHIPS** OAH; AHA; SHA; ASALH. **RESEARCH** Slavery. **SELECTED PUBLICATIONS** Auth, Black Property Owners in the South, Ill Press, 91, Ill Paperback, 97. **CONTACT ADDRESS** 807 Rankin Pl., Greensboro, NC, 37412.

SCHWIEDER, DOROTHY ANN
PERSONAL Born 11/28/1933, Presho, SD, m, 1955, 2 children **DISCIPLINE** IOWA & WOMAN'S HISTORY **EDUCATION** Dakota Wesleyan Univ, BA, 55; Iowa State Univ, MA, 68; Univ Iowa, PhD, 81. **CAREER** Instr Am govt, Dakota Wesleyan Univ, 60-62; instr, 69-81, ASST PROF AM HIST, IOWA STATE UNIV, 81- **MEMBERSHIPS** Orgn Am Hist; AAUP; Am Asn Univ Women. **RESEARCH** Communitarian studies; woman's economic history and ethnic history. **SELECTED PUBLICATIONS** Auth, The Am-W - Nothing To Do But Stay - My Pioneer Mother - Young,C/, J Of The W, Vol 0032, 1993. **CONTACT ADDRESS** Dept of Hist, Iowa State Univ, Ames, IA, 50010.

SCHWOERER, LOIS GREEN
PERSONAL Born 06/04/1927, Roanoke, VA, m, 1949, 1 child **DISCIPLINE** ENGLISH HISTORY, RENAISSANCE **EDUCATION** Smith Col, BA, 49; Bryn Mawr Col, MA, 52, PhD(hist), 56. **CAREER** Teacher, Shipley Sch, Pa, 49-51; instr hist, Bryn Mawr Col, 54-55; lectr, Univ Pittsburgh, 61-63; from lectr to assoc prof, 64-76, dept chmn, 79-81, PROF HIST, GEORGE WASHINGTON UNIV, 76-, Am Philos Soc Grant, 71-72; Nat Endowment Humanities sr fel, 75; sr fel, Folger Shakespeare Libr, 78; fel, Royal Hist Soc. **HONORS AND AWARDS** Best Bk Award, Berkshire Conf Women Historians, 75. **MEMBERSHIPS** AHA; Conf Brit Hist; Renaissance Soc Am; Int Comn Hist Rep & Parliamentary Insts. **RESEARCH** English political and intellectual history, 17th and 18th centuries; the Revolution of 1688-89; 17th & 18th century English women, especially Lady Rachel Russell. **SELECTED PUBLICATIONS** Auth, To Keep And Bear Arms - The Origins Of An Anglo-Am Right - Malcolm,Jl/, J Of Southern Hist, Vol 0061, 1995; The Attempted Impeachment Of Scroggs,William, Lord Chief-Justice Of The Court Of Kings-Bench, November-1680 March-1681/, Hist J, Vol 0038, 1995; Politics And Opinion In Crisis, 1678-81 - Knights,M/, Am Hist Rev, Vol 0101, 1996. **CONTACT ADDRESS** Dept of Hist, George Washington Univ, Washington, DC, 20052.

SCIONTI, JOSEPH NATALE
PERSONAL Born 09/25/1931, Boston, MA, m, 1955, 2 children **DISCIPLINE** EARLY MODERN EUROPEAN HISTORY **EDUCATION** Suffolk Univ, BA, 60; Tufts Univ, MA, 61; Brown Univ, PhD(reformation) 67. **CAREER** PROF HIST, UNIVERSITY MASS DARTMOUTH, 65-; Mem, Community Leaders Am, 72-; prog dir, New Eng Renaissance Conf, 73. **MEMBERSHIPS** AHA; Renaissance Soc Am **RESEARCH** Reformation in Germany, especially Luther's opponents; Renaissance in Italy, especially Florentine humanism; 19th century Italy, especially Risorgimento. **SELECTED PUBLICATIONS** Contribr, Historical Abstracts, Am Bibliog Ctr-Clio, 71-; Encyclopedia World Biography, McGraw, 73; Giuseppe Mazzini, Giuseppe Garibaldi, Huldreich Zwingli, In: Research Guide to European Historical Biography. **CONTACT ADDRESS** Dept of Hist, Univ Mass Dartmouth, 285 Old Westport Rd, North Dartmouth, MA, 02747-2300.

SCOBIE, INGRID WINTHER
PERSONAL Born 01/02/1943, Bloomington, IN, 4 children **DISCIPLINE** AMERICAN & WOMEN'S HISTORY **EDUCATION** Brown Univ, BA, 64; Univ Rochester, MA, 65; Univ Wis, PhD(Am hist), 70. **CAREER** Vis lectr hist, Princeton Univ, 75; sr Fulbright Hays prof, Univ El Salvador & Nat Inst Teacher Training, Buenos Aires, 76; lectr US hist & res assoc, Univ Calif, San Diego, 77-79 & 81-82; ASST PROF US HIST, TEX WOMAN'S UNIV, 82-, Ed & interviewer, Regional Oral Hist Off, Bancroft Libr, Univ Calif, Berkeley, 77-81; panelist & reviewer, Nat Endowment for Humanities, 79-, res grant, 81-84; Eleanor Roosevelt Inst grant, 80; Am Philos Soc grant, 80. **MEMBERSHIPS** AHA; Orgn Am Historians; Oral Hist Asn; Nat Coun Pub Hist. **RESEARCH** California; legislative activity; 20th century social and political history, especially women in politics. **SELECTED PUBLICATIONS** Auth, The Interior Castle - The Art And Life Of Stafford,Jean - Hulbert,A/, Am Hist Rev, Vol 0098, 1993; Class Conflict And Class Coalition In The Calif Woman Suffrage Movement, 1907-1912 - The San-Francisco-Wage-Earners-Suffrage-League - Englander,S/, California Hist, Vol 0073, 1994. **CONTACT ADDRESS** Dept of Hist & Govt, Tex Women's Univ, P O Box 425889, Denton, TX, 76204-5889.

SCORGIE, GLEN G.
PERSONAL Born 03/29/1952, Vancouver, BC, Canada, m, 1978, 3 children **DISCIPLINE** HISTORICAL THEOLOGY **EDUCATION** Univ of St Andrews, Scotland, PhD, 86. **CAREER** Data-processing marketing asst, 74-76; IBM Canada, Toronto; adjunct prof of theology, 84-91, Canadian Theological Seminary; dir of admissions, 76-79, asst prof, 84-88, acting dean of faculty, Jan-May 89, assoc prof 88-91, Canadian Bible Col; academic dean and vice-pres, 91-96, prof 95-96, North Amer Baptist Col; adjunct pastor for English Mininistries, 97, Chinese Bible Church of San Diego; prof, 96- , Bethel Theological Seminary. **HONORS AND AWARDS** Who's Who in America; British Government Overseas Research Student Scholarship; Regent College Church History Prize; Delta Epsilon Chi Honor Society. **MEMBERSHIPS** American Academy of Religion; Canadian Evangelical Theological Assn; Conference on Faith and History; Evangelical Theological Society. **RESEARCH** Key Determinants of Spirtual Resilience: An Interdisciplinary Perspective; Movie Theology: Thinking Christianly about Contemporary Film and Cinema; Asian theology and spirituality, Christology and pluralism. **SELECTED PUBLICATIONS** Auth, A Call for Continuity: The Theological Contribution of James Orr, 88; Directionary of Twentieth Century Christian Biography, 95; auth, A.B. Simpson, Holiness and Modernity, in Studies in Canadian Evangelical Renewal, Faith Today, 96; coauth, Human Life is Not Sheep: An Ethical Perspective on cloning, Journal of the Evangelical Theological Society, Dec 97; auth, Yearning for God: The Potential and Poverty of the Catholic Spirituality of Francis de Sales, Journal of the Evangelical Theological Society, Sept 98. **CONTACT ADDRESS** 6116 Arosa St, San Diego, CA, 92115-3902. **EMAIL** gscourgie@bethel.edu

SCOTT, ALISON M.
PERSONAL Born 02/01/1956, Dugway, UT **DISCIPLINE** AMERICAN STUDIES **EDUCATION** Whitman Coll, BA, 78; Univ Chicago, Grad Library Sch, AM, 82, Divinity Sch, AM, 82; Boston Univ, PhD, 95. **CAREER** Ref libn, Columbia Univ, Rare Book & Manuscript Library, 83-85; asst curator, rare books, Smith Coll, 85-90; head libn, Popular Culture Library, 93-, asst prof, 95-98, assoc prof, Dept Popular Culture, Bowling Green State Univ, 98-. **MEMBERSHIPS** Amer Lib Assn; Soc History Authorship, Reading, and Publishing; Soc Historians Early Amer Republic; Popular Culture Assn. **RESEARCH** History of the book in the early American republic; popular literature. **SELECTED PUBLICATIONS** Referred jour articles: "Why Aren't You Here? Postcards in the Popular Culture Library," Popular Culture in Libraries, vol 3, no 2, 95, simultaneous pub in Postcards in the Library: Invaluable Visual Resources, 95; "They Came from the Newsstand: Pulp Magazines and Vintage Paperbacks in the Popular Culture Library," Primary Sources & Their Original Works, vol 4, 96, simultaneous publication in Pioneers, Passionate Ladies, and Private Eyes: Dime Novels, Series Books, and paperbacks, 96; auth, "Vincent Starrett (26 October 1886-4 January 1974," American Book Collectors and Bibliographers, vol, 187, Dictionary of Literary Biography, 97; editor, The Writing on the Cloud: American Culture Confronts the Atomic Bomb, 97; auth, "The Paper They're Printed On," in Pulp Art: Original Cover Paintings for the Great American Pulp Magazines, 97. **CONTACT ADDRESS** Popular Culture Library, Bowling Green State Univ, Bowling Green, OH, 43403. **EMAIL** ascott@bgnet.bgsu.edu

SCOTT, CLIFFORD H.
PERSONAL Born 07/21/1937, Independence, IA, m, 1960, 2 children **DISCIPLINE** AMERICAN HISTORY **EDUCATION** Univ Northern Iowa, BA, 59; Univ Iowa, MA, 60, PhD, 68. **CAREER** Instr hist, Webster City Iowa Jr Col, 60-62; asst prof, Southeast Mo State Col, 65-68; asst prof hist, 68-75, assoc prof am hist, 75-, In Univ-Purdue Univ; proj dir, Nat Sci Found fel, 74; proj dir, Ind Comt Humanities, 77. **MEMBERSHIPS** AHA; Orgn Am Historians; AAUP. **RESEARCH** American intellectual history; gilded age America; American ethnic history. **SELECTED PUBLICATIONS** Auth, A Naturalistic Rationale For Women's Reform, Historian, winter 70; art, Images of Blackest Africa in American fiction, NDak Quart, fall 72; auth, Lester Frank Ward, Twayne, 76; auth, Fort Wayne German-Americans in WWI, Old Fort News, 77; art, Hoosier Kulturkampf, J Ger-Am Studies, 79; art, Assimilation in a German-American community, Northwest Ohio Quart, 80; art, Mission to Africa: Changing Ideas On Race And Culture, Proc Ind Acad Soc Sci, 80; art, The Amana colony: Communal Escape To The Middle Border, Proc Univ Wyo, 82. **CONTACT ADDRESS** Dept of History, Indiana Univ-Purdue Univ, Fort Wayne, 2101 Coliseum Blvd E, Ft. Wayne, IN, 46805-1445. **EMAIL** scottc@ipfw.edu

SCOTT, DARYL
DISCIPLINE UNITED STATES HISTORY **EDUCATION** Marquette Univ, BA, 84; Stanford Univ, PhD, 94. **CAREER** Assoc prof. **SELECTED PUBLICATIONS** Auth, Contempt and Pity: Social Policy and the Image of the Damaged Black Psyche 1880-1996, 97. **CONTACT ADDRESS** Dept of History, Columbia Col, New York, 2960 Broadway, New York, NY, 10027-6902.

SCOTT, DONALD M.
DISCIPLINE HISTORY **EDUCATION** Harvard Univ, BA, 62; Univ Wis, MS, 64, PhD, 68. **CAREER** Assoc prof, hist, NC State Univ; PROF, HIST & DEAN FAC, DIV SOC SCI, QUEENS COLL, CUNY. **MEMBERSHIPS** Am Antiquarian Soc **SELECTED PUBLICATIONS** Auth, From Office to Profession: New England Ministry, 1750-1850, 78; auth, "The Popular Lecture and the Creation of a Public in Mid-Nineteenth Century America," Jour of Am Hist 66, 80; auth, America's Families: A Documentary History, 82; auth, "Print and the Public Lecture System, 1840-1860," in Printing and Society in Early America, AAS 83; auth, "Itinerant Lectures and Lecturing in New England, 1800-1850," in Hierarchy in New England and New York, 86; auth, "Knowledge and the Marketplace," in The Mythmaking Frame of Mind: Social Imagination and American Culture, 93. **CONTACT ADDRESS** Dean of the Social Sciences, Queens Col, CUNY, 6530 Kissena Blvd, Flushing, NY, 11367-1597. **EMAIL** Donald_Scott@QC.edu

SCOTT, JOHN SHERMAN
PERSONAL Born 07/20/1937, Bellaire, Ohio, m, 1982 **DISCIPLINE** ETHNIC STUDIES **EDUCATION** SC State U, BA 1961; Bowling Green U, MA 1966; PhD 1972. **CAREER** Bowling Green State Univ OH, prof ethnic studies & resident-writer beginning 1970, prof emeritus, currently; director, Ethnic Cultural Arts Program. **HONORS AND AWARDS** Governor's Award for the Arts, State of Ohio, 1990; produced play (TV), CURRENTS, 1991, produced docu-drama (TV), Hats & Fans, 1991, PBS. **MEMBERSHIPS** Consultant Toledo Model Cities Prog 1969-72; consult Toledo Bd Edn; mem NY Dramatists League 1971-; Speech Comm Assn 1966-73; Eugene O'Neill Memorial Theatre Center 1970-; Frank Silvera Writer's Wrkshp 1973-. **SELECTED PUBLICATIONS** Pub articles Players Black Lines; plays performed, Off-Broadway, NYC; Ride a Black Horse, Negro Ensemble Company 1972; Karma and The Goodship Credit, Richard Allen Center 1978-79. **CONTACT ADDRESS** Prof of Ethnic Studies & Resident-Writer, Bowling Green State Univ, Shatzel Hall, Bowling Green, OH, 43402.

SCOTT, KERMIT
DISCIPLINE MEDIEVAL PHILOSOPHY **EDUCATION** Columbia Univ, PhD. **CAREER** Assoc prof, Purdue Univ. **RESEARCH** Social and political philosophy; Marxism. **SELECTED PUBLICATIONS** Published articles, a translation, and a critical text on medieval philosophy. **CONTACT ADDRESS** Dept of Philos, Purdue Univ, 1080 Schleman Hall, West Lafayette, IN, 47907-1080.

SCOTT, OTIS L.
PERSONAL Born 12/27/1941, Marion, Ohio, m, 1963 **DISCIPLINE** ETHNIC STUDIES **EDUCATION** University of MD & Eastern Washington State College, Cheney, WA; Central State College, Wilberforce, OH; California State University, Sacramento, BA, 1971, MA, 1973; Union Graduate School, Cincinnati, OH, PhD, 1982. **CAREER** California State University, Sacramento, CA, professor, 1974-. **HONORS AND AWARDS** Co-Project Director, Beyond the Canon, 1990-; CSUS Exceptional Merit Award, 1984. **MEMBERSHIPS** Member, National Conference of Black Political Scientists, 1989-; member, National Council for Black Studies, 1979-; member, National Association of Ethnic Studies, 1985-; member, Sacramento Area Black Caucus, 1974-; National Association for Ethnic Studies, 1996-98, pres, 1998. **SELECTED**

PUBLICATIONS Author, The Veil: Perspectives on Race & Ethnicity in the US, West Publishing Co, 1994; co-author, Teaching From A Multicultural Perspective, Sage, 1994; author, "Lines, Borders and Corrections," Kendall Hunt, 1997; Journal article, Ethnic Studies Past and Present Explorations in Ethnic Studies Vol 11, No 2, 1988; Journal article, Coping Strategies of Women in Alice Walkers Novels Explorations in Ethnic Studies, Vol 10, No 1, 1987. **CONTACT ADDRESS** Ethnic Studies Department, California State Univ, Sacramento, 6000 J St, Sacramento, CA, 95819.

SCOTT, PETER DALE
PERSONAL Born 01/11/1929, Montreal, PQ, Canada, m, 1956, 3 children **DISCIPLINE** ENGLISH, POLITICAL SCIENCE **EDUCATION** McGill Univ, BA, 49, PhD(polit sci), 55. **CAREER** Lectr polit sci, McGill Univ, 55-56; foreign serv off, Can Foreign Serv, 56-61; lectr speech, 61-62, acting asst prof, 62-63, asst prof, 63-66, asst prof, 66-68, assoc prof, 68-80, PROF ENGLISH, UNIV CALIF, BERKELEY, 80-, Humanities res fel, Univ Calif, Berkeley, 68; Guggenheim fel, 69-70. **RESEARCH** Covert Politics; medieval Latin poetry; literature and politics. **SELECTED PUBLICATIONS** Auth, Mcnamara And Vietnam - Reply/, New York Rev Of Books, Vol 0042, 1995. **CONTACT ADDRESS** 2823 Ashby Ave, Berkeley, CA, 94705.

SCOTT, REBECCA JARVIS
PERSONAL Born 07/18/1950, Athens, GA, m, 1978 **DISCIPLINE** LATIN AMERICAN HISTORY **EDUCATION** Harvard Univ, BA, 71; London Sch Econ, MPhil, 73; Princeton Univ, PhD(hist), 82. **CAREER** ASST PROF HIST, UNIV MICH, 80-, Mich Soc Fellows jr fel, 80- **MEMBERSHIPS** AHA; Latin Am Studies Asn. **RESEARCH** Slave emancipation and transition to free labor in Cuba, 1868-1895; comparative study of emancipations and postemancipation societies, Cuba, Brazil, Louisiana; the formation of the Cuban rural working class in the late 19th and early 20th centuries. **SELECTED PUBLICATIONS** Auth, Defining The Boundaries Of Freedom In The World Of Cane - Cuba, Brazil, And Louisiana After Emancipation/, Am Hist Rev, Vol 0099, 1994. **CONTACT ADDRESS** Dept Hist, Univ Mich, 435 S State St, Ann Arbor, MI, 48109-1003.

SCOTT, ROY V.
PERSONAL Born 12/26/1927, Wrights, IL, m, 1959, 3 children **DISCIPLINE** AMERICAN HISTORY **EDUCATION** Iowa State Univ, BS, 52; Univ Ill, MA, 53, PhD, 57. **CAREER** Asst prof hist, Univ Southwestern La, 57-58; res assoc, Bus Hist Found 58-59; asst prof hist, Univ Mo, 59-60; from asst prof to assoc prof, 60-64, prof hist, Miss State Univ, 64-, assoc, Bus Hist Found, 63-64; William L Giles distinguished prof of hist, 74-. **HONORS AND AWARDS** Cert Commendation, Am Asn State & Local Hist, 77. **MEMBERSHIPS** AHA; Orgn Am Historians; Agr Hist Soc (vpres, 77-78, pres, 78-79); Econ Hist Asn; Miss Hist Soc, pres, 89-90. **RESEARCH** Farm life in the Middle West. **SELECTED PUBLICATIONS** Auth, Agrarian Movement in Illinois, 1880-1896, Univ Ill, 62; American railroads and agricultural extension, 1900-1914, Bus Hist Rev, spring 65; The Reluctant Farmer: The Rise of Agricultural Extension to 1914, Univ Ill, 71; coauth, The Public Career of Cully A Cobb: A Study in Agricultural Leadership, Univ Miss, 73; coed, Southern agriculture since the Civil War, Agr Hist Soc, 79; auth, Railroad development Programs in the Twentieth Century, Iowa State Univ Press, 85; Eugene Beverly Ferris and Agricultural Science in the Lower South, Center for the Study of Southern Culture, 91; coauth, The Great Northern Railway: A History, Harvard Business School Press, 88; Wal-Mart: A History of Sam Walton's Retail Phenomenon, Twayne, 94; Old Main: Images of a Legend, Miss State Univ Alumni Asn, 95. **CONTACT ADDRESS** Dept of History, Mississippi State Univ, PO Box H, Mississippi State Univ, MS, 39762-5508.

SCOTT, SAMUEL FRANCIS
PERSONAL Born 01/10/1938, Quincy, MA, m, 1961, 2 children **DISCIPLINE** MODERN EUROPEAN & FRENCH HISTORY **EDUCATION** Boston Col AB, 59; Univ Wis-Madison, MA, 62, PhD(hist), 68. **CAREER** From instr to asst prof, 67-76, assoc prof, 76-81, PROF HIST, WAYNE STATE UNIV, 81-, Wayne State Univ fac res award, 70 & 76; Soc Sci Res Coun fac res grant, 71; Nat Endowment for Humanities res grant, 76. **MEMBERSHIPS** AAUP; Soc Etudes Robespierristes; Soc Fr Hist Studies; fel Inter-Univ Sem Armed Forces & Soc; Am Soc 18th Century Studies. **RESEARCH** French Revolution; social history; military history. **SELECTED PUBLICATIONS** Auth, Revolution And Political-Conflict In The Fr Navy, 1789-1794 - Cormack,Ws/, J Of Mil Hist, Vol 0060, 1996; War, Revolution, And The Bureaucratic State - Politics And Army Administration In France, 1791-1799 - Brown,Hg/, Am Hist Rev, Vol 0102, 1997. **CONTACT ADDRESS** Dept of Hist, Wayne State Univ, 838 Mackenzie, Detroit, MI, 48202-3919.

SCOTT, SUSAN C.
PERSONAL Born 07/13/1942, Drexel Hill, PA, s **DISCIPLINE** ART HISTORY; ARCHITECTURAL HISTORY **EDUCATION** Penn St Univ, BS, 64; Penn St Univ, MA, 78; Penn St Univ, PhD, 95 **CAREER** Teacher public schools, Pa & Delaware, 64-70; instr, Penn St Univ, 85-94; asst prof, Penn St Univ, 95 **HONORS AND AWARDS** Founding Member, Intl Soc Study of Chinese Archit Hist; Penn St Univ Panhellenic Soc Award for outstanding teaching; Louise Purcell/Knight Ridder Travel Grant; **MEMBERSHIPS** College Art Assoc; Amer Soc for 18th Cent Studies; Soc of Architectural Historians; American Fulbright Soc; Int Soc for Chinese Architectural Studies **RESEARCH** Oriental Art and Architecture; Baroque Architecture in Italy; Renaissance Architecture in Italy **SELECTED PUBLICATIONS** Co-ed, Rembrandt, Rubens, and the Art of their Time: Recent Perspectives, Pa State Univ, 97; review of Elisabeth Blair MacDougall, "Fountains, Statues, and Flowers: Studies in Italian Gardens of the Sixteenth and Seventeenth Centuries," Jrnl Soc Archit Historians, 97; co-ed, The Art of Interpreting, Pa State Univ, 96 **CONTACT ADDRESS** Dept Art Hist, Pennsylvania State Univ, 229 Arts Building, University Park, PA, 16802. **EMAIL** ssm117@psu.edu

SCOTT, WILLIAM BUTLER
PERSONAL Born 02/27/1945, Charleston, SC, m, 1966 **DISCIPLINE** HISTORY **EDUCATION** Presby Col, BA, 67; Wake Forest Univ, MA, 68; Univ Wis, Madison, PhD(hist), 73. **CAREER** Asst prof, 73-80, ASSOC PROF HIST, KENYON COL, 80- **MEMBERSHIPS** AHA; Orgn Am Historians; Southern Hist Asn; Inst Early Am Hist & Cult. **RESEARCH** American intellectual and legal history. **SELECTED PUBLICATIONS** Auth, Royce,Josiah - From Grass Valley To Harvard - Hine,Rv/, Am Hist Rev, Vol 0098, 1993; Veblen,Thorstein And His Critics, 1891-1963 - Conservative, Liberal, And Radical Perspective - Tilman,R/, J Of Am Hist, Vol 0080, 1993; The Chicago Pragmatists And Am Progressivism - Feffer,A/, Am Hist Rev, Vol 0099, 1994; Intellectuals In Exile - Refugee Scholars And The New-School-For-Soc-Research - Krohn,Cd/, Am Hist Rev, Vol 0100, 1995. **CONTACT ADDRESS** Kenyon Col, Seitz House, Gambier, OH, 43022-9623.

SCOTT, WILLIAM CLYDE
PERSONAL Born 09/14/1937, Oklahoma City, OK, m, 1964, 3 children **DISCIPLINE** CLASSICS **EDUCATION** Princeton Univ, AB, 59, MA, 62, PhD(classics), 64. **CAREER** Instr classics, Phillips Acad, Andover, 59-60; asst prof, Haverford Col, 64-66; asst prof classics, 66-70, assoc prof classics & drama, 70-75, assoc dean fac, 70-72, chemn dept, 70-76, prof classics & drama, 75-, humanities res prof, 88-, Dartmouth prof of classics, Dartmouth Col, 94-, Dartmouth fac fel, 67-68; mem managing comt, Am Sch Class Studies Athens. **HONORS AND AWARDS** Goodwin Award of Merit, Am Philol Asn, 86. **MEMBERSHIPS** Am Philol Asn; Am Inst Archaeol. **RESEARCH** Greek epic; Greek drama; Roman lyric. **SELECTED PUBLICATIONS** Auth, The confused chorus (Agamemnon 975-1034), Phoenix, 69; Catullus and Caesar (c 29), Class Philol, 71; A repeated episode at Odyssey 1 125-48, TAPha, 71; The Oral Nature of the Homeric Simile, Leiden, 74; Lines for Clytemnestra (Ag 489-502), 78 & Non-Strophic Elements in the Oresteia, 82, TAPhA; Musical Design in Aeschylean Theater, 84; Plato's The Republic, 85; Musical Design in Sophoclean Theater, 96. **CONTACT ADDRESS** Dept of Classics, Dartmouth Col, 6086 Reed Hall, Hanover, NH, 03755-3506. **EMAIL** william.c.scott@dartmouth.edu

SCOTT, WILLIAM R.
DISCIPLINE AFRICAN-AMERICAN HISTORY **EDUCATION** PhD, Princeton Univ. **CAREER** Prof, Lehigh Univ **HONORS AND AWARDS** Director of the African-American Studies Program **MEMBERSHIPS** Inst Int Educ S African Educ Prog; dir, United Negro Col Fund/Mellon Minorities Fels Prog. **RESEARCH** Black American thought; African-U.S. interaction. **SELECTED PUBLICATIONS** Auth, Sons of Sheba's Race: African-Americans and the Italo-Ethiopian War. **CONTACT ADDRESS** Lehigh Univ, Bethlehem, PA, 18015.

SCOTT, WILLIAM RICHARD
PERSONAL Born 12/18/1932, Parsons, KS, m, 1955, 3 children **DISCIPLINE** SOCIOLOGY **EDUCATION** Parsons Jr Coll, AA, 52; Univ Kansas, BS, 54, MA, 55; Univ Chicago, PhD, 61. **CAREER** Asst prof, Stanford Univ, 60; vice ch, Soc, SU, 68-72; ch, Soc, SU, 72-75; vis sr res, nat Ctr Health Servs Res, Dept Health Educ & Welfare, 75-76; dir, Stanford Ctr Orgs Res, 88-96; adj prof, Public Pol & Admin, Univ Tromso, Norway, 91-92; vis prof, Copenhagen Bus Sch, 92; vis prof, Kellogg Grad Sch Mgt, Northwestern Univ, 97; PROF, STANFORD UNIV, SOC. **MEMBERSHIPS** Am Soc Asn; Acad Mgt; Macro-Org Behav Soc; Soc Res Asn; Inst Medicine **RESEARCH** Effects of institutional facets of environments on organizations; Structure & performance of public & nonprofit organizations. **SELECTED PUBLICATIONS** Institutions and Organizations, Sage; coauth, Organizational Environments: Ritual and Rationality, Sage, 92; ed, Organisational Sociology, Dartmouth Publ, 94; co-edr, Institutional Environments and Organizations: Structural Complexity and Individualism, Sage, 94; The Institutional Construction of Organizations: International and Longitudinal Studies, Sage 95; Organizations: Rational,Natural and Open Systems, Prentice Hall, 98. **CONTACT ADDRESS** Dept Sociol, Stanford Univ, Stanford, CA, 94305. **EMAIL** scottwr@leland.stanford.edu

SCOTT JENKINS, VIRGINIA
DISCIPLINE AMERICAN STUDIES/HISTORY **EDUCATION** Wheaton Col, BA, 73; George WA Univ, PhD, 91. **RESEARCH** Material cult studies. **SELECTED PUBLICATIONS** Auth, Early Nineteenth Century Road Food: What People Ate When They Traveled in the United States, Mid-Atlantic Almanack 2, 93; A Green Velvety Carpet: The Front Lawn in America, Jour Amer Cult, 94; The Lawn: A History of An American Obsession, Smithsonian Inst Press, 94; Slipping Up: Bananas and American Humor, Columbia Jour Amer Stud, 98; Fairway Living, Princeton Architecture Press, in companion volume to an exhibit at the Canadian Arch Ctr, 98. **CONTACT ADDRESS** Am Stud Dept, Univ MD, Col Park, College Park, MD, 20742. **EMAIL** vjenkins@mnsinc.com

SCRANTON, PHILIP
PERSONAL Born 09/11/1946, New Brighton, PA, m, 1983, 1 child **DISCIPLINE** AMERICAN HISTORY, HISTORY OF TECHNOLOGY **EDUCATION** Univ Penn, BA, 68, MA, 71, PhD, 75. **CAREER** Instr to assoc prof, Phil Col of Textiles and Science, 74-84; assoc prof to prof, Rutgers Univ, 84-97; Kranzberg Prof, Georgia Inst Tech, 87- ; dir, Ctr Hist Bus, Hagley Mus and Lib, 92- ; ed, Stud in Industry and Soc, Rutgers Univ Pr, 94- . **HONORS AND AWARDS** President's Awd for Tchg Excellence, PCT&S; Soc for the Hist of the Early Republic book awd; Taft Prize in labor hist book awd; Newcomen prize in bus hist, article awd; NEH fel; Mellon res fel. **MEMBERSHIPS** Am Hist Asn; Org of Am Hist; Soc for the Hist of Tech; Bus Hist Conf; So Hist Asn. **RESEARCH** American industrialization, 1860-1980. **SELECTED PUBLICATIONS** Auth, Proprietary Capitalism: the Textile Manufacture at Philadelphia, 1800-1885, Cambridge Univ Pr, 83; coauth, Work Sights: Industrial Philadelphia, 1890-1950, Temple Univ Pr, 86; auth, Figured Tapestry: Markets, Production, and Power in Philadelphia Textiles, 1885-1941, Cambridge Univ Pr, 89; auth, Diversity in Diversity: Flexible Production and American Industrialization; 1870-1930, in Bus Hist Rev, 91; auth, Large Firms and Industrial Restructuring: the Philadelphia Region, 1900-1980, in Pa Mag of Hist and Bio, 92; auth, Manufacturing Diversity: Production Systems, Markets, and American Consumer Society, Tech and Culture, 94; auth, Determinism and Indeterminacy in the History of Technology, in Machines and History, MIT, 94; auth,Have a Heart for the Manufacturers, in Flexibility and Mass Production in Western Industrialization, Cambridge, 97; auth, Endless Novelty: Specialty Production and American Industrialization, 1865-1925, Princeton, 97. **CONTACT ADDRESS** School of History, Technology and Society, Georgia Inst of Tech, Atlanta, GA, 30332-0345. **EMAIL** philip.scranton@hts.gatech.edu

SCRUGGS, OTEY MATTHEW
PERSONAL Born 06/29/1929, Vallejo, California, m **DISCIPLINE** HISTORY **EDUCATION** Univ of CA Santa Barbara, BA 1951; Harvard U, MA 1952, PhD 1958. **CAREER** Univ of CA Santa Barbara, instr to asso prof 1957-69; Syracuse Univ, prof of history 1969-94, emeritus, 1994-, chair, dept of history 1986-90. **HONORS AND AWARDS** Syracuse Univ, Chancellor's Citation for Exceptional Academic Achievement. **MEMBERSHIPS** Mem Assn for Study of Afro/Am Life & Hist; editl Bd Afro-ams in NY Life & Hist 1977-; mem Orgn of Am Historians; mem bd of dir Onondaga Historical Assn 1988-92.

SCULLION, SCOTT
DISCIPLINE CLASSICS **EDUCATION** Univ Toronto, BA, 82; Harvard Univ, PhD, 90. **MEMBERSHIPS** Am Philol Asn. **RESEARCH** Greek religion; Greek literature, especially drama. **SELECTED PUBLICATIONS** Auth, Three Studies in Athenian Dramaturgy, Teubner, 94; auth, Olympian and Chthonian, Class Antiquity, 94; auth, Dionysos and Katharsis in Antigone, Class Antiquity, forthcoming; auth, Three Notes on Attic Sacrificial Calendars, Zeitschrift fur Papyrologie und Epigraphik, forthcoming; auth, Saviours of the Father's Hearth: Olympian and Chthonian in the Oresteia, in Hagg, ed, Greek Sacrificial Ritual, Olympian and Chthonian, Stockholm, Paul Astroms Forlag, forthcoming. **CONTACT ADDRESS** Dept of Classics, Union Col, Schenectady, NY, 12308.

SCULLY, PAMELA F.
DISCIPLINE HISTORY **EDUCATION** Univ Cape Town, BA,85; MA, 87; Univ Mich, PhD, 93. **CAREER** Visiting instr, 92-93 Kenyon Coll; visiting scholar, Stanford Univ, 94-95; asst prof, 93- Kenyon Coll. **HONORS AND AWARDS** Fac Devel Grant, Kenyon Col, 94; NEH Fel, 95-96; Fac Devel Grant, 96-97. **RESEARCH** South African History; Sub-Saharan African History; Race, Sexuality and Empire. **SELECTED PUBLICATIONS** Auth, Narratives of Infanticide in the Aftermath of Slave Emancipation in the Rural Western Cape, South Africa, 1838-1848, Can Jour of African Studies, 96; Rape, Race, and Colonial Culture: The Sexual Politics of Identity in the Nineteenth Century Cape Colony, South Africa, Am Hist Rev, 95; Liquor and Labor in the Western Cape, Liquor and labor in Southern Africa, Ohio Univ Press, 92; rev, Elizabeth Schmidt, Peasants, Traders, and Wives, Soc Hist 21, 96; P.J. van der Merwe, The Migrant Farmer in the History of the Cape Colony, 1657-1842, Soc Hist 20, 95; Les Switzer, Power and Resistance in an African Society, Intl Jour of African Hist Studies 28, 95; Elizabeth Eldredge and Fred Morton, Slavery in South Africa,

IJAHS 30, 96; Robert C-H Shell, Children of Bondage, Am Hist Rev 101, 96. **CONTACT ADDRESS** Dept of Hist, Kenyon Col, Gambier, OH, 43022. **EMAIL** scully@kenyon.edu

SCULLY, STEPHEN P.
PERSONAL Born 06/04/1947, m, 3 children **DISCIPLINE** CLASSICAL STUDIES **EDUCATION** NY Univ, BA, 71; U NC Chapel Hill, MA, 75; Brown Univ, PhD, 78. **CAREER** Mellen Fellow, 78-80, John Hopkins Univ; Assoc Prof, 80-, Boston Univ. **HONORS AND AWARDS** NEH Summer Stipend; Jasper Whiting Fellowship; Honor and the Sacred City; Best Acad Books, Choice. **MEMBERSHIPS** Amer Philos Assoc; New England Class Assoc. **RESEARCH** Epic; Tragedy; Near Eastern Lit; Renaissance Stud. **SELECTED PUBLICATIONS** Coauth, Arion, 3rd Series, 3.1 and 4.1, Special Issue, The Chorus in Greek Tragedy and Culture, 96 & 96; auth, Homer and The Sacred City, Ithaca, NY, Cornell Univ, 90; coauth, Euripides Suppliant Women, Oxford, Oxford Univ Press, 95. **CONTACT ADDRESS** Dept Classics, Boston Univ, Boston, MA, 02215. **EMAIL** sscully@bu.edu

SEADLE, MICHAEL S.
DISCIPLINE HISTORY **EDUCATION** Earlham Col, BA, 72; Univ Mich, MS, 97; Univ Chicago, MA, 73, PhD, 77. **CAREER** Asst dir, Acad Computing Svcs, E Mich Univ, 87-89; online oper mgr, asst dir, Libr Tech Dept, Cornell Univ, 89-92; pres, Seadle Consult, 92-96; digital info assoc, Univ Mich, 96-97; DIGITAL SVCS LIBRN, MICH STATE UNIV, 98-. **CONTACT ADDRESS** Michigan State Univ, 100 Library, East Lansing, MI, 48224-1048. **EMAIL** seadle@mail.lib.msu.edu

SEAGER, SHARON HANNUM
PERSONAL Born 10/24/1938, Amarillo, TX **DISCIPLINE** HISTORY **EDUCATION** Trinity Univ, BA, 60; Rice Univ, PhD(hist), 65. **CAREER** Asst prof hist, Southeast Mo State Col, 64-66; assoc prof, 66-80, PROF HIST, BALL STATE UNIV, 80- **MEMBERSHIPS** Orgn Am Historians; Southern Hist Asn. **RESEARCH** Ideology of the Southern Confederacy; history of the South; women in American history. **SELECTED PUBLICATIONS** Auth, Thomas Chilton--lawyer, politician, preacher, Filson Club Hist Quart, 64; contribr, History from a feminist perspective, In: Conspectus of History, Cambridge Univ, 78. **CONTACT ADDRESS** Dept of History, Ball State Univ, Muncie, IN, 47306-0002. **EMAIL** sseager@gw.bsu.edu

SEALE, WILLIAM
PERSONAL Born 08/07/1939, Beaumont, TX, m, 1966, 2 children **DISCIPLINE** AMERICAN HISTORY **EDUCATION** Southwestern Univ, BA, 61; Duke Univ, MA, 64, PhD, 65. **CAREER** Lectr US hist, 64-65, Univ Houston; lectr, Univ SC, 69-71; asst prof hist, 65-69, Lamar State Univ; adj prof archit, 79-, Columbia Univ; curator, 74-75, Smithsonian Institution; free-lance writer & consult on hist restor & proj in Am hist, 77-. **MEMBERSHIPS** AHA; Soc Archit Historians; Assn Preservation Technol. **RESEARCH** American cultural history, particularly as it relates to architecture and customs of living. **SELECTED PUBLICATIONS** Auth, The President's House: A History, White House Hist Assn, 87; auth, Of Houses and Time, Harry Abrams, 91; auth, The White House; History of an American Idea, Am Inst of Archit Press, 92; auth, The White House Garden, White House Hist Assn, 95. **CONTACT ADDRESS** 805 Prince St, Alexandria, VA, 22314. **EMAIL** oeconomy@aol.com

SEALEY, B. RAPHAEL
PERSONAL Born 08/14/1927, Middlesbrough, United Kingdom, d, 1 child **DISCIPLINE** ANCIENT HISTORY **EDUCATION** Univ Oxford, England, MA, 51. **CAREER** Various positions in British and American Universities, 54-67; PROF HIST, UNIV CA, BERKELEY, 67-. **MEMBERSHIPS** Am Philol Asn; Asn Ancient Historians. **RESEARCH** Greek hist; Greek and Roman law. **SELECTED PUBLICATIONS** Auth, Demosthenes and His Time: a Study on Defeat, Oxford Univ Press, 93; The Justice of the Greeks, Univ MI Press, 94. **CONTACT ADDRESS** Dept Hist, Univ California, Berkeley, CA, 94720-2550. **EMAIL** squiley@socrates

SEARS, ELIZABETH ANN
DISCIPLINE AFRICAN AMERICAN MUSIC, AMERICAN MUSICAL THEATER, PIANO **EDUCATION** New Eng Conserv Mus, BM; Ariz State Univ, MM; Cath Univ Am, PhD. **CAREER** Music, Wheaton, Col. **RESEARCH** European and American art song, piano performance. **SELECTED PUBLICATIONS** Ed, bk of essays on Amer pop song; co-writer, textbook on Amer musical theater. **CONTACT ADDRESS** Dept of Mus, Wheaton Col, 26 East Main St, Norton, MA, 02766. **EMAIL** asears@wheatonma.edu

SEATON, DOUGLASS
PERSONAL Born 06/08/1950, Baltimore, MD, m, 1972 **DISCIPLINE** HISTORICAL MUSICOLOGY **EDUCATION** Columbia Univ, PhD, 77. **CAREER** Fla State Univ, 78- . **MEMBERSHIPS** Am Musicol Soc; The Col Mus Soc; 19th Cent Stud Asn; Lyrica Soc Word-Music Rel. **RESEARCH** Felix Mendelssohn Bartholdy, song, criticism. **SELECTED PUBLICATIONS** The Art Song: A Research and Information Guide, 87; Ideas and Styles in the Western Musical Tradition, 91. **CONTACT ADDRESS** School of Music, Florida State Univ, Tallahassee, FL, 32306-1180. **EMAIL** seaton_d@cmr.fsu.edu

SEAVY, WILLIAM
DISCIPLINE CLASSICS **EDUCATION** Univ NC, PhD, 93. **CAREER** Vis asst prof, E Carolina Univ, 94-98. **HONORS AND AWARDS** Outstanding hist prof, E Carolina Univ, 97. **MEMBERSHIPS** APA, CAMWS, Ploutarchos. **RESEARCH** Roman War law; Greek and Roman intellectual history. **CONTACT ADDRESS** Dept of History, East Carolina Univ, Brewster A-340, Greenville, NC, 27858-4353. **EMAIL** seaveyw@mail.ecu.edu

SEBESTA, JUDITH LYNN
PERSONAL Chicago, IL **DISCIPLINE** CLASSICAL LANGUAGES AND LITERATURE, ANCIENT HISTORY, WOMEN IN ANTIQUITY **EDUCATION** Univ Chicago, AB, 68; Stanford Univ, PhD, 72. **CAREER** From instr to asst prof, 72-77, Assoc Prof Classics, Univ S Dak, 77-, Dir, Integrated Humanities Prof, Univ SDak, 81, Dir Classics, 81, Chair, Dept Hist, 97-. **HONORS AND AWARDS** Phi Beta Kappa, 67; Harrington Lectr, Col Arts & Sci, 94. **MEMBERSHIPS** Am Philol Asn; Class Asn Midwest & South; Am Classical League. **RESEARCH** The Roman army; provinces of the Roman empire; classical philology. **SELECTED PUBLICATIONS** Auth, Carl Orff Carmina Burana, Bolchazy-Carducci Publ, 84, 96; Mantles of the Gods and Catullus 64, Syllectu Classica 5, 93; coauth, The World of Roman Costume, Univ Wis Press, 94; auth, Women's Costume and Feminine Civic Morality in Augustan Rome, Gender & Hist 9, 97; Aliquid Sem per Novi: New Challenges & New Approaches, in Latin for the 21st Century, Addison-Wesley, 97. **CONTACT ADDRESS** Dept of Hist, Univ of SDak, 414 E Clark St, Vermillion, SD, 57069-2390. **EMAIL** jsebesta@sunbird.usd.edu

SEDGWICK, ALEXANDER
PERSONAL Born 06/08/1930, Boston, MA, m, 1961, 2 children **DISCIPLINE** EARLY MODERN AND MODERN EUROPEAN HISTORY **EDUCATION** Harvard Univ, AB, 52, PhD(hist), 63. **CAREER** Instr hist, Dartmouth Col, 62-63; from asst prof to assoc prof, 63-74, Prof hist, Univ VA, 74-95, Univ prof 95-97, Dept ChPerson, 79-85,Dean Col A&S, 85-90; Dean GSAS 90-95; Emer prof, 97-. **HONORS AND AWARDS** Am Coun Learned Soc grant-in-aid, 67-68, Am Phil Soc grant-in-aid, 71. **MEMBERSHIPS** AHA; Soc Fr Hist Studies (execsecy, 79-84, pres 84); AAUP (nat coun 76-79). **RESEARCH** Early and mod French hist. **SELECTED PUBLICATIONS** Auth, The Ralliement in French Politics, 1890-98, Harvard Univ, 65; The Third French Republic, 1870-1914, Crowell, 68; Jansenism in 17th Century France: Voices from the Wilderness, Univ VA, 77; Seventeenth-Century French Jansenism and the Enlightenment, Fr Relig & Soc, 82; Voltaire: I'd Rather Be in Philadelphia, 85; The Nuns of Port-Royal, A Study in Female Spirituality, 90; The Gentle Strength, 90; Prophets Without Honor, 90; La revolutionn francaise et le caractere de la Democratie francaise, 90; La famille Arnauld a travers le Port-Royal de Saaainte-Beuve, Chroniques de Port Royal, 95; Travails of Conscience, Harvard Univ, 98. **CONTACT ADDRESS** Dept of History, Univ of VA, Randall Hall, Charlottesville, VA, 22903. **EMAIL** as6d@virginia.edu

SEDLAR, JEAN WHITENACK
PERSONAL Born 02/02/1935, South Milwaukee, WI, d, 2 children **DISCIPLINE** EUROPEAN & WORLD HISTORY **EDUCATION** Univ Chicago, MA, 56, PhD(hist), 70. **CAREER** Lectr hist, Ill Inst Technol, 71-72; asst prof to prof hist, Univ Pittsburgh, Johnstown, 72-. **HONORS AND AWARDS** NEH Inst 87, 89; summer Fulbright to Germany, 92. **MEMBERSHIPS** Am Asn Advan Slavic Studies; Midwest Slavic Asn. **RESEARCH** East-central Europe; history from medieval period to present; cross cultural influences in history; East-Central Europe: World War II. **SELECTED PUBLICATIONS** Co-ed, The Origins of Civilization, Vol I, The Ancient Near East, Vol II, The Classical Mediterranean World, Vol III, Classical India, Vol IV, Classical China, Vol V & India, China and Japan: The Middle Period, Vol VII, In: Readings in World History, Oxford Univ Press, 69-71; auth, India and the Greek World: A Study in the Transmission of Culture, Rowman & Littlefield, 80; India in the Mind of Germany: Schelling, Schopenhauer and Their Times, Univ Press Am, 82; auth, East Central Europe in the Middle Ages, 1000-1500, In: Vol III of History of East Central Europe, Univ Wash Press, 94. **CONTACT ADDRESS** Dept of Hist, Univ of Pittsburgh, 450 Schoolhouse Rd, Johnstown, PA, 15904-2912. **EMAIL** sedlar@pitt.edu

SEEBASS, TILMAN
PERSONAL Born 09/08/1939, Basel, Switzerland **DISCIPLINE** MUSICOLOGY **EDUCATION** Humanistisches Gymnasium, MA, 59; Univ of Basel and Heidelberg, PhD, 70. **CAREER** Swiss Nat Res Fund Fellow, 70-75; Asst/Assoc/Full Prof, Duke Univ, 77-93; Prof, Chmn, Inst of Musicol, Innsbruck, 93- ; Pres Austrian Soc of Musicol, 96- . **MEMBERSHIPS** AMS; Int Soc Musicol; Int Council Trad Mus; Austrian Soc Musicol; Soc Ital di Musicol. **RESEARCH** Musicology general; musical iconography; Indonesian music. **SELECTED PUBLICATIONS** The visualization of music through pictorial imagery and notation in late medieval France, in Studies in the Performance of Late Medieval Music, Cambridge, 83, 19-33; Ed, Imago Musicae, The Int Yrbook of Mus Iconography, 84; A note on kebyar in modern Bali, in Orbis Musicae, Tel-Aviv, IX, 85, 103-121; Notes and paradigms: vocal and instrumental practice in ritual music, contradiction and agreement, in La mus et le rite, sacre et profane, Actes du XIIIe, Congres de la Soc Int de Musicol Strasbourg, 86, 207-221; Between oral and written tradition: the function of notation in Indonesia, in The oral and the literate in music, Tokyo, Acad Mus, 86, 414-427; The relationship of theory to practice in non-Western musical traditions, in Report of the XIVth Int. Congress of the Intl Musicol Soc at Bologna 87, Bologna, 89, 200-21; Classical and Romantic principles in Schubert's Lieder, in Studies in musical sources and style. Madison, WI: A-R, 90, 481-504; The illustration of music theory in the late middle ages: some thoughts on its principles and a few examples, in Music Theory and its Sources: Antiquity and the Middle Ages, Univ Notre Dame Press, 90, 197-234; Idyllic Arcadia and Italian musical reality: experiences of German writers and artists (1770-1835), Imago Mus, 7, 90, 149-187; Iconography and dance research, Yearbk Trad Mus, 23, 91, 33-51; Presence and absence of Portuguese musical elements in Indonesia: an essay on the mechanisms of music acculturation, Portugal and the world-the encounter of cultures in music, Lisbon, Publ m Quixote, 97, 201-225; The power of music in Greek vase painting: reflections on the visualization of rJuqmov and ejpaw/dhv, Imago Mus 8, 91, 11-37; Change in Balinese music life: Kebiar in the 1920s and 1930s, in Being Modern in Bali: Image and Change, New Haven, Yale Univ Press, 96, 171-191. **CONTACT ADDRESS** Inst of Musicology, Univ of Innsbruck, Karl-Schoenherr-Str 3, Innsbruck, ., A-6020. **EMAIL** tilman.seebass@uibk.ac.at

SEED, PATRICIA
PERSONAL Baltimore, MD **DISCIPLINE** LATIN AMERICAN HISTORY **EDUCATION** Fordham Univ, BA, 71; Univ Tex, Austin, MA, 75; Univ Wis-Madison, PhD(Latin Am hist), 80. **CAREER** Vis lectr, Ohio Univ, 79; asst prof, Col Charleston, 80-82; ASST PROF HIST, RICE UNIV, 82- **MEMBERSHIPS** AHA; Conf Latin Am Hist; Latin Am Studies Asn. **SELECTED PUBLICATIONS** Auth, Transatlantic Encounters, Europeans And Andeans In The 16th-Century - Andrien,Kj, Adorno,R/, Hisp Am Hist Rev, Vol 0073, 1993; New Worlds, Ancient Texts - The Power Of Tradition And The Shock Of Discovery - Grafton,A, Shelford,A, Siraisi,N/, Ethnohistory, Vol 0040, 1993; Narratives Of Don-Juan - The Language Of Seduction In 17th-Century Hisp Lit And Society/, J Of Soc Hist, Vol 0026, 1993; Are These Not Also Men - The Indians Humanity And Capacity For Spa Civilization/, J Of Latin Am Studies, Vol 0025, 1993; The Conquest Of Mexico - The Incorporation Of Indian Societies Into The Western World, 16th-Century 18th-Century - Gruzinski,S/, J Of Latin Am Studies, Vol 0026, 1994; Europ Encounters With The New-World - From Renaissance To Romanticism - Pagden,A/, Am Hist Rev, Vol 0099, 1994; The Hist Of Capitalism In Mexico - Its Origins, 1521-1763 - Semo,E/, J Of Latin Am Studies, Vol 0026, 1994; The Indians Of The Discovery - Evangelism, Marriage And Sexuality In 16th-Century Mexico - Fr - Ragon,P/, Hisp Am Hist Rev, Vol 0074, 1994; The Devil In The New-World - The Impact Of Diabolism In New-Spain - Cervantes,F/, J Of Latin Am Studies, Vol 0027, 1995; New-World Encounters - Greenblatt,S/, Ethnohistory, Vol 0044, 1997; Women On The Margins - 3 17th-Century Lives - Davis,Nz/, William And Mary Quart, Vol 0054, 1997; Utopia And Hist In Mexico - The First Chronicles Of Mexican Civilization, 1520-1569 - Baudot,G/, J Of Latin Am Studies, Vol 0029, 1997 **CONTACT ADDRESS** Hist Dept, Rice Univ, Houston, TX, 77001.

SEELY, BRUCE E.
PERSONAL Born 01/10/1953, Chicago, IL, m, 1985, 2 children **DISCIPLINE** HISTORY **EDUCATION** St. Lawrence Univ, BA, 75; Univ Delaware, MA, 77; PhD, 82. **CAREER** US Dept of the Interior, NPS, historian, 76-78; Texas A&M Univ, asst prof, 81-86; Mich Tech Univ, asst prof, assoc prof, prof, 86-, Pres Univ Senate, 97-. **HONORS AND AWARDS** Soc Indust Archeo, Norton Prize, 84; Rail & Loco Hist Soc, Rail Hist Award, 85-86; Soc Hist of Tech, Abbott Payson Usher Award, 87; PWHS & APWA, Abel Wolman Award, 88; MTU, Omicron Delta Kappa, Copper Scroll Award, 90; MIT, Dibner Inst, Fellow, 96. **MEMBERSHIPS** SHT, SIA, OAH, PWHS, BHC **RESEARCH** Hist of tech and eng; eng edu; rail and hwy transport; iron and steel indust. **SELECTED PUBLICATIONS** Auth, Encyclopedia of American Business History and Biography: The Iron and Steel Industry in the Twentieth Century, ed and contrib, Bruccoli Clark Layman Inc, 94; Building the American Highway System: Engineers as Policy Makers, Temp Univ Press, 87; Teaching the History of Technology, in: Studies in History of Sciences, The Asiatic Society, 97; The Diffusion of Science into Engineering: Highway Research at the Bureau of Public Roads, in: The Transfer and Transformation of Ideas and Material Culture, Tex A and M Univ Press 88. **CONTACT ADDRESS** Dept of Social Sciences, Michigan Tech Univ, 1400 Townsend Dr, Houghton, MI, 49931-1295. **EMAIL** bseely@mtu.edu

SEELY, GORDON M.
PERSONAL Born 04/14/1930, San Mateo, CA, m, 1958, 2 children **DISCIPLINE** HISTORY OF EDUCATION **EDUCATION** Stanford Univ, AB, 51, MA, 54 & 58, PhD, 63. **CAREER** Teacher, High Schs & Jr Col, Calif, 54-55, 56-57, 59-60; from asst prof to assoc prof, 60-69, prof History, San Francisco State Univ, 69-. **RESEARCH** American social and intellectual history, especially education; California history. **SELECTED PUBLICATIONS** Ed, Education and Opportunity, Prentice-Hall, 1st ed, 71, 2nd ed, 75. **CONTACT ADDRESS** Dept Hist, San Francisco State Univ, 1600 Holloway Ave, San Francisco, CA, 94132-1740. **EMAIL** evgor@worldnet.att.net

SEELYE, JOHN D.
DISCIPLINE HISTORY **CAREER** GRAD RES PROF, UNIV FLA **MEMBERSHIPS** Am Antiquarian Soc **SELECTED PUBLICATIONS** Auth, Melville: The Ironic Diagram, 70; auth, Prophetic Waters: The River in Early American Life and Literature, 77; auth, "Rational Exultation: The Erie Canal Celebration of 1825," Procs of the AAS 84, 84; auth, Monumental Trivia: The Rhetorical History of Plymouth Rock," paper, SE AM Stud Asn, 87; auth, Beautiful Machine: Rivers and the Republican Plan, 1755-1828, Oxford Univ Press, 91. **CONTACT ADDRESS** PO Box 2199, Hawthorne, FL, 32640.

SEEMAN, ERIK R.
DISCIPLINE HISTORY **EDUCATION** Harvard Univ, AB, 89, Univ MIch, PhD. **CAREER** ASST PROF, HIST, STATE UNIV NY BUFFALO **MEMBERSHIPS** Am Antiquarian Soc **SELECTED PUBLICATIONS** Auth, "She Died Like Good Old Jacob, Deathbed Scenes and Inversions of Power in New England, 1675-1775," Procs of the AAS 104; auth, The Spiritual Labour of John Barnard: An Eighteenth-Century Artisan Constructs His Piety, Rel & Am Cult: A Jour of Interp 5, Summer 95. **CONTACT ADDRESS** Dept of Hist, SUNY-Buffalo, Park Hall, Buffalo, NY, 14260. **EMAIL** seeman@acsu.buffalo.edu

SEFTON, JAMES EDWARD
PERSONAL Born 07/29/1939, San Francisco, CA **DISCIPLINE** UNITED STATES HISTORY **EDUCATION** Univ Calif, Los Angeles, AB, 61, PhD, 65. **CAREER** From instr to assoc prof, 65-73, PROF HIST, CALIF STATE UNIV, NORTHRIDGE, 73-, Nat Col Athletics Asn, Fac Athletics Rep, 81-90; Am Philos Soc Penrose Fund grant, 68-69. **HONORS AND AWARDS** Distinguished Teaching Award, Calif State Univ, Northridge, 70. **MEMBERSHIPS** AHA; Southern Hist Asn; Orgn Am Historians; US Naval Inst. **RESEARCH** Military and naval history; Civil War and Reconstruction; United States constitutional history; Fine arts and historical photography. **SELECTED PUBLICATIONS** Auth, The United States Army and Reconstruction, 1865-77, La State Univ, 67; The impeachment of President Johnson: A century of historical writing, 6/68 & Aristotle in blue and braid: General John M Schofield's essays on Reconstruction, 3/71, Civil War Hist; Black slaves, red masters, white middlemen: A congressional debate of 1852, Fla Hist Quart, 10/72; Tribute pennies and tribute clauses: Religion in the first constitutions of Trans-Mississippi States, 1812-1912, in The American West and the Religious Experience, 74; auth, Andrew Johnson and the Uses of Constitutional Power, Little, 80; Admiral Royal Eason Ingersoll, in Dictionary of American Military Biography, Greenwood Press, 84; Ulysses S Grant, in Encyclopedia of the American Presidency, Simon & Schuster, 94; Reconstruction, Photography and War, and Naval Operations in the Pacific in World War II, in: Oxford Companion to American Military History, 98. **CONTACT ADDRESS** Dept of Hist, California State Univ, Northridge, 18111 Nordhoff St, Northridge, CA, 91330-8250.

SEGAL, ALAL FRANKLIN
PERSONAL Born 08/02/1945, Worcester, MA, m, 1970, 2 children **DISCIPLINE** JUDAICA, HISTORY OF RELIGION **EDUCATION** Amherst Col, BA, 67; Brandeis Univ, MA, 69; Hebrew Union Col, BHL, 70; Yale Univ, MPhil, 72, PhD(Judaica), 75. **CAREER** Asst prof Judaica, Princeton Univ, 74-78; assoc prof, Univ Toronto, 78-81; Assoc Prof Judaica, Barnard Col & Grad Fac, Columbia Univ, 81-, Woodrow Wilson fel, 67-68; Jewish Mem Found fel, 73 & 78; Guggenheim fel, 78; chairperson Judaica Sect IAHR, Winnipeg, 80; Mellon fel, Aspen Inst, 81; chmn relig dept, Barnard Col, 81. **MEMBERSHIPS** Soc Bibl Lit; Asn Jewish Studies; Asn Sci Study Relig. **RESEARCH** Judaica; early Christianity. **SELECTED PUBLICATIONS** Auth, Revelation And Mystery In Ancient Judaism And Pauline Christianity - Bockmuehl,Mna/, J Of Bibl Lit, Vol 0111, 1992; Disinheriting The Jews - Abraham In Early-Christian Controversy - Siker,Js/, J Of Rel, Vol 0073, 1993; Dangerous Food - 1-Corinthians 8-10 In Its Context - Gooch,Pd/, Studies In Rel-Sci Religieuses, Vol 0024, 1995. **CONTACT ADDRESS** Dept of Relig Barnard Col, Columbia Univ, New York, NY, 10027.

SEGAL, DAVID R.
PERSONAL Born 05/22/1941, New York, NY, m, 1967, 1 child **DISCIPLINE** SOCIOLOGY **EDUCATION** Harper Col, BA, 62; Univ Chicago, MA, 63, PhD, 67. **CAREER** Asst to Assoc Prof, Univ Mich, 66-75; Prof, Univ Md, 75-; Dir, Ctr for Res on Military Org, 95-. **HONORS AND AWARDS** Mid Career Award, Am Soc for Pub Admin, 84; Dept of Army Medal for Outstanding Civ Service, 89; Morris Rosenberg Award, DC Sociol Soc, 97; Grad Mentorship Award, 98. **MEMBERSHIPS** Soiciol Res Asn; Am Sociol Asn; DC Sociol Soc; Inter-Univ Seminar on Armed Forces & Soc; Int Sociol Asn. **RESEARCH** Military manpower, personnel, and organization; peacekeeping operations. **SELECTED PUBLICATIONS** Auth, Five phases of United Nations peacekeeping: an evolutionary typology, J of Polit and Mil Sociol, 25, 65-79, 95; auth, The social construction of peacekeeping by US soldiers, Tocqeville Rev, 17, 7-21, 96; co-auth, Attitudes of citizen-soldiers toward military missions in the post Cold War world, Armed Forces & Soc, 23, 373-390, 97, co-auth, The all-volunteer force in the 1970s, Soc Sci Quart, 79, 390-411, 98; auth, The all-volunteer force, The Oxford Companion to Am Mil Hist, in press. **CONTACT ADDRESS** Dept of Sociol, Univ Md, College Park, MD, 20742. **EMAIL** segal@bss1.umd.edu

SEGAL, N.L.
DISCIPLINE PSYCHOLOGY **EDUCATION** Boston Univ BA 73; Univ Chicago ma 74, PhD 82. **CAREER** California State Univ Fullerton, prof 91-; MN Center for Twins Adoption Research, asst dir 82-91. **HONORS AND AWARDS** Dist alumni Boston U 90 **MEMBERSHIPS** APA; APS; ISTS; BGA **RESEARCH** Twin studies **CONTACT ADDRESS** Dept of Psychology, California State Univ, Fullerton, Fullerton, CA, 92634.

SEGEL, EDWARD BARTON
PERSONAL Born 12/25/1938, Boston, MA **DISCIPLINE** HISTORY **EDUCATION** Harvard Univ, AB, 60; Univ Calif, Berkeley, MA, 62, PhD(hist), 69. **CAREER** Actg asst prof hist, Univ Calif, Berkeley, 65-67, from lectr to asst prof, 67-73, humanities res fel, 70-71; asst prof hist, Reed Col, 73-76, prof hist & humanities, Reed Col, 76-. **HONORS AND AWARDS** Teaching Award, Univ Calif, Berkeley, 67. **MEMBERSHIPS** AHA; SHAFR **RESEARCH** European diplomatic history, 19th and 20th centuries; British foreign policy, 1919-1939. **SELECTED PUBLICATIONS** Auth, A J P Taylor and history, Rev Politics, 10/64 & In: The Origins of the Second World War: A J P Taylor and His Critics, Wiley, 72; Paul Tillich and the unbelievers, Humanity, 12/65. **CONTACT ADDRESS** Dept of History, Reed Col, 3203 SE Woodstock Blvd, Portland, OR, 97202-8199. **EMAIL** Edward.Segel@reed.edu

SEGGER, MARTIN
PERSONAL Born 11/22/1946, United Kingdom, m, 1970, 3 children **DISCIPLINE** ART HISTORY **EDUCATION** Univ Victoria Canada, BA, 69, DspEd, 70; London Univ, UK, M. Phil, 73. **CAREER** Royal British Columbia Museum, 74-77; adj prof, dir, 77-, Hartwood Art Museum & Gallery, Univ of Victoria. **HONORS AND AWARDS** Harvey J McKee/Apr; Natl Comm Award 7 Lieut Gov's Award, Heritage Canada Found; AASLH Award of Merit. **MEMBERSHIPS** ICOM/ICTOP; Soc for Stud of Arch in Canada; Asn for Preservation Tech; ICOMOS-Canada; Can Museum Dir Org. **RESEARCH** Architectural history 19th century, European & Amer, Europe dec arts, cult resource management. **SELECTED PUBLICATIONS** Auth, City of Victoria Heritage Conservation Report, 75; auth, Victoria, A Primer for Regional History in Architecture, 79; auth, The British Columbia Parliament Buildings, 79; auth, Heritage Canada, 81; auth, Introduction to Museum Studies, 85; auth, In Search of appropriate Form, 86; auth, The Development of Gordon Head Campus, 88; auth, Introduction to Heritage Conservation, 89; auth, Exploring Victoria's Architecture, 96. **CONTACT ADDRESS** Hartwood Gallery, Univ of Victoria, PO Box 3025, Victoria, BC, V8W 3P2. **EMAIL** msegger@uvic.ca

SEGRE, CLAUDIO GIUSEPPE
PERSONAL Born 03/02/1937, Palermo, Italy, m, 1967, 2 children **DISCIPLINE** MODERN HISTORY **EDUCATION** Reed Col, BA, 57; Stanford Univ, MA, 61; Univ Calif, Berkeley, MA, 64, PhD(hist), 70. **CAREER** Instr hist, Stanford Univ, 67-70 asst prof, 70-77, ASSOC PROF HIST, UNIV TEX, AUSTIN, 77-, Nat Endowment for Humanities fel, 73-74; Air Force Hist Found grant, 76. **HONORS AND AWARDS** Marraro Prize, Soc Ital Hist Studies, 75. **MEMBERSHIPS** Soc Ital Hist Studies. **RESEARCH** Modern Italy; fascism; imperialism. **SELECTED PUBLICATIONS** Auth, The Italian Navy In World-War-Ii - Sadkovich,Jj/, Am Hist Rev, Vol 0100, 1995. **CONTACT ADDRESS** Dept of Hist, Univ of Tex, Austin, TX, 78712.

SEHLINGER, PETER J.
PERSONAL Born 08/18/1940, Louisville, KY, m, 1977 **DISCIPLINE** HISTORY **EDUCATION** Univ of South, BA, 62; Tulane Univ, MA, 64; Univ Ky, PhD(hist), 69. **CAREER** Assoc dean overseas study, Ind Univ, Bloomington, 76-79; assoc prof hist, 69-79, prof hist, Ind Univ, Indianapolis, 79-, Orgn Am States, Chilean res fel, 75-76. **MEMBERSHIPS** Andean Sect, Coun Latin Am Hist; Latin Am Studies Asn; AHA; Midwest Asn Latin Am Studies; Soc Iberian & Latin Am Thought. **RESEARCH** Chilean intellectual history; international investment and the War of the Pacific; US Diplomatic History. **SELECTED PUBLICATIONS** Auth, El Desarrollo Intelectual y la Influencia de Valentin Letelier, Revista Chilena de Historia y Geografia, 69; La Realidad Chilena Vista por Lord James Bryce y Arnold Toynbee, Mapocho, 70; Raul Silva Castro, Professor, Boletin de la Academia Chilena, 70; The City in Chilean Politics, 1952-1970, Proc Ind Acad Social Sci, 71; Cien Anos de la Obra de Letelier, 71 & La Correspondencia de Valentin Letelier, 72, Revista Chilena de Historia y Geografia; The Peruvian Population Problem, 1962-1972, Proc Ind Acad Social Sci, 73; Valentin Letelier y la Historiografia Positiva en Chile Durante el S XIX, Revista Chilena de Historia y Geografia, 77. **CONTACT ADDRESS** Dept of History, Indiana Univ-Purdue Univ, Indianapolis, 425 University Blvd, Indianapolis, IN, 46202-2880.

SEIBERLING, GRACE
DISCIPLINE ART HISTORY/VISUAL AND CULTURAL STUDIES **EDUCATION** Yale Univ, PhD, 76. **CAREER** Assoc prof, Univ of Rochester. **RESEARCH** 19th century painting and photography, espec Impressionism; early Brit photography; mus(s). **SELECTED PUBLICATIONS** Auth, Monet in London, Atlanta: High Mus, 88; Amateurs, Photography, and the Mid-Victorian Imagination, Chicago, Univ Chicago Press, 86 & Naturaleza y tecnica en las series de Monet, In Claude Monet, Madrid, Museo Espanol de Arte Comtemporaneo, 86; coauth, A Vision Exchanged: Amateurs and Photography in Mid- Victorian England, London Victoria and Albert Mus, 85. **CONTACT ADDRESS** Dept of Art and Art Hist, Univ of Rochester, 601 Elmwood Ave, Ste. 656, 422 Morey , Rochester, NY, 14642. **EMAIL** seib@troi.cc.rochester.edu

SEIBERT-MCCAULEY, MARY F.
PERSONAL Born 06/21/1930, Louisiana, w **DISCIPLINE** EDUCATION **EDUCATION** TN State Univ, BS 1952, MA 1961; Northwestern Univ, 1957; Vanderbilt, 1966, 1967, 1977; George Peabody Vanderbilt, PhD 1983. **CAREER** Future City Sch, teacher 1952-57; Roosevelt HS, English teacher 1957-62; Bruce HS, English teacher 1963-66; Dyersburg City High School, English teacher, 1966-69; Dyersburg Comm Coll, assoc prof 1969-, chmn of English 1974-84; prof of English 1985, chmn of humanities 1976-84; Union City Ford, Lincoln Mercury, Union City, TN, part owner, 1988-; Math Contracting Co, Dyersburg, TN, president, 1977-90; Dyersburg State College, Dyersburg, TN, Humanities Dept, chair, professor of English, 1969-94. **HONORS AND AWARDS** Outstanding Teacher Awd, TN Governor's Comm on Handicapped 1966; First Black Teacher Dyersburg HS & DSCC 1966-; Certificate Outstanding Educator of Amer 1975; Stipend Natl Endowment for Humanities 1976. **MEMBERSHIPS** Mem Delta Sigma Theta Sor 1951-; WDSG, first African-American disc-jockey, WJRO, 1953-57; pres NAACP Dyersburg Chap 1963-64; pres Math Inc Construction Co 1977-; mem 1st Woman Dyer Co Bd of Educ 1977-; bd mem Dyer Co Mentally Retarded Assn 1980-; bd mem Dyer Co Cancer Assn 1982-; mem Tabernacle Bapt Ch; real estate holdings; mem Kiwanis Club 1988-; 1st Black Dyersburg City Bd of Educ 1988-; 1st Black director, First Citizen National Bank, 1991; mem, Dyersburg Dyer County Modernization Committee, 1990; West Tennessee Habitat; director, Tennessee State Alumni; Board for Dyersburg Dyer County Crimstoppers, 1990-; Dyersburg Dyer County Consolidation Committee, 1993-94; Aurora Civic and Social Club. **SELECTED PUBLICATIONS** Wrote first dissertation on and with assistance from Alex Haley: Alex Haley: A Southern Griot, 1988; First African-American Jury Commissioner, 1994. **CONTACT ADDRESS** Chmn of Humanities, Dyersburg State Comm Col, Dyersburg, TN, 38024.

SEIDEL, ROBERT NEAL
PERSONAL Born 10/10/1936, New York, NY, m, 1957, 3 children **DISCIPLINE** HISTORY **EDUCATION** State Univ NY, Cortland, BA, 68; Cornell Univ, MA, 71, PhD, 73. **CAREER** Lectr hist, Cornell Univ, 72-73; from asst prof to prof, 74-90, Distinguished Teaching Prof Hist, Empire State Col, Rochester, 90-, actg assoc dean, 81-82, interim dean, 90-91; res assoc policy studies, Prog Policies Sci & Technol in Develop Nations, Cornell Univ, 73-74. **HONORS AND AWARDS** Earhard Found, Ann Arbor, Mich fel res grant, 78. **MEMBERSHIPS** AHA; OAH; APSA. **RESEARCH** History of American foreign relations; United States-Latin American relations; 20th century United States history. **SELECTED PUBLICATIONS** Auth, American reformers abroad: The Kemmerer Missions in South America, in J Econ Hist, 6/72; Progressive Pan Americanism: Development and United States Policy Toward South America, 1906-1931, 73 & Toward an Andean Common Market for Science and Technology, 74, Cornell Univ; Latin America: The Burden of Derivative Modernization, in Third World Rev, fall 76; coauth, Learning Contracts as Aids to Independent Study in History, in Teaching Hist: J Methods, spring 77; Neighborly Affection and the Common Good, Saratoga Springs, 90. **CONTACT ADDRESS** SUNY, Empire State Col, 8 Prince St, Rochester, NY, 14607-1440. **EMAIL** rseidel@sescva.esc.edu

SEIFMAN, ELI
PERSONAL Born 08/04/1936, Brooklyn, NY, m, 1990, 2 children **DISCIPLINE** EDUCATION **EDUCATION** Queens Col, CUNY, BA, 55, MS, 59; New York Univ, PhD, 65. **CAREER** Lect, 64-65, asst prof, 65-68, assoc prof, 68-71, asst prof, 71-75,

prof, 75-, chair soc sci interdisc prog, 78-, dir, Center for Excellence & Innovation in Education, 88-, dist serv prof, 92- prof, 96-, SUNY, Stony Brook. **HONORS AND AWARDS** Phi Beta Kappa; Phi Alpha Theta; Kappa Delta Pi; The Royal Soc for Asian Affairs of Great Britain; Dante Medal, Long Island Chap, Amer Assoc of Teachers of Italian. **MEMBERSHIPS** Assoc for Asian Stud; Royal Soc for Asian Affairs; Nat Counc for the Soc Stud. **RESEARCH** Cont Chinese ed; soc stud teacher ed. **SELECTED PUBLICATIONS** Art, The Formation of China's Educational Policy for the 1990s: The Ten-Year program of the Eighth Five-Year Plan of the People's Republic of China, Proceedings of the 13th International Symposium on Asian Studies, 91; art, China: The Anti-Child Labor Regulations, Asian Thought & Society, Aug, 92; art, China, The Law for the Protection of Minors, Asian Thought & Society, Jan-Apr 92; art, The Law for the Protection of the Handicapped, Asian Thought & Society, Jan-Apr, 94; coauth, Chinese Education in the Decade of Socialist Modernization, Asian Thought & Society, Set-Dec, 96. **CONTACT ADDRESS** 11 Royalston Ln, Centereach, NY, 11720-1414.

SEIGFRIED, CHARLENE
DISCIPLINE CLASSICAL AMERICAN PHILOSOPHY, 19TH-CENTURY PHILOSOPHY, FEMINIST PHILOSOPHY **EDUCATION** Loyola Univ, Chicago, PhD. **CAREER** Prof, Purdue Univ. **RESEARCH** Pragmatism and feminism. **SELECTED PUBLICATIONS** Published works in the areas of social and political philosophy, metaphysics, and aesthetics. **CONTACT ADDRESS** Dept of Philos, Purdue Univ, 1080 Schleman Hall, West Lafayette, IN, 47907-1080.

SEIP, TERRY L.
DISCIPLINE HISTORY **EDUCATION** La State Univ, PhD, 74. **CAREER** Assoc prof, Univ Southern Calif. **HONORS AND AWARDS** AHA Nancy Lyman Roelker Mentorship awd, 96. **RESEARCH** American South; Civil War &Reconstruction; quantitative methods. **SELECTED PUBLICATIONS** Auth, The South Returns to Congress: Men, Economic Measures & Intersectional Relationships, 1868-1879, La State Univ, 83. **CONTACT ADDRESS** Dept of History, Univ Southern Calif, University Park Campus, Los Angeles, CA, 90089. **EMAIL** rseip@bcf.usc.edu

SEIPP, DAVID J.
PERSONAL Born 10/19/1955, Dubuque, IA, m, 1994 **DISCIPLINE** LEGAL HISTORY **EDUCATION** Harvard Col, AB, 77; Merton Col Oxford, BA, 79; St. Johns' Col Cambridge, LLB, 80; Harvard Law Sch, JD, 82. **CAREER** Law clerk, U.S. Court of Appeals, 82-83; assoc, Foley, Hoag, and Eliot, 83-86; assoc prof, Boston Univ Sch Law, 86-92; prof, 92- . **MEMBERSHIPS** Selden Soc; Am Soc for Legal Hist; Am Law Inst. **RESEARCH** Legal history. **SELECTED PUBLICATIONS** Auth, The Concept of Property in the Early Common Law, Law and Hist Rev, 94; auth, Crime in the Year Books, Law Reporting in Britain: Proceedings of the Eleventh British Legal History Conference, 95; auth, The Distinction Between Crime and Tort in Early Common Law, Boston Univ Law Rev, 96; auth, Holmes's Path, Boston Univ Law Rev, 97; auth, The Mirror of Justices, Learning the Law: Proceedings of the Thirteenth British Legal History Conference, 99. **CONTACT ADDRESS** School of Law, Boston Univ, 765 Commonwealth Ave, Rm 934B, Boston, MA, 02215. **EMAIL** dseipp@bu.edu

SELBY, JOHN EDWARD
PERSONAL Born 01/01/1929, Boston, MA, m, 1954, 4 children **DISCIPLINE** EARLY AMERICAN HISTORY **EDUCATION** Harvard Univ, AB, 50; Brown Univ, MA, 51, PhD(hist), 55. **CAREER** From instr to asst prof hist, Univ Ore, 55-61; asst dir res, Colonial Williamsburg, 61-65; assoc prof, 65-70, actg dean grad studies, 68-70, grad dean arts & sci, 71-81, PROF HIST, COL WILLIAM & MARY, 70-, Book rev ed, William & Mary Quart, 65-70, 71-, actg ed, 70-71. **MEMBERSHIPS** AHA **RESEARCH** The American Revolution; 18th century Virginia. **SELECTED PUBLICATIONS** Auth, The Blackwell Encycl Of The Am-Revolution - Greene,Jp, Pole,Jr/, J Of Southern His, Vol 0059, 1993; The Am-Revolution, 1775-1783 - An Encycl - Blanco,Rl, Sanborn,Pj/, J Of Am Hist, Vol 0082, 1996. **CONTACT ADDRESS** Dept of Hist, Col of William and Mary, Williamsburg, VA, 23185.

SELFRIDGE-FIELD, ELEANOR
DISCIPLINE MUSIC **EDUCATION** Drew Univ, BA, 62; Columbia Univ, MSC, 63; Oxford Univ, DPhil, 69. **CAREER** Consult prof, Stanford Univ; admin, Ctr for Computer Asst Res in the Hum. **HONORS AND AWARDS** Am Coun of Learned Soc Grant; Ford Found; Gladys Krieble Delmas Found. **MEMBERSHIPS** IMS, AMS, SMT, IEEE CS **RESEARCH** Techology for classical music research; Vivaldi; Venetian music; history of instrumental music; melodic similarity. **SELECTED PUBLICATIONS** Venetian Instrumental Music from Gabrieli to Vivaldi, Oxford, 75; Pallade Veneta: Writings on Music in Venetian Society, Venice 85; The Works of Benedetto and Alessandro Marcello, Oxford Univ Press, 90; Ed, Beyond MIDI: The Handbook of Musical Codes, MIT Press, 97. **CONTACT ADDRESS** CCARH, Standford Univ, Braun Music Center 129, Stanford, CA, 94305-3076. **EMAIL** esf@ccrma.stanford.edu

SELFRIDGE-FIELD, ELEANOR
DISCIPLINE MUSIC; JOURNALISM; MUSIC HISTORY **EDUCATION** Magna cum laude, Drew Univ, 62; MSc, Columbia Univ, 63; DPHIl, Oxford Univ, 69. **CAREER** Consulting prof, Stanford Univ, admin, Center for Computer Asst Research in the Hum; lectr, writer, tchr and music technologist. **HONORS AND AWARDS** Research Grants: Am Council of Learned Soc; Ford Found, Gladys Krieble Delmas Found. **MEMBERSHIPS** IMS, AMS,SMT, IEEE CS. **RESEARCH** Tech for class music research; Vivaldi; Venetian music; hist of instrumental music; melodic similarity. **SELECTED PUBLICATIONS** The Handbook of Musical Codes, 97, ed The Works of Benedetto and Alessandro Marcello, 90, Writings on Music in Venetian Soc, 85-Venetian Instrumental Music form Gabrieli to Vivaldi, var ed, articles program and liner notes. **CONTACT ADDRESS** Stanford Univ, Stanford, CT, 94305-3076.

SELINGER, SUZANNE
PERSONAL Born 01/31/1940, New York, NY **DISCIPLINE** HISTORY **EDUCATION** Vassar Col, BA, 60; Yale Univ, MA, 61, PhD, 65; Columbia Univ, MSLS, 74. **CAREER** Asst prof, hist, Douglass Col, 66-70; ref librn, Yale Univ Libr, 74-81; asst ed, Frederick Douglass Papers, Yale Univ, 83-84; theol librn, assoc prof, hist theol, Drew Univ, 87- . **MEMBERSHIPS** AHA; AAR; Sixteenth Century Stud Conf; Karl Barth Soc of N Am. **RESEARCH** Twentieth-century theology; twentieth-century intellectual and cultural history; feminist theory. **SELECTED PUBLICATIONS** Auth, Calvin Against Himself: An Inquiry in Intellectual History, Archon, 84; asst ed, The Frederick Douglass Papers, Series One: Speeches, Debates, and Interviews, v.4, 1864-80, Yale, 91; auth, Charlotte von Kirschbaum and Karl Barth: A Study in Biography and the History of Theology, Penn State, 98. **CONTACT ADDRESS** University Library, Drew Univ, Madison, NJ, 07940. **EMAIL** sselinge@drew.edu

SELLER, MAXINE SCHWARTZ
PERSONAL Born 05/23/1935, Wilmington, NC, m, 1956, 3 children **DISCIPLINE** AMERICAN HISTORY **EDUCATION** Bryn Mawr Col, BA, 56; Univ Pa, MA, 57, PhD(hist), 65. **CAREER** From instr to asst prof hist, Temple Univ, 64-66; from assoc prof to prof, Bucks County Community Col, 66-74; asst prof, 74-77, assoc prof, 77-82, PROF SOCIAL EDUC, STATE UNIV NY, BUFFALO, 82-, Mem teaching div, Am Hist Asn, 74-77; secy, Hist Educ Div, Am Educ Res Asn, 78-79. **MEMBERSHIPS** Am Hist Asn; Am Educ Res Asn; Immigration Hist Soc; Orgn Am Historians; Am Jewish Hist Soc. **RESEARCH** History of ethnic groups in United States; history of women in United States; history of education of women and minorities in United States. **SELECTED PUBLICATIONS** Auth, Japanese-Am Ethnicity - The Persistence Of Community - Fugita,Ss, Obrien,Dj/, Am Hist Rev, Vol 0097, 1992; Ethnicity, Ethnic-Identity, And Lang Maintenance, Vol 16, Of Am Immigration And Ethnicity - Pozzetta,Ge/, J Of Am Ethnic Hist, Vol 0013, 1994; Family Tightrope - The Changing Lives Of Vietnamese Americans - Kibria,N/, Am Hist Rev, Vol 0100, 1995. **CONTACT ADDRESS** Dept Social Found, SUNY, PO Box 601000, Buffalo, NY, 14260-1000.

SELVIDGE, MARLA J.
PERSONAL Born 11/11/1948, Gross Pt, MI, m, 1982 **DISCIPLINE** BIBLICAL LANGUAGES AND LITERATURE **EDUCATION** Taylor Univ, BA, 70; Wheaton Col, MA, 73; St. Louis Univ, PhD, 80. **CAREER** Asst prof, John Wesley Col, 73-74; pers dir, Thalhimers, 74-76; res asst, Cts for Reformation Res, 76-77; dir evening div, St Louis Univ, 77-80; lect, St. Louis Univ, 78-80; asst prof, Carthage Col, 80-81; ast prof, Univ Dayton, 81-84; asst prof, Converse Col, 84-87; chemn Relig and Philos, Converse Col, 84-85; coordr grant writing, Cheshire Public Sch, 87-89; asst prof, Marist Col, 89-90; dir, assoc prof, Central Missouri St Univ, 90-94; prof, dir, Center for Relig Stud, Central Missouri St Univ, 94- . **HONORS AND AWARDS** Tenney Awd, Best Thesis, 73; Fac of the Year, 74; nominated Outstanding Women in America, 80; res grant, William R. Kenan Fund and Natl Endowment for the Hum, 84-87; res grant CMSU, 91-92; Missouri Hum Council Grant, 92-94. **MEMBERSHIPS** Soc Bibl Lit; Am Acad Relig; Missouri St Tchr Asn. **SELECTED PUBLICATIONS** Auth, "Chautauqua Revival Brings to Life Religious Figures," Relig Stud News, 93; "Mennonites and Amish," Women in American Religious History, Kathryn Kuhlman, Missouri Chautauqua, 93; "Magic and Menses," Explorations, 93; "Discovering Women," Teacher Created Materials, 95; "Notorious Voices," Continuum, 96; "Reflections on Violence and Pornography," A Feminist Companion to the Bible, Sheffield, 96; The New Testament, PrenticeHall, 98. **CONTACT ADDRESS** Center For Religious Studies, Central Missouri State Univ, Martin 118, Warrensburg, MO, 64093.

SEMMENS, RICHARD
DISCIPLINE MUSIC **EDUCATION** Stanford Univ, PhD, 80. **CAREER** Assoc prof **RESEARCH** Theory and practice of French baroque music; baroque dance and dance music; 17th century music and science; history of woodwind instruments; history of theory. **SELECTED PUBLICATIONS** Auth, The Bassons in Mersenne's Harmonie universelle, Jour Am Musical Instrument Soc, 84; Etienne Loulie and the New Harmonic Counterpoint, Jour Music Theory, 84; Joseph Sauveur's Treatise of the Theory of Music, UWO, 87; Music and Poetry in a Chanson by Gilles Binchois, Inst Medieval Music, 90; Joseph Sauveur and the Absolute Frequency of Pitch, Theoria, 91; Such Sweet Harmonie: Mozart's Chamber Music for Wind Instruments, UWO, 93; Dancing and Dance Music in Purcell's Operas, Oxford, 96. **CONTACT ADDRESS** Dept of Music, Western Ontario Music, London, ON, N6A 5B8. **EMAIL** musrts@julian.uwo.ca

SEMONCHE, JOHN ERWIN
PERSONAL Born 02/09/1933, Alpha, NJ, m, 1962, 1 child **DISCIPLINE** AMERICAN HISTORY **EDUCATION** Brown Univ, AB, 54; Northwestern Univ, MA, 55, PhD, 62; Duke Univ, LLB, 67. **CAREER** Instr hist, Univ Conn, 60-61; from instr to asst prof hist & mod civilization, 61-68, assoc prof, 68-73, PROF HIST, UNIV NC, CHAPEL HILL, 73-, Lectr sch law, Univ NC, Chapel Hill, 67-78; attorney, 67- **MEMBERSHIPS** AHA; Orgn Am Historians. **RESEARCH** American legal and constitutional history; jurisprudence. **SELECTED PUBLICATIONS** Auth, Laws Promise, Laws Expression - Visions Of Power In The Politics Of Race, Gender, And Rel - Karst,Kl/, J Of Am Hist, Vol 0081, 1995; Shaping The 18th Amendment - Temperance Reform, Legal Cult, And The Polity, 1880-1920 - Hamm,Rf/, Am J Of Legal Hist, Vol 0040, 1996; The Godless Constitution - The Case Against Religious Correctness - Kramnick,I, Moore,Rl/, J Of Am Hist, Vol 0083, 1996. **CONTACT ADDRESS** Dept of Hist, Univ of NC, Chapel Hill, NC, 27514.

SENGUPTA, GUNJA
PERSONAL Born 04/02/1962, Calcutta, India **DISCIPLINE** HISTORY **EDUCATION** Tulane Univ, PhD, 91. **CAREER** Asst to assoc prof, Texas A&M Univ, Commerce, 91-98; asst prof, Brooklyn Col, CUNY, 98- . **HONORS AND AWARDS** Paul Barrus Distinguished Faculty Award, 98. **MEMBERSHIPS** Am Hist Asn; Orgn of Am Hist; Southern Hist Assoc. **RESEARCH** African Americans; US social. **SELECTED PUBLICATIONS** Auth, For God & Mammon: Evangelicals and Entrepreneurs, Masters & Slaves in Territorial Kansas, 1854-1860, Univ Georgia, 96. **CONTACT ADDRESS** History Dept, Brooklyn Col, CUNY, Bedford Ave and Avenue H, Brooklyn, NY, 11210. **EMAIL** SenGupta@brooklyn.cuny.edu

SENIE, HARRIET F.
PERSONAL Born 09/23/1943, New York, NY, d, 1 child **DISCIPLINE** ART HISTORY, CONTEMPORARY ART **EDUCATION** Brandeis Univ, BA, 64; Hunter Col, MA, 71; Inst of Fine Arts, PhD, 81. **CAREER** Gallery dir, asst prof of art hist, SUNY at Old Westbury, 79-82; assoc dir, The Art Museum, Princeton Univ, 82-85; VISITING PROF, 94-97, PROF, CUNY GRAD CENTER, 97-; DIR, MUSEUM STUDIES PROG, PROF OF ART HIST, CITY COL, NY, 86-. **HONORS AND AWARDS** PSC CUNY Res Grant, 88, 91, 94, & 96; Rifkind Scholars Award, City Col, 93; Eisner Scholars Award, 89; NEA Museum Studies Grant, 87; Pres Grant for Innovative Teaching, 86; Princeton Univ Spears Fund Res Grant, 83; Kress Found Res Grant, 78-79; Inst of Fine Arts, 74-78; NY Univ, 73-74. **MEMBERSHIPS** Col Art Asn; Am Studies Asn; Am Asn of Museums; Art Table; Coun of SUNY Gallery and Exhibition Dirs. **SELECTED PUBLICATIONS** Auth, Dangerous Precedent? Richard Serra's Titled Arc in Context, Univ of Calif Press, forthcoming; auth, Contemporary Public Sculpture: Tradition, Transformation, and Controversy, Oxford Univ Press, 92; Public Art in Brazil, Sculpture, 98; coed & contrib, Public Art and the Legal System, Public Art Rev, 94; auth, Eden Revisited: The Contemporary Garden as Public Art, Urban Paradise, Public Art Issues, 94; auth, USA: Offentliche Kunst un republikanische Administration, Orte, 92; contribur, Encycl of New York City, Yale Univ Press, 95; contrib, Dictionary of Women Artists, Fitzroy Dearborn Pub, 97; co-ed & contribur, Critical Issues in Public Art: Content, Context, and Controversy, Harper & Collins, 92. **CONTACT ADDRESS** 215 Sackett St., Brooklyn, NY, 11231-3604. **EMAIL** hfsenie@interport.net

SENN, ALFRED ERICH
PERSONAL Born 04/12/1932, Madison, WI, m, 1957, 3 children **DISCIPLINE** MODERN EUROPEAN HISTORY **EDUCATION** Univ Pa, BA, 53; Columbia Univ, cert & MA, 55, PhD(mod Europ hist), 58. **CAREER** Lectr hist, Hunger Col, 58; from instr to asst prof, Newark Col Arts & Sci, Rutgers Univ, 58-61; from asst prof to assoc prof, 61-67, chmn Russ area studies prog, 66-69, PROF HIST, UNIV WIS-MADISON, 67-, Vis lectr, Princeton Univ, 60; adj asst prof, Fordham Univ, 61; Fulbright res fel, Ger, 63-64; Guggenheim Found fel, 69-70. **MEMBERSHIPS** Am Asn Advan Slavic Studies. **RESEARCH** Twentieth century Eastern Europe. **SELECTED PUBLICATIONS** Auth, Sport, Politics, And Communism - Riordan,J/, Am Hist Rev, Vol 0097, 1992; Lithuanian Religious Life In Am - A Compendium Of 150 Roman-Cath Parishes And Institutions, Vol 1, Eastern United-States - Wolkovichvalkavicius,W/, Cath Hist Rev, Vol 0079, 1993; The Olympics - A Hist Of The Modern Games - Guttmann,A/, Am Hist Rev, Vol 0098, 1993; Comparing The Circumstances Of Lithuanian Independence, 1918-1922 And 1988-1992/, J Of Baltic Studies, Vol 0025, 1994; Thinking Theoretically About Soviet Nationalities - Hist And Comparison In The Study Of The Ussr - Motyl,Aj/,

Russian Hist-Histoire Russe, Vol 0021, 1994; Lithuanias 1st 2 Years Of Independence + 1991-1993/, J Of Baltic Studies, Vol 0025, 1994; Utopia Or Alpine Dream - Swiss Travelogs On The Soviet-Union 1917-1941 - Ger - Uhlig,C/, Am Hist Rev, Vol 0099, 1994; The Bolsheviks Ger Gold Revisited - An Inquiry Into The 1917 Accusations - Lyandres,S/, Russian History-Histoire Russe, Vol 0022, 1995; Playing Politics - Soviet Sport Diplomacy To 1992 - Peppard,V, Riordan,J/, Slavic Rev, Vol 0054, 1995; Beria - Stalin 1st Lieutenant - Knight,A/, Historian, Vol 0057, 1995; Serious Fun - A History Of Spectator Sports In The Ussr - Edelman,R/, Russian Hist-Histoire Russe, Vol 0022, 1995; Philos And Romantic Nationalism - The Case Of Poland - Walicki,A/, Historian, Vol 0058, 1996. **CONTACT ADDRESS** Dept of Hist, Univ of Wis, 455 North Park St, Madison, WI, 53706-1483.

SENTILLES, RENEE M.
DISCIPLINE HISTORY **EDUCATION** Mt. Holyoke Coll, BA, 88; Utah State Univ, MA, 91; Wm & Mary Coll, PhD, 97. **CAREER** VIS ASST PROF, HIST, FRANKLIN & MARSHALL COLL **MEMBERSHIPS** Am Antiquarian Soc **RESEARCH** Adah Isaacs Menken **CONTACT ADDRESS** Hist & Am Stud, Franklin and Marshall Col, PO Box 3003, Lancaster, PA, 17604-3003.

SERAILE, WILLIAM
PERSONAL Born 03/12/1941, New Orleans, LA, m, 1970, 2 children **DISCIPLINE** AFRICANAMERICAN & AMERICAN HISTORY **EDUCATION** Cent Wash State Univ, BA, 63; Columbia Univ, MA, 67; City Univ New York, PhD(Am hist), 77. **CAREER** Lectr, 71-77, ASST PROF AFRICAN-AM HIST, HERBERT H LEHMAN COL, 77-, Assoc ed, Silver Burdette Company, Morristown, 70-71; contrib ed, Afro-Am NY Life & Hist, 82- **MEMBERSHIPS** Asn Study Afro-Am Life & Hist. **RESEARCH** African-American politics. **SELECTED PUBLICATIONS** Auth, Bright Radical Star - Black-Freedom And White Supremacy On The Hawkeye Frontier - Dykstra,Rr/, Montana-The Mag Of Western Hist, Vol 0045, 1995. **CONTACT ADDRESS** Dept Black Studies, Lehman Col, CUNY, 250 Bedford Park W, Bronx, NY, 10468-1527.

SEREBRENNIKOV, NINA EUGENIA
DISCIPLINE ART HISTORY **EDUCATION** George Washington Univ, BA; Univ NC Chapel Hill, MSLS, MA, PhD. **CAREER** Assoc prof, Davidson Col. **RESEARCH** Medieval, Renaissance, and Baroque art; issues of gender. **SELECTED PUBLICATIONS** Auth, publ(s) about 16th-century Flemish painting, espec the work of Peter Bruegel the Elder. **CONTACT ADDRESS** Davidson Col, 102 N Main St, PO Box 1719, Davidson, NC, 28036. **EMAIL** niserebrennikov@davidson.edu

SERELS, M. MITCHELL
PERSONAL Born 01/12/1948, New York, NY, m, 1979, 4 children **DISCIPLINE** PSYCHOLOGY; HISTORY **EDUCATION** Yeshiva Univ, BA, 67, MS, 70; Hunter Col, MA, 71; NY Univ, PhD, 90. **CAREER** Assoc Dir, Jacob E Safea Inst of Sephardic Stud, Yeshiva Univ, 73-; Univ Dir of Foreign Stud Svcs, Yeshiva Univ, 92-. **HONORS AND AWARDS** Knighted, Caballero de order de Merito Civil, by King Juan Carlos I of Spain. **MEMBERSHIPS** Am Soc of Sephardic Stud; Nat Asn of Foreign Stud Advisors. **RESEARCH** Jews of Spanish origin; Morocco; W Africa. **SELECTED PUBLICATIONS** Auth, Sephardim and the Holocaust, NY, 94; auth, Historia de los Judios de Tanger, Caracos, 96; auth, Jews of Cape Verde: A Brief History, NY, 97. **CONTACT ADDRESS** Yeshiva Univ, 500 W 185th St, New York, NY, 10033. **EMAIL** m.serels@ymail.yu.edu

SERVLNIKOV, SERGIO
PERSONAL Born 05/09/1961, Argentina **DISCIPLINE** HISTORY **EDUCATION** Universidad de Buenos Aires, Licencido, 98; New York State Univ, PhD, 98 **CAREER** Asst prof, Univ Ky **HONORS AND AWARDS** James D. Robertson Memorial Prize; Conference of Latin Am Hist **MEMBERSHIPS** Am Hist Asn **RESEARCH** Latin Am Hist **SELECTED PUBLICATIONS** Auth, art, When Looting Became a Right. Food Riots and Urvan Poverty in Argentina, 94; Auth, art, Disputed Images of Colonialism. Spanish Rule in Indian Subversion in Northern Potosi, 1777-1780, 96; auth, art, Su verdad y su justicia. Tomas Katari y la in **CONTACT ADDRESS** Dept of History, Univ of Kentucky, Lexington, KY, 40506-0027. **EMAIL** sseruln@pop.uky.edu

SESSIONS, KYLE CUTLER
PERSONAL Born 07/06/1934, Malad, ID, m, 1959, 3 children **DISCIPLINE** REFORMATION & RENAISSANCE HISTORY **EDUCATION** Ohio State Univ, BA, 56, MA, 59, PhD(Reformation hist), 63. **CAREER** Lectr hist, Huron Col, Ont, 63-64, asst prof, 64-67; dir honors, 73-78, ASSOC PROF HIST, ILL STATE UNIV, 67- **MEMBERSHIPS** Conf on Faith & Hist; Am Soc Reformation Res; 16th Century Studies Conf (pres, 69-71); Western Assoc for Ger Studies. **RESEARCH** Lutheran Reformation; music of the Reformation; Peasants' revolt. **SELECTED PUBLICATIONS** Auth, The Ger Peasants War And Anabaptist Community Of Goods - Stayer,Jm/, Am Hist Rev, Vol 0097, 1992; Germania-Illustrata - Essays On Early-Modern Germany Presented To Strauss,Gerald - Fix,Ac, Karantnunn,Sc/, Cath Hist Rev, Vol 0080, 1994. **CONTACT ADDRESS** Dept of Hist, Illinois State Univ, Normal, IL, 61761.

SETTLES, ROSETTA HAYES
PERSONAL Born 11/16/1920, Little Rock, Arkansas, m **DISCIPLINE** EDUCATION **EDUCATION** Wiley Coll, BA 1948; Harvard U, EdM 1951; Walden U, PhD 1977; Oakland U, Grad Study 1970; Summer Sch, Overseas Study 1971; Great Britain Sch, TourStudy 1973. **CAREER** Oakland Univ, asso prof 1969-; Garden City Public School, rdng supr 1967-, first black teacher 1967-; Clintondale Public School, rdng spec, clinician 1965-67; Little Rock, remedial rdng elem teacher 1945-56; Harvard Boston Summer School Prog, team teacher 1965; Summer School Prog, asst dir; Detroit Public School, rdng consultant 1972; Garden City Summer School Prog, prin, dir 1974. **HONORS AND AWARDS** Originator, sponsor Lena D Hayes Schlrshp Award 1950; Harvard Univ Schlrshp 1951; Top Ten Outstndng Dunbar HS Alumni Nation 1973; Tribute Award 1977; Top Ten Outstndng Dunbar HS Alumni Nat, Little Rock AR Conv 1979; **MEMBERSHIPS** Fdr org Nat Dunbar HS Alumni Reunion of Classes; vice pres Detroit Chap Dunbar High Alumni 1980-; mem Nat Bd of Dir Dunbar HS Alumni Assn 1977-; mem IRA; NCTE; MRA; del NEA; mem NAACP. **SELECTED PUBLICATIONS** Auth, "Reading & Rhythm" 1970. **CONTACT ADDRESS** 31753 Maplewood St, Garden City, MI, 48135.

SEWELL, RICHARD HERBERT
PERSONAL Born 04/11/1931, Ann Arbor, MI **DISCIPLINE** AMERICAN HISTORY **EDUCATION** Univ Mich, AB, 53; Harvard Univ, MA, 54, PhD(hist), 62. **CAREER** Asst prof hist, Northern Ill Univ, 62-64; vis lectr, Univ Mich, 64-65; from asst prof to assoc prof, 65-74, PROF HIST, UNIV WIS-MADISON, 74- **MEMBERSHIPS** Orgn Am Historians. **RESEARCH** United States political and social history, 1815-1877. **SELECTED PUBLICATIONS** Auth, Sherman - Merchant Of Terror, Advocate Of Peace - Vetter,Ce/, J Of Southern H, Vol 0059, 1993; When The Yankees Came - Conflict And Chaos In The Occupied South, 1861-1865 - Ash,Sv/, Revs In Am Hist, Vol 0024, 1996; The Hard Hand Of War - Union Policy Toward Southern Civilians, 1861-1865 - Grimsley,M/, Revs In Am Hist, Vol 0024, 1996. **CONTACT ADDRESS** Dept of Hist, Univ of Wis, Madison, WI, 53706.

SEXTON, DONAL J.
PERSONAL Born 07/13/1939, Buffalo, NY, m, 1962, 2 children **DISCIPLINE** HISTORY **EDUCATION** Univ of TN, PhD, 75; MI St Univ, MA, 65, BA, 63 **CAREER** Tch Asst, 72-73, Univ of TN; Asst Prof, Ful Prof, 65-, Tusculum Col **HONORS AND AWARDS** Nat Alumni Facul Awd, 98; Moncado Prize awd, 94; Tenured, 70 **MEMBERSHIPS** WW2 Studs Asn **SELECTED PUBLICATIONS** Coauth, Glimpses of Tusculum Col, 94 **CONTACT ADDRESS** Tusculum Col, Greenville, TN, 37743-6126. **EMAIL** dsexton@tusculum.edu

SEXTON, JAMES D.
PERSONAL m, 1 child **DISCIPLINE** ANTHROPOLOGY **EDUCATION** UCLA, BA 67, MA 71, PhD 73. **CAREER** Northern Arizona Univ, asst, assoc, prof, Regent's prof, 73 to 98-. **HONORS AND AWARDS** NAU Pres Awd for Tchg; Phi Kappa Phi **MEMBERSHIPS** AAA; SWAA **RESEARCH** Latin Amer **SELECTED PUBLICATIONS** Auth, Heart of Heaven Heart of Earth, 99; Mayan Folktales, 92; Ignacio, 92; Campesino, 85; Son of Tecun Uman, 81. **CONTACT ADDRESS** Dept of Anthropology, No Arizona Univ, PO Box 15200, Flagstaff, AZ, 86014-5200.

SEYMOUR, JACK L.
PERSONAL Born 10/27/1948, Kokomo, IN, m, 1997, 2 children **DISCIPLINE** HISTORY AND PHILOSOPHY OF EDUCATION **EDUCATION** Ball State Univ, BS; Vanderbilt Divinity School, DMin & MDiv; George Peabody Col of Vanderbilt, PhD. **CAREER** Asst prof Church & Ministry, Vanderbilt Univ 74-78; Dir Field Educ, Chicago Theol Sem, 78-82; prof Christian Educ, assoc prof, asst prof, Scarritt Grad School, 82-88; prof Relig Educ, 88-, acad dean, 96-, Garrett-Evangelical Theol Sem, 88-. **RESEARCH** Theology of people of God; Ethnographic Research in education; Theological education. **SELECTED PUBLICATIONS** Coauth Educating Christians: The Intersection of Meaning, Learning, and Vocation, Abdington Press, 93; For the Life of a Child: The 'Religious' in the Education of the Public, Relig Educ, 94; Contemporary Approaches to Christian Education, Theological Perspectives on Christian Formation, W B Eerdmans, 96; The Ethnographer as Minister: Ethnographic Research in the Context of Ministry Vocations, Relig Educ, 96; Temples of Meaning: Theology and the People of God, Lib Relig Educ, 96; rev Essays on Religion and Education: An Issue in Honor of William Bean Kennedy, Relig Educ, 96; The Cry for Theology: Laity Speak about the Church, and The Cry for Theology: Laity Speak about Theology, PACE: Professional Approaches for Christian Education, 96; auth Mapping Christian Education: Approaches to Congregational Learning, Abingdon Press, 97; Thrashing in the Night: Laity Speak about Religious Knowing, Relig Educ, 97. **CONTACT ADDRESS** Garrett-Evangelical Theol Sem, 2121 Sheridan Rd, Evanston, IL, 60201. **EMAIL** Kack/Seymour@nwu.edu

SHACKLEY, M. STEVEN
PERSONAL San Diego, CA, m, 1995, 1 child **DISCIPLINE** ANTHROPOLOGY **EDUCATION** San Diego State Univ, BA, 79, MA, 81; PhD, 90, Arizona State Univ. **CAREER** Tchg asst, anthrop, San Diego State Univ, 80-81; tchg asst, lectr, anthrop, 83-84, 85-86, Arizona State Univ; lectr archaeol, Calif State Univ, Fullerton, 87-91; adj asst prof, anthrop, San Diego State Univ, 89-90; fac memb Archaeol Res Facil, Univ Calif, Berkeley, 90- ; adj asst prof, anthrop, Univ Calif, Berkeley, 94-95; adj assoc prod, anthrop, Univ Calif, Berkeley, 95- . **HONORS AND AWARDS** Phi Beta Kappa; Regents Grad Acad Scholar, 84-86; ARCS Fel, 84-85; listed Who's Who in the West & Who's Who in Science and Engineering. **MEMBERSHIPS** AAAS; Geol Soc Am; Az Archaeol and Hist Soc; Int Asn for Obsidian Stud; Soc for Am Archaeol; Soc for Archaeol Sci; Soc for Calif Archaeol; Soc of Prof Archaeol. **SELECTED PUBLICATIONS** Contribur, Current Issues and Future Directions in Archaeological Volcanic Glass Studies: An Introduction; contribur, Intrasource Chemical Variability and Secondary Depositional Processes in Sources of Archaeological Obsidian: A Case Study from the American Southwest; contribur, Factors Affecting the Energy-Dispersive X-Ray Fluorescence Analysis of Archaeological Obsidian; auth, Archaeological Obsidian Studies: Method and Theory, Plenum, 98. **CONTACT ADDRESS** Phoebe Hearst Museum of Anthropoloty, Univ of California, 103 Kroeber Hall, Berkeley, CA, 94720-3712. **EMAIL** shackley@qal.berkeley.edu

SHADBOLT, DOUGLAS
PERSONAL Born 04/18/1925, Victoria, BC, Canada **DISCIPLINE** ARCHITECTURE/HISTORY **EDUCATION** Univ BC; McGill Univ; Univ Ore, BArch, 57. **CAREER** Asst to assoc prof, McGill Univ, 58-61; prof & founding dir, sch archit, NS Tech Col, 61-68; prof & founding dir, sch archit, Carleton Univ, 68-79; dir, sch archit, 79-90, PROF EMER ARCHITECTURE, UNIV BC, 90-. **HONORS AND AWARDS** DEng(hon), NS Tech Col, 69; DEng(hon), Carleton Univ, 82; ACSA Distinguished Prof, 87. **SELECTED PUBLICATIONS** Auth, Ron Thom, The Shaping of an Architect, 95. **CONTACT ADDRESS** 4525 Gothard St, Vancouver, BC, V5K 3K8.

SHADE, BARBARA J.
PERSONAL Born 10/30/1933, Armstrong, Missouri, m **DISCIPLINE** EDUCATION **EDUCATION** Pittsburg St Univ Pittsburg KS, BS 1955; Univ of WI Milwaukee, MS 1967; Univ of WI Madison, PhD 1973. **CAREER** Univ of WI, asst prof dept Afro-am Studies 1975; Dane Co Head Start, exec dir 1969-71; Milwaukee WI Pub Schs, tchr 1960-68; Consult parent Devel Regn V, 1973-75; Dept of Pub Instr WI, urban ed consult 1974-75; Univ of WI Parkside, assoc prof/chair div of educ; professor/dean, school of education. **HONORS AND AWARDS** Postdoctorial Fellow, Nat Endwmnt for Hmnties 1973-74. **MEMBERSHIPS** Mem Delta Sigma Theta Sor 1952-; mem Am Psychol Assn; bd pres St Mary's Hosp Med Cntr 1978; vice pres priorities Dane Co United Way 1979; mem Assoc of Black Psychologists, Amer Educ Rsch Assoc. **SELECTED PUBLICATIONS** Publ Jour of Psychol Jour of Social Psychol; Negro Educ Rvw; Review of Educational Rsch; Journal of Negro Educ; Journal of School Psychology. **CONTACT ADDRESS** Dean of Education, Univ of Wisconsin Parkside, Kenosha, WI, 53141.

SHADE, WILLIAM G.
PERSONAL Born 04/05/1939, Detroit, MI, m, 1962, 2 children **DISCIPLINE** AMERICAN HISTORY **EDUCATION** Brown Univ, AB, 61, MAT, 62; Wayne State Univ, PhD, 66. **CAREER** Instr hist, Temple Univ, 66-67; from instr to assoc prof, 67-76, prof hist Lehigh Univ, 76-, ed, Pa Hist, 68-72; mem adv bd nat parks, monuments & hist sites, Secy Interior, 71-77; vis assoc prof, Univ Va, 72-73. **HONORS AND AWARDS** Avery O Craven Award, Org of Am Hist, 97; Eleanor and Joseph F Libsch Res Award, Lehigh Univ, 97. **MEMBERSHIPS** AHA; Orgn Am Historians; Survey Studies Habits & Attitudes. **RESEARCH** Civil War and Reconstruction; American political development; 19th century social history. **SELECTED PUBLICATIONS** Auth, The Evolution of American Electoral Systems, Greenwood, 81; co-ed, Our American Sisters: Women in American Life and Thought, D C Heath, 82; auth, Democratizing the Old Dominion: Virginia and the Second Party System, 1824-1861, Univ Press of Virginia, 96. **CONTACT ADDRESS** Dept of History, Lehigh Univ, Bethlehem, PA, 18105. **EMAIL** wgs@lehigh.edu

SHADISH, W.R.
PERSONAL Born 03/11/1949, Brooklyn, NY, m, 1981 **DISCIPLINE** CLINICAL PSYCHOLOGY **EDUCATION** Santa Clara Univ, BA, 72; Purdue Univ, MA, 75, PhD, 78. **CAREER** Staff asst, State of Calif Legis, Joint Comt on the Master Plan for Higher Educ, 72; core staff therapist, Purdue Univ Psychol Svc Ctr, 75-77; intern, Memphis Clin Psychol Internship Consortium, 77-78; instr part-time, Dept of Psychol, Northwestern Univ, 79-81; post-doctoral res fel, Ctr for Health Svc and Policy

Res, Northwestern Univ, 78-81; vis res assoc, Vanderbilt Inst for Pub Policy Studies, Vanderbilt Univ, 85-90; vis scholar, Inst for Policy Res, Northwestern Univ, spring quarter, 97; dir, Ctr for Appl Psychol Res, Dept of Psychol, Univ Memphis, 90-97; dir, res design and stat prog, Dept of Psychol, Univ Memphis, 87-; prof, Dept of Psychol, Univ Memphis, 90-. **HONORS AND AWARDS** Outstanding Res Publ Award, Amer Asn for Marriage and Family Therapy, 94; Paul F. Lazarsfeld Award for Eval Theory, Amer Eval Asn, 94; Outstanding Res Publ Award, Amer Asn for Marriage and Family Therapy, 96; James McKeen Cattell Fund Sabattical Award, 96-97; Pres elect, 96; pres, 97, past-pres, 98, Amer Eval Asn; Svc award, Amer Eval Asn, 93; bd of visitors eminent facul award, Univ Memphis, 95; distinguished res award, Univ Memphis, 88; Merit Facul award, Col of Arts and Sci, Univ Memphis, 91; SPUR award (Superior Performance in Univ Res), Univ Memphis, 87, 88, 90, 93, 94. **MEMBERSHIPS** Amer Asn for Appl and Preventive Psychol; Amer Eval Asn; Amer Psychol Asn; Amer Psychol Soc; Amer Stat Asn; Soc for Clin Trials. **RESEARCH** Experimental and Quasi-experimental design; Program evaluation; Meta-analysis. **SELECTED PUBLICATIONS** Co-ed, with E. Chelimsky, Evaluation for the 21st Century: A Handbook, Thousand Oaks, Calif, Sage Publ, 97; with D. L. Newman, M. A. Scheirer & C. Wye, Guiding Principles for Evaluators, San Francisco, Jossey-Bass, 95; with S. Fuller, The Social Psychology of Science, NY, Guilford Publ, 94; jour articles, Evaluation theory is who we are, Amer Jour of Eval, 19, 1-19, 98; with X. Hu, R. R. Glaser, R. J. Kownacki & T. Wong, A method for exploring the effects of attrition in randomized experiments with dichotomous outcomes, Psychol Methods, 3, 3-22, 98; with M. D. Stanton, Outcome, attrition and family-couples treatment for drug abuse: A meta-analysis and review of the controlled, comparative studies, Psychol Bulletin, 122, 170-191; with G. Matt, A. Novaro, G. Siegle, P. Crits-Christoph, M. Hazelrigg, A. Jorm, L. S. Lyons, M. T. Nietzel, H. T. Prout, L. Robinson, M. L. Smith, M. Svartberg & B. Weiss, Evidence that therapy works in clinically representative conditions. Jour of Cons and Clin Psychol, 65, 355-365, 97; with R. C. Klesges, S. E. Winders, A. W. Meyers, L. H. Eck, K. D. Ward, C. M. Hulquist & J. W. Ray, How much weight gain occurs following smoking cessation? A comparison of weight gain using both continous and point prevalence abstinence, Jour of Cons and Clin Psychol, 65, 286-291, 97. **CONTACT ADDRESS** Dept. of Psychology, The Univ of Memphis, Memphis, TN, 38152. **EMAIL** shadish@mail.psyc.memphis.edu

SHAFFER, ARTHUR
DISCIPLINE HISTORY **EDUCATION** Univ Calif Los Angeles, BA, 59; MA, 62; PhD, 66. **CAREER** Prof **HONORS AND AWARDS** SC Hist Soc Awd, 91. **SELECTED PUBLICATIONS** Auth, The Politics of History: Writing the History of the American Revolution, 1783-1815, 75; To Be An American: David Ramsay and the Making of an American National Consciousness, 91; Edmund Randolph's History of Virginia, Univ Va, 70; co-ed, Politics and Patronage in the Gilded Age: The Garfield-Henry Correspondence, Univ Wis Madison, 70. **CONTACT ADDRESS** History Dept, Univ of Missouri, St. Louis, 484 Lucas Hall, St. Louis, MO, 63121. **EMAIL** Shaffer@umslvma.umsl.edu

SHAFFER, ARTHUR H.
PERSONAL Born 03/18/1936, Pittsburgh, PA, m, 1958, 3 children **DISCIPLINE** EARLY AMERICAN HISTORY **EDUCATION** Univ Calif, Los Angeles, AB, 59, PhD(hist), 66. **CAREER** From asst prof to assoc prof, 66-76, PROF HIST, UNIV MO, ST LOUIS, 76-, Nat Endowment for Humanities fel, 72-73. **RESEARCH** Political and legal biography of Edmund Randolph, 1753-1813; David Ramsey, 1749-1815. **SELECTED PUBLICATIONS** Auth, Quakers And Baptists In Colonial Mass - Pestana,Cg/, Historian, Vol 0055, 1993. **CONTACT ADDRESS** Dept of Hist, Univ of Mo, 8001 Natural Bridge, Saint Louis, MO, 63121-4499.

SHAFFER, NANCY E.
PERSONAL Los Angeles, CA **DISCIPLINE** THE HISTORY AND PHILOSOPHY OF SCIENCE **EDUCATION** Graceland Col, BS, 85; Rice Univ, MA, 87; Ariz State Univ, MA, 91; Univ Calif, Davis, PhD, 96. **CAREER** Instr, Concordia Univ, Montreal, Quebec; asst prof, Univ Nebr, Omaha. **MEMBERSHIPS** Philos of Sci Asn; Am Asn of Philos Tchr. **SELECTED PUBLICATIONS** Auth, Bias in Scientific Practice, Philos of Sci. **CONTACT ADDRESS** Univ Nebr, Omaha, Omaha, NE, 68182.

SHAFFER, THOMAS LINDSAY
PERSONAL Born 04/04/1934, Billings, MT, m, 1954, 8 children **DISCIPLINE** HISTORY **EDUCATION** Univ Albuquerque, BA, 58; Univ Notre Dame, JD, 61; St. Mary's Univ, Tex, LLD (honorary), 84. **CAREER** Univ Notre Dame, asst prof of law, 63-66, prof of law, 66-80, assoc dean, 69-71, dean, 71-75, Robert and Marion Short prof of law, 88-97, Robert and Marion Short prof of law emer, 97-, supv atty, Notre Dame Legal Aid Clinic, 91-; Univ Calif Los Angeles, visiting prof of law, 70-71; Univ Va, visiting prof of law, 75-76; Washington and Lee Univ, Frances Lewis scholar, fall 79, prof of law, 80-87, Robert E. R. Huntley prof of law, 87-88, dir, Frances Lewis Law Ctr, 83-85; Univ Maine, visiting prof of law, summer 82 & 86, fall 98; Bos-

ton Col, Richard Huber Distinguished Visiting Prof of Law, fall, 92; **HONORS AND AWARDS** Phi Beta Kappa; Order of the Coif; Emil Brown Prize in preventive law, 66; pres citation, Univ Notre Dame, 75; Gallagher lectr, Soc for Adolescent Med, 76; Or Emet lectr, York Univ, 79; Rightor Lectr, Loyola Univ, 79; Seegers lectr, Valparaiso Univ, 81; Sullivan lectr, Capital Univ, 82; Cunningham lectr, Queen's Univ, 84; Burch lectr, Vanderbilt Univ, 84; Blankenbaker lectr, Univ Mont, 85; Law Forum lectr, Oh State Univ, 88; Currie lectr, Univ Miss, 89; Vasey Symposium lectr, Univ Dayton, 89; Lichtenstein lectr, Hofstra Univ, 89; Tabor lectr, Valparaiso Univ, 97; Law and Soc lectr, William Mitchell Col of Law, 91; St. Thomas More award and honorary doctorate, St. Mary's Univ of Tex, 83; Law medal, Gonzaga Univ, 91; Reinhold Niebuhr award, Univ Notre Dame, 91; Teacher of the year, Notre Dame Law Sch, 91; Jour of Law and Relig award, 93; Hon Order of Ky Colonels; Admiral of the Tex Navy; Honorary Oakie From Muskogee. **MEMBERSHIPS** Nat Lawyers Asn; Amer Law Inst; Amer Col of Probate Coun; Amer Bar Asn; Asn of Amer Law Sch; Univ of Miami Sch of Law; Practicing Law Inst; Bar Asn of the Seventh Fed Circuit; Soc for Values in Higher Educ; Christ Legal Soc; Ind State Bar Asn; Cath Comn on Intellectual and Cultural Affairs; St. Joseph County Bar Asn; Soc of Christ Ethics; Jewish Law Asn. **RESEARCH** Property, ethics, law and poverty. **SELECTED PUBLICATIONS** Auth, Sermon, Red Mass for the judges and lawyers of the Twin Cities, St. Paul, 28 sep, 97; auth, The Christian Jurisprudence of Robert E. Rodes, Jr.; auth, Professor Frank Booker: A Colleague's Reflection, Notre Dame Lawyer, 12, spring, 97; auth, On Living One Way in Town and Another Way at Home, Inaugural Glenn Tabor Lecture in Legal Ethics, Valparaiso Univ, 31 feb, 97; auth, The Ethical Preparation of Lawyers, Seventh Circuit Judicial Conf, 13 oct, 96; auth, Morality in the Practice of Law, Faith and Ethics Series, First Presbyterian Church, Bethlehem, Penn, 29 sep, 96; auth, Stories of Legal Order in American Business, Univ Notre Dame, 30 sep-1 oct, 96; auth, H. Jefferson Powell on The American Constitutional Tradition: A Conversation, 72, Notre Dame Law Rev, 11, 96; rev, Greenawalt, Private Consciences and Public Reasons, 38, Jour of Church and State, 413, 96; auth, Surprised by Joy on Howard Street, CSC, Labors from the Heart: Mission and Ministry in a Catholic Univ, 96; auth, On Teaching Legal Ethics in the Law Office, 71, Notre Dame Law Rev, 605, 96; co-auth, Is This Appropriate?, 46, Duke Law Jour, 781, 97; co-auth, A Reply to Professor Sammons: Lawyers As Strangers and friends, 18, Univ Ark Little Rock Law Rev, 69, 95; auth, Maybe a Lawyer Can Be a Servant; If Not...., 27, Tex Tech Law Rev, 1345, 96; auth, On Lying for Clients, Conference on Legal Ethics, Hofstra Univ, mar, 96; rev, Kellerman, A Keeper of the Word, Christ Legal Soc Quart, summer, 95; rev, Kronman, The Lost Lawyer: Failing Ideals of the Legal Profession, 41, Loyola Univ Law Rev, 387, 95. **CONTACT ADDRESS** Law School, Univ of Notre Dame, Notre Dame, IN, 46556.

SHAHID, IRFAN ARIF
PERSONAL Nazareth, Palestine, m **DISCIPLINE** HISTORY, LITERATURE **EDUCATION** Oxford Univ, BA, 51; Princeton Univ, PhD, 54. **CAREER** Jr fel Arab-Byzantine rel, Ctr Byzantine Studies, 59-60; assoc prof, Ind Univ, Bloomington, 60-62; assoc prof, 62-66, prof Arabic, Georgetown Univ, 66-, Fulbright-Hays fel Arabic-Am lit, US Off Educ, 68-69; vis fel, Inst Advan Studies, Princeton, 76; Sultanate of Oman prof Arabic & Islamic lit, Georgetow Univ, 81- **HONORS AND AWARDS** Andrew W Mellon Fund Distinguished Lectureship in Lang & Ling, Sch Lang & Ling, Georgetown Univ, 77-79; Life mem, Clare Hall, Cambridge Univ, Engl, 89. **MEMBERSHIPS** Am Orient Soc; Mediaeval Acad Am; Mid East Studies Asn NAm; Mid East Inst; Am Asn Tchr(s) Arabic. **RESEARCH** Arab hist; Arab-Byzantine rel; Arabic lit. **SELECTED PUBLICATIONS** Auth, The martyrs of Najran: new documents, In: Subsidia Hagiographica, 71; Epistula de re publica genereda, In: Themistii Orationes, Vol III, Teubner Class Ser, 74; Rome and the Arabs, 84, Byzantium and the Arabs in the Fourth Century, 84, Byzantium and the Arabs in the Fifth Century, 89, Byzantium and the Arabs in the Sixth Century, 95, Dumbarton Oaks. **CONTACT ADDRESS** Dept of Arab Lang, Lit & Ling, Georgetown Univ, Washington, DC, 20057-1046. **EMAIL** arabic@guvax.georgetown.edu

SHALHOPE, ROBERT E.
PERSONAL Born 02/24/1941, Kansas City, MO, m, 1963, 2 children **DISCIPLINE** HISTORY **EDUCATION** DePauw Univ, BA, 63; Univ MO, MA, 64, PhD, 67. **CAREER** Univ OK, 67-, George Lynn Cross prof of Hisstory, 91-. **HONORS AND AWARDS** Fel, Charles Warren Center for Studies in American History, Harvard Univ; NEH fel; member, Am Antiquarian Soc; NEH summer fel. **MEMBERSHIPS** Org of Am Hist; Omohunduo Inst of Am Hist and Culture. **RESEARCH** Am history, 1763-1848. **SELECTED PUBLICATIONS** Auth, The Roots of Democracy: American Culture and Thought, 1760-1800, Twayne, 90; Bennington and the Green Mountain Boys: The Emergence of Liberal Democracy in Vermont, 1760-1850, Johns Hopkins Univ Press, 96. **CONTACT ADDRESS** Dept of History, Univ of Oklahoma, Norman, OK, 73019. **EMAIL** robert-schalhope@ou.edu

SHANK, WESLEY I.
PERSONAL Born 03/01/1927, San Francisco, CA, m, 1949, 3 children **DISCIPLINE** ARCHITECTURE **EDUCATION**

Univ Calif - Berkeley, BA, 51; McGill Univ, MArch, 65. **CAREER** Draftsman, architect, architectural specifications writer in San Francisco Bay area, 51-63; Prof, 64-92, Prof Archit Emeritus, Iowa State Univ, 92-; architect and architectural historian, Nat Park Service, Historic Am Buildings Survey field offices across the U.S., 67-82. **MEMBERSHIPS** Soc Archit Hist; Am Inst Archit. **RESEARCH** Historic American architecture and architects. **SELECTED PUBLICATIONS** Auth, Hugh Garden in Iowa, Prairie Sch Rev 5, 68; The Residence in Des Moines, J Soc Archit Hist 29, 70; Eighteenth-Century Architecture of the Upper Delaware River Valley of New Jersey and Pennsylvania, J Soc Archit Hist 31, 72; compiler, The Iowa Catalog: Historic American Buildings Survey, Univ Iowa Press, 79; Cochrane & Piquenard, Edmond Jacques Eckel, Edward Townsend Mix, and John Francis Rague, entries in: Macmillan Encyclopedia of Architects, The Free Press, 82; The Demise of the County Courthouse Tower in Iowa: A Study in Early Twentieth Century Cultural and Architectural Change, The Annals of Iowa, Spring 92; Eckel & Mann, In: Dictionary of Art, Grove, 96; Iowa's Historic Architects: A Biographical Dictionary, Univ Iowa Press, 98; Edward Townsend Mix, In: American National Biography, Oxford Univ Press (forthcoming 99). **CONTACT ADDRESS** 1904 Northcrest Cir, Ames, IA, 50010-5113. **EMAIL** wshank@iastate.edu

SHANNON, CATHERINE BARBARA
PERSONAL Hingham, MA **DISCIPLINE** HISTORY **EDUCATION** Univ Toronto, BA, 60; Nat Univ Ireland, Dublin, MA, 63; Univ Mass, PhD(hist), 75. **CAREER** Teacher hist, Holbrook High Sch, 64-67; PROF BRIT & IRISH HIST, WESTFIELD STATE COL, 67- . **HONORS AND AWARDS** Westfield State Col fac res grant, 74. **MEMBERSHIPS** AHA; Irish Hist Soc; Am Comt Irish Studies; Northeast Asn Irish Studies. **RESEARCH** Political and social history of modern Ireland; Northern Ireland 1820-1922; British Unionist party politics, 1885-1922. **SELECTED PUBLICATIONS** Auth, Ulster Liberal Unionists and Local Government Reform, 1885-1898, Irish Hist Studies, 3/73. **CONTACT ADDRESS** 577 Western Ave, Westfield, MA, 01085-2501.

SHANNON, SYLVIA C.
DISCIPLINE HISTORY **EDUCATION** Georgetwon Univ, AB, 74; Boston Univ, PhD, 88. **CAREER** Asst prof, 91-, St Anselm Col. **RESEARCH** Early mod Europ hist, espec Renaissance and Reformation hist; confessional struggle between Calvinists and Cath(s) in France on the colonial efforts made by the French Crown in Brazil. **SELECTED PUBLICATIONS** Auth, Military Outpost or Religious Refuge?: the Expedition of Villegagnon to Rio de Janeiro in 1555, Proceedings Fr Colonial Hist Soc, 96. **CONTACT ADDRESS** St Anselm Col, 100 Saint Anselm Dr, Manchester, NH, 03102-1310. **EMAIL** sshannon@anselm.edu

SHANNON, TIMOTHY J.
DISCIPLINE AMERICAN HISTORY **EDUCATION** Northwestern Univ PhD, 93. **CAREER** Asst Prof hist, Gettysburg College. **MEMBERSHIPS** OAH **RESEARCH** Native American History; American Colonial History. **SELECTED PUBLICATIONS** Auth, The Crossroads of Empire: Indians Colonists and the Albany Congress of 1754, Cornell Univ Press, forthcoming; auth, Dressing for Success on the Mohawk Frontier: Hendrick William Johnson and the Indian Fashion, William and Mary Qtly, 96; This Unpleasant Business: The Transformation of Land Speculation in the Ohio Country, in: The Pursuit of Public Power: The Origins of Politics in Ohio, eds, Jeffrey P Brown, Andrew R L Clayton, Kent State Univ Press, 94; auth, The Ohio Company and the Meaning of Opportunity in the American West, New Eng Qtly, 91. **CONTACT ADDRESS** History Dept, Gettysburg Col, Gettysburg, PA, 17325. **EMAIL** tshannon@gettysburg.edu

SHANTZ, DOUGLAS H.
PERSONAL Born 01/11/1952, Kitchener, ON, Canada, m, 1974, 4 children **DISCIPLINE** HISTORY **EDUCATION** Wheaton Col, BA, 73; Westminster Theol Sem, MA; Univ of Waterloo, PHD **CAREER** Asst Prof of Theol, 83-86, NW Baptist Theol; Assoc Prof of Relig Studies, 86-98, Trinity West Univ **HONORS AND AWARDS** SSHRC Small Grant; **MEMBERSHIPS** AAR; Soc for Reformation Res; Am Soc of Church Hist **RESEARCH** Radical reform; German Pietism and Millenialism **SELECTED PUBLICATIONS** Auth, "Crautwald, Valentin," Oxford Encyclopedia of the Reformation, Oxford Univ Press, 96; Auth, "The Crautwald-Bucer Correspondence 1528 A Family Feud Within the Zwingli Circle," Mennonite Quarterly Review, 94, 79-94 **CONTACT ADDRESS** Trinity Western Univ, 7600 Glove, Langley, BC, V2Y 1Y1. **EMAIL** shantz@twu.ca

SHAPIRO, EDWARD S.
PERSONAL Born 01/14/1938, Washington, DC, m, 1965, 4 children **DISCIPLINE** HISTORY **EDUCATION** Georgetown Univ,BA 59; Univ NC; Harvard Univ PhD 68. **CAREER** St John's Univ, instr asst prof 65-69. **HONORS AND AWARDS** Oxford Cen Fell; Ecumenical Res Fell. **MEMBERSHIPS** AHA; AMJHS; OAH. **RESEARCH** Am Jewish hist, 20th century Am hist, Am ethnic hist. **SELECTED PUBLICATIONS** The Letters of Sydney Hook: Democracy, Communism and the

Cold War; A Time for Healing: American Jewry Since World War II. **CONTACT ADDRESS** 4 Forest Dr, West Orange, NJ, 07052. **EMAIL** shapired@lanmailshu.edu

SHAPIRO, H. ALAN
PERSONAL Born 08/03/1949, New York, NY, s **DISCIPLINE** CLASSICAL ARCHAEOLOGY **EDUCATION** Princeton Univ, PhD, 77. **CAREER** Asst Prof, Columbia Univ, 77-78; Mellon Fel & Asst Prof, Tulane Univ, 78-81; Asst Prof to Assoc Prof, Stevens Inst Technol, 81-92; Prof, Univ Canterbury, 94-96; Prof, Johns Hopkins Univ, 97-. **HONORS AND AWARDS** Phi Beta Kappa; NEH grant, 89; Parker Vis Scholar, Brown Univ, 90; Vis Scholar, Deutsches Archaologisches Institut, 92; Guggenheim Fel, 92-93. **MEMBERSHIPS** Archaeol Inst Am; Am Philol Asn. **RESEARCH** Greek art and archaeology; mythology. **SELECTED PUBLICATIONS** Auth, Myth into Art. Poet and Painter in Classical Greece, Routledge, 94; coauth, Women in the Classical World, Oxford, 94; co-ed, The Archaeology of Athens and Attica under the Democracy, Oxbow Bks, 94; Mother City and Colony. Classical Athenian and South Italian Vases in New Zealand and Australia, Exhibition Catalogue, Robert MacDougall Art Gallery, Christchurch, 95; Greek Vases in the San Antonio Museum of Art, 96; series ed, Cambridge Studies in Classical Art and Iconography, 92-; transl, The Mask of Socrates, Univ Calif, 95. **CONTACT ADDRESS** Classics Dept, Johns Hopkins Univ, 3400 N Charles St, Baltimore, MD, 21218-2690. **EMAIL** ashapiro@jhu.edu

SHAPIRO, HENRY D.
PERSONAL Born 05/07/1937, New York, NY, m, 1963, 3 children **DISCIPLINE** AMERICAN INTELLECTUAL HISTORY **EDUCATION** Columbia Col, AB, 58; Cornell Univ, MA, 60; Rutgers Univ, PhD(hist), 66. **CAREER** Teaching asst hist, Cornell Univ, 58-60; asst instr, Rutgers Univ, 60-62; instr, Ohio State Univ, 63-66; asst prof, 66-71, assoc prof, 71-80, PROF HIST, UNIV CINCINNATI, 80-, CO-DIR, CTR NEIGHBORHOOD & COMMUNITY STUDIES, 81-, Charles Warren fel, Harvard Univ, 71-72; Fulbright sr lectr Am hist, John F Kennedy Inst Am Studies, Free Univ Berlin, 77-78. **HONORS AND AWARDS** Moses Coit Tyler Prize, Cornell Univ, 61; W D Weatherford Prize, Berea Col, 79. **MEMBERSHIPS** Am Studies Asn. **RESEARCH** American intellectual history; history of American culture; American science in the 19th century. **SELECTED PUBLICATIONS** Auth, Pluralism And Progressives - Hull-House And The New Immigrants, 1890-1919 - Lissak,Rs/, American Jewish Archives, Vol 0045, 1993; Front Yard Am - The Evolution And Meanings Of A Vernacular Domestic Landscape - Schroeder,Feh/, Technology And Cult, Vol 0036, 1995; The Lawn - A Hist Of An Am Obsession - Jenkins,Vs/, Technology And Cult, Vol 0036, 1995; Appalachia In The Making - The Mountain South In The 19th-Century - Pudup,Mb/, Appalachian J, Vol 0024, 1996. **CONTACT ADDRESS** Dept of Hist, Univ of Cincinnati, Cincinnati, OH, 45221.

SHAPIRO, HENRY L.
PERSONAL New York, NY **DISCIPLINE** ANCIENT PHILOSOPHY, AESTHETICS **EDUCATION** Univ Toronto, BA, 60; Columbia Univ, PhD, 69. **CAREER** Preceptor philos, Columbia Univ, 64-66; actg asst prof, Univ Calif, Riverside, 66-68; chmn dept, 70-73, Asst Prof Philos Univ Mo-St Louis, 68-. **RESEARCH** Greek philosophy; 19th century continental philosophy; philosophy of literature. **SELECTED PUBLICATIONS** Auth, The Oxford Book Of Gothic Tales - Baldick,C/, Studies In Short Fiction, Vol 0030, 1993; 'Proofs And Three Parables' - Steiner,G/, Studies In Short Fiction, Vol 0031, 1994; The Oxford Book Of Sea Stories - Tanner,T/, Studies In Short Fiction, Vol 0032, 1995. **CONTACT ADDRESS** Dept of Philos, Univ of Mo, 8001 Natural Bridge, Saint Louis, MO, 63121-4499.

SHAPIRO, HERBERT
PERSONAL Born 06/14/1929, Jamaica, NY, m, 1957, 2 children **DISCIPLINE** AMERICAN HISTORY **EDUCATION** Queens Col, BA, 52; Columbia Univ, MA, 58; Univ Rochester, PhD(hist), 64. **CAREER** Asst prof hist, Morehouse Col, 62-66; from Asst Prof to Assoc Prof, 66-88, PROF HIST, UNIV CINCINNATI, 88-. **MEMBERSHIPS** AHA; Orgn Am Historians; Southern Hist Asn. **RESEARCH** The populist-progressive period; African-American history. **SELECTED PUBLICATIONS** Coauth, The World of Lincoln Steffens, Hill & Wang, 62; auth, The Ku Klux Klan during Reconstruction--South Carolina episode, J Negro Hist, 1/64; The Muckrakers in American Society, Heath, 68; The Populists and the Negro: A reconsideration, In: The Making of Black America, Atheneum, 68; Steffens, Lippmann and Reed: The muckraker and his proteges, Pac Northwest Quart, 10/71; Muckracking in America, Forum, 76; Lincoln Steffens and the McNamara Case, Am J Econ & Sociol, 10/80; Eugene Genovese, Marxism and the Study of Slavery, J Ethnic Studies, Vol 9, No 4; White Violence and Black Response: From Reconstruction to Montgomery, 88; co-ed, American Communism and Black Americans, 1930-1934, 91; I Belong to the Working Class: The Unfinished Autobiography of Rose Pastor Stokes, 92; Northern Labor and Antislavery: A Documentary History, 94; ed, African American History and Radical Historiography: Essays in Honor of Herbert Aptheker, 98. **CONTACT ADDRESS** Dept of Hist, Univ of Cincinnati, PO Box 210373, Cincinnati, OH, 45221-0373. **EMAIL** shapirh@ucbeh.san.uc.edu

SHAPIRO, LINN
DISCIPLINE HISTORY **EDUCATION** American Univ, PhD, 96. **CAREER** Mgr, res proj develop, Am Hist Asn. **MEMBERSHIPS** Am Hist Asn. **RESEARCH** History of the American Left, African American culture. **CONTACT ADDRESS** American Historical Assn.

SHAPIRO, STANLEY
PERSONAL Born 10/16/1936, New York, NY, m, 1964 **DISCIPLINE** RECENT AMERICAN HISTORY **EDUCATION** Brooklyn Col, AB, 58; Univ CA, Berkeley, AM, 59, PhD, 67. **CAREER** Instr, 65-67, Asst prof hist, Wayne State Univ, 68-, dir, honors prog, Wayne State Univ, 94. **MEMBERSHIPS** AHA; Orgn Am Historians; Labor Historians, 70. **RESEARCH** Polit, soc, and intellectual hist of the First World War period. **SELECTED PUBLICATIONS** Auth, The great war and reform: Liberals and labor, 1917-1919, Labor Hist, 71; The twilight of reform: Advanced liberals after the armistice, Historian, 71; The passage of power: Labor and the new social order, Proc Am Philos Soc, 12/76. **CONTACT ADDRESS** Dept of Hist, Wayne State Univ, 3139 FAB, Detroit, MI, 48202-3919. **EMAIL** s_shapiro@wayne.edu

SHAPIRO, STUART CHARLES
PERSONAL Born 12/30/1944, New York, NY, m, 1972 **DISCIPLINE** COMPUTER SCIENCE **EDUCATION** MIT, SB, Math, 66; Univ Wis, MS, Comput Sci, 68, PhD, 71. **CAREER** Tchg asst, Univ Wis, 66-67, res asst, Univ Wis, 67-70, lectr, Univ Wis, Comput Sci, 71; vis asst prof, Ind Univ, 71-72; asst prof, Ind Univ, 72-77; assoc prof, Ind Univ, 77-78; asst prof, SUNY-Buffalo, 77-78; assoc prof, SUNY, 78-83; PROF, SUNY, COMP SCI & ENGG, 83.; **MEMBERSHIPS** An Asn Artificial Intel; Asn for Comput Machinery; Cognitive Sci Soc; IEEE **RESEARCH** Artificial intelligence; Cognitive science; Computational linguistics; Sematics networks; Belief systems; Logic program. **SELECTED PUBLICATIONS** Coauth, "Knowledge-Based Multimedia Systems," Multimedia Systems, ACM Press, 94; coauth, Proceedings of the Seventh Florida Artificial Intelligence Research Symposium, Fla AI Res Soc, 94; coauth, Deixis in Narrative: A Cognitive Science Perspective, Lawrence Erlbaum, 95; coauth, Readings in Intelligent user Interfaces, Morgan Kaufmann, 98; coauth, Principles of Knowledge Representation and Reasoning: Proceedings of the Sixth International Conference, Morgan Kaufmann, 98; auth, Mind 107, 98; coauth, Thought, Language, and Ontology: Essays in Memory of Hector-Neri Castaneda, Kluwer Academic Publ, 98. **CONTACT ADDRESS** Dept Computer Sci & Engg, SUNY-Buffalo, 226 Bell Hall, Box 602000, Buffalo, NY, 14260-2000. **EMAIL** shapiro@cs.buffalo.edu

SHARFMAN, GLENN
PERSONAL Born 09/06/1961, Chicago, IL, m, 1985, 3 children **DISCIPLINE** HISTORY **EDUCATION** Univ Miami, BA, 83; Univ NC, MA, 85, PhD, 89. **CAREER** ASSOC PROF HISTORY, HIRAM COL, 90-. **HONORS AND AWARDS** Michael Starr Award; Paul Martin Award. **MEMBERSHIPS** AHA; Leo Baeck Inst; Ohio Acad Hist. **RESEARCH** Modern Jewish; modern German; Holocaust. **SELECTED PUBLICATIONS** The Dilemma of Jewish Youths in Nazi Germany, Shafer, 92; Various Solutions to the Juderfrage: A Look back at 19th century antisemitism, Festschift for Richard Rubenstein; "Integration or Exclusion?: Bavarian Jews in the 19th Century," Jour Relig Hist, 95; Jewish Emancipation in 1848, Revolutions of 1848, 96. **CONTACT ADDRESS** Dept. Of History, Hiram Col, Pendleton House, Hiram, OH, 44234. **EMAIL** SharfmanGR@Hiram.edu

SHARMA, JAGDISH P.
PERSONAL Born 01/04/1934, m, 1962, 2 children **DISCIPLINE** ANCIENT HISTORY & RELIGION **EDUCATION** Agra Univ, BA, 55; Univ London, BA(hons), 59, PhD(ancient hist), 62. **CAREER** Vis asst prof Indian hist, Univ Va, 63-64; vis asst prof sch int serv, Am Univ, 64; asst prof, 64-68, assoc prof, 68-76, prof Indian hist, Univ Hawaii, Manoa, 76-; dir undergrad majors in Asian studies, Univ Hawaii, 69-71, chm hist forum, Hist Fac Res Sem, 69-75, 97-; adv, Jainas Am. **MEMBERSHIPS** Asn Asian Studies; life fel Royal Asiatic Soc; Am Orient Soc; AAUP. **RESEARCH** Ancient republics; ancient politics and democracy in the ancient world; Jainism; comparative religions. **SELECTED PUBLICATIONS** Auth, Republics in Ancient India, c 1500 BC-500 BC, E J Brill, Leiden, 68; coauth, Hinduism, Sarvodaya and Social Change, In: Religion and Political Modernization, Yale Univ, 74; auth, Jaina and Buddhist Traditions Regarding the Origins of Ajatasattu's War within Vajjians: A New Interpretation, Shramana, Vol 25, No 9 & 10; Hemacandra: The Life and Scholarship of a Jaina Monk, Asian Profile, Vol 3, No 2; Jainas as a Minority in Indian Society and History, Jain J, Vol 10, No 4; coauth, Dream-Symbolism in the Sramanic Tradition, Firma KLM-Calcutta, 80; ed & contribr, Individuals and Ideas in Modern India; auth, Nine Interpretative Studies, Firma KLM-Calcutta, 82; Time Perspective in the Study of Culture, J Soc Res, 3/79; Life-Pattern of the Jinas in Bibliography: East & West, ed by Carol Ramalb, Hon, 89; Jawaharlal Nehru--A Biographical Sketch, in Foreign Visitors to Congress: Speeches and History for US Capitol Society, Wash, DC, Millwood, NY, Karaus Int Pubs, 2 vols, 89; August 15 (1947)-India in Book of Days-1987: An Encyclopedia, Ann Arbor: The Reirian Press, 88; Japan as Seen From America and India: My First Impressions in Japanese with Eng Summary in Japan in the World Vol XIII Takushoku Univ, Tokyo, 94; Indian Thinking and Thinkers in Perspectives on History & Culture (in honor of Prof D P Singhal), ed by Arvind Sharma, Indian Books Centre, Delhi, 92; Individuals and Ideas in Traditional India, ed with contribution, MRML, New Delhi (in press); Jaina Yakshas, Kusumanjali, Meerut, India, 89, 93; The Jinasattvas: Class and Gender in the Social Origins of Jaina Heroes, ed by N. K. Wagle, Univ Toronto Press, (forthcoming); Political History in the Historiography of Ancient India: New Trends and Prospects in Political History in a Changing World, ed by G C Pande, et al Kusumanjali, Jodhpur, 92; Ambapali's Vesali about 500 B C in City in Pre-Modern Asia, ed by Leslie Gunawardana (forthcoming). **CONTACT ADDRESS** Dept Hist, Univ Hawaii at Manoa, 2530 Dole St, Honolulu, HI, 96822-2383. **EMAIL** jpsharma@hawaii.edu

SHARMA, R.N.
PERSONAL Born 10/22/1944, Punjab, India, m, 1972, 2 children **DISCIPLINE** LIBRARY AND INFORMATION SCIENCE; HIGHER EDUCATION; HISTORY **EDUCATION** Univ Delhi, BA, 63, MA, 66; N TX State Univ, MLS, 70; SUNY, Buffalo, PhD, 82. **CAREER** Asst librn, Col Ozarks, 70-71; ref librn, Colgate Univ, 71-81; head librn, Penn State Univ, Beaver Campus, 81-85; asst dir, Univ WI, 85-89; dir, Univ Evansville, 89-95; dir, WV State Col, 96-. **HONORS AND AWARDS** Who's Who Among Asian Am, 92-94; advisory bd, 94-98, Asian Lit; Humprhy/OCLC/Forest Press Award, 97, ALA; chair, Am Librns Delegation to Palestine, 97; Am Librns Delegation to Northern Ireland, 97; Benjamin Franklin Award, 98, Publishers Marketing Asn. **MEMBERSHIPS** Am Libr Asn; Asn Col Res Libr; Int Relations Round Table; Indian Libr Asn; Asian/Pacific Am Librn Asn. **RESEARCH** International librarianship; history of libraries; library administration; reference services. **SELECTED PUBLICATIONS** Auth, Indian Academic Libraries and Dr. S. R. Ranganathan: A Critical Study, Sterling, 86; Ranganathan and the West, Sterling, 92; Research and Academic Librarians: A Global View, Resources in Education, 92; Changing Dimensions: Managing Library and Information Services for the 1990's: A Global Perspective, Ed Resources Infor Center, 94; Linking Asian/Pacific Collections to America, Educational Resources Infor Center, 95. **CONTACT ADDRESS** Drain-Jordan Library, West Virginia State Col, PO Box 1002, Institute, WV, 25112-1002. **EMAIL** sharmarn@mail.wvsc.edu

SHARONI, SIMONA
DISCIPLINE MIDDLE EASTERN STUDIES **EDUCATION** George Mason Univ, PhD. **CAREER** Prof, Am Univ. **RESEARCH** Conflict resolution, gender; Israeli-Palestinian conflict. **SELECTED PUBLICATIONS** Auth, Gender and the Israeli-Palestinian Conflict: The Politics of Women's Resistance, Syracuse Univ Press, 95. **CONTACT ADDRESS** American Univ, 4400 Massachusetts Ave, Washington, DC, 20016.

SHARP, BUCHANAN
PERSONAL Born 09/25/1942, Dumbarton, Scotland, m, 1964, 2 children **DISCIPLINE** BRITISH & DUTCH HISTORY **EDUCATION** Univ Calif, Berkeley, AB, 64, PhD(hist), 71; Univ Ill, Urbana-Champaign, MA, 65. **CAREER** Asst prof, 70-77, ASSOC PROF HIST, UNIV CALIF SANTA CRUZ, 77-. **MEMBERSHIPS** Econ Hist Soc; Past & Present Soc, Eng; Scottish Hist Soc; AHA. **RESEARCH** Economic and social history of Tudor-Stuart England; economic and social history of the Dutch Republic in the 16th and 17th centuries. **SELECTED PUBLICATIONS** Auth, The Making Of An Industrial-Society - Whickham 1560-1765 - Levine,D, Wrightson,K/, Am Hist Rev, Vol 0098, 1993; A Community Transformed - The Manor And Liberty Of Havering, 1500-1620 - Mcintosh,Mk/, J Of Economic Hist, Vol 0053, 1993; The Battle Of The Frogs And Fairfords Flies, Miracles And The Pulp Press During The English-Revolution - Friedman,J/, Albion, Vol 0026, 1994; Hunters And Poachers - A Cult And Soc-History Of Unlawful Hunting In Eng, 1485-1640 - Manning,Rb/, Am Hist Rev, Vol 0100, 1995. **CONTACT ADDRESS** Dept of Hist, Stevenson Col Univ of Calif, 1156 High St, Santa Cruz, CA, 95064-0001.

SHARP, JAMES ROGER
PERSONAL Born 08/08/1936, Troy, KS, m, 1957, 2 children **DISCIPLINE** AMERICAN HISTORY **EDUCATION** Univ Mo, BA, 58, MA, 60; Univ Calif, Berkeley, PhD(hist), 66. **CAREER** Asst prof, 66-70, assoc prof, 70-81, PROF HIST, SYRACUSE UNIV, 79-, CHAIRPERSON DEPT, 76-, Soc Sci Res Coun res grant, 69; Nat Endowment for Humanities fel, 70-71; consult, Nat Endowment for Humanities Panel for Younger Humanist Fels, 71 & 72; Am Coun Learned Soc fel, 79-80. **MEMBERSHIPS** AHA; Orgn Am Historians; Southern Hist Asn. **RESEARCH** Early national and middle periods of United States history. **SELECTED PUBLICATIONS** Auth, The Origins Of Jeffersonian Commercial-Policy And Diplomacy - Benatar,Ds/, J Of Southern Hist, Vol 0060, 1994; Original Intentions - On The Making And Ratification Of The United-States Constitution - Bradford,Me/, J Of Interdisciplinary Hist, Vol 0026, 1995; Clinton,George - Yeoman Politician Of The New Republic - Kaminski,Jp/, Am Hist Rev, Vol 0100, 1995; The Papers Of Jackson,Andrew, Vol 4, 1816-1820 - Moser,Hd,

Hoth,Dr, Hoeman,Gh, Eds/, Penn Mag Of Hist And Biog, Vol 0119, 1995; The Presidency Of Jackson,Andrew - Cole,Db/, Penn Mag Of Hist And Biog, Vol 0119, 1995; Devising Liberty - Preserving And Creating Freedom In The New Am Republic - Konig,Dt/, William And Mary Quart, Vol 0053, 1996; Jefferson And Madison - 3 Conversations From The Founding - Banning,L/, J Of Am Hist, Vol 0082, 1996; The Jacksonian Promise - Am 1815-1840 - Feller,D/, Am Hist Rev, Vol 0102, 1997; The Papers Of Madison,James, Secretary-Of-State Series, Volume 3 - March 1, 1802 October 6, 1802 - Mattern,Db, Stagg,Jca, Cross,Jk, Perdue,Sh/, Penn Mag Of Hist And Biog, Vol 0121, 1997. **CONTACT ADDRESS** Dept of Hist, Syracuse Univ, Syracuse, NY, 13210.

SHARP, MIKE
DISCIPLINE POLITICAL SCIENCE **EDUCATION** Northwest Mo State Univ, BA, 72; Univ Okla, MA, 89, PhD, 90. **CAREER** Vis asst prof, 87-88, asst prof, 88-94, ASSOC PROF, 94-, CHAIR POL SCI, 97-, NORTHEASTERN STATE UNIV. **CONTACT ADDRESS** Dept of Pol Sci, Northeastern State Univ, Tahlequah, OK, 74464. **EMAIL** shapr@cherokee.nsuok.edu

SHARRER, GEORGE TERRY
PERSONAL Born 12/30/1944, Baltimore, MD **DISCIPLINE** UNITED STATES AND AGRICULTURAL HISTORY **EDUCATION** Univ Md, College Park, BA, 66, MA, 68, PhD(hist), 75. **CAREER** Technician agr, 69-72, specialist mfg, 72-75, CUR FOOD TECH, SMITHSONIAN INST, 75-, ed, Living Historical Farm Bull, 76- **MEMBERSHIPS** Agr Hist Soc; Asn Living Hist Farms & Agr Mus (secy-treas, 76-80). **RESEARCH** History of American food technology; history of museums. **SELECTED PUBLICATIONS** Auth, Cole,Robert World - Agriculture And Soc In Early Maryland - Carr,Lg, Menard,Rr, Walsh,Ls/, Technol And Cult, Vol 0034, 1993; 75 Years Of Service - Cooperative Extension In Iowa - Schweider,D/, J Of Am Hist, Vol 0081, 1994; An Anxious Pursuit - Agricultural Innovation And Modernity In The Lower South, 1730-1815 - Chaplin,Je/, Technol And Cult, Vol 0036, 1995; The Great Glanders Epizootic, 1861-1866 - A Civil-War Legacy/, Agricultural Hist, Vol 0069, 1995. **CONTACT ADDRESS** Mus of Am Hist, Smithsonian Inst, Rm 5035, Washington, DC, 20650.

SHARY, TIMOTHY
PERSONAL Born 08/17/1967, Cheverly, MD, s **DISCIPLINE** FILM HISTORY **EDUCATION** Hampshire Col, BA, 91; Ohio Univ, MA, 92; Univ of Mass, PhD, 98. **CAREER** VIS LECTR, CLARK UNIV, 97-. **HONORS AND AWARDS** Phi Kappa Phi. **MEMBERSHIPS** Soc for Cinema Studies; Univ Film & Video Asn. **RESEARCH** Film hist, theory, and criticism; media studies; media production. **SELECTED PUBLICATIONS** Auth, Reification and Loss in Postmodern Puberty: The Cultural Logic of Fredric Jameson and Young Adult Movies, Postmodernism in the Cinema, Berghahn Books, 98; The Teen Film and its Methods of Study, J of Popular Film and Television, 97; The Only Place To Go Is Inside: Confusions of Sexuality and Class in Clueless and Kids, Pictures of a Generation on Hold: Youth in Film and Television of the 90s, Media Studies Working Group, 96; Exotica: Atom Egoyan's Neurotic Thriller, Point of View, 95; Video as Accessible Artifact and Artificial Access: The Early Films of Atom Egoyan, Film Criticism, 95; Viewing Experience: Structures of Subjectivity in East and West European Films, Echoes and Mirrors, 94; Present Personal Truths: The Alternative Phenomenology of Video in I've Heard the Mermaids Singing, Wide Angle, 93. **CONTACT ADDRESS** Dept of Commun, Univ of Massachusetts, Machmer Hall, Amherst, MA, 01003. **EMAIL** shary@comm.umass.edu

SHASHKO, PHILIP
PERSONAL Born 03/27/1936, m, 1971, 2 children **DISCIPLINE** RUSSIAN & BALKAN HISTORY **EDUCATION** Mich State Univ, BA, 60; Univ Calif, Berkeley, MA, 61; Univ Mich, Ann Arbor, cert Russ studies, 63, PhD(hist), 69. **CAREER** Asst prof, 68-74, assoc prof, 74-82, PROF HIST, UNIV WIS-MILWAUKEE, 82-, Int Res & Exchanges Bd fel, Bulgaria, 69-70; Univ Wis Grad Sch res grant, 69-70; Am Coun Leraned Socs travel grant, Warsaw, 73; Nat Endowment for Humanities grant, 78. **HONORS AND AWARDS** Standard Oil Teaching Excellence Award, Univ Student Govt, 73. **MEMBERSHIPS** Am Asn Advan Slavic Studies; AHA; Am Asn Southeast Europ Studies; Bulgarian Studies Asn (vpres, 75-78). **RESEARCH** Russian intelligentsia; modern Balkans; Russian-Balkan relations. **SELECTED PUBLICATIONS** Auth, Scholar, Patriot, Mentor - Historical Essays In Honor Of Djordjevic,Dimitrije - Spence,Rb, Nelson,Ll/, Slavic Rev, Vol 0053, 1994; The Macedonian Conflict - Ethnic Nationalism In A Transnational World - Danforth,Lm/, Am Hist Rev, Vol 0102, 1997. **CONTACT ADDRESS** Dept of Hist, Univ of Wis, Po Box 413, Milwaukee, WI, 53201-0413.

SHATTUCK, ROGER
PERSONAL Born 08/20/1923, New York, NY, m, 1949, 4 children **DISCIPLINE** HISTORY **EDUCATION** Yale Univ, BA, 1947. **CAREER** Info officer, film sect, UNESCO, Paris, Fr, 47-48; asst trade ed, Harcourt, Brace & Co, 49-50; jr fel, Soc Fel, Harvard Univ, 50-53; instr, fr, Harvard Univ, 53-56; asst prof to prof, fr and eng, Univ Tex Austin, 56-71; Commonwealth prof, Fr, Univ Va, 74-88; Fulbright prof, Amer lit, Univ Dakar, Senegal, 84-85; prof and prof emer, mod foreign lang, 86-97. **RESEARCH** Literature; A public morality; The fine arts. **SELECTED PUBLICATIONS** Auth, Forbidden Knowledge: From Prometheus to Pornography, 96; auth, The Innocent Eye: On Modern Literature and the Arts, 84; auth, The Forbidden Experiment: the Story of the Wild Boy of Aveyron, 80; auth, Marcel Proust, 74; auth, Half Tame, 64; auth, Proust's Binoculars, 63; auth, The Banquet Years, 58. **CONTACT ADDRESS** 231 Forge Hill Rd., Lincoln, VT, 05443.

SHAVELL, S.
PERSONAL Born 05/29/1946, Washington, DC **DISCIPLINE** ECONOMICS **EDUCATION** Univ Michigan, AB 68; MIT, PhD 73. **CAREER** Harvard Univ, asst prof, assoc prof, 74-80; Harvard Law school, asst prof 80-82, prof 82-. **HONORS AND AWARDS** Guggenheim Fel; Fel Econ Soc **MEMBERSHIPS** AEA; ALEA **RESEARCH** Law and economics **SELECTED PUBLICATIONS** Auth, Economic Analysis of Accident Law, Harvard Univ Press, Cam MA, 87; The Fundamental Divergence Between the Private and the Social Motive to Use the Legal System, Jour of Legal Stud, 97; Acquisition and Disclosure of Information Prior to Sale, Rand Jour of Econ, 94; The Optimal Structure of Law Enforcement, Jour of Law and Econ, 93. **CONTACT ADDRESS** School of Law, Harvard Univ, Cambridge, MA, 02138. **EMAIL** shavell@law.harvard.edu

SHAW, BARTON CARR
PERSONAL Born 06/06/1947, Annapolis, MD, m, 1 child **DISCIPLINE** AMERICAN HISTORY **EDUCATION** Elon Col, AB, 69; Univ WI-Milwaukee, MA, 72; Emory Univ, PhD, 79. **CAREER** Asst prof hist, Ga Inst Technol, 79-80; from Asst Prof to Prof Hist, Cedar Crest Col, 80-; Fulbright Sr Lectr, Univ Sheffield (UK), 87. **HONORS AND AWARDS** Ford Found Fel, 72-76; Frederick Jackson Turner Award, Org Am Hist, 85; Cedar Crest Col Alumnae Award for Excellence in Tchg, 89; NEH Summer Inst on the Southern Civil Rights movement, Harvard Univ, 93. **MEMBERSHIPS** Orgn Am Historians; Southern Hist Asn. **RESEARCH** Hist of the Am South; hist of Am populism. **SELECTED PUBLICATIONS** Auth, The Hobson Craze, US Naval Inst Proc, 2/76; From the user's perspective: Research in Georgia archives, Ga Archive, spring 80; The wool-hat boys: A history of the populist party in Georgia, 1892 to 1910, Proc Ninty-Fifth Annual Meeting Am Hist Asn, 80; The Wool-Hat Boys: Georgia's Populist Party, LSU Press, 84. **CONTACT ADDRESS** Dept of Hist, Cedar Crest Col, 100 College Dr, Allentown, PA, 18104-6196. **EMAIL** bcshaw@cedarcrest.edu

SHAW, DONALD LEWIS
PERSONAL Born 10/27/1936, Raleigh, NC, m, 1960, 4 children **DISCIPLINE** MASS COMMUNICATIONS HISTORY **EDUCATION** Univ NC, Chapel Hill, AB, 59, MA, 60; Univ Wis, PhD(mass commun), 66. **CAREER** From asst prof to assoc prof, 66-76, prof jour, 76- ,KENAN PROF, 92- , UNIV NC, CHAPEL HILL. **MEMBERSHIPS** Asn Educ in Jour; AJHA; AAPOR; WAPOR. **RESEARCH** Relationship among technology, mass communication and culture. **SELECTED PUBLICATIONS** Coauth, The Agenda-Selling Function of Mass Media, Publ Opinion Quart, summer 72; coauth (with McCombs), The Emergence of American Political Issues: The Agenda-Setting Function of the Press, West Pub Co, 77; coauth, Communication and Democracy. **CONTACT ADDRESS** Sch of Journalism, Univ North Carolina, Chapel Hill, NC, 27514.

SHAW, JOSEPH WINTERBOTHAM
PERSONAL Born 07/06/1935, Chicago, IL, m, 1965, 2 children **DISCIPLINE** BRONZE AGE AEGEAN & CLASSICAL GREEK ARCHEOLOGY **EDUCATION** Brown Univ, BA, 57; Wesleyan Univ, MAT, 59; Univ Pa, PhD(classical archaeol), 70. **CAREER** Excavation architect Greek architecture, Kenchreai Excavations, Univ Chicago, 63-70 & Kato Zakros Excavations, Greek Archaeol Serv, 64-70; from asst prof to assoc prof, 70-77, assoc chmn dept, 77-79, PROF FINE ART, UNIV TORONTO, 77-, Adj prof underwater archaeol, Am Inst Nautical Archaeol, 72-; adv ed, Am J Field Archaeol, 73-; dir Aegean archaeol, Kommos Excavations, ROM & Univ Toronto, 75-; numerous res grants and fels in Can & Am. **MEMBERSHIPS** Archaeol Inst Am; Can Mediter Inst. **RESEARCH** Minoan archaeology; Aegean architecture and archaeology; investigation of prehistoric and historic harbors and harbor works in the Aegean and Eastern Mediterranean. **SELECTED PUBLICATIONS** Auth, Excavations At Kommos Crete During 1986-1992/, Hesperia, Vol 0062, 1993; Excavations In The Southern Area At Kommos, Crete, 1993/, Am J Of Archaeol, Vol 0098, 1994; 2 3-Holed Stone Anchors From Kommos, Crete - Their Context, Type And Origin/, Int J Of Nautical Archaeol, Vol 0024, 1995. **CONTACT ADDRESS** Dept of Fine Art, Univ of Toronto, Toronto, ON, M5S 1A1.

SHAW, MICHAEL
DISCIPLINE CLASSICS **EDUCATION** Univ TX, PhD, 71. **CAREER** Assoc prof, Univ KS. **HONORS AND AWARDS** Mem, Ad hoc Comm for Women's Stud, 72-77. **RESEARCH** Greek and Roman lit. **SELECTED PUBLICATIONS** Auth, The Female Intruder: Women in Fifth-century Drama, Class Philol 70, 75; The ethos of Theseus in The Suppliant Women, Hermes ll0, 82. **CONTACT ADDRESS** Dept of Class, Univ Kansas, Admin Building, Lawrence, KS, 66045. **EMAIL** gorgo@kuhub.cc.ukans.edu

SHAY, ROBERT
DISCIPLINE MUSIC HISTORY, CHORAL MUSIC **EDUCATION** Wheaton Col, BMus; NEngl Conserv Mus, MMus; Univ NC, Chapel Hill, MA, PhD. **CAREER** Assoc prof, Lyon Col. **SELECTED PUBLICATIONS** Auth, Henry Purcell: The Early Manuscript Sources, Cambridge UP. **CONTACT ADDRESS** Dept of Music, Lyon Col, 300 Highland Rd, PO Box 2317, Batesville, AR, 72503. **EMAIL** shay@lyon.edu

SHEA, GEORGE W.
PERSONAL Born 10/07/1934, Paterson, NJ, m, 1956, 3 children **DISCIPLINE** CLASSICAL LANGUAGES **EDUCATION** Fordham Univ, BA, 56; Columbia Univ, MA, 60, PhD(-classics), 66. **CAREER** Asst prof Latin & Greek, St John's Univ, NY, 61-65; asst prof classics, asst dean, Fordham Col & dir jr year abroad prog, 67-70, assoc prof classics & dean Col at Lincoln Ctr, Fordham Univ, 70-. **MEMBERSHIPS** Am Philol Asn; Am Conf Acad Deans. **RESEARCH** Latin epic poetry and Roman history; Johannis of Flavius Cresconius Corippus. **SELECTED PUBLICATIONS** Auth, The Poems of Alcimus Avitus, MRTS, 97; The Iohannis of Flavius Crescorius Corippus, Mellon, 98; Delia and Nemesis, UPA, 98. **CONTACT ADDRESS** Classics Dept, Fordham Univ, 113 W 60th St, New York, NY, 10023-7484.

SHEA, WILLIAM LEE
PERSONAL Born 08/22/1948, Breaux Bridge, LA, m, 1971, 1 child **DISCIPLINE** AMERICAN HISTORY **EDUCATION** La State Univ, Baton Rouge, BA, 70; Rice Univ, PhD(hist), 75. **CAREER** ASSOC PROF HIST, UNIV ARK, MONTICELLO, 74- **HONORS AND AWARDS** Moncado Prize, Am Military Inst, 78. **MEMBERSHIPS** AHA; Southern Hist Asn; Am Military Inst; Civil War Round Table Assoc. **RESEARCH** Early American history; military history; American Civil War. **CONTACT ADDRESS** Social Sci Dept, Univ of Ark, Monticello, AR, 71655.

SHEDD, D.
PERSONAL Born 08/04/1922, New Have, CT, m, 1946, 4 children **DISCIPLINE** HISTORY OF MEDICINE **EDUCATION** Yale Univ, BS, 44; Yale Univ Sch Med, MD, 46 **CAREER** Inst, asst prof, assoc prof, dept surgery, Yale Univ Sch Med, 53-67; chief, dept head, neck surgery, Roswell Pk Cancer Inst, 67-96; res prof, dept surgery, 67-97, EMERITUS, 97-, STATE UNIV NY, BUFFALO. **HONORS AND AWARDS** Markle Scholar Med, 53-58; Alpha Omega Alpha Hon Med Soc,; Sigma Xi hon sci soc. **MEMBERSHIPS** Soc Univ Surgeons; New England Surgical Soc; Soc Head, Neck Surgeons; Am Col Surgeons; Soc Surgical Oncology; Am Asn Hist Med; Am Head, Neck Soc. **SELECTED PUBLICATIONS** Co-auth, Nicholas Senn: Outrider of Modern Head and Neck Oncology, Bull Am Col Surgeons, 81:20-24, 96; auth, The Work of Henry T. Butlin, an Early Head and Neck Surgeon, Am J Surgery, forthcoming; co-auth, The Work of George Washington Crile in Head and Neck Surgery, Bull Am Col Surgeons, 81:27; co-auth, Contributions of Grant E. Ward to Head and Neck Oncology, Bull Am Col Surgeons, 82:18, 97. **CONTACT ADDRESS** NY State Dept Health, Roswell Pk Mem Inst, Buffalo, NY, 14263. **EMAIL** pkhv30a@prodigy.com

SHEDEL, JAMES P.
PERSONAL Born 04/10/1947, Oakland, CA, m, 1983, 1 child **DISCIPLINE** HISTORY, ART & SOCIETY **EDUCATION** Univ of Calif at Santa Cruz, BA, 69; Univ of Rochester, MA, 70, PhD, 78. **CAREER** Lectr, Univ of Rochester, 75; tchg/res fel, Stanford Univ, 76-77; vis asst prof, Northwestern Univ, 78-79; ASST PROF TO ASSOC PROF, GEORGETOWN UNIV, 79-. **HONORS AND AWARDS** Fulbright fel, 73-74. **MEMBERSHIPS** Am Hist Asn; Am Catholic Hist Asn; German Studies Asn; Soc of Architectural Historians. **RESEARCH** Austria (18th-20th centuries); Germany; art and society. **SELECTED PUBLICATIONS** Auth, Art and Society, the New Art Movement in Vienna: 1897-1914, The Soc for the Promotion of Sci and Scholar, 81; Austria and Its Polish Subjects, 1866-1914: A Relationship of Interests, Austrian Hist Yearbook, 89; A Question of Identity: Kokoschka, Austria, and the Meaning of the AnschluB, 1938: Understanding the Past, Overcoming the Past, Ariadne Press, 91; Art and Idnetity: The Wiener Secession 1897-1938, Sucession: Permanence of an Idea, Verlag Gerd Hatje, 97. **CONTACT ADDRESS** Dept of Hist, Georgetown Univ, Washington, DC, 20057. **EMAIL** shedelj@gunetl.georgetown.edu

SHEEHAN, BERNARD W.
PERSONAL Born 02/24/1934, New York, NY, m, 1957, 3 children **DISCIPLINE** HISTORY **EDUCATION** Fordham Univ, BS, 57; Univ Mich, MA, 58; Univ Va, PhD, 65. **CAREER** Instr hist, Regis Col, 58-62; asst prof, Univ Ala, 65-66; asst prof, Col William & Mary, 66-69, fel, Inst Early Am Hist

& Cult, 66-69; assoc prof, 69-80, prof hist, IN Univ, Bloomington, 80, Assoc ed, J Am Hist, 69-73, actg ed, 73-74; Henry E Huntington Libr fel, 75-76; adj scholar, Heritage Found; ed, Ind Mag Hist, 96-. **HONORS AND AWARDS** Earhart Found fels, 77, 78, 81 & 82; dir, Nat Endowment Hum Summer Sem, 80. **RESEARCH** The Indian in early Am hist; Am intellectual hist. **SELECTED PUBLICATIONS** Auth, Indian-White Relations in Early America: A Review Essay, 4/69 & Paradise and the Noble Savage in Jeffersonian Thought, 7/69, William & Mary Quart; Seeds of Extinction: Jeffersonian Philanthropy and the American Indian, Chapel Hill, 73; Savagism and Civility: Indians and Englishmen in Colonial Virginia, Cambridge, 80; The Problem of moral Judgements in History, SAtlantic Quart 84, 85; The Indian Problem in the Northwest: From Conquest to Philanthropy, In: Launching the Extended Republic: The Federalist Era, 96. **CONTACT ADDRESS** Dept of Hist, Indiana Univ, Bloomington, 1 Indiana University, Bloomington, IN, 47405.

SHEEHAN, JAMES JOHN
PERSONAL Born 05/31/1937, San Francisco, CA, m, 1960, 1 child **DISCIPLINE** MODERN EUROPEAN HISTORY **EDUCATION** Stanford Univ, AB, 58; Univ Calif, Berkeley, MA, 59, PhD(hist), 64. **CAREER** Instr hist, Stanford Univ, 62-64; from asst prof to assoc prof, Northwestern Univ, Evanston, 64-72, prof, 72-79; PROF HIST, STANFORD UNIV, 79-, Vis fel, Inst Advan Studies, 73-74 & Wolfson Col, Oxford, 81; fels, Nat Endowment for Humanities, summer, 72 & Am Coun Learned Soc, 81-82. **MEMBERSHIPS** AHA **RESEARCH** German social and political history. **SELECTED PUBLICATIONS** Auth, Ger Professions, 1800-1950 - Cocks,G, Jarausch,K/, Central Europ Hist, Vol 0025, 1992; Regulating The Soc - The Welfare-State And Local-Politics In Imperial Germany - Steinmetz,G/, Central Europ Hist, Vol 0026, 1993; The Politics Of Technological-Change In Prussia - Out Of The Shadow Of Antiquity, 1809-1848 - Brose,Ed/, Central Europ Hist, Vol 0026, 1993; Weber,Max - Correspondence 1906-1908 - Ger - Lepsius,Mr, Mommsen,Wj/, J Of Modern Hist, Vol 0065, 1993; The Authoritarian Nation-State - Constitution, Soc And Cult Of The Ger Empire - Ger - Mommsen,Wj/, EuropHist Quart, Vol 0023, 1993; The Germans And The Final-Solution - Public-Opinion Under Nazism - Bankier,D/, J Of Interdisciplinary Hist, Vol 0024, 1994; Europe Between Restoration And Revolution, 1815, Oldenbourg, Hist Outlines - Ger - Bleicken,J/, Europ Hist Quart, Vol 0025, 1995; On Looking Into The Abyss - Untimely Thoughts On Cult And Soc - Himmelfarb,G/, Am Hist Rev, Vol 0100, 1995. **CONTACT ADDRESS** Dept of Hist, Stanford Univ, Stanford, CA, 94305-1926.

SHEETS, GEORGE ARCHIBALD
PERSONAL Born 08/18/1947, Buenos Aires, Argentina, m, 1969, 2 children **DISCIPLINE** CLASSICAL LANGUAGES, HISTORICAL LINGUISTICS **EDUCATION** Univ NC, BA, 70; Duke Univ, PhD(class studies), 74; JD W. Mitchell Col of Law, 90. **CAREER** Instr classics, Univ TX, Austin, 74-75; Mellon fel classics, Bryn Mawr Col, 76-77; asst prof, 77-82, ASSOC PROF CLASSICS, UNIV MN, MINNEAPOLIS, 82-. **MEMBERSHIPS** Am Philol Asn; Class Asn Mid West & South; Minnesota State Bar. **RESEARCH** Historical linguistics; Roman literature; legal history. **SELECTED PUBLICATIONS** Auth, Palatalization in Greek, Indoger Forsch, 75; Secondary midvowels in Greek, Am J Philol, 79; The dialect gloss, Hellenistic poetics and Livius Andronicus, 81, Am J Philol; Grammatical commentary to Book I of the Histories of Herodotus, Bryn Mawr Commentaries, 81; Ennius Lyricus, 8 IL Class Studies; Plautus and early Roman Tragedy, 8 Ill Class Studies, Rome Prize, Am Academy, 85; Conceptualizing International Law in Thucydides, 115, Am J Philol. **CONTACT ADDRESS** Classical and NE Studies, Univ of MN, 9 Pleasant St S E, 330 Folwel, Minneapolis, MN, 55455-0194. **EMAIL** gasheets@umn.edu

SHEIDLEY, HARLOW W.
DISCIPLINE HISTORY **EDUCATION** Stanford Univ, AB, 63; Univ Conn, MA, 78, PhD, 90. **CAREER** ASST PROF, HIST, UNIV COLO, COLO SPRINGS **MEMBERSHIPS** Am Antiquarian Soc **SELECTED PUBLICATIONS** Auth, Dialogues of a New Republic: An Exhibition of Selected Items from the Pierce Welch Gaines Collection of Americana, 80; auth, "Preserving the Old Fabrick: The Massachusetts Conservative Elite and the Constitutional Convention of 1820-1821," Procs of the Mass Hist Soc 103, 91; auth, "The Webster-Hayne Debate: Recasting New England's Sectionalism," New Eng Quart 67, 94; auth, Sectional Nationalism: Massachusetts Conservative Leaders and America, 1815-1836, Northeastern Univ Press. **CONTACT ADDRESS** Dept of Hist, Univ of Colo at Colo Springs, 1420 Austin Bluffs Pkwy., Colorado Springs, CO, 80933-7150. **EMAIL** hsheidle@mail.uccs.edu

SHEIDLEY, WILLIAM E.
PERSONAL Born 05/29/1940, Kansas City, MO, m, 1962, 2 children **DISCIPLINE** EMGLISH **EDUCATION** Stanford Univ, AB, 62, AM, 66, PhD, 68. **CAREER** Teach asst, Standord Univ, 63-65; asst prof, 66-72, assoc prof, 72-81, prof Eng, 81-94, Univ Conn; vis lectr, 92-93, assoc prof, 94-95, PROF ENG, 95-, CHAIR DEPT ENG, FOR LANG, 95-, UNIV S COLO; asst prof Eng, US Air Force Acad, 93-94. **HONORS AND AWARDS** Phi Beta Kappa; Sigma Tau Delta., Cofounder, dir, Conn Writing Project, 82-87. **RESEARCH** English Renaissance lit; the Hamlet tradition. **SELECTED PUBLICATIONS** Auth, Barnabe Googe, G. K. Hall, 81; auth, George Gascoigne and The Spoyle of Antwerpe (1576), War, Literature, and the Arts 8.1, 96; auth, The Play(s) within the Film: Tom Stoppard's Rosencrantz & Guildenstern Are Dead, Screen Shakespeare, Univ Aarhus Press, 94; auth, Making Hamlet Pirouette: The 1816 Pantomime Tragique by Louis Henry (and trans), Hamlet Studies 15, 93; auth, Born in Imitation of Someone Else: Reading Turgenev's Hamlet of the Shchigrovsky District as a Version of Hamlet, Studies in Short Fiction 27, 90; auth, Hamlet as a Vision of Renewal, Hamlet Studies 12, 90; auth, The Autor Penneth, Wherof He Hath No Proofe: The Early Elizabethan Dream Poem as a Defense of Poetic Fiction, Studies in Philol 81, 84. **CONTACT ADDRESS** Dept of English & For Langs, Univ of So Colorado, 2200 Bonforte Blvd, Pueblo, CO, 81001-4901. **EMAIL** sheidley@uscolo.edu

SHELDON, MARIANNE BUROFF
PERSONAL Born 07/16/1946, Brooklyn, NY, 1 child **DISCIPLINE** AMERICAN HISTORY **EDUCATION** Rutgers Univ, BA, 68; Univ Mich, MA, 70, PhD, 75. **CAREER** Instr Hist, Univ Mich, 75; asst prof, 75-81, from assoc prof to prof Hist, Mills Col, 81-88. **MEMBERSHIPS** AHA; Southern Hist Asn; Orgn Am Historians. **RESEARCH** American history ot 1820; Antebellum South; American urban history. **SELECTED PUBLICATIONS** Auth, Black-White relations in Richmond, Virginia, 1782-1820, J Southern Hist, XLV: 27-44; Social stratification in Richmond, Virginia, 1788-1817, SAtlantic Urban Studies, IV: 177-197; Women in the Labor Force, with Nancy Thornborrow in Women: A Feminist Perspective, ed, Jo Freeman, 5th edition, 95. **CONTACT ADDRESS** Mills Col, 5000 MacArthur Blvd, Oakland, CA, 94613-1000. **EMAIL** mshel@mills.edu

SHELDON, ROSE MARY
DISCIPLINE HISTORY **EDUCATION** Col NJ, BA; Hunter Col, MA; Univ Mich, PhD. **CAREER** Assoc prof, VMI; Amer Acad fel in Rome, 80; ed bd, Int J Intel and Counterintel. **HONORS AND AWARDS** Nat Intel Bk Awd, 87. **SELECTED PUBLICATIONS** Contribu, Stud in Intel, Intel and Nat Security, Amer Intel J, Intel Quart, Foreign Intel Lit Scene, Small Wars and Insurgenies, J Mil Hist, The Washington Post. **CONTACT ADDRESS** Dept of History, Virginia Military Inst, Lexington, VA, 24450.

SHELLEY, BRUCE
DISCIPLINE HISTORICAL THEOLOGY **EDUCATION** Columbia Bible, BA; Fuller Sem, M.Div; Iowa Univ, Ph.D. **CAREER** Sr prof, Denver Sem. **HONORS AND AWARDS** Ed adv bd, Christian Hist; consult ed, InterVarsity's popular Dictionary of Christianity in Am. **SELECTED PUBLICATIONS** Auth, Church History in Plain Language; All the Saints Adore Thee; The Gospel; and the American Dream and The Consumer Church; corresponding ed, Christianity Today; pub(s), articles in Encycl Am; Evangel Dictionary of Theol; New Intl Dictionary of the Christian Church. **CONTACT ADDRESS** Denver Conservative Baptist Sem, PO Box 10000, Denver, CO, 80250. **EMAIL** bruces@densem.edu

SHELMERDINE, CYNTHIA WRIGHT
PERSONAL Born 01/07/1949, Boston, MA **DISCIPLINE** CLASSICS; CLASSICAL ARCHAEOLOGY **EDUCATION** Bryn Mawr Col, AB, 70; Cambridge Univ, BA, 72, MA, 80; Harvard Univ, AM, 76, PhD, 77. **CAREER** Asst prof Classics, Univ Tex, Austin, 77-84; assoc prof, 84-97; prof, 97-; chair, 98-. **HONORS AND AWARDS** Marshall scholar, 70-72; Ctr. for Hellenic Studies, jr fel, 81-82; Pres assocs tchg award, Univ of Texas, 88. **MEMBERSHIPS** Archaeol Inst Am; Am Philol Asn; Am Sch Class Studies Athens Alumni Asn; Class Asn Middle West & South. **RESEARCH** Mycenaean Greek; Bronze Age Archaeology. **SELECTED PUBLICATIONS** Auth, The Pylos Ma tables reconsidered, Am Jour Archaeol, 73; contribur, Excavations at Nichoria (vol II), Univ Minn, (in press); Nichoria in context, Am Jour Archeol, 81; coauth, The Pylos Regional Archaeological Project. Part1: Overview and the Archaeological Survey, Hesperia 66, 97; auth, Review of Aegean Prehistory VI: The Palatial Bronze Age of the Central and Southern Greek Mainland, Am Jour of Archeol 101, 97; contribur, Sandy Pylos. From Nestor to Navarino, Univ Texas, 98. **CONTACT ADDRESS** Dept of Classics, Texas Univ, Austin, TX, 78712-1181. **EMAIL** cwshelm@mail.utexas.edu

SHELMERDINE, SUSAN C.
PERSONAL Born 04/21/1954, Boston, MA, s **DISCIPLINE** CLASSICAL STUDIES **EDUCATION** Smith Col, BA, 76; Univ Mich, MA, 77, PhD, 81. **CAREER** Lect, Univ N Carolina, 81-82, ast prof, 82-88; vis asoc prof, Univ Mich, 88-89; asoc prof, Univ N Carolina, 88- , dept head, 89-92, asoc dean, 92-95. **HONORS AND AWARDS** Jr fel, Ctr Hellenic Stud, Washington DC, 95-86; NEH Fel, 96-97. **MEMBERSHIPS** APA; Class Asn Middle West & South. **RESEARCH** Greek poetry; language pedagogy. **SELECTED PUBLICATIONS** Co-auth, Greek for Reading, Univ Mich, 94; auth, The Homeric Hymns, Focus Information Grp, 95; contribur, HarperCollins Dictionary of Religion, HarperCollins, 95; auth, "Greek Studies Today," Class Jrnl, 96 **CONTACT ADDRESS** Dept of Classical Studies, Univ of North Carolina Greensboro, PO Box 26170, Greensboro, NC, 27402-6170. **EMAIL** shelmerd@uncg.edu

SHELTON, JO-ANN
DISCIPLINE ROMAN AND GREEK HISTORY **EDUCATION** Univ Calif, Berkeley, PhD, 74. **CAREER** PROF, UNIV CALIF, SANTA BARBARA. **RESEARCH** Roman and Greek tragedy; Roman social hist; Roman epistol. **SELECTED PUBLICATIONS** Auth, Seneca's Hercules Furens: Theme, Structure, and Style, Gottingen, 78; As the Romans Did, Oxford, 88; The Madness of Hercules, Lawrence, 91. **CONTACT ADDRESS** Dept of Classics, Univ Calif, Santa Barbara, CA, 93106-7150. **EMAIL** jshelton@humanitas.ucsb.edu

SHENTON, JAMES
DISCIPLINE UNITED STATES HISTORY **EDUCATION** Columbia Univ, BA, 49; Columbia Univ, PhD, 55. **CAREER** Prof. **RESEARCH** Immigration and ethnic history. **SELECTED PUBLICATIONS** Auth, Robert John Walker: A Politician from Jackson to Lincoln, 61; The Reconstruction: A Documentary History of the South after the Civil War, 63; The Historian's History of the United States, 66; Free Enterprise Forever!, 77; Ethnic Groups in American Life, 78. **CONTACT ADDRESS** Dept of History, Columbia Col, New York, 2960 Broadway, New York, NY, 10027-6902.

SHEON, AARON
PERSONAL Born 10/07/1937, Toledo, OH, m, 1963, 2 children **DISCIPLINE** HISTORY OF ART **EDUCATION** Univ Mich, AB, 59, MA, 60; Princeton Univ, MFA, 62, PhD(hist of art), 66. **CAREER** Staff officer, UNESCO, Paris, 63-66; asst prof, 66-68, assoc prof, 69-78, prof Hist of Art & Actg chmn dept, Univ Pittsburg, 79-, vis exhib cur, Mus Art, Carnegie Inst, Pittsburgh, 77-81; prog consult, Nat Endowment for Arts & Humanities, 78-; vis prof, Carnegie-Mellon Univ, 81; consult, Pa Arts Coun, 81-; Nat Endowment Humanities grant, 79. **HONORS AND AWARDS** Chancellor Bowman Award, 76. **MEMBERSHIPS** Col Art Asn Am; Soc Hist Fr Art. **RESEARCH** Nineteenth century French art; art and scientific thought; French decorative arts. **SELECTED PUBLICATIONS** Auth, The Gosman Collection, Univ Pittsburgh, 69; Monticelli, His Contemporaries, His Influence, Mus Art, Pittsburgh, 78; Organic Vision, the Architecture of Peter Berndtson, Horizon Press, 80; Octave Tassaert's Le Suicide: Early realism and the plight of women, Arts, 5/81; Monticelli Centennial, Marseille Museum, 86; Van Gogh's Understanding of Theories of Neurosis and Degeneration, 96. **CONTACT ADDRESS** Dept of Fine Arts, Univ of Pittsburgh, 104 Frick Fine Arts, Pittsburgh, PA, 15260-7601.

SHEPHERD, JOHN
DISCIPLINE HISTORY OF POPULAR MUSIC **EDUCATION** Carleton Univ, BA, BM; Royal Col of Mus, ARCM; Univ York, UK, DPhil. **CAREER** Prof. **HONORS AND AWARDS** Davidson Dunton res lectrship, 92., Adj res prof, Grad Prog in Musicology, York Univ; dept of mus, Univ Ottawa. **SELECTED PUBLICATIONS** Auth, Music as Social Text, Polity Press, 91; co-auth, Rock and Popular Music: Politics, Policies, Institutions, Routledge, 93; Music and Cultural Theory, Polity Press of Cambridge, 97; Popular Music Studies: A Select International Bibliography, 97; co-ed, Relocating Cultural Studies: Developments in Theory and Research, Routledge, 93. **CONTACT ADDRESS** Carleton Univ, 1125 Colonel By Dr, Ottawa, ON, K1S 5B6.

SHEPPARD, THOMAS FREDERICK
PERSONAL Born 06/05/1935, Indianapolis, IN **DISCIPLINE** HISTORY, MODERN EUROPE **EDUCATION** Vanderbilt Univ, AB, 57; Univ Nebr, MA, 62; Johns Hopkins Univ, PhD(hist), 69. **CAREER** Instr hist, Western Ky Univ, 62-65; from asst prof to assoc prof, 69-77, chmn dept, 75-81, PROF HIST, COL WILLIAM & MARY, 77-, Nat Endowment for Humanities younger humanists fel, France, 72-73; mem coun, Inst Early Am Hist & Cult, 78-81. **MEMBERSHIPS** AHA; Soc Fr Hist Studies. **RESEARCH** French Social and economic history, local history. **SELECTED PUBLICATIONS** Auth, Justice In The Sarladais 1770-1790 - Reinhardt,Sg/, Am Hist Rev, Vol 0098, 1993. **CONTACT ADDRESS** Dept of Hist, Col of William and Mary, Williamsburg, VA, 23185.

SHERIDAN, JENNIFER A.
PERSONAL Born 04/01/1962, Englewood, NJ **DISCIPLINE** CLASSICS **EDUCATION** Montclair State Col, BA, 84; Columbia Univ, MA, 85, PhD, 90. **CAREER** Asst prof, St Joseph's Univ, 90-95; Asst prof, Wayne State Univ, 95-. **MEMBERSHIPS** APA, ANS, ASP, AIP, DCA, MCC, CAMWS **RESEARCH** Papyrology; Women in the ancient world. **SELECTED PUBLICATIONS** co-auth, Greek and Latin Documents from 'Abu Sha'ar, 1990-1991, Jour Amer Res Ctr In Egypt 31, 94; Greek and Latin Documents from 'Abu Sha'ar, 1992-1993, Bull Amer Soc Papyrologists 31, 94; auth, Women without Guardians: An Updated List, Bull Amer Soc Papyrologists 33, 96; Papyri numbers 257, 259, 286, Columbia Papyri X, 96; Not at a Loss for Words: The Economic Power of

Literate Women in Late Antique Egypt, Transactions of Amer Philol Asn, 98; Columbia Papyri IX: The Vestis Militaris Codex, 98. **CONTACT ADDRESS** Dept of Greek and Latin, Wayne State Univ, 431 Manoogian Hall, Detroit, MI, 48202. **EMAIL** j.Sheridan@wayne.edu

SHERIFF, CAROL
DISCIPLINE HISTORY **EDUCATION** Wesleyan, BA, 85; Yale Univ, MA, 88, MPhil, 90, PhD, 93. **CAREER** ASST PROF, HIST, COLL WM & MARY **HONORS AND AWARDS** NY State Hist Asn Prize, 96; Award For Excellence in Res using holdings of the NY State Arch, 96. **MEMBERSHIPS** Am Antiquarian Soc **SELECTED PUBLICATIONS** Auth, The Artificial River: The Erie Canal and the Paradox of Progress, 1817-1862, Hill & Wang, 96. **CONTACT ADDRESS** Hist Dept, The Coll of Wm & Mary, Box 8795, Williamsburg, VA, 23187-8795. **EMAIL** cxsher@facstaff.wm.edu

SHERIFF, MARY D.
DISCIPLINE ART HISTORY **EDUCATION** Univ DE, PhD. **CAREER** Prof, Univ NC, Chapel Hill. **RESEARCH** 18th and 19th century art; critical theory. **SELECTED PUBLICATIONS** Auth, J.-H. Fragonard: Art and Eroticism, Univ Chicago Press, 90; coed, Eighteenth-Century Studies (1993-1998) The Exceptional Woman: Elisabeth Vigee-Lebrun and the Cultural Politics of Art, Univ Chicago Press, 96. **CONTACT ADDRESS** Univ N. Carolina, Chapel Hill, Chapel Hill, NC, 27599. **EMAIL** msheriff@email.unc.edu

SHERK, ROBERT K.
DISCIPLINE CLASSICS **EDUCATION** Johns Hopkins Univ, PhD, 50. **CAREER** Fac, 62; to prof emer, present, SUNY Buffalo. **RESEARCH** Hellenistic and Roman hist; epigraphy; ancient biog; Roman empire from Augustus to Hadrian. **SELECTED PUBLICATIONS** Auth, Roman Documents from the Greek East, Johns Hopkins, 69; Municipal Decrees of the Roman West, Buffalo, 70; The Roman Empire from Augustus to Hadrian, Cambridge, 88; articles on Hellenistic and Roman history; co-ed, Translated Documents of Greece and Rome, Cambridge, 177-85. **CONTACT ADDRESS** Dept Classics, SUNY Buffalo, 712 Clemens Hall, Buffalo, NY, 14260.

SHERKAT, DARREN E.
PERSONAL Born 12/31/1965, Tulsa, OK, d, 1 child **DISCIPLINE** SOCIOLOGY **EDUCATION** Univ Tulsa, BA, 87; MA, 89, PhD, 91, Duke Univ. **CAREER** Asst Prof, 91-96, Assoc Prof, 96-, Vanderbilt Univ. **MEMBERSHIPS** Amer Sociological Assoc; Southern Sociological Assoc; Soc for the Scientific Study of Religion; Religious Research Assoc; Assoc for the Sociology of Religion; Intl Sociological Assoc. **RESEARCH** Sociology of religion; social movements; statistics and methods; contemporary sociological theory **SELECTED PUBLICATIONS** Coauth, Conservative Protestantism and Support for Corporal Punishment, American Sociological Review, 93; Theory and Method in Religious Mobility Research, Social Science Research, 93; The Political Development of Sixties Activists: Identifying the Influence of Class, Gender, and Socialization on Protest Protestantism, Social Forces, 94; Preferences, Constraints, and Choices in Religious Markets: An Examination of Religious Switching and Apostasy, 95; The Semi-Involuntary Institution Revisited: RegionalVariations in Church Participation Among Black Americans, Social Forces, 95; Auth, Embedding Religious Choices: Integrating Preferences and Social Constraints into Rational Choice Theories of Religious Behavior, Rational Choice Theory and Religion: Summary and Assessment, 97; Coauth, The Cognitive Structure of a Moral Crusade: Conservative Protestantism and Oppostion to Pornography, Social Forces, 97; Explaining the Political and Personal Consequences of Protest, Social Forces, 97; The Impact of Fundamentalism on Educational Attainment, American Sociological Review, 97; Auth, Counterculture or Continuity? Examining Competing Influences on Baby Boomers' Religious Orientations and Participation, Social Forces, 98. **CONTACT ADDRESS** Dept of Sociology, Vanderbilt Univ, Nashville, TN, 37235. **EMAIL** sherkade@ctrvax.vanderbilt.edu

SHERMAN, RICHARD B.
PERSONAL Born 11/16/1929, Somerville, MA, m, 1952, 2 children **DISCIPLINE** AMERICAN HISTORY **EDUCATION** Harvard Univ, AB, 51, PhD, 59; Univ PA, MA, 52. **CAREER** Instr hist, PA State Univ, 57-60; from asst prof to assoc prof, 60-70, prof Hist, 70-87, Chancellor Prof Hist, 87-92, :Pullen Prof Hist, 92-94, PROF EMERITUS, COL WILLIAM & MARY, 94-; Fulbright prof hist, Univ Stockholm, 66-67. **HONORS AND AWARDS** PBK **MEMBERSHIPS** AAUP. **RESEARCH** Recent American history. **SELECTED PUBLICATIONS** Ed, The Negro and the City, Prentice-Hall, 70; auth, The Republican Party and Black America, from McKinley to Hoover, 1896-1933, Univ VA, 73; The Case of Odell Wallen and Virginia Justice, 1940-1942, Univ TN, 92; co-auth, The College of William and Mary: A History, King and Queen Press, 93; articles in New England Quart, Mid-America, Polit Sci Quart, PA Hist, J Negro Hist, Historian, Proloque, J Southern Hist, VA Mag Hist and Biography. **CONTACT ADDRESS** Dept of Hist, Col of William and Mary, Williamsburg, VA, 23185. **EMAIL** rbsher@facstaff.wm.edu

SHERMAN, ROGER
PERSONAL Born 09/10/1930, Jamestown, NY, m, 2 children **DISCIPLINE** ECONOMICS **EDUCATION** Harvard Univ, MBA, 59; Carnegie-Mellon Univ, MS, 65, PhD, 66. **CAREER** Asst, assoc prof, and Brown-Forman prof of Economics, Univ VA, 65-, economics dept chair, 82-90. **HONORS AND AWARDS** Fulbright lect, 72; Rockefeller Found vis scholar, 85; VA Social Science Asn Outstanding Scholar, 94. **MEMBERSHIPS** Am Economic Asn; Economic Science Asn; Industrial Org Soc; Royal Economic Soc; Southern Economic Asn. **RESEARCH** Experimental economics; industrial org and regulation. **SELECTED PUBLICATIONS** Auth, A Private Ownership Bias in Transit Choice, Am Economic Rev, 67; Risk Attitude and Cost Variability in a Capacity Choice Experiment, Rev of Economic Studies, 69; Congestion Interdependence and Urban Transit Fares, Econometrica, 71; Oligopoly: An Empirical Approach, D C Heath, 72; The Psychological Difference between Ambiguity and Risk, Quart J of Economics, 74; Second-Best Pricing with Stochastic Demand, with Michael Visscher, Am Economic Rev, 78; Waiting-Line Auctions, with Charles A Holt, J of Political Economy, 82; Nonprice Rationing and Monopoly Price Structures when Demand is Stochastic, with Michael Visscher, Bell J of Economics, 82; The Regulation of Monopoly, Cambridge Univ Press, 89; The Loser's Curse, with Charles A Holt, Am Economic Rev, 94. **CONTACT ADDRESS** Dept of Economics, Univ of Virginia, Rouss Hall, Charlottesville, VA, 22903. **EMAIL** rs5w@virginia.edu

SHERMAN, WILLIAM LEWIS
PERSONAL Born 04/09/1927, Pasadena, CA, m, 1960, 3 children **DISCIPLINE** COLONIAL LATIN AMERICAN HISTORY **EDUCATION** Univ of the Americas, MA, 58; Univ NMex, PhD(hist), 67. **CAREER** Foreign serv, US Dept State, 51-53; instr & asst to pres, Mex City Col, 59-60; coord Latin Am area studies, Peace Corps, Univ NMex, 63-65; asst prof hist, Calif Western Univ, 65-66 & Colo State Univ, 66-68; from asst prof to assoc prof, 68-76, PROF HIST, UNIV NEBR-LINCOLN, 76-, Fac Improv Comt res grant, Spain, 67; Woods res grant, Cent Am, 70; Nebr Found res grant, Cent Am, 72; Del Amo grant, Spain, 64-65; Univ Nebr grant, Spain, 80. **MEMBERSHIPS** Int Cong Americanists; Int Congr Americanists; corresp mem Geog & Hist Soc Guatemala. **RESEARCH** Central America and Mexico in the 16th century. **SELECTED PUBLICATIONS** Auth, Indigenous Rulers - An Ethnohistory Of Town Government In Colonial Cuernavaca - Haskett,R/, Am Hist Rev, Vol 0098, 1993; Encomienda Politics In Early Colonial Guatemala, 1524-1544 - Dividing The Spoil - Kramer,W/, Am Hist Rev, Vol 0101, 1996. **CONTACT ADDRESS** Dept of Hist, Univ of Nebr, Lincoln, NE, 68508.

SHERR, RICHARD JONATHAN
PERSONAL Born 03/25/1947, New York, NY **DISCIPLINE** MUSIC HISTORY **EDUCATION** Columbia Univ, BA, 69; Princeton Univ, MFA, 71, PhD(Musicol), 75. **CAREER** Lectr music, Univ Calif, Los Angeles, 73-74; vis lectr, Univ Wis-Madison, 74-75; asst prof, 75-80, from assoc prof Music, Smith Col, 80-86. **MEMBERSHIPS** Am Musicol Soc; Renaissance Soc Am; Int Musicol Soc. **RESEARCH** Music and musicians in Rome in the late 15th and early 16th centuries; music in Mantua in the late 16th century; Arthur Sullivan and popular music of the 19th century. **SELECTED PUBLICATIONS** Auth, New archival data concerning the Chapel of Clement VII, J Am Musicol Soc, 76; contribr, Josquin des Prez: Proc Int Josquin Festival-Cong, 76; auth, Notes on two Roman manuscripts of the early sixteenth century, Musical Quart, 77; The publications of Guglielmo Gonzaga, J Am Musicol Soc, 78; From the diary of a 16th century papal singer, Current Musicol, 78; ed, Bertrandi Vaqueras: Opera Omnia, Hanssler Verlag, 79; auth, Guglielmo Gonzaga and the Castrati, Renaissance Quart, 80; Schubert, Sullivan and Grove, Musical Times, 80; auth, Papal Music Manuscripts in Late Fifteenth and Early Sixteenth Century Rome, Hanssler Verlag, 96; ed, Papal Music and Musicians in Late Medieval and Renaissance Rome, Oxford Univ Press, 98. **CONTACT ADDRESS** Dept of Music, Smith Col, 98 Green St, Northampton, MA, 01063-0001. **EMAIL** rsherr@smith.edu

SHERRICK, REBECCA LOUISE
PERSONAL Born 05/28/1953, Carthage, IL **DISCIPLINE** AMERICAN HISTORY, WOMEN'S STUDIES **EDUCATION** IL Wesleyan Univ, BA, 75; Northwestern Univ, PhD(hist), 80. **CAREER** Asst prof hist to provost, Carroll Col, 80-. **MEMBERSHIPS** AHA; Orgn Am Historians. **RESEARCH** Father-daughter relationship as a factor in identity formation; female friendships among late-Victorian women; autobiography and womens identity. **SELECTED PUBLICATIONS** Auth, Toward Universal Sisterhood, Women's Studies Int Forum, 9/82. **CONTACT ADDRESS** Dept Hist, Carroll Col, Wisconsin, 100 N East Ave, Waukesha, WI, 53186-5593.

SHERRILL, NED
PERSONAL Born 09/09/1956, m, 1979, 3 children **DISCIPLINE** POLITICAL SCIENCE **EDUCATION** Macalester Col, BA, 79; Yale Divinity Sch, MDiv, 83. **CAREER** Teacher & Chaplain, St. Paul's Sch, 83-86; Teacher & Chaplain, Wooster Sch, 86-90; Dean of chapel, St. Paul's Sch, 90-98; Vicar/Headmaster. St. John's Sch, 98-. **MEMBERSHIPS** AAR; SBL; NAES. **RESEARCH** Religion in education. **CONTACT ADDRESS** 911 N. Marine Dr., Tamuning, GU, 96911. **EMAIL** esherrill@stjohns.edu.gu

SHERRILL, VANITA LYTLE
PERSONAL Born 02/23/1945, Nashville, Tennessee, s **DISCIPLINE** EDUCATION **EDUCATION** Fisk U, BA 1966; Fisk U, MA 1971; Vanderbilt U, 1985. **CAREER** Volunteer State Comm Coll, instr/field supr 1973-; Vocational Diagnostic Component Nashville CE Program, coord 1973; Metro Health Dept, social worker consult 1971-72; TN State Planning Commn, research asst 1970-71; Hubbard Hosp MeHarry Med Center, asst proj adminstr 1966-69; Gerontology TN State U, instr 1977; Univ of TN, educ intern 1977; Vanderbilt Univ Com for the Behavioral Sci, review bd 1985; Dede Wallace Center, treas 1985; Samaritan Center, sec bd of dirs, 1985; Nashville Urban League, bd of dirs 1985. **HONORS AND AWARDS** Grant Educ & Research Tour of W Africa Phelps-Stokes Found 1979; Commr Century III 1985; Charter Mem Leadership Nashville 1985. **MEMBERSHIPS** Mem Delta Sigma Theta Soc 1985; mem Intl Curr Devel Prog; mem Am Personnel & Guidance Assn; mem Am Psychol Assn; mem Nat Assn of Black Social Wkrs; mem Jack & Jill Inc Nashville Chap 1985; mem Hendersonville Chap of Links Inc 1985; bd of dirs Alive-Hospice 1985; bd of dirs Council of Comm Servs 1985. **CONTACT ADDRESS** Volunteer State Comm Coll, Nashville Pike, Gallatin, TN, 37066.

SHERRY, LEE F.
PERSONAL Born 08/22/1954, Marietta, OH, m, 1992 **DISCIPLINE** CLASSICS **EDUCATION** Univ Texas, Austin, BA, 79; Columbia Univ, MA, 82, MPhil, 84; PhD, 91. **CAREER** Instr, Columbia Univ, 82-89; instr, NY Univ, 86-87; lectr, Queens Col, 88; tchr Latin, Trinity School, 87-91; lectr, Catholic Univ, 92-96; res assoc, Dumbarton Oaks, 91-96; tchr Latin, Kent Place School, Summit NJ, 96- . **HONORS AND AWARDS** Phi Beta Kappa, 79; Summa Cum Laude, 79; Phi Kappa Phi, 78. **MEMBERSHIPS** APA; Am Class League; Class Asn of the Atlantic States; NJ Class Asn. **RESEARCH** Greek language and literature; Latin language and literature; Medieval and Byzantine studies; patristics; computers and the humanities. **SELECTED PUBLICATIONS** Coauth, Barbarians and Politics at the Court of Arcadius, in Transformation of the Classical Heritage, Univ Calif, 93; cotrans, Christ the Lamb and the Enotion of the Law in a Wall Painting of Araka on Cyprus, Deltion Chr Arch Het, 94; coauth, Dumbarton Oaks Hagiography Database of the Ninth Century, 95; cotrans, The Poem of Maria Komnene Palaiologina to the Virgin and Mother of God, the Chorine, Cahiers Archeologiques, 95; coauth, Thesaurus Pseudo-Nonni quondam Panopolitani, Paraphrasis Evangelii S. Ioannis, Corpus Christianorum, 95; coauth, The Dumbarton Oaks Byzantine Hagiography Database Project, Medieval Prosopography, 96; trans, Vita of Athanasia of Aegina, in Talbot, ed, Byzantine Saints' Lives in Translation Series, Dumbarton Oaks, 96; auth, The Paraphrase of St. John Attributed to Nonnus, Byzantion, 96; coauth, The Tale of a Happy Fool: The Vita of St. Philaretos the Merciful, Byzantion, 96. **CONTACT ADDRESS** Kent Place Sch, 42 Norwood, Summit, NJ, 07902-0308. **EMAIL** sherryl@kentplace.summit.nj.edu

SHERRY, MICHAEL STEPHEN
PERSONAL Born 01/08/1945, Indianapolis, IN **DISCIPLINE** AMERICAN HISTORY **EDUCATION** Washington Univ, BA, 67; Yale Univ, MA, 69, PhD(hist), 75. **CAREER** Teacher hist, Hamden Hall Country Day Sch, Conn, 69-71 & Yale Psychiat Inst, Yale Univ, 74-76; assoc prof Am hist, Northwestern Univ, 76-79; Nat Endowment for Humanities res fel, 79-80; ASST PROF AM HIST, NORTHWESTERN UNIV, 80-, Lectr Am hist, Yale Univ, 75-76. **MEMBERSHIPS** Orgn Am Historians; Am Mil Inst. **RESEARCH** The institutions, values and impact of American military and national security policy in the 20th century. **SELECTED PUBLICATIONS** Auth, Fortress Calif, 1910-1961 - From Warfare To Welfare - Lotchin,Rw/, Am Hist Rev, Vol 0098, 1993; The Origins Of Sdi, 1944-1983 - Baucom,Dr/, Diplomatic Hist, Vol 0018, 1994; Cardinal Choices - Presidential Sci Advising From The Atomic-Bomb To Sdi - Herken,G/, Diplomatic Hist, Vol 0018, 1994; The Devil We Knew - Americans And The Cold-War - Brands,Hw/, J Of Am Hist, Vol 0081, 1994; Projections Of War - Hollywood, Am Cult, And World-War-Ii - Doherty,T/, Diplomatic Hist, Vol 0019, 1995; We Value Teaching Despite - And Because Of - Its Low Status/, J Of American Hist, Vol 0081, 1994; Untitled/, J Of Am Hist, Vol 0083, 1996; The New Winter Soldiers - Gi And Veteran Dissent During The Vietnam Era - Moser,R/, Revs In Am Hist, Vol 0025, 1997; Masters Of War - Military Dissent And Politics In The Vietnam Era - Buzzanco,R/, Revs In Am Hist, Vol 0025, 1997. **CONTACT ADDRESS** Dept of Hist, Northwestern Univ, Evanston, IL, 60201.

SHERWIN, MARTIN J.
PERSONAL Born 07/02/1937, New York, NY, m, 1963, 2 children **DISCIPLINE** HISTORY **EDUCATION** Dartmouth Col, BA, 59; UCLA, PhD, 71 **CAREER** Walter S Dickson prof, Tufts Univ **HONORS AND AWARDS** Bernath Bk Prize; Amer Hist Bk Prize; Guggenheim Fel; NETT Fel; Rockefeller Found Fel; MacArthur Found Peace Fel; Soc Amer Hist; Amer Acad Arts Sci; UNESCO Distinguished Fel **MEMBERSHIPS** AHA; OAH; ASA **RESEARCH** Cold War **SELECTED PUBLICATIONS** A World Destroyed: Hiroshima and the Origins of the Arms Race **CONTACT ADDRESS** Tufts Univ, Medford, MA, 02155. **EMAIL** msherwin@tufts.edu

SHESGREEN, SEAN NICHOLAS
PERSONAL Born 12/05/1939, Derry City, Ireland, d, 1 child **DISCIPLINE** ENGLISH LITERATURE, ART HISTORY **EDUCATION** Loyola Univ Chicago, BA, 62, MA, 66; Northwestern Univ, PhD(English), 70. **CAREER** Teaching asst English, Northwestern Univ, 68-69; asst prof, 69-74, assoc prof, 74-82, PROF ENGLISH, NORTHERN IL UNIV, 82-, Presidential Res Prof, 90-95; Vis fac mem, Univ CA, Riverside, 74-75; Am Philos Soc grant-in-aid, 76; exchange prof English, Xian Foreign Lang Inst, People's Repub China, 81-82. **HONORS AND AWARDS** Huntington Library Summer fel, 98; Yale Univ Center for Art fel, 90; Ball Brothers Found fel, Lilly Library , IN Univ, Bloomington; NEH Newberry Library Sr fel, 98-99. **MEMBERSHIPS** MLA; Am Soc 18th Century Studies. **RESEARCH** Eighteenth century novel with emphasis on Henry Fielding; 18th century graphic art with emphasis on William Hogarth; criers of London. **SELECTED PUBLICATIONS** Auth, Literary Portraits in the Novels of Henry Fielding, Northern Ill Univ, 72; ed, Engravings by Hogarth, Dover, 73; auth, A Harlot's Progress and the Question of Hogarth's Didacticisms, 18th Century Life, 75; Hogarth's Industry and Idleness, 18th Century Studies, 76; Hogarth and the Times-of-the-Day Tradition, Cornell Univ Press, 82; Marcellus Laroon's Cryer of the City of London, Studies Bibliog, 82; The Crier and Hawkers of London, Stanford Univ Press, 90. **CONTACT ADDRESS** No Illinois Univ, 1425 W Lincoln Hwy, De Kalb, IL, 60115-2825. **EMAIL** shesgreen@niu.edu

SHEWMAKER, KENNETH EARL
PERSONAL Born 06/26/1936, Los Angeles, CA, m, 1960, 2 children **DISCIPLINE** AMERICAN DIPLOMATIC HISTORY **EDUCATION** Concordia Teachers Col, BS, 60; Univ Calif, Berkeley, MA, 61; Northwestern Univ, PhD(US-Chinese rels), 66. **CAREER** Instr hist, Northwestern Univ, 65-66; asst prof, Col William & Mary, 66-67; from asst prof to assoc prof, 67-78, prof hist, Dartmouth Col, 78-, Soc Sci Res Coun/Am Coun Learned Soc Joint Comt Contemp China res grant, 67-68; Nat Hist Publ Comn res grant, 72-73; Dartmouth Col sr fac grant, 82. **HONORS AND AWARDS** Stuart L Bernath Prize, Soc Hist Am Foreign Rels, 72; Distinquished Teaching Award, Dartmouth Col, 86 & 96. **MEMBERSHIPS** New Hampshire Hist Soc; Orgn Am Historians; Soc Hist Am Foreign Rels. **RESEARCH** American diplomatic history; United States-China relations; Daniel Webster and American foreign policy. **SELECTED PUBLICATIONS** Auth, The war of words: The Cass-Webster Debate of 1842-43, Diplomatic Hist, spring 81; Daniel Webster, Angler, The American Fly Fisher, Fall 92; Forgeing the Great Chain: Daniel Webster and the Origins of American Foreign policy Toward East Asia and the Pacific 1841-1852, Proceedings of the Am Philos Soc, 85; Hook and line, and bob and sinder: Daniel Webster and the Fisheries Dispute of 1852, Diplomatic History, Spring 85; contribur, Encyclopedia of US Foreign Relations, Oxford Univ Press, 97; Commercial Expansionism in China, Hawaii, and Japan, Major Problems in American Foreign Relations Vol 1: To 1920, 95; ed, Daniel Webster: The Completest Man, Univ Press New England, 90. **CONTACT ADDRESS** Dept of History, Dartmouth Col, 6107 Reed Hall, Hanover, NH, 03755-3506. **EMAIL** shewmaker@dartmouth.edu

SHEY, HOWARD JAMES
PERSONAL Born 07/21/1935, m, 1962, 2 children **DISCIPLINE** CLASSICS **EDUCATION** Creighton Univ, BA, 62; Ind Univ, Bloomington, MA, 63, Univ Iowa, PhD(classics), 68. **CAREER** From instr to asst prof classics, 66-72, Assoc Prof Classics, Univ Wis-Milwaukee, 72-, Bk rev ed, Class J, 68-73. **MEMBERSHIPS** Am Philol Asn; Class Asn Mid W & S. **RESEARCH** Latin and Greek lyric poetry; Latin epic. **SELECTED PUBLICATIONS** Auth, Petronius and Plato's Gorgias, Class Bull, 5/71; The poet's progress: Horace Ode 1 1,9/71 & Tyrtaeus and the art of propaganda, 5/76, Arethusa; Petrarch's Secretum, 89. **CONTACT ADDRESS** Dept of Classics, Univ of Wis, PO Box 413, Milwaukee, WI, 53201-0413.

SHI, MINGZHENG
PERSONAL Born 11/03/1963, Beijing, China, m, 1994, 1 child **DISCIPLINE** HISTORY **EDUCATION** Peking Univ, BA, 86; Univ CT, MA, 88; Columbia Univ, M Phil, 90, PhD, 93. **CAREER** Asst prof, Univ Houston, 92-97; asst prof, Univ HI, 97-. **HONORS AND AWARDS** ACLS; NEH; Mellon grants recipient. **MEMBERSHIPS** Asian Studies Asn; Urban Hist Asn. **RESEARCH** Modern China, social, cultural and urban. **SELECTED PUBLICATIONS** Auth, Minds of the Sages: A Comparative Study of the Political Philosophies Between Confucius and Plato, The J of Cultural Studies 1:1, May 86; The Development of Municipal Institutions and Public Works in Early Twentieth Century Beijing, Chinese Historians 5:2, fall 92; The Transformation of Beijing: Urban Development and Social Change, Peking Univ Press, 95 (Chinese); America as an Idea: a Historical Inquiry of the Chinese Perceptions of the United States, The J of Am Studies 28:2, Dec 96; Rebuilding the Chinese Capital: Beijing in the Early Twentieth Century, Urban Hist 25:1, May 98; From Imperial Gardens to Public Parks: The Transformation of Space in Early Twentieth Century Beijing, Modern China 24:3, July 98; Remaking Beijing: Urban Space, Infrastructure, and Social Change in the Chinese Capital, 1900-1928, English manuscript, in prep. **CONTACT ADDRESS** Dept of Hist, Univ HawaiiI, Honolulu, HI, 96822. **EMAIL** mingzhen@hawaii.edu

SHIELDS, JOHANNA NICOL
PERSONAL Born 07/12/1942, Mobile, AL, m, 1968, 2 children **DISCIPLINE** AMERICAN HISTORY **EDUCATION** Univ Ala, BA, 64, MA, 65, PhD(hist), 72. **CAREER** From instr to asst prof, 67-77, ASSOC PROF HIST, UNIV ALA, HUNTSVILLE, 77- **MEMBERSHIPS** Orgn Am Historians; AHA; Southern Hist Asn; Soc Sci Hist Asn; Am Studies Asn. **RESEARCH** Antebellum United States history; 19th century Southern history. **SELECTED PUBLICATIONS** Auth, The Fire-Eaters - Walther,Eh/, Am Hist Rev, Vol 0098, 1993; White Honor, Black Humor, And The Making Of A Southern Style/, Southern Cultures, Vol 0001, 1995; The Literary Percys - Family Hist, Gender And The Southern Imagination - Wyatt-brown,B/, J Of Southern Hist, Vol 0062, 1996; Southern Writers And Their Worlds - Morris,C, Eacker,Sa, Jones,Ag, Wyattbrown,B, Joyner,C/, J Of Southern Hist, Vol 0063, 1997. **CONTACT ADDRESS** Dept of Hist, Univ of Ala, Huntsville, AL, 35807.

SHIELS, RICHARD DOUGLAS
PERSONAL Born 04/05/1947, Detroit, MI, m, 1972 **DISCIPLINE** AMERICAN AND RELIGIOUS HISTORY **EDUCATION** Hope Col, BA, 68; Yale Univ, MAR, 71; Boston Univ, PhD, 76. **CAREER** Asst prof, Boston Univ, 75-76; asst prof, 76-82, assoc orof hist, Ohio St Univ, Newark, 82-. **MEMBERSHIPS** Orgn Am Historians; AHA. **RESEARCH** American intellectual and social history. **SELECTED PUBLICATIONS** Auth, "Second Great Awakening in Connecticut," Church History, Vol 49, 80; Feminization of American congregationalists, 1730-1835, Am Quart, Vol 33, 81. **CONTACT ADDRESS** History Dept, Ohio State Univ, 1179 University Dr, Newark, OH, 43055-1797. **EMAIL** shiels.1@osu.edu

SHIFF, RICHARD
DISCIPLINE ART AND ART HISTORY **EDUCATION** Yale Univ, PhD. **CAREER** Prof; Effie Marie Cain Regents Chr in Art & dir, Ctr Study Modernism. **RESEARCH** Mod art from the early 19th century to the present, with emphasis on French painting and post-war Am art. **SELECTED PUBLICATIONS** Auth, Cezanne and the End of Impressionism & stud of critical and methodological issues; publ on, artists Edouard Manet, Willem de Kooning, Richard Serra, Vija Celmins, Jasper Johns, Roger Fry's social theories, and on Walter Benjamin's theory of aura. **CONTACT ADDRESS** Dept of Art and Art Hist, Univ of Texas at Austin, 2613 Wichita St, FAB 2.106, Austin, TX, 78705.

SHINGLETON, ROYCE GORDON
PERSONAL Born 10/25/1935, Stantonsburg, NC, m, 1962, 2 children **DISCIPLINE** HISTORY **EDUCATION** East Carolina Univ, BS, 58; Appalachian St Univ, MA, 64; Fla State Univ, PhD, 71. **CAREER** Ga State Univ, 68-74; Oglethorpe Univ, 74-77; Prof Hist, Darton Col. **HONORS AND AWARDS** Darton Col Found Commun Service Award, 79; SE Writers' Asn award for best non-fiction manuscript, 81; Atlanta Foundation Grant, 85; Atlanta Hist Soc Franklin Garrett Award, 85; Darton Col Foundation Advising Award, 93; Nat Inst for Staff and Org Dev Award for Excellence in Tchng, 94; recipient of the Clarendon Award, 95. **MEMBERSHIPS** US Civil War Ctr; Ga Asn of Hist; Univ System of Ga Advisory Committee on Hist; Thronateeska Heritage Ctr of Albany. **RESEARCH** Civil War and Reconstruction; 19th century US; Southern history; US Survey. **SELECTED PUBLICATIONS** Auth, The Sword and the Cross of Giles B Cooke: A Christian Soldier with Lee and Jackson, Blue and Gray X, 5, 32-35, 6/93; auth, High Seas Confederate, The Life and Times of John Newland Maffitt, Univ SC Press, 94, 95; auth, Confederate Mike Usina: Boy Sea Fox, Civil War, XLV, 50-57, 6/94; co-auth, The Confederate States Navy: The Ships, Men and Organization, 1861-65, Naval Inst Press & Conway Maritime Press, 97. **CONTACT ADDRESS** Soc Sci Div, Darton Col, Albany, GA, 31707. **EMAIL** rshingle@mail.dartnet.peachnet.edu

SHIPLEY, NEAL ROBERT
PERSONAL Pittsburgh, PA **DISCIPLINE** HISTORY **EDUCATION** Grove City Col, AB, 59; Harvard Univ, AM, 60, PhD(hist), 67. **CAREER** Asst prof hist, Univ Tenn, Knoxville, 67-78; assoc prof, 68-85, PROF HIST, UNIV MASS, AMHERST, 85-, assoc dean, humanities & fine arts, 85-92; dir, UMass Amherst-Trinity Col, Oxford, Oxford Summer Seminar Brit Studies, 87-92. **RESEARCH** Tudor-Stuart history; Victorian studies **SELECTED PUBLICATIONS** Auth, Full hand and worthy purposes: The foundation of Charter House, 1606-1616, Guildhall Studies, 4/75; History of a manor: Castle Campes, 1580-1629, Bull Inst Hist Res, 11/75; Thomas Sutton: Tudor-Stuart moneylender, Bus Hist Rev, winter 76; London's City Lands Committee, 1592-1644, Guildhall Studies, spring 77. **CONTACT ADDRESS** Dept of Hist, Univ of Mass, Amherst, MA, 01003-0002. **EMAIL** nrs@oitunix.oit.umass.edu

SHIVERS, JAY SANFORD
PERSONAL Born 07/07/1930, New York, NY, m, 1994, 1 child **DISCIPLINE** EDUCATION, RECREATIONAL SERVICE EDUCATION **EDUCATION** BS, IN Univ, 52; MA 53, Re Dir 55, NY Univ; PhD, Univ WI, 58. **CAREER** Coordr Nstl Rec and Park Assoc Dept Accreditation Univ Conn Baccalaureate Prog in Rec Scv Edu, with options in Natural Res Rec Mge and Therapeutic Rec, 91; Visiting Prof Wingate Inst, Israel, 76; Vis Prof Moorehead State Col, MN, 70; Vis Prof and Acting Ch Calif State Col, Hayward, 67; Asst Prof and Supvr of Rec Svc Edu, Assoc Prof, 67, Prof 70-, Prof Consul Keystone Training and Rehabil Inst Scranton, PA, 64-66. **HONORS AND AWARDS** Who's Who in Am Edu, Intl Dictionary of Biog, World Dictinary of Bio, Outstanding Am Edu, Contemporary Am Auth, Intl Dir of Auth, Natl Lit Award from the Natl Rec and Park Assoc, Distinguishes Svc Award, Natl Therapeutic Rec Soc. **MEMBERSHIPS** Natl Rec and Park Assoc, Int Playground Assock Intl Federation of Park and Rec Admin, Leisure Res Section Intl Sociol Assoc, Am Assoc Univ Prof Natl Consortium on Physical Edu and Rec for the Disabled. **SELECTED PUBLICATIONS** Shivers, Jay S Introduction to Recreational Service, Springfield, IL, Himan Kinetics, 97; Shivers, Jay S and L DeLisle, The Story of Leisure, Champaigne, IL: Human Kinetics, 97; Shivers Jay S and H F Fait, Therapeutic and Adapted Recreational Service, Lea and Febiger, 78; Shivers, Jay S and G Hjelte, Public Administration of Recreational Service, 2nd ed, Lea and Febiger, 78; Shivers, Jay S, Essentials of Recreational Service, Lea and Febiger, 78. **CONTACT ADDRESS** Dept Sport, Leisure and Excerise Sci., Univ CT, Storrs, CT, 06268. **EMAIL** Shivers@Uconnvm.Uconn.edu

SHLOSSER, FRANZISKA E.
DISCIPLINE MEDIEVAL HISTORY **EDUCATION** McGill Univ, MA, PhD. **CAREER** Assoc prof. **RESEARCH** History of costume and interiors. **SELECTED PUBLICATIONS** Pub(s), ancient Greek Numismatics, Late Antiquity and Byzantine History; auth, The Reign of the Emperor Maurikios (582-602): A Reassessment, Hist Monogr 14, Athens: Hist Publ St D Basilopoulos, 94. **CONTACT ADDRESS** Dept of Hist, Concordia Univ, Montreal, 1455 de Maisonneuve W, Montreal, PQ, H3G 1M8. **EMAIL** shlosse@vax2.concordia.ca

SHNEIDMAN, J. LEE
PERSONAL Born 06/20/1929, New York, NY, m, 1961, 2 children **DISCIPLINE** MEDIEVAL HISTORY **EDUCATION** NY Univ, BA, 51, MA, 52; Univ Wis, PhD, 57. **CAREER** Vis instr hist, 56-57, CUNY; lectr hist & govt, 57-58, Univ Md Overseas Prog; from instr to asst prof hist, 57, 58-62, Fairleigh Dickinson Univ; asst prof, 62-63, Brooklyn Col, 62-63; from asst prof to assoc prof, 63-71, prof hist, 71-, Adelphi Univ; mem ed bd, Indice Historico Espanol. **MEMBERSHIPS** AHA; Mediaeval Acad Am; Group for Use of Psychol in Hist; chmn, Columbia Univ Seminar; Hist of Legal and Polit Thought and Institutions. **RESEARCH** Political thought and nationalism in the Middle Ages; psychohistory; psychobiography of Aaron Burr. **SELECTED PUBLICATIONS** Auth, Eastern Europe and the Soviet Union, Spain in the Twentieth Century World, Greenwood, 80; coauth, The Burr-Hamilton Duel: Suicide or Murder?, J Psychohist, vol 8, 80. **CONTACT ADDRESS** 161 W 86th St, New York, NY, 10024.

SHOEMAKER, REBECCA SHEPHERD
PERSONAL Born 05/10/1947, Franklin, NC, m, 1981, 1 child **DISCIPLINE** US HISTORY **EDUCATION** Berea Col, BA, 69; Ind Univ, Bloomington, MA, 70, PhD, 76. **CAREER** From assoc to asst instr US hist, Ind Univ, Bloomington, 70-73; instr, Univ NC, Wilmington, 73-74; asst prof US hist, Ill State Univ, Normal, 74-77; sr res hist, Centennial Hist Ind Gen Assembly, 77-79; asst prof, 79-82, assoc prof, 82-87, prof, Ind State Univ, Terre Haute, 87-; Res Fel Ind Hum Counc, 86. **HONORS AND AWARDS** Clio Grant Ind Hist Soc, 92. **MEMBERSHIPS** Orgn Am Historians; Ind Assoc Hist; Ind Acad Soc Sci; Ind Hist Soc. **RESEARCH** US constitutional history; US civil liberties history. **SELECTED PUBLICATIONS** Auth, Restless Americans: the geographic mobility of farm laborers in the Old Midwest 1850-1870, Ohio Hist, winter 80; Edna Belle Scott Sewell, In: Notable American Women, The Modern Period, Cambridge, 80; James D Williams, Indiana's farmer Governor, In: Their Infinite Variety, Ind Hist Bureau, 82; rev The Effective Republic: Administration and Constitution in the Thought of Alexander Hamilton, Hist Rev New Books, 93; rev The Constitution in Conflict, Hist: Rev New Books, 93; Indiana Civil Liberties Union, Encycl Ind, 94; Justice Willis Van Devanter, A Biographical Directory US Supreme Court Justices, 94; James D Williams, Traces of Indiana and Midwestern History, VIII, 96; rev Explicit and Authentic Acts: Amending the Constitution, 1776-1995, Hist: Rev New Books, 97; rev Friendly Fire: The ACLU in Utah, Jour Church State, 98; James Britt Donovaqn and Edith Spurlock Sampson, Am Nat Biog, 99. **CONTACT ADDRESS** Dept Hist, Indiana State Univ, Terre Haute, IN, 47809. **EMAIL** hishoema@ruby.indstate.edu

SHORROCK, WILLIAM IRWIN
PERSONAL Born 06/16/1941, Milwaukee, WI, m, 1964, 2 children **DISCIPLINE** MODERN EUROPEAN & EUROPEAN DIPLOMATIC HISTORY **EDUCATION** Denison Univ, BA, 63; Univ Wis, MA, 65, PhD, 68. **CAREER** From instr to asst prof Europ hist, Univ Wis, Marathon County Campus, 67-69; assoc prof, 69-82, prof hist, Cleveland State Univ, 82-. **MEMBERSHIPS** AHA; Fr Colonial Hist Soc. **RESEARCH** Nineteenth and twentieth century French diplomatic history; Third Republic French political history. **SELECTED PUBLICATIONS** Auth, The French presence in Syria and Lebanon before the First World War, 1900-1914, in Historian, 2/72; An-

ticlericalism and French policy in the Ottoman Empire, in Europ Studies Rev, 1/74; France and the rise of facism in Italy, 1919-1923, in J Contemp Hist, 10/75; French Imperialism in the Middle East: The Failure of Policy in Syria and Lebanon, 1900-1914, Univ Wis, 76; French suspicion of British policy in Syria, 1900-1914, in J Europ Studies, 76; La France, l'Italie fasciste et la question de l'Adriatique, 1922-1924, in Rev d'hist diplomatique, 80; Prelude to empire: French Balkan policy, 1878-1881, in East Europ Quart, 81; The Jouvenel mission to Rome and the origins of the Laval-Mussolini accords, 1933-1935, in Historian, 82; From Ally to Enemy: The Enigma of Fascist Italy in French Diplomacy, 1920-1940, Kent State Univ Press, 88. **CONTACT ADDRESS** Office Acad Affairs, Cleveland State Univ, 1983 E 24th St, Cleveland, OH, 44115-2440. **EMAIL** w.shorrock@popmail.csuohio.edu

SHORTRIDGE, JAMES R.
PERSONAL Born 03/14/1944, Kansas City, MO, m, 1967, 2 children **DISCIPLINE** GEOGRAPHY **EDUCATION** Dartmouth Col, AB 66; Univ Kansas, MA 68, PhD 72. **CAREER** Univ Kansas, asst prof 72-77, assoc prof 77-84, prof 84-. **HONORS AND AWARDS** OBK 66; Guggenheim fel 79-80. **MEMBERSHIPS** AAG; Kansas State Hist Soc. **RESEARCH** Historical and cultural geography of US. **SELECTED PUBLICATIONS** The Taste of American Place, with Barbara G Shortridge and James R Shortridge, Rowman Littlefield, 98; Peopling the Plains, Univ Press Kansas, 96; The Middle West, Univ Kansas Press, 89. **CONTACT ADDRESS** Dept Geography, Univ Kansas, Lawrence, KS, 66045. **EMAIL** shortrid@falcon.cc.ukans.edu

SHOTWELL, CLAYTON M.
PERSONAL Born 07/27/1946, Libby, MT, m, 1974, 2 children **DISCIPLINE** MUSIC **EDUCATION** Hastings Col, BA, 70; Univ Minn, MA, 74, PhD, 87. **CAREER** Asst Dean, asst prof, Univ of the Pacific, 89-94; assoc prof, chemn of dept, Augusta State Univ, 94-99. **MEMBERSHIPS** Col Music Soc; Soc for Ethnomusicology; Africah Stud Asn; Int Asn for the Study of Popular Music. **RESEARCH** Music in West Africa; Latin America; Chicano music; technology. **SELECTED PUBLICATIONS** Auth, Ethnic Enclaves in America: Teaching Resources on Native American and Mexican Music and Culture, in, Teaching World Music; Proceedings of the Second International Symposium on Teaching Musics of the World, Basel, 93; auth, Corridos, Mariachi Music, in, Encyclopedia of the Latino Experience, Salem Press, 95. **CONTACT ADDRESS** Dept of Fine Arts, Augusta State Univ, Augusta, GA, 30904-2200. **EMAIL** cshotwel@aug.edu

SHOWALTER, DENNIS EDWIN
PERSONAL Born 02/12/1942, Delano, MN, m, 1965, 2 children **DISCIPLINE** HISTORY **EDUCATION** Univ Minn, PhD, 69. **CAREER** US Air Force Acad, 91-93; distinguished vis prof, US Mil Acad, 97-98; Asst prof to prof, Colorado Col, 69- . **HONORS AND AWARDS** Paul Birdsall Prize, Am hist Asn, 92. **MEMBERSHIPS** Soc for Mil Hist. **RESEARCH** Military history; modern German history. **SELECTED PUBLICATIONS** Auth, Tannenberg: Clash of Empires, Archon Books, 1990; co-ed, Vietnam 1964-1973: An American Dilemma, Imprint, 93; auth, Caste, Skill and Training: The Evolution of Cohesion in European Armies from the Middle Ages to the 16th Century, in J of Mil Hist, 93; auth, The Political Soldiers of Imperial Germany: Myths and Realities, in Ger Stud Rev, 94; auth, Hubertusberg to Auerstaedt: The Prussian Army in Decline? in Ger Hist, 94; auth, The Convenient Opponent: German Preparations for D-Day, Dwight D Eisenhower Lect in War and Peace, Kansas State, 95; auth, Wars of Frederick the Great, Longmans, 96; auth, German Military Elites in the Twentieth Century, in Neilsen, ed, Military Elites in War and Peace, Praeger, 96; auth, Past and Future: The Military Crisis of the Weimar Republic, War and Soc, 96; co-ed, The What Ifs of World War II, Emperor, 97; auth, Gunpowder and Regional Military Systems, in Bradford, ed, Military Conflict between Cultures, Texas A&M, 97; auth, The German Soldier in World War I: From Langemarck to St. Mihiel, in Votaw, ed, A Weekend with the Great War, White Mane, 97; auth, Manoeuvre Warfare: The Eastern and Western Fronts, 1914-1915, in Oxford Illustrated History of the First World War, 98; auth, Dien Bien Phu in Three Cultures, War and Soc, 98; auth, Mass, Technology, and Warfighting, in The Great War and Total War, 99. **CONTACT ADDRESS** Colorado Col, Colorado Springs, CO, 80903. **EMAIL** Dshowalter@ColoradoCollege.edu

SHRADER, CHARLES R.
PERSONAL Born 07/03/1943, Nashville, TN, m, 1963, 2 children **DISCIPLINE** HISTORY **EDUCATION** Vanderbilt Univ, BA, 64; Columbia Univ, MA, 70, MPhil, 74, PhD, 76; US Army Command and Gen Staff Col, 78; US Army War Col, 82; NATO Defense Col, 84. **CAREER** Comn Off, US Army 64-87; asst prof, US Mil Acad; fac, US Army Command and Gen Staff Col, 77-80; act dir/dep dir, Combat Stud Inst, 78-80; chief, Orah Hist Br/asst dir, US Army Mil Hist Inst, 80-84; Fac, US Army War Col, 80-84; Fac, NATO Defense Col, 84-85; chief, Hist Svcs Div, US Army Ctr Mil Hist, 85-87; adj fac, Univ Md, 74-76; adj fac, Elizabethtown Col, 88-89; adj fac, Pa State Univ, Harrisburg, 88-90; INDEPENDENT SCHOLAR, 87-; EXEC DIR, SOC MIL HIST, 92-. **HONORS AND AWARDS** Army War Col Fac Writing Prize, 82; Harold L. Peterson Award hon men, 93; Marshall Chair of Mil Stud, US Army War Col, 83-84. **MEMBERSHIPS** AHA; Phi Beta Kappa; Medieval Acad Am; US Comn Mil Hist; Soc Historians For Rel; Nat Coalition Independent Scholars. **RESEARCH** Am mil biography; ins and intellectual his of US Army; hist mil logistics; medieval ms stud; ecclesiastical, intellectual, mil hist Middle Ages. **SELECTED PUBLICATIONS** Gen ed, Reference Guide to United States Military History, Facts on File, 91-94; auth, U.S. Military Logistics, 1607-1990: A Research Guide, Greenwood Press, 92; auth, Friendly Fire: The Inevitable Price, Parameters: US Army War Col Q, XXII:3, Autumn 92; auth, Communist Logistics in the Korean War, Greenwood Press, 95; auth, From Vietnam to the Gulf and After: Logistics and US Army Strategic Planning Since 1945, in Serving Vital Interests: Australia's Strategic Planning in Peace and War, DARA, 96; auth, United States Army Logistics, 1775-1992: An Anthology, US Army Ctr of Mil Hist, 97; auth, The First Helicopter War: Logistics and Mobility in Algeria, 1954-1962, Praeger, forthcoming; auth, Logistical Support of the Communist Insurgency in Greece, 1945-1949, Praeger, forthcoming. **CONTACT ADDRESS** 910 Forbes Rd, Carlisle, PA, 17013. **EMAIL** Heriger@aol.com

SHRIMPTON, G.S.
DISCIPLINE GREEK HISTORY **EDUCATION** Univ Brit Col, BA, 63, MA, 65; Stanford Univ, PhD, 70. **CAREER** Prof, 67-. **HONORS AND AWARDS** Pres, Fac Assn, 82-83, 83-84; CUFA/BC, 83-84, 92-93; Victoria Choral Soc, 86-87; Class Assn of Pacific Northwest, 88-89; act ch, Hisp and Ital dept, 84-85. **RESEARCH** History and historians of fifth and fourth-century Greece. **SELECTED PUBLICATIONS** Ed, Classical Contributions: Essays in Honour of M.F. McGregor, Toronto, 81; auth, Theopompus the Historian, Montreal, 91. **CONTACT ADDRESS** Dept of Greek and Roman Studies, Victoria Univ, PO Box 1700 STN CSC, Victoria, BC, V8W 2Y2. **EMAIL** gshrimpt@uvic.ca

SHRIVER, GEORGE HITE
PERSONAL Born 10/26/1931, Jacksonville, FL, m, 1953, 4 children **DISCIPLINE** MEDIEVAL HISTORY **EDUCATION** Stetson Univ, AB, 53; Southeastern Baptist Theol Sem, NC, BD, 56; Duke Univ, PhD(hist & church hist), 61. **CAREER** Instr relig, Duke Univ, 58-59; assoc prof church hist, Southeastern Baptist Theol Sem, NC, 59-68, prof hist, 68-73; assoc prof, 73-76, PROF HIST, GA SOUTHERN COL, 76-, Am Asn Theol Schs fel & Swiss-Am exchange scholar, 65-66; consult, Choice, 70- **MEMBERSHIPS** Am Soc Church Historians; AHA; Am Acad Relig. **RESEARCH** Philip Schaff and Mercersburg theology; American religious dissent; the ecumenical movement. **SELECTED PUBLICATIONS** Auth, Schaff,Philip - Historian And Ambassador Of The Universal Church - Penzel,K/, Church Hist, Vol 0061, 1992; Telling The Churches Stories - Ecumenical Perspectives On Writing Christian Hist - Wengert,Tj, Brockwell,Cw/, Church Hist, Vol 0065, 1996; Cosmos In The Chaos - Schaff,Philip Interpretation Of 19th-Century Am Rel - Graham,Sr/, J Of Presbyterian Hist, Vol 0075, 1997. **CONTACT ADDRESS** Dept of Hist, Georgia So Univ, Statesboro, GA, 30458.

SHUBERT, HOWARD
PERSONAL Born 11/15/1954, Montreal, Canada, m, 1986, 2 children **DISCIPLINE** HISTORY OF ARCHITECTURE **EDUCATION** McGill Univ, BComm, 77, BA, 79; Univ Toronto, MA, 80, MPhil, 83. **CAREER** Assoc cur, Can Ctr for Archit, 85- . **MEMBERSHIPS** Soc of Archit Hist; Soc for the Stud of Archit in Can. **RESEARCH** Sports architecture. **SELECTED PUBLICATIONS** Auth, Toys and the Modernist Tradition, Canadian Centre for Architecture, 93; auth, Richard Henriquez: Memory Theatre, Canadian Centre for Architecture, 93; auth, Frank Lloyd Wright and Quebec, ARQ, 96; auth, making History Become Memory: The Architecture of Richard Henriquez, Soc for the Stud of Archit in Can, Bull, 96; auth, Introducing Other Soundings, Archit and Urbanism, 97; auth, The Architects and Designers of Lincoln Center, New York, Casabella, 98; auth, Sports Facilities in Canada, in, 1999 Canadian Encyclopedia World Edition, CD-ROM, McClelland & Stewart, 98. **CONTACT ADDRESS** 1920 Baile St, Montreal, PQ, H3H 2S6. **EMAIL** howards@cca.qc.ca

SHULTIS, CHRISTOPHER
DISCIPLINE MUSIC HISTORY **EDUCATION** Univ NMex, PhD. **CAREER** Prof, Univ N Mex. **HONORS AND AWARDS** Deems Taylor Awd, 96. **SELECTED PUBLICATIONS** Auth, Silencing the Sounded Self: John Cage and the Intentionality of Non-Intention, Musical Quarterly, 95; Cage in Retrospect: A Review Essay, J Musicol, 96. **CONTACT ADDRESS** Music Dept, Univ NMex, 1805 Roma NE, Albuquerque, NM, 87131. **EMAIL** paaffair@unm.edu

SHUMSKY, NEIL LARRY
PERSONAL Born 05/28/1944, Dayton, OH, m, 1966, 2 children **DISCIPLINE** AMERICAN URBAN & SOCIAL HISTORY **EDUCATION** Univ Calif, Los Angeles, AB, 66; Univ Calif, Berkeley, PhD(hist), 72. **CAREER** Instr hist, San Francisco State Col, 68-72; asst prof, 72-78, ASSOC PROF HIST, VA POLYTECH INST & STATE UNIV, 78- **MEMBERSHIPS** AHA; Am Studies Asn; Orgn Am Historians. **RESEARCH** American urban and social history; American ethnic relations. **SELECTED PUBLICATIONS** Auth, The Market Revolution - Jacksonian Am, 1815-1846 - Sellers,C/, J Of Interdisciplinary Hist, Vol 0024, 1993; The Metropolitan Frontier - Cities In The Modern Am-W - Abbott,C/, Pac Histl Rev, Vol 0064, 1995. **CONTACT ADDRESS** Dept of Hist, Va Polytech Inst & State Univ, Blacksburg, VA, 24061.

SHUMWAY, LARRY V.
PERSONAL Born 11/25/1934, Winslow, AZ, m, 1971, 6 children **DISCIPLINE** MUSIC **EDUCATION** Brigham Young Univ, BA, 60; Seton Hall Univ, MA, 64; Univ Washington, PhD. **CAREER** Assoc Prof, Brigham Young Univ, 75-. **MEMBERSHIPS** Soc for Ethnomusicology; Natl Assoc for Humanities Education **RESEARCH** Music of Japan, Tonga, traditional USA **SELECTED PUBLICATIONS** Auth, Non-Western Humanities in the Undergraduate Curriculum: Developing an International Perspective, Interdisciplinary Humanities, 97; auth, Dancing the Buckles of Their Shoes in Pioneer Utah (bundled with CD recording including 7 of Mr. Shumway's fiddle tunes), BYU Studies, 97-98. **CONTACT ADDRESS** Brigham Young Univ, JKHB 2007B, Provo, UT, 84602. **EMAIL** larry_shumway@byu.edu

SIBALIS, MICHAEL
DISCIPLINE CULTURE; HISTORY OF MODERN FRANCE **EDUCATION** McGill, BA; , Sir George Williams, MA; Concordia, PhD. **CAREER** Prof **SELECTED PUBLICATIONS** Coauth, The Regulation of Male Homosexuality in Revolutionary and Napoleonic France, Oxford UP, 96. **CONTACT ADDRESS** Dept of History, Wilfrid Laurier Univ, 75 University Ave W, Waterloo, ON, N2L 3C5. **EMAIL** msibalis@mach1.wlu.ca

SICHEL, WERNER
PERSONAL Born 09/23/1934, Munich, Germany, m, 1959, 2 children **DISCIPLINE** ECONOMICS **EDUCATION** Northwestern Univ, PhD, 64. **CAREER** PROF & CHR DEPT ECONOMICS, W MICH UNIV, 85-; Fulbright sr lectr, Univ Belgrade, 68-69; vis schol Hoover Inst, Stanford Univ, 84-85. **MEMBERSHIPS** Midwst Bus Econ Asn; Midwst Econ Asn. **RESEARCH** Telecommunication industry **SELECTED PUBLICATIONS** auth Basic Economic Concepts, Chicago: Rand McNally, 74; Economics, Boston: Houghton Mifflin, 84; Economics Journals and Serials: An Analytical Guide, Westport: Greenwood Press, 86; coauth The State of Economic Science: The Views of Six Nobel Laureates, W E Upjohn Inst for Employment Res, 89; Networks, Infrastructure and the New Task for Regulation, Univ Mich Press, 96; Promoting Competition in Michigan Telecommunication Markets Through Innovative Legislation, Mich State Univ, 98. **CONTACT ADDRESS** Dept of Economics, W Mich Univ, Kalamazoo, MI, 49008. **EMAIL** WERNER.SICHEL@WMICH.EDU

SICHER, ERWIN
PERSONAL Born 12/05/1935, Kuhnsdorf, Austria, m, 1959, 3 children **DISCIPLINE** HISTORY **EDUCATION** Collonges-Sous-Saleve, THB, 57; Pacific Union Col, MA, 59; Univ South Calif, PhD, 70; Texas Women Univ, PhD, 91. **CAREER** From assoc prof to prof to chem, 70-, Andrews Univ. **HONORS AND AWARDS** Tchr Year, SWAU, 81; Presidential citation for service to SWAU, 82; Zapara Award for excellence in tchg, 88., Pres, Asn SDA Historians; Secy, Keene Independent Sch District; Chemn, Odyssey Harbor. **MEMBERSHIPS** Am Hist Asn **RESEARCH** Twentieth Century Europe, Third Reich. **SELECTED PUBLICATIONS** Auth, art, Adult Education in the Third Reich, 95. **CONTACT ADDRESS** Southwestern Adventist Univ, Keene, TX, 76059. **EMAIL** sichere@swau.edu

SICIUS, FRANCIS
DISCIPLINE WESTERN CIVILIZATION **EDUCATION** State Univ, BA, MA, Loyola Univ Chicago PhD, 89. **CAREER** History, St. Thomas Univ. **SELECTED PUBLICATIONS** Area: Cath soc. **CONTACT ADDRESS** St Thomas Univ, 16400 N.W. 32nd Ave, Miami, FL, 33054-9913. **EMAIL** fsicius@stu.edu

SICK, DAVID
PERSONAL Born 01/24/1966, Lancaster, PA, s **DISCIPLINE** CLASSICS **EDUCATION** Univ MN, PhD, 96. **CAREER** Instr, Macalester Col, 96-97; ASST PROF, RHODES COL, 97-. **MEMBERSHIPS** Amer Philol Assoc; Amer Academy Relig; Soc Biblical Lit. **RESEARCH** Graeco-Roman relig; comparative myth. **SELECTED PUBLICATIONS** Auth, Cattle-Theft and the Birth of Mithras, JIES 24, 96. **CONTACT ADDRESS** Greek and Roman Studies, Rhodes Col, 2000 North Parkway, Memphis, TN, 38112-1690. **EMAIL** sick@rhodes.edu

SIDEBOTHAM, STEVEN EDWARD
PERSONAL Born 03/23/1951, Berlin, Germany, m, 1981 **DISCIPLINE** ANCIENT HISTORY, CLASSICAL ARCHEOLOGY **EDUCATION** Univ Pa, BA, 74; Univ Mich, MA(-class archeol) & MA(hist), 77, PhD(hist), 81. **CAREER** ASST

PROF HIST, UNIV DEL, 81- **MEMBERSHIPS** Archaeol Inst Am; Soc for the Promotion Hellenic Studies; Soc for the Promotion Roman Studies. **RESEARCH** Roman economic and trade policy in the Red Sea, Persian Gulf and Indian Ocean; Roman numismatics; Roman lamps and terra sigillata stamps. **SELECTED PUBLICATIONS** Auth, Travelers To An Antique Land - The Hist And Lit Of Travel To Greece - Eisner,R/, Classical World, Vol 0086, 1992; Univ-Of-Delaware Survey Of The Berenice-Nile Road/, Am J Of Archaeol, Vol 0098, 1994. **CONTACT ADDRESS** Dept of Hist, Univ of Del, Newark, DE, 19711.

SIDER, DAVID
DISCIPLINE GREEK POETRY AND PHILOSOPHY **EDUCATION** Columbia Univ, PhD. **CAREER** Prof, Fordham Univ. **SELECTED PUBLICATIONS** Ed, The Fragments of Anaxagoras, Introduction and Commentary, 81; auth, Parmenides, The Fragments, Bryn Mawr Commentaries, 86; co-ed, The New Simonides, Arethusa volume 26 2, 96. **CONTACT ADDRESS** Dept of Class Lang and Lit, Fordham Univ, 113 W 60th St, New York, NY, 10023.

SIDER, E. MORRIS
PERSONAL Born 11/20/1928, Cheapside, ON, Canada, m, 1951, 2 children **DISCIPLINE** ENGLISH AND MODERN EUROPEAN HISTORY **EDUCATION** Upland Col, BA, 52, BTheol, 53; Univ Western Ont, MA, 55; State Univ NY Buffalo, PhD, 66. **CAREER** Teacher elem sch, Walpole Sch Bd, Ont, 47-49; prin hist & English, Niagara Christian Col, 55-61; prof hist, Messiah Col, 63-, Ed, J Brethren in Christ Hist & Life, 78-; archivist, Brethren in Christ Arch, Messiah Col, 79. **HONORS AND AWARDS** Can Council Fellows, 58-59; Alumnus of the Year, Niagara Christian Coll, 82; Excellence in tchg Award, Messiah Col; 87; Distinguished Alumnus Award, Messiah col, 97; Sears Roebuck Found Tchg Excellence and Campus Award, 97. **MEMBERSHIPS** Can Hist Asn; AHA; Hist Asn, Eng. **RESEARCH** Eng dissenters; Anabaptist hist. **SELECTED PUBLICATIONS** Auth, Fire in the Mountains, privately publ, 76; A Vision for Service: A History of Upland College, 76 & Nine Portraits, 78, Evangel Press; ed, Lantern in the Dawn: Selections from the Writings of John Zercher, 80, Niagara Christian College: A History, 82, Messenger of Grace: A Biography of C N Hostetter J, Evangel Press, 82; Messiah College: A History, 84; The Brethren Christ in Canada, 88; Leaders Among Brethren, 87. **CONTACT ADDRESS** Dept of Hist, Messiah Col, Grantham, PA, 17027. **EMAIL** msider@messiah.edu

SIDER, ROBERT DICK
PERSONAL Born 03/10/1932, Cheapside, ON, Canada, m, 1959, 3 children **DISCIPLINE** CLASSICS, RELIGION **EDUCATION** Univ Sask, BA, 55, MA, 56; Oxford Univ, BA, 58, MA, 64, PhD, 65, DPhil, 65. **CAREER** Assoc prof bibl and class lit, Messiah Col, 62-68; from asst prof to assoc prof, 68-77, prof class studies, 77-81, Charles A Dana Prof Class Lang, 81-97, Charles A Dana prof emeritus, 97-, Dickinson Col; adj prof Col of Grad Stud, Univ Sask, 97-; Am Coun Learned Soc fel, 74-75; vis prof Greek & Latin, Cath Univ Am, 78-79; vis prof Univ Col, Univ Toronto, 82-83; fel-in-residence, Netherlands Inst for Adv Stud, 89-90; gen ed, New Testament Scholarship of Erasmus for Collected Works of Erasmus, Univ Toronto Press. **MEMBERSHIPS** Can Asn Rhodes Scholars;Asn Am Rhodes Scholars; NAm Patristic Soc (vpres, 72, pres, 73). **RESEARCH** Classical rhetoric; Christian Latin literature in antiquity and Renaissance; Christian humanism. **SELECTED PUBLICATIONS** Auth, Ancient Rhetoric and the Art of Tertullian, Oxford Univ, 71; coauth, A Decade of Patristic Studies, 2 v, Classical World, 82, 83; auth, The Gospel and its Proclamation, Michael Glazier, 83; ed, Paraphrase on Romans (CWE 42), Toronto, 84; ed, Annotations on Romans (CWE 56), Toronto, 94; transl, Paraphrase on Acts (CWE 50), Toronto, 95. **CONTACT ADDRESS** 304 Arthur Ave, Saskatoon, SK, S7N 1J3. **EMAIL** sider@skyway.usask.ca

SIDRAN, BEN H.
PERSONAL Born 08/14/1943, Chicago, IL, m, 1969, 1 child **DISCIPLINE** AMERICAN STUDIES **EDUCATION** Univ Wis, BA, 65; Univ Sussex, MA philos, 67, PhD, 70. **CAREER** Author **HONORS AND AWARDS** Fel, Wisc Acad Arts Sci Winner, ACE Award. **MEMBERSHIPS** ASCAP; NARAS; AFTRA; AF of M. **SELECTED PUBLICATIONS** Talking Jazz, Da Capo Press; Black Talk, Da Capo Press. **CONTACT ADDRESS** Box 763, Madison, WI, 53701. **EMAIL** bensidran@aol.com

SIEBER, GEORGE WESLEY
PERSONAL Born 11/16/1930, Evansville, IN, m, 1961, 2 children **DISCIPLINE** HISTORY **EDUCATION** Carroll Col (Wis), BA, 52; Univ Wis, MS, 53; Univ Iowa, PhD, 60. **CAREER** Asst prof hist, Lakeland Col, 59-62; from asst prof to assoc prof, 62-66, PROF HIST, UNIV WIS-OSHKOSH, 66-, CHMN DEPT, 74- **MEMBERSHIPS** Econ Hist Asn; Nat Asn Interdisciplinary Ethnic Studies; Forest Hist Soc. **RESEARCH** Sawmilling in the Mississippi Valley; Indians of Wisconsin. **SELECTED PUBLICATIONS** Auth, Great-Lakes Lumber On The Great-Plains - The Laird-Norton-Lumber-Company In South-Dakota - Vogel,Jn/, J Of Am Hist, Vol 0080, 1994. **CONTACT ADDRESS** Dept of History, Univ of Wis, Oshkosh, WI, 54901.

SIEBER, JOHN HAROLD
PERSONAL Born 09/19/1935, Janesville, WI, m, 1960, 2 children **DISCIPLINE** RELIGION, CLASSICS **EDUCATION** Luther Col, BA, 58; Luther Theol Sem, BD, 62; Claremont Grad Sch, PhD(relig), 66. **CAREER** Asst prof classics, 65-67, asst prof relig, 67-72, assoc prof, 72-80, Prof Relig & Classics, Luther Col, 80-, Am Philos Soc res grant, 72. **MEMBERSHIPS** Soc Bibl Lit. **RESEARCH** Theology of Rudolf Bultman; Gnostic library from Nag-Hammdi, Egypt. **SELECTED PUBLICATIONS** Auth, Conflict And Community In Corinth - A Socio-Rhetorical Commentary On 1-Corinthians And 2-Corinthians - Witherington,B/, Interpretation-A J Of Bible And Theol, Vol 0051, 1997. **CONTACT ADDRESS** Dept of Relig, Luther Col, 700 College Dr, Decorah, IA, 52101-1045.

SIEBER, ROY
DISCIPLINE AFRICAN AND OCEANIC ART **EDUCATION** Univ Iowa, PhD. **CAREER** Prof emer. **RESEARCH** Northern Nigeria and western Ghana; exhibiting African art; the roles of conoisseurship. **SELECTED PUBLICATIONS** Auth, African Textiles and Decorative Arts; African Furniture and Household Objects and African Art in the Cycle of Life. **CONTACT ADDRESS** Dept of History and Art, Indiana Univ, Bloomington, 300 N Jordan Ave, Bloomington, IN, 47405. **EMAIL** sieber@indiana.edu

SIEGEL, ADRIENNE
PERSONAL Born 06/10/1936, New York, NY, m, 1972 **DISCIPLINE** AMERICAN HISTORY, POPULAR LITERATURE **EDUCATION** Univ Pa, BS, 57; Columbia Univ, MA, 59; New York Univ, PhD(hist), 73. **CAREER** Teacher, James Madison High Sch, 62-82; asst prof hist, Long Island Univ, 77-93: Fel, New York Univ, 71-72; assoc, Danforth Found, 72-82; Fulbright fel India, 78; fel, Inst Res in Hist, 81-82; ASST PROF, CITY UNIV NY, COL STATEN ISLAND, 93-. **HONORS AND AWARDS** Phi Delta Kappa Scholarship, 90; Phi Delta Kappa Chapter Editor & Fdn Rep, 88-93; Phi Delta Kappa Cert Rec, 89; NY Univ Alumnae Award, 74; Bronx Educ Endowment Fund Board 84-93. **MEMBERSHIPS** Orgn Am Historians; Popular Cult Asn. **RESEARCH** History of the American city. **SELECTED PUBLICATIONS** Auth, When cities were fun, J Popular Cult, 75; Philadelphia: A Chronological and Documentary History, Oceana, 75; Brothels, bets and bars, NDak Quart, 76; The Image of the American City in Popular Literature, Kennikat, 81; auth, The Marshall Court, Associated Faculty Press, 87; auth, Visions for the Reconstruction of the NYC School System, in Urban Education, Jan 86; auth, Incubator of Dreams: Directing College Guidance at America's Most Elite Minority High School, Education, Winter 89; auth, A Case for Colaboratives: Turning Around Bronx Public Schools, Urban Review, 88; auth, Mission Possible: The Rescue of Bronx Public Schools, Phi Delta Kappa Fastback, 88; auth, Don't Wait, Communicate: Helping Teachers to Talk Shop, The Effective School Report, 87; auth, Collective Dreams or Urban Realities: Psychohistory, Persons & Communities, 83; auth, The Myth of Mobility in the Media of Another Century, in The Many Faces of Psychohistory, Intl. Psychohistorical Assn, 84. **CONTACT ADDRESS** 330 W Jersey St, Elizabeth, NJ, 07202. **EMAIL** Siegel@postbox.CSI.CUNY.edu

SIEGEL, PETER E.
PERSONAL Born 11/06/1953, Ann Arbor, MI, m, 1991, 2 children **DISCIPLINE** ANTHROPOLOGY AND ENTONOLOGY **EDUCATION** Univ Del, BA, Anthrop, 78; Univ Del, AS, Entonology, 78; SUNY Binghamton Univ, MA, Anthrop, 81; SUNY Binghamton Univ, PhD, Anthrop, 92. **CAREER** Princ archeol, John Milner Asn; res assoc, Field Mus of Natural Hist; res assoc, Ctr de Invest Indigenas de Puerto Rico. **HONORS AND AWARDS** Heinz Family Found grant for archeol fieldwork in Latin Amer; Wenner-Gren grant for fieldwork in Puerto Rico; Natl Sci Found Diss Improvement grant. **MEMBERSHIPS** Soc Amer Archeol; Amer Anthrop Asn. **RESEARCH** Latin American Archeol; Eastern North America; Complex Society. **SELECTED PUBLICATIONS** Rev, The Indigenous People of the Caribbean, ed Samuel M. Wilson, Univ Press Fl, Gainesville, Latin Amer Antiquity, 9, 180-182, 98; auth, Ancestor Worship and Cosmology among the Tainos, Taino: Pre-Columbian Art and Culture from the Caribbean, ed Fatima Bercht, Estrellita Brodsky, John Alan Farmer and Dicey Taylor, pp 106-111, The Monacelli Press and El Museo del Barrio, New York, 97; An Interview with Irving Rouse, Current Anthrop, 37, 671-689; 96; Ideology and Culture Change in Prehistoric Puerto Rico: A View from the Community, Jour of Field Archaeol, 23, 313-333, 96; The Archaeology of Community Organization in the Tropical Lowlands: A Case Study from Puerto Rico, Archaeol in the Amer Tropics: Current Analytical Methods and Appln, ed Peter W. Stahl, pp 42-65, Cambridge Univ Press, Cambridge, 95; rev, The Archaeology of Pacific Nicaragua, Frederick W. Lange, Payson D. Sheets, Anibal Martinez and Suzanne Abel-Vidor, Univ Nmex Press, Albuquerque, The Latin Amer Anthrop Rev, spring 1993, 5, 1, 45-46, 95; auth, The First Documented Prehistoric Gold-Copper Alloy Artefact from the West Indies, Jour Archaeol Sci, 20, 67-79, 93; Saladoid Survivial Strategies: Evidence from Site Locations, Proceedings of the Intl Congress for Caribbean Archaeol, 14, 315-337, Barbados, 93. **CONTACT ADDRESS** John Milner Associates, 535 N Church St, West Chester, PA, 19380. **EMAIL** psiegel@johnmilnerassociates.com

SIEVENS, MARY BETH
DISCIPLINE HISTORY **EDUCATION** Mt Holyoke, BA, 86; Boston, MA, 92, PhD, 97. **CAREER** INSTR, CHAMPLAIN COLL **MEMBERSHIPS** Am Antiquarian Soc **SELECTED PUBLICATIONS** Co-ed, Yankee Correspondence: Civil War Letters between New England Soldiers and the Home Front, 96. **CONTACT ADDRESS** PO Box 472, Enosburg Falls, VT, 05450. **EMAIL** msievens@together.net

SIGMUND, PAUL EUGENE
PERSONAL Born 01/14/1929, Philadelphia, PA, w, 1964, 3 children **DISCIPLINE** POLITICAL SCIENCE **EDUCATION** Georgetown Univ, BA, 50; Harvard Univ, MA, 54, PhD 59. **CAREER** Instr, sr tutor, Harvard Univ, 59-63; assoc prof, Polit, 63-70; PROF, POLIT,PRINCETON UNIV, 1970-. **HONORS AND AWARDS** Tappan Thesis Prize, Harvard. **MEMBERSHIPS** Am Polit Sci Asn, Latin Am Studies Asn, Conf for the Study of Polit Thought, Phi BetaKappa. **RESEARCH** History of Political Theory, 1200-1700; Latin American Politics; Religion and Politics **SELECTED PUBLICATIONS** auth, Liberation Theology at the Crossroads: Democracy or Revolution?, 90; auth, The United States and Democracy in Chile, 93; transl, Nicholas of Cusa, The Catholic Concordance, 96; ed, Evangelization and Religious Freedom in Latin America, 99. **CONTACT ADDRESS** Dept of Polit, Princeton Univ, Princeton, NJ, 08540. **EMAIL** paulsig@princeton.edu

SILBER, NINA
PERSONAL Born 06/12/1959, New York, NY, m, 1989, 2 children **DISCIPLINE** U.S. HISTORY **EDUCATION** Univ of CA, Berkeley, PhD, 89. **CAREER** Vis asst prof, Univ of Delaware, 89-90; from asst prof to assoc prof, Boston Univ, 90-. **HONORS AND AWARDS** Smithsonian fel, 87-89; Charles Warren fel, Harvard Univ, 96-97. **MEMBERSHIPS** Org of Am Hists; Southern Hist Asn. **RESEARCH** Civil War; Women. **SELECTED PUBLICATIONS** Auth, The Romance of Reunion: Northerners and the South, 1865-1900, 93; Yankee Correspondence: Civil War Letters between New England Soldiers and the Homefront, 96; introd to new ed of M. Livermore, My Story of the War, 95; The Northern Myth of the Rebel Girl, Women of the American South: A Multicultural Reader, Christie Anne Farnham; coed, Divided Houses: Gender and the Civil War, 92. **CONTACT ADDRESS** Dept of History, Boston Univ, 226 Bay State Rd., Boston, MA, 02215. **EMAIL** nsilber@bu.edu

SILBERMAN, SARA LEE
DISCIPLINE HISTORY **EDUCATION** Brown Univ, AB; John Hopkins Univ, MA, PhD. **CAREER** Assoc prof; Conn Col, 66-. **HONORS AND AWARDS** Amer Asn Univ Women, post doc fel; Danforth Found Assoc, 81. **RESEARCH** Late 19th and 20th century US history; history of women in the US. **SELECTED PUBLICATIONS** Auth, The Curious Pattern of a Distinguished Medical Career: A Psychoanalytic Protrait of Edith Banfield Jackson, MD, in Biography: An Interdisciplinary Quarterly, 94; Pioneering in Family-Centered Maternity and Infant Care: Edith B. Jackson and the Yale Rooming-In Research Project, Bull Hist Med, 90. **CONTACT ADDRESS** Dept of History, Connecticut Col, 270 Mohegan Ave, Box 5615, New London, CT, 06320. **EMAIL** slsil@conncoll.edu

SILBEY, JOEL H.
PERSONAL Born 08/16/1933, Brooklyn, NY, m, 1959, 2 children **DISCIPLINE** AMERICAN HISTORY **EDUCATION** Brooklyn Col, BA, 55; Univ Iowa, MA, 56, PhD, 63. **CAREER** Asst prof hist, San Francisco State Col, 60-64; vis asst prof, Univ Pittsburgh, 64-65; asst prof, Univ Md, 65-66; from asst prof to assoc prof, 66-68, prof Am History, 68-86, PRES WHITE PROF HISTORY, 86- , CORNELL UNIV, 68-, Soc Sci Res Coun & Am Philos Soc fel, 69-70; NSF fel, 70-74; Nat Endowment for Humanities sr fel, 80-81; vis fel Ctr Advan Study in Behav Sci, 85-86; vis scholas Russell Sage Found, 88-89; John Simon Guggenheim Mem fel, 89-90. **MEMBERSHIPS** AHA; Orgn Am Historians; Southern Hist Asn. **RESEARCH** Political history; slavery controversy; Civil War and reconstruction. **SELECTED PUBLICATIONS** Auth, The Civil War synthesis in American political history, Civil War Hist, 6/64; The Shrine of Party: Congressional Voting Behavior, 1841-1852, Univ Pittsburgh, 67 & Greenwood, 81; The Transformation of American Politics, 1840-1860, Prentice Hall, 67; co-ed, Voters, Parties and Elections, Xerox, 72; Clio and computers: moving into Phase II, 1970-1972, Comput & Humanities, 11/72; Political Ideology and Voting Behavior in the Age of Jackson, Prentice-Hall, 73; A Respectable Minority: The Democratic Party in the Civil War Era, Norton, 77; co-ed, A History of American Electoral Behavior, Princeton Univ, 78; The Partisan Imperative: The Dynamics of American Politics Before the Civil War, Oxford, 85; The American Political Nation, 1838-1893, Stanford, 91; ed Encycl of Am Legis System, Scribners, 93. **CONTACT ADDRESS** Dept of Hist, Cornell Univ, McGraw Hall, Ithaca, NY, 14853-0001.

SILBIGER, ALEXANDER
DISCIPLINE MUSIC **EDUCATION** Brandeis Univ, PhD. **CAREER** Musicol prof, Duke Univ. **RESEARCH** Hist and performance of early keyboard music. **SELECTED PUBLICATIONS** Auth, publ(s) on Renaissance and Baroque music.

CONTACT ADDRESS Dept of Music, Duke Univ, Mary Duke Biddle Music Bldg, Durham, NC, 27706. **EMAIL** lexsilb@duke.edu

SILCOX, DAVID P.
PERSONAL Born 01/28/1937, Moose Jaw, SK, Canada **DISCIPLINE** ART HISTORY **EDUCATION** Univ Toronto, BA, 59, MA, 66; Courtauld Inst, Univ London, 62-63. **CAREER** Arts off, Can Coun, 65-70; asst to assoc dean fine arts, 70-73, assoc prof, York Univ, 70-77; dir cultur affairs, Municipality Metro Toronto, 74-83; asst to deputy min, Dept Communications, Ottawa, 83-91; SR RESIDENT AND ASSOC FELLOW, MASSEY COL, UNIV TORONTO, 91-. **HONORS AND AWARDS** Sir Frederick Banting Award, 62; Can Coun arts bursary, 62, res grant, 73, res fel, 74-75; McLean Found res grant, 70; York Univ res grant, 72. **SELECTED PUBLICATIONS** Auth, Christopher Pratt, 82, 95; auth, Painting Place: The Life and Work of David B. Milne, 96; coauth, Tom Thomson: The Silence and the Storm, 77; contribur, Jack Bush, 84; guest ed, Canadian Art, 62; int ed bd, Studio Int, 68-75. **CONTACT ADDRESS** Massey Col, Univ Toronto, Toronto, ON, M5S 3G3.

SILET, CHARLES LORING PROVINE
PERSONAL Born 04/25/1942, Chicago, IL, m, 1976, 4 children **DISCIPLINE** AMERICAN STUDIES, LITERATURE **EDUCATION** Butler Univ, BA, 66; Ind Univ, MA, 68, PhD(English & Am studies), 73. **CAREER** Instr, 73-74, asst prof, 74-79 PROF ENGLISH, IOWA STATE UNIV, 79-, Dir Grad Studies, Dept English, Iowa State Univ, 81- **MEMBERSHIPS** MLA; Am Studies Asn; Midcontinent Am Studies Asn. **RESEARCH** American culture and literature 1880-1930; contemporary cinema; bibliography. **SELECTED PUBLICATIONS** Auth, Fuller,Henry,Blake - Further Additions And Corrections/, Resources For Am Literary Study, Vol 0019, 1993; Hitchcock Rereleased Films - From 'Rope' To 'Vertigo' - Raubicheck,W, Srebnick,W/, Film Criticism, Vol 0018, 1993; Matthews,Brander, Roosevelt,Theodore And The Politics Of Am Lit, 1880-1920 - Oliver,Lj/, J Of Am Hist, Vol 0080, 1993; The Hunt For Willie-Boy - Indian-Hating And Popular-Cult - Sandos,Ja, Burgess,Le/, J Of Am Hist, Vol 0082, 1995. **CONTACT ADDRESS** Dept of English, Iowa State Univ, Ames, IA, 50011-0002.

SILK, GERALD
PERSONAL Born 12/29/1947, Fall River, MA, m, 1983, 1 child **DISCIPLINE** ART HISTORY **CAREER** Asst prof, Columbia Univ, 76-83; asst prof, Univ Pennsylvania, 83-87; assoc prof, Tyler Sch of Art, Temple Univ, 98-. **HONORS AND AWARDS** Amer Acad in Rome Prize, 81-82; Ailsa Mellon Bruce Senior Fel CASUA, Natl Gallery of Art, 87-88; NEH Summer Stipend 91. **MEMBERSHIPS** Coll Art Assn; Soc of Fel the Amer Acad in Rome; Amer Culture/Popular Culture Assn. **RESEARCH** Modern cotemporary art **SELECTED PUBLICATIONS** Auth, Museums discovered: The Wadsworth Atheneum, 82; Automobile and Culture, 84; Refrains and Reframes: Artists Rethink Art History, Art Journal, Fall 95; Fascist Modernism and the Photo-Collages of Bruno Munari, in Cummer Studies: Cultural and Artistic Upheavals in Modern Europe, 1848-1945, 96; Censorship and Controversy in the Career of Edward Kienholz, in Suspended License: Essays in the History of Censorship and the Visual Arts, 97; All by Myself: Piero Manzoni's Autobiographical Use of his Body, its Parts, and its Products, in True Relations: Essays on Autobiography and the Postmodern, 98 **CONTACT ADDRESS** Dept of Art Hist, Temple Univ, Philadelphia, PA, 19122. **EMAIL** gsilk@nimbus.occs.temple.edu

SILLIMAN, ROBERT HORACE
PERSONAL Born 01/26/1935, Waterbury, CT, m, 1956 **DISCIPLINE** HISTORY OF SCIENCE **EDUCATION** Cornell Univ, BA, 56, MA, 59; Princeton Univ, MA, 64, PhD(hist), 68. **CAREER** From instr to asst prof hist, 64-71, ASSOC PROF HIST, EMORY UNIV, 71- **MEMBERSHIPS** Hist Sci Soc. **RESEARCH** European intellectual history; history of optics; early 19th century physics. **SELECTED PUBLICATIONS** Auth, Syphilis, Puritanism And Witch-Hunts - Historical Explanations In The Light Of Medicine And Psychoanalysis With A Forecast About Aids - Andreski,S/, Hist And Philos Of The Life Sciences, Vol 0015, 1993; The Hamlet-Affair - Lyell,Charles And The N-Americans/, Isis, Vol 0086, 1995. **CONTACT ADDRESS** Dept of History, Emory Univ, 1364 Clifton Rd N E, Atlanta, GA, 30322-0001.

SILVERA, ALAIN
PERSONAL Born 09/19/1930, Alexandria, Egypt, m, 1955, 1 child **DISCIPLINE** MODERN HISTORY **EDUCATION** Cornell Univ, AB, 52; Ecole Normale Superieure, Paris, 55; Harvard Univ, AM, 53, PhD, 63. **CAREER** Lectr govt, Univ Md, Paris, France, 56-57; tutor hist & lit, Harvard Univ, 58-59; lectr, 61-63, from asst prof to assoc prof, 63-74, PROF HIST, CHR HIST, 93- ,BRYN MAWR COL, 74-, Am Asn Mid East Studies traveling fel, Cairo, 63; Fulbright vis prof, Univ Lille, 66-67, 68-69; vis prof, Bryn Mawr Inst Avignon, 67, 69 & 71; fels, Am Philos Soc, 71 & Am Coun Learned Socs, 74-75; vis prof, Temple Univ, 74-75; sr fel, Am Res Ctr Egypt, Cairo, 77-78, sr Fulbright, Egypt, 82-83. **MEMBERSHIPS** AHA; Fr Soc Mod Hist; MidE Studies Asn NAm. **RESEARCH** Modern Near East; 19th and 20th century France. **SELECTED PUBLICATIONS** Auth, Daniel Halevy and His Times, Cornell Univ, 66; Jomard and Egyptian reforms in 1839, Mid Eastern Studies, 71; The French Revolution of May 1968, Va Quart Rev, 71; ed, The End of the Notables, Wesleyan Univ, 74; auth, The origins of the French Expedition to Egypt, Islamic Quart, 74; The first Egyptian student mission to France under Muhammad Ali, Mod Egypt, Frank Cass, London, 80; Kemalism and the origins of Egyptian Nationalism, Atatnrk, Istanbul, 81; Egypt and the French Revolution, Revue Francaise d'histoire d'outre-Mer, 82; Colonizing Egypt, Victorian Studies, 89; The Guide to the Labyrinth, Times Lit Suppl, 96; Of Caliphs and Sultans, The New Criterion, 96; North African Jewry, The Jewish Jour Sociol, 96; ed The Encyclopedia of Revolution and Revolutionaries: from Anarchism to Zhou en Lai, Facts on File, 96; The Jews of Egypt, Mid E Stud, 98; Elie Kedourie, politique et moraliste, Frank Cass, 97; Moshe Sharett, Mid E Stud, 98. **CONTACT ADDRESS** Dept of Hist, Bryn Mawr Col, 101 N Merion Ave, Bryn Mawr, PA, 19010-2899. **EMAIL** asilvera@bmc.edu

SILVERBERG, JOANN C.
PERSONAL Born 05/19/1940, New York, NY, 1 child **DISCIPLINE** CLASSICAL PHILOLOGY **EDUCATION** Barnard, AB, 60; Radcliffe, AM, 62; Harvard, PhD, 67. **CAREER** Sweet Brian Col, 64-65; from asst prof to assoc prof, 67-, Conn Col. **HONORS AND AWARDS** Phi Beta Kappa; Woodrow Wilson Fel; Mellon, Fulbright, Dartmouth-Dana, NYS Regents Grants. **MEMBERSHIPS** APA; CANE. **RESEARCH** Latin and Greek language and literature; historiography comedy and love poetry; linguistics, gender and women's studies. **SELECTED PUBLICATIONS** Auth, for, A Feminist Classicist Reflects on Athena; auth, rev, The Chilly Classroom Climate: A Guide to Improve the Education of Women, 98. **CONTACT ADDRESS** Connecticut Col, 270 Mohegan Ave, Box 5551, New London, CT, 06320. **EMAIL** jcsil@conncoll.edu

SILVERMAN, KENNETH EUGENE
PERSONAL Born 02/05/1936, New York, NY, 2 children **DISCIPLINE** ENGLISH, AMERICAN STUDIES **EDUCATION** Columbia Univ, BA, 56, MA, 58, PhD(English), 64. **CAREER** Instr English, Univ WY, 58-59; preceptor, Columbia Col, 62-64; PROF ENGLISH, NY UNIV, 64-, Danforth assoc, 68-71; Nat Endowment for Humanities Bicentennial grant, 72-74; Am Coun Learned Soc grant-in-aid, 86; Am Philos Soc grant, 86. **HONORS AND AWARDS** Ambassador of Honor Book Award, 84; Bancroft Prize in Am Hist, 85; Pulitzer Prize for Biography, 85; John Simon Guggenheim Memorial Found fel, 89-90; Edgar Award, The Mystery Writers of America, 92; Christopher Literary Award, Soc of Am Magicians, 97. **MEMBERSHIPS** Fel, Am Antiqn Soc; The Authors' Guild; fel, Soc Am Hist; The Century Asn; Soc Am Magicians. **RESEARCH** American culture. **SELECTED PUBLICATIONS** Ed, Colonial American Poetry, Hafner, 68; auth, Timothy Dwight, Twayne, 69; ed, Literature in America I: The Founding of a Nation, Free Press, 71; Selected Letters of Cotton Mather, La State Univ, 71; auth, A Cultural History of the American Revolution, Crowell, 76; A Cultural History of the American Revolution, Thomas Y. Crowell, 76; co-ed, Adventures in American Literature, Harcourt Brace Jovanovich, 80, rev eds, 85, 89; auth, The Life and Times of Cotton Mather, Harper & Row, 84; Edgar A. Poe. Mournful and Never-ending Remembrance, HarperCollins, 91; ed, New Essays on Poe's Major Tales, Cambridge Univ Press,93, with intro; HOUDINI!!! The Career of Ehrich Weiss, HarperCollins, 96. **CONTACT ADDRESS** Dept of English, New York Univ, 19 University Pl, New York, NY, 10003-4556. **EMAIL** ks2@is2.nyu.edu

SILVERMAN, VICTOR
PERSONAL New York, NY **DISCIPLINE** HISTORY **EDUCATION** Univ CA, Berkeley, BA, 84, MA, 86, PhD, 90. **CAREER** Lect, St. Mary's Col of CA, 92; vis prof, SAIS-Nanjing Univ, China, 92-93; ASST PROF, POMONA COL, 93-. **HONORS AND AWARDS** Fulbright fel; Excellence in European Studies fel; Kaiser Found Award. **MEMBERSHIPS** OAH; AHA; Soc for Historians of Am Foreign Relations; Southwest Labor Studies Asn; Social Sci Hist Asn. **RESEARCH** US labor; diplomacy; sexuality; CA/San Francisco; film. **SELECTED PUBLICATIONS** Auth, Popular Bases of the International Labor Movement in the United States and Britain, 1939-1949, Int Rev of Social Hist 38, 93; Is National History a Thing of the Past?: On the Growing Reality of World History in the 20th Century, European Legacy 1:2, summer 96; Imagining Internationalism in America and British Labor, 1939-1949, Univ IL Press, forthcoming 99; Insider-Outsider-No-Sider: Life and Death of Rose Cohen, The Stanger/Lo Straniero, forthcoming, 99; reviews and opinion pieces in a variety of academic and popular publications, film and creative work. **CONTACT ADDRESS** Dept of Hist, Pomona Col, 551 N. College Ave., Claremont, CA, 91711. **EMAIL** vsilverman@pomona.edu

SILVERSTEIN, JOSEF
PERSONAL Born 05/15/1922, Los Angeles, CA, m, 1954, 2 children **DISCIPLINE** GOVERNMENT, POLITICAL SCIENCE **EDUCATION** Univ Calif, LA, BA, 52; Cornell Univ, PhD, 60. **CAREER** Asst prof, Wesleyan Univ, 59-64; assoc prof, 64-67; prof, 67-78; chm, Polit Sci dept, Rutgers Col, 77-80; prof, Rutgers Col, 78-92; prof emer, Rutgers Univ, 92-98; PROF, RUTGERS UNIV, 98-. **HONORS AND AWARDS** Fulbright Sr Lectr, Univ Malaysia, 67-68, Mandalay Univ, Burma, 61-62. **MEMBERSHIPS** APSA; AAS. **RESEARCH** Comparative politics; Foreign policy; International relations. **SELECTED PUBLICATIONS** auth, "Change in Burma," Current Hist, 95; auth, "Federalism as a Solution to the Ethnic Problem in Burma," Verlag Rugler, 97; auth, "Burma's Uneven Struggle," Jour of Democracy, 96; auth, "The Civil War, the Minorities and Burma's New Politics," in Burma: the Challenge of Change in a Divided Society, St. Martin's Press, 97; auth, "Forty Years of Failure in Burma," in Government, Politics and Ethnic Relations in Asia and the Pacific, MIT Press, 97; auth, "The Idea of Freedom in Burma and the Political Thought of Daw Aing San Suc Ky" in Asian Freedoms: The Idea of Freedom in East and Southeast Asia, Cambridge Univ Press, 98; auth, "East Asia: A Year of Uneven Progress," in Freedom is the World 1997-1998, New York, 98; auth, "Evolution and Salience of Burma's National Culture," in Burma: Prospects for a Democratic Future, Wash Brookings Inst Press, 98. **CONTACT ADDRESS** Josef Silverstein, 93 Overbrook Dr, Princeton, NJ, 08540. **EMAIL** josefs@rutgers.edu

SILVIA, STEPHEN J.
DISCIPLINE POLITICAL ECONOMICS **EDUCATION** Cornell Univ, BS; Yale Univ, MA, PhD. **CAREER** Prof, Am Univ. **HONORS AND AWARDS** Fulbright Res Fel; Nat Endowment Humanities grant; Robert Bosch Fel. **RESEARCH** Comparative industrial politics and comparative economic systems. **SELECTED PUBLICATIONS** Articles, Bus Contemp World; Comp Polit; German Polit; German Studies Rev; Gewerkschaftliche Monatshefte; Industrial & Labor Relations Rev; Int Joul Politl Econ; New German Critique and W European Polit. **CONTACT ADDRESS** American Univ, 4400 Massachusetts Ave, Washington, DC, 20016.

SIMMONS, JEROLD LEE
PERSONAL Born 08/30/1941, Lexington, NE, m, 1967 **DISCIPLINE** AMERICAN HISTORY **EDUCATION** Kearney State Col, BA, 63; Univ Nebr, Omaha, MA, 67; Univ Minn, PhD(hist), 71. **CAREER** Instr US hist, Ill Col, 71-72; lectr, Univ Ill, 72-73; asst prof, Bellevue Col, 73-79, chair, Div Social & Behav Sci, 74-79; assoc prof US hist, Univ Nebr, Omaha, 79-, consult, Western Heritage Mus, 82. **MEMBERSHIPS** Orgn Am Hist. **RESEARCH** Hist of Am civil liberties; local hist; film hist. **SELECTED PUBLICATIONS** Ed, La Belle Vue: Studies in the History of Bellevue, Nebraska, Walsworth, 76; auth, Dawson County responds to the new deal, 1933-1940, Nebr Hist, spring 81; The county courthouse as an archives, Govt Publ Rev, 12/81; The American Civil Liberties Union and the Dies Committee, Harvard Civil Rights/Civil Liberties Rev, 7/82; Uses of local history in the college American history class, Teaching Hist, 82; Origins of the campaign to abolish HUAC, 1956-1961, Southern Calif Quart (in prep). **CONTACT ADDRESS** Dept of History, Univ of Nebraska, 6001 Dodge St, Omaha, NE, 68182-0002.

SIMMONS, MICHAEL
PERSONAL Born 06/15/1952, Raleigh, NC, m, 1973, 2 children **DISCIPLINE** ANCIENT HISTORY **EDUCATION** Univ S AL, BA, 76; Duke, MDiv, 80; Yale, STM, 82; New Col Univ of Edinburgh, PhD, 85 **CAREER** Asst Prof, Auburn Univ **HONORS AND AWARDS** Res Grant Oxford Univ, 95; Res Grant Oxford Univ, 99 **MEMBERSHIPS** Assoc Internationale des Etudes Patristiques; Am Philo Assoc; Am Hist Assoc; N Am Patristics Assoc **SELECTED PUBLICATIONS** Auth, Arnobius of Sicca, in Religious Conflict & Competition in the Age of Diocletian, Oxford, 95 **CONTACT ADDRESS** History Dept, Auburn Univ, Montgomery, PO Box 244023, Montgomery, AL, 36124-4023. **EMAIL** mbsimmons@1-a-net.net

SIMMONS, RICHARD C.
DISCIPLINE HISTORY **EDUCATION** Cambridge Univ, BA, 58, MA, 62; Univ Calif, Berkeley, PhD, 65. **CAREER** Reader to PROF, AM HIST, UNIV BIRMINGHAM **MEMBERSHIPS** Am Antiquarian Soc **SELECTED PUBLICATIONS** Auth, The American Colonies from Settlement to Independence, 76; coauth, Proceedings and Debates of the British Parliaments Respecting North America, 1754-1783, 82-87; auth, "Massachusetts and the Glorious Revolution, 1689-92: Select Documents," Publ of the Colonial Soc of Mass, 88; ed, The U.S. Constitution: The First Two Hundred Years, Procs of the Fulbright Colloquium, 1987, Manchester Univ Press, 89; British Imprints Relating to North America 1621-1760: An Annotated Checklist, British Lib, 96. **CONTACT ADDRESS** School of Hist, Univ of Birmingham, Birmingham, ., B15 2TT. **EMAIL** r.c.simmons@bham.ac.uk

SIMMONS, SYLVIA Q.
PERSONAL Born 05/08/1935, Boston, Massachusetts, m, 1957 **DISCIPLINE** EDUCATION **EDUCATION** Manhattanville Coll, BA 1957; Boston Coll, MED 1962, PhD, 1990. **CAREER** ABCD Headstart Program, soc serv suprv 1965; Charles River Park Nursery School, Montessori teacher 1965-66; Boston Coll, reg school of mgmt 1966-70; Harvard Univ, assoc dean of admissions & financial aid, faculty arts & sci 1974-76; Radcliffe Coll, assoc dean of admissions, financial aid & wom-

ens educ, dir financial aid 1972-76; Univ of MA Central Office, assoc vice pres academic affairs 1976-81; MA Higher Educ Asst Corp, sr vice pres 1982-; American Student Assistance, exec vp, 1992-95, president, 1995-96; lecturer in education, Boston Univ. **HONORS AND AWARDS** Women in Politics; Outstanding Young Leader Boston Jr Chamber of Commerce 1971; Boston Coll Bicentennial Award 1976; Black Achiever Award 1976; President's Award, Massachusetts Educ Opportunity Program 1988; Human Rights Award, Massachusetts Teachers Assn, 1988; Educator of the Year, Boston Chapter Assn of Negro Business & Professional Women's Club, 1989; Recognition of Contributions to Higher Educ, College Club, 1988; Honorary Degree, St Joseph's College, 1994; Sojournore Daughters, 25 African-American Women Who Have Made A Difference, 1990; Bishop James Healey Award, 1997. **MEMBERSHIPS** Past mem Exec Council Natl Assoc of Student Financial Aid Admin; past 1st vice pres Eastern Assoc of Financial Aid Admin; mem MA Assoc of Coll Minority Admin; consult Dept of HEW Office of Educ Reg I; consultant Coll Scholarship Serv, MA Bd of Higher Educ; past mem Rockefeller Selection Comm Harvard Univ; mem Delta Sigma Theta Natl; bd mem Family Serv Assoc Boston, Wayland Fair Housing, Concerts in Black & White, past pres Newton Chapter of Jack & Jill Inc, Boston Chapter Links Inc, Boston Manhattanville Club; mem bd of trustees Manhattanville Coll; past bd trustees Rivers Country Day School; past bd mem Cambridge Mental Health Assn; past bd trustees Simons Rock Coll; North Shore CC, chmn bd of trustees; William Price Unit of American Cancer Soc, past pres; bd of dir Amer Cancer Soc MA Div 1-90; board of trustees, Boston College; past mem board, Mass Foundation for the Humanities, 1990-91; Merrimack Coll, bd of trustees; Mt Ida Coll, bd of overseers; Grimes-King Foundation, bd of dirs; Regis College, bd of trustees; Anna Stearns Foundation, board of directors; Exec Service Corps, bd of dir.

SIMON, JANICE
DISCIPLINE ART HISTORY **EDUCATION** SUNY, Buffalo, BA, 78; Univ Mich, MA, 81, PhD, 90. **CAREER** Asst prof to ASSOC PROF, ART, UNIV GEORGIA **MEMBERSHIPS** Am Antiquarian Soc **SELECTED PUBLICATIONS** Auth, "Imaging a New Heaven on a New Earth: The Crayon and Nineteenth-Century America Periodical Covers," Am Per 1, 91; "Seeking to Keep that Earlier, Wilder Image Bright," Winterthur Portfolio 27, 92; auth, Sanford R Gifford's Kaaterskill Falls: A Place of Intimate Immensity," Bull Det Inst of Arts 67, Spring 93; auth, "Glimpses of Eternity: The Mythic Late Paintings of Charles Burchfield," Extending the Golden Year: The Charles Burchfield Centenary, Hamilton College, 93; co-ed, "Introduction, The Promise of 1893;" Crosscurrents in American Art at the Turn of the Century, Georgia Mus Art, 94; cont, essays Am Paintings in the Det Inst of Arts v 2, Fall, 97; auth, "Nature's Forest Volume: The Aldine, The Adirondacks, and the Sylvan Landscape" in The Call of the Wild: Printmakers in the Adirondacks, Syracuse Univ Press, 98; auth, essays on The Aldine and The Crayon for Am & Intl Art Per, Greenwood Press, 98; "Naked wastes...glorious woods: The Forest View of the White Mountains," in Images of the Hills: The Visual Arts and the White Mountains, New Hampshire Hist Soc and N.E. Press, 98. **CONTACT ADDRESS** School of Art, Univ of Georgia, Visual Arts Bldg., Athens, GA, 30602. **EMAIL** jsimon@uga.cc.uga.edu

SIMON, JOHN Y.
PERSONAL Born 06/25/1933, Highland Park, IL, m, 1956, 2 children **DISCIPLINE** AMERICAN HISTORY **EDUCATION** Swarthmore Col, BA, 55; Harvard Univ, MA, 56, PhD, 61. **CAREER** Instr hist, OH State Univ, 60-64; assoc prof, 64-71, Prof Hist, S IL Univ, Carbondale, 71-, Exec Dir Ulysses S Grant Asn, 62. **MEMBERSHIPS** AHA; Orgn Am Historians. **RESEARCH** Am Civil War. **SELECTED PUBLICATIONS** Auth, Ulysses S Grant Chronology, Ohio Hist Soc, 63; ed, General Grant by Matthew Arnold with a rejoinder by Mark Twain, 66 & The Papers of Ulysses S Grant, vol 1-22, Southern Ill Press, 67-98; The Personal Memoirs of Julia Dent Grant, Putnam, 75. **CONTACT ADDRESS** Ulysses S Grant Asn Morris Libr, Southern Illinois Univ, Carbondale, IL, 62901-6632. **EMAIL** jsimon@lib.siu.edu

SIMON, PAUL L.
PERSONAL Born 07/05/1936, Cincinnati, OH, m, 1965, 3 children **DISCIPLINE** MODERN UNITED STATES HISTORY **EDUCATION** Villa Madonna Col, BA, 58; Xavier Univ, OH, MA, 59; Univ Notre Dame, PhD, 65. **CAREER** From instr to assoc prof, 63-73, Prof Hist, Xavier Univ, OH, 73-, Chmn Dept, 65. **MEMBERSHIPS** MALAS **RESEARCH** Mexico, Central Am, Caribbean. **SELECTED PUBLICATIONS** Auth, The appointing powers of the President, Cithara, 63; Frank Walker, New Dealer, 1933-1935, Univ Microfilms, 65; Cincinnati's unique immigrant experience, Ill Quart, spring 72; Source Book: Cincinnati's Ethnic Heritage, Xavier Univ, Ohio, 78. **CONTACT ADDRESS** Dept of Hist, Xavier Univ, 3800 Victory Pky, Cincinnati, OH, 45207-1092. **EMAIL** simon@admin.xu.edu

SIMON, ROGER DAVID
PERSONAL Born 07/05/1943, Indianapolis, IN, m, 1977, 2 children **DISCIPLINE** AMERICAN HISTORY **EDUCATION** Rutgers Univ, New Brunswick, AB, 65; Univ WI-Madison, MA, 66, PhD, 71. **CAREER** From instr to prof, 70-86, assoc prof hist, Lehigh Univ, 86. **MEMBERSHIPS** AHA; Orgn Am Historians; Soc Hist Technol; Urban Hist Asn. **RESEARCH** Urban hist; soc hist. **SELECTED PUBLICATIONS** Auth, Housing and services in an immigrant neighborhood, J Urban Hist, 76; The City-Building Process, Am Philos Soc, 78, rev ed 96; coauth, Migration, Kinship, and Urban Adjustment: Blacks and Poles in Pittsburgh, 1900-1930, J Am Hist, 79; Lives of Their Own, Univ IL Press, 82. **CONTACT ADDRESS** Dept of Hist, Lehigh Univ, 9 W Packer Av, Bethlehem, PA, 18015-3081. **EMAIL** rds2@lehigh.edu

SIMON, SHELDON W.
PERSONAL Born 01/31/1937, St. Paul, MN, m, 1962, 1 child **DISCIPLINE** POLITICAL SCIENCE **EDUCATION** Univ Minnesota, PhD 64. **CAREER** Arizona State Univ, prof 75-, dir Asian Stud 80-88, ch Poli Sci 75-79. **HONORS AND AWARDS** Phi Beta Kappa; Summa cum laude; Outstanding Fac Awd; Phi Kappa Phi. **MEMBERSHIPS** AAUP; APSA; ISA. **RESEARCH** Asian security; regionalism in Asia. **SELECTED PUBLICATIONS** Auth, Asian Political Economy and Security Toward the 21st Century: A Review Essay, Intl Politics, 98; auth, Security Prospects in Southeast Asia: Collaborative Efforts and the ASEAN Regional Forum, The Pacific Rev, 98; auth, The Limits of Defense and Security Cooperation in Southeast Asia, The Jour of Asian and African Studies, 98; auth, Alternative Visions of Security in Northeast Asia, The Jour of NE Asian Studies, 96; auth, Alternate Visions of Security in the Asia-Pacific, Pacific Affs, 96; auth, Security Economic Liberalism and Democracy: Asian Elite Perceptions of Post Cold War Foreign Policy Values, NBR Analysis, 96; auth, Southeast Asian Security in the New Millenium, co-ed, Armonk NY, M E Sharpe, 96. **CONTACT ADDRESS** Political Science Dept, Arizona State Univ, Tempe, Tempe, AZ, 85287-2001.

SIMON, STEPHEN JOSEPH
PERSONAL Born 07/02/1939, Clay Center, OH, m, 1970, 2 children **DISCIPLINE** ANCIENT HISTORY **EDUCATION** Xavier Univ (Ohio), BA,61; Loyola Univ of Chicago, PhD(hist), 73. **CAREER** Instr hist, St Procopius Col, 67-69 & Loyola Univ, Italy, 69-70; asst prof, 70-77, dir foreign studies, 72-73, Prof Hist, Appalachian State Univ, 77-. **MEMBERSHIPS** AHA; Class Asn Atlantic States; Am Philol Asn. **RESEARCH** Roman religion; the Roman Empire; Etruscan art. **SELECTED PUBLICATIONS** Auth, Euripides defense of women & Domitianpatron of letters, 11/73, Class Bull; The Boeotian concept of democracy, Tertesius, spring 74. **CONTACT ADDRESS** Dept of History, Appalachian State Univ, 1 Appalachian State, Boone, NC, 28608-0001.

SIMPSON, CHRIS
DISCIPLINE EARLY ROMAN IMPERIAL HISTORY **EDUCATION** Alberta, PhD. **CAREER** Assoc Prof **SELECTED PUBLICATIONS** Auth, The Excavations of San Giovanni di Ruoti, 77; Caligula's cult: immolation, immortality, intent, 96; The Original Site of the Fasti Capitolini, 93s. **CONTACT ADDRESS** Dept of Classics, Wilfrid Laurier Univ, 75 University Ave W, Waterloo, ON, N2L 3C5. **EMAIL** csimpson@mach1.wlu.ca

SIMPSON, DICK
PERSONAL Born 11/08/1940, Houston, TX, m, 1985, 2 children **DISCIPLINE** POLITICAL SCIENCE **EDUCATION** Univ Texas, BA, 63; Indiana Univ, MA, 64, PhD, 68; McCormick Theol Sem, MDiv, 84. **CAREER** For Area Fel, Ford Found, Sierra Leone, 66-67; from instr, assist, assoc and full prof, 67- , Univ Illinois, Chicago; dir, Office of Chicago Studies, 87-90; dir Chicago Political Studies Project, 92-95; dir Graduate Stud Polit Sci, 95-96. **HONORS AND AWARDS** Silver Circle Award for excellence in teaching, 71; Outstanding Young Men of America Award, 72; Emmy nomination for documentary film, 89; Teaching Recognition Program Award, 97. **MEMBERSHIPS** Am Polit Sci Asn; Midwest Polit Sci Asn; Ill Polit Sci Asn. **RESEARCH** Urban politics; American politics; religion and politics; electoral politics. **SELECTED PUBLICATIONS** Coauth, Political Action: The Key to Understanding Politics, Ohio Univ, 84; auth, The Politics of Compassion and Transformation, Ohio University, 89; ed, Blueprint of Chicago Government: 1989, Univ Illinois at Chicago, 89; co-ed, The Crazy Quilt of Government: Units of Government in Cook County, 1993, University of Illinois at Chicago, 94; auth, Winning Elections: A Handbook of Modern Participatory Politics, HarperCollins, 96. **CONTACT ADDRESS** Dept of Political Science, Univ of Illinois at Chicago Circle, PO Box 4348, Chicago, IL, 60680. **EMAIL** simpson@uic.edu

SIMPSON, MICHAEL
DISCIPLINE CLASSICAL STUDIES **EDUCATION** Yale Univ, PhD, 64. **CAREER** Prof. **SELECTED PUBLICATIONS** Auth, Gods and Heroes of the Greeks: The Library of Apollodorus, Univ Mass, 95; Manners as Morals: Hospitality in the Odyssey, Art Inst, 92; Artistry in Mood: Iliad 3.204-224, Class Jour, 88; Cosmologies and Myths, Charles Scribner's Sons, 88. **CONTACT ADDRESS** Dept of Classics, Richardson, TX, 75083-0688. **EMAIL** msimpson@utdallas.edu

SIMPSON, PETER L.P.
PERSONAL England **DISCIPLINE** CLASSICS, PHILOSOPHY **EDUCATION** Victoria Univ Manchester, UK, PhD **CAREER** Asst prof, Univ Col Dublin, Ireland, 82-84; asst prof, Catholic Univ Am, DC, 84-88; Full prof, City Univ NY, 88- . **HONORS AND AWARDS** Earhart found fel, 95; Jr fel, Ctr Hellenic stud, 92. **MEMBERSHIPS** APA; ACPA; APSA; SAGP. **RESEARCH** Ancient and medieval philosophy; moral and political philosophy. **SELECTED PUBLICATIONS** Auth, The Politics of Aristotle, U of North Carolina P, 97; A Philosophical Commentary on the Politics of Aristotle, U of North Carolina P, 98. **CONTACT ADDRESS** Dept of Philosophy, Staten Island Col, 2800 Victory Blvd, 2N, Staten Island, NY, 10314. **EMAIL** simpson@postbox.csi.cuny.edu

SIMS, AMY R.
DISCIPLINE MODERN EUROPEAN HISTORY, EUROPEAN INTELLECTUAL HISTORY, POLITICAL THEORY, G **EDUCATION** Queens Col, BA, Magna Cum Laude; Cornell Univ, MA, PhD. **CAREER** Instr, asst to dir of Overseas Stud, Stanford Univ; instr, Boston Col; asst prof Hist, Golden Gate Univ; tchg fel, Harvard Univ, Cornell Univ. **MEMBERSHIPS** Am Hist Asn. **SELECTED PUBLICATIONS** Auth of article on historians in Nazi Germany. **CONTACT ADDRESS** Golden Gate Univ, San Francisco, CA, 94105-2968.

SIMS, HAROLD DANA
PERSONAL Born 10/19/1935, Fort Myers, FL, m, 1965, 2 children **DISCIPLINE** LATIN AMERICAN HISTORY **EDUCATION** Stetson Univ, BA, 62; Univ Fla, MA, 63, PhD, 68. **CAREER** From instr to asst prof, 66-72, assoc prof, 72-82, prof hist, Univ of Pittsburgh; Whitaker Prize for best book, MACLAS, 91. **RESEARCH** Nineteenth century Mexican social history; Japanese immigration to Latin America; Napoleonic Latin American policy. **SELECTED PUBLICATIONS** Auth, A House Divided: Ideological Divisions in Cuban Labor and the U.S. Role, 1944-1949, Cuban Studies 21, 91; The Expulsion of Mexico's Spaniards, 1821-1836, Pittsburgh, 91; Cuba, in Latin America Between the Second World War and the Cold War, Cambridge Univ Press, 93; coauth, Las minas de plata en el distrito minero de Guanajuato, Guanajuato, 93; co-ed, MACLAS Latin American Essays Vols 8-12, 95-99; author of numerous other articles and chapters. **CONTACT ADDRESS** Dept of Hist, Univ of Pittsburgh, 3K38 Forbes Quad, Pittsburgh, PA, 15260-0001. **EMAIL** dana1@pitt.edu

SIMS, LOWERY STOKES
PERSONAL Born 02/13/1949, Washington, DC, s **DISCIPLINE** ART HISTORY **EDUCATION** Queens Coll, BA 1970; Johns Hopkins Univ, MA 1972; CUNY, New York, NY, MA, philosophy, 1990, PhD, 1995. **CAREER** Metro Museum of Art, asst museum educ 1972-75; Queens Coll Dept Art, adjunct instructor 1973-76; Sch Visual Arts, instructor 1975-76, 1981-86; METRO MUSEUM OF ART, assoc curator beginning 1979-, CURATOR, currently. **HONORS AND AWARDS** Fellowship for Black Dr Students, Ford Found, 1970-72; Employee Travel Grant, Metro Museum Art, 1973; numerous publications; Amer Artists & Exhibition Catalogs; Hon Doctor of Humane Letters, Maryland Inst Coll of Art, 1988; Frank Jewett Mather Award, College Art Association, 1991; One of Crain's Magazine Top 100 Minortiy Executives, 1998; Lifetime Achievement in the Arts, Queens Museum of Art, 1998. **MEMBERSHIPS** Mem grants comm, Metro Museum Art, 1975-77; museum aid panel, NY State Council on Arts, 1977-79; mem, Art Table, College Art Assn 1983-, Assn of Art Critics, Amer Sect Intl Art Critics Assn 1980-, Natl Conf of Artists; visual arts panel, New York State Council on Arts 1984-86; council mem, New York State Council on Arts, 1987-92; bd, College Art Association, 1994-97; bd, Tiffany Foundation, 1995-97; advisory bd, Center for Curational Studies, 1995-; chair, Forum of Curators and Conservator, Metro Museum of AA, 1996-97. **CONTACT ADDRESS** Dept of 20th Century Art, Metro Museum of Art, New York, NY, 10028.

SIMS, ROBERT CARL
PERSONAL Born 12/26/1936, Ft Gibson, OK, m, 1963, 3 children **DISCIPLINE** UNITED STATES HISTORY **EDUCATION** Northeastern Okla State Col, BA, 63; Univ Okla, MA, 65; Univ Colo, PhD(hist), 70. **CAREER** Assoc prof, 70-80, PROF HIST, BOISE STATE UNIV, 80-, Nat Endowment for Humanities fel race & ethnicity, Columbia Univ, 77-78. **MEMBERSHIPS** AHA; Orgn Am Historians. **RESEARCH** Japanese-Americans; Idaho and Pacific Northwest history; United States economic history. **SELECTED PUBLICATIONS** Auth, In Mountain Shadows - A History Of Idaho - Schwantes,Ca/, Ore Hist Quart, Vol 0096, 1995; Jewel Of The Desert - Japanese-Am Internment At Topaz - Taylor,Sc/, Int Hist Rev, Vol 0017, 1995. **CONTACT ADDRESS** Dept of Hist, Boise State Univ, 1910 University Dr, Boise, ID, 83725-0399.

SINCLAIR, MICHAEL LOY
PERSONAL Born 08/13/1939, Hendersonville, NC, m, 1961, 1 child **DISCIPLINE** MODERN CHINA, CHINA AND THE WEST **EDUCATION** Wake Forest Univ, BA, 63; Stanford Univ, AM, 65, PhD, 73. **CAREER** Instr, 68-73, asst prof, 73-76, assoc prof, 76-84, prof horf hist, Wake Forest Univ, 84-; Woodrow Wilson Fel, 63, Ford Found East Asian Studies Fel,

66-68. **MEMBERSHIPS** Asn Asian Studies. **RESEARCH** China and the West; the French settlement of Shanghai; Sino-French War 1883-85; computers in historical research. **SELECTED PUBLICATIONS** Auth, Through the Bamboo Curtain: Changing European conceptions of China from Marco Polo to the present, In: Asian Studies III, 78; How China Sees the World, In: China: The Challenge of the '80s, Charlotte, NC, 80. **CONTACT ADDRESS** Dept of Hist, Wake Forest Univ, Box 7806, Winston Salem, NC, 27109-7806. **EMAIL** sinclair@wfu.edu

SINGAL, DANIEL JOSEPH
PERSONAL Born 11/17/1944, Boston, MA, m, 1969, 2 children **DISCIPLINE** AMERICAN INTELLECTUAL HISTORY **EDUCATION** Harvard Col, BA, 66; Columbia Univ, MA, 67, PhD(hist), 76. **CAREER** Mellon fel hist, Tulane Univ, 77-79, asst prof, 79-80; ASST PROF HIST, HOBART & WILLIAM SMITH COL, 80-; NIMH fel social hist, Columbia Univ, 66-70. **HONORS AND AWARDS** Charles W Ramsdell Award, 81. **MEMBERSHIPS** Orgn Am Historians; Am Studies Asn. **RESEARCH** Intellectual and cultural history of the South; American historiography; American political thought. **SELECTED PUBLICATIONS** Auth, Ulrich B Phillips: The Old South as the New, J Am Hist, 3/77; Broadus Mitchell and the Persistence of New South Thought, J Southern Hist, 8/79; The War Within: From Victorian to Modernist Thought in the South, Univ NC Press, 82; William Faulkner: The Making of a Modernist, Univ NC Press, 10/97. **CONTACT ADDRESS** Dept of History, Hobart & William Smith Cols, 300 Pulteney St, Geneva, NY, 14456-3382. **EMAIL** singal@hws.edu

SINGELIS, T.M.
PERSONAL Born 06/29/1949, Warren, OH, s **DISCIPLINE** PSYCHOLOGY **EDUCATION** Yale Univ, BA Psychology, 71; Univ Hawaii, MA, 92; Univ Hawaii, PhD, 95 **CAREER** Assoc prof, California State Univ, Chico, 95-98 **MEMBERSHIPS** Intl Assoc for Cross-Cult Psychol; Intl Communication Assoc **RESEARCH** Cultural Influences on Self; Intercultural Communication **SELECTED PUBLICATIONS** Coauth, "Unpackaging culture's influence on self-esteem and embarrassability: The role of self-construals," Jrnl Cross-Cultural Psychol; auth, Teaching about culture, ethnicity, and diversity: Exercises and planned activities," Sage; auth, "The context of intergroup communication," Jrnl Lang Soc Psychol, 96 **CONTACT ADDRESS** Dept Psychol, California State Univ, Chico, Chico, CA, 95929. **EMAIL** tcds@ecst.csuchico.edu

SINGER, DAVID G.
PERSONAL Born 04/23/1932, Cleveland, OH, m, 1975, 2 children **DISCIPLINE** UNITED STATES HISTORY **EDUCATION** Loyola Univ of Chicago, PhD, 73. **CAREER** Instr, hist, Spertus Inst of Judaica, De Vry Tech Inst; instr, ESL, CRT Tech Inst, De Vry Tech Inst. **HONORS AND AWARDS** Teaching fel, Loyola Univ of Chicago. **MEMBERSHIPS** Midwest Jewish Stud Asn; National and Illinois Teachers of Eng as a Second Lang. **RESEARCH** Judaism, Amer Jewish Hist. **SELECTED PUBLICATIONS** Auth, From St. Paul's Abrogation of the Old Covenant to Hitler's War Against the Jews, Anti-Semitism in American History, Urbana, 87. **CONTACT ADDRESS** 6749 Drake, Lincolnwood, IL, 60645.

SINGER, JOEL DAVID
PERSONAL Born 12/07/1925, New York, NY, m, 1991, 2 children **DISCIPLINE** POLITICAL SCIENCE **EDUCATION** BA, Duke Univ, 46; PhD, NY Univ, 56; Dr of Laws,(Hon), NW Univ, 83. **CAREER** NY Univ, Inst, 54-55; Vassar Coll, Inst, 55-57; Univ MI, Mental Health Res Inst, Sr Sc, 61-83; Univ of Oslo, Inst for Soc Res, Fullbright Fellow, 63-64; Univ MI, Assoc Prof, 65-65; Prof of Political Sci, 65-; Carnegie Endowment and Grad Inst of Intl Studies, Geneva, 67-68; ZUMA and the Univ of Mannheim, W Germany, 67-68; Graduate Inst of Intl Studies, Geneva, 83-84; Netherlands Inst for Advanced Studies, Wassenaar, 84; Intl Inst for Peace, Vienna; Polemological Inst, Univ of Groningen, 91-. **HONORS AND AWARDS** Fird Fekkiw Iowa Seninar in Intl Relations, 56; Ford Found Training Grant, Harvard Univ, 57-58; Fullbright Res Scholar, Univ of Oslo, 63-64; Natl Sci Found Res Grant, 78-83; Phoenix Memorial Fund Res Grant, 81-82; World Soc Found Res Grant, 88-90; Lifetime Achievement Award, APSA Conflict Process Section, 90; Natl Sci Found Res Grant, 92-94; Chair Helen Dwight Reid Award Comm APSA, 95-96. **SELECTED PUBLICATIONS** Peace in the Global System: Displacement,Interregnum or Transformation?, in Kegley; ed, The Long Post-War Peace, NY Harper Collins, pp56-84, 91; Toward a Behavioral Science of World Politics, in Jessor; ed, Perspectives on Behavioral Science: The Colorado Lectures, Boulder CO Westview Press, pp131-147 91; Nuclear Confrontation: Ambivalence, Rationality and the Doomsday Machine, in Bornschier and Lengyes; Formations and Values in the World System: World Society Studies, New Brunswick NJ, Transaction Publ, pp257-281, 92; Conflict Research, the Security Divemma and Learning from History, in Behavior, Culture and Conflict in World Politics, William Zimmerman and Harold K. Jacobson, Univ MI Press, pp79-92, 93; Early Warning Indicators for Cultural Groups in Danger, Journal of Ethno-Development, pp105-110, 94; Armed Conflict in the Former-Colonial Regions: From Classification to Explanation, in van der Goor et al, ed Between Development and Destruction, pp35-49, NY St Martins, 96. **CONTACT ADDRESS** Dept of Political Sci, Univ of MI, Ann Arbor, MI, 49109. **EMAIL** jdsinger@umich.edu

SINGER, MARTIN
DISCIPLINE HISTORY OF EAST ASIA **EDUCATION** Hunter Col, BA; Univ Mich, MA, PhD. **CAREER** Assoc prof; dept ch, 94-97; dean, Fac Arts and Sci, 97. **HONORS AND AWARDS** Ass provost, 77-80; provost, 80-85; founding dir, Concordia Univ Coun Intl Coop, 86-89. **RESEARCH** China and Japan. **SELECTED PUBLICATIONS** Auth, Educated Youth and the Cultural Revolution in China, 71; The Revolutionization of Youth in The People's Republic of China, 77; Canadian Academic Relations with the People's Republic of China Since 1970, 2 vol(s), 86; China's Academic Relations With Canada: Past, Present and Future, 92; Academic Relations Between Canada and China, 1970-1995, 96. **CONTACT ADDRESS** Dept of Hist, Concordia Univ, Montreal, 1455 de Maisonneuve W, Montreal, PQ, H3G 1M8. **EMAIL** msinger@vax2.concordia.ca

SINGER, WENDY F.
DISCIPLINE SOUTH ASIAN HISTORY **EDUCATION** Univ Va, BA, 82; MA,84; PhD, 91. **CAREER** Assoc prof, Kenyon Coll; dir of International Studies. **HONORS AND AWARDS** Fel, A. N. Sinha Institute, India, 86; NEH travel grant, 93; Fulbright Fac Res Abroad, 95-96; Visiting Res, Moscow, 94; PEW Grant, 94. **RESEARCH** British imperialism, oral history methodology. **SELECTED PUBLICATIONS** Auth, Creating History: Oral Narrative and Political Resistance, Oxford Univ Press, 97; Indian Peasants and the Communist International International Communism and the Communist International, Manchester Univ Press, 97; In Pursuit of Dignity, Jour of Women's Hist, 96; rev, Eldrid Mageli, Organizing Women's Protest; A Study of Political Styles in Two South Indian Activist Groups, Curzon Press, 97. **CONTACT ADDRESS** Dept of Hist, Kenyon Col, Gambier, OH, 43022. **EMAIL** singerw@kenyon.edu

SINGLETON, GREGORY HOLMES
PERSONAL Born 10/04/1940, Florence, AL, m, 1995 **DISCIPLINE** AMERICAN HISTORY **EDUCATION** San Fernando Valley State Col, BA, 67; Univ CA, Los Angeles, PhD, 76. **CAREER** Instr hist, Northwestern Univ, 70-72; from Asst Prof to Assoc Prof, 72-83, prof hist, Northeastern IL Univ, 83. **HONORS AND AWARDS** Fel, Univ Chicago, 77; sr res fel, Inst for Advan Study Relig, Divinity Sch, Univ Chicago, 81-82. **MEMBERSHIPS** AHA; Orgn Am Historians; Am Studies Asn; Am Soc Church Hist. **RESEARCH** Am cult hist Am soc hist; hist of Christianity. **SELECTED PUBLICATIONS** Auth, Mere middle-class institutions: Urban protestantism in nineteenth century America, J Social Hist, summer 73; The genesis of suburbia: A complex of historical trends, In; The Urbanization of the Suburbs, Sage, 73; Fundamentalism and urbanization; a quantitative critique of impressionist interpretation, In; The New Urban History, Princeton, 75; Protestant voluntary associations and the shaping of Victorian America, Am Quart, winter 76; Popular culture or the culture of the populace?, J Popular Cult, summer 77; Religion in the City of Angels: American Protestant Culture and Urbanization, Los Angeles 1850-1930, UMI, Studies in Am Hist and Culture 2, 79; Ecumenism Revisited: Eulogy for the '60s, Ekklesia, Spring 97. **CONTACT ADDRESS** Dept of Hist, Northeastern Illinois Univ, 5500 N St Louis Ave, Chicago, IL, 60625-4625. **EMAIL** g-singleton@neiu.edu

SINKLER, GEORGE
PERSONAL Born 12/22/1927, Charleston, SC, m, 1949 **DISCIPLINE** HISTORY **EDUCATION** Augustana Coll (RI, IL), AB 1953; Columbia Univ (Tchrs), MA 1954; Columbia Univ (Tchrs), Ed D (History) 1966. **CAREER** Bluefield State Coll, instr 1954-55; Prairie View A&M Coll, instr assoc prof 1955-65; Morgan State Univ, prof history 1965-88, PROFESSOR EMERITUS, HISTORY. **HONORS AND AWARDS** Phi Beta Kappa, Phi Alpha Theta, Kappa Delta Augustiana Coll 1953; Mr Friednship 1953; Augustana Grad Flwshp 1953; Post Doctoral Flw Johns Hopkins Univ 1972-73; NEH Summer Stipend for Coll Tchrs 1980; John Hay Whitney Opportunity Fellow, 1958; Southern Fellowship Fund Grant 1957; Danforth Fellowships 1961, 1964. **MEMBERSHIPS** Visiting prof Jackson State Coll 1969; visiting prof Amherst 1969, Baltimore Comm Coll 1972, Frostburg State Univ 1969, Youngstown State Univ 1969, Univ of NE (Omaha) 1971, Catonsville Comm Coll 1971; mem Govans United Meth Church 1967-; cncl mem Govans Comm 1967-79; mem York Road Plng Comm 1967; Amer Hist Assoc; Orgn of Amer Historians. **SELECTED PUBLICATIONS** Racial Attitudes of Amer Pres, Doubleday 1971; articles in OH Hist, Vol 77 1968; IN Magazine of Hist Vol 65 1969; newspapers Afro-Amer Baltimore 1972; Amsterdam News 1976; "What History Tells Us About Presidents and Race" Afro-American Feb 19, 1972; "Blacks and American Presidents" New York Amsterdam News Summer 1976.

SINNETTE, ELINOR DESVERNEY
PERSONAL Born 10/08/1925, New York, NY, m, 1949 **DISCIPLINE** AFRICAN-AMERICAN STUDIES **EDUCATION** Hunter Coll of the City Univ of New York, AB, 1947; Pratt Inst School of Library Serv, MLS, 1959; Columbia Univ School of Library Serv, DLS, 1977. **CAREER** The New York City Public Library, New York NY, librarian, 1947-54; New York City Bd of Educ, New York NY, school librarian, 1960-65; Inst of African Studies, Univ of Ibadan, Nigeria, lecturer, Institute of Librarianship, 1965-69; Ahmadu Bello Univ, Zaria, Nigeria, lecturer, 1969-70; MOORLAND-SPRINGAN RESEARCH CENTER, HOWARD UNIV, 1980-. **HONORS AND AWARDS** Distinguished Service Award, 92nd Infantry Div, World War II Assn, 1986; The Forrest C Pogue Award for Significant Contributions to Oral History, OHMAR, 1991; The BCALA Professional Achievement Award, 1992; **MEMBERSHIPS** Life mem, The Oral History Assn, Oral History Middle Atlantic Region, mem, Black Caucus of the American Library Assn. **SELECTED PUBLICATIONS** Author of "Arthur Alfonso Schomburg, Black Bibliophile and Collector, A Biography," The New York Public Library and Wayne State Univ Press, Detroit MI, 1989; editor "Black Bibliophiles and Collectors; Preservers of Black History," Wash, DC, Howard University Press, 1990.

SIPORIN, STEVE
DISCIPLINE ENGLISH; HISTORY **EDUCATION** Stanford Univ, BA, 69; Univ Ore, MA, 74; Ind Univ, PhD, 82. **CAREER** Lectr, Ind Univ, 76; folklore consult to Iowa Arts Coun, 77-78; folk arts coordr, Ore Arts Comn, 80-81; folk arts coordr, Idaho Comn on the Arts, 82-86; from asst prof to assoc prof, Utah State Univ, 90-. **HONORS AND AWARDS** Fulbright Lectureship, Portugal, 92-93; Hon. Mention, Giuseppe Pitre Internat Folklore Prize. **MEMBERSHIPS** Int Soc for Folk Narrative Res; Am Folklore Soc; Folklore Soc Utah; Int Conf Group on Portugal. **SELECTED PUBLICATIONS** Auth, We Came To Where We Were Supposed To Be: Folk Art of Idaho, 84; Our Way of Life Was Very Clear, Northwest Folklore 8, 90; The Fruit Jobber's Tales, Int Folklore Rev 7, 90; Immigrant and Ethnic Family Folklore, Western States Jewish Hist 22, 90; A Jew Among Mormons, Dialogue: A J of Mormon Thought 24, 91; Public Folklore: A Bibliographic Introduction, Public Folklore, Wash., D.C.: Smithsonian Inst. Press, 92; Folklife and Survival: The Italian- Americans of Carbon County, Utah, Old Ties, New Attachments: Italian-American Folklife in the West, Wash., D.C.: Libr. Of Congress, 92; American Folk Masters: The National Heritage Fellows, 92; The Sephardim: Field Report From Portugal, Jewish Folklore and Ethnology Review 15, 93; Memories of Jewish Life, New Horizons in Sephardic Studies, Albany: State Univ of NY Press, 93; From Kashrut to Cucina Ebraica: The Recasting of Italian Jewish Foodways, Jour of Am Folklore 107, 94; Halloween Pranks: Just a Little Inconvenience, Halloween and Other Festivals of Death and Life, Knoxville: Univ of Tenn. Press, 94; National Heritage Fellows, Am Folklore: An Encyclopedia, New York: Garland, 96. **CONTACT ADDRESS** Dept of English, Utah State Univ, Logan, UT, 84322-3200. **EMAIL** siporin@cc.usu.edu

SIRACUSA, JOSEPH M.
PERSONAL Born 07/06/1944, Chicago, IL, m, 1 child **DISCIPLINE** HISTORY **EDUCATION** Univ Denver, BA, 66, MA, 68; Univ Colo, Boulder, PhD(hist), 71. **CAREER** Instr hist, Univ Colo, Boulder, 69-71; mem exec training prog, Merrill Lynch, Pierce, Fenner & Smith, Inc, 72-73; lectr, 73-75, sr lectr, 76-80, READER AM DIPLOMATIC HIST, UNIV QUEENSLAND, 80-, Univ Queensland res grant, 73-82; Australian Govt res grants, 75 & 76; Harry S Truman Libr Inst grant-in-aid, 75 & 77; act ed, Australian J Polit & Hist, 76-77, assoc ed, 77-. **MEMBERSHIPS** AHA; Organ Am Historians; Soc Historians of Am Foreign Rels; Australian Inst Int Affairs; Asn Contemporary Historians. **SELECTED PUBLICATIONS** Auth, Problems In Australian Foreign-Policy, January-July 1994/, Australian J Of Politics And Hist, Vol 0040, 1994; Independence And Foreign-Policy - New-Zealand And The World Since 1935 - Mckinnon,M/, AmHist Rev, Vol 0099, 1994; Evatt - A Life - Crockett,P/, Am Hist Rev, Vol 0100, 1995; Determinism And Am Foreign-Relations During The Roosevelt,Franklin,D. Era - Cole,Ws/, J Of Am Hist, Vol 0083, 1997. **CONTACT ADDRESS** Dept of Hist, Univ of Queensland, St Lucia 4067, Queensland, ..

SIRAISI, NANCY GILLIAN
PERSONAL Born 07/06/1932, Catterick, England, 2 children **DISCIPLINE** MEDIEVAL HISTORY **EDUCATION** Oxford Univ, BA, 53, MA, 58; City Univ New York, PhD(medieval hist), 70. **CAREER** Asst prof, 70-75, assoc prof, 70-79, PROF HIST, HUNTER COL, 80- **MEMBERSHIPS** Mediaeval Acad Am; Hist Sci Soc; AHA; Renaissance Soc Am; Am Asn Hist Med. **RESEARCH** Intellectual history; the universities; science and medicine. **SELECTED PUBLICATIONS** Auth, Botany In Medieval And Renaissance Univs - Reeds,Km/, Renaissance Quart, Vol 0046, 1993; Masters Of Med And Arts At The Univ-Of-Ferrara, 1391-1950 - Italian - Raspadori,F/, Isis, Vol 0084, 1993; Med And The 5 Senses - Bynum,Wf, Porter,R/, Soc Hist Of Med, Vol 0007, 1994; The Med Consilia - Fr - Agrimi,J, Crisciani,C, Viola,C/, Isis, Vol 0086, 1995; The Codices Of Campagna,Bernardo - Philos And Med In The Late 1300s - Italian - Caroti,S/, Isis, Vol 0086, 1995; Early Anatomy

In Comparative Perspective - Introd/, J Of The Hist Of Med And Allied Sciences, Vol 0050, 1995; Vesalius And The Reading Of Galen Teleology + An Examination Of The Philos And Cult Influences Of Classical Literature On Renaissance Representations Of The Human-Body And On The History Of Anatomical Studies/, Renaissance Quart, Vol 0050; Gehennical Fire - The Lives Of Starkey,George, An Am Alchemist In The Scientific Revolution - Newman,Wr/, Renaissance Quart, Vol 0050, 1997. **CONTACT ADDRESS** Dept Hist, Hunter Col, CUNY, 695 Park Ave, New York, NY, 10021-5085.

SIRHANDI, MARCELLA
DISCIPLINE CONTEMPORARY AND 20TH CENTURY SOUTH ASIAN ART **EDUCATION** Ohio State Univ, PhD, 95. **CAREER** Engl, Okla St Univ. **SELECTED PUBLICATIONS** Auth, Contemporary Painting in Pakistan, 92. **CONTACT ADDRESS** Oklahoma State Univ, 101 Whitehurst Hall, Stillwater, OK, 74078.

SIRRIDGE, MARY
DISCIPLINE ANCIENT AND MEDIEVAL PHILOSOPHY, PHILOSOPHY OF ART **EDUCATION** St Mary's Col, Notre Dame, BA, 67; Ohio State Univ, MA, PhD, 72. **CAREER** Prof, La State Univ. **RESEARCH** Philosophy of language in ancient and medieval thought. **SELECTED PUBLICATIONS** Auth, Donkeys, Stars and Illocutionary Acts, J of Aesthet and Art Criticism; The Moral of the Story: Exemplification and the Literary Work, The Brit J of Aesthet; Can Est' Be Used Impersonality?, in Sophisms in Medieval Logic and Grammar. **CONTACT ADDRESS** Dept of Philos and Relig Stud, Louisiana State Univ, 106 Coates Hall, Baton Rouge, LA, 70803.

SISHAGNE, SHUMET
PERSONAL Born 01/20/1950, Ethiopia, m, 1980, 1 child **DISCIPLINE** HISTORY **EDUCATION** Harile Selassie Univ, BA, 73; Addis Ababa Univ, MA, 84; Univ Ill, PhD, 91. **CAREER** Lect, Addis Ababa Univ, 84-86; from asst prof to assoc prof, 91-, Christopher Newport Univ. **HONORS AND AWARDS** Swedish Agency for Res Cooperation with the Developing Countries; Instituto Italo-Africano; Arms Control; Disarmament and Int Security; MacArthur Fel. **MEMBERSHIPS** Asn Third World Stud; Asn Am Univ Prof. **RESEARCH** Modern Ethiopia **SELECTED PUBLICATIONS** Auth, Remembering a Glorious but Incomplete Victory: Adwa; auth, Accumulation of Land in Northern Ethiopia; auth, Ethiopia Irredentism in Ethiopia. **CONTACT ADDRESS** Dept of History, Christopher Newport Univ, Newport News, VA, 23606. **EMAIL** sishagne@cnu.edu

SITKOFF, HARVARD
DISCIPLINE HISTORY **EDUCATION** Columbia Univ, PhD. **CAREER** Prof, Univ NH, 76. **HONORS AND AWARDS** Charles Warren Ctr fel, Harvard Univ; Mary Ball Washinton Prof Am Hist in Ireland; NEH fel; Allen Nevins Award, Columbia Univ; John Adams Prof Am Civilization in the Neth; Nat Fac of Hum, Arts and Sci; Rutgers Ctr for Hist Anal Scholar-in-Residence; Fletcher M Green Award, Southern Hist Asn; Robert Starobin Mem fel. **RESEARCH** Race riots of the 1960s. **SELECTED PUBLICATIONS** Auth, A New Deal for Blacks, 78; The Struggle for Black Equality, 81, 93; Fifty Years later: The New Deal Evaluated, 85; coauth, The Enduring Vision: A History of the American People, 90, 92, 96; ed, A History of Our Time, 82, 87, 91,95. **CONTACT ADDRESS** Univ NH, Durham, NH, 03824. **EMAIL** his@christa.unh.edu

SIVIN, NATHAN
PERSONAL Born 05/11/1931, Clarksburg, WV, m, 1962 **DISCIPLINE** HISTORY OF SCIENCE, CHINESE HISTORY **EDUCATION** Mass Inst Technol, BS, 58; Harvard Univ, AM, 60, PhD(hist of sci), 66. **CAREER** Vis lectr, Univ Singapore, 62-63; instr humanities, Mass Inst Technol, 64-65, from asst prof to assoc prof hist sci, 66-73, prof hist of sci & Chinese cult, 73-77; PROF CHINESE CULT & HIST OF SCI, UNIV PA, 77-, Nat Sci Found res grant, 67-70 & 79-81; res assoc, Res Inst Humanistic Studies, Kyoto Univ, 67-68 & 71-72, vis prof, 74 & 79-80; Guggenheim Found fel, 71-72; ed & publ, Chinese Sci, 75; gen ed, Science, Medicine & Technology in East Asia, monogr series, Univ Mich, 80. **HONORS AND AWARDS** MA, Univ Pa, 78. **MEMBERSHIPS** Fel Am Acad Arts & Sci; Hist Sci Soc; Am Soc Study Relig; corresp mem Int Acad Hist Sci. **RESEARCH** Traditional Chinese science. **SELECTED PUBLICATIONS** Auth, The Discourse Of Race In Modern China - Dikotter,F/, Soc His Of Med, Vol 0006, 1993; State, Cosmos, And Body In The Last 3-Centuries-Bc/, Harvard J Of Asiatic Studies, Vol 0055, 1995; Divination, Mythology And Monarchy In Han China - Loewe,M/, J Of Interdisciplinary Hist, Vol 0027, 1996. **CONTACT ADDRESS** Dept of Orient Studies/CU, Univ Pa, Philadelphia, PA, 19174.

SIZEMORE, BARBARA A.
PERSONAL Born 12/17/1927, Chicago, Illinois **DISCIPLINE** EDUCATION **EDUCATION** Northwestern Univ Evanston IL, BA 1947, MA 1954; Univ of Chicago IL, PhD 1979. **CAREER** Chicago Pub Schl Chicago IL, tchr, elem prin, hs prin dir of Woodlawn Exper Schl Proj 1947-72; Amer Assc of Schl Admin, assc sec 1972-73; Washington DC, supt of schls 1973-75; Univ of Pittsburgh, assc prof 1977-89, prof, 1989-92; DePaul University, School of Education, dean, 1992-98, prof emerita, 1998-. **HONORS AND AWARDS** Honorary Doctor of Letters Central State Univ 1974; Honorary Doctor of Laws DE State Coll 1974; Honorary Doctor of Humane Letters Baltimore Coll of the Bible 1974; Honorary Doctor of Pedagogy, Niagara Univ, 1994; Northwestern Univ Merit Alumni Awd 1974; United Nations Assoc of Pittsburgh Human Rights Awd 1985; Racial Justice Awd, YWCA, 1995; The Ruptured Diamond: The Politics of the Decentralization of the DC Public Schools, Lanham, MD: Univ Press of America, l981. **MEMBERSHIPS** Consult, Chicago Public Schools, 1992-; University of Alabama at Birmingham AL, 1992-; mem Delta Sigma Theta; Natl Alliance of Black Schl Educ; bd mem Journal of Negro Educ 1974-83. **CONTACT ADDRESS** School of Education, DePaul Univ, Chicago, IL, 60614.

SKAGGS, DAVID CURTIS
PERSONAL Born 03/23/1937, Topeka, KS, m, 1961, 2 children **DISCIPLINE** HISTORY **EDUCATION** Univ Kansas, BSEd, 59, MA, 60; Georgetown Univ, PhD, 66. **CAREER** Instr to prof hist, 65-98; prof emer, 98-; vis prof mil hist & strategy, Air War Col, Maxwell AFB, 90-91, 95-96. **HONORS AND AWARDS** William C Foster vis fel, US Arms Control & Disarmament Agency, 85-86. **MEMBERSHIPS** Orgn Am Hist, Soc for Mil Hist, Assoc Inst Early Am Hist & Culture, Soc for Hist of the Early Am Republic. **RESEARCH** Colonial Brit Am & Early US; Am mil hist. **SELECTED PUBLICATIONS** Author, Roots of Maryland Democracy, 1753-1776, Greenwood, 73; co-author, A Signal Victory: The Lake Erie Campaign, 1812-1813, Naval Inst Press, 97; co-ed, Johann Ewald's Treatise on Partisan Warfare, Greenwood, 91; ed, The Poetic Writings of Thomas Cradock, 1718-1770, Univ Del Press, 83. **CONTACT ADDRESS** Dept of History, Bowling Green State Univ, Bowling Green, OH, 43403-0220. **EMAIL** dskaggs@bgnet.bgsu.edu

SKAGGS, JIMMY M.
PERSONAL Born 06/13/1940, Gorman, TX, 3 children **DISCIPLINE** AMERICAN STUDIES, ECONOMICS **EDUCATION** Sul Ross State Col, Tex, BS, 62; Tex Tech Univ, MA, 65, PhD(hist), 70. **CAREER** From asst prof to assoc prof econ, 70-77, assoc prof Am studies, 75-77, CHMN DPET AM STUDIES, WICHITA STATE UNIV, 75-, PROF AM STUDIES & ECON, 77- **MEMBERSHIPS** Southwestern Soc Sci Asn; Mid-Continent Am Studies Asn. **SELECTED PUBLICATIONS** Auth, Chisholm,Jesse - Ambassador Of The Plains - Hoig,S/, J Of The W, Vol 0032, 1993; The Frontier World Of Fort-Griffin - The Life And Death Of A Western Town - Robinson,C/, Pac Hist Rev, Vol 0062, 1993; Tex Crossings - The Lone Star State And The Am Far W, 1836-1986 - Lamar,Hr/, Pac Hist Rev, Vol 0062, 1993; Imagining Development - Economic Ideas In Peru Fictitious Prosperity Of Guano, 1840-1880 - Gootenberg,P/, Agricultural Hist, Vol 0069, 1995. **CONTACT ADDRESS** Dept of Am Studies, Wichita State Univ, Wichita, KS, 67208.

SKALITZKY, RACHEL IRENE
PERSONAL Born 02/07/1937, Waterloo, WI **DISCIPLINE** COMPARATIVE LITERATURE, MEDIEVAL STUDIES **EDUCATION** Mt Mary Col, BA, 62; Fordham Univ, MA, 66, PhD(class lang & lit), 68. **CAREER** Teacher 6th grade, St Boniface Sch, Milwaukee, 58-62; teacher Latin & music, St Anthony High Sch, Detroit, 62-63; instr classics, Mt Mary Col, 68-69, asst prof & chmn, 69-72; lectr classics, 72-73, asst prof, 73-76, Assoc Prof Comp Lit, Univ WI-Milwaukee, 76-, Coordr Women's Studies, 75-. **MEMBERSHIPS** Am Comp Lit Asn; Am Philol Asn; Nat Women's Studies Asn; MLA; Am Asn Univ Women. **RESEARCH** Classical philology; literary criticism; patristic lit. **SELECTED PUBLICATIONS** Auth, Good wine in a new vase, Horace, Epistles 1.2, Trans & Proc Am Philol Asn, 68; Annianus of Celeda: His Text of Chrysostom's Homilies on Matthew, Aevum, 71; Horace on travel, Epistles 1.11, Class J, 73; Plotinian Echoes in Peri Hypsous 7.2 and 9.7-10, Class Bull, 2/77. **CONTACT ADDRESS** Dept of Comp Lit, Univ of Wisconsin, Po Box 413, Milwaukee, WI, 53201-0413. **EMAIL** rachelsk@uwm.edu

SKEEN, CARL EDWARD
PERSONAL Born 07/28/1937, Williams Mountain, WV, m, 1961, 2 children **DISCIPLINE** EARLY AMERICAN HISTORY **EDUCATION** Ohio Univ, BS, 59; Ohio State Univ, MA, 60, PhD(hist), 66. **CAREER** Asst prof hist, Ohio State Univ, 66-67; asst prof, 68-75, assoc prof hist, Memphis State Univ, 75-81, prof, 81-, Nat Hist Publ Comn fel, Papers of John C Calhoun Proj, 67-68. **HONORS AND AWARDS** Distinguished Teaching Service Award, 83-84. **MEMBERSHIPS** Orgn Am Historians; Soc Historians Early Am Repub. **RESEARCH** Jeffersonian America; War of 1812 and War Department; era of good feelings. **SELECTED PUBLICATIONS** Auth, Calhoun, Crawford, and the Politics of Retrenchment, SC Hist Mag, 7/72; Monroe and Armstrong: A Study in Political Rivalry, New York Hist Soc Quart, 4/73; The Newburgh Addresses Reconsidered, William & Mary Quart, 4/74; Mr Madison's Secretary of War, Pa Mag of Hist & Biog, 7/76; The Year Without a Summer: A Historical View, J Early Repub, spring 81; John Armstrong, Jr, 1758-1843: A Biography, Syracuse Univ Press, 81; Vox Populi, Vox Dei: The Compensation Act of 1816 and the Rise of Popular Politics, J Early Repub, fall 86; A 'Bulwark of Liberty?' Militia Reform Proposals in the Early Republic, Valley Forge Journal, 12/90; An Uncertain 'Right": State Legislatures and the Doctrine of Instruction, Mid-America, 1/91; Citizen Soldiers in the War of 1812, Univ Press of Ky, 98. **CONTACT ADDRESS** Dept of Hist, Memphis State Univ, Campus Box 5261, Memphis, TN, 38152-6120. **EMAIL** ceskeen@memphis.edu

SKELNAR, ROBERT JOHN
PERSONAL Born 04/20/1963, Detroit, MI **DISCIPLINE** CLASSICS **EDUCATION** Univ Mich, BA, 85; Princeton Univ, MA, 88; Univ Mich, JD, 91, PhD, 96. **CAREER** Asst Inst, Princeton Univ, 87-88; tchg asst, 91-95; lect Class Studs, 96-97, Univ Mich; inst, Latin, The Emerson Sch, 96-97; Mellon postdoc fel, vis asst prof Classics, Swarthmore Col. **HONORS AND AWARDS** Phi Beta Kappa; Mellon Fellow Humanities; Mellon Diss Grant. **MEMBERSHIPS** Amer Philol Asn; Class Asn Middle West and South. **RESEARCH** Greek and Roman civilization, Greek Mythology. **SELECTED PUBLICATIONS** Auth, The Death of Priam: Aeneid 2.506-558, Hermes 118, 90, 67-75; Horace, Odes 1, 3, AC 60, 91, 266-269; Multiple Structural Divisions in Horace, Odes 1.38, pp 46, 91, 444-448; Rullus' Colonies: Cicero, De Lege Agraria 1.16-17 and 2.73-75, Eos 80, 92, 81-82; Recusatio and Praeteritio in American Judicial Rhetoric, Acta Univ Carolinae, 38, 92, 97-114; Charles Baudelaire: Meditation, The Formalist, 3,1,92; SEG XXXII 1243, 13-15, RhM 136, 93, 93-94; Rainer Maria Rilke: Autumn Day, The Formalist, 4,1, 93; Papinian on the Interdict unde vi, RiDA 41, 94, 379-389; Catullus 36: Beyond Literary Polemics, RBPh 74, 96, 57-59; The Centrality of the Civic Image in Droste's Mondesaufgang, Droste-Jahrbuch 3, 97, 127-134. **CONTACT ADDRESS** Dept of Classics, Swarthmore Col, Swarthmore, PA, 19081. **EMAIL** rsklenal@swarthmore.edu

SKELTON, WILLIAM B.
PERSONAL Born 05/14/1939, Syracuse, NY, m, 1968, 1 child **DISCIPLINE** MODERN HISTORY **EDUCATION** Bowdoin Col, BA, 61; Northwestern Univ, MA, 63, PhD, 68. **CAREER** Instr hist, Ohio State Univ, 65-69; assoc prof, 69-80, prof Us hist, Univ Wis-Stevens Point, 80-. **HONORS AND AWARDS** Soc Mil 1st Distinguished Book Award, 94. **MEMBERSHIPS** Orgn Am Historians; AHA. **RESEARCH** US hist, 19th century; soc hist US Army, 19th century. **SELECTED PUBLICATIONS** Auth, The commanding general and the problem of command in the US Army, 1821-1841, Mil Affairs, 12/70; Professionalization in the US Army Officer Corps during the Age of Jackson, Armed Forces & Soc, summer 75; Army officers' attitudes toward Indians, 1830-1860, Pacific Northwest Quart, 7/76; An American Profession of Arms: The Army Officer Corps, 1783-1861, 92; The Confederation's Regulars: A Social Profile of Enlisted Service in America's First Standing Army, William and Mary Quart, 89; High Army Leadership in the Era of the War of 1812: The Making and Reamking of the Officer Corps, William & Mary Quart, 94; Samuel P. Huntington and the Roots of the American Military Tradition, Jour Mil Hist, 96. **CONTACT ADDRESS** Dept of History, Univ of Wisconsin, 2100 Main St, Stevens Point, WI, 54481-3897. **EMAIL** wskelton@uwsp.edu

SKEMP, SHEILA LYNN
PERSONAL Born 08/21/1945, Melrose Park, IL **DISCIPLINE** AMERICAN HISTORY **EDUCATION** Univ MT, BA, 67; Univ IA, MA, 70, PhD, 74. **CAREER** Asst prof hist, Ripon Col, 75-76; asst prof, Western CT State Col, 77-79; asst prof, Univ IA, 79-80; asst prof hist, Univ MS, 80-88, assoc prof, Univ MS, 88-97, prof hist, Univ MS, 97-, Consult, Univ Mid-Am, 77. **HONORS AND AWARDS** Outstanding Tchr in Lib Art, Univ MS, 93; Mortar Board Outstanding Faculty Women, Univ MS, 97. **MEMBERSHIPS** Am Studies Asn; Southern Asn Women Historians. **RESEARCH** Am colonial puritanism; Am revolution-RI; 18th century Am, the growth of Southern nationalism. **SELECTED PUBLICATIONS** Auth, George Berkeley's Newport experience, RI Hist, 5/78; coed, Foundations of Am Nationalism, Univ Mid-Am Press, 78; Co-ed, Sex, Race, & the Role of Women in the South, Univ Press MS, 83; Co-ed, Race & Family in the South, Univ Press MS, 99; Auth, William Franklin: Son of a Patriot, Servant of a King, Oxford, 90; Auth, Benjamin & William Franklin: Patriot & Loyalist, Father & Son, Bedford Press, 94; Auth, Judith Sargent Murray: A Brief Biography with Documents, Bedford Press, 98. **CONTACT ADDRESS** Hist Dept, Univ of MS, General Delivery, Univ, MS, 38677-9999. **EMAIL** sskemp@olemiss.edu

SKLAR, KATHRYN K.
DISCIPLINE HISTORY **EDUCATION** Radcliffe/Harvard, BA, 65; Univ Mich, PhD, 69. **CAREER** Assoc prof, hist, Univ Calif Los Angeles; DIST PROF, HIST, State Univ NY, BINGHAMTON **MEMBERSHIPS** Am Antiquarian Soc **SELECTED PUBLICATIONS** Auth, Catherine Beecher: A Study in American Domesticity, 73; ed, Notes of Sixty Years: The Autobiography of Florence Kelley, 1859-1926, 85; auth, "The Greater Part of the Petitioners are Female: The Reduction by Statute of Women's Working Hours in the Paid Labor Force, 1840-1917," in The International History of the Shortening of the Work Day, Temple Univ Press, 88; auth, "Who Funded Hull

House?," in Lady Bountiful Revisited: Women, Philanthropy, and Power, Rutgers Univ Press, 90; co-ed, Women and Power in American History: A Reader, 2 vols., Prentice Hall, 91; co-ed & contrib, The Social Survey Movement in Historical Perspective, Cambridge Univ Press, 92; auth, "Coming to Terms with Florence Kelley: The Tale of a Reluctant Biographer," in The Challenge of Feminist Biography: Writing the Lives of Modern American Women, Univ Ill Press, 92; auth, "The Historical Foundations of Women's Power in the Creation of the American Welfare State, 1830-1930," in Mothers of a New World: Maternalist Politics and the Origins of Welfare States, Routledge, 93; auth, "The Schooling of Girls and Community Values In Massachusetts Towns, 1750-1820," Hist of Educ Quart, 94. **CONTACT ADDRESS** Dept of Hist, SUNY-Binghamton, Binghamton, NY, 13902. **EMAIL** kksklar@binghamton.edu

SKLAR, KATHRYN KISH
PERSONAL Born 12/16/1939, Columbus, OH, m, 2 children **DISCIPLINE** HISTORY **EDUCATION** Radcliffe Col, BA, 65; Univ Mich, PhD, 69. **CAREER** Asst prof, Univ Mich, 69-74; assoc prof, Univ Calif, Los Angeles, 74-81; prof hist, Univ Calif, LA, 81-88; DIST PROF HISTORY, SUNY, BINGHAMTON, 88-. **HONORS AND AWARDS** Berkshire Conf Book Prize, 74, 95; Asn Res on Nonprofit Orgs and Vol Action, Outstanding Contr award. **MEMBERSHIPS** Berkshire Conf Women Historians; Org Am Historians; AHA. **RESEARCH** Hist Am women and social movements. **SELECTED PUBLICATIONS** Co-ed, Social Justice Feminists in the United States and Germany: A Dialogue in Documents, 1885-1933, Cornell Univ Press, 98; auth, Florence Kelley and the Nation's Work: the Rise of Women's Political Culture, 1830-1900, Vol I, Yale Univ Press, 95; co-ed U.S. History as Women's History: New Feminist Essays, Univ NC Press, 95; auth, The Consumers' White Label of the National Consumers' League, 1898-1918, in Getting and Spending: American and European Consumption in the Twentieth Century, Cambridge Univ Press, 98; auth, Hull House Maps and Papers: Social Science as Women's Work in the 1890's, in The Social Survey Movement in Historical Perspective, Cambridge Univ Press, 92, reprint in Gender and American Social Science: The Formative Years, Princeton Univ Press, 98; auth, Women Who Speak for an Entire Nation: American and British Women Compared at the World Anti- Slavery Convention, London, 1840, in The Abolitionist Sisterhood: Women's Political Culture in Antebellum America, Cornell Univ Press, 94. **CONTACT ADDRESS** Dept of History, SUNY, Binghamton, Binghamton, NY, 13902. **EMAIL** kksklar@binghamton.edu

SKLAR, RICHARD LAWRENCE
PERSONAL Born 03/22/1930, New York, NY, m, 1992, 2 children **DISCIPLINE** POLITICAL SCIENCE **EDUCATION** Univ of Utah, AB, 52; Princeton Univ, MA, 57, PhD, 61. **CAREER** Asst prof, Brandeis Univ, 61-63; lectr, univ of Ibadan, 63-65; sr lectr, Univ of Zambia, 66-68; PROF, 69-94, PROF EMERITUS, UCLA, 94-. **HONORS AND AWARDS** Past pres, African Studies Asn, 81-82; UCLA Distinguished Teaching Award, 88. **MEMBERSHIPS** African Studies Asn; Am Political Sci Asn. **RESEARCH** Developmental democracy; postimperialism; politics in Africa. **SELECTED PUBLICATIONS** Auth, Nigerian Political Parties, 63, 83; auth, Corporate Power in an African State, 75; coauth, Postimperialism, 87; coauth, African Politics and Problems in Development, 91. **CONTACT ADDRESS** Dept of Political Sci, Univ of Calif, Los Angeles, CA, 90095-1472.

SKLAR, ROBERT ANTHONY
PERSONAL Born 12/03/1936, New Brunswick, NJ, m, 1958, 2 children **DISCIPLINE** CINEMA STUDIES, CULTURAL HISTORY **EDUCATION** Princeton Univ, AB, 58; Harvard Univ, PhD, 65. **CAREER** From asst prof to prof hist, Univ Mich, Ann Arbor, 65-76; PROF CINEMA STUDIES & CHMN DEPT, NY UNIV, 77-; Rackham fel, 67; Fulbright lectr, USEC, Japan, 71; distinguished vis prof, Bard Col, 75-76; Rockefeller Found humanities fel, 76-77; contribr ed, Am Film Mag, 77-. **HONORS AND AWARDS** Theatre Libr Asn Award, 75. **MEMBERSHIPS** Am Studies Asn (vpres, 71); Soc Cinema Studies; Nat Film Preserv Bd; New York Film Fest Selec Cmt; Mich Am Stu Asn; ed bd, Am Qrt. **RESEARCH** American movies and television; twentieth century American culture and society. **SELECTED PUBLICATIONS** Auth, F Scott Fitzgerald, Oxford Univ, 67; ed, The Plastic Age: 1917-1930, Braziller, 70; auth, Movie-Made America: A Cultural History of American Movies, Random House, 75; auth, Prime Time America: Life On and Behind the Television Screen, Random House, 82; co-ed, Resisting Images: Essays on Cinema and History, Temple Univ, 90; auth, City Boys: Cagney, Bogart, Garfield, Princeton Univ, 92; auth, Film: An International History of the Medium, Prentice Hall, 93; auth, Movie-Made AmericaL A Cultural History of American Movies, Vintage Bks, 94; co-ed, Frank Capra: Authorship and the Studio System, Temple Univ, 98. **CONTACT ADDRESS** Dept of Cinema Studies, New York Univ, 721 Broadway, Rm 600, New York, NY, 10003-6807. **EMAIL** rs9@is2.nyu.edu

SKOLNIKOFF, EUGENE B.
PERSONAL Born 08/29/1928, Philadelphia, PA, m, 1957, 2 children **DISCIPLINE** POLITICAL SCIENCE **EDUCATION** M.I.T., SM/SB, 50; Oxford, BA/MA, 52; M.I.T., Phd, 65 **CAREER** Prof, M.I.T., 65-; visiting lctr, Yale Univ, 97; visiting Res Scholar, Balliol Col, 89; dir, M.I.T. Center Intl Studies, 72-87; senior consultant, White House Office Sci & Tech, 77-81 **HONORS AND AWARDS** Rhodes Scholar; Rockefeller Found Scholar; Tau Beta Pi; Eta Kappa Nu; Sigma Xi; Amer Acad Arts Sci Fel; Amer Assoc Advancement Sci Fel; Carnegie Endowment Intl Peace; Commander's Cross of the Order of Merit of the Fed Repub Germany, 86; Order of the Rising Sun, Gold Rays, Neck Ribbon, Japanese Govt, 89 **MEMBERSHIPS** Amer Assoc Advan Sci; Amer Assoc Rhodes Scholars; Amer Pol Sci Assoc; Amer Acad Arts Sci; Amer Council Germany; Coun For Rel; Fed Amer Sci; Soc Social Studies Sci; United Nations Assoc; World Assoc Int Rel **RESEARCH** Science; Technology and International Affairs; Environment; Foreign Policy; Science Policy; International Organizations **SELECTED PUBLICATIONS** Coauth, The Implementation and Effectiveness of International Environmental Commitments: Theory and Practice, MIT, 98; auth, The Elusive Transformation: Science, Technology and the Evolution of International Politics, Princeton, 93; co-ed, Visions of Apocalypse: End or Rebirth?, Holmes & Meier, 85 **CONTACT ADDRESS** Building E53-473, Cambridge, MA, 02139.

SLAGLE, JUDITH BAILY
PERSONAL Born 11/20/1949, Kingsport, TN, m, 1969 **DISCIPLINE** CLASSICAL LITERATURE **EDUCATION** East Tenn State Univ, MA, 85; Univ Tenn, PhD, 91. **CAREER** Asst Prof, Middle Tenn State Univ, 93-97; Chr Humanities, Roane State Col, 97-. **HONORS AND AWARDS** Honorary Research Fel, Univ of Edinburgh Inst for Advanced Studies in the Humanities, 96. **MEMBERSHIPS** Amer Soc for Eighteenth Century Studies; Eighteenth Century Scottish Studies Soc. **RESEARCH** Thomas Shadwell (Restoration Dramatist); Joanna Baillie (Scottish playwright) **SELECTED PUBLICATIONS** Auth, The Collected Letters of Joanna Baillie, 99. **CONTACT ADDRESS** 907 Pintail Rd, Knoxville, TN, 37922. **EMAIL** slagle_jb@a1.rscc.cc.tn.us

SLANE, ANDREA
DISCIPLINE FILM HISTORY **EDUCATION** Rutgers Univ, BA; Univ Calif, PhD. **CAREER** Engl, Old Dominion Univ. **RESEARCH** Video and Multimedia. **SELECTED PUBLICATIONS** Area: Kinks in the System: Six Shorts About People Left to their own Devices; Six short videos on the human processing of information received by machines; Irresistible Impulse (feature length video); Research on images of fascism. **CONTACT ADDRESS** Old Dominion Univ, 4100 Powhatan Ave, Norfolk, VA, 23058. **EMAIL** ASlane@odu.edu

SLATE, PHILIP
DISCIPLINE EUROPEAN MISSIONS, COMMUNICATION, HISTORICAL MISSIOLOGY **EDUCATION** David Lipscomb Univ, BA, 57; Harding Grad Sch, MA, 61; Oxford Univ, England, 68-71, Fuller Theological Seminary , Dmiss, 76. **CAREER** Instr, Harding Grad Sch Rel, 72-93; prof, Missions and Homiletics; dean, 86-92; chm; prof, 93-. **MEMBERSHIPS** Mem, Am Soc Missiology; Evangelical Missiological Soc. **SELECTED PUBLICATIONS** Auth, Perspectives on Worldwide Evangelism, Resource Publ, 88; co-auth, Reaching Russia, ACU Press, 94; articles, Culture Concept and Hermeneutics: Quest to Identify the Permanent in Early Christianity. Encounter 53, 92; The Deceiving Nature of Adaptation in E-1 Situations, J Applied Missiology 3, 95; Two Features of Irenasus' Missiology. Missiology 23, 96; numerous articles. **CONTACT ADDRESS** Dept of Missions, Abilene Christian Univ, Abilene, TX, 79699-9000. **EMAIL** slate@bible.acu.edu

SLATER, PETER GREGG
PERSONAL Born 06/03/1940, New York, NY, m, 1963, 1 child **DISCIPLINE** AMERICAN SOCIAL & INTELLECTUAL HISTORY **EDUCATION** Cornell Univ, BA, 62; Brown Univ, MA, 65; Univ Calif, Berkeley, PhD(hist), 70. **CAREER** Actg instr hist, Univ Calif, Berkeley, 66-67; from instr to asst prof, Dartmouth Col, 68-77; assoc prof, 77-81, PROF HIST, MERCY COL, NY, 81-, Chmn Dept, 77-89, Special Asst to Provost, 93-94, DEAN, WHITE PLAINS CAMPUS, 94-. **HONORS AND AWARDS** Phi Beta Kapp, 62; Sears-Roebuck Fnd Teaching Excellence, 96; Mercy Col, 98. **MEMBERSHIPS** Am Studies Asn; Council Col Arts Scis White Plains Bus Dev Corp. **RESEARCH** Family history; cultural modernism. **SELECTED PUBLICATIONS** Auth, Ben Lindsey and the Denver Juvenile Court: A Progressive look at human nature, Am Quart, summer 68; Ethnicity in the Great Gatsby, Twentieth Century Lit, 1/73; Children in the New England Mind: In Death and in Life, Archon Bks, 77; From the cradle to the coffin: Patental bereavement and the shadow of infant damnation in Puritan society, Psychohistory Rev, Fall-winter 77-78; The negative secularism of the modern temper: Joseph Wood Krutch, Am Quart, summer 81; auth, The Egg, Modernsense, Spring-Summer, 84; auth, Joseph Wood Krutch, A Companion to American Thought, 95; High Wire column, White Plains Watch, 97-. **CONTACT ADDRESS** Mercy Col, 277 Martine Ave, White Plains, NY, 10601. **EMAIL** pslter@bestweb.net

SLATERY, WILLIAM PATRICK
PERSONAL Born 01/10/1943, Watts Bar Dam, TN, m, 1969, 2 children **DISCIPLINE** ART **EDUCATION** Univ Chattanooga, AB, 65; E Tenn St Univ, MA, 67 **CAREER** SR instr, art, 68-, Palm Beach Comm Col; adj art instr, 67-68, Univ Tenn, Chattanooga; profes News Photographer, 78-, Chattanooga Free Press; chmn, 78-, Town Council, Cloud Lake, FL. **RESEARCH** Computer graphics & Univ studio applications **CONTACT ADDRESS** PO Box 42, Lake Worth, FL, 33460. **EMAIL** slateryp@pbcc.cc.fl.us

SLATKIN, LAURA M.
DISCIPLINE CLASSICAL PHILOLOGY **EDUCATION** Radcliffe Col, BA, 68; Cambridge Univ, MA, 70; Harvard Univ, PhD, 79. **CAREER** Asst prof, Univ Calif, 76-80; Vis Asst Prof, Yale Univ, 80-81; Lectr, Columbia Univ, 81-83; Asst prof to Assoc prof, Columbia Univ, Colubia Univ, 83-90; Assoc prof, Univ Chicago, 93- . **HONORS AND AWARDS** NEH Fel; Columbia Univ Coun Res Hum Fel; Mellon Fel; ACLS Fel; Am Asn Univ Women Fel. **SELECTED PUBLICATIONS** Auth, Oedipus at Colonus: Exile and Integration, Univ Calif Press, 86; The Wrath of Thetis, TAPA, 86; Genre and Generation in the Odyssey, METIS, 87; Univ Calif Press, 92; auth, The Power of Thetis: Allusion and Interpretation in the Iliad, Univ Calif Press, 92; auth, Myth in Homer, Leiden, 95; Composition by Theme and the Metis of the Odyssey, Princeton Univ Press, 96; auth, the Poetics of Exchange in the Iliad, The Iliad and Its Contexts, 97; auth, Measure and mortality in Hesiod's Works and Days, Metis, 97. **CONTACT ADDRESS** Dept of Classics, Univ Chicago, 1050 E 59th St, Chicago, IL, 60637.

SLATTA, RICHARD WAYNE
PERSONAL Born 10/22/1947, Powers Lake, ND, m, 1982 **DISCIPLINE** LATIN AMERICAN HISTORY **EDUCATION** Pac Lutheran Univ, BA, 69; Portland State Univ, MA, 74; Univ Tex, Austin, PhD(hist), 80. **CAREER** Instr US hist, Concordia Lutheran Col, 75-76; instr hist, Univ Colo, Boulder, 79-80; ASST PROF HIST, NC STATE UNIV, 80-, Vis researcher, Inst Torcuato DiTella, Argentina, 77-78. **MEMBERSHIPS** AHA; Conf Latin Am Hist; Latin Am Studies Asn; Western Hist Asn. **RESEARCH** Horsemen of the Americas; comparative frontiers; banditry and crime in the Americas. **SELECTED PUBLICATIONS** Auth, Under Western Skies - Nature And Hist In The Am W - Worster,D/, Midwest Quart-A J Of Contemporary Thought, Vol 0034, 1993; Revolution And Restoration, The Rearrangement Of Power In Argentina, 1776-1860 - Szuchman,Md, Brown,Jc/, Hisp Am Hist Rev, Vol 0075, 1995; Cowboys And The Wild W - An A-Z Guide From The Chisholm-Trail To The Silver-Screen - Cusic,D/, Montana-The Mag Of Western Hist, Vol 0046, 1996; The Drifting Cowboy - James,W/, Great Plains Quart, Vol 0017, 1997; I See By Your Outfit - Hist Cowboy Gear Of The Northern Plains - Lindmier,T, Mount,S/, Great Plains Quart, Vol 0017, 1997; Heroes On Horseback - A Life And Times Of The Last Gaucho Caudillos - Chasteen,Jc/, Am Hist Rev, Vol 0102, 1997. **CONTACT ADDRESS** Hist Dept, No Carolina State Univ, Raleigh, NC, 27650.

SLAUGHTER, THOMAS PAUL
DISCIPLINE EARLY AMERICAN HISTORY **EDUCATION** Univ Md, BA, 76, MA, 78; Princeton Univ, MA, 80, PhD(hist), 82. **CAREER** ASST PROF HIST, RUTGERS UNIV, 82-, Fel, Am Bar Found, 82- **MEMBERSHIPS** Orgn Am Historians; Soc for Historians Early Am Repub. **RESEARCH** Whiskey rebellion; social banditry in the era of the American Revolution; the case of Aaron Burr. **SELECTED PUBLICATIONS** Auth, The Correspondence Of Bartram,John, 1734-1777 - Berkeley,E, Berkeley,Ds/, William And Mary Quart, Vol 0050, 1993; Bartram,William On The Southeastern Indians - Waselkov,Ga, Hollandbraund,Ke/, Penn Mag Of Hist And Biog, Vol 0120, 1996; Franklin,Benjamin And His Enemies - Middlekauff,R/, J Of Interdisciplinary Hist, Vol 0028, 1997. **CONTACT ADDRESS** Hist Dept, Rutgers Univ, P O Box 5059, New Brunswick, NJ, 08903-5059.

SLAVIN, ARTHUR J.
PERSONAL Born 02/15/1933, Brooklyn, NY **DISCIPLINE** ENGLISH HISTORY & HUMANITIES **EDUCATION** La State Univ, BA, 58; Univ NC, PhD, 61. **CAREER** Asst prof hist, Bucknell Univ, 61-65; from asst prof to prof, Univ Calif, Los Angeles, 65-73; prof & chmn dept, Univ Calif, Irvine, 73-74; dean col arts & sci, 74-77, JUSTUS BIER DISTINGUISHED PROF HUMANITIES & PROF HIST, UNIV LOUISVILLE, 77-, Guggenheim fel, 67-68; sr res fel, Fogler Libr, 70-71; Henry Huntington Libr res fel, 75; mem, Bd Consults, Nat Endowment Humanities, 76-; Clark lectr, William A Clark Libr, 77-78; distinguished lectr hist, Brigham Young Univ, 80; Nat Endowment for Humanities fel, 80-81; distinguished lectr, NC Asn Col Universities, 82. **MEMBERSHIPS** AHA; Conf Brit Studies; Medieval Acad Am; Am Soc Reformation Res; Renaissance Soc Am. **RESEARCH** Tudor England; The Holocaust and imaginative literature; literature, politics and modern culture. **SELECTED PUBLICATIONS** Auth, The Idea Of Hist In Early-Stuart Hist - Woolf,D/, Sixteenth Century J, Vol 0023, 1992; The Mental World Of The Jacobean Court - Peck,Ll/, J Of Interdisciplinary Hist, Vol 0023, 1993; Consilium-Et-Timor-Mortis + More,Thomas - On Speaking, Writing

And Silence In 'Utopia'/, Renaissance And Reformation, Vol 0016, 1993; The English - Elton,Gr/, Sixteenth Century J, Vol 0025, 1994; The Royal Palaces Of Tudor Eng - Architecture And Court Life 1460-1547 - Thurley,S/, Sixteenth Century J, Vol 0026, 1995; The Problem Of Ireland In Tudor Foreign-Policy, 1485-1603 - Palmer,W/, Am Hist Rev, Vol 0101, 1996. **CONTACT ADDRESS** 502 Club Lane, Louisville, KY, 40207.

SLAVIN, ROBERT EDWARD
PERSONAL Born 09/17/1950, Bethesda, MD, m, 1973, 3 children **DISCIPLINE** PSYCHOLOGY, SOCIAL RELATIONS **EDUCATION** Reed Coll, BA, Psychol, 72; Johns Hopkins Univ, PhD, 75. **CAREER** Student tchr, Soc Stud, Aloha High Sch, 70-71; tchr, Aloha Children's center, 72-73; assoc res sci, Center Social Org Schs, Johns Hopkins Univ, 75-78; res sci, 78-85; dir, elem Sch Prog, Center Res Elem & Middle Schs, Johns Hopkins Univ, 85-90; prin res sci, Center Res Effective Schooling for Disadvantaged Students, Johns Hopkins Univ, 89-94; PRIN RES SCI, CTR RES ON EDUC OF STUDENTS PLACED AT RISK, JOHNS HOPKINS UNIV, 94-; ch, Success for All Found, 97-. **MEMBERSHIPS** Am Educ Res Asn; Asn Supervision & Curric Dept; Int Asn Study of Coop in Educ **RESEARCH** School reform; Cooperative learning; Educational psychology; Research review; Students at risk. **SELECTED PUBLICATIONS** Co-edr, Preventing Early School Failure: Research , Policy, and Practice, Allyn & Bacon, 94; auth, Cooperative Learning: Theory, Research, and Practice, Allyne & Bacon, 95; coauth, Every Child, Every School: Success for All, Corwin, 96; auth, Education for All, Swets & Zeitlinger, 97; coauth, Show Me the Evidence: Proven and Promising Programs for Americas Schools, Corwin 98. **CONTACT ADDRESS** Ctr for Res on the Educ of Students Placed at Risk, Johns Hopkins Univ, 3003 N Charles St, Baltimore, MD, 21218. **EMAIL** bslavin@jhu.csos.edu

SLAVIN, STEPHEN L.
PERSONAL Born 07/29/1939, Brooklyn, NY **DISCIPLINE** ECONOMICS **EDUCATION** New York Univ, PhD 73. **CAREER** Dept Econ, Union Col **MEMBERSHIPS** AEA **SELECTED PUBLICATIONS** Auth, Chances Are: The Only Statistic Book You'll Ever Need, UP of Amer, 98; Math Essentials, Learning Express, Random House, 98; Math For Your First and Second Grader, Wiley, 95; Quick Business Math, Wiley, 95; Quick Algebra Review, with Peter Selby, Wiley, 92. **CONTACT ADDRESS** Dept of Economics, Union Col, 564 Marlborough RD, Brooklyn, NY, 11226.

SLAWEK, STEPHEN
DISCIPLINE MUSIC AND ASIAN STUDIES **EDUCATION** Univ IL at Urbana-Champaign, PhD. **CAREER** Assoc prof & div & head; Univ TX at Austin, 83-; dir, N Indian Class Music Ensemble. **RESEARCH** Musical traditions of South Asia. **SELECTED PUBLICATIONS** Auth, Sitar Technique in Nibaddh Forms, Delhi, Motilal Banarsidass, 87; coauth, Musical Instruments of North India: Eighteenth century Portraits by Baltazard Solvyns, Delhi, Manohar Publ, 97. **CONTACT ADDRESS** School of Music, Univ of Texas at Austin, 2613 Wichita St, Austin, TX, 78705.

SLIND, MARVIN G.
DISCIPLINE MODERN EUROPEAN, SCANDINAVIAN AND WORLD HISTORY **EDUCATION** Wash State Univ, PhD, 78. **CAREER** Asst prof, Washington State Univ. **SELECTED PUBLICATIONS** Coauth, Norse to the Palouse: Sagas of the Selbu Norwegians; co-ed, NAFSA's Guide to Education Abroad for Advisers and Administrators. **CONTACT ADDRESS** Dept of History, Washington State Univ, 301 Wilson Hall, PO Box 644030, Pullman, WA, 99164-4030. **EMAIL** slind@wsu.edu

SLOAN, DAVID
DISCIPLINE HISTORY **EDUCATION** Univ Calif Santa Barbara, PhD. **CAREER** Assoc prof. **RESEARCH** Colonial America; early national period. **SELECTED PUBLICATIONS** Auth, The Expedition of Hernando de Soto: A Post-Mortem Report, Part I, Ark Hist Quarterly, 92; The Expedition of Hernando de Soto: A Post-Mortem Report, Part II, Ark Hist Quaterly, 92. **CONTACT ADDRESS** History Dept, Univ of Arkansas, Fayetteville, 408 Old Main, Fayetteville, AR, 72701. **EMAIL** dsloan@comp.uark.edu

SLOAN, EDWARD WILLIAM
PERSONAL Born 10/19/1931, Cleveland, OH, m, 5 children **DISCIPLINE** HISTORY **EDUCATION** Yale Univ, BA 53, MA 54; Harvard Univ, MA 60, PhD 63. **CAREER** Trinity College, inst to Charles P. Northam Prof of Hist, 1963 to present. **HONORS AND AWARDS** Phi Beta Kappa. **MEMBERSHIPS** AHA; OAH; ASA; US Naval Inst; IMEHA; BHC; NASOH. **RESEARCH** Maritime and Naval Hist; Business and Entrepreneuria Hist; Hist of Technology. **SELECTED PUBLICATIONS** Auth, America and the Sea, coauth, Mystic CT, Mystic Seaport Press, 98; Glasgow's Response to New Yorks Challenge: The Cunard Steamship Persia Confronts America's Collins line in the Race for Transatlantic Supremacy, paper pres at Bus Hist Conf Glasgow, Scotland, 97; Diving in to History: Unraveling the Mystery of a Lost Transatlantic Liner, Conn Acad of Arts and Sciences, Hartford CT, 95; The Wreck of the Collins Liner Pacific: A Challenge for Maritime Historians and Nautical Archaeologists, Bermuda Jour of Archae and Maritime Hist, 93; The Nightingale and the Steamship: Jenny Lind and the Collins Liner Atlantic, The Amer Neptune, 91. **CONTACT ADDRESS** Dept of History, Trinity Col, 300 Summit ST, Hartford, CT, 06106. **EMAIL** edward.sloan@mail.trincoll.edu

SLOAN, HERBERT
DISCIPLINE UNITED STATES HISTORY **EDUCATION** Stanford Univ, BA, 69; Columbia Univ, PhD, 88. **CAREER** Assoc prof. **SELECTED PUBLICATIONS** Auth, Principle and Interest: Thomas Jefferson and the Problem of Debt, 95; The Earth Belongs to the Living, 93. **CONTACT ADDRESS** Dept of History, Columbia Col, New York, 2960 Broadway, New York, NY, 10027-6902.

SLOAN, PHILLIP R.
DISCIPLINE HISTORY **EDUCATION** Univ Utah, BS, 60; Scripps Inst of Ocean, MS, 64; Univ Calif San Diego, MA, 67, PhD, 70. **CAREER** Prof, 74-. **RESEARCH** History of biology; Buffon studies; history of natural history; evolution; recent human genetics. **SELECTED PUBLICATIONS** Auth, The Gaze of Natural History, 95; Lamarck from an English-Language Perspective, 97; Lamarck in Britain: Trans-forming Lamarck's Transformism, 97; ed, Richard Owen's Hunterian Lectures at the Royal College of Surgeons, 92. **CONTACT ADDRESS** History and Philosophy of Science Dept, Univ of Notre Dame, Notre Dame, IN, 46556. **EMAIL** Phillip.R.Sloan.1@nd.edu

SLOAN, THOMAS
DISCIPLINE ART HISTORY **EDUCATION** Univ NE, BFA, 60; Northwestern Univ, MA, 62, PhD, 72. **CAREER** Instr, Princeton Univ; Northwestern Univ; Univ VA; Northeastern IL, Univ; ch, assoc prof, 86-. **HONORS AND AWARDS** Fel grant, Northwestern Univ; travel grant, Fulbright-Hays. **SELECTED PUBLICATIONS** Pub(s), Arts mag; Scandinavian Rev; Psychoanalytic Perspectives On Art. **CONTACT ADDRESS** Dept of Art Hist, Sch of the Art Inst of Chicago, 37 S Wabash Ave, Chicago, IL, 60603.

SLOAN, TOD STRATTON
PERSONAL Born 07/06/1952, Washington, DC, d, 1 child **DISCIPLINE** PERSONALITY PSYCHOLOGY **EDUCATION** Univ MI, PhD (personality psychology). **CAREER** Asst prof, 82-89, assoc prof, Univ Tulsa, 89-. **HONORS AND AWARDS** Fulbright awards for Venezuela and Nicaragua. **MEMBERSHIPS** Int Soc for Theoretical Psychology; Am Psychol Asn. **RESEARCH** Social theory; psychoanalysis; modernization. **SELECTED PUBLICATIONS** Auth, Life Choices, Westview, 96; Damaged Life, Routledge, 96. **CONTACT ADDRESS** Dept of Psychology, Univ of Tulsa, Tulsa, OK, 74104. **EMAIL** tod-sloan@utulsa.edu

SLOTKIN, RICHARD S.
PERSONAL Born 11/08/1942, New York, NY, m, 1963, 1 child **DISCIPLINE** AMERICAN STUDIES **EDUCATION** Brooklyn Col, BA, 63; Brown Univ, PhD, 67. **CAREER** From asst prof to assoc prof to prof, 66-81, OLIN PROF AM STUD, 81- , Dir Am Stud, 76-94, PROF ENGLISH & CHMN DEPT AM STUDIES, WESLEYAN UNIV, 76-, Wesleyan Ctr Humanities fel, 69-70; Nat Endowment for Humanities younger humanist fel, 73-74; Rockefeller Found fel, 77; Nat Endowment for Humanities grant, 81. **HONORS AND AWARDS** A J Beveridge Award, AHA, 73; Nat Book Award Finalist, 73 & 93; Little Big Horn Asn Lit Award, 85., MA, Wesleyan Univ, 76. **MEMBERSHIPS** Am Studies Asn; Orgn Am Hist; Soc Am Hist; PEN; Writers Guild; Am Hist Asn; Am Film Inst. **RESEARCH** American popular culture; mythology; literature. **SELECTED PUBLICATIONS** Auth, Literature and cultural history, Col English, 8/72; Narratives of Negro crime, Am Quart, 4/73; Regeneration through Violence, Wesleyan Univ, 73; And then the mare will go: Black Hills scheme by Custer, J of West, 7/76; So Dreadful a Judgment, Wesleyan Univ, 78; The Crater (novel), 80; Buffalo Bill's Wild West, Univ Pittsbugh & Brooklyn Museum, 81; Theodore Roosevelt's Myth of the Frontier, Am Quart, 4/82; Prologue to a Study of Movie Gebresm 85; The Fatal Environment, Atheneum, 85; Myth and the Production of History, in Ideology and Classic Am Lit, Cambridge Univ, 86; Return of Henry Starr, 88; Gunfighters & Green Berets, RHR, 89; Gunfighter Nation, Atheneum, 92; Buffalo Bills Wild West & the Mythologization of American History, Cultures of US Imperialsim, Duke Univ, 94; Movie Western, Updating the Literary West, 97. **CONTACT ADDRESS** Ctr for the Americas, Wesleyan Univ, Middletown, CT, 06459. **EMAIL** rslotkin@wesleyan.edu

SMAIL, DANIEL L.
DISCIPLINE MEDIEVAL SOCIAL HISTORY **EDUCATION** MI Univ, PhD. **CAREER** Asst prof, Fordham Univ. **HONORS AND AWARDS** Fel, ACLS., Bd mem, W Soc Fr Hist. **SELECTED PUBLICATIONS** Auth, Common Violence: Vengeance and Inquisition in Fourteenth-Century Marseille, Past and Present, 96; Demonter le patrimoine: les femmes et les biens dans la Marseille medievale, Annales, 97; Angevin courts , Fr Hist Stud, 97. **CONTACT ADDRESS** Dept of Hist, Fordham Univ, 113 W 60th St, New York, NY, 10023.

SMALL, JOCELYN PENNY
DISCIPLINE ART HISTORY **EDUCATION** Princeton Univ, PhD. **CAREER** Prof, Rutgers Univ. **RESEARCH** Greek, Etruscan and Roman art; mythology and iconography; cognitive studies. **SELECTED PUBLICATIONS** Auth, Wax Tablets of the Mind: Cognitive Studies of Literacy and Memory in Classical Antiquity; Routledge, 97; Scholars, Etruscans, and Attic Painted Vases, Jour Roman Archaeol, 94; The Etruscan View of Greek Art, Boreas, 94; SIBYL: The US Database of Classical Iconography: Issues of Simplicity and Complexity of Design, Revue Informatique et Statistique dans les Sciences humaines, 93; coauth, Murlo and Etruscan Studies in Essays in Memory of Kyle Meredith Phillips, Jr, Univ Wis P, 94. **CONTACT ADDRESS** Dept of Art Hist, Rutgers Univ/Rutgers Col, Hamilton St., New Brunswick, NJ, 08903. **EMAIL** small@rci.rutgers.edu

SMALL, KENNETH ALAN
PERSONAL Born 02/09/1945, m, 1968, 1 child **DISCIPLINE** ECONOMICS **EDUCATION** Univ of Calif at Berkeley, PhD, 76. **CAREER** Asst prof, Princeton Univ, 76-83; ASSOC PROF TO PROF, UNIV OF CALIF AT IRVINE, 83-. **MEMBERSHIPS** Am Economic Asn; Econometric Soc; Royal Economic Soc; Transportation Res Board; Regional Sci Asn Int; Am Real Estate & Urban Economics Asn. **RESEARCH** Urban economics; transportation economics; environmental economics. **SELECTED PUBLICATIONS** Auth, Approximate Generalized Extreme Value Models of Discrete Choice, J of Econometrics, 94; auth, Urban Transportation Economics, Harwood Acad Pub, 92; co-ed, Transport Economics: Selected Readings, Harwood Acad Pub, 97; coauth, Environment and Transport in Economic Modelling, Kluwer Acad Press, 98; coauth, The Economics of Traffic Congestion, Am Scientist, 94; coauth, Urban Spatial Structure, J of Economic Lit, 98; coauth, Urban Transportation, Handbook of Regional and Urban Economics, North-Holland, forthcoming. **CONTACT ADDRESS** Dept of Economics, Univ of Calif, Irvine, CA, 92697-5100. **EMAIL** ksmall@uci.edu

SMALL, LAWRENCE FARNSWORTH
PERSONAL Born 12/30/1925, Bangor, ME, m, 1947, 4 children **DISCIPLINE** HISTORY, POLITICAL SCIENCE **EDUCATION** Univ Maine, BA, 48, MA, 51; Bangor Theol Sem, BD, 48; Harvard Univ, PhD, 55. **CAREER** Asst minister, All Souls Church, Lowell, Mass, 50-52 & First Congregational Church, Winchester, Mass, 52-55; minister, Paramus Congregational Church, NJ, 55-59; assoc prof hist & polit sci, 59-61, dean & registr, 61-65, actg pres, 65-66, PROF HIST, ROCKY MOUNTAIN COL, 61-, PRES, 66- **MEMBERSHIPS** AHA; Am Polit Sci Asn. **RESEARCH** American intellectual and religious history, especially Unitarianism and Fundamentalism. **SELECTED PUBLICATIONS** Auth, Golden Opportunities - A Biog Hist Of Montana Jewish Communities - Coleman,Jl/, Am Jewish Archives, Vol 0047, 1995. **CONTACT ADDRESS** 7320 Sumatra Pla, Billings, MT, 59102.

SMALL, MELVIN
PERSONAL Born 03/14/1939, New York, NY, m, 1958, 2 children **DISCIPLINE** AMERICAN DIPLOMATIC HISTORY **EDUCATION** Dartmouth Col, BA, 60; Univ Mich, MA, 61, PhD, 65. **CAREER** From asst prof to assoc prof, 65-76, prof hist, Wayne State Univ, 76, Chmn Dept Hist, 79-86; Co-investr correlates of war proj, Univ MI, 67-; vis prof Univ MI, Ann Arbor, 68; vis prof, Marygrove Col, 71; vis lectr, Aarhus Univ, 72-74, 83; vis prof, Univ Windsor, 77-78. **HONORS AND AWARDS** Fel, Ctr Advan Studies Behav Sci, 69-70; Am Coun Learned Soc studies fel, 69-70; **MEMBERSHIPS** AHA; Orgn Am Historians; Soc Hist Am Foreign Rels. **RESEARCH** Mod international war 1815-1980; public opinion and foreign policy; Vietnam war. **SELECTED PUBLICATIONS** Ed, Public Opinion and Historians, Wayne State Univ, 70; coauth, The Wages of War, 1816-1965, Wiley, 72; auth, America and the German Threat to the Hemisphere, 1905-1914, The Americas, 1/72; Some Suggestions from the Behavioral Sciences for Historians Interested in the Study of Attitudes, Societas, winter 73; How We Learned to Love the Russians, 5/74 & The Applicability of Quantitative International Politics to Diplomatic History, 2/76, Historian; Was War Necessary, Sage, 80; coauth, Resort to Arms, Sage, 82; auth, Johnson, Nixon, and the Doves, 88. **CONTACT ADDRESS** Dept Hist, Wayne State Univ, 3119 FAB, Detroit, MI, 48202-3919.

SMALLS, JAMES
DISCIPLINE MODERN ART, AFRICAN-AMERICAN ART **EDUCATION** UCLA, PhD. **CAREER** Asst prof, Rutgers, The State Univ NJ, Univ Col-Camden. **RESEARCH** Nineteenth-century French art with special interest in the representation of blacks, women, colonized peoples; nineteenth and twentieth-century African-American art and culture. **SELECTED PUBLICATIONS** Auth, Public face, Private Thoughts: Fetish, Interracialism, and the Homoerotic in Some Photographs by Carl Van Vechten, in Sex Positives?: The Cultural Politics of Dissi-

dent Sexualities, Yale UP, 91; Food for Thought: African-American Visual Narration, in Dream Singers, Story Tellers: An African-American Presence, exh cat, Fukui Fine Art Mus, Japan, and NJ State Mus, 92; America the Beautiful, America the Ugly, Benny Andrews, The Am Ser, exh cat, NJ State Mus, 93; A Ghost of a Chance: Invisibility and Eli sion in African-American Art Historical Practice, in Art and Doc 13, 94; Separating the Men from the Men: (Re)defining Masculinity in and out of the Artist's Studio, in Semiotics, 94; Making Trouble for Art History: The Queer Case of Girodet, in Art J 55, no 4, 96. **CONTACT ADDRESS** Dept of Art Hist, Rutgers, The State Univ NJ, Univ Col-Camden, Voorhees Hall, 71 Hamilton St, New Brunswick, NJ, 08903.

SMALLWOOD, JAMES MILTON
PERSONAL Born 07/10/1944, Terrell, TX, m, 2 children **DISCIPLINE** HISTORY, POLITICAL SCIENCE **EDUCATION** ETex State Univ, BS, 67, MA, 69; Tex Tech Univ, PhD(hist, polit sci), 74. **CAREER** Instr hist, ETex State Univ, 67-69, Southeastern Okla State Univ, 69-70 & Tex Tech Univ, 70-74; dir Will Rogers Res Proj, 76-81, PROF HIST, OKLA STATE UNIV, 75-, Consult, Okla Humanities Coun & Okla Heritage Asn, 77- **MEMBERSHIPS** AHA; Orgn Am Historians; Southern Hist Asn; Western Hist Asn. **RESEARCH** Recent United States history; Southern United States history; Civil War, Reconstruction. **SELECTED PUBLICATIONS** Auth, Codes Of Conduct - Race, Ethics And The Color Of Our Character - Holloway,Kfc/, Miss Quart, Vol 0049, 1996; A Black Educator In The Segregated South - Kentucky Atwood,Rufus,B. - Smith,Gl/, Miss Quart, Vol 0049, 1996. **CONTACT ADDRESS** Dept of Hist, Oklahoma State Univ, Stillwater, OK, 74074.

SMEINS, LINDA
DISCIPLINE ART HISTORY **EDUCATION** Univ Denver, BFA; Calif State, MA; Univ Brit Columbia, PhD. **CAREER** Dept Art, Western Wash Univ **MEMBERSHIPS** Mem, Col Art Assn; Soc Arch Hist(s). **SELECTED PUBLICATIONS** Auth, Stopovers in the Flight of Time, Jet Dreams Art of the Fifties in the Northwest Seattle/London: Univ Washn Press, Tacoma Art Museum, 95; National Rhetoric, Public Discourse, and Spatialization: Middle Class America and the Pattern Book House, Nineteenth-Century Contexts, 92. **CONTACT ADDRESS** Dept of Art, Western Washington Univ, 516 High St, Bellingham, WA, 98225. **EMAIL** lsmeins@cc.wwu.edu

SMETHURST, MAE J.
PERSONAL Born 05/28/1935, Houghton, MI, m, 1956 **DISCIPLINE** CLASSICS **EDUCATION** Dickinson Col, BA, 57; Univ Mich, MA, 60, PhD(classics), 68. **CAREER** Instr classics, Univ Mich, 66-67; from instr to asst prof, 67-76, Assoc Prof Classics, Univ Pittsburgh, 76- **MEMBERSHIPS** Am Philol Asn. **RESEARCH** Aeschylus; tragedy; Oresteia. **SELECTED PUBLICATIONS** Auth, The Appeal Of A Plotless Tragedy + Aeschylus And Zeami, A Comparative-Study Of Greek Tragedy And No/, Coll Lit, Vol 0023, 1996. **CONTACT ADDRESS** Dept of Classic, Univ of Pittsburgh, 207 Hillman Libr, Pittsburgh, PA, 15260-0001.

SMETHURST, RICHARD JACOB
PERSONAL Born 10/05/1933, Carlisle, PA, m, 1956 **DISCIPLINE** JAPANESE HISTORY **EDUCATION** Dickinson Col, AB, 55; Univ Mich, Ann Arbor, MA, 61, PhD, 68. **CAREER** From Asst Prof to Assoc Prof, 67-85, prof hist, Univ Pittsburgh, 85-, Dept Chair, Univ Ctr for Int Studies Res Prof, 88-. **MEMBERSHIPS** Asn Asian Studies; Columbia Univ Mod Japan Seminar. **RESEARCH** Japanese social and economic history; Japanese rural history; comparative military history. **SELECTED PUBLICATIONS** Auth, The Military Reserve Association and the Minobe Crisis of 1935, in Crisis Politics in Prewar Japan, Sophia Univ, 70; The Creation of the Military Reserve Association in Japan, J Asian Studies, 8/71; A Social Basis for Prewar Japanese Militarism: The Army and the Rural Community, Univ Calif, 74; Agricultural Development and Tenancy Disputes in Japan, 1870-1940, Princeton, 87; Japan's First Experiment with Democracy, 1870-1940, in The Social Meaning of Democracy, NYU, 95; The Self-Taught Bureaucrat: Takahashi Korekiyo and Economic Policy during the Great Depression, in Learning in Likely Places: Varieties of Apprenticeship in Japan, Cambridge, 98. **CONTACT ADDRESS** Dept History, Univ Pittsburgh, 3M38 Forbes Quad, Pittsburgh, PA, 15260-0001. **EMAIL** rsmett@pitt.edu

SMILEY, DAVID LESLIE
PERSONAL Born 03/17/1921, MS, m, 1945, 1 child **DISCIPLINE** HISTORY **EDUCATION** Baylor Univ, AB, 47, MA, 48; Univ Wis, PhD, 53. **CAREER** Asst prof, 50-56, assoc prof, 57-63, PROF HIST, WAKE FOREST UNIV, 63-, Fulbright lectr, Univ Strasbourg, 68-69. **MEMBERSHIPS** Orgn Am Historians; Southern Hist Asn; Agr Hist Soc. **RESEARCH** United States history, especially the national period; the South in American history; the southern antislavery movement. **SELECTED PUBLICATIONS** Auth, The Ky Encycl - Kebler,Je, Clark,Td, Harrison,Lh, Klotter,Jc/, Miss Quart, Vol 0046, 1993. **CONTACT ADDRESS** 1060 Polo Rd NW, Winston-Salem, NC, 27106.

SMILEY, RALPH
PERSONAL Born 03/24/1927, New York, NY, m, 1964, 4 children **DISCIPLINE** EUROPEAN HISTORY, THE MIDDLE EAST **EDUCATION** Brooklyn Col, BA, 51; Rutgers Univ, MA, 63, PhD(mod Europe), 71. **CAREER** Asst hist, Rutgers Univ, 63-65, teaching asst, Douglass Col, 65-66; assoc prof, Indiana Univ of Pa, 66-69; assoc prof, 69-80, PROF HIST, BLOOMSBURG STATE COL, 80-, ADJ PROF MASS COMMUN, 77-, Instr film, Pa State Univ, 76-77. **MEMBERSHIPS** Am Film Inst; AHA; Conf Group Cent Europ Hist; Am Asn Advan Slavic Studies; MidE Inst. **RESEARCH** Twentieth century European inter-war period, 1919-1939; European imperialism; film semiotics. **SELECTED PUBLICATIONS** Auth, Democracy, Development, And The Countryside - Urban-Rural Struggles In India - Varshney,A/, Historian, Vol 0059, 1997. **CONTACT ADDRESS** Dept of Hist, Bloomsburg Univ of Pennsylvania, Bloomsburg, PA, 17815.

SMIT, J.W.
DISCIPLINE EARLY MODERN EUROPEAN HISTORY **EDUCATION** Univ Utrecht, MA, 53, PhD, 58. **CAREER** Queen Wilhelmina prof. **RESEARCH** Social and economic history of the 16th and 17th-centuries. **SELECTED PUBLICATIONS** Fruin en de Partijen Tijdens de Republiek, 58; History of Art, Art in History, History in Art, Stud in 17th Century Dutch Cult, 91. **CONTACT ADDRESS** Dept of Hist, Columbia Col, New York, 2960 Broadway, New York, NY, 10027-6902.

SMITH, BILLY G.
DISCIPLINE HISTORY **EDUCATION** UCLA, BA, 71, MA, 73, PhD, 81. **CAREER** PROF, HIST, MONTANA STATE UNIV **MEMBERSHIPS** AM Antiquarian Soc **SELECTED PUBLICATIONS** Auth, "The Vicissitudes of Fortune: The Careers of Laboring Men in Philadelphia, 1750-1800," Univ NC Press, 88; auth, The Lower Sort: Philadelphia's Laboring People, 1750-1800, Cornell Univ Press, 1990; coauth, Blacks Who Stole Themselves: Advertisements for Runaways in the Pennsylvania Gazette, 1728-90, Univ Penn, 89; auth, coauth, The Unfortunate: The Voyage and Adventures of William Moraley, an Indentured Servant, Penn State Press, 91; auth, Life in Early Philadelphia: Documents from the Revolutionary and Early National Periods, Penn State Univ Press, 95; coauth, "A Melancholy Scene of Devastation": The Public Response to the 1793 Philadelphia Yellow Fever Epidemic, 97; auth, "Runaway Slaves in the Mid-Atlantic Region during the Revolutionary Era," in The Transforming Hand of Revolution: Reconsidering the American Revolution as a Social Movement, Univ Press Va. **CONTACT ADDRESS** Hist & Phil, Montana State Univ, Bozeman, MT, 59717. **EMAIL** uhibs@msu.oscs.montana.edu

SMITH, BRIAN H.
PERSONAL Born 08/01/1940, Freeport, NY, m, 1980, 2 children **DISCIPLINE** POLITICAL SCIENCE **EDUCATION** Fordham Univ, Ab, 64; Woodstock Col, Mdiv, 70; Union Theolog Sem, STM, 71; Yale Univ, PhD, 79. **CAREER** From asst prof to assoc prof, MIT, 80-87; prof, Ripon Col, 87-. **HONORS AND AWARDS** Outstanding Acad Book; Best Prof Book; Catholic Press Asn. **MEMBERSHIPS** Latin Am Stud Asn; Am Acad Relig. **RESEARCH** Religion and politics, NGO's and development in Latin Am. **SELECTED PUBLICATIONS** Auth, art, Non governmental Organisations in International Development: Trends and Future Research Priorities, 93; auth, art, Religion and Politics: A New Look Through an Old Prism, 95; coauth, The Catholic Church and Democracy in Chile and Peru, 97; auth, art, Nongovernmental Organizations, 98; auth, Religious Politics in Latin America, Pentecostal vs. Catholic, 98. **CONTACT ADDRESS** Dept of Religion, Ripon Col, Ripon, WI, 54971-0248. **EMAIL** smithb@mail.ripon.edu

SMITH, C. S.
PERSONAL Born 10/23/1960, PA, m, 1983, 3 children **DISCIPLINE** SOCIOLOGY **EDUCATION** Harvard, MA, PhD, 90. **CAREER** Dept Sociology, Univ NC. **MEMBERSHIPS** ASR; ASA; SSSR. **RESEARCH** Religion; social movements; Latin America. **SELECTED PUBLICATIONS** Auth, The Emergence of Liberation Theology: Radical Religion and Social Movement Theory, Univ Chicago Press, 91; Disruptive Religion: The Fare of Faith in Social Movement Activism, Routledge Pubs, 96; Resisting Reagan: The US Central America Peace Movement, Univ Chicago Press, 96; American Evangelicalism: Embattled and Thriving, Univ of Chicago Press, 98. **CONTACT ADDRESS** Dept of Sociol, Univ North Carolina, Chapel Hill, Chapel Hill, NC, 27599. **EMAIL** cssmith@email.unc.edu

SMITH, CHARLES F., JR.
PERSONAL Born 01/05/1933, Cleveland, Ohio, m **DISCIPLINE** EDUCATION **EDUCATION** Bowling Green State Univ, BS 1960; Kent State Univ, EdM 1963; Harvard Univ Grad School Ed, CAS 1965; MI State Univ, EdD 1969. **CAREER** Elementary School Teacher Lorain OH 1960-62; Peace Corps Field Trgn Ctr Puerto Rico, dir 1962-63; Peace Corps, spec asst 1963; Flint Publ Schools, asst dir elem ed 1965-66; MI State Univ, instr ed 1966-68; Boston Coll, assoc prof ed, prof emeritus, currently. **HONORS AND AWARDS** Phi Delta Kappa Teaching Fellow Harvard Univ Grad School Ed 1963-65, Danforth Assoc 1974; Traveling Fellowships Cameroons & Nigeria, Africa, 1958, 1960, Canada 1957, Germany 1954, Jamaica 1953; Visiting Scholar Univ of MI, 1988, Atlanta Univ, 1991, Yale Univ, 1995. **MEMBERSHIPS** Mem adv task force MA Comm Crim Justice; adv council MA Council Bilingual Ed; adv comm MA Comm Minority Higher Ed; bd of dir School Vols Boston; adv task force, implement phase I deseg Boston Publ School; chmn Area Welfare Bd; vice pres Black Citizen of Newton; chmn Black Faculty Staff and Administrators Assoc of Boston Coll; mem Curriculum Comm Natl Cncl for the Social Studies; bd of dir MA Council of the Social Studies; bd of dir, Natl Council for the Social Studies. **CONTACT ADDRESS** Professor Emeritus, Education, Boston Col, Campion Hall, 140 Commonwealth Ave, Chestnut Hill, MA, 02167.

SMITH, CHARLIE CALVIN
PERSONAL Born 06/12/1943, Brickeys, Arkansas, m **DISCIPLINE** HISTORY **EDUCATION** AM & N Coll Pine Bluff AR, BA history 1966; AR State Univ Jonesboro, MSE social science 1971; Univ of AR Fayetteville, PhD US history 1978. **CAREER** AR State Univ, asst prof of History 1978-; AR State Univ, instructor in History 1970-78; Lee Co Public School Marianna AR, Social Studies teacher, asst football coach 1966-70; Arkansas State Univ, assoc prof of History, 1982-86, asst dean 1986-. **MEMBERSHIPS** Comm mem AR Endowment for the Humanities 1975-77; gov appointee bd mem AR Student Loan Assn 1975-76; gov appointee bd mem AR Historic Preservation Program 1979-84; mem Jonesboro Rotary Club, 1987-; pres Southern Conference on Afro-Amer Studies, 1988-. **SELECTED PUBLICATIONS** Published "The Oppressed Oppressors Negro Slavery among the choctaws of OK" red river valley history review vol 2 1975; published "the civil war letters of John G Marsh" Upper OH Valley History Review 1979; published "The Diluting of an Inst the social impact of WWII on the AR family" AR history quarter (spring) 1980; published biographical sketches of AR Governors J Marion Futrell & Homer M Adkins AR Ednowment for the Humanities 1980; Presidential Fellow, Arkansas State Univ, 1982; Outstanding Black Faculty Member/Teacher, Black Student Body ASU, 1984-86, 1988; War and Wartime Changes; The Transformation of Arkansas, 1940-45, U of A Press, 1987. **CONTACT ADDRESS** Professor of History, Arkansas State Univ, PO Box 1030, State University, AR, 72467.

SMITH, DALE CARY
PERSONAL Born 07/02/1951, Orlando, FL, m, 1973, 1 child **DISCIPLINE** HISTORY OF MEDICINE **EDUCATION** Duke Univ, BA, 73; Univ Minn, PhD, 79. **CAREER** Instr & res fel hist med, Univ Minn, 79-81, Asst Prof, 81-82; from Asst Prof to Assoc Prof, 82-97, Prof and Chair Med Hist, Uniformed Serv Univ of the Health Sci, 97-; Book rev ed, J Hist Med & Allied Sci, 79-82, Assoc ed, 83-87; Ed, Am Asn Hist Med Newsletter, 97-. **HONORS AND AWARDS** Laurance D. Redway, MD, Award for Excellence in Medical Writings of the Med Soc of the State of NY, 87; named Outstanding Teacher by 1st year med students: 96, 97, 98. **MEMBERSHIPS** Am Asn Hist Med; AHA; Orgn Am Historians; AAAS; Soc Mil Hist; U.S. Naval Inst. **RESEARCH** Changing concepts of disease; development of clinical medicine and surgery; history of military medicine. **SELECTED PUBLICATIONS** Auth, Quinine and fever: The development of the effective dosage, J Hist Med, 76; The rise and decline of typhomalarial fever, J Hist Med, 82; ed, On the Causes of Fever by William Budd, Johns Hopkins Univ Press, 84; auth, An Historical Overview of the Recognition of Appendicitis, NY State J Med, 86; Military Medicine, in Encyclopedia of the American Military, Charles Scribners Sons, 94; Appendicitis Appendectomy and the Surgeon, Bull Hist Med, 96; The American Gastroenterological Association: A Centennial History, Am Gastroenterological Asn. 98. **CONTACT ADDRESS** Dept of Med Hist, Uniformed Serv Univ of the Health Sci, 4301 Jones Bridge Rd, Bethesda, MD, 20814-4799. **EMAIL** dcsmith@usuhs.mil

SMITH, DANIEL B.
PERSONAL Born 08/12/1950, Kansas City, MO, s, 1 child **DISCIPLINE** HISTORY **EDUCATION** Okla State Univ, BA, 72; Univ Va, PhD, 78. **CAREER** Prof, Univ Ky, 78-. **HONORS AND AWARDS** NEH Screenwriting Fel, 85, 90, 95; Emmy, Alamance, 96. **RESEARCH** Early America; history of the family; film and history. **SELECTED PUBLICATIONS** Auth, Inside the Great House: Planter Family Life in Eighteenth-Century Chesapeake Society, 80; auth, art, Cotton Mather and Children in the Puritan Heart, 95; auth, art, This Heaven in Idea: Image and Reality on the Kentucky Frontier, 98. **CONTACT ADDRESS** Dept of History, Univ of Kentucky, Lexington, KY, 40506. **EMAIL** dbsmit01@pop.nky.edu

SMITH, DANIEL SCOTT
PERSONAL Born 09/24/1942, Galesburg, IL, m, 1967, 2 children **DISCIPLINE** AMERICAN & DEMOGRAPHIC HISTORY **EDUCATION** Univ Fla, BA, 63; Univ Calif, Berkeley, MA, 65, PhD(hist), 73; Princeton Univ, cert demog, 74. **CAREER** From instr to asst prof hist, Univ Conn, 71-74; asst prof, 74-77, ASSOC PROF HIST, UNIV ILL, CHICAGO, 77-, Instr, Newberry Libr Inst Quant Hist, 72-; Pop Coun fel, Off Pop Res, Princeton, 73-74; assoc dir, Family & Community Hist Ctr, Newberry Libr, 74-; Am Coun Learned Socs fel, 77-78; Ed,

Historical Methods, 80- **MEMBERSHIPS** Pop Asn Am; AHA; Econ Hist Asn; Orgn Am Historians. **RESEARCH** American historical demography. **SELECTED PUBLICATIONS** Auth, The Journey Of Life - A Cult Hist Of Aging In Am - Cole,Tr/, Soc Hist Of Med, Vol 0006, 1993; That Noble Dream - The Objectivity Question And The Am Hist Profession - Novick,P/, Hist Methods, Vol 0026, 1993; Continuity And Discontinuity In Puritan Naming, Mass, 1771/, William And Mary Quart, Vol 0051, 1994; Female Householding In Late 18th-Century Am And The Problem Of Poverty/, J Of Soc Hist, Vol 0028, 1994; Friends In Life And Death - The British And Irish Quakers In The Demographic-Transition, 1650-1900 - Vann,Rt, Eversley,D/, J Of Modern Hist, Vol 0066, 1994; Sexual Customs In Rural Norway - A 19th-Century Study - Sundt,E/, J Of Soc Hist, Vol 0028, 1994; Birth-Weight And Economic-Growth - Womens Living Standards In The Industrializing W - Ward,Wp/, J Of Am Hist, Vol 0081, 1994; Behind And Beyond The Law Of The Household/, William And Mary Quart, Vol 0052, 1995; Cult Demography - New-Eng Deaths And The Puritan Perception Of Risk/, J Of Interdisciplinary Hist, Vol 0026, 1996; The Number And Quality Of Children - Educ And Marital Fertility In Early 20th-Century Iowa/, J Of Soc Hist, Vol 0030, 1996; Family And Soc-Change - The Household As A Process In An Industrializing Community - Janssens,A/, J Of Interdisciplinary Hist, Vol 0026, 1996; Delinquent Daughters - Protecting And Policing Adolescent Female Sexuality In The United-States, 1885-1920 - Odem,Me/, J Of Interdisciplinary Hist, Vol 0027, 1997. **CONTACT ADDRESS** Dept of Hist, Univ of Ill, Chicago, IL, 60680.

SMITH, DAVID CLAYTON
PERSONAL Born 11/14/1929, Lewiston, ME, m, 1953, 2 children **DISCIPLINE** MODERN & AGRICULTURAL HISTORY **EDUCATION** Farmington State Col, BS, 55; Univ ME, M Ed, 56, MA, 58; Cornell Univ, PhD(hist), 65. **CAREER** Instr hist, Hobart & William Smith Col, 60-63, instr hist & econ, 63-65; from asst prof to assoc prof, 65-75, prof hist, Univ ME, Orono, 75-, chemn dept, 80-, Mem & chemn, Maine Hist Preserv Comn, 70-75; pres, Penobscot Heritage Mus Living Hist, 72-76; coop prof, Inst Quaternary Studies, 78-. **HONORS AND AWARDS** James Madison Prize, 94. **MEMBERSHIPS** AHA; Orgn Am Historians; Forest Hist Soc; Agr Hist Soc; Asn Can Studies US. **RESEARCH** Forest hist; agr hist; climate hist; H.G. Wells; World War II. **SELECTED PUBLICATIONS** Auth, Lumbering and the Maine Woods: A Bibliography, Maine Hist Soc, 70; History of United States Papermaking 1690-1970, Lockwood, 71; History of Maine Lumbering 1869-1960, 72, A History of the Univ ME, 78, History of the Maine Agricultural Experiment Station, 80 & Long Time Series Temperature and Precipitation Maine 1808-1980, 81, Univ ME; auth, Desperately Mortal: A Life of H.G. Wells, 86; coauth, Miss You, 90; coauth, Since You Went Away, 92; coauth, We're In This War, Too, 93; ed, Collected Correspondence of H.G. Wells, 98. **CONTACT ADDRESS** Dept of History, Univ of ME, Orono, ME, 06973. **EMAIL** dcsmith@maine.maine.edu

SMITH, DAVID E.
PERSONAL Born 08/08/1936, Springhill, NS, Canada **DISCIPLINE** POLITICAL SCIENCE/HISTORY **EDUCATION** Univ Western Ont, BA 59; Duke Univ, MA, 62, PhD, 64; Univ Sask, DLitt, 95. **CAREER** Asst prof, 66-69, assoc prof, 69-74, PROF POLITICAL SCIENCE, UNIV SASK, 74-, asst dean grad stud, 75-78; vis prof, Can stud, Japan, 81-82. **HONORS AND AWARDS** Jules and Gabrielle Leger fel, 92-93; Killam res fel, 95-97; fel, Royal Soc Can. **RESEARCH** Saskatchewan; Prairie provinces; Liberal Party; political history. **SELECTED PUBLICATIONS** Auth, Prairie Liberalism: The Liberal Party in Saskatchewan 1905-71, 75; auth, Regional Decline of a National Party: Liberals on the Prairies, 81; coauth, James G. Gardiner: Relentless Liberal, 90; coauth, Building a Province: A History of Saskatchewan in Documents, 92; coauth, The Invisible Crown: The First Principles of Canadian Government, 95. **CONTACT ADDRESS** Dept of Political Science, Univ of Saskatchewan, Saskatoon, SK, S7N 5A5.

SMITH, DAVID FREDRICK
PERSONAL Born 06/11/1941, Liverpool, England, m, 1968, 2 children **DISCIPLINE** MODERN BRITISH HISTORY **EDUCATION** Bristol Univ, BA, 63; Wash Univ, AM, 65; Univ Toronto, PhD, 72. **CAREER** Lectr hist, Webster Col, 65-67; lectr, Univ Toronto, 71-72; asst prof, 72-80, assoc prof history, Univ Puget Sound, 80-. **MEMBERSHIPS** Conf Brit Studies. **RESEARCH** The home office in 19th century Britain; penal reform in mid 19th century Britain; administrative reform of the Victorian period. **CONTACT ADDRESS** Dept Hist, Univ Puget Sound, 1500 N Warner St, Tacoma, WA, 98416-0005. **EMAIL** DFSMITH@ups.edu

SMITH, DAVID RICHARD
PERSONAL Born 04/24/1942, Jersey City, NJ, m, 1989, 5 children **DISCIPLINE** CLASSICAL STUDIES **EDUCATION** David Lipscomb Col, BA, 64; Vanderbilt Univ, MA, 66; Univ PA, PhD(class studies), 68. **CAREER** Asst prof classics, Univ CA, Riverside, 68-70; asst prof, 70-75, assoc prof, 75-80, prof hist, CA State Polytech Univ Pomona, 80-; assoc ed, Helios J Class Asn Southwest, 75-77. **MEMBERSHIPS** Class Asn Southwest; Am Philol Asn; AHA; WHA. **RESEARCH** Greek history, religion and philosophy of history; world history and teaching methodologies. **SELECTED PUBLICATIONS** Auth, Hieropoioi and Hierothytai on Rhodes, L'Antiquite Classique, 72; The Hieropoioi on Kos, Numen, 73; The Coan Festival of Zeus Polieus, Class J, 10/73; Review of G S Kirk, Myth: Its Meaning and Function in Ancient and Other Cultures, Helios, 5/76; The Poetic Focus in Horace, Odes 3.13, Latomus, 76; Teaching Religion in the Medieval Period, World Hist Bull, 90-91; Teaching and Assessing the Doing World History Method in the World History Survey, Aspen World Hist Handbook, vol 2, 97; Technology in the World History Survey, Aspen World Hist Handbook, vol 2, 97. **CONTACT ADDRESS** Dept Hist, California State Polytech Univ, 3801 W Temple Ave, Pomona, CA, 91768-4001. **EMAIL** drsmith2@csupomona.edu

SMITH, DENIS
PERSONAL Born 10/03/1932, Edmonton, AB, Canada **DISCIPLINE** POLITICAL SCIENCE/CANADIAN STUDIES **EDUCATION** McGill Univ, BA, 53; Oxford Univ, BA, 55, MA, 59, BLitt, 59; Trent Univ, LittD, 89. **CAREER** Instr, 56-57, lectr, polit econ, Univ Toronto, 57-58; lectr, 60-61, asst prof, polit sci, York Univ, 61-63; assoc prof, 64-68, vice pres, 64-67, dept ch, 66-70, prof, 68-96, dean soc sci, 82-88, PROF EMER POLITICAL SCIENCE, UNIV WESTERN ONT, 96-. **HONORS AND AWARDS** Univ BC Medal Can Biog 73, 95; JW Dafoe Found Bk Prize, 73, 95. **SELECTED PUBLICATIONS** Auth, Bleeding Hearts, Bleeding Country, 71; auth, Gentle Patriot, 73; auth, Diplomacy of Fear, 88; auth, Rogue Tory, 95; ed, J Can Stud, 66-75; ed, Can Forum, 75-79. **CONTACT ADDRESS** 64 Augusta St, Port Hope, ON, L1A 1G9. **EMAIL** dsmith@eagle.ca

SMITH, DENNIS P.
PERSONAL Born 02/09/1949, Kittery, ME, m, 1982, 4 children **DISCIPLINE** HISTORY **EDUCATION** Northeastern St Univ, BA, 85, MS, 87. **CAREER** Asst prof, Ok St Univ **HONORS AND AWARDS** Regents Distinguished Teaching Award, 97, Estab Ok Film Repository, USAO, 90; actively worked with St Teacher Training in the Arts; Campus co-ord for cooperative agreements with St vocational tech inst. **MEMBERSHIPS** Comm Col Humanities Assoc; Nat Assoc for Humanities Educ. **RESEARCH** Biblical hist; oral hist; visual arts. **CONTACT ADDRESS** Humanities Dept, Oklahoma State Univ, 900 N Portland, Oklahoma City, OK, 73107-6195. **EMAIL** smithdp@okway.okstate.edu

SMITH, DIANE E.
PERSONAL Born 02/27/1959, Grand Rapids, MI, m, 1981, 4 children **DISCIPLINE** CLASSICS, LATIN **EDUCATION** Villanova Univ, MA 86; Univ of Michigan, BA, 80; Richmond Coll, 76-77; Intercollegiate Center for Classical Stud, Rome, 79-80; Amer School of Classical Stud, Athens, 82. **CAREER** Tchr, 86-88, School of the Holy Child, Rye NY; Scholar and Typesetter, in Greek, Latin, Linguistics and Modern Lang, 88-, Teacher, 87-, Waco Christian Sem, Waco, TX. **HONORS AND AWARDS** Graduate Fellowship, Villanova Univ. **MEMBERSHIPS** Classical Assoc of Midwest and South; Amer Classical League. **SELECTED PUBLICATIONS** Typesetting in the following; Bolchazy-Carducci, Schemling, Gareth and Jon D. Mikalson, eds, Qui Miscuit Utile Dulci, Festschrift Essays for Paul Lachlan MacKendrick, 98; L & L Enterprises/Bolchazy-Carducci, DuBose, Gaylan, Farrago, 97; Franz Steiner Verlag, Linderski, J., Ed, Imperium Sine Fine, Festschrift for T.R.S. Broughton, Historia-Einzelschrift, 105, 96; Rowmand and Littlefield, Edmunds, Lowell, Oedipus at Colonus, 96; Oxford University Press, Battye, Adriand and Ian Roberts, eds, Clause Structure and Language Change, 95; Longman Publishing Group, Davis, Sally, Review and Test Preparation Guide for the beginning Latin Student, 94. **CONTACT ADDRESS** 5801 Fairview Dr, Waco, TX, 76710.

SMITH, DONALD HUGH
PERSONAL Born 03/20/1932, Chicago, Illinois, d **DISCIPLINE** EDUCATION **EDUCATION** Univ of IL, AB 1953; DePaul, MA 1959; Univ of WI, PhD 1964. **CAREER** Baruch Coll, prof, chairman, dept of educ; Chicago Pub Sch, tchr 1956-63; Cntr for Inner City Studies Northeastern IL U, asst prof asso prof dir 1964-68; Univ Comm Educ Prgms Univ of Pitts, prof dir 1968-69; Nat Urban Coalition Washington DC, exec asso 1969-70; Educ Devel Baruch Coll Cty of NY, prof dir 1970-97, associate provost, retired. **HONORS AND AWARDS** Recip Chicago Bd of Educ Flwshp 1962; Univ of WI Flwshp 1963; del White House Conf on the Disadvantaged 1966; Disting Leadership Awd Natl Alliance of Black School Educators 1986; Awd for Distinguished Serv NY State Black & Puerto Rican Legislation, 1986. **MEMBERSHIPS** Exec dir Chancellor's Task Force on SEEK Cty Univ of NY 1974-; Nat Adv Counc Voc Educ 1968-70; adv Doctoral Prgm in Educ Adminstrn Atlanta Univ 1975; chairman of Black Faculty of Cty Univ of NY, 1989-92; mem InterAm Congress of Psychology 1972-; advisor Martin Luther King Jr Ctr for Social Change; mem Nat Study Commn of Tchr Educ 1972-75; chmn task force NY State Dropout Problem; bd of dir NY Serv to Older People; consult to numerous schools & univs; pres Natl Alliance of Black School Educators 1983-85; advisory board, African Heritage Studies Assn.

SMITH, DUANE ALLAN
PERSONAL Born 04/20/1937, San Diego, CA, m, 1960, 1 child **DISCIPLINE** UNITED STATES HISTORY **EDUCATION** Univ Colo, BA, 59, MA, 61, PhD(Hist), 64. **CAREER** From asst prof to assoc prof, 64-72, prof Hist, Ft Lewis Col, 72-, Am Asn State & Local Hist grant-in-aid, 67; Huntington Libr res grant, 68, 73 & 78. **HONORS AND AWARDS** Colorado Prof of Year, 90. **MEMBERSHIPS** Mining Hist Assoc; Western Hist Asn. **RESEARCH** Western mining camps; mining history; Colorado history. **SELECTED PUBLICATIONS** Auth, Rocky Mountain Mining Camps: The Urban Frontier, Ind Univ 67; coauth, A Colorado History, Pruett, 72, 76, 88, 95; auth, Horace Tabor, His Life and the Legend, Colo Assoc Press, 73; Silver Saga, Pruett, 74; Colorado Mining, Unix NMex, 77; Rocky Mountain Boom Town, Univ NMex, 80; Secure the Shadow, Colo Sch Mines, 80; coauth, A Land Alone, Pruett, 81; Mining America Univ Press Kansas, A Tale of Two Towns, Univ Press Colo, 97. **CONTACT ADDRESS** Southwest Center, Fort Lewis Col, 1000 Rim Dr, Durango, CO, 81301-3999. **EMAIL** smith_d@fortlewis.edc

SMITH, DWIGHT L.
DISCIPLINE HISTORY **EDUCATION** Indiana Central Univ, AB, 40; Indiana, AM, 41, PhD, 49; Indianapolis, LittD, 87. **CAREER** Prof to PROF EMER, HIST, MIAMI UNIVERSITY OHIO **MEMBERSHIPS** Am Antiquarian Soc **RESEARCH** War of 1812 **SELECTED PUBLICATIONS** Auth, Indians of the United States and Canada: A Bibliography, vol 1, 74, vol 2, 83; auth, The War of 1812: An Annotated Bibliography, Garland, 85; The History of Canada: An Annotated Bibliography, 83; coauth, The Colorado River Survey: Robert B. Stanton and the Denver, Colorado Canyon & Pacific Railroad, 87; auth, Survival on a Westward Trek, 1858-1859: The John Jones Overlanders, Ohio Univ Press, 89; coauth, A Journey through the West: Thomas Rodney's 1803 Journey from Delaware to the Mississippi Territory, Ohio Univ Press, 97. **CONTACT ADDRESS** Dept of Hist, Miami Univ, Oxford, OH, 45056.

SMITH, ELEANOR JANE
PERSONAL Born 01/10/1933, Circleville, OH, m, 1972 **DISCIPLINE** EDUCATION **EDUCATION** Capital Univ, BSM 1955; Ohio St Univ, 1966; The Union Graduate School/UECU, PhD 1972. **CAREER** Board of Ed, Columbus, OH 2nd-6th grd tchr 1956-64; Board of Ed, Worthington OH 6 & 7th grd tchr 1964-69; Univ of Cinn, prof, Afro-Am Studies 1972-82; vice provost Faculty & Acad Affairs; Smith Coll, dean of institutional affairs, 1988-90; William Paterson College, vice president for academic affairs and provost, 1990-94; UNIV OF WISCONSIN-PARKSIDE, CHANCELLOR, currently. **HONORS AND AWARDS** Historical Presentation, Black Heritage, History, Music & Dance written & produced 1972-; numerous publications; YWCA Career Women of Achievement 1983; Capital Univ, Alumni Achiev Awd 1986. **MEMBERSHIPS** Assoc of Black Women Historians, natl co-founder & co-director 1978-80; mem Natl Council for Black Studies 1982-88; mem Natl Assn Women in Education, 1986-; American Assn for Higher Education; American Council on Education; American Assn of State Colleges and Universities. **CONTACT ADDRESS** Univ of Wisconsin, Parkside, 900 Wood Rd, 2000, Kenosha, WI, 53141-2000.

SMITH, F. TODD
PERSONAL Born 11/21/1957, New Orleans, LA, m, 1996 **DISCIPLINE** HISTORY **EDUCATION** Univ Mo, BA, 79; Univ SD, MA, 83; Tulane Univ, PhD, 89. **CAREER** Asst prof, Xavier Univ La, 91-96; asst prof, Univ W Fl, 96-97; asst prof, Univ of N Tx, 97- . **HONORS AND AWARDS** Ray A. Billington Award, Western His Assoc, 92; Ottis Lock Award, East Tx Hist Assoc, 96. **MEMBERSHIPS** Amer Hist Assoc **RESEARCH** Southern plains native amer; colonial Tx & La. **SELECTED PUBLICATIONS** Auth, The Kadohadacho Indians and the Louisiana-Texas Frontier, 1803-1815, Southwestern Hist Quart, 91; The Red River Caddos: A Historical Overview to 1835, Bull of the Tx Archeol Soc, 94; A Native Response to the Transfer of Louisiana: The Red River Caddos and Spain, 1762-1803, La Hist, 96; The Caddo Indians: Tribes at the Convergence of Empires, 1542-1854, Tx A & M Univ Press, 95; The Caddos, the Wichitas, and the United States, 1846-1901, Tx A& M Univ Press, 96; The Wichita Indians: Southern Plains Farmers, Hunters, and Traders, 1541-1845, forthcoming. **CONTACT ADDRESS** History Dept, Univ of N Tx, Denton, TX, 76203. **EMAIL** ftsmith@UNT.edu

SMITH, F. WILSON
PERSONAL Born 08/23/1922, Malden, MA, m, 1949, 2 children **DISCIPLINE** HISTORY **EDUCATION** Amherst Col, AB 47; Univ Cal Berk, MA 48; Columbia Univ, PhD 55. **CAREER** Princeton Univ, inst 53-58; John Hopkins Univ, asst prof, assoc prof, 58-64; Univ Cal Davis, prof, 64-90; Univ Cal Acad Sen, vice ch, ch, Ac Rep to Regents, 83-85; Phillip D. Reed Found, member, 90-96. **HONORS AND AWARDS** Beveridge Prize; SSRC res Awds; Henry Huntington Lib Gnt. **MEMBERSHIPS** AHA; OAH; HES; AAUP **RESEARCH** US intellectual history; history of Amer higher EDU. **SELECTED PUBLICATIONS** Auth, Essays in American Intellectual History, Dryden 75; Theories of Education in Early America,

Bobbs, 73; articles, book revs, encyc essays and contributions to American National Biography. **CONTACT ADDRESS** 1215 West 8th St, Davis, CA, 95616.

SMITH, GLENN R.
PERSONAL Born 07/14/1945, Topeka, Kansas, m **DISCIPLINE** EDUCATION **EDUCATION** Adams State Coll, BA 1968; Univ CO, MA 1971; Univ CO, PhD 1975. **CAREER** Community Coll Denver, instr; Met State Coll, asst dir financial aid; Urban Educ Prog, asst dir. **MEMBERSHIPS** Mem Am Educ Studies Assn; Black Eductors Denver; phi Delta Kappa; mem & Greater Park Hill; US Civil Serv Commn CU Fellowship Univ CO 1972-74. **CONTACT ADDRESS** 250 W 14 Ave, PO Box 375, Denver, CO, 80204.

SMITH, HAROLD L.
PERSONAL Born 11/25/1942, Ottumwa, IA **DISCIPLINE** EUROPEAN INTELLECTUAL HISTORY **EDUCATION** Univ Northern Iowa, BS, 65; Univ Iowa, MA, 67, PhD, 71. **CAREER** Asst prof hist, Univ Mo-Kansas City, 71, Univ Mont, 72-73, Univ Iowa, 75-76; from Asst Prof to Assoc Prof, 76-84, Prof Hist, Univ Houston-Victoria, 85-, asst to chancellor acad affairs, 81-82. **HONORS AND AWARDS** Nat Endowment for Humanities fel, 77, 93; Am Philos Soc grant, 79, 85, 94; NEH Grant, 90; Vis Fel, Univ Oxford, 94. **MEMBERSHIPS** AHA; Western Conf Brit Studies (pres 87-88). **RESEARCH** British women's history; 20th century Britain. **SELECTED PUBLICATIONS** Ed, War and Social Change: British Society in the Second World War, Manchester Univ Press, 86; British Feminism in the Twentieth Century, Univ Mass Press, 90; auth, Britain in the Second World War: A Social History, Manchester Univ Press, 96; The British Women's Suffrage Campaign, 1866-1928, Longman, 98; author of several journal articles. **CONTACT ADDRESS** Dept of Hist, Univ of Houston-Victoria, 2506 E Red River, Victoria, TX, 77901-4450. **EMAIL** smithH@cobalt.vic.uh.edu

SMITH, HENRY
DISCIPLINE JAPANESE HISTORY AND ART **EDUCATION** Yale Univ, BA, 62; Harvard Univ, PhD, 70. **CAREER** Prof. **SELECTED PUBLICATIONS** Ed, Learning from Shogun: Japanese History and Western Fantasy, 80. **CONTACT ADDRESS** Dept of Hist, Columbia Col, New York, 2960 Broadway, New York, NY, 10027-6902.

SMITH, JAMES DAVID
PERSONAL Born 06/23/1930, Monroe, Louisiana, m **DISCIPLINE** ART **EDUCATION** So U, BA 1952; Univ CA, 1954-55; Univ So CA, MFA 1956; Chouinard Art Inst, 1962; CO Coll, 1963; Univ OR, PhD 1969. **CAREER** Santa Barbara County Schools, consultant, 1970, 1974, 1975; Univ of CA, Dept of Studio Art, prof, 1969-, Dept of Black Studies, chmn, 1969-73; Univ OR, vis asst prof 1967-69; Santa Barbara HS, instr 1966-67; So Univ, asst prof 1958-66; Prairie View Coll, instr 1956-58; So Univ, vis prof 1954-55. **HONORS AND AWARDS** Selected John Hay Whitney Fellow in the Humanities 1963; exhibited in Dallas Mus of Art; Santa Barbara Mus of Art 1973; Award of Merit, CA Art Educ, 1983; Eugene J Grisby Jr Art Award, Natl Art Educ Assn, 1981; CA Art Educ of the Year, Natl Art Educ Assn, 1986; numerous shows in galleries throughout US; University Distinguished Professor in the Arts & Humanities, 1992-93. **MEMBERSHIPS** Nat Art Educ Assn 1963-; past pres CA Art Educ Assn 1977-79; mem Kappa Alpha Psi; Phi Delta Kappa; NAACP; bd dir Self Care Found of Santa Barbara 1974-; bd dir Children's Creative Proj Santa Barbara 1975-84; pres CA Art Educ Assn 1975-77; co-orgnr Spl Art Exhibition for Hon Edmond Brown Jr, Governor of the State of California, 1975. **CONTACT ADDRESS** Dept of Studio Art, Univ of California, Santa Barbara, CA, 93106.

SMITH, JAMES HOWELL
PERSONAL Born 07/17/1936, Farmersville, TX, m, 1958, 2 children **DISCIPLINE** AMERICAN HISTORY **EDUCATION** Baylor Univ, BA, 58; Tulane Univ, MA, 61; Univ Wis, PhD, 68. **CAREER** Faculty, WAKE FOREST UNIV, 65-, ch dept hist, 87-95; So Fel Fund Col Tchg Fel, 58-61; NEH Summer Fel oward Univ, 69; Duke Univ Lilly Found Schol 77-78; Tx Christian Univ Res Leave Adjunct Fac, 97-98; **HONORS AND AWARDS** ODK Award Contrib Stud Life, 89; Schoonmaker Fac Prize Contrib Comm Serv, 97; Leadership Winston-Salem, 98. **MEMBERSHIPS** AHA; Orgn Am Historians. **RESEARCH** Afro- Am hist; hist of Am philanthropy; 20th century Am hist; Presidential Disability and the 25th Amendment. **SELECTED PUBLICATIONS** Auth, Mrs Ben Hooper: Peace worker and politician, Wis Mag Hist, winter 62-63; Texas, 1893, Southwestern Hist Quart, 10/66; Industry and Commerce 1896-1975: Winston-Salem in History, Vol VIII, 77; coed Disability in US Presidents: Report, Recommendations and Commentaries by the Working Group, Bowman Gray Sci Press, 97. **CONTACT ADDRESS** PO Box 7806, Winston Salem, NC, 27109-7806. **EMAIL** smithhow@wfu.edu

SMITH, JAMES MORTON
PERSONAL Born 05/28/1919, Bernie, MO, m, 1945, 2 children **DISCIPLINE** HISTORY **EDUCATION** Univ Southern Ill, BEd, 41; Univ Okla, MA, 46; Cornell Univ, PhD(hist), 51. **CAREER** Instr hist, Butler Univ, 46-48; res assoc int indust & labor rels, Cornell Univ, 51-52; instr hist, Ohio State Univ, 52-55, Howard fac fel, 54-55; lectr hist & ed pub, Inst Early Am Hist & Cult, Col William & Mary, 55-66; prof AM hist, Cornell Univ, 66-70; prof, Univ Wis-Madison, 70-76; PROF AM HIST, UNIV DEL, 76-; DIR, WINTERTHUR MUS, 76-, Grants-in-aid, Inst Early Am Hist & Cult, 52, Soc Sci Res Coun, 53, Am Philos Soc, 54, Fund for Republic, 55, Thomas Jefferson Mem Found, 59 & Am Coun Learned Soc, 60; consult, Conf Nature & Writing of Hist, Kans, 55; Guggenheim fel, 60-61; vis prof Am hist, Duke Univ, 62-63 & Univ Wis, 64-65; chmn, Coun Inst Early Am Hist & Cult, 70-76; dir, State Hist Soc Wis, 70-76; prin investr proj, Nat Endowment for Humanities, 72-73; mem admin bd, Papers John Marshall, 72-74; bd mem, Papers of James Madison & Black Abolitionist Ed Proj; gen ed, Bicentennial State Hist. **MEMBERSHIPS** Orgn Am Historians; Southern Hist Asn; Am Asn Mus; Asn Art Mus Dirs; Am Asn State & Local Hist. **RESEARCH** Early American constitutional development and civil liberties. **SELECTED PUBLICATIONS** Auth, Freedom's Fetters: The Alien and Sedition Laws and American Civil Liberties, Cornell Univ, 56; coauth, Liberty and Justice: A Historical Record of American Constitutional Development, Knopf, 58; ed, Seventeenth Century America: Essays in Colonial History, Univ NC, 59; auth, George Washington: A Profile, Hill & Wang, 69; ed, The Constitution, Harper, 71; Politics and Society in American History (2 vols), Prentice-Hall, 73; Documentary History Of The 1st Federal Congress, 1789-1791, Vol 4; Legislative Histories, Amendments To The Constitution Through Foreign-Officers-Bill, Vol 5; Legislative Histories, Funding-Act Through Militia-Bill, Vol 6; Legisla, Pennsylvania Magazine. **CONTACT ADDRESS** Winterthur Mus, Winterthur, DE, 19735.

SMITH, JEFFREY
DISCIPLINE ART OF NORTHERN EUROPE FROM 1400 UNTIL 1700 **EDUCATION** Columbia Univ, MA, MPhil, PhD. **CAREER** Prof; Univ TX at Austin, 79-; fel 3 occasions, Zentralinstitut f r Kunstgeschichte in Munich. **HONORS AND AWARDS** Alexander von Humboldt-Stiftung of Bonn, Ger, 24 month fel; ACLS, NEH, & Getty grant Prog. **MEMBERSHIPS** Bd dir, Historians Netherlandish Art, 89-94 & bd of dir, Cole Art Asn, 96-2000. **RESEARCH** Jesuit contrib to Ger art and on Ger sculpt from 1580 until 1648. **SELECTED PUBLICATIONS** Auth, Nuremberg, A Renaissance City, 1500-1618, Austin, 83 & German Sculpture of the Later Renaissance, c. 1520-1580: Art in an Age of Uncertainty, Princeton, 94, ed, New Perspectives on the Art of Renaissance Nuremberg: Five Essays, Austin, 85. **CONTACT ADDRESS** Dept of Art and Art Hist, Univ of Texas at Austin, 2613 Wichita St, FAB 2.120, Austin, TX, 78705.

SMITH, JESSE OWENS
PERSONAL Born 12/05/1942, Comer, Alabama, m, 1987 **DISCIPLINE** POLITICAL SCIENCE **EDUCATION** California State University, Los Angeles, CA, BA, 1971; University of Chicago, Chicago, IL, MA, 1973, PhD, 1976. **CAREER** University of Wisconsin, Oshkosh, WI, professor, 1974-76; San Diego State University, San Diego, CA, professor, 1977-84, California State University, Fullerton, CA, professor, 1984-. **MEMBERSHIPS** California Black Faculty and Staff Association, 1978-; National Conference of Black Political Scientists, 1972-; National Council of Black Studies, 1976-; American Political Science Association, 1976-; National Association for the Advancement of Black Studies. **CONTACT ADDRESS** Professor of Political Science, California State Univ, Fullerton, 800 State College Dr, Fullerton, CA, 92631.

SMITH, JOANNA S.
PERSONAL Born 07/17/1965, Brooklyn, NY **DISCIPLINE** ARCHAEOLOGY **EDUCATION** Princeton Univ, BA, 87; Bryn Mawr Col, MA, 89, PhD, 94. **CAREER** Inst, Brookline Adult Ed, 95; res fel, lectr, dept archaeol, Boston Univ, 95; NEH fel, Cyprus Am Archaeol Res Inst, 96; Archaeol res, Leventis Found, Cyprus, 96-98; res fel, archaeol, Boston Univ, 98; vis asst prof, archaeol, Bryn Mawr Col, 99. **HONORS AND AWARDS** Summa Cum Laude, 87; Seeger grant, Am School of Class Stud, Athens, 87; Fulbright grant, 91-92; Jacob K Javits fel, 88-91, 92-93; Whiting fel, 93-94; NEH fel, 96; Kress fel, 97. **MEMBERSHIPS** Am Anthrop Asn; Am Philol Asn; Am Sch of Class Stud, Athens; Am Sch of Oriental Res; Archaeol Inst Am; Cyprus Am Archaeol Res Inst. **RESEARCH** The Eastern Mediterranean in the Bronze and Iron Ages; Cyprus; socio- economic and administrative structures; cult and ritual; cylinder and stamp seals; linear scripts (Cypro-Minoan, Linear B, Cypriot Syllabic); metal, textile, and ceramic technology; spatial, contextual, and functional analysis. **SELECTED PUBLICATIONS** Auth, The Cylinder Seal and the Inscribed Sherd, in Todd, ed, Excavations at Sanida, Report of the Dept of Antiquities, Cyprus, 92; auth, From Writing to Weaving, CAARI News, 93; auth, The Pylos Jn Series, Minos, 92/93; auth, Preliminary Comments on a Rural Cypro-Archaic Sanctuary in Polis-Peristeries, Bull of the Am Sch of Oriental Res, 97; auth, Cylinder Seal, in South, ed, Vasilikos Valley Project 4: Kalavasos- Ayios Dhimitrios III: Tombs 8, 9, 11-20, Stud in Mediterranean Archaeol, 98. **CONTACT ADDRESS** Dept of Archaeology, Boston Univ, 167 Clinton Rd, Brookline, MA, 02445-5815.

SMITH, JOANNE HAMLIN
PERSONAL Born 10/19/1954, Pittsburgh, PA, m, 1986 **DISCIPLINE** EDUCATION **EDUCATION** Edinboro Univ of Pennsylvania, Edinboro, PA, BS, 1972-76; Wichita State Univ, Wichita, KS, MEd, 1977-79; Kansas State University, Manhattan, KS, PhD, 1983-86. **CAREER** McPherson College, director of housing, assistant in student services, 1976-86; Arizona State Univ, assistant director of residence life, 1986-91; SOUTHWEST TEXAS STATE UNIV, DIRECTOR OF RESIDENCE LIFE, 1992-. **HONORS AND AWARDS** Women Helping Women Honoree, Soroptomist International, 1979; NASPA Region IV West Award for Outstanding Contributions, 1978. **MEMBERSHIPS** Treasurer, president-elect, president, Arizona College Personnel Assn, 1986-91; Association of College & University Housing Officers, 1986-; American College Personnel Association, 1986-; Phi Delta Kappa, 1976-; Natl Bd of Certified Counselors, certified counselor, 1980-. **CONTACT ADDRESS** Residence Life, Southwest Texas State Univ, San Marcos, TX, 78666.

SMITH, JOHN DAVID
PERSONAL Born 10/14/1949, Brooklyn, NY, m, 1971 **DISCIPLINE** HISTORY **EDUCATION** Baldwin-Wallace Col, AB, 71; Univ Ky, AM, 73, PhD(hist), 77. **CAREER** Cur, Louis A Warren Lincoln Libr & Mus, 77-79; dir, Hist Columbia Found, 79-80; instr, Southeast Mo State Univ, 80-81, asst prof, 81-82; ASST PROF, NC STATE UNIV, 82-, Assoc fac hist, Ind Univ-Purdue Univ, Fort Wayne, 78-79; lectr, Univ SC, 79-80; vis asst prof, Univ Ky, summer, 81; fel, Am Coun Learned Soc, 81-82; James Still fel, Univ Ky, 82. **MEMBERSHIPS** AHA; Orgn Am Historians; Southern Hist Asn. **RESEARCH** History of the South; Civil War and Reconstruction; Afro-American history. **SELECTED PUBLICATIONS** Coauth, History Comes To Life--Collecting Historical Letters And Documents, J Of The West, Vol 35, 96; The Confederate Republic--A Revolution Against Politics, J Of Am Hist, Vol 82, 95; The End Of Racism--Principles For A Multicultural Society, J Of Southern Hist, Vol 62, 96; The Papers Of Vance,Zebulon,Baird, Vol 2, Civil War Hist, Vol 42, 96; Black Confederates And Afro-Yankees In Civil-War Virginia, Am Hist Rev, Vol 101, 96; Woodson,Carter,G.--A Life In Black-History, Reviews In Am Hist, Vol 22, 94; Emancipation In Virginias Tobacco Belt, 1850-1870, Am Hist Rev, Vol 99, 94; Before Freedom Came--African-American Life In The Antebellum South, J Of Southern Hist, Vol 59, 93; Grimke,Archibald--Portrait Of A Black Independent, Rev In Am Hist, Vol 22, 94; The Fleming Lectures, 1937-1990--A Historiographical Essay, J Of Southern Hist, Vol 60, 94; Surveying The South--Studies In Regional Sociology--, Southern Cultures, Vol 2, 96; A Government Of Our Own--The Making Of The Confederacy, J Of Am Hist, Vol 82, 95. **CONTACT ADDRESS** Dept of Hist, No Carolina State Univ, Raleigh, NC, 27607.

SMITH, JONATHON ZITTELL
PERSONAL Born 11/21/1938, New York, NY, m, 1965 **DISCIPLINE** HISTORY OF RELIGION, HELLENISTIC RELIGIONS **EDUCATION** Haverford Col, BA, 60; Yale Univ, PhD(hist relig), 69. **CAREER** Instr relig, Dartmouth Col, 65-66; actg asst prof, Univ Calif, Santa Barbara, 66-68; asst prof, 68-73, William Benton prof relig & human sci, 74-82, dean col, 77-82, Robert O Anderson Distinguished Serv Prof Humanities, Univ Chicago, 82-, Co-ed, Hist Relig, 68-81. **MEMBERSHIPS** Soc Relig Higher Educ; Soc Bibl Lit; Am Acad Relig; Soc Study Relig. **RESEARCH** Hellenistic religions; anthropology of religion; method and theory of religion. **SELECTED PUBLICATIONS** Auth, Map is not Territory: Studies in the History of Religions, E J Brill, 78; Imagining Religion: From Babylon to Jonestown, Univ Chicago, 82; Nothing Human Is Alien To Me: Polygenesis And Human-Diversity As Characterizations Of Enlightenment Universalism In Early Anthropological Discourse, Religion, Vol 26, 96; A Matter Of Class: An Examination Of The Relationship Of Classification And Typology To Religious Thought--Taxonomies Of Religion, Harvard Theological Rev, Vol 89, 96. **CONTACT ADDRESS** Univ of Chicago, 1116 E 59th St, Chicago, IL, 60637.

SMITH, LACEY BALDWIN
PERSONAL Born 10/03/1922, Princeton, NJ **DISCIPLINE** HISTORY **EDUCATION** Bowdoin Col, BS, 46; Princeton Univ, MA, 49, PhD(hist), 51. **CAREER** Instr hist, Princeton Univ, 51-53; asst prof, Mass Inst Technol, 53-55; assoc prof, 55-62, chmn dept, 71-72, 74-77, PROF HIST, NORTHWESTERN UNIV, EVANSTON, 62-, Sr Fulbright scholar & Guggenheim fel, 63-64; Nat Endowment for Humanities sr fel, 73-74 & 82-83; chmn grad rec exam comt, Educ Testing Serv, 73-75; chmn, Ill Humanities coun, 82. **HONORS AND AWARDS** Lit Award, Chicago Found, 76., LittD, Bowdoin Col, 77. **MEMBERSHIPS** Midwestern Conf Brit Studies (pres, 70-72); Conf Brit Studies (pres, 77-79); fel Royal Hist Soc; fel Royal Soc Lit UK; AHA. **RESEARCH** English history, especially 16th century. **SELECTED PUBLICATIONS** Auth, Elizabeth I: Problems in Civilization, Forum Press, 80; The Past Speaks, Sources and Problems in English History to 1688, Heath, 81; coauth, Elizabeth-I--War And Politics, 1588-1603, J Of Interdisciplinary Hist, Vol 24, 94; Going To The Wars--The Experience Of The British Civil-Wars, 1638-1651, JOf Interdisciplinary Hist, Vol 26, 96; Law-Making And Society In Late Elizabethan England--The Parliament Of England, 1584-1601, J Of Interdisci-

plinary Hist, Vol 28, 1998; The Royal Palaces Of Tudor England, Architecture And Court Life, 1460-1547, Albion, Vol 26, 94. **CONTACT ADDRESS** 225 Laurel Ave, Wilmette, IL, 60091.

SMITH, LAURENCE D.
PERSONAL Born 10/28/1950, Iowa City, IA, m, 1981 **DISCIPLINE** HISTORY **EDUCATION** Univ New Hampshire, PhD 83. **CAREER** Univ Maine, asst prof, assoc prof, 83 to 98-. **MEMBERSHIPS** HSS; CS; APA; APS **RESEARCH** History of psychology; philosophy of science; graphical data displays. **SELECTED PUBLICATIONS** Co-ed with W. R. Woodward, B. F. Skinner and Behaviorism in American Culture, Beth PA, Lehigh Univ Press, 96; The role of data and theory in covariation assessment: Implications for the theory-ladenness of observation, Coauth, Jour of Mind and Behav, 96; Behaviorism, in: R. Fox and J. Kloppenberg, eds, A companion to American thought, Cambridge MA, Blackwell, 95. **CONTACT ADDRESS** Dept of Psychology, Maine Univ, Orono, ME, 04469. **EMAIL** ldsmith@maine.maine.edu

SMITH, MARK
DISCIPLINE PRE-MODERN EUROPEAN HISTORY **EDUCATION** Westmont Col, BA, summa cum laude; Denver Sem, MDiv; Univ Calif, Santa Barbara, MA, PhD. **CAREER** Instr, Albertson Col, 89-; bd supvr, Bethsaida Excavations, Israel. **SELECTED PUBLICATIONS** Auth, A Hidden Use of Porphyry's History ofPhilosophy in Eusebius' Praeparatio Evangelica, J of Theol Stud, 88; In Search of Santa, Timeline, 91; Ancient Bisexuality and the Interpretation of Romans 1:26-27, J of Am Acad of Relig, 96; Eusebius and the Religion of Constantius I, Studia Patristica, 97; A Tale of Two Julias: Julia, Julias and Josephus, in Bethsaida Excavations Rpt, Vol 2; Paul and Ancient Bisexuality, J of Am Acad of Relig, 97. **CONTACT ADDRESS** Albertson Col, Idaho, Caldwell, ID, 83605. **EMAIL** msmith@stimpy.acofi.edu

SMITH, MERRITT ROE
PERSONAL Born 11/14/1940, Waverly, NY **DISCIPLINE** HISTORY OF TECHNOLOGY **EDUCATION** Georgetown Univ, AB, 63; Pa State Univ, MA, 65, PhD, 71. **CAREER** Asst prof, Ohio State Univ, 70-75, assoc prof hist, 75-78; Prof hist technol , Prof Science Tech & Soc, MIT, 78-, Adv ed, Technol & Cult, 72-; Am Philos Soc res grant, 74; Harvard-Newcomen fel, Grad Scb Bus Admin, Harvard Univ, 74-75; fel, Regimal Econ Hist Res Ctr, Eleutherian Mills Libr, 78-79. **HONORS AND AWARDS** F J Turner Award, Orgn Am Historians, 77; Pfizer Award, Hist Sci Soc, 78; Hon Mention, Thomas Newcomen Award in Bus Hist, Newcomen Soc North Am & Bus Hist Rev, 80; Guggenheim Fel, 83; NSF Scholar, NSF, 84; Regents Fel, Smithsonian Inst, 84-85; Leonardo da Vinci Medal, Soc Hist Technol, 94; Hon Dr Humane Lett, Rensselaer Polytechnic Inst, 97. **MEMBERSHIPS** Soc Hist Technol; Orgn Am Historians; Soc Indust Archaeol; Hist Sci Soc; Am Hist Asm; Am Antiq Soc; Ma Hist Soc. **RESEARCH** Nineteenth century metalworking technologies; transfer of technology; comparative study of early industrial communities. **SELECTED PUBLICATIONS** Auth, George Washington and the establishment of the Harpers Ferry Armory, Va Mag Hist & Biog, 10/73; From craftsman to mechanic, Technological Innovation and the Decorative Arts, Univ Va, 73; The American Precision Museum, Technol & Cult, 74; Harpers Ferry Armory and the New Technology, Cornell Univ, 77; contribr, Military arsenals and industry before World War I, War Business and American Society, Kennikat, 77; Eli Whitney and the American system, Technology in America, VOA Forum Ser, 78; Does Technology Drive History, MIT Press, 94; Major Problems in the History of American Technology, Houghton Mifflin, 98. **CONTACT ADDRESS** Dept Hist, Massachusetts Inst of Tech, 77 Massachusetts Ave, Cambridge, MA, 02139-4307. **EMAIL** Roesmith@MIT.edu

SMITH, MICHAEL MYRLE
PERSONAL Born 11/02/1940, Springfield, IL, m, 1964, 3 children **DISCIPLINE** HISTORY **EDUCATION** Southern Ill Univ, BA, 63, MA, 67; Tex Christian Univ, PhD(hist), 71. **CAREER** Asst prof, 70-76, ASSOC PROF HIST, OKLA STATE UNIV, 76-, ACTG CHMN DEPT, 78- **RESEARCH** Colonial Mexico; 19th century Brazil; Colonial Latin American medicine. **SELECTED PUBLICATIONS** Auth, The real expedicion maritima de la Vacuna in New Spain and Guatemala, Am Philos Soc, 74; Carrancista Propaganda And The Print Media In The United-States--An Overview Of Institutions, Americas, Vol 52, 95. **CONTACT ADDRESS** Dept of Hist Math Sci, Oklahoma State Univ, Stillwater, OK, 74074.

SMITH, NELSON C.
DISCIPLINE AMERICAN; CANADIAN LITERATURE **EDUCATION** Princeton Univ, AB; Oberlin Col, MAT; Univ Wash, PhD. **CAREER** Assoc prof; dir, Lit Prog. **HONORS AND AWARDS** Can Coun Leave fel, 73-74. **RESEARCH** 19th-century British fiction; mystery fiction; the novel. **SELECTED PUBLICATIONS** Pub(s), articles and rev(s), Col Composition and Commun, Melville Soc Newsl, SEL, ESC, Prairie Forum, Supernatural Fiction Writers, Sci Fiction Writers, Pop Fiction in Am, Dictionary of Lit Biogr, A Trollope Companion, Encycl of Can Lit; coauth, Language BC, 76; The Art of Gothic, 80; James Hogg, 80; co-ed, Wilkie Collins to the Forefront, 95. **CONTACT ADDRESS** Dept of English, Victoria Univ, PO Box 3070, Victoria, BC, V8W 3W1. **EMAIL** ncsmith@uvic.ca

SMITH, PAMELA H.
PERSONAL Born 11/30/1957, CA, m, 1994, 2 children **DISCIPLINE** HISTORY **EDUCATION** Univ Wollongong, New South Wales, Australia, BA (First Class Honors), 79; Johns Hopkins Univ, PhD, 91. **CAREER** Teaching asst, Dept of Hist of Science, Johns Hopkins Univ, 84-86; asst prof, 90-97, ASSOC PROF, DEPT OF HIST, POMONA COL, CLAREMONT, CA, 97-; DIR OF EUROPEAN STUDIES, CLAREMONT GRAD UNIV, 96-. **HONORS AND AWARDS** Fel, Dept of Hist of Science, Johns Hopkins Univ, 83-85, 88-90; German Academic Exchange Service Summer Lang Scholarship, Bremen, Ger, 85; Frederic C. Lane Fel, Advanced Prog in Comparative European Hist, Villa Spelman, Johns Hopkins Univ, Florence, Italy, 85; German Academic Exchange Service Grad Res Fel, Munich, Ger, 86-88; Long & Widmont Memorial Found Award for Grad Res, 89; Pew Liberal Arts Enrichment Prog grant, Pomona Col, NEH Res Asst grant, 92; Steele Fel Res Leave, Pomona Col, 93-94; fel, Wissenschaftskolleg-Inst of Advanced Study, Berlin, 94-95; Pfizer Prize for The Business of Alchemy, Hist of Science Soc, 95; Irvine grant for Curriculum Development, Pomona Col, NEH Res asst grant, 96; NEH res asst grant, 97; John S. Guggenheiom fel, NEH Res fel, Sidney M. Edelstein Int fel, 97-98. **MEMBERSHIPS** Am Hist Asn; Hist of Science Soc; West Coast Hist of Science Soc; British Asn for the Hist of Science; Historians of Netherlandish Art; Am Asn for Netherlandic Studies. **SELECTED PUBLICATIONS** Auth, Review, Gareth Roberts, The Mirror of Alchemy, British Library, 95, Bul of the Hist of Medicine, 71, 97; review, Stanton J. Linden, Darke Hierogliphicks: Alchemy in English Literature from Chaucer to the Restoration, Univ Press KY, 96, Isis, 88, 97; review, Edward G. Ruestow, The Microscope in the Dutch Republic, Cambridge Univ Press, 96, Technology and Culture, forthcoming; review, Andrew Weeks, Paracelsus (SUNY Pr., 97), Bul for the Hist of Medicine, 72, 98; review, Edward Muir, Ritual in Early Modern Europe, Cambridge Univ Press, 97, Central European Hist, forthcoming; four entries in Encyclopedie der Alchemie, ed Claus Priesner and Karin Figala, C. H. Beck, 98; Giving Voice to the Hands: The Articulation of Material Literacy in the Sixteenth Century, in Popular Literacies, ed John Trimbur, Univ Pittsburgh Press, forthcoming; Vital Spirits: Alchemy, Redemption, and Artisanship in Early Modern Europe, in Rethinking the Scientific Revolution, ed Margaret Osler, Cambridge Univ Press, forthcoming; The House that Sylvius Built: Painting, the New Philosophy, and Modernity in Seventeenth-century Leiden, or, the Ivory Lathe in the Attic, Isis, forthcoming; Scholars, Scientists, Merchants, and Kings: Kuntskammern in the Making of Social Status in Early Modern Europe, Looking Through the Habsburg Glasses: America's Presence in Seventeenth-Century Art and Science, ed Ineke Phaf-Rheinberger, under review; Laboratories, The Cambridge History of Science, Vol 3: Early Modern Europe, ed Lorraine Daston and Katharine Park, forthcoming; numerous other publications. **CONTACT ADDRESS** Hist Dept, Pomona Col, 551 N. College Ave., Claremont, CA, 91711. **EMAIL** psmith@pomona.edu

SMITH, PATRICK
DISCIPLINE MODERN AND CONTEMPORARY ART **EDUCATION** Notre Dame Univ, BA; Univ NC, MA; Northwestern Univ, PhD. **CAREER** Assoc prof **RESEARCH** American modern and post-modern art. **SELECTED PUBLICATIONS** Publ, Andy Warhol's Art and Films; Warhol: Conversations about the Artist. **CONTACT ADDRESS** Dept of art., Wichita State Univ, 1845 Fairmont, Wichita, KS, 67260-0062.

SMITH, PAUL HUBERT
PERSONAL Born 06/21/1931, East Sparta, OH, m, 1954, 2 children **DISCIPLINE** AMERICAN HISTORY **EDUCATION** Bowling Green State Univ, BA, 54, MA, 55; Univ Mich, PhD, 62. **CAREER** Asst prof hist, Memphis State Univ, 60-62; from asst prof to assoc prof, Univ Nev, 62-66, chmn dept, 65-66; assoc prof, Univ Fla, 66-69; ed, Letters Of Delegates To Cong, 1774-89, Libr Cong, 69-. **MEMBERSHIPS** AHA; Orgn Am Historians; Am Studies Asn; Inst Early Am Hist & Cult; Asn for Doc Ed. **RESEARCH** American colonial and revolutionary history; 18th century British history. **SELECTED PUBLICATIONS** Auth, Loyalists and Redcoats, Univ NC, 64; Sir Guy Carleton, George Washington's Opponents, Morrow, 68; ed, English Defenders of American Freedoms, Libr Congr, 72; ed, Manuscript Sources...on the American Revolution, Libr Congr, 75; auth, Letters of Delegates to Congress, US Govt Printing Off, 76-97. **CONTACT ADDRESS** 15320 Pine Orchard Dr, Silver Spring, MD, 20906.

SMITH, PAUL M., JR.
PERSONAL Born 08/10/1920, Raleigh, North Carolina, m, 1972 **DISCIPLINE** EDUCATION **EDUCATION** St Augustine's Coll, BA 1941; NC Central Univ, BLS 1947; Univ IL, MLS 1949; Indiana Univ, EdD 1957. **CAREER** Shepard High School, teacher, 1941-42; Shaw University, assistant librarian, 1947-48; Dillard University, head librarian/instructor, 1950-53; Claflin College, head librarian, 1954-55; A & T State University, chief librarian, 1957-58; Albany State Coll, prof 1958-59; SC State Coll, prof 1959-60; NC Central Univ, prof 1960-69; Columbia Univ, adj prof 1969-70; Univ of Cincinnati, prof Afro-Amer Studies/prof psychology, professor emeritus. **HONORS AND AWARDS** Licensed Psychologist OH 1973-; publns in many nationally known journals. **MEMBERSHIPS** Mem Assn of Black Psychologists 1980-85. **CONTACT ADDRESS** Professor Emeritus, Univ of Cincinnati, Cincinnati, OH, 45221.

SMITH, PETER LAWSON
PERSONAL Born 03/31/1933, Victoria, BC, Canada, m, 1957, 3 children **DISCIPLINE** CLASSICS **EDUCATION** Univ BC, BA, 53; Yale Univ, MA, 55, PhD, 58. **CAREER** Instr classics, Univ BC, 55-56 & Yale Univ, 58-59; lectr, Carleton Univ, 59-60; from asst prof to assoc prof, 60-75, chmn dept, 63-69, assoc dean arts & sci, 70-71, dean fine arts, 72-80, Prof Classics, Univ Vivtoria, 75- **MEMBERSHIPS** Am Philol Asn; Class Asn Can; Class Asn Pac Northwest; Cambridge Philol Soc: Vergil Soc Am. **RESEARCH** Latin lyric poetry; Vergil; Roman drama. **SELECTED PUBLICATIONS** Auth, A symbolic pattern in Vergil's Eclogues, Phoenix, winter 65; Poetic tensions in the Horatian Recusatio, Am J Philol, 1/68; Vergil's Avena and the pipes of pastoral poetry, Trans Am Philol Asn, 70; Resonance in Vergil's Eclogues, Humanities Asn Rev, 77; coauth, Death And Rebirth In Virgil Arcadia, Phoenix-The J Of The Classical Assn Of Canada, Vol 46, 92. **CONTACT ADDRESS** Dept of Classics, Univ of Victoria, Victoria, BC, V8W 2Y2.

SMITH, PHILIP CHADWICK FOSTER
PERSONAL Born 02/17/1939, Salem, MA, 2 children **DISCIPLINE** MARITIME HISTORY **EDUCATION** Harvard Col, BA, 61. **CAREER** Asst cur, 63-66, cur maritime hist, Peabody Mus, Salem, 66-78; managing ed, Am Neptune, 69-79; ed mus publ, 78-79; CUR, PHILADELPHIA MARITIME MUS, 79-, Curator Maritime hist, Bostonian Soc, 67-78; mem bd ed, Hist Collections, Essex Inst, Salem, 75-; consult, Seafarers ser, Time-Life Bks Inc, 77-; assoc ed, Colonial Soc Mass, 78-; pres & chmn, Corinthian Historical Found, 81; ed, Am Neptune, 80-; vis lectr, Univ Pa, 81- **MEMBERSHIPS** US Comn Maritime Hist; Coun N Am Soc Oceanic Hist; Coun Am Maritime Mus; Soc Nautical Res; Int Cong Maritime Mus. **RESEARCH** Maritime history. **SELECTED PUBLICATIONS** Ed, Seafaring in Colonial Massachusetts, 80; Sibley's Heir: A Volume in Memory of Clifford Kenyon Shipton, Colonial Soc Mass, 82; auth, Big Muddy--Down The Mississippi Through America Heartland--Hall,Bc, Wood,Ct, Am Neptune, Vol 53, 93; United-States Trade With China, 1784-1814--Foreword/, American Neptune, Vol 54, 94; Growing-Up In A Shipyard--Reminiscences Of A Shipbuilding Life In Essex, Massachusetts--Story,Da, New England Quart-A Hist Rev Of New England Life And Letters, Vol 66, 93. **CONTACT ADDRESS** Philadelphia Maritime Mus, 321 Chestnut St, Philadelphia, PA, 19106.

SMITH, RANDALL BRIAN
PERSONAL Born 07/31/1959, Upper St. Clair, PA, s **DISCIPLINE** MEDIEVAL PHILOSOPHY; MEDIEVAL THEOLOGY **EDUCATION** Cornell Col, BA, 81; Univ Dallas, MA, 87; Univ Notre Dame, MMS, 91; PhD, 98. **CAREER** Post-Doctoral Res Assoc, Univ Notre Dame, 98-99. **HONORS AND AWARDS** Bradley Fel; Strake Found Grant. **MEMBERSHIPS** Amer Philos Assoc **RESEARCH** Thomas Aquinas; Medieval Philosophy & Theology; Natural Law; History of Biblical Exegesis. **CONTACT ADDRESS** Dept of Theology, Univ Notre Dame, Notre Dame, IN, 46556. **EMAIL** rsmith.11@nd.edu

SMITH, REBEKAH M.
DISCIPLINE CLASSICS **EDUCATION** Univ S, BA, 82; Univ NC, Chapel Hill, PhD, 91. **CAREER** Lectr, Univ NC, Chapel Hill. **HONORS AND AWARDS** Phi Beta Kappa, 80-82; tchg fel, Univ S, 80-82; Wilkins scholar, 80-81; Salutatorian, Class of 82; Green Latin Medal, 82. **SELECTED PUBLICATIONS** Auth, Photius on the Ten Attic Orators, Greek, Roman and Byzantine Stud 33, 92; Two Fragments of 'Longinus' in Photius, Class Quart 44, 94; A Hitherto Unrecognized Fragment of Caecilius, Am J of Philol 115, 4, 94; A New Look at the Canon of the Ten Attic Orators, Mnemosyne 48, 95. **CONTACT ADDRESS** Univ N. Carolina, Chapel Hill, Chapel Hill, NC, 27599.

SMITH, REUBEN W.
DISCIPLINE HISTORY **EDUCATION** Univ CA, BA, 51; MA, 52; Harvard Univ,PhD, 63. **CAREER** Prof emer, Univ Pacific. **RESEARCH** Islamic civilization; Near and Middle East. **SELECTED PUBLICATIONS** Auth, publ(s) on Islam. **CONTACT ADDRESS** Hist Dept, Univ Pacific, Pacific Ave, PO Box 3601, Stockton, CA, 95211.

SMITH, RICHARD J.
DISCIPLINE HISTORY, CHINESE CULTURE **EDUCATION** Univ CA, Davis, PhD, 72. **CAREER** Master, Hanszen Col, 82-87; adj prof, Univ TX, Austin; prof, 73-, dir, Asian Stud, Rice Univ. **HONORS AND AWARDS** Piper Professorship, 87; George R. Brown Cert of Highest Merit, 92; Sarofim Distinguished Tchg Professorship, 94-96; Nicolas Salgo Distin-

guished Tchg Prize, 96. **MEMBERSHIPS** Pres, TX Found for China Stud; pres, Southwest Conf of the Asn for Asian Stud. **RESEARCH** Contemp Chinese cult. **SELECTED PUBLICATIONS** Auth, China's Cultural Heritage: The Qing Dynasty, 1644-1912, 83; Fortune-tellers and Philosophers: Divination in Traditional Chinese Society, 91; Chinese Almanacs, 92; Chinese Maps: Images of All Under Heaven, 96; coauth, Robert Hart and China's Early Modernization, 91; H.B. Morse, Customs Commissioner and Historian of China, 95; coed, Cosmology, Ontology, and Human Efficacy: Essays in Chinese Thought, 93. **CONTACT ADDRESS** Rice Univ, PO Box 1892, Houston, TX, 77251-1892. **EMAIL** smithrj@ruf.rice.edu

SMITH, ROBERT FREEMAN
PERSONAL Born 05/13/1930, Little Rock, AR, m, 1951, 2 children **DISCIPLINE** UNITED STATES HISTORY **EDUCATION** Univ Ark, BA, 52, MA, 53; Univ Wis, PhD(Hist), 58. **CAREER** Instr Hist, Univ Ark, 53; assoc prof, Tex Lutheran Col, 58-62; from asst prof to assoc prof, Univ RI, 62-66; vis assoc prof, Univ Wis, 66-67; assoc prof, Univ Conn, 67-69; prof Hist, Univ Toledo, 69-; disting univ prof, 86; Tom L Evans res award, Harry S Truman Libr Inst, 76-77. **HONORS AND AWARDS** Tex Writer's Roundup Award, 61; Bk Award, Ohio Acad Hist, 73. **MEMBERSHIPS** Orgn Am Historians; Soc Historians Am Foreign Rels; Am Mil Inst; US Naval Inst; Southern Hist Asn. **RESEARCH** United States diplomatic history; history of inter-American relations; American military history. **SELECTED PUBLICATIONS** Auth, United States and Cuba: Business and Diplomacy, 1917-1960, 60 & What Happened in Cuba?, 63, Twayne; Background to Revolution: The Development of Modern Cuba, Knopf, 66; The United States and Revolutionary Nationalism in Mexico, 1916-1932, Univ Chicago, 72; Republican policy and the Pax Americana, 1921-1933, In: From Colony to Empire: Essays in the History of American Foreign Relations, Wiley, 72; The good neigbor policy: The liberal paradox in United States relations with Latin America, In: Watershed of Empire: Essays on New Deal Foreign Policy, Inst Humane Studies, 76; Reciprocity, In: Dictionary of the History of American Foreign Policy, Scribner, 78; auth, Era of Caribbean Intervention, Vol I, In: The United States and the Latin American Sphere of Influence, Kreiger Publ Co, 81; The Caribbean World and the United States: Mixing Rum and Coca Cola, Twayne Publ, 94; Estados Unidos y la Revolucion Mexicana, 1921-1959, in: Mitos en las Relaciones Mexico-Estados Unidos, Secretaria de Relaciones Exteriores de Mexico, 95. **CONTACT ADDRESS** Dept of History, Univ of Toledo, 2801 W Bancroft St, Toledo, OH, 43606-3390.

SMITH, ROBERT J.
DISCIPLINE HISTORY **EDUCATION** Yale Univ, BA, 57; Univ Pa, MA, 61, PhD, 67. **CAREER** Prof. **RESEARCH** Capitalism; education in Europe. **SELECTED PUBLICATIONS** Auth, The Ecole Normale Superieure and the Third Republic, SUNY, 82; The Making of the Modern World, St Martin's; Patron, Famille, et Entreprise: Bouchayer et Viallet De Grenoble, 96. **CONTACT ADDRESS** Dept of History, State Univ NY Col Brockport, Brockport, NY, 14420. **EMAIL** rjsmith@acspr1.acs.brockport.edu

SMITH, SHERRY L.
PERSONAL Born 03/19/1951, Hammond, IN, m, 1986 **DISCIPLINE** HISTORY **EDUCATION** Purdue Univ, BA, 72, MA, 74; Univ of Washington, PhD, 84. **CAREER** Asst prof to assoc prof, Univ Texas, 85- . **HONORS AND AWARDS** NEH fel for Col Tchrs, 96-97; NEH Summer Stipend, 94; Fulbright Found Sr lectruship, NZ, 93. **MEMBERSHIPS** AHA; Western Hist Asn; Am Soc for Ethnohistory. **RESEARCH** American Indians; American West. **SELECTED PUBLICATIONS** Auth, Sagebrush Soldier: William Earl Smith's View of the Sioux War of 1876, Univ Oklahoma Pr, 89; auth, The View from Officers' Row: Army Perceptions of Indians, Univ Arizona Pr, 91; auth, A Woman's Life in the Teton Country: Geraldine A. Lucas, in Montanam, the Mag of West Hist, 94; auth, Reimagining the Indian: Charles Erskine Scott Wood and Frank Linderman, in Pacific Northwest Q, 96; auth, Frontier Army: Military Life on the Frontier, Women and the Frontier Army, and, George Crook, in Encyclopedia of the American West, Macmillan, 96; auth, Lost Soldiers: Re-Searching the Military in the West, in Western Hist Q, 98; auth, Introduction, Covered Wagon Women, Univ Nebraska, forthcoming. **CONTACT ADDRESS** Dept of History, Univ of Texas, El Paso, El Paso, TX, 79968. **EMAIL** ssmith@utep.edu

SMITH, STEVEN G.
DISCIPLINE HISTORY OF WESTERN PHILOSOPHY AND ABRAHAMIC RELIGIOUS THOUGHT, PHILOSOPHY O **EDUCATION** Fla State Univ, BA, 73; Vanderbilt Univ, MA, 78; Duke Univ, PhD, 80. **CAREER** Dept Philos, Millsaps Col **SELECTED PUBLICATIONS** Auth, The Argument to the Other: Reason Beyond Thought in Karl Barth and Emmanuel Levinas, 83; The Concept of the Spiritual: An Essay in First Philosophy, 88 & Gender Thinking, 92. **CONTACT ADDRESS** Dept of Philosophy, Millsaps Col, 1701 N State St, Jackson, MS, 39210. **EMAIL** smithsg@okra.millsaps.edu

SMITH, THOMAS G.
PERSONAL Born 11/10/1945, Binghampton, NY, m, 1968, 4 children **DISCIPLINE** HISTORY **EDUCATION** SUNY, Cortland, BA, 67; Univ Connecticut, MA, 69, PhD, 77. **CAREER** Nichols Col, asst prof, 75-81, assoc prof, 82-86, prof, 87-. **HONORS AND AWARDS** Nichols Col ser awd for contrib to the college, 86. **MEMBERSHIPS** Org Am Historians; Environmental Hist Asn. **RESEARCH** US Foreign Policy; Environ Hist. **SELECTED PUBLICATIONS** Robert Frost, Stuart Udall, and the Last Go-Down, New Eng Quart, 97; John Kennedy, Stuart Udall, New Frontier Conservation, Pacific Hist Rev, 95; Negotiating With Castro: The Bay of Pigs Prisoners and a Lost Opportunity, Diplomatic Hist, 95; The Canyon Lands National Park Controversy, 1961-1964, Utah Hist Quart, 91; Independent: A Biography of Lewis W Douglas, with Robert Brower, NY, Knopf, 86. **CONTACT ADDRESS** Dept History, Nichols Col, Dudley, MA, 01570. **EMAIL** smith.t.9@nichols.com

SMITH, TOM W.
PERSONAL PA, m, 1969, 3 children **DISCIPLINE** AMERICAN HISTORY **EDUCATION** Univ Chicago, PhD, 79. **CAREER** Dir of General Social Survey, Nat Opinion Res Center, Univ Chicago, 80-; Secretary General, Int Social Survey Prog, 97-. **HONORS AND AWARDS** Worcestor Prize, 94. **MEMBERSHIPS** Am Asn for Public Opinion Res; A, Soc Asn; Mid-West Asn for Public Opinion Res. **RESEARCH** Social change; survey methods. **SELECTED PUBLICATIONS** Auth, Holocaust Denial: What the Survey Data Reveal, Working Papers in Contemporary Anti-Semitism, Am Jewish Committee, 95; A Political Profile of Italian Americans: 1972-1994, Nat Italian Am Found, 96; Annotated Bibliography of Papers Using the General Social Survey, 11th ed, with James A Davis, NORC, 96; General Social Surveys, 1972-1996: Cumulative Codebook, with James A Davis, NORC, 96; Marriage and Divorce, American Demographics, 19, Oct 97; Tall Oaks from Little Acorns Grow: The General Social Surveys, 1971-1997, The Public Perspective, 8, Feb/March 97; Why Our Neck of the Woods is Better Than the Forest, The Public Perspective, 9, June/July 98; The 1997-1998 National Gun Policy Survey of the National Opinion Research Center: Research Findings, NORC Report, March 98; Standard Definitions: Final Disposition of Cases Codes and Outcome Rates for RDD Telephone Surveys and In-Person Household Surveys, AAPOR, 98; National Pride: A Cross-National Analysis, GSS Cross-National Report no 19, with Lars Jarkko, NORC, 98; numerous other publications. **CONTACT ADDRESS** Nat Opinion Research Center, Univ of Chicago, 1155 E 60th St, Chicago, IL, 60637. **EMAIL** smitht@norcmail.uchicago.edu

SMITH, W. WAYNE
PERSONAL Born 11/30/1936, Laurel, DE, m, 1960, 2 children **DISCIPLINE** AMERICAN HISTORY **EDUCATION** Md State Teachers Col, Salisbury, BS, 58; Univ Md, MA, 61, PhD(hist), 67. **CAREER** Instr hist, Frostburg State Col, 61-63; asst prof, Southern Conn State Col, 66-68; assoc prof, 68-71, PROF HIST, IND UNIV PA, 71-, Nat Endowment for Humanities fel, 76; Newberry fel, 77. **MEMBERSHIPS** AHA; Orgn Am Historians; Southern Hist Asn. **RESEARCH** Jacksonian America; Civil War. **SELECTED PUBLICATIONS** Auth, Jacksonian Democracy on the Chesapeake, Md Hist Mag, 12/67 & 3/68; An Experiment in Counterinsurgency, J Southern Hist, 8/69; Politics and Democracy in Maryland, 1800-1856, In: Maryland, A Modern History, Md Hist Soc; 74; coauth, New Approaches in Teaching Local History, Newberry Libr, 78; The critical election in Indiana County, People, Poverty, Politics, 82; coauth, The Capture Of New-Orleans, 1862, Penn Magazine Of Hist And Biography, Vol 120, 96; The Fredericksburg Campaign--Decision On The Rappahannock, Penn Magazine Of Hist And Biography, Vol 120, 96. **CONTACT ADDRESS** Dept Hist, Univ Pa, Indiana, PA, 15701.

SMITH, WALLACE CALVIN
PERSONAL Born 05/12/1941, Pembroke, GA, m, 1964, 2 children **DISCIPLINE** AMERICAN HISTORY **EDUCATION** Emory Univ, AB, 63; Univ NC, Chapel Hill, MA, 65, PhD, 71. **CAREER** Asst prof hist, LaGrange Col, 65-67; teaching assoc, Univ NC, 67-71; asst prof, Jacksonville Univ, 71-72; asst prof, 72-75, assoc prof, 75-83, , PROF HIST UNIV SC AIKEN, 83-, Chmn Social & Behav Sci Div, 81-85. **HONORS AND AWARDS** Phi Beta Kappa, Pi Gamma Mu, Phi Alpha Theta, Who's Who Among American Teachers. **MEMBERSHIPS** Southern Hist Asn; Soc Hist Early Am Repub; GA Hist Soc; SC Hist Asn. **RESEARCH** Colonial American history; revolution and early national era; Antebellum Southern Unitarians, William Gregg. **SELECTED PUBLICATIONS** Auth, Utopia last chance? The Georgia silk boomlet of 1751, GA Hist Quart, spring 75; Habersham Family, In: Encycl of Southern History, 79; James Habersham et al, articles, in Dictionary of Georgia Biography, 83; The Habershams in Forty Years of Diversity, UGA Press, 84; David Wallace & Graniteville Centennial, proceedings of SCHA, 97; co-auth, African-Americans and the Palmetto State, 94. **CONTACT ADDRESS** Div of Hist and Political Science, Univ of S. Carolina, 471 University Pky, Aiken, SC, 29801. **EMAIL** Calvins@aiken.sc.edu

SMITH, WALTER L.
PERSONAL Born 05/14/1935, Tampa, FL **DISCIPLINE** EDUCATION **EDUCATION** FL A&M Univ, BA Biology & Chem 1963, MEd Admin & Supv 1966; FL State Univ PhD Higher Ed Admin 1974. **CAREER** Natl Educ Assn, assoc regional dir for NEA 1969-70; FL Educ Assn, admin asst 1970, asst exec sec 1970-73; Hillsborough Comm Coll, collegium dir 1973, dean employee relations 1973-74, provost 1974; Roxbury Comm Coll, pres 1974-77; FL A&M Univ, prof, president 1977-85; Education Development in South Africa, international team leader; founding rector, Funda Comm Coll, South Africa currently; UNIV OF FL, VISITING PROFESSOR, currently. **HONORS AND AWARDS** Red-X Awd Cape Kennedy IBM Corp 1966; Scholarly Distinction Awd Natl Urban League 1974; Meritorious Serv Awd Amer Assoc State Colleges & Univs 1984; President's Award, Natl Conf of Black Mayors; Jackson Memorial Awd Assoc of Classroom Teachers 1984; Fulbright Senior Scholar 1985; Congressional recognition for international leadership. **MEMBERSHIPS** Chairperson FL Supreme Ct Judicial Nominating Comm 1980-83; FL Supreme Ct Article V Comm 1983; chmn State Bd of Educ US Dept of Interior 1984; bd of dirs Natl Assoc for Equal Opportunity HE 1982-; bd dir Amer Assn of State Colleges and Univs; Urban League, chairman of the board. **CONTACT ADDRESS** Dept Ed Leadership, Univ of Florida, 258 Norman Hall, Gainesville, FL, 32611.

SMITH, WOODRUFF DONALD
PERSONAL Born 03/22/1946, Missoula, MT, m, 1967, 2 children **DISCIPLINE** MODERN EUROPEAN & AFRICAN HISTORY **EDUCATION** Harvard Univ, AB, 67; Univ Chicago, AM, 68, PhD(hist), 72. **CAREER** Asst prof hist, Roosevelt Univ, 68-69; sr analyst, Sparcom, Inc, Va, 72-73; asst prof, 73-77, assoc prof, 77-81, PROF HIST, UNIV TEX, SAN ANTONIO, 81-, Am Philos Soc grant, 76-77; Ger Acad Exchange Serv grant, 78; Fulbright fel, Netherlands, 80; Nat Endowment for Humanities grant, 81. **MEMBERSHIPS** AHA **RESEARCH** Modern German history; history of imperialism; African history. **SELECTED PUBLICATIONS** Coauth, The social and political origins of German diffusionist ethnology, J Hist Behav Sci, 78; The German Colonial Empire, Univ NC, 78; The emergence of German urban sociology, 1900-1910, J Hist Soc, 80; European Imperialism in the 19th and 20th Centuries, Nelson-Hall, 82; The German Experience Of Professionalization--Modern Learned Professions And Their Organizations From The Early 19th-Century To The Hitler Era, J Of Interdisciplinary Hist, Vol 23, 93; Nicolai,Helmut And Nazi Ideology, Am Hist Rev, Vol 98, 93 **CONTACT ADDRESS** Div of Soc Sci, Univ of Tex, San Antonio, TX, 78285.

SMITH FAVIS, ROBERTA
DISCIPLINE ART HISTORY **EDUCATION** Bryn Mawr Col, BA; Univ Pa, PhD. **CAREER** Assoc prof, 85-. **RESEARCH** 19th and 20th century American painting. **SELECTED PUBLICATIONS** Auth, pubs on historical and contemporary art. **CONTACT ADDRESS** Dept of Art, Stetson Univ, Unit 8378, DeLand, FL, 32720-3771.

SMITH JR., C. SHAW
DISCIPLINE ART HISTORY **EDUCATION** Univ NC Chapel Hill, AB, MA, PhD. **CAREER** Assoc prof and dept chr, Davidson Col. **RESEARCH** 18th and 19th-century painting; mod and contemp art; art and theory; French art hist. **SELECTED PUBLICATIONS** Auth, publ(s) in Eugene Delacroix and French Romanticism, Southern cult, art criticism. **CONTACT ADDRESS** Davidson Col, 102 N Main St, PO Box 1719, Davidson, NC, 28036. **EMAIL** shsmith@davidson.edu

SMITH NELSON, DOROTHY J.
PERSONAL Born 06/24/1948, Greenville, Mississippi, s **DISCIPLINE** EDUCATION **EDUCATION** Tufts University, BA, 1970, MEd, 1971; Southern Illinois University at Carbondale, PhD, 1981. **CAREER** Southern Illinois University at Carbondale Office of Student Development, coordinator of student development, 1979-81; Mississippi Valley State University, assistant vice pres for academic affairs & director academic skills parlor, 1971-. **HONORS AND AWARDS** Clark Doctoral Scholar Award for Research, Southern Illinois University, 1981; NAACP, Education Award, 1981; Education Achievement Award, Progressive Art & Civic Club, 1982; Outstanding Young Women of America, 1979-. **MEMBERSHIPS** Board, NAACP, 1982-84; Post Doctoral Academy of Higher Education, 1979-; financial sec, Les Modernette Social Club, 1981-; International Reading Assoc, 1985; Southern Illinois University Alumni Assoc; Concerned Educators of Black Students; Southeast Regional Reading Conference; Alpha Kappa Alpha; Progressive Art and Civic Club, Mississippi Reading Assoc, Natl Assoc of Develop Educators, Mississippi Assoc of Develop Educators. **CONTACT ADDRESS** Director, Student Counseling, Mississippi Valley State Univ, 14000 Highway 82 W #7232, Itta Bena, MS, 38941-1400.

SMITH, JR, JOHN K.
DISCIPLINE HISTORY OF TECHNOLOGY AND BUSINESS HISTORY **EDUCATION** PhD,Univ Del. **CAREER** Asso prof, Lehigh Univ. **RESEARCH** History of industrial research and development and the chemical industry. **SELECT-**

ED PUBLICATIONS Co-auth, Science and Corporate Strategy: DuPont R&D,1902-1980. **CONTACT ADDRESS** Lehigh Univ, Bethlehem, PA, 18015.

SMITH-ROSENBERG, CARROLL
DISCIPLINE HISTORY & PSYCHIATRY **EDUCATION** Conn Coll for Women, BA, 75; Columbia Univ, MA, 58, PhD, 68. **CAREER** Assoc prof, hist & psych, Univ Penn; PROF, HIST & WOMEN'S STUD, GRAD CH, AM CULT PROG, UNIV MICH. **MEMBERSHIPS** Am Antiquarian Soc **SELECTED PUBLICATIONS** Auth, "Sex as Symbol in Jacksonian America," Am Jour of Soc 84, 78; auth, "Davy Crockett as Trickster: Pornography, Liminality and Perversion in Victorian America," Jour of Contemp Hist 17, 82; auth, Disorderly Conduct; Visions of Gender in Victorian America, Alfred A. Knopf, 85; auth, "Domesticating Virtue: Coquettes and Rebels in Young America," in Literature and the Body, Johns Hopkins Univ Press, 88; auth, "Dis-covering the Subject of the Great Constitutional Discussion 1786-1789," Jour of Am Hist 79, 91; auth, "Subject Female: Engendering American Identity," Am Lit Hist, 93. **CONTACT ADDRESS** 2010 Hall Ave, Ann Arbor, MI, 48104. **EMAIL** csmithis@umich.edu

SMITHER, HOWARD ELBERT
PERSONAL Born 11/15/1925, Pittsburg, KS, m, 1946, 2 children **DISCIPLINE** HISTORICAL MUSICOLOGY **EDUCATION** Hamline Univ, AB, 50; Cornell Univ, MA, 52, PhD(musicol), 60. **CAREER** From instr to asst prof music, Oberlin Col, 55-60; asst prof, Univ Kans, 60-63; assoc prof, Tulane Univ, 63-68; assoc prof, 68-71, prof music, 71-79, dir grad studies music, 77-79, HANES PROF OF HUMANITIES IN MUSIC, UNIV NC, CHAPEL HILL, 79-, Fulbright res grant, Italy, 65-66; Nat Endowment for Humanities sr res fel, Italy, 72-73 & England, 79-80. **HONORS AND AWARDS** Deems Taylor Award, Am Soc Composers, Authors & Publ, 78. **MEMBERSHIPS** Am Musicol Soc (pres, 80-82); Libr Asn; Col Music Soc; Ital Soc Musicol; Int Musicol Soc. **RESEARCH** History of the oratorio; music in the Italian baroque; rhythmic techniques in 20th century music. **SELECTED PUBLICATIONS** Auth, The rhythmic analysis of twentieth century music, J Music Theory, 64; The Latin dramatic dialogue, J Am Musicol Soc, 67; Narrative and dramatic elements in the Laude Filippine, 1563-1600, Acta Musicologica, 69; Domenico Alaleona's Studi su la storia dell'oratorio, Notes, 75; Carissimi's Latin oratorios, Analecta Musicologica, 76; The baroque oratorio: A report on research, Acta Musicologica, 76; A History of the Oratorio (vols 1 & 2), Univ NC, 77; Oratorio and sacred opera, 1700-1825, Proc Royal Musicol Asn, 79-80; Il-Tempio-Armonico--Music From The Oratorio-Dei-Filippini Of Rome: 1575-1705, Music & Letters, Vol 74, 93. **CONTACT ADDRESS** Dept of Music, Univ of NC, Chapel Hill, NC, 27514.

SMITHERMAN, GENEVA
PERSONAL Brownsville, Tennessee, m **DISCIPLINE** EDUCATION **EDUCATION** Wayne State University, BA, 1960, MA, 1962; University of Michigan, PhD, 1969. **CAREER** Detroit Public Schools, teacher, 1960-66; Eastern Michigan University & Wayne State University, instructor, 1965-71; Wayne State University, assistant professor; Afro-American studies, Harvard University, lecturer, 1971-73; University of Michigan, adjunct professor, 1973; Wayne State University, professor, 1973-. **HONORS AND AWARDS** Dean's List of Honor Students, Wayne State University; University of Michigan, Pre-Doctoral Fellowship; Award for Scholarly Leadership in Language Arts Instruction, 1980. **MEMBERSHIPS** National Council Teachers of English, 1979-82; Executive Committee Conference College Composition, 1971-73; chairman, Black Literature Section, Midwest Language Association, 1972; Modern Language Association Committee, Minorities, 1976-77; Oral History Committee, Afro Museum, 1967-68; judge, Scholastic Writing Awards Contest, 1975; advisory board, Ethnic Awareness Project, 1977-78; founding member, African-American Heritage Association, 1976. **CONTACT ADDRESS** English, Michigan State Univ, 201 Morrill Hall, East Lansing, MI, 48824-1036.

SMOCOVITIS, V.B.
PERSONAL Born 11/15/1955, El Mansura, Egypt **DISCIPLINE** HISTORY OF SCIENCE **EDUCATION** Univ West Ont, BSC, 79; Cornell Univ, PhD, 80. **CAREER** Asst prof to Assoc Prof, Dept Hist, Univ Fla, 88-. **HONORS AND AWARDS** Mellon Fel, Hum, Stanford Univ 90-92. **MEMBERSHIPS** Hist Sci Soc; Soc for Study of Evolution; Am Asn for Advancement of Sci; Botanical Soc of Am. **RESEARCH** History of evolutionary biology, botany. **SELECTED PUBLICATIONS** coauth, Unitzy Biology: The Evolutionary Systems and Evolutionary Biology, Princeton Univ Press, 96. **CONTACT ADDRESS** Dept Hist, Univ of Florida, 4131 Turlington Hall, Gainesville, FL, 32611. **EMAIL** bsmocovi@history.olf.edu

SMOKER, PAUL L.
DISCIPLINE PEACE STUDIES AND INTERNATIONAL RELATIONS **EDUCATION** Lancaster Univ, Eng, MSc, PhD. **CAREER** Lloyd Prof Peace Stud and World Law, Antioch Col. **MEMBERSHIPS** Int Peace Res Asn; World Future Soc; World Futures Stud Fedn. **RESEARCH** The evolution of holistic peace theory. **SELECTED PUBLICATIONS** Auth, Peacekeeping, in Encyclopedia of the Future, MacMillan, 96; coauth, A Reader n Peace Studies, Pergamon Press, 90; Collected Papers of Lewis Fry Richardson, Cambridge UP, 1993; Inadvertent Nuclear War: The Implications of the Changing Global Order, Pergamon Press, 93; Towards Global/Local Cultures of Peace, in UNESCO Readings in Peace and Conflict Stud, 96; Exploring the Foundations for Inner-Outer Peace in the Twenty-First Century, Int J of Peace Stud, 96. **CONTACT ADDRESS** Antioch Col, Yellow Springs, OH, 45387.

SMYLIE, JAMES HUTCHINSON
PERSONAL Born 10/20/1925, Huntington, WV, m, 1952, 3 children **DISCIPLINE** AMERICAN CHURCH HISTORY **EDUCATION** Washington Univ, BA, 46; Princeton Theol Sem, BD, 49, ThM, 50, PhD(church hist), 58. **CAREER** Asst minister, First Presby Church, St Louis, 50-52; instr church hist, Princeton Theol Sem, 56-59, asst prof, 59-62, dir studies, 60-62; alumni vis prof church hist, 62-64, assoc prof, 64-67, PROF AM CHURCH HIST, UNION THEOL SEM, VA, 67-, Advan Relig Studies Found grant, 67; ed, J Presby Hist, 68- **MEMBERSHIPS** AHA; Am Cath Hist Asn; Am Studies Asn; Am Soc Church Historians (secy, 63-). **RESEARCH** Religion and politics; religion and culture. **SELECTED PUBLICATIONS** Auth, Into All the World, 65 & A Cloud of Witnesses, 65, John Knox; ed, Presbyterians and the American Revolution: A documentary account, 74 & Presbyterians and the American Revolution: An interpretive account, 76, J Presby Hist; Presbyterians And Aging--Perspectives From Our Past, American Presbyterians-J Of Presbyterian Hist, Vol 73, 95; Nisbet,Charles, 2nd Thoughts On A Revolutionary Generation, American Presbyterians-J Of Presbyterian Hist, Vol 73, 95; Ecumenist--The Reunion Of Protestantism And Roman-Catholicism, American Presbyterians-J Of Presbyterian Hist, Vol 73, 95; 'Uncle Toms Cabin' Revisited, The Bible, The Romantic Imagination, And The Sympathies Of Christ, Am Presbyterians--J Of Presbyterian Hist, Vol 73, 95; Religion And Politics In The Early Republic--Adams, Jasper And The Church-State Debate, Catholic Hist Rev, Vol 83, 1997; Ungodly Women, Gender, And The 1st-Wave Of American Fundamentalism, Interpretation-A J Of Bible And Theology, Vol 49, 95; Encyclopedia Of The Reformed Faith, American Presbyterians-J Of Presbyterian Hist, Vol 72, 1994; Baptist Theologians, Church Hist, Vol 64, 95; American Religious Bodies, Just War, And Vietnam, American Presbyterians-J Of Presbyterian Hist, Vol 73, 95; Fundamentalism And Gender, 1875 To The Present, Interpretation--A J Of Bible And Theology, Vol 49, 95; The Presbyterian Hymnal Companion, American Presbyterians-J Of Presbyterian Hist, Vol 72, 1994; Preface, American Presbyterians-J Of Presbyterian Hist, Vol 74, 96; Revolution And Religion--American Revolutionary War And The Reformed Clergy, J Of Presbyterian Hist, Vol 75, 1997; Baptist Theologians, Church Hist, Vol 64, 95; Church Growth And Decline In Historical-Perspective, Protestant Quest For Identity, Leadership, And Meaning, American Presbyterians-J Of Presbyterian Hist, Vol 73, 95; Images Of American Presbyterians In The Mirror Of Humor, American Presbyterians-J Of Presbyterian Hist, Vol 71, 93; coauth, 1st-Lady Between 2 Worlds, Am Presbyterians--J Of Presbyterian Hist, Vol 71, 93. **CONTACT ADDRESS** 1220 Rennie Ave, Richmond, VA, 23227.

SNEAD, DAVID L.
PERSONAL Born 02/21/1969, Charleston, SC, m, 1991, 2 children **DISCIPLINE** HISTORY **EDUCATION** BA, 90, MA, 91, Virginia Tech; Univ Virginia, PhD, 97. **CAREER** Visiting Asst Prof, Univ Richmond, 96-. **MEMBERSHIPS** Soc of Historians of Amer Foreign Relations; Amer Historical Assoc. **RESEARCH** Diplomatic and military history **SELECTED PUBLICATIONS** Auth, The Gaither Committee, Eisenhower, and the Cold War, 99. **CONTACT ADDRESS** 2601 Rudolph Rd, Richmond, VA, 23294. **EMAIL** dsnead2@richmond.edu

SNETSINGER, JOHN
PERSONAL Born 05/12/1941, Santa Barbara, CA **DISCIPLINE** AMERICAN HISTORY **EDUCATION** Univ Calif, Los Angeles, AB, 63; Univ Calif, Berkeley, MA, 66; Stanford Univ, PhD(hist), 69. **CAREER** Instr hist, San Jose State Univ, 67-70; PROF HIST, CALIF POLYTECH STATE UNIV, SAN LUIS OBISPO, 70-, Researcher, Harry S Truman Inst Nat & Int Affairs, 68 & 73. **RESEARCH** Recent American foreign policy; ethnic history. **SELECTED PUBLICATIONS** Auth, Truman, the Jewish Vote and the Creation of Israel, Hoover Inst, Stanford Univ, 74; ; American Consuls In The Holy-Land 1832-1914, Am Hist Rev, Vol 101, 96; Truman, Palestine, And The Press--Shaping Conventional Wisdom At The Beginning Of The Cold-War, Am Hist Rev, Vol 98, 93. **CONTACT ADDRESS** Dept of Hist, California Polytech State Univ, San Luis Obispo, CA, 93407.

SNOW, D. R.
DISCIPLINE ANTHROPOLOGY **EDUCATION** Univ Minn, BA, 62; Univ Ore, PhD, 66. **CAREER** Teach asst, 65-66; asst prof, 66-69; asst prof, 69-72, assoc prof, 72-80, chair, dept anthrop, 74-80, PROF, ANTHROP, 80-95, 89-91, SUNY, ALBANY; assoc dean Soc & Beh Scis, 80-83, Act Dean Col Soc & Beh Scis, 83; vis prof, Univ Am, Mexico, 78; PROF, HEAD DEPT ANTHROP, PA STATE UNIV, 95-. **CONTACT ADDRESS** Dept of Anthrop, Pennsylvania State Univ, 409 Carpenter Bldg, University Park, PA, 16801. **EMAIL** drs17@psu.edu

SNOW, GEORGE EDWARD
PERSONAL Born 01/13/1939, Miami, FL, m, 1958, 4 children **DISCIPLINE** MODERN EUROPEAN HISTORY **EDUCATION** Ohio State Univ, BA, 62, MA, 64; Ind Univ, PhD(hist), 70. **CAREER** From asst prof to assoc prof, 67-73, PROF HIST, SHIPPENSBURG STATE COL, 73-, CHMN DEPTS HIST & PHILOS, 80-, Am Philos Soc res grant, 73; co-holder Nat Endowment for Humanities prog develop grant, 76-77. **MEMBERSHIPS** Soc Sci-Hist Asn; AHA; Am Asn Advan Slavic Studies; Can Asn Slavists. **RESEARCH** Imperial Russian bureaucracy under Nicholas II; imperial Russian labor policy in the 19th and 20th centuries. **SELECTED PUBLICATIONS** Auth, The Kokovtsov Commission: An abortive attempt at labor reform in Russia in 1905, Slavic Rev, 12/72; The Peterhof Conference and the Bulygin Duma, Russ Hist/Hist Russe, 75; ; Alcoholism In The Russian Military--The Public Sphere And The Temperance Discourse, 1883-1917, Jahrbucher Fur Geschichte Osteuropas, Vol 45, 1997; The Engineer Of Revolution--Krasin, L.B. And The Bolsheviks, 1870-1926, Historian, Vol 55, 93; The Soldiers Story--Soviet Veterans Remember The Afghan-War, Slavic Rev, Vol 55, 96; A History Of Vodka, Russian Hist--Histoire Russe, Vol 20, 93; Russia Goes Dry--Alcohol, State And Society, Slavic Rev, Vol 56, 1997. **CONTACT ADDRESS** Dept of Hist, Shippensburg State Col, 1871 Old Main Dr, Shippensburg, PA, 17257-2299.

SNYDER, ARNOLD C.
DISCIPLINE HISTORY **EDUCATION** Univ Waterloo, BA, 74; McMaster Univ, MA, 75; PhD, 81. **CAREER** Assoc prof **HONORS AND AWARDS** Ed, Conrad Grebel Rev. **SELECTED PUBLICATIONS** Auth, pub(s) on church history, Anabaptist history and thought, and spirituality and peace. **CONTACT ADDRESS** Dept of History, Conrad Grebel Col, 200 Westmount Rd, Waterloo, ON, N2L 3G6. **EMAIL** casnyder@uwaterloo.ca

SNYDER, DAVID W.
PERSONAL Born 03/21/1961, IN **DISCIPLINE** MUSIC EDUCATION **EDUCATION** Doctorate of music EDU , 96. **CAREER** Illinois state Univ, asst prof, 95-. **HONORS AND AWARDS** Teaching, Res, Ser Initiative Awds. **MEMBERSHIPS** MENC **RESEARCH** Teacher EDU ; pre-student teaching exp; classroom mgmt. **CONTACT ADDRESS** Dept of Music, Illinois State Univ, Campus Box 5660, Normal, IL, 61790. **EMAIL** dsnyder@ilstu.edu

SNYDER, GLENN HERALD
PERSONAL Born 10/08/1924, Superior, WI, m, 1951, 3 children **DISCIPLINE** POLITICAL SCIENCE **EDUCATION** Univ Oregon, BS, 48; Columbia Univ, PhD, 56. **CAREER** Tchg fel, Wesleyan Univ, 53-55; lectr, res assoc, Columbia Univ, 55-58; res assoc, Princeton Univ, 58-60; assoc prof, Univ Denver, 60-62; vis assoc prof, Univ Calif, Berkeley, 62-64; assoc prof, prof, SUNY Buffalo, 64-84; prof, prof emer, Univ North Carolina, 84-. **HONORS AND AWARDS** Fel, Woodrow Wilson Ctr, 81-82; fel, Guggenheim Found, 90-91. **MEMBERSHIPS** Am Polit Sci Asn; Int Inst for Strategic Stud; Triangle Inst for Strategic Stud. **RESEARCH** International relations; military affairs. **SELECTED PUBLICATIONS** Auth, Deterrence and Defense, Princeton, 61; coauth, Strategy, Politics and Defense Budgets, Columbia, 62; auth, Stockpiling Strategic Materials, Chandler, 67; coauth, Conflict Among Nations, Princeton, 77; auth, Alliance Politics, Cornell, 97. **CONTACT ADDRESS** Dept of Political Science, Univ of No Carolina, 520 Morgan Creek Rd, Chapel Hill, NC, 27514. **EMAIL** gsnyder1@email.unc.edu

SNYDER, LEE DANIEL
PERSONAL Born 06/04/1933, Waterbury, CT, m, 1961, 2 children **DISCIPLINE** CHURCH HISTORY **EDUCATION** Williams Col, AB, 55; Harvard Univ, AM, 56, PhD(Europ hist), 66; Union Theol Sem, BD, 61. **CAREER** Asst prof hist, Ithaca Col, 63-64 & Ohio Wesleyan Univ, 64-69; assoc prof hist, 69-80, PROF SOC SCI, NEW COL, UNIV S FLA, 80-, DIR MEDIEVAL-RENAISSANCE STUDIES, 77-, Vis prof, Methodist Theol Sch Ohio, 68. **MEMBERSHIPS** AHA; Mediaeval Acad Am; Am Soc Church Hist; Soc Values Higher Educ; Am Soc Reformation Res. **RESEARCH** Renaissance and Reformation church history; Christian devotion in 15th and 16th centuries; humanism. **SELECTED PUBLICATIONS** Auth, Seeking insight on insight, Soundings, 74; Some thoughts on a theology of resurrection, Encounter, 75; Erasmus on prayer, Renaissance & Reformation, 76; ; The Social Dimension Of Piety--Associative Life And Devotional Change In The Penitent Confraternities Of Marseilles: 1499-1792, Church Hist, Vol 65, 96; Patronage In Renaissance Italy From 1400 To The Early 16th-Century, Church Hist, Vol 66, 1997; Religion, Political-Culture And The Emergence Of Early-Modern Society --Essays In German And Dutch History, Church Hist, Vol 64, 95; translator, Macrobius,Ambrosius,Aurelius,Theodosius--Commentary On The Dream Of Scipio, Church Hist, Vol 61, 92. **CONTACT ADDRESS** Div of Soc Sci, New Col of the Univ of So Florida, Sarasota, FL, 33580.

SNYDER, ROBERT EDWARD
PERSONAL Born 03/27/1943, Amsterdam, NY, m, 1961, 2 children **DISCIPLINE** AMERICAN HISTORY **EDUCATION** Union Col, BA, 67, MA, 71; Syracuse Univ, PhD(Am Studies), 80. **CAREER** ASST PROF AM STUDIES, UNIV SOUTH FLA, 80- **MEMBERSHIPS** AHA; Orgn Am Historians; Southern Hist Asn. **RESEARCH** Modern America; American South; labor. **SELECTED PUBLICATIONS** Auth, Huey Long and the presidential election of 1936, La Hist, spring 75; The concept of demagoguery: Huey P Long and his literary critics, La Studies, spring 76; Huey Long and the Cotton Holiday Plan of 1931, La Hist, spring 77; The Cotton Holiday Movement in Mississippi, J Miss Hist, 2/78; Women, Wobblies, and workers' rights: The 1912 textile strike in Little Falls, New York, NY Hist, 1/79; contribr, At the Point of Production, Greenwood Press, 81; ; The Kingfish And His Realm--The Life And Times Of Long, Huey, P., J Of Southern Hist, Vol 59, 93; Messiah Of The Masses--Long, Huey, P. And The Great-Depression, J Of Southern Hist, Vol 60, 94; Huey At 100--Centennial Essays On Long, Huey, J Of Southern Hist, Vol 63, 97; A Southern Life--Letters Of Green,Paul, 1916-1981, J Of Southern Hist, Vol 61, 95; Secure The Shadow--Death And Photography In America, Am Hist Rev, Vol 101, 96. **CONTACT ADDRESS** Dept of Am Studies, Univ of South Fla, Tampa, FL, 33620.

SOARES, ANTHONY T.
DISCIPLINE EDUC PSYCHOLOGY **EDUCATION** Univ Ill, DEd, 62. **CAREER** PROF EDUC, Univ Bridgeport, 65-. **MEMBERSHIPS** AERA; APS; PDK; EERO; AAER; KDP; CPA; ASCD. **RESEARCH** Self perceptins, assessment, learning growth and develop. **SELECTED PUBLICATIONS** Self Perceptions Inventories, SPI; Apperception Inventories, API. **CONTACT ADDRESS** Univ of Bridgeport, University Ave, Bridgeport, CT, 06602.

SOBEL, ROBERT
PERSONAL Born 02/19/1931, New York, NY, m, 1958, 1 child **DISCIPLINE** BUSINESS HISTORY **EDUCATION** City Col NY, BSS, 51; NY Univ, MA, 52, PhD, 57. **CAREER** Instr hist, NY Univ, 56-57; from asst prof to assoc prof, 57-76, prof hist, New Col, Hofstra Univ, 76-, Cordell Hull fel, 61-63; Econ-in-Action fel, 62; NY State fel African hist, 66-67; bus hist ed, Greenwood Press, 66-. **MEMBERSHIPS** AHA; Bus Hist Asn; Am Econ Asn. **RESEARCH** American financial history; history of American foreign policy and public opinion. **SELECTED PUBLICATIONS** Auth, The Origins of Interventionism, Bookman Assoc, 60; A guide to American History, 62 & A History of the New York Stock Market, 63, Collier; The Big Board: A History of the New York Stock Exchange, Free Press, 65, The American Revolution, Am RDM, 67; The Great Bull Market: Wall Street in the 1920's, Norton, 68; Panic on Wall Street, Macmillan, 68. **CONTACT ADDRESS** Dept of History, Hofstra Univ, 1000 Fulton Ave, Hempstead, NY, 11550-1091.

SOCHEN, JUNE
PERSONAL Born 11/26/1937, Chicago, IL **DISCIPLINE** HISTORY **EDUCATION** Univ Chicago, AB, 58; Northwestern Univ, AM, 60, PhD(hist), 67. **CAREER** Ed, Carnegie Corp Proj on Guide & Motivation Super Studies, 60-61; teacher English & hist, NShore Country Day Sch, Ill, 61-64; PROF HIST, NORTHEASTERN ILL UNIV, 64-, Nat Endowment for Humanities younger humanist grant, 71-72. **MEMBERSHIPS** AHA; Am Studies Asn. **RESEARCH** Women's history; 20th century United States intellectual history; popular culture. **SELECTED PUBLICATIONS** Ed, The New Feminism in Twentieth Century America, Heath, 71; The Black Man and the American Dream, 1900-1930, 71 & auth, The New Woman: Feminism in Greenwich Village, 1910-1920, 72, Quadrangle; co-ed, Destroy to Create: Readings on the American Environment, Dryden, 72; auth, The Unbridgeable Gap: Blacks and Their Quest for the American Dream, 1900-1930, Rand McNally, 72; Movers and Shakers: American Women Thinkers and Activists, 1900-1970, Quadrangle, 73; Her story: A Woman's View of American History, Alfred, 74, 2nd ed, 81; Consecrate Every Day: The Public Lives of Jewish American Women, 1880-1980, State Univ NY, 81; Enduring Values: Women in Popular Culture, Praeger Publ, 87; Cafeteria America: New Identities in Contemporary Life, Iowa State Univ Press, 88; ed, Women's Comic Visions, Wayne State Univ Press, 91; auth, She Who Laughs Lasts: The Life and Times of Mae West, Harlan Davidson, Inc, 92. **CONTACT ADDRESS** Dept of History, Northeastern Illinois Univ, 5500 N St Louis Ave, Chicago, IL, 60625-4625. **EMAIL** jsochen@neiu.edu

SOCOLOFSKY, HOMER EDWARD
PERSONAL Born 05/20/1922, Tampa, KS, m, 6 children **DISCIPLINE** HISTORY **EDUCATION** Kans State Univ, BS, 44, MS, 47; Univ Mo, PhD, 54. **CAREER** Asst, 46, from instr to assoc prof, 47-63, PROF HIST, KANS STATE UNIV, 63-, Vis asst prof, Yale Univ, 54-55; Woods fel, Nebr Hist Soc, 61-; actg chmn dept, Kans State Univ, 64-65 & 69-70; comnr, Kans Am Revolution Bicentennial Comn, 75-76; sr context consult, Univ Mid-Am, 75; Fulbright lectr, India, 81-82. **MEMBERSHIPS** Orgn Am Historians; Agr Hist Soc (vpres, 67-68, pres, 68-69); Western Hist Asn; Great Plains Hist Asn. **RESEARCH** Agricultural history; public land disposal and land policy; history of the Great Plains. **SELECTED PUBLICATIONS** Auth, Mary Donoho--New First-Lady Of The Santa-Fe-Trail, J Of The West, Vol 32, 93; Wagon-Wheel Kitchens--Food On The Oregon-Trail, J Of The West, Vol 35, 96; Rooted In Dust--Surviving Drought And Depression In Southwestern Kansas, Agricultural History, Vol 69, 95; Final Harvest And Other Convictions And Opinions, J Of The West, Vol 34, 95; Faded Dreams--More Ghost Towns Of Kansas, J Of The West, Vol 35, 96; The Career Of Elmer Mccurdy, Deceased--An Historical Mystery, J Of The West, Vol 32, 93; Populism, Its Rise And Fall, Great Plains Quarterly, Vol 13, 93; Western-History-Association Prize Recipient, 92, Western Historical Quarterly, Vol 24, 93; Rooted In Dust--Surviving Drought And Depression In Southwestern Kansas, Agricultural Hist, Vol 69, 95; Talking Mysteries--A Conversation With Tony Hillerman, J Of The West, Vol 32, 93; Oregon-Trail--Last Of The Pioneers, J Of The West, Vol 35, 96; The Last Conquistador--Juan,De Onate And The Settling Of The Far Southwest, J Of The West, Vol 0032, 1993. **CONTACT ADDRESS** Dept of Hist, Kansas State Univ, Manhattan, KS, 66506.

SOCOLOW, SUSAN M.
DISCIPLINE HISTORY **EDUCATION** Barnard Col, BA, 62; Columbia Univ, MA, 64, PhD, 73. **CAREER** Samuel Candler Dobbs Prof Lat Am Hist. **RESEARCH** Latin American social history and quantitative techniques. **SELECTED PUBLICATIONS** Auth, The Merchants of Viceregal Buenos Aires: Family and Commerce; The Bureaucrats of Buenos Aires, 1769-1810: Amor Al Real Servicio; Women in Colonial Latin America; ed, The Atlantic Staple Trade; co-ed, Cities and Society in Colonial Latin America; The Countryside in Colonial Latin America. **CONTACT ADDRESS** Dept History, Emory Univ, 221 Bowden Hall, 561 Kilgo Cir, Atlanta, GA, 30322-1950. **EMAIL** socolow@emory.edu

SODEN, DALE
DISCIPLINE HISTORICAL, POLITICAL, AND INTERNATIONAL STUDIES. **EDUCATION** Univ Wash, MA, 76; PhD, 80. **CAREER** Asso dean acad aff; assoc prof, 85-. **HONORS AND AWARDS** Corp bd, YMCA; bd of trustees, Pacific Lutheran theol sem, Berkeley. **MEMBERSHIPS** St Mark's Lutheran Church. **RESEARCH** Relationship between religion and public policy in the history of the Pacific Northwest. **SELECTED PUBLICATIONS** Auth, history of Whitworth College; articles for scholarly jour(s) on topics in American religious history. **CONTACT ADDRESS** Dept of Hist, Whitworth Col, 300 West Hawthorne Rd, Spokane, WA, 99251. **EMAIL** dsoden@whitworth.edu

SOFFER, REBA NUSBAUM
PERSONAL Born 12/22/1934, Nashville, TN, m, 1956, 1 child **DISCIPLINE** MODERN EUROPEAN HISTORY **EDUCATION** Brooklyn Col, BA, 55; Wellesley Col, MA, 57; Radcliffe Col, PhD, 62. **CAREER** From instr to assoc prof, 61-71, PROF HIST, CALIF STATE UNIV, NORTHRIDGE, 71-, Vis lectr, Univ Calif Los Angeles, 67-68, vis prof, 80; fel, Nat Endowment Humanities, 71 & 81-82, Am Counc Learned Soc, 72, Am Philos Soc, 74; Munro Humanities lectr, Calif Inst Technol, 77; vis fel, Mansfield Col, Oxford & vis prof, Selwyn Col, Cambridge, 81; lectr, Northern Ariz Univ, 80, Inst Educ, Univ Calif, Berkeley, 82. **HONORS AND AWARDS** Pac Coast Br Award, AHA, 78. **MEMBERSHIPS** AHA; Conf Brit Studies (assoc exec secy, 78-83); Pac Coast Conf Brit Studies (pres, 76-78); Inst Hist Res; Soc Hist Soc Sci. **RESEARCH** British history of the 19th and 20th centuries: intellectual, social and institutional. **SELECTED PUBLICATIONS** Auth, Popular Anti-Catholicism In Mid-Victorian England, J Of Modern Hist, Vol 66, 94; The Conservative Historical Imagination In The 20th-Century, Albion, Vol 28, 96; Philosophers And Kings, Education For Leadership In Modern England, Albion, Vol 24, 92; Public Moralists--Political-Thought And Intellectual Life In Britain, 1850-1930, Am Hist Rev, Vol 97, 92. **CONTACT ADDRESS** Dept of Hist, California State Univ, Northridge, Northridge, CA, 91324.

SOKAL, MICHAEL MARK
PERSONAL Born 10/06/1945, Brooklyn, NY, m, 1968, 2 children **DISCIPLINE** HISTORY OF SCIENCE & TECHNOLOGY **EDUCATION** Cooper Union, BE, 66; Case Western Reserve Univ, MA, 68, PhD(Hist of Sci & Technol), 72. **CAREER** Res asst Hist of Sci, Ctr Hist Physics, Am Inst Physics, New York, 66; asst prof, 70-75, assoc prof, 75-81, prof Hist, Worchester Polytech Inst, 81-, vis res fel, Div Med Sci, Nat Mus Hist & Technol, Smithsonian Inst, 73-74; affil assoc prof Hist of Sci & Technol, Clark Univ, 75-80; nat lectr, Sigma Xi, 79-81; vis scholar Hist of Sci, Harvard Univ, 81-82. **HONORS AND AWARDS** WPI Pres Fletcher Disting Prof in Humanities, 93-95; chmn elect, chmn & Immediate Chmn Sextion on Hist and Philo of Science, Am Assn for the Advan of Science, 97-99. **MEMBERSHIPS** Hist Sci Soc; Soc for Hist of Tech; Cheiron; Am Asn Advan Sci. **RESEARCH** History of psychology; history of American science and technology. **SELECTED PUBLICATIONS** Auth, The unpublished autobiography or James McKeen Cattell, Am Psychologist, 71; auth, Science and James McKeen Cattell, 1894 to 1945, Science, 80; ed, An education in psychology: James McKeen Cattell's journal and letters from Germany and England, 1880-1888, Mass Inst Tech Press, 81; auth, ed, Psychological Testing and Am Soc, 1890-1930, Rutgers Univ Press, 87. **CONTACT ADDRESS** Dept of Humanities, Worcester Polytech Inst, 100 Institute Rd, Worcester, MA, 01609-2247. **EMAIL** msokal@wpi.edu

SOKOL, DAVID M.
DISCIPLINE ART HISTORY **EDUCATION** NY Univ, PhD. **CAREER** Prof, Univ IL at Chicago. **RESEARCH** Am art; mod art; museology. **SELECTED PUBLICATIONS** Auth, American Vision: Paintings from a Century of Collecting; Life in 19th Century America; co-auth, American Art: Painting-Sculpture-Architecture-Decorative Arts-Photography. **CONTACT ADDRESS** Art Hist Dept, Univ Illinois Chicago, S Halsted St, PO Box 705, Chicago, IL, 60607.

SOLBERG, WINTON UDELL
PERSONAL Born 01/11/1922, Aberdeen, SD, m, 1952, 3 children **DISCIPLINE** AMERICAN HISTORY **EDUCATION** Univ SDak, AB, 43; Harvard Univ, MA, 47, PhD, 54. **CAREER** From instr to asst prof soc sci, US Mil Acad, 51-54; from instr to asst prof hist, Yale Univ, 54-58; James Wallace prof Am hist, Macalester Col, 58-62; vis prof, 61-62, assoc prof, 62-67, chmn dept hist, 70-72, PROF AM HIST, UNIV ILL, URBANA, 67-, Morse fel, Yale Univ, 57-58; consult & lectr, US Army War Col, Carlisle Barracks, 59, 60 & 62; res fel, Ctr Study Hist of Liberty in Am, Harvard Univ, 62-63; Fulbright-Hays lectr, Johns Hopkins Sch Adv Int Studies, Bologna, 67-68; mem, Ill Coun Humanities, 73-75; Nat Endowment Humanities sr fel, 74-75; dir, Nat Endowment Humanities Residential Sem, 76-77; vis prof, Konan Univ, Kobe, Japan, 81. **HONORS AND AWARDS** Fulbright-Hays lectr, Moscow Univ, USSR, 78. **MEMBERSHIPS** Orgn Am Hist; Am Studies Asn; Southern Hist Asn; AHA; AAUP (first vpres, 74-76). **RESEARCH** American intellectual history; American religious and scientific thought; political and constitutional thought. **SELECTED PUBLICATIONS** Auth, Cotton Mather's indebtedness to Marcello Malpighi, J Hist Med & Allied Sci, 7/81; auth & ed, John Cotton's Treatise on the Duration of the Lord's Day, Publ Colonia Soc Mass, 82; The Seventh-Day-Men--Sabbatarians And Sabbatarianism In England And Wales, 1600-1800, Church Hist, Vol 64, 1995; The Founders And The Classics--Greece, Rome, And The American Enlightenment, Am Hist Rev, Vol 100, 95; The Documentary History Of The Ratification Of The Constitution, J Of Southern Hist, Vol 61, 95; The Secularization Of The Academy, Catholic Hist Rev, Vol 79, 93. **CONTACT ADDRESS** Dept of Hist, Univ of Ill, Urbana, IL, 61801.

SOLBRIG, OTTO THOMAS
PERSONAL Born 12/21/1930, Buenos Aires, Argentina, m, 1969, 2 children **DISCIPLINE** BOTANY **EDUCATION** Liceo Militar, General San Martin, Argintina, 45-48; Univ of La Plata, Argentina, 50-54; Univ of Calif, Berkeley, PhD, 59; Harvard Univ, MA (honoris causa), 69. **CAREER** Res asst in botany and genetics, Univ of La Plata, 51-54; teaching fel in Botany, Univ of Calif, Berkeley, 56-58; asst to assoc curator, Gray Herbarium of Harvard Univ, 60-66; assoc prof to prof, Univ of Michigan, Ann Arbor, 66-69; visiting prof, Dept of Biology, Univ de los Andes, Venezuela, 83-84; BUSSEY PROF OF BIOLOGY, HARVARD UNIV. **HONORS AND AWARDS** Fel, Third World Acad of Sci, 96; Silver Medal, Univ Complutense de Madrid, 93; fel, San Pablo Found of Torino, 90-91; Willdenow Medal, Berlin Botanical Gardens, 79; Guggenheim Fel, 75-76; fel, Am Acad of Arts and Scis, 74; Congressional Antarctic Medal, 67; Cooley Prize, Am Soc of Plant Taxonomy, 61; James Gowey fel in Botany, Univ of Calif, Berkeley, 58-59. **MEMBERSHIPS** Rockefeller Latin Am Center; Comt on Special Concentrations; Interdisciplinary Coordinating Comt on Latin Am and Iberian Studies; Common Room, Lowell House; Am Asn for the Advancement of Sci; Third World Acad of Sci; Am Soc of Naturalists; Ecological Soc of Am; Am Soc of Plant Taxonomists; Soc for the Study of Evolution; British Ecological Soc; Asn Argentina de Ecologia; Soc Argentina de Botanica; New England Botanical Club. **RESEARCH** Population Ecology; biodiversity; evolution and ecology of desert, savanna, and forest floor plants; natural resources and land use. **SELECTED PUBLICATIONS** Coauth, So Shall you Reap, Island Press, 94; coauth, Biodiversity and Global Change, CAB Int, 94; coauth, Biodiversity and Savanna Ecosystem Processes, Spring Verlag, 95; coauth, Gramero del Mundo, hasta cuando?, Grafica Editora, 97; Hacia una Agricultura Productiva y Sostenible en la Pampa Argentina, DRCLAS-CPIA, 98; Estilos de Desarrollo y Conservacion de la Biodiversidad en America Latina y el Caribe, UDEBA, in press; auth, Biodiversity and the World's Food Crises, Plant Production in a New Century, Kluver-Acad pub, 94; auth, The Diversity of the Savanna Ecosystem, in Biodiversity and Savanna Ecosystem Processes: A Global Perspective, Springer-Verlag, 95; auth, Biodiversity: An Introduction, Seminario Int sobre el Ambiente Vol 1, Univ Autonoma del Estado de Mexico, 96. **CONTACT ADDRESS** Dept of Biology, Harvard Univ, 22 Divinity Ave, Cambridge, MA, 02138. **EMAIL** solbrig@fas.harvard.edu

SOLDON, NORBERT C.
PERSONAL Born 08/04/1932, Nanticoke, PA, m, 1959, 3 children **DISCIPLINE** MODERN EUROPEAN HISTORY **EDUCATION** Pa State Univ, BA, 54, MA, 59; Univ Del, PhD(hist), 69. **CAREER** Teacher soc sci, High Sch, Del, 59-63; from asst prof to assoc prof, 63-69, PROF EUROP HIST, WEST CHESTER STATE COL, 69- **MEMBERSHIPS** AHA; Conf Brit Studies; Res Soc Victorian Periodicals; Soc Study Labour Hist; Study Group Int Labor & Working Class Hist. **RESEARCH** British history, 1815 to the present; European economic history; European intellectual history; comparative women's trade union history. **SELECTED PUBLICATIONS** Auth, Victorian periodicals: The crisis of late Victorian liberalism, Victorian Periodical News, 12/73; Laissez-faire as dogma: The story of the liberty and property defence league, In: Essays in Anti-Labour History, Macmillan, 74; Women in British Trade Unions, 1874-1976, Gill & Macmillan, 78; On Her Their Lives Depend--Munitions Workers In The Great-War, Am Hist Rev, Vol 100, 95. **CONTACT ADDRESS** 957 Cloud Lane, West Chester, PA, 19380.

SOLIDAY, GERALD
DISCIPLINE HISTORY **EDUCATION** Harvard Univ, PhD, 69. **CAREER** Assoc prof. **RESEARCH** European social and cultural history; social history of literature; historiography. **SELECTED PUBLICATIONS** Auth, A Community in Conflict: Frankfurt Society in the Seventeenth and Early Eighteenth Centuries, Brandeis Univ, 74; Principal Editor and one contribution, The History of Kinship and the Family: A Select International bibliography, Kraus Int, 80; Stadtische Fuhrungsschichten in Marbur l560-l800, Marburg, 80; Aus schlechten Christen werden gemeiniglich auch schlechte Unterthanen: Die Schulbildung der Marburger Handwerker in der fruhen Neuzeit, Hessisches Jahrbuch fur Landesgeschichte, 93. **CONTACT ADDRESS** Dept of History, Richardson, TX, 75083-0688. **EMAIL** soliday@utdallas.edu

SOLNICK, BRUCE B
PERSONAL Born 09/07/1933, New York, NY, m, 1959, 1 child **DISCIPLINE** LATIN AMERICAN HISTORY **EDUCATION** NY Univ, AB, 54, AM, 55, PhD(mod hist), 60. **CAREER** Instr hist, Hunter Col, 59-61; asst prof, 61-64, ASSOC PROF HIST, STATE UNIV NY ALBANY, 64-, State Univ NY res grant-in-aid, Caribbean, 62; vis asst prof hist, NY Univ, 64; Res Found State Univ NY fac res fels, 67-68; exec ed, Terrae Incognitae Ann Soc Hist of Discoveries, 67-78; fel, John Carter Brown Libr, Brown Univ, 68; vis assoc prof hist Grad Sch, NY Univ, 68, Union Col, 70; Fulbright prof hist, UK, 79-80. **MEMBERSHIPS** AHA; Conf Latin Am Hist; Latin Am Studies Asn; Soc Hist Discoveries (vpres, 81-); corresp mem Brazilian Hist & Geog Inst. **RESEARCH** West Indies; United States-Latin American relations; history of discoveries. **SELECTED PUBLICATIONS** Auth, Early Images Of The Am--Transfer And Invention, Hispanic Am Hist Rev, Vol 77, 97; Medinaceli And Columbus--The Other Alternative To The Discovery, Hispanic Am Hist Rev, Vol 77, 97; The Armature Of Conquest--Spanish Accounts Of The Discovery Of America, 1492-1589, Hispanic Am Hist Rev, Vol 77, 97; The Desoto Chronicles, Hispanic Am Hist Rev, Vol 74, 94; The Conquerors Of The New-Kingdom Of Granada, Am Hist Rev, Vol 101, 96. **CONTACT ADDRESS** Dept of Hist, State Univ of NY, 1400 Washington Ave, Albany, NY, 12222-1000.

SOLOMON, HOWARD MITCHELL
PERSONAL Born 06/27/1942, New Castle, PA **DISCIPLINE** HISTORY OF STEREOTYPING, LESBIAN/GAY HISTORY, EARLY MODERN EUROPE **EDUCATION** Univ Pittsburgh, AB, 64; Northwestern Univ, Evanston, MA, 67, PhD, 69. **CAREER** Teaching asst hist, Northwestern Univ, 65-67; from instr to asst prof, NY Univ, 68-71; asst prof, 71-74, assoc prof, 74-92, dean undergrad studies & acad affairs, 78-82, academic dean, Center for European Studies (Talloires, France), 92; dir, writing across the cirriculum, 92-94; PROF HIST, TUFTS UNIV, 92-. **HONORS AND AWARDS** Lesbian/Gay Campus Service Award, 92. **MEMBERSHIPS** AHA; Soc Fr Hist Studies; Nat Coalition Bldg Inst; Center for Millennial Studies. **RESEARCH** History of stereotyping; lesbian/gay history; health and medicine; early modern France. **SELECTED PUBLICATIONS** Auth, Public Welfare, Science and Propaganda in 17th Century France, Princeton Univ, 72; The Gazette and Anti-statist Propaganda: the Medium of Print in the First Half of the 17th century, CAN J Hist, 74; Teaching about Health in Preindustrial Europe, Radical Teacher, 81; What a Shame You Don't Publish: Crossing the Boundaries as a Public Intellectual Activist, Dangerous Territories: Struggles for Difference and Equality in Education, Routledge, 97; Nebuchadnezzar, the Cripple, and Ground Hog Day: a Mediation on Tu B'Shvat, Tu B'Shvat Anthology, Jewish Pub Soc, 98. **CONTACT ADDRESS** Dept of Hist, Tufts Univ, Medford, MA, 02155. **EMAIL** hsolom01@emerald.tufts.edu

SOLOMON, P.
PERSONAL Born 12/06/1945, Hartford, CT **DISCIPLINE** SOCIAL WORK **EDUCATION** Russell Sage Col BA 68; Case Western Reserve Univ MA 70 and PhD 78. **CAREER** Univ Penn, prof School of Social Work 94-, School of Med prof Social Work in Psychiatry 95-; Allegheny Univ, adj prof psychiatry 94-97; Hahnemann Univ, sch med prof 88-94, dir Men Health Ser and Sys Res 88-94. **HONORS AND AWARDS** Outstanding People of the 20th Century, Dict of Intl Biography, Who's Who in the following, Amer Women, of Women, Medicine and Health Care, America, The World, Intellectuals, Prof and Business Women, Amer EDU , in the East, Finance and Industry **MEMBERSHIPS** Society for Social Work and Research; Intl Assoc of Psychosocial Rehab Serv **RESEARCH** Ser Delivery Sys of Severe Mental Illness and Families; Fam EDU and Psychiatric Rehab; Criminal Justice and Mental Health. **SELECTED PUBLICATIONS** Coauth, Psychiatric rehabilitation in practice, And over Med Pub, 93, New Developments in Psychiatric Rehabilitation: New directions for mental health serv, Jossey-Bass, 90; Consumer Providers in psychiatric rehabilitation, in: P. Corrigan, D. Giffort, Building Teams and Programs for Effective Psychiatric Rehabilitation, Jossey-Bass, in press; Evolution of service innovation for adults with severe mental illness. In: D. Biegal, A Blum, Innovation and Practice and Service Delivery across the Life Span, NY Oxford Press, in press; Families Coping with Mental Illness,: The Cultural Context, Jossy-Bass, 98; Recent Advances in Mental Health Research: Implications for Social Work Practice, NASW Press, 98. **CONTACT ADDRESS** School of Social Work, Univ of Pennsylvania, 3701 Locust Walk, Philadelphia, PA, 19104. **EMAIL** solomonp@ssw.upenn.edu

SOLOWAY, RICHARD ALLEN
PERSONAL Born 03/04/1934, Boston, MA, m, 1957 **DISCIPLINE** HISTORY **EDUCATION** Univ Iowa, BA, 55; Univ Wis, MA, 56, PhD(hist), 60. **CAREER** Asst prof hist, Univ Mich, 62-68; assoc prof, 68-71, PROF HIST, UNIV NC, CHAPEL HILL, 71- **MEMBERSHIPS** AHA; Conf British Studies. **RESEARCH** Modern English history; European social and intellectual history. **SELECTED PUBLICATIONS** Auth, Darwinism, War And History--The Debate Over The Biology Of War From The Origin Of Species To The First-World-War, Histoire Sociale-Social Hist, Vol 29, 96; The Perfect Contraceptive, Eugenics And Birth-Control Research In Britain And Am In The Interwar Years, J Of Contemporary Hist, Vol 30, 95; Measuring The Mind--Education And Psychology In England, C.1860-C.1990, Amn Hist Rev, Vol 101, 96; Fertility, Class And Gender In Britain, 1860-1940, Albion, Vol 29, 97; Contraception And Abortion From The Ancient-World To The Renaissance, J Of Interdisciplinary Hist, Vol 24, 94; The Facts Of Life, The Creation Of Sexual Knowledge In Britain, 1650-1950, Albion, Vol 28, 96. **CONTACT ADDRESS** Dept of Hist, Univ of NC, Chapel Hill, NC, 27514.

SOLTOW, JAMES HAROLD
PERSONAL Born 07/01/1924, Chicago, IL, m, 1946 **DISCIPLINE** HISTORY **EDUCATION** Dickinson Col, AB, 48; Univ Pa, AM, 49, PhD(hist), 54. **CAREER** Asst hist, Univ Pa, 50-52; lectr, Hunter Col, 52-55; res assoc, Colonial Williamsburg, Inc, 55-56; instr hist & sociol, Russell Sage Col, 56-58; fel bus hist, Grad Sch Bus Admin, Harvard Univ, 58-59; from asst prof to assoc prof, 59-68, chmn dept, 70-75, PROF HIST, MICH STATE UNIV, 68-, Nat Rec Mgt Coun res fel, 54; Found Econ Educ fel, 60; Fulbright res fel, Univ Louvain, 65-66. **MEMBERSHIPS** AHA; Econ Hist Asn; Orgn Am Historians; Econ & Bus Hist Soc; Bus Hist Conf. **RESEARCH** American economic and social history. **SELECTED PUBLICATIONS** Auth, Foundations of Regional Industrialization, In: Regional Economic History: The Mid-Atlantic Area Since 1700, Hagley Found, 76; coauth, The Evolution of the American Economy: Growth, Welfare, and Decision Making, Basic Books, 79; Origins of Small Business and the Relationships Between Large and Small Firms, In: Small Business in American Life, Columbia Univ Press, 80; Cotton As Religion, Politics, Law, Economics And Art, Agricultural Hist, Vol 68, 94; A Hist Of Small Business In Am, J Of Am Hist, Vol 80, 93; Cotton As Religion, Politics, Law, Economics And Art, Agricultural Hist, Vol 68, 94. **CONTACT ADDRESS** Dept of Hist, Michigan State Univ, East Lansing, MI, 48823.

SOLTOW, LEE
PERSONAL Chicago, IL, m, 1949, 3 children **DISCIPLINE** ECONOMICS **EDUCATION** Univ Wisconsin, PhD **CAREER** Ohio Univ, prof econo, 50-98. **HONORS AND AWARDS** Distg prof. **MEMBERSHIPS** AEA; ASA. **RESEARCH** Income and wealth distribution. **SELECTED PUBLICATIONS** Income and Wealth Inequality in the Netherlands, 16th to 20th Century, with Luiten van Zander, Amsterdam, Het Spinhuis, 98; Property and Inequality in Victorian Ontario: Structural patterns and Cultural Communities in the 1871 Census, with Gordon Darroch, Univ Toronto Press, 94. **CONTACT ADDRESS** Dept Economics, Ohio Univ, Athens, OH, 45701.

SOMERVILLE, JAMES KARL
PERSONAL Born 05/02/1935, Racine, WI, m, 1960 **DISCIPLINE** AMERICAN HISTORY **EDUCATION** Univ Wis, Milwaukee, BS, 57; Univ Wis, Madison, MS, 59; Western Reserve Univ, PhD, 65. **CAREER** Teacher, high sch, Ill, 59-61; instr hist, Ohio State Univ, 65-67; asst prof, 67-90, ASSOC PROF HIST, STATE UNIV NY COL GENESEO, 90-97, PROF EMER, 97-. **MEMBERSHIPS** Inst Early Am Hist & Cult; AHA; Orgn Am Historians. **RESEARCH** The colonial family; Women in colonial America; Childhood and adolescence in American history; The Vietnam War. **SELECTED PUBLICATIONS** Auth, Family demography and the published record: An analysis of the vital statistics of Salem, Massachusetts, Essex Inst Hist Collections, 10/70; The Salem (Massachusetts) woman in the home, 1660-1770, Eighteenth Century Life, 9/74; Homesick in upstate New York: The sala of Sidney Roby, 1843-1847, NY Hist, 4/91. **CONTACT ADDRESS** Dept of Hist, State Univ of NY Col, 1 College Cir, Geneseo, NY, 14454-1401. **EMAIL** somerville@uno.cc.geneseo.edu

SOMKIN, FRED
PERSONAL Born 05/12/1924, Detroit, MI, m, 1959 **DISCIPLINE** AMERICAN HISTORY **EDUCATION** Wayne Univ, BA, 46; Columbus Law Sch, LLB, 52; Am Univ, MA, 62; Cornell Univ, PhD, 67. **CAREER** Lawyer, Washington, DC, 52-59; lectr hist, Queen's Univ, Ont, 62-65, from asst prof to assoc prof, 65-68; assoc prof history, 68-91, prof, 92-94, PROF EMER, 94- , CORNELL UNIV, 68-, Res fel, Charles Warren Ctr Study Am Hist, Harvard Univ, 67-68; pub mem, Prof Standards Rev Comt, NY State Psychol Asn, 77-79. **MEMBERSHIPS** Am Soc Legal Hist; Am Cult Asn; Jean Bodin Soc; Asn Jewish Stud. **RESEARCH** American intellectual history; Jewish immigrant culture; American legal history. **SELECTED PUBLICATIONS** Auth, The contributions of Sir John Lubbock, FRS, to the origin of species, Royal Soc London Notes & Rec, 12/62; Unquiet Eagle: Memory and Desire in the Idea of American Freedom, 1815-60, Cornell Univ, 67; Sir John Lubbock (Lord Avebury), In: Dictionary of Scientific Biography, (16 vols), Scribners, 70-78; Love's body, USA, Rev Am Hist, 12/79; Scripture notes to Lincoln's second inaugural, Civil War Hist, 6/81; How Vanzetti said goodbye, J Am Hist, 9/81; The Strange Careet of Fugitivity in the History of Interstate Extradition, Utah Law Rev, 84; Zions Harp by the East River: Jewish-American Popular Songs in Columbus Golden Land, 1890-1914, Perspectives in Am Hist, 85; Where have all the Chazonim gone?, Kolenu, 86; HO-WA-HO-SA-WA-KA: Chief Wolf Paw on the Airwaves, A Memoir and Meditation, Consumable Goods: Papers from the NE Pop Cult Asn Mtg, 86; A Constitutional Parable, The Cresset, 88; A Note on the Wit of the Hermit of Prague, Notes and Queries, 94; Joseph Campbells Old Woman and Ben Sirahs Wisdom, ANQ, 98. **CONTACT ADDRESS** Dept of Hist, Cornell Univ, McGraw Hall, Ithaca, NY, 14853-4601.

SOMMERFELDT, JOHN R.
DISCIPLINE HISTORY **EDUCATION** Univ Mich, AB, MA, PhD. **CAREER** Prof, Dallas Univ. **RESEARCH** Medieval intellectual history; medieval spirituality and ecclesiastical history. **SELECTED PUBLICATIONS** Auth, The Spiritual Teachings of Bernard of Clairvaux, 91. **CONTACT ADDRESS** Dept of History, Univ of Dallas, 1845 E Northgate Dr, Braniff 236, Irving, TX, 75062.

SOMMERS, LAURIE.
DISCIPLINE WORLD MUSIC, FOLK AND ETHNIC MUSIC **EDUCATION** Univ Mich, BA; Ind Univ, MA, PhD. **CAREER** Adj prof, Valdosta State Univ; pub sector folklorist, ethnomusicologist, Ind Div of State Parks, Bur of Fla Folklife, Smithsonian Inst; folklife spec, cur, Mich State Univ Mus, 87-95; dir, S Ga folklife proj. **RESEARCH** Musics of the Americas; regional and ethnic music traditions of North America. **SELECTED PUBLICATIONS** Auth, Beaver Island House Party; Fiesta, Fe, y Cultura: Celebrations of Faith and Culture in Detroit's Colonia Mexicana; Anatomy of a Folklife Festival: Michigan on the Mall. **CONTACT ADDRESS** Dept of Mus, Valdosta State Univ, 1500 N. Patterson St, Valdosta, GA, 31698.

SOMMERVILLE, CHARLES JOHN
PERSONAL Born 08/15/1938, Lawrence, KS, m, 1964, 2 children **DISCIPLINE** ENGLISH CULTURAL HISTORY **EDUCATION** Univ Kansas, BA, 60, MA, 63; Univ Iowa, PhD, 70; Univ Reading, ND UK. **CAREER** Prof, 71- Univ FA; Instr, 68-70, Stanford Univ. **HONORS AND AWARDS** Ids Mem; SWR Sr Fel. **RESEARCH** Secularization; Popular Religion. **SELECTED PUBLICATIONS** Auth, The News Revolution in England: Cultural Dynamics of Daily Information, 96; The Secularization of Early Modern England: From Religious Culture to Religious Faith, 92; The Discovery of Childhood in Puritan England, 92; The Rise and Fall of Childhood, 90; Popular Religion in Restoration England, 77. **CONTACT ADDRESS** History Dept, Univ Fla, Box 117320, Gainesville, FL, 32611. **EMAIL** jsommerv@history.ufl.edu

SOMMERVILLE, JOSEPH C.
PERSONAL Born 12/28/1926, Birmingham, Alabama, m **DISCIPLINE** EDUCATION **EDUCATION** Morehouse College, BS, 1949; Univ of Michigan, MS, 1956, EdS, 1966, PhD, 1969. **CAREER** Ohio AARP, president, 1996-; College of Education, prof emeritus, 1992; Department of Educational Leadership, department chairman, prof of Adm & Supr; Univ of Toledo, prof of educ, dir of adminstrative internships, 1970-75; Wayne Co Intermediate School Dist, The Assist Center, staff development specialist, 1968-70; Dougals and Woodson School, Inkster, MI, prin, 1961-68, teacher, 1949-61. **HONORS AND AWARDS** Citation of Outstanding Serv to Wayne

Co; speaker many natl & local professional confs. **MEMBERSHIPS** State Pres Ohio AARP; OH Assn of Elem Sch Principals; Assn for Sch Curriculum Development; Phi Kappa Phi; Am Educ Research Assn; exec bd, Natl Urban Educ Assn; past pres, bd trustees, Toledo-Lucas Co Library; Westmoreland Assn; Phi Delta Kappa; Sigma Pi Phi Fraternity Model Comm Sch Com; scholarship com chmn, Omega Psi Phi. **SELECTED PUBLICATIONS** Author several articles in natl & state journals & books.

SONKOWSKY, ROBERT PAUL
PERSONAL Born 09/16/1931, Appleton, WI, m, 1956, 3 children **DISCIPLINE** CLASSICS **EDUCATION** Lawrence Col, AB, 54; Univ NC, PhD, 58. **CAREER** Teaching asst, Univ NC, 55-56, teaching fel, 57-58; from instr to asst prof classics, Univ Tex, 58-61; assoc prof, Univ Mo, 62-63; chmn dept, 64-78, assoc prof Classics, Speech & Theatre Arts, Univ Minn, Minneapolis, 63-, Johnson fel, Inst Res Humanities, 61-62; selection juror, Am Acad Rome Fels, 70. **MEMBERSHIPS** Am Philol Asn: Class Asn Mid W & S; Speech Commun Asn; Am Theatre Asn; Int Soc Chronobiol. **RESEARCH** Ancient rhetoric and drama; Latin literature; oral performance. **SELECTED PUBLICATIONS** Auth, An Aspect of Delivery in Ancient Rhetorical Theory, Trans & Proc Am Philol Asn, 59; Scholarship and Showmanship, 61 & Greek Euphony and Oral Performance, 67, Arion; A Fifteenth Century Rhetorical Opusculum, Class Medieval & Renaissance Studies for B L Ullman, 69; Euphantastik Memory and Delivery in the Classical Rhetorical Tradition, Rhetoric, Brown & Steinmann, 79; Recordings: selections from Cicero, Vergil, Cattulus, Horace, Ovid, Jeffrey Norton, In: Oedipus in Oedipus Rex, Digital Excellence, Inc. **CONTACT ADDRESS** Dept of Classics, Univ of Minn, 9 Pleasant St S E, Minneapolis, MN, 55455-0194. **EMAIL** sonko001@tc.umn.edu

SONN, RICHARD D.
DISCIPLINE HISTORY **EDUCATION** Univ Calif Berkeley, PhD. **CAREER** Assoc prof. **RESEARCH** France history; modern European history. **SELECTED PUBLICATIONS** Auth, Culture and Anarchy, Drunken Boat, 94; Anarchism, Twayne, 92; Anarchists, Artists and Aesthetes (rev), Nineteenth C Contexts, 91; The Early Political Career of Maurice Barres: Anarchist, Socialist, or Protofascist?, Clio, 91; British Anarchism, Garland, 93. **CONTACT ADDRESS** History Dept, Univ of Arkansas, Fayetteville, 416 Old Main, Fayetteville, AR, 72701. **EMAIL** rsonn@comp.uark.edu

SORELLE, JAMES MARTIN
PERSONAL Born 02/01/1950, Waco, TX, m, 1973 **DISCIPLINE** AMERICAN HISTORY **EDUCATION** Univ Houston, BA, 72, MA, 74; Kent State Univ, PhD(hist), 80. **CAREER** Asst prof Afro-Am hist, Ball State Univ, 79-80; LECTR AM HIST, BAYLOR UNIV, 80- **MEMBERSHIPS** Orgn Am Historians; Southern Hist Asn. **RESEARCH** Afro-American history; urban history; 20th century United States. **SELECTED PUBLICATIONS** Auth, An de po cullud man is in de wuss fix uv awl: Black occupational status in Houston, Texas, 1920-1940, Houston Rev, spring 79; Watkin,William,Ward And The Rice-Institute, J Of Southern Hist, Vol 60, 94; Houston, The Unknown City, 1836-1946, J Of Southern Hist, Vol 60, 94; Houston Forgotten Heritage--Landscape, Houses, Interiors, 1824-1914, J Of Southern Hist, Vol 60, 94. **CONTACT ADDRESS** Dept of Hist, Baylor Univ, Waco, TX, 76798.

SORIN, GERALD
PERSONAL Born 10/23/1940, Brooklyn, NY, m, 1962, 1 child **DISCIPLINE** AMERICAN HISTORY **EDUCATION** Columbia Univ, BA, 62, PhD(Am hist), 69; Wayne State Univ, MA, 64. **CAREER** From asst prof to assoc prof, 65-77, prof hist, State Univ NY Col New Paltz, 77-, Danforth assoc, 70-; John Adams Distinguished Chair in American History (Fulbright, Netherlands), 98; Distinguished Teaching Prof, 94-. **MEMBERSHIPS** Orgn Am Historians; Am Jewish Hist Soc. **RESEARCH** Abolitionism; 19th century radicalism; Civil War; American Jewish experience. **SELECTED PUBLICATIONS** Auth, New York Abolitionists, Greenwood, 71; Abolitionism: A New Perspective, Praeger, 72; The Prophetic Minority, Indiana, 85; The Nurturing Neighborhood, New York Univ, 90; A Time for Building, John Hopkins, 92; Tradition Transformed, John Hopkins, 97. **CONTACT ADDRESS** Dept of Hist, State Univ of NY Col, 75 S Manheim Blvd, New Paltz, NY, 12561-2400. **EMAIL** soring@matrix.newpaltz.edu

SORKIN, DAVID
PERSONAL Born 09/22/1953, Chicago, IL, m, 1976, 4 children **DISCIPLINE** HISTORY **EDUCATION** Univ Cal Berk, PhD 83, MA 77; Univ Wisconsin Madison, BA 75. **CAREER** Univ Wisconsin Madison, Frances and Laurence Weinstein prof 92-; Oxford Univ St Anthony's Col, res fel, HB lectr, 86-92; Brown Univ, asst prof, 83-86. **HONORS AND AWARDS** Joel H Cavior Lit Awd **MEMBERSHIPS** AHA; AJS **RESEARCH** Modern Jewish Hist; European intellectual and religious hist. **SELECTED PUBLICATIONS** Profiles in Diversity: Jews in a Changing Europe, 1750-1870, co-ed, 90, 97; Moses Mendlessohn and the religious Enlightenment, 96; The Transformation of German Jewry, 87, pbk 90, 98. **CONTACT ADDRESS** Dept of History, Univ of Wisconsin, Madison, 455 N. Park St, Madison, WI, 53706-1483. **EMAIL** sorkind@macc.wisc.edu

SORRENSON, RICHARD J.
DISCIPLINE HISTORY OF PHILOSOPHY **EDUCATION** Auckland Univ, MS, 84; Princeton Univ, PhD, 93. **CAREER** Asst prof. **MEMBERSHIPS** Am Philos Soc. **SELECTED PUBLICATIONS** Auth, The ship as a scientific instrument in the eighteenth century, Osiris. 96; Towards a history of the Royal Society of London in the 18th century, 96. **CONTACT ADDRESS** Dept of History and Philosophy of Science, Indiana Univ, Bloomington, 300 N Jordan Ave, Bloomington, IN, 47405. **EMAIL** rjs@indiana.edu

SORTOR, M.
PERSONAL Born 07/25/1957, New York, NY, m, 1981, 1 child **DISCIPLINE** HISTORY **EDUCATION** Univ CAL SD, PhD, 89. **CAREER** Assoc Prof, Asst Prof, teach/res, 89 to 95-, Grinnell College; Fel, 87-89, Stanford. **HONORS AND AWARDS** NEH Fel; Best Article in Urban Hist; Harris Fel. **MEMBERSHIPS** AHA; MA; RSA; SCS; SLCS; UHA. **RESEARCH** France and Flanders, 1250-1550; Urban History; Economic History. **SELECTED PUBLICATIONS** Auth, The Ieperleet Affair: The Struggle for Market Position in Late Medieval Flanders, Speculum, 98; auth, Saint-Omer and Its Textile Trades in the Late Middle Ages: A Contribution to the Proto-Industrialization Debate, Amer Hist Rev, 98; coed, The Other side of Western Civilization, 92. **CONTACT ADDRESS** Dept of History, Grinnell Col, Grinnell, IL, 50112. **EMAIL** sortor@ac.grin.edu

SORUM, CHRISTINA ELLIOTT
DISCIPLINE CLASSICS **EDUCATION** Wellesley Col, BA, 67; Brown Univ, PhD, 75. **CAREER** Asst prof, for lang and lit, North Carolina State Univ, 75-82; chemn, 82-91, assoc prof, 82-86, Frank Bailey Assoc Prof, 86-92, Frank Bailey Prof, Classics, 92- , Dean of Arts and Sci, 94- , Union Col. **HONORS AND AWARDS** Outstanding Teacher Award, 82; Fac Merit Service Award, 94. **MEMBERSHIPS** Am Philol Asn; Class Asn of the Atlantic States; Class Asn of the Middle W and S; Class Asn of the Empire State; Asn of Am Col and Univ; Asn of General and Liberal Studies; AAUW. **RESEARCH** Greek and Latin language and literature; Greek and Latin drama and epic in translation; classical mythology. **SELECTED PUBLICATIONS** Auth, Monsters and the Family: The Exodos of Sophocles' Trachiniae, Greek, Roman and Byzantine Stud, 78; auth, The Family in Sophocles' Antigone and Electra, the Classical World, 82; auth, The Authorship of the Agesilaus, La Parola del Passato, 84; auth, Sophocles' Ajax in Context, The Classical World, 86; auth, Myth, Choice, and Meaning in Euripides: Iphigenia at Aulis, Am J of Philology, 92; auth, Euripides' Judgment: Literary Creation in Andromache, Am J of Philology, 95. **CONTACT ADDRESS** Dept of Classics, Union Col, Schenectady, NY, 12308. **EMAIL** sorumc@idol.union.edu

SOSIN, JACK MARVIN
PERSONAL Born 04/17/1928, Hartford, CT, m, 1965, 1 child **DISCIPLINE** AMERICAN COLONIAL HISTORY **EDUCATION** Univ Conn, BA, 50, MA, 51; Ind Univ, PhD, 58. **CAREER** Lectr hist, Ind Univ, 57-58; from instr to assoc prof, 58-65, prof hist, Univ Nebr, Lincoln, 65-. **MEMBERSHIPS** AHA; Orgn Am Historians; Conf Brit Studies; fel Royal Hist Soc. **RESEARCH** British imperial history and administration. **SELECTED PUBLICATIONS** Auth, Whitehall and the Wilderness, Univ Nebr, 61; The proposal in the pre-Revolutionary decade for establishing bishops in the colonies, J Ecclesiastical Hist, 4/62; The Massachusetts Acts of 1774, Huntington Libr Quart, 5/63; Imperial regulation of colonial paper money, Penn Mag Hist, 4/64; Agents and Merchants, Univ Nebr, 65; The Revolutionary Frontier, Holt, 67. **CONTACT ADDRESS** Dept Hist, Univ Nebr, Lincoln, NE, 68508.

SOSNOWSKI, THOMAS C.
PERSONAL Born 09/28/1945, MI, m, 1980, 2 children **DISCIPLINE** HISTORY **EDUCATION** Univ Detroit, BA, 67; Kent State Univ, MA, 70, PhD, 75; Laval Univ Quebec, 70. **CAREER** ASSOC PROF HIST, KENT STATE UNIV, STARK CAMPUS, 76-. **HONORS AND AWARDS** Dist Teaching Award, Kent State Univ, 78, 85. **MEMBERSHIPS** Soc Fr Hist Stud; Western Soc Fr Hist; Ohio Acad Hist; Ohio Hist Soc; Stark County Hist Soc. **RESEARCH** Fr revolution; emigres; Ohio hist. **SELECTED PUBLICATIONS** various **CONTACT ADDRESS** 6000 Frank Ave NW, Canton, OH, 44720. **EMAIL** tososnowski@stark.kent.edu

SOTO, GILBERTO D.
PERSONAL Born 05/09/1961, Torreon, Mexico, m, 1986, 2 children **DISCIPLINE** MUSIC **EDUCATION** Universidad Antonomo del Noneste, BA, 83; Abilene Christian Univ, BA, 86; Univ Lutheran Ms, MM, 88, PhD, 98. **CAREER** Instr, 86-90, Ms Gulf Coast Commun Col; instr, 90-, Loredo Commun Col. **HONORS AND AWARDS** Tepsichorean Award, 93; Nisod Teaching Excellence Award, 95; LU Presidential Award, 98., Performed at the White House, Washington, DC, 96. **MEMBERSHIPS** TMEA; MENC; TAMS. **RESEARCH** Music educ for young children. **CONTACT ADDRESS** 8627 Northridge, Loredo, TX, 78045.

SOUCY, ROBERT J.
PERSONAL Born 06/25/1933, Topeka, KS, m, 1957, 2 children **DISCIPLINE** MODERN EUROPEAN HISTORY **EDUCATION** Washburn Univ, AB, 55; Univ Kans, MA, 57; Univ Wis, PhD(hist), 63. **CAREER** Instr hist, Harvard Univ, 63-64; asst prof, Kent State Univ, 64-66; asst prof, 66-76, assoc prof, 76-79, PROF HIST, OBERLIN COL, 79- **MEMBERSHIPS** AHA; Soc Fr Hist Studies. **RESEARCH** French fascism; late 19th and early 20th century French intellectual history. **SELECTED PUBLICATIONS** Auth, Barres and fascism, Fr Hist Studies, spring 67; Romanticism and realism in the fascism of Drieu La Rochelle, J Hist Ideas, 1-3/70; French fascism as class conciliation and moral regeneration, Societas Rev Soc Hist, autumn 71; Fascism in France: The Case of Maurice Barres, Univ Calif, 72; Family, Dependence, And The Origins Of The Welfare-State--Britain And France, 1914-1945, J Of Interdisciplinary Hist, Vol 26, 95; From Fascism To Libertarian Communism--Valois,Georges Against The Third-Republic, Am Hist Rev, Vol 99, 94; France Hollow Years--An Exchange, NY Rev Of Books, Vol 43, 96. **CONTACT ADDRESS** Dept of Hist, Oberlin Col, Oberlin, OH, 44070.

SOUTHALL, GENEVA H.
PERSONAL Born 12/05/1925, New Orleans, Louisiana, d **DISCIPLINE** MUSIC **EDUCATION** Dillard University, BA, 1945; National Guild Pianist, Artist Diploma, 1954; American Conservatory of Music, MusM, 1956; University of Iowa, PhD, 1966. **CAREER** University of Minnesota, professor Afro-American Music Culture in New World, 1970-; Grambling College, professor, 1966-70; South Carolina State College, associate professor, 1962-64; Knoxville College, assistant music professor, 1959-61; United States Information Service, chamber pianist, 1955. **MEMBERSHIPS** American Student Faculty Assembly, University of Minnesota; Womens Student Assembly, University of Minnesota; Field Research Activ, Haiti & Jamaica; graduate faculty, Music Department, University of Minnesota; African Studies Council, University of Minnesota; music editor, Howard University Press; board directors, Urban League; NAACP; board of directors, Urban Coalition of Minneapolis; life member, board directors, Association for the Study of Afro-American Life & History; Metropolitan Cultural Arts Center; admissions board, Park Avenue Unit Methodist Church; board directors, National Women Helping Offenders; Society for Ethnomusicology; American Musicol Society; Crusade Scholar, Methodist Church, 1961-62; Pi Kappa Lamda, National Honors Music Society. **SELECTED PUBLICATIONS** Published in "Reflections in Afro-American Music", "Black Perspectives in Music". **CONTACT ADDRESS** Afro-American Studies, Univ of Minnesota, 808 Social Science, Minneapolis, MN, 55455.

SOUTHARD, EDNA CARTER
PERSONAL Born 02/09/1945, Cairo, Egypt, m, 1969, 2 children **DISCIPLINE** RENAISSANCE ART HISTORY **EDUCATION** Barnard Col, BA, 66; Univ Chicago, MA, 73; Ind Univ, PhD(art hist-Renaissance), 78. **CAREER** Asst & researcher, New York Times, Brussels Bur, 67-69; asst manuscript ed, Univ Chicaago Press, 70-71; adj instr jour & art hist, Earlham Col, 74-76; adj assoc prof, Wright State Univ, 79-80; educ & prog coordr, 80-82, ASST PROF ART HIST, ASSOC CUR & EDUC COORDR, MIAMI UNIV, 82-, Proj dir, Democracy in Peace & War: Great Books in Political Values, 78-79; adj asst prof, Ind Univ, 80-81 & Miami Univ, 81; US rep, Conf Int Negociants Oeuvres Art Competition, 79 & 80. **MEMBERSHIPS** Col Art Asn; Am Asn Mus; Renaissance Soc Am. **RESEARCH** Italian Renaissance painting; 19th and 20th century European art; Sienese art and the Palazzo Pubblico. **SELECTED PUBLICATIONS** Auth, The earliest known decorations for the Palazzo Pubblico, Siena, Burlington Mag, 8/79; The Frescoes in Siena's Palazzo Pubblico, 1289-1539, Garland, 79; Simone Martini's lost Marcus Regulus: Document rediscovered and a subject clarified, Zeitschrift f?r Kunstgeschichte, XLII, No 2-3, 79; Ambrogio Lorenzetti's Frescoes in the Sala della Pace: a change of names, Mitteilungen des Kunsthistorischen Institutes in Florenz, No 3, 80; Kings And Connoisseurs--Collecting Art In 17th-Century Europe, Sixteenth Century J, Vol 27, 96; The Sienese Trecento Painter Bartolo-Di-Fredi, Sixteenth Century J, Vol 26, 95. **CONTACT ADDRESS** Art Mus, Miami Univ, Patterson Ave, Oxford, OH, 45056.

SOUTHARD, ROBERT FAIRBAIRN
PERSONAL Born 07/27/1945, Baltimore, MD, m, 1969, 2 children **DISCIPLINE** MODERN EUROPEAN HISTORY **EDUCATION** Columbia Univ, BA, 66; Univ Chicago, PhD, 74. **CAREER** Asst prof, 71-77, assoc prof, 77-81, prof hist, Earlham Col, 81- **MEMBERSHIPS** AAUP; AIS; MWJSA. **RESEARCH** History; European historiography; modern Jewish history. **SELECTED PUBLICATIONS** Auth, Marxist Rhetoric, Fascist Behavior, Alternative, 6-7/76; Theology in Droysen's early political historiography: Free will, necessity, and the historian, Hist & Theory, Vol XVIII, No 3; Droysen and the Prussian School of History, Lexington, 94. **CONTACT ADDRESS** Dept of Hist, Earlham Col, 801 National Rd W, Richmond, IN, 47374-4095. **EMAIL** bobs@earlham.edu

SOUTHERLAND, JAMES EDWARD
PERSONAL Born 06/14/1942, Houston County, AL, m, 1964, 2 children **DISCIPLINE** LATIN AMERICAN HISTORY **EDUCATION** Univ Ga, AB, 65, MA, 67, PhD(Hist), 70. **CAREER** Asst prof, 69, assoc prof Hist, Brenau Univ, 82-, chmn, Humanities & Comm Arts, 71-89; Nat Endowment for Humanities grants, 73-74. **HONORS AND AWARDS** BFA Outstanding faculty, 83; Outstanding faculty, 84; Panhellemc faculty Member of the year, 91. **MEMBERSHIPS** Southern Hist Asn; Southeast Council Latin Am Studies; AHA; OOK, 93. **RESEARCH** Mexican-United States relations. **SELECTED PUBLICATIONS** Auth, John Forsyth and the frustrated 1857 loan and land grab, WGa Col Studies in Soc Sci, 6/72; Samuel Adams in American Portraits, Vol I to 1877, Kendall/Hunt Publishing Co, 93; Biographical sketches of Eugene McCarthy, Joseph and Daniel Berrigan in The Vietnam War: An Encyclopedia, Garland Press, 96. **CONTACT ADDRESS** Div of Soc & Behav Sci, Brenau Univ, 204 Boulevard, Gainesville, GA, 30501-3697. **EMAIL** jsoutherland@lib.brenau.edu

SOUTHERN, DAVID WHEATON
PERSONAL Born 02/19/1938, Great Bend, KS, m, 1961, 1 child **DISCIPLINE** AMERICAN HISTORY **EDUCATION** Alderson-Broaddus Col, BA, 64; Wake Forest Univ, MA, 65; Emory Univ, PhD, 71. **CAREER** Instr hist, NC Wesleyan Col, 65-67; from asst prof to assoc prof, 70-86, prof hist, Westminster Col, Mo, 86-. **HONORS AND AWARDS** NEH fel, 82-83; res grant, Am Coun Learned Soc, 85, Am Philos Soc, 88; Cushwa Grant, Univ Notre Dame, 87; Gustavus Myers Award - an outstanding book on intolerance, 87 & 96. **MEMBERSHIPS** Orgn Am Historians; AHA; Southern Hist Asn; Asn for Study of Negro Life and Hist. **RESEARCH** Black-white relations in America since the Civil War; American politics and reform, 1890 to 1988. **SELECTED PUBLICATIONS** Auth, An American Dilemma: Gunnar Myrdal and the civil rights cases of 1944-1954, J Hist Soc, spring 81; Beyond Jim Crow liberalism: Judge Waring and the fight against segregation in South Carolina, 1942-1952, J Negro Hist, fall 81; Gunnar Myrdal and Black-White Relations: The Use and Abuse of An American Dilemma, 1944-1969, Baton Rouge, 87; An American Dilemma after Fifty Years: Putting the Myrdal Study and Black-White Relations in Perspective, Hist Teacher, 2/95; John LaFarge and the Limits of Catholic Interracialism, 1911-1963, Baton Rouge, 96; But Think of the Kids: Catholic Interracialists and the Great American Taboo of Race Mixing, U.S. Cath Hist (forthcoming Fall 98); author of a number of book chapters and reviews. **CONTACT ADDRESS** Dept of Hist, Westminster Col, 501 Westminster Ave, Fulton, MO, 65251-1299. **EMAIL** southed@jaynet.wcmo.edu

SOUTHERN, EILEEN JACKSON
PERSONAL Born 02/19/1920, Minneapolis, Minnesota, m **DISCIPLINE** MUSIC **EDUCATION** Univ of Chicago, BA 1940, MA 1941; New York Univ, PhD 1961. **CAREER** Prairie View State Coll, lecturer, 1941-42; Southern Univ, asst prof 1943-45, 1949-51; Alcorn Coll, asst prof 1945-46; Claflin Univ, asst prof 1947-49; City Univ of New York, asst to full prof 1960-75; Harvard Univ, full prof 1975-87, prof emeritus. **HONORS AND AWARDS** Alumni Achievement Award, Univ of Chicago 1971; Achievement Award, Natl Assn Negro Musicians 1971; Citation Voice of Amer, 1971; Deems Taylor Awrd ASCAP 1973; Bd of Dir, Amer Musicological Soc, 1974-76; Honorary MA, Harvard Univ 1976; Honorary Phi Beta Kappa Radcliffe/Harvard Chapter 1982. **MEMBERSHIPS** Concert pianist Touring in USA, Haiti 1942-54; co-founder/editor, The Black Perspective in Music scholarly journal 1973-; mem, Assn for Study of Afro-Amer Life & History; mem, Alpha Kappa Alpha; bd, New York City YWCA, 1950; leader, Girl Scouts of Amer, 1950-1960; American Musicological Society; Sonneck Society for American Music, International Musicological Society. **SELECTED PUBLICATIONS** Readings in Black American Music WW Norton 1971, revised 1983; The Buxheim Organ Book (Brooklyn, NY) 1963; The Music of Black Amer (New York) 1971, 2nd Ed 1983, 3rd ed, 1997; Anonymous Pieces in the Ms El Escorial IVa24 Basel, Switzerland 1981; author, Biographical Dictionary of Afro-Amer & African Musicians (Westport) 1982; author of articles in The New Grove Dictionary of Music and Musicians (Macmillan) 1980 and The New Grove Dictionary of American Music (Macmillan), 1986; Honorary DA Columbia College, Chicago,1; bd of dirs Sonneck Soc of Ame Music 1986-88; co-editor, African-American Traditions: An Annotated Bibliography, Westport: Greenwood Press, 1990; Peabody Medal, Johns Hopkins Univ, 1991; African-American Musical Theater, Nineteenth Century, 1994. **CONTACT ADDRESS** PO Drawer I, Cambria Heights, NY, 11411.

SOWARDS, JESSE KELLEY
PERSONAL Born 05/12/1924, Clintwood, VA, m, 1946, 2 children **DISCIPLINE** EARLY MODERN EUROPEAN HISTORY **EDUCATION** Univ Wichita, AB, 47; Univ Mich, MA, 48, PhD(hist), 52. **CAREER** Instr hist, William Woods Col, 50-51; assoc prof hist & humanities, Northwest Mo State Col, 51-56; from asst prof to prof, 56-73, DISTINGUISHED PROF HIST, WICHITA STATE UNIV, 73-, DEAN LIB ARTS & SCI, 65-, Ford Found fac res grant, 53-54. **MEMBERSHIPS** AHA; Renaissance Soc Am; Mediaeval Acad Am; Cent Renaissance Conf (pres, 72). **RESEARCH** Renaissance and Reformation, especially intellectual history; Erasmus studies. **SELECTED PUBLICATIONS** Auth, Interpretations Of Erasmus C. 1750-1920--Man On His Own, Renaissance Quarterly, Vol 47, 94; Annotated Catalog Of Early Editions Of Erasmus At The Center-For-Reformation-And-Renaissance-Studies, Toronto, Sixteenth Century J, Vol 27, 96; Erasmus Annotations On The New-Testament, Galatians To The Apocalypse, Sixteenth Century J, Vol 25, 94; Historia And Fabula--Myths And Legends In Hist Thought From Antiquity To The Modern-Age, Sixteenth Century J, Vol 27, 96; Bibliotheca-Erasmiana-Bruxellensis--Catalog Of Erasmus Works Published In The 16th-Century Belonging To The Bibliotheque-Royale-Albert-1er, Sixteenth Century J, Vol 24, 93. **CONTACT ADDRESS** Dept of Hist, Wichita State Univ, Wichita, KS, 67208.

SOWARDS, STEVEN W.
DISCIPLINE HISTORY, LIBRARY SCIENCE **EDUCATION** Stanford Univ, BA, 73; Ind Univ, MA, 76, PhD, 81, MLS, 86. **CAREER** Ref librn, Hanover Col, 86-88; hum librn, Swarthmore Col, 88-96; soc scis & hum ref, 96-98, head, main libr ref, Mich State Univ librs, 98-. **HONORS AND AWARDS** Fulbright res fel, Vienna, 77-78 **MEMBERSHIPS** ALA, Libr Hist Round Table, MLA. **RESEARCH** Mod Balkan hist; hist lib-rs; web-based ref tools. **SELECTED PUBLICATIONS** Auth, A Typology for Ready Reference Web Sites in Libraries, First Monday: Peer-Reviewed J on the Internet 3/5. May 98; auth, Save the Time of the Surfer: Evaluating Web Sites for Users, Library Hi Tech 15/3-4, 97; auth, Austria's Policy of Macedonian Reform, East European Monographs, 89; auth, Historical Fabrications in Library Collections, Collection Management 10/3- 4, 88. **CONTACT ADDRESS** Libraries, Michigan State Univ, 100 Library, East Lansing, MI, 48224. **EMAIL** sowards@pilot.msu.edu

SOYER, DANIEL
DISCIPLINE AMERICAN IMMIGRATION AND ETHNICITY **EDUCATION** NY Univ, PhD. **CAREER** Asst prof, 97, Fordham Univ. **HONORS AND AWARDS** Thomas J Wilson prize, Harvard UP, 97., Res fel, Lower E Side Tenement Mus; consult, E Europ migration; arch consult, Jewish Hist Inst, Warsaw. **RESEARCH** Documentation of immigrant lives through autobiography. **SELECTED PUBLICATIONS** Auth, Jewish Immigrant Associations and American Identity in New York, 1880-1939, Harvard UP, 97 **CONTACT ADDRESS** Dept of Hist, Fordham Univ, 113 W 60th St, New York, NY, 10023.

SPAETH, BARBETTE S.
DISCIPLINE GREEK AND ROMAN RELIGION, MYTHOLOGY, LATIN LITERATURE **EDUCATION** John Hopkins Univ, PhD, 87. **CAREER** Class, Tulane Univ. **HONORS AND AWARDS** Phi Beta Kappa, 76; Lord fel,Amer Sch Class Stud at Athens, 83; Robinson travel fel, John Hopkins Univ, 86; fel, Am Sch Class Stud at Athens, 86-87; Broneer fel, Am Acad, Rome, 90-91. **SELECTED PUBLICATIONS** Auth, The Goddess Ceres and the Death of Tiberius Gracchus, Hist, 90; Athenians and Eleusinians in the West Pediment of the Parthenon, Hesperia, 91; The Goddess Ceres and Roman Women, Newcomb Ctr for Res on Women Newsletter, 93; The Goddess Ceres in the Ara Pacis Augustae and the Carthage Relief, Amer Jour Archaeol 98, 94. **CONTACT ADDRESS** Dept of Class, Tulane Univ, 6823 St Charles Ave, New Orleans, LA, 70118. **EMAIL** spaeth@mailhost.tcs.tulane.edu

SPAGNOLO, JOHN PETER
PERSONAL Born 08/01/1934, Jerusalem, Palestine, m, 1965, 2 children **DISCIPLINE** HISTORY **EDUCATION** Am Univ, Beirut, BA, 57, MA, 62; Oxford Univ, DPhil, 65. **CAREER** From instr to asst prof hist, Am Univ, Beirut, 60-66; asst prof, 66-70, ASSOC PROF HIST, SIMON FRASER UNIV, 70-**MEMBERSHIPS** Mid East Studies Asn North Am, Brit Soc Mid East Studies; Mid East Inst; Can Inst Int Affairs. **RESEARCH** Franco-British Imperialism in the Middle East; modern Middle East; political modernization. **SELECTED PUBLICATIONS** Auth, The definition of a style of Imperialism: The internal politics of the French educational investment in Ottoman Beirut, Fr Hist Studies, 74; France and Ottoman Lebanon: 1861-1914, Ithaca, 77; The Long Peace--Ottoman Lebanon, 1861-1920, Am Hist Rev, Vol 100, 95; The Syrian Involvement In Lebanon Since 1975, Int Hist Rev, Vol 16, 94; The Multinational Force In Beirut, 1982-1984, Int Hist Rev, Vol 16, 94. **CONTACT ADDRESS** Dept of Hist, Simon Fraser Univ, Burnaby, BC, V5A 1S6.

SPALL, RICHARD
PERSONAL Born 12/01/1952, Logansport, IN, m, 1972, 2 children **DISCIPLINE** HISTORY OF BRITAIN **EDUCATION** Wittenberg Univ, BA, 77; Univ Ill, AM, 79; Univ Ill, PhD, 85. **CAREER** Grad teaching asst, Univ Ill, 78-82; Babcock res fel, Univ Ill, 82-83; grad col fel/Von Mises Fel, 83; vis lectr, Univ Ill, 83-84; vis instr, OWU, 84-85; vis asst prof, OWU, 85-86; asst prof, OWU, 85-89; assoc prof, OWU, 89-96; book review ed, The Historian, 93-; Cornelia Coles Fairbanks prof of hist, 96-. **HONORS AND AWARDS** Cornelia Coles Fairbanks Endowed Professorship, Ohio Wesleyan Univ; Sherwood Dodge Shanklin Teaching Award, Ohio Wesleyan Univ; All-Campus Award for Excellence in Teaching, Univ Ill; Col of Humanities Outstanding Teaching Award, Univ Ill; Phi Kappa Phi Academic Honor Soc; Laurence Marcellus Larson Prize, Univ Ill; Joseph Ward Swain Prize, Univ Ill; Margaret S. Ermarth Award, Wittenberg Univ; Paul F. Bloomhardt Award, Wittenberg Univ; Phi Alpha Theta. **MEMBERSHIPS** Anglo Am Conference of Historians; British History Asn; Conference of Historical Journals; Healey Institute; Historical Asn; Inst of Historical Res; Midwest Conference on British Studies; Ohio Academy of History; Phi Alpha Theta. **RESEARCH** Free trade radicalism; Victorianism; 19th-Century British political and social reform. **SELECTED PUBLICATIONS** Auth, "John Bright", in Research Guide to European Historical Biography 1450 to the Present, Beacham, 93; auth, "Anthony Ashley Cooper, 7th earl of Shaftsbury", "Henry John Temple, 3rd Viscount Palmerston", "Sir Robert Peel", in Historical Leaders of the World, Gale Research, 94; auth, "Review of the 'Victorian World Picture'", in Albion 30, Rutgers Univ Press, 97. **CONTACT ADDRESS** Ohio Wesleyan Univ, 10 Elliott Hall, Delaware, OH, 43015. **EMAIL** rfspal@cc.owu.edu

SPANN, EDWARD KENNETH
PERSONAL Born 04/12/1931, Fair Lawn, NJ, m, 1961, 4 children **DISCIPLINE** UNITED STATES HISTORY **EDUCATION** Iona Col, BA, 52; NY Univ, MA, 53, PhD, 57. **CAREER** Grad asst, NY Univ, 56-57; lectr, Hunter Col, 58, instr hist, 58-60; instr, NY Univ, 61; from asst prof to assoc prof, 61-69, PROF HIST, IND STATE UNIV, TERRE HAUTE, 69-, Dir, Eugene V Debs Soc. **HONORS AND AWARDS** Annual Manuscript Award, NY State Hist Asn, 77. **MEMBERSHIPS** Orgn Am Historians; Soc Historians of Early Repub. **RESEARCH** Jacksonian and antebellum intellectual history; United States urban history; modernization with special reference to utopianism. **SELECTED PUBLICATIONS** Auth, The New Metropolis: New York City, 1840-1857, Columbia Univ Press, 81; Historikal Crotchets--Suggestions For Appalachian-Trail Users--Trail Etiquette, NY Hist, Vol 74, 93; The Unbounded Community--Neighborhood Life And Social-Structure In New-York, 1830-1875, NY Hist, Vol 74, 93; Franklin Delano Roosevelt And The Regional-Planning-Association-Of-Am, 1931-1936, NY Hist, Vol 74, 93; Celebrating The New-World--Chicago Columbian Exposition Of 1893, J Of Am Hist, Vol 81, 94. **CONTACT ADDRESS** 2705 S 25th St, Terre Haute, IN, 47802.

SPARKS, ESTHER
DISCIPLINE AMERICAN WORKS ON PAPER, FOLK ART OF THE AMERICAS **EDUCATION** Univ Chicago, BA; Northwestern Univ, MA, PhD. **CAREER** Instr, Univ MS; dir, W Graham Arader III Gallery, Chicago; cur, Northwestern Univ; actg cur, Art Inst of Chicago. **SELECTED PUBLICATIONS** Auth, Universal Limited Art Editions: A History of the First 25 Years, Harry N Abrams, 89. **CONTACT ADDRESS** Univ MS, Oxford, MS, 38677.

SPATZ, NANCY
PERSONAL Born 03/05/1961, Chicago, IL **DISCIPLINE** MEDIEVAL STUDIES **EDUCATION** Northwestern Univ, BA, 83; Cornell Univ, MA, 86, PhD, 92 **CAREER** Lect, 90-91, Alfred Univ; Asst Prof, 91-96, Univ of N CO; Visit Asst Prof, 94-95, CO Col; Assoc Prof, 96-, Univ of N CO **HONORS AND AWARDS** NEH Summer Seminar in Rome **MEMBERSHIPS** Medieval Acad of Am **RESEARCH** Medieval Hist **CONTACT ADDRESS** Dept of History, Univ of No Colorado, Greeley, CO, 80639. **EMAIL** nancyspatz@aol.com

SPEAR, ALLAN H.
DISCIPLINE HISTORY **EDUCATION** Yale Univ, MA, PhD. **CAREER** Assoc prof **RESEARCH** Recent American history; Afro-American history; Minnesota history. **SELECTED PUBLICATIONS** Auth, Black Chicago: The Making of a Negro Ghetto, 1890-1920, 67. **CONTACT ADDRESS** History Dept, Univ of Minnesota, Twin Cities, 614 Social Sciences Tower, 267 19th Ave S, Minneapolis, MN, 55455. **EMAIL** spear001@tc.umn.edu

SPECTOR, JACK
DISCIPLINE MODERN ART **EDUCATION** Columbia Univ, PhD. **CAREER** Prof II, Rutgers, The State Univ NJ, Univ Col-Camden. **SELECTED PUBLICATIONS** Auth, Surrealist Art and writing, 1919 to 1939, The Gold of Tome, Cambridge UP, 96; Medusa on the Barricades, in Am Image, Vol 53, no 1, 96; Delacroix's Liberty on the Barricades in 1815 and 1830, in Source, Notes on the Hist of Art, vol xv no 3, 96; ed, American Image, Vol 53, nos 1 and 2, 96. **CONTACT ADDRESS** Dept of Art Hist, Rutgers, The State Univ NJ, Univ Col-Camden, Voorhees Hall, 71 Hamilton St, New Brunswick, NJ, 08903.

SPECTOR, R.H.
PERSONAL Born 01/17/1943, Pittsburgh, PA, m, 1998, 2 children **DISCIPLINE** HISTORY **EDUCATION** Johns Hopkins Univ, BA, 64; Yale Univ, MA, 66, PhD, 67. **CAREER** Yale Univ, asst inst, 66-67; Louisiana State Univ, asst prof, 69-71; U.S. Army Center of Military History, Southeast Asian Branch, historian, 71-84, acting chief, 79-80, 82-83; Smithsonian Inst, lectr, 80, 86-87; Univ Alabama, assoc prof, prof, 84-90; Navy Dept, Dir & curator Naval Hist., 86-89; Woodrow Wilson Int

Center for Scholars, Guest Scholar, 90; Princeton Univ, vis prof, 91; George Washington Univ, Elliot School of Int Affairs, prof, 90-; National War Col, Distinguished vis prof, 95-96. **HONORS AND AWARDS** Roosevelt Prize for Naval History, USIA Visiting Lecturer, Fulbright-Hays sr lectr, Fulbright sr lectr. **MEMBERSHIPS** AHA, SMH, OAH, NASOH, Authors' Guild, USNI, Naval Rev UK. **RESEARCH** History of US foreign and national security policy; US - East Asian relations, modern military history. **SELECTED PUBLICATIONS** Auth, After Tet: The Bloodiest Year in Vietnam, NY: Free Press, 93; auth, Eagle Against the Sun: The American War with Japan, NY: Free Press, 84; Strategy: Causes, Conduct and Termination in the War, coauth, Security Studies for the 21st Century, ed. R. Shultz, NY: Brassey's, 97; auth, The Pacific War and the Fourth Dimension Strategy, The Pacific War Revisited, ed. G. Bischof and R.L. Dupont, Baton Rouge LSU Pr, 97; Korea in the Mirror of Vietnam, Security in Korea: War Stalemate and Negotiation, ed. D. Goldstein, Boulder CO: Westview Press, 94. **CONTACT ADDRESS** Dept of History, George Washington Univ, Washington, DC, 20052. **EMAIL** spector@gwu.edu

SPECTOR, SCOTT
DISCIPLINE HISTORY **EDUCATION** John Hopkins Univ, PhD, 93 **CAREER** Asst Prof, 94-, Univ Michigan **CONTACT ADDRESS** Dept of History, Univ of Michigan, Ann Arbor, MI, 48109-1003. **EMAIL** spec@umich.edu

SPECTOR, SHERMAN DAVID
PERSONAL Born 05/07/1927, Andover, MA, m, 1955, 3 children **DISCIPLINE** HISTORY OF RUSSIA & EAST CENTRAL EUROPE **EDUCATION** Bowdoin Col, AB, 49; Columbia Univ, AM, 51, PhD, 60. **CAREER** Lectr polit sci, George Washington Univ, 53-55; lectr hist, Pace Col, 56-57; asst prof, State Univ NY, Albany, 57-60; asst prof, 60-68, coordr spec events, 77-82, PROF HIST, RUSSELL SAGE COL, 68-, State Univ NY Res Found grant-in-aid, 57; consult foreign area studies, NY State Educ Dept, 63-70; Fulbright-Hays prof hist, Univ Bucharest, 70; dir, Sage Soviet Summer Sem, E Europe, 71 & 72. **MEMBERSHIPS** AHA **RESEARCH** History of modern Rumania; 20th century Russia. **SELECTED PUBLICATIONS** Auth, Rumania at the Paris Peace Conference, Twayne, 62; Rumania, Encycl American, 64-76; ed, A History of the Balkan Peoples, Twayne, 72; auth, Rumania & Bulgaria at (the) Paris Peace Conference, In: A History of First World War, Purnell, London, 72; ed, A History of the Romanian Peoples, GK Hall, 74; auth, Soviet Moldavia, In: Nationalism in the USSR, Univ Detroit, 77; Romanian Cassandra--Antonescu,Ion And The Struggle For Reform, 1916-1941, Amhist Rev, Vol 99, 94. **CONTACT ADDRESS** Dept of Hist, Russell Sage Col, Troy, NY, 12180.

SPEER, DONALD
PERSONAL Born 06/15/1961, Grand Rapids, MI, m, 1984, 3 children **DISCIPLINE** MUSIC - PIANO; PIANO PEDAGOGY **EDUCATION** Louisiana Col, BM, 1983; Southern Ill Univ-Edwardsville, MM, 85; Lousiana State Univ, PhD, 91. **CAREER** Assoc Prof, Western KY Univ, 91- . **MEMBERSHIPS** Ky Music Teachers Asoc; Music Teachers Nat Asoc. **RESEARCH** Piano pedagogy **SELECTED PUBLICATIONS** auth with C. Yarbrough and S. Parker, Perception and Performance of Dynamics and Articulation among Young Pianists, Bull of the Coun for Res in Music Educ, 93; auth, An Analysis of Sequential Patterns of Instruction in Piano Lessons, Jour of Res in Music Educ, 94. **CONTACT ADDRESS** Western Kentucky Univ, Bowling Green, KY, 42101. **EMAIL** donald.speer@wku.edu

SPEIDEL, MICHAEL PAUL
PERSONAL Born 05/25/1937, Pforzheim, Germany, m, 1966, 2 children **DISCIPLINE** ROMAN HISTORY **EDUCATION** Univ Freiburg, PhD, 62. **CAREER** Lectr hist & Ger, Chulalongkorn Univ, Bangkok, 62-64; dir studies, Ger lang, Goethe House, Montreal, 65-68; assoc prof, 68-73, prof ancient hist, Univ Hawaii, Manoa, 73-, lectr Ger, McGill Univ, 66-68; Am Coun Learned Soc grant-in-aid, 73-74; vis prof Roman Hist, Univ S Africa, 75; Nat Endowment for Humanities res tool grant, 76; vis prof under Wien/Austria. **MEMBERSHIPS** Ger Archaeol Inst. **RESEARCH** Greek and Roman epigraphy and papyrology; history of the Roman Empire; history of the Roman Army. **SELECTED PUBLICATIONS** Auth, Equites Singulares, Habelt, Bonn, 65; The Captor of Decebalus, a New Inscription from Philippi, J Roman Studies, 70; Die Schlussadlocutio der Trajanssaule, Romische Mitteilungen, 71; The Pay of the Auxilia, J Roman Studies, 73; The Religion of Lupiter Delichemus in the Roman Army, Brill-Leyden, 77; Guards of the Roman Armies, Habelt-Bonn, 78; Roman Army Studies I, Sieber-Amsterdam, 84; Roman Army Studies II, Sieber-Amsterdam, 92. **CONTACT ADDRESS** Dept of Hist, Univ of Hawaii at Manoa, 2530 Dole St, Honolulu, HI, 96822-2303. **EMAIL** Speidel@hawaii.edu

SPELLMAN, JOHN WILLARD
PERSONAL Born 07/27/1934, Tewksbury, MA **DISCIPLINE** HISTORY, ASIAN STUDIES **EDUCATION** Northeastern Univ, BA, 56; Univ London, PhD(Indian hist), 60. **CAREER** Vis asst prof hist, Wesleyan Univ, 61-62; vis lectr Indian polit, Univ Kerala, 62-64; asst prof, Univ Wash, 64-67; head dept, 67-79, PROF ASIAN STUDIES, 67-, Ford Found Non-Western study grant, 64-66; consult, Peace Corps Training Prog, India, 64-68; Can Univ Serv Overseas, 66-68; consult & regional field dir, Asia Develop, Madras India, Can Univ Serv Overseas, 82. **MEMBERSHIPS** Fel Royal Asiatic Soc; Am Orient Soc; Asn Asian Studies; Indian Polit Sci Asn; Can Soc Asian Studies. **RESEARCH** Religion and society in ancient India; Indian cultural values; Indian healing and witchcraft. **SELECTED PUBLICATIONS** Auth, Political Theory of Ancient India, Oxford Univ, 64; An analysis of the 1963 Trivandrum II by-election, Polit Sci Rev, Rajasthan, 65; The Beautiful Blue Jay and Other Tales of India, Little, 67; An annotated bibliography of ancient Indian politics, Motilal Banarsidass, New Delhi; Symbolic significance of the number twelve in ancient India, J Asian Studies, Vol XXII, No 1; The Construction Of Religious Boundaries--Culture, Identity And Diversity In The Sikh Tradition, Studies In Religion-Sciences Religieuses, Vol 25, 96. **CONTACT ADDRESS** Dept of Asian Studies, Univ of Windsor, Windsor, ON, N9B 3P4.

SPELLMAN, LYNNE
DISCIPLINE ANCIENT GREEK PHILOSOPHY **EDUCATION** Unv Ill, PhD. **CAREER** Philos, Univ Ark **HONORS AND AWARDS** Vis fel, Cambridge Univ.s **SELECTED PUBLICATIONS** Auth, Substance and Separation in Aristotle, Cambridge Univ Press, 95. **CONTACT ADDRESS** Univ Ark, Fayetteville, AR, 72701. **EMAIL** lspellm@comp.uark.edu

SPENCE, CLARK CHRISTIAN
PERSONAL Born 05/25/1923, Great Falls, MT, m, 1953, 2 children **DISCIPLINE** AMERICAN HISTORY **EDUCATION** Univ Colo, BA, 48, MA, 51; Univ Minn, PhD(hist), 55. **CAREER** Instr hist, Carleton Col, 54-55; from instr to assoc prof, Pa State Univ, 55-60; vis lectr, Univ Calif, Berkeley, 60-61; assoc prof, 61-64, chmn dept, 67-70, PROF HIST, UNIV ILL, URBANA, 64-, Ford Found fac fel, soc sci res on bus, 63-64; Guggenheim fel, 70-71. **HONORS AND AWARDS** Beveridge Award, AHA, 56; Bk Award, Agr Hist Soc, 59. **MEMBERSHIPS** AHA; Orgn Am Historians; Agr Hist Soc; Western Hist Asn(Pres, 69-70). **RESEARCH** Western American; agricultural and mineral history. **SELECTED PUBLICATIONS** Auth, The Rainmakers: American Pluviculture to World War II, Univ Nebr, 80; Cradle To Grave--Life, Work, And Death At The Lake-Superior Copper Mines, Montana-The Magazine Of Western Hist, Vol 44, 94; I-Was-A-Stranger-And-Ye-Took-Me-In + Fraud And Con-Artists In Mining Of The American-West, Montana-The Magazine Of Western Hist, Vol 44, 94; No Duty To Retreat--Violence And Values In Amn Hist And Society, Pacific Hist Rev, Vol 62, 93. **CONTACT ADDRESS** Dept of HIst, Univ of Ill, Urbana, IL, 61801.

SPENCE, JONATHAN DERMOT
PERSONAL Born 08/11/1936, Surrey, England, m, 1962, 3 children **DISCIPLINE** HISTORY OF CHINA **EDUCATION** Cambridge Univ, BA, 59; Yale Univ, PhD(hist), 65. **CAREER** Mem fac, 56-71, PROF HIST, YALE UNIV, 71-, CHMN, COUN E ASIAN STUDIES, 77-, Ed, Ch'ing-shih wen-t'i, 66-73; rev ed, J Asian Studies, 73-75; dir, Nat Endowment for Humanities Sem 77. **MEMBERSHIPS** Asn Asian Studies; AHA. **SELECTED PUBLICATIONS** Auth, Ts'ao Yin and the K'ang-hse Emperor: Bondservant and Master, Yale Univ, 66; To Change China: Western Advisers in China, 1620-1960, Little, 69; Emperor of China: Self-portrait of K'ang-hsi, 1654-1722, Knopf, 74; The Death of Woman Wang, Viking, 78; Soulstealers--The Chinese Sorcery Scare Of 1768, Harvard J Of Asiatic Studies, Vol 52, 92. **CONTACT ADDRESS** Dept of Hist, Yale Univ, P O Box 208324, New Haven, CT, 06520-8324.

SPENCER, ELAINE GLOVKA
PERSONAL Born 09/17/1939, Rice Lake, WI, m, 1966, 1 child **DISCIPLINE** HISTORY **EDUCATION** Lewis & Clark Col, BA, 61; Univ Calif, Berkeley, MA, 62, PhD(hist), 69. **CAREER** Asst prof 69-81, assoc prof, 81-91, prof, Northern Ill Univ, 92-, dept ch, 95- **HONORS AND AWARDS** Newcomen Special Award, Bus Hist, 79; Hermann E Krooss Prize, Bus Hist Conf, 81. **MEMBERSHIPS** AHA **RESEARCH** Modern German social history. **SELECTED PUBLICATIONS** Auth, Rulers of the Ruhr: Leadership and authority in German big business before 1914, Bus Hist Rev, 79; Workers In The German Empire 1871-1914--German, Am Hist Rev, Vol 98, 93; Workers Culture In Imperial Germany--Leisure And Recreation In Rhineland And Westphalia, Histoire Sociale-Social Hist, Vol 26, 93; Industrial-Policy In The Third-Reich--German Labor Front, Entrepreneurs And State Bureaucracy In West-German Heavy Industry, Am Hist Rev, Vol 100, 95; Street Politics--Social-History Of Public-Order In Berlin 1900-1914, Am Hist Rev, Vol 102, 97; Regimenting Revelry--Rhenish Carnival In The Early-19th-Century, Central European Hist, Vol 28, 95; auth, Custom, Commerce, and Contention, Rhenish Carnival Celebrations, 1890-1914, German Stu Rev, 98. **CONTACT ADDRESS** Dept of Hist, No Illinois Univ, 1425 W Lincoln Hwy, De Kalb, IL, 60115-2825. **EMAIL** espencer@niu.edu

SPENCER, GEORGE W.
PERSONAL Born 08/30/1939, Wooster, OH, m, 1966, 1 child **DISCIPLINE** SOUTH ASIAN HISTORY **EDUCATION** Univ Md, BA, 61; Univ Calif, Berkeley, MA, 63, PhD(hist), 67. **CAREER** From Asst Prof to Assoc Prof, 67-84, PROF HIST, NORTHERN ILL UNIV, 84-, Dept Chair, 90-95. **MEMBERSHIPS** Asn Asian Studies; AHA. **RESEARCH** Political, social and economic implications of religious movements and institutions in early South India. **SELECTED PUBLICATIONS** Coauth (with K R Hall), The economy of Kancipuram: A sacred center in early South India, J Urban Hist, 80; auth, Sons of the sun: The solar generalogy of a Chola king, Asian Profile, 82. **CONTACT ADDRESS** Dept of History, No Illinois Univ, De Kalb, IL, 60115-2893. **EMAIL** gspencer@eniu.edu

SPENCER, HEATH A.
PERSONAL Born 09/26/1966, Seattle, WA, m, 1988, 3 children **DISCIPLINE** HISTORY **EDUCATION** Univ Ky, BA, 88, MA, 92, PhD, 97 **CAREER** Asst prof, Ks Wesleyan Univ, 95- **MEMBERSHIPS** German Stud Assoc; Conf Group on Cent Eur Hist; Phi Alpha Theta. **RESEARCH** German social & religious hist in the nineteenth & twentieth cent **CONTACT ADDRESS** Dept of History, Kansas Wesleyan Univ, Salina, KS, 67401. **EMAIL** spencerh@kwu.edu

SPERBER, JONATHON
PERSONAL Born 12/26/1952, New York, NY, m, 1990, 2 children **DISCIPLINE** HISTORY **EDUCATION** Cornell Univ, AB, 73; Univ Chicago, MA, 74, PhD, 80. **CAREER** Archivist, Leo Baeck Inst, New York, 79-82; vis asst prof, Northwestern Univ, 82-84; Asst prof to assoc prof to prof, Univ Mo Columbia, 84- . **HONORS AND AWARDS** Fel, Alexander von Humboldt-Stiftung, 87-88; Fel, John Simon Guggenheim Memorial Found, 88-89; Herbert Baxter Adams Prize, Amer Hist Assoc, 85; German Stud Assoc/German Acad Exchange Svc book prize, 93; Allan Sharlin Memorial Award, Soc Sci Hist Assoc, 98., Phi Beta Kappa, 73; Grad Student Fel of the German Acad Exchange Svc, 76-78. **MEMBERSHIPS** Amer Hist Assoc; German Stud Assoc. **RESEARCH** Soc, polit & relig hist of nineteenth century Germany & modern Europe. **SELECTED PUBLICATIONS** Auth, Popular Catholicism in Nineteenth Century German, Princeton Univ Press, 84; Rhineland Radicals: The Democratic Movement and the Revolution of 1848-1849, Princeton Univ Press, 91; The European Revolutions, 1848-1851, Cambridge Univ Press, 94; The Kaiser's Voters: Electors and Elections in Imperial Germany, Cambridge Univ Press, 97. **CONTACT ADDRESS** Dept of History, Univ of Mo, Read Hall, Columbia, MO, 65211. **EMAIL** sperberj@missouri.edu

SPETTER, ALLAN BURTON
PERSONAL Born 12/24/1939, Brooklyn, NY, m, 1966 **DISCIPLINE** AMERICAN DIPLOMATIC HISTORY **EDUCATION** Rutgers Univ, BA, 60, MA, 61 PhD(hist), 67. **CAREER** Asst prof hist, 67-71, asst dean, Col Lib Arts, 71-74, ASSOC PROF HIST, WRIGHT STATE UNIV, 71- **MEMBERSHIPS** AHA; Orgn Am Historians; Soc Hist Am Foreign Rels. **RESEARCH** American diplomacy, 1865-1900. **SELECTED PUBLICATIONS** Auth, Harrison and Blaine: Foreign policy, 1889-1893, Ind Mag Hist, 69; The US, the Russian Jews, and the Russian Famine of 1891-1892, Am Jewish Hist Quart, 5/75; Harrison and Blaine: No reciprocity for Canada, Can Rev Am Studies, fall 81; Distant Friends--The United-States And Russia, 1763-1867, Diplomatic Hist, Vol 18, 94. **CONTACT ADDRESS** 731 Torrington Pl, Dayton, OH, 45406.

SPIEGEL, GABRIELLE MICHELE
PERSONAL Born 01/20/1943, New York, NY, m, 1965, 2 children **DISCIPLINE** MEDIEVAL HISTORY, HISTORIOGRAPHY **EDUCATION** Bryn Mawr Col, BA, 64; Harvard Univ, MAT, 65; John Hopkins Univ, MA, 70, PhD(hist), 74. **CAREER** Lectr hist, Bryn Mawr Col, 72-73; asst prof, 74-79, ASSOC PROF HIST, UNIV MD, 79-, Nat Endowment Humanities fel, 79. **MEMBERSHIPS** Medieval Acad Am; Southeastern Medieval Asn; AHA; Berkshire Conf Women Historians (pres, 81-83). **RESEARCH** Capetian history; historiography; French historiography. **SELECTED PUBLICATIONS** Auth, The Reditus Regni ad Stripem Karoli Magni: A new look, Fr Hist Studies, 71; The Cult of Saint Denis and Capetian Kingship, J Medieval Hist, 75; Political utility in medieval historiography: A sketch, Hist & Theory, 75; Defense of the Realm: Evolution of a Capetian propaganda slogan, J Medieval Hist, 77; The Chronicle Tradition of Saint-Denis: A survey, Medieval Classics: Texts and Studies, 78; coauth, The Fleurs-de-Lis Frontispieces to Guillaume de Nagis Chronique Abregee: Political Iconography in Late 15th Century France, Viator, 81; Medieval Canon Formation And The Rise Of Royal Historiography In Old French Prose, Mln-Modern Language Notes, Vol 108, 93. **CONTACT ADDRESS** Dept of Hist, Univ of Md, College Park, MD, 20742.

SPIGNER, CLARENCE
PERSONAL Born 03/19/1946, Orangeburg, SC, s **DISCIPLINE** SOCIOLOGY **EDUCATION** Santa Monica College, Santa Monica, CA, AA, social studies, 1974-76; University of California, Berkeley, CA, AB, sociology, 1977-79, MPH, health, 1980-82, DrPH, health, 1983-87. **CAREER** American

Heart Assn, Marin, CA, evaluator, 1981-82; National Health Service, London, England, researcher/planner, 1982-83; University of California, Berkeley, CA, fitness superv, 1983-86, teaching asst/post-doc/lecturer, 1984-88; UNIVERSITY OF OREGON, EUGENE, OR, assistant professor, ASSOC PROF, currently. **HONORS AND AWARDS** Phi Beta Kappa, Phi Beta Kappa Honor Society, 1979-; Chancellor's Post-Doctoral Fellow, Univ of California-Berkeley, 1987; Henrik Blum Distinguished Service Award, Univ of California-Berkeley, 1987; Outstanding Faculty Award, Office of Multicultural Affairs, Univ of Oregon, 1990; Friars Senior Honor Society, University of Oregon, 1990. **MEMBERSHIPS** Board mem, Womanspace, 1989-91; steering committee member, Clergy and Laity Concerned, 1990-; University of Oregon, Substance Abuse Advisory Board, 1990-92, Affirmative Action Task Force, 1990-, Council for Minority Education, chair, 1990-91. **CONTACT ADDRESS** Dept of Health Services, Univ of Washington, H681 Health Sciences Ctr, Seattle, WA, 98195.

SPILLER, ROGER JOSEPH
PERSONAL Born 10/19/1944, Bonham, TX, m, 1971 **DISCIPLINE** AMERICAN MILITARY HISTORY **EDUCATION** Southwest Tex State Univ, BA, 69, MA, 71; La State Univ, PhD(Am hist), 77. **CAREER** Instr US hist, Southwest Tex State Univ, 74-78; vis assoc prof, 78-80, ASSOC PROF MIL HIST, US ARMY COMMAND & GEN STAFF COL, 80-, Command historian, US Army Combined Arms Ctr & Ft Leavenworth, 80-**MEMBERSHIPS** Orgn Am Historians; Am Mil Inst; Southern Hist Asn. **SELECTED PUBLICATIONS** Auth, Some implications of Ultra, Mil Affairs, 4/76; Assessing Ultra, Mil Rev, 8/79; Calhoun's expansible army: The history of a military idea, SAtlantic Quart, winter 80; ed, S L A Marshall at Leavenworth: Five lectures presented at the US Army Command and General Staff College, 80, ed & contribr, A Brief History of the US Army Command and General Staff College, 81 & auth, Not war but like war: The American intervention in Lebanon, 1958, In: Leavenworth Paper No 3, 81, US Army Command & Gen Staff Col; ed, Dict of American Military Biography, Greenwood Press; auth, Soldiers Of The Sun, The Rise And Fall Of The Imperial Japanese Army, J Of Military Hist, Vol 57, 93; Crossing The Deadly Ground--United-States-Army Tactics, 1865-1899, J Of Southern Hist, Vol 62, 96. **CONTACT ADDRESS** PO Box 3173, Ft Leavenworth, KS, 66027.

SPILLMAN, LYNETTE P.
DISCIPLINE SOCIOLOGY **EDUCATION** BA, Australian Nat Univ, 82; MA, Univ Calif Berkeley, 85; PhD, 91. **CAREER** Soc, Notre Dame Univ. **HONORS AND AWARDS** Vis fel, Res Sch of Soc Sci, Australian Nat Univ, spring, 98; Inst for Scholar in the Liberal Arts, Prep of New Course summer stipend, Found of Social Theory, 95; Inst for Scholar in the Liberal Arts, Travel grant, Book manuscript res, 94; Univ of Queensland, travel grant, 93; Univ Notre Dame Facul Res Prog award, 93; Lilly Endowment Tchg fel, 93; Chancellor's Dissertation year fel, Univ Calif Berkeley, 90; Eli Sagan prize, Sociol Dept, Univ Calif Berkeley; Outstanding grad student instr award, 87; Regents' fel, grad div, Univ Calif Berkeley, 83; Fulbright travel award, Australian-Amer Educ Found, 83; Quentin Gibson prize in Philos, Australian Nat Univ, 79. **MEMBERSHIPS** Soc Sci Hist Asn; Amer Sociol Asn; Amer Hist Asn. **RESEARCH** Comparative historical sociology; Cultural sociology; National identity; Markets; Immigration & diversity. **SELECTED PUBLICATIONS** Auth, When Do Collective Memories Last? Founding Moments in the United States and Australia, Soc Sci Hist, 22, 4, 98; Nation and Commemoration: Creating National Identities in the United States and Australia, Cambridge and NY, Cambridge Univ Press, 97; How are Structures Meaningful? Cultural Sociology and Theories of Social Structure, Humboldt Jour of Soc Rel, spec issue, Recent Advances in Theory and Research in Social Structure, 22, 2, 31-45, 96; Neither the Same Nation Nor Different Nations: Constitutional Conventions in the United States and Australia, Comp Studies in Soc and Hist, 38, 1, 149-81, jan 96; Culture, Social Structure, and Discursive Fields, Current Perspectives in Soc Theory, 15, 129-54, 95; Imagining Community and Hoping For Recognition: Bicentennial Celebrations in 1976 and 1988, Qual Soc, 17, 1, 3-28, 94; rev, Sarah M. Corse, Nationalism and Literature: The Politics of Culture in Canada and the United States, NY, Cambridge Univ Press, Contemporary Soc, 27, 3, 279-280, may 98; Karen A. Cerulo, Identity Designs: The Sights and Sounds of a Nation, The Arnold and Caroline Rose Book Series of the American Sociological Association, New Brunswick, NJ, Rutgers Univ Press, Contemporary Soc, 26, 2, 244-45, mar 97; John R. Searle, The Construction of Social Reality, NY, The Free Press, Contemporary Soc, 25, 4, 57-48, jul 96. **CONTACT ADDRESS** Dept of Sociology, Univ of Notre Dame, 325 O'Shaughnessy Hall, Notre Dame, IN, 46556-5639. **EMAIL** spillman.1@nd.edu

SPINDEL, DONNA JANE
PERSONAL Born 07/13/1949 **DISCIPLINE** EARLY AMERICAN HISTORY **EDUCATION** Mount Holyoke Col, AB, 71; Duke Univ, PhD(hist), 75. **CAREER** Ed asst, NC State Arch, 74, admin asst to dir, 75-76; ASST PROF HIST, MARSHALL UNIV, 76-, Res grants, Am Philos Soc & Marshall Univ, 78. **MEMBERSHIPS** Orgn Am Historians; Am Soc Legal Hist. **RESEARCH** Early American legal history; colonial American history. **SELECTED PUBLICATIONS** Auth, Anchors of empire: Savannah, Halifax and the Atlantic frontier, Am Rev Can Studies, autumn 76; ed, North Carolina Indian Records, NC Div Arch & Hist, 77; auth, The Stamp Act crisis in the British West Indies, J Am Studies, 8/77; Law and disorder: The North Carolina Stamp Act crisis, NC Hist Rev; Law And Liberty In Early New-England--Criminal-Justice And Due-Process, 1620-1692, J Of Am Hist, Vol 81, 94; The Law Of Words--Verbal Abuse In North-Carolina To 1730, Am J Of Legal Hist, Vol 39, 95; Slavery In North-Carolina, 1748-1775, J Of Southern Hist, Vol 62, 96; Law And People In Colonial Am, J Of Southern Hist, Vol 59, 93; Assessing Memory--20th-Century Slave Narratives Reconsidered, J Of Interdisciplinary Hist, Vol 27, 96. **CONTACT ADDRESS** Dept of Hist, Marshall Univ, Huntington, WV, 25701.

SPINK, WALTER M.
PERSONAL Born 02/16/1928, Worcester, MA, m, 1952, 3 children **DISCIPLINE** HISTORY OF ART **EDUCATION** Amherst Col, AB, 49; Harvard Univ, MA, 50, PhD, 54. **CAREER** From instr to asst prof hist art & cur art collection, Brandeis Univ, 56-61, actg chmn dept fine arts, 59-60; assoc prof, 61-68, prof hist, Univ of Mich, Ann Arbor, 68-, Dir, Asian Art Arch, Univ Mich, 62- & India photographic exped, 64-68; trustee, Am Inst Indian Studies, 62-65, 73-74, sr res fel, 66 & mem comt art & archaeol, 69-; co-ed, Ars Orientalis, 63-; consult, Foreign Area Mat Ctr, State Univ YN, 63-68; prin investr, India color slide proj, US Dept State, 64-65; Bollingen Found res grant Indian art, 64-65; bd dir, Am Acad Benares, 65-71; Am Coun Learned Soc grant, 72-; mem, S Asia Regional Coun, 72-76; Rackham grants, 74, 77. **MEMBERSHIPS** Asn Asian Studies; Asia Society; Col Art Asn Am; Am Comt S Asian Art(-pres, 72-76); Conf Relig S India. **RESEARCH** Indian sculpture and architecture of early Buddhist, Gupta, and early medieval periods; the God Krishna; art and worship. **SELECTED PUBLICATIONS** Auth, Ajanta to Ellore, 67 & Krishnamandala, 71, Ctr S & Southeast Asian Studies, Univ Mich; The Axis of Eros, Schocken, 73, Penguin, 75; Ajanta's chronology: The crucial cave, Ars Orientalis, 9/75; Elephanta: Relationships with Ajanta and Ellora, Motichandra Festschrift, Prince of Wales Mus, Bombay, 77; Bagh: A study, Arch Asian Art, Vol XXX, 76-77; The great cave at Elephanta: A study of sources, in Gupta Period, 77; Jogeswari, J Indian Soc Orient Art, 77. **CONTACT ADDRESS** Dept of Hist of Art, Univ of Mich, 519 S State St, Ann Arbor, MI, 48109-1357. **EMAIL** wspink@umich.edu

SPITZ, LEWIS W.
PERSONAL Born 12/14/1922, Bertrand, NE, m, 1948 **DISCIPLINE** HISTORY **EDUCATION** Concordia Col, AB, 44; Concordia Sem, BD, 47; Univ Mo, AM, 48; Harvard Univ, PhD, 54. **CAREER** Asst prof hist, Univ Mo, 53-60; assoc prof, 60-65, PROF HIST, STANFORD UNIV, 65-, WILLIAM R KENAN, JR CHAIR HIST, 74-, Soc Relig Higher Educ Kent fel; Guggenheim fel, 56; Huntington Libr fel, 59; Am Coun Learned Soc fel & Fulbright prof, Univ Mainz, 60-61; Am ed, Arch Reformation Hist, 67-; Nat Endowment for Humanities sr fel, 68-69; pres, Friends of Reformation Res, 76-; sr fel, Inst Advan Study, Princeton, 79-80; vis prof, Columbia Univ, 80-81. **HONORS AND AWARDS** Trenholme Award, 48., DD, Concordia Theol Sem, 77; LLD, Valparaiso Univ, 78. **MEMBERSHIPS** AHA; Am Soc Church Hist (pres, 76-); Am Soc Reformation Res (pres, 63-64); Renaissance Soc Am; Cent Renaissance Conf (pres, 56-57). **RESEARCH** Renaissance and Reformation. **SELECTED PUBLICATIONS** Ed, The Religious Renaissance of the German Humanists, Harvard, 63; The Protestant Reformation, Prentice Hall, 66; Life in Two Worlds--Biography of William Sihler, Concordia, 68; The Reformation--Basic Interpretations, Heath, 72; co-ed, Discord, Dialogue and Concord, Fortress, 77; Widerspruch, Dialog und Einigung, Calwer, 77; ed, The Renaissance and Reformation Movements (2 vols), Concordia, 80; Humanisms and Reformation in der deutschen Geschichte, de Gruyter, 81; The Humanist-Scholastic Debate In The Renaissance And Reformation, Speculum-A J Of Medieval Studies, Vol 72, 97. **CONTACT ADDRESS** Dept of Hist, Stanford Unic, Stanford, CA, 94305.

SPITZER, ALAN B
PERSONAL Born 03/27/1925, Philadelphia, PA, m, 1950, 2 children **DISCIPLINE** MODERN EUROPEAN & FRENCH HISTORY **EDUCATION** Swarthmore Col, BA, 48; Columbia Univ, MA, 49, PhD(hist), 55. **CAREER** Instr gen educ, Boston Univ, 53-54, asst prof, 55-57; from asst prof to assoc prof, 57-63, PROF HIST, UNIV IOWA, 63- **MEMBERSHIPS** AHA; Conf Fr Studies; AAUP. **RESEARCH** The social history of 19th century France; the politics of the French Restoration. **SELECTED PUBLICATIONS** Auth, Citizens--A Chronicle Of The French-Revolution, J Of Modern Hist, Vol 65, 93; The 1830 Revolution In France, Am Hist Rev, Vol 98, 93; The Invisible Code--Honor And Sentiment In Postrevolutionary France, 1814-1848, J Of Interdisciplinary Hist, Vol 28, 98. **CONTACT ADDRESS** Dept of Hist, Univ of Iowa, Iowa City, IA, 52240.

SPITZER, JOHN
DISCIPLINE MUSIC HISTORY **EDUCATION** Harvard Univ, BA; Cornell Univ, PhD. **CAREER** Prof, John Hopkins Univ. **MEMBERSHIPS** Am Musicol Soc. **SELECTED PUBLICATIONS** Auth, pubs in Journal of Musicology; Early Music; Harvard Dictionary of Music. **CONTACT ADDRESS** Dept of Musicology, Johns Hopkins Univ, 1 E Mt Vernon Pl, Baltimore, MD, 21202-2397.

SPITZER, LEO
PERSONAL Born 09/11/1939, La Paz, Bolivia, 1 child **DISCIPLINE** AFRICAN HISTORY, COMPARATIVE WORLD HISTORY **EDUCATION** Brandeis Univ, BA, 61; Univ Wis, Madison, MA, 63, PhD(African hist), 69. **CAREER** From instr to asst prof, 67-75, assoc prof, 75-81, PROF HIST, DARTMOUTH COL, 81-, Mem, Nat Humanities Fac, 70-74; Dartmouth fac fel, 71 & 78; Soc Sci Res Coun fel, Brazil, 72; consult, Inst Contemp Curric Develop, 73-; Comp World Hist Prog fel, Univ Wis, 74-75; Am Coun Learned Soc grant, 78; Nat Endowment Humanities fel, 81. **MEMBERSHIPS** African Studies Asn; AHA. **RESEARCH** African and Afro-Brazilian reactions to Western culture; assimilation and identity--a comparative historical inquiry; Sierra Leone, Brazil; Austria. **SELECTED PUBLICATIONS** Contribr, Africa and the West, Univ Wis, 72; auth, Interpreting African intellectual history: A critical review of the past decade, African Studies Rev, 72; coauth, ITA Wallace-Johnson and the West African Youth League (2 parts), Int J African Hist Studies, 73; auth, The Sierra Leone Creoles, Univ Wis, 74; Assimilation and identity in comparative perspective, Biography, 80; Os Dois Mundos de Andre Rebongas, Cornelius May, e Stefan Zweig, Estudos Afro-Asiatices, 80; Into the bourgeoisie: A study of Stefan Zweig and Jewish social mobility, 1750-1880, In: Stefan Zweig's Time, Life and Work, State Univ NY Press, 82; Persistant Memory--Central-European Refugees In An Andean Land, Poetics Today, Vol 17, 96; H.C. Bankolebright And Politics In Colonial Sierra-Leone, 1919-1958, Am Hist Rev, Vol 98, 93. **CONTACT ADDRESS** Dept of Hist, Dartmouth Col, 6107 Reed Hall, Hanover, NH, 03755-3506.

SPRAGUE, PAUL EDWARD
PERSONAL Born 02/28/1933, Cumberland, MD, m, 1956, 2 children **DISCIPLINE** ARCHITECTURAL & ART HISTORY **EDUCATION** Rutgers Univ, BA, 54; Princeton Univ, MFA, 62; PhD, 69. **CAREER** Asst prof art hist, Lake Forest Univ, 63-64; asst prof archit hist, Univ Notre Dame, 64-68; asst prof art & archit hist, Univ Chicago, 68-74; adj asst prof archit hist, Univ Ill, Chicago, 74-77; Assoc Prof, 77-84; Prof Archit Hist, 84-97, Prof Emer, 97- , Univ Wis, Milwaukee; vis prof, Univ Cincinnati, 80; vis prof, Seijo Univ, Tokyo, 90. **MEMBERSHIPS** Soc Archit Historians; Victorian Soc in Am; Midwest Art Hist Soc; Soc for Industrial Archaeol; Frank Lloyd Wright Conservancy; Southeast Chapter Soc of Archit Hist. **RESEARCH** Early modern architecture in the Midwest; Sullivan-Wright, their students and colleagues; conservation of historic architecture (historic preservation). **SELECTED PUBLICATIONS** Auth, Adler & Sullivan's Schiller Building, 65; auth, The National Farmer's Bank, Prarie Sch Rev, 67; auth, Griffin Rediscovered in Beverly, Prarie Sch Rev, 73; auth, Frank Lloyd Wright and Prarie School Architecture in Oak Park, Oak Park Landmarks Comn, 76; auth, The Drawings of Louis Sullivan, Princeton, 79; auth, The Origin of Baloon Framing, J Soc Archit Historians, 81; auth, Chicago Baloon Frame, The Technology of Historic American Buildings, 84; auth, Louis Sullivan and Adler & Sullivan, in Macmillan Encyclopedia of Architecture, 82; ed, contribur, Frank Lloyd Wright in Madison, Elvehjem Museum, 90; auth, Frank Lloyd Wright, in The Dictionary of Art, Macmillan, 96; coauth, Two American Architects in India: Walter B. Griffin and Marion M. Griffin, 1935-1937, Univ Ill, 97; auth, Marion Mahony as Originator of Griffin's Mature Style: Fact or Myth? in Beyond Architecture: Marion Mahony and Walter Griffin, Powerhouse Museum, Sydney, 98. **CONTACT ADDRESS** Dept of Art History, Univ Wisconsin, Milwaukee, WI, 53211.

SPRAGUE, STUART SEELY
PERSONAL Born 06/24/1937, Norwalk, CT, m, 1966, 4 children **DISCIPLINE** AMERICAN URBAN HISTORY **EDUCATION** Yale Univ, BA, 60, MAT, 62; NY Univ, PhD(hist), 72. **CAREER** Master hist, Hatch Sch, Newport, RI, 60-61; teacher, Jurupa Jr High Sch, Riverside, Calif, 62-63; from asst prof to assoc prof, 68-75, PROF HIST, MOREHEAD STATE UNIV, 75- **MEMBERSHIPS** Spelean Hist Asn. **RESEARCH** Early national period; Appalachian history; Kentucky history. **SELECTED PUBLICATIONS** Auth, The names the thing: Ohio town promotion in the Era of Good Feelings, Names, 77; The great Appalachian iron and coal town boom, 1889-1893, Appalachian J, 77; contribr, The lure of the city: New York's great hotels in the Golden Age, 1873-1907, Conspectus of Hist, Cities in Hist, 78; auth, Postcard Ancestors, Family Heritage, 79; Kentucky politics and the heritage of the American Revolution: The early years, 1783-1788, Regist Ky Hist Soc, 80; Yale of yore: Learning by osmosis, a hidden curriculu, Yale Alumni Mag, 80; coauth (with E Perkins), Frankfort: A Pictorial History, 80; auth, Eastern Kentucky: A Pictorial History, spring 82; Kentucky Road To Statehood, J Of Southern Hist, Vol 59, 93. **CONTACT ADDRESS** Dept of Hist, Morehead State Univ, UPO 846, Morehead, KY, 40351.

SPRING, DAVID
PERSONAL Born 04/29/1918, Toronto, ON, Canada **DISCIPLINE** HISTORY **EDUCATION** Univ Toronto, BA, 39; Harvard Univ, AM, 40, PhD, 48. **CAREER** Lectr hist, Univ Toronto, 46-48; from asst prof to assoc prof, 49-62, PROF HIST, JOHNS HOPKINS UNIV, 62-, Vis prof Victorian studies, Univ Leicester, 68-69; Nat Endowment for Humanities sr fel, 76-77. **HONORS AND AWARDS** Guggenheim fel, 57-58; Tawney Mem lectr, Brit Econ Hist Soc, 81. **MEMBERSHIPS** AHA; Conf Brit Studies; fel Royal Hist Soc. **RESEARCH** Modern English history; English landed classes in the 19th century; English social and political thought of 19th and 20th centuries. **SELECTED PUBLICATIONS** Auth, English Landed Estate in the 19th Century: Its Administration, Johns Hopkins Univ, 63; contrib, Land and Industry: The Landed Estate and the Industrial Revolution, David & Charles, 71; Great Landowners of Great Britain and Ireland, Univ Leicester, 71; co-ed, Ecology and Religion in History, Harper & Row, 74; coauth, The First Industrial Society, Macmillan, 75; ed & contrib, European Landed Elites in 19th Century, Johns Hopkins Univ, 77; contribur, Jane Austen: New Perspectives, Holmes & Meier, 83; contrib, Land and Society in Britain, 1700-1914, Manchester, 96. **CONTACT ADDRESS** Dept of History, Johns Hopkins Univ, 3400 N Charles St, Baltimore, MD, 21218.

SPRING, HOWARD
PERSONAL Born 11/20/1947, Toronto, ON, Canada, m, 1977, 2 children **DISCIPLINE** MUSICOLOGY **EDUCATION** York Univ, Toronto, BA, 76; York Univ, Toronto, MFA, 83; Univ of Ill at Urbana-Champaign, PhD, 93. **CAREER** Asst prof, Univ Guelph, 1992-. **MEMBERSHIPS** Soc for Ethnomusicology; Am Musicological Soc; Ctr for Black Music Res. **SELECTED PUBLICATIONS** Auth, "The Use of Formulas in the Improvisation of Charlie Christian", in Jazzforschung 22, 90; auth, "Swing and the Lindy Hop: Dance, Venue, Media, and Tradition", in American Music 15, 97. **CONTACT ADDRESS** School of Fine Art and Music, Univ of Guelph, Guelph, ON, N1G 2W1. **EMAIL** hspring@arts.uoguelph.ca

SPRINGER, CARL P. E.
PERSONAL Born 11/28/1954, San Diego, CA, m, 1980, 4 children **DISCIPLINE** CLASSICS **EDUCATION** Univ of Wis Madison, PhD, 84. **CAREER** Asst prof, Ill State Univ, 84-90; assoc prof, Ill State Univ, 91-96; prof and chair dept of Foreign Lang, Ill State Univ, 96-. **HONORS AND AWARDS** Fulbright res Grant, 90; Alexander von Humboldt Fel, 93-94. **MEMBERSHIPS** Am Philos Asn; N Am Patristic Soc. **RESEARCH** Late Antiquity; Latin Epic; Biblical Poetry. **SELECTED PUBLICATIONS** Auth, Fannius and Scaevola in Cicero's De Amicitia, Studies in Latin Lit and Roman Hist VII, 94; The Concinnity of Ambrose's Illuminans Altissimus, Panchaia, Festschrift fur Professor Klaus Thraede, 95; The Manuscripts of Sedulius, A Provisional Handlist, 95; rev, early Christian Poetry, J of Early Christian Studies, 96. **CONTACT ADDRESS** Dept of Foreign Languages, Illinois State Univ, Normal, IL, 61790-4300. **EMAIL** cpsproner@stu.edu

SPRY, IRENE
PERSONAL Transvaal, South Africa **DISCIPLINE** ECONOMIC HISTORY **EDUCATION** London Sch Econ, 24-25; Girton Col, Cambridge, BA, 28; Bryn Mawr Col, MA, 29. **CAREER** Lectr, asst prof, Univ Toronto, 29-38; lectr, writer & reviewer, 45-67; assoc prof/prof, 68-73, PROF EMER, UNIV OTTAWA, 74-. **HONORS AND AWARDS** Res Fel, Can Plains Res Ctr; Can Coun Res Award, 65; Distinguished Can Citizen Award, Univ Regina, 87; Off, Order Can, 93; LLD Univ Toronto, 71; DU Univ Ottawa, 85. **SELECTED PUBLICATIONS** Auth, The Palliser Expedition, 64; auth, The Papers of the Palliser Expedition, 1857-1860, 68; auth, The Transition from a Nomadic to a Settled Society in Western Canada, 1856-1896, in Trans Royal Soc Can, 68. **CONTACT ADDRESS** Univ Ottawa, Ottawa, ON, K1N 6NS.

SPURLOCK, JOHN C.
DISCIPLINE AMERICAN HISTORY **EDUCATION** Univ Calif-Riverside, BA, 76, MA, 77; Rutgers Univ, PhD, 87. **CAREER** Asst Prof, Bloomsburg Univ, 87-89; Asst Ed, Papers of Albert Gallatin, Baruch Col, CUNY, 89-90; Asst Prof to Assoc Prof, Seton Hill Col, 90-. **MEMBERSHIPS** Am Hist Asn; Org Am Hist. **RESEARCH** Social and cultural history. **SELECTED PUBLICATIONS** Auth, Free Love: Marriage and Middle-Class Radicalism in America, 1825-1860, NY Univ, 88; coauth, New and Improved: The Transformation of American Women's Emotional Culture, NY Univ, 98. **CONTACT ADDRESS** History Dept, Seton Hill Col, Greensburg, PA, 15601. **EMAIL** jspurloc@setonhill.edu

SPYRIDAKIS, STYLIANOS V.
PERSONAL Born 01/27/1937, Crete, Greece, 2 children **DISCIPLINE** ANCIENT HISTORY **EDUCATION** Univ Calif, Los Angeles, BA, 60, PhD(ancient hist), 66. **CAREER** Instr ancient hist, Univ Calif, Santa Barbara, 64-65; asst prof, Calif State Univ, Los Angeles, 65-66; asst prof, Univ Nebr, Lincoln, 66-67; asst prof to prof Ancient History, Univ Calif, Davis, 67-, vis prof, Univ Crete, Greece, 79-80. **HONORS AND AWARDS** Walter Lowey Fel, Heidelberg, 63-64; elector, Univ of Crete, 80-; Distinguished Teaching Award, Univ Calif, Davis, 70; Honorary Member, Cretan Hist and Archaeol Soc; Board of Dir, S. B. Vryonis Center for the Study of Hellenism, Sacto, Calif, 89-. **MEMBERSHIPS** Cretan Hist & Archaeol Soc; Asn Ancient Hist. **RESEARCH** Hellenistic history; Crete and the Aegean. **SELECTED PUBLICATIONS** Auth, Ptolemaic Itanos and Hellenistic Crete, Univ Calif, 70; Cretica: Studies on Ancient Crete, New Rochelle, 92; Mantinades: Selected Love Distichsof Crete, New Rochelle, 97; coauth and translator, Ancient Greece: Documentary Perspectives, Kendall-Hunt, 85; Ancient Rome: Documentary Perspectives, Kendall-Hunt, 90; numerous journal articles and monographs. **CONTACT ADDRESS** Dept of Hist, Univ of Calif, Davis, CA, 95616-5200. **EMAIL** svspyridakis@ucdavis.edu

ST CLAIR HARVEY, ARCHER
DISCIPLINE ART HISTORY **EDUCATION** Princeton Univ, PhD. **CAREER** Assoc prof, Rutgers Univ. **HONORS AND AWARDS** Assoc dir, Am Acad Rome/Soprintendenza Archeologica di Roma Palatine East Excavation. **RESEARCH** Early Christian and Byzantine art; late antique art; Byzantine influence on Western art; liturgical and topographical influence on Early Christian and Medieval art. **SELECTED PUBLICATIONS** Auth, A Byzantine Source for the San Paolo Bible, Festschrift Kurt Weitzmann, Princeton, 95; coauth, A Late Roman Domus with Apsidal Hall on the Northeast Slope of the Palatine, Rome Papers (Jour Roman Archaeol), 94; Scavi di un complesso tardo romano sul versante nord ovest dei Palatino, Bolletino di archeologia, 91. **CONTACT ADDRESS** Dept of Art Hist, Rutgers Univ/Rutgers Col, Hamilton St., New Brunswick, NJ, 08903. **EMAIL** astch@rci.rutgers.edu

ST. CLAIR HARVEY, ARCHER
DISCIPLINE EARLY CHRISTIAN AND BYZANTINE ART **EDUCATION** Princeton Univ, PhD. **CAREER** Assoc prof, Rutgers, The State Univ NJ, Univ Col-Camden; assoc dir, Am Acad in Rome/Soprintendenza Archeologica di Roma Palatine East Excavation. **RESEARCH** Late Antique and early Christian Art; Byzantine influence on Western art. **SELECTED PUBLICATIONS** Auth, A Byzantine Source for the San Paolo Bible, Princeton, 95; coauth, Scavi di un complesso tardo romano sul versante nord ovest dei Palatino (1990), Bolletino di archeologia IX, 91; A Late Roman Domus with Apsidal Hall on the Northeast Slope of the Palatine, Rome Papers (J of Roman Archaeol, suppl ser), 94; coed, The Carvers Art: Medieval Sculpture in Ivory, Bone, and Horn, Jane Voorhees Zimmerli Art Mus, 89. **CONTACT ADDRESS** Dept of Art Hist, Rutgers, The State Univ NJ, Univ Col-Camden, Voorhees Hall, 71 Hamilton St, New Brunswick, NJ, 08903. **EMAIL** astch@rci.rutgers.edu

ST. GEORGE, ROBERT B.
DISCIPLINE AMERICAN CIVILIZATION **EDUCATION** Hamilton, AB, 76; Delaware, MA, 78; Univ of Penn, MA, 80, PhD, 82. **CAREER** ASSOC PROF & CH, GRAD GROUP, AM CIVILIZATION, UNIV PENN **HONORS AND AWARDS** Fred Kniffer Prize, 88; George Wittenborn Award of the Art Libraries of North America, 88; Charles F. Montgomery Prize, 88. **MEMBERSHIPS** Am Antiquarian Soc **RESEARCH** Lit and reading in Mass, 1640-1720. **SELECTED PUBLICATIONS** Auth, "From Nature to Culture," Portfolio: The Mag of the Fine Arts 4, 82; auth, "Set Thine House in Order: The Domestication of the Yeomanry in Seventeenth-Century New England," in New England Begins: The Seventeenth Century, Museum of Fine Arts, 82; auth, "Heated Speech and Literacy in Seventeenth-Century New England," in 17th-Century New Eng, 84; auth, Material Life in America, 1600-1860, Northeastern Univ Press, 88; ed, American Seating Furniture, 1630-1730: An Interpretive Catalogue of the Winterthur Collection, W W Norton, 88; auth, "Bawns and Beliefs: Architecture, Commerce, and Conversion in Early New England," Winterthur Portfolio, Winter 90; Conversing by Signs: Place and Performance in Early New England Culture, 95. **CONTACT ADDRESS** 215 College Ave, Swarthmore, PA, 19081.

STABILE, DONALD ROBERT
PERSONAL Born 03/07/1944, New York, NY **DISCIPLINE** ECONOMIC HISTORY AND HISTORY OF ECONOMIC THOUGHT **EDUCATION** Univ of MA, Amherst MA, 72; PhD, 79. **CAREER** Prof of Econ, St. Mary's College of MD, 89-; Chair Dept of Econ , St. Mary's Coll of MD, 94-96; Assoc Provst for Academic Services, St. Mary's Coll of MD, 96-98; Assoc Prof of Econ, St Mary's Coll of MD, 85-89; Asst Prof of Econ, St. Mary's Coll of MD, 80-85; Asst Prof of Econ, Drury Coll, 78-80. **MEMBERSHIPS** Econ and Bus Hist Soc; Assoc for Evolutionary Econ; Assoc for Soc Econ. **RESEARCH** Hist of Econ Thought; Political Economy; Hist of Federal Fin; Interdisciplinary Soc Sci **SELECTED PUBLICATIONS** The Origins of American Public Finance: The Debates Over Money, Debts and Taxes in the Costitutional Era,1776-1836, Greenwood Press, 98; Work and Welfare: The Social Costs of Labor in the History of Economic Thought, Greenwood Press 96; Activist Unionism: The Institutional Econimics of Solomon Barkin, M.E.Sharpe, Inc 93; Adam Smith and the Natural Wage: Sympathy,Subsistence and Social Distance, Review of Social Economy, 97; Thorstein Veblen's Intellectual Antecedents: A Case for John Bates Clark, Journal of Economic Issues, 97; Theories of Consumption and Waste: Institutional Foreshadowings in Classical Writings, Journal of Economic Issues, 96; Pigou, Clark and Modern Economics, Cambridge Journal of Economic Issues, 96; Pigou's Influence on Clark: Work and Welfare, Journal of Economic Issues, 95; Henry George's Influence on John Bates Clark, American Journal of Economics and Sociology, 95. **CONTACT ADDRESS** St. Mary's Coll of Maryland, St. Marys City, MD, 20686. **EMAIL** drstabile@osprey.smcm.edu

STACKHOUSE, JOHN G., JR.
DISCIPLINE THEOLOGY; PHILOSOPHY OF RELIGION; CHURCH HISTORY **EDUCATION** Queen's Univ Kingston, BA, 80; Wheaton Col Grad Sch, 82; Univ Chicago, PhD, 87. **CAREER** Instr, Wheaton Col Grad Sch, 84-86; Asst Prof, NWestern Col, Iowa, 87-90; from Asst Prof to Prof Religion, Univ Manitoba, 90-98; Sangwoo Youtong Chee Prof Theology, Regent Col, Vancouver, 98-. **HONORS AND AWARDS** Prof of the Year (Award for Teaching Excellence), NWestern Col, 89; Rh Found Award for Outstanding Contributions to Schol and Res in the Humanities, Univ Manitoba, 93; Outreach Award for Community Service, Univ Manitoba, 97; First Place for Editorial Writing, Canadian Church Press, 98. **MEMBERSHIPS** Am Acad Relig; Am Soc Church Hist; Canadian Soc Church History; Canadian Evangelical Theol Asn. **RESEARCH** Epistemology; philosophy of religion; religion in North America. **SELECTED PUBLICATIONS** Auth, Canadian Evangelicalism in the Twentieth Century: An Introduction to Its Character, Univ Toronto Press, 93; Can God Be Trusted? Faith and the Challenge of Evil, Oxford Univ Press, 98; author of over 200 journal articles and reviews. **CONTACT ADDRESS** Regent Col, 5800 University Blvd., Vancouver, BC, V6T 2E4. **EMAIL** jgs@regent-college.edu

STADTER, PHILIP AUSTIN
PERSONAL Born 11/29/1936, Cleveland, OH, m, 1963, 3 children **DISCIPLINE** CLASSICAL LITERATURE **EDUCATION** Princeton Univ, AB, 58; Harvard Univ, MA, 59, PhD, 63. **CAREER** From instr to assoc prof, 62-71, PROF CLASSICS, 71- , EUGENE FALK PROF OF HUMANITIES, 91- , UNIV NC, CHAPEL HILL, 71- ; Chmn Dept, 76-86, Guggenheim fel, 67-68; Nat Endowment for Humanities sr fel, 74-75; Am Coun-Learned Soc fel, 82-83; Nat Hum Ctr fel, 89-90. **MEMBERSHIPS** Am Philol Asn; Class Asn Midwest & South; Asn Ancient Historians. **RESEARCH** Plutarch, Arrian, Greek in Renaissance; Greek historiograph **SELECTED PUBLICATIONS** Auth, Plutarch's Historical Methods, Harvard Univ, 65; Flavius Arrianus: The new Xenophon, Greek, Roman & Byzantine Studies, 67; The structure of Livy's history, Historia, 72; coauth, The Public Library of Renaissance Florence, Antenore, Italy, 72; ed, The Speeches of Thucydides, Univ NC, 73; auth, Pace, Planudes, and Plutarch, Ital Medioevale e Umanistica, 73; Arrianus, Flavius, In: Catalogus Translationum et Commentariorum, Vol III, Cath Univ Am, 76; Arrian of Nicomedia, Univ NC, 80; A Commentary on Plutarch's Pericles, Univ NC, 89; ed Plutarch and the Historical Tradition, Routledge, Eng, 92. **CONTACT ADDRESS** Dept of Classics, Univ of N. Carolina, Chapel Hill, NC, 27514. **EMAIL** stadter@unc.edu

STADTWALD, KURT
PERSONAL Born 12/03/1957, Omaha, NE, m, 1990, 2 children **DISCIPLINE** HISTORY **EDUCATION** William Jewell Col, BA, 80; Univ Nebr, MA, 82; Univ Minn, PhD, 91. **CAREER** Vis Prof, Denison Univ, 90-91; assoc prof, 91-, chemn, 96-, Concordia Univ. **HONORS AND AWARDS** Who's Who in Am Cols and Univs, 80., Grad Fel, Ctr Austrian Stud, 85-86; Fulbright Fel, Austria, 87-88; Disseration Fel, Univ Minn, 89-90. **MEMBERSHIPS** Sixteenth Century Society; Friends of the Society of Reformation Res. **RESEARCH** German Humanism; the Holy Roman Empire; sixteenth century political opinions. **SELECTED PUBLICATIONS** Auth, article, Pope Alexander III's Humiliation of Emperor Frederick Barbarossa as an Episode in Sixteenth-Century German History, 93; auth, article, Patriotism and Antipapalism in the Politics of Conrad Celtis's Vienna Circle, 93. **CONTACT ADDRESS** Dept of History, Concordia Univ, Illinois, 7400 Augusta St, River Forest, IL, 60305. **EMAIL** crfstadtwkw@curf.edu

STAFFORD, BARBARA MARIA
PERSONAL Born 09/16/1941, Vienna, Austria, m **DISCIPLINE** ART HISTORY **EDUCATION** Northwestern Univ, BA, 64, MA, 66; Sorbonne, 61-62; Univ Chicago, PhD, 72. **CAREER** Instr, Nat Coll of Educ, 69-70, 71-72; asst prof, Loyola Univ, 72-73; from asst to assoc prof, Univ Del, 73-81; PROF, UNIV CHICAGO, 81-. **HONORS AND AWARDS** Univ Del Excellence-in-Teaching Award, 76; ACLS Summer Grant, 76; Univ Del Summer Grants, 74, 78; NEH Fel, 79-80; Am Soc for 18th Century Studies Clifford Prize, 79; Ctr for Adv Stud in the Visual Arts Fel, 79-80; Millard Meiss Publ Awd, CAA, 83; Smithsonian Inst Fel, 84-85; Joh Simon Guggenheim Fel, 89-90; Alexander von Humboldt Sr Fel, 89-91; Univ Cal Humanities Res Inst Fel, 91; Co-recip Gottschalk Prize for best book on an 18th century topic, 92; Univ Mich Fel, 93; Getty Ctr Schol, 95-96; Honorary Doctorate, Maryland Inst, 96. **MEMBERSHIPS** Amer Soc for 18th-Century Studies; Brit Assn for 18th-Century Studies; Coll Art Assn; Hist of Sci Soc; Int Soc for 18th Century Studies; Soc francaise de l'histoire de la der-

matologie; Soc de l'hsitoire d'art francais; Soc of Archit Hist; Society for Sci, Lit & Soc. **SELECTED PUBLICATIONS** Auth, Symbol and Myth: Humber de Superville's Essay on Absolute Signs in Art, Associated Univ Presses, 79; Voyage into Substance: Art Science, Nature and the Illustrated Travel Account, 1760-1840, MIT, 84; Body Criticism: Imaging the Unseen in Enlightenment Art and Medicine, MIT, 91; Artful Science, Enlightenment Entertainment and the Eclipse of Visual Education, MIT, 91; Good Looking: Essays on the Virtue of Images, MIT, 96; catalogues: Imaging the Body: From Fragment to Total Display, Art Inst of Chicago, 92; Metaphors of Biological Structure/Architecture Construction, Art Inst of Chicago, 92; Depth Studies: Illustrated Anatomies from Vesalius to Vicqd'Azyr, Univ Chicago, 92; coed: The Blackwell Companion to the Enlightenment, Blackwell, 91; European Cultures, Studies in Literature and the Arts, DeGruyter, 93-; consulting ed: Advances in Visual Semiotics, Univ Ind, 95; coed, Reflecting Senses, Perception and Appearance in Literature, Culture and the Arts, DeGruyter, 95; articles: Art of Conjuring, or How the Romantic Virtuoso Learned from the Enlightened Charlatan, Art J, summer 92; Present Image, Past Text, Post Body: Educating the Late Modern Citizen, Semiotica, 92; Presuming Images and Consuming Words: The Visualization of Knowledge from the Enlightenment to Postmodernism, Consumption and the World of Goods, Routledge, 93; Images of Ambiguity: Eighteenth-Century Microscopy and the Neither/Nor, Visions of Empire, Cambridge Univ, 93; Instructive Games: Apparatus and the Experimental Aesthetics of Imposture, Reflecting Senses, Perception and Appearance inLiterature, Culture and the Arts; Critic's Voice, Sculpture Mag, 95; Medical Ethics as Postmodern Aesthetics: Reflections on Biotehnological Utopia, Utopian Visions, Univ Mich, 95; Eighteenth-Century at the End of Modernity: Towards the Re-Enlightenment, Past Prologue, AMS Press, 94; Making Images Real: Toward a Pragmatic Aesthetics and an Applied Interdisciplinarity, J. Pual Getty Trust Newsletter, spring 94; Interview, Sculpture Mag, May 94; Pain under Pane, Beyond Ars Medica, Thread Waxing Space, 95-96; Cross-Cortical Romance: Analogy, Art, and Consciousness, Art Issues, Mar/Apr 96; Display and the Rhetoric of Contamination, Visualization in the Sciences, Princeton Univ, 96; Digital Imagery and the Practices of Art History, Art Bulletin, 97. **CONTACT ADDRESS** Dept of Art, Univ of Chicago, Cochrane-Woods Art Ctr, Chicago, IL, 60637. **EMAIL** bms6@midway.uchicago.edu

STAFFORD, WILLIAM SUTHERLAND
DISCIPLINE CHURCH HISTORY **EDUCATION** Stanford Univ, BA, 65-69; Yale Univ, MA, Mphil, 69-74, PhD, 75; Univ de Strasbourg: Fac de theol protestante, 73-74. **CAREER** Tchg fel, Yale Col, 71-73; vis asst prof, Brown Univ, 74-76; asst prof, 76-82; assoc prof, Va Theol Sem, 82-90; David J. Ely prof, 90-; associate dean for Acad Aff, VP. **SELECTED PUBLICATIONS** Auth, Disordered Loves: Healing the Seven Deadly Sins, Cowley Publ, 94; Sexual Norms in the Medieval Church, A Wholesome Example: Sexual Morality in the Episcopal Church, 91; The Eve of the Reformation: Bishop John Fisher, 1509, Hist Mag Protestant Episcopal Church, 85. **CONTACT ADDRESS** Va Theol Sem, 3737 Seminary Rd, Alexandria, VA, 22304. **EMAIL** WSStafford@vts.edu

STAGER, LAWRENCE E.
PERSONAL Born 01/05/1943, Kenton, OH, m, 1970, 1 child **DISCIPLINE** NEAR EASTERN ARCHEOLOGY & HISTORY **EDUCATION** Harvard Univ, BA, 65, MA, 72, PhD(Syro-Palestinian archaeol & hist), 75. **CAREER** Instr, 73-74, asst prof, 74-75, ASSOC PROF SYRO-PALESTINIAN ARCHAEOL, ORIENT INST, UNIV CHICAGO, 76-, Co-dir, Am Exped Idalion, Cypress, 72-74; ed, Am Schs Orient Res Newslett, 75-76; dir, UNESCO Save Carthage Proj, Am Pumic Archaeol Exped, 75-80; assoc trustee, Am Schs Orient Res, 77-80; assoc ed, Bull Am Schs Orient Res, 78- **MEMBERSHIPS** Am Schs Orient Res; Archaeol Inst Am; Am Orient Soc; Soc Bibl Lit. **RESEARCH** Phoenician colonization; agriculture in the Bronze and Iron Age Levant; Bronze Age urbanization in the eastern Mediterranean. **SELECTED PUBLICATIONS** Auth, Farming in the Judean Desert during the Iron Age, Bull Am Schs Orient Res, 76; coauth, A metropolitan landscape: The late Punic port of Carthage, World Archaeol, 77; auth, The rite of child sacrifice at Carthage, In: New Light on Ancient Carthage, Univ Mich Press, 80; Highland village life in Palestine some three thousand years ago, Orient Inst News & Notes, 81; The archaeology of the east slope of Jerusalem and the terraces of the Kidron, J Near Eastern Studies, 82; The first fruits of civilization, In: Olga Tufnell Festschrift, Inst Archeol Occasional Papers, 82; The Dating Of Ancient Water-Wells By Archaeological And 14c Methods--Comparative-Study Of Ceramics And Wood, Israel Exploration J, Vol 44, 94; coauth, Production and commerce in temple courtyards, Bull Am Schs Orient Res, 82. **CONTACT ADDRESS** Orient Inst, Univ of Chicago, Chicago, IL, 60637.

STAHL, ALAN MICHAEL
PERSONAL Born 08/07/1947, Providence, RI **DISCIPLINE** MEDIEVAL HISTORY, NUMISMATICS **EDUCATION** Univ Calif, Berkeley, BA, 68; Univ Pa, PhD(hist), 77. **CAREER** Asst cur, 80-82, ASSOC CUR MEDIEVAL COINS, AM NUMISMATIC SOC, 82-, Assoc, Sem Medieval Studies, Columbia Univ, 81- **MEMBERSHIPS** Am Hist Asn; Am Numismatic Soc; Mediaeval Acad Am; Soc Study Crusades. **RESEARCH** Medieval numismatics; European economic history. **SELECTED PUBLICATIONS** Auth, The Merovingian CA coinage of Austrasia, Am Numismatic Soc Mus Notes, 76; A numerical taxonomy of Merovingian coins, Comput & Humanities, 78; The Melgorien penny, Medieval Coins, 78; The Merovingian Coinage of the Region of Metz, Publ d'hist d'art d'archeol l'Univ Cath, Louvain, 82; The circulation of European coins in the crusader states, In: The Meeting of Two Worlds, Medieval Inst, 82; Changing Values In Medieval Scotland--A Study Of Prices, Money, And Weights And Measures, Speculum-A J Of Medieval Studies, Vol 72, 97. **CONTACT ADDRESS** Am Numismatic Soc, Broadway & 155th St, New York, NY, 10032.

STALEY, ALLEN
PERSONAL Born 06/04/1935, Mexico, MO, m, 1968, 2 children **DISCIPLINE** HISTORY OF ART **EDUCATION** Princeton Univ, BA, 57; Yale Univ, MA, 60, PhD(Art Hist), 65. **CAREER** Lectr, The Frick Collection, 62-65; asst cur Paintings, Phila Mus Art, 65-68; from asst prof to assoc prof Art Hist, 69-76, prof Art Hist & Archaeol, Columbia Univ, 76-. **RESEARCH** English painting. **SELECTED PUBLICATIONS** Coauth, Romantic Art in Britain: 1760-1860, Phila Mus Art, 68; ed, From Realism to Symbolism: Whistler & Hist World, Columbia Univ, 71; auth, The Pre-Raphaelite Landscape, Oxford Univ, 73; The Post-Pre-Raphaelite Print: Etching, Illustration, Reproductive Engraving, and Photography in England in and around the 1860's, Wallach Art Gallery, Columbia University, 95. **CONTACT ADDRESS** Dept of Art History, Columbia Univ, 2960 Broadway, New York, NY, 10027-6900.

STALEY, GREGORY A.
PERSONAL Born 08/12/1948, Hagerstown, MD, m, 1979, 1 child **DISCIPLINE** CLASSICS **EDUCATION** Dickinson Col, AB, 70; Princeton Univ, MA, 73, PhD, 75. **CAREER** Instr, Dickinson Col, 74-75; Asst Prof, Fordham Univ at Lincoln Center, 75-76; Sessional Lectr, Univ Alberta, 76-78; Asst Prof, Dickinson Col, 78-79; Asst Prof to Assoc Prof Classics, Univ Md, 79-. **HONORS AND AWARDS** NEH Grants, Div Educ, 80, 89; Rome Prize Fel, Am Acad Rome, 83-84. **MEMBERSHIPS** Am Philol Asn; Am Classical League; Int Soc Classical Tradition. **RESEARCH** Classical tradition in America; Latin literature; mythology. **SELECTED PUBLICATIONS** Auth, But Ancient Violence Longs to Breed: Robinson Jeffers' The Bloody Sire and Aeschylus' Orestia, Classical & Mod Lit, 83; The Literary Ancestry of Sophocles' Ode to Man, The Classical World, 85; Aeneas' First Act, The Classical World, 90. **CONTACT ADDRESS** Classics Dept, Univ of Maryland Col Park, 2407 Marie Mount Hall, College Park, MD, 20742-4811. **EMAIL** gs32@umail.umd.edu

STALLS, M.
PERSONAL Born 10/22/1947, Metropolis, Illinois **DISCIPLINE** AFRICAN-AMERICAN STUDIES **EDUCATION** Southern IL Univ, BA 1970, MS 1976, PhD 1991. **CAREER** IL Dept of Children & Family Svcs, child welfare worker 1970-75; IL Farmers Union, manpower coordinator 1976-78; SIU-C School of Tech Careers, researcher/service coord 1978-80; SIU-C Ctr for Basic Skills, coord of supple inst, developmental skills specialist/instructor, visiting assistant professor, Black American studies, developmental skills training specialist, currently. **HONORS AND AWARDS** Service Awd Eurma C Hayes Comp Child Care Services/PAC 1977; Fellow IL Comm on Black Concerns in Higher Educ 1984; Cert of Appreciation SIU-C HEADSTART Carbondale, IL 1986; Iota Phi Theta Quintessence Award 1984; SIU-C-BAC Academic Excellence Award 1987, Paul Robeson Award; Faculty Staff Award 1988; 5 Poems published in Literati 1989; coord Southern Region IC-BCHE Regional Fall Seminar 1988; George S. Counts Doctoral Award 1990; ICBCHE, Dedicated Service Award, 1990; Alton Metropolitan Human Development Recognition Award, 1991; Humanitarian Award, SIUC Black Affairs Council, 1996; Southern Illinois University at Carbondale, Academic Excellence Award, Black Affairs Council, 1991; nominee, Outstanding Professor, Graduate & Professional Education, 1994, Univ Woman of Distinction Award, Univ Administrative/Professional, 1998. **MEMBERSHIPS** Founder/coord Black Women's Coalition 1983; mentor SIU-C Project Magic 1984-; consultant Jack Co Public Housing Initiatives Training Prog 1985; IL Committee on Black Concerns in Higher Educ steering committee mem, 1985-, vice chair, Southern Region, 1997, 1998; consultant SIU-C Women's Studies Film Project 1986-; American Assn of Counseling and Devel; National Council of Black Studies; executive director Star Human Serv Devel Corp Inc, 1987-; Founder/convener Assembly of African, African-American Women, 1989, Kappa Delta Pi, 1987. **CONTACT ADDRESS** Center for Basic Skills, Southern Illinois Univ at Carbondale, Woody Hall, C-7, Carbondale, IL, 62901.

STAMBROOK, FRED
PERSONAL Born 11/16/1929, Vienna, Austria **DISCIPLINE** HISTORY **EDUCATION** Oxford Univ, BA, 50; Univ London, BS, 51, PhD, 60. **CAREER** Educ Off, RAF, 50-52; mem, Ger War Doc Proj, 54-59; lectr hist, Univ Sydney, 60-68; PROF HISTORY, UNIV MANITOBA, 68-, assoc dean, arts, 75-77, dean 77-82, vice pres acad, 82-91; vis prof, Univ Ky, 67. **HONORS AND AWARDS** Queen's Silver Jubilee Medal, 77; Canada 125 Medal, 92. **SELECTED PUBLICATIONS** Auth, European Nationalism in the Nineteenth Century, 69; co-ed, Documents on German Foreign Policy 1918-1945, Ser C & D, 56-66; co-ed, A Modern History Sourcebook, 66. **CONTACT ADDRESS** Univ Col, Univ Manitoba, Winnipeg, MB, R3T 2M8.

STAMP, ROBERT M.
PERSONAL Born 02/11/1937, Toronto, ON, Canada **DISCIPLINE** HISTORY **EDUCATION** Univ Western Ont, BA, 59, PhD, 70; Univ Toronto, MA, 62. **CAREER** Tchr, London Sec Sch, 60-65; asst prof, Univ Western Ont, 65-69; assoc prof 69-73, prof 73-83, dir Can stud 80-83, PROF, UNIV CALGARY, 95. **SELECTED PUBLICATIONS** Auth, School Days: A Century of Memories, 75; auth, The Schools of Ontario 1876-1976, 82; auth, The World of Tomorrow, 85; auth, QEW: Canada's First Superhighway, 87; auth, Kings, Queens and Canadians, 87; auth, Royal Rebels, 88; auth, Riding the Radials, 89; auth, Early Days in Richmond Hill, 91; auth, Bridging the Border, 92; auth, Turning 100 Together, 94. **CONTACT ADDRESS** 123 - 34A St NW, Calgary, AB, T2N 2Y4. **EMAIL** stamp@acs.ucalgary.ca

STANDRING, TIMOTY
DISCIPLINE ITALIAN RENAISSANCE AND BAROQUE **EDUCATION** Univ Chicago, PhD, 82. **CAREER** Assoc prof-. **RESEARCH** Pousiin, Castiglione, Cassiano dal Pozzo, British landscape painting. **SELECTED PUBLICATIONS** Pub(s), Burlington Mag, Print Quart, Art Jour, Sixteenth Century Stud, Renaissance Quart. **CONTACT ADDRESS** Dept of Art Hist, Univ Denver, 2199 S Univ Blvd, Denver, CO, 80208.

STANISLAWSKI, MICHAEL
DISCIPLINE JEWISH, RUSSIAN, AND EUROPEAN INTELLECTUAL HISTORY **EDUCATION** Harvard Univ, 73, PhD, 79. **CAREER** Nathan J Miller prof. **SELECTED PUBLICATIONS** Auth, Tsar Nicholas I and the Jews, 83; For Whom Do I Toil?, 88; Psalms for the Tsar, 88; co-auth, Heritage: Civilization and the Jews: Study Guide, 84; ed, Heritage: Civilization and the Jews: Source Reader, 84. **CONTACT ADDRESS** Dept of Hist, Columbia Col, New York, 2960 Broadway, New York, NY, 10027-6902.

STANLEY, DELLA M.M.
PERSONAL Born 08/21/1950, Kingston, ON, Canada **DISCIPLINE** CANADIAN STUDIES **EDUCATION** Mt Allison Univ, BA, 73; Univ NB, MA, 74, PhD, 80. **CAREER** Asst prof, Queen's Univ, 78-81; Asst prof, Saint Mary's Univ, 84-90; asst prof, 82-92, COORDR, CANADIAN STUDIES PROGRAMME, 88-, ASSOC PROF, 92-, CHAIR, POLITICAL & CANADIAN STUDIES, MT ST VINCENT UNIV, 97-. **MEMBERSHIPS** Asn Can Stud; Can Hist Asn; Adminrs Can Stud Progs; Osgoode Soc; Heritage Can. **SELECTED PUBLICATIONS** Auth, Au Service de deux peuples: Pierre Landry, 76; auth, Louis Robichaud: A Decade of Power, 84; auth, A Man for Two Peoples: Judge Pierre Landry, 88; auth, A Victorian Lady's Album: Kate Shannon's Halifax and Boston Diary of 1892, 94. **CONTACT ADDRESS** Can Stud Prog, Mount Saint Vincent Univ, 106 Shore Dr, Bedford, NS, B4A 2E1.

STANLEY, JULIAN CECIL
PERSONAL Born 07/09/1918, Macon, GA, m, 1980, 1 child **DISCIPLINE** PSYCHOLOGY **EDUCATION** Ga So Univ, BS, 37; Harvard Univ, EdM, 1946; EdD, 50. **CAREER** Teacher, Fulton and West Fulton high schs, Atlanta, 37-42; instr, Newton Jr Col, 46-48; instr, Harvard Univ, 48-49; assoc prof, George Peabody Teacher's Col, 49-57; prof, 57-67; prof, Johns Hopkins Univ, 67- . **HONORS AND AWARDS** Phi Beta Kappa; Sigma Xi; Phi Delta Kappa; Social Sci Res Coun Inst Math for Soc Sci, Univ Mich, 55; Postdoctoral fel, Univ Chicago, 55-56; Fulbright res scholar, Univ Louvain, Belgium, 58-59; Fulbright lectr, New Zealand and Autralia, 74. **MEMBERSHIPS** AAAS; Am Statis Asoc; Am Psychol Soc; Am Educ Res Asoc; Nat Asoc for Gifted Children; AAUP; Psychometric Soc; Tenn Psychol Asoc. **SELECTED PUBLICATIONS** Co-ed with W.C. George and C.H. Solano, The Gifted and the Creative: A Fifty-Year Perspective, 77; ed, Educational Programs and Intellectual Prodigies, 78; co-ed with W.C. George and S.J. Cohn, Educating the Gifted: Acceleration and Enrichment, 79; co-ed with C.P. Benbow, Academic Precocity; Aspects of Its Develoment, 83; co-auth with K.D. and B. Hopkins, Educational and Psychological Measurement and Evaluation, 90. **CONTACT ADDRESS** Dept. of Psychology, Johns Hopkins Univ, 3400 N Charles St., Baltimore, MD, 21218.

STANLEY-BLACKWELL, LAURIE
PERSONAL Kingston, ON, Canada **DISCIPLINE** HISTORY **EDUCATION** Mt Allison Univ, BA, 77; Dalhousie Univ, MA, 80; Queen's Univ, PhD, 89. **CAREER** Instr, Queen's Univ, 86-88; asst prof, 89-94, ASSOC PROF HISTORY, ST. FRANCIS XAVIER UNIV, 94-. **HONORS AND AWARDS** Federated Alumni Life Mem Prize, 77; Tweedle Memorial Gold Medal, 77; Groiler Award Hist, 78, Outstanding Tchr Award, Fac Arts, Mt Allison Univ, 95,; Killam Memorial Scholar, Dalhousie Univ, 78-79. **MEMBERSHIPS** Can Hist Asn; Asn Can Studs;

Atlantic Asn Hist. **SELECTED PUBLICATIONS** Auth, Unclean! Unclean! Leprosy in New Brunswick, 1844-1880, 82; auth, The Well-Watered Garden: The Presbyterian Church in Cape Breton, 1798-1860, 83; contribur, Dictionary of Canadian Biography. **CONTACT ADDRESS** Dept of History, St. Francis Xavier Univ, Antigonish, NS, B2G 2W5. **EMAIL** lstanley@juliet.stfx.ca

STANSIFER, CHARLES LEE
PERSONAL Born 12/13/1930, Garden City, KS, m, 1954, 4 children **DISCIPLINE** LATIN AMERICAN HISTORY **EDUCATION** Wichita State Univ, BA, 53, MA, 54; Tulane Univ, PhD, 59. **CAREER** Ed asst, Miss Valley Hist Rev, 55-58; asst prof hist, Univ Southwestern La, 58-63; asst prof, 63-65, dir jr year prog, Costa Rica, 66 & 74, assoc prof, 65-79, prof hist, Univ KS, 79-, Dir, Ctr Latin Am Studies, 75-89, Doherty Found fel, 62-63; dir, Tri-Univ Ctr Latin Am Studies, KS, 76-82. **MEMBERSHIPS** Conf Latin Am Hist; Lat Am Studies Asn. **RESEARCH** Central Am and Mex hist; US-Latin Am diplomatic rel(s). **SELECTED PUBLICATIONS** Auth, E George Squier and the Honduras Interoceanic Railroad Project, Hisp Am Hist Rev, 2/66; Application of the Tobar Doctrine to Central America, The Americas, 1/67; E George Squier: Varios aspectos de su carrera in Centro America, Rev Pensamiento Centroam, 68; National Latin America: A topical approach, Univ Kans, 74; Jose Santos Zelaya: A new look at Nicaragua's liberal dictator, Rev Interam, fall 77; Ruben Dario and his relationship to the Dictator Zelaya, Ann, Southeastern Asn Latin Am Studies, 3/79; The Nicaraguan national literacy crusade, No 6, 81 & Cultural Policy in the old and the new Nicaragua, No 41, 81, Am Univs Field Staff Reports; Costa Rica, Clio Press, 91; Nicaragua's prolonged contra war, In: Prolonged war: a post-nuclear challenge, Air Univ Press, 94; Elections and democracy in Central America: the cases of Costa Rica and Nicaragua, In: Assession democracy in Latin America, Westview Press, 98. **CONTACT ADDRESS** Dept of Hist, Univ Kansas, Lawrence, KS, 66045-0001. **EMAIL** cstan@ukans.edu

STANTON, PHOEBE BAROODY
PERSONAL Born 12/05/1914, Freeport, IL, m, 1948, 1 child **DISCIPLINE** HISTORY OF ART **EDUCATION** Mt Holyoke Col, BA, 37; Radcliffe Col, MA, 39; Univ London, PhD, 50. **CAREER** Instr humanities, Reed Col, 45-47; spec employee, US Embassy, London, 50-51, asst cult off, 51-53; lectr hist of art, Bryn Mawr Col, 53-54; educator, Walters Gallery, Baltimore, Md, 54-55; lectr hist of art, eve col, 55-57, from asst prof to prof, 62-71, William R Kenan, Jr prof hist of art, Johns Hopkins Univ, 71-80, mem fac fine arts, eve col, 57-80. Lectr, Goucher Col, 55-60, adj prof, 60-63; consult urban design, Dept Housing & Community Develop & Charles Ctr-Inner Harbor Mgt Admin, City of Baltimore, 70-; Nat Endowment for Humanities sr fel, 72-73. **HONORS AND AWARDS** Calvert Prize for Historic Preservation, 76; Emmarv Award, critical writing, 76; Col Art Assoc Distinguished teaching award, 80., LittD, Mt Holyoke Col, 71. **MEMBERSHIPS** Col Art Asn Am; Victorian Soc; Soc Archit Hist, Gt Brit; Soc Archit Historians. **RESEARCH** History of architecture, Great Britain and the United States; history of urban design. **SELECTED PUBLICATIONS** Auth, The Gothic Revival and American Church Architecture: An Episode in Taste 1840-1856, Johns Hopkins Univ, 68; Pugin, Thames & Hudson, 71; Pugin--A Gothic Passion, Albion, Vol 27, 95. **CONTACT ADDRESS** 100 W University Pkwy, Baltimore, MD, 21210.

STAPLES, ROBERT EUGENE
PERSONAL Born 06/28/1942, Roanoke, VA, d **DISCIPLINE** SOCIOLOGY **EDUCATION** LA Valley Coll, AA, 60; Calif State Univ-Northridge, AB, 63; San Jose State Univ, MA, 65; Univ Minn, PhD, 70. **CAREER** PROF, SOCIOL, UNIV CALIF-SAN FRAN, 72-. **MEMBERSHIPS** Nat Coun Family Relations; Asn Black Nurs Fac **RESEARCH** Family, Human sexuality. **CONTACT ADDRESS** Dept Sociol, Univ Calif-San Fran, Box 0612, San Francisco, CA, 94143.

STARK, GARY DUANE
PERSONAL Born 06/27/1948, St. Paul, MN **DISCIPLINE** MODERN GERMAN HISTORY **EDUCATION** Hamline Univ, BA, 70; Johns Hopkins Univ, MA, 72, PhD(hist), 74. **CAREER** Vis asst prof hist, Dalhousie Univ, 74-75; asst prof, 75-81, ASSOC PROF HIST, UNIV TEX, ARLINGTON, 81-**MEMBERSHIPS** AHA; Southern Hist Asn; Conf Group Cent Europ Hist; Western Asn Ger Studies. **RESEARCH** German cultural history; German social and political history; sociology of knowledge. **SELECTED PUBLICATIONS** Auth, Censorship And Literary-Life In Wilhelmine Germany--A Research Report, Intes Archiv Fur Sozialgeschichte Der Deutschen Literatur, Vol 17, 92; Political Censorship Of The Arts And The Press In 19th-Century Europe, J Of Modern Hist, Vol 64, 92; The Politics Of The Unpolitical--German Writers And Power 1770-1871, Central European Hist, Vol 27, 94; Censorship Of Political Caricature In 19th-Century France, J Of Modern Hist, Vol 64, 92; Public-Libraries In Nazi Germany, Amn Hist Rev, Vol 98, 93. **CONTACT ADDRESS** Dept of Hist, Univ Tex, Arlington, TX, 76019.

STARK, JAMES A.
DISCIPLINE MUSIC **EDUCATION** Univ Minn, BA; Univ Toronto, MA, PhD. **CAREER** Prof. **HONORS AND AWARDS** Assoc ed, Jour Res Singing. **CONTACT ADDRESS** Mount Allison Univ, 63D York St, Sackville, NB, E4L 1E4.

STARN, RANDOLPH
PERSONAL Born 04/03/1939, Modesto, CA, m, 1960, 2 children **DISCIPLINE** EARLY MODERN EUROPEAN HISTORY **EDUCATION** Stanford Univ, BA, 60; Univ Calif, Berkeley, MA, 61; Harvard Univ, PhD(Hist), 67. **CAREER** Asst prof, 66-71, assoc prof, 71-78, prof Hist, Univ Calif, Berkeley, 78-; Marian E Koshland Disting prof and dir Townsend Cen for Humanities, 96; prof Italian Studies; Fulbright lectr, Univ Perugia, 73-74; vis mem, Inst Advan Study, Princeton Univ, 79-80; Guggenheim Fel, 84; dir Ecole des Haules Ehedes, Paris, 86. **MEMBERSHIPS** AHA; Renaissance Soc Am. **RESEARCH** Renaissance Italy; historiography; history. **SELECTED PUBLICATIONS** Auth, Donato Giannotti and His Epistolae, Droz, Geneva, 68; A Renaissance Likeness: Art and Culture in Raphael's Julius II, 80 & Contrary Commonwealth: The Theme of Exiles in Medieval and Renaissance Italy, 82, Univ Calif; Arts of Power 92, Univ Calif, Ambrogio Lorenzetti Soc, 94. **CONTACT ADDRESS** Dept of History, Univ of California, Berkeley, 3229 Dwinelle Hall, Berkeley, CA, 94720-2551.

STARR, CHESTER G.
PERSONAL Born 10/05/1914, Centralia, MO, m, 1940, 4 children **DISCIPLINE** ANCIENT HISTORY **EDUCATION** Univ Mo, AB, 34, AM, 35; Cornell Univ, PhD, 38. **CAREER** Am Acad Rome fel, 38-40; from instr to prof hist, Univ Ill, Urbana-Champaign, 40-70; PROF HIST, UNIV MICH, ANN ARBOR, 70-, BENTLEY PROF, 73-, Guggenheim fel, 50-51, 58-59. **HONORS AND AWARDS** Citation of Merit, Univ Mo, 63., LLD, Univ Mo, 81. **MEMBERSHIPS** AHA; Soc Promotion Roman Studies; Asn Ancient historians (pres, 74-78); fel, Am Acad Arts & Sci. **RESEARCH** Roman Empire; ancient civilization; early Greece. **SELECTED PUBLICATIONS** Auth, Civilization and the Caesars, Cornell Univ, 54; Origins of Greek Civilization, Knopf, 61; Roman Imperial Navy, Heffer, Cambridge, 2nd ed, 61; History of the Ancient World, Oxford Univ, 65, 3rd ed, 82; Awakening of the Greek Historical Spirit, Knopf, 68; Athenian Coinage, 480-449 BC, Clarendon, 70; Political Intelligence in Classical Greece, Brill, 74; Economic and Social Growth in Early Greece, Oxford Univ, 77; Beginnings of Imperial Rome, Univ Mich, 80; Essays on Ancient History, Brill, 79; The Roman Empire: A Study in Survival, Oxford Univ, 82; Ships And Sea-Power Before The Great-Persian-War--The Ancestry Of The Ancient Trireme, Am Hist Rev, Vol 99, 94. **CONTACT ADDRESS** Dept of Hist, Univ of Mich, Ann Arbor, MI, 48109.

STARR, JOSEPH BARTON
PERSONAL Born 12/24/1945, Pensacola, FL, m, 1966, 2 children **DISCIPLINE** AMERICAN HISTORY, INTERNATIONAL AFFAIRS **EDUCATION** Samford Univ, AB, 66; Fla State Univ, MA, 67, PhD(hist), 71. **CAREER** Asst prof Am hist, Troy State Univ, Dothan/Ft Rucker, 70-77, assoc prof, 78-80; SR LECTR & MISSIONARY AM STUDIES, HONG KONG BAPTIST COL, 82-, Vpres, Ala Baptist Hist Soc, 73-74; consult, Nat Endowment for Humanities, 77-78; Fulbright-Hays sr scholar Am studies, Hong Kong Baptist Col, 78-79. **HONORS AND AWARDS** Ala Hist Comn merit award, 76. **MEMBERSHIPS** AHA; Southern Hist Asn; Orgn Am Historians. **RESEARCH** American loyalists, especially on the frontier; antebellum Southern culture; early missionaries to China. **SELECTED PUBLICATIONS** Auth, Campbell Town: French Huguenots in British West Florida, Fla Hist Quart, 76; The spirit of what is there called liberty: The Stamp Act in British West Florida, Ala Rev, 76; Tories, Dons and Rebels: The American Revolution in British West Florida, 1775-1783, Univ Presses Fla, 76; coauth, Alabama: A Place, A People, A Point of View, Kendall/Hunt Publ Co, 77; auth, To live (and die) in Dixie, In: Perspectives: The Alabama Heritage, Troy State Univ Press, 78; Left as a gewgaw: The impact of the American Revolution on British West Florida, In: Eighteenth Century Florida: The Impact of the American Revolution, 78, intro & index to John Pope's A Tour Through the Southern and Western Territories of the United States (1792), 79, Univ Presses Fla; The rattletrap raid, Am Hist Illustrated, 82; James Grant--Scottish Soldier And Royal-Governor Of East-Florida, J Of Southern Hist, Vol 60, 94; Alabama--The Hist Of A Deep South State, J Of Am Hist, Vol 82, 95. **CONTACT ADDRESS** 169 Boundary St, Hong Kong, ..

STARR, KEVIN
DISCIPLINE HISTORY **EDUCATION** PhD. **CAREER** Prof, Sch Urban and Regional Plan, Univ Southern Calif. **RESEARCH** History of California & the West. **SELECTED PUBLICATIONS** Auth, Americans & the California Dream, 1850-1915, Oxford, 73; Inventing the Dream: California Through the Progressive Era, Oxford, 85; Material Dreams: Southern California Through the 1920s, Oxford, 90; The Dream Endures: California Through the Great Depression, Oxford, 96. **CONTACT ADDRESS** Dept of History, Univ Southern Calif, University Park Campus, Los Angeles, CA, 90089. **EMAIL** kstarr@library.ca.gov

STARR, LARRY
PERSONAL Born 04/17/1946, Brooklyn, NY, m, 1968, 3 children **DISCIPLINE** MUSIC HISTORY **EDUCATION** BA, Queens Col, CUNY, 67, PhD, Univ of CA at Berkeley. **CAREER** Asst prof, SUNY, Stony Brook, 70-77; at Univ of WA 77, full prof 93. **RESEARCH** Am music, espec in the 20th century. **SELECTED PUBLICATIONS** A Union of Diversities: Style in the Music of Charles Ives, 92. **CONTACT ADDRESS** Univ of Washington, Box 353450, Seattle, WA, 98195. **EMAIL** lstarr@u.washington.edu

STARR, RAYMOND JAMES
PERSONAL Born 05/17/1952, Grand Rapids, MI, m, 1975 **DISCIPLINE** CLASSICAL LANGUAGES **EDUCATION** Univ Mich, BA, 74; Princeton Univ, MA, 76, PhD(class), 78. **CAREER** Lectr class, Princeton Univ, 78-79; Asst Prof Greek & Latin, Wellesley Col, 79-, Fel, Am Coun Learned Soc, 82-83. **MEMBERSHIPS** Am Philol Asn; Class Asn Can; Class Asn New England. **RESEARCH** Social context of ancient literature; Roman historiography; comedy. **SELECTED PUBLICATIONS** VERGIL 'SEVENTH ECLOGUE' AND ITS READERS - BIOGRAPHICAL ALLEGORY AS AN INTERPRETATIVE STRATEGY IN ANTIQUITY AND LATE-ANTIQUITY/, CLASSICAL PHILOLOGY, Vol 0090, 1995 **CONTACT ADDRESS** Dept of Greek & Latin, Wellesley Col, 106 Central St, Wellesley, MA, 02181-8204.

STARR-LEBEAU, GRETCHEN D.
DISCIPLINE HISTORY **EDUCATION** Univ Virginia, BA, 90; MA, 92, PhD, 96, Univ Michigan. **CAREER** Adjunct faculty, Suffolk Univ, 96-97; Asst Prof, Univ Kentucky, 97-. **CONTACT ADDRESS** Dept of History, Univ of Kentucky, 1715 Patterson Office Tower, Lexington, KY, 40506-0027. **EMAIL** starrle@pop.uky.edu

STARTT, JAMES DILL
PERSONAL Born 07/26/1932, Baltimore, MD, m, 1960, 2 chiidren **DISCIPLINE** BRITISH COMMONWEALTH & BRITISH HISTORY **EDUCATION** Univ Md, BA, 57, MA, 61, PhD(hist), 65. **CAREER** Asst prof hist, Murray State Univ, 64-66; assoc prof, 66-71, PROF HIST, VALPARAISO UNIV, 71- **MEMBERSHIPS** AHA; MidWest Conf Brit Studies; Am Comt Irish Studies. **RESEARCH** History of Journalism; British history. **SELECTED PUBLICATIONS** Auth, American Propaganda In Britain During World-War-I, Prologue-Quarterly Of The National Archives, Vol 28, 96; Winning The Peace--British Diplomatic Strategy, Peace Planning, And The Paris-Peace-Conference, 1916-1920, Historian, Vol 55, 93; Lord Beaverbrook--A Life, Historian, Vol 56, 94; Henry R. Luce--A Political Portrait Of The Man Who Created The Amn Century, Am Hist Rev, Vol 100, 95. **CONTACT ADDRESS** 822 Brosn St, Valparaiso, IN, 46383.

STAUDENMAIER, JOHN M.
DISCIPLINE HISTORY OF AMERICA **EDUCATION** St Louis Univ, BA, MA; Univ Pa, PhD. **CAREER** Prof, 81. **HONORS AND AWARDS** Bannon scholar, Santa Clara Univ; Dibner fel, MIT. **RESEARCH** Studying Henry Ford and the Ford Motor Company. **SELECTED PUBLICATIONS** Auth, Technology's Storytellers: Reweaving the Human Fabric; ed, Technology and Culture. **CONTACT ADDRESS** Dept of Hist, Univ Detroit Mercy, 4001 W McNichols Rd, PO BOX 19900, Detroit, MI, 48219-0900.

STAUDER, JACK
PERSONAL Born 03/02/1939, Pueblo, CO, d, 2 children **DISCIPLINE** SOCIAL ANTHROPOLOGY **EDUCATION** Cambridge Univ, PhD 68; Harvard Univ, BA 62. **CAREER** Harvard Univ, instr, 68-71; Northeastern Univ, asst prof, 71-73; Univ Massachusetts, prof, 73-. **RESEARCH** Environmental Issues; Ranching. **SELECTED PUBLICATIONS** Auth, The Majangir: Cultural Ecology of a Southwestern Ethiopian People, Cambridge, 70; Changing Course: Teaching Both Sides of Environmental Issues, Liberal Edu, 95; auth, Under Siege: Arizona Cowboys and Endangered Species, Range, 98. **CONTACT ADDRESS** Dept of Sociology and Anthropology, Univ of Massachusetts, North Dartmouth, MA, 02747. **EMAIL** jstauder@umassd.edu

STAUDINGER LANE, EVELYN
DISCIPLINE ART HISTORY **EDUCATION** Wellesley Coll, BA, 77; MA, 80; Brown Univ, PhD, 87. **CAREER** Asst Prof Art, Wheaton Coll **MEMBERSHIPS** CAA; Medieval Acad of Amer; ICMA; Corpus Vitrearum Medii Aevi. **RESEARCH** Gothic Art and Architecture; Medieval Stained Glass **CONTACT ADDRESS** 11 Pine Needle Rd., Wayland, MA, 01778. **EMAIL** elane@wheatonma.edu

STAUFFER, GEORGE B.
DISCIPLINE MUSIC HISTORY AND LITERATURE **EDUCATION** Columbia Univ, PhD. **CAREER** Prof & dept ch; gen ed, Monuments Western Mus ser at Macmillan. **MEMBERSHIPS** Pres, Amer Bach Soc. **RESEARCH** Baroque music; works and life of J.S. Bach in particular. **SELECTED PUBLICATIONS** Auth, J.S. Bach as Organist; Bach Perspectives 2 &

Bach: The Mass in B Minor; articles in, Early Mus, Mus Quart, J Musicol, Bach-Jahrbuch. **CONTACT ADDRESS** Dept of Music, Hunter Col, CUNY, 695 Park Ave, New York, NY, 10021.

STAVE, BRUCE M.

PERSONAL Born 05/17/1937, New York, NY, m, 1961, 1 child **DISCIPLINE** AMERICAN HISTORY **EDUCATION** Columbia Univ, AB, 59, MA, 61; Univ Pittsburgh, PhD(hist), 66. **CAREER** From instr to asst prof hist, Univ Bridgeport, 65-70; from asst prof to assoc prof, 70-75, res found grants, 70-82, dir, oral hist proj, 79-81, prof hist, 75- , chemn, 85-94, Univ CT, dir, Ctr Oral Hist, 81-, Fulbright lectr, India, 68-69; Nat Endowment Hum fel, 74; dir, Peoples CT Oral Hist Proj, 74-76; guest fel & vis lectr, Yale Col, 76; ed, Oral Hist Rev, 96-99, assoc ed, J Urban Hist, 76-; Fulbright prof, New Zealand, Australia, Indonesia & Philippines, 77, Fulbright prof, Peoples Rep of China, 84-85. **HONORS AND AWARDS** Harvey Kantor Mem Award for Significant Work in Oral Hist, New Eng Asn Oral Hist, 77; Homer Babbidge Jr Award for best bk, Asn for Study of CT Hist. **MEMBERSHIPS** AHA; Orgn Am Historians; Oral Hist Asn; Soc Sci Hist Asn; Immigrant Hist Soc; New Eng Hist Asn; CT Acad of Arts & Sci; New Eng Asn of Oral Hist; CT Coord Comt for the Promotion of Hist. **RESEARCH** Am urban hist; recent Am hist; oral hist. **SELECTED PUBLICATIONS** Auth, The New Deal and the Last Hurrah, Univ Pittsburgh, 70; ed, Urban Bosses, Machines and Progressive Reformers, Heath, 72; co-ed, The Discontented Society, Rand McNally, 72; auth, Urban bosses and reform, In: The Urban Experience, Wadworth, 73; Series of oral history conversations on urban history, J Urban Hist, 74-78; ed & contribr, Socialism & the Cities, Kennikat, 75, 77; auth, The Making of Urban History, 77 & ed, Modern Industrial Cities: History, Policy & Survival, 81, Sage; co-ed, Talking about Connecticut: Oral History in the Nutmeg State, Conn Humanities Council, 85, rev, 90; coauth, Mills and Meadows: A Pictorial History of Northeastern Connecticut, Donning Co, 91; coauth, From the Old Country: An Oral History of European Migration to America, Twayne, 94; coauth, Witnesses to Nuremberg: An Oral History of American Participants at the War Crimes Trials, Twayne, 98. **CONTACT ADDRESS** Dept of History, Univ of CT, Storrs, CT, 06269-2103. **EMAIL** stave@uconnvm.uconn.edu

STAVIG, WARD

PERSONAL Born 11/30/1948, Ukiah, CA, m, 1986, 2 children **DISCIPLINE** HISTORY **EDUCATION** Univ Calif Davis, PhD, 91 **CAREER** Instr, Sacramento City Col, 75-78; lectr, Calif St Univ Hayword, 89; vis lectr, Univ Calif Santa Cruz, 91; lectr, Univ Calif Davis, 90, 92; vis prof, Universidad Catolica Boliviana, 93; asst prof to assoc prof, Univ S Fl, 93- . **HONORS AND AWARDS** Fulbright Fel, 83-84, 92-93. **MEMBERSHIPS** AHA; CLAH. **RESEARCH** Colonial Andes; indigenous society. **SELECTED PUBLICATIONS** Auth, Conflict, Violence, And Resistance, in The Countryside in Colonial Latin America, Univ NM Press, 96; America and the People Truly Without History, review essay, Colonial Latin American, 97; Culture, Technology and Social Change: Selected Proceedings of the Third Biennial conf, Univ S Fl, 96; Amor y Violencia Sexual, Valores indigenas en la sociedad colonial, Instituto de Estudios Peruanos, 96; The World of Tupac Amaru: Cultural Identity, community and Conflict in Colonial Peru, Univ Nb Press, 99. **CONTACT ADDRESS** Dept of History, Univ of S Fl, 4202 E Fowler Ave, Tampa, FL, 33620-8100. **EMAIL** stavig@lluna.cas.usf.edu

STAVRIANOS, LEFTEN STAVROS

PERSONAL Born 02/05/1913, Vancouver, BC, Canada **DISCIPLINE** HISTORY **EDUCATION** Univ BC, AB, 33; Clark Univ, AM, 34, PhD, 37. **CAREER** Lectr, Queen's Univ, Can, 37-38, instr, Smith Col, 39-43, asst prof, 43-44, 45-46; from assoc prof to prof, 46-73, EMER PROF HIST, NORTHWESTERN UNIV, 73-; ADJ PROF, UNIV CALIF, SAN DIEGO, 76-, Royal Soc Can fel, Europe, 38-39; Guggenheim fel, 51-52; fel, Ctr Advan Study Behav Sci, 72-73. **MEMBERSHIPS** AHA; Nat Educ Asn. **RESEARCH** World history; modern Balkan history. **SELECTED PUBLICATIONS** Auth, Balkan Federation; The Balkans Since 1453; World Since 1500, 66, World to 1500, 70 & Man's Past and Present, 70, Prentice-Hall; The Promise of the Coming Dark Age, W H Freeman, 76; Global Rift: The Third World Comes of Age, William Morrow, 81; The Global Condition--Conquerors, Catastrophes, And Community, J Of World Hist, Vol 5, 94. **CONTACT ADDRESS** Dept Hist, Univ Calif San Diego, La Jolla, CA, 92093.

STAYER, JAMES MENTZER

PERSONAL Born 03/15/1935, Lancaster, PA, m, 1958, 3 children **DISCIPLINE** HISTORY **EDUCATION** Juaniata Col, AB, 57; Univ Va, AM, 58; Cornell Univ, PhD(hist), 64. **CAREER** Instr hist, Ithaca Col, 59-61; asst prof, Bridgewater Col, 62-65; asst prof early mod Europ hist, Bucknell Univ, 65-68; asst prof Renaissance & Reformation hist, 68-72, assoc prof, 72-78, PROF HIST, QUEEN'S UNIV, ONT, 78-, Am Philos Soc grant-in-aid, 67-68; Alexander von Humboldt Found res grant, Ger, 67-67 & 79-80; publ subvention, Humanities Res Coun Can, 72; Can Coun leave fel, 74-75; Soc Sci Humanities Res Coun Can, 82-83. **MEMBERSHIPS** Sixteenth Century Studies Conf; Am Soc Reformation Res. **RESEARCH** Ulrich Zwingli; Renaissance and Reformation history; radical reformation. **SELECTED PUBLICATIONS** Auth, Oldeklooster and Menno, Sixteenth Century J, 4/78; The Swiss brethren: An exercise in historical definition, Church Hist, 6/78; Zwingli before Zurich, Humanist reformer and papal partisan, Archiv f?r Reformationsgeschichte, 81; Conflicting Visions Of Reform--German Lay Propaganda Pamphlets, 1519-1530, Sixteenth Century J, Vol 27, 96; The German Peasants-War--A History In Documents, Sixteenth Century J, Vol 24, 93. **CONTACT ADDRESS** Dept of Hist, Queen's Univ, Kingston, ON, K7L 3N6.

STEARNS, PETER N.

PERSONAL Born 03/03/1936, London, England, m, 1964, 4 children **DISCIPLINE** MODERN HISTORY **EDUCATION** Harvard Univ, AB, 57, AM, 59; PhD, 63. **CAREER** From instr to assoc prof hist, Univ Chicago, 62-68; prof, Rutgers Univ, New Brunswick, 68-73, chmn dept, 69-73; HENIZ PROF, CARNEGIE-MELLON UNIV, 73-, DEAN, COL OF HUMANITIES AND SOCIAL SCIENCES, 91-; Vis asst prof, Northwestern Univ, 65; managing ed, J Social Hist, 67-; Am Philos Soc & Soc Sci Res Coun grants, 67-68; vis prof, Sir George William Univ, 70; Guggenheim fel, 73-74; vis prof polit sci, Univ Houston, 78. **HONORS AND AWARDS** Koren Prize, Soc Fr Hist Studies, 66; Newcomen Spec Award Bus Hist, Newcomen Soc, 67. **MEMBERSHIPS** AHA, vice-pres, 95-98; Soc Fr Hist Studies; Soc Sci Hist Asn. **RESEARCH** Modern social history; comparative European history; applied history; world history. **SELECTED PUBLICATIONS** Auth, European Society in Upheaval, Macmillan, 67, rev ed, 75; 1848: The Tide of Revolution in Europe, Norton, 74; Lives of Labor: Works in Maturing Industial Society, 75 & Old Age in European Society, 77, Holmes & Meier; Face of Europe, Forum, 77; Paths to Authority, Middle Class Consciousness, Univ IL, 78; Be a Man! Males in Society, 80 & Old Age in Preindustrial Society, 82, Holmes & Meier; Anger: the Struggle for Emotional Control in America's History, Chicago, 86; World History: Patterns of Change and Continuity, Harper & Row, 87; Jealousy: The Evolution of an Emotion in American History, NYU, 89; Meaning Over Memory: Recasting the Teaching of Culture and History, NC, 93; The Industrial Revolution in World History, Westview, 93; American Cool: Developing the Twentieth-Century Emotional Style, NYU, 94; Millenium III, Century XXI: A Retrospective on the Future, Westview, 96; Fat History: Bodies and Beauty in Western Society, NYU, 97. **CONTACT ADDRESS** Dept of Hist, Carnegie Mellon Univ, 5000 Forbes Ave, Pittsburgh, PA, 15213-3890. **EMAIL** ps0q@andrew.cmu.edu

STEBBINS, ROBERT E.

PERSONAL Born 07/28/1931, Lima, OH, m, 1954, 3 children **DISCIPLINE** MODERN EUROPEAN HISTORY **EDUCATION** Bowling Green State Univ, BA, 53; Yale Univ, BD, 56; Univ Minn, MA, 60, PhD(hist), 65. **CAREER** Assoc prof, 63-71, prof Hist, Eastern KY Univ, 71-. **MEMBERSHIPS** AHA **RESEARCH** Nineteenth century France; European intellectual history. **CONTACT ADDRESS** Dept of Hist, Eastern Kentucky Univ, 521 Lancaster Ave, Richmond, KY, 40475-3102. **EMAIL** Hisstebb@acs.eku.edu

STEBENNE, DAVID

PERSONAL Born 07/04/1960, Providence, RI **DISCIPLINE** HISTORY, LAW **EDUCATION** Yale Univ, BA, 82; Columbia Univ, JD, MA, 86, PhD, 91. **CAREER** Lectr, Hist, Yale Univ, 91-93; asst prof, Hist, Ohio State Univ, 93-97; ASSOC PROF, HIST, OHIO STATE UNIV, 97-. **MEMBERSHIPS** Am Hist Asn; Org Am Hist; Bus Hist Conf; DC Bar; Md Bar **RESEARCH** Modern US history; politics, economics, labor & legal history **SELECTED PUBLICATIONS** Arthur J. Goldberg: New Deal Liberal, Oxford Univ Press, 96. **CONTACT ADDRESS** Hist Dept, Ohio State Univ, 106 Dulles Hall, 230 w 17th, Columbus, OH, 43210-1367. **EMAIL** stebenne.1@osu.edu

STECKEL, RICHARD H.

PERSONAL Born 06/28/1944, Milledgeville, GA, m, 1972, 2 children **DISCIPLINE** ECONOMICS **EDUCATION** Oberlin College, BA, 66; Univ OK, MA, 70; Univ Chicago, MA, 73, PhD, 77. **CAREER** Instr, Asst Prof, Assoc Prof, Prof, 74 to 89-, Ohio State Univ. **HONORS AND AWARDS** Charles Warren Fel; OSU Dist Lectr, . **MEMBERSHIPS** EHA; SSHA; PAA; AHA; EHA; AEA; AAPA. **RESEARCH** Long term trends in health care and nutrition. **SELECTED PUBLICATIONS** Coed, Health and Welfare During Industrialization, Univ Chicago Press, 97. **CONTACT ADDRESS** Economics Dept, Ohio State Univ, 1945 N High St, Columbus, OH, 43210. **EMAIL** steckel.1@osu.edu

STEEGER, WM P.

PERSONAL Born 05/26/1945, Brooklyn, NY, m, 1968, 4 children **DISCIPLINE** OLD TESTAMENT ARCHEOLOGY **EDUCATION** Univ Florida, BA, 67; Southern Baptist Theol Sem, Louisville, Mdiv 70, PhD, 83; Univ of Louisville, KY, MA, 72. **CAREER** Instr, 69-73, Univ of Louisville; Prof, 76-86, Baptist Theol of Southern Africa, Johannesburg, S Africa; Prof, 78-86, Die Theol Sem van die Baptist; Prof, 83-84, Oakland City Coll; Prof, 86-, Ouachita Baptist Univ, Arkadelphia, AR, Chr Div of Rel and Philos. **HONORS AND AWARDS** Phi Kappa Phi; Phi Alpha Theta; Amer Ed, KY, South; Biblical Stud and Archaeol; Man of Achievement; Vis Prof of OT-Southern Baptist Theol Sem, KY. **MEMBERSHIPS** Soc of Biblical Lit; Evangelical Theol Soc; Inst of Biblical Res; Natl Assoc of Baptist Prof of Rel. **RESEARCH** Old Testament; Biblical Archaeology. **SELECTED PUBLICATIONS** Contrib auth, Anchor Bible Dictionary, Doubleday & Co; Contrib auth, Mercer Commentary of the Bible, Mercer Univ Press; auth, Joshua: An Exposition, Baptist Theological College of Southern Africa, Johannesburg, South Africa; Psalms: An Exposition, Old Testament Theology, Old Testament Introduction, Baptist Theo College of S Africa, Johannesburg, S Africa. **CONTACT ADDRESS** Ouachita Baptist Univ, OBU 3720, Arkadelphia, AR, 71998. **EMAIL** steeger@alpha.edu

STEEL, DAVID WARREN

DISCIPLINE MUSIC HISTORY **EDUCATION** Harvard Univ, AB, 68; Univ Mich, AM, 76, PhD, 82. **CAREER** ASSOC PROF, MUS & SOUTHERN CULT, UNIV MISS **MEMBERSHIPS** Am Antiquarian Soc **SELECTED PUBLICATIONS** Auth, "Truman S. Wetmore and His Republican Harmony," Conn Hist Soc Bull 45, 80; auth, "L.L. Jones and The Southern Minstrel (1849)," Am Mus 6, 88; auth, "John Wyeth and the Development of Southern Folk Hymnody," in Music from the Middle Ages through the 20th Century, Gordon & Breach, 88; auth, Stephen Jenks, in New Grove Dict of Am Music; ed, Stephen Jenks: Collected Works, A-R Editions, 95. **CONTACT ADDRESS** Dept of Music, Univ of Miss, Meek Hall, University, MS, 38677. **EMAIL** mudws@olemiss.edu

STEELE, IAN KENNETH

PERSONAL Born 09/10/1937, Edmonton, AB, Canada, m, 1961, 2 children **DISCIPLINE** MODERN HISTORY **EDUCATION** Univ Alta, BA, 61; Univ London, PhD(hist), 64. **CAREER** From lectr to assoc prof, 64-75, PROF HIST, UNIV WESTERN ONT, 75-, Can Coun leave fel, 70-71, 77-78; Killam fel, 80-81. **MEMBERSHIPS** Can Hist Asn. **RESEARCH** British imperial and American Colonial history. **SELECTED PUBLICATIONS** Auth, The Widening Gate--Bristol And The Atlantic Economy, 1450-1700, Am Hist Rev, Vol 98, 93; The American-Revolution In Indian Country--Crisis And Diversity In Native-American Communities, Int Hist Rev, Vol 18, 96; The Intellectual Construction Of America--Exceptionalism And Identity From 1492 To 1800--Greene,Jp/, J Of Imperial And Commonwealth Hist, Vol 22, 94; The Sense Of The People--Politics, Culture And Imperialism In England 1715-1785, J Of Imperial And Commonwealth Hist, Vol 25, 97; Lord-Churchill Coup--The Anglo-Am Empire And The Glorious-Revolution Reconsidered, Int Hist Rev, Vol 18, 96; A Passion For Government--The Life Of Sarah-Of-Marlborough, Historian, Vol 56, 93; Negotiated Authorities--Essays In Colonial Political And Constitutional Hist, Pennsylvania Magazine Of Hist And Biography, Vol 120, 96; The Public Prints--The Newspaper In Anglo-American Culture, 1665-1740, J Of Am Hist, Vol 81, 95; Sojourners In The Sun--Scottish Migrants In Jamaica And The Chesapeake, 1740-1800, Virginia Magazine Of Hist And Biography, Vol 101, 93; Making The Empire Work, London And Am Interest-Groups, 1690-1790, Eighteenth-Century Studies, Vol 26, 93; Colonial Am--A Hist, 1607-1760, J Of Imperial And Commonwealth Hist, Vol 22, 94; Atlantic Am Societies--From Columbus To Abolition, 1492-1888, Int Hist Rev, Vol 16, 94; The Pueblo Revolt Of 1680--Conquest And Resistance In 17th-Century New-Mexico, Am Hist Rev, Vol 101, 96. **CONTACT ADDRESS** Dept of Hist, Univ of Western Ont, London, ON, N6A 5C2.

STEELE, MARTA N.

PERSONAL Born 05/20/1949, Trenton, NJ, d, 1 child **DISCIPLINE** CLASSICAL PHILOLOGY **EDUCATION** Wellesley Col, BA, 71; Univ CA, Los Angelos, MA, 73; Boston Univ, PhD candidate, 80-. **CAREER** Full-time and freelance newspaper reporter, 83-85; adjunct instr, English composition, res and exposition, business writing, Rider Col Dept of English, 84-85; copy chief, NJ Network, Trenton, NJ, 85; freelance manuscript ed, indexer, and proofreader, 87-91; freelance trans/author, 95-97; manuscript ed, series ed, Princeton Univ Press, 91-. **HONORS AND AWARDS** Listed in Who's Who in the East and Int Who's Who of Professionals; honored at Royal Danish Embassy, Washington, DC, and Princeton Univ Press, 5/98, for completeion of the 25 text volumes of the Kierkegaard's Writings series. **MEMBERSHIPS** Am Philol Asn; Am Classical League. **RESEARCH** Homeric philology (PhD thesis topic); poetics, epic in general; computer programs to facilitate various aspects of Classics editing and indexing. **SELECTED PUBLICATIONS** Editor, R Rehm, Marriage to Death: The Conflagation of Wedding and Funeral Rituals in Greek Tragedy, 94; P C Miller, Dreams in Late Antiquity: Studies in the Imagination of a Culture, 94; D J Furley and A Nehamas, eds, Aristotle's Rhetoric: Philosophical Essays, 94; G Vlastos, ed by D Graham, Studies in Greek Philosophy: Volume 1: The Presocratics; Volume II, Socrates, Plato, and Their Tradition, 95; M W Gleason, Making Men: Sophists and Self-Presentation in Ancient Rome, 95; N Loraux, trans Paula Wissing, The Experiences of Tiresias: The Feminine and the Greek Man, 95; E Stehle, Performance and Gender in Ancient Greece, 96; S Schein, Reading the Odyssey: Selected Interpretive Essays, 96; J Ober and C Hendrick, eds, Demokratia: A Conversation on Democracies,

Ancient and Modern, 96; D Lyons, Gender and Immortality: Heroines in Ancient Greek Myth and Cult, 97; Patricia Curd, The Legacy of Parmenides: Eleatic Monism and Later Presocratic Thought, 98; Johanna Prins (Yopi), Victorian Sappho, forthcoming 99; Sidney Alexander, trans and commentator, The Complete Odes and Satires of Horace, forthcoming 99; editor of numerous other publications. **CONTACT ADDRESS** Univ Press, Princeton Univ, 41 William St, Princeton, NJ, 08540. **EMAIL** marta_steele@pupress.princeton.edu

STEELE, RICHARD WILLIAM
PERSONAL Born 01/28/1934, New York, NY, m, 1958, 2 children **DISCIPLINE** AMERICAN HISTORY **EDUCATION** Queens Col, NY, AB, 56; Univ Wis, MA, 59; Johns Hopkins Univ, MA, 66, PhD(Am hist), 69. **CAREER** Archivist, Nat Arch, 60-61; historian, Off Joint Chiefs Staff, 62-63; from asst prof to assoc prof hist, 67-75, PROF HIST, SAN DIEGO STATE UNIV, 75- **MEMBERSHIPS** AHA; Orgn Am Historians. **RESEARCH** World War II American home front; Franklin D Roosevelt and public opinion; Roosevelt subversion and dissent. **SELECTED PUBLICATIONS** Auth, Arming Military-Justice--The Origins Of The United-States-Court-Of-Military-Appeals, 1775-1950, Historian, Vol 56, 93; The Propaganda Warriors--Am Crusade Against Nazi Germany, Int Hist Rev, Vol 19, 97; Am Unbound, World-War-2 And The Making Of A Superpower, Pacific Hist Rev, Vol 63, 94; Fear Of The Mob And Faith In Government In Free Speech Discourse, 1919-1941, Am J Of Legal Hist, Vol 38, 94. **CONTACT ADDRESS** Dept of Hist, San Diego State Univ, San Diego, CA, 92182.

STEELMAN, JOSEPH F.
PERSONAL Born 12/22/1922, Wilkesboro, NC, m, 1947, 2 children **DISCIPLINE** AMERICAN HISTORY **EDUCATION** Univ NC, AB, 43, MA, 47, PhD, 55. **CAREER** Instr hist, Univ NC, 47-52; instr hist & govt, Tex A&M Univ, 52-53; asst prof hist, State Univ NY Cortland, 53-54; from asst prof to assoc prof, 55-63, Southern fel, 58, PROF HIST, E CAROLINA UNIV, 63-, Pres, NC Lit & Hist Asn, 70- & Hist Soc NC, 76- **HONORS AND AWARDS** R D W Connor Award, 66, 67, 70. **MEMBERSHIPS** AHA; Orgn Am Historians; Southern Hist Asn. **RESEARCH** North Carolina in the Progressive Era, 1884-1917; Republican Party politics in North Carolina, 1884-1917; Joseph Hyde Pratt and North Carolina Conservation Movements, 1884-1917. **SELECTED PUBLICATIONS** Auth, Republicanism in North Carolina: John Motley Morehead's Campaign to Revive a Moribund Party, 1908-1910, Vol XLII: 153-168; The Trials of a Republican State Chairman: John Motley Morehead and North Carolina Politics, 1910-1912, Vol XLIII: 31-42; Richmond Pearson, Roosevelt Republicans, and the Campaign of 1912 in North Carolina, Vol XLIII: 122-139; The Progresive Democratic Convention of 1914 in North Carolina, Vol XLVI: 83-104; Republican Party Strategists and the Issue of Fusion with Populists in North Carolina, 1893-1894, Vol XLVII: 244-269; Edward J Justice: Profile of a Progressive Legislator, 1899-1913, Vol XLVIII: 147-160 &; Origins of the Campaign for Constitutional Reform in North Carolina, 1912-1913, Vol LVI: 396-418, NC Historical Rev; ed, Of Tar Heel Towns, Shipbuilders, Reconstructionists, and Alliancemen: Papers in NC Hist, 81; The Papers Of William,Alexander Graham, Vol 8, 1869-1875, J Of Southern Hist, Vol 60, 94. **CONTACT ADDRESS** Dept of Hist, East Carolina Univ, Greenville, NC, 27834.

STEELY, MELVIN T.
DISCIPLINE HISTORY **EDUCATION** Vanderbilt Univ, PhD, 71. **CAREER** Prof. **RESEARCH** Modern German history; Cold War; 20th century Europe; oral history. **SELECTED PUBLICATIONS** Auth, pubs on East Germany; Versailles Treaty, and the Nazis in the Spanish Civil War. **CONTACT ADDRESS** History Dept, State Univ of West Georgia, Carrollton, GA, 30118. **EMAIL** msteely@westga.edu

STEEN, IVAN DAVID
PERSONAL Born 09/06/1936, New York, NY, m, 1958, 2 children **DISCIPLINE** AMERICAN HISTORY **EDUCATION** NY Univ, BA, 57, MA, 59, PhD(hist), 62. **CAREER** Instr hist, Hunter Col, 62-65; ASST PROF HIST, STATE UNIV NY ALBANY, 65-, Consult historian, Historic Rome Develop Proj, NY, 66-67. **MEMBERSHIPS** AHA; Orgn Am Historians. **RESEARCH** American social history; history of the American city. **SELECTED PUBLICATIONS** Auth, America's first World's Fair, NY Hist Soc Quart, 7/63; Philadelphia in the 1850's: As described by British travelers, Pa Hist, 1/66; Palaces for travelers: New York City's hotels in the 1850's as viewed by British visitors, NY Hist, 4/70; Cleansing the Puritan city: The Reverend Henry Morgan's antivice crusade in Boston, New Eng Quart, 9/81; Before The Mayor Was Mayor--The Education And Early Career Of Erastus Corning, Ny Hist, Vol 073, 92. **CONTACT ADDRESS** McKown Rd, RD 1 Box 196G, Albany, NY, 12203.

STEEVES, PAUL DAVID
PERSONAL Born 06/20/1941, Attleboro, MA, m, 1962, 2 children **DISCIPLINE** RUSSIAN MODERN & ECCLESIASTICAL HISTORY **EDUCATION** Washington Univ, AB, 62; Univ Kans, MA, 72, PhD(Russ hist), 76. **CAREER** Asst instr Western civilization, Univ Kans, 66-68; vis lectr hist, Kans State Teachers Col, 71-72; asst prof, 72-78, PROF HIST, STETSON UNIV, 78-, DIR RUSS STUDIES, 76-, DIR HONORS PROG, 78-, Ed, Newsletter, Conf Faith & Hist, 79. **HONORS AND AWARDS** O P Backus Award, Univ Kans, 76; W H McInery Award, Stetson Univ, 79. **MEMBERSHIPS** AHA; Conf Faith & Hist; Am Asn Advan Slavic Studies; Soc Study Relig Under Communism; Southern Conf Slavic Studies. **RESEARCH** Evangelical Baptist movement in Russia. **SELECTED PUBLICATIONS** Auth, Baptists as subversives in the contemporary Soviet Union, In: God and Caesar, Conf Faith & Hist, 71; ed, Church and State in USSR, A sourcebook, Stetson Univ, 73; auth, Alexander Karev, evangelical in a Communist land, Fides et Historia, 76; Amendment of Soviet law concerning religious association, J Church & State, 77; Old-Believers In Modern Russia, Russian Rev, Vol 56, 97; A Long Walk To Church--A Contemporary-History Of Russian Orthodoxy, Russian Rev, Vol 56, 97; Out Of The Red Shadows--Anti-Semitism In Stalin Russia, J Of Church And State, Vol 38, 96. **CONTACT ADDRESS** Dept of Hist, Stetson Univ, 421 N Woodland Blvd, Deland, FL, 32720-3761.

STEFFEN, JEROME ORVILLE
PERSONAL Born 02/26/1942, WI, m, 1966, 2 children **DISCIPLINE** AMERICAN HISTORY **EDUCATION** Univ Wis, BS, 66; Eastern Michigan Univ, MA, 68; Univ Mo-Columbia, PhD(hist), 71. **CAREER** ASSOC PROF HIST, UNIV OKLA, 74- **MEMBERSHIPS** Org Am Historians; Western Historical Asn. **RESEARCH** American frontier; comparative frontiers. **SELECTED PUBLICATIONS** Ed, Mid-American Frontiers Ser, 47 vols, Arno Press, 75; auth, William Clark Jeffersonian Man on the Frontier, 77, co-ed, Frontiers: A Comparative Approach, 77, auth, Comparative Frontiers: A Proposal for Studying the American West, 80, ed, American West: New Perspectives New Dimensions, 81 & auth, Stages of development in Oklahoma history, In: Oklahoma: New Viewpoints, 82, Univ Okla Press; Gold Seeking--Victoria And California In The 1850s, Pacific Hist Rev, Vol 65, 96; Were In The Money--Depression Am And Its Films, J Of The West, Vol 34, 95; Cycles Of Myth Restoration--One Approach To Understanding Amn Culture, J Of Am Culture, Vol 16, 93. **CONTACT ADDRESS** Dept of Hist, Univ of Olka, Norman, OK, 73019.

STEFFENSEN-BRUCE, INGRID A.
PERSONAL Born 05/12/1967, Lewisburg, PA, m, 1992, 1 child **DISCIPLINE** HISTORY OF ART AND ARCHITECTURE **EDUCATION** Univ VA, BA, 88; Yale Univ, MA, 89; Univ DE, PhD, 94. **CAREER** Instr (Tenure Track), Brookdale Col, 96-. **HONORS AND AWARDS** Wilbur Owen Sypherd Award for Outstanding Dissertation in the Humanities, Univ DE, 95; Phi Beta Kappa, Univ VA, 95. **MEMBERSHIPS** Col Art Asn; Soc of Architectural Hist; Am Culture Asn. **RESEARCH** 19th century Am art and architecture. **SELECTED PUBLICATIONS** Auth, The World's Columbian Exposition and Its Influence on the Milwaukee Public Library and Museum Competition, 1893, Nineteenth Century, spring 97; Portrait of the PhD as a Young Woman, in On the Market: Surviving the Academic Job Search, eds Christina Boufis and Victoria Olsen, Riverhead Books, 97; Nineteenth-Century Women as Architects: the Ladder Question, Nineteenth Century, spring 98; Marble Palaces, Temples of Art: Art Museums, Architecture, and American Culture, 1890-1930, Bucknell Univ Press, 98. **CONTACT ADDRESS** 64 Whitney Rd, Short Hills, NJ, 07078. **EMAIL** iasbruce@aol.com

STEGGLES, MARY ANN
DISCIPLINE ART **EDUCATION** Univ Manitoba, BA, 87, MA, 90; Univ Leicester, PhD. **CAREER** Art, Acadia Univ. **RESEARCH** Art and politics nineteenth century art public monuments; patronage indian art and architecture. **SELECTED PUBLICATIONS** Auth, The Myth of the Monuments, 94; Bombay: A City of Imperial Statues, 96. **CONTACT ADDRESS** Dept of Art, Acadia Univ, Wolfville, NS, B0P 1XO.

STEGMAIER, MARK JOSEPH
PERSONAL Born 08/27/1945, Cumberland, MD, m, 1971, 2 children **DISCIPLINE** AMERICAN HISTORY **EDUCATION** Univ Santa Clara, BA, 67; Univ Calif, Santa Barbara, MA, 70, PhD(hist), 75. **CAREER** Asst prof, 75-82, assoc prof am hist, Cameron Univ, 82-. **MEMBERSHIPS** AHA; Orgn Am Historians. **RESEARCH** United States History, 1840-1860. **SELECTED PUBLICATIONS** Auth, The kidnapping of Generals Crook and Kelley by the McNeill Rangers, Feb 21, 1865, WVa Hist, 67; Maryland's fear of insurrection at the time of Braddock's defeat, Md Hist Mag, 75. **CONTACT ADDRESS** Dept of Soc Sci, Cameron Univ, 2800 Gore Blvd, Lawton, OK, 73505-6377.

STEIMAN, LIONEL BRADLEY
PERSONAL Born 07/12/1941, Winnipeg, MB, Canada, m, 1967, 1 child **DISCIPLINE** EUROPEAN HISTORY **EDUCATION** Univ Man, BA, 64; Univ Pa, MA, 65, PhD(hist), 70. **CAREER** Lectr, 70-72, asst prof, 72-78, ASSOC PROF HIST, UNIV MAN, 78- **MEMBERSHIPS** Western Asn Ger Studies. **RESEARCH** German exile studies. **SELECTED PUBLICATIONS** Auth, The agony of humanism, J Europ Studies, 6/76; The eclipse of humanism: Zweig between the wars, Mod Austrian Lit, 12/81; The worm in the rose: Historical destiny and individual action in Stefan Zweig's Vision of History, In: Proceedings of the Stefan Zweig Symposium at Fredonia, NY, 1981, State Univ NY Press; From Prejudice To Persecution--A History Of Austrian Anti-Semitism, Modern Austrian Lit, Vol 26, 93. **CONTACT ADDRESS** Dept of Hist, Univ of Man, Winnipeg, MB, R3T 2N2.

STEIN, BURTON
PERSONAL Born 08/01/1926, Chicago, IL, m, 1966 **DISCIPLINE** INDIAN HISTORY **EDUCATION** Univ Chicago, MA, 53, PhD(hist), 58. **CAREER** Instr soc sci, Wilson Jr Col, 55-56; from asst prof to assoc prof hist, Univ Minn, 58-66; PROF HIST, UNIV HAWAII, MANOA, 67-, Am Coun Learned Soc grant-in-aid, 61; Fulbright res fel, India, 61-62; mem scholarly resources comt, AHA, 63-64; exec comt & bd trustees, Am Inst Indian Studies, 64-66, res fel & sr fel, Madras, 66-68; vis prof hist, Univ Chicago, 74-75; vis prof South Asia, Univ Pa, 77. **MEMBERSHIPS** Asn Asian Studies; AHA. **RESEARCH** South Indian history; Indian economic history; Asian peasant history. **SELECTED PUBLICATIONS** Auth, The Ruhela Chieftaincies--The Rise And Fall Of Ruhela Power In India In The 18th-Century, Bullet Of The School Of Oriental And African Studies-Univ Of London, Vol 60, 97; Money And The Market In India 1100-1700, Bulletin Of The School Of Oriental And African Studies-Univ Of London, Vol 59, 96; Tiruvannamalai, A Saiva Sacred Complex Of South-India, Vol 4, The Sociological Configuration Of The Hindu Temple, J Of The American Oriental Society, Vol 113, 93; Dalit Movements And The Meaning Of Labor In India, Bulletin Of The School Of Oriental And African Studies-Univ Of London, Vol 58, 95; Land And Local Kingship In 18th-Century Bengal, Bulletin Of The School Of Oriental And African Studies-Univ Of London, Vol 58, 95. **CONTACT ADDRESS** Dept of Hist, Univ of Hawaii Manoa, Honolulu, HI, 96822.

STEIN, KENNETH W.
DISCIPLINE HISTORY **EDUCATION** Franklin Marshall Col, BA, 68; Univ Mich, MA, 69/71, PhD 76. **CAREER** Prof/ Dir Mid East Res Prog. **HONORS AND AWARDS** Carter Ctr Mid East Fellow. **RESEARCH** Modern Near-Eastern history; social and economic history of Palestine in the twentieth century; inter-Arab political history; the Arab-Israeli peace process and the Mediterranean littoral states of the Near East. **SELECTED PUBLICATIONS** Auth, The Intifadah and the 1936-39 Uprising: A Comparison; The Study of Middle Eastern History in the United States; coauth, The Land Question in Palestine 1917-1939: The Blood of Abraham; Making Peace Between Arabs and Israelis: Lessons from Fifty Years of Negotiating Experience. **CONTACT ADDRESS** Dept History, Emory Univ, 221 Bowden Hall, 561 Kilgo Cir, Atlanta, GA, 30322-1950. **EMAIL** kstein@emory.edu

STEIN, LEON
PERSONAL Born 03/28/1941, New York, NY, m, 1965, 1 child **DISCIPLINE** EUROPEAN INTELLECTUAL HISTORY **EDUCATION** NY Univ, BA, 62, MA, 64, PhD(hist), 66. **CAREER** Instr hist, NY Univ, 65-66; asst prof, 66-70, assoc prof, 70-80, PROF HIST, ROOSEVELT UNIV, 80- **MEMBERSHIPS** AHA; Conf Group Cent Europ Historians. **RESEARCH** Modern European intellectual history; Germany 1500-1815. **SELECTED PUBLICATIONS** Auth, Patriotism and religion in the Thirty Years' War, Cent Europ Hist, 72; A Desperate Embrace-The Holocaust And The Ideas Of Existentialism, Proteus, Vol 12, 95. **CONTACT ADDRESS** Dept of Hist, Roosevelt Univ, 430 S Michigan, Chicago, IL, 60605.

STEINBERG, LEO
PERSONAL Born 07/09/1920, Moscow, USSR **DISCIPLINE** HISTORY OF ART **EDUCATION** NY Univ, PhD(art), 60. **CAREER** Prof art hist, Hunter Col, 61-75; BENJAMIN FRANKLIN PROF HIST OF ART & UNIV PROF, UNIV PA, 75-, Soc Fels, Am Acad in Rome. **HONORS AND AWARDS** DFA, Philadelphia Col Art, 81. **MEMBERSHIPS** Col Art Asn Am. **RESEARCH** Renaissance, baroque and contemporary art. **SELECTED PUBLICATIONS** Auth, The Philosophical Brothel (Picasso's Demoiselles d' Avignon), Art News, 9-10/72; Other Criteria, Confrontations with Twentieth-Century Art, Oxford Univ, 72; Leonardo's Last Supper, Art Quart, 73; Michelangelo's Last Judgment as Merciful Heresy, Art in Am, 11-12/75; Michelangelo's Last Paintings, Phaidon & Oxford Univ, 75; Borromini's San Carlo alle quattro Fontane, Garland, 77; A corner of the Last Judgment, Daedalus, spring 80; The Line of Fate in Michelangelo's painting, Critical Inquiry, spring 80; Max Ernst-Dada And The Dawn Of Surrealism, Ny Rev Of Books, Vol 40, 93. **CONTACT ADDRESS** Univ of Pa, Philadelphia, PA, 19104.

STEINBERG, MARK D.
DISCIPLINE HISTORY **EDUCATION** Univ Calif Berkeley, PhD, 87. **CAREER** Assoc prof, Univ Ill Urbana Champaign, 96-. **HONORS AND AWARDS** Dir, Russian E Europ Center. **RESEARCH** Cultural and social history of the nineteenth and twentieth centuries. **SELECTED PUBLICATIONS** Auth, Moral Communities: The Culture of Class Relations in the Russian Printing Industry, 1867-1907, Univ Calif, 92; The Fall of the Romanovs: Political Dreams and Personal Struggles in a

Time of Revolution, Yale, 95; co-ed, Cultures in Flux: Lower Class Values, Practices and Resistance in Late Imperial Russia, Princeton, 94. **CONTACT ADDRESS** History Dept, Univ Ill Urbana Champaign, 52 E Gregory Dr, Champaign, IL, 61820. **EMAIL** steinb@uiuc.edu

STEINBERG, SALME HARJU
PERSONAL Born 02/21/1940, New York, NY, m, 1963, 2 children **DISCIPLINE** AMERICAN HISTORY **EDUCATION** Hunter Col, City Univ New York, BA, 60, MA, 62; Johns Hopkins Univ, PhD(hist), 71. **CAREER** Instr hist, Towson State Col, 64-66; lectr, Goucher Col, 71-72; asst prof, Northwestern Univ, 72-75; asst prof, 75-78, ASSOC PROF HIST, NORTHEASTERN ILL UNIV, 78- **MEMBERSHIPS** Orgn Am Historians; Bus Hist Conf; Econ Hist Asn. **RESEARCH** United States economic and social history; United States business history; non-profit institutions. **SELECTED PUBLICATIONS** Auth, Reformer in the Marketplace: Edward W Bok and the Ladies Home Journal, La State Univ Press, 79; Magazines For The Millions--Gender And Commerce In The Ladies-Home-J And The Saturday-Evening-Post 1880-1910, Am Hist Rev, Vol 101, 96; The Republic Of Mass-Culture--Jism, Filmmaking, And Broadcasting In Am Since 1941, Am Hist Rev, Vol 98, 93. **CONTACT ADDRESS** 2708 Harrison St, Evanston, IL, 60201.

STEINER, BRUCE E.
DISCIPLINE HISTORY **EDUCATION** St Thomas, AB, 56; Univ Virg, MA, 59, PhD, 62. **CAREER** PROF, HIST, OHIO UNIV **MEMBERSHIPS** Am Antiquarian Soc **SELECTED PUBLICATIONS** Auth, "Anglican Office-Holding in Pre-Revolutionary Connecticut: The Parameters of New England Community," Wm & Mary Quart 31, 74; auth, Connecticut Anglicans in the Revolutionary Era: A Study in Communal Tensions, 79. **CONTACT ADDRESS** Dept of Hist, Ohio Univ, Athens, OH, 45701.

STEINHARDT, NANCY SHATZMAN
PERSONAL Born 07/14/1954, St. Louis, MO, m, 1979, 4 children **DISCIPLINE** EAST ASIAN ART; ARCHAEOLOGY **EDUCATION** Wash Univ, AB, 74; Harvard Univ, AM, 75, PhD, 81. **CAREER** Lectr, Bryn Mawr Col, 81-83; lectr, Univ Pa, 82-86; asst prof, 86-91, assoc prof, 91-98, prof, 98-, Univ Pa. **HONORS AND AWARDS** Soc Sci Res Found fel, 97; Nat Endow for the Humanities fel, 94; Asian Cultural Coun grant, 93; Amer Philos Soc grant, 92; Getty Grant Prog Sr fel, 90; Amer Coun of Learned Soc fel, 89; Graham Found for Adv Studies in the Fine Arts, grant, 89. **MEMBERSHIPS** Col Art Asn; Asn of Asian Studies; Soc of Archit Hist; Hist of Islamic Art; Soc of East Asian Archaeol; Northeast China Studies Asn. **RESEARCH** Chinese art and architecture from Han through Yuan; Central Asian art & archaeology; Northeast Asian art & architecture. **SELECTED PUBLICATIONS** Article, The Temple to the Northern Peak in Quyang, Artibus Asiae, 58, 1/2, 69-90, 98; auth, Liao Architecture, Univ Hawaii Press, 97; article, Chinese Cartography and Chinese Calligraphy, Oriental Art, 43, 1, 10-20, 97; article, Chinese Architecture, Chinese City Planning, Dict of Art, vol 6, 646-666, 96; article, Chinese Architecture, 963-966, Orientations, 26, 2, 46-52, 95; article, Liao: An Architectural Tradition in the Making, Artibus Asiae, 54, 1/2, 5-39, 94; article, The Tangut Royal Tombs near Yinchuan, Essays in Honor of Oleg Grabar, Muqarnas, 10, 369-381, 93; auth, Chinese Imperial City Planning, Univ Hawaii Press, 90; auth, Chinese Traditional Architecture, China Inst, 84. **CONTACT ADDRESS** Dept. of Asian & Middle Eastern Studies, Univ of Pennsylvania, 847 Williams Hall, Philadelphia, PA, 19104-6305. **EMAIL** nssteinh@sas.upenn.edu

STEINMETZ, DAVID CURTIS
PERSONAL Born 06/12/1936, Columbus, OH, m, 1959, 2 children **DISCIPLINE** CHURCH HISTORY **EDUCATION** Wheaton Col, Ill, AB, 58; Drew Univ, BD, 61; Harvard Univ, ThD(church hist), 67. **CAREER** From asst prof to assoc prof church hist, Lancaster Theol Sem, 66-71; assoc prof, 71-79, Prof Church Hist & Doctrine, Divinity Sch, Duke Univ, 79-, Am Asn Theol Schs fac fel, Oxford Univ, 70-71; vis prof church hist, Harvard Univ, 77; Guggenheim fel, Cambridge Univ, 77-78. **MEMBERSHIPS** Am Soc Church Hist; Am Soc Reformation Res; Mediaeval Acad Am; Renaissance Soc Am; Soc Bibl Lit. **RESEARCH** History of Christian thought in the late Middle Ages and Reformation. **SELECTED PUBLICATIONS** Auth, The Superiority of Pre-Critical Exegesis, Theol Today, 80; Luther and Staupitz: An Essay in the Intellectual Origins of the Protestant Reformation, Duke, 80; Calvin on Isaiah 6: A Problem in the History of Exegeis, Interpretation, 82; The Theory And Practice Of Exegesis--Proceedings Of The 3rd Int-Colloquium On The Hist Of Biblical Exegesis In The 16th-Century: Geneva, August 31 September 2, 88, Sixteenth Century J, Vol ; An Exploration Of The Human Imagination As An Instrument Of Spiritual Nurture And Theological Reform, Interpretation-A J Of Bible And Theology, Vol 47, 93; Divided By A Common Past--The Reshaping Of The Christian Exegetical Tradition In The 16th-Century, J Of Medieval And Early Modern Studies, Vol 27, 97. **CONTACT ADDRESS** Divinity Sch, Duke Univ, Durham, NC, 27706.

STEINWEIS, ALAN
DISCIPLINE EUROPEAN, JEWISH HISTORY **EDUCATION** Univ NC, Chapel Hill, PhD, 88. **CAREER** Hyman Rosenberg Assoc Prof Hist, dir, Judaic Stud, Univ Nebr, Lincoln. **HONORS AND AWARDS** Fulbright award, 96. **SELECTED PUBLICATIONS** Art, Ideology, and Economics in Nazi Germany, Univ NC Press, 93. **CONTACT ADDRESS** Univ Nebr, Lincoln, 637 Oldfat, Lincoln, NE, 68588-0417. **EMAIL** aes@unlinfo.unl.edu

STELTER, GILBERT ARTHUR
PERSONAL Born 06/13/1933, Lamont, AB, Canada, m, 1961, 3 children **DISCIPLINE** MODERN HISTORY **EDUCATION** Moravian Col, BA, 56; Univ Alta, BD, 59, PhD(urban hist), 68. **CAREER** Lectr hist, Univ Alta, 63-64; from asst prof to assoc prof urban hist, Laurentian Univ, 64-74, chmn dept hist, 69-72; assoc prof urban hist, 72-80, PROF URBAN HIST, UNIV GUELPH, 80-, Can ed rep, Urban Hist Yearbk, Univ Leicester, 74- **HONORS AND AWARDS** Silver Jubilee Medal, Govt Can, 78. **MEMBERSHIPS** Can Hist Asn; Asn Study Hist Archit Can. **RESEARCH** Canadian urban history; Canadian resource towns; city-building process in Canada. **SELECTED PUBLICATIONS** Auth, Urbanization in the Americas: The Background in Comparative Perspective, Nat Mus of Man, 80; coauth, Canada's Urban Past: A Bibliography to 1980 and Guide to Canadian Urban Studies, Univ of BC Press, 81; co-ed, Shaping the Urban Landscape: Aspects of the Canadian City-Building Process, Carleton Univ Press, 82; Regina--An Illustrated Hist, Canadian Hist Rev, Vol 75, 94; The City Beyond--A Hist Of Nepean, Birthplace Of Canada Capital, 1792-1990, Histoire Sociale-Social Hist, Vol 27, 94. **CONTACT ADDRESS** Dept of Hist, Univ of Guelph, Guelph, ON, N1G 2W1.

STENECK, NICHOLAS H.
PERSONAL Born 05/08/1940, Jersey City, NJ, m, 1963, 2 children **DISCIPLINE** HISTORY OF SCIENCE, SCIENCE POLICY **EDUCATION** Rutgers Univ, BS, 62; Univ Wis-Madison, MA, 69, PhD(hist, hist sci), 70. **CAREER** Asst prof, 70-76, ASSOC PROF HIST, UNIV MICH, ANN ARBOR, 76-, Am Coun Learned Soc study fel, 72-73. **MEMBERSHIPS** Hist Sci Soc. **RESEARCH** Scientific revolution, 17th century England; contemporary science-values disputes. **SELECTED PUBLICATIONS** Ed, Science and Society: Past, Present and Future, Univ Mich, 74; auth, Science and Creation in the Middle Ages, Medieval & Renaissance Colleqium, 76, co-ed, Society and History: Essays by Silvia L Thrupp, Univ Mich, 77; coauth, Early research on the biological effects of microwave radiation: 1940-1960, Annals of Sci, 37: 323-351; auth, The origins of US safety standards for microwave radiation, Science, 208: 1230-1237; The Ballad of Robert Crosse and Joseph Glanvill and the background to Plus Ultra, Brit J Hist Sci, 14: 159-74; Greatrakes the stroker: The interpretations of historians, Isis, 6/82; Impure Science--Fraud, Compromise, And Political Influence In Scientific Research, Isis, Vol 84, 93; Stealing Into Print--Fraud, Plagiarism, And Misconduct In Scientific Publishing, Isis, Vol 84, 93. **CONTACT ADDRESS** Dept of Hist, Univ of Mich, Ann Arbor, MI, 48104.

STENNIS-WILLIAMS, SHIRLEY
DISCIPLINE EDUCATION **EDUCATION** Loyola & Chicago Teachers College; Jackson State Univ, Valedictorian BS 1958; Peabody Coll of Vanderbilt Univ, MA 1964, EdD 1972; Harvard Management Development Program, 1990. **CAREER** Jackson State Lab School, teacher 1958-59; Chicago Public Schools, teacher 1959-64; Peabody Coll of Vanderbilt Univ, teaching assistant 1964-66; UNIV OF WI OSHKOSH, asst prof 1966-72, coord of field experience 1975-83, assoc prof 1972-83, professor 1982-85, asst vice chancellor, 1985-91; SENIOR SYSTEM ACADEMIC PLANNER, DEAN OF EDUCATION, 1992-. **HONORS AND AWARDS** Natl Defense Education Act Doctoral Fellowship 1963-66. First African-American asst prof, assoc prof and coordinator of field experience at the Univ of Wisconsin, Oshkosh. **MEMBERSHIPS** State delegate Founding Conv Natl Women's Studies Conf 1980; board of directors Wisc Council of Teachers of Engl 1981-83; district dir Wisc Council of Teachers of Engl 1981-83; founding president Wisc State Human Relations Assn 1982-83; board of directors Midwest Human Relations Assn 1982-83; American Association for Higher Education, Black Caucus secretary, treasurer, member of executive board, 1985-1992. **CONTACT ADDRESS** Education, Edinboro Univ of Pennsylvania, Meadville St, Edinboro, PA, 16444.

STEPHAN, JOHN JASON
PERSONAL Born 03/08/1941, Chicago, IL, m, 1963 **DISCIPLINE** RUSSIAN & EAST ASIAN HISTORY **EDUCATION** Harvard Univ, AB, 63, MA, 64; Univ London, PhD(hist), 69. **CAREER** Res assoc int rel, Soc Sci Res Ctr, Waseda Univ, Japan, 69-70; from asst prof to assoc prof, 70-77, chmn EAsian studies comt, Asian Studies Prog, 73-74, PROF HIST, UNIV HAWAII, MANOA, 77-; Trustee, Libr Int Rels, Chicago, 75-; Japan Found prof fel, 77; sr assoc mem, St Antony's Col, Oxford Univ, 77; vis prof, Inst Far E, Moscow, 82; Sanwa Distinguished Scholar in Residence, Fletcher School of Law and Diplomacy, Tufts Univ, 89. **HONORS AND AWARDS** Kenneth W. Baldridge Prize, Hawaii Chapter, Phi Alpha Theta, 96. **MEMBERSHIPS** Asn Asian Studies; Am Asn Advan Slavic Studies; AHA; Canadian Hist Asn. **RESEARCH** Modern Japanese foreign relations, especially Soviet-Japanese relations; history of Soviet Far East and northern Japan; Japanese-Americans in East Asia. **SELECTED PUBLICATIONS** Auth, Sakhalin: A History, Oxford, 71; Korean Minority in the Soviet Union, Mizan, 12/71; Japanese Studies in the Soviet Union, Asian Studies Prof Rev, spring 73; The Kuril Islands: Russo-Japanese Frontier in the Pacific, Oxford, 74; Japan and the Soviet Union: The Distant Neighbours, Asian Affairs, 10/77; The Russian Fascists, Harper & Row, 78; Asia in the Soviet Conception, In: Soviet Policy in Asia, Yale, 82; Hawaii Under the Rising Sun, Univ HI Press, 84; Soviet-American Horizons on the Pacific, with V. P. Chichkanov, Univ HI Press, 86; The Russian Far East: A History, Stanford Univ Press, 94; Highjacked in Utopia: American Nikkei in Manchuria, Amerasia J, vol 23, no 3, winter 97-98. **CONTACT ADDRESS** Dept of Hist, Univ of Hawaii Manoa, 2530 Dole St, Honolulu, HI, 96822-2303. **EMAIL** stephan@hawaii.edu

STEPHANSON, ANDERS
DISCIPLINE UNITED STATES HISTORY **EDUCATION** Gothenburg Univ, BA, 75; Columbia Univ, PhD, 86. **CAREER** Assoc prof. **SELECTED PUBLICATIONS** Auth, Kennan and the Art of Foreign Policy, 89; Manifest Destiny, 95. **CONTACT ADDRESS** Dept of History, Columbia Col, New York, 2960 Broadway, New York, NY, 10027-6902.

STEPHENS, LESTER DOW
PERSONAL Born 02/18/1933, Gatesville, TX, m, 2 children **DISCIPLINE** HISTORY **EDUCATION** Univ Corpus Christi, BS, 54; Univ Tex, MEd, 59; Univ Miami, PhD, 64. **CAREER** Teacher pub schs, Tex, 54-57; asst prof hist, Univ Corpus Christi, 57-61; social studies ed, 63-66, assoc prof, 66-67, assoc prof social studies, educ & hist, 67-69, assoc prof hist, 69-78, prof, 78-98, dept hd, 81-91, emeritus prof, Univ Ga, 98-. **HONORS AND AWARDS** Eight awards for distinguished teaching, Univ Ga. **MEMBERSHIPS** AHA; Orgn Am Hist; Hist of Sci Soc; Soc Stu of Natural Hist; Southern Hist Asn. **RESEARCH** History of science, historiography **SELECTED PUBLICATIONS** Auth, Probing the Past: A Guide to the Study and Teaching of History, Allyn & Bacon, 74; Historiography: A Bibliography, Scarecrow, 75; Evolution and woman's rights in the 1890's, Historian, 76; Joseph LeConte on evolution, education and the structure of knowledge, J Hist Behav Sci, 76; Farish Furman's formula: Scientific farming and the new South, Agr Hist, 76; Joseph LeConte's evolutional idealism, J Hist Ideas, 78; Joseph LeConte and the development of the physiology and psychology of vision in the United States, Anals of Sci, 80; Joseph LeConte: Gentle prophet of evolution, La State Univ Press, 82; The Evolution Controversy In America, J Of Southern Hist, Vol 62, 96; Ancient Animals and other Wondrous Things, Charleston Museum, 88; Scientific Societies in the Old South, Sci and Med in the Old South, La State Univ, 89; John Edwards Holbrook and Lewis R. Gibbes, Col Bldg in Ichthyology and Heptetology, Am Soc of Ichthyologists and Herpetologists, 97. **CONTACT ADDRESS** Dept of Hist, Univ of Ga, Georgia University, Athens, GA, 30602-0001. **EMAIL** lsteohen@arches.ugov.edu

STEPHENS, SUSAN A.
DISCIPLINE CLASSICS **EDUCATION** BA, 65; Columbia Univ, MA, 67; Stanford Univ, PhD, 72. **CAREER** Prof, Stanford Univ. **RESEARCH** Ancient novel; attic prose; Greek prose compos; papyrology. **SELECTED PUBLICATIONS** Auth, Yale Papyri in the Beinecke Library II, 85; Who Reads Ancient Novels? in Search for the Ancient Novel, 94; coauth, Ancient Greek Novels--the Fragments, 95. **CONTACT ADDRESS** Stanford Univ, Bldg 20, Main Quad, Stanford, CA, 94305.

STEPHENS, WILLIAM RICHARD
PERSONAL Born 01/02/1932, Ashburn, MO, m, 1952, 3 children **DISCIPLINE** AMERICAN SOCIAL & EDUCATIONAL HISTORY **EDUCATION** Greenville Col, BS, 53; Univ Mo, Columbia, MEd, 57; Wash Univ, EdD, 64. **CAREER** Assoc prof, Greenville col, 57-61; assoc prof, Ind State Univ, 64-70; prof, Ind Univ, Bloomington, 70-71; vpres & dean fac, 71-77, pres, 77-, Greenville Col; retired as Pres Emeritus, 93; dir of Pres Fel Inst, 95-. **HONORS AND AWARDS** Award of Merit, Nat Voc Guid Assn, 73; Distinguished Alumnus Award, Greenville Col, 81. **MEMBERSHIPS** Hist Educ Soc; Philos Educ Soc. **RESEARCH** Social and intellectual sources of American educational theory and systems, 1885-1920; progressive and reform values in American public education, 1890-1920. **SELECTED PUBLICATIONS** Coauth, Jesse Hewlon, Educ Forum, 11/67; art, Schools and wars, Teachers Col J, 5/67; art, The junior high school, a product of reform values, 1890-1920, 11/67, Teachers Col J; art, Social Reform and the Origins of Vocational Guidance, 1890-1925, Nat Voc Guid Assn, 70; coauth, Education in American Life, Houghton, 71. **CONTACT ADDRESS** 516 N Elm St, Greenville, IL, 62246-1199. **EMAIL** wstephen@greenville.edu

STERLING, DAVID L.
PERSONAL Born 07/04/1929, Brooklyn, NY, m, 1963 **DISCIPLINE** AMERICAN HISTORY **EDUCATION** NY Univ,

BA, 51, MA, 52, PhD, 58; Ohio State Univ, JD, 67. **CAREER** Asst prof Am hist, Albany State Teachers Col, 57-59; instr, Ohio State Univ, 59-64; asst prof, 64-69, ASSOC PROF AM HIST, UNIV CINCINNATI, 69- **MEMBERSHIPS** AAUP **RESEARCH** Life of John Pintard, 1759-1844. **SELECTED PUBLICATIONS** Auth, A Federalist opposes the Jay Treaty: The letters of Samuel Bayard, William & Mary Quart, 7/61; Police interrogation and the psychology of confession, J Pub Law, 65; The naive liberal, the devious Communist and the Johnson Case, Ohio Hist, spring 69; The Legacy Of Oliver,Wendell Holmes, Historian, Vol 56, 94; The United-States Military Under The Constitution Of The United-States, 1789-1989, J Of Military Hist, Vol 58, 94. **CONTACT ADDRESS** Dept of Hist, Univ of Cincinnati, Cincinnati, OH, 45221.

STERN, FRANCES MERITT
PERSONAL m **DISCIPLINE** PSYCHOLOGY **EDUCATION** Newark State Col, BA, 60, MA, 62; New York Univ, PhD, 72. **CAREER** ASSOC PROF, DEPT OF PSYCHOLOGY, KEAN COL OF NEW JERSEY, 69-; LICENSED PRACTICING PSYCHOLOGIST, 80-; DIR, INST FOR BEHAVIORAL AWARENESS, 73-. **HONORS AND AWARDS** Founder's Day Award, NYU; Who's Who of Am Women; Who's Who in The East., Temple Univ School of Medicine, Dept of Psychiatry, 76-80. **MEMBERSHIPS** APA; Asn for the Advancement of Behavior Therapy; NJ Psychol Asn; Am Soc for Training and Development. **RESEARCH** Test anxiety; stress reduction; behavioral modification. **SELECTED PUBLICATIONS** Coauth, Wash Away Stress-and Find the Gold in Gritty Situations, Veterinary Economics, 96; How Do You Handle a Stress Carrier?, Managing Stress in a Jewish Family, 94; Need for Achievement: Jewish love of Learning or Reflection of a Test-Crazed Society?, Jewish Family, 94; Taking the Angst Out of Test Anxiety, NJEA Rev, 94 Mind Trips to Help You Lose Weight, Playboy Press, 76; Stressless Selling, Prentice-Hall, 81; Stressless Selling-Revised Edition, Amacom, 90; Turning Visions Into Reality & Mind Over Body, Mind Over Matter, Time-Life Books, 88; auth, How to Live With Psychology and Maybe Learn to Like It, I.I.I., 72. **CONTACT ADDRESS** Inst for Behavioral Awareness, 810 Springfield Ave, Springfield, NJ, 07081. **EMAIL** flashtrst@aol.com

STERN, FRITZ
DISCIPLINE MODERN EUROPEAN AND GERMAN HISTORY **EDUCATION** Columbia Univ, BA, 46; Columbia Univ, Phd, 53. **CAREER** Prof emeri. **SELECTED PUBLICATIONS** Ed, The Varieties of History, 56; The Politics of Cultural Despair, 65; The Failure of Illiberalism: Essays on the Political Culture of Modern Germany, 72; Gold and Iron: Bismarck, Bleichrder and the Building of the German Empire, 77; Dreams and Delusions: the Drama of German History, 87. **CONTACT ADDRESS** Dept of Hist, Columbia Col, New York, 2960 Broadway, New York, NY, 10027-6902.

STERN, MARVIN
DISCIPLINE HISTORY **EDUCATION** Brandeis Univ, AB, AM, PhD; Harvard Univ, AM; Yale Univ, AM. **CAREER** PROF HIST, LAWRENCE TECH UNIV **MEMBERSHIPS** Am Hist Asn; Soc Mil Hist; British Soc 18th Century Stud. **RESEARCH** Edward Gibbon, family of Sir Henry Clinton; British hist, ancient hist, Jap hist. **SELECTED PUBLICATIONS** Auth, Death, Grief and Friendship in the 18th Century, 84; auth, Thorns and Briars: Bonding, Love and Death, 91. **CONTACT ADDRESS** Lawrence Tech Univ, Southfield, MI, 48075.

STERN, NANCY B.
PERSONAL Born 07/15/1944, NY, m, 1964, 2 children **DISCIPLINE** HISTORY OF SCIENCE, COMPUTER INFO SYS **EDUCATION** SUNY, Stony Brook, PhD, 77. **CAREER** Brodlieb Distinguished Prof Business, Hofstra Univ, 77-. **HONORS AND AWARDS** Beta Gamma Sigma; Citibank, Hist Comp; IFIP Pioneer Day. **MEMBERSHIPS** ACM; ISIS. **RESEARCH** Multimedia, hist of computing. **SELECTED PUBLICATIONS** Computers and Information Processing, Cobol Programming, 8th ed, John Wiley and Sons, Inc. **CONTACT ADDRESS** Hofstra Univ, BAS Dept, Hempstead, NY, 11550. **EMAIL** acsnns@hofstra.edu

STERN, ROBIN
DISCIPLINE ART HISTORY **EDUCATION** State Univ NY, AB, 74; Univ Chicago, AM, 77, PhD, 84. **CAREER** Instr, DePaul Univ; Univ Chicago; Northwestern Univ; vis asst prof, 84-. **HONORS AND AWARDS** Wrtg fel, Univ Chicago; res grant, Metropolitan Ctr Far E Art Stud. **SELECTED PUBLICATIONS** Auth, Emaki; Masterworks in Wood: China and Japan by Donald Jenkins. **CONTACT ADDRESS** Dept of Art Hist, Sch of the Art Inst of Chicago, 37 S Wabash Ave, Chicago, IL, 60603.

STERN, STEVE JEFFEREY
PERSONAL Born 12/28/1951, Brooklyn, NY **DISCIPLINE** LATIN AMERICAN HISTORY **EDUCATION** Cornell Univ, BA, 73; Yale Univ, MPhil, 76, PhD, 79. **CAREER** Asst prof hist, Univ Wis-Madison, 79-, Vis asst prof hist, Yale Univ, 82. **MEMBERSHIPS** Latin Am Studies Asn; Conf Latin Am Hist. **RESEARCH** History of indigenous peoples--Andean South America; colonial Latin American history. **SELECTED PUBLICATIONS** Auth, The rise and fall of Indian-White alliances: A regional view of conquest history, Hisp Am Hist Rev, 81; contribur, chap, In: The Inca and Aztec States, 1400-1800, Acad Press, 82; auth, Peru's Indian Peoples and the Challenge of Spanish Conquest: Huamanga to 1640, Univ Wis, 82. **CONTACT ADDRESS** Dept of History, Univ of Wisconsin, Madison, 455 North Park St, Madison, WI, 53706-1483.

STERNFELD, FREDERICK WILLIAM
PERSONAL Born 09/25/1914, Vienna, Austria, m, 1943 **DISCIPLINE** MUSICOLOGY **EDUCATION** Yale Univ, PhD, 43; Dartsmouth Col, MA, 55. **CAREER** From instr to asst prof music, Wesleyan Univ, 40-46; asst prof, Dartmouth Col, 46-55, prof, 55-56; lectr, 56-72, READER, OXFORD UNIV, 72-, Ed, Renaissance News, 46-54, music ed, 54-; Guggenheim fel, 54; mem, Inst Advan Studies, 55; vis Mellon prof, Univ Pittsburgh, 63-64; res fel, Folger Shakespeare Libr, 64. **MEMBERSHIPS** Am Musicol Soc; Music Libr Asn; Royal Music Asn (vpres, 71-). **RESEARCH** Relationship between music and words; Renaissance music; dramatic music. **SELECTED PUBLICATIONS** Auth, Goethe and Music, New York Pub Libr, 54 & Da Capo, 79; Music in Shakespearean Tragedy, Dover, 63; coauth, English Madrigal Verse, 3rd ed, 67 & ed, New Oxford History of Music, Vol 7, 73, Oxford Univ; ed, History of Western Music, Praeger, Vol 1, 73. **CONTACT ADDRESS** Fac Music, Univ Oxford, Oxford, ., OX11DB.

STEVENS, CAROL B.
PERSONAL Born 12/28/1950, Corpus Christi, TX, m, 1980, 1 child **DISCIPLINE** HISTORY **EDUCATION** Univ Mich, Ann Arbor, PhD, 85. **CAREER** Assoc prof, 92- , actg chemn Hist Dept, 98-99, Colgate Univ. **MEMBERSHIPS** AHA; AAASS; WASS; ESSA. **RESEARCH** Early modern military history; medieval Russia; banditry. **SELECTED PUBLICATIONS** Auth, Soldiers on the Steppe, Northern Illinois, 95; auth, Policing and Provincial Order, Calif Slavic Stud, 97; auth, Evaluating the Petrine Military, Study Group on the 18th Century Newsl, 98. **CONTACT ADDRESS** Dept of History, Colgate Univ, Hamilton, NY, 13346. **EMAIL** KStevens@mail.colgate.edu

STEVENS, DONALD G.
PERSONAL Born 02/14/1939, Boston, MA, m, 1964, 2 children **DISCIPLINE** MODERN EUROPEAN HISTORY **EDUCATION** St Anselm's Col, BA, 60; Niagara Univ, MA, 62; St Johns Univ, NY, PhD, 67. **CAREER** Asst, Niagara Univ, 61; Asst Prof to Prof Hist, 64-90, John Whitman Distinguished Service Prof, King's Col, Pa, 90-. **MEMBERSHIPS** AHA; SHAFR; WWII Studies Asn. **RESEARCH** American relations with the League of Nations; Anglo-American relations WWII; economic warfare. **CONTACT ADDRESS** Dept of Hist, King's Col, 133 N River St, Wilkes Barre, PA, 18711-0801. **EMAIL** dgsteven@rs01.kings.edu

STEVENS, JOHN A.
PERSONAL Born 09/11/1963, Elmhurst, IL, m, 1988, 2 children **DISCIPLINE** CLASSICS **EDUCATION** Univ Iowa, BA, 86, MA, 88; Duke Univ, PhD, 92. **CAREER** Vis asst prof, NY Univ, 92-93; vis asst prof, E Carolina Univ, 93-94; asst prof, E Carolina Univ, 94-. **MEMBERSHIPS** Soc Ancient Greek Philos; Am Philos Asn; Classical Asn Middle W & S; Vergilian Soc. **RESEARCH** Latin literature; ancient philosophy; lyric poetry. **SELECTED PUBLICATIONS** Auth, Posidonian Polemic and Academic Dialectic: The Impact of Carneades Upon Posisonius, GRBS, 95; Friendship and Profit in Xenophon's Oeconomicus in The Socratic Movement, 94. **CONTACT ADDRESS** Classical Studies Dept FLL, East Carolina Univ, General Classroom Bldg., Greenville, NC, 27858-4353. **EMAIL** stevensj@mail.ecu.edu

STEVENS, KEVIN M.
DISCIPLINE HISTORY **EDUCATION** Univ Wis - Madison, PhD, 92. **CAREER** Asst Prof Hist, Univ Nev, 90-. **MEMBERSHIPS** Soc Ital Hist Studies. **RESEARCH** Printing/publishing - 16th century Italy. **SELECTED PUBLICATIONS** Auth, Printing and Politics: Carlo Borromeo and the Seminary Press of Milan, Stampa, libri e letture a Milan nell'eta di Carlo Borromeo, Vita e Pensiero, 92; coauth, Giovanni Battista Bosso and the Paper Trade in late Sixteenth-Century Milan, La Bibliofilia, XCVI, 94; auth, Printing and Patronage in Sixteenth-Century Milan: The Career of Francesco Moscheni (1547-66), Gutenberg-Jahrbuch, 95; Vinceno Girardone and the Popular Press in Counter-Reformation Milan: A Case Study (1570), 16th Century J 3, 95; A Bookbinder in Early Seventeenth-Century Milan. The Shop of Pietro Martire Locarno, The Library, Univ Oxford Press, 96; Liturgical Publishing in mid-Sixteenth-Century Milan: The Contracts for the Breviarium Humiliatorum (1548) and the Breviarium Ambrosianum (1556), La Bibliofilia 2, 97. **CONTACT ADDRESS** History Dept, Univ Nevada, Reno, NV, 89557-0037. **EMAIL** kstevens@scs.unr.edu

STEVENS, KIRA
DISCIPLINE MEDIEVAL, MODERN AND CONTEMPORARY RUSSIAN HISTORY **EDUCATION** Univ SC, AB; Univ MI, PhD. **CAREER** Assoc prof, Colgate Univ. **RESEARCH** Mil affairs and soc life in early mod Russ. **SELECTED PUBLICATIONS** Auth, Soldiers on the Steppe: Army Reform and Social Change in Early Modern Russia, N Ill UP, 95. **CONTACT ADDRESS** Dept of Russ Stud, Colgate Univ, 13 Oak Drive, Hamilton, NY, 13346.

STEVENS, WESLEY MACCLELLAND
PERSONAL Born 08/25/1929, Ft Worth, TX, m, 1954, 4 children **DISCIPLINE** MEDIEVAL HISTORY, HISTORY OF SCIENCE **EDUCATION** Tex A&M Univ, BA, 51; Southern Methodist Univ, MDiv, 55; Union Theol Sem, NY, STM, 59; Emory Univ, PhD(medieval hist), 68. **CAREER** Managing ed, Christian Scholar, 57-60; from instr to asst prof hist, Oxford Col, Emory Univ, 60-67; asst prof, 68-71, assoc prof, 71-78, PROF HIST, UNIV WINNIPEG, 78-, Can Coun res grant, 71-73, 77-78, 79-80 & 82-, leave fel, 74-75. **MEMBERSHIPS** Medieval Acad Am; Hist Sci Soc; Can Hist Asn; Can Soc Hist & Philos Sci; Can Soc Hist & Philos Math (pres, 81-). **RESEARCH** Medieval schools; computus; Latin paleography. **SELECTED PUBLICATIONS** Auth, The figure of the Earth in Isidore's De natura rerum, Isis, 80; Compotistica et astronomica in the Fulda school, In: Saints, Scholars and Heroes: Studies...in honour of C W Jones, 79; Scientific instruction in early insular schools, In: Insular Latin Studies, 81; Cuthbert--His Cult And His Community To Ad1200, Speculum-A J Of Medieval Studies, Vol 68, 93; Studies On The Forged Documents Of The Cloister-Of-St-Maximin-Near-Trier From The 10th- To The 12th-Century, Speculum-A J Of Medieval Studies, Vol 68, 93; Technology And Religion In Medieval Sweden, Historisk Tidsskrift, Vol 73, 94; Time, Number And Image--Studies On The Connections Of Philosophy And Science According To Abbo-Of-Fleury, Speculum-A J Of Medieval Studies, Vol 70, 95. **CONTACT ADDRESS** 269 Overdale St, James Winnipeg, MB, R3J 2G2.

STEVENSON, JOHN A.
PERSONAL Born 11/06/1952, Clinton, SC, m **DISCIPLINE** ENGLISH AND HISTORY **EDUCATION** Duke Univ, BA, 75; Univ Va, PhD, 83. **CAREER** Asst prof, 82-90, assoc prof, 90-, chair, 96-, eng, Univ Colo. **HONORS AND AWARDS** Nat Merit Scholar; AB Duke Scholar; Phi Beta Kappa; Boulder Facul Teaching Award, 90. **MEMBERSHIPS** MLA. **RESEARCH** 18th century British literature. **SELECTED PUBLICATIONS** Auth, Tom Jones and the Stuck, ELH, 94; auth, The British Nonl, Defoe to Austen, 90; auth, A Vampire in the Mirror, PMLA, 88; auth, Clarissa and the Harlowes Once More, ELH, 81. **CONTACT ADDRESS** Dept. of English, Univ of Colorado, Box 226, Boulder, CO, 80309. **EMAIL** john.stevenson@colorado.edu

STEVENSON, LOUISE L.
DISCIPLINE AMERICAN STUDIES **EDUCATION** Columbia Univ, BA, 70; New York Univ, MA, 73; Boston Univ, PhD(Am studies), 81. **CAREER** Assoc teacher Am studies, Mass Bay Communities Col, 75; lectr Am hist & studies, Univ NH, 76; admin dir, Am & New England Studies Prog, Boston Univ, 77-79; vis lectr hist, Univ NH, Durham, 79-82; ASST PROF HIST & AM STUDIES DEPT, FRANKLIN & MARSHALL COL, 82-, Asst ed, Continuity, 79-81. **SELECTED PUBLICATIONS** Auth, Women anti-suffragists in the 1915 Massachusetts campaign, New England Quart, 3/79; A conservative critique of Victorian culture: The New Haven set, 1840-1890, Continuity, fall 80; Sarah Porter and her school, 1843-1900, Winterthur Portfolio; The Secularization Of The Academy, J Of Am Hist, Vol 80, 93; Harriet Beecher Stowe--A Life, J Of Am Hist, Vol 81, 94; The 1st Woman In The Republic--A Cultural Biography Of Lydia Child, Pa Magazine Of Hist And Bio, Vol 120, 96; Am Women-Writers And The Work Of Hist, 1790-1860, William And Mary Quart, Vol 53, 96. **CONTACT ADDRESS** Hist & Am Studies Dept, Franklin and Marshall Col, PO Box 3003, Lancaster, PA, 17604-3003.

STEVENSON, WALT
PERSONAL Born 08/03/1961, Philadelphia, PA, m, 1989, 2 children **DISCIPLINE** CLASSICAL PHILOLOGY **EDUCATION** Carleton Col, BA (classical philol), 83; Brown Univ, PhD (classical philol), 90. **CAREER** Lect, Univ RI, 88-89; instr, Dickinson Col, 89-90; vis prof, L'rivskaj Derzhavni Universitet/L'rivska Bohoslorska Akademia, 97-98; assoc prof, Univ Richmond, 90-. **HONORS AND AWARDS** Fulbright fel, 97-98. **MEMBERSHIPS** Am Philol Asn; Classical Asn of the Midwest and South. **RESEARCH** Greek and Latin lit; Roman Imperial Social History. **SELECTED PUBLICATIONS** Auth, Plato's Symposium 190d7, Phoenix 47, 93; The Rise of Eunuchs in Greco-Roman Antiquity, J of the Hist of Sexuality 5, 95; De Italia: Italy Goes Multimedia, New England Classical Newsletter & J 23, 95; Professional Poets and Poetic Heroes in Homeric Greece, Usna Epika: Etnichni Tradytsii ta Vykonavstvo II, Kiev, 97. **CONTACT ADDRESS** Dept of Classics, Univ of Richmond, Richmond, VA, 23173. **EMAIL** wstevens@richmond.edu

STEWARD, DICK HOUSTON
PERSONAL Born 12/11/1942, Jefferson City, MO, m, 1969, 2 children **DISCIPLINE** AMERICAN DIPLOMATIC HISTORY **EDUCATION** Southeast Mo State Col, BS, 64; Univ Mo-Columbia, MA, 65, PhD(Hist), 69. **CAREER** Instr Hist,

Univ Mo-Columbia, 68-69; asst prof, 71-75, assoc prof Hist, Lincoln Univ, 75-. **RESEARCH** Recent United States history; Latin American history; United States economic diplomacy. **SELECTED PUBLICATIONS** Contribr, It Actually Costs Us Nothing: US-Colombian Economic Policy, Houghton, 73; auth, Trade a Hemisphere: The Good Neighbor Policy & Reciprocal Trade, Univ Mo, 75; Money, Marines, and Mission: Recent US-Latin American Policy, Univ Press Am, 80. **CONTACT ADDRESS** Dept of Soc Sci, Lincoln Univ, 820 Chestnut St, Jefferson City, MO, 65101-3500.

STEWART, CHARLES CAMERON
PERSONAL Born 12/19/1941, Evanston, IL, 3 children **DISCIPLINE** AFRICAN HISTORY, ISLAMIC HISTORY **EDUCATION** Hanover Col, BA, 63; Univ Ghana, MA, 65; Oxford Univ, DPhil(Orient Studies), 70. **CAREER** Asst prof, 71-74, actg dir African Studies Prog, 77-78 & 80-81, assoc prof Hist, Univ Ill, Urbana-Champaign, 74- & dir African Studies Prog, 81-84, from lectr to sr lectr Hist, Ahmadu Bello Univ, Nigeria, 73-76; chmn Dept Hist, Univ Ill, Urbana-Champaign 92-97; exec assoc dean, Coll Lib Arts, 97-. **MEMBERSHIPS** African Studies Asn. **RESEARCH** Recent Mauritanian history; history of Islamic Africa; historiography of Northern Nigeria. **SELECTED PUBLICATIONS** Auth, Notes on North and West African manuscript material, Res Bull Ctr Arabic Doc, 68; New source on the book market in Morocco in 1830, Hesperis-Tamuda, 70; co-ed, Julien, History of North Africa, Routledge/ Praeger, 70; auth, Political authority and social stratification in Mauritania, In: Arabs and Berbers, Heath, 72; coauth, Islam and Social Order in Mauritania, Clarendon, 73; auth, Southern Saharan scholarship and the bilad al-sudan & Frontier disputes and problems of legitimation, J African Hist, 76; co-ed, Modes of Production in Africa, Sage, 81; co-ed Imagining the Twentieth Century, U Ill Press, 97. **CONTACT ADDRESS** Dept of History, Univ of Illinois, Urbana-Champaign, 810 S Wright St, Urbana, IL, 61801-3611. **EMAIL** cc@uiuc.edu

STEWART, CHARLES TODD
PERSONAL Born 05/13/1922, New York, NY, m, 1953, 3 children **DISCIPLINE** ECONOMICS **EDUCATION** George Wash Univ, BA, 46, MA, 48, PhD, 54. **CAREER** Asst prof, 47-49, Utah St Univ; Sr res analyst, 52-58, Georgetown Univ Grad School; Sr economist, 58-62, Dir of Economic Res, 62-63, US Chamber of Commerce; prof of econ, 63-92, prof emeritus, 92-, George Wash Univ **HONORS AND AWARDS** Ohira Memorial Prize for 1987. **MEMBERSHIPS** AAAS; Am Economic Asn. **RESEARCH** Discovery and invention; health care policy; inequality and its causes. **SELECTED PUBLICATIONS** Auth, Low Wage Workers in an Affluent Society, The Nelson Hall Co, 74; auth, Air Pollution, Human Health, and Public Policy, Lexington Bks, 79; coauth, Technology Transfer and Human Factors, Lexington Bks, 87; auth, Healthy, Wealthy, or Wise?, M. E. Sharpe, 95; auth, Inequality and Equity: Economics of Greed, Politics of Envy, Ethics of Equality, Greenwood Pubs, 98. **CONTACT ADDRESS** 5147 Macomb St NW, Washington, DC, 20016.

STEWART, GORDON THOMAS
PERSONAL Born 07/06/1945, Newport-on-Tay, Scotland, m, 1967, 2 children **DISCIPLINE** MODERN HISTORY **EDUCATION** Univ St Andrews, MA, 67; Queen's Univ, Ont, PhD(mod hist), 70. **CAREER** Asst prof, 70-73, ASSOC PROF HIST, MICH STATE UNIV, 73- **RESEARCH** British Empire since the 18th century; Canadian-American studies; American colonial history. **SELECTED PUBLICATIONS** Coauth, A People Highly Favoured of God, the Nova Scotia Yankees and the American Revolution, Archon Bks, 72; The Contribution Of Methodism To Atlantic Canada, Canadian Hist Rev, Vol 74, 93; The Siege Of Fort Cumberland, 1776--An Episode In The American-Revolution William And Mary Quart, Vol 54, 97; Canada And The United-States--Ambivalent Allies, Am Hist Rev, Vol 101, 96; Revolution Downeast--The War For Amn Independence In Maine, Am Hist Rev, Vol 100, 95; After The Rebellion--The Later Years Of William Lyon Mackenzie , NY Hist, Vol 73, 92. **CONTACT ADDRESS** Dept of Hist, Michigan State Univ, 301 Morrill Hall, East Lansing, MI, 48824-1036.

STEWART, JAMES BREWER
PERSONAL Born 08/08/1940, Cleveland, OH, m, 1965, 2 children **DISCIPLINE** AMERICAN HISTORY **EDUCATION** Dartmouth Col, BA, 62; Case Western Reserve Univ, MA, 66, PhD(hist), 68. **CAREER** Asst prof, Carroll Col, Wis, 68-69; from Asst Prof to Prof, 69-82, JAMES WALLACE PROF HIST, MACALESTER COL, 82-; res & teaching fel, Newberry Libr, 72-73; vis dist prof hist, Univ S Carolina, 78-79; Provost, Macalester Col, 87-90. **HONORS AND AWARDS** Fel, Am Coun of Learned Soc, 80; Soc of Midland Authors Best Biography Award, 86; fel Am Coun Learned Socs. **MEMBERSHIPS** Orgn Am Historians; Southern Hist Asn; Soc Hist of Early Am Republic. **RESEARCH** Pre-civil War U.S. political and social history; antislavery and African American history; comparative slavery and emancipation. **SELECTED PUBLICATIONS** Auth, Joshua R. Giddings and the Tactics of Radical Politics, Case Western Reserve Univ, 70; Holy Warriors: The Abolitionists and American Slavery, Hill & Wang, 76, rev ed, 97, Japanese transl, 94; Wendell Phillips: Liberty's Hero, La State Univ, 86; William Lloyd Garrison and the Challenge of Emancipation, Harlan Davidson, 92; coauth, One Blood: The Life and Collected Writings of Hosea Easton, Univ Mass, 98; ed, The Constitution and the Problem of Freedom of Expression, Southern Ill Univ, 86. **CONTACT ADDRESS** Dept of History, Macalester Col, 1600 Grand Ave, St. Paul, MN, 55105-1899. **EMAIL** stewart@macalester.edu

STEWART, MAC A.
PERSONAL Born 07/07/1942, Forsyth, Georgia, m **DISCIPLINE** EDUCATION **EDUCATION** Morehouse Coll, BA 1963; Atlanta Univ, MA 1965; The Ohio State Univ, PhD 1973. **CAREER** Jasper County Training School, teacher/counselor 1963-64; Crispus Attucks HS, teacher 1965-66; Morehouse Coll, dir of student financial aid 1966-70; The Ohio State Univ, asst dean 1973-75, assoc dean 1975-90, acting dean, 1990-91, dean 1991-. **HONORS AND AWARDS** Distinguished Affirmative Action Awd The Ohio State Univ 1984; Outstanding Alumni Awd Hubbard School 1986; Distinguished Service Award, Negro Educational Review, 1992; Frederick D Patterson Award, United Negro College Fund, 1992. **MEMBERSHIPS** Consultant KY State Univ 1978; mem bd dirs Buckeye Boys Ranch 1979-85; mem bd dirs Bethune Center for Unwed Mothers 1980-83; consultant Wilberforce Univ 1980; faculty mem Ohio Staters Inc 1982-91; consultant The Ohio Bd of Regents 1986; consultant, US Department of Education, 1990; consultant, Temple University, 1991; board of trustees, Columbus Academy, 1991-; consultant, Virginia Commonwealth University, 1992; mem Amer Personnel and Guidance Assoc, Amer Coll Personnel Assoc, Natl Assoc of Student Personnel Administrators, Mid-Western Assoc of Student Financial Aid Administrators, Alpha Kappa Delta Natl Hon Sociological Soc, Phi Delta Kappa Natl Hon Educ Frat, Phi Kappa Phi Natl Honor Soc, Amer Assoc of Higher Educ; bd mem, Human Subjects Research Committee Children's Hospital. **CONTACT ADDRESS** Dean, The Ohio State Univ, 154 W 12th Ave, Columbus, OH, 43210.

STHELE, EVA
DISCIPLINE GREEK AND ROMAN LITERATURE **EDUCATION** Univ Cincinnati, PhD. **CAREER** Instr, Wheaton Col; prof-. **HONORS AND AWARDS** Coord, dept's Latin Day. **RESEARCH** Ancient relig(s). **SELECTED PUBLICATIONS** Auth, Performance and Gender in Ancient Greece: Nondramatic Poetry in its Setting, Princeton UP, 96; Women Looking at Women: Women's Ritual and Temple Sculpture, Sexuality in Ancient Art, Cambridge UP, 96; Help Me to Sing, Muse, of Plataia, The New Simonides, Arethusa 29, 96. **CONTACT ADDRESS** Dept of Class, Univ MD, 4229 Art-Sociology Building, College Park, MD, 20742-1335. **EMAIL** es39@umail.umd.edu

STIEGLITZ, ROBERT R.
PERSONAL Born 04/14/1943, Bershad, Ukraine, m, 1975, 2 children **DISCIPLINE** ANCIENT MEDITERRANEAN STUDIES **EDUCATION** Brandeis Univ, PhD 71; City Col NY, BA 67. **CAREER** Rutgers Univ, assoc prof, 78-; New York Univ, adj assoc prof, 80-90; Ntl Maritime Museum Israel, curator, adj prof, 71-74. **HONORS AND AWARDS** Sachar Intl Awd; Israel Ntl Acad; AIA; ACLS; Earthwatch; RU Res Coun. **MEMBERSHIPS** ASOR; AIA; IES; HIMA. **RESEARCH** History of Ancient Seafaring; Biblical Archaeology; NW Semitic Philo. **SELECTED PUBLICATIONS** Auth, A Late Byzantine Reservoir and Piscina at Tel Tanninim, Israel Exploration Jour, 98; Illustrated Dictionary of Bible Life and Times, contr, NY, Reader's Digest, 97; The Minoan Origin of Tyrian Purple, Biblical Archi, 94; Migrations in the Ancient Near East, 3500-500 BC, Anthropol Science, 93; Phoenicians on the Northern Coast of Israel, coauth, Haifa, Hecht Museum, Univ Haifa, 93; Ptolemy IX Soter II Lathtrus on Cyprus and the Coast of the Levant, Res Maritima: Cyprus and the Eastern Med from Prehistory to Late Antiquity, ed, S. Swiny et al, CARRI Mono Ser, Atlanta, Scholar's Press, 97. **CONTACT ADDRESS** Dept of Classical, Modern Languages, and Literatur, Rutgers Univ, Newark, NJ, 07102-1814. **EMAIL** stieglit@andromeda.rutgers.edu

STILES, KRISTINE
DISCIPLINE ART HISTORY **EDUCATION** Univ CA Berkeley, PhD. **CAREER** Assoc prof, Duke Univ. **RESEARCH** Contemp art. **SELECTED PUBLICATIONS** Auth, Theories and Documents of Contemporary Art, 96. **CONTACT ADDRESS** Dept of Art and Art Hist, Duke Univ, East Duke Building, Durham, NC, 27706.

STILLMAN, DAMIE
PERSONAL Born 07/27/1933, Dallas, TX, m, 1960, 2 children **DISCIPLINE** ART HISTORY **EDUCATION** Northwestern Univ, BS, 54; Univ Del, MA, 56; Columbia Univ, PhD(art hist), 61. **CAREER** Asst librn, W P Beklnap, Jr, Res Libr Am Painting, H F duPont Winterthur Mus, 57-59; asst prof art hist, Oakland Univ, 61-65; assoc prof, 65-68, prof art hist, Univ Wis-Milwaukee, 68-77, chm dept, 75-77; PROF ART HIST, 77-89, JOHN W SHIRLEY PROF ART HIST, UNIV DEL, 89- & CHM DEPT, 81-86, 93-98; ed-in-chief, Buildings of the United States, 96- . **HONORS AND AWARDS** Am Coun Learned Soc grant-in-aid, 68; Nat Endowment for Humanities younger humanist fel, 70-71; Am Philos Soc res grant, 73; Soc Archit Historians Award, 75; NEH fel, 86-87; Univ Del Ctr for Advanc Stud fel, 88-89; Gottschalk Prize, Am Soc Eighteenth Century Stud, 88. **MEMBERSHIPS** Col Art Asn Am; Soc Archit Historians (pres, 82-84); Soc Archit Hist, Gt Brit; Am Soc Eighteenth Century Studies; Northeast Am Soc for Eighteenth Century Stud, (pres 95-96); Am Stud Asn; Victorian Soc in Am. **RESEARCH** Eighteenth century English and American architecture; American and English art; neo-classical architecture and decoration. **SELECTED PUBLICATIONS** Auth, New York City Hall: Competition and Execution, J Soc Archit Hist, 11/64; The Decorative Work of Robert Adam, Tiranti, London, 66; English Painting: The Great Masters, 1730-1860, McGraw, 66; The Gallery at Lansdowne House: International Architecture and Decoration in Microcosm, Art Bull, 3/70; British Architects and Italian Architectural Competitions, 1758-1780, J Soc Archit Hist, 3/73; The Pantheon Redecorated, VIA III, 77; Death Defied and Honor Upheld: the Mausoleum in Neo-Classical England, Art Quart, 78; Church Architecture in Neo-Classical England, J Soc Archit Hist, 5/79; auth, English Neo-Classical Architecture, Zwemmer, 88; auth, The Neo-Classical Transformation of the English Country House, in Stud in the Hist of Art, 89; auth, City Living Federal Style, in Everyday Life in the Early Republic, Winterthur, 94. **CONTACT ADDRESS** Dept of Art Hist, Univ Del, Newark, DE, 19716.

STILLMAN, NORMAN ARTHUR
PERSONAL Born 07/06/1945, New York, NY, m, 1967, 2 children **DISCIPLINE** ORIENTAL STUDIES, MIDDLE EASTERN HISTORY **EDUCATION** Univ Pa, BA, 67, PhD(Orient studies), 70. **CAREER** Asst prof Near Eastern lang & lit, NY Univ, 70-73; ASSOC PROF HIST & ARABIC, STATE UNIV NY BINGHAMTON, 73-, Jewish Theol Sem fel, 70-71; consult, Soc Sci Res Coun, 72-77 & Nat Geog Soc, 79-80; vis assoc prof Mid Eastern & Jewish hist, Haifa Univ, 79-80. **MEMBERSHIPS** Am Orient Soc; Mid East Studies Asn NAm; Asn Jewish Studies; Conf Jewish Social Studies; Societe de l'histoire du Maroc. **RESEARCH** History of the Jews under Islam; North African history; semitic languages and literatures. **SELECTED PUBLICATIONS** Auth, The story of Cain and Abel in the Qur'an and the Muslim commentators: Some observations, J Semitic Studies, autumn 74; A new source for eighteenth-century Moroccan history in the John Rylands University Library of Manchester: The Dombay Papers, Bull John Rylands Univ Libr Manchester, spring 75; Charity and social service in Medieval Islam, Societas, spring 75; New attitudes toward the Jew in the Arab world, Jewish Social Studies, summer-fall 75; coauth, The art of a Moroccan folk poetess, ZDMG, 78; auth, The Jews of Arab Lands, Jewish Publ Soc Am, 79; co-ed, Studies in Judaism and Islam, 81 & asst ed, Studies in Geniza and Sepharad: Heritage, 81, Magnes Press; Sephardi Entrepreneurs In Eretz Israel--The Amzalak Family 1816-1918, Am Hist Rev, Vol 97, 92. **CONTACT ADDRESS** Dept of Hist, State Univ NY, Binghamton, NY, 13901.

STINGER, CHARLES LEWIS
PERSONAL Born 03/19/1944, Waverly, NY, m, 1968, 2 children **DISCIPLINE** ITALIAN RENAISSANCE HISTORY **EDUCATION** Hobart Col, BA, 66; Stanford Univ, MA, 67, PhD(hist), 71. **CAREER** Instr Europ social & cult prog, Stanford Univ, 70-72; Harvard Ctr Renaissance Study fel, Villa I Tatti, Florence, Italy, 72-73; asst prof, 73-77, ASSOC PROF HIST, STATE UNIV NY BUFFALO, 77-, Am Coun Learned Socs grant-in-aid, 77. **MEMBERSHIPS** Renaissance Soc Am; Am Soc Reformation Res; AHA. **RESEARCH** The Renaissance in Rome; religious thought in Italian Renaissance humanism. **SELECTED PUBLICATIONS** THE LATIN MANUSCRIPTS OF NICHOLAS-V - INVENTORY EDITION AND MANUSCRIPT IDENTIFICATION - ITALIAN - MANFREDI,A/, SPECULUM-A JOURNAL OF MEDIEVAL STUDIES, Vol 0072, 1997 **CONTACT ADDRESS** Dept of Hist, SUNY, Buffalo, Buffalo, NY, 14261.

STINSON, ROBERT WILLIAM
PERSONAL Born 09/12/1941, Elmhurst, IL, m, 1966, 2 children **DISCIPLINE** AMERICAN HISTORY; HISTORIOGRAPHY **EDUCATION** Allegheny Col, BA, 64; Ind Univ, MA, 66, PhD(hist), 71. **CAREER** From Asst Prof to Assoc Prof, 70-88, PROF HIST, MORAVIAN COL, 88-. **HONORS AND AWARDS** Lindback Award for Distinguished Teaching, Christian and Mary Lindback Found, 72. **RESEARCH** United States, 1865 to the present; history of journalism; history of film; historiography. **SELECTED PUBLICATIONS** Auth, S S McClure's My autobiography: The progressive as self-made man, Am Quart, summer 70; McClure's road to McClure's: How revolutionary were the 1890's magazines?, Jour Quart, summer 70; Ida Tarbell and the ambiguities of feminism, Pa Mag Hist & Biog, 4/77; Lincoln Steffens' Shame of the Cities reconsidered, New Republic, 7/77; How they kept the trust: Ida Tarbell's John D Rockefeller, Nation, 11/77; On the death of a baby, Atlantic Monthly, 7/79; Lincoln Steffens, Ungar, 79; The Long Dying of Baby Andrew, Little, Brown, 83; The Faces of Clio, Nelson-Hall, 87. **CONTACT ADDRESS** Dept of History, Moravian Col, 1200 Main St, Bethlehem, PA, 18018-6650. **EMAIL** merws01@moravian.edu

STINSON, RUSSELL
DISCIPLINE MUSIC **EDUCATION** Stetson Univ, Bmus; Univ Chicago, MA, PhD. **CAREER** Assoc prof & Col organist, Lyon Col. **RESEARCH** Music hist; theory; performance. **SELECTED PUBLICATIONS** Auth, The Bach Manuscripts of Johann Peter Kellner and His Circle, Duke UP, 90. **CONTACT ADDRESS** Dept of Music, Lyon Col, 300 Highland Rd, PO Box 2317, Batesville, AR, 72503.

STITES, FRANCIS NOEL
PERSONAL Born 12/25/1938, Indianapolis, IN, m, 1966, 2 children **DISCIPLINE** AMERICAN CONSTITUTIONAL HISTORY **EDUCATION** Marian Col, Ind, BA, 60; Ind Univ, MA, 65, PhD(hist), 68. **CAREER** Instr hist, Eastern Ind Ctr, Earlham Col, 66-67; from asst prof to assoc prof, 68-77, PROF HIST, SAN DIEGO STATE UNIV, 77- **MEMBERSHIPS** Orgn Am Historians; AHA; Am Soc Legal Hist. **RESEARCH** Early American legal and social history. **SELECTED PUBLICATIONS** Auth, Private Interest and Public Gain, the Dartmouth College Case, 1819, Univ Mass, 72; John Marshall: Defender of the Constitution, Little, Brown & Co, 81; Constitutional Hist Of The Amn-Revolution--The Authority Of Law, Am Hist Rev, Vol 100, 95; The Wheeling Bridge Case--Its Significance In American Law And Technology, Am J Of Legal Hist, Vol 38, 94. **CONTACT ADDRESS** Dept of Hist, San Diego State Univ, 5500 Campanile Dr, San Diego, CA, 92182-0002.

STOCKMAN, ROBERT H.
PERSONAL Born 10/06/1953, Meriden, CT, m, 1992, 1 child **DISCIPLINE** HISTORY OF RELIGION **EDUCATION** Wesleyan Univ, BA, 75; Brown Univ, MSc, 77; Harvard Divinity School, MTS, 82, ThD, 90. **CAREER** Grad res asst, Brown Univ, 75-77; instr, Geology and Oceanography, Comm Col of RI, 77-80; instr, Geology, Boston State Col, 80-82; instr, Geology, Univ Lowell, 83-84; instr, Geology and Astronomy, Bentley Col, 83-90; teaching asst, Harvard Univ, 86-89; asst prof relig, DePaul Univ, 95-96; INSTR RELIG, DEPAUL UNIV, 90-95, 96-98. **MEMBERSHIPS** Amer Academy Relig; Middle East Studies Assoc; Soc Iranian Studies; Amer Hist Assoc; Assoc Baha i Studies, member, ex comm, 90-, member and chair, Study of Religions Section, 89-. **RESEARCH** Amer Bahai hist; Amer relig hist. **SELECTED PUBLICATIONS** Auth, The Bahai i Faith in America, vol 1, Origins, 1862-1900, Baha i Pub Trust, 85, vol 2, Early Expansion, 1900-1912, George Ronald, 95; The Baha i Faith in America: One Hundred Years, in World Order, vol 25, no 3, spring 94; Paul Johnson's Theosophical Influence in Baha i History: Some Comments, in Theosophical Hist, vol 5, no 4, Oct 94; The Baha i Faith: A Portrait, in Joel Beversluis, ed, A Sourcebook for the Earth's Community of Religions, 2nd ed, CoNexus Press, 95; The Baha i Faith in the 1990's, article in Dr Timothy Miller, ed, America's Alternative Religions, SUNY Press, 95; The Vision of the Baha i Faith, in Martin Forward, Ultimate Visions: Reflections on the Religions We Choose, One World, 95; The Baha i Faith in England and Germany, 1900-1913, in World Order, vol 27, no 3, spring 96; The Baha i Faith section of the Pluralism Project, CD Rom, Columbia Univ Press, 97; many other articles, several forthcoming publications. **CONTACT ADDRESS** 1067 Woodward Ave., South Bend, IN, 46616. **EMAIL** rstockman@usbnc.org

STOCKWELL, EDWARD G.
PERSONAL Born 06/11/1933, Newburyport, MA, m, 1956, 3 children **DISCIPLINE** SOCIOLOGY **EDUCATION** Harvard Univ, BA 55; Univ Conn, MA 57; Brown Univ, PhD 60. **CAREER** US Bureau of the Census, population analyst, 60-61; Univ Conn, faculty, 61-71; Bowling Green state Univ, faculty, 71-. **MEMBERSHIPS** PAA; IUSSP **RESEARCH** Population problems **SELECTED PUBLICATIONS** Auth, Several books and monographs, over 150 prof journal articles. **CONTACT ADDRESS** Dept of Sociology, Bowling Green State Univ, Bowling Green, OH, 43403. **EMAIL** estockw@bgnet.bgsu.edu

STODDARD, WHITNEY S.
PERSONAL Born 03/25/1913, Greenfield, MA, m, 3 children **DISCIPLINE** ART HISTORY **EDUCATION** Williams, BA, 35; Harvard Univ, MA, 36; PhD, 41. **CAREER** Instr, Williams Col, 38; asst prof, 43; assoc prof, 49; prof, 55. **HONORS AND AWARDS** Col Art Asoc, Outstanding Teacher Award, 89. **MEMBERSHIPS** Col Art Asoc; Soc of Archit Hist **RESEARCH** Middle Ages--France **SELECTED PUBLICATIONS** The West Portals of Saint-Denis and Chartres, 52; Adventure in Architecture, 58; Monastery and Cathedral in France, 66; The Facade of Saint-Gilles du-Gard, 73; The Sculptors of the West Portals of Chartres, 87. **CONTACT ADDRESS** 1611 Cold Spring Rd., Apt. 227, Williamstown, MA, 01267-2777.

STOEFFLER, FRED ERNEST
PERSONAL Born 09/27/1911, Happenbach, West Germany, m, 1941, 2 children **DISCIPLINE** RELIGION, HISTORY OF CHRISTIANITY **EDUCATION** Temple Univ, BS, 38, STM, 45, STD, 48; Yale Univ, BD, 41. **CAREER** Pastor, Methodist Church, 39-51; from asst prof to prof hist Christianity, 51-62, Prof Relig, Temple Univ, 62-, Mem coun, Am Soc Church Hist, 77-79. **MEMBERSHIPS** Am Soc Church Hist; Am Soc Reformation Res; AHA; Acad Polit Sci; Am Acad Relig. **RESEARCH** Reformation; mysticism; pietism. **SELECTED PUBLICATIONS** Auth, Mysticism in the Devotional Literature of Colonial Pennsylvania, Pa Ger Folklore Soc, 49; The Rise of Evangelical Pietism, Brill, Leiden, 65; transl, B Lohse, History of Doctrine, Fortress, 66; auth, German Pietism During the 18th Century, Brill, Leiden, 73; ed & contribr, Continental Pietism and Early American Christianity, Wm B Eerdmans, 76; Anton Wilhelm Bohme: Studies On The Ecumenical Thought And Dealings Of A Pietist From Halle, Church Hist, Vol 61, 92. **CONTACT ADDRESS** Dept of Relig, Temple Univ, Philadelphia, PA, 19122.

STOETZER, O. CARLOS
PERSONAL Born 06/28/1921, Buenos Aires, Argentina, m, 1955, 2 children **DISCIPLINE** HISTORY OF LATIN AMERICA & AFRICA **EDUCATION** Univ Perugia, cert Ital civ, 42; Debrecen Univ, cert Hungarian civ, 43; Freiburg Univ, Dr iur-(law), 45; Georgetown Univ, PhD(int rels), 61. **CAREER** Asst cult dept, Pan Am Union, Orgn Am States, DC, 50-51, philatelic div, 51-53, travel div, 53-56, coun, 56-61; actg secy, Inter-Am Inst Agr Sci, 58-61; assoc prof polit sci, Manhattanville Col, 61-63, 64-66; chief div law & hist, Inst Latin Am Studies, Hamburg, Ger, 63-64; assoc prof, 66-79, Prof Hist, Fordham Univ, 79-91, RETIRED PROF EMERITUS. **HONORS AND AWARDS** Knight Comdr Order Isabella the Catholic, Span Govt, 59; prof honorario Universidad del Salvador, Buenos Aires, Argentina, 82. **MEMBERSHIPS** Soc for Iberian & Latin Am Thought (pres, 77-79); Latin Am Studies Asn; Caribbean Studies Asn; Conf Latin Am Hist; Argentine Asn Am Studies. **RESEARCH** Hispanic world, especially intellectual history and international relations. **SELECTED PUBLICATIONS** Auth, The Organization of American States, an Introduction, Praeger, 65, 93; El Pensamiento Politico en la America Espanola Durante el Periodo de la Emancipacion, 1789-1825 (2 vols), Inst Estud Polit, Madrid, 66; Die geistigen Grundlagen der spanischamerikanischen Unabhangigkeit, In: Idee und Wirklichkeit in Iberoamerika, Beitrage zur Politik und Geistesgeschichte, Hoffman & Campe, Hamburg, 69; Grundlagen des spanischamerischen Verfassungsdenkens, Verfassung und Recht in Ubersee, 69; Nineteenth-century traditionalism in Spanish America, Int Philos Quart, 78; Benjamin Constant and the Doctrinaire Liberal Influence in Hispanic America, Verfassung und Recht in Ubersee, 78; The Scholastic Roots of the Spanish-American Revolution, Fordham Univ, 79; Positivism and Idealism in the Hispanic World: The Positivist Case of Brazil and the Krausean Influence in Spanish America, Rev Interam, summer 79; numerous entries, Historical Dictionary of the Spanish Empire, 1402-1975, Westport, CT: Greenwood Press, 92; Complejidades regionales en la formacion de las naciones de la America Central y del Caribe, South Eastern Latin Americanist, XXXVII, 4, spring 94; The HispanicTradition, Latin American Revolutions, 1808-1826, Old and New World Origins, ed and with an intro by John Lynch, Univ OK Press, 94; Der mittelamerianische Indigo und Echo in Europa in der Fruhen Neuzeit, Jahrbuch fur Geschichte von Staat, Wirtschaft und Geschichte Lateinamerikas, Cologne, GER, vol 32, 95; Krausean Philosophy as a Major Political and Social Force in the Modern Argentina and Guatemala, Bridging the Atlantic. Toward a Reassessment of Iberian and Latin American Cultural Ties, ed and with intro by Marina Perez de Mendiola, Albany, State Univ NY Press, 96; Iberoamerica. Historia politica y cultural, vol I: Los Gobiernos Peninsulares (1492/1500-1808), vol II: Periodo de la Independencia (1808-1826), vol III: Organizatcion y constitucion de las naciones iberoamericanas (1826-1880), Buenos Aires: Fundacion Universidad a Distancia Hernandarias, Editorial Docencia, 96; vol IV: Marco politico de Iberoamerica en el siglo XX (1880-1945), vol V: Corrientes de pensamiento en Iberoamerica, 98; numerous other articles including a collection of twelve Haitian presidential biographies that appeared in Haiti Philately, Port Townsend, WA, from June 95 through June 98. **CONTACT ADDRESS** PO Box 7484, Wilton, CT, 06897.

STOEVER, WILLIAM K.B.
PERSONAL Born 06/20/1941, Riverside, CA, m, 1971 **DISCIPLINE** HISTORY OF RELIGION **EDUCATION** Pomona Col, BA, 63; Yale Univ, MDiv, 66, MPhil, 69, PhD(relig studies), 70. **CAREER** Asst prof, 70-75, assoc prof, 76-80, prof humanities, Western Wash Univ, 80-, Chemn, Dept Lib Studies 78-, Nat Endowment for Humanities res fel, 74-75. **MEMBERSHIPS** AHA; Am Soc Church Hist; Am Acad Relig; Am Studies Asn. **RESEARCH** History and historiography of religion in Amica; 17th century Puritanism; Jonathan Edwards; religion and cultural change. **SELECTED PUBLICATIONS** Auth, Henry Boynton Smith and the German theology of history, Union Sem Quart Rev, fall 69; Nature, grace, and John Cotton: The theological dimension in the New England antinomian controversy, Church Hist, 3/75; A Faire and Easie Way to Heaven: Covenant Theology and Antinomianism in Early Massachusetts, Wesleyan Univ Press, 78; The Godly Will's Discerning: Shepard, Edwards, and the Identification of True Godliness, Jonathan Edwards's Writings: Text, Context, Interpretation, Ind Univ Press, 97. **CONTACT ADDRESS** Dept of Lib Studies, Western Washington Univ, M/S 9084, Bellingham, WA, 98225-5996.

STOFF, MICHAEL B.
PERSONAL Born 05/12/1947, New York, NY, 2 children **DISCIPLINE** HISTORY **EDUCATION** Rutgers College, BA, 69; Yale Univ, MPhil, 72, PhD, 77. **CAREER** Act instr, 74-75, lectr, 76-79, Yale Univ; asst prof, 79-86, ASSOC PROF HIST, UNIV TEX, AUSTIN, 86-. **HONORS AND AWARDS** Lane Cooper Scholar, Rutgers, 67-69; Univ fel, Yale Univ, 69-74; res grant, Concilium Int, Area Stud, Yale Univ, 73-74; summer res award, Univ Res Inst, Univ Tex, Austin, 80-81; acad dev grant, Univ Tex, Austin, 80-81; Summer Inst Grant, NEH, Bard Col, Vassar Col, Franklin D Roosevelt Libr, 86, 88, 90, 92; Walter Prescott Webb fel, Univ Tex, Austin, 89; Dean's fel, Col Lib Arts, Univ Tex, Austin, 97. **SELECTED PUBLICATIONS** Co-auth, Nation of Nations: A Narrative History of the American Republic, McGraw Hill, 98, 99; co-auth, American Journey: The Quest for Liberty, Prentice Hall, 94; co-auth, The American Nation, Prentice Hall, 96; auth, 1945: Dawn of the American Century, forthcoming; auth, The Tragedy of Herbert Hoover, in The Reader's Companion to the American Presidency, Houghton Mifflin & Co, forthcoming. **CONTACT ADDRESS** Dept of History, Univ of Texas, Austin, Austin, TX, 78712. **EMAIL** mbstoff@mail.utexas.edu

STOIANOVICH, TRAIAN
PERSONAL Born 07/23/1921, Yugoslavia, m, 1945, 2 children **DISCIPLINE** HISTORY **EDUCATION** Univ Rochester, BA, 42; NY Univ, MA, 49. **CAREER** Instr hist, NY Univ, 52-55; from instr to assoc prof, 55-67, fel, 65-66, prof I, 67-75, PROF II HIST, RUTGERS UNIV, 75-, Am Philos Soc res fel, Paris & Belgrade, 58; Fulbright res fel, Salonika, Greece, 58-59; vis asst prof, Univ Calif, Berkeley, 60 & Stanford Univ, 60-61; vis assoc prof, NY Univ, 63 & 66-67; Am rep, Comn Econ & Social Hist, Int Asn SE Europe Studies, 66-71; Fulbright res fel, Paris, 77. **MEMBERSHIPS** AHA; Econ Hist Asn; Am Asn Advan Slavic Studies; AAUP. **RESEARCH** Modern European history; economic history; social history. **SELECTED PUBLICATIONS** Auth, An Economic And Social-Hist of The Ottoman-Empire, 1300-1914, Historian, Vol 59, 96; The Uskoks of Senj--Piracy, Banditry, And Holy-War In The 16th-Century Adriatic, Am Hist Rev, Vol 98, 93; Social-History of Siberia 1815-1941--Sustainable Progress During Industrialization, Am Hist Rev, Vol 101, 96; Elementary-Education In Yugoslavia: 1918-1941--Social Modernization, Am Hist Rev, Vol 102, 97. **CONTACT ADDRESS** Dept of Hist, Rutgers Univ, New Brunswick, NJ, 08903.

STOKES, GALE
PERSONAL Born 10/05/1933, Orange, NJ, m, 1958, 2 children **DISCIPLINE** HISTORY **EDUCATION** Colgate Univ, BA, 54; IN Univ, MA, 65, PhD, 70. **CAREER** To Mary Gibbs Jones prof of History, Rice Univ, 68-. **HONORS AND AWARDS** Wayne S Vucinich Prize, AAASS, 94; Russ E Europe Inst, IN Univ, Distinguished Alumnus, 95. **MEMBERSHIPS** Am Hist Asn (member, res coun, 98-); Am Asn for Advancement of Slavic Studies (bd, 97-98). **RESEARCH** 19th and 20th century Eastern Europe; Balkans; Natsanacism. **SELECTED PUBLICATIONS** Auth, The Politics of Development: the Emergence of Political Parties in Nineteenth Century Serbia, Duke Univ Press, 90; The Walls Came Tumbling Down: The Collapse of Communism in Eastern Europe, Oxford Univ Press, 93; From Stalinism to Pluralism, 2nd ed, Oxford Univ Press, 95; Three Eras of Political Change in Eastern Europe, Oxford Univ Press, 97; The West Transformed, with Warren Hollister and Sears McGee, Harcourt Brace, 99. **CONTACT ADDRESS** History Dept, Rice Univ, 6100 S Main St, Houston, TX, 77005-1892. **EMAIL** gstokes@rice.edu

STOKES, LAWRENCE DUNCAN
PERSONAL Born 01/10/1940, Toronto, ON, Canada, m, 1964, 2 children **DISCIPLINE** MODERN EUROPEAN & GERMAN HISTORY **EDUCATION** Univ Toronto, BA, 62; Johns Hopkins Univ, MA, 64, PhD(hist), 72. **CAREER** Asst prof, 67-73, ASSOC PROF HIST, DALHOUSIE UNIV, 73-, Can Coun res grant, 73, 76, fel, 74-75; Humboldt fel, 79-80. **MEMBERSHIPS** Can Hist Asn; Conf Group Cent Europe Hist; Hist Asn, England; Can Comt Hist 2nd World War; Interuniv Ctr Europ Studies. **RESEARCH** Twentieth century German history; history of European fascist movements. **SELECTED PUBLICATIONS** Auth, The Nazi Impact On A German Village, Am Hist Rev, Vol 99, 94; Hitler Army--Soldiers, Nazis And The War In The 3rd-Reich, Int Hist Rev, Vol 15, 93; The Politics Of The Body In Weimar Germany--Womens Reproductive Rights And Duties, German Studies Rev, Vol 17, 94; Hitler Panzers East--World-War-Ii Reinterpreted, Int Hist Rev, Vol 15, 93; The Path To Genocide--Essays On Launching The Final-Solution, Central European Hist, Vol 26, 93; Opposition And Resistance In Gdansk 1933-1939, Am Hist Rev, Vol 101, 96; Reevaluating The Third-Reich, German Studies Rev, Vol 18, 95; The Rise And Rule Of The Nazis In A Small Industrial-City--Osterode 1918-1945, Histoire Sociale-Social Hist, Vol 26, 93; Hitler Followers--Studies In The Sociology Of The Nazi-Movement, English Hist Rev, Vol 109, 94; Nazism And Modernization, J Of Modern Hist, Vol 65, 93; Those Were Our School Years--Volksschule In Bremen Under National-Socialism, Am Hist Rev, Vol 100, 95; The Barbed-Wire College--Re-Educating German Pows In The United-States During World-War-II, Dalhousie Rev, Vol 75, 95; The Racial State--Germany 1933-1945, Central European Hist, Vol 25, 92. **CONTACT ADDRESS** Dept of Hist, Dalhousie Univ, Halifax, NS, B3H 3J5.

STOKSTAD, MARILYN JANE
PERSONAL Born 02/16/1929, Lansing, MI **DISCIPLINE** ART HISTORY **EDUCATION** Carleton Col, BA, 50; Mich St Univ, MA, 53, PhD, 57; Oslo Univ, post grad, 51-52. **CAREER** Instr, 56-58, Univ Mich; fac mem, 58-, assoc prof, 61-66, dir, mus art, 61-67, prof, 66-80, dist prof, art, 80-94, Judith Harris Murphy dist prof, 94-, res assoc, sum, 65-66, 67, 71, 72, assoc dean, Col Liberal Arts & Sci, 72-76, Univ Kans; res cur, 69-80, Nelson-Atkins Mus Art; consult curator, medieval art, 80, bd dir, 72-75, 81-84, 88-96, vice pres, 90-93, pres, 93-96, sr adv, 96-97, Intl Ctr Medieval Art. **HONORS AND AWARDS** Dist Svc Award, Alumni Assn Carleton Col, 83; Kans Gov's Arts Award, 97; Fulbright Fel, 51-52; NEH grantee, 67-68; Fel AAUW. **MEMBERSHIPS** AAUW; Midwest Col Art Conf; Col Art Assn; Soc Archit Hist. **RESEARCH** Medieval art. **SELECTED PUBLICATIONS** Auth, Santiago de Compostela, 78; auth, The Scottish World, 81; auth, Medieval Art, 86; auth, Art History, 95. **CONTACT ADDRESS** Dept of Art History, Univ of Kansas, Lawrence, KS, 66045. **EMAIL** stokstad@eagle.cc.ukans.edu

STOLER, MARK A.
PERSONAL Born 03/02/1945, New York, NY, m, 1991, 1 child **DISCIPLINE** HISTORY **EDUCATION** City Col of New York, BA, 66; Univ WI, Madison, MA, 67, PhD, 71. **CAREER** Lect, Univ WI, Milwaukee, 68-69; PROF HIST, UNIV VT, 70-; vis prof, Strategy Dept, US Naval War Col, 81-82; vis prof Hist, Univ Haita, Israel, 84-85; vis prof Hist, US Military Academy, 94-95. **HONORS AND AWARDS** Phi Alpha Theta; Army Civilian Service Award and Commander's Award for Public Service, 81, 95; Kidder Outstanding Faculty Award, Univ VT, 84; Dean's Lecture Award, Univ VT, 92; Univ Scholar Award, Univ VT, 93. **MEMBERSHIPS** Soc for Historians of Am Foreign Relations; Am Hist Asn; Org of Am Historians; Soc for Military Hist; World War II Studies Asn; Vermont Historical Soc; Committee on Peace Res in History; Center for Res on VT. **RESEARCH** US diplomatic and military history. **SELECTED PUBLICATIONS** Auth, The Politics of the Second Front: American Military Planning and Diplomacy in Coalition Warfare, 1941-1943, Greenwood Press, 77; The Origins of the Cold War (ed Microfiche collection), Scholarly Resources, 82; Explorations in American History: A Skills Approach, 2 vols, with Marshall True, IDC Pubs, 80, 2nd ed, Alfred A. Knopf, 86; George C. Marshall: Soldier-Statesman of the American Century, Twayne Pubs, 89; George C. Marshall, Robert Murphy, Edmund Muskie, and Lend-Lease, in Encyclopedia of US Foreign Relations, ed Bruce W. Jentleson and Thomas G. Paterson, Council of Foreign Relations, Oxford Univ Press, 97; Why George C.Marshall: A Biographical Assessment, in The Marshall Mission to China, ed Larry I. Bland, George C. Marshall Found, 98; Allied Summit Diplomacy, in World War II in Asia and the Pacific and the War's Aftermath, with General Themes: A Handbook of Literature and Research, ed Lloyd Lee. Greenwood Press, 98; George Marshall and Henry Stimson, in Oxford Companion to United States History, Oxford Univ Press, 98; George C. Marshall, Joint Chiefs of Staff and Diplomatic and Military Course of World War II, in The Oxford Companion to American Military History, ed John Whiteclay Chambers II, Oxford Univ Press, 98; The Joint Chiefs of Staff Assessment of Soviet-American Relations in the Spring of 1945, in Victory in Europe, 1945: the Allied Triumph over Germany and the Opening of the Cold War, ed Arnold A. Offner and Theodore A. Wilson, Univ Press KS, forthcoming 99. **CONTACT ADDRESS** Dept of Hist, Univ Vermont, Wheeler House- 442 Main St., Burlington, VT, 05405. **EMAIL** mstoler@zoo.uvm.edu

STOLER, MARK ALAN
PERSONAL Born 03/02/1945, New York, NY, m, 1991, 1 child **DISCIPLINE** HISTORY **EDUCATION** City Coll NY, BA, 66; Univ Wis Madison, MA, 67; PhD, 71. **CAREER** Res and archival asst, Univ Wis Madison, 67-68; lectr, Univ Wis Milwaukee, 68-69; vis prof, US Naval War Coll, 81-82; Fulbright lectr, Univ Haifa Israel, 84-85; vis prof, US Mil Acad, 94-95; instr, 70-71; asst prof, 71-76; assoc prof, 76-84; prof, Univ VT, 84-. **HONORS AND AWARDS** Phi Alpha theta, 66; danforth assoc, 79; Dept of the Army, Civilian Service Award and Commander's award for Public Service, 81, 95; George V Kidder Outstanding Fac, Univ Vt, 84; Dean's Lecture Award for Outstanding Scholar and Tchg, Univ Vt, 92; Univ Scholar Award, Univ Vt, 93; numerous grants, Univ Vt. **MEMBERSHIPS** Soc for Hist of Am Foreign Rel; Am Hist Asn; Orgn of Am Hist; Soc for Milit Hist; World War II Studies Asn; Vt Hist Soc; Comm on Peace Res in Hist; Center for Res on Vt. **RESEARCH** US diplomatic and military history; World War II. **SELECTED PUBLICATIONS** Auth, Dwight D Eisenhower: Architect of Victory, in D-Day: The Normandy Invasion After Fifty Years, 94; The 'Wise Old Owl': George D Aiken and Foreign affairs, 1941-1975, in The Political Legacy of George D Aiken: Wise Old Owl of the US Senate, 95; A Half Century of Conflict: Interpretations of US World War II Diplomacy, in America and the World: the Historiography of American Foreign Relations Since 1941, 96; Strategy, Grand and Otherwise: A Commentary, in World war II in Europe: the Final Year, 98; Why George C Marshall: A Bibliographical Assessment, in The Marshall Mission to China, 98. **CONTACT ADDRESS** History Dept, Univ of Vt, Burlington, VT, 05401. **EMAIL** mstoler@zoo.uvm.eduremark: this entry contains additions to DAS 8th edition

STOLL, STEVEN
DISCIPLINE HISTORY **EDUCATION** Univ Calif, Berkeley, BA, 88; Yale Univ, MA, 90, MPhil, 92, PhD, 94. **CAREER** ASST PROF, HIST, YALE UNIV **MEMBERSHIPS** Am Antiquarian Soc **CONTACT ADDRESS** Hist Dept, Yale Univ, PO Box 208234, New Haven, CT, 06520-8324.

STONE, BAILEY S.
PERSONAL Born 06/08/1946, Schenectady, NY, s **DISCIPLINE** HISTORY **EDUCATION** Bowdoin Col, BA, 68; Princeton Univ, PhD, 73. **CAREER** From asst prof to prof, Univ Houston, 75- . **MEMBERSHIPS** AHA; Soc for French Hist Stud; Phi Alpha Theta. **RESEARCH** Eighteenth-century and Revolutionary Europe; modern revolutions. **SELECTED PUBLICATIONS** Auth, The Parliament of Paris, 1774-1789, Univ N Carolina, 81; auth, The French Parliaments and the Crisis of the Old Regime, U N Carolina, 86; auth, The Genesis of the French Revolution: A Global-Historical Interpretation, Cambridge, 94. **CONTACT ADDRESS** Dept of History, Univ of Houston, Houston, TX, 77204-3785. **EMAIL** BSStone@jetson.uh.edu

STONE, DAVID M.
DISCIPLINE SOUTHERN BAROQUE ART **EDUCATION** Harvard Univ, PhD. **CAREER** Assoc prof. **SELECTED PUBLICATIONS** Auth, Guercino, Master Draftsman: Works from North American Collections, Harvard, 91; Guercino: Catalogo completo dei dipinto, Cantini, 91. **CONTACT ADDRESS** Dept of Art Hist, Univ Delaware, 162 Ctr Mall, Newark, DE, 19716. **EMAIL** dmstone@udel.edu

STONE-MILLER, REBECCA
PERSONAL Born 07/17/1958, Manchester, NH, m, 1989, 2 children **DISCIPLINE** ART HISTORY **EDUCATION** Yale Univ, PhD, 87. **CAREER** Asst Prof, 90-96, Assoc Prof, Emory Univ, 96-. **HONORS AND AWARDS** Getty Grant for Catalogue Preparation, 98-99. **MEMBERSHIPS** Inst Andean Studies; Phi Beta Kappa; Col Art Asn. **RESEARCH** Andean art; textiles; Central American art; shamanism. **SELECTED PUBLICATIONS** Auth, To Weave for the Sun: Ancient Andean Textiles, Thames & Hudson, 94; Art of the Andes, Thames & Hudson (World of Art Series), 96. **CONTACT ADDRESS** Art Hist Dept, Emory Univ, Carlos Hall, Atlanta, GA, 30322. **EMAIL** rstonem@emory.edu

STONE-RICHARDS, MICHAEL
DISCIPLINE 20TH CENTURY EUROPEAN ART **EDUCATION** Courtauld Inst Art, PhD. **CAREER** Prof, Northwestern Univ. **RESEARCH** 20th-century European art from symbolism to Viennese Actionism; Situationist International with special emphasis on surrealism in its international dimension, art and phenomenology in post-World War II Europe. **SELECTED PUBLICATIONS** Auth, essays in Ger & Engl on, Picasso; Breton; Reverdy. **CONTACT ADDRESS** Dept of Art History, Northwestern Univ, 1801 Hinman, Evanston, IL, 60208.

STORCH, NEIL T.
PERSONAL Born 05/15/1940, New York, NY **DISCIPLINE** HISTORY **EDUCATION** Seton Hall Univ, AB, 63; Univ Wis-Madison, MA, 64, PhD(hist), 69. **CAREER** Asst prof, 69-75, from assoc prof Hist, Univ Minn, Duluth, 75-83. **MEMBERSHIPS** Orgn Am Historians; Am Cath Hist Asn; Am Cath Hist Soc, Amer Con of Cath Hist; Amer Academy of Rel; College Theol Soc. **RESEARCH** Early American history; diplomatic history; American Catholic history. **SELECTED PUBLICATIONS** Auth, The recall of Silas Deane, Conn Hist Soc Bull, 1/73; Convoys for our envoys, US Naval Inst Proc, 10/75; Adams, Franklin and the origin of consular representation, Foreign Serv J, 10/75; Guide to the archives and manuscripts of the Diocese of Duluth, Soc Sci Res, 77; with Ken Moran, UMD comes of Age: The First One Hundred Years, 96. **CONTACT ADDRESS** Dept of History, Univ of Minnesota, 10 University Dr, Duluth, MN, 55812-2496.

STORER, NORMAN WILLIAM
PERSONAL Born 06/08/1930, Middletown, CT, m, 1975, 2 children **DISCIPLINE** SOCIOLOGY **EDUCATION** Univ KS, BA, 52, MA, 56; Cornell Univ, PhD, 61. **CAREER** Instr-asst prof, Harvard Univ, 60-66; staff assoc, Social Science Res Coun, New York City, 66-70; prof, Baruch Col, CUNY, 70-88; prof Emeritus, 89-. **HONORS AND AWARDS** Phi Beta Kappa, 52; Sigma Xi, 95. **MEMBERSHIPS** AAAS. **RESEARCH** Sociology of science; academic organization; domestic violence. **SELECTED PUBLICATIONS** Auth, The Social System of Science, Holt, Rinehart & Winston, 66; ed, The Sociology of Science: Theoretical and Empirical Investigation, by Robert K Merton, Univ Chicago Press, 73; auth, Focus on Society: An Introduction to Sociology, Addison-Wesley, 2nd ed, 80; The Teaching Relationship: A Hypothesized Model and Its Consequences, in Mid-American Review of Sociology, vol 14, no 1-2, winter 90; The Department of Sociology and...: The Significance of Disciplinary Purity on American Campuses, in Gale Miller, ed, Studies in Organizational Sociology: Essays in Honor of Charles K Warriner, JAI Press, 91; How Alcohol Affects DV Calls, in Law Enforcement Quart, Nov 93-Jan 94; Domestic Violence in Suburban San Diego, with William D Flores, Conimar Press, 94. **CONTACT ADDRESS** 1417 Van Buren Ave, San Diego, CA, 92103-2339. **EMAIL** Nwstorer@compuserve.com

STORRS, LANDON R.Y.
PERSONAL Born 05/29/1962 **DISCIPLINE** HISTORY **EDUCATION** Yale Univ, BA, 83; Univ Wisc, Madison, MA, 89, PhD, 94. **CAREER** Tchg asst, Univ Wisc, Madison, 90-93; vis asst prof, Middlebury Col, 94-95; asst prof, hist, Univ Houston, 95- . **HONORS AND AWARDS** Magna cum laude, 83; Univ Wisc Grad Sch fel, 89-90; Mellon fel, 87-88, 88-89, 92; Univ Houston Res Initiation grant, 96; finalist, Lerner-Scott Prize, Orgn of Am Hist, 96; limited grant-in-aid, Univ Houston, 98. **MEMBERSHIPS** Orgn of Am Hist; AHA; Coord Coun for Women in Hist; Social Sci Hist Asn; S Hist Asn; S Asn for Women Hist; AAUP. **SELECTED PUBLICATIONS** Auth, An Independent Voice for Unorganized Workers: The Consumers' League Speaks to the Blue Eagle, Labor's Heritage, 95; auth, Gender and the Development of the Regulatory State: The Controversy over Restricting Women's Night Work in the Depression-Era South, J of Policy Hist, 98; auth, Civilizing Capitalism: The National Consumers' League and the Politics of Fair Labor Standards in the New Deal Era, Univ N Carolina, forthcoming. **CONTACT ADDRESS** Dept of History, Univ of Houston, Houston, TX, 77204-3785.

STORTZ, GERRY
DISCIPLINE HISTORY **EDUCATION** Univ Waterloo, BA, 73; MA, 76; Univ Guelph, PhD, 80. **CAREER** Assoc prof **RESEARCH** Canadian religious history; Canadian labour history; immigration history. **SELECTED PUBLICATIONS** Auth, A Canadian Veterinarian Overseas in the First World War; Archbishop Lynch and New Ireland: An Unfulfilled Dream for Canada's Northwest; Archbishop Lynch and the Knights of Labor; Archbishop Lynch and Toronto's Anglicans; Arthur Palmer: Founder and First Rector of St. George's Anglican Church, Guelph. **CONTACT ADDRESS** Dept of History, St. Jerome's Univ, Waterloo, ON, N2L 3G3.

STORTZ, MARTHA ELLEN
DISCIPLINE HISTORICAL THEOLOGY; ETHICS **EDUCATION** Carleton Col, BA; Univ Chicago, MA, PhD. **CAREER** Prof **HONORS AND AWARDS** Mem, convener, GTU Core Dr fac; adv comm, LCA Study on Issues Concerning Homosexuality, 86; bd mem,, Ctr for Women and Rel, GTU; ELCA rep, Intl Consult of Lutheran Women Theologians, Helsinki, 91. **MEMBERSHIPS** Mem, Ctr for Global Edu, Augsburg Col; ELCA Task Force on Theol Edu; ELCA Commn for Church in Soc Bd. **SELECTED PUBLICATIONS** Auth, PastorPower, Abingdon Press, 93. **CONTACT ADDRESS** Dept of Historical Theology and Ethics, Pacific Lutheran Theol Sem, 2770 Marin Ave, Berkeley, CA, 94708-1597. **EMAIL** mstortz@autobahn.org

STORY, RONALD
DISCIPLINE HISTORY **EDUCATION** NY State Univ, PhD, 72. **CAREER** Prof, Univ MA Amherst. **SELECTED PUBLICATIONS** Auth, Forging of an Aristocracy: Harvard and the Boston Upper Class 1800-1870, 80; co-auth, Generations of Americans: A History of the United States, 76; co-ed, A More Perfect Union: Documents in American History, 84; Sports in Massachusetts: Historical Essays, 91; Five Colleges: Five Histories, 93. **CONTACT ADDRESS** Dept of Hist, Univ Massachusetts Amherst, Mass Ave, Amherst, MA, 01003.

STOTT, ANNETTE
DISCIPLINE ART **EDUCATION** Boston Univ, PhD, 86; Univ of WI-Madison, MA, 80; Concordia Col, BA, 77 **CAREER** Prof, 94-, Asst Prof, 91-94, Univ of Denver; Asst Prof, 87-91, Winthrop Univ; Asst Prof, 868-87 Univ of Maine-Orono **HONORS AND AWARDS** NEH Fel, 97-98; Fulbright Fel, Netherlands, 83-84, Summa cum laude; Boston Univ Fel **MEMBERSHIPS** Col Art Asn; Am Culture Assoc; Am Studies Asn **RESEARCH** Am Art and Architecture; Women's Studies **SELECTED PUBLICATIONS** Auth, Holland Mania: The Unknown Dutch Period in American Art and Culture, New York: Overlook Press, 98; Transformative Triptychs in Multicultural America, The Art Journal, 98 **CONTACT ADDRESS** Sch of Art, Univ of Denver, Denver, CO, 80208. **EMAIL** astott@du.edu

STOTT, WILLIAM MERRELL
PERSONAL Born 06/02/1940, New York, NY, m, 1962, 2 children **DISCIPLINE** AMERICAN STUDIES, ENGLISH **EDUCATION** Yale Univ, AB, 62, MPh, 70, PhD(Am studies), 72. **CAREER** Foreign serv officer, US Info Agency, 64-68; asst prof, 71-74, assoc dean, Div Gen & Comp Studies, 75-77, assoc prof, 74-80, prof Am Studies & English, Univ Tex, Austin, 80-, dir, Am Studies Prog, 81-84, Guggenheim Mem Found Fel, 78; Fulbright lectr, Polytechnic of Cent London, 80-81; Univ of London, 86-87. **MEMBERSHIPS** Am Studies Asn. **RESEARCH** Journalism; mass culture; autobiography. **SELECTED PUBLICATIONS** Auth, Documentary Expression and Thirties America, Oxford Univ, 73, Chicago UP, 86; coauth, On Broadway, Univ Tex, 78; Write to the Point, Columbia UP, 90;

Facing the Fire: Experiencing and Expressing Anger Appropriately, Doubleday, 93. **CONTACT ADDRESS** Dept of Am Studies, Univ of Texas, Austin, TX, 78712-1026. **EMAIL** wstott@mail.utexas.edu

STOUT, HARRY S.
DISCIPLINE HISTORY **EDUCATION** Calvin Coll, BA, 69; Kent State Univ, MA, 72, PhD, 74. **CAREER** Assoc prof, hist, Univ Conn; MASTER, BERKELEY COLL & JONATHAN EDWARDS PROF, AM CHRISTIANITY, YALE UNIV **MEMBERSHIPS** Am Antiquarian Soc **SELECTED PUBLICATIONS** Auth, The New England Soul: Preaching and Religious Culture in Colonial New England, Oxford, 86; co-ed, Jonathan Edwards and the American Experience, Oxford, 88; auth, The Divine Dramatist: George Whitefield and the Rise of Modern Evangelicalism, Eardmans Press, 91. **CONTACT ADDRESS** Berkeley Col, 403 Yale Station, New Haven, CT, 06520.

STOUT, JOSEPH ALLEN
PERSONAL Born 05/27/1939, Sioux City, IA, m, 1975, 2 children **DISCIPLINE** SPANISH, HISTORY **EDUCATION** PhD, Hist Oklahoma State Univ, 71; MA, Hist, TX A&M Univ, 68; BA, Angelo State Col, 67. **CAREER** San Angelo TX Public Sachools, Inst Hist, 68-69; Missouri Southern State College Asst Prof, 71-72; Oklahoma State Univ, Asst to Prof, 72-. **HONORS AND AWARDS** Phi Kappa Phi; Phi Alpha Theta. **MEMBERSHIPS** Conf of US-Mexican Historians; TX State Hist Assoc; Southwest council of Latin Am Area Studies. **RESEARCH** US Mexican Frontier; US Mexican Military; Mexican Revolutionary period. **SELECTED PUBLICATIONS** The United States and the Native Americans in John A Carroll, and Colin Baxter; The American Military Tradition from Colonial Times to the Present, Wilmington, Delaware, Scholarly Resources Inc, 96; Historiography and Sources in Mexico for Frontier History, in Jaime E Rodriguez and Virginia Guedea, Cinco Siglos en las Historia de Mexico, 2 vols, Mexico, D F, Instituto Mora and Irvine CA, Univ of CA, Irvine, 92; Deadly Crossings: Carrancistas, Villistas, and the Punitive Expedition, 1915-1920, in press, Texas Christian Univ Press, 99. **CONTACT ADDRESS** Dept Hist, Oklahoma State Univ, Stillwater, OK, 74074. **EMAIL** JAS1624@OKWAY.OKSTATE.EDU

STOUT, NEIL R.
PERSONAL Born 08/12/1932, Marietta, OH, m, 1956, 2 children **DISCIPLINE** AMERICAN HISTORY **EDUCATION** Harvard Univ, AB, 54; Univ Wis, MS, 58, PhD, 62. **CAREER** From instr to asst prof hist, Agr & Mech Col Tex, 61-64; from asst prof to assoc prof, 64-72, prof hist, Univ Vermont, 72- . **MEMBERSHIPS** New Eng Hist Asn (vpres, 78-79, pres, 79-80); Orgn Am Historians. **RESEARCH** American Revolution; biography. **SELECTED PUBLICATIONS** Auth, Spies who went out in the cold, Am Heritage, 2/72; Royal Navy in America, 1760-1775, US Naval Inst, 73; The Perfect Crisis, NY Univ, 76; auth, History Student's Vade Mecum, 90, 93, 94, 96. **CONTACT ADDRESS** 129 Robinson Pkwy, Burlington, VT, 05401. **EMAIL** nstout@zoo.uvm.edu

STOVER, JOHN FORD
PERSONAL Born 05/16/1912, Manhattan, KS, m, 1937, 3 children **DISCIPLINE** HISTORY **EDUCATION** Univ Nebr, AB, 34, MA, 37; Univ Wis, PhD(Am hist), 51. **CAREER** From instr to assoc prof, 47-59, prof, 59-78, EMER PROF HIST, PURDUE UNIV, 78-, Mem, Ind Sesquicentennial Comn Exec Comt & chmn, Educ Comt, 62; consult, Midwest Prog Airborn TV Instr, 63-64; consult & contribr suppl, Dictionary Am Biog, 66-67. **MEMBERSHIPS** AHA; Orgn Am Historians; Southern Hist Asn; Soc Am Hist; Western Hist Asn. **RESEARCH** American transportation history; American social history; Civil War and Reconstruction. **SELECTED PUBLICATIONS** Auth, Railroads of the South, 1865-1900, Univ NC, Chapel Hill, 55; American Railroads, Univ Chicago, 61; A History of American Railroads, 67 & Turnpikes, Canals, and Steamboats, 69, Rand McNally; The Life and Decline of the American Railroad, Oxford Univ, 70; Transportation in American History, Am Hist Asn, 70; History of the Illinois Central Railroad, Macmillan, 75; Iron Road to the West, Columbia Univ, 78; Politics And Industrialization--Early Railroads In The United-States And Prussia, J Of Am Hist, Vol 82, 95. **CONTACT ADDRESS** Dept Hist, Purdue Univ, Lafayette, IN, 47907.

STOW, GEORGE BUCKLEY
PERSONAL Born 03/17/1940, Camden, NJ, m, 1974, 1 child **DISCIPLINE** MEDIEVAL ENGLISH HISTORY **EDUCATION** Lehigh Univ, BA, 67; Univ Southern Calif, MA, 68; Univ Ill, Urbana, PhD(hist), 72. **CAREER** From instr to assoc prof, 72-83, PROF HIST, LA SALLE UNIV, 83- **HONORS AND AWARDS** Phi Beta Kappa, Phi Kappa Phi; Phi Alpha Theta; Eta Sigma Phi; Joseph Ward Swain Prize, 70; Lawrence M Larsen Award, 70; NDEA Fel 68; Woodward Wilson Dissertation Fel, 70; La Salle Univ Summer Res Grant, 75, 85 & 88; La Salle Univ Res Leave Sabbatical 88; Amer Philos Soc Res Grant, 88 & 89. **MEMBERSHIPS** Fel Royal Hist Soc. **RESEARCH** Medieval Europe; Ancient Rome; England to 1688. **SELECTED PUBLICATIONS** Auth, Historia Vitae et Regni Ricardi Secundi, Univ Pa. 77; The Vita Ricardi Secundi as a Source for the Reign of Richard II, Vale Evesham Hist Soc Res Papers, 73; Some New Manuscripts of the Vita Ricardi Secundi, 1377-1402, Manuscripta, 75; Thomas Walsingham, John Malvern and the Vita Ricardi Secundi, 1377-1381, Mediaeval Studies, 77; ed, Historia Vitae et Regni Ricardi Secundi, Univ Pa, 77; auth, Bodleian Library Ms Bodley 316 and the Dating of Thomas Walsingham's Literary Career, Manuscripta, 81; Richard II in Thomas Walsingham's Chronicles, Speculum, 84; Richard II in Jean Foissart's Chroniques, J of Medieval Hist, 85; Chronicles versus Record Sources: The Character of Richard II, Documenting the Past, 89; Richard II in John Gower's Confessio Amantis: Some Historical Perspectives, Mediaevalia, 93; Richard II Leader and Tyrant, Great Leaders, Great Tyrants, Greenwood, 1995; Richard II and the Invention of the Pocket Handkerchief, Albion, 95; Stubbs, Steel, and Richard II as Insane: The Origin and Evolution an English Historiographical Myth, Proceedings of the Amer Philos Soc, Forthcoming. **CONTACT ADDRESS** Dept of History, La Salle Univ, 1900 W Olney Ave, Philadelphia, PA, 19141-1199. **EMAIL** stow@alpha.lasalle.edu

STOWERS, STANLEY KENT
PERSONAL Born 02/24/1948, Munice, IN, m, 1968, 2 children **DISCIPLINE** HISTORY OF EARLY CHRISTIANITY **EDUCATION** Abilene Christian Univ, AB, 70; Princeton Theol Sem, MA, 74; Yale Univ, PhD(relig studies), 79. **CAREER** Asst prof relig studies, Phillips Univ, 79-80; Asst Prof Relig Studies, 81-91, PROF REL STUDIES, BROWN UNIV, 91-. **HONORS AND AWARDS** Sheridan Teaching Award, 97; Woodrow Wilson fel, 92; NEH fel, 91; FIAT fel, 90. **MEMBERSHIPS** Am Acad Relig; Soc Bibl Lit. **RESEARCH** Early Christianity; Hellenistic philosophy; early Christian literature; Greek Religion. **SELECTED PUBLICATIONS** Auth, The Diatribe and Paul's Letter to the Romans, Scholars Press, 81; auth, A Rereading of Romans, Yal Univ Press, 94; auth, Letter Writing in Greco-Roman Anqiquity, Westminster Press, 86. **CONTACT ADDRESS** Dept of Relig Studies, Brown Univ, Box 1927, Providence, RI, 02912-9127. **EMAIL** Stanley_Stowers@brown.edu

STRANAHAN, PATRICIA
PERSONAL Born 10/07/1949, New Castle, PA **DISCIPLINE** MODERN CHINESE & JAPANESE HISTORY **EDUCATION** Westminster Col, BA, 71; Univ Pa, MA, 74, PhD(Orient studies), 79. **CAREER** ASST PROF HIST, TEX A&M UNIV, 80- **MEMBERSHIPS** Asn Asian Studies. **RESEARCH** History of Chinese Communist Party; development of policy for women in Yanan (1937-1947). **SELECTED PUBLICATIONS** Auth, Changes in Policy for Yanan Women, 1935-1937, Mod China, 1/81; The Communist-Party In Shanghai--Introduction, Chinese Studies In Hist, Vol 28, 95. **CONTACT ADDRESS** Hist Dept, Tex A&M Univ, College Station, TX, 77843.

STRANGE, JAMES F.
PERSONAL Born 02/02/1938, Pampa, TX, m, 1960, 4 children **DISCIPLINE** BIBLICAL STUDIES, ARCHEOLOGY **EDUCATION** Rice Univ, BA, 59; Yale Univ, MDiv, 64; Drew Univ, PhD, 70. **CAREER** Asst prof, 72-75, assoc prof, 75-80, prof relig studies, Univ S Fla, Tampa, 80-, dean col arts & lett, 81-89, Montgomery fel, William F Albright Inst Archaeol Res, Jerusalem, 70-71; fel Off Judeo-Christian Studies, Duke Univ, 71-72; asoc dir, Joint Exped to Khirbet Shema', Israel, 71-73; assoc dir, Meiron Excavation Proj, Israel, 73-78; vis lectr, Univ of the Orange Free State, Repub S Africa, 79; Nat Endowment for Humanities fel, Jerusalem, 80; dir, Survey in Galilee, 82; dir USF Excavations at Sepphoris, Israel, 83; dir, Excavations Qumran, 96; McMannis Lect, Wheaton Col, 96; Benjamin Meaker vis prof Inst Advan Stud, Univ Bristol, 97. **HONORS AND AWARDS** Samuel Robinson Lect, Wake Forest Univ, 81. **MEMBERSHIPS** Soc Bibl Lit; Israel Explor Soc; Am Schs Orient Res; NY Acad Sci; Soc Sci Explor. **RESEARCH** Archaeology of Israel in Roman to Arab times; Roman and Byzantine ceramics in the Eastern Mediterranean; computer models for Roman-Byzantine archaeology and historical geography. **SELECTED PUBLICATIONS** Coauth, Archaeology and rabbinic tradition at Khirbet Shema, the 1970 and 1971 campaigns, Bibl Archaeologist, 72; Excavations at Meiron in Upper Galilee--1971, 1972, 74 & auth, Late Hellenistic and Herodian ossuary tombs at French Hill, Jerusalem, 75, Bull of Am Schs of Orient Res; coauth, Ancient Synagogue Excavations at Khirbet Shema, Upper Galilee, Israel 1970-1972, Duke Univ, 76; auth, Capernaum, Crucifixion, Methods of, & Magdala, Interpreter's Dictionary of Bible, suppl vol, 76; Excavations at Meiron, in Upper Galilee--1974, 1975: A second preliminary report, 78 & coauth, Excavations at Meiron, 81, Am Schs of Orient Res; Archaeology and the religion of Judaism, Aufstieg und Niedergang der Roemischen Welt, 81; coauth, The Excavations at the Ancient Synagogue of Gush Halav, Israel, 90. **CONTACT ADDRESS** Dept Relig Studies, Univ SFla, 4202 Fowler Ave, CPR 107, Tampa, FL, 33620-9951. **EMAIL** strange@chuma.cas.usf.edu

STRANGE, STEVEN K.
DISCIPLINE ANCIENT PHILOSOPHY **EDUCATION** Univ TX, PhD, 81. **CAREER** Philos, Emory Univ. **SELECTED PUBLICATIONS** Transl, Porphyry, On Aristotle's Categories. **CONTACT ADDRESS** Emory Univ, Atlanta, GA, 30322-1950.

STRASSBERG, BARBARA
PERSONAL Born 08/22/1945, Krakow, Poland, 2 children **DISCIPLINE** SOCIOLOGY **EDUCATION** MA, 67, 70, PhD, 75, Jagiellonian Univ, Cracow, Poland; post-doct stud, Univ Chicago, 77-78. **CAREER** Lectr, Teachers Col, Cracow, 70-72; asst prof, 72-76, assoc prof 78-84, Jagiellonian Univ; hon fel, 84-86, vis scholar, 87, Univ Chicago; lect, Triton Col, 85, 86, Univ Chicago, 86, Coll of Du Page, 86- , De Paul Univ, 89, Columbia Col, 90, 91; asst prof, 91-94, assoc prof, 94- , Aurora Univ. **HONORS AND AWARDS** F. Ananiecki Awd of the Polish Acad of Sci for The Church in the Process of Assimilation of Polish Americans, 85; Who's Who in the Midwest, 94; World Who's Who of Women, 95; Who's Who of Am Women, 95. **MEMBERSHIPS** Am Asn Univ Women; Midwest Sociol Soc; Illinois Sociol Asn; Soc for Sci Study of Jewry; Am Sociol Asn; Illinois Sociol Asn; Asn for Sociolog of Relig; Soc for Sci Study of Relig. **SELECTED PUBLICATIONS** Auth, "The Origins of the Polish National Catholic Church," PNCC Stud, 86; "Polish Catholicism in Transition," ed. Gannon,World Catholicism in Transition, Macmillan, 88; "Changes in Religious Culture in Post-World War II Poland," Sociol Analysis, 88; "Religion and Patriotism," ed Hadden, Religion and Politics (in printing); trans, Malinowski, Coral Gardens, Polish Scientific Pub, 85; Magic, Science and religion, Polish Scientific Pub, 85; Polish Americans, Ossolineum, 85; The Polish National Catholic Church in Relation to Modern Theological Ecumenical and Social Issues, Kosciol Polskokatolicki, 84. **CONTACT ADDRESS** Dept of Sociology, Aurora Univ, Aurora, IL, 60605. **EMAIL** bstrass@admin.aurora.edu

STRATER, HENRY A.
PERSONAL Born 10/28/1934, Cleveland, OH, m, 3 children **DISCIPLINE** ENGLISH, CLASSICAL LANGUAGES **EDUCATION** John Carroll Univ, AB, 56, MA; Case Western Univ, MA, 59; Ohio State Univ, PhD, 71. **CAREER** Tchr, Shaker Heights Sch, Ohio, 56-84; holder of Waldron ch in Classics, Univ Sch, 84- . **HONORS AND AWARDS** Good tchr awd, Class Asn Mid W and S; Seelbach awd for excel in tchg. **MEMBERSHIPS** Amer Class League; Ohio Class Conf; Amer Philol Asn; Class Asn Mid W and S. **RESEARCH** Vergil; Methods of teaching Classical Languages. **SELECTED PUBLICATIONS** Auth, Greek to Me: An Introduction to Classical Greek. **CONTACT ADDRESS** Univ Sch, 1131 Blanchester Rd, Lyndhurst, OH, 44124. **EMAIL** hastrater@aol.com

STRATTON, JOHN RAY
PERSONAL Born 03/12/1935, Sandwich, IL, m, 1957, 2 children **DISCIPLINE** SOCIOLOGY **EDUCATION** Univ IL, BA, 57, MA, 69, PhD, 63. **CAREER** Instr, Bradley Univ, Peoria, IL, 61-64; asst prof, 64-68, assoc prof, Univ IA, 68-; vis asst prof, San Diego State Univ, summer 67. **HONORS AND AWARDS** NIMH, 66; Univ IA Old Gold Award, summer 68; US Dept of Justice, Office of Law Enforcement Assistance, 68, 69; NSF Dissertation grants, two in 73; IA Dept of Social Services grants, two in 80; IA Criminal and Juvenile Justice Agency Quick Stop Evaluation, 84; Governors Volunteer Award, 84; Potstanding Citizen Award, IA Correctional Asn, 87; Correctional Center, 6th Judicial District, dedicated in honor of Dr Stratton, 92; Distinguished Service Award, Midwest Psychoil Sco, 941; SROP Distinguished Mentor Award, Commitee on Inst Cooperation, 95. **MEMBERSHIPS** Midwest Sociol Asn. **RESEARCH** Corrections; sexual assault. **SELECTED PUBLICATIONS** Ed, with Robet Leger, Sociology of Corrections, Wiley & Sons, 77; auth, with David A Parton and Michael Shanahan, The Use of Discretion in Prison Discipline Committees, Am J of Criminal Justice, 12:1, fall 87; auth, with David A Parton and Mark Hansel, Measuring Crime Seriousness: Lessons from the National Survey of Crime Severity, British J of Criminology, 91; numerous other publications. **CONTACT ADDRESS** Dept of Sociol, Univ of Iowa, Iowa City, IA, 52246. **EMAIL** JohnStratton@blue.weeg.UIowa.edu

STRAUSBERG, STEPHEN FREDERICK
PERSONAL Born 09/03/1943, Brooklyn, NY **DISCIPLINE** ECONOMIC HISTORY **EDUCATION** Brooklyn Col, BA, 64; Cornell Univ, PhD(hist), 70. **CAREER** Res historian, US Pub Land Law Rev Comn, 66-67; asst prof, 68-82, ASSOC PROF HIST, UNIV ARK, FAYETTEVILLE, 82-, Proj planner, Ark Humanities Prog, 76-78. **HONORS AND AWARDS** Outstanding Humanist, Ark Humanities Prog, 76. **MEMBERSHIPS** AHA; Orgn Am Historians. **RESEARCH** Southern economic history; history of public lands; Arkansas history. **SELECTED PUBLICATIONS** Contribr, History of the Public Domain, US Govt Printing Off, 69; Historical Abstracts, 72-76 & America, 73-76, ABC-Clio; auth, Federal Stewardship on the Frontier, Arno, 78; Swamplands in Indiana, Ind J Hist, 78; The New Deal in Arkansas, The Depression in the Southwest, Kennikat Press, 80; Public Values, Private Lands--Farmland Preservation Policy, 1933-1985, J Of Am Hist, Vol 82, 95. **CONTACT ADDRESS** Dept of Hist, Univ of Ark, Fayetteville, AR, 72701-1202.

STRAUSS, DAVID
DISCIPLINE HISTORY **EDUCATION** Amherst Col, BA, 59; Columbia Univ, MA, 63, PhD, 68. **CAREER** Vis prof, Univ Lyon, France, 70-71; Instr, 67-68, asst prof, 68-74, Colgate Univ; vis prof, 83-84, vis scholar, 88, Waseda Univ,

Tokyo; assoc prof, 74-80, PROF HIST, 80-, KALAMAZOO COL. **CONTACT ADDRESS** Dept of History, Kalamazoo Col, 1200 Academy St, Kalamazoo, MI, 49006.

STRAUSS, GERALD
PERSONAL Born 05/03/1922, Frankfurt am Main, Germany **DISCIPLINE** HISTORY **EDUCATION** Boston Univ, AB, 49; Columbia Univ, AM, 50, PhD, 57. **CAREER** Instr hist, Phillips Exeter Acad, 51-57; asst prof, Univ Ala, 57-59; from asst prof to assoc prof, 59-71, PROF HIST, IND UNIV, BLOOMINGTON, 71-, Am Coun Learned Soc grants-in-aid, 60, 62; Fulbright exchange prof, Trinity Col, Univ Dublin, 61-62; Guggenheim fel, 65-66, 72-73; mem, Inst Advan Study, Princeton Univ, 75-76. **RESEARCH** Early modern European history; German humanism. **SELECTED PUBLICATIONS** Auth, Martin Bucer--Reforming Church And Community, Central European Hist, Vol 28, 95; Religion, Political-Culture And The Emergence Of Early-Modern Society--Essays In German And Dutch Hist, J Of Modern Hist, Vol 66, 94; Wondrous In His Saints--Counterreformation Propaganda In Bavaria, J Of Modern Hist, Vol 67, 95; The Harvest Of Humanism In Central-Europe--Essays In Honor of Lewis W. Sptitz, Catholic Hist Rev, Vol 79, 93. **CONTACT ADDRESS** Dept of Hist, Indiana Univ, Bloomington, Bloomington, IN, 47405.

STRAUSS, WALLACE PATRICK
PERSONAL Born 03/17/1923, St. Louis, MO, m, 1951, 1 child **DISCIPLINE** AMERICAN HISTORY **EDUCATION** Occidental Col, AB, 48; Stanford Univ, MA, 49; Columbia Univ, PhD, 58. **CAREER** Historian, Peabody Mus Exped, Polynesia, 51; lectr Am hist, Columbia Univ, 58; instr soc sci, San Francisco State Col, 58-60; asst prof hist, Dakota State Col, 60-61; asst prof Am thought & lang, Mich State Univ, 61-66; assoc prof, 66-70, PROF AM HIST, OAKLAND UNIV, 70-, Fulbright lectr, Univ Hong Kong, 64-65, sr Fulbright lectr Am hist, 70-71. **MEMBERSHIPS** Am Studies Asn; AHA; Soc Historians Am Foreign Rels. **RESEARCH** Nineteenth century American diplomatic history; American naval history; international rivalries in the Pacific in the 19th century. **SELECTED PUBLICATIONS** Auth, Preparing the Wilkes Expedition: A study in disorganization, Pac Hist Rev, 8/59; Americans in Polynesia, 1783-1842, Mich State Univ, 63; Paradoxical cooperation: Sir Joseph Banks and the London Missionary Society, Hist Studies Australia & NZ, 4/64; ed, Stars and Spars: The American Navy in the Age of Sail, Blaisdell, 68; auth, Isolation and Involvement: An Interpretive History of American Diplomacy, Xerox, 72; coauth, Lands below the Horn, In: America Spreads Her Sails, Naval Inst, 73; The Voyage Of The Peacock--A Journal By Benajah Ticknor Naval Surgeon, Pacific Hist Rev, Vol 61, 92. **CONTACT ADDRESS** Dept of Hist, Oakland Univ, Rochester, MI, 48063.

STRAUSS CLAY, JENNY
DISCIPLINE CLASSICAL STUDIES **EDUCATION** Univ Wash, PhD. **CAREER** Prof. **SELECTED PUBLICATIONS** Auth, Wrath of Athena, Princeton, 83; The Politics of Olympus, Princeton, 89; pubs on Greek and Roman poetry. **CONTACT ADDRESS** Dept of Classics, Virginia Univ, Charlottesville, VA, 22903. **EMAIL** jsc2t@virginia.edu

STRAWSER, SHERRI C.
DISCIPLINE SCHOOL PSYCHOLOGY, ASSESSMENT IN SPECIAL EDUCATION, LEARNING DISABILITIES **EDUCATION** Univ Utah, PhD, 85. **CAREER** Dir, except children's serv, Univ Nev, Las Vegas. **HONORS AND AWARDS** Educ of the Yr, State Asn for Retarded Citizens of Utah, 90; fed res grant, US Dept of Educ; fed trng pers prep grant, US Dept of Educ; Utah Ctr of Excellence grant, Off of Econ Develop of Utah. **SELECTED PUBLICATIONS** Auth, Assessment and identification practices, in W. N. Bender, ed, Learning disabilities: Best practices professionals, Andover Med Publ, 93; coauth, Assessment of subtypes of learning disabilities: A practical approach to diagnosis and intervention, Spec Serv in Sch, 6 (1/2), 90. **CONTACT ADDRESS** Dept of Spec Educ, Univ Nev, Las Vegas, 4505 Maryland Pky, Las Vegas, NV, 89154-3014. **EMAIL** strawser@nevada.edu

STRAYER, ROBERT WILLIAM
PERSONAL Born 10/22/1942, Pittsburgh, PA **DISCIPLINE** SOVIET, WORLD, & AFRICAN HISTORY **EDUCATION** Wheaton Col, Ill, BA, 64; Univ Wis-Madison, MA, 66, PhD(hist), 71. **CAREER** PROF HIST, STATE UNIV NY COL BROCKPORT, 70-. **HONORS AND AWARDS** Chancellor's Award for Excellence in Teaching. **MEMBERSHIPS** African Studies Asn. **RESEARCH** Modern imperialism in Africa; missionary history in Africa; the recruitment of chiefs in colonial Kenya. **SELECTED PUBLICATIONS** Auth, The dynamics of mission expansion, Int J African Hist Studies, 73; The making of mission schools in Kenya, Comp Educ Rev, 73; Mission history in Africa, African Studies Rev, 76; The Making of Mission Communities in East Africa, State Univ NY, 78; Kenya: Focus on Nationalism, Prentice-Hall, 75; The Making of the Modern World, St. Martin's Press, 95; Why Did the Soviet Union Collapse, M.E. Sharpe, 98. **CONTACT ADDRESS** Dept of Hist, State Univ of NY Col, 350 New Campus Dr., Brockport, NY, 14420-2914. **EMAIL** rstrayer@po.brockport.edu

STREETS, HEATHER
DISCIPLINE MODERN BRITISH HISTORY **EDUCATION** Duke Univ, PhD, 98. **CAREER** Asst prof, Washington State Univ. **SELECTED PUBLICATIONS** Auth, Side By Side in Generous Rivalry: Highlanders, Sikhs, and the Making of Modern Martial Race Ideology in the 1857 Indian Uprising, J Brit Stud. **CONTACT ADDRESS** Dept of History, Washington State Univ, 301 Wilson Hall, PO Box 644030, Pullman, WA, 99164-4030. **EMAIL** streetsh@mail.wsu.edu

STRICKLAND, ARVARH E.
PERSONAL Born 07/06/1930, Hattiesburg, Mississippi, m, 1951 **DISCIPLINE** HISTORY **EDUCATION** Tougaloo Coll, Tougaloo, MS, BA, history, English, 1951; Univ of Illinois, Urbana, IL, MA, education, 1953, PhD, history 1962. **CAREER** Chicago State Coll, asst prof, 1962-65, assoc prof, 1965-68, prof, 1968-69; Univ of Missouri at Columbia, prof, 1969-95, prof emeritus, 1995-, chmn dept of history, 1980-83, interim dir black studies program, 1986, 1994-95, Office of the Vice President for Academic Affairs, sr faculty assoc, 1987-88; interim assoc vice pres for academic affairs, 1989, assoc vice pres for academic affairs, 1989-91. **HONORS AND AWARDS** Kappa Delta Pi (education), 1953; Phi Alpha Theta (history), 1960; Kendric C Babcock Fellow in History, Univ of Illinois, 1961-62; Distinguished Serv Award, Illinois Historical Soc, 1967 Honor Soc of Phi Kappa Phi, Univ of Missouri, 1973; Assoc of the Danforth Found, 1973; Omicron Delta Kappa Natl Leadership Honor Soc, 1978; Martin Luther King Memorial Comm Award for Outstanding Community Serv, 1982; Faculty-Alumni Award, Alumni Assn of the Univ of Missouri, 1983; Serv Appreciation Award, Missouri Comm for the Humanities, 1984; Thomas Jefferson Award, Univ of Missouri, 1985; Office of Equal Opportunity Award for Exemplary Serv in Enhancing the Status of Minorities, Univ of Missouri, 1985; Distinguished Alumni Award (Tougaloo Coll), Natl Assn for Equal Opportunity in Higher Educ, 1986; N Endowment for the Humanities, Travel to Collections Grant, 1986; Byler Distinguished Professor Award, Univ of Missouri, Columbia, 1994; St Louis American's Educator of the Year Award, 1994. **MEMBERSHIPS** Amer Assn of Univ Prof; Missouri Advisory Commn on Historic Preservation, 1976-80; Gen Bd of Higher Educ and Ministry, The United Methodist Church, 1976-80, mem exec comm; commr, Columbia Planning and Zoning Comm, 1977-80; Assn for the Study of Afro-Amer Life and History; Southern Historical Assn; bd of trustees, State Historical Soc of Missouri; co-chmn, Mayor's Steering Comm for Commemorating the Contribution of Black Columbians, Columbia, MO, 1980; mem, Fed Judicial Merit Selection Comm for the Western Dist of Missouri, 1982; Kiwanis Club of Columbia; Missouri Historical Records Advisory Bd; commr, Peace Officers Standards and Training Commn, 1988-89. **SELECTED PUBLICATIONS** History of the Chicago Urban League, Univ of Illinois Press, 1966; Building the United States, author with Jerome Reich and Edward Biller, Harcourt, Brace Jovanovich Inc, 1971; The Black American Experience, co-author with Jerome Reich, Harcourt, Brace Jovanovich Inc, 1974; Vol I, From Slavery through Reconstruction to 1877; Vol 11, From Reconstruction to the Present Since 1877; Edited with an Introduction, Lorenzo J Greene, Working With Carter G Woodson, The Father of Black History: A Diary, 1928-30, Louisiana State Univ Press, 1989; Edited with an introduction, Lorenzo J Greene, Selling Black History for Carter G Woodson: A Diary, 1930-33, Univ of Missouri Press, 1996. **CONTACT ADDRESS** Department of History, Univ of Missouri-Columbia, 101 Read Hall, Columbia, MO, 65211.

STRICKLAND, DOROTHY S.
PERSONAL Born 09/29/1933, Newark, New Jersey, m, 1955 **DISCIPLINE** EDUCATION **EDUCATION** Kean Coll, BS; NY Univ, MA, PhD, l951-55; New York Univ, NY, MA, 1956-58, PH.D., 1967-71. **CAREER** Kean Coll, prof 1970-80; NY Univ, adj prof; Jersey City State Coll, asst prof; Learning Disability Spec E Orange, teacher, reading consultant; Teachers Coll Columbia Univ, prof of Educ 1980-; Rutgers University, prof (state prof of reading) 1990; Teachers College, prof 1980-90. **HONORS AND AWARDS** Woman of the Year Zeta Phi Beta 1980; Natl Rsch Award Natl Council Teachers English 1972; Founders Day Recognition NY Univ 1971; Outstanding Teacher Educ Reading, Intl Reading Assn, 1985; Award for Outstanding Contribution to Ed, Natl Assn of Univ Women, 1987; emerging literacy, Intl Reading assn, 1989; admin & supvr, reading programs, Teachers Coll Press, 1989; Elected Reading Hall of Fame, International Reading Assn, 1990; Distinguished Alumni Award, New York University, 1990; Outstanding Alumni Award, Kean College of NJ, 1990; National Council of Teachers of English Award for Research; Rewey Bell Inglis Award as Outstanding Woman in English Education; Recipient, IN Univ Citation, Outstanding Contributions to Literacy, 1998. **MEMBERSHIPS** Teacher, East Orange, NJ, 1955-61; reading specialist, East Orange, NJ, 1961-66; Jersey City State Coll, Jersey City, NJ, 1966-70; bd of dir Natl Council Teachers English; Educ advisory bd Early Years Magazine; chmn Early Childhood Educ; mem Journal Reading Instructor, Websters New World Dictionary, commission Sprint Magazine; pres Intl Reading Assoc 1978-79; mem Natl Comm Ed Migrant Children; trustee, Research Found, Natl Council Teachers English, 1983-86. **SELECTED PUBLICATIONS** Author, editor, or co-editor, Language Literacy and the Child, Process Reading and Writing: A Literature Based Approach, Emerging Literacy: Young Children Learn to Read and Write, The Administration and Supervision of Reading Programs, Educating Black Children: America's Challenge, Family Storybook Reading, Listen Children: An Anthology of Black Literature, Families: An Anthology of Poetry for Young Children; Publications: Literacy Instruction in Half Day and Full Day Kindergartens, Newark, DE Intl Reading Assn, Morrow LM, Strickland, DS, & Woo, D, 1998; Teaching Phonics Today, Newark, DE, Intl Reading Assn, Strickland DS, 1998. **CONTACT ADDRESS** Professor of Reading, Rutgers Univ, 10 Seminary Place, New Brunswick, NJ, 08903.

STRICKLAND, RUTH ANN
PERSONAL Born 09/23/1959, Goldsboro, NC **DISCIPLINE** POLITICAL SCIENCE **EDUCATION** Univ of Southern California, PhD, 89. **CAREER** Prof, Appalachian State Univ, 10 years. **HONORS AND AWARDS** Inducted into the Acad of Outstanding Teachers, Coll of Arts and Sciences, 98. **MEMBERSHIPS** Amer Political Science Assn; NC Political Sci Assn. **RESEARCH** Amer natl government; public policy analysis; judicial process. **SELECTED PUBLICATIONS** Auth, "The Incivility of Mandated Drug Treatment through Civil Commitments," Politics and Life Sciences, Mar 96; coauth, "North Carolina v. Robert Lee Carter: Good Faith Exceptions and New Judicial Federalism in North Carolina," Albany Law Review, v 59, n 5, 96; coauth, "The NAFTA(-ization) of Sexual Harassment: The Experiences of Canada, Mexico, and the United States," NAFTA: Law and Business Review Jour of the Americas, Spring 97; coauth, Contemporary World Issues: Campaign and Election Reform: A Reference Handbook, 1997; auth, "Abortion: Pro-choice versus Pro-life, " in Moral Controversies in American Politics: Cases in Social Regulatory Policy, 1998. **CONTACT ADDRESS** Dept of Political Sci & Criminal Justice, Appalachian State Univ, Boone, NC, 28608. **EMAIL** strcklndra@appstate.edu

STRICKLIN, DAVID
DISCIPLINE HISTORY **EDUCATION** Baylor Univ, BA, MA; Tulane Univ, PhD. **CAREER** Asst prof, Lyon Col. **RESEARCH** Southern cult; Am relig; vernacular music. **SELECTED PUBLICATIONS** Auth, A Genealogy of Dissent: The Culture of Southern Baptist Protest in the Twentieth Century, UP KY. **CONTACT ADDRESS** Dept of Hist, Lyon Col, 300 Highland Rd, PO Box 2317, Batesville, AR, 72503.

STRIKER, CECIL LEOPOLD
PERSONAL Born 07/15/1932, Cincinnati, OH, m, 1968 **DISCIPLINE** HISTORY OF ART, ARCHAEOLOGY **EDUCATION** Oberlin Col, BA, 56; NY Univ, MA, 60, PhD, 68. **CAREER** From instr to asst prof hist of art, Vassar Col, 62-68; assoc prof, 68-78, prof hist of art, Univ Penn, 78-; field rep, Dumbarton Oaks Ctr Byzantine Studies, 66-, vis fel, 70-71; co-dir, Kalenderhane Archaeol Proj, Turkey, 66-; art historian in residence, Am Acad Rome, 70-71; co-investr, Greek Medieval Dendrochronological Proj, 76-; pres, Am Res Inst Turkey, 77-. **HONORS AND AWARDS** Am Acad Rome, Art Historian in Residence, 71; Koldewey Gesellschaft, 80; German Archaeol Inst, corresp mem, 85. **MEMBERSHIPS** Col Art Asn Am; Archaeol Inst Am; Asn Field Archaeol; Koldewey Gesellschaft. **RESEARCH** Early Christian, Byzantine and early medieval art, architecture and archaeology. **SELECTED PUBLICATIONS** Auth, Applied Proportions in Later Byzantine Architecture, Studien zur Byzantinischen Kunstgeschichte, Amsterdam, 95; ed, Architectural Studies in memory of Richard Krautheimer, Mainz, 96; auth, Richard Krautheimer and the Study of Early Christian and Byzantine Architecture, In Memoriam Richard Krautheimer: Relazioni della Giornata di Studi, Roma, Palazzo dei Conservatori, 97; auth and co-ed, Kalenderhane in Istanbul: The Buildings, Their history, Architecture and Decoration, Mainz, 97. **CONTACT ADDRESS** Dept of Hist of Art, Univ of Pa, 3405 Woodland Walk, Philadelphia, PA, 19104-6208. **EMAIL** cstriker@sas.upenn.edu

STRIPLING, LUTHER
PERSONAL Born 08/25/1935, Tingnall, Georgia, w, 1957 **DISCIPLINE** MUSIC **EDUCATION** Clark Coll, AB 1957; Atlanta Univ, attended 1960-65; Univ KY, MMus 1968; Univ CO, DMus 1971. **CAREER** Hamilton HS, teacher 1957-66, chmn music dept 1960-66; GA Interscholastic Assn, chmn vocal div 1964-66; Univ KY, instructor 1966-68; Univ CO, 1970-71; Macalester Coll, coordinator vocal activities 1971; So IL Univ at Edwardsville, assoc prof of music/dir of opera workshop; Tarrant County Jr Coll NE Campus, 1984-95; professor of vocal music/dir, Bel Canto Singles, currently. **MEMBERSHIPS** Pres MN chapter Natl Opera Assn Inc; general dir Macalester Coll Opera Workshop; assn general dir Assoc Coll of the Twin Cities Opera Workshop; minister of music Pilgrim Baptist Church; pres St Louis Dist Chapter of Natl Assn of Teachers of Singing 1980-82; numerous performances orchestral appearances directing papers in field; mem, bd of governors, NE Trinity Arts Council, 1989-91. **SELECTED PUBLICATIONS** Contributor Burkhart Charles Anthology for Musical Analysis 3rd Ed NY Holt Rinehart & Winston 1978. **CONTACT ADDRESS** Professor of Music, Tarrant Cnty Jr Coll NE, 828 Harwood Rd, FAB 147, Hurst, TX, 76053.

STROCCHIA, SHARON T.
DISCIPLINE HISTORY **EDUCATION** Stanford Univ, BA, 72; Univ Calif Berkeley, MA, 73, PhD, 81. **CAREER** Assoc prof **RESEARCH** Social and cultural history of Renaissance Italy; women, gender, and family in 15th-century Florence; the use of feminist theory for Renaissance studies; social history of nuns and nunneries in Renaissance Florence. **SELECTED PUBLICATIONS** Auth, Death and Ritual in Renaissance Florence. **CONTACT ADDRESS** Dept History, Emory Univ, 221 Bowden Hall, 561 Kilgo Cir, Atlanta, GA, 30322-1950. **EMAIL** sstrocc@emory.edu

STROHL, JANE E.
DISCIPLINE CHURCH HISTORY **EDUCATION** Vassar Col, BA; Lutheran Theol Sem at Gettysburg, MDiv; Univ Chicago Divinity Sch, MA, PhD. **MEMBERSHIPS** Mem, Intl Lutheran-Orthodox Joint Comm; Amer Acad Rel; Amer Soc of Church Hist; Lutheran Women's Caucus. **RESEARCH** Reformation history. **SELECTED PUBLICATIONS** Auth, God's Life-Giving Promise, Creation Is a Continuing Event, 87; The Call to Ministry of Word and Sacrament, Serving the Word: Lutheran Women Consider Their Calling, Marilyn Preus, 88; Martin Luther, Daily Readings from Spiritual Classics, Paul Ofstedal, 90; Ministry in the Middle Ages and Reformation, Called and Ordained: Lutheran Perspectives on the Office of the Ministry, 90. **CONTACT ADDRESS** Dept of Church History, Pacific Lutheran Theol Sem, 2770 Marin Ave, Berkeley, CA, 94708-1597. **EMAIL** jstrohl@plts.edu

STROKER, WILLIAM DETTWILLER
PERSONAL Born 05/23/1938, Paris, KY, m, 1967, 1 child **DISCIPLINE** NEW TESTAMENT STUDIES, HELLENISTIC RELIGIONS, EARLY CHRISTIANITY **EDUCATION** Transylvania Univ, BA, 60; Yale Univ, BD, 63, MA, 66, PhD, 70. **CAREER** From instr to asst prof, 69-76, assoc prof Relig, 76-82, PROF RELIG, DREW UNIV, 82-. **HONORS AND AWARDS** Scholar-Teacher of the Year, Drew Univ, 89. **MEMBERSHIPS** Soc Bibl Lit. **RESEARCH** Post-Canonical traditions about Jesus; religious thought of the hellenistic period; Pauline theology and influence. **SELECTED PUBLICATIONS** Auth, Postcanonical Sayings of Jesus, 89. **CONTACT ADDRESS** Dept of Relig, Drew Univ, 36 Madison Ave, Madison, NJ, 07940-1493. **EMAIL** WStroker@Drew.edu

STROM, SHARON HARTMAN
PERSONAL Born 12/24/1941, Oakland, CA, 4 children **DISCIPLINE** AMERICAN SOCIAL HISTORY **EDUCATION** Whittier Col, BA, 63; Cornell Univ, MA, 69, PhD(hist), 70. **CAREER** Lectr hist, State Univ NY Stony Brook, 69-70; asst prof, 70-75, assoc prof hist, Univ RI, 75-80, full prof, 80-. **MEMBERSHIPS** Orgn Am Historians. **RESEARCH** Labor history; history of women. **SELECTED PUBLICATIONS** Auth, Leadership and Tactics in the American Woman Suffrage Movement, J Am Hist, 9/75; coauth, Moving the Mountain: Women Working for Social Change, Feminist Press, 80; Beyond the Typewriter: Gender, Class, and Office Work, Univ of Ill, 92. **CONTACT ADDRESS** Dept of Hist, Univ of RI, Kingston, RI, 02881. **EMAIL** csstrom@uri.acc.uri.edu

STROMBERG, PETER G.
PERSONAL Born 10/28/1952, Minneapolis, MN, m, 1992, 2 children **DISCIPLINE** CULTURAL ANTHROPOLOGY **EDUCATION** Purdue Univ, BS/BA, 74; Stanford Univ, PhD, 81. **CAREER** Vis Asst Prof, Univ Ariz, 84-87; Asst Prof, Univ Tulsa, 87-92; Assoc Prof, Dept of Anthrop, Univ Tulsa, 92-; Ch, Dept of Anthrop, 97-. **HONORS AND AWARDS** MINH Post-doctoral Fellow, Univ Calif, san Diego, 81; NIMH Postdoc Fellow, Univ Calif-Berkeley, 83. **MEMBERSHIPS** Am Anthrop Asn. **RESEARCH** Religion; contemporary society; social theory; psychological anthropology. **SELECTED PUBLICATIONS** Auth, Language and Self-Transformation: A Study of the Christian Conversion Narrative, Cambridge Univ Press, 93; co-auth, Representation and Reality in the Study of Culture, Am Anthrop, 99, 123-124, 97; Theories of the Transcendent, Rev in Anthrop, in press. **CONTACT ADDRESS** Dept of Anthrop, Univ Tulsa, Tulsa, OK, 74104. **EMAIL** peter-stromberg@utulsa.edu

STRONG, DOUGLAS HILLMAN
PERSONAL Born 10/07/1935, San Francisco, CA, m, 3 children **DISCIPLINE** AMERICAN & ENVIRONMENTAL HISTORY **EDUCATION** Univ Calif, Berkeley, BA, 58, MA, 59; Syracuse Univ, PhD(soc sci), 64. **CAREER** From asst prof to assoc prof, 64-68, PROF HIST, SAN DIEGO STATE UNIV, 71- **RESEARCH** California environmental history; national park history. **SELECTED PUBLICATIONS** Auth, The Sierra Forest Reserve: The movement to preserve the San Joaquin Valley watershed, Calif Hist Soc Quart, 3/67; Trees--or Timber? The Story of Sequoia and Kings Canyon National Parks, Sequoia Natural Hist Asn, 68; The Conservationists, Addison-Wesley, 71; These Happy Grounds: A History of the Lassen Region, Loomis Mus, 73; Teaching American environmental history, Social Studies, 10/74; Ethics or expediency: An environmental question, Environ Affairs, spring 76; Ralph H Cameron and the Grand Canyon, Arizona & the West, spring/summer 78; Preservation efforts at Lake Tahoe, Forest Hist, 4/81; Stopping Time--A Rephotographic Survey Of Lake-Tahoe, Calif Hist, Vol 72, 93; The Birth Of The Sierra-Club, Calif Hist, Vol 71, 92. **CONTACT ADDRESS** Dept of Hist, San Diego State Univ, San Diego, CA, 92182.

STRONG, DOUGLAS M.
PERSONAL Born 09/27/1956, Buffalo, NY, m, 1986, 2 children **DISCIPLINE** HISTORY OF CHRISTIANITY **EDUCATION** Houghton Col, BA, 78; Princeton Theological Seminary, Mdiv, 81, PhD, 90. **CAREER** PROF OF HIST OF CHRISTIANITY, WESLEY THEOLOGICAL SEMINARY, 89-. **MEMBERSHIPS** Am Acad of Religion; Am Soc of Church Hist; Am Hist Asn; Wesleyan Theological Soc. **RESEARCH** 19th Century American religious history. **SELECTED PUBLICATIONS** Auth, Reading Christian Ethics: A Historical Sourcebook, Westminster John Knox, 96; auth, They Walked in the spirit: Personal Faith and Social Action in America, Westminster John Knox, 97; auth, Perfectionist Politics: Abolitionism and the Religious Tensions of American Democracy. **CONTACT ADDRESS** Wesley Theol Sem, 4500 Massachusetts Ave NW, Washington, DC, 20016.

STRONG, JOHN A.
PERSONAL Born 10/03/1935, Cooperstown, NY, m, 1961, 2 children **DISCIPLINE** HISTORY **EDUCATION** Syracuse Univ, MA, 59, PhD(hist), 68. **CAREER** Assoc prof, 65-80, PROF HIST & AM STUDIES, SOUTHAMPTON COL, LONG ISLAND UNIV, 80- **MEMBERSHIPS** AHA; African Studies Asn. **RESEARCH** African history; American social and cultural history. **SELECTED PUBLICATIONS** Auth, Indian-White relations in seventeenth century Virginia, Maxwell Rev, 12/64; Emerging ideological patterns among Southern African refugees, Africa Today, summer 67; The Imposition Of Colonial Jurisdiction Over The Montauk Indians Of Long-Island, Ethnohist, Vol 41, 94. **CONTACT ADDRESS** Dept of Soc Sci, Southampton Col Long Island Univ, 239 Montauk Hwy, Southampton, NY, 11968-4198.

STRONG, JOHN S.
PERSONAL Born 08/28/1956, Philadelphia, PA, m, 1996 **DISCIPLINE** ECONOMICS **EDUCATION** Washington & Lee Univ, BA, 78; Harvard Univ, MPP, 81, Phd, 86. **CAREER** PROF, SCHOOL OF BUSINESS, COL OF WILLIAM AND MARY, 85-; visiting prof, Harvard Univ, 89-90; visiting scholar, Harvard Inst for Int Development, 93. **HONORS AND AWARDS** Fulbright Scholar, 78-79; Phi Beta Kappa; Nat Sci Found Grad Fel, 79-82. **MEMBERSHIPS** Am Economic Asn; Am Fin Asn. **RESEARCH** Transport economics. **SELECTED PUBLICATIONS** Coauth, Moving to Market: Restructuring Transport in the Former Soviet Union, Harvard Univ Press, 96; coauth, Why Airplanes Crash: Aviation Safety in a Changing World, Oxford Univ Press, 92. **CONTACT ADDRESS** School of Business, Col of William and Mary, Williamsburg, VA, 23187. **EMAIL** jsstro@dogwood.tyler.wm.edu

STRONG-BOAG, VERONICA
PERSONAL Born 07/05/1947, Scotland **DISCIPLINE** HISTORY/WOMEN'S STUDIES **EDUCATION** Univ Toronto, BA, 70; Carleton Univ, MA, 71; Univ Toronto, PhD, 75. **CAREER** Hist/Women's Stud School, dept hist, Trent Univ, 74-76; Concordia Univ, 76-80; dept hist & women's stud prog, Simon Fraser Univ, 80-91; dir, Ctr Res Women's Stud & Gender Rel, 91-97, PROF EDUCATIONAL STUDIES, UNIV BC, 91-. **HONORS AND AWARDS** John A. Macdonald Prize, Can Hist Asn **MEMBERSHIPS** Can Hist Asn (pres, 93-93) **SELECTED PUBLICATIONS** Auth, The Parliament of Women, 76; auth, A Woman with a Purpose, 80; auth, The New Day Recalled: Lives of Girls and Women in English Canada 1919-1939, 88; co-ed, True Daughters of the North, 80; co-ed, Rethinking Canada, 86, 91, 98; co-ed, British Columbia Reconsidered, 92; co-ed, Janey Canuck: Women in Canada 1919-1939, 94. **CONTACT ADDRESS** Dept Educ Stud, Univ BC, Vancouver, BC, V6T 1Z1. **EMAIL** stbg@unixg.ubc.ca

STROUD, RONALD SIDNEY
PERSONAL Born 07/08/1933, Toronto, ON, Canada, m, 1963, 2 children **DISCIPLINE** CLASSICS **EDUCATION** Univ Toronto, BA, 57; Univ Calif, Berkeley, PhD(classics), 65. **CAREER** Secy, Am Sch Class Studies Athens, 60-63; from asst prof to assoc prof, 65-72, Prof Classics, Univ Calif, Berkeley, 72-, Am Philos Soc, Am Coun Learned Socs & Guggenheim fels, 77-78. **RESEARCH** Greek history; Greek epigraphy; classical archaeology. **SELECTED PUBLICATIONS** Auth, Tribal Boundary Markers from Corinth, Calif Studies Class Antiq, 68; Drakon's Law on Homicide, Univ Calif, 68; An Ancient Fort on Mt Oneion, 71 & Inscriptions from the North Slope of the Acropolis, 71 & 72, Hesperia; Thucydides and the Battle of Solygeia, Calif Studies Class Antiq, 71; An Athenian Law on Silver Coinage, Hesperia, 74; The Axones and Kyrbeis of Drakon and Solon, Univ Calif, 79; Athenian Economy And Society--A Banking Perspective, Mnemosyne, Vol 49, 96; co-ed, Supplementum Epigraphieum Graecum, Vol 26, 79, Vol 27, 80 & Vol 28, 82. **CONTACT ADDRESS** Dept Classics, Univ Calif, Berkeley, CA, 94720.

STROUP, RODGER EMERSON
PERSONAL Born 10/04/1946, St. Louis, MO, m, 1968, 1 child **DISCIPLINE** AMERICAN HISTORY **EDUCATION** Wofford Col, BA, 68; Univ SC, MA, 72, PhD(hist), 80. **CAREER** Grad asst Am hist, Univ SC, 70-72, teaching asst world & US hist, 72-74; dir & cur, Hist Columbia Found, 74-79; CUR HIST, SC STATE MUS, 79-, Consult, Am Asn State & Local Hist, 79-. **RESEARCH** South Carolina material culture studies. **SELECTED PUBLICATIONS** Auth, Before and after: Three letters from E B Heyward, SC Hist Mag, 4/73; The naval policy of England's liberal government 1906, 73 & John L McLaurin: Independent Tillmanite, 75, Proc SC Hist Asn; Upcountry patron: Wade Hampton II, In: Artist in the Lives of South Carolina, Carolina Art Asn, 78; Columbia And Richland County--A South-Carolina Community, 1740-1990, J Of Am Hist, Vol 81, 94. **CONTACT ADDRESS** Dept of Hist, SC State Mus, Columbia, SC, 29211.

STRUEVER, NANCY SCHERMERHORN
PERSONAL La Salle, IL **DISCIPLINE** RENAISSANCE INTELLECTUAL HISTORY **EDUCATION** Univ Rochester, BA, 54, MA, 57, PhD(hist), 66. **CAREER** Inst hist, Rochester Inst Technol, 62-63; from instr to assoc prof, Hobart & William Smith Cols, 64-73; assoc prof, 73-78, PROF HIST, JOHNS HOPKINS UNIV, 78-, Am Coun Learned Soc fel, 72-73; fel, Ctr Humanities, Wesleyan Univ, 73. **MEMBERSHIPS** AHA **RESEARCH** Linguistics and history. **SELECTED PUBLICATIONS** Auth, The Language of History in the Renaissance, Princeton Univ, 70; The study of language and the study of history, J Interdisciplinary Hist, 74; Perfect Friendship--Studies In Literature And Moral-Philosophy From Boccaccio To Corneille, Sixteenth Cent J, Vol 26, 95. **CONTACT ADDRESS** Dept of Hist, Johns Hopkins Univ, 3400 N Charles St, Baltimore, MD, 21218.

STRUM, PHILIPPA
PERSONAL Born 12/14/1938, New York, NY, 1 child **DISCIPLINE** POLITICAL SCIENCE **EDUCATION** Grad Facul of the New Sch, PhD, 64. **CAREER** Res fel, Harvard Univ, summer, 60; lectr to instr, Brooklyn Col, 62-64; lectr, The New Sch, summer 62 & 63; instr to assoc prof, Rutgers Univ, Newark, 64-72; assoc prof, Brooklyn Col, 72-75; acting chair, Brooklyn Col, 74-75; vis prof, Barnard Col, 78-79; vis scholar, NY Univ, 82-83; res fel, Truman Inst of Hebrew Univ, 85-86; Dubach Vis Distinguished Prof, Ore State Univ, Apr 11-15, 88; Fulbright sr lectr, Bogazici Univ, Istanbul, Spr, 95; Lyons Distinguished Vis Prof, Va Commonwealth Univ, Apr, 97; fel, Woodrow Wilson Intl Ctr for Scholars, 97-98; prof, City Univ of NY, Brooklyn Col and the Grad Ctr, 74-98; Broeklundian prof, polit sci, City Univ of NY, Brooklyn Col and the Grad Ctr, 98-. **HONORS AND AWARDS** Fel, Woodrow Wilson Ctr, 97-98; Scholar's Incentive Award, Brooklyn Col, Spr 96-Aut 97; Fulbright Tchg Fel, Turkey, Spr, 95; Hughes-Gosset Award for Hist Excellence, Jour of Supreme Ct Hist, 94; fel, Woodrow Wilson Ctr, Wash, DC, 97-98; City Univ of NY Facul Res Award Prog, 94-95. **MEMBERSHIPS** Amer Polit Sci Asn; Amer Civ Liberties Un. **RESEARCH** Civil liberties and human rights; American constitutional law and government; Women and politics; Women in U.S., Israel and Palestine. **SELECTED PUBLICATIONS** Auth, West Bank Women and the Intifada: Revolution within the Revolution, ed Suha Sabbah, Palestinian Women of Gaza and the West Bank, Ind Univ Press, 98; Rights, Responsibilities and the Social Contract, ed Hunter and Mack, Intl Rights and Responsibilities for the Future, Praeger, 96; Human Rights and Gender Issues, Women's Studies Rev, Istanbul, 95; The Road Not Taken: Constitutional Non-decision Making in 1948-1950 and Its Impact on Civil Liberties in the Israeli Political Culture, ed Troen and Lucas, Israel: The First Decade of Independence, SUNY Press, 95; Harry Andrew Blackmun, Ruth Bader Ginsburg, Louis Dembitz Brandeis, ed Melvin I. Urofsky, Biog Dict of US Supreme Ct Justices, Garland Publ, 94; Civil Liberties, ed Bacon, Davidson and Keller, The Encycl of the US Congress, Simon & Schuster, 94; American Civilization and the Social Contract, occasional paper, Brandeis Univ Women's Studies Prog, 94; Louis D. Brandeis: The People's Attorney, 81, Amer Jewish Hist, 94; Louis D. Brandeis as Lawyer and Judge, Jour of Supreme Ct Hist, 93; Louis Dembitz Brandeis, ed Cushman, The Supreme Court Justices, 1789-1993, Supreme Ct Hist Soc/Cong Quart, 93. **CONTACT ADDRESS** 124 W. 79th St., New York, NY, 10024. **EMAIL** pstrum@broadway.gc.cuny.edu

STRUVE, WALTER
PERSONAL Born 05/06/1935, Somers Point, NJ, m, 1959 **DISCIPLINE** EUROPEAN HISTORY, GERMAN STUDIES **EDUCATION** Lafayette Col, AB, 55; Yale Univ, MA, 57, PhD(mod Europ hist), 63. **CAREER** Instr hist, Princeton Univ, 61-64; from instr to assoc prof, 64-82, PROF HIST, CITY COL NEW YORK, 82-, Res grants, City Univ New York, 67, 71, 73-76 & 81, Am Philos Soc, 68-69, Ger Acad Exchange Serv, 78, Fulbright, Ger, 78-79 & Fritz Thyssen Found, 79-80. **MEMBERSHIPS** Conf Group Cent Europ Hist; AHA; Immigration Hist Soc; Conf Group Int Labor & Working-Class Hist; Soc Ger-Am Studies. **RESEARCH** German history; US immigration; history of white-collar unionism. **SELECTED PUBLICATIONS** Auth, Elites Against Democracy: Leadership Ideals in Bourgeois Political Thought in Germany, 1890-1933, Princeton Univ, 73; The Republic of Texas, Bremen, and the

Hildesheim District: A Contribution to the History of Emigration, Commerce, and Social Change in the Nineteenth Century, August Lax, Hildesheim, Ger, 82; Jews And The German State--The Political-History Of A Minority, 1848-1933, German Studies Rev, Vol 19, 96; Emigrant Agencies And Emigrant Associations In The 19th-Century And 20th-Century, German Studies Rev, Vol 16, ; The German Communists And The Rise Of Nazism, German Studies Rev, Vol 15, 92. **CONTACT ADDRESS** 2727 Palisade Ave, Bronx, NY, 10463.

STUART, JACK
PERSONAL Born 04/24/1937, Brooklyn, NY **DISCIPLINE** UNITED STATES HISTORY **EDUCATION** Brooklyn Col, AB, 59; Columbia Univ, PhD(hist), 68. **CAREER** Asst prof, 67-72, assoc prof, 72-78, PROF HIST, CALIF STATE UNIV, LONG BEACH, 78- **MEMBERSHIPS** AHA; Study Group Int Labor & Working Class Hist. **RESEARCH** United States social history; labor history; radical history. **SELECTED PUBLICATIONS** Auth, William English Walling and the search for an American socialist theory, Sci & Soc, summer 71; Realities of the Truman Presidency, 75; Man Of The People--A Life Of Harry S. Truman, Am Hist Rev, Vol 102, 97. **CONTACT ADDRESS** Dept of Hist, California State Univ, Long Beach, 1250 N Bellflower, Long Beach, CA, 90840-0001.

STUEWER, ROGER H.
PERSONAL Born 09/12/1934, Shawano, WI, m, 1960, 2 children **DISCIPLINE** HISTORY OF PHYSICS **EDUCATION** Univ Wis, PhD(hist sci & physics), 68. **CAREER** Instr physics, Heidelberg Col, 60-62; from asst prof to assoc prof hist physics & physics, Univ Minn, Minneapolis, 67-71; assoc prof hist sci, Boston Univ, 71-72; assoc prof hist physics & physics, 72-74, prof hist sci, Univ Minn, Minneapolis, 74-, Am Coun Learned Soc fel, 74-75; hon res assoc, Harvard Univ, 74-75; ed, Am J Physics Resource Letters. **HONORS AND AWARDS** AAAS fel, 83; Am Phyts Soc fel, 91; George Taylor Distinguised Service Award, Univ Minnesota, 90; Am Assn Phy Teachers Distinguished Service Citation, 90; Sigma Xi Distinguished Lecturer, 97-99. **MEMBERSHIPS** Hist Sci Soc (secy, 72-77); Am Physics Soc; Brit Soc Hist Sci; AAAS. **RESEARCH** History of 19th and 20th century physics; history of quantum theory; optics; nuclear physics. **CONTACT ADDRESS** Sch of Physics and Astron, Univ of Minnesota, 116 Church St SE, Minneapolis, MN, 55455-0149. **EMAIL** rstuewer@physics.spa.umn.edu

STUNKEL, KENNETH REAGAN
PERSONAL Born 09/08/1932, Ft Worth, TX, m, 1971, 3 children **DISCIPLINE** ASIAN & EUROPEAN INTELLECTUAL HISTORY **EDUCATION** Univ Md, BA, 54, MA, 59, PhD, 66. **CAREER** Assoc prof, 65-75, PROF HIST, MONMOUTH COL NJ, 75-, DEAN, SCH HUMANITIES & SOC SCI, 80-86, 93-; Lectr hist & philos, Univ Col, Far E Div & Univ Md, 73-74. **MEMBERSHIPS** Asn Asian Studies; AHA; Int Studies Asn. **RESEARCH** Impact of Sanskrit scholarship on European culture, 1785-1840; comparative Chinese and European intellectual history, especially with respect to science; Japanese environmental problems; Skepticism in early Modern Europe; The Thought of Lewis Mumford; Coherence in the humanities. **CONTACT ADDRESS** Dept of Hist, Monmouth Univ, 400 Cedar Ave, West Long Branch, NJ, 07764-1898. **EMAIL** kstunkel@mondec.monmouth.edu

STURGEON, MARY C.
DISCIPLINE ART HISTORY **EDUCATION** Bryn Mawr Col, PhD. **CAREER** Prof, ch, dept Art, Univ NC, Chapel Hill. **RESEARCH** Archaic, class and hellenistic sculpture; Greek painting. **SELECTED PUBLICATIONS** Auth, The Reliefs from the Theater in Ancient Corinth, Princeton Univ, 77; Sculptures from the Sanctuary of Poseidon at Isthmia, Princeton Univ, 87; The Corinth Amazon: Formation of a Roman Classical Sculpture, Am J of Archaeol 99, 95. **CONTACT ADDRESS** Univ N. Carolina, Chapel Hill, Chapel Hill, NC, 27599. **EMAIL** sturgeon@email.unc.edu

STURGILL, CLAUDE C.
PERSONAL Born 12/09/1933, Glo, KY **DISCIPLINE** EARLY MODERN EUROPE **EDUCATION** Univ Ky, AB, 56, MA, 59, PhD, 63. **CAREER** Instr, Univ Ky, 61; asst prof Europ hist, Western Ky State Col, 62-64; asst prof early mod Europe, Wis State Univ, Oshkosh, 64-66; assoc prof French hist, E Carolina Univ, 66-69; assoc prof, 69-77, PROF 18th CENTURY EUROP HIST, UNIV, FLA, 77-, Wis State Univ Regents' grant, 64-65; Nat Endowment for Humanities fel, 68; councilor, Int Comn Mil Hist, 71-; secygen, US Comn Mil Hist, 73-79; Fulbright prof, France 80; prof Centre de Recherches sur la Civilisation de l'Europe Moderne, Univ de Paris IV (Sorbonne), 80. **HONORS AND AWARDS** Int Comn Mil Hist medal for fostering int cooperation, 76. **MEMBERSHIPS** AHA; Soc Hist France; US Comn Mil Hist. **RESEARCH** Administrative history of the French army, 1700-1730. **SELECTED PUBLICATIONS** Auth, Marshal Villars in the War of the Spanish Succession, Univ Ky, 65; coauth, A Guidebook to the History of the Western World, Heath, 67, 69 & 76; ed-in-chief, Proceedings on the Interuniversity Consortium on Revolutionary Europe, 1750-1850, 73, 74, 75 & auth, Claude Le Blanc: Civil Servant of the King, 76, Univ Fla; La Formation de la Milice Permanente en France, 1726-1730, Ser Hist de l'Armee, Paris, 77; ed, Rolle's Petition, Univ Fla, 78; L'Organisation et l'Administration de la Marechaussee et de la Justice Prevotale, 1720-1730, Ser Hist de l'Armee, Paris, 80; Soldiers--Disciplinary Laboratory--The Army Of Piedmont In The 18th-Century, Am Hist Rev, Vol 98, 93; The War Of The Austrian Succession, Am Hist Rev, Vol 100, 95. **CONTACT ADDRESS** Div of Humanities Dept of Hist, Univ of Fla, 4131 GPA, Gainesville, FL, 32611.

STURSBERG, PETER
PERSONAL Born 08/31/1913, Chefoo, China **DISCIPLINE** CANADIAN STUDIES **EDUCATION** McGill Univ **CAREER** Journalist, 34-40; ed & war correspondent, CBC, 41-45; foreign correspondent, var publs, 45-57, 73-80; commentator, CTV, 60-73; instr, Can stud, 80-88, adj prof, Simon Fraser Univ, 82-88 (RETIRED). **HONORS AND AWARDS** Can Radio Award, 50; mem, Order Can, 96. **RESEARCH** Canadian studies; communications; political history. **SELECTED PUBLICATIONS** Auth, Journey Into Victory, 1944; auth, Agreement in Principle, 61; auth, Those Were The Days, 69; auth, Mister Broadcasting, 71; auth, Diefenbaker Leadership Gained 1956-62, 75; auth, Diefenbaker Leadership Lost 1962-67, 76; auth, Lester Pearson and the American Dilemma, 80; auth, EXTRA! When the Papers Had the Only News, 82; auth, Gordon Shrum, 86; auth, The Golden Hope, 87; auth, Roland Michener: The Last Viceroy, 89; auth, The Sound of War, 93. **CONTACT ADDRESS** 5132 Alderfield Pl, West Vancouver, BC, V7W 2W7.

STURTEVANT, DAVID REEVES
PERSONAL Born 09/20/1926, Zanesville, OH, m, 1947, 3 children **DISCIPLINE** HISTORY **EDUCATION** Muskingum Col, BA, 50; Stanford Univ, MA, 51, PhD, 58. **CAREER** From Asst Prof to Prof, 55-94, Prof Emeritus Hist, Muskingum Col, 94-; conducted grad seminars, Ataneo de Manila Univ & Univ Philippines; vis prof Philippine hist, Univ Hawaii, 76-77. **HONORS AND AWARDS** Fulbright res grant, Philippines, 65-66; Am Coun Learned Soc-Soc Sci Res Coun res grant, Asia, 70. **MEMBERSHIPS** Asn Asian Studies. **RESEARCH** East Asian history, especially southeast Asia, particularly the Philippine Islands. **SELECTED PUBLICATIONS** Auth, Sakdalism and Philippine radicalism, J Asian Studies, 2/62; Guardia de Honor: Revitalization within the revolution, Asian Studies, 8/66; No uprising fails, Solidarity, 10/66; Epilog for an old Colorum, Solidarity, 8/68; Agrarian Unrest in the Philippines, Ctr Int Studies, Ohio Univ, 69; Popular Uprisings in the Philippines, 1840-1940, Cornell Univ, 76. **CONTACT ADDRESS** Dept of Hist, Muskingum Col, 153 Stormont St, New Concord, OH, 43762-1199.

SUCHLICKI, JAIME
PERSONAL Born 12/08/1939, Havana, Cuba, m, 1964, 3 children **DISCIPLINE** MODERN HISTORY **EDUCATION** Univ Miami, AB, 64, MA, 65; Tex Christian Univ, PhD(Hist), 67 Pr. **CAREER** Res asst, Ctr Advan Int Studies, 64-65, asst prof Hist & res assoc, 67-70, lectr, Caribbean Area Studies sem, 67-68, assoc prof & assoc dir, Inst Inter Am Studies, 70-76, prof Hist & dir Latin Am Studies, Univ Miami, 76-. **MEMBERSHIPS** Conf Latin Am Hist; Am Acad Polit Sci; Latin Am Studies Asn. **RESEARCH** Latin American history; Caribbean affairs; student movements. **SELECTED PUBLICATIONS** Auth, The Cuban Revolution: A Documentary Bibliography, 1952-1968, Ctr Advan Int Studies, 68; University Students and Revolution in Cuba, 1920-1968, 69 & ed, Cuba, Castro and Revolution, 72, Univ Miami; auth, Recent research on student violence in Latin America, Latin Am Res Rev, Fall 72; A Documentary Guide to the Cuban Revolution, Univ Miami, 73; Cuba: From Columbus to Castro, Brassey's, 97; Mexico: From Montezuma to Nafta, Brassey's, 96. **CONTACT ADDRESS** Sch of Int Studies, Univ of Miami, PO Box 248106, Miami, FL, 33124-8106. **EMAIL** wooobie777@aol.com

SUDERBURG, ROBERT
DISCIPLINE MUSIC **EDUCATION** Univ Minnesota, BA; Yale Sch Mus, MM; Univ Pa, PhD. **CAREER** Prof; composer-in-residence; dir, Group for 20th century Mus, Nat Young Composers Competition, Williams Col; taught at, Bryn Mawr, Univ Pa, Philadelphia Mus Acad; co-dir, Contemp Mus Group, Univ Wash; chancellor, NC Sch of the Arts; pres, Cornish Inst; Williams Col 85-; NEA, Composers Panel, 75-81. **HONORS AND AWARDS** Guggenheim fel (2); NEA prizes (2); awd(s) & commissions, BMI, ASCAP, Rockefeller Found, Amer Mus Ctr, Hindemith Found, Seattle Symphony, Washington State Arts Commn, ITG (2)., Bio appeared, Amer Grove Dictionary of Mus. **SELECTED PUBLICATIONS** Comp, Chamber Musics I-XI; SIX MOMENTS for solo piano; rec(s), Concerto, within the mirror of time, for piano and orchestra, Columbia; Chamber Music II, Concerto, voyage de nuit d'apres Baudelaire, for voice and chamber orchestra, Vox-Turnabout; Chamber Musics III, Night Set IV, V Steven son, for voice, string quartet and tape, Amer Rec Soc; Chamber Music VII, Rituals, for trumpet and piano, 4 rec(s) Vox, ITG, Coronet & Okla; Chamber Music VIII, 3 rec(s), Vox, Coronet & Okla; Chamber Music XI, Strophes of Night and the Dawn, Fla & Coronet. **CONTACT ADDRESS** Music Dept, Williams Col, Williamstown, MA, 01267.

SUDHIR, PILLARISETTI
DISCIPLINE HISTORY **EDUCATION** Univ London, PhD. **CAREER** Mng ed, Perspectives, Am Hist Asn; previous adj lectr, George Mason Univ. **MEMBERSHIPS** Am Hist Asn. **RESEARCH** Cultural history, computer technology. **SELECTED PUBLICATIONS** Co-ed, Interrogating Modernity: Culture and Colonialism in Modern India, Seagull, 93. **CONTACT ADDRESS** American Historical Assn.

SUELFLOW, AUGUST ROBERT
PERSONAL Born 09/05/1922, Rockfield, WI, m, 1946, 2 children **DISCIPLINE** HISTORY **EDUCATION** Concordia Theol Sem, BA, 44, BD, 46, STM, 47, DD, 67. **CAREER** Asst cur, 46-48, DIR, CONCORDIA HIST INST, 48-95, consult, 95-97, ASSOC ED, QUART, 50-, Asst pastor, Lutheran Mem Church, Richmond Heights, Mo, 48-56; archivist, Western Dist, Lutheran Church-Mo Synod, 48-66, res secy church govt, Surv Comn, 60-62, archivist, Lutheran Church-Mo Synod, Mo Dist, 66-; guest lectr, Concordia Sem, 52-69; asst pastor, Immanuel Lutheran Church, Olivette, 56-58, Mt Olive Lutheran Church, St Louis, Mo, 58-63, interim pastor, 63-65 & 70-72; trustee, Am Microform Acad, 62-75; instr, Wash Univ, 67-; adj prof, Concordia Sem, St Louis, 75-, chmn hist theol dept, 75-81; ed, Heritage in Motion, Concordia, 98. **MEMBERSHIPS** Am Soc Church Hist; fel Soc Am Archivists; Orgn Am Historians; Lutheran Hist Conf (vpres, 62-64, pres, 64-68 & 70-78); Lutheran Soc Worship, Music & Arts. **RESEARCH** History of the Lutheran church in America; church polity; union movements within the church. **SELECTED PUBLICATIONS** Auth, Heart of Missouri, Concordia, 54; contribr, Lutheran Encycl, Augsburg, 54; coauth, Moving Frontiers, Concordia, 64; contribr, Encycl Lutheran Church, Augsburg, 65; ed, Microfilm Index and Bibliography, Concordia Sem, 66; A Preliminary Guide to Church Records Repositories, 69 & auth, Religious archives: An introduction, 80, Soc Am Archivists; ed & transl, Walther's Convention Essays, 81; ed, Walther's Select Writings, 5 vol, Concordia, 81; auth/compiler, Bibliography of Concordia Publ House publ, 1847-1970, cd-rom, 98. **CONTACT ADDRESS** 7249 Northmoor Dr., Saint Louis, MO, 63105.

SUGAR, PETER FRIGYES
PERSONAL Born 01/05/1919, Budapest, Hungary, m, 1955, 3 children **DISCIPLINE** HISTORY **EDUCATION** City Col New York, BA, 54; Princeton Univ, MA, 56, PhD, 59. **CAREER** Instr hist, Princeton Univ, 57-59; from asst prof to assoc prof, 59-71, assoc dir, Inst Comp & Foreign Area Studies, 74-80, PROF HIST, UNIV WASH, 72-, Wilson fel, 54; Am Coun Learned Soc grant-in-aid, 61; Guggenheim fel, 64; mem, Int Sci Bd Bulgarian Res Inst, Vienna. **MEMBERSHIPS** AHA; Am Orient Soc; Am Asn Advan Slavic Studies. **RESEARCH** Eastern European history, especially nationalism; the Ottoman Empire in Near Eastern history. **SELECTED PUBLICATIONS** Auth, Nationalism in Eastern Europe, Univ Wash, 69; ed & coauth, Native Fascism in the Succession States, 1918-1945, ABC-Clio, 71; auth, Southeastern Europe Under Ottoman Rule, 1354-1804, Univ Wash, 77; ed & coauth, Ethnic Diversity and Conflict in Eastern Europe, ABC-Clio, 80; Dynasty, Politics And Culture--Selected Essays, Slavic Rev, Vol 52, 93; Donald W. Treadgold, 1922-94, Slavic Rev, Vol 54, 95; South Slav Nationalisms--Textbooks And Yugoslav Union Before 1914, Slavic Rev, Vol 53, 94; Bosnia-Herzegovina Under The Austro-Hungarian Empire: 1878-1918, The Intelligentsia Between Tradition And Ideology, Am Hist Rev, Vol 101, 96; Sandor Wokerle 1848-1921--The Political-Biography Of A Hungarian Statesman Of The Danube Monarchy, Am Hist Rev, Vol 100, 95; Habsburgs And Ottomans Between Vienna And Belgrade: 1683-1739, Slavic Rev, Vol 56, 97; Jews Of Hungary 1825-1849--Problems Of Assimilation and Emancipation, Am Hist Rev, Vol 102, 97. **CONTACT ADDRESS** Dept of Hist, Univ of Wash, Seattle, WA, 98195.

SUGGS, ROBERT CHINELO
PERSONAL Born 12/23/1943, Newport, Rhode Island, m **DISCIPLINE** EDUCATION **EDUCATION** Barrington Coll, BA 1967; State Univ of NY at Albany, MS 1971, EdD 1979. **CAREER** Dept of Counselor Ed State Univ, asst prof 1972-80; Comm Bible Church, pastor 1974-80; Dept of Counselor Ed Millersville Univ, adjunct asst prof 1982-85; Psychophysiological Clinic Univ of MD, clinical asst prof 1983-85; Crossroads Counseling Assocs, therapist 1983-; Christian Assoc of Psych Studies, newsletter editor 1983-; Messiah Coll, assoc prof of psychology, professor of psychology, director of personnel, 1986-; Cornerstone College, vp for academic affairs. **HONORS AND AWARDS** Doctoral fellow State Univ of NY at Albany 1971-73; outstanding teacher Messiah Coll 1981; Named to Top 500 High School Basketball Players in the US Dell Mag 1963. **CONTACT ADDRESS** Cornerstone Col, Vice President for Academic Affairs, Grand Rapids, MI, 49505.

SUINN, RICHARD MICHAEL
PERSONAL Born 05/08/1933, Honolulu, HI, m, 1958, 4 children **DISCIPLINE** PSYCHOLOGY **EDUCATION** Ohio State Univ, BA, 55; Stanford Univ, PhD, 59. **CAREER** Counselor, Stanford Counseling Center, 58; asst prof, Whitman Col, 59-64; res assoc, Stanford Medical School, 64-66; assoc prof, Univ of Hawaii, 66-68; PROF OF PSYCHOLOGY, COLO STATE UNIV, 68-. **HONORS AND AWARDS** Who's Who

in Am; Career Contribution to Ed and Training, Am Psychol Asn. **MEMBERSHIPS** Am Psychol Asn; Asn for Advancement of Behavior Therapy; Board of Professional Psychology. **RESEARCH** Behavior therapy; stress management. **SELECTED PUBLICATIONS** Auth, Anxiety Management Training: A Behavior Therapy, Plenum, 90; auth, The Seven Steps to Peak Performance, Hans Huber Pubs Inc, 86; auth, Psychology in Sports: Methods and Applications, Burgess Pub Co, 90; auth, Fundamentals of Behavior Pathology, John Wiley & Sons, 70 & 75; coauth, The Innovative Medical-Psychiatric Therapies, Univ Park Press, 76; auth, The Innovative Psychological Therapies: Critical and Creative Incidents, Harper & Row, 75; auth, The Predictive Validity of Projective Measures, C.C. Thomas, 69. **CONTACT ADDRESS** Dept of Psychology, Colorado State Univ, Fort Collins, CO, 80523. **EMAIL** Suinn@Lamar.colostate.edu

SUITS, THOMAS ALLAN
PERSONAL Born 04/05/1933, Milwaukee, WI, m, 1955, 2 children **DISCIPLINE** CLASSICAL PHILOLOGY **EDUCATION** Yale Univ, AB, 55, MA, 56, PhD(classics), 58. **CAREER** From instr to assoc prof Greek & Latin, Columbia Univ, 58-66; assoc prof classics, 66-72, Prof Classics, Univ Conn, 72-Mem class jury, Am Acad in Rome, 77-79. **MEMBERSHIPS** Am Philol Asn; Class Asn New England (pres, 80-81). **RESEARCH** Latin literature, especially Elegy; Propertius. **SELECTED PUBLICATIONS** Coauth, Latin Selections, Bantam, 61; auth, Mythology, address, and structure in Propertius 2.8, 65 & The Vertumnus elegy of Propertids, 69, Trans & Proc Am Philol Asn; ed, Macrobius: The Saturnalia, Columbia Univ, 69; auth, The structure of Livy's 32nd book, Philologus, 74; The knee and the shin: Seneca, Apocolocyntosis 10.3, Class Philol, 75; The iambic character of Propertius 1.4, Philologus, 76; Tibullus, Elegies Ii--With Introduction And Commentary, Am J Of Philology, Vol 117, 96. **CONTACT ADDRESS** 12 Hillyndale Rd, Storrs, CT, 06268.

SULEIMAN, MICHAEL W.
PERSONAL Born 02/26/1934, Tiberia, Palestine, m, 1963, 2 children **DISCIPLINE** POLITICAL SCIENCE **EDUCATION** Bradley Univ, BA 60; Univ Wis, MS 62, PhD 65. **CAREER** Kansas State Univ, Dept hd pol sci, AESF, prof, Dist Prof, 75 to 90-; Univ Calif Berk, vis sch, 79; KSU, assoc prof, 68-72; Univ London, vis sch, 69-70; KSU, asst prof, 65-68; Abbotsholme Sch, tchr, 55-56; Bishop's Sch Jordan, tchr, 53-55. **HONORS AND AWARDS** Princeton Inst Adv Stud; 2 NEH Fel; Fulbright-Hays Fel; Phi Kappa Phi; Dist Grad Fac Mem; MASUA Hon Mem; Smithsonian Inst Gnt; APS Fel; ARCE Fel; Ford Fac Res Fel; KSU Fac Res Fel; Phi Eta Sigma Schshp. **MEMBERSHIPS** APSA; MESA; MEI; IAMCR; AIMS; ASA; AISA. **RESEARCH** Comparative politics; Middle East politics; Political socialization in developing countries esp Middle East; Parties and political development; Amer images of Middle East Peoples; the Arab-American Community. **SELECTED PUBLICATIONS** Auth, Arabs in America: Building a New Future, ed, coauth, Philadelphia PA, Temple Univ Press, forthcoming; US Policy on Palestine form Wilson to Clinton, ed, coauth, Belmont MA, AAUG Press, 95; auth, Arab Americans: Continuity and Change, co-ed, coauth, Belmont MA, AAUG Press, 89; The Arabs in the Mind of America, Brattleboro VT, Amana Books, 88; auth, American Images of Middle East Peoples: Impact of the High School, Middle East Studies Assoc, NY, 77; auth, Political Parties in Lebanon: The Challenges of a Fragmented Political Culture, Ithaca NY, Cornell U Press, 67; Tunisia and the World: Attitudes of Turkish Youths Towards Other Countries, Maghreb Rev, 97; auth, Arab Immigration to America, 1880-1940, Awraq, Madrid, 96; auth, The Arab-American Left, in: Paul Buhle, Dan Geogakas, eds, The Immigrant Left, Albany NY, SUNY Pr, 96; auth, Arab Americans and the Political Process, Ernest Mccarus, ed, Arab-Americans: An Evolving Identity, Ann Arbor, U of Michigan Press, 94; auth, Political Orientation of Young Tunisians: The Impact of Gender, Arab Studies Quart, 93. **CONTACT ADDRESS** Dept of Political Science, Kansas State Univ, Manhattan, KS, 66506. **EMAIL** suleiman@ksu.edu

SULLIVAN, CHARLES R.
DISCIPLINE HISTORY **EDUCATION** George Mason Univ, BA; Columbia Univ, MA, MPil, PhD. **CAREER** Asst prof, Dallas Univ. **RESEARCH** Modern European intellectual history, history of political economy and classical Liberalism. **SELECTED PUBLICATIONS** Auth, The First Chair of Political Economy in France: Alexandre Vandermonde and the Principles of Sir James Steuart at the Ecole Normale of the Year III, Fr Hist Stud, 97; Western Histories in Invitation to the Classics, Baker, 98. **CONTACT ADDRESS** Dept of History, Univ of Dallas, 1845 E Northgate Dr, Braniff 238, Irving, TX, 75062. **EMAIL** sullivcr@acad.udallas.edu

SULLIVAN, DENIS
DISCIPLINE GREEK, LATIN, CLASSICAL PHILOLOGY AND ANCIENT HISTORY **EDUCATION** Tufts Univ, AB, 66; Univ NC Chapel Hill, PhD, 72; Cath Univ, MS, 75. **CAREER** Libr staff, Univ Md, 75-78; asst dean, Univ Md, Univ Col, 78-82; asst prof, Univ Md Col Pk, 82-88; assoc prof, Univ Md Col Pk, 88-. **HONORS AND AWARDS** Phi Beta Kappa; NDEA Title IV Fel; Woodrow Wilson Dissertation Fel; Dumbarton Oaks Byzantine Fel, 91-92 and 98-99. **MEMBERSHIPS** Amer Philol Asn; Ctr for Byzantine Studies; US Nat Comt on Byzantine Studies. **RESEARCH** Byzantine studies; Textual criticism. **SELECTED PUBLICATIONS** Auth, The Life of St. Ioannikios in Byzantine Defenders of Images, ed A. M. Talbot, Dumbarton Oaks, Wash, DC, 243-351, 98; Tenth Century Byzantine Offensive Siege Warfare: Instructional Prescriptions and Historical Practice, Byzantium at War, Athens, Nat Hellenic Res Foun, 179-200, 97; Was Constantine VI Iassoed at Markellai?, Greek, Roman and Byzantine Studies, 35, 3, 287-291, 94; Legal Opinion of Eustathios (Romaios) the Magistros, A. Laiou, Consent and Coercion to Sex and Marriage in Ancient and Medieval Societies, Wash, 175-175, 93; The Life of Saint Nikon: Text, Translation and Commentary, Brookline, Ma, Hellenic Col Press, 87; The Versions of the Vita Niconis, Dumbarton Oaks Papers, 32, 157-173, 78. **CONTACT ADDRESS** Dumbarton Oaks, 1703 32nd St. Northwest, Washington, DC, 20007-2961. **EMAIL** ds77@umail.umd.edu

SULLIVAN, DONALD DAVID
PERSONAL Born 05/11/1930, Denver, CO, m, 1964, 3 children **DISCIPLINE** MEDIEVAL & RENAISSANCE HISTORY **EDUCATION** Univ Chicago, BA, 56, MA, 57; Univ Colo, PhD(hist), 67. **CAREER** Asst prof hist, San Diego State Col, 65-67; ASST PROF HIST, UNIV NMEX, 67- **MEMBERSHIPS** AHA; Renaissance Soc Am; Mediaeval Acad Am; Am Soc Church Hist. **RESEARCH** German religious and ecclesiastical history of the 15th century; early humanism in Northern Europe, especially Nicholas of Cusa; periodization. **SELECTED PUBLICATIONS** Auth, Nicholas of Cusa as Reformer, Mediaeval Studies, 74; Innuendo & the Weighted Alternative in Tacitus, Class J, 76; The end of the Middle Ages, Hist Teacher, 81; Kaiser And Pope In Conflict--On The Relationship Of State And Church In The Late-Middle-Ages, Church Hist, Vol 62, 93; The Impact Of Humanism On Western-Europe, Church Hist, Vol 62, 93; Corpus-Christi--The Eucharist In Late-Medieval Culture, Church Hist, Vol 63, 94. **CONTACT ADDRESS** Dept Hist, Univ of NMex, Albuquerque, NM, 87110.

SULLIVAN, SHIRLEY DARCUS
PERSONAL Vancouver, BC, Canada **DISCIPLINE** CLASSICAL LANGUAGES, EARLY GREEK PHILOSOPHY **EDUCATION** Univ BC, BA, 66, MA, 68; Univ Toronto, PhD(class), 73. **CAREER** Assoc Prof Class, Univ BC, 72- **MEMBERSHIPS** Am Philol Asn; Class Asn Can; Soc Ancient Greek Philos; Class Asn Pac NW; Class Asn Can West. **RESEARCH** Presocratic philosophers; Greek lyric poets; Homer. **SELECTED PUBLICATIONS** Auth, Daimon parallels the Holy Phren in Empedocles, Phronesis, 77; Noos precedes Phren in Greek lyric poetry, L'Antiquite Classique, 77; Thumos and Psyche in Heraclitus B 85, Rivista di Studi Classici, 77; The Phren of the Noos in Xenophane's God, Symbolae Osloenses, 78; What death brings in Heraclitus, Gymnasium, 78; A Person's Relation to Psyche in Homer, Hesiod and the Greek Lyric Poets, 79 & How a Person Relates to Noos in Homer, Hesiod and the Greek Lyric Poets, 80, Glotta; A Strand of Thought in Pindar, Olympians 7, TAPA, 82; THE WORD-FIELD SEELE-GEIST IN THE VOCABULARY OF HOMER, PHOENIX-THE J OF THE CLASSICAL Assn OF CANADA, Vol 45, 91. **CONTACT ADDRESS** Dept of Class, Univ of BC, Vancouver, BC, V6T 1W5.

SULLIVAN, ZOLA JILES
PERSONAL Born 11/05/1921, Tallahassee, Florida, m, 1956 **DISCIPLINE** EDUCATION **EDUCATION** FL A M Univ Tllhs, BS MS 1950; Fisk Univ Nshvl; Univ of MI Ann Arbor; University of Miami, Miami, FL, post masters work, 1961; Oxfrd Univ Engl, 1965; Univ of IL Urbn Champ, PhD 1970. **CAREER** Broward Co Public School Sys Ft Lauderdale, teacher 1942-43; Palm Beach Co Elementary School, teacher 1943-50; FL A&M Univ, instructor 1950-53; Dade Co Public Sys, prin elementary teacher 1953-71; FL Intl Univ Miami FL, asst prof educ 1971-74, assoc prof educ 1974-90; Florida Memorial College, adjunct professor, 1990-91; retired. **HONORS AND AWARDS** Recip num schol & career opport cert; NDEA Fellwshp Univ of IL 1969-70; inttr various prog & Univ class; recip num plqs & cert for outstndng work; FL Governor's Awd for Outstanding Achievement 1986; Outstanding Serv to African Educators Political Leaders and Students, recognized by FL Chapter of the Natl Council of Intl Visitors; First Black Female to receive a PhD in Miami, Fl, Univ of IL, 1970; Consultant Ministry of Education, Nassau, BS, 1971. **MEMBERSHIPS** Chmn Num Chldhd Educ Com; consult Num Educ Assn; spkr lectr Num Elmntry Schs; coor Num Educ Wrkshps; mem Num Educ Assns; spkr Num Ch Grps; mem Rchmnd Hghts Women's Club FL; mem Alpha Phi Alpha Frat; Iota Pi Lambda Chap Miami; mem FL Intl Task Force on Needs Assessment to Improve Educational Opportunities in Guinea; advisory board, Black Heritage Museum of Dade Count, 1989-; member, Primary Readers and Evaluators in First Editions of Eric Early Childhood; founding member, Second Baptist Church, Miami, FL, 1963; founding professor, Florida International University, 1971. **SELECTED PUBLICATIONS** pub num papers on educ

SUMIDA, JON TETSURO
PERSONAL Born 07/07/1949, Washington, DC, m, 1975 **DISCIPLINE** BRITISH & MILITARY HISTORY **EDUCATION** Univ Calif, Santa Cruz, BA, 71; Univ Chicago, MA, 74, PhD, 82. **CAREER** Lectr Europ hist, Roosevelt Univ, 80; asst lectr, 80-82, Asst Prof, 82-88, ASSOC PROF EUROP & MIL HIST, UNIV MD, COLLEGE PARK, 88-. **HONORS AND AWARDS** Archives Fel Commoner, Churchill Col Cambridge, 83; Fel, Woodrow Wilson Ctr, 86, 96-96; Fel, Guggenheim Found, 90-91; Hooper Res Grant, U.S. Naval Hist Ctr, 92; Moncado Prizes for articles in the J Military Hist, 93, 95; Naval Hist Auth of the Year, U.S. Naval Inst, 96. **MEMBERSHIPS** Int Naval Res Orgn; Navy Records Soc. **RESEARCH** Nineteenth and 20th century British naval history; 19th and 20th century British political history. **SELECTED PUBLICATIONS** Auth, British capital ship design and fire control in the Dreadnought era, J Mod Hist, 6/79; The Pollen Papers: The Privately Circulated Printed Works of Arthur Hungerford Pollen, 1901-1916, 84; In Defence of Naval Supremacy: Finance, Technology and British Naval Policy, 1889-1914, 89; Inventing Grand Strategy and Teaching Command: The Classic Works of Alfred Thayer Mahan Reconsidered, 97. **CONTACT ADDRESS** Dept of Hist, Univ Md, College Park, MD, 20742-0001.

SUMNER, GREGORY D.
DISCIPLINE AMERICAN HISTORY AND CULTURE **EDUCATION** Ind Univ, BA, MA, PhD; University Mich Law Sch, JD. **CAREER** Assoc prof, 93. **HONORS AND AWARDS** Fel(s), Andrew Mellon Found; John D and Catherine T MacArthur Found; NEH. **SELECTED PUBLICATIONS** Auth, Dwight Macdonald and the Politics Circle: The Challenge of Cosmopolitan Democracy, Cornell Univ Press, 96. **CONTACT ADDRESS** Dept of Hist, Univ Detroit Mercy, 4001 W McNichols Rd, PO BOX 19900, Detroit, MI, 48219-0900. **EMAIL** SUMNERGR@udmercy.edu

SUN, RAYMOND
DISCIPLINE EUROPEAN HISTORY **EDUCATION** Johns Hopkins Univ, PhD, 91. **CAREER** Asst prof, Washington State Univ. **SELECTED PUBLICATIONS** Auth, Catholic-Marxist Competition in the Working-Class Parishes of Cologne during the Weimar Republic, in Cath Hist Rev 83, 97 & Arbeiter Priester und die 'Roten': Kulturelle Hegemonie im Katholischen Milieu, 1885-1933, Workers, Priests and 'Reds': Cultural Hegemony in the Catholic Milieu, 1885-1933, in Geschichte zwischen Kultur und Gesellshaft: Beitraege zur Theoriedebatte, History Between Culture and Society: Contributions to the Debate Over Theory, Munich: Beck Verlag, 97. **CONTACT ADDRESS** Dept of History, Washington State Univ, 301 Wilson Hall, PO Box 644030, Pullman, WA, 99164-4030. **EMAIL** sunray@wsu.edu

SUNDBERG, WALTER
DISCIPLINE CHURCH HISTORY **EDUCATION** S.t Olaf Col, BA, 69; Princeton Theol Sem, MDiv, 73, PhD, 81; Univ Tubingen, Ger, 71-72. **CAREER** Instr, Augsburg Col, 81-84; US Army Chaplains prog, 77; Lutheran Theol Sem, Philadelphia, 76; vis prof, Col St. Catherine, 85-86; asst prof, 84; assoc prof, 86; prof, 94-; act ch, hist dept, 87-88. **HONORS AND AWARDS** Rockefeller Theol fel; grad fel; Amer Lutheran Church., Asst minister, Como Park Lutheran Church; ed bd(s), Lutheran Quart; Lutheran Commentator; bd mem, Great Commn Network; Lutheran Bible Ministries; Lutheran Bible Inst; ALC Inter-Church Relations Comm. **MEMBERSHIPS** Mem adv coun, Interpretation. **SELECTED PUBLICATIONS** Contrib, Ministry in 19th Century European Lutheranism, Called and Ordained: Lutheran Perspectives on the Office of Ministry, 90; pub(s), articles in First Things, Lutheran Quart, Lutheran Forum; coauth, The Bible in Modern Culture: Theology and Historical Critical Method from Spinoza to Kasemann, 95. **CONTACT ADDRESS** Dept of Church History, Luther Sem, 2481 Como Ave, St. Paul, MN, 55108. **EMAIL** wsundber@luthersem.edu

SUNDSTROM, ROY ALFRED
PERSONAL Born 02/24/1934, Mineola, NY, m, 1963, 2 children **DISCIPLINE** ENGLISH & EARLY MODERN EUROPEAN HISTORY **EDUCATION** Univ Mass, Amherst, AB, 56; Western Mich Univ, MA, 66; Kent State Univ, PhD(Hist), 72. **CAREER** Asst prof, 69-73, assoc prof, 73-79, prof Hist, Humboldt State Univ, 79-, Am Philos Soc res grant, 74 & 75. **MEMBERSHIPS** AHA; Conf Brit Historians; Huguenot Soc London. **RESEARCH** Late Stuart England; biography of Sidney Godolphin, 1645-1712. **SELECTED PUBLICATIONS** Auth, Some original sources relating to Huguenot refugees in England, 1680-1727, Brit Studies Monitor, Summer 76; The French Huguenots and the Civil List, 1696-1727: A study of alien assimilation in England, Albion, Fall 76; Sidney Godolphin: Servant of the State, Univ of Delaware, Press, 92. **CONTACT ADDRESS** Dept of History, Humboldt State Univ, 1 Harps St, Arcata, CA, 95521-8299.

SUNSERI, ALVIN RAYMOND
PERSONAL Born 02/11/1925, New Orleans, LA, m, 1952, 6 children **DISCIPLINE** HISTORY OF WARS & REVOLUTIONS **EDUCATION** Southeast La Univ, BA, 53; La State Univ, MA, 55, PhD(hist), 73. **CAREER** Instr hist, St Paul's

Col, 54-56 & NMex Mil Inst, 56-59; asst prof, Col Santa Fe, 59-61 & NMex Highlands Univ, 61-63; teaching asst, La State Univ, 63-65; asst prof, Western State Col Colo, 65-67; from asst prof to assoc prof, 67-75, PROF HIST, UNIV NORTHERN IOWA, 75- **MEMBERSHIPS** AHA; Orgn Am Historians; Southern Hist Asn; Hist Asn England. **RESEARCH** Military-industrial complex; Civil War & reconstruction. **SELECTED PUBLICATIONS** Auth, Baron von Steuben and the reeducation of the American Army, Armor, 65; The Ludlow Massacre, American Chronicle, 1/72; Anglo-American attitudes toward the Hispanos, 1946-1961, J Mex-Am Hist, 12/73; The army and the economy: Iowa as a case study, In: The United States Army in Peacetime: Essays in Honor of the Bicentennial 1775-1975, 75; The Chicano studies program in Northern New Mexico: Broken promises and future prospects, In: Identitiy and Awareness in the Minority Experience, La Crosse, 75; The migrant workers of Iowa, In: Essays on Minority Cultures, Univ Wis-La Crosse, 76; The Military-Industrial Complex in Iowa, In: War, Business and American Society, Kennikat, 77; Seeds of Discord: New Mexico Following the Anglo-American Conquest, 1846-1861, Nelson-Hall, 78; Forgotten Frontier--The Story Of Southeastern New-Mexico, J Of The West, Vol 35, 96. **CONTACT ADDRESS** Dept of Hist, Univ of Northern Iowa, Cedar Falls, IA, 50613.

SUNY, RONALD GRIGOR
PERSONAL Born 09/25/1940, Philadelphia, PA, m, 1971, 2 children **DISCIPLINE** RUSSIAN & ARMENIAN HISTORY **EDUCATION** Swarthmore Col, BA, 62; Columbia Univ, MA & Russ Inst Cert, 65, PhD(hist), 68. **CAREER** Spec lectr hist, Columbia Univ, 67-68; asst prof, Oberlin Col, 68-72, assoc prof, 72-81; ALEX MANOOGIAN PROF MOD ARMENIAN HIST, UNIV MICH, ANN ARBOR, 81-, Int Res & Exchanges Bd grant, USSR, 71-72; prof mod Armenian hist, Univ Mich, Ann Arbor, 77-78. **MEMBERSHIPS** Am Asn Advan Slavic Studies; Study Group Hist Europ Labor & Working Class Hist; Soc Armenian Studies. **RESEARCH** Russian social history; labor movement and social democracy in Transcaucasia; nationality problems in the USSR. **SELECTED PUBLICATIONS** Auth, Journeyman for the revolution: Stalin and the labour movement in Baku, Soviet Studies, 1/72; The Baku Commune, 1917-1918: Class and Nationality in the Russian Revolution, Princeton Univ, 72; Armenia in the Twentieth Century, Columbia Armenian Studies; Workers Of The World And Oppressed Peoples, Unite--Proceedings And Documents Of The 2nd Congress, 1920, Slavic Rev, Vol 51, 92; Revision And Retreat In The Historiography Of 1917, Social-Hist And Its Critics, Russian Rev, Vol 53, 94; Stalinist Simplifications And Soviet Complications--Social Tensions And Political Conflicts In The USSR, 1933-1953, Russian Rev, Vol 53, 94; Lenin, Trotsky, And Stalin--The Intelligentsia And Power, J Of Modern Hist, Vol 66, 94. **CONTACT ADDRESS** 1723 Wells, Ann Arbor, MI, 48104.

SURRENCY, ERWIN C.
PERSONAL Born 05/11/1924, Jesup, GA, m, 1945, 2 children **DISCIPLINE** LEGAL HISTORY **EDUCATION** Univ Ga, AB, 47, AM, 48, LLB, 49; George Peabody Col, MALS, 50. **CAREER** Librn, Charles Klein Law Libr, Temple Univ, 50-78, from asst prof to assoc prof law, 54-60, prof, 60-78; Prof Law & Dir Law Libr, Univ Ga, 79-, Ed, Am J Legal Hist, 57-; lectr, Queen's Univ, Belfast, 63-64; mem, Asn Am Law Schs; consult, Nigerian Govt on Law Libr, 75-76. **MEMBERSHIPS** Am Soc Legal Hist (pres, 57-59); Am Hist Asn; Stair Soc; Selden Soc; Am Asn Law Libr (pres, 73-74). **RESEARCH** History of the legal profession in America; history of the federal courts; legal history of Georgia. **SELECTED PUBLICATIONS** Auth, Marshall Reader, 55; How The United-States Perfects An International Agreement, Law Libr J, Vol 85, 93; coauth, Research in Pennsylvania Law, 55; Guide to Legal Research, 59, Oceana. **CONTACT ADDRESS** Dept of Law, Univ of Ga, Athens, GA, 30601.

SUSSMAN, LEWIS ARTHUR
PERSONAL Born 06/26/1941, New York, NY, m, 1965 **DISCIPLINE** CLASSICS **EDUCATION** Princeton Univ, AB, 64; Univ NC, Chapel Hill, PhD(classics), 69. **CAREER** Asst prof classics, Univ CA, Irvine, 69-76, chm dept, 72-75; assoc prof classics, 76-94, prof, Univ FL, 94-,chm dept, 93-; Univ FL Humanities Coun grant, 77; Nat Endowment for Humanities summer sem, Rome, 79. **MEMBERSHIPS** Am Philol Asn; Class Asn Mid West & South (secy-treas, 77-78). **RESEARCH** Ancient rhetoric; Ovid; Roman literature of the Augustan Age. **SELECTED PUBLICATIONS** Auth, Early imperial declamation: A Translation of the Elder Seneca's Prefaces, Speech Monogr, 6/70; The Artistic Unity of the Elder Seneca's First Preface & Controversiae as a Whole, Am J Philol, 4/71; The Elder Seneca's Discussion of the Decline of Roman Eloquence, CA Studies Class Antiq, 72; The Elder Seneca, E J Brill, 78; Latin and Basic Skills, Class J, 78; Arellius Fuscus and the Unity of Seneca's Suasoriae, Rheinisches Mus, 78; The Major Declamations Ascribed to Quintilian, Peter Lang, 87; The Declamations of Calpurnius Flaccus, E J Brill, 94. **CONTACT ADDRESS** Dept Classics, Univ FL, 3c Daver Hall, Gainesville, FL, 32611-7435. **EMAIL** sussman@classics.ufl.edu

SUTHERLAND, DANIEL E.
PERSONAL Born 03/05/1946, Detroit, MI, m, 1993, 3 children **DISCIPLINE** HISTORY **EDUCATION** Wayne St Univ, BS, 68, MA, 73, PhD, 76. **CAREER** Vis asst prof, 76, Univ Alabama; adj asst prof, 76-77, Wayne St Univ; asst prof, 77-83, assoc prof, 83-86, prof, 88-89, dept head, 83-89, McNeese St Univ; assoc prof, 89-91, prof, 91-, dept chmn, 92-98, Univ Arkansas; **RESEARCH** 19th century US hist **CONTACT ADDRESS** Dept of History, Univ of Arkansas, Fayetteville, AR, 72701. **EMAIL** dsutherl@comp.uark.edu

SUTHERLAND, ELIZABETH H.
PERSONAL Born 07/05/1963, Princeton, NJ, s **DISCIPLINE** CLASSICS **EDUCATION** Univ of Calif Berk, PhD, 94. **CAREER** Univ Calif Santa Cruz, lectr, 95; Univ Calif Irvine, lectr, 95-96; Univ Tenn Knoxville, asst prof, 96-. **MEMBERSHIPS** APA, CAMWS. **RESEARCH** Augustan poetry; feminist theory **SELECTED PUBLICATIONS** Auth, Visions and Desire in Horace's Carm 2.5, Helios, 97; auth, Audience Manipulation and Emotional Experience in Horace's Pyrrha Ode, AJP, 95. **CONTACT ADDRESS** Dept of Classics, Tennessee Univ, 1101 McClung Tower, Knoxville, TN, 37996. **EMAIL** ehsuther@utk.edu

SUTTON, DONALD SINCLAIR
PERSONAL Born 11/08/1938, London, England, m, 1967, 1 child **DISCIPLINE** CHINESE HISTORY **EDUCATION** Cambridge Univ, BA, 62, PhD(Orient studies), 71; Columbia Univ, MA, 64. **CAREER** Res historian mod China, Ctr Chinese Studies, Univ Mich, Ann Arbor, 67-69; instr, 69-71, asst prof, 71-77, ASSOC PROF HIST, CARNEGIE-MELLON UNIV, 77-, Soc Sci Res Coun res & travel grant, 71-72; Am Coun Learned Soc anthrop & res grant, 80-81. **MEMBERSHIPS** Asn Asian Studies; AHA. **RESEARCH** Modern Chinese armies as social institutions; early modern Chinese; popular mentalities. **SELECTED PUBLICATIONS** Auth, Taoist Ritual and Popular Cults Of Southeast China, J Of Social Hist, Vol 28, 95; Consuming Counterrevolution--The Ritual And Culture Of Cannibalism In Wuxuan, Guangxi, China, May To July 1968, Comparative Studies In Society And Hist, Vol 37, 95; Ritual, History, And The Films Of Yimou Zhang, East-West Film J, Vol 8, 94; Body, Subject And Power In China, J Of Social Hist, Vol 28, 95; Statecraft And Political-Economy On The Taiwan Frontier, 1600-1800, J Of Social Hist, Vol 28, 95; Ethnography And The Hist Imagination, J Of Social Hist, Vol 28, 94. **CONTACT ADDRESS** Dept of Hist & Philos, Carnegie Mellon Univ, 5000 Forbes Ave, Pittsburgh, PA, 15213-3890.

SUTTON, ROBERT MIZE
PERSONAL Born 12/15/1915, Bunker Hill, IL **DISCIPLINE** AMERICAN HISTORY **EDUCATION** Shurtleff Col, AB, 37; Univ Ill, AM, 38, PhD, 48. **CAREER** From instr to assoc prof Am hist, 48-63, assoc dean grad col, 58-65, chmn dept hist, 72-74, PROF HIST, UNIV ILL, URBANA, 63-, DIR ILL HIST SURV, 65-, Mem, Ill Bicentennial Comn, 74-76. **HONORS AND AWARDS** DHL, Wheaton Col, 71. **MEMBERSHIPS** AHA; Orgn Am Historians; Am Asn State & Local Hist; Conf Faith & Hist. **RESEARCH** History of railroad transportation; Lincoln and the railroads of Illinois; westward movement and state development. **SELECTED PUBLICATIONS** Coauth, Lincoln Images, Augustana Col, 60; auth, The Illinois Central: thoroughfare for freedom, Civil War Hist, 9/61; The origin of American land-grand railroad rates, Bus Hist Rev, spring 66; A History of Illinois in Paintings, Univ Ill, 68; The Heartland: Pages from Illinois History, Deerpath, 75; coauth, Manuscripts Guide to Collections at the University of Illinois at Urbana-Champaign, Univ Ill, Urbana, 76; The Illinois Central Railroad in Peace and War, 1858-1868, Arno Press, 81; High On The Okaw Western Bank--Vandalia, Illinois, 1819-39, Western Hist Quart, Vol 24, 93. **CONTACT ADDRESS** Dept of Hist, Univ of Ill, Urbana, IL, 61801.

SUTTON, ROBERT PAUL
PERSONAL Born 09/21/1940, Altoona, PA, m, 1963, 3 children **DISCIPLINE** UNITED STATES HISTORY **EDUCATION** Juniata Col, BA, 62; Col William & Mary, MA, 64; Univ Va, PhD(hist), 67. **CAREER** Lectr hist, Christopher Newport Col, 62-64; instr, Univ Va, 64-67; assoc prof, Mansfield State Col, 67-70, chmn dept, 68-70; dir local & regional arch/collections, 76-79, from assoc prof to prof hist, Western Ill Univ, 70-82; dir Ctr Icarian Studies, 79-; Bd Dir communcal Studies Assoc, 93-; Nat Endowment for Humanities fel, 70. **HONORS AND AWARDS** Western Ill Univ Faculty Excellence Awards 76-77, 86-95; Western Ill Univ Outstanding Research Award, College of Arts & Sciences, 94. **MEMBERSHIPS** AHA; Southern Hist Asn; Am Soc Legal Hist; Soc Am Archivists. **RESEARCH** Intellectual and social history of early national era, History of American Law, Communcal Societies. **SELECTED PUBLICATIONS** Auth, Nostalgia, pessimism, and malaise: the doomed aristocrat in late-Jeffersonian Virginia, 1/68 & Sectionalism and social structure: a case study of Jeffersonian democracy, 1/72, Va Mag Hist & Biog; ed, The Prairie State: A Documentary History of Illinois (2 vols), Eerdmans, 76; co-ed, Mon Cher, Emile: The Cabet Baxter Letters, 1854-55, Western Ill Regional Studies, spring 79; Voyage in Icaria: A message to the world, In: Humanistic Values of the Icarian movement, Ill Humanities Coun, 81; Morris Birkbak and Prairre Albion: A Critical Bibliography, Midwest Bibliography, Univ Iowa Press, 81; Les Icariens: The Utopian Dream in Europe and America, 94; **CONTACT ADDRESS** Dept of History, Western Illinois University, 1 University Cir, Macomb, IL, 61455-1390. **EMAIL** Robert_Sutton@ccmai.wiu.edu

SUTTON, SHARON EGRETTA
PERSONAL Born 02/18/1941, Cincinnati, Ohio **DISCIPLINE** MUSIC **EDUCATION** Univ of Hartford, B Mus 1963; Columbia Univ, March 1973; City Univ of NY, M Phil 1981, MA Psychology 1982, PhD Psychology 1982. **CAREER** Musician, orchestras of "Fiddler on the Roof," "Man of La Mancha," the Bolshoi, Moiseiyev and Leningrad Ballet Companies 1963-68; architect, Pratt Institute, visiting asst prof 1975-81; Columbia Univ, adj asst prof 1981-82; Univ of Cincinnati, asst prof 1982-84; SE Sutton Architect, private practice 1976-; Univ of MI, assoc prof, 1984-94, prof of architecture and urban planning, 1994-97; Univ of Washington, prof of architecture, dir CEEDS; Exhibitions, The Evans-Tibbs Collection in Washington, DC, fine artist, 1985; Your Heritage House in Detroit, MI 1986, June Kelly Gallery in NYC 1987, Univ of MI Musuem of Art 1988; Art included in collections of, The Mint Museum, The Baltimore Museum of Art, Baltimore, MD, The Wadsworth Atheneum, Hartford, CT. **HONORS AND AWARDS** Danforth Foundation, Post baccalaureat Award 1979-81; Design Rsch Recognition Awd Natl Endowment for the Arts 1983; group VII Natl Fellowship, WK Kellogg Foundation, 1986-1989; project director Natl Endowment for the Arts, "Design of Cities" Grant; American Planning Assn Education Award, 1991; University of Michigan Regent's Award for Distinguished Public Service; first African-American woman to be named a full professor of architecture in the US; Second African-American Woman to be advanced to fellowship in the Amer Inst of Architects; Distinguished Professor, Association of Collegiate Schools of Architecture; Life Achievement Awd, Michigan Women's Hall of Fame, 1997. **MEMBERSHIPS** Founder/coordinator, Urban Network: An Urban Design Program for Youth; fellow, Amer Institute of Architects; Amer Psychological Assn; American Educational Research Association; president-elect, National Architecture Accrediting Board. **CONTACT ADDRESS** Prof of Architecture, Univ of Washington, 208 T Gould Hall, PO Box 355720, Seattle, WA, 98195-5720.

SUTTPN, DANA F.
DISCIPLINE CLASSICAL STUDIES, PHILOLOGY **EDUCATION** New School for Social Research, BA, 65; Univ Wisc, MA, 66, PhD, 70. **CAREER** Lectr, CUNY, Herbert Lehman Coll, 69-72; asst prof, Univ Ill, 75-79; asst to assoc to PROF, UNIV CALIF, IRVINE, 79-. **HONORS AND AWARDS** Guggenheim fel, 75; Adele Mellon Prize, disting scholarship, 96. **RESEARCH** Greek, Latin, Neolatin poetry and drama. **SELECTED PUBLICATIONS** Auth, Sophocles' Inachus, in Beitrage zur klassischen Philologie, Verlag Anton Hain, Meisenheim am Glan, 79; auth, The Greek Satyr Play, in Beitrage zur klassischen Philologie, Verlag Anton Hain, Meisenheim am Glan, 80; auth, Self and Society in ARitsophanes, Univ Press Am, 80; auth, The Dramaturgy of the Octavia, in Beitrage zur klassischen Philologie, Verlag Anton Hain, Konigstein/Taunus, 83; auth, The Lost Sophocles, Univ Press Am, 84; auth, The Satyr Play, in Cambridge History of Classical Literature I, 85; auth, Seneca on the Stage, in Mnemosyne, E. J. Brill, 86; auth, The Greek Dithyrambographers, Georg Olms Verlag, 89; auth, Thomas Legge: The Complete Plays, Peter Lang Verlag, 93; auth, Ancient Comedy: The Conflict of the Generations, in Twaynes' Literary Genres and Themes Series, Macmillan, 93; auth, The Catharsis of Comedy, in Greek Studies: Interdisciplinary Approaches, Rowman and Littlefield, 94; auth, William Gager: The Complete Works, Garland Press, 94; auth, Oxford Poetry by Richard Eedes and George Peele, Garland Press, 95; auth, The COmplete Works of Thomas Watson (1556-1592), Edwin Mellen Press, 96; auth, Homer in the Papyri, hypertext version, http://eee/uci.edu/üpapyri, 97; Matthew Gwinne's tragedy Nero, hypertext, http://eee/uci/edu/üpapyri/Nero, 97; Edward Forsett's comedy Pedantius, hypertext, http://eee/uci.edu/üpapyri.forsett, 98; Geroge Ruggle's comedy Ignoramus, hypertext, http://eee/uci.edu/üpapyri.ruggle, 98; William Alabaster's tragedy Roxana, hypertext, http://eee/uci.edu/üpapyri.alabaster, 98; auth, The Complete Latin Poetry of William Savage Landor, Edwin Mellen Press, forthcoming. **CONTACT ADDRESS** Dept of Classics, Univ of California, Irvine, 120 HOB II, Irvine, CA, 97692-2000. **EMAIL** DanaS64562@aol.com

SVEJDA, GEORGE J.
PERSONAL Born 03/12/1927, Horni Vilimec, Czechoslovakia, m, 1967, 4 children **DISCIPLINE** MODERN MEDIEVAL, DIPLOMATIC & IMMIGRATION HISTORY **EDUCATION** St Procopius Col, BA, 52; Georgetown Univ, PhD, 59; postdoc study, Univ Penn, 61-63. **CAREER** Res assoc polit sci, Columbia Univ, 58-59; European exchange specialist, Libr Cong, 59-61; tech writer sci, Franklin Inst, Pa, 62; historian, US Dept Interior, 62-80; res analyst, Dept of Justice, Dept of Navy. **HONORS AND AWARDS** Phi Alpha Theta; Dict of Int Biog, 72; Who's Who Among Authors and Journalists, 74. **MEMBERSHIPS** Orgn Am Historians; Am Acad Polit & Soc Sci. **RESEARCH** Modern, medieval and United States diplomatic and immigration history. **SELECTED PUBLICATIONS**

Auth, Carl Sandburg: Literary Liberty Bell, Nat Park Serv, 71; auth, Furnishing Study for the Castle Clinton Officer's Quarters, 72, Nat Park Serv; art, The Czech Catholic immigration to the United States of America, Czech Catholics at the 41st International Eucharistic Congress Philadelphia, 76; art, George Washington, Encycl Southern History, La State Univ, 79. **CONTACT ADDRESS** 1007 Cliftonbrook Lane, Silver Spring, MD, 20905. **EMAIL** Svejda@erols.com

SVINGEN, ORLAN
DISCIPLINE UNITED STATES HISTORY **EDUCATION** Univ Toledo, PhD,82. **CAREER** Assoc prof, Washington State Univ. **RESEARCH** Native American history. **SELECTED PUBLICATIONS** Auth, The Northern Cheyenne Indian Reservation 1877-1900, UP Colo, 94. **CONTACT ADDRESS** Dept of History, Washington State Univ, 301 Wilson Hall, PO Box 644030, Pullman, WA, 99164-4030. **EMAIL** svingen@wsu.edu

SWAIN, CHARLES W.
PERSONAL Born 07/30/1937, Des Moines, IA, m, 1958, 2 children **DISCIPLINE** HISTORY OF RELIGION **EDUCATION** State Univ Iowa, AB, 59; Brown Univ, PhD(relig), 65. **CAREER** Instr relig, Oberlin Col, 63-65; from asst prof to assoc prof, 65-77, Prof Relig, Fla State Univ, 77-, Soc Relig Higher Educ Asian relig fel, 67-68; vis lectr, Ctr Study World Relig, Harvard Univ, 67-68; Helmsley lectr, Brandeis Univ, 68. **MEMBERSHIPS** Am Acad Relig; AAUP; Soc Values Higher Educ. **RESEARCH** History of western religious thought; history of western philosophy; phenomenology of religion. **SELECTED PUBLICATIONS** Auth, The Bible Through the Ages, World Publ, 67; People of the Earth, 76; Hamann and the philosophy of David Hume, J Hist Philos, Vol V, No 4; Doubt in defense of faith, J Am Acad Relig, Vol XXXVI, No 2; Buddhist Spirituality--Indian, Southeast-Asian, Tibetan, And Early Chinese, J Of Ecumenical Studies, Vol 32, 95; Wonhyo And Christianity--Ilshim As A Central Category, J Of Ecumenical Studies, Vol 30, 93; Theology From Asiatic Sources--The Theological Path Of Song,Choan,Seng Prior To The Budding Of Asiatic Ecumenical Discussion, J Of Ecumenical Studies, Vol 33, 96; 7 Dilemmas In World Religions, J Of Ecumenical Studies, Vol 33, 96; A Hist Of Christianity In Asia, Vol 1--Beginnings To 1500, J Of Ecumenical Studies, Vol 31, 94. **CONTACT ADDRESS** Dept of Relig, Florida State Univ, 600 W College Ave, Tallahassee, FL, 32306-1096.

SWAIN, JOSEPH
PERSONAL Born 05/19/1955, Malden, MA, m, 3 children **DISCIPLINE** MUSIC **EDUCATION** Dartmouth Col, AB, 77; Harvard Univ, AM, 80; Harvard Univ, PhD, 83. **CAREER** Assoc Prof Mus, Colgate Univ. **MEMBERSHIPS** Am Musicol Soc; Soc Mus Percept and Cognition; Am Bach Soc. **RESEARCH** Music criticism and critical theory. **SELECTED PUBLICATIONS** Sound Judgment: Basic Ideas About Music, San Francisco Press, 87; The Broadway Musical: A Critical Survey, NY, Oxford Univ Press, 90; Leonard Meyer's New Theory of Style, Mus Anal, 11, (2-3), Jul-Oct 92, 335-354; The Practicality of Chant in Modern Liturgy, The Diapason, Jul 92; How They Do It in Venice, Italy, Past Mus 16:3, 15-17; What is Meant by 'Musical Structure', Crit Mus, 2:1-2, Summer 94, 20-44; Musical Communities and Music Perception, Mus Percep, 11(3), Spring 94, 307-320; Operatic Conventions and the American Musical, in Opera and the Golden West: The Past, Present, and Future of Opera in the USA, London, Assoc Univ Press, 94, 296-301; The Concept of Musical Syntax, Mus Quart, 77:2, Summer 95, 285-308; The Range of Musical Semantics, The Jour Aesthet and Art Crit, 54.2, Spring 96, 135-152; Missalettes: Wrong Idea, Mod Liturgy, Oct 96, 6-7; Musical Languages, NY, WW Norton, 97; Bowdlerizing the Liturgy, Am, Aug 16-23; Musical Disguises in Mozart's Late Comedies, The Opera Quart 13.4, 97, 47-58; Liturgy as Artwork, Celebration 27.6, 1998, 285-287; Dimensions of Harmonic Rhythm, Music Theory Spectrum 20.1, 98,48-71; Finding a Way to Cure Sing-Song Syndrome, Pastoral Mus, Feb-Mar 98, 16-17. **CONTACT ADDRESS** Music Dept., Colgate Univ, 13 Oak Dr, Hamilton, NY, 13346-1298. **EMAIL** jswain@mail.colgate.edu

SWAIN, MARTHA HELEN
PERSONAL Born 06/21/1929, Cape Girardeau, MO **DISCIPLINE** HISTORY **EDUCATION** Miss State Univ, BS, 50; Vanderbilt Univ, MA, 54, PhD(hist), 75. **CAREER** Teacher social studies, pub schs, Miss & Fla, 50-69; from instr to asst prof hist, 74-78, chmn dept, 78-81, ASSOC PROF, TEX WOMAN'S UNIV, 78-, Asst prof social studies, Fla State Univ, 63-64. **MEMBERSHIPS** AHA; Orgn Am Historians; Southern Hist Asn; Nat Coun Social Studies. **RESEARCH** New Deal; social welfare history; 20th century Mississippi. **SELECTED PUBLICATIONS** Auth, The lion and the fox: Franklin D Roosevelt and Senator Pat Harrison, J Miss Hist, 76; Pat Harrison and the Social Security Act, Southern Quart, 77; Joseph H Short, In: Dictionary of American Biography, Suppl V, Scribners, 77; The Harrison Education Bills, 1935-1941, Miss Quart, 78; Pat Harrison: The New Deal Years, Univ Press Miss, 78; Ellen Woodward, In: Notable American Women, Harvard Univ, 80; Love And Politics In Wartime--Letters To My Wife, 1943-45, J Of Am Hist, Vol 80, 93. **CONTACT ADDRESS** Tex Woman's Univ, Box 23974, Denton, TX, 76204.

SWAINSON, DONALD
PERSONAL Born 11/23/1938, m, 1963, 2 children **DISCIPLINE** CANADIAN HISTORY **EDUCATION** Univ Man, BA, 60; Univ Toronto, MA, 61, PhD(hist), 69. **CAREER** Lectr, 63-65, asst prof, 65-70, assoc prof, 70-79, PROF HIST, QUEEN'S UNIV, 79. **MEMBERSHIPS** Can Hist Asn. **RESEARCH** Ontario history; prairie (Canadian) history; Canadian political parties. **SELECTED PUBLICATIONS** Auth, Ontario and Confederation, Centennial Comn Can, 67; The North-West Transportation Company: Personnel and attitudes, Hist & Sci Soc Man Trans, 69-70; ed, Historical Essays on the Prairie Provinces, 70 & J C Dent: The Last Forty Years, 71, McClelland & Stewart; auth, John A Macdonald: The Man and the Politician, Oxford Univ, 71; ed, Oliver Mowat's Ontario, Macmillan, 72; auth, Sir Henry Smith and the politics of the Union, Ont Hist, 74; Macdonald of Kingston, Thomas Nelson, 79; Agnes, The Biography Of Lady Macdonald, Canadian Hist Rev, Vol 74, 93; Liberty And Community--Canadian Federalism And The Failure Of The Constitution, Am Hist Rev, Vol 98, 93. **CONTACT ADDRESS** Dept of Hist, Queen's Univ, Kingston, ON, K7L 3N6.

SWANSON, BERT E.
PERSONAL Born 08/15/1924, Tacoma, WA, w, 1968 **DISCIPLINE** POLITICAL SCIENCE **EDUCATION** George Washington Univ, BA, 50; Univ Oregon, MA, 56; PhD, 59. **CAREER** Hunter Col, 59-61; Sarah Lawrence, 61-71; Univ Fla, 71-. **RESEARCH** Urban policy and politics. **SELECTED PUBLICATIONS** Auth, Dialogued Community, in, Commun Econ Develop, 81. **CONTACT ADDRESS** Dept of Political Science, Univ of Florida, Gainsville, FL, 32601. **EMAIL** bes@nervm.nerdc.ufl.edu

SWANSON, MAYNARD WILLIAM
PERSONAL Born 09/04/1929, Worcester, MA, m, 1958, 3 children **DISCIPLINE** MODERN HISTORY, AFRICAN HISTORY **EDUCATION** Amherst Col, BA, 52; Harvard Univ, MA, 57, PhD(hist), 65. **CAREER** Lectr hist, Univ Natal, 62; instr, Yale Univ, 63-65, asst prof, 65-70; ASSOC PROF HIST, MIAMI UNIV, 70-, Morse fel, Yale Concilium Int Studies, 67-68, travel & res grants, 69; Am Philos Soc travel & res grant, 69; Soc Sci Res Coun & Am Coun Learned Soc res grant, SAfrica, 74; vis lectr, Univ Natal, 82. **MEMBERSHIPS** AHA; African Studies Asn. **RESEARCH** South Africa, history of native policy; race relations; urban history. **SELECTED PUBLICATIONS** Auth, South West Africa, in trust, 1915-1939, In: Britain and Germany in Africa: Imperial Rivalry and Colonial Rule, Yale Univ, 67; Urban origins of separate development, Race, 68; Reflections on urban history in South Africa, In: Focus on Cities, Inst Social Res, Univ Natal, 70; The Durban System: Roots of urban apartheid in colonial Natal, African Studies, 12/76; The sanitation syndrome: Bubonic Plaque and urban native policy in the Cape Colony, 1900-1909, J African Hist, 77; The Views of Mahlathi: Writings of a Black South African, Natal Univ Press, 82; The Making Of Modern South-Africa--Conquest, Segregation And Apartheid, J Of African Hist, Vol 36, 95. **CONTACT ADDRESS** Dept of Hist, Miami Univ, Oxford, OH, 45056.

SWANSON, RANDY
PERSONAL Born 03/13/1953, Chicago, IL, m, 1974, 2 children **DISCIPLINE** ARCHITECTURE **EDUCATION** Univ Ill-Urbana-Champaign, BS, 76, MA, 81; Univ Penn, MS, 87, PhD, 93. **CAREER** Archit, Sole Proprietor; Assoc Prof Archit, UNC-Charlotte. **MEMBERSHIPS** HCARB; SHOT; SBSE; SAH **RESEARCH** History and theory technology and design; scientific facilities. **SELECTED PUBLICATIONS** Coauth, The Philadelphia Waterworks: An Eotechnic Quenching of Thirst and Place, Making Environments: Technology and Design, ACSA Press, 92; Two Directions of Technical Innovation in Late 19th Century Laboatory Design, Architecture: Design Implementation, ACSA Press, 93; Comfronting the Barrier Between Qualitiative and Quantitative Research, Conference Proceedings, 96; Changing Concepts of Early Twentieth-Century Laboratory Design: Technological Risk and Innovation at New Haven, Ct and Blackley, England, Int Conf London, 96; l'Observatoire de Paris, (1667-1672) by Claude Perrault: A Preliminary Report of an Architectural Examination, Nat Conf Baltimore, 98. **CONTACT ADDRESS** College of Architecture, UN. Carolina-Charlotte, Charlotte, NC, 28223. **EMAIL** RSWANSON@EMAIL.UNCC.EDU

SWANSON, ROY ARTHUR
PERSONAL Born 04/07/1925, St. Paul, MN, m, 1946, 4 children **DISCIPLINE** CLASSICS, COMPARATIVE LITERATURE **EDUCATION** Univ Minn, BA, 48, BS, 49, MA, 51; Univ Ill, PhD, 54. **CAREER** Instr educ, Univ Ill, 52-53; instr classics, Ind Univ, 54-57; from asst prof to prof classics & humanities, Univ Minn, 57-65, chm dept comp lit, 64-65; prof English, Macalester Col, 65-67, coordr humanities, 66-67; chm dept classics, 67-70, 86-89; chm dept comp lit, 69-73, 76-82, Prof Classics & Comp Lit, Univ Wis-Milwaukee, 67-, Chm Dept Comp Lit, 76-, Fulbright scholar, Rome, 53; fel, Univ Ill, 54; ed, Minn Rev, 60-67; Lilly Found fel, Stockholm, 65-66; ed, Class J, 68-73. **HONORS AND AWARDS** Distinguished Teacher Award, Univ Minn, 62 & Univ Wis- Milwaukee, 74, 91; grad sch res grant, 68-69, 74 & 81. **MEMBERSHIPS** Am Philol Asn; MLA; Am Comp Lit Asn; Int Comp Lit Asn; Southern Comp Lit Asn. **RESEARCH** Lyric poetry, especially Greek and Roman; mediaeval studies; literary criticism. **SELECTED PUBLICATIONS** Auth, Odi et Amo: the complete poetry of Catullus, Lib Arts Press, 59; Heart of reason: Introductory essays in modern-world humanities, Denison, 63; The humor of Don Quixote, Romanic Rev, 10/63; Evil and love in Lagerkvist's crucifixion cycle, Scand Studies, 11/66; Pindar's odes, Bobbs, 74; Love is the function of death: Forster, Lagerkvist, and Zamyatin, Can Rev Comp Lit, 76; Deceptive symmetry: Classical echoes in the poetry of Richard Emil Braun, Mod Poetry Studies, 76; Ionesco's classical absurdity, In: The Two Faces of Ionesco, Whitston, 78; Pur Lager-Kvist: Five Early Works, Lewiston, 89; De nuptis metamorphoseon et mechanicorum quantorum, Stone Soup (London), 97. **CONTACT ADDRESS** Depts of Fr, Ital, & Comp Lit, For Lang and Li, Univ of Wis, PO Box 413, Milwaukee, WI, 53201-0413. **EMAIL** rexcy@uwm.edu

SWART, PAULA
PERSONAL The Hague, Netherlands **DISCIPLINE** ASIAN STUDIES **EDUCATION** Lang Inst, Beijing, Chinese Lang, 78; Univ Leiden, BA, 79; Univ Nanjing, China, 79; Univ Amsterdam, MA, 82. **CAREER** Participant, res proj Witte Leeuw, 79-81; res asst, Montreal Mus Fine Arts, 83-89; CURATOR, ASIAN STUDIES, VANCOUVER MUSEUM, 89-. **HONORS AND AWARDS** Undergrad Scholar, 74-77; Holland China Exchange Scholar, 77-78; Grad Scholar, 79-81, Dutch Gov. **MEMBERSHIPS** Japan Sword Appreciation Soc; Can Soc Asian Art; Am Museum Asn. **SELECTED PUBLICATIONS** Auth, Bronze Carriages from the Tomb of China's First Emperor, in Archaeol, Vol 37, 84; auth, Art from the Roof of the World: Tibet, 89; coauth, In Search of Old Nanking, 82; coauth, Chinese Jade Stone for the Emperors, 86. **CONTACT ADDRESS** Curator Asian Studies, Vancouver Museum, 1100 Chestnut St, Vancouver, BC, V6J 3J9.

SWARTZ, MARVIN
DISCIPLINE HISTORY **EDUCATION** Yale Univ, PhD, 67. **CAREER** Prof, Univ MA Amherst. **SELECTED PUBLICATIONS** Auth, The Union of Democratic Control in British Politics during the First World War, 71; The Politics of British Foreign Policy in the Era of Disraeli and Gladstone, 85; co-ed, Disraeli's Reminiscences, 75. **CONTACT ADDRESS** Dept of Hist, Univ Massachusetts Amherst, Mass Ave, Amherst, MA, 01003.

SWEARER, DONALD K.
PERSONAL Born 08/02/1934, Wichita, KS, m, 1964, 2 children **DISCIPLINE** HISTORY OF RELIGION **EDUCATION** Princeton Univ, BA, cum laude 56, MA, 65, PhD, 67; Yale Univ, BD, 62, STM, 63. **CAREER** Assoc Prof 70-75, Prof 75-, Eugene M Lang Res Prof 87-92, Charles and Harriet Cox McDowell Prof of Religion 92-, Swarthmore College; Instr, Asst Prof 65-70, Oberlin College. **HONORS AND AWARDS** Phi Beta Kappa; Lent Fel; 3 NEH Fels; Fulbright Fel; Guggenheim Fel; 2 Fulbright Fels. **MEMBERSHIPS** AAAS; AAR; ASSR; SBCS; AAUP. **RESEARCH** Buddhism; Comparative Religious Ethics. **SELECTED PUBLICATIONS** Auth, Holism and the Fate of the Earth, Rel and Ecology: Forging an Ethic Across Traditions, forthcoming; Center and Periphery: Buddhism and Politics in Modern Thailand, Buddhism and Politics in Modern Asia, ed, Ian Harris, Cassell's 98; Buddhist Virtue Voluntary Poverty and Extensive Benevolence, J of Rel Ethics, 98; The Worldliness of Buddhism, Wilson Qtly, 97; Bhikkhu Buddhadasa's Interpretation of the Buddha, J of the American Acad of Religion, 96; Hypostasizing the Buddha: Buddha: Image Consecration in Northern Thailand, Hist of Religions, 95; coauth, The Legend of Queen Cama, Camadevivamsa, Albany NY, SUNY Press, 98; auth, The Buddhist World of Southeast Asia, Albany, SUNY Press, 95; Ethics Wealth and Salvation, A Study in Buddhist Social Ethics, coed, Columbia, Univ S Carolina Press, pbk ed, 92. **CONTACT ADDRESS** Dept of Religion, Swarthmore Col, Swarthmore, PA, 19081. **EMAIL** dsweare1@swarthmore.edu

SWEENEY, JOHN ALBERT
PERSONAL Born 06/03/1925, Columbus, Ohio, m **DISCIPLINE** MUSICOLOGY, ETHNOMUSICOLOGY **EDUCATION** New York University, BA, 1949; Trinity College, London, LTCL, 1951; American Guild of Organists, AAGO, 1953; New York University, MA, 1953; State College of Music, Munich, Germany, graduate certificate, 1954; Free University, West Berlin, Germany, PhD, 1961; Johns Hopkins University, Ed, 1965; African Studies, University of Nairobi & Kenya, East Africa, graduate certificate, 1971. **CAREER** Morgan State University, professor of music, instruments, theory, musicology, ethnomusicology, 1962; University of Maryland, Extension Program, USAF, Berlin, Germany, teacher music theory, 1955-60; West Germany, guest lecturer, musicology, 1954-61; New York City St Mark's, Morgan State University, 1962-; New York, Munich, Baltimore, french hornist, bands, orchestras, 1945-70; Music Education's National Conference; Society for Ethnomusicology; Morgan State University & Baltimore Area, advanced international studies. **HONORS AND AWARDS** Fulbright Scholar, Germany, 1953-54. **MEMBERSHIPS** Ping Council for Annual Black Music Week, Morgan State University; Ad-

vanced Council, Left Bank & Jazz Society, Baltimore; India Forum; Dedicated to Dissemination of Indian Culture; Organist, Union Baptist Church Elected to Following Honor Society; Mu Sigma, New York University, 1968; Phi Beta Kappa, New York University, 1949; Phi Delta Kappa, Johns Hopkins University, 1965. **SELECTED PUBLICATIONS** Published Anthem: "134th Psalm", 1951; Book: The Trumpets in the cntatas of J S Bach, 1961; Book Reviews; Article: "Guyanea & the African Diaspora", 1976. **CONTACT ADDRESS** Fine Arts, Morgan State Univ, 1700 E Cold Spring, Baltimore, MD, 21239.

SWEENEY, KEVIN
DISCIPLINE COLONIAL AMERICAN HISTORY **EDUCATION** Yale Univ, PhD, 86. **CAREER** Instr, Amherst Col, 89. **RESEARCH** The hist and material cult of 17th and 18th-century New Engl. **SELECTED PUBLICATIONS** His writing has focused on the hist and material cult of seventeenth and eighteenth-century New Engl. **CONTACT ADDRESS** Amherst Col, Amherst, MA, 01002-5000.

SWEENEY, THOMAS JOHN
PERSONAL Born 08/25/1936, Akron, OH, m, 5 children **DISCIPLINE** EDUCATION **EDUCATION** Univ Akron, BA, 59; Univ Wisc, MS, 60; Ohio St Univ, PhD, 64 **CAREER** Commd 2nd lt, through grades to capt, 58-66, U.S. Army; tchr, 58-61, Ohio St Pub schls; instr, 61-63, Ohio St Univ; couns, 63-64, S.W. City schls, Grove City OH; prof, 64-72, Univ SC; prof, 72-, Ohio Univ; couns, 69-86, Gen Electric Found; prof emer, 72-, Ohio Univ. **HONORS AND AWARDS** ACA Dist Svc Award, 84; Dist Legis Svc Award, 86; Stripling Excel Award, 92; Couns Vision & Innov Award, 98. **MEMBERSHIPS** ACA; Asn Couns Edn & Supervision; Chi Sigma Iota **SELECTED PUBLICATIONS** Auth, Adlerian Counseling, 98; auth, prod, telecourse series, Coping with Kids, 78. **CONTACT ADDRESS** Ohio Univ, McCracken Hall, Athens, OH, 45701.

SWEET, PAUL ROBINSON
PERSONAL Born 03/14/1907, Willow Grove, PA, m, 1937, 2 children **DISCIPLINE** HISTORY **EDUCATION** DePauw Univ, AB, 29; Univ Wis, PhD, 34. **CAREER** Mem fac, Birmingham-Southern Col, 34-36, Bates Col, 36-46, Univ Chicago, 46-47 & Colby Col, 47-48; US ed-in-chief, Documents Ger Foreign Policy, 1918-1945, US Dept State, 48-59, first secy polit affairs, Am Embassy, Bonn, 59-63, consul gen, US Consulate Gen, Stuttgart, 63-67; prof hist, 68-76, EMER PROF HIST, MICH STATE UNIV, 76-, Chmn Atlantic affairs sem, Foreign Serv Inst, US Dept State, 67-68. **MEMBERSHIPS** AHA **RESEARCH** Modern German and Austrian history; European diplomatic history. **SELECTED PUBLICATIONS** Coauth, The Tragedy of Austria, Gollancz, London, 48; Festschrift fur Heinrich Benedikt, Vienna, 57; auth, Friedrich von Gentz: Defender of the Old Order, Greenwood, 70; The historical writing of Heinrich von Srbik, Hist & Theory, 70; Wilhelm von Humboldt (1767-1835): His legacy to the historian, Centennial Rev, 71; Young Wilhelm von Humboldt's writings reconsidered, J Hist Ideas, 73; Wilhelm von Humboldt: A Biography 1767-1808, Ohio State Univ, Vol I, 78; The Windsor File + British Government Efforts To Suppress Publication Of Documents From The German-Foreign-Ministry-Archives, Historian, Vol 59, 97; Fichte And The Jews--A Case Of Tension Between Civil-Rights And Human-Rights, German Studies Rev, Vol 16, 93. **CONTACT ADDRESS** Dept of Hist, Michigan State Univ, East Lansing, MI, 48824.

SWEETS, JOHN FRANK
PERSONAL Born 07/18/1945, Knoxville, TN, m, 1967, 1 child **DISCIPLINE** MODERN EUROPEAN HISTORY **EDUCATION** Fla State Univ, BA, 67; Duke Univ, MA, 69, PhD, 72. **CAREER** Asst prof, 72-77, assoc prof, 77-84, PROF HIST, UNIV KANS, 85-; Ed, Proc Western Soc Fr Hist, 82-; NEH fel, 78-79 & 87-88 **MEMBERSHIPS** AHA; Soc Fr Hist Studies; Western Soc Fr Hist. **RESEARCH** Social and political history of 20th century France; lacemakers of LePuy in 19th Century; resistance and occupation in France 1940-1944; Vichy France. **SELECTED PUBLICATIONS** Auth, The Politics of Resistance in France, Northern Ill Univ Press, 76; Choices in Vichy France, Oxford Univ Press, 86 & 94; Clermont-Ferrand a l'heure allemande, Plon, 96 **CONTACT ADDRESS** Dept of Hist, Univ of Kans, Lawrence, KS, 66045-0001. **EMAIL** jfsweets@falcon.cc.ukans.edu

SWENSON, EDWARD
DISCIPLINE MUSIC HISTORY **EDUCATION** Oberlin Col, BM; Univ Ky, MM; Cornell Univ, PhD. **CAREER** Prof. **SELECTED PUBLICATIONS** Auth, pubs on history of music. **CONTACT ADDRESS** Dept of Music History, Theory and Composition, Ithaca Col, 100 Job Hall, Ithaca, NY, 14850. **EMAIL** swensone@ithaca.edu

SWERDLOW, AMY
PERSONAL New York, NY, 4 children **DISCIPLINE** AMERICAN HISTORY **EDUCATION** New York Univ, BA, 63; Sarah Lawrence Col, MA, 73. **CAREER** Assoc dir, 73-76, PROF WOMEN'S HIST, SARAH LAWRENCE COL, 81-, Fel, Rutgers Univ & Woodrow Wilson Found, 80. **MEMBERSHIPS** AHA; Orgn Am Historians. **RESEARCH** Women's history; peace movements. **SELECTED PUBLICATIONS** Coauth, Household & Kin: Families in Flux, Feminist Press, McGraw Hill, 81; co-ed, Class, Race & Sex: The Dynamics of Control, G K Hall, 83; Ladies Day at the Capitol, Women Strike for Peace, Feminist Studies, fall 82; Polite Protesters--The Amn Peace Movement Of The 1980s, J Of Am Hist, Vol 81, 95; The Women And The Warriors--The US Section Of The Womens-International-League-For-Peace-And-Freedom, 1911-1946, J Of Am Hist, Vol 83, 96. **CONTACT ADDRESS** Dept Women's Hist, Sarah Lawrence Col, 80 CPW, New York, NY, 10023.

SWIDLER, LEONARD
PERSONAL Born 01/06/1929, Sioux City, IA, m, 1957, 2 children **DISCIPLINE** RELIGION; HISTORY **EDUCATION** St Norbert Col, BA, 50; Marquette Univ, MA, 55; Univ Tubingen, STL, 59; Univ Wis, PhD(hist), 61. **CAREER** From asst prof to assoc prof hist, Duquesne Univ, 60-66; Prof Relig, Temple Univ, 66-, Founder & co-ed, J Ecumenical Studies, 64-; mem, Comt Educ for Ecumenism & Presby/ Reformed and Roman Cath Consultation, 65-; fel, Inst Ecumenical & Cult Res, 68-69; Fulbright res grant, Ger, 72-73; guest prof Cath & Protestant theol, Univ Tubingen, 72-73; guest prof Philos, Nankaiv, Tianjin, 87. **HONORS AND AWARDS** LLD, La Salle Col, 77. **MEMBERSHIPS** Am Soc Church Hist; Am Acad Relig; Cath Theol Soc, Am; Church Hist Soc. **RESEARCH** Inter-religious dialogue; modern church history; women in religion and society; global ethics. **SELECTED PUBLICATIONS** Ed, Ecumenism, the Spirit and Worship, 66 & auth, The Ecumenical Vanguard, 66, Duquesne Univ; Freedom in the Church, Pflaum, 69; coauth, Bishops and People, Westminster, 71; Isj en Isjah, 73; auth, Women in Judaism, 76; Blood witness for peace and unity, 77; coauth, Women priests, 77; Yeshua: A Model for Moderns, 87; After the Absolute, 90; Toward a Catholic Constitution, 96; THEORIA, Praxis, 98. **CONTACT ADDRESS** Dept of Religion, Temple Univ, 1114 W Berks St, Philadelphia, PA, 19122-6090. **EMAIL** dialogue@vm.temple.edu

SWIERENGA, ROBERT PETER
PERSONAL Born 06/10/1935, Chicago, IL, m, 1956, 5 children **DISCIPLINE** AMERICAN HISTORY **EDUCATION** Calvin Col, AB, 57; Northwestern Univ, MA, 58; State Univ Iowa, PhD(hist), 65. **CAREER** Instr high sch, Iowa, 58-61; instr hist, Calvin Col, 61-62, asst prof, 65-68; assoc prof, 68-72, PROF HIST, KENT STATE UNIV, 72-, Am Coun Learned Soc grant-in-aid, 67-68; managing ed, Soc Sci Hist, 76; Fulbright-Hays Silver Opportunity res scholar, Netherlands, 76; Am Coun Learned Soc fel, 81. **MEMBERSHIPS** Orgn Am Historians; Econ Hist Asn; Agr Hist Soc; Soc Sci Hist Asn; Immigration Hist Soc. **RESEARCH** American land, immigrant, and quantitative history. **SELECTED PUBLICATIONS** Auth, Bright Radical Star--Black-Freedom and White Supremacy on the Hawkeye Frontier, Agricultural Hist, Vol 68, 94; Evangelicals and Politics in Antebellum America, Civil War Hist, Vol 40, 94; Untitled, J Am Hist, Vol 83, 96; Odyssey-Of-Woe--The Journey of the Immigrant Ship April from Amsterdam to New-Castle, 1817-1818, Penn Magazine Hist Biography, Vol 0118, 94; Out on the Wind--Poles and Danes in Lincoln County, Minnesota, 1880-1905, Historian, Vol 55, 93; Born in the Country--A History Of Rural America, J Am Hist, Vol 83, 96; Strategic Factors in 19th-Century American Economic-History--A Volume to Honor Robert Fogel, J Interdisciplinary Hist, Vol 24, 94. **CONTACT ADDRESS** Dept of Hist, Kent State Univ, Kent, OH, 44242.

SWIETEK, FRANCIS ROY
PERSONAL Born 04/17/1946, La Salle, IL **DISCIPLINE** MEDIEVAL HISTORY, LATIN **EDUCATION** St John's Univ, Minn, BA, 68; Univ Ill, Urbana-Champaign, MA, 71, PhD(hist), 78. **CAREER** Libr manuscript cataloguer & asst to dir Latin studies, St John's Univ, Minn, 71-74; ASST PROF HIST, UNIV DALLAS, 78- **MEMBERSHIPS** Medieval Acad Am; AHA; Midwest Medieval Conf. **RESEARCH** Medieval intellectual and ecclesiastical history; Medieval Latin literature; Latin paleography. **SELECTED PUBLICATIONS** Auth, Ab-Antiquo-Alterius-Ordinis-Fuerit--An Examination of 12th-Century Papal Exemptions from the Monastic Ban on So-Called Spiritualia Ownership--Alexander-III on the Reception of Savigny into the Cistercian Order, Rev Hist, Vol 89; Christendom and Christianity in the Middle-Ages--The Relations Between Religion, Church, and Society, Cath Hist Rev, Vol 81, 95. **CONTACT ADDRESS** Dept of Hist, Univ of Dallas, Irving, TX, 75061.

SWIFT, LOUIS JOSEPH
PERSONAL Born 08/01/1932, Scranton, PA, m, 1964, 3 children **DISCIPLINE** CLASSICS **EDUCATION** St Mary's Univ, Md, AB, 54; Pontif Gregorian Univ, STB, 56; Johns Hopkins Univ, MAT, 58, PhD(classics), 63. **CAREER** From asst prof to assoc prof classics, State Univ NY Buffalo, 63-70; assoc prof, 70-76, PROF CLASSICS & CHMN DEPT, UNIV KY, 82-, Am Philos Soc grant-in-aid, 64; State Univ NY Res Found fac fel, 68. **MEMBERSHIPS** Am Philol Asn; Arch Archaeol Inst Am; Class Asn Mid West & South; NAm Patristic Soc; AAUP. **RESEARCH** Latin literature; pastristics; ancient rhetoric. **SELECTED PUBLICATIONS** Auth, The Concise Dictionary of Early Christianity, Cath Hist Rev, Vol 79, 93; Christian Intolerance in Face of Pagans, Cath Hist Rev, Vol 80, 94. **CONTACT ADDRESS** Dept of Classics, Univ of Ky, 500 S Limestone St, Lexington, KY, 40506-0003.

SWIFT, MARY GRACE
PERSONAL Born 08/03/1927, Bartlesville, OK **DISCIPLINE** RUSSIAN HISTORY & GOVERNMENT **EDUCATION** Creighton Univ, BS, 56, MA, 60; Notre Dame Univ, PhD(Soviet area studies), 67. **CAREER** ASSOC PROF HIST, LOYOLA UNIV, LA, 66- **HONORS AND AWARDS** De la Torre Bueno Prize, 73. **MEMBERSHIPS** Am Asn Advan Slavic Studies. **RESEARCH** Dance history, especially Russian ballet. **SELECTED PUBLICATIONS** Auth, Sisters in Arms--Catholic Nuns Through 2 Millennia, New Orleans Rev, Vol 23, 97. **CONTACT ADDRESS** Dept of Hist, Loyola Univ, New Orleans, LA, 70118.

SWINDELL, WARREN C.
PERSONAL Born 08/22/1934, Kansas City, MO, m, 1967 **DISCIPLINE** MUSICOLOGY **EDUCATION** Lincoln Univ of MO, BS Music Educ 1956; The Univ of MI Ann Arbor, MM 1964; The Univ of IA, PhD Music Educ 1970. **CAREER** Central High Sch Hayti MO, band and choir dir 1956-57, dir of musical act 1959-60; Hubbard High Sch, dir of music act 1960-61; Flint MI Public Schools, inst mus specialist 1961-67; KY State Univ, chair/prof of music 1970-79, prof of music 1979-80; INDIANA STATE UNIV, CHAIR, DIR/PROF CTR, DEPT OF AFRICAN AND AFRICAN AMERICAN STUDIES, 1980-96, prof, currently. **HONORS AND AWARDS** Numerous Service Awds NAACP 1978-94; NEH Summer Seminar for College Teachers Grant 1984; Faculty Rsch Grant Indiana State Univ 1985; IN State Univ Research Grant 1987-88; Amer Philosophical Society Research Grant 1988; Lilly Endowment Faculty Open Fellowship 1993-94; Caleb Mills Award for Distinguished Teaching. **MEMBERSHIPS** Evaluator Natl Assoc of Schools of Music Accred 1977-78; screening panel KY Arts Commn Project 1977-79; chaired State, Div & Natl MENC meetings 1979-80; worshipful master, Prince Hall Lodge #16, 1991-92; president, Region V, National Council for Black Studies, 1989-91; secretary, Indiana Coalition of Blacks in Higher Education, 1992-93; first vp, Indiana Coalition of Blacks in Higher Educ, 1994-95; pres, Indiana Coalition, 1996-; Prince Hall Grand Lodge Jurisdiction of Indiana, chairman of masonic history & education; chairman, School of Instruction, Prince Hall Masons; Terre Haute, Indiana Branch NAACP, first vp 1995-96, pres, 1997. **CONTACT ADDRESS** Africana Studies, Indiana State Univ, Stalker Hall 204, Terre Haute, IN, 47809.

SWINDEN, KEVIN J.
PERSONAL Born 03/04/1970, Toronto, ON, Canada, m, 1998 **DISCIPLINE** MUSIC **EDUCATION** Univ W On, BM, 92; St Univ NY Buffalo, PhD, 97. **CAREER** Vis asst prof, St Univ NY Buffalo, 97; vis asst prof, St Univ NY Potsdam, 98; asst prof, Univ Ms, 98- . **HONORS AND AWARDS** Thomas J. Clifton Mem Award, 97 **MEMBERSHIPS** SMT; CUMS; SCSMT. **RESEARCH** Nineteenth century chromatic harmony; Bruckner, theory pedogogy. **SELECTED PUBLICATIONS** Auth, Bruckner's Perged Prelude-A dramatic revue of Wagner?, Music Anal, 99 **CONTACT ADDRESS** PO Box 6835, University, MS, 38677. **EMAIL** kswinden@olemiss.edu

SWINNEY, EVERETTE
PERSONAL Born 09/09/1933, Lima, OH, m, 1953, 4 children **DISCIPLINE** AMERICAN HISTORY **EDUCATION** OH Northern Univ, BA, 55; PA State Univ, MA, 57; Univ TX, PhD, 66. **CAREER** Grad asst, PA State Univ, 55-57; from instr to assoc prof, 57-67, prof hist, Southwest TX State Univ, 67-96, prof emeritus, 96-, chmn dept, 67-80. **MEMBERSHIPS** Orgn Am Historians; Southern Hist Asn. **RESEARCH** Civil War and reconstruction; computers and hist; historiography. **SELECTED PUBLICATIONS** Auth, Enforcing the Fifteenth Amendment, 1870-1877, J Southern Hist, 5/62; United States v Powell Clayton, Ark Hist Quart, summer 67, Suppressing the Klu Klux Klan: Re Enforcement of the Reconstruction Amendments 1870-1877, gorland pub, 87. **CONTACT ADDRESS** Dept of Hist, Southwest Texas State Univ, 601 University Dr, San Marcos, TX, 78666-4685. **EMAIL** es08@academia.swt.edu

SWINTH, KIRSTEN
DISCIPLINE AMERICAN CULTURAL HISTORY **EDUCATION** Yale Univ, PhD. **CAREER** Asst prof, Fordham Univ. **HONORS AND AWARDS** John Paul Getty postdoc fel. **RESEARCH** Women artists and the develop of Am art. **SELECTED PUBLICATIONS** Pub(s), rev(s) and articles on women artists and on turn-of-the-century aesthetic debates. **CONTACT ADDRESS** Dept of Hist, Fordham Univ, 113 W 60th St, New York, NY, 10023.

SWINTON, GEORGE
PERSONAL Born 04/17/1917, Vienna, Austria **DISCIPLINE** HISTORY OF ART **EDUCATION** McGill Univ, BA, 46; Montreal Sch Art Design, 46-47; Art Students' League, 49-50. **CAREER** Cur, Saskatoon Art Ctr, 47-49; instr, Smith Col, 50-53; artist-in-res, Queen's Univ, 53-54; prof art, Univ Man, 54-74; prof, 73-81, adj prof, 81-85, PROF EMER ART HISTORY,

CARLETON UNIV, 86-; vis prof, Simon Fraser Univ, 72; vis prof, Univ Wisconsin, 74; vis prof, Univ Leningrad, 81. **HONORS AND AWARDS** Centennial Medal, 67; mem, Order of Can, 79; Canada 125 Medal; LLD(hon), Univ Man, 87. **SELECTED PUBLICATIONS** Auth, Eskimo/Sculpture/Esquimaude, 65; auth, Sculpture of the Eskimo, 72, 2nd ed 75, 3rd ed 82; auth, Sculpture Esquimaude, 76; auth, Sculpture of the Inuit, 92; coauth, What is Good Design?, 54; illusr/des, Red River of the North, 69. **CONTACT ADDRESS** 202-21 Roslyn Rd, Winnipeg, MB, R3L 2S8.

SWINTON, GEORGE

PERSONAL Born 04/17/1917, Vienna, Austria **DISCIPLINE** ART HISTORY **EDUCATION** McGill Univ, BA, 46; Montreal Sch Art Design, 46-47; Art Students' League, 49-50. **CAREER** Cur, Saskatoon Art Ctr, 47-49; instr, Smith Col, 50-53; artist-in-residence, Queen's Univ, 53-54; prof art, Univ Man, 54-74; prof, 73-81, adj prof, 81-85, PROF EMER ART HISTORY, CARLETON UNIV, 86-; vis prof, Simon Fraser Univ, 72; vis prof, Univ Wisconsin, 74; vis prof, Univ Leningrad, 81. **HONORS AND AWARDS** Centennial Medal, 67; mem, Order of Can, 79; Canada 125 Medal; LLD(hon), Univ Man, 87. **SELECTED PUBLICATIONS** Auth, Eskimo/Sculpture/Esquimaude, 65; auth, Sculpture of the Eskimo, 72, 2nd ed, 75, 3rd ed, 82; auth, Sculpture Esquimaude, 76; auth, Sculpture of the Inuit, 92; coauth, What is Good Design?, 54; illusr/des, Red River of the North, 69. **CONTACT ADDRESS** 202 - 21 Roslyn Rd, Winnipeg, MB, R3L 2S8.

SWINTON, KATHERINE E.

PERSONAL Born 08/14/1950, East York, ON, Canada **DISCIPLINE** LAW/HISTORY **EDUCATION** Univ Alta, BA, 71; Osgoode Hall Law Sch, York Univ, LLB, 75; Yale Univ, LLM, 77. **CAREER** Parliamentary intern, House of Commons, 71-72; law clerk, Supreme Court Can, 75-76; asst prof, Osgoode Hall Law Sch, 77-79; asst prof, 79-82, assoc prof, 82-87, prof fac law, Univ Toronto, 88-97; JUSTICE, ONTARIO COURT (GENERAL DIVISION), 97-. **SELECTED PUBLICATIONS** Auth, The Supreme Court and Canadian Federalism: The Laskin-Dickson Years, 90; co-ed, Studies in Labour Law, 83; co-ed, Competing Constitutional Visions: The Meech Lake Accord, 88; co-ed, Rethinking Federalism, 95. **CONTACT ADDRESS** Ontario Court, 361 University Ave, Toronto, ON, M5G 1T3.

SYED, JASMIN

DISCIPLINE CLASSICS **EDUCATION** Staatsexamen, PhD, 91. **CAREER** Asst prof, Stanford Univ. **RESEARCH** Latin lit; Roman cult hist; lit theory; gender in the ancient world. **SELECTED PUBLICATIONS** Auth, The Construction of Roman Identity in Vergil's Aeneid; Creating Roman Identity: Subjectivity and Self-Fashioning in Latin Literature, 97. **CONTACT ADDRESS** Stanford Univ, Bldg 20, Main Quad, Stanford, CA, 94305.

SYLIOWICZ, JOSEPH S.

PERSONAL Born 12/07/1931, Belgium, m, 1960, 2 children **DISCIPLINE** INTERNATIONAL STUDIES **EDUCATION** BA Univ of Denver, 53; MA School of Adv Intl Studies, John Hopkins Univ, 55; PhD Columbia Univ, 61. **CAREER** Univ MD, Extension Div, 60; Hunter Col, 61-62; Brooklyn Col, 61-64; Long Island Univ, 66; Univ Mich 80; Univ Utah, 80; Oxford Univ, Michaelmas Term, 84; Dir Intermodal Trans Inst and Prof, Graduate School of Intl Studies, Univ Denver, present. **HONORS AND AWARDS** Intl Award for Dci and Ethics in Trans Res, Alliance for Trans Res, 97; Outstanding Scholar, Burlington Northern Found Award, 86; Sr Assoc St Anthony's Col and Fel Dept of External Studies, Oxford Univ, 84-85; Fulbright Sr Res Fellowship, 83; Soc Sci Res Council, 68-69. **MEMBERSHIPS** Phi Beta Kappa; Pi Gamma Mu; Tau Kappa Alpha; Phi Delta Rho; Am Men of Sci; Who's Who in the West; Dictionary of Intl Bio; Intl Scholars Dir; Intl Auth; Writer Who's Who. **SELECTED PUBLICATIONS** Denver International Airport: Lessons Learned, McGraw Hill,96, Co-auth; Politics, Technology and Development: Decision Making in the Turkish Iron and Steel Industry, NY: St Martins Press and London: The Manmillan Press Ltd/St Antony's College Series, 91; Education in L C Brown, ed, The Imperial Legacy: The Ottoman Imprint on the Balkans and the Middle East, NY, Coumbia Univ Press, 95; Education and Political Development in M Heper ed, Politics in the 3rd Turkish Republic, Westview, 93; Revisiting Transportation Planning and Decision Making Theory, co-auth, 74. **CONTACT ADDRESS** Graduate School of Intl Studies, Univ Denver, Denver, CO, 80210. **EMAIL** JSZYLIOW@DU.EDU

SYLLA, EDITH DUDLEY

PERSONAL Born 08/15/1941, Cleveland, OH, m, 1963, 2 children **DISCIPLINE** HISTORY OF SCIENCE, MEDIEVAL PHILOSOPHY **EDUCATION** Radcliffe Col, AB, 63; Harvard Univ, AM, 64, PhD(hist of sci), 71. **CAREER** Instr social studies, 68-70, asst prof hist, 70-75, assoc prof, 75-81, PROF HIST, NC STATE UNIV, 81-, Reviewer, Zentralblatt fur Math, 73; NSF res grant, Oxford, Eng, 75-76; fel, Andrew D White Ctr for Humanities, Cornell Univ, 78-79, Inst Advan Studies, Princeton, 82-83. **MEMBERSHIPS** Hist Sci Soc; Mediaeval Acad Am; AAAS; AHA; Int Soc Study Mediaeval Philos. **RESEARCH** History of 14th century philosophy; medieval logic, mathematics and science. **SELECTED PUBLICATIONS** Auth, Thomas Bradwardine--A View of Time and a Vision of Eternity in 14th-Century Thought, ISIS, Vol 87, 96; The 'Sophismata' of Richard Kilvington, Speculum, Vol 68, 93. **CONTACT ADDRESS** Dept of Hist, No Carolina State Univ, Box 5941, Raleigh, NC, 27650.

SYLVAS, LIONEL B.

PERSONAL Born 05/10/1940, New Orleans, LA **DISCIPLINE** EDUCATION **EDUCATION** Southern Univ, BS 1963; Univ of Detroit, MA 1971; Nova Univ, EdD 1975. **CAREER** Ford Motor Co, indust rsch analy 1967-69, ed training spec 1969-71; Miami Dade Comm Coll, assoc acad dean 1971-74; Miami Dade Comm Coll, asst to pres 1974-77; NORTHERN VA COMM COLL, CAMPUS PROVOST. **HONORS AND AWARDS** Outstanding Educator Miami Dade Comm Coll 1975. **MEMBERSHIPS** Consult Southern Assoc of Coll & Schools Eval Team 1974-; mem advisory bd Black Amer Affairs, Natl School Volunteer Prog 1974-78; pres Southern Reg Couns 1977-88; field reader for Titles III & IV Office of Educ 1979-; mem advisory bd Amer Red Cross 1982-; consult advisory group VA Power Co 1983-87; panelist on the VA Commission of the Arts; mem Constitution Bicentennial Commiss VA. **CONTACT ADDRESS** No Virginia Comm Coll, 15200 Neabsco Mills Rd, Woodbridge, VA, 22191-4006.

SYLVESTER, JOHN ANDREW

PERSONAL Born 12/20/1935, Springfield, MA **DISCIPLINE** UNITED STATES HISTORY & DIPLOMACY **EDUCATION** Harvard Univ, AB, 57; Univ Wis, MA, 59, PhD(hist), 67. **CAREER** Asst prof, 66-70, ASSOC PROF HIST, OKLA STATE UNIV, 70- **MEMBERSHIPS** AHA; Orgn Am Historians; Soc Historians Am Foreign Rel. **RESEARCH** Recent United States diplomacy; historical methods; political geography. **SELECTED PUBLICATIONS** Auth, Taft, Dulles and Ike--New Faces For 1952, Mid-Am Hist Rev, Vol 76, 94. **CONTACT ADDRESS** Dept of Hist, Oklahoma State Univ, Stillwater, OK, 74078.

SYLWESTER, HAROLD JAMES

PERSONAL Born 09/23/1934, Roseburg, OR, m, 1965, 2 children **DISCIPLINE** AMERICAN DIPLOMATIC HISTORY **EDUCATION** Concordia Teachers Col, BS, 56: Univ Ore, MEd, 60; Univ Kans, MA, 64, PhD(Am hist), 70. **CAREER** Instr Am hist, Concordia Teachers Col, 64-65; asst prof, 69-75, ASSOC PROF HIST, CENT MO STATE UNIV, 75-. **HONORS AND AWARDS** Res grant, Harry S Truman Inst, 70, Kansas City Regional Coun Higher Educ, 70 & Am Philos Soc, 71; US Dept Educ grant, 81-82; NEH fel, 79, 88; Constitution - Bicentennial Commission, 89; Fel, Mid-America Japan in the school, U.S.-Japan Found, Univ Kans, 92; Fulbright-Hayes, Russia and the Baltic States, 94. **MEMBERSHIPS** AHA; Orgn Am Historians; Soc for Hist of Am For Policy; Nat Coun for the Soc Studies; Concordia Hist Inst; Nat Coun of Geog Educ. **RESEARCH** Focus on the Truman administration; public opinion and American foreign policy; relationship between domestic developments and foreign affairs. **SELECTED PUBLICATIONS** Auth, The Swedish Lutherans on the Delaware and their interest in schools, Concordia Hist Quart, 7/67; The Kansas press and the coming of the Spanish-American War, Historian, 2/69. **CONTACT ADDRESS** Dept of History, Central Missouri State Univ, Warrensburg, MO, 64093-8888. **EMAIL** sylwest@cmsuvmb@cmsu.edu

SYMEONOGLOU, SARANTIS

PERSONAL Born 02/14/1937, Athens, Greece, m, 1965, 2 children **DISCIPLINE** CLASSICAL ARCHEOLOGY **EDUCATION** Univ Athens, Greece, BA, 61; Columbia Univ, PhD(archaeol), 71. **CAREER** Asst cur archaeol, Greek Archaeol Serv, 63-66; asst prof, 69-76, Assoc Prof Archaeol, WA Univ, 77-, Field dir excavation, Columbia Univ Archaeol Exped, 70-74; WA Univ res fel archaeol, 73-74; Am Philos Soc fel archaeol, 76; Founder and Dir, Odyssey Project, 84-. **MEMBERSHIPS** Archaeol Inst Am; Asn Field Archaeol; Am Schs Oriental Res; Am Oriental Soc; Archaeol Soc of Athens. **RESEARCH** Minoan-Mycenaean art and archaeol; class art; Near-Eastern art and archaeol, Archael Soc of Athens. **SELECTED PUBLICATIONS** Auth, Excavations in Boeotia, 1965, 66 & coauth, Antiquities and monuments of Boeotia, 67, Archaeologikon Deltion; auth, A chart of Minoan and Mycenaean pottery, Am J Archaeol, 70; Archaeological survey in the area of Phlamoudhi Cyprus, Report Dept Antiq Cyprus, 72; Thebes, Greece: an archaeological and sociological problem, Architectura, 72; coauth, Ancient Collections in WA Univ, WA Univ, 73; auth, Kadmeia I; Mycenaean Finds from Thebes, Greece, Studies Mediterranean Archaeol, 73; contribr, Excavations at Phlamoudhi & the form of the Sanctuary in Bronze Age Cyprus, Archaeol Cyprus, Recent Develop, 75; The Topography of Thebes, Princeton Univ Press, 85; The Island of Odysseus, in The Sciences, Nov-Dec, 88; The Masters of Olympia, in press. **CONTACT ADDRESS** Dept of Art & Archaeol, Washington Univ, 1 Brookings Dr, Box 1189, St. Louis, MO, 63130-4899. **EMAIL** ssymeono@artsci.wustl.edu

SYMONDS, CRAIG LEE

PERSONAL Born 12/31/1946, Long Beach, CA, m, 1969, 1 child **DISCIPLINE** AMERICAN HISTORY **EDUCATION** Univ Calif, Los Angeles, BA, 67; Univ Fla, MA, 69, PhD, 76. **CAREER** Asst prof strategy, US Naval War Col, 74-75; from Asst Prof to Assoc Prof, 76-86, prof hist, US Naval Acad, 86-, Chair, Dept Hist, 88-92. **HONORS AND AWARDS** Teaching Excellence Award, USNA, 88; Johnson Lyman Book Award, NASOH, 95; S.A. Cunningham Award for Literary Achievement, 97; Research Excellence Award, USNA, 98; Superior Civilian Service Award (2 awards); Civilian Meritorious Service Award. **MEMBERSHIPS** Am Mil Inst; US Naval Inst; North Am Soc Oceanic Hist; Soc Historians Early Am Repub. **RESEARCH** 19th century American Naval Policy; United States Civil War. **SELECTED PUBLICATIONS** Ed, Charleston Blockade, NNC Press, 76; auth, Navalists and Antinavalists, Univ Del Press, 80; ed, A Year on a Monitor, USC Press, 88; Civil War Reminiscences of William H. Parker, Naval Inst Press, 90; auth, Joseph E. Johnston: A Civil War Biography, W.W. Norton, 92; U.S. Naval Institute's Historical Atlas of the U.S. Navy, 95; Stonewall of the West: Patrick Cleburne and the Civil War, Univ Press Kans, 97. **CONTACT ADDRESS** Dept of Hist, US Naval Acad, Annapolis, MD, 21402. **EMAIL** symonds@nadn.navy.mil

SYMONS, T.H.B

PERSONAL Born 05/30/1929, Toronto, ON, Canada, m, 1963, 3 children **DISCIPLINE** MODERN HISTORY **EDUCATION** Univ Toronto, BA, 51; Oxford Univ, MA, 53. **CAREER** Instr mod hist & dean men, Trinity Col, Univ Toronto, 54-56, instr & dean, Devonshire House, 56-63; asst prof, 63-66, founding pres & vchancellor, 61-72, ASSOC PROF HIST, TRENT UNIV, 66-, Charter mem, World Univ Serv Can; mem, Adv Comt Confederation to Prime Minister Ont, 65-72; chmn, Ministerial Comn Fr Lang Educ Ont, 71-72; chmn, Asn Commonwealth Univs, 71-72; chmn, Nat Comn Can Studies, 72-; mem, Ont Arts Coun, 74-76; chmn, Ont Human Rights Comn, 75-78; spec adv higher educ to Govt of Can, 76; mem, Can Coun, 76-. **HONORS AND AWARDS** Officer of Order of Can, 76., LLD, Waterloo Lutheran Univ, 71, Univ NB, 72, York Univ, 73, Trent Univ, 75 & Lawrentian Univ, 77; DU, Univ Ottawa, 74. **MEMBERSHIPS** Fel Royal Soc Arts; Can Hist Asn; Champlain Soc; Asn Can Studies US; fel Royal Soc Can. **RESEARCH** Canadian history and contemporary Canadian studies; local history; Canadian-American relations. **SELECTED PUBLICATIONS** Auth, Canadian Studies and the Canadian University in the 21st-Century, J Can Studies, Vol 30, 95. **CONTACT ADDRESS** Trent Univ, Peterborough, ON, K9J 7B8.

SYMONS, VAN J.

PERSONAL Born 06/05/1945, Logan, UT, m, 1971, 5 children **DISCIPLINE** HISTORY **EDUCATION** Brigham Young Univ, AB, 70; Brown Univ, PhD, 75. **CAREER** Asst prof, Whittier Col, 74-78; vis Mansfield Prof, The Maureen and Mike Mansfield Center, Univ of Mont, 90-91; ASST TO FULL PROF OF HIST, 78-, DIR OF ASIAN STUDIES PROG, 78-90, CHEMN OF HIST DEPT, AUGUSTANA COL, 83-86 & 92-95. **HONORS AND AWARDS** Dir, ASIANetwork Consultancy Advisory Prog, 98-99; NEH summer inst, Univ of Mich, 94, Univ of Mont, 95. **MEMBERSHIPS** Asn for Asian Studies; ASIANetwork. **RESEARCH** Late Ming-Early Qing Chinese dynastic history. **SELECTED PUBLICATIONS** Auth, Moral Judgment in War and Crimes Against Humanity, America's Wars in Asia: A Cultural Approach to Hist and Memory, M.E. Sharpe Inc., 98; Near the Vortex of the Storm: Ming Chinese Frontier Politics and the 1627 Manchu Invasion of Korea, Ch'ing-chu Cha-ch'I Ssu-ch'in chiao-shou pa-shih shou-ch'en hsueh-shu lun-wen chi, 95; Peace, War, and Trade Along the Great Wall: Nomadic-Chinese Interaction Through Two Millennia, Ind Univ Press, 89; Ch'ing Ginseng Management: Ch'ing Monopolies in Microcosm, Az State Univ, Center for Asian Studies, 81. **CONTACT ADDRESS** Dept of Hist, Augustana Col, Rock Island, IL, 61201. **EMAIL** hisymons@augustana.edu

SYNAN, EDWARD A.

PERSONAL Born 04/13/1918, Fall River, MA **DISCIPLINE** PHILOSOPHY, MEDIEVAL STUDIES **EDUCATION** Seton Hall Univ, AB, 38; Cath Univ Am, STL, 42; Univ Toronto, MA, 50, PhD, 52; Pontif Inst Medieval Studies, Toronto, LMS, 51. **CAREER** Prof philos & chmn dept, Seton Hall Univ, 52-59; pres, 73-79, Prof Philos, Pontif Inst Medieval Studies, Toronto, 59-, Can Coun grant, 65; PROF, UNIV TORONTO, 59-. **HONORS AND AWARDS** LLD, Seton Hall Univ, 73; DLitt, Univ Dallas, 79; ThD, Darlington Sem, 79. **MEMBERSHIPS** Am Cath Philos Asn; Mediaeval Acad Am; Renaissance Soc Am; Am Soc Polit & Legal Philos; Can Philos Asn. **RESEARCH** Medieval philosophy; theology; Christian-Jewish relations. **SELECTED PUBLICATIONS** Auth, The Church and the Jews in the 13th-Century, 1254-1314, Cath Hist Rev, Vol 79, 93; 4 Quodlibets by Pecham,John, Quodlibeta-I-III, Quodlibeta-IV-Romanum, Speculum, Vol 68, 93; Alienated Minority--The Jews of Medieval Latin Europe, Cath Hist Rev, Vol 80, 94; Thomas Aquinas and the Jews, Cath Hist Rev, Vol 82, 96. **CONTACT ADDRESS** Pontifical Inst of Medieval Studies, 59 Queen's Park, Toronto, ON, M5S 2C4.

SYNAN, VINSON
DISCIPLINE CHURCH HISTORY **EDUCATION** Univ Richmond, BA; Univ Ga, MA, PhD. **CAREER** Dean; prof, 94. **SELECTED PUBLICATIONS** Auth, Emmanuel Col:The First Fifty Years, MA thesis, N Wash Press, 68; The Holiness-Pentecostal Movement in the U.S., PhD dissertation, Eerdmans, 71; The Old-Time Power: History of the Pentecostal Holiness Church, Advocate Press, 73; Charismatic Bridges, Word of Life, 74; Aspects of Pencostal/Charismatic Origins, Logos, 75; Azusa Street, Bridge Publ, 80; In the Latter Days, Servant, 85; The Twentieth-Century Pentecostal Explosion, Creation House, 87; Launching the Decade of Evangelization, N Amer Renewal Srv Comm, 90; Under His Banner: A History of the FGBMFI, Gift Publ, 92; The Spirit Said Grow, MARC, World Vision, 92. **CONTACT ADDRESS** Dept of Church History, Regent Univ, 1000 Regent Univ Dr, Virginia Beach, VA, 23464-9831.

SYNNOTT, MARCIA G.
PERSONAL Camden, NJ, m, 1979, 2 children **DISCIPLINE** HISTORY (UNITED STATES) **EDUCATION** Radcliffe Col, BA, 61; Brown Univ, AM (Am civilization), 64; Univ MA, Amherst, PhD (Hist), 74. **CAREER** History teacher, The MacDuffie School, Springfield, MA, 63-68; instr hist, Univ SC, 72-74, asst prof hist, 74-79, assoc prof Hist, 79-97, prof Hist, Univ SC, 97-. **HONORS AND AWARDS** Fulbright lect in Am civilization, English dept, Univ Oslo, Norway, spring 88; res grants-in-aid from Rockefeller Univ, Am Coun of Learned Soc; Southern Regional Ed Board, and the Am Philos Soc. **MEMBERSHIPS** Hist of Ed Soc (member ed bd, Hist of Ed Quart, 96, 97, 98); Southern Asn for Women Historians; Southern Hist Asn; Am Hist Asn; Org of Am Hist; Nat Coun on Public Hist. **RESEARCH** Am higher ed; desgregation; women's hist; anti-semitism; race and ethnic relations; historic site interpretation. **SELECTED PUBLICATIONS** Auth, Anti-Semitism and American Universities: Did Quotas Follow the Jews?, in Anti-Semtism in American History, ed by David A Gerber, Univ IL Press, 86; Desegregation in South Carolina, 1950-1963: Sometime Between the Now and the Never, in Looking South: Chapters in the Story of an American Region, ed by Winfred B Moore, Jr, & Joseph F Tripp, Contributions in American History, No 136, Greenwood Press, 89; Federalism Vindicated: University Desegregation in South Carolina and Alabama, 1962-1963, J of Policy History Vol, no 3, July 89; Disney's America: Whose Patrimony, Whose Profits, Whose Past?, The Public Historian Vol 17, no 4, fall 95; Race, Gender, and Personal Place in the Desegregation of State Universites in the American South, chapter in Women and Higher Education: Past, Present, and Future, ed by Mary R Masson and Deborah Simonton, Aberdeen Univ Press, 96; Alica Norwood Spearman Wright: Civil Rights Apostle to South Carolinians, in Beyond Image and Convention: Explorations in Southern Women's History, ed by Janet Lee Coryell, Martha H Swain, Sandra Gioia Treadway, and Elizabeth Hays Turner, in the Southern Women Series, Univ MO Press, 98; The Half-Opened Door: Discrimination and Admissions at Harvard, Yale, and Princeton, 1900-1970, foreword by Arthur S Link, Contributions in American History, no 80, Greenwood Press, 79. **CONTACT ADDRESS** Dept of History, Univ of South Carolina, Columbia, SC, 29208. **EMAIL** synnott@garnet.cla.sc.edu

SYRETT, DAVID
PERSONAL Born 01/08/1939, White Plains, NY, m, 1962, 3 children **DISCIPLINE** BRITISH EIGHTEENTH CENTURY NAVAL HISTORY **EDUCATION** Columbia Univ, BA, 61, MA, 64; Univ London, PhD(hist), 66. **CAREER** Asst prof, 66-71, assoc prof, 71-80, PROF HIST, QUEENS COL, NY, 80-. **MEMBERSHIPS** Navy Rec Soc, Eng; Royal Hist Soc; Soc Nautical Res; AHA. **RESEARCH** British naval history in the 18th century. **SELECTED PUBLICATIONS** Auth, The Procurement of Shipping by the Board of Ordnance During the American War, 1775-1782, Mariners Mirror, Vol 81, 95; Shooting the War--The Memoir and Photographs of a U-Boat Officer in World-War-II, Am Neptune, Vol 54, 94; The Operations of the Drossel Group Of U-Boats, April-28-May-8-1943, Mariners Mirror, Vol 79, 93; The U-Boat War in The Caribbean, Am Neptune, Vol 56, 96; Communications Intelligence and the Sinking of the U-1062--30-September-1944, J Military Hist, Vol 58, 94; The Battle for Convoy Sc-121, March 6-10, 1943, Am Neptune, Vol 57, 97; The Victualling Board Charters Shipping, 1775-82, Hist Res, Vol 68, 95. **CONTACT ADDRESS** Dept of Hist, Queens Col, CUNY, 6530 Kissena Blvd, Flushing, NY, 11367-1597.

SZABO, FRANZ A.J.
DISCIPLINE HISTORY **EDUCATION** Univ Montreal, BA; Univ Alberta, MA, 70; PhD, 76. **CAREER** Prof. **HONORS AND AWARDS** Barbara Jelavich prize, AAASS. **RESEARCH** Enlightened Absolutism in the Habsburg Monarchy. **SELECTED PUBLICATIONS** Auth, Kaunitz and Enlightened Absolutism, 1753-1780, Cambridge UP, 94; Wenzel Anton Kaunitz-Rietberg und Seine Zeit: Bemerkungen zum 200. Todestag des Staatskanzlers, Staatskanzler Wenzel Anton von Kaunitz-Rietberg (1711-1794): Neue Perspektiven zu Politik und Kultur der europaischen Aufklarung, Schnider Verlag, 96; Reflections on the Austrian identity in the Old World and the New, A History of the Austrian migration to Canada, Carleton UP, 96; co-ed, Staaskanzler Wenzel Anton von Kaunitz-Rietberg(1711-1794): Neue Perspektiven und Kuitur der europaischen Aufklarung, Schnider Verlag,96; A History of the Austrian Migration to Canada, Carleton UP, 96; ed, Austrian Immigration to Canada: Selected Essays, Carleton UP, 96. **CONTACT ADDRESS** Dept of Hist, Carleton Univ, 1125 Colonel By Dr, Ottawa, ON, K1S 5B6. **EMAIL** fszabo@ccs.carleton.ca

SZABO, JOYCE
DISCIPLINE ART **EDUCATION** Wittenberg Univ, BA, 73; Vanderbilt Univ, MA, 78; Univ NMex, PhD, 83. **CAREER** Assoc prof, Univ N Mex. **SELECTED PUBLICATIONS** Auth, Mapped Battles and Visual Narratives: The Arrest and Killing of Sitting Bull, Am Indian Art Magazine, 96; Narrative Captions for Howling Wolf Entries in Plains Indian Drawings 1865-1935: Pages from a Visual History, Harry N. Abrams, 96; Review of Modern by Tradition: American Indian Painting in the Studio Style (rev), NMex Hist Rev, 96; Howling Wolf and the History of Ledger Art, Univ NMex, 94; People of the Members-Exhibition Review, Museum Anthropol, 94; Shields and Lodges, Warriors and Chiefs: Kiowa Drawings as Historic Records, Ethnohist, 94; Chief Killer and a New Reality: Narration and Description in Fort Marion Art, Am Indian Art Magazine, 94; Howling Wolf: An Autobiography of a Plains Warrior-Artist, Albuquerque, 94. **CONTACT ADDRESS** Art Dept, Univ NMex, 1805 Roma NE, Albuquerque, NM, 87131. **EMAIL** paaffair@unm.edu

SZASZ, FERENC MORTON
PERSONAL Born 02/14/1940, Davenport, IA, m, 1969, 3 children **DISCIPLINE** HISTORY **EDUCATION** Ohio Wesleyan Univ, BA, 62; Univ Rochester, PhD, 69. **CAREER** From vis instr to Prof of Hist, Univ New Mexico. **HONORS AND AWARDS** Phi Beta Kappa, 62; Univ New Mexico teaching awards; three book awards. **MEMBERSHIPS** Orgn of Am Hist; Western Hist Asn; Soc of Church Hist. **RESEARCH** History of religion in America; the early Atomic Age; popular culture. **SELECTED PUBLICATIONS** Auth, The Day the Sun Rose Twice: The Story of the Trinity Site Nuclear Explosion, July 16, 1945, Univ New Mexico, 84; auth, The British Scientists and the Manhattan Project: The Los Alamos Years, St Martins, 92; ed, Great Mysteries of the West, Fulcrum, 93; co-ed, Religion in Modern New Mexico, Univ New Mexico, 97. **CONTACT ADDRESS** Dept of History, Univ of New Mexico, Albuquerque, NM, 87131.

SZASZ, MARGARET CONNELL
PERSONAL Pasco, WA, 3 children **DISCIPLINE** UNITED STATES HISTORY **EDUCATION** Univ Wash, BA, 57, MA, 68; Univ N Mex, PhD(hist), 72. **CAREER** Teacher English, US Army High School, Ger, 57-58; teaching asst hist, 68-71, res asst hist, Am Indian Hist Res Proj, 71-72, VIS SCHOLAR, UNIV NMEX, 81-, Mem, Ad Hoc Comn Basics Educ, NMex Humanities Coun, 77-81. **MEMBERSHIPS** Western Hist Asn; Orgn Am Historians. **RESEARCH** History of American Indian education; American Indian ethnohistory; social history of the American West. **SELECTED PUBLICATIONS** Auth, The Enduring Indians of Kansas--A Century and a Half of Acculturation, Pacific Hist Rev, Vol 61, 92; Apache Mothers and Daughters--4 Generations of a Family, Am Hist Rev, Vol 99, 94; Social-Order and Political-Change--Constitutional Governments Among the Cherokee, the Choctaw, the Chickasaw, and the Greek, NMex Hist Rev, Vol 69, 94; Survival of the Spirit--Chiricahua Apaches in Captivity, Am Indian Cult Res J, Vol 18, 94; Promises of the Past--A History of Indian Education in the United-States, Western Hist Quart, Vol 25, 94; They Called It Prairie-Light--The Story of Chilocco-Indian-School, NMex Hist Rev, Vol 71, 96; Spain and the Plains--Myths and Realities of Spanish Exploration and Settlement on the Great-Plains, Ethnohist, Vol 43, 96. **CONTACT ADDRESS** 1312 Lafayette Dr NE, Albuquerque, NM, 87106.

SZUCHMAN, MARK DAVID
PERSONAL Born 06/21/1948, Havana, Cuba, m, 1969, 2 children **DISCIPLINE** LATIN AMERICAN HISTORY **EDUCATION** Brandeis Univ, BA, 69; Univ Tex, Austin, MA, 71, PhD(hist), 76. **CAREER** Asst prof, 76-81, ASSOC PROF HIST, FLA INT UNIV, 81-, Soc Sci Res Coun res grant family hist, 78-79. **MEMBERSHIPS** Conf Latin Am Hist; Latin Am Studies Asn; Soc Sci Hist Asn; Chile-Rio Plata Studies Comt. **RESEARCH** Latin American urban history; 19th century Argentina; the family. **SELECTED PUBLICATIONS** Auth, Order and Virtue--The Republican Discourse in the Rosas Regime, Hisp Am Hist Rev, Vol 76, 96; Handbook of Latin-American Studies CD-Rom, Hisp Am Hist Rev, Vol 77, 97; Workers in Buenos-Aires--Experience of the Market 1850-1880, J Interdisciplinary Hist, Vol 25, 94. **CONTACT ADDRESS** Dept of Hist, Florida Intl Univ, 1 F I U South Campus, Miami, FL, 33199-0001.

T

TABBERNEE, WILLIAM
PERSONAL Born 04/21/1944, Rotterdam, Netherlands, m, 3 children **DISCIPLINE** EARLY CHURCH HISTORY **EDUCATION** Coburg Tchrs Col, TPTC, 65; Melbourne Col of Divinity, DipRE, 68, LTh, 68; Univ Melbourne, BA, 72, PhD, 79; Yale Divinity Sch, STM, 73. **CAREER** Lectr, Church history and systematic theol, 73-76, chemn Dept of Christian Thought and Hist, 77-80, Col of the Bible, Melbourne, Australia; dean, Evangelical Theol Asn, Melbourne, Australia, 79-80; prin, Col of the Bible of Churches of Christ in Australia, 81-91; pres, prof of Christian Thought and Hist, 91-94, Stephen J. England prof of Christian Thought and History, 95-, Phillips Grad Sem. **HONORS AND AWARDS** DDiv, Phillips Univ, 93. **MEMBERSHIPS** AAR; NAPS; Australian and New Zealand Soc for Theol Stud. **RESEARCH** Early Christianity; Montanism. **SELECTED PUBLICATIONS** Auth, Montanist Regional Bishops: New Evidence from Ancient Inscriptions, Jour of Early Christian Stud, 93; auth, Evangelism Beyond the Walls, Impact, 95; auth, Lamp-bearing Virgins: An Unusual Episode in the History of Early Christian Worship based on Mt25:1-13, Europ Evangel Soc, 95; auth, Paul of Tarsus: Church Planter Par Excellence, Australian Christian, 96; auth, 25 December, Christmas? Australian Christian, 96; auth, Unfencing the Table: Creeds, Councils, Communion and the Campbells, Mid-Stream, 96; auth, Augustine: Doctor of Love, Australian Christian, 97; auth, Archaeology; Revelation Revelations, Australian Christian, 97; auth, Athanasius: Champion of Orthodoxy, Australian Christian, 97; auth, Eusebius' Theology of Persecution: As Seen in the Various Editions of His Church History, Jour of Early Christian Stud, 97; auth, Ignatius, the Letter- Writing Martyr, Australian Christian, 97; auth, Learning to Handle the Gospel and the Fire Simultaneously: Ministerial Education for the Twenty-First Century, in Exploring Our Destiny, World Convention of Churches of Christ, 97; auth, Montanist Inscriptions and Testimonia: Epigraphic Sources Illustrating the History of Montanism, Patristic Monograph Ser, Mercer Univ, 97; auth, Our Trophies Are Better Than Your Trophies: The Appeal to Tombs and Reliquaries in Montanist- Orthodox Relations, Studia Patristica, 97; auth, Perpetua; The First Woman Journalist, Australian Christian, 97; auth, Eusebius: Chronicler of a Golden Age, Australian Christian, 98; auth, Francis of Assisi: Preacher to the Birds, Australian Christian, 98; auth, Mary Magdalene: A Saint with an Undeserved Reputation, Australian Christian, 98; auth, Restoring Normative Christianity: Episkope and the Christian Church, Mid-Stream, 98. **CONTACT ADDRESS** Phillips Theol Sem, 4242 S Sheridan Rd, Tulsa, OK, 74145. **EMAIL** ptspres@fullnet.net

TABER, JOHN
DISCIPLINE CLASSICAL INDIAN PHILOSOPHY, 19TH CENTURY GERMAN PHILOSOPHY **EDUCATION** Univ Kans, BA, 71; Univ Hamburg, PhD, 79. **CAREER** Assoc prof, Univ NMex. **SELECTED PUBLICATIONS** Auth, Transformative Philosophy: A Study of Sankara, Fichte, and Heidegger, Univ Hawaii Press, 83; contribur, articles on Indian Philos, Routledge Encycl of Philos, 95. **CONTACT ADDRESS** Univ NMex, Albuquerque, NM, 87131.

TABILI, LAURA
PERSONAL WI **DISCIPLINE** HISTORY **EDUCATION** Univ Wisconsin, Milwaukee, BS, 78, MA, 82; Rutgers Univ, PhD, 88. **CAREER** Asst prof, 88-94, assoc prof, 94- , Univ Arizona. **HONORS AND AWARDS** Am Philos Soc res grant, 97; German Marshall Found res grant, 98. **MEMBERSHIPS** Am Hist Asn; N Am Conf on British Stud; Coun for European Stud. **RESEARCH** Migration; British and European history; women's history; race. **SELECTED PUBLICATIONS** Auth, The Construction of Racial Difference in Twentieth Century Britain: The Special Restriction (Coloured Alien Seamen) Order, 1925, J of Brit Stud, 94; auth, We Ask for British Justice: Workers and Racial Difference in Late Imperial Britain, Cornell, 94; auth, Labour Migration, Racial Formation, and Class Identity: Some Reflections on the British Case, North West Labour Hist, 95-96; auth, Women of a Very Low Type: Crossing Racial Boundaries in Late Imperial Britain, in Frader, ed, Gender and Class in Modern Europe, Cornell, 96; auth, A Maritime Race: Masculinity and the Racial Division of Labor in British Merchant Ships, 1900-1939, in Creighton, ed, Iron Men, Wooden Women: Gender and Seafaring in the Atlantic World, 1700-1920, Johns Hopkins, 96. **CONTACT ADDRESS** History Dept, Univ of Arizona, Tucson, AZ, 85721. **EMAIL** tabili@u.arizona.edu

TABORN, JOHN MARVIN
PERSONAL Born 11/07/1935, Carrier Mills, IL, m **DISCIPLINE** PSYCHOLOGY **EDUCATION** Southern IL Univ, BS 1956; Univ of IL, MA 1958; Univ of MN, PhD 1970; Harvard Business Sch, Mgmt Certificate 1971. **CAREER** Minneapolis Public Schools, psychologist 1966-70; Univ of MN, youth develop consultant 1971-73; J TABORN ASSOCS INC, PRES 1979-; UNIV OF MN, ASSOC PROF 1973-. **HONORS AND AWARDS** Bush Leadership Fellow 1970; Monitor of the Year Monitors Minneapolis 1980. **MEMBERSHIPS** Mem Natl Assoc of Black Psychologists 1970-; professional mem Amer Psychological Assoc 1972-; consultant State of MN 1973-82; bd of dirs Minneapolis Urban League 1974-80; consultant Honeywell Inc 1981-84; mem Sigma Pi Phi Frat 1983-; consultant Natl Assoc Black Police 1984-, State of CA Education 1986-. **SELECTED PUBLICATIONS** Numerous scholarly publications. **CONTACT ADDRESS** Univ of Minnesota, 808 Social Science Bldg, Minneapolis, MN, 55455.

TAGER, JACK
PERSONAL Born 10/18/1936, Brooklyn, NY, m, 1969, 2 children **DISCIPLINE** MODERN UNITED STATES & URBAN HISTORY **EDUCATION** Brooklyn Col, BA, 58; Univ CA, Berkeley, MA, 59; Univ Rochester, PhD(hist), 65. **CAREER** Asst prof hist, OH State Univ, 64-67; asst prof, 67-70, assoc prof, 70-77, Prof hist, Univ MA, Amherst, 77-, Dir honors, Univ MA, Amherst, 78-. **MEMBERSHIPS** AHA, Orgn Am Historians. **SELECTED PUBLICATIONS** Auth, Progressives, conservatives and the theory of the status revolution, Mid-America, 7/66; The Intellectual as Urban Reformer: Brand Whitlock and the Progressive Movement, Case Western Reserve Univ, 68; co-ed, The Urban Vision: Selected Interpretations of the Modern American City, Dorsey, 70; auth, Partners in design: architects and entrepreneurs, S Atlantic Quart, spring 77; Tweed's New York: another look, Forum, Am Legal Studies Asn, 12/77; The Skyscraper, the architect and the corporation, Ill Quart, summer 80; Massachusetts and the Gilded Age, Umass Press, 85; co-ed, Historical Atlas of Massachusetts, Umass Press 1991; Massachusetts Politics, Inst for Mass Studies, 98. **CONTACT ADDRESS** Dept of History, Univ of MA, Amherst, MA, 01002.

TAGG, JAMES
DISCIPLINE HISTORY **EDUCATION** Western Mich Univ, BA, 64; Wayne State Univ, MA, 68; PhD, 73. **RESEARCH** Early American Republic. **SELECTED PUBLICATIONS** Auth, Benjamin Franklin Bache and the Philadelphia Aurora, Univ Pa, 91; American response to the French Revolution 1789-1799. **CONTACT ADDRESS** Dept of History, Lethbridge Univ, 4401 University Dr W, Lethbridge, AB, T1K 3M4. **EMAIL** tagg@hg.uleth.ca

TAGG, JOHN
DISCIPLINE ART HISTORY **EDUCATION** Royal Col Art London. **CAREER** Art Dept, SUNY, Bingham **RESEARCH** Hist and theory of photography; mod Europ and Am cult hist; contemp critical theory (Marxism, semiotics, poststructuralism); curatorial practice. **SELECTED PUBLICATIONS** Auth, The Discontinuous City: Picturing and the Discursive Field in Visual Culture: Images and Interpretations, 94; The Pencil of History in Fugitive Images: From Photography to Video, 95; A Discourse (With Shape of Reason Missing) in Vision and Textuality, 95; The Currency of the Photograph in Representation and Photography: The Screen Education Reader, vol II; A Change of Skin in (Un)Fixing Representation; The World of Photography or Photography of the World? in Camerawork: A Reader. **CONTACT ADDRESS** SUNY Binghamton, PO Box 6000, Binghamton, NY, 13902-6000. **EMAIL** jt33@cornell.edu

TAIT, ALAN A.
PERSONAL Born 07/01/1934, Edinburgh, Scotland, m, 1963, 1 child **DISCIPLINE** ECONOMICS **EDUCATION** Univ Edinburgh, MA, 57; Trinity Col, Univ Dublin, PhD, 66. **CAREER** Trinity Col Dublin, Prof, 59-71; Univ Strathclyde, Prof, 71-76; Asst Dir, Dep Dr, Dir, IMF, Wash DC Geneva, 76-98. **HONORS AND AWARDS** Trinity Col Dublin, Hon fel, 96. **RESEARCH** Pub Fin; Trade Policy. **SELECTED PUBLICATIONS** Value Added Tax: International Practice and Problems, IMF, 88; Excess Wages tax, with N Erbas, in Fiscal Policy and Economic Reforms, edit, 96. **CONTACT ADDRESS** 58 Rue de Moillebeau, Geneva, ., 1209.

TAKAKI, RONALD TOSHIYUKI
PERSONAL Born 04/12/1939, Honolulu, HI, m, 1961, 2 children **DISCIPLINE** UNITED STATES HISTORY **EDUCATION** Col Wooster, BA, 61; Univ CA, Berkeley, MA, 62, PhD(hist), 67. **CAREER** Instr Am hist, Col San Mateo, 65-67; asst prof hist, Univ Calif, Los Angeles, 67-72; prof ethnic studies, Univ CA, Berkeley, 72-; Nat Humanities Found fel, 70-71; Rockefeller Found fel, 81-82. **HONORS AND AWARDS** Distinguished Teaching Award, Berkeley, 81; Messenger Lecturer, Cornell Univ, 93; fel, Soc Am Hist, 95. **RESEARCH** Ethnic studies; race relations; American social and intellectual history. **SELECTED PUBLICATIONS** Auth, A Pro-Slavery Crusade: The Agitation to Reopen the African Slave Trade, Free, 71; Violence in the Black Imagination, Putnam, 72; Iron Cages: Race and Culture in 19th Century America, Knopf, 79; Strangers from a Different Shore: A History of Asian Americans, Little, Brown, 95; A Different Mirror: A History of Asian Americans, Little, Brown, 93; Hiroshima: Why America Dropped the Atomic Bomb, Little, Brown, 95; A Larger Memory: A History of Our Diversity, with Voices, Little, Brown, 98. **CONTACT ADDRESS** Dept Ethnic Studies, Univ California, 506 Barrows Hall, Berkeley, CA, 94720-2571. **EMAIL** rtakaki@uclink4.berkeley.edu

TALBOT, CHARLES
DISCIPLINE NORTHERN EUROPEAN ART OF THE GOTHIC, RENAISSANCE, AND BAROQUE **EDUCATION** Yale Univ, PhD. **CAREER** Alice Pratt Brown distinguished prof. **SELECTED PUBLICATIONS** Pub(s), area of Ger art; Span Colonial Art and Arch in Mex and Latin Am. **CONTACT ADDRESS** Dept of Art Hist, Trinity Univ, 715 Stadium Dr, San Antonio, TX, 78212.

TALBOTT, JOHN EDWIN
PERSONAL Born 09/25/1940, Grinnell, IA, 3 children **DISCIPLINE** MODERN EUROPEAN HISTORY **EDUCATION** Univ Mo, BA, 62; Stanford Univ, MA, 63, PhD(hist), 66. **CAREER** From instr to asst prof hist, Princeton Univ, 66-71; assoc prof, 71-79, PROF MOD EUROP HIST, UNIV CALIF, SANTA BARBARA, 79-, Class of 1931 bicentennial preceptor, Princeton Univ, 69-71; mem bd human resources, Nat Acad Sci, 71-74; mem, Inst Advan Study, 75-76; vis prof hist, Stanford Univ, 80-81; vis prof strategy, Naval War Col, 81-82. **HONORS AND AWARDS** Best Book Award, Pac Coast Branch AHA, 81. **MEMBERSHIPS** AHA; Soc Fr Hist Studies; US Naval Inst. **RESEARCH** Modern France; history of education; European social history. **SELECTED PUBLICATIONS** Auth, Soldiers, Psychiatrists, and Combat Trauma, J Interdisciplinary Hist, Vol 27, 97; Big Business and Industrial-Conflict in 19th-Century France--A Social-History of the Parisian-Gas-Company, Tech Cult, Vol 35, 94. **CONTACT ADDRESS** Dept of Hist, Univ of Calif, 552 University Rd, Santa Barbara, CA, 93106-0001.

TALBOTT, ROBERT DEAN
PERSONAL Born 02/18/1928, Centralia, IL, m, 1957, 1 child **DISCIPLINE** LATIN AMERICAN HISTORY **EDUCATION** Univ Ill, BA, 50, MA, 55, PhD, 59. **CAREER** Teaching asst, Univ Ill, 55-58; instr hist, Kans State Teachers Col, Emporia, 58-59; assoc prof soc sci, NDak State Teachers Col, Valley City, 59-62; assoc prof hist, Kearney State Col, 62-67; from asst prof to assoc prof, 67-74, PROF LATIN AM HIST, UNIV NORTHERN IOWA, 74- **MEMBERSHIPS** Conf Latin Am Hist; AHA; Latin Am Studies Asn; Midwest Asn Lat Am Studies (pres, 81-82). **RESEARCH** Chilean boundaries and associated political problems. **SELECTED PUBLICATIONS** Auth, Castro,Fidel, the Full Story of His Rise to Power, His Regime, His Allies, and His Adversaries, J Military Hist, Vol 58, 94. **CONTACT ADDRESS** Dept of Hist, Univ of Northern Iowa, Cedar Falls, IA, 50613.

TALL, EMILY
PERSONAL Born 05/22/1940, New York, NY **DISCIPLINE** RUSSIAN **EDUCATION** Cornell Univ, BA, 61; Middlebury Col, MA, 67; Brown Univ, PhD(Slavic lang & lit), 74. **CAREER** Asst prof, 73-80, ASSOC PROF RUSS, STATE UNIV NY BUFFALO, 80- **MEMBERSHIPS** Am Asn Teachers Slavic & EEurop Lang; Am Asn Advan Slavic Studies; Am Coun Teachers Russ. **RESEARCH** Russian language teaching; Soviet literary criticism; Soviet literature. **SELECTED PUBLICATIONS** Auth, James Joyce and the Russians, Slavic E Europ J, Vol 37, 93. **CONTACT ADDRESS** State Unif of NY, Buffalo, NY, 14261.

TALLEY, WILLIAM B.
PERSONAL Born 09/22/1955, Sumter, South Carolina, m, 1993 **DISCIPLINE** EDUCATION **EDUCATION** South Carolina State, BS, 1976, MS, 1978; Southern Illinois Univ, PhD, 1986 . **CAREER** State of South Carolina, counselor, trainee, 1976-78, vocational rehab coun selor, 1978-80, disability examiner, 1980-82; State of Louisiana, LSU, educator, 1986-88; PSI Inc, counselor, 1988-90; Univ of Maryland, Eastern Shore, educator, dir of rehabilitation services; Coppin State College, asst prof, currently. **MEMBERSHIPS** Natl Rehab Assn, 1978-; Amer Asn of Counseling & Devt, 1982-; NAACP , 1973-; Alpha Phi Alpha, vp, Delta Omicron Lambda Chapter, 1994-; Univ of MD-E astern Shore Faculty Assembly, chair, 1993-; MD Rehab Counseling Assn, chair, m em comm, 1994-; Assn of Black Psychologists, 1988-; Amer Personnel & Guidance A ssn, 1984-; Natl Assn of Certified Hypnotherapists, 1988-; MD Rehab Assn, 1990- ; numerous other past and present memberships. **SELECTED PUBLICATIONS** Certified Rehabilitation Counselor; Nationally Certified Counselor; License d Professional Counselor; Publications: The Predictors of Case Outcome for Clie nts in a Private Rehabilitation Program in Illinois, Dissertation Abstracts Int l, 1982; The Predictors of Case Outcome for Clients in Private Rehabilitation: An Illinois Study, The Journal of Private Sector Rehabilitation, 1988. **CONTACT ADDRESS** Coppin State Col, 2500 W North Ave, Baltimore, MD, 21216.

TAMBS, LEWIS
PERSONAL Born 07/07/1927, San Diego, CA, d, 7 children **DISCIPLINE** LATIN AMERICAN & IBERIAN HISTORY **EDUCATION** Univ Calif, Berkeley, BS, 53, Santa Barbara, MA, 62, PhD, 67. **CAREER** Asst plant engr, Standard Brands, Calif, 53-54; pipeline engr, Creole Petroleum Corp, Caracas, Venezuela, 54-57; gen mgr, CACYP, Instalaciones Petroleras, Maracaibo, 57-59; from instr to asst prof hist, Creighton Univ, 65-69; assoc prof, 69-75, dir, Ctr Latin Am Studies, 72-75, prof hist, Ariz State Univ, 75-80 & 87-; fac res grant, Amazon, 70 & Washington, DC & Madrid, 71; vis prof mod Brazil, Am Grad Sch Int Mgt, 72-79; consult NSC, 82-83; US Ambassador Colombia, 83-85; US Ambassador Costa Rica, 85-87. **MEMBERSHIPS** Coun Foreign Rels; Pac Coast Coun Latin Am Studies (pres, 75-76). **RESEARCH** Amazon rubber boom, 1890-1912; geopolitics of the Pacific basin; conflict in the southern cone of South America. **SELECTED PUBLICATIONS** Auth, Brazil's expanding frontiers, Americas, 10/66; Latin American geopolitics: A basic bibiliography, Rev Geog, 12/70; co-ed, Academic Writer's Guide to Periodicals: Latin America, Kent State Univ, 71 & coauth, Vol II: East European and Slavic Studies, 73 & Vol III: African and Black American Studies, 75, Kent State Librs; ed, United States Policy Towards Latin America, Ctr Latin Am Studies, Ariz State Univ, 76; coauth, Hitler's Spanish Legion: The Blue Division in Russia, Univ Southern Ill, 78. **CONTACT ADDRESS** Dept Hist, Arizona State Univ, Tempe, PO Box 872501, Tempe, AZ, 85287-2501. **EMAIL** history@asuvm.inre.asu.edu

TANDY, DAVID
PERSONAL Born 04/19/1950, New York, NY, 2 children **DISCIPLINE** CLASSICAL PHILOLOGY **EDUCATION** Yale, PhD, 79 **CAREER** Distinguished Prof in Humanities, Univ TN, 98-; Asst Prof, 80-pres, Univ of TN **MEMBERSHIPS** Am Philol Assoc; Econ Hist Assoc; Karl Polanyi Inst of Polit Econ **RESEARCH** Forms of Domination & Resistance in the Classical World; Social & Economic History of Ancient Greece & Rome **SELECTED PUBLICATIONS** Auth, Warriors into Traders, Univ of CA, 97 **CONTACT ADDRESS** Dept of Classics, Univ of TN, Knoxville, TN, 37996-0413. **EMAIL** dtandy@utk.edu

TANENBAUM, JAN KARL
PERSONAL Born 12/21/1936, Chicago, IL, m, 1958, 3 children **DISCIPLINE** MODERN EUROPEAN HISTORY **EDUCATION** Univ Mich, BA, 58; Univ Calif, Berkeley, MA, 60, PhD, 69. **CAREER** From instr to asst prof, 66-74, assoc prof, 74-79, prof history, Fla State Univ, 79-. **MEMBERSHIPS** AHA; Soc Fr Hist Studies; Soc Histoire Moderne; Fr Colonial Hist Soc. **RESEARCH** Modern French history. **SELECTED PUBLICATIONS** Auth, General Maurice Sarrail 1856-1929, The French Army and Left-Wing Politics, Univ NC, 74; France and the Arab Middle East, 1914-1920, Am Philos Soc, 78; The French army and the Third Republic, In: Trends in History, winter 81; French Estimates of Germany's Operational War Plans in Knowing One's Enemies, Princeton Univ Press, 84. **CONTACT ADDRESS** Dept of History, Florida State Univ, 600 W College Ave, Tallahassee, FL, 32306-1096.

TANKARD, JUDITH B.
PERSONAL Born 02/18/1942, New York, NY, m, 1969 **DISCIPLINE** ART HISTORY **EDUCATION** Univ NC, BA, 63; NY Univ, MA, 67. **CAREER** Instr Landscape Hist, Radcliffe Seminars, 87-; independent scholar, writer, lecturer, editor, and consultant on historic gardens. **HONORS AND AWARDS** Am Horticultural Soc Bk Award, 98. **MEMBERSHIPS** Soc Archit Hist; Garden Writers Asn Am; New England Garden Hist Soc; The Garden Hist Soc; The Southern Garden Hist Soc; SPNEA. **RESEARCH** Anglo-American historic gardens and garden makers. **SELECTED PUBLICATIONS** Coauth, Gertrude Jekyll: A Vision of Garden and Wood, Sagapress-Abrams, 89; Gertrude Jekyll at Munstead Wood, Sutton-Sagapress, 96; auth, The Gardens of Ellen Biddle Shipman, Sagapress-Abrams, 97; author of numerous articles. **CONTACT ADDRESS** 1452 Beacon St., Newton, MA, 02468. **EMAIL** jtankard@concentric.net

TANNENBAUM, REBECCA J.
DISCIPLINE HISTORY **EDUCATION** Wesleyan, BA, 84; Yale Univ, MA, 93, PhD, 96. **CAREER** Asst prof History, Univ Ill, Chicago. **RESEARCH** Practice of medicine in American history. **SELECTED PUBLICATIONS** Fel Publ, A Woman's Calling: Women Medical Practitioner in New England, 1650-1750, Yale, 96; auth, Earnestness, Temperance, Industry: The Definitions and Uses of Professional Character Among Nineteenth Century American Physicians, Jour of the Hist of Med and Life Sci 49, 94; What is Best to be Done for these Fevers: Elizabeth Davenport's Medical Practice in New Haven Colony, The New Eng. Quart, 97. **CONTACT ADDRESS** Dept of History, M/L 198, Univ Illinois, 913 University Hall, 601 S Morg, Chicago, IL, 60607-7109. **EMAIL** tannen@panter.cis.yale.edu

TANNER, HELEN HORNBECK
PERSONAL Born 07/05/1916, Northfield, MN, m, 1940, 4 children **DISCIPLINE** ETHNOHISTORY **EDUCATION** Swarthmore Col, AB, 37; Univ Fla, MA, 49; Univ Mich, PhD, 61. **CAREER** Lectr, exten serv, Univ Mich, Ann Arbor, 61-67 & 71-72, asst dir, Ctr Continuing Educ of Women, 64-68; dir, Atlas Great Lakes Indian Hist Proj, Newberry Libr, 76-81. Consult & expert witness, Sisseton & Wahpeton Sioux Tribe, 70, Caddo Tribe of Okla, 71-72, US Dept Justice, 74-78; Sioux Tribe, 80-82. **MEMBERSHIPS** Can Cartographic Asn; Conf Latin Am Historians; Am Soc Ethnohist; Soc Hist Discoveries; Am Soc Ethnohist (pres, 82-). **RESEARCH** Indian history of Great Lakes; Spanish borderlands; historical cartography. **SELECTED PUBLICATIONS** Auth, Calumet and Fleur-De-Lys, Archaeology of Indian and French Contact in the Midcontinent, Western Hist Quart, Vol 24, 93; Commoners, Tribute, and Chiefs--The Development of Algonquian Culture in the Potomac Valley, J Southern Hist, Vol 61, 95; The Ojibway-Jesuit Debate at Walpole-Island, 1844, Ethnohist, Vol 41, 94; Countering Colonization--Native-American Women and Great-Lakes Missions, 1630-1900, Ethnohist, Vol 41, 93; The Middle Ground--Indians, Empires, and Republics in the Great-Lakes Region, 1650-1815, Ethnohist, Vol 40, 93; Powhatan Foreign-

Relations, 1500-1722, Va Magazine Hist Biography, Vol 0102, 94. **CONTACT ADDRESS** Newberry Libr, 60 W Walton St, Chicago, IL, 60610.

TANNER, WILLIAM RANDOLPH
PERSONAL Born 09/11/1933, Keokuk, IA, m, 1961, 1 child **DISCIPLINE** CONSTITUTIONAL UNITED STATES HISTORY **EDUCATION** Western Ill Univ, BS, 55; Univ Kans, MA, 67, PhD(hist), 71. **CAREER** Teacher social studies, Bushnell-Prairie City High Sch, Ill, 57-59; teacher US hist, Shawnee Mission WHigh Sch, Kans, 62-66; asst instr, Univ Kans, 66-69; asst prof, 70-74, chmn dept, 71-73, assoc prof, 74-80, prof US Hist, Humboldt State Univ, 81-, retired, 94. **MEMBERSHIPS** AHA; Orgn Am Historians. **RESEARCH** Post-World War II United States history; 20th century political and economic history; the presidency. **SELECTED PUBLICATIONS** Ed, Liberty and the Supreme Court, Univ Kans, 69; contribr, The Specter: Original Essays on the Cold War and the Origins of McCarthyism, New Viewpoints, 74; co-ed, Herbert Hoover and the Republican Era, Univ Press, 84; auth, A View from the Hill: A History of Humboldt State University, 93. **CONTACT ADDRESS** Dept of Hist, Humboldt State Univ, 1 Harps St, Arcata, CA, 95521-8299.

TANSEY, CHARLOTTE
PERSONAL Montreal, PQ, Canada **DISCIPLINE** EDUCATION **EDUCATION** Univ Montreal, BA, 43; McGill Univ, MA, 48. **CAREER** Ch, publicity, Newman Club McGill Univ, 47-48; found dir/sec, 45-48, registrar, 48-66, acad VP, 62-81, PRES/DIR STUDS, THOMAS MOORE INSTITUTE, 81-. **HONORS AND AWARDS** Citizen of the Year Award, Montreal Citizenship Coun, 75; LLD Concordia Univ, 85; DL Burlington Col, Vermont, 95. **MEMBERSHIPS** Can Fedn Hum; Asn Continuing Higher Educ; Nontraditional Educ Comt. **SELECTED PUBLICATIONS** Auth, The Assumptions of Adult Learning in Culture, 57; auth, Other Voices, Other Classrooms, in Can Forum, 68; auth, Creativity and Method: Essays in Honor of Bernard Lonergan, 81; auth, Liberal Arts in the Post Classical World, in Temoignages: Reflections on the Humanities, 93. **CONTACT ADDRESS** Pres & Dir of Studies, Thomas Moore Inst, 3405 Atwater Ave, Montreal, PQ, H3H 1Y2.

TAO, TIEN-YI
PERSONAL Born 01/24/1919, China **DISCIPLINE** CHINESE HISTORY **EDUCATION** Nat Taiwan Univ, BA, 52, MA, 56; Univ Chicago, PhD(Chinese hist), 73. **CAREER** Res assoc Chinese hist, Inst Hist & Philol, Academia Sinica, 57-60; ASST PROF HIST, HIST DEPT, UNIV HAWAII, 68- **MEMBERSHIPS** Asn Asian Studies. **RESEARCH** China government and China bureaucracy. **SELECTED PUBLICATIONS** Auth, 'Yen Tieh Lun' Discourses on Salt and Iron--As a Historical Source, Bul Inst Hist Philol Acad Sinica, Vol 67, 96. **CONTACT ADDRESS** Dept of Hist, Univ of Hawaii, 2530 Dole St, Honolulu, HI, 96822-2303.

TARAN, LEONARDO
PERSONAL Born 02/22/1933, Galarza, Argentina, m, 1971, 1 child **DISCIPLINE** CLASSICS, ANCIENT PHILOSOPHY **EDUCATION** Princeton Univ, PhD, 62. **CAREER** Fel res, Inst Res Humanities, Univ Wis, 62-63; jr fel res, Ctr Hellenic Studies, 63-64; asst prof classics, Univ Calif, Los Angeles, 64-67; assoc prof, 67-71, chmn dept, 76-79, Prof, 71-87, JAY PROF GREEK & LATIN LANGS, COLUMBIA UNIV, 87-; Am Philos Soc grant, 63, 71 & 75; fel Am Coun Learned Soc, 66-67, 71-72; Guggenheim Found fel, 75; mem Inst Advan Study, Princeton, 66-67 & 78-79. **MEMBERSHIPS** Am Philol Asn; Soc Ancient Greek Philos. **RESEARCH** Ancient philosophy; Greek literature. **SELECTED PUBLICATIONS** Auth, Parmenides, Princeton Univ, 65; Asclepius of Tralles: Commentary to Nicomachus' introduction to arithmetic, Am Philos Soc, 69; The creation myth in Plato's Timaeus, in Essays in Greek Philosophy, State Univ NY, 71; coauth, Eraclito, testimonianze e imitazioni, La Nuova Italia Editrice, 72; auth, Academica: Plato, Philip of Opus and the Pseudo-Platonic Epinomis, Am Philos Soc Memoirs, 75; Anonymous Commentary on Aristotle's de Interpretatione, Anton Hain, 78; Speusippus and Aristotle on homonymy and synonymy, Herme, 106: 73-99; Speusippus of Athens, Leiden, Brill, 81. **CONTACT ADDRESS** Dept of Classics, Columbia Univ, 2960 Broadway, New York, NY, 10027-6900. **EMAIL** lt1@columbia.edu

TARANOW, GERDA
PERSONAL New York, NY **DISCIPLINE** THEATRE HISTORY & ENGLISH **EDUCATION** NY Univ, BA, 52, MA, 55; Yale Univ, PhD, 61. **CAREER** From instr to asst prof, Univ KY, 63-66; asst prof, Syracuse Univ, 66-67; from asst prof to assoc prof, 67-76, prof English, Conn Col, 76-; fel, Yale Univ, 62-63; NEH fel, 80-81, referee, 72-. **MEMBERSHIPS** MLA; Am Soc Theatre Res; Int Fed Theatre Res; Asn Recorded Sound Collections; Societe d'histoire du Theatre (France); Soc for Theatre Res (England). **RESEARCH** Shakespeare; drama. **SELECTED PUBLICATIONS** Auth, Sarah Bernhardt: The Art Within the Legend, Princeton Univ, 72; The Bernhardt Hamlet: Culture and Context, Peter Lang, 97. **CONTACT ADDRESS** Dept English, Connecticut Col, 270 Mohegan Ave, Box 5567, New London, CT, 06320-4125. **EMAIL** gtar.@conncoll.edu

TARBELL, ROBERTA K.
DISCIPLINE RENAISSANCE, BAROQUE, 19TH/20TH CENTURY ART AND ARCHITECTURE **EDUCATION** Cornell Univ, BS, 65; Univ Del, MA, 68; PhD, 76 **CAREER** Asst cur, Del Art Mus, 67-69; guest dir, Whitney Mus of Am Art, Nat Mus of Am Art, Rutgers Univ Art Gallery, Jewish Mus, 74-85; asst prof Art Hist, 84-90, actg chp 90-92, assoc prof, Rutgers, State Univ NJ, Camden Col of Arts and Sci, 90-; adj asso prof Art Hist, Winterthur Mus/Univ Del, 86-. **HONORS AND AWARDS** Grad fel, Univ Del, 69-72; Smithsonian Inst predoctoral fel, 72-74; NEH res summer stipend 82-84; John Sloan Mem Found res grant, 85; Rutgers Univ res coun grant, 85-92; Merit Awards, Rutgers Univ, 86, 89, 90, 91; fac acad stud prog, Rutgers Univ, 88, 89, 93, 97; Smithsonian Inst sr postdoctoral fel, Hirshhorn Mus and Sculpture Garden, Wash, DC, 89; John Sloan Mem Found res grant, 89-90; Spec Award, Bd of Gov, Rutgers Univ, 90; Scholar in Residence, Pollock-Krasner House and Res Ctr, East Hampton, Long Island, 94. **MEMBERSHIPS** Bd mem, Walt Whitman Asn, 89-; bd mem, Ctr of the Creative Arts, Yakys, Del, 95-; Col Art Asn; Catalogue RaisonnQ Scholars' Asn; Asn of Hist of Am Art; Soc of Archit Hist; Women's Caucus for Art. **RESEARCH** Twentieth-century sculpture. **SELECTED PUBLICATIONS** Auth, John Storrs and the Spirit of Walt Whitman, in Walt Whitman and Robert Laurent and American Figurative Sculpture 1910-1960, David and Alfred Smart Mus of Art, Univ Chicago, 94; Mahonri Young's Sculptures of Laboring Men, Walt Whitman, and Jean Frantois Millet, in Walt Whitman and Robert Laurent and American Figurative Sculpture 1910-1960, David and Alfred Smart Mus of Art, Univ Chicago, 94; Primitivism, Folk Art, and the Exotic, in The Human Figure in American Sculpture: The Question of Modernity, 1890-1945. Univ Wash Press and the Los Angeles County Mus of Art, 95; Marguerite and William Zorach, Peggy Bacon, Robert Laurent, and Hugo Robus, in The Dictionary of Art, Macmillan Publ Ltd, 96.; William Zorach's Kiddie Kar, 1994 Annual Report of the Middlebury Col Mus of Art, 96; coed, Walt Whitman and Robert Laurent and American Figurative Sculpture 1910-1960, David and Alfred Smart Mus of Art, Univ Chicago, 94. **CONTACT ADDRESS** Rutgers, State Univ NJ,, Camden Col of Arts and Sci, New Brunswick, NJ, 08903-2101. **EMAIL** tarbell@camden.rutgers.edu

TARKOW, THEODORE A.
DISCIPLINE CLASSICAL STUDIES **EDUCATION** Oberlin Col, AB, 66; Univ Mich, MA, 67; Univ Mich, PhD, 71. **CAREER** Asst prof to prof, class studies, Univ Mo Columbia, 70-; assoc dean, col of arts and sci; Univ Mo Columbia, 82-. **HONORS AND AWARDS** Woodrow Wilson fel, 67; Amer Philos Asn award for excellence in teaching of the classics, 81; pres, Class Asn of Middlewest & South, 87. **MEMBERSHIPS** Amer Philol Asn; Archaeol Inst of Amer; Class Asn of Middlewest & South. **RESEARCH** Greek comedy & tragedy; Greek lyric poetry. **SELECTED PUBLICATIONS** Auth, Scan of Orestes, Rheinisches Mus fur Philol, 124; auth, Ainthes & the ghost of Aeschylus in Aristophanes Frogs, Traditio, 38; auth, Tyrtaeus 9D, L'antiquite Classique, 52; auth, Sight & Seeing in the Prometheus Board, Eranus, 89. **CONTACT ADDRESS** Univ of Missouri, 317 Lowry Hall, Columbia, MO, 65211. **EMAIL** tarkowt@missouri.edu

TARR, JOEL A.
PERSONAL Born 05/08/1934, Jersey City, NJ, m, 4 children **DISCIPLINE** AMERICAN HISTORY **EDUCATION** Rutgers Univ, BS, 56, MA, 57; Northwestern Univ, PhD(hist), 63. **CAREER** Teaching asst, Northwestern Univ, 57-59; lectr hist, Chicago campus, 59-61; from instr to asst prof, Calif State Col Long Beach, 61-66; vis prof Am hist, Univ Calif, Santa Barbara, 66-67; from asst prof to prof hist & urban affairs, 67-76, prof hist, technol & urban affairs, 76-79, Prof Hist & Pub Policy, 79-90, Richard S. Caliguiri Prof Hist & Policy, Carnegie-Mellon Univ, 90-, dir, Prog Technol & Humanities, 75-, co-dir, Prog Applied Hist & Soc Sci, 77-. **HONORS AND AWARDS** Am Philos Soc grant, 64-65; Scaife fel, Carnegie-Mellon Univ, 67-69; Nat Endowment for Humanities jr fel, 69-70; Gen Elec Found grant, 72-73; NSF grant, 75 & 78; Exxon Found, 81-82; Andrew W Mellon Found grant, 75-80 & 80-85; NSF grants, 85, 95; Abel Wolman Prize of the Public Works Hist Soc for the Best Book Published in Public Works Hist, 88; Carnegie-Mellon Univ Robert Doherty Prize for "Substantial and Sustained Contributions to Excellence in Education", 92; Choice Distinguished Academic Book Award, 97. **MEMBERSHIPS** Org Am Hist; Am Soc Environmental Hist; Soc Hist Tech; Urban Hist Asn (pres-elect, 97). **RESEARCH** Technology and the city; urban environmental history. **SELECTED PUBLICATIONS** Auth, A Study in Boss Politics: William Lorimer of Chicago, Univ Ill, 71; coauth, Technology and the Rise of the Networked City in Europe and America, Temple Univ Press, 88; auth, The Search for the Ultimate Sink: Urban Pollution in Historical Perspective, Series in Technology and the Environment, Univ Akron Press, 96; Searching for a Sink for an Industrial Waste, In: Out of the Woods: Essays in Environmental History, Univ Pittsburgh Press, 97; coauth, The Horse and the City, In: The Making of Urban American, SR Publ, 97; author of numerous other book chapters and journal articles. **CONTACT ADDRESS** Prog in Technol & Soc, Carnegie Mellon Univ, 5000 Forbes Ave, Pittsburgh, PA, 15213-3890. **EMAIL** jt03@andrew.cmu.edu

TARR, ZOLTAN
PERSONAL Hungary **DISCIPLINE** SOCIOLOGY, HISTORY **EDUCATION** Univ Ill, PhD, 74. **CAREER** CUNY; New School; Rutgers Univ. **HONORS AND AWARDS** Two Fullbright fel; two NEH fel. **MEMBERSHIPS** ASA; APSA; AHA. **RESEARCH** Intellectual history; history of European Jewry. **SELECTED PUBLICATIONS** Auth and coeditor, ten books, fifty articles. **CONTACT ADDRESS** 134 West 93rd St., #5-B, New York, NY, 10025.

TARRANT, RICHARD JOHN
PERSONAL Born 04/04/1945, New York, NY, m, 1968 **DISCIPLINE** CLASSICS **EDUCATION** Fordham Univ, BA, 66; Oxford Univ, DPhil, 72. **CAREER** From lectr to prof classics, Univ Toronto, 70-82; PROF GREEK & LATIN, HARVARD UNIV, 82-, Rev ed, Phoenix, Class Asn Can, 75-78, ed, 78-82. **MEMBERSHIPS** Am Philol Asn; Class Asn; Class Asn Can. **RESEARCH** Greek and Latin drama; Latin poetry; textual criticism. **SELECTED PUBLICATIONS** Auth, Thematic and Narrative Structure in Ovid 'Metamorphosen'--The Relationship Between Frame Stories and Enclosed Stories in the 5th, 10th and 15th Books of Ovid 'Metamorphosen', J Roman Studies, Vol 82, 92; The Silence of Cephalus--Text and Narrative Technique in Ovid, Metamorphoses 7.685ff, Transactions Am Philol Asn, Vol 0125, 95. **CONTACT ADDRESS** Dept of Greek & Latin, Harvard Univ, 319 Boylston Hall, Cambridge, MA, 02138-3800.

TARTER, BRENT
PERSONAL Born 10/06/1948, Austin, TX **DISCIPLINE** HISTORY OF VIRGINIA, AMERICAN REVOLUTION **EDUCATION** Angelo State Col, San Angelo, BA, 70; Univ Va, MA, 72. **CAREER** Hist ed, Va Independence Bicentennial Comn, 74-82. **MEMBERSHIPS** Southern Hist Asn. **RESEARCH** History of Virginia; history of the United States, 1900-1945; American revolution. **SELECTED PUBLICATIONS** Auth, David Humphrey Life of General Washington, with Washington,George Remarks, J Southern Hist, Vol 59, 93. **CONTACT ADDRESS** Va State Libr, Richmond, VA, 23219.

TARVER, LEON R., II
PERSONAL m **DISCIPLINE** POLITICAL SCIENCE **EDUCATION** Southern University, BA, political science; Harvard University, John F Kennedy School of Government, MA, public administration; Union Institute, PhD, public administration. **CAREER** SOUTHERN UNIVERSITY SYSTEM, BATON ROUGE, LA, vice-chancellor for administration, prof of public administration, PROF OF PUBLIC POLICY AND URBAN AFFAIRS, pres, currently. **CONTACT ADDRESS** So Univ, Baton Rouge, LA, 70813.

TATAREWICZ, JOSEPH N.
DISCIPLINE HISTORY **EDUCATION** IN Univ, PhD. **CAREER** Asst prof, Univ MD Baltimore County. **RESEARCH** Hist of sci; sci policy; public hist. **SELECTED PUBLICATIONS** Auth, Space Technology and Planetary Astronomy. **CONTACT ADDRESS** Dept of Hist, Univ MD Baltimore County, Hilltop Circle, PO Box 1000, Baltimore, MD, 21250. **EMAIL** tatarewicz@.umbc.edu

TATE, MICHAEL LYNN
PERSONAL Born 01/24/1947, Big Spring, TX, m, 1972, 2 children **DISCIPLINE** AMERICAN HISTORY **EDUCATION** Austin Col, BA, 69; Univ Toledo, MA, 70, PhD(Am hist), 74. **CAREER** Asst prof Am hist, Concordia Col, MN, 73-74 & Austin Col, summer, 74; asst prof, 74-78, assoc prof Am hist, Univ NE, Omaha, 78-; Contrib ed, Am Indian Quart, 76-; exec ed hist, Govt Publ Rev, 81-. **HONORS AND AWARDS** Muriel H. Wright Award from OK Hist Soc; Diamond Professorship, Univ NE at Omaha; Burlington Northern Faculty Achievement Award; Univ NE Great Teacher Award. **MEMBERSHIPS** Orgn Am Historians; Western Hist Asn; Soc Am Indian Studies & Res; Center for Great Plains Study. **RESEARCH** American Indian history and legal questions; Am frontier. **SELECTED PUBLICATIONS** Auth, The Indians of Texas, Scarecrow Press, 86; The Upstream People: An Annotated Research Bibliography of the Omaha Tribe, Scarecrow Press, 91; Nebraska History: An Annotated Bibliography, Greenwood Press, 95; Civilization's Guardian: The Multi-Purpose Army in the Settlement of the West, Univ OK Press, 99. **CONTACT ADDRESS** Dept of Hist, Univ NE, 6001 Dodge St, Omaha, NE, 68182-0002.

TATE, THAD W.
DISCIPLINE EARLY AMERICAN HISTORY **EDUCATION** Univ NC, AB, 47, MA, 48; Brown Univ, PhD, 60. **CAREER** Retired. **SELECTED PUBLICATIONS** Fel Publ, The Discovery and Development of the Southern Colonial Landscape, Procs of the AAS 92, 83; auth, The Negro in Eighteenth-Century Williamsburg, Univ Va, 66, repr 85; co-ed and contrib, The Chesapeake in the Seventeenth Century, Univ NC Press, 79; coauth, Colonial Virginia: A History, KTO Press, 86; auth, Transformation of the Land in Colonial America, In: Our American Land: 1987 Yearbook of Agriculture, US Govt Printing Off, 87; coauth and ed, The College of William and Mary: A History, King and Queen Press, 93. **CONTACT ADDRESS** 313 1/2 Burns Lane, Williamsburg, VA, 23185-3908.

TATHAM, DAVID FREDERIC
PERSONAL Born 11/29/1932, Wellesley, MA, m, 1979 **DISCIPLINE** ART HISTORY **EDUCATION** Univ Mass, AB, 54; Syracuse Univ, MA, 60, PhD(humanities), 70. **CAREER** Lectr fine arts, 62-71, dean students, 66-71, assoc prof, 72-78, PROF ART HIST, SYRACUSE UNIV, 78-, CHMN, 80-86. **HONORS AND AWARDS** Henry A Moe Prize, 91; John Ben Snow Award, 96; Am Philos Soc fel; NEH fel; life fel, Atheneum of Philadelphia. **MEMBERSHIPS** Col Art Asn Am; Am Antiqn Soc. **RESEARCH** American painting and graphic arts of 19th and 20th centuries. **SELECTED PUBLICATIONS** Auth, Lure of the Striped Pig: The Illustration of Popular Music in America 1820-1870, Imprint Soc, 73; Winslow Homer's Library, 5/77, Am Art J; Winslow Homer and the New England Poets, Proceedings of the Am Antiquarian Soc, 10/79; Samuel F B Morse's Gallery of the Louvre, Am Art J, fall 81; auth, Prints and Printmakers of New York State, Syracuse, 86; auth, Winslow Homer and the Illustrated Book, Syracuse, 92; auth, Winslow Homer in the Adirondacks, Syracuse, 96. **CONTACT ADDRESS** Dept of Fine Arts, Syracuse Univ, Syracuse, NY, 13244.

TATUM, GEORGE B.
PERSONAL Born 08/01/1917, Cleveland, OH, m, 1942, 3 children **DISCIPLINE** ART AND ARCHAEOLOGY **EDUCATION** Princeton Univ, AB, 40; MFA, 47; PhD, 50. **CAREER** Prof, Univ Pa, 48-68; prof, Univ Del, 68-78; visiting prof, Williams Col, 81; adj prof, Columbia Univ, 79-82. **HONORS AND AWARDS** Phi Beta Kappa; Sr Fel in Landscape Archit, Dumbarton Oaks (Harvard Univ), 67-68. **MEMBERSHIPS** Am Inst of Archit; Athenaeum of Philadelphia; Soc of Archit Historians. **RESEARCH** American architecture (eighteenth and nineteenth centuries); history of garden design (American and English). **SELECTED PUBLICATIONS** Auth, Penn's Great Town; Two Hundred Fifty Years of Philadelphia Architecture in Prnts and Drawings, 61; auth, Architecture, The Arts in America: The Colonial Period, 66; auth, Philadelphia Georgian: The City House of Samuel Powel and Some of its Eighteenth-Century Neighbors, 76; ed with E.B. MacDougall, Prophet with Honor: The Career of Andrew Jackson Downing, 1815-1852, 89; auth with William Alex, Calvert Vaux: Architect and Planner, 94. **CONTACT ADDRESS** 9102 Chester Village West, Chester, CT, 06412-1047.

TATUM, NANCY R.
PERSONAL Born 08/14/1930, Pittsburg, KS **DISCIPLINE** ENGLISH LITERATURE & HISTORY **EDUCATION** Univ Ark, BA, 52; Bryn Mawr Col, MA, 54, PhD, 60. **CAREER** Instr English & asst to dean, Lake Erie Col, 58-59; from instr to assoc prof, 60-69, PROF ENGLISH, WASHINGTON COL, 69-, Ernest A Howard Prof, 79-. **MEMBERSHIPS** MLA; Shakespeare Asn Am. **RESEARCH** Restoration drama; Shakespearean stage technique; seventeenth century English social and economic history. **CONTACT ADDRESS** Dept of English, Washington Col, 300 Washington Ave, Chestertown, MD, 21620-1197.

TAUBER, ALFRED I.
PERSONAL Born 06/24/1947, Washington, DC, m, 1966, 4 children **DISCIPLINE** PHILOSOPHY; HISTORY OF SCIENCE **EDUCATION** BS, 69, Tufts Univ; MD, 73, Tufts Univ School of Medicine **CAREER** Instr, 78-80, Asst Prof, 80-82, Harvard Medical School; Assoc Prof Medicine, 82-86, Assoc Prof Biochemistry, 82-86; Assoc Prof Pathology, Prof of Medicine, 84-87, Prof of Pathology, 87-, Boston Univ School of Medicine; Prof Philosophy, 92-, College of Arts and Sciences, Boston Univ. **HONORS AND AWARDS** Research Fel in Medicine, Harvard Medical School, 77-78; Clinical Fel in Medicine, Tufts-New England Medical Center Hospital, 75-77. **RESEARCH** Philosophy and the history of science **SELECTED PUBLICATIONS** Coauth, Metchnikoff and the Origins of Immunology: From Metaphor to Theory, 91; Auth, The Immune Self: Theory or Metaphor, 94; Coauth, The Generation of Diversity: Clonal Selection Theory and the Rise of Molecular Immunology, 97; Auth, Confessions of A Medicine Man: An Essay in Popular Philosophy, 99. **CONTACT ADDRESS** Center for Philosophy and History of Science, Boston Univ, Boston, MA, 02115. **EMAIL** atauber@bu.edu

TAWA, NICHOLAS E.
PERSONAL Born 10/22/1923, Boston, MA, m, 1947, 2 children **DISCIPLINE** MUSICOLOGY **EDUCATION** Harvard Univ, BA, 45; Boston Univ, MA, 47; Harvard Univ, PhD, 74. **CAREER** Full Prof to 94, Prof Emeritus, Univ Mass-Boston, 94-. **HONORS AND AWARDS** Distinguished School Award, Univ Mass, 90 **MEMBERSHIPS** Sonneck Soc. **RESEARCH** Music in America. **SELECTED PUBLICATIONS** Auth, The Way to Tin Pan Alley: American Popular Song, 1886-1910, Schirmer, 90; auth, The Coming-of-Age of American Art Music, Greenwood, 91; auth, Mainstream Music of Early Twentieth-Century America: The Composers, Their Words, and Their Times, Greenwood, 92; auth, American Composers and Their Public: A Critical Look, Scarecrow, 95; auth, Arthur Foote: A Musician in the Frame of Time and Place, Scarecrow Press, 97; author of numerous and book chapters. **CONTACT ADDRESS** 69 Undine Rd., Boston, MA, 02135-3811. **EMAIL** ntawa@worldnet.att.net

TAYLOR, ALAN S.
DISCIPLINE HISTORY **EDUCATION** Colby, BA, 77; Brandeis, PhD, 86. **CAREER** Prof History, Univ Calif, Davis. **HONORS AND AWARDS** Winner Bancroft, Beveridge, and Pulitzer Prizes for 'William Cooper's Town,' 96. **SELECTED PUBLICATIONS** Fel publ, From Fathers to Friends of the People, Jour of the Early Repub 11, 91; auth, Liberty Men and Great Proprietors: The Revolutionary Settlement on the Maine Frontier, Univ NC, 90; Who Murdered Judge William Cooper? NY Hist, 91; William Cooper's Town: Power and Persuasion on the Frontier of the Early Republic, Knopf, 97. **CONTACT ADDRESS** Dept of History, Univ Calif, Davis, CA, 95616. **EMAIL** astaylor@ucdavis.edu

TAYLOR, ARNOLD H.
PERSONAL Born 11/29/1929, Regina, Virginia **DISCIPLINE** HISTORY **EDUCATION** VA Union U, BA cum laude 1951; Howard U, MA 1952; The Cath Univ of Am, PhD 1963. **CAREER** Howard Univ, prof History 1972-; Univ of CT at Sterrs, prof history 1970-72; NC Central Univ, prof History 1965-70; So Univ in New Orleans, prof history chmn div of soc sci 1964-65; Benedict Coll, instr to prof of history 1955-64. **HONORS AND AWARDS** Recip post doc res grants Nat Endowment on the Humanities 1968, Am Council of Learned Societies 1969, Ford Found 1969-70, Univ of CT res found 1971-72. **MEMBERSHIPS** Mem assn for the study of Afro Am Life & History; So Historical Assn; Am Historical Assn; Orgn of Am Historians; author Am Diplomacy & the Narcotics Traffic 1900-39, A Study in InternatlHumanitarian Reform Duke Univ Press 1969, "Travail & Triumph Black Life & Culture in the South Since the Civil War" Greenwood Press 1976; author several articles in scholarly journals Fulbright Hays Sr Lectr, Am Hist at Jadavpur Univ Calcutta India 1967-68. **CONTACT ADDRESS** Prof of History & Dept Chrmn, Howard Univ, Washington, VT, 20059.

TAYLOR, CHARLES AVON
PERSONAL Baltimore, MD, m, 1982 **DISCIPLINE** EDUCATION **EDUCATION** Univ of Maryland, Baltimore MD, BA, 1973; Johns Hopkins Univ, Washington DC, 1976; Loyola Univ of Chicago, Chicago IL, EdD, 1984. **CAREER** Univ of Maryland, Baltimore MD, counselor, resident life dept, 1971-73; Univ of Kentucky, Minority Affairs Accreditation Team, consultant, 1975; Catonsville Community Coll, Catonsville MD, student activities specialist, 1973-76; Loyola Univ of Chicago, Chicago IL, asst dean of students, 1976-86, instructor in counseling, psychology, and higher education, 1983-88, instructor in African American studies, 1984-88; Chicago State Univ, Chicago IL, dean of student development, 1986-88; KELLOGG COMMUNITY COLL, BATTLE CREEK MI, VICE PRES FOR STUDENT SERVICES, 1988-. **HONORS AND AWARDS** Advisor of the Year, Loyola Univ of Chicago, 1980; Community Leadership Award, Neighborhood Housing Services of Chicago, 1984; Black & Hispanic Achievers of Industry Award, YMCA of Metropolitan Chicago, 1984; Outstanding Citizens Award, Chicago Junior Assn of Commerce & Industry, 1986. **MEMBERSHIPS** Chmn, education committee, NAACP of Battle Creek MI; exec bd mem, Michigan Assn of Community Coll Student Personnel Administrators; American Association for Higher Education, AAHE Black Caucus; Battle Creek Area Urbn League; Parent Teachers Association, River Side Elementary, Lakeview School District PTA, Battle Creek, MI; National Council on Student Development, A Council of the American Association of Community and Junior Colleges; American Association for Counseling and Development; National Association of Student Personnel Administrators; American College Personnel Association; ACU-I Region 8 Representative Committee on Minority Programs; John Hopkins Alumni Assocation; Battle Creek Community Foundation. **CONTACT ADDRESS** Student Services, Kellogg Comm Col, 450 North Ave, Battle Creek, MI, 49017.

TAYLOR, CHARLES L.
PERSONAL Born 11/08/1935, SC, m, 1958, 2 children **DISCIPLINE** POLITICAL SCIENCE **EDUCATION** Yale Univ, PhD, 63. **CAREER** Asst prof, William and Mary, 62-66; dir Polit Sci res Libr, Yale Univ, 66-70; assoc prof and prof, Virginia Polytech Inst and State Univ, 70- . **HONORS AND AWARDS** John Marshall prof, Budapest Univ of Ec Sci. **MEMBERSHIPS** Am Polit Sci Asn; Int Stud Asn. **RESEARCH** European politics; cross-national political events measurement. **SELECTED PUBLICATIONS** Coauth, Partisanship, Candidates and Issues: Attitudinal Components of the Vote in German Federal Elections, in von Beyme, ed, German Political Studies III, Sage, 78; coauth, World Handbook of Political and Social Indicators, 3d ed, Yale, 83; coauth, Mapping Mass Political Conflict and Civil Society: Issues and Prospects for the Automated Development of Event Data, J of Conflict Resolution, 97. **CONTACT ADDRESS** Dept of Political Science, Virginia Polytechnic Univ, Blacksburg, VA, 24061. **EMAIL** clt@vt.edu

TAYLOR, CLEDIE COLLINS
PERSONAL Born 03/08/1926, Bolivar, AR **DISCIPLINE** ART HISTORY **EDUCATION** Wayne State U, BS 1948, MA 1957; L'Universita Per Stranieri, Cert etruscology 1968; Wayne State U, SP cert humanities/art/hist 1970; Union Grad Sch, PhD art hist 1978. **CAREER** DETROIT PUB SCH, art tchr 1979, SUPR OF ART 1980-; Metal Processes WSU, instructor fashion design 1981; Arts Extended Gallery Inc, dir, currently; Pri Jewelry Design, practicing metal craftsperson; Children's Museum, asst dir, 1987-91. **HONORS AND AWARDS** Contribution to Black Artist Nat Conf of Artist 1984, 1994; Spirit of Detroit Award City of Detroit 1983; curator "African Tales in Words And Wood" 1984; curator "Tribute to Ernest Hardman" Exhibit Scarab Club 1985; award, Spirit of Detroit, City of Detroit for Small Business 1988; One Hundred Black Women for Art and Literature 1989; Governor's Award for Contribution to Art Education, 1989. **MEMBERSHIPS** 1st chmn Detroit Cncl of the Arts 1977-81; 1st chmn Minority Arts Advisory Panel MI Cncl for the Arts 1982-; mem bd of trustees Haystack Mountain Sch of Crafts 1982-; mem Detroit Scarab Club 1983-; DPS advisor/liason Detroit Art Tchrs Assn 1983-; mem/art advisor Nat Assn of the African Diaspora 1980-; dir Art Symposium Surinam NAAD Conf 1982; mem Berea Lutheran Ch; mem Alpha Kappa Alpha Sor; dir Art Symposium Barbados; appointed Michigan Council for the Arts 1987-; Board of Michigan Arts Foundation, 1988-. **SELECTED PUBLICATIONS** Publ "Journey to Odiamola" 1978; "Words in a SketchBook" 1985; **CONTACT ADDRESS** Arts Extended Gallery, 1553 Woodward, Ste 212, Detroit, MI, 48226.

TAYLOR, DANIEL JENNINGS
PERSONAL Born 09/01/1941, Covington, KY, m, 1966, 2 children **DISCIPLINE** CLASSICS, LINGUISTICS **EDUCATION** Lawrence Col, BA, 63; Univ Wash, MA, 65, PhD(classics), 70. **CAREER** From instr to asst prof classics, Univ Ill, Urbana, 68-74; asst prof, 74-78, ASSOC PROF CLASSICS, LAWRENCE UNIV, 78-, Chmn Dept, 75-, Actg vpres & dean for Campus life, Lawrence Univ, 77-78, 79-80; Nat Endowment for Humanities fel, 80-81. **MEMBERSHIPS** Am Philol Asn; Am Class League; Archaeological Inst Am. **RESEARCH** Syntax of Greek and Latin; history of linguistics; Varro. **SELECTED PUBLICATIONS** Auth, Studies on the Text of Suetonius 'De Grammaticis Et Rhetoribus', Hist Ling, Vol 21, 94; Desperately Seeking Syntax--Rewriting the History of Syntactic Theory in Greece and Rome, Lang Commun, Vol 13, 93; Theories of the Sign in Classical Antiquity, Hist Ling, Vol 21, 94. **CONTACT ADDRESS** 115 S Drew St, Appleton, WI, 54911-5798.

TAYLOR, DAVID VASSAR
PERSONAL Born 07/13/1945, St Paul, Minnesota, m, 1976 **DISCIPLINE** EDUCATION **EDUCATION** Univ of Minnesota, BA 1967; Univ of Nebraska, MA 1971, PhD 1977; Harvard Univ, IEM Program 1985. **CAREER** St Olaf Coll, Northfield MN, dir Amer minority studies program 1974-76; State Univ of New York New Paltz Campus, chairperson black studies dept 1977-78; Hubert Humphrey Collection Minnesota Historical Soc, curator 1978-79; Macalester Coll, dir minority/special serv program 1979-83; The Coll of Charleston, dean of undergraduate studies 1983-86; Minnesota State Univ System Office, assoc vice chancellor for academic affairs 1986-89; Univ of Minnesota Gen Coll, Minneapolis MN, dean 1989-. **HONORS AND AWARDS** Research Fellow-Dissertation Fellowship Fund for Black Americans 1975-77; consultant historian "Blacks in Minnesota" film for Gen Mills 1980. **MEMBERSHIPS** Bd of dirs Hallie Q Brown Comm Center St Paul 1978-79; bd of advisors Perrie Jones Library Fund St Paul 1979-80, Minnesota Quality of Life Study 1979-80; vestry St Phillip's Episcopal Church 1978-81; bd of trustees Seabury Western Theological Seminary 1985-90; chairman, board of directors, Penumbra Theatre Co; board, Friends of the Saint Paul Public Libraries; treasurer, Jean Covington Foundation. **SELECTED PUBLICATIONS** Author bibliography/3 articles/chapter in book. **CONTACT ADDRESS** Dean, General College, Univ of Minnesota, 128 Pleasant St, SE, Minneapolis, MN, 55455.

TAYLOR, HERMAN DANIEL
PERSONAL Born 02/26/1937, Yazoo City, Mississippi, m **DISCIPLINE** MUSIC **EDUCATION** Chicago Musical Coll of Roosevelt Univ, BMus 1963; Univ of MI, MMus 1974, AMusD 1976. **CAREER** Southern Univ, instr of music 1963-67; Dillard Univ, instr of music 1969-73; Prairie View A&M Univ, assoc prof of music 1976-77; Dillard Univ, prof ofmusic 1977-. **HONORS AND AWARDS** Artist Fellowship Awd LA State Arts Council 1984; Performing from memory all the organ works of JS Bach in US & in Europe 1984-85; UNCF Disting Faculty Scholar 1985-86 **MEMBERSHIPS** State chmn Amer Guild of Organists; volunteer for the Heart Fund 1978-; asst club scout master 1984-85. **CONTACT ADDRESS** Professor of Music, Dillard Univ, 2601 Gentilly Blvd, New Orleans, LA, 70122.

TAYLOR, HOWARD F.
PERSONAL Born 07/07/1939, Cleveland, Ohio, m **DISCIPLINE** AFRICAN-AMERICAN STUDIES **EDUCATION** Yale, PhD 1966; Yale, MA 1964; Hiram Coll, AB 1961. **CAREER** Princeton Univ, prof 1973; Syracuse Univ, 1968-73; IL Inst of Tech, 1966-68; Natl Acad of Scis, cons. **HONORS AND AWARDS** Various grants. **MEMBERSHIPS** NAAS; Am Sociol Assn; E Sociol Soc; Am Assn of Univ Profs; Assn of Black Sociologists. **SELECTED PUBLICATIONS** Publ two books num articles. **CONTACT ADDRESS** Afro-Amer Studies Prog, Princeton Univ, Princeton, NJ, 08544.

TAYLOR, IRA DONATHAN
PERSONAL Born 08/12/1962, Hot Springs, AR, m, 1986, 3 children **DISCIPLINE** HISTORY **EDUCATION** Hardin-Simmons Univ, BFA, 85, MA, 89; Univ Ark, Fayetteville, PhD, 97. **CAREER** Asst prof, Hardin-Simmons Univ, 95-. **HONORS AND AWARDS** Phi Kappa Phi, Alpha Chi, Nat Scholar Soc. **MEMBERSHIPS** Asn Ancient Hist; W Tex Hist Asn; Taylor County Hist Commission; Tex Medieval Asn; World Hist Asn; Hist Soc. **RESEARCH** Ancient, medieval and military history. **SELECTED PUBLICATIONS** Auth, art, A Comparitive Study of the Post-Alexandrian Macedonian Phalanx and the Roman Manipular Legend to the Battle of Pydna, 93; coauth, A Long the Texas Forts Trail, 97; auth, art, Some Living Conditions at Forts in the American Southwest, 98. **CONTACT ADDRESS** Hardin-Simmons Univ, Box 16125, Abilene, TX, 79698. **EMAIL** dtaylor.hist@hsutx.edu

TAYLOR, JAMES COLERIDGE
PERSONAL Born 12/21/1922, Henderson, North Carolina, m, 1982 **DISCIPLINE** EDUCATION **EDUCATION** Maryland University, European Div, BA, 1958, BS, 1963; Boston University, Boston, MA, MA, 1966; USC, Los Angeles, CA, PhD, 1972-73; International Inst of Human Rights, Strasbourg, France, 1973-75. **CAREER** US Army Medical Service, hospital administrator, 1943-68; Monterey Peninsula College, Monterey, CA, division chairman, 1970-71; University of Maryland, European Div, lecturer, 1972; assistant director, 1973-74. **MEMBERSHIPS** President, NAACP, Monterey, CA, Branch 1968-70; vice-president, UNA, NAACP Monterey, CA, Branch, 1969-71; Representative, Baha'i Intl Community, Human Rights Commission, Geneva, Switzerland, 1978, 1987; member, United Nations Assn Human Rights Committee, London, 1984-90; member, Univ of Maryland, Speakers Bureau, Europe; member, NCOBPS, APSA: Amer Academy Pol & Soc Scientist, ASALH. **CONTACT ADDRESS** Lecturer, Univ of Maryland, Box 2187, APO New York, NY, 09238.

TAYLOR, JAMES S.
DISCIPLINE HISTORY **EDUCATION** Stanford Univ, PhD, 66. **CAREER** Prof. **RESEARCH** Britain history; modern Europe; world history. **SELECTED PUBLICATIONS** Auth, pubs on English philanthropy and the Poor Law system. **CONTACT ADDRESS** History Dept, State Univ of West Georgia, Carrollton, GA, 30118. **EMAIL** jtaylor@westga.edu

TAYLOR, JEROME
PERSONAL Born 01/26/1940, Waukegan, Illinois, m **DISCIPLINE** AFRICAN-AMERICAN STUDIES **EDUCATION** Univ of Denver, BA 1961; IN Univ, PhD 1965. **CAREER** Mental Health Unit Topeka, dir 1968-69; Univ of Pittsburgh Clinical Psych Ctr, dir 1969-71; Univ of Pittsburgh, assoc prof of black studies and education, dir, Inst for the Black Family, currently. **HONORS AND AWARDS** Postdoctoral fellow, Menninger Found, 1965-67. **MEMBERSHIPS** Mem Amer Psychol Society, Assoc of Black Psych, Omicron Delta Kappa, Sigma Xi, Psi Chi; member, National Black Child Development Institute; member, National Council on Family Relations. **CONTACT ADDRESS** Dir, Inst for the Black Family, Univ of Pittsburgh, Pittsburgh, PA, 15260.

TAYLOR, KAREN
DISCIPLINE HISTORY **EDUCATION** Univ Utah, BA, 80; Clark, MA, 82; Duke Univ, PhD, 88. **CAREER** Assoc prof. **SELECTED PUBLICATIONS** Auth, Moral Motherhood and the Suppression of Corporal Punishment, Jour Psychohistory, 87; The Cult of True Motherhood and the Expansion of the Domestic Sphere, The Study of Women: History, Religion, Literature and the Arts, Greenwood Press, 89. **CONTACT ADDRESS** Dept of Hist, Col of Wooster, Wooster, OH, 44691.

TAYLOR, KENNETH LAPHAM
PERSONAL Born 05/16/1941, Los Angeles, CA, m, 1969, 3 children **DISCIPLINE** HISTORY OF SCIENCE **EDUCATION** Harvard Col, AB, 62; Harvard Univ, AM, 65, PhD(hist of sci), 68. **CAREER** Asst prof, 67-72, assoc prof hist of sci, Univ Okla, 72-, dept chemn, 79-, Nat Ctr Sci Res fel, 73-74. **HONORS AND AWARDS** S T Friedman Medal, Geol Soc London, 98. **MEMBERSHIPS** Brit Soc Hist Sci; Hist Sci Soc; Soc Hist Technol; Hist of Earth Sci Soc; Geol Soc Am; Soc Hist Nat Hist. **RESEARCH** History of geology; science in the 18th century. **CONTACT ADDRESS** Dept of Hist of Sci, Univ of Oklahoma, 601 Elm Ave, Norman, OK, 73019-0315. **EMAIL** ktaylor@ou.edu

TAYLOR, QUINTARD, JR.
PERSONAL Born 12/11/1948, Brownsville, Tennessee **DISCIPLINE** HISTORY **EDUCATION** St Augustine's Coll, BA 1969; Univ of MN, MA 1971, PhD 1977. **CAREER** Univ of MN, instructor 1969-71; Gustavus Adolphus Coll, instructor 1971; WA State U, asst prof 1971-75; CA Polytechnic State U, prof of history; Univ of Lagos, Akoka Nigeria, visiting Fulbright prof 1987-88; Univ of OR, prof, 1990-96, dept head, 1997-. **HONORS AND AWARDS** Carter G Woodson Award ASALH 1980; Kent Fellowship The Danforth Found 1974-77; Bush Fellowship Univ of MN 1971-77; NEH Travel & Collections Grant, National Endowment for the Humanities 1988; The Emergence of Afro-American Communities in the Pacific Northwest 1865-1910; Carter G Woodson Award for best article published in the Journal of Negro History 1978-79. **MEMBERSHIPS** Consult Great Plains Black Museum 1980-85; consult Afro-Am Cultural Arts Ctr 1977-78; reviewer Nat Endowment for the Humanities 1979-83; pres Martin Luther Fund 1983-85, mem 1979-; mem Endowment Comm "Journal of Negro History" 1983-; mem, California Black Faculty Staff Assn 1985-, Golden Key Natl Honor Society 1987-, Phi Beta Delta Society for International Scholars 1989-; bd of governors, Martin Luther King Vocational-Technical Coll, Owerri Nigeria 1989-, African-American Vocational Institute, Aba Nigeria 1989-. **SELECTED PUBLICATIONS** Written: In Search of the Racial Frontier: African Americans in the American West, 1528-1990; The Forgiving of A Black Community Seattles, Central District from 1870 Through the Civil Rights Era. **CONTACT ADDRESS** Dept of History, Univ of Oregon, Eugene, OR, 97403-1288.

TAYLOR, RICHARD STUART
PERSONAL Born 06/24/1942, Chicago, IL **DISCIPLINE** AMERICAN HISTORY, HISTORY OF RELIGION **EDUCATION** Wheaton Col, Ill, BA, 64; Northern Ill Univ, MA, 70, PhD(hist), 77. **CAREER** Publ ed, 78-80, DIR OFF RES & PUBL, HIST SITES DIV, ILL DEPT CONSERV, 80- **MEMBERSHIPS** AHA; Am Soc Church Hist; Orgn Am Historians; Soc Historians Early Am Repub. **RESEARCH** Evangelicalism in 19th century America; antebellum reform; new thought in the 1920s. **SELECTED PUBLICATIONS** Auth, Preachers--Billy Sunday, and Big-Time American Evangelism, J Am Hist, Vol 80, 93; Between Memory and Reality--Family and Community in Rural Wisconsin, 1870-1970, J Interdisciplinary Hist, Vol 26, 95. **CONTACT ADDRESS** Illinois Historical Preservation Agency, 523 W Monroe Apt 1, Springfield, IL, 62704.

TAYLOR, ROBERT R.
DISCIPLINE TWENTIETH-CENTURY EUROPE HISTORY **EDUCATION** Brit Columbia Univ, BA, MA; Stanford Univ, PhD. **CAREER** Prof. **RESEARCH** History of the Welland Canals. **SELECTED PUBLICATIONS** Auth, The Word in Stone: The Role of Architecture in the National Socialist Ideology, Univ Calif Press; Hohenzollern Berlin: Construction and Reconstruction, Meany. **CONTACT ADDRESS** Dept of Hist, Brock Univ, 500 Glenridge Ave, St Catharines, ON, L2S 3A1. **EMAIL** rtaylor@spartan.ac.BrockU.CA

TAYLOR, SANDRA C.
PERSONAL Sacramento, CA, m **DISCIPLINE** AMERICAN FOREIGN RELATIONS **EDUCATION** Stanford Univ, AB, 58; Univ Colo, MA, 63, PhD(hist), 66. **CAREER** Teacher social studies, Denver Pub Schs, 59-62; instr hist, Univ Colo, Denver Ctr, 63; instr, Colorado Springs Ctr, 66; asst prof, 66-72, asst dean lib educ, 76-78, assoc dean lib educ, 78-81, ASSOC PROF HIST, UNIV UTAH, 73-, Vis asst prof hist & Asian studies, Univ Hawaii, Hilo Col, 72-73. **MEMBERSHIPS** Orgn Am Historians; Soc Historians of Am Foreign Rels; Asn for Asian Studies. **RESEARCH** American relations with Meiji Japan; biography of Sidney L Gulick; relocation of Japanese Americans. **SELECTED PUBLICATIONS** Auth, The Hood-River Issei--An Oral-History of Japanese Settlers in Oregon Hood-River-Valley, Pacific Hist Rev, Vol 64, 95; Righting a Wrong--Japanese-Americans and the Passage of the Civil-Liberties-Act of 1988, Western Hist Quart, Vol 25, 94; Breaking the Silence--Redress and Japanese-American Ethnicity, J Am Hist, Vol 82, 96; Democracy on Trial--The Japanese-American Evacuation and Relocation in World-War-II, J Am Hist, Vol 83, 96. **CONTACT ADDRESS** Dept of Hist, Univ of Utah, 217 Carlson Hall, Salt Lake City, UT, 84112-3124.

TAYLOR, SUE
DISCIPLINE ART HISTORY **EDUCATION** Roosevelt Univ, BA; Univ Chicago, MA, PhD. **SELECTED PUBLICATIONS** Auth, Lessons in Hysteria: Louise Bourgeois in the Nineties, New Art Examiner, 97. **CONTACT ADDRESS** Portland State Univ, PO Box 751, Portland, OR, 97207-0751.

TAYLOR, THOMAS TEMPLETON
PERSONAL Born 01/08/1955, Columbia, SC, m, 1975, 3 children **DISCIPLINE** HISTORY **EDUCATION** UnivNC-Greensboro, BA, 76, MA, 78; Univ Ill at Urbana-Champaign, PhD, 88. **CAREER** Lect, Residential Col, Univ NC-Greensboro, 84-88; asst prof, 88-93, assoc prof, 93- ,Wittenberg Univ. **HONORS AND AWARDS** Phi Alpha Theta, 75; Univ Diss Fellow, Univ Ill, 82-83; ODK Disting Tchg Award Wittenberg, 91. **MEMBERSHIPS** Am Soc Legal Hist; Soc Cinema Stud; Am Soc Church Hist; Assoc Inst for Early Am Hist and Culture; Conf Faith and Hist. **RESEARCH** Legal, film, religious, early American history. **SELECTED PUBLICATIONS** Law and Justice, in Jessica Kross, ed., American Eras, 1600-1754, Gale Res, 98. **CONTACT ADDRESS** Dept of History, Wittenberg Univ, PO Box 720, Springfield, OH, 45501. **EMAIL** ttaylor@wittenberg.edu

TAYLOR, TOM
DISCIPLINE HISTORY **EDUCATION** St John's Univ, BA, 78; Univ MN, MA, 83, PhD, 88. **CAREER** Hist, Seattle Univ. **MEMBERSHIPS** AHA; Ger Stud Asn; Soc Sci Hist Asn. **SELECTED PUBLICATIONS** Auth, Children in Mod German History, Children in Historical and Comparative Perspective; Images of Youth and the Family in Wilhelmine Germany: Toward a Reconsideration of the German Sondring, Ger Stud Rev, 92. **CONTACT ADDRESS** Dept of Hist, Seattle Univ, 900 Broadway, Seattle, WA, 98122-4460. **EMAIL** twtaylor@seattleu.edu

TAYLOR, VERTA
PERSONAL Born 01/15/1948, Jonesboro, AR **DISCIPLINE** SOCIOLOGY **EDUCATION** Ohio State Univ, PhD 76, MA 71; Indiana State Univ, BA 70. **CAREER** Ohio State Univ, asst prof, assoc prof, prof, 76 to 97-, co-dir Disaster Res Cen 76-78, grad fac 80 to 98-, act dir WS 84-85. **HONORS AND AWARDS** Dist Tchr; Grad Tchg Awd; Mentoring Awd; Fem Lectr. **MEMBERSHIPS** ASA; SSSP; NASA; SWS. **RESEARCH** Gender; Social movements; Women's studies; Gay and lesbian studies. **SELECTED PUBLICATIONS** Auth, Rock-a-by Baby: Feminism Self-Help and Postpartum Depression, NY, Routledge, 96; auth, Survival in the Doldrums: The American Women's Rights Movement, 1945-1960's, NY, Oxford Univ Press, 87; auth, Feminist Frontiers IV: Rethinking Sex Gender and Society, co-ed, NY, McGraw Hill, 97; Women's Self Help and the Reconstruction of Gender: The Postpartum Support and Breast Cancer Movements, coauth, Mobilization: An Intl Jour, 96; auth, Identity Politics as High Risk Activism: Career Consequences for Lesbian Gay and Bisexual Sociologists, Social Problems, 95; auth, Women's Culture and Lesbian Feminist Activism: A Reconsideration of Cultural feminism, coauth, Signs: Jour of Women in Culture and Soc, 93. **CONTACT ADDRESS** Dept of Sociology, Ohio State Univ, 190 North Oval Hall, Columbus, OH, 43210. **EMAIL** vat@ohstsoca.sbs.ohio-state.edu

TAYLOR GUTHRIE, DANILLE
DISCIPLINE AFRO AMERICAN STUDIES **EDUCATION** Brown Univ, PhD, 84. **CAREER** Asst prof. **RESEARCH** African American literature and culture; black cultural studies; race ethnic studies; women's studies; native American literature; literature by American women of color; folklore and arts; black music. **SELECTED PUBLICATIONS** Auth, Conversations with Toni Morrison, Univ Miss, 94; Scholar In Residence-Rockerfeller Fellow at Integrative Studies Conference for Balck Musi Research, Columbia Col, 97; Who Are The Beloved?a Old and New Testaments, Old and New Communities of Faith in Toni Morrison's Beloved; Looking Beneath the Wings of Two Wings to Veil My Face (rev), Callalloo. **CONTACT ADDRESS** Dept of Minority Studies, Indiana Univ, Northwest, 3400 Broadway, Gary, IN, 46408.

TAYLOR-MITCHELL, LAURIE
PERSONAL Born 06/01/1956, Houston, TX, m, 1990, 1 child **DISCIPLINE** HISTORY OF ART **EDUCATION** Univ MI, PhD, 88 **CAREER** Asst prof, 91-96, Univ of Incamate Word, San Antonio, TX **HONORS AND AWARDS** Phi Beta Kappa **MEMBERSHIPS** Coll Art Assn; Italian Art Soc; Midwest Art Hist Soc; ICMA; South Central Renaissance Conf **RESEARCH** Painting and sculpture, 14th and 15th century, Florence and Tuscany **SELECTED PUBLICATIONS** Auth, Images of St. Matthew Commissioned by the Arte del Cambio for Orsanmichele in Florence: Some Observations on Conservatism in Form and Patronage, Gesta, 92; Guild Commissions at Orsanmichele: Some Relationships Between Interior and Exterior Imagery in the Trecento and Quattrocento, Explorations in Renaissance Culture, 94; A Florentine Source for Verrocchio's Figure of St. Thomas at Orsanmichele, Zeitschrift fur Kunstgeschichte, 94; Botticelli's San Barnaba Altarpiece: Guild Patronage in a Florentne Context, The Search for a Patron in the Middle Ages and the Renaissance, 96. **CONTACT ADDRESS** 110 Sunnycrest Dr, San Antonio, TX, 78228-2913.

TE, JORDAN
PERSONAL Born 07/23/1929, Leeds, England **DISCIPLINE** EDUCATIONAL PSYCHOLOGY **EDUCATION** Indiana Univ, EdD, 55. **CAREER** DEAN, GRAD SCHOOL, ASSOC VICE CHANCELLOR FOR ACAD AFFAIRS, CURATORS' PROF, UNIV OF MO, 68-. **RESEARCH** Longitudinal research; Victorian childhood. **SELECTED PUBLICATIONS** Auth, The Degeneracy Crisis and Victorian Youth, State Univ of NY Press, 93; auth, The Arrow of Time: Longitudinal Study and its Applications, Genetic, Social, and General Psychol Monographs, 94; auth, Ireland and the Quality of Life: The Famine Era, Mellen Press, 97; auth, The First Decade of Life Vol 1 & 2, Mellen Press, 97; auth, Ireland's Children: Stress, Quality of Life, and Child Development in the Famine Era, Greenwood Press, 98; The Census of Ireland 1821-1911: General Reports and Extracts (Three volumes), Mellen Press, 98; auth, Victorian-Edwardian Child-Savers and Their Culture: A Thematic Appraisal, Mellen Press, 98; auth, A Weighted Index of Quality of Life for Irish Children: 1841, 1851, & 1861, Soc Indicators Res, 96; auth, An Almighty Visitation of Providence: The Irish Famine 1845-1849, J of the Royal Soc of Health, 97; auth, Questioning the Predictive Validity of Historical Quality of Life Measures: The IREQUAL Index, Int Test Comn Newsletter, 97; A Century of Irish Censuses 1812-12911, New Hibernia Rev, 97. **CONTACT ADDRESS** 925 Woods Mill Rd., Ballwin, MO, 63011.

TEAFORD, JON C.
PERSONAL Columbus, OH **DISCIPLINE** HISTORY **EDUCATION** Oberlin Col, BA, 69; Univ of Wis, MA, 70, PhD, 73. **CAREER** Vis asst prof of Hist, Iowa State Univ, 73-75; asst prof, 75-79, assoc prof, 79-84, prof, Purdue Univ, 84-. **MEMBERSHIPS** Urban Hist Asn; Soc of Am City & Regional Planning Hist. **SELECTED PUBLICATIONS** Auth, The Municipal Revolution in America, 75; City and Suburb: The Political Fragmentation of Metropolitan America, 79; The Unheralded Triumph: American Urban Government 1870-1900, 84; The Twentieth-Century American City, 86; The Rough Road to Renaissance: Urban Revitalization in America 1940-1985, 90; Cities of the Heartland: The Rise and Fall of the Industrial Midwest, 93; Post-Suburbia: The Politics and Government of Edge Cities, 97. **CONTACT ADDRESS** History Dept, Purdue Univ, West Lafayette, IN, 47907.

TEBBEN, JOSEPH RICHARD
PERSONAL Born 11/26/1943, Columbus, OH, m, 1968, 6 children **DISCIPLINE** CLASSICS **EDUCATION** Duquesne Univ, BA, 65; Univ Pittsburgh, MA, 66; OH State Univ, PhD, 71. **CAREER** From instr to asst prof, 70-77, Assoc Prof Classics, OH State Univ, 77. **RESEARCH** Ancient Greek epic; Computing and class. **SELECTED PUBLICATIONS** Auth, A Course in Medical and Technical Terminology, Burgess, 79; Verba: A computer-assisted course in terminology, Class World, 75; Hesiod Konkordanz, 77 & Homer Konkordanz, 77, Georg Olms; Computer restoration of Greek diacritical symbols, Relo Rev, 77; Alkinoos and Phaiakian Security, Symbolae Osloenses, 91; Concordantia Homerica: Odyssea, Georg Olms, 94; Concordantia Homerica: Ilias, Georg Olms, 98. **CONTACT ADDRESS** Dept of Class, Ohio State Univ, 1179 University Dr, Newark, OH, 43055-1797. **EMAIL** tebben.1@osu.edu

TEBBENHOFF, EDWARD H.
PERSONAL Born 04/14/1949, Suffren, NY, m, 1980, 1 child **DISCIPLINE** HISTORY **EDUCATION** Univ Minn, PhD, 92 **CAREER** Assoc prof, Luther Col. **RESEARCH** Early Amer, hist methods **CONTACT ADDRESS** History Dept, Luther Col, 700 College Dr, Decorah, IA, 52101.

TEGEDER, VINCENT GEORGE
PERSONAL Born 10/01/1910, La Crosse, WI **DISCIPLINE** HISTORY POLITICAL SCIENCE **EDUCATION** St John's Univ, Minn, BA, 33; Univ Wis, MA, 42, PhD, 49. **CAREER** Prof hist, 46-79, EMER PROF HIST, ST JOHN'S UNIV, MINN, 79-, ARCHIVIST, 75-, Vis prof hist, Sacramento State Col, 65-66 & 67 & Int Div, Sophia Univ, Tokyo, 73-74. **MEMBERSHIPS** Am Cath Hist Asn. **RESEARCH** American West during the Civil War; culture on the frontier; colonization. **SELECTED PUBLICATIONS** Auth, Obituary (rev), Cath Hist Rev, Vol 80, 94. **CONTACT ADDRESS** St John's Univ, Archives Collegeville, MN, 56321.

TEICH, ALBERT HARRIS
PERSONAL Born 12/17/1942, Chicago, IL, m, 1989, 3 children **DISCIPLINE** SCIENCE AND POLICY PROGRAMS **EDUCATION** PhD, MIT, 69; BS, MIT 64. **CAREER** Dir Directorate for Sci and Policy Programs, Amer Asso for the Advancement of Sci, 90-; Head Office of Public Sector Program, Amer Assoc for the Advancement of Sci, 84-89; Manager Sci Policy Studies Amer Assoc for the Advancement of Sci, 80-84; Deputy Dir, Graduate Program in Sci Tech and Public Policy, Assoc Prof, Public Affairs George Washington Univ, 76-80; Vis Res Prof, Graduate School of Publc Affairs, State Univ NY, Albany, 75-76; Dir of Res Inst for Public Policy Alternative, State Univ NY, 74-75. **MEMBERSHIPS** Amer Assoc for the Advancement of Sci Elected Fellow, 86; Elected Chm Section X, 88-89; Tech Transfer Soc Elected VP, 86-91; Elected Member Board of Dir, 91-95; Assoc for Public Policy; Analysis and Mgt Elected Member, Policy Board, 96-; Amer Soc for Public Admin Member, Ed Board Pub, Admin Rev, 83-86; Sigma Xi. **RESEARCH** US and Intl Sci and Tech policy; budgeting and priority setting; Sci Tech and Soc; mutual impacts of Tech and Soc; Soc and ethical aspects of Info Tech and computer networking. **SELECTED PUBLICATIONS** Akbert H.Teich, Science and Society in The World Book Science Year 99, Chicago World Book Publishng Co, 98; Albert H. Teich, The Political Context of Science Priority Setting, in the United States, chapter 1, in Mark S.Frankel and Jane Cave eds; Evaluating Science and Scientists, Budapest, Central Euro Univ Press, 97; Albert H.Teich ed, Competitiveness in Academic Research, AAAS, 97 ; Albert H.Teich, Cost, Funding and Budget Issues in Megascience Projects; The Case of the United States Chapter 5 in Organization for Economic Cooperation and Development Megascience Policy Issues, OECD, 95; Albert H.Teich, ed, Technology and the Future, St.Martin's Press, first published, 72, 7th ed, 97; Albert H.Teich, US Science Policy in the 1990s: New Institutional Arrangements, Procedures and Legitmations, in Susan E.Cozzens et al, The Research System in Transition, Kluwer Academic Publ 90. **CONTACT ADDRESS** American Assn for the Advancement of Sci., 1200 New York Ave NW, Washington, DC, 20005. **EMAIL** ATEICH@AAAS.ORG

TELESCA, WILLIAM JOHN
PERSONAL Born 08/01/1931, Port Chester, NY, m, 1958, 4 children **DISCIPLINE** MEDIEVAL HISTORY, CLASSICAL CIVILIZATION **EDUCATION** Fordham Univ, BA, 58, MS, 61, PhD(medieval hist), 68. **CAREER** Teacher soc studies, Port Chester High Sch, NY, 58-67; asst prof medieval hist, 67-80, prof hist, Le Moyne Col, NY, 80-. **HONORS AND AWARDS** Regents War Service Scholar, 58-61; Fulbright Scholar in Rome, 66-67. **MEMBERSHIPS** Mediaeval Acad Am; Asn Cistercian Studies; AAUP. **RESEARCH** Western monasticism; 15th century French monarchy and the papacy. **SELECTED PUBLICATIONS** Auth, The Problem of the Commendatory Monasteries and the Order of Citeaux, Citeaux, 71; The Cistercian Dilemma at the Close of the Middle Ages: Gallicanism or Rome, In: Studies in Medieval Cistercian History, 71 & Jean de Cirey, an Abbot General of the Fifteenth Century, In: Studies in Medieval Cistercian History, Vol II, 73, Cistercian Publ; Papal Reservations and Provisions of Cistercian Abbeys, Citeaux, 75; The Cistercian Abbey in Fifteenth Century France: A Victim of Competing Jurisdictions of Sovereignty, Suzerainty, and Primacy in Cistercians in the Late Middle Ages, Cistercian Publ, 81; The Order of Citeaux during the Council of Basel, 1431-1449, In: Citeaux Com Cist, Vol II, 17-36; Cistercian 'Transfers' and Papal Provisions in the Fifteenth Century, Citeaux, pp279-293, 90; Tasse pagate dagli ordini religiosi alla Santa Sede nel medioevo, in Dizionario degli istituti di perfezione, pp 27-39, 94. **CONTACT ADDRESS** Dept of Hist, LeMoyne Col, 1419 Salt Springs Rd, Syracuse, NY, 13214-1300.

TEMPERLEY, NICHOLAS
PERSONAL Beaconsfield, England, m, 1960, 3 children **DISCIPLINE** MUSIC, MUSICOLOGY **EDUCATION** Royal Col of Music, London, ARCM, 52; Cambridge Univ, King's Col, MA, PhD, 59. **CAREER** Post-doctoral fel, Univ Il, 59-61; asst lect music, Cambridge Univ and fel of Clare Col, 61-66; asst prof music, Yale Univ, 66-67; assoc prof, 67-72, prof Music, Univ IL, 72-96, chair, musicology, 72-75, 92-96. **HONORS AND AWARDS** John Stewart of Rannoch Scholarship in Sacred Music, 53-57; Otto Kinkeldey Award in Musicology, 80; Univ Scholar, Univ IL; Hon fel, Guild of Church Musicians. **MEMBERSHIPS** Am Musicology Soc; Royal Musical Asn; Midwest Victorian Asn; Hymn Soc of Am. **RESEARCH** Classical and early Romantic music; English music; rise and development of piano music and the art song; hymnology. **SELECTED PUBLICATIONS** Auth, Critical Edition of Berlioz, Symphonie fantastique, 71; The Music of the English Parish Church, 79; The Athlone History of Music in Britain, vol 5, The Romantic Age 1800-1914, 81; The London Pianoforte School, 20 vols, 82-85; The Lost Chord: Essays in Victorian Music; Haydn: The Creation; The Hymn Tune Index, 4 vols, 98. **CONTACT ADDRESS** Univ of Illinois, Urbana-Champaign, 1114 W Nevada, Urbana, IL, 61801. **EMAIL** ntemp@uiuc.edu

TENENBAUM, SERGIO
DISCIPLINE ETHICS, HISTORY OF MODERN PHILOSOPHY, PRACTICAL REASON **EDUCATION** Hebrew Univ Jerusalem, BA, 88; Univ Pittsburgh, MA, 93, PhD, 96. **CAREER** Asst prof, Univ NMex. **SELECTED PUBLICATIONS** Auth, Hegel's Critique of Kant in the Philosophy of Right, in Kant Studien; Realists without a Cause: Deflationary Theories of Truth and Ethical Realism, Can J of Philos. **CONTACT ADDRESS** Univ NMex, Albuquerque, NM, 87131.

TENG, TONY
DISCIPLINE EAST ASIAN HISTORY, MODERN CHINA AND JAPAN **EDUCATION** Tunghai Univ, Taiwan, BA; Occidental Col, MA; Univ WI, Madison, PhD. **CAREER** Instr, RI Col. **RESEARCH** Mod Chinese diplomatic hist. **SELECTED PUBLICATIONS** Publ entries in National Dictionary of Revolutionary China, 1838-1926 and Nationalism in East Asia, an Encyclopdia Study. **CONTACT ADDRESS** Rhode Island Col, Providence, RI, 02908.

TEPASKE, JOHN J.
PERSONAL Born 12/08/1929, Grand Rapids, MI, m, 1951, 2 children **DISCIPLINE** LATIN AMERICAN HISTORY **EDUCATION** Mich State Univ, BA, 51; Duke Univ, MA, 53, PhD, 59. **CAREER** Asst prof hist, Memphis State Univ, 58-59; from instr to assoc prof, Ohio State Univ, 59-67; assoc prof, 67-69, prof hist, Duke Univ, 69-; Foreign area training fel & res fel, Univ Calif, Berkeley, 62-63; Tinker Found fel, 75-77; Nat Endowment for Humanities fel, 77; Am Philos Soc fel, 81; chmn, Conf Latin Am Hist, 81; Soc Sci Res Coun Fel, 85-86; Bank Spain Fel, 86-87; Nat Hum Ctr Fel, 89-90; Guggenheim Fel, 95-96; Distinguished Serv Award, Conf Latin Am Hist, 96. **MEMBERSHIPS** AHA; Conf Latin Am Hist; Latin Am Studies Asn; Soc Span & Port Studies. **RESEARCH** Quantitative history; vice-royalty of Peru; comparative colonial history. **SELECTED PUBLICATIONS** Auth, The Governorship of Spanish Florida, 1700-1763, Duke Univ, 63; Three American Empires, Harper, 67; auth, La Real Hacienda de Nueva Expana: La Real Caja de Mexico, 1576-1816, Inst Nacional de Antropologia e Historia, 76; ed, Discourse and Political Reflections on the Kingdoms of Peru, Univ Okla Press, 78; Research Guide to Andean History: Bolivia, Chile, Ecuador and Peru, Duke Univ Press; coauth, The Royal Treasuries of the Spanish Empire in America, Peru 1; Upper Peru 2; Chile and the Rio de la Plata, Duke Univ Press, 82; coauth, The Royal Protomedicato: The Regulation of the Medical Professions in the Spanish Empire, Duke Univ Press, 95; coauth, Ingresos y egresos de la Real Hacienda de Nueva Espana, Instituto Nacional de Antropologia e Historia, 86 & 88; coauth The Royal Treasuries of the Spanish Empire in America, Eighteenth-Century Ecuado, Duke Univ Press, 90. **CONTACT ADDRESS** Dept of History, Duke Univ, PO Box 90719, Durham, NC, 27708-0719. **EMAIL** jjay@acpub.duke.edu

TERBORG-PENN, ROSALYN M.
PERSONAL Born 10/22/1941, Brooklyn, New York, d **DISCIPLINE** HISTORY **EDUCATION** Queens Coll CUNY, BA 1963; George Washington U, MA 1967; Howard U, PhD 1977. **CAREER** Morgan State U, prof of history, coordinator of graduate programs in history, 1986-. **HONORS AND AWARDS** Grad History Essay Award Rayford Logan, Howard Univ 1973; Grad Fellowship in History Howard Univ 1973-74; Post Doct Fellowship for Minorities Ford Found 1980-81; Visiting Scholar Grant Smithsonian Inst 1982, 1994; Travel to Collections Grant Nat Endowment for the Humanities 1984; Association of Black Women Historians, Letitia Woods Brown Award for Best Article Published on Black Women, 1987-88, for Best Anthology, 1995, for Best Book, 1998; Lorraine A Williams Leadership Award, 1998; The Sage Womens Educational Press, Anna Julia Cooper Award for Distinguished Scholarship, 1995. **MEMBERSHIPS** History editor Feminist Studies, 1984-89; commr Howard Cty MD Commn for Women 1980-82; chair, American Historical Association Comm on Women Historians, 1991-93; Research & Publications Comm, Maryland Historical Soc, 1989-96; Alpha Kappa Alpha Sorority, Inc; Association of Black Women Historians, founder, 1978. **SELECTED PUBLICATIONS** Author: Afro-American Woman-Struggles and Images, 1978, 1981, 1997; Women in Africa and the African Dispora, 1987, 1996; African-American Women in the Struggle for the Vote, 1998. **CONTACT ADDRESS** Professor of History, Morgan State Univ, Baltimore, MD, 21251.

TERCHEK, RONALD JOHN
PERSONAL Born 07/29/1936, Cleveland, OH, m, 1998, 2 children **DISCIPLINE** POLITICAL SCIENCE **EDUCATION** Univ Chicago, BA, 58, MA, 60; Univ Maryland, PhD, 65. **CAREER** From Asst prof to prof, Univ Maryland, 65- . **HONORS AND AWARDS** Omicron Delta Kappa; Lilly Fel, 93-94; University Teaching Excellence Awards, 85, 89, 92; listed, Who's Who in the East, 98. **MEMBERSHIPS** Am Polit Sci Asn; Foundations on Polit Theory; Conf for the Study of Polit Theory; Pi Sigma Alpha; Phi Kappa Phi; Int Asn for Philos of Law and Social Philos. **RESEARCH** Classical liberalism: Locke, Smith, and J.S. Mill; liberal democratic theory; Gandhi's political theory with special emphasis on his critique of modernity and modernization; civic realism. **SELECTED PUBLICATIONS** Ed, Interactions; Foreign Policy as Public Policy, Am Enterprise Inst, 83; auth, Republican Paradoxes and Liberal Anxieties: Retrieving Neglected Fragments in Political Theory, Rowman & Littlefield, 96; auth, Leo Strauss and the Republican Tradition, in Deutsch, ed, Leo Strauss, the Straussians, and the Study of the American Regime, Rowman & Littlefield, 97; auth, the Political Thought of Mahatma Gandhi, Rowman & Littlefield, 98. **CONTACT ADDRESS** Dept of Government and Politics, Univ of Maryland, College Park, MD, 20740. **EMAIL** rterchek@bss2.umd.edu

TERPSTRA, VERN
PERSONAL Born 08/20/1927, Grand Rapids, MI, m, 1950, 2 children **DISCIPLINE** INTERNATIONAL BUSINESS, MARKETING **EDUCATION** BA 50, MBA 51, PhD 65, all Univ of Michigan. **CAREER** Prof of International Business Univ of Michigan 66-92, Asst Prof Marketing Wharton School 64-66, Dir Mormal School Congo 53-61. **HONORS AND AWARDS** Fellow-Academy of International Business; Fellow -Marketing Sci Institute;Fellow-Ford Foundation. **MEMBERSHIPS** Academy of International Business-President 70-72, Amer Marketing Assoc **RESEARCH** International Marketing, International Business, Cross Cultural Issues **SELECTED PUBLICATIONS** International Marketing 7th ed, Dryden Press, 97; International Dimensions of Marketing Kent 3rd ed, 93; Cultural Enviornment of International Business 3rd ed, Southwestern, 91; Lectures in International Marketing(Chinese) National Center for Management Development Dalian China, 86: Univ Educ for International Business AEIB 69; Amer Marketing in the Common Market Praeger, 67; Co-auth Comparative Analysis for International Marketing, Allyn&Bacon, 67; Co-auth Marketing Development in the European Economic Community, McGraw-Hill, 64; Co-auth, Patents and Progress, Irwin, 65. **CONTACT ADDRESS** Graduate School of Business, Univ of Michigan, Ann Arbor, MI, 48109. **EMAIL** vterp@umich.edu

TERRELL, MELVIN C.
PERSONAL Born 10/05/1949, Chicago, Illinois, s **DISCIPLINE** EDUCATION **EDUCATION** Chicago State Univ, BSEd 1971; Loyola Univ of Chicago, MEd 1974; Southern Illinois Univ at Carbondale, PhD 1978; Inst for Educ Mgmt Harvard Univ, Post-Doctoral Study/Mgmt Devel Program summer 1986; Univ of Virginia Annual Summer Professional Dept

Workshop Educ Mgmt Strategies, 1987; Natl Assn of Student Personnel Admin, Richard F Stevens Inst, 1989; Amer Council on Educ, Fellow, Florida State Univ, 1993-94. **CAREER** Kennedy-King Coll Chicago, student devel specialist, counseling instructor 1973-75; Eastern New Mexico Univ, coordinator/counselor of black affairs & asst prof ethnic studies 1977-78; Chicago State Univ, project director/asst professor of education, 1978-79; Univ of Arkansas at Monticello, dir learning devel center 1979-80; Univ of Wisconsin-Oshkosh, dir multicultural educ center 1981-85; Univ of Toledo, dir of minority affairs & adjunct asst prof 1985-88; Northeastern Illinois Univ, full professor of counselor education, 1988-, vice president for student affairs, 1988-; Illinois State Univ, visiting prof, summer 1991. **HONORS AND AWARDS** Outstanding Admin, Univ of Toledo 1985, 1986, Administrator of the Year, 1986-88; recipient of a Ford Foundation Grant on Cultural Diversity, co-principal investigator, 1992-94; Identified as an Exemplary Leader in "Effective Leadership in Student Services," written by Linda M Clement & Scott T Rickard, Jossey-Bass, 1992. **MEMBERSHIPS** Past Vice chmn of educ comm NAACP Toledo Branch 1985-88; educ bd Natl Assoc of Student Personnel Admin Journal 1986-89 on Leadership Educ, 1986-; chair educ comm Alpha Phi Alpha 1986-88; natl chmn, Ethnic Minority Network, Natl Assn of Student Personnel Assn, 1988-90; vice chmn, Amer Assn of Higher Educ, 1989; chmn, Amer Assn of Higher Educ, Black Caucus Exec, 1991-93; life mem, Alpha Phi Alphi Fraternity, Inc; evaluation team mem, Middle States Assn of Colls & Univs; consultant evaluator, North Central Assn of Colleges & Universities, 1988-; member, National Assn of Student Personnel Administrators; past natl coord, Minority Undergraduate Fellows Program, Natl Assn of Student Personnel Admini, 1994-98; chair, exec comm, Ill Comm on Blacks Concerned in Higher Ed (ICBCHE), 1995-. **SELECTED PUBLICATIONS** "Diversity, Disunity and Campus Community," National Association of Student Personnel Administrators Monograph, 1992; Source of funding for minority student programming and its implications; Fund raising and development for student affairs; "Developing Student Government Leadership," New Directions for Student Services Monograph, Summer, 1994; author, "From Isolation to Mainstream, An Institutional Committment" 1987; co-author, Model Field Based Program in Multicultural Educ for Non-Urban Univs 1981, "Multicultural Educ Centers in Acad Marketplace" 1987; author, Racism: Undermining Higher Education, 1988; editor, NASPA Journal Series on Cultural Pluralism, 1988; Scott Goodnight Award for Outstanding Performance of a Dean, 1990; co-editor, From Survival to Success: Promoting Minority Student Retention, 1988; **CONTACT ADDRESS** Vice Pres for Student Affairs/Public Affairs & Professor of Counselor Education, 5500 N St Louis Ave, Rm B-104, Chicago, IL, 60625.

TERRILL, ROSS
PERSONAL Melbourne, Australia **DISCIPLINE** ASIAN STUDIES **EDUCATION** Weley Col Melbourne, 56; BA, First Class Hon, Univ of Melbourne, 62; PhD, Polit Sci, Harvard Univ, 70; **CAREER** Austialian Army, 57-58; Tutor in Polit Sci, Univ of Melbourne, 62-63; Staff Sec Australian Student Christian Movement, 62, 64-65; Res Fel Asia Sic, 68-70, Lectr on Govt, 70-74, Dir Student Prog in Intl Affairs, 74-77, Assoc Prof Govt, Harvard Univ, 74-78; Vis Prof, Monash Univ, 96-98; Res Assoc, Fairbank Center for East Asian Res, Harvard Univ 70-. **HONORS AND AWARDS** Natl Mag Award for Reporting Excellence, 72; George Polk Memoria Award for Outstanding Mag Reporting, 72; Summer Prize for PhD Thesis, Harvard Univ, 70; Exhibition in Polit Sci, Univ of Melbourne, 57; Frank Knox Memorial Fellowship, Harvard Univ, 65-66. **SELECTED PUBLICATIONS** China in Our Time, Simon & Schuster, 92; The Australians, Simon & Schuster, 87; The White-Boned Demon: A Biography of Madame Mao Zedong, William Morrow, 84; Mao in History, The Natl Interest, 98; China Under Deng, Foreign Affairs, Vol 73 No 5, 94; United States-China Relations, Australian Journal of Chinese Affairs, No 3, 80; China Quarterly, No 139, 94; Journal of Asian Studies, Vol 48, No 4, 89; Bulletin of Australian Political Studies Associations, Vol 8 No 2, Political Sci Quarterly, No 40, 69. **CONTACT ADDRESS** Fairbank Center for East Asian Res, Harvard Univ, Cambridge, MA, 02138. **EMAIL** terr@compuserve.com

TERRILL, TOM E.
PERSONAL Born 09/15/1935, Oklahoma City, OK, m, 1961, 2 children **DISCIPLINE** AMERICAN HISTORY **EDUCATION** Westminster Col, Mo, BA, 57; Princeton Theol Sem, BD, 61; Univ Wis-Madison, MA, 63, PhD(Am hist), 66. **CAREER** Vis asst prof Am & African hist, Hiram Col, 65-66; asst prof Am hist, 66-70, assoc prof, 70-80, PROF HIST, UNIV SC, 80-, Vis lectr, Allen Univ, 67 & 70; vis prof church hist, Lutheran Southern Theol Sem, 72; Nat Endowment for Humanities younger humanist fel, 73-74; grant, SC Comt for Humanities, 73, 76 & 78-; Rockefeller Found Humanities fel, 79-80. **MEMBERSHIPS** AHA; Econ Hist Asn; Southern Hist Asn; Orgn Am Historians. **RESEARCH** Late 19th century United States; Southern textile workers; Southern economic and labor history. **SELECTED PUBLICATIONS** Auth, The South--A Bibliographical Essay, Am Studies Int, Vol 31, 93. **CONTACT ADDRESS** Dept of Hist, Univ of SC, Columbia, SC, 29208.

TERRY, ANN R.
DISCIPLINE ART HISTORY **EDUCATION** Eastern Mich Univ, BFA, 71; Univ Ill, MA, PhD. **CAREER** Asso pro, **HONORS AND AWARDS** Fel(s): Int Res & Exchanges Board; The Kress Found; Am Philos Soc; Dumbarton Oaks Fel; Omicron Delta Kappa Award. **RESEARCH** Archaeology,art and architecture of early Christian period. **SELECTED PUBLICATIONS** Areas: Late Roman grave stelae, Byzantine architectural history, marble intarsia from antiquity. **CONTACT ADDRESS** Wittenberg Univ, Springfield, OH, 45501-0720.

TERRY, JAMES L.
PERSONAL Born 09/12/1949, Terre Haute, IN **DISCIPLINE** LIBRARY SCIENCE; SOCIOLOGY **EDUCATION** Long Island Univ, MLS, 90; Purdue Univ, PhD, 88. **CAREER** Libr, Assoc Curator, New York Univ, 90-. **HONORS AND AWARDS** Louis Schneider Memorial Award for Outstanding Dissertation, 88. **MEMBERSHIPS** Amer Libr Assoc; Amer Sociological Assoc. **RESEARCH** Political economy of information technology; information literacy; sociology of work and labor **SELECTED PUBLICATIONS** Auth, Authorship in College and Research Libraries revisited: Gender, Institutional Affiliation, Collaboration, College and Research Libraries, 96; auth, Automated Library Systems: A History of Constraints and Opportunities, Advances in Librarianship, 98. **CONTACT ADDRESS** Bobst Library, New York Univ, 70 Washington Sq S, New York, NY, 10012. **EMAIL** terryj@elmer4.bobst.nyu.edu

TERRY, JANICE J.
PERSONAL Born 03/29/1942, Cleveland, OH **DISCIPLINE** MODERN MIDDLE EAST HISTORY **EDUCATION** Col Wooster, BA, 64; Am Univ Beirut, MA, 66; Univ London, PhD, 68. **CAREER** Assoc prof hist, 68-76, assoc prof hist & philos, 76-80, prof hist, Eastern Mich Univ, 80-, US Dept Health, Educ & Welfare res grant, Egypt, 73. **MEMBERSHIPS** Mid East Studies Asn N Am; Mid East Inst. **RESEARCH** Modern Egypt. **SELECTED PUBLICATIONS** Auth, Official British reaction to Egyptian nationalism, al-Abhath, 68; Israel's policy toward the Arab states, in The Transformation of Palestine, Northwestern Univ, 71; co-ed, The Arab World From Nationalism to Revolution, Medina Univ, 71; auth, Struggle for independence in Aden, MidE Forum, winter & summer 73; The consequences of economic abstention: The Aswan Dam, in Intervention or Abstention, Univ Press Ky, 75; Zionist Attitudes Toward Arabs: Palestine Studies, 76; The Wafd 1919-1952: Cornerstone of Egyptian Political Power, Third World Ctr, 82; coauth (with professors Goff, Moss & Upshur), The World in the 20th Century, McGraw Hill, 5th ed; coauth, World History, West, 3rd ed. **CONTACT ADDRESS** Dept of Hist, Eastern Michigan Univ, 701 Pray Harrold, Ypsilanti, MI, 48197-2201.

TERRY, MICKEY THOMAS
DISCIPLINE MUSICOLOGY **EDUCATION** East Carolina University; Georgetown University, PhD, Late Medieval and Early Modern European History. **CAREER** Organ recitalist; GEORGETOWN UNIV, PROF; ST. LUKE'S EPISCOPAL CHURCH, ORGANIST, currently. **HONORS AND AWARDS** Ninth Annual Clarence Mader National Organ Competition, second prize, 1985; Michigan International Organ Competition, finalist, 1987; Flint competition, Flint, MI, finalist, 1989. **MEMBERSHIPS** American Guild of Organists, District of Columbia Chapter, sub-dean; "ECS/AGO African-American Organ Music Series", advisory bd. Held many concerts across US; broadcasted on Public Radio International's "Pipedreams" several times; John F. Kennedy Center for the Performing Arts, featured artist; Piccolo-Spoleto Music Festival, Charleston, SC, organ recitalist; St. Paul's Chapel, Columbia Univ, presented lecture-recital, 1996; Region III American Guild of Organists Convention, featured recitalist; American Guild of Organists National convention, featured recitalist, 1998; Performed with George Walker and others on "George Walker-A Portrait". **SELECTED PUBLICATIONS** Written articles for "The American Organist Magazine", "The Diapason." **CONTACT ADDRESS** St. Luke's Episcopal Church, Washington, DC.

TEUTE, FREDRIKA J.
PERSONAL Born 10/16/1947, Rochester, NY, m, 1985 **DISCIPLINE** AMERICAN HISTORY **EDUCATION** Radcliffe Col, BA, 69; Col of William & Mary, MA, 76; Johns Hopkins Univ, PhD, 88. **CAREER** Assoc ed, Papers of James Madison, 71-76; Ed of Publ, Virginia Hist Soc, 81-84; assoc ed, Papers of John Marshall, 84-89; Ed of Publ, Omohundro Inst of Early Am Hist and Cult, 89- . **HONORS AND AWARDS** Butler Prize, Johns Hopkins Univ; Bunting Inst Fel; Mellon fel; NEH-Am Antiq Soc Fel. **MEMBERSHIPS** Am Antiq Soc; AHA; OAH; ASECS; SHA; ASA; ADE; SEA. **RESEARCH** Early American frontiers; early Kentucky; early national political culture. **CONTACT ADDRESS** Omohundro Inst of Early American History and Culture, PO Box 8781, Williamsburg, VA, 23187-8781. **EMAIL** fjteut@facstaff.wm.edu

TEVIOTDALE, ELIZABETH C.
PERSONAL Born 11/15/1955, New York, NY, s **DISCIPLINE** ART HISTORY **EDUCATION** BA, State Univ of NY at Buffalo, 79; MA, Univ of NC, 81; MA, Tulane Univ, 85; PhD, Univ of NC, 91. **CAREER** 97-, Assoc Curator of Manuscripts, The J. Paul Getty Mus 92-97, Asst Curator of Manuscripts, The J. Paul Getty Mus 91-92, vis asst prof, Davidson Col Spring 91, vis instru, Univ of IA. **HONORS AND AWARDS** Samuel H. Kress Found Predoctoral Fel Summer 89; Swedish Institute Guest Scholarship 83-84; Fulbright Travel Grant 83-84; For Exchange Fel, Freie Universitat Berlin. **MEMBERSHIPS** UCLA Center of Medieval and Renaissance Studies Am Musicological Soc Col Art Assoc International Center of Medieval ARt Medieval Acad of Am. **RESEARCH** Western medieval liturgical manuscripts and their illumination. **SELECTED PUBLICATIONS** A Pair of Franco-Flemish Cistercian Antiphonals of the 13th Century and Their Programs of Illumination- forthcoming in Fragments as Witnesses to Medieval Bks and Bkmaking (Anderson-Lovelace) And Episode in the Medieval Afterlife of the Caligula Troper, in Anglo-Saxon Manuscripts and Their Heritage, ed Phillip Pulsiano and Elaine Treharne, Ashgate, 98, pp 219-226; Latin Verse Inscriptions in Anglo-Saxon Art, Gesta 35, 96, 99-110; 750 Years in the Life of a Pair of Cistercian Antiphonals Pastoral Music 20/2, 96, 38-40; The Invitation to the Puy d'Evreux, Current Musicology 52, 93, 7-26; Some Classified Catalogues of the Cottonian Library, The British Library Jour 18, 92, 74-87; Music and Pictures in the Middle Ages, in Companion to Medieval and Renaissance Music, ed Tess Knighton and David Fallows, JM Dent, 92, pp 179-188; The Filiation of the Music Illustrations in a Boethius in Milan and in the Piacenza Codice magno, Imago Musicae 5, 88, 7-22; A Speculation on an Affinity between Ruskin's Seven Lamps of Architecture and Monet's Cathedrals, The Rugers Art Review 4, 83, 68-77. **CONTACT ADDRESS** The J. Paul Getty Museum, 1200 Getty Center Drive, Ste. 1000, Los Angeles, CA, 90049-1687. **EMAIL** eteviotdale@getty.edu

THACKERAY, FRANK W.
PERSONAL Born 03/16/1943, Pittsburgh, PA, m, 1971, 2 children **DISCIPLINE** RUSSIAN & EASTERN EUROPEAN HISTORY **EDUCATION** Dickinson Col, BA, 65; Temple Univ, MA, 71, PhD, 77. **CAREER** Prof hist, IN Univ Southeast, 77. **HONORS AND AWARDS** Outstanding Research/Creativity Activity Award, Ind Univ SE, 98. **MEMBERSHIPS** AHA; Am Asn Advan Slavic Studies; NAm Asn Sport Hist. **SELECTED PUBLICATIONS** Auth, Antecedents of Revolution: Alexander I and the Polish Congress Kingdom, East Europ Quart, 80; co-ed, Events That Changed the World series, Greenwood, 95-; Events That Changed America series, Greenwood, 95. **CONTACT ADDRESS** Dept of Hist, Indiana Univ, Southeast, New Albany, IN, 47150-2158. **EMAIL** fthacker@iusmail.ius.indiana.edu

THADEN, EDWARD C.
PERSONAL Born 04/24/1922, Seattle, WA, m, 1950 **DISCIPLINE** HISTORY **EDUCATION** Univ Wash, BA, 44; Univ Zurich, Cert, 48; Univ Paris, PhD, 50. **CAREER** Instr to prof, Pa State Univ, 52-68; vis prof, Univ Marburg, 65; prof, Univ Ill, 68; vis prof, Martin Luther Univ, 88-; vis res prof to instr, Moscow, 88-90. **HONORS AND AWARDS** Fulbright Fel, Finland, 57-58, Germany, 65, Poland/Finland, 68; Carnegie Grant; ACLS Res Awards, 63, 75; IREX/USSR Acad Awards, 75, 88, 90; Woodrow Wilson Int Ctr Scholar, 80., Pres, Comm Internationale des Etudies Historques Slaves, 95-00. **MEMBERSHIPS** Am Hist Asn; Asn Adv Baltic Stud; Am Asn Adv of Slavic Studies; Com Int des Etudes Historique Slaves. **RESEARCH** Russian; Balkan; Baltic and Scandinav history. **SELECTED PUBLICATIONS** Auth, The Western Borderland of Russia, 1710-1870, 84; auth, Interpretting History: collected Essays on the Relations of Russia with Europe, 90; auth, Essays in Russian and East European History: Festschrift in Honor of Edward C. Thaden, 95; auth, art, Der Sowjetische Historismus und Ostmitteleuropa Nach 1939, 95; auth, The Rise of Historicism in Russia, 99. **CONTACT ADDRESS** PO Box 31786, Seattle, WA, 98103-1786. **EMAIL** engvik@worldnet.att.net

THAYER, JOHN A.
DISCIPLINE HISTORY **EDUCATION** Univ Wis, PhD, 60. **CAREER** Prof **RESEARCH** Nineteenth and twentieth century Italian and European cultural-political history. **SELECTED PUBLICATIONS** Auth, Italy and the "Great War": Politics and Culture, 1870-1915, 73; History As Logic and As Explanation, Studies Modern Italian Hist, 86. **CONTACT ADDRESS** History Dept, Univ of Minnesota, Twin Cities, 614 Social Sciences Tower, 267 19th Ave S, Minneapolis, MN, 55455. **EMAIL** thaye001@tc.umn.edu

THEILE, KARL H.
PERSONAL St. Louis, MO **DISCIPLINE** HISTORY; INTERNATIONAL RELATIONS **EDUCATION** Univ Rochester, BS, 61; Calif State Univ, LA, MA, 63; Univ Southern Calif, PhD, 81. **CAREER** Prof, dept chemn, LA T-TCC, 70-. **MEMBERSHIPS** Hum Asn Calif **RESEARCH** World War II **SELECTED PUBLICATIONS** Auth, Beyond Monsters and Clowns, 96. **CONTACT ADDRESS** 3940 Fairway Ave, Studio City, CA, 91604.

THEODORATUS, ROBERT JAMES
PERSONAL Born 06/24/1928, Bellingham, WA, m, 1962, 3 children **DISCIPLINE** SOCIO-CULTURAL ANTHROPOLOGY **EDUCATION** Wash State Univ, BA, 50; Univ Wash, MA, 53, PhD, 61. **CAREER** Res anal, HRAF, 61-62; asst prof

Anthropology, Sacremento State Col, 62-66; assoc prof, 66-80, PROF ANTHROPOLOGY, 80-; COL STATE UNIV, 66-; Phi Beta Kappa, 50; Phi Kappa Phi, 50. **MEMBERSHIPS** Am Anthrop Assoc; Royal Anthrop Inst; Polynesian Soc; Spc Folk Life Stud. **RESEARCH** Immigrant ethnic cultures in North America; Ethnology of Europe; Comparative religion; Folk religion; Food; Culture. **SELECTED PUBLICATIONS** auth Europe: A selected Ethnographic Bibliography, HRAF Press, 69; A Greek Community in America: Tacoma, Washington, Sacremento Anthrop Soc, 71; Patterns in Welsh Culture, Studies in Modern British Society, Az State Univ, 80; Orcadians, Shetlanders, Welsh, Encyclo World Cult, 92; British Isles, Encyclo Cult Anthrop, Henry Holt, 96; Shamanism in the Columbia-Fraser Plateau Region, Ancient Traditions: Shamanism in Central Asia and the Americas, Univ Press Col, 94. **CONTACT ADDRESS** Robert James Theodoratus, 3349 Oregon Trail, Fort Collins, CO, 80526-4206. **EMAIL** B Theo@ Pageplus.com

THEOHARIS, ATHAN

PERSONAL Born 08/03/1936, Milwaukee, WI, m, 1966, 2 children **DISCIPLINE** RECENT UNITED STATES HISTORY **EDUCATION** Univ Chicago, AB, 56, AB, 57, AM, 59, PhD(hist), 65. **CAREER** Instr hist, Tex A&M Univ, 62-64; asst prof, Wayne State Univ, 64-68; assoc prof, Staten Island Community Col, 68-69; assoc prof, 69-76, PROF HIST, MARQUETTE UNIV, 76-, Wayne State Univ fac res fel, 67; grant, Johnson Found, 77, Nat Endowment for Humanities, 76, Warsh-Mott Fund, 80 & Field Found, 80; Albert Beyeridge res grant, 80; fel, Laveiligelire journalism, 80; Thomas P Lockwood prof Am hist, State Univ NY, Buffalo, 82-83. **HONORS AND AWARDS** Binkley-Stephenson Award, 79; Certificate of Merit, Am Bar Asn, 72. **MEMBERSHIPS** AHA; Orgn Am Historians; Acad Polit Sci. **RESEARCH** Truman administration; the cold war; civil liberties in the years and after and federal surveillance policy. **SELECTED PUBLICATIONS** Auth, Exposed--Federal-Bureau-Of-Investigation FBI--Unclassified Reports on Churches and Church Leaders, J Am Hist, Vol 80, 94; For the Presidents Eyes Only--Secret Intelligence and the American Presidency from Washington to Bush, Am Hist Rev, Vol 0101, 96; Owen Lattimore and the Loss of China, J Am Hist, Vol 79, 93; Unlocking the Files of the FBI--A Guide to Its Records and Classification-System, J Am Hist, Vol 80, 94; Inside-Out--A Memoir of the Blacklist, NY Hist, Vol 77, 96; Intelligence Intervention in the Politics of Democratic-States--The United-States, Israel, and Britain, Am Hist Rev, Vol 0102, 97; American Intelligence, 1775-1990--A Bibliographical Guide, J Am Hist, Vol 80, 94; The Central-Intelligence-Agency--An Instrument of Government to 1950, Am Hist Rev, Vol 98, 93; Foreign-Relations of the United-States, 1958-1960, J Am Hist, Vol 80, 93. **CONTACT ADDRESS** Dept of Hist, Marquette Univ, Milwaukee, WI, 53233.

THERIAULT, MICHEL

PERSONAL Born 12/02/1942, Toronto, ON, Canada **DISCIPLINE** CANON LAW/HISTORY **EDUCATION** Univ Montreal, Bphil, 62; McGill Univ, MLS, 76; Pontif Univ St Thomas (Rome), JCD, 71. **CAREER** Head acquisitions dept, Univ Montreal Libr, 69-75; chief, Retrospective Nat Biblio Div, Nat Libr Can, 75-85; asst prof, 85-92, ASSOC PROF CANON LAW, ST PAUL UNIV, 92-. **MEMBERSHIPS** Can Canon Law Soc (secy-treas, 88-90, vice-pres, 95-97); Soc Law Eastern Churches (deleg Can, 87-97); Bibliog Soc Can (assoc secy, 81-86). **SELECTED PUBLICATIONS** Auth, Neo-vagin et impuissance, 71; auth, Le livre religieux au Quebec depuis les debuts de l'imprimerie jusqu'a la Confederation 1764-1867, 77; auth, The Institutions of Consecrated Life in Canada from the Beginning of New France up to the Present, 80; ed, Choix et acquisition des documents au Quebec, vol 1, 77; co-ed, Proceedings of the 5th International Congress of Canon Law, 86; co-ed, Code de droit canonique, 90; co-ed, Canonical Studies Presented to Germain Lesage, 91; co-ed, Studia Canonica, Index 1-25 1967-1991, 92; co-ed, Code of Canon Law Annotated, 93; transl, A Manual for Bishops, 94. **CONTACT ADDRESS** Faculty of Canon Law, St Paul Univ, 223 Main St, Ottawa, ON, K1S 1C4.

THERNSTROM, STEPHAN ALBERT

PERSONAL Born 11/05/1934, Port Huron, MI, m, 1959, 2 children **DISCIPLINE** AMERICAN HISTORY **EDUCATION** Northwestern Univ, BS, 56; Harvard Univ, AM, 58, PhD, 62. **CAREER** Instr hist & lit, Harvard Univ, 62-66, asst prof hist, 66-67; assoc prof, Brandeis Univ, 67-69; prof, Univ Calif, Los Angeles, 69-73; prof, 73-81, WINTHROP PROF HIST, HARVARD UNIV, 81-, Res mem, Mass Inst Technol-Harvard Univ Joint Ctr Urban Studies, 62-69; Am Coun Learned Soc fel, 65-66; Guggenheim Found fel, 69-70; mem hist adv comt, Math Soc Sci Bd, 72-; bd dirs, Soc Sci Res Coun, 77-80; Pitt prof Am hist, Cambridge Univ, 78-79; dir, Charles Warren Ctr for Study Am Hist, 80-83. **HONORS AND AWARDS** Bancroft Prize Am Hist, 74; Harvard Univ Press Faculty Prize, 74; Leland Prize, Am Hist Asn, 81. **MEMBERSHIPS** Soc Am Historians. **RESEARCH** American social, urban and ethnic history. **SELECTED PUBLICATIONS** Auth, Poverty and Progress, Harvard Univ, 64; Poverty, Planning and Politics in the New Boston, Basic Bks, 68; co-ed, Nineteenth Century Cities: Essays in the New Urban History, Yale Univ, 69; auth, Reflections on the new urban history, Daedalus, 9/71; coauth, Men in motion: Urban population mobility in 19th century America, J Interdisciplinary Hist, fall 71; ed, The Harvard Studies in Urban History, 71, auth, The Other Bostonians: Poverty and Progress in the American Metropolis, 1880-1970, 73 & ed, The Harvard Encyclopedia of American Ethnic Groups, Harvard Univ, 79; co-auth, America in Black and White: One Nation, Indivisible, 97. **CONTACT ADDRESS** 1445 Massachusetts Ave, Lexington, MA, 02173. **EMAIL** thernstr@fas.harvard.edu

THOLFSEN, TRYGVE RAINONE

PERSONAL Born 04/05/1924, Philadelphia, PA, m, 1947, 3 children **DISCIPLINE** MODERN EUROPEAN & ENGLISH HISTORY **EDUCATION** Yale Univ, BA, 48, MA, 49, PhD(hist), 52. **CAREER** From instr to asst prof hist, Univ Calif, Los Angeles, 52-59; assoc prof & chmn dept, La State Univ, 59-62; assoc prof, 62-67, PROF HIST, TEACHERS COL, COLUMBIA UNIV, 67-, Guggenheim fel, 68-69. **MEMBERSHIPS** AHA; Conf Brit Studies. **RESEARCH** Victorian England; history and philosophy of history. **SELECTED PUBLICATIONS** Auth, The Victorians and the Stuart Heritage--Interpretations of a Discordant Past, Am Hist Rev, Vol 0102, 97; Return to Essentials--Some Reflections on the Present State of Historical Study, J Interdisciplinary Hist, Vol 24, 94. **CONTACT ADDRESS** Teachers Col Columbia Univ, Box 217, New York, NY, 10027.

THOMAIDIS, SPERO T.

PERSONAL Born 12/14/1928, Highland Falls, NY **DISCIPLINE** MODERN EUROPEAN HISTORY **EDUCATION** City Col NY, BA, 47; Columbia Univ, MA, 48, PhD(Hist), 65. **CAREER** Assoc prof Hist, Bemidji State Univ, 65-. **MEMBERSHIPS** AHA. **RESEARCH** German Reformation; modern European intellectual history. **CONTACT ADDRESS** Dept of History, Bemidji State Univ, 1500 Birchmont Dr NE, Bemidji, MN, 56601-2699.

THOMAS, CAROL G.

PERSONAL Born 08/11/1938, Oak Park, IL, m, 1960 **DISCIPLINE** ANCIENT HISTORY **EDUCATION** Northwestern Univ, AM, 61, PhD(hist), 65. **CAREER** Instr hist, 64-65, acting asst prof, 65-67, asst prof, 67-71, assoc prof, 71-81, PROF ANCIENT HIST, UNIV WASH, 81-, Am Coun Learned Soc study fel, 75. **MEMBERSHIPS** Soc Prom Hellenic Studies; Am Philol Asn. **RESEARCH** Greek political institutions, especially Homeric period; continuity between Mycenaean Age and classical Greek history; the Greek polis. **SELECTED PUBLICATIONS** Auth, The Orientalizing Revolution--Near-Eastern Influence on Greek Culture in the Early Archaic Age, Am Hist Rev, Vol 99, 94; The Homeric Epics--'Iliad' and 'Odyssey'--Strata Or A Spectrum, Colby Quart, Vol 29, 93; Origins of the Greek Miracle--Populating and Population in Northern Greece, Am Hist Rev, Vol 98, 93; The Discovery of the Greek Bronze-Age, Am J Archaeol, Vol 0101, 97; Reading Greek Death--To the End of the Classical-Period, Am Hist Rev, Vol 0102, 97. **CONTACT ADDRESS** Dept of Hist, Univ of Wash, Seattle, WA, 98195.

THOMAS, DIANA

PERSONAL Phoenix, AZ **DISCIPLINE** ARCHITECTURAL HISTORIAN **EDUCATION** York Univ, BA(Art Hist), 79; Ariz State Univ, MA (Archit Hist), 83. **CAREER** Consultant & Archit Hist, 83-85; archit hist, Alta Community Dev, 85-92; archit hist, Preservation Office, State of Ariz, 92-94; PRESERVATION PLANNER, CITY PHOENIX, 94-. **MEMBERSHIPS** Soc Stud Archit Can; Am Soc Archit Hist; Edmonton Soc Urban & Archit Studs. **SELECTED PUBLICATIONS** Auth, Traditions in a New World: Ukrainian-Canadian Churches in Alberta, in Soc Stud Archit Can Bull, 88; auth, Ukrainian Churches in Alberta: A Look at Tradition in Transition, in Proc Ukrainian Festival, 88; auth, The Alberta Inventory of Historic Sites: Recording Ukrainian Church Architecture, in Pamiatky Ukrainy, 92. **CONTACT ADDRESS** Soc Study Architecture Canada, PO Box 2302, Stn. D, Ottawa, ON, K1P 5W5.

THOMAS, DONALD E.

DISCIPLINE HISTORY **EDUCATION** Univ Mich, BA; Univ Chicago, MA, PhD. **SELECTED PUBLICATIONS** Auth, Diesel: Technology and Society in Industrial Germany, Univ Ala Press, 87; articles on, 19th and 20th century Ger technologival history. **CONTACT ADDRESS** Dept of History, Virginia Military Inst, Lexington, VA, 24450.

THOMAS, EMORY M.

PERSONAL Born 11/03/1939, Richmond, VA, m, 1962, 2 children **DISCIPLINE** AMERICAN HISTORY **EDUCATION** Univ Va, BA, 62; Rice Univ, PhD, 66. **CAREER** From asst prof to assoc prof, 67-77, PROF HIST, UNIV GA, 77-87, REGENTS PROF HIST, UNIV GA, 87-; Douglas Southall Freeman Prof Hist, Univ Richmond, 9; Lamar lectr, Wesleyan Col, 72; Fulbright sr lectr, Univ Genoa, 74. **HONORS AND AWARDS** John S Longscope Prize, Rice Univ, 66; Albert Christ-Janer Award, Creativity Res, Univ GA, 80; Univ GA Alumni Soc, Fac Serv Award, 82; Sea Grant, Oral hist Georgia coast, 82-84; Joseph H Parks-Alf A Heggoy Award, Excellence Teaching, 88; Mellon res fel, VA Hist Soc, 89. **MEMBERSHIPS** Southern Hist Asn; Orgn Am Historians; Ctr Study Southern Cult. **RESEARCH** Southern history; Confederacy; Maritime history. **SELECTED PUBLICATIONS** Auth, Rebel nationalism: E H Cushing and the Confederate experience, Southwest Hist Quart, 1/70; The Confederate State of Richmond: A Biography of the Capitol, Univ Tex, 71; Honest to Clio: The New History of the Old South, Wesleyan Col, 72; The Confederacy as a Revolutionary Experience, 71 & The American War and Peace, 1860-1877, 73, Prentice-Hall; Different Drums -- The Civil War Era, in Men, Women, and Issues in American History, Dorsey Press, 75; The Best of Bicentennial Times, King William County His Soc Bull, 10/76; A Virginian Ambassador in Turin: John Moncure Daniel, in First Intl Conf Am Hist, Italy and the United States, 1776-1976, Genoa, Italy, 5/76; The Confederate States of America, in The American Destiny, vol 7, Danbury Press, 76; Jefferson Davis and the American Revolutionary Tradition, J Ill State Hist Soc, 2/77; The Confederate Nation, 1861-1865, Harper, 79; The Peninsular Campaign, in The Image of War: 1861-1865, vol II, Doubleday, 82; The Paradoxes of Confederate Historiography, in The Southern Enigma: Essays on Race, Class, and Folk Culture, Greenwood Press, 83; Reckoning with Rebels, The Old South in the Crucible of War, Univ Press Miss, 83; The South and the Sea: Some Thoughts on the Southern maritime Traditions, GA Hist Quart, summer 83; Richmond, City and Captial at War, in The Image of War, 1861-65, vol VI, Doubleday, 84; Bold Dragoon: The Life of J E B Stuart, Harper Collins, 86; The Greatest Service I Rendered the State, J E B Stuart's Account of the Capture of John Brown, VA Mag Hist and Biogr, 7/86; Slavery and the Confederacy, in Dictionary of Afro-American Slavery, Westport, 88; Civil War, in Encyclopedia of Southern Culture, Chapel Hill, 89; Marse Robert at Midlife, in The Confederate High Command & Related Topics, White Mane Press, 90; The Confederacy as a Revolutionary Experience, in American Negro Slavery: A Modern Reader, Oxford Univ Press, 73, in Major Problems in the History of the American South, vol 1, D C Heath, 90, and in Major Problems in the Civil War and Reconstruction, D C Heath, 90; Everyone's War, in Touched By Fire, vol 2, Little Brown, 90; God and General Lee, Anglican and Episcopal Hist, 3/91; ed bd, Encyclopedia of the Confederacy, 4 vol, Simon & Schuster, 93; Secession, Succession, and Sumter: the Crisis of 1860-61, in The Davis A Sayre History Symposium: Collected Essays, 1985-89, Sayre School, 93; Rethinking Robert E Lee, Douglas Southall Freeman Hist Rev, Univ Richmond, spring 94; Introduction, Georgia Hist Quart, special ed, spring 95; Robert E Lee: A Biography, W W Norton, 95; Eggs, Aldie, Shepherdstown and J E B Stuart, in the Gettysburg Nobody Knows, Oxford Univ Press, 97; Killing Yankees: Confederate Strategy and Military Policy, in Writing the Civil War: The Quest to Understand, Univ SC Press, 10/98; The Lees, in Intimate Strategies: Military Marriages of the Civil War, Oxford Univ Press, in press; Ambivalent Visions of Victory: Jefferson Davis, Robert E Lee, and Confederate Grand Strategy, in Jefferson Davis and His Generals, Oxford Univ Press, in press. **CONTACT ADDRESS** Univ of Ga, Georgia University, Athens, GA, 30602-0001. **EMAIL** et68@webtv.org

THOMAS, GARY CRAIG

PERSONAL Born 11/20/1944, Long Beach, CA **DISCIPLINE** GERMAN LITERATURE, MUSICOLOGY **EDUCATION** Univ Calif, Los Angeles, AB, 66; Harvard Univ, MA, 70, PhD, 73. **CAREER** Asst prof, Humanities & Ger, 71-91, ASSOC PROF CULTURAL STUDIES & GER, UNIV MINN, MINNEAPOLIS, 91-. **MEMBERSHIPS** MLA; Am Soc Study 16th & 17th Century Ger Lit; Renaissance Soc Am; Am Guild Organists. **RESEARCH** Gay studies; musical-literary relations; cultural studies. **SELECTED PUBLICATIONS** Auth, Philipp von Zesen's German Madrigals, Argenis, 78; Zesen, Rinckart and the Musical Origins of the Dactyl, Argenis, 78; Dance Music and the Origins of the Dactylic Meter, in Daphnis, Zeitschrift fur Mittlere Deutsche Literatur, 87; Die Aelbianische Musen-Lust, Peter Lang, 91; Musical Rhetoric and Politics in the Early German Lied, in Music and German Literature: Their Relationship since the Middle Ages, Camden House, 92; Philipp von Zesen's German Madrigals, in Daphnis: Zeitschrift fur Mittlere Deutsche Literatur, 92; co-ed, Queering the Pitch: The New Gay and Lesbian Musicology, Routledge, 93; Was George Frideric Handel Gay? - On Closet Questions and Cultural Politics, in Queering the Pitch: The New Gay and Lesbian Musicology, Routledge, 94. **CONTACT ADDRESS** Dept of Cultural Studies & Comp Lit, Univ of Minn, 9 Pleasant St SE, Minneapolis, MN, 55455-0194. **EMAIL** thoma002@tc.umn.edu

THOMAS, GERALD EUSTIS

PERSONAL Born 06/23/1929, Natick, MA, m, 1954 **DISCIPLINE** HISTORY **EDUCATION** Harvard Univ, BA 1951; George Washington Univ, MS 1966; Yale Univ, PhD 1973. **CAREER** US Navy, commanding officer USS Impervious, 1962-63; College Training Programs Bureau of Naval Personnel, head, 1963-65; US Navy, commanding officer USS Bausell, 1966-68; Prairie View A&M Coll Naval ROTC Unit, prof of naval science & commanding officer, 1968-70; US Navy, commander Destroyer Squadron Five, 1973-75, rear admiral, 1974-81; US Dept of Defense, acting deputy asst sec of defense for intl security affairs & dir of Near East, South Asia, & Africa Region, 1976-78, Comtrapac, US Pacific Fleet, 1978-81, retired, 1981; State Dept, US ambassador to Guyana 1981-83, US ambassador to Kenya 1983-86; YALE UNIV, LECTURER,

DAVENPORT COLLEGE, MASTER, currently. **MEMBERSHIPS** Overseer, Bd of Overseers, Harvard Univ, 1981-88; bd of trustees, Univ of San Diego, 1981-86; life mem, Org of Amer Historians. **CONTACT ADDRESS** Master of Davenport Col, Yale Univ, 271 Park St, New Haven, CT, 06511-4751.

THOMAS, JACK RAY
PERSONAL Born 12/23/1931, Youngstown, OH, m, 1957 **DISCIPLINE** LATIN AMERICAN HISTORY **EDUCATION** Youngstown Univ, BA, 54; Kent State Univ, MA, 60; Ohio State Univ, PhD(hist), 62. **CAREER** Asst prof Latin Am hist, Univ Wis-Eau Claire, 62-65; asst prof, 65-69, assoc prof, 69-79, PROF LATIN AM HIST, BOWLING GREEN STATE UNIV, 79-, Nat Found Arts & Humanities res fel, 68. **MEMBERSHIPS** AHA; Midwest Coun Latin Am Studies; Conf Latin Am Hist; Latin Am Studies Asn; Soc Hist Am Foreign Rel. **RESEARCH** Nineteenth century Latin American historiography; Latin American accounts of travels in the United States in the 19th century; United States-Chilean relations, 1891-1945. **SELECTED PUBLICATIONS** Auth, The Dictatorship of Ibanez and the Labor Unions, Americas, Vol 53, 97; The Coca Boom and Rural Social-Change in Bolivia, Historian, Vol 57, 94. **CONTACT ADDRESS** Dept of Hist, Bowling Green State Univ, Bowling Green, OH, 43402.

THOMAS, JEAN D'AMATO
PERSONAL Born 07/20/1945, Boston, MA, m, 1989, 3 children **DISCIPLINE** CLASSICAL TRADITION **EDUCATION** Tufts Univ, BA, 67; Middlebury Col, MA, 69; Johns Hopkins Univ, PhD, 76. **CAREER** Vis lectr, Univ Pittsburgh, 74-75; vis lectr Williams Col, 75-76; dir, Vergillian Soc of Am summer sessions, Rome, 78; asst prof, Univ So Calif, 76-81; dir, prof-in-charge, Intercollegiate Ctr for Class Stud, Rome, 82-83; adj asst prof, Brandeis Univ, 83; lectr, NEH funding, Summer Inst for High Sch Tchrs, 83, 84; adj instr, Univ Md, 87; humanist adm, NEH, 84-87; dir, lib arts progs for adults, Tufts Univ, 87-88; columnist, Natchitoches Times, 96- ; assoc prof, prof, Louisiana Scholars Col, Northwestern State Univ, 88- . **HONORS AND AWARDS** Diss fel, AAU, 72; Am Council of Learned Soc fel, 77; NEH travel grant, 89; APA res grant, 91 Louisiana Endow Hum grant, 92; Il Premio Giornalistico Theodor Mommsen, 93. **MEMBERSHIPS** Am Philol Asn; Int Inst for Class Tradition; Louisiana Class Asn; Vergillian Soc Am. **RESEARCH** Classical tradition, both in literature and art and archaeology, as it applies to the Phlegraean Fields near Naples; the classical tradition in the United States. **SELECTED PUBLICATIONS** Auth, Cicero's Property in the Phlegraean Fields and Antiquarian Investigation in the Naples Area, VIATOR, 93; auth, The Apocryphal Lighthouse at Capo Miseno: A Creation of Medieval Scholarship, VIATOR, 96. **CONTACT ADDRESS** 332 Henry Ave, Natchitoches, LA, 71457. **EMAIL** damato@nsula.edu

THOMAS, JOHN LOVELL
PERSONAL Born 10/28/1926, Portland, ME, m, 1951, 2 children **DISCIPLINE** AMERICAN HISTORY **EDUCATION** Bowdoin Col, BA, 47; Columbia Univ, MA, 50; Brown Univ, PhD(Am civilization), 60. **CAREER** Lectr English, Barnard Col, Columbia Univ, 50-52; instr Am civilization, Brown Univ, 54-56, asst prof hist, 61-62; asst prof, Harvard Univ, 62-64; assoc prof, 64-72, PROF HIST, BROWN UNIV, 72- **RESEARCH** American intellectual history. **SELECTED PUBLICATIONS** Auth, All Over the Map--Rethinking American Regions, J Am Hist, Vol 83, 96; Positivist Republic--Auguste Comte and the Reconstruction of American Liberalism, 1865-1920, Am Hist Rev, Vol 0101, 96; Through the Avenue of Art (rev), William Mary Quart, Vol 53, 96. **CONTACT ADDRESS** Dept of Hist, Brown Univ, 1 Prospect St, Providence, RI, 02912-9127.

THOMAS, NIGEL J.T.
PERSONAL Born 02/07/1952, Rochester, United Kingdom, m, 1992, 2 children **DISCIPLINE** HISTORY AND PHILOSOPHY OF SCIENCE **EDUCATION** Leeds Univ, PhD, 87. **CAREER** Instr, Calif Inst Techol, 90-92; instr, Rio Hondo Coll, 96-97; adj asst prof Calif State Univ, 95-. **MEMBERSHIPS** Am Philos Asn; Soc for Philos and Psychol; Cognitive Sci Soc; Hist of Sci Soc; Soc for Machines and Mentality; Cheiron; Am Psychol Asn; Asn for the Scientific Study of Consciousness, Soc for the Multidisciplinary Study of Consciousness. **RESEARCH** Philosophy of Mind; Imagination; Cognitive Science; History of Psychology. **SELECTED PUBLICATIONS** Auth, Imagery and the coherence of Imagination: a Critique of White, J of Philos Res, 97; A Stimulus to the Imagination, Psyche, 97; Mental Imagery, the Stanford Encycl of Philos, 97; entries on Sir Frederick Gowland Hopkins and Marshall W Nirenberg, The Biographical Encycl of Sci, 98; Are Theories of Imagery Theories of Imagination? An Active perception Approach to Conscious Mental Content, Cognitive Sci, forthcoming, rev, The Imagery Debate, 94. **CONTACT ADDRESS** 86 South Sierra Madre Blvd #5, Pasadena, CA, 91107. **EMAIL** nthomas@calstateca.edu

THOMAS, NORMAN C.
PERSONAL Born 02/16/1932, Sioux Falls, SD, m, 1953, 4 children **DISCIPLINE** POLITICAL SCIENCE **EDUCATION** Univ Michigan, BA 53; Princeton Univ, MA 58, PhD 59. **CAREER** Univ Cincinnati, Charles Phelps Taft Prof, Prof Emeritus, 80 to 98-; Duke Univ, prof 72-80; Univ Mich, inst, asst prof ,assoc prof, 59-72. **HONORS AND AWARDS** Phi Beta Kappa; U of Cin, Grad Fel, Dist Tchg Prof **MEMBERSHIPS** APSA; MPSA; SPSA; ASPA **RESEARCH** Amer polit institution; Us Presidency; Amer pub policy and admin. **SELECTED PUBLICATIONS** Auth, The Politics of the Presidency, coauth, 4th ed, C Q Press, 97; Education in National Politics, 75; Rule 9: Politics Administration and Civil Rights, 66. **CONTACT ADDRESS** 510 Oliver Court, Cincinnati, OH, 45215-2505. **EMAIL** ncthomas@gateway.net

THOMAS, ORLAN E.
DISCIPLINE MUSIC HISTORY AND LITERATURE, MUSIC THEORY **EDUCATION** Univ NE, BME, MM; Eastman Sch Mus, DMA. **CAREER** Assoc prof Mus, TX Tech Univ. **SELECTED PUBLICATIONS** Auth, So You Want to Write a Song? Fundamentals of Songwriting. **CONTACT ADDRESS** Texas Tech Univ, Lubbock, TX, 79409-5015. **EMAIL** a5sjm@ttuvm1.ttu.edu

THOMAS, SAMUEL JOSEPH
PERSONAL Born 09/06/1941, Cleveland, OH, m, 1965, 3 children **DISCIPLINE** AMERICAN & MODERN EUROPEAN HISTORY **EDUCATION** Kent State Univ, BA, 64; MI State Univ, MA, 66, PhD, 71. **CAREER** Asst instr, 66-69, instr, 70-71, asst prof, 71-77, assoc prof, 77-, prof Am hisy, MI State Univ, 77. **HONORS AND AWARDS** Cushwa res travel grants; M Thomas Inge Award for Comic Arts Scholarship, 97. **MEMBERSHIPS** Am Cath Hist Asn; Orgn Am Historians; Am Soc Church Hist. **RESEARCH** Nineteenth and 20th century Am relig hist; 19th and 20th century Am family hist; role of the press in Am relig hist. **SELECTED PUBLICATIONS** Auth, The American Press Response to the Death of Pope Pius IX and the Election of Pope Leo XIII, Records of the Am Cath Hist Soc of Philadelphia, 75; The American Periodical Press and the Apostolic letter Testem Benevolentiae, The Cath Hist Rev, 7/76; The American Press and the Church-State Pronouncements of Pope Leo XIII, U S Cath Hist, fall 80; The American Press and the Encyclical Longinqua Oceani, Jour Church State, autumn 80; Catholic Journalists and the Ideal Woman in Late Victorian American, Int Jour Women's Studies, 1/81; Nostrum Advertising and the Image of Woman as Invalid in Late Victorian America, Jour Am Culture, fall 82; Portraits of a Rebel Priest: Edward McGlynn in Caricature, 1886-1893, Jour Am Culture, winter 84; The Tattooed Man Caricatures and the Presidential Campaign of 1884, Jour Am Culture, winter 87; After Vatican II: The American Catholic Bishops and the Syllabus from Rome, 1966-1968, Cath Hist Rev, 4/97. **CONTACT ADDRESS** Dept of Hist, Michigan State Univ, 301 Morrill Hall, East Lansing, MI, 48824-1036. **EMAIL** Sthomas@hs1.hst.msu.edu

THOMASSON, GORDON C.
PERSONAL Born 12/28/1942, Santa Monica, CA, m, 1975, 4 children **DISCIPLINE** HISTORY, RELIGION **EDUCATION** UCLA, AB, 66; UCSB, AM, 72; Cornell Univ, PhD, 87. **CAREER** Asst prof, 80-82, Cuttington Univ; world stud fac, 88-93, Marlboro Col & Schl for Intl Training; asst prof, 93-, Broome Com Col (SUNY); intl stud adj, 96-98, CCNY **RESEARCH** Globval hist, world relig, anthropology of development, Liberia, Southeast Asia, Mormonism. **CONTACT ADDRESS** 280 Academy Dr., Vestal, NY, 13850. **EMAIL** thomasson_g@mail.sunybroome.edu

THOMPSON, ALAN SMITH
PERSONAL Born 01/13/1939, Mobile, AL, m, 1966, 2 children **DISCIPLINE** AMERICAN HISTORY **EDUCATION** Auburn Univ, BA, 61; Univ AL, MA, 63, PhD, 79. **CAREER** Tchr Am hist, Vigor High Sch, 63-64; tchg asst, Univ AL, 65-66, 67-68 & instr, 66-67; instr, 68-70, asst prof, 70-80, assoc prof, 80-86, prof Am hist, La State Univ, Shreveport, 86-, dir, LSUS Oral Hist Prog, 85-90, 93-97, ed, North LA Hist Asn Jour, 90. **HONORS AND AWARDS** NEH Summer Inst Grants, 77 & 87; LSUS Res Grant, 82; LSUS Am Studies Grant, 85, 87 - 88; Community Found Shreveport-Bossier Grants, 85-88, 90-92 & 95; Cath Diocese of Alexandria-Shreveport Grant, 83-84; LA Div of Arts Grant, 94. **MEMBERSHIPS** Southern Hist Asn; LA Hist Asn; North LA Hist Asn; Nat Trust Hist Preserv; Ala Hist Asn; Nat Coun on Pub Hist; LA Pres Alliance. **RESEARCH** Antebellum south; Antebellum Ala; Shreveport; Antebellum Mobile; Am archit hist; Caddo Indians. **SELECTED PUBLICATIONS** Auth, The Caspiana Big House: Its history and restoration, NLa Hist Asn J, summer 78; Historic and cultural resources of Coushatta, Louisiana, Red River Bridge and Approaches, Coushatta, La, Report 2, 2/79; Physical impacts: Historic background of Coushatta, environmental assessment for Red River Bridge and Approaches, Coushatta, La, 3/81, La Dept Transp; Southern rights and nativism as issues in Mobile politics, 1850-1861, Ala Rev, Ala Hist Asn, 4/82; Shreveport 1878-1900, Shreveport Jour, 9/85; Shreveport Transportation: Riverboats & Railroads, Glimpses of Shreveport, 85; thomas Jefferson-President, The Rating Game in American Politics, 86; Populism in Shreveport, North La Hist Asn Jour, winter 86; The Shreveport Rate Case, Grassroots Constitutionalism, 88; History of Community Foundation of Shreveport-Bossier, 96. **CONTACT ADDRESS** Dept Hist & Social Sci, Louisiana State Univ, 1 University Pl, Shreveport, LA, 71115-2301. **EMAIL** athompso@pilot.lsus.edu

THOMPSON, CYNTHIA L.
PERSONAL Born 06/03/1943, Buffalo, NY **DISCIPLINE** CLASSICS IN GREEK NEW TESTAMENT **EDUCATION** Yale Univ, PhD, 73, MA, 68; Wellesley Coll, BA, 66. **CAREER** Res, 73-75, Harvard Divinity School; Asst Prof of Classics & Religion, 75-80, Denison Univ, Granville, DH; Editor, 80-94, 97-, Westminster John Knox Press; Editor, 94-97, Fortress Press, Minneapolis, Philadelphia, Louisville. **HONORS AND AWARDS** Phi Beta Kappa **MEMBERSHIPS** APA, SBL. **RESEARCH** Women's Adornment in Greek-Roman World; Classical and Biblical Heritage. **SELECTED PUBLICATIONS** Auth, Hairstyles, Head Coverings and St Paul's Portraits From Roman Corinth, Biblical Archaeologist, 88; Rings of Gold-Neither Modest Nor Sensible, Bible Review, 93. **CONTACT ADDRESS** 39 Roslin St, #3, Dorchester, MA, 02124. **EMAIL** cynthom@aol.com

THOMPSON, DOROTHY GILLIAN
PERSONAL Born 02/25/1943, Duncan, BC, Canada **DISCIPLINE** MODERN FRENCH HISTORY **EDUCATION** Univ BC, BA, 64, PhD(Fr hist), 72; Stanford Univ, MA, 65. **CAREER** Instr Europ Hist, Purdue Univ, 68-70; lectr, Univ Windsor, 71-72; asst prof, 72-77, ASSOC PROF EUROP HIST, UNIV NB, FREDERICTON, 77- **MEMBERSHIPS** AHA; Soc Fr Hist Studies. **RESEARCH** Confiscation of ecclesiastical property in 18th century France; 18th century French Jesuits. **SELECTED PUBLICATIONS** Auth, The Sisters of Saint-Joseph in the 17th and 18th Centuries, Am Hist Rev, Vol 98, 93. **CONTACT ADDRESS** Dept of Hist, Univ of NB, PO Box 4400, Fredericton, NB, E3B 5A3.

THOMPSON, GLEN L.
PERSONAL Born 04/14/1950, LaCrosse, WI, m, 1977, 2 children **DISCIPLINE** ANCIENT HISTORY **EDUCATION** Northwestern Col, BA, 72; Wisconsin Lutheran Sem, MDiv, 77; Columbia Univ, MA, 84, PhD, 90. **CAREER** Prof, Michigan Lutheran Sem, 92-96; prof, Martin Luther Col, 97- . **MEMBERSHIPS** Soc Bibl Lit; Am Philol Asn; N Am Patristics Soc; Asn Ancient Historians; Inst for Bibl Res; Evangel Theol Soc. **RESEARCH** Roman social history; early Christian Church; Greek and Latin in manuscripts. **SELECTED PUBLICATIONS** Auth, A Dike Certificate from Tebtunis, Bul of Am Soc of Papyrologists, 91; auth, Jesus and the Historical Jesus, Wisc Lutheran Q, 95; auth, Teaching the Teachers: Pastoral Training in the Early Church, Wisc Lutheran Q, 97. **CONTACT ADDRESS** Martin Luther Col, 1995 Luther Ct, New Ulm, MN, 56073. **EMAIL** thompsgl@mlc-wels.edu

THOMPSON, JANET ANN
PERSONAL Born 08/01/1944, Balboa, Panama Canal Zone **DISCIPLINE** HISTORY **EDUCATION** Univ Cincinnati, BA, 74, MA, 76, PhD, 87; Case Western Reserve Univ, MSLS, 84. **CAREER** Asst prof librarianship, Univ New Mexico, 86-88; asst prof hist, Southwest Texas State Univ, 88-90; hist fac, Tallahassee Commun Col, 90- . **RESEARCH** Women; witchcraft; English West country. **SELECTED PUBLICATIONS** Auth, Wives, Widows, Witches and Bitches: Women in 17th Century Devon, Peter Lang, 93. **CONTACT ADDRESS** Div of Social Sciences, Tallahassee Community Col, Tallahassee, FL, 32304. **EMAIL** thompsja@mail.tallahassee.cc.fl.us

THOMPSON, JEWEL T.
PERSONAL Kinsale, VA, w, 1961, 2 children **DISCIPLINE** MUSIC THEORY AND COMPOSITION **EDUCATION** Virgina State Univ, BS, 56; Eastman Sch of Music of Univ of Rochester, MA, 60, PhD, 82. **CAREER** Asst prof, Virginia State Univ, 60-62; West Virginia Inst of Technology, 68-72; adjunct lect, Hunter Coll of City Univ of NY 72-75, adjunt asst prof, 75-85, asst prof 85-91, assoc prof 91-96, prof 96-. **HONORS AND AWARDS** Hattie Mistrong Found Fel; Ford Found Grant; Supreme Charitable Found of Ancient and Accepted Scottish Rite of Freemasonry Grant; Dame of Honour of the Grand Sovereign Dynastic Hospitalier of St John (Knights of Malta). **MEMBERSHIPS** Amer Soc of Composers, Authors, and Publishers (ASCAP); Music Theory Society of NY State; The Amer Music Ctr. **RESEARCH** Analytical studies **SELECTED PUBLICATIONS** Auth, Samuel Coleridge-Taylor: The Development of His Compositional Style Metuelen, Scarecrow Press, 94; The International Dictionary of Black Composers, Five Critical Essays on Samuel Coleridge Taylor, Fitzroy/ Dearborn Publishers, spring 99. **CONTACT ADDRESS** Hunter Col, CUNY, 695 Park Ave, New York, NY, 10021.

THOMPSON, JOHN H.
PERSONAL Born 09/18/1946, Winnipeg, MB, Canada **DISCIPLINE** HISTORY **EDUCATION** Univ Winnipeg, BA, 68; Univ Man, MA, 69; Queen's Univ, PhD, 75. **CAREER** Prof hist, McGill Univ, 71-90; exch prof, Simon Fraser Univ, 82-83; exch prof, 87-88, PROF HISTORY, DUKE UNIV, 90-; DISTINGUISHED VIS PROF, UNIV ALTA, 97-. **HONORS AND AWARDS** Margaret McWilliams Medal, Man Hist Soc, 68; W L Morton Gold Medal, Univ Man, 69; Can Hist Asn Reg Hist Prize, 81. **MEMBERSHIPS** Can Hist Asn **SELECTED PUBLICATIONS** Auth, Ethnic Minorities During Two World Wars, 91; auth, The Harvests of War: the Prairie West, 1914-1918, 78; sr auth, Canada 1922-39: Decades of Discord, 85; auth, Forging the Prairie West, 98; co-ed, Loyalties in Conflict:

Ukrainians in Canada During the Great War, 83. **CONTACT ADDRESS** 6420 Ada Blvd, Edmonton, AB, T5W 4P2. **EMAIL** jhtl@gpu.srv.ualberta.ca

THOMPSON, LARRY
PERSONAL Born 02/09/1967, El Paso, TX, m, 1996 **DISCIPLINE** ART EDUCATION Univ Tx San Antonio, BFA, 93; Univ N Tx, MFA, 95. **CAREER** Teaching Fel, Univ N Tx, 93-95; Art Teacher, Irving Independent Sch Distr, Irving, Tx, 96-98; Asst prof, La Col, 98-. **HONORS AND AWARDS** Best of Show, 94; Juror's Award, 93, 95, 96., Univ Tx San Antonio Dean's list 90-93. **MEMBERSHIPS** Col Art Assoc. **RESEARCH** Painting **CONTACT ADDRESS** 920 Twin Bridges, No 144, Alexandria, LA, 71303. **EMAIL** thompson@lacollege.edu

THOMPSON, MARGARET SUSAN
PERSONAL Born 01/25/1949, Brooklyn, NY **DISCIPLINE** HISTORY, POLITICAL SCIENCE **EDUCATION** Smith Col, AB, 70; Univ Wis-Madison, MA, 72, PhD(hist), 79. **CAREER** Instr, Knox Col, 77-78, asst prof, 79-81; ASST PROF HIST, SYRACUSE UNIV, 81-, Nat Endowment for Humanities res grant, summer, 80; J Franklin Jameson fel, AHA, 80-81. **MEMBERSHIPS** Orgn Am Historians; Am Polit Sci Asn; Soc Sci Hist Asn; AHA. **RESEARCH** American political history; Civil War and Reconstruction; 20th century politics. **SELECTED PUBLICATIONS** Auth, Cultural Conundrum--Sisters, Ethnicity, and the Adaptation of American-Catholicism, Mid Am Hist Rev, Vol 74, 92; Rose Hawthorne Lathrop--Selected-Writings, Cath Hist Rev, Vol 81, 95. **CONTACT ADDRESS** 333 Fellows Ave, Syracuse, NY, 13210.

THOMPSON, ROBERT FARRIS
PERSONAL Born 12/30/1932, El Paso, Texas, m **DISCIPLINE** AFRICAN-AMERICAN HISTORY **EDUCATION** Yale U, BA 1955, MA 1961, PhD 1965. **CAREER** African & Afro-Amer Art History Yale Univ, prof 1964-. **SELECTED PUBLICATIONS** Authored "African Influence on the Art of the United States" 1969; "Black Gods & Kings" 1971; "African Art in Motion" 1974; "Four Moments of the Sun" 1981; "Flash of the Spirit" 1983. **CONTACT ADDRESS** Professor History of Art, Yale Univ, 63 Wall St, New Haven, CT, 06510.

THORELLI, HANS BIRGER
PERSONAL Born 09/18/1921, Newark, NJ, m, 1948, 2 children **DISCIPLINE** POLITICAL ECONOMY **EDUCATION** Univ Stockholm, Swe, MA, 44, LLB, 45, PhD, 54; Northwestern Univ, 46-47. **CAREER** Prof, Bus Admin, Univ Chicago, 59-64; vis prof, IMD, Lausanne, 64-65; vis prof, London Grad Sch Bus, 69-70; PROF, BUS ADMIN, IND UNIV, 64-. **MEMBERSHIPS** Am Econ Asn; Am Mktg Asn; Acad Mgt **RESEARCH** International Business Strategy, Public Policy; Marketing; Management **SELECTED PUBLICATIONS** International Operations Simulation Mark 2000 Administrator's Compendium, Prentice-Hall, 94; edr, Integral Strategy: Concepts and Dynamics, JAI Press, 95; edr, Integral Strategy: Integration as Focus, JAI Press, 95. **CONTACT ADDRESS** Kelley Sch Bus, Indiana Univ, Bloomington, Marketing 328L, Bloomington, IN, 47401. **EMAIL** thorelli@indiana.edu

THORMANN, GERARD CHARLES
PERSONAL Born 09/30/1922, Frankfurt, Germany, m, 1953, 4 children **DISCIPLINE** HISTORY **EDUCATION** Univ Aix-Marseille, BesL, 41; Columbia Col, BA, 46; Columbia Univ, MA, 47, PhD(hist), 51. **CAREER** From instr to assoc prof hist, Notre Dame Col Staten Island, 48-59; assoc prof, 59-68, PROF HIST, MANHATTANVILLE COL, 68- **MEMBERSHIPS** AHA; Am Cath Hist Asn; Soc Fr Hist Studies. **RESEARCH** Modern European history; Christian democratic parties; Christian trade unionism. **SELECTED PUBLICATIONS** Auth, History of French Christian trade unionism, 1887-1951; History of the Belgian-Christian Workers Movement, Cath Hist Rev, Vol 0082, 96; The Thought of Pottier, Antoine 1849-1923 in Contribution to the History of Christian Democracy in Belgium, Cath Hist Rev, Vol 0080, 94. **CONTACT ADDRESS** Dept of Hist, Manhattanville Col, Purchase, NY, 10577.

THORNTON, ARCHIBALD PATON
PERSONAL Born 10/21/1921, Glasgow, Scotland, m, 1948, 2 children **DISCIPLINE** HISTORY **EDUCATION** Glasgow Univ, MA, 47; Oxford Univ, DPhil(hist), 52. **CAREER** Lectr hist, Oxford Univ, 48-50; lectr, Aberdeen Univ, 50-57; prof and chmn, Univ W Indies, 57-60, dean fac arts, 59-60; chmn dept, 67-72, PROF HIST, UNIV TORONTO, 60-, Her Majesty's Colonial Serv App Bd, 52-57; Smuts fel, Cambridge Univ and Commonwealth fel, St John's Col, 65-66 and 70. **MEMBERSHIPS** AHA; Can Hist Asn; fel Royal Hist Soc; fel Royal Soc Can. **RESEARCH** British history; commonwealth history; imperial history. **SELECTED PUBLICATIONS** Auth, In the City of the Heart--Reflections on Jerusalem, A Unique Imperial City Beyond Europe, Queens Quart, Vol 0103, 96; A Summer Crossing--The Landing-Craft Tank which Crossed the English-Channel on Sunday June 4, 1944 to Invade and Liberate Hitler-Occupied Europe, Queens Quart, Vol 0101, 94; The Travelers Tale, Queens Quart, Vol 0101, 94; Rights As A European Export, Queens Quart, Vol 0102, 95. **CONTACT ADDRESS** Dept of Hist, Univ of Toronto, Toronto, ON, M5S 1Aa.

THORNTON, JOHN K.
PERSONAL Fort Monroe, VA **DISCIPLINE** AFRICA AND WORLD HISTORY **EDUCATION** Univ Mich, BA, 71; UCLA, MA, PhD. **CAREER** Prof; taught at,Univ Zambia in Lusaka, 80-81; part time, Allegheny Col, 81-84 & Univ Va, 84-86. **RESEARCH** Central Africa particularly on the Kingdom of Kongo, northern Angola during the period 1500-1800. **SELECTED PUBLICATIONS** Auth, The Kingdom of Kongo: Civil War and Transition, 1641-1718, Univ Wis Press, 83; Africa and Africans in the Making of the Atlantic World, 1400-1680, Cambridge UP, 92. **CONTACT ADDRESS** Dept of History, Millersville Univ, Pennsylvania, PO Box 1002, Millersville, PA, 17551-0302. **EMAIL** lin@cldc.howard.edu

THORNTON, RICHARD C.
PERSONAL Born 03/22/1936, Camden, NJ, m, 1981 **DISCIPLINE** HISTORY, INTERNATIONAL AFFAIRS **EDUCATION** Colgate Univ, BA, 61; Univ WA, PhD, 66. **CAREER** Res assoc hist, Univ WA, 66-67; prof hist & int affairs, George Washington Univ, 67. **RESEARCH** Sino-Soviet rel; US for policy; international communism. **SELECTED PUBLICATIONS** Auth, The Comintern and Li Li-san Line in 1930, The China Quart, 64; Soviet Histoirans and China's Past, Problems of Communism, 68; The Comintern and the Chinese Communists: 1928-1931, Univ of Wash Press, 69; China and the Communist World, In: Communist China, 1949-1968: A Twenty Year Assessment (Frank Trager and William Henderson, ed), NY Univ Press, 70; Bear and Dragon: Sino-Soviet Relations, 1949-1971, Am-Asian Educ Exchange Monogr Series, 71; The Structure of Communist Politics, World Politics, 7/72; The Soviet Policy Toward China, In: Soviets in Asia (Norton L Dodge, ed), Washington, DC, 72; China, the Struggle for Power, 1917-1972, Ind Univ Press, 73; Problems and Prospects for Research on China, Int Studies Newsletter, Univ Pittsburgh, winter 73; Soviet Strategy in the Vietnam War, Asian Affairs, 74; South Asia: Imbalance on the Subcontinent, Orbis, fall 75; Teng Hsiao-ping and Peking's Current Political Crisis: A Structural Interpretation, Issues and Studies, 7/76; Toward a New Equilibrium? Tripolar Politics, 1964-1976, Naval War Col Rev, winter 77; Soviet Strategy in Asia since World War II, In: The USSR/US Defense: A Critical Comparison, Am Inst of Aeronautics and Astronatics, 77; The Political Succession to Mao Tse-tung, Issues and Studies, 6/78; The Chinese Revolution in Global Perspectives, In: China, A Balance Sheet (Jurgen Domes, ed), Univ Saarbrucken, 79; Sino-Soviet Rivalry in Southeast Asia, Issues and Studies, 10/80; US-Soviet Strategic Balance in the Middle East, 1977-1981, Korea and World Affairs, winter 81; China: A Political History, 1917-1980, Westview Press, 82; Arms Control and Heavy Missiles, The Naval War Col Rev, 84; Distant Connections: US-Soviet Rivalry in the Middle East and Southeast Asia, Asian Affairs, fall 84; Is Detente Inevitable?, Wash Inst for Values in Public Policy, 85; Soviet Asian Strategy in the Brezhnev Era and Beyond, Wash Inst for Values in Public Policy, 85; Strategic Change and American Foreign Policy: Perceptions of the Sino-Soviet conflict, Jour of Northeast Asian Studies, spring 86; The Grand Strategy Behind Renewed Sino-Soviet Ties, The World and I, 12/86; Nuclear Superiority, Geopolitics and State Terrorism, Global Affairs, fall 86; Detente II-SALT III, American Dream or Nightmare? The World and I, 1/87; The Nixon-Kissinger Years, The Reshaping of American Foreign Policy, Paragon House, 11/89; Defense/Aerospace: The United States in an Emerging New World, The Wash Res Group, 7/90; Deng's Middle Kingdom Strategy, In: The Broken Mirror: China after Tiananmen (George Hicks, ed), Longman Group UK Ltd, 90; Middle East Oil: Dividing the Spoils, Defense and Diplomacy, 90; The Carter Years: Toward a New Global Order, Paragon House, 91; Co-auth (with Alan Capps), New Light on the Iran Hostage Rescue Mission, Marine Corps Gazette, 12/91; Co-auth (with John Newman), A Comparative Plitical-Economic History of the Peoples Republic of China: A Short Course, In Depth, 12/92; John King Fairbank: An Assessment, The World and I, 6/92; Co-auth (with Bruce A Babcock), Japan's Response to Crisis: Not with a Bang but with a Buck, Global Affairs, winter 93; Mikhail Gorbachev: A Preliminary Strategic Assessment, The World and I, 1/93; Co-auth (with Alan Capps), Somalia's Iranian Connection, Washington Commentary, 10/8/93; Nixon's Foreign Policy was Undercut by Kissinger, The Wash Times, 5/3/94; The Sino-Russian Struggle for Hegemony in Northeast Asia, Problems of Post-Communism, 95; China at the Crossroads, The World and I, 4/96; Russo-Chinese Detente and the Emerging New World Order, In: The Roles of the United States, Russia and China in the New World Order (Hafeez Malik, ed), St Martin's Press, 97; The Secretary's History Lesson, The Wash Post, 6/29/97; Reagan Versus Volcker: Economic Policy Conflict in the First Year, In: Kurt London Occasional Papers, Inst for European, Russian and Eurasian Studies, George Wash Univ, 98; The Falklands Sting: Reagan, Thatcher and the Argentine Bomb, Brassey's, 98. **CONTACT ADDRESS** Inst for Europ, Russ & Eurasian Studies, George Washington Univ, 2013 G St N W, Ste. 401, Washington, DC, 20052-0001.

THORPE, WAYNE L.
DISCIPLINE HISTORY **EDUCATION** Univ Wash, BA; Portland State Univ, BA; Univ Colo, MA; Univ British Columbia, PhD. **HONORS AND AWARDS** Vis res fel, Intl Inst Soc Hist, Amsterdam. **RESEARCH** European hist. **SELECTED PUBLICATIONS** Auth, The Workers Themselves: Revolutionary Syndicalism and International Labour 1919-1923; co-ed, Revolutionary Syndicalism: An International Perspective. **CONTACT ADDRESS** History Dept, McMaster Univ, 1280 Main St W, Hamilton, ON, L8S 4L9.

THORSON, J.A.
PERSONAL Born 10/08/1946, Chicago, IL, m, 1966, 2 children **DISCIPLINE** ADULT EDUCATION, GERONTOLOGY **EDUCATION** Northern IL Univ, BS, 67; Univ NC, Chapel Hill, M Ed, 71; Univ GA, Ed D, 75. **CAREER** Asst prof of Adult ed, Univ GA, 75-77; prof and chmn, Dept of Gerontology, Univ NE at Omaha, 77-. **HONORS AND AWARDS** Fel, Gerontological Soc of Am, 76; Award for Distinguished Res, Univ NE at Omaha, 91. **MEMBERSHIPS** Gerontological Soc of Am **RESEARCH** Humor; death anxiety; social gerontology. **SELECTED PUBLICATIONS** Auth, Aging in a Changing Society, Wadsworth Pub Co, 95; Note on Forced Institutional Relocation of Nursing Home Residents, Psychological Reports, 78, 96; Qualitative Thanatology, Mortality, 1, 96; Elder Abuse and Neglect, AARC Times, 21, 97; with F C Powell, I Sarmany-Schuller, and W Hampes, Psychological Health and Sense of Humor, J of Clinical Psychology, 53, 97; with H Sorenson, Geriatric Respiratory Care, Delmar Pubs, 98; Clarifying the Confusion Associated with Delerium, AARC Times, 22, March 98; Understanding the Aspects of Dementia, AARC Times, 22, April 98; Religion and Anxiety: Which Anxiety? Which Religion?, in H G Koenig, ed, Handbook of Religion and Mental Health, Academic Press, 98; numerous other publications. **CONTACT ADDRESS** Dept of Gerontology, Univ of Nebraska, Omaha, Omaha, NE, 68182. **EMAIL** jthorson@unomaha.edu

THRASHER, WILLIAM
PERSONAL Born 06/08/1934, Foreman, AR, s **DISCIPLINE** ART EDUCATION Boston Univ, MA, 61; Henderson St niv, BA, 56 **CAREER** Inst, 96-, MA Col of Art **HONORS AND AWARDS** John E Thayer Awd, 97; Fulbright Fel, 91 **RESEARCH** Contemporary Japanese craftmanship **CONTACT ADDRESS** Wellesley, MA, 02481. **EMAIL** wmthras@aol.com

THREATTE, LESLIE LEE
PERSONAL Born 02/01/1943, Miami, FL **DISCIPLINE** CLASSICAL PHILOLOGY **EDUCATION** Oberlin Col, BA Harvard Univ, PhD(Class Philol), 69. **CAREER** Asst prof Class, Cornell Univ, 68-70; asst prof 70-75; assoc prof Class, 75-80; Univ Calif, Berkeley. **MEMBERSHIPS** Am Philol Assn. **SELECTED PUBLICATIONS** Auth, The Grammar of Attic Inscriptions I, de Gruyter, Berlin, 79, II, 96. **CONTACT ADDRESS** Dept of Classcs, Univ of California, Berkeley, 7211 Dwinelle Hall, Berkeley, CA, 94720-2520.

THRO, LINUS J.
PERSONAL Born 01/15/1913, St. Charles, MO **DISCIPLINE** MEDIEVAL PHILOSOPHY **EDUCATION** St Louis Univ, AB, 34, lic theol, 45; Col Immaculate Conception, lic phil, 38; Univ Montreal, MA, 38; Univ Toronto, PhD, 48. **CAREER** Instr, Regis Col, 38-41; from instr to assoc prof, 49-72, chmn dept, 68-74, PROF MEDIAEVAL PHILOS, ST LOUIS UNIV, 72- **MEMBERSHIPS** Am Philos Asn; Metaphys Soc Am; Am Cath Philos Asn. **RESEARCH** Thought and influence of John Duns Scotus; philosophy and religion in relation to science. **SELECTED PUBLICATIONS** Auth, A Note on Universals, Mod Schoolman: Gilson and Duns Scotus, New Scholasticism; Questions on Aristotle 'Metaphysics X and Xii' by Dymsdale,John in Latin Text and Analysis of 13th-Century Philosophical Work, Manuscripta, Vol 0036, 1992. **CONTACT ADDRESS** Dept of Philos, St Louis Univ, St Louis, MO, 63103.

THURMAN, ALFONZO
PERSONAL Born 10/24/1946, Mayfield, KY, m **DISCIPLINE** EDUCATION **EDUCATION** Univ of Wisconsin-LaCrosse, BS 1971, Univ of Wisconsin-Madison, MA 1973, PhD 1979. **CAREER** Univ of Wisconsin-Whitewater, coordinator minority affairs 1971-75; Univ of Wisconsin-Oshkosh, dir academic devel program 1975-80; NORTHERN ILLINOIS UNIV, dir special projects 1980-84, asst to the provost 1984-87, ASSOC DEAN, COLL OF EDUC, PROF, ED POLICY STUDIES, 1987-. **HONORS AND AWARDS** Outstanding Leadership Award ILAEOPP 1985; **MEMBERSHIPS** Pres Illinois Assn of Educ Opportunity Program 1983-84; chairman DeKalb Human Relations Comm 1983-86; Parliamentarian Mid-America Assn of Educ Opportunity Programs, 1989-90; bd of dirs, IL Assn of Colleges of Teacher Education. **SELECTED PUBLICATIONS** Author: "Establishing Special Services on Campus" (chapter) IN Handbook of Minority Student Services, "Policy Making, Higher Education's Paradox" (article) in Thresholds 1986; Leadership of the Governing Board and Central Administration: Providing the Policy and Budgetary Framework for Incorporating Multicultural Elements into College and University Curriculum, co-authored with Carol Floyd, chapter, 1991; Trio Programs: A Proposal for Accrediting Programs Designed to Increase Underrepresented Groups in Higher Education, chapter, 1993. **CONTACT ADDRESS** Col of Educ, No Illinois Univ, Graham Hall 321, De Kalb, IL, 60115.

THURSTON, GARY L.
DISCIPLINE HISTORY OF MODERN EUROPE AND OF RUSSIA **EDUCATION** Columbia Univ, PhD, 73. **CAREER** Dept Hist, Univ of RI **RESEARCH** Juxtaposition of public and private space in Russian theater in the half-century before the revolution of 1917. **SELECTED PUBLICATIONS** Auth, bk on the hist of Russ popular theater. **CONTACT ADDRESS** Dept of Hist, Univ of RI, 8 Ranger Rd, Ste. 1, Kingston, RI, 02881-0807.

THURSTON, ROBERT
DISCIPLINE MODERN RUSSIAN HISTORY **EDUCATION** Univ Mich, PhD, 80. **CAREER** Miami Univ, prof hist, 96-. **RESEARCH** Mod Russian hist; Europ witch hunts; Am lynching. **SELECTED PUBLICATIONS** Liberal City, Conservative State: Moscow and Russia's Urban Crisis, 1906-1914, Oxford Univ Press, 87; Life and Terror in Stalin's Russia, 1934-1940, Yale Univ Press, 96; ed & contrib, The People's War: Popular Response to World War II in the Soviet Union, forthcoming, Univ Ill Press. **CONTACT ADDRESS** Miami Univ, Oxford, OH, 45056. **EMAIL** thurstrw@muohio.edu

THYM, JURGEN
PERSONAL Born 07/02/1943, Bremervoerde, Germany, m, 1992 **DISCIPLINE** MUSICOLOGY **EDUCATION** Athenaeum Stade, Abitur, 63; Hochschule fuer Musik Berlin, Diploma Schulmusik, 67; Freie Universitaet Berlin, Diploma Hist, 69; Case Western Reserve Univ, PhD Musicology, 74. **CAREER** 73, Vis Instr, Oberlin Col-Conservatory; Eastman School of Music, Univ Rochester, Instr, 73, Asst Prof 74, Assoc Prof 80, Prof 89-, Ch Musicol 82-. **MEMBERSHIPS** Am Musicol Soc; Am Liszt Soc; Lyrica; Int Musicol Soc; Int Asn for Word and Music Studies; WMA. **RESEARCH** German Lied; Text/Music Relations; Beethoven; Analysis; Second Viennese School. **SELECTED PUBLICATIONS** Articles and Reviews in MLA Notes; Comparative Literature; J Music Theory; J Musicol Res; Fontes Artis Musicae; Am Choral Rev; Mendelssohn and Schumann Essays, ed Jon Finson and Larry Todd; German Lieder in the Nineteenth Century, ed Rufus Hallmark; Music Hist Through Sources, ed Alfred Mann; Translations of Kirnberger's Kunst des reinen Satzes in der Musik (with David Beach) and Schenker's Kontrapunkt (with John Rothgeb); Editions: Schoenberg Gesamtausgabe (4 v with Nikos Kokkinis), 100 Years of Eichendorff Songs. **CONTACT ADDRESS** Eastman Sch of Music, 26 Gibbs St, Rochester, NY, 14604. **EMAIL** jthy@aol.com

THYRET, ISOLDE
PERSONAL Born 02/11/1955, Stuttgart, Germany **DISCIPLINE** HISTORY **EDUCATION** Univ of WA, PhD, 92, MA, 86, BA, 85, BA, 81 **CAREER** Asst Prof, 94-, Kent St Univ; Visit Prof, 93-94, CO Col **HONORS AND AWARDS** Lib and media Svcs Res Collection Awd, 98 **MEMBERSHIPS** Am Hist Asn; Assn for Women in Slavic Studies; Hagiography Soc **RESEARCH** Women and Relig in medieval Russia **SELECTED PUBLICATIONS** Auth, Muscovite Miracle Stories as Sources for Gender-specific Religious Experience, DeKalb: N IL Press, 97; Blessed is the Tsarisa's Womb: The Myth of Miraculous Birth and Royal Motherhood in Muscovite Rusia, Russian Review, 94 **CONTACT ADDRESS** Dept of History, Kent State Univ, Kent, OH, 44242. **EMAIL** ithyret@kent.edu

TICK, JUDITH
PERSONAL Born 01/04/1943, Winthrop, m **DISCIPLINE** MUSIC HISTORY **EDUCATION** City Univ New York, PhD, 78. **CAREER** Asst-assoc prof music, Brooklyn Col, 75-91; prof, Northeastern Univ, 91-. **HONORS AND AWARDS** Humanities Fel, Nat Endowment for the Arts, 91; Rockefeller Found Nat Fel, 86. **MEMBERSHIPS** Sonneck Soc for Study of Am Music; Am Musicol Soc. **RESEARCH** Am music; hist of women in music. **SELECTED PUBLICATIONS** Ruth Crawford Seeger, A Composer's Search for American Music,Oxford Univ Press, 97; Charles Ives and Gender Ideology, in Musicology and Difference, UC Press, 93; Ruth Crawford's Spiritual Concept: The Sound Ideals of an Early American Modernist, JAMS, 91; Women and Music, New Grove Dictionary of Am Music, 86; Women Making Music, The Western Art Tradition 1150-1950, Univ Ill Press, 86; American Women Composers Before 1870, UMI, 83, Univ Rochester Press, 95. **CONTACT ADDRESS** Dept of Music, Northeastern Univ, 360 Huntington Ave, Boston, MA, 02115.

TIERNEY, BRIAN
PERSONAL Born 05/07/1922, Scunthorpe, England, m, 1949, 4 children **DISCIPLINE** HISTORY **EDUCATION** Cambridge Univ, BA, 48, PhD(hist), 51. **CAREER** From instr to assoc prof hist, Cath Univ Am, 51-59; prof, 59-67, Goldwin Smith prof medieval hist, 67-77, BRYCE & EDITH M BOWMAR PROF HUMANISTICS STUDIES, CORNELL UNIV, 77-92, Guggenheim fel, 55-57; vis lectr, Univ Calif, Los Angeles, 56; mem Inst Advan Study, Princeton, 61-62; Am Coun Learned Soc fels, 61-62 & 66-67; Soc Relig Higher Educ fel, 66-67; Nat Endowment for Humanities fel, 77-78 & 85-86. **HONORS AND AWARDS** DTh, Uppsala Univ, 64; DHL, Cath Univ Am, 81. **MEMBERSHIPS** AHA; Am Cath Hist Asn (pres, 64); fel Mediaeval Acad Am; fel Am Acad Arts & Sci; fel Am Philos Soc. **RESEARCH** Mediaeval representative government; mediaeval law; mediaeval church history. **SELECTED PUBLICATIONS** Auth, Foundations of the Conciliar Theory, Cambridge Univ, 55; Crisis of Church and State 1050-1300, Prentice-Hall, 64; Origins of Papal Infallibility, E J Brill, 72; Religion, Law, and the Growth of Constitutional Thought, 1150-1650, Cambridge Univ, 82; The Idean of Natural Rights, Scholars Press, 97. **CONTACT ADDRESS** 201 Willard Way, Ithaca, NY, 14850. **EMAIL** bt20@cornell.edu

TIERNEY, KEVIN HUGH
PERSONAL Born 09/22/1942, Bristol, United Kingdom, s **DISCIPLINE** HISTORY; LAW **EDUCATION** Cambridge Univ, BA, 64, LLB, 65, MA, 68; Yale Univ, LLM, 67. **CAREER** Lawyer, Donovan Leisure Newton & Irvine, NYC, 68-70; assoc prof to prof, Wayne State Univ Law School, 71-79; vis prof to PROF, HASTINGS COL LAW UNIV CALIF, 79-. McMahon Law Studentship, St John's Col, 65; Lord Mansfield Schol, Lincoln's Inn, 66; Sterling fel Yale Law School, 67; Ransom Ctr fel Univ Texas, 92 & 95. **MEMBERSHIPS** MI State Bar; ALI. **RESEARCH** Conflict of laws; Jurisprudence; Legal history; Biography in general. **SELECTED PUBLICATIONS** Courtroom Testimony: A Policeman's Guide, 71; How to be a Witness, 72; Darrow: A Biography, 79. **CONTACT ADDRESS** 200 McAllister St, Rm 353, San Francisco, CA, 94102. **EMAIL** tierneyk@uchastings.edu

TIERSTEN, LISA
DISCIPLINE MODERN EUROPEAN CULTURAL HISTORY **EDUCATION** Univ Mass, BA; Yale Univ, PhD, 91. **CAREER** Asst prof, Bernard Col. **SELECTED PUBLICATIONS** Auth, Consumer Culture and the European Bourgeoisie, Il Bollettino del diciannovesimo secolo, 97. **CONTACT ADDRESS** Dept of Hist, Columbia Col, New York, 2960 Broadway, New York, NY, 10027-6902.

TIGAY, JEFFREY HOWARD
PERSONAL Born 12/25/1941, Detroit, MI, m, 1965, 4 children **DISCIPLINE** BIBLICAL STUDIES, ANCIENT NEAR EASTERN LITERATURE **EDUCATION** Columbia Col, BA, 63; Jewish Theol Sem, Am, MHL, 66; Yale Univ, PhD(comp Blbl & Ancient Near East Studies), 71. **CAREER** Jewish Studies Ellis asst prof, 71-77, M Ellis assoc prof to prof Hebrew & Semitic Lang & Lit, Univ Pa, 77-86, Grantee, Nat Sci Found, 72; assoc, Univ Sem on Studies Hebrew Bible, Columbia Univ, 72; Am Coun Learned Soc fel, 75-76; fel, inst Advan Studies, Hebrew Univ, Jerusalem, 78-79; grant, Am Philos Soc, 80 & Am Coun Learned Soc, 80-81; Nat Endowment for Humanties summer res fel, 80; Mem Fedn Jewish Cult fel, 81-82; vis assoc prof, Bible Jewish Theol Sem Am. **HONORS AND AWARDS** Elected fel, Am Acad for Jewish Research, 86; Lindback Award for disting teaching, Univ of Pennsylvania. **MEMBERSHIPS** Am Acad for Jewish Research, Am Schools of Oriental Res; Assoc for Jewish Studies; The Biblical Colloquium; Soc of Biblical Lit. **RESEARCH** Biblical literature; comparative Biblical and ancient Near Eastern studies; ancient Judaism. **SELECTED PUBLICATIONS** Tehilla Le-Moshe Biblical and Judaic Studies in Honor of Moshe Greenberg, Winona Lake, Indiana, Eisenbraun's, coed with M Cogan and B I Eichler. **CONTACT ADDRESS** Dept Orient Studies, Univ of Pennsylvania, 255 S 36th St, Philadelphia, PA, 19104-3805. **EMAIL** jtigay@sas.upenn.edu

TIGNOR, ROBERT L.
PERSONAL Born 11/20/1933, Philadelphia, PA, m, 1956, 1 child **DISCIPLINE** MIDDLE EASTERN HISTORY **EDUCATION** Col Wooster, BA, 55; Yale Univ, MA, 56, PhD, 60. **CAREER** From instr to assoc prof, 60-76, PROF HIST, PRINCETON UNIV, 76-, CHMN DEPT, 77- **MEMBERSHIPS** Mid E Studies Asn. **RESEARCH** Modern African and Middle Eastern history. **SELECTED PUBLICATIONS** Auth, The Social Origins of Egyptian Expansionism During the Muhammad Ali Period, J Interdisciplinary Hist, Vol 0024, 93; Race, Nationality, and Industrialization in Decolonizing Kenya, Int J African Hist Studies, Vol 0026, 93; Colonialism and Revolution in the Middle-East in Social and Cultural Origins of Egypt Urabi Movement, J Interdisciplinary Hist, Vol 0025, 94; South Asians in East-Africa in an Economic and Social-Hist, 1890-1980, Am Hist Rev, Vol 0099, 94; Rebel and Saint in Muslim Notables, Populist Protest, Colonial Encounters Algeria and Tunisia, 1800-1904, J Interdisciplinary Hist, Vol 0027, 96; Green Imperialism in Colonial Expansion, Tropical Island Edens and the Origins of Environmentalism, J Interdisciplinary Hist, Vol 0027, 96; Redefining the Egyptian Nation, J Interdisciplinary Hist, Vol 0027, 97; Pragmatism and Vision in 20th-Century Egypt, J Imperial and Commonwealth Hist, Vol 0025, 97; Manji, Madatally--Memoirs of A Biscuit Baron, J African Hist, Vol 0038, 97; Merchant Capital and Economic Decolonization--The United-Africa-Company, J African Hist, Vol 0038, 97 **CONTACT ADDRESS** Dept of Hist, Princeton Univ, Princeton, NJ, 08540.

TILLIS, FREDERICK C.
PERSONAL Born 01/05/1930, Galveston, Texas, m **DISCIPLINE** MUSIC **EDUCATION** Wiley College, BA 1949; Univ of Iowa, MA, 1952, PhD, 1963. **CAREER** Wiley College, instructor/director of instrumental music, 1949-51, assistant professor/chairman of the dept of music, 1956-61, associate professor/chairman of the dept of music, 1963-64; Grambling College, professor of music/head of theory dept, 1964-67; Kentucky State University, professor/head of the music dept, 1967-69; University of Massachusetts, associate professor of music, 1970-73, professor of music theory and composition/director of Afro American music & jazz program, 1973-, director of UMass jazz workshop, 1974-80, director of fine arts center, 1978-, associate chancellor for affirmative action and equal opportunity, 1990-. **HONORS AND AWARDS** Recip United Negro Coll Fund Fellowship 1961-63; recip Rockefeller Fund Grant for Devl Compstn 1978; recip Nat Endowment for the Arts, Composers Grant 1979; Chancellor of the University of Massachusetts, Distinguished Lecturer, 1980; MA Cultural Council, Commonwealth Award in organizational leadership, 1997. **MEMBERSHIPS** Music or DA board of dir, 1995; Chancellor's Executive Advisory Council, 1994-; ALANA Honor Society Board, 1994-; Faculty Senate Council on the Status of Minorities, 1984-; Academy of American Poets; American Composers Alliance; American Federation of Musicians; Broadcast Music Industry; Center for Black Music Research; International Association of Jazz Educators; Music Educators National Conference; TransAfrica Forum; American Music Center; Massachusetts Music Educators Association; United Negro College Fund. **SELECTED PUBLICATIONS** Composer of more than 120 compositions spanning both the European classical & jazz traditions; Albums: "Freedom," 1973; "Fantasy on a Theme by Julian Adderley," 1975; "The Music of Frederick Tillis, Vol I," 1979; "Quintet for Brass," 1980; "Kcor Variations," 1980; "Elegy," 1983; "Swing Low, Deep River," 1984; "Contrasts and Diversions: The Tillis-Holmes Jazz Duo," 1987; "Voices of Color," 1989; "Crucificion," 1990; "Paintings in Sound," 1990; "The Second Time Around: The Tillis-Holmes Jazz Duo," 1991; "Among Friends-The Billy Taylor Trio and Fred Tillis," 1992; author: In the Spirit and the Flesh, 1989; Images of Mind and Heart, 1991; In Celebration, 1993; Of Moons, Moods, Myths, and the Muse, 1994; "Free as a Feather," Jazz Educators Journal, Dec 1994; Harlem Echoes, 1995. **CONTACT ADDRESS** Director, Fine Arts Center, Univ of Massachusetts, 129 Herter Hall, Amherst, MA, 01003-3910.

TILLMAN, HOYT CLEVELAND
PERSONAL Born 07/08/1944, Crestview, FL, m, 1970, 2 children **DISCIPLINE** HISTORY, CHINESE THOUGHT **EDUCATION** Belhaven Col, BA, 66; Univ Va, MA, 68; Harvard Univ, PhD(hist and East Asian lang), 76. **CAREER** From sophomore tutor to head tutor East Asian studies, Harvard Univ, 74-76; asst prof, 76-81, ASSOC PROF HIST, ARIZ STATE UNIV, 81- **MEMBERSHIPS** AHA; Asn Asian Studies; Soc Asian and Comp Philos. **SELECTED PUBLICATIONS** Auth, Divergent philosophic orientations toward values, J Chinese Philos, 12/78; The Idea and Reality of the Thing During the Sung: Philosophical Attitudes, Bull Sung-Yuan Studies, 78; Proto-nationalism in 12th-century China? The Case of Ch'en Liang, Harvard J Asiatic Studies, 12/79; The Development of Tension Between Virtue and Achievement in Early Confucianism: Attitudes Toward Kwan Chung and Hegemon (pa) as Conceptual Symbols, Philos E and W, 1/81; Utilitarian Confucianism: Ch'en Liang's Challenge to Chu Hsi, Harvard, 82; Chu,Hsi Family Rituals in a 12th-Century Chinese Manual for the Performance of Cappings, Weddings, Funerals, and Ancestral Rites, Philos E and W, Vol 0043, 93; Confucianism and Family Rituals in Imperial China in A Social-History of Writings About Rites, Philos E and W, Vol 0043, 93; The Uses of Neo-Confucianism Revisited in A Reply to Debary, Philos E and W, Vol 0044, 94; co-ed, Selected Papers in Asian Studies, Wern Conf Asn Asian Studies, 77. **CONTACT ADDRESS** Dept of Hist, Arizona State Univ, Tempe, Tempe, AZ, 85281.

TILLSON, ALBERT H., JR.
PERSONAL Born 11/12/1948, Arlington, VA, m, 1988 **DISCIPLINE** HISTORY **EDUCATION** George Mason Univ, BA, 71; John Hopkins Univ, MA, 74; Univ Texas, PhD, 86. **CAREER** Asst Prof, Assoc Prof, 86 to 92-, Univ Tampa; Instr, 86, Pan Amer Univ; Instr, 84-85, St Norbert College. **HONORS AND AWARDS** U of Tampa Sabbatical Leave; Andrew Mellon Res Fels; NEH. **MEMBERSHIPS** AHA; OIEAHC; SHA; VHA; SASECS; THA. **RESEARCH** Colonial and revolutionary US history, esp the 18th century Chesapeake slavery in the early British and Spanish America. **SELECTED PUBLICATIONS** Rev, New Light on the Chesapeake, Flowerdew Hundred: The Archaeol of a VA Plantation 1619-1864, by James Deetz, and From Gentleman to Townsfolk: The Gentry of Baltimore Cnty, MD 1660-1776, by Charles Steffen, Revs in Amer Hist, 94; auth, The Southern Back Country: A Survey of Current Research, Virginia Mag of History and Biography, 90. **CONTACT ADDRESS** Dept of History, Univ Tampa, Box 2F, Tampa, FL, 33606.

TILLY, LOUISE A.
DISCIPLINE HISTORY **EDUCATION** Univ Toronto, PhD, 55. **CAREER** Michael E Gellert Prof Hist and Sociol and chr Comm on Hist Studies. **RESEARCH** Global perspectives on industrialization and gender inequality. **SELECTED PUBLICATIONS** Auth, The European Experience of Declining Fertility, 92; Politics and Class in Milan, 1881-1901, 92; coauth, Women, Work, and Family, 78; The Rebellious Century, 75; co-ed, Women, Politics, and Change, 90; co-ed and co-trans, Meme Santerre, A French Woman of the People, 85. **CON-**

TACT ADDRESS Eugene Lang Col, New Sch for Social Research, 66 West 12th St, New York, NY, 10011.

TIMBERLAKE, CHARLES
PERSONAL Born 09/09/1935, South Shore, KY, m, 1958, 3 children **DISCIPLINE** HISTORY **EDUCATION** Berea Col, BA, 57; Claremont Grad Sch, MA, 62; Univ Wash, PhD, 68. **CAREER** From asst prof to assoc prof to prof to chemn, 67-, asst dir 88-90, Univ Mo; vist prof, Univ Manchester, 87-88; ed, Inter Documentation Co, 92-95; consult, ed, Univ Helsinki Press, 93-94. **HONORS AND AWARDS** Phi Kappa Phi, 94; Nat Science Found, 95; Who's Who in Am, 95; Fulbright-Hayes Fac Res Abroad Program, 95; Byler Distinguished Prof Award, 96. **MEMBERSHIPS** Asn Am Univ/Asn Res Libr; Am Asn for the Advancement of Slovic Stud; Am Hist Asn; Central Slavic Conference; Mo Conference on Hist; State Hist Society of Mo. **SELECTED PUBLICATIONS** Ed, Religious and Secular Forces in Late Tsarist Russia, 92; ed, A Brief History of Modern Finland, 92; ed, A Study Guide to Martti Hiakio, A Brief History of Modern Finland, 93; auth, Waterways in the Russian Heartland, 95; auth, The Fate of Russian Orthodox Monasteries and Convents Since 1917, 95. **CONTACT ADDRESS** Dept of History, Univ of Missouri, Columbia, MO, 65211. **EMAIL** histcet@showme.missouri.edu

TIMBERLAKE, CONSTANCE HECTOR
PERSONAL St John, New Brunswick, Canada, m **DISCIPLINE** EDUCATION **EDUCATION** Syracuse Univ, Doctorate in Educ Admin, 1979; MS; BA (cum laude); NYS, cert. **CAREER** Syracuse Univ, assoc prof Col Human Develop; Syracuse Sch Dist, chief counselor & admin ABE prog; Neighborhood Ctr, exec dir; Syracuse Pub Sch Dist, commiss of educ; Adolescent Pregnancy Prevention Program, project dir, 1987-. **HONORS AND AWARDS** Citations, Meritorious Srvs 1972, March Wash 1963, Ldrshp Agway 1974; Jefferson Award, WTVH-TV/Amer Inst for Public Service, 1989. **MEMBERSHIPS** NY Sch Brds Assc; mem Prog Com; Central NY Sch Bd Inst mem planning com; AERA; AAUP; Syracuse Prof Women; HEW Task Force Social Justice Natl Literacy Volunteers Amer; Human Rights Comm of Syracuse & Onondaga Co; vice pres Syracuse NAACP; v chrprsn Coalition Quality Educ; v chrprsn Onondaga Urban League Guild; Natl Org Women; Adv Bd Onondaga Comm Clge; Neighborhood Health Ctr adv council; Metr Ch Bd Human Srv Com; Fair-Employ Review Bd Onondaga Co; PEACE Head Start Self-Evaluation & Performance Stand Improvement Plan; exec mem Black Political Caucus; numerous vol srvs; trust Pi Lambda Theta Inc; pres elect NYS Council Family Relations Council; mem SUNY at Oswego Adv Council Oswego NY; pres, New York State Council on Family Relations, 1988-89; honoraryadvisory bd mem, For Kids Sake, 1987; mem & program dir, Syracuse Boys Club of Syracuse; vice chair, Syracuse Univ Black & Latino Faculty Org, 1986-89. **SELECTED PUBLICATIONS** Author of 30 journal articles & reviews, 1974-; more than 20 media presentations & documentaries, 1980-. **CONTACT ADDRESS** Chair Child Family Comm Study, Syracuse Univ, 201 Slocum Hall CFCS Dept, Syracuse, NY, 13244-5300.

TIMBIE, JANET ANN
PERSONAL Born 10/17/1948, San Francisco, CA, m, 1969, 1 child **DISCIPLINE** HISTORY OF CHRISTIANITY, COPTIC LANGUAGE **EDUCATION** Stanford Univ, AB, 70; Univ Pa, PhD(relig studies), 79. **CAREER** Reader hist and relig, Am Univ, 71-72 and prof lectr relig, 80-81; Dumbarton Oaks Ctr for Byzantine Studies fel, 78-79; Mellon fel, Cath Univ, 79-80; RES AND WRITING, 82-, Ed and transl, US Cath Conf Bishops, 79-82. **MEMBERSHIPS** Cath Bibl Asn; Soc Bibl Lit; Am Acad Relig; Int Asn Coptic Studies. **RESEARCH** Christianity in Egypt through 5th century; development of early Christian monasticism; Coptic language and literature. **SELECTED PUBLICATIONS** Auth, The dating of a Coptic-Sahidic Psalter codex from the University Museum in Philadelphia, Le Museon, 75; Dualism and the Concept of Orthodoxy in the Thought of the Monks of Upper Egypt, Edwin Mellen P; The Status of Women and Gnosticism in Irenaeus and Tertullian, Cath Biblical Quart, Vol 0058, 96; coauth, The Nag Hammadi library in English, Religious Studies Rev, 82; co-ed, The Testament of Job, Scholars Press, 75. **CONTACT ADDRESS** 4608 Merivale Rd, Chevy Chase, MD, 20815.

TINDALL, GEORGE BROWN
PERSONAL Born 02/26/1921, Greenville, SC, m, 1946, 2 children **DISCIPLINE** AMERICAN HISTORY **EDUCATION** Furman Univ, AB, 42; Univ NC, MA, 48, PhD(hist), 51. **CAREER** Asst prof hist, Eastern Kent State Col, 50-51, Univ Miss, 51-52, Woman's Col Univ NC, 52-53 and La State Univ, 53-58; assoc prof, 58-64, prof hist, 64-69, KENAN PROF, UNIV NC, CHAPEL HILL, 69-, Guggenheim fel, 57-58; Soc Sci Res Coun fac res grant, 59-60; mem, Inst Advan Study, Princeton, 63-64; Fulbright Gast prof, Interpreters Inst, Univ Vienna, 67-68; vis prof, Kyoto Am Studies summer sem, 77; Nat Endowment for Humanities and Ctr Adv Study Behav Sci fels, 79-80. **HONORS AND AWARDS** LittD, Furman Univ, 72. **MEMBERSHIPS** AHA; Orgn Am Historians; Southern Hist Asn (vpres, 72, pres, 73); Soc Am Historians. **RESEARCH** United States history; history of the South. **SELECTED PUBLICATIONS** Auth, South Carolina Negroes, 1877-1900, Univ SC, 52; Mythology: A New Frontier in Southern History in The Idea of the South, Univ Chicago, 64; The Emergence of the New South, 1913-1945, La State Univ, 67; The Disruption of the Solid South, Univ Ga, 72 and Norton, 72; The Persistent Tradition in New South Politics, 75 and The Ethnic Southerners, 76, La State Univ; Lone Star Rising Johnson, Lyndon and His Times, 1908-1960, J Am Hist, Vol 0079, 93; ed, The Pursuit of Southern History, La State Univ, 64; A Populist Reader, Harper Torchbks, 66. **CONTACT ADDRESS** Dept Hist, Univ NC, Chapel Hill, NC, 27514.

TINGLEY, DONALD FRED
PERSONAL Born 03/13/1922, Marshall, IL, m, 1944, 1 child **DISCIPLINE** HISTORY **EDUCATION** Eastern Ill State Col, BS, 47; Univ Ill, MA, 48, PhD(hist), 52. **CAREER** Hist res ed, Ill State Hist Soc, 52-53; asst prof soc sci, 53-56, assoc prof, 56-62, PROF HIST, EASTERN ILL UNIV, 62- **MEMBERSHIPS** Orgn Am Historians. **RESEARCH** Intellectual, religious and social history of the United States; Illinois history. **SELECTED PUBLICATIONS** Auth, Flower, Eliza Julia--Letters Of An English Gentlewoman in Life on the Illinois-Indiana Frontier, 1817-1861, J Am Hist, Vol 0079, 93; coauth and ed, Essays in Illinois History, Southern Ill Univ, 68; The Emerging University, Eastern Ill Univ, 74; Social History of the United States, Gale Res, 79; The Structuring of a State: The History of illinois, 1899-1928, Univ Ill, 80; Women and Feminism in American History, Gale Res, 81. **CONTACT ADDRESS** Eastern Illinois Univ, 98 Harrison St, Charleston, IL, 61920.

TINSLEY, JAMES AUBREY
PERSONAL Born 01/02/1924, Haynesville, LA, m, 1948, 3 children **DISCIPLINE** AMERICAN HISTORY **EDUCATION** Baylor Univ, BA, 47; Univ NC, MA, 48; Univ Wis, PhD, 54. **CAREER** Instr Am hist, Agr and Mech Col Tex, 48-49; instr, NTex State Col, 49-50, asst prof, 51-52; from asst prof to assoc prof, 53-61, chmn dept hist, 67-69, PROF AM HIST, UNIV HOUSTON, 61-, ASSOC DEAN COL ARTS and SCI, 69-, ED, PUBL SER, TEX GULF COAST HIST ASN, 56-; vis prof, Vanderbilt Univ, 63-64. **MEMBERSHIPS** Orgn Am Historians; Southern Hist Asn; Am Studies Asn; Am Asn State and Local Hist. **RESEARCH** Progressive movement in Texas; United States business and economic history. **SELECTED PUBLICATIONS** Auth, Hist Organizations as Aids to History--in Support of Clio, State Hist Soc Wis, 58; Texas Society of Certified Public Accountants: A History, Tex Soc Cert Pub Acct, 62; The Paradox of Southern Progressivism, 1880-1930--, Southwestern Hist Quart, Vol 0097, 94; Cartooning For Suffrage, Southwestern Hist Quart, Vol 0098, 94; Cartooning Texas--100 Years of Cartoon Art in The Lone-Star State, Southwestern Hist Quart, Vol 0098, 94. **CONTACT ADDRESS** Dept of Hist, Univ of Houston, Houston, TX, 77004.

TIPPETT, MARIA W.
PERSONAL Born 12/09/1944, Victoria, BC, Canada **DISCIPLINE** HISTORY **EDUCATION** Simon Fraser Univ, BA, 62; Univ London, PhD, 82. **CAREER** Lectr, Simon Fraser Univ, 76-82, 84-85; lectr, Univ BC, 83-85; Robarts prof Can stud, York Univ, 86-87; vis fel, Clare Hall, 91, elected FAC HIST, 92-, res assoc, Scott Polar Res Inst, 93-95, SR RES FEL, CHURCHHILL COL, CAMBRIDGE UNIV, 95-. **HONORS AND AWARDS** Eaton's BC Bk Award, 78; Gov Gen Award (non-fiction), 79; Sir John A. Macdonald Prize Can Hist, 79; Can Stud Writing Award, 82; Hon mention, Francois-Xavier Garneau Medal, 85; BC Bk Prize finalist, 93; Canada 125 Medal; Royal Soc Can, 92; LLD(hon), Windsor Univ, 94 **MEMBERSHIPS** Adv Bd Can Hist Rev (bd chmn, 86-87); Royal Over-Seas League; BC Writers Fedn. **SELECTED PUBLICATIONS** Auth, Emily Carr, 79; auth, Art at the Service of War, 84; auth, The Making of English-Canadian Culture 1900-1939: The External Influences, 88; auth, Breaking the Cycle and other stories from a Gulf Island, 89; auth, Making Culture, English-Canadian Institutions and the Arts before the Massey Commission, 90; auth, By A Lady: Celebrating Three Centuries of Art by Canadian Women, 92; auth, Between Two Cultures: A Photographer Among the Inuit, 94; auth, Becoming Myself: A Memoir, 96; coauth, From Desolation to Splendour, 77; coauth, Phillips in Print, 82; ed bd, Art Focus. **CONTACT ADDRESS** Churchill Col, Cambridge Univ, Cambridge, ., CB3 0DS.

TIRADO, ISABEL A.
DISCIPLINE HISTORY **EDUCATION** Hunter Col, CUNY, BA, 69; MA, 73; Univ Calif-Berkeley, PhD, 85. **CAREER** Assoc prof & ch, Hist Dept, William Paterson Col, 85-; ch, Hist dept, 93-96; mem, Provost Search Comt, 95; mem, Comprehensive Anal Ranking Comt, 94-95; Hist Dept Exec Coun, 90-91 & 92-93; Freshman Sem instr, 92-93; Search Comt, Distinguished Vis Hisp Scholar, 93; Search Comt, Acad Coordr, Off of Minority Educ, 93; Campus-wide Sabbatical Comt, 92; Local Arrangements Comt, AHA, 90; ch, Curric Comt, 89-91; Search Comt for Assoc VP, WPC, 87; ch, Western Civilization Comt, 87-89; fac adv, Stud Advisement Ctr, WPC, 87; NJ Humanities Grant, 86-87; Writing Across Curric prog, 86-87; fac mentor to minority stud, 86-87; NJ Endowment for the Humanities, 86; Curric & Activ Comt, 85-86; act instr, Univ Calif-Berkeley, 85; grad instr, Univ Calif-Berkeley, 82-84; lectr, Lehman Col, CUNY, 71-72; coordr, Women's and Minorities' Proj, Grad Assembly, Univ Calif-Berkeley, 82-83; res asst, Univ Ccalif-Berkeley, 77-78. **HONORS AND AWARDS** NEH, Columbia Univ, 96; IREX Individual Advan Res Opportunities in Eurasia grant, 96-97; Amer Philos Soc travel grant, 95; IREX Short Term Travel Grants, 93, 94 & 95; IREX Collab Grant, 92; NEH, Stanford Univ 92; Nat Coun for Soviet and E Europ Res fel, 91-92; sr fel, Harriman Inst, Columbia Univ, 91-92; Fulbright-Hays fel, 90; IREX sr scholar exchange, Soviet Acad Sci, Inst Hist, 90; Ford Found Postdr fel, 88-89; vis sch, Harriman Inst, Columbia Univ, 85-86 & 88-89; NEH, Fordham Univ, 86; Mellon Found Dissertation fel, 84-85; Dean's fel, Univ Calif-Berkeley, 83-84; IREX-Leningrad State Univ Exchange, 82; IREX Dissertation Grant, 80-81; Ford Found Doctoral fel, 77-79; Michael Gurevich Awd, 75; Dean's List, Hunter Col, 67-69. **MEMBERSHIPS** Amer Asn for the Advan of Slavic Stud; AHA; Asn of Women in Slavic Stud; Peasant Consortium; Lat Amer Network of Col Empls. **SELECTED PUBLICATIONS** Auth, Books Young Guard: The Petrograd Komsomol Organizations 1917-1920, Greenwood Press, 88; The Komsomol and Young Peasant Women: The Polit Mobilization of Young Women in the Russian Village, 1921-1927, Russ Hist, 23, 96; Nietzschean Images in the Komsomol's Vanguardism, in Nietzsche and Soviet Culture: Ally and Adversary, Cambridge Univ Press, 94; The Village Voice: Women's Views of Themselves and Their World in Russian Chastushki of the 1920s, The Carl Beck Papers, 93; The Komsomol and Young Peasants: the Dilemma of Rural Expansion, 1921-1925, Slavic Rev, 93; The Revolution, Young Peasants, and the Komsomol's Anti-Religious Campaigns 1920-1928, Can-Amer Slavic Stud, 92; rev, Peasant Icons: Representations of Rural People in Late 19th Century Russia, Slavic Rev, 94; New Directions in Soviet History, Cambridge Univ Press, 94; Russia's Women: Accommodation, Resistance, Transformation, Amer Hist Rev, 93; Peasant Russia, Civil War: The Volga Countryside in Revolution, 1917-1921, The Historian, 90. **CONTACT ADDRESS** Dept of History, William Paterson Col, 300 Pompton Rd., Wayne, NJ, 07470. **EMAIL** tirado@frontier.wilpaterson.edu

TIRADO, THOMAS C.
DISCIPLINE LATIN AMERICAN HISTORY, COLUMBUS AND THE AGE OF DISCOVERY, AND WORLD CIVILI **EDUCATION** Univ Ill, BA, 61; Georgetown Univ, MA, 66; Temple Univ, PhD, 77. **CAREER** Prof; Millersville Univ, 65-; rural commun develop, Peace Corps, 62-63, Proj Colombia; tchg asst, Univ Ill; dir, Comput Information Retrieval Syst on Columbus & the Age of Discovery. **SELECTED PUBLICATIONS** Auth, Publication of Celsa's World: Conversations with a Mexican Peasant Woman, Ctr for Latin Amer Stud, Ariz State UP, 91; Celsa's World: Conversations with a Mexican Peasant Woman, Ariz State Univ, 95; rev, Cristoforo Colombus: God's Navigator, Hisp Amer Hist Rev, 95; Portugal and Columbus--Old Drives in New Discoveries, Mediter Stud, 93; Not 'Just Another Reader,' rev Marvin Lunenfeld's 1492: Discovery, Invasion, Encounter: Sources and Interpretations, in the Int Columbian Quincentenary Alliance Newsl, 91; Discovery Five Hundred, Newsle Int Columbian Quincentenary Alliance, Inc, rev Marvin Lunenfeld's 1492: Discovery, Invasion, Encounter: Sources and Interpretations, 91; Bul, Soc for Span and Portuguese Hist Stud, Not 'Just Another Reader,' rev Marvin Lunenfeld's 1492: Discovery, Invasion, Encounter: Sources and Interp(s), 91. **CONTACT ADDRESS** Dept of History, Millersville Univ, Pennsylvania, PO Box 1002, Millersville, PA, 17551-0302. **EMAIL** tctirado@marauder.millersv.edu

TIRRO, FRANK PASCALE
PERSONAL Born 09/20/1935, Omaha, NE, m, 1961, 2 children **DISCIPLINE** MUSIC THEORY **EDUCATION** Univ NE, BME, 60; Northwestern Univ, MM, 61; Univ Chicago, PhD, 74. **CAREER** Tchr & chmn dept music, Univ Chicago Lab Schs, 61-70; vis lectr music hist, Univ KS, 72-73; asst prof, 73-74, assoc prof, 74-80, Dean Yale Sch Music & prof musicol, Yale Univ, 80, dir, Southeastern Inst Medieval & Renaissance Studies, 77-80. **HONORS AND AWARDS** Am Coun Learned Socs travel grant, 68; fel Villa I Tatti, Harvard Univ, 71-72; Duke Univ Res Coun grant, 75, 76 & 78. **MEMBERSHIPS** Am Musicol Soc; Int Musicol Soc; Int Soc Jazz Res; Medieval Acad Am; Renaissance Soc Am. **RESEARCH** Music of the Renaissance; hist of jazz; music theory. **SELECTED PUBLICATIONS** Auth, The silent theme tradition in jazz, Music Quart, 67; Jazz improvisation, Proc Sixth Int Cong Aesthetics, 68; Jazz, In: Dictionary of Contemporary Music, Dutton, 74; Constructive elements in jazz improvisation, J Am Musicol Soc, 74; Jazz: A History, Norton, 77, 2nd ed, 93; Lorenzo di Giacoma da Prato's organ at San Petronio and its use during the fifteenth and sixteenth centuries, Myron P Gilmore Festschrift, Sansoni, 78; The Humanities: Cultural Roots and Continuities, Houghton Mifflin, 80, 5th ed, 97; Royal 8 G VII: Strawberry Leaves, Single Arch, and Wrong-Way Lions, Music Quart, 81; La Stesura del Testo nei Manoscritti di Giovanni Spataro, Rivista Italiana di Musicologia, 80; Music of the Renaissance, Musical Quart, 82; Renaissance musical sources in the archive of San Petronio, Haensaler-Verlag, 86; Melody and the Mark-off-Chain model, Leonard B Meyer Festschrift, 88; Culture and the cultivated mind, The Arts in Lutheran Higher Educ, 89; Music of the American dream, Eileen Southern Festschrift, 92; Censorship and the arts, Wittenberg Rev, 92; Medieval retentions in music of the 20th Century, Medievalism, 96; Living with jazz, Harcourt Brace, 96. **CONTACT ADDRESS** Sch of

Music, Yale Univ, PO Box 208246, New Haven, CT, 06520-8246. **EMAIL** frank.tirro@yale.edu

TIRYAKIAN, EDWARD A.

PERSONAL Born 08/06/1929, Bronxville, NY, m, 1953, 2 children **DISCIPLINE** SOCIOLOGY **EDUCATION** Princeton Univ, BA, 52; Harvard Univ, MA, 54, PhD, 56. **CAREER** Instr to asst prof, Princeton Univ, 56-57; lecturer, Harvard univ, 62-65; Assoc prof, Duke Univ, 65-67; prof, Duke Univ, 67-. **HONORS AND AWARDS** Summa cum laude, Phi beta Kappa, Princeton; doctuer honoris causa Univ Paris V; fellow, Ctr for Adv Stud in the Behavioral Sci, 97-98., Ch, Dept Sociol & Anthrop, Duke Univ, 69-72; Dir of Int Stud, 88-91. **MEMBERSHIPS** Int Sociol Asn; Am Soc for the Stud of Relig (past pres); Int Asn of French-speaking Sociol (AISLF, past pres); Am Sociol Asn; Eastern Sociol Soc; Southern Sociol Soc. **RESEARCH** Sociology of religion; comparative nationalism; sociological theory. **SELECTED PUBLICATIONS** Ed, The 100th Anniversary of Durkheim's Division of Labor in Society, Sociol Forum, 9, 1, 3/94; Revisiting Sociology's First Classic: The Division of Labor in Society and its Actuality, Sociol Forum, 9, 3-16, 3/94; auth, Collective Effervescence, Social Change and Charisma: Durkheim, Weber, and 1989, Int Sociol, 10, 269-81, 9/95; auth, Three Metacultures of Modernity: Christian, Gnostic, Chthonic, Theory Culture & Society, 13, 99-118, 2/96; auth, The Wild Cards of Modernity, Daedalus, 126, 147-81, Spring 97. **CONTACT ADDRESS** Dept of Sociol, Duke Univ, Box 90088, Durham, NC, 27708-0088. **EMAIL** durkhm@soc.duke.edu

TISCHLER, HANS

PERSONAL Born 01/18/1915, Vienna, Austria, m, 1938, 4 children **DISCIPLINE** MUSIC HISTORY AND THEORY **EDUCATION** Vienna State Acad, MusB, 33, MusM, 36; Univ Vienna, PhD(musicol), 37. **CAREER** Prof music, Wesleyan Col, W Va, 45-47; assoc prof, Roosevelt Univ, 47-65; PROF MUSICOL, IND UNIV, BLOOMINGTON, 65-, Am Philos Soc grants, 55-56, 62-63, 64-65 and 81-82; guest prof musicol, Univ Chicago, 56-57; Roosevelt Univ res grant, 58; Guggenheim fel, 64-65; Chapelbrook Found and Ind Univ res grants, 65-66 and 69-70; guest prof musicol, Tel Aviv Univ, 72; Nat Endowment for Humanities fel, 75-76. **MEMBERSHIPS** Am Musicol Soc; Mediaeval Acad Am; Int Musicol Soc; Medieval Asn Midwest; AAUP. **RESEARCH** Medieval and 20th century music; music aesthetics; musical forms. **SELECTED PUBLICATIONS** Auth, The Perceptive Music Listener, Prentice-Hall, 55; Practical Harmony, Allyn and Bacon, 64; Structural Analysis of Mozart's Piano Concertos, Inst Mediaeval Music, 66; The Montpellier Codex, 3 vols, A-R Editions, 78; Complete Comparative Edition of the Earliest Motets, 3 vols, Yale Univ, 82; Complete Comparative Edition of the Parisian Two-Part Organa, Pendragon P; The Earliest Motets: Their Style and Evolution, Inst of Mediaeval Music; Interpreting the 'Roman De Fauvel' in Monophonic Song, Early Music, Vol 0021, 93; Mode, Modulation, and Transposition in Medieval Songs, J Musicology, Vol 0013, 95; Brule, Gace and Melodic Formulas, Acta Musicologica, Vol 0067, 95; coauth and ed, Essays in Musicology for W Apel, Festschrift, 68; ed, Willi Apel: The History of Keyboard Music to 1700, Ind Univ, 73. **CONTACT ADDRESS** Sch of Music, Indiana Univ, Bloomington, Bloomington, IN, 47401.

TITLEY, EDWARD B.

PERSONAL Born 01/08/1945, Cork, Ireland **DISCIPLINE** HISTORY **EDUCATION** Nat Univ Ireland, BA, 66; Univ Man, BEd, 70, MEd, 75; Univ Alta, PhD, 80. **CAREER** Sec sch tchr, Man, 67-70; elem sch prin, Dept Indian Affairs, 71-74; lectr, 80-86, asst prof, 86-89, assoc prof, Univ Alta, 89-90; assoc prof, 91-93, PROF EDUCATION, UNIV LETHBRIDGE, 93-. **MEMBERSHIPS** Can Hist Asn; Can Hist Educ Asn (pres, 90-92); Can Soc Study Educ; Writers Guild Alta. **SELECTED PUBLICATIONS** Auth, Church, State and the Control of Schooling in Ireland, 1900-1944, 83; auth, A Narrow Vision: Duncan Campbell Scott and the Administration of Indian Affairs in Canada, 86; auth, Dark Age: The Political Odyssey of Emperor Bokassa, 97; ed, Canadian Education: Historical Themes and Contemporary Issues, 90; co-ed, Education in Canada: An Interpretation, 82. **CONTACT ADDRESS** Faculty of Education, Univ Lethbridge, Lethbridge, AB, T1K 3M4. **EMAIL** brian.titley@uleth.ca

TITON, JEFF TODD

PERSONAL Born 12/08/1943, Jersey City, NJ **DISCIPLINE** AMERICAN STUDIES **EDUCATION** Amherst College, BA, 65; Univ Minn, MA, 70, PhD, 71. **CAREER** Prof music, 86-, Brown Univ; vis Prof at: 85, Carleton College, 90, Berea College, 93, Amherst College; Asst Prof, Assoc Prof, 71-86, Tufts Univ. **HONORS AND AWARDS** NEH Fels; ASCAP Deems Taylor Awd. **MEMBERSHIPS** Soc for Ethnomusicology; AFS; ASA. **RESEARCH** American Music, old time fiddle and string band music, blues; Lined-out hymnody of Old Regular Baptists; Black Preaching. **SELECTED PUBLICATIONS** Auth, Knowing Fieldwork, Shadows in the Field, ed, Gregory Barz, Timothy Cooley, NY, Oxford Univ Press, 96; ed, Worlds of Music: An Introduction to Music of the World's Peoples, NY Schirmer Books, 84, rev 2nd edition, 92, 3rd ed, 96; Text, J Amer Folklore, 95; Bi-musicality as Metaphor, J Amer Folklore, 95; Blues and Franklin Rev CL, Encyc of African-American Culture and History, ed, Jack Saltzman, David L Smith, Cornel West, NY, MacMillan, 95; Early Downhome Blues: A Musical and Cultural Analysis, Urbana IL, Univ IL Press, 77, pbk, Illini Books 79, Winner ASCAP Deems Taylor Award, rev 2nd ed, Univ N C Press, 95. **CONTACT ADDRESS** Dept of Music, Brown Univ, College Stn, Box 1924, Providence, RI, 02912. **EMAIL** Jeff_Titon@brown.edu

TITTLER, ROBERT

PERSONAL Born 12/07/1942, New York, NY **DISCIPLINE** HISTORY **EDUCATION** Oberlin Col, BA, 64; New York Univ, MA, 65; PhD, 71. **CAREER** Asst prof, 69-74, assoc prof, Loyola Col, 74-75; assoc prof, 75-81, chmn hist, Loyola campus, 76-77, co-chmn, united dept, 77-78, PROF HISTORY, CONCORDIA UNIV, 81-, dir, hist grad prog, 86-89; Andrew H. Mellon lectr, Princeton, 87; vis prof, Yale Univ, 98. **HONORS AND AWARDS** Haskell fel & Penfield fel, England, 68-69; Can Coun leave fel, 74-75; SSHRC res grants 82-83, 87-89, 91-94, 97-99; NEH fel, 91. **MEMBERSHIPS** Ctr Renaissance Reformation Stud; Inst Hist Res; N Am Conf Brit Stud; Econ Hist Soc; Soc 16th Century Stud; Rec Early Eng Drama; Past Present Soc. **RESEARCH** Renaissance and Reformation studies **SELECTED PUBLICATIONS** Auth, Nicholas Bacon, The Making of a Tudor Statesman, 76; auth, The Reign of Mary I, 83, 2nd ed, 91; auth, Architecture and Power, the Town Hall and the English Urban Community 1500-1640, 91; auth, The Reformation and the Towns, 98; Acad ed-in-chief, History of Urban Society in Europe, 5 vol ser; ed, Accounts of the Roberts Family of Ticehurst, Sussex, 79; co-ed, The Mid-Tudor Polity, c. 1540-1560, 80. **CONTACT ADDRESS** Dept of History, Concordia Univ, Montreal, 7141 Sherbrooke St W, Montreal, PQ, H4B 1R6. **EMAIL** tittler@vax2.concordia.ca

TIYAMBE ZELEZA, PAUL

DISCIPLINE HISTORY **EDUCATION** Dalhousie Univ, PhD, 82. **CAREER** Prof, Univ Ill Urbana Champaign. **HONORS AND AWARDS** Dir, Center African Studies. **RESEARCH** African economic and labor history; imperialism and colonialism. **SELECTED PUBLICATIONS** Auth, Labor, Unionization and Women's Participation in Kenya, 1965-1987, Friedrich Ebert Found, 88; A Modern Economic History of Africa, Codesria, 93; Smouldering Charcoal, Oxford, 92. **CONTACT ADDRESS** History Dept, Univ Ill Urbana Champaign, 52 E Gregory Dr, Champaign, IL, 61820. **EMAIL** zeleza@uiuc.edu

TOBEY, RONALD CHARLES

PERSONAL Born 10/25/1942, Plymouth, NH, 1 child **DISCIPLINE** HISTORY OF SCIENCE AND TECHNOLOGY **EDUCATION** Univ NH, BA, 64; Cornell Univ, MA, 66, PhD, 69. **CAREER** Vis asst prof Am hist, Univ Pittsburgh, 69-70; asst prof, 70-75; assoc prof, 75-81, prof hist of sci, Univ CA, Riverside, 81, dir prog hist resources mgt, 72, Nat Endowment for Hum fel, 75; mem adv coun, Nat Arch Region 9, 76-77; mem bd trustees, Riverside Munic Mus, 77-83; Pres, Board of Dir, Mission Inn Found, 85-93. **MEMBERSHIPS** AHA; Orgn Am Historians; Hist Sci Soc; Soc Hist Tech. **RESEARCH** Hist of Am sci; Am soc hist; Hist Am Sci & Tech. **SELECTED PUBLICATIONS** Auth, American Ideology of National Science, 1919-1930, Univ Pittsburgh, 71; How Urbane is the Urbanite? An Historical Model of the Urban Hierarchy and The Social Motivation of Service Classes, Hist Methods Newslett, 9/74; Theoretical Science and Technology in American Ecology, Technol & Cult, 10/76; American Grassland Ecology, 1895-1955: The Life Cycle of a Professional Research Community, In: History of American Ecology, Arno, 77; Technology and culture, Vol 17, 76; Saving the Prairies, In: The Life Cycle of the Founding of American Plant Ecology, 1895-1955, Univ Calif, 81; The Citrus Industry and the Revolution of Corporate Capitalism in Southern California, 1887-1944, California History p6-21, 95; Moving Out and Settling In: Residential Mobility, Home Owning and The Public Enframing of Citizenship, 1921-1950, American Historical Review p13595-1422, 90; Technology as Freedom: The New Deal and the Electrical Modernization of the American Home, Univ CA, 96. **CONTACT ADDRESS** Dept Hist, Univ California, 900 University Ave, Riverside, CA, 92521-0204. **EMAIL** rtobey@lucknow.com

TOBIN, EUGENE MARC

PERSONAL Born 03/23/1947, Newark, NJ, m, 1979, 2 children **DISCIPLINE** AMERICAN HISTORY **EDUCATION** Rutgers Univ, BA, 68; Brandeis Univ, MA, 70, PhD(Am hist), 72. **CAREER** Instr hist, Jersey City State Col, 72-74; asst prof, Kutztown State Col, 75-76; vis asst prof, Miami Univ, 77-79 & Ind Univ, Bloomington, 79-80; asst prof hist, Hamilton Col, 80-, Nat Endowment for Humanities fel hist, Vanderbilt Univ, 76-77; Am Philos Soc res grant, 78 & 82; Miami Univ Fac res appointment, 78; dir, Am Studies, Hamilton Col, 82-; asst prof, 80-83; assoc prof, 83-88; prof hist, 880; publius virgilius Rogers prof Am hist, 88-90. **HONORS AND AWARDS** William Adee Whitehead Award, NJ Hist Soc, 76. **MEMBERSHIPS** AHA; Orgn Am Historians; Am Studies Asn. **RESEARCH** Recent American political history; Natl Assoc Independent Colleges & Univ,; Commission of Independent Coll and Univ, New York. **SELECTED PUBLICATIONS** Auth, The progressive as politician: Jersey City 1896-1907, NJ Hist, spring 73; Mark Fagan, the progressive as single taxer, 7/74 & In pursuit of equal taxation: Jersey City's struggle against corporate arrogance, 4/75, Am J Econ & Sociol; The progressive as humanitarian: The search for social justice in Jersey City 1890-1917, NJ Hist, fall-winter, 75; The political economy of George L Record: A progressive alternative to socialism, Historian, 8/77; co-ed, The Age of Urban Reform: New Perspectives on the Progressive Era, Kennikat, 77; Direct action and conscience: The 1913 Paterson strike as example of the relationship between labor radicals and liberals, Labor Hist, winter 79; George L Record and the progressive spirit, NJ Hist Comn; America's Independent Progressives, 1913-1933, Greenwood Press, 1986; co-editor, The National Lawyers Guild: From Roosevelt through Reagan, Temple University Press, 88. **CONTACT ADDRESS** President's Office, Hamilton Col, 198 College Hill Rd, Clinton, NY, 13323-1292. **EMAIL** etobin@hamilton.edu

TOBY, RONALD P.

PERSONAL Born 12/06/1942, White Plains, NY, m, 1987 **DISCIPLINE** HISTORY **EDUCATION** Columbia Univ, BA, 65, MA, 74, PhD, 77 **CAREER** Preceptor, 72-73, Columbia Univ; lectr, 77-78, Univ Calif Berkeley; asst prof to prof, dept head, 78-, Univ Il Urbana-Champaign; vis prof, 84-85, Keio Univ; vis prof, 95-96, Kyoto Univ. **HONORS AND AWARDS** Fulbright-Hays Fel, 74-76, 84-85; Univ Scholar Univ Il, 86-89; LAS Faculty Fel, 87-88; Nat Endow for the Human Sr Fel, 88-89; Japan Found Prof Fel, 89-90; Toyota Found Res Grant, 89-91; JSPS Sr Res Fel, 93; Nat Endow for the Humanities Summer Res Fel, 94. **MEMBERSHIPS** Amer Hist Assoc; Assoc for Asian Stud; Early Modern Japan Group; Chosen Gakkai(-Korean Stud Assoc); Int Soc for Ryukyuan Stud. **RESEARCH** Notions of ethnicity & identity at the intersection of cultural hist & int relations **SELECTED PUBLICATIONS** Auth, State and Diplomacy in Early Modern Japan: Asia in the Development of the Tokugawa Bakufu, Stanford, 91; co-auth, Gyoretsu to misemono (Parades & Entertainments), Asahi Shinbunsha, 94; auth, Imagining and Imaging 'Anthropos' in Early-modern Japan, Visual Anthrop Rev, 98; auth, Gazing at 'Man': the Early-Modern Japanese Imaginary and the Birth of a Visual Anthropology, Wanami world history, Iwanami Shoten, 99; auth, From 'sangoku' to 'bankoku': The Iberian Irruption and Japanese cosmology, Mare Liberum, 99. **CONTACT ADDRESS** Dept of History, Univ Il, 309 Gregory Hall, 810 S Wright St, Urbana, IL, 61801. **EMAIL** rptoby@uiuc.edu

TODD, IAN ALEXANDER

PERSONAL Born 09/24/1941, West Kirby, England, m, 1981 **DISCIPLINE** ARCHAEOLOGY **EDUCATION** Univ Birmingham, BA, 63, PhD(archaeol), 67. **CAREER** Asst prof, 69-77, ASSOC PROF ARCHAEOL, BRANDEIS UNIV, 77-, Dir archeol excavation at Neolithic Cypriote site, Kalavasos-Tenta, 76-; comt mem and chmn, Cyprus Archaeol Res Inst sect, Am Schs Orient Res, 78; dir, Cyprus Am Archaeol Res Inst, 79-80. **MEMBERSHIPS** Brit Inst Archaeol Ankara; Brit Inst Persian Studies; Int Inst Conserv Hist and Artistic Works; Prehist Soc; Israel Explor Soc. **RESEARCH** Early prehistory of Near and Middle East and archaeology of areas of the Aegean, Near and Middle East; archaeology of Anatolia; archaeology of Cyprus. **SELECTED PUBLICATIONS** Auth, Asikli Huyuk: A Protoneolithic Site in Central Anatolia, Anatolian Studies, 66; Preliminary Report on a Survey of Neolithic Sites in Central Anatolia, Turk Arkeoloji Dergisi, 66; Anatolia and the Khirbet Kerak Problem, Alter Orient Altes Testament, 73; Catal Huyuk in Perspective, Cummings, 76; Vasilikos Valley Project: First Preliminary Report, 1976, Report Dept Antiq Cyprus, 77; Vasilikos Valley Project: Second Preliminary Report, 1977, 79 and Vasilikos Valley Project: Third preliminary report, 1978, 79, J Field Archaeol; The Neolithic Period in Central Anatolia, 80; Neutron-Activation Analysis of Obsidian from Kalavasos-Tenta, J Field Archaeol, Vol 0022, 95. **CONTACT ADDRESS** Dept of Class and Orient Studies, Brandeis Univ, Waltham, MA, 02254.

TODD, LARRY

DISCIPLINE MUSIC **EDUCATION** Yale Univ, PhD. **CAREER** Musicol prof, Duke Univ. **RESEARCH** 19th century music and Mendelssohn. **SELECTED PUBLICATIONS** Ed, Schirmer Studies in Musical Genres and Repertories. **CONTACT ADDRESS** Dept of Music, Duke Univ, Mary Duke Biddle Music Bldg, Durham, NC, 27706. **EMAIL** rltodd@duke.edu

TODD, MARGO

PERSONAL Born 07/24/1950, Peoria, IL, m, 1970, 3 children **DISCIPLINE** HISTORY **EDUCATION** Tufts, BA, 72; Washington Univ, MA, 77, PhD, 81. **CAREER** Vanderbilt Univ, asst prof, 81-87, assoc prof, 87-. **HONORS AND AWARDS** Royal Historical Society, Fel; Univ of Edinburg, NEH & ACLS Fellowships **MEMBERSHIPS** NACBS, ASCH **RESEARCH** Hist early modern England and Scotland; Reformation and culture of protestantism. **SELECTED PUBLICATIONS** Auth, Christian Humanism and the Puritan Social Order, Cambridge Press, 87;A Captive's Story: Puritans, Pirates, and the Drama of Reconciliation, The Seventeenth Century, 97; All One With Tom Thumb: Arminianism, Popery and the Story of the Reformation in Early Stuart Cambridge, Church Hist, 95; Puritan Self-fashioning: The Diary of Samuel Ward,

Jour of Brit Stud, 92; Providence, Chance and the New Science in Early Stuart Cambridge, The Hist J, 86. **CONTACT ADDRESS** Dept of History, Vanderbilt Univ, Nashville, TN, 37235. **EMAIL** margo.todd@vanderbilt.edu

TODOROVA, M.
PERSONAL Born 01/05/1949, Sofia, Bulgaria, m, 1976, 2 children **DISCIPLINE** HISTORY **EDUCATION** Sofia Univ Bulgaria, PhD 77. **CAREER** Univ Sofia, asst prof, assoc prof, 73-92; Univ Florida, asst, assoc, full prof, 92 to 96-. **HONORS AND AWARDS** Wilson Cen Sch fel, 88&94; Mellon Dist Prof; Fulbright Prof, 88-89. **MEMBERSHIPS** AHA; AAASS **RESEARCH** Balkan; East European Hist; Anthropology. **SELECTED PUBLICATIONS** Auth, Imagining the Balkans, Oxford Univ Press, 97; Balkan Family Structure and the European Pattern, Amer Univ Press, 93; English Travelers' Accounts on the Balkans, Sofia, 87. **CONTACT ADDRESS** Dept of History, Univ of Florida, Gainesville, FL, 32611. **EMAIL** mtodorv@history.ufl.edu

TOFT, ROBERT
DISCIPLINE MUSIC **EDUCATION** King's Col, PhD, 83. **CAREER** Prof **HONORS AND AWARDS** Ed, Studies in Music. **SELECTED PUBLICATIONS** Auth, Traditions of Pitch Content in the Sources of Two Sixteenth-Century Motets, Music Letters, 88; Aural Images of Lost Traditions: Sharps and Flats in the Sixteenth Century, Toronto, 92; Tune thy Musicke to thy Hart: The Art of Eloquent Singing in England 1597-1622, Toronto, 93; The Expressive Pause: Punctuation, Rests, and Breathing in England 1770-1850, Performance Practice Rev, 94; The Vocal Appoggiatura in England c1780-c1830: A Regional Perspective Amidst a Pan-European Debate, Irish Musical Stud, 96; Action and Singing in Late 18th- and Early 19th-Century England, Performance Practice Rev, 96; The Promethean Fire of Eloquent Expression: Vocal Delivery in Handel's Oratorios in the Early 19th Century, Jour Musicol Res, 97. **CONTACT ADDRESS** Dept of Music, Western Ontario Univ, London, ON, N6A 5B8. **EMAIL** rtoft@julian.uwo.ca

TOHER, MARK
DISCIPLINE CLASSICS **EDUCATION** Brown Univ, BA, 74, PhD, 85; Univ Oxford, BA, 76. **CAREER** Chemn, Dept of Classics, St George's Sch, 77-80; asst prof, 83-89, assoc prof, Classics, 89- , chemn dept, 91-94, Union College. **HONORS AND AWARDS** Phi Beta Kappa; Brown Univ Sr Scholarship, 74-76; dir of sem for NEH summer inst, 87; NEH summer inst, 88; NEH travel grant, 92; mem Managing Comm of Am School of Class Stud, Athens, 84- . **SELECTED PUBLICATIONS** Auth, The Tenth Table and the Conflict of the Orders, in Raaflaug, ed, Social Struggles in Archaic Rome: New Perspectives on the Roman Conflict of the Orders, Los Angeles, 86; auth, On the Terminal Date of Nicolaus' Universal History, Ancient Hist Bull, 87; auth, On the Use of Nicolaus' Historical Fragments, Class Antiquity, 89; auth, Augustus and the Evolution of Roman Historiography, in Raaflaub, ed, Between Republic and Empire: Interpretations of Augustus and His Principate, Los Angeles, 90; auth, Greek Funerary Legislation and the Two Spartan Funerals, in Flower, ed, Georgica: Studies in Honor of George Cawkwell, London, 91. **CONTACT ADDRESS** Dept of Classics, Union Col, Schenectady, NY, 12308.

TOHIDI, NAYEREH E.
PERSONAL Born 09/24/1957, Tehran, Iran, m, 1974 **DISCIPLINE** EDUCATIONAL PSYCHOLOGY & SOCIOLOGY **EDUCATION** Univ Tehran, BS, 75; Univ Ill Champaign-Urbana, MA, 78, PhD, 83. **CAREER** Vis lectr & res assoc, Harvard Divinity School, 93-94; vis scholar & res fel Hoover Inst, Stanford Univ, 94-95; adj prof, UCLA, 95-97; asst prof, Calif State Univ, Northridge, 97-; **HONORS AND AWARDS** Fulbright prof USSR, 91-92; Postdr fel, Stanford Univ, 94-95. **MEMBERSHIPS** Mid E Studies Asn; W Sociol Asn; Amer Acad Relig. **RESEARCH** Women and gender in Muslim societies; Islamic fundamentalism; Women and development in the Middle East; Islam and nationalism in the newly independent republics of Central Asia and the Caucasus (Azerbaijan in particular). **SELECTED PUBLICATIONS** Auth, Memoirs of Baku: An Oral History of a Woman Writer, Iran Nameh, 93; auth, Immigrant Iranians and Gender Relations: Irangeles: Iranians in Los Angeles, Univ Calif Press, 93; A Review of the Events in the Field, Central Asia Monitor, 94; Gender, Religion, and National Identity in Azerbaijan, Central Asia and Caucasia Rev, 94; Cultural and Political Dimensions of Development in Azervaijan: the Quest for Identity, Int Affairs, 94; Modernization, Islamization, and Gender in Iran, Gender and National Identity: Women and Politics in Muslim Societies, Oxford Univ Press, 94; Fundamentalist Backash and Muslim Women in the Bejing Conference, Canadian Women Studies, 96; Soviet in Public, Azeri in Private: Gender, Islam, and Nationalism in Soviet and Post-Soviet Azerbaijan, Womens Studies Int Forum, 96; Feminism, Demokracy ve Islamgarayi, Ketabsara, 96; auth, The Intersection of Gender, Ethnicity and Islam in Azerbaijan, Nationalities Papers, 97; Islamic Feminism: A Democratic Challenge or a Theocratic Ploy? Knakash, 97; coed, Diversity Within Unity: Gender Dynamics and Change in Muslim Societies, Lynne Rienner Publ, 98. **CONTACT ADDRESS** Womens Studies Dept, California State Univ, Northridge, 18111 Nordhoff St, Northridge, CA, 91330-8251. **EMAIL** nayereh.tohidi@csun.edu

TOKER, FRANKLIN K.
PERSONAL Born 04/29/1944, Montreal, PQ, Canada, m, 1972, 3 children **DISCIPLINE** ARCHITECTURAL HISTORY, MEDIEVAL ARCHEOLOGY **EDUCATION** McGill Univ, BA, 64; Oberlin Col, AM, 66; Harvard Univ, PhD(fine arts), 72. **CAREER** Dir archaeol excavation, Cathedral of Florence, 69-74; vis Mellon prof archit, Carnegie-Mellon Univ, 74-76, assoc prof hist of archit, 76-80; prof Hist Of Art, Univ Pittsburgh, 80-, Harvard Univ Ctr Ital Renaissance Studies fel, 72-74; vis prof, Univ Florence, 88-89, Univ Rome, 91-, Univ Reggio Calabria, 96; mem, Inst for Advanced Study, Princeton, NJ, 85. **HONORS AND AWARDS** Kress Fel, 65; Can Coun Fel, 66; Fel Comt to Rescue Italian Art, Florence, 69; Alice Davis Hitchcock Bk Award, Soc Archit Historians, 70; fel I Tatti-Harvard Univ Ctr for Italian Renaissance Studies, Florence, 72; Guggenheim fel, 79; NEH grants, 79, 92; Arthur Kingsley Porter Prize, Col Art Asn, 80; NEH sr fel, 85; Pittsburgh Hist and Landmarks Found award for Pittsburgh: An Urban Portrait, 87; fel Bellagio Study and Conf Ctr, Rockefeller Found, 94; life mem Col Art Asn, Arthur Kingsley Porter prize, 80; life mem, Medieval Acad; life mem Soc Archit Hist (pres 93-94, board dir 85-88). **MEMBERSHIPS** Col Art Asn; Nat Trust Hist Preserv; Soc Archit Historians; Int Ctr Medieval Art. **RESEARCH** Medieval architecture in Italy; architecture of the nineteenth century; history of the architectural profession. **SELECTED PUBLICATIONS** Auth, The Church of Notre-Dame in Montreal, McGill-Queen's Univ, 70, Fr ed, 81, rev ed, 91; James O'Donnell: An Irish Georgian in America, J Soc Archit Historians, 70; coauth, An Umbrian Abbey: San Paolo di Valdiponte, Papers Brit Sch Rome, 73; S Reparata: L'Antica Cattedrale Fiorentina, Bonechi, Florence, 74; auth, Excavations below the Cathedral of Florence, Gesta, 75; A baptistery below the Baptistery of Florence, Art Bull, 76; Richardson en concours: The Pittsburgh courthouse, Carnegie Mag, 77; Florence Cathedral: The design stage, Art Bull, 78; Pittsburgh: An Urban Portrait, 86, 2nd ed, 95. **CONTACT ADDRESS** Dept of History and Art, Univ of Pittsburgh, 104 Frick Fine Arts, Pittsburgh, PA, 15260-7601. **EMAIL** ftoker@pitt.edu

TOKUNAGA, EMIKO
PERSONAL Born 09/28/1939, San Francisco, CA, s **DISCIPLINE** HISTORY OF DANCE **EDUCATION** Harvard, Admin Fel, 95-96; NY Univ, MA, 66; Univ UT, BFA, 61 **CAREER** Coord, 94-98, Harvard-Radcliffe; Art Dir, 98-, Boston Conserv; Adj Assoc Prof, 93-94, Hofstra Univ **HONORS AND AWARDS** 2,000 Performances with Tokunaga dance **RESEARCH** Dance dialogues **CONTACT ADDRESS** PO Box 1008 Astor Sta, Boston, MA, 02123.

TOLBERT, ELIZABETH D.
DISCIPLINE MUSIC HISTORY **EDUCATION** FL State Univ, BM; Univ CO, MM; Univ CA, PhD. **CAREER** Prof, John Hopkins Univ. **RESEARCH** Intercultural approaches to aesthetics; music theory; music cognition. **SELECTED PUBLICATIONS** Auth, pubs in Embodied Voices; World of Music; Notes; Ethnomusicology; Yearbook for Traditional Music. **CONTACT ADDRESS** Dept of Musicology, Johns Hopkins Univ, 1 E Mt Vernon Pl, Baltimore, MD, 21202-2397.

TOLCHIN, SUSAN JANE
PERSONAL Born 01/14/1941, New York, NY, m, 1965, 2 children **DISCIPLINE** POLITICAL SCIENCE **EDUCATION** Bryn Mawr Col, BA, 61; Univ Chicago, MA, 62; New York Univ, PhD, 68. **CAREER** Asst prof to prof, Public Administration, 78-98, prof Public Policy, George Washington Univ, 98-. **HONORS AND AWARDS** Marshall Dimock Award, Am Soc for Public Administration, 97. **MEMBERSHIPS** Nat Academy of Public Administration; Am Soc for Public Administration; Am Political Science Asn. **RESEARCH** US competiveness and trade policy; US government; Congress. **SELECTED PUBLICATIONS** Co-auth, Buying Into America-How Foreign Money is Changing the Face of Our Nation, Times Books/Random House, 88, Berkeley paperback ed, 89, new paperback ed, Farragut Pubs, 93, Taiwan & Japan eds, 89, Korean ed, 90; co-auth, Selling Our Security-The Erosion of America's Assets, Alfred A Knopf, 92, Penguin paperback, 93; auth, Halting the Erosion of America's Critical Assets, Issues in Science and Technology, J of the Nat Academy of Sciences, vol IX, no 3, spring 93; Women in the US Congress and Jeanette Rankin, published in The Encyclopedia of the United States Congress, Simon & Schuster, 94; The Angry American-How Voter Rage is Changing the Nation, Westview/HarperCollins, 96; Missles to Plowshares: The Switch from War to Peace, J of Socio-Economics, vol 25, no 4, 96; The Globalist from Nowhere: Making Governance Competitive in the International Environment, Public Administration Rev, Jan/Feb 96, vol 56, no 1 (Received the Marshall Dimock award for the best lead article of the Public Administration Review for 1996, annual convention, Am Soc Public Admin, Philadelphia, PA, July 97). **CONTACT ADDRESS** Inst of Public Policy, George Washington Univ, Fairfax, VA, 22030. **EMAIL** stolchi1@gmu.edu

TOLLES JR, BRYANT F.
DISCIPLINE ART HISTORY **EDUCATION** Boston Univ, PhD. **CAREER** Assoc prof. **RESEARCH** Museum studies; American architecture. **SELECTED PUBLICATIONS** Co-auth, New Hampshire Architecture, New Eng, 79; The Architecture of Salem, Essex, 83. **CONTACT ADDRESS** Dept of Art Hist, Univ Delaware, 162 Ctr Mall, Newark, DE, 19716.

TOLMACHEVA, MARINA
DISCIPLINE ISLAMIC CIVILIZATION AND MIDDLE EAST HISTORY **EDUCATION** Inst Ethnog, Acad Sci USSR, Leningrad, PhD, 70. **CAREER** Prof & dir Asia Prog, Washington State Univ. **SELECTED PUBLICATIONS** Auth, The Pate Chronicle, Mich State UP, 93; The Muslim Women in Soviet Central Asia, Central Asian Survey, 93 & Ibn Battuta on Women's Travel in the Dar al-Islam, Women and the Journey, Wash State UP, 93. **CONTACT ADDRESS** Dept of History, Washington State Univ, 301 Wilson Hall, PO Box 644030, Pullman, WA, 99164-4030. **EMAIL** tolmache@wsu.edu

TOLSON, ARTHUR L.
PERSONAL Born 10/15/1924, Sweet Springs, MO, m, 1954, 1 child **DISCIPLINE** AMERICAN & BLACK AMERICAN HISTORY **EDUCATION** Wiley Col, AB, 46; Okla State Univ, MA, 52; Univ Okla, PhD(hist), 66. **CAREER** Head, soc sci dept & dean instr, Butler Col, 57-60; assoc prof hist, Tex Col, 60-62; prof, Jarvis Col, 62-67; prof hist, Southern Univ, Baton Rouge, 67-. **MEMBERSHIPS** Asn Studies Afro-Am Life & Hist; Southern Conf Afro-Am Studies. **SELECTED PUBLICATIONS** Articles in Black Scholar, Black Collegian, J Soc & Behav Sci, Materials & Sources African & Afro-Am Studies & Black Hist in Okla; auth, The Black Oklahomans, A History 1541-1972. **CONTACT ADDRESS** Dept of History, Southern Univ, PO Box 9200, Baton Rouge, LA, 70813.

TOLZMANN, DON HEINRICH
PERSONAL Born 08/12/1945, Granite Falls, MN, m, 1971, 3 children **DISCIPLINE** HISTORY **EDUCATION** Univ Minnesota, BA; United Theologisic Seminary; Univ Kentucky, MA; Univ Cincinnati, PhD. **CAREER** Curator, German Am Collection and Director German Am Studies Prog, Univ Cincinnati, 74-. **HONORS AND AWARDS** Fed Ser Cross, (FRG); German Am Tricent Medal; German Am of the year award. **MEMBERSHIPS** Soc for Ger Am Studies; SM Hist Asn. **SELECTED PUBLICATIONS** German-Americans and the World Wars, Muenchen, K G Saur, 95; In der Neuen Welt, Deutsche-Amerikanische Festschrift fur die 500-Jahrfeier der Entdecking von Amerika, NY, Peter Lang, 92; Cincinnati's German Heritage, Bowie, MD, Heritage Books Inc, 94; The First Germans in America, with NY Germans, Bowie, MD, Heritage Books, 92; The Cincinnati Germans after the Great War, NY, Peter Lang, 87; German American Literature, Metuchen, NJ, Scarecrow Pr, 77; German-Americana, Metuchen, NJ, Scarecrow Pr, 75. **CONTACT ADDRESS** Univ Cincinnati, PO Box 210113, Cincinnati, OH, 45221. **EMAIL** Don.Tolzmann@uc.edu

TOMASINI, WALLACE JOHN
PERSONAL Born 10/19/1927, Brooklyn, NY, m, 1953, 2 children **DISCIPLINE** ART HISTORY **EDUCATION** Univ Mich, BA, 49, MA, 50, PhD(hist), 53. **CAREER** Instr art hist, Finch Col, 54-57; from asst prof to assoc prof, 57-64, prof Art Hist, 64- , dir Sch Art & Art Hist, 72-94, Univ Iowa; Belg-Am Found fel, 53; Am Philos Soc grant, 57-58; Univ Iowa fac res grants, 59-60 & 66-68. **MEMBERSHIPS** Am Numis Soc; AHA; Col Art Asn Am; Midwest Art Hist Soc; Renaissance Soc Am. **RESEARCH** Visigothic numismatics; social and economic status of Renaissance artists; Giotto studies. **SELECTED PUBLICATIONS** Auth, The Barbaric Tremissis in Spain and Southern France; Anastasivs to Leovigliid, Am Numis Soc, 64; Drawing and the Human Figure, 1400-1964, Univ Iowa, 64; coauth, Paintings From Midwestern University Collections, Comt Instnt Coop, 73. **CONTACT ADDRESS** Sch of Art & Art Hist, Univ of Iowa, 100 Art Building, Iowa City, IA, 52242-1706.

TOMAYKO, JAMES EDWARD
PERSONAL Born 07/08/1949, Charleroi, PA, m, 1972 **DISCIPLINE** CHINESE LANGUAGE, HISTORY OF TECHNOLOGY **EDUCATION** Carnegie-Mellon Univ, BA, 71, DA, 80; Univ Pittsburgh, MA, 72. **CAREER** Headmaster, Self-Directed Learning Ctr, 75-80; instr hist, Garden City Community Col, 80-81; tech pub specialist, NCR Corp, 81; ASST PROF COMP SCI, HIST AND CHINESE, WICHITA STATE UNIV, 82-. **MEMBERSHIPS** Soc for the Hist of Technol; Asn Comput Mach; Chinese Lang Teachers Asn; Am Asn Artificial Intelligence; Asn Comput Ling. **RESEARCH** History of computing; Chinese natural language processing. **SELECTED PUBLICATIONS** Auth, The Ditch Irrigation Boom in Southwest Kansas, J West, fall 82; A Simple, Comprehensive Input/Output System for Chinese Natural Language Processing, Comp Sci Dept, Wichita State Univ, 5/82; The Relationship Between the N-BU-N and V-BU-V Constructions in Chinese, Proc of the Mid-Am Ling Conf, 82; Memories of Turing, Alan in Annals of the History of Computing, Vol 0015, 93. **CONTACT ADDRESS** 828 S Holyoke, Wichita, KS, 67218.

TOMBERLIN, JOSEPH A.
PERSONAL Born 05/02/1937, Nashville, GA, m, 1963 **DISCIPLINE** AMERICAN HISTORY **EDUCATION** Valdosta State Col, AB, 62; Fla State Univ, MA, 64, PhD(hist), 67. **CAREER** From asst prof to assoc prof, 67-74, PROF HIST, VALDOSTA STATE COL, 74-, ACTG HEAD DEPT, 80- **MEMBERSHIPS** Orgn Am Historians; Southern Hist Asn. **RESEARCH** Twentieth century United States; the new South.

SELECTED PUBLICATIONS Auth, Florida Whites and the Brown Decision of 1954, Fla Hist Quart, 7/72; Florida and the School Desegregation Issue, 1954-1959, J Negro Educ, fall 74; A Common Thread in African-Americans, the Civil-Rights Movement, and the United States Supreme Court, Miss Quart, vol 0047, 94; For the Sake of My Country, the Diary of Ward, WW, 9th Tennessee Cavalry, Morgans Brigade CSA, Southern Hum Rev, vol 0029, 95; Living Monuments, Confederate Soldiers Homes in the New South, Southern Hum Rev, vol 0029, 95; coauth, John Doe Alias God: A note on Father Divine's Georgia career, Ga Hist Quart, spring 76. **CONTACT ADDRESS** Dept of Hist, Valdosta State Col, Valdosta, GA, 31601.

TOMES, NANCY JANE
PERSONAL Born 10/25/1952, Louisville, KY, m, 1979 **DISCIPLINE** AMERICAN HISTORY **EDUCATION** Univ Ky, BA, 74; Univ Pa, PhD(hist), 78. **CAREER** ASST PROF AM HIST, HIST DEPT, STATE UNIV NY STONY BROOK, 78-, NIMH trainee, Rutgers and Princeton Prog Ment Health Res, 81- **MEMBERSHIPS** AHA; Orgn Am Historians; Social Sci Hist Asn. **RESEARCH** Medical history; history of women in the professions. **SELECTED PUBLICATIONS** Auth, A Torrent of Abuse, J Social Hist, Spring 78; Little World of Our Own, J Hist Med and Allied Sci, 10/78; A Generous Confidence in Madhouses, Mad Doctors and Madmen, Univ Pa P, 81; The Quaker Connection in Friends and Neighbors, Temple Univ P, 82; Am Attitudes toward the Germ theory of Disease, J Hist Med Allied Sci, Vol 52, 97; Introduction to Special Issue on Rethinking the Reception of the Germ Theory of Disease--Comparative Perspectives, J Hist Med Allied Sci, Vol 52, 97. **CONTACT ADDRESS** Dept of Hist, State Univ NY, 100 Nicolls Rd, Stony Brook, NY, 11794-0002.

TOMLINS, CHRISTOPHER L.
PERSONAL Born 04/02/1951, Beaconsfield, England, m, 1980, 2 children **DISCIPLINE** HISTORY; LEGAL STUDIES **EDUCATION** Oxford Univ, BA, 73; Sussex Univ, MA, 74; Oxford Univ, MA, 77; Jonhs Hopkins Univ, MA, 77; PhD, 81. **CAREER** La Trobe Univ, lectr, 80-85; sr lectr, 86-88; reader, 89-94; res fel, Am Bar Found, 92-96; sr res fel, 96- . **HONORS AND AWARDS** Fulbrigh Fel, 75; Am Bar Found Legal Hist Fel, 84; Am Hist Asoc Littleton-Griswold Fund Fel, 88; Erwin W. Surrency Prize, Am Soc for Legal Hist, 89; James willard Hurst Pirze of the Law and Soc Asoc, 94; Littleton-Griswold Prize of the Am Hist Asoc and the Am Soc for Legal Hist, 94. **MEMBERSHIPS** Am Hist Asoc; Orgn of Am Hist; Econ Hist Asoc; Am Soc for Legal Hist. **RESEARCH** American legal history and the history of legal culture, 16th-20th centuries; history of work and labor. **SELECTED PUBLICATIONS** Auth, Law, Labor, and Ideology in the Early American Republic, 93; auth, How Who Rides Whom: Recent 'New' Histories of American Labor Law and What They May Signify, Social Hist, 95; auth, Subordination, Authority, Law: Subjects in Labor History, Int Labor and Working Class Hist, 95; auth, Why Wait for Industrialism? An Historiographical Argument, Labor Hist, 99; co-ed with Bruce H. Mann, The Many Legalities of Early American, forthcoming. **CONTACT ADDRESS** American Bar Foundation, 750 N Lake Shore Dr, Chicago, IL, 60611. **EMAIL** clt@abfn.org

TOMLINSON, ROBERT
PERSONAL Born 06/26/1938, Brooklyn, New York **DISCIPLINE** ART **EDUCATION** Pratt Inst, Brooklyn, BFA 1961; Columbia Univ Teachers Coll NY, 1963; CUNY Graduate Center NY, PhD 1977. **CAREER** Emory Univ Atlanta, asst prof 1978-84, assoc prof, 1984-93, prof, 1994-; Hunter Coll NY, adj asst prof 1972-78; HS of Art & Design NY, French instr 1968-72; Ministere de l'Education Nationale Paris, Eng instr 1963-68; This Week Mag, asst art dir 1961-63. **HONORS AND AWARDS** Number 1 man exhibit of Painting Paris, London, NY, Washington 1968, 1971, 1979, 1984; rep in private coll; Advanced Study Fellow Ford Found, 1972-76; fellow, CUNY 1975-77; Amer Council of Learned Societies Grant 1979. **MEMBERSHIPS** Mem Am Soc for Eighteenth Cent Stud mem Mod Lang Assoc; chmn Emory Univ Commn on the Status of Minorities 1980-81, 1984-85. **CONTACT ADDRESS** Emory Univ, Atlanta, GA, 30322.

TOMPSON, G. RAY
DISCIPLINE HISTORY **EDUCATION** Fort Hays State Univ, AB, 65; MA, 67, PhD, 72, Univ Kansas. **CAREER** Asst/Assoc/Full Prof, 72-, Salisbury State Univ. **CONTACT ADDRESS** Salisbury State Univ, Salisbury, MD, 21801. **EMAIL** grthompson@ssu.edu

TOMPSON, RICHARD STEVENS
PERSONAL Born 01/21/1935, Glen Ridge, NJ, m, 1960, 3 children **DISCIPLINE** BRITISH & IRISH HISTORY **EDUCATION** Yale Univ, BA, 57; Villanova Univ, MA, 62; Univ Mich, PhD(hist), 67. **CAREER** Lectr Hist, Univ Mich, 66-67; from asst prof to assoc prof, 67-76, chmn dept, 75-80, prof Hist, Univ Utah, 76-. **MEMBERSHIPS** Conf Brit Studies. **RESEARCH** British legal history. **SELECTED PUBLICATIONS** Auth, The Leeds grammar school case, J Educ Admin & Hist, 70; Classics or Charity? The Dilemma of the 18th Century Grammar School, Manchester Univ, 71; English grammar school curriculum in the 18th century: A reappraisal, Brit J Educ Studies, 71; English and English education in the eighteenth century, Studies Voltaire & The Eighteenth Century, CLXVII, 77; The Charity Commission and the Age of Reform, Routledge, 79; Scottish Judges and the Birth of British Copyright, Juridical Review, 92. **CONTACT ADDRESS** Dept of History, Univ of Utah, 211 Carlson Hall, Salt Lake City, UT, 84112-3124. **EMAIL** richard.tompson@m.cc.utah.edu

TOMS-ROBINSON, DOLORES C.
PERSONAL Born 12/26/1926, Washington, District of Columbia, m **DISCIPLINE** EDUCATION **EDUCATION** Howard Univ, BS cum laude 1947, MS 1948; Univ of MI, PhD 1957; Univ of IL Inst for Study of Mental Retardation, post doctoral study 1956-57. **CAREER** Univ of UT, rsch child psychology, 1957-58; Jarvis Christian Coll, dir of psychol testing 1960-62; Jackson State Coll, dir fresh studies 1962-64; TX So Univ, prof of psychology 1964-70; Central MI Univ, chmn 1974-76, prof 1970-. **MEMBERSHIPS** Mem Council for Exceptional Children; NEA; Phi Delta Kappa. **CONTACT ADDRESS** Professor, Counseling & Special Education, Central Michigan Univ, Rowe Hall 208, Mount Pleasant, MI, 48859.

TOOLEY, T. HUNT
PERSONAL Born 02/19/1955, Vernon, TX, m, 1977, 3 children **DISCIPLINE** HISTORY **EDUCATION** Texas A & M Univ, BA, 77, MA, 78; Univ Virginia, PhD, 86. **CAREER** Instr History, Univ Virginia, 85-86; Lectr, Univ N Carolina-Wilmington, 86-87; asst prof history, Erskine Col, 87-91; asst prof, 91, assoc prof history, 94, DIR HONORS PROG & HIST DEPT CHR, 94- , AUSTIN COL; Pres Endowed Schol Texas A & M, 73-77. **HONORS AND AWARDS** Dupont fel, Univ Virginia, 79-80; DAAD fel Germany, 82-83; Erskine Col Exc Tchg Award, 88. **MEMBERSHIPS** Am Hist Asn; Hist Soc; German Stud Asn. **RESEARCH** 20thCentury Europe; Germany since 1871; Comparative war and peacemaking. **SELECTED PUBLICATIONS** Auth, Nazi Technocracy nd Coerced Labor: A Case Study of the Synthetic Fuel Industry, The Red River Valley Hist Jour of World History, 78; German Political Violence and the Border Plebiscite in Upper Silesia, 1919-1921, Cent Europ Hist, 88; The Internal Dynamics of Changing Frontiers: The Plebiscites on Germany's Borders, 1919-1921, The Establishment of European Frontiers After the Two World Wars, Peter Lang, 96; The Polish-German Ethnic Dispute in the 1921 Upper Silesian Plebiscite, Can Rev Stud Nat, 97; National Identity and Weimar Germany: Upper Silesia and the Eastern Border, 1918-1922, Univ Nebraska Press, 97. **CONTACT ADDRESS** Dept History, Austin Col, Sherman, TX, 75090. **EMAIL** htooley@austinc.edu

TOPLIN, ROBERT B.
PERSONAL Born 09/26/1940, Philadelphia, PA, m, 1962, 2 children **DISCIPLINE** UNITED STATES AND LATIN AMERICAN HISTORY **EDUCATION** Pa State Univ, BA, 62; Rutgers Univ, MA, 65, PhD(hist), 68. **CAREER** Teaching asst hist, Rutgers Univ, 64-67; from asst prof to assoc prof hist, Denison Univ, 68-78; assoc prof, 78-79, PROF HIST, UNIV NC, WILMINGTON, 80-, Nat Endowment for Humanities younger humanist fel, 70-71, sr fel, 77, media grant, 78, production grant, 80 and script grant, 82; proj dir, PBS Television ser Slavery in America. **HONORS AND AWARDS** Fel, Va Ctr Hum, 94; fel, ACLS, 91; UNC-W summer res initiative, 96; NEH summer inst, Brazil, 92; NEH prod grant, 91. **MEMBERSHIPS** Orgn Am Historians; AHA; Southern Hist Asn, Lat Am Stud Asn; IAMHIST. **RESEARCH** Film and history **SELECTED PUBLICATIONS** Auth, Upheaval, Violence, and the Abolition of Slavery in Brazil: The Case of Sao Paulo, Hisp Am Hist Rev, 11/69; Reinterpreting Comparative Race Relations: the United States and Brazil, J Black Studies, 12/71; The Abolition of Slavery in Brazil, Atheneum, 72; The Specter of Crisis: Slaveholder Reactions to Abolitionism in the United States and Brazil, Civil War Hist, 6/72; ed, Slavery and Race Relations in Latin America, 74 and auth, Unchallenged Violence: An American Ordeal, 75, Greenwood; Between Black and White: Attitudes Toward Southern Mulattoes, 1830-1861, J Southern Hist, 79; Freedom and Prejudice: The Legacy of Slavery in the United States and Brazil, Greenwood, 81; ed, Ken Burns' The Civil War, Oxford Univ Press, 96; auth, History by Hollywood: The Use and Abuse of the American past, Univ Ill Press, 96; auth, Hollywood as Mirror; Changing Views of Outsiders and Enemies in American Movies, Greenwood Press, 82. **CONTACT ADDRESS** Dept of Hist, Univ of NC, Wilmington, NC, 28403. **EMAIL** toplinrb@uncwil.edu

TOPPIN, EDGAR ALLAN
PERSONAL Born 01/22/1928, New York, New York, m **DISCIPLINE** SOCIAL SCIENCES **EDUCATION** Howard Univ, AB cum laude 1949, MA 1950; Northwestern Univ, PhD 1955. **CAREER** AL State Coll, instr 1954-55; Fayetteville State Coll, chmn Soc Sci Div 1955-59; Univ Akron, asst assc prof 1959-64; VA State Coll, full prof 1964-; NC Coll, vis prof 1959, 1963; Western Res Univ, 1962; Univ Cincinnati, 1964; San Francisco State Coll, 1969; IN Univ, 1971. **HONORS AND AWARDS** Grad flwshps from Howard Univ 1949-50; Hearts Fnd 1950-51, 1952-53; John Hay Whitney Fnd opport Flwship History 1964; research grants from Amer Assn State Local History 1964; Old Dominion Fnd 1968; Ford Fnd 1970; Comtemporary Authors. **MEMBERSHIPS** Natl Pres Assc study Afro-Amer life & history 1973-76; editorial bd Journal Negro History 1962-67; exec bd Orgn Amer Historians 1971-74; mem Natl Hist Pub Commn 1972- 1st black mem; adv bd Natl Parks Historic Sites Bldgs & Monuments 1st black mem; bd dir So Flwshps Fund 1966-; World Book Encyclopedia Socl Sci Adv Com 1968-; vice pres bd Akron Urban League 1961-64; bd dir Fayetteville United Fund 1957-59. **SELECTED PUBLICATIONS** Author books, Pioneer Patriots 1954; Mark Well Made 1967; Unfinished March 1967; Blacks in Amer 1969; Biog History of Black in Amer 1971; Black Amer in US 1973; 30 lesson educ TV Course Amer from Africa. **CONTACT ADDRESS** VA State Coll, Petersburg, VA, 23803.

TORBENSON, CRAIG L.
DISCIPLINE HISTORICAL-CULTURAL GEOGRAPHY, HISTORIC PRESERVATION **EDUCATION** Brigham Young Univ, BS, 82; MS, 85; Univ Okla, PhD, 92. **CAREER** Dept Hist, Wichita State Univ **RESEARCH** Norwegian-American nigration and settlement; historical and cultural geography. **SELECTED PUBLICATIONS** Auth, A Geography of Social Fraternities and Sororities, Nat Soc Sci Jour, 97; Themes in Geography: An Interactive Study Guide, Kendall/Hunt, 94; World Regional Geography; An Atlas Study Guide, Kendall/Hunt. **CONTACT ADDRESS** Dept of Hist, Wichita State Univ, 1845 Fairmont, Wichita, KS, 67260-0062.

TORODASH, MARTIN
PERSONAL Born 03/13/1928, Brooklyn, NY, m, 1967 **DISCIPLINE** AMERICAN AND LATIN AMERICAN HISTORY **EDUCATION** Univ Pa, AB, 50; NY Univ, MA, 55, PhD(hist), 66. **CAREER** From asst prof to assoc prof, 61-73, PROF HIST, FAIRLEIGH DICKINSON UNIV, 73-, Assoc, Columbia Univ sem Early Am hist and cult, 67- **MEMBERSHIPS** AHA; Orgn Am Historians; Hakluyt Soc; Soc Hist Discoveries. **RESEARCH** Woodrow Wilson's Administration; Discovery and Exploration: Samoa. **SELECTED PUBLICATIONS** Auth, the Am Presidency Since 1789, Wheeler's Rev, Fall 60; Columbus Historiography Since 1939, 11/66 and Magellan Historiography, 5/71, Hisp Am Hist Rev.; Columbus and the Ends of the Earth--Europe Prophetic Rhetoric As Conquering Ideology, Hisp Am Hist Rev, Vol 73, 93; The Geographical Conceptions of Columbus--A Critical Consideration of 4 Problems, Hisp Am Hist Rev, Vol 74, 94; Columbus, Christopher and the Discovery of America--Realities, Imaginings, and Reinterpretations, Hisp Am Hist Rev, Vol 76, 96; Cosmographers and Pilots of the Spanish Maritime Empire, Hisp Am Hist Rev, Vol 77, 97; Lamb, Ursula 1914-96 in Memoriam, Hisp Am Hist Rev, Vol 77, 97. **CONTACT ADDRESS** Dept of Hist and Polit Sci, Fairleigh Dickinson Univ, Teaneck, NJ, 07666.

TORRECILLA, JESUS
DISCIPLINE CULTURAL IDENTITY AND COLLECTIVE IMITATION, MARGINALITY, TIME AND POWER **EDUCATION** Univ Southern Calif, LA, PhD, 91. **CAREER** Asst prof Span, grad adv, La State Univ. **RESEARCH** Spanish peninsular literature-18th to 20th centuries. **SELECTED PUBLICATIONS** Auth, La imitaci?n colectiva: modernidad vs. autenticidad en la literatura espa?ola, Gredos, 96; coed, Raz?n, tradici?n y modernidad: Revision de la Ilustraci?n hisp?nica, Tecnos, 96. **CONTACT ADDRESS** Dept of For Lang and Lit, Louisiana State Univ, 149 B Prescott Hall, Baton Rouge, LA, 70803. **EMAIL** torrecil@homer.forlang.lsu.edu

TORRES, HECTOR
DISCIPLINE CHICANO/CHICANA LITERATURE, LITERARY THEORY **EDUCATION** Univ Tex, PhD, 86. **CAREER** Instr, Univ NMex, 86-. **SELECTED PUBLICATIONS** Coauth, Dialogic Structure and Levels of Discourse in Steinbeck's The Grapes of Wrath, Ariz Quart, 89. **CONTACT ADDRESS** Univ NMex, Albuquerque, NM, 87131.

TORREY, GLENN E.
PERSONAL Born 12/04/1930, Yuba City, CA, m, 1959, 3 children **DISCIPLINE** MODERN EUROPEAN HISTORY **EDUCATION** Univ Ore, BS, 53, MA, 57, PhD, 60. **CAREER** From asst prof to assoc prof, 59-65, PROF HIST, EMPORIA STATE UNIV, 65-, US Dept State exchange scholar, Rumania, 61-62, sr res award, 66-67; Am Coun Learned Soc Slavic and EEurop grant, 61-62; Am Philos Soc grant-in-aid, 62, grant, 76; Am Coun Learned Soc-Soc Sci Res Coun Slavic and EEurop grant, 66-67; assoc ed, Yearbk Rumanian Studies, 68-; Int Res and Exchanges Bd res prof, Romania, 72 and 76. **MEMBERSHIPS** AHA; Am Asn Advan Slavic Studies. **RESEARCH** German-Rumanian relations, 1914-1918; Rumania during the First World War. **SELECTED PUBLICATIONS** Auth, Rumania and the Belligerents, 1914-1916, J Contemp Hist, 6/66; The Central Powers and Rumania, August-November 1914, Suedost-Forsch, 66; Rumania's Decision to Intervene: 1916 in Yearbook of Rumanian Studies, Vol II, 72; Rumania and the Allied Offensive at Salonika, August 1916, Rev Roumaine d'Hist, 75; The Entente and the Rumanian campaign of 1916 in Rumanian Studies, Vol IV, 77; The Rumanian Campaign of 1916: Its Impact on the Belligerents, Slavic Rev, Vol 39, 80.; Romania and Its War for National Unity--The Campaign of 1918-1919, Am Hist Rev, Vol 102, 97. **CONTACT ADDRESS** Div of Soc Sci, Emporia State Univ, Emporia, KS, 66801.

TOTTEN III, GEORGE OAKLEY
PERSONAL Born 07/21/1922, Washington, DC, m, 1976, 2 children **DISCIPLINE** POLITICAL SCIENCE; ASIAN COMPARATIVE GOVERNMENT; ASIAN POLITICAL THOUGHT. **EDUCATION** Univ Mich, AB, 43; Columbia, AB, 46, AM, 49; Yale Univ, MA, 50, PhD, 54; Univ Stockholm, Docentur-i-Japanologi, 77. **CAREER** Lect in Govt, E Asian Inst, 54-55; res assoc E Asian Affairs, Fletcher School Law & Dipl, 55-58; asst prof Political Science, MIT, 58-59; asst prof Political Science & History, Boston Univ, 59-61; assoc prof Political Science, Univ Rhode Island, 61-64; assoc to full prof Political Science, 65-92, DISTINGUISED PROF EMER, 95-, USC, 65-; vis prof, Univ Stockholm, 77-79 & 85-88, Waseda Univ, 70-73, Univ Hawaii, 92. **MEMBERSHIPS** Am Polit Sci Asn; Int Polit Sci Asn; Asn E Asian Studies; Asn Polit Sci NA; Los Angeles-Guangzhan Sister City Asn; Japan Soc S Calif; US-China Peoples Friendship Asn; Comt US-China Rel. **RESEARCH** Reintegration of North and South Korea; Reintegration Taiwan and Mainland China; Relations among Korea, Japan, China, and the US; Multiethnic and Transnational Studies. **CONTACT ADDRESS** Dept of Political Science, US. Carolina, VKC 327, Los Angeles, CA, 90089-0044. **EMAIL** totten@usc.edu

TOULOUSE, MARK G.
PERSONAL Born 02/01/1952, Des Moines, IA, m, 1976, 3 children **DISCIPLINE** AMERICAN RELIGIOUS HISTORY **EDUCATION** Howard Payne Univ, BA, 74; Southwestern Baptist Theol Sem, MDiv, 77; Univ Chicago, PhD, 84. **CAREER** Instr, relig stud, Ill Benedictine Col, 80-82, asst prof, 82-84; asst prof of hist, Phillips Univ Grad Sem, 84-86; asst prof, Brite Divinity Sch, Texas Chr Univ,86-89, assoc prof, 89-91, assoc dean, 91-94, prof, 94- . **HONORS AND AWARDS** Henry Luce III Fel, 97-98; Who's Who in Relig, 89-90, 92-93; Men of Achievement, 93; Who's Who in Am Educ, 96-97. **MEMBERSHIPS** Am Acad Relig; Am Soc of Church Hist; Disciples of Christ Hist Soc. **RESEARCH** American theology; American religion and culture; history of Christian Church (Disciples of Christ). **SELECTED PUBLICATIONS** Auth, The Christian Century and American Public Life: The Crucial Years,1956-1968, in New Dimensions in Modern American Religious History, 93; auth, A Case Study: Christianity Today and American Public Life, in J of Church and State, 93; auth, W.A. Criswell, in Dictionary of Baptists in America, 94; auth, The Braunschweiger-Bibfeldts: the Metaphysical Incarnation of Wo/Man, in The Unrelieved Paradox, 94; auth, The Christian Church (Disciples of Christ), in Encyclopedia Americana, 94; auth, What is the Role of a Denomination in a Post-Denominational Age, in Lexington Theol Q, 94; auth, Sojourners, in Popular Religious Magazines of the United States, 95; auth, several entries in Encylopedia of Religious Controversies in the United States, 97; auth, The Problem and Promise of Denominational History, in Discipliana, 97; auth, Joined in Discipleship: The Shaping of Contemporary Disciples Identity, Chalice, rev ed, 97; coed, Makers of Christian Theology in America, Abingdon, 97. **CONTACT ADDRESS** Brite Divinity School, Texas Christian Univ, TCU Box 298130, Fort Worth, TX, 76129. **EMAIL** M.Toulouse@tcu.edu

TOUMAZOU, MICHAEL K.
PERSONAL Born 12/11/1952, Famagusta, Cyprus, m, 1978, 3 children **DISCIPLINE** CLASSICS **EDUCATION** Marshall Col, BA, 77; Loyola Univ Chicago, MA, 80; Bryn Mawr Col, MA, 83, PhD, 87. **CAREER** Asst prof, classics, 87-93, ASSOC PROF CLASSICS, 93-, DEPT CHAIR, 95-, DAVIDSON COL. **HONORS AND AWARDS** Whiting Fnd fel, 86-87; NEH senior fel, 1994-95; Trustee of Cyprus Am Archeol Res Inst, 96-. **MEMBERSHIPS** Archeol Inst Am; Am Schs Oriental Res; Soc Promotion Hellenic Stud; Classical Asn Midwest & South; NC Class Asn. **RESEARCH** Classl & Cypriote Archeol **SELECTED PUBLICATIONS** Articles in Zeitsmrift fur Papyrologie und Epigraphic, 41, 81, Am J Archeol, 91-99, Bulletin de Correspondence Hellenique, J Field Archeol 25, 98; auth, Aspects of Burial Practices in Prehistoric Cypriote Site, c. 7,000-25,000 B.C., Univ Mich, 87. **CONTACT ADDRESS** Dept of Classics, Davidson Col, Davidson, NC, 28036. **EMAIL** mitoumazou@davidson.edu

TOUPIN, ROBERT
PERSONAL Born 02/05/1924, Montreal, PQ, Canada **DISCIPLINE** MODERN HISTORY **EDUCATION** Univ Montreal, BA, 52; Immaculate-Conception Col, Montreal, LPh, 53, LTh, 60; Univ Toronto, MA, 56; Sorbonne, DUniv(hist), 65. **CAREER** From lectr to asst prof, 61-69, ASSOC PROF HIST, LAURENTIAN UNIV, 69-, Dir and ed-in-chief, Laurentian Univ Rev, 73-77 and 79- **MEMBERSHIPS** Asn Int des Docteurs de l'Univ Paris; Renaissance Soc Am; Soc d'etudes de la Renaissance. **RESEARCH** Relations between church and state in France in late 16th century; documents relating to the Jesuits in New France in the 18th century; French society and intellectual life. **SELECTED PUBLICATIONS** Ed, Correspondance du nonce en France G B Castelli, 1581-1583, Pontif Gregorian Univ and DeBoccard, Paris, 67; The Prairie in New France 1647-1760, Histoire Sociale-Soc Hist, Vol 26, 93; co-ed, Correspondance du nonce en France A M Salviati, t II 1574-1578, Pontif Gregorian Univ, Rome, 75. **CONTACT ADDRESS** Dept of Hist, Laurentian Univ, 935 Ramsey Lake Rd, Sudbury, ON, P3E 2C6.

TOVELL, ROSEMARIE
PERSONAL Lima, Peru **DISCIPLINE** ART HISTORY **EDUCATION** Queen's Univ, BA, 68; Univ Toronto, MA, 72. **CAREER** Cur asst, 72-73, asst cur, 73-82, CURATOR, PRINTS DRAWINGS, NAT GALLERY CAN, 82-. **MEMBERSHIPS** Print Coun Am; Can Eskimo Arts Coun. **SELECTED PUBLICATIONS** Auth, Reflections in a Quiet Pool: The Prints of David Milne, 80; auth, Berczy, 91; auth, A New Class of Art: the Artist's Print in Canadian Art, 1877-1920, 96; coauth, An Engraver's Pilgrimage: James Smillie Jr. in Quebec 1821-1830, 89. **CONTACT ADDRESS** National Gallery of Canada, 380 Sussex Dr, Ottawa, ON, K1N 9N4.

TOWNSEND, GAVIN
PERSONAL Born 06/16/1956, Santa Monica, CA, m, 1981, 1 child **DISCIPLINE** ART HISTORY **EDUCATION** Hamilton Col, Clinton, NY, BA, 78; Univ CA, Santa Barbara, MA, 81, PhD, 86. **CAREER** Asst prof, 86-92, assoc prof of Art, UTC, 92-; dir, Univ Honors Prog, Univ TN at Chattanooga, 97-. **HONORS AND AWARDS** Outstanding Prof Award, Student Govt Asn, UTC; Samuel Kress Found Fel. **MEMBERSHIPS** Soc of Am Architectural Historians. **RESEARCH** Architectural hist. **SELECTED PUBLICATIONS** Auth, The Tudor Houses of the Prairie School, Arris, 3, 92; Helmut Jahn, for the 20th Century Supplement to the Encyclopedia of World Biography, Jack Heraty & Assoc, 94; Frank Forster and the French Provincial Revival in America, Arris, 6, 95; Max von Pettenkofer, The Macmillan Dictionary of Art, Macmillan, 96; Lamb and Rich, and Kirby, Petit and Green, in Robert MacKay, ed, Long Island Country Estates and Their Architects, 1860-1940, Norton, 97; several other publications. **CONTACT ADDRESS** Dept of Art, Univ of Tennessee, Chattanooga, Chattanooga, TN, 37403. **EMAIL** Gavin-Townsend@vtc.edu

TOWNSEND, RICHARD
DISCIPLINE HISTORY OF ART **EDUCATION** Univ New Mex, BA, 64; Univ of the Amer, Mex City, MA, 66; Harvard Univ, PhD, 75. **CAREER** Instr, art hist, Univ Neb, 67-69; asst prof, art hist, Univ Tex Austin, 74-79; cur, dept of African and Amerindian Arts, Art Inst of Chicago, 82-. **HONORS AND AWARDS** Fulbright, 64-65; Grand Prize Fel, Harvard, 67-75. **RESEARCH** Pre-Columbian fields, especially the Aztecs; West Mexico; The United States southwestern peoples. **SELECTED PUBLICATIONS** Ed, The Ancient Americas: Art from Sacred Landscapes, Landscape and Symbol, The Renewal of Nature at the Temple of Tlaloc, Art Inst of Chicago, 92; auth, The Aztecs, Thames and Hudson, 91; auth, Sacred Geography, Sacred Lakes, Encycl of World Relig, MacMilland and Co, 86; auth, Coronation at Tenochtitlan, The Aztec Templo Mayor, Dumbarton Oaks Ctr for Pre-Columbian Studies, 86; auth, Deciphering the Nazca World: Ceramics Images from Ancient Peru, Mus Studies, Art Inst and the Univ of Chicago Press, 85; auth, The Art of Tribes and Early Kingdoms: Selections from Chicago Collections, Art Inst of Chicago, 84; auth, Pyramid and Sacred Mountain, Ethnoastronomy and Archaeoastronomy in the American Tropics, NY Acad of Sic, v 385, 82; auth, Malinalco and the Lords of Tenochtitlan, The Art and Iconography of Late Post-Classic Central Mexico, Dumbarton Oaks Ctr for Pre-Columbian Studies, 82; auth, State and Cosmos in the Art of Tenochtitlan, Dumbarton Oaks Ctr for Pre-Columbian Studies, 79. **CONTACT ADDRESS** Dept of African and Amerindian Arts, Art Inst of Chicago, 111 S. Michigan Av., Chicago, IL, 60603. **EMAIL** rtownsend@artic.edu

TRACE, JACQUELINE BRUCH
PERSONAL Buffalo, NY, 2 children **DISCIPLINE** RENAISSANCE LITERATURE, HISTORY OF BUFFALO **EDUCATION** Bowling Green State Univ, BA, 57; OH Univ, MA, 59; Univ MA, PhD, 75. **CAREER** Prof lit, State Univ NY Fredonia, 78; dealer in bks. **MEMBERSHIPS** AAUW **RESEARCH** Historical influence on Shakespearean drama; the rhetoric of technical and business commun; parapsychological lit. **SELECTED PUBLICATIONS** Auth, The supernatural element in Barbour's Bruce, Mass Studies English, spring 68; Shakespeare's bastard Faulconbridge: An early Tudor hero, Shakespeare Studies Vol XIII, 80; Style and Strategy of the Business Letter, Prentice-Hall, 85; Dark Goddesses: Black Feminist Theology in Morrisons Beloved, Obsidian II, no 3, 91. **CONTACT ADDRESS** SUNY at Fredonia, Fredonia, NY, 14063-1143. **EMAIL** traceja@buffalostate.edu

TRACEY, DONALD RICHARD
PERSONAL Born 01/24/1932, Baltimore, MD, m, 1962, 2 children **DISCIPLINE** MODERN EUROPEAN HISTORY **EDUCATION** Univ Md, BA, 54, MA, 62, PhD(hist), 67. **CAREER** From instr to asst prof hist, Temple Univ, 65-72; assoc prof and chmn dept hist and polit sci, 72-77, PROF HIST, ILL COL, 77- **MEMBERSHIPS** Conf Group Cent Europ Hist. **RESEARCH** Modern European history; German history. **SELECTED PUBLICATIONS** Auth, Reform in the Early Weimar Republic: The Thuringian Example, J Mod Hist, 6/72; Development of National Socialist Party in Thuringia, Cent Europ Hist, 3/75; Target Hitler in The Plots To Kill Hitler, Historian, Vol 55, 93. **CONTACT ADDRESS** Dept of Hist and Polit Sci, Illinois Col, Jacksonville, IL, 62650.

TRACHTENBERG, ALAN
PERSONAL Born 03/22/1932, Philadelphia, PA, m, 1952, 3 children **DISCIPLINE** ENGLISH, AMERICAN STUDIES **EDUCATION** Temple Univ, AB, 54; Univ Minn, PhD(Am studies), 62. **CAREER** Instr English, Gen Col, Univ Minn, Minneapolis, 56-61; from instr to assoc prof, Pa State Univ, University Park, 61-69; assoc prof, 69-71, PROF AM STUDIES and ENGLISH, YALE UNIV, 72-, CHMN DEPT AM STUDIES, 80-, Am Coun Learned Soc grant-in-aid, 64-65, study fel, 68-69; fel, Ctr Adv Studies Behav Sci, 68-69. **MEMBERSHIPS** MLA; Am Studies Asn. **RESEARCH** American literature; American cultural history. **SELECTED PUBLICATIONS** Auth, The Park and the People--A Hist of Central-Park, Am Hist Rev, Vol 98, 93; Mystic Chords of Memory--The Transformation of Tradition in American Culture, Am Hist Rev, Vol 98, 93; Land of Desire--Merchants, Power, and the Rise of a New American Culture, Am Hist Rev, Vol 100, 95; Morris, Wright Photo-Texts, Yale J Criticism, Vol 9, 96; The Lasting of the Mohicans--Hist of an American Myth, J Am Hist, Vol 84, 97; Seeing and Believing--Hawthorne Reflections on the Daguerrotype in the 'House of the Seven Gables,' Am Lit Hist, Vol 9, 97; Wild West Shows and the Images of American-Indians, 1883-1933, J Am Hist, Vol 84, 97; Dressing in Feathers--The Construction of the Indian in American Popular-Culture, J Am Hist, Vol 84, 97. **CONTACT ADDRESS** Am Studies Prog, Yale Univ, P O Box 208302, New Haven, CT, 06520-8302.

TRACHTENBERG, MARC
PERSONAL Born 02/09/1946, New York, NY, m, 1973, 1 child **DISCIPLINE** HISTORY **EDUCATION** Univ Calif, Berkeley, AB, 66, MA, 67, PhD(hist), 74. **CAREER** Asst prof, 74-80, ASSOC PROF HIST, UNIV PA, 80-, Social Sci Res Coun res training fel econ, 77-78. **MEMBERSHIPS** AHA; Societe d'Histoire Moderne. **RESEARCH** International politics 1914 to present. **SELECTED PUBLICATIONS** Auth, Etienne Clementel and French Economic Diplomacy During the First World War, French Hist Studies, 77; The Origins of United States Nuclear Strategy, 1945-1953, J Am Hist, Vol 81, 94; The Arming of Europe and the Making of the First-World-War, J Modern Hist, Vol 69, 97. **CONTACT ADDRESS** Dept of Hist, Univ Pa, Philadelphia, PA, 19174.

TRACY, JAMES
PERSONAL Born 02/14/1938, St. Louis, MO, m, 1997, 3 children **DISCIPLINE** HISTORY **EDUCATION** St. Louis Univ, BA, 59; Johns Hopkins Univ, MA, 60; Notre Dame, MA, 61; Princeton Univ, PhD, 67. **CAREER** From instr to prof, Univ Minn, 66- . **HONORS AND AWARDS** Fel, Netherlands Inst for Advanc Stud, 93-94. **MEMBERSHIPS** Am Hist Asn; Am Cath Hist Asn; Soc for Reformation Res; Sixteenth Century Stud Conf. **RESEARCH** Sixteenth century Europe; Low Countries; Europeans overseas. **SELECTED PUBLICATIONS** Co-ed, Handbook of European History in the Late Middle Ages, Renaissance and Reformation, 2 v, Brill, 93-94; auth, Studies in Eighteenth Century Mughal and Ottoman Trade, J of the Econ and Soc Hist of the Orient, 94; auth, Lords, Peasants, and The Beginnings of Calvanist Preaching in Holland's Noorderkwartier, in Thorpe, ed, Politics, Religion and Diplomacy in Early Modern Europe: Essays in Honor of De La Mar Jensen, St Louis, 94; auth, Erasmus among the Post-Modernists: Dissimulatio, Bonae Literae, and Docta Pietas Revisited, in Pagel, ed, Erasmus' Vision of the Church, St. Louis, 95; auth, Lineration through the Philosophia Christi: Erasmus as a Reformer of Doctrine, Luther Jahrbuch, 95; auth, Erasmus of the Low Countries, California, 96; auth, Die Civitates in der Christlicher Rewchtsordnung bei Erasmus von Rotterdam, in Blickle, ed, Theorien Kommunaler Ordnung, Munich, 96; auth, Erasmus, Coornhert, and the Acceptance of Religious Disunity in the Body Politic: A Low Countries Tradition? in Berkvens-Stevelink, ed, The Emergence of Tolerance in the Dutch Republic, Leiden, 97. **CONTACT ADDRESS** History Dept, Univ of Minnesota, 614 Social Sciences, Minneapolis, MN, 55455. **EMAIL** tracy001@tc.umn.edu

TRACY, PATRICIA JUNEAU
PERSONAL Born 03/09/1947, Hartford, CT, m, 1969 **DISCIPLINE** AMERICAN HISTORY **EDUCATION** Smith Col, BA, 69; Univ Mass, Amherst, PhD, 77. **CAREER** ASST PROF TO PROF AM HIST, WILLIAMS COL, 78-. **RESEARCH** Social hist of colonial New England; cross cultural family hist; gender. **SELECTED PUBLICATIONS** Auth, Jonathan Edwards, Pastor: Religion and Society in 18th Century Northampton, Hill & Wang, 80. **CONTACT ADDRESS** Dept of Hist, Williams Col, Stetson Hall, Williamstown, MA, 01267-2600. **EMAIL** patricia.j.tracy@williams.edu

TRAFZER, CLIFFORD EARL
PERSONAL Born 03/01/1949, Mansfield, OH **DISCIPLINE** AMERICAN INDIAN AND AMERICAN HISTORY **EDUCATION** Northern Ariz Univ, BA, 70, MA, 71; Okla State Univ, PhD(hist), 73. **CAREER** Archivist, Northern Ariz Univ Libr, 70-71; mus cur, Ariz Hist Soc, 73-76; instr Am Indian hist, Navajo Community Col, 76-77; asst prof Am Indian hist, 77-82, ASSOC PROF AM HIST, WASH STATE UNIV, 82- **MEMBERSHIPS** Western Hist Asn; Am Indian Hist Soc; Orgn Am Historians. **RESEARCH** American Indian history; the South-

west and the Columbia Plateau. **SELECTED PUBLICATIONS** Auth, Indian Country, Los-Angeles--Maintaining Ethnic-Community in Complex Society, J Calif Hist, Vol 71, 92; Earth, Animals, and Acads, Plateau Indian Communities, Culture, and the Walla-Walla-Council of 1855, Am Indian Cult Res J, Vol 17, 93; A Time of Gathering--Native Heritage in Washington-State, Mont- Mag Western Hist, Vol 43, 93; Always Getting Ready, Upterrlainarluta--Yupik Eskimo Subsistence in Southwest Alaska, Western Hist Quart, Vol 25, 94; Once They Moved Like the Wind--Cochise, Geronimo, and the Apache Wars, J Am Hist, Vol 81, 94; Native-American Dance--Ceremonies and Social Traditions--Heth,C, Am Indian Cult Res J, Vol 18, 94; Chiefs, Agents and Soldiers--Conflict on the Navajo Frontier, 1868-1882, Am Hist Rev, Vol 100, 95; Nchi-Wana the Big River--Mid-Columbia Indians and Their Land, Am Indian Cult Res J, Vol 19, 95; Magic in the Mountains, the Yakima Shaman--Power and Practice, Pacific Northwest Quart, Vol 86, 95; The Campo Indian Landfill War--The Fight for Gold in California Garbage, J Am Hist, Vol 83, 96; Invisible Enemies--Ranching, Farming, and Quechan Indian Deaths at the Fort-Yuma Agency, California, 1915-1925, Am Indian Cult Res J, Vol 21, 97. **CONTACT ADDRESS** Native Am Prog Dept of Hist, Wash State Univ, Pullman, WA, 99163.

TRAILL, DAVID ANGUS
PERSONAL Born 01/28/1942, Helensburgh, Scotland **DISCIPLINE** LATIN, GREEK **EDUCATION** Univ St Andrews, MA, 64; Univ Calif, Berkeley, PhD(classics), 71. **CAREER** Asst prof, 70-78, ASSOC PROF CLASSICS, UNIV CALIF, DAVIS, 78- **MEMBERSHIPS** Am Philol Asn; Medieval Asn Pac; Am Inst Archaeol. **RESEARCH** Classical and medieval Latin poetry; Schliemann. **SELECTED PUBLICATIONS** Auth, Ovid, 'Tristia' 2.8, 2.296, and 2.507--Happier Solutions, Hermes-Zeitschrift Fur Klassische Philologie, Vol 120, 92; The Text of Catullus 64.24, Class Philol, Vol 87, 92; The Text of Catullus 64.24, Class Philol, Vol 87, 92; Frazer,J.G.--His Life and Work, Class J, Vol 87, 92; Between Scylla and Charybdis at 'Aeneid' 3.684-86--A Smoother Passage, Am J Philology, Vol 114, 93; Horace 'Carmen 1,30'--Glyceras Problem, Class Philol, Vol 88, 93; Horace 'Carmen 1,30'--Glyceras Problem, Class Philol, Vol 88, 93; Propertius 'Elegy Book-1, Number-21'--The Sister, The Bones, and The Wayfarer, Am J Philology, Vol 115, 94; Troia--Bridge Between East and West, Am J Archaeol, Vol 98, 94; The Spoken Language of Orazio, Class World, Vol 90, 97. **CONTACT ADDRESS** Dept Classics, Univ of Calif, Davis, CA, 95616.

TRANI, EUGENE PAUL
PERSONAL Born 11/02/1939, Brooklyn, NY, m, 1962, 2 children **DISCIPLINE** AMERICAN HISTORY **EDUCATION** Univ Notre Dame, BA, 61; Ind Univ, MA, 63, PhD(hist), 66. **CAREER** Instr hist, Ohio State Univ, 65-67; from asst prof to prof hist, Southern Ill Univ, Carbondale, 67-76; prof and vpres acad affairs, Univ Nebr-Lincoln, 76-80; PROF HIST and VCHANCELLOR ACAD AFFAIRS, UNIV MO-KANSAS CITY, 80-, Southern Ill Univ Off Res and Proj grant, 67-69 and 70-72; vis res assoc, Papers of Woodrow Wilson, Princeton Univ, 69-70; Nat Endowment for Humanities younger humanist award, 72-73; Woodrow Wilson Int Ctr Scholars fel, 72-73; Lilly Endowment fel, 75-76. **HONORS AND AWARDS** Sr Fulbright lectr, Moscow State Univ, USSR, 81. **MEMBERSHIPS** AHA; Orgn Am Historians; Am Asn Advan Slavic Studies; Soc Historians Am Foreign Rels; Coun Foreign Rels. **RESEARCH** American diplomatic history; recent American history. **SELECTED PUBLICATIONS** Auth, Notes for Charles Sawyer's Concerns of a Conservative Democrat, Southern Ill Univ, 68; Russia in 1905: The View from the American Embassy, Rev Politics, 69; The Treaty of Portsmouth: An Adventure in American Diplomacy, Univ Ky, 69; Woodrow Wilson, China, and the Missionaries, 1913-1921, J Presby Hist, 71; The foreign policy of Nebraska, Washington Quart, summer 80; The United States in the Pacific in Private Interests and Public Policies, 1784-1899, Int Hist Rev, Vol 18, 96; coauth, The American YMCA and the Russian Revolution, Slavic Rev, 74; auth, The Secretaries of the Department of the Interior, 1849-1969, Smithsonian Inst, 75; Woodrow Wilson and the Decision to Intervene in Russia: A Reconsideration, J Mod Hist, 76; The Presidency of Warren G Harding, Regents P, 77. **CONTACT ADDRESS** Office of VChancellor, Univ of Mo, Kansas City, MO, 64110.

TRAPP-DUKES, ROSA LEE
PERSONAL Born 12/19/1942, Bishopville, South Carolina, m **DISCIPLINE** EDUCATION **EDUCATION** Madonna Coll, BA 1965; Univ of MI, EdS 1970; E MI, MA 1969; Univ of MI, PhD 1973. **CAREER** Univ of MI, teacher, training coord, lecturer 1970-71; Natl Inst Mental Health, dept of HEW fellow 1971-72; Dept of HEW, soc sci res analyst 1972-74; Howard Univ Center for Study of Handicapped Children & Youth, dir 1978-81; DC Parent Child Center, exec dir 1981-82; Howard Univ, assoc prof. **HONORS AND AWARDS** Participant DHEW Fellowship Prgm 1971-72; Awarded $100,000 Title I Preschool Eval Contract DC Pub Sch 1975-76; elected Outstanding Young Women of AmerPrgm 1976; publ "Cognitive & Perceptual Devel in Low SES Minority Urban Children, Preschool Prgm Impact" Abstracts Soc for Res in Child Devel 1977; Awarded approx $300,000 by USDOE Office of Sp Ed for Interdisciplinary Model for Parent and Child Training Project IMPACT 1978-81. **MEMBERSHIPS** Mem bd dir Dist Hghts Youth Club 1975; mem Soc for Res in Child Dev 1976-77; mem adv bd Early & Periodic Screening Diag & Treatment Prog Natl Child Day Care Assn 1976-77; consult Natl Educ in res proposal & prgm devel; sr collaborator Inst for Child Devel & Family Life; vice pres for Health Aff Howard Univ; 3 year mem bd dir Day Care & Child Devel Coun of Amer; mem Soc for Res in Child Devel; Natl Assn for Educ of Young Children; Amer Ed Res Assn; Natl Coun for Black Child Devel. **CONTACT ADDRESS** Sch of Ed, Howard Univ, 2400 Sixth St, Washington, VT, 20059.

TRASK, DAVID F.
PERSONAL Born 05/15/1929, Erie, PA, m, 1965 **DISCIPLINE** AMERICAN HISTORY **EDUCATION** Wesleyan Univ, BA, 51; Harvard Univ, AM, 52, PhD, 58. **CAREER** Instr polit econ, Boston Univ, 56-58; from instr to assoc prof hist, Wesleyan Univ, 58-62; from asst prof to assoc prof, Univ Nebr, Lincoln, 62-66; from assoc prof to prof hist, State Univ NY Stony Brook, 66-76, chmn dept, 69-74; dir, Off Historian, Dept State, Washington, DC, 76-81; CHIEF HISTORIAN, US ARMY CTR MIL HIST, WASHINGTON, DC, 81-, Dir, NDEA Inst, 65; mem, Nat Hist Publ and Rec Comn, 76-81 and Senate Hist Off Adv Comt, 77-78. **MEMBERSHIPS** AHA; Orgn Am Historians; Soc Historians of Am Foreign Rel; Soc Hist Fed Govt; Nat Coun Pub Hist. **RESEARCH** Recent American history; American diplomatic history; American military history. **SELECTED PUBLICATIONS** Auth, General Tasker Howard Bliss and the Sessions of the World, 1919, Am Philos Soc, 66; Victory Without Peace: American Foreign Relations in the Twentieth Century--World War I at Home: Readings on American Life 1914-1920, 70, Wiley; Captains and Cabinets: Anglo-American Naval Relations 1917-1918, Univ Mo, 72; The War with Spain in 1898, Macmillan, 81; The Spanish-American War--Conflict in the Caribbean and the Pacific, 1895-1902,, Int Hist Rev, Vol 17, 95; Trial By Friendship--Anglo-American Relations, 1917-1918, J Mil Hist, Vol 57, 93; coauth, A Bibliography for the Study of United States-Latin American Relations Since 1810, Univ Nebr, 68; The Unfinished Century: America Since 1900, 73 and The Ordeal of World Power: American Diplomacy Since 1900, 75, Little, Brown. **CONTACT ADDRESS** 3223B Sutton Pl NW, Washington, DC, 20016.

TRASK, KERRY A.
PERSONAL Born 10/17/1941, Orillia, ON, Canada, d, 2 children **DISCIPLINE** HISTORY **EDUCATION** Hamline Univ, St. Paul, MN, BA (Hist, cum laude), 65; Univ MN, MA (Hist), 68, PhD (Hist), 71. **CAREER** ASST, ASSOC, PROF, UNIV WI COLLEGES, STATIONED AT UNIV WI, MANITOWOC, 72-. **HONORS AND AWARDS** Teacher of the Year, Univ WI, Manitowoc, 76; Coun for WI Writers, Leslie Cross Book-Length Nonfiction Award, 96; State Hist Soc of WI Distinguished Service to History Book Award of Merit; WI Library Asn Literary Award of Outstanding Achievement by a WI Author, 96. **MEMBERSHIPS** Am Soc Ethnohistory; Inst of Early Am Hist and Culture; State Hist Soc of WI. **RESEARCH** Ethnohistory of the early Great Lakes region; Colonial Am; early WI and the Am Civil War. **SELECTED PUBLICATIONS** Auth, In the Pursuit of Shadows: Massachusetts, Millelialism, and the Seven Years War, Garland Pub, Inc, 89; Fire Within: A Civil War Narrative From Wisconsin, Kent State Univ Press, 95; I Have Been Brave But Wicked-Pray For Me, Voyageur, spring/summer, 98; numerous articles published before 90, and many book reviews for MI Hist Rev, Ethnohistory, William and Mary Quart, Voyageur, and The Old Northwest. **CONTACT ADDRESS** Univ Wis, Manitowoc, 705 Viebauh St., Manitowoc, WI, 54220. **EMAIL** ktrask@uwc.edu

TRASK, ROGER R.
PERSONAL Born 09/14/1930, Erie, PA, m, 1956, 3 children **DISCIPLINE** AMERICAN HISTORY **EDUCATION** Thiel Col, BA, 52; Pa State Univ, MA, 54, PhD(hist), 59. **CAREER** From instr to asst prof hist, Upsala Col, 59-62; asst prof, Thiel Col, 62-64; from asst prof to prof US hist, Macalester Col, 64-74; PROF US HIST, UNIV S FLA, 74-, Vis lectr US diplomatic hist, Univ Ill, Champaign, 67-68; chief historian, US Nuclear Regulatory Comn, 77-78. **MEMBERSHIPS** AHA; Orgn Am Historians; Soc Historians Am Foreign Rels. **RESEARCH** United States diplomatic history, 20th century; Turkish-American relations; United States-Latin American relations. **SELECTED PUBLICATIONS** Auth, the United States and Turkish Nationalism: investments and Technical Aid During the Ataturk Era, Bus Hist Rev, spring 64; Joseph C Grew and Turco-American Rapprochement, 1927-1932--Studies on Asia 1967, Univ Nebr, 67; The United States Response to Turkish Nationalism and Reform, 1914-1939, Univ Minn, 71; The Impact of the Cold War on United States-Latin American Relations, 1945-1949, Diplomatic Hist, Summer 77; Film and Media Revs in Recent Videos on Columbus and the Discovery of America, Pub Hist, Vol 14, 92; Foreign Relations of the United States, 1958-1960, Vol 6, J Am Hist, Vol 79, 93; contribr, Latin Am Scholarship Since World War II, Univ Nebr, 71; co-ed, The Gilded Age and After, Scribner, 72; A Bibliography of United States-Latin American Relations Since 1810, 68, Univ Nebr; Selected Readings in Am Hist (2 Vols), Scribner, 69. **CONTACT ADDRESS** Dept of Hist, Univ of SFla, Tampa, FL, 33620.

TRATTNER, WALTER IRWIN
PERSONAL Born 07/26/1936, New York, NY, m, 1958, 3 children **DISCIPLINE** AMERICAN HISTORY **EDUCATION** Williams Col, AB, 58; Harvard Univ, AMT, 59; Univ Wis, MS, 61, PhD, 64. **CAREER** Teaching asst, Univ Wis, 60-62, res asst, 62-63; asst prof hist, Northern Ill Univ, 63-65; asst prof hist, 65-67, assoc prof hist and social welfare, 67-71, PROF HIST, UNIV WISMIL WAUKEE, 71-, Dept Health, Educ and Welfare grant, 68-69. **HONORS AND AWARDS** Outstanding Educator of Am, Outstanding Educr Am, 71 and 75. **MEMBERSHIPS** Nat Conf Social Welfare; AHA; Orgn Am Historians; Social Welfare Hist Group. **RESEARCH** American social history; history of social welfare in America; recent American history. **SELECTED PUBLICATIONS** Auth, In the Web of Class--Delinquents and Reformers in Boston, 1810s-1930s, J Am Hist, Vol 79, 93; Brutal Need--Lawyers and the Welfare Rights Movement, 1960-1973, Am Hist Rev, Vol 100, 95; Safety Net--Welfare and Social-Security, 1929-1979, Am Hist Rev, Vol 102, 97. **CONTACT ADDRESS** 4719 N Elkhart Ave, Milwaukee, WI, 53211.

TRAUPMAN, JOHN CHARLES
PERSONAL Born 01/02/1923, Nazareth, PA, m, 1949, 1 child **DISCIPLINE** CLASSICAL LANGUAGES **EDUCATION** Moravian Col, BA, 48; Princeton Univ, MA, 51, PhD(classics), 56. **CAREER** From instr to assoc prof, 51-61, Prof Classics, 61-89, chemn 57-89, St Joseph's Univ; Assoc ed, Scribner Bantam English Dictionary, 77. **HONORS AND AWARDS** Magna cum laude, 48; Schulze Greek Award, 48; Robbins Scholar, Princeton Univ, 50-51; Faculty Merit Award for Research, 82; St Joseph's Univ Col Tchg Award, 86; Award of the Class Asn of the Atlantic States, 90; Special Award of the Class Asn of the Atlantic States, 96. **MEMBERSHIPS** Am Philol Asn; Archaeol Inst Am; Am Class League. **RESEARCH** Archaeology; Latin lexicography. **SELECTED PUBLICATIONS** Auth, New Collegiate Latin and English Dictionary, Bantam, 66, rev ed, 95; The New College Latin and English Dictionary, Amsco 68; ed, German-English Dictionary, Bantam, 82; auth, latin is Fun,, book I, Amsco, 88, book II, Amsco, 94; assoc ed, Scribner English Dictionary, Scribner, 77; auth, German Fundamentals, Barron's, 92; auth, Conversational latin for Oral Proficiency, 2d ed, Bolchazy-Carducci, 97; auth, Lingua Latina, book I, Amsco, 98. **CONTACT ADDRESS** Dept of Classics, St. Joseph's Univ, Philadelphia, PA, 19131. **EMAIL** traupman@sju.edu

TRAUTMANN, THOMAS ROGER
PERSONAL Born 05/27/1940, Madison, WI, m, 1962, 2 children **DISCIPLINE** HISTORY OF ANCIENT INDIA **EDUCATION** Beloit Col, BA, 62; Univ London, PhD(hist), 68. **CAREER** Lectr early hist S Asia, Sch Orient & African Studies, Univ London, 65-68; from asst prof to assoc prof, 68-77, prof hist, Univ Mich, Ann Arbor, 77-. **MEMBERSHIPS** Am Orient Soc; fel Royal Asiatic Soc; Asn Asian Studies. **RESEARCH** Kinship and marriage; statecraft. **SELECTED PUBLICATIONS** Auth, Length of generation and reign in ancient India, J Am Orient Soc, 69; Kautilya and the Arthasastra, Brill, 71; Hinduism, In: Man and His Gods, Grosset, 71; Licchavi-dauhitra, J Royal Asiatic Soc, 72. **CONTACT ADDRESS** Dept Hist, Univ Mich, 435 S State St, Ann Arbor, MI, 48109-1003.

TREADGOLD, DONALD WARREN
PERSONAL Born 11/24/1922, Silverton, OR, m, 1947, 3 children **DISCIPLINE** RUSSIAN HISTORY **EDUCATION** Univ Ore, AB, 43; Harvard Univ, AM, 47; Oxford Univ, DPhil, 50. **CAREER** From asst prof to assoc prof, 49-59, chmn dept, 72-82, PROF HIST, UNIV WASH, 59-, Ford Found fel, Harvard Univ, 54-55; chmn region XIV, Wilson Fel Found, 57-60; vis prof, Taiwan Univ, 59; consult, Ford Found, 60-61; mem, Joint Comt Slavic Studies, 60-64, chmn, 62-64; ed, Slavic Rev, 61-65 and 68-75; Guggenheim fel, 64-65; vis res prof, USSR Acad Sci, Inst Hist, Moscow, 65 and Toyo Bunko, Tokyo, 68; chmn, Conf Slavic and E Europ Hist, 66; chmn orgn comt, XIV Int Cong Hist Sci, 73; mem, Coun Nominating Comt, Phi Beta Kappa, 73-78, chmn, 77-78; mem acad coun, Kennan Inst Advan Russ Studies, 77-81; fac lectr, Univ Wash, 80; Rockefeller Found grant, 82; MEM BD TRUSTEES, NAT COUN SOVIET AND EAST EUROP RES, 77- **HONORS AND AWARDS** Harbison Distinguished Teaching Award, Danforth Found, 68; Distinguished Serv Award, Am Asn Advan Slavic Studies, 75. **MEMBERSHIPS** AHA; Am Asn Advan Slavic Studies (pres, 77-78); Asn Am Rhodes Scholars. **RESEARCH** Nineteenth and twentieth century Russia; modern China. **SELECTED PUBLICATIONS** Auth, Christianity Encounters With Nonwestern Cultures in A Brief Commentary on Missionary Interactions Globally from the Apostle Paul to the Present, J Relig Hist, Vol 17, 93; A Hist of the Peoples of Siberia--Russia North Asian Colony, 1581-1990, Russian Hist-Histoire Russe, Vol 20, 93; New Perspectives in Modern Russian Hist--Selected Papers from the 4th World Congress for Soviet and East European Studies, Harrogate, 1990, Slavic Rev, Vol 52, 93; No Religion Higher Than Truth--A History of the Theosophical Movement in Russia, 1876-1922, Am Hist Rev, Vol 99, 94; Science in Russia and the Soviet-Union--A Short Hist, Slavic Rev, Vol 53, 94. **CONTACT ADDRESS** Dept of Hist, Univ of Wash, Seattle, WA, 98195.

TREADGOLD, WARREN
PERSONAL Born 04/30/1949, Oxford, England, m, 1982 **DISCIPLINE** HISTORY, CLASSICS **EDUCATION** Harvard Univ, AB, 70, PhD, 77. **CAREER** Lectr, UCLA, 77-78; Humboldt res fel, Univ Munich, 78-80; Mellon fel, Stanford Univ, 80-82; Humboldt res fel, Free Univ Berlin, 82-83; asst prof, Hillsdale Col, 83-88; asst prof to prof, Fla Int Univ, 88-97; PROF, SAINT LOUIS UNIV, 97-; Phi Beta Kappa, 70; Dumbarton Oaks Jr fel, 75-77; NEH fel, 87 & 96-97; Wilbur Found fel, 89; vis fel All Souls Col, 89; Earhart Found fel, 92-93. **HONORS AND AWARDS** Woodrow Wilson Int Ctr Scholars. **MEMBERSHIPS** Am Philol Asn; Am Hist Asn; Medieval Acad Am; US Nat Comm Byzantine Stud; Am Asn Univ Prof. **RESEARCH** Byzantine and late ancient history and literature. **SELECTED PUBLICATIONS** Auth The Nature of the Bibliotheca of Photius, Wash DC, 80; The Byzantine State Finances in the Eighth and Ninth Centuries, NY, 82; ed Renaissances Before the Renaissance: Cultural Revivals of Late Antiquity and the Middle Ages, Stanford, 84; auth The Byzantine Revival, 780-842, Stanford, 88; Byzantium and Its Army, 284-1081, Stanford, 95; A History of the Byzantine State and Society, Stanford, 97. **CONTACT ADDRESS** Dept of History, St Louis Univ, 3800 Lindell Blvd, PO Box 56907, St. Louis, MO, 63156-0907.

TREADWAY, JOHN DAVID
PERSONAL Born 06/30/1950, San Bernardino, CA, m, 1976, 1 child **DISCIPLINE** HISTORY **EDUCATION** Fla State Univ, BA, 72; Univ Va, PhD(hist), 80. **CAREER** From asst to assoc prof, 80-98, prof hist, 98- , Univ Richmond. **HONORS AND AWARDS** Fulbright fel, 85, 90; Woodrow Wilson Ctr, 89; Virginia Outstanding Faculty Award, 93; Univ Richmond Distinguished Educator Award, 85, 88, 91, 95; vis Fulbright res prof, Univ Belgrade, 90. **MEMBERSHIPS** Am Hist Asn; Am Asn for the Advanc of Slavic Stud; N Am Soc for Serbian Stud; Soc for Austrian and Habsburg hist; Southeast European Stud. **RESEARCH** Central and Eastern Europe; Yugoslavia. **SELECTED PUBLICATIONS** Auth, The Falcon and the Eagle: Montenegro and Austria-Hungary, 1908-1914, Purdue Univ Press, 83; co-ed, The Soviet Union under Gorbachev: Assessing the First Year, Praeger, 87. **CONTACT ADDRESS** History Dept, Univ of Richmond, Richmond, VA. **EMAIL** jtreadwa@richmond.edu

TRECKEL, PAULA ANN
PERSONAL Born 03/15/1953, Youngstown, OH, m, 1980 **DISCIPLINE** COLONIAL AMERICAN HISTORY **EDUCATION** Kent State Univ, BA, 73; Syracuse Univ, MA, 76, PhD(Am studies), 78. **CAREER** Asst prof hist, Col St Benedict, 78-81; ASST PROF HIST, ALLEGHENY COL, 81-, Consult, American Women Writers Prog, Ungar Publ Co, Inc, 79-81. **MEMBERSHIPS** Orgn Am Historians. **RESEARCH** Women and families on the colonial American frontier; women and medicine in Early America; Ida Tarbell and the age of reform. **SELECTED PUBLICATIONS** Auth, Subjects of Slavery, Agents of Change--Women and Power in Gothic Novels and Slave Narratives, 1790-1865, J Southern Hist, Vol 60, 94; Wilderness at Dawn--the Settling of the North-American Continent, J Southern Hist, Vol 60, 94; Barton, Clara--In the Service of Humanity, J Southern Hist, Vol 62, 96; A Social-Hist of Wet Nursing in America--From Breast to Bottle, J Interdis Hist, Vol 28, 97. **CONTACT ADDRESS** Dept of Hist, Allegheny Col, Box 131, Meadville, PA, 16355.

TREDWAY, JOHN THOMAS
PERSONAL Born 09/04/1935, North Tonawanda, NY, m, 1950, 2 children **DISCIPLINE** CHURCH & INTELLECTUAL HISTORY **EDUCATION** Augustana Col, BA, 57; Univ Ill, MA, 58; Garrett Theol Sem, BD, 61; Northwestern Univ, PhD, 64. **CAREER** From asst prof to prof hist, 64-75, dean col, 70-75, pres, 75-, Augustana Col, Ill; vis prof, Waterloo Lutheran Sem, 67-68; chmn, Nat Lutheran-Methodist Theol Dialogs, 77-. **MEMBERSHIPS** Am Soc Church Historians; AHA. **RESEARCH** Nineteenth century American and British church history; modern European intellectual history. **SELECTED PUBLICATIONS** Auth, Newman: Patristics, ecumenics and liberalism, Christian Century, 65; co-ed, The Immigration of Ideas, Augustana Hist Soc, 68. **CONTACT ADDRESS** Augustana Col, Rock Island, IL, 61201.

TREFOUSSE, HANS L.
PERSONAL Born 12/18/1921, Frankfurt, Germany, m, 1947, 1 child **DISCIPLINE** HISTORY **EDUCATION** City Col NY, BA, 42; Columbia Univ, MA, 47, PhD(hist), 50. **CAREER** Instr hist, Hunter Col, 47-48; instr, Adelphi Col, 49-50; from instr to assoc prof, 50-65, PROF HIST, BROOKLYN COL, 66-, Mem grants-in-aid selection comt, Am Coun Learned Soc, 62-64; PROF HIST, GRAD CTR, CITY UNIV NY, 64-; ASSOC, SEM AM CIVILIZATION, COLUMBIA UNIV, 68-; Guggenheim fel, 77-78. **MEMBERSHIPS** AHA; Orgn Am Historians; Southern Hist Asn. **RESEARCH** American history; Civil War and Reconstruction; international relations. **SELECTED PUBLICATIONS** Auth, The Spirit of 1848--German Immigrants, Labor Conflict, and the Coming of the Civil-War, Revs Am Hist, Vol 21, 93; Let Us Have Peace--Grant, Ulysses S. and the Politics of War and Reconstruction, 1861-1868, J Southern Hist, Vol 59, 93; The Culture of Sentiment--Race, Gender, and Sentimentality in 19th-Century America, Historian, Vol 56, 94; The Papers of Johnson, Andrew, Vol 10--February-July 1866, Civil War Hist, Vol 40, 94; The Jewel of Liberty--Lincoln,Abraham Re-Election and the End of Slavery, J Southern Hist, Vol 62, 96; The Capture of New Orleans, 1862, Civil War Hist, Vol 42, 96; The Papers of Johnson,andrew, Vol 11, August 1866 January 1867, Civil War Hist, Vol 42, 96; The Federal Impeachment Process--A Constitutional and Historical-Analysis, Am Hist Rev, Vol 102, 97; State of Rebellion--Reconstruction in South-Carolina, J Am Hist, Vol 84, 97; Lincoln,Abraham--From Skeptic to Prophet, Civil War Hist, Vol 43, 97. **CONTACT ADDRESS** Dept of Hist, Brooklyn Col, CUNY, 2901 Bedford Ave, Brooklyn, NY, 11210-2813.

TREGGIARI, SUSAN M.
DISCIPLINE CLASSICS **EDUCATION** BA, 62; MA, 65; BLitt, 67; Oxford Univ, DLitt, 93. **CAREER** Anne T. and Robert M. Bass Prof Schl Hum and Sci; prof class/hist. **RESEARCH** Roman hist; Roman soc in the late Republic and Principate; lit, epigraphic and juristic sources. **SELECTED PUBLICATIONS** Auth, Roman Freedmen During the Late Republic, 69; Roman Marriage: Iusti Coniuges from the Time of Cicero to the Time of Ulpian, 91; Social Status And Social Legislation in the Cambridge Ancient History X, 96. **CONTACT ADDRESS** Stanford Univ, Bldg 20, Main Quad, Stanford, CA, 94305.

TREHUB, ARNOLD
PERSONAL Born 10/19/1923, Malden, MA, m, 1950, 3 children **DISCIPLINE** PSYCHOLOGY **EDUCATION** Boston Univ, PhD, 54. **CAREER** Res pyschol, dir of res, VA Medical Center, Northampton, Ma, 54-82; ADJUNCT PROF OF PSYCHOL, UNIV OF MASS AT AMHERST, 71-. **MEMBERSHIPS** Soc for Neuroscience; NY Acad of Sci; AAAS. **RESEARCH** Brain mechanisms of cognition. **SELECTED PUBLICATIONS** Auth, The Cognitive Brain, MIT Press, 91. **CONTACT ADDRESS** Dept of Psychology, Univ of Mass at Amherst, Amherst, MA, 01003. **EMAIL** trehub@psych.umass.edu

TRELEASE, ALLEN WILLIAM
PERSONAL Born 01/31/1928, Boulder, CO, 2 children **DISCIPLINE** HISTORY **EDUCATION** Univ IL, AB, 50, MA, 51; Harvard Univ, PhD(hist), 55. **CAREER** Teaching fel, Harvard Univ, 53-55; from instr to prof hist, Wells Col, 55-67, acting dean fac, 62-63, dept head, 63-67; head dept, 84-92, prof Hist, Univ NC, Grennsboro, 67-94, RETIRED 94. **HONORS AND AWARDS** Charles S Sydnor Award, Southern Hist Asn, 72. **MEMBERSHIPS** AHA; Orgn Am Historians; Southern Hist Asn. **RESEARCH** American history; Southern history; Civil War and Reconstruction periods. **SELECTED PUBLICATIONS** Auth, Indian Affairs in Colonial New York: The 17th Century, Cornell Univ, 60; The Iroquois and the Western fur trade, Miss Valley Hist Rev, 6/62; Who were the scalawags?, J Southern Hist, 11/63; contribr, Attitudes of Colonial Powers Toward the American Indian, Univ Utah, 69; auth, White Terror: The Ku Klux Klan Conspiracy and Southern Reconstruction, 71 & Reconstruction: The Great Experiment, 71, Harper & Row; Republican Reconstruction in North Carolina, J Southern Hist, 8/76; The Fusion Legislatures of 1895 and 1897: A roll-call analysis of the North Carolina House of Representatives, NC Hist Rev, 7/80; The North Carolina Railroad, 1849-1871, and theModernization of North Carolina, Univ NC Press, 91; Changing Assignments: A Pictorial History of the University of North Carolina, Univ NC G, 91. **CONTACT ADDRESS** 307 Kirk Rd, Greensboro, NC, 27455.

TRENN, THADDEUS JOSEPH
PERSONAL Born 01/16/1937, Chicago, IL, m, 1969, 1 child **DISCIPLINE** HISTORY AND PHILOSOPHY OF SCIENCE **EDUCATION** St Mary's Col, Minn, BA, 59; Univ Notre Dame, MS, 61 and MA, 62; Univ Wis-Madison, PhD(hist of sci), 72. **CAREER** Instr philos, Univ Santa Clara, Calif, 64-65; asst prof, St Norbert Col, 65-69; tutor hist of sci, Cambridge Univ, 70-71; res assoc, Max-Planck Inst, Ger, 71-73; prof hist sci, Univ Regensburg, West Ger, 73-79; RES ASSOC, MAX PLANCK INST FUR PHYSIK, MUNICH, 79- **HONORS AND AWARDS** American Oxonian, 68; Kurschners Deutscher Gelehrten-Kalender, 77. **MEMBERSHIPS** Sigma Xi; Philos Sci Asn; Am Philos Asn; Hist Sci Soc; NY Acad Sci. **RESEARCH** History of modern experimental physical science; science and public policy; scientific method. **SELECTED PUBLICATIONS** Auth, Brooks,Harriet--Pioneer Nuclear Scientist, Annals Sci, Vol 0050, 1993 **CONTACT ADDRESS** Max-Planck Inst fur Physik, Fohringer Ring 6 8000 Munich 40.

TRENNERT, ROBERT ANTHONY
PERSONAL Born 12/15/1937, South Gate, CA, m, 1965, 2 children **DISCIPLINE** AMERICAN HISTORY **EDUCATION** Occidental Col, BA, 61; Los Angeles State Col, MA, 63; Univ Calif, Santa Barbara, PhD(hist), 69. **CAREER** From instr to asst prof hist, Temple Univ, 67-74; asst prof, 74-76, assoc prof, 76-81, PROF HIST, ARIZ STATE UNIV, 81-. **MEMBERSHIPS** Western Hist Asn; Orgn Am Historians; Westerners Int. **RESEARCH** American Indian policy; American Indian education; popular images of the American Indian. **SELECTED PUBLICATIONS** Auth, Exploring the Hohokam--Prehistoric Desert Peoples of the Southwest, Jour West, Vol 0032, 93; Desert Lawmen--the High Sheriffs of New-Mexico and Arizona, 1846-1912, Southwestern Hist Quart, Vol 0097, 93; A Spirited Resistance--the North-American Indian Struggle for Unity, 1745-1815, Historian, Vol 0055, 93; American-Indian Children at School, 1850-1930, Pacific Hist Rev, Vol 0063, 94; Anasazi Places--the Photographic Vision of Current, William, Jour West, Vol 0034, 95; A Friend to Gods Poor--Smith, Edward, Parmalee, West Hist Quart, Vol 0026, 95; Indians and a Changing Frontier--the Art of George Winter, Jour Amer Hist, Vol 0081, 94; Untitled--Reply, Amer Hist Rev, Vol 0100, 95; Apache Reservation--Indigenous Peoples and the American State, Amer Hist Rev, Vol 0100, 95; Islands in the Desert--A History of the Uplands of Southwestern Arizona, New Mexico Hist Rev, Vol 0071, 96; The Federal-Government and Indian Health in the Southwest--Tuberculosis and the Phoenix-East-Farm-Sanatorium, 1909-1955, Pacific Hist Rev, Vol 0065, 96; Living in the Shadow of Death--Tuberculosis and the Social Experience of Illness in American History, Pacific Hist Rev, Vol 0065, 96; Disease and Class--Tuberculosis and the Shaping of Modern North-American Society, Jour Amer Hist, Vol 0083, 96; Parading Through History--the Making of the Crow Nation in America, 1805-1935, Montana-Mag West Hist, Vol 0047, 97. **CONTACT ADDRESS** Dept of Hist, Arizona State Univ, Tempe, Tempe, AZ, 85281.

TREXLER, RICHARD C.
DISCIPLINE HISTORY **EDUCATION** Baylor Univ, AB; Johan Goethe Univ, Frankfurt, PhD, 64. **CAREER** Asst prof, UTEP, 64-6; asst prof, Occidental Col, 66-68; assoc prof, Univ Ill, Champaign-Urbana, 70-78; PROF, 78-, DISTING PROF, 95-, SUNY, BINGHAMTON. **SELECTED PUBLICATIONS** Auth, A Saint in the Family--Religious Vocation and Social Resistance in Medieval Latin Hagiography--Italian, Amer Hist Rev, Vol 0098, 93; Madonnas That Maim--Popular Catholicism in Italy Since the 15th-Century, Jour Interdisciplinary Hist, Vol 0025, 94; The Evolution of Womens Asylums Since 1500--From Refuges for Exprostitutes to Shelters for Battered Women, Jour Soc Hist, Vol 0028, 94; Death and Ritual in Renaissance Florence 1992, Soc Hist, Vol 0019, 94; Law, Family, and Women--Toward a Legal Anthropology of Renaissance Italy, Speculum-Jour Medieval Stud, Vol 0069, 94; A New-World in a Small Place--Church and Religion in the Diocese of Rieti, 1188-1378, Cath Hist Rev, Vol 0081, 95; Francis-of-Assisi, His Mothers Son--Defense of the Authors Radical Interpretation of Francis Renunciation, Studi Medievali, Vol 0036, 95; Mary--Virgin, Mother, Our Lady--German, Speculum-Jour Medieval Stud, Vol 0071, 96; Thread of Blood--Colonialism, Revolution, and Gender on Mexico Northern Frontier, Jour Amer Hist, Vol 0083, 96; The Elect Nation--the Savonarolan Movement in Florence, 1494-1545, Amer Hist Rev, Vol 0101, 96; Ceremonies of Possession in Europes Conquest of the New-World, 1492-1640, Jour Soc Hist, Vol 0030, 97. **CONTACT ADDRESS** Dept of History, SUNY, Binghamton, Binghamton, NY, 13902-6000. **EMAIL** trexler@binghamton.edu

TRIBE, IVAN MATHEWS
PERSONAL Born 05/01/1940, Albany, OH, m, 1966 **DISCIPLINE** AMERICAN HISTORY **EDUCATION** Ohio Univ, BSEd, 62, MA, 66; Univ Toledo, PhD(hist), 76. **CAREER** Lectr, 76-77, asst prof history, Rio Grande Col, 77-84, assoc prof, 84-90, prof, 90-, Fel, Berea Col Appalachian Studies, 80. **MEMBERSHIPS** AHA; Orgn Am Historians. **RESEARCH** Appalachian culture; industrial communities; Ohio and Midwest. **SELECTED PUBLICATIONS** Auth, Rise and Decline of Private Academies in Albany, Ohio, Ohio Hist, 69; coauth, Molly O'Day and the Cumberland Mountain Folks, John Edwards Memorial Found, Univ Calif, Los Angeles, 75; auth, West Virginia Country Music During the Golden Age of Radio, Goldenseal, 77; Dream and Reality in Southern Ohio: The Development of the Columbus and Hocking Railroad, The Old Northwest, 78; Songs of the Silver Bridge, Goldenseal, 79; co-ed, An Encyclopedia of East Tennessee, Children's Mus Oak Ridge, 81; Mountaineer Jamboree: Country Music in West Virginia, Lexington: Univ Press of Kentucky, 84; The Stonemans: An Appalachian Family and the Music That Shared Their Lives, Univ of Illinois Press, 93; co-auth, Definitive Country: The Ultimate Encyclopediaof Country Music and Its Performers, Penguin Books, 95. **CONTACT ADDRESS** Dept of Hist, Univ of Rio Grande, Rio Grande, OH, 45674-9999.

TRISCO, ROBERT FREDERICK
PERSONAL Born 11/11/1929, Chicago, IL, s **DISCIPLINE** HISTORY & RELIGION **EDUCATION** St. Mary of the Lake Seminary, BA, 51; Pontifical Gregorian Univ, STL, 55, Hist. Eccl.D, 62. **CAREER** INST, 59-63, ASST PROF, 63-65, ASSOC PROF, 65-75, PROF, 75-96, VICE-RECTOR FOR ACADEMIC AFFAIRS, 66-68, CHEMN, DEPT OF CHURCH HIST, 75-78, PROF, DEPT OF CHURCH HIST, THE CATHOLIC UNIV OF AM, 76-. **HONORS AND AWARDS** Honorary degree, Doctor of Humane Letters, Belmont Abbey Col, 92; Honorary Prelate of His Holiness (Monsignor), 92. **MEMBERSHIPS** Am Catholic Hist Asn; Am Soc of Church Hist; Pontifical Commt for Hist Sci. **RESEARCH** History of the Catholic Church in the United States. **SELECTED PUBLICATIONS** Ed, The Catholic Hist Rev, 63-. **CONTACT ADDRESS** Cath-

olic Univ of America, Curley Hall, Washington, DC, 20064. **EMAIL** TRISCO@cua.edu

TROLANDER, JUDITH ANN
PERSONAL Born 05/31/1942, Minneapolis, MN **DISCIPLINE** AMERICAN HISTORY **EDUCATION** Univ Minn, BA, 64; Case Western Reserve Univ, MSLS, 66, MA, 69, PhD(hist), 72. **CAREER** Lectr US hist, Cleveland State Univ, spring, 71; instr, Univ Akron, summer, 71; asst prof, Western Ill Univ, 71-75; from assoc prof to prof US Hist, Univ Minn, Duluth, 75-, Dir, Northeast Minn Hist Ctr, 76-87. **MEMBERSHIPS** Orgn Am Historians; Social Welfare Hist Group. **RESEARCH** Social history in the United States. **SELECTED PUBLICATIONS** Auth, Twenty years at Hiram House, Ohio Hist, winter 69; The response of settlements to the Great Depression, Social Work, 9/73; Settlement Houses and the Great Depression, Wayne State Univ Press, 75; Anna Lane Lingelbach, 77, Lavinia Lloyd Dock, 80, Lillie Peck, 80 & Emily Greene Balch, 81, In: Dict of American Biography; Social action: Settlement houses and Saul Alinsky, 1939-65, Social Serv Rev, 9/82; Fighting Racism and Sexism: The Council on Social Work Education, Social Service Review, March, 97. **CONTACT ADDRESS** Dept of History, Univ of Minnesota, 10 University Dr, Duluth, MN, 55812-2496. **EMAIL** jtroland@d.umn.edu

TRONZO, WILLIAM
DISCIPLINE MEDIEVAL ART, EARLY CHRISTIAN AND BYZANTINE ART **EDUCATION** Haverford Col, BA, 73; Harvard Univ, PhD, 82. **CAREER** Instr, Dumbarton Oaks and Am Univ, 82-84; Johns Hopkins, 84-90; Duke Univ, 92-96; Williams Col, 96-97; Tulane Univ, 97-. **HONORS AND AWARDS** Robert Woods Bliss fel, Dumbarton Oaks, 75-76; Arthur Lehman fel, Harvard, 76-77; Rome prize fel, 76-77; 1977-79, Copeland fel, Amherst Col, 96-97. **SELECTED PUBLICATIONS** Auth, The Prestige of St. Peters. Observations on the Function of Monumental Narrative Cycles in Italy, Stud Hist of Art of the Nat Gallery of Art, 16, 85; The Medieval Object-Enigma, and the Problem of the Cappella Palatina in Palermo, Word & Image, 9, 93; Mimesis in Byzantium: Notes Towards a History of the Function of the Image, RES: Jour Anthrop and Aesthet, 25, 94; I grandi cicli pittorici romani e la loro influenza, La Pittura in Italia: L'Altomedioevo, Milan, 94. **CONTACT ADDRESS** Dept of Art, Tulane Univ, 6823 St Charles Ave, New Orleans, LA, 70118. **EMAIL** wtronzo@mailhost.tcs.tulane.edu

TROY, NANCY J.
DISCIPLINE MODERN ART **EDUCATION** Yale Univ, PhD. **CAREER** Prof, Univ Southern Calif; past ed-in-ch and bd mem, Art Bull; organizes, Getty Res Institute's Work in Progress lect ser. **RESEARCH** Relationship between art, theater & haute couture fashion in early 20th-century France & America. **SELECTED PUBLICATIONS** Co-ed, Architecture and Cubism, MIT Press, 97. **CONTACT ADDRESS** Col Letters, Arts & Sciences, Univ Southern Calif, University Park Campus, Los Angeles, CA, 90089.

TROY, VIRGINA GARDNER
PERSONAL Albuquerque, NM, m, 1990, 1 child **DISCIPLINE** ART HISTORY **EDUCATION** W Wa Univ, BA, 79; Univ Wa Seattle, MA, 86; Emery Univ, PhD, 97. **CAREER** Instr, 80-83, Bellevue Art Museum Sch; teaching asst, 84-86, Univ Wa; instr, 89-91, Brenau Univ; instr, 89-93, Art Inst Atlanta; instr, 89-93, Amer Col Applied Art; teaching asst to teaching assoc, 92-96, Emory Univ; adj faculty, 95-97, Atlanta Col Art; adj faculty, 97-98, N Ga Col & St Univ, Dahlonega; adj faculty, 89-98, Kennesaw St Univ Ga; asst prof, 98-, Berry Col. **HONORS AND AWARDS** Betty Park Award, 96,98; Berry Col Overseas Summer Res Grant, 99. **MEMBERSHIPS** Col Art Assoc; SE Col Art Assoc; Hist Central & E Europ Art. **RESEARCH** Bauhaus; Anni Albers; primitivism. **SELECTED PUBLICATIONS** Auth, Anni Albers at Black Mountain College, Mid-Atlantic Col Art Conf, 98; art, Anni Albers and the Andean Textile Paradigm, Artiest Dialogues-Resonances: Josef and Anni Albers, Kunstmuseum Bern, 98; art, The Great Weaver of Eternity: Dynamic Symmetry and Utopian Ideology in the Art and Writing of Mary Hambidge, Surface Design J, 99. **CONTACT ADDRESS** PO Box 6083, Rome, GA, 30162. **EMAIL** vtroy@berry.edu

TRUDEL, MARCEL
PERSONAL Born 05/29/1917, St-Narcisse de Champlain, Canada, m, 1942, 3 children **DISCIPLINE** HISTORY OF CANADA **EDUCATION** Seminaire des Trois-Rivieres, AB, 38; Laval Univ, L es L, 41, D es L, 45. **CAREER** Secy fac lett, Laval Univ, 52-55, dir hist inst, 55; dir inst Can Studies, Carleton Univ, Can 55-64; RES PROF HIST, UNIV OTTAWA, 65-, Speaker, French Can Inst Sorbonne; Poitiers, Genes, Messine. **MEMBERSHIPS** Inst Fr-Am Hist; Can Hist Asn (pres); Fr-Can Acad. **SELECTED PUBLICATIONS** Auth, The Explorers of North-America, 1492-1795--French, Rev Hist Amer Fr, Vol 0047, 94; The Testimonies of Canadian and Quebecois Historians--A Century and a Half After the Publication of the 1st Volume of L Histoire du Canada by Garneau, Francois,Xavier, Etudes Francaises, Vol 0030, 94. **CONTACT ADDRESS** 5 Dollard, Aylmer, PQ, J9H 1G1.

TRUMBACH, RANDOLPH
PERSONAL Born 12/06/1944, Belize, Honduras **DISCIPLINE** ENGLISH & EUROPEAN HISTORY **EDUCATION** Univ New Orleans, BA, 64; Johns Hopkins Univ, MA, 66, PhD(hist), 72. **CAREER** Intern hist, Univ Chicago, 69-71; asst prof, 73-78, assoc prof hist, 78-84, prof, 85-, Baruch Col & CUNY Grad School, CUNY res awards, 73-74, 77-80, & 85-86; Nat Endowment Humanities fel, 79. **MEMBERSHIPS** AHA; Am Soc 18th Century Studies; Soc Sci Hist Asn; Conf Brit Studies. **RESEARCH** English social history; the family, sex, religion. **SELECTED PUBLICATIONS** Auth, London's sodomites, J Social Hist, 9/77; The Rise of the Egalitarian Family, Acad Press, 78; Sex and the Gender Revolution Vol 1, Univ Chicago Press, 98. **CONTACT ADDRESS** Dept of History, Baruch Col, CUNY, 17 Lexington Ave, New York, NY, 10010-5518.

TRUMPENER, ULRICH
PERSONAL Born 03/24/1930, Berlin, Germany, m, 1954, 3 children **DISCIPLINE** MODERN EUROPEAN HISTORY **EDUCATION** Univ Ore, BA, 54; Univ Calif, Berkeley, MA, 57, PhD(hist), 60. **CAREER** Instr hist, Stanford Univ, 60-61; asst prof, Univ Iowa, 61-66; from asst prof to assoc prof, 66-71, PROF HIST, UNIV ALTA, 71-, Can Coun fel, 70-71, res grant, 74. **MEMBERSHIPS** AHA; Conf Group Cent Europ Hist; Can Hist Asn. **RESEARCH** Modern German history; military history; international relations. **SELECTED PUBLICATIONS** Auth, Pforzheim Code-Yellowfin--An Analysis of the Air Attacks 1944-1945--German, Ger Stud Rev, Vol 0016, 93; The National Question in Europe in Historical Context, Intl Hist Rev, Vol 0017, 95; Position as a Major Power and World-Politics--Foreign-Policy of Imperial Germany, 1870 until 1914-German, Intl Hist Rev, Vol 0017, 95; The Great-Powers, Imperialism, and the German Problem, 1865-1925, Intl Hist Rev, Vol 0018, 96. **CONTACT ADDRESS** Dept of Hist, Univ of Alta, Edmonton, AB, T6G 2E1.

TRUSS, RUTH SMITH
DISCIPLINE HISTORY **EDUCATION** Univ Ala, PhD, 92. **CAREER** ASST PROF HIST, UNIV MONTEVALLO, 98-. **CONTACT ADDRESS** Univ of Montevallo, Station 6180, Montevalle, AL, 35115. **EMAIL** trussr@um.montevallo.edu

TRUSTY, NORMAN LANCE
PERSONAL Born 09/26/1933, Ancon, Czechoslovakia, m, 1956, 2 children **DISCIPLINE** AMERICAN HISTORY **EDUCATION** Col William & Mary, AB, 56; Boston Univ, AM, 57, PhD, 64. **CAREER** Instr Hist, Ohio State Univ, 60-64; from asst prof to assoc prof, 64-77, chmn Dept Hist & Polit Sci, 67-74, prof Hist, Purdue Univ, Calumet Campus, 77-, dir, Regional Studies Inst, Purdue Univ, Calumet Campus. **MEMBERSHIPS** Orgn Am Historians. **RESEARCH** Antislavery: Revolutionary War; Northwest Indiana. **SELECTED PUBLICATIONS** Ed, Black America: A Bibliography, Purdue Univ, 76; auth, War by the book: the defense of Yorktown, IASS Proc, 77; contribr, Calumet region since 1930, In: The Calumet Region, Ind Hist Bur, 77. **CONTACT ADDRESS** Dept of History, Purdue Univ, Calumet, 2233 171st St, Hammond, IN, 46323-2094. **EMAIL** trustyl@aol.com

TRYMAN, MFANYA DONALD
PERSONAL Born 01/26/1948, Montclair, NJ, m **DISCIPLINE** POLITICAL SCIENCE **EDUCATION** Pasadena City Coll, AA Liberal Art 1969; CA State Polytechnic Univ, BS Political Science 1971; FL State Univ, MA 1972, MSPA 1974, PhD 1975. **CAREER** TX Southern Univ, assoc prof 1975-81; Univ of Houston, prof 1981-82; Jackson State Univ, assoc prof 1981-85, dir MPPA program 1981-; PRAIRIE VIEW A&M UNIV, ASSOC PROF 1985-. **HONORS AND AWARDS** CA State Polytechnic Univ Magna Cum Laude 1971; Outstanding Black Sr Scholar Awd 1971; Outstanding Educator Legislative Black Caucus of TX Awd 1979; fellow, Dept of Labor & Howard Univ 1980; Scholar Spotlight on Scholars Awd 1983; Cert of Merit NASA Johnson Space Center 1986. **MEMBERSHIPS** Mem conf of minority Public Admin 1976-; mem Natl conf of Black Political Scientists 1976-; natl campaign adv St Rep El Franco Lee 1978; bd mem advbd Congressman Mickey Leland 1978-80; voluntary boxing dir Hester House Comm Org 1979; vice pres Demographic Environs Rsch Inc 1980-85; project mgr Comm & Economic Develop Work Study Prog 1983-; dir Master of Public Policy & Admin Prog Jackson State Univ 1983-85; mem Natl Forum of Black Public Admins 1983-85, natl Conf of Black Studies 1985-87. **SELECTED PUBLICATIONS** 1 of over 40 articles & two books on Black Politics Affirmative Action Public Policy and Econ Devel in professional journals & mags. **CONTACT ADDRESS** Political Science, Prairie View A&M Univ, 14543 Leacrest Dr, Houston, TX, 77049.

TSAI, SHIH-SHAN HENRY
DISCIPLINE ASIAN STUDIES **EDUCATION** Nat Taiwan Normal Univ, BA, 62; Univ Ore, MA, 67, PhD, 70. **CAREER** Vis assoc prof, Nat Taiwan Univ, 70-71; vis assoc prof, Univ Calif, Los Angeles, 79; vis assoc prof, Univ Calif, Berkely, 81; PROF, DIR ASIAN STUDIES, UNIV ARK, 83-. **SELECTED PUBLICATIONS** Auth, Organizing Asian-American Labor--The Pacific Coast Canned-Salmon Industry, 1870-1942, Jour Amer Hist, Vol 0082, 95; Margins and Mainstreams--Asians in American History and Culture, Pacific Hist Rev, Vol 0064, 95; The Asian-American Movement, Pacific Hist Rev, Vol 0064, 95; In Search of Equality--The Chinese Struggle Against Discrimination in 19th-Century America, Pacific Hist Rev, Vol 0065, 96. **CONTACT ADDRESS** 2105 Austin Dr, Fayetteville, AR, 72703. **EMAIL** HTSAI@comp.uark.edu

TSIN, MICHAEL
DISCIPLINE CHINESE HISTORY **EDUCATION** Univf Essex, BA, 82; Princeton Univ, PhD, 91. **CAREER** Asst prof. **RESEARCH** Cultural history of revolution in twentieth-century China. **SELECTED PUBLICATIONS** Auth, Imagining Society' in Early Twentieth-Century China, The Idea of the Citizen, 97; Nation, Governance and Modernity in Early Twentieth-Century China. **CONTACT ADDRESS** Dept of Hist, Columbia Col, New York, 2960 Broadway, New York, NY, 10027-6902.

TSIRPANLIS, CONSTANTINE NICHOLAS
PERSONAL Born 03/18/1935, Cos, Greece **DISCIPLINE** HISTORY, PHILOSOPHY **EDUCATION** Greek Theol Sch Halki, Istanbul, Lic theol, 57; Harvard Univ, STM, 62; Columbia Univ, AM, 66; Fordham Univ, PhD(hist), 73. **CAREER** Instr mod Greek, NY Univ, 64-70; teacher classics and chmn dept, Collegiate Sch, NY, 67-69; instr mod Greek, New Sch Social Res, 68-70; res and writing, 70-72; adj prof world hist, NY Inst Technol, 72-75; ASSOC PROF CHURCH HIST and GREEK STUDIES, UNIFICATION THEOL SEM, 76-, Lectr class philol, Hunter Col, 66-67; lectr medieval and ancient hist, Mercy Col, 72; adj prof Western civilization, Delaware County Community Col, 75, Dutchess County Community Col, 76. **HONORS AND AWARDS** Nat Medal Greek Rebirth, Greek Govt, 72. **MEMBERSHIPS** NAm Acad Ecumenists; Am Soc Neo-Hellenic Studies (exec vpres, 67-69); Am Philol Asn; Medieval Acad Am; NAm Patristic Soc. **RESEARCH** Late Byzantine intellectual history and theology; early Byzantine theology and philosophy; Greek patristics. **SELECTED PUBLICATIONS** Auth, Photian Studies, Church Hist, Vol 0063, 94; Church, Nation and State in Russia and Ukraine, Church Hist, Vol 0066, 97; Heretics, Dissidents, Muslims and Jews in Byzantium, 12th-Century Heresiology-Italian, Church Hist, Vol 0066, 97. **CONTACT ADDRESS** Unification Theol Sem, 10 Dock Rd, Barrytown, NY, 12507.

TSUNODA, ELIZABETH
DISCIPLINE MODERN JAPAN **EDUCATION** Univ Ill, BA, 62, Columbia Univ, MA, 84, MPhil, 86; PhD, 93. **CAREER** Vis adj prof, NY Univ, 85-87; Vis adj prof, Smith Col, 87; Profeceptor, Columbia Univ, 91; Asst prof, Washington Univ, 93 **SELECTED PUBLICATIONS** Coed & contribr, Contemporary Japan: Teaching Workbook, Columbia Univ, 88. **CONTACT ADDRESS** Washington Univ, 1 Brookings Dr, St. Louis, MO, 63130.

TSURUMI, ELIZABETH PATRICIA
PERSONAL Born 02/19/1938, North Vancouver, BC, Canada **DISCIPLINE** JAPANESE HISTORY **EDUCATION** Univ BC, BA, 59; Tenri Univ, Nara Japan, cert Japanese lang, 61; Harvard Univ, AM, 66, PhD(hist and E Asian lang), 71. **CAREER** Asst prof hist, Univ Western Ont, 71-72; asst prof, 72-77, ASSOC PROF HIST, UNIV VICTORIA, 77-, Res assoc Japanese hist, EAsian Res Ctr, Harvard Univ, 74-75; Can Coun leave fel, 74-75; Japan Soc Prom Sci fel, 79; Soc Sci and Humanities Res Coun Can leave fel, 79-80. **HONORS AND AWARDS** Kyoto Nat Essay Prize foreign scholars, Int Cult Asn, Japan, 79. **MEMBERSHIPS** Can Soc Asian Studies; Comp and Int Educ Soc Can; Asn Asian Studies; BC Women's Studies Asn; Anarcho Inst. **RESEARCH** Japanese colonialism; Japanese education; history of Japanese women in a comparative focus. **SELECTED PUBLICATIONS** Auth, Office Ladies Factory Women--Life and Work at a Japanese Company, Labor Hist, Vol 0036, 95. **CONTACT ADDRESS** Dept of Hist, Univ of Victoria, Victoria, BC, V8W 2Y2.

TU, WEI-MING
PERSONAL Born 02/26/1940, Kunming, China, m, 1963, 1 child **DISCIPLINE** HISTORY, RELIGIOUS PHILOSOPHY **EDUCATION** Tunghai Univ, Taiwan, BA, 61; Harvard Univ, MA, 63, PhD(hist), 68. **CAREER** Vis lectr humanities, Tunghai Univ, Taiwan, 66-67; lectr EAsian studies, Princeton Univ, 67-68, asst prof, 68-71; from asst prof to assoc prof hist, Univ Calif, Berkeley, 71-77, prof, 77-81; PROF CHINESE HIST and PHILOS, HARVARD UNIV, 81-, Consult-panelist, Nat Endowment for Humanities, 75; Am Coun Learned Soc fel, 77; mem bd dirs, Chinese Cult Found San Francisco, 79- **MEMBERSHIPS** Asn Asian Studies; Soc Asian and Comp Philos; Am Acad Polit Sci. **RESEARCH** Chinese intellectual history; Confucianism in East Asia; religious philosophy. **SELECTED PUBLICATIONS** Auth, Introduction--Cultural Perspectives, Daedalus, Vol 0122, 93; Destructive Will and Ideological Holocaust--Maoism as a Source of Social Suffering in China, Daedalus, Vol 0125, 96. **CONTACT ADDRESS** Dept of EAsian Lang and Civilizations, Harvard Univ, Cambridge, MA, 02138.

TUCHER, ANDREA J.
DISCIPLINE HISTORY, JOURNALISM **EDUCATION** Princeton, AB, 76; Columbia, MSLS, 77; NewYork Univ, MA, 82, PhD, 90. **CAREER** Assoc ed, Columbia Jour Rev; adj prof Columbia Grad Sch of Journalism. **HONORS AND AWARDS** Allan Nevins Prize of the Soc of Amer Hist. **RESEARCH** Early American murder news. **SELECTED PUBLICATIONS** Fel Publ, Froth and Scum: Truth, Beauty, Goodness, and the Ax-Murder in America's First Mass Medium, Univ NC, 94; coauth, Moyers: Report from Philadelphia: The Constitutional Convention of 1787, Ballantine, 87; ed, Bill Moyers' World of Ideas II, Doubleday, 90. **EMAIL** andiet@earthlink.net

TUCK, DONALD RICHARD
PERSONAL Born 04/24/1935, Albany, NY, m, 1957, 2 children **DISCIPLINE** HISTORY OF RELIGIONS, ASIAN STUDIES **EDUCATION** Nyack Col, BS, 57; Wheaton Col, MA, 65; Univ Iowa, PhD(relig and cult), 70. **CAREER** Minister of youth, Presby Church, Ill, 63-65; interim minister, Methodist Church, Fed Church and United Church of Christ, Iowa, 65-69; teaching and res asst, Sch Relig, Univ Iowa, 67-68; from instr to assoc prof relig, 69-78, PROF RELIG, WESTERN KY UNIV, 78-, Fac res grant, Radhakrishnan and Tagore, 70; fac res grant, Tagore, 72; consult, Choice, 76-, Nat Endowment Humanities, 77- and South Asia in Rev, 78-; fac res grant, Santal Relig, 76 and soc aspects, Bhagavata, Purana, 78. **MEMBERSHIPS** Am Acad Relig; Asn Asian Studies. **RESEARCH** Religion and culture of Modern India; Sarvepalli Radhakrishnan and Rabindranath Tagore; Bengal Vaisnavism-Caitanya. **SELECTED PUBLICATIONS** Auth, Lacuna in Sankara Studies--A Thousand Teachings Upadesasahasri, Asian Philos, Vol 0006, 96. **CONTACT ADDRESS** Dept of Relig and Philos, Western Kentucky Univ, 1 Big Red Way St, Bowling Green, KY, 42101-3576.

TUCKER, BRUCE
DISCIPLINE HISTORY **EDUCATION** Univ Toronto, BA, 70, MA, 72; Brown Univ, PhD, 79. **CAREER** Assoc prof and dept ch; taught at, Dalhousie Univ; Univ Cincinnati and Univ Windsor; assoc ed, Can Rev of Amer Stud. **MEMBERSHIPS** Pres, Can Assn for Amer Stud. **RESEARCH** American cultural and intellectual history; urban history and historiography. **SELECTED PUBLICATIONS** Auth, Beyond Synthesis: The Problem of Coherence in American History, Can Rev Amer Stud 26, 96; The New American Intellectual History: A Review Essay, Can Rev Amer Stud, vol 22, 91; Oral History: An Interview with Virginia Rock, Can Rev Amer Hist 27, 97; The Politics of Culture in Provincial New England, Reviews in Amer Hist 25, 97;Oral History: An Interview with Robert Martin, Can Rev Amer Stud 26, 96; Oral History: An Interview with Bruce Daniels, Can Rev Amer Stud 25, 95 & Assessing the Field: An Oral History Interview, Can Rev Amer Stud 23, 92; coauth, Changing Plans for America's Inner Cities: Cincinnati's Over-the-Rhine and Twentieth-Century Urbanism, Ohio UP, 98; contrib, Roscoe Giffin and the First Cincinnati Workshop on Urban Appalachians, in Phillip Obermiller, Down Home, Downtown: Urban Appalachians Today, Dubuque, Iowa: Kendall/Hunt, 96; Michael T. Maloney, rep in Interviewing Appalachia, Knoxville: U of Tennessee P, 94 & Towards a New Ethnicity: Urban Appalachian Ethnic Consciousness in Cincinnati, 1950-1987, Ethnic Diversity and Civic Identity: Patterns of Conflict and Cohesion in Cincinnati Since the Nineteenth Century, Chicago and Urbana: U of Illinois P, 92. **CONTACT ADDRESS** Dept of History, Philosophy and Political Science, Univ of Windsor, 401 Sunset Ave, Windsor, ON, N9B 3P4. **EMAIL** history@uwindsor.ca

TUCKER, DAVID MILTON
PERSONAL Born 11/28/1937, Pottsville, AR, m, 1966, 2 children **DISCIPLINE** AMERICAN HISTORY **EDUCATION** Col Ozarks, BA, 59; OK State Univ, MA, 61; Univ IA, PhD(hist), 65. **CAREER** PROF HIST, MEMPHIS STATE UNIV, 65-. **MEMBERSHIPS** Orgn Am Historians; Am Hist Asn. **RESEARCH** Recent American history; African American history. **SELECTED PUBLICATIONS** Auth, Justice Horace Harmon Lurton: the Shaping of a National Progressive, Am J Legal Hist, 7/69; Black pride and Negro business in the 1920's, Bus Hist Rev, winter 69; Lieutenant Lee of Beale Street, Vanderbilt Univ, 71; Black Pastors and Leaders, Memphis State Univ, 75; Memphis Since Crump: Bossism, Blacks and Civic Reformers, Univ TN, 81; Arkansas: A People, Memphis State, 85; Decline of Thrift in America, Praeger, 90; Kitchen Gardening in America, IA State, 93; Mugwumps: Public Moralists of the Gilded Age, MO, 98. **CONTACT ADDRESS** Dept of Hist, Memphis State Univ, Memphis, TN, 38152-6120. **EMAIL** dtucker@cc.memphis.edu

TUCKER, LOUIS LEONARD
PERSONAL Born 12/06/1927, Rockville, CT, m, 1953, 2 children **DISCIPLINE** EARLY AMERICAN HISTORY **EDUCATION** Univ Wash, BA, 52, MA, 55, PhD, 57. **CAREER** Instr hist, Univ Calif, Davis, 57-58; instr, Col William and Mary, 58-60; dir, Cincinnati Hist Soc, 60-66; asst comnr state hist and state historian, State Educ Dept NY, 66-76; DIR, MASS HIST SOC, BOSTON, 77-, Fel hist, Inst Early Am Hist and Cult, Williamsburg, Va, 58-60; lectr, Univ Cincinnati, 60-65; Churchill fel, English Speaking Union, 69; adj prof, Boston Univ, 77-; Nat Archiv Adv Coun, 77- **MEMBERSHIPS** Am Asn State and Local Hist (pres, 72-74). **RESEARCH** Colonial American and New York State history. **SELECTED PUBLICATIONS** Auth, The New-York-Historical-Society--Lessons from One Nonprofits Long Struggle for Survival, NY Hist, Vol 0077, 96. **CONTACT ADDRESS** Massachusetts Historical Society, 1154 Boylston St, Boston, MA, 02215.

TUCKER, MARK
DISCIPLINE LIBRARY AND INFORMATION SCIENCE, HISTORY **EDUCATION** Lipscomb Univ, BA, 67; George Peabody Col Teach, Vanderbilt Univ, MLS, 68, EdS, 72; Univ Ill, Urbana-Champaign, PhD, 83. **CAREER** Head Librarian, Fred-Hardeman Univ, 68-71; ref librn, Wabash Col, 73-79; ref librn, Purdue Univ, 79-82; asst prof, libr sci, Purdue Univ, 79-85; sen ref librn, Purdue Univ, 82-90; assoc prof, libr sci, Purdue Univ, 85-89; PROF, LIBR SCI, 89-, HUM, SOC SCI, EDUC LIBRN, 90-, PURDUE UNIV. **RESEARCH** Hist, biog, related to librarianship and higher educ. **SELECTED PUBLICATIONS** Auth, Sabin, Joseph (6 Dec 1821-5 June 1991), Am Nat Biography, 18: 168-69, Oxford Univ Press, 99; auth, Work, Monroe Nathan (1866-1945), in Notable Black American Men, 1262-66, Gale Research, 98; auth, Wide Awakening: Political and Theological Impulses for Reading and Libraries at Oberlin College, 1883-1908, Univ Ill Occasional Papers, 207, 97; coauth, Change and Tradition in Land Grant University Libraries, in For the Good of the Order: Essays Written in Honor of Edward G. Holley, JAI Press, 94. **CONTACT ADDRESS** Hum, Soc Sci & Educ Libr, Purdue Univ, Stewart Ctr, West Lafayette, IN, 47907. **EMAIL** jmark@purdue.edu

TUCKER, MARY EVELYN
PERSONAL Born 06/24/1949, New York, NY, m, 1978 **DISCIPLINE** HISTORY, RELIGION **EDUCATION** Trinity Col, BA, 71; SUNY, Fredonia, MA, 72; Fordham Univ, MA, 77; Columbia Univ, PhD, 85. **CAREER** Lectr, Eng, Erie Commun Col, 72; lectr Eng, Notre Dame Seishin Univ, Japan, 73-75; lectr relig, Elizabeth Seton Col, 76-78; preceptor, Columbia Univ, 79-80, 83; asst prof hist, Iona Col, 84-89; assoc prof relig, Bucknell Univ, 89- . **HONORS AND AWARDS** Phi Beta Kappa; HEW fel, 71-72; NEH fel, 77; Columbia Pres fel, 80-81, 81-82; Japan Found fel, 83-84; Mellon fel, 85-86; Columbia Univ postdoctoral res fel, 87-88; Person of the Year Award, Bucknellian, 92; NEH Chair in the Hum, 93-96; sr fel, Center for the Study of World Relig, Harvard Univ, 95-96; Trinity Col Centennial Alumnae Award for Academic Excellence, 97; assoc in res, Reischauer Inst of Japanese Stud, Harvard Univ, 95-99. **MEMBERSHIPS** Neo-Confucian Stud, Columbia Univ. Regional Sem on Japan, Columbia Univ; Am Teilhard Asn; Environ Sabbath, UN Environ Prog; AAR; Asn Asian Stud; Soc for Values in Higher Educ; Asn for Relig and Intellectual Life. **SELECTED PUBLICATIONS** Auth, Moral and Spiritual Cultivation in Japanese Neo-Confucianism: The Life and Thought of Kaibara Ekken (1630-1714), SUNY, 89; coauth, Worldviews and Ecology, Bucknell Univ, 93; co-ed, Buddhism and Ecology: The Interaction of Dharma and Deeds, Harvard Univ, 97; co-ed, Confucianism and Ecology: The Interrelation of Heaven, Earth, and Humans, Harvard Univ, 98. **CONTACT ADDRESS** Dept of Religion, Bucknell Univ, Lewisburg, PA, 17837. **EMAIL** mtucker@bucknell.edu

TUCKER, MELVIN JAY
PERSONAL Born 03/03/1931, Easthampton, MA, m, 1953, 3 children **DISCIPLINE** HISTORY **EDUCATION** Univ Mass, BA, 53, MA, 54; Northwestern Univ, PhD, 62. **CAREER** Teaching asst, Northwestern Univ, 57-58; instr Europ hist, Colby Col, 59-60; instr hist, Mass Inst Technol, 60-63; asst prof, 63-66, ASSOC PROF HIST, STATE UNIV NY BUFFALO, 66-, DIR GRAD STUDIES, 79-, Fel, Medieval Sev, Ctr Medieval and Early Renaissance Studies, State Univ NY Binghampton, 70-77; contrib ed hist of childhood, J Psychohist, 73- **HONORS AND AWARDS** Certificate of Merit, Buffalo and Erie Co Hist Soc, 74. **MEMBERSHIPS** AHA; Conf Brit Studies; Asn Bibliog of Hist. **RESEARCH** Tudor-Stuart history; Late Medieval English and European history; history of childhood. **SELECTED PUBLICATIONS** Auth, The Paston Family in the 15th-Century--The 1st Phase, Speculum-Jour Medieval Stud, Vol 0068, 93. **CONTACT ADDRESS** 107 Willow Green Dr, Tonawanda, NY, 14150.

TUCKER, NANCY BERNKOPF
PERSONAL New York, NY, m **DISCIPLINE** HISTORY **EDUCATION** Hobart & William Smith Col, BA, 70; Columbia Univ, MA, 73, MAPhil, 76, PhD, 80. **CAREER** Asst Prof, 80-86, assoc prof, 86-87, Colgate Univ; assoc prof, 87-94, prof, 94-, Georgetown Univ. **RESEARCH** Amer foreign rel; Amer East Asian rel, esp rels with China, Taiwan, Hong Kong & Korea. **CONTACT ADDRESS** Dept of History, Georgetown Univ, Washington, DC, 20057-1058. **EMAIL** tuckern@gusun.gerogetown.edu

TUCKER, RICHARD PHILIP
PERSONAL Born 09/17/1938, Morristown, NJ **DISCIPLINE** MODERN ASIAN HISTORY **EDUCATION** Oberlin Col, AB, 60; Harvard Univ, MA, 61, PhD(hist), 66. **CAREER** Asst prof, 66-72, assoc prof, 72-82, PROF HIST, OAKLAND UNIV, 82-, Mem bd trustees, Am Inst Indian Studies, 68-71 and 76-83, fac fel, 69-70 and 80-82; Am Coun Learned Soc res grant, 69-70; mem, Nat Humanities Fac, 71-74, chmn, Maharashtra Study Group, 71-73. **MEMBERSHIPS** Asn Asian Studies; Soc Relig Higher Educ; Am Asn Advan Sci; Am Soc Environmental Hist; Forest Hist Soc. **RESEARCH** South Asian and comparative environmental history. **SELECTED PUBLICATIONS** Auth, Imperialism and Medicine in Bengal--A Sociohistorical Perspective, Jour Interdisciplinary Hist, Vol 0024, 94; Conservation of Neotropical Forests--Working from Traditional Resource Use, Americas, Vol 0051, 95; Human Impact on the Environment--Ancient Roots, Current Challenges, Jour Interdisciplinary Hist, Vol 0025, 95. **CONTACT ADDRESS** Dept of Hist, Oakland Univ, Rochester, MI, 48063.

TUCKER, ROBERT ASKEW
PERSONAL Born 03/23/1930, Atlanta, GA **DISCIPLINE** LATIN, GREEK **EDUCATION** Emory Univ, BBA, 51, MAT, 62; Johns Hopkins Univ, PhD(classics), 67. **CAREER** Teacher Latin, Cross Keys High Sch, DeKalb County, Ga, 62-65; asst prof classics, 67-72, ASSOC PROF CLASSICS, UNIV GA, 72-. **MEMBERSHIPS** Class Asn Mid W and S (secy-treas, 71-73); Am Philol Asn; Vergilian Soc Am; Am Archaeol Inst; Am Class League. **RESEARCH** Roman epic, especially Lucan. **SELECTED PUBLICATIONS** Auth, Vergil, Class Bulletin, Vol 0070, 94. **CONTACT ADDRESS** Dept of Classics, Univ of Georgia, Athens, GA, 30602.

TUCKER, SPENCER C.
DISCIPLINE HISTORY **EDUCATION** Va Mil Inst, BA, 59; Univ NC, hapel Hill, MA, 62; PhD, 66. **CAREER** John Biggs ch Mil Hist, Va Mil Inst, 97-; Fulbright fel, Univ Bordeaux, 59-60; capt, Army Intel, 65-67; prof, Tex Christian Univ, 67-97, ch hist dept, 92-97; vis res assoc, Smithsonian Inst, 69-70. **SELECTED PUBLICATIONS** Auth, Arming the Fleet: US Naval Ordnance in the Muzzle-Loading Era, Naval Inst Press, 89; The Jeffersonian Gunboat Navy, Univ SC Press, 93; Raphael Semmes and the Alabama, Ryan Place, 96; coauth, Injured Honor: The Chesapeake-Leopard Affair of June 22, 1807, Naval Inst Press, 96; The Great War, 1914-18, Univ Col London Press, 98; The Big Guns, Civil War Siege, Seacoast and Naval Cannon, Mus Restoration Serv, 98; ed, The European Powers in the First World War, An Encycl, Garland, 96. **CONTACT ADDRESS** Dept of History, Virginia Military Inst, Lexington, VA, 24450.

TUCKER, WILLIAM E.
PERSONAL Born 06/22/1932, Charlotte, NC, m, 1955, 3 children **DISCIPLINE** AMERICAN RELIGIOUS & CHURCH HISTORY **EDUCATION** Atlantic Christian Col, BA, 53, LLD, 78; Tex Christian Univ, BD, 56; Yale Univ, MA, 58, PhD(relig), 60. **CAREER** From assoc prof to prof relig & philos, Atlantic Christian Col, 59-66, chmn dept, 62-66; assoc prof church hist & asst dean, Brite Divinity Sch, Tex Christian Univ, 66-69, prof church hist, 69-76, assoc dean, 69-71, dean, 71-76; pres, Bethany Col, 76-79; chancellor, Tex Christian Univ, 79-98, trustee, Disciples of Christ Hist Soc, 69-; mem bd, Christian Church (Disciples of Christ), 71-, dir bd higher educ, 73-, chmn bd, 75-77; pres, Coun Southwestern Theol Schs, 75-76; vpres, WVa Found Independent Cols, 77-. **HONORS AND AWARDS** LLD, Atlantic Christian Col, 78; DHL, Chapman Col, 81; DHu, Bethany Col, 82. **RESEARCH** American church history since 1865; history and thought of the Christian Church (Disciples of Christ) and related religious groups; Fundamentalism and the Church in America. **SELECTED PUBLICATIONS** Auth, J H Garrison and Disciples of Christ, Bethany, 64; contribr, The Word We Preach, Tex Christian Univ, 70; Westminster Dictionary of Church History, Westminster, 71; Dictionary of American Biography, suppl 3, Scribner's, 73; coauth, Journey in Faith: A History of the Christian Church (Disciples of Christ), Bethany, 75; contribr, Encycl of Southern History, La State Univ Press, 79. **CONTACT ADDRESS** Chancellor Emeritus, Tex Christian Univ, PO Box 297080, Fort Worth, TX, 76129-0002.

TUCKER, WILLIAM F.
PERSONAL Born 04/27/1941, Whiteville, NC, m, 1967, 1 child **DISCIPLINE** HISTORY **EDUCATION** Univ NC Chapel Hill, AB, 64; Ind Univ, MA, 66, PhD, 71. **CAREER** Asst prof to assoc prof, 71-99, Univ Ark. **HONORS AND AWARDS** Fulbright-Hayes Faculty Res Abroad, 74-75., Dean's list **MEMBERSHIPS** Middle East Stud Assoc; Middle East Medievalists. **RESEARCH** Shiite Islam; ecological & soc hist; pre-modern Islamic world. **SELECTED PUBLICATIONS** Auth, Ibn Battuta, Abu Abd Allah Muhammad (1304-1377), Arab Traveler, The Discoverers: an Encyclopedia of Explorers and Exploration, McGraw Hill Co, 80; art, Abd Allah ibn Mauwiya and the Janahiyya: Rebels and Ideologues of the Late Umayyad Period, Studia Islamica, 80; contr, Charismatic Leadership and Shiite Sectarianism, Middle East and Islamic societies, Amana Books, 87; contr, The Emergence of Kurdish Nationalism and the Sheikh Said Rebellion, 1880-1925, Univ Tx Press, 89; art, Environmental Hazards, Natural Disasters, Economic Loss and Mortality in Mamiuk Syria, Mamluk Stud Rev, 99. **CONTACT ADDRESS** 108 Hartman Ave, Fayetteville, AR, 72701. **EMAIL** jtucker@comp.uark.edu

TULCHINSKY, GERALD J.J.
PERSONAL Born 09/09/1933, Brantford, ON, Canada **DISCIPLINE** HISTORY **EDUCATION** Univ Toronto, BA, 57; McGill Univ, MA, 60; Univ Toronto, PhD, 71. **CAREER** Lectr, Loyola Col (Montreal), 60-62; asst prof, Univ Sask, 65-66; asst prof, 66-73, assoc prof, 73-83, PROF HISTORY, QUEEN'S UNIV, 83-. **SELECTED PUBLICATIONS** Auth, River Barons: Montreal Business Men and Development of Industry and Transportation 1837-1953, 77; auth, Taking Root: The Origins of the Canadian Jewish Community, 92; ed, Immigration in Canada; To Preserve and Defend; contribur, Dictionary of Canadian Biography; contribur, Canadian Encyclopedia. **CONTACT ADDRESS** Dept of History, Queen's Univ, Kingston, ON, K7L 3N6.

TULIS, JEFFREY K.
PERSONAL Born 10/01/1950, Long Branch, NJ, m, 1998, 2 children **DISCIPLINE** POLITICAL SCIENCE **EDUCATION** Bates Col, BA, 72; Brown Univ, MA, 74; Univ Chicago, PhD, 82. **CAREER** Asst prof polit, Princeton Univ, 81-87; Asn prof of govt, Univ Tex at Austin, 88-. **HONORS AND AWARDS** Claire E Turner Award, Bates Col; Fellow, Am Coun of Learned Stud (pres); Asn Teaching Award; Phi Beta Kappa. **MEMBERSHIPS** Am Polit Sci Asn. **RESEARCH** American politics; Constitutional theory; political philosophy. **SELECTED PUBLICATIONS** Co-ed, The Presidency in the Constitutional Order, La State Univ Press, 81; auth, The Rhetorical Presidency, Princeton Univ Press, 87; auth, The Constitutional Presidency and American Political Development, The Constitution and the American Presidency, SUNY Press, 91; auth, Riker's Rhetoric of Ratification, Stud in Am Polit Dev, 5, 2, Fall 91; auth, Revising the Rhetorical Presidency, Beyond the Rhetorical Presidency, Tex AM Press, 96; auth, Constitutional Abdication: The Senate, the President, and Appointments to the Supreme Court, Case West Law Rev, 47, 4, Sum 97; auth, Reflections on the Rheetorical Presidency in American Political Development, Speaking to the People: The Rhetorical Presidency in Historical Perspective, Univ Mass Press, 98. **CONTACT ADDRESS** 7105 Running Rope, Austin, TX, 78731. **EMAIL** jtulis@gov.utexas.edu

TULL, CHARLES JOSEPH
PERSONAL Born 08/28/1931, Runnemede, NJ, m, 1953, 6 children **DISCIPLINE** UNITED STATES HISTORY **EDUCATION** Creighton Univ, BS, 55; Univ Notre Dame, MA, 57, PhD(hist), 62. **CAREER** Instr hist, St Vincent Col, 59-61; asst prof, DePaul Univ, 61-65; assoc prof US hist, 66-71, chmn dept hist, 68-70, PROF HIST, IND UNIV, SOUTH BEND, 71-, Vis assoc prof, Univ Notre Dame, 65-66, 67-68. **MEMBERSHIPS** Oral Hist Asn; AHA; Am Cath Hist Asn; Orgn Am Historians; Southern Hist Asn. **RESEARCH** Recent United States political and diplomatic history. **SELECTED PUBLICATIONS** Auth, The Coughlin-Fahey Connection--Coughlin, Charles,E., Fahey,Denis, Cssp, and Religious Anti-Semitism in the United-States, 1938-1954, Cath Hist Rev, Vol 0079, 93. **CONTACT ADDRESS** 118 Wakewa Ave, South Bend, IN, 46617.

TULL, HERMAN
PERSONAL Born 10/27/1955, Philadelphia, PA, m, 1978, 2 children **DISCIPLINE** HISTORY AND LITERATURE OF RELIGIONS **EDUCATION** Hobart Col, BA, 78; Northwestern Univ, PhD, 85. **CAREER** Asst prof, Rutgers Univ; lectr, Princeton Univ. **HONORS AND AWARDS** Univ fel, Northwestern Univ; Getty Postdoctoral fel. **RESEARCH** Vedic ritual; Gnomic literature in Sanskrit. **SELECTED PUBLICATIONS** Auth, Hinduism, Harper's Dictionary of Religious Education, 90; auth, F. Max Muller and A.B. Keith: 'Twaddle,' the 'Stupid' Myth, and the Disease of Indology, NUMEN, 91; auth, The Tale of 'The Bride and the Monkey': Female Insatiability, Male Impotence, and Simian Virility in Indian Literature, J Hist of Sexuality, 93; auth, The Killing That Is Not Killing: Men, Cattle, and the Origins of Non-Violence (ahimsa) in the Vedic Sacrifice, Indo-Iranian J, 96; auth, The Veduic Origins of Karma: Cosmos as Man in Ancient Indian Myth and Ritual. **CONTACT ADDRESS** 228 Terhune Rd., Princeton, NJ, 08540. **EMAIL** hwtull@msn.com

TULLOS, ALLEN E.
DISCIPLINE HISTORY AND LIBERAL ARTS **EDUCATION** Univ Ala, BA, 72; Univ NC, MA, 76; Yale Univ, MA, 79, PhD, 85. **CAREER** Affl prof dept hist/Grad Inst Lib Arts. **HONORS AND AWARDS** Charles S. Syndor Prize, So Hist Assn; coprod, A Singing Stream: Chronicle of a Black Family; Best Indep Prod, Corp Pub Broadcasting. **RESEARCH** US popular culture; American regional cultures; 19th- and 20th-century Southern studies, history and film; geography and justice in the Black Belt region of the American South since the civil rights movement. **SELECTED PUBLICATIONS** Auth, Habits of Industry: White Culture and the Transformation of the Carolina Piedmont; **CONTACT ADDRESS** Dept History, Emory Univ, 221 Bowden Hall, 561 Kilgo Cir, Atlanta, GA, 30322-1950. **EMAIL** ilaat@emory.edu

TULLY, JAMES H.
PERSONAL Born 04/17/1946, Nanaimo, BC, Canada **DISCIPLINE** POLITICAL SCIENCE/PHILOSOPHY **EDUCATION** Univ BC, BA, 74; Univ Cambridge, PhD, 77. **CAREER** Prof, philos & polit sci, McGill Univ, 77-96; adv, Royal Comn Aboriginal Peoples, 92-96; PROF POLITICAL SCIENCE, UNIV VICTORIA, 96-. **SELECTED PUBLICATIONS** Auth, A Discourse on Property, 80; auth, An Approach to Political Philosophy, 93; auth, Strange Multiplicity, 95; ed, John Locke, 83; ed, Meaning and Context, 88; ed, Pufendorf, 91; ed, Philosophy in an Age of Pluralism; ser ed, The Complete Works of John Locke; ser ed, Ideas in Context. **CONTACT ADDRESS** Dept of Political Science, Univ of Victoria, PO Box 3050, Victoria, BC, V8W 3P5.

TUMASONIS, ELIZABETH
PERSONAL Charleston, WV **DISCIPLINE** ART HISTORY **EDUCATION** Col William & Mary, BA, 63; New York Univ, MA, 67; Univ Calif Berkley, PhD, 79. **CAREER** Instr, Univ Missouri, 66-67; instr, DePauw Univ, 67-69; tchg assoc, Univ Calif Berkeley, 69-72; instr, Univ S Calif, 73-75; prof, Calif State Univ, 78-81; asst prof, 81-91, ch, 91-94, ASSOC PROF, HIST ART, UNIV VICTORIA, 91-. **HONORS AND AWARDS** Award Excellence Tchg, Univ Victoria Alumni, 89; Tchg Fel, 3M, 92. **MEMBERSHIPS** Univ Art Asn Can; German Studs Asn; Victoria Horticultural Soc. **SELECTED PUBLICATIONS** Auth, The Image of the Centaur in the Painting of Arnold Bocklin, in New Mexico Studs Fine Arts, 78; auth, The Piper Among the Ruins: The Image of the God Pan in the Painting of Arnold Bocklin, in RACAR: The Can Art Rev, 91; auth, Max Klinger's Christ on Olympus: The Confrontation between Christianity and Paganism, in RACAR: The Can Art Rev, 95. **CONTACT ADDRESS** Dept of History in Art, Univ Victoria, Victoria, BC, V8W 3P4. **EMAIL** dpouliot@finearts.uvic.ca

TURINO, THOMAS
DISCIPLINE MUSIC **EDUCATION** Colgate Univ, BA; Univ TX, PhD. **CAREER** Assoc prof, 87-, Univ IL Urbana Champaign. **RESEARCH** Musics of Latin Am. **SELECTED PUBLICATIONS** Auth, Moving Away from Silence, 93; pubs in Ethnomusicology; the New Groves Dictionary of Musical Instruments; Latin American Music Review. **CONTACT ADDRESS** Dept of Music, Univ Illinois Urbana Champaign, E Gregory Dr, PO Box 52, Champaign, IL, 61820. **EMAIL** t-turino@uiuc.edu

TURK, ELEANOR L.
PERSONAL Born 09/09/1935, Charlottesville, VA, d, 1 child **DISCIPLINE** GERMAN HISTORY **EDUCATION** Ohio Wesleyan Univ, BA, 57; Univ Ill, MA, 70; Univ Wis-Madison, PhD(hist), 75. **CAREER** Asst to exec vchancellor, Univ Kans, 75-76, asst to dean, Lib Arts & Sci, 76-77, asst dean, 77-78; ASST DEAN, HUMANITIES & SCI, ITHACA COL, 78-, Lectr Western civilization, Univ Kans, 76-78, courtesy asst prof hist, 77-78 & Lib Arts Placement dir, 77-78; instr hist, Ithaca Col, 79-80. **MEMBERSHIPS** Western Asn Ger Studies; Soc Ger Am Studies; Am Asn Higher Educ; Soc Gen & Lib Studies. **RESEARCH** The press of Imperial Germany; civil liberty in Imperial Germany; German immigration in the 19th century. **SELECTED PUBLICATIONS** Auth, The press of Imperial Germany: A new role for a traditional resource, Cent Europ Hist, 12/77; The Germans of Atchison, Kansas 1854-1859: The development of an ethnic community, Kans Hist, fall 79; Holding the line: The National Liberal Party and the Prussian Association law of 1897, Ger Studies Rev, 10/79; The Immigrant experience in Kansas, 1860-1900, Occas Papers Soc Ger-Am Studies, Vol 10, 80; The Battenberg affair: Chancellor crisis or media event, Ger Studies Rev, 5/82. **CONTACT ADDRESS** Sch of Humanities & Sci, Ithaca Col, Ithaca, NY, 14850.

TURK, RICHARD WELLINGTON
PERSONAL Born 02/10/1938, Ann Arbor, MI, m, 1963, 2 children **DISCIPLINE** AMERICAN NAVAL AND DIPLOMATIC HISTORY **EDUCATION** Albion Col, BA, 60; Fletcher Sch Law, MA, 61, MALD, 62, PhD(int affairs), 68. **CAREER** Asst prof, 68-76, assoc prof, 76-80, PROF HIST, ALLEGHENY COL, 80-. **MEMBERSHIPS** AHA; Soc Historians Am Foreign Rels. **RESEARCH** American Naval Nistory, 1865-1914. **SELECTED PUBLICATIONS** Auth, Lucky Lady and the Navy Mystique, the Chenango in World-War-II, Jour Military Hist, Vol 0057, 93; Mahan Is Not Enough-The Proceedings of a Conference on the Works of Sir Corbett, Julian, and Admiral-Sir Richmond,Herbert, Amer Neptune, Vol 0055, 95; The War in the Pacific--From Pearl-Harbor to Tokyo-Bay, Jour Military Hist, Vol 0060, 96; Victory at Sea--World-War-II in the Pacific, Jour Military Hist, Vol 0060, 96; All at Sea--Coming of Age in World-War-II, Jour Military Hist, Vol 0061, 97. **CONTACT ADDRESS** Dept of Hist, Allegheny Col, 520 N Main St, Meadville, PA, 16335-3902.

TURNBAUGH, WILLIAM A.
PERSONAL Born 06/01/1948, Williamsport, PA, m, 1974 **DISCIPLINE** ANTHROPOLOGY/ARCHAEOLOGY **EDUCATION** Lycoming Col, BA, 70; Harvard Univ, PhD. **CAREER** Res asst, Harvard Univ, 73-74; asst prof, Univ RI, 74-78; assoc prof, 78-83; prof, 83- . **HONORS AND AWARDS** Woodrow Wilson fel, 70-71; Nat Sci Found fel, 70-73. **MEMBERSHIPS** Soc for Am Archaeol; Soc for Hist Archaeol; Soc of Prof Archaeol; Explores Club; Sigma Xi; Phi Alpha Theta; Phi Kappa Phi. **RESEARCH** North American prehistoric and historic archaeology; Native American material culture and craft arts. **SELECTED PUBLICATIONS** Auth, Man, Land, and Time, 77; auth, The Material Culture of RI-1000, A Mid-17th-Century Narragansett Indian Burial Site, 84; auth with Sarah Peabody Turnbaugh, Indian Baskets, 86; auth with Sarah Peabody Turnbaugh, Indian Jewelry of the American Southwest, 96; auth with Robert Jurmain, Harry Nelson, and Lynn Kilgore, Understanding Physical Anthropology and Archaeology, 99. **CONTACT ADDRESS** Dept. of Sociology and Anthropology, Univ of Rhode Island, Kingston, RI, 02881. **EMAIL** waturnba@uriacc.uri.edu

TURNBULL, CHARLES WESLEY
PERSONAL Born 02/05/1935, Charlotte Amalie, St Thomas, Virgin Islands of the United States, s **DISCIPLINE** EDUCATION **EDUCATION** Hampton University, Hampton, VA, BS, 1958, MA, 1959; University of Minnesota, Minneapolis, MN, PhD,1976. **CAREER** Virgin Island Department of Education, St Thomas, VI, social studies teacher, 1959-61, assistant principal, 1961-65, principal, 1965-67, assistant commissioner of education, 1967-79; commissioner of education, 1979-87; University of the Virgin Islands, St Thomas, VI, professor of history, 1988-. **HONORS AND AWARDS** Ford Foundation Scholar, Ford Foundation, 1954-59; President Senior Class of 1958, Hampton University, 1957-58; Delegate to Four Constitutional Conventions of the US Virgin Islands, 1964-65; 1972-73; 1977-78; 1980-81; Citation for Excellence, Leadership and Service in the Field of Education, Iota Phi Lambda Sorority, 1989; Citation for Contributions to Virgin Islands History & Culture, Cultural Education Division Virgin Island Department of Education, 1987; Citation for Excellence in Teaching, Charlotte Amalie High School Class of 1964, 1989; Citation for Excellence in the Service of Humanity, Alpha Phi Alpha Fraternity Inc, Theta Epsilon Lambda Chapter, 1992. **MEMBERSHIPS** Member, Alpha Phi Alpha Fraternity Inc, 1958-; member, Association of Caribbean Historians; member, Organization of American Historians; member, Council of Chief State School Officers, 1979-87; member, Board of Trustees, University of the Virgin Islands, 1979-87; member, Virgin Islands Board of Elections, 1974-76; member, Virgin Islands Humanities Council, 1989-; member, Virgin Islands Board of Education, 1988-; president, Virgin Islands Historical Society, 1976-; member, American Historical Association. **CONTACT ADDRESS** Social Sciences Division, Univ of the Virgin Islands, St Thomas, 00802.

TURNBULL, PAUL
DISCIPLINE HISTORY **CAREER** Sr res fel, Ctr Cross-Cult Res, Australian Natl Univ. **RESEARCH** Enlightenment Historiography; the production of History in multimedia. **CONTACT ADDRESS** Dept of Education, Australian National Univ. **EMAIL** Paul.Turnbull@anu.edu.au

TURNER, ELDON R.
DISCIPLINE HISTORY **EDUCATION** Washburn, BA, 63; Univ Kans, MA, 67, PhD, 73. **CAREER** Asst prof History, Univ Fla. **RESEARCH** Early New England. **SELECTED PUBLICATIONS** Auth, Gender, Abortion, and Testimony: A Textual Look at the Martin Cases, Middlesex County, Massachusetts, 1681-83, Procs of Mass Hist Soc, 87; Statute for the Times: Two Hundred Years of Virginia's Statute for Religious Liberty, Amer Hist Today, 87. **CONTACT ADDRESS** Dept of History, Univ Florida, 4131 Turlington Hall, Gainesville, FL, 32611.

TURNER, FRANK MILLER
PERSONAL Born 10/31/1944, Springfield, OH **DISCIPLINE** BRITISH & MODERN INTELLECTUAL HISTORY **EDUCATION** Col William & Mary, AB, 66; Yale Univ, PhM, 70, PhD, 71. **CAREER** Instr to asst prof, 71-77, dir undergrad studies, 75-78, assoc prof, 77-82, prof hist, Yale Univ, 82-; dir, spec humanities prog, 80-, Nat Endowment for Humanities fel younger humanist, 74-75, fel independent study, 78-79; Mellon fel, Aspen Inst, 75. **MEMBERSHIPS** AHA; Conf Brit Studies, Royal Hist Soc. **RESEARCH** Victorian intellectual history; science and religion; influence of classical thought; The Oxford Monument. **SELECTED PUBLICATIONS** Auth, Lucretius among the Victorians, Victorian Studies, 73; auth, Between Science and Religion: The Reaction to Scientific Naturalism in Late Victorian England, Yale Univ, 74; art, Rainfall, plagues and the Prince of Wales: A chapter in the conflict of science and religion, J Brit Studies, 74; art, Victorian scientific naturalism and Thomas Carlyle, Victorian Studies, 75; art, The Victorian conflict between science and religion in professional dimension, Isis, 78; coauth, The Western Heritage, Macmillan, 79; art, Public Science in Britain, 1880-1919, Isis, 80; auth, The Greek Heritage in Victorian Britain, Yale Press, 81. **CONTACT ADDRESS** Dept of History, Yale Univ, PO Box 208324, New Haven, CT, 06520-8324. **EMAIL** fmturner@minerra.cis.yale.edu

TURNER, JAMES
DISCIPLINE HISTORY **EDUCATION** Harvard Univ, BA, 68, AM, 71, PhD, 75. **CAREER** Prof. **RESEARCH** British and American intellectual history; history of universities. **SELECTED PUBLICATIONS** Auth, Reckoning with the Beast: Animals, Pain, and Humanity in the Victorian Mind, 80; With-

out God, Without Creed: The Origins of Unbelief in America, 86; The German Model and the Graduate School, 93; Religion et langage dans l'Amerique du XIXeme sicle, 93. **CONTACT ADDRESS** History and Philosophy of Science Dept, Univ of Notre Dame, Notre Dame, IN, 46556. **EMAIL** Turner.36@nd.edu

TURNER, JAMES HILTON
PERSONAL Born 04/19/1918, Woodville, ON, Canada, m, 1945, 3 children **DISCIPLINE** CLASSICAL LANGUAGES **EDUCATION** Univ Toronto, BA, 40; Univ Cincinnati, PhD, 44. **CAREER** Mem fac, Bishop's Col Sch, 44-45 McCallie Sch, 45-47; from instr to asst prof class lang, Univ Vt, 47-51; asst prof, Heidelberg Col, 51-52; from asst prof to assoc prof, 52-57, chmn dept lang, 53-62, PROF CLASS LANG, WESTMINSTER COL, 57-, Assoc ed, Class World, 57-60. **MEMBERSHIPS** Class Asn Atlantic States; Am Class League (vpres, 58-59); AAUP. **RESEARCH** Aristophanes. **SELECTED PUBLICATIONS** Auth, Aristophanes, Lysistrata, Class World, Vol 0086, 93; Introduction to Attic Greek, Class World, Vol 0089, 96. **CONTACT ADDRESS** Dept of Foreign Languages, Westminster Col, New Wilmington, PA, 16142.

TURNER, JOHN D.
PERSONAL Born 07/15/1938, Glen Ridge, NJ, m, 1992, 2 children **DISCIPLINE** HISTORY OF RELIGION **EDUCATION** Dartmouth Col, AB, 60; Union Theol Sem, BD, 65, ThM, 66; Duke Univ, PhD, 70. **CAREER** Asst prof, Univ Montana, 71-75; COTNER COL PROF RELIG, 76- , Assoc prof History, 76-83, CHR, PROG RELIG STUD, 78- , PROF CLASSICS & HISTORY, 84- , UNIV NEBRASKA-LINCOLN. **HONORS AND AWARDS** Rockefeller Doctoral fel, 68, Phi Beta Kappa, 69, Duke Univ; Am Soc Learned Soc fel, 76. **MEMBERSHIPS** Soc Bibl Lit; Studiorum Novi Testamenti Soc; Int Soc Neoplatonic Stud; Int Asn Coptic Stud; Corresp Inst Antiq & Christianity. **RESEARCH** Biblical studies; History of Hellenistic/Graeco-Roman Religion and Philosophy; Gnosticism; History of Later Greek Philosophy; Codicology and Papyrology; Greek, Coptic, Egyptian and Hebrew language and literature. **SELECTED PUBLICATIONS** Auth, Typologies of the Sethian Gnostic Treatises from Nag Hammadi, Les textes de Nag Hammadi et le probleme de leur classification: Actes du colloque tenu a Quebec du 15 au 22 Septembre, 1993, Peeters and Univ Laval, 95; ed, The Nag Hammadi Library After Fifty Years: Proceedings of the 1995 Society of Biblical Literature Commemoration, E.J. Brill, 97; auth, To See The Light: A Gnostic Appropriation of Jewish Priestly Practice and Sapiential and Apocalyptic Visionary Lore, Mediators of the Divine: Horizons of Prophecy and Divination on Mediterranean Antiquity, Scholars Press, 98; The Gnostic Seth, Biblical Figures Outside the Bible, Trinity Int Press, 98; Introduction & Commentaire, Zostrien, Presses de l'Universite Laval/Editions Peeters, 99. **CONTACT ADDRESS** Dept of Classics, Univ Nebraska, Lincoln, 238 Andrews Hall, Lincoln, NE, 68588-0337. **EMAIL** jturner@unlinfo.unl.edu

TURNER, RALPH V.
PERSONAL Born 08/27/1935, Forrest City, AR **DISCIPLINE** MEDIEVAL HISTORY **EDUCATION** Univ Ark, BA, 57, MA, 58; Johns Hopkins Univ, PhD, 62. **CAREER** Jr instr hist, Johns Hopkins Univ, 60-62; from instr to asst prof, Fla State Univ, 62-66; from asst prof to assoc prof, Ohio Univ, 66-70; assoc prof, 70-73, PROF HIST, FLA STATE UNIV, 73-, Am Bar Found legal hist fel, 80-81; vis fel, St Edmund's House, Cambridge Univ, 80-81. **MEMBERSHIPS** AHA; Conf Brit Studies; Am Soc Legal Hist; Selden Soc; Pipe Roll Soc. **RESEARCH** Medieval English constitutional and legal history; the judiciary in late 12th and early 13th century England. **SELECTED PUBLICATIONS** Auth, John-Lackland 1199-1216--Military Reputation Reconsidered--Defining Characteristics of a 12th-Century Medieval King Through His Continental Campaign of 1214-1215, Jour Medieval Hist, Vol 0019, 93; Vassals, Heiresses, Crusaders, and Thugs--The Gentry of Angevin Yorkshire, 1154-1216, Amer Hist Rev, Vol 0099, 94; The Problem of Survival for the Angevin Empire--Henry-II and His Sons Vision Versus Late 12th-Century Realities, Amer Hist Rev, Vol 0100, 95; John, King Concept of Royal Authority, History of Political Thought, Vol 0017, 96; The Accession of Henry-II in England--Royal Government Restored 1149-1159, Amer Hist Rev, Vol 0101, 96; Richard-Lionheart and English Episcopal Election, Albion, Vol 0029, 97; The English and the Norman-Conquest, Amer Hist Rev, Vol 0102, 97. **CONTACT ADDRESS** Dept of Hist, Florida State Univ, Tallahassee, FL, 32306.

TURNER, TERENCE S.
PERSONAL Born 12/30/1935, Philadelphia, PA, m, 1980, 2 children **DISCIPLINE** ANTHROPOLOGY **EDUCATION** Harvard Col, BA, 57; Univ Calif Berkeley, MA, 59; Harvard Univ, PhD, 65. **CAREER** Asst prof Anthrop, 66-68, Prof Anthrop, Cornell Univ, 99- ; asst prof , 68, prof, 82-98, Univ Chicago. **HONORS AND AWARDS** Forman lectr, Royal Anthrop Inst, 92; Solon T Kimball Award, Am Anthrop Soc, 98. **MEMBERSHIPS** Am Anthrop Asn; Am Ethnol Soc; Royal Anthrop Inst Gr Brit & Ireland; Asn Soc Anthrop Gr Brit & Commonwealth; Soc Cult Anthrop; Soc Lat Am Anthrop; Soc des Am; Associacao Brasileir a de Antropologia. **RESEARCH** Compar-

ative social organization; kinship; political systems; cultural and symbolic forms ; Marxist social theory and political economy; semiotics and literary theory; visual anthropology and indigenous media; rights of indigenous peoples; human rights as anthropological issue; political and cultural aspects of interethnic contact. **SELECTED PUBLICATIONS** Auth, Indigenous Rights vs Neo-Liberal Developmentalism in Brazil, Dissent, 96; Social Complexity and Recursive Hierarchy in Indigenous South American Societies, Structure, knowledge, and representation in the Andes, Jour Steward Anthrop Soc, 97; Il sacro come alienzzione della coscienza sociale: riti e cosmologia dei Cayapo, Culture e religioni indigine in Americhe, Trattato di Antropologia del Sacro, Editoriale Jaca Book, 97; coauth, Universal Human rights versus Cultural Relativity, Jour Anthrop Res, 97; Human Rights, human difference, and anthropology's contribution to an emancipatory cultural politics, Jour Anthrop Res, 97; Indigenous rights, environmental protection and the struggle over forest resources in the Amazon: the case of the Brazilian Kayapo, Earth, air, fire and water: the humanities and the environment, Univ Mass Press, 98; The poetics of play: ritual clowns, masking and performative mimesis among the Kayapo, The play of gods and men: Essays in Play and Performance,Lit Verlag, 98; Mineral extraction by and for indigenous Amazonian Communities: Gold Mining by the Walapi and Kayapo, Mining, Oil, Environment, People and Rights in the Amazon, 98. **CONTACT ADDRESS** 115 Eddy St., Ithaca, NY, 14850. **EMAIL** tst3@cornell.edu

TURNER, THOMAS REED
PERSONAL Born 08/19/1941, Cambridge, MA, m, 1969, 2 children **DISCIPLINE** CIVIL WAR HISTORY **EDUCATION** Boston Univ, BA, 63, MA, 64, PhD(hist), 71. **CAREER** Assoc prof, 71-80, PROF HIST, BRIDGEWATER STATE COL, 81-. **MEMBERSHIPS** AHA; Orgn Am Historians. **RESEARCH** Lincoln and Civil War; American assassinations; American foreign relations. **SELECTED PUBLICATIONS** Auth, Lincoln Loyalists--Union Soldiers from the Confederacy, Civil War Hist, Vol 0039, 93; American-Gothic--The Story of America Legendary Theatrical Family, Junius, Edwin, and Booth, John, Wilkes, Jour So Hist, Vol 0060, 94; April 65 Confederate Covert Action in the American Civil-War--Author Reply, Va Mag Hist and Biog, Vol 0104, 96. **CONTACT ADDRESS** Dept of Hist, Bridgewater State Col, Bridgewater, MA, 02324.

TURNER, WES
DISCIPLINE EARLY CANADA AND THE NINETEENTH-CENTURY BRITISH EMPIRE HISTORY **EDUCATION** Univ Toronto, BA, MA; Duke Univ, PhD. **CAREER** Assoc prof. **RESEARCH** Canadian immigration history. **SELECTED PUBLICATIONS** Auth, The War of 1812: the War that Both Sides Won, Dundurn, 90; The Early Settlement of Niagara, Niagara's Changing Landscape, Carleton UP, 94. **CONTACT ADDRESS** Dept of Hist, Brock Univ, 500 Glenridge Ave, St Catharines, ON, L2S 3A1. **EMAIL** wturner@spartan.ac.BrockU.CA

TURNER CENSER, JANE
PERSONAL Born 07/13/1951, Glasgow, KY, m, 1976, 2 children **DISCIPLINE** HISTORY **EDUCATION** Transylvania Univ, AB, 73; Johns Hopkins Univ, MA, 75 PhD, 80. **CAREER** Asst to assoc ed, Frederick Law Olmsted Papers, 79-89; asst prof to assoc prof, George Mason Univ, 89-. **HONORS AND AWARDS** A. Elizabeth Taylor Prize, 97; RDW Conner Award, 96; Nat Endowment Hum Fel Col Tchrs, 98-99; Fel, Nat Hum Ctr, 83-84; Am Coun Learned Societies Fel, 83-84., Bd ed, Jour Southern Hist, 92-96; bd ed, H-Civ War, 93-; coun, Int Exchange Scholar; Am Cult Advisory Comt, 89-92. **MEMBERSHIPS** Am Hist Asn; Org Am Hist; Southern Hist Asn; Southern Asn Women's Hist. **RESEARCH** Nineteenth Century America with emphasis on southern social, cultural and women's history. **SELECTED PUBLICATIONS** Auth, North Carolina Planters and Their Children, 1800-1860, 90; coed, The Years of Olmsted, Vaux and Company, 1865-1874, 92; auth, art, A Changing World of Work: North Carolina Elite Women, 1865-1895; auth, art, the Nineteenth Century Bookshelf, 96; auth, Like Unto Like: A Novel, 97. **CONTACT ADDRESS** Dept of History and Art History, George Mason Univ, MSN 3G1, Fairfax, VA, 22030-4444. **EMAIL** jcensel@gmu.edu

TUSA, MICHAEL
DISCIPLINE 19TH CENTURY MUSIC **EDUCATION** Princeton Univ, PhD. **CAREER** Assoc prof; Univ TX at Austin, 81-; served as, bk review ed, Beethoven Forum & J Am Musicol Soc. **RESEARCH** 19th-century opera; the study of the compos process; the hist of piano music. **SELECTED PUBLICATIONS** Auth, Euryanthe' and Carl Maria von Weber's Dramaturgy of German Opera Oxford, Clarendon Press, 91; publ on Weber, Wagner, Schubert & Beethoven in 19th-century Music, J Amer Musicol Soc, Archiv Fuer Musikwissenschaft, Music Rev, Beethoven Forum & New Grove. **CONTACT ADDRESS** School of Music, Univ of Texas at Austin, 2613 Wichita St, Austin, TX, 78705.

TUSHINGHAM, ARLOTTE DOUGLAS
PERSONAL Born 01/19/1914, Toronto, ON, Canada, m, 1948, 2 children **DISCIPLINE** ARCHAEOLOGY **EDUCATION**

Univ Toronto, BA, 36; Univ Chicago, BD, 41, PhD(Near East studies), 48. **CAREER** Instr Old Testament, Pine Hill Divinity Hall, NS, 41-42, 46; instr, Univ Chicago, 48-50; ann prof, Am Sch Orient Res, Jerusalem, 51-52, dir, 52-53; assoc prof, Queen's Univ, Ont, 53-55; assoc prof, 55-64, prof Near Eastern studies, Univ Toronto, 64-79; chief archaeologist, 64-79, CONSULT, ROYAL ONT MUS, 79-, Head art and archaeol div, Royal Ont Mus, 55-64. **HONORS AND AWARDS** Gold Medal, Iran, 66. **MEMBERSHIPS** Can Mus Asn (pres, 63-65); fel Royal Soc Can; fel Soc Antiq London. **RESEARCH** Near Eastern archaeology, particularly Palestine. **SELECTED PUBLICATIONS** Auth, The Walls of Jerusalem--From the Canaanites to the Mamlukes, Jour Amer Oriental Soc, Vol 0116, 96. **CONTACT ADDRESS** Royal Ont Mus, 100 Queen's Park, Toronto, ON, M5S 2C6.

TUSHNET, MARK VICTOR
PERSONAL Born 11/18/1945, Newark, NJ, m, 1969, 2 children **DISCIPLINE** LAW, AMERICAN LEGAL HISTORY **EDUCATION** Harvard Col, BA, 67; Yale Univ JD & MA, 71. **CAREER** Asst prof, 73-76, assoc prof, 76-79, prof law, Univ Wis, 79-; prof law, Georgetown Univ Law Ctr, 81-. **MEMBERSHIPS** Orgn Am Historians; Am Soc Legal Hist; Am Hist Assn; Conf Critical Legal Studies. **RESEARCH** Constitutional law; federal jurisdiction; American legal history. **SELECTED PUBLICATIONS** Auth, The Warren Court in Historical Perspective, ec, University of Press of Virginia, 93; auth, Making Civil Rights Law: Thurgood Marshall and the Supreme Court, 1936-1961, Oxford University Press, 94; auth, Brown v Board of Education, Franklin Watts, 95; coauth, Remnants of Belief: Contemporary Constitutional Issues, Oxford University Press, 96; auth, Making Constitutional Law: Thurgood Marshall and the Supreme Court, 1961-1991, Oxford University Press, 97. **CONTACT ADDRESS** Law Ctr, Georgetown Univ, 600 New Jersey NW, Washington, DC, 20001-2022. **EMAIL** tushnet@law.georgetown.edu

TUTTLE, RICHARD J.
PERSONAL Born 06/22/1941, Oakland, CA, d, 1 child **DISCIPLINE** HISTORY OF ART **EDUCATION** Stanford Univ, PhD, 76. **CAREER** Asst Prof, Assoc Prof, 77 to 83-, Tulane Univ; res Asst, 72-76, Bibliothela Hertziawa, Rome. **HONORS AND AWARDS** SAH Founders Awd; Rome Prize Fel. **MEMBERSHIPS** SAH **RESEARCH** Italian Renaissance Architecture and Urbanism. **SELECTED PUBLICATIONS** Auth, On Vignola's Rule of the Five Orders, in:" Paper Palaces: The Rise of the Renaissance Architectural Treatise, ed, Vaughn Hart, Peter Hicks, London, Yale, 98; Bologna in: Storia dell'architettura italiana: il Qattrocento, ed, Forthcoming; Paolo Fiore, Milan, Electa, 98; Vignola and Villa Giulia: the white drawing, Casabella, 97; Jacopo Vignola, in: The Dictionary of Art, London and NY, MacMillan, 96; Piazza Desing Strategies in Renaissance Bologna: Piazza Maggiore, Annali di Archi, 94; The Basilica os S Petronio in Bologna, in: The Renaissance from Brunelleschi to Michelangelo: The Representation of Architecture, ed, H A Millon, V Magnag Lampugnani, Milan, Bompiani, 94. **CONTACT ADDRESS** Newcomb Art Dept, Tulane Univ, New Orleans, LA, 70118-5698. **EMAIL** rjtuttle@mailhost.tcs.tulane.edu

TWETON, D. JERONE
PERSONAL Born 05/08/1933, Grand Forks, ND, m, 1957, 3 children **DISCIPLINE** AMERICAN HISTORY **EDUCATION** Gustavus Adolphus Col, BA, 55; Univ NDak, MA, 56; Univ Okla, PhD(hist), 64. **CAREER** From asst prof to prof hist, Dana Col, 59-65; from asst prof to assoc prof, 65-71, PROF HIST, UNIV N DAK, 71-, CHMN DEPT, 65-, Vis scholar, Gen Beadle State Col, 67. **MEMBERSHIPS** AHA; Orgn Am Historians; Econ Hist Asn; Western Hist Asn; Agr Hist Soc. **RESEARCH** The American West; the Populist era. **SELECTED PUBLICATIONS** Auth, Boileau, Gerald, J. and the Progressive Farmer Labor Alliance--Politics of the New-Deal, Amer Hist Rev, Vol 0100, 95. **CONTACT ADDRESS** Dept of Hist, Univ of NDak, Grand Forks, ND, 58202.

TWINAM, ANN
PERSONAL Born 04/23/1946, Cairo, IL, m, 1973 **DISCIPLINE** LATIN AMERICAN HISTORY **EDUCATION** Northern Ill Univ, BA, 68; Yale Univ, MPhil, 71, PhD(hist), 76. **CAREER** Teaching asst, Yale Univ, 71-72; asst prof, 74-81, ASSOC PROF HIST, UNIV CINCINNATI, 81-. **MEMBERSHIPS** Latin Am Studies Asn; Conf Latin Am Hist; Midwest Asn Latin Americanists; AAUP. **RESEARCH** Latin American social and economic colonial period; Colombian 18th and 19th centuries; Antioqueno (Colombian) regional history. **SELECTED PUBLICATIONS** Auth, The Colonial Elite of Early Caracas--Formation and Crisis, 1567-1767, Amer Hist Rev, Vol 0097, 92. **CONTACT ADDRESS** Dept Hist, Univ Cincinnati, P O Box 210373, Cincinnati, OH, 45221-0373.

TWOHIG, DOROTHY ANN
PERSONAL Born 05/10/1927, Charleston, WV **DISCIPLINE** AMERICAN AND ECONOMIC HISTORY **EDUCATION** Morris Harvey Col, BA, 52; Columbia Univ, MA, 54. **CAREER** Ed staff, Dict American Biography, Columbia Univ, 57-59, asst ed, Papers of Alexander Hamilton, 59-69; ASSOC PROF, UNIV VA, 80-, ASSOC ED, PAPERS OF GEORGE

WASHINGTON, 69-, Lectr, Dept Hist, Univ Va, 78-; co-ed, The Diaries of George Washington, 6 vols, Univ Press Va, 76-79. **HONORS AND AWARDS** Philip M Hamer Award, Soc Am Archivists, 77. **MEMBERSHIPS** AHA; Soc Historians Early Am Repub. **RESEARCH** George Washington; history of early American public finance; Colonial economic history. **SELECTED PUBLICATIONS** contribr, Dict American History, Scribner's, 78; ed, J Proc of the President, Univ Press Va, 81. **CONTACT ADDRESS** Papers of George Washington, Univ of Virginia, 1 Randall Hall, Charlottesville, VA, 22903-3244.

TYLER, DANIEL
PERSONAL Born 08/09/1933, Abington, PA, m, 1955, 3 children **DISCIPLINE** HISTORY **EDUCATION** Harvard Univ, AB, 55; Colo State Univ, MA, 67; Univ NMex, PhD(hist), 70. **CAREER** PROF HIST, COLO STATE UNIV, 70-, Fulbright lectr, Univ Autonoma de Mexico, 74-76, Univ de Cuyo, Argentina, 79. **MEMBERSHIPS** Western Hist Asn. **RESEARCH** Mexico period of the American Southwest, 1821-1848; Colorado since 1932. **SELECTED PUBLICATIONS** Auth, River of Traps--A Village Life, NMex Hist Rev, Vol 0068, 93; A River Too Far--The Past and Future of the Arid West, Jour West, Vol 0032, 93; Going-Like-A-Boy-Australia--Making-Up Girls in the 1930s Kindergarten, Australian Hist Stud, Vol 0025, 93; Temptations--Sex, Selling and the Department Store, Australian Hist Stud, Vol 0026, 94; The Spanish Colonial Legacy and the Role of Hispanic Custom in Defining New-Mexico Land and Water Rights, Colonial Latin Amer Hist Rev, Vol 0004, 95; Historical Atlas of Colorado, Pacific Hist Rev, Vol 0064, 95; Crossing the Next Meridian--Land, Water, and the Future of the West, Jour West, Vol 0034, 95; Building Hoover-Dam--An Oral-History of the Great-Depression, Jour West, Vol 0035, 96; Water, Land, and Law in the West--The Limits of Public-Policy, 1850-1920, West Hist Quart, Vol 0028, 97. **CONTACT ADDRESS** Dept of Hist, Colorado State Univ, Fort Collins, CO, 80523-0001.

TYLER, GERALD DEFOREST
PERSONAL Born 02/28/1946, Louisa Co, VA **DISCIPLINE** EDUCATION **EDUCATION** Norfolk State Univ, BS (honors) 1977, MA (highest honors) 1983; Old Dominion Univ, pursuing PhD 1983. **CAREER** Dalmo Sales Co, salesman 1964-66; US Marine Corps, admiral's orderly 1966-69; Tidewater Regional Transit System, bus oper 1969-77; Elizabeth City State Univ, spec asst to chancellor 1977-84; NORFOLK STATE UNIV, DIR OF UNIV RELATIONS, 1984-. **HONORS AND AWARDS** Safe Driving Awd for operating 32 passenger bus free of accidents while employed at TRT 1969-77; Certificate of Appreciation UNCF New York 1979; Outstanding Boxer Awd USMC; First Awd Cert as Asst Head Coach for ECSU's Lady Vikings Softball Team 1980-81; NCSEA Inc Employee of the Year Awd 1981-82; Awd for Outstanding Leadership Unselfish and Dedicated Serv rendered as Sr Class Advisor 1982-84. **MEMBERSHIPS** Mem, NAACP, 1979-; Adv ECSU Student Chap NAACP 1980-84; mem NC State Employees Assn Inc 1980-84; pres Prof Business Assn 1980-81; alternate delegate 35th Annual NCSEA Convention Comm 1980-81; mem S Humanities Conf 1980-82; chmn NC State Employees Assoc Inc 1981-82; mem Greater Bibleway Temple 120 Club 1981; 1st vice pres Pasquotank Co Branch NAACP 1981-84; mem NCSEA Inc Area 24 Exec Bd 1981-84; adv ECSU Sr Class 1981-84; 1st vice chmn Pasquotank Co Voting Precinct 3B 1981-82; mem NCSEA Inc Bd of Governors 1981-82; chmn NCSEA Inc Area 24 1981-82; bd mem Gov's FOTC Assn 1982-84; bd mem Albemarle Develop Auth 1982-84; head adv ECSU Sr Class 1982-84; mem NCSEA Inc State Organ Study Comm 1982-83; mem Pasquotank Co Voting Precinct 3B 1983-84; mem Pasquotank Co Improvement Assn 1983-84; mem New Towne Civic League 1984-86; mem Tidewater Media Prof Assn 1984-89; bd mem New Towne Civic League 1984-86; mem VA Social Sci Assn 1984-94; mem Virginia Assn of Printing, Publications & Public Relations, 1986-; bd of dirs & advisors, Pepper Bird Found, 1988; bd mem, Miss Black Virginia Pageant, 1986-88; mem bd of advisors, Miss Collegiate African American Pageant, 1989-93; mem board of directors, Tidewater Charter, American Red Cross, 1990-92; Hampton Roads Black Media Professionals, 1990-; The Council for the Advancement and Support of Education District III, board of directors and nominating committee, 1993-95. **CONTACT ADDRESS** University Relations, Norfolk State Univ, Wilson Hall, Ste 340, Norfolk, VA, 23504.

TYLER, JOHN W.
PERSONAL Born 05/21/1951, Wilmington, DE **DISCIPLINE** EARLY AMERICAN HISTORY **EDUCATION** Trinity Col, BA, 73; Princeton Univ, MA, 75, PhD(hist), 80. **CAREER** CHMN HIST DEPT, GROTON SCH, 78-. **MEMBERSHIPS** AHA; Orgn Am Historians; Inst Study Early Am Hist and Culture. **RESEARCH** 18th century mercantile history; causation of the American revolution; 18th century social history and material culture. **SELECTED PUBLICATIONS** Auth, The Secret-6--The True Tale of the Men Who Conspired with Brown, John, New Eng Quart-Hist Rev of New Eng Life and Letters, Vol 0068, 95; In Public Houses, Drink and the Revolution of Authority in Colonial Massachusetts, , New Eng Quart-Hist Rev of New Eng Life and Letters, Vol 0069, 96. **CONTACT ADDRESS** Groton Sch, Farmers Row, Groton, MA, 01450.

TYLER, PAMELA
DISCIPLINE HISTORY **EDUCATION** Tulane Univ, PhD, 89 **CAREER** Asst prof, 90-96, Assoc Prof, 96-, NC State Univ. **HONORS AND AWARDS** Gen L Kemper Williams Prize in La Hist, 96 **MEMBERSHIPS** Southern Asn Women Historians; Southern Hist Asn. **RESEARCH** Women in 20th cent Am South **SELECTED PUBLICATIONS** Auth, Silk Stockings and Ballot Boxes: New Orleans Women and Politics, 1920-1963, Univ Ga Press, 96. **CONTACT ADDRESS** No Carolina State Univ, Box 8108, Raleigh, NC, 27695-8108.

TYLER MAY, ELAINE
DISCIPLINE HISTORY **EDUCATION** Univ Calif Los Angeles, PhD. **CAREER** Prof **HONORS AND AWARDS** Pres, Am Studies Asn. **RESEARCH** Family history; gender issues. **SELECTED PUBLICATIONS** Auth, Great Expectations: Marriage and Divorce in Post-Victorian America, Univ Chicago, 80; Homeward Bound: American Families in the Cold War Era, Basic Bk, 88; Pushing Limits: American Women, 1940-1961, Oxford, 94; Barren in the Promised Land: Childless Americans and the Pursuit of Happiness, Basic Bk, 95. **CONTACT ADDRESS** History Dept, Univ of Minnesota, Twin Cities, 614 Social Sciences Tower, 267 19th Ave S, Minneapolis, MN, 55455. **EMAIL** mayxx002@tc.umn.edu

U

UBBELOHDE, CARL
PERSONAL Born 11/04/1924, Waldo, WI, m, 1952, 4 children **DISCIPLINE** HISTORY **EDUCATION** Wis State Col, Oshkosh, BS, 48; Univ Wis, MS, 50, PhD, 54. **CAREER** From instr to assoc prof hist, Univ Colo, 54-65; from assoc prof to prof, 65-75, actg chmn dept, 67-68, chmn dept, 73-76, HENRY ELDRIDGE BOURNE PROF HIST, CASE WESTERN RESERVE UNIV, 75-, CHMN DEPT, 80-. **HONORS AND AWARDS** Harfurth Award, Univ Wis, 55; Carl Frederick Wittke Distinguished Teacher, Case Western Reserve Univ, 67-69 and 73. **MEMBERSHIPS** Orgn Am Historians; AHA; Asn Can Studies in US. **RESEARCH** American Colonial and Revolutionary history. **SELECTED PUBLICATIONS** Auth, The Context of Colonization--Selected Articles on Britain in the Era of American Colonization, Jour Amer Hist, Vol 0079, 93; A Rage for Liberty--Selected Articles on the Immediate Causes of the American-Revolution, Jour Amer Hist, Vol 0079, 93; The Stresses of Empire--Selected Articles on the British-Empire in the 18th-Century, Jour Amer Hist, Vol 0079, 93; An Empire Takes Shape--Selected Articles on the Origins of the Old-English Colonial System, Jour Amer Hist, Vol 0079, 93; A Nation in the Womb of Time--Selected Articles on the Long-Term Causes of the American-Revolution, Jour Amer Hist, Vol 0079, 93. **CONTACT ADDRESS** Dept of Hist, Case Western Reserve Univ, Cleveland, OH, 44106.

UDOVITCH, ABRAHAM L
PERSONAL Born 05/31/1933, Winnipeg, MB, Canada, m, 1956, 2 children **DISCIPLINE** ISLAMIC HISTORY **EDUCATION** Columbia Univ, BS, 58, MA, 59; Jewish Theol Sem, BHL, 59; Yale Univ, PhD, 65. **CAREER** Asst prof Islamic studies, Brandeis Univ, 64-65 and Cornell Univ, 65-67; chmn dept, Near Eastern Studies, 73-76, assoc prof, 67-71, PROF ISLAMIC HIST, PRINCETON UNIV, 71-, Soc Sci Res Coun res grant, 67-68; Guggenheim fel, 70-71; Fulbright-Hays grant, 71-72. **MEMBERSHIPS** Am Orient Soc; Mid E Studies Asn; Am Res Inst Turkey. **RESEARCH** Economic and social history of the medieval Islamic world. **SELECTED PUBLICATIONS** Auth, Vision of Yemen Between Habshush and Halevi--Arabic, Annales-Hist Sci Soc, Vol 0049, 94. **CONTACT ADDRESS** Dept of Near Eastern Studies, Princeton Univ, 110 Jones Hall, Princeton, NJ, 08540.

UEDA, REED T.
PERSONAL Born 09/14/1949, Honolulu, HI, m, 1970, 2 children **DISCIPLINE** AMERICAN HISTORY **EDUCATION** Univ Calif, Los Angeles, BA, 70; Univ Chicago, MA, 73; Harvard Univ, MA, 76, PhD, 81. **CAREER** Res ed, Harvard Encycl Am Ethnic Groups, Harvard Univ, 77-79; instr hist, 80-81; vis prof, Brandeis Univ, 85; vis prof, Harvard Univ, 87-89, 96; asst prof, 81-88, ASSOC PROF HIST, TUFTS UNIV, 88-, Issue ed, Harvard Educ Rev, fall, 77; co-ed, J Interdisciplinary Hist; assoc, Charles Warren Center Studies in Am Hist. **HONORS AND AWARDS** Woodrow Wilson Intl Center fel; NEH fel; Am Counc Learned Soc fel. **MEMBERSHIPS** AHA; Orgn Am Hist. **RESEARCH** History of immigration; history of urbanization; history of ethnic groups. **SELECTED PUBLICATIONS** Auth, West Indians & naturalization and citizenship & coauth, Central and South Americans & policies against prejudice and discrimination, Harvard Encycl American Ethnic Groups, Harvard Univ Press, 80; West End House 1906-1981, West End House, 81; Avenues to Adulthood, 87; Postwar Immigrant American, 94 **CONTACT ADDRESS** Dept of Hist, Tufts Univ, 520 Boston Ave, Medford, MA, 02155-5555. **EMAIL** rueda@emerald.tufts.edu

UFFORD, LETTIA W.
PERSONAL Born 07/30/1936, Durham, NC, m, 1961, 3 children **DISCIPLINE** HISTORY **EDUCATION** Radcliffe Col, AB, 58; Columbia Univ, MA, 62, PhD, 77. **CAREER** Independent **HONORS AND AWARDS** MDEA Title IV fel, 59-61 **MEMBERSHIPS** Middle East Stud Asn; Am Hist Asn; Princeton Res Forum. **RESEARCH** 19th cent Middle East **SELECTED PUBLICATIONS** Auth, Imperials at Work and Play: The Papers of General Sir John and Lady Maxwell, Princeton Univ Library Chronicle, Nol LI:2; Winter 90. **CONTACT ADDRESS** 150 Mercer St., Princeton, NJ, 08540. **EMAIL** cufford@aol.com

UHR, HORST
PERSONAL Born 01/03/1934, Wiesbaden, Germany **DISCIPLINE** HISTORY OF ART **EDUCATION** Wayne State Univ, BA, 69; Columbia Univ, MA, 70, PhD(art hist), 75. **CAREER** Asst prof, 75-80, assoc prof, 81-87, PROF RENAISSANCE ART & ARCHIT, WAYNE STATE UNIV, 87-. **MEMBERSHIPS** Col Art Asn Am **RESEARCH** Northern painting 15th and 16th centuries; 19th century German painting **SELECTED PUBLICATIONS** Auth, The Late Drawings of Lovis Corinth: The Genesis of his Expressionism, Arts Mag, 11/76; Pink Clouds Walchensee: The apotheosis of a mountain landscape, Bull Detroit Inst Arts, 12/77; Lovis Corinth's Formation in the Academic Tradition: The evidence of the Kiel sketchbook and other related student drawings, Arts Mag, spring 78; coauth, Aureola and Fructus: Distinctions of beatitude in scholastic thought and the meaning of some crowns in early Flemish painting, Art Bull, 6/78; auth, Masterpieces of German Expressionism in the Detroit Institute of Arts, Hudson Hill Press, 82; auth, Lovis Corinth, Univ Calif Press, Berkeley-London, 90. **CONTACT ADDRESS** Dept of Art & Art Hist, Wayne State Univ, 150 Art, Detroit, MI, 48202-3103. **EMAIL** aa5202@wayne.edu

ULERY, ROBERT
PERSONAL Born 04/02/1944, Goshen, IN **DISCIPLINE** CLASSICS **EDUCATION** BA, 66, MA, 68, PhD, 71, Yale Univ. **CAREER** Asst Prof, 71-78, Assoc Prof, 78-89, Prof, 89-, Wake Forest Univ. **HONORS AND AWARDS** Ovatio, Classical Assoc of the Middle West and South, 94. **MEMBERSHIPS** Amer Assoc of Neo-Latin Studies; Amer Philological Assoc; Classical Assoc of the MiddleWest and South; Renaissance Soc of Amer. **RESEARCH** C. Sallustius Crispis and Cornelius Tacitus: manuscript tradition and Nachleben **SELECTED PUBLICATIONS** Auth, The Text of Tacitus in 15th-Century Italy and the Guarneri Brothers, Studies in Classical Tradition 12, 89; Constantius Felicius Durantinus and the Renaissance Origins of Anti-Sallustian Criticism, International Journal of the Classical Tradition 1.3, 95; Approaches to Cicero, Teacher's Guide to Cicero, 95. **CONTACT ADDRESS** Winston-Salem, NC, 27109. **EMAIL** ulery@wfu.edu

ULLMAN, JOAN CONNELLY
PERSONAL Born 07/08/1929, New York, NY, m, 1967 **DISCIPLINE** MODERN SPANISH HISTORY **EDUCATION** Univ Calif, Berkeley, AB, 51; Bryn Mawr Col, MA, 53, PhD(hist and mod Spanish lit), 63. **CAREER** Polit asst foreign serv, US Dept State, 53-57; dir, Int Inst for Girls, Spain, 58-61 and 78-79; dean students and asst prof hist, Elbert Covell Col, Univ of the Pac, 63-66; from asst prof to assoc prof, 66-74, PROF HIST, UNIV WASH, 74-, Guggenheim Found fel, 72-73; ed, Soc Spanish and Poruguese Hist Studies Bull, 73-77. **MEMBERSHIPS** AHA **RESEARCH** Spanish history, especially restoration, 1875-1923; labor history, both socialism, anarcho-syndicalism, 19th and 20th century, and anticlericalism; socialism. **SELECTED PUBLICATIONS** Auth, A Social-History of Modern Spain, Hist Soc-Soc Hist, Vol 0026, 93. **CONTACT ADDRESS** Dept of Hist, Univ of Wash, Seattle, WA, 98195.

ULRICH, HOMER
PERSONAL Born 03/27/1906, Chicago, IL, m, 1934, 3 children **DISCIPLINE** HISTORY OF MUSIC, MUSICOLOGY **EDUCATION** Univ Chicago, MA, 39. **CAREER** Cellist and bassoonist, Chicago Symphony Orchestra, 29-35; head music dept, Monticello Col, 35-38; from assoc prof to prof music lit, Univ Tex, 39-53; prof and head dept music, 53-72, EMER PROF MUSIC LIT and MUSIC, UNIV MD, COLLEGE PARK, 72-, Ed, Am Music Teacher, 72- **MEMBERSHIPS** Music Teachers Nat Asn; Am Musicol Soc. **RESEARCH** Music history, chamber music; symphonic music. **SELECTED PUBLICATIONS** Auth, Literature and Music in Social Circles--The Formation of Taste, Conversational Topics and Musical Entertainment in Bourgeois Salons--German, Musikforschung, Vol 0049, 96. **CONTACT ADDRESS** 3587 S Leisure World Blvd, Silver Spring, MD, 20906.

ULRICH, LAUREL THATCHER
PERSONAL Born 07/11/1938, Sugar City, ID, m, 1958, 5 children **DISCIPLINE** AMERICAN HISTORY **EDUCATION** Univ Utah, BA, 60; Simmons Col, MA, 71; Univ New NH, PhD(hist), 80. **CAREER** Instr English, 72-73, instr hist, 76-80, ASST PROF HIST, HUMANITIES PROG, UNIV NH, 80-. **MEMBERSHIPS** Orgn Am Historians; Mormon Hist Asn; Nat Women Studies Asn. **RESEARCH** Women and family in America; early American cultural history; women and religion.

SELECTED PUBLICATIONS Auth, Cole, Robert World--Agriculture and Society in Early Maryland, Jour Interdisciplinary Hist, Vol 0023, 93. **CONTACT ADDRESS** Humanities Prog, Univ NH, 125 Technology Dr, Durham, NH, 03824-4724.

ULTEE, J. MAARTEN
PERSONAL Born 01/13/1949, Utrecht, Netherlands, m, 1994, 1 child **DISCIPLINE** EUROPEAN HISTORY **EDUCATION** Reed Col, BA, 69; Johns Hopkins Univ, MA, 72, PhD, 75. **CAREER** Lecturer, Stanford Univ, 74-75; Asst Prof, Hobart & William Smith Col, 75-78; NEH Fellow, Univ NC, 78-79; Vis Asst Prof, Davidson Col, 79-80; Asst Prof, Univ Ala, 80-83; Assoc Prof, 83-91; Prof, 91-. **HONORS AND AWARDS** Woodrow Wilson Nat Fellow, 69-70; NEH Fellow, 78-79; DAAD Fellow, 84; Acad Vis, London Sch of Econ, 87-88. **MEMBERSHIPS** Am Asn for the Hist of Med; Am Catholic Hist Asn; Renaissance Soc of Am; W Soc for French Hist (gov counc 97-00). **RESEARCH** History of surgery; Dutch history; French history 1500-1800. **SELECTED PUBLICATIONS** Tr, The Nobility of Holland: From Knights to Regents, 1500-1650, Cambridge Univ Press, 93; co-ed, The Low Countries and Switzerland, Am Hist Asn Guide to Hist Lit, Oxford Univ Press, 1, 870-88, 95; tr, Four Windows of Opportunity: A Study in Publishing, Amsterdam, 95; auth, sections in Oxford Encycl of the Reformation, Oxford Univ Press, 95; auth, Religion and Surgery in Sixteenth-Century France, Proceedings of the West Soc for French Hist, 23, 40-55, 96; auth, Illustrating Amputation, Treasures of the Reynolds Historical Library, 9/98. **CONTACT ADDRESS** Dept of Hist, Univ Ala, Box 870212, Tuscaloosa, AL, 35487-0212. **EMAIL** multee@history.as.ua.edu

UNDERWOOD, TED LEROY
PERSONAL Born 07/22/1935, Agra, KS, m, 1958, 2 children **DISCIPLINE** EARLY MODERN EUROPEAN HISTORY **EDUCATION** Univ Calif, Berkeley, BA, 59; Berkeley Baptist Divinity Sch, BD, 62; Univ London, PhD, 65. **CAREER** Asst prof ecclesiastical hist, Bishop Col, 65-67; from asst prof to assoc prof, 67-73, PROF HIST, UNIV MINN, MORRIS, 73-, CHMN SOC SCI DIV, 78-, Co-dir, WCent Minn Hist Res Ctr, 72-74. **MEMBERSHIPS** Am Soc Church Hist; Friends Hist Soc; Conf British Studies. **RESEARCH** Seventeenth century English Puritanism. **SELECTED PUBLICATIONS** Auth, Bunyan in Our Time, Church Hist, Vol 0063, 94; 1st Among Friends--Fox, George and the Creation of Quakerism, Cath Hist Rev, Vol 0081, 95. **CONTACT ADDRESS** Dept of Hist Soc Sci Div, Univ of Minn, 600 E 4th St, Morris, MN, 56267-2134.

UNGER, IRWIN
PERSONAL Born 05/02/1927, Brooklyn, NY, m, 1956, 3 children **DISCIPLINE** HISTORY **EDUCATION** City Col New York, BSS, 48, Columbia Univ, MA, 49, PhD, 58. **CAREER** Instr hist, Columbia Col, 56-58; spec lectr, Univ PR, 58-59; asst prof, Long Beach State Col, 59-62; asst prof, Univ Calif, Davis, 62-66; PROF HIST, WASH SQ COL, NY UNIV, 66-, Grants-in-aid, Soc Sci Res Coun, 59, Am Philos Soc, 60 & 62; Am Coun Learned Soc fel, 65-66; Guggenheim fel, 72-73; Rockefeller Humanities Found fel, 80-81. **HONORS AND AWARDS** Pulitzer Prize Hist, 65. **MEMBERSHIPS** AHA; Orgn Am Historians; Econ Hist Asn. **RESEARCH** Civil War and Reconstruction; United States economic history; U.S. in the 1960s. **SELECTED PUBLICATIONS** Auth, The business community and the origins of the 1875 Resumption Act, Bus Hist Rev, 61; The Greenback Era: A Social and Political History of American Finance, 1865-1879, Princeton Univ, 64; The New Left and American history, Am Hist Rev, 7/67; A History of the New Left, Dodd, 74; coauth, The Vulnerable Years: The United States, 1896-1917, Holt, 77; Best of Intentions, Doubleday, 97. **CONTACT ADDRESS** Dept of History, Wash Sq Col, NY Univ, 19 University Pl, New York, NY, 10003-4556.

UNGER, RICHARD W.
PERSONAL Born 12/23/1942, Huntington, WV, m, 1966, 1 child **DISCIPLINE** ECONOMIC HISTORY, HISTORY OF TECHNOLOGY **EDUCATION** Haverford Col, BA, 63; Univ Chicago, MA, 65; Yale Univ, MA, 67, MPhil, 69, PhD(hist), 71. **CAREER** Asst prof, 69-76, assoc prof, 76-81, PROF HIST, UNIV BC, 81-. **MEMBERSHIPS** Econ Hist Soc; Soc Hist Technol; Soc Nautical Res; Medieval Asn Pac; NAm Soc Oceanic Hist. **RESEARCH** History of Dutch brewing; history of European long distance commerce to 1800; maritime history, 1350-1850. **SELECTED PUBLICATIONS** Auth, The Worlds of Columbus, Christopher, Speculum-Jour Medieval Stud, Vol 0068, 93; Northern Ships and the Late-Medieval Economy--The Maritime History Northern Europe, Amer Neptune, Vol 0053, 93; Medieval Ships and Shipping, American Neptune, Vol 0055, 95; Mahan, Alfred,Thayer, Ship Design, and the Evolution of Sea Power in the Late-Middle-Ages, Intl Hist Rev, Vol 0019, 97; 4 Centuries of Producing Peat, Jour Econ Hist, Vol 0057, 97; Naval Policy and Politics of the Dukes of Burgundy, 1384-1482--French, Speculum-Jour Medieval Stud, Vol 0072, 97. **CONTACT ADDRESS** Dept Hist, Univ BC, Vancouver, BC, V6T 1W5.

UNRAU, WILLIAM ERROL
PERSONAL Born 08/19/1929, Goessel, KS, m, 1952, 2 children **DISCIPLINE** AMERICAN HISTORY **EDUCATION** Bethany Col, Kans, BA, 51; Univ Wyo, MA, 56; Univ Colo, PhD, 63. **CAREER** Assoc prof hist and chmn dept, Bethany Col, Kans, 57-64; assoc prof, 65-68, PROF HIST, WICHITA STATE UNIV, 68-. **MEMBERSHIPS** AHA; Orgn Am Historians; Western Hist Asn. **RESEARCH** American Indian and federal Indian policy; settlement and economic development of the Great Plains and American west. **SELECTED PUBLICATIONS** Auth, Indian Law Race Law--A 500-Year History, Historian, Vol 0055, 93; Tribal Wars of the Southern Plains, West Hist Quart, Vol 0024, 93; Bloody Dawn--The Story of the Lawrence Massacre, Jour So Hist, Vol 0059, 93; State and Reservation--New Perspectives on Federal Indian Policy, Pacific Hist Rev, Vol 0063, 94; Between Indian and White Worlds--The Cultural Broker, Montana-Mag West Hist, Vol 0045, 95; The White Earth Tragedy--Ethnicity and Dispossession at a Minnesota-Anishinaabe-Reservation, 1889-1920, Amer Hist Rev, Vol 0100, 95; The Northern Cheyenne Indian Reservation, 1877-1900, Amer Hist Rev, Vol 0100, 95; Our Hearts Fell to the Ground--Plains Indian Views of How the West Was Lost, Jour Early Rep, Vol 0017, 97. **CONTACT ADDRESS** Dept of Hist, Wichita State Univ, Wichita, KS, 67208.

UNTERBERGER, BETTY MILLER
PERSONAL Born 12/27/1923, Scotland, m, 1944, 3 children **DISCIPLINE** HISTORY **EDUCATION** Syracuse Univ, AB, 43; Radcliffe Col, MA, 46; Duke Univ, PhD(Hist), 50. **CAREER** Asst prof Hist, ECarolina Col, 48-50; dir Lib Arts Ctr Adults, Whittier Col, 54-57, assoc prof Hist, 57-61; from assoc prof to prof, Calif State Col, Fullerton, 61-68, grad coordr, 66-68; prof Hist, Tex A&M Univ, 68-, Ford Found res grant, 59; Am Philos Soc res grants, 60-61; nat examr, Advan Placement Am Hist; Tex A&M Univ Orgn Res Fund grant, 69-70; partic, Nat Security Forum, US Air Force, 73; mem Adv Comt on Foreign Rels of US, State Dept, 78-81, chmn, 81; comnr, Nat Hist Publ & Records Comn, 81-83. **HONORS AND AWARDS** Pac Coast Br AHA Award, 56. **MEMBERSHIPS** AHA; Rocky Mountain Asn Slavic Studies (vpres, 72-); Soc Historians Am Foreign Rels; Orgn Am Historians; Conf Peace Res Hist. **RESEARCH** American diplomatic history; Soviet American relations; American Far Eastern relations. **SELECTED PUBLICATIONS** Auth, Woodrow Wilson and the decision to send American troops to Siberia, Pac Hist Rev, 55; America's Siberian Expedition, 1918-1920: A Study of National Policy, Duke Univ, 56, Greenwood, 69; Russian revolution and Wilson's Far Eastern policy, Russ Rev, 57; American Intervention in the Russian Civil War, Heath, 68; The arrest of Alice Masaryk, Slavic Rev, 74; The American image of Mohamed Ali Jinnah, Pakistan Affairs, 12/76; National self-determination, In: Dictionary of the History of American Foreign Policy, Scribner's, 78; American Image of Mohammed Ali Jinnah another Pakistan Liberation Movement, Diplomatic Hist, 81; The United States and National Self Determination, Presidential Studies Quarterly, Fall, 96; Woodrow Wilson and the Cold War, in the Liberal Persuasion: Arthur Schlesinger, Jr and the Challenge of the American Past, ed, John Patrick Digging, Princeton University Press, 97. **CONTACT ADDRESS** Dept of History, Texas A&M Univ, 1 Texas A&M Univ, College Station, TX, 77843.

UPSHUR, JIU-HWA LO
DISCIPLINE HISTORY **EDUCATION** Univ Mich, PhD. **CAREER** Prof, Eastern Michigan Univ. **RESEARCH** Modern China. **SELECTED PUBLICATIONS** Coauth, The Twentieth Century: A Brief Global history; World History; co-ed, Lives and Times: A World History Reader. **CONTACT ADDRESS** Dept of History and Philosophy, Eastern Michigan Univ, 701 Pray-Harrold, Ypsilanti, MI, 48197.

UPTON, DELL
PERSONAL Born 06/24/1949, Ft. Monmouth, NJ, d **DISCIPLINE** HISTORY, ENGLISH, AMERICAN CIVILIZATION **EDUCATION** Colgate Univ, BA, 70; Brown Univ, MA, 75; PhD, 80. **CAREER** Archit Hist, Va Hist Landmarks Commission, 74-79; Museum and Hist Preservation Consultant, 79-82; asst prof, Case Western Reserve Univ, 82-83; asst, full, prof Univ Calif Berkeley, 83-. **HONORS AND AWARDS** Summer Res Fel, 87; Alice Davis Hitchock, Soc of Archit Hist, 87; John Hope Franklin Award, Am Studies Asn, 87; Award Abbott Lowell Cummings Award, 87; Rachal Award Va Hist Soc, 88; Vis Sr Fel, Nat Gallery of Art, 88; Guggenheim Fel, 90-91; Getty Sr Res Grant in Art Hist, 90-91; Louisiana Lit award, 96. **MEMBERSHIPS** Soc of Archit Hist; Vernacular Archit Forum; Orgn of Am Hist; Am Hist Asn; Am Studies Asn; Urban Hist Asn. **RESEARCH** Vernacular architecture; Cultural landscapes; Material culture; Urban cultural landscapes of the early republic; Black main streets in the early 20th-century South. **SELECTED PUBLICATIONS** Auth, Madaline: Love and Survival in Antebellum New Orleans, 96; Architecture in the United Statesm 98. **CONTACT ADDRESS** Dept of Architecture, Univ of Calif, Berkeley, CA, 94720-1800. **EMAIL** dell_upton@msn.com

URBAN, MICHAEL
PERSONAL Born 05/28/1947, Los Angeles, CA, m, 1971, 2 children **DISCIPLINE** POLITICAL SCIENCE **EDUCATION** Univ Kansas, PhD 76. **CAREER** Univ Cal SC, prof. **HONORS AND AWARDS** NCEEES Gnt; NEH; NSF. **MEMBERSHIPS** AAASS. **RESEARCH** Russian Politics and Culture. **SELECTED PUBLICATIONS** Auth, The Rebirth of Politics in Russia, Cambridge Univ Press, 97; auth, Ideology and System Change in the USSR and East Europe, ed, St Martins, 92; More Power to the Soviets, Edward Elgar, 90; **CONTACT ADDRESS** Dept of Politics, Univ of California, Santa Cruz, Santa Cruz, CA, 95064. **EMAIL** urban47@cats.ucsc.edu

URBAN, WILLIAM LAWRENCE
PERSONAL Born 12/31/1939, Monroe, LA, m, 1965, 3 children **DISCIPLINE** MEDIEVAL HISTORY **EDUCATION** Univ Tex, BA, 61, MA, 63, PhD(hist), 67 **CAREER** Asst prof hist, Univ Kans, 65-66; asst prof, 66-71, chmn dept, 70-74, assoc prof, 71-78, PROF HIST, MONMOUTH COL, ILL, 78-, CHMN DEPT, 81-, LEE L MORGAN PROF HIST; Vis prof, Knox Col, 71 & 73; dir Florence prog, Assoc Cols Midwest, 74-75; dir Zagreb prog, ACM, 86; dir, Olomouc prog, ACM, 91; Fulbright res fel, Ger, 75-76; fac fel, Univ Chicago, 76-77; Nat Endowment for Humanities grants, 77, 78-79 & 81. **MEMBERSHIPS** AHA; Mediaeval Acad Am; AAUP **RESEARCH** Crusades; medieval Baltic. **SELECTED PUBLICATIONS** Co-auth, A History of Monmouth College, 79; The Samogitian Crusade, 89; Dithmarschen, A Medieval Peasant Republic, Mellen, 91; The Baltic Crusade, 2nd ed, 94. **CONTACT ADDRESS** Dept of Hist, Monmouth Col, 700 E Broadway, Monmouth, IL, 61462-1963. **EMAIL** urban@monm.edu

URNESS, CAROL
PERSONAL Born 04/08/1936, Wilmington, CA **DISCIPLINE** HISTORY **EDUCATION** Univ Minn, Minneapolis, BA, 57, MA, 60. **CAREER** From jr librn to sr librn, Univ Libr, 59-64, ASST CUR RARE BKS, JAMES FORD BELL LIBR, UNIV MINN, MINNEAPOLIS, 64-. **MEMBERSHIPS** Soc Hist Discoveries; Hakluyt Soc; Soc Bibliog Natural Hist; Asn Bibliog Hist. **RESEARCH** Geographical exploration to 1800; history of science. **SELECTED PUBLICATIONS** Auth, Native-American Communities in Wisconsin, 1600-1960--A Study of Tradition and Change, West Hist Quart, Vol 0027, 96; The Ojibway of Western Canada, 1780 to 1870, West Hist Quart, Vol 0027, 96. **CONTACT ADDRESS** 1026 23rd Ave NE, Minneapolis, MN, 55418.

UROFSKY, MELVIN IRVING
PERSONAL Born 02/07/1939, New York, NY, m, 1961, 2 children **DISCIPLINE** AMERICAN HISTORY **EDUCATION** Columbia Univ, AB, 61, MA, 62, PhD(hist), 68. **CAREER** Instr hist, Ohio State Univ, 64-67; asst prof, State Univ NY, Albany, 67-70, dean innovative educ, 70-72, asst prof hist, Allen Ctr, 72-74; chmn dept, 74-81, PROF HIST, VA COMMONWEALTH UNIV, 74-, Nat Endowment for Humanities grant, 67-74, sr fel, 76; consult, Inst Advan Urban Educ, 71-72; co-chmn, Am Zionist Fedn Ideological Comt, 76-78; chmn, Zionist Acad Coun, 77-79; chmn, Acad Coun Am Jewish Historical Soc, 79. **HONORS AND AWARDS** Kaplan Award, Jewish Bk Coun, 76. **MEMBERSHIPS** Orgn Am Historians; AHA; Am Jewish Hist Soc. **RESEARCH** American history; history of American Jewry. **SELECTED PUBLICATIONS** Auth, Cardozo--A Study in Reputation, Amer Jewish Archv, Vol 0045, 93; After Tragedy and Triumph--Modern Jewish Thought and the Amer Experience, Jour Amer Ethnic Hist, Vol 0012, 93; Fair Trial--Rights of the Accused in Amer Hist, Amer Hist Rev, Vol 0098, 93; Jews in Christian America--The Pursuit of Religious Equality, Historian, Vol 0056, 94; To Guide by the Light of Reason--An Appreciation, Amer Jewish Hist, Vol 0081, 94; The Lonely Days Were Sundays, Reflections of a Jewish Southerner, Miss Quart, Vol 0047, 94; Liberty and Sexuality--The Right to Privacy and the Making of Roe V Wade, Amer Hist Rev, Vol 0099, 94; Bone of Bone and Flesh of Flesh--Recent Publications on the Study of the Jewish People in America, Rev(s) in Amer Hist, Vol 0022, 94; The Constitution, Law and Amer Life--Critical Aspects of the 19th-Century Experience, Jour So Hist, Vol 0060, 94; Of Laws and Limitations--An Intellectual Portrait of Brandeis, Louis, Dembitz, Amer Jewish Hist, Vol 0084, 96. **CONTACT ADDRESS** 1500 Careybrook Dr, Richmond, VA, 23233.

URY, M. WILLIAM
PERSONAL Born 04/05/1956, Cleveland, OH, m, 1984, 4 children **DISCIPLINE** HISTORICAL THEOLOGY **EDUCATION** Asbury Col, BA, 78; Asbury/Theolog Seminary, M.Div, 83; Drew Univ, PhD, 91. **CAREER** Prof, Wesley Theolog Seminary, 89-98. **HONORS AND AWARDS** Tchr of the Year, 94-95; Who's Who in Amer Univ & Col; Phi Alpha Theta; Theta Phi. **MEMBERSHIPS** Amer Acad Relig; Evangel Theolog Seminary; Wesley Theolog Soc. **RESEARCH** Theology; Historical Theology; Philosophy; Languages. **SELECTED PUBLICATIONS** Coauth, Loving Jesus: A Guidebook for Mature Discipleship, Discipleship Manual Vol III, 98; coauth, Following: A Guidebook for Mature Discipleship Vol II, Discipleship Manual, 97; The World is Still Our Parish, Good News Mag, 96. **CONTACT ADDRESS** Wesley Biblical Sem, Box 9928, Jackson, MS, 39286. **EMAIL** 103533,3144@compuserve.com

USCHER, NANCY
DISCIPLINE MUSIC **EDUCATION** Yale Univ, BA; Univ NY, MA; PhD. **CAREER** Prof, Univ N Mex. **SELECTED PUBLICATIONS** Auth, The Schirmer Guide to Schools of Music; Conservatories Throughout the World; Your Own Way

in Music: A Career and Resource Guide. **CONTACT ADDRESS** Music Dept, Univ NMex, 1805 Roma NE, Albuquerque, NM, 87131.

USILTON, LARRY
DISCIPLINE MEDIEVAL ENGLAND, MEDIEVAL EUROPE, ANCIENT GREECE AND ROME, ANCIENT NEAR EA **EDUCATION** Miss State Univ, BA, MA, PhD. **CAREER** Instr, Univ NC, Wilmington. **MEMBERSHIPS** Medieval Acad Am; Royal Hist Soc London. **RESEARCH** English monasticism. **SELECTED PUBLICATIONS** Auth, The Worlds of Medieval Women, Creativity, Influence, and Imagination, WVa Univ Press, 85; The Kings of Medieval England, C.560-1485: A Survey and Research Guide, Scarecrow Press, 96; articles on corrodies in The American Benedictine Rev, June, 80. **CONTACT ADDRESS** Univ N. Carolina, Wilmington, 232 Morton Hall, Wilmington, NC, 28403-3297. **EMAIL** usiltonl@uncwil.edu

UTLEY, ROBERT MARSHALL
PERSONAL Born 10/31/1929, Bauxite, AR, m, 1956, 2 children **DISCIPLINE** MODERN HISTORY **EDUCATION** Purdue Univ, BS, 51; Ind Univ, MA, 52. **CAREER** Historian, Joint Chiefs Staff, US Dept Defense, 54-57; historian, Nat Surv Hist Sites and Bldgs, Southwest Region, Nat Park Serv, 57-62, regional historian, 62-64, chief historian, 64-72, dir off archeol and hist preserv, 72-73, asst dir park hist preserv, 73-76; dep exec dir, Adv Coun Hist Preserv, 77-80; WRITING and CONSULT, 80- **HONORS AND AWARDS** Distinguished Serv Award, Dept Interior, 71., LittD, Purdue Univ, 74, Univ NMex, 76. **MEMBERSHIPS** Orgn Am Historians; Western Hist As-n(vpres, 66-67, pres, 67-68). **RESEARCH** American frontier; American Indian; historic preservation. **SELECTED PUBLICATIONS** Auth, Maclean and Custer, Montana-Mag West Hist, Vol 0043, 93; Desert Lawmen--The High Sheriffs of New-Mexico and Arizona, 1846-1912, NMex Hist Rev, Vol 0069, 94; Untitled, Montana-Mag West Hist, Vol 0045, 95. **CONTACT ADDRESS** 5 Vista Grande Ct Eldorado, Santa Fe, NM, 87501.

V

VACCARO, JOSEPH
PERSONAL Born 02/07/1935, Cambridge, MA, m, 1963, 4 children **DISCIPLINE** MARKETING **EDUCATION** Boston Coll, BSBA, 57; Suffolk Univ, MBA, 69; Suffolk Univ Law Sch, JD, 76. **CAREER** Prof of marketing, 71-present, Suffolk Univ. **HONORS AND AWARDS** Dean's Teaching Award; Certificate of recognition from Amer Marketing Assn; Amer Advertising Fedn; MA Press Assn; Faculty Advisor of the year award from Boston chapter of the Amer Marketing Assn; Hugh G. Wales Advisor of the Year from the Amer marketing Assn **MEMBERSHIPS** Amer Marketing Assn; Amer Advertising Fedn; Assn of Marketing Educators; Amer Acad of Advertising; Amer Assn of Advertising Agencies. **RESEARCH** Sales and self management; advertising; marketing laws; media planning; ethics; counter trade. **SELECTED PUBLICATIONS** Auth, Managing Sales Professionals - The Reality of Profitabiltiy, 95; Taking Advantage of Barter in Radio, The Journal of Services Marketing, 97; Assessing Attitudes and Opinions of Parents and Non-parent Adults Toward Television Exposure to Kids, Journal of Association of Marketing Educators, Spring 98. **CONTACT ADDRESS** 36 Oakwood Rd., Auburndale, MA, 02466-2248. **EMAIL** jvaccaro@suffolk.edu

VADNEY, THOMAS EUGENE
PERSONAL Born 07/01/1939, Lowville, NY **DISCIPLINE** RECENT AMERICAN AND WORLD HISTORY **EDUCATION** Univ Toronto, BA, 63; Univ Wis, MA, 65, PhD(Am hist), 68. **CAREER** Vis asst prof Am hist, Univ Minn, Minneapolis, 68-70; asst prof, 70-72, ASSOC PROF AM HIST, UNIV MAN, 72-, Can Coun res grants, 71-72, 74 and leave fel, 76-77; Univ Man Res Bd res grants, 72-74; co-ed, Can Rev Am Studies, 77-78. **MEMBERSHIPS** Orgn Am Historians; AHA; Can Hist Asn; Can Asn Univ Teachers. **RESEARCH** Recent American history; post-1945 world history; Canadian-American urban history. **SELECTED PUBLICATIONS** Auth, The 20th-Century World--An International History, Intl Hist Rev, Vol 0015, 93; Conceptualizing Global History, Intl Hist Rev, Vol 0016, 94. **CONTACT ADDRESS** Dept of Hist, Univ of Man, Winnipeg, MB, R3T 2N2.

VALAIK, J. DAVID
PERSONAL Born 06/09/1935, Hazleton, PA, m, 1960, 3 children **DISCIPLINE** AMERICAN HISTORY **EDUCATION** Univ Notre Dame, BA, 57; Univ Rochester, PhD, 64. **CAREER** From asst prof to assoc prof, 60-71, dean continuing studies, 70-80, prof hist, Canisius Col, 71-. **MEMBERSHIPS** AHA; Am Cath Hist Asn; Orgn Am Historians. **RESEARCH** Twentieth century and United States diplomatic history; Latin American relations. **SELECTED PUBLICATIONS** Auth, Catholics, Neutrality and the Spanish Embargo, 1937-39, in J Am Hist, 6/67; American Catholic Dissenters and the Spanish Civil War, in Cath Hist Rev, 1/68; American Catholics and the Spanish Republic 1931-1936, in J Church & State, winter 68; Col Paul D Bunker, Assembly, US Military Acad, 12/80; Theodore Roosevelt: An American Hero in Caricature, Western NY Inst Press, 93; A History of the Diocese of Buffalo, Western NY Heritage Press, 97. **CONTACT ADDRESS** Dept of Hist, Canisius Col, 2001 Main St, Buffalo, NY, 14208-1098. **EMAIL** valaik@canisius.edu

VALDES, DENNIS N.
PERSONAL Born 08/30/1946, Detroit, MI, s **DISCIPLINE** SOCIOLOGY **EDUCATION** Univ Mich, PhD, 78. **CAREER** Asst prof, 78-80, Wayne St Univ; asst, assoc prof, 80-, Univ Minn. **RESEARCH** Chicano/Mexican labor & social hist. **SELECTED PUBLICATIONS** Auth, Al Norte: Agricultural Workers in the Great Lakes Regions, Univ Tex, 91. **CONTACT ADDRESS** Dept of Chicano History, Univ of Minnesota, 107 Scott Hall, Minneapolis, MN, 55455. **EMAIL** valde001@maroon.tc.umn.edu

VALENZE, DEBORAH
DISCIPLINE 18TH AND 19TH-CENTURY BRITISH HISTORY **EDUCATION** Brandeis Univ, PhD, 82. **CAREER** Assoc prof, Bernard Col. **RESEARCH** Commoditization of culture in eighteenth-century Britain. **SELECTED PUBLICATIONS** Auth, Prophetic Sons and Daughters: Female Preaching and Popular Religion in Industrial England, Princeton, 85; The First Industrial Woman, Oxford, 95. **CONTACT ADDRESS** Dept of Hist, Columbia Col, New York, 2960 Broadway, New York, NY, 10027-6902.

VALKENIER, ELIZABETH KRIDL
PERSONAL Born 11/13/1926, Warsaw, Poland, m, 1951, 1 child **DISCIPLINE** RUSSIAN HISTORY **EDUCATION** Smith Col, BA, 48; Yale Univ, MA, 49; Columbia Univ, PhD, 73. **CAREER** Ref Asst & Res Assoc, Couns on Foreign Rel, 53-62; European Inst Res Asst to P.E. Mosely, Dir, 62-72; Asst Curator, Bakhmeteff Archive, 75-78; Res Scholar, Harriman Inst, 81-; Adj Prof, Political Science, 82-, Columbia Univ. **HONORS AND AWARDS** Phi Beta Kappa; BA Cum Laude; PhD with dist, MacArthur Fdn, Fac Res Prog, 85-86; Natl Coun for Soviet & Europe Res, 79-81, 89-90; IREX Sr Scholar Res & Trvl Grants, 74-98; Pew Fdn, 91, Kennan Inst , 91. **MEMBERSHIPS** AAASS; Pol Inst of Arts and Sci; Mid Atl Slavic Stud Assn; SHERA. **RESEARCH** Russian Central Asian Relations, Biography, Valentin Serov (1865-1911), Russian Painter **SELECTED PUBLICATIONS** Auth,The Soviet Union and the Third World: An Economic Bind, Praeger, 83&85; Auth, The Wanderers, Master of the l9th Century Russian Painting, Univ of Tx Press, 91; Auth, Art and Culture in Nineteenth Century Russia, Ind Univ Press, 83; Auth, East-West Tensions in the Third World, W.W. Norton, 86; Auth, Russian Realist Art, the State of Society, The Peredvizhniki and Their Tradition, Columbia Univ Press, 89; Auth, Ilya Repin and the World of Russian Art, Columbia Univ press , 90; Stalinizing Polish History: What Soviet Archives Disclose, E Europ Pol and Soc, V 7, No 1, 93; The Writer an Artist's Model: Repin's Portrait of Garshin, Metro Mus of Art J, V28, 93; Contr, Russian Art and Architecture, Acad Amer Encl, 93; Contr, The Birth of Realism, The Move Toward Decorativism, Cambridge Ency of Russia and Soviet Union, 93; The Changing Face of Oriental Studies in Russia, Central Asia Monitor, 4/94; The Birth of National Style, The Russian Stravinsky (Brklyn Acad Music, 94); Repin Tetrospective, Tretiakov Gallery, Slavic Rev, V54 No1, 94; Repin za rubezhom , Nashe Nasledi/Moscow/ No31, 94; Repin in Emigration, Har Inst Rev, V8 No4, 95; Contrib, Russian l9th Century Painters, Dict of Art, 95; Contrib, Russian Art and Architecture, Collier Ency, 95. **CONTACT ADDRESS** Columbia Univ, Harriman Inst, 420 West 1, NY, NY, 10027.

VALLETTA, CLEMENT LAWRENCE
PERSONAL Born 07/31/1938, Easton, PA **DISCIPLINE** AMERICAN CIVILIZATION, ENGLISH **EDUCATION** Univ Scranton, BA, 61; Univ Pa, MA, 62, PhD(Am Civilization), 68. **CAREER** From instr to assoc prof, 64-77, chmn dept, 71-80, prof English, King's Col, PA, 77-. **MEMBERSHIPS** MLA; Am Studies Asn; Am Folklore Soc; Christianity and Literature. **RESEARCH** Americanization of ethnic groups; influence of relativity physics in non-scientific aspects; American civilization, folk, rhetorical, literary aspects. **SELECTED PUBLICATIONS** Auth, Friendship and games in Italian American life, Keystone Folklore Quart, 70; Einstein, Edison and the conquest of irony, Cithara, 72; contrib, The ethnic experience in Pennsylvania, Bucknell Univ, 73; Studies in Italian American social history, Rowman & Littlefield, 75; auth, A study of Americanization in Carneta, Arno, 75; ed, Ethnic Drama: Video-Text and Study Guide, ERIC, 81; Pennsylavania History, 92; with Robert Paoletti In-Determindcy in Science and Discourse, Technical Writing and Communication, 95; Caring and Christian Irony in Ann Tyler's Novels, Repis Collage Proceedings, 96; A Christian Dispersion in Don DeLillo's The Names, Christianity and Literature, 98. **CONTACT ADDRESS** Dept of English, King's Col, 133 N River St, Wilkes Barre, PA, 18711-0801. **EMAIL** clvallet@kings.edu

VALONE, CAROLYN
DISCIPLINE ITALIAN RENAISSANCE ART **EDUCATION** Northwestern Univ, PhD. **CAREER** Prof, Trinity Univ. **SELECTED PUBLICATIONS** Pub(s), area of Roman and Venetian art and patronage of the sixteenth and seventeenth centuries. **CONTACT ADDRESS** Dept of Art Hist, Trinity Univ, 715 Stadium Dr, San Antonio, TX, 78212.

VALONE, JAMES S.
PERSONAL Born 12/29/1934, Warren, PA, m, 1959, 4 children **DISCIPLINE** EARLY MODERN EUROPEAN HISTORY **EDUCATION** Pa State Univ, AB, 56, MA, 58; Univ Mich, PhD, 65. **CAREER** From instr to asst prof, 61-68, assoc prof hist, Canisius Col, 68-, assoc dean, sch bus, 80-. **MEMBERSHIPS** AHA; Soc Fr Hist Studies; Am Cath Hist Soc. **RESEARCH** The political affairs of the Huguenots from 1598-1629. **SELECTED PUBLICATIONS** Auth, The Huguenots and the War of the Spanish Marriages: 1615-1616, Univ Microfilms, 66; Huguenot Politics, 1601-1622, The Edwin Mullen Press, 94. **CONTACT ADDRESS** Dept of Hist, Canisius Col, 2001 Main St, Buffalo, NY, 14208-1098. **EMAIL** valone@canisius.edu

VAN APPLEDORN, MARY JEANNE
PERSONAL Born 10/02/1927, Holland, MI **DISCIPLINE** MUSIC THEORY, COMPOSITION **EDUCATION** Univ Rochester, Eastman Sch of Music, BM 48, MM theory 50, PhD music 66. **CAREER** Texas Tech Univ, Sch of Music, Paul Whitfield Horn Prof, 50-98. **HONORS AND AWARDS** ASCAP, Stnd Panel Awds, Intl Trumpet Awd, Brit Trombone Asn Awd., Will be listed in New Grove Dictionary of Music and Musicians. **MEMBERSHIPS** ASCAP; SCI. **RESEARCH** Musicology, Theory, Composition. **SELECTED PUBLICATIONS** Music of Enchantment, for native american flute, Colorado Springs CO, ZaloJP Pub, 98; Cycles of Moons and Tides, San Antonio TX, Southern Music Co, 98; Les Hommes Vides, Bryn Mawr PA, Hildegard Pub, 98; Passages, Warwick UK, Warwick Music, 97; numerous others. **CONTACT ADDRESS** Dept Comp and Music, Texas Tech univ, Box 1583, Lubbock, TX, 79408-1583. **EMAIL** a5sjm@techmail.admin.ttu.edu

VAN BROEKHOVEN, DEBORAH
PERSONAL Born 02/15/1950, Toccoa, GA, m, 1978 **DISCIPLINE** AMERICAN STUDIES; HISTORY **EDUCATION** Barrington Col, BA, 72 Bowling Green State Univ, MA, 73, PhD, 77. **CAREER** Grand Rapids Baptist Col, asst prof of hist, 76-78; Barrington Col, asst prof, 78-85; Pembroke Center, Brown Univ, vis assoc prof, 85-87; OH Wesleyan Univ, assoc prof, 87-98; Am Baptist Hist Soc, exec dir, 98-. **HONORS AND AWARDS** NEH Fel, 86-87, Am Antiquarian Soc. **MEMBERSHIPS** Soc for Historians of the Early Am Republic, Friends Hist Assoc, OH Acad of Hist, Southern Hist Assoc, Organization of Am Historians, Am Hist Assoc. **RESEARCH** Relig, Soc and Cult Hist. **SELECTED PUBLICATIONS** Articles: Better than a Clay Club; The Organization of Women's Anti-Slavery Fairs, 1835-60, Slavery & Abolition 19, 98; 24-45; Needles, Pens and Petitions: Reading Women into Antislavery History, in The Meaning of Slavery in the North, Garland, 98, 125-155; Suffering with Slaveholders: Francis Wayland and the Politcs of Baptist Antislavery Positions, Religion and the Antebellum Debate Over Slavery, Univ of GA Press, 98; Abolitionists Were Female: Rhode Island Women and the Antislavery Network, 1830-1860, Urbana and Chicago: Univ of IL Press, 99. **CONTACT ADDRESS** American Baptist Hist Soc, Valley Forge, PA, 19482-0851. **EMAIL** deborah.vanbro@abc-usa.org

VAN BROEKHOVEN, DEBORAH B.
DISCIPLINE HISTORY **EDUCATION** Bowling Green, PhD. **CAREER** Assoc prof History, Ohio Wesleyan. **RESEARCH** Women's studies, women in the Anti-Slavery Movement. **SELECTED PUBLICATIONS** Fel Publ, 'Let Your Name be Enrolled': Process and Ideology in Female Anti-Salvery Petitioning, In: The Abolitionist Sisterhood: Women's Political Culture in Antebellum America, Cornell Univ, 94; auth, Crisis in the Life of a Literary Patriot: Brockden Brown's Shift from Cosmopolitan to Chronicler, Psychohist Rev 12, 84; 'A Determination to Labor': Female Antislavery Activity in Rhode Island, RI Hist, 85; Needles, Pens, and Petitions: Reading Women into Antislavery History, In: The North Looks at Slavery, Garland Press, 97; Francis Wayland and Baptist Schism Over Slavery, In: Slavery, Religion, and Sectionalism, Univ Tenn, 97; Abolitionists Were Female: Rhode Island's Women Organize Against Slavery, Univ Ill, 98. **CONTACT ADDRESS** Dept of History, Ohio Weslayan Univ, Delaware, OH, 43015. **EMAIL** dbvanbro@cc.owu.edu

VAN DE MIEROOP, MARC
DISCIPLINE ANCIENT NEAR EASTERN HISTORY **EDUCATION** Katholieke Universiteit, BA, 78; Yale, PhD, 83. **CAREER** Hist, Columbia Univ **SELECTED PUBLICATIONS** Auth, Society and Enterprise in Old Babylonian Ur, 92. **CONTACT ADDRESS** Columbia Univ, 2960 Broadway, New York, NY, 10027-6902.

VAN DEBURG, WILLIAM L.
PERSONAL Born 05/08/1948, Kalamazoo, MI, m, 1967, 2 children **DISCIPLINE** AFRO-AMERICAN HISTORY **EDUCATION** Western Mich Univ, BA, 70; Mich State Univ, MA,

71, PhD, 73. **CAREER** Asst prof, 73-79, assoc prof Afro-Amer studies, 79-, dept chmn, 81-84, Univ Wis-Madison; Danforth assoc, Danforth Found, 75-81; consult, Educ Testing Serv, 79-81, Ctr Study Southern Cult, 79-. **MEMBERSHIPS** Southern Hist Assn. **RESEARCH** Slavery and plantation studies; Black American historiography; Black Popular cultural studies, Black Nationalism. **SELECTED PUBLICATIONS** Auth, Modern Black Nationalism: From Markus Garvey to Louis Farrakhan, New York, University Press, 97; auth, Black Camelot: African-American Culture Heroes in Their Times, 1960-1980, University of Chicago Press, 97. **CONTACT ADDRESS** Afro-Am Studies Dept, Univ of Wisconsin, 600 N Park St, Madison, WI, 53706-1403. **EMAIL** wlvandeb@faccstaff.wisc.edu

VAN DEN BERGHE, PIERRE L.
PERSONAL Born 01/30/1933, Lubumbashi, Congo, m, 1956, 3 children **DISCIPLINE** SOCIOLOGY **EDUCATION** Stanford Univ, BA, 52, MA, 53; Harvard Univ, MA, 59, PhD, 60. **CAREER** Teaching Fel, Harvard Univ, 57-60; Ford Found Res Fel and Lectr, Univ Natal, 60-61; Vis Lectr, Sorbonne, 62; Asst Prof, Wesleyan Univ, 62-63; Assoc Prof, SUNY - Buffalo, 63-65; Assoc Prof, 65-67, Prof, 67-98, Prof Emeritus, Univ Wash, 98-; Vis Rockefeller Prof, Univ Nairobi & Univ Ibadan, 67-69; Vis Prof, Univ Haifa, 76; Sr. Fulbright Fel, Univ New South Wales, 82; Vis Prof, Univ Louis Pasteur, 83; Fel, Ctr Advanced Study Behavioral Sci, 84-85; Vis Prof, Univ Tuebingen, 86; Vis Prof, Univ Tel Aviv, 88; Vis Prof, Univ Cape Town, 89. **RESEARCH** Sociobiology; race and ethnic relations; kinship; tourism; genocide geographical specialization; sub-saharan Africa and Latin America. **SELECTED PUBLICATIONS** Ed & coauth, The Liberal Dilemma in South Africa, St. Martin's Press/Croom Helm, 79; auth, The Ethnic Phenomenon, Elsevier, 81, 2nd ed, Praeger, 87; co-ed, Tourism and Ethnicity, Special Issue of Annals of Tourism Research, 11, no 3, 84; auth, Stranger in their Midst, Univ Press Colo, 89; ed & coauth, State Violence and Ethnicity, Univ Press Colo, 90; auth, The Quest for the Other: Ethnic Tourism in San Cristobal, Mexico, Univ Wash Press, 94; Power Differentials and Language, The Encyclopedia of Language and Linguistics (in press); author of numerous other chapters, journal articles, and other publications. **CONTACT ADDRESS** Sociology Dept, Univ Wash, 202 Savery Hall, Box 353340, Seattle, WA, 98195-3340. **EMAIL** pludb@u.washington.edu

VAN DER MERWE, NIKOLAAS JOHANNES
PERSONAL Born 08/11/1940, Cape Province, South Africa, m, 2 children **DISCIPLINE** ARCHAEOLOGY **EDUCATION** BA, 62, MA, 65, PhD, 66, Yale. **CAREER** Curatorial and Lab Asst, Yale Uni, 62-66; Asst Prof Anthro, 66-69, Assoc Prof Anthro, 69-74, State Univ NY, Binghamton; Prof Archeol, 74-, Dir African Studies, 76-78, Dir Archeometry Res Unit, Found for Res Devel, 93-98, Univ Cape Town; Clay Orof of Sci Archaeol, Dept Anthro, 88-, Prof, Dept Earth and Planetary Sci, Harvard Univ. **SELECTED PUBLICATIONS** A L Cohen, J E Parkington, G B Brundit & N J van der Merwe, 92, A Holocene marine climate record in mollusc shells from the southwest African coast, Quanternary Research 38, 379-385; N J van der Merwe, J A Lee-Thorp & J S Raymond, 93, Light stable isotopes and the subsistence base of Formative cultures at Valdivia, Ecuador in J B Lambert and G Grupe eds, Prehistoric Human Bone-Archaeology at the Molecular Level, pp 63-98, Berlin: Springer-Verlag; Lee-Thorp, N J van der Merwe, & C K Brain, 94, Diet of Australopithecus robustus at J A Swartkrans from stable carbon siotope analysis, J Human Evolution 27, 361-372. **CONTACT ADDRESS** Peabody Museum, Harvard Univ, Cambridge, MA, 02138. **EMAIL** vanderme@fas.harvard.edu

VAN DER MIEROOP, MARC
DISCIPLINE ANCIENT NEAR EASTERN HISTORY **EDUCATION** Katholieke Univ, Leuven, BA, 78; Yale Univ, PhD, 83. **CAREER** Prof. **RESEARCH** Imperialism in the ancient Near East. **SELECTED PUBLICATIONS** Auth, Society and Enterprise in Old Babylonian Ur, 92. **CONTACT ADDRESS** Dept of Hist, Columbia Col, New York, 2960 Broadway, New York, NY, 10027-6902.

VAN DER SLIK, JACK RONALD
PERSONAL Born 12/14/1936, Kalamazoo, MI, m, 1963, 3 children **DISCIPLINE** POLITICAL SCIENCE AND EDUCATION **EDUCATION** Calvin College, BA, 58; Western Michigan Univ, MA; Michigan State Univ, 67 MA, PhD. **CAREER** Instructor, Michigan State Univ, 67, Asst Prof to Assoc Prof, Southern Illinois Univ 67-78, Visiting Assoc Prof, Calvin College, 72-73, Academic Dean, Trinity Christian College, 78-81, Assoc Dean of Liberal Arts, Carbondale 75-78, Prof, Sangamon State Univ since 95, named Univ of Illinois at Springfield 81-present. **HONORS AND AWARDS** Pi Sigma Alpha-political science honorary society, life member, Biography in Contemporary Authors, Listed in Who's Who in the Midweest; Who's Who Among Teachers 96. **MEMBERSHIPS** Amer Political Sci Assoc; Academy of Ploitical Sci; Midwest Political Sci Assoc; Policy Studies Assoc; Christians in Political Sci. **RESEARCH** Amer national and state politics; Illinois politics; legislatures; religion and politics. **SELECTED PUBLICATIONS** Almanac of Illinois Politics, Institute for Public Affairs, editor, 90, 92, 94, 96, 98; Politics in the Amer States and Communities, A Contemporary Reader, Allyn & Bacon, 96; One for All and All for Illinois: Representing the Land of Lincoln in Congress Institute for Public Affairs, 95; Lawmaking in Illinois: Legislative Politics,People and Processes, 86; Amer Legislative Processes New York: Thomas Y. Crowell Co, 77; Clinton and the New Convenant: Theology Shaping a New Politics or Old Politics in Religious Dress?, Journal of Church and State, forthcoming; The Democratization of Legislative Politics in Korea, Korea Journal 37, No 4 p39-64, Doh C. Shin and Van Der Slik, 97; Contrain Congressional Behavior: Bipartisan Cooperation in the Illinois Delegation, Illinois Political Sci Review 2, no 1, p5-19, 96; A Polemic on Educ Reform in the Amer States, Social Indicators Research 27, no 3, p205-220, Doh C. Shinn and Van Der Slik, 92. **CONTACT ADDRESS** Dept of Political Studies, Univ of Illinois at Sprinfield, PO Box 19243, Springfield, IL, 62794-9243. **EMAIL** vanderslik.jack@uis.edu

VAN HELDEN, ALBERT
PERSONAL Born 03/07/1940, The Hague, Netherlands **DISCIPLINE** HISTORY OF SCIENCE **EDUCATION** Univ London Imp College, PhD, 70. **CAREER** Lynette S Autrey Prof, currently, 70-, Rice Univ. **MEMBERSHIPS** AAAS; HSS. **RESEARCH** History of Astronomy **SELECTED PUBLICATIONS** Auth, A Catalog of Early Telescopes, Isituto e Museo di Storia della Scienza, Florence, 98; coauth, The History of Science in the Netherlands, Leiden, Brill, 98; The Galileo Project, http://www.rice.edu/Galileo, 95, hypertext resource on the life and work of Galileo Galilei 1564-1642; coed, Scientific Instruments, Osiris, 94; coed, Julian Huxley 1887-1975: Biologist and Statesman of Science, RUP 93. **CONTACT ADDRESS** Dept of History, Rice Univ, 6100 S Main St, Houston, TX, 77005-1892. **EMAIL** helden@rice.edu

VAN MIEGROET, HANS J.
DISCIPLINE ART HISTORY **EDUCATION** Univ CA, PhD. **CAREER** Assoc prof, Duke Univ. **RESEARCH** Economic, soc and polit hist of early mod Europ art with emphasis on Burgundy, France, the Netherlands and Germany. **SELECTED PUBLICATIONS** Auth, on Konrad Witz and Gerard David; co-auth, studies on econ arts, 96; Markets and Novelty, 98. **CONTACT ADDRESS** Dept of Art and Art Hist, Duke Univ, East Duke Building, Durham, NC, 27706. **EMAIL** hvm@acpub.duke.edu

VAN NUS, WALTER
DISCIPLINE HISTORY **EDUCATION** Univ Toronto, BA, MA, PhD. **CAREER** Assoc prof. **HONORS AND AWARDS** Dir, undergrad hist prog(s); act assoc dean. **RESEARCH** Canadian urban development and urban architecture. **SELECTED PUBLICATIONS** Pub(s), series of papers on urban aesthetics, the history of urban planning thought in Can, urban development in Montreal. **CONTACT ADDRESS** Dept of Hist, Concordia Univ, Montreal, 1455 de Maisonneuve W, Montreal, PQ, H3G 1M8. **EMAIL** vannus@vax2.concordia.ca

VAN PATTEN, JAMES J.
PERSONAL Born 09/09/1925, North Rose, NY, m, 1961 **DISCIPLINE** HISTORY **CAREER** Asst, assoc prof, 62-69, Cent Mo St Univ; assoc prof, 69-71, Univ Okla; assoc prof, 71-98, Univ Ark. **MEMBERSHIPS** APA; Amer Ed Res Assn; Ed Law Assn; Phil of Ed Soc; Amer Ed Stud Assn. **RESEARCH** Futurism; history of Amer educ; global educ, phil/history. **SELECTED PUBLICATIONS** Auth, What's Really Happening in Education, Univ Press Amer, 97; auth, The Culture of Higher Education, Univ Press Amer, 96; auth, Watersheds in Higher Education, Mellon Press NY, 97; coauth, History of Education in America, Prentice Hall/Merrill, 99. **CONTACT ADDRESS** Education Leadership, Univ of Arkansas, GE 248 Education, Fayetteville, AR, 72701. **EMAIL** jvanpatt@com.uark.edu

VAN STEEN, GONDA ALINE HECTOR
PERSONAL Born 04/08/1964, Aalst, Belgium, m, 1996 **DISCIPLINE** CLASSICS **EDUCATION** Princeton Univ, MA, 90, PhD, 95. **CAREER** Asst Prof, 95-97, Cornell Univ; Asst Prof, Classic & Modern Greek, 97-, Univ of Ariz. **HONORS AND AWARDS** Undergrad full tuition fel Govt Belgium, Undergrad Dissertation Awd, J D & C T MacArthur Found Grant, Alexander Papamarkou Awd, Gennadeion Fel, AGTE Awd, Stanley J Seeger Fel, Mary Isabel Sibley Fel, MGSA PhD Dissertation Prize. **MEMBERSHIPS** APA, MGSA, MLA. **RESEARCH** Ancient & modern Greek drama, film & performance criticism, gender studies, language instruction, foreign studies program. **SELECTED PUBLICATIONS** Auth, Venom in Verse, Aristophanes and Transgression in Modern Greece, Princeton Univ Press, forthcoming 99; Destined to Be? - Tyche in Chariton's Chaereas and Callirhoe and in the Byzantine Romance of Kallimachos and Chrysorroi, in: L'Antiquite Classique, 88; Aristophanes Revival on the Modern Greek Stage, in: Dialogos, Hellenic Studies Review, Kings Coll London, 95; Aspects of Public Performance in Aristophanes' Acharnians, AC, 94. **CONTACT ADDRESS** Dept of Classics, Univ of Arizona, Mod Lang Bldg, Box 210067, Tucson, AZ, 85721-0067. **EMAIL** gonda@u.arizona.edu

VAN TINE, WARREN R.
PERSONAL Born 08/28/1942, Philadelphia, PA, m, 1983, 1 child **DISCIPLINE** HISTORY **EDUCATION** Baldwin-Wallace Col, BA, 65; Northern Ill Univ, MA, 67; Univ Mass, PhD,72. **CAREER** From asst prof to assoc prof to prof, 70-, Ohio State Univ. **HONORS AND AWARDS** Fulbright Sen Lectr, 78; Grant Aid, Ohio State Univ, 72-74, 84, 86; Seed Grant, Ohio State Univ, 85-86; Ctr Labor Res Grant, 90-91; Univ Distinguished Affirmation Action Award, 93; Outstanding Tchg Award, Sigma Chi Fraternity, 94-95; Ctr Labor Res Grant, 96-97. **MEMBERSHIPS** Ohio Acad Hist; Labor and Working Class Hist Asn. **RESEARCH** US labor, African American, Ohio. **SELECTED PUBLICATIONS** Auth, The Making of the Labor Bureaucrat: Union Leadership in the United States, 1870-1920, 73; coauth, John L. Lewis: A Bibliography, 77; auth, art, Joe Hill, 83; coauth, John L. Lewis, 86; coauth, In the Workers' Interests: A History of the Ohio AFL-CIO, 1958-1998, 98. **CONTACT ADDRESS** 230 W 17th Ave, Columbus, OH, 43202. **EMAIL** vantine.1@osu.edu

VAN ZANTEN, DAVID
DISCIPLINE HISTORY **EDUCATION** Vis student Courtauld Inst of Art, London, 63-64; Princeton Univ, BA, 65; Harvard Univ, MA, 66, PhD, 70. **CAREER** Vis Prof, 76, Cornell Univ; Vis Prof, 79, Univ of California/Berkley; Vis Prof, 80, Columbia Univ; Asst Prof, 70-71, McGill Univ; Asst Prof/Assoc Prof, 71-79, University of Pennsylvania; Assoc Prof/Prof, 79-, Northwestern Univ. **HONORS AND AWARDS** NEH Sr Fel, 97-98/89-90; Chevalier of the Ordre des Arts et des Lettres, France, 95; Alice Davis Hitchcock Awd, 88; Prix Bernier Academie des Beaux-Arts, Paris; Fulbright Fel, Paris, 68-69. **SELECTED PUBLICATIONS** Auth, Walter Burley Griffin Selected Designs, 70; auth, The Architectural Polychromy of the 1830s, Garland, 77; auth, The Beaux-Arts tradition in French Architecture, Princeton, 82; auth, Designing Paris The Architecture of Duban Labrouste Vaudoyer and Duc, MIT Press, 87; auth, Building Paris Architectural Institutions and the Transformation of the French Capital 1830-1870, Cambridge, 95. **CONTACT ADDRESS** Dept of Art History, Northwestern Univ, Evanston, IL, 60208. **EMAIL** d-van@nwu.edu

VANAUKEN, SHELDON
DISCIPLINE HISTORY, ENGLISH **EDUCATION** Oxford Univ, BLitt, 57. **CAREER** From asst prof to assoc prof, 48-73, PROF HIST and ENGLISH, LYNCHBURG COL, 73- **RESEARCH** Nineteenth century England. **SELECTED PUBLICATIONS** Auth, Employment Law Survey, Denver Univ Law Rev, Vol 0072, 95. **CONTACT ADDRESS** 100 Breckenbridge, Lynchburg, VA, 24501.

VANDERPOOL, HAROLD YOUNG
PERSONAL Born 06/28/1936, Port Arthur, Tex, m, 1960, 3 children **DISCIPLINE** AMERICAN HISTORY, ETHICS **EDUCATION** Harding Col, BA, 58; Abilene Christian Univ, MA, 60; Harvard Univ, BD, 63, PhD(relig & hist), 71, ThM, 76. **CAREER** From instr to asst prof relig & Am studies, Wellesey Col, 66-75; Harvard Univ Interfac Prof Med Ethics fel, 75-76; Assoc Prof Hist Med & Med Ethics, Univ Tex Med BR, Galveston, 76- **HONORS AND AWARDS** Kennedy Fnd Fel; Outstand Acad Bk, Assn of Col and Res Lib; Special Govt Emp for the NIH and US FDA **MEMBERSHIPS** Am Asn for Hist Med; AHA; Am Soc Church Hist; Soc Health & Human Values; Am Studies Asn. **RESEARCH** Ethics of reseach with Human Subjects; medical ethics; hisoty of medicine in American society; religion and society. **SELECTED PUBLICATIONS** Auth, The ethics of terminal care, JAMA, 78; auth, Responsibility of Physicians Toward Dying Patients, Medical Complications in Cancer Patients, Raven, 81; auth, Medicine and Religion: How Are They Related? J Relig & Health, 90; auth, Death and Dying: Euthanasia and Sustaining Life: Historical Perspective, Ency of Bioethics, Simon & Schuster MacMillan, 95; coauth, The Ethics of Research Involving Human Subjects, U Pub Group, 96; auth, Doctors and the Dying of Patients in American History, Physician Assisted Suicide, Indiana Univ, 97; auth, Critical Ethical Issues in Clinical Trials with Xenotransplants, The Lancet, 98. **CONTACT ADDRESS** Inst of Med Humanities, Univ of Tex Med Br, 301 University Blvd, Galveston, TX, 77555-1311. **EMAIL** hvanderp@utmb.edu

VANDERVORT, BRUCE
DISCIPLINE HISTORY **EDUCATION** Univ Va, PhD, 89. **CAREER** Prof, Va Mil Inst.. **HONORS AND AWARDS** Asst ed, J Mil Hist. **RESEARCH** Modern French history after1789; the history of European imperialism. **SELECTED PUBLICATIONS** Auth, Victor Griffuelhes and French Syndicalism, 1895-1922, La State Univ Press, 96; Wars of Imperial Conquest in Africa, 1830-1914, Univ Col London Press, 98. **CONTACT ADDRESS** Dept of History, Virginia Military Inst, Lexington, VA, 24450.

VANDERWOOD, PAUL JOSEPH
PERSONAL Born 06/03/1929, Brooklyn, NY **DISCIPLINE** LATIN AMERICAN HISTORY **EDUCATION** Bethany Col, BA, 50; Memphis State Univ, MA, 57; Univ Tex, Austin, PhD(hist), 70. **CAREER** Journalist, Memphis Press Scimitar, 54-63; evaluator, US Peace Corps, 63-64; PROF HIST, SAN DIEGO STATE UNIV, 69-. **HONORS AND AWARDS** Nat Asn State and Local Hist Award, 71; Hubert B Herring Award, Pac Coast Coun Latin Am Studies, 76 and 81. **MEMBERSHIPS** AHA; Conf Latin Am Hist; Am Film Inst; Pac Coast

Coun Latin Am Studies. **RESEARCH** Mexican revolution; film and history; social banditry. **SELECTED PUBLICATIONS** Auth, The Hisp Image on the Silver-Screen, an Interpretive Filmography from Silents to Sound, 1898-1935, Hisp Amer Hist Rev, Vol 0073, 93; Manet, the Execution of Maximilian, Painting, Politics, and Censorship, Hisp Amer Hist Rev, Vol 0073, 93; Political Protest and Street Art--Popular Tools for Democratization in Hisp Countries, Hisp Amer Hist Rev, Vol 0074, 94; Forge of Progress, Crucible of Revolt, the Origins of the Mexican-Revolution in La Comarca-Lagunera, 1880-1911, Hisp Amer Hist Rev, Vol 0075, 95; Peasant and Nation--The Making of Postcolonial Mexico and Peru, Hisp Amer Hist Rev, Vol 0076, 96; Memo from Zanuck,Darryl,F.--The Golden Years at Twentieth-Century-Fox, Jour West, Vol 0035, 96; Eastwood, Clint--A Cultural Production, Jour West, Vol 0035, 96; New-Kingdom of the Saints--Religious Art of New-Mexico, 1780-1907 - Frank,L/, Hisp Amer Hist Rev, Vol 0076, 96; History of Indigenous Rebellions in the Tarahumara--Spanish, Hisp Amer Hist Rev, Vol 0077, 97. **CONTACT ADDRESS** Dept of Hist, San Diego State Univ, San Diego, CA, 92182.

VANDIVER, ELIZABETH
DISCIPLINE CLASSICS **EDUCATION** Univ Tex, Austin, PhD, 90. **CAREER** Vis asst prof, 96-98; assoce head, Willard Residential Col; co-organizer, 3-yr Colloquium on Translation in Context. **RESEARCH** A Reader's Guide to Shakespeare's Mythology. **SELECTED PUBLICATIONS** Auth, Heroes in Herodotus: The Interaction of Myth and History, Studien zur klassische philol, 91; Fireflies in a Jar, Sappho in Translation, Poetry in Rev, 96; Ex hoc ingrato gaudia amore tibi: Catullus' Unhappy Love and the Modern Reader, The New Engl Class Newsletter and J, 92; Greek Heroic Mythology and the Ritual Theory of Tragedy's Origin, Text and Presentation, 91; Sound Patterns in Catullus 84, Class J, 90. **CONTACT ADDRESS** Dept of Classics, Northwestern Univ, 1801 Hinman, Kresge 10A, Evanston, IL, 60208. **EMAIL** e-vandiver@nwu.edu

VANDIVER, FRANK EVERSON
PERSONAL Born 12/09/1925, Austin, TX, m, 1955 **DISCIPLINE** HISTORY **EDUCATION** Univ Tex, MA, 49; Tulane Univ, PhD(hist), 51. **CAREER** Historian, US Civil Serv, Tex, 44-45; Air Force historian, Ala, 51-52; instr hist, exten, Univ Ala, 52; from instr to asst prof, Wash Univ, 52-55; from asst prof to prof, 55-65, chmn dept hist, 62 and 68-69, acting pres, 69-70, Harris Masterson, Jr prof hist, Rice Univ, 65-79, provost, 70-79, vpres, 75-79; pres, North Tex State Univ, 79-81; PRES, TEX AandM UNIV, 81-, Am Philos Soc res grants, 54, 55 and 60; Guggenheim fel, 55-56; lectr, Va Civil War Centennial Comn, Richmond, 62; Harmon Mem lectr, US Air Force Acad, 63, mem, Harmon Mem Lect Serv Selection Comt, 71-; Harmsworth prof, Oxford Univ, 63-64; pres, Jefferson Davis Asn, 63-, chief adv ed, Papers of Jefferson Davis; master, Margarett Root Brown Col, 64-66; mem adv coun, Off Chief Mil Hist, Dept Army, 69-74, selection comt, Ft Leavenworth Hall of Fame Asn of US Army, 71-80; chmn, US Army Mil Hist Res Collection Adv Comt, 72-; mem, Nat Coun on Humanities, 72-78, chmn educ subcomt, 73-76, chmn planning and analysis subcomt, 76-78, vchmn, 76-78; vis prof mil hist, US Mil Acad, 73-74; bd dirs, Inst Civil War Studies, 75-; Fulbright-Hays fel, 76; hon chmn, Pershing Mem Mus, 77- **HONORS AND AWARDS** Carr P Collins Prize, Tex Inst Lett, 58; Harry S Truman Award, 66; Jefferson Davis Award, Confederate Mem Lit Soc, 71; Fletcher Pratt Award, NY Civil War Round Table, 71; Best Bk Award for Non-fiction, Tex Bks Rev, 77., MA, Oxford Univ, 63. **MEMBERSHIPS** Orgn Am Historians; AHA (vpres, 74-75, pres, 75-76); Southern Hist Asn; fel Soc Am Historians; Am Comt Hist 2nd World War. **RESEARCH** American history; military history; Civil War history. **SELECTED PUBLICATIONS** Auth, Lee and Jackson--Confederate Chieftains, Jour Amer Hist, Vol 0080, 93; Lee Considered--Lee,Robert,E. and Civil-War History, Jour So Hist, Vol 0059, 93; Uncertain Warriors--Johnson,Lyndon and His Vietnam Advisers, Jour So Hist, Vol 0061, 95; Pay Any Price--Johnson,Lyndon and the Wars for Vietnam, Jour So Hist, Vol 0063, 97; Burns,Ken the Civil War--Historians Respond, Jour So Hist, Vol 0063, 97; Fulbright--A Biography, Jour So Hist, Vol 0063, 97. **CONTACT ADDRESS** Texas Aandm Univ, College Stn, TX, 77843.

VANN, RICHARD T.
PERSONAL Born 06/25/1931, Belton, TX, m, 1954, 1 child **DISCIPLINE** SOCIAL AND INTELLECTUAL HISTORY **EDUCATION** Southern Methodist Univ, BA, 52; Oxford Univ, BA, 54, MA, 58; Harvard Univ, MA, 57, PhD(hist), 59. **CAREER** Instr hist, Harvard Univ, 59-61; asst prof, Carleton Col, 61-64; assoc prof, 64-69, PROF HIST and LETT, WESLEYAN UNIV, 69-, Exec ed, Hist and Theory, 65-; Soc Relig Higher Educ cross-disciplinary fel, 66-67; Soc Sci Res Coun grant, 66-67 and fel, 70-71; Am Coun Learned Socs grant, 66-68; prin investr, Nat Endowment for Humanities grant, 74-77; Guggenheim fel, 76-77. **MEMBERSHIPS** Fel Royal Hist Soc. **RESEARCH** Historical demography; theory of history; history of the family. **SELECTED PUBLICATIONS** Auth, Patients, Power, and the Poor in 18th-Century Bristol, Jour Interdisciplinary Hist, Vol 0024, 93; History and Social-Theory, Amer Hist Rev, Vol 0099, 94; The Largest Amount of Good--Quaker Relief in Ireland, 1654-1921, Amer Hist Rev, Vol 0099, 94; History, Historians, and the Dynamics of Change, Clio-Jour Lit Hist and Philos Hist, Vol 0024, 95; Telling the Truth About History, Amer Hist Rev, Vol 0100, 95; Commoners, Common Right, Enclosure and Social-Change in England, 1700-1820, Jour Interdisciplinary Hist, Vol 0026, 96. **CONTACT ADDRESS** Dept of Hist and Lett, Wesleyan Univ, Middletown, CT, 06457.

VANN, ROBERT LINDLEY
PERSONAL Born 08/08/1945, Greenville, TX **DISCIPLINE** ARCHITECTURE **EDUCATION** Univ Tex, Austin, BS, 68; Cornell Univ, PhD, 76. **CAREER** Lectr, 74-75, asst prof archit, Univ Md, College Park, 75-, vis mem archit, Cornell Summer Prog in Rome, 79-80. **MEMBERSHIPS** Soc Archit Historians; Archaeol Inst Am; Soc Hist Archaeol; Asn Field Archaeol. **RESEARCH** Aspects of construction in Roman archaeology; underwater archaeology; architecture of the Roman provinces. **SELECTED PUBLICATIONS** Auth, A discussion of the cisterns, Excavations at Carthage, Vol III, 77; auth, A note on the building mortars at Carthage, Excavations at Carthage, 1976,Vol IV, 78; auth, Problems and procedures in architectural recording at Carthage, Roman cisterns in the Michigan field, Univ Mich, 77; auth, Byzantine street construction in the southwest quarter, Caesarea Studies, 82. **CONTACT ADDRESS** Sch of Architecture, Univ MD, College Park, MD, 20742-0001. **EMAIL** rv6@umail.umd.edu

VANSINA, JAN
PERSONAL Born 09/14/1929, Antwerp, Belgium, m, 1954, 1 child **DISCIPLINE** AFRICAN HISTORY AND ANTHROPOLOGY **EDUCATION** Univ Leuven, PhD(mod hist), 57. **CAREER** Researcher, Inst Cent African Res, Belgium, 52-60, dir ctr, 57-60; assoc prof hist, 60-64, prof anthrop and hist, 64-73 and 75-77, VILAS RES PROF, UNIV WIS-MADISON, 77-, Vis lectr, Univ Lovanium, Leopoldville, 57-59 and Northwestern Univ, 62-63; vis prof, Univ Lovanium Kinshasha, 66-67, prof, 71; mem, Int Sci Comt Drafting Gen Hist Africa, UNESCO, 70-78, vpres, 81-; vis prof, Univ Pa, 82. **HONORS AND AWARDS** Quinquennial Prize, 67; Herskovits Prize, African Studies Asn, 67. **MEMBERSHIPS** Fel African Studies Asn; Royal Acad Overseas Sci, Belgium; AHA; Int African Inst; Int Soc Folk Narrative Res. **RESEARCH** General social anthropology; African history; techniques and methods in culture history. **SELECTED PUBLICATIONS** Auth, Catastrophe and Creation--The Transformation of an African Culture, Jour African Hist, Vol 0034, 93; Ethnography and the Hist Imagination, Intl Jour African Hist Stud, Vol 0026, 93; Bantu Roots--French and English, Intl Jour African Hist Stud, Vol 0026, 93; History Making in Africa, Intl Jour African Hist Stud, Vol 0027, 94; Africa and the Disciplines--The Contribution of Research in Africa to the Social-Sciences and the Humanities, Intl Jour African Hist Stud, Vol 0027, 94; History in Popular Songs and Dances--The Bemba Cultural Zone of Upper Shaba Zaire--French, Jour African Hist, Vol 0035, 94; Valleys of the Niger--French, Jour African Hist, Vol 0036, 95; New Linguistic Evidence and the Bantu Expansion, Jour African Hist, Vol 0036, 95; Iron, Gender, and Power--Rituals, of Transformation in African Societies, Amer Hist Rev, Vol 0100, 95; African Masterworks in the Detroit-Institute-of-Arts, Jour African Hist, Vol 0038, 97; South-Pacific Oral Traditions, Jour Interdisciplinary Hist, Vol 0027, 97. **CONTACT ADDRESS** 2810 Ridge Rd, Madison, WI, 53705.

VAPORIS, CONSTANTINE N.
DISCIPLINE HISTORY **EDUCATION** Princeton Univ, PhD. **CAREER** Assoc prof, Univ MD Baltimore County. **HONORS AND AWARDS** Fulbright Sch Awd. **RESEARCH** Japanese and East Asian hist. **SELECTED PUBLICATIONS** Auth, Breaking Barriers: Travel and the State in Early Modern Japan. **CONTACT ADDRESS** Dept of Hist, Univ MD Baltimore County, Hilltop Circle, PO Box 1000, Baltimore, MD, 21250. **EMAIL** vaporis@research.umbc.edu

VARDAMAN, JAMES WELCH
PERSONAL Born 11/26/1928, Dallas, TX, m, 1955, 3 children **DISCIPLINE** MODERN EUROPEAN HISTORY **EDUCATION** Baylor Univ, BA, 51; Univ Minn, MA, 52; Vanderbilt Univ, PhD, 57. **CAREER** Instr Hist, La Col, 54-56; asst prof, Howard Payne Col, 56-58 & Tex Christian Univ, 58-62; assoc prof, Va Mil Inst, 62-66; prof Hist, Baylor Univ 66-; Jo Murphy chairholder, Int Ed; dir Cen Int Affairs. **MEMBERSHIPS** AHA; Southern Hist Asn; Nat Assn for Foreighn Student Affairs; Assn of Int Ed Admin. **RESEARCH** English history; 20th century European history; 17th century Europe. **CONTACT ADDRESS** Dept of History, Baylor Univ, PO Box 97306, Waco, TX, 76706-7306. **EMAIL** James_Vardaman@baylor.edu

VARDY, STEVEN BELA
PERSONAL Born 07/03/1936, Hungary, m, 1962, 3 children **DISCIPLINE** HISTORY; EAST EUROPEAN STUDIES **EDUCATION** John Carroll Univ, BS, 59; Indiana Univ, MA, 61, PhD, 67. **CAREER** Instr, Washburn Univ, 63-64; from asst prof to distinguished prof, Duquesne Univ, 64-; IREX vis scholar, Hung Acad of Scis & Univ of Budapest, 69-70, 75-76; adj prof, Univ of Pittsburgh, 78-96; chemn, Dept of Hist, Duquesne Univ, 83-96. **HONORS AND AWARDS** Res Grants from IREX, NEH, Ford Found, Hunkele Found, Noble J. Dick Found, W. Penn Asn, German Am Nat Cong; Hillman Found, 63-97; Presidential Award for Excellence in Scholar, Duquesne Univ, 84; Hungary's Berzsenyi Prize, 92; Elected Mem of the Hungarian Writers' Found, 97; Gold Medal for Hist Scholar, Arpad Acad of Arts and Scis, 97; McAnulty Distinguished Prof of Hist, Duquesne Univ, 98. **MEMBERSHIPS** Am Asn for the Advan of Slavic Studies; Am Asn for the Study of Hungarian Hist; AHA; Am Hungarian Educators' Asn; Arpad Acad of Arts and Scis; Hungarian Writers' Fedn; Int Asn of Hungarian Hists; Int Asn of Hungarian Lang and Cult; Int PEN. **RESEARCH** Central European/Hungarian historiography; modern central European/Habsburg/Hungarian history; immigration history with emphasis on Hungarian immigration. **SELECTED PUBLICATIONS** Auth, Modern Hungarian Historiography, 76; Clio's Art in Hungary and in Hungarian-America, 85; The Hungarian-Americans, 85; Baron Joseph Eoetvoes: A Literary Biography, 87; The Austro-Hungarian Mind: At Home and Abroad, 89; Attila the Hun, 90; Historical Dictionary of Hungary, 97; Hungarians in the New World, 98. **CONTACT ADDRESS** Dept of History, Duquesne Univ, Pittsburgh, PA, 15282. **EMAIL** Svardy@aol.com

VARDY, STEVEN BELA
PERSONAL Born 07/03/1935, Bercel, Hungary, m, 1962, 1 child **DISCIPLINE** EUROPEAN HISTORY **EDUCATION** John Carroll Univ, BS, 59; Ind Univ, MA, 61, PhD(hist), 67. **CAREER** Instr hist, Washburn Univ, 63-64; from asst prof to assoc prof, 64-71, PROF HIST, DUQUESNE UNIV, 71-98, DIST PROF HIST, 98-, DIR HIST FORUM, 78-83, 86-96, Partic, Carnegie Corp instnl grant, 67-70; founding mem, Inter-Univ Teaching & Res Prog Comp Communism, Univ Pittsburgh, 67-; Int Res & Exchanges Bd fel, Eastern Europe, 69-70, sr fel, 75-76; vis scholar, Inst Hist, Hungarian Acad Sci, 69-70 & 75-76; ethnic studies comt, Pittsburgh Coun Higher Educ, 71-; Am Hungarian Studies Found res grant, 73; partic, Hillman Found res grant for ethnic studies, 73-75; Hungarian Cult Found res & publ grant, 75; vis scholar hist, Eotvos Univ Budapest, 75-76; adj prof Hungarian, Univ Pittsburgh, 79-; Uralic and Altaic res grant, 80 & 82; Hunkele Found res grant, 80. **HONORS AND AWARDS** Res grants, Dusquene Univ Pres Awd for Excel in Scholarship; Berzsenyi Prize for Schol Ach of Hunagrian Stu; Gold Medal for Hist Schol; McAnulty Dist Prof of Hist **MEMBERSHIPS** AAASS; AASHH; AHA; Am Hungarian Educ Assn; HWF; IAHH; IAHLC. **RESEARCH** East European history, with emphasis on the Habsburg Empire and the Ottoman Empire in the Balkans; East European historiography; East Europeans in the United States. **SELECTED PUBLICATIONS** Auth, Hungarian studies at American and Canadian universities, Can-Am Rev Hungarian Studies, 75; The origins of Jewish emancipation in Hungary, Ungarn-Jahrbuch, Munich, 76; Modern Hungarian Historiography, Columbia Univ, 76; The development of East European historical studies in Hungary prior to 1945, Balkan Studies, Thessaloniki, 77; Ethnicity and Politics among Hungarian-Americans, In: America's Ethnic Politics, Greenwood Press, 82; ed, Society in Change, Columbia Univ Press, 82; co-ed, Louis the Great of Hungary and of Poland (1342-1382), Duquesne Univ Press, 82; auth, Attila the Hun, Chelsea House, 90; auth, Historical Dictionary of Hungary, Scarecrow Pub, 97; auth, Hungarians in the New World, Mundus, 98. **CONTACT ADDRESS** Dept of Hist, Duquesne Univ, Pittsburgh, PA, 15219.

VARG, PAUL ALBERT
PERSONAL Born 03/20/1912, Worcester, MA, m, 1936, 1 child **DISCIPLINE** HISTORY **EDUCATION** Clark Univ, BA, 35, MA, 37; Univ Chicago, PhD, 47. **CAREER** Teacher, Publ Schs, Iowa, 36-37; critic teacher hist, Nebr State Teachers Col, Kearney, 37-38; instr, NPark Col, 39-43; assoc prof, Ohio State Univ, 46-58; prof, 58-62, Dean, Col Arts and Lett, 62-69, PROF HIST, MICH STATE UNIV, 69-, Fulbright lectr, Univ Stockholm, 55-56; vis prof, Univ Ore, 57-58. **MEMBERSHIPS** AHA; Orgn Am Historians. **RESEARCH** American diplomatic history. **SELECTED PUBLICATIONS** Auth, Encountering the Dominant Player--United-States Extended Deterrence Strategy in the Asia-Pacific, Intl Hist Rev, Vol 0014, 92; United-States Attitudes and Policies Toward China--The Impact of American Missionaries, Cath Hist Rev, Vol 0079, 93. **CONTACT ADDRESS** Dept of Hist, Michigan State Univ, East Lansing, MI, 48824.

VARGA, NICHOLAS
PERSONAL Born 09/13/1925, Elizabeth, NJ, m, 1951, 3 children **DISCIPLINE** AMERICAN HISTORY **EDUCATION** Boston Col, BS, 51, MA, 52; Fordham Univ, PhD, 60. **CAREER** From instr to prof, 55-92, chmn dept, 62-67, prof emer hist, Loyola Col, Md, 92-, archivist, 77-. **MEMBERSHIPS** AHA; NY State Hist Asn. **RESEARCH** New York colonial history; 19th and 20th century Baltimore. **SELECTED PUBLICATIONS** Auth, The New York Restraining Act ..., in NY Hist, 7/56; Robert Charles, New York agent, 1748-1770, in William & Mary Quart, 4/61; The Reverend Michael Houdin (1706-1776) ..., in Hist Mag Protestant Episcopal Church, 12/64; Crisis in the Great Republic, Fordham Univ, 69; Town and County, Weslyan Univ, 78; Baltimore's Loyola, Loyola's Baltimore, Md Hist Soc, 90. **CONTACT ADDRESS** Dept of Hist, Loyola Col, 4501 N Charles St, Baltimore, MD, 21210-2694.

VARGAS, JULIE S.
PERSONAL Born 04/28/1938, Minneapolis, MN, m, 1962, 2 children **DISCIPLINE** BEHAVIOROLOGY **EDUCATION** Harvard Univ, AB, 60; Columbia Univ, MA, 62; Univ Pittsburgh, PhD, 69. **CAREER** Elementary school teacher, New York City and Morceville, PA, 60-62; res assoc, Am Inst for Res, 62-64; res asst, Univ Pittsburgh, 64-66; fac member to prof, WV Univ, 66-. **HONORS AND AWARDS** Vis Scholar, Dept of Psychology, Harvard Univ, 93. **MEMBERSHIPS** Asn for Behavior Analysis; Sigma Xi; Int Behaviorology Soc; Phi Delta Kappa. **RESEARCH** Instructional design; verbal behavior; life and work of B F Skinner. **SELECTED PUBLICATIONS** Auth, Writing Worthwhile Behavioral Objectives, Harper & Row, 73; Behavioral Psychology for Teachers, Harper & Row, 77; with B M Stewart, Teaching Behavior to Infants: A Manual for Childcare Workers and Parents, Charles C Thomas, 90; with D Shanley, Academic Skills, in W O'Donohue and Leonard Krasner, eds, Handbook of Psychological Skills Training, Allyn and Bacon, 95; with E A Vargus, B F Skinner and the Origins of Programmed Instruction, in L D Smith and W R Woodward, eds, B F Skinner and Behaviorism in American Culture, Associated Univ Presses, 96; From Aircrib to Walden Two: B F Skinner as Social Inventor, in J P Cautela and W Ishaq, eds, Contemporary Issues in Behavior Therapy,: Improving the Human Condition, Plenum, 96; Problems in Vargas, J, Contributions of Verbal Behavior to Instructional Technology, The Analysis of Verbal Behavior, 15, 98; Commentary: Problems in the New Millenium, Contemporary Education, in press, several other publications. **CONTACT ADDRESS** Dept of Educational Psychology, West Virginia Univ, Box 6122, Morgantown, WV, 26506. **EMAIL** JVargas2@wvu.edu

VARNELIS, KAZYS
PERSONAL Born 09/20/1967, Chicago, IL, m, 1995 **DISCIPLINE** HISTORY OF ARCHITECTURE AND URBANISM **EDUCATION** Simon's Rock Col, AA; Cornell Univ, BS, MA, PhD. **CAREER** Facul, hist/theory, Southern Calif Inst of Archit, 96-. **RESEARCH** Modern architecture. **SELECTED PUBLICATIONS** Auth, The Education of the Innocent Eye, Jour of Archit Educ, 98; auth, You Cannot Not Know History: Philip Johnson's Politics and Cynical Survival, Jour of Archit Educ, 95. **CONTACT ADDRESS** S. Carolinal-ARC, 5454 Beethoven St., Los Angeles, CA, 90048. **EMAIL** kazys@sciarc.edu

VARNER, ERIC R.
DISCIPLINE ANDEAN ART AND ARCHITECTURE **EDUCATION** Yale Univ, PhD, 93. **CAREER** Art, Emory Univ. **SELECTED PUBLICATIONS** Auth, Damnatio Memoriae and Roman Imperial Portraiture. **CONTACT ADDRESS** Emory Univ, Atlanta, GA, 30322-1950. **EMAIL** evarner@emory.edu

VASSBERG, DAVID ERLAND
PERSONAL Born 03/13/1936, Harlingen, TX, m, 1962, 2 children **DISCIPLINE** SPANISH & LATIN AMERICAN HISTORY **EDUCATION** Univ Tex, Austin, BA, 58, MA, 66, PhD(Hist), 71. **CAREER** Asst prof, 71-77, assoc prof Hist, 77-83, Univ Tex-Pan Am, 83-98; vis scholar Univ Texas, Austin, 86, 94-96; vis research prof, Univ of Valladolid, Spain, 91; Nat Endowment for Humanities fel, 74-75; Joint Hispano-American Council fel, 78-79; Nat Institutes for Health fel, 95-96; Span Ministry of Foreign Affairs fel, 95. **HONORS AND AWARDS** Europ Hist Prize, Southwestern Social Science Assn, 77; Pan American Distinguished Faculty Awards, 83, 85. **MEMBERSHIPS** Soc Span & Port Hist Studies; American Hist Assn; Soc Science Hist Assn; Asociacion de Demografia Historica, Spanish. **RESEARCH** Early modern Spanish history; rural history; family history. **SELECTED PUBLICATIONS** Auth, The Tierras Baldias: community property and public lands in 16th century Castile, Agr Hist, 7/74; Villa-Lobos as pedagogue: music in the service of the state, J Res Music Educ, Fall 75; The sale of Tierras Baldias in 16th century Castile, J Mod Hist, 12/75; African influences on the music of Brazil, Luso-Brazilian Rev, Summer 76; coauth, Regionalism and the musical heritage of Latin America, Inst Latin Am Studies, Univ Tex Austin, 80; El campesino castellano frente al sistema comunitaro: Usurpaciones de tierras concejiles y baldias durante el siglo XVI, Boletin de la Real Academia de la Historia, Spring 78; auth, Concerning Pigs, the Pizzaros, and the agro-pastoral background of the conquerors of Peru, Latin Am Res Rev, Fall 78; The Village and the Outside World in Golden Age Castile: Mobility and Migration in Everyday Rural Life, Cambridge Univ Press, 96. **CONTACT ADDRESS** Dept of History, Univ of Texas-Pan American Univ, 1201 W University Dr, Edinburg, TX, 78539-2999. **EMAIL** vassberg@prc.utexas.edu

VAUGHAN, ALDEN T.
DISCIPLINE HISTORY **EDUCATION** Amherst, BA, 50; Columbia Teacher's Col, MA, 56; Columbia, MA, 58, PhD, 64. **CAREER** Emer Prof History, Columbia. **RESEARCH** British North American heritage. **SELECTED PUBLICATIONS** Fel Publ, Frontier Banditti and the Indians: The Paxton Boys' Legacy, 1763-75, Penn Hist 51, 84; auth, New England Frontier: Puritans and Indians, 1620-1675, 65; American Genesis: Captain John Smith and the Founding of Virginia, 75; Shakespeare's Indian: The Americanization of Caliban, Shakespeare Quart 39, 88; Roots of American Racism: Essays on the Colonial Experience, Oxford Univ, 95; coauth Shakespeare's Caliban: A Cultural History, Cambridge Univ, 91. **CONTACT ADDRESS** 50 Howland Ter, Worcester, MA, 01602.

VAUGHAN, MARY KAY
DISCIPLINE CULTURAL HISTORY **EDUCATION** PhD. **CAREER** Prof History and Latin American Studies, Univ Ill, Chicago. **MEMBERSHIPS** Latin Am Stud Asn. **SELECTED PUBLICATIONS** Co-ed, Women from the Mexican Countryside (1850-1990); auth, Creating Spaces, Shaping Transitions, 94; The State, Education and Social Class in Mexico, 1880-1928, 82; Cultural Politics in Revolution: Teachers, Peasants and Schools in Mexico, 1930-1940, nd.

VAUGHN, BARRY
PERSONAL Born 10/29/1955, Mobile, AL, s **DISCIPLINE** CHURCH HISTORY **EDUCATION** Harvard Univ, BA, 78; Yale Univ, MDiv, 82; Univ of St Andrews, UK, PhD, 90. **CAREER** Asst prof, Samford Univ, 88-90; asst prof, 90-91, adj prof, 93-98, Univ Alabama. **HONORS AND AWARDS** Day fel, 82; Rotary Grad Fel, 84-85. **MEMBERSHIPS** AAR; AHA. **SELECTED PUBLICATIONS** Auth, Benjamin Keach's The Gospel Minister's Maintenance Vindicated and the Status of Ministers among Late Seventeenth Century Baptists, Baptist Rev of Theol, 93; auth, Reluctant Revivalist: Isaac Watts and the Evangelical Revival, Southeastern Comn on the Study of Relig, 93; auth, Resurrection and Grace: The Sermons of Austin Farrer, Preaching, 94; auth, Sermon, Sacrament, and Symbol in the Theology of Karl Rahner, Paradigms, 95; auth, The Glory of a True Church: Benjamin Keach and Church Order among Late Seventeenth Century Particular Baptists, Baptist Hist and Heritage, 95; auth, The Pilgrim Way: A Short History of the Episcopal Church in Alabama, in, Our Church: The Diocese of Alabama in history and Photographs, 96; auth, Gospel Songs and Evangelical Hymnody: Evaluation and Reconsideration, Am Organist, 96; auth, When Men Were Numbered, Anglican Dig, 97; auth, Sermons for Advent and Christmas, Clergy J, forthcoming. **CONTACT ADDRESS** 1600 E 3rd Ave, Apt 3002, San Mateo, CA, 94401-2160. **EMAIL** anglcan@aol.com

VAUGHN, MICHAEL S.
PERSONAL Born 05/24/1962, Springfield, MO, m, 1989, 1 child **DISCIPLINE** CRIMINAL JUSTICE **EDUCATION** Sam Houston State Univ, PhD, 93 **CAREER** Asst prof, dept of criminal justice, georgia state univ, 93-. **HONORS AND AWARDS** Phi Kappa Phi **MEMBERSHIPS** Acad Criminal Justice Sci; Amer Soc Criminol; Amer Judicature Soc **RESEARCH** Legal issues in criminal justice; Cross-cultural crime and social control. **SELECTED PUBLICATIONS** Auth, Prison Civil Liability for Inmate-Against-Inmate Assault and Breakdown/Disorganization Theory, Jour Criminal Justice, 96; coauth, Drug Crime in Taiwan: A Time-Series Analysis From 1965 to 1994, Deviant Behavior, 96; The Fourth Amendment as a Tool of Actuarial Justice: The Special Needs Exception to the Warrant and Probable Cause Requirements, Crime and Delinquency, 97; auth, Prison Officials Liability for Inmate-to-Inmate Assault: A Review of Case Law, Jour Offender Rehabil, 97; Civil Liability Against Prison Officials for Prescribing and Dispensing Medication and Drugs to Prison Inmates, Jour Legal Med, 97; First Amendments Civil Liability Against Law Enforcement Supervisors for Violating their Subordinates Rights to Engage in Overt Political Expression, Policing: An Int Jour of Police Strategies and Mgt, 97; Political Patronage in Law Enforcement: Civil Liability Against Police Supervisors for Violating their Subordinates First Amendment Rights, Jour Criminal Justice, 97; coauth, Drugs in Thailand: Assessing Police Attitudes, Int Jour Offender Ther & Comp Criminol, 98; Separate and Unequal: Prison Versus Free-World Medical Care, Justice Quart, 98. **CONTACT ADDRESS** Dept of Criminal Justice, Georgia State Univ, Box 4018, Atlanta, GA, 30302-4018. **EMAIL** mvaughn@gsu.edu

VAUGHN, STEPHEN LEE
PERSONAL Born 01/03/1947, Poplar Bluff, MO, m, 1974, 1 child **DISCIPLINE** AMERICAN HISTORY **EDUCATION** Southeast Mo State Univ, BA, 68; Ind Univ, MA, 69; Ind Univ, PhD, 77. **CAREER** Lectr Am hist, Ind Univ, 77-78, asst prof, 78-79; assoc ed, J Am Hist, 79-80; asst prof diplomatic hist, Univ Ore, Eugene, 80-81; asst prof hist jour & mass commun, Univ of Wis-Madison, 81-, Hist asst to exec secy, Orgn Am Historians, 77-80, actg exec secy, 82-; asst prof, Ind Univ, 81. **MEMBERSHIPS** Orgn Am Historians; AHA; Asn Educ Jour. **RESEARCH** Late 19th and 20th century America, social, intellectual, diplomatic history; nationalism; history of mass communications. **SELECTED PUBLICATIONS** Auth, Holding Fast the Inner Lines: Democracy, Nationalism and the Committee on Public Information, Univ NC Press, 80; ed, The Vital Past: Writings on the Uses of History, Univ Ga Press, 85; auth, Morality and Entertainment, J Am Hist, 6/90; Ronald Reagan in Hollywood: Movies and Politics, Cambridge Univ Press, 94; assoc ed, Dictionary of American History, Scribner's, 96. **CONTACT ADDRESS** Univ of Wis, 821 University Ave, Madison, WI, 53706-1497. **EMAIL** slvaughn@facstaff.wisc.edu

VAZQUEZ, OSCAR E.
DISCIPLINE ART HISTORY **EDUCATION** Univ CA Santa Barbara, PhD, 89. **CAREER** Assoc prof/dir undergrad studies, SUNY Binghamton. **RESEARCH** Mod Europ art, collections, patronage and art market systems; 18th and 19th century art criticism and theory; Span art and cult hist; Latin Am 19th and 20th century art. **SELECTED PUBLICATIONS** Auth, Beauty Buried in its own Cemetery: Santiago Rusinol's 'Jardins d'Espanya'" as Reliquaries of Aristocratic History, Word & Image, 95; Defining Hispanidid: Allegories, Genealogies and Cultural Politics in the Madrid Academy Competitions of 1893, Art Hist, 97. **CONTACT ADDRESS** SUNY Binghamton, PO Box 6000, Binghamton, NY, 13902-6000. **EMAIL** frances@binghamton.edu

VECOLI, RUDOLPH JOHN
PERSONAL Born 03/02/1927, Wallingford, CT, m, 1959, 3 children **DISCIPLINE** AMERICAN SOCIAL HISTORY **EDUCATION** Univ Conn, BA, 50; Univ Pa, MA, 51; Univ Wis, PhD, 63. **CAREER** For affairs officer, US Info Agency, US Dept State, 51-54; instr hist, Ohio State Univ, 57-59 and Pa State Univ, 60-61; lectr Am civilization, Rutgers Univ, 61-63, asst prof hist, 63-65; assoc prof Am hist, Univ Ill, Urbana, 65-67; PROF AM HIST and DIR, IMMIGRATION HIST RES CTR, UNIV MINN, MINNEAPOLIS, 67-, Mem bd dirs, Am Immigration and Citizenship Conf, 69-; Am Coun Nationalities Serv; vis prof Am hist, Univ Uppsala, 70; Am-Scand Found fel, 70; sr res scholar, Fulbright-Hays Prog, Italy, 73-74. **HONORS AND AWARDS** Gold Medal, Lucchesi che hanno onorato l'Italia nel mondo, 71; Medallion from City Coun Ljubljana, 81; Cavaliere Ufficiale nell'Ordine al Merito della Repubblica Italiana, Pres Ital repub, 82. **MEMBERSHIPS** AHA; Orgn Am Historians; Am Ital Hist Asn (pres, 66-70); Immigration Hist Soc (pres, 82-). **RESEARCH** History of American immigration and ethnic groups; Italian American history; history of the American labor movement. **SELECTED PUBLICATIONS** Auth, Making a New-Deal--Industrial-Workers in Chicago, 1919-1939, Rev(s) Amer Hist, Vol 0020, 92; Poverty, Ethnicity, and the Amer City, 1840-1925--Changing Conceptions of the Slum and the Ghetto, Soc Hist, Vol 0018, 93; An Interethnic Perspective on Amer Immigration Hist, Mid-America-An Hist Rev, Vol 0075, 93; Italian Immigrants and Working-Class Movements in the United-States--A Personal Reflection on Class and Ethnicity, Jou Can Hist Assn-Rev Soc Hist Can, Vol 0004, 93; Immigrant Radicals--The View from the Left, Vol 9, of Amer Immigration and Ethnicity, Jour Amer Ethnic Hist, Vol 0013, 94; The Little Slaves of the Harp--Italian Child Street Musicians in 19th-Century Paris, London, and New-York, Amer Hist Rev, Vol 0099, 94; Crossings, the Great Transatlantic Migrations, 1870-1914 Intl Hist Rev, Vol 0016, 94; The Formation of the United-States--Society and Nation From independence to the Civil-War--French, Jour Amer Hist, Vol 0082, 95; The Contemporary-World--Encyclopedia of Hist and Soc-Sciences, Vol 5, Hist of North-America--French, Jour Amer Hist, Vol 0082, 95; Race, Religion, and Nationality in Amer Society--A Model of Ethnicity --From Contact to Assimilation, Jour Amer Ethnic Hist, Vol 0014, 95; Postethnic America--Beyond Multiculturalism, Rev(s) in Amer Hist, Vol 0024, 96. **CONTACT ADDRESS** Immigration Hist Res Ctr, Univ of Minn, St Paul, MN, 55114.

VECSEY, CHRISTOPHER
DISCIPLINE RELIGION, NATVE AMERICAN STUDIES **EDUCATION** PhD, 77, Northwestern Univ. **CAREER** Prof, Colgate Univ. **SELECTED PUBLICATIONS** Auth, American Indian Catholics, Padres' Trail, Univ Notre Dame Press, 96; ed, Religion in Native North America, Idaho Press, 90; Handbook of American Indian Religious Freedom, Crossroad/Continuum, 91. **CONTACT ADDRESS** Dept of Philos and Relig, Colgate Univ, 13 Oak Drive, Hamilton, NY, 13346. **EMAIL** wkelly@mail.colgate.edu

VEENKER, RONALD ALLEN
PERSONAL Born 05/13/1937, Huntington Park, CA, m, 1960, 1 child **DISCIPLINE** OLD TESTAMENT; ANCIENT NEAR-EASTERN STUDIES **EDUCATION** Bethel Col, Minn, BA, 59; Bethel Theol Sem, BDiv, 63; Hebrew Union Col, PhD(Ancient NE), 68. **CAREER** Asst prof, Univ Miami, 67-68; assoc prof, 68-76, PROF BIBL STUDIES, WESTERN KY UNIV, 76-, Fel, Hebrew Union Col, Jewish Inst Relig, 77-78. **MEMBERSHIPS** Am Orient Soc; Soc Bibl Lit. **RESEARCH** Old Babylonian economic and legal texts; computer assisted analysis of Old Babylonian economic texts. **SELECTED PUBLICATIONS** Auth, Stages in the Old Babylonical legal process, Hebrew Union Col Annual, 76; contribr, Interpreter's Dictionary of the Bible: Supplement, Abingdon, 76; auth, Gilgamesh and the Magic Plant, Bibl Archaeol, Fall 81; A Response to W.G. Lambert, Bibl Archaeol, Spring 82; Noah, Herald of Righteousness, Proceedings of the Eastern Great Lakes and Midwest Bibl Soc, vol VI, 86; coauth, Me m, the First Ur III Ensi of Ebla, In: Ebla 1975-1985: Dieci anni di studi linguistici e fililogici, Atti del Convegno Internazionale, Napoli, 10/85; auth, Texts and Fragments: The Johnstone Collection, J of Cuneiform Studies, vol 40, no 1, 88; A critical review of Karl van Lerberghe, Old Babylonian Legal and Administrative Texts from Philadelphia, Orientalia Lovaniensia Analecta 21, Uitgeverij Peeters, 86, for the J of the Am Orient Soc, 92; Texts and Fragments: Collection of the Erie Historical Museum, J of

Cuneiform Studies, vol 43, no 1, 93. **CONTACT ADDRESS** Dept of Philos & Relig, Western Kentucky Univ, 1 Big Red Way St, Bowling Green, KY, 42101-3576. **EMAIL** ronald.veenker@wku.edu

VEHSE, CHARLES T.
PERSONAL Born 03/07/1961, Huntington, WV, m, 1984, 1 child **DISCIPLINE** HISTORY OF RELIGIONS **EDUCATION** Univ of Chicago, PhD, 98, MA, 85; Brown Univ, AB, 83. **CAREER** Vis Asst Prof, 96-, West VA Univ; lectr, 88-91, Dept of Theo, Loyola Univ Chicago; Tutor for German Lang, 82-83, Brown Univ. **HONORS AND AWARDS** Dean's Prof Travel Grant; Solomon Goldman Lecture; Vis Res Fellow; Fellow, Interuniversity Prog for Jewish Stud; Arie and Ida Crown Mem Res Grant; Lucius N. Littauer Found Res Grant; Bernard H. and Blanche E. Jacobson Found Res Grant; Stipendium des Landes Baden-Wurtemberg. **RESEARCH** Religious and Judaic Studies, German Judaism of the modern era, History and Methods in the History of Religion, Ritual Studies and Comp Liturgy, History and Interpretaion of the Hebrew Bible; Humanities and Social Sciences, German Language and Literature. **SELECTED PUBLICATIONS** Auth, Religious Practice and Consciousness, A Case Study of Time from the 19th century, Consciousness Research Abstracts, Thorverton, UK, J of Consci Stud, 98; Were the Jews of Modern Germany as Emancipated and Assimilated as We Think?, The Solomon Goldman Lectures, 96-97, Spertus Institute of Jewish Studies, Forthcoming; Long Live the King, Historical Fact and Narrative Fiction in 1 Samuel 9-10, The Pitcher Is Broken, Memorial Essays for Gosta WW. Ahlstrom, Sheffield Academic Press, 95. **CONTACT ADDRESS** 742 Ridgeway Ave, Morgantown, WV, 26505-5746. **EMAIL** veh@midway.uchicago.edu

VELIMIROVIC, MILOS
DISCIPLINE MUSIC HISTORY **EDUCATION** Harvard Univ, PhD. **CAREER** Dept Music, Va Univ **RESEARCH** Byzantine music; history of Slavonic music; history of Italian opera in the 18th century. **SELECTED PUBLICATIONS** Auth, The Melodies of the Ninth century Kanon for St. Demetrius, 84; Dr. Charles Burney and Russian Music, 93. **CONTACT ADDRESS** Dept of Music, Virginia Univ, Charlottesville, VA, 22903. **EMAIL** mmv@virginia.edu

VENEZIANO, CAROL
PERSONAL Born 02/02/1952, Quincy, IL, m, 1978, 2 children **DISCIPLINE** CRIMINAL JUSTICE **EDUCATION** DePauw Univ, BA, 74; Auburn Univ, MS, 77; Sam Houston State Univ, PhD, 82. **CAREER** Asst prof to assoc prof, Memphis State Univ, 81-88; prof, Southeast Missouri State Univ, 88-98. **HONORS AND AWARDS** Two teaching awards; three research awards. **MEMBERSHIPS** Acad of Criminal Justice Sci; Am Soc of Criminol; Am Correctional Asn; Midwestern Criminal Justice Asn; Southern Criminal Justice Asn. **RESEARCH** Criminological theory; correlates of delinquency; correctional institutions. **SELECTED PUBLICATIONS** Coauth, Evaluating Investigator Job Performance: An Analysis of Practitioner Opinions, in The Justice Prof, 93; coauth, Psychosocial and Sociodemographic Characteristics of DWI Offenders, in J of Addictions & Offender Counseling, 93; coauth, Are Victimless Crimes Actually Harmful?, in J of Contemp Criminal Justice, 93; coauth, Project REACH: A Therapeutic Club Model, in New Designs for Youth Development, 94; coauth, Stress-related Factors Associated with Driving While Intoxicated, in J of Alcohol and Drug Educ, 94; coauth, The Development of an Exit Exam in Criminal Justice for Graduating Seniors: A Case Study, in J of Criminal Justice Ed, 94; coauth, Attitudes Toward Community Based Corrections as an Alternative to Incarceration, in Corrections Today, 95; coauth, A Survey of Inmates with Disabilities, in Encyclopedia of American Prisons, Garland, 95; coauth, A Comparison of the Dispositions of Juvenile Offenders Certified as Adults with Juvenile Offenders Not Certified, in Juvenile and Family Court J, 95; coauth, Reasons for Refraining from Criminal Activity, in Am J of Criminal Justice, 96; coauth, Factors Accounting for Not Engaging in Illegal Acts in Relationship to Type of Crime, in J of Crime and Justice, 96; coauth, Correlates of Assertiveness among Institutionalized Juvenile Delinquents, in J of Crime and Justice, 97; coauth, The Academic Achievement of Juvenile Delinquents Relative to Intellectual Ability: Implications for Research and Educational Program Development, in Practical Applications for Criminal Justice Statistics, Butterworth-Heinemann, 98. **CONTACT ADDRESS** Dept of Criminal Justice, Southeast Missouri State Univ, MS 8200, Cape Girardeau, MO, 63701. **EMAIL** cveneziano@semovm.semo.edu

VERBRUGGE, MARTHA HELEN
PERSONAL Born 07/19/1949, Northfield, MN **DISCIPLINE** MEDICAL AND AMERICAN SOCIAL HISTORY **EDUCATION** Carleton Col, BA, 71; Harvard Univ, PhD(sci hist), 78. **CAREER** ASST PROF MED and SCI HIST, BUCKNELL UNIV, 78-, Nat Endowment for Humanities grant, summer, 79; Am Coun Learned Soc grant, 80; res fel, Charles Warren Ctr Studies for Am Hist, Harvard Univ, 81-82. **MEMBERSHIPS** AHA; Am Asn Hist Med; Hist Sci Soc; Orgn Am Historians; Am Asn Advan Sci. **RESEARCH** History of women's health and medical care in America; history of popular health and hygienic habits; history of non-orthodox systems of medicine and personal health. **SELECTED PUBLICATIONS** Auth, Babe--The Life and Legend of Zaharias, Babe, Didrikson, Amer Hist Rev, Vol 0102, 97; Recreating the Body--Womens Physical-Education and the Science of Sex-Differences in America, 1900-1940, Bulletin Hist Med, Vol 0071, 97. **CONTACT ADDRESS** Dept of Hist, Bucknell Univ, Lewisburg, PA, 17837-2029.

VERGE, ARTHUR C.
PERSONAL Born 03/14/1956, Santa Monica, CA, s **DISCIPLINE** HISTORY **EDUCATION** Univ Calif, Santa Barbara, BA, 78; Univ Southern Calif, MA, MPA, 84, PhD, 88. **CAREER** Prof, El Camino, 89-. **HONORS AND AWARDS** Presidential Leadership Award, 95, Doane Col. **MEMBERSHIPS** Am Hist Asn; Calif Hist Soc; Southern Calif Hist Soc. **RESEARCH** California history; second world war; beach and surf culture. **SELECTED PUBLICATIONS** Auth, art, The Scandinavian-Americans, 90; auth, Paradise Transformed: Los Angeles During the Second World War, 93; auth, art, The Impact of the Second World War on Los Angeles, 94; auth, art, Daily Life in Wartime California, 99. **CONTACT ADDRESS** Dept of History, El Camino Col, 16007 Crenshaw Blvd, Torrance, CA, 90506.

VERKAMP, BERNARD
PERSONAL Born 02/20/1938, Huntingburg, IN **DISCIPLINE** HISTORICAL THEOLOGY **EDUCATION** St. Louis Univ, PhD, 72. **CAREER** Prof philos, Vincennes Univ, 72-98. **HONORS AND AWARDS** Phi Beta Kappa, 86. **MEMBERSHIPS** APA; AAUP. **RESEARCH** Philosophy of religion; ethics. **SELECTED PUBLICATIONS** Auth, The Moral Treatment of Returning Warriors, Associated Univ Pr, 93; auth, The Evolution of Religion: A Re-Examination, Univ Scranton, 95; auth, Senses of Mystery: Religious and Nonreligious, Univ Scranton, 97. **CONTACT ADDRESS** 408 N 5th St, Vincennes, IN, 47591. **EMAIL** bverkamp@vunet.vinu.edu

VERNON BURTON, ORVILLE
DISCIPLINE HISTORY **EDUCATION** Princeton Univ, PhD, 76. **CAREER** Prof,Univ Ill Urbana Champaign. **RESEARCH** Race relations,;American South; family community history; politics; agrarian societie; religion, quantitative techniques; advanced information technologies. **SELECTED PUBLICATIONS** Auth, In My Father's House Are Many Mansions: Family and Community in Edgefield, Univ NC, 85; A Gentleman and an Officer:" A Social and Military History of James B. Griffin's Civil War, Oxford, 96. **CONTACT ADDRESS** History Dept, Univ Ill Urbana Champaign, 52 E Gregory Dr, Champaign, IL, 61820. **EMAIL** o-burton@uiuc.edu

VERRETT, JOYCE M.
PERSONAL Born 05/26/1932, New Orleans, Louisiana, m **DISCIPLINE** HISTORY **EDUCATION** Dillard U, BA 1957; NY U, MS 1963; Tulane U, PhD 1971. **CAREER** Orleans Parsih LA, hs teacher 1958-63; Dillard Univ Div of Ntrl Sci, instr prof chmn. **HONORS AND AWARDS** HS Vldctn 1948; Alpha Kappa Mu Nat Hon Soc 1956; Beta Kappa Chi Nat Sci Hon Soc 1956; Grad Summa Cum Laude Dillard Univ 1957; NSF Fllwshp for Adv Study 1960-62; 1st blk wmn to recv PhD in Bio from Tulane Univ 1971; Otstndng Educ of Am 1972. **MEMBERSHIPS** Ent Soc Am; Nat Inst Sci; Beta Beta Beta Bial & Hon Soc; Beta Kappa Chi Sci Hon Soc Cncr Assn Grtr ND 1974; LA Hrt Assn 1973-; NAACP 1960-; Reg 9 Sci Fair 1958-. **CONTACT ADDRESS** Dillard Univ, 2601 Gentilly Blvd, New Orleans, LA, 70122.

VERVOORT, PATRICIA
PERSONAL Boston, MA **DISCIPLINE** ART HISTORY **EDUCATION** St. Mary's Univ, BA, 63; Univ Iowa, MA, 70. **CAREER** Lectr, art hist, 75-89, asst prof, 89-92, ch, dept visual arts, 90-95, ASSOC PROF, ART HISTORY, LAKEHEAD UNIV, 92-. **MEMBERSHIPS** Univ Art Asn Can; Soc Stud Archit Can. **SELECTED PUBLICATIONS** Auth, Meaning in Old Buildings, in Thunder Bay Hist Mus Soc Papers and Records V, 77; auth, Sunrise on the Saguenay: Popular Literature and the Sublime, in Mosaic: J Interdisciplinary Stud Lit, 88; auth, Lakehead Terminal Elevators: Aspects of Their Engineering History, in Can J Civil Engg, 90; auth, Re-Constructing van Gogh: Paintings as Sculptures in Low Countries and Beyond, 93. **CONTACT ADDRESS** Dept of Visual Arts, Lakehead Univ, Thunder Bay, ON, P7B SE1. **EMAIL** pveroor@cs_acd_Ian.lakeheadu.ca

VETROCQ, MARCIA E.
DISCIPLINE ART HISTORY **EDUCATION** Princeton Univ, BA; Stanford Univ, MA, PhD; Columbia Univ, postdoctoral work. **CAREER** Prof, Univ New Orleans; corresp ed, Art in Am. **HONORS AND AWARDS** Wolfsonian Found sr fel, Am Acad, Rome, 96. **MEMBERSHIPS** Int Asn of Art Critics. **SELECTED PUBLICATIONS** Articles on art history and contemporary criticism in Europe and the United States in Art in America; catalogue essay for the Guggenheim Museum's exhibition The Italian Metamorphosis, 1943-1968, NY, 94; a major article on contemporary American art for the Encyclopedia Italiana, Rome, 96. **CONTACT ADDRESS** Univ New Orleans, New Orleans, LA, 70148. **EMAIL** clrfa@uno.edu

VETTES, WILLIAM GEORGE
PERSONAL Born 10/29/1920, Chicago, IL **DISCIPLINE** MODERN HISTORY **EDUCATION** Roosevelt Col, BA, 49; Northwestern Univ, MA, 51, PhD, 58. **CAREER** From asst prof to assoc prof, 58-67, PROF HIST, UNIV WIS,LA CROSSE, 67-. **MEMBERSHIPS** Am Asn Mid E Studies; AHA. **RESEARCH** Balkans and near east; Balkan labor movement. **SELECTED PUBLICATIONS** Auth, The Greek Civil-War--1945-1950, Jour Military Hist, Vol 0058, 94. **CONTACT ADDRESS** Dept of Hist, Univ of Wis, La Crosse, WI, 54601.

VIAULT, BIRDSALL SCRYMSER
PERSONAL Born 09/20/1932, Mineola, NY, m, 1970 **DISCIPLINE** NINETEENTH & TWENTIETH CENTURY EUROPEAN HISTORY **EDUCATION** Adelphi Univ, BS, 55, MA 56; Univ Tubingen, dipl, 54; Duke Univ, MA, 57, PhD, 63. **CAREER** From instr to asst prof hist, Adelphi Univ, 59-68; assoc prof, 68-72, PROF HIST, WINTHROP COL, 72-97, PROF EMER, 98-, CHMN, 79-89; vis assoc prof, Duke Univ, 70. **HONORS AND AWARDS** Ford Found coop prog Humanities postdoctoral fel, Univ NC, Duke Univ, 69-70. **MEMBERSHIPS** Am Cath Hist Asn; Southern Hist Asn; Soc Hist of Am Foreign Relations; SC Hist Asn; Phi Kappa Phi, Phi Alpha theta, Zeta Beta Tau. **RESEARCH** German history, 1919-1945; European diplomatic history, 1919-1940; the Cold War. **SELECTED PUBLICATIONS** Auth, Les demarches pour le retablissement de la paix (Septembre 1939-Aout 1940), 7/67 & Mussolini et la Recherche d'une Paix Negociee (1939-1940), 7/77, Rev d'Hist de la Deuxieme Guerre Mondiale; World History in the 20th Century, 69; American History since 1865, 89, rev ed, 93; Western Civilization since 1600, 90; Modern European History, 90; English History, 92. **CONTACT ADDRESS** Dept of Hist, Winthrop Univ, 701 W Oakland Ave, Rock Hill, SC, 29733-0001. **EMAIL** viaultb@winthrop.edu

VICK-WILLIAMS, MARIAN LEE
PERSONAL Newton Grove, NC **DISCIPLINE** EDUCATION **EDUCATION** Fayetteville State Univ, BS 1948; Univ of MI, MA 1954; Syracuse Univ, CAGS 1961; Duke Univ, EdD 1968. **CAREER** NC Public Schools, elementary teacher 1948-60; Bennett Coll, dir of reading center 1961-62; Winston-Salem State Univ, asst prof of reading 1962-66; NC A&T State Univ, assoc prof of Reading Edu 1968-70, prof of Reading Educ 1970-77, Dept of Elementary Educ, acting chairperson 1977-80, chairperson 1980-83, prof of reading educ and graduate advisor of reading majors, 1984-90. **HONORS AND AWARDS** NAFEO's 1985 Distinguished Alumni Award 1985; FSU National Alumni Association, Alumni Queen, 1993-94, Alumni Achievement Award; recipient of Southern Education Foundation Award. **MEMBERSHIPS** Life mem NAACP 1979-; Alpha Kappa Alpha, Beta Iota Omega Chapter; Kappa Delta Pi; Phi Delta Kappa; NEA-NCAE; Intl Reading Assoc; St James Presbyterian Church; FSU Natl Alumni Assn; NAFEO; Coll Reading Assn; Amer Educational Research Assn; Natl Reading Conference; ASCD. **SELECTED PUBLICATIONS** SPA Author of nine published articles in professional journals and books.

VIERECK, PETER
PERSONAL Born 08/05/1916, New York, NY, m, 1972, 2 children **DISCIPLINE** POETRY, HISTORY **EDUCATION** Harvard Univ, BS, 37, AM, 39, PhD, 42. **CAREER** Instr hist and lit, Harvard Univ, 46-47; asst prof hist, Smith Col, 47-48; assoc prof, 48-49, assoc prof Europ and Russ hist, 49-55, alumni found prof Europ and Russ hist, 55-80, WILLIAM R KENAN JR PROF HIST, MT HOLYOKE COL, 80-; Vis lectr, Smith Col, 48-49; Guggenheim fels, 49 and 55; vis lectr, Poet's Conf, Harvard Univ, 53 and Univ Calif, Berkeley, 57 and 64; Whittal lectr poetry, Libr Cong, 54 and 63; Fulbright prof Am poetry, Univ Florence, 55; Elliston poetry lectr, Univ Cincinnati, 56; US Dept State cult exchange poet, USSR, 61; Twentieth Century Fund travel and poetry res grant, Russia, 62; lectr poetry, City Col New York and New Sch Social Res, 64; dir poetry workshop, NY Writer's Conf, 65-67. **HONORS AND AWARDS** Garrison Prize for Poetry, Phi Beta Kappa, 36; Harvard Bowdoin Medal for Prose, 39; Tietjens Prize for Poetry, 48; Pulitzer Prize for Poetry, 49., DHL, Olivet Col, 59. **MEMBERSHIPS** AHA **RESEARCH** Modern European and Russian history; Anglo-American poetry; modern Russian culture. **SELECTED PUBLICATIONS** Auth, Anti Form or Neo and Essay in a Curse on Both Houses, Parnassus Poetry Rev, Vol 18, 93; Dumped, Parnassus Poetry Rev, Vol 18, 93; Anyhow, Parnassus Poetry Rev, Vol 18, 93; Sinew, Parnassus Poetry Rev, Vol 18, 93; Where Find Us, Parnassus Poetry Rev, Vol 18, 93; Metrics, Not Hour Hand, Parnassus Poetry In Rev, Vol 18, 93; My Seventy-Seventh Birthday, Parnassus Poetry Rev, Vol 18, 93; Slack A While, Parnassus Poetry Rev, Vol 18, 93; ... and Sometimes Not, Parnassus Poetry Rev, Vol 18, 93; Invocation, Parnassus Poetry Rev, Vol 18, 93; Threnody Reversals, Parnassus Poetry Rev, Vol 18, 93; Moon Ode, Parnassus Poetry Rev, Vol 18, 93; Second Moon Ode, Parnassus Poetry Rev, Vol 18, 93; Topsy Turvy, Parnassus Poetry Rev, Vol 18, 93; Why I Sometimes Believe in God, Parnassus Poetry Rev, Vol 18, 93. **CONTACT ADDRESS** Dept of Hist, Mount Holyoke Col, South Hadley, MA, 01075.

VIETOR, RICHARD HENRY KINGSBURY
PERSONAL Born 04/22/1945, Minneapolis, MN, m, 1968, 3 children **DISCIPLINE** HISTORY **EDUCATION** Union Col, NY, BA, 67; Hofstra Univ, MA, 71; Univ Pittsburgh, PhD (hist), 75. **CAREER** Vis asst Am hist, Va Polytechnic Inst and State Univ, 75; asst prof recent US hist, Univ Mo-Columbia, 75-78; ASSOC PROF BUS ADMIN, HARVARD BUS SCH, 78-; Consult energy policy, Hudson Inst, 75-77. **HONORS AND AWARDS** Newcomen Award, 81. **MEMBERSHIPS** Orgn Am Historians. **RESEARCH** Twentieth century American energy policy and environmental policy. **SELECTED PUBLICATIONS** Auth, Containing the Atom in Nuclear Regulation in a Changing Environment, 63-71, Am Hist Rev, Vol 99, 94 **CONTACT ADDRESS** Business Sch, Harvard Univ, 232 Baker, Boston, MA, 02163.

VIGIL, RALPH HAROLD
PERSONAL Born 09/06/1932, Vigil, CO, m, 1969 **DISCIPLINE** COLONIAL LATIN AMERICAN HISTORY **EDUCATION** Pac Lutheran Univ, BA, 58; Univ NMex, MA, 65, PhD (hist), 69. **CAREER** Instr hist, Washburn Univ, 65-69; asst prof, Fresno State Col, 69-71; assoc prof, Univ Tex, El Paso, 71-72; ASSOC PROF HIST, UNIV NEBR, LINCOLN, 73-. **MEMBERSHIPS** AHA; Asn Borderlands Scholars; Conf Latin am Hist. **RESEARCH** Sixteenth century Spanish New World Society; Spanish borderlands. **SELECTED PUBLICATIONS** Auth, Spanish Borderlands Sourcebooks in The Spanish Missions of New Mexico, Great Plains Quart, Vol 13, 93; Spanish Texas, 1519-1821, Southwestern Histl Quart, Vol 97, 93; Entrada in The Legacy of Spain and Mexico in the United-States, Southwestern Histl Quart, Vol 99, 95; Guatemala in the Spanish Colonial Period, Cath Hist Rev, Vol 82, 96. **CONTACT ADDRESS** Dept of Hist, Univ of Nebr, Lincoln, NE, 68506.

VILES, PERRY
PERSONAL Born 10/19/1932, Boston, MA, m, 1959, 5 children **DISCIPLINE** EARLY MODERN EUROPEAN HISTORY **EDUCATION** Harvard Univ, AB, 54, MA, 57, PhD(hist), 65. **CAREER** From instr to asst prof hist, Univ Pa, 63-71; asst prof, 71-74, chmn dept, 73-74, asst to pres develop, 74-78, asst dean, Lyndon State Col, 78-, Am Antiq Soc vis fel, 72; Gov's Comn Admin Justice, State Vt, 74-77. **RESEARCH** European and American social history, 1700-1850; family and adolescent in Western society. **SELECTED PUBLICATIONS** Auth, The slaving interest in the Atlantic ports, 1763-1792, Fr Hist Studies, fall 72. **CONTACT ADDRESS** Off of the Dean, Vail Ctr, Lyndon State Col, Lyndonville, VT, 05851.

VILES, PERRY
DISCIPLINE HISTORY **EDUCATION** Harvard, AB, 54, MA, 57, PhD, 65. **CAREER** Retired asst prof History, Lyndon State. **RESEARCH** Adolescence in American history. **CONTACT ADDRESS** The Kings Rose, 1747 Moore, South Kingston, RI, 02879.

VINCENT, CHARLES
PERSONAL Born 10/19/1945, Hazlehurst, MS, m, 1971, 3 children **DISCIPLINE** MODERN HISTORY **EDUCATION** Jackson State Univ, BA, 66; La State Univ, Baton Rouge, MA, 68, PhD, 73. **CAREER** Instr soc sci, TJ Harris Jr Col, 67-68; instr, 68-69, asst prof, 69-70, 73-75, assoc prof, 75-78, Prof History, Southern Univ, Baton Rouge, 78-, Moton Ctr Independent Studies fel, 78-. **HONORS AND AWARDS** Eminent Scholar, Va State Univ, 90-91; Pres Fac Excellence Award, 94; Found Hist La Preserv Award, 96. **MEMBERSHIPS** Asn Study Afro-Am Life & Hist; Southern Hist Asn; Orgn Am Historians. **RESEARCH** Reconstruction history; Southern history; Afro-American history. **SELECTED PUBLICATIONS** Auth, Two Articles, Dictionary of Negro Biography, Crowell, 75; Laying the cornerstone at Southern University, La Hist, summer 76; Louisana's Black Legislators and Their Efforts to Pass a Blue Law during Reconstruction, J Black Studies, 9/76; Black Legislators in Louisana during Reconstruction, La State Univ, 76; Southern University and World War I: Aspects of the University and its Leadership, J Soc & Behav Scientists, 79; Antoine Dubuclet: Louisana's Black State Treasure, 1868-1978, J Negro Hist, spring 81; Booker T Washington's tour of Louisiana, April 1915, La Hist, spring 81; A Centennial History of Southern University & A&M College, 1880-1980, Moran Industs, 81; Black Constitution Makers: In Search of Fundamental Law, Lafayette), 93; Blacks in Louisiana, in Vol 3, Encyclo of African-American Culture & History, (NY) 96. **CONTACT ADDRESS** Dept Hist, Southern Univ, PO Box 9491, Baton Rouge, LA, 70813.

VINE, BRENT
DISCIPLINE CLASSICS **EDUCATION** Phillips Exeter Acad, Class Dipl, 69; Harvard Col, AB, 73; Harvard Univ, AM, 75, PhD, 82. **CAREER** Tchg fel, Harvard Univ, 74-80; vis instr, Tex Tech Univ, 81-82; sec, Mass Inst Tech, 82-83; instr, Phillips Acad, 83-86; asst prof, Yale Univ, 86-91; asst prof, Princeton Univ, 91-94; assoc prof, Princeton Univ, 91-94; ASSOC PROF, UCLA, 95-. **SELECTED PUBLICATIONS** Auth, "On the 'Missing' Fourth Stanza of Catullus 51," Harvard Stud Class Philol 92; "On Phonetic Repetition in Moby-Dick," Lang and Style 22, 89; Gk. -isko: and Indo-European *-iske/o-, Hist Sprachforschung 106, 93; "Catullus 76.21: ut torpor in artus," Rheinisches Museum fur Philol 136, 94; "Greek opeas/opear 'awl'," Glotta 72, 94/95; rev(s), J. Gager, "Curse Tablets and Binding Spells from the Ancient World," Bryn Mawr Class Rev 4, 91-94; comment on P. Keyser, review of J. Riddle, "Contraception and Abortion from the Ancient World to the Renaissance," Bryn Mawr Classl Rev 5, 95. **CONTACT ADDRESS** Dept of Classics, Univ Calif, PO Box 951436, Los Angeles, CA, 90095-1436.

VINOVSKIS, MARIS A.
PERSONAL Born 01/01/1943, Riga, Latvia, m, 1966, 1 child **DISCIPLINE** AMERICAN HISTORY **EDUCATION** Wesleyan Col, BA, 65; Harvard Univ, AM, 66, PhD, 75. **CAREER** Asst prof hist, Univ Wis, 72-74; asst prof, 74-77, assoc prof, 77-80, prof hist, 80-, A.M & H.P. Bentley Prof of Hist, 97-, fac mem, School of Public Policy, 98-, Univ Mich; mem demog, Ctr Demog & Ecol, Univ Wis, 72-74; Clark Univ & Am Antiqn Soc fel family hist, 73-74; Harvard Ctr Population Studies res fel, 73-75; fac assoc polit sci, Inst Social Res, Univ Mich, 74-81; asst staff dir pop, US House Select Comt on Pop, 77-78; res scientist, Inst Soc Res, Univ Mich, 81-; Guggenheim fel, 81; res advisor to OERI, US Dept of Educ, 92-93. **HONORS AND AWARDS** Elected mem Nat Acad of Educ, 96; elected pres Hist of Educ Soc, 94-95. **MEMBERSHIPS** AHA; Social Sci Hist Asn; Econ Hist Asn; Orgn Am Historians; Pop Asn Am. **RESEARCH** Demographic history; family history; educational history. **SELECTED PUBLICATIONS** Coauth, Religion, Family, and the Life Course: Explorations in the Social History of Early America, Michigan, 92; co-ed, Learning from the Past: What History Teaches Us About School Reform, Johns Hopkins, 95; auth, Education, Society, and Economic Opportunity: A Historical Perspective on Persistent Problems, Yale, 95; auth, History and Educational Policymaking, Yale, 99. **CONTACT ADDRESS** Dept of History, Univ Mich, 1029 Tisch Hall, Ann Arbor, MI, 48109-1003. **EMAIL** vinovski@umich.edu

VINYARD, JOELLEN
DISCIPLINE HISTORY **EDUCATION** Univ Mich, PhD. **CAREER** Prof, coop and internship adv, Eastern Michigan Univ. **RESEARCH** US Michigan,US, Urban. **SELECTED PUBLICATIONS** Auth, The Irish on the Urban Frontier: Nineteenth-Century Detroit; Michigan: The World Around Us. **CONTACT ADDRESS** Dept of History and Philosophy, Eastern Michigan Univ, 701 Pray-Harrold, Ypsilanti, MI, 48197.

VINZ, WARREN LANG
PERSONAL Born 12/04/1932, Washington, IA, m, 1960, 1 child **DISCIPLINE** EUROPEAN AND UNITED STATES HISTORY **EDUCATION** Sioux Falls Col, BA, 54; Berkeley Baptist Divinity Sch, BD, 57; Univ Utah, MA, 66, PhD (hist), 68. **CAREER** Assoc minister, First Baptist Church, Utah, 57-61, minister, Idaho, 61-65; from asst prof to assoc prof, 68-72, PROF HIST and CHMN DEPT, BOISE STATE UNIV, 72-; Consult, John Wiley and Sons, 69-71. **MEMBERSHIPS** AHA **RESEARCH** American church history; church history. **SELECTED PUBLICATIONS** Auth, the Role of Religion in The Making of Public, Church Hist, Vol 63, 94; How Does America Hear the Gospel, Church Hist, Vol 63, 94; The Role of Religion in The Making of Public Policy, Church Hist, Vol 63, 94; The Fundamentalist Phenomenon, Church Hist, Vol 63, 94; Icons of American Protestantism in The Art of Sallman, Warner, Church Hist, Vol 66, 97. **CONTACT ADDRESS** Dept of Hist, Boise State Univ, 07 University Blvd, Boise, ID, 83707.

VIOLA, HERMAN JOSEPH
PERSONAL Born 02/24/1938, Chicago, IL, m, 1964, 3 children **DISCIPLINE** AMERICAN HISTORY **EDUCATION** Marquette Univ, BA, 56, MA, 60; Ind Univ, Bloomington, PhD (hist), 70. **CAREER** Archivist, Nat Arch, 67-68; Nat Hist Publ Comn, 68; ed, Prologue, J Nat Arch, 68-72; DIR NAT ANTHROP ARCH, SMITHSONIAN INST, 72-; Dir, Human Studies Film Arch, Smithsonian Inst, 82-. **MEMBERSHIPS** Soc Am Archivists; Orgn Am Historians; Western Hist Asn. **RESEARCH** American Indian policy; frontier movement. **SELECTED PUBLICATIONS** Auth, Sacred Encounters in Father Desmet and the Indians of the Rocky-Mountain West, Mo-Mag Western Hist, Vol 45, 95; Undaunted Courage in Lewis, Meriwether, Jefferson, Thomas, and the Opening of the American-West, William Mary Quart, Vol 54, 97. **CONTACT ADDRESS** Nat Anthrop Arch, Smithsonian Inst, Washington, DC, 20560.

VIOLAS, PAUL CONSTANTINE
PERSONAL Born 05/04/1937, Rochester, NY, m, 1957, 4 children **DISCIPLINE** HISTORY OF EDUCATION **EDUCATION** Univ Rochester, BA, 59, MA, 66, EdD 69. **CAREER** Teacher US hist, Canandaigua Acad, 59-66; PROF HIST OF EDUC, UNIV ILL, 68-; ASSOC DEAN, 82-; Assoc ed, Educ Theory, 70-. **MEMBERSHIPS** Hist Educ Soc. **RESEARCH** History of urban education United States; history of working class; class consciousness. **SELECTED PUBLICATIONS** Auth, Literacy and Paideia in ancient Greece, J Aesthetic Educ, Vol 29, 95. **CONTACT ADDRESS** Univ Ill, 375 Educ Bldg, Urbana, IL, 61801.

VIOLETTE, AURELE J.
DISCIPLINE HISTORY **EDUCATION** Ohio State Univ, PhD, 71. **CAREER** Prof. **RESEARCH** Russian history. **SELECTED PUBLICATIONS** Auth, French in Peopling Indiana: the Ethnic Experience, 96; pubs in Slavonic and East European Review, European Studies Review, Indiana Magazine of History. **CONTACT ADDRESS** Dept of History, Indiana Univ-Purdue Univ, Fort Wayne, 2101 Coliseum Blvd, Fort Wayne, IN, 46805. **EMAIL** violette@fwa.cioe.com

VIPOND, MARY
DISCIPLINE HISTORY **EDUCATION** Queen's Univ, BA; Univ Toronto, MA, PhD. **CAREER** Prof. **MEMBERSHIPS** Mem, Concordia's Ctr for Broadcasting Stud. **RESEARCH** Twentieth century English Canadian intellectual, cultural and media history. **SELECTED PUBLICATIONS** Auth, The Mass Media in Canada, 89; 2nd ed, 92; Listening In: The First Decade of Canadian Broadcasting, 1922-1932. **CONTACT ADDRESS** Dept of Hist, Concordia Univ, Montreal, 1455 de Maisonneuve W, Montreal, PQ, H3G 1M8. **EMAIL** vipond@vax2.concordia.ca

VIPPERMAN, CARL
PERSONAL Born 03/27/1928, Sophia, WV, m, 1957, 1 child **DISCIPLINE** AMERICAN HISTORY **EDUCATION** Univ NC, Chapel Hill, AB, 55; Univ Ga, MA, 61; Univ Va, PhD (hist), 66. **CAREER** From asst prof to assoc prof Am hist, Col Charleston, 64-67; asst prof, 67-79, ASSOC PROF AM HIST, UNIV GA, 79-. **MEMBERSHIPS** Southern Hist Asn. **RESEARCH** Middle period of American history; Lowndes family in colonial and antebellum South Carolina politics; Georgia politics and Indian removal. **SELECTED PUBLICATIONS** Auth, Spalding, Billups, Phinizy, In Memoriam, J Southern Hist, Vol 60, 94. **CONTACT ADDRESS** Dept of Hist, Univ of Ga, Athens, GA, 30601.

VISSER, DERK
DISCIPLINE HISTORY **EDUCATION** Bryn Mawr Col, PhD. **CAREER** Prof, Ursinus Col. **HONORS AND AWARDS** Lindback Award for Excellence in Tchg; Laughlin Prof Achievement Award. **RESEARCH** Medieval European history; the history of the Renaissance and Reformation. **SELECTED PUBLICATIONS** Published widely on the Reformation in Germany and the Netherlands, including the standard biography of Zacharius Ursinus as well as several books and numerous articles on medieval church history. **CONTACT ADDRESS** Ursinus Col, Collegeville, PA, 19426-1000.

VITA, STEVEN
PERSONAL Born 07/16/1960, Chicago, IL, s **DISCIPLINE** ART **EDUCATION** Univ of Chicago Lab Sch, 74-76; Latin Sch of Chicago, 76-78; Denison Univ, BA, 78-82 **CAREER** Ed and Founder, 91-pres, Veery Journ **MEMBERSHIPS** Am Philos Assoc **CONTACT ADDRESS** Veery, Suite 2044, Chicago, IL, 60602.

VITZ, ROBERT C.
PERSONAL Born 12/26/1938, Minneapolis, MN, m, 1964, 3 children **DISCIPLINE** HISTORY **EDUCATION** Depauw Univ, BA, 60; Miami Univ, MA, 67; UNC-Chapel Hill, PhD, 71. **CAREER** Visiting Asst Prof, 71-72, Purdue Univ; Asst Prof, 72-75, Assoc Prof, 75-87, Prof, 87-, Chr Dept History and Geography, Northern Kentucky Univ, 95-. **HONORS AND AWARDS** Post Corbett Award (finalist), 89. **MEMBERSHIPS** Cincinnati History Museum; Kentucky Assoc of Teachers of History **RESEARCH** U.S. cultural and intellectual history; U.S. urban history **SELECTED PUBLICATIONS** Auth, Introduction, Cincinnati Symphony Orchestra: Centennial Portraits, 95; auth, The Troubled Life of James Handasyd Perkins, Queen City Heritage, 95. **CONTACT ADDRESS** Dept of History and Geography, No Kentucky Univ, Highland Heights, KY, 41099. **EMAIL** vita@nku.edu

VIVIAN, JAMES FLOYD
PERSONAL Born 08/25/1934, Phoenix, AZ, m, 1964, 2 children **DISCIPLINE** US HISTORY, LATIN AMERICAN & UNITED STATES DIPLOMATIC HISTORY **EDUCATION** Coe Col, BA, 60; Univ Nebr-Lincoln, MA, 64; Am Univ, PhD(-US Diplomacy), 71. **CAREER** Archivist, Nat Arch, Washington, DC, 69-70; asst prof US & Latin Am Hist, Univ Wis-Platteville, 70-73; assoc prof Hist, 73-80, prof Hist, Univ NDak, 80-. **MEMBERSHIPS** AHA; Orgn Am Historians; Soc Historians Am Foreign Rels: AAUP; Conf Latin Am Hist. **RESEARCH** US political, Inter-American affairs; United States-Latin American relations. **SELECTED PUBLICATIONS** Auth, The Taking of Panama Canal Zone: Myth and reality, Diplomatic Hist, Winter 80; US Policy during Brazilian Naval Revolt, 1893-94: Case for American neutrality, Am Neptune, 10/81; ed, William Howard Taft: Collected Editorials, 1917-1921, NY: Praeger Publishers, 90; The President's Salary: A Study in constitutional Declension, 1789-1990, NY: Garland Press, 93. **CONTACT ADDRESS** Dept of History, Univ of North Dakota, Box 8096, Grand Forks, ND, 58202-8096.

VIVONI-FARAGE, ENRIQUE
PERSONAL Born 11/14/1949, San German, PR, m, 1972, 3 children **DISCIPLINE** ARCHITECTURE **EDUCATION** Univ Puerto Rico, M Arch, 73; Univ Penn, PhD, 85. **CAREER** Univ Puerto Rico, prof, 86-, Arch and Construction Archives, dir. **MEMBERSHIPS** AAP; SAH; SAA **RESEARCH** Twentieth Century Architecture **SELECTED PUBLICATIONS** Auth, Alarife de suenos: Pedro Adolfo de Castro y Besosa, San Jaun, AACUPR, 99; The Architecture of Power, pub electronically in: ARIS3 Jour of Carnegie Mellon Univ; Hispanofilia: arquitecura y vida en Puerto Rico, co-ed, San Jaun, Ed de la Univ Puerto Rico y AACUPR, 98; San Jaun of Puerto Rico: De plaza fuerte a ciudad bella, in: Arcos de la memoria, SJ, Asso Puertorriquena de Hist, 98; Ilusion de Francia: arquitectura y afrancesamiento en Puerto Rico, co ed, SJ, AACUPR, 97; El'98 y la creacion de tres imaginarios: isla pasado isla paraiso e isla progreso, Claridad, 96; La academia y la arquitectura en Puerto Rico, Cap rev de Col of Arch de Puerto Rico, 95; Lo internacional de la arquitectura puertorriquena, Claridad, 95; Rafael Carmoega y su pasion por la arquitectura, Cap Rev del Col of Arch de Puerto Rico, 94. **CONTACT ADDRESS** Dept of Architecture, Puerto Rico Univ, UPR Station, PO Box 21909, Rio Piedras, PR, 00931. **EMAIL** evivoni@upracd.upr.cln.edu

VLAM, GRACE A.H.
PERSONAL Born 12/17/1930, Netherlands, s **DISCIPLINE** ART HISTORY **EDUCATION** Univ Utah, MA, 60; Univ Mich, Ann Arbor, PhD, 76. **CAREER** Cur and Actg Dir, Salt Lake Art Ctr, 66-68; instr, Univ Utah, 69-70; tchg fel, Univ Mich, 71-73; vis asst prof, SUNY Buffalo, 76-77; indep res, Yale Univ, 77-78; vis asst prof, Weber State Col, 81-82; adj instr, 82-88, assoc instr, 89- , Univ Utah; Assoc Prof Art Hist and Hum, Salt Lake Commun Col. **HONORS AND AWARDS** Plantin-Moretus Mus Res Grant, Antwerp, Belgium, 72; Samuel B. Kress grant, 73-74; Horace Rackham res grant, 74-75; A. and S. Krissoff Res Grant, 74-75; NEH summer stipend, 77, 83. **MEMBERSHIPS** Col Art Asn of Am. **RESEARCH** Archaeo-Art history. **SELECTED PUBLICATIONS** Coauth, The Poet-Painters: Buson and His Followers, Univ Michigan, 74; coauth, Namban Byobu (Namban Screens), Kodansha, 79; contribur, Muller, ed, Encyclopedia of Dutch Art, 97. **CONTACT ADDRESS** Humanities Dept, Salt Lake Community Col, 4600 S Redwood Rd, PO Box 30808, Salt Lake City, UT, 84130-0808.

VLASICH, JAMES ANTHONY
PERSONAL Born 04/19/1944, Hillsboro, IL, 2 children **DISCIPLINE** AMERICAN INDIAN HISTORY, AMERICAN WEST, SPORTS HISTORY. **EDUCATION** Southern Ill Univ, BA, 67; Ft Lewis Col, BA, 75; Univ Utah, MA, 77, PhD, 80. **CAREER** Assoc engr & comput programmer, McDonnel Douglas Corp, 67-68; United States Army, 68-69; Comput Programmer, State of Colo, 70-73; asst US hist, Univ Utah, 75-77, res asst Am Indians, Am West Ctr, 78-79; instr US hist, Westminster Col, 79; historian Western hist, Archaeol Ctr, Univ Utah, 80-81; asst prof Indians, Southern Utah Univ, Lake City, Utah, 74-77. **HONORS AND AWARDS** Teacher of the Year, Southern Utah Univ, 86; Southern Utah Univ Award for best published article of the year (Alexander Cleland and the Origin...), 92; Distinguished Educator, Southern Utah Univ, 98. **MEMBERSHIPS** Orgn Am Historians; Western Hist Asn; Soc Am Baseball Res. **RESEARCH** Southwest Indians; New Mexico history. **SELECTED PUBLICATIONS** Auth, Transitions in pueblo agriculture, 1938-1948, NMex Hist Rev, 1/80; The history of the Bayhorse mining district, 9/80, History of the Elko and Ely districts, 4/81 & History of the Escalante Desert, 8/81, Univ Utah Archaeol Ctr; Assimilation or extermination: A cooperative study of Indians of the US in 19th century and Brazilian Indians in the 20th century, Occas Papers, No 19, Am West Ctr, Univ Utah, 81; A Legend for the Legendary: The Origin of the Baseball Hall of Fame, Bowling Green Univ Press, 90; Alexander Cleland and the Origin of the Baseball Hall of Fame, in Cooperstown Symposium on Baseball and American Culture, Meckler Publ, 89; Bob Broeg, in The Dictionary of Literary Biography: Twentieth Century Sportswriters, Gale Res, 96. **CONTACT ADDRESS** Southern Utah Univ, 225 Centrum, Cedar City, UT, 84720-2470. **EMAIL** vlasich@sw.edu

VOEGELI, VICTOR JACQUE
PERSONAL Born 12/21/1934, Jackson, TN, m, 1956, 2 children **DISCIPLINE** UNITED STATES HISTORY **EDUCATION** Murray State Col, BS, 56; Tulance Univ, MA, 61, PhD(hist), 65. **CAREER** Instr US Hist, Tulane Univ, 63-65, asst prof, 65-67; from asst prof to assoc prof, 67-73, chmn dept, 73-75, prof Hist, Vanderbilt Univ, 73-, dean, Col Arts & Sci, 76-92; acting Dean, Col Arts & Sciences, 96-97; Nat Endowment for Humanities res grant, 69-70 & 72. **MEMBERSHIPS** Southern Hist Asn Orgn Am Historians. **RESEARCH** Southern History; Civil War and reconstruction; 19th century United States. **SELECTED PUBLICATIONS** Auth, The Northwest and the race issue, 1861-1862, Miss Valley Hist Rev, 9/63; Free But Not Equal: The Midwest and the Negro During the Civil War, Univ Chicago, 67. **CONTACT ADDRESS** Vanderbilt Univ, Box 1863, Nashville, TN, 37240-0001.

VOELTZ, RICHARD ANDREW
PERSONAL Born 12/04/1948, Chicago, IL **DISCIPLINE** MODERN EUROPEAN HISTORY **EDUCATION** Univ Calif, Santa Cruz, BA, 71; Univ Ore, MA, 74; Univ Calif, Los Angeles, PhD (hist), 80. **CAREER** Teaching asst western civilization, Univ Calif, Los Angeles, 79-80; LECTR HIST, CALIF STATE UNIV, FULLERTON, 80-. **MEMBERSHIPS** AHA; NAm Soc Sport Hist. **RESEARCH** British and German colonial companies; South Africa; comparative social history. **SELECTED PUBLICATIONS** Auth, Our Great Solicitor in Wedgewood, Josiah, C and the Jews, Historian, Vol 55, 93; Studies in the Economic History of Southern Africa, Vol II, South Africa, Lesotho and Swaziland, Int J African Hist Stud, Vol 26, 93; Machinery, Money, and the Millennium, from Moral Economy to Socialism, 1815-1860, Labor Hist, Vol 34, 93; The Occupation of Namibia in Afrikanerdoms Attack on the British Empire, Int J African Hist Stud, Vol 27, 94; Image as Artifact in the Historical Analysis of Film and Television, Hist J Film Radio TV, Vol 14, 94; Black Country Elites in the Exercise of Authority in an Industrialized Area 1830-1900, J Soc Hist, Vol 29, 95; The Epidemic Streets in Infectious Disease and the Rise of Preventive Medicine 1856-1900, J Soc Hist, Vol 28, 95; from Empire to International Commonwealth in a Biography of Curtis,Lionel, Am Hist Rev, Vol 102, 97; The First Teenagers in the Life Style of Young Wage Earners in Interwar Britain, Albion, Vol 29, 97. **CONTACT ADDRESS** 11005 Sardis Ave, Los Angeles, CA, 90064.

VOGAN, NANCY F.
DISCIPLINE MUSIC **EDUCATION** Univ Rochester, MA, PhD. **CAREER** Prof. **RESEARCH** Hist of music instruction; hist of music in Canada. **SELECTED PUBLICATIONS** Auth, Music Education and Music Festivals: A Case Study, Can Music Edu, 94; co-auth, Music Education in Canada: A Historical Account, Univ Toronto, 91. **CONTACT ADDRESS** Mount Allison Univ, 63D York St, Sackville, NB, E4L 1E4.

VOGEL, MORRIS J
PERSONAL Born 08/24/1945, Kazakhstan, USSR, m, 1968, 2 children **DISCIPLINE** AMERICAN AND SOCIAL HISTORY **EDUCATION** Brandeis Univ, BA, 67; Univ Chicago, PhD (hist), 74. **CAREER** Inst, 73-79, ASSOC PROF HIST, TEMPLE UNIV, 79-; Res assoc, Philadelphia Soc Hist Proj, Univ Pa, 80-82; Nat Sci Found, Ethics and Values in Sci and Technol, Interdisciplinary Incentive Award, 80-82. **MEMBERSHIPS** Orgn Am Historians; Am Studies Asn. **RESEARCH** Social history of American medicine; history of Philadelphia. **SELECTED PUBLICATIONS** Auth, Making a Place for Ourselves in the Black Hospital Movement 1920-1945, Am Hist Rev, Vol 102, 97; Technology in the Hospital in Transforming Patient Care in the Early 20th Century, Am Hist Rev, Vol 102, 97. **CONTACT ADDRESS** 637 Foxcroft Rd, Elkins Park, PA.

VOGEL, ROBERT
PERSONAL Born 11/04/1929, Vienna, Austria, 1 child **DISCIPLINE** MODERN HISTORY **EDUCATION** Sir George Williams Univ, BA, 52; McGill Univ, MA, 54, PhD (hist), 59. **CAREER** Lectr, 58-61, from asst prof to assoc prof, 61-69, chmn dept, 66-71, PROF HIST, McGILL UNIV, 69-; DEAN FAC ARTS, 71-. **MEMBERSHIPS** AHA; Orgn Hist Asn. **RESEARCH** British foreign policy in the nineteenth and twentieth centuries; war and society in modern Europe. **SELECTED PUBLICATIONS** Auth, Earthworms, Smithsonian, Vol 24, 93; From Consecutio Temporum to Aktionsart, Lingua E Stile, Vol 31, 96; Alienation in Studies on the Early Works of Boll, Etudes Germaniques, Vol 52, 97. **CONTACT ADDRESS** Fac of Arts, McGill Univ, 853 Sherbrooke St, Montreal, PQ, H3A 2T6.

VOGELER, MARTHA SALMON
PERSONAL New York, NY, m, 1962 **DISCIPLINE** ENGLISH LITERATURE, INTELLECTUAL HISTORY **EDUCATION** Jersey City State Col, BA, 46; Columbia Univ, MA, 52, PhD (English), 59. **CAREER** Lectr French Columbia Univ, 55-60; lectr, NY Univ, 56-59; instr, Vassar Col, 59-62; asst prof, Long Island Univ, 62-66; assoc prof, 69-73, PROF ENGLISH, CALIF STATE UNIV, FULLERTON, 73-; Am Coun Learned Soc grant, 67; Am Philos Soc grants, 67 and 70. **MEMBERSHIPS** MLA; AAUP; Tennyson Soc; Res Soc Victorian Periodicals; Pac Coast Conf British Studies. **RESEARCH** Victorian biography, aesthetics and religious thought. **SELECTED PUBLICATIONS** Auth, Gissing, George in Lost Stories from America, Eng Lit Transition, Vol 36, 93; Bridges, Robert in a Biography, Eng Lit Transition, Vol 36, 93; The Collected Letters of Gissing, George, Vol 4, 1889-1891,, Eng Lit Transition, Vol 37, 94; The Collected Letters of Gissing,George, Vol 5, 1892-1895, Eng Lit Transition, Vol 38, 95; The Collected Letters of Gissing, George, Vol 6, 1895-1897, Eng Lit Transition, Vol 38, 95; The Collected Letters of Gissing, George, Vol 7, 1897-1899, Eng Lit Transition, Vol 39, 96; Thomas,Edward in Selected Letters, Eng Lit Transition, Vol 40, 97; The Collected Letters of Gissing, George, Vol 8, 1900-1902, Eng Lit Transition, Vol 40, 97. **CONTACT ADDRESS** Dept of English, California State Univ, Fullerton, Fullerton, CA, 92831.

VOGT, GEORGE LEONARD
PERSONAL Belleville, IL **DISCIPLINE** AMERICAN HISTORY **EDUCATION** Yale Univ, AB, 66; Univ Va, MA, 70 PhD (hist), 78. **CAREER** From asst to exec dir, 74-78, ASST DIR PUBL, NAT HIST PUBL and REC COMN, 78-. **MEMBERSHIPS** Asn State and Local Hist; Southern Hist Asn; Manuscript Soc (vpres, 81-); Nat Micrographics Asn. **RESEARCH** Twentieth century southern politics; historical editing; American cultural history. **SELECTED PUBLICATIONS** Auth, Richmond Times Dispatch in the Story of a Newspaper, Va Mag Hist Biog, Vol 104, 96. **CONTACT ADDRESS** Nat Hist Publ and Rec Comn, National Archives, Washington, DC, 20408.

VOIGT, DAVID QUENTIN
PERSONAL Born 08/09/1926, Reading, PA, m, 1951, 2 children **DISCIPLINE** HISTORY, SOCIOLOGY, ANTHROPOLOGY **EDUCATION** Albright Col, BS (history), 48; Columbia Univ, MA (Am hist), 49; Syracuse Univ, PhD (Hist, Socl Sci), 62. **CAREER** Teacher, state of NY, social studies, 50-56; assoc prof hist and social science, Millerville State Univ, PA, 56-63; assoc prof, sociology & anthroplogy, Muskingum Col, New Concord, OH, 63-64; prof of sociology & anthropology at Albright Col, Reading, PA, 64-95, prof Emeritus, 96-. **HONORS AND AWARDS** Winner of Lindback Distinguished Teaching Award; Alumnus of the Year, Milton Hershey School, PA, 93. **MEMBERSHIPS** PA Sociol Soc (past pres); Am Anthropol Asn; Am Sociol Asn; Soc for Am Baseball Res (past pres); North Am Soc for Sports Hist. **RESEARCH** Am baseball studies--author of seven books on Am major league baseball; leisure in AM; Civil War hist. **SELECTED PUBLICATIONS** Auth, Thenk God for Nuts, in The Perfect Game, Marl Alvarez, ed, Dallas, TX, 93; The History of Major League Baseball, in 3rd ed of Total Baseball, 93; The League That Failed, Scarecrow Press of MD, 98. **CONTACT ADDRESS** Dept of Sociol, Albright Col, Reading, PA, 19603.

VOIGTS, LINDA EHRSAM
PERSONAL Born 05/09/1942, Abilene, KS, m, 1963, 1 child **DISCIPLINE** OLD AND MIDDLE ENGLISH, HISTORY OF MEDICINE **EDUCATION** William Jewell Col, BA, 63; Univ Mo-Kansas City, MA, 66; Univ Mo-Columbia, PhD (English), 73. **CAREER** Teacher Ger and English, North Kansas City High Sch, 63-65; instr English, William Jewell Col, 65-69; instr compos, Univ Mo-Columbia, 72; vis asst prof English, William Jewell Col, 73-74 and Univ Mo-Columbia, 74-75; asst prof, 75-79, ASSOC PROF ENGLISH, UNIV MO-KANSAS CITY, 79-; Am Coun Learned Soc grant-in-aid, 75; Andrew W Mellon fac fel humanities, Harvard Univ, 78-79; vis instr, Harvard Univ, summer, 80. **HONORS AND AWARDS** Zeitlin-VerBrugge Prize, Hist of Sci Soc, 81. **MEMBERSHIPS** Mediaeval Acad Am; MLA; Hist of Sci Soc; Am Asn Hist Med; New Chaucer Soc. **RESEARCH** Old English; Middle English. **SELECTED PUBLICATIONS** Auth, Memorials of the Book Trade in Medieval London in the Archives of Old London Bridge, Anglia Zeitschrift fur Englische Philologie, Vol 111, 93; The Authorship of the Equatorie of the Planetis, Isis, Vol 86, 95; Anglo-Saxon Medicine, Isis, Vol 86, 95; What's the Word and the Vernacularization of Science and Medicine in England from 1375 To 1475, Bilingualism in Late Medieval England, Speculum J Medieval Stud, Vol 71, 96. **CONTACT ADDRESS** Dept of English, Univ of Mo, 5100 Rockhill Rd, Kansas City, MO, 64110-2499.

VOLL, JOHN OBERT
PERSONAL Born 04/20/1936, Hudson, WI, m, 1965, 2 children **DISCIPLINE** MIDDLE EASTERN HISTORY **EDUCATION** Darmouth Col, AB, 58; Harvard Univ, AM, 60, PhD (hist and Mid E studies), 69. **CAREER** From instr to asst prof, 65-73, ASSOC PROF HIST, UNIV NH, 73-; Nat Endowment for Humanities younger humanist fel, 71-72. **MEMBERSHIPS** Mid E Studies Asn NAm; Am Orient Soc; Mid E Inst; African Studies Asn; New Eng Hist Asn (secy 75-78). **RESEARCH** Modern Islamic history; Sudanese history; methodology of world history. **SELECTED PUBLICATIONS** Auth, Historical Discord in the Nile Valley, Int J African Hist Stud, Vol 27, 94; Islam as a Special World System, J World Hist, Vol 5, 94; The Sufi Brotherhoods in the Sudan, Int J African Hist Stud, Vol 29, 96; Civil War in the Sudan, Int J African Hist Stud, Vol 29, 96; Islam in the View from the Edge, Int Hist Rev, Vol 18, 96; Merchants and Faith in Muslim Commerce and Culture in the Indian Ocean, J World Hist, Vol 8, 97. **CONTACT ADDRESS** Dept of Hist Soc Sci Ctr, Univ of NH, Durham, NH, 03824.

VOLPE, VERNON L.
PERSONAL Born 03/24/1955, New Orleans, LA, m, 1982, 2 children **DISCIPLINE** HISTORY **EDUCATION** Youngstown State Univ, BA, 77, MA, 79; Univ Nebr, PhD, 84. **CAREER** Vis Asst Prof, Tex A & M Univ, 86-87; Univ Nebr at Kearney, Prof Hist, 87-, Dept Ch, 93-96. **HONORS AND AWARDS** Pratt-Heins Foundation Fac Award, Res & Schol, 91; Fellow, Ctr for Great Plains Stud, Univ Nebr. **MEMBERSHIPS** Org of Am Hist; S Hist Asn; Soc for Hist of the Early Am Republic; Nebr Hist Soc. **RESEARCH** 19th century US Civil War & Reconstruction; American exploration. **SELECTED PUBLICATIONS** Auth, Forlorn Hope of Freedom: The Liberty Party in the Old Northwest, 1838-1848, Kent State Univ Press, 90; auth, The Liberty Party and Polk's Election, 1844, The Hist, 53, 691-710, 91; auth, Theodore Dwight Weld's Antislavery Mission in Ohio, Ohio Hist, 100, 5-18, 91; auth, The Fremonts and Emancipation in Missouri, The Hist, 56, 339-354,

53; auth, Origins of Republican Dominance: John C Fremont's 1856 Victory in Ohio, The Pursuit of Public Power: Political Culture in Ohio, 1787-1861, Kent St Univ Press, 94. **CONTACT ADDRESS** Dept Hist, Univ Nebr at Kearney, Kearney, NE, 68849. **EMAIL** volpe@lotus.unk.edu

VOLZ, CARL
PERSONAL Born 10/07/1933, Faribalt, MN, m, 1958, 5 children **DISCIPLINE** ANCIENT MEDIEVAL CHURCH HISTORY **EDUCATION** Concordia Seminary, MO, BA 55; Mdiv 58, STM 59; WA Univ, MA 61; Fordham Univ, PhD 66. **CAREER** Concordia Coll, NY, instr 59-62; Christ Lutheran Church, NY pastor 61-64; Concordia Seminary, MO, prof church hist 64-74; Luther Seminary, MN, prof church hist 74. **HONORS AND AWARDS** Phi Beta Kappa **MEMBERSHIPS** Am Soc of Church Hist; NAPS. **RESEARCH** Hist, worship, church and state rel(s) 300-1300 AD. **SELECTED PUBLICATIONS** The Medieval Church, Abingdon, 97; Pastoral Life and the Practice in the Early Church, Augsbury, 90, re-issued, Sigler Press, 98. **CONTACT ADDRESS** Luther Sem, 2481 Como Av, St Paul, MN, 55108. **EMAIL** cvolz@luthersem.edu

VOLZ, CARL A.
DISCIPLINE CHURCH HISTORY **EDUCATION** Concordia Sem, BA, 55, MDiv, 58, STM, 59; Wash Univ, MA, 61; Fordham Univ, PhD, 66; post dr, Cambridge Univ; Trinity Col, Dublin; fel, Univ Chicago, Inst Advan Stud Rel. **CAREER** Instr, Concordia Sem, 64-74; registar, 71-74; guest prof, Martin Luther Sem, Papua, New Guinea, 87; United Theol Col, Bangalore, S India, 88; Luther Sem, Seoul, Korea; Tokyo, Japan, 95; vis prof, Meramec Community Col, 67-71; Concordia Sem, Springfield, 67; Concordia Col, St Paul, 81-83; instr, 74; dept ch, 85-91; dean of stud (s), 75-76; prof, 82-. **HONORS AND AWARDS** Fel(s), John W. Behnken; Lutheran Brotherhood; AAL., Pastor, Christ Lutheran Church, 61-64; ELCA rep, Lutheran-Orthodox Dialogs; bd mem, Ecumenical Inst; dir, Jerusalem House of Studies. **MEMBERSHIPS** Mem, Minn Coun of Churches Comm on Ecumenicity; Comm on Ecumenical Relations of the ELCA Saint Paul Area Synod. **SELECTED PUBLICATIONS** Auth, Pastoral Life and Practice in the Early Church, 90; Faith and Practice in the Early Church, 83; The Church and the Middle Ages, 70; ed, Teaching the Faith, 67. **CONTACT ADDRESS** Dept of Church History, Luther Sem, 2481 Como Ave, St. Paul, MN, 55108. **EMAIL** cvolz@luthersem.edu

VON ARX, JEFFERY P.
PERSONAL Born 05/12/1947, Bellefonte, PA, s **DISCIPLINE** HISTORY **EDUCATION** Princeton Univ, AB, 69; Yale Univ, MA, 73, Mphil, 74, PhD, 80; Weston Sch of Theol, Mdiv, 81. **CAREER** Asst Prof History, Assoc Prof, Dept Chair, Georgetown Univ, 82-98; Dean, Fordham Coll, 98-. **HONORS AND AWARDS** Visiting Fel, Research Sch of the Social Sci, Australian Natl Univ, 90; Georgetown Univ Summer Academic Grant, 86; Grant-in-Aid, Concilium on Area and Internatl Studies, Yale Univ, 75; Phi Beta Kappa, Princeton Univ, 69; Natl Merit Scholar, Princeton Univ, 65-69. **MEMBERSHIPS** Amer Hist Assoc; Amer Catholic Hist Assoc; member, Joint Commission of Bishops and Scholars; North Amer Conf on British Studies; Amer Conf for Irish Studies; Australian Studies Assoc of North Amer. **RESEARCH** British and Irish 19th century hist; church hist, Australian hist. **SELECTED PUBLICATIONS** auth, Victorian Faith in Crisis, The Victorian Crisis of Faith as Crisis of Vocation, Macmillan, London, 90; Recusant Studies, Archbishop Manning and the Kulturkampf, Oct 92; ed, Varieties of Ultramontanism, Catholic Univ Press, Washington D.C., 97. **CONTACT ADDRESS** Dean's Office, Fordham Col, Rose Hill, Bronx, NY, 10458. **EMAIL** vonarx@murray.fordham.edu

VON BAEYER, EDWINNA L.
PERSONAL Born 08/22/1946, Detroit, MI **DISCIPLINE** HISTORY **EDUCATION** Univ Mich, BA, 68; Univ Pa, MA, 70. **CAREER** Independent writer/researcher **HONORS AND AWARDS** Can Coun Explor grant, 81; SSHRCC grant, 83. **MEMBERSHIPS** Bd dir, Ottawa Independent Writers Asn, 89-94; Friends of Cent Exp Farm, 96-. **RESEARCH** Canadian landscape history. **SELECTED PUBLICATIONS** Auth, Rhetoric and Roses: A History of Canadian Gardening 1900-1930, 84; Garden of Dreams, Kingsmere and Mackenzie King, 90; coauth, The Reluctant Gardener, 92; co-ed, Garden Voices-Two Centuries of Canadian Garden Writing, 95. **CONTACT ADDRESS** 131 Sunnyside Ave, Ottawa, ON, K1S 0R2.

VON BORSTEL, FEDERICO
PERSONAL Born 02/22/1950, Mexico, m, 1979, 1 child **DISCIPLINE** EDUCATION **EDUCATION** Univ Minn, BA, 72; Allende Inst, MA, 74; Univ of Americas, MA, 77; Univ Toronto, PhD, 82. **CAREER** Prof, 74-79, Metropolitan Univ; dir, planning & devel, 82-83, IberoAmerican Univ; chief acad off, 82-83, Univ Baja Calif; coord, Latin Amer rel, 84-86, assoc/adj prof, 86-97, dir, 86-89, career devel, dir, 84-89, So Bay Reg Ctr, US Intl Univ; principal, 89-99, Ed Planning & Devel Corp, San Diego, CA; prof, chmn, lib stud, dir res, 94-99, New School Architecture. **RESEARCH** Educational planning, productive education, curriculum development. **CONTACT ADDRESS** 13527 Mountainside Dr, Poway, CA, 92064. **EMAIL** gvonb@sdcoe.k12.ca.us

VON HAGEN, MARK L.
DISCIPLINE HISTORY **EDUCATION** Georgetown Univ, BSFS, 76; Indiana Univ, MA, Slavic Lang aand Lit, 78; Stanford Univ, MA, Hist, 80, PhD, 85. **CAREER** Instr, Assoc Dir, Indiana Univ, 81-82; Visiting Prof, Yale Univ, Jan 88-May 88; Asst Prof, Columbia Univ, Jan 85- June 89; Visiting Prof, Osteuropa-Inst, Sept 91-Dec 91; Assoc Dir, Columbia Univ, W. Averell Harriman Inst for the Advanced Study of the Soviet Union, July 89-June 92; Visiting Assoc Prof, Stanford Univ, Jan 95-June 95; Dir, The Harriman Inst, Columbia Univ, July 95-present; Prof, Columbia Univ, July 89-present. **SELECTED PUBLICATIONS** Auth, Post-Soviet Political Order: Conflict and State Building, The Great War and the Mobilization of Ethnicity in the Russian Empire, 98; ConAuth, Forging the Sword: Selecting, Educating and Training Cadets and Junior Officers in the Modern World, Confronting Backwardness: Dilemmas of Soviet Officer Education in the Interwar Years, 1918-1941, forthcoming 1998; Peoples, Nations, Identies: The Russian-Ukrainian Encounter, Introduction and States, Nations and Identities: The Russian-Ukrainian Encounter in the First Half of the 20th Century, forthcoming 1998; Kazan, Moscow, St. Petersburg: Multiple Faces of the Russian Empire, Writing the History of Russia as Empire, 97. **CONTACT ADDRESS** The Harriman Institute, Columbia Univ, 420 W. 118, New York, NY, 10027. **EMAIL** mlv2@columbia.edu

VON LAUE, THEODORE HERMAN
PERSONAL Born 06/22/1916, Frankfurt am Main, Germany **DISCIPLINE** HISTORY **EDUCATION** Princeton Univ, AB, 39, PhD, 44; Columbia Univ, cert, 48. **CAREER** Instr, Princeton Univ, 43-45; asst prof, Univ PA, 48-49 & Swarthmore Col, 49-51; lectr, Bryn Mawr Col, 52-54; prof hist, Univ CA, Riverside, 54-64 & Wash Univ, 64-70; FRANCES & JACOB HIATT PROF EUROP HIST, CLARK UNIV, 70-: Fulbright scholar, Finland, 54-55; Guggenheim fel, 62-63, 74-75; Ford vis prof, Mass Inst Technol, 67-68. **MEMBERSHIPS** AHA; Am Asn Advan Slavic Studies; African Studies Asn. **RESEARCH** Russian and Soviet history; history of Ghana; perspectives of global history. **SELECTED PUBLICATIONS** Auth, Leopold Ranke, Princeton Univ, 50; Sergei Witte and the Industrialization of Russia, Columbia Univ, 63; Why Lenin? Why Stalin?, 64 & The Global City, 69, Lippincott; contribr, Man's Unfinished Journey, A World History, 71, & World Civilization, 81, Houghton; The World Revolution of Westernization. The Twentieth Century in Global Perspective, Oxford Univ Press, 87. **CONTACT ADDRESS** Dept of Hist, Clark Univ, 950 Main St, Worcester, MA, 01610.

VONFALKENHAUSEN, L.
DISCIPLINE ART HISTORY **EDUCATION** Harvard Univ, PhD 88. **CAREER** Stanford Univ vis prof; Univ Cal Riverside, asst prof, assoc prof; U of Calif LA, prof. **HONORS AND AWARDS** Andrew W Miller Postdoc Fel; Getty Rex Fel. **MEMBERSHIPS** AAA; AAS; CAA. **RESEARCH** Chinese Bronze Age Archaeology. **SELECTED PUBLICATIONS** Auth, Suspended Music: Chime-Bells in the Culture of Bronze Age China, Berk and LA, U of Calif Press, 93; auth, The Waning of the Bronze Age: Material Culture and Social Developments, 770-481 bc, The Cambridge History og Bronze Age China, Edward L Shaughnessy, Michael Loewe, eds, Cambridge, Cambridge U Press, forthcoming; auth, Reflections on the Political Role of Spirit Mediums in Early China: The wu Officials in the Zhou li, Early China, 95; auth, The Moutuo Bronzes: New Perspectives on the Late Bronze Age in Sichuan, Arts Asiatiques, 96; auth, The Concept of wen in the Ancient Chinese Ancestral Cult, Chin Lit: Essays Article and Rev, 96; auth, Inscribed and Decorated Objects, coauth, in: Down by the Station: The Los Angeles Chinatown 1850-1933, by Roberta S Greenwood, LA, UCLA Inst of Archaeol, 96; rev, Monumentally in Early Chinese Art and Architecture, by Wu Hung, Early China, 96; auth, Early Chinese Texts: A Bibliographic Guide, ed, Michael J. Loewe, China Rev Intl, 96; auth, Art and Political Expression in Early China, by Martin Powers, Harvard Jour of Asiatic Stud, 95; translations from Chinese, Teng Shu-p'ing, The Original Significance of bi Disks: Insights Based on Liangzhu Jade bi with Incised Symbolic Motifs, co-ed, Jour of East Asian Archaeol, forthcoming. **CONTACT ADDRESS** Dept of Art History, Univ of California, Los Angeles, Los Angeles, CA, 90024-1417. **EMAIL** lothar@hamnet.ucla.edu

VOS, ARVIN G.
PERSONAL Born 07/28/1942, Taintor, IA, m, 1967, 5 children **DISCIPLINE** MEDIEVAL PHILOSOPHY **EDUCATION** Calvin Col, AB, 64; Univ Toronto, MA, 66, PhD(philos), 70. **CAREER** Asst prof, 70-75, assoc prof, 75-80, Prof Philos, Western KY Univ, 81-, Adj prof, Sch Theol, Fuller Theol Sem, 78-79; vis prof philos, Calvin Col, 80-81. **MEMBERSHIPS** Soc Christian Philosophers. **RESEARCH** Thomas Aquinas; Augustine; Dante **SELECTED PUBLICATIONS** Auth, Aquinas, Calvin & Contemporary Protestant Thought, 85. **CONTACT ADDRESS** Dept of Philos & Relig, Western Kentucky Univ, 1 Big Red Way, Bowling Green, KY, 42101-3576. **EMAIL** arvin.vos@wku.edu

VRYONIS, SPEROS, JR.
PERSONAL Born 07/18/1928, Memphis, TN, m, 3 children **DISCIPLINE** HISTORY (ANCIENT, BYZANTINE, BALKAN, ISLAMIC, TURKISH) **EDUCATION** Southwestern Col (now Rhodes Col), BA, 50; Harvard, MA, 52, PhD, 56. **CAREER** Jr Fulbright fel, Am, School of Classical Studies Athens, 50-51; jr fel, Dumbarton Oaks, Washington, DC, 54-56; instr, Harvard Univ, 56-60; prof, UCLA, 60-88; prof, Univ Athens, 76-83; Alexander S Onassis Prof of Hellinic Civilization & Culture, New York Univ; dir, G E von Grunebaum Center of Near Eastern Studies UCLA, dir, Onassis Center for Hellenic Studies, NYU, dir, Vryonis Center, Sacramento, 96-. **HONORS AND AWARDS** Fel, Medieval Academy of Am; fel, Am Philos Soc; fel, Am Academy of Arts and Scirnces; Haskins Medal, Am Med Academy; Kokkinos Award, Academy of Athens. **RESEARCH** Classical antiquity; Byzantium; Ottoman-Turkish hist; Islamic hist; hist of Balkans; immigration hist. **SELECTED PUBLICATIONS** Auth, Byzantium and Europe, London, 70; The Decline of Medieval Hellenism in Asia Minor and the Process of Islamization from the Eleventh through the Fifteenth Century, Berkeley, 71; Byzantium: Its Internal History and Relations with the Muslim World, London, 71; ed, The Past in Medieval and Modern Greek Culture, Malibu, 78; auth, Studies on Byzantium, Seljuks and Ottomans, Malibu, 81; St. George Greek Community of Memphis, Malibu, 82; The Turkish State and History. Cleo Meets the Grey Wolf, Thessalonika, 91; ed, Greece on the Road to Democracy: From the Junta to PASOK 1974-1986; ed, The Greeks and the Sea, New Rochelle, 93; auth, Byzantine Institutions, Society and Culture, vol I, The Imperial Institution and Society, New Rochelle, 97. **CONTACT ADDRESS** 3140 Gold Camp Dr, Ste 50, Rancho Cordova, CA, 95670-6023.

VUCINICH, WAYNE S.
PERSONAL Born 06/23/1913, Butte, MT **DISCIPLINE** HISTORY **EDUCATION** Univ Calif, AB, 36, AM, 37, PhD, 41. **CAREER** Res analyst, Off Strategic Serv, 41-45 and US Dept State, 45-46; From instr to prof hist, 46-77, cur and dir Russ and East Europe studies, Hoover Inst, 74-77, ROBERT and FLORENCE MCDONNELL PROF EASTERN EUROP STUDIES, STANFORD UNIV, 77-; DIR CTR RUSS and EASTERN EUROP STUDIES, 72-. **MEMBERSHIPS** AHA; Am Asn Adv Slavic Studies (pres). **RESEARCH** East Europe and Near East history. **SELECTED PUBLICATIONS** Auth, Russian Refugees in France and the United States Between the World Wars, Russian History Histoire Russe, Vol 20, 93; Js of the Priest Veniaminov, Ioann in alaska, 1823 to 1836, Western Hist Quart, Vol 25, 94; The Great Russian Navigator, Chirikov, A, I, Western Hist Quart, Vol 25, 94; Imperial Legacy in the Ottoman Imprint on the Balkans and the Middle East, Am Hist Rev, Vol 102, 97. **CONTACT ADDRESS** Dept of Hist, Stanford Univ, Stanford, CA, 94305.

W

WACHOLDER, BEN ZION
PERSONAL Born 09/21/1924, Dzarow, Poland, m, 1993, 4 children **DISCIPLINE** ENGLISH LITERATURE; CLASSICS; HISTORY **EDUCATION** Yeshiva Univ, BA, 51; UCLA, PhD, 60. **CAREER** Prof, Hebrew Union Col, 56-98. **HONORS AND AWARDS** Pursuing the Text: Studies in Honor of Ben Zion Wacholder on the Occasion of his Seventieth Birthday **MEMBERSHIPS** Soc of Bibl Lit; Asoc of Jewish Studies **RESEARCH** Judaism during the second temple period; Hellenistic Judaism; Dead Sea Scrolls; Talmudic Studies; ancient historiography, ancient calendars **SELECTED PUBLICATIONS** auth, Nicolaus of Damascus, 62; auth, Eupolemus, 74; Essays in Jewish Chronology and Chronography, 84; The Dawn of Qumran, 84; A Preliminary Edition of the Unpublished Dead Sea Scrolls, 96. **CONTACT ADDRESS** 7648 Greenland Pl., Cincinnati, OH, 45237. **EMAIL** ben648@aol.com

WACHTEL, ALBERT
PERSONAL Born 12/20/1939, Queens, NY, m, 1958, 7 children **DISCIPLINE** MODERN BRITISH & AMERICAN LITERATURE **EDUCATION** Queens Col, NY, BA, 60; State Univ NY Buffalo, PhD(English Lit), 68. **CAREER** Instr English, State Univ NY Buffalo, 63-66, asst to dean, 66-68; asst prof English, Univ Calif, Santa Barbara, 68-74; assoc prof, 74-78, prof English, Pitzer Col, 78-. **HONORS AND AWARDS** National Defense Education Act Fel 60-63; Creative Arts Inst Fel, 70; Danforth Assoc, 79; NEH grants, 86, 98. **MEMBERSHIPS** James Joyce Soc; MLA. **RESEARCH** Theory of tragedy; Shakespeare; modern fiction. **SELECTED PUBLICATIONS** Auth, On Analogical Action, J Aesthet & Art Criticism, 63; The Boundaries of Narrative, J Aesthet Educ, 68; The Burden, 71 & The Genesis of Constructive Self-Destruction Dubliners, 74, Spectrum; Ripe for Peaching: Stephen Dedalus and the Chain of Command, James Joyce Quart, 76; A Clean Slate, 76 & Retreating Forward, 78, Moment; Cradle and all, Southern Rev, 82; Why Leam? Why Live? LA Times, 88; co-ed Modernism, 86; The Cracked Looking Glass, 92; Ham, Gettysburg Review, 96; A Malignant Metaphor, Wall Street Journal, 97. **CONTACT ADDRESS** Pitzer Col, 1050 N Mills Ave, Claremont, CA, 91711-6101. **EMAIL** awachtel@pitzer.edu

WACK, JOHN THEODORE
PERSONAL Born 12/18/1934, South Bend, IN **DISCIPLINE** AMERICAN HISTORY **EDUCATION** Univ Notre Dame, AB, 55, MA, 57, PhD, 67. **CAREER** From instr to assoc prof, 61-79, prof hist, Wheeling Col, 79- chmn dept, 75-. **MEMBERSHIPS** AHA; Orgn Am Historians. **RESEARCH** American social history; native American history; history of Appalachia. **CONTACT ADDRESS** Dept of Hist, Wheeling Jesuit Col, 316 Washington Ave, Wheeling, WV, 26003-6243. **EMAIL** jtwack@wju.edu

WADDAMS, STEPHEN M.
PERSONAL Born 09/30/1942, England **DISCIPLINE** HISTORY **EDUCATION** Trinity Col, BA, 63; King's Col, Cambridge, MA, 69, PhD, 94; Univ Toronto, LLB, 67; Univ Michigan, LLM, 68, SJD, 72. **CAREER** Asst prof, 68, assoc prof, 71, fel, Trinity Col, assoc fel, Massey Col, PROF LAW, UNIV TORONTO 76-. **HONORS AND AWARDS** Hurst Prize in Law, 65; Angus MacMurchy Gold Medal, 67; Law Reform Comn Can Award, 89; David W Mundell Medal, 96. **MEMBERSHIPS** Mem, Law Soc Upper Can; Can Bar Asn: Can Asn Law Tchrs; fel, Royal Soc Can, 88. **SELECTED PUBLICATIONS** Auth, The Law of Contracts, 77, 84, 93; auth, Introduction to the Study of Law, 79, 83, 87, 92, 97; auth, Law Politics and the Church of England: the Career of Stephen Lushington 1782-1873, 92. **CONTACT ADDRESS** 58 Russell Hill Rd, Toronto, ON, M4V 2T2.

WADDELL, LOUIS MORTON
PERSONAL Bronxville, NY, 2 children **DISCIPLINE** HISTORY **EDUCATION** Princeton Univ, AB, 53; NY Univ, MA, 61; Univ NC, Chapel Hill, PhD (hist), 71. **CAREER** Instr hist and polit sci, Davis and Elkins Col, 61-63; assoc prof social sci, La Polytech Inst, 66-68; asst prof, Paul D Camp Community Col, 72-73; ASSOC HISTORIAN, PA HIST and MUS COMN, 73-. **RESEARCH** Pennsylvania history; late Stuart England; economic history. **SELECTED PUBLICATIONS** Auth, the Storm Gathering in the Penn Family and the American Revolution, William Mary Quart, Vol 50, 93; Untitled, Virginia Magazine of History and Biography, Vol 103, 95. **CONTACT ADDRESS** Div of Hist, Pennsylvania Historical and Mus Commission, PO Box 1026, Harrisburg, PA, 17120.

WADE, JACQUELINE E.
PERSONAL Born 09/07/1940, Murfreesboro, Tennessee **DISCIPLINE** AFRICAN-AMERICAN STUDIES **EDUCATION** Fisk Univ, BA 1962; Univ of PA, MSW 1972, PhD 1983. **CAREER** Univ of PA, dir Penn Children's Ctr 1973-80, assoc dir of student life 1980-84, faculty school of social work 1973-88, dir Afro Amer studies prog 1984-88; Bennett College, Women's Research Training and Development, director, 1988-90; Ohio State University, National Council for Black Studies, exec dir, 1990-. **HONORS AND AWARDS** Challenge Grant, St Peter's Coll Urban Educ, 1988-. **MEMBERSHIPS** Consultant Trenton State Coll AFAMS Dept 1984-, Philadelphia Sch Dist Desegregation Office 1985-, Benj Bannekar Honors Coll Prairie View A&M 1985-, Conrad Hilton Foundation 1985-88. **CONTACT ADDRESS** Executive Director, Natl Council for Black Studies, Ohio State Univ, 208 Mount Hall, 1050 Carmack Rd, Columbus, OH, 43210.

WADE, LOUISE CARROLL
PERSONAL Born 02/22/1928, Toledo, OH **DISCIPLINE** AMERICAN SOCIAL & URBAN HISTORY **EDUCATION** Wellesley Col BA, 48; Univ Rochester, PhD(hist), 54. **CAREER** Lectr hist, Univ Rochester, 55-60 & Univ Chicago, 63-67; assoc prof hist,75-80, prof hist, 80-93, prof emer, Univ Ore, 93-, adv counc, Ill Bicentennial Publ, 74-75, mem Social Welfare Hist Group (secy-treas, 62-66); AHA; Orgn Am Historians; Fulbright Award, Australia, 80. **HONORS AND AWARDS** Newberry Lib Fel, 89-90. **MEMBERSHIPS** AHA; Orgn Am Historians; Western Asn Women Historians. **RESEARCH** American Urban social and labor history. **SELECTED PUBLICATIONS** Auth, Graham Taylor: Pioneer for Social Justice, 1851-1938, Univ Chicago, 64; The social gospel impulse and Chicago settlement-house founders, Chicago Theol Sem Regist, 4/65; coauth, A History of the United States, Houghton Mifflin, 66; auth, The heritage of Chicago's early settlement houses, J Ill State Hist Soc, winter 67; Julia Lathrop, Florence Kelley, Mary McDowell & Margaret Haley, In: Notable American Women: A Biographical Dict, Harvard Univ, 71; We are something more than packers, Chicago Hist, fall-winter 73; Graham Taylor, Mary McDowell & Mary Church Terrell, In: Dict of American Biography, Scribner, 74; Burnham & root's stockyards connection, Chicago Hist, fall 75; Chicago's Pride: The Stockyards, Packing Town, and Environs in the Nineteenth Century, Univ of Ill Press, 87; The Problem with Classroom use of Upton Sinclair's The Jungle, Am Studies, 91. **CONTACT ADDRESS** Dept of History, Univ of Oregon, Eugene, OR, 97403-1288. **EMAIL** lwade@darkwing.uoregon.edu

WADE, MICHAEL G.
PERSONAL Born 10/01/1946, Oakland, CA, m, 1970, 3 children **DISCIPLINE** HISTORY **EDUCATION** Maryland, BA, 68; SW LA, MA, 71, PhD, 78 **CAREER** Inst, 78-83, MS Co Cmnty Col; Asst Prof, 83-87, Assoc Prof, 87-92, Prof, 92-95, Chair, 95-, Appalachain St Univ; **HONORS AND AWARDS** Beveridge Res Grant, 84, Phi Alpha Theta; Phi Kappa Phi; Pi Gamma Mu; Sigma Tau Delia **MEMBERSHIPS** LA Hist Asn; Southern Hist Asn **RESEARCH** College desegregation; New Deal **SELECTED PUBLICATIONS** Ed, Education in Louisiana through the Integration Era, CLS, 99; Auth, Sugar Dynasty: M.A. Patout and Son, ltd., 1791-1993, CLS, 95 **CONTACT ADDRESS** Dept of History, Appalachian State Univ, Boone, NC, 28608. **EMAIL** wademg@appstate.edu

WADE, REX ARVIN
PERSONAL Born 10/09/1936, Piedmont, KS, m, 1957, 3 children **DISCIPLINE** RUSSIAN HISTORY **EDUCATION** Southwestern Col, BA, 58; Univ Nebr, MA, 60, PhD, 63. **CAREER** From asst prof to prof hist, Wis State Col, La Crosse, 63-68; chmn dept, 77-80; PROF HIST, UNIV HAWAII, 68-; DEAN FAC ARTS and HUMANITIES, 80-; Nat Defense Foreign Lang fel, 61; vis prof, Univ NC, 71, Nat Endowment for Humanities sr fel, 72, Univ Nebr, 73 and Portland State Univ, 76; Fulbright-Hays fel, Findland, 72; Am Coun Learned Soc Sr fel, 74-75; Int Res and Exchanges Bd, 75 and 82. **MEMBERSHIPS** AHA; Am Asn Advan Slavic Studies; AAUP. **RESEARCH** Russian Revolution. **SELECTED PUBLICATIONS** Auth, Reed, John and the Russian Revolution in Uncollected Articles, Letters and Speeches on Russia, 1917-1920, Rus Rev, Vol 52, 93; Notes of a Red-Guard, Slavic Rev, Vol 53, 94; The Bolsheviks German Gold Revisited in an Inquiry Into the 17 Accusations, Slavic Rev, Vol 55, 96; Dear Comrades in Menshevik Reports on the Bolshevik Revolution and the Civil War, Rus Hist-Hist Russe, Vol 23, 96. **CONTACT ADDRESS** Fac Arts and Humanities, Univ of Hawaii, Honolulu, HI, 96822.

WADE, WILLIAM JUNIUS
PERSONAL Born 10/12/1927, Little Rock, AR, m, 1953, 3 children **DISCIPLINE** AMERICAN HISTORY **EDUCATION** Southwestern at Memphis, BA, 49; Univ NC, MA, 50, PhD, 59. **CAREER** Asst prof, 52-53, dean fac, 62-77, prof hist, King Col, 53-; assoc ed, Journal Presby Hist, 69-77. **MEMBERSHIPS** AHA; Orgn Am Historians; Southern Hist Assn; Am Soc Church Hist. **RESEARCH** History of the Presbyterian Church in the United States; religion in American culture. **CONTACT ADDRESS** Dept of History, King Col, 1350 King College Rd, Bristol, TN, 37620-2635.

WAGAR, W. WARRAN
PERSONAL Born 06/05/1932, Baltimore, MD, m, 1953, 4 children **DISCIPLINE** HISTORY **EDUCATION** Franklin & Marshall Col, AB (magna cum laude), 53; Ind Univ, MA, 54; Yale Univ, PhD, 59. **CAREER** Inst to assoc prof of hist, Wellesley Col, 58-66; assoc prof to prof of hist, Univ of NMex, 66-71; PROF OF HIST, 71-86, DISTINGUISHED TCHG PROF OF HIST, SUNY-BINGHAMTON, 86-. **HONORS AND AWARDS** Fulbright Scholar, 57-58; ACLS Fel, 63-64; NEH Sr Fel, 74-75; Univ and Chancellor's Awds for Excellence in Tchg, SUNY, 85; honorary Doctor of Humane Letters, Univ of Maine, 96. **MEMBERSHIPS** Am Hist Asn; Soc for Utopian Studies; Sci-Fiction Res Asn; H.G. Wells Soc. **RESEARCH** European intellectual history; futures studies; world history. **SELECTED PUBLICATIONS** Auth, World Views: A Study in Comparative History, Dryden Press & Holt Rinehart, 77; Terminal Visions: The Lit of Last Things, Ind Univ Press, 82; The Next Three Futures: Paradigms of Things to Come, Praeger, 91, Adamantine Press, 92, Greenwood Press, 91; ed, The Secular Mind: Transformations of Faith in Modern Europe, Holmes & Meier, 82; The Open Conspiracy: H.G. Wells on World Revolution, Praeger, 99. **CONTACT ADDRESS** Dept of Hist, SUNY, Binghamton, PO Box 6000, Binghamton, NY, 13902. **EMAIL** wwagar@binghamton.edu

WAGNER, DAVID
PERSONAL Born 01/31/1950, Brooklyn, NY, m, 1980 **DISCIPLINE** SOCIAL WORK **EDUCATION** Columbia, BA, 72, MS, 76; Univ Mass, MA, 80; CUNY, PhD, 88. **CAREER** Lectr & asst dir field work, School Soc Work, Columbia Unive, 85-88; ASSOC PROF SOCIAL WORK & SOCIOLOGY, COCHR DEPT SOCIAL WORK, UNIV S MAINE, 88- . **HONORS AND AWARDS** C Wright Mills Award **MEMBERSHIPS** Am Sociol Asn; Int Sociol Asn; Soc Study Sociol Problems; E Sociol Soc; Coun Soc Work Eval. **RESEARCH** Poverty and inequality; Social control and deviance; Social welfare policy and history. **SELECTED PUBLICATIONS** Checkerboard Square, Westview Press, 93; The New Temperance, Westview/Harper-Collins, 97. **CONTACT ADDRESS** Univ S Maine, 96 Falmouth St, Portland, ME, 04103. **EMAIL** Wagner@usm.maine.edu

WAGNER, ROY
PERSONAL Born 10/02/1938, Cleveland, OH, d, 2 children **DISCIPLINE** MEDIEVAL HISTORY, CULTURAL ANTHROPOLGY **EDUCATION** Harvard Coll, AB, 61; Univ Chicago, AM, 62, PhD, 66. **CAREER** Asst prof, South Ill Univ, 66-68; assoc prof, Northwest Univ, 68-74; PROF, UNIV VA, 74-. **MEMBERSHIPS** Am Anthrop Asn **RESEARCH** Myth, cultural & religious conceptualization; Holographic world perspectives in Melanesia. **SELECTED PUBLICATIONS** The Curse of Souw, Chicago Press, 67; Habu, Chicago, 72; Lethal Speech, Cornell, 78; The Invention of Culture, Chicago Press, 81; Asiwinarong, Princeton, 86. **CONTACT ADDRESS** Dept Anthrop, Univ Va, Brooks Hall, Charlottesville, VA, 22903.

WAGNER, WALTER HERMANN
PERSONAL Born 11/21/1935, Germany, m, 1958, 1 child **DISCIPLINE** CHURCH HISTORY, BIBLICAL STUDIES **EDUCATION** Gettysburg Col, BA, 57; Lutheran Sem, Pa, BD, 60; Drew Univ, PhD (church hist), 68. **CAREER** Asst prof relig and philos, Calif Lutheran Col, 63-65; assoc prof relig and hist, Upsala Col, 65-73; adj prof church hist, Drew Univ, 73-74; Dir Theol Educ, Lutheran Church Am, 77-; Co-pastor, Calvary Lutheran Church, Cranford, NJ, 60-63; adj prof church hist, Lutheran Sem, Pa, 70-71; chmn Div Ecumenical Rels, Lutheran Church Am, NJ Synod, 72-77; pastor, Epiphany Lutheran Church, Warren, NJ, 73-77. **HONORS AND AWARDS** Distinguished Teaching Award, Lindback Found and Upsala Col, 69. **MEMBERSHIPS** Am Soc Church Hist; Soc Bibl Lit; Am Soc Reformation Hist; Soc Reformation Res. **RESEARCH** New Testament; patristics; Reformation. **SELECTED PUBLICATIONS** Auth, Toward Understanding Justin Martyr, Cithara Essays Judeo-Christian Tradition, Vol 34, 95; Interpretations of Genesis VI, 1-4 in 2nd Century Christianity, J Religious Hist, Vol 20, 96; Clement of Alexandria Self-Understanding and Addressing the Christian Concepts of Theology, Ethics, and Mysticism, Cithara Essays Judeo-Christian Tradition, Vol 36, 96; Scripture and the Church in Selected Essays Sasse, Herman, Church Hist, Vol 66, 97; Journeying to God in Muhammad Isra and Miraj, Cithara Essays Judeo-Christian Tradition, Vol 36, 97. **CONTACT ADDRESS** Div for Prof Leadership, Lutheran Church in America, 2900 Queen Lane, Philadelphia, PA.

WAGNER, WILLIAM GILSON
PERSONAL Born 05/28/1950, Erie, PA, m, 1972, 1 child **DISCIPLINE** RUSSIAN AND EUROPEAN HISTORY **EDUCATION** Haverford Col, BA, 72; Oxford Univ, BPhil, 74, DPhil-(mod hist), 81. **CAREER** Res lectr, Christ Church, Oxford Univ, 78-80; ASST PROF HIST, WILLIAMS COL, 81-; Exam hist, Oxford and Cambridge Sch Exam Bd, 75-80; grad adv, Inter-Fac Liason Comt Russ and East Europ Studies, Oxford Univ, 78-80, tutor hist, Balliol Col, 78-80. **MEMBERSHIPS** AHA; Am Asn Advan Slavic Studies. **RESEARCH** Russian socio-legal and economic history; general socio-legal history, particularly in property, inheritance, and family law; women's and family history. **SELECTED PUBLICATIONS** Auth, Genesis and Development of Plekhanov Theory of Knowledge in a Marxist Between Anthropological Materialism and Physiology, Rus Rev, Vol 52, 93; The Corporation Under Russian Law, 1800-17 in a Study in Czarist Economic Policy, Rus Rev, Vol 52, 93; An Introduction to 19th Century Russian Slavophilism, J Mod Hist, Vol 66, 94; The Russian City Between Tradition and Modernity, 1850-1900, Engl Hist Rev, Vol 109, 94; The Keys to Happiness in Sex and The Search for Modernity in Fin De Siecle Russia, Rus Rev, Vol 54, 95; Family Law, the Rule of Law, and Liberalism in Late Imperial Russia, Jahrbucher Geschichte Osteuropas, Vol 43, 95. **CONTACT ADDRESS** Hist Dept, Williams Col, 880 Main St, Williamstown, MA, 01267-2600.

WAGSTAFF, GRAYSON
DISCIPLINE MUSICOLOGY AND MUSIC HISTORY **EDUCATION** James Madison Univ, BM; Univ TX, PhD. **CAREER** Music Dept, Univ Ala **HONORS AND AWARDS** Fulbright Fel; Musicol adv, Gabrieli Consort and Players. **SELECTED PUBLICATIONS** Articles: Revista de Musicologea, Encomium Musicae, Musical Quart, Revised New Grove Dictionary. **CONTACT ADDRESS** Univ AL, Box 870000, Tuscaloosa, AL, 35487. **EMAIL** gwagstaf@music.ua.edu

WAHL, JIM
DISCIPLINE HISTORY **EDUCATION** Univ Western Ontario, BA, 62; Louis Univ, MA, 64; PhD, 68. **CAREER** Assoc prof **RESEARCH** Legal history; nineteenth century religious history. **SELECTED PUBLICATIONS** Auth, Baldus de Ubaldis and the Foundations of the Nation-State; Baldus de Ubaldis: A Study in Reluctant Conciliarism; Father Louis Funcken's Contribution to German Catholicism: in Waterloo County, Ontario; Looking Back: The Early Days, Louis Funcken and St. Jerome's College. **CONTACT ADDRESS** Dept of History, St. Jerome's Univ, Waterloo, ON, N2L 3G3.

WAIDA, MANABU
PERSONAL Osaka, Japan **DISCIPLINE** HISTORY OF RELIGION **EDUCATION** Univ Chicago, PhD (hist relig), 74. **CAREER** Asst prof hist relig, St Mary's Univ, Halifax, 70-73; ASSOC PROF HIST RELIG, UNIV ALTA, 74-; Vis asst prof hist relig, Univ Rochester, 74; Can Coun leave fel, 78-79; EXEC, CAN CORP STUDIES IN RELIG, 80-. **MEMBERSHIPS** Can Soc Study Relig (treas, 76-80); Am Acad Relig; Can Asn Asian Studies; Am Asn Asian Studies. **RESEARCH** Myths and symbols; sacrad kingship; religions in Circumpacific Regions. **SELECTED PUBLICATIONS** Auth, Shamanism, History, and the State, Asian Folklore Studies, Vol 54, 95. **CONTACT ADDRESS** Dept of Relig Studies, Univ of Alta, Edmonton, AB, T6G 2E6.

WAITE, GARY K.
PERSONAL Born 03/20/1955, Vancouver, BC, Canada **DISCIPLINE** HISTORY **EDUCATION** Ont Bible Col, BTh, 78; Univ Waterloo, BA, 80, MA, 81, PhD, 87. **CAREER** Lectr, Univ Waterloo, 86-87; asst prof, 87-91, PROF HISTORY, UNIV NEW BRUNSWICK, 91-. **HONORS AND AWARDS** SSHRCC grants; Univ Waterloo Alumni Gold Medal Acad Excellence, 87. **MEMBERSHIPS** Can Soc Renaissance Stud; Sixteenth Century Stud Conf Asn; Can Hist Asn. **RESEARCH** Religion & culture in 16th century Netherlands. **SELECTED PUBLICATIONS** Auth, David Joris and Dutch Anabaptism 1524-1543, 90; ed & transl, The Anabaptist Writings of David Joris 1535-1543, 94. **CONTACT ADDRESS** History Dept, Univ of New Brunswick, Fredericton, NB, E3B 5A3. **EMAIL** waite@unb.ca

WAITE, PETER B.
PERSONAL Born 07/12/1922, Toronto, ON, Canada **DISCIPLINE** HISTORY **EDUCATION** Univ BC, BA, 48, AM, 50; Univ Toronto, PhD, 54. **CAREER** Lectr 51-55, asst prof, 55-60, assoc prof, 60-61, head dept 60-68, prof, 61-88, PROF EMER HISTORY, DALHOUSIE UNIV, 88-; vis prof, 63-64, J.B. Smallman Prof, Univ Western Ont, 88-89; vis prof, Dartmouth Col, 67. **HONORS AND AWARDS** BC Hist Fedn Medal, 89; 50th Anniversary Cert Merit, Soc Sci Fedn Can, 90; off, Order Can; DLitt(hon), Univ NB; DLitt(hon), Memorial Univ Nfld; DLitt(hon), Carleton Univ; LLD(hon), Dalhousie Univ. **MEMBERSHIPS** Can Hist Asn (pres, 68-69); Hum Res Coun (chmn, 68-70). **RESEARCH** Canadian history; Canadian Confederation. **SELECTED PUBLICATIONS** Auth, The Life and Times of Confederation 1864-1867, 62; auth, The Confederation Debates in the Province of Canada 1865, 63; auth, Pre-Confederation (vol II Can Hist Doc), 65; auth, Canada 1874-1896: Arduous Destiny(vol 13 Can Centenary Ser), 71; auth, Confederation 1854-1867, 72; auth, Macdonald: His Life and World, 75; auth, Years of Struggle 1867-1896(vol 1 Century Can Ser), 85; auth, The Man from Halifax: Sir John Thompson, Prime Minister, 85; auth, Lord of Point Grey: Larry MacKenzie of U.B.C., 87; auth, The Loner: Three Sketches of the Personal Life and Ideas of R.B. Bennett, 1870-1947, 92; auth, The Lives of Dalhousie University, 1818-1980, vol I 94, vol II 97. **CONTACT ADDRESS** 960 Ritchie Dr, Halifax, NS, B3H 3P5.

WAITE, ROBERT GEORGE LEESON
PERSONAL Cartwright, MB, Canada, m, 1943, 2 children **DISCIPLINE** MODERN HISTORY **EDUCATION** Macalester Col, BA, 41; Univ Minn, MA, 46; Harvard Univ, PhD (hist), 49. **CAREER** From asst prof to prof, 49-60, chmn dept, 68-73, BROWN PROF HIST, WILLIAMS COL, 60-; Fulbright and Guggenheim scholars, 53-54; Am Coun Learned Soc and Soc Sci Res Coun grants, 66-67, 68 and 82; MEM COL ENTRANCE BD, BD EXAM FOR ADVAN PLACEMENT IN EUROP HIST, 67-; sr mem hist, St Antony's Col, Oxford Univ, 78 and 82. **MEMBERSHIPS** AHA **RESEARCH** Modern German history; psychoanalysis and history--the case of Kaiser William II. **SELECTED PUBLICATIONS** Auth, Old Dreams of a New Reich in Volkish Utopias and National Socialism, Cent European Hist, Vol 26, 93; Assassinating Hitler in Ethics and Resistance in Nazi Germany, Cent European Hist, Vol 26, 93; Hitler Mind in a Plunge into Madness, J Interdisciplinary Hist, Vol 24, 93; The Nazi Elite, J Interdisciplinary Hist, Vol 25, 95; Death and Deliverance in Euthanasia in Germany 1900-1945, J Interdisciplinary Hist, Vol 27, 96. **CONTACT ADDRESS** Talcott Rd, Williamstown, MA, 01267.

WAJDA, SHIRLEY TERESA
PERSONAL Born 05/28/1958, Warren, OH, s **DISCIPLINE** AMERICAN CIVILIZATION **EDUCATION** Boston Univ, BA, 82; Univ of Penn, AM, 89, PhD, 92. **CAREER** Instr, Clarion Univ of Penn, 89-91; asst prof, Boston Univ, 91-94; vis asst prof, Univ of Iowa, 95; asst prof, Kent State Univ, 96-. **HONORS AND AWARDS** Smithsonian Institution Grad Student Fel, 88; Educ Press of Am Distinguished Achievement Award, 90; Andrew W. Mellon Found Res Fel, 91-92; Junior Fac Fel, Boston Univ Soc of Fels, 93-94; Winterthur Museum and Library-Nat Endowment for the Hums Fel, 93-94; Teaching Development Award, Kent State Univ, 96; V. and R. Morgan Res Fel, Western Reserve Hist Soc, 96; Hagley Winterthur Arts and Industries Res Fel, 97; A. W. Mellon Found Res Fel, Library Company of Philadelphia, 97; Student Advisory Coun Award forOutstanding Teaching in Arts and Scis, Col of Arts and Scis, Kent State Univ, 97-98. **MEMBERSHIPS** Am Studies Asn; Great Lakes Am Studies Asn; New England Am Studies Asn; Mid- America Studies Asn; Org of Am Hists; Ohio Acad of Hist; Western Reserve Hist Soc; Am Asn of Museums; Nineteenth-Century Studies Asn; Soc for the Hist of Authorship, Reading and Publishing; Soc for Hists of the Early Am Republic; Vernacular Architecture Forum; Asn of Hists of Am Art. **RESEARCH** American material culture and art; nineteenth-century American social and cultural history. **SELECTED PUBLICATIONS** Auth, A Room With a Viewer: The Parlor Steroscope, Comic Stereographs, and the Psychic Role of Play in Late Victorian America, in Hard at Play: Leisure in America, 1840-1940, 92; The Artistic Portrait Photograph, in The Arts and the American Home, 1890-1930, 94; The Commercial Photographic Parlor, 1839-1889, in Shaping Communities: Perspectives in Vernacular Architecture, VI, 97; 'And a little child shall lead them': Children's Cabinets of Curiosities, 1790-1860, in Reader: Essays in Reader-Oriented Theory, Criticism and Pedagogy, 38/39, 97-98. **CONTACT ADDRESS** Dept of History, Kent State Univ, 305 Bowman Hall, Box 5190, Kent, OH, 44242-0001. **EMAIL** swadja@kent.edu

WAKELYN, JON L.
PERSONAL Born 08/19/1938, Tampa, FL, m, 1990, 2 children **DISCIPLINE** HISTORY **EDUCATION** Long Island Univ, BA, 62; Rice Univ, PhD, 66. **CAREER** Asst to assoc prof, Washington Col, 66; asst to prof, Cath Univ Am, 70-96; vis prof, Univ Md, 74-75; vis prof, Maynoth Col, Ireland, 92, 94; PROF, KENT STATE UNIV, 96-. **HONORS AND AWARDS** NDEA fel; NEH fel, 68; ALA outstanding ref work, 78; outstanding teach, Cath Uni, 83. **MEMBERSHIPS** Org Am Historians; So Hist Asn. **RESEARCH** 19th cent U.S.; Old South. **SELECTED PUBLICATIONS** Auth, Leaders of the American Civil War, 98; auth, Southern Pamphlets on Secession, 96; auth, Biographical Dictionary of State Leaders, 89; auth, Web of Southern Social Relations, 85; auth, Catholics in the Old South, 83; auth, Politics of A Literate Man, 73; Biographical Dictionary of the Confederacy, 78. **CONTACT ADDRESS** 126 E Strretsboro St, Hudson, OH, 44236. **EMAIL** jwakelyn@kent.edu

WAKEMAN, FREDERIC EVANS, JR.
PERSONAL Born 12/12/1937, Kansas City, KS, 3 children **DISCIPLINE** CHINESE HISTORY **EDUCATION** Harvard Col, BA, 59; Univ Calif, Berkeley, MA, 62, PhD, 65. **CAREER** Asst prof, 65-67, assoc prof, 69-71, prof, hist, 71- , Univ Calif, Berkeley; dir, Inter-Univ Prog for Chinese Lang Stud, Taipei, 67-68; pres, Social Sci Res Coun, 86-89; Walter and Elise Haas Prof Asian Stud, Univ Calif, Berkeley, 89- ; dir, Inst of East Asian Stud, 90- . **HONORS AND AWARDS** Phi Beta Kappa; Levenson Prize, Berkeley Prize, 87; pres, Am Hist Asn, 92; Phi Beta Kappa Vis Scholar, 94-95. **MEMBERSHIPS** Am Hist Asn; Asn of Asian Stud; Am Acad of Arts and Sci; APA. **RESEARCH** History of early Republican China; Shanghai history. **SELECTED PUBLICATIONS** Auth, Strangers at the Gate: Social Disorder in South China, 1839-1861, Univ Calif, 66; auth, Nothing Concealed: Essays in Honor of Liu Yu-yun, Taipei: CMRASC, 70; auth, History and Will: Philosophical Perspectives of the Thought of Mao Tse-tung, Univ Calif, 73; coauth, Conflict and Control in Late Imperial China, Univ Calif, 75; auth, The Fall of Imperial China, Free Press, 75; auth, The Great Enterprise: The Manchu Reconstruction of Imperial Order in Seventeenth-Century China, Univ Calif, 85; co-ed, Perspectives on Modern China: Four Anniversaries, M.E. Sharpe, 91; co-ed, Shanghai Sojourners, Institute of East Asian Studies, 92; auth, Policing Shanghai, 1927-1937, Univ Calif, 95; auth, The Shanghai Badlands: Wartime Terrorism and Urban Crime, 1937-1941, Cambridge, 96; co-ed, China's Quest for Modernization, Institute of East Asian Studies, 97. **CONTACT ADDRESS** Institute of East Asian Studies, Univ of California, 2223 Fulton St, No 2318, Berkeley, CA, 94720-2318. **EMAIL** jingcha@socrates.berkeley.edu

WALBANK, MICHAEL BURKE
PERSONAL Born 04/14/1933, Bristol, England, m, 1978 **DISCIPLINE** CLASSICS, ARCHEOLOGY **EDUCATION** Univ Bristol, BA, 54; Univ BC, MA, 65, PhD (classics), 70. **CAREER** Asst prof, 70-76, ASSOC PROF CLASSICS, UNIV CALGARY, 76-; Can Coun fels, 71-72 and 76-77; consult, BBCOpen Univ Prod, 78. **MEMBERSHIPS** Am Sch Class Studies Athens; Class Asn of Can; Archaeol Inst of Am; Soc Prom Hellenic Studies; Soc Prom of Roman Studies. **RESEARCH** Greek epigraphy; Greek archaeology; ancient science and technology. **SELECTED PUBLICATIONS** Auth, A Lex Sacra of the State and of the Deme of Kollytos, Hesperia, Vol 63, 94; Greek Inscriptions from the Athenian Agora in Lists of Names, Hesperia, Vol 63, 94; Greek Inscriptions from the Athenian-Agora in Building Records, Hesperia, Vol 64, 95; An Inscription from the Athenian Agora in Thasian Exiles at Athens, Hesperia, Vol 64, 95; Greek Inscriptions from the Athenian Agora Financial Documents, Hesperia, Vol 65, 96; Greek Inscriptions from the Athenian Agora, Hesperia, Vol 66, 97. **CONTACT ADDRESS** 14 Harcourt Rd SW, Calgary, AB, T2V 5J1.

WALBERG, GISELA
DISCIPLINE ANCIENT HISTORY **EDUCATION** Univ Stockholm, Fil Kand, 66; Univ Uppsala, PhD, 76. **CAREER** Asst, Medelhavsmuseet, 64-67, 69-70; Asst, Swedish Inst, Athens, 67-69; Asst prof, Uppsala Univ, 76-78; Asst prof, Univ Cincinnati, 79-82; Assoc prof, Univ Cincinnati, 82-84; Prof, Univ Cincinnati, 84-. **HONORS AND AWARDS** Alexander von Humboldt-Stiftung Grant; Alexander-von-Humboldt-Stiftung Fel; Swedish Nat Endowment Hum; Lerici-Found. **SELECTED PUBLICATIONS** Auth, Kamares. A Study of the Character of Palatial Middle Minoan Pottery, Uppsala, 76; auth, Kamares Style. The Overall Effects of Palatial Middle Minoan Pottery, Uppsala, 78; auth, Tradition and Innovation. Essays in Minoan Art, Mainz, 86; auth, Illustration Volume to Furumark, Swedish Coun, 92; **CONTACT ADDRESS** Dept of Classics, Univ Cincinnati, PO Box 0226, Cincinnati, OH, 45210-0226. **EMAIL** Giswalberg@aol.com

WALCH, TIMOTHY G.
PERSONAL Born 12/06/1947, Detroit, MI, m, 1978, 2 children **DISCIPLINE** US HISTORY **EDUCATION** Univ Notre dame, BA 70; Northwester Univ, PhD 75. **CAREER** Assoc dir, Soc Amer Archivists, 75-79; prog analy, Nat Archive Records Admin, 79-83; Ed Br Chief, Nat Archive Rec Admin, 83-88; Asst dir Herbert Hover Pres Lib, 88-93; and Director, 93. **MEMBERSHIPS** OAH; US Cath Hist Soc. **RESEARCH** Hist of the US Presidency, Hist of Amer Catholicism. **SELECTED PUBLICATIONS** Herbert Hoover and Franklin D Roosevelt: A Documentary History, 98; At the President's Side: The Vice Presidency in the Twentieth Century, 97; Parish School: American Catholic Parochial Education from Colonial times to the Present, 96. **CONTACT ADDRESS** National Archives, Washington, DC, 20408. **EMAIL** timothy.walch@hoover.nara.gov

WALCOTT, ROBERT
PERSONAL Born 01/24/1910, Boston, MA **DISCIPLINE** HISTORY **EDUCATION** Harvard Univ, AB, 31, AM, 32, PhD, 38. **CAREER** Asst hist, Harvard Univ, 36-38, instr and tutor, 38-41; instr, Westminster Col, Pa, 41-42 and Black Mountain Col, 45-46; From asst prof to prof, 46-75, EMER PROF HIST, COL WOOSTER, 75-; Fulbright award, UK, 53-54; Soc Sci Res Coun fel, 55-56. **MEMBERSHIPS** Fel Royal Hist Soc. **RESEARCH** English history; European history, especially 17th and 18th centuries; economic history. **SELECTED PUBLICATIONS** Auth, Out of The Kumbla in Morrison, Toni Jazz and Pedagogical Answerability, Cult Studies, Vol 9, 95. **CONTACT ADDRESS** 14 Whig Rd, Dennis, MA, 02638.

WALD, ALAN MAYNARD
PERSONAL Born 06/01/1946, Washington, DC, w, 1975, 2 children **DISCIPLINE** AMERICAN STUDIES, ENGLISH LITERATURE **EDUCATION** Antioch Col, BA, 69; Univ Calif, Berkeley, MA, 71, PhD(English), 74. **CAREER** Lectr English, San Jose State Univ, 74; teaching assoc, Univ Calif, Berkeley, 75; asst prof English Lit & Am Cult, Univ Mich, Ann Arbor, 75-, from assoc prof to prof, 81-86; Am Coun Learned Soc grant-in-aid, 75-76; Rackham Fac Res grant, 76-77. **HONORS AND AWARDS** ACLS Natl Fel, 83-84; Beinecke llow, Yale, 89; Michigan Humanities fell, 85; Excellence in Research Award from UM, 96; A Bartlett Giamatti Faculty fel at UM Institut for Humanities, 97-98. **MEMBERSHIPS** MLA. **RESEARCH** American literary radicalism; Marxist aesthetics; the New York intellectuals. **SELECTED PUBLICATIONS** Auth, James T Arrell: The Revolutionary Socialist Years, 78; The Responsibility of Intellectuals, 92; Writing From the Left, 94. **CONTACT ADDRESS** Dept of English, Univ of Michigan, 317 Angell Hall, Ann Arbor, MI, 48109-10003.

WALDBAUM, JANE C.
PERSONAL New York, NY **DISCIPLINE** CLASSICAL ARCHEOLOGY, ANCIENT ART **EDUCATION** Brandeis Univ, AB, 62; Harvard Univ, AM, 64, PhD, 68. **CAREER** Res fel class art & archaeol, Harvard Univ, 68-70 & 72-73; asst prof, 73-78; Univ WI-Milwaukee, assoc prof art hist, 78-84, Prof, 84, Dorcot Research Prof, W F Albright Inst of Archaeol Research, 90-91; Am Philos Soc grant, 72; Nat Endowment for Hum fel, summer, 75; vis assoc prof art hist, IN Univ, Bloomington, 78-79; exec comt, Archaeol Inst Am, 74-77, chmn, comt on mem prog, 77-81, nominating comm, 84, chmn comm on lecture prog, 85-87, academic trustee 93-98, comm prof responsibilities, 93, fellowship comm, 93, gold metal comm, 93, chair, 96-97, ancient near east comm, 93; Vis schol, Univ Penn, 85-86; vis schol, Inst of Archaeol, Hebrew Univ of Jerusalem, Israel, 89-90 and 90-91; Prof, Dept of Art History, Univ WI-Milwaukee, 84-, Ch, 82-85, 86-89, 91-92. **HONORS AND AWARDS** Dorot Research Professorship, W F Albright Inst for Archaeol Research, Jerusalem, 90-91; Am Sch(s) of Oriental Research-NEH Post Doct Research Fel, 89-90. **MEMBERSHIPS** Archaeol Inst Am, National, Boston Society, Pres, Milwaukee Soc, 83-85, 91-95, 97-; Am Schs Orient Res; Soc for Archaeol Sci; Asn for Field Archaeol; Soc for Archaeol Sciences; Israel Exploration Soc; Milwaukee Area Biblical Archaeol Soc, Bd of Dir, 87-; WI Soc for Jewish Learning, Bd member, 93. **RESEARCH** Early Iron Age in the Eastern Mediterranean; ancient metalwork and metallurgy; archaeol of Sardis. **SELECTED PUBLICATIONS** Auth, Philistine tombs from Tell Fara and their Aegean prototypes, 66 & 68, Am J Archaeol; coauth, New excavations at Sardis and some problems in Western Anatolian archaeology, In: Near Eastern Archaeology in the Twentieth Century, Studies in Honor of Nelson Glueck, Doubleday, 70; auth, A bronze and iron Iranian axe in the Fogg Art Museum, In: Studies Presented to George M A Hanfmann, Philipp von Zabern, 71; The Luristan bronzes, Princeton Mus Rec, 73; coauth, A survey of Sardis and major monuments outside the city walls, Sardis Report 1, Harvard Univ, 75; auth, From bronze to iron: The Transition from the Bronze Age to the Iron Age in the Eastern Mediterranean, Paul Astroms Forlag, Studies in Mediter Archaeol, 78; The first archaeological appearance of iron and the transition to the Iron Age, In: The Coming of the Age of Iron, A Festschrift for Cyril Stanley Smith, 80; Sardis Monograph 8, Metalwork from Sardis, the finds through 1974, Harvard Univ Press, 83; Bimetallic objects from the eastern Mediterranean and the question of the dissemination of iron, In: Proc the Archaeol Symnposium, Early Metallurgy on Cyprus, Larnaca, 82; Metalwork and Metalworking at Sardis, in E Guralnick ed, pp 36-45, 87; The Coming of Iron,

Wisconsin Academy Rev, pp 8-21, 87; Metalwork from Idalion, 1971-1980, in L E Stager and A M Walker, eds, Oriental Inst of the Univ Chicago, pp 328-355, 89; Copper, Iron, Tin, Wood: The Start of the Iron Age in the Eastern Mediterranean, pp 111-122, 89; Early Greek Contacts with the Southern Levant, c 1000-600BC: The Eastern Perspective, Bulletin of the Am Schs of Oriental Research 305, pp 1-17, 97; The Chronology of Early Greek Pottery: New Evidence from Seventh Century BC Destruction Levels in Israel, with Jodi Magness, Am J Archaeol 101, pp 23-40, 97. **CONTACT ADDRESS** Dept Art Hist, Univ Wisconsin, PO Box 413, Milwaukee, WI, 53201-0413. **EMAIL** jcw@uwm.edu

WALDEN, DANIEL
PERSONAL Born 08/01/1922, Philadelphia, PA, m, 1957, 2 children **DISCIPLINE** AMERICAN STUDIES **EDUCATION** City Col New York, BA, 59; Columbia Univ, MA, 60; New York Univ, PhD, 64. **CAREER** Asst prof, New Sch Soc Res, 60-63; asst prof, Mich State Univ, 63-66; prof Am Stud, 66-, Penn State Univ; instr hist, Queens Col, NY, 60-63; Univ Col grant, Mich State Univ, 65-66; res grant, Pa State Univ, 67-68; Truman Libr grant, 67-68; consult, US Inform Agency, 73-; ed, Studies Am Jewish Lit, 75- **HONORS AND AWARDS** ALA distinguished award, 97; distinguished service award, Soc Am Jewish Lit, 92. **MEMBERSHIPS** MLA; Am Studies Asn; Popular Cult Asn; Am Cult Asn; ALA; Soc Am Jewish Lit; Soc for utopian Stud. **RESEARCH** American ethnic literature; American culture; technology and culture. **SELECTED PUBLICATIONS** Co-ed, New Voices in an Old Tradition: A New Look, 95; co-ed, The Tragedy of Joy, 96; co-ed, A Significant Pattern, 97; co-ed, The Resonance of Twoness, 98. **CONTACT ADDRESS** Dept of English and American Studies, Pennsylvania State Univ, University Park, PA, 16802. **EMAIL** dxw8@psu.edu

WALDMAN, MARTIN
PERSONAL Born 03/10/1940, Brooklyn, NY, m, 1962 **DISCIPLINE** HISTORY OF MODERN FRANCE **EDUCATION** Brandeis Univ, BA, 60; Syracuse Univ, PhD (hist), 68. **CAREER** Asst Europ hist, Syracuse Univ, 62-64; lectr, 66-68, asst prof, 68-80, ASSOC PROF EUROP HIST, CITY COL NEW YORK, 80-; City Univ Res Found fel, 74-75. **MEMBERSHIPS** AHA; Soc Fr Hist Studies; Soc Mod Hist, France. **RESEARCH** French social history; the Paris Commune of 1871. **SELECTED PUBLICATIONS** Auth, Eliminating the Market for Secondhand Goods in an Alternative Explanation for Leasing, J Law Econ, Vol 40, 97. **CONTACT ADDRESS** Dept of Hist, City Col, CUNY, 138th St and Convent Ave, New York, NY, 10031.

WALDREP, CHRISTOPHER
PERSONAL Born 11/19/1951, Oak Ridge, TN, m, 1976, 2 children **DISCIPLINE** HISTORY **EDUCATION** Eastern IL Univ, BS 73; PurdueUniv, MA 74; OH State, PhD 90. **CAREER** Eastern IL Univ, assoc prof 90. **HONORS AND AWARDS** NEH, APS, AHA, fellowships and endowments. **MEMBERSHIPS** AHA; OAH; SHA; Amer Soc for Legal Hist. **RESEARCH** Vigilantism, lynching, law enforcement. **SELECTED PUBLICATIONS** Night Riders: Defending Community in the Black Patch: 1890-1915, Durham, Duke Univ Press, 93; Roots of Disorder: Race and Criminal Justice in the American South, 1817-1880, Urbana, Univ IL Press, 98. **CONTACT ADDRESS** Dept of Hist, Eastern Illinois Univ, Charleston, IL, 61920. **EMAIL** cfcrw@eiu.edu

WALDSTREICHER, DAVID L.
DISCIPLINE HISTORY **EDUCATION** Yale Univ, PhD, 94. **CAREER** Asst prof American Studies, Yale Univ. **SELECTED PUBLICATIONS** Fel Publ, In the Midst of Perpetual Fetes: The Making of American Nationalism, 1776-1820, IEAHAC & UNC Press, pending; auth, 'Fallen under My Observation: Vision and Virtue in The Coquette, Early Amer Lit 27, 92; Federalism and the Politics of Style, In: Federalism Revisited, pending. **CONTACT ADDRESS** Dept of American Studies, Yale Univ, PO Box 208236, New Haven, CT, 06520-8236. **EMAIL** david.waldstreicher@yale.edu.

WALKEN, CHRISOPHER
DISCIPLINE HISTORY OF AFRICAN-AMERICAN MUSIC **EDUCATION** Hamilton Col, BA; Rutgers Univ, MA, PhD. **CAREER** Assoc prof. **HONORS AND AWARDS** Summer stipend and a travel-to-collections grant, NEH; fel, media grants, W Va Hum Coun; res grants, W Va Univ fac senate. **RESEARCH** Jazz; Multicultural study of the history of art music. **SELECTED PUBLICATIONS** Publ, articles in Black Mus Res Jour, Col Mus Symposium, Contrib to Mus Edu, Mus and Letters, The New Grove Dictionary of Mus and Musicians; George Crumb: Profile of a Composer; and Oratorios of the Italian Baroque. **CONTACT ADDRESS** Dept of Mus, W Va Univ, PO Box 6009, Morgantown, WV, 26506-6009. **EMAIL** cwilkin2@wvu.edu

WALKER, ANDREW DAVID
DISCIPLINE CLASSICS **EDUCATION** Univ Wash, BA, 82; Univ NC, Chapel Hill, BA, 84, PhD, 93. **CAREER** Lectr, class, 91-92, Univ Va; lectr, class, Univ S Calif, 93-94. **MEMBERSHIPS** APA. **RESEARCH** Cultural stud; gender & comparative lit. **SELECTED PUBLICATIONS** Art, Eros and the Eye in the Love Letters of Philostratus, PCPS, 92; art, Enargeia and the Spectator in Greek Historiography, TPAP, 93; art, Lucan's Legends of the Fall, Ramus, 96; art, Oedipal Narratives and the Exilic Ovid, Ramus, 97. **CONTACT ADDRESS** 3444 Glenhurst Ave, Los Angeles, CA, 90039. **EMAIL** adwalker@usc.edu

WALKER, DAVID ALLAN
PERSONAL Born 04/14/1941, Alexandria, VA, m, 1967, 2 children **DISCIPLINE** AMERICAN HISTORY **EDUCATION** Missouri Valley Col, BA, 63; La State Univ, MA, 65; Univ Wis-Madison, PhD (hist), 73. **CAREER** Instr hist, Lakeland Col, 66-68; asst prof hist, Mankato State Univ, 71-75; asst prof, 75-78, ASSOC PROF HIST, UNIV NORTHERN IOWA, 78-; Minn Hist Soc res fel hist, 73-74; vis prof Univ Wyoming, 81-82. **HONORS AND AWARDS** Charles J Kennedy Award, Econ and Bus Hist Soc, 477. **MEMBERSHIPS** Western Hist Asn; Orgn Am Historians; Econ and Bus Hist Soc; Social Sci Hist Asn. **RESEARCH** American West: mining, conservation, territorial. **SELECTED PUBLICATIONS** Auth, Sespe Gunsmoke, an Epic Case of Rancher Versus Squatters, J W, Vol 32, 93; Encyclopedia of Western Railroad History in The Desert States, J W, Vol 33, 94; Encyclopedia of Western Railroad History, Vol 3, the Mountain States, J W, Vol 33, 94; The Taos Indians and the Battle for Blue Lake, J W, Vol 35, 96; The Cartwrights of San Augustine J W, Vol 35, 96; Railroad Crossing in Californians and the Railroad 1850-1910, J W, Vol 35, 96; Backwoods Railroads in Branchlines and Shortlines of Western Oregon, J W, Vol 35, 96. **CONTACT ADDRESS** Dept of Hist, Univ Northern Iowa, Cedar Falls, IA, 50613.

WALKER, ERNESTEIN
PERSONAL Born 05/26/1926, McDonough, Georgia, m **DISCIPLINE** HISTORY **EDUCATION** Spelman Coll, AB 1949; Atlanta U, MA 1953; Univ Edinburgh, 1958; Western Res U, PhD 1964. **CAREER** Morgan State U, prof hist 1965-; SC State Coll, instr prof 1956-65; Fort Valley State Coll, instr 1955-56; KY State U, 1954-55. **MEMBERSHIPS** Mem Am Hist Assn; Assn Study Afro Life & Hist; So Hist Assn; medieval acad pres Baltimore Chap Nat Alumnae Assn, Spelman Coll Publ, "Disestablishment of the Ch of Ireland", Jour Social Sci 1960; "Age of Metternick a study in nonmenclature" exploration educ 1962; "the influence of Lord Liverpool 1815-1827" Jour Higher Educ 1967; "The Struggle for Parliamentary Reform" 1977; "The Black Woman" The Black Am Ref Book 1976. **CONTACT ADDRESS** Morgan State Univ, Baltimore, MD, 21239.

WALKER, FORREST A.
PERSONAL Born 10/08/1929, Pittsburg, KS, m, 1956, 2 children **DISCIPLINE** AMERICAN HISTORY **EDUCATION** Tex Col Arts and Indust, BA, 51, MA, 52; Univ Okla, PhD (hist), 62. **CAREER** Asst prof hist, Florence State Col, 61-63; assoc prof, 63-70, chmn dept, 70-76, PROF HIST, EASTERN NMEX UNIV, 70-; CHMN DEPT HIST, 80-. **MEMBERSHIPS** Orgn Am Historians. **RESEARCH** Twentieth century American history. **SELECTED PUBLICATIONS** Auth, Russia in the Age of Reaction and Reform, 1801-1881, Slavic Rev, Vol 52, 93; Catholics at the Gathering Place in Historical Essays on the Archdiocese of Toronto, 1841-91, Cath Hist Rev, Vol 80, 94; The Texas City Horror and the Explosion of April-16,1947, Am Heritage, Vol 47, 96. **CONTACT ADDRESS** Dept of Hist, Eastern New Mexico Univ, Portales, NM, 88130.

WALKER, GEORGE KONTZ
PERSONAL Born 07/08/1938, Tuscaloosa, AL, m, 1966, 2 children **DISCIPLINE** LAW, HISTORY **EDUCATION** Univ AL, BA, 59; Vanderbilt Univ, LLB, 66; Duke Univ, MA, 68; Univ VA, LLM, 72. **CAREER** From asst prof to assoc prof, 72-76, Prof Law, Wake Forest Univ, 77-, Woodrow Wilson fel, Duke Univ, 62-63; Sterling fel, Yale Law Sch, 75-76; vis prof law, Marshall-Wythe Sch Law, Col William & Mary, 79-80; vis prof Law, Univ Ala Sch Law, 85; Charles H Stockton Prof Intl Law, Naval War Col, 92-93. **HONORS AND AWARDS** Phi Beta kappa, Order of Barristers (hon), Order of the Coif (hon), Am Law Inst. **MEMBERSHIPS** Virginia, North Carolina Bars; Am Soc Int law; Int law Asn, Am Bar Asn; Maritime Law assoc, VA, NC Bar Asns; admitted to practice in federal courts. **RESEARCH** International law; federal jurisdiction; admiralty; conflict of laws; civil procedure; alternative dispute resolution. **SELECTED PUBLICATIONS** Auth of 10 bks, over 40 bk chpts, articles. **CONTACT ADDRESS** Sch of Law, Wake Forest Univ, PO Box 7206, Winston Salem, NC, 27109-7206.

WALKER, HUGH D.
PERSONAL Born 02/21/1934, Plymouth, NH, m, 1957, 5 children **DISCIPLINE** KOREAN HISTORY **EDUCATION** Univ NH, BA, 56; Univ Calif, Los Angeles, MA, 60, PhD, 71. **CAREER** Lectr hist & Chinese, Far East Div, Univ Md, 62-65; from asst prof to assoc prof hist & Chinese, 65-76, PROF HIST, UNIV WIS STEVENS POINT, 76-, Mem, Korean Res Ctr, Seoul, 62-. **MEMBERSHIPS** Asn Asian Studies; Korean Hist Asn. **RESEARCH** Korean history; Sino-Korean diplomatic relations; East Asian history. **SELECTED PUBLICATIONS** Auth, Korea and the Chinese imperium, Orient-West, 3-4/64; Traditional Sino-Korean diplomatic relations, Monumenta Serica, 65; The weight of tradition, in Korea's Response to the West, Korean Res Publ, 68. **CONTACT ADDRESS** Dept of Hist, Univ of Wis Stevens Point, 2100 Main St, Stevens Point, WI, 54481-3897.

WALKER, JULIET ELISE KIRKPATRICK
PERSONAL Born 07/18/1940, Chicago, IL, d, 2 children **DISCIPLINE** AFRO-AMERICAN HISTORY **EDUCATION** Roosevelt Univ, BA, 63; Univ Chicago, AM, 70, PhD(US hist), 76. **CAREER** Teacher hist & curric writer, Chicago Bd Educ, 63-69; lectr, dept of hist, Roosevelt Univ, 72-73; instr Black Studies, Univ Wis-Milwaukee, 73-76; asst prof Am Hist, Univ Ill, Urbana, 76-82, assoc prof, 82-90, prof, 90-; vis prof, Univ Tx Austin, spring 79; consult, Nat Endowment for Humanites, 76-78 & People's Heritage, Milwaukee, 77-78; Newberry Libr Chicago fel, 77; Harvard Univ, W. E. B. DuBois Institute, research assoc, 86-87; Princeton Univ, Shelby Cullom Davis Center for Hist Studies, fel, fall 94; Univ Witwatersrand, Johannesburg, South Africa, vis senior Fulbright prof, dept of hist, 95. **HONORS AND AWARDS** Newberry Lib Fellowship for the Study of State and Local Hist, summer 77; Karl E Mundt educational and Historical Found Prize, 78; Univ Illinois Undergraduate Instructional Award, 81; Nat Endowment for the Humanities (NEH) Fellowship for Independent Study and Research, 82-83; Am Hist Asn, Albert J. Beveridge Grant for Research in Am Hist, April, 84; Honorable Mention, Otto A. Rothert Award for best article published in each vol of The Filson Club History Quart, Jan 84; Asn of Black Women Historians Brown Publication Prize, Special Citation for Free Frank, Oct 85; Berkshire Fellowship in Hist, Radcliffe Col Mary Ingraham Bunting Institute, summer 85; Newcomen Prize for the best article "Racism, Slavery, and Free Enterprise: Black Entrepreneurshipo in the United States before the Civil War," to be published in the Harvard Business History Review for 1986; Asn of Black Women Historians, Brown Publication Prize for the best article "Racism, Slavery, and Free Enterprise," published by or on Black Women in 1986; Rockefeller Found Fellowship, 86-87; E. Franklin Frazier Vis Scholar for 88-89 at Clark Univ, Worchester, Ma, declined; Ralph Metcalfe Prof, Oct 3-6, 89, Marquette Univ, Milwaukee, WI; Ga Interdepartmental Univ Hist Program Vis Distinguished Scholar, 90; George Rogers Clark Award, Sept 90; Key to the City of Barry, Ill, Oct 90; Carter G. Woodson Award forbest article punblished 1983-1985, Journal of Negro Hist, Oct 91; Incomplete List of Faculty Rated as Excellent, 91; Finalist, Oakley-Kunde Award for Excellence to Undergraduate Education, 93; Princeton Univ, Shelby Cullom Davis Center for Hist Studies, Fellowship, fall semester, 94; Fulbright Fellowship for Teaching and Research, South Africa, 95; United States Information Agency Fulbright Certificate of award, 96; and numerous grants from the Univ of Ill at Urbana from 85-94. **MEMBERSHIPS** Asn for Study Afro-Am Life & Hist; AHA; Southern Hist Asn; Orgn Am Historians. **RESEARCH** African American business history, Black Intellectual History, Black Women and Peace Activism. **SELECTED PUBLICATIONS** Auth, Occupational Distribution of Frontier Towns in Pike County: An 1850 Census Survey, Western Ill Regional Studies 5, 2: 146-171, fall 82; Black Entrepreneurship: An Historical Inquiry, Essays in Economic and Business Hist, 1: 37-55, 83; Pioneer Slave Entrepreneurship on the Kentucky Pennyroyal Frontier, Journal of Negro Hist 68, 2: 289-308, summer 83; Entrepreneurial Ventures in the Origin of Agricultural Towns in Nineteenth Century Illinois, Ill Hist Journal 78, 1: 289-303, spring 83; Legal Processes and Judicial Challenges: Black Land Ownership on the Western Illinois Frontier, Western Ill Reg Studies 6, 2: 22-38, fall 83, reprinted, ed Paul Finkelman, Race and Law Before Emancipation, Hamden, Ct: Garland Pubs, 91;The Legal Status of Free Blacks in Early Kentucky, 1792-1825, the Filson Club Hist Quart 57: 383-395, Oct 83, reprinted, ed Paul Finkelman,. Race and Law Before Emancipation, Hamden, Ct: Garland Pubs, 91; Racism, Slavery, and Free Enterprise: Black Entrepreneurship in the United States before the Civil War, Harvard Business Hist Rev 60, 3: 343-382, autumn 86; Whither Liberty, Legality, or Equality: Slavery, Race, Property and the 1787 American Constitution, New York Law School Journal of Human Rights 6, 2: 299-352, spring 89; Prologue to Capitalism: Free Enterprise and Black Entrepreneurship. A Comparative History of Black Business in the United States and South Africa, Johannesburg, South Africa: Univ of the Witwatersrand, Institute for Advances Social Research, 95; Entrepreneurs, Jack Salzman, David Lionel Smith and Cornel West, eds, Encyclopedia of African-American Culture and History, vol 2, New York: Simon & Schuster Macmillan, 96; Banking, Jack Salzman, David Lionel Smith and Cornel West, eds, Encyclopedia of African-American Culture and History, vol 1, New York: Simon & Schuster Macmillan, 96; The Promised Land: The Chicago Defender and the Black Press in Illinois, 1862-1970, in H. Lewis Suggs, ed, The Black Press in the Midwest, Westport Ct: Greenwood Press Pubs Group, 96; Promoting Black Entrepreneurship and Business Enterprise in Antebellum America: The National Negro Convention, 1830-1855, in Thomas D. Boston, ed, A Different Vision: Race and Public Policy: 2 vols, London: Routledge Press, 97; Trade and Markets in Precolonial West and West Central Africa: The Cultural Foundation of the African American Business Tradition, in Thomas D. Boston, ed, A Different Vision: Race and Public Policy, 2 vol, London: Routledge Press, 97; African Americans, in Elliot Barkan, ed, A Nation of Peoples: A Sourcebook on America's Multicultural Heritage, Westport, Cn: Greenwood Pub, 98; ed, African Amer-

icans in Business: The Path Towards Empowerment, Washington, D. C.:The Assoc Pubs, Inc, 98;ed, Encyclopedia of African American Business History, Westport, Cn: Greenwood Pub Group, forthcoming 98; auth, The History of Black Business in America: Capitalism, Race, Entrepreneurship, New York: Macmillan/Twayne. 98; Free Frank: A Black Pioneer on the Antebellum Frontier, Lexington: The Univ Press of Ky, 83, 85, paper, 95; War, Peace, and Structural Violence: Peace Activism and the African American Experience, Bloomington: Indiana Univ , Center on Global Change and World Peace, 92; African-American Business and Entrepreneurship: Critical Historiographical Assessments in the Economic and Cultural Life of Blacks and Capitalism, contract, Westport, Ct: Greenwood, forthcoming 99. **CONTACT ADDRESS** Dept of Hist, Univ of Ill, 810 S Wright St, Urbana, IL, 61801-3611. **EMAIL** jewalker@uiuc.edu

WALKER, KENNETH R.
PERSONAL Born 12/19/1930, East Providence, Rhode Island, m **DISCIPLINE** EDUCATION **EDUCATION** Providence Coll, AB 1957; Rhode Island Coll, MEd, 1962; Boston Univ, EdD, 1976; Providence Coll, Hon SocD, 1983. **CAREER** East Providence Rhode Island School Dept, teacher, 1957-68, asst principal, 1968-70; Rhode Island Coll, assoc prof, dir, Early Enrollment Program, beginning 1970; Johnson/Wales Univ, prof, currently. **HONORS AND AWARDS** Exemplary Citizenship Award, 1974; IBA Man of Year Award, 1967; Recip Afro-Am Award EPHS, 1971; Serv to Youth Award No Kingston Jr HS 1969; RI Big Brother of Yr Award, 1963; Educ Award NAACP, 1980; East Providence High School Hall of Fame, 1987. **MEMBERSHIPS** Consult HEW Title IV; mem Guidance & Personnel Assn; Intl Assn of Approved Basketball Officials; Collegiate Basketball Officials Assn; Assn Curriculum Devel Specialist; Amer Fedn Teachers; Rhode Island State Parole Bd; consult, Rhode Island State Dept Educ; Omega Psi Phi Fraternity; mem, Governor's Task Force, 1991 Report on Education Rhode Island.

WALKER, LAWRENCE DAVID
PERSONAL Born 10/04/1931, Las Animas, CO, m, 1954, 2 children **DISCIPLINE** EUROPEAN HISTORY **EDUCATION** Stanford Univ, AB, 53, MA, 57; Univ Calif, Berkeley, PhD (Europ hist), 65. **CAREER** Instr hist Western civilization, Stanford Univ, 61-63; asst prof mod Europ hist, Univ Southern Calif, 64-69; assoc prof, 69-81, PROF HIST, ILL STATE UNIV, 81-; Nat Endowment for Humanities younger humanist fel, 71-72; Nat Endowment for Humanities residential fel, Northwestern Univ, 81-82. **MEMBERSHIPS** AHA; Group Use Psychol Hist; Cath Hist Asn. **RESEARCH** Historiography; quantitative history. **SELECTED PUBLICATIONS** Auth, Volkish History in Methodological Innovation and Volkish Ideologization in German Historiography 1918-1945, Am Hist Rev, Vol 99, 94; Generations in Conflict in Youth Revolt and Generation Formation in Germany, 1770-1968, Ger Studies Rev, Vol 20, 97. **CONTACT ADDRESS** Dept of Hist, Illinois State Univ, Normal, IL, 61761.

WALKER, MACK
PERSONAL Born 06/06/1929, Springfield, MA, m, 1954, 3 children **DISCIPLINE** MODERN EUROPEAN HISTORY **EDUCATION** Bowdoin Col, AB, 50; Harvard Univ, PhD, 59. **CAREER** Instr hist, RI Sch Design, 57-59; from instr to asst prof, Harvard Univ, 59-66; from assoc prof to prof, Cornell Univ, 66-74; prof of hist, Johns Hopkins Univ, 74-, dept chm, 79-82, fel, Inst Advan Study, 77. **MEMBERSHIPS** AHA; Conf Group Cent Europ Hist; Am Acad Arts & Sci. **RESEARCH** German social and political history. **SELECTED PUBLICATIONS** Auth, Germany and the emigration, 1816-1885, Harvard Univ, 64; ed, Metternich's Europe, Harper, 68; Plombieres, Oxford Univ, 68; auth, German Home Towns, Cornell Univ, 71; auth, Johann Jakob Moser and the Holy Roman Empire of the German Nation, NC Univ, 81; auth, The Salzburg Transaction, NC Univ, 92; auth, Der Salzberg Handel Vandenhoeck and Rupprecht, 97. **CONTACT ADDRESS** Dept of Hist, Johns Hopkins Univ, 3400 N Charles St, Baltimore, MD, 21218-2680.

WALKER, NANCY A.
PERSONAL Born 09/05/1942, Shreveport, LA, m, 1976 **DISCIPLINE** ENGLISH, AMERICAN STUDIES **EDUCATION** La State Univ, BA, 64; Tulane Univ, MA, 66; Kent State Univ, PhD(Am lit), 71. **CAREER** INSTR ENGLISH & AM STUDIES, STEPHENS COL, 71- **MEMBERSHIPS** MLA; Am Studies Asn; Midcontinent Am Studies Asn; Popular Cult Asn; Am Humor Studies Asn. **SELECTED PUBLICATIONS** Auth, A novel in the form of a comic strip: Nathanael West's Miss Lonelyhearts, Serif, 66; coauth, An Analytical Index to American Quarterly, Norwood, 76; auth, Feminist or naturalist: The social context of Kate Chopin's, The Awakening, Southern Quart, 79; All that you need to know: John O'Hara's achievement in the novella, John O'Hara J, 81; Do feminists ever laugh?, Women's humor and women's rights, Int J Women's Studies, 81; Wit, sentimentality and the image of women in the Nineteenth century, Am Studies, 81; Phyllis McGinley, Dict of Lit Biog, 82. **CONTACT ADDRESS** Vanderbilt Univ, 65201.

WALKER, PAMELA J.
DISCIPLINE NINETEENTH-CENTURY BRITISH HISTORY **EDUCATION** Concordia Univ, BA; York Univ, MA, 84; Rutgers Univ, PhD, 91. **CAREER** Assoc prof. **RESEARCH** Trans-Atlantic religious and cultural movements. **SELECTED PUBLICATIONS** Auth, I Live But Yet Not I For Christ Liveth in Me: Men and Masculinity in the Salivation Army, 1865-1890, Asserting Manliness, 91; Proclaiming Women's Right to Preach, Harvard Divinity Bulletin, 94. **CONTACT ADDRESS** Dept of Hist, Carleton Univ, 1125 Colonel By Dr, Ottawa, ON, K1S 5B6. **EMAIL** pjwalker@ccs.carleton.ca

WALKER, PHILIP ALFRED
PERSONAL Winston-Salem, NC, m, 1957, 4 children **DISCIPLINE** MODERN EUROPEAN HISTORY **EDUCATION** Univ NC, AB, 40, PhD (recent Europe), 55; Emory Univ, MA, 42. **CAREER** Instr hist, Emory Univ, 47-48; From asst prof to assoc prof, Univ Southern Miss, 51-58; assoc prof, La Polytech Inst, 58-63; chmn div humanities, 66-71, PROF HIST and HEAD DEPT, UNIV NC, ASHEVILLE, 63-; Fel, Inst Asian Studies, Duke Univ, 67. **MEMBERSHIPS** AHA; Southern Hist Asn. **RESEARCH** Paris peace conference of ; general intellectual history. **SELECTED PUBLICATIONS** Auth, the Current Canon in British Romantics Studies, Col Eng, Vol 55, 93; Reflections on the Practical and Legal Implications of School-Based Management and Teacher Empowerment, J Law Educ, Vol 22, 93; 2 Comments on Taking It Personally - Reading Derrida Responses, College English, Vol 57, 95; Racial Protest, Identity, Words, and Form In Angelou, Maya I Know Why the Caged Bird Sings, Col Lit, Vol 22, 95. **CONTACT ADDRESS** Dept of Hist, Univ of NC, Asheville, NC, 28804.

WALKER, ROBERT HARRIS
PERSONAL Born 03/15/1924, Cincinnati, OH, m, 1953, 3 children **DISCIPLINE** AMERICAN CIVILIZATION **EDUCATION** Northwestern Univ, BS, 45; Columbia Univ, MA, 50; Univ Pa, PhD (Am civilization), 55. **CAREER** Educ spec, US War Dept, Shizuoka, Japan, 46-47; instr English, Carnegie Inst Technol, 50-51; instr Am civilization and ed, Am Quart, Univ Pa, 53-54; asst prof, Univ Wyo, 55-59, actg dir Am studies, 56-59; assoc prof Am lit, 59-63, dir Am Studies Prog, 59-65 and 68-70, PROF AM CIVILIZATION, GEORGE WASHINGTON UNIV, 63-; Ed, Am Quart, 53-54, Am Studies Int, 70-81 AND CONTRIB IN AM STUDIES SER, 70-; consult, US Info Agency and US Foreign Serv Inst, 59-66 and Peace Corps, 61-62; dir, Div Educ and Pub Prog, Nat Endowment for Humanities, 66-68; fels, Woodrow Wilson Int Ctr, 72-73, Rockefeller Ctr, Bellagio, 79, Huntington Libr, 80 and Hoover Inst, 80; comnr, Japan-US Friendship Comn, 77-81; AM COUN LEARNED SOC DELEG TO UNESCO, 78-; Am specialist grants, Thailand, Greece and Iran, 79, Israel, 80 and Brazil, 81. **MEMBERSHIPS** Am Studies Asn (pres, 70-71); Orgn Am Historians; Cosmos Club. **RESEARCH** Reform; literature and society. **SELECTED PUBLICATIONS** Auth, Crossings in the Great Transatlantic Migrations, 1870-1914, Am Studies Int, Vol 31, 93; Cincinnati, Queen City of the West, 1819-1838, Am Studies Int, Vol 31, 93; Bode, Carl in In Memoriam, Am Quart, Vol 45, 93; Sporting with the Gods in The Rhetoric of Play and Game in american Culture in Oriard, M, Am Studies Int, Vol 31, 93; Small Craft Advisory, Am Studies Int, Vol 31, 93; The American Pacific in from the Old China Trade to the Present, Am Studies Int, Vol 31, 93; Remembering Bode, Carl, 1911-1993, Am Studies Int, Vol 31, 93; Too Marvelous For Words in The Life and Genius of Tatum, Am Studies Int, Vol 32, 94; Beyond the Rising Sun in Nationalism in Contemporary Japan, Am Studies Int, Vol 33, 95. **CONTACT ADDRESS** 3915 Huntington St NW, Washington, DC, 20015.

WALKER, ROBERT MILLER
PERSONAL Born 12/10/1908, Flushing, NY **DISCIPLINE** ART HISTORY **EDUCATION** Princeton Univ, AB, 32, MFA, 36; Harvard Univ, PhD, 41. **CAREER** Instr fine arts, Williams Col, 35-38; asst, Harvard Univ, 39-40; From asst prof to prof, 41-74, chmn dept, 41-71, EMER PROF ART HIST, SWARTHMORE COL, 74-; Lectr, Pa Acad Fine Arts, 46 and 47 and Johns Hopkins Univ, 49. **MEMBERSHIPS** Col Art Asn Am; Soc Archit Hist (treas, 55-63); Archaeol Inst Am; Print Coun Am. **RESEARCH** Art history; architecture; prints and drawings. **SELECTED PUBLICATIONS** Auth, 2 Unpublished Portuguese Sonnets on the Battle of Ameixial and June 8 1663, Port Studies, Vol 9, 93; Fanshawe,Richard Lusiad and Fariaesousa, Manuel, De Lusiadas Comentadas and The Probable Source in Castilian Prose of the 1st English Translation of Camoes Os Lusiadas in New Documentary Evidence, Port Studies, Vol 10, 94. **CONTACT ADDRESS** Six Fox Hollow, Wayland, MA, 01778.

WALKER, SUE SHERIDAN
PERSONAL Born 08/11/1935, Chicago, IL, m, 1959, 1 child **DISCIPLINE** MEDIEVAL HISTORY **EDUCATION** Loyola Univ, BA, 58, MA, 61; Univ Chicago, PhD(hist), 66. **CAREER** Asst prof hist, Univ Windsor, 66-68; asst prof, 68-71, assoc prof, 71-79, prof hist, Northeastern Ill Univ, 79-, Am Asn Univ Women fel, 65-66; chmn, Northeastern Ill Univ & Am Soc Legal Hist Conf on English Plea Rolls, 73; bk rev ed, Am J Legal Hist, 77-82; Nat Endowment for Humanities fel, 82-83. **HONORS AND AWARDS** Elected a Fellow of the Royal Historical Society, 86; named to the Council of the Pipe Roll Society, 96; Newberry Library/National Endowment for the Humanities Fellowship, 90-91. **MEMBERSHIPS** Am Soc for Legal Hist; AHA; Medieval Acad Am; Selden Soc. **RESEARCH** Medieval English Family Law and Society: Inheritance, dower and wardship; rights of women and legal process in the royal courts esp concerning widows as litigants in dower pleas and the impact of an increasingly professional royal court. **SELECTED PUBLICATIONS** Auth, Violence and the exercise of Feudal guardianship: The action of ejectio custodia, Am J Legal Hist, Vol XVI, 72; Proof of age of Feudal heirs in Medieval England, Mediaeval Studies, Vol XXXV, 73; Widow and ward: The Feudal Law of child custody in Medieval England, Feminist Studies No 3, 34/76; ed, Checklist of Research in British Legal Manuscripts, Vol I & II, Northeastern Ill Univ; The Action of Waste in the Early Common Law, Legal Records and the Historian, Royal Hist Soc, 78; Feudal Constraint and Free Consent in the Making of Marriages in Medieval England: Widows in the King's Gift, Can Hist Soc, 79; Wife and Widow in Medieval England, Ann Arbor, 93; a series of articles on Wardship, Marriage and Legal Remedies including Free Consent and Marriage of feudal wards in medieval England, J of Medieval Hist 8, pp 123-134, 92; Punishing convicted ravishers: statutory strictures and actual practice..., J of Medieval Hist 13, pp 237-250, 87; guest ed and contrib to an issue of family law (papers from one session of the 1986 Conference on British Legal Manuscripts, J of Medieval Hist 14, no 1, 88; Common Law Juries and Feudal Marriage Customs..., Univ of Ill Law Review 1984, no 3, pp705-718; Wrongdoing and Compensation: The Pleas of Wardship..., The J of Legal Hist 9, 88; Wager of Law and Judgment by Default in Pleas of Dower in the Royal Courts of Late Thirteenth-and Fourteenth Century England, The Life of the Law, ed Peter Birks, London, 93. **CONTACT ADDRESS** Dept of Hist, Northeastern Illinois Univ, 5500 N St Louis Ave, Chicago, IL, 60625-4625.

WALKER, VALAIDA SMITH
PERSONAL Darby, PA, d **DISCIPLINE** EDUCATION **EDUCATION** Howard University, Washington, DC, BS, 1954; Temple University, Philadelphia, PA, MED, 1970, EdD, 1973. **CAREER** TEMPLE UNIVERSITY, PHILADELPHIA, PA, PROF, 1974-, chairperson, 1980-83, associate dean, 1983-84, assoc vice provost, 1984-90, vice provost, 1987-90, VICE PRES FOR STUDENT AFFAIRS, 1990-. **HONORS AND AWARDS** Chapel of the Four Chaplains Service Award; Special Educator of the Year, Sigma Pi Epsilon Delta, 1983. **MEMBERSHIPS** Former member, President's Commission on Mental Retardation; past president, American Association on Mental Retardation; PA Advisory Board on Special Education; William Penn Adult Community School Advisory Board, 1976-; Knoll/Shaffer Bi-Partisan Commission, 1989-; exec advisor, Caribbean Association on Mental Retardation. **CONTACT ADDRESS** Student Affairs, Temple Univ, Conwell Hall, 4th Fl, Philadelphia, PA, 19122.

WALKER, WILLARD
PERSONAL Born 07/29/1926, Boston, MA, m, 1952, 2 children **DISCIPLINE** ANTHROPOLOGY, LINGUISTICS **EDUCATION** Harvard Univ, AB, 50; Univ Ariz, MA, 53; Cornell Univ, PhD (gen ling), 64. **CAREER** Res assoc, Univ Chicago Carnegie Cross-Cult Educ Proj, Tahlequah, Okla, 64-66; From asst prof to assoc prof anthrop, 66-77, PROF ANTHROP, WESLEYAN UNIV, 77-. **MEMBERSHIPS** Am Anthrop Asn; Ling Soc Am; Soc Appl Anthrop; Am Ethnol Soc; Am Soc Ethnohist. **RESEARCH** North American Indian languages; ethnology of North America; native writing systems. **SELECTED PUBLICATIONS** Auth, the Early History of the Cherokee Syllabary, Ethnohistory, Vol 40, 93; Pamela and Skepticism, Eighteenth Century Life, Vol 16, 92; Deadlock, Or, the Two Titles, Parnassus Poetry Rev, Vol 18, 93; As A Man Grows Older and Svevo Senilita in Translation, NY Rev Books, Vol 41, 94; The Way Home, Parnassus Poetry Rev, Vol 20, 95; Tlooth, Parnassus Poetry Rev, Vol 20, 95; Cigarettes, Parnassus Poetry Rev, Vol 20, 95; Singular Pleasures, Parnassus Poetry Rev, Vol 20, 95; Out of Bounds, Parnassus Poetry Rev, Vol 20, 95; Armenian Papers in Poems 1954-1984, Parnassus Poetry Rev, Vol 20, 95; Machiavellian Rhetoric in from the Counterreformation To Milton, Philos Lit, Vol , 95; The Sinking of the Odradek Stadium and Other Novels, Parnassus Poetry Rev, Vol 20, 95; Immeasurable Distances, Parnassus Poetry Rev, Vol 20, 95; 20 Lines A Day, Parnassus Poetry Rev, Vol 20, 95; Selected Declarations of Dependence, Parnassus Poetry Rev, Vol 20, 95; The Jist, Parnassus Poetry Rev, Vol 20, 95; Mikmaq Hieroglyphic Prayers in Readings in North America First Indigenous Script, Am Indian Cult Res J, Vol 20, 96; The Determination of Locke, Hume and Fielding, Eighteenth Century Life, Vol 20, 96; Professional Correctness in Literary Studies and Political Change, Philos Lit, Vol 20, 96; Reason and Rhetoric in the Philosophy of Hobbes, Philos Lit, Vol 21, 97; Fair New World, Int Fiction Rev, Vol 24, 97. **CONTACT ADDRESS** Dept of Anthrop, Wesleyan Univ, Middletown, CT, 06457.

WALKER BYNUM, CAROLINE
DISCIPLINE MEDIEVAL HISTORY **EDUCATION** Univ Mich, BA, 62; Harvard Univ, PhD, 69. **CAREER** Prof. **SELECTED PUBLICATIONS** Auth, Docere Verbo et Exemplo, 79; Jesus as Mother, 82; Holy Feast and Holy Fast, 87; Fragmentation and Redemption, 91; The Resurrection of the Body

in Western Christianity: 200-1336, 95; ed, Gender and Religion, 86. **CONTACT ADDRESS** Dept of Hist, Columbia Col, New York, 2960 Broadway, New York, NY, 10027-6902.

WALKOWITZ, DANIEL JAY
PERSONAL Born 11/25/1942, Paterson, NJ, m, 1965, 1 child **DISCIPLINE** AMERICAN HISTORY **EDUCATION** Univ Rochester, AB, 64; PhD (hist), 72. **CAREER** Instr hist, Rensselaer Polytech Inst, 69-71; lectr univ col, Rutgers Univ, New Brunswick, 71-72, asst prof, 72-78; asst prof, 78-80, ASSOC PROF HIST, NY UNIV, 80-; CO-DIR GRAD PROG PUB HIST, 81-; Proj dir, Nat Endowment for Humanities Media Grant, 76-78 and 80; consult, Cabin Creek Films, 78-81, the Wobblies, 79, Saratoga Co Hist Mus, 79, Red Hill Films, 80, Am Film Inst, 80-81, Chinatown Hist Proj, 81-82. **MEMBERSHIPS** Orgn Am Historians; Soc Sci Hist Asn; AHA; Pub Hist Asn. **RESEARCH** Working-class history; comparative urban and social history. **SELECTED PUBLICATIONS** Auth, Social Work and Social Order in The Settlement Movement in 2 Industrial Cities, 1889-1930, J Social Hist, Vol 28, 94; The Wages of Whiteness in Race and The Making of the American Working Class, J Am Ethnic Hist, Vol 14, 94; Success While Others Fail in Social Movement Unionism and the Public Workplace, Labor Hist, Vol 38, 97; Working on the Bomb in an Oral History of Wwii Hanford, J Soc Hist, Vol 31, 97. **CONTACT ADDRESS** Dept of Hist, New York Univ, 715 Broadway, New York, NY, 10003-6806.

WALL, BENNETT HARRISON
PERSONAL Born 12/07/1914, Raleigh, NC, m, 3 children **DISCIPLINE** HISTORY **EDUCATION** Wake Forest Col, AB, 33; Univ NC, AM, 41, PhD, 46. **CAREER** From instr to assoc prof hist, Univ Ky, 44-65; assoc prof, 65-69, head dept, 68-73, prof hist, Tulane Univ, 69-80; LECTR HIST, UNIV GA, 81-. **MEMBERSHIPS** Econ Hist Asn; Agr Hist Soc; Orgn Am Historians; Southern Hist Asn (secy-treas, 52-); Newcomen Soc. **RESEARCH** Southern history; United States business and economic history, 00-72; United States local and regional politics, 1865-20. **SELECTED PUBLICATIONS** Auth, Kentucky and the Bourbons in The Story of Allen Dale Farm, J Southern Hist, Vol 59, 93; The History of Belle Meade in Mansion, Plantation, and Stud, J Southern Hist, Vol 59, 93. **CONTACT ADDRESS** Dept of Hist, Univ of Ga, Athens, GA, 30602.

WALL, HELENA M.
PERSONAL Born 11/22/1955, New York, NY **DISCIPLINE** HISTORY **EDUCATION** Brandeis Univ, BA (Hist), 77; Harvard Univ, MA (Hist), 78, PhD (Hist), 83. **CAREER** Lect in Hist and Hist and Lit, Harvard Univ, 83-84; asst prof Hist, 84-90, assoc prof Hist, 90-98, PROF OF HIST, POMONA COLL, 98-. **HONORS AND AWARDS** NEH fel for Coll Teachers; NEH Summer fel; fel, Charles Warren Center, Harvard Univ; Phi Beta Kappa. **MEMBERSHIPS** AHA; OAH. **RESEARCH** Colonial Am; Am social hist; early modern hist. **SELECTED PUBLICATIONS** Auth, Fierce Communion: Family and Community in Early America, Harvard Univ Press, 90. **CONTACT ADDRESS** Dept of Hist, Pomona Col, Claremont, CA, 91711. **EMAIL** hwall@pomona.edu

WALL, IRWIN M.
PERSONAL Born 04/21/1940, New York, NY, m, 1961, 1 child **DISCIPLINE** FRENCH, EUROPEAN, AND INTERNATIONAL HISTORY **EDUCATION** Columbia Univ, BA, 61, MA, 62, PhD, 68. **CAREER** PROF HIST, Univ of Calif, Riverside, 70-. **MEMBERSHIPS** Western Soc Fr Hist (pres, 94-95) **RESEARCH** French Left; French-American relations. **SELECTED PUBLICATIONS** Auth, French Communism in the Era of Stalin, 83; L'Influence Americaine sur la politique francaise, Paris, 89; The United States and the Making of Postwar France, 91; numerous book chapters and articles on French history and politics. **CONTACT ADDRESS** Dept of Hist, Univ of Calif, 900 University Ave, Riverside, CA, 92521-0001. **EMAIL** irwin.wall@ucr.edu

WALL, JOSEPH FRAZIER
PERSONAL Born 07/10/1920, Des Moines, IA, m, 1944, 3 children **DISCIPLINE** HISTORY **EDUCATION** Grinnell Col, BA, 41; Harvard Univ, MA, 42; Columbia Univ, PhD (hist), 51. **CAREER** From instr to prof hist, Grinnell Col, 47-60, chmn dept, 54-57 and 63-64, Roberts honor prof, 60-61, Parker prof, 62-78, chmn fac, 66-69, dean col, 69-73, Earl Strong Distinguished prof, 72-78; prof and chmn dept, State Univ NY, Albany, 78-80; ROSENFIELD PROF HIST and DIR ROSENFIELD PROG PUB AFFAIRS, GRINNELL COL, 80-; Sr Fulbright scholar, Edinburgh Univ, 57-58; Fulbright prof Am studies, Gothenburg Univ, 64-65; mem comn accreditation, N Cent Asn Cols and Sec Schs, 70-74. **HONORS AND AWARDS** Bancroft Prize in Hist, 71., Grinnell Col, LHD, 78; LLD, Simpson Col, 78; LHD, Luther Col, 82. **MEMBERSHIPS** AHA; Orgn Am Historians; Am Studies Asn; Western Hist Asn; Soc Am Hist. **RESEARCH** American history since the Civil War, political and cultural; Andrew Carnegie. **SELECTED PUBLICATIONS** Auth, the Battle for Homestead 1880-1892 in Politics, Culture, And Steel, J Econ Hist, Vol 54, 94; Merchant Adventurer in The Story of Grace, W.R., J Am Hist, Vol 81, 94; Luce, Henry, R. in a Political Portrait of the Man Who Created the American Century, J Am Hist, Vol 82, 95. **CONTACT ADDRESS** Dept of Hist, Grinnell Col, Grinnell, IA, 50112.

WALLACE, ANDREW
PERSONAL Born 11/18/1930, Springfield, IL, m, 1958, 2 children **DISCIPLINE** AMERICAN HISTORY **EDUCATION** Univ Ariz, BA, 53, PhD (hist), 68. **CAREER** Ed, J Ariz Hist, Ariz Pioneers Hist Soc, 64-68; asst prof, 68-80, ASSOC PROF HIST, NORTHERN ARIZ UNIV, 80-. **MEMBERSHIPS** AHA; Orgn Am Historians; Western Hist Asn. **RESEARCH** Nineteenth century United States history; history of the American West; American military history. **SELECTED PUBLICATIONS** Auth, Deposit Account Developments in Truth in Savings, Business Lawyer, Vol 48, 93; A Vast Amount of Trouble in a History of the Spring Creek, Western Histl Quart, Vol 26, 95; Hadrians Villa and Its Legacy, Archaeol, Vol 49, 96; Arizona in a History, NMex Histl Rev, Vol 71, 96. **CONTACT ADDRESS** Dept of Hist, No Arizona Univ, Flagstaff, AZ, 86001.

WALLACE, CARL M.
DISCIPLINE HISTORY **EDUCATION** Univ New Brunswick, MA; Univ Alberta, PhD. **CAREER** Prof. **SELECTED PUBLICATIONS** Auth, Communities in the Northern Ontario Frontier, Dundern, 92; co-ed, Reappraisals in Canadian History: Pre-Confederation, Scarborough, 92; co-ed, Reappraisals in Canadian History: Post-Confederation, Scarborough, 92; co-ed, Sudbury: Railtown to Regional Capital, Dundurn, 93. **CONTACT ADDRESS** Dept of History, Laurentian Univ, 935 Ramsey Lake Rd, Sudbury, ON, P3E 2C6.

WALLACE, PAUL
PERSONAL Born 07/21/1931, Los Angeles, CA, m, 1976, 2 children **DISCIPLINE** POLITICAL SCIENCE **EDUCATION** Univ CA, Berkeley, AB, 53, MA, 57, PhD, 66. **CAREER** Univ MO-Columbia, asst to full prof 64, ch 81-82, 84-85, dir 79-80, ch intl affs 87-88, lectr 81, 83, CA State Univ, vis lectr 61, 63; Asia Found, superv ref scvs 57-60. **HONORS AND AWARDS** MiddleBush Prof; Facul Alumni Awd; 5 Smithsonian funded stud; Ford Found Gnt; Provost Gnt; Sr RES Fell; AIIS Fell; Fulbright Fell; Smithsonian and Ford bk project. **MEMBERSHIPS** APSA; MPSA; AAS. **RESEARCH** Politics of South Asia. **SELECTED PUBLICATIONS** Region and Nation in India, ed Paul Wallace, New Delhi, Oxford &IBH, 85; General Elections, 1996, Economic and Political Weekly, India, 97; Sikh Nationalist Terrorism in India, NY, M E Sharpe, 97; Problems of Partitions in Europe and South Asia, Slavic Rev, 96; Political Violence and Terrorism in India, in: Martha Crenshaw, ed, Terrorism in Context, PA State Univ Press, 95. **CONTACT ADDRESS** Dept of Polit Sci, Univ of MO, Columbia, MO, 65201.

WALLACE, ROBERT
DISCIPLINE CLASSICS **EDUCATION** Columbia Col, BA, 72; Oxford Univ, MA, 77; Harvard Univ, PhD, 84. **CAREER** Asso prof, Class dpt ch, Northwestern Univ,91-; master, Chapin Humanities Residential Col. **RESEARCH** Music, Philosophy, and Politics in 5th-Century Athens. **SELECTED PUBLICATIONS** Auth, The Areopagos Council, to 307 BC, Hopkins, 89; co-ed, Poet, Public and Performance in Ancient Greece, Hopkins, 97; Studies in Greco-Roman History 360-146 BC in Honor of Ernst Badian, Okla, 96; coauth, Harmonia Mundi: Music and Philosophy in the Ancient World, Quaderni Urbinati di Cultura Classica, 91. **CONTACT ADDRESS** Dept of Classics, Northwestern Univ, 1801 Hinman, Kresge 11, Evanston, IL, 60208. **EMAIL** rwallace@nwu.edu

WALLACE, WALTER L.
PERSONAL Born 08/21/1927, Washington, DC, d, 3 children **DISCIPLINE** SOCIOLOGY **EDUCATION** Columbia Univ, BA, 54; Atlanta Univ, MA, 55; Univ Chicago, PhD, 63. **CAREER** Instr, Dept Hist & Soc Sci, Spelman Col, 55-57; assoc study dir Nat Opinion Res Ctr, Univ Chicago, 60-62; instr to prof, Dept Sociol, Northwestern Univ, 62-71; vis adj prof Dept Sociol, Columbia Univ, 69-71; staff sociol, Russell Sage Found, 69-77; Prof Dept Sociol, Princeton Univ, 71-. **HONORS AND AWARDS** Vis scholar Russell Sage Found, 68-69; fel Ctr Adv Study Behav & Soc Sci, 74-75; Sociol Res Asn fel. **MEMBERSHIPS** Am Sociol Asn **RESEARCH** Sociological theory; Ethnic, racial, nationality relations. **SELECTED PUBLICATIONS** Auth Principles of Scientific Sociology, 83; Toward a Disciplinary Matrix for Sociology, 88; A Weberian Theory of Human Society, 94; The Future of Ethnicity, Race, & Nationality, 97. **CONTACT ADDRESS** Sociology Dept, Princeton Univ, Princeton, NY, 08544. **EMAIL** wwallace@princeton.edu

WALLACE, WILLIAM
DISCIPLINE PAINTING, SCULPTURE, AND ARCHITECTURE ITALY FROM 1300 TO 1700 **EDUCATION** Columbia Univ, PhD, 83. **CAREER** Art, Washington Univ. **SELECTED PUBLICATIONS** Auth, ; Michelangelo at San Lorenzo: The Genius as Entreprofeneur, Cambridge Univ Profess, 94; Michelangelo: Selected Scholarship in English, 5 volumes, Garland Profess, 95. **CONTACT ADDRESS** Washington Univ, 1 Brookings Dr, St. Louis, MO, 63130.

WALLACE, WILLIAM A.
PERSONAL Born 05/11/1918, New York, NY **DISCIPLINE** PHILOSOPHY & HISTORY **EDUCATION** Manhattan Col, BEE, 40; Cath Univ Am, MS, 52; Univ Fribourg, PhD(philos), 59 DrTheol, 61. **CAREER** Lector philos, Dominican House Philos, 54-62; lectr philos & ed, New Cath Encycl, Cath Univ Am, 62-65; prof theol, Dominican House Studies, 67-70; Prof Philos & Hist, Cath Univ Am, 70-88; prof philos, Univ Maryland, College Park, 88- ; Assoc ed, Thomist, 62-; NSF res grants, 65-67, 72-77 & 80-83; trustee, Providence Col, 67-84; mem adv panel, Frog Hist & Philos Sci, NSF, 75-77; mem, Inst Advan Study, Princeton, 76-77; dir gen, Leonine Comn, 76-89; consult, Nat Endowment for Humanities, 76- **HONORS AND AWARDS** DSc, Providence Col, 73; D Litt, Molloy Col, 74; LHD, Manhattan Col, 75; LHD, Fairfield Univ, 86., DSc, Providence Col, 73; DLitt, Molloy Col, 74; LHD, Manhattan Col, 75. **MEMBERSHIPS** Am Cath Philos Asn (vpres, 68, pres, 69); Hist Sci Soc; Philos Sci Asn; Renaissance Soc Am. **RESEARCH** Scientific methodology; medieval and early modern science; Galileo. **SELECTED PUBLICATIONS** Auth, Galileo and His Sources, Princeton, 84; ed, Reinterpreting Galileo, Catholic Univ, 86; ed, Galileo Galilei, Tractactio de demonstratione, Antenore, 88; auth, Galileo, The Jesuits and the Medieval Aristotle, Variorum, 91; auth, Galileo's Logic of Discovery and Proof, Kluwer, 92; ed and transl, Galileo's Logical Treatises, Kluwer, 92; auth, The Modeling of Nature, Catholic Univ, 96. **CONTACT ADDRESS** 3407 Cool Spring Rd, Adelphi, MD, 20983. **EMAIL** wallacew@wam.umd.edu

WALLACH, ALAN
PERSONAL Born 06/08/1942, Brooklyn, NY, m, 1988 **DISCIPLINE** ART HISTORY **EDUCATION** Columbia Univ, PhD, 73. **CAREER** Asst to Assoc Prof, Kean Col, 74-88; Ralph H Ward Prof of Art & Art Hist, Prof Am Stud, Col of William & Mary. **HONORS AND AWARDS** Smithsonian Inst Sr Postdoctoral Fellow, 85-86. **MEMBERSHIPS** Col Art Asn; Am Stud Asn. **RESEARCH** 9th century American art; museums & art institutions. **SELECTED PUBLICATIONS** Auth, Making a Picture of the View from Mt Holyoke, American Iconology: New Approaches to Nineteenth Century Art and Literature, Yale Univ Press, 80-91, 310-312, 93; co-ed, auth, Thomas Cole: Landscape into History, Yale Univ Press, 94; auth, Wadsworth's Tower: An Episode in the History of American Landscape Vision, Am Art, 10:3, 8-27, 96; auth, Long-term Visions, Short-term Failures: Art Institutions in the United States, 1800-1860, Art in Bourgeois Society, 1790-1850, Cambridge Univ Press, 303-319, 98; Exhibiting Contradiction: Essays on the Art Museum in the United States, Univ Mass Press, 98. **CONTACT ADDRESS** Dept of Art/Art Hist, Col of William and Mary, PO Box 8795, Williamsburg, VA, 23187. **EMAIL** axwall@facstaff.wm.edu

WALLACH, LUITPOLD
PERSONAL Born 02/06/1910, Munich, Germany, m, 1970 **DISCIPLINE** CLASSICS, MEDIEVAL LATIN **EDUCATION** Univ Tuebingen, DPhil(hist), 32; Cornell Univ, PhD (classics), 47. **CAREER** Asst prof classics, Hamilton Col, 51-52; asst prof hist, Univ Ore, 53; asst prof classics, Cornell Univ, 53-55; asst prof, Univ Okla, 55-57; asst prof, Harpur Col, 57-62; prof, Marquette Univ, 62-67; prof, 67-78, EMER PROF CLASSICS, UNIV ILL, URBANA, 78-; Fund Advan Educ fel, 52; Am Coun Learned Soc grant, 60; mem bd, Grad Sch, Marquette Univ, 63-67, fac fel, 67; Leo Baeck Inst fel, 67; assoc, Ctr Advan Studies, Univ Ill, 69-70. **HONORS AND AWARDS** Festschrift: Beitraege Luitpold Wallach Gewidmet, Hiersemann, Stuttgart, 75. **MEMBERSHIPS** Am Philol Asn; AHA; Mediaeval Acad Am. **RESEARCH** Philology; mediaeval Latin and history. **SELECTED PUBLICATIONS** Auth, Coercive Uses of Mandatory Reporting in Therapeutic Relationships, Behavioral Scis Law, Vol 11, 93. **CONTACT ADDRESS** Dept of Classics, Univ of Ill, Urbana, IL, 61801.

WALLENSTEIN, PETER
PERSONAL Born 05/22/1944, East Orange, NJ, m, 1986 **DISCIPLINE** U.S. HISTORY **EDUCATION** Columbia Univ, BA, 66; Johns Hopkins Univ, PhD, 73. **CAREER** Instr and asst prof, Sarah Lawrence Col, 70-75; vis asst prof, Univ Toronto, 75-77; asst prof, Univ Maryland in East Asia, 79-82; asst prof and assoc prof, Va Polytechnic Inst and State Univ, 83-. **MEMBERSHIPS** Southern Hist Asn; Orgn Amer Hist. **RESEARCH** Southern History; Virginia; Race and Policy: Higher Education. **SELECTED PUBLICATIONS** Auth, Virginia Tech, Land-Grant University, 1872-1997: History of a School, a State, a Nation, Blacksburg, Va, Pocahontas Press, 97; From Slave South to New South: Public Policy in Nineteenth-Century Georgia, Chapel Hill, Univ NC Press, 87; essays, Laissez Faire and the Lunatic Asylum: State Welfard Institutions in Georgia-The First Half Century, 1830s-1880s, ed Elna C. Green, Before the New Deal: Essays in Southern Social Welfare History, 1830-1930, Athens, Univ Ga Press, 98; Indian Foremothers: Race, Sex, Slavery, and Freedom in Early Virginia, ed Catherine Clinton and Michele Gillespie, The Devil's Lane: Sex and Race in the Early South, New York, Oxford Univ Press, 57-73, 97; Helping to Save the Union: The Social Origins, Wartime Experience, and Military Impact of White Union Soldiers from East Tennessee, eds Kenneth W. Noe and Shannon H. Wilson, Appalachia in the Civil War, Knoxville, Univ of Tenn Press, 1-29, 97; Incendiaries All: Southern Politics and the Harpers Ferry Raid, ed Paul Finkelman, His Soul Goes Marching On: Responses to John Brown and the Harpers Ferry Raid, Charlottesville, Univ Press of Va, 149-73, 95; Race, Marriage, and the Law of Freedom: Alabama and Virginia, 1860s-1960s, Chica-

go-Kent Law Rev, 70, no 2, special issue The Law of Freedom, 371-437, 94; Flawed Keepers of the Flame: The Interpreters of George Mason, Va Mag of Hist and Bio, 102, April, 229-60, 94; These New and Strange Beings: Women in the Legal Profession in Virginia, 1890-1990, Va Mag of Hist and Bio, 101, April, 193-226, 93; Cartograms and the Mapping of Virginia History, 1790-1990, Va Soc Sci Jour, 28, 90-110, 93. **CONTACT ADDRESS** History Dept., Virginia Tech, Blacksburg, VA, 24061. **EMAIL** pwallens@vt.edu

WALLERSTEIN, I.
PERSONAL Born 09/28/1930, New York, NY, m, 1964, 3 children **DISCIPLINE** SOCIOLOGY **EDUCATION** Columbia Univ, BA, 51, MA, 54, PhD, 59. **CAREER** Columbia Univ, 58-71; prof, McGill Univ, 71-76; distinguished prof, Binghamton Univ, 76-. **HONORS AND AWARDS** Honorary degrees, Univ Paris, 76, York Univ, 95, Univ Libre du Bruxelles, 96, Univ Nac Aut de Mexico, 98; mem, Amer Acad of Arts and Sci, 98; **MEMBERSHIPS** African Studies Assn (president 72-73); Amer Sociology Assn; International soc Assn (president, 94-98); Eco Hist Assn. **RESEARCH** Hist capitalism; modern-world system; structures of knowledge **SELECTED PUBLICATIONS** Auth, The Modern World-System, 3 vol, 74, 80, 89; Unthinking Social Science, 91; After Liberatism, 95; Utopistics: Or Historical Choices for the 21st Century, 98. **CONTACT ADDRESS** Fermamd Braudel Ctr, SUNY, Binghamton, Binghamton, NY, 13901. **EMAIL** iwaller@binghamton.edu

WALLOT, JEAN-PIERRE
PERSONAL Born 05/22/1935, Valleyfield, PQ, Canada **DISCIPLINE** HISTORY **EDUCATION** Univ Montreal, BA, 54, LL, 57, MA, 57, PhD, 65. **CAREER** Lectr & asst prof, Univ Montreal, 61-66; hist, Mus Man, 66-69; assoc prof, Univ Toronto, 69-71; prof, Concordia Univ, 71-73; chmn, 73-75, vice dean arts & sci, 75-82, vice pres, 82-85, Univ Montreal; guest lectr, Univ Sherbrooke, 67, 68; guest lectr, Univ Que Montreal, 72; guest lectr, Univ BC, 72; guest lectr, Laval Univ, 73, 77; guest lectr, Univ Ottawa, 86-98; ; Nat Archivist, 85-97; mem, secy, Acad I, Royal Soc Can (sect pres, 85-87, pres-elect, 96-97, pres, 97-99). **HONORS AND AWARDS** Fel, Royal Soc Can, 78; Tyrrell Medal Royal Soc, 82; Acad des lettres du Quebec, 83; Doctorate hon) & Univ Medal, Univ Rennes (France), 87; Off, Ordre des Arts et Lettres de la Republique francaise, 87; Am Antiquarian Soc, 87; Off, Order Can, 91; Centenary Medal, Royal Soc, 94; Doctorate (hon), Univ Ottawa, 96; Jacques-Ducharme Prize, Asn Archivistes Que, 97. **MEMBERSHIPS** Can Hist Asn; Inst d'histoire de l'amerique francaise; Chevaliers de colomb. **RESEARCH** Economic and social history of Quebec **SELECTED PUBLICATIONS** Auth, Intrigues francaises et americaines au Canada 1800-1802, 65; auth, Un Quebec qui bougeait 1801-1810, 73; coauth, Les Imprimes dans le Bas-Canada 1794-1812, 73; ed, Memoires d'un Bourgeois de Montreal, 80; ed, France de l'Ouest et Quebec, 82; ed, Evolution et eclatement du monde rural, 86. **CONTACT ADDRESS** 395 Wellington St, Ottawa, ON, K1A 0N3.

WALSH, DAVID A.
DISCIPLINE ART HISTORY AND HISTORY **EDUCATION** Univ MN, PhD, 74. **CAREER** Assoc prof, Univ of Rochester. **HONORS AND AWARDS** NEH res grant, 89-91. **RESEARCH** Medieval art; archaeology; hist; art hist. **SELECTED PUBLICATIONS** Auth, Reconstructions of the Mill Buildings, In A Medieval Industrial Complex and its Landscape: The Metalworking, Watermills, and Workshops of Bordesley Abbey, York: Counc for Brit Archaeol Res Report, 93; Regionalism and Localism in Early Cistercian Architecture in England, Arte Medievale, II, vol 2; The Excavations of Cluny III by K.J. Conant, Le gouvernement d'Hugues de Semur Cluny, Actes du Colloque scientifique int, Cluny, 88 & The Iconography of the Bronze Doors of Barisanus of Trani, Gesta, XXI/2; coauth, Architecture of Cowdery's Down: a Reconsideration, Archaeol J, 150, 93. **CONTACT ADDRESS** Dept of Art and Art Hist, Univ of Rochester, 601 Elmwood Ave, Ste. 656, 414 Morey , Rochester, NY, 14642. **EMAIL** dwls@db1.cc.rochester.edu

WALSH, ELIZABETH
PERSONAL Born 05/30/1933, Cumberland, MD **DISCIPLINE** ENGLISH LITERATURE, MEDIEVAL STUDIES **EDUCATION** Manhattanville Col, BA, 55, MA, 63; Harvard Univ, PhD (English and Am lit), 73. **CAREER** Sec sch teacher English and related subjects, Acad of the Sacred Heart, Conn, 59-63 and Albany, NY, 64-67; dean freshman class, Manhattanville Col, 67; teaching fel English, Harvard Univ, 70-72, resident tutor, 72-73, instr, 73-74; asst prof, La State Univ, Baton Rouge, 74-75; asst prof, 75-78, ASSOC PROF ENGLISH, UNIV SAN DIEGO, 78-; Am Coun Learned Soc travel grant, 78. **MEMBERSHIPS** MLA; Medieval Acad Am; Asn Scottish Lit Studies; Dante Soc Am; Medieval Asn Pac. **RESEARCH** The concept of the hero in epic and romance; cultural influences on fifteenth and sixteenth century Scottish literature. **SELECTED PUBLICATIONS** Auth, 3 Middle English Charlemagne Romances in The Sultan of Babylon, the Siege of Milan, and The Tale of Ralph the Collier,J Medieval Studies, Vol 68, 93. **CONTACT ADDRESS** Dept of English, Univ of San Diego, 5998 Alcala Park, San Diego, CA, 92110-2492.

WALT, JOSEPH W.
PERSONAL Born 04/21/1924, Los Angeles, CA **DISCIPLINE** MODERN EUROPEAN HISTORY **EDUCATION** Univ Tenn, AB, 47, AM, 51; Northwestern Univ, PhD, 60. **CAREER** Teacher, High Sch, Tenn, 50-52; instr Europ hist, Univ Tenn, 52-63; teaching asst, Northwestern Univ, 53-55; from asst prof to assoc prof, 55-64, prof hist, 64-94, emer, Simpson Col, 94-. **MEMBERSHIPS** AHA; Mid E Inst; Hist Asn Liechtenstein. **RESEARCH** Modern Middle East; Swiss-Liechtenstein. **SELECTED PUBLICATIONS** Auth, Don Berry, Iowan, Herzberg, 74; Era of Levere, Banta, 75; ed, The Phoenix, Benson, 76; Beneath the Whispering Maples: The Hisotry of Simpson College, Simpson Col Press, 95. **CONTACT ADDRESS** Dept of History, Simpson Col, 701 N C St, Indianola, IA, 50125-1297.

WALTER, JOHN C.
PERSONAL Born 05/05/1933 **DISCIPLINE** HISTORY **EDUCATION** AR AM&N Coll, BS (Cum Laude) Mech Engrg, History; Univ of Bridgeport, MA Amer History; Univ of ME at Orono, PhD Afro-Amer & US History. **CAREER** Purdue Univ, instr history 1970-72, asst prof history 1972-73; IN Univ at Kokomo, vstg asst prof black politics 1971-73; John Jay Coll of Criminal Justice CUNY, assoc prof history, chmn black studies 1973-76; Bowdoin Coll, dir, asst prof history Afro-Amer Studies Prog 1976-80; Smith Coll, assoc prof Afro-Amer Studies 1980-. **MEMBERSHIPS** Dir Afro-Amer Studies Prog Bowdoin Coll 1976-80; org, 1st chmn 1976-80, exec bd mem 1978- New England Conf of the Natl Council for Black Studies; exec comm Five Coll Black Studies 1982-; bridge comm & instr Smith Coll 1980-; devel & org Bridges to Pluralism 1983-; contrib ed Jrnl of Afro-Amer inNY Life & History State Univ Coll NY 1976-, UMOJA A Scholarly Jrnl of Afro-Amer Affairs Univ of CO 1976-, Review of Afro-Amer Issues & Culture Syracuse Univ 1976-, New England Jrnl of Black Studies Hampshire Coll 1981-; mem Amer Historical Assoc, Assoc of Caribbean Historians, Assoc for the Study of African-Amer Life & History, Caribbean Studies Assoc, Coll Lang Assoc, New England Historical Assoc, Natl Assoc of Interdisciplinary Ethnic Studies, Org ofAmer Historians,So Historical Assoc; consultnison Univ 1979, Wesleyan Univ 1978; reader Natl Endowment for the Humanities, Univ Press of Amer. **SELECTED PUBLICATIONS** Num rsch, book reviews & publ incl, A Passion for Equality 1977, Politics & Africanity in West Indian Soc Brown Univ 1983, The Black Immigrant & PoliticalRadicalism in the Harlem Renaissance 61st Annual Conf of the Assoc for the Study of Afro-Amer Life & History 1976, Franklin D Roosevelt & the Arms Limitation 1932-41 Hofstra Univ Conf 1982, Politics & Africanity in West Indian Soc Brown Univ 1983, The Transformation of Afro-Amer Politics, The Contribs of theWest Indian Immigrant Colby Coll 1983, Women & Identity in the Caribbean Smith Coll Women's Studies Cluster Comm Sem 1983, Enterprise Zones, Conservative Ideology or Free-Floating Political Fantasy? Simon's Rock of Bard Coll Bulletin 1984. **CONTACT ADDRESS** Department of Afro-American Studies, Univ of Cincinnati, Cincinnati, OH, 45221.

WALTER, JOHN CHRISTOPHER
PERSONAL Born 05/05/1933, Oracabessa, Jamaica **DISCIPLINE** HISTORY **CAREER** From instr to asst prof hist, Purdue Univ, 70-73; chmn dept Black studies, John Jay Col Criminal Justice, 73-76; asst prof hist, 76-80, ASSOC PROF AFRO-AM STUDIES, 80-; Chmn, Ind Higher Educ Comt Afro-Am Studies, Ind State Dept Educ, 73. **MEMBERSHIPS** Asn Studies Afro-Am Life and Hist; Southern Hist Asn; AHA; Orgn Am Historians; Caribbean Hist Asn. **RESEARCH** Role of West Indians in american Black Leadership, 1900-2970; blacks and technology, 00-60; race and American foreign relations in the 20th century. **SELECTED PUBLICATIONS** Auth, Working People of California, Western Hist Quart, Vol 27, 96. **CONTACT ADDRESS** Afro-Am Ctr, Bowdoin Col, Brunswick, ME, 04011.

WALTER, RICHARD JOHN
PERSONAL Born 05/03/1939, Champaign, IL, m, 1969, 1 child **DISCIPLINE** HISTORY **EDUCATION** Duke Univ, BA, 61; Stanford Univ, PhD(hist), 66. **CAREER** From asst prof to assoc prof, 68-77, prof hist, Wash Univ, 77-, consult Latin Am hist, Fulbright-Hays Prog, 72-76. **MEMBERSHIPS** Latin Am Studies Asn; Conf Latin Am Hist. **RESEARCH** Latin American political history, with special concentration on Argentina. **SELECTED PUBLICATIONS** Auth, Student Politics in Argentina, Basic Bks, 68; The intellectual background of the 1918 University Reform in Argentina, Hisp Am Hist Rev, 5/69; Municipal politics and government in Buenos Aires: 1918-1930, J InterAmerican Studies & World Affairs, 5/74; The Socialist Party of Argentina, 1890-1930, Univ Tex, 77; Elections in the city of Buenos Aires during the first Yrigoyen Administration, Hisp Am Hist Rev, 78; Politics and Urban Growth in Buenos Aires, 1910-1942, Cambridge, 93; The Province of Buenos Aires and Argentine Politics, 1912-1943, Cambridge, 85. **CONTACT ADDRESS** Dept of History, Washington Univ, 1 Brookings Dr, St. Louis, MO, 63130-4899. **EMAIL** rjwalter@artsci.wustl.edu

WALTERS, E. GARRISON
PERSONAL Born 02/07/1944, Atlantic City, NJ, m, 1976 **DISCIPLINE** HISTORY **EDUCATION** Boston Univ, BA, 67, MA, 68; Ohio State Univ, PhD (hist), 72. **CAREER** Spec asst Provost admin, 72-74, ASST DEAN HUMANITIES, 74- and LECTR INT STUDIES, OHIO STATE UNIV, 75-; Asst dir, Ctr Slavic and East European Studies, Ohio State Univ, 77-78; ADJ ASST PROF, SLAVIC AND EAST EUROP LANG AND LIT, OHIO STATE UNIV, 78-; ED, BALKANISTICA, 80-. **RESEARCH** Contemporary Eastern Europe; the history of Southeastern Europe; Romanian history. **SELECTED PUBLICATIONS** Auth, of Walls and Bridges in the United States and Eastern Europe, Diplomatic Hist, Vol 17, 93. **CONTACT ADDRESS** Col of Humanities, Ohio State Univ, Columbus, OH, 43210.

WALTERS, ELIZABETH J.
DISCIPLINE ANCIENT EGYPTIAN, GREEK AND ROMAN ART AND ARCHITECTURE **EDUCATION** Vassar Col, BA; Inst Fine Arts, NY, MA, PhD. **CAREER** Assoc prof, Pa State Univ, 82-. **HONORS AND AWARDS** Norbert Schimmel fel, Metropolitan Museum Art; dir, Temple-Town Hierakonpolis Proj, Egypt. **MEMBERSHIPS** Assoc mem, Am Scho Class Stud, Athens. **RESEARCH** Greek sculpture for the Agora excavations. **SELECTED PUBLICATIONS** Auth, Attic Grave Reliefs that Represent Women in the Dress of Isis; Hesperia Supp XXII, Princeton. **CONTACT ADDRESS** Pennsylvania State Univ, 201 Shields Bldg, University Park, PA, 16802. **EMAIL** DrWalters@aol.com

WALTERS, GWENFAIR
DISCIPLINE CHURCH HISTORY **EDUCATION** Wellesley Col, BA; Gordon-Conwell Theol Sem, MDiv; Cambridge Univ, PhD. **CAREER** Consult, hist archv proj, Cambridge Univ; asst prof, 93-; adv to Women; dir, Edu Tech Develop, Gordon-Conwell Theol Sem, 93-. **RESEARCH** History of worship, spirituality, media, technology, and the arts in the Church. **SELECTED PUBLICATIONS** Ed, Towards Healthy Preaching. **CONTACT ADDRESS** Gordon-Conwell Theol Sem, 130 Essex St, South Hamilton, MA, 01982.

WALTERS, HUBERT EVERETT
PERSONAL Born 04/27/1933, Greenville, North Carolina, d **DISCIPLINE** MUSIC EDUCATION **EDUCATION** NC Central Univ, BA 1951-55; vA State Univ, 1959; E Carolina Univ, MM 1963-65; Boston Univ, DMA (pending) 1969-; Boston University, School of Theology, pursing MDiv. **CAREER** TX Coll Tyler, TX, chrmn dept of Music 1965-66; Shaw Univ Raleigh, NC, asst prof Music 1966-69; Harvard Univ, lctr on Black Music 1970-74; Goddard Coll VT, lecturer on Black Music 1971-73; Boston State Coll, asst proj of Music 1971-82; Boston Coll, lecturer on Black Music 1982-; Univ of MA-Boston, asst prof of Music 1982-. **HONORS AND AWARDS** LO Kelly Award Excell in Music NC Central Univ 1955; mem Pi Kappa Lambda; Natl Music Honor Soc; Martin Luther King, Jr flwshp Award from Woodrow Wilson Fdn 1969. **MEMBERSHIPS** V pres NC State Music Teachers 1963; mem Music Educators Natl Conf; mem Amer Choral Dir Assoc; Omega Psi Phi Frat; deacon Emmanuel Bapt Church; minister, Worship at Peoples Baptist Church, Boston MA. **CONTACT ADDRESS** Univ of MA, Harbor Campus Columbia Pt, Boston, MA, 02125.

WALTERS, RONALD
PERSONAL Born 07/20/1938, Wichita, Kansas, m **DISCIPLINE** AFRICAN-AMERICAN STUDIES **EDUCATION** Fisk Univ, BA History 1963; Amer Univ, MA 1966, PhD 1971. **CAREER** Georgetown & Syracuse Univ, instr; Brandeis Univ African & Afro-Amer Studies, chmn 1969-71; Howard Univ, chmn pol sci 1971-74, prof of pol sci; Univ of Maryland, prof and sr fellow, currently. **HONORS AND AWARDS** The Ida B Wells Barnett Awd Natl Alliance of Black School Educators 1985; Rockefeller Foundation Rsch Grant 1985; The Congressional Black Associates Awd 1986. **MEMBERSHIPS** Past pres African Heritage Studies Assoc; mem bd Natl Black Election Study, Inst of Social Rsch, Univ of MI; mem adv bd Southern Christian Leadership Conf; founder Natl Black Independent Political Party; secty/founding mem Natl Black Leadership Roundtable; founder/past mem Bd of TransAfrica; consultant United Nations Special Comm Against Apartheid of the Security Cncl. **SELECTED PUBLICATIONS** Speaks & writes on US Foreign Policies toward Africa & Black Amer Politics; over 70 articles in several scholarly jrnls; three books in press; Disting CommServ Awd Howard Univ 1982; Disting Scholar/Activists Awd The Black Scholar Magazine 1984. **CONTACT ADDRESS** Afro-American Studies Program, Univ of Maryland, Lefrak Hall, Ste 2169, College Park, MD, 20742. **EMAIL** rwalters@bss2.umd.edu

WALTERS, RONALD GORDON
PERSONAL Born 04/23/1942, Sacramento, CA, m, 1965, 1 child **DISCIPLINE** AMERICAN SOCIAL & CULTURAL HISTORY **EDUCATION** Stanford Univ, AB, 63; Univ CA, Berkeley, MA, 65, PhD, 71. **CAREER** Actg instr hist, Univ CA, Berkeley, 67-68; from instr to asst prof, 70-75, assoc prof, 75-81, prof hist, Johns Hopkins Univ, 81-, Nat Endowment for Humanities younger humanist fel, 74-75; Rockefeller Found hum fel, 77-78. **MEMBERSHIPS** Southern Hist Asn; AHA;

Orgn Am Historians. **RESEARCH** Am reform movements; sexual attitudes and behavior; popular entertainment. **SELECTED PUBLICATIONS** Ed, Primers for Prudery: Sexual Advice to Victorian America, Prentice-Hall, 73; The Antislavery Appeal: American Abolitionism After 1830, Johns Hopkins Univ, 76; American Reformers: 1815-1860, Hill & Wang, 78, rev ed, 97; Signs of the times: Clifford Geertz and historians, Social Res, autumn 80; Popular Culture, In: Encyclopedia of the United States in the Twentieth Century (Kutler, ed), Scribner's, 96; ed, Scientific Authority in Twentieth-Century America, Johns Hopkins Univ, 97. **CONTACT ADDRESS** Dept Hist, Johns Hopkins Univ, 3400 N Charles St, Baltimore, MD, 21218-2680. **EMAIL** rgw1@jhu.edu

WALTHER, THOMAS ROBERT
PERSONAL Born 02/26/1938, Placedo, TX, m, 1963, 3 children **DISCIPLINE** HISTORY **EDUCATION** Tex A&I Univ, BA, 59, MA, 64; Univ Okla, PhD(hist), 71. **CAREER** Field worker, State Dept Pub Welfare, Tex, 61-62; investr, US Civil Serv Comn, Tex, 62-64; from asst prof to assoc prof, 68-79, Prof Hist and Dept Chmn, Pittsburg State Univ, 79-. **MEMBERSHIPS** Orgn Am Historians; Western Hist Asn; Southern Hist Asn; Kans State Hist Soc. **RESEARCH** The American West; American economic history; 19th century United States history. **SELECTED PUBLICATIONS** Auth, Some aspects of economic mobility in Barrett Township of Thomas County, 1885-1905, Kans Hist Quart, autumn 71; Native white American emigrants to Kansas, Bull Kans State Col Pittsburg, 12/75; coauth, Crawford County: From coal to soybeans, 1900-1941, Heritage of Kans, spring 78; Industrialization in southeastern Kansas, 1870-1915, Heritage Great Plains, spring 81; Industrialization on the Frontier: A Case Study, Crawford County, Kansas, 1870-1915, Red River Hist Rev, Fall 81; Two Architects of Industrialization in Southeast Kansas: Morris Cliggitt and George Nicholson, The Little Blakans Rev, Winter 82-83; 100 Years of Excellence, A History of the Pittsburg & Midway Coal Company, 1885-1985, P&M Coal Company, 85; auth, The Governors and Lieutenent Governors from Southeast Kansas, The Little Balkans Rev, Winter 88-89. **CONTACT ADDRESS** Dept of History, Pittsburg State Univ, 1701 S Broadway St, Pittsburg, KS, 66762-7500. **EMAIL** twalther@pittstate.edu

WALTMAN, JEROLD LLOYD
PERSONAL Born 07/26/1945, Monroe, LA, m, 1986, 3 children **DISCIPLINE** POLITICAL SCIENCE **EDUCATION** La Tech, BA; Denver Univ, MA; Ind Univ, PhD. **CAREER** Kenkaker Community Col, 69-72; La Col, 76-78; Univ Southern Miss, 78-. **RESEARCH** Comparative public administration; labor market policy. **SELECTED PUBLICATIONS** Auth, American Government: Politics and Citizenship, Am Press, 98; The Political Origins of the U.S. Income Tax, Univ Press of Miss, 85; Copying Other Nations' Policies, Schenkman, 80; coauth, Minimum Wage Increases and the Business Failure Rate, J of Economic Issues, Spring 98. **CONTACT ADDRESS** Dept of Political Sci, Univ Southern Miss, Box 5108, Hattiesburg, MS, 39406.

WALTNER, ANN
DISCIPLINE HISTORY **EDUCATION** Univ Calif Berkeley, PhD. **CAREER** Assoc prof **RESEARCH** Chinese fiction. **SELECTED PUBLICATIONS** Auth, The Grand Secretary's Family: Three Generations of Women in the Family of Wang Hsi-Chueh, 92; Learning from a Woman: Ming Literati Responses to Tanyangzi, Int J Am Oriental Hist, 90; On Not Becoming a Heroine: Lin Dai-Yu and Cui Ying-ying, Signs, 89; The Moral Status of the Child in Late Imperial China: Childhood in Ritual and Law, Social Res, 86. **CONTACT ADDRESS** History Dept, Univ of Minnesota, Twin Cities, 614 Social Sciences Tower, 267 19th Ave S, Minneapolis, MN, 55455. **EMAIL** waltn001@tc.umn.edu

WALTON, BRIAN G.
DISCIPLINE JACKSONIAN PERIOD **EDUCATION** Vanderbilt Univ, PhD. **CAREER** Hist Dept, Western Carolina Univ **HONORS AND AWARDS** Coordr, Hist Day. **SELECTED PUBLICATIONS** Auth, The Greek and Roman Worlds, 80. **CONTACT ADDRESS** Western Carolina Univ, Cullowhee, NC, 28723.

WALTON, GUY E.
PERSONAL Born 10/18/1935, New York, NY, m, 1970, 1 child **DISCIPLINE** ART HISTORY **EDUCATION** Wesleyan Univ, BA, 57; NY Univ, MA, 62, PhD(art hist), 67. **CAREER** Prof, fine arts, Col of Arts and Sci, NY Univ. **HONORS AND AWARDS** Knight, 1st class, Royal Order of the Polar Star, Sweden. **MEMBERSHIPS** Col Art Asn; Soc of Archit Hist; Soc de Phistoire de l'art francais. **RESEARCH** 17th century Frank, Italy, Sweden and Russia. **SELECTED PUBLICATIONS** Auth, Versailles, the view from Sweden, NY, 88; Louis XIV's Versailles, Chicago, 86. **CONTACT ADDRESS** 100 Bleecker St., Apt 23A, New York, NY, 10012.

WALTZ, KENNETH NEAL
PERSONAL Born 06/08/1924, Ann Arbor, MI, m, 1949, 3 children **DISCIPLINE** POLITICAL SCIENCE **CAREER** Ford Prof, Univ CA, Berkeley, 71-94, Emeritus, 94-; res assoc, inst of War and Peace Studies and adjunct prof, Columbia Univ, 97-; vis appointments at various institutions, including Columbia, Harvard, the London School of Economics, Australian Nat Univ, Kings Col (London), the Woodrow Wilson Center, Peking and Fudan Universities. **SELECTED PUBLICATIONS** Auth, Man, the State, and War, 59; Foreign Policy and Democratic Politics, 67, 92; co-ed and co-auth, Conflict in World Politics, 71; co-ed, The Use of Force, 71, 4th ed 93; auth, Theory of International Politics, 79; The Spread of Nuclear Weapons, Adelphi Paper No 171, 81; Nuclear Myths and Political Realities, Am Political Science Rev, Sept 90, Heinz Eulau award for best article in the Review; The Emerging Structure of International Politics, Int Security, fall 93; co-auth, The Spread of Nuclear Weapons: A Debate, 95; auth, Evaluating Theories, Am Political Science Rev 91, Dec 97; Thoughts About Virtual Nuclear Arsenals, in Michael J Mazarr, ed, Nuclear Weapons in a Transformed World: The Challenge of Virtual Nuclear Arsenals, St Martin's, 97; Kant, la democratie et la paix, in Pierre Laberge, Guy Lafrance, and Denis Dumas, eds, L'annee 1795-Kant: Essai sur la Paix, Paris: Librarie Philosophique J Vrin, 97; Intimations of Multipolarity, Copenhagen: DUPI, in press; several translations into Chinese, Spanish, and Italian. **CONTACT ADDRESS** Inst of War and Peace Studies, Columbia Univ, 420 W 118th St, New York, NY, 10027.

WALZ, JOHN D.
PERSONAL Born 09/23/1929, Milbank, SD **DISCIPLINE** RUSSIAN AND EAST EUROPEAN HISTORY **EDUCATION** Univ Wyo, BA, 51; Syracuse Univ, MA, 61; PhD (hist), 67. **CAREER** Instr hist, Syracuse Univ, 62-64; From asst prof to assoc prof, 65-73, PROF HIST, CALIF STATE UNIV, HAYWARD, 73-; Exchange prof hist, Middlesex Polytech, London, 80-81. **MEMBERSHIPS** AHA; Am Asn Advan Slavic Studies. **RESEARCH** Twentieth century Russia; Russian armed forces before and during the revolution. **SELECTED PUBLICATIONS** Auth, Soviet Military Doctrine from Lenin to Gorbachev,1915-1991, Russ Hist Hist Russe, Vol 21, 94. **CONTACT ADDRESS** Dept of Hist, California State Univ, Hayward, Hayward, CA, 94542.

WALZER, MICHAEL
PERSONAL Born 03/03/1935, m, 2 children **DISCIPLINE** POLITICAL SCIENCE **EDUCATION** Brandeis Univ, BA, 56; Harvard Univ, PhD, 61. **CAREER** Prof Government, Harvard Univ, 66-80; PROF SOCIAL SCIENCE, INST ADVAN STUDY, 80-. **RESEARCH** Politics; Political theory; Moral philosopht. **SELECTED PUBLICATIONS** On Toleration, Yale Univ Press, 87. **CONTACT ADDRESS** School of Social Science, Inst for Advanced Studies, Princeton, NJ, 08540.

WANDYCZ, PIOTR STEFAN
PERSONAL Krakow, Poland **DISCIPLINE** MODERN EUROPEAN HISTORY **EDUCATION** Univ Grenoble, cert, 42; Cambridge Univ, BA, 48, MA, 52; Col of Europe, cert and London Sch Econ, PhD, 51. **CAREER** Res assoc, Mid-Europ Studies Ctr, 52-54; From instr to assoc prof hist, Ind Univ, 54-66; assoc prof, 66-68, PROF HIST, YALE UNIV, 68-; Soc Sci Res Coun grant, 58; Am Philos Soc grants, 60, 64 and 81; Ford Int Prog grant, 63; res fel, Russ Ctr, Harvard Univ, 63-65; Rockefeller Found grant, 63; vis prof, Columbia Univ, 67, 69 and 75; partic acad exchange with Poland and Czech, Int Res and Exchange Bd, 72-73; Guggenheim Mem Found fel, 77-78. **HONORS AND AWARDS** George L Beer Prize, AHA, 62; Alfred Jutzykowski Found Prize, 76., MA, Yale Univ, 68. **MEMBERSHIPS** AHA; Polish Hist Asn Gt Brit; Int Free Acad Sci and Lett, Paris; Polish Inst Arts and Sci in am; Czech Soc Arts and Sci in am. **RESEARCH** Twentieth century East European diplomatic history. **SELECTED PUBLICATIONS** Auth, the Popular Front and Central Europe in the Dilemmas of French Impotence, 1918-1940, Am Hist Rev, Vol 98, 93; Untitled, Am Hist Rev, Vol 99, 94; Untitled, Am Hist Rev, Vol 102, 97. **CONTACT ADDRESS** Dept of Hist, Yale Univ, New Haven, CT, 06520.

WANG, AIHE
DISCIPLINE HISTORY; LANGUAGE **EDUCATION** Higher Education Examination Committee, P.R.C., BA, 83; Chinese Acad of Social Sciences, MA, 86; MA, 90, PhD, Harvard Univ **CAREER** Asst prof, Purdue Univ, 95-. **CONTACT ADDRESS** Dept of History, Purdue Univ, 1358 University Hall, West Lafayette, IN, 47907-1358. **EMAIL** aihewang@purdue.edu

WANG, K.W.
PERSONAL Born 11/22/1954, Taipei, Taiwan **DISCIPLINE** HISTORY **EDUCATION** Stanford Univ, PhD, 85. **CAREER** Vis Assoc Prof, 96-97, Ntl Chengchi Univ Taiwan; vis Lectr, 93, Hong Kong Univ. **MEMBERSHIPS** AAS; Soc Stud 20th Century China in NA; AACS. **RESEARCH** Nationalist Party; Wartime China, 1937-1945. **SELECTED PUBLICATIONS** Auth, Modern China: An Encyclopedia of History Culture and Nationalism, NY, Garland Pub, 98. **CONTACT ADDRESS** History Dept, St Michael's Col, Colchester, VT, 05439. **EMAIL** kwang@smcvt.edu

WANG, LIPING
DISCIPLINE HISTORY **EDUCATION** Univ Calif San Diego, PhD, 97. **CAREER** Asst prof **RESEARCH** Social and cultural history of the Late Imperial China and the Republican China (1911-1949). **SELECTED PUBLICATIONS** Auth, Tradition as a Modern Invention: Tourism and Spatial Changes in Hangzhou: 1900-1927, Univ Hawaii. **CONTACT ADDRESS** History Dept, Univ of Minnesota, Twin Cities, 614 Social Sciences Tower, 267 19th Ave S, Minneapolis, MN, 55455. **EMAIL** lipin003@tc.umn.edu

WANG, Q. EDWARD
DISCIPLINE MODERN CHINESE AND JAPANESE HISTORY, CHINESE CULTURAL HISTORY **EDUCATION** East China Normal Univ, Shanghai, BA, MA; Syracuse Univ, PhD, 92. **CAREER** Instr, chp, dept Hist, coordr, Asian/Asian Am Stud prog, Rowan Col of NJ. **RESEARCH** Chinese cultural and intellectual history; comparative historiography. **SELECTED PUBLICATIONS** Boks and articles on Chinese cultural and intellectual history and comparative historiography in both Chinese and English. **CONTACT ADDRESS** Rowan Col of NJ, Glassboro, NJ, 08028-1701.

WANK, SOLOMON
PERSONAL Born 03/16/1930, Brooklyn, NY, m, 1955, 2 children **DISCIPLINE** MODERN EUROPEAN HISTORY **EDUCATION** NY Univ, BA, 51; Columbia Univ, MA, 52, PhD (hist), 61. **CAREER** Lectr hist, Brooklyn Col, 57-58, 59-60; lectr, City Col New York, 60-61; From asst prof to assoc prof hist, 61-73, chmn dept, 65-71, PROF HIST, FRANKLIN and MARSHALL COL, 73-; Lectr, Pace Col, 57-58, 59; Franklin and Marshall Col fac res grant, 64, 73-75 and 76-78; Fulbright fel, Vienna, 64-65; Am Coun Learned Soc fel, 67-68; mem Mid Atlantic Regional Evaluating Comt for younger scholar fels and summer stipends, Nat Found for Humanities, 67-71; vis scholar, Inst ECent Europe, Columbia Univ, 79-80; distinguished vis prof liberal arts, Concordia Univ. **MEMBERSHIPS** AHA; Conf Group Cent Europ Hist; Conf Peace Res in Hist; AAUP; Conf Group for Study Nationalism. **RESEARCH** Europe in the th and 20th centuries; diplomatic history of Europe, 1871-14; Habsburg monarchy, 1867-18. **SELECTED PUBLICATIONS** Auth, the Habsburg Monarchy Among the Great Powers, Ctrl European Hist, Vol 26, 93; The Decline and Fall of the Habsburg Empire 1815-, Ctrl European Hist, Vol 26, 93; Desperate Counsel in Vienna in July 14 And Full-Text of Promemoria with Translation ApPENded - Molden,Berthold Unpublished Memorandum, Ctrl European Hist, Vol 26, 93; The Protocols of the Ministerial Council of the Austro Hungarian Monarchy 1896-1907, J Modern Hist, Vol 66, 94; Vienna Washington in a J of Diplomatic Relations, 1838-1917, Ctrl European Hist, Vol 27, 94; Between Berlin and St Petersburg in Foreign Policy of the Austro Hungarian Empire Under Kalnoky, Gustave, 1881-1895, Ctrl European Hist, Vol 28, 95. **CONTACT ADDRESS** Dept of Hist, Franklin and Marshall Col, Lancaster, PA, 17604.

WAPNER, PAUL
DISCIPLINE GLOBAL ENVIRONMENTAL POLITICS **EDUCATION** Univ Colo, BA, Univ Chicago, MA, Princeton Univ, PhD. **CAREER** Asst prof, Am Univ. **HONORS AND AWARDS** Exec dir, Public Int Law & Policy Gp **RESEARCH** Social movements and international relations theory. **SELECTED PUBLICATIONS** Auth, Environmental Activism and World Civic Politics, Albany: State Univ NY, 96. **CONTACT ADDRESS** American Univ, 4400 Massachusetts Ave, Washington, DC, 20016.

WARD, DAVID
PERSONAL Born 07/08/1938, Manchester, United Kingdom, m, 1964, 2 children **DISCIPLINE** GEOGRAPHY **EDUCATION** Univ Leeds, UK, BA, MA; Univ Wisconsin Madison, MSc, PhD. **CAREER** Univ Wis Mad, Andrew H Clark Prof, geog, 69-, Chanc, 93-. **HONORS AND AWARDS** Guggenheim fel, Alls fel, Fulbright fel. **MEMBERSHIPS** Asn Am Geog. **RESEARCH** Hist geog, urban geog. **SELECTED PUBLICATIONS** Cities and Immigrants: A Geography of change in Nineteenth Century America, NY, Oxford Univ Press, 71; Poverty, Ethnicity and the American City, Changing Conceptions of the Slum and the Ghetto, 1840-1920, NY, Cambridge Univ Press, 89; numerous articles and dissertations. **CONTACT ADDRESS** Dept Geography, Univ Wisconsin, Bascom Hall, Madison, WI, 53706. **EMAIL** ward@mail.bascom.wisc.edu

WARD, HARRY M.
PERSONAL Born 07/30/1929, Lafayette, IN **DISCIPLINE** AMERICAN HISTORY **EDUCATION** William Jewell Col, BA, 51; Columbia Univ, MA, 54, PhD, 60. **CAREER** Asst prof hist, Georgetown Col, 59-61; from asst prof to assoc prof, Morehead State Col, 61-65; assoc prof hist, 65-78, chmn dept, Univ Col, 70-74, PROF AM HIST, UNIV RICHMOND, 78-, Wm Binford Vest prof his, 93-, Vis assoc prof, Southern Ill Univ, 67-68; res grants, Plimoth Plantation, 68-69, Va Soc Cincinnati, 70, 73 & City of Richmond, 73; mem comt Am hist, col level exams, Educ Testing Serv, Princeton, NJ, 69; mem Richmond Bicentennial Comn, 72-80; consult, US Bicentennial Media Corp, 74-76. **HONORS AND AWARDS** Frances Tav-

ern Museum Book Award, 90; Va Soc Sci Asn Scholar Award, 92. **MEMBERSHIPS** AHA; Southern Hist Asn; Orgn Am Historians; Va Hist Soc; fel Pilgrim Soc. **RESEARCH** American colonial and Revolutionary history; American frontier; early Virginia history. **SELECTED PUBLICATIONS** Auth, The United Colonies of New England, 1643-90, Vantage, 61; Department of War, 1781-1795, Univ Pittsburgh, 62; Dominion interlude, In: The Colonial Experience, Houghton, 66; Unite or Die: Intercolony Relations, 1690-1763, 71 & Statism in Plymouth Colony, 73, Kennikat; Search for American identity: Early historians of New England, In: Perspectives On Early American History, Harper, 73; coauth, Richmond During the Revolution, 1775-1783, Univ Va, 78; Auth, Duty, Honor or Country: General George Weedon and the American Revolution, Am Philos Soc, 79; auth, Richmond: An Illustrated History, Windsor, 85; auth, Charles Scott and the Spirit of 76, University of Virginia, 88; auth, Major General Adams Stephen and the Cause of America Liberty, Univ Va, 89; auth, Colonial America, 1607-1763, Prentice Hall, 91; auth, The American Revolution: Nationhood Achieved, 1763-1788, St. Martin's, 95; auth, General William Maxwell and the New Jersey Continentals, Greenwood Press, 97. **CONTACT ADDRESS** Dept of Hist, Univ of Richmond, 28 Westhampton Way, Richmond, VA, 23173-0002.

WARD, JAMES A.
DISCIPLINE HISTORY **EDUCATION** Purdue Univ, BA, 64, MA, 65; La State Univ, PhD, 69. **CAREER** Prof. **SELECTED PUBLICATIONS** Auth, That Man Haupt: A Biography of Herman Haupt Baton, La State Univ, 73; Edgar Thomson: Master of the Pennsylvania, Greenwood, 80; Railroads and the Character of America, Univ Tennessee, 86; coauth, American History: A Brief View, Brown, 78; ed, Southern Rallroadman: Conductor Nimrod I. Bell's Memoirs, Northern Ill Univ, 93; The Fall of the Packard Motor Car Company, Stanford, 95; co-ed, Railroads in America, Northern Ill Univ. **CONTACT ADDRESS** Dept of History, 615 McCallie, Chattanooga, TN, 37403. **EMAIL** univrel@cecasun.utc.edu

WARD, JAMES RANDOLPH
PERSONAL Born 10/14/1939, Jacksonville, TX, m, 1970, 2 children **DISCIPLINE** AMERICAN HISTORY **EDUCATION** Tex Christian Univ, BA, 61, MA, 63, PhD (hist), 72. **CAREER** Instr hist, Navarro Jr Col, 63-67; asst prof, 70-74, assoc prof, 74-80, PROF HIST, ANGELO STATE UNIV, 80-. **MEMBERSHIPS** Orgn Am Historians; Southwestern Soc Sci Asn. **RESEARCH** American frontier history; American diplomatic history; Texas history. **SELECTED PUBLICATIONS** Auth, the Nahuas After the Conquest in a Social and Cultural History of the Indians of Central Mexico, 16th Through 18th Centuries, Hist, Vol 78, 93; The Floundering of Delivery Under Section of Cogsa in a Proposal to Steady Its Meaning in Light of Its Legislative History, J Maritime Law Commerce, Vol 24, 93; The British in Java, 1811-1816, Hist, Vol 78, 93; Region and State in Latin america Past, Hist, Vol 79, 94; Society, Economy and Defense in 17th Century Peru in the Administration of the Count of Alba De Liste, Hist, Vol 79, 94; The Industrial Revolution and British Imperialism, 1750-1850, Econ Hist Rev, Vol 47, 94; Land Without Evil in Utopian Journeys Across The South American Watershed, Hist, Vol 79, 94; Aguirre in the Re Creation of a 16th Century Journey Across South America, Hist, Vol 79, 94; Historical Dictionary of Indonesia, Hist, Vol 79, 94; Mariategui and Latin american Marxist Theory, Hist , Vol 79, 94; The PENguin History of Latin america, Hist, Vol 79, 94; Portuguese Trade in asia Under the Habsburgs, 1580-1640, Hist, Vol 79, 94; Trade, War and Revolution in Exports from Spain to Spanish America 1797-1820, Hist, Vol 79, 94; The Origins of Industrial Capitalism in India in Business Strategies and the Working Classes in Bombay,1900-1940, Econ Hist Rev, Vol 48, 95; Slave Society in the Danish West Indies, Econ Hist Rev, Vol 48, 95; The Economy and Material Culture of Slaves in Goods and Chattels on the Sugar Plantations of Jamaica and Louisiana, Econ Hist Rev, Vol 48, 95; Local Suppliers of Credit in the Third World, 1750-1960, Hist, Vol 80, 95;The World of Maluku in Eastern Indonesia in the Early Modern Period, Hist, Vol 80, 95; Engines of Growth in the State and Transnational Auto Companies in Brazil, Econ Hist Rev, Vol 48, 95; A World on the Move in the Portuguese in africa, Asia, and America, 1415-1808, Hist, Vol 80, 95; Africa and Africans in the Making of the Atlantic World, 1400-1680, Hist, Vol 80, 95;The Economics of Emancipation in Jamaica and Barbados, 1823-1843, J Imperial Commonwealth Hist, Vol 24, 96; The America in the Spanish World Order, the Justification for Conquest in the 17th Century, Hist, Vol 81, 96; Religious Regimes in Peru in Religion and State Development in a Long Term Perspective and the Effects in the Andean Village of Zurite, Hist, Vol 81, 96; The Armature of Conquest in Spanish Accounts of the Discovery of America, 1492-1589, Hist, Vol 81, 96; Frontier Development in Land, Labor, and Capital on the Wheatlands of Argentina and Canada 1890-1914, Hist, Vol 81, 96; The British in the America 1480-1815, History, Vol 81, 96; Africa, Asia and South America Since 1800 -1900, A Bibliographical Guide, Hist, Vol 82, 97; Governance and Society in Colonial Mexico in Chihuahua in the 18th Century, Hist, Vol 82, 97; Encountering Development in the Making and Unmaking of the Third World, Hist, Vol 82, 97. **CONTACT ADDRESS** Dept of Hist, Angelo State Univ, San Angelo, TX, 76901.

WARD, JOHN WILLIAM
PERSONAL Born 12/21/1922, Boston, MA, m, 1949, 3 children **DISCIPLINE** AMERICAN CIVILIZATION **EDUCATION** Harvard Col, AB, 45; Univ Minn, MA, 50, PhD (Am civilization), 53. **CAREER** From instr to assoc prof English and Am civilization, Princeton Univ, 52-57, assoc prof hist, 58-64, chmn Am civilization prog, 61-64; prof hist, Amherst Col, 64-79, pres, 71-79; PRES, AM COUN LEARNED SOC, 82-; Coun Humanities fel, Princeton Univ, 54-55; Guggenheim fels, 58 and 68; fel, Inst Advan Studies Behav Sci, 63-64; Fulbright lectr Am hist, Univ Reading, 67-68; Phi Betta Kappa distinguished lectr, 70-71. **HONORS AND AWARDS** LLD, Amherst Col, 79. **MEMBERSHIPS** Am Studies Asn; AHA: Soc Am Historians. **RESEARCH** Relation of ideas and expressive forms to social forces in america. **SELECTED PUBLICATIONS** Auth, Down Deep in Dixie in Black South Fiction in the Privileged Place of Story, African Am Rev, Vol 27, 93; Black South Literature in Before Day Annotations for Jackson, Blyden, African Am Rev, Vol 27, 93; Southern Visions in What We Seen, What We Foresee in from the Lions View, African Am Rev, Vol 27, 93; Black Southern Culture in 1st Words, African Am Rev, Vol 27, 93; Afterword and Black Southern Culture and the Reason Its Music Was Not Examined in This Issue in Why No Music, African Am Rev, Vol 27, 93; Introduction and the Culture of the Black South in Seeing Instead of Just Looking, African Am Rev, Vol 27, 93; Sayings, Sermons, Tall Tales and Lies in Contemporary Black Poetry, African Am Rev, Vol 27, 93; Reading South in Poets Mean and Poems Signify, A Note on Origins, African Am Rev, Vol 27, 93; We Aint Playing and the Concept of a Black Theater of the South, African Am Rev, Vol 27, 93; Serious, Georgia Rev, Vol 48, 94; Denizens Vieux Carre, Mississippi Quart, Vol 48, 95; Triangulation, Lit Med, Vol 15, 96; The Norton Anthology of African American Literature, Am Book Rev, Vol 18, 97. **CONTACT ADDRESS** Am Coun Learned Soc, 800 Third Ave, New York, NY, 10022.

WARD, ROBERT DAVID
PERSONAL Born 02/15/1929, Montevallo, AL, m, 1953, 3 children **DISCIPLINE** AMERICAN HISTORY **EDUCATION** Auburn Univ, BS, 50, MS, 51; Univ NC, PhD, 57. **CAREER** From asst prof to assoc prof Am hist, 55-60, head dept, 69-71, PROF AM HIST, GA SOUTHERN COL, 60-. **MEMBERSHIPS** Southern Hist Asn; Am Mil Inst; Co Mil Historians. **RESEARCH** American military policy, 00 to present; Alabama history, 1865-00; new South. **SELECTED PUBLICATIONS** Auth, Alabama in the History of a Deep South State, J Am Hist, Vol 82, 95. **CONTACT ADDRESS** Dept of Hist, Georgia So Univ, Statesboro, GA, 30458.

WARD, TOM R.
DISCIPLINE MUSIC **EDUCATION** Univ Pittsburgh, MA, PhD. **CAREER** Prof, 69-, Univ IL Urbana Champaign. **MEMBERSHIPS** Am Musicol Soc. **RESEARCH** Music and liturgy in the Middle Ages and Renaissance; music and music theory in univ(s) of the fourteenth and fifteenth centuries. **SELECTED PUBLICATIONS** Auth, The Polyphonic Office Hymn 1400-1520: A Descriptive Catalog; pubs in Musica Disciplina; Journal of the American Musicological Society; Early Music History. **CONTACT ADDRESS** Dept of Music, Univ Illinois Urbana Champaign, E Gregory Drive, PO Box 52, Champaign, IL, 61820. **EMAIL** t-ward2@uiuc.edu

WARD, WILLIAM R.
DISCIPLINE MODERN HISTORY **EDUCATION** Oxford, BA, 46, MA, 51, PhD, 51. **CAREER** Emer Prof Modern History, Durham. **RESEARCH** Church history. **SELECTED PUBLICATIONS** Fel Publ, Pastoral Office and the General Priesthood in the Great Awakening, Studies in Church Hist 26, 89; auth, Religion and Society in England, 1790-1850, 72; Early Victorian Methodism, 76; Theology, Sociology, and Politics: The German Protestant Social Conscience, 79, Journals and Dioceses of John Wellesley, 86; The Protestant Evangelical Awakening, 1725-50: A European View, 92; Faith and Faction, 93; Parson and Parish in 18th Century Surrey, 94; Parson and Parish in 18th Century Hampshire, 95. **CONTACT ADDRESS** 21 Grenehurst Way, Petersfield, ., GU31 4AZ.

WARDLE, LYNN DENNIS
DISCIPLINE INTERNATIONAL RELATIONS AND POLITICAL SCIENCE **EDUCATION** Brigham Young Univ, BA, 71; J D Duke Univ, JD, 74. **CAREER** Assoc, Streigh, Lang, Weeks & Cardon, 75-78; Law clerk, Hon Jon Sinca, US Dist Crt, Dist Col, 74-75; Assoc Prof, J Reuben Clark Law school, Brigham Young Univ. **MEMBERSHIPS** Intl Soc of Fam Law, Am Law Inst. **RESEARCH** Fam Law, Legal Hist. **CONTACT ADDRESS** Brigham Young Univ, Dept Law, Provo, UT, 84602. **EMAIL** wardlel@lawgate.byu.edu

WARE, RONALD DEAN
PERSONAL Born 10/05/1928, Dayton, KY, m, 1968, 2 children **DISCIPLINE** MEDIEVAL HISTORY **EDUCATION** Univ Cincinnati, BA, 50; Univ Wis, MS, 56, PhD(hist), 60. **CAREER** Res assoc hist, Univ Wis, 59-60; asst prof, Tex Technol Col, 60-61 & Ill State Univ, 61-64; from asst prof to assoc prof, 64-78, prof hist, Univ Mass, Amherst, 78-, Fulbright vis prof medieval hist, Trinity Col, Dublin, 70-71. **HONORS AND AWARDS** Outstanding Teacher, Col of Humanities and Fine Arts, 94-95. **MEMBERSHIPS** Mediaeval Acad Am; New England Medieval Conf (Pres, 93-94); New Eng Hist Asn; Renaissance Society of Am; Midwest Medieval Conf (Pres, 89-90). **RESEARCH** Medieval economic and social history; Anglo-Saxon diplomatics; medieval historiography. **SELECTED PUBLICATIONS** Auth, Hisperic Latin and Hermeneutic Tradition, In: Studies in Medieval Culture, Western Mich Univ, 66; 14 articles in New Catholic Encyclopedia, McGraw, 67; Chronology, Theory and Practice, In: Medieval Studies: An Introduction, Syracuse Univ, 76, sub ed, 92. **CONTACT ADDRESS** Dept of Hist, Univ of Mass, Amherst, MA, 01003-0002.

WARE, THOMAS C.
PERSONAL Born 04/07/1929, Louisville, KY, m, 1953, 5 children **DISCIPLINE** ENGLISH INTERDISCIPLINARY STUDIES **EDUCATION** Univ Louisville, BA, 57; Univ NC, Chapel Hill, MA, 60, PhD (English), 69. **CAREER** From instr to asst prof, Univ Cincinnati, 62-67; asst prof, Univ Chattanooga, 67-69; assoc prof, 69-74, PROF ENGLISH and HEAD DEPT, UNIV TENN CHATTANOOGA, 74-; Nat Endowment for Humanities summer grants, Columbia Univ, 77 and 81. **MEMBERSHIPS** Asn Depts English; SAtlantic Mod Lang Asn. **RESEARCH** Anglo-Irish literature; British literature 1800-20; modern British novel. **SELECTED PUBLICATIONS** Auth, Naturalism in the European Novel in New Critical Perspectives, Eng Lit Transition, Vol 36, 93. **CONTACT ADDRESS** Dept of English, Univ of Tenn, Chattanooga, TN, 37401.

WARGA JR., RICHARD G.
DISCIPLINE GREEK, LATIN, MYTHOLOGY, SCIENTIFIC TERMINOLOGY **EDUCATION** Univ Ill, Urbana-Champaign, PhD, 88. **CAREER** Instr Classics, coordr, elem Lat crse, La State Univ. **RESEARCH** Epigraphy; papyrology; Coptic studies. **SELECTED PUBLICATIONS** Auth, A Coptic-Greek Stele from Memphis, Tennessee, in Chronique d'Egypte LXVI, 91; A Repayment of a Loan, in Zeitschrift f(r Papyrologie und Epigraphik 100, 94. **CONTACT ADDRESS** Dept of For Lang and Lit, Louisiana State Univ, 122 A Prescott Hall, Baton Rouge, LA, 70803. **EMAIL** warga@homer.forlang.lsu.edu

WARING, STEPHEN P.
PERSONAL Born 10/04/1958, NE, s **DISCIPLINE** HISTORY **EDUCATION** Doane Col, BA, 80; Univ Iowa, MA, 82, PhD, 88. **CAREER** Asst prof, 88-94, ASSOC PROF HIST, 94-, UNIV ALA, HUNTSVILLE. **HONORS AND AWARDS** Fel Aerospace hist, AHA; Outstanding Teach, 95-96; UAH Alumni Fdn, 97-98. **MEMBERSHIPS** AHA **RESEARCH** Hist tech; labor hist; intellectual hist; policy hist. **SELECTED PUBLICATIONS** Auth, Taylorism Transformed: Scientific Management Theory Since 1945, Univ NC Press, 91; auth, At the Center: The History of NASA's Marshall Space Flight Center, 1960-1990, under rev by NASA-MSFC; auth, The Challenger Investigations: Engineering Knowledge, and Politics, 1971-1988, forthcoming; Peter Drucker, MBO, and the Corporatist Critique of Scientific Management in A Mental Revolution: The Scientific Management Movement After Taylor, Ohio State Univ Press, 92; Cold Calculus: The Impact of the Cold War on Operations Research, in Radical History Review 63, 95. **CONTACT ADDRESS** History Dept, Univ of Alabama, Huntsville, Huntsville, AL, 35899. **EMAIL** warings@email.uah.edu

WARK, ROBERT RODGER
PERSONAL Born 10/07/1924, Edmonton, AB, Canada **DISCIPLINE** HISTORY OF ART **EDUCATION** Univ Alta, BA, 44, MA, 46; Harvard Univ, MA, 49, PhD (fine arts), 52. **CAREER** Sessional instr English, Univ Alta, 46-48; teaching fel fine arts, Harvard Univ, 50-51, instr, 52-54; instr hist art, Yale Univ, 54-56; CUR, ART COLLECTIONS, HUNTINGTON LIBR and ART GALLERY, 56-; Lectr art, Calif Inst Technol, 60 and Univ Calif, Los Angeles, 67-81. **MEMBERSHIPS** Col Art Asn Am; Asn Art Mus Dir. **RESEARCH** British art of the Georgian period. **SELECTED PUBLICATIONS** Auth, the Gentle Pastime of Extra Illustrating Books and Relationships Between Visual and Verbal Communication and the Increase of Book Illumination in Mid 18th Century, Huntington Libr Quart, Vol 56, 93; Thackeray Drawings for Cornhill To Cairo in the Huntington Library, Huntington Libr Quart, Vol 57, 94. **CONTACT ADDRESS** Henry E. Huntington Libr and Art Gallery, San Marino, CA, 91108.

WARK, WESLEY K.
PERSONAL Born 12/31/1952, Edmonton, AB, Canada **DISCIPLINE** INTERNATIONAL RELATIONS **EDUCATION** Carlton Univ, BA, 75; Cambridge Univ, MA, 77; London Sch Econ, PhD, 84. **CAREER** Vis prof, McGill Univ, 83-84; assoc prof, Univ Calgary, 84-88; ASSOC PROF INTERNATIONAL RELATIONS, UNIV TORONTO 88-. **HONORS AND AWARDS** Alta Heritage Scholar, 79-83 **MEMBERSHIPS** Founding mem, Can Asn for Security & Intelligence Studies; mem, Brit Stud Group on Intelligence. **SELECTED PUBLICATIONS** Auth, The Ultimate Enemy, 85; auth, Spy Fiction, Spy Films and Real Intelligence, 91; auth, Espionage Past, Present, Future?, 93; ed, Intelligence Nat Security J, 86-. **CONTACT ADDRESS** Trinity Col, Univ of Toronto, Toronto, ON, M5S 1H8.

WARKENTIN, LARRY R.
PERSONAL Born 08/14/1940, Reedley, CA, m, 1962, 2 children **DISCIPLINE** MUSIC **EDUCATION** Tabor Col, BA, 62; Calif St Univ, MA, 64; Univ So Ca, DMA, 67. **CAREER** Chmn, tchr, music dept, 66-, Fresno Pacific Univ. **HONORS AND AWARDS** Calif Music Tchrs, 1st place comp, 84; ASCAP, classical comp, 88-. **MEMBERSHIPS** Amer Soc of Composers Authors & Pub; Calif Music Tchrs Asn. **RESEARCH** Music composition; church music **SELECTED PUBLICATIONS** Auth, How Wondrous Great, Lorenz Music, OH, 90; auth, From the Hands, What does the Lord Require, Wonder of Wonders, When Grief is Raw, Hymnal: a Worship Book, Brethren Press, 92; art, Caring about Music in the Church, Dir Jour, 93; art, guest ed, Caring about Music in the Church, Direction Jour, 93; rev, On The Aisle, Fresno Bee, 88-95; auth, Huldrich Zwingli, Dict of Art, Macmillan, 96; auth, Alleluia, Moon of Hope Pub, 96; auth, When Grief is Raw, Covenant Hymnal, Covenant Press, 96; auth, Like Candle Flame, Lumina Music, 98. **CONTACT ADDRESS** Fresno Pacific Col, 1717 S Chestnut Ave, Fresno, CA, 93702-9863. **EMAIL** lwarkent@fresno.edu

WARLICK, M.E.
DISCIPLINE 18TH THROUGH 20TH CENTURY EUROPEAN ART, CONTEMPORARY ART **EDUCATION** Univ Md, PhD, 84. **CAREER** Assoc prof-. **RESEARCH** Max Ernst, Gustav Klimt, alchemy, surrealism, contemporary women artists. **SELECTED PUBLICATIONS** Publ, Art Jour, Leonardo, Art Bulletin, The Philosopher's Stones. **CONTACT ADDRESS** Dept of Art Hist, Univ Denver, 2199 S Univ Blvd, Denver, CO, 80208.

WARMBRUNN, WERNER
DISCIPLINE HISTORY **EDUCATION** Cornell Univ, BA; Stanford Univ, MA, PhD. **CAREER** Prof emer; dir, Pitzer Hist and Archiv Proj. **RESEARCH** German History, History of the Second World War. **SELECTED PUBLICATIONS** Auth, The German Occupation of Belgium, 1940 - 1949, Peter Lang, 93. **CONTACT ADDRESS** Dept of Hist, Pitzer Col, 1050 N. Mills Ave., Claremont, CA, 91711-6101.

WARNER, R. STEPHEN
PERSONAL Born 12/07/1941, Oakland, CA, m, 1979, 2 children **DISCIPLINE** SOCIOLOGY **EDUCATION** Univ Calif Berkeley, PhD, 72. **CAREER** Asst prof Sociology, Sonoma State Col, 67-78; actg asst prof, Univ Calif Berkely, 69-70; lectr to asst prof Sociology, Yale Univ, 70-76; asst prof to Prof of sociology, Univ ILL Chicago, 76-.. **HONORS AND AWARDS** Guggenheim fel, 74-75; NEH, 91-92; Inst Advanced Study, 88-89 **MEMBERSHIPS** Am Sociol Asn; Asn for Sociol Relig; Soc for Sci Study Relig. **RESEARCH** Contemporary American religion. **SELECTED PUBLICATIONS** Auth, A Work in Progress Toward a New Paradigm for the Sociological Study of Religion in the United States, Am Jour Sociol, 93; The Place of the Congragation in the American Religious Configuration, New Perspectives in the Study of Congregations, Am Congregations, Univ Chicago Press, 94; The Metropolitan Community Churches and the Gay Agenda: The Power of Pentecostalism and Essentialism, Sex, Lies, and Sanctity: Religion and Deviance in Contemporary North America, JAI Press, 95; Religion, Boundaries, and Bridges: The 1996 Paul Hanly Furfey Lecture, Sociol Relig, 97; Approaching Religious Diversity: Barriers, Byways, and Beginnings, Sociol Relig, 98; coed Gatherings in Disapora: Religious Communities and the New Immigration, Temple Univ Press, 98. **CONTACT ADDRESS** Sociology Dept M/C 312, Univ Chicago, 1007 W Harrison, Chicago, IL, 60607-7140. **EMAIL** RSWARNER@U/C.EDU

WARNER, ROBERT MARK
PERSONAL Born 06/28/1927, Montrose, CO, m, 1954, 2 children **DISCIPLINE** AMERICAN HISTORY **EDUCATION** Muskingum Col, BA, 49; Univ Mich, MA, 53, PhD, 58. **CAREER** Teacher high sch, Colo, 49-50; asst cur, 57-61, asst dir, 61-66, dir, Mich Hist collections, Univ Mich, Ann Arbor, 66-71, from lectr to prof hist, 71-96, prof libr sci, 74-96; Archivist of US, 80-85, Mem, Int Coun Arch, 76-; bd dirs, Woodrow Wilson Int Ctr Scholars; LHD DePaul Univ, 83; Exec Comt 84-88. **HONORS AND AWARDS** HHD, Westminster Col, 81; LLD, Muskingum, 81; Dean, Univ of Mich, Sch of Infor, 85-92; Univ Hist, 95-; Dean Emeritus, 96-; Prof Emeritus of Infor, 96-; Prof Emeritus of Hist, 96-. **MEMBERSHIPS** AHA; Orgn Am Historians; fel Soc Am Archivists (vpres, 75-76, pres, 76-77). **RESEARCH** Progressive movement; Michigan history; archival management. **SELECTED PUBLICATIONS** Auth, Profile of a Profession: A History of the Michigan State Dental Association, Wayne State Univ, 63; coauth, The Modern Manuscript Library, Scarecrow, 66; co-ed, A Michigan Reader: 1865 to the Present, Eerdmans, 74. **CONTACT ADDRESS** School of Information, Univ of Mich, 550 E University Ave, Ann Arbor, MI, 48109-1092. **EMAIL** archlib@umich.edu

WARNER, TED J
PERSONAL Born 03/02/1929, Ogden, UT, m, 1953, 3 children **DISCIPLINE** WESTERN AMERICAN HISTORY **EDUCATION** Brigham Young Univ, BS, 55, MS, 58; Univ NMex, PhD (hist), 64. **CAREER** Instr hist, Col Eastern Utah, 56-58; spec col librn, Univ NMex, 60-62; assoc prof, 62-72, PROF HIST AND CHMN DEPT, BRIHAM YOUNG UNIV, 72-; MEM, COLONIAL NMEX HIST FOUND AND MEM, BD UTAH STATE HIST, 77-. **MEMBERSHIPS** Western Hist Asn; AHA; Orgn Am Historians; Mormon Hist Asn. **RESEARCH** Spanish borderlands; Indian in american history. **SELECTED PUBLICATIONS** Auth, On Rims and Ridges, the Los Alamos Area Since 1880, Pac Hist Rev, Vol 63, 94; Baca, Elfego in Life and Legend, J W, Vol 34, 95. **CONTACT ADDRESS** Dept of Hist, Brigham Young Univ, Provo, UT, 84602.

WARNICKE, RETHA MARVINE
PERSONAL Born 10/05/1939, McLean Co, KY, m, 1961, 1 child **DISCIPLINE** TUDOR-STUART HISTORY **EDUCATION** Ind Univ, Bloomington, BA, 61; Harvard Univ, MA, 63, PhD (hist), 69. **CAREER** From lectr to asst prof, 69-76, ASSOC PROF HIST, ARIZ STATE UNIV, 76-. **MEMBERSHIPS** AHA; AAUP **RESEARCH** Constitutional history; women's history; local British history. **SELECTED PUBLICATIONS** Auth, the Fall of Boleyn, Anne Revisited, Eng Hist Rev, Vol 108, 93; The Pursuit of Stability in Social Relations in Elizabethan London, Sixteenth Century J, Vol 24, 93; The 6 Wives of Henry VIII, Sixteenth Century J, Vol 24, 93; Elizabeth Glass, with the Glass of the Sinful Soul by Elizabeth I and Epistle Dedicatory and Conclusion by Bale, John, Albion, Vol 25, 93; The Prince and the Law, 1200-1600 in Sovereignty and Rights in the Western Legal Tradition, Renaissance Quart, Vol 47, 94; Cardinal Wolsey in Church, State, and Art, J of Modern Hist, Vol 66, 94; Gender and Authority in 16th Century England in the Knox Debate, Albion, Vol 27, 95; Henry VIII Greeting of Anne of Cleves and Early Modern Court Protocol, Albion, Vol 28, 96; Drake, Francis in the Lives of a Hero, Sixteenth Century J, Vol 27, 96; Women According to Men in the World of Tudor Stuart Women, Renaissance Quart, Vol 50, 97. **CONTACT ADDRESS** Dept of Hist, Arizona State Univ, Tempe, Tempe, AZ, 85281.

WARREN, ANN KOSSER
PERSONAL Born 04/13/1928, Jersey City, NJ, m, 1949, 5 children **DISCIPLINE** MEDIEVAL AND RELIGIOUS HISTORY **EDUCATION** City Univ New York, BA, 49; Case Western Reserve Univ, MA, 76, PhD (hist), 80. **CAREER** LECTR HIST, CASE WESTERN RESERVE UNIV, 80-; Vis asst prof, Hiram Col, fall, 80. **MEMBERSHIPS** Mediaeval Acad Am; AHA; Soc Church Hist; Midwest Medieval Asn. **RESEARCH** Medieval English recluses: anchorites and hermits; medieval spirituality: pilgrimage phenomena; medieval social history: will studies and family history. **SELECTED PUBLICATIONS** Auth, the Black Death and Pastoral Leadership in the Diocese of Hereford in the 14th Century, Church Hist, Vol 65, 96; A History of Canterbury Cathedral, Albion, Vol 28, 96; Contemplation and Action in the Other Monasticism, Cath Hist Rev, Vol 83, 97. **CONTACT ADDRESS** Dept of Hist, Case Western Reserve Univ, Cleveland, OH, 44106.

WARREN, DONALD R
PERSONAL Born 09/27/1933, Waco, TX, m, 1957, 3 children **DISCIPLINE** HISTORY OF EDUCATION **EDUCATION** Univ Tex, BA, 56; Harvard Univ, ThM, 60; Univ Chicago, PhD (hist educ), 68. **CAREER** Prog dir social serv, Cambridge Neighborhood House, 56-60; dean students tutorials and social issues, College House, 60-62; dir studies adult educ, Ecumenical Inst, 62-64; asst prof hist and philos educ, Chicago State Univ, 65-69; assoc prof, Univ Ill, Chicago, 69, head dept policy studies, 70-79; PROF and CHMN DEPT EDUC POLICY, PLANNING and ADMIN, UNIV MD, COLLEGE PARK, 79-; Consult educ res, US Office Educ, 71-73; consult educ policy and hist educ, Holt, Rinehart, and Winston Inc, 72-79; chmn, Task Force Acad Stand, Am Educ Studies Asn, 76-78; Assoc ed, Educ Theory, 76-69; bd scholars, Potomac Educ Resources, 80-. **MEMBERSHIPS** Am Educ Studies Asn (pres, 75-76); Am Educ Res Asn (secy, 74-76); Ctr Study Democratic Inst; AHA; Hist Educ Soc. **RESEARCH** History of American education; history of federal education policy; education policy. **SELECTED PUBLICATIONS** Auth, Run for Office, Trial, Vol 29, 93. **CONTACT ADDRESS** Dept of Educ Policy Planning and Admin, Univ of Maryland, College Park, MD, 20742.

WARREN, J. BENEDICT
PERSONAL Born 06/30/1930, Waterflow, NM, m, 1968 **DISCIPLINE** COLONIAL MEXICAN AND LATIN AMERICAN HISTORY **EDUCATION** Duns Scotus Col, BA, 53; Univ NMex, MA, 60, PhD (hist), 63. **CAREER** Ed, Americas, Acad Am Franciscan Hist, Washington, DC, 63-66; From asst prof to assoc prof, 68-77, PROF HIST, UNIV MD, COLLEGE PARK, 77-; Fel, John Carter Brown Libr, Brown Univ, 65; consult, Hisp Found, Libr Cong, 67-72; Fulbright res award, Mexico, 81-82. **MEMBERSHIPS** Conf Latin am Hist; Latin am Studies Asn. **RESEARCH** Sixteenth century Michoacan; Bishop Vasco de Quiroga; intellectual history of 16th century Mexico. **SELECTED PUBLICATIONS** Auth, Chimalpahin and the Kingdoms of Chalco, Am, Vol 49, 93; The Encomenderos of New Spain, 1521-1555, Am, Vol 50, 93; Mexico and the Spanish Conquest, Hist, Vol 57, 95; Lascasas in Mexico in Unknown History and Work, Cath Hist Rev, Vol 81, 95. **CONTACT ADDRESS** Dept of Hist, Univ of Md, College Park, MD, 20742.

WARREN, JOSEPH DAVID
PERSONAL Born 04/02/1938, New York, New York, d **DISCIPLINE** EDUCATION **EDUCATION** North Carolina A&T Univ, Greensboro NC, BS 1969; Brandeis Univ, Waltham MA, MA 1973, PhD 1983. **CAREER** United Planning Org, Washington DC, dir of comm organization, 1965-67; Policy Management System, New York NY, natl VISTA training coordinator, 1967-69; Brandeis Univ, Waltham MA, exec dir of Upward Bound, 1970-74; Commonwealth of Massachusetts, Boston MA, asst sec of educational affairs, 1975-79; Northeastern Univ, Boston MA, urban asst to president 1979-82, dir of community affairs 1982-90, associate professor of African-American Studies, 1990-. **HONORS AND AWARDS** MA Black Achievers Awards; Phi Kappa Phi Society Award; First Annual MA Affirmative Action Award; award for minority business from Gov of MA; Award for Youth Service from Mayor of Boston; created & directed univ-based academy for pre-high schools; created & directed special higher educ opportunity for public housing residents; chaired Blue Ribbon Panel on Racial Incident, Newton MA; lead devel of MA business set-aside program. **MEMBERSHIPS** Pres, Devel & Training Associates; chair, Industrial Sites Devel Assn, Boston Mayor's Minority Business Advisory Council, MA Human Resource Center; mem, United Way of Greater Boston, Roxbury Multi-Service Center; trustee, Emmanual Coll. **CONTACT ADDRESS** Northeastern Univ, 132 Nightingale, Boston, MA, 02115.

WARREN, MORRISON FULBRIGHT
PERSONAL Born 12/06/1923, Marlin, Texas, s **DISCIPLINE** EDUCATION **EDUCATION** AZ State Univ, BA 1948; AZ State Univ, MA 1951, EdD 1959. **CAREER** Phoenix Elem School Dist 1, teacher 1948-53, principal 1953-68; AZ State Univ Explt Progs Coll Ed, dir 1968-84, prof emeritus of education 1984-. **HONORS AND AWARDS** Named one of four Outstanding Young Men of Phoenix Jr C of C 1958; Recipient of Natl Conference of Christians and Jews, Human Relations Award w/Sandra O'Connor, (Western Region, Arizona). **MEMBERSHIPS** Mem 1966-70, vice mayor 1969, Phoenix City Council; pres Fiesta Bowl 1981-; life mem NEA; dir 1st Interstate Bank of AZ NA 1981-86; bd of dir Samaritan Health Svc until 1992, AZ Publ Svc, until 1994; State Bd of Education, Arizona, 1991-94; Far West Regional Laboratory for Educ, Res and Service, 1992-95. **CONTACT ADDRESS** Prof Emeritus of Education, Arizona State Univ, Tempe, Suite E728, Tempe, AZ, 85287.

WARREN, NAGUEYALTI
PERSONAL Born 10/01/1947, Atlanta, Georgia, m **DISCIPLINE** EDUCATION **EDUCATION** Fisk Univ, BA 1972; Simmons Coll, MA 1974; Boston Univ, MA 1974; Univ of Mississippi, PhD 1984. **CAREER** Northeastern Univ, instructor 1977-78; Univ of Calabar, lecturer 1979; Fisk Univ, asst prof and chairperson, Dept of English 1984-88; Emory University, asst dean, assoc prof, 1988-. **HONORS AND AWARDS** Awd for Contribution to Black History Month Meharry Medical Coll 1984; Golden Poet Awd World Poetry Assoc 1985; poetry published in the following The American Poetry Anthology, Mississippi Earthworks, Janus, Riders of the Rainbow, Earthshine. **MEMBERSHIPS** Mem College Language Assoc, Modern Language Assoc, Natl Council of Teachers of English, Southern Conf on Afro-Amer Studies; advisory board member, W E B Du Bois Foundation. **SELECTED PUBLICATIONS** Book: Lodestar and Other Night Lights, New York, Mellen, 1992. **CONTACT ADDRESS** Emory Univ, 215 White Hall, Atlanta, GA, 30322.

WARREN, STANLEY
PERSONAL Born 12/18/1932, Indianapolis, Indiana **DISCIPLINE** EDUCATION **EDUCATION** Indiana Central Coll, BS 1959; Indiana Univ, MAT 1964; Indiana Univ, EdS; Indiana Univ, EdD 1973. **CAREER** DePauw Univ, dir black studies prof educ; Indianapolis Publ Sch, ctr admin; Indiana-Purdue Univ; Indiana Univ; Indiana Commn for Humanities, assoc; DePauw Univ, assoc dean. **MEMBERSHIPS** Fellowship & Grant, Carnegie; Wingspread; Eli Lilly; NSF; Natl Def Educ Act; John Hay; NEH; State Ethnic Studies Advisory Council; bd mem, Indiana Historical Society. **CONTACT ADDRESS** DePauw Univ, Asbury Hall, Greencastle, IN, 46135.

WARTH, ROBERT DOUGLAS
PERSONAL Born 12/16/1921, Houston, TX **DISCIPLINE** HISTORY **EDUCATION** Univ Ky, BS, 43; Univ Chicago, AM, 45, PhD, 49. **CAREER** Instr hist, Univ Tenn, 50-51; instr, Rutgers Univ, 51-54, asst prof, 54-58; vis prof, Paine Col, 60; assoc ed, Grolier Soc, 60-62 and 63-64; lectr hist, Hunter Col, 62-63; assoc prof, Staten Island Community Col, 64-68; PROF HIST, UNIV KY, 68-. **MEMBERSHIPS** AHA; Am Asn Advan Slavic Studies; Southern Conf Slavic Studies (pres, 82-83). **RESEARCH** Modern Russian history; Soviet foreign relations; international communism. **SELECTED PUBLICATIONS** Auth, Nicholas and Alexandra in the Family Albums, Russ Hist Histoire Russe, Vol 20, 93; Survival and Consolidation in the Foreign Policy of Soviet Russia, 1918-1921, Rus Rev, Vol 53, 94; American Soviet Relations in from the Russian Revolution to the Fall of Communism, J Am Hist, Vol 82, 95; The Fall of the Romanovs in Political Dreams and Personal

Struggles in a Time of Revolution, Rus Rev, Vol 56, 97. **CONTACT ADDRESS** Dept of Hist, Univ of Ky, Lexington, KY, 40506.

WARTLUFT, DAVID J.
DISCIPLINE AMERICAN LUTHERAN HISTORY **EDUCATION** BA, Muhlenberg Col, 1960; MDiv, LTSP, 1964; MA, Univ Pa, 1964; MS in Library Science, Drexel Univ, 1968; Pastorate in Pa, 1964-65. **CAREER** Dir of the Library; cord, Small Group prog. **HONORS AND AWARDS** Bd of dir(s), treasurer, Lutheran Hist Conf; exec sec, Amer Theol Library Assn. **RESEARCH** Exploring the Lutheran heritage. **SELECTED PUBLICATIONS** Pub(s), on American Lutheranism. **CONTACT ADDRESS** Dept of Practical Theology, Lutheran Theol Sem, 7301 Germantown Ave, Philadelphia, PA, 19119 1794. **EMAIL** Dwartluft@ltsp.edu

WASERMAN, MANFRED
PERSONAL Born 03/21/1933, Free City of Danzig, Poland, 1 child **DISCIPLINE** AMERICAN HISTORY, LIBRARY SCIENCE **EDUCATION** Univ Md, BA, 59, MA, 61; Cath Univ Am, MS, 63, PhD (hist), 82. **CAREER** Teacher hist, Prince Geofe's County, Md, Pub Sch, 60-62; librn, Library, Yale Univ, 63-65; CURATOR, MOD MANUSCRIPTS, NAT LIBR MED, 65-. **MEMBERSHIPS** Am Asn Hist Med; AHA; Am Libr Asn; Oral Hist Asn. **RESEARCH** History of medicine and public health; history of child health care; primitive medicine and ethnology. **SELECTED PUBLICATIONS** Auth, Montefiore, Moses, A Hebrew Prayer Book, and Medicine in the Holy Land, Judaism, Vol 45, 96. **CONTACT ADDRESS** Hist Med Div, National Libr of Med, Bethesda, MD, 20209.

WASHBURN, WILCOMB EDWARD
PERSONAL Born 01/13/1925, Ottawa, KS, m, 1951, 2 children **DISCIPLINE** HISTORY **EDUCATION** Dartmouth Col, AB, 48; Harvard Univ, MA, 51, PhD (Am civilization), 55. **CAREER** Civil inform and educ off, US Mil Govt, Japan, 46-47; teaching fel hist and lit, Harvard Univ, 54-55; instr hist, Col William and Mary and fel, Inst Early Am Hist and Cult, 55-58; actg cur div polit hist, 58-59, cur, 59-65, chmn dept Am studies, 65-68, DIR AM STUDIES PROG, SMITHSONIAN INST, 68-; LECTR, AM UNIV, 61-; adj prof, 63-68; ADJ PROF, UNIV MD, 75- AND GEORGE WASHINGTON UNIV, 76-. **HONORS AND AWARDS** LittD, St Mary's Col, Md, 70. **MEMBERSHIPS** AAAS; Am Studies Asn (pres, 78-80); Am Soc Ethnohist (pres, 57-58); AHA; Soc Hist Discoveries (pres, 65-66). **RESEARCH** Indian-white relations; colonial American history; political theory. **SELECTED PUBLICATIONS** Auth, Smith Goes to Tokyo in Japanese Cinema Under the American Occupation, 1945-1952, Am Stud Intl, Vol 31, 93; The Skulking Way of War in Technology and Tactics Among the New England Indians, Tech Cult, Vol 34, 93; The Public Trust and the First Americans, Public Indians, Tech Cult, Vol 34, 93; The American Indian in the Civil War, 1862-1865, Ethnohist, Vol 41, 93; Reading Football in How the Popular Press Created an American Spectacle, Am Stud Intl, Vol 32, 94; Art of the American Indian Frontier, Pac Hist Rev, Vol 63, 94; A Biography of Mcnickle, Darcy in Singing an Indian Song, Pac Hist Rev, Vol 63, 94; An American in Japan, 1945-1948 in a Civilian View of the Occupation, Am Stud Intl, Vol 33, 95; Desoto, Hernando and the Indians of Florida, J Interdisciplinary Hist, Vol 25, 95; Retained by the People in History of American Indians and the Bill of Rights, Pac Hist Rev, Vol 64, 95; America in European Consciousness, 1493-1750, Am Stud Intl, Vol 33, 95; Un American Activities in the Trials of Remington, William, Am Stud Intl, Vol 33, 95; The Quotable Johnson, Paul in a Topical Compilation of His Wit, Wisdom and Satire, Am Stud Intl, Vol 33, 95; Indians at Hampton Institute, 1877-1923, Va Mag Hist Biog, Vol 104, 96; Untitled, Am Hist Rev, Vol 101, 96; Indian Depredation Claims, 1796-1920, Pac Hist Rev, Vol 66, 97; Between 2 Fires in american Indians in the Civil War, Pac Hist Rev, Vol 66, 97. **CONTACT ADDRESS** Off of Am Studies, Smithsonian Inst, Washington, DC, 20560.

WASHINGTON, EARL MELVIN
PERSONAL Born 06/22/1939, Chicago, Illinois, m **DISCIPLINE** EDUCATION **EDUCATION** Western MI Univ, BA 1963, MA 1968; Univ of MI, 1971; Western MI Univ EdD. **CAREER** Cleveland Public Schools, teacher 1963-68; Kalamazoo Valley CC, instructor 1968-70; Western MI Univ, asst prof communications 1975-82, assoc prof communications, dir black faculty devel prog 1982-, asst dean 1984-, associate professor, communications; The Institute for the Study of Race and Ethnic Relations, director, consultant, workshop presenter. **HONORS AND AWARDS** 2nd vice pres Kalamazoo PTA; various articles publ in communication, educ and communication quartery and black issues in higher education 1980-; press/publ dir Kalamazoo Metro Branch NAACP 1984-84; vice pres 100 men of Kalamazoo 1983-85; papers presented including at Natl Assn for Equal Oppty; Phi Kappa Phi. **MEMBERSHIPS** Knappen Voight Co, consultant 1977; Kalamazoo Valley Int Schl Dist, consultant 1979; WMU, dir blk college prog 1984. **SELECTED PUBLICATIONS** Several papers presented; co-author, College: The First Two Years. **CONTACT ADDRESS** Western Michigan Univ, 2020 Friedmann Hall, Kalamazoo, MI, 49008.

WASHINGTON, MICHAEL HARLAN
PERSONAL Born 09/25/1950, Cincinnati, Ohio **DISCIPLINE** EDUCATION **EDUCATION** Raymond Walters Coll, AA 1971; Univ of Cincinnati, BS 1973, MEd 1974, EdD 1984. **CAREER** Univ of Cincinnati, learning skills specialist 1974-79; Northern KY Univ, learning skills specialist 1979-80, dir of Afro-Amer Studies program 1986-, assoc prof of history 1980-. **HONORS AND AWARDS** Staff Developement grant, KY Council on Higher Educ 1979, 1980; Outstanding Professor of the Year, Northern Kentucky Univ, Professor of the Year, 1996; Raymond Walters College, Distinguished Alumni Award, Raymond Walters College, 1996. **MEMBERSHIPS** Consultations Office of In-Service Educ No KY University 1980; United Christian Ministeries and Black Campus Ministries, University of Cincinnati 1980-81; University of Cincinnati Medical Ctr 1980; No KY Univ Div of Continuing Educ 1980-81; Inservice Tchr Training, Southwestern Business Coll 1982; Diocesan Secondary Social Studies Tchr, Thomas Moore Coll 1982; KY Assoc of Teachers of History 1981-; Black History Archives Comm 1985-; Phi Alpha Theta 1985-; Minority Students Retention Scholarship, No KY University, founder, 1986; African-American Studies Prog, No KY University, founder, 1986. **SELECTED PUBLICATIONS** Auth, poem "On Time," publ in American Poetry Anthology, 1986; author of book "Academic Success & the College Minority Student," 1986; co-author, "Undoing Racism," 1997. **CONTACT ADDRESS** Dir Afro American Studies Prog, Northern Kentucky Univ, 440 Landrum, Highland Heights, KY, 41076.

WASHINGTON, ROBERT ORLANDA
PERSONAL Born 02/08/1935, Newport News, Virginia, m, 1955 **DISCIPLINE** EDUCATION **EDUCATION** Hampton Institute, Hampton, VA, BS, 1956; Marquette University, Milwaukee, WI, MA, 1966; University of Missouri, Columbia, MO, MS, 1968; Brandeis University, Waltham, MA, PhD, 1973. **CAREER** Greenleigh Assoc, New York, NY, sr research assoc, 1968-72; University of Wisconsin-Milwaukee, Milwaukee, WI, assoc dean, 1972-76; Ohio State University, Columbus, OH, dean, 1976-82; University of Illinois, Champaign-Urbana, IL, dean, 1982-86; Social Policy Research Group, Boston, MA, pres, 1986-88; University of New Orleans, vice chancellor, 1988-93, professor, currently; co-editor, Journal of Planning Education and Research. **HONORS AND AWARDS** Outstanding Teacher of the Year, 1975; Phi Kappa Phi, 1992; NDEA Fellow, 1968. **MEMBERSHIPS** Member, National Assn of Social Worker, 1976-90; commissioner, Council on Social Work Education Commission on Accreditation, 1978-81; Association of Collegiate Schools of Planning; URban Affairs Association. **CONTACT ADDRESS** Professor, College of Urban & Public Affairs, Univ of New Orleans, Lakefront Campus, New Orleans, LA, 70148.

WASON, ROBERT W.
DISCIPLINE MUSIC **EDUCATION** Hartt Sch Music, MusB, 67, MusM, 69; Yale Univ, MPhil, 78, PhD, 81. **CAREER** Teaching Asst, 67-69, Piano Instr and Teaching Assoc, 69-70, Instr Theory/Compos, Hartt Sch Music, 70-76, 77-79; Teaching Asst, Yale Univ, 76-77; Lectr Music, Clark Univ, 80; Asst Prof, Univ N Texas, 81-83; Asst Prof to Assoc Prof, 83-97, Prof Music Theory, Eastman Sch Music, 97-; Heinrich Strobel Found Vis Prof, Univ Basel, 91; Vis Prof, Univ Brit Columbia, 92; Vis Prof, SUNY - Buffalo, 94. **HONORS AND AWARDS** Bronze Medal, Concours Int de Guitare, Radio France, 75; Fulbright Schol, 79-80; Paul Sacher Found Stipend, 89-90; NEH Fel Univ Teachers, 89-90; Guggenheim Fel, 90; UR Bridging Fel, 97; Special Opportunity Stipend, Arts and Cultural Coun Greater Rochester, 97; DAAD Study Visit, Ger Acad Exchange, 97. **SELECTED PUBLICATIONS** Auth, Viennese Harmonic Theory from Albrechtsberger to Schenker and Schoenberg, UMI Press, 85, repr U of R Press, 95; coauth, On Preparing Anton Webern's Early Songs for Performance: A Collaborators' Dialogue, Theory and Practice, vol 20, 95; auth, A Pitch-Class Motive in Webern's Op.3 George Lieder, Webern Studies, Cambridge Univ Press, 96; coauth, Die Harmonik des Jazz (forthcoming); author of several other articles, reviews, publications, and musical compositions. **CONTACT ADDRESS** Eastman Sch Music, Univ Rochester, 26 Gibbs St., Rochester, NY, 14604. **EMAIL** rwsn@theory.esm.rochester.edu

WASSERMAN, MARK
PERSONAL Born 01/29/1946, Boston, MA, m, 1968, 2 children **DISCIPLINE** HISTORY **EDUCATION** Univ of Chicago, PhD **CAREER** Asst prof, Northern Ill Univ, 76-77; from asst prof to prof, Rutgers Univ, 78-. **HONORS AND AWARDS** Arthur P. Whitaker Award, 84, 87. **MEMBERSHIPS** AHA; LASA; MACLAS; PCCLAS; RMCLAS. **RESEARCH** Mexico **SELECTED PUBLICATIONS** Auth, Persistent Oligarchs: Elites and Politics in Chihuahua, Mexico, 1910-1949, 93. **CONTACT ADDRESS** Dept of History, Rutgers Univ, 16 Seminary Place, New Brunswick, NJ, 08901. **EMAIL** wasserm@rci.rutgers.edu

WASSON, ELLIS ARCHER
PERSONAL Born 12/31/1947, Rye, NY **DISCIPLINE** HISTORY **EDUCATION** Johns Hopkins Univ, BA, 72, MA, 72; Univ Cambridge, PhD (hist), 75. **CAREER** Chmn dept hist, 77-

78, HIST MASTER, RIVERS SCH, MASS, 76-; DEAN FAC, 78-. **MEMBERSHIPS** AHA; Eng Hist Asn; New Eng Hist Teachers (secy-treas, 78). **RESEARCH** Nineteenth century English history. **SELECTED PUBLICATIONS** Auth, Broughman, Henry, the Later Years 1830-1868, the Great Actor, Albion, Vol 26, 94; The Great Reform Bill in the Boroughs in English Electoral Behavior, Albion, Vol 27, 95; British Non Elite Mps, , Albion, Vol 28, 96; The Rockingham Connection and the 2nd Founding of the Whig Party, Am Hist Rev, Vol 102, 97. **CONTACT ADDRESS** The Rivers Sch, 333 Winter St, Weston, MA, 023.

WASWO, ANN
PERSONAL Born 05/17/1940, Los Angeles, CA, m, 1964 **DISCIPLINE** JAPANESE HISTORY **EDUCATION** Stanford Univ, BA, 61, MA, 64, PhD (hist), 69. **CAREER** Lectr East Asian civilization, Stanford Univ, 68-69, actg asst prof hist, 69-70; asst prof, Univ Va, 71-76; ASST PROF, PRINCETON UNIV, 79-. **MEMBERSHIPS** Asn Asian Studies. **RESEARCH** Social history of modern Japan. **SELECTED PUBLICATIONS** Auth, Rice as Self in Japanese Identities Through Time, Monumenta Nipponica, Vol 49, 94; The Autobiography of Shibusawa Eiichi in from Peasant to Entrepreneur, Eng Hist Rev, Vol 111, 96; Eastern Asia in an Introductory History, Eng Hist Rev, Vol 111, 96; Japan and the World Since 1868, Eng Hist Rev, Vol 112, 97. **CONTACT ADDRESS** East Asian Studies, Princeton Univ, Princeton, NJ, 08540.

WATANABE, MORIMICHI
PERSONAL Born 08/08/1926, Yamagata, Japan, m, 1954, 1 child **DISCIPLINE** LATE MEDIEVAL HISTORY, POLITICAL SCIENCE **EDUCATION** Univ Tokyo, LLB, 48; Columbia Univ, MA, 56, PhD (polit theory), 61. **CAREER** Lectr polit sci, Meiji Gakuin Jr Col, Tokyo, 48-50, prof, 50; instr, Meiji Gakuin Col, 49-51, lectr, 51-54; vis asst prof, Kans State Col Pittsburg, 60-61; instr, Queens Col, NY, 61-63; From asst prof to assoc prof, 63-71, PROF HIST and POLIT SCI, C W POST CTR, LONG ISLAND UNIV, 71-; Am Philos Soc res grants, 64, 70 and 77; Am Coun Learned Soc res grant, 66; Found Reformation Res grant-in-aid, 70; vis prof, Fac Law, Univ Tokyo, 76 and Fac Law, Keio Univ, 76. **MEMBERSHIPS** AHA; Mediaeval Acad Am; Renaissance Soc Am; Am Cath Hist Asn; Am Soc Church Hist. **RESEARCH** History of legal and political thought; Conciliar Movement; Nicholas of Cusa. **SELECTED PUBLICATIONS** Auth, the Japanese Question in Power and Purpose in a New Era, Japan Quart, Vol 40, 93. **CONTACT ADDRESS** C W Post Ctr, Long Island Univ, 720 Northern Blvd, Greenvale, NY, 11548-1300.

WATELET, HUBERT
PERSONAL Born 09/14/1932, La Louviere, Belgium, m, 1958, 5 children **DISCIPLINE** MODERN EUROPEAN HISTORY **EDUCATION** Univ Louvain, MA, 57, PhD (mod hist), 69. **CAREER** Librn, Univ Lovanium, Kinshasa, 58-61; archivist, State Archiv, Belg, 62-64; lectr Europ hist, 64-67, asst prof, 67-71, ASSOC PROF HIST, UNIV OTTAWA, 71-. **MEMBERSHIPS** Can Hist Asn; Soc for Fr Hist Studies. **RESEARCH** Industrial revolution; 20th century French historiography. **SELECTED PUBLICATIONS** Auth, the Social Sciences in Canada in 50 Years of Action on a National Scale by the Social Science Federation of Canada, Rev D Histoire De L Am Fr, Vol 47, 93. **CONTACT ADDRESS** Dept of Hist, Univ of Ottawa, Ottawa, ON, K1N 6N5.

WATERMAN, THELMA M.
PERSONAL Born 06/10/1937, Hartford, Connecticut, d **DISCIPLINE** EDUCATION **EDUCATION** Hartford Coll for Women, Hartford CT, AA 1969; Trinity Coll, Hartford CT, BA 1971; Yale Univ Divinity School, MDiv 1978. **CAREER** Proof oper bank 1956-57; dept store salesgirl 1959-61; Headstart Prog, teacher aide 1964-67; Trinity Coll, resident counselor of grad & undergrad students; City Hartford, teacher 1971; coll admin 1971-; Office of Community Affairs, Connecticut Coll, dir; New Haven Boys and Girls Club, New Haven CT, admin, 1984-85; United Way of Southeastern Connecticut, Gales Ferry CT, assoc exec dir, 1985-. **HONORS AND AWARDS** Delta Sigma Theta Sorority Award, 1965; citationist, Lane Byrant Annual Awards Competition, 1965; Rudolph Haffner Award for Community Service, Hartford Coll for Women, 1969; Samuel S Fishzoln Award, Trinity Coll, 1971; Community Service Recognition, Norwich Branch NAACP, Norwich CT, 1980; Martin Luther King Jr Community Service Award, Club Cosmos, New London CT, 1980; Certificate, Connecticut Advisory Council on Vocational and Career Education, 1985; Martin Luther King Jr Community Service Award, Club Cosmos, New London, CT, 1980. **MEMBERSHIPS** Conducted leadership training sessions, community leaders devel manpower prog, workshops, seminars, conf prog evaluation; co-organizer of 1st public housing proj pre-school ctr 1963; group counselor, Parker Memorial Ctr Hartford 1967-68; counselor, Drop Outs Anonymous Hartford 1967-69; comm rep, Hartford Bd of Educ 1970; vice pres, Dwight School PTA Hartford 1970-71; pres, POWER Hartford 1970-71; bd mem, OIC 1972; United Way 1972; Connecticut Talent Asst Coop 1973-76; Southeastern Connecticut Youth Serv 1973-74; Info & Referral Agency 1974-77; vice pres, Black Seminarians 1974-75; Yale Univ Divinity School Comp Youth Serv 1972-75; Catholic Charities

1971-74; Educ Task Force Model City 1972-75; Minority Navy Wives Scholarship Comm 1972-74. **CONTACT ADDRESS** United Way of Southeathern Connecticut, Gales Ferry, CT, 06335.

WATERS, JOHN J.
PERSONAL Born 04/22/1937, New York, NY, m, 2 children **DISCIPLINE** AMERICAN COLONIAL HISTORY **EDUCATION** Manhattan Col, AB, 57; Columbia Univ, PhD (hist), 65. **CAREER** Res asst John Jay papers, Columbia Univ, 61-65; asst prof, 65-69, assoc prof, 69-77, PROF HIST, UNIV ROCHESTER, RIVER CAMPUS, 78-; Mem, Inst Early Am Hist and Cult, Williamsburg, Va and Jamestown Prize, 68; John Carter Brown res fel, Brown Univ, 68; Charles Warren fel, Harvard Univ, 70-71. **MEMBERSHIPS** AHA; Orgn Am Historians; Soc Sci Hist Asn. **RESEARCH** Social history of pre-industrial America; historical and quantitative methodology. **SELECTED PUBLICATIONS** Auth, Inheritance and Family Life in Colonial New York City, J Interdisciplinary Hist, Vol 26, 95. **CONTACT ADDRESS** Dept of Hist, Univ of Rochester River Campus, 500 Joseph C Wilson, Rochester, NY, 14627-9000.

WATERS, NEIL L.
DISCIPLINE JAPANESE HISTORY, US-JAPAN RELATIONS, EAST ASIAN CIVILIZATION **EDUCATION** Pac Lutheran Univ, BA; Wash State Univ, MA; Univ Hawaii, PhD. **CAREER** Prof, 90-; Kawashima prof Japanese Stud, 90; dept ch. **RESEARCH** Japanese social, intellectual and regional history in the Meiji and Taisho eras. **SELECTED PUBLICATIONS** Auth, Japan's Local Pragmatists Council on East Asian Studies, Harvard UP, 83; The Second Transition: Early to Mid-Meiji in Kanagawa Prefecture, J Asian Stud, 49 2, 90 & The Village Consolidation of 1889: theInstitutionalization of Contradiction, Asian Cult Stud 18, 92. **CONTACT ADDRESS** Dept of History, Middlebury Col, Middlebury, VT, 05753. **EMAIL** nwaters@panther.middlebury.edu

WATKINS, ANDREA
DISCIPLINE MUSIC **EDUCATION** Brigham Young Univ, BA; George Wash Univ, MA; Union Grad Sch, PhD. **CAREER** Prof. **SELECTED PUBLICATIONS** Co-author, Dancing Longer, Dancing Stronger, 90. **CONTACT ADDRESS** Music and Dance Dept, Univ of Massachusetts, Amherst, 720 Massachusetts Ave, Amherst, MA, 01003.

WATKINS, JOHN C.
PERSONAL Born 04/02/1935, Mobile, AL, m, 1972, 4 children **DISCIPLINE** CRIMINAL JUSTICE **EDUCATION** Univ AL, BS 57, JD 62; FL State Univ, MS 64; Northwestern Univ, LL M 68. **CAREER** Univ AL, Col Arts Sci, prof founding ch, dept crim just 71-; Sam Houston State Univ, Col Crim Just, assoc prof crimin 69-71; Univ AL, Culverhouse, asst prof law 65-69. **HONORS AND AWARDS** NIMH Fell; Alpha Kappa Delta; Omicron Delta Kappa. **MEMBERSHIPS** AM Bar Assn; AL St Bar Assn. **RESEARCH** Juvenile law, policy and practice, criminology and war crimes, war crime trials in the twentieth century. **SELECTED PUBLICATIONS** The Juvenile Justice Century: A Sociolegal Commentary on American Juvenile Courts, CAP, 98; Encyclopedic Essays on World war II, German Propaganda, War Crimes, Nuremberg, My Lai, & Bosnia, Magill's Ready ref. **CONTACT ADDRESS** University Station, University, AL, 35486. **EMAIL** jwatkins@cj.as.ua.edu

WATKINS, MELVILLE H.
PERSONAL Born 05/15/1932, McKellar, ON, Canada **DISCIPLINE** POLITICAL SCIENCE/HISTORY **EDUCATION** Univ Toronto, BComm, 52; MIT, grad stud econ. **CAREER** Fac mem, 58, PROF ECONOMICS & POLITICAL SCIENCE, UNIV TORONTO, 70-; head, Fed Govt Task Force, Structure Can Industry, 67-68; pres, Harold Innis Found, 69-70; consult, Indian Brotherhood NWT, 74-76; consult, Can Labour Cong, 87-88. **RESEARCH** Canadian economic history and policy. **SELECTED PUBLICATIONS** Auth, Madness and Ruin: Politics and the Economy in the Neoconservative Age, 92; ed, Dene Nation-The Colony Within, 77; ed, Canada: Handbooks to the Modern World, 93; co-ed, Economics Canada, 63; co-ed, Approaches to Canadian Economic History, 67; co-ed, Gordon to Watkins to You, 70; co-ed, Canadian Economic History, 93; co-ed, Canada Under Free Trade, 93. **CONTACT ADDRESS** Dept of Economics, Univ of Toronto, Toronto, ON, M5S 1A1.

WATKINS-OWENS, IRMA
DISCIPLINE AFRICAN-AMERICAN HISTORY **EDUCATION** Univ MI, PhD. **CAREER** Assoc prof, Fordham Univ. **RESEARCH** Study of African Am women. **SELECTED PUBLICATIONS** Auth, Blood Relations: Caribbean Immigrants and the Harlem Community, 1900-1930, Ind UP, 96. **CONTACT ADDRESS** Dept of Hist, Fordham Univ, 113 W 60th St, New York, NY, 10023.

WATROUS, LIVINGSTON V.
DISCIPLINE ART HISTORY **EDUCATION** Univ PA, PhD. **CAREER** Fac, SUNY Buffalo; to chr art hist dept and dir grad studies; Whitehead Prof, Am Schl Class Studies Athens, 93-94; prof, present, SUNY Buffalo. **HONORS AND AWARDS** Grants, Archaeol Inst Am, NEH, Nat Geog Soc, Fulbright comm, and Inst Aegean Studies., Dir, Gournia Survey Project; Elizabeth A. Whitehead Prof, Am Schl Classical Studies Athens, 93-94. **RESEARCH** Greek art and archaeol; Bronze Age Aegean art; archaeol. **SELECTED PUBLICATIONS** Auth, The Sanctuary of Zeus at Psychro, 96; The Plain of Phaistos; Kommos III: The Late Bronze Age Pottery, Princeton UP, 92. **CONTACT ADDRESS** Dept Art, SUNY Buffalo, 202 Center for the Arts, Buffalo, NY, 14260-6010.

WATROUS, MARY A.
DISCIPLINE LATIN AMERICA AND WORLD HISTORY **EDUCATION** Wash State Univ, PhD, 91. **CAREER** Asst prof, Washington State Univ. **RESEARCH** Food and cuisines in world history. **SELECTED PUBLICATIONS** Auth, Mexican Banking and Finance, 1940-96 & Short Term Miracles: Long Term Paradox, in The Encyclopedia of Mexico: History, Society, and Culture, Fitzroy Dearborn Publ, 98. **CONTACT ADDRESS** Dept of History, Washington State Univ, 301 Wilson Hall, PO Box 644030, Pullman, WA, 99164-4030. **EMAIL** watrous@wsu.edu

WATSON, ALAN
PERSONAL Born 10/27/1933, Hamilton, Scotland, 2 children **DISCIPLINE** COMPARATIVE LAW, CLASSICAL STUDIES **EDUCATION** Univ Glasgow, MA, 54, LLB, 57; Univ Oxford, DPhil, 60, DCL, 73. **CAREER** Lectr law, Wadham Col, Oxford Univ, 57-59; fel law, Oriel Col, Oxford Univ, 59-65; Douglas prof civil law, Univ Glasgow, 65-68; proof civil law, Univ Edinburgh, 68-79; PROF LAW AND CLASS STUDIES, UNIV PA, 79-; Gen ed, transl Justinian's Digest, Commonwealth Fund, 78. **HONORS AND AWARDS** LLD, Univ Edinburgh, 80. **RESEARCH** Society and legal change; Roman law. **SELECTED PUBLICATIONS** Auth, the Importance of Nutshells, Am J Comp Law, Vol 42, 94; Wilhelm Strad and Bow and the Instrument Dated 1725 and the Tubbs Bow of 1885, Strad, Vol 106, 95; From Legal Transplants to Legal Formants, Am J Comp Law, Vol 43, 95; Introduction to Law For 2nd Year Law Students, J Legal Educ, Vol 46, 96; Aspects of Reception of Law, Am J Comp Law, Vol 44, 96; A History of Private Law in Europe, with Particular Reference to Germany, Am Hist Rev, Vol 102, 97. **CONTACT ADDRESS** Law School, Univ Pa, Philadelphia, PA.

WATSON, ALAN DOUGLAS
PERSONAL Born 05/03/1942, Rocky Mount, NC, m, 1964, 3 children **DISCIPLINE** COLONIAL AMERICAN HISTORY **EDUCATION** Duke Univ, AB, 64; E Carolina Univ, MA, 66; Univ SC, PhD(hist), 71. **CAREER** Instr hist, Danville Div, Va Polytech Inst, 66-68; asst prof, 71-74, assoc prof, 74-79, PROF HIST, UNIV NC, WILMINGTON, 79- **MEMBERSHIPS** NC Hist Asn; Southern Hist Asn. **RESEARCH** Colonial American society and economy; United States economic history. **SELECTED PUBLICATIONS** Auth, Society and economy in colonial Edgecombe County, NC Hist Rev, summer 73; Orphanage in Colonial North Carolina: Edgecombe County as a case study, NC Hist Rev, 4/75; Society in Colonial North Carolina, NC Archives, 75; ed, A letter from Charles Williamson to Lord Dartmouth, July 1766, SC Hist Mag, 1/76; auth, The Quitrent System in Royal South Carolina, William & Mary Quart, 4/76; auth, A History of New Bern and Craven County NC, Tryon Palace Commission, 87; auth, Wilmington: Port of North Carolina, Univ SC Press, 92; auth, A Brief History of Onslow County (NC), NC Arch, 95. **CONTACT ADDRESS** Dept of Hist, Univ of N. Carolina, 601 S College Rd, Wilmington, NC, 28403-3201. **EMAIL** watsona@uncwil.edu

WATSON, HARRY LEGARE
PERSONAL Born 07/10/1949, Greensboro, NC, m, 1977, 1 child **DISCIPLINE** HISTORY **EDUCATION** Brown Univ, AB, 71; Northwestern Univ, PhD (hist), 76. **CAREER** Asst prof, 76-82, ASSOC PROF HIST, UNIV NC, CHAPEL HILL, 82-. **MEMBERSHIPS** AHA; Orgn Am Historians; Soc Hist Early Am Repub. **RESEARCH** Society and politics of the antebellum South; North Carolina history. **SELECTED PUBLICATIONS** Auth, the Venturous Conservative Reconsidered and Meyer, Marvin the Jacksonian Persuasion, Politics and Belief in Social History and Political Culture in the Market Revolution, Rev Am Hist, Vol 22, 94; Boats Against the Current, American Culture Between Revolution and Modernity, Nineteenth Century Prose, Vol 21, 94; The Image and Definition of Southern Culture and Introduction, Southern Cults, Vol 1, 95; The Common Rights of Mankind in Subsistence, Shad, and Commerce in the Early Republican South, J Am Hist, Vol 83, 96. **CONTACT ADDRESS** Dept of Hist, Univ NC, Chapel Hill, NC, 27514.

WATSON, JUDGE
PERSONAL Born 06/12/1926, Carver, KY, m, 1952, 3 children **DISCIPLINE** AMERICAN SOUTH, MEDIEVAL EUROPEAN HISTORY **EDUCATION** Asbury Col, BA, 52; Ind Univ, Bloomington, MA, 57, PhD (hist), 63. **CAREER** Asst prof hist, Glenville State Col, 58-64; assoc prof, Asbury Col, 64-67; lectr, Ariz State Univ, 67-68; assoc prof, ETex State Univ, 68-69; mem fac hist, Fla Southern Col, 71-78. **MEMBERSHIPS** Orgn Am Historians; AHA; Southern Hist Soc; AHA; Southern Hist Soc. **RESEARCH** Broad form mineral deed: its impact on the coal fields of Eastern North America; Eastern Kentucky: a subregion of Appalachia in the 20th century. **SELECTED PUBLICATIONS** Auth, Shaffer, Peter in a Casebook Theatre J, Vol 46, 94; American Autobiography in Retrospect and Prospect, Biography Interdisciplinary Quart, Vol 16, 93;Voters Choice in Electoral Change in New Zealand, Australian J Politics Hist, Vol 39, 93; Arabic Adeni Textbook in arabic Dialect Series Yemen, J Semitic Stud, Vol 38, 93; The Rhetoric of Exhaustion and the Exhaustion of Rhetoric in Caldwell, Erskine in the 30s, Miss Quart, Vol 46, 93;1st Person Singular in Studies in american Autobiography, Biog Interdisciplinary Quart, Vol 16, 93; Arabic Adeni Reader in arabic Dialect Series, J Semitic Stud, Vol 38, 93; The New Art of Autobiography, An Essay on the Life of Giambattista Vicon Written by Himself, Philosophy Lit, Vol 17, 93;Lewis, Wyndham, Religion and Modernism, Relig Lit, Vol 26, 94; Distinguo in Reading Montaigne Differently, Renaissance Quart, Vol 47, 94; The Holy Land in american Religious Thought, 1620-1948 in the Symbiosis of American Religious Approaches to Scriptures Sacred Territory, Am Jewish Archives, Vol 47, 95; American Consuls in the Holy Land, , Am Jewish Archives, Vol 47, 95; Wire and Wireless in a History of Telecommunications in New Zealand, , New Zealand J Hist, Vol 29, 95; Guys and Dolls and Psychoanalysis in Exploratory Repetition and Maternal Subjectivity in the Fort Da Game, Am Imago, Vol 52, 95; To See a Promised Land in american and the Holy Land in the 20Th Century, Am Jewish Archives, Vol 47, 95; Among the White Moon Faces in Media Arabic, J Semitic Stud, Vol 40, 95;An Asian American Memoir of Homelands, Am J, Vol 22, 96; The Gendered Political Economy of Zola La Curee, Nineteenth Century Fr Stud, Vol 25, 96; Uncovering the Body, Discovering Ideology in Segregation and Sexual Anxiety in Smith, Lillian Killers of the Dream, Am Quart, Vol 49, 97; Unruly Bodies in autoethnography and Authorization in Diallo, Nafissatou De Tilene Au Plateau A Dakar Childhood, Res African Lit, Vol 28, 97; Versions of Deconversion in autobiography and the Loss of Faith, Relig Lit, Vol 29, 97; Versions of Deconversion in autobiography and the Loss of Faith, Relig Lit, Vol 29, 97. **CONTACT ADDRESS** 5604 Scott Lake Rd, Lakeland, FL, 33803.

WATSON, PATTY JO
PERSONAL Born 04/26/1932, Superior, NE, m, 1955, 1 child **DISCIPLINE** ARCHAEOLOGY **EDUCATION** Univ Chicago, MA, 56, PhD (anthrop), 59. **CAREER** Archeol field asst, Iraq-Jarmo Proj, Orient Inst, Univ Chicago, 54-55, archeologist and ethnographer, Iranian Prehist Proj, 59-60; res assoc, Orient Inst, Univ Chicago, 64 and 67; From asst prof to assoc prof, 69-73, actg chmn dept anthrop, 71-72, PROF ANTHROP, WASHINGTON UNIV, 73-; NSF grant, Univ ChicagoOrient Inst Exped, Iran, 59-60; Ill State Mus Soc grant, Ky, 63; proj assoc and unit dir, Anthrop Curric Study Proj, Am Anthrop Asn, 65-67; NSF res grants, Univ ChicagoOrient Inst-Istanbul Univ, Turkey, 68 and 70; NSF sr res grant and NSFUndergrad Res Partic Proj grant, Ky and NMex, 69-72; fel, Cave Res Found; ed, Am Anthropologist, 73-77; mem adv panel, NSF, 74-76; Nat Endowment for Humanities res grant, 77; Ctr Advan Study in Behav Sci fel, 81-82. **MEMBERSHIPS** Fel Am Anthrop Asn; Soc Am Archaeol; Archaeol Inst Am; Am Schs Orient Res; Mid East Studies Asn. **RESEARCH** Ethnoarcheology; archeological theory and method; beginnings of food production in the Old World and in the Eastern United States. **SELECTED PUBLICATIONS** Auth, A Communitarian Defense of Liberalism in Durkheim, Emile and Contemporary Social Theory, Rev Relig Res, Vol 35, 93; 8,000 Year Old Man Discovered, Archaeol, Vol 47, 94; Age and Velopharyngeal function During Speech Production, J Speech Hearing Res, Vol 37, 94; Glock, Albert, Ernest 1925-1992 in Obituary, Am Antiquity, Vol 59, 94; Martin and Malcolm as Cultural Icons in an Empirical Study Comparing Lower Class African American and White Males, Rev Relig Res, Vol 36, 95; Religion and the Self as Text in Toward a Christian Translation of Self Actualization, J Psychol Theol, Vol 23, 95; Nomads of Luristan in History, Material Culture, and Pastoralism in Western Iran, J Am Oriental Soci, Vol 116, 96; Cognitive Linguistic Demands and Speech Breathing, J Speech Hearing Res, Vol 39, 96; Violence Unveiled in Humanity at the Crossroads, J Scientific Stud Relig, Vol 35, 96; **CONTACT ADDRESS** Dept of Anthrop, Washington Univ, 1 Brookings Dr, Saint Louis, MO, 63130-4899.

WATSON, PAUL FRASER
PERSONAL Born 03/17/1940, Toronto, ON, Canada, m, 1969 **DISCIPLINE** HISTORY OF ITALIAN RENAISSANCE ART **EDUCATION** Univ Toronto, BA, 62; Yale Univ, MA, 64, PhD (hist of art), 70. **CAREER** Asst instr hist of art, Yale Univ, 63-65; From instr to asst prof, 68-76, ASSOC PROF HIST OF ART, UNIV PA, 76-; External evaluator art dept, Dickinson Col, 81; vis assoc prof, Univ Calif Berkeley, spring 82. **MEMBERSHIPS** Col Art Asn Am; Renaissance Soc Am. **RESEARCH** Quattrocento secular art; Boccaccio illustration. **SELECTED PUBLICATIONS** Auth, Poets Seeing Artists Work in Instances in the Italian Renaissance, Italica, Vol 70, 93. **CONTACT ADDRESS** Dept Hist Art, Univ Pa, 3405 Woodland Walk, Philadelphia, PA.

WATSON, THOMAS DAVIS
PERSONAL Born 10/29/1929, Lake Charles, LA, m, 1953, 2 children **DISCIPLINE** LATIN AMERICAN & UNITED

STATES HISTORY **EDUCATION** N Mex State Univ, BA, 51; Univ Southwestern La, MA, 69; Tex Tech Univ, PhD(hist), 72. **CAREER** Asst prof, 72-76, assoc prof, 76-80, Prof Hist, Mcneese State Univ, 80-, Mem, La Bicentennial Comn, 73-77. **MEMBERSHIPS** Western Hist Asn; Southern Hist Asn; Conf Latin Am Hist. **RESEARCH** Spanish Colonial Louisiana and Florida; United States diplomacy. **SELECTED PUBLICATIONS** Auth, The PWA comes to the Red River Valley, Red River Valley Hist Rev, summer 74; A scheme gone awry: Bernardo do Galvez, Gilberto Antonio de Maxent and the Southern Indian trade, La Hist, winter 76; Continuity in commerce: Development of the Panton, Leslie and Company trade monopoly in West Florida, Fla Hist Quart, 4/76; The troubled advance of Panton, Leslie and Company into Spanish West Florida, In: Eighteenth Century Florida and the Revolutionary South, Univ Press Fla, 78; Strivings for sovereignty: Alexander McGillivary, creek warfare and diplomacy, 1783-1790, Fla Hist Quart, 4/80; coauth (with Samuel Wilson Jr), A lost landmark revisited: The William Panton House of Pensacola, Fla Hist Quart, 7/81; Bouligny,Francisco - A Bourbon Soldier In Spanish Louisiana - Din,Gc/, Journal Of Southern History, Vol 0060, 1994. **CONTACT ADDRESS** Dept of Hist, McNeese State Univ, Lake Charles, LA, 70609.

WATSON, WILBUR H.
PERSONAL Born 04/14/1938, Cleveland, m **DISCIPLINE** SOCIOLOGY **EDUCATION** Kent St U, BA 1964, MA 1966; Univ of PA, PhD 1972. **CAREER** Temple Univ Phila, asst prof of Soc 1973-; Rutgers Coll, asst prof of Soc 1970-74; Cheyney St Coll, asst prof of soc 1969-70; Kent St Univ, instr 1966-68; Lincoln Univ, instr 1966-68. **HONORS AND AWARDS** Numerous flwshps & awards. **MEMBERSHIPS** Mem Am Soclgcl Assn; Soc for Study of Soc Problems; Assn of Black Soclgsts; Assn for Study of African Am Life & Hist; Assn of Soc & Behvrl Scientests; mem bd govs Ctr for Rsrch on Acts of Man Univ of PA 1969-70; chmn steering com Proj-Learn;Exprmntl Elem Sch 1970-71; steering com Nat Black Alliance for Grad Level Ed 1972-74; cnsltng rsrch soclgst Stephen Smith Geriatric Ctr Philadelphia 1972-; founding ed The Black Soclgst 1975-. **SELECTED PUBLICATIONS** Author of "Hum Aging & Dying" (with RJ Maxwell) 1977; "Stress & Old Age" 1980; other Publications. **CONTACT ADDRESS** Department of Sociology, Temple Univ, Philadelphia, PA, 19122.

WATT, JEFFREY R.
PERSONAL Born 04/25/1958, Connellsville, PA, m, 1987, 2 children **DISCIPLINE** EUROPEAN HISTORY **EDUCATION** Grove City Col, BA, 80; Ohio Univ, MA, 82; Univ Wisc, Madison, PhD, 87. **CAREER** Lectr, hist, Univ Wisc, Madison, 87-88; asst prof, 88-94, assoc prof, 94- , hist, Univ Miss. **HONORS AND AWARDS** Cora Lee Graham Award for Outstanding Teacher of Freshmen, 91; NEH summer stipend, 92. **MEMBERSHIPS** Am Hist Asn; Calvin Stud Soc; Renaissance Soc of Am; Soc for Reformation Res. **RESEARCH** Early modern Europe; social history. **SELECTED PUBLICATIONS** Auth, The Making of Modern Marriage: Matrimonial Control and the Rise of Sentiment in Neuchatel, 1550-1800, Cornell Univ, 92; auth, Women and the Consistory in Calvin's Geneva, Sixteenth Century J, 93; auth, The Control of Marriage in Reformed Switzerland, 1600-1800, in Graham, ed, Later Calvinism: International Perspectives, Sixteenth Century Journal Publ, 94; auth, The Marriage Laws Calvin Drafted for Geneva, in Neuser, ed, Calvinus Sacrae Scripturae Professor, Eerdman's, 94; auth, The Family, Love, and Suicide in Early Modern Geneva, J of Family Hist, 96; auth, Calvin on Suicide, Church Hist, 97; auth, Reformed Piety and Suicide in Geneva, 1550-1800, in Roney, ed, The Identity of Geneva: The Christian Commonwealth, 1564-1864, Greenwood, 98; auth, Suicide in Reformation Geneva, Archive for Reformation Hist, 98; auth, The Impact of the Reformation and the Counter-Reformation, in Barbagli, ed, The History of the European Family, v.1: Family Life in Early Modern Times, Yale Univ, forthcoming. **CONTACT ADDRESS** Dept of History, Univ of Mississippi, University, MS, 38677. **EMAIL** hswatt@olemiss.edu

WATTS, ANNE WIMBUSH
PERSONAL Born 01/01/1943, Grambling, Louisiana, m, 1967 **DISCIPLINE** EDUCATION **EDUCATION** Grambling State University, BS, 1962; University of Wisconsin, MA, 1964; Atlanta University, MA, 1966; Georgia State University, PhD, 1982. **CAREER** Grambling State University, instructor, 1964-65; Jackson State University, instructor, 1965-66; Atlanta University, instructor, 1966-67; Spelman College, visiting professor, 1991; Morehouse College, class dean, professor, 1967-, director, summer academy, 1991-. **HONORS AND AWARDS** Phi Beta Kappa Honor Society, honorary member, 1992; Grambling State University Hall of Fame, inducted member, 1991; Golden Key National Honor Society, 1992; NAFEO Distinguished Alumni Award, nominated by GSU, 1990. **MEMBERSHIPS** National Cancer Institute Advisory Committee, chairperson of curriculum committee, 1988-90; National Black Political Action Forum, consultant, 1987-89; Alpha Kappa Alpha Sorority, Inc, internat consultant, 1991-; Atlanta Job Corps Center, advisory committee, 1992-; National Council of Negro Women, 1990-; 100 Women of Atlanta, internat pub editor, 1988-. **SELECTED PUBLICATIONS** The Litteratus, founder and editor, 1984-; Three Voices, 1988; M J: Modern Job, 1991, 1992. **CONTACT ADDRESS** Dean, Professor, Director of Summer Academy, Morehouse Col, 830 Westview Dr, Atlanta, GA, 30314.

WAUGH, DANIEL CLARKE
PERSONAL Born 12/12/1941, Philadelphia, PA **DISCIPLINE** MEDIEVAL & EARLY MODERN RUSSIAN HISTORY **EDUCATION** Yale Univ, BA, 63; Harvard Univ, AM, 65, PhD(hist), 72. **CAREER** Asst prof, 72-80, Assoc Prof Hist & Russ & East Europ Studies, Univ Wash, 80-. **MEMBERSHIPS** Am Asn Advan Slavic Studies; Int Asn Paper Historians. **RESEARCH** Cultural history of Muscovite Russia; Russian diplomatics; paleography and codicology; filigranology. **SELECTED PUBLICATIONS** Contribr, Appendix I, In: The Kurbskii-Groznyi Apocrypha, Harvard Univ, 71; auth, Neizvestnyi pamiatnik drevnerusskoi literatury, Arkheograficheskii ezhegodnik za 1971 god, 72; K izucheniiu istorii rukopisnogo sobraniia P M Stroeva, Trudy Otdela drevnerusskoi literatury, 76 & 77; Slavianskie rukopisi Sobraniia Grafa F A Tolstogo, Inter Doc Co, 77; The lessons of the Kurbskii Controversy regarding the study and dating of old Russian manuscripts, In: Russian and Slavic History, 77 & The Great Turkes Defiance: On the History of the Apocryphal Correspondence of the Ottoman Sultan in Its Muscovite and Russian Variants, 78, Slavica; Two Unpublished Muscovite Chronicles, Oxford Slavonic Papers, 79; News of the False Messiah: Reports on Shabbetai Zevi in Ukraine and Muscovy, Jewish Social Studies, 79; Semiotics Of History - German - Uspenskij,Ba, Speculum-A Journal Of Medieval Studies, Vol 0069, 1994; Semiotics Of History - German - Uspenskij,Ba, Speculum-A Journal Of Medieval Studies, Vol 0069, 1994; In Appreciation Of Keenan,Ned Warm Tribute To Lure,Yakov,Solomonovich/, Slavic Review, Vol 0056, 1997. **CONTACT ADDRESS** Dept of Hist, Univ Wash, Seattle, WA, 98195.

WAUGH, EARLE HOWARD
PERSONAL Born 11/06/1936, Regina, SK, Canada, m, 1970, 3 children **DISCIPLINE** HISTORY OF RELIGION **EDUCATION** McMaster Univ, BA, 59, MA, 65; Univ Chicago, MA, 68, PhD(hist relig), 72. **CAREER** Asst prof relig, Cleveland State Univ, 72-74; Assoc Prof Relig Studies, Univ of Alta, 76-, Chmn Dept, 74-, Mem nat alumni coun, Divinity Sch, Univ Chicago, 73- **MEMBERSHIPS** Am Acad Relig; Mid East Studies Asn; Can Soc Study Relig. **RESEARCH** Islam; Eastern religions; religion in Canada. **SELECTED PUBLICATIONS** Auth, Jealous angels: Aspects of Muslim religious language, Ohio J Relig Studies, Vol 1 No 2; coauth, Religious Encounters with Death, Pa State Univ, 77; auth, Metaphors of death in ecstatic religion, Listening, 78; The Imam in the New World: Models and modification, Festschrift, Univ Chicago, 78; The Other Sides Of Paradise - Explorations Into The Religious Meanings Of Domestic Space In Islam - Campo,Je, History Of Religions, Vol 0033, 1993; The Arab Christian - A History In The Middle-East - Cragg,K, Journal Of Religion, Vol 0073, 1993; The Other Sides Of Paradise - Explorations Into The Religious Meanings Of Domestic Space In Islam - Campo,Je, History Of Religions, Vol 0033, 1993; Muslims, Their Religious Beliefs And Practices, Vols 1-2 - Rippin,A, Studies In Religion-Sciences Religieuses, Vol 0024, 1995; Fundamentalism - Harbinger Of Academic Revisionism/, Journal Of The American Academy Of Religion, Vol 0065, 1997; Sufism, Mystics, And Saints In Modern Egypt - Hoffman,Vj, History Of Religions, Vol 0037, 1997; Sufism, Mystics, And Saints In Modern Egypt - Hoffman,Vj, History Of Religions, Vol 0037, 1997. **CONTACT ADDRESS** Dept of Relig Studies, Univ of Alta, Rm 322 Arts Bldg, Edmonton, AB, T6G 2Ey.

WAXMAN, CHAIM I.
PERSONAL Born 02/26/1941, New York, NY, m, 1962, 3 children **DISCIPLINE** SOCIOLOGY **EDUCATION** BA, 63, MHL, 65, Yeshiva Univ; MA, 65, PhD, 74, New Sch for Soc Res. **CAREER** Vis prof sociol and polit sci, Telaviv Univ, 82-84; vis prof, Yeshiva Univ, 76-; asst prof and prof of sociol, Rutgers Univ, 75-. **HONORS AND AWARDS** Pres, Asn for the Sociol Study of Jewry, 79-81. **MEMBERSHIPS** Amer Sociol Asn; Soc for the Sci Study of Relig; Eastern Sociol Asn; Asn for the Sociol of Relig; Asn for Jewish Studies; Asn for Israel Studies. **RESEARCH** Sociology of Religion; Ethnicity; Jewish Studies; Israel Studies. **SELECTED PUBLICATIONS** Auth, The Stigma of Poverty: A Critique of Poverty Theories and Policies, Pergamon Press, 77, 2nd ed, 80; America's Jews in Transition, Temple Univ Press, 82; American Aliya: Portrait of an Innovative Migration Movement, Wayne State Univ Press, 89. **CONTACT ADDRESS** Sociology Dept, Rutgers Univ, Piscataway, NJ, 08854-8045. **EMAIL** waxmanci@rci.rutgers.edu

WAY, PETER J.
DISCIPLINE HISTORY **EDUCATION** Trent Univ, Can, BA, 81; Queen's Univ, Can, MA, 83; Univ Md, PhD, 91. **CAREER** Reader Amer hist, Sussex, Eng. **RESEARCH** Canal construction labor. **SELECTED PUBLICATIONS** Fel Publ, Common Labour: Workers and the Digging of North American Canals 1780-1860, Cambridge Univ, 97; auth, Shovel and Shamrock: Irish Workers and Labor Violence in the Digging of the Chesapeake and Ohio Canal, Labor Hist 30, 89; Evil Humors and Ardent Spirits: The Rough Culture of Canal Construction Laborers, Jour of Amer Hist 79, no 4, 93; Labour's Love Lost: Observations on the Historiography of Class and Ethnicity in the Nineteenth Century, Jour of Amer Stud 28, 94; Canal Wars: The Making of the Chesapeake and Ohio Canal, In: True Stories from the American Past,Vol 1, McGraw-Hill, 97. **CONTACT ADDRESS** School of English and American Studies, Univ of Sussex, Falmer, ., BNI 9QN. **EMAIL** p.j.way@sussex.ac.uk

WEAKLAND, JOHN EDGAR
PERSONAL Born 05/11/1932, Mansfield, OH, m, 1960, 3 children **DISCIPLINE** MEDIEVAL & RENAISSANCE HISTORY **EDUCATION** John Carroll Univ, BSS, 54; Kent State Univ, MA, 60; Western Reserve Univ, PhD, 66. **CAREER** Instr hist, Kent State Univ, 60-66; from asst prof to assoc prof, 66-73, prof hist, Ball State Univ, 73; vis scholar, St Edmund's House, Cambridge, 73, 83; dir, London Ctr, Ball State Univ, 74-75; ed, Int J Soc Educ, 84-98. **HONORS AND AWARDS** Am Philos Soc res grant, 68-69 & 71-72; Andrew W Mellon fel, 82; Outstanding Fac Serv Award, Ball State Univ, 96. **MEMBERSHIPS** AHA; Am Cath Hist Asn; Mediaeval Acad Am; Renaissance Soc Am; Am Soc Church Hist. **RESEARCH** Early Renaissance church; Avignon Papacy; medieval witchcraft. **SELECTED PUBLICATIONS** Auth, John XXII before his pontificate, 1244-1316: Jacques Duese and his family, Archivum Hist Pontificiae, 72; ed & contribr, Society in ferment: medieval and modern, 72 & Focus on religion, 72, Ind Soc Studies Quart; auth, Renaissance Paideia: some ideals in Italian humanism and their relevance today, Social Studies, 4/73; ed & contribr, Myths-past and present, Indians Social Studies Quart, 75; auth, Pastorelli, Pope and persecution, Jewish Social Studies, 76; coauth, Wing Chun: Sil Lim Tao, Crompton, London, 76; coauth, Wing Chun: Chum Kil, Crompton, London, 81; Wang Chun: Bil Jee, Crompton, 83. **CONTACT ADDRESS** Dept of Hist, Ball State Univ, 2000 W University, Muncie, IN, 47306-0480. **EMAIL** 00jeweakland@bsu.edu

WEARE, WALTER BURDETTE
PERSONAL Born 12/26/1938, Denver, CO, m, 1955, 2 children **DISCIPLINE** UNITED STATES HISTORY **EDUCATION** Univ Colo, BA, 63, MA, 64; Univ NC, PhD(hist), 70. **CAREER** From instr to asst prof, 68-74, assoc prof hist, Univ Wis-Milwaukee, 74-, Nat Endowment for Humanities fel Afro-Am hist & cult, Stanford Univ, 70-71; Am Coun Learned Soc fel, 76-77. **MEMBERSHIPS** Southern Hist Asn; Asn Study Afro-Am Life & Hist; Orgn Am Historians. **RESEARCH** History of the South; Afro-American history; United States social and intellectual history since 1865. **SELECTED PUBLICATIONS** Auth, Black Business in the New South: A Social History of the North Carolina Mutual Life Insurance Company, Univ Ill, 73. **CONTACT ADDRESS** Dept of History, Univ of Wisconsin, PO Box 413, Milwaukee, WI, 53201-0413. **EMAIL** BWeare@csd.uwm.edu

WEARING, J.P.
PERSONAL Birmingham, England **DISCIPLINE** ENGLISH LITERATURE, THEATRE HISTORY **EDUCATION** Univ Wales, Swansea, BA, 67, PhD(English), 71; Univ Sask, MA, 68. **CAREER** Lectr English, Univ Alta, 71-74; asst prof, 74-77, assoc prof English, Univ Ariz, 77-84, Killam fel English, Univ Alta, 71-73; ed, Nineteenth Century Theatre Res, 72-; Guggenheim fel Theatre Hist, 78-79; prof English, Univ Ariz, 84-. **HONORS AND AWARDS** NEH Research Grant 87-91. **MEMBERSHIPS** Nineteenth Century Theatre Res; English Lit Transition. **RESEARCH** English theatre history; 19th and 20th century English drama; Shakespeare. **SELECTED PUBLICATIONS** Auth, Two early absurd plays in England, Mod Drama, 73; ed, The Collected Letters of Sir Arthur Pinero, Univ Minn, 74; auth, The London Stage 1890-1899: A Calendar of Plays and Players, Scarecrow, 76; The West End London Stage in the 1890's, Educ Theatre J, 77; coauth, English Drama and Theatre, 1800-1900, Gale Res, 78; auth, American and British Theatrical Biography: A Directory, Scarecrow, 78; Henry Arthur Jones: An Annotated Bibliography of Writings about Him, English Lit in Transition, 79; The London Stage 1900-1909: A Calendar of Plays and Players, Scarecrow, 81; The London Stage 1950-1959: A Calendar of Plays and Players, 2 vols, Metuchen, NJ & London: the Scarecrow Press, 93. **CONTACT ADDRESS** Dept of English, Univ of Arizona, 1 University of Arizona, Tucson, AZ, 85721-0001. **EMAIL** jpwearing@aol.com

WEART, SPENCER R.
PERSONAL Born 03/08/1942, Detroit, MI, m, 1971, 2 children **DISCIPLINE** HISTORY OF SCIENCE **EDUCATION** Cornell Univ, BA, 63, Univ Colo, PhD(physics & astrophysics), 68. **CAREER** Fel solar physics, Calif Inst Technol, 68-71; res specialist hist, Univ Calif, Berkeley, 71-74; Dir, Ctr Hist Physics, Am Inst Physics, 74-. **MEMBERSHIPS** Am Astron Soc; Hist Sci Soc; Soc Social Studies Sci. **RESEARCH** History of nuclear physics, astronomy and French science. **SELECTED PUBLICATIONS** Co-ed, Leo Szilard: His Version of the Facts, MIT Press, 78; Scientists in Power, Harvard Univ Press, 79; Global Warming, Cold-War, And The Evolution Of Research Plans/, Historical Studies In The Physical And Biological Sciences, Vol 0027, 1997; Global Warming, Cold-War, And The Evolution Of Research Plans/, Historical Studies In The Physical And Biological Sciences, Vol 0027, 1997. **CONTACT ADDRESS** Am Inst of Physics, 335 East 45 St, New York, NY, 10017.

WEAVER, GARRETT F.
PERSONAL Born 06/17/1948, Durham, NC, s **DISCIPLINE** HISTORY **EDUCATION** NC Cntrl, Attend; Univ of NC, PhD 1987. **CAREER** Univ of NC, lectr Afro-Amer studies 1985; Univ of WI, 1973-74; St Augustine Coll, 1972-73; NC St Univ, 1972-73; Rio Grande Coll; Marshall Univ; WV Univ, 1968-72; Afro-Amer & African Studies, 1985; Jackson State Univ, asst prof of history 1975-88. **MEMBERSHIPS** Mem Am Historical Assn; Assn for Study of Afro-Am & Life & History; Nat Geo Soc; pres NAACP Charleston; mem Kanawha Co Div Comm Wlfr Bd; NASALH Biecennial Com; Phi Beta Sigma Frat; Afro-Am Studies Cons; Black Geneological Rsrchr; dir Public & Applied History Prop; dir of history English Link Proj Jackson State Univ. **CONTACT ADDRESS** UNC Chapel Hill, 301 Peabody, Chapel Hill, NC, 27514.

WEAVER, JOHN CHARLES
PERSONAL Born 05/11/1946, Stratford, ON, Canada, m, 1971, 1 child **DISCIPLINE** URBAN & CANADIAN HISTORY **EDUCATION** Queens Univ, BA Hons, 69; Duke Univ, MA, 70, PhD(hist), 73. **CAREER** Lectr hist, Queens Univ, 72-74; asst, 74-77, Assoc Hist, Mcmaster Univ, 78-, Res assoc urban studies, Inst Local Gov, Queens Univ, 73-74. **MEMBERSHIPS** Can Hist Asn. **RESEARCH** Urban land use; urban social. **SELECTED PUBLICATIONS** Auth, The reconstruction of the Richmond District: An episode in Canadian planning and public housing, Plan Can, 75; Tomorrow's metropolis revisited: A critical assessment of Canadian urban reform, Can City, 77; Shaping the Canadian City, 1890-1920, Inst Pub Affairs, Can, 77; Policing Morals, The Metropolitan Police And The Home-Office - Petrow,S, Urban History Review-Revue D Histoire Urbaine, Vol 0023, 1995; Beyond The Fatal Shore - Pastoral Squatting And The Occupation Of Australia, 1826 To 1852, American Historical Review, Vol 0101, 1996. **CONTACT ADDRESS** 66 St Margarets Rd, Lancaster, ON, L9G 2K9.

WEBB, GEORGE ERNEST
PERSONAL Born 06/17/1952 **DISCIPLINE** AMERICAN HISTORY, HISTORY OF SCIENCE **EDUCATION** Univ AZ, BA, 73, MA, 74, PhD, 78. **CAREER** Asst Prof Hist, TN Technol Univ, 78-83; Assoc Prof Hist, TN Technol Univ, 83-88; Prof Hist, TN Technol Univ, 88-. **HONORS AND AWARDS** Phi Beta Kappa, Phi Kappa Phi, Outstanding Fac Award in Tchg, TN Technol Univ, 90; Caplenor Faculty Research Award, TN Technol Univ, 93. **MEMBERSHIPS** AHA; Hist Sci Soc; West Hist Assoc; AAAS. **RESEARCH** Hist of Am science. **SELECTED PUBLICATIONS** Auth, A E Douglass and the canals of Mars, 1890-1907, The Astron Quart, spring 79; Space Colonization, Alternative Futures, summer 80; The planet Mars and science in Victorian America, J Am Cult, winter 80; Douglass, Andrew Ellicott & Nicholson, Seth Barnes, Dict American Biography, Supplement 7, Scribner, 81; Tree Rings and Telescopes: The Scientific Career of A.E. Douglass, Univ AZ, 83; The Evolution Controversy in America, KY Univ, 94. **CONTACT ADDRESS** Dept of History, TN Technol Univ, Cookeville, TN, 38505. **EMAIL** gwebb@tntech.edu

WEBB, ROBERT KIEFER
PERSONAL Born 11/23/1922, Toledo, OH, m, 2 children **DISCIPLINE** HISTORY **EDUCATION** Oberlin Col, AB, 47; Columbia Univ, AM, 48, PhD, 51. **CAREER** Instr hist, Wesleyan Univ, 51-53; from asst prof to prof, Columbia Univ, 53-70; ed, Am Hist Rev, 68-75; Prof hist, Univ MD, Baltimore County 75-93, Guggenheim fel, 59-60, 73-74; Am Coun Learned Soc fel, 66-67; ed, AAUP Bull, 75-81; Nat Endowment for Humanities res grant, 78-80; Mem, Instit for Ad Stud, 82-83; Vis fel, Australian Natl Univ, 86; Christensen Res Fel, St. Catherine's Coll, Oxford, 92; Emer Prof, 93-. **HONORS AND AWARDS** Hon fel, Australian Acad of the Hum; Hon fel, Harris Manchester Col, Oxford. **MEMBERSHIPS** Fel Royal Hist Soc. **RESEARCH** Nineteenth century Brit soc hist. **SELECTED PUBLICATIONS** Auth, The British Working Class Reader, 1790-1848, 55 & Harriet Martineau, A Radical Victorian, 60, Columbia Univ; Modern England, 68, 2nd ed, 80 & coauth, Modern Europe, 73, Harper. **CONTACT ADDRESS** Dept of History, Univ of MD, 1000 Hilltop Cir, Baltimore, MD, 21250.

WEBB, ROSS ALLAN
PERSONAL Born 07/22/1923, Westchester, NS, Canada, m, 1954, 2 children **DISCIPLINE** AMERICAN DIPLOMATIC RECONSTRUCTION & BRITISH HISTORY **EDUCATION** Acadia Univ, BA, 49; Univ Pittsburgh, MA, 51, PhD, 56. **CAREER** Lectr hist, Univ Pittsburgh, 50-56; from asst prof to assoc prof, Univ Ky, 56-57; dean fac, 68-75, vpres acad affairs, 71-75, chmn dept hist, 67-68 **HONORS AND AWARDS** Distinguished Prof Award, Winthrop Univ, 77; Algernon Sydney Sullivan Award, 81. **MEMBERSHIPS** AHA; Southern Hist Asn; Orgn Am Hist. **RESEARCH** The British provincial press and the coming of the American Revolution. **SELECTED PUBLICATIONS** Auth, The Alaskan Boundary Dispute, 1779-1903, US Dept State, 51; coauth, A Book of Remembrance, Univ Pittsburgh, 56; auth, A Yankee from Dixie: Benjamin Helm Bristow, 3/64 & Benjamin H Bristow, civil rights champion, 1866-1872, Civil War Hist, 69; Benjamin Helm Bristow, Border State Politician, Univ Ky, 69; contribr, Radicalism, Racism and Party Realignment: The Border States During Reconstruction, Johns Hopkins Univ, 69; auth, Kentucky in the Reconstruction Era, Univ Press Ky, 79. **CONTACT ADDRESS** Dept of History, Winthrop Univ, 701 W Oakland Ave, Rock Hill, SC, 29733-0001. **EMAIL** WEBBR@winthrop.edu

WEBB, RUTH H.
DISCIPLINE CLASSICAL AND BYZANTINE RHETORIC AND EDUCATION **EDUCATION** Oxford Univ, MA, 86; London, PhD, 92. **CAREER** Asst prof, Princeton Univ. **RESEARCH** Literary narrative in late antique texts. **SELECTED PUBLICATIONS** Areas: Byzantine education, female entertainers,rhetorical ekphrasis. **CONTACT ADDRESS** Princeton Univ, 1 Nassau Hall, Princeton, NJ, 08544. **EMAIL** rhwebb@princeton.edu

WEBB, STEPHEN S.
PERSONAL Born 05/25/1937, Syracuse, NY, m, 1959, 2 children **DISCIPLINE** AMERICAN COLONIAL HISTORY **EDUCATION** Williams Col, BA, 59; Univ Wis-Madison, MS, 61, PhD(hist), 65. **CAREER** Asst prof, St Lawrence Univ, 64-65 & Col William & Mary, 65-68; assoc prof, 68-79, fac chmn, master soc sci degree prog, 74-80, Prof Hist, Syracuse Univ, 79-, Inst Early Am Hist & Cult fel, 65-68; assoc, Columbia Univ Sem Early Am Hist & Cult, 68-, chmn, 76-77; fel, Charles Warren Ctr, Harvard Univ, 71-72 & 74-75; Nat Endowment for Humanities fel, 71-72; assoc, Inst Early Am Hist & Cult, 77-. **RESEARCH** British imperial and American colonial history. **SELECTED PUBLICATIONS** Auth, The strange career of Francis Nicholson, 66, William Blathwayt, imperial fixer, 68 & Muddling through to empire, 69, William & Mary Quart; The household of James Stuart, Perspectives Am Hist, 74; The trials of Sir Edmund Andros, Human Dimensions of Nation-Making, 76; Army and Empire: English Garrison; Government in Britain & America, William & Mary Quart, 77, & Harper & Row, 78; The 'Madness Of King George' - Hytner,N, William And Mary Quarterly, Vol 0052, 1995; The Governors-General, Univ NC & Inst Early Am Hist & Cult, 79; Fields Of Battle - The Wars For North-America - Keegan,J, Reviews In American History, Vol 0025, 1997. **CONTACT ADDRESS** Dept of Hist, Syracuse Univ, Syracuse, NY, 13210.

WEBBER, RANDALL C.
PERSONAL Born 11/28/1961, Oak Ridge, TN, s **DISCIPLINE** HISTORY; RELIGIOUS STUDIES/SOCIOLOGY **EDUCATION** Furman Univ, BA, 82; Southern Baptist Theological Seminary, MDiv, 85, PhD, 89. **CAREER** Manuscript editor, 87-89, Paradigms; asst ed, 89-92, Univ MI; dir, emergency housing, Salvation Army, 92- ; proprietor, Webber Church Consulting, 97- . **HONORS AND AWARDS** Who's Who in Biblical Studies and Archaeology, 93. **MEMBERSHIPS** Soc of Biblical Lit; Amer Academy of Bereavement. **RESEARCH** Early Christianity; Grief; Politics **SELECTED PUBLICATIONS** Auth, Successful Grief and Chronic Homelessness: Is There a Relationship? Grief Work, 95; auth, Kentucky Reader Proposes Ethics Code for Churches, Baptist Today, 95; auth, Reader-Response Analysis of the Epistle of James, 96; Apocalyptic as a Second Language, in Teaching Apocalyptic, forthcoming. **CONTACT ADDRESS** 325 E Kentucky St, Louisville, KY, 40203-2709.

WEBER, CLIFFORD WHITBECK
PERSONAL Born 04/22/1943, Scranton, PA, m, 1967 **DISCIPLINE** CLASSICS **EDUCATION** Harvard Univ, AB, 65; Univ Calif, Berkeley, PhD, 75. **CAREER** Asst prof, 69-78, assoc prof classics, Kenyon Col, 78-89. **HONORS AND AWARDS** Harvard Col, Detur Prize for acad distinc, Louis Curtis Prize, Phi Beta Kappa; Kenyon Col Fac Develop Grants, 71, 72; NEH Sum Sem Grant at the Univ of Tex, 76. **MEMBERSHIPS** Am Philol Assn. **RESEARCH** Latin poetry. **SELECTED PUBLICATIONS** Art, Dodona Reneges: A Neglected Oxymoron in Georgics 1, Classical Philology, 91; auth, The Allegory of Virgil's Golden Bough, 95; art, Roscius and the Roscida Dea, Classical Quarterly, 96. **CONTACT ADDRESS** Kenyon Col, Ascension Hall, Gambier, OH, 43022-9623. **EMAIL** weberc@kenyon.edu

WEBER, DAVID J.
PERSONAL Born 12/20/1940, Buffalo, NY, m, 1962, 2 children **DISCIPLINE** LATIN AMERICAN & AMERICAN SOUTHWEST HISTORY **EDUCATION** State Univ NY Col, Fredonia, BS, 62; Univ NM, MA, 64, PhD, 67. **CAREER** From asst prof to prof hist, San Diego State Univ, 67-76; PROF HIST, SOUTHERN METHODIST UNIV, 76-, DEPT CHMN, 79-86, ROBERT AND NANCY DEDMAN PROF HIST, 86-, DIR, WILLIAM P. CLEMENTS CENTER FOR SOUTHWEST STUDIES, 95-; Fulbright-Hays lectr, Univ Costa Rica, 70; Danforth Assoc, 73; NEH Younger Humanist fel hist, 74-75; Am Coun Learned Soc fel, 80; Fellow, Center for Advanced Study in the Behavioral Sciences, Stanford Univ, 86-87, NEH Fellowship, 90-91. **HONORS AND AWARDS** Herbert E Bolton Award, Western Hist Asn, 81; Ray Allen Billington Award from the Org of Am Hist for the best book to appear on the American frontier in the previous two years, 83; elected to membership in the Academia Mexicana de la Historia, 83; Outstanding Art Book Award from the Nat Cowboy Hall of Fame and Western Heritage Center, 85; elected a Fellow of the Soc of Am Hist, 86; Honorary President, 8th Conference of Mexican and North American Historians, San Diego, Oct 90; Caughey Western History Asn Prize, for the outstanding book on the American West in 92; Premio Espana y America, from the Spanish Ministry of Culture, 92. **MEMBERSHIPS** Orgn Am Historians; Conf Latin Am Hist; Western Hist Asn, pres 90-91; AHA. **RESEARCH** Spanish-Mexican borderlands; Chicano history; fur trade. **SELECTED PUBLICATIONS** Ed, The Extranjeros: Selected Documents from the Mexican Side of the Trail, 1825-1828, Stagecoach Press, 67; The Lost Trappers, Univ NM, 70; auth, The Taos Trappers: The Fur Trade in the Far Southwest, 1540-1846, Univ OK, 71; Foreigners in Their Native Land: Historical Roots of the Mexican Americans, Univ NM, 73; ed, Northern Mexico on the Eve of the United States Invasion: Rare Imprints Concerning California, Arizona, New Mexico and Texas, 1821-1846, Arno, 76; co-ed, Fortunes are for the Few: Letters of a Forty-Niner by Charles William Churchill, San Diego Hist Soc, 77; ed, New Spain's Far Northern Frontier: Essays on Spain in the American West, 1540-1821, 79 & auth, The Mexican Frontier, 1821-1846: The American Southwest Under Mexico, 82, Univ NM; Richard H. Kern: Expeditionary Artist in the Far Southwest, 1848-1853, Univ of NM Press, 85; Myth and the History of the Hispanic Southwest: Essays by David J. Weber, Univ of NM Press, 88, paperback reprint 90; The Californios vs. Jedediah Smith: A New Cache of Documents, Arthur H. Clark Co, 90; The Spanish Frontier in North America, Yale Univ Press, 92; co-ed, Trading in Santa Fe: John Kingsbury's Correspondence with James Josiah Webb, 1853-1861, SMU Press for the DeGolyer Lib, 96; On the Edge of Empire: The Taos Hacienda of Los Martinez, Museum of NM Press, 96. **CONTACT ADDRESS** Hist Dept, Southern Methodist Univ, Dallas, TX, 75275-0176. **EMAIL** dweber@mail.smu.edu

WEBER, RONALD
PERSONAL m, 3 children **DISCIPLINE** AMERICAN STUDIES **EDUCATION** Univ Notre Dame, BA, 57; Univ Iowa, MFA, 60; Univ Minn, PhD, 67. **CAREER** Instr, Loras Col, 60-62; asst prof, 63-66, assoc prof, 67-76, prof, Am Stud, 76- , chemn, 70-77, Univ Notre Dame. **HONORS AND AWARDS** Fulbright lectr, Univ Coimbra, Portugal, 68-69, 82, Univ Lisbon, 82; res fel, NEH, 72-73; Faculty Award, 76; CHOICE Outstanding Academic Book of 81-82; res award, Univ Notre Dame 83, 88; res fel, Freedom Forum Center for Media Stud, Columbia Univ, 85-86; Bronze Medal, Council for Advancement and Support of Ed, 88; exec committee, Catholic Comn on Intellectual and Cult Affairs, 93-96. **SELECTED PUBLICATIONS** Auth, O Romance Americano, Libraria Almedina, 69; ed and contribur, America in Change: Reflections on the 60s and 70s, Univ Notre Dame, 72; ed and contribur, The Reporter as Artist: A Look at The New Journalism Controversy, Hastings, 74; co-ed and contribur, An Almost Chosen People: The Moral Aspirations of Americans, Univ Notre Dame, 76; auth, The Literature of Fact: Literary Nonfiction in American Writing, Ohio Univ, 80; auth, Seeing Earth: Space Exploration in American Writing, Ohio Univ Pr, 84; auth, Company Spook, St Martins, 86; auth, Troubleshooter, St Martins, 88; auth, Hemingway's Art of Nonfiction, St Martins, 90; auth, The Midwestern Ascendancy in American Writing, Indiana Univ, 92; auth, Hired Pens: Professional Writers in America's Golden Age of Print, Ohio Univ, 97; auth, The Aluminum Hatch, Write Way, 98. **CONTACT ADDRESS** Dept of American Studies, Univ of Notre Dame, 228 Decio Hall, Notre Dame, IN, 46556.

WEBER, SHIRLEY NASH
PERSONAL Born 09/20/1948, Hope, AR, m **DISCIPLINE** AFRICAN-AMERICAN STUDIES **EDUCATION** Univ of CA LA, BA 1966-70, MA 1970-71, PhD 1971-75. **CAREER** Episcopal City Mission Soc LA, caseworker 1969-72; CA State Coll LA, instructor 1972; SAN DIEGO STATE UNIV, PROF 1972-; San Diego City Schools, San Diego, CA, president, board of education, 1990-91. **HONORS AND AWARDS** Fellow Woodrow Wilson Fellowship 1970; Black Achievement Action Enterprise Develop 1981; Women of Distinction Women Inc 1984; Natl Citation Award, Natl Sorority of Phi Delta Kappa, Inc. July 1989; Citizen of the Year, Omega Psi Phi Fraternity, 1989; Carter G Woodson Education Award, NAACP, San Diego, 1989. **MEMBERSHIPS** Bd mem CA Black Faculty & Staff 1976-80; pres Black Caucus Speech Comm Assoc 1980-82; pres Natl Comm Assn 1983-85; regional editor Western Journal of Speech 1979-; adv bd Battered Women's Serv YWCA 1981-; Council of 21 Southwestern Christian Coll 1983-; 1st vice pres Natl Sor of Phi Delta Kappa Delta Upsilon Chapt; trustee Bd of Educ San Diego Unified School District 1988-96. **CONTACT ADDRESS** Afro-American Studies, San Diego State Univ, San Diego, CA, 92182.

WEBRE, STEPHEN
PERSONAL Born 10/13/1946, m **DISCIPLINE** HISTORY **EDUCATION** Univ Southwestern La, BA, 68; Tulane Univ, MA, 75, PhD, 80. **CAREER** Cur Manuscript, La State Mus, 80-82; asst prof hist, 82-85, assoc prof hist, 85-90, prof hist, La Tech Univ, 90-. **MEMBERSHIPS** Am Hist Asn; Latin Am Studies Asn; La Hist Asn; N La Hist Asn; SW Hist Asn; Southwestern Soc Sci Asn. **RESEARCH** Soc and polit hist of Colonial Latin Am; emphasis on Central Am; 20th-century polit movements in Mod Latin Am. **SELECTED PUBLICATIONS** Auth, Guerre et pouvoir au Salvador: Ideologies du changement

et changement ideologique, by Ivon Grenier, 96; The Banana Men: American Mercenaries and Entrepreneurs in Central America, 1880-1930, by Lester D. Langley and Thomas Schoonover, La Hist, 96. **CONTACT ADDRESS** Dept of Hist, Louisiana Tech Univ, PO Box 3178, Ruston, LA, 71272.

WEBSTER, DONALD B.
PERSONAL Born 10/14/1933, Rochester, NY **DISCIPLINE** CURATOR/HISTORIAN **EDUCATION** Univ Maine, BA, 59; Univ RI, MA, 61. **CAREER** NY State Hist Asn, 61-63; Robertson Mus Arts & Sci, 63-66; PROF, UNIV TORONTO, 66-; CURATOR EMER, CANADIANA DEPT, ROYAL ONT MUS; ch, Nat Portrait Gallery. **HONORS AND AWARDS** Fel, Royal Soc Arts **MEMBERSHIPS** Co Mil Hist; Am Ceramic Cir; Soc Hist Archaeol; Soc Post-Medieval Archaeol. **SELECTED PUBLICATIONS** Auth, Georgian Canada, Conflict & Culture, 84; auth, Military Bolt Action Rifles 1841-1918, 93; auth, Canfake, 97; ed, Book of Canadian Antiques, 74. **CONTACT ADDRESS** Canadiana Dept, Royal Ont Mus, 100 Queen's Park, Toronto, ON, M5S 2C6.

WEBSTER, JAMES
DISCIPLINE MUSIC **EDUCATION** Harvard Col, BA, 63; Princeton Univ, MFA, 65, PhD, 74. **CAREER** Goldwin Smith prof **HONORS AND AWARDS** Fulbright fel, 65-67; Alfred Einstein awd, Amer Musicol Soc, 77; Otto Kinkeldey awd, AMS, 92; NEH, sr res fel, 78-79; Guggenheim fel, 92-93. **MEMBERSHIPS** Pres, Amer Musicol Soc, 96-98; Int Musicol Soc; Soc Music Theory; Amer Soc 18th-Century Stud. **RESEARCH** Haydn; Mozart; Beethoven; Schubert; Brahms; opera buffa; analysis; theory of music; historiography; aesthetics. **SELECTED PUBLICATIONS** Auth, Haydn's Farewell Symphony and the Idea of Classical Style: Through-Composition and Cyclic Integration in his Instrumental Music, Cambridge Univ Press, 91; ed, Opera Buffa in Mozart's Vienna, Cambridge UP, 97; The Analysis of Mozart's Arias, In Cliff Eisen, Mozart Studies, Oxford UP, 91; The Form of the Finale of Beethoven's Ninth Symphony, Beethoven Forum, 92. **CONTACT ADDRESS** Dept of Music, Cornell Univ, 104 Lincoln Hall, Ithaca, NY, 14853. **EMAIL** jcw4@cornell.edu

WEBSTER, JILL
PERSONAL Born 09/29/1931, London, England **DISCIPLINE** HISTORY **EDUCATION** Univ Liverpool, BA, 78, post-grad cert educ, 65; Univ Nottingham, MA, 64; Univ Toronto, PhD, 69. **CAREER** Prof, 68-95, assoc dean arts & sci, 78-81, dir ctr medieval stud, 89-94, ch grad dept Span & Port, 93-94, PROF EMER, UNIV TORONTO, 95-. **HONORS AND AWARDS** Fel, Royal Soc Can, 91. **MEMBERSHIPS** Pres, Am Acad Res Hist Medieval Spain, 90-95; Corres mem, Seccio Historica-Arqueologica, Inst d'Estudis Catalans, Barcelona, 96-. **SELECTED PUBLICATIONS** Auth, Els Menorets: The Franciscans in the Realms of Aragon from St. Francis to the Black Death(1348), 93. **CONTACT ADDRESS** Ctr Medieval Stud, Univ Toronto, 81 St. Mary St, Toronto, ON, M5S 1J4. **EMAIL** jwebster@epas.uoftoronto.ca

WEBSTER, NIAMBI DYANNE
DISCIPLINE HISTORY **EDUCATION** Drake Univ, BA, English/drama, 1973; Mankato State Coll, MS, curriculum & instruction, 1975; University of Iowa, PhD, curriculum & instruction, 1991. **CAREER** Des Moines Public Schools, instructor 1975-78; Iowa Bystander, freelance writer, associate editor, 1976-80; Univ of IA, coord minority progs 1978-83, grad asst instructor 1980-83; IA Arts Council, touring music/theatre folk artist 1978-; Coe Coll, instr dir special servs; dir, multicultural & international student affairs, Skidmore College 1989-91; SONOMA STATE UNIVERSITY, ASSISTANT PROFESSOR, AMERICAN MULTICULTURAL STUDIES DEPARTMENT, currently. **HONORS AND AWARDS** Comm Service in the Fine Arts NAACP Presidential 1978; Black Leadership Awd Univ of IA 1979; Social Action Awd Phi Beta Sigma Frat 1980; Outstanding Young Woman in the Arts NAACP Natl Women Cong 1981; Women Equality & Dedication Comm on the Status of Women 1981; Trio Achievers Awd Natl Cncl of Educ Oppor Assoc 1985; Outstanding Woman of the Year Awd Linn Co Comm 1986. **MEMBERSHIPS** Outreach counselor YMCA Des Moines 1974-78; instr Gateway Oppor Pageant 1975-78; press & publicity chair NAACP Des Moines Chap 1976-78; founder/dir Langston Hughes Co of Players 1976-82; co-chair Polk Co Rape/Sexual Assault Bd 1977-80; artist-in-the schools IA Arts Council 1978-; 6th Judicial Dist Correctional Serv CSP & News Editor Volunteer 1984-; chairperson Mid-Amer Assoc of Ed Oppty Prog Personnel Cultural Enrichment Comm 1984-; mem Delta Sigma Theta Sor, Berkeley Alumnae; Iowa City Comm Schools Equity Comm mem 1985-87. **CONTACT ADDRESS** American Multicultural Studies Department, Sonoma State Univ, 1801 E Cotati Ave, Rohnert Park, CA, 94928-3613.

WEBSTER, RICHARD J.
PERSONAL Born 04/28/1939, Towanda, PA, m, 1966, 1 child **DISCIPLINE** AMERICAN CIVILIZATION **EDUCATION** Lafayette Col, AB, 61; Univ of Delaware, MA, 63; Univ of Pennsylvania, MA, 65, PhD, 77. **CAREER** Inst, 63-67, Temple Univ; Asst Prof, 67-69, Assoc Prof, 69-78, Prof, 78-, West Chester Univ. **HONORS AND AWARDS** Pi Delta Epsilon (Journalism) Awd, Lafayette Col; Winterthur Fel, Univ of Del. **MEMBERSHIPS** Soc of Architectual Historians, Vernacular Architecture Forum, Penn Hist Assoc **RESEARCH** American architecture and material culture, Pennsylvania in particular. **SELECTED PUBLICATIONS** Auth, Philadelphia Preserved Catalog of the Historic American Buildings Survey, Temple Univ Press, 76 rev ed 81; CoAuth Philadelphia Three Centuries of American Art, Phil Musuem of Art, 76; Introduction Philadelphia A Guide to the Nations Birthplace, Univ of Penn Press, 88; Cultural Stability on a Moving Frontier Germanic Domestic Architecture from Eighteenth Century Pennsylvania to Nineteenth Century Missouri, Proc of Soc for the Interdisciplinary Stud of Soc Imagery, Univ of South Colorado, 97; CoAuth, Pennsylvania Catalog Historic American Buildings Survey, Penn Hist and Museum Com, 99. **CONTACT ADDRESS** 1249 Surrey Rd, West Chester, PA, 19382. **EMAIL** rwebster@wcupa.edu

WECKMAN, GEORGE
PERSONAL Born 03/20/1939, Philadelphia, PA **DISCIPLINE** HISTORY OF RELIGION **EDUCATION** Philadelphia Lutheran Sem, BD, 63; Univ Chicago, PhD, 69. **CAREER** Asst prof Philos, 68-72, assoc prof, 72- , Ohio Univ. **MEMBERSHIPS** AAR. **RESEARCH** Monasticism. **SELECTED PUBLICATIONS** Auth, My Brothers' Place: An American Lutheran Monastery, Lawrenceville, VA, Brunswick Publ Corp, 92; Reduction in the Classroom, in Religion and Reductionism: essays on Eliade, Segal, and the Challenge of the Social Sciences for the Study of Religion, ed, Thomas A. Idinopulos and Edward Yonan, Leiden, E.J. Brill, 94, 211-219; Respect of Ohters' Sacreds, in The Sacred and its Scholars, ed Thomas A. Idinopulos and Edward Yonan, Leiden, E.J. Brill, 96. **CONTACT ADDRESS** Dept of Philosophy, Ohio Univ, 19 Park Pl, Athens, OH, 45701. **EMAIL** gweckman@ohiou.edu

WEEKS, T.R.
PERSONAL Born 09/05/1959, Okinawa, Japan **DISCIPLINE** HISTORY **EDUCATION** Univ California Berk, PhD 92; Univ Colorado Boul, MA 84, BA 80. **CAREER** SIUC, asst prof and assoc prof 93 to 97-. **HONORS AND AWARDS** Vitols Prize; SSRC fel; Golda Meir fel; Fulbright fel; Fulbright-Hays fel; FLAS fel; Mellon Grant; Patrick fel; Phi Beta Kappa. **MEMBERSHIPS** AHA; Assoc Adv Slavic Studies; CAS; Ntl Yiddish Bk Cen; ASN **RESEARCH** Nationalism; Min Ntlists E/C Europe, Russian Empire and USSR; Ntl Movements East Cen Europe and Russia; Ethnic Relations and Assimilation. **SELECTED PUBLICATIONS** Auth, Nation and State in Late Imperial Russia: Nationalism and Russification on Russia's Western Frontier 1863-1914, Dekalb, Northern IL Univ Press 96; Polish Jews and Jewish Poles: Assimilation in Russian Poland, 1863-1914, Polin: A Jour of Polish-Jewish Studies, 99; Fanning the Flames: Jews in the Warsaw Press, 1905-1912, East European Jewish Affairs, 98; Intl Jewish Conspiracy Reaches Poland: Teodor Jeske-Choinski and His Works, East European Quart, 97. **CONTACT ADDRESS** Dept of History, South Illinois Univ, Carbondale, IL, 62901-4519. **EMAIL** tadeusz@siu.edu

WEGS, JAMES ROBERT
PERSONAL Born 04/23/1937, Quincy, IL, m, 1964, 1 child **DISCIPLINE** MODERN EUROPEAN SOCIAL HISTORY **EDUCATION** Western Ill Univ, BA, 64; Northern Ill Univ, MA, 66; Univ Ill, PhD(hist), 70. **CAREER** Asst prof Europ hist, New York Univ, 69-76; asst prof, Vanderbilt Univ, 76-77; Assoc Prof Europ Hist, Univ Notre Dame, 77-. **MEMBERSHIPS** AHA **RESEARCH** Modern European social history; working class history. **SELECTED PUBLICATIONS** Auth, Europe Since 1945, St Martin's Press, 77; Die "sterreichische Kriegswirtschaft, 1914-1918, Verlag A Schendl, 79; Working class respectability: The Viennese experience, J Social Hist, summer 82; Images Of Youth - Age, Class, And The Male Youth Problem 1880-1920 - Hendrick,H, Journal Of Social History, Vol 0027, 1993; Fascism And The Working-Class In Austria, 1918-1934 - The Failure Of Labor In The 1st Republic - Lewis,J, Journal Of Modern History, Vol 0066, 1994. **CONTACT ADDRESS** 1024 E Napoleon, South Bend, IN, 46617.

WEHTJE, MYRON FLOYD
PERSONAL Born 10/21/1938, Longview, WA, m, 1962, 3 children **DISCIPLINE** EARLY AMERICAN HISTORY **EDUCATION** Andrews Univ, BA, 62, MA, 63; Univ Va, PhD, 78. **CAREER** Instr hist, Plainview Acad, SDak, 63-64 & Can Union Col, 64-67; from instr to asst prof, 68-71, assoc prof, 71-79, prof hist, Atlantic Union Col, 79-. **HONORS AND AWARDS** Thomas Jefferson Found Fel, 68-69; ZAPARA Excellence in Teaching Award, 88. **MEMBERSHIPS** The Soc for Hist of the Early Am Repub. **RESEARCH** Boston in the Revolutionary and early national periods; the age of Jefferson; American church history. **SELECTED PUBLICATIONS** Auth, The Congressional Elections of 1799 in Virginia, WVa Hist, 7/68; Charles Willson Peale and his Temple, Pa Hist, 4/69; Opposition in Virginia to the War of 1812, Va Mad Hist & Biog, 1/70; approx 20 articles for Hist J of Mass, including: Boston's First Response to Disorder in the Commonwealth, 1/84; Boston and the Calling of the Federal Convention of 1787, 6/87; The Ideal of Virtue in Post-Revolutionary Boston, winter/89; Controversy over the Legal Profession in Post-Revolutionary Boston, summer/92; Factionalism in Post-Revolutionary Boston, summer/95. **CONTACT ADDRESS** Dept of Hist, Atlantic Union Col, Box 1000, South Lancaster, MA, 01561-9999.

WEI, WILLIAM
DISCIPLINE HISTORY **EDUCATION** Marquette Univ, BA, 69; Univ Mich, MA, 71; PhD, 78. **CAREER** Prof. **HONORS AND AWARDS** Eugene M. Kayden Fac Bk Manuscript Prize, 85. **SELECTED PUBLICATIONS** Auth, Hmong American Youth: American Dream, American Nightmare, Univ NY, 98; The Anti-Chinese Movement in Colorado: Inter-Ethnic Competition and Conflict on the Eve of Exclusion, Chinese Am, 95; Insurgency by the Numbers: A Reconsideration of the Ecology of Communist Success in Jiangxi Province, China, 94; The Asian American Movement, Asian American History and Culture Series, Temple Univ, 93; Counterrevolution in China: The Nationalists in Jiangxi during the Soviet Period, Univ Mich, 85. **CONTACT ADDRESS** History Dept, Univ of Colorado, Boulder, Boulder, CO, 80309. **EMAIL** william.wei@colorado.edu

WEIGEL, RICHARD DAVID
PERSONAL Born 02/01/1945, Teaneck, NJ, m, 1968, 1 child **DISCIPLINE** HISTORY, CLASSICS **EDUCATION** Dickinson Col, BA, 66; Univ Del, MA, 68, PhD, 73. **CAREER** From instr to asst prof hist, Univ Del, 72-76; asst prof, Univ RI, 75; from Asst Prof to Assoc Prof, 76-84, Prof Hist, Western Ky Univ, 84-, Dept Head Hist, 98-. **HONORS AND AWARDS** Nat Endowment for Humanities summer sem grants, 77 & 80; Vis Schol, Wolfson Col, Oxford Univ, 93-; Am Acad in rome Advisory Coun, 94-. **MEMBERSHIPS** Am Philol Asn; Am Numismatic Soc Soc Ancient Numis; Soc Prom Roman Studies; Royal Numismatic Soc. **RESEARCH** Roman Republic; ancient numismatics; Roman religion. **SELECTED PUBLICATIONS** Coauth, Peace in the Ancient World, McFarland, 81; auth, Lepidus: The Tarnished Triumvir, Routledge, 92; Roman History in the Age of Enlightenment: The Dassier Medals, Revue Numismatique 36, 95; Roman Coins: An Iconographical Approach, Annali dell Istituto di Numismatica 42, 95; Roman Republican Generals and the Vowing of Temples, Classica et Medievalia (forthcoming 98); author of numerous other articles. **CONTACT ADDRESS** Dept of Hist, Western Kentucky Univ, 1 Big Red Way, Bowling Green, KY, 42101-3576. **EMAIL** Richard.Weigel@wku.edu

WEIGERT, ANDREW JOSEPH
PERSONAL Born 04/08/1934, New York, NY, m, 1968, 2 children **DISCIPLINE** SOCIOLOGY **EDUCATION** St. Louis Univ, BA, Philos, 58, PhL, 59, MA, Econ, 60; Woodstock Col, BTh, Theol, 64; Univ of Minn,PhD, Sociol, 68. **CAREER** Tchr, Mat, Sociol, Colegio San Ignacio, 60-62; asst prof, sociol, Univ of Notre Dame, 68-72; assoc prof, Univ of Notre Dame, 72-76; vis assoc prof, Sociol, Yale Divinity Sch, 73-74; res dir, Notre Dame London Prog, 86-87; PROF, SOCIOL, UNIV of NOTRE DAME, 76-. **HONORS AND AWARDS** Who's Who listing. **MEMBERSHIPS** Soc for the Sci Study of Relig; Asn for the Sociol of Relig; Soc for the Study of Symbolic Interaction. **RESEARCH** Social Psychology; Eschatology. **SELECTED PUBLICATIONS** Coauth, "Vital Realism and Sociology: A Metatheoretical Grounding in Mead, Ortega, and Schultz", Sociol Theory, 93; auth, "Lawn of Weeds," The Am Sociologist, 94; auth "Jose Ortega y Gasset on Life and Meaning,: Ultimate Reality and Meaning, 95; auth, "Moral Reasoning at the Interface of Philosophy and Sociology: A Comment on Dornbush and Thomas on Adolescent Values," Family Perspective, 95; coauth, "Multiplicity and Dialogue in Social Psychology: An Essay in Metatheorizing," Jour for the Theory of Soc Behav, 95; auth, "Definitional and Responsive Meanings: A Meadian look at Landscapes and Droughts," Jou for the Theory of Soc Behav, 97; auth, Self, Interaction, and Natural Environment, SUNY Press, 97. **CONTACT ADDRESS** Dept of Sociol, Univ of Notre Dame, Notre Dame, IN, 46556.

WEIGLEY, RUSSELL FRANK
PERSONAL Born 07/02/1930, Reading, PA, m, 1963, 2 children **DISCIPLINE** HISTORY **EDUCATION** Albright Col, BA, 52; Univ Penn, MA, 53, PhD, 56. **CAREER** Instr, Univ Penn, 56-58; asst prof,Drexel Inst Tech, 58-60, assoc prof, 60-62; assoc prof, Temple Univ, 62-64, prof, 64-84, dist univ prof, 84- ; vis prof, Dartmouth Col, 67-68; vis prof Mil Hist Res, US Army War College, 73-74. **HONORS AND AWARDS** Guggenheim Fel, 68-69; pres, 75-76, Soc for Mil hist; pres, 75-78, Penn Hist Asn; Athenaem of Phila Awd for Dist Work of Non-Fiction by a Phila Auth, 83; Samuel Eliot Morison Awd of Am Mil Inst, 89; Soc for Mil Hist Awd, 92; Inaugural George C Marshall Found Soc for Mil Hist, 99. **MEMBERSHIPS** Am Philos Soc; Am Hist Asn; Soc of Am Hist; Orgn of Am Hist; Soc for Mil Hist; Interuniversity Sem on Armed Forces and Soc; Southern Hist Asn; PA Hist Asn; Hist Soc of PA. **RESEARCH** US and European military history; World War II; American Civil War. **SELECTED PUBLICATIONS** Auth, Quartermaster General of the Union Army: A Biography of M.C. Meigs, 59; auth, Towards an American Army: Military Thought from Washington to Marshall, 62; auth, History of the United States Army, 67; auth, The Partisan War: The South Carolina Campaign of 1780-1782, 70; auth, The American Way of War : A History of United States Military Strategy and Policy, 73; auth, Eisenhower's Lieutenants : The Campaign of

France and Germany, 1944-1945, 81; ed, Philadelphia: a 300 Year History, 82; auth, The Age of Battles : the Quest for Decisive Warfare from Breitenfeld to Waterloo, 91. **CONTACT ADDRESS** 327 S Smedley St, Philadelphia, PA, 19103-6717.

WEIKEL, ANN
PERSONAL Born 12/26/1935, New York, NY **DISCIPLINE** ENGLISH & MEDIEVAL HISTORY **EDUCATION** Mt Holyoke Col, AB, 57; Yale Univ, MA, 59, PhD(hist), 66. **CAREER** Instr hist, Mt Holyoke Col, 63-64; from instr to asst prof, Knox Col, 64-67; asst prof, 67-70, assoc prof, 70-79, Prof Hist, Portland State Univ, 80-. **MEMBERSHIPS** Mediaeval Acad Am; Conf Brit Studies. **RESEARCH** Tudor England; Med-Tudor government and society. **SELECTED PUBLICATIONS** Auth, The Mariau Council Revisited, The Med-Tudor Politie 1540-1560, Macmillan, 80; Studies In Tudor And Stuart Politics And Government, Vol 4, Papers And Reviews, 1982-1990 - Elton,Gr, Albion, Vol 0025, 1993; Elizabeth-I - Maccaffrey,W, Albion, Vol 0027, 1995; Piracy And The English Government, 1616-1642 - Hebb,Dd, American Neptune, Vol 0055, 1995. **CONTACT ADDRESS** Dept of Hist, Portland State Univ, PO Box 751, Portland, OR, 97207-0751.

WEIL, MARK S.
DISCIPLINE NORTHERN RENAISSANCE ART, RENAISSANCE ARCHITECTURE **EDUCATION** Columbia Univ, PhD, 68. **CAREER** Art, Washington Univ. **HONORS AND AWARDS** Nat Endowment Hum fel. **SELECTED PUBLICATIONS** Auth; The History and Decoration the Ponte S. Angelo, 74; Coauth, Master Drawings from the Nelson-Atkins Museum Art, Washington Univ Gallery Art,89; Men, Women, and God: German Renaissance Profints from St. Louis Collections, The Saint Louis Art Mus, 97. **CONTACT ADDRESS** Washington Univ, 1 Brookings Dr, St. Louis, MO, 63130. **EMAIL** msweil@artsci.wustl.edu

WEINBERG, GERHARD LUDWIG
PERSONAL Born 01/01/1928, Hanover, Germany, 1 child **DISCIPLINE** HISTORY **EDUCATION** State Univ NY Albany, BA, 48; Univ Chicago, MA, 49, PhD, 51. **CAREER** Res asst hist, Univ Chicago, 51; res analyst, Columbia Univ, 51-54; lectr mod hist, Univ Chicago, 54-55; vis lectr hist, Univ Ky, 55-56, asst prof, 57-59; dir, Am Hist Asn Microfilm Proj, Alexandria, Va, 56-57; from assoc prof to prof hist, Univ Mich, Ann Arbor, 59-74; KENAN PROF HIST, UNIV NC, 74-, Consult war doc, AHA, 57-60; Rockefeller Found Int Rel Prog & Soc Sci Res Coun fel, 62-63; Am Coun Learned Soc fel, 65-66; Guggenheim fel, 71-72; Nat Endowment for Humanities fel, 78-79; vpres res, AHA, 82-84. **HONORS AND AWARDS** George Louis Beer Prize, AHA, 71 & 94; Halverson Prize, Western Asn Ger Studies, 81; Dr Hum Letters, Univ Albany, 89; **MEMBERSHIPS** AHA; Conf Group Cent Europ Hist; Am Comt Hist of Second World War; Coord Comt Women Hist Profession; Am Acad Arts & Sci; German Stud Asn. **RESEARCH** Modern German history; modern diplomatic history; World Wars I and II. **SELECTED PUBLICATIONS** Auth, Guide to Captured German Documents, Maxwell AFB, 52; Germany and the Soviet Union, Brill, 54; ed, Hitlers Zweites Buch, Deut Verlags-Anstalt, 61; coauth, Soviet Partisans in World War II, Univ Wis, 64; auth, The Foreign Policy of Hitler's Germany, 1933-36, Univ Chicago, 70; The Foreign Policy of Hitler's Germany, 1937-39, Univ Chicago, 80; World in the Balance: Behind the Scenes of World War II, New England Univ Press, 81; A World at Arms: A Global History of World War II, Cambridge Univ Press, 94; Germany Hitler, and World War II, Cambridge Univ Press, 95. **CONTACT ADDRESS** Dept of Hist, Univ of N. Carolina, Chapel Hill, NC, 27599-3195. **EMAIL** GWEINBER@email.unc.edu

WEINBERGER, STEPHEN
PERSONAL Born 09/03/1942, Boston, MA, m, 1966, 2 children **DISCIPLINE** MEDIEVAL HISTORY **EDUCATION** Northeastern Univ, BA, 65; Univ WI-Madison, MA 66, PhD, 69. **CAREER** Asst prof, 69-73, assoc prof hist, Dickinson Col, 73-83, prof hist, 83, dir, Ctr int Studies, Bologna, Italy, 73-75. **MEMBERSHIPS** Mediaeval Acad Am; AHA. **RESEARCH** Medieval soc and economic hist; medieval demography. **SELECTED PUBLICATIONS** Auth, Peasant households in Provence, ca 800-1100, Speculum; Les conflicts entre clercs et laics dans la Provence du XIe siecle, Annales du Midi, 92:269-279; Nobles et noblesse dans la Provence medievale (ca 850-1100), Annales: econ, soc, civilisations, 81; Aristocratic families and social stability in eleventh century Provence, J Medieval Hist; Law courts, justice, and social responsibility in Medieval Provence, Revue Hist.. **CONTACT ADDRESS** Dept of Hist, Dickinson Col, 1 Dickinson Col, Carlisle, PA, 17013-2897.

WEINER, LYNN
PERSONAL Born 02/08/1951, Detroit, MI, m, 1974, 2 children **DISCIPLINE** HISTORY; AMERICAN STUDIES **EDUCATION** Univ Mich, AB, 72; Boston Univ, MA, 75, PhD, 81. **CAREER** Vis Prof, Northwestern Univ, 90-91; Prof Hist, Roosevelt Univ, 91-, Assoc Dean, Col Arts & Sci, 93-. **HONORS AND AWARDS** NEH Fel, 89; Binkley-Stephansen Award, Org Am Hist, 95. **MEMBERSHIPS** Am Hist Asn; Org Am Hist; Am Studies Asn; Coord Comt Women Hist. **RESEARCH** U.S. social history; women's history; history of the family. **SELECTED PUBLICATIONS** Auth, Our Sister's Keepers': The Minneapolis Woman's Christian Association & Housing for Working Women, Minn Hist, Spring 79; Sisters of the Road: Women Transients & Tramps, Walking to Work: Tramps in America, 1790-1935, Nebraska, 84; From Working Girl to Working Mother: The Female Labor Force in the United States, 1920-1980, NC, 85; Women and Work, Reclaiming Our Past: Landmarks of Women's History, Ind, 92; Reconstructing Motherhood: The La Leche League in Postwar America, J Am Hist, 3/94; There's a Great Big Beautiful Tommorrow: Historic Memory and Gender in Walt Disney's Carousel of Progress, J Am Cult, Spring 97; Domestic Constraints, Voices of Women's Historians, Ind (forthcoming 99); author of numerous encyclopedia entries, book reviews, and other publications. **CONTACT ADDRESS** History Dept, Roosevelt Univ, 430 S. Michigan Ave., Chicago, IL, 60605. **EMAIL** lweiner@roosevelt.edu

WEINGARTNER, JAMES JOSEPH
PERSONAL Born 08/21/1940, Bethlehem, Pa, m, 1966, 1 child **DISCIPLINE** HISTORY **EDUCATION** Muhlenberg Col, AB, 62; Univ Wis, MS, 63, PhD(hist), 67. **CAREER** Proj asst, Univ Wis, 64-65, teaching asst, 65-67; asst prof hist, Univ NH, 67-69; from asst prof to assoc prof, 69-77, PROF HIST, SOUTHERN ILL UNIV, EDWARDSVILLE, 77- **HONORS AND AWARDS** Air Force Hist Res Agen Res Assoc **MEMBERSHIPS** AHA; Conf Group Cent Europ Hist; Am Comt Hist 2nd World War. **RESEARCH** Twentieth century Germany; recent military history. **SELECTED PUBLICATIONS** Auth, Sepp Dietrich, Heinrich Himmler, and the Leibstandarte SS Adolf Hitler, Cent Europ Hist, 9/68; The role of the Schulungsleiter in the SS-Verfugungstruppe, Study Hist & Soc, fall 69 & spring 70; The SS race and settlement main office, Historian, 11/71; Hitler's Guard: The Story of the Leibstandarte SS Adolf Hitler, 1933-1945, Southern Ill Univ, 74; Massacre at Mechterstadt: The case of the Marburger Studentencorps, 1920, Historian, 8/75; Crossroads of Death: The Story of the Malmedy Massacre and Trial, Univ Calif, 78; auth, Law and Justics in the Nazi SS: The Case of Konrad Morgen, Cent Europ Hist, 83; auth, The Buchenwald Trial of 1947: Comprehending Mass Murder, Midwest Qrt; auth, Massacre at Biscari: Parrow and an American War Crime, Historian, 89; auth, Otto Skorzeny and the Laws of War, Jou of Milit Hist, 91; auth, Trophies of War: US Troops and the Mutiliation of Japanese War Dead, Pacific Hist Rev, 92. **CONTACT ADDRESS** Dept of Hist, Southern Ill Univ, 6 Hairpin Dr, Edwardsville, IL, 62026-0001.

WEINRIB, ERNEST JOSEPH
PERSONAL Born 04/08/1943, Toronto, ON, Canada, m, 1970 **DISCIPLINE** LAW, ANCIENT HISTORY **EDUCATION** Univ Toronto, BA, 65, LLB, 72; Harvard Univ, PhD(classics), 68. **CAREER** Asst prof classics, 68-70, asst prof law, 72-75, assoc prof, 75-81, Prof Law, Fac Law, Univ Toronto, 81-. **MEMBERSHIPS** Class Can Asn; Asn Can Law Teachers. **RESEARCH** Tort law; Roman law; jurisprudence. **SELECTED PUBLICATIONS** Auth, Judiciary law of M Livius Drusus, Historia, 70; Obnuntiatio: two problems, Z Savigny-Stuftung, 70; A step forward in factual causation, Mod Law Rev, 75; The fiduciary obligation, 75 & Illegality as a tort defense, 76, Univ Toronto; Contribution in a contractual setting, Can Bar Rev, 76; Utilitarianism, Economics, and Legal Theory, Univ Toronto Law J, 80; The Case for a Duty to Rescue, Yale Law J, 80; Obedience to the Law in Plato's Crito, Am J Jurisprudence, 82; The Jurisprudence Of Legal Formalism, Harvard Journal Of Law And Public Policy, Vol 0016, 1993. **CONTACT ADDRESS** Fac of Law, Univ of Toronto, Toronto, ON, M5S 1A1.

WEINSTEIN, FRED
PERSONAL Born 10/19/1931, Brooklyn, NY, m, 1962, 5 children **DISCIPLINE** MODERN HISTORY **EDUCATION** Brooklyn Col, BA, 54, MA, 57; Univ Calif, Berkeley, PhD, 62. **CAREER** Instr hist, Univ Calif, Berkeley, 63-65; asst prof Russ hist, Univ Ore, 65-66; asst prof humanities & Russ hist, San Jose State Col, 66-69; assoc prof, 69-73, Prof Hist, State Univ Ny Stony Brook, 73-, Fel, Inst Advan Study, 70-71; chmn, Group for Uses of Psychol in Hist, 74-. **MEMBERSHIPS** AHA; Group for Uses of Psychol in Hist. **SELECTED PUBLICATIONS** Coauth, The Wish to be Free, Univ Calif, Berkeley, 69; Psychoanalytic Sociology, Johns Hopkins Univ, 73; auth, The Dynamics of Nazism, Acad Press, 80; The Powers Of The Past - Reflections On The Crisis And The Promise Of History - Kaye,Hj, American Historical Review, Vol 0098, 1993; Mythical Past, Elusive Future - History And Society In An Anxious Age - Furedi,F, American Historical Review, Vol 0099, 1994; The Fin-De-Siecle Culture Of Adolescence - Neubauer,J, Journal Of Interdisciplinary History, Vol 0024, 1994; Freud Russia - National Identity In The Evolution Of Psychoanalysis - Rice,Jl, Russian Review, Vol 0053, 1994; Psychohistory And The Crisis Of The Social-Sciences, History And Theory, Vol 0034, 1995; Fantasy And Reality In History - Loewenberg,P, American Historical Review, Vol 0102, 1997. **CONTACT ADDRESS** Dept of Hist, State Univ of NY, Stony Brook, NY, 11790.

WEIR, DAVID A.
DISCIPLINE HISTORY **EDUCATION** Haverford, BA, 80; Princeton, MA, 83, PhD, 92; St. Andrews, PhD, 84. **CAREER** Assoc prof History, Centenary Col. **HONORS AND AWARDS** Frank S. and Elizabeth D. Brewer Prize of the Amer Soc of Church Hist, 84. **SELECTED PUBLICATIONS** Fel Publ, Covenant and Covenanting in Seventeenth-Century New England, Scholars Press, 97; auth, The Origins of the Federal Theology in Sixteenth-Century Reformation Thought, Clarendon Press, 90. **CONTACT ADDRESS** Dept of History, Centenary Col, 400 Jefferson St., Hackettstown, NJ, 07840.

WEIR, ROBERT MCCOLLOCH
PERSONAL Born 08/26/1933, Philadelphia, PA, m, 1955, 2 children **DISCIPLINE** MODERN HISTORY **EDUCATION** Pa State Univ, BA, 58; Western Reserve Univ, MA, 61, PhD(hist), 66. **CAREER** From instr to asst prof hist, Univ Houston, 65-67; from asst prof to assoc prof, 67-78, PROF HIST, UNIV, SC, 78-, Nat Endowment for Humanities fel, 67-68. **HONORS AND AWARDS** Annual Essay Awards, William & Mary Quart, 69 & Southeastern Am Soc Eighteenth Century Studies, 80. **MEMBERSHIPS** AHA; Orgn Am Historians; Southern Hist Asn. **RESEARCH** American colonial and revolutionary history. **SELECTED PUBLICATIONS** Coauth, The scandalous history of Sir Egerton Leigh, 1/69 & auth, The harmony we were famous for: An interpretation of pre-revolutionary South Carolina politics, 10/69, William & Mary Quart; The South Carolinian as extremist, S Atlantic Quart, winter 75; Portrait of a hero, Am Heritage, 4/76; Who shall rule at home: The American revolution as a crisis of legitimacy for the colonial elite, J Interdisciplinary Hist, spring 76; Rebelliousness: Personality development and the American revolution in the southern colonies, In: The Southern Experience in the American Revolution, Univ NC Press, 78; The role of the newspaper press in the southern colonies on the eve of the revolution: An interpretation, In: The Press and the American Revolution, Am Antiquarian Soc, 80; Inseparable Loyalty - A Biography Of Bull,William - Meroney,Gm, Journal Of Southern History, Vol 0059, 1993; The Radicalism Of The American-Revolution - Wood,Gs, Journal Of Southern History, Vol 0060, 1994; General Grant,James - Scottish Soldier And Royal Governor Of East Florida - Nelson,Pd, Mississippi Quarterly, Vol 0049, 1996. **CONTACT ADDRESS** Dept of Hist, Univ of SC, Columbia, SC, 29208.

WEISBERG, DAVID B.
PERSONAL Born 11/15/1938, New York, NY, M, 1958, 4 children **DISCIPLINE** ASSYRIOLOGY **EDUCATION** Columbia Col, AB, 60; Jewish Theol Sem Am, BHL, 60; Yale Univ, PhD, 65. **CAREER** Res Assoc Assyriol, Orient Inst, Univ Chicago, 65-67; from asst prof to assoc prof, 67-71, Prof Bible & Semitic Lang, Hebrew Union Col, 71-. **MEMBERSHIPS** Am Orient Soc; Soc Bibl Lit. **RESEARCH** Bible; Assyriology. **SELECTED PUBLICATIONS** Auth, Guild Structure and Political Allegiance in Early Achaemenid Mesopotamia, Near Eastern Res, No. 1, Yale Univ, 67; A neo-Babylonian temple report, J Am Orient Soc, 67; Rare accents of the 21 books, Jewish Quart Rev, 67; Texts from the Time of Nebuchadnezzar, Yale, Vol 17, 80; Uruk - Late Babylonian Economic Texts From The Eanna Archive, Pt 1, Texts Of Varied Contents - German And Akkadian - Gehlken,E, Journal Of Near Eastern Studies, Vol 0055, 1996; Uruk - Late Babylonian Economic Texts From The Eanna Archive, Pt 1, Texts Of Varied Contents - German And Akkadian - Gehlken,E, Journal Of Near Eastern Studies, Vol 0055, 1996; Images Of Nebuchadnezzar - The Emergence Of A Legend - Sack,Rh, Journal Of Near Eastern Studies, Vol 0055, 1996; Images Of Nebuchadnezzar - The Emergence Of A Legend - Sack,Rh, Journal Of Near Eastern Studies, Vol 0055, 1996. **CONTACT ADDRESS** Dept of Bible & Semitic Lang, Hebrew Union Col, Cincinnati, OH, 45220.

WEISBERGER, BERNARD A
PERSONAL Born 08/15/1922, Hudson, NY, 3 children **DISCIPLINE** UNITED STATES HISTORY **EDUCATION** Columbia Univ, AB, 43; Univ Chicago, MA, 47, PhD(US hist), 50. **CAREER** Asst prof hist, Antioch Col, 52-54 & Wayne State Univ, 54-59; assoc prof, Univ Chicago, 59-63; prof, Univ Rochester, 63-68; assoc ed, 70-72, Contrib Ed, Am Heritage Co, New York, 72-; Res & Writing, 79-, Am Coun Learned Soc fel, 59-60; vis prof hist, Vassar Col, 72-79. **HONORS AND AWARDS** Ramsdell Prize, Southern Hist Asn, 62. **RESEARCH** American journalism; United States, 1877-1917. **SELECTED PUBLICATIONS** Auth, The American heritage history of the American people, Am Heritage, 71; Pathways to the Present, Harper, 76; The Dream-Maker: William C Durant, Founder of General Motors, Little, Brown, 79; Speaking Of Speakers + Some Former Great Speakers-Of-The-House, American Heritage, Vol 0046, 1995; The Fbi Unbound - How The Bureau Got Those Restrictions That So Many People Today Want To See Abolished, American Heritage, Vol 0046, 1995; Genes, Brains, And Bunk + The Dillingham-Commission Report Findings Of 1910, American Heritage, Vol 0046, 1995; What Makes A Marriage + The Courts Are Taking Up The Question Of What Can And Cannot Constitute Legal Wedlock, American Heritage, Vol 0047, 1996; Election In Silver And Gold + The Bryan,William,Jennings Mckinley,William Electoral Contest Of 1896, American Heritage, Vol 0047, 1996; The Frozen Republic - How The Constitution Is Paralyzing Democracy - Lazare,D, American Heritage, Vol 0047, 1996; Big-Bang At Bikini + Worries Surrounded These Early Atomic-Bomb Tests, American Heritage, Vol 0047, 1996; The Mckinley Era

Mega-Merger - Our Century Ends As It Began, With Corporations Rushing Into Wedlock, American Heritage, Vol 0047, 1996; Old Years New Years + History Of Some New Years Traditions In The United-States, American Heritage, Vol 0047, 1996; The Amateur Diplomats + Morrow,Dwight, Daniels,Josephus, And Us-Mexican Relations, 1927-1941, American Heritage, Vol 0048, 1997; Righteous Fists + The Boxer Rebellion And The Light It Casts On America Long, Complex Relationship With China, American Heritage, Vol 0048, 1997; The Kids Judge + Juvenile-Delinquency Corrections History, American Heritage, Vol 0048, 1997; What Made The Government Grow + Some Interesting Facts Concerning American History, American Heritage, Vol 0048, 1997; Terms Of No Endearment + The Usually Difficult 2nd Terms Of 2-Term American Presidents, American Heritage, Vol 0048, 1997; The Bank War + Jackson,Andrew And The 2nd-Bank-Of-The-United-States, American Heritage, Vol 0048, 1997. **CONTACT ADDRESS** 55 W 55th St, New York, NY, 10019.

WEISBERGER, WILLIAM
PERSONAL Born 06/25/1942, Steubenville, OH, m, 1968, 1 child **DISCIPLINE** EUROPEAN INTELLECTUAL HISTORY **EDUCATION** Georgetown Univ, BSFS, 64; Duquesne Univ, Masters, 67; Univ Pittsburgh, PhD(Europ cult hist), 80. **CAREER** Assoc Prof Europ Hist & Sociol, Butler Community Col, 69-. **MEMBERSHIPS** Am Hist Asn. **RESEARCH** The Enlightenment and Freemasonry in London, Paris, Prague and Vienna. **SELECTED PUBLICATIONS** Auth, Enlightened Men, Standard Press, 67; Studies in Central European Freemasonry, Iowa Res Lodge, 73; The World of John T Desaguliers, Pfeifer Press, 80; Living The Enlightenment - Freemasonry And Politics In 18th-Century Europe - Jacob,Mc, Journal Of Social History, Vol 0028, 1994. **CONTACT ADDRESS** 107 Crosslands Rd, Butler, PA, 16001.

WEISBORD, ROBERT G.
DISCIPLINE AFRICAN-AMERICAN HISTORY AND THE HISTORY OF THE EUROPEAN HOLOCAUST **EDUCATION** NY Univ, PhD, 66. **CAREER** Dept Hist, Univ of RI **HONORS AND AWARDS** URI Tchg & Res Excellence awd(s). **SELECTED PUBLICATIONS** Publ on, Jewish-Black relations; Pan-Africanism & the Papacy's polit position during WWII. **CONTACT ADDRESS** Dept of Hist, Univ of RI, 8 Ranger Rd, Ste. 1, Kingston, RI, 02881-0807.

WEISBROT, ROBERT S.
PERSONAL New York, NY, m, 1995 **DISCIPLINE** HISTORY **EDUCATION** Harvard Univ, PhD 80, MA 75; Princeton Univ grad fell 73-74; BrandeisUniv BA 73. **CAREER** Colby Col, prof 80-, Christian A Johnson Dist Prof, 93. **RESEARCH** Civil rights, for policy, Am polit reform. **SELECTED PUBLICATIONS** Freedom Bound: A History of America's Civil Rights Movement, W W Norton, 90, reprint, Penguin, 91; Father Divine and the Struggle for Racial Equality, Univ IL Press, 83, reprint Beacon Press, 84; The Jews of Argentina: From the Inquisition to Peron, Jewish Pub Soc, 79; Hercules: The Legendary Journeys: The Official Companion, NY, Doubleday, 98; Xena: Warrior Princess: The Official Guide to the Xenaverse, NY, Doubleday, 98; Cry for Them: The Roots of Argentie Anti-Semitism, The New Repub, 94. **CONTACT ADDRESS** Dept of Hist, Colby Col, Waterville, ME, 04901. **EMAIL** rsweisbr@colby.edu

WEISS, ELLEN B.
DISCIPLINE HISTORY OF ARCHITECTURE **EDUCATION** Univ Ill, PhD, 84. **CAREER** Prof, Tulane Univ, 87- . **MEMBERSHIPS** Soc of Archit Hist; Vernacular Archit Forum. **RESEARCH** American architecture and urbanism; camp meetings; African-American architects. **SELECTED PUBLICATIONS** Auth, City in the Woods: The Life and Design of an American Camp Meeting, 98. **CONTACT ADDRESS** School of Architecture, Tulane Univ, New Orleans, LA, 70118. **EMAIL** eweiss@mailhost.tcs.tulane.edu

WEISS, JAMES MICHAEL
PERSONAL Born 12/02/1946, Chicago, IL **DISCIPLINE** RENAISSANCE & REFORMATION HISTORY **EDUCATION** Loyola Univ, Chicago, BA, 67; Univ Chicago, MA, 70, PhD(hist), 79. **CAREER** Instr, Ludwig- Maximilians Univ, Munich, 75-76; vis instr humanities, Univ Notre Dame, 78-79; Asst Prof Church Hist, Boston Col, 79-, Res fel, Inst Europ Geschichte, Mainz, WGer, 74-78. **MEMBERSHIPS** Am Soc Church Hist; Am Soc Reformation Res; Cath Hist Soc; Renaissance Soc Am; 16th Century Conf. **RESEARCH** Renaissance and reform humanism (Erasmus); history of biography; history of spirituality. **SELECTED PUBLICATIONS** Auth, Ecclesiastes and Erasmus: The mirror and the image, Arch Refomationsgeshichte, 74; Johannes Fichardus & the uses of humanistic biography, Acta Conventus Neo-Latini, 80; the six lives of Rudolph Agricola: Forms & funciton of humanist biography, Humanistica Lovaniensia, 81; The technique of faint praise: Johann Sturm's Life of Beatus Rhenanus, Bibliotheque d'Humanisme & Renaissance, 81; The role of religious studies in a liberal education, Commonweal, 4/82; The Age of Reform, Moreana, 82; Biography Between Renaissance And Baroque - 12 Studies - German - Berschin,W, Arcadia, Vol 0029, 1994; The Bible In The 16th-Century - Steinmetz,Dc, Editor, Catholic Historical Review, Vol 0080, 1994. **CONTACT ADDRESS** Dept of Theol, Boston Col, 140 Commonwealth Ave, Chestnut Hill, MA, 02167-3800.

WEISS, JOHN
PERSONAL Born 03/31/1927, Dearborn, MI, m, 1952, 2 children **DISCIPLINE** HISTORY **EDUCATION** Wayne State Univ, BA, 50; Columbia Univ, MA, 53, PhD, 58. **CAREER** Asst prof Europ hist, Wayne State Univ, 56-68; Prof Mod Europ Hist, Lehman Col, 69-. **RESEARCH** Modern European intellectual, political and social history; history of ideas and ideologies. **SELECTED PUBLICATIONS** Auth, Moses Hess: Utopian Socialist, Wayne State Univ, 60; The university as corporation, New Univ Thought, 9-10/62; Lorenz Von Stein and dialectical idealism, Int Rev Social Hist, 63; ed, The Origins of Modern Consciousness, Wayne State Univ, 65; auth, The Fascist Tradition, Radical Right Wing Extremism in Modern Europe, Harper, 67; Adam Smith and the philosophy of anti-history, In: The Uses of History, 68; ed, Nazis and Fascists in Europe, Quadrangle, 70; auth, Conservatism in Europe: Traditionalsim, Reaction and Counter-Revolution, Harcourt, Brace & Jovanovich, 77; The Readers Repentance - Women Preachers, Women-Writers, And 18th-Century Social Discourse - Krueger,Cl, Journal Of American History, Vol 0081, 1995. **CONTACT ADDRESS** Dept of Hist, Lehman Col, CUNY, Bronx, NY, 10468.

WEISS, MICHAEL L.
DISCIPLINE CLASSICS **EDUCATION** Univ PA, BA, 87; Univ Vienna, extra-mural stud, 91-92; Cornell Univ, PhD, 93. **CAREER** Asst prof, Univ NC, Chapel Hill. **RESEARCH** Class linguistics; Greek and Latin linguistics; Indo-Europ linguistics. **SELECTED PUBLICATIONS** Auth, Old Church Slavonic spodu and Avestan spada-, Die Sprache 35,1, 93; On the Non-Verbal Origin of the Greek Verb naefein," Historische Sprachforschung, 94; Life Everlasting: Latin iugis 'everflowing', Greek Igiaew 'healthy', Gothic ajukduKs 'eternity' and Avestan yauuaeji- 'living forever', Munchener Studien zur Sprachwissenschaft 55 (94), 96; An Oscanism in Catullus 53, Class Philol, 96; Greek muriow'countless,' Hittite muri- 'bunch (of fruit),' Historische Sprachforschung 96. **CONTACT ADDRESS** Univ N. Carolina, Chapel Hill, Chapel Hill, NC, 27599. **EMAIL** mweiss@email.unc.edu

WEISS, PIERO
DISCIPLINE MUSIC HISTORY **EDUCATION** Columbia Univ, AB, PhD. **CAREER** Prof, John Hopkins Univ. **SELECTED PUBLICATIONS** Auth, Letters of Composers Through Six Centuries, 67; co-auth, Music in the Western World: A History in Documents, 84. **CONTACT ADDRESS** Dept of Musicology, Johns Hopkins Univ, 1 E Mt Vernon Pl, Baltimore, MD, 21202-2397.

WEISS, SUSAN FORSCHER
PERSONAL Born 07/22/1944, New York, NY, m, 1967, 2 children **DISCIPLINE** MUSICOLOGY **EDUCATION** Goucher Col, BA, 65; Smith Col, MA, 67; Univ Md, PhD, 85. **CAREER** Chair, Music Dept, Garrison Forest Sch, 74-94; Faculty, Dept Musicol, Peabody Conserv of The Johns Hopkins Univ, 87-. **HONORS AND AWARDS** NEH Summer Stipend, 84; Cleveland Dodge Found Grant; ACLS Travel Grant, 86; Mu Phi Epsilon Res Contest Winner, 87; John M. Ward Fellow, 90; Short-term Fellow, 91; Distinguished Tchr Yr, 94; Provost's Award for Distance Ed, JHU, 95. **MEMBERSHIPS** Chair, Acad Issues Subcomt of the Provost's Comt on Status of Women; Am Musicol Soc; Int Musicol Soc; Renaissance Soc of Am, Am Assoc of Univ Women; Fac Adv, Mu Phi Epsilon; AAUP. **RESEARCH** Medieval and Renaissance Music; Musical Pedagogy; Instruments and Instrumental Music; Musical Notation; use of computers in the study of early music; Musical Iconography. **SELECTED PUBLICATIONS** Musical Patronage of the Bentivoglio Signoria, 1465-1512, in Atti del XIV Congresso della Societa Internazionale de Musicologia, Transmissione e recezione delle forme di cultura musicale, Bologna, 87, vol 3, ch XI, p703-715;Bologna Q 18: Some Reflections on Content and Context, The Jour Am Musicol Soc,vol 41, 88,p63-101; What Do We Give Them This Time?, in Early Mus Am, vol. 1, no 2, wint 95, p20-24; Singing Along with Guido and Friends: Music In Manuscripts at the Walters Art Gallery, Bull of the Walters Art Gallery, Oct 96. **CONTACT ADDRESS** Peabody Conserv, Johns Hopkins Univ, 1 E Mt. Vernon, Baltimore, MD, 21202. **EMAIL** sweiss@peabody.jhu.edu

WEISS, T.G.
PERSONAL Born 02/26/1946, Detroit, MI, m, 1975, 2 children **DISCIPLINE** POLITICAL SCIENCE **EDUCATION** Harvard Univ, BA; Princeton Univ, MA, PhD. **CAREER** Res Prof, 90-98, Brown's Univ; exec Dir, 85-89, Intl Peace Acad; Sr Econ Affs Officer, 75-85, United Nations Conf Switz. **HONORS AND AWARDS** Council of Foreign Relations Member; Chairs Intl Org Section of the Intl Studies Assoc; Intl Inst for Strategic Studies Mem; External Research Advisory Bd of the UN High Commissioner for Refugees in Geneva; Trustee of Moses Brown Friends Sch RI. **SELECTED PUBLICATIONS** Ed, UN Subcontracting: Task-sharing with Regional Security Arrangements and Service-providing NGOs, 98; coed, Collective Conflict Mgmt and Changing World Politics, 98; coauth, The United Nations and Changing World Politics, 97; coed, Political Gain and Civilian Pain: Humanitarian Impacts of Economic Sanctions, 97; coauth, The News Media Civil War and Humanitarian Action, 96; coed, NGOs the UN and Global Governance, 96; coed, Volunteers Against Conflict, 96; coed, From Massacres to Genocide: The Media Public Policy and the Humanitarian Crises, 96; ed, The United Nations and Civil Wars, 95; coauth, Humanitarian Politics, 95; coauth, Humanitarian Action in Times of War: A Handbook for Practitioners, 93. **CONTACT ADDRESS** Graduate Sch & Univ Center, City Univ, 33 W 42nd St, New York, NY, 10036. **EMAIL** tweiss@gc.cuny.edu

WEISSER, HENRY G.
PERSONAL Born 05/21/1935, New York, NY, d, 4 children **DISCIPLINE** BRITISH & IRISH HISTORY **EDUCATION** Hartwick Col, BA, 57; Columbia Univ, MA, 58, PhD, 65. **CAREER** Teacher, Clymer Cent Sch, 57, Robert Louis Stevenson Sch, 60-61 & East Brunswick High Sch, 61-62; instr hist, Luther Col, Iowa, 62-64; from asst prof to assoc prof, 65-74, prof hist,, Colo State Univ 74-, Fac Improve Comt grants, Colo State Univ, 67-68, 68-69 & 72; res assoc, Grad Sch Int Studies, Soc Sci Found, Univ Denver, 68-69; Am Philos Soc res grant, 72; vis fel, Univ Warwick, 80-81; Nat Endowment for Humanities fel, 80-81. **MEMBERSHIPS** AHA; Rocky Mountain Conf Brit Studies (pres, 79-80); Am Conf Inst Studies. **RESEARCH** British working class history, especially Chartism; Victorian social history; modern African development. **SELECTED PUBLICATIONS** Auth, Polonophilism and the British working class, 1830-1845, Polish Rev, spring 67; Chartist internationalism, 1845-1848, Hist J, Vol XIV, No 1; British Working Class Movements and Europe, 1815-1848, Manchester Univ, 75; Ireland, Travel Culture, Society Politics and History, Hippocrene Books, 2nd ed, 94. **CONTACT ADDRESS** Dept of Hist, Colorado State Univ, Fort Collins, CO, 80523-0001. **EMAIL** hweisser@vines.colostate.edu

WEISSMAN, NEIL BRUCE
PERSONAL Born 12/10/1948, Rome, NY, m, 1970, 1 child **DISCIPLINE** RUSSIAN & COMPARATIVE HISTORY **EDUCATION** Colgate Univ, BA, 70; Princeton Univ, MA, 72, PhD(hist), 76. **CAREER** Asst prof, 75-82, Assoc Prof Hist & Comp Civilizations, Dickinson Col, 82-. **MEMBERSHIPS** Am Asn Advan Slavic Studies; Int Soc Comp Study Civilizations. **RESEARCH** Russian history and government; comparative bureaucracy. **SELECTED PUBLICATIONS** Auth, Rural crime in Tsarist Russia: The question of hooliganism, Slavic Rev, 6/78; Reform in Tsarist Russia, Rutgers Univ Press, 81; Easter In Kishinev - Anatomy Of A Pogrom - Judge,Eh, Slavic Review, Vol 0053, 1994; New Order In Postcommunist Eurasia - Ieda,O, Slavic Review, Vol 0053, 1994. **CONTACT ADDRESS** Dept of Hist, Dickinson Col, 1 Dickinson College, Carlisle, PA, 17013-2897.

WELBORN, L.L.
PERSONAL Born 10/04/1954, Memphis, TN, m, 1976, 2 children **DISCIPLINE** RELIGION, NEW TESTAMENT AND EARLY CHRISTIAN LITERATURE **EDUCATION** Harding Col, BA, 76; Yale Divinity School, MAR, 79; Univ Chicago, MA, 83; Vanderbilt Univ, MA, 84, PhD, 93. **CAREER** Asst prof, McCormick Theol Sem, 85-91; assoc prof, United Theol Sem, 91-98. **HONORS AND AWARDS** National Merit scholarship; Tew Prize; Rotary fel; Harold Stirling Vanderbilt fel. **MEMBERSHIPS** Soc of Biblical Lit. **RESEARCH** Pauline Epistles; Apostolic Fathers; Greco-Roman World. **SELECTED PUBLICATIONS** Auth, Politics and Rhetoric in the Corinthian Epistles, Mercer, 97. **CONTACT ADDRESS** United Theol Sem, 1810 Harvard Blvd, Dayton, OH, 45406.

WELCH, ASHTON WESLEY
PERSONAL Born 06/17/1947, m, 1976 **DISCIPLINE** AFRICAN-AMERICAN STUDIES **EDUCATION** Univ of Hull, UK, 1966-67; Wilberforce Univ, BA, 1968; Univ of Wisconsin, Madison, certificate, 1971, MA, 1971; Univ of Birmingham, UK, PhD, 1979. **CAREER** Richmond College, UK, 1987-88; Creighton Univ, coordinator of black studies, 1975-, history chairman, 1986-93, assoc prof, 1975-. **HONORS AND AWARDS** Creighton Univ, Robert F Kennedy Award, 1992; Creighton Univ, College of Arts and Sciences, Dean's Award, 1993; AK-SAR-BEN, Nebraska Educator Award, 1992. **MEMBERSHIPS** African Studies Assn, 1971-; Assn for the Study of Afro-Amer Life & Culture, 1973-; Natl Council on Black Studies, Committee on Ethics, 1976-; Natl Assn of Ethnic Studies, bd of dirs 1977-; Great Plains Black Museum, bd of dirs, 1975-88; Creighton Federal Credit Union, bd of dirs, 1986-. **SELECTED PUBLICATIONS** "The National Archives of the Ivory Coast," 1982; "Omaha: Positve Planning for Peaceful Integration," 1980; "The Making of an African-American Population: Omaha," 1993; "Emancipation in the United States," 1993; "Jihad," Just War: Three Views, 1991; "The Civil Rights Act of 1968," 1992; "Ethnic Definitions as Reflections of Public Policy," 1983. **CONTACT ADDRESS** Dept of Hist, Creighton Univ, 2500 California Plaza, 341 Administration, Omaha, NE, 68178.

WELCH, JUNE R.
DISCIPLINE HISTORY **EDUCATION** Tex Christian Univ, BA; Univ Tex Arlington, BA; Tex Technol Col, MA; George Washington Univ, JD. **CAREER** Assoc prof, Dallas Univ. **RESEARCH** Texas and Southwest, American Indian, 19th-century America. **SELECTED PUBLICATIONS** Auth, O Ye Legendary Texas Horned Frog, 93; A Family History, 66; The Texas Courthouse, 71; Texas: New Perspectives, 71; Historic Sites Of Texas, 72; Dave's Tune, 73; People And Places In The Texas Past, 74; And Here's To Charley Boyd, 75; The Glory That Was Texas, 75; Going Great In The Lone Star State, 76; The Texas Governor, 77; The Texas Senator, 78; All Hail The Mighty State, 79; The Colleges Of Texas, 81; Riding Fence, 83; The Texas Courthouse Revisited, 84; A Texan's Garden Of Trivia, 85; Tell Me a Texas Story, 91. **CONTACT ADDRESS** Dept of History, Univ of Dallas, 1845 E Northgate Dr, Braniff 204, Irving, TX, 75062. **EMAIL** jwelch@acad.udallas.edu

WELKE, BARBARA Y.
DISCIPLINE HISTORY **EDUCATION** Univ Chicago, PhD, 95. **CAREER** Asst prof **HONORS AND AWARDS** Erwin C. Surrency Prize, 97; Lerner-Scott Prize, 96. **RESEARCH** Twentieth-century U.S. history; U.S. legal and constitutional history. **SELECTED PUBLICATIONS** Auth, When All the Women Were White, and All the Blacks Were Men: Gender, Class, Race, and the Road to Plessy, 1855-1914, Law Hist Rev, 95; Unreasonable Women: Gender and the Law of Accidental Injury, 1870-1920, Law Social Inquiry, 94. **CONTACT ADDRESS** History Dept, Univ of Minnesota, Twin Cities, 614 Social Sciences Tower, 267 19th Ave S, Minneapolis, MN, 55455. **EMAIL** welke004@tc.umn.edu

WELLMAN, JUDITH
DISCIPLINE HISTORY **EDUCATION** Univ VA, PhD. **CAREER** Prof, SUNY Oswego. **RESEARCH** Local and soc hist; Women's hist, 19th century US. **SELECTED PUBLICATIONS** Auth, Landmarks Of Oswego County, Syracuse UP, 88; many articles on women's history. **CONTACT ADDRESS** Dept Hist, SUNY Oswego, 109 Mahar Hall, Oswego, NY, 13126.

WELLS, CAMILLE
DISCIPLINE ARCHITECTURAL HISTORY **EDUCATION** Wake Forest Univ, BA, 74; Univ Va, MA, 76; William and Mary Col, PhD, 94. **CAREER** Asst prof. **RESEARCH** Architecture and historic landscapes of early America. **SELECTED PUBLICATIONS** Auth, pubs on emphasizes Virginia from early settlement to the Civil War. **CONTACT ADDRESS** Dept of Architectural History., Virginia Univ, Charlottesville, VA, 22903. **EMAIL** cwells@virginia.edu

WELLS, COLIN
DISCIPLINE CLASSICAL STUDIES **EDUCATION** Univ Oxford, BA, MA, PhD. **CAREER** Instr, Univ Ottawa; T Frank Murchison distinguished prof, 87-; dept ch. **HONORS AND AWARDS** Dir, Sec Can Team excavations, Carthage, Tunisia, 76-86; dir, Trinity Univ excavations, 90-. **RESEARCH** Roman frontier studies. **SELECTED PUBLICATIONS** Auth, The German Policy of Augustus, 72; The Roman Empire, Harvard UP, 95. **CONTACT ADDRESS** Dept of Class, Trinity Univ, 715 Stadium Dr, San Antonio, TX, 78212.

WELLS, DAVID FALCONER
PERSONAL Born 05/11/1939, Bulawayo, Zimbabwe, m, 1965, 2 children **DISCIPLINE** SYSTEMATIC THEOLOGY, CHURCH HISTORY **EDUCATION** Univ London, EngL, BD, 66; Trinity Evangel Divinity Sch, ThM, 67; Univ Manchester, PhD, 69. **CAREER** From asst prof to prof church hist, Trinity Evangel Divinity Sch, 69-77, prof syst theol, 78-79; Prof Syst Theol, Gordon-Conwell Theol Sem, 79-, Acad dean, Gordon-Conwell Theol Sem, Charlotte, 98-; Res fel, Divinity Sch, Yale Univ, 73-74; mem, Int Evangel Roman Cath Dialog Missions, 81-; chmn, Task Force Roman Cath, World Evangel Fel Theol Comn, 81-84. **HONORS AND AWARDS** Distinguished lectr, London Inst for Contemp Christianity, London, 85. **RESEARCH** Contextualization; Christology; Roman Cath modernism. **SELECTED PUBLICATIONS** Ed, Toward a Theology for the Future, Creation House, 71; auth, Revolution in Rome, Inter-Varsity Press, 73; ed, The Evangelicals, Abingdon Press, 75; auth, Search for Salvation, Inter-Varsity Press, 78; The Prophetic Theology of George Tywell, Scholars Press, 81; ed, The Eerdmans Handbook of American Christianity, Eerdmans, 83; auth, The Person of Christ: A Biblical and Historical Analysis of the Incarnation, Crossway, 84; ed, Reformed Theology in America: A History of Its Modern Development, Eerdmans, 85; ed, God the Evangelist: How the Holy Spirit Words to Bring Men and Women to Faith, Eerdmans, 87; ed, Christian Faith and Practice in the Modern World: Theology from an Evangelical Point of View, Eerdmans, 88; ed, Turning to God: Biblical Conversion in the Modern World, Baker, 89; ed, The Gospel in the Modern World: A Tribute to John Stott, InterVarsity, 91; auth, No Place for Truth, Or, Whatever Happened to Evangelical Theology, Eerdmans, 93; auth, God in the Wasteland: The Reality of Truth in a World of Fading Dreams, Eerdmans, 94; auth, Losing Our Virtue: Why the Church Must Recover Its Moral Vision, Eerdmans, 98. **CONTACT ADDRESS** Gordon-Conwell Theol Sem, 130 Essex St, South Hamilton, MA, 01982-2395.

WELLS, JEROME C.
PERSONAL Born 05/08/1936, Detroit, MI, m, 1963, 1 child **DISCIPLINE** ECONOMICS **EDUCATION** Univ Mich, BA, 58; John Hopins Univ, MA, 61; Univ Mich, PhD, econo, 64. **CAREER** Univ Pittsburg, Prof, econo, pub admin, 90-; Ahmadu Bello Univ, Nigeria, vis prof, econ, 75-76; Univ Pittsburg, Assoc Prof, econo, 69-90; Univ Ibadan, Nigeria, Research Assoc, vis lectr, econ, 65-67; Univ Pitts, Asst Prof, econo, 64-69; Univ Ibadan, Nigeria, vis asst lectr, 61-62. **HONORS AND AWARDS** Am Farm Eco Dissert Award, 65. **MEMBERSHIPS** AEA; AAEA; African Studies Asn; Intl Asn Agri Econ. **RESEARCH** Agri performance, econ devel; cross sec charac econo growth; measuring agri output; media econo; macroecono behavior. **SELECTED PUBLICATIONS** Structural Analysis of Manufacturers-led Growth in Asia, with James H Cassing, Ru-Zhong Wang, Paper, conf Eastern Economic Asn, Washington DC, 97; African Economic Growth-Lack Of it-Revisited, Univ Pittsburg, Dept Econ, 96. **CONTACT ADDRESS** Univ Pittsburgh, Dept Economics, Pittsburgh, PA, 15213. **EMAIL** wells01+@pitt.edu

WELLS, ROBERT VALE
PERSONAL Born 07/14/1943, Bridgeport, CT, m, 1964, 2 children **DISCIPLINE** AMERICAN COLONIAL HISTORY **EDUCATION** Denison Univ, BA, 65; Princeton Univ, PhD(hist), 69. **CAREER** From instr to assoc prof, 69-80, Prof Hist, Union Col, NY, 80-, US Dept Health, Educ & Welfare grant, 72-73; fel, Charles Warren Ctr for Studies Am Hist, Harvard Univ, 74-75; John Simon Guggenheim Found fel, 77-78. **MEMBERSHIPS** AHA; Pop Asn Am; Orgn Am Historians. **RESEARCH** Demographic history; American demographic history. **SELECTED PUBLICATIONS** Auth, Family size and fertility control in eighteenth century America, Pop Studies, 71; Demographic change and the life cycle of American families, J Interdisciplinary Hist, 71; Quaker marriage patterns in a colonial perspective, William & Mary Quart, 72; The Population of the British Colonies in America Before 1776, Princeton Univ, 75; Family history and demographic transition, J Social Hist, 75; On the dangers of constructing artificial cohorts in times of rapid social change, J Interdisciplinary Hist, 78; Population dynamics in the eighteenth-century Mississippi River Valley, J Soc Hist, 78; Revolutions in Americans' Lives, Greenwood, 82; Inheritance And Family-Life In Colonial New-York - Narrett,De, New York History, Vol 0075, 1994; The Mortality Transition In Schenectady, New-York, 1880-1930, Social Science History, Vol 0019, 1995. **CONTACT ADDRESS** Dept of Hist, Union Col, 807 Union St, Schenectady, NY, 12308-3107.

WELLS, WALTER
PERSONAL Born 12/13/1937, New York, NY, m, 1961, 3 children **DISCIPLINE** ENGLISH, AMERICAN STUDIES **EDUCATION** NY Univ, BS, 60, MA, 63; Univ Sussex, DPhil, 71. **CAREER** Instr lang arts, CA State Polytech Col, 63-66; from asst prof to assoc prof, 67-77, prof English & Am Studies, 77-98, chmn Am Studies, 71-85, PROF EMERITUS, CA STATE UNIV, DOMINGUEZ HILLS, 98-; gen consult ed in humanities, Educulture, Inc, 77-80. **RESEARCH** Twentieth century Am; narrative nonfiction; stylistics. **SELECTED PUBLICATIONS** Auth, Communications in Business, Wadsworth, 68, 2nd ed, 77; Tycoons and Locusts: A Regional Look at Hollywood Fiction of the 1930's, Southern IL Univ, 73; Mark Twain's Sure-Fire Programmed Guide to Backgrounds in American Literature, Educulture, 77-80. **CONTACT ADDRESS** Dept of English, California State Univ, Dominguez Hills, 1000 E Victoria, Carson, CA, 90747-0005. **EMAIL** walterwells@earthlink.net

WELSH, MICHAEL EDWARD
PERSONAL Born 04/16/1934, Cape Town, South Africa, m, 1962, 2 children **DISCIPLINE** CLASSICS **EDUCATION** Rhodes Univ, S Africa, BA, 54; Univ Cape Town, BA, 63; Univ London, PhD(Latin), 66. **CAREER** Asst teacher, Potchefstroom Boys' High Sch, 55 & Rondebosch Boys' High Sch, 55-64; lcctr classics, Rhodes Univ, S Africa, 67; asst prof, Brock Univ, 67-68; asst prof, 68-70, Assoc Prof Classics, Carleton Univ, 70-. **RESEARCH** Latin rhetoric; Latin drama; Horace. **SELECTED PUBLICATIONS** Auth, The transmission of Aquila Romanus, Classics et Mediaevalia, 69; Whom Gods Destroy - Elements Of Greek And Tragic Madness - Padel,R, Arachne, Vol 0003, 1996; In And Out Of The Mind - Greek Images Of The Tragic Self - Padel,R, Arachne, Vol 0003, 1996. **CONTACT ADDRESS** 2071 Niagara Dr, Ottawa, ON, K1H 6G9.

WELSH-OVCHAROV, BOGOMILA
PERSONAL Sofia, Bulgaria **DISCIPLINE** FINE ART **EDUCATION** Univ Toronto, BA, 64, MPhil, 71; Univ Utrecht, PhD, 76. **CAREER** PROF FINE ART, UNIV TORONTO. **HONORS AND AWARDS** Chevalier, L'Ordre Palmes Acad, 94. **RESEARCH** Vincent Van Gogh. **SELECTED PUBLICATIONS** Auth, The Early Work of Charles Amgrand and his Contact with Van Gogh, 71; auth, Van Gogh in Perspective, 73; auth, Van Gogh: His Paris Period: 1886-88, 76; auth, Vincent Van Gogh and the Birth of Cloisonism, 81; auth, Emile Bernard: Bordellos and Prostitutes in Turn-of-the-Century French Art, 88; auth, Charles Pachter, 92. **CONTACT ADDRESS** Dept of Fine Art, Univ Toronto, Mississauga, ON, L5L 1C6.

WEMPLE, SUZANNE FONAY
PERSONAL Born 00/00/1927, Veszprem, Hungary, m, 1957, 3 children **DISCIPLINE** MEDIEVAL HISTORY **EDUCATION** Univ Calif, Berkeley, BA, 53; Columbia Univ, MLS, 55, PhD(medieval hist), 67. **CAREER** Instr hist, Stern Col Women, 62-64; lectr soc sci, Teachers Col, Columbia Univ, 64-68; instr hist, 66-67, asst prof, 68-72, assoc prof, 72-80, chair women's studies, 78-80, actg chair dept, 81, Prof Hist, Barnard Col, 80-, Dir, Nat Endowment for Humanities grants medieval & renaissance studies, 77-78 & 78-81; actg chair medieval & renaissance studies, Barnard Col, 78-79; Fulbright travel grant, Italy, spring, 82; Spivack grant, Barnard Col, 81. **HONORS AND AWARDS** Best Bk Prize, Berkshire Conf Women Historians, 82. **MEMBERSHIPS** Mediaeval Acad Am; AHA; AAUP; Inst Res Hist. **RESEARCH** Middle Ages; medieval women; law. **SELECTED PUBLICATIONS** Coauth (with JoAnn McNamara), The power of women through the family, Feminist Studies, I: 726-741; auth, Metaphor or the Carolingian doctrine of corporations, Speculum, 49: 222-237; coauth (with JoAnn McNamara), Sanctity and power: The pursuit of medieval women, In: Becoming Visible: History of European Women, Houghton & Mifflin, 76; auth, Claudius of Turin's Organic, Edizioni di Storia e Letteratura, Rome, 79; Women in Frankish Society: Marriage and the Cloister, 500-900, Univ Pa Press, 81; Becket,Thomas In The Medieval Latin Preaching Tradition - An Inventory Of Sermons About Becket,Thomas C. 1170-1400 - Roberts,Pb, Albion, Vol 0025, 1993. **CONTACT ADDRESS** Dept of Hist, Barnard Col, New York, NY, 10027.

WENDELKEN, CHERIE
DISCIPLINE ARCHITECTURAL HISTORY OF JAPAN, ART HISTORY OF JAPAN **EDUCATION** BA, 77; MArch, 80; PhD, 94. **CAREER** Asst prof, Harvard Univ. **MEMBERSHIPS** CAA; SAH. **RESEARCH** Japanese architecture and art, 1868 to present. **CONTACT ADDRESS** Dept of History of Art and Architecture, Harvard Univ, 480 Broadway, Cambridge, MA, 02138. **EMAIL** wendelk@fas.harvard.edu

WENDORFF, LAURA C.
DISCIPLINE AMERICAN CULTURE **EDUCATION** Univ Wis, BA, 81; Univ Mich, MA, 84, PhD, 92. **CAREER** Tchg asst, Univ Mich, 83-84; asst prof, 94-. **SELECTED PUBLICATIONS** Auth, Demonic Males: Apes and the Origins of Human Violence (rev), 98; Eric Heiden, Pierian, 88. **CONTACT ADDRESS** Dept of Humanities, Univ of Wisconsin, Platteville, 1 University Plaza, Platteville, WI, 53818-3099. **EMAIL** wendorff@uwplatt.edu

WENGERT, TIMOTHY J.
DISCIPLINE REFORMATION HISTORY **EDUCATION** Univ Mich, BA, 72, MA, 73; Luther Sem, MDiv, 77; Duke Univ, PhD, 84. **CAREER** Prof **SELECTED PUBLICATIONS** Auth, Philip Melanchthon's interpretation of John's Gospel; ed, Telling the Churches' Stories, Eerdmans; co-ed, The Book of Concord, Augsburg Fortress Publ; transl, Luther's Small Catechism; auth, Human Freedom, Christian Righteousness, Oxford UP; Law and Gospel, Baker Bk(s). **CONTACT ADDRESS** Dept of Hisory and Systematic Theology, Lutheran Theol Sem, 7301 Germantown Ave, Philadelphia, PA, 19119 1794. **EMAIL** Twengert@ltsp.edu

WENTE, EDWARD FRANK
PERSONAL Born 10/07/1930, New York, NY, m, 1970 **DISCIPLINE** EGYPTOLOGY **EDUCATION** Univ Chicago, AB, 51, PhD(Egyptol), 59. **CAREER** Dir Egyptol, Am Res Ctr Egypt, 57-58; res assoc, 59-63, from asst prof to assoc prof, 63-70, chmn, Dept Near Eastern Lang & Civilization, 75-79, Prof Egyptol; Orient Inst, Univ Chicago, 70-, Mem, Am Res Ctr Egypt, 57-; field dir epigraphic surv, Orient Inst, Luxor, Egypt, 72-73; mem archeol adv coun, Smithsonian Inst, 79-82. **RESEARCH** Epigraphy; Egyptian philology; history of the Egyptian New Kingdom. **SELECTED PUBLICATIONS** Coauth, Medinet Habu, Vol VI, 63, Vol VII, 64; auth, Late Ramesside Letters, 67 & coauth, The Beit el-Wali Temple of Ramesses II 67, Univ Chicago; The Literature of Ancient Egypt, Yale Univ, 72; A chronology of the New Kingdom, In: Studies in Honor of George R Hughes, Univ Chicago, 76; The Temple of Khonsu, Vol I, 79, Vol II 81; The Tomb of Kheruef, 80; co-ed, An X-Ray Atlas of the Royal Mummies, Univ Chicago, 80; Egyptian Historical Inscriptions Of The 20th-Dynasty - Peden,Aj, Journal Of The American Oriental Society, Vol 0116, 1996. **CONTACT ADDRESS** Orient Inst, Univ of Chicago, 1155 E 58th St, Chicago, IL, 60637.

WERCKMEISTER, O.K.
DISCIPLINE ART HISTORY **EDUCATION** Freie Universitat Berlin, PhD. **CAREER** Mary Jane Crowe distinguished prof, Northwestern Univ. **RESEARCH** Political history of art in the middle ages and during the decade of the Great Depression, especially the art of totalitarian regimes in the Soviet Union, Germany, and Italy. **SELECTED PUBLICATIONS** Auth, The Making of Paul Klee's Career, 1914-1920; Citadel Culture. **CONTACT ADDRESS** Dept of Art History, Northwestern Univ, 1801 Hinman, Evanston, IL, 60208.

WERLICH, DAVID P.
PERSONAL Born 11/02/1941, Minneapolis, MN, m, 1960, 3 children **DISCIPLINE** LATIN AMERICAN HISTORY **EDUCATION** Univ Minn, BA, 63, MA, 67, PhD(hist), 68. **CAREER** Asst prof, 68-78, Assoc Prof Hist, Southern Ill Univ, Carbondale, 78-. **MEMBERSHIPS** Conf Latin Am Hist; Midwestern Asn Latin Am Studies. **RESEARCH** Peruvian history; Amazonian history. **SELECTED PUBLICATIONS** Auth, Peru: A Short History, Southern Ill Univ, 78; Research Tools for Latin American Historians: A Select, Annotated Bibliography, Garland, 80; Peru, The Evolution Of A Crisis - Rudolph,Jd, Hispanic American Historical Review, Vol 0073, 1993; Militarism And Politics In Latin-America - Peru From Sanchezcerro To Sendero-Luminoso - Masterson,Dm, Hispanic American Historical Review, Vol 0075, 1995; Mirages Of Transition - The Peruvian Altiplano, 1780-1930 - Jacobsen,N, Historian, Vol 0057, 1995; Amazonian Indians From Prehistory To The Present - Anthropological Perspectives - Roosevelt,A, Historian, Vol 0058, 1996. **CONTACT ADDRESS** Dept of Hist, Southern Ill Univ, Carbondale, IL, 62901-4300.

WERLY, JOHN MCINTYRE
PERSONAL Born 11/06/1939, Rochester, NY, m, 1961, 3 children **DISCIPLINE** UNITED STATES HISTORY **EDUCATION** Trinity Col, CT, BA, 61, MA, 66; Syracuse Univ, PhD(hist), 72. **CAREER** Teacher hist, Robinson Sch, West Hartford, Conn, 63-68; teaching asst, Syracuse Univ, 69-70; instr, State Univ NY Cortland, 70-72; asst prof, 72-78, assoc prof Hist, Southeastern MA Univ, 78-84; full prof hist, Univ MA Dartmouth, 84-. **HONORS AND AWARDS** Leo Sullivan Teacher of Yr Award, Southeastern MA Univ Fac Fedn, 77; Who's Who in the East; Commonwealth Citation for Outstanding Performance, 87; Col of Arts and Sciences Distinguished Teaching Award, 92. **MEMBERSHIPS** Orgn Am Historians. **RESEARCH** American nativist movements; American millenarian movements. **SELECTED PUBLICATIONS** Auth, The Millenarian Right, SAtlantic Quart, 72; The Irish of Manchester, 1832-49, Irish Hist Studies, 73; Premillennialism and the Paranoid Style, Am Studies, 77; The Reform and Radical Millenial Alternatives in Colonial New England, Amerika Studien/ Am Studies , 84. **CONTACT ADDRESS** Dept Hist, Univ Massachusetts at Dartmouth, 285 Old Westport Rd, North Dartmouth, MA, 02747-2300. **EMAIL** jwerly@umassd.edu

WERTHEIMER, JACK
DISCIPLINE JEWISH HISTORY **EDUCATION** Queens Col CUNY, BA, MA; Columbia Univ, MPhil; PhD, 78. **CAREER** Adj lectr, City Col and Queens Col CUNY; vis asst prof, Vassar College; adj assoc prof, US Mil Acad West Point; dir, Joseph and Miriam Ratner Ctr Study Conser Judaism; provost/chief acad off, Jewish Theol Sem Am; Joseph and Martha Mendelson Prof Am Jewish Hist. **HONORS AND AWARDS** Grant, Pew Charitable Trusts; Nat Jewish Bk Awd, 93-94. **RESEARCH** History and the contemporary state of Conservative Judaism. **SELECTED PUBLICATIONS** Auth, Unwelcome Strangers East European Jews in Imperial Germany, Oxford Univ Press, 87; A People Divided: Judaism in Contemporary America, Basic Bks and Univ Press New England, 97; ed, The American Synagogue--A Sanctuary Transformed, Cambridge Univ Press, 87; The Uses of Tradition: Jewish Continuity in the Modern Era, JTS/Harvard,93; The Modern Jewish Experience--A Reader's Guide, NYU Press, 93. **CONTACT ADDRESS** Jewish Theol Sem of America, 3080 Broadway, New York, NY, 10027. **EMAIL** jawertheimer@jtsa.edu

WESCOTT, ROGER WILLIAMS
PERSONAL Born 04/28/1925, Philadelphia, PA, m, 2 children **DISCIPLINE** LINGUISTIC ANTHROPOLOGY **EDUCATION** Princeton Univ, AB, 44 & 45, MA, 47, PhD(ling sci), 48; Oxford Univ, BLitt, 52. **CAREER** Ed & interviewer, Gallup Poll, 52; asst prof hist & human rels, Mass Inst Technol & Boston Univ, 53-57; assoc prof English & soc sci, Mich State Univ, 57-62, dir African lang prog, 59-62; prof anthrop & hist & chmn, Div Soc Sci, Southern Conn State Col, 62-63; lectr sociol & anthrop, Wilson Col, 64-66; co-dir behav studies prog, 73-76, Prof Anthrop & Ling & Chmn Dept Anthrop, Drew Univ, 66-, Ford fel, Univ Ibadan, Nigeria, 55-56; foreign lang consult, US Off Educ, 61; West African Ling Surv grant, Ibadan, 61-62; consult ed, J African Lang, 62-; poetry ed, The Interpreter, 62-; ling fieldworker, Sierra Leone, 63; linguist, Bur Appl Social Res, Columbia Univ, 63-64; rev ed, Int Soc Studies Comp Civilizations, 73-; pres prof humanities & soc sci, Colo Sch Mines, 80-81. **MEMBERSHIPS** Fel African Studies Asn; fel Am Anthrop Asn; fel AAAS; Int Ling Asn; Int Soc Comp Study of Civilizations. **SELECTED PUBLICATIONS** Auth, The Divine Animal: An Exploration of Human Potentiality, Funk, 69; coauth, A Pre-Conference Volume on Cultural Futurology, Am Anthrop Asn, 70; Human Futuristics, Univ Hawaii, 71; The Experimental Symposium on Comparative Futurology, Univ Minn, 71; auth, Traditional Greek conceptions of the future, In: The Experimental Symposium on Comparative Futurology, Univ Minn, 71; coauth, The Highest State of Consciousness, Anchor Bks, 72; auth, Seven Bini charms, Folklore Forum, 10/ 72; Metaphones in Bini and English, In: Studies in Linguistics in Honor of George L Trager, Mouton, The Hague, 73; Sound and Sense, Jupiter Press, 80; Toward A More Concise Inventory Of Proto-Indo-European Roots, Word-Journal Of The International Linguistic Association, Vol 0044, 1993. **CONTACT ADDRESS** Dept of Anthropology, Drew Univ, Madison, NJ, 07940.

WESSEL, THOMAS ROGER
PERSONAL Born 09/28/1937, Belmond, IA, m, 1964, 1 child **DISCIPLINE** AMERICAN HISTORY, ANTHROPOLOGY **EDUCATION** Iowa State Univ, BS, 63; Univ Md, MA, 68, PhD(hist), 72. **CAREER** Res asst hist, Smithsonian Inst, 65-68; asst prof, 72-75, head dept hist & philos, 79, Assoc Prof Hist, Mont State Univ, 75-, Nat Endowment for Humanities fel anthrop, 73-74. **HONORS AND AWARDS** Res Achievement, Smithsonian Inst, 74. **MEMBERSHIPS** Agr Hist Soc; Orgn Am Historians; Western Hist Asn. **RESEARCH** American agricultural history; American Indian history. **SELECTED PUBLICATIONS** Auth, Prologue to the Shelterbelt, 1870-1934, J West, 68; Roosevelt and the Great Plains Shelterbelt, Great Plains J, 69; Agriculture and Iroquois hegemony in New York, 1604-1779, Md Historian, 70; A History of the Rocky Boy's Reservation, Bur Indian Affaris, 74; Agriculture, Indians and American history, Agr Hist, 76; Agriculture in the Great Plains, 1876-1930, Agr Hist Soc, 77; 4-H, An American Idea, 1900-1980, Nat 4-H Counc, 82; Centennial West - Essays On The Northern Tier States - Lang,Wl, Montana-The Magazine Of Western History, Vol 0043, 1993; The Northern-Cheyenne Indian Reservation, 1877-1900 - Svingen,Oj, Western Historical Quarterly, Vol 0025, 1994; Rooted In Dust - Surviving Drought And Depression In Southwestern Kansas - Rineykehrberg,P, Great Plains Quarterly, Vol 0016, 1996. **CONTACT ADDRESS** Dept of Hist, Montana State Univ, Bozeman, MT, 59715.

WESSELSCHMIDT, QUENTIN F.
PERSONAL Born 02/03/1937, Washington, MD, m, 1963 **DISCIPLINE** THEOLOGY, CLASSICS (GREEK AND LATIN) **EDUCATION** St Paul's Jr Coll, Concordia, MO, 57; Concordia Sr Coll, BA, 59; Concordia Sem, BD, 63; Marquette Univ, MA, 69, Univ Iowa, PhD, 79. **CAREER** Pastor, Our Savior Lutheran Church, IL, 63-65; prof, Concordia Coll, WI, 65-73; instr, Milwaukee Lutheran High Schhol, WI, 74-77; prof, Concordia Sem, Mo, 77-. **MEMBERSHIPS** North Am Patristic Soc; Am Philol Asn; Class Asn of the Mid w and s. **RESEARCH** Patristics. **SELECTED PUBLICATIONS** Auth, chapter, Heritage, Motion; Chapter, Light from Above; articles, Concordia J. **CONTACT ADDRESS** 801 De Mun Ave, St. Louis, MO, 63105.

WESSER, ROBERT F.
PERSONAL Born 02/18/1933, Buffalo, NY, m **DISCIPLINE** UNITED STATES HISTORY **EDUCATION** Univ Buffalo, BA, 54, MA, 56; Univ Rochester, PhD(hist), 61. **CAREER** From instr to asst prof Am studies, State Univ NY Buffalo, 59-66, dir Am studies prog, 63-66, asst dean, Col Arts, & Sci, 56-66; assoc prof, 66-72, dir grad studies hist, 75-77 & 79-80, prof hist, 72-95, chemn dept, 80-83, 87-90, prof emeritus, 95- , SUNY Albany; Am Asn State & Local Hist grant-in-aid, 64; consult, Albany Inst Hist & Art & NY State Senate, 77-78. **HONORS AND AWARDS** Chancellor's Award for Excellence in Teaching, State Univ NY, 74. **MEMBERSHIPS** AHA; Orgn Am Historians. **RESEARCH** Twentieth century United States history; latter 19th century United States history; New York State history. **SELECTED PUBLICATIONS** Auth, Charles Evans Hughes and the urban sources of political progressivism, NY Hist Soc Quart, 10/66; Charles Evans Hughes: Politics and Reform in New York, 1905-1910, Cornell Univ, 67; Conflict and compromise: The workmen's compensation movement in New York, 1890 s-1913, Labor Hist, summer 71; Election of 1888, In: History of American Presidential Elections, 1789-1968 (4 vols), Chelsea House & McGraw, 71; contribr ed (with David M Ellis), Two Hundred Years of the New York state legislature, Albany Inst of Hist and Art, 78; auth, The impeachment of a governor: William Sulzer and the politics of excess, NY Hist, 10/79; Woman suffrage, prohibition, and the New York experience in the progressive era, In: An American Historian: Essays to Honor Selig Alder, State Univ NY, Buffalo, 80; New York state and regulation of the insurance industry, In: American Industrialization, Economic Expansion, and the Law: 1870-1914, Sleepy Hollow Press, 81; auth, A Response to Progressivism: The Democratic Party in New York Politics, 1902-1918, NY Univ, 86. **CONTACT ADDRESS** 235 Lenox Ave, Albany, NY, 12208.

WESSLEY, STEPHEN EUGENE
PERSONAL Born 10/29/1944, Mahopac, NY, m, 1966, 2 children **DISCIPLINE** MEDIEVAL HISTORY **EDUCATION** St John's Univ, BA, 66; Columbia Univ, MA, 67, PhD(medieval hist), 76. **CAREER** Instr hist, State Univ NY, New Paltz, 70-73; asst prof, 73-80, assoc prof, Hist, York Col Pa, 80- **HONORS AND AWARDS** Lehman Fel; Fulbright Res Fel; Gladys Krieble Delmas Fdn Fel; Am Coun of Learned Soc Grant-in-Aid; Am Phil Soc Grant; Prog for Cultural Cooperation Bet Spain's Min of Culture and Educ and U.S. Univ Grant. **MEMBERSHIPS** Medieval Acad Am; AHA; Ecclesiastical Hist Soc; Soc Ital Hist Studies. **RESEARCH** Medieval heresy; history of women. **SELECTED PUBLICATIONS** Auth, The thirteenth-century Guglielmites: Salvation through women, In: Medieval Women, Oxford, 78; The composition of Georgius' Disputatio inter Catholicum et parterinum hereticum, Archivum Fratrum Praedicatorum, 78; Bonum est Benedicto mutare locum: The role of the life of Saint Benedict in Joachim of Fiore's monastic reform, Rev Benedictine, 80; auth, Joachim of Fiore and Monastic Reform, New York, 90; auth, Study Guide, 2 Vols, 98; Western Civilizations, Norton Study Guide. **CONTACT ADDRESS** Dept of History, York Col, Pennsylvania, PO Box 15199, York, PA, 17405-7199. **EMAIL** swessley@ycp.edu

WEST, C. S'THEMBILE
PERSONAL Born 05/21/1949, Harlem, NY **DISCIPLINE** AFRICAN AMERICAN STUDIES **EDUCATION** City College, CUNY, BS, 71; Columbia Univ Teachers Col, MA, 74; Temple Univ, PhD, 94. **CAREER** Guest prof, Bryn Mawr, 92, 94, 97; adj prof, instr, Temple Univ, 97-99; adjunct prof, asst prof, Theatre, LeHigh Univ, 98-99. **HONORS AND AWARDS** Fulbright-Hays Award, 91; Faculty Recognition Award, CUNY, 91; St. Louis Public Schools, Role Model Experiences Award, 93; Pan-African Stud Educ Prog, Temple Univ, Appreciation Award, 97. **MEMBERSHIPS** Am Acad Relig; Women in Relig and Soc Group; Natl Assn of Black Journalists. **RESEARCH** African American women; social protest movements; womanism; women and religion; African American religious expression; performance and prayer. **SELECTED PUBLICATIONS** Auth, Dianne McIntyre: Twentieth Century African American Griot, in African Dance: A Historical and Philosophical Inquiry, African World Press, 96; auth, Nation Builders: The Role of Women in the Nation of Islam 1960-1990s, Garland, 99. **CONTACT ADDRESS** Franklin #43, Conshohocken, PA, 19428. **EMAIL** swest001@astro.ocis.temple.edu

WEST, DELNO C.
PERSONAL Born 04/08/1936, IA, m, 1959, 3 children **DISCIPLINE** MEDIEVAL & CHURCH HISTORY **EDUCATION** Northeast MO State Univ, BS, 60; Univ Denver, MA, 61; Univ Calif, Los Angeles, PhD(medieval hist), 70. **CAREER** Asst prof, 69-75, assoc prof, 75-78, asst to acad vpres, 76-80, Prof Medieval Hist, Northern Ariz Univ, 78-, Chmn Dept Hist, 80-, Mem, Ariz-Mex Comn, 76- & Flagstaff Airport Comn, 77-; chmn, Ariz Medieval & Renaissance Ctr, 81. **MEMBERSHIPS** AHA; Mediaeval Acad Am; Rocky Mountain Medieval & Renaissance Asn (pres, 81-82). **RESEARCH** Franciscans; Joachimism; 13th century Italy. **SELECTED PUBLICATIONS** Auth, The Reformed Church and the Friars Minor: The moderate Joachite position of Fra Salimbene, Archivum Franciscanum Historicum, 71; The present state of Salimbene studies with a bibliographic appendix of the major works, Franciscan Studies, 72; ed, Joachim of Fiore in Christian Thought, B Franklin, 74; co-ed, On Pre-Modern Technology and Science, Undene, 76; auth, Between flesh and spirit: Joachite themes in the cronics of Fra Salimbene, J Medieval Hist, 77; The Education of a Joachite-Franciscan, In: Prophecy and Millenarianism: Essays in Honour of Marjorie Reeves, Longman's Press, 80; A note on the date of the expositio super regulum by Hugh J Degue, Rocky Mountain Medieval & Renaissance J, 80; Columbus And The Ends Of The Earth - Europe Prophetic Rhetoric As Conquering Ideology - Kadir,D, Cithara-Essays In The Judeo-Christian Tradition, Vol 0032, 1993; The Portuguese Columbus - Secret-Agent Of King-John-Ii - Barreto,M, American Historical Review, Vol 0098, 1993; Reading Columbus - Zamora,M, Americas, Vol 0051, 1994; The Apocalypse In The Middle-Ages - Emmerson,Rk, Mcginn,B, Catholic Historical Review, Vol 0080, 1994; The Classical-Tradition And The America, Vol 1 - European Images Of The America And The Classical-Tradition, Pt 1 - Haase,W, Reinhold,M, Journal Of American History, Vol 0082, 1995. **CONTACT ADDRESS** Dept of Hist, No Arizona Univ, Flagstaff, AZ, 86001.

WEST, ELLIOTT
PERSONAL Born 04/19/1945, Dallas, TX, m, 1983, 5 children **DISCIPLINE** HISTORY **EDUCATION** Univ Texas, Austin, BA, 67; Univ Colorado, MA, 69, PhD, 71. **CAREER** Asst prof, 71-75, assoc prof, 75-79, Univ Texas, Arlington; assof prof, 79-81, prof, 81- , Univ Arkansas. **HONORS AND AWARDS** Western Heritage Award, best non-fiction book, 90, 96; Arkansas Prof of the Year, Carnegie Found for Advancement of Tchg, 95; George Perkins Marsh Prize, 97. **MEMBERSHIPS** Western Hist Asn; Am Soc of Environ Hist. **SELECTED PUBLICATIONS** Auth, The Way West: Essays on the Central Plains, New Mexico, 95; auth, Growing Up in Twentieth Century America: A History and Resource Guide, Greenwood, 96; auth, The Contested Plains: Indians, Goldseekers and the Rush to Colorado, Kansas, 98. **CONTACT ADDRESS** Dept of History, Univ of Arkansas, Fayetteville, AR, 72701. **EMAIL** ewest@comp.uark.edu

WEST, FRANKLIN CARL
PERSONAL Born 08/17/1934, Portland, OR, m, 1963, 1 child **DISCIPLINE** MODERN GERMAN HISTORY **EDUCATION** Reed Col, BA, 56; Univ Ore, MA, 58; Univ Calif, Berkeley, PhD(hist), 70. **CAREER** Instr hist, Northwestern Univ, 63-64; instr & asst prof humanities, Reed Col, 64-66; from instr to asst prof, 66-75, assoc prof, 75-80, Prof Hist, Portland State Univ, 81-. **MEMBERSHIPS** AHA; Western Asn German Studies; Am Comt Hist Second World War. **RESEARCH** Political and cultural history of the Weimar Republic; fascism. **SELECTED PUBLICATIONS** Auth, The Parties, the Princes,

and the People: A Study of the German Referendum of June 20, 1926, Univ Calif, Berkeley, 70; Elections And Voter Tradition In Germany - Cultural Basis Of German Parties And Party Systems In The 19th And 20th Centuries - German - Rohe,K, American Historical Review, Vol 0098, 1993. **CONTACT ADDRESS** Dept of Hist, Portland State Univ, Portland, OR, 97207.

WEST, GRACE STARRY
PERSONAL Born 10/05/1946, Oklahoma City, OK, m, 1974, 4 children **DISCIPLINE** CLASSICS **EDUCATION** Scripps Col, BA, 68; Univ Calif, Los Angeles, CPhil, 72, PhD, 75. **CAREER** Univ of Dallas, 75- . **HONORS AND AWARDS** Fulbright full grant, 72-74, Univ Heidelberg. **MEMBERSHIPS** APA; Vergilian Soc; CAMWS; TCA; ACL. **RESEARCH** Greek and Roman literature and its survival to present times; teaching of Latin; myth; women in antiquity. **SELECTED PUBLICATIONS** Transl, Plato, Aristophanes; transl, Cornelius Nepos, Dion, 85; transl Cicero, Pro Archia, 87; coauth, Four Texts on Socrates, rev ed, Cornell, 98. **CONTACT ADDRESS** Dept of Classics, Univ of Dallas, 1845 E Northgate Dr, Irving, TX, 75062. **EMAIL** gwest@acad.udallas.edu

WEST, HERBERT LEE, JR.
PERSONAL Born 05/04/1947, Warrenton, North Carolina, m **DISCIPLINE** EDUCATION **EDUCATION** NC Central Univ, BA 1969; Univ of MN, MA 1972, PhD 1974. **CAREER** Teacher asst, Univ of Minnesota, 1972; asst prof, Univ of Maryland Baltimore County, 1974-1980; asst prof, Howard University, 1980-1985; faculty intern, House Urban Devel, 1980; advisor, Summer Work Program-Prince Georges County, Maryland; educator/admin, Howard County Bd of Education, 1985-; adjunct faculty Univ of Maryland Baltimore County, 1986-. **HONORS AND AWARDS** Ford Found Fellow 1971; NEH Fellow Atlanta Univ 1978; Outstanding Teacher Univ of MD Baltimore Cty 1978,79; Smithsonian Fellow Smithsonian Inst 1985; NEH Fellow Univ of NC 1983; Summer Fellow UMTA/Atlanta Univ 1984; Univ of Indiana guest lecturer 1988; NEH Fellow Columbia Univ 1989; Comga Graduate Fellowship Univ of Minnesota 1969; moderator, braodway show Sarifina, Kennedy Center, 1990. **MEMBERSHIPS** Mem NAACP, Triangle Geographers, Natl Council of Black Studies, Assoc for the Study of Afro-Amer Life; Black Student Achievement Program, Howard County, Maryland. **CONTACT ADDRESS** Educator, Howard Cty Bd of Educ, 10910 Route 108, Ellicott City, MD, 21043.

WEST, JAMES
DISCIPLINE HISTORY **EDUCATION** Princeton Univ, AB, MA, PhD. **CAREER** Vis prof, 95-. **RESEARCH** Peasant cultures; European and Russian cultural history. **SELECTED PUBLICATIONS** Ed, Between Tsar and People: Educated Society and the Quest for Public Identity in Late Imperial Russia. **CONTACT ADDRESS** Dept of History, Middlebury Col, Middlebury, VT, 05753. **EMAIL** west@panther.middlebury.edu

WEST, MARTHA S.
PERSONAL Born 02/05/1946, Pomona, CA, 3 children **DISCIPLINE** HISTORY; LAW **EDUCATION** Brandeis Univ, BA, 67; Indiana Univ, JD, 74. **CAREER** Atty, 74-82; asst prof, Univ Calif Davis Law Sch, 82-88; prof and assoc dean, 88-92; prof, 92- . **HONORS AND AWARDS** The 1981 Redding Scholar, Indianapolis Chamber of Com, Lacy Exec Leadership Series, 81-82; The Ruth E. Anderson Award from Women's Res and Resources Ctr and Women's Studies Prog, UC Davis, for outstanding service on behalf of campus women, 90; Sacramento YWCA Outstanding Woman of the Year in Educ, 91; The Deanna Falge Award for diversity and affirmative action, UC Davis, 96; The William & Sally Rutte Distinguished Teaching Award, UCD Law Sch, 97. **MEMBERSHIPS** AAUP; NLG; ABA. **RESEARCH** Women's legal rights; sex discrimination in higher education. **SELECTED PUBLICATIONS** Auth, Women Faculty: Frozen in Time, Academe, 95; auth, History Lessons: Affirmative Action, The Women's Rev of Books, 96; auth, The Hictorical Roots of Affirmative Action, La Raza Law J, 96; co-auth with H.H. Kay, Sex-Based Discrimination: Text, Cases, and Materials, 96; auth, Equitable Funding of Public Schools under State Constitutional Law, J Gender, Race, and Justice, 98. **CONTACT ADDRESS** School of Law, Univ of Calif.-Davis, Davis, CA, 95616. **EMAIL** mswest@ucdavis.edu

WEST, WILLIAM ELLIOTT
PERSONAL Born 04/19/1945, Dallas, TX, m, 1962, 3 children **DISCIPLINE** UNITED STATES HISTORY **EDUCATION** Univ Tex, Austin, BJ, 67; Univ Colo, MA, 69, PhD(hist), 71. **CAREER** Asst prof, Univ Tex, Arlington, 71-76, assoc prof hist, 76-79; Prof Hist, Univ Tex, 79-. **HONORS AND AWARDS** Louis Knott Koontz Award, Pac Coast Br, AHA, 74; Danforth Teaching Assoc, Danforth Found, 77. **MEMBERSHIPS** Orgn Am Historians; Western Hist Asn. **RESEARCH** United States frontier social history; United States progressive political history; westward expansion and progressive era. **SELECTED PUBLICATIONS** Auth, Cleansing the queen city: Prohibition and urban reform in Denver, Ariz & the West, winter 72; coauth, Patron society at the crossroads: Southern Colorado in the late 19th century, Pac Hist Rev; auth, The saloon in territorial Arizona, J of the West, 7/74; Dirty tricks in Denver, Colo Mag, summer 75; co-ed, Essays on Urban America, 75 & Essays on Walter Prescott Webb, 76, Univ Tex; Saloon on the Rocky Mountain Mining Frontier, Univ Nebr, 79; Wondrous Times On The Frontier - Brown,D, Journal Of The West, Vol 0034, 1995. **CONTACT ADDRESS** Dept of Hist, Univ of Tex, Arlington, TX, 76019.

WEST III, WILLIAM C.
DISCIPLINE CLASSICS **EDUCATION** Univ NC, Chapel Hill, PhD. **CAREER** Prof, Univ NC, Chapel Hill. **RESEARCH** Greek prose; Greek historians. **SELECTED PUBLICATIONS** Auth, The Public Archives in Fourth Century Athens, Greek, Roman, and Byzantine Stud 30, 89; M. Ulpius Domesticus and the Athletic Synod at Ephesus, Ancient Hist Bull 4.4, 90; The Decrees in Demosthenes' Against Leptines, Zeitschrift fur Papyrologie und Epigraphik 107, 95; New Light on an Opisthographic Lead Tablet in Chapel Hill, Preatti: Preliminary Publ, XI Int Cong of Greek and Latin Epigraphy, Ed Quasar, 97. **CONTACT ADDRESS** Univ N. Carolina, Chapel Hill, Chapel Hill, NC, 27599. **EMAIL** wwest@email.unc.edu

WESTERMANN, MARIET
DISCIPLINE ART HISTORY **EDUCATION** Williams Col, BA, 84; NY univ, Inst Fine Arts, MA, 89, PhD, 97. **CAREER** Res asst, Metrop Mus Art, 89; adj lectr, NY Univ, 89; adj lectr, Goldsmiths' Col, Univ London, 93; ASST PROF ART HIST, RUTGERS UNIV, 95-. **CONTACT ADDRESS** Dept of Art History, Rutgers Univ, Voorhees Hall, New Brunswick, NJ, 08901. **EMAIL** mwestermann@home.com

WESTERMEYER, JOSEPH JOHN
PERSONAL Born 04/08/1937, Chicago, IL, m, 1962, 2 children **DISCIPLINE** PSYCHOLOGY **EDUCATION** Notre Dame Univ and St Thomas Col 55-57, BS Biochem 59, MD Medicine 61, MA Anthro 69, MPH Pub Health 70, PhD Psychol/Anthro 70, Univ MN, NIDA-NIAAA Career Tchr/Res 74-77. **CAREER** Rotating Internship St Paul-Ramsey Hosp, 61-62; Gen Practive Payne Aven Medical Clin St Paul MN, 62-65; Deputy Chief Div Pub Health Agency Intl Devel Laos, 62-65; Memnrt Psychol Staff Univ MN Hosp and Clin, 70-present; Prof and Chair Dept Psychol and Behavioral Sci, Univ OK Health Sci Center OK 89-92; Residency in Psychol /grad stud in Anthro/Pub Health 67-70, Univ MN, Chief of Psychol MN VA Hosp; Prof Dept Psychol, 92-. **HONORS AND AWARDS** AOA Hon Medical Soc, 61; Fel Am Anthro Assoc, 76; Fel Am Assoc of Family Practice, 76; Fel Am Psychol Assoc, 77; Who's Who in Am, 85-present; Fel Am Psychopathological Assoc, 89; Fel Am Col Psychol, 91; Best Drs Am, Alcoholism-Addictions Psychol, Good Housekeeping, 93; Intl Who's Who in Medicine, Cambridge UK, 94-present; Intl Who's Who Prof, Jacksonville NC, 95-present. **MEMBERSHIPS** Am Acad Psychol in Alcoholism and Addictions; Am Anthro Assoc; Am Assoc for Advancement of Sci; Am Assoc of Soc Psychol; Am Col Psychol; Am Medical Assoc; Am Psychol Assoc; Am Pub Health Assoc; MN Council for Preventive Medicine; MN Psychol Assoc; OK Psychol Assoc; OK Medical Assoc; Soc of Biol Psychol; Soc for Traumatic Stress Studies. **RESEARCH** Substance abuse; psychol disorder; treatemnt outcome of same; Cross cultural epidemiology of Psychol disorder; diagnostic reliability/validity; methodology; theory. **SELECTED PUBLICATIONS** Westermeyer J, Neider J, Wetermeyer M, Culture Medicine Psychiatry 16(4): 519-529, 98; Westermeyer J, Cutural aspects of substance abuse and alcoholism, Assessment and Management; Psychiatric Clinics North America 18(3): 110-123, 96; Westermeyer J: Ethnic and cultural factors in dual disorder, Double Jeopardy: Chronic Mental Illness and Substance Abuse, eds, A D Lehman and L B Dixon, Univ Toronto Press, 95; Westermeyer J Bouafeuly-Kersey M, Her C: Hmong Children in Transcultural Child Development, eds, G Johnson-Powell and J Yamamoto, NY: John Wiley & Sons, 97; Westermeyer J: Cross-cultural aspects, Textbook of Substance Abuse, Vol(14) eds, M, Galanter and H D Kleber, Washington DC: American Press, in process. **CONTACT ADDRESS** Univ of Minnesota, Minneapolis, MN, 55455. **EMAIL** weste010@email.umn.edu

WESTERMEYER, PAUL
DISCIPLINE CHURCH MUSIC **EDUCATION** Univ Elmhurst, BA, 62; Lancaster Theol Sem, 65; Sch Sacred Mus, Union Theol Sem, SMM, 66; Univ Chicago, MA, 74, PhD, 78; additional study, Sch Cantorum; Concordia Theol Sem, 66; liturgical stud prog, Notre Dame, 69; Lutheran Gen Hospital, 83. **CAREER** Vis prof, Yale Univ Inst Sacred Mus, 89-90; prof, dept ch, choir dir, organist, Elmhurst Col, 68-90; prof, 90-. **HONORS AND AWARDS** Cantor, Ascension Lutheran Church, 82-90; ast pastor, Ascension Lutheran Church, 86-90; **MEMBERSHIPS** Mem, Amer Choral Dir(s) Assn; Amer Guild of Organists; Amer Soc of Church Hist; Evangel and Reformed Hist Soc; Hymn Soc Am; Intl Arbeitsgemeinschaft fur Hymnologie; Liturgical Conf; Mercersburg Soc; N Amer Acad of Liturgy. **SELECTED PUBLICATIONS** Auth, With Tongues of Fire, 95; The Church Musician, 88. **CONTACT ADDRESS** Dept of Music, Luther Sem, 2481 Como Ave, St. Paul, MN, 55108. **EMAIL** pwester@luthersem.edu

WESTFALL, CARROLL W.
PERSONAL Born 12/23/1937, Fresno, CA, m, 1982, 2 children **DISCIPLINE** ART HISTORY **EDUCATION** Univ Calif, BA, 61; Univ Manchester, MA, 63; Columbia Univ, PhD, 67. **CAREER** Amherst Col, 66-72; Univ Ill Chicago, 72-82; Univ Va, 82-98; Frank Montana prof and chair, Sch of Archit, Univ Notre Dame, 98-. **MEMBERSHIPS** Col Art Asn; Soc of Archit Hist; Congress for New Urbanism. **RESEARCH** History of urbanism; Theory of classical and traditional architecture; History of the classical tradition. **SELECTED PUBLICATIONS** Auth, Renewing the American City, Urban Renaissance, Intl Conf on Innovative Urban and Archit Policies: A Vision of Europe, Univ Bologna, Italy, 52-69, 96; auth, The Classical American City in Image and in Chicago, Modulus 23: The Archit Rev at the Univ of Va, 52-71, 95; auth, Allan Greenberg and the Difficult Whole of Architecture, Allan Greenberg: Selected Works, Archit Monogr, no 39, London, Acad Editions, 6-10, 95; auth, Thinking about Modernism and Classicism, The Classicist, I, 6-10, 94-95; auth, The True American City, The New City: The American City, Univ Miami Sch of Archit, II, 8-25, 93-94. **CONTACT ADDRESS** Univ of Notre Dame, 110 Bond Hall, Notre Dame, IN, 46617. **EMAIL** westfall.z@nd.edu

WESTFALL, RICHARD SAMUEL
PERSONAL Born 04/22/1924, Ft Collins, CO, m, 1952, 3 children **DISCIPLINE** HISTORY **EDUCATION** Yale Univ, BA, 48, MA, 49, PhD, 55. **CAREER** Instr hist, Calif Inst Technol, 52-53; from instr to asst prof, State Univ Iowa, 53-57; from asst prof to assoc prof, Ginnell Col, 57-63; prof, 63-76, Distinguished Prof Hist, Ind Univ, Bloomington, 76-, NSF res grants, 61-62 & 63-68; Am Coun Learned Soc fel, 72; Nat Endowment Humanities fel, 77. **HONORS AND AWARDS** Leo Gershoy award, AHA, 81. **MEMBERSHIPS** AHA; Hist Sci Soc; cor mem Int Acad Hist Sci. **RESEARCH** History of science in the 17th century; Isaac Newton; mechanics in the 17th century. **SELECTED PUBLICATIONS** Auth, Science and Religion in Seventeenth Century England, Yale Univ, 58; Development of Newton's theory of color, Isis, 62; Foundations of Newton's philosophy of nature, 62 & Hooke and the law of universal gravitation, 67, Brit J Hist Sci; coauth, Steps in the Scientific Tradition, 68 & auth, The Construction of Modern Science, 71, Wiley; Force in Newton Physics, Macdonalds, 71; Never at Rest, A Biography of Isaac Newton, Cambridge Univ Press (in prep); Newton,Isaac - A Catalog Of Manuscripts And Papers Collected And Published On Microfilm By Chadwyckhealey - Jones,P, Isis, Vol 0084, 1993; The Investigation Of Difficult Things - Essays On Newton And The History Of The Exact Sciences In Honor Of Whiteside,D.T. - Harman,Pm, Shapiro,Ae, Annals Of Science, Vol 0051, 1994; The Rise Of Public Science - Rhetoric, Technology, And Natural-Philosophy In Newtonian Britain, 1660-1750 - Stewart,L, American Historical Review, Vol 0099, 1994; Fits, Passions, And Paroxysms - Physics, Method, And Chemistry And Newtons Theories Of Colored Bodies And Fits Of Easy Reflection - Shapiro,Ae, American Historical Review, Vol 0099, 1994; Key To Newtons Dynamics - The Kepler-Problem And The Principia - Brackenridge,Jb, Isis, Vol 0087, 1996; The Principia By Newton - French - Blay,M, Isis, Vol 0087, 1996. **CONTACT ADDRESS** 2222 Browncliff Rd, Bloomington, IN, 47401.

WESTHAUSER, KARL E.
DISCIPLINE HISTORY **EDUCATION** Cornell Univ, BA, 83; Brown Univ, AM, 85, PhD, 94. **CAREER** ASST PROF HIST, ALA STATE UNIV, 95. **CONTACT ADDRESS** Alabama State Univ, Campus Box 25, Montgomery, AL, 36101.

WESTON, CORINNE COMSTOCK
PERSONAL Born 12/08/1919, Castle Hill, ME, m, 1947 **DISCIPLINE** HISTORY **EDUCATION** Univ Maine, BA, 41; Columbia Univ, MA, 44, PhD, 51. **CAREER** Instr hist, Univ Maine, 46-47; instr, Columbia Univ, 47-48; instr, Univ Maine, 48-49; lectr, Columbia Univ, 49-51; instr, Brooklyn Col, 51-52; prof, Univ Houston, 52-63; from vis assoc prof to assoc prof, Hunter Col, 64-68, assoc prof, Lehman Col, 68-69, PROF HIST, LEHMAN COL, 69-, Am Coun Learned Soc grant, 62; grants in United Kingdom, 74, 75, 78; mem, Inst Hist Res, Univ London. **HONORS AND AWARDS** Fac Res Award, City Univ New York, 70-72, 76-77, 79-80. **MEMBERSHIPS** AHA; Conf Brit Studies; Am fel Royal Hist Soc. **RESEARCH** British constitutional theory and history; Stuart and Victorian England. **SELECTED PUBLICATIONS** Auth, Beginnings of the classical theory of the English constitution, Proc Am Philos Soc, 4/56; The Royal mediation in 1884, English Hist Rev, 4/67; Liberal leadership and the Lords' veto, Hist J, 68; Concepts of estates in Stuart political thought, In: Representative Institutions in Theory and Practice, Vol XXXIX, Studies Presented to the International Commission for History of Representative and Parliamentary Institutions, Libr Encycl, Brussels, 70; Legal sovereignty in the Brady Controversy, Hist J, 72; coauth, Subjects and sovereigns: The grand controversy over legal sovereignty in Stuart England, Cambridge Univ Press, 81; auth, The authorship of the Freeholders Grand Inquest, English Hist Rev, 1/80; Sir Robert Holbourne, Henry Powle & Thomas Hunt, In: Biographical Dict of British Radicals in the Seventeenth Century, Vol 1, Harvester Press, 82; auth, The House of Lords and Ideological Politics: Lord Salisbury's Referendal Theory and the Conservative Party, 1846-1922, Am Phil Soc, 95; auth, Lord

Selborne, Bonar Law, and the Tory Revolt, in Lords of Parliament: Studies, 1714-1914, Stanford Univ Press. **CONTACT ADDRESS** 200 Central Park S, New York, NY, 10019.

WESTON, TIMOTHY B.
DISCIPLINE HISTORY **EDUCATION** Univ Wis Madison, BA, 86; Univ Calif Berkeley, MA, 89; PhD, 95. **CAREER** Prof. **SELECTED PUBLICATIONS** Auth, Corrupt Capital, Reformed Academy: Beijing and the Identity of Beijing University, 1898-1919, Kluwer, 98; America must face true cost of China Policy, 97; New Beijing Municipal Archives Building Welcomes Researchers, Chinese Urban Hist News, 96; Anarchism and Chinese Political Culture (rev), 94; co-auth, U.S., China Face Future In Which Fates Intertwine, Rocky Mountain News, 97. **CONTACT ADDRESS** History Dept, Univ of Colorado, Boulder, Boulder, CO, 80309. **EMAIL** weston@stripe.colorado.edu

WETHERELL, CHARLES W.
DISCIPLINE HISTORY **EDUCATION** St Lawrence, BA, 69; Univ NH, PhD, 80. **CAREER** Dir, Lab for Hist Res, Univ Calif, Riverside. **SELECTED PUBLICATIONS** Fel Publ, 'For These and Such Like Reasons': John Holt's Attack on Benjamin Franklin, Procs of the AAS 88, 78; coauth, The New Hampshire Committees of Safety and Revolutionary Republicanism, 1775-1784, Hist of NH 35, 80; coauth, Wealth and Renting in Pre-Revolutionary Philadelphia, Jour of Amer Hist 71, 85; coauth, The Kinship Domain in an Eastern European Peasant Community: Pinkenhof, 1833-50, Amer Hist Rev 93, 88; coauth, The Measure of Maturity: The Pennsylvania Gazette, 1728-65, William and Mary Quart, 89. **CONTACT ADDRESS** Dept of History, Lab for Hist Res, Univ California, Riverside, CA, 92121.

WEXLER, ALICE RUTH
PERSONAL Born 05/31/1942, New York, NY **DISCIPLINE** AMERICAN HISTORY **EDUCATION** Stanford Univ, BA, 64; Georgetown Univ, MA, 66; Ind Univ, PhD(hist), 72. **CAREER** Asst to assoc prof, hist, Sonoma State Univ, 72-82; vis scholar, Univ Calif, Riverside, 82-85, 87; lectr Univ Calif, Riverside, 85-86; vis lectr, Calif Inst Technol, 93; adj lectr, hist, Claremont Grad Sch, 94; adj lectr, hist, Occidental Col, 94-95; lectr, UCLA, 94, 96, 97; res scholar, Ctr for the Study of Women, UCLA, 94- . **HONORS AND AWARDS** Fulbright fel, 64-65; NEH summer stipends, 79, 86; NEH fel, 87; fel, ACLS, 97-98. **MEMBERSHIPS** AHA; West Coast Asn of Women Historians; PEN; Am Stud Asn. **RESEARCH** American social history, 1890-1920; American women's biography; psychoanalysis in America. **SELECTED PUBLICATIONS** Auth, Pain and prejudice in the Santiago campaign of 1898, J Inter-Am Studies & World Affairs, 2/76; The early life of Emma Goldman, Psychohist Rev, spring 80; Emma Goldman on Mary Wollstonecraft, Feminist Studies, spring 81; Emma Goldman: A Radical in America, Pantheon, 89; auth, Emma Goldman in Exile, Beacon, 89; auth, Mapping Fate: A Memoir of Family, Risk, and Genetic Research, Times, 95. **CONTACT ADDRESS** 225 Santa Monica Blvd, #412, Santa Monica, CA, 90401. **EMAIL** arwexler@ucla.edu

WEXLER, VICTOR G.
PERSONAL Born 11/26/1941, New York, NY **DISCIPLINE** EUROPEAN INTELLECTUAL HISTORY **EDUCATION** Univ Mich, UA, 63; Columbia Univ, MA, 65, PhD(hist), 71. **CAREER** Instr humanities, Stevens Inst Technol, 69-71; asst prof, 72-77, Assoc Prof Hist, Univ Md, Baltimore County, 77-, Nat Endowment Humanities fel, 78-79. **MEMBERSHIPS** AHA; Am Soc 18th Century Studies; East Cent Soc (pres). **RESEARCH** Eighteenth-century France and Britain. **SELECTED PUBLICATIONS** Co-ed, Historians at Work, Vol II, 73, Vol III, 76, Harper & Row; auth, Made of man's delight: Rousseau as Antifeminist, Am Hist Rev, 4/76; David Hume's discovery of a new scene of historical thought, Eighteenth-Century Studies, winter 77; Partisanship of progress: Hume on Scotland, Eighteenth-Century Life, fall 78; David Hume and the History of England, Am Philos Soc, 79; The Battle Of The Books - History And Literature In The Augustan Age - Levine,Jm, American Historical Review, Vol 0098, 1993. **CONTACT ADDRESS** Dept of Hist, Univ of MD Baltimore Co, Hilltop Circle, PO Box 1000, Baltimore, MD, 21228.

WHALEY, LINDSAY
DISCIPLINE LINGUISTICS AND CLASSICS **EDUCATION** SUNY Buffalo, PhD, 93. **CAREER** Asst prof, Dartmouth Col. **RESEARCH** Lang typology; syntactic theory; word order variability; Bantu linguistics; Tungus linguistics. **SELECTED PUBLICATIONS** Auth, An Introduction to Language Typology: The Unity and Diversity of Language, Sage, 97; Manchu-Tungus languages, Encyclopedia Britannica, 97; The Effect of Non-Surface Grammatical Relations on the Genitive Absolute in Koine Greek in Grammatical Relations: A Cross Theoretical Perspective, CSLI, 90;coauth, Endangered Languages: Current Issues and Future Prospects, Int Jour Soc Lang, 96; Kinyarwanda Multiple Applicatives and the 2-AEX in Papers from the 28th Regional Meeting of the Chicago Linguistic Society, Univ Chicago, 93; Locatives vs. Instrumentals in Kinyarwanda in Proceedings of the 17th Annual Meeting of the Berkeley Linguistic Society: Special Session on African Language Structure, 91. **CONTACT ADDRESS** Dartmouth Col, 3529 N Main St, #207, Hanover, NH, 03755. **EMAIL** lindsay.j.whaley@dartmouth.edu

WHARTON, ANNABEL
DISCIPLINE ART HISTORY **EDUCATION** London Univ, PhD. **CAREER** Prof, Duke Univ. **SELECTED PUBLICATIONS** Auth, Refiguring the Post Classical City: Dura, Jerash, Jerusalem and Ravenna, Cambridge, 95; Art of Empire treat Early Christian and Byzantine painting and architecture as an expression of the social and cultural assumptions of their audiences. **CONTACT ADDRESS** Dept of Art and Art Hist, Duke Univ, East Duke Building, Durham, NC, 27706. **EMAIL** wharton@acpub.duke.edu

WHAYNE, JEANNIE
DISCIPLINE HISTORY **EDUCATION** Univ Calif San Diego, BA, 79, MA, 81, PhD, 89. **CAREER** Asst prof, 90-96, assoc prof, Univ Ark, 96-. **SELECTED PUBLICATIONS** Auth, A New Plantation South: Land, Labor, and Federal Favor in Twentieth Century Arkansas, Univ Va, 96; The Significance of Race, Class, and Family in the Battle for Prohibition in Small Town Arkansas, Locus, 95; ed, Cultural Encounters in the Early South: Indians and Europeans in Arkansas, Univ Ark, 95; co-ed, The Governors of Arkansas, Univ Ark, 95. **CONTACT ADDRESS** History Dept, Univ of Arkansas, Fayetteville, 411A Old Main, Fayetteville, AR, 72701. **EMAIL** jwhayne@comp.uark.edu

WHEALEY, ROBERT H.
PERSONAL Born 05/16/1930, Freeport, NY, m, 1954, 3 children **DISCIPLINE** HISTORY **EDUCATION** Univ Mich, PhD,63. **CAREER** Univ Maine, 61-64; Ohio Univ, 64-. **HONORS AND AWARDS** Fulbright Scholar **MEMBERSHIPS** AHA; Soc Span Port Studies; Int Studies Asn, Ohio Acad Hist; Ger Studies Asn. **RESEARCH** Spanish Civil War; European Diplomatic History since 1914. **SELECTED PUBLICATIONS** Auth, Economic Influence of the Great Powers in Spain Civil War: From the Popular Front to the Second World War,Int Hist Rev, 83; Anglo-American Oil Confronts Spanish Nationalism 1927-31, Diplomatic Hist,88; Hitler & Spain: The Nazi Role in the Spanish Civil War, 1936-1939, 89; Selected Biographies and Interpretations of Hitler, Greenwood, 93; Francisco Franco y Bahomande, 1882-1975, Great Leaders, Great Tyrants,Greenwood, 95. **CONTACT ADDRESS** Dept of History, Ohio Univ, Athens, OH, 45701.

WHEATON, BRUCE R.
DISCIPLINE HISTORY OF SCIENCE **EDUCATION** Stanford Univ, BS; Univ Cal-Berkeley, MA; Princeton Univ, MA & PhD. **CAREER** Tchr Science & Tech, Univ Cal-Berkeley; PRIN, TECHNOL & PHYS SCI HIST ASSOC; George Mayr Educ Found Schol. **MEMBERSHIPS** US Hist Sci Soc **RESEARCH** Cultural history of science and technology **SELECTED PUBLICATIONS** auth The Tiger and the Shark: Empiricial roots of wave-particle dualism, Cambridge, 91; Inventory fo Sources for History of Twentieth-Century Physics: Report and Microfiche Index to 700,000 Letters. **CONTACT ADDRESS** Technol & Phys Sci Hist Assoc, 1136 Portland Ave, Albany, CA, 94706. **EMAIL** wheaton@tapsha.edu

WHEELER, DOUGLAS L.
DISCIPLINE WORLD HISTORY, SOUTHERN EUROPE AND IBERIA, INTERNATIONAL AFFAIRS **EDUCATION** Boston Univ, PhD. **CAREER** Prince Henry the Navigator Prof of Port Hist and the Discoveries, Univ NH, 65-. **HONORS AND AWARDS** Richard Welch Mem fel, Harvard Univ; Fulbright-Hays fel; Sr Key Soc Tchg Award. **RESEARCH** History of Portugal's role in World War II. **SELECTED PUBLICATIONS** Auth, Republican Portugal, 78; Angola, 81; A Ditadura Militar, 88; Historical Dictionary of Portugal, 93; coed, In Search of Modern Portugal. **CONTACT ADDRESS** Univ NH, Durham, NH, 03824. **EMAIL** dwheeler@christa.unh.edu

WHEELER, GERALD EVERETT
PERSONAL Born 08/16/1924, Everett, WA, m, 1948, 1 child **DISCIPLINE** AMERICAN HISTORY **EDUCATION** Univ Calif, Berkeley, AB, 48, MA, 49, PhD(Am & Far Eastern hist), 54. **CAREER** Instr hist, Col Holy Names, 50; teaching asst, Univ Calif, Berkeley, 50-52; asst prof, US Naval Acad, 52-57; assoc, 57-80, PROF HIST, SAN JOSE STATE UNIV, 80-, DEAN SOC SCI, 76-, Ed jour, Am Aviation Hist Soc, 59-60; Fulbright-Hays teaching grant, Philippines, 63-64; prof hist, Univ Calif, Berkeley, 64-65; E J King prof maritime hist, US Naval War Col, 68-69; ed, Newslett, Soc Hist Am Foreign Rels, 69-72. **MEMBERSHIPS** AHA; Orgn Am Historians; Am Aviation Hist Soc (pres, 66-67); Soc Hist Am Foreign Rels; Am Mil Inst. **RESEARCH** American diplomatic history, 1920-1970; American naval history, 1900-1970; Philippine history, 1900-1946. **SELECTED PUBLICATIONS** Coauth, Outline of world naval history, Acad Press, 56; auth, Prelude to Pearl Harbor: US Navy and the Far East, 1921-1931, Univ Mo, 63; National policy planning between the World Wars, Naval War Col Rev, 69; Admiral William Veazie Pratt, US Govt Printing Off, 74; The Road to War: The United States and Japan, 1931-1941, Forum Press, 77; Edwin Denby, 1921-1924 and Charles Francis Adams III, 1929-1933, In: The American Secretaries of the Navy (2 vols), US Naval Inst, 80; Eyewitness To Infamy - An Oral-History Of Pearl-Harbor - Travers,Pj, Journal Of The West, Vol 0033, 1994; War, Wings And A Western Youth, 1925-1945 - Hinckley,Tc, Pacific Historical Review, Vol 0066, 1997. **CONTACT ADDRESS** Dept of Hist, San Jose State Univ, San Jose, CA, 95192.

WHEELER, RACHEL
PERSONAL Born 09/11/1969, Fondulac, WI, s **DISCIPLINE** HISTORY **EDUCATION** Yale Univ, PHD, 98 **CAREER** Asst Prof, 98-pres **MEMBERSHIPS** AAR; AHA **RESEARCH** Religious Hist; Missions; Colonial America; Native American History **CONTACT ADDRESS** Dept of Relig Studies, Lewis & Clark Col, 0615 SW Palatine Hill Rd, Portland, OR, 97219. **EMAIL** rwheeler@lclark.edu

WHEELER, STANTON
PERSONAL Born 09/27/1930, Pomona, CA, m, 1951, 3 children **DISCIPLINE** SOCIOLOGY OF LAW **EDUCATION** Pomona Col, BA, 52; Univ Wash, MA, 56, PhD(sociol), 58. **CAREER** Acting instr, Univ Wash, 56-58; instr social rel, Harvard Univ, 58-60; Fulbright res scholar, Insts Sociol & Criminol, Univ Oslo, 60-61; asst prof social rel, Harvard Univ, 61-63; assoc prof sociol, Univ Wash, 63-64; sociologist, Russell Sage Found, 64-68; adj assoc prof sociol & law, 66-68, Prof Sociol & Law, Yale Law Sch, 68-, Mem, Russell Sage Found, 68-; fel, Ctr Advan Studies Behav Sci, 70-71; mem, Comt on Incarceration, 71-. **MEMBERSHIPS** Am Sociol Asn; Soc Studies Social Probs (pres-elect); Law & Soc Asn. **RESEARCH** Sociology of crime, deviance and incarceration; sociology of sport and leisure. **SELECTED PUBLICATIONS** Coauth, Socialization After Childhood: Two Essays, 66, auth, Deviant behavior, In: Sociology: An Introduction, 67, rev ed, 73 & coauth, Controlling Delinquents, 68, Wiley; auth, On Record: Files and Dossiers in American Life, Russell Sage Found, 69; Socialization in correctional institutions, In: Handbook of Socialization Theory and Research, Rand McNally, 69; The Prospects For Large-Scale Collaborative Research - Revisiting The Yale White-Collar Crime Research-Program, Law And Social Inquiry-Journal Of The American Bar Foundation, Vol 0018, 1993. **CONTACT ADDRESS** Russell Sage Prog, Yale Univ, PO Box 208215, New Haven, CT, 06520-8215.

WHEELER, WILLIAM BRUCE
DISCIPLINE HISTORY **EDUCATION** Univ Va, PhD. **CAREER** Prof. **RESEARCH** Early national period; American urban history. **SELECTED PUBLICATIONS** Coauth, Continuity and Change in an Appalachian City, Univ Tennessee; TVA and the Tellico Dam 1936-1979, Univ Tennessee; Discovering the American Past, Houghton Mifflin, 98. **CONTACT ADDRESS** Dept of History, Knoxville, TN, 37996.

WHEELOCK, ARTHUR K., JR.
DISCIPLINE ART HISTORY **EDUCATION** Harvard Univ, PhD, 73. **CAREER** CURATOR, NORTHERN BAROQUE PAINTINGS, NAT GALLERY ART **CONTACT ADDRESS** Dept Northern Baroque Painting, National Gallery of Art, Washington, DC, 20565. **EMAIL** a-wheelock@nga.gov

WHELAN, STEPHEN T.
PERSONAL Born 07/28/1947, Philadelphia, PA, m, 1971, 1 child **DISCIPLINE** LAW/HISTORY **EDUCATION** Princeton Univ, BA, 68; Harvard Univ, JD, 71. **CAREER** Atty, 75-, partner, 78, Thacher Proffitt & Wood, Mudge Rose Guthrie & Alexander. **HONORS AND AWARDS** Magna cum laude, Princeton Univ; Outstanding Sr, student pol org, Princeton Univ. **MEMBERSHIPS** Amer Bar Asn; Fel, Amer Col of Investment Counsel; The Economic Club, NY. **RESEARCH** Financial law; econ history **SELECTED PUBLICATIONS** Auth, New York's Uniform Commercial Code New Article 2A, Matthew Bender & Co., 94; art, American Bar Association Annual Survey: Leases, Bus Lawyer, Vol 49, 94 & Vol 50, 95 & Vol 51, 96 & Vol 52, 97; art, Securitization of Medical Equipment Finance Contracts, Med Finance & Tech Yearbook, Euromoney Pub, 95; art, Securitization of Medical Equipment Finance Contracts, World Leasing Yearbook, Euromoney Pub, 96; coauth, The ABC's of the UCC: Article 2A (Leases), Amer Bar Asn, 97; art, Asset Securitization, Comm Finance Guide, Matthew Bender, 98. **CONTACT ADDRESS** Thacher Proffitt & Wood, 2 World Trade Ctr, New York, NY, 10048. **EMAIL** swhelan@thacherproffitt.com

WHITE, BARBARA EHRLICH
PERSONAL New York, NY, m, 1961, 2 children **DISCIPLINE** ART HISTORY **EDUCATION** Smith, BA, 58; Columbia, MA, 60, PhD, 65. **CAREER** Adj prof, 65-, Tufts Univ. **HONORS AND AWARDS** NEH; Kress. **MEMBERSHIPS** Col Art Asn. **RESEARCH** Impressionism; P.A. Renoir. **SELECTED PUBLICATIONS** Ed, Impressionism in Perspective, Prentice-Hall, 78; auth, Renoir: His Life, Art, and Letters, Abrams, 85; auth, Impressionists Side by Side: Their Friendships, Rivalries, and Artistic Exchanges, Knopf, 96 **CONTACT ADDRESS** Dept of Art History, Tufts Univ, Medford, MA, 02155.

WHITE, CHARLES SIDNEY JOHN
PERSONAL Born 09/25/1929, New Richmond, WI **DISCIPLINE** HIST OF RELIGIONS, HINDUISM & MEDIEVAL & MODERN HINDI POETRY **EDUCATION** Univ WI, BA, 51; Univ of the Am, MA, 57; Univ Chicago, MA, 62, PhD, 64. **CAREER** Asst prof Indian studies, Univ WI, 65-66; asst prof, relig thought & S Asian studies, Univ PA, 66-71; coordr, ctr Asian Studies, 73-76, assoc prof, Am Univ, 71-78, Dir Ctr Asian Studies, 76-78, Prof Philos & Relig, Am Univ 78-94, Prof Emer Philos & Relig, 95-, chmn dept philos & relig, 84-87 & 88-94, Dir Inst Vaishnava Studies, 71-; Vis lectr Hist Relig, Princeton Univ, 68; Vis prof world relig, Lakehead Univ, Thunder Bay, Ontario, 74, 77, 80, 82, 84 & 88 (summers); Vis prof, Wesley Sem, Fall 85; Jr fel, Am Inst Indian Studies, Poona, India, 64-65 & res fel, Agra, 68-69, trustee, 73-; Kern Found Fel, 72. **HONORS AND AWARDS** Inst Int Educ graduate award, Span lang and lit, Universidad nacional de Mexico; Rockefeller Doctoral fel, relig, hon, Univ Chicago, 61; NDEA fel, Hindu-Urdu, Univ Chicago 61-64; Am Philos Soc fel, 66-67; Summer res grant, Univ PA, India, 70; Col Arts & Sci travel res grant, summer 74; Am Univ travel grant, India, summer 76; Center for Asian Studies, Am Univ, summer grant, 78; Smithsonian Grant, prin investigator, India, 82-83; Am Univ Col Arts & Sci Award fro Outstanding Scholar, 84; Am Univ Senate Comt Res, India, summer 87; CAS Mellon Award; Am Inst Indian Studies fac res fel, India, 95, spring 97. **MEMBERSHIPS** Am Asn Asian Studies; Am Acad Relig; Am Orient Soc; Soc Sci Study Relig. **RESEARCH** Hist of relig methodology; Hindu lit; Islam. **SELECTED PUBLICATIONS** Auth, Sufism in Hindi literature, 64 & Krishna as divine child, 70, Hist Relig; Heaven, In: The Encyclopedia Britannica, 65; Resources for the study of Medieval Hindu devotional religion,, Am Philos Soc Yearbk 67; A Note Toward Understanding in Field Method, In: Understanding in History of Relition, Univ Chicago Press, 67; Bhakti, In: The Encyclopedia Britannica, 68; Devi, Dharma, Dayanand Saraswati, Durga, Diwali, The Encyclopedia Americana, 68; Krsna as divine child, Hist Relig, 70; The Sai Baba movement, J Asian Studies, 72; Henry S Olcott: A Buddhist apostle, Theosophist, 4/73; co-auth, Responses to Jay J Bim on Bernard Meland, Jour Relig, 4/73; Swami Muktananda, Hist Relig, 74; Caurasi Pad of Sri Hit Harivams (transl), Univ Hawaii, 77; Structure in history of religions, Hist Relig, 78; Ramayana, Ramanuja, Ram Mohan Roy, Ramakrishna, Encyclopedia Americana, 79; Ramakrishna's Americans, Yugantar Prakashan, 79; Madhva, Mahavira, Mantra, Mandala, Manu, Encyclopedia Americana, 79; Mother Guru: Jnanananda of Madras, India, In: Unspoken Worlds: Women's Religious Lives, Harper and Row, 80, 2nd ed, Wadsworth, 88; The Hindu Holy Person, Ramakrishna, Satya Sai Baba, J Krishnamurti, Ramana Maharshi, Sadhu, Guru, Rsi, Acarya, Meher Baba, In: Abingdon Dictionary of Living Religions, 81, Perennial Dictionary of World Religions, Harper and Row, 89; Untouchables, Parsis, Encyclopedia Americana, 81; Kuan Yin, Juggernaut, Kali, Kama Sutra, Karma, Kautilya, Krishna, Jiddu Krishnamurti, Kshatriya, Kumbha Mela, Lakshmi, In: Encyclopedia Americana, 82; coauth, The Religious Quest, Univ Md. 83, 2nd ed, 85; Religion in Asia, In: Funk and Wagnall's Yearbook, 85-93, and Collier's International Yearbook; Almsgiving, Gift Giving, Jiddu Krishnamurti: A Biograhy, In: Encyclopedia of Religion, Macmillan Co, 86; Inwardness and privacy: Last bastions of religious life, Theosophis, 86 & Holistic Human Concern for World Welfare, 87; Indian developments: Sainthood in Hinduism, In: Sainthood: Its Manifestations in World Religions, Univ Calif Press, 88, paperbk, 8/90; co-auth, Joseph Campbell: Transformations of Myth Through Time, and An Anthology of Readings, Harcourt Brace Jovanovich, 89; co-ath (with David Haberman), rev, Sonic Theology: Hinduism and Sacred Sound by Guy L Beck, Jour Vaisnava Studies, spring 94; Nimbarka Sampradaya, Anandamayi Ma, Ramana Marsi, Sadhu, Swami, svamin, In: HarperCollins Dictionary of Religion, 95; The remaining Hindi works of Sri Hit Harivams, Jour Vaisnava Studies, fall 96; Mircea Eliade, Bengal Nights ... Maitreyi Devi, It Does Not Die, rev, Love and Politics for Eliade, Annals of Scholarship, summer 97; Muhammad as Spiritual Master, In: The Quest, 8/98. **CONTACT ADDRESS** Dept of Philos & Relig, American Univ, 4400 Massachusetts Ave NW, Washington, DC, 20016-8200.

WHITE, DAN SELIGSBERGER
PERSONAL Born 05/30/1939, Oakland, CA, m, 1963, 2 children **DISCIPLINE** MODERN EUROPEAN HISTORY **EDUCATION** Stanford Univ, BA, 61; Harvard Univ, MA, 63, PhD(hist), 67. **CAREER** Instr hist, Harvard Univ, 66-69; from asst prof to assoc prof, Mass Inst Technol, 69-76; lectr hist, Univ Mass, Boston, 76-77; assoc prof, 77-93, chem dept, 94-, PROF HIST, UNIV AT ALBANY, 93- . **MEMBERSHIPS** AHA **RESEARCH** Modern German history; modern European history; history of the European socialist and labor movement. **SELECTED PUBLICATIONS** Co-ed, The Thirteenth of May: The Advent of de Gaulle's Republic, Oxford Univ, 68; auth, The Splintered Party: National Liberalism in Hessen and the Reich 1867-1918, Harvard Univ, 76; auth, Lost Comrades: Socialists of The Front Generation 1918-1945, Harvard, 92. **CONTACT ADDRESS** Dept of History, Univ Albany, Ten Broeck 105, Albany, NY, 12222.

WHITE, DAVID ANTHONY
PERSONAL Born 02/17/1937, Boston, MA, m, 1961, 2 children **DISCIPLINE** LATIN AMERICAN & MODERN SPANISH HISTORY **EDUCATION** Stanford Univ, BA, 58; Univ Calif, Berkeley, MBA, 61; Univ Calif, Los Angeles, PhD, 68. **CAREER** PROF HIST, SONOMA STATE UNIV, 68-, Danforth Found assoc, 69-; Fel Col Teachers, Nat Endowment for Humanities, 81. **MEMBERSHIPS** AHA; Conf Latin Am Hist; Pac Coast Coun Latin Am Studies. **RESEARCH** Mexico in the 20th Century; Modern Mexican Art, American Ex-patriots in Mexico, 20-40; United States-Latin American relations. **SELECTED PUBLICATIONS** Creative history: Writing historical fiction, Proc Pac Coast Coun Latin Am Studies, Vol VII, 80-81; Siqueiros: A Biography, Floricanto Press, 94. **CONTACT ADDRESS** Dept Hist, Sonoma State Univ, 1801 E Cotati Ave, Rohnert Park, CA, 94928-3609. **EMAIL** tony.white@sonoma.edu

WHITE, DON LEE
PERSONAL Born 1025, Los Angeles, California **DISCIPLINE** MUSIC **EDUCATION** Los Angeles City Coll, AA 1949; CA State Coll, AB 1952; Univ of S CA, MM 1959; Stanford Univ, study toward Dr of Musical Arts 1968-69; Univ of So CA, study toward Dr of Musical Arts 1970-72; Hon D Law Monrovia Coll 1984. **CAREER** Prairie View A&M Coll, organist 1955-61; Los Angeles City Coll, instructor music 1961-62; Jefferson High Adult School, instructor 1961-63; Trade Tech Coll, instructor 1962-63; CA State Coll LA, lecturer 1962-64; CA State Univ LA, assoc prof 1964, prof of music, beginning 1983-. **HONORS AND AWARDS** Resolution City of Los Angeles Tribute Tenth Dist Councilman Thomas Bradley 1967; Los Angeles Philharmonic Orchestra 1974; lecture, "The Black Experience in Art, Aestetic meaning of Black Religious Music" presented at CA State Polytechnic Univ 1983; conductor for the Third annual Choral Festival for the Ecumenical Center for Black Church Studies 1983; elected First Vice Pres of the Natl Assn of Negro Musicians Inc 1983; an Annotated Biography of Negro Composers State LA Found Grant; The Afro-Amer Hymnal 1978; Organs in Historic Black Churches; choral arrangements, Blessed Are the Meek, When Shall I (we) Meet Him?, O for a Thousand Tongues (all published by Marvel Press), Rejoice the Lord is King, How Great the Wisdom, Glorious Things of Thee, The AME Hymn, Ye Are Baptised, Introit andA; organ compositions, Christmas Fantasy, Jesus Keep Me Near The Cross, Thanksgiving Prelude, Chorale Prelude on Fairest Lord Jesus, By the Waters of Babylon, Magnificat for organ; cantata "Jesus Said from the Cross"; A Musical Masque SATB Children Choir, Adult, Dancing and educ instruments; Dance elegy for Bass solo and piano. **MEMBERSHIPS** Dir Music So CA Conf AME Church; dir Music Fifth Dist AME Church (14 states); 1st vice pres, 1990-92, 2nd vice pres, 1980-84, Natl Assn of Negro Musicians western regional dir Natl Assn of Negro Musicians 1984-87.

WHITE, DONALD
PERSONAL Born 04/02/1935, Boston, MA, m, 1968, 3 children **DISCIPLINE** CLASSICAL ARCHAEOLOGY **EDUCATION** Harvard Univ, AB, 57; Princeton Univ, MA, 61, PhD(class archaeol), 64. **CAREER** From instr to assoc prof class archaeol, Univ Mich, 63-73; assoc prof class archaeol & assoc curator, Univ Museum, Univ Pa, 73-87; prof class archaeol and curator, Univ Mus, Univ Pa, 88-, Dir, Excavations, Apollonia and Cyrene, eastern Libya, Marsa Matruh, NW Egypt. **HONORS AND AWARDS** Honorary fellow, Wolfson Col, Oxford. **MEMBERSHIPS** Life member, Archaeol Inst Am; Associazione Internazione di Archeologia Classica, Philadelphia; numismatic and Antiquarian Soc. **RESEARCH** Excavation and publication of 3 N African sites, ancient architecture, curating greek and Roman collections. **SELECTED PUBLICATIONS** Coauth, Apollonia, the Port of Cyrene, 77; The Extramural Sanctuary of Demeter and Persephone at Cyrene I 1984 and V 1993; 70 articles and reviews. **CONTACT ADDRESS** Mus of Archaeol and Anthropol, Univ of Pa, 33 and Spruce Sts, Philadelphia, PA, 19104. **EMAIL** donwhite@sas.upenn.edu

WHITE, DONALD WALLACE
PERSONAL Summit, NJ **DISCIPLINE** AMERICAN HISTORY, INTERNATIONAL RELATIONS **EDUCATION** Hartwick Col, BA, 69; City Col, City Univ New York, MS, 72; NY Univ, MA, 72, PhD(hist), 79. **CAREER** Asst res scientist, 76-80, Assoc Res Scientist, NY Univ, 80-, Instr NY Univ, 72-73 & 79, asst ed, Papers William Livingston, 76-79, assoc ed, 79-80, asst to McGeorge Bundy, nuclear weapons & energy hist, 79-, adj asst prof, 82. **RESEARCH** Ideology of post-World War II United States foreign affairs; nuclear weapons and energy policy; local history. **SELECTED PUBLICATIONS** Auth, A local history approach to the American Revolution: Chatham, New Jersey, NJ Hist, spring/summer 78; A Village at War: Chatham, New Jersey, and the American Revolution, Fairleigh Dickinson Univ Press, 79; co-ed, The Papers of William Livingston, Vol I, 79, Vol II, 80, NJ Hist Comn; Postwar Politics In The G-7 - Orders And Eras In Comparative Perspective - Shafer,Be, Journal Of Interdisciplinary History, Vol 0028, 1998. **CONTACT ADDRESS** Dept of Hist, New York Univ, New York, NY, 10003.

WHITE, ELIZABETH
DISCIPLINE HISTORY **EDUCATION** Yale Univ, PhD, 95. **CAREER** Asst prof, Univ Nev Las Vegas. **SELECTED PUBLICATIONS** Auth, pubs on civil war and reconstruction, and American culture. **CONTACT ADDRESS** History Dept, Univ Nev Las Vegas, 4505 Md Pky, Las Vegas, NV, 89154.

WHITE, G. EDWARD
PERSONAL Born 03/19/1941, Northampton, MA, m, 1966, 2 children **DISCIPLINE** AMERICAN STUDIES; LAW **EDUCATION** Amherst Col, BA, 63; MA, 64, PhD, 67, Yale Univ; Harvard Law School, JD, 70. **CAREER** Univ Va, Sch Law **RESEARCH** American constitutional and legal history **CONTACT ADDRESS** Univ of Virginia School of Law, 580 Massie Rd., Charlottesville, VA, 22903-1789. **EMAIL** gewhite@law1.virginia.edu

WHITE, JOHN CHARLES
PERSONAL Born 04/14/1939, Washington, DC, m, 1963 **DISCIPLINE** MODERN HISTORY **EDUCATION** Washington & Lee Univ, BA, 60; Duke Univ, MA, 62, PhD(hist), 64. **CAREER** From asst prof to assoc prof, 67-76, Prof Hist, Univ Ala, Huntsville, 76-, Chmn Dept, 70-, Duke Univ res grant, 64; mem bd dirs, Consortium Revolutionary Europe, 73. **MEMBERSHIPS** Am Soc 18th Century Studies; AHA. **RESEARCH** French colonial policy in 18th century; careers of P V Malouet and Marechal de Castries; Fifth French Republic. **SELECTED PUBLICATIONS** Auth, L'Hopital Maritime de Toulon, Annales du Midi, 12/71; Aspects of reform of the French Navy under Castries: A case for humanity and justice, Univ GA, 75; ed, Proceedings Consortium on Revolutionary Europe, Univ GA, 77; Revolution And Political-Conflict In The French-Navy, 1789-1794 - Cormack,Ws, American Historical Review, Vol 0102, 1997. **CONTACT ADDRESS** Dept of Hist, Univ of Ala, Huntsville, AL, 35807.

WHITE, JOHN D.
PERSONAL Born 07/23/1948, Benham, KY **DISCIPLINE** MUSIC; PHILOSOPHY **EDUCATION** Univ Ky, BM, 70; Univ Idaho, MM, 72; Univ Iowa, PhD, 77. **CAREER** Sabbatical replacement, Willamette Univ, spring, 74; asst prof, 76-78, interim chair, 78-79, assoc prof, 78-80, dept chair, fall, 80, Western Wy Community Col, driver, Webb's Trucking, spring, 81; assoc prof, Benedict Col, 81-82; assoc prof, Chattahoochee Valley State Community Col, 82-83; grad study in philos, Univ Ky, spring, 84; lectr, Okla State Univ, 84-85; grad asst, Univ Tex Austin, 85-86; grad study in philos, Univ Iowa, spring, 87; assoc prof, Col of the Ozarks, 87-88; pianist, Univ Iowa, 88-89; prof, philos/humanities, Talladega Col, 89-. **SELECTED PUBLICATIONS** Auth, The Pythagorean Derivation and Theories of Truth, 96; auth, The Substance Argument, 95; auth, The Confluence of Deism, African Creation Myth, and Thomas Hobbes, 94; auth, Philosophy of Law, 94; auth, The Origin of Number, 93; auth, The Antigone Effect, 92; auth, Belief System Internal Inconsistency, 91; auth, The Maker's Mind Model in Aesthetics, 91; auth, The Analysis of Law and the Nesting of the Philosophy of History in the History of Empiricism, 88; auth, Some Remarks on Some Remarks on Logical Form, 87; auth, Considerations on Infinity Derived from Spinozist Theory, 87; auth, Empiricism, Hume, Quantum Mechanics, and Universe Models, 86. **CONTACT ADDRESS** Dept. of Philosophy, Talladega Col, Campus Box 165, Talladega, AL, 35160.

WHITE, JOHN HOXLAND
PERSONAL Born 11/10/1933, Cincinnati, OH **DISCIPLINE** AMERICAN RAILROAD HISTORY **EDUCATION** Miami Univ, BA, 58. **CAREER** Curator Transp, Smithsonian Inst, 58-, Lectr, Univ Pa, 66, Univ Calif, 70 & Univ Moscow, 73; consult, Calif State RR Mus, 70- & Pa State RR Mus, 68-; ed, RR Hist, 70-79. **HONORS AND AWARDS** RR Hist Award, RR & Locomative Hist Soc, 82. **MEMBERSHIPS** Soc Hist Technol; RR & Locomotive Hist Soc. **RESEARCH** Railroad technology particulary 19th century. **SELECTED PUBLICATIONS** Auth, Cincinnati Locomotive Builders, Smithsonian Inst Pres, 65; American Locomotives, 1830-1880, Johns Hopkins Univ Press, 68; ed, Development of the Locomotive Engine, Mass Inst Technol Press, 70; auth, Early American Locomotives, 72 & Horse Cars, Cable Cars and Omnibuses, 74, Dover Publ; American Railroad Passenger Car, Johns Hopkins Press, 78; John Bull: 150 Years a Locomotives, Smithsonian Inst Press, 81; The Death Of Steam + Reply To Nelson,Andrew Article Critique, American Heritage, Vol 0047, 1996; The Power Of Live Steam + All Across The Country Steam Locomotives Are Pulling Trainloads Of Passengers Into The Past, American Heritage, Vol 0047, 1996. **CONTACT ADDRESS** Div Transp, Smithsonian Inst, Washington, DC, 20560.

WHITE, KEVIN
DISCIPLINE AQUINAS, MEDIEVAL PHILOSOPHY **EDUCATION** Univ Ottawa, PhD. **CAREER** Philos, Catholic Univ Am. **RESEARCH** Thomistic psychology; Aquinas; Augustine. **SELECTED PUBLICATIONS** Auth, The Meaning of Phantasia in Aristotle's De anima, III, 3-8, Dialogue 24, 85; St Thomas Aquinas and the Prologue to Peter of Auvergne's Quaestiones super De sensu et sensato, Documenti e studi sulla tradizione filosofica medievale 1, 90; three previously unpublished chapters from St Thomas Aquinas's Commentary on Ar-

istotle's Meteora: Sentencia super Meteora 2;13-15, Mediaeval Studies 54 , 92; The Virtues of Man the Animal sociale: Affabilitas and Veritas in Aquinas, The Thomist 57, 93; Individuation in Aquinas's Super Boetium De Trinitate, Q;4, American Catholic Philosophical Quarterly 69, 95; Aquinas on the Immediacy of the Union of Soul and Body, in Paul Lockey, ed;, Studies in Thomistic Theology, Houston: Center for Thomistic Studies, 96; Ed, Hispanic Philosophy in the Age of Discovery, Catholic Univ Am Press, 97; Coed, Jean Capreolus et son temps, Cerf, 97. **CONTACT ADDRESS** Catholic Univ of America, 620 Michigan Ave Northeast, Washington, DC, 20064. **EMAIL** whitek@cua.edu

WHITE, LONNIE JOE
PERSONAL Born 02/12/1931, Knox City, TX, m, 1951, 2 children **DISCIPLINE** AMERICAN HISTORY **EDUCATION** WTex State Col, BA, 50; Tex Tech Col, MA, 55; Univ Tex, PhD(Am hist), 61. **CAREER** Teaching asst hist, Univ Tex, 57-61; from asst prof to assoc prof, 61-67, PROF AM HIST, MEMPHIS STATE UNIV, 67- **MEMBERSHIPS** AHA; Western Hist Asn; Southern Hist Asn. **RESEARCH** American frontier; military history of the Southwest. **SELECTED PUBLICATIONS** Auth, Politics on the southwestern frontier: Arkansas territory, 1819-1936, Memphis State Univ, 64; White women captives of Southern Plains Indians 1866-1875, J of West, 7/69; Indian raids the Kansas frontier, 1869, Kans Hist Quart, winter 71; coauth, Hostiles and horse Soldiers: Indian Battles and Campaigns in the West, Pruett, 72; co-ed, By Sea to San Francisco, 1849-50: The Journal of Dr James Morison, Memphis State Univ, 77; auth, Indian soldiers of the 36th division, Mil Hist of Tex & Southwest, 79; From Desert To Bayou - The Civil-War Journal And Sketches Of Merrick,Morgan,Wolfe - Thompson,Jd, Journal Of The West, Vol 0032, 1993. **CONTACT ADDRESS** Dept of Hist, Memphis State Univ, Memphis, TN, 38152.

WHITE, MICHAEL J.
PERSONAL Born 02/25/1948, Canton, IL **DISCIPLINE** ANCIENT PHILOSOPHY **EDUCATION** Ariz State Univ, BA, 70; Univ Calif, San Diego, MA, 73, PhD(philos), 74. **CAREER** Asst prof, 74-79, Assoc Prof Philos, Ariz State Univ, 79-, Vis asst prof, Univ Tex, Austin, 76-77; vis assoc prof, Univ Ariz, fall, 81. **MEMBERSHIPS** Am Philos Asn. **RESEARCH** Ancient philosophy; mathematical logic; philosophy of language. **SELECTED PUBLICATIONS** Auth, A suggestion regarding the semantical analysis of performatives, Dialectica, 30: 2-3; Aspects of Megarian fatalism: Aristotelian criticisms and the Stoic doctrine of eternal recurrence, Can J Philos, 6/80; Aristotle's temporal interpretation of necessary coming-to-be and Stoic determinism, Phoenix, 34: 3; Aristotle's concept of theoria and the energeia-kinesis distinction, J Hist Philos, 7/80; Necessity and unactualized possibilities in Aristotle, Philos Studies, Vol 38, 80; On some ascending chains of Brouwerian modal logics, Studia Logica, 40: 1; Fatalism and causal determinism: An Aristotelian essay, Philos Quart, St Andrews, 7/81; Time and determinism in the Hellenistic philosophical schools, Arch Geschichte Philos (in press); Political Liberalism - Rawls,J, Law And Philosophy, Vol 0015, 1996. **CONTACT ADDRESS** Dept of Philos, Arizona State Univ, Tempe, 1126 N Scottsdale Rd, Tempe, AZ, 85281-1700.

WHITE, PETER
PERSONAL Born 09/24/1941, Washington, DC, m, 1968, 2 children **DISCIPLINE** CLASSICAL PHILOLOGY **EDUCATION** Boston Col, BA, 63; Harvard Univ, PhD, 72. **CAREER** Asst prof, 68-74, assoc prof, 74-92, prof 93-, chmn dept classics, 80-83, 97-98, Assoc Prof Classics, Univ Chicago, 74-, Ed, Classical Philology, 74-78; Am Coun Learned Soc fel, 78-79; chmn comt publ, vice pres publ, 85-87, Am Philol Asn, 82-84,natl endow human fel, 94-95. **HONORS AND AWARDS** Goodwin award merit, Am Philol Asn, 95. **MEMBERSHIPS** Am Philol Asn. **RESEARCH** Latin lit of the early Empire; Greek and Roman historiography. **SELECTED PUBLICATIONS** Auth, The authorship of the Historia Augusta, J Roman Studies, 67; Vibius Maximus the friend of Statius, Historia, 73; The presentation and dedication of the Silvae and the Epigrams, J Roman Studies, 74; The friends of Martial, Statius and Pliny, Harvard Studies in Class Philol, 75; Amicitia and the profession of poetry in early Imperial Rome, J Roman Studies, 78; Julius Caesar in Rome, Pheonix, 88; Maecenas Retirement, univ press, 91; Promised Verse: Poets in the Society of Augustan Rome, harvard univ press, 93; Julius Caesar and the Publication of Acta in Late Republican rome, chiron, 97. **CONTACT ADDRESS** Dept of Class, Univ of Chicago, 1010 E 59th St, Chicago, IL, 60637-1512. **EMAIL** pwhi@midway.uchicago.edu

WHITE, PHILIP LLOYD
PERSONAL Born 07/31/1923, Akron, OH, m, 1958, 5 children **DISCIPLINE** AMERICAN HISTORY **EDUCATION** Baldwin-Wallace Col, AB, 47; Columbia Univ, MA, 49, PhD(Am Hist & Govt), 54. **CAREER** Lectr World Hist, City Col New York, 54-55; asst prof Am Hist, Univ Tex, 55-58; Fulbright lectr, Univ Nottingham, Eng, 58-59; asst prof, Univ Chicago, 59-62; assoc prof, 62-75, prof Hist, Univ Texas, Austin, 75-, Mem, inst Early Am Hist & Cult, Williamsburg, Va; fel, Charles Warren Ctr, Harvard Univ, 64-65. **MEMBERSHIPS** Orgn Am Historians; Soc Historians Early Am Repub. **RESEARCH** Commerce of pre-revolutionary New York; origins of American nationality; frontier community development in New York and Pennsylvania. **SELECTED PUBLICATIONS** Auth, Beekmans of New York in Politics and Commerce & ed, Beekman Mercantiel Papers (3 vols) NY Hist Soc, 56; coauth, A History of the American People, McGraw, 70; contribr, Perspectives on Early American History, Harper, 73; auth, Beekmantown, New York, Univ Tex, 79. **CONTACT ADDRESS** Dept of History, Univ of Texas, Austin, TX, 78712-1026. **EMAIL** philwhite@mail.utexas.edu

WHITE, SHANE
DISCIPLINE HISTORY **EDUCATION** Univ Sydney, BA, 79, PhD, 89. **CAREER** Sr lectr History, Univ Sydney, Australia **RESEARCH** African American slavery, African American culture **SELECTED PUBLICATIONS** Fel Publ, 'It was a Proud Day'; African Americans, Festivals, and Parades in the North, 1741-1834, Jour Amer Hist 81, 94); auth, Somewhat More Independent: The End of Slavery in New York City, 1770-1810, Univ Ga, 91; coauth, Slave Hair and African American Culture in the Eighteenth and Nineteenth Centuries, Jour of Southern Hist 61, 95; coauth, Slave Clothing and African-American Culture in the Eighteenth and Nineteenth Centuries, Past and Present 148, 95; Slavery in New York State in the Early Republic, Australasian Jour of Amer Stud 14, 95; coauth, Reading the Slave Body: Gesture, Demeanor and African-American Culture, In: Varieties of Southern History: New Essays on a Region and Its People, Greenwood Press, 96. **CONTACT ADDRESS** Dept of History, Univ of Sydney, Sydney, NW, 2006. **EMAIL** shane.white@history.usyd.edu.au.

WHITE, STEVEN D.
DISCIPLINE HISTORY **EDUCATION** Harvard Col, AB, 65; PhD, 72. **CAREER** Asa G. Candler Prof Medieval Hist. **RESEARCH** Medieval French and English history; premodern European legal history. **SELECTED PUBLICATIONS** Auth, Custom, Kinship, and Gifts to Saints: the Laudatio Parentum in Western France, 1050-1150; Sir Edward Coke and the Grievances of the Commonwealth, 1621-1628. **CONTACT ADDRESS** Dept History, Emory Univ, 221 Bowden Hall, 561 Kilgo Cir, Atlanta, GA, 30322-1950. **EMAIL** histsdw@emory.edu

WHITEHEAD, JOHN S.
DISCIPLINE WESTWARD MOVEMENT **EDUCATION** Yale Univ, PhD, 71. **CAREER** Univ Alaska **SELECTED PUBLICATIONS** Auth, The Separation of College and State: Columbia, Dartmouth, Harvard, and Yale, 1776-1876, 73; Alaska Statehood: The Memory of the Battle, 93. **CONTACT ADDRESS** Univ AK Fairbanks, PO Box 757480, Fairbanks, AK, 99775-7480. **EMAIL** ffjsw@aurora.alaska.edu

WHITEHEAD, RUTH
PERSONAL Charleston, SC **DISCIPLINE** ART HISTORY **EDUCATION** Apprentice, The Charleston Museum, 61-65; registr, 70-71, cur asst, hist, staff ethnologist, 72-86, ASST CUR, HISTORY, & STAFF ETHNOLOGIST, NOVA SCOTIA MUSEUM 87-. **HONORS AND AWARDS** Award Merit, Am Asn State Local Hist, 81; Reg'l Hist Cert Merit, Can Hist Soc, 82; Award Merit, Can Museums Asn, 82, 89. **MEMBERSHIPS** Bata Shoe Museum Found. **SELECTED PUBLICATIONS** Auth, Leonard Paul: Portrait of a People/Traditional Micmac Crafts, 78; auth, International Inventory of Micmac, Maliseet and Beothuk Material Culture, 5 vols, 88; auth, The Old Man Told Us: Excerpts from Micmac History, 1500-1950, 91. **CONTACT ADDRESS** Dept of History & Staff Ethnologist, The Nova Scotia Museum, Halifax, NS.

WHITEHOUSE, DAVID BRYN
PERSONAL Born 10/15/1941, Worksop, England **DISCIPLINE** ARCHAEOLOGY **EDUCATION** Cambridge Univ, Eng, BA, 63; MA, 65, PhD, 67. **CAREER** Wainwright Fel, Oxford Univ, 66-73; dir, Brit Inst Afghan Stud, 73-74; dir, Brit Sch at Rome, 74-84; chief cur, Corning Museum Glass, 84-87; dep dir, Corning Museum Glass, 87092; DIR, CORNING MUSEUM GLASS, 92-. **MEMBERSHIPS** Int Asn Hist Glass; Soc Antiq London; Am Asn Museums **RESEARCH** Early glass & glassmaking; Late antiquity; Islamic art & archaeology **SELECTED PUBLICATIONS** "Byzantine Gilded Glass," Gilded and Enamelled Glass from the Middle East, Brit Mus Press, 98; Excavations at d-Dur (Umm al-Qaiwain, United Arab Emirates), The Glass Vessels, Peeters, 98; rev, "The Islamic Baths of Palestine," Bibliotheca Orientalis, 98; rev, "The Von Post Collection of Cypriote Late Byzantine Glazed Pottery," Bibliotheca Orientalis, 98. **CONTACT ADDRESS** The Corning Museum of Glass, One Museum Way, Corning, NY, 14830-2253. **EMAIL** dwhiteho@servtech.com

WHITEHOUSE, EUGENE ALAN
PERSONAL Born 07/15/1931, Augusta, ME, m, 1955, 1 child **DISCIPLINE** MODERN EUROPEAN HISTORY **EDUCATION** Pa State Univ, BA, 53; Univ Mich, MA, 56, PhD, 62. **CAREER** Prof Europ Hist, Nothern Mich Univ, 59-, assoc dean sch Arts & Sci, 67-74. **MEMBERSHIPS** AHA **RESEARCH** Germany in the 1860's. **CONTACT ADDRESS** Sch Arts & Sci, No Michigan Univ, 1401 Presque Isle Ave, Marquette, MI, 49855-5301. **EMAIL** ewhiteho@nmu.edu

WHITFIELD, STEPHEN JACK
PERSONAL Born 12/03/1942, Houston, TX, m, 1984 **DISCIPLINE** AMERICAN STUDIES **EDUCATION** Tulane Univ, BA, 64; Yale Univ, MA, 66; Brandeis Univ, PhD, 72. **CAREER** Instr hist, 66-68, Southern Univ New Orleans; asst prof, 72-79, assoc prof, 79-85, prof, 85-, am studies, Brandeis Univ **HONORS AND AWARDS** Kayden Prize in the Humanities, 81. **MEMBERSHIPS** Am Studies Assn; Orgn Am Historians; Am Jewish Hist Soc. **RESEARCH** American political and intellectual history in 20th century; post-WW II US hist, Amer Jewish Hist. **SELECTED PUBLICATIONS** Auth, Voices of Jacob, Hands of Esau, Archon, 84; auth, A Critical American: The Politics of Dwight Macdonald, Archon, 84; auth, A Death in the Delta: The Story of Emmett Till, Free Press, 88; auth, American Space, Jewish Time, Archon, 88; auth, The Culture of the Cold War, John Hopkins Univ, 91. **CONTACT ADDRESS** Dept of Am Studies, Brandeis Univ, Waltham, MA, 02254-9110. **EMAIL** switfield@binah.cc.brandeis.edu

WHITING, STEVEN
PERSONAL Chicago, IL **DISCIPLINE** MUSICOLOGY **EDUCATION** Univ Ill, PhD 91. **CAREER** Ed A-R Editions (Madison), 89-91; vis lectr, Univ Ill, 91-; asst prof of Musicol, Univ Mich. **HONORS AND AWARDS** Phi Beta Kappa. **MEMBERSHIPS** Am Musicol Soc. **RESEARCH** 18th-century music; Beethoven; Satie; musical narratology. **SELECTED PUBLICATIONS** Satie the Bohemian: From Cabaret to Concert Hall, Oxford Univ Press, 98; Erik Satie, Neuf chansons de cabaret et de caf conc, pour chant et piano, Edition etablie et prefacee par Steven Moore Whiting. Paris: Editions Salabert, 96, pl. nos. E.A.S. 19340-49, 19350; Symmetry and Process in Two Variation Works by Beethoven, Katachi U Symmetry, ed T. Ogawa et al., 301-5. Tokyo, Springer-Verlag, 96; Music on Montmartre, In The Spirit of Montmartre: Cabarets, Humor, and the Avant-Garde, 1875-1905, ed Phillip Dennis Cate & Mary Shaw, 159-97. New Brunswick, NJ: Rutgers Univ Press, 96; Erik Satie and Vincent Hyspa: Notes on a Collaboration; Music & Letters 77, 96:64-91; Three Marchen-Medieval, Musical, and Modern: Fouque's Undine, Mozart's Die Zauberflote, and Hoffmann's Der goldne Topf; Symmetry: Culture and Science 7, 96: 361-76; Musical Parody and Two 'uvres posthumes' of Erik Satie: The 'Reverie du pauvre' and the 'Petite musique de clown triste.'41 Revue de Musicologie 81 (95): 215-34.Carl Dahlhaus, Albrecht Riethmuller, and Alexander L. Ringer, eds., Beethoven: Interpretationen seiner Werke, 2 vols. Laaber: Laaber-Verlag, 94, 1:600-603, 2:404-8, 443-64. (Articles on seven of Beethoven's variation works for piano.)Alexander L. Ringer, Musik als Geschichte: Gesammelte Aufsatze. Herausgegeben von Albrecht Riethmuller und Steven Moore Whiting, Laaber: Laaber-Verlag, 93; Computers and Scholarly Publication, Mod Music Librarianship: In Honor of Ruth Watanabe, edited by Alfred Mann, 133-36, New York: Pendragon, 89; 'Hort ihr wohl': Zu Funktion und Programm von Beethovens Chorfantasie, Archiv fur Musikwissenschaft 45, 88:132-47; Pianos, In Bruno Nettl, The Western Impact on World Music, 51-54, New York: Schirmer, 85. **CONTACT ADDRESS** Sch of Music, Univ of Mich, Ann Arbor, Ann Abor, MI, 48109 2085.

WHITLEY, DAVID S.
PERSONAL Born 03/05/1953, Williams AFB, AZ, m, 1987, 1 child **DISCIPLINE** ANTHROPOLOGY, ARCHAEOLOGY **EDUCATION** UCLA, PhD, 82. **CAREER** Chiel Archaeologist, Inst of Archaeology, UCLA, 83-87; post-doc res fel, Archaeology dept, Univ of the Witwatersrand, 87-89; principle, WIS Consultants, 89-. **HONORS AND AWARDS** Special appreciation awards: CA Indian Found, 93; Simi Valley Hist Soc, 91; Canadian Tribal Coun, 89. **MEMBERSHIPS** Fel, Am Antropological Asn; Soc for Am Archaeology; Soc of Prof Archaeologists; Int Coun of Monuments and Sites. **RESEARCH** Western, northern Am archaeology; prehistoric religion; rock art; neuropsychology. **SELECTED PUBLICATIONS** Auth, New Light in Old Art: Recent Advances in Hunter-Gatherer Rock Art Research, co-ed with L L Loendorf, UCLA Inst of Archaeology, Monograph 36, 94; Guide to Rock Art Sites: Southern California and Southern Nevada, Mountain Press Pub Co, 96; Following the Shaman's Path, Maturango Museum, 98; Reader in Gender Archaeology, co-ed with K Hayes-Gilpen, Routledge, 98; ed, Reader in Archaeological Theory: Post-processual and Cognitive Approaches, Routledge, 98; Les Chamanes de Californie: Art Rupestre Amerindien de Californie, Editions du Seuil, in press; numerous other scholarly articles, book reviews, and other publications. **CONTACT ADDRESS** 447 Third St, Fillmore, CA, 93015. **EMAIL** huitli@isle.net

WHITMAN, T. STEPHEN
PERSONAL Born 02/08/1950, Rexmont, PA, m, 1997 **DISCIPLINE** HISTORY **EDUCATION** Mich State Univ, BA, 71; Drexel Univ, MS, 73; Johns Hopkins Univ, MA, 90, PhD, 93. **CAREER** Adj Prof, Univ Houston, 83; Human Resources Mgr, US Dept State, 75-90; Mem, Comn US State Dept Personnel Mgt, 92-93; Asst Prof Hist, St. Mary's Col, 94-; Consult, US State Dept, 97. **HONORS AND AWARDS** Superior Honor Award, US Dept State, 90; Md Hist Soc Bk Award, 97. **SELECTED PUBLICATIONS** Auth, Industrial Slavery at the Margin: The Maryland Chemical Works, J Southern Hist, 93; Diverse Good Causes: Manumission and the Transformation of Urban Slavery, Soc Sci Hist, 95; The Price of Freedom: Slavery

and Manumission in Baltimore and Early National Maryland, Univ Press Ky, 97. **CONTACT ADDRESS** History Dept, Mount St. Mary's Col, Emmitsburg, MD, 21727. **EMAIL** whitman@msmary.edu

WHITNEY, ELSPETH
DISCIPLINE HISTORY **EDUCATION** City Univ NY, PhD, 85. **CAREER** Assoc prof, Univ Nev Las Vegas; 90-. **RESEARCH** Medieval Europe history; science and technology history; European women history; environment history. **SELECTED PUBLICATIONS** Auth, Paradise Restored: The Mechanical Arts from Antiquity Through the Thirteenth Century, 90. **CONTACT ADDRESS** History Dept, Univ Nev Las Vegas, 4505 Md Pky, Las Vegas, NV, 89154.

WHITTAKER, CYNTHIA HYLA
PERSONAL Born 05/15/1941, Niagara Falls, NY, m, 2 children **DISCIPLINE** RUSSIAN HISTORY **EDUCATION** Marymount Col, NY, BA, 62; Ind Univ, Bloomington, MA, 64, PhD(Russ hist), 72. **CAREER** Asst Prof Russ Hist, Baruch Col, 73-, Res grant & partic, Young Fac Exchange Prog with Soviet Union, 73; City Univ New York fac res award, 74-75; ed, Slavic & Europ Educ Rev, 76-. **MEMBERSHIPS** AHA; Am Asn Advan Slavic Studies. **RESEARCH** Conservatism and education in Imperial Russia. **SELECTED PUBLICATIONS** Auth, The white Negro: Russian and American abolition, NDak Quart, 65; co-ed, The American bibliography of Russian and East European studies for 1963, 66 & The American bibliography of Russian and East European studies for 1964, 66, Ind Univ; auth, The women's movement during the reign of Alexander II: A case study in Russian liberalism, J Mod Hist, 76; The ideology of Sergei Uvarov: An interpretive essay, Russ Rev, 78; The impact of the Oriental Renaissance in Russia, Jahrbuecher fuer Geschichte Osteuropas, 78; One use of history in education: A translation and analysis of Uvarov's speech of 1818, Slavic & Europ Educ Rev, 78; From promise to purge: The first years of St Petersburg University, Paedagogica Historica, 79; To The Editor + Cracraft,James Review Of Alexander,John Biography Of Catherine-The-Great, Slavic Review, Vol 0053, 1994; Political-Ideas And Institutions In Imperial Russia - Raeff,M, Slavic Review, Vol 0054, 1995; Scenarios Of Power - Myth And Ceremony In Russian Monarchy, Vol 1, From Peter-The-Great To The Death Of Nicholas-I - Wortman,Rs, American Historical Review, Vol 0101, 1996. **CONTACT ADDRESS** 531 Main St, New York, NY, 10044.

WHITTENBURG, JAMES PENN
PERSONAL Born 10/26/1946, Rome, GA, m, 1970, 1 child **DISCIPLINE** AMERICAN HISTORY **EDUCATION** Univ Chattanooga, AB, 69; Wake Forest Univ, MA, 71; Univ Ga, PhD(hist), 74. **CAREER** Asst prof hist, Univ Mo-Columbia, 74-77; asst prof, 77-80, Assoc Prof Hist, Col William & Mary, 80-. **MEMBERSHIPS** Southern Hist Asn; Orgn Am Historians. **RESEARCH** Colonial America; Southern history; quantification. **SELECTED PUBLICATIONS** Auth, The computer as a teaching aid: a report on two class projects, Hist Teacher, 5/76; coauth, Measuring inequality: a FORTRAN Program for the Gini Index, Schutz Coefficient, and Lorenz Curve, Hist Methods Newsletter, spring 77; auth, Planters, lawyers, and merchants: social change and the origins of the North Carolina Regulation, 4/77 & The common farmer: Herman Husband's plan for peace between the United States and the Indians, 1792, 10/77, William & Mary Quart; Primal Forces, 3 Interlocking Themes In The Recent Literature On 18th-Century Virginia, Virginia Magazine Of History And Biography, Vol 0104, 1996. **CONTACT ADDRESS** Dept of Hist, Col of William and Mary, Williamsburg, VA, 23185.

WICKBERG, DANIEL
DISCIPLINE HISTORY **EDUCATION** Yale Univ, PhD, 93. **CAREER** Asst prof. **RESEARCH** Modern American cultural and intellectual history; American studies; history of social thought; historiography **SELECTED PUBLICATIONS** Auth, The Senses of Humor: Self, Laughter and Bourgeois Consciousness in Modern America, Cornell, 97. **CONTACT ADDRESS** Dept of History, Richardson, TX, 75083-0688. **EMAIL** wickberg@utdallas.edu

WICKER, KATHLEEN O'BRIEN
PERSONAL Born 05/24/1937, Buffalo, NY **DISCIPLINE** NEW TESTAMENT, CLASSICAL LANGUAGES **EDUCATION** Mundelein Col, BA, 59; Loyola Univ, Chicago, PhD(hist western origins), 66. **CAREER** From instr to asst prof hist & classics, Mundelein Col, 65-71; asst prof, 71-77, assoc prof, 76-84, prof, 84- , New Testament, Mary W Johnson and J Stanley Johnson prof in Hum, 96- , Scripps Col. **HONORS AND AWARDS** Lectr classics, Loyola Univ Chicago, 70-71; partic, Corpus Hellenisticum Novi Testamenti Proj, 71-77; actg dean fac, Scripps Col, 79-81. **MEMBERSHIPS** Soc Bibl Lit. **RESEARCH** Plutarch; Hellenistic philosophy and religion. **SELECTED PUBLICATIONS** Auth, De Defectu Oraculorum, In: Plutarch's Theological Writings and the Early Christian Literature, E J Brill, Leiden, 74; First Century Marriage Ethics, In: No Famine in the Land, Scholars, 75; Plutarch: Mulierum Virtutes, In: Plutarch's Ethical Writings and the Early Christian Literature, E J Brill, Leiden, 78. **CONTACT ADDRESS** Dept of Religion, Scripps Col, 1030 Columbia Ave, Claremont, CA, 91711-3948.

WICKHAMCROWLEY, TIMOTHY P.
PERSONAL Born 11/12/1951, Elizabeth, NJ, m, 1981 **DISCIPLINE** SOCIOLOGY **EDUCATION** Princeton Univ, AB, 73; Cornell Univ, MA, 75, PhD, 82. **CAREER** Vis prof, 83-84, Hamilton Col; vis prof, 84-86, Univ Rochester; asst prof, 86-92, assoc prof, 92-, Georgetown Univ. **HONORS AND AWARDS** NEH Fel, sum inst, 95. **MEMBERSHIPS** Latin Amer Stud Assn; Amer Sociol Assn; E Sociol Soc. **RESEARCH** Latin Amer; revolution; development; theory. **SELECTED PUBLICATIONS** Art, The Rise (and Sometimes Fall) of Guerrilla Governments in Latin America, Sociol Forum 2, 87; auth, Winners, Losers, and Also-rans: Toward a Comparative Sociology of Latin American Guerrilla Movements, Power & Popular Protest: Latin Amer Soc Movements, Univ Calif Press, 89; art, Understanding Failed Revolution in El Salvador: A Comparative Analysis of Regime Types and Social Structures, Politics & Soc 17, 89; art, Terror and Guerrilla Warfare in Latin America 1956-1970, Comparative Stud in Soc & Hist 32, 90; auth, Exploring Revolution: Essays on Latin American Insurgency and Revolutionary Theory, Armonk: Sharpe, 91; auth, Guerrillas and Revolution in Latin America: A Comparative Study of Insurgents and Regimes Since 1956, Princeton Univ Press, 92; art, A Qualitative Comparative Approach to Latin American Revolutions, Intl J of Comparative Soc 32, nos 1&2, 91; art, Elites, Elite Settlements and Revolutionary Movements in Latin America 1950-1980, Soc Science Hist 18, 94; art, Concerning Foxes and Hedgehogs: Tilly on State-Incited and State-Seeking Violence, Pol Powr & Soc theory, vol 9, JAI Press, 95; art, Structural Theories of Revolution, Theorizing Revolutions, Routledge, 97. **CONTACT ADDRESS** Dept of Sociology, Georgetown Univ, Box 571037, Washington, DC, 20057. **EMAIL** Wickhamt@gunet.georgetown.edu

WICKSTROM, JOHN B.
PERSONAL Born 07/23/1941, Lansing, MI, m, 1996 **DISCIPLINE** HISTORY **EDUCATION** Mich St Univ, BA, 59; Yale Univ, MA, 64, PhD, 69. **CAREER** Asst prof to assoc prof to prof, 68-, Kalamazoo Col. **HONORS AND AWARDS** Lucasse Lectorship Award, 82. **MEMBERSHIPS** Medieval Acad; Medieval Acad of Midwest. **RESEARCH** Medieval church hist; monastic hist. **SELECTED PUBLICATIONS** Auth, ICS MS 34: A 15th Cent Cistercian Breviary, Manuscripta, 84; auth, The Antiphons ad psalmos of Carthusian Lauds, Analecta Cartusiana, 88; auth, The Humiliati: Liturgy and Identity, Archivum Fratres Praedicatorum, 92; auth, St. Maurus of Glanfueil: Text and Image in the Making of a Holy Man, Stud in Iconography, 94; auth, Pope Gregory's Life of Benedict and the Illustrations of Abbot Desiderius of Monte Cassino, Stud in Iconography, 98. **CONTACT ADDRESS** Dept of History, Kalamazoo Col, 1200 Academy St, Kalamazoo, MI, 49006. **EMAIL** wickstro@cc.kzoo.edu

WICKWIRE, MARY B.
DISCIPLINE HISTORY **EDUCATION** Yale Univ, PhD, 63. **CAREER** Prof, Univ MA Amherst. **SELECTED PUBLICATIONS** Co-auth, Cornwallis: The American Adventure, 70; Cornwallis: The Imperial Years, 80. **CONTACT ADDRESS** Dept of Hist, Univ Massachusetts Amherst, Mass Ave, Amherst, MA, 01003.

WIDENOR, WILLIAM C.
DISCIPLINE HISTORY **EDUCATION** Univ Calif Berkeley, PhD, 75. **CAREER** Prof, Univ Ill Urbana Champaign. **RESEARCH** History of the foreign relations of the United States. **SELECTED PUBLICATIONS** Auth, American Planning for the United Nations: Have We Been Asking the Right Questions?, Dipl Hist, 82; Henry Cabot Lodge and the Search for an American Foreign Policy, Univ Calif, 83; The Role of Electoral Politics in American Foreign Policy Formulation: Are Historians Meeting the Conceptual Challenge?, Soc Hist Am For Rel Newsletter, 85. **CONTACT ADDRESS** History Dept, Univ Ill Urbana Champaign, 52 E Gregory Dr, Champaign, IL, 61820.

WIDER, SARAH ANN
DISCIPLINE AMERICAN RENAISSANCE **EDUCATION** Univ NM, BA, 81; Cornell Univ, MA, PhD, 84, 86. **CAREER** Assoc prof, Colgate Univ, 86. **RESEARCH** Emerson, congregation response to early 19th century Am sermons. **SELECTED PUBLICATIONS** Publ, ESQ, Studies in the Am Renaissance. **CONTACT ADDRESS** Dept of Eng, Colgate Univ, 13 Oak Drive, Hamilton, NY, 13346.

WIECEK, WILLIAM MICHAEL
PERSONAL Born 01/31/1938, Cleveland, OH, 3 children **DISCIPLINE** UNITED STATES LEGAL & CONSTITUTIONAL HISTORY **EDUCATION** Cath Univ Am, BA, 59; Harvard Univ, LLB, 62; Univ Wis-Madison, PhD(hist), 68. **CAREER** From asst prof to assoc prof, 68-77, PROF HIST, UNIV MO-COLUMBIA, 77-, Nat Endowment for Humanities fel, 75. **MEMBERSHIPS** Orgn Am Historians. **RESEARCH** American legal and constitutional development; slavery; nuclear power. **SELECTED PUBLICATIONS** Auth, The reconstruction of federal judicial power, 1863-1875, Am J Legal Hist, 69; The great writ and reconstruction: The Habeas Corpus Act of 1867, J Southern Hist, 70; The Guarantee Clause of the US Constitution, Cornell Univ, 72; Somerset: Lord Mansfield and the legitimacy of slavery in the Anglo-American World, Univ Chicago Law Rev, 74; The law of slavery and race in the thirteen mainland colonies of British America, William & Mary Quart, 77; The Sources of Antislavery Constitutionalism in America, 1760-1848, Cornell Univ Press; Equal Justice Under Law: Constitutional Development, 1835-1875, Harper & Row; Debt, Investment, Slaves - Credit Relations In East-Feliciana Parish - Kilbourne,Rh, American Journal Of Legal History, Vol 0039, 1995. **CONTACT ADDRESS** Dept of Hist, Syracuse Univ, Syracuse, NY, 13244.

WIECZYNSKI, JOSEPH LEON
PERSONAL Born 04/13/1934, Baltimore, MD, m, 1962, 4 children **DISCIPLINE** HISTORY OF RUSSIA **EDUCATION** St Mary's Sem & Univ, BA, 56; Georgetown Univ, PhD, 66. **CAREER** Analyst Soviet studies, 64-66, US Libr Cong; asst prof hist, 66-68, Edgewood Col; from asst prof to assoc prof, 68-74, prof hist, 74-, Va Polytech Inst & State Univ; Am Philos Soc res grants, 69-70, 71 & 73; res grants, Va Polytech Inst & State Univ, 71-72 & 74-75; vis prof, 76-77, Oxford Univ; vis prof, 89, Univ London; pres, Southern Conf on Slavic Stud, 89; vice pres, 89-92, Amer Catholic Hist Assn; ed, 90-95, J Soviet and Post Soviet Review. **MEMBERSHIPS** AHA; Am Assn Advan Slavic Studies; Am Cath Hist Assn; Southern Slavic Conf; Am Renaissance Soc. **RESEARCH** Russian intellectual history; early Russian history. **SELECTED PUBLICATIONS** Auth, Economic Consequences of Disarmament: The Soviet View, Russ Rev, 68; auth, Donation of Constantine in Medieval Russia, Cath Hist Rev, 69; auth, Archbishop Gennadius and the West, Can-Am Slavic Studies, 72; ed, Moscow and the West, 72 & Ivan the Terrible, 74, Acad Int; auth, Hermetism and Cabalism in The Heresy of the Judaizers, Renaissance Quart, 75; auth, The Russian Frontier, Univ Va, 76; ed, The Modern Encyclopedia of Russian and Soviet History, Acad Int, 76-90; ed, 54 vols, The Gorbachev Encyclopedia, Ross, 93; ed, The Gorbachev Reader, Ross, 93; ed, The Gorbachev Bibliography, Ross, 96. **CONTACT ADDRESS** 803 Preston Ave, Blacksburg, VA, 24060.

WIENER, JOEL H.
PERSONAL Born 08/23/1937, New York, NY, m, 1961, 3 children **DISCIPLINE** BRITISH HISTORY **EDUCATION** NY Univ, BA, 59; Cornell Univ, PhD, 65. **CAREER** From instr to asst prof hist, Skidmore Col, 64-67; asst prof, 67-72, from asst prof hist to assoc prof, 72-78, prof hist, 78-, chemn dept, 81-85, City Col NY; vis lectr hist, Univ York, Eng, 71-73. **MEMBERSHIPS** AHA; Conf Brit Studies; fel Royal Hist Soc; Res Soc Victorian Periodicals (pres 83-85). **RESEARCH** Modern British history; history of journalism. **SELECTED PUBLICATIONS** Auth, Radicalism and Freethought in Nineteenth-Century England: The Life of Richard Carlile, Greenwood, 82; ed, Innovators and Preachers: The Role of the Editor in Victorian England, Greenwood, 85; ed, Papers for the Millions; The New Journalism in Britain, 1850s to 1914, Greenwood, 88; auth, William Lovett, Manchester, 89. **CONTACT ADDRESS** Dept of History, City Col, CUNY, Convent Ave & 138th St, New York, NY, 10031. **EMAIL** jwiener@idt.net

WIENER, JONATHAN M.
PERSONAL Born 05/16/1944, St. Paul, MN **DISCIPLINE** SOCIAL HISTORY **EDUCATION** Princeton Univ, BA, 66; Harvard Univ, PhD(govt), 72. **CAREER** Actg asst prof polit, Univ Calif, Santa Cruz, 72; lectr sociol & polit sci, Univ Calif, Los Angeles, 72-73; asst prof, 73-77, prof hist, Univ Calif, Irvine, 84- ; Am Coun Learned Socs fel, 78; Rockefeller Found humanities fel, 78. **RESEARCH** Social history of American South; history and social theory; recent United States history. **SELECTED PUBLICATIONS** Auth, Planter-merchant conflict in reconstruction Alabama, Past & Present, 75; Social origins dictatorship and democracy, Hist & Theory, 76; Social Origins of the New South, La State Univ, 78; Class Structure and Economic Development in the American South, Am Hist Rev, 79; auth, Come Together: John Lennon in His Time, Random, 84; auth, Professors, Politics & Pop, Verso, 94; auth, Gimme Some Truth: The John Lennon FBI Files, Univ Calif, 99. **CONTACT ADDRESS** Dept of History, Univ of Calif, Irvine, CA, 92697. **EMAIL** jmwiener@uci.edu

WIENER, MARTIN J.
PERSONAL Born 06/01/1941, Brooklyn, NY, 2 children **DISCIPLINE** MODERN BRITISH HISTORY **EDUCATION** Brandeis Univ, BA, 62; Harvard Univ, MA, 63, PhD(hist), 67. **CAREER** Asst prof, 67-72, assoc prof, 72-80, Prof Hist, Rice Univ, 80-, Nat Endowment for Humanities younger humanist fel, 73-74; Am Coun Learned Soc fel, 82. **HONORS AND AWARDS** Schuyler Prize, Am Hist Asn, 81. **MEMBERSHIPS** AHA; Conf Brit Studies. **RESEARCH** Nineteenth and 20th century British social and intellectual history. **SELECTED PUBLICATIONS** Auth, Between Two Worlds: The Political Thought of Graham Wallas, Clarendon, Oxford, 71; English Culture and the Decline of the Industrial Spirit 1850-1980, Cambridge, 81; Gentlemen Capitalists, The Social And Political World Of The Victorian Businessman - Malchow,Hl, Victorian Studies, Vol 0036, 1993; Crime In 19th-Century Wales - Jones,Djv, Victorian Studies, Vol 0037, 1993; Women, Crime And Custody In Victorian England - Zedner,L, Victorian Studies, Vol 0037, 1993; The Unloved State - 20th-Century Politics In The Writing Of 19th-Century History, Journal Of British Studies, Vol 0033, 1994. **CONTACT ADDRESS** Dept of Hist, Rice Univ, Houston, TX, 77001.

WIGEN, KAREN
DISCIPLINE HISTORY **EDUCATION** Univ MI Ann Arbor, BA, 80; Univ CA Berkeley, PhD, 90. **CAREER** Assoc prof, Duke Univ. **RESEARCH** Japan hist with an emphasis on the class, medieval, and early mod periods. **SELECTED PUBLICATIONS** Auth, The Making of a Japanese Periphery 1750-1920, Univ Ca, 95; Politics and piety in Japanese native-place studies: The rhetoric of solidarity in Shinano, 96; co-auth, The Myth of Continents: A Critique of Meta-Geography, Univ Ca, 97; ed, Mirror of Modernity: Japan's Invented Traditions, Univ Ca, 98. **CONTACT ADDRESS** Dept of Hist, Duke Univ, Carr Bldg, Durham, NC, 27706. **EMAIL** kwigen@acpub.duke.edu

WIGGINS, JACQUELINE D.
DISCIPLINE MUSIC EDUCATION **EDUCATION** Univ IL, Ed D, 92. **CAREER** Public school music teacher, 72-94; coordinator of Music Ed, Oakland Univ, Rochester, MI, 94-. **MEMBERSHIPS** MENC; NASM; AERA. **RESEARCH** Creative process and connections to cognitive process. **SELECTED PUBLICATIONS** Auth, Children's Strategies for Solving Compositional Problems with Peers, J of Res in Music Ed, vol 42, no 3, 94; Teacher-Research in a General Music Classroom: Effects on the Teacher, Bul of the Coun for Res in Music Ed, no 123, winter 94/95; Building Structural Understanding: Sam's Story, The Quart J of Music-Teaching and Learning, vol 6, no 3, 96; with Karen Bodoin, Painting a Big Soup: Teaching and Learning in a Second Grade General Music Classroom, J of Res in Music Ed, vol 46, no 2, 98. **CONTACT ADDRESS** Dept of Music, Theatre and Dance, Oakland Univ, Rochester, MI, 48063. **EMAIL** jwiggins@oakland.edu

WIGGINS, JAMES BRYAN
PERSONAL Born 08/24/1935, Mexia, TX, m, 1956, 2 children **DISCIPLINE** RELIGION; HISTORY **EDUCATION** Tex Wesleyan Col, BA, 57; Southern Methodist Univ, BD, 59; Drew Univ, PhD(hist theol), 63. **CAREER** Instr English, Union Jr Col, 60-63; from asst prof to assoc prof relig, 63-75, Prof Relig, Syracuse Univ, 75-, Chmn, 81-, Soc Relig Higher Educ fel; Found Arts, Relig & Cult fel. **MEMBERSHIPS** Am Acad Relig; Am Soc Church Hist. **RESEARCH** Interaction of theology with other strands of intellectual history, particularly since Reformation; Narrative language in religious discourse; religion and Culture studies. **SELECTED PUBLICATIONS** Auth, The Methodist episcopacy: 1784-1900, Drew Gateway, 63; John Fletcher: The embattled saint, Wesleyan Col, 65; coauth, The foundations of Christianity, Ronald, 69; auth, Theological reflections on reflecting on the future, Crosscurrents, winter 71; Story, In: Echoes of the Wordless Word, Am Acad Relig, fall 73; ed, Religion as Story, Harper & Row, 75; auth, Re-visioning psycho-history, Theology Today, 76; contribr, Death and Eschatology, In: Introduction to Study of Religion, Harper & Row, 78; Christianity: A Cultural Perspective, Prentice Hall, 84; In Praise of Religion Diversity, Routledge, 96. **CONTACT ADDRESS** Dept of Religion, Syracuse Univ, 501 HL, Syracuse, NY, 13244.

WIGGINS, SARAH WOOLFOLK
PERSONAL Montgomery, AL, m, 1967 **DISCIPLINE** AMERICAN HISTORY **EDUCATION** Huntingdon Col, BA, 56; La State Univ, MA, 58, PhD(hist), 65. **CAREER** Instr English, hist & govt, Southern Sem Jr Col, 59-61; from instr to asst prof, 61-69, assoc prof, 69-77, Prof Hist, Univ Ala, 77-, Mem, Ala State Capitol Preserv Comn, 69-75; ed, Ala Rev, 76-; mem, Ala Adv Bd, Nat Hist Publ & Rec Comn, 77-. **MEMBERSHIPS** AHA; Southern Hist Asn; Orgn Am Historians. **RESEARCH** Southern and Alabama history. **SELECTED PUBLICATIONS** Auth, The Pig Iron Kelly riot in Mobile, May 14, 1867, 1/70 & What is a scalawag?, 1/72, Ala Rev; The Scalawag in Alabama Politics, 1865-1881, Univ Ala, 77; Tumult And Silence At 2nd Creek - An Inquiry Into A Civil-War Slave Conspiracy - Jordan,Wd, Civil War History, Vol 0039, 1993; Historical Dictionary Of Reconstruction - Trefousse,Hl, Journal Of Southern History, Vol 0059, 1993; Holding The Line - The 3rd Tennessee Infantry, 1861-1864 - Barber,Fc, Civil War History, Vol 0041, 1995; Alabama - The History Of Deep-South State - Rogers,Ww, Journal Of Southern History, Vol 0062, 1996. **CONTACT ADDRESS** 10 Cherokee Hills, Tuscaloosa, AL, 35404.

WIGODSKY, MICHAEL M.
DISCIPLINE CLASSICS **EDUCATION** BA, 57; MA, 59; Princeton Univ, PhD, 64. **CAREER** Assoc prof, Stanford Univ. **RESEARCH** Latin poetry; Hellenistic and Roman philos. **SELECTED PUBLICATIONS** Auth, Vergil and Early Latin Poetry, 72; Horace's Miser (Sat.. 1.1.108) and Aristotelian Self-love, 80; The Alleged Impossibility of Philosophical Poetry, in Philodemus and Poetry, 94. **CONTACT ADDRESS** Stanford Univ, Bldg 20, Main Quad, Stanford, CA, 94305.

WILCOX, DEAN
PERSONAL Born 04/20/1964, Mt. Kisco, NY, m, 1987, 1 child **DISCIPLINE** THEATRE HISTORY, THEORY, AND CRITICISM **EDUCATION** Glasboro State College (now Rowan Univ), NJ, BA (Theatre Arts), 86; Univ SC, MFA (Lighting Design), 89; Univ WA School of Drama, Seattle, PhD (Theatre Hist, Theory, and Criticism), 94. **CAREER** Teaching asst, Dept of Drama, Univ WA, 91-94; lect, Theatre Hist, Univ CA, San Diego, spring 95; vis asst prof, Dartmouth Col, June-Aug 98; ASST PROF, THEATRE HISTORY, THEORY, AND CRITICISM, TX TECH UNIV, 96-. **HONORS AND AWARDS** Univ WA Fowler Graduate travel grant, 93; Univ WA Grad School Dissertation Fel, 93; Mellon Postdoctoral Fel at Cornell Univ, 95-96; accepted to Teaching Academy at TX Tech Univ, April 98. **MEMBERSHIPS** Asn of Theatre in Higher Ed; Int Federation for Theatre Res; Am Soc for Theatre Res; Am Soc for Aesthetics. **RESEARCH** Performance studies; postmodernism; semiotics; deconstruction; design hist and theory; chaos theory; performance art. **SELECTED PUBLICATIONS** Auth, book review of Phillip B. Zarilli's Acting (Re)Considered and Mariellen R. Sanford's Happenings and Other Acts, Theatre Survey, Vol 37, no 2, Nov 96; Political Allegory or Multimedia Extravaganza? A Historical Reconstruction of the Opera Company of Boston's Intolleranza, Theatre Survey, Vol 37, no 2, Nov 96; What Does Chaos Theory Have to Do with Art?, Modern Drama, Vol XXXIX, no 4, winter 96; book review of Alma Law and Mel Gordon's Meyerhold, Eisenstein and Biomechanics, Theatre Res Int, Vol 22, no 2, Autumn 97; book review of Marvin Carlson's Performance: A Critical Introduction and Richard Schechner's The Future of Ritual, Theatre Survey, Vol 38, no 2, Nov 97; Karen Finley's Hymen, Theatre Res Int, Vol 22, no 1, spring 97; A Complex Tapestry of Text and Imagery: Karen Finley, The American Chestnut, Cornell University, May 10, 1996, The Jour of Dramatic Theory and Criticism, Vol XII, no 1, fall 97; book review of Colin Counsell's Signs of Performance and Walter Gropius' The Theatre of the Bauhaus, Theatre Jour, Vol 50, no 3, Oct 98; book review of William Demastes' Theatre of Chaos: Beyond Absurdism, Into Orderly Disorder, Theatre Survey, Vol 39, no 2, Nov 98; book review of Arthur Holmberg's The Theatre of Robert Wilson, Theatre Res Int, Vol 23, no 3, Autumn 98; book review of Jonathan Kalb's The Theatre of Heiner Muller, Theatre Res Int, forthcoming; The Historical Nature of Time: Dramatic Criticism and New Historicism, Theatre Insight, forthcoming. **CONTACT ADDRESS** Dept of Theatre and Dance, Texas Tech Univ, Box 42061, Lubbock, TX, 79409-2061. **EMAIL** thdea@ttu.edu

WILCOX, LARRY DEAN
PERSONAL Born 09/03/1942, West Lafayette, OH, m, 1960, 2 children **DISCIPLINE** MODERN EUROPEAN & GERMAN HISTORY **EDUCATION** Ohio Univ, AB, 64; Univ Va, MA 66, PhD(hist), 70. **CAREER** From instr to asst prof, 68-75, assoc prof hist, Univ Toledo, 75-, prof, 85-. **HONORS AND AWARDS** Phi Beta Kappa, 63; NDEA, 64-7; DAAD Study Awards, 76, 83, 94; Outstanding Teacher Award, 85. **MEMBERSHIPS** AHA; Conf Group Cent Europ Hist; Ger Studies Assoc; Ohio Acad of History. **RESEARCH** Twentieth century Germany; press and propaganda in the rise of National Socialism; contemporary world. **SELECTED PUBLICATIONS** Auth, Hitler and the Nazi Concept of the Press, J of Newspaper and Periodical History, Winter 85; coed, Germany and Europe in the Era of Two World Wars, Univ Press of Virginia, 86; The Nazi Press Before the Third Reich, in Germany & Europe. **CONTACT ADDRESS** Dept of History, Univ of Toledo, 2801 W Bancroft St, Toledo, OH, 43606-3390. **EMAIL** lwilcox@uoft02.utoledo.edu

WILD, ROBERT ANTHONY
PERSONAL Born 03/30/1940, Chicago, IL **DISCIPLINE** NEW TESTAMENT, HISTORY OF RELIGION **EDUCATION** Loyola Univ Chicago, BA, 62, MA, 67; Jesuit Sch Theol, STL, 70; Harvard Univ, PhD(Study relig), 77. **CAREER** Teacher Latin & Greek, St Xavier High Sch, Cincinnati, 64-67; instr New Testament, 75-77, asst prof, 77-82, Assoc Prof New Testament, Marquette Univ, 82-. **MEMBERSHIPS** Cath Bibl Asn; Soc Bibl Lit. **RESEARCH** Graeco-Roman mystery cults, the Pauline writings and gnosticism; the development of the traditions about Jesus. **SELECTED PUBLICATIONS** Auth, The Serapeum at Soli, Cyprus, Numina Aegaea 2, 75; Diversification in Roman Period Isis worship: The Nile water pitcher, Soc Bibl Lit 1977 Sem Papers, 77; The known Isis-Sarapis sanctuaries of the Roman period, In: Aufstieg und Niedergang der Romischen Welt, Religion, Principat; The Isis-Sarapis Cult, Relig & Ethics Inst, 78; Water in the Cultic Worship of Isis and Sarapis, E J Brill, Leiden, 81; The Sentences of Sextus, Scholars Press, 81; And Sarapis In The Roman World - Takacs,Sa, Catholic Biblical Quarterly, Vol 0059, 1997. **CONTACT ADDRESS** Dept of Theol, Marquette Univ, Milwaukee, WI, 53233.

WILDBERG, CHRISTIAN
PERSONAL Born 02/12/1957, Flensburg, Germany, m, 1997 **DISCIPLINE** CLASSICS, ANCIENT PHILOSOPHY **EDUCATION** Cambridge Univ, PhD, 84; Marburg Univ, MThL, 85. **CAREER** Res Fellow, 84-87, Caius Coll Cambridge; Vis Lectr, 87-88, Univ of TX at Austin; Asst Prof, 88-94, Freie Univ Berlin; Res Fellow, 95-96, Center for Hellenistic, Washington; Assoc Prof of Classics 96-, Princeton Univ. **HONORS AND AWARDS** Res Grant-DFG. **MEMBERSHIPS** Amer Philos Assoc; Amer Philo Assoc. **RESEARCH** Aristotle, Tragedy. **SELECTED PUBLICATIONS** Auth, Philoponus against Aristotle on the Eternity of the World, London, Duckworth, 87; John Philoponus Criticism of Aristotle's Theory of Aether, Peripatio vol 6, pp 274, Berlin, NY, 86; Simplicius against Philpopnus on the Eternity of the World, London, Duckworth, pp 95-135, 91; Hyperesie und Epiphanie, Zur Bedeutung und Funkiton der Gotter in den Dramen des Euripdes, in prog; Aristoteles, DeCaelo, Translation, into German and Commentary, in prog. **CONTACT ADDRESS** Dept of Classics, 108 East Pyne, Princeton, NY, 08544. **EMAIL** wildberg@princeton.edu

WILE, KIP
DISCIPLINE MUSIC **EDUCATION** Clark Univ, BA; Univ Chicago, MA, PhD. **CAREER** Asst prof, Sam Houston State Univ, 95-. **HONORS AND AWARDS** M. Giles Whiting dissertation fel. **MEMBERSHIPS** Mem, TSMT exec bd. **RESEARCH** Music of late 19th- and early 20th-century Russia and France. **SELECTED PUBLICATIONS** Auth, Communication and Interaction in Stravinsky's Scherzo Fantastique 1907-8, Ind Theory Rev. **CONTACT ADDRESS** Dept of Music, Sam Houston State Univ, Huntsville, TX, 77341. **EMAIL** mus_kdw@shsu.edu

WILEY, RAYMOND A.
PERSONAL Born 10/30/1923, New York, NY, m, 1948, 8 children **DISCIPLINE** GERMAN, MYTHOLOGY & CLASSICAL LITERATURE **EDUCATION** Fordham Univ, AB, 46, MA, 48; Goethe Inst, Munich, cert, 56; Syracuse Univ, PhD(humanities), 66. **CAREER** Instr Ger & English, Boston Col, 47-48; from instr to assoc prof Ger, 48-71, dir lang lab, 70-77, actg chm dept mod lang, 76, actg chm dept classics, 76-78, Prof , 71-89, Adjunct Prof Emeritus Foreign Lang & Lit, Le Moyne Col, 89-, chm, Dept For Lang & Lit, 86-89. **HONORS AND AWARDS** Fordharn Univ Encaenia award, 56; Fulbright Summer Teachers Award to Germany, 56; NEH Summer Seminar, Stanford Univ, 80. **MEMBERSHIPS** Am Asn Teachers Ger. **RESEARCH** The Correspondence between John Mitchell Kemble and Jakob Grimm, 1832-52; 19th century German-English literary relations; Teutonic mythology. **SELECTED PUBLICATIONS** Auth, Four unpublished letters of Jacob Grimm to John Mitchell Kemble, 1832-40, J English & Ger Philol, 7/68; ed, John Mitchell Kemble and Jacob Grimm, a Correspondence: 1832-1852, Brill, Leiden, 71; auth, From letters to life, Heights Mag, Le Moyne Col, fall 71; The German-American verse of Dr Franz Lahmeyer, Ger-Am Studies, spring 74; ed, Austausch, Cent NY Chap Am Asn Teachers Ger Newslett, Vols 1-5, 70-74; auth, Dear Harriet: Fanny Kemble's View of Centennial America, Pa Gazette, 7/76; Anglo-Saxon Kemble, The Life and Works of John Mitchell Kemble 1807-57: Philologist, Historian, Archaeologist, Brit Archaeol Rec, No 72: Anglo-Saxon Studies Archaeol & Hist, I: 165-273; ed, John Mitchell Kemble's Review of Jacob Grimm's Deutsche Grammatik, State Univ NY Ctr Medieval & Early Renaissance Studies, 81; transl, On the Origin of Language, Leiden, Brill, 84; auth, Tints and Texts, A Comparison of the Nibelungenlied's MS Illustrations with Its Narrative, Acta, X, 86; Grimm's Grammar Gains Ground in England, In: The Grimm Brothers & The Germanic Past, J. Benjamins, 90. **CONTACT ADDRESS** Dept of Foreign Lang, LeMoyne Col, 1419 Salt Springs Rd., Syracuse, NY, 13214-1300.

WILHELMSEN, ALEXANDRA
DISCIPLINE HISTORY **EDUCATION** Univ Dallas, BA, 67; Rice Univ, MA, 69; Univ Navarra, PhD, 71. **CAREER** Adj prof, Dallas Univ, 71-. **HONORS AND AWARDS** Luis Hernando de Larramendi awd in Spain, 95. **RESEARCH** Spanish history, Spain's Camino de Santiago, Catholic Church, monarchy, and romanesque art. **SELECTED PUBLICATIONS** Auth, La formacion del pensamiento politico del Carlismo 1810-1875, Madrid, Editorial Actas. **CONTACT ADDRESS** Dept of History, Univ of Dallas, 1845 E Northgate Dr, 206 Carpenter Hall, Irving, TX, 75062. **EMAIL** awilhel@acad.udallas.edu

WILKIE, JACQUELINE S.
PERSONAL Born 11/28/1956, Albany, NY, s, 1 child **DISCIPLINE** HISTORY **EDUCATION** Col of St Rose, BA, 78; Northeastern Univ, MA, 79; Carnegie-Mellon Univ, PhD, 82. **CAREER** Tchng, res asst, 78-79, Northeastern Univ; curr designer, 79-81, exec asst, 81-82, proj soc hist, instr, hist, 81, adj asst prof, 82-83, Carnegie-Mellon Univ; asst prof, hist, 83-87, Central Mich Univ; women's stud coord, 92-97, dept head, 98, assoc prof, hist, 87-, Luther Coll. **RESEARCH** US popular medicine & nursing, oral hist. **CONTACT ADDRESS** History Dept, Luther Col, Decorah, IA, 52101-1045. **EMAIL** wilkieja@luther.edu

WILKIE, JAMES WALLACE
PERSONAL Born 03/10/1936, Idaho Falls, ID, m, 1963, 2 children **DISCIPLINE** LATIN AMERICAN HISTORY **EDUCATION** Mex City Col, BA, 58; Univ Calif, Berkeley, MA, 59, PhD(hist), 66. **CAREER** Teacher, High Sch, Calif, 59-60; instr hist, Mex City Col, 60; from asst prof to assoc prof, Ohio State Univ, 65-68; assoc prof, 68-71, assoc dir Latin Am Ctr, 70-76, PROF HIST, UNIV CALIF, LOS ANGELES, 71-, Dir, Latin Am Oral Hist Res Proj, 63-; Ohio State Univ fac res grant, 66-67; pres, Hist Res Found, 68-; mem, Robertson Prize Comt, Conf Latin Am Hist, 68, comt on activities & proj, 68-; Ford Found grant, 68-69; mem orgn & prog comt, Third Int Cong Mex Hist, 69, distinguished serv award comt, 70; fel, Latin Am Ctr, Univ Calif, Los Angeles, 70, 72 & 73; Soc Sci Res Coun-Am Coun Learned Soc grant, 71; chmn comt Mex studies &

cochmn, Fourth Int Cong Mex Hist, 73; chmn, Conf Latin Am Studies Asn, 76; Univ wide coordr, Consortium Mex & US, Univ Calif, 81-; ed, Statistical Abstract of Latin America, 77- **HONORS AND AWARDS** Ohio Acad Hist Bk Award, 67; Bolton Prize, 68. **MEMBERSHIPS** Latin Am Studies Asn; Conf Latin Am Hist Asn. **RESEARCH** Mexico, Bolivia, Costa Rica, and Venezuela; comparative Latin American historical statistics; oral history of twentieth-century Latin America. **SELECTED PUBLICATIONS** Auth, The Mexican Revolution: Federal Expenditure and Social Change Since 1910, Univ Calif, 67, rev ed, 70; coauth, Mexico en el Siglo XX: Entrevistas de Historia Oral, Instituto Mex Investigationes Econ, 69; auth, Elitelore, 73, Measuring Land Reform 74 & Statistics and State Policy in Latin America, 74, UCLA Latin Am Ctr; coed, Contemporary Mexico, Univ Calif, 75; ed, Money and Politics in Latin America, UCLA Latin Am Ctr, 77; The Public Treasury And Economic-Policy 1929-1958 - Spanish - Cardenas,E, American Historical Review, Vol 0101, 1996. **CONTACT ADDRESS** Dept of Hist, Univ of Calif, Los Angeles, CA, 90024.

WILKIE, NANCY C.
PERSONAL Born 12/27/1942, Milwaukee, WI **DISCIPLINE** GREEK ARCHEOLOGY, CLASSICS **EDUCATION** Stanford Univ, AB, 64; Univ Minn, MA, 67, PhD(Greek), 75. **CAREER** Instr classics, Macalester Col, 72-75; adj instr, 74-75, adj asst prof classics, 75-79, Asst Prof Classics & Socioanthrop, Carleton Col, 79-, Field dir, Phocis-Doris Exped, Loyola Univ, Chicago, 77-80. **MEMBERSHIPS** Archaeol Inst Am; Am Philol Asn; Soc Prof Archaeologists; Asn Field Archaeol; Soc Am Archaeol. **RESEARCH** Prehistoric Greek archaeology; archeological sampling. **SELECTED PUBLICATIONS** Auth, The Nichoria Tholos & Area-IV-6, Hesperia, 75; Area I, Evacuations at Nichoria in Southwest Greece, Vol I, Minn, 78; Early Helladic Pottery from Phokis and Doris, Teiresias, 79; Shaft Graves at Nichoria, Temple Univ Aegean Symp, 81; The Earliest Farmers In Macedonia, Antiquity, Vol 0071, 1997. **CONTACT ADDRESS** Carleton Col, 1 N College St, Northfield, MN, 55057-4044.

WILKIE, WILLIAM E.
PERSONAL Born 01/19/1936, Marshalltown, IA **DISCIPLINE** HISTORY **EDUCATION** Cath Univ Am, MA, 57; Univ Fribourg, PhD, 66; Cambridge Univ, MA, 72. **CAREER** From Instr to Assoc Prof, 57-80, PROF HIST, LORAS COL, 80-; Vis fel, Cambridge Univ, 72-73, 81. **HONORS AND AWARDS** NEH jr res fel, Italy, 72-73; Mellon Fel Humanities, Kans Univ, 82; Fulbright Fel Ger, 84, 89; Cert Comm, Am Asn State & Local Hist Soc. **MEMBERSHIPS** Fel Royal Hist Soc. **RESEARCH** History of Mississippi valley 1500-. **SELECTED PUBLICATIONS** Auth, Rome and the Tudors Before the Reformation, Cambridge Univ, 74 ; Dubuque on the Mississippi 1788-1988. **CONTACT ADDRESS** Dept Hist, Loras Col, PO Box 178, Dubuque, IA, 52004-0178.

WILKINS, ANN THOMAS
PERSONAL Born 01/23/1944, Portsmouth, NH, m, 1966, 2 children **DISCIPLINE** CLASSICS **EDUCATION** Wellesley Col, BA 66; Univ Pittsburgh, MA 75, PhD 90. **CAREER** Vassar Col, inst, 78-79; Univ Michigan SLC, inst 79-81; Winchester-Thurston Sch, inst 80-87, ch, 83-86; Univ Pitts, lectr 86-94; Univ Pitts Sem at Sea, faculty 88-93; Duquesne Univ, asst prof 94-. **HONORS AND AWARDS** Teach of the Year Awd; AAUW; Apple for the Tchr Awd; Mellon Fel; Tchg Asstshps and Felshps; Thomas Lawrence Fel; Presidential Sch awd; Noble K Dick Gnt; NEH. **MEMBERSHIPS** CAPV; PCA; CAAS; APA. **RESEARCH** Roman art archaeology/literature; classical tradition. **SELECTED PUBLICATIONS** Auth, Villain or Hero: Saullust's Portrayal of Catiline, Baltimore, Peter Lang Pub, 94; Dictionary entries: six entries for, The Dictionary of Art, Macmillan Pub, London, 96: Olympia Sculpture, Epidaurus Sculpture, Julio Claudian Sculpture, Roman Painting Collections and Collectors, Greek Sculpture Collections and Collectors, Roman Sculpture Collections and Collectors; two entries on classical sites for the International Dictionary of Architects and Architecture, ed Randall J. Van Vynckt, Gale Research Pub, 93: Epidaurus and Olympia; revs: Murlo and the Etruscans, eds Richard Daniel De Puma, Jocelyn Penny Small, for Classical World, 98; Introduction to Attic Greek: an Electronic Workbook, by Donald J. Mastronarde, J ourof Early Christianity, 97; Uppity Women of Ancient Times, by Vicki Leon, Penn Classical Assoc Bull, 96. **CONTACT ADDRESS** Dept of Classics, Duquesne Univ, College Hall 404, Pittsburgh, PA, 15282-1704. **EMAIL** wilkins@duq2.cc.duq.edu

WILKINS, LEONA B.
PERSONAL Born 02/09/1922, Winston-Salem, North Carolina **DISCIPLINE** MUSIC EDUCATION **EDUCATION** NC Central Univ, BA 1941; Univ MI, MMus 1944, PhD 1971; Sorbonne Univ Paris, France, cert 1968. **CAREER** Raleigh NC, teacher 1942-44; St Louis, teacher 1952-55; Detroit, teacher 1955-64; Bluefield State, 1944-45; Hampton Inst, 1945-48; TN State Univ, 1948-52; E MI Univ 1964-68; Temple Univ, 1968-72; Northwestern Univ, assoc prof 1972-; Northwestern Univ, assoc prof emeritus, 1988-; Trinity Episcopal Church, Chicago, IL, dir, children's music educ, 1990-. **HONORS AND AWARDS** Consult Silver Burdett Music Series 1970-71. **MEMBERSHIPS** Mem Music Educ Conf; Intl Soc of Music Educators; Amer Assn of Univ Profs, Am Orff-Schulwerk Assn; Coll Music Soc; Alpha Kappa Alpha; mem Bicentennial Commn for MENC 1974-76; Comn for Revision of Natl Tchrs Exam for Music Educ 1974-75; consult IL State Arts Plan; Comn for Revision of Music Objectives for Natl Assessment of Educ Progress Task Force; Role of the Arts Comm USOE; MENC; consult Evanston Public School Dist 65. **CONTACT ADDRESS** Sch of Music, Northwestern Univ, Evanston, IL, 60201.

WILKINS, MIRA
PERSONAL Born 06/01/1931, New York, NY **DISCIPLINE** BUSINESS HISTORY **EDUCATION** Radcliffe Col/Harvard Univ, AB, 53; Cambridge Univ England, PhD, 57. **CAREER** Res assoc, Weyerhaeuser Enterprises Hist, Columbia Univ, 57-58, res assoc, Ford Motor Co Hist, 58-60, co-dir, Ford Overseas Hist Proj, 60-62, proj dir Hist Am Bus Abroad, Grad Sch Bus, 62-66, adj asst prof, 64-66; assoc prof Hist & Indust Admin, Union Col, 66-68; vis lectr Hist, Smith Col, 68-70; prof Econ, Fla Int Univ, 74-, supvr, Corpus Christi Col, Cambridge Univ, 56-57; instr, Wayne State Univ, 58-59; lectr Econ Hist, Univ Mass, Amherst, 72; dir, Foreign Investment Fla Proj, 75-80; Guggenheim fel, 81-82. **HONORS AND AWARDS** Fla Int Univ Prof Exc Award, 94; 93 Cass Prize for best article in Business History, 92. **MEMBERSHIPS** Am Econ Asn; AHA; Acad Int Bus; Bus Hist Conf; Econ Hist Assn. **RESEARCH** International business history; economic history; history of foreign investment in the United States. **SELECTED PUBLICATIONS** Auth, American Business Abroad: Ford on Six Continents, Wayne State Univ, 64; The Emergence of Multinational Enterprise: American Business Abroad from the Colonial Era to 1914, Harvard Univ, 70; The role of private business in the international diffusion of technology, J Econ Hist, 3/74; Multinational oil companies in South America in the 1920s: In Argentina, Bolivia, Brazil, Chile, Colombia, Ecuador, Peru, Bus Hist Rev, Fall 74; The Maturing of Multinational Enterprise: American Business Abroad from 1914 to 1970, Harvard Univ, 74; The oil companies in perspective, In: Daedalus, Fall 75; Modern European economic history and the multinationals, J Europ Econ Hist, Winter 77; Multinational automobile enterprises and regulation: An historical overview, In: Government, Technology, and the Future of the Automobile, McGraw-Hill, 80; The History of Foreign Investment in the United States to 1914, Cambridge, Mass: Harvard Univ Press, 1989. **CONTACT ADDRESS** Dept of Economics, Florida Intl Univ, Miami, FL, 33199-0001. **EMAIL** Wilkinsm@fiu.edu

WILKINSON, DORIS
PERSONAL Lexington, Kentucky, s **DISCIPLINE** SOCIOLOGY **EDUCATION** Univ of Kentucky, BA, 1958; Case Western Univ, MA, 1960, PhD, 1968; Johns Hopkins Univ, MPH, 1985; Harvard Univ, postdoctoral study, 1998. **CAREER** Macalester Coll, assoc/full, professor 1970-77; Amer Soc Assn, exec associate, 1977-80; Howard Univ, professor, 1980-84; Univ of Virginia, Charlottesville, VA, visiting professor, 1984-85; Univ of Kentucky, Lexington, KY, professor, 1985-94; Harvard Univ, Cambridge, MA, visiting scholar, 1989-90, visiting professor, summers 1992, 1993, 1994, 1997. **HONORS AND AWARDS** NIH Fellow, 1963-66; Woodrow Wilson Fellow, 1959-61; NIE Grant, 1978-80; NCI, research contract, 1985-88; Dubois-Johnson-Frazier Award, Amer Sociological Assn, 1988; Omicron Delta Kappa Natl Leadership Hon, 1987; Grant from the Kentucky Humanities Commission for a project on Afro-Amer physicians, 1988-89; Women's History Month Award, Midway College, 1991; Public Humanities Award, Kentucky Humanities Council, 1990; Hall of Distinguished Alumni, Univ of Kentucky, 1989; Ford Fellow, Harvard Univ, 1989-90; Great Teacher Award, 1992; Distinguished Professorship, 1992; Distinguished Scholar, Assoc of Black Sociologists, 1993. **MEMBERSHIPS** President Eastern Sociological Soc, 1993; pres, District of Columbia Sociological Soc, 1982-83; bd of overseers, Case Western Reserve Univ, 1982-85; public educ, Comm Amer Cancer Soc, 1982-85; exec office budget comm, American Sociological Assn, 1985-88; pres, Soc for the Study of Social Problems, 1987-88; vice president, American Sociological Assn, vice pres, 1991-92, council, 1995-97; Kentucky Commission on Women, 1993-96; Kentucky African-American Commission, 1994-. **CONTACT ADDRESS** Department of Sociology, Univ of Kentucky, Lexington, KY, 40506.

WILL, W. MARVIN
PERSONAL Born 03/25/1937, Peace Valley, MO, m, 1962 **DISCIPLINE** POLITICAL SCIENCE **EDUCATION** McPherson Col, BA, 60; Univ Missouri, Columbia, MA, 64, PhD, 72. **CAREER** Instr, Univ Missouri, Columbia, 62-64, 67-69; instr, Florissant Valley Commun Col, 64-69; asst prof, 69-79, assoc prof, 79- , Univ Tulsa; dir, Civic Educ Ctr, St Louis, 76-78; adj prof, Washington Univ, 76-78; vis prof, Univ of the West Indies, 91-92; vis prof Col of Micronesia, 99-2000. **HONORS AND AWARDS** Fel, US Dept of State, 81; Fulbright res scholar, 91-92; Oklahoma Polit Sci Scholar of the Year, 92; Citation of Merit, Bd of Trustees, McPherson Col, 95; Rotary Int Fel, 98; NEH grant; Ford Found grant; Mellon grant. **MEMBERSHIPS** Int Studies Asn; Caribbean Stud Asn; Midwest LA Stud Asn; Latin Am Stud Asn; Am Polit Stud Asn; Am Prof for Peace in the Middle East; Okla Polit Sci Asn; UNAU. **RESEARCH** Authoritarianism and democracy in the Caribbean Basin; non-governmental and international organizations as promoters of democracy and human rights. **SELECTED PUBLICATIONS** Co-ed, The Restless Caribbean, Praeger, 79; coauth, The Caribbean in the Pacific Century, Lynne Rienner, 93; auth, Seizing the Moment: Caribbean Integration and the Role of Economic Crisis, in Sullivan, ed, The Caribbean Basin, Congressional Research Service, GPO, 93; auth, Beyond the Cold War: Security and Policy Projections from the Pacific and Caribbean Basins, in Crotty, ed, Post-Cold War Policy, Nelson-Hall, 95; auth, NGOs and IGOs as Promoters of Liberal Democracy: Cases from Nicaragua and Guyana, in Griffith, ed, Democracy and Human Rights in the Caribbean, Westview, 97; auth, From Rebellion to Institutional Development and Democracy in the Caribbean, in Kelly, ed, Assessing Democracy in Latin America, Westview, 98. **CONTACT ADDRESS** 1136 S Pittsburg Ave, Tulsa, OK, 74112-5104. **EMAIL** wmwill@utulsa.edu

WILLEY, GORDON R.
PERSONAL Born 03/07/1913, Chariton, IA, m, 1938, 2 children **DISCIPLINE** ANTHROPOLOGY, ARCHAEOLOGY **EDUCATION** Univ AZ, AB, 35, AM, 36; Columbia Univ, PhD, 42. **CAREER** Sr anthropologist, Smithsonian Inst, 43-50; Bowdirch Prof of Archaeology, 50-87, prof Emeritus, Harvard Univ, 87-. **HONORS AND AWARDS** Litt D (honorary), Cambridge Univ, 77, Univ AZ, 81, Univ NM, 84; Gold Medal, Archaeol Inst of Am, 71; Huxley Medal, Royal Anthropol Inst, 84. **MEMBERSHIPS** Am Anthropol Asn; Soc for Am Archaeology. **RESEARCH** Mexican and Central American archaeology. **SELECTED PUBLICATIONS** Auth, Archaeology of the Florida Gulf Coast, Smithsonian Misc Colls, vol 113, Smithsonian Inst, 49; Prehistoric Settlement Patterns in the Viru Valley, Peru, Bul 155, Bureau of Am Ethnology, Smithsonian Inst, 53; Method and Theory in American Archaeology, with Phillip Phillips, Univ Chicago Press, 58; Prehistoric Maya Settlements in the Belize Valley, with W R Bullard, J B Glass, and J C Gifford, Peabody Museum Papers, Harvard Univ, 65; An Introduction to American Archaeology: Vol I North and Middle America, 66, Vol II, South America, 71, Prentice-Hall; The Altar de Sacrificios Excavations: General Summary and Conclusions, Peabody Museum Papers, vol 64, no 3, Harvard Univ, 73; A History of American Archaeology, with J A Sabloff, Thames and Hudson, Ltd, and W H Freeman and Co, 74, 80, 93; New World Archaeology and Culture History: Collected Essays and Articles, republished with intro comments and annotations, Univ NM Press, 90; Excavations at Seibal, Department of Peten, Guatemala: General Summary and Conclusions, Memoirs, vol 17, no 4, Peabody Museum, Harvard Univ, 90; The Copan Residential Zone: Ceramics and Artifacts, with R M Leventhal, A A Demarest, and W L Fash, Jr, Papers Peabody Museum, vol 80, Harvard Univ, 94. **CONTACT ADDRESS** Peabody Museum, Harvard Univ, Cambridge, MA, 02138.

WILLHEIM, IMANUEL
DISCIPLINE MUSIC **EDUCATION** St Scholastica Col, BM; Northwestern Univ, MM, Univ Ill, MA, PhD. **CAREER** Prof emer, Hartt School Music. **SELECTED PUBLICATIONS** Auth, pubs on aesthetics of music & history of performance practices. **CONTACT ADDRESS** Hartt Sch Music, Univ Hartford, 200 Bloomfield Ave, West Hartford, CT, 06117.

WILLIAMS, ALAN JOHN
PERSONAL Born 01/16/1944, Ossining, NY **DISCIPLINE** FRENCH HISTORY **EDUCATION** Stanford Univ, BA, 66; Yale Univ, PhD(hist), 74. **CAREER** Asst Prof French Hist, Wake Forest Univ, 74-. **HONORS AND AWARDS** Excellence in Teaching Award, Wake Forest Univ, 78. **MEMBERSHIPS** Soc French Hist Studies. **RESEARCH** Parisian police; 18th century charlatans; the relationship between political structures and systems of patronage or protection in 18th century France. **SELECTED PUBLICATIONS** Auth, The police and public health in eighteenth century Paris, Soc Sci Quart, 75; The police and the poor of Paris, In: Transactions of the Fourth International Congress on the Enlightenment, Voltaire Found, Oxford, 76; The police and the administration of eighteenth century Paris, J Urban Hist, 78; The Police of Paris, 1718-1789, La State Univ, spring 79; The Rise Of Modern Police And The European State System From Metternich To The World-War-2 - Liang,Hh, Journal Of Interdisciplinary History, Vol 0025, 1995. **CONTACT ADDRESS** 95 Beechwood Dr, Lewisville, NC, 27023.

WILLIAMS, BERNARD D
PERSONAL Born 07/16/1930, Philadelphia, PA **DISCIPLINE** MODERN EUROPEAN HISTORY **EDUCATION** LaSalle Col, BA, 54; Niagara Univ, MA, 55. **CAREER** Instr hist, Niagara Univ, 56-60, asst prof & acting chmn dept mil sci, 60-61; from asst prof to assoc prof, 62-76, dir adv studies adv off, 66-68, PROF HIST, UNIV SCRANTON, 76-, Vis prof, Univ Ottawa, summer, 62. **MEMBERSHIPS** AHA; Acad Polit Sci; Am Mil Inst; US Naval Inst; Soc Historians of Am Foreign Rels. **RESEARCH** Diplomatic and military history of World War I and World War II; diplomatic history of the 19th century; the drought in West Africa, 1968-1975. **SELECTED PUBLICATIONS** Auth, BS degree in military science, Army, 12/67; Long Days Journey Into War - December 7, 1941 - Wein-

traub,S, Historian, Vol 0056, 1993; Living With Africa - Vansina,J, Historian, Vol 0058, 1995. **CONTACT ADDRESS** Dept of Hist, Univ of Scranton, Scranton, PA, 18510.

WILLIAMS, C. FRED
PERSONAL Born 12/24/1943, Allen, OK, m, 1971, 3 children **DISCIPLINE** AMERICAN WEST **EDUCATION** E Cent State Col, BAE, 65; Wichita State Univ, MA, 66; Univ OK, PhD, 70. **CAREER** From asst prof to assoc prof, 69-78, head dept, 73-80, prof hist, Univ AR, Little Rock, 78, assock dean, Col Lib Arts, 80-83; Assoc vite chancellor for edu prog, 83-88. **MEMBERSHIPS** Orgn Am Historians; Western Hist Asn; Agr Hist Soc. **RESEARCH** Agricult; AR state hist; historical novels. **SELECTED PUBLICATIONS** Auth, William M Jardine: Secretary of Agriculture for the business side of farming, Wichita State Studies, 70; The bear state image: Arkansas in the nineteenth century, Ark Hist Quart, 80; ed, A Documentary History of Arkansas, 84; Arkansas: An Illustrated History of the Land of Opportunity, 86. **CONTACT ADDRESS** Dept of Hist, Univ of AR, 2801 S University Av, Little Rock, AR, 72204-1000. **EMAIL** cfwilliams@ualr.edu

WILLIAMS, CAROLYN CHANDLER
PERSONAL Born 01/13/1947, Maben, Mississippi, m **DISCIPLINE** EDUCATION **EDUCATION** MS Valley State Univ, BA 1968; MS State Univ, MEd 1973, PhD 1975. **CAREER** Aberdeen Pub Schs, eng teach 1968-70; Oktibbeha Co Schs, eng teach 1970-71; Mary Holmes Coll, inst 1971-73; MS State Univ, inst 1974-75, asst prof 1975-78; assoc prof 1978-82; prof 1982-; Mississippi State Univ, Starkville, MS, administrative intern 1987. **HONORS AND AWARDS** Outstanding Univ Prof Assn of Univ Prof 1977; Outstanding Young Woman State Jaycees MS 1981; Outstanding Young Woman Starkville Jaycees local 1981; Outstanding Young Educator Phi Delta Kappa local 1982; Starkville Area Hall of Fame, Starkville Area Chamber of Commerce, 1990. **MEMBERSHIPS** Bd of dirs Mid South Educ Rsch Assn 1982-; pres, Midsouth Educational Research Assn, 1988-89; pres, Mississippi Reading Assn, 1990-91. **CONTACT ADDRESS** Prof of Instruction, Mississippi State Univ, PO Box 6331, Mississippi State, MS, 39762.

WILLIAMS, DAVID R.
PERSONAL Born 02/28/1923, Kamloops, BC, Canada **DISCIPLINE** HISTORY **EDUCATION** Univ BC, BA, 48, LLB, 49. **CAREER** ADJ PROF/WRITER-IN-RESIDENCE, FAC LAW, UNIV VICTORIA 80-. **HONORS AND AWARDS** Univ BC Medal Can Bibliog, 78; Crime Writers Can Award, 93. **MEMBERSHIPS** Law Soc BC; Writers Union Can. **SELECTED PUBLICATIONS** Auth, 100 Years at St Peter's Quamichan, 77; auth, The Man for a New Country: Sir Matthew Baillie Begbie, 77; auth, Duff: A Life in the Law, 84; auth, Pioneer Parish: The Story of St Peter's Quamichan, 91; auth, With Malice Aforethought: Six Spectacular Canadian Trials, 93. **CONTACT ADDRESS** Faculty of Law, Univ Victoria, 3355 Gibbins Rd, Duncan, BC, V9L 1N9.

WILLIAMS, EDDIE R., JR.
PERSONAL Born 01/06/1945, Chicago, IL, m, 1969 **DISCIPLINE** EDUCATION **EDUCATION** Ottawa University, Ottawa, Kansas, BA (highest honors), mathematics, 1966; Columbia University, PhD, mathematics, 1971. **CAREER** NORTHERN ILLINOIS UNIVERSITY, associate professor of mathematics, 1970-91, associate director, operating budgets, 1978-83, budget and planning, deputy director, 1983, director, 1983-85, assistant vice pres, administrative affairs, vice pres, division of finance and planning, 1985-96; SENIOR VICE PRESIDENT, FINANCE & FACILITIES, 1996-. **MEMBERSHIPS** South Park Baptist Church, assistant pastor, director, youth activities, 1970-, senior pastor, 1997-; University Resource Advisory Committee; Presidential Commission on Status of Minorities; University Affirmative Action Committee, 1974-; American Mathematical Society. **CONTACT ADDRESS** No Illinois Univ, Lowden Hall, Rm 109, De Kalb, IL, 60115.

WILLIAMS, GARETH D.
PERSONAL Born 05/29/1965, Wales, s **DISCIPLINE** CLASSICS **EDUCATION** Cambridge Univ England, BA 86. **CAREER** Columbia Univ, asst prof, 95-98. **MEMBERSHIPS** APA **RESEARCH** Silven Latin; Pros and Poetry. **SELECTED PUBLICATIONS** Auth, Banished Voices: Readings in Ovid's Exile Poetry, Cambridge, 94. **CONTACT ADDRESS** Dept of Classics, Columbia Univ, 614 Hamilton Hall, New York, NY, 10027. **EMAIL** gdws@columbia.edu

WILLIAMS, HARRY M.
DISCIPLINE HISTORY **EDUCATION** Lincoln, BA, 71; Univ Mo, MA, 82; Brown, MA, 84, PhD, 88. **CAREER** Assoc prof History, Carleton Col. **RESEARCH** Charles Lenox Remond, female abolitionists. **SELECTED PUBLICATIONS** Diss, When Black Is Right: The Life and Writings of George S. Schuyler, Brown, 88. **CONTACT ADDRESS** Dept of History, Carleton Col, Northfield, MN, 55057.

WILLIAMS, JAMES CALHOUN
PERSONAL Born 09/24/1942, San Francisco, CA, s, 1 child **DISCIPLINE** HISTORY OF AMERICAN TECHNOLOGY **EDUCATION** Univ Ore, BA, 64; San Jose State Univ, MA, 71; Univ Calif at Santa Barbara, PhD, 84. **CAREER** Prof, Gavilan Col, 71-85; expert witness and historical consultant, 78-; exec dir, Calif Hist Ctr Foundation, 85-93; prof, De Anza Col, 93-. **HONORS AND AWARDS** Certificate of Commendation for the book Energy and the Making of Modern California, Am Asn for State and Local Hist; Distinguished Service Award, Calif Council for the Promotion of Hist; Award of Distinction, Calif Council for the Promotion of Hist; Sourisseau Academy Local History Award; Rockefeller Fel, Univ Calif at Santa Barbara; Summer Studies Fel, Nat Endowment for the Humanities, Univ of Calif at Los Angeles. **MEMBERSHIPS** AHA; Am Soc for Environmental Hist; Calf Council for the Promotion of Hist; Calif Historical Soc; Int Committee for the Hist of Technology; Nat Council on Public Hist; Org of Am Historians; Soc for the Hist of Technology. **RESEARCH** Technology and the environment; earthquake engineering; energy systems; technology and gender. **SELECTED PUBLICATIONS** Auth, "The Trolley: Technology and Values in Retrospect", in San Jose Studies, 3, 77; auth, "Cultural Conflict: The Origins of American Santa Barbara", in The Southern Calif Quart, 60, 78; auth, "Television--Reflection of American Society", in The Evolution of Mass Culture in America, 1877 to Present, Forum Press, 82; auth, "Otherwise a Mere Clod: California Rural Electrification", in IEEE Technology and Society Mag, 7, 88; auth, "Standards of Professional Conduct in California", in Ethics and Public History: An Anthology, in Robert E. Krieger Publ Co., 90; auth, "Engineering California Cities", in Science-Technology Relationships/Relations Science-Technique, San Francisco Press, 93; auth, "Earthquake Engineering: Designing Unseen Technology against Invisible Forces", in ICON: Journal of the Int Committee for the Hist of Technology, 1, 95; auth, "Fuel at Last: Oil and Gas for California, 1860s-1940s" in Calif Hist 75, 96; auth, "California's First High-Head Turbine Installation", in IA: The Journal of the Soc for Industrial Archeology, 22:1, 96; auth, Energy and the Making of Modern California, University of Akron Press, 97; auth, "Energy, conservation, and Modernity: The Failure to Electrify Railroads in the American West", in Technology and Western Landscapes, Halcyon Imprint, 98; auth, "Frederick E. Terman and the Rise of Silicon Valley", in Int Journal of Technology Management, 16:8. 98; auth, "Getting Housewives the Electric Message: Gender and Energy Marketing in the Early Twentieth Century", in His & Hers: Gender, Consumption, and Technology, Univ of Va Press, 98. **CONTACT ADDRESS** De Anza Col, 21250 Stevens Creek Blvd., Cupertino, CA, 95014. **EMAIL** JCW1@netcom.com

WILLIAMS, JAMES HIAWATHA
PERSONAL Born 09/10/1945, Montgomery, AL, m, 1994 **DISCIPLINE** EDUCATION **EDUCATION** Los Angeles City Coll, Los Angeles CA, AA, 1967; California State Univ, Los Angeles CA, BA, 1973; Pepperdine Univ, Los Angeles Ca, MS, 1974; Washington State Univ, Pullman WA, PhD, 1983. **CAREER** California State Polytechnic Univ, Pomona CA, asst prof 1977-81, assoc dean & assoc prof 1980-85, dean of Coll of Arts & full prof 1988; SPOKANE COMMUNITY COLLEGE, PRES, currently. **HONORS AND AWARDS** Prism of Excellence Award, Jerry Voorhis Claremont Democratic Club, 1986; Martin Luther King Jr Humanitarian Award, Pomona Valley NAACP, 1987; Services to Youth, Claremont Area Chapter Links Inc, 1988. **MEMBERSHIPS** Mem, Phi Delta Kappa, 1977-; pres, Pomona Valley NAACP, 1984-86; mem, Phi Beta Delta, 1988-; National Association for Ethnic Studies, executive board member, 1988-, president, 1992-; Phi Kappa Phi, 1989-; pres-elect, Council of Colleges of Arts & Sciences, 1994. **CONTACT ADDRESS** Spokane Community Col, 1810 N Greene St, MS 2150, Spokane, WA, 99207-5399.

WILLIAMS, JOAN C.
DISCIPLINE HISTORY **EDUCATION** Yale Univ, BA, 74; Harvard Law Sch/Mass Inst Technol, JD/MS, 80. **CAREER** Asst Planner, SOM Environmental Study Group, 74-75; Project Hist, Nat Park Service, Hist Am Engineering Record, Puerto Rico, 76; Law Clerk, Legal Action Ctr, 77; Law Clerk to Lawyer, Lane & Edson, P.C., 79-82; Prof Law, Am Univ, 82-; Vis Prof, Univ Va Law Sch, 92; Vis Prof, Harvard Law Sch, 93-94. **HONORS AND AWARDS** Deconstructing Gender cited as one of the most cited law review articles ever written, The Most-Cited Law Review Articles Revisited, Chicago-Kent Law Rev 751, 96; cited as one of the most prolific law professors in the country, The Most Prolific Law Professors and Faculties, Chicago-Kent Law Rev 751, 96. **SELECTED PUBLICATIONS** Auth, Deconstructing Gender, Mich Law Rev 797, 89; At the Fusion of Horizons: Incommensurability and the Public Interest, Vt Law Rev 625, 96; Restructuring Work and Family Enticements Around Family Values, Harvard J Law & Public Policy 753, 96; Recapturing the Full Complexity of Our Traditions: New Developments in Property Theory, J Legal Educ 596, 96; coauth, Land Ownership and Use, Aspen Law & Bus, 4th ed, 97; auth, Make Way for Mothers: Using Title VII to Deconstruct and Reconstruct Work, Perspectives 15, 97; The Rhetoric of Property, Iowa Law Rev, 98; Reconstructing Gender, Oxford Univ Press (in progress); author of numerous articles and other publications. **CONTACT ADDRESS** Washington Col Law, American Univ, 4801 Massachusetts Ave. NW, Washington, DC, 20016-8181. **EMAIL** Williams@american.edu

WILLIAMS, JOHN HOWARD
PERSONAL Born 11/19/1946, Louisville, KY, m, 1969, 2 children **DISCIPLINE** FRENCH LANGUAGES & LITERATURE, CLASSICS. **EDUCATION** David Lipscomb Col, BA, 67; Univ Wis-Madison, MA, 68, PhD(French), 72. **CAREER** Instr French, Tenn Technol Univ, 68-69; Fulbright advan teaching fel Am lit, Univ Besancon, 71-72; asst prof French, Eastern Ky Univ, 72-74; asst prof, 74-76, assoc prof, 76-82, Prof French & Chmn Dept, Abilene Christian Univ, 82-. **MEMBERSHIPS** MLA; Am Asn Teachers Fr. **RESEARCH** Contemporary French culture; 16th century French Poetry. **CONTACT ADDRESS** Abilene Christian Univ, Station Box 824, Abilene, TX, 79601.

WILLIAMS, JOHN W.
PERSONAL Born 02/25/1928, Memphis, TN, m, 1955, 6 children **DISCIPLINE** ART HISTORY **EDUCATION** Yale Univ, BA, 52; Univ MI, MA, 53, PhD, 62. **CAREER** From instr to assoc prof art hist, Swarthmore Col, 60-72; PROF ART HIST, UNIV PITTSBURGH, 72-, Fulbright res grants, Spain, 63-64, 68-69; proj grant, Nat Endowment for Hum, 71-73. **MEMBERSHIPS** Col Art Asn Am; Int Ctr Medieval Art. **RESEARCH** Span medieval art. **SELECTED PUBLICATIONS** Auth, A Spanish tradition of Bible illustration, J Warburg & Courtald Insts, 65; The Monastery of Valeranica, Madrider Mitteilungn, 70; San Isidoro de Leon, Art Bull, 73; Marcialis Pincerna, In: Hortus Imaginum, Univ KS, 74; Generationes Abrahae: Reconquest iconography in Leon, Gesta, 77; Early Spanish Manuscript Illumination, Braziller, 77; A Spanish Apocalype, Braziller, 91; The Illustrated Beatus, 5 vols, Harvey Miller, 94. **CONTACT ADDRESS** Dept of Hist of Art & Archit, Univ of Pittsburgh, 104 Frick Fine Arts, Pittsburgh, PA, 15260-7601. **EMAIL** jww23@pitt.edu

WILLIAMS, L. PEARCE
PERSONAL Born 09/08/1927, Marmon, NY, m, 1949, 4 children **DISCIPLINE** HISTORY OF SCIENCE **EDUCATION** Cornell Univ, BA, 49, PhD, 52. **CAREER** Instr hist, Yale Univ, 52-56; asst prof, Univ Del, 56-59; from asst prof to prof, 60-71, chmn dept, 69-74, John Stambaugh Prof Hist, Cornell Univ, 71-, Assoc historian, Nat Found Infantile Paralysis, 56-57; Nat Sci Found fel, 59-60; pres comn teaching, Int Union Hist & Philos Sci, 64-80. **HONORS AND AWARDS** Pfizer Award, Hist Sci Soc, 66. **MEMBERSHIPS** AHA; Hist Sci Soc; Royal Inst Gr Brit; Acad Int Hist Sci. **RESEARCH** Science during the French Revolution and First Empire; physical sciences in the 19th century. **SELECTED PUBLICATIONS** Auth, Michael Faraday, A Biography, Chapman & Hall, London & Basic Bk, 65; The Origins of Field Theory, 66 & coauth, Great Issues in Western Civilization, 67, Random; ed, Selected Correspondence of Michael Faraday (2 vols), Cambridge Univ, 72; coauth, A History of Science in Western Civilization (3 vols), Univ Press Am, 77-78; auth, Album of Science: The Nineteenth Century, Scribner, 78; Faraday,Michael - Sandemanian And Scientist - A Study Of Science And Religion In The 19th-Century - Cantor,G, Isis, Vol 0085, 1994; Faraday,Michael And The Royal-Institution - The Genius Of Man And Place - Thomas,Jm, Isis, Vol 0085, 1994; The Biographical Dictionary Of Scientists - Porter,R, Isis, Vol 0086, 1995. **CONTACT ADDRESS** Dept of Hist, Cornell Univ, Ithaca, NY, 14850.

WILLIAMS, LAWRENCE H.
PERSONAL Born 09/14/1943, Louisville, KY, m, 1965, 3 children **DISCIPLINE** HISTORY **EDUCATION** Univ Iowa, PhD, 85. **CAREER** Prof, 85-99, African stud & hist, Luther Col. **RESEARCH** African Amer hist from slavery to contemporary. **CONTACT ADDRESS** Luther Col, 700 College Dr, Decorah, IA, 52101. **EMAIL** williala@luther.edu

WILLIAMS, LEE ERSKINE, II
PERSONAL Born 04/02/1946, Jackson, MS, m, 1973, 1 child **DISCIPLINE** HISTORY **EDUCATION** Knoxville Col, TN, BA, 68; East TN State Univ, MA, 70; MS State Univ, PhD, 75. **CAREER** Instr, Middle TN State Univ, 69-72; prof, History, UAH, 74-, dir, Multicultural Affairs, 91-. **MEMBERSHIPS** AL Hist Asn; AL Asn of Historians; Southern History Asn. **RESEARCH** African-Am hist; AL hist; Southern hist. **SELECTED PUBLICATIONS** Auth, Anatomy of Four Race Riots, 73; Post-War Riots in America, 91. **CONTACT ADDRESS** History Dept, Univ of Alabama, Huntsville, Huntsville, AL, 35807. **EMAIL** Willial@email.UAH.edu

WILLIAMS, LEROY THOMAS
PERSONAL Born 10/20/1944, Camden, AR, m, 1969, 1 child **DISCIPLINE** AMERICAN HISTORY, AFRO-AMERICAN STUDIES **EDUCATION** Ark AM&N Col, BS, 70; Univ Toledo, MA, 71, PhD(Am hist), 77. **CAREER** Asst prof hist, Cleveland State Univ, 76-77; asst prof, 77-81, assoc prof hist, Univ Ark, Little Rock, 81-. **MEMBERSHIPS** Asn Study Afr-Am Life & Hist; Nat Asn Black Prof. **RESEARCH** American social history; Afro-American urban history; Afro-American social history. **SELECTED PUBLICATIONS** Auth, Newcomers to the city, Ohio Hist, 81; ed, A Documentary History of Arkansas, 82. **CONTACT ADDRESS** Dept Hist, Univ of Ark, 2801 S University Ave., Little Rock, AR, 72204-1000.

WILLIAMS, NUDIE EUGENE

PERSONAL Born 10/16/1936, Fairfield, AL, 1 child **DISCI-PLINE** MINORITY AND AFRICAN HISTORY **EDUCA-TION** Clark Col, BS, 59; Okla State Univ, MA, 73, PhD(hist), 77. **CAREER** Instr, 76-77, Asst Prof Hist, Univ Ark, 77-, Coord Black studies, Univ Ark. **MEMBERSHIPS** Western Hist Soc; Southern Hist Asn; Orgn Am Historians; Asn Study Negro Life & Hist; Assoc Soc & Behav Sci. **RESEARCH** American minorities in the Southwest (Black lawmen); Black Western newspapers; West African comparative history. **SE-LECTED PUBLICATIONS** Auth, Cassius McDonald Barnes, governor of Oklahoma Territory, 1897-1901, Chronicles Okla, spring 75 & chap IV, In: Territorial Governors of Oklahoma, Okla Hist Soc, 75; A summary: Black newspapers in Oklahoma, 1889 to 1929, Okla Publ, 3/78; Black men who wore the star, The Chronicles of Oklahoma, Vol LIX, No 1; Black men who wore white hats: Grant Johnson, United States Deputy Marshall, Red River Valley Historical Rev, Vol V, No 3; Bass Reeves: Lawman in the Western Ozarks, Negro Hist Bull, Vol 42, No 2; A summary: Black newspapers in Oklahoma, 1889-1929, The Okla Publ, 678; Cassius McDonald Barnes, 1897-1901, Chronicles of Okla, Vol LII, No 1; Turner,James,Milton And The Promise Of America - The Public-Life Of A Post-Civil-War Black-Leader - Kremer,Gr, Journal Of Southern History, Vol 0059, 1993. **CONTACT ADDRESS** Main Campus, Univ of Ark, Fayetteville, AR, 72701-1202.

WILLIAMS, ORA

PERSONAL Born 02/18/1926, Lakewood, NJ, s **DISCI-PLINE** AFRICAN-AMERICAN STUDIES **EDUCATION** Virginia Union University, Richmond, VA, AB, 1950; Howard University, Washington, DC, MA, 1953; University of California, Irvine, CA, PhD, 1974. **CAREER** Southern University, Baton Rouge, LA, instructor, 1953-55; Tuskegee Institute, Tuskegee, AL, instructor, 1955-57; Morgan State University, Baltimore, MD, instructor, 1957-65; Camp Fire Girls, Inc, New York, NY, program advisor, 1965-68; CALIFORNIA STATE UNIVERSITY, LONG BEACH, CA, professor, 1968-88, PRO-FESSOR EMERITA, 1988-; Virginia Union University, visiting professor, 1990-91. **HONORS AND AWARDS** Second Annual Achievement Award in Humanities and Performing Arts Research, Virginia Union University Alumni Association of Southern California, 1983; Pillar of the Community Award, Long Beach Community Improvement League, 1988; Outstanding Service Award, Mayor of Long Beach, 1988; Consortium of Doctors, Savannah, GA, 1993. **MEMBERSHIPS** College Language Association; BEEM-Black Experience as Expressed in Music, board of directors, 1982; NAACP; Afro-American Youth Association, 1984; Delta Sigma Theta Sorority. **SELECTED PUBLICATIONS** Co-author of article "Johnny Doesn't/Didn't Hear," Journal of Negro History, spring, 1964; author, American Black Women in the Arts and Social Sciences: A Bibliographical Survey, Scarecrow Press, 1973, 1978, 1994; Author: Just Like Meteor: A Bio-Bibliography of the Life and Works of Charles William Williams. **CONTACT ADDRESS** English Dept, California State Univ, Long Beach, 1250 Bellflower Blvd, Humanities Office Bldg, Long Beach, CA, 90840.

WILLIAMS, PETER

DISCIPLINE MUSIC **EDUCATION** Cambridge Univ, PhD. **CAREER** Musicol prof, Duke Univ. **HONORS AND AWARDS** Center Performance Pract Studies dir. **SELECTED PUBLICATIONS** Auth, The Organ Music of J.S. Bach. **CONTACT ADDRESS** Dept of Music, Duke Univ, Mary Duke Biddle Music Bldg, Durham, NC, 27706.

WILLIAMS, RHYS H.

PERSONAL Born 08/15/1955, Muncie, IN, m, 1993 **DISCI-PLINE** SOCIOLOGY **EDUCATION** Univ Mass Amherst, PhD, 88 **CAREER** Assoc prof, Southern Illinois Univ, present; visiting asst prof, Yale Divinity School, 92-94 **MEMBER-SHIPS** Amer Socio Assoc; Soc Sci Study Relig; Soc Study Soc Prob **RESEARCH** Religion and American Politics **SELECT-ED PUBLICATIONS** Co-ed, Sacred Companies: Organizational Aspects of Religion and Religious Aspects of Organizations, Oxford, 98; Cultural Wars in American Politics: Critical Reviews of a Popular Myth, Aldine de Gruyter, 97; "Is America in a Culture War? Yes-No-Sort of." Christian Century, 97; "Politics, Religion, and the Analysis of Culture." Theory and Soc, 96 **CONTACT ADDRESS** Dept of Sociology, Southern Illinois Univ, m/c 4524, Carbondale, IL, 62901-4524. **EMAIL** willrhys@siu.edu

WILLIAMS, RICHARD HAL

PERSONAL Born 10/07/1941, Beeville, TX, m, 1963, 2 children **DISCIPLINE** HISTORY **EDUCATION** Princeton Univ, AB, 63; Yale Univ, MA, 64, PhD, 68. **CAREER** From asst prof to assoc prof hist, Yale Univ, 68-75; prof & chmn dept hist, 75-79, dean, Dedman Col, Southern Methodist Univ, 80, Morse fel, Yale Univ, 71-72; res grant, Southern Methodist Univ, 77, 79-80; evaluator/prin investr, Nat Endowment Hum, 76-78; Am Philos Soc grant, 79-80; fel, Univ Col, Oxford, 80. **HONORS AND AWARDS** Everett Eugene Edwards Award, Agr Hist Soc, 67; Outstanding Prof, Southern Methodist Univ, 77, 79, 94. **MEMBERSHIPS** AHA; Orgn Am Historians; Western Hist Asn; Southwestern Soc Sci Asn. **RESEARCH** Gilded Age; Progressive Era. **SELECTED PUBLICATIONS** Auth, George W Julian and land reform in New Mexico, 1885-1889, Agr Hist, 1/67; Dry bones and dead language: The Democratic Party, In: The Gilded Age, Syracuse Univ, 70; The Democratic Party and California Politics, 1880-1896, Stanford Univ, 73; Years of Decision: American Politics in the 1890s, John Wiley & Sons, 78; co auth, The Manhattan Project, Temply, 91; auth, Dear Tom, Dear Theodore: The Letters of Theodore Roosevelt and Thomas B. Reed, Theodore Roosevelt Association Journal, 95; auth, The Politics of the Gilded Age, Essays in Honor of Vincent P. DeSantis, Univ Notre Dame, 97; co auth, America: Past and Present, Addison Wesley, 5th ed, 98. **CONTACT ADDRESS** Dept of Hist, Southern Methodist Univ, PO Box 750001, Dallas, TX, 75275-0001. **EMAIL** hwilliam@mail.smu.edu

WILLIAMS, RICHARD S.

DISCIPLINE HISTORY OF ANCIENT GREECE, ROME AND MEDIEVAL EUROPE **EDUCATION** Mich State Univ, PhD, 73. **CAREER** Assoc prof, Washington State Univ. **HON-ORS AND AWARDS** President's Fac Excellence Award for Instruction, 92; 2 NEH Summer Inste awards. **RESEARCH** Roman mathematics. **SELECTED PUBLICATIONS** Coauth, Finger Numbers in the Greco-Roman World and Early Middle Ages, in Isis, 95. **CONTACT ADDRESS** Dept of History, Washington State Univ, 301 Wilson Hall, PO Box 644030, Pullman, WA, 99164-4030. **EMAIL** sarek@wsu.edu

WILLIAMS, ROBERT CHADWELL

PERSONAL Born 10/14/1938, Boston, MA, m, 1960, 2 children **DISCIPLINE** MODERN HISTORY **EDUCATION** Wesleyan Univ, BA, 60; Harvard Univ, AM, 62, PhD(hist), 66. **CAREER** From lectr to asst prof hist, Williams Col, 65-70; assoc prof, 70-77, Prof Hist, Washington Univ, 77-; Dean, Univ College, 81-; Kennan Inst Advan Russ Studies sr fel, 76-77. **MEMBERSHIPS** Am Asn Advan Slavic Studies. **RE-SEARCH** Russian-German relations; origins of Bolshevism; nuclear energy history. **SELECTED PUBLICATIONS** Auth, Russians in Germany: 1900-1914, J Contemp Hist, 10/66; Russian wars prisoners and Soviet-German relations 1918-1921, Can Slavic Papers, 10/67; Changing landmarks in Russian Berlin: 1922-1924, Slavic Rev, 69; Culture in Exile: Russian Emigres in Germany, 1881-1941, Cornell Univ, 72; Artists in Revolution: Portraits of the Russian Avante-Garde, 1905-1925, Ind Univ, 77; Russian Art and American Money: 1900-1940, Harvard Univ, 80. **CONTACT ADDRESS** Dept of Hist, Washington Univ, St Louis, MO, 63130.

WILLIAMS, ROBIN B.

DISCIPLINE ARCHITECTURAL HISTORY; MODERN **EDUCATION** Univ Penn, PhD 93, MA 90; Univ Toronto, BA 87. **CAREER** Savannah Col Art & Design, dir, VHS project 97-, Ch dept arch hist, 96-, prof, dept art/hist, 93-96; Univ Penn, tchg asst, 87-90. **HONORS AND AWARDS** GA Humanities Coun Gnt; Who's Who Amer Tchrs; Sch Arts Sci Diss Fel; Mellon Fel; Soc Sci Hum Res Coun Canada Doctoral Fel; Isaac Perry essay Prize; Thom Ustick Walter Essay Prize. **MEM-BERSHIPS** SAH; SCSAH; CAA; IAS; GHS. **RESEARCH** 19TH CENTURY ARCH AND URBANISM IN Italy, US and Canada; Savannah arch and urbanism; City sqs; computer tecno for stud of archi and urbanism. **SELECTED PUBLICA-TIONS** Auth, The Image of Secular Power: The romanita of Italian State Architecture under the Sinistra, 1876-1890, in: Guglielmo Calderini: La costruzione di un architettura nel progetto di una Capitale, ed Giorgio Muratore, Perugia, 96; Creating the National Capital: the Urban Works of the Royla Italian Government, Can Med Inst Bull, 92. **CONTACT ADDRESS** Dept of Architectural History, Savannah Col of Art and Design, PO Box 3146, Savannah, GA, 31402-3146. **EMAIL** rwilliam@scad.edu

WILLIAMS, SEAN

PERSONAL Born 08/17/1959, Berkeley, CA, m, 1984, 1 child **DISCIPLINE** MUSIC; ETHNOMUSICOLOGY **EDUCA-TION** Univ Cal-Berkeley, BA, 81; Univ Wash, MA, 85, PhD, 90. **CAREER** Columbia Univ, asst Prof, 90-91, Evergreen State Col, Mem Fac, 91-; Managing Ed, Asian Mus J, 96-. **HONORS AND AWARDS** Fulbright-Hays Doctoral Dissertation fel; Ford Found Dissertation fel. **MEMBERSHIPS** Soc Ethnomusicology, reg ch, 83-84, 98-99; Soc Asian Music. **RE-SEARCH** Music & language; music and urbanization; popular music; issues of race, class and gender, identity and ethnicity in music; Sundanese (Indonesian) music; Irish music. **SE-LECTED PUBLICATIONS** Co-ed & author several articles, The Garland Encyclopedia of World Music, Southeast Asia, v4, Garland Publishing, 98; Constructing Gender in Sundanese Music, in Yearbook for Traditional Music, v30, 98; Competition in the Sundanese Performing Arts of West Java, Indonesia, in Current Musicology, v62, 98; World Beat: Modern Colonialism or Indigenous Synthesis? ReView 17/1:31, 95; Our Laughter Balances Our Tears: Humor in Sundanese Arts, Balungan 5/2, 93; The Urbanization of Tembang Sunda, an Aristocratic Musical Genre of West Java, Indonesia, Univ Wash, 90; Current Developments in Sundanese Popular Music, Asian Music 21/1, 90. **CONTACT ADDRESS** Evergreen State Col, 2700 Evergreen Pky NW, Olympia, WA, 98505. **EMAIL** williams@elwha.evergreen.edu

WILLIAMS, WILLIAM HENRY

PERSONAL Born 06/09/1936, Port Jervis, NY, m, 1959, 2 children **DISCIPLINE** EARLY AMERICAN HISTORY **ED-UCATION** Drew Univ, AB, 58; Yeshiva Univ, MA, 59; Univ Del, PhD(hist), 71. **CAREER** Instr, 67-71, asst prof, 71-77, assoc prof hist, 77-85, PROF HIST, 85- , PARALLEL PROG, UNIV DEL; southern coord, Master of Arts in Liberal Stud, Univ Del, 88- . **HONORS AND AWARDS** Consult, Pa Hosp, 75-76; chmn, Del Humanities Forum, 76-77, consult, 77-81; proposal reviewer, Nat Endowment Humanities, 79- . **MEM-BERSHIPS** Orgn Am Historians. **RESEARCH** Early American social history. **SELECTED PUBLICATIONS** Auth, Early Days of the Anglo-Americans First Hospital, J Am Med Asn, 3/65; The Industrious Poor and the Founding of the Pennsylvania Hospital, Pa Mag Hist & Biog, 10/73; ed, Sixteen Miles from Anywhere: A History of Georgetown, Delaware, Countian Press, 76; auth, Independence and Early American Hospitals, Bicentenary Issue, J Am Med Asn, 5/7/76; Anglo-Americas First Hospital: The Pennsylvania Hospital, 1751-1841, Haverford House, 76; A Means to an End: Oregon's Protestant Missionaries View the Indian, Pac Historian, Summer 76; ed, Oral History Project: Education in Sussex County, Delaware, Sussex County Bicentennial Comt, 78; contrib, Dict American Medical Biography & Dict of American Biography; auth, The Garden of American Methodism: The Delmarva Peninunsula, 1769-1820, Scholarly Resources, 84; auth, The First State: An Illustrated History of Delaware, Windsor, 85; auth, Slavery and Freedom in Delaware, 1639-1865, Scholarly Resources, 96; auth, The Delmarva Chicken Industry: 75 Years of Progress, Delmarva Poultry Industry, 98. **CONTACT ADDRESS** 238 W Pine, Georgetown, DE, 19947.

WILLIAMS, WILLIAM J.

PERSONAL Born 12/25/1935, Montgomery, Alabama, s **DIS-CIPLINE** POLITICAL SCIENCE **EDUCATION** Morehouse Coll, bachelor's degree, 1952; NY Univ, master's degree, 1954; Univ of So CA, PhD, 1966. **CAREER** NY State Com/Govtl Operations NY City, admin adv 1959-60; Bldg Serv Union, rsch dir joint council #8 1960-61; CA State Legislature, consult 1961-62; US Congressman Augustus F Hawkins, congressional field dir 1962-66; US Equal Employment Oppor Comm, dep staff dir 1966-67; US Commn on Civil Rights, dir western progs 1967-68; LA Co/LA City, employee relations bd mediator 1974; Univ So CA, prof, currently. **HONORS AND AWARDS** Teaching Excellence Award, School of Public Admin, USC, 1978; Man of the Year, Alpha Phi Omega; Distinguished Prof Award, USC Graduate Student Assn, 1989. **MEMBERSHIPS** Exec dir Negro Polit Action Assn CA 1964-66; dem candidate Sec of State of CA 1966; pres, USC Chapter, Amer Assn Univ Profs, 1974-75; Pres, Inst for Applied Epistemics; Dir, Educ Consulting & Counseling Serv; Pres, Diversified Servs. **SE-LECTED PUBLICATIONS** Publications: "The Miracle of Abduction," Epistemics Institute Press, 1985; "Semantic Behavior & Decision Making," Monograph Publishing Series, A subsidiary of Univ Microfilms Intl, 1978; "Epistemics: Personalizing the Process of Change," Univ Publishers, 1975; "Selections from Semantic Behavior & Decision Making," 1975; "Uncommon Sense & Dimensional Awareness," Univ Publishers, 1973; "General Semantics & the Social Sciences," Philosophical Library, 1972. **CONTACT ADDRESS** Univ of Southern California, University Park, Los Angeles, CA, 90007.

WILLIAMS-MYERS, ALBERT J.

PERSONAL Born 03/10/1939, Edison, GA, m, 1962 **DISCI-PLINE** AFRICAN-AMERICAN STUDIES **EDUCATION** Wagner College, BA, 1962; UCLA, life-time teaching certificate, 1969, MA, 1971, PhD, 1978. **CAREER** Mobilization for Youth, work group leader, 1962-63; All Saints Parish School, teacher, 8th thru 11th grade, 1963-64; College of the Virgin Islands, head resident, director of activities, 1964-65; New York City Youth Board, street club worker, 1965-66; US Peace Corps, Malawi, Africa, volunteer, 1966-68; Carleton College, professor, 1976-79; SUNY Albany African-American Institute, executive director, 1990-91; SUNY COLL AT NEW PALTZ, PROF, currently. **HONORS AND AWARDS** Ford Foundation, Research in Africa & the Middle East Graduate Fellowship, 1973-74; Historic Hudson Valley, Distinguished African-American Researcher Award, 1992. **MEMBERSHIPS** African Studies Association, 1971-80; New York African Studies Association, president, 1985-88; NAACP, Ellenville, Chapter, 1985-. **SELECTED PUBLICATIONS** Writer, "Slavery, Rebellion and Revolution in The Americas: A Historiographical Scenario on the Theses of Genovese and Others," Journal of Black Studies 26, 4 March 1996; Making The Invisible Visible: African-Americans in New York History, 1994; "A Portrait of Eve: History of Black Women in Hudson Valley," 1987; NY City, African Americans and Selected Memory: An Historiographical Assessment of a Black Presence Before 1877; Journal of Afro-Americans in New York Life and History, July 1997; Books Published: "Long Hammering: Essays on the forging of an African American Presence in the Hudson River Valley to the Early Twentieth Century," Africa World Press, 1994; "Destructive Impulses: An Examination of An American Secret in Race Relations: White Violence," University Press of America, 1995. **CONTACT ADDRESS** SUNY, New Paltz, College Hall F-106, New Paltz, NY, 12561.

WILLIAMSON, ARTHUR H.

PERSONAL Born 12/14/1943, Cleveland, OH, m, 1970, 1 child **DISCIPLINE** HISTORY **EDUCATION** Carleton Col,

BA, 65; Wash Univ-St Louis, MA, 68, PhD, 74. **CAREER** Vis asst prof of Hist, Wash Univ-St Louis, 74-75; Asst prof of Hist, Univ Chicago, 75-78; Asst Dean Grad School Arts & Sci, NY Univ, 78-88; Dean Grad Stud, 88-91, PROF HIST, 88- , CALIF STATE UNIV-SACRAMENTO. **HONORS AND AWARDS** Fulbright Sr Schol, 93-94; Hon prof Hist, Dept Hist, Univ Aberdeen (UK); Brit Acad Travel grant, 98; Sr fel, Inst Advan Stud, Univ Edinburgh, 93-94; Danforth Tchg fel, 65-68; Woodrow Wilson Diss fel, 68-69; Univ (Ford) grant, 69-70. **MEMBERSHIPS** Am Hist Asn; 16th Century Conf; Pac Coast Conf Brit Stud. **RESEARCH** Early modern Britain; History of political thought; Reformation. **SELECTED PUBLICATIONS** Co-ed, The Expulsion of the Jews: 1492 and After, Garland Publ, 94; The Crying Game: Identity and Ambiguity, Symposium, 94; Apocalypse Now, Apocalypse Then: Prophecy and the Modern World, The Tchg Co, 95; Images of Blood: Ethnic Identity and the Destruction of the Left in Europe and America, 1972-1992, CSUS, 95; Union with England Traditional, Union with England Radical: Sir James Hope and the Mid 17th-Century British State, Engl Hist Rev, 95; Scots, Indians, and Empire: the Scottish Politics of Civilization, 1519-1609, Past and Present, 96; Reason and the Ethnic Impulse, In These Times, 96; George Buchanan, Civic Virtue, and Commerce: European Imperialism and Its 16th-Century Critics, Scottish Hist Rev, 96; Unnatural Empire: George Buchanan, Anti-Imperialism, and the 16th-Century Syphilis Pandemic, Everything Connects: In Conference with Richard H. Popkin, Brill, 98; Patterns of British Identity: 'Britain' and its Rivals in the 16th and 17th Centuries, The New British Hist c.1500-1707: A Reader, I B Tauris, 98. **CONTACT ADDRESS** Dept of Hist, California State Univ, Sacramento, Sacramento, CA, 95819-6059. **EMAIL** williamsonah@csus.edu

WILLIAMSON, JERRY WAYNE
PERSONAL Born 03/17/1944, Dallas, TX, m, 1965 **DISCIPLINE** APPALACHIAN HISTORY AND CULTURE **EDUCATION** Wayland Col, BA, 66; Univ Utah, MA, 70, PhD(English), 70. **CAREER** Asst prof, 70-75, assoc prof, 75-80, prof English, Appalachian State Univ, 80-, ed, Appalachian J: A Regional Studies Rev, 72-. **MEMBERSHIPS** MLA; Conf Editors Learned Jour; Appalachian Studies Conf. **RESEARCH** Seventeenth-century studies; Appalachian studies. **SELECTED PUBLICATIONS** Auth, The Myth of the Conqueror, Prince Henry Stuart: A Study of Seventeenth-Century Personation, AMS, 78; ed, An Appalachian Symposium, 77 & co-ed, A Guide to Appalachian Studies, 78, Appalachian State Univ; auth, Interviewing Appalachia: The Appalachian Journal Interviews, 1978-1992, Univ Tenn Press, 94; Southern Mountaineers in Silent Films, McFarland, 94; Hillbillyland: What the Movies Did to the Mountains and What the Mountains Did to the Movies, Univ NC Press, 95. **CONTACT ADDRESS** Dept of English, Appalachian State Univ, Belk Library, Boone, NC, 28608-0000. **EMAIL** willimsonjw@appstate.edu

WILLINGHAM, WILLIAM FLOYD
PERSONAL Born 09/21/1944, Pendleton, OR, m, 1968 **DISCIPLINE** EARLY AMERICAN HISTORY **EDUCATION** Willamette Univ, BA, 66; Northwestern Univ, Evanston, MA, 69, PhD(hist), 72. **CAREER** Asst prof hist, Lafayette Col, 70-72; asst prof hist, Univ Ky, 72-77; LECTR HIST, LEWIS & CLARK COL, 78-, CONSULT HIST, CITY OF PORTLAND & US CORP OF ENGRS. **MEMBERSHIPS** Orgn Am Historians. **RESEARCH** American Revolutionary history; early American local history; family and community history. **SELECTED PUBLICATIONS** Auth, Oregon Trail Symposium 1989, Pt 2, History and Interpretation, Public Historian, Vol 0015, 93; Cultural Resources and the Oregon Trail, Pt 1, Historical Archaeology, Public Historian, Vol 0015, 93; Interpreting the Oregon Trail, Public Historian, Vol 0016, 94; Family and Community on the Eastern Oregon Frontier + American Pioneer History, Oregon Hist Quart, Vol 0095, 94; The Need For Historical Research on the United States Army Corps of Engineers Protection of the Salmon, Public Historian, Vol 0017, 95; Structures in the Stream, Water, Science, snd the Rise of United States Army Corps of Engineers, Public Historian, Vol 0017, 95; Grand Coulee, Harnessing a Dream, Ore Hist Quart, Vol 0097, 96; Tangled Webs of History, Pac Northwest Quart, Vol 0087, 96; A Common Fate, Pac Northwest Quart, Vol 0088, 97. **CONTACT ADDRESS** N Pacif Div, USA Corps Eng, Portland, OR.

WILLIS, ALFRED
PERSONAL Born 06/07/1955, Atlanta, GA, s **DISCIPLINE** ART HISTORY AND ARCHAEOLOGY **EDUCATION** Clemson Univ, BA, 76; Columbia Univ, PhD (art hist/archaeol), 84; Univ Chicago, MA (library sci), 86. **CAREER** Asst prof, Syracuse Univ, 84-85; adj instr, Univ Ill at Chicago, 85-86; res, Canadian Ctr fro Archit, 86-87; actg dir, Resource Ctr, Univ Ill at Chicago, 87-88; librn, Found for Doc of Archit, Nat Gallery of Art, 88-89; cataloger, 89-90; archit librn, Kent State Univ, 90-93; head, Art Libr, Univ Cal Los Angeles, 93- . **HONORS AND AWARDS** Columbia Univ Pres Fel, 79-81; Belgian-American Educ Found Fel, 81-82; Belgian Minsitry for Netherlandish Cult Fel, 83-84. **MEMBERSHIPS** Art Libr Soc of North Am; Asoc of Archit Librns; ALA; Col Art Asoc; Sco of Archit Hist. **RESEARCH** Belgian architecture and decorative arts; theosophical architecture; Los Angeles architecture; architectural drawings; aesthetics of architecture; library science. **SELECTED PUBLICATIONS** Auth, The Exoteric and Esoteric Functions of Le Corbsier's Mundanem (1929), Modulus, 81; auth, The Gates in the Brialmont Fortifications of Antwerp as Architectural Monuments, Revue belge d'histoire militaire, 83; auth, Mannerism, Nature, and Abstraction in the Early Architectural Designs of Victor Horta, Horta: Art Nouveau to Modernism, 96; auth, The Place of Archives in the Universe of Architectural Documentation, Am Archivist, 96; auth, L'Ommegang de Bruxelles en 1930: Le contexte historique d'un cortege historique, Pleins feux sur l'Ommegang, 97. **CONTACT ADDRESS** 435 S. Curson Ave., Apt. 1-C, Los Angeles, CA, 90036. **EMAIL** awills@library.ucla.edu

WILLIS, FRANK ROY
PERSONAL Born 07/25/1930, Prescot, England, m, 1959, 3 children **DISCIPLINE** MODERN HISTORY **EDUCATION** Cambridge Univ, BA, 52; Stanford Univ, PhD, 59. **CAREER** Instr hist civilization, Stanford Univ, 59-60; from instr to assoc prof hist, Univ Wash, 60-64; assoc prof, 64-67, PROF HIST, UNIV CALIF, DAVIS, 67-, Am Coun Learned Soc grant-in-aid, 61; Rockefeller Found res grant int rels, 62-63; Guggenheim Found fel, 66-67; vis prof int rels, Stanford Univ, 71-72; Soc Sci Res Coun res training fel, 73-74. **MEMBERSHIPS** AHA **RESEARCH** France since 1750; Germany and Italy since 1945; European integration. **SELECTED PUBLICATIONS** Auth, Germany Divided--From the Wall to Reunification, Amer Hist Rev, Vol 0099, 94; We Were The People--Voices from East-Germany Revolutionary Autumn of 1989, Amer Hist Rev, Vol 0099, 94; German Unification in the European Context, Amer Hist Rev, Vol 0100, 95. **CONTACT ADDRESS** Dept of Hist, Univ of Calif, Davis, CA, 95616.

WILLIS, JAMES F.
PERSONAL m, 1 child **DISCIPLINE** HISTORY **EDUCATION** Southern State Col Magnolia, BA, 67; Duke Univ, MA, 68, PhD, 76. **CAREER** Instr, Little Rock Univ, 68-69; instr, 69-71; asst prof, Southern State Col, 73-74; asst prof, 74-93; prof polit sci, Southern AR Univ, 93-. **HONORS AND AWARDS** Best Paper Prize, 94. **MEMBERSHIPS** Ark Hist Asn; Ark Polit Sci Asn; Ark Asn Col Hist Tchr; Soc Hist Am For Rel; Int Studies Asn; Southern Polit Sci Asn; SW Soc Sci Asn; Am Hist Asn; Am Polit Sci Asn; Orgn Am Hist; Am Asn Univ Prof. **RESEARCH** Am for rel(s); international Law; Latin Am hist; East Asia hist. **SELECTED PUBLICATIONS** Auth, Breckinridge Clifton Rodes, Oxford, Univ, 95; The SAU Poll, Southern AR Univ; The SAU Poll # 2, Southern AR Univ. **CONTACT ADDRESS** Hist Dept, Southern AR Univ, East University, PO Box 100, Magnolia, AR, 71753-5000. **EMAIL** jfwillis@saumag.edu

WILLIS, WILLIAM HAILEY
PERSONAL Born 04/29/1916, Meridian, MS, m, 1943, 4 children **DISCIPLINE** CLASSICAL PHILOLOGY **EDUCATION** Miss Col, AB, 36; Columbia Univ, AM, 37; Yale Univ, PhD(Greck), 40. **CAREER** Instr classics, Yale Univ, 40-42; assoc prof Greek & Latin, Univ Miss, 46-47; prof Greek & Latin & chmn dept classics, 47-63; PROF GREEK, DUKE UNIV, 63-, Fund Advan Educ fac fel, Harvard Univ, 52-53; mem managing comt, Am Sch Class Studies Athens, 53-, vchmn, 79-81; vis prof class lang, Univ Tex, 57-58; vis prof classics, Univ NC, 59, 63-64, 66; fac fel theol, Church Divinity Sch Pac, 59; sr ed, Greek, Roman & Byzantine Studies, 59-79; vis scholar, Fac of Relig, Oxford Univ, 61-62, vis mem, Brasenose & Queen's Cols, 61-62; Am Philos Soc Penrose Fund res grant, 62; Am Coun Learned Soc fac res grant, 62; corresp mem, Inst Antiquity & Christianity, 68-; Guggenheim fel, 80-81. **MEMBERSHIPS** Archaeol Inst Am; Am Philol Asn (pres, 72-73); Southern Class Asn (pres, 58-60); Southern Humanities Conf (secy, 56-58); Class Asn Mid W & S (pres, 66-67). **RESEARCH** Greek philology; papyrology; Coptic studies. **SELECTED PUBLICATIONS** Auth, Comoedia Dukiana + Fragment of Greek Comedy among Duke University Papyri, Greek Roman and Byzantine Stud, Vol 0032, 91; Dow, Sterling--19 Nov 1903 9 Jan 1995, Greek Roman and Byzantine Stud, Vol 0036, 95. **CONTACT ADDRESS** Duke Station, Box 4715, Durham, NC, 27706.

WILLS, GREGORY A.
DISCIPLINE CHURCH HISTORY **EDUCATION** Duke Univ, BS; Gordon-Conwell Theol Sem, MDiv; Duke Univ, ThM; Emory Univ, PhD. **CAREER** Archives and spec coll(s) libn, Boyce Centennial Lib, asst prof, S Baptist Theol Sem. **SELECTED PUBLICATIONS** Auth, dissertation, Democratic Religion: Freedom, Authority, and Church Discipline in the Baptist South, 1785-1900, Oxford UP; entries on Basil Manly, Jr. and Jesse Mercer, Amer Nat Biography. **CONTACT ADDRESS** Dept of Church History, Southern Baptist Theol Sem, 2825 Lexington Rd, Louisville, KY, 40280. **EMAIL** gwills@sbts.edu

WILLS, JEFFREY
DISCIPLINE CLASSICS **EDUCATION** Harvard Univ, PhD, 88 **CAREER** Assoc Prof, 88-pres, Univ of WI **HONORS AND AWARDS** Fulbright Scholar, Ukraine, 97-98 **RESEARCH** Latin Literature **CONTACT ADDRESS** Dept of Classics, Van Hise Hall, Madison, WI, 53706. **EMAIL** wills@macc.wisc.edu

WILLS, JOHN E.
PERSONAL Born 08/08/1936, Urbana, IL, m, 1958, 5 children **DISCIPLINE** HISTORY **EDUCATION** Univ Ill, AB, 56; Harvard Univ, MA, 58; PhD, 67. **CAREER** Instr, Stanford Univ, 64-65; instr, Univ Southern Calif, 65-67; asst prof, 67-72; assoc prof, 72-84; prof, 84- . **MEMBERSHIPS** Asoc for Asian Studies; Am Hist Asoc. **RESEARCH** The Ming-Qing transition in 17th-century China; pre-modern Chinese foreign relations; China's coastal regions and their overseas connections; the maritime interconnections of Europeans ad Asians in early modern times; comparative history; philosophy of history. **SELECTED PUBLICATIONS** Auth, Pepper, Guns, and Parlelys: The Dutch East India Company and China, 1662-1681, 74; co-ed with Jonathan D. Spence, From Ming to Ch'ing: Conquest, Region, and Continuity in Seventeenth-Century China, 79; Embassies and Illusions: Dutch and Portuguese Envoys to K'ang-his, 1666-1687, 84; auth, Mountain of Fame: Portraits in Chinese History, 94. **CONTACT ADDRESS** History Dept, Univ of Southern California, Los Angeles, CA, 90089-0034. **EMAIL** jwills@usc.edu

WILLUMSON, GLENN GARDNER
PERSONAL Born 06/22/1949, Glendale, CA, m, 1970, 2 children **DISCIPLINE** ART HISTORY; ENGLISH **EDUCATION** St. Mary's Col, BA, 71; Univ Calif Davis, MA, 84; Univ Calif Santa Barbara, PhD, 88. **CAREER** Teacher, Calif Secondary Sch, 71-81; cur, Amer Art and Photog, Getty Res Inst, 88-92; affil prof, Dept of Art Hist, Pa State, 93-; cur, Palmer Mus of Art, Pa State, 92-. **HONORS AND AWARDS** Nat Endow for the Humanities fel, 97-98; Haynes fel, Huntington Libr, fac res grant, 94; J. Paul Getty Publ grant, 91; Annette Baxter prize, Amer studies, 87; Kress found fel, 87; Nat Writing Proj fel, 87; teaching resources grant, 84. **MEMBERSHIPS** Col Art Asn; Amer Studies Asn; Asn of Hist of Amer Art; Asn of Univ Mus and Galleries. **RESEARCH** History of photography; American art. **SELECTED PUBLICATIONS** Auth, The Getty Research Institute: Materials for a New Photo-History, Hist of Photog, XXII, 1, 31-39, Spring, 98; auth, Clement Greenberg, Encycl of World Bio, Jan, 95; auth, A Family Album: Portraits by John Sloan, Amer Art Rev, 116-117, June-July, 94; auth, Collecting with a Passion: Selections from the Pincus Collection of Contemporary Art, Univ Pk, Palmer Mus of Art, 93; auth, Silver Salts and Blueprints, London Times Lit Suppl, 19 Mar, 93; auth, W. Eugene Smith and the Photographic Essay, NY, Cambridge Univ Press, 92; essays, Van Dyck's Iconographie, Mus Plantin-Moretus, Stedelijk Prenteenkabinet, 376-387, 91; auth, Alfred Hart: Photographer of the Transcontinental Railroad, Hist of Photog, XII, 1, 61-75, Jan-Mar, 88. **CONTACT ADDRESS** Palmer Museum of Art, Pennsylvania State Univ, University Park, PA, 16802-2507. **EMAIL** ggw2@psu.edu

WILMARTH, ARTHUR E.
PERSONAL Born 02/16/1951, Olean, NY, m, 1983, 2 children **DISCIPLINE** HISTORY **EDUCATION** Yale Univ, BA, 72; Harvard Univ, JD, 75 **CAREER** Assoc, Arent, Fox, Kinter, Plotkin & Kahn, 75-79; assoc, Jones, Day, Reavis & Pogue, 79-85; partner, Jones, Day, Reavis & Pogue, 79-85; assoc prof law, George Washington Univ, 86-; partner, Barley, Snyder, Senft & Cohen, 92-94. **HONORS AND AWARDS** Phi Beta Kappa, Yale Univ; Who's Who in American Law; Who's who in the East; rated "av" by Martindale-Hubbell. **MEMBERSHIPS** ABA; District of Columbia Bar. **RESEARCH** Banking law; corporate law; Am legal hist. **SELECTED PUBLICATIONS** Auth, "The Case for the Validity of State Regional Banking Laws", in 18 Loyola of Los Angeles Law Review, 85; auth, "The Original Purpose of the Bill of Rights: James Madison and the Founders' Search for a Workable Balance between Federal and State Power", in 26 Am Criminal Law Review, 89; auth, "The Expansion of State Bank Powers, the Federal Response and the Case for Preserving the Dual Banking System", in 58 Fordham Law Review, 90; auth "The Potential Risks of Nationwide Consolidation in the Banking Industry: A Reply to Professor Miller", in 77 Iowa Law Review, 92; auth "Too Big to Fail, Too Few to Serve? The Potential Risks of Nationwide Banks", in 77 Iowa Law Review, 92; auth, "Too Good to be True? The Unfulfilled Promises Behind Big Bank Mergers", in 2 Stanford Journal of Law, Business & Finance, 95; coauth, Corporations and Alternative Business Vehicles, 4th ed, 97. **CONTACT ADDRESS** Law Sch, George Washington Univ, 720 20th St, NW, Washington, DC, 20052. **EMAIL** awilmarth@main.nlc.gwe.edu

WILMETH, DON B.
PERSONAL Born 12/15/1939, Houston, TX, m, 1963, 1 child **DISCIPLINE** THEATRE HISTORY, POPULAR CULTURE **EDUCATION** Abilene Christian Col, BA, 61; Univ AR, MA, 62; Univ IL, PhD, 64. **CAREER** Asst prof theatre, Eastern NM Univ, 64-65, head dept drama, 65-67; from Asst Prof to Prof, 67-98, The Asa Messer Prof of Theatre & English, Brown Univ, 98-, actg chmn theatre arts prog, 72-73, exec officer, Theatre Arts Dept, 73-, Chmn Dept, 79-87, Coordr, Grad Prog in Theatre Studies, 87-, Honorary Curator, H. Adrian Smith Collection of Conjuring Books & Magiciana (In Brown Special Collections); consult, Asn Col & Res Libr, 70-; theatre ed, Intellect Mag, 74-; bk rev ed, The Theatre J, 78-80; assoc ed, Mod Lang Studies, 80; consult, Libr Congress Am theatre project, 92-94; Vis Schol, Osaka Univ and Japan Found, Summer 93; Selection

Comt, Robert Lewis Medal for Lifetime Achievement in Theater Res, 94-99; O.R. and Eva Mitchell Distinguished Vis Prof, Trinity Univ, 95; Dean, Col Fels Am Theatre, 96-98; Corresponding Schol, Shaw Festival, Ontario, 95. **HONORS AND AWARDS** Eastern NM Univ res grants, 66-68; George Freedley Theatre Bk Award, Theatre Libr Asn, 71-72; Guggenheim fel, 82., MA, Brown Univ, 70. **MEMBERSHIPS** Theatre Libr Asn (vpres, 81); Am Theatre Asn; Am Soc Theatre Res (pres 91-94, secy 95-01); Int Fedn Theatre Res (exec comt 94-97); New Engl Theatre Conf; Am Theatre & Drama Soc (exec bd 95-99). **RESEARCH** Popular entertainment; life and art of the 19th century actor, G F Cooke; Am theatre of the 19th century. **SELECTED PUBLICATIONS** Contribr, Drama/theatre, In: Books for College Libraries, 2nd ed, Am Libr Asn, 74; auth, The American Stage to World War I, 78 & American and English Popular Entertainment, 80, Gale Res Co; The Language of American Popular Entertainment, 81 & Variety Entertainment and Outdoor Amusements, 82, Greenwood Press; co-ed, Plays by William Hooker Gillette, Cambridge Univ Press, 83; auth, Mud Show: American Tent Circus Life, Univ NMex Press, 88; co-ed and contribr, Cambridge Guide to World Theatre, Cambridge Univ Press, 88; contribr, Theatre in the Colonies and United States, 1750-1915: A Documentary History, Cambridge Univ Press, 96; co-ed, The Cambridge Guide to the American Theatre, Cambridge Univ Press, 93; auth, Staging the Nation: Plays from the American Theatre, 1787-1909, Bedford Bks, 98; co-ed, The Cambridge History of American Theatre, Beginnings to 1870, Cambridge Univ Press, 98. **CONTACT ADDRESS** Dept of Theatre Arts, Brown Univ, 1 Prospect St, Providence, RI, 02912-9127. **EMAIL** donwilmeth@brown.edu

WILSON, B.
PERSONAL Born 03/30/1947, Tampa, FL **DISCIPLINE** HISTORY **EDUCATION** Benedictine Col, BA 69; MSU, MA 72, PhD. **CAREER** General Motors Inst, assoc prof, 75; Western Mich Univ, prof, 90. **HONORS AND AWARDS** Who's Who in: The Midwest, Amer, The World. **MEMBERSHIPS** Assoc for the Study of African Amer Life and History. **RESEARCH** The Afri/Amer Experience; topics in Pan African **SELECTED PUBLICATIONS** Auth, Some Thoughts on the Black Roots of American Pop Culture, in: Amer Pop Cult at Home and Abroad, 96; African Americans in Michigan, in: Ethnic Mich, 96. **CONTACT ADDRESS** Dept of Black American Studies, Western Michigan Univ, 331 Moore Hall, Kalamazoo, MI, 49008-5093. **EMAIL** benjamin.wilson@wmich.edu

WILSON, BLAKE
DISCIPLINE MUSICOLOGY **EDUCATION** Univ Calif, Berkeley, BA, 79; Ind Univ, MM, 82, PhD, 87. **CAREER** Asst prof, Colby Col, 88-89; asst prof, Vanderbilt Univ, 89- 93; asst prof, 93-95, ASSOC PROF MUSIC, DICKINSON COL, 95-. **CONTACT ADDRESS** Music Dept, Dickinson Col, Carlisle, PA, 17013. **EMAIL** wilson@dickinson.edu

WILSON, CHARLES REAGAN
PERSONAL Born 02/02/1948, Nashville, TN **DISCIPLINE** AMERICAN HISTORY, RELIGION **EDUCATION** Univ Tex, El Paso, BA, 70, MA, 72; Univ Tex, Austin, PhD(hist), 77. **CAREER** Vis prof Am studies, Univ Wuerzburg, West Ger, 77-78; lectr, Univ Tex, El Paso, 78-80; vis prof, Tex Tech Univ, 80-81; ASST PROF AM HIST, UNIV MISS, 81-, Co-ed, Encycl Southern Cult, 81- **RESEARCH** Southern culture; American religion; popular culture. **SELECTED PUBLICATIONS** Auth, Bishop Thomas Frank Gailor: Celebrant of Southern tradition, Tenn Hist Quart, fall 79; The religion of the lost cause: Southern civil religion, J Southern Hist, 5/80; Baptized in Blood: The Religion of the Lost Cause, 1865-1920, Univ Ga Press, 80; Robert Lewis Dabney: Religion and the Southern holocaust, Va Mag Hist & Biog, 1/81; Southern funerals, cemeteries, the lost cause, Thomas Frank Gailor and Charles Todd Quintard, Encycl Southern Relig (in prep). **CONTACT ADDRESS** Univ of Miss, Box 6640, University, MS, 38655.

WILSON, CHRISTOPHER M.
PERSONAL Born 12/23/1951, Iowa City, IA **DISCIPLINE** ARCHITECTURAL HISTORY **EDUCATION** Univ New Mex, MA, 81. **CAREER** Adj Assoc Prof, 87-, Univ NM, Sch Archit Plan; Consulting Archit Historian, 83-. **HONORS AND AWARDS** Villagra Awd for Best Book, Myth of Santa Fe. **MEMBERSHIPS** VAF; SAH; ASA; WHA; OAH; NTHP. **RESEARCH** Historic and contemporary architecture and cultural landscapes of the US-Mexico borderlands; the history and politics of cultural tourism and historic preservation. **SELECTED PUBLICATIONS** Auth, The Myth of Santa Fe: Creating a Modern Regional Tradition, Albuquerque, Univ New Mexico Press, 97; Spatial Mestizaje on the Pueblo-Mexicano-Anglo Frontier, J Sch of Archit and Plan, 94; When a Room is the Hall, MASS 84, reprinted in: Images of an American Land: Vernacular Architecture in the Western US, ed, Thomas Carter, Albuquerque, U of NM Press 97. **CONTACT ADDRESS** 1208 Marquette Pl NE, Albuquerque, NM, 87106-4742. **EMAIL** cwillie6@aol.com

WILSON, CONSTANCE MARALYN
PERSONAL Born 10/07/1937, Woonsocket, RI **DISCIPLINE** SOUTHEAST ASIAN AND ASIAN HISTORY **EDUCATION** Swarthmore Col, BA, 59; Cornell Univ, PhD(hist), 70. **CAREER** Instr Asian hist, San Francisco State Col, 66-67; instr, 67-68, asst prof, 68-79, ASSOC PROF SOUTHEAST ASIAN HIST, NORTHERN ILL UNIV, 79-, Ford Found Southeast Asia fel, 71-72; Nat Endowment for Humanities younger humanist fel, 73-. **MEMBERSHIPS** Asn Asian Studies (vchairperson prog comt, 80-81, chairperson, 81-82); Siam Soc; Burma Res Soc; AHA. **RESEARCH** Economic and social history of Thailand. **SELECTED PUBLICATIONS** Auth, Toward a Bibliography of the Life and Times of Mongkut, King of Thailand, 1851-1868, In: Southeast Asian History and Historiography: Essays Presented to DGE Hall, Ithaca and London, Cornell Univ, 76; Thai and Western Studies of Thai History: Interaction and Growth, In: The Study of Thailand: Analyses of Knowledge, Approaches, and Prospects in Anthropology, Art History, Economics, History and Political Science, Ctr Int Studies, Ohio Univ, Athens, 79; coed (with C S Smith & G V Smith), Royalty and Commoners: Essays in Thai Administrative, Economic and Social History, In: Contributions to Asian Studies, Vol 15, 80. **CONTACT ADDRESS** Dept of Hist, No Illinois Univ, 1425 W Lincoln Hwy, De Kalb, IL, 60115-2825.

WILSON, DANA
DISCIPLINE MUSIC **EDUCATION** Bowdoin Col, BA; Univ Conn, MA; Eastman Sch Music, PhD. **CAREER** Prof. **HONORS AND AWARDS** Ostwald Composition Prize. **SELECTED PUBLICATIONS** Auth, pubs on Klavier, Albany, Open Loop, Summit, Redwood, and Kosei; co-auth, Contemporary Choral Arranging, Prentice Hall, 86. **CONTACT ADDRESS** Dept of Music History, Theory and Composition, Ithaca Col, 100 Job Hall, Ithaca, NY, 14850. **EMAIL** wilson@ithaca.edu

WILSON, DANIEL JOSEPH
PERSONAL Born 12/19/1949, Wausau, WI **DISCIPLINE** AMERICAN INTELLECTUAL HISTORY **EDUCATION** Univ Wis, Whitewater, BA, 72; Johns Hopkins Univ, MA, 74, PhD(Hist), 76. **CAREER** Instr, Univ Md, Baltimore County, 76-77, Johns Hopkins Univ, 77-78; asst prof US Hist, Muhlenberg Col, 78-, from assoc prof to prof, 85-94; res asst, Papers of Benjamin Henry Latrobe, 78; fel, Am Coun Learned Soc, 81-82. **HONORS AND AWARDS** Class of 1932 Res Prof, 86-87; Phi Beta Kappa, 77. **MEMBERSHIPS** AHA; Orgn Am Historians; Am Studies Asn; Am Philos Asn; Am Assoc for the His of Medicine. **RESEARCH** The impact of science and professionalization of American philosophy; history of American philosophy; a cultural hist of the polio epidemics in Am; hist of disability. **SELECTED PUBLICATIONS** Auth, Nature in Western popular literature from the dime novel to Zane Grey, NDak Quart, 76; Professionalization and organized discussion in the APA, 1900-1922, J Hist Philos, 79; Arthur O Lovejoy and the moral of The Great Chain of Being, J Hist Ideas, 80; Arthur O Lovejoy and the Quest for Intelligibility, Univ NC Press, 80; co-ed, The Cause of the South: Selections from De Bow's Review, La State Univ Press, 82; auth, Arthur O Lovejoy: An Annotated Bibliography, Garland Publ, 82; Covenants of Work and Grace; Themes of Recovery and Redemption in Polio Narratives, Literature and Medicine, 94; A Crippling Fear: Experiencing Polio in the Era of FDR, Bulletin of the History of Medicine, 98. **CONTACT ADDRESS** Dept of History, Muhlenberg Col, 2400 W Chew St, Allentown, PA, 18104-5586. **EMAIL** dwilson@muhlenberg.edu

WILSON, DAVID
PERSONAL Born 11/02/1954, Thomaston, Alabama, s **DISCIPLINE** HISTORY **EDUCATION** Tuskegee University, Tuskegee, AL, BS, 1977, MS, 1979; Harvard University, Cambridge, MA, EdM, 1984, PhD, 1987. **CAREER** Research & Development Institute of Philadelphia, Philadelphia, PA, project dir, 1979-82; Kentucky State University, Frankfurt, KY, exec asst to vice pres for business affairs, 1984-85; Woodrow Wilson National Fellowship Foundation, Princeton, NJ, 1985-88; Rutgers University, Camden, NJ, assoc provost, 1988-94; Auburn Univ, vp for univ outreach, assoc provost, currently. **HONORS AND AWARDS** Kellogg Fellow, WK Kellogg Foundation, 1988-92; Woodrow Wilson Fellow, Woodrow Wilson Natl Fellowship Foundation, 1984-85; One of America's Best and Brightest Young Business and Professional Men, Dollars and Sense Magazine, 1987; Certificate of Appreciation, Governor of Alabama, 1987; Certificate of Appreciation, Governor of Tennessee, 1988. **MEMBERSHIPS** Member, board of directors, Afro-American Historical & Cultural Museum, Philadelphia, PA, 1988-, Walt Whitman Association, Camden, NJ, 1988-, Princeton Ballet, 1988-, Optimist Club of Lower Bucks, Bensalem, PA, 1986-91; member, Alpha Phi Alpha Fraternity, Inc, 1975-. **CONTACT ADDRESS** VP for Univ Outreach, Auburn Univ, Auburn, AL, 36849.

WILSON, DAVID B.
PERSONAL Born 02/12/1941, Louisville, KY, m, 1964, 1 child **DISCIPLINE** HISTORY OF SCIENCE **EDUCATION** Wabash Col, AB, 63; Johns Hopkins Univ, PhD(hist sci), 68. **CAREER** Asst prof hist sci, Univ Okla, 67-75; archivist, Libr, Cambridge Univ, 71-75; ASSOC PROF HIST & MECH ENG, IOWA STATE UNIV, 75-. **MEMBERSHIPS** Hist Sci Soc. **RESEARCH** Nineteenth century British science. **CONTACT ADDRESS** Dept of Hist, Iowa State Univ, Ames, IA, 50011-0002.

WILSON, DAVID L.
PERSONAL Born 06/04/1943, Fort Wayne, IN, 2 children **DISCIPLINE** AMERICAN HISTORY **EDUCATION** Univ Kans, BA, 65, MA, 67; Univ Tenn, PhD(hist), 74. **CAREER** Res, Ulysses S Grant Asn, 73-74; vis asst prof hist, Southern Ill Univ, Carbondale, 76-78; asst ed, 78-81, ASSOC ED, ULYSSES S GRANT ASN, 82-, Instr Am hist, John A Logan Col, 73-80; adj asst prof hist, Southern Ill Univ, Carbondale, 74-76 & 78-; Nat Hist Publ & Records Comt fel, 75-76; consult, US Dept State Hist Off, 79. **MEMBERSHIPS** Asn Doc Ed; Soc Historians Am For Rel; Orgn Am Historians. **RESEARCH** American Civil War era; Sino-American relations. **SELECTED PUBLICATIONS** Auth, The Lloyd Lewis-Bruce Catton research notes, Ulysses S Grant Asn, 73; coauth, The Presidency of Warren G Harding, Regents Press of Kans, 77; asst-ed, The Papers of Ulysses S Grant, Vol 8, April 1-July 6, 1863, 74, Vol 9, July 7-Dec 31, 1863, 82 & Vol 10, Jan 1-May 31, 1864, 82, Southern Ill Univ Press, 79; contribr, Encycl of Southern History, La State Univ Press, 79; coauth, Samuel H Beckwith: Grant's Shadow, Ulysses S Grant: Essays & Doc, 81; co-ed, Ulysses S Grant: Essays & Documents, Southern Ill Univ Press, 81. **CONTACT ADDRESS** Ulysses S Grant Asn, Southern Ill Univ, Carbondale, IL, 62901.

WILSON, GEORGE MACKLIN
PERSONAL Born 04/27/1937, Columbus, OH, m, 1960, 2 children **DISCIPLINE** MODERN JAPANESE HISTORY **EDUCATION** Princeton Univ, AB, 58; Harvard Univ, AM, 60, PhD(hist, Far Eastern lang), 65. **CAREER** Vis lectr Japanese hist, Univ Mich, 63-64; asst prof hist, Univ Ill, 64-67; assoc prof hist, 67-76, dir E Asian Studies Prog, 68-73, from assoc dean to dean int prog, 72-78, PROF HIST & E ASIAN LANG & CULT, IND UNIV, BLOOMINGTON, 76-, Res fel, Am Coun Learned Soc, 71; sr researcher, Fulbright-Hays, 71-72; ed adv Japanese hist, Encycl Britannica, 69-; consult, Ford Found, 74-80. **MEMBERSHIPS** AHA; Asn Asian Studies. **RESEARCH** Modern Japanese and Chinese history; comparative history. **SELECTED PUBLICATIONS** Auth, Japan Orient, Amer Hist Rev, Vol 0099, 94; Tokyo, Amer Hist Rev, Vol 0102, 97. **CONTACT ADDRESS** Dept of Hist, Indiana Univ, Bloomington, Bloomington, IN, 47405.

WILSON, GLEE EVERITT
PERSONAL Born 11/25/1935, Webb City, MO, m, 1959 **DISCIPLINE** ANCIENT HISTORY, ROMANIAN CIVILIZATION **EDUCATION** Univ Kans, BA, 59, MA, 63; Univ Washington, PhD(hist), 71. **CAREER** Asst prof hist, Okla State Univ, 66-69; asst prof, 69-79, ASSOC PROF HIST, KENT STATE UNIV, 79-, Coordr, Romanian Studies Prog, Kent State Univ. **MEMBERSHIPS** Archaeol Inst Am; Soc Romanian Studies; Am Asn Southeast Europ Studies. **RESEARCH** Athenian topography and monuments; Greek cities and shores of the Black Sea; Graeco-Roman world in the third century AD. **CONTACT ADDRESS** Dept of Hist, Kent State Univ, PO Box 5190, Kent, OH, 44242-0001.

WILSON, HAROLD STACY
PERSONAL Born 06/22/1935, Neva, TN, m, 2 children **DISCIPLINE** AMERICAN HISTORY **EDUCATION** King Col, BA, 57; John Hopkins Univ, MA, 59; Emory Univ, PhD, 66. **CAREER** Asst prof hist, Wesleyan Col, Ga, 63-66; asst prof, 66-68, Col Found grant, 67-68, Assoc Prof hist, Old Dominion Univ, 68-, Assoc ed, Textile Hist Rev, 62-64, ed, 64-66; assoc ed, Wesleyan Quart Rev, 64-67; Fulbright sr lectr, Comt Int Exchange of Persons, Taiwan, 71-72, Singapore, 78-80; coordr, First Ann Urban S Conf, 74-75, chair, local arrange, committ, SHA, 88; chair, hist dept, 91-98. **HONORS AND AWARDS** Sigma Delta Chi book award, 70. **MEMBERSHIPS** AHA; Southern Hist Asn; Civil War Hist Asn. **RESEARCH** Civil War and Reconstruction; American South; progressive era; Res proj, A Very Peculiar Institution: Cotton Manufacturing in the Slave States during the Era of the Civil War. **SELECTED PUBLICATIONS** Auth, Basil Manly: Apologist for slavocracy, Ala Rev, 1/62; The role of Carter Glass in the disfranchisement of the Virginia Negro, Historian, 1/69; McClure's Magazine and the Muckrakers, Princeton Univ, 70; President Jimmy Carter and a philosophy of the sea-- Mahonist Doctrines in a modern setting, Commentary, 12/78; The chastening of the imperial president, J Hist Soc, 6/79; Mary White Ovington, First Person Singular, Whiston, 80; Circulation and Survival: McClure's Magazine and the Strange Death of Muckraking Journalism, W IL Reg Stud, 88; contrib, The Historical Dictionary of the Progressive Era,1890-1920, Greenwood,88; Matthew Fontaine Maury, The Encyclopedia of Southern Culture, UNC Press, 89; The Cruise of the C.S.S. Alabama in Southeast Asian Waters, The Journ of Confed Hist, 90. **CONTACT ADDRESS** Dept of History, Old Dominion Univ, Norfolk, VA, 23529-0091. **EMAIL** hwilson@odu.edu

WILSON, IAN E.
PERSONAL Born 04/02/1943, Montreal, PQ, Canada **DISCIPLINE** HISTORY/ARCHIVAL STUDIES **EDUCATION** Queen's Univ, BA, 67, MA, 74. **CAREER** Univ archv, Queen's Univ, 70-76; archv, City Kingston, 72-76; prov archv, Sask Arch Bd, 76-86; chmn, Sask Heritage Adv Bd, 78-83; ARCHIVIST OF ONT, 86-; dir gen, Info Rsrc Mgt Div, Ont Ministry Cult Commun, 90-93; ADJ PROF, INFO STUD, UNIV TO-

RONTO, 93-. **HONORS AND AWARDS** Woodrow Wilson fel(hon), 67; W. Kaye Lamb Prize, 83. **MEMBERSHIPS** Secy & vice pres, Kingston Hist Soc, 67-76; pres, Ont Hist Soc, 75-76; Ont dir, Forum Young Can, 95-; pres, Champlain Soc, 95-. **SELECTED PUBLICATIONS** Coauth, Heritage Kingston, 73; coauth, Canadian Archives, 80; ed, Kingston City Hall, 75; ed, Regina Before Yesterday, 78. **CONTACT ADDRESS** Ontario Archives, 77 Grenville St, Unit 300, Toronto, ON, M5S 1B3.

WILSON, JAMES HUGH
PERSONAL Born 04/17/1934, Charleston, MO, m, 1958, 2 children **DISCIPLINE** MODERN EUROPEAN HISTORY **EDUCATION** Southeast Mo State Col, BSEd, 59; Univ Mo, MA, 60, PhD(hist), 66. **CAREER** Asst prof hist, Bemidji State Col, 66-68; ASSOC PROF HIST, NEWBERRY COL, 68-, CHMN, DEPT HIST, 72-, CHMN, DEPT EDUC, 81-. **MEMBERSHIPS** Soc French Hist Studies; AHA. **RESEARCH** Modern France; French revolutionary tribunal. **CONTACT ADDRESS** Dept of Hist, Newberry Col, Newberry, SC, 29108.

WILSON, JEAN C.
DISCIPLINE ART HISTORY **EDUCATION** The Johns Hopkins Univ, PhD, 84. **CAREER** Assoc prof/dir grad studies, SUNY Binghamton. **RESEARCH** Renaissance and early mod visual cult in Italy and Northern Europe (1300-1700); art markets and socio-economic circumstances of production. **SELECTED PUBLICATIONS** Auth, Painting in Bruges at the Close of the Middle Ages in Studies in Society and Visual Culture, The Pennsylvania State P; Adriaen Isenbrant and the Problem of his Oeuvre: Thoughts on Authorship, Style, and the Methodology of Connoisseurship, Oud Holland, 95; Enframing Aspirations: Albrecht Durer's Self-Portrait of 1493 in the Musee du Louvre, Gazette des Beaux-Arts, 95; Reflections on St Luke's Hand: Icons and the Nature of Aura in the Burgundian Low Countries during the Fifteenth Century in The Sacred Image, East and West, Univ IL P, 95. **CONTACT ADDRESS** SUNY Binghamton, PO Box 6000, Binghamton, NY, 13902-6000. **EMAIL** jcwilson@binghamton.edu

WILSON, JEFFREY R.
DISCIPLINE ECONOMICS **EDUCATION** University of West Indies, St Augustine, W.I., BA, Mathematics, 1977; Iowa State University, Ames, IA, MS, Statistics 1980, PhD, Statistics, 1984. **CAREER** Iowa State University, Ames, IA, graduate research assistant, 1980-83; Oklahoma State University, Stillwater, OK, visiting asst prof of statistics, 1983-84; ARIZONA STATE UNIVERSITY, TEMPE, AZ, asst professor of statistics, 1985-91, assoc prof of statistics, DIR OF INTERDISCIPLINARY PROGRAM IN STATISTICS, PROFESSOR OF ECONOMICS, currently. **HONORS AND AWARDS** Teaching Award, Golden Key Honor Society, Arizona State University; Faculty Research Development Award, College of Business, AZ, 1990; Outstanding Graduate Teaching Award, College of Business, AZ, 1986; Distinguished Service Award, Minority Student Affairs, Ames, IA, Iowa State Univ, 1983, Final Year Book Prize, Math & Econ, Univ of West Indies, 1977; Mathematics Scholarship, Univ of West Indies, 1974-77; George Washington Carver Achievement Award, Iowa State Alumni Assn, 1995. **MEMBERSHIPS** American Statistical Association, 1980; Royal Statistical Society, 1985. **CONTACT ADDRESS** Economics, Col of Bus, Arizona State Univ, Tempe, Tempe, AZ, 85287-3806.

WILSON, JOHN
DISCIPLINE HISTORY **EDUCATION** Northwestern Univ, PhD. **CAREER** Prof, Southern CA Col. **RESEARCH** Aviation hist; mil hist hist of Am for policy. **SELECTED PUBLICATIONS** Auth, A New Research Guide in History, Turbulence Aloft: The Civil Aeronautics Administration Amid Wars and Rumors of Wars, 1938-1953; Herbert Hoover and the Armed Forces; Forging the American Character: Readings in United States History. **CONTACT ADDRESS** Dept of Hist and Polit Sci, Southern California Col, 55 Fair Dr., Costa Mesa, CA, 92626.

WILSON, JOHN BARNEY
PERSONAL Born 03/12/1930, Gainesville, FL, m, 1952, 2 children **DISCIPLINE** RUSSIAN AND EUROPEAN HISTORY **EDUCATION** Univ Fla, BA, 53; Boston Univ, AM, 54, PhD(hist), 66. **CAREER** From instr to assoc prof, 57-73, PROF HIST, DePAUW UNIV, 73-, Great Lakes Col Asn res grant, USSR, 65; vis prof, Ill State Univ, summer, 68, Univ RI, summer, 72 & Butler Univ, summer 79. **MEMBERSHIPS** AHA; Am Asn Advan Slavic Studies; Midwest Asn Latin Am Studies. **RESEARCH** Soviet and 19th century Russian history; Central Asia; eastern Europe. **CONTACT ADDRESS** Dept of Hist, DePauw Univ, Greencastle, IN, 46135.

WILSON, JOHN ELBERT
PERSONAL m **DISCIPLINE** CHURCH HISTORY **EDUCATION** Emory Univ, BA, 64; Drew Univ, MDiv, 67; Claremont Grad Univ, PhD, 75. **CAREER** PD, church hist, Univ of Basel, Switzerland, 83-84; PROF OF CHURCH HIST, PITTSBURGH THEOLOGICAL SEMINARY, 84-. **MEMBERSHIPS** Am Acad of Relig; Am Soc of Church Hist; Int Schelling Soc. **SELECTED PUBLICATIONS** Auth, Schellings Mythologie. Zur Auslegung der Philosophie der Mythologie und der Offenbarung, Frommann-Holzboog, 93; auth, Schelling und Nietzsche. Zur Auslegung der freuhen Werke Friedrich Nietzsches, W. de Gruyter, 96. **CONTACT ADDRESS** Pittsburgh Theol Sem, 616 N Highland Ave, Pittsburgh, PA, 15206-2596. **EMAIL** jewilson@pts.edu

WILSON, JOHN FREDERICK
PERSONAL Born 04/01/1933, Ipswich, MA, m, 1954, 4 children **DISCIPLINE** AMERICAN RELIGIOUS HISTORY **EDUCATION** Harvard Col, AB, 54; Union Theol Sem, NY, MDiv, 57, PhD, 62. **CAREER** Lectr relig, Barnard Col, 57-58; from instrto prof, 60-77,asst dean, 65-72, chmn dept, 74-81, COLLORD PROF RELIG, PRINCETON UNIV, 77-, Mem bd dirs, Union Theol Sem, NY, 77-. **MEMBERSHIPS** AHA; Am Soc Church Hist (pres, 76); Soc Values Higher Educ; Asn Document Editing; Am Studies Asn. **RESEARCH** Puritan studies; religion in American history; Jonathan Edwards. **SELECTED PUBLICATIONS** Auth, The Churching of America, 1776-1990, J Church and State, Vol 0035, 93; When Time Shall be no More, J Interdisciplinary Hist, Vol 0024, 94; A New Denominational Historiography + The Importance of Continuing Study of Denominations for American Religious History, Relig and Amer Culture J of Int, Vol 0005, 95; Cosmos in the Chaos, Theol Today, Vol 0053, 96; Religious Melancholy and Protestant Experience in America, J Interdisciplinary Hist, Vol 0026, 96; The Politics of Revelation and Reason, J Interdisciplinary Hist, Vol 0028, 97. **CONTACT ADDRESS** Dept of Relig, Princeton Univ, 13 1879 Hall, Princeton, NJ, 08544.

WILSON, JOSEPH F.
PERSONAL Born 12/02/1951, Chicago, Illinois, m, 1984 **DISCIPLINE** POLITICAL SCIENCE **EDUCATION** Columbia College, New York, NY, BA, 1973; Columbia University, New York, NY, MA, 1975, MPh, 1978, PhD, 1980. **CAREER** Rutgers University, New Brunswick, NJ, assistant professor, 1980-86; Brooklyn College, Brooklyn, NY, associate professor, 1986-94, prof, 1994-; Brooklyn Coll Center for Diversity and Multicultural Education, currently. **HONORS AND AWARDS** Distinguished Tow Professor of Political Science, 1993-95. **MEMBERSHIPS** Director, Brooklyn College Multicultural Center, 1990-95; appoints committee, Political Sceince Dept, 1989-95; executive committee, Black Faculty & Staff Association, 1987-95. **SELECTED PUBLICATIONS** Author, Tearing Down the Color Bar, Columbia University Press, 1989, The Re-education of The American Working Class, Greenwood Press, 1990, Black Labor in America, Greenwood Press, 1986. **CONTACT ADDRESS** Political Science Dept, Brooklyn Col, CUNY, James Hall, Brooklyn, NY, 11210.

WILSON, LEONARD GILCHRIST
PERSONAL Born 06/11/1928, Orillia, ON, Canada, m, 1969, 1 child **DISCIPLINE** HISTORY OF MEDICINE **EDUCATION** Univ Toronto, BA, 49; Univ London, MSc, 55; Univ Wis, PhD(hist of sci), 58. **CAREER** Vis instr, Univ Calif, Berkeley, 58-59; asst prof, Cornell Univ, 59-60; from asst prof to assoc prof hist of sci & med, Yale Univ, 60-67; prof hist of med & head dept, 67-98, prof emer hist of med, Univ Minn, Minneapolis, 98-; ed, J Hist Med & Allied Sci, 73-. **MEMBERSHIPS** AAAS; Am Asn Hist Med; Int Acad Hist Sci; Geol Soc Am; Brit Soc Hist Sci. **RESEARCH** Charles Lyell, history of concepts of fever; history of physiology. **SELECTED PUBLICATIONS** Coauth, Selected Readings in the History of Physiology, C C Thomas, 66; auth, Sir Charles Lyell's Scientific Journals on the Species Question, 70 & Charles Lyell, the Years to 1841: The Revolution in Geology, 72, Yale Univ; ed, Benjamin Silliman and His Circle, Sci Hist Publ, 79; auth, Medical Revolution in Minnesota, St. Paul Midewiwin Press, 89; Lyell in Amica: Transatlantic Geology, 1841-1853, Johns Hopkins Univ Press, 98. **CONTACT ADDRESS** Dept of Hist of Med, 420 Delaware St SE, Minneapolis, MN, 55455-0374. **EMAIL** wilso004@maroon.tc.umn.edu

WILSON, LEWIS
DISCIPLINE HISTORY **EDUCATION** Univ CA at Berkeley, PhD. **CAREER** Prof, Southern CA Col. **SELECTED PUBLICATIONS** Auth, A History of the Western World, Revive Us Again; contrib(s) to, Dictionary of the Pentecostal & Charismatic Movement. **CONTACT ADDRESS** Dept of Hist and Polit Sci, Southern California Col, 55 Fair Dr., Costa Mesa, CA, 92626.

WILSON, LISA H.
DISCIPLINE HISTORY **EDUCATION** Franklin and Marshall Col, BA; Temple Univ, MA, PhD. **CAREER** Assoc prof; Conn Col, 87-; past actg dir, Gender and Women's Stud Prog, Conn Col. **HONORS AND AWARDS** Richard L. Morton awd; Andrew W. Mellon Fac fel Hum, Harvard Univ & Charles Warren Ctr fel, Harvard Univ. **RESEARCH** Early Amer hist; Gender studies. **SELECTED PUBLICATIONS** Auth, Life After Death: Widows in Pennsylvania, 1750-1850, 91; A 'Man of Business': The Widow of Means in Southeastern Pennsylvania, 1750-1850, William and Mary Quart, 87. **CONTACT ADDRESS** Dept of History, Connecticut Col, 270 Mohegan Ave, Box 5526, New London, CT, 06320. **EMAIL** lhwil@conncoll.edu B1282. University of Wisconsin-Stevens Point URL: http://www.uwsp.edu/ University of Wisconsin-Stevens Point Stevens Point, WI 54481 Phone: 715-346-0123 Direct comments to webmaster@uwsp.edu

WILSON, MAJOR L.
PERSONAL Born 08/26/1926, Vilonia, AR, m, 1956, 2 children **DISCIPLINE** UNITED STATES SOCIAL AND INTELLECTUAL HISTORY **EDUCATION** Vanderbilt Univ, BA, 50; Univ Ark, MA, 53; Univ Kans, PhD(hist), 64. **CAREER** Assoc prof, 64-67, assoc prof, 67-70, PROF HIST, MEMPHIS STATE UNIV, 70-. **MEMBERSHIPS** Southern Hist Asn; Orgn Am Historians; Soc Historians Early Am Repub. **RESEARCH** United States intellectual history, 1800-1865; Jacksonian period. **SELECTED PUBLICATIONS** Auth, The concept of time and the political dialogue in the United States, 1828-1848, winter 67 & The free soil concept of progress and the irrepressible conflict, winter 70, Am Quart; The repressible conflict: Seward's concept of progress and the free-soil movement, J Southern Hist, 11/71; Space, Time and Freedom: The Quest for Nationality and the Irrepressible Conflict, Greenwood, 74; Paradox lost: order and progress in evangelical thought, Church Hist, 75; The Presidency of Martin Van Buren, Kansas, 82. **CONTACT ADDRESS** Dept of Hist, Memphis State Univ, Memphis, TN, 38152.

WILSON, MARY C.
DISCIPLINE HISTORY **EDUCATION** Oxford Univ, PhD, 84. **CAREER** Prof, Univ MA Amherst . **SELECTED PUBLICATIONS** Auth, King Abdullah Britain and the Making of Jordan, 87; The Modern Middle East: A Reader, 94. **CONTACT ADDRESS** Dept of Hist, Univ Massachusetts Amherst, Mass Ave, Amherst, MA, 01003.

WILSON, MICHAEL
DISCIPLINE HISTORY **EDUCATION** Cornell Univ, PhD, 93. **CAREER** Asst prof. **RESEARCH** Modern European cultural; intellectual and social history; history of gender and sexuality; historiography. **SELECTED PUBLICATIONS** Auth, Consuming History: The Nation, the Past and the Commodity of L'Exposition Universelle de 1900, Am Jour Semiotics, 91; Gender and Transgression in Bohemian Montmartre, Routlege, 91; Lessons of the Master: The Artist and Sexual Identity in Henry James, Henry James Rev, 93. **CONTACT ADDRESS** Dept of History, Richardson, TX, 75083-0688. **EMAIL** mwilson@utdallas.edu

WILSON, PATRICIA I.
PERSONAL Born 06/07/1940, Belmont, North Carolina, m, 1961 **DISCIPLINE** EDUCATION **EDUCATION** North Carolina A&T State University, Greensboro, NC, BS, 1961; University of Kentucky, Lexington, KY, MA, 1979, EdD, 1984. **CAREER** Morris Township Junior High, Morristown, NJ, teacher, 1963-65; Roxbury High, Succasunna, NJ, teacher, 1965-67; Morris Hills Regional High, Rockaway, NJ, teacher, 1968-71; Central High, Joliet, IL, teacher, 1972-73; Davenport West High School, Davenport, IA, teacher, 1974-77; University of Kentucky, Lexington, KY, instructor, 1979-81; Eastern Kentucky Univ, Richmond, KY, assistant professor, 1981-85; University of Kentucky, Lexington, KY, assistant professor, 1985-92; Alabama A&M University, associate professor, 1992-. **HONORS AND AWARDS** President's Award, ARMA, 1986-87; Outstanding Researcher Award, A & M School of Business, 1994. **MEMBERSHIPS** President, Delta Pi Epsilon, 1988-90; president, Association of Records Managers Administrators, 1988-89; secretary/treasurer, Phi Delta Kappa, 1990-91, membership vice pres, 1991-92; secretary, Alabama Business Ed Assn, 1994-, pres elect, 1996-97; treasurer, Gamma Nu chapter, Delta Pi Epsilon, 1997-; president, Alabama Business Educator Assoc, 1998-; pres, Alabama Business Education Assn, 1998-; editor, Southern Business Education Assn Newsletter, 1999-. **CONTACT ADDRESS** Alabama A&M Univ, PO Box 429, Normal, AL, 35762.

WILSON, RICHARD GUY
PERSONAL Born 05/16/1940, m, 2 children **DISCIPLINE** HISTORY OF ARCHITECTURE; ART HISTORY **EDUCATION** Univ Co, BA, 63; Univ Mi, MA, 68, PhD, 72. **CAREER** Teaching asst hist of art, Univ Mich, 69 & 70; from asst prof to assoc prof archit, Ia State Univ, 72-76; Assoc Prof Commonwealth Prof Archit Hist, Univ Va, 76 & Chemn Archit Hist, 79-, NSF res grant, 74; Iowa State Design Ctr grant, 73-74 & 75; Iowa Arts Coun, Nat Endowment Arts grant, 75-76; asst ed newslett, Soc Archit Historians, 75-78; guest cur, Brooklyn Mus, 77-80; Univ Va res grant, 78; Am Philos Soc res grant, 81; vis lectr, Polytechnic South Bank, London, 81. **HONORS AND AWARDS** Phi Beta Phi, 70, Hon mem AIA, 86; Am Hist Asn, Pac Coast Br, Best Article, 86; W Hist Asn, Best Article, 86; Charles Montgomery Prize, Most Distinguished Contrib Decorative Arts Soc, 87; Best Book of Year, Am Libr Asn, 87; Soc of Archit Hist Catalogue Award, 93; Award Excellence, 93; Best Essay of Year, S Libr Asn, 93. **MEMBERSHIPS** Soc Archit Historians; Nat Trust Hist Preserv; Col Art Asn. **RESEARCH** The architecture of McKim, Mead and White; the American Renaissance; design in the 1920s and 1930s. **SELECTED PUBLICATIONS** The Making of Virginia Architecture, Univ Va, 92; Thomas Jefferson's Academical Village: The Making of an Architectural Masterpiece, Univ Va, 93. **CONTACT ADDRESS** Dept Archit Hist, Univ Va, Campbell Hall, Charlottesville, VA, 22903. **EMAIL** rgw4h@virginia.edu

WILSON, ROBERT ARDEN
PERSONAL Born 07/17/1910, Des Moines, IA, m, 1940, 3 children **DISCIPLINE** HISTORY **EDUCATION** Willamette Univ, BA, 39; Univ Wash, MA, 42, PhD, 49. **CAREER** Instr US & Far Eastern hist, Willamette Univ, 39-41; from instr to assoc prof, 49-72, prof far eastern hist, 72-80, EMER PROF HIST, UNIV CALIF, LOS ANGELES, 80-, Fulbright res scholar, Japan, 52-53. **MEMBERSHIPS** Asn Asian Studies; AHA. **RESEARCH** Japanese political history, especially late Tokugawa and early Meiji periods. **SELECTED PUBLICATIONS** Auth, Genesis of the Meiji Government, Univ Calif; J of Henry Heusken, Rutgers, 63. **CONTACT ADDRESS** Dept of Hist, Univ of Calif, Los Angeles, CA, 90024.

WILSON, ROBERT SYDNEY
PERSONAL Born 07/23/1943, Moncton, NB, Canada, m, 1965, 2 children **DISCIPLINE** HISTORY **EDUCATION** Gordon Col, BA, 64; Univ Guelph, MA, 67, PhD(Brit hist), 73. **CAREER** Lectr Brit hist, Univ Guelph, 70-71; LECTR HIST & DEAN ARTS, ATLANTIC BAPTIST COL, 71-. **MEMBERSHIPS** Am Soc Church Hist; Can Soc Church Hist; Conf Faith & Hist. **RESEARCH** Nineteenth century British history; nineteenth and twentieth century Atlantic Baptist history. **SELECTED PUBLICATIONS** Contribr, Thirty-six articles, In: New International Dictionary of the Christian Church, Zondervan, 74; auth, The decline of preaching, Atlantic Baptist, 74; Alexander Crawford, In: Scottish Tradition, Univ Guelph, Ont, 82. **CONTACT ADDRESS** Atlantic Baptist Col, Salisbury Rd, Box 1004, Moncton, NB, E1C 8P4.

WILSON, RUDOLPH GEORGE
PERSONAL Born 06/17/1935, River Rouge, Michigan, m **DISCIPLINE** EDUCATION **EDUCATION** Los Angeles City Coll, AA, BA 1962, MA 1964; Washington Univ, PhD **CAREER** Southern Illinois Univ, assoc prof 1975-; Second Educ, lecturer 1969-72; Claremont High School, English teacher dept chmn 1964-69, master English teacher 1967-69; Juv Hall Couns 1961-63; Consult Affect Educ Drug Use & Abuse, Moral Educ, Val Educ, Ald Psychology, Methods of Teaching, Adult Educ, Flex Schedule, Humanistic Educ, Motiv of Reluctant Learner, English Educ, Supvr of Student Teachers, Teaching Learn Ctrs, Disc in the Sec Schools, Parent Effect Train, Transact Analy, Devel Teacher Compet; Southern IL Univ, dept chairperson curriculum instructor/prof, currently. **HONORS AND AWARDS** Teaching Excellence Award 1971; Great Teacher Award 1974; Danforth Leadership Award; Danforth Fellow; Kimmel Leadership Award; Martin Luther King Award; St Louis American Outstanding Educator Award. **MEMBERSHIPS** Mem Kappa Alpha Psi; funder, pres Southern IL Adoptive Parents Assn; bd mem Sr Citizens Inc; bd mem SW IL Area Agency on Aging; mem Edwardsville Dist 7 Bd of Educ 1972-; past pres Natl Assn for African Educ 1970-71; pres Faculty Sen, Southern IL Univ 1975-76; elected mem Pres Search Com, SIUE; vice pres Business Affairs Search Com; chmn Search Com for vice pres for student affairs. **SELECTED PUBLICATIONS** Auth, "Inner City Teaching Training Program" Office of Educ Journal 1972 **CONTACT ADDRESS** Professor, Southern Illinois Univ, Box 1122, Edwardsville, IL, 62026.

WILSON, THEODORE A.
PERSONAL Born 09/27/1940, Evansville, IN, m, 1962, 2 children **DISCIPLINE** UNITED STATES DIPLOMATIC HISTORY **EDUCATION** Ind Univ, AB, 62, MA, 63, PhD(hist), 66. **CAREER** Actg asst prof, 65-66, from asst prof to assoc prof, 66-73, chmn dept, 79-81, PROF HIST, UNIV KANS, 73-, ASSOC DEAN, COL LIB ARTS & SCI, 76-, Sr res assoc, Harry S Truman Libr Inst Nat & Int Affairs, 69-72; Nat Endowment for Humanities Younger fel, 71-72; Guggenheim fel, 72-73; vis prof Am hist, Univ Col, Dublin, 75-76; pres, Past & Present Inc, 79- **HONORS AND AWARDS** Francis Parkman Prize, Soc Am Historians, 69. **MEMBERSHIPS** Orgn Am Historians; AHA; Soc Historians Am Foreign Rels; Soc Am Historians. **RESEARCH** United States diplomacy, 1933-1953; history of the Second World War. **SELECTED PUBLICATIONS** Auth, Coalitions, Politicians and Generals, J Mil Hist, Vol 0060, 96. **CONTACT ADDRESS** Dept of Hist, Univ of Kans, Lawrence, KS, 66045.

WILSON, WILLIAM HENRY
PERSONAL Born 11/03/1935, St. Joseph, MO, m, 1960, 2 children **DISCIPLINE** UNITED STATES HISTORY **EDUCATION** Univ Mo, BJ, 57, MA, 58, PhD, 62. **CAREER** Instr, Univ Mo, 58-60; res assoc, Hist Kansas City Res Proj, 60-62; asst prof hist, Univ SDak, 62-63; from asst prof to assoc prof, Univ Alaska, 63-67; assoc prof, 68-75, PROF HIST, NTEX STATE UNIV, 75-90, REGENTS PROF HIST, 90-; Truman Libr Inst grant, 64; Am Philos Soc grant, 66 & 75; Am Asn State & Local Hist grant, 66; NEH Younger Scholars fel, 68. **HONORS AND AWARDS** Lewis Mumford Prize, 89. **MEMBERSHIPS** Orgn Am Historians; Southern Hist Asn; Soc Am City & Regional Planning; Tex State Hist Asn; Wash State Hist Asn. **RESEARCH** U S Urban history. **SELECTED PUBLICATIONS** Auth, The City Beautiful Movement in Kansas City, Univ Mo, 64; Coming of Age: Urban America, 1915-1945, Wiley, 74; Railroad in the Clouds: The Alaska Railroad in the Age of Steam, 1914-1945, Pruett, 77; The City Beautiful Movement, Johns Hopkins, 89; co-auth, Carl F Gould: A Life in Architecture in the Arts, Washington, 95; Hamilton Park: A Planned Black Community in Dallas, Johns Hopkins, 98. **CONTACT ADDRESS** Dept of Hist, No Texas State Univ, P O Box 310650, Denton, TX, 76203-0650. **EMAIL** bwilson@unt.edu

WILSON, WILLIAM JERRAM
PERSONAL Born 06/04/1928, Salt Lake City, UT, m, 1959, 2 children **DISCIPLINE** ARABIC, MIDDLE EAST HISTORY **EDUCATION** Univ UT, BA, 46, MA, 59, PhD, 65. **CAREER** Asst prof, 65-70, actg head dept, 76-77, 88-89, ASSOC PROF NEAR EASTERN STUDIES, UNIV AZ, 70-; Univ Az subsistence & travel res grant, 66, res grant, 68; vis asst prof Arabic, Univ UT, 67. **MEMBERSHIPS** Mid E Studies Asn; Am Asn Teachers Arabic; Royal Asiatic Soc. **RESEARCH** Arabic contribution to the life sciences. **CONTACT ADDRESS** Dept of Near Eastern Studies, Univ AZ, Franklin 509, Tucson, AZ, 85721-0001. **EMAIL** wjw@u.arizona.edu

WILT, ALAN FREESE
PERSONAL Born 05/14/1937, Nappanee, IN, m, 1963, 2 children **DISCIPLINE** MODERN EUROPEAN HISTORY **EDUCATION** DePauw Univ, BA, 59; Univ Mich, MA, 60, PhD(hist), 69. **CAREER** Instr hist, Midwestern Univ, 61-62; from instr to asst prof, 67-76, assoc prof, 76-81, PROF HIST, IOWA STATE UNIV, 81-, Vis prof, Air War Col, 82-83. **MEMBERSHIPS** AHA; Conf Group Cent Europ Hist; Am Comt Hist 2nd World War; Western Asn Ger Studies. **RESEARCH** Twentieth century Europe; military history; German history. **SELECTED PUBLICATIONS** Auth, Hitler Panzers East, Amer Hist Rev, Vol 0098, 93; Riviera to the Rhine, J Mil Hist, Vol 0057, 93; Churchill, J Mod Hist, Vol 0066, 94; D-Day June 6, 1944, Amer Hist Rev, Vol 0100, 95; Why the Allies Won, J Mil Hist, Vol 0060, 96; Frontsoldaten, Amer Hist Rev, Vol 0102, 97. **CONTACT ADDRESS** Dept of Hist, Iowa State Univ, Ames, IA, 50011-0002.

WILTENBURG, JOY
DISCIPLINE EARLY MODERN EUROPE AND WOMEN'S HISTORY **EDUCATION** Univ Rochester, BA; Univ Va, PhD, 84. **CAREER** Instr, Rowan Col of NJ. **RESEARCH** Social history, especially in early modern Germany and England. **SELECTED PUBLICATIONS** Published a book and several articles on social history in early modern Germany and England. **CONTACT ADDRESS** Rowan Col of NJ, Glassboro, NJ, 08028-1701.

WILTSHIRE, SUSAN FORD
PERSONAL Born 10/13/1941, Amarillo, TX, m, 1969, 2 children **DISCIPLINE** CLASSICS **EDUCATION** Univ Texas, Austin, BA, 63; Columbia Univ, MA, 64, PhD, 67. **CAREER** Asst prof classics, Univ Ill, Champaign-Urbana, 67-69; asst prof English & dir Honors Program, Fisk Univ, 69-71; asst prof to prof classics, 71- , chemn Dept of Class Stud, 89-95, Vanderbilt Univ. **HONORS AND AWARDS** Phi Beta Kappa; Woodrow Wilson Fel, Dissertation Fel, 63-64, 66-67; Madison Sarratt Prize for Excellence in Undergrad Tchg, 79; Phi Beta Kappa Assoc Lctr Panel, 91-92, 92-93; listed in Contemp Auth; Alex Haley Mem Award, 93; Overall Award of Excellence, So Books Competition, 98. **MEMBERSHIPS** Nat Coun on Hum; Am Philol Asn; Class Asn of the Middle West and South; Overseers' Comm to Visit the Dept of Classics, Harvard Univ, 96-99; Int Bonhoeffer Soc. **RESEARCH** Latin poetry; Greek epic and drama; the classical tradition in America. **SELECTED PUBLICATIONS** Auth, Seasons of Grief and Grace: A Sister's Story of AIDS, Vanderbilt, 94; coauth, Classical Nashville: Athens of the South, Vanderbilt, 96; auth, The Authority of Experience, in Hallett, ed, Compromising Traditions: The Personal Voice in Classical Scholarship, Routledge, 97; auth, Athena's Disguises: Mentors in Everyday Life, John Knox, 98; ed, Prairie Laureate: The Collected Poems of Robert Lee Brothers, Eakin, 98. **CONTACT ADDRESS** Vanderbilt Univ, PO Box 18 Station B, Nashville, TN, 37235. **EMAIL** Susan.F.Wiltshire@vanderbilt.edu

WINCH, JULIE P.
DISCIPLINE HISTORY **EDUCATION** Cambridge, BA, 75; London, MA, 76; Bryn Mawr, MA, 79, PhD, 82. **CAREER** Assoc prof History and Black Studies, Univ Mass, Boston. **RESEARCH** Black studies, American free blacks, emigration to Haiti. **SELECTED PUBLICATIONS** Fel Publ, Philadelphia's Black Elite: Activism, Accommodation, and the Struggle for Autonomy, 88; auth, Philadelphia and the Other Underground Railroad, Penn Mag of Hist and Biog 3, 87; Virginia Pindell Trotter, Trotter Inst Rev 2,88; auth, paper, American Free Blacks and Emigration to Haiti, Eleventh Carib Cong, Carib Inst and Stud Ctr for Latin Amer, 88; You Have Talents - Only Cultivate Them: Philadelphia's Black Female Literary Societies and the Abolitionist Crusade, In: The Abolitionist Sisterhood: Women's Political Culture in Antebellum America, Cornell Univ, 94. **CONTACT ADDRESS** Dept of History, Univ Massachusetts, 100 Morrissey Blvd., Boston, MA, 02125. **EMAIL** winch@umbsky.cc.umb.edu.

WIND, BARRY
DISCIPLINE ART HISTORY **EDUCATION** City Col NY, BA, 62; Univ NY, MA, 64, PhD, 72. **CAREER** Asst instr, Rutgers, 65-66; asst prof, Univ Ga, 67-71; asst prof, 71-77; assoc prof, Univ Wis, 77-87; vis assoc prof, Newberry Libr, 85; prof, 87-. **HONORS AND AWARDS** Distinguished Schr Awd. **SELECTED PUBLICATIONS** Auth, Genre in the Age of the Baroque, Garland, 91; Piccolo Ridicolo: A Little Bit on Bocchi, 94; A Quaker in Jan Steen, 95. **CONTACT ADDRESS** Dept of Art History, Univ of Wisconsin, Milwaukee, PO Box 413, Milwaukee, WI, 53201.

WINDSOR-LISCOMBE, RHODRI
PERSONAL Born 02/05/1946, Rhiwbina, Wales, m, 1990, 2 children **DISCIPLINE** ART HISTORY **EDUCATION** Clifton Col, Univ of London, BA, PhD, 72. **CAREER** Lectr, Univ London, extra-mural stud, 68-74; asst prof, McGill Univ, 74-76; asst, assoc, prof, Univ British Columbia, 76- . **HONORS AND AWARDS** Campden Charities Scholar, 68-72; fel, Soc of Antiquaries; sr fel, Green Col, Univ British Columbia; Vancouver Book Award, Int Writers Festival, 98. **MEMBERSHIPS** Soc for Stud of Archit in Canada; Soc of Archit Hist; Walpole Soc. **RESEARCH** Eighteenth to twentieth century architecture engineering and design; history of art and architecture in Europe and North America, Renaissance to modern; modernism in architecture and design. **SELECTED PUBLICATIONS** Auth, William Wilkins, Cambridge, 80; coauth, Francis Rattenbourg and British Columbia, British Columbia, 83; auth, The Church Architecture of Robert Mills, Southern Historical, 85; auth, Nationalism or Cultural Imperialism: The Chateau Style in Canada, Archit Hist, 93; auth, Altogether American: Robert Mills Architect and Engineer, Oxford, 94; auth, The New Spirit Modern Architecture in Vancouver, 1938-1965, Canadian Center for Architecture, MIT, 97; auth, A Cultural Archaeology of the Greek Revival, Choice, 99. **CONTACT ADDRESS** Dept of Fine Arts, Univ of British Columbia, 6333 Memorial Rd, Vancouver, BC, V6T 1W5. **EMAIL** iisgp@mowry.ubc.ca

WINELAND, JOHN D.
PERSONAL Born 11/09/1958, Gary, IN, m, 1993, 1 child **DISCIPLINE** ANCIENT HISTORY, ARCHAEOLOGY **EDUCATION** Valparaiso Univ, BS, 80; Cincinnati Christian Sem, MA, 87, MDiv, 88; Miami Univ, MA, 88, PhD, 96. **CAREER** Assoc prof, Bibl Stud and Archaeol, Roanoke Bible Col, 95-98; assoc prof Hist, Ky Christian Col, 98- ; adj instr, Cincinnati Bible Col, 91, 94; adj instr, N Ky Univ, 93-94; adj instr, Miami Univ, Middletown Campus, 91-94, Hamilton Campus, 91-94. **HONORS AND AWARDS** Who's who of Bibl Stud and Archael, 1993; Grad Acievement Awd, Miami Univ, 89-90; Endow BiblRes Travel Grant, 88, 90; Editor, Near East Archaeol Soc Bulletin, 96- ; Trustee, near East Archaeol Soc, 92- . **MEMBERSHIPS** AHA; ASOR; NEAS; CFH; AAH; SBL; IBR. **RESEARCH** Near Eastern History and Archaeology. **SELECTED PUBLICATIONS** Auth, Area A, Tell Abil: Preliminary Report of the 1988 Excavation Season, Near East Archaeological Soc Bull, 32-33, Winter 89; The 1990 Excavation Season Area A Tell Abil: Preliminary Report, Near East Archaeol Soc Bull, 35-36, winter 90; The Sixthe Season of Excavation, Area A, Tell Abila: Area Supervisor Preliminary Report, Near East Archaeol Soc Bull, 38, 93, 2-10; Tiberius, in Historic World Leaders, vol 3, 1250-1253, Detroit, Gale, 94; Anchor Bible Dictionary, 18 minor entries, including: Adramyttium, Amphipolis; Attalia; Beroea; Cauda; Cimmerians; Derbe; Fair Havens; Forum of Appius; Lasea; Mitylene; Patara; Phaselius; Thegium; Salome; Samos; Sepharad; Three Taverns, New York, Doubleday, 92; Archaeological and Numismatic Evidence of Greco-Roman Religions of the Decapolis, with Particular Emphasis on Gerasa and Abila, ARAM, 4, 92, 329-342, proceedings frfrom the Third Intl Conf of ARAM Soc for Syro-Mesopotamian Stud, The Oriental Inst, Univ Oxford, Eng; Oxford Encyclopedia of Near Eastern Archaeology, two biographical entries, K. A.C. Creswell, George Adam Smith, New York, Oxford Univ Press, 97. **CONTACT ADDRESS** Dept of History, Kentucky Christian Col, 100 Academic Pkwy, Grayson, KY, 41143-2205. **EMAIL** wineland@email.kcc.edu

WINES, ROGER
DISCIPLINE HISTORY **EDUCATION** Columbia Univ, PhD **CAREER** Prof, Fordham Univ. **SELECTED PUBLICATIONS** Auth, Enlightened Despotism: Reform or Reaction?, Heath, 67; ed, Leopold von Ranke's The Secret of World History: Selected Writings on the Art and Science of History Fordham UP, 81; publ, articles on the hist of the Bronx. **CONTACT ADDRESS** Dept of Hist, Fordham Univ, 113 W 60th St, New York, NY, 10023.

WINGARD, EDWARD L.
DISCIPLINE EDUCATION **EDUCATION** Miami Univ, BS; MEd; Ohio State Univ, PhD. **CAREER** Prof. **SELECTED PUBLICATIONS** Auth, The Experience of Historically Black Colleges in Serving Diversely Prepared Students, 82; Annual Meeting, 81; Self-Study Report, National Council for Accreditation of Teacher Education, Central State Univ, 82. **CONTACT ADDRESS** Dept of Education, Union Inst, 440 E McMillan St, Cincinnati, OH, 45206-1925.

WINK, ANDRE
PERSONAL Born 09/18/1953, Hollandia, Netherlands, s **DISCIPLINE** HISTORY **EDUCATION** PhD, Univ Leiden, Netherlands, 94. **CAREER** Prof, hist, Univ Wisc Madison, 89-.

HONORS AND AWARDS CSC Huygens award, Netherlands. **RESEARCH** South and southeast Asia. **SELECTED PUBLICATIONS** Auth, Al-Hind: The making of the Indo-Islamic world, vol 1-2, 90-97. **CONTACT ADDRESS** Dept. of History, Univ of Wisconsin, 3211 Humanities Bldg., 455 North , Madison, WI, 53706. **EMAIL** awink@macc.wisc.edu

WINKLE, KENNETH
DISCIPLINE U. S. 19TH CENTURY HISTORY **EDUCATION** Univ Wis, Madison, PhD, 84. **CAREER** Assoc prof, Univ Nebr, Lincoln. **HONORS AND AWARDS** Cora Friedline fac summer fel, 91; NEH summer stipend, 92. **RESEARCH** Social history of Abraham Lincoln and his Illinois roots. **SELECTED PUBLICATIONS** Auth, The Politics of Community: Migration and Politics in Antebellum Ohio, Cambridge UP, 88. **CONTACT ADDRESS** Univ Nebr, Lincoln, 617 Oldfat, Lincoln, NE, 68588-0417. **EMAIL** kwinkle@unlinfo.unl.edu

WINKLER, ALLAN M.
PERSONAL Born 01/07/1945, Cincinnati, OH, m, 2 children **DISCIPLINE** AMERICAN HISTORY **EDUCATION** Harvard Univ, BA, 66; Columbia Univ, MA, 67; Yale Univ, MPhil, 72, PhD, 74. **CAREER** Prof Hist, Miami Univ, 86- ; Vis Prof Hist, Univ Nairobi, Kenya, 95-96; Assoc Prof Hist, Univ Ore, 81-86; John Adams Prof Am Civ, Univ Amsterdam, 84-85; Asst Prof Hist, Univ Ore, 70-81; Bicent Prof Am Stud, Helsinki Univ, 78-79; Asst Prof Hist, Yale Univ, 75-78. **HONORS AND AWARDS** Dist Ed Award, Col Arts and Science, Miami Univ, 98; Sen Fulbright Lectureship, Univ Nairobi, Kenya, 95-96; Am Coun Ed Fellow Award, 91-92; Am Coun Learned Soc Travel Grant, Germany, 88; Outstanding Tchg Award, Miami Univ, 87-88; GTE Found Lectureship Prog Award, 88; Fulbright Chair, Netherlands, 84-85; Ore Comt for the Human Summer Res Fellow Award, 84; Nat Endow Human fellow, 81-82; Fulbright Travel Grant, Finland, 78-79. **MEMBERSHIPS** Am Hist Assoc; Org Am Hist; Am Stud Asn. **RESEARCH** 20th American history; Post-World War II US History; The World War II Period; The Nuclear Age. **SELECTED PUBLICATIONS** The Politics of Propaganda: The Office of War Information, 1942-1945, Yale Univ Press, 78; Modern America: The United States from World War II to the Present, Harper & Row, 85; Home Front, USA: America during World War II, Harlan Davidson, 86; Ed, The Recent Past: Readings on America Since World War II, Harper and Row, 89; The American People: Creating a Nation and a Society, Harper & Row, 86; Life Under a Cloud: American Anxiety about the Atom, Oxford Univ Press, 93; Cassie's War, Royal Fireworks Press, 94; America: Pathways to the Present, Prentice Hall, 96. **CONTACT ADDRESS** Dept of History, Miami Univ, Oxford, OH, 45056. **EMAIL** winkleam@muohio.edu

WINKLER, HENRY RALPH
PERSONAL Born 10/27/1916, Waterbury, CT **DISCIPLINE** HISTORY **EDUCATION** Univ Cincinnati, AB, 38, AM, 40; Univ Chicago, PhD, 47. **CAREER** From asst prof to assoc prof, Rutgers Univ, 47-58, chmn dept hist, 60-64, dean fac lib arts, 67-71, vprovost, 68, vpres acad affairs, 71-72, sr vpres acad affairs, 73-76, prof hist, 58-77, exec vpres, 76-77; exec vpres, 77, UNIV PROF HIST & PRES, UNIV CINCINNATI, 77-, Info analyst, Off War Info, 42-43; Fulbright vis prof, London Sch Econ, 53-54; vis prof, Bryn Mawr Col, 59-60; chmn Europ hist, Nat Col Entrance Exam, 60-64; fac mem, Hays Fels Summer Inst Humanities, Williams Col, 60, 62 & Colo Col, 61; managing ed, Am Hist Rev, 64-68; mem, Joint Comt Bibliog Aids to Hist, 66-; mem Comn Humanities in Schs, 67-; adv comt foreign copying, Libr Cong, 67-; mem bd trustees, Nat Humanities Fac, 69-, pres, 71-; mem exec comt, Nat Asn State Univ & Lang-Grant Col, 78-81; bd dirs, Am Coun Educ, 79-81. **HONORS AND AWARDS** Lindbach Award Distinguished Teaching, Rutgers Univ, 63., LittD, Lehigh Univ, Rutgers Univ & St Thomas Inst; LHD, NKy Univ, Hebrew Union Col & City Univ Manila; LLD, Xavier Univ. **MEMBERSHIPS** AHA; Orgn Am Historians; Conf Brit Studies. **RESEARCH** British diplomacy and foreign relations; British history in the nineteenth and twentieth centuries. **SELECTED PUBLICATIONS** Auth, National Crisis and National Government--British Politics, the Economy, and Empire, 1926-1932, Amer Hist Rev, Vol 0098, 93. **CONTACT ADDRESS** Off of the Pres, Univ of Cincinnati, Cincinnati, OH, 45221.

WINKLER, MARTIN M.
PERSONAL Born 05/24/1952, Germany **DISCIPLINE** CLASSICS **EDUCATION** Univ of Southern CA, PhD, 82 **CAREER** Lectr, Univ CA-Riverside, 81-82; asst prof, Univ Utah, 82-83; asst prof, Univ Wisconsin-Madison, 83-87; asst prof, Bucknell Univ, 87-89; assoc prof, prof, 89-, George Mason Univ **HONORS AND AWARDS** Mellon Found post doctoral research fel, 89-90 **MEMBERSHIPS** Amer Assoc of Univ Profs; Amer Philological Assoc; Classical Assoc of the Middle West and South; Vergician Soc of Amer **RESEARCH** Roman satire; classical tradion; classics and cinema **SELECTED PUBLICATIONS** Ed, Classics and Cinema, 91; auth, Der lateinische Eulenspiegel des Ioannes Nemius: Text und Ubersetzung, Kommentar und Untersuchungen, 95; Alogia and emphasis in Juvenal's Fourth Satire, Ramus: Critical Studies in Greek and Roman Literature, 95; Cinema and the Fall of Rome, Transactions of the American Philological Association, 95; Homeric Kleos and the Western Film, Syllecta Classica, 96; The Roman Empire in American Cinema After 1945, The Classical Journal, 98. **CONTACT ADDRESS** Dept of Modern and Classical Languages, George Mason Univ, Fairfax, VA, 22030. **EMAIL** mwinkler@osf1.gru.edu

WINKS, ROBIN WILLIAM EVERT
PERSONAL Born 12/05/1930, West Lafayette, Ind, m, 1952, 2 children **DISCIPLINE** COMPARATIVE IMPERIAL & DIPLOMATIC HISTORY **EDUCATION** Univ Colo, BA, 52, MA, 53; Johns Hopkins Univ, PhD, 57. **CAREER** Instr hist, Conn Col Women, 56-57; from instr to assoc prof, 57-67, Morse fel, 59-60, sr fac fel, 65-66, prof, 67-83, Randolph W. Townsend Jr. Prof, Yale Univ, 83-, ADV COMMONWEALTH HIST & LIT LIBR, 61-, MASTER, BERKELEY COL, 77-90, Vis lectr, Univ Alta, 59; fel, Berkeley Col, 59-; Soc Sci Res Coun grant, 59-60; Smith-Mundt vis prof, Univ Malaya, 62-63; vis prof, Univ Sydney, 63; State Dept lectr, Mid East, 66, W Africa, 72, E Africa, 74, Iran, 76, Europe, 81; mem, Fulbright Selection Comt, 67 & 72, chmn, 68; cult attache to Am Embassy, London, US Dept State, 69-71; adv State Dept, 71-; dir, off spec progs, Yale Univ, 74-76; mem, Marshall Comn, 76-; mem bd gov, Inst Soc & Policy Studies, Coun Foreign Rels; Guggenheim fel, 76-77; mem, Nat Park Serv adv bd, 80-, chmn, 81-. **HONORS AND AWARDS** Fel, Royal Hist Soc., MA, Yale Univ, 67; DLitt, Univ Nebr, 76. **MEMBERSHIPS** AHA; Orgn Am Historians; Can Hist Asn; Royal Commonwealth Soc; Athenaeum. **RESEARCH** Canadian-American diplomatic and cultural relations; Australia, New Zealand Britain in the Pacific; comparative history race relations. **SELECTED PUBLICATIONS** Auth, The Blacks in Canada, Yale Univ, 71; ed, Slavery: A Comparative Perspective, NY Univ, 72; auth, An American's Guide to Britain, Scribner's, 77; Other Voices, Other Views, Greenwood, 78; Western Civilization, 79 & Detective Fiction, 80, Prentice-Hall; The Relevance of Canadian History, Macmillan, 79; Modus Operandi, Godine, 82; auth, Cloak and Gown, Morrow, 87; auth, Asia in Western Language Fiction, Manchester, 90; auth, Frederick Billings, Oxford, 91; auth, Laurance S. Rockefells, Islad, 97. **CONTACT ADDRESS** Dept of Hist, Yale Univ, P O Box 208324, New Haven, CT, 06520-8324. **EMAIL** robin.winks@yale.edu

WINNIK, HERBERT CHARLES
PERSONAL Born 08/19/1938, Hartford, CT, m, 1994, 2 children **DISCIPLINE** HISTORY OF AMERICAN SCIENCE & THOUGHT **EDUCATION** Purdue Univ, BS, 60; Yale Univ, MA, 61; Univ Wis, Madison, PhD(Am hist), 68. **CAREER** Asst prof hist, Va Polytech Inst, 65-69; assoc prof hist, St Mary's Col, MD, 69-; consult to dean of arts & sci, Slippery Rock State Col, 68-. **MEMBERSHIPS** Orgn Am Historians; AHA; Soc Hist Sci; AAUP. **RESEARCH** American intellectual history; history of science and of American science. **SELECTED PUBLICATIONS** Auth, Summary View of AFOSR Solid State Science Program, Air Force Off Sci Res, 61; Science and Morality in TC Chamberlin, J Hist Ideas, 7-9/70; A Reconsideration of Henry A Rowland: The Man, Ann Sci, 6/72. **CONTACT ADDRESS** Dept Hist, St Mary's Col, Box 384, Leonardtown, MD, 20650. **EMAIL** hcwinnik@osprey.smcm.edu

WINPENNY, THOMAS REESE
PERSONAL Born 07/23/1941, Philadelphia, PA, m, 1967, 2 children **DISCIPLINE** AMERICAN ECONOMIC HISTORY **EDUCATION** Pa State Univ, University Park, BA, 64, MA, 65; Univ Del, PhD(hist), 72. **CAREER** From instr to asst prof, 68-74, assoc prof, 74-80, PROF HIST, ELIZABETHTOWN COL, 81-. **MEMBERSHIPS** Orgn Am Historians; Bus Hist Conf; Soc Historians Technol. **RESEARCH** Economic history; history of technology. **SELECTED PUBLICATIONS** Auth, In Service to American Pharmacy--The Professional Life of Procter, William, Pa Mag Hist and Biog, Vol 0117, 93; Early American Technology--Making and Doing Things from the Colonial Era To 1850, Pa Mag Hist and Biog, Vol 0119, 95. **CONTACT ADDRESS** Elizabethtown Col, Elizabethtown, PA, 17022.

WINQUIST, ALAN HANSON
PERSONAL Born 06/07/1942, Astoria, NY, s **DISCIPLINE** MODERN EUROPEAN, SCANDINAVIAN, AND AFRICAN HISTORY **EDUCATION** Wheaton Col, AB, 64; Northwestern Univ, MAT, 65; NY Univ, PhD, 76. **CAREER** Tchr soc studies, Grove Jr High Sch, IL, 64-65 & Weber Jr High Sch, NY, 66-67; teacher hist, Martin Luther High Sch, NY, 67-69; instr hist, Nassau Community Col, NY, 69-74; assoc prof, 74-80, prof hist, Taylor Univ, 80. **HONORS AND AWARDS** Tchg Excellence and Campus Leadership Award, The Sears Roebuck Found, 91. **MEMBERSHIPS** AHA; Conf Faith & Hist. **RESEARCH** Nineteenth and twentieth century South African and Scandinavian hist. **SELECTED PUBLICATIONS** Auth, Scandinavians and South Africa, A A Balkema, 78; Swedish American Landmarks: Where to Go and What to See, Swedish Coun Am, 95; coauth, God's Ordinary People. No Ordinary Heritage, Taylor Univ Press, 96. **CONTACT ADDRESS** Dept of Hist, Taylor Univ, 236 W Reade Ave, Upland, IN, 46989-1002. **EMAIL** alwinquis@tayloru.edu

WINSECK, DWAYNE
DISCIPLINE POLITICAL ECONOMY OF COMMUNICATION, MEDIA HISTORY **EDUCATION** Univ Oregon, PhD. **CAREER** Instr, universities in the People's Rep of China; US; Turkish Rep of N Cyprus; UK; assoc prof. **RESEARCH** Communication policy, theories of democracy and global communication. **SELECTED PUBLICATIONS** Co-ed, Democratizing Communication?: Comparative Perspectives on Information and Power, Hampton Press, 97; Media in Global Context, Edward Arnold, 97; Reconvergence: A Political Economy of Telecommunications in Canada, Hampton Press, 98; pub(s), several articles in the Can Jour of Commun; Gazette; Media, Cult and Soc; Information Soc; Europ Jour Commun. **CONTACT ADDRESS** Dept of Commun, Carleton Univ, 1125 Colonel By Dr, Ottawa, ON, K1S 5B6.

WINSHIP, PETER
PERSONAL Pensacola, FL, m, 1966, 2 children **DISCIPLINE** HISTORY; LITERATURE (18TH -20TH CENTURIES-EUROPE) **EDUCATION** Harvard, AB, 64, LLB, 68; London Univ, London Sch of Economics and political sci, LLM, 73. **CAREER** Lectr, 70-72, Addis Ababa Univ; 74-present, Southern Methodist Univ **MEMBERSHIPS** American Law Inst. **RESEARCH** Legal history; Comparative law; International law **SELECTED PUBLICATIONS** Auth, The U.N. Sales Convention and the Emerging Caselaw, in EMPTIO-VENDITIO INTER NATIONES: IN ANERKENNUNG FUR LEHRTATIGKEIT KARL HEINZ NEUMAYER, 97; auth, Selected Security Interests in the United States, Emerging Financial Markets and Secured Transactions, Kluwer, 98; auth, Karl Llewellyn in Rome, 98. **CONTACT ADDRESS** Dallas, TX, 75275-0116. **EMAIL** pwinship@mail.smu.edu

WINSLOW III, RICHARD E.
PERSONAL Born 12/21/1934, Boston, MA, s **DISCIPLINE** AMERICAN HISTORY **EDUCATION** Union Col, BS, 57; Univ NH, MA, 65; Pa State Univ, PhD, 70. **CAREER** Asst Prof, Pa State Univ, 70-71, Behrend Col, 71-77; Adjunct Assoc Prof, Univ Md, 78-79; Assoc Ed, Univ Ky, 79-81; Lib, Rochester Pub Lib, 81-83; Lib, Portsmouth Pub Lib, 83-. **HONORS AND AWARDS** Fellow, Civil War Rnd Table, 70. **MEMBERSHIPS** Portsmouth Marine Soc; Thoreau Soc; Melville Soc; Naval Hist Fnd. **RESEARCH** Marine/maritime/naval history; Henry David Thoreau; Herman Melville. **SELECTED PUBLICATIONS** Auth, Constructing Munitions of War: The Portsmouth Navy Yard Confronts the Confederacy, 1861-1865, Portsmouth Marine Soc, 95; contrib, various periodicals, including Portsmouth Herald, Historical New Hampshire. **CONTACT ADDRESS** 1 Harborview Dr, Rye, NH, 03870.

WINSOR, MARY PICKARD
PERSONAL Born 08/25/1943, New York, NY, m, 1975 **DISCIPLINE** HISTORY OF SCIENCE **EDUCATION** Radcliffe Col, AB, 65; Yale Univ, PhD(hist sci), 71. **CAREER** Lectr, 69-70, asst prof, 70-74, ASSOC PROF HIST BIOL, INST HIST & PHILOS SCI & TECHNOL, UNIV TORONTO, 74-. **MEMBERSHIPS** Hist Sci Soc; Can Soc Hist & Philos Sci. **RESEARCH** History of taxonomy; history of the Museum of Comparative Zoology at Harvard Univ; history of invertebrate zoology. **SELECTED PUBLICATIONS** Auth, An Agenda for Antiquity, Amer Hist Rev, Vol 0098, 93; The Expansion of American Biology, Isis, Vol 0084, 93; Haldane, J.B.S. Darwinism in its Religious Context, Brit J Hist Sci, Vol 0028, 95; The English Debate on Taxonomy and Phylogeny, 1937-1940, Hist and Philos of the Life Sci, Vol 0017, 95; Baird, Spencer of the Smithsonian, Amer Hist Rev, Vol 0100, 95. **CONTACT ADDRESS** Inst Hist and Philosophy Sci and Tech, Univ Toronto, Victoria Coll, 73 Queens, Toronto, ON, M5S 1K7. **EMAIL** mwinsor@chass.utoronto.ca

WINSTON, MICHAEL R.
PERSONAL Born 05/26/1941, New York, New York, m **DISCIPLINE** EDUCATION **EDUCATION** Howard Univ, BA 1962; Univ CA, MA 1964, PhD 1974. **CAREER** Howard Univ, instr 1964-66; Inst Serv Edn, exec asst & assoc dir 1965-66; Educ Asso Inc, educ consult 1966-68; Langston Univ, devel consult 1966-68; Howard Univ, asst dean liberal arts 1968-69, dir res hist dept 1972-73; Moorland-Spingarn Res Ctr, dir 1973-83; Howard Univ, vice pres academic affairs 1983-90, Alfred Harcourt Foundation, vice president, 1992-93, president, 1993-. **HONORS AND AWARDS** Fellow Woodrow Wilson Intl Ctr for Scholars-Smithsonian Inst 1979-80. **MEMBERSHIPS** Mem Amer Historical Assn, Assn Study Afro-Amer Life & Hist; co-author "Negro in the US"; co-editor "Dict Amer Negro Biography"; co-editor, Historical Judgements Reconsidered, 1988 **CONTACT ADDRESS** President, 8401 Colesville Rd, Ste 503, Silver Spring, MD, 20910.

WINT, ARTHUR VALENTINE NORIS
PERSONAL Born 10/26/1950, Kingston, Jamaica, m, 1971 **DISCIPLINE** CRIMINAL JUSTICE **EDUCATION** Washington State University, Pullman, WA, BA, 1973; University of Washington School of Law, Seattle, WA, JD, 1976; Harvard University, Institute for Educational Management, 1993. **CAREER** Evergreen Legal Services, Seattle, WA, legal asst, 1976-77; City of Seattle, Seattle, WA, eo investigator, 1977-79; Washington State University, Pullman, WA, dir of aff action,

1979-86; California State University, Fresno, Fresno, CA, asst to the president, dir of affirmative action, 1986-92; CALIF STATE UNIVERSITY, FRESNO, EXECUTIVE ASSISTANT TO PRES, 1992-; ASSOC PROF OF CRIMINOLOGY, 1991-. **HONORS AND AWARDS** Teaching Leadership Award, NAACP, Fresno, 1989; Pew Teaching Award, University of Washington, 1989; Senate Intern, Washington State Senate, 1972. **MEMBERSHIPS** Academy of Criminal Justice Sciences, American Association for Affirmative Action, director Region IX, 1990-91; Public Info Committee, 1988-90, director Region X, 1985-86; California Association of AA Officers, 1986-; board member, Golden Valley Girl Scouts, 1987-90; NAACP, 1976-; Church of Christ, 1975-; Central California Employment, round table, 1989-. **CONTACT ADDRESS** Human Resources, California State Univ, Fresno, 5150 N Maple Ave, Fresno, CA, 93740-0041.

WINTER, JAY MURRAY
PERSONAL Born 05/28/1945, Merrick, NY, m, 1970 **DISCIPLINE** SOCIAL HISTORY **EDUCATION** Columbia Univ, BA, 66; Cambridge Univ, PhD(hist), 70. **CAREER** Lectr soc hist, Univ Warwick, 70-79; LECTR HIST, PEMBROKE COL, UNIV CAMBRIDGE, 79-, Lectr mod hist, Hebrew Univ Jerusalem, 70-73. **MEMBERSHIPS** Fel, Royal Hist Soc. **RESEARCH** Social history of war; population history; labour history. **SELECTED PUBLICATIONS** Auth, The Impact of Air Power on the British People and Their Government, 1909-14, Engl Hist Rev, Vol 0107, 92; The Politics of State Expansion, Hist, Vol 0078, 93; Demography and Degeneration, J Mod Hist, Vol 0065, 93; The Great War, 1914-1918, Engl Hist Rev, Vol 0109, 94; British and French Writers of the 1st World War, Engl Hist Rev, Vol 0109, 94. **CONTACT ADDRESS** Dept of Hist, Univ Cambridge, Pembroke Coll, Cambridge, ., CB2 1RF.

WINTER, JERRY ALAN
PERSONAL Born 07/23/1937, Bronx, NY, m, 1964, 2 children **DISCIPLINE** SOCIOLOGY/SOCIAL PSYCHOLOGY **EDUCATION** BA, New York Univ, cum laude, 54-58; MA, Univ MI, 58-60; PhD, Univ MI, 60-64. **CAREER** Prof, Dept of Sociology, Connecticut College, 77-; Research Consultant, Dept of Research, Council of Jewish Federations, 90-91; Assoc Prof, Dept of Sociology, Connecticut College, 70-77; Asst Prof, Sociology Dept, Temple Univ, 68-70; Director, Research on Training for Metropolitan Ministry, Ministry Studies Board, 67-69; Asst Prof, Sociology Dept; Rutgers: The State Univ, 65-68; Instructor, Sociology Dept, The Univ of Michigan, 64-65; Editor, Contemporary Jewry, 92-97; Chair, Dept of Sociology, Conn College, 92-95; Fellow, NEH Summer Seminar, Yale Univ, 81; Acting Editor, MIMH Fellowship Program, Dept of Sociology, Temple Univ, 69-70. **HONORS AND AWARDS** Alpha Kappa Delta, Phi Beta Kappa, Psi Chi. **MEMBERSHIPS** Amer Sociological Assoc, Amer Assoc of Univ Prof, Religious Research Assoc, Assoc for the Sociological Study of Jewry. **SELECTED PUBLICATIONS** B. Lazerwitz, J. Winter, A Dashefskjy and E. Tabory, Jewish Choices: American Jewish Senominationalism, Albay NY, SUNY Press, 98; J. Winter Continues in the Sociology of Religion: Creed, Congregation and Community, NY, Harper and Row, 77; B. Lazerwitz, J.Alan Winter, A. Dashefsky and E. Tabory, A Study of Jewish Denominational Preferences: Summary Findings, American Jewish Year Book 97, 115-137, 97; Symbolic Ethenticity or Religion Among Jews in the US: A Test of Gansian Hypotheses, Review of Religious Research 37-233-247, 96; Not by Bread Alone: A National Replication and Refinement of a Study of Income, Identity and Household Composition and Jewish Involvement, Journal of Jewish Communal Service 69,75-81, 93; Jewish Giving and Strategies for Strengthening Campaigns, pp 361-377, In David M Gordis and Dorit P. Gary American Jewry: Portrait and Prognosis, Behrman House, 97. **CONTACT ADDRESS** Dept of Sociology, Connecticut Col, Box 1302, New London, CT, 06320.

WINTER, ROBERT W.
PERSONAL Born 07/17/1924, Indianapolis, IN, s **DISCIPLINE** HISTORY **EDUCATION** Dartmouth, AB, 47; Johns Hopkins, PhD, 57. **CAREER** Inst, 51-53, Bowdoin Col; inst, 54-56, Dartmouth; asst prof, 56-63, UCLA; prof, 63-94, Occidental Col. **HONORS AND AWARDS** Pres Award, CA Preserv Found. 96; Pflueger Award, local history, Historical Soc of S CA; Pres Award, Amer Inst of Architects, LA, 79. **MEMBERSHIPS** Soc of Architect Hist; Natl Trust for Historic Preserv; Victorian Soc; Hist Soc of S CA; CA Hist Soc, Pasadena Hist Musuem. **RESEARCH** Architectural history; arts & crafts movement. **SELECTED PUBLICATIONS** Auth, American Bungalow Style, 96; ed, Toward a Simpler Way of Life, 97; auth, Hidden LA, 98. **CONTACT ADDRESS** 626 South Arroyo Blvd., Pasadena, CA, 91105.

WINTER, THOMAS NELSON
PERSONAL Born 01/27/1944, m, 1964, 2 children **DISCIPLINE** CLASSICS **EDUCATION** Mich State Univ, BA, 64; Northwestern Univ, MA, 65, PhD, 68. **CAREER** Guest lectr, Adler Planetarium, 67; asst prof, 68-70, actg hd, Classics Div, Univ Hawaii, 69; asst prof, 70-75, assoc prof, Univ Nebr, Lincoln, 76-. **HONORS AND AWARDS** Merit Increment for Excellence in Tchg and Res, Univ Hawaii, 69; NEH summer sem, Am Acad Rome, 78; Parents Assn Award for Serv to Stud, Univ Nebr, Lincoln, 95, 96. **RESEARCH** Circumstantial case-assignment in the Latin of Caesar. **SELECTED PUBLICATIONS** Auth, When Quod is 'Which' and When Quod is 'Because', Class Outlook 72, 95. **CONTACT ADDRESS** Univ Nebr, Lincoln, 233 Andrew, Lincoln, NE, 68855-0337. **EMAIL** twinter@unlinfo.unl.edu

WINTERS, DONALD LEE
PERSONAL Born 08/11/1935, Ft Dodge, IA, m, 1960, 2 children **DISCIPLINE** UNITED STATES ECONOMIC HISTORY **EDUCATION** Univ Northern Iowa, BA, 57, MA, 63; Univ Wis, Madison, PhD(hist), 66. **CAREER** From asst prof to assoc prof hist, Univ Northern Iowa, 66-70; assoc prof, 70-79, PROF HIST, VANDERBILT UNIV, 79-. **HONORS AND AWARDS** Agr Hist Soc Bk Award, 69. **MEMBERSHIPS** Orgn Am Historians; Southern Hist Asn; Agr Hist Soc; Econ Hist Asn; Soc Sci Hist Asn. **RESEARCH** United States economic and agricultural history. **SELECTED PUBLICATIONS** Auth, Agriculture and Slavery in Missouri Little Dixie, J Amer Hist, Vol 0080, 93; Uncle Henry, Agr Hist, Vol 0068, 94; A New Lease on Life, Agr Hist, Vol 0069, 95; Southern Agriculture During the Civil War Era, 1960-1880, Civil War Hist, Vol 0042, 96. **CONTACT ADDRESS** Dept of Hist, Vanderbilt Univ, Nashville, TN, 37240.

WINTERS, STANLEY B.
PERSONAL Born 06/05/1924, New York, NY **DISCIPLINE** MODERN HISTORY **EDUCATION** NY Univ, AB, 48; Columbia Univ, AM, 50; Rutgers Univ, PhD(hist), 66. **CAREER** Instr hist, NY Univ, 49-50; from instr to assoc prof, 57-68, assoc chmn dept humanities, 65-72, PROF HIST, NJ INST TECHNOL, 68-, Res assoc, Rutgers Univ Urban Studies Ctr, 61-62; NSF Workshop Environ & Technol fel, 69; assoc ed, Studies E Europ Soc Hist, 71-; consult, Newark Off Pub Info, 72-; managing ed, E Cent Europe, 75-; NJ Comt for Humanities grant, 76; S & H Found grant, 77; CO-ADJ PROF HIST, GRAD FAC, RUTGERS UNIV, 80-. **HONORS AND AWARDS** Overseers Pub Serv Award, NJ Inst Technol Found, 82. **MEMBERSHIPS** AHA; Am Asn Advan Slavic Studies; Czech Soc Arts & Sci; Soc Hist of Technol. **RESEARCH** Habsburg monarchy and modern Czechoslavakia; Euro-American urban history; war and society. **SELECTED PUBLICATIONS** Auth, A History of Russian and East European Studies in the United States, Slavic Rev, Vol 0054, 95; Origins of the Czech National Renascence, Cent Europ Hist, Vol 0028, 95; Jonas, Charles 1840-1896, Amer Hist Rev, Vol 0100, 95; Masaryk, T.G--Against the Current, 1882-1914, Amer Hist Rev, Vol 0101, 96. **CONTACT ADDRESS** New Jersey Inst of Tech, 323 High St, Newark, NJ, 07102.

WINTLE, THOMAS
DISCIPLINE CHURCH HISTORY **EDUCATION** Chicago Theol Sem, DMN, 75 **CAREER** Par Minist, 75-95, Par Minist, 95-pres **MEMBERSHIPS** AAR; ASCH **RESEARCH** New England Church Hist **SELECTED PUBLICATIONS** Auth, A New England Village Church, 85 **CONTACT ADDRESS** 3 Conant Rd, Weston, MA, 02193-1625.

WINTZ, CARY DECORDOVA
PERSONAL Born 02/12/1943, Houston, TX, m, 1974, 1 child **DISCIPLINE** HISTORY **EDUCATION** Rice Univ, BA, 65; Kansas St Univ, MA, 68, PhD, 74. **CAREER** Instr, 71-74, asst prof, 74-77, assoc prof, 77-82, prof, 82-, chmn, dept hist, geography & econ, 95-, dir, acad comput, 88-94, Texas So Univ; asst dir, fac instruct & support, Frederick Douglass Inst, 87-88. **HONORS AND AWARDS** Phi Alpha Theta, Hist Hon Soc; Who's Who in S & SW, 89, 91, 94; Who's Who in the W, 90; Dist Svc Award, 88, Res Scholar of Year, 96, Texas Southern Univ; Mobil Fac Fel, Intl Fac Develop Sem, Ghana, 98. **MEMBERSHIPS** AHA; Org of Amer Hist; So Hist Assn. **RESEARCH** African-Amer hist; Texas hist; late 19th & early 20th century US. **SELECTED PUBLICATIONS** Auth, The Politics and Poetry of Claude McKay, Claude McKay: Centennial Stud, Sterling Pub, 92; co-ed, Black Dixie: Essays on Afro-Texan History and Culture in Houston, Texas A&M Univ Press, 92; coauth, The Economic Impact of Residential Desegregation on Historically Black Neighborhoods in Houston, Texas 1950-1990, J of Econ & Bus Hist Soc 13, 95; ed, The Harlem Renaissance 1920-1940: Interpretation of an African American Literary Movement, Garland Pub, 96; ed, African American Political Thought, 1890-1930: Washington, DuBois, Garvey, and Randolph, Sharpe, 96; auth, W.E.B. DuBois, The NAACP, and the Struggle for Racial Equality, Amer Reform & Reformers, Greenwood Pub, 96; auth, Women in Texas, Texas Heritage, 97. **CONTACT ADDRESS** History Dept, Texas Southern Univ, Houston, TX, 77004. **EMAIL** aaschdwintz@tsu.edu

WIRTH, JOHN DAVIS
PERSONAL Born 06/17/1936, Dawson, NM, m, 1960, 3 children **DISCIPLINE** MODERN LATIN AMERICAN HISTORY **EDUCATION** Harvard Univ, BA, 58; Stanford Univ, PhD(Latin Am hist), 66. **CAREER** Teacher hist, Putney Sch, Vt, 59-61; asst prof, 65-71, vchmn dept, 72-74, assoc prof, 71-77, PROF HIST, STANFORD UNIV, 77-, DIR, CTR LATIN AM STUDIES, 75-, Soc Sci Res Coun res fels, 69-70 & 72; Fulbright res grant, 80. **HONORS AND AWARDS** Bolton Prize, Conf Latin Am Hist, 71; Bolton Prize honorable mention, 78. **MEMBERSHIPS** AHA; Conf Latin Am Hist; Latin Am Studies Asn. **RESEARCH** Brazilian regionalism in the Old Republic; transfrontier migration in modern Latin America; comparative history of Latin America. **SELECTED PUBLICATIONS** Auth, Latin American Federalisms, Mexico, Brazil, Argentina, Hisp Amer Hist Rev, Vol 0075, 95; Black Cinderella, the Saga of Dejesus, Carolina, Maria, Hispanic Amer Hist Rev, Vol 0076, 96; The Life and Death of Dejesus, Carolina, Maria, Hisp Amer Hist Rev, Vol 0076, 96; The Trail Smelter Dispute--Canadians and Americans Confront Transboundary Pollution, 1927-41, Env Hist, Vol 0001, 96; The Environment and NAFTA, Env Hist, Vol 0002, 97; A New Name For Peace, Env Hist, Vol 0002, 97. **CONTACT ADDRESS** Dept of Hist, Stanford Univ, Stanford, CA, 94305-1926.

WISE, SYDNEY F.
PERSONAL Toronto, ON, Canada **DISCIPLINE** HISTORY **EDUCATION** Univ Toronto, BA, 49, BLS, 50; Queen's Univ, MA, 53; Univ Guelph, LLD, 87. **CAREER** Lectr, Royal Mil Col, 50-55; lectr to prof hist, 55-66, Queen's Univ, R. Samuel McLaughlin res prof, 64-65; dir hist, Dept Nat Defence, 66-73; prof, 73, dir, Inst Can Stud, Carleton Univ, 78-81, dean grad stud & res, Carleton Univ, 81-90 (RETIRED), dir, univ press, 83-90, gov, 80-83. **HONORS AND AWARDS** Cruickshank Gold Medal, Ont Hist Soc; fel, Royal Soc Can; mem, Order Can. **MEMBERSHIPS** Can Hist Asn; UN Asn Can; Ont Hist Soc. **RESEARCH** War & military history. **SELECTED PUBLICATIONS** Coauth, Men in Arms: a history of the interrelationships of warfare and western society, 56, 2nd ed 62, 3rd ed 70, 4th ed 79, 5th ed 91; coauth, Task Force Report to Federal Cabinet on Sport for Canadians, 69; coauth, Canada's Sporting Heroes: Their Lives & Times, 74; coauth, Canadian Airmen in the First World War, vol 1 80; coauth, God's Peculiar Peoples, Essays in the Political Culture of 19th Century Canada, 93; coauth, The Valour and the Horror Revisited, 94; coauth, East to Adventure: The Flight of Wild Oats 1933, 97. **CONTACT ADDRESS** 562 Lisgar St, Ottawa, ON, K1R 5H5.

WISEMAN, JAMES RICHARD
DISCIPLINE CLASSICS **RESEARCH** Classical Languages & Archeology.

WISEMAN, JOHN BAILES
PERSONAL Born 02/10/1938, Alliance, NE, m, 1964, 2 children **DISCIPLINE** AMERICAN HISTORY **EDUCATION** Linfield Col, BA, 60; Univ Md, MA, 62, PhD(Am hist), 67. **CAREER** Asst prof Am hist, Keene State Col, 66-69 & Morgan State Col, 69-71; assoc prof, 71-77, PROF AM HIST, FROSTBURG STATE COL, 77-, Danforth Found fel Black studies, 70-71. **MEMBERSHIPS** Orgn Am Historians; AHA; Asn Studies Afro-Am Life & Hist. **RESEARCH** Twentieth-century American history; Afro-American history. **SELECTED PUBLICATIONS** Auth, Racism in Democratic Party Politics, 1904-1912, Mid-America, 1/69; collabr, Allegany County, Maryland: A History, McClain, 76; auth, Dilemmas of a Party Out of Power: the Democracy, 1904-1912, Garland, 88; coauth, Maryland: Unity in Diversity, 90. **CONTACT ADDRESS** Dept of History, Frostburg State Univ, Frostburg, MD, 21532-1715. **EMAIL** jwiseman1@mindspring.com

WISEMAN, MARY BITTNER
PERSONAL Born 08/21/1936, Philadelphia, PA, m, 1989, 1 child **DISCIPLINE** AESTHETICS; FEMINISM **EDUCATION** St John's Col, Md, AB, 59; Harvard Univ, AM, 63; Columbia Univ, PhD, 74. **CAREER** From Instr to Prof Philos, Brooklyn Col of the City of New York, 72-, Prof of Philos and Comparative Lit, Grad Sch of the City Univ of New York; Dep exec officer, Humanities Inst, Brooklyn Col, 81-. **MEMBERSHIPS** Am Philos Asn; Am Soc Aesthet; Soc Women Philos; Col Art Asn. **RESEARCH** Philosophy of art; interpretation; theory of criticism. **SELECTED PUBLICATIONS** Auth, The Ecstasies of Roland Bartles, Routledge, 89; numerous articles in Am Philos Quart, Brit J of Aesthetics, J Aesthetics & Art Criticism, and others. **CONTACT ADDRESS** Dept of Philos, Brooklyn Col, CUNY, 2901 Bedford Ave, Brooklyn, NY, 11210-2813. **EMAIL** hagold@aol.com

WISER, VIVIAN
PERSONAL Born 06/17/1915, Lyndonville, NY **DISCIPLINE** AMERICAN HISTORY **EDUCATION** Univ Md, BA, 38, MA, 39, PhD, 63. **CAREER** Archivist, Nat Arch, 43-46, 48-56; HISTORIAN, USDA, 56-. **MEMBERSHIPS** Soc Am Archivists; AHA; Agr Hist Soc; Orgn Am Historians; Soc Personnel Admin. **RESEARCH** History of the United States Department of Agriculture; agricultural changes in antebellum Maryland; history of agricultural marketing. **SELECTED PUBLICATIONS** Auth, History of the Flower Bulb Industry in Washington State, Agr Hist, Vol 0068, 94. **CONTACT ADDRESS** Agr Hist, Group ES CS USDA, Washington, DC, 20250.

WISHNE, BRIAN
DISCIPLINE ARCHITECTURE **EDUCATION** Knox Col, BA, 71; Univ Boston, MA, 76; Princeton Univ, 80. **CAREER** Tchg asst, Princeton Univ, 79-80; vis prof, Univ Miami, 85; asst prof, Univ Cinn, 81-86; assoc prof, 88-. **MEMBERSHIPS**

ACSA; Soc Archit Hist. **SELECTED PUBLICATIONS** Auth, The Architecture of Herbert W. Tullgren 1889-1944: Modern Apartments in Depression-Era Milwaukee, 93; Magazine, 1993; The Architecture of Connection: Spatial Formation in the Public Architecture of Louis I. Kahn, 92; International Paradox: An Examination of the Boundary Between Architecture and Sculpture, 92. **CONTACT ADDRESS** Sch of Architecture and Urban Planning, Univ of Wisconsin, Milwaukee, PO Box 413, Milwaukee, WI, 53201. **EMAIL** bwishne@uwm.edu

WITCOMBE, CHRISTOPHER L.C.E.
DISCIPLINE ART HISTORY **EDUCATION** Univ MA, BA; MA; Bryn Mawr Col, PhD. **CAREER** Fac, 83-; Chr and prof art hist, Sweet Briar Col. **RESEARCH** Ancient Greek and Roman art; Renaissance and Baroque art; 16th century Italian art. **SELECTED PUBLICATIONS** Auth, publ(s) about painting, archit and prints of 16th century Italian art in Journal of the Society of Architectural Historians, The Burlington Magazine, and Gazette des Beaux-Arts. **CONTACT ADDRESS** Sweet Briar Col, Sweet Briar, VA, 24595. **EMAIL** witcombe@sbc.edu

WITEK, JOHN W.
PERSONAL Born 09/13/1933, Chicago, IL **DISCIPLINE** EAST ASIAN HISTORY **EDUCATION** Loyola Univ, IL, AB, 57, PhL, 59, MA, 64, STL, 66; Georgetown Univ, PhD, 73. **CAREER** Asst prof hist, Xavier Univ, 73-75; asst prof, 75-81, Asoc prof History, Georgetown Univ, 81-. **HONORS AND AWARDS** Phi Beta Kappa; Eugene Asher Distinguished Teaching Award (Hon Mention), Am Hist Soc, 91. **MEMBERSHIPS** AHA; Am Oriental Soc; Asia Soc; Asn Asian Studies; Soc Ch'ing Studies; Pres, Mid-Atlantic Reg/Asn Asian Studies, 89-90. **RESEARCH** China and Japan, 16th to 18th centuries; Christian missions in China and Japan; Chinese intellectual history, 16th century to the present. **SELECTED PUBLICATIONS** Auth, Manchu Christians at the Court of Peking in the Early Eighteenth Century, ed, E Malatesta & Y Raguid, Succes et echecs de la rensontre Chine et Occident du XVIe au XXe siecle Varietes sinologiques, Nouvelle, serie, col 74 (Taipei & Paris) 93; Eliminating Misunderstandings: Antoine de Beauvollier (1657-1708) and his Eclaircissements sur les controverses de la Chine D E Mungello, ed, The Chinese Rites Controversy: Its History and Meaaning, Monumenta Serica Monograph Series (Nettetal) 94; J Witek, ed Ferdinand Verviest (1623-1688), Jesuit Missionary, Scientist, Engineer and Diplomat, Monumenta Serica Monograph Series XXX (Nettetal) 94; The Seventeenth-Century Advance into Asia: A Review Article, Journal of Asian Studies, 94; Claude Visdelou and the Chinese Paradox, Images de la Chine: Le Contexte occidental de la sinologie naissante, Varietes sinologiiques, Nouvelle serie, vol 78 (Taipei & Paris: Institut Ricci) 95; Reporting to Rome: Some Major Events in the Christian Community in Peking, 1686-1687, Echanges culturels et e¤religieux entre la Chine et l'Occident, Varietes sinologiques, Nouvelle serie, vol 83 (San Francisco, Taipei & Paris, Institut Ricci) 95; A Dialogue on Astronomical Phenomena and Natural Theology in Early Eighteenth-Century China, F Masini ed, Western Humanistic Culture Presented to China by Jesuit Missionaries (XVII-XVIII) Centuries (Rome) 96; The Jesuits in China During the Seventeenth and Eighteenth Centuries, Archivum Historicum Societatis Jesu, 96; Principles of Scholasticism in China: A Comparison of Giulio Aleni's Wanwu zhenyuan with Matteo Ricci's Tianzhu shiyi, Tiziana Lippiello & R Malek, ed Scholas from the Est, Giulio Aleni SJ (1582-1649) and the Dialogue between Christianity and China (Nettetal) 97. **CONTACT ADDRESS** Dept Hist, Georgetown Univ, PO Box 571035, Washington, DC, 20057-1035.

WITHINGTON, ANNE F.
DISCIPLINE HISTORY **EDUCATION** Harvard, BA, 66; Univ Calif, MA, 72; Yale Univ, PhD, 83. **CAREER** Assoc prof History, SUNY, Albany. **RESEARCH** American political history. **SELECTED PUBLICATIONS** Auth, The Trial of Anne Hutchinson: A Political Trial, New Eng Quart, 78; Republican Bees: The Political Economy of the Beehive in Eighteenth Century America, Studies in Eighteenth-Century Culture 18, 88; Plays Cocks, Horses, and Funerals: Morality and Ideology in the American Revolution, Oxford Univ, pending; Consumption and Republican Ideology in the Early Republic, In: Everyday Life in the Early Republic, Norton, pending. **CONTACT ADDRESS** Dept of History, SUNY at Albany, Albany, NY, 12222.

WITHINGTON, WILLIAM ADRIANCE
PERSONAL Honolulu, HI, m, 1955, 2 children **DISCIPLINE** GEOGRAPHY **EDUCATION** Harvard Univ, BA 46; Northwestern Univ, MA 48, PhD 55. **CAREER** Geo Washington Univ, inst, asst prof, 48-53; Univ Kentucky, inst, asst prof, assoc prof, 55-89; Nommenson Univ North Sumatra Indonesia, vis Ford Foun prof, 57. **HONORS AND AWARDS** Ford Foun Fel. **MEMBERSHIPS** AAS; AAG; AGS; ANS; SE Conf AAS; Sigma Xi. **RESEARCH** Sumatra Indonesia; Southeast Asia; Human cultural geog; urban geog. **SELECTED PUBLICATIONS** Auth, Editor for Indonesia entries for Gazetteer, Columbia Univ Press, 98; Kentucky Encycl, contributor, Lexington KY, Univ Press KY, 92; Southeast Asia, Grand Rapids MI, Fidden, editor from 61-80's. **CONTACT ADDRESS** Dept of Geography, Univ of Kentucky, 113 Johnston Blvd, Lexington, KY, 40503-2028.

WITHROW, WILLIAM
PERSONAL Born 09/30/1926, Toronto, ON, Canada **DISCIPLINE** ART HISTORY **EDUCATION** Univ Toronto, BA, 50, Art Spec, OCE, 51, BEd, 55, MEd, 58, MA, 61. **CAREER** Art dept head, Earl Haig Col, 51-59; prin & res dir, Ont Dept Educ, 57-59; dir, 61-91, DIR EMER, ART GALLERY ONTARIO. **HONORS AND AWARDS** Mem, Order Can, 80. **MEMBERSHIPS** Fel, Can Mus Asn; fel, Ont Col Art; life mem, Asn Art Mus Dirs; past pres, Can Art Mus Dir Orgn. **SELECTED PUBLICATIONS** Auth, Sorel Etrog/Sculpture, 67; auth, Contemporary Canadian Painting, 72. **CONTACT ADDRESS** 7 Malabar Pl, Don Mills, ON, M3B 1A4.

WITKE, E.C.
PERSONAL Born 09/22/1931, Los Angeles, CA, m, 1975 **DISCIPLINE** CLASSICAL AND MEDIEVAL LATIN LITERATURE **EDUCATION** UCLA, BA, 53; Harvard Univ, AM, 57, PhD, 62. **CAREER** Asst prof, Univ Chicago, 62-63; asst to assoc prof Univ Cal Berkeley, 63-70; prof SUNY Binghamton, 70-71; prof, Univ Mich, 71-. **HONORS AND AWARDS** Am Acad Rome Prize, 60-62. **MEMBERSHIPS** Am Philol Asn; Medieval Acad Amer. **RESEARCH** Classical tradition in Middle Ages; Medieval theology; Erasmus. **SELECTED PUBLICATIONS** Auth, Enarratio Catulliana, Mnemosyne Supplementa, Leiden, 68; Latin Satire: The Structure of Persuasion, Leiden, 70; Numen Litterarum: The Old and the New in Latin Poetry from Constantine to Gregory the Great, Leiden & Cologne, 71; Horace's Roman Odes: A Critical Examination, Mnemosyne Supplementa, Leiden, 83. **CONTACT ADDRESS** Dept of Classical Studies, Univ Mich, Ann Arbor, MI, 48109. **EMAIL** frchas@umich.edu

WITKIN-NEW HOLY, ALEXANDRA
PERSONAL Born 05/08/1963, Denver, CO, m, 2 children **DISCIPLINE** ETHNIC STUDIES **EDUCATION** Univ Calif-Berkeley, PhD, 97. **CAREER** Asst prof, Mont State Univ, 97-. **HONORS AND AWARDS** Am Coun of Learned Soc Contemplative Pract Fel, 98-99; Influential Teacher Award, Mont State Unv, 98; Phi Beta Kappa. **MEMBERSHIPS** AAR. **RESEARCH** Ethnic studies; Native American identities, lands, and religions. **SELECTED PUBLICATIONS** Auth, "Termination, Self-Determination, Zoning, and the Pinoleville Rancheria: The Governing Council of Pinoleville Indian Community vs. Mendocino County," 89; "To Silence a Drum: The Imposition of United States Citizenship on Native Peoples," 95; The Heart of Everything That Is: Paha Sapa, Treaties, and Lakota Identity, 98; "Black Elk and the Spiritual Significance of Paha Saps (the Black Hills)," 99. **CONTACT ADDRESS** Center for Native American Studies, Montana State Univ, 20186 Wils Hall, PO Box 172340, Bozeman, MT, 59717-2340. **EMAIL** anewholy@montana.edu

WITT, RONALD GENE
PERSONAL Born 12/23/1932, Wayne, MI, m, 1965, 3 children **DISCIPLINE** RENAISSANCE AND REFORMATION HISTORY **EDUCATION** Univ Mich, BA, 54; Harvard Univ, PhD(hist), 65. **CAREER** Fulbright lectr Am civilization, Univ Strasbourg, 55-56; from instr to asst prof hist, Harvard Univ, 65-71; assoc prof, 71-80, PROF HIST, DUKE UNIV, 80-, Old Dom Fund fel, 68-69; mem univ sem Renaissance, Columbia Univ, 72-; Nat Endowment for Humanities grant, 74; Guggenheim Found fel, 77; Coun Learned Soc grant, 79. **MEMBERSHIPS** Mediaeval Acad Am; Renaissance Soc Am; AHA; Soc Ital Hist Studies. **RESEARCH** Italian humanism. **SELECTED PUBLICATIONS** Auth, Biondo 'Italia Illustrata', Summa or Creative Work, Renaissance Quart, Vol 0045, 92; Ironia, Renaissance Quart, Vol 0046, 93; The Semantic Study of the Florentine Use of the Iconography of Hercules up to the Time of Cosimo Dei Medici, Renaissance Quart, Vol 0047, 94; Still the Matter of the 2 Giovannis + 2 Humanists from Ravenna, Rinascimento, Vol 0035, 95; Medieval and Renaissance Letter Treatises and Form Letters, Cath Hist Rev, Vol 0082, 96. **CONTACT ADDRESS** Dept of Hist, Duke Univ, Durham, NC, 27706.

WITTE, ANN DRYDEN
DISCIPLINE ECONOMICS **EDUCATION** Univ Fla, BA, 63; Columbia Univ, MA, 65; North Carolina State Univ, PhD, 71. **CAREER** Instr, econ, Tougaloo Col, 67-68; instr, econ, 70-72, vis asst prof, econ, 72-73, vis asst prof, public law and govt, 73-74; asst prof, 74-79, assoc prof, 79-83, prof, 83-95, Univ North Carolina, Chapel Hill; fel law and econ, Harvard Law School, 87-88; res assoc, Natl Bur Econ Res, 84- ; prof, econ, Wellesley Col, 85- ; prof econ, Fla Int Univ, 92- . **HONORS AND AWARDS** Fel, Am Statistic Asn; fel, Royal Statistic Soc; Dist scholar, Ariz State Univ; fel Am Soc of Criminol; Phi Beta Kappa. **MEMBERSHIPS** Am Econ Asn; Am Statistical Asn; Int Inst Public Finance; Europ Asn of Law and Econ; Am Law and Econ Asn. **RESEARCH** International taxation;Regulation; Effects of information; Welfare reform; Child care and well-being; Crime and criminal justice. **SELECTED PUBLICATIONS** Coauth, Provision of Child Care: Cost Functions for Profit- Making and Not-for-Profit Day Care Centers, J of Productivity Anal, 93; coauth, Tax Compliance: An Investigation Using Individual Tax Compliance Measurement Program Data, J of Quantitative Criminol, 93; coauth, Work and Crime: An Exploration Using Panel Data, Pub Finance, 94; coauth, Criminal Deterrence: Revisiting the Issues with a Birth Cohort, Rev of Econ and Statist, 94; coauth, Economic Effects of Quality Regulations in the Day Care Industry, Am Econ Rev, 95; coauth, Childcare in Massachusetts: Where the Supply Is and Isn't, Wellesley Res Center, 97. **CONTACT ADDRESS** Dept of Economics, Wellesley Col, Wellesley, MA, 02181-8260. **EMAIL** awitte@wellesley.edu

WITTE, JOHN
PERSONAL Born 08/14/1959, St. Catherines, ON, Canada, m, 1995, 2 children **DISCIPLINE** LAW; LEGAL HISTORY **EDUCATION** Harvard Law Sch, JD, 85. **CAREER** Asst prof, Emory Univ, 89-91; assoc, 91-93; prof, 93; Jonas Robitscher prof, 93- . **HONORS AND AWARDS** Most Outstanding Prof, SBA, 92-93, 94-94, 97-98; Most Outstanding Educator Award, United Methodist Found for Christian Higher Educ, 94; Max Rheinstein Fel, Alexander von Humboldt-Stiftung, Bonn, 95; Prof of the Year, Black Law Students Asoc, 97-98; Abraham Kuyper Prize for Excellence in Theology and Public Life, Princeton Theol Sem, 99. **MEMBERSHIPS** ABA; State Bar of Georgia; Soc of Christian Ethics. **RESEARCH** European legal history; American legal history; church-state relations; religious liberty; law and religion; religion and human rights; Protestant Reformation; Canon law. **SELECTED PUBLICATIONS** Co-ed with Johan D. Van der Vyver, Religious Human Rights in Global Perspective: Religious Perspectives, 96; auth, From Sacrament to Contract: Marriage, Religion and Law in the Western Tradition, 97; Co-ed with Michael Bourdeaux, Orthodoxy and Proselytism in Russia: The War for New Souls, 99; auth, Essentia Liberty: The American Experiment in Religious Freedom, 99. **CONTACT ADDRESS** School of Law, Emory Univ, 1301 Clifton Rd., Atlanta, GA, 30322-2770. **EMAIL** jwitte@law.emory.edu

WITTIG, JOSEPH SYLVESTER
PERSONAL Born 08/18/1939, Pittsburgh, PA, m, 1969 **DISCIPLINE** ENGLISH, MEDIEVAL STUDIES **EDUCATION** Wheeling Col, BA, 63; Univ Scranton, MA, 65; Cornell Univ, PhD(English, medieval studies), 69. **CAREER** Asst prof, 69-76, ASSOC PROF ENGLISH, UNIV NC, CHAPEL HILL, 76-. **MEMBERSHIPS** MLA; Mediaeval Acad Am; New Chaucer Soc; AAUP; Southern Atlantic Mod Lang Asn. **RESEARCH** Middle English literature; Old English literature; medieval studies. **SELECTED PUBLICATIONS** Auth, The Yearbook of Langland Studies, Vol 3, Anglia-Zeitschrift fur Engl Philol, Vol 0110, 92; A Glossarial Concordance to the Riverside Chaucer, 2 Vols, Speculum-J Medieval Stud, Vol 0070, 95. **CONTACT ADDRESS** Dept of English, Univ of NC, Chapel Hill, NC, 27514.

WITTNER, LAWRENCE STEPHEN
PERSONAL Born 05/05/1941, Brooklyn, NY, m, 1963, 1 child **DISCIPLINE** AMERICAN FOREIGN POLICY, MODERN AMERICAN HISTORY **EDUCATION** Columbia Col, AB, 62; Univ Wis, MA, 63; Columbia Univ, PhD, 67. **CAREER** Asst prof hist, Hampton Inst, 67-68 & Vassar Col, 68-73; Fulbright sr lectr, Japan, 73-74; lectr, 74-76, from asst to assoc prof, hist, 76-83, prof Hist, 83-, SUNY Albany; vis assoc prof, Columbia Univ, 76; res grants, Harry Truman Libr, 75 & Eleanor Roosevelt Inst, 77; fel & grant, Res Found, State Univ NY, 77-78 & 80-81; Nat Endowment for Humanities fel, 80-81; co-exec ed, Peace and Change: A Journal of Peace Res, 84-87. **HONORS AND AWARDS** Univ Award for Excellence in Research, SUNY Albany, 85; SUNY Albany Fac Res Awards Program grant, 86-87; ACLS/Ford fel, 87-88; NEH grant, 88; Council on peace Res in Hist, Charles DeBenedetti prize, 89; NY State/United Univ Professions Excellence Award, 90; US Int of Peace res grant, 90-92; Am Philos Soc res grant, 92; Soc for Hist of Am For Rel, Warren F. Kuehl prize, 95; NEH stipend 98; SUNY Albany Fac Res Awards, 98-99. **MEMBERSHIPS** Conf Peace Res in Hist (pres, 77-79); Soc Historians Am Foreign Rels; Orgn Am Historians. **RESEARCH** History of American foreign policy; international history. **SELECTED PUBLICATIONS** Auth, Blacklisting Schweitzer, Bull of the Atomic Scientists, 95; auth, The Menace of the Maidens, Fellowship, 95; auth, Resisting the Bomb: A History of the World Nuclear Disarmament Movement, 1954-1970, Stanford, 97; auth, Merle Curti and the Development of Peace History, Peace and Change, 98; auth, The Nuclear Threat Ignored: How and Why the Campaign Against the Bomb Disintegrated in the Late 1960s, 1968: The World Transformed, Cambridge, 98; coauth, How Western Peace Activists Lifted the Iron Curtain in 1961, International Hist Rev, 98. **CONTACT ADDRESS** Dept of History, SUNY, Albany, 1400 Washington Ave, Albany, NY, 12222. **EMAIL** wittner@csc.albany.edu

WLATER, OTIS M.
PERSONAL Born 04/20/1921, Chicago, IL, d **DISCIPLINE** CLASSICAL RHETORIC **EDUCATION** Northwestern Univ, PhD, 48. **CAREER** PROF OF COMMUN, UNIV OF PITTSBURGH, 58-84. **HONORS AND AWARDS** Phi Kappa Phi **MEMBERSHIPS** Nat Commun Asn. **RESEARCH** Classical rhetoric. **SELECTED PUBLICATIONS** Auth, Speaking Intelligently: Communication for Problem Solving, Macmillan Pub Co., 76; The Improvement of Attitute Research, J of Social Psychol, 51; Toward an Analysis of Motivation, Quart J of Speech, 55; On Views of Rhetoric, Whether Conservative or

Progressive, Quart J of Speech, 63; The Value of the Classics in Rhetoric, Col Composition and Commun, 98; Plato's Idea of Rhetoric for Contemporary Students, Col Composition and Commun, 84; The Measurement of Ethos, Northwestern Univ, 84; coauth, Toward an Analysis of Ethics for Rhetoric, Quart J of Speech, 55. **CONTACT ADDRESS** 1115 Kenoyer Dr., Bellingham, WA, 98226-2333.

WOBST, H. MARTIN
PERSONAL Born 12/12/1943, Eickelborn, Germany, m, 1981, 2 children **DISCIPLINE** EUROPEAN PRE-HISTORY **EDUCATION** Univ Mich, Ann Arbor, BA, 66, MA, 68, PhD(anthrop), 71. **CAREER** Asst, prof, 71-77, assoc prof, 77-84, prof 84-, chemn dept anthrop, Univ Mass, Amherst, 74-80, ed, Memoirs, Soc Am Archaeol, 71-75. **MEMBERSHIPS** Fel Am Anthrop Asn; Soc Am Archaeol; fel Royal Anthrop Inst. **RESEARCH** Pre-history of Eastern Europe and the Union of Soviet Socialist Republics; computer simulations of Paleolithic societies; archaeological theory and cultural ecology. **SELECTED PUBLICATIONS** Auth, The Butterfield Site, Mich Anthrop Papers, 68; Boundary Conditions for Paleolithic Cultural Systems, Am Antiq, 74; The Demography of Finite Populations and the Origins of the Incest Taboo, Am Antiq, 75; Locational Relationships in Paleolithic Society, J Human Evolution, 76; Stylistic Behavior and Information Exchange, Mich Anthrop Papers, 77. **CONTACT ADDRESS** Dept of Anthrop, Univ of Massachusetts, Amherst, Machmer, Amherst, MA, 01003-0002. **EMAIL** wobst@anthro.umass.edu

WOEHRMANN, PAUL JOHN
PERSONAL Born 04/01/1939, Lakewood, OH, m, 1965, 1 child **DISCIPLINE** AMERICAN HISTORY **EDUCATION** Ohio State Univ, BA, 61, MA, 62; Kent State Univ, PhD, 67. **CAREER** Asst, Kent State Univ, 62-66; asst prof hist, WVa Wesleyan Col, 66-68 & Univ Tenn, Nashville, 68-70; res fel, Papers of Henry Clay, Univ Ky, Nat Hist Publ Comn, 70-71; Librn Hist & Marine Collection, Milwaukee Pub Libr, 72-, Milwaukee Area Tech Col, 89-; WVa Wesleyan Col res grant, 68; proj dir, Nat Endowment for Humanities, The Papers of Carl & Frank Ziedlen, 81-. **MEMBERSHIPS** Orgn Am Historians; Soc Historians Early Am Repub. **RESEARCH** Early national period, United States history; military history. **SELECTED PUBLICATIONS** Auth, At the Headwaters of the Maumee, a History of the Forts of Fort Wayne, Ind Hist Soc, 71; National Response to the Sack of Washington, Md Hist Mag, 71; ed, A Guide to the Socialist Party-Social Democratic Federation Collection of the Milwaukee Public Library, Milwaukee Pub Libr, 76; ed, The autobiography of Abraham Snethen, frontier preacher, Filson Club Hist Quart, 10/77. **CONTACT ADDRESS** Milwaukee Pub Libr, 814 W Wisconsin Ave, Milwaukee, WI, 53233-1443. **EMAIL** p.woehr@mpl.org

WOHL, ANTHONY STEPHEN
PERSONAL Born 03/28/1937, London, England, m, 1964, 2 children **DISCIPLINE** HISTORY **EDUCATION** Cambridge Univ, BA, 58; Brown Univ, PhD(hist), 66. **CAREER** Teaching asst hist, Brown Univ, 59-62; from instr to assoc prof, 63-77, PROF HIST, VASSAR COL, 77-, Vis lectr hist, Leicester Univ, Eng, 68-69; chmn nat prog, Conf Brit Studies, 77-. **MEMBERSHIPS** Conf Brit Studies; NE Victorian Studies Asn. **RESEARCH** Social history, Victorian England; housing reform and policy; public health. **SELECTED PUBLICATIONS** Auth, Disraeli, J Interdisciplinary Hist, Vol 0026, 95; Dizzi Ben Dizzi--Disraeli as Alien, J Brit Stud, Vol 0034, 95; The Jews in the History of England, 1485-1850, Historian, Vol 0058, 95. **CONTACT ADDRESS** Dept of Hist, Vassar Col, Poughkeepsie, NY, 12601.

WOHL, ROBERT
PERSONAL Born 02/13/1936, Butte, MT, m, 1966, 1 child **DISCIPLINE** MODERN HISTORY **EDUCATION** Univ Calif, Los Angeles, AB, 57; Princeton Univ, AM, 59, PhD(hist), 63. **CAREER** From instr to asst prof hist, Univ Southern Calif, 61-64; from asst prof to assoc prof, 64-69, chmn dept, 70-73, PROF HIST, UNIV CALIF, LOS ANGELES, 69-, Soc Sci Res Coun grant, 68-69; Nat Endowment for Humanities fel, 78-. **HONORS AND AWARDS** George Louis Beer Prize, 67. **MEMBERSHIPS** AHA; Soc Ital Hist Studies. **RESEARCH** International communism; modern Italy; comparative European intellectual and social history 1870 to the present. **SELECTED PUBLICATIONS** Auth, Russian Lindbergh, Amer Hist Rev, Vol 0097, 92; Liberalism, Fascism, or Social Democracy, J Mod Hist, Vol 0066, 94. **CONTACT ADDRESS** Dept of Hist, Univ of Calif, Los Angeles, CA, 90024.

WOJCIK, DANIEL
PERSONAL Born 12/21/1955, Detroit, MI **DISCIPLINE** ENGLISH; FOLKLORE **EDUCATION** BA, anthrop, Univ Calif Santa Barbara, 78; MA, folklore and myth, Univ Calif Los Angeles, 86; PhD, folklore and myth, Univ Calif Los Angeles, 92. **CAREER** Asst prof, 91-97, assoc prof, 97-, dept of eng, Univ Ore. **HONORS AND AWARDS** Amer Acad of Relig individual res grant, 96; summer res award, Office of Res and Sponsored Prog, Univ Ore, 95; Arnold Rubin award, Fowler Mus of Cultural Hist, Univ Calif Los Angeles, 90. **MEMBERSHIPS** Amer Acad of Relig; Amer Culture Asn; Amer Folklore Soc; Amer Studies Asn; Calif Folklore Soc; Intl Soc for Contemp Legend Res; Popular Culture Asn. **RESEARCH** Millennialist movements and apocalyptic beliefs; Contemporary American folklore; Popular culture; Subcultures and youth cultures; Body art; Popular religion. **SELECTED PUBLICATIONS** Auth, The End of the World As We Know It: Faith, Fatalism, and Apocalypse in America, NY Univ Press, 97; article, Embracing Doomsday: Faith, Fatalism, and Apocalyptic Beliefs in the Nuclear Age, Western Folklore, 55, no 4, 297-330, 96; article, Polaroids from Heaven: Photography, Folk Religion, and the Miraculous Image Tradition at a Marian Apparition Site, Jour of Amer Folklore, 109, no 432, 129-148, 96; auth, Punk and Neo-Tribal Body Art, Folk Art and Artists Series, Univ Press of Miss, 95. **CONTACT ADDRESS** English and Folklore Studies, Univ of Oregon, 1286 University of Oregon, Eugene, OR, 97403-1286. **EMAIL** dwojcik@oregon.uoregon.edu

WOLF, EUGENE KENDRICK
PERSONAL Born 05/25/1939, New York, NY, m, 1964, 2 children **DISCIPLINE** MUSICOLOGY **EDUCATION** Univ Rochester, BMus, 61; NY Univ, MA, 64, PhD, 72. **CAREER** Lectr fine arts, Syracuse Univ, 67-72, asst prof, 72-73; asst prof, 73-75, chmn dept, 77-80, ASSOC PROF MUSIC, UNIV PA, 75-, Rev ed, J Am Musicol Soc, 72-77; Guggenheim fel, 75-76; Am Coun Learned Soc fel, 81-82. **HONORS AND AWARDS** Alfred Einstein Award, Am Musicol Soc, 75. **MEMBERSHIPS** Col Music Soc; Am Musicol Soc; Int Musicol Soc; Music Libr Asn; Am Soc 18th Century Studies. **RESEARCH** Symphonies of Johann Stamitz; early classical symphony; 18th century musicology. **SELECTED PUBLICATIONS** Auth, Studies on Richter, Franz, Xaver Church Music 1709-1789, Notes, Vol 0051, 94; Newly Identified Manuscripts of Opera and Related Works From Mannheim + 18th-Century Electoral Court Music, J Amer Musicol Soc, Vol 0047, 94; The 18th-Century Symphony, Notes, Vol 0052, 96; Studies on the Musical Relations Between Mannheim, Bohemia and Moravia in the Late 18th and Early 19th Centuries, Notes, Vol 0052, 96. **CONTACT ADDRESS** Dept of Music, Univ Penn, 201 S 34th St, Philadelphia, PA, 19104-6313.

WOLF, GEORGE D.
PERSONAL Born 06/04/1923, Corry, PA, m, 1948, 3 children **DISCIPLINE** AMERICAN CIVILIZATION **EDUCATION** Muskingum Col, BA, 47; Bucknell Univ, MA, 53; Univ Pa, PhD(Am civilization), 64. **CAREER** High sch teacher, Pa, 48-56; assoc prof Am hist, Lock Haven State Col, 57-64, prof hist, 64-66; assoc prof, 66-69, head div humanities, soc sci & educ, 71-73, dean fac, 73-78, PROF AM STUDIES & HIST, PA STATE UNIV, CAPITOL CAMPUS, 69-, Instr, Lycoming Col, 54-56; Danforth assoc, 60-64; fac fel, Nat Ctr Educ Polit, 65-66; spec asst to Gov Pa, 65-66; historian, Pa Const Conv, 67-68; consult to Lt Gov Pa, 67-70; mem, Bd State Col & Univ Dir, 70-71. **MEMBERSHIPS** Orgn Am Historians; AAUP; Am Studies Asn. **RESEARCH** Pennsylvania history and politics: the Scranton administration, 1963-1967; Pennsylvania constitutional convention, 1967-1968; politics in America. **SELECTED PUBLICATIONS** Auth, The Politics of Fair Play, Pa Hist, 1/65; The Scranton Papers, Western Pa Hist Mag, 10/68; State Constitutional Revision, Dept Pub Instr, 68; The Fair Play Settlers of the West Branch Valley, 1769-1784, Pa Hist & Mus Comn, 69; Constitutional Revision in Pennsylvania, Nat Munic League, 69; Introd & Index for Debates of the Pennsylvania Constitutional Convention, Publ Bur, 69; The fair play settlers of the West Branch Valley, In: Pennsylvania 1776, 75 & William Scranton Pennsylvania Statesman, 81, Pa State Univ Press. **CONTACT ADDRESS** 304 Deerfield Rd, Camp Hill, PA, 17011.

WOLF, KENNETH BAXTER
PERSONAL Born 06/01/1957, Santa Barbara, CA, 2 children **DISCIPLINE** HISTORY, RELIGIOUS STUDIES **EDUCATION** Stanford, BA (Religious Studies), 79, PhD (History), 85. **CAREER** Asst prof, 85-92, ASSOC PROF, POMONA COL, 92-, chair, Hist Dept, 95-98. **HONORS AND AWARDS** Phi Beta Kappa; Inst for Advanced Study, member 89-91; Wig Distinguished Prof, Pomona Col, 88, 93, 98. **MEMBERSHIPS** Medieval Academy; Medieval Asn of the Pacific; Assoc Members of the Inst for Advanced Study. **RESEARCH** Medieval Mediterranean hist; late antique/medieval Christianity; saints. **SELECTED PUBLICATIONS** Auth, The Earliest Spanish Christian Views of Islam, Church Hist 55, 86; Conquerors and Chroniclers of Early Medieval Spain, Liverpool Univ Press, 90, revised ed, forthcoming; The Earliest Latin Lives of Muhammad, in Michael Gervers and Ramzi Jibran Bikhazi, eds, Conversion and Continuity: Indigenous Christian Communities in Islamic Lands, Eighth to Eighteenth Centuries, Pontifical Inst of Mediaeval Studies, 90; Crusade and Narrative: Bohemond and the Gesta Francorum, J of Medieval Hist, 17, 91; The 'Moors' of West Africa and the Beginnings of the Portuguese Slave Trade, J of Medieval and Renaissance Studies 24, 94; Making History: The Normans and Their Historians in Eleventh-century Italy, Univ PA Press, 95; Christian Views of Islam in Early Medieval Spain, in John Tolan, ed, Medieval Christian Perspectives of Islam: A Collection of Essays, Garland, 96; Christian Martyrs in Muslim Spain, Cambridge Univ Press, 88, Japanese ed, K. Hayashi, trans, Tosui Shobou Press, 98; Muhammad as Antichrist in Ninth-century Cordoba, in Mark Meyerson, ed, Christians, Muslims and Jews in Medieval and Early Modern Spain: Interaction and Cultural Change, Univ Notre Dame Press, forthcoming. **CONTACT ADDRESS** 551 N. College Ave., Claremont, CA, 91711. **EMAIL** kwolf@pomona.edu

WOLF, THOMAS PHILLIP
PERSONAL Born 09/27/1933, Norton County, KS, m, 1953, 3 children **DISCIPLINE** POLITICAL SCIENCE **EDUCATION** Wichita State Univ, AB, 59; MA, 61, PhD, 67, Stanford Univ. **CAREER** Asst Prof, 63-70, Assoc Prof, 70, Univ New Mexico; Assoc Prof, 70-75, Prof, Chr, 71-80, Dean Social Sciences, Indiana Univ Southeast,92-98. **HONORS AND AWARDS** Woodrow Wilson Fel, 59-60; NEH Col Faculty in Residence, 76-77; Joseph J. Malone Fel, 86. **MEMBERSHIPS** Amer Political Science Assoc; Amer Assoc of Univ Prof; Hansard Soc for Parliamentary Govt; British Politics Group; Western Social Science Assoc; Midwest Political Science Assoc; North Amer Conference on British Studies; English speaking Union; Indiana Consortium on International Programs; Southwest Political Science Assoc; Louisville Committee on Foreign Reltions; Indiana Acad of Social Sciences; Indiana Political Science Assoc; Kentucky Political Science Assoc. **RESEARCH** British politics; American presidency; public opinion **SELECTED PUBLICATIONS** Auth, Winston Leonard Spencer Churchill, Statesman Who Changed the World, 93; auth, Harold Macmillan, Leaders of Contemporary Europe, 95; auth, The Cold War, Events that Changed the World in the 20th Century, 95. **CONTACT ADDRESS** Division of Social Sciences, Indiana Univ, Southeast, New Albany, IN, 47150-2158. **EMAIL** tpwolf@ius.edu

WOLFE, CHRISTOPHER
PERSONAL Born 03/11/1949, Boston, MA, m, 1972, 10 children **DISCIPLINE** POLITICAL SCIENCE **EDUCATION** Univ Notre Dame, BA, 71; Boston Col, PhD, 78. **CAREER** Instr, 75-78, Assumption Col; Asst prof, 78-85, assoc prof, 85-92, PROF 92- & CHR 97-, MARQUETTE UNIV, 78-; Woodrow Wilson Fel, 71; Phi Beta Kappa, 71; NEH Fel, 94. **HONORS AND AWARDS** Benchmark Book Year Award, 87; Templeton Honor Rolls Educ Free Soc, 97. **MEMBERSHIPS** Am Polit Sci Assoc; Fel Cath Scholars; Federalist Soc. **RESEARCH** Constitutional law and judicial politics; Liberal Legal Theory; Natural Law. **SELECTED PUBLICATIONS** auth, "Liberalism and Paternalism: A Critique of Ronald Dworkin," Rev of Politics, 94; The Rise of Modern Judicial Review: From Constitutional Interpretation to Judge-Made Law, Rowman & Littlefield, 94; Liberalism at the Crossroads: An Introduction to Contemporary Liberal Political Theory and Its Critics, Rowman and Littlefield, 94; Being Worthy of Trust: A Response to Joseph Raz in Natural Law, Liberalism, and Morality, Oxford Univ Press, 96; How to Interpret the Constitution: Originalist Essays on Constitutional Interpretation and Judicial Review, Rowman & Littlefield, 96; "Natural Law and Liberal Public Reason," Am Jour of Jurisprudence, 97; Judicial Activism: Bulward of Freedom or Precarious Security?, Rowman & Littlefield, 97; Natural Law and Judicial Review in Natural Law and Contemporary Public Policy, Georgetown Univ Press, 98; **CONTACT ADDRESS** Dept of Political Science, Marquette Univ, Box 1881, Milwaukee, WI, 53201-1881. **EMAIL** christopher.wolfe@marquette.edu

WOLFE, DAVID L.
PERSONAL Born 03/07/1939, Lock Haven, PA, m, 1962, 3 children **DISCIPLINE** ANTHROPOLOGY, THEOLOGY, PHILOSOPHY, PHILOSOPHY OF EDUCATION **EDUCATION** Wheaton Col, BA, 61, MA, 64; NY Univ, PhD, 69. **CAREER** Inst to assoc prof of Philos, The Kings Col, NY, 63-70; asst to assoc prof of Philos, Wheaton Col, 70-74; assoc to prof of Philos, Gordon Col, 74-87; pastor, The Tunbridge Church, Tunbridge, VT, 87-. **MEMBERSHIPS** Am Philos Asn **RESEARCH** Religious epistemology' Philosophy of education; Philosophy of science. **SELECTED PUBLICATIONS** Auth Epistemology: The Justification of Belief, InterVarsity Press, 82; coed The Reality of Christian Learning, Christian Univ Press, 87; coed Slogans or Distinctives: Reforming Christian Education, Univ Press Am, 93. **CONTACT ADDRESS** Rivendell, 6 Wolfe Dr, Tunbridge, VT, 05077. **EMAIL** rivendell5@juno.com

WOLFE, ETHYLE RENEE
PERSONAL Born 03/14/1919, Burlington, VT, m, 1954 **DISCIPLINE** CLASSICAL LANGUAGES AND LITERATURE **EDUCATION** Univ Vt, BA, 40, MA, 42; NY Univ, PhD, 50. **CAREER** Lectr classics, eve session, 47-49, from instr to assoc prof, 49-67, acting chmn dept classics & comp lit, 62-63, chmn, 67-72, PROF CLASSICS, BROOKLYN COL, 68-, Dean Sch Humanities, 71-, Assoc ed, Class World, 65-70; co-ed, Am Class Rev, 70-. **MEMBERSHIPS** Am Philol Asn; Archaeol Inst Am; Am Soc Papyrologists. **RESEARCH** Latin poetry; Greek tragedy; papyrology. **SELECTED PUBLICATIONS** Auth, The Brooklyn College Core Curriculum, Arethusa, Vol 0027, 94; Cicero 'De Oratore' and the Liberal Arts Tradition in America, Class World, Vol 0088, 95. **CONTACT ADDRESS** Brooklyn Col, CUNY, Brooklyn, NY, 11210.

WOLFE, MARGARET RIPLEY
PERSONAL Born 02/03/1947, Kingsport, TN, m, 1966, 1 child **DISCIPLINE** HISTORY **EDUCATION** E Tn St Univ,

BS, 67, MA, 69; Univ Ky, PhD, 74. **CAREER** Instr to asst prof to assoc prof to prof, 69-, E Tn St Univ. **HONORS AND AWARDS** Distinguished Faculty Award, 77; E Tn St Univ Found Res Award, 79; E Tn St Univ Alumni Cert of Merit, 84; E Tn St Univ Commencement Speaker, 95., Haggin Fel, Univ Ky, 72-73; Outstanding Grad Stud in Hist, 68. **MEMBERSHIPS** St of Franklin Coun for Soc Stud; E Tn Hist Soc; Tn Hist Soc; Appalachian Stud Assoc; S Hist Assoc; S Assoc for Women Hist; S Amer Stud Assoc; St George Tucker Soc; Amer Soc for Environ Hist; Org of Amer Hist; Coordinating Coun for Women in Hist; Nat Hist Assoc; Amer Stud Assoc; Amer Hist Assoc; Amer Assoc Univ Prof; Tn St Employ Assoc. **RESEARCH** Amer soc hist; Amer urban, South, Appalachia women. **SELECTED PUBLICATIONS** Auth, Kingsport, Tennessee: A Planned American City, Univ Press Ky, 87; auth, Daughters of Canaan: A Saga of Southern Women, Univ Press Ky, 95; art, Tennessee at Two Hundred, J E Tn Hist, 96; art, World War I, Tennessee Encyclopedia of History and Culture, 98; art, Rumors of a Little Rebellion in Dixie: Real Women and Their Region, Mo Hist Rev, 98. **CONTACT ADDRESS** 175 Ripley Ln, Church Hill, TN, 37642. **EMAIL** wolfem@etsu.edu

WOLFE, MARTIN
PERSONAL Born 07/06/1920, Newark, NJ, m, 1942, 1 child **DISCIPLINE** HISTORY **EDUCATION** Univ Ill, BA, 41; Columbia Univ, MA, 46, PhD, 50. **CAREER** From instr to asst prof hist, Wayne Univ, 48-53; from asst prof to assoc prof, 53-71, PROF HIST, UNIV PA, 71-, Fulbright lectr, 56-57; assoc ed, J Econ Hist, 53-55; vis lectr, Yale Univ, 64-65. **MEMBERSHIPS** Econ Hist Asn; Soc Fr Hist Studies. **RESEARCH** Western imperialism; European economic history; French history. **SELECTED PUBLICATIONS** Auth, Highroad to the Stake, Church Hist, Vol 0062, 93; Rebel Daughters, Historian, Vol 0055, 93; Feeding Mars, 16th Century J, Vol 0025, 94; War and Government in the French Provinces, 16th Century J, Vol 0025, 94; The Lit De Justice, 16th Century J, Vol 0026, 95; Blood and Belief, Cath Hist Rev, Vol 0081, 95; A Clear and Present Danger + How Professor Fabrikant, Valery Overwhelmed Concordia University, Lingua Franca, Vol 0005, 95; A History of France, 1460-1560, 16th Century J, Vol 0027, 96; City and Spectacle in Medieval Europe, Comp Lit Stud, Vol 0033, 96; The Royal French State 1460-1610, 16th Century J, Vol 0027, 96; Arms and Military Technologies in the Medieval Universe, Speculum-J Medieval Stud, Vol 0072, 97; Law and Citizenship in Early Modern France, Renaissance Quart, Vol 0050, 97; French Renaissance Monarchy, 16th Century J, Vol 0028, 97. **CONTACT ADDRESS** Altoona Commonwealth Campus, Pennsylvania State Univ, Altoona, PA, 16601.

WOLFENSOHN, JAMES DAVID
PERSONAL Born 12/01/1933, Sydney, Australia, m, 1961, 3 children **DISCIPLINE** INVESTMENT BANKING **EDUCATION** Univ of Sydney, BA & LLB; Harvard Grad School of Business, MBA. **CAREER** Australian Olympic Fencing Team, 56; lawyer, Allen Allen & Hemsley; board member to chemn emeritus, Carnegie Hall, 70-; chemn of the board of trustees, 90-96, chemn emeritus, John F. Kennedy Center for the Performing Arts, 96-; head of investment banking, exec partner, Salomon Brothers; exec deputy chemn and managing dir, Schroders Ltd; pres, J. Henry Schroders Banking Corp; managing dir, Darling & Co; PRES, WORLD BANK GROUP, 95-; CHEMN OF THE BOARD, INST FOR ADVANCED STUDY AT PRINCETON UNIV. **HONORS AND AWARDS** David Rockefeller Prize, Museum of Modern Art; Honorary Knighthood, 95; decorated by the governments of Australia, France, Germany, Morocco, and Norway. **MEMBERSHIPS** Am Acad of Arts and Sci; Am Philos Soc. **SELECTED PUBLICATIONS** Speeches include: Concluding Remarks to the Plenary at the 1997 Annual Meeting, 97; The Challenge of Inclusion: 1997 Annual Meetings Address, 97; Towards Global Sustainability, 97; Address to the International Labour Conference, 97; The World Bank and the Evolving Challenges of Development, 97; Attracting Capital to Africa, 97; Livable Cities for the 21st Century: The Post Habitat II Agenda for the World Bank, 97; Address to the Closing Plenary Session of the Microcredit Summit, 97; The International Development Conference Keynote Address, 97; 1996 Annual Meetings Address, 96; Statement to the Press in Russia, 96; Emerging Trends in East Asia: New Directions in the World Bank's Partnership, 96; 1995 Annual Meetings Address, 95; Women and the Transformation of the 21st Century, 95. **CONTACT ADDRESS** 1818 H St NW, Washington, DC, 20433.

WOLFENSTEIN, E. VICTOR
PERSONAL Born 07/09/1940, Cleveland, OH, m, 1969, 4 children **DISCIPLINE** HISTORY; POLITICS; PSYCHOANALYSIS **EDUCATION** Columbia Col, BA, 62; Princeton Univ, MA, PhD, politics, 64, 65. **CAREER** UCLA, asst prof, 65-70, assoc prof, 70-79, prof, pol sci, 79-; Southern Cal Psychoanalytic Inst, PhD, psychoanalysis, 84, mem faculty, 84-. **HONORS AND AWARDS** UCLA, Mortor bd, Facult excell awd; Outstanding teacher awd, Southern Univ Psychoanal Inst; UCLA, Harriet Charles Luckman Distinguished teaching Awd; Guggenheim fel. **MEMBERSHIPS** APSA; Intl Psychoanal Asn; Intl Soc Pol Psychol; Western Pol Sci Asn. **RESEARCH** Pol Theory; Psychoanal Marxism; Race and gender theory. **SELECTED PUBLICATIONS** Nietzsche, Psychoanalysis and Gender, under review; Black Liberation and the Jewish Question, in: Marcus & Helmreich, eds, Black and Jews on the Couch, Praeger-Greenwood Pub, forth coming; Psychoanalytic-Marxism: Groundwork, London NY, Free Assoc Books, 90 and Guilford Pub, 93; other books and many articles. **CONTACT ADDRESS** Univ California, Los Angeles, CA, 90095-1472. **EMAIL** evw@ucla.edu

WOLFF, JANET
DISCIPLINE ART HISTORY/VISUAL AND CULTURAL STUDIES **EDUCATION** Univ Birmingham, UK, PhD. **CAREER** Dir, grad prog in Visual and Cult Stud & prof. **HONORS AND AWARDS** Guggenheim fel, 93-94. **RESEARCH** Sociology of art and cult; gender and cult; memoir, soc hist, and cult theory; modernism and modernity. **SELECTED PUBLICATIONS** Auth, Resident Alien: Feminist Cultural Criticism, New Haven: Yale UP, 95; Feminine Sentences: Essays on Women and Culture, Berkeley: Univ Calif Press, 90; Aesthetics and the Sociology of Art, London and Boston: Allen & Unwin, 83, 2nd ed, Ann Arbor: Univ Mich Press, 93; The Social Production of Art, NY UP, 81, 2nd ed, 93 & Hermeneutic Philosophy and the Sociology of Art, London and Boston: Routledge & Kegan Paul, 75. **CONTACT ADDRESS** Dept of Art and Art Hist, Univ of Rochester, 601 Elmwood Ave, Ste. 656, 423A Morey, Rochester, NY, 14642. **EMAIL** jwlf@db1.cc.rochester.edu

WOLLMAN, DAVID HARRIS
PERSONAL Born 06/20/1936, Boston, MA, m, 1967, 2 children **DISCIPLINE** BRITISH & EARLY MODERN EUROPEAN HISTORY **EDUCATION** Northeastern Univ, AB, 58; Univ Wis-Madison, MA, 61, PhD, 70. **CAREER** Instr Europ hist, Univ Md, Europ Div, 64; instr to asst prof hist, Knox Col, Ill, 67-71; asst prof to assoc prof, 71-78, coordr humanities courses, 73-76, prof hist, Geneva Col, 78-, Chmn Dept, 74-. **HONORS AND AWARDS** Nat Endowment for Humanities grant, summer 80 **MEMBERSHIPS** Conf Faith & Hist; Conf Brit Studies; Exec Dir, Beaver Co Ind Museum **RESEARCH** Stuart England, especially parliament and foreign policy; Amer Indus Hist **CONTACT ADDRESS** Dept of History, Geneva Col, 3200 College Ave, Beaver Falls, PA, 15010-3599. **EMAIL** dwollman@geneva.edu

WOLOCH, GEORGE MICHAEL
PERSONAL Born 06/01/1934, Akron, OH **DISCIPLINE** CLASSICS **EDUCATION** Yale Univ, BA, 56; Oxford Univ, BA, 60, MA, 63; Johns Hopkins Univ, PhD(classics), 66. **CAREER** Instr Latin, Pomfret Sch, 56-57; lectr sch gen studies, Brooklyn Col, 61; instr classics, McGill Univ, 61-63; jr instr, Johns Hopkins Univ, 63-64; asst prof, 66-70, ASSOC PROF CLASSICS, McGILL UNIV, 70-, Res assoc, Ctr Medieval Studies, Univ Calif, Los Angeles, 70; Can Coun leave fel, 70-71; hon cur, McGill Univ Coin Collection. **MEMBERSHIPS** Am Philol Asn; Class Asn Can; fel Royal Numis Soc. **RESEARCH** Roman cities; Ostrogothic Italy, AD 489-552; Ammianus Marcellinus. **SELECTED PUBLICATIONS** Auth, Mediterranean Cities, Phoenix-J Class Asn Can, Vol 0046, 92; Emperors and Gladiators, Amer Hist Rev, Vol 0099, 94. **CONTACT ADDRESS** Dept of Classics, McGill Univ, 855 Sherbrooke St W, Montreal, PQ, H3A 2T5.

WOLOCH, ISSER
PERSONAL Born 10/16/1937, New York, NY, m, 1962, 2 children **DISCIPLINE** MODERN EUROPEAN HISTORY **EDUCATION** Columbia Col, AB, 59; Princeton Univ, MA, 61, PhD, 65. **CAREER** Lectr hist, IN Univ, 63-64, asst prof, 65-66; asst prof, Univ CA, Los Angeles, 66-69; assoc prof, 69-75, PROF HIST, COLUMBIA UNIV, 75-, MOORE COLLEGIATE PROF OF HIST, 98-; Fel comt int & comp studies, Univ CA, Los Angeles, 68; Am Coun Learned Soc fel, 73-74; mem, Inst Advan Studies, 73-74, 88; NEH fel, 80-81; Guggenheim fel, 81-82; Ecole des Hautes Etudes Fellow, 86; Fellow, Center for the History of Freedom, DC, 94. **HONORS AND AWARDS** Leo Gershoy Award (Am Hist Asn), 95. **MEMBERSHIPS** AHA; Soc Fr Hist Studies. **RESEARCH** Eighteenth and nineteenth centuries; French Revolution; French social history. **SELECTED PUBLICATIONS** Auth, Jacobin Legacy: The Democratic Movement Under the Directory, Princeton Univ, 70; ed, The Peasantry in the Old Regime: Conditions and Protests, Holt, 70; auth, French economic and social history, J Interdisciplinary Hist, 74; coauth, The Western Experience, Knopf, 74, 6th ed, 94; auth, The French Veteran, from the Revolution to the Restoration, Univ NC, 79; Eighteenth-Century Europe: Tradition and Progress, 1715-1789, W W Norton, 82; The New Regime: Transformations of the French Civic Order, 1789-1820's, W. W. Norton, 94; ed, Revolution and the Meanings of Freedom in the Nineteenth Century, Stanford Univ Press, 96. **CONTACT ADDRESS** Dept of Hist, Columbia Univ, 2960 Broadway, New York, NY, 10027-6900. **EMAIL** iw6@columbia.edu

WOLOCH, NANCY
DISCIPLINE UNITED STATES HISTORY **EDUCATION** Wellesley Univ, BA; 61; Ind Univ, PhD, 68. **CAREER** Adj assoc prof. **SELECTED PUBLICATIONS** Auth, Women and the American Experience, 84; Early American Women: A Documentary History, 92; Muller v. Oregon: A Brief History with Documents, 96; co-auth, The American Century, 86; The Enduring Vision: A History of the American People, 90. **CONTACT ADDRESS** Dept of History, Columbia Col, New York, 2960 Broadway, New York, NY, 10027-6902.

WOLOHOJIAN, STEPHAN S.
DISCIPLINE RENAISSANCE ART **EDUCATION** Harvard Univ, PhD. **CAREER** Asst prof. **RESEARCH** Amrogio Lorenzetti. **SELECTED PUBLICATIONS** Pub(s), Burlington Mag; Speculum. **CONTACT ADDRESS** Dept of Art Hist, Univ Delaware, 162 Ctr Mall, Newark, DE, 19716. **EMAIL** stephanw@udel.edu

WOLPER, ETHEL SARA
DISCIPLINE HISTORY OF THE MIDDLE EAST, HISTORY OF ISLAM **EDUCATION** UCLA, PhD. **CAREER** Asst prof, Univ NH, 96-. **HONORS AND AWARDS** Mellow fel in Near Eastern Lit and Islamic Art Hist; Cornell Univ fel; Ittleson fel, Nat Gallery of Art; AAUW fel. **RESEARCH** Dervish lodges in pre-Ottoman Anatolia. **SELECTED PUBLICATIONS** Auth, Religious conversion and Social Transformation, Al 'Usur al-Wusta, 94; The Politics of Patronage: Political Change and the Construction of Dervish Lodges in Silvas, Mugarnas, 95. **CONTACT ADDRESS** Univ NH, Durham, NH, 03824. **EMAIL** esw@hopper.unh.edu

WOLSEY, MARY LOU MORRIS
PERSONAL Born 02/21/1936, Baltimore, MD, m, 1965, 2 children **DISCIPLINE** MEDIEVAL FRENCH LANGUAGE & LITERATURE **EDUCATION** Mary Washington Col, BA, 58; Univ Kans, MA, 61; Univ Besancon, cert etudes super, 64; Univ Minn, PhD(French), 72. **CAREER** Asst instr French, Univ Kans, 58-61; instr, Mary Washington Col, 61-63; asst English, Teachers Col, Besancon, France, 63-64; teaching assoc French, Univ Pa, 64-65 & Univ Minn, 65-67; instr, Macalester Col, 67-68, adj prof, 72-78; part-time asst prof, 76-81, Asst Prof French, Col St Thomas, 81-, Vis prof, Univ Bristol, England, 78-79. **MEMBERSHIPS** Am Asn Teachers French; Am Coun Teaching Foreign Lang; Mediaeval Acad Am; Alliance Francaise; Midwest Mod Lang Asn Am. **RESEARCH** Medieval French romance; the French novel; computer research in French. **SELECTED PUBLICATIONS** Auth, The Eracle of Gautier d'Arras: A critical study, Diss Abstr Int, 10/72. **CONTACT ADDRESS** 2115 Summit Ave, St. Paul, MN, 55105-1096. **EMAIL** mpwopsey@stthomas.edu

WOLTER, JOHN A.
PERSONAL Born 07/25/1925, St. Paul, MN, m, 1956, 4 children **DISCIPLINE** GEOGRAPHY **EDUCATION** Univ Minn, BA, 56, MA, 65, PhD, 75 **CAREER** Map Libr and Lectr, 61-64, Asst to Dir Libraries, Univ Minn Libr, 64-65; Asst Prof, Univ Wi Wis-River Falls, 66-68, Actg Dept Chair, 68; Asst Chief to Division Chief, Geog & Map Division, Libr Congress, 68-91. **HONORS AND AWARDS** Award for Distinguished Service, Libr Congress, 92. **MEMBERSHIPS** NMex Geog Soc; Asn Am Cartog; Am Libr Asn; Am Congress Surveying and Mapping; Soc Nautical Res; Hakluyt Soc; Int Soc Hist Cartog; Wash Map Soc; N Am Soc Oceanic Hist; Explorer's Club. **RESEARCH** History of cartography and nautical science. **SELECTED PUBLICATIONS** Auth, Johann Georg Kohl in America, Progress of Discovery: Johann Georg Kohl. Auf Den Spuren Der Entdecker, Akademische Druck-und Verlaganstalt, 93; coauth, Progress of Discovery: Johann George Kohl. Auf Den Spuren Der Entdecker, Akademische Druck-und Verlaganstalt, 93; co-ed, Images of the World: The Atlas Through History, McGraw Hill/Libr Congress, 97. **CONTACT ADDRESS** 5430 Ring Dove Ln., Columbia, MD, 21044-1716.

WOLTERS, OLIVER WILLIAM
PERSONAL Born 06/08/1915, Reading, England, m, 1955, 2 children **DISCIPLINE** HISTORY OF SOUTHEAST ASIA **EDUCATION** Oxford Univ, BA, 37, MA, 45; Univ London, PhD, 62. **CAREER** Malayan Civil Serv, 37-57; lectr hist, Sch Orient & African Studies, Univ London, 57-63; prof, 63-75, chmn dept Asian studies, 70-72, Goldwin Smith Prof Southeast Asian Hist, 75-, Cornell Univ; trustee, Breezewood Found, Baltimore, 64-. **MEMBERSHIPS** Asn Asian Studies. **RESEARCH** Earlier Southeast Asian history with a special interest in earlier Vietnamese history. **SELECTED PUBLICATIONS** Art, Assertions of Cultural Well-being in 14th century Vietnam, J Southeast Asian Studies, 79-80; art, Studying Srivijaya, J Malaysian Branch Royal Asiatic Soc, 80. **CONTACT ADDRESS** Dept of History, Cornell Univ, Ithaca, NY, 14853.

WOLTERS, RAYMOND
PERSONAL Born 07/25/1938, Kansas City, MO, m, 1962, 3 children **DISCIPLINE** AMERICAN HISTORY **EDUCATION** Stanford Univ, AB, 60; Univ Calif, PhD(hist), 67. **CAREER** From instr to assoc prof, 65-75, PROF HIST, UNIV DEL, 75-, Am Coun Learned Soc res grant, 70, fel, 78-79; Nat Endowment for Humanities fel, 71-72; Am Philos Soc res grant, 74; Ctr Advanced Study, Univ Del, 82-83. **MEMBERSHIPS** Asn Studies Afro-Am Life & Hist; Orgn Am Historians; AHA. **RESEARCH** United States and American Negro history. **SELECTED PUBLICATIONS** Auth, Frazier, E. Franklin Reconsidered, J Amer Hist, Vol 0080, 93; TVA and Black Ameri-

cans, Labor Hist, Vol 0035, 94; Greek and Latin Sources for the Early History of Central Europe Until 500-AD, Vol 3, from Tacitus to Ausonius 2nd-4th-Century-AD, Historische Zeitschrift, Vol 0259, 94; Washington, Booker, T. and the Adult Education Movement, Amer Hist Rev, Vol 0100, 95; On the Limits of the Law, Amer J Legal Hist, Vol 0040, 96; The Boundary of the Roman Empire from the Mosel River to the North Sea Coast, Historische Zeitschrift, Vol 0264, 97. **CONTACT ADDRESS** Dept of Hist, Univ of Del, Newark, DE, 19718.

WOLVERTON, ROBERT E.
PERSONAL Born 08/04/1925, Indianapolis, IN, m, 1952, 4 children **DISCIPLINE** CLASSICS **EDUCATION** Hanover Col, AB, 48; Univ MI, MA, 49; Univ NC, PhD(Latin, Greek & ancient hist), 54. **CAREER** Asst prof classics, Univ GA, 54-59; from asst to assoc prof classics & hist, Tufts Univ, 59-62; assoc prof classics & dir hon prog, FL State Univ, 62-67; assoc dean grad col, Univ Ill, 67-69; dean grad sch, Miami Univ, OH, 69-72; prof classics & pres, Col of Mt St Josephs on the OH, 72-77; Prof Classics & Educ Leadership & Vpres Acad Affairs, MS State Univ, 77-86, Title IV consult-reader of langs, NDEA, 67-72; consult-reviewer admin, NCent Asn Cols & Schs, 67-77; instr personnel mgt, Main Event Mgt Inc, 76-; mem exec comt, Nat Coun Chief Acad Officers, 81-; Head dept. For Lang, Miss State Univ, 91-96. **HONORS AND AWARDS** Alumni Achievement Award, Hanover Col, 71; hon life pres, Am Class League, 77, Outstanding Tchr Award, 91; John Grisham Master Tchr, 91., LittD, Col of Mt St Joseph on the OH, 77. **MEMBERSHIPS** Am Class League (pres, 72-76); Am Philol Asn; Class Asn Mid West & South; Am Asn Higher Educ. **RESEARCH** Administration in higher educ; class mythology; etymology. **SELECTED PUBLICATIONS** Auth, Classical Elements in English Words, 66 & An Outline of Classical Mythology, 67, Littlefield; contribr, Graduate Programs and Admission Manual, 4 vols, Grad Record & Exam Bd & Coun Grad Schs USA, 71 & 72; auth, The future of classics, Class Outlook, 76; contrib auth & translr, A Life of George Washington, in Latin Prose, George Washington Univ, 76; The future of graduate studies in the humanities, Nat Forum, 79; contribr, Mythological References, Arete Publ, 80. **CONTACT ADDRESS** Dept of Foreign Langs, Mississippi State Univ, PO Drawer FL, Mississippi State, MS, 39762. **EMAIL** REW1@RA.MSSTATE.EDU

WOMACK, MORRIS M.
DISCIPLINE CLASSICAL RHETORIC, SPEECH **EDUCATION** Butler Univ, BA, Butler Univ, BD, 58; Wayne State Univ, PhD, 67. **CAREER** Prof, Mich Christian Col, 59-66; REGISTRAR, PROF SPEECH, MICH CHRISTIAN COL, 67-; minister, Church of Christ, 47-. **CONTACT ADDRESS** 409 Vista Dorado Ln, Oak Park, CA, 91377. **EMAIL** womack@pepperdine.edu

WOOD, CAROLYN B.
DISCIPLINE ART HISTORY **EDUCATION** Univ NC, Chapel Hill, PhD. **CAREER** Educr for univ audiences, Univ NC, Chapel Hill. **RESEARCH** Baroque art. **SELECTED PUBLICATIONS** Coed, The Craft of Art: Originality and Industry in the Italian Renaissance and Baroque Workshop, Univ GA Press, 95. **CONTACT ADDRESS** Univ N. Carolina, Chapel Hill, Chapel Hill, NC, 27599.

WOOD, CHARLES B., III
PERSONAL Born 09/29/1936, Hartford, CT, m, 1990, 2 children **DISCIPLINE** HISTORY OF ART AND ARCHITECTURE **EDUCATION** Univ Penn, MA, 65. **CAREER** Antiquarian bookseller, 67-, Charles B Wood III Inc. **MEMBERSHIPS** AAS; SAH. **RESEARCH** History of the Architectural Book. **SELECTED PUBLICATIONS** Collaborator of, 100 Rare Book Catalogues, 67-; auth, The New Pattern Books and the Role of the Agricultural Press, in: Prophet with Honor, The Career of Andrew Jackson Downing, eds, George B Tatum, Elizabeth MacDougal, Dum Barton Oaks, 89. **CONTACT ADDRESS** Box 2369, Cambridge, MA, 02238. **EMAIL** cbw@world.std.com

WOOD, CHARLES TUTTLE
PERSONAL Born 10/29/1933, St. Paul, MN, m, 1955, 4 children **DISCIPLINE** HISTORY **EDUCATION** Harvard Univ, AB, 55, AM, 57, PhD, 62. **CAREER** Instr hist, Harvard Univ, 61-64; from asst prof to assoc prof, 64-71, actg chmn dept, 71-72, chmn prog comp lit, 77, Prof hist, 71-80, Chmn Dept, 76-89, Daniel Webster prof Hist, 80-96, EMERITUS, 96, DARTMOUTH COL. **HONORS AND AWARDS** ACLS fel, 80-81; Am Bar Fdn fel, 81-82; Medieval Acad Am fel, 84-; John Simon Guggenheim fel, 86-87. **MEMBERSHIPS** AHA; Am Soc Legal Hist; Int Comn for Hist of Rep & Parliamentary Inst; Mediaeval Acad Am; Conf Brit Studies. **RESEARCH** Medieval history, especially England and France. **SELECTED PUBLICATIONS** Auth, French apanages and the Capetian monarchy 1224-1328, Harvard Univ, 66; The age of chivalry: Manners and morals 1000-1450, Weidenfeld & Nicolson, 70; ed, Philip the Fair and Boniface VIII: State vs Papacy, 2nd ed, Krieger, 76; auth, Joan of Arc and Richard III, Oxford, 88; co-ed, The Trial of CHarles I, UPNE, 89; co-ed, Fresh Verdicts on Joan of Arc, Garland, 96; and various articles. **CONTACT ADDRESS** 7 N Balch St, Hanover, NH, 03755. **EMAIL** charles.t.wood@dartmouth.edu

WOOD, CURTIS W.
DISCIPLINE APPALACHIAN STUDIES **EDUCATION** Univ NC, PhD. **CAREER** Hist Dept, Western Carolina Univ **SELECTED PUBLICATIONS** Auth, Ulster and North America: Transatlantic Perspectives on the Scotch-Irish, 97s. **CONTACT ADDRESS** Western Carolina Univ, Cullowhee, NC, 28723.

WOOD, FORREST GLEN
PERSONAL Born 03/15/1931, Oak Park, IL, m, 1978, 2 children **DISCIPLINE** AMERICAN NEGRO AND ECONOMIC HISTORY **EDUCATION** Sacramento State Col, AB, 57, MA, 58; Univ Calif, Berkeley, PhD(hist), 63. **CAREER** Asst prof hist, Bakersfield Ctr, 63-70, found res grant, 68, assoc prof, 70-80, PROF HIST, CALIF STATE COL, BAKERSFIELD, 80-, Vis prof Univ Iowa, summer 68 & Univ Calif, Santa Cruz, 71; Nat Endowment for Humanities, Brown, 76, Harvard, 81; consult, Nat Endowment for Humanities, 77-79. **MEMBERSHIPS** AHA; Orgn Am Historians; Southern Hist Asn; Asn Studies Negro Life & Cult. **RESEARCH** History of racism in America; Negro history; Civil War and Reconstruction. **SELECTED PUBLICATIONS** Auth, The Persistence of Racism in America, J Amer Hist, Vol 0080, 93. **CONTACT ADDRESS** Dept of Hist, California State Univ, Bakersfield, Bakersfield, CA, 93309.

WOOD, GORDON STEWART
PERSONAL Born 11/27/1933, Concord, MA, m, 1956, 3 children **DISCIPLINE** EARLY AMERICAN HISTORY **EDUCATION** Tufts Univ, AB, 55; Harvard Univ, AM, 59, PhD, 64. **CAREER** Asst prof early Am hist, Harvard Univ, 66-67; assoc prof, Univ Mich, 67-69; prof hist, Brown Univ, 69-; fel, Inst Early Am Hist & Cult, Williamsburg, Va, 64-66; mem educ bd, J Am Hist, 71-74; Guggenheim fel, 80-81; Pitt prof, Cambridge Univ, 82-83. **HONORS AND AWARDS** Bancroft Prize, 70; John H Dunning Prize, AHA, 70; Pulitzer Prize, 93. **MEMBERSHIPS** AHA; Orgn Am Hist; Soc Am Historians; Am Antiquarian Soc. **RESEARCH** Early American history. **SELECTED PUBLICATIONS** Auth, The Creation of the American Republic, 1776-1787, Univ NC, 69; ed, Rising Glory of America, 1760-1820, Braziller, 71; coauth, The Great Republic, 77 & 81; auth, The Radicalism of the American Revolution. **CONTACT ADDRESS** Dept of History, Brown Univ, Providence, RI, 02912. **EMAIL** GORDON_WOOD@BROWN.EDU

WOOD, JAMES BRIAN
PERSONAL Born 03/13/1946, Sandersville, GA, m, 1968, 3 children **DISCIPLINE** EARLY MODERN EUROPEAN HISTORY, MILITARY HISTORY **EDUCATION** Eckerd Col, BA, 68; Emory Univ, PhD(hist), 73. **CAREER** Asst prof, 73-80, assoc prof, 80-85, prof hist, Williams Col, 85-, chair, 94-98. **HONORS AND AWARDS** Nancy Roelker Prize, 84; Baxter Prof Hist, 94-97; Wilmott Family Third Century Prof Hist, 97-; Soc for Military Hist, Distinguished Book Award, 98. **RESEARCH** Early modern French nobility; French wars of religion; French social and economic history; military history. **SELECTED PUBLICATIONS** Auth, La structure sociale de la Noblesse dans le bailliage de Caen et ses modifications (1463-1666), Annales de Normandie, 72; The decline of the nobility in sixteenth and early seventeenth century France: Myth or reality?, J Mod Hist, 76; Demographic pressure and social mobility among the nobility of early modern France, 16th Century J, 77; Endogamy and mesalliance: The marriage patterns of the nobility of the election of Bayeaux, 1430-1669, Fr Hist Studies, 78; The Nobility of the Election of Bayeaux, 1463-1666: Social Continuity and Change Among the Provincial Nobility of Early Modern France, Princeton Univ Press, 80; the Impact of Wars of Religion: A View of France in 1581, 16th Century Jour, 84; The Royal Army During the Early Wars of Religion, In: Society and Institutions in Early Modern France, Univ Ga Press, 91; The King's Army: Warfare, Soldiers, and Society during the Wars of Religion in France, 1562-76, Cambridge Univ Press, 96. **CONTACT ADDRESS** Dept of Hist, Williams Col, 880 Main St, Williamstown, MA, 01267-2600. **EMAIL** james.b.wood@williams.edu

WOOD, KIRK
DISCIPLINE HISTORY **EDUCATION** Frederick Col, BA, 68; Va Polytech Inst, MA, 70; Univ SC, PhD, 78. **CAREER** Assoc dir grad stud, Col Bus, Univ SC, 79-86; dead grad stud, 86-89, ASSOC PROF HIST, 95-, ALA STATE UNIV. **CONTACT ADDRESS** 300 Cheekwood Ln, Montgomery, AL, 36116. **EMAIL** mamafresh@aol.com

WOOD, MARCUS
DISCIPLINE ENGLISH, AMERICAN STUDIES **EDUCATION** St. Catherine's Col, Oxford, BA, 80; Royal Col of Art, MA, 86; Worcester Col, Oxford, PhD, 91. **CAREER** Sr res fel, Univ Manchester. **RESEARCH** Abolition propaganda. **CONTACT ADDRESS** Dept of English & American Studies, Univ of Manchester, Oxford Rd, Manchester, ., M13 9PL.

WOOD, PETER H.
DISCIPLINE HISTORY **EDUCATION** Harvard Univ, PhD, 72. **CAREER** Prof, 75-, Duke Univ. **HONORS AND AWARDS** Albert J. Beveridge Awd, 74; James Harvey Robinson Prize, 84. **MEMBERSHIPS** Am Gourd Soc. **RESEARCH** Early Am hist. **SELECTED PUBLICATIONS** Auth, Black Majority: Negroes in Colonial South Carolina from 1670 through the Stono Rebellion, 74; Strange New Land: African Americans 1617-1776, 96; co-auth, Natives and Newcomers: The Way We Lived in North Carolina before 1770, 83; Winslow Homer's Images of Blacks: The Civil War and Reconstruction Years, 88; co-ed, Powhatan's Mantle: Indian's in the Colonial Southeast, 89. **CONTACT ADDRESS** Dept of Hist, Duke Univ, Carr Bldg, Durham, NC, 27706. **EMAIL** pwood@acpub.duke.edu

WOODARD, FREDRICK
PERSONAL Born 01/29/1939, Kingfisher, OK, w **DISCIPLINE** EDUCATION **EDUCATION** Iowa Wesleyan College, Mt. Pleasant, IA, BA, 1961; University of Iowa, Iowa City, IA, MA, 1972, PhD, 1976. **CAREER** West High School, Davenport, IA, teacher, 1961-66; Black Hawk Community College, Moline, IL, instructor, 1967-69; Cornell College, Mt. Vernon, IA, instructor, 1972-76; UNIV OF IOWA, IOWA CITY, IA, instructor, 1973-76, assistant professor, 1976-79, associate professor, 1979-80, acting associate dean of the Faculties, Office of Academic Affairs, 1981-83, associate dean of the Faculties, Office of the Vice President for Academic Affairs, 1983-90, ASSOC VICE PRESIDENT FOR ACADEMIC AFFAIRS, 1990-, Museum of Art, interim director, 1990-92; Univ of California at San Diego, visiting assoc prof, 1980. **MEMBERSHIPS** Chair of session, Council on College Composition, 1975, 1977, 1981, 1983, 1985; chair of session, Midwest Modern Language Association, 1970, 1972, 1973, 1977-79, 1981-83; chair of session, National Council of the Teachers of English, 1985; member, American Library Association, 1980-; member, Modern Language Association, 1980-; committee member, Big 10 Academic Personnel Officers, 1985; committee member, Professional and Organizational Development Network in Higher Education, 1985-. **CONTACT ADDRESS** Office of Academic Affairs, Univ of Iowa, 111 Jessup Hall, Iowa City, IA, 52242.

WOODHOUSE, EDWARD JAMES
PERSONAL Born 12/25/1946, Durham, NC, 4 children **DISCIPLINE** POLITICAL SCIENCE **EDUCATION** Yale 83 PhD **CAREER** Assoc Prof, Rensselaer Polytechnic Institute, 18 years. **HONORS AND AWARDS** Woodrow Wilson Fell; Intl Studies; Assoc Sprout Award in Intl Ecology. **MEMBERSHIPS** Am Pol Sci; Soc for Soc Studies of Sci. **RESEARCH** Wiser Steeing of Tech **SELECTED PUBLICATIONS** The Polic-Making Process, 3rd ed, Englewood Cliffs Prentice Hall, 93(with Charles E. Lindblom); When Expert Advice Works and When it Does Not, IEEE Technology and Society Magazine, 97, pp 23-29(with Dean Nieusma); Science, Government and the Politics of Knowledge, in Handbook of Science and Technology Sutdies, Sage, 95, pp 533-553(with Susan Cozzensï; Can Science Be More Useful In Politics? The Case of Ecological Risk Assessment, Human and Ecological Risk Assessment vol 1, 95, pp 395-406; Incrmentalism,Intelligent Trial-and -Error and the Future of Ploitical Decision Theory, in H. Redner ed, An Heretical Heir of the Enlightenment Westview, 93(with David Collingridge). **CONTACT ADDRESS** Rensselaer Polytech Inst, Troy, NY, 12180-3590. **EMAIL** woodhouse@RPI.EDU

WOODLAND, CALVIN EMMANUEL
PERSONAL Born 11/03/1943, LaPlata, Maryland, s **DISCIPLINE** EDUCATION **EDUCATION** Morgan State Univ, BS 1965; Howard Univ, MA 1970; Rutgers Univ, EdD 1975; Southern California for Professional Studies, Psy D, 1997. **CAREER** MD Dept of Health & Mental Hygiene, music & rehab therapist 1966-70; Essex Co Coll, counselor/dir of educ advisement 1970-74; Morgan State Univ Sch of Educ, dir of teacher corps, assoc prof of educ asst dean 1974-81; Coppin State Coll, dir of spec svcs, acting dean of students 1981-82; Charles County Comm Coll, dean 1982-86; Northern Virginia Comm Coll, dean beginning 1986; vp of student dev, Bergen Comm Coll, vp of student services, currently. **HONORS AND AWARDS** HEW Fellow US Dept of Health, Educ Welfare 1976; ERIC Publications on Data Base as a Tool for Recruitment of Minority Students 1979, 85; Innovations in Counseling Psychology Book Review Journal of Contemporary Psychology 1979; Outstanding Achievement and Comm Serv Southern MD Chain Chap of Links 1986. **MEMBERSHIPS** Evaluator Middle States Assoc of Colleges & Schools 1979-; Amer Psychological Assoc, Amer Assoc for Counseling Dev, Amer Assoc of Rehab Therapists, Natl Commission for African-American Education; Health & Human Services Board for Volusia/Flagler Counties, children & family's service committee; Volusia/Flagler Counties, juvenile justice board. **CONTACT ADDRESS** VP Student Serivces, Bergen Comm Col, 400 Paramus Rd, Paramus, NJ, 07652-1595.

WOODMAN, HAROLD DAVID
PERSONAL Born 04/21/1928, Chicago, IL, m, 1954, 2 children **DISCIPLINE** UNITED STATES ECONOMIC HISTORY **EDUCATION** Roosevelt Univ, BA, 57; Univ Chicago, MA, 59, PhD(hist), 64. **CAREER** Lectr hist, Roosevelt Univ, 62-63; from asst prof to prof, Univ Mo-Columbia, 63-71; PROF

HIST, PURDUE UNIV, WEST LAFAYETTE, 71-, Soc Sci Res Coun fac fel, 69-70; fel, Woodrow Wilson Int Ctr Scholars, Washington, DC, 77. **HONORS AND AWARDS** Everett E Edwards Award, Agr Hist Soc, 63; Ramsdell Award, South Hist Asn, 65. **MEMBERSHIPS** AHA; Econ Hist Asn; Orgn Am Historians; Southern Hist Asn; Agr Hist Soc. **RESEARCH** United States economic history of the 19th century; history of the American South. **SELECTED PUBLICATIONS** Auth, Favorites of Fortune, J Interdisciplinary Hist, Vol 0023, 93; The Meaning of Freedom, J Amer Hist, Vol 0080, 93; Cotton and Capital, Civil War Hist, Vol 0039, 93; Without Consent or Contract--The Rise and Fall of American Slavery, J Econ Hist, Vol 0055, 95; Masters and Lords, J Interdisciplinary Hist, Vol 0026, 95; Without Consent or Contract--The Rise and Fall of American Slavery--Markets and Production--Technical Papers, Vol 1, J Econ Hist, Vol 0055, 95; Poor Whites of the Antebellum South, Revs in Amer Hist, Vol 0023, 95; The Burden of Dependency, Revs in Amer Hist, Vol 0023, 95; The Agrarian Origins of American Capitalism, Revs in Amer Hist, Vol 0023, 95; The Work of Reconstruction, Ark Hist Quart, Vol 0055, 96; Class, Race, Politics, and the Modernization of the Postbellum South, J Southern Hist, Vol 0063, 97. **CONTACT ADDRESS** Dept of Hist, Purdue Univ, West Lafayette, IN, 47907.

WOODMAN, TAYLOR
DISCIPLINE ART HISTORY **EDUCATION** Univ Chicago, PhD, 97. **CAREER** Asst prof, Univ IL at Chicago. **RESEARCH** Southeast Asian art; Islamic art. **SELECTED PUBLICATIONS** Auth, Bibliography of South and Southeast Asian Art and Archaeology 1989-1991. **CONTACT ADDRESS** Art Hist Dept, Univ Illinois Chicago, S Halsted St, PO Box 705, Chicago, IL, 60607.

WOODRUFF, NAN ELIZABETH
PERSONAL Born 08/25/1949, Anniston, AL **DISCIPLINE** AMERICAN HISTORY **EDUCATION** Jacksonville State Univ, BA, 71; Univ Ark, MA, 73; Univ Tenn, PhD(hist), 77. **CAREER** Asst ed, Booker T Washington Papers, 77-78; ASST PROF HIST, COL CHARLESTON, 79-. **MEMBERSHIPS** Southern Hist Asn; AHA; Orgn Am Historians. **RESEARCH** Social history; southern agricultural history. **SELECTED PUBLICATIONS** Auth, Mississippi Delta Planters and Debates Over Mechanization, Labor, and Civil-Rights in the 1940s, J Southern Hist, Vol 0060, 94; The Most Southern Place on Earth, Reviews in American History, Vol 0022, 94; The Politics of Despair, J Amer Hist, Vol 0081, 95; Night Riders, J Amer Hist, Vol 0081, 95; Days of Hope, J Amer Hist, Vol 0083, 97; Political Culture in the 19th-Century South, J Amer Hist, Vol 0084, 97. **CONTACT ADDRESS** Pennsylvania State Univ, 104 Davey Lab, University Pk, PA, 16802.

WOODS, ALAN LAMBERT
PERSONAL Born 11/23/1942, Philadelphia, PA, m, 1967, 1 child **DISCIPLINE** THEATRE HISTORY **EDUCATION** Columbia Univ, AB, 64; Univ Southern Calif, MA, 69, PhD(theatre), 72. **CAREER** Lectr drama, Univ Southern Calif, 68-71; instr theatre, Long Beach City Col, 71-72; asst prof to assoc prof Theatre, Ohio State Univ, 72-, Lectr theatre, Calif State Univ, Los Angeles, 70; ed, Theatre Studies, 72-77; coordr res panel Comt Instnl Coop, 73-; lectr, Am Asn Health, Phys Educ & Recreation, 74; co-ed, Educ Theatre J, Univ Col Theatre Asn, 78-80; mem, res comn Am Theatre Asn, 78 & exec comt, Am Soc Theatre Res, 76-78, 89-92; visiting prof, Ind Univ, 78-79; dir, Lawrence and Lee Theatre Res Inst, 79-; pres, Ohio Theatre Alliance, 90-91. **HONORS AND AWARDS** Fel, Col of the Am Theatre, 96. **MEMBERSHIPS** Am Theatre Asn; Am Soc Theatre Res. **RESEARCH** Ancient theatre; 19th century popular theatre; theatre historiography. **SELECTED PUBLICATIONS** Coauth, A note on the symmetry of Delphi, Theatre Surv, 5/72; auth, Popular theatre in Los Angeles, Players, 5/73; A quantification approach to popular American theatre, Res in Educ, 1/74; James J Corbett, theatrical star, J Sports Hist, 76; Theatre historiography, Ohio Speech J, 76; Reconstructions of performances, Copenhagen, Royal Libr, 76; Frederick B Warde, tragedian, Educ Theatre J, 77; The Ohio Theatre, 80; Selected Plays of Jerome Lawrence and Robert E. Lee, Ohio State Univ Press, 95. **CONTACT ADDRESS** Dept of Theatre, Ohio State Univ, 1806 Cannon Dr, Columbus, OH, 43210-1230. **EMAIL** woods1@osu.edu

WOODS, DANIEL
DISCIPLINE HISTORY **EDUCATION** Emmanuel Col, AA; Roanoke Col, BA; Univ Ga, MA; Univ Miss, PhD. **CAREER** Assoc prof. **RESEARCH** Religion in American life. **SELECTED PUBLICATIONS** Auth, rev of The Apostle, The Jour Southern Rel, 98. **CONTACT ADDRESS** Dept of Hist, Ferrum Col, PO Box 1000, Ferrum, VA, 24088-9000. **EMAIL** dgwoods@ferrum.edu

WOODS, JOSEPH MICHAEL
PERSONAL Born 05/19/1927, Wilmington, DE **DISCIPLINE** MODERN BRITISH AND IRISH HISTORY **EDUCATION** Univ Del, BA, 48; Harvard Univ, MA, 49, PhD(hist), 67. **CAREER** Instr, Mass Inst Technol, 63-65; asst prof, Univ NH, 65-66; asst prof, Northeastern Univ, 67-68; ASSOC PROF HIST, YORK UNIV, 68-, Vis scholar, Menninger Found, Topeka, Kans, 72-73. **MEMBERSHIPS** Am Comt Irish Studies. **RESEARCH** Charles Stewart Parnell; psychohistory; English social history. **SELECTED PUBLICATIONS** Auth, Some considerations on psychohistory, The Historian, 8/74; Toward a psychoanalytic interpretation of Charles Stewart Parnell, Bull Menninger Clinic, 11/78. **CONTACT ADDRESS** York Univ, 20 Fashion Roseway Ste 518W, Willowdale, ON, M2N 6B5.

WOODS, RANDALL B.
PERSONAL Born 10/10/1944, Galveston, TX, m, 1966, 2 children **DISCIPLINE** HISTORY **EDUCATION** Univ Tex Austin, PhD. **CAREER** Prof. **HONORS AND AWARDS** Robert H. Ferrel Prize, 96; Va Ledbetter Prize, 96. **RESEARCH** United States diplomatic history; 20th century United States. **SELECTED PUBLICATIONS** Auth, Fulbright: A Biography, Cambridge, 95; A Changing of the Guard: Anglo-American Relations, 1941-1946, Univ NC, 90; A Black Odyssey: John Lewis Waller and the Promise of American Life, 1878-1900, Univ Kans, 81; co-auth, The Dawning of the Cold War: America's Quest for Order, 1945-1950, Univ Ga, 91. **CONTACT ADDRESS** History Dept, Univ of Arkansas, Fayetteville, 403 Old Main, Fayetteville, AR, 72701. **EMAIL** rwoods@comp.uark.edu

WOODS, JR., ROBERT L.
PERSONAL Born 02/17/1945, CA, m, 1975, 1 child **DISCIPLINE** HISTORY **EDUCATION** Pomona Col, BA (Hist), 67; UCLA, PhD (Hist), 74. **CAREER** Lect, Hist, UCLA, 73-74; asst prof Hist, 74-80, ASSOC PROF, HIST, POMONA COL, 81-. **HONORS AND AWARDS** Haynes Found Grant, 79; Fel in Legal Hist, Am Bar Asn, 83; Am Coun of Learned Socs Fel, 96-97. **MEMBERSHIPS** Conference on British Studies; Economic History Soc; Past & Present Soc; Am Soc for Legal Hist; Renaissance Soc of Am; Selden Soc. **RESEARCH** English legal hist; 15th & 16th century English legal culture; Justices of the Peace; Tudor political order. **SELECTED PUBLICATIONS** Auth, Politics and Precedent: Wolsey's Parliment of 1523, Huntington Library Quart, XL; six signed entries in R. Zaller and R. Greaves, eds, Biographical Dictionary of British Radicals in the Seventeenth Century, 3 vols, Harvester Press, 81-83; Individuals in the Rioting Crowd: A New Approach, J of Interdisciplinary Hist XIV:I, 83; Programmers, Computers, and Computer Languages: Some Implications for History, Computers and the Humanities, 16, 82; Skills for Historians, in Peter Denley and Deian Hopkins, History and Computing, Manchester Univ Press, 87; Large Scale Text Operations on Microcomputers, in Thomas Moberg, ed, The Ninth International Conference on Data Bases in the Humanities and Social Sciences, Paradigm Press, 88; Thoughts Rescued: An Historian's Use of APL, in Edward Shaw, ed, APL as a Tool of Thought, VIII, Conference Proceedings, NYSIGAPL, 93; ed with Charles Carlton, Mary Robertson, and Joseph Block, State, Sovereigns and Society, Stroud GLOUCS and Allan Sutton and St. Martin's Press, 97; Charles II and the Politics of Sex and Scandal, in Carlton, Woods, Robertson and Block, eds, State, Sovereigns and Society, Stroud GLOUCS, Allan Sutton and St. martin's, 97; numerous book reviews. **CONTACT ADDRESS** Dept of Hist, Pomona Col, Pearsons Hall 111, Claremont, CA, 91711. **EMAIL** RWoods@Pomona.edu

WOODSON, LINDA
DISCIPLINE FINE ARTS AND HUMANITIES **EDUCATION** TX Christian Univ, BS, PhD. **CAREER** Assoc prof; taught at, TX Tech Univ, Southern Methodist Univ & TX Christian Univ; mem, Nominating Comt, Conf Col Composition and Commun, 85 & Exec Coun of CCTE; admin exp as, Coordr of Composition, UTSA, 86-; served as, dir Core Curric, UTSA. **HONORS AND AWARDS** Co-developed, R-WISE, Functional Skills Reading and Writing Tutor, 92. **RESEARCH** Contemp rhetorical theory; hist of rhetoric; compos theory; tchg of compos; tech writing and other kinds of writing; Am lit and the lit of TX and the Southwest. **SELECTED PUBLICATIONS** Auth, A Handbook of Rhetorical Terms, NCTE, 79; From Cases to Composition, Scott Foresman, 82; The Writer's World, HBJ, 85; essay in, Sacred Violence: A Reader's Companion to Cormac McCarthy, Tex Western Press, 95; coauth, Writing in Three Dimensions, Allyn and Bacon, 96; publ in, Style, Col Composition and Commun, JAEPL, Freshman Engl News. **CONTACT ADDRESS** Col of Fine Arts and Hum, Univ Texas at San Antonio, 6900 N Loop 1604 W, San Antonio, TX, 78249.

WOODWARD, COMER VANN
PERSONAL Born 11/13/1908, Vanndale, AR, m, 1937, 1 child **DISCIPLINE** AMERICAN HISTORY **EDUCATION** Emory Univ, PhB, 30; Columbia Univ, AM, 32, PhD, 37. **CAREER** Instr English, Ga Inst Technol, 30-31 & 32-33; asst prof soc sci, Univ Fla, 37-39; vis asst prof hist, Univ Va, 39-40; assoc prof Am hist & biog, Scripps Col, 40-43; from assoc prof to prof Am hist, Johns Hopkins Univ, 46-61; Sterling prof, 61-77, EMER PROF HIST, YALE UNIV, 77-, Rosenwald fel, 40-41; Guggenheim fels, 46-47 & 60-61; Richard lectr, Univ Va, 54; Commonwealth lectr, Univ London, 54; Harmsworth prof, Oxford Univ, 54-55; mem, Soc Sci Res Coun, 56-61; Am Coun Learned Soc award, 62; dir, Am Coun Learned Soc award, 63-. **HONORS AND AWARDS** Bancroft Hist Prize, 52; Nat Inst Arts & Lett Award, 54., LLD, Emory Univ, 60, Univ Ark, 61, Northwestern Univ, 77; LittD, Princeton Univ, 71, Cambridge Univ, England, 75; LHD, Columbia Univ, 72, Pa State Univ, 82. **MEMBERSHIPS** AHA (pres, 69); Am Philos Soc; Southern Hist Asn (pres, 52); Orgn Am Historians (pres, 69). **RESEARCH** Modern American history; Southern history. **SELECTED PUBLICATIONS** Auth, The Ideal of the University, Partisan Rev, Vol 0060, 93; The Idea of a University--A Reexamination, Partisan Rev, Vol 0060, 93; Loose Canons, Partisan Rev, Vol 0060, 93; Wallace, George, NY Rev Bks, Vol 0041, 94; The Vacant Chair, NY Rev Bks, Vol 0041, 94; The Real War Will Never Get in the Books, NY Rev Bks, Vol 0041, 94; Wallace Redeemed, an Exchange--Reply, NY Rev Bks, Vol 0041, 94; The House of Percy, NY Rev Bks, Vol 0042, 95; The Literary Percys, NY Rev Bks, Vol 0042, 95; Americans, J Southern Hist, Vol 0063, 97; The Aging of Democracies, Amer Scholar, Vol 0066, 97. **CONTACT ADDRESS** Dept of Hist Studies, Yale Univ, Hall of Grad, New Haven, CT, 06520.

WOODWARD, DAVID
PERSONAL Born 08/29/1942, Leamington, United Kingdom, m, 1966, 3 children **DISCIPLINE** GEOGRAPHY **EDUCATION** Univ Wisconsin Madison, PhD 70; Univ Wales Swansea, BA 64. **CAREER** Smith Cen Newberry Library, dir 69-80; Univ Wisconsin Madison, prof 80-. **HONORS AND AWARDS** Guggenheim Fel; Fel Brit Acad. **MEMBERSHIPS** AAG; RGS **RESEARCH** History of cartography **SELECTED PUBLICATIONS** Auth, The History of Cartography: Cartography in the Traditional African, American, Arctic, Australian and Pacific Societies, co ed, Chicago, U of Chi Press, 98; Cartography in Indigenous Societies, Mercator's World, 98; Maps as Popular Prints, Mercator's World, 98; The Description of the Four Parts of the World: Camoco's Wall Maps in the Bell Library and Their Place in the Italian Tradition, Minnea, James Ford Bell Library, 98; History of Maps, in: UK ed of Microsoft Encarta Encyclopedia, 97; Roger Bacon on Geography and Cartography, coauth, in: RogerBacon and the Sciences: Commemorative Essays, ed Jeremiah Hackett, Leiden, Brill, 97; A Map for Getting Lost: The Cultural Map of Wisconsin, Mercator's World, 97. **CONTACT ADDRESS** Dept of Geography, Univ of Wisconsin, Madison, %50 N. Park St, Madison, WI, 53706-1491. **EMAIL** dawoodwa@facstaff.wisc.edu

WOODWARD, DAVID REID
PERSONAL Born 10/09/1939, Clarksville, TN, m, 1966, 1 child **DISCIPLINE** MODERN EUROPEAN & RUSSIAN HISTORY **EDUCATION** Austin Peay State Univ, BA, 61; Univ Ga, MA, 63, PhD, 65. **CAREER** Asst prof hist, 65-70, Tex A&M Univ; assoc prof, 70-73, prof hist, 73-, Marshall Univ. **HONORS AND AWARDS** Research Award Soc Sci, 76, 86, 89, tchng award, 93, Marshall Univ. **MEMBERSHIPS** N Amer Conf Brit Studies; Western Front Assn; Army Records Soc; Soc for Mil Hist; fel, Royal Hist Soc. **RESEARCH** Military and diplomatic history of World War I, British and US. **SELECTED PUBLICATIONS** Auth, Trail by Friendship: Anglo-American Relations 1917-1918, Univ Kentucky Press, 93; auth, Field Marshal Sir William Robertson: Chief of the Imperial General Staff in the Great War, Praeger, 98; co-ed, The Military Correspondence of Field-Marshal Sir William Robertson, Army Records Soc, 89; ed, America and World War I: A Selected Annotated Bibliography of English-Language Sources, Garland, 85; ed, Britain in a Continental War: Civil-Military Debate Over the Stategical Direction of the Great War of 1914-1918, Albion, 80; ed, Did Lloyd George Starve the British Army of Men Prior to the German March 21st Offensive, Hist J, 84. **CONTACT ADDRESS** Dept of History, Marshall Univ, 400 Hal Greer Blvd, Huntingdon, WV, 25755. **EMAIL** Woodwadr@Marshall.edu

WOODWARD, RALPH L.
PERSONAL Born 12/02/1934, New London, CT, m, 1996, 3 children **DISCIPLINE** HISTORY **EDUCATION** Cent Col Mo, AB, 55; Tulane Univ, MA, 59, PhD, 62. **CAREER** Asst Prof Hist, Univ Witchita, 61-62; Asst Prof Hist, Univ SW La, 62-63; Asst to Assoc Prof of Hist, Univ NC, 63-70; Prof Hist, Tulane Univ, 70-. **HONORS AND AWARDS** Alfred B Thomas Book Award, 95; La Humanist of the Yr, 96; Waldo G Leland Award, 97. **MEMBERSHIPS** Am Hist Asn; Conf on Latin Am Hist; SE Coun on Latin Am Stud; La Hist Asn. **RESEARCH** Latin Am econ hist; Cent Am. **SELECTED PUBLICATIONS** Auth, Rafael Carrera and the Emergence of the Republic of Guatemala, 1821-1871, Univ Ga Press, 93, Spanish translation, 99; Asn ed, Encyclopedia of Latin American History and Culture, 5 vols, Charles Scribner's Sons, 96; auth, Central America, A Nation Divided, 3rd ed, Oxford Univ Press, 99. **CONTACT ADDRESS** 206 Boardman Ave, Bay St Louis, MS, 39520. **EMAIL** woodward@datasync.com

WOOLEY, ALLAN D.
PERSONAL Born 01/01/1936, Rumford, ME **DISCIPLINE** CLASSICAL PHILOLOGY **EDUCATION** Bowdoin Col, BA, 58; Princeton Univ, PhD, 62. **CAREER** Asst prof, Duke Univ, 62-67; dept chair, Gould Acad, 67-68; instr, Greek and Latin, Phillips Exeter Acad, 68-84; instr and coord, acad computing, Phillips Exeter Acad, 84-89; dept chair, Phillips Exeter Acad, 91-96; Bradbury Longfellow Gilley prof, Greek, Phillips Exeter Acad, 96-. **MEMBERSHIPS** Class Asn of New England; Amer Class League; Amer Philol Asn. **RESEARCH** Classical philology. **SELECTED PUBLICATIONS** Article, Ideographic Imagery in Aeneid and Vergil's Philosophizing, New Eng

Class Jour, may, 98. **CONTACT ADDRESS** Phillips Exeter Acad, 20 Main St., MSC 81420, Exeter, NH, 03833. **EMAIL** awooley@exeter.edu

WOOLEY, WESLEY THEODORE
PERSONAL Born 01/18/1942, Champaign, IL, m, 1964, 2 children **DISCIPLINE** AMERICAN HISTORY **EDUCATION** Univ Ill, Urbana, BA, 63; Univ Chicago, MA, 64, PhD(hist), 71. **CAREER** NDEA fel, 66-68; instr, 68-71, ASST PROF HIST, UNIV VICTORIA, 71-. **MEMBERSHIPS** AHA; Orgn Am Historians; Soc Hist Am Foreign Rels. **RESEARCH** American diplomatic history. **SELECTED PUBLICATIONS** Auth, American Foreign Relations Reconsidered, 1890-1993, Int Hist Rev, Vol 0018, 96. **CONTACT ADDRESS** Dept Hist, Univ Victoria, Victoria, BC, V8W 2Y2.

WOOLLEY, PETER J.
PERSONAL Born 02/23/1960, New York, NY, m, 1994 **DISCIPLINE** COMPARATIVE POLITICS; SOCIAL SCIENCES; HISTORY **EDUCATION** St. Joseph's Univ, BA, 81; Univ Pittsburgh, MA, 83, PhD, 89. **CAREER** Book review editor, Journal of Conflict Studies, 97-; CHAIR, DEPT OF SOCIAL SCIENCES AND HISTORY, PROF OF COMPARATIVE POLITICS, FAIRLEIGH DICKINSON UNIV, MADISON, NJ, 98-. **HONORS AND AWARDS** Edwin Miller History Prize, US Naval War College. **MEMBERSHIPS** APSA. **RESEARCH** Japanese defense policy, maritime powers and decline. **SELECTED PUBLICATIONS** Auth, Geography and the Limits of US Military Intervention, in Conflict Quart, vol XI, no 4, fall 91; Japan's Security Policies: Into the Twenty-First Century, Jour East and West Studies, vol 22, no 2, Oct 92; Low-Level Military Conflict and the Future of Japan's Armed Forces, Conflict Quart, vol XIII, no 4, fall 93; Geography Revisited: Expectations of US Military Intervention in the Post-Cold War Era, in Peacemaking, Peacekeeping and Coalition Warfare, Fariborz L. Mokhtari, ed, Nat Defense Univ Press, 94; The Role of War and Strategy in the Transformation and Decline of Great Powers, Naval War Col Rev, Vol XLIX, no 1, winter 96; with Cdr. Mark S. Woolley, USN, The Kata of Japan's Naval Forces, Naval War Col Rev, Vol XLIX, no 2, spring 96; Japan's Minesweeping Decision 1991: An Organizational Response, Asian Survey, Vol XXXVI, no 8, Aug 96, reprinted in Edward R. Beauchamp, ed, Dimensions of Contemporary Japan, Vol II, Garland Pub, forthcoming 99; Japan's Sealane Defense Revisited, Strategic Rev, Vol XXIV, no IV, fall 96; Arguing From the Same Premises: the Ideology is Intact, American Politics: Core Argument and Current Controversy, P. J. Woolley and A. R. Papa, eds, Prentice Hall Pubs, 98; In Defense of Pacific Rim Democracies: the US-Japan Alliance, Aiding Democracies Under Seige, Gabriel Marcela and Anthony Joes, eds, Praeger Pubs, forthcoming 99; Japan's Navy: Politics and Paradox, 1971-2001, Lynne-Reinner Pubs, 99. **CONTACT ADDRESS** Dept of Social Sciences and History, Fairleigh Dickinson Univ, Madison, NJ, 07940. **EMAIL** Woolley@alpha.fdu.edu

WOOSTER, RALPH ANCIL
PERSONAL Born 11/09/1928, Baytown, TX, m, 1947, 1 child **DISCIPLINE** HISTORY **EDUCATION** Univ Houston, BA & MA, 50; Univ Tex, PhD(Hist), 54. **CAREER** Head dept Hist, 66-70, from instr to prof, 55-72, Regents prof Am Hist, Lamar Univ, 72-, dean Fac & Grad Studies, 76-91. **MEMBERSHIPS** AHA; Orgn Am Historians; Southern Hist Asn; Texas State Hist Assoc. **RESEARCH** Secession movement in the United States; Civil War Terms; state and local government in Old South. **SELECTED PUBLICATIONS** Auth, Analysis of membership of secession conventions in Lower South, J Southern Hist, 8/58; Secession of the Lower South, Civil War Hist, 6/61; Secession Conventions of the South, Princeton Univ, 62; The People In Power, Univ Tenn, 69; Early Texas statehood, Southwestern Hist Quart, 10/72; coauth, Texas and Texans, Steck-Vaughn, 72; auth, Politicians, Planters and Plain Folk, Univ Tenn, 75; co-ed, Texas Vistas, Tex State Hist Asn, 80; Texas and Texans in the Civil War, Eakin Press, 95; ed, Lone Star Blue & Gray, Tex State Hist Assoc, 95. **CONTACT ADDRESS** Dept of History, Lamar Univ, PO Box 10048, Beaumont, TX, 77710-0048.

WOOSTER, ROBERT
PERSONAL Born 08/27/1956, Beaumont, TX, m, 1993 **DISCIPLINE** HISTORY **EDUCATION** Univ TX, Austin, PhD 85. **CAREER** TX A M Univ, prof hist, 86-, ch dept of hum, 97. **HONORS AND AWARDS** Civ Depu Dir, USMA rotc Mili Hist Fell; Piper Prof; Vis Schol TX ST Hist Assn. **MEMBERSHIPS** OAH; TSHA; SMH. **RESEARCH** 19th Century Military Hist; West. **SELECTED PUBLICATIONS** Fort Davis: Out Post on the Texas Frontire, TX State Hist Assn, 94; The Civil War 100, Carol Pub, 98; Nelson A Miles and the Twilight of the Frontier Army, Univ Nebraska Press, 93; The Military and the United States Indian Policy, 1865-1903, Yale Univ Press, 88. **CONTACT ADDRESS** Dept of Hist, Texas A+M Univ, 6300 Ocean Dr, Corpus Christi, TX, 78412. **EMAIL** rwooster@falcon.tamucc.edu

WOOTEN, CECIL W.
DISCIPLINE CLASSICS **EDUCATION** Davidson Col, AB, 67; Univ NC, Chapel Hill, MA, 68; Middlebury Col and Univ Paris, AM, 73; Univ NC, Chapel Hill, PhD, 72. **CAREER** Prof, Univ NC, Chapel Hill. **RESEARCH** Greek and Latin rhetoric and oratory; the ancient novel. **SELECTED PUBLICATIONS** Auth, The Elusive 'Gay' Teenagers of Classical Antiquity, The High Schl J 77, 93/94; The Peripatetic Tradition in the Literary Essays of Dionysius of Halicarnassus, in Peripatetic Rhetoric after Aristotle, eds, W. Fortenbaugh and D. Mirhady, New Brunswick, 94. **CONTACT ADDRESS** Univ N. Carolina, Chapel Hill, Chapel Hill, NC, 27599. **EMAIL** cwwooten@email.unc.edu

WORCESTER, DONALD EMMET
PERSONAL Born 04/29/1915, Tempe, AZ **DISCIPLINE** LATIN AMERICAN HISTORY **EDUCATION** Bard Col, AB, 39; Univ Calif, AM, 40, PhD, 47. **CAREER** From asst prof to prof hist & head dept, Univ Fla, 47-59; prof, 63-71, chmn dept, 63-71, Lorin A Boswell prof hist, 71-80, IDA & CECIL GREEN EMER PROF, TEX CHRISTIAN UNIV, 81-, Vis prof, Univ Madrid, 56-57; managing ed, Hisp Am Hist Rev, 60-65. **HONORS AND AWARDS** Southwest Bk Award, 79; Western Writers Am Spur Award, 75 & 79. **MEMBERSHIPS** AHA; Paraguayan Inst Hist Res; Western Writers Am (vpres, 72-73, pres, 73-74); Western Hist Asn (pres, 74-75); Westerners Int (pres, 78-79). **RESEARCH** Brazilian history; Latin American colonial institutions; plains Indians. **SELECTED PUBLICATIONS** Auth, Chisholm, Jesse, NMex Hist Rev, Vol 0068, 93; Parker, Quanah, Comanche Chief, J Amer Hist, Vol 0081, 94; Buffalo Soldiers, Braves, and the Brass, J Amer Hist, Vol 0081, 94; Apache Reservation, Pac Hist Rev, Vol 0063, 94; North American Cattle Ranching Frontiers, Western Hist Quart, Vol 0025, 94; The Jumanos, Amer Indian Culture and Res J, Vol 0019, 95; Spanish Expeditions Into Texas, 1689-1768, Amer Indian Culture and Res J, Vol 0020, 96. **CONTACT ADDRESS** Dept of Hist, Tex Christian Univ, Fort Worth, TX, 76129-0002.

WORKS, JOHN A.
PERSONAL Born 08/25/1944, St. Paul, MN **DISCIPLINE** HISTORY **EDUCATION** Yale Univ, BA, 66; Wi Univ, MA, 68, PhD, 72. **CAREER** Lectr Northeast Col of Arts & Sci Maiduguri, Nigeria, 72-75; lectr, Univ of Maiduguri, Nigeria, 75-77; asst lectr to assoc prof, Univ Mo St. Louis, 77- . **MEMBERSHIPS** African Stud Assoc; Societe des Africanistes. **RESEARCH** W Africa; Islam, Christianity, Hausa States; Chad. **SELECTED PUBLICATIONS** Auth, Pilgrims in a Strange Land, Columbia Univ Press, 76; The Muslim Maha of Wadai, in Islamic Peoples, Greenwood Press, 83. **CONTACT ADDRESS** Dept of History, Univ Mo St. Louis, Lucas Hall, St. Louis, MO, 63121. **EMAIL** HISTORYWORKS@umsl.edu

WORRALL, ARTHUR JOHN
PERSONAL Born 08/22/1933, Havelock, ON, Canada, m, 1967, 3 children **DISCIPLINE** UNITED STATES COLONIAL HISTORY **EDUCATION** Univ the South, BA, 55; Ind Univ, MA, 64, PhD(hist), 69. **CAREER** From instr to asst prof, 67-77, ASSOC PROF HIST, COLO STATE UNIV, 77-. **MEMBERSHIPS** AHA; Orgn Am Historians; Friends Hist Asn; Am Soc Church Hist. **RESEARCH** Quaker history. **SELECTED PUBLICATIONS** Auth, Quakers and Baptists in Colonial Massachusetts, Amer Hist Rev, Vol 0098, 93; Malone, J., Walter, Church Hist, Vol 0065, 96. **CONTACT ADDRESS** Dept of Hist, Colorado State Univ, Ft Collins, CO, 80523.

WORRALL, JANET EVELYN
PERSONAL Born 12/16/1940, Minneapolis, MN, m, 1967, 3 children **DISCIPLINE** LATIN AMERICAN HISTORY, AMERICAN IMMIGRATION HISTORY **EDUCATION** Hamline Univ, BA, 64; Ind Univ, MA, 66, PhD(hist), 72. **CAREER** From instr to asst prof, 68-78, ASSOC PROF HIST, UNIV NORTHERN COLO, 78-. **MEMBERSHIPS** Conf Latin Am Hist; Immigration Hist Soc; Am Ital Hist Asn; Soc Ital Hist Studies. **RESEARCH** Peru; immigration to North and South America. **SELECTED PUBLICATIONS** Auth, The Ausentes, the Social Process of International Migration in Western Mexico, Hisp Amer Hist Rev, Vol 0073, 93; European Expansion and Migration, Essays on the Intercontinental Migration from Africa, Asia, and Europe, Hisp Amer Hist Rev, Vol 0075, 95; Italian Prisoners of War in America 1942-1946, Captives or Allies, J Amer Ethnic Hist, Vol 0015, 95; Revolution by Decree--Peru, 1968-1975, Hisp Amer Hist Rev, Vol 0076, 96; Family, Church, and Market, J Amer Ethnic Hist, Vol 0015, 96. **CONTACT ADDRESS** Univ No Colorado, Greeley, CO, 80639.

WORRILL, CONRAD W.
PERSONAL Born 08/15/1941, Pasadena, California, m **DISCIPLINE** EDUCATION **EDUCATION** George Williams Coll, BS 1968; Univ of Chicago, MA 1971; Univ of WI, PhD 1973. **CAREER** Northeastern IL Univ Ctr for Inner City Studies Education, program coordinator. **HONORS AND AWARDS** Received numerous awds for community involvement; AKA Monarch Awards. **MEMBERSHIPS** Weekly columnist Chicago Defender 1983-, and other black newspapers in Chicago and around the country; chmn Natl Black United Front 1985-; bd mem IL Black United Fund 1985-; mem Woodlawn Preservation Investment Corp 1987-; mem Chicago Housing Authority 1987-; talk show host WVON-AM, 1988-; Assn for Study of Classical African Civilizations; bd mem, Temple of the African Community of Chicago. **SELECTED PUBLICATIONS** Worrill's World Book of Newspaper columns/articles have appeared in numerous African Amer publications. **CONTACT ADDRESS** Ctr for Inner City Studies, Northeastern Illinois Univ, 00 E George H. Clements Blvd., Chicago, IL, 60653.

WORSFOLD, VICTOR
DISCIPLINE HISTORY **EDUCATION** Harvard Univ, PhD, 75. **CAREER** Assoc prof. **RESEARCH** Ethics; social and political philosophy; philosophy of education. **SELECTED PUBLICATIONS** Auth, Billy Budd: a humanities approach to professional ethics, 94; Tolerance: an antidote to political correctness, 93; MacIntyre and Bloom: Two Complementary Communitarians, Ill State Univ, 92; The Possibility of Liberal Education: MacIntyrean Skepticism, 90; Isreal Scheffler's Ethics: Theory and Practice, Studies Philos Edu, 96; Teaching Democracy Democratically, Edu Theory, 97. **CONTACT ADDRESS** Dept of History, Richardson, TX, 75083-0688. **EMAIL** worsfold@utdallas.edu

WORTH, SARAH ELIZABETH
PERSONAL Born 03/12/1970, Ann Arbor, MI **DISCIPLINE** PHILOSOPHY, AESTHETICS, ANCIENT PHILOSOPHY, BIOMEDICAL ETHICS **EDUCATION** Furman Univ, BA, 92; Univ of Louisville, MA, 94; SUNY Buffalo, PhD, 97. **CAREER** Asst prof, Allegheny Col, 97-98; asst prof, Miami Univ, 98-99. **RESEARCH** Aesthetics; ancient philosophy. **SELECTED PUBLICATIONS** "Wittgenstein's Musical Understanding," British J of Aesthet, v 37, no 2. **CONTACT ADDRESS** Dept of Philosophy, Miami Univ, 212 Hall Auditorium, Oxford, OH, 45056. **EMAIL** worthse@muohio.edu

WORTHEN, THOMAS
DISCIPLINE ART HISTORY **EDUCATION** Univ IA, PhD. **CAREER** Assoc prof, Drake Univ. **RESEARCH** Europ art and archit; Italian Renaissance. **SELECTED PUBLICATIONS** Auth, articles in The Art Bulletin on Poussin and Tintoretto. **CONTACT ADDRESS** Drake Univ, University Ave, PO Box 2507, Des Moines, IA, 50311-4505.

WORTHEN, THOMAS DE VOE
PERSONAL Born 08/18/1937, Salt Lake City, UT, 4 children **DISCIPLINE** CLASSICS **EDUCATION** Univ Utah, BA, 59; Univ Wash, MA, 63, PhD, 68. **CAREER** Lectr, 65-68, asst prof, 68-72, Assoc Prof Greek, Univ Ariz, 72-. **MEMBERSHIPS** AAS (HAD div); AAAS. **RESEARCH** Greek science and proto science. **SELECTED PUBLICATIONS** Auth, Pneumatic Action in the Klepsydra and Empedocles' Account of Breathing, Isis, 70; Note on Ajax 494-5, Class Philol, 72; co-auth, The Thucydides Syndrome: A New Hypothesis for the Cause of Plague of Athens, NEJM, 86; rev, English Words from latin and Greek Elements by Donald Ayers, Univ Ariz Press, 86; Ideas of Sky in Archaic Greek Poetry, Glotta, 88; The Myth of Replacement: Stars, Gods and Order in the Univers, Univ Ariz Press, 91; contribr, Stalking the Second Tier, An Occasional Paper on Neglected Problems in Science Education, Res Corp, 91; Eclipses by the Semester, Griffith Observer, 93; Pleiades and Hesperides, Vistas in Astronomy, 95; Herodotos's Report on Thales' Eclipes, Electronic Antiquity, 97. **CONTACT ADDRESS** Dept of Classics, Univ Ariz, Tucson, AZ, 85721-0001. **EMAIL** tdw@u.arizona.edu

WORTHY, BARBARA ANN
PERSONAL Born 11/01/1942, Thomaston, Georgia, s **DISCIPLINE** HISTORY **EDUCATION** Morris Brown Coll, Atlanta GA, BA, 1964; Atlanta Univ, Atlanta GA, MA, 1970; Tulane Univ, New Orleans LA, PhD, 1983. **CAREER** Camilla High School, Camilla GA, social science teacher, 1964-69; Southern Univ at New Orleans LA, history teacher, 1970-, social sciences dept chair, currently. **HONORS AND AWARDS** Overdyke History Award, North Louisiana Historical Assn, 1981; one of 14 participants selected from six institutions of higher educ in Louisiana to participate in six-week Intl Curriculum Seminar in Kenya & Tanzania, East Africa, summer, 1985. **MEMBERSHIPS** Mem, Southern Historical Assn, 1983-; mem, Assn for Study of Afro-Amer Life & History, 1984-85; mem, Friends of Amistad, 1986-; bd of dir, Soc for the Study of Afro-LA & History, 1988-; mem, New Orleans League of Women Voters, 1988-; mem, Delta Sigma Theta. **CONTACT ADDRESS** History Department, Southern Univ at New Orleans, 6400 Press Drive, New Orleans, LA, 70126.

WORTMAN, RICHARD
DISCIPLINE RUSSIAN AND EAST CENTRAL EUROPEAN HISTORY **EDUCATION** Cornell Col, BA, 58; Univ Chicago, PhD, 64. **CAREER** Prof. **SELECTED PUBLICATIONS** Auth, The Crisis of Russian Populism, 67; The Development of a Russian Legal Consciousness, 76; Scenarios of Power: Myth and Ceremony in Russian Monarchy, 95. **CONTACT ADDRESS** Dept of History, Columbia Col, New York, 2960 Broadway, New York, NY, 10027-6902.

WORTMAN, ROY THEODORE
PERSONAL Born 11/23/1940, New York, NY, m, 1967, 2 children **DISCIPLINE** AMERICAN SOCIAL HISTORY **EDUCATION** Colo State Univ, AB, 62; Univ Colo, Boulder, MA, 65; Ohio State Univ, PhD(hist), 71. **CAREER** Woodrow Wilson Found Teaching Fel and Instr, Cent State Univ, Ohio, 65-66; teaching assoc, Ohio State Univ, 67-71, res asst, Child & State Proj, 69-70; from asst prof to assoc prof, 71-87, PROF HIST, KENYON COL, 87-; Fel, Newberry Library Program in the Humanities, 86; vis res prof, Sas katchewan Indian Federated Col, 92; **HONORS AND AWARDS** Jr and Sr Schol, Colo State Univ; Doctoral Dissertation Travel Grant, The Ohio State Univ, 70; Kenyon-Ford Found Fac Development Grant for Course Development, 72, 73, 74; Citation for Research and Service, Ohio Farmer's Union, 83; Lyndon Baines Johnson-Moody Found Presidential Library Grant, 85; Newberry Library Fac Fel in the Humanities, 86; NEH Fel, 89-90; Occassional Fel, Univ Chicago, Midwest Fac Seminar for independent study for N Am Urban Indian history, 90; Fel, Canadian Plains Res Ctr, 92; recipient of numerous other grants and fellowships. **RESEARCH** Social history; North American Indian history. **SELECTED PUBLICATIONS** Ed, A volunteer wobbly hunter, Hist Musings, fall 71; auth, The Akron Rubber Strike of 1912, In: At the Point of Production: The Local History of the IWW, Greenwood Press, 81; Let the Hunter Speak: Ken Eyster as Hunter, Craftsman, and Unreconstructed Jeffersonian, Cynegeticus, 1/82; Progress and Parity: The Ohio Farmer's Union, 1910-1982, Ohio Farmer's Union, 83; From Syndicalism to Trade Unionism: The IWW in Ohio, 1913-1950, Garland Press, 85; Populism's Stepchildren: The National Farmers Union and Agriculture's Welfare in the Twentieth Century, In: For the General Welfare (co-ed), Peter Lang Publ, 89; Gray (Salter), John Hunter, In: Encyclopedia of Native American Civil Rights, Greewood Press, 97; author of several journal articles. **CONTACT ADDRESS** Dept of Hist, Kenyon Col, Seitz House, Gambier, OH, 43022-9623.

WRAY, DAVID L.
PERSONAL Born 05/25/1959, Atlanta, GA, m, 1997 **DISCIPLINE** CLASSICAL PHILOLOGY **EDUCATION** Emory Univ, BA, 80; Harvard Univ, PhD, 96. **CAREER** Asst prof, class lang and lit, Univ Chicago, 97-. **MEMBERSHIPS** Am Philol Asn; Am Class League. **RESEARCH** Latin poetry; Hellenistic poetry; literary criticism. **SELECTED PUBLICATIONS** Auth, Catullus: Sexual Personae and Invective Tradition, Cambridge, forthcoming; auth, Lucretius, in Briggs, ed, Roman Authors vol of Dictionary of Literary Biography, Bruccoli Clark Layman, forthcoming; auth, Apollonius Masterplot: A Reading of Argonautical in Harder, ed, Apollonius Rhodius: Hellenistica Groningana IV, Groningen, forthcoming. **CONTACT ADDRESS** Dept of Classics, Univ of Chicago, 1010 E 59th St, Chicago, IL, 60637. **EMAIL** d_wray@uchicago.edu

WREN, DANIEL ALAN
PERSONAL Born 01/08/1932, Columbia, MO, w, 1962, 3 children **DISCIPLINE** MANAGEMENT **EDUCATION** Univ Mo, BS, 54, MS, 60; Univ Ill, PhD, 64. **CAREER** Asst prof to prof, Fla State Univ, 63-73; PROF, MGT, UNIV OKLA, 73-. **HONORS AND AWARDS** Educator of the Year, Acad of Mgt, 91. **MEMBERSHIPS** Acad Mgt; Southern Mgt Asn; Bus Hist Conf. **RESEARCH** Management history; Business history; Business strategy. **SELECTED PUBLICATIONS** auth, "Learning from Experience: Henri Fayol", Jour of Mgt hist; auth, The Evolution of Management Thought, John Wiley & Sons, 94; ed, Early Managment Thought, Dartmouth Publ Ltd, 97; coauth, Management Innovators: The People and Ideas That Shaped Modern Business, Oxford Univ Pr, 98. **CONTACT ADDRESS** Div of Mgt, Univ Okla, Norman, OK, 73019. **EMAIL** dwren@ou.edu

WRESZIN, MICHAEL
PERSONAL Born 10/09/1926, Glen Ridge, NJ, m, 1951, 2 children **DISCIPLINE** MODERN AMERICAN HISTORY **EDUCATION** Syracuse Univ, BA, 51; Colgate Univ, MA, 55; Brown Univ, PhD(hist), 61. **CAREER** Instr Am hist, Wayne State Univ, 59-62; asst prof, Brown Univ, 62-64; instr, 62-63, asst prof, 64-66, assoc prof, 66-80, PROF AM HIST, QUEENS COL, NY, 80-. **MEMBERSHIPS** AHA; Orgn Am Historians; Am Studies Asn. **RESEARCH** American political history of the twentieth century; American intellectual history. **SELECTED PUBLICATIONS** Auth, Letters + Response to Phillips,William Comments on my Biography of Macdonald, Dwight, Partisan Rev, Vol 0062, 95; The Lively Arts, Amer Hist Rev, Vol 0102, 97. **CONTACT ADDRESS** Dept of Hist, Queens Col, CUNY, 6530 Kissena Blvd, Flushing, NY, 11367-1597.

WRIGHT, DONALD R.
DISCIPLINE HISTORY **EDUCATION** DePauw Univ, BA; Univ Ind, MA, PhD. **CAREER** Prof. **HONORS AND AWARDS** Excellence Tchg Awd, 89. **RESEARCH** Colonial and post colonial West Africa. **SELECTED PUBLICATIONS** Auth, The World and a Very Small Place in Africa, 97; African Americans in the Early Republic, 93; African Americans in the Colonial Era, 89; That Hell-Hole of Yours¤Franklin Roosevelt in the Gambia, 1943l. **CONTACT ADDRESS** Dept of History, State Univ NY Cortland, PO Box 2000, Cortland, NY, 13045-0900. **EMAIL** wright@cortland.edu

WRIGHT, GEORGIA SOMMERS
PERSONAL m, 1967, 1 child **DISCIPLINE** ART HISTORY **EDUCATION** Swarthmore Col, BA 59; Columbia Univ, MA 61, PhD 66. **CAREER** Limestone Sculpture Provenance Project, co-dir 95-; Amer Univ, Paris, vis prof 90; Stanford Univ, vis prof 86-88; Mills College, asst prof 68-76; Univ Cal, Davis, vis lect 67-68; Univ Cal, Berk, vis lect 66-67. **HONORS AND AWARDS** Chevalier dans l'Order des Palmes Academiques. **MEMBERSHIPS** HIS; ICMA; NCIS **RESEARCH** Gothic sculpture **SELECTED PUBLICATIONS** Auth, Three articles in press for Dictionary of Art, MacMillan; Videos, Light On the Stones: The Medieval Church of Vezelay, 91, Three English Cathedrals: Norwich, Lincoln, Wells, 94, Medieval Sculpture and Nuclear Science, 96; Gothic Sculpture, Dictionary of the Middle Ages, Scribner, 90. **CONTACT ADDRESS** 105 Vicente Rd, Berkeley, CA, 94705. **EMAIL** wrightga@msn.com

WRIGHT, GWENDOLYN
DISCIPLINE UNITED STATES HISTORY **EDUCATION** NY Univ, BA, 69; Univ Ca, PhD, 80. **CAREER** Prof. **SELECTED PUBLICATIONS** Auth, Moralism and the Model Home: Domestic Architecture and Cultural Conflict in Chicago 1873-1913, 80; Building the Dream: A Social History of American Housing, 81; The History of History in American Schools of Architecture 1865-1975, 91; The Politics of Design in French Colonial Urbanism, 91. **CONTACT ADDRESS** Dept of History, Columbia Col, New York, 2960 Broadway, New York, NY, 10027-6902.

WRIGHT, HARRISON MORRIS
PERSONAL Born 10/06/1928, Philadelphia, PA, m, 1957, 5 children **DISCIPLINE** AFRICAN HISTORY **EDUCATION** Harvard Univ, AB, 50, MA, 53, PhD(hist), 57. **CAREER** From instr to assoc prof, 57-68, chmn dept, 68-79, prof hist, 68-79, Provost, 79-84, Isaac H. Clothier Prof of Hist & Int Rel, 87- , emeritus, 93- , Swarthmore Col; Ford Foreign Area training fel, England & Ghana, 61-62; Am Philos Soc res grant, S Africa, 66-67. **MEMBERSHIPS** AHA; Conf Brit Studies; African Studies Asn; Newport Hist Soc; Bd of Dir, Newport Hist Soc, 73-89; Bd of Counc, Hist Soc of Penn, 84-91, chemn, 89-91, emeritus, 91- ; Bd of Trustees, RI Hist Soc, 98- . **RESEARCH** Expansion of Europe; British Empire. **SELECTED PUBLICATIONS** Auth, New Zealand, 1769-1840: Early Years of Western Contact, Harvard Univ, 59; ed, The New Imperialism, Analysis of Late Nineteenth Century Expansion, Heath, 61, 2nd ed, 76; auth & contribr, British West Africa, Duke Univ, 66; auth, Imperialism: The Word and Its Meaning, Social Res, winter 67; ed, Sir James Rose Innes: Selected Correspondence, 1884-1902, Van Riebeeck Soc, 72; auth, The Burden of the President: Liberal-Radical Controversy Over Southern African History, D Philip & Collings, 77; The Burden of the Present and its Critics, Social Dynamics, 6/80. **CONTACT ADDRESS** PO Box 209, Jamestown, RI, 02835.

WRIGHT, JAMES EDWARD
PERSONAL Born 08/16/1939, Madison, WI, 3 children **DISCIPLINE** AMERICAN HISTORY **EDUCATION** Univ Wis-Platteville, BS, 64; Univ Wis-Madison MS, 66, PhD, 69. **CAREER** Asst prof, 69-72, assoc prof, 74-80, prof hist, Dartmouth Col, 80-, assoc dean fac, 81-85; dean of fac, 89-97; provost, 97-98; pres, 88. **HONORS AND AWARDS** Soc Sci Res Coun grant, 70-71; Guggenheim fel, 73-74; sr historian, Great Plains Hist Proj, Univ Mid-Am, 76-78; Charles Warren fel, Harvard Univ, 80-81. **MEMBERSHIPS** Orgn Am Historians; Western Hist Assn; Soc Sci Hist Assn. **RESEARCH** American political history; frontier movement; United States, 1877-1914. **SELECTED PUBLICATIONS** Auth, The Galena Lead District, State Hist Soc Wis, 67; co-ed, The West of the American People, Peacock, 70; auth, The Ethnocultural Model of Voting, Am Behav Sci, 6/73; The Politics of Populism, Yale Univ, 74; auth & co-ed, Great Plains Experience: Readings in the History of a Region, Univ Mid-Am, 78; auth, The Progressive Yankees: Republican Reformers in New Hampshire, 1906-1916, University Press at New England, 87. **CONTACT ADDRESS** Dartmouth Col, Parkhurst Hall, Hanover, NH, 03755-3529.

WRIGHT, JOHN
DISCIPLINE LATIN LANGUAGE AND LITERATURE **EDUCATION** Swarthmore, BA, 62; Ind Univ, MA, 64; Am Acad Rome, FAAR, 68; Ind Univ, PhD, 71. **SELECTED PUBLICATIONS** Auth, Dancing in Chains, Rome, 74; The Life of Cola di Rienzo, Toronto, 75; rev, Homeric Greek: A Book for Beginners, Okla, 85; rev, ed, Plautus' Curculio, Okla, 93. **CONTACT ADDRESS** Dept of Classics, Northwestern Univ, 1801 Hinma, Evanston, IL, 60208.

WRIGHT, JOHN ROBERT
PERSONAL Born 10/20/1936, Carbondale, IL **DISCIPLINE** PATRISTIC & MEDIEVAL CHURCH HISTORY **EDUCATION** Univ of the South, BA, 58; Emory Univ, MA, 59; Gen Theol Sem, MDiv, 63; Oxford Univ, DPhil, 67. **CAREER** Instr church hist, Episcopal Theol Sch, MA, 66-68; asst prof ecclesiastical hist, 68-72, prof church hist, Gen Theol Sem, 72-, res assoc, Pontifical Inst Mediaeval Studies, Toronto, 76 & 81; mem, Comn Faith & Order, World Coun Churches & Standing Ecumenical Comn of Episcopal Church, 77-; mem, Anglican/Roman Cath Consult in US, 70-; res scholar, Huntington Libr, 77. **MEMBERSHIPS** AHA; Mediaeval Acad Am; Am Soc Church Hist; Church Hist Soc. **RESEARCH** Fourteenth century church-state and Anglo-Papal relations; Walter Reynolds, Archbishop of Canterbury 1314-1327; Lambert of Auxerre, mid-thirteenth century Dominican commentator on Aristotle. **SELECTED PUBLICATIONS** Ed, Handbook of American Orthodoxy, Forward Movement, 72; co-ed, Episcopalians and Roman Catholics: Can They Ever Get Together?, Dimension, 72; coauth, A Pope for All Christians?, Paulist, 76 & SPCK, 77; auth, A Communion of Communions: One Eucharistic Fellowship, Seabury, 79; The Church and The English Crown 1305-1334, Pontifical Inst Mediaeval Studies, Toronto, 80; The Canterbury Statement and the Five Priesthoods, One in Christ, Vol 11: 3 & Anglican Theol Rev, Vol 57: 4; Anglicans and the Papacy, J Ecumenical Studies, Vol 13: 3; The Accounts of the Constables of Bordeaux 1381-1390, with Particular Notes on their Ecclesiastical and Liturgical Significance, Mediaeval Studies, 42: 238-307; An Anglican Commentary on Selected Documents of Vatican II, Ecumenical Trends, Vol 9: 8 & 9. **CONTACT ADDRESS** General Theol Sem, 175 9th Ave, New York, NY, 10011-4924. **EMAIL** wright@gts.edu

WRIGHT, JOSEPHINE
DISCIPLINE MUSIC HISTORY AND LITERATURE **EDUCATION** Univ Mo, BM, Pius XII Acad, Italy, MM; Univ Mo, MA; NY Univ, PhD. **CAREER** Instr, Harvard Univ; York Col; City Univ NY; prof, 81-. **HONORS AND AWARDS** Ed, New Music, The Black Perspective in Mus, 79-90; Amer Mus, 93-97; ed, Garland Publ's new Music In African American Culture series, 95-. **SELECTED PUBLICATIONS** Auth, articles in Amer Mus; The Black Perspective in Mus; Black Mus Res Newsletter; The New Grove Dictionary of Mus and Musicians; The New Grove Dictionary of Amer Mus; The New Grove Dictionary of Opera, Notes, and Women's Studies Quart; ed, Ignatius Sancho, 1729-1780: An Early African Composer in England, Garland Press, 81; co-author African-American Traditions in Song, Sermon, Tale, and Dance: An Annotated Bibliography, Greenwood Press, 90; principal ed, New Perspectives in Music: Essays in Honor of Eileen Southern, Harmonie Park Press, 91. **CONTACT ADDRESS** Dept of Mus, Col of Wooster, Wooster, OH, 44691. **EMAIL** jwright@acs.wooster.edu

WRIGHT, MARCIA
DISCIPLINE EASTERN AND SOUTHERN AFRICAN HISTORY **EDUCATION** Wellesley, BA, 57;, PhD, 66. **CAREER** English and Lit, Columbia Univ **SELECTED PUBLICATIONS** Coed, African Women and the Law: Historical Perspectives, 82; Women's Health and Apartheid : the Health of Women and Children and the Future of Progressive Primary Health Care in Southern Africa, 88; Auth, German Missions in Tanganyika, 1891-1941, 71; Strategies of Slaves & Women: Life-Stories from East/Central Africa, 93; An Old Nationalist in New Nationalist Times, Zambia: 1948-1963, 97. **CONTACT ADDRESS** Columbia Univ, 2960 Broadway, New York, NY, 10027-6902.

WRIGHT, SCOTT KENNETH
PERSONAL Born 10/12/1942, St. Paul, MN, m, 1967, 4 children **DISCIPLINE** AMERICAN HISTORY **EDUCATION** Univ Minn, BA, 63, MA, 68, PhD(Am studies), 73. **CAREER** Acquisitions librn, 68-71, assoc dir & ref librn, 71-74, libr dir, 74-80, asst prof hist, col St Thomas, 78-, Fulbright lectr, Kyushu Univ & Seinan Gakuin Univ, Fukuoka, Japan, 79-80. **MEMBERSHIPS** Orgn Am Historians; Am Studies Asn; Popular Cult Asn. **RESEARCH** American popular culture. **SELECTED PUBLICATIONS** Coauth, Slide & sound projects in history, AV Instr, 11/73; auth, The role of Indiana in the works of George Barr McCutcheon, Ind English, fall 80; contribr, A Bibliographic Guide to Midwestern Literature, Univ Iowa, 81. **CONTACT ADDRESS** Hist Dept, Col of St. Thomas, 2115 Summit Ave, St. Paul, MN, 55105-1096. **EMAIL** skwright@stthomas.edu

WRIGHT, THOMAS C.
DISCIPLINE HISTORY **EDUCATION** Univ Calif Berkeley, PhD, 71. **CAREER** Prof, Univ Nev Las Vegas. **RESEARCH** Latin American history. **SELECTED PUBLICATIONS** Auth, Latin America in the Era of the Cuban Revolution, Univ NY, 91; Landowners and Reform in Chile: The Sociedad Nacional de Agricultura, 1919-1940, Urbana, 82; co-auth, Flight from Chile: Voices of Exile, Albuquerque, 98; co-ed, Food, Politics, and Society in Latin America, Lincoln, 85. **CONTACT ADDRESS** History Dept, Univ Nev Las Vegas, 4505 Md Pky, Las Vegas, NV, 89154.

WRIGHT, WILLIAM JOHN
PERSONAL Born 04/07/1942, Chicago, IL, m, 1964, 2 children **DISCIPLINE** HISTORY **EDUCATION** Stetson Univ, BA, 64, MA, 65; Ohio State Univ, PhD(hist), 69. **CAREER** Asst prof, 69-75, ASSOC PROF HIST, UNIV TENN, CHATTANOOGA, 75-, Nat Endowment for Humanities fel, 79-80. **MEMBERSHIPS** Am Soc Reformation. **RESEARCH** Sixteenth Cent Studies Conf; AHA; Am Asn Univ Prof. **SELECTED PUBLICATIONS** Auth, Economy Without a House--Economics of the Poor in Nuremberg in the Late 1400s--German, Amer Hist Rev, Vol 0100, 95; Ludwig-Iv, Landgrave

of Hessen-Marburg 1537-1604--Land Division and Lutheranism in Hesse-German, Amer Hist Rev, Vol 0098, 93; Commerce and Cliques--Merchants of Cologne Trading in 16th-Century England--German, Amer Hist Rev, Vol 0097, 92; Between Fasting and Feasting--Hospital-Care in Munster 1540-1650, Amer Hist Rev, Vol 0101, 96. **CONTACT ADDRESS** Dept of Hist, Univ Tenn, Chattanooga, TN, 37401.

WRIGHT MILLER, GILL
DISCIPLINE DANCE **EDUCATION** Denison Univ, BFA; Wesleyan Univ, MALS; Laban/Bartenieff Institute of Movement Studies, CMA; NY Univ, PhD. **CAREER** Assoc prof dance and women's studies, 76-77 and 81-; chr Dance Dept, 81-97; instr Eng and adj fac Dance, NY Univ. **HONORS AND AWARDS** Res funds grants, Denison Univ; Robert C Good grant, Denison Univ; Dean's Awd Outstanding Res, NY Univ, 94. **RESEARCH** Performance work; experiential anatomy/kinesiology; Bainbridge Cohen, Olsen/McHose, Juhan, Sweigard/Dowd, and Adler. **SELECTED PUBLICATIONS** Auth, publ(s) in dance criticism, Labanotation theory, women's issues in dance, and women's photography. **CONTACT ADDRESS** Denison Univ, Main St, Granville, OH, 43023. **EMAIL** millerg@denison.edu

WRIGHT, JR, THEODORE P.
PERSONAL Born 04/12/1926, Port Washington, NY, m, 1967, 3 children **DISCIPLINE** INTERNATIONAL RELATIONS; POLITICAL SCIENCE **EDUCATION** Swarthmore Col, BA, 49; Yale Univ, MA, 51, PhD, 57. **CAREER** Instr, Asst Prof, Assoc Prof, Estes Col, 55-65; Assoc Prof, Prof, Emeritus Prof, State Univ of NY at Albany, 65-95. **HONORS AND AWARDS** Phi Beta Kappa, Fulbright Awards, 61, 63-64, 83-84, 90-91; Am Inst of Indian Stud Award, 69-70; ACLS/Soc Sci Res Counc Award, 74-75. **MEMBERSHIPS** Asn for Asian Stud; NY Conf on Asian Stud; Mid-Atl AAS; Colombia Univ Fac Seminar on S Asia; Harvard Univ Fac Seminar on S Asia; S Asian Muslim Stud Asn (pres). **RESEARCH** Politics of Muslim minority in India and of Muhajirin in Pakistan. **SELECTED PUBLICATIONS** Auth, US Perception of Islam in the Post Cold War Era: the Case of Pakistan, Pakistan J of Am Stud, 11:2, 28-39, 93; auth, Can there be a melting pot in Pakistan? Interprovincial marriage and national integration, Contemp S Asia, 3:2, 131-44, 94; auth, Impact of the Iraqi Aggression on Kuwait on South Asian Muslims, Int Conf on the Effects of the Iraqi Aggression on the State of Kuwait, Vol 1, 187-200, 96; authm, A New Demand for Muslim Reservations in India, Asian Survey, XXXVII, 9, 852-858, 9/97; auth, The BJV/Shiv Sena Coalition and the Muslim Minority in Maharashtra: the Interface of Foreign and Domestic Conflict, J of S Asian & Mid-E Stud, XXI, 2, 41-50, 98; auth, The Indian State and its Muslim Minority: from Dependence to Self-Reliance?, India: Fifty Years of Democracy & Development, APH Pubs, 313-339, 98. **CONTACT ADDRESS** 27 Vandenburg Ln, Latham, NY, 12110. **EMAIL** wright15@juno.com

WROBEL, DAVID M.
PERSONAL Born 06/24/1964, London, England **DISCIPLINE** HISTORY **EDUCATION** Univ Kent-Canterbury, BA, 85; Ohio Univ, MA, 87, PhD, 91. **CAREER** Vis instr to vis asst prof hist, Col Wooster, 90-92; vis asst prof hist, Hartwick Col, 92-94; asst prof to assoc prof hist, Widener Univ, 94-. **HONORS AND AWARDS** Caillouette Fellow, Huntington Library, Summer 97; Newberry Library Fellow, 96; Am Phil Soc fellowship, 94; Mayer Fund Fellow, Huntington Library, 93. **MEMBERSHIPS** Am Hist Asn, West Hist Asn, SW Soc Sci Asn, Phi Alpha Theta Hist Honors Soc **RESEARCH** Am cult intellectual hist. **SELECTED PUBLICATIONS** Auth, The End of American Exceptionalism: Frontier Anxiety from the Old West to the New Deal, Univ Press Kans, 93; co-ed, Many Wests: Essays on Regional Consciousness, Univ Press Kans, 97; auth, "The View from Philadelphia," in Pacific Hist Rev, Aug 98; auth, "Beyond the Frontier-Region Dichotomy," in Pacific Hist Rev, Aug 96; auth, "Early Reflections on Teaching Western History," in Magazine of Hist, Fall 94; auth, "Frederick Jackson Turner," in Dictionary of Literary Biography, Nineteenth Century Western Writers, Bruccoli, Clark, 98; auth, "Arid Lands Thesis," "Frontier Thesis," "Historiography, Western," "New Western History," Safety Valve Theory," "Frederick Jackson Turner," and "West as Region School," in The Encyclopedia of the West, Macmillan, 96; auth, "Don Laughlin," in Introduction to Casino Management, Kendall/Hunt, 95. **CONTACT ADDRESS** History Dept, Widener Univ, 1 Univ Pl, Chester, PA, 19013. **EMAIL** david.m.wrobel@widener.edu

WRONG, DENNIS H.
PERSONAL Born 11/22/1923, Toronto, ON, Canada, m, 1966, 3 children **DISCIPLINE** SOCIOLOGY **EDUCATION** Columbia Univ **CAREER** Assoc prof, New School for Soc Res, 61-63; assoc prof, Brown Univ, 56-61; prof, New York Univ, 63-94. Emeritus prof, New York Univ, 94- **HONORS AND AWARDS** Guggenheim Fel, 84-85; Fel Wilson Cent for Int Scholars, 91-92 **MEMBERSHIPS** ASA; ESS **RESEARCH** Social Theory; Politics; Modern History **SELECTED PUBLICATIONS** Auth, "The Challenge to Tenure," Dissent, 98; auth, "Fated to be a Professor?" Amer Sociologist, 98; auth, The Modern Condition: Essays at Century's End, Stanford Univ, 98 **CONTACT ADDRESS** 144 Drakes Corner Rd., Princeton, NJ, 08540. **EMAIL** dhwrong@voicenet.com

WU, PEI-YI
PERSONAL Born 12/03/1927, Nanking, China **DISCIPLINE** CHINESE LITERATURE, INTELLECTUAL HISTORY **EDUCATION** Nat Cent Univ, Nanking, AB, 50; Boston Univ, MA, 52; Columbia Univ, PhD(Chinese lit), 69. **CAREER** Ibstr Chinese, Army Lang Sch, 53-58; res linguist, Univ Calif, Berkeley, 58-59; preceptor, Columbia Univ, 62-63; instr, 63-66, lectr, 66-67; vis assoc prof, 67-69, Assoc Prof Chinese, Queens Col, 69-, Mem univ fac senate, City Univ New York, 71-74; VIS ASSOC PROF, COLUMBIA UNIV, 72-; Nat Endowment for Humanities fel, 74. **MEMBERSHIPS** Am Orient Soc; Asn Asian Studies. **RESEARCH** Chinese autobiography and myth. **SELECTED PUBLICATIONS** Auth, Memories of Kai-Feng--Meng,Yuan-Lao Description of the City in Tung-Ching Meng Hua Lu, New Lit Hist, Vol 0025, 94. **CONTACT ADDRESS** Dept of Class & Orient Lang, Queens Col, CUNY, 6530 Kissena Blvd, Flushing, NY, 11367.

WUNDER, JOHN
DISCIPLINE U. S. LEGAL HISTORY, AMERICAN WEST **EDUCATION** Univ Wash, PhD, 74. **CAREER** Prof, dir, Ctr for Great Plains Stud, Univ Nebr, Lincoln, 87-97; Am Stud Ch, Univ Helsinki, Finland, 95-96. **HONORS AND AWARDS** Nat Hum Ctr fel, Australia Nat Univ, 97. **SELECTED PUBLICATIONS** Auth, The Kiowa, Chelsea House Press, 89; "Retained by the People": A History of American Indians and the Bill of Rights, Oxford UP, 94; ed, Native Americans and the Law, Garland Press, 96; Law and the Great Plains: Essays on the Legal History of the Heartland, Greenwood Press, 96. **CONTACT ADDRESS** Univ Nebr, Lincoln, 628 Oldfat, Lincoln, NE, 68588-0417. **EMAIL** jwunder@unlinfo.unl.edu

WUNDERLI, RICHARD M.
PERSONAL Born 11/15/1940, Salt Lake City, UT, m, 1967, 1 child **DISCIPLINE** HISTORY **EDUCATION** Univ Utah, BA 64, MA 66; Univ Cal Berk, PhD 75. **CAREER** Univ Colorado, asst prof, assoc prof, prof, 76-, ch of dept, 84-90, 93-96. **HONORS AND AWARDS** Outstanding Teacher; 1st Annual Bk Awd for U of Colo. **MEMBERSHIPS** MAA **RESEARCH** Medieval History **SELECTED PUBLICATIONS** Auth, London Church Courts and Society on the Eve of Reformation, Cambridge MA, 81; Peasant Fires, Bloomington IN, 92; many articles. **CONTACT ADDRESS** Dept of History, PO Box 7150, Colorado Springs, CO, 80933-7150. **EMAIL** rwunderl@brain.uccs.edu

WUNSCH, JAMES STEVENSON
PERSONAL Born 09/27/1946, Detroit, MI, m, 1983, 3 children **DISCIPLINE** POLITICAL SCIENCE, AFRICAN STUDIES **EDUCATION** Duke Univ, Hist, BA, 68; Ind Univ, Polit Sci, MA, 70, African Stud/Polit Sci, PhD, 74. **CAREER** Assoc instr, Polit Sci, Ind Univ, 69-70; res fel, Inst African Stud, Univ Ghana, 71-72; vis sch, Univ Mich, 74; assoc investr, Nat Inst Mental Health Res Proj, 75-76; eval spec, US Dept Agric, Off Int Prog, 78-79; soc sci anal, Off Rural Develop & Develop Admin, US Agency Int Develop, 78-80; assoc investr, Nat Sci Found, 86; sr fel, Ind Univ, 85-86; vis assoc prof, Polit Sci, Ind Univ, 85-86; chr, Dept Polit Sci, Creighton Univ, 83-92; act ch, Creighton Univ, 96-97; act dir, Dept Polit Sci & Int Stud, Creighton Univ, 96-97; CHR, POLIT SCI/INT STUD, CREIGHTON UNIV, 97-. **MEMBERSHIPS** Am Polit Sci Asn; Midwest Polit Sci Asn; African Stud Asn; Policy Stud Org **SELECTED PUBLICATIONS** "Review Essay: Public Administration and Local Government," African Stud Rev, 97; coauth, "Regime Transformation from Below: Decentralization, Local Governance and Democratic Reform in Nigeria," Studies in Comp Develop, Winter, 96; coauth, "Decentralization, Local Government and Primary Health Care in Nigeria: An Analytical Study," Jour of African Policy Stud, 95; coauth, The Failure of the Centralized State: Institutions and Self Governance in Africa, Inst Contemp Stud, 95; "African Political Reforms and International Assistance: What Can and Should Be Done?", Africa: Develop & Publ Policy, MacMillan Press, 94. **CONTACT ADDRESS** Dept Polit Sci, Creighton Univ, Omaha, NE, 68178. **EMAIL** jwunsch@creighton.edu

WYATT, DAVID KENT
PERSONAL Born 09/21/1937, Fitchburg, MA, m, 1959, 3 children **DISCIPLINE** SOUTHEAST ASIAN HISTORY **EDUCATION** Harvard Univ, AB, 59; Boston Univ, MA, 60; Cornell Univ, PhD(hist), 66. **CAREER** Lectr Southeast Asian hist, Sch Oriental & African Studies, Univ London, 64-68; asst prof hist, Univ Mich, Ann Arbor, 68-69; assoc prof, 69-76, prof hist, Cornell Univ, 76-; Vis Fulbright lectr hist, Univ Malaya, 66-67; sr fel, Nat Endowment Humanities, 75-76; dir, Cornell Univ Southeast Asia Prog, 76-79. **HONORS AND AWARDS** Elected honorary member, Siam Society, 97; pres, Assn Asian Studies, 93-94. **MEMBERSHIPS** Siam Soc; Asn Asian Studies; Malayan Br Royal Asiatic Soc. **RESEARCH** History of Thailand and Laos. **SELECTED PUBLICATIONS** Auth, The Politics of Reform in Thailand, Yale Univ, 69; coauth, Hikayat Patani: The Story of Patani, Martinus Nijhoff, 70; In Search of Southeast Asia: A Modern History, Praeger, 70, 2nd ed, U of Hawaii Press, 88; auth, The Crystal Sands: The Chronicles of Nagara Sri Dharrmaraja, Cornell Univ, 75; ed, The Short History of the Kings of Siam, by Jeremias van Vliet (1640), Siam Soc, Bangkok, 75; Studies in Thai History, Silkworm Bks, 94; The Chiang Mai Chronicle, Silkworm, 95. **CONTACT ADDRESS** Dept of History, Cornell Univ, Mcgraw Hall, Ithaca, NY, 14853-4601. **EMAIL** dkw4@cornell.edu

WYATT, WILLIAM F.
PERSONAL Born 07/14/1932, Medford, MA, m, 1989, 3 children **DISCIPLINE** CLASSICS **EDUCATION** Bowdon Univ, AB; Harvard Univ, PhD 62. **CAREER** Univ Washington, asst prof, assoc prof, 60-67; Brown Univ, assoc prof, prof, 67 to 98-. **RESEARCH** Homer; Linguistics **SELECTED PUBLICATIONS** Auth, Several books, many articles and reviews. **CONTACT ADDRESS** Dept of Classics, Brown Univ, Providence, RI, 02912. **EMAIL** william_wyatt_f@brown.edu

WYMAN, DAVID S
PERSONAL Born 03/06/1929, Weymouth, MA, m, 1950, 2 children **DISCIPLINE** RECENT AMERICAN HISTORY **EDUCATION** Boston Univ, AB, 51; Plymouth State Col, MEd, 61; Harvard Univ, AM, 62, PhD(hist), 66. **CAREER** Teacher, Elem Sch, NH, 57-60 & High Sch, NH, 60-61; from asst prof to assoc prof, 66-75, PROF HIST, UNIV MASS, AMHERST, 75-, Soc Sci Res Coun fac res grant, 69-70; res fel, Charles Warren Ctr, Harvard Univ, 69-70; Am Coun Learned Soc grant-in-aid, 69-70; spec adv, US Holocaust Mem Coun, 81- **MEMBERSHIPS** Orgn Am Historians; AAUP. **RESEARCH** American refugee policy, 1930's and 1940's; American society, 1930-1945; the Jewish holocaust, 1933-1945. **SELECTED PUBLICATIONS** Auth, The Bombing of Auschwitz Re-Examined, Jour Military Hist, Vol 0061, 97; The Bombing of Auschwitz Revisited, Holocaust and Genocide Stud, Vol 0011, 97. **CONTACT ADDRESS** Dept of Hist, Univ of Mass, Amherst, MA, 01002.

WYNAR, LUBOMYR ROMAN
PERSONAL Born 01/02/1932, Lviw, Ukraine, m, 1962 **DISCIPLINE** HISTORY **EDUCATION** Ukrainian Free Univ, Munich, MA, 55, PhD, 57; Western Reserve Univ, MS, 59. **CAREER** Instr bibliog, Case Inst Technol, 59-62; asst prof bibliog & head soc sci libr, Univ Colo, 62-65; head info & ref serv, Bowling Green State Univ, 65-67, assoc prof bibliog, dir, Res Ctr & assoc dir, Univ Libr, 67-69; PROF HIST LIBR SCI, KENT STATE UNIV, 69-, DIR ETHNIC STUDIES, CTR STUDY ETHNIC PUBL, 72-, Libr consult, Educ Res Coun Cleveland, 61-62; res assoc Soviet affairs, John Carroll Univ, 62-; Coun Res & Creative Work grant, Univ Colo, 63; managing ed, Bio-Bibliog Ser & ed Soc Sci Ref Ser, Univ Colo, 63-65; chief ed, Ukrainian Historian, 64-; res grant, Comt Fac Res, Bowling Green State Univ, 66 & 68 & US Off Educ, Ethnic Heritage Studies, 77-; chmn, comt Slavic mat US & Can Libr, 68-, res rev comt, Ethnic Studies, Cleveland State Univ, 73-75 & Historiographical Comn, Ukrainian Hist Asn, 75- **MEMBERSHIPS** Am Asn Advan Slavic Studies; Am Libr Asn; Shevchenko Sci Soc (secy, 61); Ukrainian Hist Asn (secy, 65-68, pres, 81-); Asn Study of Nationalities (vpres, 77-). **RESEARCH** Slavic history, 16th to the 18th century; bibliography; history of Ukraine. **SELECTED PUBLICATIONS** Auth, To The Editor--Prymak,Thomas Review of Hrushevskyi,M. Na Porozi Novoi Ukrainy, Slavic Rev, Vol 0053, 94. **CONTACT ADDRESS** Sch of Libr Sci, Kent State Univ, Kent, OH, 44242.

WYNES, CHARLES ELDRIDGE
PERSONAL Born 08/11/1929, Rectortown, VA **DISCIPLINE** UNITED STATES HISTORY **EDUCATION** James Madison Univ, BS, 52; Univ Va, MA, 57, PhD, 60. **CAREER** From instr to asst prof, Tex A&M Univ, 58-62; from asst prof to assoc prof, 62-70, dir grad studies, 66-68, asst dean arts & sci, 68-71, PROF HIST, UNIV GA, 70-, Vis scholar, James Madison Univ, 80. **MEMBERSHIPS** Southern Hist Asn. **RESEARCH** The South since 1865; American Negro history; Georgia history. **SELECTED PUBLICATIONS** Auth, Emancipation in Virginias Tobacco Belt, 1850-1870, Jour Amer Hist, Vol 0080, 94; The Way it Was in the South--The Black-Experience in Georgia, Jour Amer Hist, Vol 0082, 95. **CONTACT ADDRESS** Dept of Hist, Univ of Ga, Athens, GA, 30602.

WYRICK, FLOYD I.
PERSONAL Born 05/26/1932, Chgo **DISCIPLINE** EDUCATION **EDUCATION** Chicago State U, BE 1954; DePaul U, MA 1963; Univ of IL, PhD 1972; Phi Delta Kappa; Kappa Delta Pi. **CAREER** Calumet HS Chicago Bd Educ, prin co-dir; Chicago Public School, teacher; Chicago City Coll; Northwestern Univ; Booz Allen & Hamilton, mgmt conselor; Adam & Assoc; Mitchell Watkins & Assoc. **MEMBERSHIPS** Mem Nat Alli of Black Sch Educ; Am Assn of Sch Adminstrs; Nat Assn of Scndry Sch Prins; Samuel B Stratton Educ Assn; mem Am Civil Libs Union; People Unit to Save Human; Alpha Phi Alpha Frat; Comm Fund of Metro Chgo. **CONTACT ADDRESS** 78131 S May St, Chicago, IL, 60620.

Y

YABLONSKY, LEWIS
PERSONAL Born 11/23/1924, Irvington, NJ, s, 1 child **DISCIPLINE** SOCIOLOGY **EDUCATION** New York Univ, PhD, 58. **CAREER** Prof Sociol, Calif State Univ - Northridge, 67-. **HONORS AND AWARDS** CSU Bd Trustees Outstanding Prof Award. **RESEARCH** Criminology. **SELECTED PUBLICATIONS** Auth, Criminology, HarperCollins, 90; Gangsters, NYU Press, 97. **CONTACT ADDRESS** 2311 4th St., #312, Santa Monica, CA, 90405. **EMAIL** yablonsky@loop.com

YAMASHITA, SAMUEL HIDEO
PERSONAL Born 11/27/1946, Honolulu, HI, m, 1969 **DISCIPLINE** HISTORY, JAPANESE HISTORY **EDUCATION** Mid-Pacific Inst (col prep diploma), 64; Macalester Col, BA (Hist), 68; Univ MI, MA (Hist), 71, PhD (Hist, Japanese Hist), 81. **CAREER** Instr, Hobart & William Smith Colleges, 77-81, asst prof, 81-82; postdoctoral fel, Reischauer Inst of Japanese Studies, Harvard Univ, 82-83; sr tutor in Asian Studies, Harvard Univ, 82-83; asst prof, 83-88, assoc prof, 88-98, PROF, POMONA COL, 98-. **HONORS AND AWARDS** Woodrow Wilson fel, 68; Rackham Prize fel, 71-72; Ford Found-Social Science Res Coun Foreign Area fel, 73-75; Wig Distinguished Prof Award, Pomona Col, 86, 90, 95; Japan Foundation Prof fel, 91. **MEMBERSHIPS** Asn for Asian Studies, 70-. **RESEARCH** Japanese intellectual hist. **SELECTED PUBLICATIONS** Auth, Review of Voice of the Past: The Status of Language in Eighteenth-Century Japan, Cornell Univ Press, 91, Am Hist Rev 99, April 94; co-trans, The Four-Seven Debate: An Annotated Translation of the Most Famous Controversy in Korean Neo-Confucian Thought, SUNY Press, 93; auth, Master Sorai's Responsals: An Annotated Translation of Sorai sensei tomonsho, Univ HI Press, 94; Review of Japanese Loyalism Reconstrued: Yamagata Daini's 'Ryushi shinron' of 1759, Univ HI Press, 95, Harvard J of Asiatic Studies, winter 98; Confucianism and the Modern Japanese State, 1904-1945, in Tu Weiming, ed, Confucian Traditions in East Asian Modernity: Moral Education and Economy and Culture in Japan and the Four Mini-Dragons, Harvard Univ Press, 96; Reading the New Tokugawa Intellectual Histories, J of Japanese Studies 22, winter 96. **CONTACT ADDRESS** Dept of Hist, Pomona Col, Claremont, CA, 91711. **EMAIL** syamashita@pomona.edu

YAMAUCHI, EDWIN MASAO
PERSONAL Born 02/01/1937, Hilo, HI, m, 1962, 2 children **DISCIPLINE** ANCIENT HISTORY, SEMITIC LANGUAGES **EDUCATION** Shelton Col, BA, 60; Brandeis Univ, MA, 62, PhD(Mediter studies), 64. **CAREER** Asst prof ancient hist, Rutgers Univ, New Brunswick, 64-69; assoc prof, 69-73, dir grad studies, Hist Dept, 78-82, prof Hist, Miami Univ, 73-, Nat Endowment for Humanities fel, 68; Am Philos Soc grant, 70; consult ed hist, J Am Sci Affiliation, 70-; sr ed, Christianity Today, 92-94. **MEMBERSHIPS** Am Sci Affil (pres, 83); Archaeol Inst Am; Conf Faith & Hist (pres, 74-76); Near E Archaeol Soc (vpres, 78); Inst Bibl Res (pres, 87-89). **RESEARCH** Gnosticism; ancient magic; Old and New Testaments. **SELECTED PUBLICATIONS** Auth, Greece and Babylon, Baker Bk, 67; Mandaic incantation texts, Am Orient Soc, 67; Gnostic Ethics and Mandaean Origins, Harvard Univ, 70; The Stones and the Scriptures, Lippincott, 72; Pre-Christian Gnosticism, Tyndale Press, London & Eerdmans, 73; The Archaeology of New Testament Cities in Western Asia Minor, Baker Bk, 80; The Scriptures and Archaeology, Western Conserv Baptist Sem, 80; World of the New Testament, Harper & Row, 81; Foes from the Northern Frontier, Baker Bk, 82; coeditor, Chronos, Kairos, Christos, Eisenbrauns, 89; Persia and the Bible, Baker Bk, 90; coauth, The Two Kingdoms, Moody, 93; coed, Peoples of the Old Testament World, Baker, 94. **CONTACT ADDRESS** Dept of History, Miami Univ, 500 E High St, Oxford, OH, 45056-1602. **EMAIL** Yamauce@casmail.muohio.edu

YANCY, DOROTHY COWSER
PERSONAL Born 04/18/1944, Cherokee Cty, Alabama, s **DISCIPLINE** POLITICAL SCIENCE **EDUCATION** Johnson C Smith Univ, AB History 1964; Univ of MA Amherst, MA 1965; Atlanta Univ, PhD Polit 1978. **CAREER** Albany State Coll Albany GA, instr history 1965-67; Hampton Inst Hampton VA, instr history 1967-69; Evanston Twp HS, teacher 1969-71; Barat Coll Lake Forest IL, dir black studies 1971-72; Georgia Inst of Tech, assistant professor, 1972-78, associate professor, 1978-88, professor, 1988-94; Johnson C. Smith Univ, prof, president, 1994-. **HONORS AND AWARDS** Fulbright-Hayes Scholar 1968; collaborating author, The Fed Gov Policy & Black Enterprise 1974; mem: Omicron Delta Kappa, Phi Kappa Phi Honor Soc, Leadership Atlanta Class, 1984; Distinguished Alumnus, Johnson C Smith Univ, 1981; Outstanding Teacher of the Year, Georgia Institute of Technology, 1985; mem, People to People Delegation of Labor Experts, to Soviet Union & Europe, 1988, to London, Berlin, & Moscow, 1990; The Academy of Political and Social Sciences of the Small Hural, Ulan Bator, Mongolia, Lecturer and Consultant, 1991. **MEMBERSHIPS** Mem: Assn for the Study of Afro-Amer Life & History, Industrial Relations Res Assn, Soc of Professionals in Dispute Resolutions; mem, labor panel Amer Arbitration Assn 1980; mem exec comm Assn of Soc & Behavioral Sci; mem So Pol Sci Assn; spec master, FL Public Employees Relations Commn; bd mem Assn for the Study of Afro-Amer Life & History; mem Labor Arbitration Panel Fed Mediation & Conciliation Serv; mediator, Mediation Res & Educ Proj, Northwestern Univ, 1988-; mem, Arbitration Panel, Bd of Regents State Univ System of FL & AFSCME, 1988-; chw, Woman Power Commission, The Links, Inc, 1990-94; Johnson C Smith Univ, board of trustees, 1991-94; bd, Charlotte Chamber of Commerce, Charlotte Urban League, Metro Charlotte YMCA. **CONTACT ADDRESS** President, Johnson C Smith Univ, 100 Beatties Ford Rd, Charlotte, NC, 28216.

YANG, SUNG CHUL
DISCIPLINE DIPLOMACY **EDUCATION** PhD, 70. **CAREER** Univ Ky **CONTACT ADDRESS** Funkhouser Bldg, Univ Ky, Lexington, KY, 40506-0054.

YANG, WINSTON L.
PERSONAL Born 06/01/1935, Nanking, China, m, 1964, 2 children **DISCIPLINE** ASIAN STUDIES **EDUCATION** National Taiwan Univ, BA, 58; Stanford Univ, PhD, 70. **CAREER** Prof and chemn, Dept of Asian Stud, Seton Hall Univ, 84- . **HONORS AND AWARDS** Royal Asiatic Soc of Gt Brit and Ireland. **MEMBERSHIPS** Asn for Asian Stud. **RESEARCH** Modern China and Taiwan. **SELECTED PUBLICATIONS** Auth, Tianammon: China's Struggle for Democracy, Univ Maryland, 90; auth, The Political Journey of Lian Chan, Business Weekly, 96. **CONTACT ADDRESS** 3 Waldeck Ct, West Orange, NJ, 07052.

YANG, ZONGSUI
DISCIPLINE HISTORY **EDUCATION** West China Union Univ, BA, 51. **CAREER** Vis prof History, Harvard; assoc prof History, Sichuan Univ, China. **RESEARCH** Boston Tea Party, Chinese translation. **CONTACT ADDRESS** 2300 Hampstead Ave, #2, Richmond, VA, 23230-2337.

YANNATOS, JAMES
PERSONAL Born 03/13/1929, New York, NY, m, 1959, 2 children **DISCIPLINE** MUSIC **EDUCATION** Yale Univ, BM, 51, MM, 52; Univ of Iowa, PhD, 61. **CAREER** SENIOR LECTR/MUSIC DIR, HARVARD-RADCLIFFE ORCHESTRA, 64-. **HONORS AND AWARDS** Fulbright Grant; Wooley Fel; Ditson Award; New England Artists Award; Virgil Thomson Found Grant. **MEMBERSHIPS** BMI. **RESEARCH** Composing. **SELECTED PUBLICATIONS** Performances: Concerto for String Quartet and Orchestra, 96, CD in 99; Variations: Solo Contra Bass, 98; Haiku Cycle (voice & chamber ensemble), 95; Concerto for percussion ensemble (...of Things Past and Present), 96; Bach-anale (suite for 2 pianos), 97; Piano Trio, 95. **CONTACT ADDRESS** Dept of Music, Harvard Univ, 9 Stearns St., Cambridge, MA, 02138. **EMAIL** yannatos@fas.harvard.edu

YANNI, CARLA
PERSONAL Born 09/18/1965, Allentown, PA **DISCIPLINE** ART HISTORY, ARCHITECTURAL HISTORY **EDUCATION** Wesleyan Univ, BA (high honors), 87; Univ Pa, PhD, 94. **CAREER** Univ New Mexico, Albuquerque, asst prof, 94-97; Rutgers Univ, asst prof, 97-. **HONORS AND AWARDS** Rosann Berry Award, 91, Founders' Award, 96, Soc of Archit Historians. **MEMBERSHIPS** Coll Art Assn; Soc of Archit Historians. **RESEARCH** Archit and science; museum archit. **SELECTED PUBLICATIONS** Auth, "Divine Display or Secular Science: Defining Nature at the Natural History Museum in London," Journ of the Soc of Archit History, 97; "On Nature and Nomenclature: William Whewell and the Production of Knowledge in Victorian Britain," Archit History, 97. **CONTACT ADDRESS** Art History Dept., Rutgers Univ, Voorhees Hall, New Brunswick, NJ, 08903. **EMAIL** cyanni@rci.rutgers.edu

YARBOROUGH, RICHARD A.
PERSONAL Born 05/24/1951, Philadelphia, Pennsylvania, d **DISCIPLINE** AFRICAN-AMERICAN STUDIES **EDUCATION** Mich State Univ, E Lansing MI, BA, 1973; Stanford Univ, Stanford CA, PhD, 1980. **CAREER** Univ of California, Los Angeles CA, asst prof 1979-86, assoc prof 1986-. **HONORS AND AWARDS** US Presidential Scholar, 1969; Alumni Dist Scholar's Award, MI State Univ, 1969-73; Whiting Fellowship in Humanities, Stanford Univ, 1977-78; Natl Endowment for the Humanities fellowship, 1984-85; Dist Teaching Award, UCLA, 1987; Ford Foundation postdoctoral fellowship, 1988-89; City of Los Angeles Commendation, 1990. **MEMBERSHIPS** Faculty res assoc, UCLA Center for African-Amer Studies, 1979-; mem 1987-92, chair 1989-90, exec comm of Div of Black Amer Literature & Culture, Modern Lang Assn; bd of editorial advisors, American Quarterly, 1987-91; mem, Natl Council, Amer Studies Assn, 1988-91; member, editorial board, African American Review, 1989-; California Council for the Humanities, 1992-96. **SELECTED PUBLICATIONS** Assoc gen editor, The Heath Anthology of American Literature, 2nd ed, D C Heath, 1994, 3rd ed, Houghton Mifflin, 1998; general editor, "Library of Black Literature," Northeastern Univ Press, 1988-; coeditor, Norton Anthology of Afro-American Literature, 1996; author of scholarly essays in numerous journals & books. **CONTACT ADDRESS** Professor/Research/Writer, Univ of California, Los Angeles, 2225 Rolfe Hall, Box 951530, Los Angeles, CA, 90095-1530.

YARDLEY, J.C.
DISCIPLINE CLASSICS **EDUCATION** St Andrews, MA, 66, PhD, 76; Oxford, BA, 70. **CAREER** Asst, Assoc to Prof, 69-88, Univ of Calgary; Prof, Chr, 88-, Univ of Ottawa. **HONORS AND AWARDS** Pres, Class Assoc of Canada, 94-96. **MEMBERSHIPS** CAC; Amer Philos Assoc. **RESEARCH** Roman Poetry; The Alexander Hist; Justin. **SELECTED PUBLICATIONS** Auth, Quintus Curtis Rufus, Penguin Classics, 84; Justin, Scholars Press, 94; Justin 11-12, Oxford Univ Press, 97. **CONTACT ADDRESS** Dept Classic Studies, Univ Ottawa, Ottawa, ON, K1N 6N5. **EMAIL** JCYard@AIX1.UOTTAWA.ca

YASKO, RICHARD ANTHONY
PERSONAL Born 01/22/1931, Racine, WI, m, 1963, 3 children **DISCIPLINE** HISTORY & JAPANESE STUDIES **EDUCATION** Dominican Col, BA, 63; Univ Chicago, MA, 65, PhD, 73. **CAREER** Vis lectr Japan hist, Univ MD, College Park, 72-73; asst prof hist, Sam Houston State Univ, 73-75; Assoc Prof Hist, 76-83, prof hist Univ WI-Whitewater, 84-, Fulbright Res Scholar, Tokyo Univ, 68-70. **HONORS AND AWARDS** Excellence in Tchg in the Hum, 93; Col of Letters & Sci Tchg Award, 94. **MEMBERSHIPS** Asn Asian Studies; Western Soc Sci Asn. **RESEARCH** Prewar Showa polit hist; G.I.s in post-occupation Japan. **SELECTED PUBLICATIONS** Auth, Hiranuma Kiichiro and the New Structure Movement, 1940-1941, Asian Forum 6/73; Bribery Cases and the Rise of the Justice Ministry, In: Late Meiji Early Taisho Japan, Law in Japan, 79. **CONTACT ADDRESS** Dept of Hist, Univ Wisconsin-Whitewater, 800 W Main, Whitewater, WI, 53190-1790.

YEARSLEY, DAVID
DISCIPLINE MUSIC **EDUCATION** Harvard Univ, AB, 87; Stanford Univ, MA, 90, PhD, 94. **CAREER** Asst prof **HONORS AND AWARDS** First prize, Bruges Int Organ Competition, 94; top prize, Schnitger Int Organ Competition, 91. **MEMBERSHIPS** Amer Musicol Soc. **RESEARCH** J. S. Bach; 17th- and early 18th-century aesthetics and criticism; keyboard music before 1750; the occult in 18th-century music. **SELECTED PUBLICATIONS** Auth, JS Bach, Cambridge Guide to the Organ. **CONTACT ADDRESS** Dept of Music, Cornell Univ, 104 Lincoln Hall, Ithaca, NY, 14853. **EMAIL** dgy2@cornell.edu

YEGUL, FIKRET KUTLU
PERSONAL Born 10/27/1941, Turkey **DISCIPLINE** HISTORY OF ART AND ARCHITECTURE **EDUCATION** Mid East Tech Univ, Ankara, Turkey, BArch, 64; Yale Univ, BArch, 65; Univ Pa, MArch, 66; Harvard Univ, PhD(art hist), 75. **CAREER** Asst prof, Wellesley Col, 75-76; ASST PROF GREEK & ROMAN ART, UNIV CALIF, SANTA BARBARA, 76-, Mem excavation, Sardis Archaeol Excavation, Harvard Univ, 63-; Am Coun Learned Soc grant, 79-80; res fel, Am Res Inst, Turkey, 80-81. **MEMBERSHIPS** Am Inst Archaeol. **RESEARCH** Roman architecture, particularly bathing and the baths in classical antiquity; Greek architecture; Islamic architecture, particularly of the Mamluk Period in Cairo. **SELECTED PUBLICATIONS** Auth, Thermae-Et-Balnea--The Architecture and Cultural History of Roman Public Baths, Amer Jour Archaeol, Vol 0097, 93. **CONTACT ADDRESS** Art Hist Dept, Univ of Calif, 552 University Rd, Santa Barbara, CA, 93106-0001.

YEH, WEN-HAN
DISCIPLINE HISTORY/EAST ASIA **EDUCATION** Univ Calif, Berkeley, PhD, 84. **CAREER** Asst prof to PROF, DEPT HIST, UNIV CALIF, BERKELEY, 87-. **HONORS AND AWARDS** Mellon fel. **MEMBERSHIPS** AHA, AAS. **RESEARCH** Modern China; hist; 20th century. **SELECTED PUBLICATIONS** Auth, The Alienated Academy: Culture and Politics in Republican China, 1919-37, Harvard, 90; Provincial Passages: Culture, Space, and the Origin of Chinese Communism, Calif Univ Press, 96. **CONTACT ADDRESS** Dept Hist, Univ of California, Berkeley, CA, 94720-2550. **EMAIL** sha@socrates.berkeley.edu

YELLIN, VICTOR FELL
PERSONAL Born 12/14/1924, Boston, MA, m, 1948, 1 child **DISCIPLINE** MUSIC HISTORY, COMPOSITION **EDUCATION** Harvard Univ, AB, 49, AM, 52, PhD, 57. **CAREER** Asst prof music, NY Univ, 56-58; Williams Col, 58-60; assoc prof, OH State Univ, 60-61; assoc prof, 61-68, master, Weinstein Hall, 65-71, prof music hist, NY Univ , 68. **HONORS AND AWARDS** MacDowell Colony, Peterborough, NH, 69; Nat Endowment for Hum fel, 78. **MEMBERSHIPS** Am Musicol Soc; Sonneck Soc for Am Music; Redwood Libr, Redwood, Newport, RI. **RESEARCH** Hist of Am music; Early romantic opera; Chromatic harmony. **SELECTED PUBLICATIONS** Auth, When Is a Symphony Not a Symphony: The Symphonies of William Boyce, Musical Am, 2/53; Some Specific Advice to

Young Opera Composers, Muiscal Am, 2/54; Opera's American History, Music Jour, 3/61; he Conflic of Generations in American Music (A Yankee View), Arts and Sci, NY Univ, winter 62; The Pronunciation of Recitative, Am Sppech, 12/68; Musical Activity in Virginia before 1620, J Am Musicol Soc, 69; The Operas of Virgil Thomson, In: Virgil Thomson American Music since 1910, Holt, 71; Ives' The Celestial Country, Music Quart 7/74; George Whitefield Chadwick, American Musical Realist, Musical Quart, 1/75; Restoration, Rayner Taylor's The Aethiop, recording, New World Records, 6/78; Rayner Taylor, Am Music, fall 83; Rayner Taylor's Music for the Aethiop I, Am Music, fall 86; Rayner Taylor's Music for the Aethiop II, Am Music, spring 87; Chadwick, Yankee Cmposer, Smithsonian, 90; Prosodic Syncopation, In: A Celebration of American Music: Words and Music in Honor of H. Wiley Hitchcock (Richard Crawford, ed), Univ Mich, 90; Sullivan and Thomson, Gilbert and Stein, Jour of Musicol, fall 93; Bristow's Divorce, Am Music, fall 94; The Aethiop (1813) Orch Score Restoration, In: Nineteenth-Century American Musical Theater (Deane L Root, ed), vol 2, Garland, 94; Mrs Belmont Matthew Perry, and the Japanese Minstrels, Am Music, fall 96; The Omnibus Idea, Harmonie Park Press, 98; Compositions, Passacaglia for Strings, 52; Ballet, The Bear that Wasn't, 52; Sonata for Violin and Piano, 53; Opera, Abaylar, 65; Sonata for Violoncello and Piano, 79; Song Cycle Teasdale, Dark of the Moon, 84; Variations on Bye Bye Blues for Violoncello or violin and piano, 88. **CONTACT ADDRESS** Dept of Music, New York Univ, 24 Waverly Pl, New York, NY, 10003-6757.

YEN, DE

PERSONAL Born 03/20/1924, Wellington, New Zealand, M, 1949, 2 children **DISCIPLINE** AGRICULTURE; ANTHROPOLOGY (PREHISTORY) **EDUCATION** Massey Agricultural Coll, Univ of NZ, B Agr Sc, 47, M Agr Sc, 48; Auckland Univ NZ, D Sc, 75. **CAREER** Plant breeder, 48-53, Crop research div, dept sci and industry research, Lincoln, NZ; officer in charge of vegetable breeding, 54-66; enthnobotanist, dept anthrop, 66-80, Bishop Museum, Honolulu; prof, 80-90, Australian Natl Univ. **HONORS AND AWARDS** Fels, Australian Acad of Humanities; Linnean Soc; Foreign assoc, Natl Acad of Sci; Elsden Best Medal; Distinguished Economic Botanist, 92. **MEMBERSHIPS** Polynesian Soc; Soc for Economic Botany; Hakluyt Soc; Amer Anthrop Assoc **RESEARCH** Origins of oceanic subsistence, agriculture **SELECTED PUBLICATIONS** Auth, Pacific Subsistence systems and Aspects of Cultural Evolution, A Community of Culture, 93; Kumara remains in Pit 0 at P5/288, The Archaeology of Paat Pouerua, Northland, New Zealand, 93; The development of Sahul agriculture with Australia as bystander, Antiquity 69, 95; Melanesian arboriculture: Historical perspecitves with emphasis on the genus Canarium, South Pacific Indigenous Nuts, 96. **CONTACT ADDRESS** Dept of Anthropol, Univ Hawaii Manoa, Honolulu, HI, 96822.

YERKES, DAVID

DISCIPLINE ANGLO-SAXON LANGUAGE AND LITERATURE **EDUCATION** Yale Univ, 71; Oxford Univ, BA, 73 Dphil, 76. **CAREER** Prof, 77-. **MEMBERSHIPS** Mem, London Medieval Soc; Medieval Acad; Soc Text Scholar. **SELECTED PUBLICATIONS** Auth, An Old English Thesaurus; Syntax and Style in Old English; The Old English Life of Machutus. **CONTACT ADDRESS** Dept of Eng, Columbia Col, New York, 2960 Broadway, New York, NY, 10027-6902.

YERUSHALMI, YOSEF HAYIM

DISCIPLINE MEDIEVAL AND MODERN JEWISH HISTORY **EDUCATION** Yeshiva Univ, BA, 53; Columbia, PhD, 66. **CAREER** Hist, Columbia Univ **SELECTED PUBLICATIONS** Auth, From Spanish Court to Italian Ghetto, 71; Haggadah and History, 75; The Lisbon Massacre of 1506, 76; Zakhor: Jewish History and Jewish Memory, 82; A Jewish Classic in the Portuguese Language, 89; Freud's Moses, 91; Ein Feld in Anathoth, 93; Diener von Koenigen und nicht Diener von Dienern, 95. **CONTACT ADDRESS** Columbia Univ, 2960 Broadway, New York, NY, 10027-6902.

YERXA, DONALD A.

DISCIPLINE AMERICAN HISTORY AND HISTORICAL METHODOLOGY **EDUCATION** Eastern Nazarene Col, BA; Univ ME, MA, PhD. **CAREER** Ch, dept hist, Eastern Nazarene Col. **SELECTED PUBLICATIONS** Auth, Admirals and Empire: The US Navy and the Caribbean, 1898-1945. **CONTACT ADDRESS** Eastern Nazarene Col, 23 East Elm Ave, Quincy, MA, 02170-2999.

YETMAN, NORMAN ROGER

PERSONAL Born 01/10/1938, New York, NY, m, 1964, 2 children **DISCIPLINE** AMERICAN STUDIES, SOCIOLOGY **EDUCATION** Univ Redlands, BA, 60; Univ Pa, MA, 61, PhD(Am Civilization), 69. **CAREER** Instr sociol, Univ Redlands, 62-63; from asst prof to prof Am studies & sociol, 66-77; Chancellors Club Teaching Prof of Am Stud and Sociol, 92- , chmn Am studies, 73-81, 93-96, chair, Sociol, 86-89, Univ Kansas; Danforth assoc; Inst Southern Hist, Johns Hopkins Univ, sr res fel, 72-73; eval consult, Nat Endowment for Humanities, 75-76; Am spec, Dept State, 77, 82, 98; Fulbright prof, Odense Univ & Univ Copenhagen, 81-82. **MEMBERSHIPS** Am Sociol Asn; Orgn Am Historians; Am Studies Asn. **RESEARCH** Racial and ethnic relations; sociology of slavery; sociology of sport. **SELECTED PUBLICATIONS** Ed, Life Under the Peculiar Institution, 70 & Voices From Slavery, 70, Holt; ed, Majority and Minority, Allyn & Bacon, 71, 75, 82, 85, 91, 99; coauth, Black Americans in sports, Civil Rights Digest, 72, 77; Family planning services and the distribution of Black Americans, Social Problems, 6/74; auth, The rise and fall of time on the cross, Rev Am Hist, spring 76; The Irish experience in America, In: Irish History and Culture, 76; coauth, Sociology: Experiencing a Changing Societies, Allyn & Bacon, 97. **CONTACT ADDRESS** Dept of Am Studies, Univ of Kans, Lawrence, KS, 66045-0001. **EMAIL** norm@falcon.cc.ukans.edu

YICK, JOSEPH KONG SANG

DISCIPLINE HISTORY **EDUCATION** Univ Tex, Austin, BA, 76; Univ Calif, Santa Barbara, MA, 78, PhD, 88. **CAREER** Asst lectr, Hong Kong Baptist Col, 79-83; inst, Santa Barbara City Col, 84087; asst prof, Auburn Univ, Montgomery, 88- 89; asst, 89-95, ASSOC PROF HIST, 95-, SOUTHWEST TEX STATE UNIV. **CONTACT ADDRESS** Dept of History, Southwest Texas State Univ, San Marcos, TX, 78666. **EMAIL** jy02@swt.edu

YIP, CHRISTOPHER

DISCIPLINE ARCHITECUTE; ARCHITECTURAL HISTORY **EDUCATION** Univ of CA, Berkeley, BA, 71, MA, June 77, PhD, Dec 85. **CAREER** Asst prof, Univ of Colorado, 82-87; Assoc Prof, 88-94, Prof, Sept 94-present, CA Polytechnic State Univ,; Assoc prof, Univ of Hawaii at Manoa, 94-96. **HONORS AND AWARDS** John K. Branner Travelling Fel, 75-76; Newhouse Found Scholar, Newhouse Found, 78-79; Regent Fel, regents of the Univ CA, 79-80. **MEMBERSHIPS** Soc of Architectural Historians; Vernacular Architecture Forum **RESEARCH** Asian Amer environments; Colonial urbanism and architecture in Asia; Asia Pacific architecture **SELECTED PUBLICATIONS** Auth, Asian American and African American Environments, with Bradford Grant in Sherry Ahrentzen & Janetta McCoy, eds., Doing Diversity: A Compendium of Architectural Courses Addressing Diversity Issues in Architecture, 96; The Creation of Periodic Street Markets as a Means of Social and Ecological Betterment, in the Proceedings of the Second International Symnposium on Asia Pacific Aritecture: The Making of Public Places, 97; A Chinatown of Gold Mountain: The Chinese in Locke, California, in Images of an American Land: Vernacular Architecture in the Western United States, Thomas Carter, ed, 97; Association Building, in Encyclopedia of Vernacular Architecture of the World, 97; Chinese American Temples, in Encyclopedia of Vernacular Architecture of the World, 97; Chinese American, in Encyclopedia of Vernacular Architecuture of the World, 97. **CONTACT ADDRESS** Architecture Dept, California Polytech State Univ, 1151 Ella St, San Luis Obispo, CA, 93407. **EMAIL** cyip@calpoly.edu

YIP, KA-CHE

PERSONAL Hong Kong, China **DISCIPLINE** HISTORY **EDUCATION** Univ Hong Kong, BA, 65; Columbia Univ, MA, 67, E Asian Inst Cert, 68, PhD, 70. **CAREER** Prof, Univ MD Baltimore County. **RESEARCH** Mod Chinese hist. **SELECTED PUBLICATIONS** Auth, Religion, Nationalism; Chinese Students: the Anti-Christian Movement of 1922-1927; Health and National Reconstruction in Nationalist China. **CONTACT ADDRESS** Dept of Hist, Univ MD Baltimore County, Hilltop Circle, PO Box 1000, Baltimore, MD, 21250. **EMAIL** yip@umbc2.umbc.edu

YODER, JOHN

DISCIPLINE INTERNATIONAL POLITICS AND PEACE STUDIES, AFRICAN STUDIES **EDUCATION** Mennonite Sem, Mdiv; Northwestern Univ, PhD. **CAREER** Prof. **HONORS AND AWARDS** Fulbright grant, 87-88., Bd, Christian Scholar's Rev; Fulbright Nat Selection Comm for Africa. **RESEARCH** Relationship between the political values of ordinary citizens and the collapse of the Liberian state. **SELECTED PUBLICATIONS** Publ, articles on Dahomey, Uganda, Zaire, and colonial America; ed, Zaire, Dictionary of African Biography, Reference Publ, 79; auth, The Kanyok of Zaire, Cambridge, 92. **CONTACT ADDRESS** Dept of Hist, Whitworth Col, 300 West Hawthorne Rd, Spokane, WA, 99251. **EMAIL** johnyoder@whitworth.edu

YODER, R. PAUL

DISCIPLINE LITERARY HISTORY FROM MILTON TO KEATS **EDUCATION** Duke Univ, PhD. **CAREER** English and Lit, Univ Ark **SELECTED PUBLICATIONS** Auth, Milton's The Passion, Milton Studies; William Blake, Hanoverian Britain, 1714-1834; Coed, Critical Essays on Alexander Pope; Approaches to Teaching Alexander Pope; Wordsworth Reimagines Thomas Gray, Criticism. **CONTACT ADDRESS** Univ Ark Little Rock, 2801 S University Ave., Little Rock, AR, 72204-1099. **EMAIL** rpyoder@ualr.edu

YORK, NEIL LONGLEY

PERSONAL Born 04/21/1951, San Luis Obispo, CA, m, 1981, 2 children **DISCIPLINE** AMERICAN HISTORY **EDUCATION** Brigham Young Univ, BA, 73, MA, 75; Univ Calif, Santa Barbara, PhD(Hist), 78. **CAREER** Lect, 77-78, asst prof Hist, Bringham Young Univ, 78-84, from assoc prof to prof Hist; 84-94; dir, Am Studies, 80-84, 94-98; vis prof, Univ Calif, Davis, 80 & 81; vis prof, Univ Utah, 89. **MEMBERSHIPS** Assoc Inst Early Am Hist & Cult; Orgn Am Historians; Soc Hist Technol; Colonial Soc of Massachusetts. **RESEARCH** Revolutionary United States; history of technology; United States diplomacy. **SELECTED PUBLICATIONS** Auth, Neither Kingdom Nor Nation: The Irish Quest for Constitutional Rights, 1698-1800, Catholic University, 94; Maxims for a Petriot: Josiah Quincy Junior and his Commonplace Book, Colonial Society of Massachusetts (in press). **CONTACT ADDRESS** Dept of History, Brigham Young Univ, 323 Kmb, Provo, UT, 84602-0002. **EMAIL** neil_york@byu.edu

YOUNG, ALFRED

PERSONAL Born 02/21/1946, New Orleans, LA, m **DISCIPLINE** HISTORY **EDUCATION** Louisiana State Univ, New Orleans, LA, BA 1970; Syracuse Univ, MA 1972, PhD 1977. **CAREER** History and African-American Studies, visiting professor, 1995-97; Syracuse Univ, lecturer Afro-Amer studies 1971, instr history 1971-72, asst prof history 1972-82, assoc prof history 1982-88; SUNY Oswego; Colgate Univ, Hamilton, NY, A Lindsay O'Connor Chair, 1988-89; GEORGIA SOUTHERN UNIVERSITY, associate professor, 1989-94, PROF OF HISTORY, 1994-, director African and African-American studies program, 1991. **HONORS AND AWARDS** Afro-Amer Fellowship Syracuse Univ 1970-72; Natl Fellowship Fund Fellow 1975-76 1976-77; Outstanding Young Men of Amer Award 1979; summer research grant NY State Afro-Amer Institute 1987; certificate of appreciation Howard Univ Model OAU, 1989; numerous publs including "The Historical Origin & Significance of the Afro-Amer History Month Observance" Negro History Bulletin 1982; selected papers presented including US Department of Education Title IV, Grant 1991-93; The National Council for Black Studies Inc, Certificate of Outstanding Service Award, 1994-96. **MEMBERSHIPS** Keeper of finance, 1980-85, chapter historian, 1988-89, Omega Psi Phi Frat Inc Chi Pi chapter; adjunct prof history, Syracuse Univ/ Univ College Auburn Correctional Facility prog, 1981-89; consultant, faculty advisor, National Model OAU, Howard Univ, 1982--; bd mem, Friends of Syracuse Univ Alumni Organization, 1987-; board of directors, National Council for Black Studies, 1992-; Academic Council of the University Systems of Georgia Regents' Global Center, 1992-. **SELECTED PUBLICATIONS** Contributor to Historical Dictionary of Civil Rights in the United States, 1992; Contributing Editor, African Homefront; "Internationalizing the Curriculum: Africa and the Caribbean," International Studies Association Conference, Acapulco, Mexico, 1993; "Dr, Carter G Woodson's Legacy of Academic Excellence & Social Responsibility," Morehouse College Black History Month Lecture, February 1, 1996; Booker T Washington's Ideas on Black Economic Development: the Tuskegee Experiment," Southern Conference on African-American Studies Inc, Baton Rouge, February 1995; "The African-American Response to Post-Reconstruction Conditions in the South, Birmingham, Alabama, February, 1993. **CONTACT ADDRESS** History Dept, Georgia So Univ, PO Box 8054, Statesboro, GA, 30460.

YOUNG, ALFRED F.

PERSONAL Born 01/17/1925, New York, NY, m, 1952, 3 children **DISCIPLINE** AMERICAN HISTORY **EDUCATION** Queen's Col, NY, BA, 46; Columbia Univ, MA, 47; Northwestern Univ, PhD(hist), 58. **CAREER** Instr hist, Wesleyan Univ, 52-53; instr, Univ Conn, 55-56; from asst prof to assoc prof, Paterson State Col, 56-64; assoc prof, 64-68, PROF HIST, NORTHERN ILL UNIV, 68-, Am Philos Soc res grant, 59 & 61; Dixon Ryan Fox Fund res grant, NY Hist Asn, 61; consult, Bobbs Merrill Publ, 66-75; fels, Guggenheim, 69-70 & Nat Endowment for Humanities-Newberry Libr, 77-78; chmn, Newberry Libr Comt on Fels, 78- **HONORS AND AWARDS** Inst Early Am Hist Jamestown Prize, 67; Best article prize, Soc Daughters Colonial Wars, 81. **MEMBERSHIPS** AHA; Orgn Am Historians; Inst Early Am Hist; Am Antiquarian Soc. **RESEARCH** Early America; social-political movements; preindustrial labor. **SELECTED PUBLICATIONS** Auth, An Outsider and the Progress of a Career in History, William and Mary Quart, Vol 0052, 95. **CONTACT ADDRESS** No Illinois Univ, 215 Forest Ave, Oak Park, IL, 60302.

YOUNG, CHARLES ROBERT

PERSONAL Born 10/12/1927, Howard, KS, m, 1946, 2 children **DISCIPLINE** HISTORY **EDUCATION** Univ Kans, AB, 49, MA, 50; Cornell Univ, PhD(hist), 54. **CAREER** From instr to assoc prof, 54-70, PROF HIST, DUKE UNIV, 70-, ASSOC DEAN, GRAD SCH, 78- **MEMBERSHIPS** AHA; Mediaeval Acad Am; Conf Brit Studies; Southern Hist Asn. **RESEARCH** Mediaeval institutions. **SELECTED PUBLICATIONS** Auth, The Royal Forests of England, Speculum-Jour Medieval Stud, Vol 0068, 93; Vassals, Heiresses, Crusaders, and Thugs--The Gentry of Angevin Yorkshire, 1154-1216, Albion, Vol 0026, 94. **CONTACT ADDRESS** Duke Univ, 102 W Duke Bldg, Durham, NC, 27708.

YOUNG, DAVID CHARLES
PERSONAL Born 12/09/1937, Lincoln, NE, m, 1958, 3 children **DISCIPLINE** CLASSICS **EDUCATION** Univ Nebr, BA, 59; Univ Iowa, MA, 60 , PhD(classics), 63. **CAREER** From asst prof to assoc prof, 63-72, chmn dept, 68-72, PROF CLASSICS, UNIV CALIF, SANTA BARBARA, 72- **MEMBERSHIPS** Am Philol Asn. **RESEARCH** Greek poetry, especially choral lyric. **SELECTED PUBLICATIONS** Auth, Myths About the Ancient Games, Archaeol, Vol 0049, 96. **CONTACT ADDRESS** Dept of Classics, Univ of Calif, Santa Barbara, CA, 93106.

YOUNG, JAMES HARVEY
PERSONAL Born 09/08/1915, Brooklyn, NY, m, 1940, 2 children **DISCIPLINE** HISTORY **EDUCATION** Knox Col, AB, 37; Univ IL, AM, 38, PhD, 41. **CAREER** From instr to assoc prof, 41-58, prof hist, 58-80, Vis assoc prof, Columbia Univ, 49-50; Ford fel, 54-55; Soc Sci res fel, 60-61; US Pub Health Serv grant, 60-65; mem nat adv food & drug coun, Food & Drug Admin, 64-67; Guggenheim Mem Found fel, 66-67; Nat Libr Med grant, 67-72; mem consumers task force, White House Conf Food, Nutrit & Health, 69; mem Hist Life Soc Study Sect, Nat Insts Health, 70-73 & 79-80, chmn, 72-73; consult-panelist, Nat Endowment for Humanities, 70-; res app hist, Intergovt Exchange Act, US Food & Drug Admin, 77-81. Candler prof Am soc hist, Emory Univ, 80-84. **HONORS AND AWARDS** Edward Kremers Award, Am Inst Hist Pharmacy, 62; Logan Clendening lectr, Sch Med, Univ KS, 73; Radbill lectr, Col Physicians, Philadelphia, 78; Garrison lectr, Am Asn Hist Med, 79; Beaumont lectr, Sch Med, Yale Univ, 80., DHL, Knox Col, 71; DSc, Rush Univ, Chicago, 76. **MEMBERSHIPS** AHA; Orgn Am Historians; Am Inst Hist Pharmacy; Am Asn Hist Med; Southern Hist Asn (pres 81-82). **RESEARCH** Am soc hist; hist of Am advert; Am med hist, espec hist of food and drug regulation. **SELECTED PUBLICATIONS** Auth, The Toadstool Millionaires, Princeton Univ, 61; co-ed, Truth Myth and Symbol, Prentice-Hall, 62; auth, Social history of American drug legislation, In: Drugs in Our Society, Johns Hopkins Univ, 64; The Medical Messiahs, Princeton Univ, 67; Quacksalber, Lempp, Schwabisch Gmund, 72; American Self-Dosage Medicines: An Historical Perspective, Coronado, 74; Botulism and the ripe olive scare of 1919-1920, Bull Hist Med, 76, co-ed, Disease and Distinctiveness in the American South, Univ of TN, 88; Pure Food, Princeton Univ, 89; American Health Quackery, Princeton Univ, 92. **CONTACT ADDRESS** Dept of History, Emory Univ, Atlanta, GA, 30322. **EMAIL** jyoun62@emory.edu

YOUNG, JAMES VAN
PERSONAL Born 06/12/1936, Waterloo, IA, m, 1959, 2 children **DISCIPLINE** POLITICAL SCIENCE **EDUCATION** Univ Iowa, BA, 58, JD, 60, PhD, 64. **CAREER** Instr, 64, Univ Iowa; asst prof, polit sci, 64-68, chmn, dept polit sci, 65-68, St Olaf Col; asst prof, 68-71, assoc prof, 71-75, chmn, dept polit sci, 71-82, prof, 75-98, prof emer, 98-, Central Mo St Univ. **HONORS AND AWARDS** Byler Dist Fac Award, 98; Cert Amer Polit Sci Assn & Pi Sigma Alpha, dist tchng, 98; All-Amer Masters, Track & Field, USA Track & Field, 91-98. Big Ten Honor Medal, Scholar & Athletics, 59; Nile Kinnick Scholar, 54-58; Univ Fel, 63; Phi Beta Kappa, 59; Order of the Coif, 60; BA, Summa cum Laude, 58; JD, Magna cum Laude, 60. **MEMBERSHIPS** Amer Polit Sci Assn; Midwest Polit Sci Assn; Mo Polit Sci Assn; Supreme Court Hist Soc; Johnson County Hist Soc. **RESEARCH** Amer Constitutional law; civil rights & liberties; judicial process & politics; state government & politics; federalism & intergovernmental relations; national government **SELECTED PUBLICATIONS** Art, Venue-Transfer of Case Laying Venue in Wrong Federal District Court, Iowa Law Rev, vol 44, 59; coauth, Remembering Their Glory: Sports Heroes of the 1940s, Barnes & Co, 77; art, Freedom of the Press in the Public Schools: A Legal-Political Analysis, Persp in Schl Censorship, 77; coauth, Liberty Versus Authority: The Supreme Court 1951-1961, McCap J, CMSU, 97; auth, Judges and Science: The Case Law on Atomic Energy, Arno Press, 79; auth, Landmark Constitutional Law Decisions: Briefs and Analyses, Univ Press Amer, 93; art, Types of Law in Missouri, Govt & Polit of Mo, 95. **CONTACT ADDRESS** 320 Goodrich Drive, Warrensburg, MO, 64093-2219. **EMAIL** jyoung@inet-hwy.com

YOUNG, JORDAN MARTEN
PERSONAL Born 09/25/1920, New York, NY, m, 1952, 1 child **DISCIPLINE** HISTORY **EDUCATION** Univ Calif, Berkeley, BA, 47, MA, 48; Princeton Univ, PhD, 53. **CAREER** Investment banker, Chase Bank, Rio de Janeiro, 53-55; gen mgr, Consolidated Industs, Venezuela, 55-56; PROF HIST, PACE UNIV, 56-; Vis prof, Grad Sch, NY Univ, 59-65; vis prof, City Col NY, 64-67; Fulbright travel & res grant, Brazil, 66-67; vis prof, NY Univ, 67-68; exec dir, Inst Brazilian Am Bus Studies, World Trade Inst, Pace Univ. **MEMBERSHIPS** AHA; Int Studies Asn; Inter-Future; Americus Found (vpres); Brazilian Childrens Fund - Sloan Kettering Hosp (chmn). **RESEARCH** Contemporary political history of Latin America, especially Brazil and Chile. **SELECTED PUBLICATIONS** Auth, Brazil the 1930 Revolution, Rutgers Univ, 67; coauth, Political Forces in Latin America, Wadsworth, 68; contribr, Conflict & Continuity of a civilian cycle, Facts on File, 72; Brazil, An Emerging World Power, Krieger, 82. **CONTACT ADDRESS** Dept of Soc Sci, Pace Univ, 1 Pace Plaza, New York, NY, 10038-1598. **EMAIL** JordanYong@aol.com

YOUNG, KATHERINE K
PERSONAL Washington, DC **DISCIPLINE** HISTORY OF RELIGIONS **EDUCATION** Univ Vt, BA, 66; Univ Chicago, MA, 70; McGill Univ, PhD(hist relig), 78. **CAREER** ASSOC PROF HINDUISM, MCGILL UNIV, 75-. **MEMBERSHIPS** Am Acad Relig; Am Oriental Soc; Am Asian Studies Asn; Int Asn Buddhist Studies. **RESEARCH** Religion in South India, especially Srivaisnavism; pilgrimage in the Hindu tradition; women in the Hindu and Buddhist traditions of India. **SELECTED PUBLICATIONS** Auth, Response to Andersen, Ruth Review of the Annual Review of Women in World Religions, a Philosophy East and West Feature Review, Philos E and W, Vol 0047, 97. **CONTACT ADDRESS** Fac of Relig Studies, McGill Univ, Montreal, PQ, H3A 2A7.

YOUNG, KENNETH RAY
PERSONAL Born 11/06/1939, Lawton, OK **DISCIPLINE** ASIAN HISTORY **EDUCATION** Calif State Univ, Los Angeles, BA, 64, MA, 65; NY Univ, PhD, 70. **CAREER** Assoc prof, 66-78, PROF HIST, WESTERN CONN STATE COL, 78-97, PROF EMER, 97-; NEH fel int affairs, 76; Fulbright scholar, Phillippines, 79. **MEMBERSHIPS** Asn Asian Studies. **RESEARCH** American diplomacy in Asia; Southeast Asian history; American diplomacy in Asia. **SELECTED PUBLICATIONS** Auth, The Asia Pacific conference, Asia Forum, 71; And then there was one: Yung Wing at Yale, Conn Hist Soc Bull, 71; coauth, Harbinger to Nixon: Du Bois in China, Negro Hist Bull, 72; Adoniram Judson: The forgotten man, Commission, 74; The Stilwell controversy, Mil Affairs, 75; Guerill a warfare: Balangiga revisited, 77 & Atrocities and war crimes, 78, Leyte-Samar Studies; The General's General: Life & Times of General Arthur McArthur, Father of Douglas, Westview Press, 94, Harper Collins, 96. **CONTACT ADDRESS** Dept of Hist, Western Connecticut State Univ, 181 White St, Danbury, CT, 06810-6826.

YOUNG, M. JANE
DISCIPLINE AMERICAN STUDIES **EDUCATION** Univ Pa, PhD, 82. **CAREER** Prof, Regents' lctr, Col of Arts and Sci, Univ NMex. **HONORS AND AWARDS** Fac Scholar Award, Univ NMex, 90. **MEMBERSHIPS** Am Anthropol Asn; Am Asn for State and Local Hist; Am Folklore Soc; Am Stud Asn; Nat Women's Stud Asn. **RESEARCH** Material culture and ethnoaesthetics. **SELECTED PUBLICATIONS** Auth, Signs from the Ancestors: Zuni Cultural Symbolism and Perceptions of Rock Art, 88; coed, Feminist Theory and the Study of Folklore, 93. **CONTACT ADDRESS** Univ NMex, Albuquerque, NM, 87131.

YOUNG, MARY ELIZABETH
PERSONAL Born 12/16/1929, Utica, NY **DISCIPLINE** AMERICAN HISTORY **EDUCATION** Cornell Univ, PhD, 55. **CAREER** From instr to prof hist, Ohio State Univ, 55-73; prof hist, Univ Rochester, 73-, Robert Schalkenbach Found grant, 52-53; Soc Sci Res Coun fac res grant, 69; consult, Am Indian Policy Rev Comn, US Cong, 77. **HONORS AND AWARDS** Louis Pelzer Award, Ms Valley Hist Asn, 55; Am Studies Asn Award, 81; Ray Allen Billington Award, W Hist Asn, 82. **MEMBERSHIPS** AHA; Orgn Am Historians; Soc Historians Early Am Repub. **RESEARCH** Governmental relations with the American Indians during nineteenth century; history of United States public lands. **SELECTED PUBLICATIONS** Auth, Redskins, Ruffleshirts and Rednecks: Indian Land Allotments in Alabama and Mississippi, 1830-1860, Univ Okla, 61; co-ed & contribr, The Frontier in American Development, Cornell Univ, 69; auth, The West and American Cultural Identity, Western Hist Quart, 70; The Indian question revisited, Marxist Perspectives, 2/78; Friends of the Indian, Mary Baldwin Col, 80. **CONTACT ADDRESS** Dept Hist, Univ Rochester, 500 Joseph C Wilson, Rochester, NY, 14627-9000. **EMAIL** yngm@db1.cc.rochester.edu

YOUNG, MICHAEL BRIAN
PERSONAL Born 12/07/1943, York, PA, m, 1968, 1 child **DISCIPLINE** ENGLISH AND EUROPEAN HISTORY **EDUCATION** Moravian Col, BA, 65; Harvard Univ, MA, 66, Ph-d(hist), 71. **CAREER** Asst prof, 70-80, ASSOC PROF HIST, ILL WESLEYAN UNIV, 80-, Fulbright fel. **MEMBERSHIPS** AAUP; AHA; Midwest Conf Brit Studies. **RESEARCH** Tudor-Stuart England. **SELECTED PUBLICATIONS** Auth, Historical Dictionary of Stuart England, 1603-1689, Albion, Vol 0029, 97; Public Duty and Private Conscience in 17th-Century England--Essays Presented to Aylmer, G.E., Historian, Vol 0057, 95; The Bishops-Wars--Charles-I Campaigns Against Scotland, 1638-1640, Albion, Vol 0027, 95; Revolution and Restoration-- England in the 1650s, Historian, Vol 0056, 94; Same-Sex Unions in Premodern Europe, Historian, Vol 0058, 95. **CONTACT ADDRESS** Dept of Hist, Illinois Wesleyan Univ, Bloomington, IL, 61701.

YOUNG, OTIS E.
PERSONAL Born 10/10/1925, South Bend, IN, m, 1950 **DISCIPLINE** HISTORY **EDUCATION** Ind Univ, AB, 48, MA, 49, PhD(hist), 52. **CAREER** Instr soc sci, Alpena Community Col, 52-54; asst prof hist, Bradley Univ, 54-63; assoc prof, 63-69, PROF HIST, ARIZ STATE UNIV, 69-, Howard vis scholar, Ohio State Univ, 59-60; consult, Mining Mus, Ariz Hist Soc, 77- & Western Mus Mining Indust, 80- **RESEARCH** United States western and military history; Appalachian metal mining frontier, 1640-1870. **SELECTED PUBLICATIONS** Auth, Roaring Days--Rosslands Mines and the History of British-Columbia, Pacific Hist Rev, Vol 0065, 96; Bisbee--Urban Outpost on the Frontier, Pacific Hist Rev, Vol 0063, 94; Islands in the Desert--A History of the Uplands of Southeastern Arizona, Pacific Hist Rev, Vol 0065, 96. **CONTACT ADDRESS** Dept of Hist, Arizona State Univ, Tempe, Tempe, AZ, 85281.

YOUNG, ROBERT JOHN
PERSONAL Born 04/27/1942, Moose Jaw, SK, Canada, m, 1965, 3 children **DISCIPLINE** HISTORY **EDUCATION** Univ Sask, BA, 64, MA, 65; Univ London, PhD(hist), 69. **CAREER** Asst prof, 68-74, assoc prof, 74-81, PROF HIST, UNIV WINNIPEG, 81-, Leave fel hist, Can Coun, 74-75, Soc Sci & Humanities Res Coun Can, 81-82. **MEMBERSHIPS** Soc French Hist Studies; Western Soc for French Hist; Can Hist Asn. **RESEARCH** French foreign policy and military planning 1919-1940. **SELECTED PUBLICATIONS** Auth, Anglo-American Policy Towards the Free French, Intl Hist Rev, Vol 0019, 97; In the Eye of the Beholder, the Cultural Representation of France and Germany by the New-York-Times, 1939-40, Hist Reflections-Reflexions Historiques, Vol 0022, 96; Transforming Paris--The Life and Labors of Baron-Haussmenn, Urban Hist Rev-Rev d Hist Urbaine, Vol 0025, 97; Shanghai on the Metro--Spies, Intrigue and the French Between the Wars, Intl Hist Rev, Vol 0017, 95; The Beast in the Boudoir, Petkeeping in 19th-Century Paris, Urban Hist Rev-Rev d Hist Urbaine, Vol 0024, 96; The Republic in Danger--Gamelin,Maurice and the Politics of French Defense, 1933-1940, Intl Hist Rev, Vol 0016, 94; Arming Against Hitler--France and the Limits of Military Planning, Jour Military Hist, Vol 0061, 97; France and the German Presence, 1940-1944--French, Intl Hist Rev, Vol 0018, 96; Lost Comrades--Socialists of the Front-Generation, 1918-1945, Intl Hist Rev, Vol 0015, 93; Daladier, Edouard 1884-1970, Amer Hist Rev, Vol 0099, 94. **CONTACT ADDRESS** Dept of Hist, Univ of Winnipeg, Winnipeg, MB, R3B 2E9.

YOUNG, WILLIAM H.
PERSONAL Born 03/16/1939, Schenectady, NY, m, 1962 **DISCIPLINE** AMERICAN STUDIES **EDUCATION** Col of William & Mary, AB, 62; Duke Univ, MA, 64; Emory Univ, PhD, 69. **CAREER** Prof, Lynchburg Col, 64-. **HONORS AND AWARDS** Outstanding Educator, 74-75. **MEMBERSHIPS** PCA; ASA; AAUP; SAH; MAPCA. **RESEARCH** American popular culture; American architectural history. **SELECTED PUBLICATIONS** Auth, Queen Anne Architecture in Lynchburg, in Lynch's Ferry, vol. 7, no.1, 94; A Home for All: Lynchburg Bungalows, in Lynch's Ferry, vol. 7, no. 2, 94/95; Top Hat, White Tie, and Tails: Art Deco in Lynchburg, in Lynch's Ferry, vol. 8, no.1, 95; In My Adobe Hacienda: Spanish Revival Styles in Lynchburg Architecture, in Lynch's Ferry, vol. 8, no. 2, 95/96; A Study of Action-Adventure Fiction: The Executioner and Mack Bolan Lewiston, 96; From a Princely Palace to a Cottage in the Cotswalds: Tudor Architecture in Lynchburg, in Lynch's Ferry, vol. 9, no. 1, 96; From Stoops...to Porches...to Decks...The Evolution of 'Outdoor Rooms' in Lynchburg Architecture, in Lynch's Ferry, vol. 9, no. 2, 96/97; An Architecture of Confidence and Nostalgia: Georgian Revival in Lynchburg, in Lynch's Ferry, vol. 10, no. 2, 97; Temples of Commerce and Domesticity: The Greek Revival in Lynchburg, in Lynch's Ferry, vol. 10, no. 2, 97/98; So Old...So New: Reflections of Colonial Architecture in Lynchburg, in Lynch's Ferry, vol. 11, no. 1, 98; The American Foursquare: A Popular Home for Lynchburg, in Lynch's Ferry, vol. 11, no. 2, 98/99; Vigilante Fiction, in The Encycl of U.S. Popular Cult, 98; Articles on Warren Baby Dodds and Walter Page, in Am Nat Biog, 98; Articles on Michael Feldman, Casey Kasem, and Jazz Radio Formats, in Hist Dictionary of Am Radio, 98; coauth, A Complete Guide to Skin and Hair, 72. **CONTACT ADDRESS** American Studies Dept, Lynchburg Col, Lynchburg, VA, 24501-3199. **EMAIL** young@lynchburg.edu

YOUNG, WILLIAM ROBERT
PERSONAL Born 06/02/1947, Toronto, ON, Canada **DISCIPLINE** HISTORY **EDUCATION** York Univ, BA Hons, 69; Univ BC, Vancouver, MA, 72, PhD, 78. **CAREER** Course dir hist, York Univ, 77-78; officer, Fed Provincial Rels Office, 77-78; Vis asst prof Hist, Simon Fraser Univ, 78-. **MEMBERSHIPS** Can Hist Asn. **RESEARCH** Canadian society during World War II. **SELECTED PUBLICATIONS** Auth, Conscription, rural depopulation and the farmers of Ontario, 1917-1919, Can Hist Rev, 9/72; coauth, Development of Canadian Consular Operations in the United States, 1940-1972, Dept of External Affairs, 73. **CONTACT ADDRESS** 5-171 MacLaren St, Ottawa, ON, K2P 0K8.

YOUNG, ZENAIDA ISABEL
PERSONAL Panama City, Panama, 2 children **DISCIPLINE** INTERIOR DESIGN **EDUCATION** Fla St Univ, MS, 87. **CAREER** Jr design, 89-91, Design Firm Inc, FL; interior design, 91-, Espinosa-Young Design Group, FL; sr instr, 93-, Palm

Beach Com Col. **RESEARCH** Historic preservation, CAD **CONTACT ADDRESS** Division of Humanities, 4200 Congress Ave, Lake Worth, FL, 33461. **EMAIL** youngz@pbcc.cc.fl.us

YOUNGER, JOHN GRIMES
PERSONAL Born 09/01/1945, Columbus, OH **DISCIPLINE** PREHISTORIC GREEK ARCHEOLOGY **EDUCATION** Stanford Univ, BA, 67; Univ Cincinnati, MA, 69, PhD(classics), 73. **CAREER** Instr classics, Campion High Sch, Athens, Greece, 73-74; asst prof, 74-79, ASSOC PROF CLASSICS, DUKE UNIV, 79-. **MEMBERSHIPS** Archaeol Inst Am; assoc Brit Sch Archaeol. **RESEARCH** Engraved sealstones and finger rings of the Greek Late Bronze Age; prehistoric Greek art; Hellenistic and late Roman sculpture. **SELECTED PUBLICATIONS** Auth, Technical Observations as Evidence for Reconstructing the East Pediment of the Temple of Zeus at Olympia, Amer Jour Archaeol, Vol 0098, 94; Corpus of Mycenaean Inscriptions From Knossos, Vol 1, 1-1063, Vol 2, 1064-4495, Class Bulletin, Vol 0069, 93; The Knossos Tablets, 5th-Edition, a Transliteration, Class Bulletin, Vol 0069, 93; Corpus-Der-Minoischen-Und-Mykenischen-Siegel-V-Suppl-1a--Minor Greek Collections Aegina-Corinth--German, Amer Jour Archaeol, Vol 0100, 96; Pottery in Archaeology, Class Bulletin, Vol 0071, 95; Technical Considerations on the Planning of Minoan Stone Relief Vessels, Amer Jour Archaeol, Vol 0098, 94; Critical Issues for Classics on the Internet, Amer Jour Archaeol, Vol 0101, 97; Archives Before Writing--Proceedings of the International-Colloquium, Oriolo-Romano, 23-25 October, Amer Jour Archaeol, Vol 0100, 1996; Architectural and Administrative Change in Neopalatial Crete, Amer Jour Archaeol, Vol 0100, 1996; Corpus-Der-Minoischen-Und-Mykenischen-Siegel-V-Suppl-1b--Minor Greek Collections %Lamia-Zacynthus and Other Eastern Mediterranean Countries--German, Amer Jour Archaeol, Vol 0100, 96. **CONTACT ADDRESS** Dept of Class Studies, Duke Univ, Durham, NC, 27706.

YOUNT, WILLIAM R.
PERSONAL m, 2 children **DISCIPLINE** FOUNDATIONS OF EDUCATION **EDUCATION** Univ Md, BS, 73; Southwestern Baptist Theol Sem, MARE, 75, PhD, 78; Univ N Tex, PhD, 84. **CAREER** Adj prof, Univ N Tex; prof, Southwestern Baptist Theol Sem, 81-. **MEMBERSHIPS** N Amer Prof Christian Edu. **RESEARCH** Ministry in former Soviet Union. **SELECTED PUBLICATIONS** Auth, Christianity and Psychology: Forever Enemies?, Moscow Theol Jour, 97; Created to Learn, Broadman Holman, 96; co-auth, Teaching Ministry of the Church, Broadman Holman, 94. **CONTACT ADDRESS** Sch Edu Ministries, Southwestern Baptist Theol Sem, PO Box 22000, Fort Worth, TX, 76122-0418. **EMAIL** yount@swbts.swbts.edu

YUAN, TSING
PERSONAL Born 07/21/1937, Peking, China, m, 1972 **DISCIPLINE** ASIAN HISTORY **EDUCATION** George Washington Univ, BA, 60, MA, 62; Univ Pa, PhD(hist), 69. **CAREER** From lectr to asst prof hist, Swarthmore Col, 66-72; asst prof, 72-76, ASSOC PROF HIST, WRIGHT STATE UNIV, 76-, Am Philos Soc fel, 70-71; Am Coun Learned Soc fel, 70-71; assoc, Univ Sem Traditional China, Columbia Univ, 70-; fel, Harvard E Asian Res Crt, 71-72; vis assoc prof hist, Ohio State Univ, 76. **MEMBERSHIPS** AHA; Asn Asian Studies. **RESEARCH** Ming history; economic and social history; agricultural history. **SELECTED PUBLICATIONS** Auth, Disorder Under Heaven--Collective Violence in the Ming Dynasty, Amer Hist Rev, Vol 0099, 94; The Cambridge History of China, Vol 6, Alien Regimes and Border States, 907-1368, Historian, Vol 0058, 96. **CONTACT ADDRESS** Dept of Hist, Wright State Univ, Dayton, OH, 45431.

YUNGBLUT, LAURA
DISCIPLINE HISTORY **EDUCATION** Western Carolina Univ, BA, 83; Univ Cincinnati, MA, 85, PhD, 93; Univ Ky, MS, 90. **CAREER** Prof, Univ Dayton. **RESEARCH** Medieval Europe; British History. **SELECTED PUBLICATIONS** Auth, Strangers Settled Here Amongst Us: Policy, Perception and the Presence of Aliens in Elizabethan England, London : Routledge, 96. **CONTACT ADDRESS** Dept of History, Univ of Dayton, 300 College Park, Dayton, OH, 45469-1679. **EMAIL** yugblut@chekov.hm.udayton.edu

YUSA, M.
DISCIPLINE PHILOSOPHY OF RELIGION; HISTORY OF IDEAS; BUDDHIST-CHRISTIAN DIALOGUE, NISH **EDUCATION** Univ CA at Santa Barbara, PhD, 83. **CAREER** Asst Prof, Assoc Prof, Prof, Western Washington Univ, 93-present. **HONORS AND AWARDS** Japan Found Research Fel, 93-94. **MEMBERSHIPS** Amer Acad Rel; Assoc for Asian Studies; Amer Oriental Soc **RESEARCH** Cross-cultural hist of ideas **SELECTED PUBLICATIONS** Intl Encyclopedia of Philosophy, Zeami, 98; Monumenta Nipponica, Philosophy and Inflation, Miki Kiyoshi in Weimar Germany 1922-24, 98, Nishida and Hearn, 96; A Companion to World Philosophies, Contemporary Buddhist Philosophy, Blackwell Publishers, Oxford, 97; Eastern Buddhist, Nishida Kitaro Mem Issue, Reflections on Nishida Studies, 95; Shiso No. 857 special issue commemorating 50th aniv of death of Nishida Kitaro, A Reflection on the Study of Nishida Philosophy in America, 95; Rude Awakenings: The Kyoto School, Zen, and the Question of Nationalism, Nishida and Totalitarianism: A Philosopher's Resistance, Univ of Hawaii Press, Honolulu, 95; Religion and Women, Women in Shinto: Images Remembered, State Univ of NY Press, Albany, 94. **CONTACT ADDRESS** Dept of Modern and Classical Languages, Western Washington Univ, Bellingham, WA, 98225.

Z

ZABEL, CRAIG
DISCIPLINE AMERICAN, MODERN EUROPEAN, AND RUSSIAN ARCHITECTURE **EDUCATION** Univ Wis, BA; Univ Ill Urbana-Champaign, MA, PhD. **CAREER** Assoc prof, Pa State Univ, 85-. **HONORS AND AWARDS** Col Arts & Archit Fac Award for Outstanding Tchg., Interim Hd & Grad Off, dept History **RESEARCH** American architecture during the 1930s and 1940s. **SELECTED PUBLICATIONS** Areas: bank architecture, Prairie School architects (particularly George G. Elmslie), American public architecture, and contemporary architecture; contrib, The Midwest in American Architecture, Univ Ill Press.. **CONTACT ADDRESS** Pennsylvania State Univ, 201 Shields Bldg, University Park, PA, 16802. **EMAIL** cxz3@psu.edu

ZABEL, JAMES ALLEN
PERSONAL Born 08/07/1945, Lincoln, NE, m, 1966, 2 children **DISCIPLINE** HISTORY **EDUCATION** Grinnell Col, BA, 67; Univ Chicago, MA, 68, PhD(hist), 71. **CAREER** PROF HIST, SCH OZARKS, 71-, CHMN DEPT, 80-, Danforth assoc, Danforth Found, 78- **MEMBERSHIPS** AHA; AAUP; Western Asn Ger Studies. **RESEARCH** Churches in modern Germany. **SELECTED PUBLICATIONS** Auth, Deity and Domination--Images of God and the State in the 19th and 20th Centuries, Jour Mod Hist, Vol 0067, 95. **CONTACT ADDRESS** Dept of Hist, The Sch of the Ozarks, Point Lookout, MO, 65726.

ZACEK, JOSEPH FREDERICK
PERSONAL Born 12/18/1930, Berwyn, IL, m, 3 children **DISCIPLINE** MODERN EUROPEAN HISTORY **EDUCATION** Univ IL, AB, 52, MA, 53, PhD, 62; Columbia Univ, cert, Prog ECent Europe, 62. **CAREER** Res asst Europ hist, Univ Ill, 57-58, teaching asst Europ & Russ hist, 59-60; asst prof hist, Occidental Col, 62-65 & Univ Calif, Los Angeles, 65-68; assoc prof, 68-71, chmn dept, 74-77, Prof History, SUNY, Albany, 71-, Vis asst prof hist, Univ Calif, Los Angeles, 63-65; Duke Found grant, 67-68; State Univ NY res grants, 69-71; Nat Sci Found res grant, 72; Int Res & Exchanges Bd fel, Czech, 73; State Univ NY Res Found grants, 74 & 75; mem, Nat Bd Consult, Nat Endowment for Humanities, 75-; Rockefeller Found sabbatical res grant, 77-78; vis scholar East Europ hist, Inst ECent Europe, Columbia Univ, 77-78; mem, Columbia Univ Sem Hist Legal & Polit Thought; mem nat screening comt, East Europ exchanges, Int Res & Exchanges Bd, 78-81; Vis Scholar, Russian & E European Ctr, Univ Il, 87. **HONORS AND AWARDS** Phi Beta Kappa, 52; Fel Russian Res Ctr, Harvard Univ, 86-91; Who's Who in Am, 90-; Comenius Medal, Govt Czech & Slovak Fed Repub, 92; Medal Comenius Pedag Inst, 92; Josef Hlavka Medal, Czech Acad Sci, 92. **MEMBERSHIPS** AHA; Am Asn Advan Slavic Studies; Czech Hist Conf; Slovak Studies Asn; Consortium on Revolutionary Europ; Asn for Study Ethnicity & Nat. **RESEARCH** History of East Central Europe; Czechs and Slovaks; East European immigration in United States. **SELECTED PUBLICATIONS** Contribr, Nationalism in Eastern Europe, Univ Wash, 69; auth, The Historian as Scholar and Nationalist: Palacky, Mouton, The Hague, 70; contribr, The Czech Renascence of the Nineteenth Century, Univ Toronto, 70; Native Fascism in the Successor States, 1918-1945, ABC-Clio, 71; Der "sterreichisch-ungarische Ausgleich 1867, Slovak Acad Sci, Czech, 71; auth, Palacky's politics: The second phase, Can Slavic Studies, 71; The French Revolution, Napoleon & the Czechs, Proc Consortium Revolutionary Europe, 80; ed & contribr, Frantisek Palacky, 1798-1876: A Centennial Appreciation, East Europ Quart, 81; Contribr, Reappraising the Munich Pact: Continental Perspectives, Johns Hopkins Univ, 92; Auth, Czech National Consciousness in the Baroque Era, in the History of European Ideas, 93. **CONTACT ADDRESS** Dept Hist, SUNY, 1400 Washington Ave, Albany, NY, 12222-1000.

ZACHER, CHRISTIAN KEELER
PERSONAL Born 03/06/1941, St. Louis, MO, m, 1967, 2 children **DISCIPLINE** ENGLISH LITERATURE, MEDIEVAL STUDIES **EDUCATION** Col of the Holy Cross, BA, 63; Univ Calif, Riverside, MA, 65, PhD(English), 69. **CAREER** Teaching asst English, Univ Calif, Riverside, 64-67; asst prof, 68-74, ASSOC PROF ENGLISH, OHIO STATE UNIV, 74-. **MEMBERSHIPS** MLA; Mediaeval Acad Am; Soc Hist Discoveries; AAUP. **RESEARCH** Medieval English and Latin literature; medieval and Renaissance travel literature. **SELECTED PUBLICATIONS** Auth, Framing the Canterbury Tales--Chaucer,Geoffrey and the Medieval Frame-Narrative-Tradition, Speculum-Jour Medieval Stud, Vol 0069, 94. **CONTACT ADDRESS** Dept of English, Ohio State Univ, 164 W 17th Ave, Columbus, OH, 43210-1326.

ZACK, ARNOLD MARSHALL
PERSONAL Born 10/07/1931, Lynn, MA, m, 1969, 2 children **DISCIPLINE** GOVERNMENT, ECONOMICS **EDUCATION** Tufts Col, BA, 53; Yale Univ, LLB, 56; Harvard Univ, MPA, 61. **CAREER** Labor management arbitrator/mediator, 60; fac, visiting prof, Cornell Univ, 82-83; Harvard Univ, Trade Union Prog, 84; visiting lectr, Yale Law School, 94-96. **HONORS AND AWARDS** Distinguished Service Award of Am Arbitration Asn; Cuslying Gavin Award of Archdiocese of Boston; Whitney North Seymour Medal. **MEMBERSHIPS** Am Bar Asn; Am Arbitration Asn; Nat Acad of Arbitrators. **RESEARCH** International labor dispute settlement systems. **SELECTED PUBLICATIONS** Coauth, Mediation and Arbitration of Labor Disputes, 97; auth, The Agreement in Negotiations and Arbitration, 2nd edition, 96; auth, Labor Arbitration Cases on the Merits, 89; auth, Labor Arbitration Procedural Issues, 91. **CONTACT ADDRESS** 170 W Canton St, Boston, MA, 02118. **EMAIL** zackam@tiac.net

ZAGARRI, ROSEMARIE
DISCIPLINE HISTORY **EDUCATION** Northwestern Univ, BA, 77; Yale Univ, MA, 78, PhD, 84. **CAREER** Prof History, Geo Mason Univ. **RESEARCH** Political history. **SELECTED PUBLICATIONS** Auth, The Politics of Size: Representation in the United States, 1776-1850, 87; David Humphrey's Life of General Washington, 91; Morals, Manners, and the Republican Mother, Amer Quart 44, 92; A Woman's Dilemna: Mercy Otis Warren and the American Revolution, 95. **CONTACT ADDRESS** Dept of History, George Mason Univ, Fairfax, VA, 22206.

ZAGORIN, PEREZ
PERSONAL Born 05/29/1920, Chicago, IL, m, 1947, 1 child **DISCIPLINE** HISTORY **EDUCATION** Univ Chicago, AB, 41; Harvard Univ, MA, 47, PhD, 52. **CAREER** Instr hist, Amherst Col, 47-49; lectr, Vassar Col, 51-53; from asst prof to prof, McGill Univ, 55-64; vis prof, Johns Hopkins Univ, 64-65; chmn dept, 68-69, prof hist, 65-82, WILSON PROF HIST, UNIV ROCHESTER, 82-, Can Coun sr fel, 58-59; Soc Sci Res Coun fac res fel, 59-60 & 61-62; regional assoc, Am Coun Learned Soc, 61-69; sr fel, Folger Shakespeare Libr, 64-65; mem adv coun, Yale Ctr Parliamentary Hist, 68-; mem, Inst Advan Studies, Princeton Univ, 72-73; W A Clark Mem Libr vis prof, Univ Calif, Los Angeles, 75-76; fel, Nat Humanities Ctr, 78-79. **MEMBERSHIPS** AHA; Renaissance Soc Am; Conf Brit Studies; fel Am Acad Arts & Sci; fel Royal Hist Soc. **RESEARCH** Early modern European and British history; history of political thought. **SELECTED PUBLICATIONS** Auth, Wyatt,Thomas and the Court of Henry-VIII--The Courtiers Ambivalence, Jour Medieval and Renaissance Stud, Vol 0023, 93; Hobbes Early Philosophical Development, Jour Hist of Ideas, Vol 0054, 93; The Cambridge History of Political-Thought 1450-1700, Renaissance Quart, Vol 0046, 93; The Political Beliefs of Pym, John to 1629, Eng Hist Rev, Vol 0109, 94. **CONTACT ADDRESS** Dept of Hist, Univ of Rochester, Rochester, NY, 14627.

ZAHNISER, MARVIN RALPH
PERSONAL Born 06/29/1934, New Kensington, PA, m, 1956, 3 children **DISCIPLINE** AMERICAN HISTORY **EDUCATION** Greenville Col, AB, 56; Univ Mich, MA, 57; Univ Calif, Santa Barbara, PhD(hist), 63. **CAREER** Vis asst prof hist, Univ Wash, 63-64; vis asst prof, Univ Iowa, 64-65; from asst prof to assoc prof, 65-73, asst vprovost arts & sci, 72-73, chmn dept, 73-77, PROF HIST, OHIO STATE UNIV, 73-, CHMN DEPT, 81-, Mershon fel, Mershon Ctr Educ Nat Security, 66; vis assoc prof hist, Univ Calif, Santa Barbara, 68. **MEMBERSHIPS** AHA; Orgn Am Historians; Soc Historians of Am Foreign Rels (exec sec-treas, 81-); Conf Faith & Hist (vpres, 76-78, pres, 78-80). **RESEARCH** American early national era, especially foreign policy; history of French-American relations, 1775-1975. **SELECTED PUBLICATIONS** Auth, Roosevelt and the French, Intl Hist Rev, Vol 0017, 95; Degaulle and the United-States--A Centennial Reappraisal, Intl Hist Rev, Vol 0018, 96; Oldest Allies, Guarded Friends--The United-States and France Since 1940, Intl Hist Rev, Vol 0018, 96. **CONTACT ADDRESS** Dept of Hist, Ohio State Univ, Columbus, OH, 43210.

ZALESCH, SAUL E.
PERSONAL Born 01/07/1952, Baltimore, MD, s **DISCIPLINE** ART HISTORY **EDUCATION** Univ Del, PhD, 92. **CAREER** Asst prof, La Tech Univ, 94- . **HONORS AND AWARDS** Henry R. Luce Found Fel, 86; Nat Mus of Am Art/Smithsonian Inst, pre-doctoral fel, 88; HEH postdoctoral fel at the Winterthur Mus, 93. **MEMBERSHIPS** Col Art Asoc; Soc of Archit Hist; Southeastern Col Art Conf; Asoc of Hist of Am Art; Asoc Hist of 19th Century Art. **RESEARCH** Mass-produced secular and religious art of the late 19th century; collecting. **SELECTED PUBLICATIONS** Auth, Against the Current: Anti-Modern Images in the Work of Winslow Homer, Am Art Rev, 93; auth, Competition and Conflict in the New York Art World, 1874-1879, Winterthur Portfolio, 94; auth, What the Four Million Bought: Cheap Oil Paintings of the

1880s, Am Quart, 96. **CONTACT ADDRESS** School of Art, Louisiana Tech Univ, PO Box 3175, Ruston, LA, 71272-0001. **EMAIL** szalesch@art.latech.edu

ZANGRANDO, JOANNA SCHNEIDER
PERSONAL Hastings, MN, 2 children **DISCIPLINE** AMERICAN SOCIAL & CULTURAL HISTORY **EDUCATION** Wayne State Univ, BA, 61, MA, 63; George Washington Univ, PhD, 74. **CAREER** Hist researcher, US Atomic Energy Comn, MD, 64-66; legis asst, US Off Educ, 66-67; lectr hist, Albertus Magnus Col, 70; instr, Univ Hartford, 70-71; lectr, Univ Akron, 71-72; NEH Mus consult, Am hist & civilization prog community mus, Nat Am Studies Fac, 72-74; vis asst prof Am studies, George Washington Univ, 74-76; asst prof, 76-80, assoc prof Am Studies, 80-88, FULL PROF, 89-, CHAIR, AM STUDIES DEPT, 87-, DIR, LIBERAL STUDIES PROG, 84-87, 98-, SKIDMORE COL; F D Roosevelt Libr res grant, 74-75; panel mem pub progs & res, fels, and seminars, general progs, Higher Ed Curriculum Devel and Focus Grants, preservation, NEH, 76-; mem bd rev for grant proposals, Eleanor Roosevelt Inst, FDR Libr, 77-81; dir, Skidmore Col London Study Abroad Prog & vis prof, 83, 90, 95; Scholar in Residence, NYU, 98. **MEMBERSHIPS** AHA; Orgn Am Historians; Am Studies Asn; Am Asn State & Local Hist; Conf Group Women's History. **RESEARCH** American culture, technology and aesthetics; women's studies and women labor union organizers, 1930's to 1950's; American material culture and museum studies; women reformers; civil rights. **SELECTED PUBLICATIONS** Coauth, Black protest: A rejection of the American dream, J Black Studies, 12/70; Law, the American value system, and the black community, Rutgers-Camden Law J, spring 71; Black history in the college curriculum, In: New Perspectives on Black Studies, Univ Ill Press, 71; auth, Women and archives: An historian views the liberation of Clio, Am Archivist, 4/73; coauth, The object as subject: The role of museums and material culture collections in American studies, Am Quart, 8/74; contribr, For the duration: Working women and World War II, In: FDR's America, Forum Press, 76; auth, Women's studies: closer to reality, In: American Studies, Topics and Sources, Greenwood, 76; Women's Studies in the U. S., in Sources in Am Studies, Greenwood, 83; coauth, Eleanor Roosevelt & Black Civil Rights, in Joan Hoff and Marjorie Lightman, eds, Without Precedent. The Life and Career of Eleanor Roosevelt, IN Press, 84; book rev, Planning a New Liberal Studies Curriculum, George Mason Univ Conference on Non-Traditional Interdisc Progs, Proceedings, 86. **CONTACT ADDRESS** Am Studies Dept, Skidmore Col, 815 N Broadway, Saratoga Springs, NY, 12866-1698.

ZANGRANDO, ROBERT LEWIS
PERSONAL Born 05/16/1932, Albany, NY, m, 1969, 2 children **DISCIPLINE** UNITED STATES HISTORY **EDUCATION** Union Col, NY, BA, 58; Univ Pa, MA, 60, PhD(hist), 63. **CAREER** Asst prof hist, Rutgers Univ, Camden, 63-65, acting chmn dept, 64-65; asst exec secy, Am Hist Asn & dir, Serv Ctr for Teachers of Hist, 65-69; lectr hist & educ, Univ Press, Yale Univ, 69-71; assoc prof, 71-81, PROF HIST, UNIV AKRON, 81-, Prog coordr, State of NJ Off Econ Opportunity, 65; mem exec bd, Soc Educ, 65-69; Am Coun Learned Soc grant-in-aid, 69; Eleanor Roosevelt Found grant-in-aid, 74; consult, Nat Am Studis Fac, 74-78. **MEMBERSHIPS** AHA; Orgn Am Historians; Asn Study Afro-Am Life & Hist; Am Studies Asn; Coord Comt Women in Hist Profession. **RESEARCH** Afro-American history and studies; 20th century US history; history of women in the US. **SELECTED PUBLICATIONS** Auth, Historians and Archivists--Educating the Next-Generation, Amer Archv, Vol 0056, 93; New Day in Babylon--The Black Power Movement and American Culture, 1965-1975, Amer Hist Rev, Vol 0099, 94; Grimke, Archibald--Portrait of a Black Independent, Jour Amer Hist, Vol 0082, 95; A Festival of Violence--An Analysis of Southern Lynchings, 1882-1930, Amer Hist Rev, Vol 0101, 96. **CONTACT ADDRESS** Dept of Hist, Univ of Akron, Akron, OH, 44325.

ZASLAW, NEAL
DISCIPLINE MUSIC **EDUCATION** Harvard Col, BA, 61; Juilliard Sch, MS, 63; Columbia Univ, MA, 65, PhD, 70. **CAREER** Herbert Gussman prof **HONORS AND AWARDS** Nat Endowment for the Humanities fel; Amer Coun Learned Societies fel; Martha Baird Rockefeller Fund for Music, fel; Oesterreichische Ehrenkreuz fuer Wissenschaft u Kunst. **MEMBERSHIPS** Amer Musicol Soc; Music Libr Asn; Early Music Am; Royal Musical Asn; Gesellschaft fuer Musikforschung; Soc francaise de musicol; Int Musicol Soc; ed, Der neue Koechel. **RESEARCH** European music of the 17th and 18th centuries; performance practice; French baroque music; Mozart; history of the orchestra. **SELECTED PUBLICATIONS** Auth, Mozart as a Working Stiff, in JM Morris, On Mozart, Cambridge, 94; Mozart's European Orchestras, Musicol Australia, 94; Ornaments for Corelli's Violin Sonatas, Op 5, Early Music, 96; Audiences for Mozart's Symphonies during His Lifetime, Israel Stud in Musicol, 96; Waiting for Figaro, in S. Sadie, Wolfgang Amade Mozart: Essays on His Life and His Music, Oxford, 97; The Breitkopf Firm's Relations with Leopold and Wolfgang Mozart, Bach Perspectives, 96; Contexts for Mozart's Piano Concertos, in N. Zaslaw, Mozart's Piano concertos: Text, Context, Performance, Mich, 96; The Adagio in F major, K Anhang 206a = A65, in S. Brandenburg, Haydn, Mozart and Beethoven, Oxford, 97. **CONTACT ADDRESS** Dept of Music, Cornell Univ, 104 Lincoln Hall, Ithaca, NY, 14853. **EMAIL** naz2@cornell.edu

ZBORAY, MARY SARACINO
PERSONAL Born 10/24/1953, Bridgeport, CT, m, 1984 **DISCIPLINE** AMERICAN STUDIES **EDUCATION** Univ Bridgeport, BA, 75, MA 80. **CAREER** Hist, Georgia St Univ. **HONORS AND AWARDS** Summa cum Laude; Charles A Dana scholar, 72-73, 73-74; Smithsonian Fel, 82-83; Hon Vis Fel, Radcliffe Col, 98-99. **MEMBERSHIPS** Am Stud Asn; Am Hist Asn; Am Textile His Mus; Conn Hist Soc; Maine Hist Soc; MLA; New England Hist Geneal Soc; NH Hist Soc; Org Am Historians. **RESEARCH** United States cultural history. **SELECTED PUBLICATIONS** Auth, "Political News and Female Readership in Antebellum Boston and Its Region," Journalism Hist, 96; "Books, Reading and the World of Goods in Antebellum New England," Am Q, 96; "The Boston Book Trades, 1789-1850," Entrepreneurs, ed by Conrad Edick Wright, Mass Hist Soc, 97; "Whig Women, Politics, and Culture in the Campaign of 1840," J of the Early Republic, 97; "Reading and Everyday Life in Antebellum Boston," Libr & Culture, 97; "Have You Read...," Nineteenth-Century Lit, 97; "The Romance of Fisherwomen in Antebellum New England," Am Stud, 98; "The Mysteries of New England," Nineteenth-Century Contexts, 99; "Transcendentalism in Print," The Transient and the Permanent, ed Charles Capper, Mass Hist Soc, 99. **CONTACT ADDRESS** Dept of History, Georgia State Univ, University Plz, Atlanta, GA, 30303. **EMAIL** hisrjz@mwa.org

ZBORAY, RONALD J.
PERSONAL Born 06/23/1953, Bridgeport, CT, m, 1984 **DISCIPLINE** HISTORY **EDUCATION** Univ Bridgeport, BA, 75; NYU, MA, 77, PhD, 84. **CAREER** Assoc spec, microfilm ed, Emma Goldman Papers, Univ of Calif, Berklely, 84-89; asst prof, History, Univ Texas at Arlington, 89-92; asst prof, Ga State Univ, 92-96, assoc prof, 96 - . **HONORS AND AWARDS** Summa cum Laude, 75; Louis M Lerner scholar, NYU, 76; NYU scholarship, 76-77; Humanist-in Museum, NY Inst for the Hum, 83; hon mention, Carl Bode Awd Comm, Am Culture Asn, 87; fel NEH, Am Antiq Soc, 91; Dale Somers Mem Awd, Georgia St Univ, 93; fel Mass Hist Soc, 94; Outstanding Jr Fac Awd, Georgia State Univ, 96; Cathy Covert Prize in Mass Commun Hist, 97; NEH fel, 98; hon vis fel, Schlesinger Lib, Radcliffe Col, 89-99. **MEMBERSHIPS** Am Asn of Univ Prof; Am Hist Asn; Am Mus of Textile Hist; Am Stud Asn; Andover Hist Soc; Asn of Georgia State Univ Hist; MLA; Am Lit Gp; New England Hist Geneal Soc; Org of Am Hist; Peabody Essex Mus; Soc for the Hist of the Early Am Republic, SC Hist Soc; Vt Hist Soc. **RESEARCH** United States cultural history. **SELECTED PUBLICATIONS** Ed, The Emma Goldman Papers: A Microfilm Edition, Chadwyck-Healey, 90; auth, A Fictive People: Antebellum Economic Development and the American Reading Public, Oxford, 93; auth, Technology and the Character of Community Life in Antebellum America: The Role of Story Papers, in Communication and Change in American Religious History, Eerdmans, 93; auth, Books, in Handbook on Mass Media in the United States: The Industry and Its Audiences, Greenwood, 94; auth, Editorial Prinicples and Procedures, in Emma Goldman: A Guide to Her Life and Documentary Sources, Chadwyck-Healey, 95; coauth, Political News and Female Readership in Antebellum Boston and Its Region, in Jour Hist, 96; coauth, Books, Reading, and the World of Goods in Antebellum New England, in Am Q, 96; coauth, The Boston Book Trades, 1789-1850: A Statistical and Geographical Analysis, in Entrepreneurs: The Boston Business Community, Mass Hist Soc, 97; coauth, Reading and Everyday Life in Antebellum Boston: The Diary of Daniel F.and Mary G. Child, in Libs and Culture, 97; coauth, Whig Women, Politics, and Culture in the Campaign of 1840: Three Perspectives from Massachusetts, in J of the Early Republic, 97; coauth, Have You Read...?: Real Readers and Their Responses in Antebellum Boston and Its Region, in Nineteenth-Century Lit, 97; coauth, The Romance of Fisherwomen in Antebellum New England, in Am Stud, 98. **CONTACT ADDRESS** Dept of History, Georgia State Univ, University Plz, Atlanta, GA, 30303. **EMAIL** hisrjz@panther.gsu.edu

ZEIDEL, ROBERT F.
DISCIPLINE HISTORY **EDUCATION** Marquette Univ, PhD, 86 **CAREER** Sr. Lectr, Univ Wisconsin-Stout **MEMBERSHIPS** Amer Historical Assoc; OHA **RESEARCH** Immigration history **CONTACT ADDRESS** Social Science Dept, Univ Wisconsin-Stout, Menomonie, WI, 54751. **EMAIL** e-zeidelr@uwstout.edu

ZEITLIN, FROMA I.
DISCIPLINE GREEK LANGUAGE AND LITERATURE. **EDUCATION** Radcliffe Col, AB, 54; Catholic Univ, MA, 65; Columbia Univ, PhD, 70. **CAREER** Prof, Princeton Univ. **RESEARCH** Mythology; Greek tragedy and lyric poetry; poetics; Religion; Gender Studies. **SELECTED PUBLICATIONS** Auth, Under the Sign of the Shield: Semiotics and Aeschylus' Seven Against Thebes; Nothing to Do with Dionysos?; Playing the other: Gender and Society in Classicl Greek Literature. **CONTACT ADDRESS** Princeton Univ, 1 Nassau Hall, Princeton, NJ, 08544. **EMAIL** fiz@princeton.edu

ZEITLIN, MAURICE
PERSONAL Born 02/24/1935, Detroit, MI, m, 1959, 3 children **DISCIPLINE** SOCIOLOGY **EDUCATION** Wayne St Univ, BA, 57; UCLA, Berkeley, PhD, 64. **CAREER** Instr, 61-64, Princeton Univ; asst prof, assoc prof, prof, 64-76, Univ Wisc; prof, 76-, UCLA. **HONORS AND AWARDS** John Simon Guggenheim Fel, 81-82; Ford Fels, 59-60, 60-61, 65-67, 70-71; Dist Contr to Scholar Award, polit sociol, Amer Soc Assn, 92, 96, 97, labor sect, soc for the stud of social problems. **MEMBERSHIPS** Amer Sociol Assn. **RESEARCH** Political economy; socio-historical development. **SELECTED PUBLICATIONS** Coauth, Cuba: An American Tragedy, 64; auth, Revolutionary Politics and the Cuban Working Class, 70; auth, The Civil Wars in Chile, 84; coauth, Landlords and Capitalists, 88; auth, The Large Corporation and Contemporary Classes, 89; coauth, Talking Union, 96. **CONTACT ADDRESS** Dept of Sociology, Univ of California, Los Angeles, CA, 90095-1551. **EMAIL** zeitlin@soc.ucla.edu

ZELIN, MADELEINE
DISCIPLINE MODERN CHINESE HISTORY **EDUCATION** Cornell Univ, BA, 70; Berkeley, PhD, 79. **CAREER** Prof. **RESEARCH** Contract law and civil procedure in Qing and Republican China. **SELECTED PUBLICATIONS** Auth, The Magistrate's Tael, Rationalizing Fiscal Reform in Eighteenth Century Ch'ing China, 84; Rainbow, 92. **CONTACT ADDRESS** Dept of Hist, Columbia Col, New York, 2960 Broadway, New York, NY, 10027-6902.

ZELLER, SUZANNE
DISCIPLINE INTELLECTUAL IMPACT OF SCIENCE IN CANADA **EDUCATION** Univ Windsor, BA, MA; Toronto, PhD. **CAREER** Prof **SELECTED PUBLICATIONS** Auth, Inventing Canada: Early Victorian Science and the Idea of a Transcontinental Nation, U of Toronto P, 87; Land of Promise, Promised Land: The Culture of Victorian Science in Canada, 96. **CONTACT ADDRESS** Dept of History, Wilfrid Laurier Univ, 75 University Ave W, Waterloo, ON, N2L 3C5. **EMAIL** szeller@mach1.wlu.ca

ZELNIK, REGINALD ELY
PERSONAL Born 05/08/1936, New York, NY, m, 1956, 2 children **DISCIPLINE** MODERN RUSSIAN HISTORY **EDUCATION** Princeton Univ, AB, 56; Stanford Univ, MA, 61, PhD(Hist), 66. **CAREER** Lectr Hist, Ind Univ, Bloomington, 63-64; from asst prof to assoc prof, 64-76, chmn, Ctr Slavic & East Europ Studies, 77-80, prof Hist, Univ Calif, Berkeley, 76-, sr fel, Russ Inst, Columbia Univ, 68-69; Guggenheim Found fel, 71-72; Int Res & Exchanges Bd/Am Coun Learned Soc grant, inst Hist, Moscow, 72; fel, Hist Comn of Berlin, 76; chmn, Dept of Hist, UC Berkeley, 94-97. **HONORS AND AWARDS** AHA's Nancy Lyman Roelker Mentorship Award. **MEMBERSHIPS** AHA; Am Asn Advan Slavic Studies. **RESEARCH** Russian labor history; comparative European labor history. **SELECTED PUBLICATIONS** Auth, The Sunday-school movement in Russia: 1859-1862, J Mod Hist, 6/65; coauth, The Politics of Escalation in Vietnam, Beacon, 66; auth, Labor and Society in Tsarist Russia: The Factory Workers of St Petersburg, 1855-1870, Stanford Univ, 71; Populists and workers, Soviet Studies, 72; Russian workers and the revolutionary movement, J Social Hist, Winter 72; Russian Rebels: An introduction to the memoirs of the Russian worker, Semen Kanatchiav and Matvei Fisher, Russ Rev, 7-10/76; Passivity and protest in Germany and Russia: Barrington Moore's conception of working-class responses to injustice, J Social Hist, 3/82; Law Disorder on the Narova River: The Kreenholm Strike of 1872, Univ of Calif Press, 95. **CONTACT ADDRESS** Dept of History, Univ of California, Berkeley, 3229 Dwinelle Hall, Berkeley, CA, 94720-2551. **EMAIL** selnik@socrates.berkeley.edu

ZEMAN, JAROLD K.
PERSONAL Born 02/27/1926, Czechoslovakia **DISCIPLINE** CHURCH HISTORY **EDUCATION** Knox Col, Univ Toronto, BD, 52; Univ Zurich, DTheol, 66; McMaster Univ, DD, 85; Acadia Univ, DD, 94. **CAREER** Dir, Cont Theol Educ, 70-81, 85-91, dir confs, 81-85, PROF CHURCH HISTORY, ACADIA UNIV & ACADIA DIVINITY COL, 68-91; dir, Acadia Ctr Baptist Anabaptist Stud, Acadia Univ, 91-97. **MEMBERSHIPS** Pres, Baptist Fed Can, 79-82; mem, Rel Adv Comt CBC, 79-84; mem, Can Soc Ch Hist; Am Soc Ch Hist; Am Acad Relig. **SELECTED PUBLICATIONS** Auth, God's Mission and Ours, 63; auth, The Whole World at Our Door, 64; auth, Historical Topography of Moravian Anabaptism, 67; auth, The Anabaptists and the Czech Brethren, 69; auth, Baptists in Canada and Co-operative Christianity, 72; auth, The Hussite Movement and the Reformation, 77; auth, Baptist Roots and Identity, 78; auth, Renewal of Church and Society in the Hussite Reformation, 84; coauth, Baptists in Canada 1760-1990: A Bibliography, 89; ed, Baptists in Canada, 80. **CONTACT ADDRESS** PO Box 164, Wolfville, NS, BOP 1XO.

ZEMANS, JOYCE P.
PERSONAL Born 04/21/1940, Toronto, ON, Canada **DISCIPLINE** ART HISTORY **EDUCATION** Univ Toronto, BA, 62, MA, 66. **CAREER** Ch, dept lib arts stud, Ont Col Art, 66-75; dir, Can Coun, 89-92; ch, dept visual arts, 75-81, assoc prof art

hist, 75-95, dean, fine arts, 85-88, PROF ART HISTORY, YORK UNIV, 95-, Robarts ch can stud, 95-96. **MEMBERSHIPS** Can Asn Fine Arts Deans; Int Coun Fine Arts Deans; Univ Art Asn Can Adv; bd mem, J Can Art Hist; bd mem, Art Gallery York Univ; bd mem, Laidlaw Foundation (pres, 96-). **SELECTED PUBLICATIONS** Auth, Art, 76; auth, J.W.G. Macdonald: The Inner Landscape, 81; auth, Christopher Pratt, 85; auth, Jock Macdonald, 86; auth, Where is Here? Canadian Cultural Policy a Globalized Environment, 98; coauth, Kathleen Munn & Edna Tacon: New Perspectives on Modernism in Canada, 88. **CONTACT ADDRESS** Faculty of Fine Arts, York Univ, 4700 Keele St, Toronto, ON, M3J 1P3.

ZEMEL, CAROL
DISCIPLINE ART HISTORY **EDUCATION** Columbia Univ, PhD. **CAREER** Fac, SUNY Buffalo. **HONORS AND AWARDS** Grant, NEH; Millard Meiss grant; Col Art Assoc. **RESEARCH** 19th- and 20th-century art; feminism; art criticism. **SELECTED PUBLICATIONS** Auth, Van Gogh's Progress: Utopian Modernity in Late Nineteenth Century Art, Univ Calif, 97; The Formation of a Legend, van Gogh Criticism 1890-1900, UMI Res, 80. **CONTACT ADDRESS** Dept Art, SUNY Buffalo, 202 Center for the Arts, Buffalo, NY, 14260-6010.

ZHAO, QUANSHENG
DISCIPLINE COMPARATIVE POLITICS AND INTERNATIONAL RELATIONS **EDUCATION** Am Univ, BA; Peking Univ, BA; UC Berkeley, MA, PhD. **CAREER** Prof, Am Univ. **HONORS AND AWARDS** Grants, Japan Found, Asia Found, Pacific Cult Found; Harvard Univ., Chair, APSA's Conf Gp on China Stud, 92-; ed bd, Am Asian Rev. **RESEARCH** Comparative policymaking in East Asia; Political development and democratization; International relations theory and international security and political economy. **SELECTED PUBLICATIONS** Auth, Interpreting Chinese Foreign Policy, Oxford Univ Press, 96; Japanese Policymaking, Oxford Univ Press/ Praeger, 93; co-ed, Politics of Divided Nations: China, Korea, Germany and Vietnam. **CONTACT ADDRESS** American Univ, 4400 Massachusetts Ave, Washington, DC, 20016.

ZHUK, SERGEI I.
DISCIPLINE AMERICAN HISTORY **EDUCATION** Dniepropetrovsk Univ, Ukraine, Dipl of Hist, 81, DHist Sci, 96; Moscow Inst of Hist, Hist Sci, 87. **CAREER** Prof American History, Dneipropetrovsk Univ, Ukraine. **RESEARCH** Quakers' attitudes toward sectarian religious groups in the 17th and 18th centuries. **SELECTED PUBLICATIONS** Auth, From 'Inner Light' to 'New Canaan': The Quaker Society of the 'Middle' Colonies, Dniepropetrovsk Univ, 95; Levelling of the Extemes, In: Images of America, Free Univ of Brussels, 97. **CONTACT ADDRESS** Dept of History, Johns Hopkins Univ, 3400 N Charles St., Baltimore, MD, 21218. **EMAIL** sizl@jhunix.hcf.jhu.edu.

ZIEFLE, HELMUT WILHELM
PERSONAL Born 04/02/1939, Heilbronn-Sontheim, Germany, m, 1965, 2 children **DISCIPLINE** GERMAN LITERATURE, MODERN GERMAN HISTORY **EDUCATION** State Univ NY Albany, BA, 64, MA, 66; Univ Ill, PhD, 73. **CAREER** Teacher Ger, Bethlehem Cent High, 65-67; from instr to assoc prof, 67-82, Prof Ger, Wheaton Col, 82-, Dir, Wheaton in Ger, 77-; pres, Ger Evening Sch, Wheaton, 78-80; scholar in residence, Ger Dept, Circle Campus, fall, 79; pres, AATG Northern Ill Chapter, 89-91. **HONORS AND AWARDS** AATG/Goethe House Certificate of Merit Award, 92. **MEMBERSHIPS** Am Asn Teachers Ger; ICTFL; NACFLA. **RESEARCH** Early German baroque literature; modern German literature: Hesse, Mann and postwar German literature; history of the Third Reich especially German opposition to Hitler. **SELECTED PUBLICATIONS** Auth, Sibylle Schwarz: Life and work, in Studies in German, English and Comparative Literature, Bouvier, Bonn, 75; Opitz' influence on poetry of Sibylle Schwarz, Vol 4, 76 & Occupation of Greifswald during Thirty Years War, Vol 2, 77, Pommern; A Christian family resists Hitler, Christianity Today, Vol 6, 78; The long shadow of Hitler, The Christian Reader, 79, 2-5; ed, Sibylle Schwarz: German poetic poems, in Middle German Literature, Lang, Bern, 80; auth, One Woman Against the Reich, Bethany House Publ, 81; Dict of Modern Theological German, Baker Bk House, 82; ed, Hermann Hesse und das Christentum, R. Brockhaus Verlag, 94; auth, Modern Theological German: A Reader and Dictionary, Baker Book House, 97. **CONTACT ADDRESS** 501 College Ave, Wheaton, IL, 60187. **EMAIL** helmut w ziefle@wheaton.edu

ZIEGER, R.H.
PERSONAL Born 08/02/1938, Englewood, NJ, m, 1962, 1 child **DISCIPLINE** HISTORY **EDUCATION** Montclair State College, BA, 60; Univ Wyoming, MA, 61; Univ Maryland, PhD, 65. **CAREER** Prof, Dist Prof, 86 to 98-, Univ FL; Prof, 77-86, Wayne State Univ; Assoc Prof, 73-77, Kansas State Univ; Asst, Assoc Prof, 64-73, Univ Wisc SP. **HONORS AND AWARDS** Philip A Taft Awd for Best Book; Norman Wilinsky Grad Teach Awd; U of FL TIP; U of FL Profess Excell Awd. **MEMBERSHIPS** OAH; UFF; AHA; SHA; HAC. **RESEARCH** Modern US History; US Labor History. **SELECTED PUBLICATIONS** Ed, Southern Labor in Transition, Univ Tenn Press, 97; auth, The CIO, 1935-1955, Univ of NC Press, 95, awd for best bk in labor hist; Auth, CIO Leaders and the State, 1935-1955, in: Amer Labor in the Era of WW II, ed, Sally Miller, Daniel A Cornfield, Greenwood Press, 95; John L Lewis and the Labor Movement 1940-1960. In: The United Mine Workers of America: A Model of Industrial Solidarity?, ed, John H Laslett, Penn State Press, 96; Historians and the US Industrial Relations Regime, J Policy Hist, 97; The Quest for Ntl Goals 1957-1981, in: The Carter Presidency: Policy Choices in the Post-New Deal Era, ed, Gary M Fink, Hugh Davis Graham, Univ Press of Kansas, 97; From Primordial Folk to Redundant Workers: Southern Textile Workers and Social Observers, 1920-1990, in: S Lab in Transition 1940-1995, ed, RH Zieger, U of Tenn Press. **CONTACT ADDRESS** Dept of History, Univ Fla, Box 117320, Gainesville, FL, 32611. **EMAIL** rhagz@nersp.nerdc.ufl.edu

ZIEMKE, EARL FREDERICK
PERSONAL Born 12/16/1922, WI, m, 1949 **DISCIPLINE** HISTORY **EDUCATION** Wis State Col, BS, 48; Univ Wis, MA, 49, PhD, 51. **CAREER** Researcher, Bur Applied Social Res, Columbia Univ, 51-55; historian, Off of Chief Mil Hist, US Dept Army, 55-67; prof hist, 67-77, RES PROF HIST, UNIV GA, 77- **MEMBERSHIPS** AHA; AAUP; Am Mil Inst. **RESEARCH** Germany; Russia **SELECTED PUBLICATIONS** Auth, Eisenhower and the German Pows--Facts Against Falsehood, Jour Amer Hist, Vol 0080, 94; Moscow--The Turning-Point--The Failure of Hitler Strategy in The Winter of 1941-42, Slavic Rev, Vol 0053, 94; Weserubung--The German Attack on Denmark and Norway in April, 1940--German, Intl Hist Rev, Vol 0019, 97; Commanding the Red-Army Sherman Tanks--The World-War-II Memoirs of Hero of the Soviet-Union Loza, Dmitriy, Jour Military Hist, Vol 0061, 97. **CONTACT ADDRESS** 400 Brookwood Dr, Athens, GA, 30605.

ZIEWACZ, LAWRENCE E.
PERSONAL Born 12/23/1942, Sault Ste Marie, MI, m, 1968, 2 children **DISCIPLINE** AMERICAN HISTORY **EDUCATION** Mich State Univ, BA, 65, MA, 66, PhD(US hist), 71. **CAREER** Instr US hist, Lansing Community Col, 68-70 & Edinboro State Col, 70-71; ASSOC PROF AM THOUGHT & LANG, MICH STATE UNIV, 71-, Reviewer, Nat En dowment for Humanities, 78-82. **MEMBERSHIPS** Orgn Am Historians; Soc Hist Educ; Popular Cult Asn; Soc Study Midwestern Lit & Cult. **RESEARCH** Michigan history; sports history; United States political and social history. **SELECTED PUBLICATIONS** Auth, The eighty-first ballot: The senatorial struggle of 1883, Mich Hist, fall 72; coauth, The election of 1882: A republican analysis, J Great Lakes Hist Conf, 76; The athletic revolution reconsidered: An examination of literature of athletic protest, Sport Sociol Bull, fall 77; The progress of woman suffrage in 19th century Michigan, J Great Lakes Hist Conf, 79; auth, The Old Northwest and Gilded Age politics: An analysis, Midwestern Miscellany, Vol VIII, 80; coauth, Michigan: A History of the Great Lakes States, Forum Press, 81; Violence in sports, In: Sports in Modern America, River City Publ, 81; Sports in the Twenties, In: The Evolution of Mass Culture in America, 82. **CONTACT ADDRESS** Dept of Am Thought & Lang, Michigan State Univ, 229 Bessey Hall, East Lansing, MI, 48824-1033.

ZILFI, MADELINE CAROL
PERSONAL Norwood, MA, m, 1979, 1 child **DISCIPLINE** MIDDLE EAST HISTORY **EDUCATION** Mt Holyoke Col, AB, 64; Univ Chicago, MA, 71, PhD(hist), 76. **CAREER** ASST PROF HIST, UNIV MD, COLLEGE PARK, 76- **MEMBERSHIPS** AHA; Mid East Studies Asn; Turkish Studies Asn; Mid East Inst. **RESEARCH** Ottoman institutional history; Islamic law; Islamic fundamentalism. **SELECTED PUBLICATIONS** Auth, A Medrese for the Palace, Ottoman Dynastic Legitimation in the 18th-Century, Jour Amer Oriental Soc, Vol 0113, 93; East Encounters West--France and the Ottoman-Empire in the 18th-Century, Jour Near East Stud, Vol 0052, 93; Christians and Muslims in Ottoman Cyprus and the Mediterranean World, 1570-1640, Amer Hist Rev, Vol 0099, 94; An Economic and Social-History of the Ottoman-Empire, 1300-1914, Amer Hist Rev, Vol 0102, 97. **CONTACT ADDRESS** Dept of Hist, Univ of Md, College Park, MD, 20742-0001.

ZILVERSMIT, ARTHUR
PERSONAL Born 07/05/1932, The Hague, Netherlands, m, 1955, 2 children **DISCIPLINE** AMERICAN HISTORY **EDUCATION** Cornell Univ, BA, 54; Harvard Univ, MA, 55; Univ CA, Berkeley, PhD, 62. **CAREER** From instr to asst prof, Am hist, Williams Col, 61-66; from asst prof to assoc prof, 66-73, prof hist, Lake Forest Col, 73-, Dir Grad Prog Lib Studies, 76-90, Dir Continuing Educ, 77-90, Vis fel, Shelby Cullom Davis Ctr Hist Studies, Princeton Univ, 72-73. **MEMBERSHIPS** AHA; Orgn Am Historians; Am Studies Asn; Hist Educ Soc. **RESEARCH** Hist of Am educ; African-Am hist. **SELECTED PUBLICATIONS** Auth, The First Emancipation, Univ Chicago, 67; Mumbet, Quok Walker and the Abolition of Slavery in Massachusetts, William & Mary Quart, 68; contribr, The Abolitionists: From Patience to Militance, In: The Black Experience in America, Univ TX, 70; auth, Liberty and Property: New Jersey and the Abolition of Slavery, NJ Hist, winter 70; ed, Lincoln on Black and White: A Documentary History, Wadsworth, 71; contribr, The Failure of Progressive Education, In: Schooling and Society, Johns Hopkins Univ, 76; Lincoln and the Problem of Race: A Decade of Interpretations, In: Papers of the Abraham Lincoln Association, 81; Changing Schools: Progressive Education Theory and Practice, 1930-1960, Univ Chicago, 93. **CONTACT ADDRESS** Dept of Hist, Lake Forest Col, 555 N Sheridan Rd, Lake Forest, IL, 60045-2399. **EMAIL** zilversmit@lfc.edu

ZIMMER, LOUIS BERNARD
PERSONAL Born 01/16/1931, New Rochelle, NY, m, 1954, 2 children **DISCIPLINE** EUROPEAN HISTORY **EDUCATION** State Univ NY Col Cortland, BS, 53; NY Univ, MA, 59, PhD(English intellectual hist), 70. **CAREER** Teacher, Hackensack High Sch, 59-62; asst prof social studies, 62-64, ASSOC PROF HIST, MONTCLAIR STATE COL, 64-. **HONORS AND AWARDS** Founders' Day Award, NY Univ, 70. **MEMBERSHIPS** AHA; Am Soc Eighteenth Century Studies. **RESEARCH** English and European intellectual history; modern European history. **SELECTED PUBLICATIONS** Auth, Public Moralists--Political-Thought and Intellectual Life in Britain, 1850-1930, Victorian Stud, Vol 0036, 92. **CONTACT ADDRESS** Montclair State Univ, 127 Buckingham Rd, Upper Montclair, NJ, 07043.

ZIMMERMAN, FRANKLIN B.
PERSONAL Born 06/20/1923, Wauneta, KS, m, 1957, 4 children **DISCIPLINE** MUSIC HISTORY & LITERATURE **EDUCATION** Univ Southern Calif, BA, 49, MA, 52, PhD, 58; Oxford Univ, BLitt, 56; Univ Pa, AM, 70. **CAREER** Asst prof music, Crane Dept Music, State Univ NY Teachers Col, Potsdam, 58-60; vis assoc prof, Sch Music, Univ Southern Calif, 60-61, assoc prof, 61-64, chm dept music hist & lit, 60-64; prof music, Dartmouth Col, 64-66; prof music, dir pro musica & div music hist & musicol, Univ Ky, 67-68; CHM DEPT MUSIC & DIR PRO MUSICA, UNIV PA, 68-, Conductor & performer, var concerts in US & England, 38-; lectr, var orgn, 58-; Am Coun Learned Soc fel, London, 59-60, grant, Univ Calif, Los Angeles, 63; Dartmouth Col Res & Publ Fund grant, 64; sr res fel, Univ Calif, Los Angeles, 68; dir, Pa Pro Musica, 71- **HONORS AND AWARDS** Gold Medal for Musicol, Arnold Bax Found, 60; Ben Franklin technolol grant for visible music soundscapes, 98., MA, Dartmouth Col, 66 & Univ Pa, 71. **MEMBERSHIPS** Am Musicol Soc; Int Musicol Soc; Royal Music Asn; Renaissance Soc Am; Col Music Soc. **RESEARCH** Purcell; Baroque music; Handel. **SELECTED PUBLICATIONS** Auth, A Purcell Iconography, Henricksen, London, 58; Henry Purcell, 1659-1695: An Analytical Catalogue of his Music, 63 & Henry Purcell, 1659-1695: His Life and Times, 67, MacMillan, London; Henry Purcell, 1659-1695: A Thematic Index to His Complete Works, 73 & G F Handel: Thematic and First-Line Indexes to His Complete Works, Vienna House, 73-74; The Anthems of Henry Purcell, Am Choral Found, 73; Louis Grabu's Albion & Albanius, In: The Works of John Dryden, Vol XV, Univ Calif, 75; The William Kennedy Gostling Manuscript: A Primary Source for the Anthems of Henry Purcell, John Blow, Univ Tex, Austin, 77; auth, Invented Visible Music Soundscapes. **CONTACT ADDRESS** 225 South 42nd St, Philadelphia, PA, 19104.

ZIMMERMAN, JAMES ALLEN
PERSONAL Born 05/12/1933, Peoria, IL, m, 1956, 4 children **DISCIPLINE** UNITED STATES DIPLOMATIC HISTORY **EDUCATION** Ill State Univ, BS, 55; Univ Ill, Urbana, MA, 61, PhD(Hist), 72. **CAREER** Chmn, Dept Soc Sci, Carl Sandburg High Sch, Orland Park, Ill, 57-67; asst prof Hist, Mankato State Col, 70-73; prof Hist & vpaa, Tri-State Univ, 73-. **HONORS AND AWARDS** Gerald R Moore Award for Overall Teaching Excellence. **MEMBERSHIPS** Orgn Am Historians; Soc Hist Am Foreign Rels; NEA; Indiana Assn of Historians. **RESEARCH** American anti-imperialism and expansionism. **SELECTED PUBLICATIONS** Auth, The Chicago Liberty and Loyalty Meetings, 1899: Public attitudes toward the Philippine-American War, NDak Quart, Autumn 75; Who were the anti-imperialists and the expansionists of 1898 and 1899?, A Chicago perspective, Pac Hist Rev, 11/77. **CONTACT ADDRESS** Dept of History, Tri-State Univ, Angola, IN, 46703. **EMAIL** zimmermans@alpha.tristate.edu

ZIMMERMAN, JOSEPH F.
PERSONAL Born 06/29/1928, Keene, NH, m, 1998, 1 child **DISCIPLINE** POLITICAL SCIENCE AND ECONOMICS **EDUCATION** Univ of NH, BA, 50; Syracuse Univ, MA, 51, PhD, 54. **CAREER** Instr to prof, Worcester Polytechnic Inst, 54-65; prof, State Univ of NY at Albany, 65-. **HONORS AND AWARDS** Distinguished Citizen Award, Nat Civic League, 86; Outstanding Academician, Section On Intergovernmental Admin and Management of the Am Soc for Public Admin, 97. **MEMBERSHIPS** Am Political Sci Asn; Am Soc for Public Admin. **RESEARCH** Federalism; representation and electoral systems; state and local government, comparative local government with emphasis on the Republic of Ireland. **SELECTED PUBLICATIONS** Auth, The Recall: Tribunal of the People, 97; Interstate Relations: The Neglected Dimension of Federalism, 96; State-Local Relations: A Partnership Approach, 95;

Curbing Unethical Behavior in Government, 94; Contemporary American Federalism, 92. **CONTACT ADDRESS** Grad School of Public Affairs, State Univ of NY Albany, 135 Western Ave., Albany, NY, 12222. **EMAIL** zimmer@cnsvax.albany.edu

ZIMMERMAN, LORETTA ELLEN
PERSONAL Born 09/14/1935, Metairie, LA **DISCIPLINE** AMERICAN HISTORY **EDUCATION** Newcomb Col, BA, 57; Tulane Univ, MA, 61, PhD(hist), 64. **CAREER** Asst prof hist, Williams Wood Col, 64-65; vis prof, Augustana Col, 65-66; asst prof, Univ TX, Arlington, 66-67; assoc prof , 67-85, Prof Hist, Univ Portland, 86-, former dir Peace Studies prog. **RESEARCH** History of American feminism; history of American reformism; European and American intellectual history. **SELECTED PUBLICATIONS** Auth, five articles, In: Notable American Women 1607-1950, Belknap, 71; Woman Suffrage, a Feminist Movement, 1848-1910, spring 72 & Mary Beard: an Activist of the Progressive Era, spring 74, Review; coauth, A History of the United States with Topics, vols I and II, with Jerry R. Baydo and John Boon, Gregory Press, 94-96; coauth, Readings for a History of the United States with Topics, vol II, with Jerry R. Baydo and John Boon, Gregory Press, 94-96; coauth, A Student Workbook for History of the United States with Topics, with Jerry R. Baydo and John Boon, Gregory Press, 94-96; author of a series of articles on culture for Salem Press. **CONTACT ADDRESS** Fac of Hist, Univ of Portland, 5000 N Willamette, Portland, OR, 97203-5798. **EMAIL** Zummerma@vofport.edu

ZIMMERMAN, ZORA DEVRNJA
PERSONAL Born 05/12/1945, Marienbad, Czechoslovakia, m, 1976, 2 children **DISCIPLINE** COMPARATIVE LITERATURE, FOLKLORE **EDUCATION** State Univ NY, BA, 67, PhD, 74. **CAREER** Asst prof, 74-79, assoc prof, 80-84, PROF ENGLISH, IOWA STATE UNIV, 85-. **HONORS AND AWARDS** NEH summer fel. **MEMBERSHIPS** AAASS; Am Folklore Soc; H"lderlin Ges; CCAS; Nat Asn Ethnic Studies. **RESEARCH** Serbian traditional narrative and lyric; dynamics of change and persistence in folklore; English and European Romanticism. **SELECTED PUBLICATIONS** Co-ed, The Arc from Now (poems), Iowa State Univ, 78; auth, Moral vision in the Serbian folk epic: The foundation sacrifice of Skadas, Slavic & East Europ J, Vol 23, 79; The changing roles of the Vila in Serbian traditional literature, J of Folklore Inst, Vol 26, 79; Metrics of passion: The poetry of Carl Dennis, Poet & Critic, Vol 12, 80; transl & ed, Serbian Folk Poetry: The Oldest Epics, Kosovo Publ Co, 82; Teaching folklore in Iowa, in Teaching Folklore, Am Folklore Soc Inc, 84, rev ed, 89; Traditiona and change in a ritual feast: The Serbian Krsna Slava in America, Great Lakes Rev, fall 85; Serbian Folk Poetry: Ancient Legends, Romantic Songs, Kasovo Publ Co, 86; On the hermeneutics of oral poetry: The Uosovo Mythos, Serbian Studies, fall 90; The building of Skadar, in The Walled-Up Wife Casebook, Univ Wisc Press, 96. **CONTACT ADDRESS** Col of Lib Arts & Sci, Iowa State Univ, Ames, IA, 50011-0002. **EMAIL** zdzimme@iastate.edu

ZIMMERMANN, THOMAS C. PRICE
PERSONAL Born 08/22/1934, Bryn Mawr, PA **DISCIPLINE** RENAISSANCE HISTORY **EDUCATION** Williams Col, BA, 56; Oxford Univ, BA, 58, MA, 64; Harvard Univ, AM, 60, PhD(hist), 64. **CAREER** From asst prof to prof hist & humanities, Reed Col, 64-77, chemn dept hist, 73-75; prof hist, vpres acad affairs & dean fac, Davidson Col, 77-88, Charles A Dana prof of hist, 86-; mem region XIV selection comt, Woodrow Wilson Nat Fel Found, 67-70; fel, Harvard Int Ctr Renaissance Studies, Villa I Tatti, Florence, Italy, 70-71; mem Ore comt humanities, Nat Endowment for Humanities, 71-77; Am Coun Learned Soc fel, 75-76; mem, Board of Advisors, Lowell Observatory, 88-93; mem, Rome Prize Jury, Am Acad in Rom, 93. **HONORS AND AWARDS** Danforth Fel, 56-62; Fulbright Fel, Italy, 62-64; Am Hist Assoc Marraro Prize, 97; President's Book Prize, Am Assoc for Italian Studies, 97. **MEMBERSHIPS** AHA; Renaissance Soc Am; Soc Italian Hist Studies; Phi Beta Kappa; 16th Century Studies Conf. **RESEARCH** Sixteenth century Italian history. **SELECTED PUBLICATIONS** Auth, A note on Clement VII and the divorce of Henry VIII, Eng Hist Rev, 7/67; Girolamo Savonarola: a study in mazeway resynthesis, Soundings, J Interdisciplinary Studies, spring 68; Confession and autobiography in the early Renaissance, In: Renaissance Studies in Honor of Hans Baron, Northern Ill Univ, 71; Paolo Giovio and the evolution of Renaissance art criticism, In: Essays in Honour of P O Kristeller, Manchester Univ, 76; For Paolo Giovio: The Historian and the Crisis of 16th Century Italy, Princeton Univ Press, 95. **CONTACT ADDRESS** Davidson Col, PO Box 1719, Davidson, NC, 28036-1719.

ZINN, GROVER A.
DISCIPLINE EUROPEAN CHRISTIAN HISTORY **EDUCATION** Rice Inst, BA, 59; Duke Univ, BD, 62; PhD, 69. **CAREER** William H. Danforth prof, 66. **RESEARCH** Medieval Christian thought, mysticism, iconography. **SELECTED PUBLICATIONS** Auth, Richard of St. Victor: The Twelve Patriarchs, The Mystical Ark; Book Three of the Trinity; Medieval France: An Encyclopedia. **CONTACT ADDRESS** Dept of Relig, Oberlin Col, Oberlin, OH, 44074.

ZIOLKOWSKI, JOHN EDMUND
PERSONAL Born 06/19/1938, Montevallo, AL, m, 1958, 2 children **DISCIPLINE** CLASSICAL LANGUAGES **EDUCATION** Duke Univ, AB, 58; Univ NC, PhD(classics), 63. **CAREER** Instr Latin, Univ NC, 62-64; asst prof classics, Randolph-Macon Woman's Col, 64-67; asst prof, 67-72, ASSOC PROF CLASSICS, GEORGE WASHINGTON UNIV, 72-, CHMN DEPT 71-. **MEMBERSHIPS** Am Philol Asn; Am Inst Archeol. **RESEARCH** Greek and Roman literature; Renaissance Latin; Classical influence on Washington DC. **SELECTED PUBLICATIONS** Auth, The Parthenon Stone in the Washington Monument, Prologue-Quart Nat Archv, Vol 0025, 93; A Commentary on Thucydides, Vol 1, Books-1-3, Class World, Vol 0086, 93; City-States in Classical Antiquity and Medieval Italy, Class World, Vol 0087, 94; The Classics in American Theater of the 1960s and Early 1970s, Class World, Vol 0088, 95; Shakespeare and Classical Comedy--The Influence of Plautus and Terence, Class World, Vol 0090, 97; Sacred Geography of the Ancient Greeks--Astrological Symbolism in Art, Architecture, Class World, Vol 0090, 97. **CONTACT ADDRESS** Dept of Classics, George Washington Univ, 2035 H St N W, Washington, DC, 20052-0001.

ZIRIN, RONALD A.
DISCIPLINE CLASSICS **EDUCATION** Princeton Univ, PhD, 67; Univ Buffalo, PhD, 85. **CAREER** Fac, 66; prof, present, SUNY Buffalo. **RESEARCH** Linguistics; mythology; Sanskrit; applications of psychoanalysis to Classical traditions. **SELECTED PUBLICATIONS** Auth, The Phonological Basis of Latin Prosody, Mouton, 70; articles on Greek and Latin linguistics. **CONTACT ADDRESS** Dept Classics, SUNY Buffalo, 712 Clemens Hall, Buffalo, NY, 14260.

ZIRING, LAWRENCE
PERSONAL Born 12/11/1928, Brooklyn, NY, m, 1962, 2 children **DISCIPLINE** POLITICAL SCIENCE **EDUCATION** Columbia Univ, PhD 62, MIA 57, BS 55. **CAREER** Western MI Univ, Arnold E Schneider Prof 98-, prof 73-98, assoc 67-73; Syracuse Univ, asst prof 64-67; Lafayette Col, asst prof 61-64; Dacca Univ :now Bangladesh:, vis asst prof 59-60. **HONORS AND AWARDS** Arnold E Schneider Prof; Distg Facul Schl; Jones Facul Teach Awd. **MEMBERSHIPS** Am Inst Pakistan Stud, trustee. **RESEARCH** Comp polit, Intl Rel, for policy. **SELECTED PUBLICATIONS** The United Nations, with J C Plano, R Riggs, 3d ed, Harcourt Brace, forthcoming, 99; Pakistan in the Twentieth Century, Oxford Univ Press, 97; International Relations: A Political Dictionary, ABC-Clio, 95; The New Europe and the New World, New Issues Press, 93; Bangladesh: From Mujib to Ershad, Oxford Univ Press, 92; Pakistan's Foreign Policy, with S Burke, Oxford Univ Press, 2d ed, 90. **CONTACT ADDRESS** Dept of Polit Sci, Western Michigan Univ, Kalamazoo, MI, 49008. **EMAIL** lawrence.ziring@wmich.edu

ZIRINSKY, MICHAEL PAUL
PERSONAL Born 11/25/1942, Brooklyn, NY, m, 1965 **DISCIPLINE** HISTORY, GOVERNMENT **EDUCATION** Oberlin Col, AB, 64; Am Univ, MA, 68; Univ NC, Chapel Hill, PhD(hist), 76. **CAREER** Instr hist, Randolph Macon Col, 65-67; asst prof, 73-79, ASSOC PROF HIST, BOISE STATE UNIV, 79-. **MEMBERSHIPS** AHA; Mid East Inst; Western Soc Fr Hist; Soc Fr Hist Studies; Mid East Studies Asn. **RESEARCH** Modern Middle Eastern history (20th century); France since World War I; 20th century Iran. **SELECTED PUBLICATIONS** Auth, A Panacea for the Ills of the Country, American Presbyterian Education in Interwar Iran, Amer Presbyterians-Jour Presbyterian Hist, Vol 0072, 94. **CONTACT ADDRESS** Dept of Hist, Boise State Univ, Boise, ID, 83725.

ZIRKEL, PATRICIA MCCORMICK
PERSONAL Born 11/02/1943, m, 1968, 1 child **DISCIPLINE** HISTORICAL THEOLOGY **EDUCATION** St Thomas Aquinas Col, Sparkill, NY, BS Ed, 66; St John's Univ, MA, 78; Fordham Univ, PhD, 89. **CAREER** Assoc prof, St Vincent's Col, St John's Univ, 90-. **HONORS AND AWARDS** Faculty Merit award, 97, 98. **MEMBERSHIPS** Am Academy of Relig; Am Asn of Univ Profs; Col Theol Soc; Medieval Academy of America. **RESEARCH** Christian theol-Medieval Europe; Christian Liturgy; Theodicy-Holocaust Studies. **SELECTED PUBLICATIONS** Auth, The Ninth Century Eucharistic Controversy: A Context for the Beginnnings of Eucharistic Doctrine in the West, Worship, vol 68, no 1, Jan 94; Why Should It Be Neccessary That Christ Be Immolated Daily?, Paschasius Radbertus on Daily Eucharist, Am Benedictine Rev, Sept 96; The Body of Christ and the Future of Liturgy, Anglican Theol Rev, forthcoming. **CONTACT ADDRESS** 6 Brancatelli Ct, West Islip, NY, 11795-2502. **EMAIL** zirkelp@stjohns.edu

ZOLBERG, VERA L.
PERSONAL Vienna, Austria, m, 2 children **DISCIPLINE** SOCIOLOGY **EDUCATION** Univ Chicago, PhD, 74; Boston Univ, MA, 56; Hunter Col, NYC, BA, 53. **CAREER** New School For Social Research, Sr lectr, 84-; Purdue Univ, asst prof, assoc prof, 74-84; St Xavier Col, Instr, Asst prof, 64-67; Edgewood Col, Instr, 62-64. **HONORS AND AWARDS** Phi Beta Kappa; ACLS gnt,89; High Honors, PhD, Field; Rockefeller Gnt, 98-2002. **MEMBERSHIPS** ASA; ESA; ISA. **RESEARCH** Sociology of the Arts; Policies of Cult Support; Cultur and Soc. **SELECTED PUBLICATIONS** Outsider Art: Contesting Boundaries in Contemporary Culture, co-ed, co-auth, Cambridge Univ Press, 97; Constructing a Sociology of the Arts, Cambridge Univ Press, trans into Ital, Mulino Press; The Happy Few-en Masse: Franco_American Comparisons in Cultural Democratization, in: The Arts of Democracy, Culture, Civil Society and the State, ed Herman Lebovics Casey n Blake, Wash CD, Woodrow Wilson Cen Press, forthcoming; many essays article and revs. **CONTACT ADDRESS** New Sch for Social Research, 65 Fifth Av, NYC, NY, 10003. **EMAIL** zolberg@newschool.edu

ZONDERMAN, DAVID A.
DISCIPLINE HISTORY **EDUCATION** Amherst, BA, 80; Yale Univ, MA, 82, MPhilos, 83, PhD, 86. **CAREER** Assoc prof History, NC State Univ. **RESEARCH** Working class Activists and middle class reformers in 19th century Boston and New York **SELECTED PUBLICATIONS** Auth, Aspirations and Anxieties: New England Workers and the Mechanized Factory System, 1815-1850, Oxford Univ, 91; Foreign Pioneers: Immigrants and the Mechanized Factory System in Antebellum New England, In: Work, Recreation and Cutlure: Essays in American Labor History, Garland Publ, 96. **CONTACT ADDRESS** Dept of History, No Carolina State Univ, Box 8108, Raleigh, NC, 27695. **EMAIL** zonderman@social.chass.ncsu.edu.

ZUBER, RICHARD LEE
PERSONAL Born 04/04/1932, Allendale, FL, m, 1954, 2 children **DISCIPLINE** AMERICAN HISTORY **EDUCATION** Appalachian State Teachers Col, BS, 54; Emory Univ, MA, 57; Duke Univ, PhD, 61. **CAREER** Asst prof hist, The Citadel, 60-62; asst prof, 62-66, assoc prof, 66-75, prof hist, 75-, Wake Forest Univ; Coop Prog Humanities fel, Univ NC, 67-68; chmn dept, Wake Forest Univ, 75-83. **HONORS AND AWARDS** Award of Merit, Am Assn State & Local Hist, 66. **MEMBERSHIPS** Orgn Am Historians. **RESEARCH** Reconstruction period **SELECTED PUBLICATIONS** Auth, Jonathan Worth: A Biography of a Southern Unionist, Univ NC, 65; auth, North Carolina During Reconstruction, NC Dept Arch & Hist; auth, Conscientious Objectors in the Confederacy: The Quakers of North Carolina, Quaker Hist, 78; auth, Jonathan Worth, American National Biog, Oxford University Press, 98. **CONTACT ADDRESS** Dept of History, Wake Forest Univ, PO Box 7806, Winston Salem, NC, 27109-7806.

ZUCK, LOWELL H.
PERSONAL Born 06/24/1926, Ephrata, PA, m, 1950, 1 child **DISCIPLINE** CHURCH HISTORY **EDUCATION** Elizabethtown Col, BA, 47; Bethany Bibl Sem, BD, 50; Yale Univ, STM, 51, MA, 52, PhD(Reformation church hist), 55. **CAREER** Vis prof philos & relig, Col Idaho, 54-55; from asst prof to assoc prof, 55-62, PROF CHURCH HIST, EDEN THEOL SEM, 62-, Teacher univ col, Washington Univ, 57-; Am Asn Theol Schs grants, 64-65 & 75-76; Am Philos Soc grant, 80; Nat Endowment for Humanities summer seminar, Johns Hopkins Univ, 82. **MEMBERSHIPS** AHA; Am Soc Church Hist; Am Soc Reformation Res (treas, 69-78); 16th Century Studies Conf (treas, 69-71, pres, 71-72). **RESEARCH** Anabaptist research; Reformation church history; Puritan church history. **SELECTED PUBLICATIONS** Auth, From Reformation Orthodoxy to the Enlightenment--Geneva 1670-1737--French, Church Hist, Vol 0063, 94; Ingdoms--The Church and Culture Through the Ages, Sixteenth Century Jour, Vol 0025, 94; Sin and the Calvinists--Morals Control and the Consistory in the Reformed Tradition, Church Hist, Vol 0065, 96; Hochstift and Reformation--Studies in the History of the Imperial Church Between 1517 and 1648--German, Sixteenth Century Jour, Vol 0027, 96; Calvinism in Europe, 1540-1620, Church Hist, Vol 0065, 96; Adultery and Divorce in Calvin, John Geneva, Church Hist, Vol 0065, 96; Poverty and Deviance in Early-Modern Europe, Sixteenth Century Jour, Vol 0027, 96; A Short History of Renaissance and Reformation Europe--Dances Over Fire and Water, Sixteenth Century Jour, Vol 0027, 96; The Oxford Encyclopedia of the Reformation, 4 Vols, Sixteenth Century Jour, Vol 0028, 97; Documents on the Continental Reformation, Sixteenth Century Jour, Vol 0028, 97. **CONTACT ADDRESS** Eden Theol Sem, 475 E Lockwood Ave, St Louis, MO, 63119.

ZUCKERMAN, MARY ELLEN
PERSONAL Born 01/10/1954, Gainsville, FL, m, 1988, 2 children **DISCIPLINE** MARKETING **EDUCATION** Simmons Col, BA, 76; Columbia Univ Grad School of Business, MBA, 82; Columbia Univ Graduate School of Arts & Sci, PhD, 87. **CAREER** Res Fel, Freedom Forum Media Studies Center, 89-90; vis assoc prof, McGill Univ, 90-91; asst prof, 85-90, ASSOC PROF, SCHOOL OF BUSINESS, SUNY GENESEO, 90-; vis prof, Advertising Ed Found Prog, Time Inc, summer, 96. **HONORS AND AWARDS** Found grant, 87 & 89, mid-career summer fel, Geneseo Found, 94; Spencer Found Grant, 92-94; Who's Who in the East; res fel, Gannett Center for Media Studies, 89-90; Nuala Drescher Leave Award, 89-90; NEH Travel to Collections Grant, 89; PDQWL Travel Grant Award, SUNY Union, 89; fac advisor res grant, Am Marketing Asn, 88. **SELECTED PUBLICATIONS** Auth, Encyclopaedia of Women in Journalism, in progress; A History of Mass Circu-

lation Women's Magazines in the U.S., Greenwood Press, 98; From Voting with the Ballot to Voting with the Pocketbook: The Good Citizenship and Pro-Advertising Campaigns in the Woman's Home Companion 1920-1934, Am Periodicals, fall 95; McCall's, Family Circle, Woman's Day, Women's Periodicals in the United States, Greenwood Press, 95; The Career of Mrs. Christine Frederick, presented at the Org of Am Hist, spring 94; rev, Magazines for Millions: Gender and Commerce in the Ladies' Home Journal and The Saturday Evening Post 1880-1910, Business Hist Rev, 95. **CONTACT ADDRESS** Dept of Marketing, State Univ New York Col at Geneseo, 206-C Welles, Geneseo, NY, 14454.

ZUCKERMAN, MICHAEL
PERSONAL Born 04/24/1939, Philadelphia, PA, m, 1986, 5 children **DISCIPLINE** AMERICAN STUDIES **EDUCATION** Univ Pa, BA, 61; Harvard Univ, PhD, 67. **CAREER** Prof, Univ Penn, 65- . **HONORS AND AWARDS** SSRC fel; NEH fel; Guggenheim fel; ACLS fel; Rockefeller fel; Fulbright fel; Netherlands Inst for Advan Study fel. **RESEARCH** Early American history; American character; American community life; American family and identity. **SELECTED PUBLICATIONS** auth, The Place of Religion in Urban and Community Studies, Relig and Amer Cult, 96; Ideology and Utopia: Philosophical Fantasies of Historical Knowledge, Amer Studies, 96; Cities in the Wilderness: Derelicts of Development, Trends, 97; The Dodo and the Phoenix: A Fable of American Exceptionalism in American Exceptionalism? US Working-Class Formation in an International Context, 97; Tocqueville, Turner, and Turds: Four Stories of Manners in Early America, Jour of Amer Hist, 98. **CONTACT ADDRESS** Dept of History, Univ Pa, Philadelphia, PA, 19104.

ZUKOWSKY, JOHN
DISCIPLINE ART HISTORY **EDUCATION** NY State Univ, PhD. **CAREER** Archit cur, Art Inst Chicago; adj prof. **SELECTED PUBLICATIONS** Ed, Chicago Architecture and Design 1923-1993; Chicago Architecture, 1872-1922; Karl Friedrich Schinkel 1781-1841. **CONTACT ADDRESS** Art Hist Dept, Univ Illinois Chicago, S Halsted St, PO Box 705, Chicago, IL, 60607.

ZUNZ, OLIVIER J.
PERSONAL Born 07/15/1946, Paris, France, m, 1970, 2 children **DISCIPLINE** AMERICAN HISTORY **EDUCATION** Univ de Paris X-Nanterre, BA, 68; doctorat de troisieme cycle, Univ de Paris I, Pantheon-Sorbonne, 77; Doctorat d'Etat, Sorsonne, 82. **CAREER** Asst prof, 78-83, assoc prof, 83-88, prof, 88-, hist, Univ Va; vis appt, Ecole des Hautes Etudes en Sci Soc, Paris, 85-96; Vis prof, Col of FR, 97; dir, d'Etudes, Centre

d'Etudes Nord-Americaines, 98. **MEMBERSHIPS** OAH; AHA. **RESEARCH** Modern Amer history. **SELECTED PUBLICATIONS** Auth, Why the American Century?, Chicago, Univ Chicago Press, 98; auth, Making America Corporate, 1870-1920, Chicago, Univ Chicago Press, 90; auth, The Changing Face of Inequality: Urbanization, Industrial Development, and Immigrants in Detroit, 1880-1920, Chicago, Univ Chicago Press, 82; co-ed, The Landscape of Modernity: Essays on New York City, 1900-1940, NY, Russell Sage Found, 92; ed and coauth, Reliving the Past: The Worlds of Social History, Chapel Hill, Univ NC Press, 85; rev, History by Affirmation: The End of Democracy, Self-Rule: A Cultural History of American Democracy, Rev in Amer Hist 95; auth, Class, Encycl of the US in the Twentieth Century, NY, Charles Scribner's Sons, 96; ed, Exporting American Individualism, The Tocqueville Rev, 95; ed, Exporting American Individualism, Nat Inst for Res Advan Res Output, Tokyo, 94; auth, Producers, Brokers, and Users of Knowledge: The Institutional Matrix, Mod Impulses in the Human Sci, Johns Hopkins Univ Press, 94; auth, Recentrer l'histoire americaine, Chantiers d'histoire americaine, Belin, 94. **CONTACT ADDRESS** Corcoran Dept. of History, Univ of Virginia, Randall Hall, Charlottesville, VA, 22903. **EMAIL** oz@virginia.edu

ZUPKO, JACK
DISCIPLINE MEDIEVAL PHILOSOPHY **EDUCATION** Cornell Univ, PhD, 89. **CAREER** Philos, Emory Univ. **SELECTED PUBLICATIONS** Articles, Jour His Philos, Medieval Philos & Theol, Mediaeval Studies, Rev Metaphysics. **CONTACT ADDRESS** Emory Univ, Atlanta, GA, 30322-1950.

ZUPKO, RONALD EDWARD
PERSONAL Born 08/05/1938, Youngstown, OH, m, 1963 **DISCIPLINE** MEDIEVAL ECONOMIC AND SOCIAL HISTORY **EDUCATION** Youngstown State Univ, BA, 60; Univ Chicago, MA, 62; Univ Wis, PhD(medieval hist), 66. **CAREER** Teaching asst, Dept Integrated Lib Studies, Univ Wis, 64-66; asst prof medieval hist, 66-69, assoc prof & asst chmn, Dept Hist, 69-76, PROF MEDIEVAL HIST, MARQUETTE UNIV, 76-, Am Philos Soc res grants, 72, 73 & 80-81; NSF fel in res, 72-73; assoc mem, Inst Advan Studies, Princeton, 77-; consult, field reader & evaluator, Metric Educ Prog, US Off Educ, Washington, DC, 77- **HONORS AND AWARDS** Teaching Excellence Award, Marquette Univ, 77. **MEMBERSHIPS** Medieval Acad Am; Mid-West Medieval Asn; Am Econ Asn; Repetoire Int Medievistes; Am Econ Assoc. **RESEARCH** Medieval English history; medieval English weights and measures, including officials, legislation and all other aspects; medieval economic and social history. **SELECTED PUBLICATIONS** Auth, A Gentry Community--Leicestershire

in the 15th-Century, C.1422-C.1485, Historian, Vol 0056, 94. **CONTACT ADDRESS** Dept of Hist, Marquette Univ, Coughlin Hall, Milwaukee, WI, 53233.

ZWIEBACH, BURTON
PERSONAL Born 09/17/1933, New York, NY, m, 1962, 2 children **DISCIPLINE** POLITICS **EDUCATION** City Coll of NY, BA, 54; Columbia Law School, LLB, 57; Columbia Univ, PhD, 57. **CAREER** Assoc, 58, Stillman & Stillman; res Asst, 58-61, Advisory Comm on Prac & Proc, NY State Legislature; lect-Prof Poli-Sci, 63-, Queen's College, CUNY. **HONORS AND AWARDS** ABA Gavel Awd Cert of Merit. **MEMBERSHIPS** APA, ASPLP, Amintaphil, CSPT. **RESEARCH** Political theory, ethics. **SELECTED PUBLICATIONS** Auth, The Common Life, Temple Univ Press, 88; Civility and Disobedience, Cambridge Univ Press, 75. **CONTACT ADDRESS** Dept of Political Science, Queens Col, CUNY, 6530 Kissena Blvd, Flushing, NY, 11367. **EMAIL** BZwiebach@aol.com

ZYCHOWICZ, JAMES L.
PERSONAL Born 12/13/1955, Toledo, OH **DISCIPLINE** MUSICOLOGY **EDUCATION** Univ Toledo, BME, 77; Bowling Green State Univ, MM, 81; Univ Cincinnati, PhD, 88. **CAREER** Dean of Stud, mus tchr, Holy Spirit Seminary, Ohio, 81-83; teach asst, Univ Cincinnati, Col-Conserv Mus, 84-86; Dir Mus Engraving, A-R Editions, Madison, 88-92; Dir Prod Svcs, 92-93; Exec Dir, 93-97; Dir Sales Marketing, Mng Ed,Computer Mus and Digital Audio Series, 97-. **HONORS AND AWARDS** Fulbright Scholar, Vienna, 86-87. **MEMBERSHIPS** Am Musicol Soc; Am Musicol Soc, Midwest Ch; Int Gustav Mahler Gesellschaft; Kurt Weill Found Mus; Carl-Maria-von-Weber Ausgabe, Detmold, Ger Mem. **RESEARCH** Musicology: Nineteenth-century music, including music of Gustav Mahler, Carl- Maria von Weber; sketch and manuscript studies; also music of Kurt Weill; opera studies. **SELECTED PUBLICATIONS** Ed, The Seventh Symphony of Gustav Mahler: A Symposium, Univ Cincinnati, 91; Ed, Ein schlechter Jasager: Considerations on the Finale to Mahler's Seventh Symphony, in The Seventh Symphony of Gustav Mahler: A Symposium, Univ Cincinnati, 91, pp 98-106; Liszt and Mahler: Perspectives on a Difficult Relationship, in Jour Am Liszt Soc, vol 36, 94,pp 1-18; The Odyssey of Kurt Weill's 'Ulysses Africanus,' The Am Mus Res Ctr Jour, vol 4, 94,pp 77-97; Music Manuscripts in the Bibliotheque Musicale Gustav Mahler, Paris, Fontes Artis Mus, vol 41, no 3, pp279-95 Toward an Ausgabe letzter Hand: The Publication and Revision of Mahler's Fourth Symphony, Jour Musicol, vol 12, 95, pp260-72; Mozart by Mahler, in Neue Forschungen zu Gustav Mahler und seiner Zeit: Festschrift Henry-Louis de La Grange zum 70. Geburtstag, Berne: Peter Lang, 97, p381-412. **CONTACT ADDRESS** 803 E. Gorham St., Madison, WI, 53703. **EMAIL** JZychowicz@aol.com

Geographic Index

ALABAMA

Auburn
Bond, Gordon Crews
Flynt, Wayne
Kicklighter, Joseph Allen
Lewis, Walter David
Newton, Wesley Phillips
Wilson, David

Birmingham
Allen, Lee Norcross
Brown, James Seay, Jr.
Brown, John Andrew
Conley, Caroline A.
Davis, Jack E.
Fottler, Myron D.
Frost, Ginger S.
Glosecki, Stephen O.
Haarbauer, Don Ward
Hamilton, Virginia V.
Huddle, T.S.
Johnson, Leroy
Mayfield, John
Mcwilliams, Tennant S.
Raabe, William A.
Rikard, Marlene Hunt

Coker
McDonald, Forrest

Florence
Osborne, Thomas Robert

Huntsville
Baird, Bruce C.
Boucher, Philip P.
Dunar, Andrew J.
Ellos, Jack D.
Gerberding, Richard A.
Hull, Henry Lane
Martin, Virginia
Reaves, Benjamin Franklin
Shields, Johanna Nicol
Waring, Stephen P.
White, John Charles
Williams, Lee Erskine, II

Jacksonville
Caldwell, Ronald James
Hollis, Daniel W.
Koerper, Phillip Eldon

Livingston
Gilbert, James L.
Pate, James Paul

Loachapoka
Schafer, Elizabeth D.

Mobile
Brown, Richmond F.
Fogleman, Aaron S.
Holmes, Larry E.
Mahan, Howard F.
McKiven, Henry M., Jr.
Mohr, Clarence L.
Monheit, Michael L.
Oszuscik, Philippe

Rogers, Daniel E.

Montevallo
Fuller, Justin
Morgan, David Taft
Truss, Ruth Smith

Montgomery
Bell, Katie Roberson
Berkley, Gerald Wayne
Cheatham, Carl W.
Fair, John Douglas
Fitzsimmons, Michael P.
Futrell, Robert Frank
Harris, Willa Bing
Hicks, L. Edward
Newton, Merlin Owen
Pace, Kay Robertine
Salyer, Gregory
Simmons, Michael
Westhauser, Karl E.
Wood, Kirk

Normal
Wilson, Patricia I.

Selma
Garcia, William Burres

Talladega
White, John D.

Tuscaloosa
Clayton, Lawrence A.
Mendle, Michael J.
Monk, Dennis
Ohnuma, Reiko
Ultee, J. Maarten
Wagstaff, Grayson
Wiggins, Sarah Woolfolk

Union Springs
Lewis, Meharry Hubbard

University
Badger, Reid
Doster, James Fletcher
Jones, Howard
Pickett, Terry H.
Watkins, John C.

Vestabia Hills
McCarl, Mary F.R.

Waverly
Dodge, Timothy

ALASKA

Anchorage
Ducker, James H.

Fairbanks
Cole, Terrence M.
Cornwall, Peter G.
Falk, Marvin W.
Gold, Carol

Hunt, William Raymond
Jonaitis, Aldona
Mangusso, Mary C.
Naske, Claus-M.
Pierce, Richard A.
Whitehead, John S.

ARIZONA

Flagstaff
Cox, Joseph W.
Hassing, Arne
Hinsley, Curtis M.
Kitterman, David Harold
Kyte, George Wallace
Lubick, George Michael
Mcfarlane, Larry Allan
Mihesuah, Devon Abbott
Poen, Monte Mac
Sexton, James D.
Wallace, Andrew
West, Delno C.

Glendale
Peters, Issa

Phoenix
Corrigan, John
Cutrer, Thomas W.
Doyel, D.
Goff, John S.

Pine
Pope, Robert G.

Scottsdale
Richardson, Richard C., Jr.

Tempe
Adelson, Roger
Batalden, Stephen Kalmar
Burg, Barry Richard
Codell, Julie
Coudert, Allison P.
Davis, Thomas Joseph
Fisher, Marvin
Fullinwider, S. Pendleton
Giffin, Frederick Charles
Harris, Walter, Jr.
Kahn, B. Winston
Kintigh, Keith W.
Kleinfeld, Gerald R
Luckingham, Bradford Franklin
MacCoull, Leslie
Mackinnon, Stephen Robert
Montgomery, Toni-Marie
Simon, Sheldon W.
Tambs, Lewis
Tillman, Hoyt Cleveland
Trennert, Robert Anthony
Warnicke, Retha Marvine
Warren, Morrison Fulbright
White, Michael J.
Wilson, Jeffrey R.
Young, Otis E.

Tucson
Austin, J. Norman
Bernstein, Gail Lee
Carter, Paul Allen
Clarke, James W.
Cosgrove, Richard A.
Darling, Linda T.
Dever, William Gwinn
Dinnerstein, Leonard
Eaton, Richard Maxwell
Fishback, Price Vanmeter
Fontana, Bernard Lee
Gamal, Adel Sulaiman
Gibbs, David N.
Guy, Donna Jay
Hovendick, Kelly B.
Johnson, Harold Benjamin
Kellogg, Frederick
Kunnie, Julian
Martinez, Oscar J.
Nakhai, Beth Alpert
Nichols, Roger L.
Parezo, Nancy Jean
Romer, F.E.
Rowe, David C.
Schaller, Michael
Tabili, Laura
Van Steen, Gonda Aline Hector
Wearing, J.P.
Wilson, William Jerram
Worthen, Thomas De Voe

ARKANSAS

Arkadelphia
Steeger, Wm P.

Batesville
Shay, Robert
Stinson, Russell
Stricklin, David

Conway
Barnes, Kenneth C.
Bender, Melvin E.
Brodman, James William
Farthing, John L.
Frizzell, Robert
Schantz, Mark S.

Fayetteville
Bolsterli, Margaret Jones
Bukey, Evan Burr
Bukey, Evan Burr
Chappell, David L.
Chase, James S.
Cochran, Robert
Coon, Lynda L.
Edwards, Sandra
Eichmann, Raymond
Engels, Donald W.
Finlay, Robert
Fredrick, David
Gatewood, Willard Badgette
Henry Tsai, Shin Shan
Jacobs, Lynn F.
Kennedy, Thomas C.
Levine, Daniel

Levine, Daniel Blank
Minar, Edward
Schilcher, Linda
Sloan, David
Sonn, Richard D.
Spellman, Lynne
Strausberg, Stephen Frederick
Sutherland, Daniel E.
Tsai, Shih-shan Henry
Tucker, William F.
Van Patten, James J.
West, Elliott
Whayne, Jeannie
Williams, Nudie Eugene
Woods, Randall B.

Little Rock
Baker, Thomas H.
Bilsky, Lester James
Bolton, Sidney Charles
Brown, Dee Alexander
Jacoway, Elizabeth
Kaiser, Thomas Ernest
Levernier, James Arthur
Littlefield, Dan F.
Moneyhon, Carl Hofmann
Parins, Marylyn
Williams, C. Fred
Williams, Leroy Thomas
Yoder, R. Paul

Magnolia
Willis, James F.

Monticello
Shea, William Lee

Mountain View
Mcneil, William Kinneth

Pine Bluff
Littlejohn, Walter L.

State University
Dougan, Michael Bruce
Smith, Charlie Calvin

Tempe
Brandt, Beverly K.

CALIFORNIA

Alameda
Quivik, Fredric L.

Albany
Wheaton, Bruce R.

Arcata
Fox, Stephen C.
Ingle, Harold Norman
Johnson, Ronald William
Okin, Louis A.
Sundstrom, Roy Alfred
Tanner, William Randolph

Bakersfield
Kleinsasser, Jerome
Rink, Oliver A
Wood, Forrest Glen

Belmont
Easter, Marilyn

Berkeley
Abrams, Richard M.
Anderson, William Scovil
Banks, William Maron, III
Barnes, Thomas Garden
Barth, Gunther
Birnbaum, Lucia Chiavola
Bolt, Bruce A.
Borah, Woodrow
Bouwsma, William James
Brentano, Robert
Brucker, Gene Adam
Chinnici, Joseph Patrick
Clader, Linda
Clark, VeVe A.
Clemens, Diane Shaver
Clifford, Geraldine Joncich
Costa, Gustavo
Countryman, L. Wm
Crocker, Richard Lincoln
Daube, David
De Vries, Jan
Donovan, Mary Ann
Dundes, Alan
Edwards, Harry
Ernst, Eldon G.
Falk, Candace
Fass, Paula S.
Faulhaber, Charles Bailey
Feeley, Malcolm M.
Feldman, Gerald Donald
Gifford, Bernard R.
Greenewalt, Crawford Hallock
Groth, Paul
Gruen, Erich S.
Guinan, Michael Damon
Gumperz, John J.
Haber, Samuel
Hahn, Roger
Heilbron, John L.
Herr, Richard
Hetherington, Norriss Swigart
Hollinger, D.A.
Irschick, Eugene Frederick
Jay, Martin Evan
Joyce, Rosemary A.
Kagan, Robert A.
Keightley, David Noel
Kettner, James Harold
Kilmer, Anne Draffkorn
Kirch, Patrick V.
Kirk-Duggan, Cheryl Ann
Knapp, Arthur Bernard
Knapp, Robert Carlyle
Laguerre, Michael Saturnin
Lapidus, Ira M.
Laqueur, Thomas Walter
Leonard, Thomas Charles
Lesch, John Emmett
Lewin, Linda
Litwack, Leon F.
Long, Anthony Arthur
Lyman, J. Rebecca
Mastronarde, Donald John
May, Henry Farnham
Merchant, Carolyn
Messinger, Sheldon L.
Metcalf, Thomas R.
Middlekauff, Robert Lawrence
Miller, Stephen G.
Muir, William Ker
Murgia, Charles Edward
Nagler, Michael Nicholas
Parsons, Jed
Redmount, Carol A.
Riasanovsky, Nicholas
Richmond, Velma B.
Rose, Leo E.
Rothblatt, Sheldon
Scheiber, Harry N.
Scheiffele, Eberhard
Scheiner, Irwin
Scott, Peter Dale
Sealey, B. Raphael
Shackley, M. Steven
Starn, Randolph
Stortz, Martha Ellen
Strohl, Jane E.
Stroud, Ronald Sidney
Takaki, Ronald Toshiyuki
Threatte, Leslie Lee

Upton, Dell
Wakeman, Frederic Evans, Jr.
Wright, Georgia Sommers
Yeh, Wen-han
Zelnik, Reginald Ely

Carmel
Sarbin, Theodore R.

Carson
Garber, Marilyn
Grenier, Judson A.
Hata, Donald Teruo
Ivers, Louise H.
Wells, Walter

Chico
Boyle, John Hunter
Caldwell, Sarah
Conlin, Joseph R.
Cowden, Joanna Dunlap
Farrer, Claire Rafferty
Karman, James
Lillibridge, George Donald
Minor, Clifford Edward
Singelis, T.M.

Claremont
Barron, Hal S.
Blaine, Bradford Bennett
Camp, Roderic A.
Cressy, David
Davis, Nathaniel
Dornish, Margaret Hammond
Elliott, Ward Edward Yandell
Emerick, Judson
Geerken, John Henry
Gonzalez, Deena J.
Gorse, George L.
Greenberger, Allen Jay
Jackson, Agnes Moreland
Jaffa, Harry Victor
Levy, Leonard Williams
Lofgren, Charles Augustin
Osborn, Ronald Edwin
Post, Gaines
Rice, Albert R.
Schneider, Tammi J.
Silverman, Victor
Smith, Pamela H.
Wachtel, Albert
Wall, Helena M.
Warmbrunn, Werner
Wicker, Kathleen O'Brien
Wolf, Kenneth Baxter
Woods, Robert L., Jr.
Yamashita, Samuel Hideo

Concord
Chandler, Robert Joseph

Costa Mesa
Cerillo, Augustus
Wilson, John
Wilson, Lewis

Cupertino
Williams, James Calhoun

Daly City
Leitao, David

Davis
Bauer, Arnold Jacob
Bettinger, Robert L.
Bowsky, Martha Welborn
Bowsky, William Marvin
Brody, David
Brower, Daniel Roberts
Crummey, Robert Owen
Fleischer, Manfred Paul
Goodman, Paul
Groth, Alexander J.
Hagen, William Walter
Halttunen, Karen
Jackson, William Turrentine
Jett, Stephen C.
Poppino, Rollie Edward
Price, Don Cravens
Rosen, Ruth E.
Sarlos, Robert Karoly
Schaeffer, Peter Moritz-Friedrich
Schleiner, Winfried H.
Smith, F. Wilson
Spyridakis, Stylianos V.
Taylor, Alan S.
Traill, David Angus
West, Martha S.

Willis, Frank Roy

Del Mar
Fouquet, Patricia Root

Encinitas
Beyer, David W.
Farrell, Warren Thomas

Escondida
Neihoff, Arthur H.

Fillmore
Whitley, David S.

Fremont
Kirshner, Alan Michael

Fresno
Basden, B.H.
Benko, Stephen
Bohnstedt, John Wolfgang
Boyajian, James Charles
Dinkin, Robert J.
Kauffman, George B.
Klassen, Peter James
Warkentin, Larry R.
Wint, Arthur Valentine Noris

Fullerton
Axelrad, Allan M.
Bakken, Gordon Morris
Bellot, Leland Joseph
De Rios, Marlene Dobkin
Hansen, Debra Gold
Hardy, B. Carmon
Hobson, Wayne K.
Onorato, Michael P.
Pivar, David J.
Putnam, Jackson K.
Segal, N.L.
Smith, Jesse Owens
Vogeler, Martha Salmon

Hayward
Bowser, Benjamin P.
Bullough, William Alfred
Gilliard, Frank Daniel
Henig, Gerald S.
Morby, John Edwin
Pitts, Vera L.
Raack, Richard C.
Reuter, William C.
Roszak, Theodore
Walz, John D.

Hollywood
Samudio, Jeffrey

Irvine
Barney, Stephen Allen
Bruce, D.D.
Dickson, Bruce D., Jr.
Donlan, Walter
Fahs, Alice E.
Ferrin Sutton, Dana
Grofman, Bernard N.
Hill, Lamar Mott
Leonard, Karen Isaksen
Martin, Jay H.
Mcculloch, Samuel Clyde
Miles, Margaret M.
Nelson, Keith Lebahn
Saadoun, Mohamed
Small, Kenneth Alan
Suttpn, Dana F.
Wiener, Jonathan M.

La Jolla
Bailey, Frederick George
Briggs, Charles L.
Gollaher, David L.
Gutierrez, Ramon A.
Hughes, Judith Markham
Luft, David Sheers
Marino, John Anthony
Martin, Wayne M.
Mosshammer, Alden Adams
Neuhouser, Frederick
Pasler, Jann C.
Pomeroy, Earl
Ringrose, David R.
Schudson, Michael
Stavrianos, Leften Stavros

La Mirada
Finley, Thomas John

Long Beach
Burke, Albie
Gosselin, Edward Alberic
Hood, David Crockett
Kennett, Douglas
Lindgren, Raymond Elmer
Person, Dawn Renee
Polakoff, Keith Ian
Robinson, Jim C.
Stuart, Jack
Williams, Ora

Los Angeles
Accampo, Elinor A.
Ake, David
Alexander, Theodore Thomas, Jr.
Ando, Clifford
Appleby, Joyce
Aronson, Jonathan
Banner, Lois W.
Barnes Robinson, Susan
Becker, Marjorie R.
Benson, Robert Louis
Berger, Gordon
Bergren, Ann L.T.
Berton, Peter
Blank, David L.
Brown, Jonathan Charles
Brown, Kendall H.
Bruno, James Edward
Buccellati, Giorgio
Caiden, Gerald E.
Capron, Alexander M.
Chambers, Mortimer Hardin
Chapple, C.K.
Chaput, Donald
Chyet, Stanley F.
Coben, Stanley
Cody, Martin Leonard
Cohen, Norman Sonny
Coombs, Robert H.
Cox, Thomas C.
Crecelius, Daniel
Dales, Richard C.
Dallek, Robert
Dewey, Donald Odell
Dingman, Roger V.
Dresser, N.
Dyck, Andrew R.
Ehret, Christopher
Elman, B.A.
Ethington, Philip J.
Eubanks, Rachel Amelia
FA, Mayer
Fireman, Janet Ruth
Fisher, Raymond Henry
Frakes, Jerold C.
Free, Katherine B.
Frischer, Bernard
Funkenstein, Amos
Furth, Charlotte
Ghirardo, Diane
Gilliland-Swetland, Anne J.
Glasco, Anita L.
Glaser, Daniel
Goldberg, Sander M.
Gurval, Robert Alan
Hahn, Harlan
Harley, Maria Anna
Harper, Katherine
Hayes, Robert Mayo
Hines, Thomas S.
Hirsch, Werner Z.
Hise, Greg
Horowitz, Maryanne Cline
Hundley, Norris Cecil
Jacoby, Sanford M.
Jones, Amelia
Jones, Michael Owen
Katada, Saori
Keddie, Nikki R.
Knoll, Paul W.
Krekic, Barisa
Kroeber, Clifton Brown
Kushner, James Alan
Laslett, John Henry Martin
Lattimore, Steven
Light, Ivan
Lowenstein, Steven Mark
Malone, Carolyn
Markel, Stephen
Martines, Lauro
Matteson, Lynn Robert
May, Christopher N.
Mazon, Mauricio
Mellor, Ronald
Meyer, Richard
Moore, A. Lloyd
Morgan, Kathryn A.

Moss, Bernard Haym
Nagle, D. Brendan
Naiditch, P.G.
Nash, Gary B.
Nosco, Peter
Notehelfer, Fred G.
Nunis, Doyce Blackman
Pal, Pratapaditya
Papadopoulos, John K.
Perkins, Linda Marie
Pollini, John
Purefoy Morris, Sarah
Reill, Peter Hanns
Richlin, Amy
Rorlich, Azade-Ayse
Ross, Steven J.
Ruiz, Teofilo Fabian
Ryan, Herbert Joseph
Sanchez, George J.
Sardesai, Damodar Ramaji
Schierle, Gotthilf Goetz
Schmidhauser, John Richard
Seip, Terry L.
Sklar, Richard Lawrence
Starr, Kevin
Teviotdale, Elizabeth C.
Totten, George Oakley, III
Troy, Nancy J.
Varnelis, Kazys
Vine, Brent
Voeltz, Richard Andrew
Vonfalkenhausen, L.
Walker, Andrew David
Wilkie, James Wallace
Williams, William J.
Willis, Alfred
Wills, John E.
Wilson, Robert Arden
Wohl, Robert
Wolfenstein, E. Victor
Yarborough, Richard A.
Zeitlin, Maurice

Malibu
Baird, David
Herbert, Luft
Rowland, Rick

Manhattan Beach
Lee, Anthony A.

Marina del Rey
Levine, David Oscar

Menlo Park
Carr, Michael Harold

Mill Valley
Arbino, Gary P.
Honeycutt, Dwight A.
McCoy, Gary W.

Mission Viejo
Giacumakis, George

Modesto
Oppenheim, Samuel Aaron

Moraga
Guarneri, Carl J.
Lemke-Santangelo, Gretchen
Santiago, Myrna

Moreno Valley
Conway, Melissa

Mount View
Brennan, Mary Alethea

Newhall
Johnson, Robert C.

Northridge
Bajpai, Shiva Gopal
Baur, John Edward
Broesamle, John Joseph
Camp, Richard
Clendenning, John
Field, Earle
Herman, Phyllis
Koistinen, Paul Abraham Carl
Meyer, Michael
Schaffer, Ronald
Sefton, James Edward
Soffer, Reba Nusbaum
Tohidi, Nayereh E.

Rock, Kenneth Willett
Suinn, Richard Michael
Theodoratus, Robert James
Tyler, Daniel
Weisser, Henry G.
Worrall, Arthur John

Greeley
Bellman, Jonathan
Hall, Gene E.
Knott, Alexander W.
Larson, Robert Walter
Rowe, Gail Stuart
Spatz, Nancy
Worrall, Janet Evelyn

Gunnison
Headrick, Annabeth

Pueblo
Sheidley, William E.

USAF Academy
Macisaac, David

CONNECTICUT

Avon
Kalvoda, Josef

Bridgeport
Soares, Anthony T.

Chester
Tatum, George B.

Danbury
Roman, Eric
Young, Kenneth Ray

Fairfield
Abbott, Albert
Cross, Dolores E.
Long, R. James
Manning, Christel
Mille, Diane
Roney, John B.
Rosivach, Vincent John
Rosner, Stanley

Gales Ferry
Waterman, Thelma M.

Greenwich
Panaitescu, Adrian

Guilford
Kelley, Brooks Mather

Hamden
Glassner, Martin Ira

Hartford
Bradley, James R.
Bradley, James Robert
Desmangles, Leslie Gerald
Greenberg, Cheryl Lynn
Kaimowitz, Jeffrey H.
Kassow, Samuel D.
Maciuika, Benedict Vytenis
Macro, Anthony David
Sloan, Edward William

Middlebury
Bedford, Steven M.

Middletown
Buel, Richard (Van Wyck)
Butler, Jeffrey Ernest
Elphick, Richard
Gillmor, Charles Stewart
Greene, Nathanael
Hill, Patricia
Horgan, Paul
Johnston, William
Katz, Marilyn A.
Long, Jerome Herbert
Meyer, Donald
O'Hara, James J.
Pomper, Philip
Roberts, Michael
Slotkin, Richard S.
Vann, Richard T.
Walker, Willard

New Haven
Adams, Marilyn M.
Anderson, Michael John
Ausmus, Harry Jack
Babcock, Robert
Bers, Victor
Blassingame, John W.
Blatt, Sidney Jules
Butler, Jon
Carby, Hazel V.
Clifford, Nicholas R.
Cott, Nancy Falik
Davis, David Brion
de Bretteville, Sheila Levrant
Faragher, John Mack
Feinberg, Harvey Michael
Foos, Paul W.
Forte, Allen
Foster, Benjamin Read
Foster, Karen Polinger
Griffith, Ezra
Hersey, George Leonard
Imholt, Robert Joseph
Kazemzadeh, Firuz
Kubler, George
Lamar, Howard Roberts
Lopez, Robert Sabatino
Macmullen, Ramsay
Matthews, John F.
Merriman, John M.
Minkema, Kenneth P.
Musto, David Franklin
Pelikan, Jaroslav
Perlis, Vivian
Pollitt, Jerome J.
Prown, Jules D.
Russell, Tilden A.
Sanneh, Lamin
Spence, Jonathan Dermot
Stoll, Steven
Stout, Harry S.
Thomas, Gerald Eustis
Thompson, Robert Farris
Tirro, Frank Pascale
Trachtenberg, Alan
Turner, Frank Miller
Waldstreicher, David L.
Wandycz, Piotr Stefan
Wheeler, Stanton
Winks, Robin William Evert
Woodward, Comer Vann

New London
Burlingame, Michael A.
Despalatovic, Elinor Murray
Forster, Marc R.
Held, Dirk
Lesser, Jeffrey
Paxton, Frederick S.
Silberman, Sara Lee
Silverberg, Joann C.
Taranow, Gerda
Wilson, Lisa H.
Winter, Jerry Alan

North Haven
Katsaros, Thomas

Northampton
Aldrich, Mark

Orchard Branford
Palisca, Claude Victor

Simsbury
Frost, James Arthur

Stamford
Babson, Jane F.
Selfridge-Field, Eleanor

Storrs
Allen, Irving L.
Asher, Robert
Brown, Richard David
Clifford, John Garry
Coons, Ronald Edward
Costigliola, Frank Charles
Curry, Richard Orr
Dayton, Cornelia H.
Dickerman, Edmund H.
Greene, John C.
Hagan, Willie James
Hoglund, Arthur William
Lougee, Robert Wayne
Mchugh, Michael P.
Moynihan, Ruth Barnes
Paterson, Thomas Graham

Shivers, Jay Sanford
Stave, Bruce M.
Suits, Thomas Allan

Stratford
Fritz, Robert B.

Waterbury
O'Donnell, Kim

Waterford
Murstein, Bernard I.

West Hartford
Auten, Arthur
Azzara, Christopher D.
Braus, Ira
Breit, Peter K.
Canning, Paul
Lacey, Barbara E.
Miller, Patrick
Mori, Akane
Saunders, Clark T.
Willheim, Imanuel

West Haven
Glen, Robert Allan

Westport
Fraser, Julius Thomas
Millar, Steven

Willimantic
Carter, David G., Sr.
Dawson, Anne
Lacey, James
Pocock, Emil

Wilton
Sachs, William L.
Stoetzer, O. Carlos

DELAWARE

Dover
Caldwell, M. Milford
Flayhart, William H., III

Georgetown
Williams, William Henry

Newark
Bernstein, John Andrew
Bernstein, John Andrew
Boylan, Anne Mary
Callahan, Daniel Francis
Callahan, Raymond Aloysius
Chapman, H. Perry
Craven, Wayne
Crawford, John S.
Curtis, James C.
Direnzo, Gordon James
Duggan, Lawrence Gerald
Ferguson, Eugene S
Geiger, Reed G.
Gibson, Ann
Grubb, Farley
Herman, Bernard L.
Heyrman, Christine L.
Hoffecker, Carol E.
Homer, William I.
Kallmyer, Nina
Lopata, Roy Haywood
Meyer, Donald Harvey
Morgan, John D.
Munroe, John Andrew
Ness, Lawrence
Newton, James E.
Pellecchia, Linda
Peterson, Larry
Pong, David B.P.T.
Postle, Martin J.
Reedy, Chandra L.
Schwartz, Norman B.
Sidebotham, Steven Edward
Stillman, Damie
Stone, David M.
Tolles, Bryant F., Jr.
Wolohojian, Stephan S.
Wolters, Raymond

Wilmington
Baber, Lucky Larry
Finkelstein, Rona
Porter, Glenn

Winterthur
Smith, James Morton

DISTRICT OF COLUMBIA

Washington
Abel, Elie
Adams, Russell Lee
Andrews, Avery D.
Apostolos-Cappadona, Diane
Arnold, Steven H.
Atkin, Muriel Ann
Baker, Richard Allan
Barlow, William
Barlow, William B.
Becker, William Henry
Beckerman, Paul
Beisner, Robert L.
Bell, William Gardner
Bennet, Joel F.
Berkowitz, Edward D.
Billington, James H.
Birch, Bruce Charles
Birnbaum, Norman
Blakely, Allison
Blecker, Robert A.
Boorstin, Daniel Joseph
Borelli, John
Brautigam, Deborah
Breitman, Richard D.
Broad, Robin
Brown, Dorothy M.
Calhoun, Lee A.
Campbell, Ted A.
Cenkner, William
Cheru, Fantu
Clarke, Duncan
Cline, Catherine Ann
Cohen, Stephen P.
Coll, Blanche D
Cotman, John W.
Crawford, Michael John
Crew, Spencer R.
Cromwell, William C.
Crouch, Tom Day
Curran, Robert Emmott
Daniel, Pete
Davis, Audrey Blyman
Davison, Roderic Hollett
Delio, Ilia
Deng, Francis M.
Dennis, George Thomas
Depauw, Linda Grant
Deutscher, Irwin
Dillon, Wilton Sterlin
Dionne, E.J.
Downs, Anthony
Dudley, William Sheldon
Duncan, Richard R.
Engel, Martin
England, James Merton
Eno, Robert Bryan
Esposito, John L.
Eyck, Gunther
Fern, Alan M.
Fiema, Zbigniew
Finan, John J.
Fisher, Louis
Forman, P.
Garibaldi, Antoine Michael
Garrard, Mary
Garthoff, Raymond L.
Gawalt, Gerard Wilfred
Gephart, Ronald Michael
Goldstein, Joshua S.
Goodman, Louis
Gowans, Alan
Gravelle, Jane Gibson
Greenough, Sarah
Gregg, Robert
Gribbin, William James
Gundersheimer, W.L.
Halal, William E.
Hallion, Richard Paul
Halton, Thomas
Harris, Joseph E.
Harrison, Cynthia
Hartgrove, Joseph Dane
Hassing, Richard F.
Haynes, John E.
Heffron, Paul Thayer
Helms, John Douglas
Henning, Randall
Herber, Charles Joseph
Hill, Bennett David

Hill, Peter Proal
Hirschmann, David
Hoge, Dean R.
Hunt, Richard Allen
Jacks, Philip
Jaffe, Lorna S.
Johnson, Jacob Edwards, III
Johnson, Ronald Maberry
Karp, Stephen A.
Kim, Hyung Kook
Kinsella, David
Klaren, Peter Flindell
Klein, Ira N.
Kohler, Sue A.
Kohn, Richard Henry
Kotler, Neil G.
Kraut, Alan M.
Kurland, Jordan Emil
Kuznick, Peter J.
Langer, Erick Detlef
LeMelle, Tilden J.
Lewis, Douglas
Lewis, Peter
Lewis, V. Bradley
Liss, Peggy K korn
Loewen, James W.
Lubbers, Jeffrey S.
Lubrano, Linda L.
Lynch, John Edward
Lynn, Kenneth Schuyler
MacDonald, William L.
Mackintosh, Barry
Maisch, Christian
Mardin, Serif
Marlin-Bennett, Rene
Marty, Myron August
McCurdy, Howard Earl
McNeill, John R.
Mendelson, Johanna
Minnich, Nelson H.
Mittelman, James
Moran Cruz, Jo Ann Hoeppner
Muller, Jerry Z.
Multhauf, Robert Phillip
Murray, Shoon
Musgrove, Philip
Mutchler, David Edward
Nadell, Pamela
Needell, Allan A.
Nordquist, Barbara K.
O'Connor, Michael Patrick
O'Neill, James E.
Oppenheim, Janet
Palmer, Phyllis Marynick
Pasha, Mustapha
Payne, Deborah C.
Phillips, Ann
Pillsbury, Joanne
Pinkett, Harold Thomas
Poos, L.R.
Post, Robert C.
Prevots, Naima
Pruitt, Anne Smith
Rand, Harry
Reagon, Bernice Johnson
Reusher, Jay
Richardson, John
Riley, James Denson
Ritchie, Donald Arthur
Robinson, Lilien F.
Ross, Dorothy Rabin
Rothenberg, Marc
Ruedy, John D.
Sachar, Howard Morley
Said, Abdul Aziz
Samarasinghe, Vidyamali
Schneider, Cathy
Schwoerer, Lois Green
Shahid, Irfan Arif
Sharoni, Simona
Sharrer, George Terry
Shedel, James P.
Silvia, Stephen J.
Spector, R.H.
Stewart, Charles Todd
Strong, Douglas M.
Sullivan, Denis
Teich, Albert Harris
Terry, Mickey Thomas
Thornton, Richard C.
Trask, David F.
Trisco, Robert Frederick
Tucker, Nancy Bernkopf
Tushnet, Mark Victor
Viola, Herman Joseph
Vogt, George Leonard
Walch, Timothy G.
Walker, Robert Harris
Wapner, Paul

HAWAII

Hilo
Best, Gary Dean
Fields, Lanny Bruce
Howell, Richard Wesley

Honolulu
Ball, Robert J.
Beechert, Edward D.
Bentley, Jerry Harrell
Bilmes, Jack
Bomberger, E. Douglas
Chappell, David Wellington
Choe, Yong-ho
Cowing, Cedric Breslyn
Daniel, Marcus L.
Ellsworth, James Dennis
Finney, Ben Rudolph
Forman, Michael Lawrence
Grant, Glen
Graves, Michael W.
Hooper, Paul Franklin
Johnson, Donald Dalton
Kraft, James P.
Kwok, D.W.Y.
Ladd, Doris
Lam, Truong Buu
Littman, Robert J.
Mccutcheon, James Miller
Newby, I.A.
Rapson, Richard L.
Richards, Leon
Sharma, Jagdish P.
Shi, Mingzheng
Speidel, Michael Paul
Stein, Burton
Stephan, John Jason
Tao, Tien-Yi
Wade, Rex Arvin
Yen, De

Kailua
Johnson, Ronald C.

IDAHO

Boise
Austin, Judith
Ericson, Robert Edward
Lovin, Hugh Taylor
Ourada, Patricia K.
Sims, Robert Carl
Vinz, Warren Lang
Zirinsky, Michael Paul

Caldwell
Maughan, Steven
Smith, Mark

Lewiston
Bianchi, Robert S.

Moscow
Hackmann, William Kent
Harris, Robert Dalton
Kilmko, Ronald

Nampa
Marshman, Michelle

Pocatello
Cantrill, Dante
Ellis, Susan
Engebretsen, Terry
Hatzenbuehler, Ronald Lee

ILLINOIS

Addison
Morello, John

Aurora
Strassberg, Barbara

Bloomington
Young, Michael Brian

Carbondale
Barton, H. Arnold
Bender, Marvin Lionel
Detwiler, Donald Scaife
Dotson, John Edward

Gold, Robert Leonard
Gorman, Carma
Hill, Jonathan D.
Kilpatrick, Thomas L.
Molfese, D.L.
Simon, John Y.
Stalls, M.
Weeks, T.R.
Werlich, David P.
Williams, Rhys H.
Wilson, David L.

Champaign
Anderson, James D.
Appel, Susan K.
Barrett, James R.
Buchanan, Donna A.
Burkhardt, Richard W.
Capwell, Charles
Choldin, Marianna Tax
Cople Jaher, Frederick
Crummey, Donald E.
Davis, Peter
Dunlay, Don E.
Fehl, Philipp P.
Fu, Poshek
Garcia, Matt
Graves, Robert
Gushee, Lawrence
Hill, John Walter
Hoddeson, Lillian
Hoxie, Frederick E.
Jacobsen, Nils
Johannsen, Robert W.
Kling, Blair B.
Koenker, Diane P.
Koslofsky, Craig
Krummel, Donald William
Leff, Mark H.
Liebersohn, Harry
Littlefield, Daniel
McColley, Robert
McLaughlin, Megan
Meyer, Adolphe Erich
Michel, Sonya
Oberdeck, Kathryn J.
Pleck, Elizabeth
Prochaska, David
Pruett, John H.
Radding, Cynthia
Reagan, Leslie J.
Ringer, Alexander
Rivest, Johanne
Schroeder, Paul W.
Steinberg, Mark D.
Tiyambe Zeleza, Paul
Turino, Thomas
Vernon Burton, Orville
Ward, Tom R.
Widenor, William C.

Charleston
Bazargan, Susan
Colvin, William E.
Lehman, Cynthia L.
Marquardt-Cherry, Janet Teresa
Tingley, Donald Fred
Waldrep, Christopher

Chicago
Adkins, Arthur William Hope
Albrecht, Gary Louis
Alexander, Michael C.
Allee, Mark
Allen, Michael I.
Anderson, Greg
Asmis, Elizabeth
Austen, Ralph Albert
Austern, Linda
Bartsch, Shadi
Biggs, Robert Dale
Bireley, Robert Lee
Bledstein, Adrien
Bledstein, Burton J.
Bock-Weiss, Catherine C.
Bottoms, Bette L.
Boyer, John William
Brauer, Jerald
Brinkman, John Anthony
Brown, Richard Holbrook
Bruegmann, Robert
Buntrock, Dana
Burnell, Devin
Burnett, Anne Pippin
Burton, J.D.
Butler, Lee Hayward, Jr.
Cafferty, Pastora San Juan
Cardoza, Anthony L.
Civil, Miguel

Clark, Terry Nichols
Cohen, Sheldon S.
Cohn, Bernard Samuel
Comaroff, Jean
Craig, John Eldon
Csikszentmihalyi, Mihaly
Cumings, Bruce
Daily, Jonathan
Danzer, Gerald A.
Dee, James Howard
Dennis, David B.
DePillars, Murry Norman
Dickie, Matthew Wallace
Dietler, Michael
Dik, Helma
Dominowski, Roger L.
Draznin, Yaffa Claire
Echols, James Kenneth
Edie, Carolyn A.
Eliade, Mircea
Elkins, James
Erenberg, Lewis
Erlebacher, Albert
Eslinger, Ellen T.
Fanning, Steven
Faraone, Christopher
Fasolt, Constantin
Ferrari Pinney, Gloria
Flanagan, Maureen Anne
Floyd, Samuel Alexander
Foster, Teree E.
Fried, Richard M.
Fry, Christine L.
Gagliano, Joseph Anthony
Galush, William J.
Garner, Roberta
Gebhard, Elizabeth Replogle
Geyer, M.
Ghazzal, Zouhair
Gilbert, Bentley Brinkerhoff
Gilfoyle, Timothy J.
Glueckert, Leo
Golb, Norman
Goldman, Jean
Gordon, Milton A.
Gossett, Philip
Graber, Doris A.
Gray, Hanna Holborn
Green, Jesse Dawes
Gross, Hanns
Gross-Diaz, Theresa
Groves, Nicholas
Gutek, Gerald Lee
Hales, Peter Bacon
Hall, Jonathan M.
Harrington, Ann M.
Harrington, Kevin
Hayes, Zachary Jerome
Hays, Jo N.
Headrick, Daniel Richard
Hellie, Richard
Helmholz, R.H.
Hendel, Kurt Karl
Higgins, Hannah
Hirsch, Susan E.
John, Richard R.
Johnson, Paul B.
Johnson, W. Ralph
Johnson, Walker C.
Johnson-Odim, Cheryl
Jones, Peter D'a
Jordan, David P.
Kaegi, Walter Emil
Kang, Soo Y.
Karamanski, Theodore J.
Karl, Barry D.
Kaufman, George G.
Kaufman, Suzanne
Keenan, J.G.
Khodarkovsky, Michael
Kirshner, Julius
Knapp, Thomas A.
Krieger, Leonard
Kulczycki, John J.
Kuzdale, Ann E.
Levy, Richard S.
Lincoln, Bruce
Lopata, Helena Z.
Macdonald, J. Fred
Mann, Arthur
Margolin, Victor
Marty, Martin Emil
Mccaffrey, Lawrence John
McCullagh, Suzanne Folds
McGinn, Bernard John
McManamon, John
Mcneill, William Hardy
Mellon, Stanley
Messer, Robert Louis

Miller, Bernice Johnson
Miller, David B.
Miller, Virginia E.
Mooney-Melvin, Patricia
Morrison, Karl Frederick
Moseley, Michael Edward
Moylan, Prudence A.
Nelson, Robert S.
Nolan, Janet
Novick, Peter
O'Connell, Daniel C.
Olin, Margaret
Patton, Gerald Wilson
Perelmuter, Hayim Goren
Perman, Micheal
Pfeffer, Paula F.
Pinder, Kymberly
Platt, Harold L.
Pollak, Martha
Ramsey, John T.
Ransby, Barbara
Reardon, John J.
Redfield, James M.
Reiner, Erica
Reisch, George
Reitz, Miriam
Remini, Robert Vincent
Reynolds, Frank E.
Riess, Steve Allen
Roeder, George H.
Rosenwein, Barbara Herstein
Royster, Philip M.
Sack, James J.
Saller, Richard
Schelbert, Leo
Schmaus, Warren Stanley
Schroeder, Susan P.
Schultz, Reynolds Barton
Simpson, Dick
Singleton, Gregory Holmes
Sizemore, Barbara A.
Slatkin, Laura M.
Sloan, Thomas
Smith, Daniel Scott
Smith, Jonathon Zittell
Smith, Tom W.
Sochen, June
Sokol, David M.
Stafford, Barbara Maria
Stager, Lawrence E.
Stein, Leon
Stern, Robin
Tannenbaum, Rebecca J.
Tanner, Helen Hornbeck
Terrell, Melvin C.
Tomlins, Christopher L.
Townsend, Richard
Vita, Steven
Walker, Sue Sheridan
Warner, R. Stephen
Weiner, Lynn
Wente, Edward Frank
White, Peter
Woodman, Taylor
Worrill, Conrad W.
Wray, David L.
Wyrick, Floyd I.
Zukowsky, John

De Kalb
Atkins, E. Taylor
Blomquist, Thomas W.
Dye, James Wayne
Foster, Stephen
George, Charles Hilles
Gildemeister, Glen A.
Keen, Benjamin
Kern, Stephen
Kinser, Samuel
Kourvetaris, Yorgos A.
Lincoln, William Bruce
Meyer, Jerry D.
Moody, J. Carroll
Norris, James D.
Parot, Joseph John
Posadas, Barbara Mercedes
Resis, Albert
Schneider, Robert W.
Schwarz, Jordan A.
Shesgreen, Sean Nicholas
Spencer, Elaine Glovka
Spencer, George W.
Thurman, Alfonzo
Williams, Eddie R., Jr.
Wilson, Constance Maralyn

Deerfield
Baxter, Harold J.
Benson, Warren S.

Pointer, Steven R.

Edwardsville
Astour, Michael Czernichow
Chen, Ching-Chih
Nore, Ellen
Pearson, Samuel C.
Weingartner, James Joseph
Wilson, Rudolph George

Elgin
Broad, David B.

Elsah
Helmer, Stephen

Evanston
Berger, Martin
Binford, Henry C.
Blier, Suzanne Preston
Breen, Timothy Hall
Clayson, S. Hollis
Davis, Whitney
Dillon, Diane
Dobbs, Betty Jo (Teeter)
Eldred, Katherine O.
Fraser, Sarah
Garrison, Daniel
Garrison, David H.
Haimowitz, Natalie Reader
Harris, Robert Allen
Heyck, Thomas William
Hindman, Sandra L.
Joravsky, David
Kieckhefer, Richard
Kotler, Philip
Lowe, Eugene Y., Jr.
Mokyr, Joel
Monoson, S. Sara
Monroe, Betty I.
Moskos, Charles C.
Mueller, Martin
Muir, Edward
Murphy, Larry G.
Okoye, Ikem
Packer, James
Perry, Edmund
Petry, Carl Forbes
Reginald, Allen
Roosevelt, A.C.
Safford, Frank Robinson
Seymour, Jack L.
Sherry, Michael Stephen
Steinberg, Salme Harju
Stone-Richards, Michael
Van Zanten, David
Vandiver, Elizabeth
Wallace, Robert
Werckmeister, O.K.
Wilkins, Leona B.
Wright, John

Galesburg
Bailey, Stephen
Davis, Rodney Owen
Gold, Penny Schine
Hane, Mikiso
Hord, Frederick Lee

Greenville
Huston, Richard P.
Stephens, William Richard

Grinnell
Sortor, M.

Homewood
Gerrish, Brian Albert

Jacksonville
Burnette, Rand
Davis, James Edward
Koss, David Henry
Tracey, Donald Richard

Lake Forest
Benton, Catherine
Ebner, Michael Howard
Lemahieu, Dan Lloyd
Sadri, Ahmad
Schulze, Franz
Zilversmit, Arthur

Lincolnwood
Singer, David G.

Lombard
Dayton, Donald Wilber

Macomb
Brown, Spencer Hunter
Burton, William Lester
Leonard, Virginia Waugh
Palmer, Scott W.
Sutton, Robert Paul

Maywood
Roeber, Anthony G.

Monmouth
Cordery, Simon
Cordery, Stacy A. Rozek
Urban, William Lawrence

Naperville
Mueller, Howard Ernest

Normal
Austensen, Roy Allen
Davis, Gloria-Jeanne
Freed, John Beckmann
Holsinger, M. Paul
Homan, Gerlof Douwe
Jelks, Edward Baker
Schapsmeier, Edward Lewis
Sessions, Kyle Cutler
Snyder, David W.
Springer, Carl P. E.
Walker, Lawrence David

Oak Brook
Durnbaugh, Donald F.

Oak Park
Greenhouse, Wendy
Robinet, Harriette Gillem
Young, Alfred F.

Orland Park
Antia, Kersey H.

Ottawa
Devine, Donald J.

Peoria
Bowers, William Lavalle
Guzman, Gregory G.

Quincy
Dressler, Hermigild

River Forest
Hays, Rosalind Conklin
Holli, Melvin
Stadtwald, Kurt

Riverside
Martin, Marty

Rock Island
Calder, Lendol
Hauck, Paul A.
Kivisto, Peter
Mayer, Thomas F.
Symons, Van J.
Tredway, John Thomas

Springfield
Bridges, Roger Dean
Jackson, Jacqueline Dougan
Taylor, Richard Stuart
Van Der Slik, Jack Ronald

University Park
Kennedy, Joyce S.

Urbana
Accad, Evelyne
Bernard, Paul Peter
Bruner, Edward M.
Buckler, John
Burton, Orville Vernon
Calder, William M.
Copeland, Robert M.
Cornelius, Janet Duitsman
Cuffey, Kenneth H.
Cuno, Kenneth M.
Fritzsche, Peter
Hitchins, Keith
Irish, Sharon
Jacobson, Howard
Jaher, Frederic Cople
Jakle, John Allais
Love, Joseph L.
Lynn, John A.
Mckay, John Patrick

Mitchell, Richard E.
Nettl, Bruno
Nettl, Bruno
Newman, John Kevin
Nichols, Jalden
Nikelly, Arthur G.
Porton, Gary Gilbert
Salamon, Sonya
Sansone, David
Scanlan, Richard T.
Solberg, Winton Udell
Spence, Clark Christian
Stewart, Charles Cameron
Sutton, Robert Mize
Temperley, Nicholas
Toby, Ronald P.
Violas, Paul Constantine
Walker, Juliet Elise Kirkpatrick
Wallach, Luitpold

Wauconda
Bolchazy, Ladislaus J.

Wheaton
Hawthorne, Gerald F.
Kay, Thomas O.
Lewis, James F.
Madigan, Mary
Noll, Mark Allan
Ziefle, Helmut Wilhelm

Wilmette
Huppert, George
Smith, Lacey Baldwin

INDIANA

Anderson
Nelson, J. Douglas
Rable, George Calvin
Robertson, Patricia C.

Angola
Zimmerman, James Allen

Bloomington
Alter, George
Bannon, Cynthia J.
Bertoloni Meli, Domenico
Bodnar, John Edward
Brooks, George E.
Brown, A. Peter
Brown, Mary Ellen
Buelow, George John
Burnim, Mellonee Victoria
Burns, Sarah
Byrnes, Robert Francis
Caldwell, L.K.
Capshew, J. H.
Carmichael, Ann Grayton
Choksy, Jamsheed K.
Christ, Matthew R.
Churchill, Frederick Barton
Cohen, William B.
Cole, Bruce
Davies, Ivor Kevin
Endelman, Todd Michael
Facos, Michelle
Faries, Molly
Ferrell, Robert Hugh
Franklin, James L., Jr.
Fratianni, Michele
Gealt, Adelheid Medicus
Glowacki, Kevin T.
Grant, Edward
Gronbjerg, Kirsten Anderson
Halporn, James Werner
Hansen, William F.
Hart, Jeffrey Allen
Hudson, Herman C.
Irvine, B.J.
Jelavich, Barbara
Johnson, Owen V.
Kaplan, Herbert Harold
Katz, Irving
Kennedy, Janet
Kleinbauer, W. Eugene
Kleinbauer, W. Eugene
Koertge, Noretta
Lankford, Nelson Douglas
Leach, Eleanor W.
Lloyd, Elisabeth A.
Lohmann, Christoph Karl
Long, Timothy
Lucas, Paul Robert
Madison, James H.

Mathiesen, Thomas J.
Maultsby, Portia K.
McGerr, M.
McNaughton, Patrick
Mehlinger, Howard Dean
Nader, Helen
Nagle, Betty Rose
Nelson, Susan
Peterson, M. Jeanne
Pletcher, David Mitchell
Rabinowitch, Alexander
Riley, J.C.
Scheifele, Eleanor L.
Sheehan, Bernard W.
Sieber, Roy
Sorrenson, Richard J.
Strauss, Gerald
Thorelli, Hans Birger
Tischler, Hans
Westfall, Richard Samuel
Wilson, George Macklin

Clarksville
Kramer, Carl Edward

Crawford
Danby, Judd G.

Crawfordsville
Barnes, James John
Davis, George H.

Elkhart
Dyck, Cornelius John

Evansville
Bigham, Darrel Eugene
Pitzer, Donald Elden
Richardson, Donald

Fort Wayne
Bell, John P.
Blumenshine, Gary B.
Cantor, Louis
Fischer, Bernd
Haw, James A.
Scott, Clifford H.
Violette, Aurele J.

Gary
Cohen, Ronald Dennis
Taylor Guthrie, Danille

Goshen
Berry, Lee Roy, Jr.

Greencastle
Huffman, Carl A.
Schlotterbeck, John Thomas
Warren, Stanley
Wilson, John Barney

Hagerstown
Lambert, Byron C.

Hammond
Trusty, Norman Lance

Hanover
Caine, Stanley Paul

Indianapolis
Anderson, David L.
Ashanin, Charles B.
Divita, James John
Geib, George Winthrop
Gray, Ralph D.
Harris, Edward E.
Langsam, Miriam Zelda
Libby, Justin Harris
Little, Monroe Henry
Planeaux, Christopher
Saffire, Paula Reiner
Sehlinger, Peter J.

Lafayette
Stover, John Ford

Muncie
Edmonds, Anthony Owens
Flores, Carol A.
Greenwood, Theresa M. Winfrey
Hoover, Dwight W
Hozeski, Bruce William
Jackson, Philip Taylor
Koumoulides, John A.
Perera, Nihal

Seager, Sharon Hannum
Weakland, John Edgar

New Albany
Bowden, James Henry
Findling, John Ellis
Thackeray, Frank W.
Wolf, Thomas Phillip

North Manchester
Bishop, C. James
Brown, Kenneth Lee
Deeter, Allen C

Notre Dame
Amar, Joseph P.
Bauer, Joseph P.
Bergen, Doris
Blantz, Thomas E.
Collins, James M.
Costello, Donald Paul
Crowe, Michael J.
Cushing, James T.
Dolan, Jay P.
Donahoe, Bernard Francis
Dowty, Alan K.
Ghilarducci, Teresa
Hamlin, Christopher S.
Hare, John
Hatch, Nathan O.
Kazin, Alfred
Keselman, Thomas A.
Leyerle, Blake
Louthan, Howard
Marsden, G.M.
Moody, Peter R.
O'Boyle, Cronelius
Pike, Fredrick Braun
Reydams-Schils, Gretchen
Schlereth, Thomas J.
Shaffer, Thomas Lindsay
Sloan, Phillip R.
Smith, Randall Brian
Spillman, Lynette P.
Turner, James
Weber, Ronald
Weigert, Andrew Joseph
Westfall, Carroll W.

Rensselaer
Heiman, Lawrence Frederick

Richmond
Bailey, Jackson Holbrook
Barbour, Hugh
Blakey, George Thomas
Brown, Mark M.
Cline, Peter Knox
Goertzen, Chris
Hamm, Thomas D.
Roop, Eugene F.
Southard, Robert Fairbairn

South Bend
Block, Joyce
Brinkley, George A.
Furlong, Patrick Joseph
Marti, Donald B.
Scherer, Paul Henry
Schreiber, Roy
Stockman, Robert H.
Tull, Charles Joseph
Wegs, James Robert

Terre Haute
Baker, Ronald Lee
Bakerman, Jane Schnabel
Bone, Quentin
Christianson, Gale Edward
Clouse, Robert G.
Giffin, William Wayne
Jegede, Dele
Muyumba, Francois N.
Pierard, Richard Victor
Robinson, Ruth
Shoemaker, Rebecca Shepherd
Spann, Edward Kenneth
Swindell, Warren C.

Upland
Ringenberg, William Carey
Winquist, Alan Hanson

Valparaiso
Corazzo, Nina
Howard, Thomas A.
Krodel, Gottfried G.
Ludwig, Theodore Mark

Morgan, David
Nordling, John G.
Rast, Walter Emil
Schoppa, Robert Keith
Startt, James Dill

Vincennes
Rinderle, Walter
Verkamp, Bernard

West Lafayette
Babrow, Austin S.
Bartlett, Robert V.
Berthrong, Donald John
Contreni, John Joseph
Curd, Martin Vincent
Curd, Patricia
Curtis, Susan
Deflem, Mathieu
Fouche, Rayvon
Gordon, Leonard H.D.
Gorn, Elliott J.
Haywood, Richard Mowbray
Ingrao, Charles William
Kirby, John T.
Kuehn, Manfred
Larson, John Lauritz
May, Robert Evan
McGee, Reece Jerome
Mork, Gordon Robert
Nof, Shimon Y.
Parman, Donald L.
Parman, Donald Lee
Rajagopal, Arvind
Rothenberg, Gunther Eric
Saunders, Elmo Stewart
Scott, Kermit
Seigfried, Charlene
Teaford, Jon C.
Tucker, Mark
Wang, Aihe
Woodman, Harold David

Westville
Jablon, Howard

Worthington
Clary, David Allen

IOWA

Ames
Avalos, Hector
Bloomer, Jennifer A.
Cravens, Hamilton
Dobson, John Mccullough
Fink, Deborah R.
Keller, Clair Wayne
Madison, Kenneth Glenn
Mccarthy, Dennis Michael Patrick
Mcjimsey, George Tilden
Plakans, Andrejs
Rudge, David W.
Ruebel, James
Schofield, Robert Edwin
Schwieder, Dorothy Ann
Shank, Wesley I.
Silet, Charles Loring Provine
Wilson, David B.
Wilt, Alan Freese
Zimmerman, Zora Devrnja

Cedar Falls
Burstein, Andrew
Gilgen, Albert R.
Glenn, George
Isenberg, Nancy G.
Johnson, John W.
Maier, Donna J. E.
Sunseri, Alvin Raymond
Talbott, Robert Dean
Walker, David Allan

Cedar Rapids
Carroll, Rosemary F.
Lisio, Donald John
Mungello, David Emil

Davenport
McDaniel, George William

Decorah
Bunge, Wilfred F.
Christianson, John Robert
Cole, Richard G.
Couch, Leon W., III

KANSAS

Grewal, Joyti
Hervey, Norma J.
Iudin-Nelson, Laurie
Kemp, Henrietta J.
Kuehn, D.D.
Kurth, William Charles
Sieber, John Harold
Tebbenhoff, Edward H.
Wilkie, Jacqueline S.
Williams, Lawrence H.

Des Moines
Barton, Mike Alan
Harris, Charles David
Worthen, Thomas

Dubuque
Albin, Thomas R.
Drummond, Richard Henry
Healey, Robert Mathieu
Kang, Wi Jo
Quere, Ralph Walter
Scharnau, Ralph William
Wilkie, William E.

Forest City
Hamre, James S.

Grinnell
Kaiser, Daniel Hugh
Lalonde, Gerald Vincent
Wall, Joseph Frazier

Indianola
Walt, Joseph W.

Iowa City
Baynton, Douglas C.
Bozeman, Theodore Dwight
Ciochon, Russell L.
Cuttler, Charles David
Depuma, Richard Daniel
Detmer, Hellena R.
Duck, Steve
Eckhardt, Patricia
Folsom, Lowell Edwin
Gelfand, Lawrence E.
Hale, Charles Adams
Hanley, Sarah
Harris, Michael Wesley
Hawley, Ellis Wayne
Hornsby, Roger Allen
Horton, Loren Nelson
Horwitz, Henry Gluck
Jones, Phillip Erskine
Kaplan, Benjamin J.
Kerber, Linda Kaufman
McCloskey, Deirdre
McPherson, James Alan
Michaels, Paula A.
Nickelsburg, George William
Elmer
Rohrbough, Malcolm Justin
Schacht, John N.
Schwalm, Leslie A.
Spitzer, Alan B
Stratton, John Ray
Tomasini, Wallace John
Woodard, Fredrick

Marshalltown
Colbert, Thomas Burnell

Mount Vernon
Allin, Craig Willard

Oskaloosa
Porter, David L.

KANSAS

Baldwin
English, John Cammel

Emporia
Bonner, Mary Winstead
Dicks, Samuel Eugene
Torrey, Glenn E.

Fort Leavenworth
Spiller, Roger Joseph

Hays
Luehrs, Robert Boice
Schmeller, Helmut John

Hutchinson
Chalfant, William Y.

Lawrence
Alexander, John T.
Antonio, Robert
Bailey, Victor
Bays, Daniel Henry
Brundage, James A.
Cienciala, Anna M.
Clark, John Garretson
Clark, Walter
Corbeill, Anthony
Dardess, John Wolfe
Goodman, Grant Kohn
Gordon, Jacob U.
Greaves, Rose Louise
Katzman, David Manners
Laird, Paul
Li, Chu-Tsing
Lombardo, Stanley
Mccoy, Donald Richard
Miller, Timothy
Nelson, Lynn Harry
Paludan, Phillip Shaw
Saul, Norman Eugene
Shaw, Michael
Shortridge, James R.
Stansifer, Charles Lee
Stokstad, Marilyn Jane
Sweets, John Frank
Wilson, Theodore A.
Yetman, Norman Roger

Leavenworth
Berlin, Robert Harry

Manhattan
Carey, James Charles
Ferguson, Clyde Randolph
Frey, Marsha Lee
Hamscher, Albert Nelson
Higham, Robin
Kaufman, Burton
Kren, George M.
Linder, Robert Dean
Mcculloh, John Marshall
Nafziger, E. Wayne
Socolofsky, Homer Edward
Suleiman, Michael W.

North Newton
Juhnke, James Carlton
Piper, Jon Kingsbury

Pittsburg
Cornish, Dudley Taylor
Hurley, David
Raverty, Dennis
Schick, James Baldwin Mcdonald
Walther, Thomas Robert

Salina
Spencer, Heath A.

Topeka
Danker, Donald Floyd
Haywood, C. Robert

Wichita
Born, John D.
Chang, Dae Hong
Douglas, Donald Morse
Dreifort, John E.
Duram, James C.
Gaunt, Philip
Gleissner, Stephen
Gythiel, Anthony P.
Johnson, Judith R.
Klunder, Willard C.
McCormick, Robert B.
Merriman, Mira P.
Miner, Craig
Murdock, Katherine
Rosenthal, Lisa
Skaggs, Jimmy M.
Smith, Patrick
Sowards, Jesse Kelley
Tomayko, James Edward
Torbenson, Craig L.
Unrau, William Errol

Winfield
Mueller, Roland Martin

KENTUCKY

Berea
Bolin, John Seelye
Nelson, Paul David
Schneider, Robert J.

Bowling Green
Ardrey, Saundra Curry
Bennett, James D.
Coutts, Brian E.
Harrington, Jesse Drew
Harrison, Lowell Hayes
Jackson, Carlton Luther
Klein, Michael Eugene
Lee, David Dale
Lucas, Marion Brunson
Salisbury, Richard Vanalstyne
Speer, Donald
Tuck, Donald Richard
Veenker, Ronald Allen
Vos, Arvin G.
Weigel, Richard David

Crestview Hills
Cimprich, John V.

Danville
Brown, Richard Carl
Foreman, George
Hamm, Michael Franklin
Joyce, Jane W.
Levin, William R.
Morrison, James V.
Newhall, David Sowle

Edgewood
Borne, Lawrence Roger

Frankfort
Griffin, Betty Sue
Klotter, James Christopher

Grayson
Wineland, John D.

Highland Heights
Adams, Michael Charles C
Ramage, James Alfred
Vitz, Robert C.
Washington, Michael Harlan

Lexington
Albisetti, James C.
Alvey, Richard Gerald
Banning, Lance
Banning, Lance G.
Betts, Raymond Frederick
Cawelti, John George
Chassen-Lopez, Francie R.
Christianson, Eric Howard
Eastwood, Bruce Stansfield
Freehling, William W.
Hargreaves, Mary Wilma Massey
Harris, Joseph John, III
Heath, Robin L.
Herring, George C.
Ireland, Robert M.
Jones, Paul Henry
Krislov, Joseph
Longyear, Rey Morgan
Nugent, Donald Chrostopher
Olson, Robert
Petrone, Karen
Phillips, Jane Ellen
Popkin, Jeremy D.
Robinson, Andrew
Roland, Charles P.
Servlnikov, Sergio
Smith, Daniel B.
Starr-LeBeau, Gretchen D.
Swift, Louis Joseph
Warth, Robert Douglas
Wilkinson, Doris
Withington, William Adriance
Yang, Sung Chul

Louisville
Anderson, Marvin W.
Block, Daniel I.
Blustein, Bonnie Ellen
Burnett, Donald L.
Chancellor, James D.
Curry, Leonard Preston
Deering, Ronald F.
deZeeuw, Anne Marie
Dickson, John H.
Gouverneur, Gray Henry

Hoyt-O'Connor, Paul E.
Hudson, James Blaine, III
Kebric, Robert Barnett
Mackey, Thomas
Maloney, Thomas
Morgan, William
Mulder, John Mark
Rothenbusch, Esther H.
Slavin, Arthur J.
Webber, Randall C.
Wills, Gregory A.

Morehead
Leroy, Perry Eugene
Sprague, Stuart Seely

Murray
Cartwright, Joseph Howard

Newport
Purvis, Thomas L.

Nicholasville
Eller, Ronald D.

Richmond
Ellis, William Elliott
Forderhase, Rudolph Eugene
Graybar, Lloyd Joseph
Hay, Melba Porter
Hill, Ordelle Gerhard
Stebbins, Robert E.

Wilmore
Arnold, Bill T.
Hamilton, Victor Paul
Kinghorn, Kenneth Cain

LOUISIANA

Alexandria
Thompson, Larry

Baton Rouge
Batinski, Emily E.
Becker, Robert Arthur
Carleton, Mark Thomas
Cassidy, Jane W.
Clarke, William M.
Cooper, William
Culbert, David H.
Di Maio, Irene Stocksieker
Djebar, Assia
Edgeworth, Robert J.
Edwards, Jay D.
Gellrich, Michelle
Henderson, John B.
Holtman, Robert Barney
Lindenfeld, David Frank
Loos, John Louis
Loveland, Anne Carol
Mattingly, Carol
McGee, Patrick
Oliver, Lisi
Peoples, VerJanis Andrews
Ridgel, Gus Tolver
Royster, Charles William
Schierling, Stephen P.
Schufreider, Gregory
Sirridge, Mary
Tarver, Leon R., II
Tolson, Arthur L.
Torrecilla, Jesus
Vincent, Charles
Warga, Richard G., Jr.

Hammond
Kurtz, Michael L.
McGehee, R.V.

Lafayette
Conrad, Glenn Russell
Fackler, Herbert Vern
Garrett, Aline M.
Gentry, Judith Anne Fenner
Richard, Carl J.
Schoonover, Thomas David

Lake Charles
Goins, Scott
Watson, Thomas Davis

Monroe
James, Elridge M.
Legan, Marshall Scott

Natchitoches
Thomas, Jean D'Amato

New Orleans
Altman, Ida
Anderson, Nancy Fix
Berlin, Netta
Billings, William M.
Boles, John Bruce
Brown, Marilyn
Brumfield, William Craft
Carter, Jane B.
Clark, Michael Dorsey
Collin, Richard H.
Cook, Bernard Anthony
Cummings, Anthony M.
Desai, Gaurav Gajanan
Ebel, Roland H.
Eskew, Harry Lee
Esthus, Raymond Arthur
Fann, Willerd Reese
Frey, Slyvia Rae
Goins, Richard Anthony
Greenleaf, Richard E.
Hirsch, Arnold Richard
James, Felix
Jenkins, A. Lawrence
Jordan, Eddie Jack, Sr.
Kehoe, Dennis P.
Kuczynski, Michael
Latner, Richard Barnett
Lazzerini, Edward James
Liuzza, Roy
Logsdon, Joseph
Malone, Bill Charles
McClay, Wilfred M.
Nair, Supryia
Poe, Joe Park
Reeves, Willaim Dale
Schafer, J.K.
Schlunz, Thomas Paul
Spaeth, Barbette S.
Swift, Mary Grace
Taylor, Herman Daniel
Tronzo, William
Tuttle, Richard J.
Verrett, Joyce M.
Vetrocq, Marcia E.
Washington, Robert Orlanda
Weiss, Ellen B.
Worthy, Barbara Ann

Ruston
Attrep, Abraham M.
Bush, John M.
Cook, Philip C.
Daly, John P.
Ingram, Earl Glynn
Meade, Wade C.
Rea, Kenneth W.
Webre, Stephen
Zalesch, Saul E.

Shreveport
Pederson, William David
Thompson, Alan Smith

MAINE

Bangor
Baker, William Joseph

Brunswick
Boyd, Barbara Weiden
Helmreich, Ernst Christian
Levine, Daniel
Walter, John Christopher

Farmington
Condon, Richard Herrick
Flint, Allen Denis

Lewiston
Hochstadt, Steve
Leamon, James Shenstone

New Vineyard
Bliss, Francis Royster

Orono
Babcock, Robert Harper
Battick, John Francis
Blanke, Richard
Doty, Charles Stewart
Fries, Russell Inslee
Ives, Edward Dawson

Mooney, L.M.
Munson, Henry Lee
Pease, Jane Hanna
Petrik, Paula E.
Smith, David Clayton
Smith, Laurence D.

Portland
Wagner, David

Strong
Decker, Leslie Edward

Waterville
Fleming, James Rodger
O'Neill, Kerill
Roisman, Hanna M.
Weisbrot, Robert S.

Woolwich
Martin, Kenneth R.

York Beach
Davison, Nancy R.

MARYLAND

Adelphi
Wallace, William A.

Annapolis
Abels, Richard
Barbera, Andre
Carr, Lois Green
Cochran, Charles Leo
Coletta, Paolo E.
Culham, Phyllis
DeCredico, Mary A.
Hagan, Kenneth James
Symonds, Craig Lee

Baltimore
Albrecht, Catherine
Anderson-Tanner, Frederick T., Jr.
Arnold, Joseph L.
Baker, Jean Harvey
Baldwin, John Wesley
Bardaglio, Peter W.
Bell, John D.
Bett, Richard
Blumberg, Arnold
Boehling, Rebecca
Breihan, John R.
Brennan, Timothy J.
Brieger, Gert Henry
Browne, Gary L.
Browne, Gary Lawson
Burke, Colin B.
Catania, Anthony Charles
Cohen, Warren I.
Cooper, Jerrold Stephen
Cripps, Thomas
Curtin, Philip De Armond
Davisson, Mary H.T.
Donaghy, Thomas J.
Durham, Joseph Thomas
Elfenbein, Jessica
Faulcon, Clarence Augustus, II
Fee, Elizabeth
Forscher Weiss, Susan
Forster, Robert
Freedman, Robert Owen
Galambos, Louis Paul
Gardner, Bettye J.
Geiger, Mary Virginia
Gittlen, Barry M
Goedicke, Hans
Goldthwaite, Richard A.
Gorman, Michael J.
Greene, Jack P.
Grubb, James S.
Guy, Fred
Hall, Tom
Ham, Debra Newman
Harrison, Daphne Duval
Haynes, James H.
Herbert, Sandra
Herbert, Sandra Swanson
Higham, John
Hopkins, Fred
Hrabowski, Freeman Alphonsa, III
Irwin, John Thomas
Jacklin, Thomas M.
Jeffrey, Julie Roy
Jeffries, John W.
Jusczyk, P.W.

Kagan, Richard Lauren
Kargon, Robert
Kars, Marjoleine
Kessler, Herbert Leon
King, Ora Sterling
King-Hammond, Leslie
Knight, Franklin W.
Knight, Franklin Willis
Larew, Karl Garret
Legon, Ronald
Lidtke, Vernon Leroy
McConnell, Roland Calhoun
Mitchell, Reid
Mruck, Armin Einhard
Mulcahey, Donald C.
Murray, Mabel Lake
Neverdon-Morton, Cynthia
Papadakis, Aristeides
Pegram, Thomas R.
Phillips, Glenn Owen
Ranum, Orest
Ritschel, Daniel
Roller, Matthew B.
Russell-Wood, A.J.R.
Ryon, Roderick Naylor
Sawyer, Jeffrey K.
Scherer, Imgard S.
Shapiro, H. Alan
Slavin, Robert Edward
Spitzer, John
Spring, David
Stanley, Julian Cecil
Stanton, Phoebe Baroody
Struever, Nancy Schermerhorn
Sweeney, John Albert
Talley, William B.
Tatarewicz, Joseph N.
Terborg-Penn, Rosalyn M.
Tolbert, Elizabeth D.
Vaporis, Constantine N.
Varga, Nicholas
Walker, Ernestein
Walker, Mack
Walters, Ronald Gordon
Webb, Robert Kiefer
Weiss, Piero
Weiss, Susan Forscher
Wexler, Victor G.
Yip, Ka-che
Zhuk, Sergei I.

Bethesda
Cassedy, James Higgins
Hewlett, Richard Greening
Smith, Dale Cary
Waserman, Manfred

Bowie
Miller, M. Sammye

Burtonsville
Rothfeld, Anne

Catonsville
Loerkw, William

Chestertown
Janson-La Palme, Bayly
Tatum, Nancy R.

Chevy Chase
Gutowski, Carolyn
Patterson, David Sands
Timbie, Janet Ann

College Park
Albert, Peter J.
Bedos-Rezak, Brigitte
Belz, Herman Julius
Berlin, Adele
Berlin, I.
Bradbury, Miles L.
Breslow, Marvin A.
Brown, Richard Harvey
Brush, Stephen George
Caughey, John L.
Colantuono, Anthony
Cole, Wayne S.
Corbin Sies, Mary
Cunningham, William Dean
Darden, Lindley
Davidson, Roger Harry
Denny, Don William
Doherty, Lillian E.
Eckstein, A.M.
Evans, Emory Gibbons
Finkelstein, Barbara
Flack, J..Kirkpatrick

Friedel, Robert D.
Gerstel, Sharon E.J.
Gilbert, James Burkhart
Grimsted, David Allen
Gullickson, Gay Linda
Hallett, Judith P.
Hampton, Robert L.
Harlan, Louis R.
Harris, James F.
Henretta, James A.
Jashemski, Wilhelmina F.
Kornbluth, Geneva
Lee, Hugh Ming
Lesher, James
Lounsbury, Myron
Lyons, Clare A.
Matossian, Mary Kilbourne
Ming Lee, Hugh
Mintz, Lawrence E.
Olson, Alison Gilbert
Olson, Keith Waldemar
Paoletti, Jo
Peller Hallett, Judith
Pressly, William L.
Price, Richard
Promey, Sally M.
Ridgway, Whitman Hawley
Ritzer, George
Rutledge, Steven H.
Scott Jenkins, Virginia
Segal, David R.
Spiegel, Gabrielle Michele
Staley, Gregory A.
Sthele, Eva
Sumida, Jon Tetsuro
Terchek, Ronald John
Vann, Robert Lindley
Walters, Ronald
Warren, Donald R
Warren, J. Benedict
Zilfi, Madeline Carol

Columbia
Ligon, Doris Hillian
Mitchell, Helen Buss
Wolter, John A.

Darnestown
Knox, Bernard MacGregor Walker

Elkton
Coulet Du Gard, Rene

Ellicott City
West, Herbert Lee, Jr.

Emmitsburg
Johnson, Curtis
Kalas, Robert
Krysiek, James
Whitman, T. Stephen

Fort Washington
Demolen, Richard Lee
Gustafson, Milton Odell

Frederick
Keeler, Mary Frear

Frostburg
Clulee, Nicholas H.
Rhodes, Randall
Wiseman, John Bailes

Gaithersburg
Dierenfield, Bruce Jonathan

Largo
James, David Phillip

Leonardtown
Winnik, Herbert Charles

North Potomac
Kapsch, Robert J.

Pasadena
De Pauw, Linda Grant

Princess Anne
Harleston, Robert Alonzo

Rockville
Cantelon, Philip Louis
Kimes, Don

Salisbury
Tompson, G. Ray

Silver Spring
Abraham, Daniel
Berger, Carl
Moore, Robert Henry
Null, Elisabeth M.
Robbins, Paul Richard
Smith, Paul Hubert
Svejda, George J.
Ulrich, Homer
Winston, Michael R.

St. Mary's City
Stabile, Donald Robert

St. Michaels
McLoud, Melissa

Takoma Park
Hammond, James Matthew

Towson
Esslinger, Dean Robert
Evangeliou, Christos C.
Leahy, David G.

Westminster
Evergates, Theodore

MASSACHUSETTS

Allston
D'Agostino, Peter R.

Amherst
Altstadt, Audrey L.
Avrech Berkman, Joyce
Barton, Carlin
Benson, Jack Leonard
Berkman, Joyce A.
Bliss, Katherine
Bowman, Joye L.
Boyer, Horace Clarence
Boyle, Kevin
Brigham, John
Brown, Dennis T.
Cantor, Milton
Cheyette, Fredric Lawrence
Chrisman, Miriam Usher
Cohen, Alvin Philip
Couvares, F.G.
Davidov, Judith Fryer
Depillis, Mario Stephen
Dizard, Jan
Drake, Fred
Fabos, Julius Gyula
Gentry, Atron A.
Glassberg, David
Goldman, Sheldon
Gordon, Daniel
Guttmann, Allen
Harbison, Craig
Hawkins, Hugh Dodge
Heffernan, Charles
Higginson, John
Johnston, William M.
Jones, Byrd Luther
Jones, Robert
Jones, Robert Edward
Karpinski, Gary S.
Kitchell, Kenneth F.
Klare, Michael T.
Laurie, Bruce
Lawall, Gilbert Westcott
Levine, Sura
Levy, Barry
Levy, Barry
Love, Barbara
Marshall, Peter K.
May, Ernest
Mazor, Lester Jay
McFarland, Gerald W.
Minear, Richard H.
Nightingale, Carl
Nissenbaum, Stephen W.
Nissenbaum, Stephen Willner
Norton, Paul F.
Owens, Larry
Peiss, Kathy
Pelz, Stephen Ernest
Petropulos, John Anthony
Philippides, Marios
Platt, Gerald M.
Potash, Robert Aaron

Rausch, Jane M.
Rearick, Charles
Reck, David
Richards, Leonard
Roskill, Mark
Ryavec, Karl William
Sandweiss, Martha
Sarti, Roland
Schwartz, Marvin
Shary, Timothy
Shipley, Neal Robert
Story, Ronald
Swartz, Marvin
Sweeney, Kevin
Tager, Jack
Tillis, Frederick C.
Trehub, Arnold
Ware, Ronald Dean
Watkins, Andrea
Wickwire, Mary B.
Wilson, Mary C.
Wobst, H. Martin
Wyman, David S

Andover
Dalton, Kathleen Mary

Auburndale
Vaccaro, Joseph

Belmont
Brauer, Carl Malcolm

Boston
Amiji, Hatim M.
Bacon, Mardges
Beaudry, Mary Carolyn
Bell, James Brugler
Bennett, Norman Robert
Blaisdell, Charmarie Jenkins
Blessington, Francis Charles
Boskin, Joseph
Breines, Winifred
Bruce, Robert Vance
Burns, Carol J.
Campbell, Ballard C.
Cash, Philip
Chesson, Michael B.
Chu, Jonathan M.
Corrin, Jay Patrick
Cottle, Thomas J.
Cromley, Elizabeth
Diefendorf, Barbara Boonstoppel
El-Baz, Farouk
Foss, Clive
Fowler, William Morgan
Fredriksen, P.
Gagliardo, John G.
Gilbert, Robert Emile
Glick, Thomas F.
Green, Harvey
Greenberg, Kenneth
Hankin, Alan Lee
Hansen, Julie
Henderson, Jeffrey
Herman, Gerald Harvey
Jacobs, Donald Martin
Jefferson, Carter
Kaufman, Deborah Renee
Kee, Howard Clark
Keylor, William Robert
Larson, Calvin J.
Lepore, Jill
Leventhal, Fred Marc
Lint, Gregg Lewis
Lyman, Richard B.
Malinowski, Michael J.
Mason, Herbert Warren
Mayer, Henri Andre Van Huysen
McMullin, Thomas Austin
Miller, Naomi
Ness, Arthur J.
Nisetich, Frank
Orlow, Dietrich Otto
Parker, Simon B.
Perricone, Jack
Pruett, Gordon Earl
Psathas, George
Quitt, Martin Herbert
Riely, John C.
Rosen, Stanley H.
Rothwell, Kenneth S.
Ruck, Carl Anton Paul
Ryan, Kevin
Schachter, Gustav
Scharf, Bertram
Scully, Stephen P.
Seipp, David J.
Silber, Nina

Tauber, Alfred I.
Tawa, Nicholas E.
Tick, Judith
Tokunaga, Emiko
Tucker, Louis Leonard
Vietor, Richard Henry Kingsbury
Walters, Hubert Everett
Warren, Joseph David
Winch, Julie P.
Zack, Arnold Marshall

Bridgewater
Karavites, Peter
Turner, Thomas Reed

Brookline
Brenner, Louis
Gabel, Creighton
Perdicoyianai-Paleologou, Helene
Smith, Joanna S.

Cambridge
Aaron, Daniel
Ackerman, James Sloss
Anderson, Stanford Owen
Appiah, Kwame Anthony
Badian, Ernst
Bailyn, Bernard
Bailyn, Lotte
Baryosef, O.
Bisson, Thomas N.
Craig, Albert Morton
Daley, Brian Edward
Dominguez, Jorge Ignacio
Elliott, Clark Albert
Farmer, P.
Fideler, Paul Arthur
Field, Mark G.
Fogelson, Robert M.
Ford, Franklin Lewis
Gaskell, Ivan
Goldin, Claudia
Graham, Loren Raymond
Graham, Patricia Albjerg
Grimsted, Patricia Kennedy
Hall, David D.
Hammond, Mason
Handlin, Oscar
Harrington, Daniel Joseph
Heimert, Alan
Higonnet, Patrice
Hoffmann, Stanley
Hunt, Richard M.
Hutchison, William Robert
Jones, Christopher P.
Kahn, Jonathan
Karlsen, Carol F.
Kelman, Steven
Khoury, Philip S.
Kuhn, Thomas Samuel
Lamberg-Karlovski, Clifford Charles
Lockwood, Lewis Henry
Maccaffrey, Wallace T.
Macdougall, Elisabeth Blair
MacFarquer, Roderick
Maier, Pauline Rubbelke
Mazlish, Bruce
McGuire, Charles
Mendelsohn, Everett Irwin
Moore, Sally F.
Nagy, Gregory John
O'Malley, John William
Painter, Karen
Patterson, H. Orlando L.
Perkins, Dwight Heald
Pian, Rulan Chao
Posen, Barry R
Rabbat, Nasser O.
Ritvo, Harriet
Schafer, Elizabeth
Shavell, S.
Skolnikoff, Eugene B.
Smith, Merritt Roe
Solbrig, Otto Thomas
Tarrant, Richard John
Terrill, Ross
Tu, Wei-Ming
van der Merwe, Nikolaas Johannes
Wendelken, Cherie
Willey, Gordon R.
Wood, Charles B., III
Yannatos, James

Chestnut Hill
Braude, Benjamin
Breines, Paul
Buni, Andrew
Criscenti, Joseph Thomas

Cronin, James E.
Daly, William M.
Deleeuw, Patricia Allwin
Florescu, Radu R.
Friedman, Ellen G.
Garroutte, Eva
Green, Carol Hurd
Manning, Roberta Thompson
McDonough, Christopher Michael
Mcnally, Raymond T.
Murphy, Francis Joseph
Northrup, David Arthur
O'Connor, Thomas H.
Petillo, Carol Morris
Picklesimer, Dorman
Raelin, Joseph A.
Reinerman, Alan Jerome
Smith, Charles F., Jr.
Weiss, James Michael

Chicopee
Moriarty, Thomas Francis

Cohasset
Campbell, John Coert

Danvers
Davis, David D.

Dennis
Walcott, Robert

Dorchester
Thompson, Cynthia L.

Dudley
Smith, Thomas G.

East Orleans
Romey, William Dowden

Gorham
Schiferl, Ellen

Groton
Tyler, John W.

Hadley
Gonzalez De Leon, Fernando Javier

Harvard
Carroll, Charles Francis

Harwich Port
Berry, J. Duncan

Hatfield
Aldrich, Michele

Hingham
Bartlett, Irving Henry

Holden
Johnson, Donald Ellis

Jamaica Plain
Faxon, Alicia Craig

Leicester
Bell, Diane

Lexington
Thernstrom, Stephan Albert

Lincoln
Little, Elizabeth A.

Lincoln Center
Donald, David Herbert

Lowell
Blewett, Mary H.
De Girolami Cheney, Liana
Ogasapian, John

Marblehead
Devine, Mary E.

Marshfield
Henderson, H. James

Medford
Abramson, Daniel
Brooke, John L.
Caviness, Madeline H.

Drachman, Virginia Goldsmith
Krimsky, Sheldon
Laurent, Pierre Henri
Marcopoulos, George John
Marrone, Steven Phillip
Perry, John Curtis
Phillips, Joanne Higgins
Reid, Peter L.D.
Sherwin, Martin J.
Solomon, Howard Mitchell
Ueda, Reed T.
White, Barbara Ehrlich

Medway
Morvan, Jennifer

Milton
Hansen, Wells S.

Natick
Dolnikowski, Edith W.

New Braintree
Cooke, Nym

Newton
Porter, Jack Nusan
Tankard, Judith B.

Newtonville
Belsley, David A.

North Amherst
Greenbaum, Louis Simpson

North Andover
Ford, Peter Anthony

North Dartmouth
Huff, Toby E.
Koot, Gerard M.
Scionti, Joseph Natale
Stauder, Jack
Werly, John Mcintyre

Northampton
Ackelsbert, Martha A.
Brooks, E. Bruce
Buettner, Brigitte
Davis, John
Derr, Thomas Sieger
Felton, Craig
Ford, Andrew
Gintis, Herbert
Gregory, Justina Winston
Haddad, Robert Mitchell
Horowitz, Daniel
Houser, Caroline
Kellum, Barbara
Leibsohn, Dana
Leshko, Jaroslav
Mitchell, Betty L.
Morris-Hale, Walter
Nenner, Howard Allen
Rhie, Marylin
Salisbury, Neal
Sherr, Richard Jonathan

Norton
Bloom, Alexander
Chandra, Vipan
Coale, Samuel Chase
Crosby, Travis L.
Helmreich, Paul Christian
Manson Tomasek, Kathryn
Relihan, Joel C.
Sears, Elizabeth Ann

Oakham
Barnhill, Georgia Brady

Paxton
Bilodeau, Lorraine

Quincy
Cameron, James Reese
Yerxa, Donald A.

Roslindale
Holmes, Steven J.

Salem
Chomsky, Aviva

Sharon
Rudnick, Lois P.

Somerville
Mutschler, Ben
Race, Jeffery

South Hadley
Burns, Michael
Crosthwaite, Jane Freeman
Herbert, Eugenia Warren
Hill, Eugene David
Viereck, Peter

South Hamilton
Clark Kroeger, Catherine
Isaac, Gordon L.
Kaiser, Walter C., Jr.
Kuzmic, Peter
Rosell, Garth M.
Walters, Gwenfair
Wells, David Falconer

South Lancaster
Sbacchi, Alberto
Wehtje, Myron Floyd

Springfield
Bock, Robert L.

Sturbridge
Larkin, Jack

Sunderland
Ilardi, Vincent

Waltham
Binion, Rudolph
Black, Eugene Charlton
Freeze, Gregory L.
Geehr, Richard Stockwell
Jick, Leon Allen
Johnston, Patricia Ann
Jones, Jacqueline
Keller, Morton
Reinharz, Jehuda
Sarna, Jonathan D.
Todd, Ian Alexander
Whitfield, Stephen Jack

Wayland
Staudinger Lane, Evelyn
Walker, Robert Miller

Wellesley
Auerbach, Jerold Stephen
Cohen, Paul Andrew
Cudjoe, Selwyn Reginald
Fontijn, Claire
Hoopes, James
Jacobs, Ruth Harriet
Johnson, Roger A.
Lefkowitz, Mary Rosenthal
Malino, Frances
Martin, Tony
Merry, Sally E.
O'Gorman, James F.
Starr, Raymond James
Thrasher, William
Witte, Ann Dryden

Westfield
Ali, Kamal Hassan
Gerstein, Linda Groves
Kaufman, Martin
Kosar, Anthony J.
Leaver, Robin A.
Rife, Jerry E.
Shannon, Catherine Barbara

Weston
Grad, Bonnie L.
Laska, Vera
Meade, Catherine M.
Wasson, Ellis Archer
Wintle, Thomas

Williamstown
Beaver, Donald de Blasiis
Bloxam, M. Jennifer
Brown, Michael Fobes
Cassiday, Julie A.
Christensen, Kerry A.
Dew, Charles Burgess
Frost, Peter K.
Fuqua, Charles
Fuqua, Charles J.
Gagliardi, Frank M.
Goldstein, Darra
Hedreen, Guy
Helfant, Ian M.

Johnson, Emily
Kohut, Thomas A.
Kraus, Matthew A.
Oakley, Francis
Park, David Allen
Roberts, Kenneth C., Jr.
Rudolph, Frederick
Stoddard, Whitney S.
Suderburg, Robert
Tracy, Patricia Juneau
Wagner, William Gilson
Waite, Robert George Leeson
Wood, James Brian

Winchester
Meister, Maureen

Worcester
Attreed, Lorraine C.
Billias, George Athan
Borg, Daniel Raymond
Bullock, Steven C.
Burkett, Randall Keith
Catto, Bonnie
DeHoratius, Edmund F.
Dunn, Patrick Peter
Dykstra, Robert R.
Flynn, James Thomas
Hamilton, John Daniel Burgoyne
Hansen, Peter H.
Hench, John Bixler
Kealey, Edward J.
Kuzniewski, Anthony Joseph
Lapomarda, Vincent Anthony
Lavery, Gerard B.
Little, Douglas James
Lucas, Paul
Manfra, Jo Ann
Mcbride, Theresa Marie
Mcclymer, John Francis
Mccorison, Marcus Allen
Moynihan, Kenneth J.
Powers, James Francis
Sokal, Michael Mark
Vaughan, Alden T.
Von Laue, Theodore Herman

Worcester
Avery-Peck, Alan J.

MICHIGAN

Adrian
Fechner, Roger Jerome

Albion
Cocks, Geoffrey C.
Horstman, Allen

Allendale
Niemeyer, Glenn Alan

Alma
Massanari, Ronald Lee

Ann Arbor
Becker, Marvin Burton
Bono, Barbara Jane
Britton, Allen Perdue
Bryant, Bunyan I.
Burling, Robbins
Crawford, Richard
Eadie, John W.
Eisenstein, Elizabeth Lewishohn
Eley, Geoff
Fine, Sidney
Frier, Bruce Woodward
Goldstein, Laurence Alan
Green, Thomas Andrew
Grew, Raymond
Harrison, Don K., Sr.
King, John O.
Kirkpatrick, Diane Marie
Koenen, Ludwig
Krahmalkov, Charles R.
Lewis, David Lanier
Lindner, Rudi Paul
Malm, William P.
Marzolf, Marion Tuttle
McCarren, Vincent Paul
Moody, Charles David, Sr.
Ness, Gayl DeForrest
Patterson, Willis Charles
Pedley, John Griffiths
Perkins, Bradford
Pernick, Martin Steven

MINNESOTA

MISSISSIPPI

Kiger, Joseph Charles
Landon, Michael De Laval
Moysey, Robert Allen
Skemp, Sheila Lynn
Steel, David Warren
Swinden, Kevin J.
Watt, Jeffrey R.
Wilson, Charles Reagan

MISSOURI

Ballwin
Te, Jordan

Bolivar
Gallatin, Harlie Kay
Hooper, William Loyd

Canton
Lee, George Robert

Cape Girardeau
Hoffman, Steven J.
Veneziano, Carol

Columbia
Budds, Michael
Bullion, John Lewis
Burggraaff, Winfield J.
Camargo, Martin
Collins, Robert Maurice
Cunningham, Noble E., Jr.
Dorsey, Carolyn Ann
Estevez, Victor A.
Flader, Susan L.
Hocks, Elaine
Holland, Antonio F.
Hooley, Daniel M.
Koclitschek, Theodore
Koegel, John
Lears, T.J. Jackson
Lyman, R. Lee
Marshall, Howard Wight
Miller, Kerby A.
Nauert, Charles G.
Neff, Hector
Oglesby, James Robert
Pigg, Kenneth E.
Saylor, Charles F.
Schenker, David J.
Sperber, Jonathon
Strickland, Arvarh E.
Tarkow, Theodore A.
Timberlake, Charles
Wallace, Paul

Fulton
Lael, Richard Lee
Southern, David Wheaton

Jefferson City
Hoard, R.J.
Kremer, Gary R.
Steward, Dick Houston

Kansas City
Brodhead, Michael John
Clardy, Jesse V.
Deblauwe, Francis
Dolskaya-Ackerly, Olga
Eubanks, Eugene E.
Graham, John Thomas
Hattaway, Herman Morell
Hoffmann, Donald
Klausner, Carla Levine
LaBudde, Kenneth J.
Larsen, Lawrence H.
Lewis, Martha Hoffman
Lumin, Bernard
Moten, Chauncey Donald
Norton, Kay
Ogilvie, Leon Parker
Pogemiller, Leroy
Potts, Louis Watson
Robinson, Genevieve
Trani, Eugene Paul
Voigts, Linda Ehrsam

Kirksville
DeLancey, Julia
Orel, Sara E.
Presley, Paula
Ramsbottom, Mary Macmanus
Schnucker, Robert Victor

Maryville
Carneal, Thomas William

Point Lookout
Zabel, James Allen

Rolla
Ridley, Jack B.

Springfield
Dicke, Thomas Scott
Giglio, James Nicholas
Lewis, Andrew Wells
Luckert, Karl Wilhelm
Miller, Worth Robert
Moyer, James Carroll
Nugent, Pauline
Parsons, James

St. Louis
Allen, Garland E.
Barman, Lawrence
Beinfeld, Solon
Berger, Henry Weinberg
Bernstein, Iver
Bliss, Robert M.
Brock, Karen L.
Brown, Leslie
Burkholder, Mark A.
Childs, Elizabeth C.
Cooper, Jerry Marvin
Critchlow, D.T.
Dzuback, Mary Ann
Faherty, William Barnaby
Feuerhahn, Ronald R.
Finney, Paul Corby
Fiss, Karen A.
Fleener, Charles Joseph
Gerteis, Louis
Guentner, Frances J.
Hatch, George
Hause, Steven C.
Head, Thomas F.
Hirst, Derek M.
Hurley, Andrew J.
Izenberg, Gerald Nathan
Jenkins, Jennifer L.
Kolmer, Elizabeth
Konig, David Thomas
Korr, Charles P.
Leven, Charles Louis
Lowry, William R.
Madden, T.F.
Maltby, William Saunders
Miller, Angela L.
Miller, Howard Smith
Mitchell, Richard Hanks
Mumford, Eric
Okenfuss, Max Joseph
Ordower, Henry M.
Primm, James Neal
Riesenberg, Peter
Robbert, Louise Buenger
Roediger, Henry L.
Rosenbloom, Joseph R.
Rosin, Robert L.
Ross, Stephanie A.
Rowan, Steven
Ruddy, T. Michael
Sanchez, Jose Mariano
Schlafly, Phyllis Stewart
Schneider, Laurence
Shaffer, Arthur
Shaffer, Arthur H.
Shapiro, Henry L.
Suelflow, August Robert
Symeonoglou, Sarantis
Thro, Linus J.
Treadgold, Warren
Tsunoda, Elizabeth
Wallace, William
Walter, Richard John
Watson, Patty Jo
Weil, Mark S.
Wesselschmidt, Quentin F.
Williams, Robert Chadwell
Works, John A.
Zuck, Lowell H.

Warrensburg
Adams, Louis Jerold
Crews, Daniel A.
Crump, Gail Bruce
Foley, William Edward
Selvidge, Marla J.
Sylwester, Harold James
Young, James Van

MONTANA

Billings
Friguglietti, James
Small, Lawrence Farnsworth

Bozeman
Malone, Michael Peter
Mentzer, Raymond A.
Mullen, Pierce C.
Rydell, Robert William
Safford, Jeffrey Jaeger
Smith, Billy G.
Wessel, Thomas Roger
Witkin-New Holy, Alexandra

Great Falls
Furdell, Ellzabeth Lane

Helena
Lambert, Richard Thomas

Missoula
Flores, Dan
Fritz, Harry William
Grieves, Forest L.
Lauren, Paul Gordon
Lopach, James L.

NEBRASKA

Boys Town
Larzelere, R.E.

Crete
Hanson, Charles Parker

Kearney
Barua, Pradeep P.
Glazier, Stephen D.
Schuyler, Michael Wayne
Volpe, Vernon L.

Lincoln
Adkin, Neil
Ambrosius, Lloyd
Berger, Patrice
Braeman, John
Burnett, Amy
Burnett, Stephen G.
Burnett, Stephen G.
Cahan, David
Coble, Parks
Coope, Jessica
Cope, Esther Sidney
Dorsey, Learthen
Gorman, Vanessa
Homze, Edward L.
Ide, Harry
Kennedy, Dane Keith
Kleimola, Ann
Leinieks, Valdis
Lu, Suping
Luebke, Frederick Carl
Mahoney, Timothy
Maslowski, Peter
McClelland, James
Miller, Susan
Miller, Tice Lewis
Moulton, Gary Evan
Newman, Lex
Porsild, Charlene
Rader, Benjamin G.
Rawley, James A.
Rinkevich, Thomas E.
Sherman, William Lewis
Sosin, Jack Marvin
Steinweis, Alan
Turner, John D.
Vigil, Ralph Harold
Winkle, Kenneth
Winter, Thomas Nelson
Wunder, John

Omaha
Aikin, Roger
Arav, Rami
Beau, Bryan Le
Christensen, John E.
Dalstrom, Harl A.
Friedlander, Walter J.
Garcia, Juan Ramon
Jensen, Tim
Johansen, Bruce Elliott
Kuo, Lenore

LeBeau, Bryan
Mihelich, Dennis
Palmer, Russ
Pollak, Oliver Burt
Pratt, William C.
Schultenover, David
Shaffer, Nancy E.
Simmons, Jerold Lee
Tate, Michael Lynn
Thorson, J.A.
Welch, Ashton Wesley
Wunsch, James Stevenson

Seward
Fiala, Robert D.
Grothaus, Larry Henry

Wayne
Hickey, Donald Robert

NEVADA

Las Vegas
Babbitt, Beatrice C.
Bell, Andrew J.E.
Bell, Barbara Mosallai
Chung, Sue Fawn
Coughtry, Jay
Crank, Joe N.
Cronan Rose, Ellen
Davenport, Robert Wilson
Dil, Nasim
Eggener, Keith L.
Fawn Chung, Sue
Filler, John W.
Fry, Joseph A.
Goodwin, Joanne
Kelly, Cathie
Klein, Lawrence E.
Loader, Colin T.
Mattson, Vernon E.
Miller, Susan P.
Moehring, Eugene P.
Muccigrosso, Robert Henry
Pierce, Thomas B.
Rasmussen, Chris
Rollings, Willard H.
Rothman, Hal K.
Strawser, Sherri C.
White, Elizabeth
Whitney, Elspeth
Wright, Thomas C.

Reno
Achtenberg, Deborah
Casper, Scott E.
Hoffman, Piotr
Hulse, James W.
Marschall, John Peter
Nickles, Thomas
Reinshagen-Joho, Liane
Rusco, Elmer R.
Stevens, Kevin M.

NEW HAMPSHIRE

Bradford
Jacobsen, Thorkild

Concord
Mevers, Frank Clement

Durham
Bolster, W. Jeffrey
Brettschneider, Marla
Clark, Charles Edwin
Diefendorf, Jeffry Mindlin
Dorsey, Kurk
Fitzpatrick, Ellen
Frierson, Cathy A.
Golinski, Jan
Gould, Eliga H.
Gullace, Nicoletta F.
Harris, J. William
Kelleher, Patricia
McCann, Francis D., Jr.
McMahon, Gregory
Mennel, Robert Mckisson
Palmer, Stuart
Rouman, John Christ
Salyer, Lucy
Sitkoff, Harvard

Ulrich, Laurel Thatcher
Voll, John Obert
Wheeler, Douglas L.
Wolper, Ethel Sara

Exeter
Bedford, Henry F.
Cole, Donald Barnard
Wooley, Allan D.

Hancock
Bateson, Mary C.

Hanover
Cohen, Ada
Corrigan, Kathleen
Daniell, Jere Rogers
Doenges, Norman Arthur
Ermarth, Hans Michael
Garthwaite, Gene Ralph
Heck, Marlene
Hockley, Allen
Jordan, Jim
Kelley, Mary
Kenseth, Joy
Masters, Roger D.
McGrath, Robert
Pastor, Beatriz
Penner, Hans Henry
Randolph, Adrian W. B.
Rosenthal, Angela
Rutter, Jeremy B.
Scott, William Clyde
Shewmaker, Kenneth Earl
Spitzer, Leo
Whaley, Lindsay
Wood, Charles Tuttle
Wright, James Edward

Manchester
Cassidy, James G.
Constance, Joseph
Foster, Anne L.
Huff, Peter A.
Major, Wilfred E.
Mason, Francis M.
Pajakowski, Philip E.
Resch, John P.
Shannon, Sylvia C.

Pembroke
Garvin, James L.

Portsmouth
Hilson, Arthur Lee

Rye
Winslow, Richard E., III

NEW JERSEY

Camden
Carlisle, Rodney
Dorwart, Jeffery Michael
Hull, N.E.H.
Klinghoffer, Arthur Jay
Lees, Andrew

Cherry Hill
Bender, Henry V.
Butler, Rebecca Batts

Cranford
Hogan, Lawrence Daniel

Elizabeth
Lupia, John N.
Siegel, Adrienne

Englewood
Saloman, Ora Frishberg

Ewing
Dickinson, Gloria Harper
Gotthelf, Allan

Florham Park
Geissler, Suzanne Burr

Glassboro
Adelson, Fred B.
Applebaum, David
Grupenhoff, Richard
Hewsen, Robert
Hunter, Gary

Losada, Luis Antonio
Pascoe, Louis B.
Penella, Robert Joseph
Rogler, Lloyd H.
Ryan, James D.
Scherr, A.E.
Seraile, William
Struve, Walter
Von Arx, Jeffery P.
Weiss, John

Brooklyn
Berger, David
Bridenthal, Renate
Bridenthal, Renate
Clayman, Dee Lesser
Dorinson, Joseph
Edwards, Mary
Eisenstadt, Abraham S.
Fichtner, Paula Sutter
Fierce, Milfred C.
Filonowicz, Joseph
Fisher, Craig B.
Gabel, Jack
Gallagher, Mary A.Y.
Gisolfi, Diana
Gruber, Helmut
Haring, Lee
Hoogenboom, Ari
Karkhanis, Sharad
King, Margaret Leah
Klein, Bernard
Leeb, Isidore Leonard
Leiman, Sid Zalman
Mallory, Michael
McLaughlin, Andree Nicola
Menashe, Louis
Monteiro, Thomas
Page, Willie F.
Papayanis, Nicholas
Pile, John F.
Reguer, Sara
Schaar, Stuart H.
Sengupta, Gunja
Senie, Harriet F.
Slavin, Stephen L.
Trefousse, Hans L.
Wilson, Joseph F.
Wiseman, Mary Bittner
Wolfe, Ethyle Renee

Buffalo
Allen, William Sheridan
Ault, Bradley A.
Bobinski, George Sylvan
Broman, Per F.
Burkman, Thomas
Cardoso, Joaquin Jose
Carman, Charles
Coffta, David J.
Curran, Leo C.
De La Pedraja, Rene
Devereux, David R.
Dyson, Steven L.
Ellis, Richard E.
Fordham, Monroe
Garton, Charles
Gerber, David A.
Glass, Dorothy
Guinn, Paul
Hart, Stephen
Iggers, Georg G.
Jones, Larry Eugene
Keil, Charles M.H.
Kelly, David H.
Koginos, Manny T.
Kustus, George L.
Lamb, Charles M.
Lewis, Lionel Stanley
Lunenfeld, Marvin
Malamud, Martha A.
Mathiot, Madeleine
McGuire, Donald T., Jr.
McNutt, Paula M.
O'Connor, Eugene
Paley, Samuel M.
Palmer, Robert L., II
Peradotto, John Joseph
Podet, Allen Howard
Primack, Maxwell
Quinan, Jack
Seeman, Erik R.
Seller, Maxine Schwartz
Shapiro, Stuart Charles
Shedd, D.
Sherk, Robert K.
Stinger, Charles Lewis
Tall, Emily
Valaik, J. David

Valone, James S.
Watrous, Livingston V.
Zemel, Carol
Zirin, Ronald A.

Cambria Heights
Southern, Eileen Jackson

Canton
Coburn, Thomas Bowen
DeGroat, Judith A.

Centereach
Seifman, Eli

Clinton
Gold, Barbara K.
Kanipe, Esther Sue
Kelly, Alfred Herbert
Tobin, Eugene Marc

Cooperstown
Jones, Louis Clark

Corning
Whitehouse, David Bryn

Cortland
Best, Judith A.
Wright, Donald R.

Derby
LaMarche, Jean

Dobbs Ferry
Rosenof, Theodore Dimon

Elmsford
Rugoff, Milton

Flushing
Davis, Ellen Nancy
Erickson, Raymond Frederick
Eubank, Keith
Greenbaum, Fred
Gruder, Vivian Rebecca
Heilman, Samuel C.
Hershkowitz, Leo
Lidov, Joel
Markovitz, Irving L.
McManus, Edgar J.
Merli, Frank John
Meza, Pedro Thomas
Scott, Donald M.
Syrett, David
Wreszin, Michael
Wu, Pei-Yi
Zwiebach, Burton

Fly Creek
Kuzminski, Adrian

Forest Hills
Feldman, Louis H.

Fredonia
Browder, George C.
Huffman, James Richard
Raat, William D.
Regelski, Thomas Adam
Reiff, Daniel D.
Schoenbach, Peter J.
Trace, Jacqueline Bruch

Garden City
Cunsolo, Ronald S.
Ernst, Robert

Geneseo
Bailey, Charles Randall
Cook, William Robert
Derby, William Edward
Fausold, Martin L.
Herzman, Ronald Bernard
Somerville, James Karl
Zuckerman, Mary Ellen

Geneva
Crouthamel, James L.
Singal, Daniel Joseph

Getzville
Murphy, Orville Theodore

Great Neck
Baron, Carol K.
Bogin, Ruth

Christie, Jean
Kahn, David
Marcus, Paul
Parmet, Robert David
Peterson, Jon Alvah

Greenvale
Bush-Brown, Albert
Courtemanche, Regis Armand
Morrison, G. Grant
Watanabe, Morimichi

Hamilton
Bolland, O. Nigel
Busch, Briton Cooper
Carter, John Ross
Dudden, Faye E.
Frost, Richard Hindman
Gallucci, John
Godwin, Joscelyn
Hudson, George C., Jr.
Irwin, Joyce Louise
Olcott, Martha
Payne, Harry Charles
Plata, Fernando
Rexine, John Efstratios
Ries, Nancy
Stevens, Carol B.
Stevens, Kira
Swain, Joseph
Vecsey, Christopher
Wider, Sarah Ann

Hempstead
Cassidy, David C.
Cohen, George Michael
Moore, John Clare
Naylor, Natalie A.
Sobel, Robert
Stern, Nancy B.

Homer
Dudgeon, Ralph T.

Huntington Station
Douglass, Melvin Isadore

Ithaca
Arlin, Mary I.
Austin, William Weaver
Baljon, Neil
Baugh, Daniel Albert
Bensel, Richard F.
Benson, LeGrace
Bilson, Malcolm
Bjerken, Xak
Blumin, Stuart
Borstelmann, Thomas
Brodhead, Garry
Brumberg, Joan Jacobs
Calkins, Robert Gilmer
Clinton, Kevin
Cochran, Sherman
Colby-Hall, Alice Mary
Coleman, John E.
Colman, Gould P.
Coral, Lenore
Cummings, Craig
Daniel, Cletus Edward
Ezergailis, Andrew
Greene, Sandra E.
Gudding, Gabriel
Hanchett, Tom
Harris, Robert L., Jr.
Harris-Warrick, Rebecca
Hatch, Martin
Hester, Karlton Edward
Holloway, Thomas Halsey
John, James J.
Johnson, Timothy
Kammen, Michael
Kennedy, Kenneth Adrian Raine
Kirkwood, Gordon Macdonald
Kline, Ronald R.
Koschmann, Julien Victor
Krumhansl, Carol L.
Kuniholm, Peter Ian
Lafeber, Walter
Lewenstein, Bruce V.
Lurie, Alison
Mcbride, Paul Wilbert
McClain, John O.
Mieczkowski, Bogdan
Moore, Robert Laurence
Najemy, John Michael
Norton, Mary Beth
Norton, Mary Beth
Okihiro, Gary Y.
Owen, David I.

Pelto, William
Peraino, Judith A.
Pintner, Walter Mckenzie
Polenberg, Richard
Powers, David Stephen
Pucci, Pietro
Radice, Mark A.
Ramage, Nancy Hirschland
Rosen, David
Rossiter, Margaret W.
Salvatore, Nicholas Anthony
Scatterday, Mark Davis
Silbey, Joel H.
Somkin, Fred
Swenson, Edward
Tierney, Brian
Turk, Eleanor L.
Turner, Terence S.
Webster, James
Williams, L. Pearce
Wilson, Dana
Wolters, Oliver William
Wyatt, David Kent
Yearsley, David
Zaslaw, Neal

Jamaica
Boyer, Marjorie Nice
Butscher, Edward
Coppa, Frank John
Curran, Thomas J.
Griffin, William Denis
Hagedorn, Nancy L.
Harmond, Richard Peter
Kinkley, Jeffrey Carroll

Keuka Park
Diamond, Sander A.

Kings Point
Gardella, Robert Paul

Lake Peekskill
Cuppo Csaki, Luciana

Larchmont
Fabian, Ann

Latham
Wright, Theodore P., Jr.

Laurens
Fink, William Bertrand

Loudonville
Murphy, John C.

Millbrook
Mclaughlin, Mary Martin

Mount Vernon
Brown, Beatrice S.

New Paltz
D'Elia, Donald John
Garlick, Peter C.
Hauptman, Laurence Marc
Huang, Ray
Knapp, Ronald G.
Lee, Loyd Ervin
Rhoads, William B.
Schnell, George Adam
Sorin, Gerald
Williams-Myers, Albert J.

New Rochelle
Dunkak, Harry Matthew
Guidorizzi, Richard Peter
Pilant, Craig Wesley
Schleifer, James Thomas

New York
Abelson, Elaine S.
Abrams, Bradley
Angel, Marc D.
Armitage, David
Armstrong, Charles
Avery, Kevin J.
Avrich, Paul Henry
Bacon, Helen Hazard
Bagnall, Roger Shaler
Bailey, Adrienne Yvonne
Baker, Paul R.
Ball, Susan
Barstow, Anne Llewellyn
Barzun, Jacques
Bean, John Malcolm William
Beck, James Henry

Bellush, Bernard
Ben-Atar, Doron
Benardete, Seth Gabriel
Bender, Thomas
Berkin, Carol Ruth
Berrol, Selma Cantor
Betts, Richard Kevin
Billows, Richard A.
Blackmar, Elizabeth
Blazekovic, Zdravko
Boddewyn, Jean J.
Bonfante, Larissa
Bonomi, Patricia Updegraff
Borg, Dorothy
Brabant, Jozef M.
Brilliant, Richard
Brinkley, Alan
Bristow, Edward
Brook, Barry Shelley
Brown, Blanche Rachel
Brown, Jonathan M.
Buja, Maureen
Bulliet, Richard
Burstein, L. Poundie
Bushman, Claudia
Bushman, Richard
Bynum, Caroline Walker
Cameron, Alan
Campbell, Mary Schmidt
Cannadine, David
Cantor, Norman Frank
Carnes, Mark C.
Caroli, Betty Boyd
Carrubba, Robert W.
Casson, Lionel
Cavaglieri, Giorgio
Cazeaux, Isabelle
Chambers, John W.
Chernow, Barbara A.
Chusid, Martin
Cimbala, Paul A.
Claster, Jill Nadell
Cohen, Martin Aaron
Cohen, Myron L.
Cohen, Naomi Wiener
Colton, Joel
Cook, Blanche Wiesen
Coulter, Harris L.
Cribiore, Raffaela
Cunningham, Sarah Gardner
D'Arms, John H.
Dauben, Joseph Warren
Davis, Elliot Bostwick
Dawson, John Philip
de Grazia, Victoria
Deak, Istvan
Dean, Warren
DeFord, Ruth
Diamond, Sigmund
Dilts, Mervin R.
Dirks, Nicholas
Donhauser, Peter L.
Donohue, John Waldron
Douglas, Ann
Duncan, Carol G.
Dyson, Michael Eric
Eden, Kathy
Edwards, Lee M.
Eigen, Michael
Eisenstadt, Peter
Eisenstein, Hester
Eisler, Colin
Embree, Ainslie Thomas
Evans, Harry B.
Feinberg, Barbara Jane
Feingold, Henry L.
Felix, David
Fields, Barbara J.
Fishman, David E.
Foltz, Richard
Foner, Eric
Foner, Eric
Forman Crane, Elaine
Franklin, Phyllis
Fukuyama, Francis
Gans, Herbert J.
Gasman, Daniel E.
Gelb, Joyce
Gerber, Jane Satlow
Gerson, Kathleen
Gettleman, Marvin Edward
Gilinsky, Joshua
Glatzer Rosenthal, Bernice
Gluck, Carol
Godfrey, Mary F.
Goldberg, Barry
Goldberger, Leo
Gordon, Leonard Abraham
Goren, Arthur

Gottlieb, Beatrice
Gottlieb, Carla
Graham, William C.
Grele, Ronald J.
Grennen, Joseph Edward
Griffel, L. Michael
Gyug, Richard F.
Haddad, Mahmoud
Hampton, Barbara L.
Harris, William Vernon
Hayim Yerushalmi, Yosef
Haynes, Holly
Helly, Dorothy O.
Hicks, David L.
Himmelberg, Robert F.
Himmelfarb, Gertrude
Hobsbawm, Eric
Hoffman, Anne
Hopkins, John Orville
Howell, Martha
Hoxie, Ralph Gordon
Hull, Richard W.
Hunting, Mary Anne
Huttenbach, Henry R.
Israel, Fred L.
Jackson, Kenneth T.
Jaffe, David P.
Jalal, Ayesha
James, Winston
Jeffries, Leonard
Jeffries, Rosalind R.
Jervis, Robert
Jimenez-Ramirez, Talia
Johnson, Penelope Delafield
Kagan, Susan
Kamhi, Michelle Marder
Katznelson, Ira
Kaufmann, Frank
Kaye, Joel
Kessler-Harris, Alice
Kessner, Thomas
Klein, Herbert S.
Koenigsberg, Lisa M.
Kortepeter, Carl Max
Kostelanetz, Richard
Kosto, Adam
Kovaleff, Theodore Philip
Kowaleski, Maryanne
Kramer, Lawrence Eliot
Krinsky, Carol Herselle
Kupperman, Karen Ordahl
Lagemann, Ellen Condliffe
Landau, Sarah Bradford
Latham, Michael E.
Lavin, David E.
Lefkowitz, Joel M.
Lemay, Richard
Lerner, B. H.
Libo, Kenneth Harold
Lienhard, Joseph T.
Lindo-Fuentes, Hector
Lippman, Edward
Lipsey, Robert E.
London, Clement B. G.
London, Herbert
Lotz, David Walter
Lowrie, Michele
Lufrano, Richard
Lynch, Hollis R.
Macchiarulo, Louis
Malefakis, Edward
Malefakis, Edward Emanuel
Marable, Manning
Marcus, David
Marm, Michael
Marrin, Albert
Martin, Richard
Marx, Anthony W.
Mattingly, Paul Havey
Maxwell, Kenneth R.
Mayerson, Philip
Mbodj, Mohamed
McCaughey, Robert Anthony
Mckitrick, Eric Louis
Metcalf, William E.
Miller, James
Miller-Jones, Dalton
Mockler, Robert J.
Moore, Deborah Dash
Mueller, Claus
Muller, Priscilla Elkow
Mullin, Robert Bruce
Mundy, John Hine
Murnion, Philip Joseph
Muscarella, Oscar White
Musto, Ronald G.
Myers, David
Naison, Mark
Nash, June C.

Nathan, Andrew J.
Nichols, Mary P.
Nolan, Mary
O'Conell, Robert J.
Oliva, L. Jay
Olugebefola, Ademola
Ortner, Sherry B.
Paca, Barbara
Page, Stanley W.
Panella, Robert J.
Pasteur, Alfred Bernard
Patriarca, Silvana
Paxton, Robert O.
Paxton, Robert Owen
Peirce, Sarah
Penkower, Monty Noam
Perkins, Leeman Lloyd
Perry, Marilyn
Pessen, Edward
Peters, Francis Edward
Peters, Julie
Pflugfelder, Gregory
Piccato, Pablo
Pike, Ruth
Polk, Robert L.
Pomeroy, Sarah B.
Porada, Edith
Prager, Jonas
Preston, George Nelson
Prince, Carl E.
Purcell, E.A.
Raeff, Marc
Ragan, Bryant T., Jr.
Randall, Francis Ballard
Reff, Theodore Franklin
Reid, John Phillip
Riley, Terence
Rives, James
Roe, Mark J.
Romm, James S.
Rosand, David
Rosenberg, Rosalind Navin
Rosenblum, Robert
Rosner, David
Roth-Burnette, Jennifer
Rothman, David
Sandler, Lucy Freeman
Sappol, Michael
Scaglia, Gustina
Scammell, Michael
Schama, Simon
Scherzinger, M.
Schorsch, Ismar
Schrecker, Ellen Wolf
Schwartz, Shuly Rubin
Scott, Daryl
Segal, Alal Franklin
Serels, M. Mitchell
Shea, George W.
Shenton, James
Shneidman, J. Lee
Sider, David
Silverman, Kenneth Eugene
Sims, Lowery Stokes
Siraisi, Nancy Gillian
Sklar, Robert Anthony
Sloan, Herbert
Smail, Daniel L.
Smit, J.W.
Smith, Henry
Soyer, Daniel
Stahl, Alan Michael
Staley, Allen
Stanislawski, Michael
Stauffer, George B.
Stephanson, Anders
Stern, Fritz
Strum, Philippa
Swerdlow, Amy
Swinth, Kirsten
Taran, Leonardo
Tarr, Zoltan
Terry, James L.
Tholfsen, Trygve Rainone
Thompson, Jewel T.
Tiersten, Lisa
Tilly, Louise A.
Trumbach, Randolph
Tsin, Michael
Unger, Irwin
Valenze, Deborah
Valkenier, Elizabeth Kridl
van de Mieroop, Marc
van der Mieroop, Marc
Von Hagen, Mark L.
Waldman, Martin
Walker Bynum, Caroline
Walkowitz, Daniel Jay
Walton, Guy E.

Waltz, Kenneth Neal
Ward, John William
Watkins-Owens, Irma
Weart, Spencer R.
Weisberger, Bernard A
Weiss, T.G.
Wemple, Suzanne Fonay
Wertheimer, Jack
Weston, Corinne Comstock
Whelan, Stephen T.
White, Donald Wallace
Whittaker, Cynthia Hyla
Wiener, Joel H.
Williams, Gareth D.
Wines, Roger
Woloch, Isser
Woloch, Nancy
Wortman, Richard
Wright, Gwendolyn
Wright, John Robert
Wright, Marcia
Yellin, Victor Fell
Yerkes, David
Yerushalmi, Yosef Hayim
Young, Jordan Marten
Zelin, Madeleine
Zolberg, Vera L.

Ossining
Gocking, Roger S.

Oswego
Cheng, Weikun
Conrad, David
Deal, J. Douglas
Forbes, Geraldine May
Halbersleben, Karen I.
Kulikowski, Mark
Loveridge-Sanbonmatsu, Joan
Peterson, Luther D.
Powell, Thomas F.
Wellman, Judith

Pittsford
France, Jean R.

Plattsburgh
Abu-Ghazaleh, Adnan M.
Lindgren, James M.
Myers, John L.

Potsdam
Johnson, Arthur L.

Poughkeepsie
Adams, Nicholas
Cohen, Miriam J.
Edwards, Rebecca
Fergusson, Frances D.
Johnson, M. Glen
Kohl, Benjamin Gibbs
Libin, Kathryn
Mann, Brian
Olsen, Donald J. Ames
Pisani, Michael
Rappaport, Rhoda
Wohl, Anthony Stephen

Princeton
Wallace, Walter L.
Wildberg, Christian

Purchase
Dubin, S.C.
Howard, John Robert
Newton, Esther
Schwab, Peter
Thormann, Gerard Charles

Rhinebeck
Orlin, Eric

Ridgewood
Constantinou, Constantia

Rochester
Anderson, David Atlas
Berlo, Janet Catherine
Bond, Gerald Albert
Camp, Robert C.
Chiarenza, Carl
Crimp, Douglas
Deci, Edward Lewis
Genovese, Eugene D.
Gordon, Lynn Dorothy
Gupta, Brijen Kishore
Hahn, Thomas
Hauser, William Barry

Holly, Michael Ann
Kaeuper, Richard William
Kavork Dohanian, Diran
Kollar, Nathan Rudolph
Kowalke, Kim H.
Lemke, Werner Erich
Locke, Ralph Paul
Mann, Alfred
Meerbote, Ralf
More, Ellen Singer
Resinski, Rebecca
Seiberling, Grace
Seidel, Robert Neal
Thym, Jurgen
Walsh, David A.
Wason, Robert W.
Waters, John J.
Wolff, Janet
Young, Mary Elizabeth
Zagorin, Perez

Saratoga Springs
Clapper, Michael
Kuroda, Tadahisa
Lynn, Mary Constance
Porter, David H.
Zangrando, Joanna Schneider

Scarsdale
Nag, Moni

Schenectady
Finkelstein, Joseph
Gmelch, George
Gmelch, Sharon Bohn
Jonas, Manfred
Mace, Sarah
Scullion, Scott
Sorum, Christina Elliott
Toher, Mark
Wells, Robert Vale

Shoreham
Brinkman, John T.

Southampton
Baker, Donald G.
Strong, John A.

St. Bonaventure
Eckert, Edward K.

Staten Island
Anderson, Robert Mapes
Binder, Frederick Melvin
Cooper, Sandi E.
Frank, Sam Hager
Simpson, Peter L.P.

Stony Brook
Barnhart, Michael Andrew
Bottigheimer, Karl S.
Burner, David B.
Cowan, Ruth Schwartz
Fuller, Sarah
Godfrey, Aaron W.
Gootenberg, Paul
Guilmain, Jacques
Kuisel, Richard F.
Landsman, Ned C.
Lebovics, Herman
Lemay, Helen Rodnite
McWorter, Gerald A.
Rubin, James Henry
Tomes, Nancy Jane
Weinstein, Fred

Syracuse
Bennett, David Harry
Dixon, Laurinda S.
Donegan, Jane Bauer
Farnsworth, Beatrice
Field, Daniel
Gold, Ann G.
Gregory, Robert G.
Judge, Edward H.
Ketcham, Ralph Louis
MacDonald, Mary N.
Macdonald, Roderick James
Marsh, Peter T.
Milac, Metod M.
Miller, Patricia Cox
Powell, James Matthew
Sharp, James Roger
Tatham, David Frederic
Telesca, William John
Thompson, Margaret Susan
Timberlake, Constance Hector

Webb, Stephen S.
Wiecek, William Michael
Wiggins, James Bryan
Wiley, Raymond A.

Tarrytown
Carrillo, Elisa Anna
Goldin, Milton

Tonawanda
Naylor, John Francis
Tucker, Melvin Jay

Troy
Apena, Igho Adeline
Crouch, Dora Polk
Duchin, Faye
Edwards, George Charles III
Restivo, Sal
Spector, Sherman David
Woodhouse, Edward James

Tuchahoe
Bodling, Kurt A.

Upton
Harbottle, Garman

Verbank
Salzman, Neil

Vestal
Africa, Thomas Wilson
Thomasson, Gordon C.

Walworth
Murzaku, Ines A.

Waterport
Bucholz, Arden

West Islip
Zirkel, Patricia McCormick

West Nyack
Olin, John C.

West Point
Crane, Conrad C.
Crane, Conrad Charles
Doughty, Robert
Johnson, James M.
McDonald, Robert M.S.
Rogers, Clifford J.

White Plains
Slater, Peter Gregg

Yonkers
Lentner, Howard H.

NORTH CAROLINA

Asheville
Dvorsky-Rohner, Dorothy
Locke, Don C.
Walker, Philip Alfred

Belmont
Biggs, Anselm

Boone
Claassen, Cheryl
Hanft, Sheldon
Hay, Fred J.
Keefe, Susan E.
Keefe, Thomas Keelin
Kinsey, Winston Lee
Moore, Michael J.
Simon, Stephen Joseph
Strickland, Ruth Ann
Wade, Michael G.
Williamson, Jerry Wayne

Cary
Crow, Jeffrey Jay

Chapel Hill
Barney, William Lesko
Baron, Samuel Haskell
Baxter, Stephen Bartow
Behrends, Frederick
Bennett, Judith Mackenzie

Blau, Judith R.
Boren, Henry C.
Brooks, E. Willis
Broughton, Thomas Robert Shannon
Brown, Frank
Bullard, Melissa Meriam
Connor, Carolyn
Dessen, Cynthia Sheldon
Filene, Peter Gabriel
Finson, Jon William
Folda, Jaroslav
Folda, Jaroslav T., III
Ganz, David
Grendler, Paul F.
Haar, James
Haggis, Donald
Hall, Jacquelyn Dowd
Harris, Michael D.
Headley, John M.
Henry, Eric Putnam
Higginbotham, R. Don
Hoogland Verkerk, Dorothy
Houston, George W.
Hunt, Michael H.
Jones, Houston Gwynne
Kasson, John Franklin
Lee, Sherman E.
Linderski, Jerzy
Lotchin, Roger W.
Mack, Sara
Marks, Arthur S.
Mathews, Donald G.
Matilsky, Barbara C.
Mavor, Carol
Mcvaugh, Michael Rogers
Miller, Marla R.
Newman, William S.
Orth, John Victor
Pfaff, Richard William
Powers, Doris Bosworth
Race, William H.
Riggs, Timothy A.
Sasson, Jack Murad
Schroth, Sarah W.
Semonche, John Erwin
Shaw, Donald Lewis
Sheriff, Mary D.
Smith, C. S.
Smith, Rebekah M.
Smither, Howard Elbert
Snyder, Glenn Herald
Soloway, Richard Allen
Stadter, Philip Austin
Sturgeon, Mary C.
Tindall, George Brown
Watson, Harry Legare
Weaver, Garrett F.
Weinberg, Gerhard Ludwig
Weiss, Michael L.
West, William C., III
Wittig, Joseph Sylvester
Wood, Carolyn B.
Wooten, Cecil W.

Charlotte
Clark, Anna
Dupre, Dan
Escott, Paul David
Gabaccia, Donna
Goldfield, David
Haber, Carole
Heath, Kingston W.
Lansen, Oscar
Laurent, Jane Katherine
Patterson, Karl David
Swanson, Randy
Yancy, Dorothy Cowser

Concord
McLean, Mable Parker

Cullowhee
Anderson, William L.
Blethen, H. Tyler
Carmichael, Peter S.
Dorondo, David R.
Graham, Gael N.
Lovin, Clifford R.
Philyaw, Scott L.
Schwartz, Gerald
Walton, Brian G.
Wood, Curtis W.

Davidson
Ahrensdorf, Peter J.
Berkey, Jonathan P.
Edmonson, Clifton Earl
Krentz, Peter Martin

Levering, Ralph Brooks
Ligo, Larry L.
Mele, Alfred R.
Ratliff, Charles Edward
Serebrennikov, Nina Eugenia
Smith, C. Shaw, Jr.
Toumazou, Michael K.
Zimmermann, Thomas C. Price

Durham
Antliff, Mark
Bartlet, Elizabeth C.
Biddle, Tami Davis
Boatwright, Mary T.
Brothers, Thomas
Bruzelius, Caroline
Cell, John W.
Davis, Calvin D.
Davis, Calvin D.
Davis, Gregson
Dirlik, Arif
Druesedow, John E.
Durden, Robert Franklin
Ferguson, Arthus Bowles
Gavins, Raymond
Gilliam, Bryan
Goranson, Stephen
Holsti, Ole R.
Humphreys, Margaret
Jacobs, Sylvia Marie
Jones, Barney Lee
Jones, Beverly Washington
Keefe, Susan Ann
Keohane, Nannerl O.
Keyssar, Alexander
Koonz, Claudia
Kuniholm, Bruce Robellet
Leighten, Patricia
Lerner, Warren
Malpass, Leslie Frederick
Mauskopf, Seymour Harold
Mezzatesta, Michael P.
Mickiewicz, Ellen Propper
Miller, Martin Alan
Oates, John Francis
Peyroux, Catherine
Rice, Louise
Richardson, Lawrence Jr
Richey, Russell Earle
Rigsby, Kent Jefferson
Roland, Alex
Sasson, Sarah Diane Hyde
Silbiger, Alexander
Steinmetz, David Curtis
Stiles, Kristine
Tepaske, John J.
Tiryakian, Edward A.
Todd, Larry
Van Miegroet, Hans J.
Wharton, Annabel
Wigen, Karen
Williams, Peter
Willis, William Hailey
Witt, Ronald Gene
Wood, Peter H.
Young, Charles Robert
Younger, John Grimes

Elon College
Ellis, Clyde

Fayetteville
Andrews, Maxine Ramseur

Greensboro
Baber, Ceola Ross
Calhoon, Robert M.
Clowse, Converse Dilworth
Crowe, David M.
Current, Richard Nelson
Deagon, Ann Fleming
Goldstein, Carl
Hansen, Bob
Hayes, Charles Leonard
Hunter, Phyllis A.
Jennings, Robert Ray
Kirk, Wyatt D.
Leplin, Jarrett
Mackenzie, David
Saab, E. Ann Pottinger
Schleunes, Karl Albert
Schweninger, Loren Lance
Shelmerdine, Susan C.
Trelease, Allen William

Greenville
Adler, Philip Joseph
Chestnut, Dennis Earl
Cobb, William Henry

Holsey, Lilla G.
Nischan, Bodo
Papalas, Anthony John
Seavy, William
Steelman, Joseph F.
Stevens, John A.

Hickory
Huff, Carolyn Barbara

Lewisville
Williams, Alan John

Pembroke
Brown, Robert Warren
Hilton, Kathleen C.

Raleigh
Banker, James Roderick
Beers, Burton Floyd
Cofield, Elizabeth Bias
Crisp, James Ernest
Crumbley, Deidre H.
Harris, William C.
Holley, Linda Tarte
McMurry, Linda O.
Mcmurry, Richard Manning
Middleton, Stephen
Moorhead, James Howell
Sack, Ronald Herbert
Slatta, Richard Wayne
Smith, John David
Sylla, Edith Dudley
Tyler, Pamela
Zonderman, David A.

Research Triangle Park
Connor, Walter Robert
Gatewood, Algie C.

Southern Pines
Lemmon, Sarah McCulloh

Wilmington
Clark, Andrew
Conser, Walter H., Jr.
Janson, Anthony F.
Kimmel, Richard H.
Martin, Sherrill V.
McLaurin, Melton Alonza
Toplin, Robert B.
Usilton, Larry
Watson, Alan Douglas

Winston-Salem
Andronica, John Louis
Angelou, Maya
Barnett, Richard Chambers
Fleer, Jack David
Gokhale, Balkrishna Govind
Hendricks, James Edwin
Levy, David Benjamin
Pendergraft, Mary L.B.
Sadler, Wilbert L., Jr.
Sinclair, Michael Loy
Smiley, David Leslie
Smith, James Howell
Ulery, Robert
Walker, George Kontz
Zuber, Richard Lee

NORTH DAKOTA

Fargo
Danbom, David Byers

Grand Forks
Beringer, Richard E.
Erickson, Daniele Nathan
Iseminger, Gordon Llewellyn
Pynn, Ronald
Tweton, D. Jerone
Vivian, James Floyd

Jamestown
Bratton, Timothy L.
Cox, Sharon G.
Joy, Mark S.
Lorenzo, David J.

Mayville
Neilson, James Warren

Richardton
Forman, Mary

OHIO

Ada
Beanblossom, Ronald Edwin

Akron
Baker, Joseph Wayne
Bouchard, Constance Brittain
Brown, Ronald Paul
Clements, Barbara Evans
Fant, J. Clayton
Gerlach, Don R.
Harp, Stephen
Hixson, Walter Lawrence
Kyvig, David Edward
Liss, Sheldon Barnett
Mancke, Elizabeth
McClain, Andrew Bradley
Mushkat, Jerome
Nelson, Daniel
Patsouras, Louis
Schreiber, Mae N.
Zangrando, Robert Lewis

Alliance
Dorsey, Scott W.
Harris, Victoria
Miskell, Jerry

Athens
Alexander, Charles C.
Baxter, Douglas Clark
Booth, Alan R.
Carpenter, T.H.
Chastain, James G.
Childs, Francine C.
Collins, Elizabeth F.
Fidler, Ann
Field, Phyllis Frances
Fletcher, Marvin Edward
Frederick, William Hayward
Gaddis, John Lewis
Hamby, Alonzo Lee
Hoff, Joan
Jordan, Donald A.
Mcgeoch, Lyle Archibald
Owens, William M.
Reeves, Albert Compton
Richter, Donald Charles
Soltow, Lee
Steiner, Bruce E.
Sweeney, Thomas John
Weckman, George
Whealey, Robert H.

Berea
Moore, Edgar Benjamin

Bluffton
Gratz, Delbert L.

Bowling Green
Corrigan, Vincent
Daly, Lawrence John
Danziger, Edmund J.
Forse, James Harry
Friedman, Lawrence Jacob
Givens, Stuart R.
Hess, Gary R.
Kiple, Kenneth Franklin
Middleton, Charles
Scott, Alison M.
Scott, John Sherman
Skaggs, David Curtis
Stockwell, Edward G.
Thomas, Jack Ray

Canton
McClain, Shirla R.
Sosnowski, Thomas C.

Cedarville
McGoldrick, James Edward
Murdoch, James Murray

Cincinnati
Aeschbacher, William Driver
Amussen, Susan
Atkins, Robert
Beaver, Daniel R.
Bell Chambers, Marjorie
Burrell, Barbara
Castenell, Louis Anthony, Jr.
Cebula, James E.
Cline, Eric
Collins, Patricia Hill
Cottrell, Jack Warren
Daniel, Hershey

Davis, Jack L.
Fleming, John Emory
Foss, D. Pedar W.
Gutzwiller, Kathryn
Harris-Cline, Diane
Harrison, George Mallory
Kafker, Frank Arthur
Kaufman, Stephen Allan
Kraut, Benny
Langsam, Walter E.
Larocca, John Joseph
Laux, James Michael
Lund, Jerome A.
Marcus, Jacob Rader
Meyer, Michael Albert
Meyerowitz, Joanne
Michelini, Ann Norris
Miller, Zane L.
Murray, James
North, James Brownlee
Parker, Holt
Plank, Geoffrey
Pogue, Samuel Franklin
Ramusack, Barbara N.
Rose, Brian
Sage, Michael
Sakmyster, Thomas Lawrence
Sarason, Richard Samuel
Sato, Elizabeth Selanders
Schrier, Arnold
Shapiro, Henry D.
Shapiro, Herbert
Simon, Paul L.
Smith, Paul M., Jr.
Sterling, David L.
Thomas, Norman C.
Tolzmann, Don Heinrich
Twinam, Ann
Wacholder, Ben Zion
Walberg, Gisela
Walter, John C.
Weisberg, David B.
Wingard, Edward L.
Winkler, Henry Ralph

Cleveland
Adams, Henry
Altschul, Michael
Anderson, Earl Robert
Beatie, Bruce A.
Bergman, Robert P.
Buchanan, Harvey
Bynum, David Eliab
Clark, Sanza Barbara
Curnow, Kathy
Czuma, Stanislaw
Donaldson, Thomas
Edmonson, James Milton
Gamboni, Dario
Goist, Park Dixon
Grundy, Kenneth William
Haddad, Gladys
Helzle, Martin
Hunter, John
Landau, Ellen G.
Ledford, Kenneth F.
McHale, Vincent Edward
Mesch, Claudia
Miller, Genevieve
Morton, Marian Johnson
Neils, Jenifer
Peskin, Allan
Poduska, Donald Miles
Ramos, Donald
Rocke, Alan J.
Scallen, Catherine B.
Shorrock, William Irwin
Ubbelohde, Carl
Warren, Ann Kosser

Cleveland Heights
Manning, Roger B.

Columbus
Andrien, Kenneth James
Balcer, Jack Martin
Bartholomew, James Richard
Benedict, Michael Les
Blackford, Mansel Griffiths
Bourguignon, Erika Eichhorn
Burnham, John Chynoweth
Chu, Samuel C.
Cohen, Jeremy
Cooper, Donald B.
Cox, Kevin R.
Devine, Michael John
Dillon, Merton Lynn
Findley, Carter Vaughn
Fullmer, June Zimmerman

Reed, John Julius
Shaw, Barton Carr
Wilson, Daniel Joseph

Altoona
Wolfe, Martin

Ardmore
Bober, Phyllis Pray

Bala-Cynwyd
Keefe, Thomas M.
Murphey, Murray Griffin

Barracks Carlisle
Deutsch, Harold Charles

Beaver Falls
Copeland, Robert M.
Wollman, David Harris

Bethlehem
Aronson, Jay Richard
Baylor, Michael G.
Cooper, Gail
Cutcliffe, Stephen Hosmer
Girardot, Norman J.
Goldman, Steven
Kohls, Winfred A.
Loengard, Janet Senderowitz
Peters, Tom F.
Phillips, C. Robert, III
Radycki, Diane
Remer, Rosalind
Saeger, James Schofield
Schwartz, Eli
Scott, William R.
Shade, William G.
Simon, Roger David
Smith, John K., Jr.
Stinson, Robert William

Bloomsburg
Bryan, Jesse A.
Hickey, Michael C.
Smiley, Ralph

Bradford
Frederick, Richard G.

Bryn Mawr
Brand, Charles Macy
Cast, David Jesse Dale
Cohen, Jeffrey A.
Dickerson, Gregory Weimer
Dudden, Arthur Power
Eiteljorg, Harrison, II
Gaisser, Julia Haig
Hamilton, Richard
Lane, Barbara Miller
Lang, Mabel Louise
Lichtenberg, Phillip
Mellink, Machteld Johanna
Ridgway, Brunilde (Sismondto)
Salmon, John Hearsey Mcmillan
Silvera, Alain

Butler
Weisberger, William

California
Folmar, John Kent

Camp Hill
Wolf, George D.

Carlisle
Bullard, Truman
Emery, Ted
Garrett, Clarke W.
Jarvis, Charles Austin
Lockhart, Philip N.
Richter, Daniel K.
Schiffman, Joseph
Shrader, Charles R.
Weinberger, Stephen
Weissman, Neil Bruce
Wilson, Blake

Chambersburg
Buck, Harry Merwyn

Chester
Wrobel, David M.

Cheyney
McCummings, LeVerne

Collegeville
Akin, William Ernest
Clark, Hugh R.
Hemphill, C. Dallett
King, Richard D.
Visser, Derk

Conshohocken
West, C. S'thembile

Coopersburg
Eckardt, Alice Lyons

Dallas
Forslund, Catherine

East Stroudsburg
Donaghay, Marie
Henwood, James N.J.
Jarvis, Joseph Anthony
Mercado, Juan Carlos

Easton
Cooke, Jacob Ernest
Mattison, Robert S.

Edinboro
Hoffman, Donald Stone
Howell, Allen C.
Stennis-Williams, Shirley

Elizabethtown
Winpenny, Thomas Reese

Elkins Park
Vogel, Morris J

Ellwood City
Lambert, Lynda J.

Erie
Adovasio, J.M.
Frankforter, Albertus Daniel
Loss, Archie Krug

Fayetteville
Ross, Marilyn A.

Gettysburg
Birkner, Michael J.
Gritsch, Eric W.
Shannon, Timothy J.

Grantham
Davis, Edward B.
Kraybill, Donald B.
Sider, E. Morris

Greensburg
Spurlock, John C.

Gwynedd Valley
Duclow, Donald F.

Harrisburg
Waddell, Louis Morton

Haverford
Bronner, Edwin Blaine
Dillon, Clarissa F.
Gillis, Daniel J.
Lane, Roger
Mckenna, John William
Russo, Joseph Anthony

Havertown
Griffith, Sally F.

Hazleton
Aurand, Harold Wilson
Brown, Kenneth

Huntingdon
Nieto, Jose Constantino

Indiana
Cashdollar, Charles David
Ferro, Trenton R.
Goodrich, Thomas Day
Marcus, Irwin Murray
Smith, W. Wayne

Johnstown
Sedlar, Jean Whitenack

La Plume
Elliott, Carolyn S.

Lancaster
Andrew, John Alfred
Farber, Jay Joel
Hopkins, Thomas J.
Pearson, Edward
Schuyler, David
Schuyler, David
Sentilles, Renee M.
Stevenson, Louise L.
Wank, Solomon

Laporte
Ferguson, James Wilson

Lewisberg
Keen, J. Ernest

Lewisburg
Grim, John A.
Padilla, Mark
Tucker, Mary Evelyn
Verbrugge, Martha Helen

Lincoln University
Rowe, Patsy Baxter

Lock Haven
Jones, Laird

Malvern
Kelley, John T.

Meadville
Carr, Amelia J.
Helmreich, Jonathan Ernst
Miller, David
Ozorak, Elizabeth Weiss
Treckel, Paula Ann
Turk, Richard Wellington

Media
Carlson, Robert E.
Cimbala, Stephen J.
Clement, Priscilla Ferguson
Franz, George W.

Merion Station
Fox, Frank

Middletown
Bronner, Simon J.
Bruhn, John Glyndon

Millersville
Bremer, Francis John
Clark, Linda Loeb
Downey, Dennis B.
Thornton, John K.
Tirado, Thomas C.

Narbeth
Bizzarro, Tina W.

New Wilmington
Botzenhart-Viehe, Verena
Garrison, Roman
Heinz, Vira I.
Martin, Russell E.
Pitman, Grover A.
Rennie, Bryan S.
Turner, James Hilton

Newtown
Eyer, Diane E.

Oreland
Lyons, Joseph

Philadelphia
Asante, Molefi Kete
Azzolina, Davis S
Barker, William Shirmer, II
Bernstein, Lawrence F.
Betancourt, Philip Paul
Burton, David Henry
Carter, Edward C., II
Cochran, Thomas Childs
Collier-Thomas, Bettye
Contosta, David Richard
Cotter, John Lambert
Crane, Diana
Cutler III, William W.
Davidson, Abraham A
Davis, Allen Freeman

Davis, Daniel Clair
DeLong, David G.
Dodds, Dennis R.
Dunn, Richard Slator
Dyson, Robert Harris, Jr.
Engs, Robert Francis
Ershkowitz, Herbert J.
Fair, Theopolis
Faust, Drew Gilpin
Ferere, Gerard Alphonse
Friedman, Murray
Glazier, Ira Albert
Good, Irene Lee
Graham, A. John
Haller, Mark Hughlin
Harris, P.M.G.
Hart, Darryl Glenn
Hilty, James
Hughes, Thomas Parke
Kahn, Charles H.
Katz, Michael B.
Kay, Gersil Newmark
Kors, Alan Charles
Kraft, Robert Alan
Krey, Philip D.W.
Kuklick, Bruce
Kunreuther, Howard
Kusmer, Kenneth L.
Lees, Lynn Hollen
Leichty, Erle Verdun
Lieberman, Stephen Jacob
Logan, Samuel Talbot, Jr.
Lyons, Timothy James
Marzik, Thomas David
Matter, Edith Ann
McCoubrey, John W.
McGovern, Patrick E.
Mcgrew, Roderick Erle
Meister, Michael William
Meyer, Leonard B.
Miller, Naomi F.
Miller, Randall Martin
Myrick, Howard A., Jr.
Naquin, Susan
O'Donnell, James Joseph
Ohline, Howard Albert
Peters, Edward Murray
Pipes, Daniel
Rainey, Penelope
Rosnow, Ralph Leon
Rossi, John P.
Rouse, Donald E.
Rusch, Scott M.
Schmandt, Raymond Henry
Schuyler, Robert L.
Silk, Gerald
Sivin, Nathan
Smith, Philip Chadwick Foster
Solomon, P.
Steinberg, Leo
Steinhardt, Nancy Shatzman
Stoeffler, Fred Ernest
Stow, George Buckley
Striker, Cecil Leopold
Swidler, Leonard
Tigay, Jeffrey Howard
Trachtenberg, Marc
Traupman, John Charles
Wagner, Walter Hermann
Walker, Valaida Smith
Wartluft, David J.
Watson, Alan
Watson, Paul Fraser
Watson, Wilbur H.
Weigley, Russell Frank
Wengert, Timothy J.
White, Donald
Wolf, Eugene Kendrick
Zimmerman, Franklin B.
Zuckerman, Michael

Phoenixville
Lukacs, John Adalbert

Pittsburgh
Achenbaum, W. Andrew
Andrews, George Reid
Anise, Ladun Oladunjoye E.
Avery, Harry Costas
Biggs, Shirley Ann
Blee, K.M.
Castellano, Charlene
Chase, William John
Clack, Jerry
Clothey, Frederick Wilson
Davis, Nathan T.
Drescher, Seymour
Floyd, Edwin Douglas
Gaichas, Lawrence Edward

Gill, Mary Louise
Glasco, Laurence A.
Greenwald, Maurine Weiner
Hall, Van Beck
Hamilton, Carol
Hammond, Paul Y.
Harris, Ann Sutherland
Hays, Samuel Pfrimmer
Hsu, Cho-yun
Jones, Nicholas Francis
Karsten, Peter
Kehl, James Arthur
Krause, Corinne Azen
Lennox, James Gordon
Levy, Eugene Donald
Linduff, Katheryn Mcallister
Livezeanu, I.
Markoff, John
Mcshea, William Patrick
Meltzer, Allan H.
Miller, Andrew M.
Miller, David William
Muller, Edward K.
Newman, Kathleen
Newmyer, Stephen Thomas
Oestreicher, Richard Jules
Orbach, Alexander
Parker, Lisa S.
Porter, Curtiss E.
Rawski, Evelyn Sakakida
Richardson, Cordell
Root, Deane Leslie
Sandage, Scott A.
Schaub, Marilyn McNamara
Sheon, Aaron
Sims, Harold Dana
Smethurst, Mae J.
Smethurst, Richard Jacob
Stearns, Peter N.
Sutton, Donald Sinclair
Tarr, Joel A.
Taylor, Jerome
Toker, Franklin K.
Vardy, Steven Bela
Vardy, Steven Bela
Wells, Jerome C.
Wilkins, Ann Thomas
Williams, John W.
Wilson, John Elbert

Port Carbon
Aurand, Harold, Jr.

Radnor
Reher, Margaret Mary

Reading
Voigt, David Quentin

Saratoga Springs
Black, Brian C.

Scranton
Homer, Francis Xavier James
Hueston, Robert Francis
Kamla, Thomas A.
Kennedy, Lawrence W.
Williams, Bernard D

Shippensburg
Leighow, Susan
Offner, John L.
Quist, John W.
Reber, Vera Blinn
Rimby Meo, Susan
Snow, George Edward

Slippery Rock
Nichols, John A.
Prorok, Carolyn

Southampton
Crofts, Daniel Wallace

Springfield
Malsbary, Gerald Henry

State College
Moses, Wilson J.

Swarthmore
Blake, J. Herman
Chmielewski, Wendy E.
Cothren, Michael W.
DuPlessis, Robert S.
Friend, Theodore W.
Frost, Jerry William
Graybill, Maribeth

Hungerford, Constance Cain
Kitao, T. Kaori
Marissen, Michael
Morgan, Kathryn L.
North, Helen Florence
Ostwald, Martin
Rose, Gilbert Paul
Skelnar, Robert John
St. George, Robert B.
Swearer, Donald K.

Uniontown
Hovanec, Evelyn Ann

University Park
Borza, Eugene N.
Bradford Smith, Elizabeth
Brown, Ira Vernon
Broyles, Michael
Cross, Gary
Curran, Brian A.
Cutler, Anthony
Eggert, Gerald G.
Engel, David M.
Frantz, John B.
Golany, Gideon S.
Goldschmidt, Arthur E., Jr.
Hager, Hellmut
Knight, Isabel Frances
Kochanek, Stanley Anthony
Laporte, Robert, Jr.
Maddox, Robert James
Murray, Robert Keith
Ng, On-cho
Porter, Jeanne Chenault
Price, Robert George
Robinson, Joyce H.
Rose, Paul L.
Ruggiero, Guido
Scott, Susan C.
Snow, D. R.
Walden, Daniel
Walters, Elizabeth J.
Willumson, Glenn Gardner
Woodruff, Nan Elizabeth
Zabel, Craig

Valley Forge
Van Broekhoven, Deborah

Villanova
Bergquist, James Manning
Burke, Michael E.
Cherry, Charles L.
Cummings, Raymond L.
Gallicchio, Marc S.
Greene, Thomas R.
Heitzmann, William Ray
Hughes, Kevin L.
Johannes, John R.
Kelley, Donald B.
Malik, Hafeez
O'Brien, J. Willard
Procko, Bohdan P
Radan, George T.
Reilly, Bernard F

Wallingford
Nishimura-Jensen, Julie M.

Wayne
Hunt, John M., Jr.

West Chester
McNairy, Francine G.
Siegel, Peter E.
Soldon, Norbert C.
Webster, Richard J.

Wilkes-Barre
Cox, Harold E.
Curran, Daniel John
Hupchick, Dennis P.
Stevens, Donald G.
Valletta, Clement Lawrence

Williamsport
Golahny, Amy
Larson, Robert H.
Morris, Richard J.

York
Wessley, Stephen Eugene

RHODE ISLAND

Jamestown
Wright, Harrison Morris

Kingston
Briggs, J.M.
Cohen, Joel Alden
Findlay, James F., Jr.
Gutchen, Robert M.
Klein, Maury
Ladewig, James L.
Strom, Sharon Hartman
Thurston, Gary L.
Turnbaugh, William A.
Weisbord, Robert G.

Middletown
Demy, Timothy J.

Newport
Dimaio, Michael

Providence
Alexander, Jon
Benedict, Philip Joseph
Boegehold, Alan
Branham, Joan R.
Brown, Peter B.
Chudacoff, Howard Peter
Conley, Patrick Thomas
Cvornyek, Bob
D'Evelyn, Margaret M.
Dufour, Ron
Dupree, Anderson Hunter
Fornara, Charles William
Gleason, Abbott
Gordon-Seifert, Catherine
Graubard, Stephen Richards
Heath, Dwight Braley
Holloway, Robert Ross
Joukowsky, Martha Sharp
Kellner, George
Kertzer, David Israel
Konstan, David
Landow, George Paul
Lemons, Stanley J.
Lesko, Leonard Henry
Litchfield, Robert Burr
Lopes, William H.
Marks, Sally Jean
Monroe, William S.
Neu, Charles Eric
Nwauwa, Apollos O.
Olson, Jeanine
Patterson, James Tyler
Putnam, Michael C.J.
Raaflaub, Kurt A.
Rich, Norman
Richards, Joan Livingston
Rosenberg, Bruce
Schneider, Joanne
Schulz, Anne Markham
Schulz, Juergen
Schuster, Leslie
Stowers, Stanley Kent
Teng, Tony
Thomas, John Lovell
Titon, Jeff Todd
Wilmeth, Don B.
Wood, Gordon Stewart
Wyatt, William F.

Saunderstown
Handsman, Russell G.

Smithfield
Litoff, Judy Barrett

South Kingston
Viles, Perry

SOUTH CAROLINA

Aiken
Smith, Wallace Calvin

Central
Bross, James Beverley
Grant, H. Roger

Charleston
Addington, Larry H.
Barrett, Michael Baker
Beck, Guy
Clark, Malcolm Cameron
Heisser, David C. R.
Moore, Winfred B., Jr.

Clemson
Crosby, Margaree Seawright
Golden, Richard Martin
Mckale, Donald Marshall

Columbia
Augustinos, Gerasimos
Basil, John Duryea
Beardsley, Edward Henry
Becker, Peter Wolfgang
Beltman, Brian William
Bridwell, R. Randal
Briggs, Ward W.
Carter, Jeffrey D.R.
Clements, Kendrick Alling
Connelly, Owen
Connelly, Owen S.
Day, Richard E.
Duffy, John Joseph
Edgar, Walter Bellingrath
Greenspan, Ezra
Gregg, Edward
Herzstein, Robert Edwin
Johanson, Herbert A.
Johnson, Herbert Alan
Kegley, Charles W.
Kross, Jessica
Maney, Patrick J.
Mathisen, Ralph Whitney
Moore, Robert Joseph
Patterson, Robert Benjamin
Perkins, Kenneth J Ames
Scardaville, Michael Charles
Stroup, Rodger Emerson
Synnott, Marcia G.
Terrill, Tom E.
Weir, Robert Mccolloch

Cullowhee
Lewis, James A.

Due West
Erickson, Nancy Lou
Farley, Benjamin Wirt

Florence
Diggs, William P.

Greenville
Abrams, Douglas Carl
Beale, David Otis
Gingery, Gail Alvah
Hayner, Linda K.
Kindall, Susan Carol
Kuehmann, Karen Marie
Matzko, John Austin
McKnight, Edgar Vernon
Parker, Mark M.

Newberry
Wilson, James Hugh

Orangeburg
Hine, William Cassidy
Michaux, Henry G.
Rogers, Oscar Allan, Jr.

Rock Hill
Haynes, Edward S.
Morgan, Thomas Sellers
Viault, Birdsall Scrymser
Webb, Ross Allan

Spartanburg
Dunn, Joe Pender
Holcombe, Lee
Racine, Philip N.

Sumter
Safford, John L.

SOUTH DAKOTA

Aberdeen
King, Walter Joseph

Brookings
Funchion, Michael Francis
Miller, John Edward

Huron
Meyer, Kenneth John

Sioux Falls
Olson, Gary Duane

Vermillion
Cherry, Paul
Hilderbrand, Robert Clinton
Hoover, Herbert Theodore
Lee, Roy Alton
Lehmann, Clayton M.
Moyer, Ronald L.
Sebesta, Judith Lynn

Yankton
Kessler, S. Ann

TENNESSEE

Athens
Dunn, Durwood

Bristol
Wade, William Junius

Chattanooga
Froide, Amy
Ingle, Homer Larry
Rice, Richard
Russell, James M.
Townsend, Gavin
Ward, James A.
Ware, Thomas C.
Wright, William John

Church Hill
Ripley Wolfe, Margaret
Wolfe, Margaret Ripley

Clarksville
Butts, Michelle Tucker
Gildric, Richard P.
Muir, Malcolm, Jr.
Pesely, George E.

Cleveland
Hoffman, Daniel

Cookeville
Webb, George Ernest

Dyersburg
Seibert-McCauley, Mary F.

Gallatin
Sherrill, Vanita Lytle

Greenville
Sexton, Donal J.

Hermitage
Moser, Harold Dean

Jackson
Carls, Alice
David, Arthur LaCurtiss
Dockery, David S.
Maire-Carls, Alice-Catherine
McClure, Wesley Cornelius

Jefferson City
Hawkins, Merrill M.

Johnson City
Baxter, Colin Frank
Day, Ronnie
Drinkard-Hawkshawe, Dorothy
Essin, Emmett M.
Fritz, Stephen G.

Knoxville
Ash, Stephen V.
Banker, Mark T.
Bast, Robert
Becker, Susan D.
Bergeron, Paul H.
Bing, J. Daniel
Bohstedt, John Howard
Bradley, Owen

Breslaw, Elaine
Brummett, Palmira
Burman, Thomas
Craig, Christopher P.
Diacon, Todd
Farris, W. Wayne
Finger, John R.
Gesell, Geraldine C.
Haas, Arthur G.
Habel, Dorothy
Haiken, Elizabeth
Hao, Yen-Ping
Higgs, Catherine
Hiles, Timothy
Jackson, Charles O.
Johnson, Charles W.
Klein, Milton M.
Martinson, Fred
Moffat, Frederick
Nappa, Christopher
Neff, Amy
Norrell, Robert J.
Peek, Marvin E.
Piehler, G. Kurt
Ratner, Larry
Rutledge, Harry Carraci
Schroeder-lein, Glenna R.
Slagle, Judith Baily
Sutherland, Elizabeth H.
Tandy, David
Wheeler, William Bruce

Martin
Downing, Marvin Lee
Jones, Kenneth Paul
Parker, Henry H.

Memphis
Caffrey, Margaret M.
Crouse, Maurice Alfred
Evans, David Huhn
Hatfield, Douglas Wilford
Hawes, Joseph
Hurley, Forrest Jack
Joiner, Burnett
Melancon, Donald
Purtle, Carol Jean
Shadish, W.R.
Sick, David
Skeen, Carl Edward
Tucker, David Milton
White, Lonnie Joe
Wilson, Major L.

Milligan College
Farmer, Craig S.

Murfreesboro
Brookshire, Jerry Hardman
Ferris, Norman B.
Huhta, James Kenneth
Hutcheson, Thom
Rolater, Frederick Strickland
Rowe, D.L.

Nashville
Allen, Jack
Blasi, Anthony J.
Carlton, David L.
Cockrell, Dale
Conkin, Paul K.
Cyrus, Cynthia
Deal, Terrance E.
Delzell, Charles Floyd
Doyle, Don H.
Eakin, Marshall C.
Elliott, Derek Wesley
Enterline, Lynn
Epstein, James A.
Fryd, Vivien G.
Graham, Hugh Davis
Graham, Hugh G.
Grantham, Dewey Wesley
Haas, Peter J.
Hambrick, Charles Hilton
Helguera, J. Leon
Howell, Sarah McCanless
Isherwood, Robert M.
Jackson, Andrew
Lee, Douglas
Mcseveney, Samuel Thompson
Myers, Charles Bennett
Sherkat, Darren E.
Todd, Margo
Voegeli, Victor Jacque
Wiltshire, Susan Ford
Winters, Donald Lee

Sewanee
Goodstein, Anita Shafer
Hawkins, Ralph K.
Perry, Charles Richard

Signal Mountain
Conwell, David

TEXAS

Abilene
Cantrell, Gregg
Ellis, Laura
Ferguson, Everett
Foster, Douglas A.
Slate, Philip
Taylor, Ira Donathan
Williams, John Howard

Alpine
Elam, Earl Henry

Amarillo
Sapper, Neil Gary

Arlington
Carroll, Bret E.
Green, George N.
Kellner, Hans
Maizlish, Stephen E.
Palmer, Stanley Howard
Philp, Kenneth
Reinhartz, Dennis Paul
Richmond, Douglas Wertz
Rodnitzky, Jerome L.
Schkade, Lawrence L.
Stark, Gary Duane
West, William Elliott

Austin
Abzug, Robert Henry
Alofsin, Anthony
Antokoletz, Elliott Maxim
Baltzer, Rebecca
Barker, Nancy Nichols
Bhague, Gerard
Bowman, Shearer Davis
Boyd, Carolyn Patricia
Braisted, William Reynolds
Brown, Norman D.
Burnham, Patricia
Carter, Joseph Coleman
Charlesworth, Michael
Clarke, John
Clarke, John R.
Collins, Derek B.
Cook, Erwin
Critchlow, Donald T.
Crosby, Alfred W.
Crunden, Robert M.
Curran, Thomas F.
Davis, Donald G., Jr.
DelAntonio, Andrew
Dewar, Mary
Dietz, Hanns-Bertold
Divine, Robert Alexander
Dulles, John Watson Foster
Edlund-Berry, Ingrid E.M.
Erlmann, Veit
Falola, Toyia
Fisher, James T.
Foley, Neil
Forgie, George Barnard
Frazier, Alison
Gagarin, Michael
Galinsky, Karl
Goetzmann, William Harry
Goff, Barbara E.
Goosman, Stuart
Gould, Lewis Ludlow
Graham, Richard
Graham, Richard
Green, Douglass Marshall
Grieder, Terence
Gutmann, Myron P.
Hall, Michael G.
Henderson, Linda
Hoberman, Louisa Schell
Holz, Robert K.
Hubbard, Thomas K.
Hunt, Bruce J.
Kenny, Kevin
Kroll, John Hennig
Kruppa, Patricia Stallings
Leoshko, Janice
Lopreato, Joseph

MacNeil, Anne
Magee, S.P.
Meacham, Standish
Meikle, Jeffrey L.
Meisel, Janet Anne
Meritt, Lucy
Minault, Gail
Mourelatos, Alexander Phoebus Dionysiou
Nelson, Wanda Lee
Nethercut, William Robert
Pells, Richard Henry
Prindle, David F.
Rather, Susan
Reynolds, Ann
Romo, Ricardo
Segre, Claudio Giuseppe
Shelmerdine, Cynthia Wright
Shiff, Richard
Slawek, Stephen
Smith, Jeffrey
Stoff, Michael B.
Stott, William Merrell
Tulis, Jeffrey K.
Tusa, Michael
White, Philip Lloyd

Baytown
Maroney, James C.

Beaumont
Carroll, John Martin
Wooster, Ralph Ancil

Canyon
Culley, John Joel
Nall, Garry Lynn
Petersen, Peter Lewis

College Station
Adams, Ralph James Quincy
Anderson, Terry Howard
Atkins, Stephen E.
Austin, Scott
Baer, Judith A.
Bass, George Fletcher
Baum, Dale
Beaumont, Roger A.
Black, Shirley Jean
Bornstein, Daniel
Bradford, James Chapin
Canup, John
Dethloff, Henry Clay
Knobel, Dale Thomas
Kosztolnyik, Zoltan Joseph Desiderius
Kramer, Arnold Paul
Nance, Joseph Milton
Pejovich, Svetozar
Rowe, M.W.
Schmidt, Henry Conrad
Stranahan, Patricia
Unterberger, Betty Miller
Vandiver, Frank Everson

Commerce
Reynolds, Donald E.

Corpus Christi
Delaney, Norman Conrad
Wooster, Robert

Dallas
Babcock, William Summer
Brettell, Caroline B.
Cordell, Dennis Dale
Countryman, Edward
Davis, Ronald Leroy
McKnight, Joseph Webb
Mears, John A.
Merrifield, William R.
Niewyk, Donald Lee
Weber, David J.
Williams, Richard Hal
Winship, Peter

Denton
Campbell, Randolph Bluford
Chipman, Donald Eugene
Demoss, Dorothy Dell
Hildreth, Gladys Johnson
Hurley, Alfred Francis
Kamman, William
La Forte, Robert Sherman
Lowe, Richard Grady
Lowry, Bullitt
Marcello, Ronald E.
Odom, Edwin Dale

Pickens, Donald Kenneth
Scobie, Ingrid Winther
Smith, F. Todd
Swain, Martha Helen
Wilson, William Henry

Early
Mangrum, Robert G.

Edinburg
Bokina, John
Henggeler, Paul R.
Miller, Hubert J.
Vassberg, David Erland

El Paso
Clymer, Kenton James
Hackett, David Andrew
Jackson, Carl Thomas
Kawashima, Yasuhide
Metz, Leon Claire
Ross, David
Smith, Sherry L.

Fort Worth
Bell, Reva Pearl
Black, Wesley O.
Brisco, Thomas V.
Brown, Richard Fargo
Eldridge, Daryl
Erisman, Fred Raymond
Loud, Patricia Cummings
McBeth, Harry Leon
Newman, J.R.
Procter, Ben
Salih, Halil Ibrahim
Toulouse, Mark G.
Tucker, William E.
Worcester, Donald Emmet
Yount, William R.

Galveston
Burns, Chester Ray
Cole, Thomas Richard
Vanderpool, Harold Young

Georgetown
Gottschalk, Peter
Hobgood-Oster, Laura
Neville, Gwen K.

Hawkins
Hawkins, Dorisula Wooten

Houston
Beeth, Howard
Bilstein, Roger Eugene
Christian, Garna
Crist, Lynda Lasswell
Cunningham, James J.
Curry, Lawrence H., Jr.
Decker, Hannah S.
Dirst, Matthew
Drew, Katherine Fischer
Farge, James Knox
Fisher, Robert Bruce
Green, Leamon L., Jr.
Gruber, Ira Dempsey
Hart, John Mason
Haskell, Thomas Langdon
Hyman, Harold Melvin
Jackson, Richard A.
Jefferson, Joseph L.
Johnson, Richard Ronald
Jones, James Howard
Kitchel, Mary Jean
Levin, Donald Norman
Lindahl, Carl
Martin, James Kirby
Martin, James Kirby
Matusow, Allen Joseph
McCaffrey, James M.
Melosi, Martin V.
Miles, Edwin Arthur
Mintz, Steven
Moore, James Talmadge
Morrison, Dennis L.
Mwamba, Zuberi I.
Natunewicz, Mary Ann T.
Nogee, Joseph Lippman
O'Brien, Thomas F.
Oby, Jason B.
Parsons, Keith M.
Pitre, Merline
Rasmussen, S.J.
Reed, Linda
Schiefen, Richard John
Seed, Patricia

Smith, Richard J.
Stokes, Gale
Stone, Bailey S.
Storrs, Landon R.Y.
Tinsley, James Aubrey
Tryman, Mfanya Donald
Van Helden, Albert
Wiener, Martin J.
Wintz, Cary DeCordova

Huntsville
Barker, Rosanne M.
Bilhartz, Terry D.
Camfield, Thomas M.
Castillo Crimm, Carolina
Coffey, Joan L.
Mallard, Harry
Olm, Lee Elmer
Olson, James S.
Pappas, Nicholas C.J.
Roth, Mitchel
Wile, Kip

Hurst
Pate, J'Nell L.
Stripling, Luther

Irving
Jodziewicz, Thomas W.
Sanchez, Elizabeth D.
Sommerfeldt, John R.
Sullivan, Charles R.
Swietek, Francis Roy
Welch, June R.
West, Grace Starry
Wilhelmsen, Alexandra

Keene
Sicher, Erwin

Kingsville
Hunter, Leslie Gene

Lancaster
Christman, Calvin Lee

Livingston
O'Day, Edward Francis

Loredo
Soto, Gilberto D.

Lubbock
Barr, Chester Alwyn
Brink, James Eastgate
Check, Ed
Collins, Jacquelin
Cutter, Paul F.
Flynn, George Quitman
George, Edward V.
Hobbs, Wayne
Howe, John Mcdonald
Kuethe, Allan James
Nelson, Otto Millard
Newcomb, Benjamin H.
Niessen, James P.
Thomas, Orlan E.
Van Appledorn, Mary Jeanne
Wilcox, Dean

Mesquite
Lightner, Robert P.

Nacogdoches
Davis, Carl L.
Devine, Joseph A., Jr.
Johnson, Bobby Harold
McDonald, Archie Philip
McGrath, Sylvia Wallace
Reese, James Verdo

Odessa
Olien, Diana Davids

Plainview
Owens, Nora Estelle

Richardson
Alexander, Bobby C.
Bambach, Charles
Branson, Susan
Chandler, Joan
Channell, David
Hambly, Gavin Richard Grenville
Kain, John Forrest
Leaf, Murray John
Rabe, Stephen

Simpson, Michael
Soliday, Gerald
Wickberg, Daniel
Wilson, Michael
Worsfold, Victor

Rio Vista
Baker, Thomas Lindsay

San Angelo
Hindman, E. James
Ward, James Randolph

San Antonio
Adams, R.E.W.
Allen, Mark
Barker, Wendy
Brackenridge, Robert Douglas
Breit, William Leo
Bruster, Douglas
Burton, Joan
Caver, Christine
Garrison, Mark
Graff, Harvey J.
Hovey, Kenneth
Hutton, John
Johnson, David Ralph
Kates, Gary
Larson, Doran
Lopez, Debbie
Lyons, Bonnie
McBride, Margaret
McCusker, John J.
Mcnutt, James Charles
Mendoza, Louis
Metcalf, Alida C.
Miller, Char
Pearce, James
Reitzes, Lisa B.
Rodriguez, Clemencia
Romano, Susan
Salvucci, Linda Kerrigan
Schulte, Josephine Helen
Smith, Woodruff Donald
Talbot, Charles
Taylor-Mitchell, Laurie
Valone, Carolyn
Wells, Colin
Woodson, Linda

San Marcos
Arnoult, Sharon
Brandimarte, Cynthia A.
Brown, Ronald Conklin
de la Teja, J.F.
Dunn, Dennis John
Liddle, William D.
Makowski, Elizabeth
Margerison, Kenneth
Pohl, James William
Smith, Joanne Hamlin
Swinney, Everette
Yick, Joseph Kong Sang

Sherman
Cape, Robert W.
Carlson, Arvid John
Cummins, Light Townsend
Cummins, Victoria Hennessey
Tooley, T. Hunt

Victoria
Smith, Harold L.

Waco
Breckenridge, James
Charlton, Thomas Lee
Cresson, Bruce Collins
Hendon, David Warren
Longfellow, David Lyman
Pitts, Bill
Smith, Diane E.
Sorelle, James Martin
Vardaman, James Welch

UTAH

Blanding
Barlow, K. Renee

Cedar City
Vlasich, James Anthony

Logan
Carmack, Noel A.
Cole, Robert

Coon, David L.
Frykman, George Axel
Gough, Jerry B.
Harris, Laurilyn J.
Hirt, Paul W.
Hume, Richard L.
Johnson, Wendy Dasler
Kale, Steven D.
Kennedy, Thomas L.
Kicza, John Edward
Krantz, Grover S.
Lipe, William David
Mauss, Armand
Meyer, Kathryn E.
Peabody, Susan
Pesek, Thomas G.
Peterson, Jacqueline
Reed, T.V.
Schlesinger, Roger
Slind, Marvin G.
Streets, Heather
Sun, Raymond
Svingen, Orlan
Tolmacheva, Marina
Trafzer, Clifford Earl
Watrous, Mary A.
Williams, Richard S.

Seattle
Bacharach, Jere L.
Banks, James Albert
Benson, Keith Rodney
Bernard, J.W.
Bliquez, Lawrence J.
Burnstein, Daniel
Butow, Robert J.C.
Carlsen, James Caldwell
Clausen, Meredith L.
Conlon, Frank Fowler
Connolly, Joy P.T.
Eastman, Carol M.
Ellison, Herbert J.
Fortier, Ted
Hankins, Thomas Leroy
Harmon, Daniel P.
Johnson, Richard Rigby
Jones, Edward Louis
Leiren, Terje Ivan
Mayerfeld, Jamie
Miller, Jacquelyn C.
Ochsner, Jeffrey Karl
Ottenberg, Simon
Palais, James Bernard
Pascal, Paul
Pauwels, Heidi
Pease, Otis Arnold
Scalise, Charles J.
Spigner, Clarence
Starr, Larry
Sugar, Peter Frigyes
Sutton, Sharon Egretta
Taylor, Tom
Thaden, Edward C.
Thomas, Carol D.
Treadgold, Donald Warren
Ullman, Joan Connelly
Van Den Berghe, Pierre L.
Waugh, Daniel Clarke

Spokane
Carriker, Robert C.
Hunt, James
Migliazzo, Arlin C.
Sanford, Daniel
Schlatter, Fredric William
Soden, Dale
Williams, James Hiawatha
Yoder, John

Tacoma
Barnett, Suzanne Wilson
Block, Geoffrey
Browning, C.R.
Carp, E. Wayne
Cooney, Terry Arnold
Reigstad, Ruth
Smith, David Fredrick

Walla Walla
Breit, Frederick Joseph
Masteller, Richard N.

WEST VIRGINIA

Charleston
Casdorph, Paul Douglas
James, Betty Harris

Huntington
Palmer, William
Riddel, Frank Stephen
Spindel, Donna Jane
Woodward, David Reid

Institute
Sharma, R.N.

Montgomery
Alexander, Ronald R.
Bradford, Richard Headlee
Long, Ronald Wilson

Morgantown
Bagby, Wesley Marvin
Hood, Mantle
Hudson, Barton
Labys, Walter Carl
Maxon, Robert Mead
Mccluskey, Stephen C.
Vargas, Julie S.
Vehse, Charles T.
Walken, Chrisopher

Parkersburg
Allen, Bernard Lee

Salem
Florian, Robert Bruce

Shepherdstown
Hanak, Walter Karl
Holland, James C.

Wheeling
Laker, Joseph Alphonse
Wack, John Theodore

WISCONSIN

Appleton
Bremer, William Walling
Chaney, William Albert
Lawton, Carol
Taylor, Daniel Jennings

Beloit
Hodge, Robert White

Cross Plains
Davis, Gary A.

De Pere
Patterson, Wayne Kief

Eau Claire
Gross, Rita M.
Lauber, Jack M.

Elkhart Lake
Lydolph, Paul E.

Green Bay
Aldrete, Gregory S.
Kaye, Harvey Jordan
Lockard, Craig Alan

Kenosha
Bailey, John Wendell
Buenker, John D.
Egerton, Frank N.
Gellott, Laura S.
Greenfield, Gerald M.
Mclean, Andrew Miller
Meyer, Stephen
Noer, Thomas John
Reeves, Thomas C.
Schunk, Thom
Shade, Barbara J.
Smith, Eleanor Jane

La Crosse
Chavalas, Mark W.
Jenson, Carol Elizabeth
Kuhn, Gary G.
Pemberton, William Erwin
Pinnell, Richard

Vettes, William George

Ladysmith
Lewis, Thomas T.

Madison
Archdeacon, Thomas John
Barker, John W.
Bender, Todd K.
Bogue, Allan G.
Bowling, Kenneth R.
Boyer, Paul S.
Chamberlain, Michael
Clover, Frank M.
Coffman, Edward M.
Courtenay, William James
Coutenay, Lynn
Doane, Alger Nicolaus
Fishman, Sterling
Fox, Michael
Friedman, Edward
Frykenberg, Robert E.
Gargan, Edward T.
Gordon, Linda
Gorski, Philip
Haller, Archibald O.
Ham, F. Gerald
Hamalainen, Pekka Kalevi
Hamerow, Theodore Stephen
Hatheway, Jay
Haveman, Robert H.
Hilts, Victor L.
Hollingsworth, Joseph Rogers
Hopkins, Dianne McAfee
Hutchison, Jane Campbell
Kaminski, John Paul
Kingdon, Robert Mccune
Knipe, David Maclay
Kutler, Stanley I.
Latousek, Rob
Leavitt, Judith Walzer
Lee, Jean B.
LeMoine, Fannie J.
Lin, Yu-sheng
Lindberg, David C.
Lindstrom, Diana
Lovejoy, David Sherman
Malone, Barbara S. (Bobbie)
Mazzaoui, Maureen Fennell
McClure, Laura Kathleen
McKeown, James C.
Michels, Anthony
Mosse, George L.
Numbers, Ronald Leslie
O'Keife, J. Paul
Ormand, Kirk
Payne, Stanley George
Powell, Barry
Risjord, Norman Kurt
Schultz, Stanley Kenton
Senn, Alfred Erich
Sewell, Richard Herbert
Sidran, Ben H.
Sorkin, David
Stern, Steve Jefferey
Van Deburg, William L.
Vansina, Jan
Vaughn, Stephen Lee
Ward, David
Wills, Jeffrey
Wink, Andre
Woodward, David
Zychowicz, James L.

Manitowoc
Trask, Kerry A.

Marinette
Krog, Carl Edward

Menomonie
Kirby, Alec
Zeidel, Robert F.

Milwaukee
Aman, Mohammed M.
Bartley, Russell Howard
Baumann, Carol Edler
Bellegarde-Smith, Patrick
Bendiner, Kenneth Paul
Buck, David D.
Carey, Patrick W.
Carpenter, Joseph, II
Donnelly, John Patrick
Dziewanowski, Marian Kamil
Fetter, Bruce Sigmond
Foley, Mary Briant
Gardinier, David E.
Greene, Victor Robert

Hamdani, Abbas Husayn
Hay, Carla Humphrey
Hay, Robert Pettus
Hayes, Jeffrey R.
Hoeveler, J. David
Hoey, Lawrence R.
Horsman, Reginald
Hubbard, Nancy
Joyce Stone, Andrea
Krause, Linda R.
Levy, Ian Christopher
Marten, James
Moberg, David Oscar
Pollard, Diane S.
Prucha, Francis Paul
Ross, Ronald John
Schmidt, Martin Edward
Schroeder, John H.
Shashko, Philip
Shey, Howard James
Skalitzky, Rachel Irene
Sprague, Paul Edward
Swanson, Roy Arthur
Theoharis, Athan
Trattner, Walter Irwin
Waldbaum, Jane C.
Weare, Walter Burdette
Wild, Robert Anthony
Wind, Barry
Wishne, Brian
Woehrmann, Paul John
Wolfe, Christopher
Zupko, Ronald Edward

Monona
Anderson, Charles W.

New Berlin
Milham, Mary Ella

Oshkosh
Grieb, Kenneth J.
Linenthal, Edward Tabor
O'Shaughnessy, Andrew J.
Sieber, George Wesley

Platteville
Wendorff, Laura C.

Racine
Burckel, Nicholas C.

Ripon
Doss, Seale
Hyde, James F., Jr.
Miller, George Hall
Smith, Brian H.

River Falls
Cederberg, Herbert Renando
Peterson, Edward Norman

Shorewood
Sawkins, Annemarie

Stevens Point
Knowlton, Robert James
Mertz, Paul Eric
Overholt, Thomas William
Paul, Justus F.
Skelton, William B.
Walker, Hugh D.

Stoughton
Hatheway, Joseph G.

Waukesha
Dukes, Jack Richard
Sherrick, Rebecca Louise

Wausau
Lorence, James J.

Whitewater
Anderson, Janet A.
Haney, Richard Carlton
Quinlivan, Mary E.
Yasko, Richard Anthony

WYOMING

Cody
Bender, Nathan E.

Laramie
Denney, Colleen J.
Gressley, Gene M.
Harris, Janice Hubbard
Holt, Philip
Kohler, Eric Dave
Larson, Taft Alfred
Moore, William Howard
Schaefer, Jean Owens

GUAM

Tamuning
Sherrill, Ned

PUERTO RICO

Rio Piedras
Pico, Fernando
Vivoni-Farage, Enrique

Trujillo Alto
Garcia, Aurelio A.

VIRGIN ISLANDS

St. Thomas
Krigger, Marilyn Francis
Turnbull, Charles Wesley

CANADA

ALBERTA

Athabasca
Finkel, Alvin
Roberts, Barbara A.

Calgary
Bercuson, David Jay
Eyck, Frank
Francis, Robert D.
Knafla, Louis A.
Kome, Penny J.
Martin, John Stephen
Mastin, Catharine M.
Mcginnis, David Prentice
Mckenna, Marian Cecilia
Mcmordie, Michael J.
Osler, Margaret Jo
Rasporich, Anthony W.
Stamp, Robert M.
Walbank, Michael Burke

Edmonton
Bowker, Wilbur F.
Buck, Robert J.
Fishwick, Duncan
Jones, William J.
Jones, William John
Lightner, David Lee
Macleod, Roderick Charles
Owram, Douglas R.
Pownall, Frances Skoczylas
Thompson, John H.
Trumpener, Ulrich
Waida, Manabu
Waugh, Earle Howard

Lethbridge
Baker, William M.
Greenshields, Malcolm
Huel, Ray
Penton, Marvin J.
Robinson, Tom
Tagg, James
Titley, Edward B.

BRITISH COLUMBIA

Burnaby
Boyer, Richard
Carlson, Roy L.

French, Goldwin S.
Gentles, Ian
Gervers, Michael
Goffart, Walter A.
Golombek, Lisa
Granatstein, Jack L.
Grant, John Neilson
Greer, Allan R.
Gross Stein, Janice
Grzymski, Krzysztof A.
Gwyn, Alexandra
Harrison, Timothy P.
Hillgarth, Jocelyn Nigel
Howarth, Thomas
Hughes, Andrew
Iacovetta, Franca
Ingham, John Norman
Irwin, Eleanor
Israel, Milton
Johnson, Robert E.
Johnson, William M.
Keep, John L.H.
Klein, Martin A.
Kornberg, Jacques
Lachan, Katharine
Lee, M. Owen
Legge, Elizabeth
MacMillan, Margaret
Maniates, Maria Rika
Marrus, Michael R.
Mason, H.J.
Mason, Steve
McDonough, C.J.
Mcintire, Carl Thomas
Mertins, Detlef
Moore, Christopher H.
Morrison, Alex
Mowat, Farley
Nigosian, Solomon Alexander
Normore, Calvin Gerard
Ouellet, Fernand
Pierson, Ruth
Pothecary, Sarah
Powicke, Michael Rhys
Prentice, Alison
Reynolds, Roger Edward
Rigg, Arthur George
Rix, Brenda
Roazen, Paul
Robson, Ann W.
Rutherford, Paul F.W.
Sadlier, Rosemary
Samarin, William J.
Samuel, Alan Edouard
Saywell, John T.
Shaw, Joseph Winterbotham
Silcox, David P.
Swinton, Katherine E.
Synan, Edward A.
Thornton, Archibald Paton
Tushingham, Arlotte Douglas
Waddams, Stephen M.
Wark, Wesley K.
Watkins, Melville H.
Webster, Donald B.
Webster, Jill
Weinrib, Ernest Joseph
Wilson, Ian E.
Winsor, Mary Pickard

Zemans, Joyce P.

Waterloo
Boire, Gary
Castricano, Jodey
Comacchio, Cynthia
Copp, John T.
Cornell, Paul G.
Cristi, Renato
Enns, Leonard
Evans, Joan
Fletcher, Judith
Forsyth, Phyllis
Freed, Joann
Gray, Laura
Greene, Gordon K.
Harrigan, Patrick Joseph
Hull, Kenneth
Klaassen, Walter
Lorimer, Douglas
Lorimer, Joyce
Marr, William L.
McLaughlin, Ken
Mitchinson, Wendy
O'Dell, Leslie
Packull, Werner O.
Rummel, Erika
Santosuosso, Alma
Sawatsky, Rodney James
Schaus, Gerald
Sibalis, Michael
Simpson, Chris
Snyder, Arnold C.
Stortz, Gerry
Wahl, Jim
Zeller, Suzanne

West Hill
Eksteins, Modris

Whitby
Murray, Joan

Willowdale
Woods, Joseph Michael

Windsor
Bird, Harold Wesley
Klein, Owen
Kovarik, Edward
McCrone, Kathleen E.
Murray, Jacqueline
Sautter, Udo
Spellman, John Willard
Tucker, Bruce

Woodville
Fleming, Rae B.

PRINCE EDWARD ISLAND

Charlottetown
Arsenault, Joseph G.
Bolger, Francis W.P.
Robb, Stewart A.

QUEBEC

Aylmer
Trudel, Marcel

Hull
L'Allier, Louis
McGhee, Robert J.
Russell, Hilary A.

Laval
Roberge, Rene-Michel

Montreal
Anctil, Pierre
Asselin, Olivier
Bates, Donald G.
Bayley, C.C.
Beaudoin-Ross, Jacqueline
Belisle, Jean
Bertrand, Charles L.
Bode, Frederick August
Boker, Hans J.
Carr, Graham
Chalk, Frank
Chausse, Gilles
Coolidge, Robert Tytus
Cote, Joanne
De Moura Sobral, Luis
Decarie, Graeme
Diubaldo, Richard J.
Dunlop, Anne
Durocher, Rene
Fahmy-Eid, Nadia
Fick, Carolyn E.
Foss, Brian
Galavaris, George
Galvaris, George
Ghosh, Ratna
Gillett, Margaret
Glen, Thomas L.
Hill, John
Hoffman, Peter C.W.
Hould, Claudette
Hubbard, William H.
Hudson, Robert
Ingram, Norman
Kirby, Torrance W.
Larouche, Michel
Lehuu, Isabel
Lemieux, Lucien
Lesser, Gloria
Lusignan, Serge
McSheffrey, Shannon
Miller, Carman I.

Morton, Desmond D.P.
Nish, Cameron
Orr, Leslie
Pedersen, Diana
Robert, Jean-Claude
Rudin, Ronald
Sanders, Lionel
Sanderson, Warren
Schachter, Albert
Schade, Rosemarie
Scheinberg, Stephen
Schoenauer, Norbert
Shlosser, Franziska E.
Shubert, Howard
Singer, Martin
Tansey, Charlotte
Tittler, Robert
van Nus, Walter
Vipond, Mary
Vogel, Robert
Woloch, George Michael
Young, Katherine K

Outremont
Potvin, Gilles E.J.

Quebec
Desautels, Jacques
Desautels, Jacques
Porter, John R.

St-Joseph-de-la-rive
des Gagniers, Jean

Ste. Foy
Auger, Reginald
Dumont, Micheline
Fortin, Michel

SASKATCHEWAN

Regina
Bismanis, Maija
Conway, John F.

Saskatoon
Bietenholz, Peter Gerard
Fairbairn, Brett T.
Hayden, James Michael
Lambi, I.N.
Miller, James R.
Miquelon, Dale B.
Sider, Robert Dick
Smith, David E.

OTHER COUNTRIES

AUSTRALIA
Martin, Austin Lynn
Siracusa, Joseph M.
Halperin, David M.
White, Shane

AUSTRIA
Seebass, Tilman

ENGLAND
Simmons, Richard C.
Tippett, Maria W.
Winter, Jay Murray
Clark, Christopher F.
Ratcliffe, Donald John
Morgan, Kenneth
Baylen, Joseph Oscar
Lawson-Peebles, Robert
Way, Peter J.
Madsen, Deborah
Hall, Peter G.
Wood, Marcus
Bent, Margaret
Elliott, John Huxtable
Langford, Paul
Lewis, Jane E.
Raven, James R.
Sternfeld, Frederick William
Ward, William R.
Nicholls, David

FRANCE
Fabre, Genevieve Edith
Fabre, Michel J.
Green, Nancy Lascoe

GERMANY
Schmidt, Klaus
Lohr, Charles Henry

HONG KONG
Starr, Joseph Barton

IRELAND
Bowler, Peter John

ISRAEL
Eber, Irene
Gartner, Lloyd Philip
Gershenson, Daniel Enoch

ITALY
Brenk, Frederick Eugene
Little, Lester Knox
North, Robert

JAPAN
Rothfork, John G.
Kikuchi, Akira

NETHERLANDS
Horst, Irvin Buckwalter

SCOTLAND
Ermarth, Elizabeth D.

SWITZERLAND
Blair, John George
Tait, Alan A.
Pipkin, Harry Wayne